The Cambridge Bibliography of English Literature

VOLUME 4 · 1800–1900
Third Edition

The Cambridge Bibliography of English Literature

Edited by
JOANNE SHATTOCK

VOLUME 4 · 1800–1900

Third edition

CAMBRIDGE
UNIVERSITY PRESS

PUBLISHED BY THE PRESS SYNDICATE OF THE UNIVERSITY OF CAMBRIDGE
The Pitt Building, Trumpington Street, Cambridge CB2 1RP, United Kingdom

CAMBRIDGE UNIVERSITY PRESS
The Edinburgh Building, Cambridge CB2 2RU, UK www.cup.cam.ac.uk
40 West 20th Street, New York, NY 10011–4211, USA www.cup.org
10 Stamford Road, Oakleigh, Melbourne 3166, Australia
Ruiz de Alarcón 13, 28014 Madrid, Spain

First published 1999

Printed in Great Britain at the University Press, Cambridge

Typeset in Lexicon 7/9pt

A catalogue record for this book is available from the British Library

Library of Congress cataloguing in publication data

ISBN 0 521 39100 8

Contents summary

Editor's preface

This is the first volume of *The Cambridge Bibliography of English Literature* third edition to appear. It is the work of an international community of scholars who have collaborated to produce a definitive primary bibliography of nineteenth-century authors and texts.

The third edition of CBEL has distinguished forebears. The first edition, edited by F. W. Bateson, was published in 1940, with a supplement in 1957. The second edition, *The New Cambridge Bibliography of English Literature* (NCBEL), edited by George Watson and Ian Willison, was published in four volumes between 1969 and 1974 with an index volume in 1977. As was the case with the previous edition, the third edition has built on the strength of its predecessors. The first task in the process of revision was to update and augment the bibliographical details already available. In practical terms this has resulted in a radical recasting of a large proportion of the existing entries in line with the buoyant state of scholarship and textual criticism on Romantic and Victorian literature over the past thirty years. Equally important to the new edition has been the introduction of hundreds of entries for writers previously omitted from the Bibliography. The size of the new volume for 1800–1900, nearly fifty per cent longer than its predecessor, is a tangible pointer to the impact of the new material.

Although the new entries are spread throughout the volume, certain sections of the Bibliography have been transformed by the additions. We have extended the number of poets, particularly in the period 1800–1835, by nearly fivefold, and of novelists by an appreciable if less dramatic percentage. The section on children's books contains entries for over four hundred writers for children. There is a small but significant addition to the number of dramatists and the sections on source materials for the study of the nineteenth-century theatre have been thoroughly revised. We have introduced a new section on political economy, an acknowledgement of the large amount of writing on the 'dismal science' in which authors were engaged during the nineteenth century, and a section on household books, the domestic manuals and conduct books which were a major part of mass publishing from the mid-century onward. The section on philosophy has been expanded to include writers on science, another area in which interdisciplinary research has flourished in the last three decades. Writers of non-fictional prose are now given full entries, in which the variety of their work, editorial as well as creative, is documented.

A large proportion of new entries across all genres and subjects is devoted to women, underlining the enormous amount of recovery and rereading of women writers which has taken place since the previous edition of the Bibliography. The new entries for these writers are located not only in the traditional genres of poetry and the novel, children's literature and household books, but in history, philosophy, science, English studies, and non-fictional prose, reflecting their emergent voices and significant contributions to a variety of discourses in the nineteenth century.

CBEL is a bibliography of English literature in its broadest sense. The genre sections of poetry, the novel, drama and non-fictional prose occupy a central position. But just as the nineteenth-century reader was determinedly non-specialist and assumed that current 'literature' included history, philosophy, and scientific writing as well as poetry and fiction, so the genre sections of the Bibliography are complemented by a number of subject sections, on history, philosophy and science, religion, travel, English studies, the literature of sport, education, and newspapers and magazines. These sections are author based, and concentrate on primary texts. In addition the Bibliography contains two important and extensively revised sections on book production and distribution and on literary relations with the continent.

Any bibliography which aims to be comprehensive is inevitably implicated in the formation of a canon, however unofficially. The new entries and the revisions to this volume of CBEL have appreciably altered the existing nineteenth-century canon as well as reflecting the main focus of research over the last thirty years. The new edition has made a significant alteration to the canon in another respect by abandoning the distinction between major and minor writers which was a feature of the two previous editions. This unnecessary classification not only produced some now indefensible categorizations, but it has been recognized that a bibliography such as CBEL plays a significant part in the ongoing process which constantly revises and challenges such categorizations.

One enormous difference in circumstances separates the contributors to the third edition of CBEL from their predecessors – the development and proliferation of electronic bibliographical resources. These have had an immense impact on the new edition, and have presented some interesting problems. On the one hand they have provided immediate access to catalogues and bibliographies worldwide. On the other, the same catalogues have thrown up evidence which is contradictory, unclear, or in other ways problematic. A perennial trouble spot in nineteenth-century bibliography, the difficulty of distinguishing a new edition from a new impression, a distinction not easy to make from an examination of the books themselves, has been exacerbated by electronic catalogues. So too has the difficulty of determining the status of American 'editions', another feature of nineteenth-century publishing. Printed catalogues are not free from error, and their increased accessibility has compounded the possibility of perpetuating mistakes. Every effort has been made by contributors to verify the details of a particular edition or impression by physical examination where possible. This of course is a counsel of perfection, and not all contributors have had access to extensive collections of primary materials. But all have been aware of the need for caution where conflicting or uncorroborated dates have existed.

The proliferation of reviews and magazines and the emergence of a reviewing culture of vast proportions and variety distinguished the nineteenth-century literary world from its predecessors. The fruits of several decades of scholarship on nineteenth-century periodicals and literary reviewing are evident in this edition of the Bibliography, particularly through the inclusion of extensive listings of contemporary reviews of individual works and where possible the identification of the reviewers.

CBEL is an author-based bibliography. The focus of this volume is on authors who flourished between 1800 and 1900, who were native to, or resident in the British Isles, and whose main body of work appeared before 1900. Scottish, Welsh and Irish writers in English have not been allocated separate sections but rather are integrated into the major divisions of the Bibliography. No attempt has been made to standardize entries in terms of the amount of bibliographical detail provided. This varies according to the state of knowledge of the subject, and sometimes according to the emphasis chosen by the contributor. In the case of some entries, the emphasis is on translations. In others the focus is on contemporary responses, the posthumous history of texts, or textual criticism. For less well-known authors the task has been the more straightforward one of compiling in the first instance a full and accurate listing of primary works.

General arrangement

Authors are located within the genre or subject section in which the predominant portion of their work was published, or with which they are most closely identified. Cross-references to these main entries are provided in other sections, and an extensive system of cross-referencing is in operation throughout the volume. The organization of the Bibliography is chronological. In the sections devoted to poetry, the novel, drama and non-fictional prose, the period 1800–1900 has been sub-divided into three parts: early nineteenth century (1800–1835); mid nineteenth century (1835–1870) and late nineteenth century (1870–1900). The purpose of these divisions is to provide contextualization, and to avoid unwieldy alphabetical lists. Authors are assigned to these sections by date of birth. To be included in the 'early' division, an author normally must have been born between 1760 and 1800. The mid-nineteenth-century sections include those writers born after 1799 and before 1831, and the late period those born between 1830 and 1865, whose more important works were written before 1900. Date of birth normally determines inclusion in a particular volume of the Bibliography so that William Blake (b.1757) and William Godwin (b.1756), to name two writers who might have been expected to appear in this volume, are to be found in the preceding one, and Yeats (b.1865) and Synge (b.1871) in the following one. The entry for George Bernard Shaw (b. 1856) no longer appears in the nineteenth-century volume, as it can be convincingly argued that his most significant work was published after 1900.

Style of entries

Author entries are divided into two sections. The first is devoted to primary material (works *by* the author), and the second to secondary materials (works *about* the author), the latter selected in accordance with carefully defined principles. The emphasis is on primary material. A full author entry contains an opening note giving details of the location of major collections of manuscripts. This is followed by a list of any existing bibliographies and reference works dealing with both primary and secondary materials, and by details of collections and selections of works. The focus of the entry is a chronological list of individual works, arranged by date of first publication. These include all significant English language editions, and where known, American and continental editions, followed by contemporary reviews of the work and translations into other languages. Individual works may include contributions to periodicals and to collaborative works, letters, journals, diaries, notebooks, translations, prefaces, and introductions *by* the author, works written under pseudonyms, attributed or spurious works.

Secondary material, listed in the second section of the entries, has been assembled according to more selective principles than in the two previous editions. The availability of comprehensive bibliographies of secondary material, both in electronic and volume form, and the back-dating to 1920 of two major bibliographies, the Annual Bibliography of English Language and Literature and the Annotated Bibliography of English Studies, made it clear that it would be an unnecessary duplication for the third edition of CBEL to provide a selective list of secondary criticism for each author, as had previously been the case.

Secondary material in this edition, therefore, falls into three categories: (1) A selective listing of pre-1920 criticism which can fairly be claimed to have contributed signally to the establishment or revaluation of the writer concerned.

Where possible entries for major writers include a number of obituaries which, in the case of nineteenth-century writers, often provide important information as well as useful contemporary assessment. Contemporary reviews of individual works, as mentioned above, are listed under the work concerned in section 1 of the entry. (2) A complete and up-to-date listing of textual and bibliographical criticism of the author's works, either individually or collectively, which provides information on composition, transmission, printing and publication history, dating, and authorship, and which glosses, corrects or emends the text(s) concerned. (3) A selective list of authoritative biographies, normally one contemporary and one recent, but which in the case of significant figures, may be more extensive. In the case of major figures there are notes of periodicals devoted to the author, and areas not usually covered by the bibliography, including film, television, and radio adaptations of works.

Titles of works reproduce the wording and spelling of the title pages of first editions, but longer titles have usually been abbreviated. Capitalization has been kept to a minimum and arabic numerals preferred over roman. The number of volumes is indicated, unless it is one. The place of publication is assumed to be London unless otherwise stated. In any given entry details of place of publication and numbers of volumes apply until contradicted, whereupon 'London' and '1 vol' may be reinstated. Names of publishers are not usually provided, but the names of series are given. Periodical articles are cited by volume and year, occasionally by a complete date, but page numbers are omitted. Translations are cited by language and date.

The details of an entry for a particular work tend to be more intense during the lifetime of an author and the early years of the life of a book. In the case of those works which have undergone multiple reprints, some process of selection has been undertaken and attempts have been made to avoid the use of 'etc' for those works which were virtually never out of print. The question of what constitutes a 'significant' English language edition is a vexed one. It has not always been possible, in the case of prolific reprintings, to distinguish between a new edition and an impression. In the case of modern reprints, usually only those which contain a useful introduction or editorial materials have been included. The initials of the contributor are located in square brackets at the end of an entry. In the case of those entries which are unsigned, the revision or construction of a new entry has been undertaken in house. Every attempt has been made to make the information provided as up to date as possible.

Joanne Shattock
University of Leicester
August 1999

Acknowledgements

A project of such proportion as CBEL is indebted to the expertise and generosity of a large number of scholars worldwide. My thanks go first and foremost to the contributors to the volume, who are listed separately, and whose professionalism and persistent desire for accuracy and comprehensiveness was salutary. A number of special advisers to this volume were generous with time and their knowledge of both the subject and of individuals working in specific areas: John Barnard, Gillian Beer, Marilyn Butler, Brian Lake, David McKitterick and John Sutherland. Several individuals had a major impact on particular sections of the Bibliography. J. R. de J. Jackson undertook the task of revising what was known previously as the 'Minor Poetry 1800–1835' section, now recast and expanded beyond recognition. Elizabeth Harrisson, director of the Mellon Microfilming Project at Cambridge University Library, generously shared the results of her scrupulous and painstaking examination of texts based on the 'minor' fiction sections of NCBEL, enabling us to augment and correct existing entries before beginning the task of adding to them. Richard Foulkes ably acted as commissioning editor of the drama section, drawing together a band of scholars who have revised and significantly extended the coverage of the nineteenth-century theatre in this edition.

Many individuals shared their knowledge and gave assistance with individual entries, among them D. Baus, Monty Chisholm, K. Fagan, C. Hatt, Merlin Holland, Philip Horne, Linda Hunt, Russell Jackson, Ilona Koren-Deutsch, the late David Linton, Tony Mason, Christopher Mulvey, D. Pautz, Marie Sanderson, the late Lillian F. Shankman, Jack Stillinger, John Stokes, R. H. Super, Oscar Wellens, Rachel Wilson, Duncan Wu, Bradley Young.

Bibliographical work depends on meticulous research, and on an eye for detail. This volume is silently indebted to the work of its excellent research assistants, Jean Elliott and Rosemary Scott, who compiled many new entries and revised others. Sue Lloyd and Sue Martin, of the Victorian Studies Centre at Leicester University, were responsible for keying in and transforming the raw data into its present form. For ensuring consistency as well as clarity I am indebted to the copy editor Helen Southall, and to proof readers Caroline Burkett and Angela Warren. Many members of Cambridge University Press have given the project support at significant stages: Josie Dixon, Maureen Leach, Caroline Murray, Rod Mulvey, Lin Vasey. My special thanks go to Andrew Brown, who initiated the new edition and directed the project from the outset, and to Caroline Bundy, whose professionalism and enthusiasm steered this volume to completion in its final years.

Joanne Shattock

Contributors

AARON, JANE University of Glamorgan
ALEXANDER, CHRISTINE University of New South Wales
ALEXANDER, J.H. University of Aberdeen
ALEXANDER, LYNN University of Tennessee at Martin
ANDERSON, NANCY FIX Loyola University New Orleans
ASHTON, ROSEMARY University College London
ATKINSON, DAMIAN St Edmund Hall, Oxford
BANHAM, MARTIN University of Leeds
BARRON, DAVID J. Lancaster University
BARTHOLOMEW, BARBARA University of Houston–Downtown
BATLEY, PATRICIA London College of Printing
BECKSON, KARL City University of New York
BEETHAM, MARGARET Manchester Metropolitan University
BELCHER, MARGARET University of Canterbury, New Zealand
BELL, BILL University of Edinburgh
BLAIN, VIRGINIA Macquarie University
BLOM, J.M. Nijmegen University
BLOOM, ABIGAIL BURNHAM Independent scholar, New York
BOARDMAN, BRIGID M. Independent scholar, Bath
BRADBURY, NICOLA University of Reading
BROWN, ANDREW Cambridge University Press
BROWN, PENNY E. University of Manchester
BROWNE, JANET Wellcome Institute for the History of Medicine
BUTTS, DENNIS University of Reading
CARNALL, GEOFFREY University of Edinburgh
CHISHOLM, ROY University of Kent
CLEMIT, PAMELA University of Durham
COCHRAN, PETER Hertfordshire and Essex High School, Bishops Stortford
COHEN, MORTON N. Emeritus, City University of New York
CONNOLLY, CLAIRE Cardiff University
COOTER, R. University of East Anglia
COUSTILLAS, PIERRE University of Lille
COX, RICHARD WILLIAM University of Manchester Institute of Science and Technology
CRIPPS, ELIZABETH American Intercontinental University
CRISP, JANE Griffith University
CUTMORE, JONATHAN Independent scholar, Toronto
DAHL, CURTIS Wheaton College, Massachusetts
DAVIES, LORRAINE Liverpool Hope University College
DAY, AIDAN University of Edinburgh
DEKKERS, ODIN Independent scholar, The Netherlands
DEMOOR, MARYSA Ghent University
DENNIS, BARBARA University of Wales, Lampeter
DESMARAIS, JANE Goldsmiths College, University of London
DIXON, DIANA Loughborough University
DONALDSON, SANDRA University of North Dakota
EASSON, ANGUS University of Salford
EDWARDS, OWEN DUDLEY University of Edinburgh
EDWARDS, P.D. University of Queensland
ELIOT, SIMON The Open University
ELLIOTT, JEAN Birkbeck College, University of London
EMELJANOW, VICTOR University of Newcastle, New South Wales
EVEREST, KELVIN University of Liverpool
FARWELL, RUTH S. South Bank University
FEATHER, JOHN Loughborough University
FENWICK, GILLIAN University of Toronto
FINKELSTEIN, DAVID Napier University, Edinburgh
FRANKLIN, CAROLINE University of Wales, Swansea
FRASER, SIR ANGUS Independent scholar, Richmond, Surrey
FREDEMAN, WILLIAM E. Emeritus, University of British Columbia
GARDNER, PHILIP Memorial University of Newfoundland
GARLICK, BARBARA University of Queensland
GARRIOCK, JEAN B. Independent scholar, Kendal, Cumbria
GARSIDE, PETER Cardiff University
GASSON, ANDREW Independent scholar, London
GATRELL, SIMON University of Georgia
GAVIN, ADRIENNE Canterbury Christ Church University College
GILCHER, EDWIN Independent scholar, Cherry Plain, New York
GOODACRE, SELWYN H. Independent scholar, Woodville, Derbyshire
GRIFFIN, JOHN University of Southern Colorado
HALLORAN, WILLIAM F. University of Wisconsin-Milwaukee
HAMILTON, LEE T. University of Texas–Pan American
HANLEY, KEITH Lancaster University
HARRIS, MARGARET University of Sydney
HARRISSON, ELIZABETH Cambridge University Library
HAWES, DONALD University of Westminster
HERMANS, THEO University College London
HOLDER, HEIDI J. Central Michigan University
HUMPHERYS, ANNE City University of New York
HUNTER, LYNETTE University of Leeds
HUNTER, SHELAGH Independent scholar, New Haven, Connecticut
INMAN, BILLIE A. Emerita, University of Arizona
JACK, R.D.S. University of Edinburgh
JACKSON, J.R. DE J. University of Toronto
JAMES, W.L.G. Emeritus, University of Kent
JOHNSTON, JUDITH University of Western Australia
JONES, ALED University of Wales, Aberystwyth
†JONES, STANLEY University of Glasgow
JOUKOVSKY, NICHOLAS A. Pennsylvania State University
KAPLAN, JOEL University of Birmingham
KARLIN, DANIEL University College London
KAYE, HEIDI De Montfort University
KESTNER, J.A. University of Tulsa
KORSTEN, F.J.M. Nijmegen University
LAINE, MICHAEL University of Toronto
LARKIN, PETER University of Warwick

LEMIRE, EUGENE Flinders University, South Australia
LEONARD, TOM Independent scholar, Glasgow
LEWIS, DONALD M. Regent College, Vancouver
†LINTON, DAVID Independent scholar, Sevenoaks, Kent
LINSLEY, JOY L. University of St Thomas, Houston
MCCORMACK, W. J. Goldsmiths College, University of London
MCCOWN, ROBERT University of Iowa
MCCUE, KIRSTEEN Independent scholar, Stonehouse, Lanarkshire
MACK, DOUGLAS S. University of Stirling
MACKLIN, JOHN University of Leeds
MAIDMENT, BRIAN University of Huddersfield
MANDAL, ANTHONY Cardiff University
MAYER, DAVID University of Manchester
MAYS, J. C. C. University College Dublin
MEADOWS, PETER Cambridge University Library
MEYERS, TERRY L. College of William and Mary
MILBANK, ALISON University of Virginia
MILLER, GEORGE Independent scholar, Oswestry, Shropshire
MILLER, MARY RUTH Emerita, North Georgia College and State University
MITCHELL, SALLY Temple University
MULHOLLAND, JOAN University of Queensland
NATTRASS, LEONORA Nottingham Trent University
NORTH, JULIAN De Montfort University
O'BRIEN, KAREN University of Warwick
O'CONNOR, BARRY University of Newcastle, New South Wales
PARRY, ANN Staffordshire University
PEATTIE, ROGER University of Calgary
PERKINS, PAMELA University of Manitoba
PERRIN, ROBERT G. University of Tennessee
PHELAN, J. Kings College, University of London
POMARE, CARLA University 'Amedeo Avogadro', Vercelli
POTTER, ESTHER Independent scholar, London
REEDER, DAVID A. University of Leicester
RICHARDS, JEFFREY Lancaster University
RIGNALL, JOHN University of Warwick
ROBB, DAVID S. University of Dundee
ROCHE, NIGEL St Bride Printing Library, London
ROSENGARTEN, H. J. University of British Columbia
ROWELL, GEORGE Emeritus, University of Bristol
ROY, DONALD Emeritus, University of Hull
SALTER, DENIS McGill University
SAMUELS LASNER, MARK Independent scholar, Washington DC
SANDERS, VALERIE University of Sunderland
SCHLICKE, PAUL V. W. University of Aberdeen
SCHNEEWIND, J. B. Johns Hopkins University
SCHULTZ, R. BARTON University of Chicago
SCOTT, PATRICK University of South Carolina
SCOTT, ROSEMARY Independent scholar, Cambridge
SECORD, JAMES A. University of Cambridge
SENELICK, LAURENCE Tufts University
SHAFFER, ELINOR S. University of London
SHILLINGSBURG, PETER L. Mississippi State University
SIMONS, JOHN Edge Hill University College
SIRCAR, SANJAY JOHN Independent scholar, Canberra
SKILTON, DAVID Cardiff University
SLATER, MICHAEL Birkbeck College, University of London
STEDMAN, JANE W. Emerita, Roosevelt University
STEPHENS, JOHN RUSSELL University of Wales, Swansea
STEWART, CHRISTINA DUFF Emerita, University of Toronto
STIERSTORFER, K. University of Würzburg
STOREY, GRAHAM Trinity Hall, Cambridge
STOREY, MARK University of Birmingham
SWEARINGEN, ROGER G. Independent scholar, Santa Rosa, California
SWEET, NANORA L. University of Missouri, St Louis
TARR, RODGER L. Illinois State University
TASKER, MEG University of Ballarat
THESING, WILLIAM B. University of South Carolina
THOMAS, SUE La Trobe University
THOMPSON, DOREEN H. Independent scholar, Victoria, British Columbia
THOMSON, PETER University of Exeter
TIFFIN, CHRIS University of Queensland
TRELA, D. J. Roosevelt University
TWYCROSS-MARTIN, HENRIETTA Independent scholar, Cambridge
WADDINGTON, P. H. Emeritus, Victoria University of Wellington
WAWN, ANDREW University of Leeds
WEARING, J. P. Emeritus, University of Arizona
WELLENS, O. Free University of Brussels
WESTWATER, MARTHA Mount Saint Vincent University, Halifax, Nova Scotia
WHISTLER, NICHOLAS M. Independent scholar, Toronto
WIENER, JOEL H. City University of New York
WILKES, JOANNE University of Auckland
WINCH, DONALD N. University of Sussex
WOOLFORD, JOHN King's College, University of London
WORTH, G. J. University of Kansas
WU, DUNCAN University of Glasgow
YZEREEF, BARRY University of Calgary
ZINKHAN, ELAINE J. Independent scholar, Toronto

Abbreviations

Additional abbreviations are used in individual sections of the Bibliography. These are noted in full at the beginning of those sections.

Acad	Academy
addn	addition
Allibone	Allibone, S. A. Critical dictionary of English literature and British and American authors. 3 vols Philadelphia 1858, suppl 2 vols 1891
Amer	American
Amer SEER	American Slavic and East European Review
anon	anonymous
Archiv	Archiv für das Studium der Neueren Sprachen und Literaturen
AS	Anglo-Saxon
assoc	association
b.	born
BB	Bulletin of Bibliography
BC	Book Collector
Bibl	Bibliographical
BJRL	Bulletin of the John Rylands University Library of Manchester
bk	book
BL	British Library
BLCat	British Library Catalogue
BLJ	British Library Journal
Block	Block, A. The English Novel 1740–1850. A catalogue. rev edn 1961
BLR	Bodleian Library Record
BM	British Museum
BNYPL	Bulletin of New York Public Library (now BRH)
Bodleian	Bodleian Library, Oxford
Br	British
BRH	Bulletin of Research in the Humanities (formerly BNYPL)
Bull	Bulletin
c.	circa
Cambridge UL	Cambridge University Library
CBEL	Cambridge bibliography of English literature, ed. F.W. Bateson, 4 vols 1940, suppl 1957
CD-Rom	Compact disk read-only memory
cent	century
ch	chapter
CHEL	Cambridge history of English literature
Chron	Chronicle
CLB	Charles Lamb Bulletin
col	column
Coll	collection
comp	compiled
CP	Contemporary poets
CritQ	Critical Quarterly
Cz	Czechoslovakian
d.	died
DAI	Dissertation Abstracts International
dir	directed by
diss	dissertation
DLB	Dictionary of Literary Biography
DNB	Dictionary of National Biography
Du	Dutch
EA	Etudes Anglaises
E & S	Essays and Studies
ed	edited by
edn	edition
EETS	Early English Text Society
EHR	English Historical Review
EIC	Essays in Criticism
EL	Everyman's Library
ELH	ELH: A Journal of English Literary History
ELN	English Language Notes
ELR	English Literary Renaissance
ELT	English Literature in Transition
EM	English Miscellany
EML	English Men of Letters
EMS	English Manuscript Studies
Eng	English
engr	engravings
ES	English Studies (Netherlands)
ESTC	Eighteenth-century short-title catalogue
EStudien	Englische Studien
ET	electronic text
et al	and others
ETL	English theatrical literature 1559–1900 by R. W. Lowe 1888, updated by J. W. Arnott and J. W. Robinson 1970
facs	facsimile
facs (photo)	photographic facsimile
fl.	floruit
Folger	Folger Shakespeare Library
Fr	French
Ger	German
GM	Gentleman's Magazine
Halkett and Laing	Halkett, S. and J. Laing, Dictionary of anonymous and pseudonymous English literature. 9 vols Edinburgh 1926–62
Harvard	Harvard University Library
HLB	Harvard Library Bulletin
HLQ	Huntington Library Quarterly
HMC	Historical Manuscripts Commission
HMSO	Her Majesty's Stationery Office

HRHRC	Harry Ransom Humanities Research Center, University of Texas, Austin
HSNPL	Harvard Studies and Notes in Philology and Literature
HudR	Hudson Review
Huntington	Henry E. Huntington Library, San Marino, California
ibid	ibidem
IELM	Index of English literary manuscripts. Vol iv 1800–1900, comp B. Rosenbaum, P. White et al. 1982–
illus	illustrated
illustr	illustrated by
inst	institute
introd	introduction
Ital	Italian
Jap	Japanese
JEGP	Journal of English and Germanic Philology
JHI	Journal of the History of Ideas
Jnl	Journal
JPRS	Journal of Pre-Raphaelite Studies
jr	junior
Julian	Julian, J. A dictionary of hymnology. 1892, 1907 (rev)
KR	Kenyon Review
KSJ	Keats–Shelley Journal
Lang	Language
LC	Library of Congress
Lib	Library (not periodical *Library*)
Lit	Literature
LJ	London Journal
LR	Sutton, D. C. ed. Location Register of English literary manuscripts and letters: eighteenth and nineteenth centuries. 2 vols 1995. Location Register of twentieth-century English literary manuscripts and letters. 2 vols 1988.
Mag	Magazine
M & L	Music and Letters
ME	Middle English
MHRA	Modern Humanities Research Association
micro	Available on microfilm or microfiche
Miles	Miles, A. H. et al, (ed). The poets and poetry of the century. 10 vols [1891–7], 12 vols 1905–7 (enlarged)
misc	miscellany
ML	Muses' Library
MLA	Modern Language Association of America
MLN	Modern Language Notes
MLQ	Modern Language Quarterly
MLR	Modern Language Review
Mod	Modern
MP	Modern Philology
ms	manuscript
N & Q	Notes and Queries
nat	national
NCBEL	New Cambridge bibliography of English literature, ed. G. Watson and I. Willison, 5 vols 1969–77
NCTR	Nineteenth century theatre research (to 1986, then Nineteenth Century Theatre)
nd	no date
Nicoll	Nicoll, A. A history of English drama, 1800–1850. Vol iv Early nineteenth century drama. Cambridge 1930, 1955. Vol v Later English drama 1850–1900. 1959.
NLS	National Library of Scotland
NMM	New Monthly Magazine
no	number
np	no place of publication
NRA	National Register of Archives
n.s.	new series
NSTC	Nineteenth-century short-title catalogue
NYPL	New York Public Library
OBS	Oxford Bibliographical Society
OE	Old English
OHEL	Oxford history of English literature
o.s.	old series
OSA	Oxford Standard Authors
p.	page
pam	pamphlet
PBA	Proceedings of the British Academy
pbd	published
pbn	publication
PBSA	Papers of the Bibliographical Society of America
Pen	Penguin Classics or Penguin New English Library
PMLA	Publications of the Modern Language Association of America
PQ	Philological Quarterly
Princeton	Princeton University Library
priv	privately
Proc	Proceedings
prop	proprietor
pt	part
ptd	printed
Quart	Quarterly
REL	Review of English Literature
RES	Review of English Studies
rev	revised (by)
Rev	Review
RL	The Rothschild Library (mostly at Trinity College, Cambridge)
RMS	Renaissance & Modern Studies
Rogers	Rogers, C. (ed). The modern Scottish minstrel. 6 vols, Edinburgh 1855–7
Rosenbach	Rosenbach Library and Museum
Rus	Russian
rptd	reprinted
Sadleir	Sadleir, M. XIX century fiction. A bibliographical record. 2 vols 1951.
SAQ	South Atlantic Quarterly
SB	Studies in Bibliography (University of Virginia)
SDUK	Society for the Diffusion of Useful Knowledge
SE	Studies in English (University of Texas)
SEEJ	Slavic and East European Journal
SEER	Slavonic and East European Review
SEL	Studies in English Literature, 1500–1900 (Rice University)
ser	series
ShJE	Shakespeare-Jahrbuch
SHR	Southern Humanities Review
ShS	Shakespeare Survey
SiR	Studies in Romanticism
SN	Studia Neophilologica
Soc	Society
Sp	Spanish
SP	Studies in Philology
SPCK	Society for the Promotion of Christian Knowledge
SQ	Shakespeare Quarterly
STC	Short-title catalogue (1475–1640)
STS	Scottish Text Society
Stud	Studies
Summers	Montagu Summers, A gothic bibliography. 1941
suppl	supplement
Swed	Swedish
TCBS	Transactions of the Cambridge Bibliographical Society
TEBS	Transactions of the Edinburgh Bibliographical Society
ThR	Theatre Research International

ThS	Theatre Survey
TLS	Times Literary Supplement
TN	Theatre Notebook
TQ	Theatre Quarterly
tr	translated by
Trans	Transactions
trn	translation
TSLL	Texas Studies in Literature and Language
TStL	Tennessee Studies in Literature
TWC	The Wordsworth Circle
UCLA	University of California at Los Angeles
UCS	University of Colorado Studies
Univ	University
unpbd	unpublished
UTQ	University of Toronto Quarterly
var	variorum
VP	Victorian Poetry
VPN	Victorian Periodicals Newsletter
VPR	Victorian Periodicals Review
VS	Victorian Studies
vol	volume
Ward	Ward, W.S. Literary reviews in British periodicals 1789–1797. A bibliography. New York 1979. Ward, W.S. Literary reviews in British periodicals 1798–1820. A bibliography. 2 vols 1972. Ward, W.S. Literary reviews in British periodicals 1821–1826. A bibliography. 1977.
WC	World's Classics (hardback)
WCp	World's Classics paperback
WCSJ	Wilkie Collins Society Journal
Wellesley	Wellesley Index to Victorian Periodicals, ed W. E. Houghton, et al. 5 vols Toronto 1966–89
Wing	Short-title catalogue (1641–1700)
Wolff	Wolff, R. L. (ed). Nineteenth-century fiction: a bibliographical catalogue. 5 vols 1981–6
Yale	Yale University Library
YES	Yearbook of English Studies
YULG	Yale University Library Gazette
YWES	Year's Work in English Studies

US states:

Alabama	AL	Montana	MT
Alaska	AK	Nebraska	NE
Arizona	AZ	Nevada	NV
Arkansas	AR	New Hampshire	NH
California	CA	New Jersey	NJ
Colorado	CO	New Mexico	NM
Connecticut	CT	New York	NY
Delaware	DE	North Carolina	NC
District of Columbia	MD	North Dakota	ND
Florida	FL	Ohio	OH
Georgia	GA	Oklahoma	OK
Hawaii	HI	Oregon	OR
Idaho	ID	Pennsylvania	PA
Illinois	IL	Rhode Island	RI
Indiana	IN	South Carolina	SC
Iowa	IA	South Dakota	SD
Kansas	KS	Tennessee	TN
Kentucky	KY	Texas	TX
Louisiana	LA	Utah	UT
Maine	ME	Vermont	VT
Maryland	MD	Virginia	VA
Massachusetts	MA	Washington	WA
Michigan	MI	West Virginia	WV
Minnesota	MN	Wisconsin	WI
Mississippi	MS	Wyoming	WY
Missouri	MO		

Contents

v Children's books

5. DRAMA

i General introduction

ii Early nineteenth-century drama 1800–1835 1955–88

iii Mid-nineteenth-century drama 1835–1870 1988–2027

iv Late nineteenth-century drama 1870–1900 2028–76

6. PROSE

i Early nineteenth-century prose 1800–1835 2077–2210

ii Mid-nineteenth-century prose 1835–1870 2210–2306

12. TRAVEL

13. HOUSEHOLD BOOKS 2735–54

14. SPORT

15. EDUCATION

16. NEWSPAPERS AND MAGAZINES

1

Book Production and Distribution

GENERAL WORKS: *catalogues and surveys.*
BOOK PRODUCTION: *General works; Paper (Bibliographies and dictionaries, History of production, Technique and raw materials, Qualities and trade, Taxation, Directories, Periodicals); Ink; The manufacture of type (Typefounding, Type design, Stereotyping and electrotyping); Printing (General and literary works, Manuals, Business management, Composition, Type composing machinery, Printing machinery and presswork, Colour printing, Trade organisations); Graphic processes (General works, Intaglio surfaces, Planographic surfaces, Surfaces in relief); Printing Style (Aesthetic considerations, Legibility); Private printing (General works, Particular presses and societies); Printers and printing firms; Printing trade periodicals; Book illustration (General works, Illustrators); Bookbinding.*
BOOK DISTRIBUTION: *General works; Copyright; Authors' guides to publication; The practice of publishing; Individual publishers; General catalogues; Trade periodicals; Circulating libraries; Retail bookselling (General works and the Net Book Agreement, Individual firms); Antiquarian book trade (General works, Periodicals, Book auctions, Individual firms); Private book collecting; Public libraries (The British Museum, Accounts of other libraries, The Free Library movement); Librarianship (Periodicals).*

A. GENERAL WORKS

In addition to the works listed below, much information may be found in the general and special catalogues of the following international exhibitions: London 1851, 1862, 1871–4; New York 1853; Paris 1855, 1867, 1878, 1889, 1900; Vienna 1873; Philadelphia 1876; Brussels 1880, 1888, 1897; Amsterdam 1883; Antwerp 1886; Chicago 1893.

Timperley, C. H. A dictionary of printers and printing. 1839, 1842 (rev as Encyclopaedia of literary and typographical anecdote).
Hodson, W. H. Booksellers, publishers and stationers' directory for London and country. 1855.
Kelly's post office directory of stationers, printers, booksellers, publishers and papermakers of England, Scotland, Wales and Ireland. 1872, 1876, 1880, 1885, 1889, 1893, 1896, 1900.
Caxton Celebration, London 1877. Catalogue of the loan collection of antiquities, curiosities, and appliances connected with the art of printing. Ed G. Bullen 1877.
Katalog der Bibliothek des Börsenvereins der deutschen Buchhändler. 3 vols Leipzig 1885–1902.
Catalogue of the books in the library of the Typothetae of the city of New York. New York 1896.
St Bride Foundation, London. Catalogue of the technical reference library of works on printing and the allied arts [by R. A. Peddie]. 1919.
Catalogus der Bibliotheek van de (Koninklijke) Vereeniging ter Bevordering van de Belangen des Boekhandels te Amsterdam. 10 vols 's-Gravenhage [etc] 1920–97.
Leicester Free Public Libraries. Catalogue of works on printing, bookbinding, papermaking and related industries. Leicester 1927.
Berry, W. T. The St Bride typographical library. 1932.
Hart, H. Bibliotheca typographica: a list of books about books. Rochester NY 1933.
List of books on printing and the allied trades in the Bristol public libraries. Bristol 1936.
Jones, G. W. Catalogue of the well-known collection of rare and valuable books illustrating the history of printing, sold by Sotheby & Co 1936.
Winship, G. P. The literature of printing. Ch 15 of A history of the printed book, Dolphin 3 1938.
Hogben, L. T. From cave painting to comic strip. 1949.
Howe, E. Bibliotheca typographica. Signature n.s. 10 1950.
Steinberg, S. H. Five hundred years of printing. 1955, 1961, 1974 (rev by J. Moran), 1996 (rev by J. Trevitt).
Dictionary catalogue of the history of printing from the John M. Wing Foundation in the Newberry Library (Chicago). 6 vols Boston 1961; 1st suppl 3 vols Boston 1970; 2nd suppl 4 vols Boston 1981.
Myers, R. The British book trade from Caxton to the present day, a bibliographical guide. 1973.
Brenni, V. J. Book printing in Britain and America: a guide to the literature and a directory of printers. Westport CT 1983.
Schreyer, A. D. The history of books: a guide to selected resources in the Library of Congress. Washington 1987. [NAR]

B. BOOK PRODUCTION

(1) GENERAL WORKS

The sister arts: or a concise and interesting view of the nature and history of paper-making, printing and bookbinding. Lewes 1809. Attributed to J. Baxter.
British manufacturing industries. Ed G. P. Bevan. 1876, 1877, 1892.
Catalogue of machinery, models etc in the Machinery and Inventions Division of the South Kensington Museum. Pt 2 (Paper-making and printing machinery) 1897.
Heath, T. C. How books are made. [1900.]
Hitchcock, F. H. The building of a book. New York 1906, 1929.
Aldis, H. G. The printed book. Cambridge 1916, 1941 (rev J. Carter and B. Crutchley), 1951.
Jackson, H. The printing of books. 1938, 1947.
McCombs, C. F. Printing from the 16th to the 20th century. New York 1940 (NYPL).
Jennett, S. The making of books. 1951, 1956, 1964, 1967, 1973. [NAR]

(2) PAPER

Bibliographies and dictionaries

Munsell, J. A. A chronology of paper and paper-making. Albany NY 1857, 1860, 1864, 1870, 1876.

Akesson, L. Lexikon der Papier-Industrie: Deutsch-Englisch-Französisch. Lucerne 1895; Zürich 1905 (with H. Everling and M. Flückiger).

Hopkins, E. A. Taschen-Hilfsbuch unentbehrlicher Woerter des Papierfachs (Deutsch-Englisch). 1903.

Surface, H. E. Bibliography of the pulp and paper industries. Washington 1913 (USA Dept of Agriculture Forest Service Bull no 123).

Paper Makers' Association of Great Britain: Technical Section. Catalogue of the library. 1934.

Labarre, E. J. A dictionary of paper and paper-making terms. Amsterdam 1937; rev as Dictionary and encyclopaedia of paper and paper-making, Amsterdam (also Oxford) 1952; suppl by E. G. Loeber, Amsterdam 1967.

Leif, I. P. An international sourcebook of paper history. Hamden CT 1978.

History of production

Koops, M. Historical account of the substances which have been used to describe events and to convey ideas from the earliest date to the invention of paper. 1800 (anon), 1801.

Report [from the Select Committee of the House of Commons] on Mr Koops' petition respecting his invention for making paper from various refuse materials. 1801. (55). iii. 127.

Minutes of proceedings of the Committee [of the House of Lords] to whom was referred the Bill intituled An act for prolonging the term of certain Letters Patent assigned to Henry Fourdrinier and Sealy Fourdrinier for the invention of making paper by means of machines. 10 Aug 1807. (H. L. 36) H. L. iv.

Report from the Select Committee [of the House of Commons] on Fourdrinier's patent. (351) xx 35 1837. Report on re-committed Report, (405) xx 91 1837.

Society for Promoting Christian Knowledge. Useful arts and manufactures of Great Britain. 1848.

Herring, R. A lecture on the origin, manufacture and importance of paper. 1853.

Planche, G. De l'industrie de la papeterie. Paris 1853.

Tomlinson, C. Cyclopaedia of useful arts etc. [1854.]

Herring, R. Paper and paper making, ancient and modern. 1855, 1856, 1863.

Gamble, J. The origin of the machine for making endless paper, and its introduction into England. Jnl of Soc of Arts 27 Feb 1857.

Tomlinson, C. Illustrations of useful arts, manufactures and trades. [1858.]

Patent Office. Abridgments of specifications relating to the manufacture of paper, pasteboard and papier mâché [1665–1857]. 1858.

Patent Office. Abridgments of specifications [illustrated series]: class 96, paper, pasteboard and papier mâché [1855–1900 in 7 vols]. 1893–1905.

Report from the Select Committee [of the House of Commons] on Paper (export duty on rags). (467) xi 267 1861.

Richardson, W. H. On the manufacture of paper. In W. G. Armstrong, The industrial resources of the district of the three northern rivers, the Tyne, Wear and Tees, 1864 (2 edns).

Dropisch, B. Die Papiermaschine: ihre geschichtliche Entwicklung und Construction. Braunschweig 1878.

Routledge, T. [Memoir.] Minutes of Proc Institution of Civil Engineers 92 1888.

A brilliant page in the history of British paper making: Mill no 24, St Neot's. British and Colonial Printer 13 Sep 1888.

Vachon, M. Les arts et les industries du papier en France. Paris [1894].

The firm of John Dickinson & Co Ltd. 1896 (priv ptd).

The invention of the paper making machine. World's Paper Trade Rev 8 Oct 1897–7 Jan 1898.

Beadle, C. A short account of the history of papermaking. [1897.]

Robertson, J. Fifty years' experience in paper making. Newcastle upon Tyne 1897.

Southward, J. Progress in printing and the graphic arts during the Victorian era (ch 11 Paper making). 1897.

Beveridge, J. The progress of the British paper trade during the 19th century. Paper and Pulp 1 Jan 1900.

[Didot, A. F.] Le centenaire de la machine à papier continu. Paris [1900].

Campredon, E. Le papier: étude monographique sur la papeterie française. Paris 1901.

Fittica, F. B. Geschichte der Sulfitzellstoff-Fabrikation. Leipzig 1902.

Beadle, C. The development of watermarking in hand-made and machine-made papers. Jnl of Soc of Arts 18 May 1906.

Maddox, H. A. Paper: its history, sources and manufacture. [1916], [1928], [1930], 1933, 1936, 1939.

Craig, Robert & Sons. A century of papermaking 1820–1920. Edinburgh 1920.

Spalding & Hodge Ltd. Past and present 1796–1921. [1921.]

Renker, A. Das Buch vom Papier. Berlin 1929 (priv ptd); Leipzig [1934], [1936], Stuttgart 1950, Wiesbaden 1951.

Hunter, D. Papermaking through eighteen centuries. New York 1930.

Cormack, A. A. Our ancient and honourable craft 1750–1933: being an account of the rise and development of paper-making in Scotland, and at Culter, Aberdeenshire in particular. 1933.

Esparto papers. Edinburgh 1933 (Assoc of Makers of Esparto Papers); rev as Esparto paper 1956.

Carter, J. and H. G. Pollard. An enquiry into the nature of certain nineteenth century pamphlets. 1934, 1983. Ch 4.

Clapperton, R. H. Paper: an historical account of its making by hand from the earliest times down to the present day. Oxford 1934.

Clapperton, R. H. Paper and its relationship to books. 1934, 1935.

Althin, T. Carl Daniel Ekmans liv och person. Daedalus (Tekniska Museet, Stockholm) 1935.

Lloyd, L. C. Paper-making in Shropshire 1656–1912. Trans of the Shropshire Archaeological Soc 49 1938.

Albert Spicer 1847–1934: a man of his time, by one of his family. 1938.

The invention of the papermaking machine. Paper & Print 16–18 1943–5.

Hunter, D. Papermaking: the history and technique of an ancient craft. New York 1943, 1947.

Bettendorf, H. J. Paperboard and paperboard containers, a history. Chicago 1946.

Esk Mills jubilee 1898–1948. Penicuik [1948].

Edward Collins & Sons. Over 200 years of papermaking. Paper-Maker July 1949.

Paper making: a general account of its history, processes and applications. Kenley 1949 (Br Paper & Board Makers Assoc).

Shears, W. S. William Nash of St Paul's Cray: papermakers. 1950.

A brief history of British paper mills, paper mill machinery and raw material manufacturers. Paper Making & Paper Selling 70–2 1951–3.

Culter Mills Paper Co. History of Culter Paper Mills: two hundred years of progress. Aberdeen 1951.

Guard Bridge Paper Co. Guard Bridge panorama: the story of a great enterprise founded on the making of paper. Dundee 1951.

Shorter, A. H. The distribution of British paper mills in 1851. Paper-Maker June 1951.

Timaeus, C. E. A century and a half of wire weaving: the story of C. H. Johnson & Sons. 1952.

Balston, T. William Balston: paper maker 1759–1849. 1954.
Chambers, R. S. History of paper making. British Engineer n.s. 15 1954 (Inst of Br Engineers).
Evans, J. The endless web: John Dickinson and Co Ltd 1804–1954. 1955.
Within a mile of Edinburgh town: the history of Bertrams Ltd [papermaking machinery manufacturers]. Edinburgh 1955.
Balston, T. James Whatman, father and son. 1957.
Carter, H. Wolvercote Mill. Oxford 1957, 1974.
Owen, R. Lepard & Smiths Ltd 1757–1957. 1957.
Coleman, D. C. The British paper industry 1495–1860: a study in industrial growth. Oxford 1958.
East Lancashire Paper Mill Co Ltd. 1860–1960, one hundred years of progress. Derby 1960.
Samuel Jones and Co Ltd: 150 years on paper. [1960.]
International Association of Paper Historians (Basel). IPH Information. No 1, 1962–no 6, 1966; n.s. vol 1 no 1, 1977–v 24 no 4, 1990. Continued as International Paper History, vol 1 no 1, 1991– . IPH yearbook, no 1, 1980–no 8, 1990. Continued as IPH Congress Book, no 9, 1992– .
Portal, F. Portals: the church, the state and the people, leading to 250 years of papermaking. Oxford 1962.
Green, T. Yates Duxbury & Sons, papermakers of Bury. 1963.
Muir, A. The Kenyon tradition: the history of James Kenyon & Son Ltd 1664–1964 [papermakers' felt manufacturers]. Cambridge 1964.
Clapperton, R. H. The paper-making machine: its invention, evolution and development. Oxford 1967.
Ketelbey, C. D. M. Tullis Russell . . . 1809–1959. 1967.
Lewis, P. A numerical approach to the location of industry exemplified by the distribution of the papermaking industry in England and Wales from 1860 to 1965. Hull 1969.
Johnson, J. M. Peter Dixon, one hundred years of paper making 1871–1971. Grimsby 1971.
Shorter, A. H. Paper making in the British Isles. Newton Abbot 1971.
Muir, A. The British Paper and Board Makers Association 1872–1972. 1972.
Fuller, M. J. The watermills of the East Malling stream. Maidstone 1973.
Hampson, C. G. 150th anniversary history of Robert Fletcher & Son Ltd. Manchester [1973].
Henry Cooke, papermaker: a short history to celebrate his bicentenary 1773–1973. [1973.]
Gilbert, J. L. Wansford's paper mills, their history and romance. 1974.
Thomson, A. G. The paper industry in Scotland 1590–1861. Edinburgh 1974.
Weatherill, L. One hundred years of papermaking, an illustrated history of the Guard Bridge Paper Co Ltd 1873–1973. 1974.
Lyddon, D. and P. Marshall. Paper in Bolton. Altrincham 1975.
Chitty, J. Paper in Devon. Exeter 1976, 1985.
Chater, M. Family business, a history of Grosvenor Chater 1690–1977. 1977.
Waters, I. Mounton Valley paper mills, near Chepstow. Chepstow 1978.
Funnell, K. J. Snodland Paper Mill: C. Townsend Hook & Co from 1854. 1979.
Fuller, M. J. The watermills of the East Malling and Wateringbury streams. Maidstone 1980.
Reader, W. J. Bowater, a history. Cambridge 1981.
Isaac, P. C. G. Fourstones Paper Mill. Newcastle-upon-Tyne [1985].
Mandl, G. T. Three hundred years in paper. 1985.
Watson, N. The last mill on the Esk, 150 years of papermaking. Edinburgh 1987.
Crocker, A. Paper mills of the Tillingbourne. Oxshott 1988.
Hills, R. L. Papermaking in Britain 1488–1988. 1988.
British Association of Paper Historians. The Quarterly, no 1 July 1989– .
Crocker, A. and M. Kane. The diaries of James Simmons, paper maker of Haslemere 1831–1868. Oxshott 1990.
Pilkington, A. Frogmore and the first Fourdrinier: the British Paper Company 1890–1990. 1990.
Luker, B. G. Mill 364: paper making at St Cuthberts. 1991.
Schmoller, T. Sheffield papermakers. Wylam 1992.
Fedo, J. Mill on the Don. 1993.
Shorter, A. H. Studies on the history of papermaking in Britain. Aldershot 1993.
British Association of Paper Historians. Studies in British paper history. Vol 1, 1996– .

Technique and raw materials

Piette, L. Traité de la fabrication du papier. Paris 1831.
Le Normand, L. S. Manuel du fabricant de papiers. 3 vols Paris 1833–4.
Rüst, W. A. Die Papierfabrikation und die technischen Anwendungen des Papiers. (Die mechanische Technologie, Abthl. 3). Berlin 1838.
Müller, L. Die Fabrikation des Papiers. Berlin 1849, 1855, 1862, 1877.
Piette, L. Essais sur la coloration des pâtes à papier. Paris 1853; rev as Traité de la coloration des pâtes à papier. Paris 1863.
Planche, G. De l'industrie de la papeterie. Paris 1853.
Royle, J. F. The fibrous plants of India fitted for cordage, clothing and paper, with an account of the cultivation and preparation of flax, hemp and their substitutes. 1855.
Saunders, T. H. Illustrations of the British paper manufacture. 1855.
Herring, R. A letter on the collection of rags for the manufacture of paper. 1860.
Piette, L. Manuel du directeur, du contre-maître et des chefs d'ateliers de papeterie, contenant la description de moyens pratiques pour convertir le chiffon et diverses plantes en papier. 2 vols Paris 1861.
Prouteaux, A. Guide pratique de la fabrication du papier et du carton. Paris 1864, [1885]; tr as Practical guide for the manufacture of paper and boards, Philadelphia 1866.
Hofmann, C. A practical treatise on the manufacture of paper in all its branches. Philadelphia 1873; tr as Praktisches Handbuch der Papier-Fabrikation, Berlin 1875, [1886–97]; incomplete 2nd Eng edn New York and London [c. 1895].
Kerr, H. C. Report on the cultivation of, and trade in, jute in Bengal and on Indian fibres available for the manufacture of paper. Calcutta 1874.
Routledge, T. Bamboo considered as a paper-making material. 1875.
Archer, T. C. Paper. In G. P. Bevan, British manufacturing industries, 1876.
The art of paper making: a guide to the theory and practice of the manufacture of paper by the editor of the Paper Mills Directory. 1876 (2nd edn).
Arnot, W. The technology of the paper trade. 1878; rev J. M. Arnot, British and Colonial Printer 24 Dec 1891–15 Sep 1892.
The paper-makers handbook and guide to paper-making. By a practical paper-maker. 1878.
Routledge, T. Bamboo and its treatment. Sunderland 1879.
Dunbar, J. The practical paper-maker. Leith 1880, 1881, 1887.
Liotard, L. Memorandum on materials in India suitable for the manufacture of paper. Calcutta 1880.
Erfurt, J. Das Färben des Papierstoffs. Berlin [1881], 1900, 1912; tr as The dyeing of paper pulp (with additions by J. Hübner), 1901.
Industries of Maidstone: being a series of descriptive articles. Maidstone 1881. Describes the Balston paper mills, Hobb's printing office, Amies's paper moulds.
Hoyer, E. Das Papier: seine Beschaffenheit und deren Prüfung.

Munich 1882; tr Fr as Le papier, étude sur sa composition: analyses et essais, Paris 1884.
Stonhill, W. J. Paper pulp from wood, straw and other fibres in the past and the present. In Forestry and forest products: prize essays of the Edinburgh International Forestry Exhibition 1884, ed J. Rattray and H. R. Mill, Edinburgh 1885.
Wyatt, J. W. The art of making paper by the machine. [1885.]
Davis, C. T. The manufacture of paper. Philadelphia 1886.
Mierziński, S. Handbuch der praktischen Papier-Fabrikation. 3 vols Vienna 1886.
Parkinson, R. A treatise on paper. Preston 1886, Clitheroe 1887, 1896.
Cross, C. F. and E. J. Bevan. A text-book of paper-making. 1888, 1900, 1907, 1916, 1920.
Herzberg, W. Papier-Prüfung. Berlin 1888, 1902, 1907, 1915, 1921, 1927, 1932 (rev R. Korn and B. Schulze); tr as Paper testing 1892.
Watt, A. The art of paper-making. 1890.
Bennett, J. B. Paper-making processes and machinery. Edinburgh 1892.
Clapperton, G. Practical paper making. 1894, 1907; rev R. H. Clapperton 1926.
Dunbar, J. Notes on the manufacture of wood pulp and wood pulp papers. Leith 1894.
Griffin, R. B. and A. D. Little. The chemistry of paper making. New York 1894.
Andés, L. E. Papier-Specialitäten. Vienna 1896, 1922 (as Papier-Spezialitäten); tr as The treatment of paper for special purposes, 1907, 1923.
Kirchner, E. Das Papier. 3 vols Biberach 1897–1910.
Henderson, R. Paper making machinery. 1900.
MacNaughton, J. Factory book-keeping for paper mills. 1900, 1902.
Rübencamp, R. and P. Klemm. Farbe und Papier in Druckgewerbe (II. Theil, Papier). Frankfurt 1900.
USA Department of State, Bureau of Foreign Commerce. Paper in foreign countries: uses of wood pulp. Special Consular Reports vol 19, Washington 1900.
Beveridge, J. Papermakers' pocket book (tables, formulae, etc). 1901.
Hübner, J. Cantor lectures on paper manufacture. 1903.
Sindall, R. W. Paper technology. 1906, 1910, 1920.
Sindall, R. W. The manufacture of paper. 1908.
Strachan, J. The invention of wood pulp processes in Britain during the nineteenth century. Paper-Maker (annual no) 1949.

Qualities and trade

Dusautoy, J. A. The paper-maker's ready reckoner. Romsey 1805.
Murray, J. [On the bad composition of paper.] Gent Mag 93 July 1823.
Murray, J. Observations and experiments on the bad composition of modern paper. 1824.
Julia de Fontenelle, J. S. E. and P. Poisson. Manuel complet du marchand papetier et du régleur. Paris 1828, 1854; tr as Der vollkommene Papier- und Schreib-Materialien Händler. Ulm 1831.
Murray, J. Practical remarks on modern paper. Edinburgh 1829.
The stationer's handbook and guide to the paper trade. 1859, 1859, 1863, 1868, 1869, 1870, 1871, 1872, 1873, 1874, 1875, 1881, 1884 (13th edn), 1893 (17th edn).
Herring, R. A practical guide to the varieties and relative values of paper, illustrated with samples. 1860.
Haines, E. N. The paper makers' and stationers' calculator. 1862, 1880.
Olmer, G. Du papier mécanique et de ses apprêts dans les diverses impressions. Paris 1882.
Winkler, O. Der Papierkenner: ein Handbuch und Rathgeber für Papier-Käufer und Verkäufer, technische Lehranstalten etc. Leipzig 1887.
Society of Arts. Report of the committee on the deterioration of paper. 1898.
Spicer, A. D. The paper trade. 1907.

Taxation

Report from the Committee [of the House of Commons] on the booksellers and printers petition [relating to the high duties on paper]. 1802. (34). ii. 89.
Fourteenth Report of the Commissioners of inquiry into the Excise Establishment: paper. 1835. (Command [16]). xxxi. 159.
[McCulloch, J. R.] Observations illustrative of the practical operation and real effect of the duties on paper showing the expediency of their reduction or repeal. 1836.
Edwards, E. The duties on paper, advertisements and newspapers. 1849.
Knight, C. The struggles of a book against excessive taxation. [1850.]
Knight, C. The case of the authors as regards the paper duty. 1851.
The paper difficulty. Chambers's Jnl Nov 1854.
Bohn, H. G. The paper duty considered in reference to its action on the literature and trade of Great Britain. 1860–1 (3 edns).
Report of the Commissioners of Inland Revenue to the Treasury on the repeal of the duty upon paper, dated 1 March 1860. 1860. (122). xi. 215.
Newspaper and Periodical Press Association for Obtaining the Repeal of the Paper Duty. Free trade in paper. 1860.
Petter, G. W. Some objections to the repeal of the paper duty considered in reply to Mr H. G. Bohn's pamphlet. 1860.
Report from the Select Committee [of the House of Commons] on Paper (export duty on rags). 1861. (467). xi. 267.
Paper. Cornhill Mag Nov 1861.
The rag tax: the paper makers' grievance and how to redress it. 1863 (priv ptd).
Carey, H. C. The way to outdo England without fighting her: letters on the paper question [tariffs]. Philadelphia 1865.
Wrigley, T. The case of the paper makers. Bury [1865].
[Bruce, H. and D. Chalmers.] Mr Gladstone and the paper duties by two Midlothian paper makers. 1885.
Collet, C. D. History of the taxes on knowledge. 2 vols 1899, 1 vol 1933 (abridged).

Directories

There are minor changes of title in several of these directories.

List of paper mills in England, Scotland and Ireland. 1853. Rptd in Paper-Maker (annual no) 1921–2.
A new list of paper mills in the United Kingdom. [By G. T. Mickleburgh?] 1859.
The paper mills directory. Annually 1860–1941.
Craig, J. The paper makers' directory and diary, 1876. [1876.]
Directory of paper makers of the United Kingdom. Annually 1876–1968/9.
The paper mill directory of the world. Holyoke MA 1883.
Paper makers' directory of all nations. Annually 1884–1972.
The paper trade directory of Great Britain and the colonies. Annually 1886–1957.

Periodicals

There are minor changes of title in several of these periodicals.

The paper trades' news. No 1, 5 Oct 1860–no 22, 1 July 1861. Continued as The stationers', printers' and bookbinders' monthly journal, no 23, 1 Aug 1861–no 27, 1 Dec 1861. Weekly, later monthly.
The paper-makers' circular. No 1, 9 Sep 1861–no 16, 3 Dec 1862. Continued as The paper-makers' circular and rag price current, no 17, 3 Feb 1863–no 39, 1 Dec 1864. Monthly.
Macniven & Cameron's paper trade review (also The paper trade review). No 1, Nov 1862–vol 2 no 12, Dec 1864. Continued as The paper trade review n.s. vol 1 no 1, Feb 1866–vol 3 no 5, June 1868. Pbd in Edinburgh 1862–Feb 1866, then London. Monthly.
The paper makers' monthly journal. Vol 1 no 1, Feb 1863–vol 70 no 3, 15 Mar 1932. Monthly.
The paper and printing trades journal. No 1, Dec 1872–no 89, 1897.

Ed A. W. Tuer. Quarterly. Index to nos 1–32 by E. R. Pearce, Taunton 1881.
The paper makers' circular and rag merchants' and wholesale stationers' weekly gazette and price current. No 1, 19 Jan 1874–no 433, Mar 1907. Weekly, later monthly.
The paper consumers' circular. [No 1, 22 Feb 1879?]–no 2, 1 Mar 1879–no 182, 1 Dec 1882. Weekly, later monthly.
Paper making. [1881]–1 Nov 1895–Nov–Dec 1964. Monthly.
The paper trade review: new series. No 1, 17 Aug 1883–1 May 1891. Continued as World's paper trade review, 8 May 1891–25 May 1972. Weekly, later monthly. Continues a section (16 Sep 1879–2 Aug 1883) in the British and colonial printer.
The paper record. No 1, 26 Feb 1886–Sep 1895. Fortnightly, later weekly.
The paper-maker and British paper trade journal. No 1, 26 Jan 1891–May 1972. Monthly.
Stationery world and fancy goods review. No 1, 29 Jan 1892–July 1916. Monthly.
Amalgamated Society of Paper Makers: quarterly report. Dartford 1894–1918?.
The paper exchange news. Vol 1 no 1, Apr 1895–vol 2 no 1 June 1896.
Paper box maker. No 1, 7 Apr 1895. Continued as Paper box and bag maker. No 2, 26 May 1895–Aug 1958. Monthly.
Wood pulp. Vol 1 no 1, Jan 1896–vol 3 no 5, 9 May 1898. Continued as Paper and pulp, vol 3 no 1, 1 June 1898–vol 11 no 1, 1 Jan 1906. Incorporated with Paper-making. Fortnightly under first title, weekly under second.
World's pulp and paper industry. No 1, 21 Sep 1898–no 80, 2 May 1900. Weekly.
Paper and printing bits. No 1, Oct 1898–no 17, Mar–Apr 1900. Birmingham. Monthly, but irregular. [NAR]

(3) INK

See W. B. Gamble, Chemistry and manufacture of writing and printing inks: a list of references in the New York Public Lib, New York 1926.
Haldat du Lys, C. N. A. Recherches chimiques sur l'encre. Nancy 1802, Paris 1804, 1805.
Savage, W. Practical hints on decorative printing. 1822.
Hansard, T. C. Typographia (pt 2 ch 8 On printing ink). 1825.
Savage, W. On the preparation of printing ink, both black and coloured. 1832.
Champour, — de and F. Malepeyre. Nouveau manuel complet de la fabrication des encres. Paris 1856, 1875, 1895.
Underwood, J. The history and chemistry of writing, printing and copying inks. [1858.]
Patent Office. Abridgments of specifications relating to printing [and printing ink] [1617–1857]. 1859. Rptd with the suppl of 1878 as Printing patents (Printing Historical Soc) 1969.
Patent Office. Abridgments of specifications [illustrated series]: class 146, writing instruments [and printing ink]. 1855–1900 in 7 vols. 1893–1905.
Davids, Thaddeus & Co. The history of ink. New York [1860].
[Lorilleux, C.] Notice sur la fabrication des encres d'imprimerie noires et de couleur. Paris [1867].
Waldow, A. Kurzer Rathgeber für die Behandlung der Farben. Leipzig 1868, 1884 (3rd edn).
Stevens, C. P. The roller guide: a treatise on rollers and compositions. Boston 1877.
Bersch, J. Die Fabrikation der Mineral- und Lackfarben. Vienna 1878, 1893; tr as The manufacture of mineral and lake pigments. 1901.
Lehner, S. Die Tinten-Fabrikation. Vienna 1880; tr as The manufacture of ink. Philadelphia 1892; tr again as Ink manufacture. London 1902, 1914, 1926.
Goebel, T. Unsere Farbe. St Gallen 1886.
Andés, L. E. Oel- und Buchdruckfarben. Vienna 1889, 1921 (as Öl- etc); tr as Oil colours and printers' inks, 1903, 1918.
Bannan, J. Modern ink making. Inland Printer (Chicago). Apr, July, Nov 1896.
Southward, J. Progress in printing and the graphic arts during the Victorian era (ch 10 Ink manufacture). 1897.
Jennison, F. H. The manufacture of lake pigments from artificial colours. 1900, 1920.
Rübencamp, R. and P. Klemm. Farbe und Papier im Druckgewerbe. (I. Theil, Farbe). Frankfurt 1900.
Carvalho, D. N. Forty centuries of ink. New York 1904.
Mitchell, C. A. and T. C. Hepworth. Inks: their composition and manufacture. 1904, 1916, 1924.
Jacobi, C. T. Printing inks. Library ser 2 vol 7 1906.
Seymour, A. Modern printing inks. 1910.
Underwood, N. and T. V. Sullivan. The chemistry and technology of printing inks. 1915.
Burt, F. L. Printing inks; their history, composition and manufacture. Inland Printer (Chicago) Nov 1919–Feb 1920.
Wiborg, F. B. Printing Ink: a history. New York 1926.
Kriegel, H. G. Encyclopaedia of printing, lithographic inks and accessories. New York 1932.
Allen, A. S. Inks for printing. Dolphin 1 1933.
Wolfe, H. J. Manufacture of printing and lithographic inks. New York [1933], 1935; then as Printing and litho inks. 1941, 1949, 1957.
The story of printing inks. Paper & Print 21–2 1948–9.
Winstone, B. & Sons. Ink in the making [1848–1948]. 1948.
Hughes, J. H. Printing ink rollers: their history and manufacture. Paper & Print 23 1950.
Coates Bros. Seventy-five years 1877–1952. [1952.]
Archambeaud, P. L'encre au cours des âges. La France Graphique May 1955.
Mander Brothers. The history of Mander Brothers 1773–1955. [1955.]
Bloy, C. H. A history of printing ink, balls and rollers, 1440–1850. 1967.
Coates, J. B. M. A history of Coates Brothers & Company Limited 1877–1977. 1977.
Whittaker, F. G. Edward Marsden: the story of a company. 1978. [NAR]

(4) THE MANUFACTURE OF TYPE

Typefounding

Hansard, T. C. Typographia (pt 1 section 8, On type-founding). 1825.
Bower Bros. Proposals for establishing a graduated scale of sizes for the bodies of printing types. Sheffield 1841 (3rd edn).
Hansard, T. C. Treatises on printing and type-founding. Edinburgh 1841.
Henze, A. Handbuch der Schriftgiesserei und der verwandten Nebenzweige. Weimar 1844.
Mayhew, H. (ed). The type-foundry of Messrs James Marr & Co, Edinburgh and London. Shops & Companies of London 8/9 [1865?].
Bachmann, J. H. Die Schriftgiesserei. Leipzig 1867.
Gauthier, V. E. Concordance du point typographique avec la système métrique. Paris 1868, Nice 1871 (2nd edn), 1874 (6th edn), 1881 (7th edn).
Johnson, J. R. On certain improvements in the manufacture of printing types. Jnl of Soc of Arts 21 Mar 1873. *See* Printing Times Apr–May 1873.
Smalian, H. Practisches Handbuch für Buchdrucker im Verkehr mit Schriftgiessereien. Danzig 1874, Leipzig 1877.
Marder, Luse & Co. Illustrated type making with a descriptive article upon the American system of interchangeable type bodies. Chicago [1880].

Boussemaer, A. La fonderie typographique. Lille 1885.
Reed, T. B. A history of the old English letter foundries. 1887, 1952 (rev A. F. Johnson).
Bausa, V. Origines de la fonderie typographique et des machines à fondre. Paris 1893.
Fox, W. W. The printer and the typefounder: a modern view of an ancient grievance. [1897.]
Southward, J. Progress in printing and the graphic arts during the Victorian era (ch 7 Type-founding). 1897.
De Vinne, T. L. The practice of typography: a treatise on the processes of type-making, the point system, the names, sizes, styles and prices of plain printing types. New York 1900.
Smith, T. W. Autobiography. [c. 1900.] (Caslon foundry.)
Figgins, J. Type founding and printing during the nineteenth century. [1901.]
Haddon, W. The standardization and interchangeability of printing types. [1902.]
Stephenson, H. K. Type founding of to-day and the point system. 1904.
Wightman, J. H. A brief history of typefounding and the point system. 1910.
Haddon, W. John Haddon & Co's centenary booklet descriptive of the growth of the business and its present position, with personal reminiscences. [1914.]
Stephenson, Blake & Co. Ltd. The story of Sheffield and typefounding. Sheffield 1914.
Legros, L. A. and J. C. Grant. Typographical printing-surfaces: the technology and mechanism of their production. 1916.
McRae, J. F. Two centuries of typefounding: annals of the letter foundry established by William Caslon. 1920.
Burdon, C. S. One hundred years [of Pavyer and Bullen's Ltd]. 1922.
Bauer, F. Die Normung der Buchdrucklettern. Leipzig 1929.
Koch, P. The making of printing types. Dolphin 1 1933.
Howe, E. Typefounding and mechanical typesetting in the nineteenth century. Typography 2 1937.
Rollins, C. P. A brief and general discourse on type. Ch ix of A history of the printed book. Dolphin 3 1938.
Berry, W. T. and A. F. Johnson. The homes of the London typefounders. Paper & Print 19 1946. Rptd in Johnson's Selected essays (ed P. H. Muir). Amsterdam 1970.
Berry, W. T. and A. F. Johnson. British typefounders in 1851. Printing Rev 16 1951.
Bohadti, G. Die Buchdruckletter. Berlin 1954.
Musson, A. E. The London Society of Master Letter-Founders 1793–1820. Library 5th ser 10 1955.
Mosley, J. The typefoundry of Vincent Figgins 1792–1836. Motif 1 1958.
Morison, S. Talbot Baines Reed: author, bibliographer, typefounder. Cambridge 1960 (priv ptd).
Pollard, S. [A history of Stephenson, Blake & Co Ltd 1818–1959. Sheffield 1960?] Printed but not issued.
Avis, F. C. Edward Philip Prince, type punchcutter. 1967.
Stephenson, Blake & Co. Ltd. A century and a half: Stephenson, Blake 1819–1969. Sheffield [1969].
Birkbeck, J. A. Some notes on the nineteenth century typefounders' ring. Dundee 1970 (priv ptd).
Hopkins, R. L. Origin of the American point system for printers' type measurement. Terra Alta WV 1976.
Ovink, G. W. From Fournier to metric, and from lead to film [on typographic measurement]. Quaerendo 9 1979.
Paput, C. La gravure du poinçon typographique. Paris 1990.
Wilkes, W. Das Schriftgießen: von Stempelschnitt, Matrizenfertigung und Letternguß, eine Dokumentation. Darmstadt 1990.
Rehak, T. Practical typecasting. New Castle DE 1993.

Type design

Austin, R. Specimen of printing types cast at Austin's Imperial Letter-foundery. 1819. Address 'To printers'. Rptd in Berry, W. T. and A. F. Johnson. Catalogue of specimens of printing types 1665–1830. Oxford 1935, pp. 76–7. *See below.*
Capelle, P. Manuel de la typographie française. Paris 1826.
De Vinne, T. L. Historic printing types: a lecture. New York 1886 (Grolier Club).
Reed, T. B. Old and new fashions in typography. Jnl of Soc of Arts 18 Apr 1890.
De Vinne, T. L. The practice of typography: a treatise on the processes of type making, the point system, the names, sizes, styles, and prices of plain printing types. New York 1900.
Wyse, H. T. Modern type display and the use of type ornament. Edinburgh 1911.
Thibaudeau, F. La lettre de l'imprimerie. 2 vols Paris 1921.
Updike, D. B. Printing types: their history, forms and use. 2 vols Cambridge MA 1922, 1937; rptd as '3rd edn' 1962.
Bastien, A. and G. J. Freshwater. Printing types of the world. 1931.
Carter, J. and H. G. Pollard. An enquiry into the nature of certain nineteenth century pamphlets. Ch 5. 1934, 1983.
Johnson, A. F. Type designs: their history and development. 1934, 1959, 1966.
Berry, W. T. and A. F. Johnson. Catalogue of specimens of printing types by English and Scottish printers and founders 1665–1830. 1935. Suppl in Signature n.s. 16 1952. Rptd with the suppl, New York 1983.
Gray, N. XIXth century ornamented types and title-pages. 1938; rev as Nineteenth century ornamented typefaces. 1976.
Howe, E. and O. Vignettes in typefounders' specimen books 1780–1900. Signature 11 1939.
McLean, R. An examination of Egyptians. Alphabet & Image 1 1946.
Johnson, A. F. Fat faces: their history, forms and use. Alphabet & Image 5 1947. Rptd in his Selected essays (ed P. H. Muir). Amsterdam 1970.
Nowell-Smith, S. The phonotypes of Robert Bridges. Alphabet & Image 5 1947.
Johnson, A. F. Some English decorated initials. Alphabet & Image 7 1948.
Peddie, R. A. Subject index of books published up to and including 1880: new series. 1948. (List of type specimens).
Berry, W. T. and A. F. Johnson. Encyclopaedia of type faces. 1953, 1958 (with W. P. Jaspert), 1962, 1970.
Dowding, G. An introduction to the history of printing types. 1961.
Handover, P. M. Letters without serifs. Motif 6 1961.
Wolpe, B. Vincent Figgins type specimens 1801 and 1815 reproduced in facsimile. 1967.
19th-century type-specimen books, no 1: Anthony Bessemer, London 1830. Jnl of the Printing Historical Soc 5 1969.
Ovink, G. W. Nineteenth-century reactions against the didone type model. Quaerendo 1–2 1971–2.
Annenberg, M. A typographic journey through the Inland Printer 1883–1900. Baltimore 1977.
Gray, N. Slab-serif type design in England 1815–1845. Jnl of the Printing Historical Soc 15 1980–1.
Mosley, J. British type specimens before 1831: a hand-list. Oxford 1984.
Freeman, J. I. Founders' type and private founts at the Chiswick Press in the 1850s. Jnl of the Printing Historical Soc 19/20 1984–6.
Peterson, W. S. The type-designs of William Morris. Jnl of the Printing Historical Soc 19/20 1984–6.
Chambers, D. Specimen of modern printing types by Edmund Fry: a facsimile. 1986.
Twyman, M. The bold idea: the use of bold-looking types in the nineteenth century. Jnl of the Printing Historical Soc 22 1993.

Stereotyping and electrotyping

Camus, A. G. Histoire et procédés du polytypage et de la stéréotypie. Paris 1801; tr as History and processes of polytyping and stereotyping. In G. A. Kubler. Historical treatises, abstracts and papers on stereotyping. New York 1936.

Wilson, A. Arbitration between the University of Cambridge and A. Wilson. 1806.

Brightly, C. The method of founding stereotype as practised by Charles Brightly. Bungay 1809.

Wilson, A. Stereotype printing. [1811.]

Hodgson, T. An essay on the origin and progress of stereotype printing; including a description of the various processes. Newcastle 1820.

Le Gentil, J. P. G. (Comte de Paroy). Précis sur la stéréotypie. Paris 1822; tr as Abstract on stereotyping. In G. A. Kubler. Historical treatises, abstracts and papers on stereotyping. New York 1936.

Description des procédés de stéréotypage. Annales de l'industrie nationale et étrangère 12 1823.

Hansard, T. C. Typographia (pt 2 ch 16 Stereotype printing). 1825.

Chabert, L. Stéréotypie et polytypie. Paris 1829.

Westreenen van Tiellandt, W. H. Rapport sur les recherches relatives à l'invention première et à l'usage le plus ancien de l'imprimerie stéréotype. La Haye 1833. In French and Dutch; tr as Report on the researches relating to the first invention and the oldest practice of stereotype printing. In G. A. Kubler. Historical treatises, abstracts and papers on stereotyping. New York 1936.

Meyer, H. Handbuch der Stereotypie. Braunschweig 1838.

Jordan, C. J. Engraving by Galvanism. Mechanics' Mag 8 June 1839.

Spencer, T. An account of some experiments made for the purpose of ascertaining how far voltaic electricity may be usefully applied to the purpose of working in metal. Liverpool 1839.

Spencer, T. Instructions for the multiplication of works of art in metal by voltaic electricity. Glasgow 1840.

Jacobi, M. H. Die Galvanoplastik. St Petersburg 1840.

Netto, F. A. W. Anweisung zur Galvanoplastik. Quedlinburg 1840, 1841.

[Schoenberg, L.] Metallic engravings in relief for letter-press printing: being a greatly improved substitute for wood-engravings called acrography, by the inventor. 1841.

Smee, A. Elements of electro-metallurgy: or the art of working in metals by the galvanic fluid. 1841, 1843, 1851.

Palmer, E. Illustrations of electrotype, intended as an accompaniment to Smee's Elements of electro-metallurgy. 1841.

Walker, C. V. Electrotype manipulation. 1841, 1841 (3rd edn), 1843 (12th edn), 1850, 1859 (29th edn).

Zantedeschi, F. Della elettrotipia, memorie. Venice 1841.

Knobloch, M. Der Galvanismus in seiner technischen Anwendung seit dem Jahre 1840: oder Galvanoplastik. Erlangen 1842.

Kobell, F. von. Die Galvanographie. Munich 1842, 1846.

Sampson, T. Electrotint: or the art of making paintings in such a manner that copper plates and 'blocks' can be taken from them by means of voltaic electricity. 1842.

Palmer, E. Glyphography: or engraved drawing for printing at the type press after the manner of woodcuts. [1843], [c. 1845].

Dircks, H. Contribution towards a history of electro-metallurgy. Mechanics' Mag 3 Feb–23 Nov 1844.

La stéréotypie perfectionée et de son véritable inventeur [Durouchail]. Paris 1847.

Dircks, H. Jordantype, otherwise called 'electrotype', its early history: being a vindication of the claims of C. J. Jordan as the inventor of electro-metallurgy. 1852.

Martin, A. Repertorium der Galvanoplastik und Galvanostegie. 2 vols Vienna 1856.

Archimowitz, T. Neues französisches Stereotyp-Verfahren. 2 pts Karlsruhe 1856–8.

Collins, H. G. Electro-block printing, especially as applied to enlarging or reducing any printing surface or original drawing. Jnl of Soc of Arts 7 Dec 1860.

Archimowitz, T. Die Papier Stereotypie. Karlsruhe 1862.

Dircks, H. Contribution towards a history of electro-metallurgy, establishing the origin of the art. 1863.

Hering, A. Die Galvanoplastik und ihre Anwendung in der Buchdruckerkunst. Leipzig 1870, 1898 (rev by F. Meta).

Nicholson, T. Instructions for the manipulation of the Nicholson stereotype apparatus. 1874 (2nd edn).

Wilson, F. J. F. Stereotyping and electro-typing. [1880.]

Urquhart, J. W. Electro-typing. 1881.

Langbein, G. Vollständiges Handbuch der galvanischen Metall-Niederschläge (Galvanoplastik und Galvanostegie). Leipzig 1886, 1889, 1895, 1898; then as Handbuch der elektrolytischen (galvanischen) Metallniederschläge. 1903, 1906; tr as A complete treatise on the electro-deposition of metals (with additions by W. T. Brannt. Philadelphia 1891, 1894, 1898, 1902, 1905, 1909, 1913; then as Electro-deposition of metals. New York 1920, 1924.

Bouant, É. La galvanoplastie. Paris 1887, 1894.

Geymet, T. Traité de galvanoplastie et d'électrolyse. Paris 1888.

Kempe, C. Wegweiser durch die Stereotypie und Galvanoplastik. Nuremberg 1889.

Bolas, T. Cantor lectures on stereotyping. 1890.

Kempe, C. Die Papierstereotypie. Nuremberg 1891 (3rd edn), 1891, 1892 (5th edn), 1899 (8th edn), 1904 (10th edn).

Partridge, C. S. Stereotyping, the papier-mâché process. Chicago 1892.

Hart, H. Charles, Earl Stanhope and the Oxford University Press. Oxford Historical Soc Collectanea 3 1896, 1966 (ed J. Mosley; Printing Historical Soc).

Kempe, C. Die Galvanoplastik. Nuremberg 1897 (6th edn).

Partridge, C. S. Electrotyping: a practical treatise. Chicago 1899, 1908.

Practical notes on stereotyping and electrotyping (from The British Printer). 1901, 1914, 1927.

The centenary of stereotyping in England 1802–1902. Br and Colonial Printer 22–29 May 1902.

Langbein, G. and A. Friessner. Galvanoplastik und Galvanostegie. Leipzig 1904 (4th edn).

Pilsworth, E. S. Electrotyping in its relation to the graphic arts. New York 1923.

Kubler, G. A. Historical treatises, abstracts and papers on stereotyping. New York 1936.

Kubler, G. A. The era of Charles Mahon, third Earl of Stanhope, stereotyper, 1750–1825. New York 1938.

Kubler, G. A. A new history of stereotyping. New York 1941.

Turner, M. L. Andrew Wilson: Lord Stanhope's stereotype printer. Jnl of the Printing Historical Soc 9 1973/4.

Silver, R. G. Trans-Atlantic crossing: the beginning of electrotyping in America. Jnl of the Printing Historical Soc 10 1974/5. [NAR]

(5) PRINTING

General and Literary Works

See Bigmore, E. C. and C. W. H. Wyman. A bibliography of printing. 3 vols 1880–6.

See Bullen, H. L. The literature of typography. Inland Printer (Chicago) Feb 1913–Nov 1916.

See The history of printing from its beginnings to 1930: the subject catalogue of the American Type Founders Company Library in the Columbia University Libraries. 4 vols Millwood NY 1980.

See A bibliography of the history of printing in the Library of Congress. 2 vols New York 1987–90.

McCreery, J. The press: a poem. 2 pts Liverpool 1803–27, 1828.

Täubel, C. G. Allgemeines theoretisch-practisches Woerterbuch der Buchdruckerkunst und Schriftgießerey. 2 vols Vienna 1805. Täubel, C. G. Ergaenzungs-Band [suppl]. Vienna 1809.

Timperley, C. H. Songs of the press and other poems relative to printing. 1833, 1845.
Brimmer, G. The composing room: a serio-comico-satirico-poetico production-Oh!. 1835.
Savage, W. A dictionary of the art of printing. 1841.
'Parley, P.' Parley's visit to the printing office. [1843.]
Neubürger, H. Encyklopädie der Buchdruckerkunst. Leipzig 1844.
Knight, C. The old printer and the modern press. 1854.
Hodson's booksellers, publishers and stationers' directory for London and country. 1855, rptd 1972 (introd by G. Pollard).
Patent Office. Abridgments of specifications relating to printing 1617–1857. 1859. Rptd with the suppl of 1878 as Printing patents (Printing Historical Soc) 1969.
Patent Office. Abridgments of specifications [illustrated series], class 100: printing, letterpress and lithographic [1855–1900 in 7 vols]. 1893–1905. Class 101, printing other than letterpress or lithographic [1855–1900 in 7 vols]. 1893–1905.
Ringwalt, J. L. American encyclopaedia of printing. Philadelphia 1871.
Southward, J. A dictionary of typography. 1871, 1875.
Waldow, A. Die Buchdruckerkunst in ihren technischen und kaufmannischen Betriebe. 3 vols Leipzig 1874–7.
Printing, stationery, paper making and kindred trades exhibition and market. Official catalogue of exhibits. Ed L. Wolf. 1880.
Printing, stationery, paper making and kindred trades exhibition and market. 2nd annual exhibition. Official catalogue of exhibits. Ed L. Wolf. 1881.
Faulmann, C. Illustrierte Geschichte der Buchdruckerkunst. Vienna 1882.
Lorck, C. B. Handbuch der Geschichte der Buchdruckerkunst. 2 vols Leipzig 1882–3.
Printing, stationery, paper making and kindred trades exhibition and market. 3rd exhibition. Official catalogue of exhibits. Ed L. Wolf 1883.
Tuer, A. W. Quads for authors, editors and devils. 1884.
Waldow, A. Illustrierte Encyklopädie der graphischen Künste. Leipzig 1884.
Jacobi, C. T. The printers' vocabulary. 1888.
Paper, printing, stationery, publishing and fancy goods international exhibition and market. Official catalogue. Ed J. S. Morriss. 1891.
American dictionary of printing and bookmaking. New York 1894.
[Wilson, J. F.] A few personal recollections by an old printer. 1896 (priv ptd).
Jacobi, C. T. Gesta typographica: or a medley for printers and others. 1897.
Southward, J. Progress in printing and the graphic arts during the Victorian era. 1897.
Printers', paper makers', stationers', photographers', fine art publishers', bookbinders', etc. international exhibition and market. Official catalogue. 1897.
Thomson, T. Rhymes and songs for printers. Edinburgh 1897.
Plomer, H. R. A short history of English printing. 1900.
Morin, E. Dictionnaire typographique. Lyon 1903.
Maire, A. La technique du livre. Paris 1908.
The Times: printing number. 10 Sep 1912.
Peddie, R. A. An outline of the history of printing to which is added the history of printing in colours. 1917. Another edn as The history of printing together with printing in colours. 1917.
Arneudo, G. I. Dizionario esegetico, tecnico e storico per le arti grafiche. 3 vols Turin 1917–25.
Jones, I. A history of printing and printers in Wales to 1810, and of successive and related printers to 1923; also a history of printing and printers in Monmouthshire to 1923. Cardiff 1925.
Gentry, H. and D. Greenhood. Chronology of books and printing. San Francisco 1933.
Greenhood, D. and H. Gentry. Chronology of books and printing. New York 1936.
Beilenson, P. The nineteenth century: ch vii of A history of the printed book. Dolphin 3 1938.
The London school of printing and kindred trades: a survey of its inception, development and work, with a few historical notes on Stamford Street and the vicinity. 1939 (also in the School's year book 1938/9).
Fishenden, R. B. Printing and invention. Printing Rev 9 1941.
Corrigan, A. J. A printer and his world. 1944.
Smail, J. C. Printing. (Scottish enterprise ser). Edinburgh [1947].
Simon, O. English typography and the industrial age. Signature n.s. 7 1948.
Johnson, A. F. Typographia: or the printer's instructor. Penrose Annual 43 1949.
Berry, W. T. The printed word. In A century of technology 1851–1951, ed P. Dunsheath 1951.
Corrigan, A. J. 1851 prototypes of 1951 printing equipment. Paper & Print 24 1951.
Corrigan, A. J. Printing in 1851. Printing Rev 16 Autumn 1951.
Hasler, C. The official catalogues of the Great Exhibition of 1851. Penrose Annual 45 1951.
Hazell, R. C. Printing at the turn of the century [i.e. 1901]. Penrose Annual 45 1951.
Le livre anglais: trésors des collections anglaises. Paris 1951 (Bibliothèque Nationale).
Rosner, C. Printer's progress: a comparative survey of the craft of printing 1851–1951. 1951.
Watson, S. F. Early print in East Anglia: an exhibition tracing the development of printing in East Anglia from the sixteenth century to the early years of the nineteenth century. Eastbourne 1951.
Berry, W. T. Printing and related trades. In A history of technology. Vol 5 1850–1900, ed C. Singer et al. Oxford 1958.
Jennett, S. Pioneers in printing. 1958. With brief biographies of Senefelder, Koenig, Mergenthaler, Lanston.
Wallis, L. W. Technical and social progress in the nineteenth century. Print in Britain Aug 1959–Mar 1960.
Handover, P. M. Printing in London from 1476 to modern times: competitive practice and technical invention in the trade of book and Bible printing, periodical production, jobbing etc. 1960.
Printing and the mind of man, assembled at the British Museum and at Earls Court, London, 16–27 July 1963: catalogue of a display of printing mechanisms and printed materials arranged to illustrate the history of western civilization and the means of the multiplication of literary texts since the xv[th] century. 1963.
Clair, C. A history of printing in Britain. 1965.
Berry, W. T. and H. E. Poole. Annals of printing: a chronological encyclopaedia. 1966.
Day, K. (ed). Book typography 1815–1965 in Europe and the United States of America. 1966.
Carter, J. and P. H. Muir. Printing and the mind of man: a descriptive catalogue illustrating the impact of print on the evolution of western civilization during five centuries. 1967, 1983.
Clair, C. A chronology of printing. 1969.
Morgan, P. Warwickshire printers' notices 1799–1866. Oxford 1970. (Dugdale Soc).
Twyman, M. Printing 1770–1970: an illustrated history of its development and uses in England. 1970.
Chappell, W. A short history of the printed word. 1972.
Todd, W. B. A directory of printers and others in allied trades, London and vicinity, 1800–1840. 1972 (Printing Historical Soc.)
Hunt, C. J. The book trade in Northumberland and Durham to 1860: a biographical dictionary. Newcastle 1975. Suppl Newcastle 1981.
Rotherham, A. and M. Steele. A history of printing in north Staffordshire. Stoke-on-Trent 1975.

Sessions, W. K. and E. M. Printing in York from the 1490s to the present day. York 1976.
Skingsley, T. A. Technical training and education in the English printing industry. Jnl of the Printing Historical Soc 13–14 1978/9–1979/80.
Brown, P. A. H. London publishers and printers c. 1800–1870. 1982.
Copsey, T. Book distribution and printing in Suffolk 1534–1850. Ipswich 1994.

Manuals

See L. C. Wroth, Corpus typographicum: a review of English and American printers' manuals, Dolphin (New York) 2 1935.
See Gaskell, P. et al. An annotated list of printers' manuals to 1850. Jnl of the Printing Historical Soc 4 1968. Addenda. Jnl of the Printing Historical Soc 7 1971.
See Barber, G. French letterpress printing: a list of French printing manuals. 1969. (Oxford Bibl Soc).
See Boghardt, M. 'Der in der Buchdruckerei wohl unterrichtete Lehr-Junge': bibliographische Beschreibung der im deutschsprachigen Raum zwischen 1608 und 1847 erschienenen typographischen Lehrbücher. Philobiblon (Stuttgart) 27 1983.
Vinçard, B. L'art du typographe. Paris 1806, 1823.
Stower, C. The printer's grammar. 1808.
Stower, C. The compositor's and pressman's guide to the art of printing. 1808, 1812.
Täubel, C. G. Neues theoretisch-praktisches Lehrbuch der Buchdruckerkunst. 2 vols Vienna 1810.
Van Winkle, C. S. The printer's guide: or an introduction to the art of printing. New York 1818, 1827, 1836.
Flick, J. F. Handbuch der Buchdruckerkunst für angehende und praktische Buchdrucker. Berlin 1820.
Johnson, J. Typographia: or the printers' instructor. 2 vols 1824. Abridgement with some new material. 1 vol Boston 1828.
Brun, M. A. Manuel pratique et abrégé de la typographie française. Paris 1825, Brussels 1826 (piracy); tr as Kurzes practisches Handbuch der Buchdruckerkunst in Frankreich. Carlsruhe and Baden 1828.
Fournier, H. Traité de la typographie. Paris 1825, Brussels 1826 (piracy), Tours 1854, 1870 (2nd edn), 1904, 1919, 1925. Introd only tr C. E. Keymer, Gloucester 1866.
Hansard, T. C. Typographia: an historical sketch of the origin and progress of the art of printing; with practical directions for conducting every department in an office. 1825.
Partington, C. F. The printer's complete guide. 1825, [1831].
[Krebs, B.] Handbuch der Buchdruckerkunst. Frankfurt 1827.
Sherman, A. N. The printer's manual. New York 1834.
Frey, A. Manuel nouveau de typographie, imprimerie. Paris 1835, 1857 (as Nouveau manuel complet de typographie).
Hasper, W. Handbuch der Buchdruckerkunst. Carlsruhe and Baden 1835.
Adams, T. F. Typographia: or the printer's instructor. Philadelphia 1837, 1844, 1845, 1851, 1853, New York 1856, Philadelphia 1857, 1861, 1864.
Lefevre, P. T. Recueil complet d'impositions. Paris 1838, 1848, 1873, 1883.
Timperley, C. H. The printers' manual. 1838.
Holtzapffel and Co. Complete instructions for the management of Mr Cowper's parlour printing press. 1839 (2 edns); then as Printing apparatus for the use of amateurs. 1846.
Hansard, T. C. Treatises on printing and type-founding. Edinburgh 1841.
Neubürger, H. Praktisches Handbuch der Buchdruckerkunst. Leipzig 1841.
[Cleef Jz, P. M. Van.] Handboek ter beoefening der Boekdrukkunst in Nederland. 's Gravenhage 1844.
Grattan, E. The printer's companion. Philadelphia 1846.
Lefevre, P. T. Guide pratique du compositeur d'imprimerie. Paris 1855, 1873, 1880.
Pozzoli, G. Manuale di tipografia: ovvero guida practica pei combinatori di caratteri, pei torcolieri e pei legatori di libri. Milan 1861.
The printer. 1865, [c. 1880] (Houlston and Wright (later Houlston's) Industrial Lib no 31).
MacKellar, T. The American printer: a manual of typography. Philadelphia 1866 (2 edns), 1867, 1868, 1870, 1871, 1872, 1873, 1874, 1876, 1878 (rev), 1879, 1882, 1883, 1885, 1887, 1889, 1893.
Marahrens, A. Vollständiges theoretisch-praktisches Handbuch der Typographie. 2 vols Leipzig 1869–70, Kiel 1891.
Lefevre, P. T. Guide pratique du compositeur d'imprimerie. Deuxième partie [on presswork]. Paris 1872, 1878.
Morton, C. The art of printing simplified for the use of amateurs: the cosmopolitan amateur printing office guide. [1873.]
Pozzoli, G. Nuovo manuale di tipografia. Milano 1873, 1882.
Bachmann, J. F. Neues Handbuch der Buchdruckerkunst. Weimar 1876.
Gould, J. The letterpress printer: a complete guide to the art of printing. 1876, [1881], [1884], [1888], [1893], [1903].
Raynor, P. E. Printing for amateurs: a practical guide. [1876.]
Fischer, H. Anleitung zum Accidenzsatz. Leipzig 1877, 1893.
Trueman, H. P. The eclectic hand-book of printing. 1880 (2nd edn).
Southward, J. Practical printing: a handbook of the art of typography. 1882, 1884, 1887, 1892 (rev A. Powell), 1900, 1911 (rev G. Joyner).
Lefevre, P. T. Guide pratique du compositeur et de l'imprimeur typographes. Paris 1883.
Laynaud, L. Guide pratique de l'imposeur. Tournon-sur-Rhône 1884, 1885, Montélimar 1890.
Jacobi, C. T. The printers' handbook of trade recipes, hints and suggestions. 1887, 1891, 1905.
Bishop, H. G. The practical printer. Albany 1889, Oneonta NY 1891, 1895, 1903.
Jacobi, C. T. Printing: a practical treatise. 1890, 1898, 1904, 1908, 1913, 1917.
O'Brien, M. B. A manual for authors, printers and publishers. 1890.
Oldfield, A. A practical manual of typography. [1890], 1898, [1906].
Dumont, J. Vade-mecum du typographe. Brussels 1891, 1894, 1906.
Sala, C. Manuale pratico di tipografia. 2 vols Milan 1894.
Fisher, T. The elements of letterpress printing, composing and proof reading. Madras 1895, 1906.
Southward, J. Modern printing: a handbook of the principles and practice of typography and the auxiliary arts. 4 pts 1898–1900 (reissue 1 vol 1900), 4 pts 1904–7, 2 vols 1912–13 (rev H. Whetton), 1922, 1924–5, 1933–6, 1950–4, 1954 (8th edn vol 1 only).

Business management

Rhynd, M. Rhynd's printers' guide: being a new and correct list of master printers in London. 1804 (3rd edn).
Magrath, W. The printer's assistant. 1804, 1805.
[Mason, W.] The printer's assistant. 1810, 1812, 1814, 1821, 1823.
Stower, C. The printer's price book. 1814.
Rose, P. and J. Evans. The printer's job price book. Bristol 1814, 1824.
[Mason, W.] The printer's price book for job work in general. 1816, 1820.
Cowie, G. Cowie's printer's pocket-book and manual. 4 edns from [c. 1835] to [c. 1850], then 1866.
Day, W. J. A series of tables invented and arranged for the use of the practical printer. 1841.
Houghton, T. S. The printers' practical every-day book. Preston 1841, London 1842, 1843, 1849, Preston [1856], [1857] (rev), [1875] (rev G. Marshall).
Feeny, R. Master printer's price manual. 1845.
Howitt, F. E. The country printer's job price book. [1849] (2nd edn).

Fielding, D. The typographical ready reckoner and memorandum book. [1853], [1858].
Cobbett, T. G. The master printer's handbook of prices. Birkenhead 1860.
Ruse, G. and C. Straker. Printing and its accessories: a comprehensive book of charges for the guidance of letter-press and lithographic printers, engravers and bookbinders. [c. 1860.]
Crisp, W. F. The printer's business guide. Great Yarmouth 1866, 1868, London [1869]; then as The printers', lithographers', engravers' and bookbinders' business guide. [1873]; then as The printers', lithographers', engravers', bookbinders' and stationers' business guide. [1874], [1876]; then as Crisp's business guide for printers, lithographers, engravers, bookbinders, rulers, stationers, etc. [1881.]
[Lawton, J. W.] The printers' pocket companion. Rochdale [1870].
Bidwell, G. H. The prompt computer: for the use of book, newspaper and job printers. New York [1875].
Ellis, J. B. and W. Denton. The printers' calculator and practical companion. Leeds 1876.
[Clark, J. T.] Price lists of letterpress job printing. Stalybridge 1881, 1885 (4th edn), 1889, 1890 (6th edn).
Manning, J. The printers' vade-mecum and ready reference. Aberdeen 1881.
Ellis, J. B. Hints and tables for the printing office and paper warehouse. Leeds [1887], [c. 1890].
Rowell, G. F. How to start a printing office. 1897.
Rowell, G. F. Hints on estimating. 1897, 1901.
Gotts, J. B. Estimating, book-keeping, system for letterpress and lithographic printers, binders and stationers. 1901.
Whitehead, T. L. The ideal price list, estimate guide and cost book for commercial letterpress printing. Bury 1901.
Lakin-Smith, H. Printers' accounts. 1903, 1916.
Federation of Master Printers. Profit for printers: or what is 'cost'? 1904, 1907, 1909.
Naylor, T. E. How to start in business as a printer. [1905.]

Composition

Stower, C. Typographical marks used in correcting proofs. 1805, 1806, 1822.
Wilson, J. A treatise on grammatical punctuation. Manchester 1844; then as A treatise on English punctuation. Boston 1850, 1855. Edns 4–32, 1855–99, are reprints of 3rd edn.
Graham, J. The compositor's text book: or instructions in the elements of the art of printing. Glasgow 1848.
F[ord], T. The compositor's handbook. 1854.
Wilson, W. The compositor's assistant containing all the imposition tables now in use. Exeter 1855.
Beadnell, H. A guide to typography. 2 vols 1859–61.
Ruse, G. Imposition simplified. [1860], [1875].
Bidwell, G. H. Treatise on the imposition of forms. New York 1865; then as The printer's new hand-book: a treatise on the imposition of forms. New York [1875].
Goebel, T. Ueber den Satz des Englischen. Leipzig 1865.
Neill & Co. Guide to authors in correcting the press. Edinburgh [c. 1870], [c. 1880], 1895, 1897.
Newman, E. The author's guide for printing. 1875.
Gould, J. The compositor's guide and pocket book. 1878.
[Blades, W.] How to correct printers' proofs. [1883], [1893].
Jowett, H. Hints to authors: being a handy book of reference in all matters referring to printing. 1889 (3rd edn).
Fletcher, W. C. A simple guide to the art of punctuation for authors and printers. Oxford [c. 1890].
Hart, H. Rules for compositors and readers employed at the Clarendon Press, Oxford. Oxford 1893, 1894, 1895 (2 edns), 1896, 1897, 1898, 1899 (2 edns), 1901 (2 edns), 1902 (2 edns), 1903; then as Rules for compositors and readers at the University Press, Oxford. 1904 (4 edns), 1905, 1907, 1909, 1912, 1914, 1918, 1921 (2 edns), 1925, 1928, 1930, 1936, 1938, 1943, 1946, 1948, 1950, 1952; then as Hart's Rules for compositors and readers at the University Press, Oxford 1967, 1978, 1983.
Mitchell, J. Printers' blunders: their causes, effects and cure. Edinburgh 1894.
Teall, F. H. Punctuation: with chapters on hyphenization, capitalization and spelling. New York 1898.
Teall, F. H. Proof-reading: a series of essays for readers and their employers. Chicago 1899.
De Vinne, T. L. The practice of typography: correct composition. New York 1901.
Collins, F. H. Author and printer. 1905 (2 edns); then as Authors' and printers' dictionary. 1909, 1912 (rev H. Hart), 1921, 1928, 1933, 1938, 1946, 1956, 1973 (rev S. Beale).
Brossard, L. E. Le correcteur typographe: essai historique, documentaire et technique. Tours 1924.
Pryor, L. A. The history of the California job type case. Jnl of the Printing Historical Soc 7 1971.
Speckter, M. K. Disquisition on the composing stick. New York 1971.
Rumble, W. A time of giants: speed composition in nineteenth-century America. Printing History no 28 1992.

Type composing machinery

Gaubert, E. R. Rénovation de l'imprimerie: notice sur la gérotype, ou machine à distribuer et à composer en typographie. Paris 1843.
Bradbury, H. Hattersley's type-composing machine. Jnl of the Soc of Arts 13 May 1859.
Mitchell, W. H. Type-setting by machinery. 1863.
Yeaton, C. C. Manual of the Alden typesetting and distributing machine. New York 1865.
Brown, O. L. Types: a description of Brown's patent type setting and distributing machinery. Boston 1870.
Mackie, A. Mackie's type-composing machine. Engineering 12 May 1871.
Fraser, A. On type-setting machines with description of Fraser's patent composing and distributing machines. Trans of the Royal Scottish Soc of Arts 9 pt 3 Edinburgh 1876.
Marchal, J. Rapport sur la machine à composer de M. Kastenbein. [Nancy 1878.]
Barnes, W. C., J. W. McCann and A. Duguid. A collation of facts relative to fast typesetting. New York 1887.
Southward, J. The 'Thorne' combined type-setting & distributing machine. 1890. Rptd from the Printers' Register 6 Apr 1890.
Southward, J. Type-composing machines of the past, the present and the future. 1890, Leicester 1891.
Linotype Co Ltd. The Linotype composing machine. 1891, 1896, [1897].
Report to the American Newspaper Publishers' Association by the committee in charge of the type composition machine tournament held in Chicago Ill, October 12–17 1891. New Haven 1892.
Linotype Co Ltd. The Linotype: its history, construction and operation. [1893] (2 edns).
Southward, J. Machines for composing letterpress printing surfaces. Jnl of the Soc of Arts 20 Dec 1895.
Lanston Monotype Machine Co. The Lanston Monotype machine. Washington 1896.
An inquiry into the claims of the Lanston Monotype machine. Manchester 1897.
Steevens, G. W. The Monotype. New Rev Nov 1897.
A revolution in printing: the story of the Linotype. Chambers's Jnl 30 Jan 1897.
Evans, F. The Linotype: its mechanical details and their adjustment. [Kansas City] 1897.
Linotype Co Ltd. The solution of a problem of four centuries: the evolution of the Linotype composing machine. [1897.]

Southward, J. The Lanston Monotype machine. [1897.]
Barclay, E. J. The Linotype operator's companion. Cincinnati 1898.
Biography of Ottmar Mergenthaler and history of the Linotype. Baltimore 1898; New Castle DE 1989 (ed C. Schlesinger).
Wicks Rotary Type-Casting Co. The Wicks type setter. 1898.
Herrmann, C. Geschichte der Setzmachine und ihre Entwickelung. Vienna [1900].
The Lanston Monotype Corporation Ltd. The Lanston Monotype machine. 1901.
Card, H. C. The Lanston Monotype keyboard: its care and adjustment. 1902.
Thompson, J. S. The mechanism of the Linotype. Chicago 1902, 1905.
Thompson, J. S. History of composing machines: a complete record of the art of composing type by machinery. Chicago 1904.
De Vinne, T. L. The practice of typography: modern methods of book composition. New York 1904.
Conrardy, G. Une étude sur la machine à composer. Brussels 1904 (Fédération Typographique Belge).
Thompson, J. S. The origin and development of the Linotype. Inland Printer (Chicago) Aug 1905.
Legros, L. A. Typecasting and composing machines. Proc of the Institution of Mechanical Engineers Dec 1908.
Giraud, H. Nouveau manuel complet de linotypie. Paris 1909.
Blevins, A. E. The evolution of printing and typesetting machines. Jnl of the South African Institution of Engineers Mar 1912 (discussion in Apr 1912 issue).
Legros, L. A. and J. C. Grant. Typographical printing-surfaces: the technology and mechanism of their production. 1916.
Bullen, H. L. Linn Boyd Benton – the man and his work. Inland Printer (Chicago) Oct 1922.
Elliott, R. C. The 'Monotype' from infancy to maturity. Monotype Recorder Jan/Feb 1932.
Dreier, T. The power of print – and men: commemorating the 50 years of Linotype's contribution to printing and publishing. New York 1936.
Monotype Corporation Ltd: forty historic years and what they brought about in the composing room. Monotype Recorder Dec 1937.
'Morris, C.' The Hooker composing machine. Printing Rev Summer 1949.
Monotype Corporation Ltd. The pioneer days of 'Monotype' composing machines. Monotype Recorder Autumn 1949.
Sherman, F. M. The genesis of machine typesetting. Chicago 1950.
Scully, M. Mergenthaler and his Linotype machine. Amer Printer Feb 1953.
Ottmar Mergenthaler: the part he played in the development of the Linotype. L. & M. News Feb/Mar 1954. (Linotype and Machinery Ltd).
Moran, J. The composition of reading matter: a history from case to computer. 1965.
Moran, J. An assessment of Mackie's steam type-composing machine. Jnl of the Printing Historical Soc 1 1965.
Huss, R. E. The development of printers' mechanical typesetting methods 1822–1925. Charlottesville VA 1973 (Bibl Soc of the Univ of Virginia).
Huss, R. E. Dr Church's 'Hoax'. Lancaster PA 1976. (The first typesetting machine.)
Preece, D. A. Social aspects and effects of composing machine adoption in the British printing industry. Jnl of the Printing Historical Soc 18 1984.
Randle, J. The development of the Monotype machine. Matrix 4 1984.
Huss, R. E. The printer's composition matrix: a history. New Castle DE 1985.
Romano, F. J. Machine writing and typesetting: the story of Sholes and Mergenthaler and the invention of the Linotype. Salem NH 1986.
Wallis, L. W. A concise chronology of typesetting developments 1886–1986. 1988 (Wynkyn de Worde Soc).

Printing machinery and presswork

Giroudot, —. Notice sur les presses mécaniques et celles à la Stanhope. Paris [1835].
Bauer, A. F. The first printing machines constructed in London up to the year 1818 by Friedrich Koenig and Andreas Friedrich Bauer. Leipzig 1851. In German and English; rptd in A. F. Bauer 1783 bis 1860. Würzburg 1960.
Read, J. M. Instructions in the art of making-ready woodcuts. Reading [c. 1860].
Wittig, C. F. and C. F. Fischer. Die Schnellpresse: ihre Mechanik und Vorrichtung zum Druck aller typographischen Arbeiten. Leipzig 1861, 1866, 1878.
Mayhew, H. (ed). Conisbee's printing machine manufactory. Shops & Companies of London 8/9 [1865?].
Eisenmann, A. Die Schnellpresse: ihre Construction, Zusammenstellung und Behandlung. Leipzig 1865, 1872.
Waldow, A. Die Zurichtung und der Druck von Illustrationen. Leipzig 1867, 1879.
Myers, J. A few practical hints to printers on the treatment of rollers. 1871.
The Walter Press: descriptive and historical account. Edinburgh 1872.
Waldow, A. Die Schnellpresse und ihre Behandlung vor und bei dem Drucke. Leipzig 1872.
Monet, A. L. Le conducteur de machines typographiques. Paris 1872; then as Les machines et appareils typographiques en France et à l'étranger suivi des procédés d'impression. 1878; then as Machines typographiques et procédés d'impression. 1898.
Bachmann, J. H. Der Buchdrucker an der Handpresse. Leipzig [1873].
Cummins, R. The pressmen's guide. Brooklyn 1873.
Rigg, A. On type-printing machinery and suggestions thereon. Jnl of the Soc of Arts 13 Feb 1874.
Goebel, T. Friederich König und die Erfindung der Schnellpresse. Braunschweig 1875.
The Walter Press: reprints of descriptions. London 1876.
[Gaskill, J.] The printing-machine manager's complete practical handbook, by an old machine manager. 1877, [c. 1880], [1888].
Stevens, C. P. The roller guide: a treatise on rollers and compositions. Boston 1877.
Thompson, J. R. Printers' rollers: how to treat them. Leeds 1880.
Wilson, F. J. F. Typographic printing machines and machine printing. [1880], [1882], [1884], [1886].
[Wyman, C. W. H.] List of technical terms relating to printing machinery. 1882.
Goebel, T. Friedrich Koenig und die Erfindung der Schnellpresse: ein biographisches Denkmal. Stuttgart 1883, 1906, Würzburg 1956; tr as Frédéric König et l'invention de la presse mécanique. Paris 1885.
Noble, F. Difficulties in machine printing, and how to overcome them. 1883.
McNamara, S. The printing press. Inland Printer (Chicago) June 1884–June 1886; continued by another hand until June 1887.
Clowes, E. A. Printing machinery. Minutes of Proc Inst Civil Engineers 89 1887.
Waldow, A. Hilfsbuch für Maschinenmeister an Buchdruck-Cylinder-Schnellpressen. 3 vols Leipzig 1887–92.
Southward, J. The principles and progress of printing machinery. [1888], 1890.
Wilson, F. J. F. and D. Grey. A practical treatise upon modern printing machinery and letterpress printing. 1888.

Motteroz, C. Essai sur la mise en train typographique. Paris 1891; tr as Essay on typographical make-ready. Inland Printer (Chicago) Dec 1891–Jan 1893.
Patent Office Studies [on printing machinery]. British & Colonial Printer 3 Aug 1893–12 Apr 1894.
Powrie, W. Machinery for book and general printing. 1899.
Hoe, R. A short history of the printing press and of the improvements in printing machinery from the time of Gutenberg up to the present day. New York 1902.
Thomas, F. W. A concise manual of platen presswork. Chicago 1903.
Beschreibung des Modells der ersten von Friederich Koenig erfundenen Schnellpresse aus dem Jahre 1811. Würzburg [1908].
Haag, A. Über maschinelle Einrichtungen und Arbeitsmethoden in englischen Buchdruckereien. [Vienna 1910.]
Powell, D. T. The inking of the forme. Imprint July 1913.
Dieterichs, K. Die Buchdruckpresse von Johannes Gutenberg bis Friedrich König. Mainz 1930 (Gutenberg Gesellschaft).
Isaacs, G. A. The story of the newspaper printing press. 1931.
Burke, J. Prelum to Albion: a history of the development of the hand press from Gutenberg to Morris. San Francisco 1940.
Green, R. The iron hand press in America. Rowayton CT 1948.
Otley's 100 years' service to the printing industry. Paper & Print Winter 1949. (On Dawson, Payne & Elliott Ltd; The Bremner Machine Co Ltd; Waite & Saville Ltd.)
Liveing, E. The house of Harrild 1801–1948. 1949.
Kainen, J. George Clymer and the Columbian Press. New York 1950.
Neipp, L. Les machines à imprimer depuis Gutenberg. Paris 1951.
Berry, W. T. The autobiography of a wooden press. Typographica 8 1953.
Green, R. A history of the platen jobber. Chicago 1953.
Bisset, C. D. A short history of platen presses. Print in Britain Mar 1954.
Berry, W. T. Augustus Applegath: some notes and references. Jnl of the Printing Historical Soc 2 1966.
Stone, R. The Albion press. Jnl of the Printing Historical Soc 3 1967.
Twyman, M. The lithographic hand press 1796–1850. Jnl of the Printing Historical Soc 3 1967.
Allen, L. M. Printing with the handpress. Kentfield CA, 1969 (priv ptd), New York 1969.
Moran, J. The Columbian press. Jnl of the Printing Historical Soc 5 1969.
Silver, R. G. An early time-sharing project: the introduction of the Napier press in America. Jnl of the Printing Historical Soc 7 1971.
Tucker, S. D. History of R. Hoe & Co, 1834–1885 (ed R. G. Silver). Proc of the Amer Antiquarian Soc Oct 1972.
Moran, J. Printing presses: history and development from the fifteenth century to modern times. 1973.
Sterne, H. E. Catalogue of nineteenth century printing presses. Cincinnati 1978.
Comparato, F. E. 'Old Thunderer's' American lightning: machinework and machinations in furnishing the first Hoe rotaries to The Times, 1856–60. Jnl of the Printing Historical Soc 13 1978/9.
Comparato, F. E. Chronicles of genius and folly: R. Hoe & Co and the printing press as a service to democracy. Culver City CA 1979.
Silver, R. G. The autobiography of Stephen P. Ruggles. Printing History no 1 1979. (Inventor of printing presses.)
Logan, H. C. The American hand press, its origin, development and use. Whittier CA 1980.
Saxe, S. O. A brief history of Golding & Co. Printing History no 6 1981. (Printers' suppliers.)
Silver, R. G. The power of the press: hand, horse, water and steam. Printing History no 9 1983.
Brewer, R. Friedheim: a century of service 1884–1984. [1984.] (Printing machinery agents.)
Wood, P. Otley and the Wharfedale printing machine. Matrix 4 1984.
Harris, E. Press-builders in Philadelphia 1776–1850. Printing History no 22 1989.
Saxe, S. O. American iron hand presses. Council Bluffs IA 1991 (priv ptd); New Castle DE 1992.
175 years Koenig & Bauer. Würzburg 1992.

Colour printing

All methods of colour printing involve separate impressions for each colour used, irrespective of the process by which the printing surface has been made. The only exceptions to this are hand colouring of the plate for each impression, Congreve's patent for interlocking blocks separately inked (c. 1830), and Stenochromy (c. 1875); the last two were never successfully applied to book illustration. This section therefore covers the application of colour to all printing processes including chromolithography. Information on coloured inks is given in some of the books already mentioned cols 9–10, above; historical works not concerned with technique appear in col 40, below; and some further details will be found in the biographies of George Baxter *and* Francis Orpen Morris, *cols 44, 60, below.*

Savage, W. Practical hints on decorative printing. 1822.
The pictorial album: or cabinet of paintings for 1837. Preface.
Chevreul, M. E. De la loi du contraste simultané des couleurs. 2 vols Paris 1839, 1 vol 1889; tr as The principles of harmony and contrast of colours and their application to the arts (tr C. Martel [i.e. T. Delf]). London 1854, 1855, 1859. Also as The laws of contrast of colour (tr by J. Spanton). London 1857, 1858, 1861.
Netto, F. A. W. Das Geheimniss des Oelbilder-Drucks erfunden vom Maler Liepmann in Berlin. Quedlinburg 1840.
Liepmann, J. Der Oelgemälde-Druck erfunden und beschrieben. Berlin 1842.
Rotch, B. Hullmandel's lithotint process. Trans Soc of Arts 54 1843.
Weishaupt, H. Theoretisch-praktische Anleitung zur Chromolithographie. Quedlinburg 1848.
Digeon, R. H. Des cercles chromatiques de M. E. Chevreul reproduits au moyen de la chromo-calcographie, gravure et impression en taille-douce combinées. Paris 1855.
Maxwell, J. C. On the theory of compound colours and the relations of the colours of the spectrum. Philosophical Trans of Royal Soc 150 1860.
Chevreul, M. E. Des couleurs et de leurs applications aux arts industriels. Paris 1864.
Ihm, B. A. Die bunten Farben in der Buchdruckerei. Biel 1865, Vienna 1874.
Nature and art. No 1, June 1866–no 13, June 1867. Continued as The Chromolithograph no 1, 23 Nov 1867–no 51, 20 Mar 1869. Monthly under first title, then weekly.
Zenker, W. Lehrbuch der Photochromie. Berlin 1868.
Ducos du Hauron, L. Les couleurs en photographie. Paris 1869.
Watt, P. B. A few hints on colour and printing in colours. 1872.
[Simpson, W.] A glance at the history of chromo-lithography. Lithographer Aug 1873.
Meyerstein, E. Stenochromy: a new process for printing a number of colours at the same time. Jnl of the Soc of Arts 15 Dec 1876.
Saint-Victor, P. de. La photochromie. Paris 1876.
Ducos du Hauron, L. Traité pratique de photographie des couleurs. Paris 1878.
Weissenbach, H. von. Der xylographische Farbendruck in den verschiedenen Phasen seiner Herstellung. Nuremberg 1878 (priv ptd).
Noble, F. The principles and practice of colour printing. 1881.
Wohlfarth, A. Über Farben. Leipzig 1882 (2nd edn).
Achaintre, A. Étude sur les impressions en couleurs. Paris [1883].
Audsley, G. A. The art of chromolithography. 1883.
Waldow, A. Anleitung zum Farbendruck auf der Buchdruckpresse und Maschine. Leipzig [1883].
Die Heliochromie: das Problem des Photographirens in natürlichen Farben. Düsseldorf 1884.
Meta, O. Der Steindrucker an der Schnellpresse nebst einer

Abhandlung über die Farben in der Chromolithographie. Vienna 1884.
Richmond, W. D. Colour and colour printing as applied to lithography. [1885.]
Reich, W. Die Farbenmischung für Druckereien: Steindruck, Buchdruck, Lichtdruck. Berlin 1887.
Berget, A. Photographie des couleurs par la méthode interférentielle de M. Lippmann. Paris 1891, 1901.
Earhart, J. F. The color printer: a treatise on the use of colors in typographic printing. Cincinnati 1892.
Ives, F. E. Hand-book to the photochromoscope. 1894.
Morin, E. Essai sur les impressions en couleurs. Paris 1894; then as Les impressions en couleurs. Paris 1899.
Berthier, A. Manuel de photochromie interférentielle: procédés de reproduction directe des couleurs. Paris 1895.
Hesse, F. Die Chromolithographie mit besonderer Berücksichtigung der modernen auf photographischer Grundlage beruhenden Verfahren. Halle 1896, [1904–6]; tr as La chromolithographie et la photochromolithographie. Paris 1897.
Zander, C. G. Photo-trichromatic printing in theory and practice. Leicester [1896].
Ducos du Hauron, A. La triplice photographique des couleurs et l'imprimerie. Paris 1897.
Hübl, A. F. von. Die Dreifarbenphotographie mit besonderer Berücksichtigung des Dreifarbendruckes und der photographischen Pigmentbilder in natürlichen Farben. Halle 1897, 1902, 1912, 1921; tr as Three-colour photography, three-colour printing. London 1904, 1915.
Vidal, L. Photographie des couleurs. Paris 1897.
Mellerio, A. La lithographie originale en couleurs. Paris 1898.
Clerc, L. P. La photographie des couleurs. Paris [1899].
Ducos du Hauron, A. La photographie des couleurs et les découvertes de Louis Ducos de Hauron. Paris [1899].
Bolas, T., A. A. K. Tallent and E. Senior. A handbook of photography in colours. 1900.
Vaughan, W. E. Autobiographica, with a gossip of the art of printing in colours. [Brighton] 1900 (priv ptd).
Ives, F. E. The progress of three-colour work. Penrose's Pictorial Annual 7 1901.
Horgan, S. H. Three-colour process work. In H. Jenkins, A manual of photoengraving. 2nd edn. Chicago 1902.
Ives, F. E. The half-tone and trichromatic process theories. In H. Jenkins, A manual of photoengraving. 2nd edn. Chicago 1902.
Shepherd, S. & Co. Photography in natural colours. 1902.
Dalziel, H. Three-colour printing. Jnl of the Soc of Arts 20 Feb 1903.
Soullier, E. Nouveau traité sur les impressions modernes en couleurs. Paris 1903.
Vidal, L. Traité pratique de photochromie. Paris 1903.
Klein, H. O. Collodion emulsion and its applications to various photographic and photo-mechanical purposes, with special reference to trichromatic process work. 1905; then as The applications of collodion emulsion to three-colour photography, process work [etc.]. 1910.
Hardie, M. English coloured books. 1906.
Calmels, H. and L. P. Clerc. La reproduction photographique des couleurs. Paris [1907].
Wallon, E. La photographie des couleurs et les plaques autochromes, conférence faite devant la Société française de photographie, suivie d'une notice sur le mode d'emploi des plaques autochromes, par MM Lumière. Paris 1907.
Goldberg, E. Farbenphotographie und Farbendruck. Leipzig 1908.
Hübl, A. F. von. Die Theorie und Praxis der Farbenphotographie mit Autochromplatten. Halle 1908, 1909, 1912, 1916, 1921, 1933.
Paton, H. Colour etching. 1909.
Preissig, V. Zur Technik der farbigen Radierung und des Farbenkupferstichs. Leipzig 1909.
Prideaux, S. T. Aquatint engraving: a chapter in the history of book illustration. 1909.
Burch, R. M. Colour printing and colour printers. 1910.
Andrews, E. C. Colour and its application to printing. Chicago 1911.
Martin, L. C. Colour and methods of colour reproduction, with chapters on colour printing and colour photography by W. Gamble. 1923.
Wall, E. J. The history of three-color photography. Boston 1925.
Lewis, C. T. C. The story of picture printing in England during the nineteenth century. [1928.]
Johnson, A. F. Rudolph Ackermann and Thomas Rowlandson. Penrose Annual 37 1935.
Sexton, T. A. F. A century of colour printing. In F. R. Higgins. Progress in Irish printing. Dublin 1936.
Gray, N. The nineteenth-century chromo-lithograph. Architectural Rev 84 1938.
Tritton, F. J. A survey of colour photography. Photographic Jnl 79 1939.
Heintzelman, A. W. Early English color prints. More Books (Bull Boston Public Lib) 17 1942.
Friedman, J. S. History of color photography. Boston 1944, London 1968.
Cordingley, J. Early colour printing and George Baxter 1804–67: a monograph produced in the printing dept of the North-Western Polytechnic. 1949.
Hasler, C. Mid-nineteenth-century colour printing. Penrose Annual 45 1951.
Groschwitz, G. von. The significance of xix century color lithography. Gazette des Beaux-Arts 44 1954.
Tooley, R. V. English books with coloured plates 1790–1860. 1954.
McLean, R. Victorian book design and colour printing. 1963, 1972.
Twyman, M. The tinted lithograph. Jnl of the Printing Historical Soc 1 1965.
Wakeman, G. and G. D. R. Bridson. A guide to nineteenth century colour printers. Loughborough 1975.
Wakeman, G. The production of nineteenth century colour illustration. Loughborough 1976 (priv ptd).
Cate, P. D. and S. H. Hitchings. The color revolution: color lithography in France 1890–1900. Santa Barbara and Salt Lake City 1978.
Friedman, J. M. Color printing in England 1486–1870. New Haven CT 1978 (Yale Center for Br Art).
Wakeman, G. Victorian colour printing. Loughborough 1981.
Gascoigne, B. The earliest English chromolithographs. Jnl of the Printing Historical Soc 17 1982/3.
Gascoigne, B. Milestones in colour printing 1457–1859, with a bibliography of Nelson prints. Cambridge 1997.

Trade organisations

Head, W. W. The Victoria Press, with an account of the movement for the employment of females in printing. 1869.
Willis, F. The present position and future prospects of the London Society of Compositors. [1881.]
Hodson, J. S. A history of the printing trade charities. 1883.
Dickson, J. J. Manchester Typographical Society and branch of T. A. [Typographical Assoc] Centenary 1797–1897. 1897.
Jubilee of the London Society of Compositors: a brief record of events prior to and since its re-establishment in 1848. 1898.
Slatter, H. The Typographical Association: a fifty years' record 1849–99. Ed R. Hackett, Manchester [1899].
Scottish Typographical Association: a fifty years' record 1853–1903. Glasgow 1903.
MacDonald, J. R. Women in the printing trades. 1904.
Cork Typographical Society. Centenary 1806–1906: souvenir. Cork 1906.
Leeds Typographical Society. Centenary 1810–1910: a souvenir, compiled by R. M. Lancaster. Leeds 1910.

The history and progress of the Amalgamated Society of Lithographic Printers 1880–1930. 1930.

Suthers, R. B. The story of 'Natsopa' 1889–1929. 1930.

[Morison, S.] Hand list of printing trade documents issued by the London associations of master-printers, booksellers, compositors, press-men and machine-men 1795–1919, now preserved at the University Press Cambridge. Cambridge 1936.

Temple, H. S. Printing trade organizations. 1938.

Creasey, J. The printers' devil: an account of the history and objects of the Printers' Pension, Almshouse and Orphan Asylum Corporation, ed W. Hutchinson. 1943.

Howe, E. From craft to industry: the London printing trade 1700–1900. Printing Rev 13 1947.

Howe, E. The London compositor: documents relating to wages, working conditions and customs of the London printing trade 1785–1900. 1947 (Bibl Soc).

Howe, E. and H. E. Waite. The London Society of Compositors: a centenary history. 1948.

Rowles, G. E. The 'line' is on: a centenary souvenir of the London Society of Compositors 1848–1948. [1948.]

Monotype Casters' and Typefounders' Society. Diamond jubilee 1889–1949. Sixtieth annual report. 1949.

Sessions, M. The Federation of Master Printers: how it began. 1950.

Howe, E. and J. Child. The Society of London Bookbinders 1780–1951. 1952.

Gillespie, S. C. A hundred years of progress: the record of the Scottish Typographical Association 1853 to 1952. Glasgow 1953.

Musson, A. E. The Typographical Association. 1954.

Shane, T. N. Passed for press: a centenary history of the Association of Correctors of the Press. [1954.]

Bundock, C. J. The story of the National Union of Printing, Bookbinding and Paper Workers. 1959.

Blagden, C. The Stationers' Company: a history 1403–1959. 1960.

Moran, J. Seventy-five years of the National Society of Operative Printers and Assistants. 1964.

Child, J. Industrial relations in the British printing industry. 1967.

Reynolds, S. Britannica's typesetters. Edinburgh 1989. (Women compositors in Edinburgh 1860–1910.)

Wallis, L. W. The devil's background. [Maulden, Beds] 1991. (History of apprenticeship in printing.)

Bateman, D. A Bristol printers' chapel in the nineteenth century. Jnl of the Printing Historical Soc 24 1995. [NAR]

(6) GRAPHIC PROCESSES

Graphic processes are here divided into four categories according to the nature of the surface from which the impression is taken. Books dealing with impression from intaglio, planographic and relief surfaces are separately listed; while those dealing with more than one kind of surface have been grouped under General Works. No attempt has been made to distinguish between books dealing with the autographic and photographic production of the same kinds of surface.

General Works

See Singer, H. W. and W. Strang. Etching, engraving and the other methods of printing pictures. 1897.

See Levis, H. C. A descriptive bibliography of the most important books in the English language relating to the art and history of engraving. 1912; Suppl and index 1913.

See Subject list of works on the fine and graphic arts (excluding photo-mechanical printing and photography) in the library of the Patent Office (London). 1914.

See Subject list of works on photo-mechanical printing and photography in the library of the Patent Office (London). 1914.

See Weitenkampf, F. List of works in the New York Public Library relating to prints. New York 1916.

See Columbia University Libraries. A catalogue of the Epstean collection on the history and science of photography and its applications especially to the graphic arts. New York 1937; Indexes and additions. 1938; Accessions 1938–41. 1942.

See New York Public Library. Dictionary catalogue of the Prints Division. 5 vols Boston 1975.

See Bridson, G. and G. Wakeman. Printmaking & picture printing: a bibliographical guide to artistic & industrial techniques in Britain 1750–1900. Oxford 1984.

Partington, C. F. The engraver's complete guide, comprising the theory and practice of engraving, with its modern improvements in steel plates, lithography, etc.; forming part of The mechanics' library or book of trades. 1825.

Fielding, T. H. The art of engraving. 1841, 1844.

Auer, A. Die Entdeckung des Naturselbstdruckes = The discovery of the natural printing process. Vienna 1854. In Ger, Eng, Fr and Ital.

Donlevy, J. The rise and progress of the graphic arts elucidating the new art of chromo-glyphotype. New York 1854.

Bradbury, H. Nature printing: its origin and objects. 1856.

Kessler, G. Photographie auf Stahl, Kupfer und Stein, zur Anfertigung von Druckplatten für den Kupfer-, Stein- und Buchdruck. Berlin 1856.

Fromberg, E. O. Die graphischen oder zeichnenden Künste der Galvanoplastik. Quedlinburg 1857.

Hammann, J. H. H. Des arts graphiques destinés à multiplier par l'impression considérés sous le double point de vue historique et pratique. Geneva 1857.

Sutton, T. A dictionary of photography. 1858 (with J. Worden), 1867 (with G. Dawson).

Hardwich, T. F. A manual of photographic chemistry. 1859 (5th edn), 1861, 1864, 1873, 1883.

Stannard, W. J. The art-exemplar: a guide to distinguish one species of print from another with pictorial examples. [c. 1860.]

Poitevin, A. Traité de l'impression photographique sans sels d'argent. Paris 1862; then as Traité de l'impression photographique. 1883.

Fouqué, V. La vérité sur l'invention de la photographie. Paris 1867; tr as The truth concerning the invention of photography. New York 1935.

Davenport, S. T. On prints and their production. Jnl of the Soc of Arts 10 Dec 1869 (and Letter 17 Dec 1869).

Geymet, T. Gravure héliographique, galvano-plastie; traité pratique. Paris 1870 (with [C.?] Alker); then as Traité pratique de gravure héliographique et de galvano-plastie. 1885 (3rd edn).

Moock, L. Traité pratique complet d'impression photographique aux encres grasses. Paris 1874, 1877; then as Traité pratique d'impression photographique aux encres grasses, de phototypographie et de photogravure (rev T. Geymet). 1888.

Tissandier, G. Les merveilles de la photographie. Paris 1874; tr as A history and handbook of photography. London 1876, 1878.

Vogel, H. W. Die chemischen Wirkungen des Lichts und die Photographie in ihrer Anwendung in Kunst, Wissenshaft und Industrie. Leipzig 1874; tr as The chemistry of light and photography in their application to art, science and industry. London 1875.

Wessely, J. E. Anleitung zur Kenntniss und zum Sammeln der Werke des Kunstdruckes. Leipzig 1876.

Abney, W. de W. A treatise on photography. 1878.

Bolas, T. The application of photography to the production of printing surfaces and pictures in pigment. Jnl of the Soc of Arts 19 July–23 Aug 1878.

Davanne, A. La photographie et les arts graphiques. In Cercle de la Librairie. Catalogue de l'exposition de gravures anciennes et modernes. Paris 1881.

Hamerton, P. G. The graphic arts. 1882.

Lostalot, A. de. Les procédés de la gravure. Paris [1882].

Bolas, T. Cantor lectures on the recent improvements in photomechanical printing methods. Jnl of the Soc of Arts 10–24 Oct 1884.
Hodson, J. S. An historical and practical guide to art illustration in connection with books, periodicals and general decoration. 1884.
Pettit, J. S. Modern reproductive graphic processes. New York 1884.
Scherer, R. Neueste graphische Verfahren. Vienna 1885.
Wilkinson, W. T. Photo-engraving on zinc and copper, in line and half-tone and photo-lithography. 1886; then as Photo-engraving and photo-lithography in line and half-tone, also collotype and heliotype. 1887; then as Photo-engraving, photo-etching and photo-lithography in line and half-tone, also collotype and heliotype: Amer edn, rev E. L. Wilson. New York 1888; then as Photo-engraving, photo-litho and collotype. London 1890; then as Photo-engraving, photo-litho, collotype and photogravure. 1894; then 6th edn as 3rd. New York 1895.
Burbank, W. H. Photographic printing methods. New York 1887.
Burton, W. K. Practical guide to photographic & photo-mechanical printing. 1887, 1892.
Les procédés: traité pratique de phototypie, impression aux encres grasses, report sur bois, photolithographie, photozincographie, photogravure. Paris 1887.
Roux, V. Traité pratique de photographie décorative appliquée aux arts industriels. Paris 1887.
[Wood, H. T. W.] Modern methods of illustrating books. 1887.
Harrison, W. J. A history of photography. Bradford 1888.
Monet, A. L. Procédés de reproductions graphiques appliquées à l'imprimerie. Paris 1888.
Wall, E. J. A dictionary of photography. 1889, (17 edns to 1945; major edns only), 1890 (2nd edn), 1895 (6th edn); then as The dictionary of photography. 1897 (7th edn, rev T. Bolas), 1902 (8th edn), 1912 (9th edn, rev F. J. Mortimer), 1920 (10th edn).
Vogel, H. W. Handbuch der Photographie. 4 vols Berlin 1890–9.
Waterhouse, J. Practical notes on the preparation of drawings for photographic reproduction, with a sketch of the principal photomechanical printing processes. 1890.
Werge, J. The evolution of photography. 1890.
Duchochois, P. C. Photographic reproduction processes: a practical treatise of the photo-impressions without silver salts. New York 1891, London 1892 (with additional matter by E. J. Wall).
Schiendl, C. Geschichte der Photographie. Vienna 1891.
Brothers, A. Photography: its history, processes, apparatus and materials. 1892, 1899.
Hamerton, P. G. Drawing and engraving. 1892.
Harland, J. W. The printing arts: an epitome of engraving, lithography and printing. 1892.
Museum of Fine Arts, Boston. Exhibition illustrating the technical methods of the reproductive arts from the xvth century to the present time with special reference to the photo-mechanical processes. Boston 1892. Introd by S. R. Koehler.
Wilkinson, W. T. Photo-mechanical processes. 1892, 1897, [1904].
Woodbury, W. B. The encyclopaedia of photography. 1892.
Farquhar, H. D. The grammar of photo-engraving. New York 1893, London 1895 (with additional material by J. M. Eder).
Process work. Vols 1–3 (nos 1–33) Mar 1893–Feb 1896; continued as Process work and the printer. Vols 4–6 (nos 34–69) Mar 1896–Feb 1899; continued as Process work. n.s. nos 1–57 (vols 7–11) Apr 1899–Dec 1903; continued as Process work and electrotyping. nos 1–166 [= vols 12–26] Jan/Feb 1904–Oct/Dec 1921; continued as Process work and the printer. Vol 27 no 1, Jan/Mar 1922–vol 29 no 4, Oct/Dec 1924; continued as Process work. Vol 30 nos 1–7, Feb–Aug 1927; continued as Process work and photo-litho. Vol 30 nos 8–9, Sep–Oct 1927. Ed W. Gamble. (A. W. Penrose & Co.)
Adeline, J. Les arts de reproduction vulgarisés. Paris [1894].
Blackburn, H. The art of illustration. 1894, 1896, Edinburgh 1901 (rev J. S. Eland).
Hinton, A. H. A handbook of illustration. [1894.]
Kitton, F. G. The art of photo-etching and engraving. (On John Swain and Son.) Br Printer July/Aug 1894.
The Photogram. Vol 1 nos 1–12, Jan–Dec 1894; continued until Dec 1905 under same title, then as The Photographic Monthly Jan 1906–Oct 1911. However photomechanical interests were served from 1895 by an enlarged edn entitled The Process Photogram. Vols 2–12 (nos 13–144) Jan 1895–Dec 1905; continued as The Process Engraver's Monthly. Vols 13–63 (nos 145–747) Jan 1906–Mar 1956; continued as Process. Vols 63–7 (nos 748–803) Apr 1956–Dec 1960. Ed H. S. Ward, W. Gamble, et al.
Villon, A. M. Nouveau manuel complet du graveur en creux et en relief. 2 vols Paris 1894.
Fraipont, G. Les procédés de reproduction en creux et la lithographie: eau-forte, pointe sèche, burin, lithographie. Paris [1895].
Process Work Year Book. [Vol 1] 1895; continued as The Process Year Book. Vols 2–7 1896–1901; continued as Penrose's Pictorial Annual. Vols 8–19 1902/3–1913/14; continued as Penrose's Annual. Vols 20–37 1915–35; continued as The Penrose Annual. Vols 38–69 1936–76; continued as Penrose. Vols 70–4 1977/8–1982. Ed W. Gamble, R. B. Fishenden, et al.
Pennell, J. The illustration of books. 1896.
Bracquemond, F. Étude sur la gravure sur bois et la lithographie, Paris 1897.
Singer, H. W. and W. Strang. Etching, engraving and the other methods of printing pictures. 1897.
Hinton, A. H. Practical pictorial photography. 2 vols 1898.
Hübl, A. von. Die photographischen Reproductionsverfahren. Halle 1898.
Kampmann, C. Die graphischen Künsten. Leipzig 1898, 1905, 1909, 1927, 1932, 1941.
Urban, W. Recept-Sammlung aus dem photomechanischen Betriebe der technischen Lehr- und Versuchs-Anstalt von Klimsch & Co. [Frankfurt 1898.]
Story, A. T. The story of photography. 1899.
Albert, A. Verschiedene Reproductions-Verfahren mittels lithographischen und typographischen Druckes. Halle 1900.
Vidal, L. Traité pratique de photogravure en relief et en creux. Paris 1900.
Ward, W. H. The printing arts: a description of the methods now in use, more particularly with regard to illustration. [c. 1900.]
Fisch, A. Traité pratique des impressions photo-mécaniques. Paris [1901].
Ribette, A. Traité pratique d'héliogravure en creux sur zinc, au bitume de Judée, accompagné de notions et de quelques procédés lithographiques, zincographiques, pour la reproduction. Paris [c. 1902].
Kirkbridge, J. Engraving for illustration: historical and practical notes. 1903.
Eder, J. M. Geschichte der Photographie. Halle 1905 (3rd edn), 1932; tr as History of photography. New York 1945.
Klein, H. O. Collodion emulsion and its application to various photographic and photo-mechanical purposes. 1905.
Albert, A. Technischer Führer durch die Reproduktions-Verfahren und deren Bezeichnungen. Halle 1908.
Baker, W. H. A dictionary of engraving. Cleveland 1908.
Clerc, L. P. Les reproductions photomécaniques monochromes. Paris 1910.
Garrett, A. E. The advance of photography. 1911.
Krüger, O. F. W. Die Illustrationsverfahren. Leipzig 1914.
Richter, E. H. Prints: a brief review of their technique and history. Boston 1914.
Gamble, W. Photography and its applications. [1920.]
Hackleman, C. W. Commercial engraving and printing. Indianapolis [1921], [1924].
Ivins, W. M. Photography and the 'modern' point of view. Metropolitan Museum Stud 1 1928.

Horgan, S. H. Bringing photography to the printing press. Photographic Jnl Aug 1929.
Poortenaar, J. Van prenten en platten. Amsterdam 1931; tr as The technique of prints and art reproduction processes. 1933.
Fischer, E. 200 Jahre Naturselbstdruck. Gutenberg-Jahrbuch 1933.
Gamble, C. W. Modern illustration processes. 1933, 1938, 1950.
Groesbeck, H. A. Processes for reproduction. Dolphin 1 1933.
Curwen, H. Processes of graphic reproduction in printing. 1934, 1947, 1963 (rev C. Mayo), 1966.
Gray, B. The English print. 1937.
Newhall, B. Photography: a short critical history. New York [1938] (2nd edn); then as History of photography from 1839 to the present day. [1949], [1964], 1982.
Kainen, J. The development of the halftone screen. Smithsonian Report 1951.
Brunner, F. A handbook of graphic reproduction processes. Teufen 1962.
Roger-Marx, C. La gravure originale au xixe siècle. Paris 1962; tr as Graphic art [of] the nineteenth century. 1962.
Cleaver, J. A history of graphic art. [1963.]
Wakeman, G. Henry Bradbury's nature printed books. Library 5th ser 21 1966.
Cave, R. and G. Wakeman. Typographia naturalis [nature printing]. Wymondham 1967.
Harris, E. M. Experimental graphic processes in England 1800–1859. Jnl of the Printing Historical Soc 4–6 1968–70.
Wakeman, G. Victorian book illustration: the technical revolution. Newton Abbot 1973.
Godfrey, R. T. Printmaking in Britain: a general history from its beginnings to the present day. Oxford 1978.
Crawford, W. The keepers of light: a history and working guide to early photographic processes. New York 1979.
Griffiths, A. Prints and printmaking: an introduction to the history and techniques. 1980.
Wakeman, G. Graphic methods in book illustration. Loughborough 1981 (priv pbd).
Coe, B. and M. Haworth-Booth. A guide to early photographic processes. 1983 (Victoria and Albert Museum).
Lister, R. Prints and printmaking: a dictionary and handbook of the art in nineteenth-century Britain. 1984.
Gascoigne, B. How to identify prints: a complete guide to manual and mechanical processes. 1986.
Wakeman, G. The production of nineteenth century illustration. Loughborough 1986 (priv pbd).
Nadeau, L. Encyclopedia of printing, photographic and photomechanical processes. 2 vols Fredericton, New Brunswick 1989–90.

Intaglio surfaces

Copper- or steel-plate engraving, etching, aquatint, mezzotint, photogravure, heliogravure.

Green, J. H. The complete aquatinter. [London] 1801 (anon), 1804, 1810.
Landseer, J. Lectures on the art of engraving. 1807.
Hassell, J. Calcographia: or the art of multiplying with perfection drawings after the manner of chalk, black lead pencil, and pen and ink. 1811.
Martin, T. The circle of the mechanical arts. 1813.
Eberhard, H. W. Die Anwendung der chemischen Druckart auf Metallplatten. Mainz 1821.
Eberhard, H. W. Die Anwendung des Zinks statt der Stein- und Kupferplatten zu den vertieften Zeichnungsarten. Darmstadt 1822.
Hassell, J. Graphic delineation: a practical treatise on the art of etching. 1826, 1827.
Deleschamps, P. Des mordans, des vernis et des planches dans l'art du graveur ou traité complet de la gravure. Paris 1836.
Pye, J. Evidence relating to the art of engraving, taken before the Select Committee of the House of Commons on Arts 1836, and the Committee's report made to the House thereon; reprinted, together with the petition of engravers which led to that evidence being taken; to which is prefixed a brief account of the connexion of engraving with the Royal Academy of Arts in London. 1836.
Berthiau, —. and P. Boitard. Nouveau manuel complet de l'imprimeur en taille-douce. Paris 1837.
Alken, H. T. The art and practice of etching. 1849.
Ashley, A. The art of etching on copper. [1849.]
Chevreul, M. E. Considérations sur la reproduction par les procédés de M. Niepce de Saint-Victor des images gravées, dessinées ou imprimées. Mémoires de l'Académie des sciences de l'Institut de France. 2nd ser 20 1849.
Talbot, W. H. F. Photographic engraving. Athenaeum 9–30 Apr 1853; Jnl of the Photographic Soc 21 Apr–21 May 1853.
Niepce de Saint-Victor, C. M. F. Recherches photographiques. Paris 1855; tr as Photographic researches. Paris 1855.
Salmon, A. and H. Garnier. Process of photographic engraving. Jnl of the Photographic Soc 22 Oct 1855.
Niepce de Saint-Victor, C. M. F. Traité pratique de gravure héliographique sur acier et sur verre. Paris 1856.
Talbot, W. H. F. Mr Fox Talbot's new discovery: photoglyphic engraving. Photographic News 24 Sep 1858. Description of the process: 22 Oct 1858.
Lalanne, M. Traité de la gravure à l'eau-forte. Paris 1866, 1878; tr as A treatise on etching. Boston 1880.
Autotype Printing and Publishing Co Ltd. The autotype process (ed J. R. Sawyer). [1867], 1871, 1873, 1875, 1876, 1877 (2 edns).
Shrubsole, W. G. Etching: its principles and practice. [1870], 1889.
Hamerton, P. G. The etcher's handbook. 1871, 1875, 1881.
Hannot, A. Gravure sur cuivre au moyen de la photographie et de la galvanoplastie. Brussels 1872.
Scamoni, G. Handbuch der Heliographie nebst praktischem Wegweiser im Gebiete der bezüglichen Gravirkunst. St Petersburg 1872.
Martial, A. P. Nouveau traité de la gravure à l'eau-forte pour les peintres et les dessinateurs. Paris 1873.
Tissandier, G. Une conférence sur l'héliogravure et ses applications à la librairie. Paris 1874.
Edwards, E. The heliotype process. Boston 1876.
Haden, F. S. About etching. 1878.
Husnik, J. Die Heliographie: oder eine Anleitung zur Herstellung druckbarer Metallplatten aller Art. Vienna 1878, 1888, 1905.
Chattock, R. S. Practical notes on etching. [1882], 1883, 1886.
Delaborde, H. La gravure: précis élémentaire de ses origines de ses procédés et son histoire. Paris 1882; tr as Engraving: its origin, processes and history, with an additional chapter on English engraving by W. Walker. London 1886.
Davanne, L. A. Nicéphore Niepce, inventeur de la photographie. Paris 1885.
Geymet, T. Traité pratique de photogravure sur zinc et sur cuivre. Paris 1886.
Roux, V. Manuel de l'imprimeur héliographe. Paris 1886.
Geymet, T. Traité pratique de gravure sur verre par les procédés héliographiques. Paris 1887.
Short, F. On the making of etchings. 1888, 1893, 1898.
Ferret, J. La photogravure facile et à bon marché. Paris 1889.
Wilkinson, W. T. Photogravure. 1890, 1895.
Dubouchet, H. and G. Précis élémentaire de gravure sur cuivre. Paris 1891.
'Robert, K.' Traité pratique de la gravure à l'eau-forte. Paris 1891. [Pseud of Georges Meusnier.]
Herkomer, H. von. Etching and mezzotint engraving. 1892.
Blaney, H. R. Photogravure. New York 1895.

Paton, H. Etching, drypoint, mezzotint: the whole art of the painter-etcher. 1895, 1909.
Wedmore, F. Etching in England. 1895.
Denison, H. A treatise on photogravure in intaglio by the Talbot-Klic process. 1896.
Huson, T. Huson on photo-aquatint & photogravure to which is appended A treatise on machine printed photogravure by A. Villain and J. W. Smith. [1897.]
Maskell, A. and R. Demachy. Photo-aquatint: or the gum-bichromate process. 1897.
Brown, G. E. Ferric & heliographic processes. [1899], [1901].
Schiltz, M. Manuel pratique d'héliogravure en taille-douce. Paris 1899.
Vidal, L. Le progrès de la photogravure. Paris 1900.
Ziegler, W. Die Techniken des Tiefdruckes. Halle 1901.
Victoria and Albert Museum. Catalogue of the loan exhibition of British engraving and etching. 1903.
Hind, A. M. A short history of engraving and etching. 1908, 1911; then as A history of engraving & etching from the 15th century to the year 1914. 1923.
Prideaux, S. T. Aquatint engraving: a chapter in the history of book illustration. 1909.
Hardie, M. Frederick Goulding, master printer of copper plates. Stirling 1910.
D., A. C. A note on the art of mezzotint and mezzotint printing in colour. [1911] (priv pbd).
Short, F. Etchings and engravings: what they are and are not. 1911.
Wedmore, F. Cantor lectures: etching. Jnl of the Royal Soc of Arts 11 Aug 1911.
Cameron-Swan, D. Pioneers of photogravure. Imprint June 1913.
S[wan], M. E. and K. R. Sir Joseph Wilson Swan. 1929; rptd with appendix. Newcastle 1968.
Meier, H. The origin of the printing and roller press. Print Collector's Quart 28 1941.
Colas, H. Les origines de la photogravure. France Graphique Jan 1954.
[Nešvera, R. K. et al]. Karel Klíč, vynálezce hlubotisku. Prague 1957. On the inventor of photogravure.
Bain, I. Thomas Ross & Son: copper- and steel-plate printers since 1833. Jnl of the Printing Historical Soc 2 1966.
Lilien, O. M. History of industrial gravure printing up to 1920. 1972.
Beck, H. Victorian engravings. 1973 (Victoria and Albert Museum).
Lilien, O. M. Der Tiefdruck (Geschichte der Druckverfahren, Teil 3). Stuttgart 1978.
Engen, R. K. Dictionary of Victorian engravers, print publishers and their works. Cambridge 1979.
Hunnisett, B. A dictionary of British steel engravers. Leigh-on-sea 1980; then as An illustrated dictionary of British steel engravers. Aldershot 1989.
Dyson, A. The rolling-press: some aspects of its development from the seventeenth century to the nineteenth century. Jnl of the Printing Historical Soc 17 1982/3.
Dyson, A. Pictures to print: the nineteenth-century engraving trade. 1984.
Wax, C. The mezzotint: history and technique. New York 1990.
Heath, J. The Heath family, engravers 1779–1878. 2 vols Aldershot 1993.

Planographic surfaces

Lithography (stone, zinc, aluminium), photolithography, collotype. For chromolithography see col 24, above.

See Mohr, L. Bibliographie der Lithographie, des Steindruckes und der verwandten Zweige. [Leipzig] 1880.
See C. Kampmann, Die Literatur der Lithographie von 1798–1898. Vienna 1899.
Senefelder, J. A. Printing textile fabrics [and other surfaces, by lithography]. Patent Specification no 2518 [of] 1801. 1856.
Fisher, T. The process of polyautographic printing. GM Mar 1808.
[Rapp, H. von.] Das Geheimniss des Steindrucks. Tubingen 1810, Schweinfurt 1810.
[Bankes, H.] Lithography: or the art of making drawings on stone for the purpose of being multiplied by printing. Bath 1813; then as Lithography: or the art of taking impressions from drawings and writing made on stone. London 1816.
Fisher, T. Curious specimen of polyautography or lithography. GM Oct 1815.
Engelmann, G. Rapport sur la lithographie. [Paris 1816.]
B., L. J. D. Coup d'oeil sur la lithographie. Brussels 1818.
D***, —. Procédé actuel de la lithographie mise à la portée de l'artiste et l'amateur. Paris 1818.
Mairet, F. Notice sur la lithographie. Dijon 1818 (anon), Chatillon-sur-Seine 1824; tr as Kurzer Abriss der Lithographie oder Steindruckerey. Pesth 1819.
Senefelder, J. A. Vollstaendiges Lehrbuch der Steindruckerey. Munich 1818, 1821, 1827; tr as A complete course of lithography. London 1819; 2nd edn tr as The invention of lithography. New York 1911.
Peignot, G. Essai historique sur la lithographie. Paris 1819.
Raucourt de Charleville, A. Mémoire sur les expériences lithographiques faites à l'École Royale des Ponts et Chausées de France. Toulon 1819; tr as A manual of lithography. 1820, 1821, 1832.
Ridolfi, C. and F. Tartini. Memoria sulla litografia. Florence 1819.
Ackermann, R. Portable lithographic press. Trans of the Soc of Arts 37 1820.
Kohl, L. Practische Anleitung zur Lithographie. Vienna 1820.
Ruthven, J. A short account of lithography or the art of printing from stone. Edinburgh 1820; then as Concise account of lithography or the art of printing from stone with suitable directions. London 1821.
Williams, J. F. L. An historical account of inventions and discoveries. 2 vols 1820. Includes lithography.
Eberhard, H. W. Die Anwendung des Zinks statt der Stein- und Kupferplatten zu den vertieften Zeichnungsarten. Darmstadt 1822.
Engelmann, G. Manuel du dessinateur lithographe. Paris 1822, 1824, 1830; tr as Handbuch für Steinzeichner. Berlin 1833.
[Gaillot, —.] L'aquatinta lithographique. Paris 1824; tr as Lithographic pencil drawing: or instructions for imitating aquatinta on stone. London 1824.
Hullmandel, C. The art of drawing on stone. [1824], 1833, 1835.
Houbloup, L. Théorie lithographique: ou manière facile d'apprendre à imprimer soi-même. Paris 1825.
Brégeaut, L. R. (also R. L.). Manuel théorique et pratique du dessinateur et de l'imprimeur lithographe. Paris 1827; then as Manual complet théorique et pratique du dessinateur et de l'imprimeur lithographe. Paris 1827 (2nd edn), 1834; then as Nouveau manuel complet [etc]. Paris 1839; then as Nouveau manuel complet de l'imprimeur lithographe. Paris 1850 (rev E. Knecht and J. Desportes).
Hullmandel, C. On some important improvements in lithographic printing. [1827.]
Phillips, G. F. The art of drawing on stone. 1828.
Chevallier, J. B. A. and —. Langlumé. Mémoire sur l'art du lithographie. Paris 1829.
[Croker, T. C.] History of lithography. Foreign Rev and Continental Misc July 1829.
Hullmandel, C. On some further improvements in lithographic printing. [1829.]
Pescheck, H. E. Das Ganze des Steindrucks, von seiner artistisch-, chemisch- und mechanischen Seite. Ilmenau 1829.
Bautz, J. B. B. Die Lithographie in ihrem ganzen Umfange. Augsburg 1831, 1836.

History and process of lithography. Lib of the Fine Arts Feb 1831.
A view of the present state of lithography in England. Lib of the Fine Arts Apr 1831.
Pillon, A. C. Instruction sur l'autographie. Paris 1833.
Senefelder, K. Lehrbuch der Lithographie. Ratisbon 1833, 1834.
Tudot, E. Description de tous les moyens de dessiner sur pierre. Paris 1833; then as Traité de lithographie ou description de tous les moyens de dessiner sur pierre. Paris 1834.
Desportes, J. Manuel pratique du lithographe. Paris 1834, 1840.
Le Lithographe (Paris). Vol 1 no 1 [June] 1837–vol 6 no 5 [Mar] 1848. Ed J. Desportes.
Chevallier, J. B. A. and —. Langlumé. Traité complet de la lithographie. Paris 1838.
Engelmann, G. Traité théoretique et pratique de lithographie. Mulhouse 1840; tr as Das Gesammtgebiet der Lithographie. Chemnitz 1840.
Fielding, T. H. On the theory of painting: also an appendix containing a manual of lithography. 1842 (3rd edn).
Tissier, L. Historique de la gravure typographique sur pierre et de la Tissiérographie. Paris 1843.
Klinkhardt, F. Die anastatische Druckerei. Quedlinburg 1846.
De la Motte, P. On the various applications of anastatic printing and papyrography. 1849.
Cowell, S. H. A brief description of the art of anastatic printing. Ipswich [c. 1851], 1874.
Stanbury, G. Practical guide to lithography. 1851, 1854.
Mason, C. The practical lithographer. 1852.
Jordan, C. J. A treatise on anastatic printing, or the art of reprinting from prints on paper. 1853 (priv pbd).
Salières, P. N. Gravure diaphane: nouveau procédé à la portée de tous les peintres et de tous les dessinateurs. Montpelier 1853.
[Waterlow, A. C.] Every man his own printer; or lithography made easy. 1854, 1859.
Aresti, J. Lithozôgraphia: or aquatinta stippled gradations produced upon drawings washed or painted on stone. [1856], 1857.
Ferchl, F. M. Uebersicht der einzig bestehenden, vollständigen Incunabeln-Sammlung der Lithographie. Oberbayerisches Archiv für vaterländische Geschichte 16 1856.
Schenck, F. Short treatise on lithography. Edinburgh 1857.
James, H. Photo-zincography. Southampton 1860 (Ordnance Survey).
Ferchl, F. M. Geschichte der Errichtung der ersten lithographischen Kunstanstalt bei der Feiertags-Schule für Künstler und Techniker in München. Munich 1862.
Nagler, G. K. Alois Senefelder und der geistliche Rath Simon Schmid als Rivalen in der Geschichte der Erfindung des mechanischen Steindruckes. Munich 1862.
Scott, A. de C. On photo-zincography and other photographic processes employed at the Ordnance Survey Office, Southampton. 1862, 1863.
Berri, D. G. The art of lithography. 1864, 1872, 1879.
Straker, C. Instructions in the art of lithography. 1867.
Lemling, J. Die Photoverrotypie. Lüdenscheid 1870.
The Lithographer. Vols 1–5 (no 1–49) July 1870–July 1874. Then incorporated in The Printing Times.
Markl, A. Die neuesten Fortschritte der Phototypie. Prague 1870.
Pietsch, L. Alois Senefelder: Erfinder der Lithographie. Berlin 1871.
Sawyer, J. R. Photography in the printing press. Photographic Jnl Jan 1872; rptd in The Autotype process, 1876 (5th edn), 1877 (2 edns).
Heliotype Co. The Heliotype process described and illustrated. [c. 1872.]
Geymet, T. Photolithographie traites et demi-teintes: traité pratique. Paris 1873; then as Traité pratique de photolithographie et de phototypie. 1882; then as two separate works: Traité pratique de photolithographie. 1888 (3rd edn) and Traité pratique de phototypie. 1888 (new edn).
The history of lithography as written in the records of the Patent Office. Lithographer Jan–July 1874; The Printing Times Aug 1874; The Printing Times and Lithographer Oct–Dec 1874.
Fortier, G. La photolithographie: son origine, ses procédés, ses applications. Paris 1876.
Doyen, C. Trattato di litografia, storico, teorico, pratico ed economico. Turin 1877.
Husnik, J. Das Gesammtgebiet des Lichtdrucks. Vienna 1877, 1880, 1885, 1894, 1922.
Pumphrey, A. Collography for autographic printing. Birmingham 1878.
Richmond, W. D. The grammar of lithography. 1878.
Schnauss, J. Der Licht-Druck und die Photolithographie. Düsseldorf [1879], [1880]; tr as Collotype and photo-lithography. London 1889.
Vidal, L. Traité pratique de phototypie: ou impression à l'encre grasse sur une couche de gelatine. Paris 1879.
Allgeyer, J. Handbuch über das Lichtdruck-Verfahren. Leipzig 1881, 1896 (with F. Renner).
Weishaupt, H. Verzeichnis der lithographischen Inkunabeln-Sammlung. Munich 1884.
La gravure sur pierre: traité pratique à l'usage des écrivains et des imprimeurs lithographes. Paris 1887.
Roux, V. Formulaire pratique de phototypie. Paris 1887.
Bonnet, G. Manuel de phototypie. Paris 1889.
Lorilleux, C. & Cie. Traité de lithographie: histoire, théorie, pratique. Paris 1889.
The British lithographer. Vols 1–4 (nos 1–24) Oct/Nov 1891–Aug/Sep 1895. Then incorporated in The British printer.
Valette, A. Manuel pratique du lithographe. Lyon 1891, 1894, Paris 1903.
Villon, A. M. Nouveau manuel complet du dessinateur et de l'imprimerie lithographe. 3 vols Paris 1891.
Watt, P. B. The rise and progress of lithography in Britain. Br Lithographer Dec/Jan 1891/2–June/July 1892.
Trutat, E. Impressions photographiques aux encres grasses: traité pratique de photocollographie à l'usage des amateurs. Paris 1892.
Voirin, J. Manuel pratique de phototypie. Paris 1892, [1910].
Vidal, L. Traité pratique de photolithographie. Paris 1893.
Fritz, G. Die Photolithographie. Halle 1894; tr as Photo-lithography, London 1895.
Green, E. The beginnings of lithography. Archaeological Jnl June 1894.
Bouchot, H. La lithographie. Paris [1895].
Wilkinson, W. T. Collotype. 1895.
Grolier Club. Catalogue of an exhibition illustrative of a centenary of artistic lithography 1796–1896. New York 1896.
Spielmann, M. H. The renaissance of lithography. Scribner's Mag Nov 1896.
Spielmann, M. H. The revival of lithography: introduction – its rise and first decline. Mag of Art Dec 1896.
Watt, P. B. Early English lithography. Artist May 1896.
Wedmore, F. The revival of lithography. Art Jnl Jan–Feb 1896.
Curtis, A. Some masters of lithography. New York 1897.
Green, E. Bath and early lithography. Proc of the Bath Natural History and Antiquarian Field Club 8 1897.
Spielmann, M. H. Original lithography: the present revival in England. Mag of Art Apr 1897.
Albert, A. Der Lichtdruck an der Hand- und Schnellpresse samt allen Nebenarbeiten. Halle 1898, 1906.
Algraphy Ltd. Instructions to the trade for preparation of aluminium plates for algraphic printing. 1898.
Munier, A. Traité de lithographie. Reims 1898.
Pennell, J. and E. R. Lithography and lithographers: some chapters in the history of the art. 1898, 1915.

Aluminium Plate and Press Co. Aluminography: the aluminium plate versus the lithographic stone. New York 1899.
Pennell, J. The truth about lithography. Studio Feb 1899.
Haynié, J. Der lithographische Umdruck nach dem heutigen Stande dieser Technik. Frankfurt 1900.
Laynaud, L. La phototypie pour tous. Paris 1900.
Weilandt, C. Der Aluminiumdruck (Algraphie). Mainz 1900, Vienna 1902; tr as Algraphy: or the art of printing from aluminium plates. London [1901].
Fithian, A. W. Practical collotype. 1901.
Fritz, G. Handbuch der Lithographie. Halle 1901.
Gerber, C. H. Der praktische Steindrucker an der Hand- & Schnellpresse. Sternberg [1903].
Graul, R. and F. Dornhoffer. Die Lithographie von ihrer Erfindung bis zur Gegenwart. Vienna 1903.
Seymour, A. Practical lithography. 1903.
Cumming. D. Handbook of lithography. 1904.
Jacobi, E. The gelatine process. In F. H. Hitchcock, The building of a book, 1906.
Maurou, P. and A. Broquelet. Traité complet de l'art lithographique au point de vue artistique et pratique. Paris 1907.
Harrap, C. Text book of metalography (printing from metals). Leicester 1909; then as Metalography (printing from metals) and off-set printing. Leicester 1912; then as Offset printing from stone and plates (planography or metalography). Leicester 1927.
Harrap, C. Transferring: the practice of transferring to stone, zinc and aluminium. 1912.
Goodman, J. Practical modern metalithography. 1914.
Rhodes, H. J. The art of lithography. 1914, 1924.
Wagner, C. Alois Senefelder: sein Leben und Wirken. Leipzig 1914, 1943.
Dussler, L. Die Incunabeln der deutschen Lithographie 1796–1821. 1925.
Halbmeier, C. Senefelder: the history of lithography. New York 1926.
Peters, H. T. America on stone: a chronicle of American lithography. New York 1931.
Johnson, A. F. Early lithography in England. Penrose Annual 38 1936.
Gray, N. The nineteenth-century chromo-lithograph. Architectural Rev 84 1938.
King, A. H. English pictorial music title-pages 1820–1885: their style, evolution and importance. Library 5th ser 4 1950.
Man, F. H. 150 years of artists' lithographs 1803–1953. 1953.
Weber, W. Saxa loquuntur. 2 vols Heidelberg 1961–4; tr as A history of lithography. London 1966.
Man, F. H. Lithography in England 1801–10. In C. Zigrosser. Prints. New York 1963.
Baier, W., R. Skopec and A. Neumann. Lichtdruck 1865–1965. Dresden [1965].
Twyman, M. Lithography 1800–1850. Oxford 1970.
Wakeman, G. Aspects of Victorian lithography: anastatic printing and photo-zincography. Wymondham 1970 (priv ptd).
Twyman, M. Lithographic stone and the printing trade in the nineteenth century. Jnl of the Printing Historical Soc 8 1971.
Twyman, M. A directory of London lithographic printers 1800–1850. Jnl of the Printing Historical Soc 10 1974/5.
Twyman, M. Thomas Barker's lithographic stones. Jnl of the Printing Historical Soc 12 1977/8.
Marzio, P. C. The democratic art: pictures for a 19th-century America. Boston 1979.
Weber, W. Aloys Senefelder: Erfinder der Lithographie; Daten zum Leben ind Wirken. Frankfurt 1981.
Porzio, D. La Litografia. Milan 1982; tr as Lithography: 200 years of art, history & technique. New York 1983.
Gilmore, P. Lasting impressions: lithography as art. 1988.
Twyman, M. Early lithographed books. 1990.
Reardon, T. and K. Kirby. Collotype: prince of the printing processes. Printing History 25 1991.
Imiela, H. J. Stein- und Offsetdruck (Geschichte der Druckverfahren, Teil 4). Stuttgart 1993.

Relief surfaces

Wood engraving, steel engraving, zincography, line blocks, half tone blocks. Some works on electrotyping which deal with the conversion of intaglio into relief surfaces are listed above, under Spencer, Jacobi, Schoenberg, Sampson, Palmer et al.

Heller, J. Geschichte der Holzschneidekunst. Bamberg 1823.
Dembour, A. Description d'un nouveau procédé de gravure en relief sur cuivre, dite ectypographie métallique. Metz 1835; tr as Die Metal-Ektypographie. Braunschweig 1835.
[Cole, H.] Modern wood engraving. London & Westminster Rev Aug 1838.
Chatto, W. A. A treatise on wood engraving, historical and practical, with illustrations engraved by J. Jackson. 1839, 1861 (rev H. G. Bohn).
Palmer, E. Glyphography: or engraved drawing for printing at the type press after the manner of woodcuts. [1843] (2 edns).
Tissier, L. Historique de la gravure typographique sur pierre et de la tissiérographie. Paris 1843.
Chatto, W. A. The history and art of wood engraving. 1848.
C[hatto], W. A. Gems of wood engraving from the Illustrated London News, with a history of the art, ancient and modern. 1849.
Gillot, F. Paniconographie de Gillot. Paris 1852; then as Album de gravure paniconographique et photogravure. 1875.
Michel, V. Spécimen de clichés bitumineux inventés par V. Michel. Paris 1854.
Devincenzi, J. Électrographie: ou nouvel art de graver en relief sur métal. Paris 1856.
Wood engraving as an employment for women. Alexandra Mag Apr 1865.
Fitz-Cook, H. On the Graphotype. Jnl of the Soc of Arts 8 Dec 1865.
Gilks, T. The art of wood engraving. 1866, 1867, 1871.
Fuller, S. E. A manual of instruction in the art of wood engraving. Boston 1867, New York 1879.
Gilks, T. A sketch of the origin and progress of the art of wood engraving. 1868.
Graphotyping Co. The handbook of Graphotype. 1868.
Isermann, A. Anleitung zur Chemitypie. Leipzig 1869.
Lewis, J. Printing surfaces in relief and their production. Lithographer Feb–Apr, June 1871.
Motteroz, C. Essai sur les gravures chimiques en relief. Paris 1871.
Lefman, J. and C. Lourdel. Photo-typographie: gravure en relief. Paris 1872.
Tissandier, G. Histoire de la gravure typographique: conférence faite au Cercle de la Librairie. Journal général de la librairie, de l'imprimerie, etc. 6 Feb 1875.
Emerson, W. A. Practical instruction in the art of wood engraving. East Douglas 1876; then as Hand-book of wood engraving, with practical instruction in the art. Boston 1881.
Scherer, R. Lehrbuch der Chemigraphie und verwandten Fächer. Vienna 1877.
Linton, W. J. Some practical hints on wood engraving. Boston 1879.
Marx, G. W. The art of drawing and engraving on wood. [1881], [1882].
Vidal, L. Traité pratique de photoglyptie. Paris 1881; tr as Die Photoglyptie: oder der Woodbury-Druck. Halle 1897.
Toifel, W. F. Handbuch der Chemigraphie. Vienna 1883, 1896.
Woodberry, G. E. A history of wood-engraving. New York 1883.
Linton, W. J. Wood-engraving: a manual of instruction. 1884.
Roux, V. Traité pratique de zincographie. Paris 1885, 1891, 1904.

Böck, J. Zincography: a practical guide to the art as practised in connexion with letterpress printing. [1886] (2nd edn).

Brown, W. N. A practical manual of wood engraving, with a brief account of the history of the art. 1886; subsequent 'editions' (reprints) as Wood engraving: a practical and easy introduction to the study of the art.

Husnik, J. Die Zinkätzung (Chemigraphie, Zinkotypie). Vienna 1886, 1896, 1907, 1923.

Leslie, A. F. W. Practical instructor of photo-engraving and zinc etching processes. New York [1886].

Geymet, T. Traité pratique de gravure en demi-teinte. Paris 1888.

Schraubstadter, C. Photo-engraving: a practical treatise on the production of printing blocks by modern photographic methods. St Louis MO 1892.

'Verfasser, J.' The half-tone process. Bradford 1894, 1896, London 1904, 1907, [1912]. [Pseud of W. Gamble.]

Volkmer, O. Die Photo-Galvanographie zur Herstellung von Kupferdruck- und Buchdruckplatten nebst den nöthigen Vor- und Nebenarbeiten. Halle 1894.

Cronenberg, W. Die Praxis der Autotypie auf amerikanischer Basis. Düsseldorf 1895; tr as Half-tone on the American basis. Bradford 1896.

Cundall, J. A brief history of wood engraving. 1895.

Fraipont, G. Les procédés de reproduction en relief. Paris [1895].

Meisenbach Co. Ltd. Meisenbach improved process of photo-engraving [half tone]. [1895.]

Swan Electric Engraving Co. Specimens of reproductions, press opinions and some criticisms. [1895.]

Whittet, R. Photo-engraving by the half-tone enamel process. Ed A. C. Lamoutte, New York 1895.

Jenkins, H. A manual of photo-engraving. Chicago 1896, 1902; then as Amstutz' hand-book of photoengraving. 1907 (rev N. S. Amstutz).

Boutall, W. Process engraving: twenty-five years' progress. British and Colonial Printer 6 May 1897.

Ward, W. H. The evolution of half-tone engraving. Artist Mar 1897.

Austin, A. C. Practical half-tone and tri-colour engraving. Buffalo NY 1898.

Ives, F. E. Lectures on photo-process work. London Technical Education Gazette Jan 1899.

Cox, A. Half-tone printing. Birmingham 1903.

Victoria and Albert Museum. Catalogue of the loan exhibition of process engraving. 1905. Introd by J. Waterhouse.

Gill, E. M. Half-tone, line and colour plates. In F. H. Hitchcock, The building of a book. 1906.

Gamble, W. Line photo-engraving. [1910.]

Horgan, S. H. Photo-engraving primer. Boston 1920.

Furst, H. The modern woodcut. 1924.

McCabe, L. R. The beginnings of halftone, taken from the note book of S. H. Horgan. Inland Printer (Chicago) Mar–Apr 1924.

Horgan, S. H. More about the beginnings of halftone. Chicago 1925.

Gamble, W. The beginning of half-tone: a history of the process. Br & Colonial Printer: special quarterly no Dec 1927; rptd New York [1928].

Bliss, D. P. A history of wood-engraving. 1928.

Sleigh, B. Wood engraving since eighteen-ninety. 1932.

Howe, E. From Bewick to the half-tone: a survey of [relief] illustration processes during the nineteenth century. Typography 3 1937.

Fildes, P. Phototransfer of drawings in wood-block engraving. Jnl of the Printing Historical Soc 5 1969.

Lindley, K. The woodblock engravers. Newton Abbot 1970. On nineteenth-century 'trade' engraving.

Woodward, D. The decline of commercial wood-engraving in nineteenth-century America. Jnl of the Printing Historical Soc 10 1974/5.

Garrett, A. A history of British wood engraving. Tunbridge Wells 1978.

Sander, D. M. Wood engraving: an adventure in printmaking. 1979.

Buchanan-Brown, J. British wood-engravers c. 1820–c. 1860: a checklist. Jnl of the Printing Historical Soc 17 1982/3.

Engen, R. K. Dictionary of Victorian wood engravers. Cambridge 1985.

Pankow, D. Dungeons and dragon's blood: the development of late 19th and early 20th century platemaking processes. Printing History 19 1988.

Hamilton, J. Wood engraving & the woodcut in Britain c. 1890–1990. 1994.

Andrews, M. Hare & Co, commercial wood-engravers: Jabez Hare, founder of the firm, and his letters 1846 to 1847. Jnl of the Printing Historical Soc 24 1995. [NAR]

(7) PRINTING STYLE

Aesthetic considerations

Works on individual presses and printers are listed from col 41, below.

Hansard, T. C. Typographia (pt 2 ch 4 Fine printing). 1825.

Jacobi, C. T. On the making and issuing of books. 1891; then as Some notes on books and printing. 1892, 1902, 1903, 1912.

Southward, J. Artistic printing. 1892.

Arts and Crafts Exhibition Society. Arts and crafts essays. 1893. Printing by William Morris and Emery Walker.

Morris, W. The ideal book. Trans Bibl Soc 1 1893.

Joyner, G. Fine printing: its inception, development and practice. 1895.

Ricketts, C. and L. Pissarro. De la typographie et de l'harmonie de la page imprimée [and] William Morris et son influence sur les arts et métiers. 1898.

Ricketts, C. A defence of the revival of printing. 1899.

De Vinne, T. L. Title-pages as seen by a printer. New York 1901 (Grolier Club); then as The practice of typography: a treatise on title pages. 1902.

Cobden-Sanderson, T. J. Ecce mundus: industrial ideals and the book beautiful. Hammersmith 1902.

Steele, R. R. The revival of printing: a bibliographical catalogue of works issued by the chief modern English presses. 1912.

Pevsner, N. Pioneers of the Modern Movement. 1936; then as Pioneers of modern design. 1960.

Barman, C. Timetable typography. Typography 5 1938.

Beilenson, P. The nineteenth century. In A history of the printed book, Dolphin 3, New York 1938.

Betjeman, J. Ecclesiastical typography. Typography 6 1938.

Ridler, V. Artistic printing: a search for principles. Alphabet & Image 6 1948.

McLean, R. Modern book design from William Morris to the present day. 1951, 1958.

McLean, R. Victorian book design and colour printing. 1963, 1972.

Day, K. Book typography 1815–1965 in Europe and the United States of America. 1965.

Taylor, J. R. The art nouveau book in Britain. 1966.

Lewis, J. Anatomy of printing: the influence of art and history on its design. 1970.

Morris, W. The ideal book: essays and lectures on the arts of the book. Ed W. S. Peterson. Berkeley 1982.

Meggs, P. B. A history of graphic design. 1983, New York 1992.

Legibility

Babbage, C. Table of logarithms. 1827. Preface.

Cohn, H. L. Die Hygiene des Auges in den Schulen. Leipzig 1883; tr as Hygiene of the eye in schools, 1886.

Cattell, J. M. The inertia of the eye and brain. Brain 8 1885.

Maire, A. La technique du livre. Paris 1888.

Sanford, E. C. The relative legibility of the small letters. Amer Jnl of Psychology May 1888.

Goldscheider, A. and R. F. Müller. Zur Physiologie und Pathologie des Lesens. Zeitschrift für klinische Medizin (Berlin) 23 1893.
Griffing, H. and S. I. Franz. On the conditions of fatigue in reading. Psychological Rev (New York) 3 1896.
Dodge, R. Visual perception during eye movements. Psychological Rev (New York) 7 1900.
Javal, E. Physiologie de la lecture et de l'écriture. Paris 1905, 1906.
Huey, E. B. The psychology and pedagogy of reading. New York 1908.
Pyke, R. L. Report on the legibility of print. Medical Research Council (Special Report no 110). 1926. [NAR]

(8) PRIVATE PRINTING

General works

See Haas, I. A bibliography of material relating to private presses. Chicago 1937.
Martin, J. A bibliographical catalogue of books privately printed. 1834; then as Bibliographical catalogue of privately printed books. 1854.
Hume, A. The learned societies and printing clubs of the United Kingdom. 1847, 1853 (with a suppl by A. I. Evans).
Bohn, H. G. Appendix volume to the Bibliographer's manual by W. T. Lowndes. 1865.
Henning, F. W. J. A few words upon early printing and private presses. [1880.]
Quaritch, B. Account of the great learned societies and associations and of the chief printing clubs of Great Britain and Ireland. (Sette of Odde Volumes. Miscellany no 14.) 1886.
Plomer, H. R. Some private presses of the nineteenth century. Library 1 1900.
Dobell, B. Catalogue of books printed for private circulation. 1906.
Ashbee, C. R. The private press: a study in idealism; to which is added a bibliography of the Essex House Press. Broad Campden 1909.
Terry, C. S. A catalogue of the publications of Scottish historical and kindred clubs and societies 1780–1908. Aberdeen 1909.
Steele, R. R. The revival of printing: a bibliographical catalogue of works issued by the chief modern English presses. 1912.
Steeves, H. R. Learned societies and English literary scholarship. New York 1913.
Tomkinson, G. S. A select bibliography of the principal modern presses, public and private in Great Britain and Ireland. 1928.
Ransom, W. Private presses and their books. New York 1929.
Williams, H. Book clubs & printing societies of Great Britain and Ireland. 1929.
Balston, T. The Cambridge University Press collection of private press types: Kelmscott, Ashendene, Eragny, Cranach. Cambridge 1951 (priv ptd).
Ransom, W. Kelmscott, Doves and Ashendene: the private press credos. (Typophile Chapbook no 27) New York 1952.
Manchester Public Libraries. Reference library subject catalogue, section 094: private press books. 2 pts Manchester 1959–60.
Times Bookshop, London. English private presses 1757–1961. 1961.
Franklin, C. The private presses. 1969, Aldershot 1991.
Cave, R. The private press. 1971, New York 1983.
Ridler, W. British modern press books; a descriptive check list of unrecorded items. 1971.
British Library. Modern British and American private presses (1850–1965): holdings of the British Library. 1976.
Dreyfus, J. The Hammersmith hot-house: private presses beside the Thames. Matrix 16 1996.

Particular presses and societies

Lee Priory Press (Sir Samuel Egerton Brydges, 1812–22)
Brydges, S. E. The autobiography, times, opinions and contemporaries of Sir Egerton Brydges. 2 vols 1834.

Roxburghe Club (1812 onwards)
Haslewood, J. Roxburghe revels and other relative papers. Edinburgh 1837 (priv ptd).
Bigham, C. (Viscount Mersey). The Roxburghe Club: its history and its members 1812–1927. Oxford 1928.
Barker, N. The publications of the Roxburghe Club 1814–1962. Cambridge 1964.

Bannatyne Club (1822–67)
Bannatyne Club, Edinburgh. Lists of members and the rules, with a catalogue of the books printed for the Bannatyne Club. Ed D. Laing, Edinburgh 1867.

Abbotsford Club (1833–66)
Abbotsford Club, Edinburgh. A list of the members, the rules, and catalogue of books printed for the Abbotsford Club. Ed D. Laing, Edinburgh 1866.

Camden Society (1838–97)
Nichols, J. G. A descriptive catalogue of the works of the Camden Society. 1862, 1872.

Daniel Press (C. H. O. Daniel, 1845–1919)
Madan, F. The Daniel Press: memorials of C. H. O. Daniel with a bibliography of the press. Oxford 1921. Addenda and corrigenda, Oxford 1922.
Jacobi, C. T. The Daniel Press, 1845–1919. Penrose's Annual 27 1925.

Stanbrook Abbey Press (1876 onwards)
The Stanbrook Abbey Press: ninety-two years of its history, by the Benedictines of Stanbrook. Worcester 1970.
Butcher, D. The Stanbrook Abbey Press, 1956–90. Lower Marston 1992.

Kelmscott Press (William Morris, 1891–8)
See Walsdorf, J. J. William Morris in private press and limited editions. Phoenix 1983.
See Peterson, W. S. A bibliography of the Kelmscott Press. Oxford 1984.
See Aho, G. L. William Morris: a reference guide. Boston 1985.
I., I. H. The Kelmscott Press: an illustrated interview with Mr William Morris, printer. Bookselling, Christmas 1895.
Colebrook, F. Wm Morris, master printer. [Tunbridge Wells 1897.]
Forman, H. B. The books of William Morris described. 1897.
Cotton, A. L. The Kelmscott Press and the new printing. Contemporary Rev Aug 1898.
Morris, W. A note by William Morris on his aims in founding the Kelmscott Press, together with a short description of the press by S. C. Cockerell & an annotated list of the books printed thereat. Hammersmith 1898.
Mackail, J. W. The life of William Morris. 2 vols 1899.
Jacobi, C. T. The Kelmscott Press, 1891–1898. Penrose's Annual 24 1922.
Sparling, H. H. The Kelmscott Press and William Morris, master-craftsman. 1924.
Double Crown Club. The illuminated manuscripts of William Morris, by Graily Hewitt; The typography of William Morris, by Holbrook Jackson, and by James Shand: three papers. [1934.]
Zapf, H. William Morris: sein Leben und Werk in der Geschichte der Buch- und Schriftkunst. Scharbeutz [1949].
Gutenberg Museum, Mainz. Morris-Drucke und andere Meisterwerke englischer und amerikanischer Privatpressen. Mainz 1954.
Schmidt-Künsemüller, F. A. William Morris und die neuere Buchkunst. Wiesbaden 1955.
William Morris Society. The typographical adventure of William Morris, an exhibition. 1957.
Brown University Library. William Morris and the Kelmscott Press. Providence RI 1960.
Robinson, D. A companion volume to the Kelmscott Chaucer. 1975.
William Morris and the art of the book. New York 1976 (Pierpont Morgan Lib).

William Morris Gallery. In fine print: William Morris as book designer. 1976.
Thompson, S. O. American book design and William Morris. 1977, 1996.
Robinson, D. William Morris, Edward Burne-Jones and the Kelmscott Chaucer. 1982.
Franklin, C. Printing and the mind of Morris: three paths to the Kelmscott Press. Cambridge 1986.
Dreyfus, J. Morris and the printed book. 1989.
Peterson, W. S. The Kelmscott Press. Oxford 1991.

Eragny Press (L. and E. Pissarro, 1894–1914)
Moore, T. S. A brief account of the origin of the Eragny Press and a note on the relation of the printed book to life; [with] a bibliographical list of the Eragny books printed in the Vale type. Hammersmith 1903.
Jacobi, C. T. Eragny Press, 1894–1914. Penrose's Annual 28 1926.
Pissarro, L. Notes on the Eragny Press and a letter to J. B. Manson. Ed A. Fern, Cambridge 1957 (priv ptd).

Ashendene Press (C. H. St J. Hornby, 1895–1935)
A list of the books printed at the Ashendene Press mdcccxcv–mcmxiii. 1913.
Jacobi, C. T. The Ashendene Press, 1895–1923. Penrose's Annual 26 1924.
A hand-list of the books printed at the Ashendene Press mdcccxcv–mcmxxv. 1925.
A descriptive bibliography of the books printed at the Ashendene Press mdcccxcv–mcmxxxv. 1935.
Ward, S. The Ashendene Press. Philobiblon (Vienna) 10 1938.
C. H. St J. Hornby 1867–1946: an anthology of appreciations. 1946 (priv ptd).
Franklin, C. The Ashendene Press. Dallas 1986.

Vale Press (W. L. Hacon and C. Ricketts, 1896–1904)
Ricketts, C. and L. Pissarro. De la typographie et de l'harmonie de la page imprimée [and] William Morris et son influence sur les arts et métiers. 1898.
Ricketts, C. A bibliography of books issued by Hacon & Ricketts. 1904.

Essex House Press (C. R. Ashbee, 1898–1910)
Ashbee, C. R. The private press: a study in idealism; to which is added a bibliography of the Essex House Press. Broad Campden 1909.
Jacobi, C. T. Essex House Press, 1898–1909. Penrose's Annual 29 1927.

Doves Press (T. J. Cobden-Sanderson and Sir Emery Walker, 1900–16)
Catalogue raisonné of books printed & published at the Doves Press. Hammersmith 1908, 1911, 1916.
Cobden-Sanderson, T. J. Cosmic vision. 1922.
Jacobi, C. T. The Doves Press, 1900–1916. Penrose's Annual 25 1923.
Nash, J. H. (ed). Cobden-Sanderson and the Doves Press: the history of the press and the story of its types, told by A. W. Pollard; the character of the man set forth by his faithful scribe E. Johnston; with The ideal book, or Book beautiful, by T. J. Cobden-Sanderson; and a list of the Doves Press printing. San Francisco 1929.
Schmidt-Künsemüller, F. A. Emery Walker. Gutenberg Jahrbuch (Mainz) 1950.
Rooke, N. Sir Emery Walker 1851–1933. Penrose Annual 48 1954.
Nordlunde, C. V. Thomas James Cobden-Sanderson, bookbinder and printer. Copenhagen 1957.
Nordlunde, C. V. Sir Emery Walker and the revival of printing. Copenhagen 1959.
Franklin, C. Emery Walker: some light on his theories of printing and on his relations with William Morris and Cobden-Sanderson. Cambridge 1973 (priv ptd).
Franklin, C. Doves Press: the start of a worry. Dallas 1983. [NAR]

(9) PRINTERS AND PRINTING FIRMS

Aberdeen University Press
Keith, A. Aberdeen University Press: an account of the press from its foundation in 1840. Aberdeen 1963.

Adlard & Son, Dorking
Two hundred years in print: the company history of Adlard and Son Limited. Dorking [1966].

David Allen & Sons, Belfast
Allen, W. E. D. David Allens: the history of a family firm 1857–1957. 1957.

J. W. Arrowsmith, Bristol
Arrowsmith: 1854–1954. [Bristol] 1955.

Stephen Austin and Sons, Hertford
Moran, J. Stephen Austin's of Hertford: a bi-centenary history. Hertford 1968.

Balding & Mansell, Wisbech
Brown, R. The story of Balding + Mansell from 1892 to 1992. Wisbech 1992.

Ballantyne, Hanson & Co, Edinburgh
Lockhart, J. G. Memoirs of the life of Sir Walter Scott. 7 vols Edinburgh 1837–8, (many later edns).
[Ballantyne, J.] Refutation of the mistatements and calumnies contained in Mr Lockhart's Life of Sir Walter Scott respecting the Messrs Ballantyne. 1838 (3 edns).
[Lockhart, J. G.] The Ballantyne-humbug handled in a letter to Sir Adam Ferguson. Edinburgh 1839.
[Ballantyne, J.] Reply to Mr Lockhart's pamphlet entitled The Ballantyne-humbug handled. 1839.
The history of the Ballantyne Press and its connection with Sir Walter Scott. Edinburgh 1871.
[Dobson, W. T. and W. L. Carrie.] The Ballantyne Press and its founders 1796–1908. Edinburgh 1909.

George Baxter, London
Baxter Society. Jnl vol 1 1895. Continued as Quart Jnl vol 1 no 1, Jan 1921–vol 4 no 3, Dec 1924. Continued as Members Jnl vol 5 no 1, July 1925–vol 9 no 1, June 1929. Continued as Quart Jnl vol 10 no 1, Mar 1930–vol 11 no 5, Dec 1931. Continued as Quart Circular vol 1 no 1 (= vol 12), Apr 1932; vol 13 no 1, July 1933. Continued as Members Circular vol 14 no 1, Dec 1934–vol 17 no 6, Aug 1938.
Bullock, C. F. Life of George Baxter, engraver, artist and colour printer. Birmingham 1901.
Lewis, C. T. C. George Baxter (colour printer): his life and work. 1908.
Colebrook, F. George Baxter: his work and method. 1909.
Lewis, C. T. C. The picture printer of the nineteenth century: George Baxter, 1804–1867. 1911.
The Baxter year book, 1912. Continued as The Baxter book, 1919.
Clarke, H. G. Baxter colour prints: their history and methods of production. 1919.
Clarke, H. G. Baxter colour prints, pictorially presented. 1920–1.
The Baxter Times: a journal for nineteenth century colour print collectors vol 1 no 1, June 1923–vol 3 no 6, Nov 1925. Continued as B. P. collector and Baxter Times n.s. vol 3 no 1, Dec 1925–vol 5 no 2, July 1927. Continued as Books, prints and pictures vol 5 no 3, Aug 1927–vol 5 no 8, Jan 1928.
Lewis, C. T. C. George Baxter, the picture printer. [1924.]
Clarke, H. G. and J. H. Rylatt. The centenary Baxter book: being an appreciation of George Baxter 1804–1867. Leamington 1936.
Ball, A. and M. Martin. The price guide to Baxter prints. Woodbridge 1974.
Mitzman, M. E. George Baxter and the Baxter prints. Newton Abbot 1978.
New Baxter Society. Newsletter vol 1 no 1, Nov 1983– .

Ebenezer Baylis & Son, Worcester
A century of fine printing: the story of Ebenezer Baylis & Son Ltd,

Worcester, and Fleming & Humphreys (Baylis) Ltd, Leicester. [Worcester] 1961.
John Bell, London
Morison, S. John Bell 1745–1831: bookseller, printer, publisher, typefounder, journalist, etc. Cambridge 1930 (priv ptd).
A catalogue of books, newspapers, &c, printed by John Bell and by John Browne Bell, son of the above, exhibited at the First Edition Club. 1931.
John Bellows, Gloucester
Bellows, E. E. John Bellows: letters and memoir. 1904.
Charity, K. John Bellows of Gloucester 1831 to 1902: a many sided man. York 1993.
Bemrose & Sons, Derby
Messrs Bemrose & Sons, Derby and London. British Printer July/Aug 1892.
Bemrose, H. H. The House of Bemrose 1826–1926. Derby 1926.
Hackett, D. The history of the future: the Bemrose Corporation 1826–1976. 1976.
Thomas Bensley, London. *See* William Bulmer, *below*.
Charles Birchall, Liverpool
The house of Birchall. Liverpool [1949?].
Bradbury, Wilkinson & Co, London and New Maldon
Bradbury, Wilkinson & Co. Over a century of security printing. New Maldon [1965?].
George Bradshaw, Manchester
Katin, L. One hundred years of Bradshaw. Printing Rev Spring 1939.
Smith, G. R. The history of Bradshaw: a centenary review. 1939.
John Brown & Son, Glasgow
The firm of three generations. Glasgow 1908.
William Bulmer, London
Marrot, H. V. William Bulmer; Thomas Bensley: a study in transition. 1930.
Croft, W. The achievement of Bulmer and Bensley [with handlists of their work]. Signature n.s. 16–17 1952–3; Suppl 18 1954.
Isaac, P. C. G. William Bulmer: an introductory essay. Library 5th ser 13 1958.
Isaac, P. C. G. William Bulmer: the fine printer in context 1757–1830. 1993.
Burrup, Mathieson & Co, London
McConnell, B. At the sign of the Crane: 350 years of Burrup, Mathieson and Co Ltd 1628–1978. [1978.]
Thomas Bushill & Sons, Coventry
Howe, E. Bushills: the story of a Coventry firm of printers and box-makers 1856–1956. Coventry 1956.
Butler & Tanner, Frome
Rhode, J. A hundred years of printing 1795–1895. Frome 1927 (priv ptd).
Cambridge University Press
Bowes, R. Biographical notes on the university printers from the commencement of printing in Cambridge to the present time. Cambridge Antiquarian Soc Communications 5 1886.
Roberts, S. C. A history of the Cambridge University Press 1521–1921. Cambridge 1921.
Crutchley, E. A. A History and description of the Pitt Press erected to the memory of Mr Pitt for the use of the University Printing Press AD 1833 altered and restored AD 1937. Cambridge 1938.
Rogers, B. Report on the typography of the Cambridge University Press, prepared in 1917. Cambridge 1950 (priv ptd).
Scurfield, G. A stickful of nonpareil. Cambridge 1956 (priv ptd). On the Press in the 1890s under Charles and John Clay.
Black, M. H. Cambridge University Press 1584–1984. Cambridge 1984.
McKitterick, D. Four hundred years of university printing and publishing in Cambridge 1584–1984: catalogue of the exhibition in the University Library. Cambridge 1984.
Cassell & Co, London
McCoy, M. P. A visit to a London printing office. 1881.
Nowell-Smith, S. The house of Cassell 1848–1958. 1958.
Catnach Press, Newcastle and London
Hindley, C. The life and times of James Catnach, (late of Seven Dials), ballad monger. 1878.
Hindley, C. The history of the Catnach Press. 1886.
Cheney & Sons, Banbury
Cheney, J. John Cheney and his descendants. Banbury 1936 (priv ptd).
Cheneys of Banbury 1767–1967. Banbury 1967.
Chiswick Press, London, *see* Charles Whittingham, *below*.
Richard Clay & Co, Bungay
Moran, J. Clays of Bungay. Bungay 1978.
William Clowes & Sons, London and Beccles
Smiles, S. William Clowes: introducer of book-printing by steam. In his Men of invention and industry. 1884.
Clowes, W. B. Family business 1803–1953. 1953.
Cockayne & Co, London
Cockayne & Co. One hundred years, 1844–1944. [1944.]
William Collins, Glasgow
Keir, D. The house of Collins. 1952.
T. & A. Constable, Edinburgh
Brief notes on the origins of T. & A. Constable Ltd. Edinburgh 1937. On the Edinburgh University Press.
Co-operative Printing Society, Manchester
The origin, the history and the services of the Co-operative Printing Society. [Manchester] 1890.
Hall, F. The history of the Co-operative Printing Society, 1869–1919. [Manchester 1920.]
Mercer, T. W. Sixty years of Co-operative printing. [Manchester] 1930.
S. H. (later W. S.) Cowell Ltd, Ipswich
Illustrations to the art of printing: being a description of a visit to the steam printing works of S. H. Cowell, Ipswich. Ipswich 1876.
A walk through our works: a short account of a visit to the printing, stationery and bookbinding manufactory of S. H. Cowell, Ipswich. Ipswich 1888.
W. S. Cowell Ltd. Foundations of quality. Ipswich 1974.
Cox & Wyman, London, Fakenham and Reading
Moran, J. Cox & Wyman Ltd: a company history [1777–1977]. 1977.
Crampton & Sons, Sawston
Teversham, T. F. The story of a country printing house. Cambridge 1962.
Curwen Press, London
Harley, B. The Curwen Press: a short history. [1970.]
Simon, H. Song and words: a history of the Curwen Press. 1973.
William Davison, Alnwick
Isaac, P. C. G. William Davison of Alnwick, pharmacist and printer 1781–1858. Oxford 1968.
Dawson & Goodall, Bath
Dawson & Goodall. 200 years of printing. Bath 1970.
De La Rue & Co, London
Illustrated description of Thos De La Rue and Co's works, with an account of the employees' benefit societies. 1883.
Houseman, L. The house that Thomas built: the story of De La Rue. 1968.
Derry & Sons, Nottingham
Derry's: a century in print 1867–1967. Nottingham 1967.
William Dickes, London
Docker, A. The colour prints of William Dickes. [1924.]
Edmund Evans, London
McLean, R. (ed). The reminiscences of Edmund Evans. Oxford 1967.
John Fairfax, Leamington
Morgan, P. John Fairfax and the sale of his printing stock and equipment in Leamington in 1838. Jnl of the Printing Historical Soc 24 1995.

Emily Faithfull, London, *see* Victoria Press, *below*.
Benjamin Fawcett, Driffield
Morris, M. C. F. Benjamin Fawcett, colour printer and engraver. Oxford 1925.
Desmond, R. Benjamin Fawcett (1808–1893), printer and engraver of natural history books. Festschrift für Claus Nissen (ed E. Geck and G. Pressler). Wiesbaden 1973.
McLean, R. and A. Benjamin Fawcett, engraver and colour printer. Aldershot 1988.
Leslie Fleming, Edinburgh journeyman
Fleming, L. An octogenarian printer's recollections. Edinburgh 1893.
Forman & Sons, Nottingham
Fuller, F. History of the firm. In Forman & Sons. Centenary. Nottingham 1948.
W. J. Fowler & Son, London
W. J. Fowler & Son Ltd: 50 years of typographical progress. 1948.
Frank Gaskell, Birmingham
Gaskell, F. The experience and maxims of a practical printer. [1890.]
Henry George, Westerham
Moran, J. Henry George, printer, bookseller, stationer and bookbinder, Westerham, 1830–c. 1846. Westerham 1972.
Glasgow University Press
Maclehose, J. The Glasgow University Press 1638–1931. Glasgow 1931.
The Glasgow University Printing office in 1826. Cambridge 1953 (priv ptd).
Luke Hansard, London
Hansard, L. Biographical memoir of Luke Hansard, many years printer to the House of Commons. 1829 (priv ptd); then as The auto-biography of Luke Hansard, printer to the House 1752–1828. 1991 (ed Robin Myers; Printing Historical Soc).
Howe, E. The Hansard family. Signature n.s. 6 1948.
Trewin, J. C. and E. M. King. Printer to the House: the story of Hansard. 1952.
Harrison & Sons, London
The house of Harrison: being an account of the family and firm of Harrison and Sons, printers to the King. 1914.
Harrison and Sons. Harrison: a family imprint. [1950.]
Hazell, Watson & Viney Ltd, London and Aylesbury
Hazell, R. C. Walter Hazell 1843–1919. 1919 (2 edns (one priv ptd)).
Keefe, H. J. A century in print: the story of Hazell's 1839–1939. 1939.
Hazell, Watson & Viney. Hazells in Aylesbury 1867–1967: a scrap-book to commemorate the first hundred years at the printing works, Aylesbury. Aylesbury 1968.
Frank Horsell & Co, Leeds
Brewer, R. A sharper image: a history of the Horsell Group 1885–1989. 1989.
Jarrold & Sons, Norwich
The house of Jarrolds 1823–1923: a brief history of one hundred years. Norwich 1924.
Jarrold & Sons. History of Jarrold & Sons [1823–1948]. [Norwich 1948.]
George W. Jones, London
Jay, L. A tribute to the work of George W. Jones, master printer, on the occasion of his eightieth birthday. Birmingham 1940 (Birmingham School of Printing); also in Printing Rev no 35 1941.
Rudge, W. E. George W. Jones: superior printer, 1860–1942. Print 3 no 3 1943.
Kenrick & Jefferson, West Bromwich
Cartwright, W. H. The house of K. & J. [1878–1953]. West Bromwich [1953].
King's Printing Office, Edinburgh
Kinnear, S. Reminiscences of an aristocratic Edinburgh printing office. Edinburgh 1890.
William Kitchin, Ulverston
Benbow, J. The Kitchin collection, the work of a late 19th century jobbing printer and his son. Reading 1974.
Le Blond & Co, London
Lewis, C. T. C. The Le Blond book: being a history & detailed catalogue of the work of Le Blond & Co. 1920.
Lewis, C. T. C. The story of picture printing in England during the nineteenth century (ch 17–19 Le Blond & Co). [1928.]
M. Lownds & Son, London
M. Lownds & Son, 1855–1905: a record of fifty years' progress. [1905.]
McCaw, Stevenson & Orr, Belfast
McCabe, B. From Linenhall to Loopbridge: the story of McCaw, Stevenson & Orr Ltd, printers, 1876–1990. [Belfast] 1990.
John McCreery, Liverpool and London
Barker, J. R. John McCreery, a radical printer, 1768–1832. Library 5th ser 16 1961.
Isaac, P. C. G. John M'Creery: a tentative checklist of his printing. Wylam 1991.
W. & J. Mackay, Leith and Chatham
Whyman, J. From Leith to Lordswood: being a short history of W. & J. Mackay to mark their centenary 1875–1975. Chatham [1975].
Mark & Moody, Stourbridge (Worcs.)
Haden, H. J. The story of Mark & Moody Ltd 1840–1957. Stourbridge [1958].
Milner & Sowerby, Halifax
Bridge, D. William Milner: printer and bookseller. Trans of Halifax Antiquarian Soc 1969.
William Morris. *See col 41 above, under* Kelmscott Press
James Moyes, London
Bain, I. James Moyes and his Temple Printing Office of 1825. Jnl of the Printing Historical Soc 4 1968.
Neill & Co, Edinburgh
History of the firm of Neill & Co Ltd. Edinburgh 1900.
The printing-house of Neill. Edinburgh [1918].
McLaren, M. The house of Neill 1749–1949. Edinburgh 1949.
Thomas Nelson & Sons, Edinburgh
The story of a famous firm of printer-publishers. Br & Colonial Printer 8 June 1951, Suppl.
Bernard Newdigate, London typographer
Blackwell, B. Bernard Newdigate, typographer. 1945 (priv ptd).
Thorp, J. B. H. Newdigate: scholar-printer 1869–1944. Oxford 1950.
Nichols & Sons, London
Nichols, J. G. Memoir of John Nichols. In Illustrations of the literary history of the eighteenth century vol 8, 1858.
Nichols, J. G. Memoir of the late John Bowyer Nichols. 1864.
Nichols, R. C. Memoir of the late John Gough Nichols. 1874 (2 edns).
The house of Nichols 1699–1930. [1930.]
Smith, A. H. John Nichols, printer and publisher. Library 5th ser 18 1963.
J. W. Northend, Sheffield
Millington, R. A history of J. W. Northend Ltd, printers of Sheffield, 1889–1989. Sheffield 1989.
Novello & Co, London
Novello & Co. A century and a half in Soho: a short history of the firm of Novello, publishers and printers of music 1811–1961. 1961.
Hurd, M. Vincent Novello – and company. St Albans 1981.
Oxford University Press
Hart, H. Charles Earl Stanhope and the Oxford University Press. Oxford Historical Soc Collectanea 3 1896, 1966 (ed J. Mosley; Printing Historical Soc).
Some account of the Oxford University Press. Oxford 1922, 1926.
Batey, C. Horace Hart and the University Press, Oxford 1883–1915. Signature n.s. no 18 1954.
Batey, C. The Oxford partners: some notes on the administration of

the University Press 1780–1881. Jnl of the Printing Historical Soc 3 1967.
Barker, N. The Oxford University Press and the spread of learning 1478–1978. Oxford 1978.
Sutcliffe, P. H. The Oxford University Press: an informal history. Oxford 1978.
Petty & Sons, Leeds
[Murray, C. C.] Petty & Sons Limited 1865–1965. 1965.
Pillans & Wilson, Edinburgh
A printing house of old & new Edinburgh 1775–1925. Edinburgh 1925.
Pitman Press, Bath
An historical review of the Pitman Press [1845–1937]. Bath [1937].
John Pitts, London
Shepard, L. John Pitts, ballad printer of Seven Dials, London, 1765–1844. 1969 (Priv Libs Assoc).
Robert Pocock, Gravesend
Arnold, G. M. Robert Pocock: the Gravesend historian, naturalist, antiquarian, botanist and printer. 1883.
Raithby, Lawrence & Co, Leicester
Brewer, R. Raithby Lawrence 1876–1976 [and predecessors] 1776–1876. Leicester [1976].
Thomas Reed & Co, Sunderland
Bean, D. Thomas Reed – the first 200 years: a brief history 1782–1982. Sunderland [1982].
Andrew Reid & Co, Newcastle
A famous north country printery: Andrew Reid & Co Ltd. British Printer Mar/Apr 1896.
Reid, A. A note on the company's history. In Reid & Co. Centenary celebrations 1845–1945 [at] Edinburgh 18th September 1948. [Newcastle 1948.]
Sharp, M. Andrew Reid & Co Ltd: a famous north-country printery. Wylam 1991.
E. S. & A. Robinson, Bristol
Darwin, B. Robinsons of Bristol 1844–1944. Bristol 1945.
Thomas Ross & Son, London
Bain, I. Thomas Ross & Son, copper- and steel-plate printers since 1833. Jnl of the Printing Historical Soc 2 1966.
Dyson, A. Thomas Ross & Son, fine art printers: the nineteenth century heritage. 1983 (priv ptd).
Joseph Rounsfell, itinerant journeyman
Rounsfell, J. W. On the road: journeys of a tramping printer. Ed A. Whitehead. 1982. On trade union relief of a travelling compositor.
W. R. Royle & Son, London
Royle occasion: the first 150 years. [1976.]
William Sessions Ltd, York
The story of a printing house [1865–1965]. York 1965.
Robert Skeen, London printer's overseer
Autobiography of Mr Robert Skeen, printer 1876 (priv ptd).
Robert Smail, Innerleithen
Boyter, I. Robert Smail's printing works, established 1848, saved for the nation 1987. Edinburgh 1987 (Nat Trust for Scotland).
L. A. Smart & Son, Gloucester
Wain, D. W. L. A. Smart & Son Ltd: a century of progress in printing 1850–1950. [Gloucester 1950.]
Charles Manby Smith, itinerant journeyman
Smith, C. M. The working man's way in the world. [1853], 1854, 1857 (all anon), 1967 (ed E. Howe; Printing Historical Soc). Autobiography of a journeyman printer.
Nowell-Smith, S. Charles Manby Smith, his family & friends, his fantasies & fabrications. Jnl of the Printing Historical Soc 7 1971.
John Soulby, Ulverston
Twyman, M. John Soulby, printer, Ulverston: a study of the work printed by John Soulby, father and son, between 1796 and 1827. Reading 1966.

Spottiswoode & Co, London
History of Spottiswoode & Co Ltd, being a brief epitome of the chief events 1739–1909. 1909.
Austen-Leigh, R. A. The story of a printing house: being a short account of the Strahans and the Spottiswoodes. [1911], 1912.
Straker Bros, London
Straker Bros. 1800–1925: a brief history of the business. London [1925].
The house of Straker [1800–1950]. [1950.]
Taylor & Francis, London
Brock, W. H. and A. J. Meadows. The lamp of learning: Taylor & Francis and the development of science publishing. [1984.]
C. P. Thorn & Sons, Woolwich
Thorns of Woolwich 1881–1953. 1953.
Tillotson & Son, Bolton
Singleton, F. Tillotsons 1850–1950: centenary of a family business. Bolton 1950.
Tinlings, Liverpool
Tinlings of Liverpool: the past, the present and the future. Liverpool 1962.
A. W. Tuer, London
Johnson, A. F. Old-face types in the Victorian age. Monotype Recorder Sep/Dec 1931.
'Caxton Morris'. Andrew White Tuer. Printing Rev Summer 1950.
Tullis Press, Cupar
Doughty, D. W. The Tullis Press, Cupár, 1803–1849. Dundee 1967 (Abertay Historical Soc). On St Andrews University Press.
Unwin Brothers, London and Woking
Unwin Brothers. A century of progress: being a record of the rise and present position of the Gresham Press 1826–1926. [1926.]
Colebrook, F. The Unwins. Caxton Mag Nov 1950.
Unwin, P. The printing Unwins: a short history of Unwin Brothers, the Gresham Press, 1826–1976. 1976.
Vacher & Sons, London
At the sign of the red pale, being a short history of the house of Vacher & Sons Ltd of Westminster 1751–1926. [1926.]
Victoria Press (Emily Faithfull), London
Head, W. W. The Victoria Press: its history and vindication with an account of the movement for the employment of females in printing. 1869.
Fredeman, W. E. Emily Faithfull and the Victoria Press. Library 5th ser 29 1974.
Stone, J. S. More light on Emily Faithfull and the Victoria Press. Library 5th ser 33 1978.
Ratcliffe, E. The Caxton of her age: the career and family background of Emily Faithfull (1835–95). Upton upon Severn 1993.
Waddie & Co, Edinburgh
Waddie & Co. A centenary history, 1860–1960. [1960.]
Waterlows, London
Smalley, G. The life of Sir Sidney Waterlow. 1909.
The house of Waterlows of Birchin Lane from 1811 to 1911. [1911.]
Waterlow and Sons Ltd, 1810 to 1914. [1914.]
Boon, J. Under six reigns: being some account of 114 years of progress and development of the house of Waterlow. 1925.
George Waterston & Sons, Edinburgh
Bicentenary history: George Waterston & Sons Ltd 1752–1952. Edinburgh [1952].
Two hundred and twenty five years: a history of George Waterston & Sons Limited 1752–1977. [Edinburgh 1977.]
Wertheimer, Lea & Co, London
A romance of the printing trade. [1914.]
Charles Whittingham & Co., Chiswick Press, London
Warren, A. The Charles Whittinghams, printers. New York 1896 (Grolier Club).
Plomer, H. R. A glance at the Whittingham ledgers. Library 2 1901.
Keynes, G. William Pickering, publisher. 1924, 1969.

Buechler, J. 'Adapted from an old book': some sources for Chiswick Press woodcut initials. Printing History 7/8 1982.

Wightman & Co, London

Wightman & Co. One hundred years. [1936.]

John Wright & Sons, Bristol

Wright & Sons. A centenary souvenir 1825–1925. Bristol 1925.

Wright & Sons. 125 years of printing and publishing 1825–1950. Bristol 1952.

Wyman & Sons, London

Lawrence, A. The story of Wyman & Sons Ltd. [1907.]

Yelf Brothers, Newport IoW

Daish, A. N. Printers' pride: the house of Yelf at Newport, Isle of Wight, 1816–1966. Newport, IoW 1967. [NAR]

(10) PRINTING TRADE PERIODICALS

Although this section contains only periodicals issued in Great Britain, two others may be mentioned for their international importance: Journal für Buchdruckerkunst, Braunschweig 1834–1919; The inland printer, Chicago 1883–1978.

See Mohr, L. Die periodische Fachpresse der Typographie und der verwandten Geschaftszweige, Strasbourg 1879.

See Ulrich, C. F. and K. Küp. Books and printing: a selected list of periodicals 1800–1942. Woodstock VT 1943.

St Bride Foundation Institute. Catalogue of the periodicals relating to printing & allied subjects in the technical library. 1951.

The compositors' chronicle. No 1, Sep 1840–no 37, Aug 1843. Continued as The printer. No 1, Nov 1843–no 19, June 1845. Monthly.

The typographical gazette. No 1, Apr 1846–no 16, May 1847. Monthly.

The typographical protection circular. No 1, Jan 1849–no 59, Nov 1853. Continued as The typographical circular. No 1, Apr 1854–no 55, Sep 1858. Continued as The London press journal and general trades advocate. No 1, 1 Nov 1858–no 4, 1 Jan 1859. Monthly; ed E. S. Mantz.

Typographical societies' monthly circular. No 1, Oct 1852–no 273, June 1875. Continued as The provincial typographical circular. No 274, July 1875–no 297, June 1877. Continued as The typographical circular. No 298, July 1877–no 1332, Nov/Dec 1963. Manchester. Monthly; ed H. Slatter.

The Scottish typographical circular. No 1, Sep 1857–no 6, Feb 1858; n.s. no 1, Mar 1858–no 42, Aug 1861; third ser no 1, Sep 1861–no 568, Dec 1908. Continued as The Scottish typographical journal. No 569, Jan 1909–no 1379, Dec 1973. Edinburgh, later Glasgow. Monthly; ed D. Hunter.

Journal of the typographic arts. No 1, Jan 1860–no 29, May 1862. Monthly.

J. & R. M. Wood's typographic advertiser. No 1, June 1862–no 71, Feb 1868. Monthly.

The printers' register. No 1, July 1863–no 1111, Jan 1956. Monthly; ed W. Dorrington (1863–6), A. J. C. Powell.

The printers' journal and typographical magazine. No 1, 2 Jan 1865–no 122, 22 Mar 1869. Fortnightly.

London, provincial and colonial press news. No 1, Jan 1866–no 564, Dec 1912. Monthly; ed W. Dorrington.

The chromolithograph: a journal of art literature, decoration and the accomplishments. No 1, 23 Nov 1867–no 51, 20 Mar 1869. Weekly.

The lithographer. No 1, July 1870–no 49, July 1874. Continued as The printing times and lithographer. Aug–Dec 1874 (no 50–4 of The lithographer and no 20–4 of The printing times); n.s. no 1, Jan 1875–no 180, Dec 1889–[July 1891?]. Continued as The lithographer. No 1, Sep 1891–no 3, Nov 1891. Continued as The printing times and lithographer. n.s. Vol 1 no 1, July 1892–vol 9 [no 11], Nov/Dec 1900. Monthly.

The paper and printing trades journal. No 1, Dec 1872–no 89, 1897. Quarterly; ed A. W. Tuer. Index to nos 1–32 by E. R. Pearce, Taunton 1881.

The printing times. No 1, Jan 1873–no 19, July 1874. Monthly.

The Fleet Street gazette: a journeyman's journal. No 1, 28 Feb–no 7, 23 May 1874. Fortnightly.

Hailing's circular. No 1, Nov 1877–no 24, Autumn 1889. Cheltenham. Quarterly, then irregular.

The British and colonial printer. Vol 1 no 1, 16 Dec 1878–vol 153 no 26, 25 Dec 1953. Continued as Printing world. Vol 154 no 1, 1 Jan 1954– . Twice monthly, later weekly.

Paper and print. No 1, 2 Aug 1879–no 236, 2 Feb 1884. Weekly; ed H. F. Gough.

The printing trades diary and desk-book. 1879–86. Annual; ed C. W. H. Wyman.

The printing review. No 1, Jan 1879–no 12, Dec 1879.

The printers' friend. No 1, Nov 1880–no 8, June 1883.

The printers' international specimen exchange. Vol 1, 1880–vol 16, 1896/7. Annual; ed A. W. Tuer.

The printer: a quarterly journal devoted to the interests of printers and printing. No 1, Nov 1883–no 20, Aug 1888. Ed W. A. Coote.

The modern printer: a technical journal. Vol 1 no 1, Mar 1884–vol 2 no 4, Aug 1888. Quarterly; ed M. P. McCoy.

World's printers, stationers and kindred traders' effective advertiser. No 1, Apr 1884–no 161, May 1898. Continued as Imperial printer. No 162, June 1898. Monthly.

Salmon's Printing Trades Circular. No 1, Jan 1886–no 13, Aug 1890. Manchester.

The typographic chronicle. No 1, Feb 1887–no 14, Sep 1897; n.s. no 1, Mar 1898–no 12, Jan 1904.

Printers', lithographers', bookbinders' and stationers' sales and wants advertiser. No 1, Mar 1887–no 910, Dec 1962. Continued as Printing trades journal. No 911, Jan 1963–no 1094, Apr 1978. Incorporated with Printing world.

The British printer. Vol 1 no 1, Jan/Feb 1888– . 6 times a year 1888–1955, then monthly. In progress.

The vigilance gazette: a monthly (later quarterly) journal devoted to the interests of the London Society of Compositors. No 1, May 1888–no 6, Feb 1889. Continued as The London printers' circular and vigilance gazette. No 7, May 1889–no 11, May 1890.

The printer's exchange and sale journal. Nos 1–7, 1889–1890.

The English typographia. Vol 1 no 1, Spring 1889–vol 2 no 1, Oct 1896–[?].

The printing world. No 1, Jan 1891–vol 19 no 9, Sep 1911.

The British lithographer. No 1, Oct/Nov 1891–no 24, Aug/Sep 1895. Incorporated with The British printer.

The printing news: a monthly journal for the workers. Vol 1 no 1, Aug 1892–vol 3 no 5, Dec 1894.

Printers, stationers and kindred traders' weekly advertiser. Vol 1 no 1, 3 June 1893–vol 1 no 4, 24 June 1893. Continued as Printers and kindred traders' weekly advertiser. Vol 1 no 5, 1 July 1893–vol 1 no 25, 18 Nov 1893. Continued as Printers and kindred traders' monthly advertiser. Vol 2 no 1, Jan 1894–vol 4 no 5, May 1896.

Leeds typographical circular. [?]–no 22, Aug 1893–no 24, Feb 1894–[?]. Leeds.

The stationers' and printers' annual. 1895–1903.

The British art printer and lithographer. Vol 1 no 1, Jan/Feb 1895. Continued as The art printer and lithographer. Vol 1 no 2, Mar/Apr 1895; vol 1 no 3, May/June 1896–vol 1 no 4, July/Aug 1896.

Amateur printing. No 1, June 1895–no 76, Jan 1914. (Amateur Printers Assoc.)

The printer's engineer. No 1, Sep 1895–no 832, Oct 1939. Monthly, later quarterly. Pbd by Usher-Walker.

The printing and kindred traders' review. No 1, Mar 1896–no 3, Dec 1896. Quarterly.

Print: a journal for printing-house employés of all grades and departments. No 1, May 1896–no 6, Oct 1896. Monthly.
Barnett's weekly printing trades gazette and paper industries intelligencer. No 1, 20 Mar 1897–no 253, 5 Feb 1902. Weekly.
The Caxtonian quarterly. No 1, Feb 1898–no 22, Apr/May 1904–[?]; vol 4 no 1, Jan/Feb 1906–[?]; n.s. no 1, May 1908–no 3, May 1909.
Journal of printing and kindred trades of the British Empire. No 1, June 1898–no 32, Jan 1901. (Inst of Printers and Kindred Trades of the British Empire.)
Paper and printing bits. No 1, Oct 1898–no 17, Mar/Apr 1900. Birmingham. Monthly. Pbd by Willcocks, Wheeler & Co.
Haddon's diary and printers' guide. 1899–1901. Annual.
The printers' year book and diary. 1899–1903. Continued as The printers' and stationers' year book and diary. 1904–1926 or 1927. Continued as Caxton year book and diary. 1927 or 1928–1958–[?].
The printers' pocket guide. 1899–1914. Ed A. C. Couch. Title varies slightly.
The Press: an independent journal for pressman, proprietor, printer, publisher and stationer. Vol 1 no 1, July 1899–vol 4 no 6, June 1902. Continued as The press, paper, printing, bookbinding and stationery chronicle. n.s. Vol 4 no 1, July 1902–vol 4 no 2, Aug 1902. Continued as The Caxton magazine and the press. Vol 4 no 3, Sep 1902–vol 6, no 1, July 1904. Continued as The Caxton magazine and British manufacturing, art and fancy stationer. Vol 6 no 2, Aug 1904–vol 9 no 12, June 1908. Continued as The Caxton magazine and British stationer. Vol 10 no 1, July 1908–vol 22 no 5, May 1920. Continued as The Caxton magazine. Vol 22 no 6, June 1920–vol 61 no 5, May 1959. Monthly. [NAR]

(11) BOOK ILLUSTRATION

General works

Many of the works listed in (6) Graphic processes are also relevant here.
See Hassall, J. Wood engraving: a reader's guide. 1949.
See Bland, D. A bibliography of book illustration. 1955.
See Olmsted, J. C. and J. E. Welch. Victorian novel illustration: a selected checklist 1900–1976. New York 1979.
Orme, E. An essay on transparent prints and on transparencies in general. 1807.
[Plowman, J.] An essay on the illustration of books. 1824.
Art-circular: a monthly record of illustrated literature and art-manufactures. Nos 1–5 1850–1.
Hamerton, P. G. Etching and etchers. 1868, 1876, 1880.
Ruskin, J. Ariadne Florentina. 1873 (many edns and in sets of his collected works).
Redgrave, S. A dictionary of artists of the English School. 1874, 1878.
Carr, J. C. Cantor lectures on book illustration, old and new. 1882.
Everitt, G. English caricaturists and graphic humourists of the nineteenth century. 1886.
Tuer, A. W. 1,000 quaint cuts from books of other days. [1886.]
Crane, W. Cantor lectures on the decoration and illustration of books. 1889.
Linton, W. J. The masters of wood engraving. New Haven 1889.
Pennell, J. Pen drawing and pen draughtsmen. 1889, 1894, 1897, 1921.
Brough, W. S. Book illustration. Leek 1891.
Slater, J. H. Engravings and their value. 1891, 1897, 1900, 1912, 1921, 1929 (rev F. W. Maxwell-Barbour).
Harper, C. G. English pen artists of to-day: examples of their work, with some criticisms and appreciations. 1892.
Nisbet, H. Illustrative art: past and present. GM Mar 1892.
Blomfield, R. Of book illustration and book decoration. Arts and crafts essays by members of the Arts and Crafts Exhibition Soc. 1893.
Blackburn, H. Cantor lectures on the art of book and newspaper illustration. 1894.
Blackburn, H. The art of illustration. 1894, 1896, Edinburgh 1901 (rev J. S. Eland).
Chapin, W. O. The masters and masterpieces of engraving. New York 1894.
Harper, C. G. A practical handbook of drawing for modern methods of reproduction. 1894.
Layard, G. S. Tennyson and his Pre-Raphaelite illustrators. 1894.
Meade, E. Pen pictures and how to draw them. 1895.
Pennell, J. Modern illustration. 1895.
Vine, C. J. Hints on drawing for process reproduction. 1895.
Wedmore, F. Etching in England. 1895.
Crane, W. Of the decorative illustration of books old and new. 1896, 1901.
Pennell, J. English book illustration 1860–1870. Jnl of Royal Soc of Arts 3 Apr 1896.
Pennell, J. The illustration of books. 1896.
White, G. English illustration: 'the sixties' 1855–70. 1897.
White, G. Children's books and thier illustrators. Studio winter 1897/8.
Whitman, A. C. The masters of mezzotint, the men and their work. 1898.
Kitton, F. G. Dickens and his illustrators. 1899.
Slater, J. H. Illustrated sporting books. 1899.
Doyen, C. Origini e sviluppo della litografia durante il secolo 19. Milan 1901.
Victoria and Albert Museum. Catalogue of the loan collection of modern illustration. 1901.
Murdoch, T. The early history of lithography in Glasgow. Glasgow 1902.
Pingrenon, R. Les livres ornés et illustrés en couleur depuis le xve siècle en France et en Angleterre. Paris 1903.
Sketchley, R. E. D. English book illustration of to-day: appreciations of the work of living English illustrators with lists of their books. 1903.
Whitman, A. C. Nineteenth-century mezzotinters. 3 vols 1903–7.
'Paston, George' (E. M. Symonds). Old coloured books. 1905.
Hardie, M. English coloured books. 1906.
Spurrier, S. Black and white: a manual of illustration. 1909.
Salaman, M. C. Old English colour prints. Studio winter 1909/10.
Hammerton, J. A. The Dickens picture-book: a record of the Dickens illustrators. 1910.
Murdoch, W. G. B. The renaissance of the nineties. 1911.
Imeson, W. E. Illustrated music-titles and their delineators. [1912.]
Jackson, H. The eighteen-nineties. 1913.
Sullivan, E. J. The art of illustration. 1921.
Salaman, M. C. British book illustration: yesterday and to-day. 1923.
Tate Gallery. Catalogue: book illustration of the sixties. 1923.
Nevill, R. H. Old English sporting books. 1924.
Robinson, C. N. Old naval prints. 1924.
Siltzer, F. The story of British sporting prints. 1925, 1929.
Lewis, C. T. C. The story of picture printing in England during the nineteenth century. [1928.]
Reid, F. Illustrators of the sixties. 1928.
Newbolt, F. The history of the Royal Society of Painter-Etchers and Engravers 1880–1930. 1930.
Ruemann, A. Das illustrierte Buch des xix. Jahrhunderts in England, Frankreich und Deutschland 1790–1860. Leipzig 1930.
Balston, T. English book illustration 1880–1900. In J. Carter, New paths in book collecting, 1934.
Burke, W. J. Rudolph Ackermann: promoter of the arts and sciences. BNYPL 1934.
Thorpe, J. English illustration: the nineties. 1935.
Tooley, R. V. Some English books with coloured plates, their points, collations & values: first half of the nineteenth century. 1935.
Pevsner, N. Pioneers of the Modern Movement. 1936; then as Pioneers of modern design. 1960.

Gray, B. The English print. 1937.
Reitlinger, H. S. From Hogarth to Keene. 1938.
Sparrow, W. S. Book illustrators of the sixties. H. Hartley. Eighty-eight not out. 1939.
Bechtel, E. de T. Illustrated books of the sixties. Print 1 no 1 1940.
Piper, J. British romantic artists. 1942.
Arts Council. English book illustration since 1800. Ed P. James. 1943.
New York Public Library. Influences and trends in nineteenth-century illustration. New York 1943.
Meynell, F. English printed books. 1946.
James, P. English book illustration 1800–1900. 1947.
Miller, B. E. M., L. P. Latimer and B. Folmsbee. Illustrators of children's books 1744–1945. Boston 1947.
Wallis, N. Fin de siècle. [1947.]
Friedman, A. B. English illustrators of the 1860's. Bull Boston Public Lib 23 1948.
Smith, J. A. Children's illustrated books. 1948.
Piper, J. Picturesque travel illustrated. Signature n.s. no 11 1950.
Bland, D. The illustration of books. 1951, 1953, 1962.
Abbey, J. R. Scenery of Great Britain and Ireland in aquatint and lithography 1770–1860: a bibliographical catalogue. 1952 (priv ptd).
Abbey, J. R. Life in England in aquatint and lithography 1770–1860: a bibliographical catalogue. 1953 (priv ptd).
Ivins, W. M. Prints and visual communication. 1953.
Abbey, J. R. Travel in aquatint and lithography 1770–1860: a bibliographical catalogue. 2 vols 1956–7 (priv ptd).
Bland, D. A history of book illustration. 1958, 1969.
Barkley, H. 19th-century illustrators – and others. Penrose Annual 53 1959.
Garvey, E. M. (ed). The artist & the book 1860–1960 in Western Europe and the United States. Boston 1961, 1972.
McLean, R. Victorian book design and colour printing. 1963, 1972.
Pitz, H. Illustrating children's books: history, technique, production. New York [1963].
Sutphen, R. Old engravings & illustrations 1860–1907. Minneapolis [1965].
Turner, D. H. English book illustration 966–1846. 1965.
Taylor, J. R. The art nouveau book in Britain. 1966.
Harvey, J. R. Victorian novelists and their illustrators. 1970.
Slythe, R. M. The art of illustration. 1970.
Muir, P. Victorian illustrated books. 1971.
Wakeman, G. Victorian book illustration: the technical revolution. Newton Abbot 1973.
Peppin, B. Fantasy: book illustration 1860–1920. 1975.
Ray, G. N. The illustrator and the book in England from 1790 to 1914. New York 1976.
Anglo, M. Penny dreadfuls and other Victorian horrors. 1977.
Baker, C. Bibliography of British book illustrators 1860–1900: being an attempt to classify the first editions of books by illustrator. Birmingham 1978.
Houfe, S. The dictionary of British book illustrators and caricaturists 1800–1914 with introductory chapters on the rise and progress of the art. Woodbridge CT 1978, 1981. The dictionary portion revised as The dictionary of 19th century British book illustrators and caricaturists. 1996.
Engen, R. K. Dictionary of Victorian engravers, print publishers and their works. Cambridge 1979.
Cohen, J. R. Charles Dickens and his original illustrators. Columbus OH 1980.
De Maré, E. The Victorian woodblock illustrators. 1980.
Hall, N. J. Trollope and his illustrators. 1980.
Hunnisett, B. Steel-engraved book illustration in England. 1980.
Hunnisett, B. A dictionary of British steel engravers. Leigh-on-sea 1980; then as An illustrated dictionary of British steel engravers. Aldershot 1989.
Harthan, J. The history of the illustrated book: the Western tradition. 1981.
Hodnett, E. Image and text: studies in the illustration of English literature. 1982.
Buchanan-Brown, J. British wood-engravers c. 1820–c. 1860: a checklist. Jnl of the Printing Historical Soc 17 1982/3.
Lister, R. Prints and printmaking: a dictionary and handbook of the art in nineteenth-century Britain. 1984.
Engen, R. K. Dictionary of Victorian wood engravers. Cambridge 1985.
Alderson, B. Sing a song for sixpence: the English picture book tradition and Randolph Caldecott. Cambridge 1986.
Daniels, M. Victorian book illustration. 1988.
Felmingham, M. The illustrated gift book 1780–1930 with a checklist of 2500 titles. Aldershot 1988.
Hodnett, E. Five centuries of English book illustration. Aldershot 1988.
Dalby, R. The golden age of children's book illustration. 1991.
Houfe, S. Fin de Siècle: the illustrators of the 'nineties. 1992.
Goldman, P. Victorian illustrated books 1850–1870: the heyday of wood-engraving. 1994.
Kooistra, L. J. The artist as critic: bitextuality in Fin-de-Siècle illustrated books. Aldershot 1995.
Goldman, P. Victorian illustration: the Pre-Raphaelites, the Idyllic School and the High Victorians. Aldershot 1996.

Illustrators

Henry Alken (1784–1851)
Sparrow, W. S. Henry Alken. 1927.
Noakes, A. The world of Henry Alken. 1952.

Aubrey Beardsley (1872–98)
Symons, A. Aubrey Beardsley. 1898, 1905.
The early work of Aubrey Beardsley. 1899.
The later work of Aubrey Beardsley. 1901.
Ross, R. B. Aubrey Beardsley. 1909.
The uncollected work of Aubrey Beardsley. 1925.
Walker, R. A. (ed). Letters from Aubrey Beardsley to Leonard Smithers. 1937.
Walker, R. A. Le morte d'Arthur with Beardsley illustrations: a bibliographical essay. Bedford 1945.
Gallatin, A. E. Aubrey Beardsley: catalogue of drawings and bibliography. New York 1945 (priv ptd).
Walker, R. A. The best of Beardsley. 1948.
Hölscher, E. Aubrey Beardsley. Hamburg 1949.
Gallatin, A. E. and A. D. Wainwright. The Gallatin Beardsley Collection in the Princeton University Library: a catalogue. Princeton 1952.
Reade, B. Beardsley. 1967.
Langenfeld, R. Reconsidering Aubrey Beardsley. Ann Arbor 1989.
See also col 702.

Thomas Bewick (1753–1828)
A descriptive and critical catalogue of works illustrated by Thomas and John Bewick. 1851.
A memoir of Thomas Bewick written by himself. Newcastle 1862; ed A. Dobson, Newcastle 1887; ed M. Weekley, 1961; ed I. Bain, Oxford 1975.
Hugo, T. The Bewick collector: a descriptive catalogue of the works of Thomas and John Bewick. 1866; Suppl 1868.
Stephens, F. G. Notes on a collection of drawings and woodcuts by Thomas Bewick. 1881.
Thomson, D. C. The life and works of Thomas Bewick. 1882.
Bewick memento, with an introduction by R. Robinson: catalogue of the scarce and curious collection of Bewick relics, etc, sold by auction. 1884.
Dobson, A. Thomas Bewick and his pupils. 1884, 1889.
Bewick gleanings: being impressions from copperplates and wood

blocks, engraved in the Bewick workshop. Ed J. Boyd. Newcastle 1886.
Robinson, R. Thomas Bewick: his life and times. Newcastle 1887.
Anderton, B. Thomas Bewick, the Tyneside engraver. Library 3rd ser 7 1916.
Rayner, J. (ed). A selection of engravings on wood by Bewick. 1947.
Bingley, B. Bewickiana. Signature n.s. 9 1949.
Reynolds, G. Thomas Bewick: a résumé of his life and work. 1949.
Roscoe, S. Thomas Bewick: a bibliography raisonné of editions of The general history of quadrupeds, The history of British birds, and The fables of Aesop, issued in his lifetime. Oxford 1953.
Stone, R. (ed). Wood engravings of Bewick. 1953.
Weekley, M. Thomas Bewick. Oxford 1953.
Bewick to Dovaston: letters 1824–1828. Ed G. Williams. 1968.
Thomas Bewick vignettes. Ed I. Bain. 1978.
Bain, I. Thomas Bewick: an illustrated record of his life and work. Newcastle 1979; then as The workshop of Thomas Bewick: a pictorial survey. Stocksfield, Northumberland 1989.
The watercolours and drawings of Thomas Bewick and his workshop apprentices. Ed I. Bain. 2 vols 1981.

William Blake (1757–1827)
Gilchrist, A. Life of William Blake. 2 vols 1863, 1880, 1907 (ed W. G. Robertson), 1942 (ed R. Todd).
Langridge, I. William Blake: a study of his life and art work. 1904.
Keynes, G. A bibliography of William Blake. New York 1921.
Binyon, L. The drawings and engravings of William Blake. Ed G. Holme 1922.
Todd, R. The techniques of William Blake's illuminated painting. Print 6 no 1 1948.
Keynes, G. Blake studies. 1949, Oxford 1971.
Keynes, G. (ed). William Blake's engravings. 1950.
Keynes, G. and E. Wolf. William Blake's illuminated books: a census. New York 1953 (priv ptd).
Butlin, M. William Blake 1757–1827. 1957, 1990. Catalogue of his works in the Tate Gallery, London.
Keynes, G. William Blake's illustrations to the Bible. Clairvaux 1957.
Keynes, G. A study of the illuminated books of William Blake. 1965.
Bentley, G. E. Blake books. Oxford 1977. Bibliography of his writings and works about him.
Bindman, D. William Blake: his art and times. 1982.
Essick, R. N. William Blake's commercial book illustrations: a catalogue and study of the plates engraved by Blake after designs by other artists. Oxford 1991.
Viscomi, J. Blake and the idea of the book. Princeton 1993.
Heppner, C. Reading Blake's designs. Cambridge 1995.

Richard Parkes Bonington (1801–28)
Dubuisson, A. Richard Parkes Bonington: his life and work. 1924.
Shirley, A. Bonington. 1940.

Thomas Shotter Boys (1803–74)
Stokes, H. Thomas Shotter Boys. [1925.]
Roundell, J. Thomas Shotter Boys. 1974.

Ford Madox Brown (1821–93)
Hueffer, F. M. Ford Madox Brown: a record of his life and work. 1896.

Hablot Knight Browne (1815–82)
Kitton, F. G. Phiz (Hablot K. Browne): a memoir including a selection from his correspondence. 1882.
Thomson, D. C. Life and labours of Hablot Knight Browne, 'Phiz'. 1884.
Johannsen, A. Phiz: illustrations from the novels of Charles Dickens. Chicago [1956].
Buchanan-Brown, J. Phiz!: the book illustrations of Hablot Knight Browne. Newton Abbot 1978.
Steig, M. Dickens and Phiz. Bloomington 1978.

Sir Edward Burne-Jones (1833–98)
Vallance, A. Sir Edward Burne-Jones. Great masters of decorative art. 1900.
Harrison, M. and B. Waters. Burne-Jones. 1973, 1989.

Randolph Caldecott (1846–86)
Blackburn, H. Randolph Caldecott: a personal memoir of his early art career. 1886.
Sendak, M. Caldecott & Co. New York 1988.

Edward Calvert (1799–1883)
Lister, R. Edward Calvert. 1962.

Charles Conder (1868–1909)
Gibson, F. Charles Conder: his life and work. 1914.
Rothenstein, J. The life and death of Conder. 1938.

Samuel Cousins (1801–87)
Pycroft, G. Memoir of Samuel Cousins. Exeter 1887 (priv ptd).
Whitman, A. C. Samuel Cousins. 1904.

Walter Crane (1845–1915)
Konody, P. G. The art of Walter Crane. 1902.
Crane, W. An artist's reminiscences. 1907.
Massé, G. C. E. A bibliography of first editions of books illustrated by Walter Crane. 1923.
Smith, G. and S. Hyde. Walter Crane 1845–1915: artist, designer and socialist. 1989.

Joseph Crawhall (1821–96)
Crawhall, J. Impresses quaint. Newcastle 1889.
Felver, C. Joseph Crawhall, the Newcastle wood engraver. Newcastle [1973].

George Cruikshank (1792–1878)
Thackeray, W. M. An essay on the genius of Cruikshank. Westminster Rev June 1840; 1884.
Bates, W. George Cruikshank, the artist, the humorist and the man. 1878, 1879.
Jerrold, B. The life of George Cruikshank. 1882, 1898.
Stephens, F. G. A memoir of George Cruikshank; and An essay on the genius of George Cruikshank by W. M. Thackeray. 1891.
Douglas, R. J. H. The works of Cruikshank. [1903.]
Cohn, A. M. George Cruikshank: a catalogue raisonné. 1924.
McLean, R. Cruikshank: his life and work as a book illustrator. 1948.
Wardroper, J. The caricatures of George Cruikshank. 1977.
Jones, M. W. George Cruikshank: his life and London. 1978.
Buchanan-Brown, J. The book illustrations of George Cruikshank. Newton Abbot 1980.

George Dalziel (1815–1902); Edward Dalziel (1817–1905)
Dalziel, G. and E. The brothers Dalziel: a record of fifty years' work in conjunction with many of the most distinguished artists of the period 1840–90. 1901.
Colebrook, F. Dalziel and the Dalsprites. 1909.

Gustave Doré (1832–83)
Roosevelt, B. Life and reminiscences of Gustave Doré. 1885.
Blanchard, J. Life of Gustave Doré. 1891.
Valmy-Baysse, J. Gustave Doré: bibliographie et catalogue complet de l'oeuvre. 2 vols. Paris 1930.
Lehmann-Haupt, H. The terrible Gustave Doré. New York 1943.
Rose, M. Gustave Doré. 1946.
Richardson, J. Gustave Doré: a biography. 1980.

Richard Doyle (1824–83)
Hambourg, D. Richard Doyle. 1948.
Engen, R. Richard Doyle. Stroud Glos 1983.

George du Maurier (1834–96)
Wood, T. M. George du Maurier, the satirist of the Victorians. 1913.
Whiteley, D. P. George du Maurier's illustrations for Once a week. Alphabet & Image 5 1947.
Whiteley, D. P. George du Maurier: his life and work. 1948.
Du Maurier, D. (ed). The young George du Maurier: a selection of

his letters 1860–67, with a biographical appendix by D. P. Whiteley. 1951.
See also col 1517.
Benjamin Fawcett (1808–93)
Morris, M. C. F. Benjamin Fawcett: colour printer & engraver. Oxford 1925.
McLean, R. and A. Benjamin Fawcett, engraver and colour printer, with a list of his books and plates. Aldershot 1988.
Sir Luke Fildes (1844–1927)
Thomson, D. C. The life and work of Luke Fildes. The art annual 1895.
Fildes, L. V. Luke Fildes: a Victorian painter. 1968.
Alfred Henry Forrester (1804–72)
[Forrester, A. H.] A bundle of crowquills dropped by Alfred Crowquill in his eccentric flights over the fields of literature. 1854.
Birket Foster (1825–99)
Huish, M. B. Birket Foster: his life and work. The Art Annual 1890.
Cundall, H. M. Birket Foster. 1906.
Harry Furniss (1854–1925)
Furniss, H. The confessions of a caricaturist. 2 vols 1901.
Furniss, H. How and why I illustrated Thackeray. 1912.
Henry Fuseli (1741–1825)
Weinglass, D. H. Prints and engraved illustrations by and after Henry Fuseli: a catalogue raisonné. Aldershot 1994.
James Gillray (1757–1815)
[Grego, J.] The works of James Gillray, the caricaturist, with the history of his life and times. Ed T. Wright [1873].
Hill, D. Mr Gillray, the caricaturist: a biography. 1965.
Kate Greenaway (1846–1901)
Spielmann, M. H. and G. S. Layard. Kate Greenaway. 1905.
Muir, P. Notes on the occasion of the centenary of K. G. Alphabet & Image 1 1946.
Thomson, S. R. Kate Greenaway: a catalogue of the Kate Greenaway collection, Rare Book Room, Detroit Public Library. Detroit 1977.
Engen, R. Kate Greenaway: a biography. 1981.
Schuster, T. E. and R. Engen. Printed Kate Greenaway: a catalogue raisonné. 1986.
Taylor, I. The art of Kate Greenaway. 1991.
See col 1799.
Ernest Griset (1844–1907)
Lambourne, L. Ernest Griset: fantasies of a Victorian illustrator. 1979.
Sir Francis Seymour Haden (1818–1910)
Harrington, H. N. The engraved work of Sir Francis Seymour Haden. Liverpool 1910.
Philip Gilbert Hamerton (1834–94)
Philip Gilbert Hamerton: an autobiography 1834–58, and a memoir by his wife 1858–94. 1897.
John Hassall (1868–1948)
Cuppleditch, D. The John Hassall lifestyle. 1979.
Arthur Boyd Houghton (1836–75)
Arthur Boyd Houghton: a selection from his work in black and white, with an introductory essay by L. Housman. 1896.
Hogarth, P. Arthur Boyd Houghton. 1981.
Laurence Housman (1865–1959)
Engen, R. Laurence Housman. Stroud 1983.
William Holman Hunt (1827–1910)
Schleinitz, O. William Holman Hunt. Leipzig 1907.
Orlando Jewitt (1799–1869)
Carter, H. Orlando Jewitt. Oxford 1962.
Broomhead, F. The book illustrations of Orlando Jewitt. Pinner 1995.
Charles Keene (1823–91)
Layard, G. S. The life and letters of Charles Samuel Keene. 1892.
Pennell, J. The work of Charles Keene. 1897.
Emanuel, F. Charles Keene: etcher, draughtsman and illustrator: being a lecture delivered to the Print Collectors' Club. 1935.
Hudson, D. Charles Keene. 1947.
Piper, M. Charles Keene. Signature new ser no 16 1952.
Houfe, S. The work of Charles Samuel Keene. Aldershot 1995.
Edward Lear (1812–88)
Davidson, A. Lear: landscape painter and nonsense poet. 1938.
Lear, E. The complete nonsense of Lear. Ed H. Jackson 1947.
Reade, B. The birds of Edward Lear. Signature n.s. no 4 1947.
Murphy, R. (ed). Edward Lear's Indian journal 1873–1875. 1953.
Chitty, S. That singular person called Lear. 1988.
See also col 630.
John Leech (1817–64)
Kitton, F. G. John Leech: artist and humourist. 1883, 1884.
Frith, W. P. Leech: his life and work. 2 vols 1891.
Wilson, S. K. Catalogue of an exhibition of works by John Leech. New York 1914 (Grolier Club).
[Field, W. B. O.] John Leech on my shelves. Munich 1930 (priv ptd).
Bodkin, T. (ed). The noble science: John Leech in the hunting field. 1948.
Rose, J. The drawings of John Leech. 1950.
Houfe, S. John Leech and the Victorian scene. Woodbridge 1984.
Frederic Leighton (1830–96)
Barrington, R. The life, letters and work of Frederic Leighton. 2 vols 1906.
William James Linton (1812–97)
Linton, W. J. Threescore and ten years 1820 to 1890. New York 1894; then as Memories. London 1895.
Smith, F. B. Radical artisan: William James Linton 1812–97. Manchester 1973.
David Lucas (1802–81)
Wedmore, F. Constable, Lucas: with a descriptive catalogue of the prints they did between them. 1904.
Daniel Maclise (1806–70)
O'Driscoll, W. J. A memoir of Daniel Maclise. 1871.
John Martin (1789–1854)
Balson, T. John Martin: his life and works. 1947.
Phil May (1864–1903)
Thorpe, J. Phil May, master-draughtsman & humourist. 1932; then as Phil May. 1948.
Cuppleditch, D. Phil May: the artist & his wit. 1981.
Sir John Everett Millais (1829–96)
Millais's illustrations: a collection of drawings on wood. 1866.
Spielmann, M. H. Millais and his works. 1898.
Millais, J. G. The life and letters of Sir John Everett Millais. 2 vols 1899, 1905 (1 vol abridged).
Francis Orpen Morris (1810–93)
Morris, M. C. F. Francis Orpen Morris: a memoir. 1897.
Samuel Palmer (1805–81)
Palmer, A. H. The life and letters of Samuel Palmer. 1892.
Grigson, G. Samuel Palmer at Shoreham. Signature no 7 1937.
Grigson, G. Samuel Palmer: the visionary years. 1947.
Melville, R. Samuel Palmer. 1956.
Lister, R. Samuel Palmer: a biography. 1974.
Lister, R. Catalogue raisonné of the works of Samuel Palmer. Cambridge 1988.
Beatrix Potter (1866–1943)
The art of Beatrix Potter, with an appreciation by A. C. Moore. 1955, 1956, 1964, 1966.
Lane, M. The magic years of Beatrix Potter. 1978.
Beatrix Potter: the V & A collection: catalogue compiled by A. S. Hobbs and J. I. Whalley. 1985.
Taylor, J. Beatrix Potter: artist, storyteller and countrywoman. 1986.
Taylor, J., et al. Beatrix Potter 1866–1943: the artist and her world. 1987.

James Pryde (1866–1941)
Hudson, D. James Pryde 1866–1941. 1949.
Arthur Rackham (1867–1939)
Hudson, D. Arthur Rackham: his life and work. 1960, 1974.
Larkin, D. Arthur Rackham. 1975.
Hamilton, J. Arthur Rackham: a life with illustration. 1990.
Abraham Raimbach (1776–1843)
Raimbach, M. T. S. Memoirs and recollections of the late Abraham Raimbach, engraver. 1843 (priv ptd).
Samuel William Reynolds (1773–1835)
Whitman, A. C. Samuel William Reynolds. 1903.
Charles Ricketts (1866–1931)
Moore, T. S. Charles Ricketts. 1933.
Moore, T. S. Self-portrait, taken from the letters & journals of Charles Ricketts. Ed C. Lewis. 1939.
Calloway, S. Charles Ricketts: subtle and fantastic decorator. 1979.
Darracott, J. The world of Charles Ricketts. 1980.
Delaney, J. G. P. Charles Ricketts: a biography. Oxford 1990.
Charles Robinson (1870–1937)
De Freitas, L. Charles Robinson. 1976.
Larkin, D. Charles & William Heath Robinson. 1976.
William Heath Robinson (1872–1944)
Day, L. The life and art of W. Heath Robinson. 1947.
Lewis, J. Heath Robinson: artist and comic genius. 1973.
Larkin, D. Charles & William Heath Robinson. 1976.
Beare, G. C. The illustrations of W. Heath Robinson: a commentary and bibliography. 1983.
Robert Traill Rose (1863–1942)
Rose, M. T. S. Alexander Rose, geologist, and his grandson Robert Traill Rose, artist. Edinburgh [1956].
Dante Gabriel Rossetti (1828–82)
Marillier, H. C. Dante Gabriel Rossetti: an illustrated memorial of his art and life. 1899, 1901, 1904.
Pissarro, L. Rossetti. [1907.]
Thomas Rowlandson (1756–1827)
Grego, J. Rowlandson, the caricaturist: a selection from his works. 2 vols 1880.
Catalogue of books illustrated by Thomas Rowlandson. New York 1916 (Grolier Club).
Roe, F. G. Rowlandson: the life and art of a British genius. Leigh-on-sea 1947.
Falk, B. Thomas Rowlandson, his life and art: a documentary record. 1949.
Frederick Sandys (1829–1904)
Gray, J. M. Sandys and the woodcut designs of thirty years ago. Century Guild Hobby Horse Dec 1888.
Reproductions of woodcuts by F. Sandys 1860–1866. [1915] (priv ptd).
Charles Shannon (1863–1937)
Ricketts, C. A catalogue of Mr Shannon's lithographs. [1902.]
William Simpson (1823–99)
Simpson, W. The autobiography of William Simpson (Crimean Simpson). 1903.
Marcus Stone (1840–1921)
Baldry, A. L. Marcus Stone. The art annual 1896.
Thomas Stothard (1755–1834)
Bray, A. E. Life of Thomas Stothard. 1851.
Coxhead, A. C. Thomas Stothard, his life and work. 1909.
William Strang (1859–1921)
[Binyon, L.] William Strang: catalogue of his etched work. 1906, 1912; suppl to 1920. 1923.
Dodgson, C. The etchings of William Strang & Sir Charles Holroyd. 1933.
Edmund Joseph Sullivan (1869–1933)
Thorpe, J. E. J. Sullivan. 1948.
Sir John Tenniel (1820–1914)
Monkhouse, W. C. The life & works of Sir John Tenniel. 1901.
Sarzano, F. Sir John Tenniel. 1948.
Engen, R. Sir John Tenniel: Alice's White Knight. Aldershot 1991.
William Makepeace Thackeray (1811–63)
Buchanan-Brown, J. The illustrations of William Makepeace Thackeray. Newton Abbot 1979.
Hugh Thomson (1860–1920)
Spielmann, M. H. and W. Jerrold. Hugh Thomson: his art, his letters, his humour and his charm. 1931.
Charles Turner (1774–1857)
Whitman, A. C. Charles Turner. 1907.
Joseph Mallord William Turner (1775–1851)
Thornbury, W. The life of J. M. W. Turner. 1862, 1877.
Rawlinson, W. G. The engraved work of J. M. W. Turner. 2 vols 1908–13.
Mauclair, C. Turner. Paris 1939; tr as Turner. London 1939.
Finley, G. Landscapes of memory: Turner as illustrator to Scott. 1980.
Herrmann, L. Turner prints: the engraved work of J. M. W. Turner. Oxford 1990.
Piggott, J. Turner's vignettes (Tate Gallery, London). 1993.
James Abbott McNeill Whistler (1834–1903)
Kennedy, E. G. The etched work of Whistler. New York 1910 (Grolier Club).
Way, T. R. Memories of James McNeill Whistler, the artist. 1912.
Dodgson, C. The etchings of James McNeill Whistler. 1922.
Lochnan, K. A. Whistler's etchings and the sources of his etching style 1855–1880. New York 1988.
Joseph Wolf (1820–99)
The life of Joseph Wolf. 1895. [NAR]

(12) BOOKBINDING

Bibliographies and Reference works

Prideaux, S. T. A bibliography of bookbinding. 1892.
Grolier Club. Commercial bookbinding: an historical sketch. New York 1894.
Grolier Club. List of books and articles relating to bookbinding to be found in the library. New York 1907.
Mejer, W. Bibliographie der Buchbindereiliteratur. Leipzig 1925; H. Herbst, Supplement 1924–32, Leipzig 1933; Bucheinbandliteratur 1933–7. In Jahrbuch der Einbandkunst, iv, 1937 pp. 189–215.
Harthan, J. P. Bookbindings: select bibliography. 1950, 1961, 1985.
Hobson, A. R. A. The literature of bookbinding. Cambridge 1954.
Library book lists: bookbinding and warehouse work. London School of Printing, National Book League, St Bride Printing Library 1959.
Brenni, V. J. Bookbinding: a guide to the literature. Westport CT and London [1982].
Pollard, G. Early bookbinding manuals. Oxford 1984. With E. Potter.
Breslauer, B. H. The uses of bookbinding literature. New York 1986.

General works

The book of trades. Vol 3, 1805, 1811, 1815, 1818 etc.
New scale of prices for bookbinding. 1807. A broadside.
The corrected list of prices. 1808.
Country scale of prices for bookbinding. [1810.]
[Minshall, N.] The whole art of bookbinding. Oswestry 1811, rptd Austin TX 1987.
The bookbinders' price-book. 1813.
Martin, T. (pseudonym of John Farey). Article Bookbinding in The circle of the mechanical arts. 1813.
Sinclair, H. The whole process of marbling paper. Glasgow [c. 1815], London 1820, rptd Austin TX 1987.
Parry, H. The art of bookbinding; containing a description of the tools. 1817; tr Ger 1819.

[Martin, T.] The bookbinder's complete instructor. Peterhead 1823.
[Cowie, G.] The bookbinder's manual. [1828], 1829, 1832, [c. 1835], [c. 1852].
The reply of the journeymen bookbinders to remarks on a memorial addressed to their employers on the effects of a machine introduced to supersede manual labour. 1831.
[Hannett, J.] Bibliopegia: or the art of bookbinding in all its branches by 'J. A. Arnett'. 1835, 1836, 1842, 1848 (4th edn), 1865 (6th edn) rptd New York and London 1980.
Boteler, W. C. Songs for bookbinders. 1837.
[Hannett, J.] The bookbinders' school of design, as applied to the combination of tools in the art of finishing, by 'J. A. Arnett'. 1837.
The handbook of taste in bookbinding. [c. 1840.]
Foucaud, E. Reliure. In his Les artisans illustres. Paris 1841.
The book-finishers' friendly circular. No 1, Aug 1845–no 19, Sep 1850.
Cundall, J. On ornamental art applied to ancient and modern bookbindings. 1848.
The bookbinders' trade circular, issued by the London Consolidated Society of Journeymen Bookbinders. No 1, Oct 1850–no 154, 20 Nov 1877. Monthly. Ed T. J. Dunning.
Great Exhibition, 1851. Illustrated catalogue 2, section 3, class 17, 1851.
Great Exhibition, 1851. Reports of the Juries. 1852.
Woolnough, C. W. The whole art of marbling as applied to book edges and paper. 1853, 1881, rptd 1985.
Cyclopaedia of useful arts and manufactures. Ed C. Tomlinson. 1852–1854. Article Bookbinding.
Hodson's booksellers, publishers and stationers' directory for London and country. 1855. Rptd Oxford 1972.
Nicholson, J. B. A manual of the art of bookbinding. Philadelphia 1856, 1882, 1887.
Dunning, T. J. Account of the London Consolidated Society of Bookbinders. In Nat Assoc for the Promotion of Social Science report, 1860.
Patent Office. Abridgments of specifications relating to books, portfolios, card-cases etc 1768–1866. 1870.
The Post Office directory of stationers etc. Kelly 1872, 1876 etc.
Hatton, J. Printing and bookbinding. In G. P. Bevan, British manufacturing industries, 1876.
Crisp, W. F. Bookbinding made easy: or every man his own binder. Great Yarmouth [1877].
Cox, A. J. & Co. The making of the book: a sketch of the bookbinding art. Chicago 1878.
Lenormand, S. Nouveau manuel complet du relieur en tous genres. Paris 1879.
Zaehnsdorf, J. W. The art of bookbinding. 1880, 1890, 1903 (6th edn).
Cundall, J. On bookbindings ancient and modern. 1881.
Wheatley, H. B. Bookbinding considered as a fine art, mechanical art and manufacture. 1882.
Adam, P. Systematisches Lehr- und Handbuch der Buchbinderei. 2 vols Dresden 1883–91.
Crane, W. J. E. Bookbinding for amateurs. 1885, 1903.
The bookbinder. No 1, Jan 1887–no 36, Dec 1889. Continued as The British bookmaker, no 37, Jan 1890–no 81, Mar 1894. Monthly.
Wheatley, H. B. The principles of design as applied to bookbinding. Jnl of Royal Soc of Arts Feb 1888.
Michel, M. L'ornamentation des reliures modernes. Paris 1889.
Bosquet, E. Traité de l'art du relieur. Paris 1890.
Bouchot, H. De la reliure: exemples à imiter ou à rejeter. Paris 1891.
Burlington Fine Arts Club. Exhibition of bookbindings. 1891.
Cobden-Sanderson, T. J. Bookbinding. Eng Illustr Mag Jan 1891.
Wood, H. F. Bookbinding. In G. P. Bevan, British manufacturing industries, 1892.
Brassington, W. S. A history of the art of bookbinding. 1894.
White, G. The artistic decoration of bookcovers. In Studio, Oct 1894.
Bosquet, E. La reliure: études d'un practicien. Paris 1894.
Fletcher, W. Y. English bookbindings. In A. H. Church, Some minor arts, 1894.
Matthews, B. Bookbindings of the present. Century Mag June 1894.
Cobden-Sanderson, T. J. Bookbinding: its processes and ideals. Fortnightly Rev Aug 1894.
Zaehnsdorf. A short history of bookbinding. 1895.
Matthews, B. Books in paper covers. Century Mag July 1895.
Matthews, B. Bookbindings, old and new: notes of a book-lover with an account of the Grolier Club, New York. New York 1896.
Gruel, L. Conférence sur la reliure et la dorure des livres. Paris 1896.
Davenport, C. J. Cantor lectures on decorative bookbinding. 1898.
Goupil & Co. Catalogue of exhibition of modern English artistic bookbindings, with historical sketch of bookbinding in England by W. Y. Fletcher. 1898.
Cobden-Sanderson, T. J. Bookbinding. In Arts and Crafts Society, Arts and crafts essays. 1899.
Matthews, W. Modern bookbinding practically considered. New York 1899.
Bowdoin, W. G. Decorative achievements of pyrography in bookbindings. Artist Jun 1899.
Wood, E. et al. Modern bookbindings and their designers. Studio, winter no 1899.
Cockerell, D. Bookbinding and the care of books: a textbook for bookbinders and librarians. 1901, 1953 (5th edn), rptd 1978.
Royal Society of Arts. Report of the committee on leather for bookbinding. 1901.
Orrinsmith, H. Bookbinding design. In Practical designing. Ed G. White. 1902.
Stewart, C. J. Bookbinders' arbitration award. 1903.
Adam, P. Practical bookbinding. 1903.
Loubier, J. Der Bucheinband in alter und neuer Zeit. Berlin [1904].
MacDonald, J. Ramsay. Women in the printing trades. 1904.
Prideaux, S. T. Modern bookbindings: their design and decoration. 1906.
Stephen, G. A. Commercial bookbinding. 1910.
Harrison, T. The bookbinding craft and industry. [Before 1930.]
Sadleir, M. The evolution of publishers' binding styles 1770–1900. 1930.
Bowyer, W. Publishers' binding cloth. In The Book-Collector's Quarterly Apr 1932.
Carter, J. Binding variants in English publishing 1820–1900. 1932; More binding variants. 1938; Rptd in one vol 1989.
Sadleir, M. Yellow backs. In New paths in book collecting. Ed J. Carter 1934.
Carter, J. Publishers' cloth 1820–1900. New York [1935].
Leighton, D. Modern bookbinding: a survey and a prospect. 1935.
Carter, J. English publishers' bindings 1800–1900. In Bull of the New York Public Lib. Aug 1936.
Hobson, G. D. English bindings 1490–1940 in the library of J. R. Abbey. 1940.
Loring, R. B. Decorated book papers: being an account of their design and fashions. 1942, Cambridge MA 1952 (2nd edn rev P. Hofer).
Diehl, E. Bookbinding: its background and technique. 2 vols New York 1946, rptd 1980.
Leighton, D. Canvas and bookcloth: an essay on beginnings. In The Library 5 ser 3 1949.
Rosner, C. The art of the book jacket. 1949.
Howe, E. A list of London bookbinders 1648–1815. 1950.
Howe, E. The Society of London Bookbinders 1780–1951. 1952. With J. Child.
The Book Collector. Quart from no 1 Mar 1952.
Munby, A. N. L. Collecting English signed bindings. In Book Collector 2, 3, 1953.
Mitchell, W. S. Bookbinders' tickets. In Durham Univ Jnl Dec 1953.
Mitchell, W. S. British signed bindings in the library of King's College, Newcastle upon Tyne, Newcastle 1954.

Rosner, C. The growth of the book jacket. 1954.
Ramsden, C. Bookbinders of the United Kingdom (outside London) 1780–1840. 1954.
Ramsden, C. London bookbinders 1780–1840. 1956.
Nixon, H. M. Broxbourne library: styles and designs of bookbindings from the twelfth to the twentieth century. 1956.
Pollard, H. G. Changes in the style of bookbinding 1550–1830. In The Library 5 ser, 11, 1956.
The history of bookbinding 525–1950 AD. Exhibition catalogue ed D. Miner. Baltimore MD 1957.
Pantazzi, S. Four designers of English publishers' bindings 1850–80. In Papers of the Bibl Soc of America, no 55, 1961.
Middleton, B. A history of English craft bookbinding technique. 1963, 1978, 1996.
Metzdorf, R. Victorian book decoration. In Princeton Univ Chron Winter 1963.
Renier, A. Friendship's offering. Private Libs Assoc 1964.
Tanselle, G. T. The bibliographical description of patterns. In Stud in Bibliography 23 1970.
Barber, G. G. Rossetti, Ricketts and some English publishers' bindings of the nineties. In The Library 5 ser 25 1970.
Tanselle, G. T. Book-jackets, blurbs and bibliographers. In The Library 5 ser 26, 2 1971.
Jamieson, E. English embossed bindings 1825–50. Cambridge 1972.
Grieve, A. Rossetti's applied art designs: 2. Bookbindings. In Burlington Mag Feb 1973.
McLean, R. Victorian publishers' book-bindings in cloth and leather. 1974.
Nixon, H. M. British bookbindings presented by Kenneth H. Oldaker to the Chapter Library of Westminster Abbey. 1982.
McLean, R. Victorian publishers' book-bindings in paper. 1983.
Foot, M. M. The Henry Davis gift. Vol 2 1983.
Wakeman, G. Nineteenth century trade bindings. 2 vols Oxford 1983.
Ball, D. Victorian publishers' bindings. 1985.
Foot, M. M. Pictorial bookbindings. 1986.
Maggs Bros Ltd. Catalogues of bookbindings. No 1075 pt 2 Spring 1987; no 1098 Summer 1989.
McKay, B. Patterns and pigments in English marbled paper. Kidlington 1988.
McKay, B. Marbling methods and receipts from four centuries. Kidlington 1990.
Packer, M. Bookbinders of Victorian London. 1991.
Howsam, L. Cheap bibles: nineteenth century publishing and the British and Foreign Bible Society. Cambridge 1991.
Nixon, H. M. The history of decorated bookbindings in England. Oxford 1992 with M. M. Foot.
Foot, M. M. Studies in the history of bookbinding. Aldershot 1993.
Wakeman, G. Functional developments in bookbinding. Newcastle, Delaware and Oxford 1993. With Graham Pollard.
Potter, E. The London bookbinding trade: from craft to industry. In The Library, Dec 1993.
Tomlinson, W. Bookcloth 1823–1980. Stockport 1995. With R. Masters.
Tidcombe, M. Women bookbinders 1880–1920. 1996.

Individual binders

Bedford, Francis
Dictionary of National Biography.
Athenaeum, 16 June 1883.
Birdsall family, Northampton
Evans, E. and R. Grover. The Birdsall collection of bookbinders finishing tools. Toronto 1972.
James Burn & Company
Darley, L. S. Bookbinding then and now. 1959.
Clarke, John
Catalogue of plant and materials to be sold by auction 31 Jan 1860.
Cobden-Sanderson, T. J.
The journals of T. J. Cobden-Sanderson, 2 vols 1926.
Schmidt-Kunsemuller, F. A. T. J. Cobden-Sanderson as bookbinder. Tr I. Grafe Esher 1966.
Four lectures by T. J. Cobden-Sanderson. Ed J. Dreyfus. San Francisco 1974.
Tidcombe, M. The bookbindings of T. J. Cobden-Sanderson. 1984.
Cockerell, Douglas
Rooke, N. Douglas Cockerell. Obituary notice in Jnl of the Royal Soc of Arts 21 Dec 1945.
Edwards of Halifax
Hanson, T. W. 'Edwards of Halifax'. A family of booksellers, collectors and bookbinders. [1912.]
Edwards of Halifax, bookbinders. In Book Handbook 6 1948.
Gosden, Thomas
Andrews, W. L. An English XIX century sportsman, bibliophile and binder of angling books. New York 1906.
Munby, A. N. L. Notes on Thomas Gosden. In Book Collector 24 1975.
Guild of Women Binders
Anstruther, G. E. The bindings of to-morrow. A record of the work of the Guild of Women-Binders and of the Hampstead Bindery. 1902.
Waller, A. C. The Guild of Women-Binders. In The Private Library, 1983.
Gwynn family
Middleton, B. C. The Gwynn family: book edge gilders, paper marblers and bookbinders. In New Bookbinder 3, 1983.
Hering, Charles, James and Henry
Marks, J. G. Bookbinding practices of the Hering family 1794–1844. In Br Lib Jnl 6, 1, Spring 1980.
Hunter & Foulis
A hundred years of publishers' bookbinding 1857–1957. Edinburgh [1957].
Key & Whiting Ltd.
Key & Whiting Ltd. The years between 1799–1949. 1949.
Kitcat, G. & J.
Adams, J. The House of Kitcat: a story of bookbinding. 1948.
Leighton, John
Pantazzi, S. John Leighton 1822–1912. A versatile Victorian designer: his designs for book covers. In Connoisseur 152, Apr 1963.
Oxford University Press
Catalogue of Binding Exhibition, Paris 1900. 1900.
Prideaux, S. T.
A catalogue of books bound by S. T. Prideaux between MDCCCXC and MDCCCC. 1900, rptd New York 1979.
Westley & Clark
Dodd, George. Days at the factories. 1843. Pp 363–84.
Westley, Josiah
Southgate & Barrett. Auction sale of the bookbinding equipment of Josiah Westley. 12 and 13 Nov 1852. Catalogue no 1137.
Zaehnsdorf Limited
Middleton, B. C. The Zaehnsdorf story. In Br and Colonial Printer 25 Dec 1953.
Broomhead, F. The Zaehnsdorfs (1842–1947), craft bookbinders. 1986. [EP]

C. BOOK DISTRIBUTION

(1) GENERAL WORKS

National Book Council. Books about books: a catalogue of the books contained in the National Book Council Library. 1933, 1935, 1955 (as National Book League).
Britton. J. Autobiography. 2 vols 1850.

[Phillips, S.] The literature of the rail. 1851.
Hodson, W. H. Hodson's booksellers', publishers' and stationers' directory for London and country. 1855.
Curwen, H. A history of booksellers, the old and the new. [1873.]
'The Bookman' directory of booksellers, publishers and authors. 1893.
Mumby, F. A. The romance of bookselling. 1910, 1930 (rev as Publishing and bookselling), 1940, 1954 (rev).
Shaylor, J. The fascination of books. 1912.
Collins, A. S. The profession of letters 1780–1832. 1928.
Cruse, A. The Englishman and his books in the early 19th century. 1930.
Darton, F. J. H. Children's books in England. Cambridge 1932.
Flower, D. S. Century of best sellers 1830–1930. 1934.
Cruse, A. The Victorians and their books. 1935.
Craig, A. The banned books of England. 1937.
Cruse, A. After the Victorians. 1938.
Turner, E. S. Boys will be boys. 1948. On boys' stories.
Steinberg, S. H. Five hundred years of printing. 1955, 1961, 1974, 1996 (new edn).
Altick, R. D. The English common reader 1800–1900. Chicago 1957.
Hepburn, J. The author's empty purse and the rise of the literary agent. Oxford 1968.
Thomas, D. A longtime burning: the history of literary censorship in England. 1969.
Gaskell, P. A new introduction to bibliography. Oxford 1972.
Hendrick, D. L. (ed). The book through five thousand years. 1972.
Mumby, F. A. and I. Norrie. Book publishing 1870–1970. 1974 (5th edn).
Brown, P. London publishers and printers c. 1800–1870. 1982.
Myers, R. and M. Harris (ed). Author/publisher relations during the eighteenth and nineteenth centuries. Oxford 1983.
Cross, N. The common writer: life in nineteenth century Grub Street. Cambridge 1985.
Febvre, L. and H. J. Martin. The coming of the book: the impact of printing 1450–1800. Tr D. Gerard. 1990.
Barker, N. (ed). A potencie of life: books in society. The Clark lectures 1986–1987. 1993.
Dreyfus, J. Into print: selected writings on printing history, typography and book production. 1994.
Journal of the printing historical society 1965– .
Publishing History 1977– .

(2) COPYRIGHT

Solberg, T. Bibliography of literary property. In R. R. Bowker, Copyright: its law and its literature, New York 1886.
List of works on copyright in the Patent Office Library. 1900.
Montefiori, J. The law of copyright. 1802.
Montagu, B. Enquiries and observations respecting the [Cambridge] University Library [in relation to the Copyright Act]. 1805.
Report of the Select Committee [of the House of Commons] on copyright of printed books, and the delivery of them to the public libraries. 1812–13. (292). iv. 999.
— Minutes of evidence on the effect of the law on literary property. 1812–13. (341). iv. 1003; rptd 1818, (177). ix. 389.
[Duppa, R.] An address to the Parliament of Great Britain on the claims of authors to their own copyright. 1813, 1813; rptd in Pamphleteer 2 1813.
[Turner, S.] Reasons for a modification of the Act of Anne respecting the delivery of books and copyright. 1813.
[Duppa, R.] Enquiries respecting the proposed alteration to the law of copyright. 1813.
Murray, W., Earl of Mansfield. Argument in favour of the author's perpetual copyright. 1813.
Britton, J. The rights of literature: or an enquiry into the policy and justice of the claims of certain public libraries on all the publishers and authors for eleven copies of every new publication. 1814.
Brydges, S. E. Reasons for a further amendment of the Act of 54 Geo. III c. 156, being an Act to amend the Copyright Act of Queen Anne. 1817.
Brydges, S. E. Answer to the further statement, ordered by the Syndics of the University of Cambridge to be printed and circulated [on the Copyright Act]. 1818.
Brydges, S. E. A summary statement of the great grievance imposed on authors and publishers by the late Copyright Act. 1818.
Brydges, S. E. A vindication of the pending Bill for the amendment of the Copyright Act. 1818.
Christian, E. A vindication of the right of the universities [under the Copyright Act]. 1818.
Lackington, G. [and others]. Copyright Bill. Humble petition. [1818.]
Turner, S. To the chairman of the committee upon the copyright laws. [1818.]
Webb, W. Observations on the Copyright Bill. 1818.
Whitaker, T. D. Petitions from authors on the Copyright Act. 1818.
Observations on the Copyright Bill. 1818.
Report of the Select Committee [of the House of Commons] respecting the amendment of 54 George III. 1818. (402). ix. 249. Minutes of Evidence, 1818, (280). ix. 257.
Fearnan, W. A letter in reply to the ridiculous threats of Mr John Ballantyne. 1819.
Gentz, F. von. Reflections on the liberty of the press in Great Britain. Tr from Ger 1819, 1820 (in The pamphleteer).
A. M. Brief observations on the Copyright Bill. The pamphleteer 18 1821.
Authorship and publication: a concise guide including the law of copyright. 1822.
Godson, R. A practical treatise on the law of patents for inventions and of copyright. 1823, 1840, 1844. Suppls 1832, 1844, 1851.
Sackett, G. A. A plea for authors. New York 1823.
Espinasse, I. A treatise on the law of actions and copyright. 1824.
Maugham, R. A treatise on the laws of literary property. 1828.
Report from the Select Committee [of the House of Commons] appointed to inquire into the laws affecting dramatic literature. 1831–2. (679). vii. 2.
Bossange, H. Opinion nouvelle sur la propriété littéraire. Paris 1836.
Buckingham, J. S. Speech of J. S. Buckingham [on copyright] in the House of Commons. 1836.
Didot, A. F. Note sur la propriété littéraire et sur la répression des contrefaçons faites à l'étranger, particulièrement en Belgique. [Paris c. 1836.]
Blanc, E. Traité de contrefaçon et de sa poursuite en justice. Paris 1837, 1838, 1855.
Hood, T. Copyright and copywrong. Athenaeum 15–29 Apr 1837, 11–18 June 1842; rptd in Works, vols 4, 6, 1862.
Talfourd, T. N. Speech delivered in the House of Commons on moving to bring in a Bill to consolidate the law relating to copyright. 1837.
Tegg, T. Remarks on the speech of Sergeant Talfourd. 1837.
Blunt, H. A letter to Mr Sergeant Talfourd relating to literary copyright. 1838.
Chambers, W. and R. Brief objections to Mr Talfourd's new copyright bill. Edinburgh 1838.
[Day, W?] A proposed new law of copyright. [1838.]
Dickens, C. Proclamation [against piracy and plagiarism of Nicholas Nickleby]. [1838.]
M'Dowall, W. Serjeant Talfourd's Copyright Bill. 1838.
Mudie, R. The copyright question and Mr Sergeant Talfourd's Bill. 1838.
Nicklin, P. H. Remarks on literary property. Philadelphia 1838.
Talfourd, T. N. A speech on moving the law of copyright. 1838.

Renouard, A. C. Traité des droits d'auteurs. 2 vols Paris 1838–9.
Talfourd, T. N. Three speeches delivered in the House of Commons in favour of an extension of copyright 1838, 1840. Fr trn by P. Laboulaye, Paris 1858.
Webster, G. Observations on the law of copyright in reference to the Bill of Mr Sergeant Talfourd. 1838.
Areopagitica secunda: or speech of the shade of John Milton on Sergeant Talfourd's Copyright Extension Bill. 1838.
A few words on the copyright question. 1838.
A plea for authors. 1838.
A proposed new law of copyright of the highest importance to authors in a letter to T. N. Talfourd. [1838.]
Saunders, R. Copyright in law reports. 1839.
Talfourd, T. N. Serjeant Talfourd's speech on the copyright question. 1839.
A few words on the copyright question. [1839.]
A few words on the copyright question shewing it to be one of public interest, with some objections to Sergeant Talfourd's Bill. 1839.
Tegg, T. Copyright. 1839.
Tegg, T. Extension of copyright. 1840.
Christie, W. D. A plea for perpetual copyright. 1840.
Lahure, C. Observations sur la demande faite par les libraires, réunies en commission, de reconnaître chez nous, et sans condition, la propriété littéraire des étrangers; et moyen de paralyser les contrefaçons belges sans nuire à aucune des branches de notre industrie. Paris 1840.
Lieber, F. On international copyright. New York 1840.
Lowndes, J. J. An historical sketch of the law of copyright. 1840, 1842.
Ward, J. W., Earl of Dudley. Letters to the Bishop of Llandaff [on copyright]. 1840, 1841.
Balzac, H. de. Notes remises à MM. les Députés composant la commission de la loi sur la propriété littéraire [5 Mar 1841]. In Œuvres complètes vol 22, Paris 1872.
Objections to remarks upon Mr Serjeant Talfourd scheme of a Copyright Bill. [1840.]
Macaulay, T. B. The speech of Mr Sergeant Talfourd's Bill for the extension of copyright. 1841.
Burke, P. A treatise on the law of copyright in literature. 1842.
Dickens, C. [Printed circular on Anglo-American copyright, beginning:] You may perhaps be aware. 1842.
Stanhope, P. H., Baron Mahon [later Earl Stanhope]. Speech moving the first clause of the Bill on the law of copyright. 1842.
The law of copyright regarding authors, dramatic writers and musical composers as altered by the recent statute. 1842.
Mathews, C. An appeal to American authors and the American press in behalf of an international copyright. New York 1842; rptd in Various writings of C. Mathews, New York 1843.
Mathews, C. A speech on international copyright. New York 1842.
Mathews, C. The better interests of the country in connection with international copyright. New York 1843.
Mathews, C. The various writings. New York 1843.
Adamson, T. A reply to Considerations and arguments [by J. Campbell]. New York 1844.
Campbell, J. Considerations and arguments proving the inexpediency of an international copyright law. New York 1844.
Muquardt, C. De la contrefaçon et de son influence pernicieuse sur la littérature et la librairie. Brussels 1844.
Curtis, G. T. A treatise of the law of copyright in books. Boston 1847.
Fleugel, J. G. A call for redress in a matter of piracy committed on J. G. Fleugel's English and German dictionary. Leipzig 1847.
Jay, J. Letters to Godfrey. New York 1847.
Reid, J. Suggestions on a reform in the law of copyright. 1847.
Cocks versus Purday. The law of copyright in foreign compositions. 1848.
Jay, J. International copyright. Washington DC 1848.
Purday, Z. T. Assumed copyright in foreign authors. Report. [1848.]
Some remarks on the law of copyright. [1848?]
Boosey versus Purday. Assumed copyright in foreign authors: judgement given in the Court of Exchequer, Westminster Hall 5 June 1849. 1849.
Purday, Z. Assumed copyright in foreign authors. Judgment. [1849.]
S., G. English copyright in foreign compositions. The Jurist no 684 1850, 1850 (rptd).
A Bill to amend the law relating to the protection [in New South Wales] of works entitled to copyright in the United Kingdom. [Sydney] 1850.
A brief statement on the subject of assumed foreign copyright. 1851.
Bohn, H. G. The question of unreciprocated foreign copyright. 1851.
Norman, J. P. The law and practice of copyright. 1851.
Sheard, H. A brief statement on the subject of assumed foreign copyrights. 1851.
Villefort, A. De la propriété littéraire et artistique au point de vue internationale. Paris 1851.
Burke, P. The law of international copyright between England and France. 1852.
Conkling, A. Opinion of the Hon Alfred Conkling upon a question of copyright. 1852.
Halliwell, J. O. Observations on some of the manuscript emendations of Shakespeare and are they copyright? 1852.
Mathews, C. J. Letter from Mr Charles Mathews to the dramatic authors of France. 1852, Paris 1852 (Fr trn).
Delalain, A. H. J. Législation de la propriété littéraire. Paris 1852, 1852, 1854, 1855, 1858 (rev).
Duncan, I. M. Report of the trial of the Atlas Company against A. Fullarton and Company. Edinburgh 1853.
Thackeray, W. M. Mr Brown's letters. New York 1853. Author's preface.
Carey, H. C. Letters on international copyright. Philadelphia 1853, New York 1868.
Lacan, A. J. B. and C. P. P. Paulmier. Traité de la législation et de la jurisprudence des théatres. 2 vols Paris 1853.
Considerations on international copyright. Philadelphia 1853.
Boosey, T. A few supplemental remarks on the case, Jeffreys v. Boosey. 1854.
Boosey, T. A true statement of the case. 1854.
Boosey, T. Copyrights and patents. 1854.
Duncan, I. M. British copyright in foreign compositions. The Jurist nos 922, 923, 1854, 1854 (rptd).
Leverson, M. R. Copyright and patents: being an investigation of the principles of legal science applicable to property in thought. 1854.
Rolfe, R. M., Baron Cranworth. Report of the judgments [in Jeffreys v. Boosey]. 1854.
Sugden, E. B., Baron St Leonards. Report of the judgments [in Jeffreys v. Boosey]. 1854.
Burke, P. The copyright law and the press. 1855.
Miller, H. What is criticism? And whose property are letters? Rptd from The witness. Edinburgh 1855.
Eisenlohr, C. F. M. Sammlung der Gesetze und internationalen Verträge zum Schutze des literarischenartischen Eigenthums in Deutschland, Frankreich und England. Heidelberg 1856. 1857.
Napier, M. Note of the state of the question of literary piracy in re Napier v. Grand and Routledge. [1858?]
Wood, J. An exposure of a recent attempt at book-making [on plagiarism]. 1858.
Laboulaye, E. R. L. Études sur la propriété littéraire en France et en Angleterre. Paris 1858.
Compte rendu des travaux du congrès de Bruxelles. Paris 1858.
Thomson, A. The Bible printing patent: shall it be renewed? 1859.
Fraser, J. A handy-book of patent and copyright law. 1860.
Peele, C. The eighth commandment [on copyright in translations]. 1860.

Reade, C. The eighth commandment. 1860.
Didot, A. F. Observations présentées à la Commission de la propriété littéraire et artistique. Paris 1862.
Law, S. D. Digest of American cases relating to patents for inventions and copyrights from 1789 to 1862. New York 1862, 1870 (rev), 1877 (rev).
Gastambide, J. A. Histoire et théorie de la propriété des auteurs. Paris 1862.
Burke, P. The present state of the law of copyright with a view to its amendment. 1863.
Phillips, C. P. The law of literature and art. 1863.
Chappell, F. P. and J. Shoard. A handy book of the law of copyright. 1863.
Gambart, E. On piracy of artistic copyright. 1863.
Huard, A. Étude comparative des législations françaises et étrangères en matière de la propriété industrielle, artistique et littéraire. Paris 1863.
Reade, C. The rights and wrongs of authors. In Readiana, 1863.
A handy-book on the law of the drama and music, being an exposition of the law of dramatic copyright. 1864.
Select Committee on Copyright (No 2) Bill. 1864 (441) ix 1.
Trollope, A. On the best means of extending and securing an international law of copyright. Trans Nat Assoc for Promotion of Social Science 1867.
Delalain, A. H. J. Nouvelle législation de la propriété littéraire. Paris 1868.
Gerhard, F. Will the people of the United States be benefited by an international copyright law? New York 1868.
Le Barrois d'Orgeval, R. La propriété littéraire en France et à l'étranger. Paris 1868.
White, R. G. The American view of the copyright question. Broadway Annual (New York) May 1868; rptd New York 1880.
[Helps, Sir A.] International copyright between England and America. Macmillan's Mag June 1869.
Hazlitt, W. C. A case of plagiarism. [1869.]
Carter, T. H. International copyright with Great Britain. Boston MA [1870?]
Copinger, W. A. The law of copyright in works of literature and art. 1870, 1881, 1893, 1904 (rev J. M. Easton), 1915, 1927 (rev F. E. Skone James), 1936 (rev F. E. Skone James), 1948 (rev F. E. Skone James), 1958 (rev F. E. Skone James and E. P. Skone James), 1965 (rev F. E. Skone James and E. P. Skone James), 1971 (ed E. P. Skone James), 1980 (ed E. P. Skone James, J. F. Mummery, J. E. Raymer James), 1990 (ed E. P. Skone James et al.).
Booth, W. D. Rights of dramatic authors at Common Law. New York 1871.
Hotten, J. C. Literary copyright: seven letters addressed to Earl Stanhope. 1871.
Klostermann, R. Das Urheberrecht und das Verlagsrecht nach deutschen und ausländischen Gesetzen systematisch und vergleichend dargestellt. Berlin 1871.
Shortt, J. The law relating to literature and art. 1871, 1884.
Appleton, W. H. Letters on international copyright. New York 1872.
Carey, H. C. The international copyright question considered. Philadelphia 1872.
Longman, T. Some observations on copyright. 1872.
Lovell, J. and G. M. Adam. A letter to Sir John Rose on Canadian copyright. 1872.
Trevelyan, C. E. The compromise offered by Canada in reference to English copyright. 1872.
Memoranda on international and colonial copyright, 1872.
Coryton, J. Stageright: a compendium of the laws relating to dramatic authors. 1873.
Copyright Association. Report of the year 1874–5. 1875.
Morgan, J. H. The law of literature. 2 vols New York 1875, 1876.
Dicey, E. The copyright question. Fortnightly Rev Jan 1876.
Purday, C. H. Copyright: a sketch of its rise and progress. 1877.
[Froude, J. A.] The copyright commission. Edinburgh Rev Oct 1878.
Minutes of evidence taken before the Royal Commission on Copyright. 1878 (C.2036.-I) xxiv. 253.
The present state of literature: the Copyright Act. 1878.
Report of the [Royal Commission on copyright]. 1878 (C.2036) xxiv. 163.
Levi, L. International copyright in relation to the USA and other foreign states. 1879.
Macfie, R. A. Copyright and patents for inventions. Vol 1, Edinburgh 1879.
M[arston], E. Copyright national and international from the point of view of a publisher. 1879.
Conant, S. S. and L. H. Courtney. International Copyright. Macmillan's Mag June 1879.
Drone, E. S. A treatise on the law of property in intellectual productions in Great Britain and the USA. Boston 1879.
Morgan, J. H. Anglo-American international copyright. New York 1879.
Putnam, G. H. International copyright considered in some of its relations to ethics and political economy. New York 1879.
Harper & Bros. Memorandums on international copyright. [New York 1879], [1880] (enlarged).
'Stylus'. American publishers and English authors. Baltimore 1879.
Fliniaux, C. La propriété industrielle et la propriété littéraire et artistique en France et à l'étranger. Tours 1879.
Pouillet, E. Traité théorique et pratique de la propriété littéraire et artistique et du droit de représentation. Paris 1879.
Clunet, E. Concordance des résolutions du Congrés de la Propriété artistique tenu à Paris en 1878. Paris 1879.
Arnold, M. Copyright. Fortnightly Rev Mar 1880; rptd in his Irish essays, 1882.
Collins, W. W. Considerations on the copyright question addressed to an American friend. International Rev (New York) June 1880; rptd 1880.
Jerrold, S. A handbook of English and foreign copyright in literary and dramatic works. 1881.
Longman, C. J. A publisher's view of international copyright. Fraser's Mag Mar 1881.
Dawson, S. E. Copyright in books: an insight into its origin and the present state of the law in Canada. Montreal 1882.
Scrutton, T. E. The laws of copyright. 1883, 1890, 1896, 1903.
Thompson, G. C. Remarks on the law of literary property in various countries. 1883.
Lea, H. C. International copyright. [Philadelphia 1884.]
Newton, A. V. An analysis of the patent and copyright laws. 1884.
Slater, J. H. The law relating to copyright. 1884.
Tuer, A. W. John Bull's womankind [on the law of copyright]. [1884.]
Pitman versus Hine. Report of the trial for an infringement of the Copyright Act. 1884.
Bowker, R. R. Copyright: its law and its literature. New York 1886.
International copyright in the congress of the United States. Library Jnl 1886, 1886 (rpt).
Daldy, F. R. (ed). The articles of the International Copyright Union. 1887.
Howard, A. Copyright: a manual for authors and publishers. 1887.
Matthews, J. B. Cheap books and good books. New York 1888.
Allom, A. T. Tabulated statutes. The law of copyright. 1889.
Association Littéraire Internationale: son histoire 1878–89. Paris 1889.
Daldy, F. R. The colonial copyright acts. 1889.
Lyon-Caen, C. and P. Delalain. Lois françaises et étrangères sur la propriété littéraire. 2 vols Paris 1889.
Matthews, J. B. American authors and British pirates. New York 1889.
Cutler, E., T. E. Smith and F. E. Weatherly. The law of musical and dramatic copyright. 1890.

Bewes, W. A. Copyright, patents, designs, trade marks, etc [including copyright]. 1891.
Lely, T. M. Copyright law reform. 1891.
Putnam, G. H. The question of copyright. New York 1891, 1896.
Cooke, P. J. A handbook of the drama, with a chapter on the law of copyright. 1895.
Chamier, D. Law relating to literary copyright. 1895.
Chosson, E. La propriété littéraire. Paris 1895.
Osterreith, A. Die Geschichte des Urheberrechts in England. Leipzig 1895.
Cohen, B. A. The law of copyright. 1896.
Lancefield, R. T. Notes on copyright, domestic and international. Hamilton Ontario 1896.
Allen, C. E. Publishers' accounts, including a consideration of copyright. 1897.
Rivière, L. Protection internationale des oeuvres littéraires et artistiques. Paris 1897.
Report of the Select Committee of the House of Lords on the Copyright Bills [evidence and appendix]. 1898, 1899, 1900.
Birrell, A. Seven lectures on the law and history of copyright in books. 1899.
Briggs, W. The law of literary copyright. 1900.
Solberg, T. Copyright enactments [in USA] 1783–1900, together with the Presidential proclamations regarding international copyright. Washington 1900.
Strong, A. A. The law of copyright for actor and composer. 1901.
Macgillivray, E. J. Treatise upon the law of copyright in the United Kingdom and the Dominions of the Crown and in the USA. 1902, 1906.
Browne, T. B. An epitome of useful information relating to trade marks, letters patent, designs, copyright, and the use of the royal arms. 1903, 1905.
Hinkson, H. A. Copyright law. 1903.
Hamlin, A. S. Copyright cases: a summary of leading American decisions. New York 1904.
Recueil des conventions et traités concernant la propriété littéraire. Berne 1904.
Solberg, T. Copyright in Congress 1789–1904: a bibliography and chronological record. Washington 1905.
Briggs, W. The law of international copyright. 1906.
Colles, W. M. and H. Hardy. Playwright and copyright in all countries. 1906.
Macgillivray, E. J. A digest of the law of copyright. 1906.
Allen, G. Copyright and copywrong: the authentic and the unauthentic Ruskin. 1907.
Macgillivray, E. J. Copyright in letters. 1907.
Strahan, J. A. Notes and comments on some copyright cases. 1907.
Report of the Committee on the Law of Copyright. 1909.
Singer, B. The law of copyright. 1911, 1914.
Bowker, R. R. Copyright: its history and its law. 1912.
Putnam, G. H. George Pamer Putnam. New York 1912.
Potu, E. La convention de Berne. Paris 1914.
Flower, D. Authors and copyright in the xixth century with unpublished letters from Wilkie Collins. Book Collectors' Quart no 7 1932.
Pollard, G. Introduction. In I. R. Brussel, Anglo-American first editions, 1935.
Bader, A. L. Frederick Saunders and the early history of the international copyright movement in America. Lib Quart 8 1938.
Houtchens, L. H. Charles Dickens and international copyright. Amer Lit 13 1941–2.
Eaton, A. J. The American movement for international copyright 1837–60. Lib Quart 15 1945.
Zall, P. M. Wordsworth and the Copyright Act of 1842. PMLA 70 1955.
Barber, G. Galignani and the publication of English books in France from 1800 to 1852. Library 5th ser 16 1961.
Noyes, R. Wordsworth and the Copyright Act of 1842: an addendum. PMLA 76 1961.
Patterson, R. L. Copyright in historical perspective. Nashville TN 1968.
Nowell Smith, S. International copyright law and the publisher in the reign of Queen Victoria. Oxford 1968.
Barnes, J. J. Galignani and the publication of English books in France: a postscript. Library 5th ser 25 1970.
Whale, R. F. Copyright: evolution, theory and practice. 1971, 1983 (by R. F. Whale and J. J. Phillips), 1993 (ed J. J. Phillips, R. Durie and I. Karet).
Kent, A. and A. H. Lancour. Copyright: current viewpoints on history. New York 1972.
Barnes, J. J. Authors, publishers and politicians: the quest for an Anglo-American copyright agreement 1815–1854. 1974.
Ricketson, S. The Berne Convention and the protection of literary and artistic works 1886–1986. 1987.
Welsh, A. From copyright to Copperfield: the identity of Dickens. Cambridge MA 1987.
Todd, W. B. and A. Bowman. Tauchnitz International Editions in English 1841–1955: a bibliographical history. New York 1988.
Feather, J. Publishers and politicians: the remaking of the law of copyright in Britain 1775–1842. Publishing History 24 1988, 25 1989.
Eilenberg, S. Mortal pages: Wordsworth and the reform of copyright. ELH 56 1989.
Saunders, D. Authorship and copyright. 1992.
Feather, J. Publishing, piracy and politics: an historical study of copyright in Britain. 1994.
Sherman, B. and A. Strowel. Of authors and origins: essays on copyright law. Oxford 1994.
Woodmansee, M. and P. Jaszi (ed). The construction of authorship: textual appropriation in law and literature. Durham NC 1994.
[JF]

(3) AUTHORS' GUIDES TO PUBLICATION

The following works all profess to instruct an author how to choose and negotiate with a publisher. This function is now fulfilled by the literary agent, who was hardly established as a profession before 1880.

[H., T.] The perils of authorship; an enquiry into the difficulties of literature. [c. 1835], [c. 1840] (4th edn).
[H., T.] The author's advocate and young publishers' friend: a sequel to the perils of authorship. [c. 1840.]
The author's printing and publishing assistant. 1839, 1839, New York 1839, 1840, [c. 1848] (7th edn). Attributed to Frederic Saunders; all English edns pbd by Saunders & Otley.
Hints and directions for authors in writing, printing and publishing their works. 1842. Attributed to the publisher Edward Bull.
[Churton, E.] The author's handbook: a complete guide to the art and system of publishing on commission. 1844, 1845 (with addns).
Saunders and Otley & Co. Advice to authors, inexperienced writers and possessors of manuscripts, on the efficient publication of books intended for general circulation or private distribution with select specimens of printing. [1853.]
A description of publishing methods and arrangements. New York 1855 (4th edn).
The search for a publisher: or counsels to a young author. 1855, 1859 (4th edn), 1865, 1870, [1873], 1881 (8th edn).
[Judd, J. and A. H. Glass.] Counsels to authors and hints to advertisers. 1856, 1857.
Counsels to authors. Plans of publishing, and specimens of types. 1863.
Collingridge, W. H. and L. Collingridge. Comprehensive guide to printing and publishing. 1869, 1877 (10th edn), 1897.

Spon, E. How to publish a book, being directions and hints to authors. 1872.

[Southward, J.] Authorship and publication: a guide in matters relating to printing and publishing. 1882, 1883, 1884.

[Putnam, G. H. and J. B.] Authors and publishers: a manual of suggestions for beginners in literature. New York 1883, 1897 (7th edn), 1900.

Deacon's composition and style, a handbook for literary students, with a complete guide to all matters connected with printing and publishing. Ed R. D. Blackman [1885] (5th edn).

Russell, P. The literary manual: or a complete guide to authorship. 1886.

The author's guide to printing and publishing by a journalist. [1886] (2nd edn).

O'Brien, M. B. A manual for authors, printers and publishers. 1890.

Sprigge, S. S. The methods of publishing. 1890, 1891 (2nd edn).

The author. No 1, 15 May 1890– . The monthly organ of the Incorporated Society of Authors; ed Sir Walter Besant.

[Warren, W. T.] How to print and publish a book. Winchester 1890.

Jacobi, C. T. On the making and issuing of books. 1891.

Jacobi, C. T. Some notes on books and printing. A guide for authors, publishers and others. 1892, 1902, 1903, 1912 (4th edn).

Besant, W. The Society of Authors: a record of its action from its foundation. 1893.

Watt, A. P. Letters addressed to A. P. Watt by various writers [on his Literary agency]. 1893, 1894, 1896.

Eisemann, E. Le contrat d'édition et les autres louages d'œuvres intellectuelles. Paris 1894.

Lamb, J. B. Practical hints on writing for the press. 1897.

Wagner, L. How to publish a book or an article and how to produce a play: advice to young authors. 1898.

Besant, W. The pen and the book. 1899.

Bennett, A. How to become an author: a practical guide. 1903, [1908] 1912.

[Watson, W. L.] The author's progress; or the literary book of the road. By Adam Lorimer. Edinburgh 1906.

Booth, W. S. A practical guide to authors in their relations with publishers and printers. Boston 1907. [PB]

(4) THE PRACTICE OF PUBLISHING

Memoirs of authors have not been included in this list although they contain much relevant material, particularly the autobiographies of Anthony Trollope, Herbert Spencer, Harriet Martineau, Cyrus Redding and Edmund Yates, and the biographies of Macaulay by Sir G. O. Trevelyan and of Scott by J. G. Lockhart (as well as his Journal and Correspondence). Works relating to publishers' control of the retail price (the Net Book Agreement and its predecessors) have been listed with those on retail bookselling, col 87.

Babbage, C. On the economy of machinery and manufactures. 1832, 1835 (4th edn).

First Report from the Select Committee on Postage. Minutes of evidence. 1837–8. xx. 278.

Jerdan, W. Illustrations of the plan of a National Association for the encouragement and protection of authors and men of talent and genius. 1839.

The Aldine magazine of biography, bibliography, criticism and the arts. 1839. Ed William West.

[Grant, J.] Travels in town by the author of Random recollections of the Lords and Commons. 2 vols 1839.

Balzac, H. de. Code littéraire (May 1840). In his œuvres complètes vol 22, Paris 1872.

James, G. P. R. Some observations on the booktrade as connected with literature in England. Jnl of Statistical Soc of London Feb 1843.

[Petheram, J.] Reasons for establishing an authors publication society. 1843.

The present system of publishing. 1844.

Knight, C. The old printer and the modern press. 1854.

Spedding, J. Publishers and authors. 1867.

Ruskin, J. Fors clavigera. 1871–84. Letters 6, 11, 16, 53, 57, 62, 89; Notes and correspondence, 10, 14–15.

Walker, A. The road: leaves from the sketch book of a commercial traveller. Otley 1872.

Powell, A. The law specially affecting printers, publishers and newspaper proprietors. 1887, 1889 (2nd edn).

The grievances between authors and publishers: being the report of the conferences of the Incorporated Society of Authors with additional matter and summary. 1887.

Besant, W. Literary conferences. 1888.

Jessopp, A. A plea for the publisher. Contemporary Rev Mar 1890.

Smiles, S. Authors and publishers. Murray's Mag Jan–Feb 1890.

Sprigge, S. S. The methods of publishing. 1890, 1891 (2nd edn).

Sprigge, S. S. The society of French authors. Its foundation and history. 1890.

The Society of Authors. The cost of production. 1891. (3 edns).

Kegan Paul, C. The life and death of books. In his Faith and unfaith, 1891.

Besant, W. The Society of Authors: a record of its action from its foundation. 1893.

[Heinemann, W.] The hardships of publishing. 1893 (priv ptd).

Besant, W. Literary conferences. Contemporary Rev Jan 1894.

Jerome, J. K. et al. My first book. 1894.

Buchanan, R. W. Is Barabbas a necessity? a discourse on publishers and publishing. 1896.

Allen, C. E. Publishers' Accounts; including a consideration of copyright and the valuation of literary property. 1897.

Spencer, H. Various fragments. 1897, 1900 (rev).

Besant, W. The pen and the book. 1899.

International Publishers' Congress 1899. Report. 1899.

International Publishers' Congress 1901. Report. Leipzig 1902.

Besant, W. Autobiography. 1902.

[Bennett, E. A.] The truth about an author. 1903, 1914.

Publishers and publishing a hundred years ago, from materials collected by Aleck Abrahams, with some notes by E. Marston. Publishers' Circular 6, 13 Jan 1906.

Yard, R. S. The publisher. Boston 1913.

Putnam, G. H. Memories of a publisher 1865–95. 1915.

Unwin, S. The truth about publishing. 1926, 1929 (3rd edn rev), 1946, 1960 (7th edn), 1976 (8th edn).

'On the road' one hundred years ago: being an account of a journey made [in 1830] by a traveller of Messrs A. & C. Black's when subscribing the seventh edition of the Encyclopaedia Britannica. Ed J. Cannon, Publishers' Circular 9 Feb–13 Apr 1935.

Lawrence, C. W. (ed). A history of the printed book. Number 3 of The Dolphin: a Journal of the Making of Books. New York 1938.

Burlingame, R. and C. Scribner. Of making many books: a hundred years of reading, writing and publishing. 1946, rptd 1996.

Jennett, S. Pioneers in printing. 1958.

Flower, D. The paper-back, its past, present and future. A paper read to the Double Crown Club in April 1959. 1959.

Unwin, P. Book publishing as a career. 1965.

Bailey, H. S. The art and science of book publishing. 1970, 1990.

Kingford, R. J. L. The Publishers Association 1896–1946. Cambridge 1970.

Parsons, I. M. Book publishing, a background glance, a forward look. 1980.

Clark, C. Publishers agreements. 1984, 1988, 1993 (3rd edn).

Feather, J. A history of British publishing. 1988.

Eliot, S. Some patterns and trends in British publishing 1800–1919. 1994. [PB]

(5) INDIVIDUAL PUBLISHERS

Rudolph Ackermann (1764–1834)
P[apworth], W[yatt]. N & Q 7–14 Aug 1869.
Ford, J. Ackermann's History of Westminster Abbey. BC 30 1981.
George Allen (1832–1907)
Maidment, B. E. John Ruskin, George Allen and American pirated books. Publishing History 9 1981.
Allen & Unwin Ltd
George Allen & Unwin Ltd. 1933.
Mumby, F. A. and F. H. S. Stallybrass. From Swan Sonnenschein to George Allen and Unwin Ltd. 1955.
Edward Arnold (1857–1942)
Bennett, B. and A. Hamilton. Edward Arnold: a hundred years of publishing. 1990.
Samuel Bagster (1772–1851)
The centenary of the Bagster publishing house. 1894.
B. T. Batsford
Bolitho, H. A Batsford century: the record of a hundred years of publishing and bookselling 1843–1943. [1943.]
George Bell (1814–90)
Bell, E. George Bell, publisher. 1924 (priv ptd).
Weedon, A. A quantitative survey: George Bell & Sons. Publishing History 23 1993.
John Bell (1745–1831)
Morison, S. John Bell 1745–1831. 1930.
Richard Bentley (1794–1871)
Richard Bentley & Son: reprinted from Le Livre Oct 1885 with some additional notes. 1886 (priv ptd).
Sadleir, M. Standard novels. Colophon [New York] Apr 1932.
Gettman, R. A. A Victorian publisher: a study of the Bentley papers. Cambridge 1960.
Turner, M. L. Index and guide to the lists of Richard Bentley & Son 1829–1898. Bishops Stortford 1975.
James, E. Sale of the Standard novels. Library 5th ser 33 1978.
Bentley's advertising procedures. Publishing History 1 1982.
Adam Black (1784–1874)
Nicholson, A. Memoirs of A. Black. Edinburgh 1885, 1885.
Adam and Charles Black 1807–1957: some chapters in the history of a publishing house. 1957.
John Blackie (1782–1874)
Blackie, W. G. The origin and progress of the firm of Blackie and Son 1809–1874. 1897.
A Scottish student in Leipzig, being the letters of W. G. Blackie, his father and his brothers in the years 1839–1840. Ed W. W. Blackie. 1932.
Blackie, A. Blackie and Son 1809–1959: a short history of the firm. 1959.
100 years of publishing [exhibition catalogue]. 1959.
Dempster, J. A. H. Author–publisher agreements: some light on Blackie and Son's nineteenth century practice. Bibliotheck 12 1984–5.
William Blackwood (1776–1834); John Blackwood (1818–79)
Blackwood, J. A. A selection from the obituary notices. Ed W. Blackwood, Edinburgh 1880 (priv ptd).
Oliphant, M. O. Annals of a publishing house: W. Blackwood and his sons. 2 vols 1897. Vol 3, J. Blackwood by his daughter Mrs G. Porter, 1898.
B., I. C. The early house of Blackwood. Edinburgh 1900 (priv ptd).
Tredrey, F. D. The house of Blackwood 1804–1954. Edinburgh 1954.
Conrad, J. Letters to William Blackwood. Ed W. Blackburn. Durham NC 1958.
Haight, G. S. New George Eliot letters to William Blackwood. TLS 3 Oct 1972.
Sutherland, J. A. John Blackwood and the serialisation of Middlemarch. Bibliotheck 7 1975.
Anderson, R. F. Negotiating for The mill on the Floss. Bibliotheck 7 1975.
Anderson, R. F. Things wisely ordered: John Blackwood, George Eliot and Romola. Publishing History 11 1982.
Robinson, C. E. Percy Bysshe Shelley, Charles Ollier and William Blackwood. In Shelley revalued, ed K. Everest, Leicester 1983.
Haythornthwaite, J. A. The wages of success: Miss Marjoribanks and the house of Blackwood. Publishing History 15 1984.
Hall, N. J. Seeing Trollope's An autobiography through the press. Princeton Univ Lib Chron 47 1985–6.
Haythornthwaite, J. A. Friendly encounters: the house of Blackwood and Margaret Oliphant. Publishing History 28 1990.
Finkelstein, D. Thomas de Quincey and Robert Blackwood. N & Q 237 1992.
Martin, C. A. Two unpublished letters from John Blackwood. Publishing History 37 1995.
The Bodley Head
See also Elkin Mathews (1851–1921) and John Lane (1854–1925).
Ryder, S. C. The Bodley Head, 1857–1957. 1970.
Nelson, J. G. The early nineties: a view from The Bodley Head. Cambridge MA 1971.
Nelson, J. G. The Bodley Head and the Daniel Press. PBSA 77 1983.
Lambert, J. W. and M. Ratcliffe. The Bodley Head 1887–1987. 1987.
Stetz, M. B. and M. S. Lasner. England in the 1980s: literary publishing at The Bodley Head. Washington DC 1990.
British and Foreign Bible Society
Howsam, L. Cheap Bibles. Cambridge 1991.
Henry Butterworth (1786–1860)
Jones, H. K. Butterworths: history of a publishing house. 1980.
Burns and Oates
'Wilberforce, Wilfrid' (Wilfrid Meynell). The house of Burns and Oates. [1908.]
Early chapters in the history of Burns & Oates. 1949 (priv ptd).
Cadell and Davies
The publishing firm of Cadell and Davies: select correspondence and accounts 1793–1836. Ed T. Besterman 1938.
Cambridge University Press
See also under Printers and Printing firms.
Roberts, S. C. A history of the Cambridge University Press 1521–1921. Cambridge 1921.
Roberts, S. C. The evolution of Cambridge publishing. Cambridge 1956.
Roberts, S. C. Adventures with authors. Cambridge 1966.
Black, M. H. The Cambridge University Press in the second half of the nineteenth century. Publishing History 14 1983.
Black, M. H. Cambridge University Press 1584–1984. Cambridge 1984.
Richard Carlile (1790–1843)
Holyoake, G. J. The life and character of Carlile. 1848.
Campbell, T. C. The battle of the press as told in the story of the life of Carlile. 1899.
John Cassell (1817–65)
Kirton, J. W. John Cassell. 1891.
Pike, G. H. John Cassell. 1894.
Flower, N. Just as it happened. 1950.
Nowell-Smith, S. The house of Cassell 1848–1958. 1958.
James Catnach (1792–1841)
Hindley, C. The life and times of Catnach, balladmonger. 1878, 1970.
St Bride foundation: catalogue of an exhibition of street literature. 1954.
Muir, P. Catnachery. San Francisco CA 1955.
William Chambers (1800–83); Robert Chambers (1802–71)
Chambers, W. Memoir of Robert Chambers with autobiographic reminiscences of William Chambers. Edinburgh 1872, 1884 (12th edn), 1893 (rev).

Chambers, W. The story of a long and busy life. Edinburgh 1882, 1884 (13th edn).
Payn, J. Some literary recollections. 1886.
Collingwood, F. A notable Scottish bookman. Lib Rev 23 1971.
Chapman and Hall
Waugh, A. A hundred years of publishing: being the story of Chapman and Hall Ltd. 1930.
Waugh, A. One man's road. 1931.
John W. Chapman
Kegan Paul, C. Biographical sketches. 1883.
Chatto & Windus
A century of writers 1855–1955. 1955.
Warner, O. Chatto & Windus: a brief account. 1973.
Eliot, S. 'His generation read his stories': Walter Besant, Chatto and Windus and All sorts and conditions of men. Publishing History 21 1987.
Eliot, S. Unequal partnerships: Besant, Rice and Chatto 1876–1882. Publishing History 23 1989.
T. and T. Clark
The publishing house of T. and T. Clark. Edinburgh 1882.
Dempster, J. A. H. The T. & T. Clark story. Edinburgh 1982.
William Cobbett (1763–1833)
See col 2109.
Henry Colburn (d. 1855)
Sutherland, J. Henry Colburn. Publishing History 19 1986.
William Collins, Sons & Co.
William Collins, Sons & Co. The story of a great business 1820–1910. Glasgow 1909.
Keir, D. The house of Collins. 1952.
Archibald Constable (1774–1827)
See also Sir Walter Scott, *col 992.*
Constable, T. Constable and his literary correspondents. 3 vols Edinburgh 1873.
Quayle, E. The ruin of Sir Walter Scott. 1968.
Joseph Cundall (1818–95)
McLean, R. Joseph Cundall, a Victorian publisher. Pinner 1976.
J. M. Dent (1849–1926)
Dent, H. R. The memoirs of J. M. Dent, with some additions by H. R. Dent. 1928.
Rhys, E. Everyman remembers. 1931.
Dent, H. M. and H. R. Dent. The house of Dent 1888–1938. [1938.]
G. H. Doran
Chronicles of Barabbas 1884–1934. 1935.
Gerald Duckworth & Co.
Fifty years 1898–1948. [1948] (priv ptd).
Edinburgh University Press
See also Printers and Printing firms.
Richardson, J. Edinburgh University Press. Br Book News Jan 1991.
Richard Edwards (1768–1827)
Bentley, G. E. Richard Edwards publisher. SB 41 1988.
John Francis (1811–82)
Francis, J. C. Francis: publisher of the Athenaeum. 2 vols 1888.
Glasgow University Press
See also Printers and Printing firms.
Maclehose, J. The Glasgow University Press 1638–1931. Glasgow 1931.
William Godwin (1756–1836)
Kegan Paul, C. William Godwin: his friends and contemporaries. 2 vols 1876.
Kinnell, M. Childhood and children's literature: the case of M. J. Godwin and Co. 1805–1825. Publishing History 23 1988.
Charles Griffin & Co
The centenary volume of Griffin and Co. 1820–1920. 1920.
Robert Hardwicke (1822–75)
English, M. P. Robert Hardwicke (1822–1875) publisher. Archives of Natural History 13 1986.
English, M. P. Robert Hardwicke and T. H. Huxley. Archives of Natural History. 16 1989.
John Harris
Moon, M. John Harris's books for youth 1801–1843. Cambridge 1976.
Moon, M. A supplement. Richmond 1983, Winchester 1987.
C. Harrison
Harrison, C. From office boy to publisher: a record of 43 years of work. [1911.]
Hatchard & Co
Humphreys, A. L. Piccadilly bookmen: memorials of the house of Hatchard. 1893.
William Heinemann (1863–1920)
Heinemann, W. The hardships of publishing, 1893.
Whyte, F. Heinemann: a memoir. 1928.
Stevens, A. E. The recollections of a bookman. 1933.
Evans, C. S. 1883–1944. Obituary notices. 1945 (priv ptd).
Hill, A. In pursuit of publishing. 1988.
St John, J. William Heinemann: a century of publishing. 1890–1990. 1990.
Her Majesty's Stationery Office
Barty-King, H. Her Majesty's Stationery Office. The story of the first 200 years. 1986.
Hodder and Stoughton
Attenborough, P. A living memory: Hodder and Stoughton 1868–1975. 1975.
William Hone (1780–1842)
Hackwood, F. W. Hone: his life and times. 1912.
John Camden Hotten (1832–77)
Paley, M. D. John Camden Hotten and the first British editions of Walt Whitman. Publishing History 6 1979.
Lasner, M. S. William Rossetti's Swinburne's poems and ballads. BC 31 1982.
James Fletcher Hughes
Garside, P. J. F. Hughes and the publication of popular fiction. Library 6th ser 9 1987.
Jarrold & Co
The house of Jarrolds 1823–1923. 1924.
Paul Jerrard
Leathlean, H. Paul Jerrard: publisher of 'special presents'. BC 40 1991.
Joseph Johnson (1738–1809)
Chard, L. F. Bookseller to publisher: Joseph Johnson and the English book trade 1760–1810. Library 5th ser 32 1977.
Tyson, G. P. Joseph Johnson. Iowa City IO 1979.
W. & A. K. Johnston
One hundred years of map making: the story of W. and A. K. Johnston. 1925.
Thomas Kelly (1772–1855)
Fell, R. C. Passages from the private and official life of the late Alderman Kelly. 1856.
Henry S. King
Howsam, L. Forgotten Victorians: contracts with the authors of Henry S. King and Kegan Paul, Trench. Publishing History 34 1993.
Charles Knight (1791–1873)
Knight, C. Passages of a working life. 3 vols 1864.
Strahan, A. Knight, publisher. Good Words 1 Sep 1867.
Clowes, A. A. Knight: a sketch. 1892.
Lang, P. H. Charles Knight and The art of printing. Printing Rev 1939.
Morbey, C. C. F. Charles Knight: an appreciation. Birmingham 1979.
John Lane (1854–1925)
See also Bodley Head, The
May, J. L. John Lane and the nineties. 1936.
Ryder, S. C. The Bodley Head 1857–1957. 1970.

H. K. Lewis & Co
Lewis's 1844–1944. 1945.
E. & S. Livingstone Ltd
Eighty years of publishing 1864–1944. Edinburgh 1944.
Footprints on the sands of time 1863–1963: the story of Livingstone, medical, scientific, nursing and dental publishers. [1963.]
Edward Lloyd (1815–90)
Hoggart, P. R. Edward Lloyd. Dickensian 80 1984.
John Linnell
Bindman, D. (ed). Colour versions of William Blake's Book of Job. 1987.
Longmans, Green & Co
This is the name under which the firm traded for the greater part of the 19th century. For the many variations, see the list in Wallis *(1974), below.*
Rees, T. Reminiscences of literary London from 1779 to 1853, with additions by John Britton. New York 1896.
Cox, H. and J. E. Chandler. The house of Longman 1724–1924. 1925 (priv ptd).
'Indiaman'. Three addresses: an essay in publishing ecology 1939–1947. 1947.
Blagden, C. Fire more than water: notes for the story of a ship. 1949.
Owen, J. W. B. Letters of Longman & Co to Wordsworth 1814–1836. Library 5th ser 9 1954.
Briggs, A. (ed). Essays in the history of publishing: the house of Longman 1724–1974. 1974.
Wallis, P. At the sign of the ship. 1974 (priv ptd).
Braun, T. Thomas Longman and Lothair. Publishing History 6 1979.
James Lumsden & Son
Roscoe, S. J. Lumsden & Son of Glasgow. Private Library 3 1970.
Roscoe, S. J. and R. A. Brimmell. James Lumsden & Son of Glasgow. Pinner 1981.
Daniel Macmillan (1813–57); Alexander Macmillan (1818–96); Sir Frederic Macmillan (1851–1936)
Hughes, T. Memoir of Daniel Macmillan. 1882, 1883.
A bibliographical catalogue of Macmillan & Co's publications 1843–1889. 1891.
Macmillan G. A. Letters of Alexander Macmillan. 1908 (priv ptd).
Graves, C. L. Life and letters of Alexander Macmillan. 1910.
Morgan, C. The house of Macmillan 1843–1943. [1943.]
Nowell-Smith, S. Letters to Macmillan. 1967.
Fredeman, W. E. The bibliographical significance of a publisher's archives: the Macmillan papers. SB 23 1970.
Cohen, M. H. Lewis Carroll and the house of Macmillan. Browning Inst Stud 7 1979.
Cohen, M. H. and A. Gandolfo. Lewis Carroll and the house of Macmillan. Cambridge 1987.
Sutherland, J. Macmillans and Robert Elsemere. N & Q 232 1987.
John Macrone
Sutherland, J. John Macrone: Victorian publisher. Dickens Stud Annual 13 1984.
Edward Marston (1825–1914)
Marston, E. After work. 1904.
Elkin Mathews (1851–1921)
See also Bodley Head, The
Nelson, J. G. Elkin Mathews' Shilling garland series. PBSA 78 1984.
Nelson, J. G. Elkin Mathews, W. B. Yeats and the Celtic movement. Jnl of Modern Lit 14 1987.
Nelson, J. G. Elkin Mathews: publisher to Yeats, Joyce and Pound. Madison WI 1989.
Muir, B. Elkin Mathews celebrates its centenary. BC 37 1988.
Sir Algernon Methuen (1856–1924)
Methuen: a memoir. 1925.
Duffy, M. A thousand capricious chances: a history of the Methuen lists 1889–1989. 1989.
Minerva Press
Blakey, D. The Minerva Press 1790–1820. 1939.
R. C. Morgan
Morgan, G. E. A veteran in revival: R. C. Morgan his life and times. 1909, 1931.
Edward Moxon (1801–58)
Thomas, D. The prosecution of Moxon's Shelley. Library 5th ser 33 1978.
Hagen, J. S. Tennyson's troubled years with Moxon. Browning Inst Stud 7 1979.
John Murray (I, 1745–93; II, 1778–43; III, 1808–92; IV, 1851–1928)
Smiles, S. A publisher and his friends [JM I & II]. 2 vols 1891, 1891, 1911 (abridged).
Murray, J. [III]. The origin and history of Murray's Handbooks for travellers. Murray's Mag Nov 1889.
Murray, J. [IV]. John Murray [III] 1808–1892. 1919.
'Paston, George' (E. M. Symonds) At John Murray's: record of a literary circle 1843–1892. 1932.
Bennett, S. John Murray's Family library. SB 29 1976.
Lutyens, M. The impresario of Albemarle Street. TLS 24 Nov 1978.
Gilson, D. Jane Austen and John Murray. BC 34 1985.
Zachs, W. 'An illiterate fellow of a bookseller': John Murray [I] and his authors. In A genius for letters, ed R. Myers and M. Harris, Winchester, New Castle DE 1995.
Thomas Nelson (1780–1861); William Nelson (1816–87); Thomas Nelson (1822–92)
Wilson, Sir Daniel. Nelson: a memoir. Edinburgh 1889 (priv ptd).
Dempster, J. A. H. Thomas Nelson and sons in the late nineteenth century. Publishing History 13, 14 1983.
Sir George Newnes (1851–1910)
Friedrichs, H. The life of Sir George Newnes. 1911.
James Nisbet (1785–1854)
Wallace, J. A. Lessons from the life of the late James Nisbet, 1867.
Novello, Ewer & Co
A short history of cheap music. 1887.
Charles Ollier (1788–1859)
Robinson, C. E. Percy Bysshe Shelley, Charles Ollier and William Blackwood. In Shelley revalued, ed K. Everest, Leicester 1983.
John Cunningham Orr (1827–80)
Bolton, H. C. John Cunningham Orr: a nineteenth-century book publisher in Cupar Fife. Bibliotheck 12 1884–5.
Oxford University Press
See also Printers and Printing firms.
Hart, H. Charles Earl Stanhope and the Oxford University Press. Oxford 1896, 1966 (ed J. Mosley).
Madan, F. A brief account of the University Press at Oxford. Oxford 1908.
Some account of the Oxford University Press 1468–1921. Oxford 1922.
Eyre, F. Oxford University Press and children's books. School Lib Jnl 25 1978.
McKitterick, D. J. The Oxford press 1478–1978. BC 27 1978.
Sutcliffe, P. The Oxford University Press: an informal history. Oxford 1978.
Charles Kegan Paul (1828–1902)
Kegan Paul, C. Memories. 1899, 1971.
Dunlap, J. R. Two Victorian voices: Charles Kegan Paul. Printing History 2 1980.
Roth, L. A British publisher on galley proofs. Library 6th ser 6 1984.
Howsam, L. Forgotten Victorians: contracts with the authors of Henry S. King and Kegan Paul, Trench. Publishing History 34 1993.
George Philip
Philip, G. The story of the last hundred years: a geographical record. 1934.
Sir Richard Phillips (1767–1840)
[Phillips, R. ?] Memoirs of the public and private life of Sir Richard Phillips. 1808.
GM Aug 1840 [Obituary].

Timbs, J. Recollections of Sir Richard Phillips. In Walks and talks about London. 1864.
William Pickering (1796–1854)
Keynes, G. L. William Pickering, publisher. 1924, 1969 (rev).
Munby, A. N. L. The sales of William Pickering's publications. BC 21 1972.
Warrington, B. William Pickering and the book trade. Bull John Rylands Lib 68 1985.
Warrington, B. William Pickering, his authors and interests. Bull John Rylands Lib 69 1987.
Warrington, B. William Pickering, bookseller and book collector. Bull John Rylands Lib 71 1989.
Warrington, B. The bankruptcy of William Pickering. Publishing History 72 1990.
Sir Isaac Pitman (1813–97)
Reed, T. A. A biography of Sir Isaac Pitman. 1890.
Baker, A. The life of Sir Isaac Pitman, 1908.
The house of Pitman. 1930.
Grant Richards (1872–?)
Richards, G. Memories of a misspent youth 1872–1896. 1932.
Richards, G. Author hunting. 1934.
Rivington & Co
Rivington, S. The publishing house of Rivington. 1894.
Rivington, S. The publishing family of Rivington. 1919.
Holmes, J. C. Self and partners, mostly self. 1936.
Crumb, L. N. Publishing the Oxford Movement: Francis Rivington's letters to Newman. Publishing History 28 1990.
George Robinson (1737–1801)
Bentley, G. E. Copyright documents in the George Robinson archive. SB 35 1982.
Routledge & Co
Mumby, F. A. The house of Routledge 1834–1934. 1934.
Sir Walter Scott Bt (1826–1910)
Turner, J. R. Title-pages produced by the Walter Scott Publishing Co Ltd. SB 44 1991.
John Sharpe
Bain, I. Sharpe: Publisher and bookseller, Piccadilly: a preliminary survey of his activities in the London book trade 1800–1840. Welwyn 1960.
Joseph Shaylor (1844–1924)
Shaylor, J. Sixty years a bookman. 1923.
Simms & McIntyre
Adams, J. R. R. Simms and McIntyre, creators of the Parlour library. Linen Hall Rev 4 1987.
Simpkin, Marshall & Co
Simpkins, being some account of the origin and progress of the house of Simpkin, Marshall. 1924.
George Smith (1824–1901)
[Lee, S. and L. Stephen.] Smith: a memoir. 1902 (priv ptd).
[Huxley, L.] The house of Smith, Elder. 1923 (priv ptd).
Meredith, M. Browning and the prince of publishers. Browning Inst Stud 7 1979.
Glynn, J. Prince of publishers. 1986.
William Henry Smith (I, 1792–1865; II, 1825–91); Willian Frederick Danvers Smith (1868–1928)
Maxwell, H. The life and times of the Rt Hon William Henry Smith. 2 vols Edinburgh 1893.
Pocklington, G. R. The story of W. H. Smith & Son. 1921 (priv ptd); rev F. E. K. Foat 1932 (priv ptd), 1937, 1949, 1955 (rev edn).
Wilson, C. First with the news. The history of W. H. Smith 1792–1972. 1985.
Society for the Diffusion of Useful Knowledge
Smith, H. The Society for the Diffusion of Useful Knowledge 1826–1842. Halifax NS 1975.
Society for the Promotion of Christian Knowledge
1698 and after: the story of the SPCK. 1947.
Edward Stanford
Edward Stanford, with a note on the history of the firm 1852–1901. 1902 (priv ptd).
W. T. Stead (1849–1912)
Wood, S. W. T. Stead and his Books for bairns. Univ Edinburgh Jnl 3 1987.
Elliot Stock (1838–1911)
Pantazzi, S. Elliot Stock. BC 20 1971.
Alexander Strahan
Strahan, A. Twenty years of a publisher's life. Day of Rest Jan–Dec 1881.
Srebrnik, P. T. Alexander Strahan. Ann Arbor MI 1986.
Sweet and Maxwell
Then and now 1799–1974. 1974.
Benjamin Tabart
Moon, M. Benjamin Tabart's Juvenile Library. Winchester 1990.
Bernhard Tauchnitz
Fünfzig Jahre der Verlagshandlung Bernhard Tauchnitz, 1837 bis 1887. Leipzig 1887.
Todd, W. B. and A. Bowman. Tauchnitz International editions in English 1841–1955: a bibliographical history. New York 1988.
John Taylor (1781–1864)
Taylor, O. M. John Taylor. London Mercury June 1925.
Blunden, E. Keats's publisher: a memoir of John Taylor. 1936.
Chilcott, T. A publisher and his circle. 1972.
Taylor and Francis
Brock, W. H. and A. J. Meadows. The lamp of learning: Taylor & Francis and the development of science publishing. [1984.]
Bell, H. K. Taylor & Francis: serving science. Learned Publishing 6 1993.
Thomas Tegg (1776–1845)
[Grant, J.] In his Portraits of public characters vol 2, 1841.
Memoir of the late Thomas Tegg, abridged from his autobiography by permission of his son William Tegg. 1870 (priv ptd). Rptd from City Press 6 Aug 1870.
Temple Press Ltd
Armstrong, A. C. Bouverie Street to Bowling Green Lane: fifty-five years of specialised publishing. 1946.
William Tinsley (1831–1902)
Tinsley, W. Random recollections of an old publisher. 2 vols 1900.
Downey, E. Twenty years ago. 1905.
Nicholas Trubner (1817–84)
Axon, W. E. A. In memoriam Nicholas Trubner. Lib Chron Apr 1884.
Henry Vizetelly (1820–94)
Vizetelly, H. Glances back through seventy years. 2 vols 1893.
Ward Lock & Co
Liveing E. Adventure in publishing: the house of Ward, Lock 1854–1954. [1954.]
Frederick Warne & Co
King, A. and A. F. Stuart. The house of Warne: one hundred years of publishing. 1965.
Joseph Whitaker (1820–95)
Publisher's circular, 18–25 May 1895.
Effingham Wilson (1783–1868)
[Bagehot, W.] In memoriam Effingham Wilson. 1868 (priv ptd). Rptd from City Press 18 July 1868.
Nye, F. W. Effingham Wilson. Publishing History 36 1994. [JF]

(6) GENERAL CATALOGUES

This section lists general catalogues of books in print over a specified period; it does not include catalogues of individual publishers or any limited to particular subjects. Catalogues issued regularly at intervals of less than a year are listed in cols 85–86 below in the section on Periodicals.

Growoll, A. and W. Eames. Three centuries of English book trade bibliography. New York 1903.

Pollard, G. General lists of books printed in England. Bull Inst of Hist Research Feb 1935.
[Bent, W.] The modern catalogue of books (1792–1803). 1803.
— The new London catalogue (1800–5). 1805.
— The new London catalogue (1800–7). 1807.
— The London catalogue (1700–1811). 1811.
— A modern catalogue of books (1811–12). 1812.
— The London catalogue (1800–14). 1814.
— A catalogue of books (1814–16). 1816.
— The modern London catalogue (1800–18). 1818.
— A catalogue of books (1818–20). 1820.
— The London catalogue (1800–22). 1822.
[Bent, R.] A catalogue of books (1822–4). 1824.
— The London catalogue (1800–27). 1827; Suppl, 1829.
— The London catalogue (1810–31). 1831; Suppl, 1833.
— The London catalogue (1814–34). 1835; Suppl, 1837.
— The London catalogue (1814–39). 1839.
[Low, S.] A catalogue of books. 1838–59. Annually. Incorporated in The English catalogue, below.
— The British catalogue. Vol 1 (1837–52), 1853. Index to the British Catalogue (1837–57), 1858.
— The English catalogue. 1860– . An annual.
— The English catalogue of books (1835–63). 1864. Vol 2 (1863–72), 1873; index to vol 2 (1856–76), 1876; vol 3 (1872–80), 1882; Index to vol 3 (1874–80), 1884; vol 4 (1881–9), 1891; Index to vol 4 (1881–9), 1893; vol 5 (1890–7), 1898; vol 6 (1898–1900), 1901.
[Hodgson, T.] Supplement to the London catalogue (1839–44). 1844.
— The London catalogue (1814–46). 1846; Bibliotheca Londiniensis: a classified index, 1848; Suppl, 1849.
— The London catalogue (1816–51). 1851; Classified index, 1853.
— The London catalogue (1831–55). 1855.
[Whitaker, J.] The reference catalogue of current literature. 1874– . Until 1936 this consisted of publishers' catalogues bound together and indexed. Since 1936 it comprises catalogues of *Authors* and *Titles* compiled from publishers' lists.
Peddie, R. A. and Q. Waddington. The English catalogue of books (1801–36). 1914.

(7) TRADE PERIODICALS

The following periodicals contain either current lists of books pbd or comment and correspondence on trade affairs. Some contain both; but no periodicals of literary criticism intended for general circulation have been included.

The monthly literary advertiser. No 1, 10 May 1805–10 Dec 1828. Continued as Bent's literary advertiser, 10 Jan 1829–16 June 1860. Monthly. Incorporated in Bookseller. Ed William Bent (1805–23), Robert Bent (1823–42), Thomas Hodgson (1842–60).
The retail booksellers' and bookbuyers' advocate. No 1, 1 Dec 1836; no 2, Jan 1837; no 3 [Feb 1837]. Probably ed Edward J. Portwine.
The publishers' circular. No 1, 2 Oct 1837– . Fortnightly at first, then weekly; ed Sampson Low.
The intelligencer for publishers and booksellers. No 1, July 1854–no 7, Jan 1855. Monthly.
The bookseller. Jan 1858–30 Mar 1928. Continued as Publisher and bookseller 6 Apr 1928–29 Sep 1933. Continued as Bookseller, 6 Oct 1933– . Weekly. Ed Edward Tucker, Joseph Whitaker.
The stationer. No 1, 1 May 1859–10 Aug 1865. Continued as Stationer, printer, and fancy trades register, 1 Sep 1865–Feb 1912.
Index to current literature. No 1, 30 Sep 1859–no 8, 31 Dec 1860. Quarterly; ed Sampson Low.
The booksellers' record. No 1, 19 Nov–no 7, 31 Dec 1859. Weekly.
The books of the month. No 1, Apr 1861–no 17, Aug 1862.
The literary gazette: a monthly record of literature. No 1, 14 Jan–no 7, 10 July 1865.
The bookbuyer's guide: being a list of the principal books published in the various departments of literature. No 1, Dec 1869–no 9, Mar 1872. Quarterly; ed Thomas J. Fenwick from no 4.
The stationer's and bookseller's circular. No 1, 4 Mar–no 4, 25 Mar 1871. Weekly.
The booksellers' circular and bookbuyers' guide. No 1, 20 Oct 1874. Monthly; ed W. E. Goulden.
The bookbuyer: a chronicle of, and guide to current literature. N.s. no 1, Feb; no 2, Mar 1875.
The book circular: a monthly record of new books and new editions classified according to subjects. No 1, 1 Jan–no 6, 1 June 1877.
The stationery trades journal. No 1, 18 Mar 1880– . Monthly; ed J. Whitaker.
The stationery trade review (Edinburgh). No 1, Jan 1881–Dec 1887. Continued at London as Stationery, bookselling and fancy goods, vol 1, no 1, Jan 1888–Sep 1897. Continued as Morriss's Trade journal Oct 1897–Apr 1903. Continued as British Empire paper, stationery and printing trades journal, vol 23, no 5, May 1903–June 1913. Monthly; ed J. S. Morriss from 1888.
The stationer and bookseller. No 1, 8 May 1883. Continued as Stationers' and booksellers' journal, no 2, 23 June 1883–no 12, 30 Apr 1884. Monthly; incorporated in Stationery review.
Books. A weekly journal for those who buy them, sell them and read them. No 1, 18 Apr–no 3, 4 July 1889.
The newsagent and advertisers' record. No 1, July 1889–Dec 1890. Continued as Newsagent and booksellers' review, 31 Jan 1891. Weekly.
The book world: a journal for publishers and booksellers. No 1, Aug 1890–Apr 1899. Ed 'Boswell'.
The newsman and publication register. No 1, 25 Oct 1890–no 10, 1 Sep 1891. Monthly.
The stationery world and fancy goods review. No 1, 29 Jan 1892– . Monthly; ed S. Phillips.
The book review index. No 1, June 1892. Quarterly.
The book and news trade gazette. [No 1, 1893]–1 Jan 1898–29 Sep 1907.
Bookselling. No 1, Jan 1895–Dec 1896. Continued as Books and bookselling. Jan–Dec 1897. Monthly; ed 'Temple Scott' (J. H. Isaacs).
New book list for bookbuyers, librarians and booksellers. No 1, Sep 1895–Aug 1898. Monthly; ed Cedric Chivers and Armistead Cay.
The stationers' and printers' annual trade book of reference. 1895–1903.
The January monthly part of the English catalogue of books for 1897, Jan 1897–Dec 1900. Monthly.
The booksellers' review. No 1, 11 Mar 1897–27 Jan 1898.
The Aldine Newsagents' trade journal. Nos 1–92, Dec 1897–Dec 1904. Monthly.

(8) CIRCULATING LIBRARIES

Friswell, J. H. Circulating libraries: their contents and their readers. London Soc Dec 1871.
Moore, G. Literature at nurse: or circulating morals. 1885.
Preston, W. C. Mudie's library. Good Words Oct 1894.
Preston, W. C., W. H. Smith's library. Good Words Nov 1895.
Shaylor, J. Fiction: its issue and classification. Publishers' Circular 14 May 1898; rptd in his Fascination of books, 1912.
Tinsley, W. Random recollections of an old publisher. 2 vols 1900.
John and A. Hallam Murray *v.* Walter and others. 1908 (priv ptd).
Society of Bookmen. Report on the commercial circulating libraries. 1928 (priv ptd).
Griest, G. L. Mudie's circulating library and the Victorian novel. Newton Abbott 1971.

(9) RETAIL BOOKSELLING

General works and the Net Book Agreement

The stationers' price-book: being a catalogue of every article used or vended in that business. 1800.

Pickering, W. Booksellers' monopoly: address to the trade and to the public. 1832.

Paternoster Row and the bookselling trade. Pinnock's Guide to Knowledge Aug 1834.

The retail booksellers' and bookbuyers' advocate. No 1, Dec 1836; no 2, Jan 1837; no 3, [Feb 1837]. Ed Edward Portwine?

A manual of book-keeping for booksellers, publishers and stationers, by a bookseller. 1850.

Chapman, J. W. The commerce of literature. Westminster Rev Apr 1852; rptd as Cheap books and how to get them, 1852, 1852 (rev).

A report of the proceedings at a meeting (consisting chiefly of authors) held 4 May 1852 at the House of Mr John Chapman for the purpose of hastening the removal of the trade restrictions on the commerce of literature. 1852.

The opinions of certain authors on the bookselling question. [Ed John W. Parker & Son] [1852]. Additional letters on the bookselling question, 1852.

[Bigg, J.] The bookselling system: a letter to Lord Campbell respecting the late inquiry into the regulations of the booksellers' Association in reference to the causes which led to its dissolution, by a retired bookseller. 1852.

The intelligencer for publishers and booksellers. No 1, July 1854–no 7, Jan 1855.

Ridge, L. L. Ridge's scheme for promoting the interests of the country booksellers and publishers. Grantham 1868.

[Wyman, C. W. H.] Wyman's dictionary of stationery and compendium of useful information for the office, counting house & library. [1875], 1876, 1881.

Prouting, F. J. The stationer's guide and practical handbook to the art of window dressing. 1881.

Growoll, A. The profession of bookselling: a handbook of practical hints for the apprentice and bookseller. 2 pts New York 1893–5.

Stott, D. The decay of bookselling. Nineteenth Century Dec 1894.

Heinemann, W. Bookselling: the system adopted in Germany for the prevention of underselling and for promoting the sale of books. Taunton 1895.

Bowes, R. The friends of literature. In E. Marston, Sketches of some booksellers of the time of Dr Johnson, 1902.

Bowes, R. Booksellers' associations, past and present. Taunton 1905.

The successful bookseller: a complete guide to success to all engaged in a retail bookselling, stationery and fancy goods business. 1906.

Net Books Committee. Net books question. 1908.

Bowes, R. Cambridge bookshops and booksellers 1846–1858. Cambridge 1912.

Macmillan, Sir F. The Net Book Agreement 1899 and the book war 1906–8. Glasgow 1924.

Gray, G. J. Cambridge bookselling and the oldest book-shop in the United Kingdom. Cambridge 1925.

Simpson, W. Old Inverness booksellers. Man and memories of bygone days. Inverness 1931.

Blackwell, B. The nemesis of the Net Book Agreement: an address. 1933.

Corp, W. G. Fifty years: a brief account of the Associated Booksellers of Great Britain and Ireland 1895–1945. Oxford 1945.

Barnes, J. J. Free trade in books. Oxford 1964.

Plant, M. The English book trade: an economic history of the making and sale of books. 1965 (2nd edn), 1974 (3rd edn).

Barker, R. E. and G. R. Davies (ed). Books are different. An account of the defence of the Net Book Agreement. 1966.

Williams, H. Book clubs and printing societies of Great Britain and Ireland. 1929, rptd Detroit 1971.

Taraporevala, R. J. Competition and its control in the British book trade 1850–1939. With a foreword and chapter on retail price competition and the origins of the Net Book Agreement. 1973.

Myers, R. and M. Harris (ed). Development of the English book trade. Oxford 1981.

Myers, R. Economics of the British book trade 1605–1939. 1985.

Myers, R. and M. Harris (ed). Spreading the word: the distribution networks of print 1550–1850. Winchester 1990.

Individual firms

Booksellers in alphabetical order

J. Brown & Son. The firm of three generations. Glasgow 1908.

Blackwell, B. H. Blackwell's 1879–1979, the history of a family firm. Oxford 1983.

Cowan, S. Humorous episodes in the life of a provincial publisher extending over 50 years. Birmingham 1912.

Fitzgerald, J. The recollections of a book collector (1848–58). Liverpool 1903.

MacAndrew, I. F. Memoir of Isaac Forsyth, bookseller in Elgin 1768–1859. 1889.

Humphreys, C. The life of Charles Humphreys, bookseller, told by himself. [c. 1910.]

H. K. Lewis & Co. Ltd. Lewis's 1844–1931: an illustrated account of its foundation and development. 1931.

Miller, G. Later struggles in the journey of life. 1833.

Couper, W. J. The Millers of Haddington, Dunbar and Dunfermline. A record of Scottish bookselling. 1914.

The Parkers of Oxford. Oxford 1914.

Simpson, W. Old Inverness booksellers: men and memories of bygone days. Inverness 1931.

John Smith & Son, Ltd. A short note on a long history 1751–1925. Glasgow 1925.

Burdekin, R. Memoirs of the life and character of Mr R. Spence of York, bookseller. York 1827.

[Thin, J.] Reminiscences of booksellers and bookselling in Edinburgh in the time of William IV. 1905.

Thin, J. A note on the centenary of the firm of J. Thin bookseller 1848–1948. Edinburgh 1948.

West, W. Fifty years' recollections of an old bookseller. Cork 1835, 1837 (2nd edn).

David Wyllie & Sons. A century of bookselling 1814–1914. Aberdeen 1914. [PB]

(10) THE ANTIQUARIAN BOOK TRADE

General works

[Dibdin, T. F.] Bibliophobia: remarks on the present languid and depressed state of literature and the book trade. 1832.

The directory of second-hand booksellers. Ed A. Gyles, Nottingham 1886; rev J. Clegg, Rochdale 1888, 1891, 1894, 1899, 1903 etc. Later continued by A. J. Philip at Gravesend. Continued as The librarian. International directory of booksellers, publishers, binders, papermakers, printers, agents, etc. Ed A. Philip 1927. Continued as Clegg's international directory of booksellers, publishers, binders 1930–1, 1936–7, 1940–1. Continued as Clegg's international directory of world book trade 1950.

Wheatley, H. B. Prices of books. 1898.

Block, A. A short history of the principal London antiquarian booksellers and book auctioneers. 1933.

Lewis, R. H. Antiquarian books: an insider's account. 1978.

Periodicals

The book exchange: or monthly list of books, odd volumes, mss, wanted to buy, sell or exchange. No 1, Sep 1863–no 11, July 1864.

The literary mart and book exchange. A monthly journal for pub-

lishers & booksellers. No 1, July 1874–no 22, Mar 1876. Ed W. E. Goulden.
The clique. Derby. No 1, June 14 1890– . Weekly; ed F. E. Murray. Later at London, and twice a week.

Book auctions

Sotheby & Co. A list of the original catalogues of the principal libraries which have been sold by auction [1744–1818] by Mr Sotheby. 1818, 1828 (continued to 1828).
Book prices current. 1887. Annually since; ed J. H. Slater. Index, 1887–96, 1906; index 1897–1907, 1909.
Book sales of 1895 [–1897/8]. A record of the most important books sold at auction and the prices realised. 4 vols 1896–9. Ed 'Temple Scott' (J. H. Isaacs).
Book auction records. 1903. Annual; ed W. Heath.
Hodgson & Co. One hundred years of book auctions 1807–1907: being a brief record of the firm of Hodgson's. 1907 (priv ptd).
List of catalogues of English book sales 1676–1900, now in the British Museum. 1915.
Hobson, G. D. Notes on the history of Sotheby's. 1917 (priv ptd).

Individual Firms

Block, A. The book collector's vade mecum. 1932. Appendix B (also rptd separately) contains accounts of many antiquarian booksellers active before 1900.
James Bain Ltd
Booksellers since 1816: retrospectus and prospectus. 1861.
H. G. Bohn
The Times 25 Aug 1884.
Book Monthly Apr 1904.
Gustave David, Cambridge
David of Cambridge: some appreciations. Cambridge 1937.
Bertram Dobell
Bradbury, S. Dobell: bookseller and man of letters. 1909.
Dobell, P. J. In memoriam Bertram Dobell 1842–1914. [1915.]
Ellis
Smith, G. and F. Benger. The oldest London bookshop: a history of 200 years. 1928.
Bernard Quaritch
[Wyman, C. W. H.] BQ: a biographical and bibliographical fragment. 1880.
Junk, W. [Memoir in] Internationales Addressbuch der Antiquar-Buchhändler. Berlin 1906.
Thomas Rodd
GM June 1849.
Sotheran & Co
Stonehouse, J. H. In his Piccadilly notes, 1934.
Walter T. Spencer
Spencer, W. T. Forty years in my bookshop. Ed T. Moult 1923.
B. F. Stevens
Fenn, G. M. Memoir of B. F. Stevens. 1903.
Henry Stevens
Parker, W. W. Henry Stevens of Vermont: American rare book dealer in London 1845–86. Amsterdam 1963.
Waverley Book Store, Edinburgh
Williamson, R. M. Bits from an old book shop. 1904. [PB]

(11) PRIVATE BOOK COLLECTING

Dibdin, T. F. Bibliomania: or book-madness, a bibliographical romance containing some account of the history, symptoms and cure of the fatal disease. 1809, 1811 (enlarged), 1842 (rev), 1876 (rev), 4 vols Boston 1903.
—The bibliographical decameron. 3 vols 1817.
—A bibliographical, antiquarian and picturesque tour in France and Germany. 3 vols 1821, 1829; tr Fr 1825.
—The library companion: or the young man's guide and the old man's comfort in the choice of a library. 2 vols 1824, 1825 (2nd edn).
—Reminiscences of a literary life. 2 vols 1836.
—A bibliographical, antiquarian and picturesque tour in the northern counties of England and in Scotland. 3 vols 1838.
[Beresford, J.] Bibliosophia: or Book-wisdom, containing some account of the pride, pleasure and privileges of that glorious vocation, book-collecting. 1810.
[Clarke, W.] Repertorium bibliographicum: or some account of the most celebrated British libraries. 1819.
Goodhugh, W. The English gentleman's library manual. 1827.
Haslewood, J. Roxburghe revels and other relative papers. Ed J. Maidment, Edinburgh 1837 (priv ptd).
The book collector's handbook: a modern library companion. 1845.
Burton, J. H. The book-hunter. Edinburgh 1862, 1863, New York 1863, Edinburgh 1882 (with memoir of the author by K. Burton); ed J. H. Slater [1908].
Power, J. A handy book about books for book-lovers, book-buyers, and book-sellers. 1870.
Lang, A. The library. 1881.
Lang, A. Books and bookmen. 1887, 1892, 1912.
Slater, J. H. The library manual: a guide to the formation of a library and the valuation of books. [1883], 1892 (enlarged).
—Round and about the bookstalls. A guide for the book-hunter. 1891.
—Book collecting: a guide for amateurs. 1892.
—Early editions: a bibliographical survey of some popular modern authors. 1894.
—The romance of book collecting. 1898.
—How to collect books. 1905.
Wheatley, H. B. How to form a library. 1886.
Fitzgerald, P. The book fancier: or the romance of book collecting. 1886, 1887.
Ireland. A. The book-lovers enchiridion. 1890.
Quaritch, B. Contributions towards a dictionary of English book collectors. 14 pts 1892–1921.
Roberts, W. The book hunter in London. 1895.
Roberts, W. Rare books and their prices. 1896.
Hazlitt, W. C. The confessions of a collector. 1897.
Fletcher, W. Y. English book collectors. 1902.
Hazlitt, W. C. Memoirs of book collecting. 1904.
Jerrold, W. C. The Autolycus of the bookstalls. 1902.
de Ricci, S. The book collector's guide. A practical handbook of British and American bibliography. New York 1921.
Bigham, C. The Roxburghe Club: its history and its members 1812–1927. 1928.
de Ricci, S. English collectors of books and mss. Cambridge 1930.
Carter, J. W. and H. G. Pollard. An enquiry into the nature of certain nineteenth-century pamphlets. 1934.
Partington, W. Thomas J. Wise in the original cloth: the life and records of the forger of nineteenth-century pamphlets, with an appendix by G. B. Shaw. 1946.
Sadler, M. T. H. Book collecting: a reader's guide. 1947.
Winterich, J. T. The Grolier Club 1884–1950; an informal history. New York 1950, 1967 (as The Grolier Club 1884–1967; an informal history).
Munby, A. N. L. Phillipps studies. 5 vols Cambridge 1951–60; abridged by N. Barker 1967; 2 vols 1971 (reissued).
Carter, J. ABC for book-collectors. 1952, 1953, 1961, 1967 (4th edn), 1973, 1980 (6th edn).
Carter, J. Books and book collectors. 1956.
Barker, N. The publication of the Roxburghe Club 1814–1962. Cambridge 1964.
Carter, J. Taste and technique in book collecting. 1970 (3rd edn).
National book league: the British as collectors. Catalogue and exhibition of books selected by Frank Herrmann. 1972.

Thomas, A. G. Great books and book collectors. 1975.
Franklin, C. Book collecting as one of the fine arts and other essays. 1996. [PB]

(12) PUBLIC LIBRARIES

The British Museum

Acts and votes of Parliament relating to the British Museum with the statutes and rules relating thereof, and the succession of trustees and officers. 1805, 1828.
Report from the Select Committee on the condition, management and affairs of the British Museum [minutes of evidence and appendix] 6 Aug 1835; 14 July 1836.
Edwards, E. A letter to B. Hawes: being strictures on the minutes of evidence taken before the Select Committee on the British Museum. 1836, 1839 (priv ptd as Remarks on the minutes).
Millard, J. A. A letter containing a plan for the better management of the British Museum. 1836 (priv ptd).
Panizzi, A. On the collection of printed books at the British Museum: its increase and arrangement. [1845] (priv ptd).
Panizzi, A. On the supply of printed books from the Library to the Reading Room of the British Museum. 1846.
Nicolas, N. H. Animadversions on the Library and catalogues of the British Museum. 1846.
Report of the Commissioners appointed to inquire into the constitution and government of the British Museum [minutes of evidence and appendix]. 2 vols 1850.
Edwards, E. Lives of the founders of the British Museum with notices of its chief augmentors, and other benefactors. 1870.
Cowtan, R. Memories of the British Museum. 1872.
Cowtan, R. A biographical sketch of Sir Anthony Panizzi. 1873.
Fagan, L. The life of A. Panizzi, late Principal Librarian of the British Museum. 2 vols 1880.
Friggeri, E. La vita, le opere e i tempi di Antonio Panizzi. Belluno 1897.
Rawlings, G. B. The British Museum Library. 1916.
Barwick, G. F. The Reading Room of the British Museum. 1929.
Brooks, C. Antonio Panizzi, scholar and patriot. Manchester 1931.
Esdaile, A. The British Museum Library: a short history and survey. 1946, 1948.
Miller, E. Prince of librarians: The life and times of Antonio Panizzi, of the British Museum. 1967.
Brodie, A. British library history: bibliography 1985–1988. 1991.
Day, A. E. The new British library. 1994.

Accounts of other libraries

Hartshorne, C. H. The book rarities in the University of Cambridge. 1829.
Edwards, E. Memoirs of libraries: including a handbook of library economy. 2 vols 1859.
Edwards, E. Libraries and founders of libraries. 1865.
Macray, W. D. Annals of the Bodleian Library. 1868, Oxford 1890 (enlarged).
Axon, W. E. A. Handbook of the public libraries of Manchester and Salford. 1877.
Mason, T. The public and private libraries of Glasgow. Glasgow 1885 (priv ptd).
[Sutton, C. W. (ed).] Manchester public libraries. Handbook, historical and descriptive. 1887.
Greenwood, T. Greenwood's library year book. 1897. Continued as British library year book. 1900–1. Continued as The libraries, museums and art galleries year book. 1910–11.
Credland, W. R. Manchester free libraries. 1899.
Mathews, E. R. N. A survey of the Bristol public libraries. Bristol 1900.
Hunt, F. W. Libraries of Devonport, naval, military and civil. Devonport 1901.
Cowell, P. Liverpool public libraries: a history of fifty years. Liverpool 1903.
Rye, R. A. The libraries of London: a guide for students. 1908, 1927 (enlarged).
Savage, E. A. The story of libraries and book collecting. 1908.
Guppy, H. The John Rylands Library, Manchester 1899–1924. Manchester 1924.
Rye, R. A. The students' guide to the libraries of London. 1928.
Kenyon, F. G. Libraries and museums. 1930.
Esdaile, A. J. K. (ed). The world's great libraries. Vol 1: National libraries, 1934; vol 2: Famous libraries (by M. Burton), 1937.
Davies, W. L. The National Library of Wales: a survey of its history, its contents and its activities. 1937.
Thornton, J. L. The chronology of librarianship. 1941.
Craster, E. History of the Bodleian Library 1845–1945. Oxford 1952.
Birmingham Public Library. Notes on the history of the Birmingham public libraries 1861–1961. Birmingham 1962.
Ker, N. R. Medieval libraries of Great Britain. 1964.
Philip, I. The Bodleian library in the seventeenth and eighteenth centuries. The Lyell lectures. Oxford 1983.

The Free Library movement

Brougham, H. P. (Baron Brougham). Practical observations on the education of the people. 1825 (5th edn).
Edwards, E. A letter to the Earl of Ellesmere on the desirability of a better provision of public libraries in the British Empire, and particularly in the metropolis. 1848, 1849 (priv ptd as Remarks on the paucity of libraries freely open to the public).
Report of the Select Committee on Public Libraries. 5 pts 1849–52.
Hole, J. An essay on the history and management of literary and scientific and mechanics' institutions. 1853.
Papworth, J. W. and W. Museums, libraries and picture galleries, public and private. 1853.
Reed, C. Why not? a plea for a free public library and museum in the City of London. 1855.
Traice, W. H. J. Handbook of Mechanics' Institutions with priced catalogue of books suitable for libraries prepared for the Yorkshire Union of Institutes. 1856.
Feilde, M. H. On the advantage of free public news rooms and lending libraries. 1858.
De Peyster, J. F. The moral and intellectual influence of libraries upon social progress. 1866.
Phillips, J. H. An essay on the advantages of free libraries. 1867.
Edwards, E. Free town libraries: their formation, management and history. 1869.
Mullins, J. D. Free libraries and news rooms; their formation and management. 1869, 1879 (3rd edn).
Fowler, J. C. On public libraries. 1871.
Chambers, G. F. and H. W. Fovargue. The law relating to public libraries and museums. 1879, 1899 (4th edn).
Hibbert, J. Notes on free public libraries and museums. Preston 1881.
Jevons, W. S. The rationale of free libraries. Contemporary Rev Mar 1881.
Southward, J. Technical literature in free public libraries. 1883.
Manners, Lady J. Some of the advantages of easily accessible reading and recreation rooms and free libraries with remarks on starting and maintaining them. [1885.]
Greenwood, T. Public libraries: a history of the movement and a manual for the organisation and management of rate-supported libraries. [1886], 1894 (rev).
Greenwood, T. Sunday schools and village libraries. 1892.
MacAlister, J. Y. W. and T. Mason. Library Association: public library manual, part 1: library legislation 1855–90. 1892.
Fovargue, H. W. Adoption of the Public Library Acts in England and Wales. 1896.
Verney, E. Village libraries. [1897.]

Ogle, J. J. The free library: its history and present condition. 1897.
Mullen, B. H. Salford and the inauguration of the public free libraries movement. Salford 1899.
Greenwood, T. Edward Edwards: the chief pioneer of municipal public libraries. 1902.
Morel, E. Essai sur le développement des bibliothèques publiques et de la librairie dans les deux mondes. 2 vols Paris 1909.
Morel, E. La librairie publique. Paris 1910.
Greenborough, W. H. The public libraries: a retrospect of 30 years 1882–1912. Reading 1913.
Baker, E. A. The public library. 1924.
Cruse, A. The Englishman and his books in the nineteenth century. New York 1930.
Shirley, G. W. William Ewart: pioneer of public libraries. Dumfries 1930.
Minto, J. A history of the library movement in Great Britain and Ireland. 1932.
Bostwick, A. E. (ed). Popular libraries of the world. Chicago 1933.
Hendrick, B. J. The life of Andrew Carnegie. 1933.
Smith, G. A. The British benefactions of Andrew Carnegie. New York 1936.
Leyland, E. The public library: its history, organization and functions. 1937.
Wellard, J. H. The public library comes of age. 1940.
Thornton, J. L. Selected readings in the history of librarianship. 2 pts 1948–57, 1966 (2nd edn).
Clough, E. A. On being a hundred years old. 1950.
Munford, W. A. Penny rate: aspects of British public library history 1850–1950. 1951.
Altick, R. D. The English common reader: a social history of the mass reading public 1800–1900. Chicago 1957.
Tylecote, M. The Mechanics' Institutes of Lanchashire and Yorkshire before 1851. Manchester 1957.
Irwin, R. The origins of the English library. 1958.
Munford, W. A. William Ewart 1798–1869: portrait of a radical. 1960.
Irwin, R. The heritage of English library. 1964.
Irwin, R. The English library: sources and history. 1966.
Kelly, T. Early public libraries: a history of public libraries in Great Britain before 1850. 1966.
Black, A. M. A new history of the public library: social and intellectual contexts 1850–1914. 1996. [PB]

(13) LIBRARIANSHIP

See M. O. Burton and M. E. Vosburgh. A bibliography of librarianship. 1934.
Namur, P. Manuel du bibliothécaire. Brussels 1834.
Schmidt, J. A. F. Handbuch der Bibliothekwissenschaft, der Litteratur und Bücherkunde. Weimar 1840.
Jewett, C. C. Smithsonian report on the construction of catalogues of libraries and their publication by means of separate stereotyped titles. Washington 1853 (2nd edn).
de Morgan, A. On the difficulty of the correct description of books. Companion to Br Almanack 1853; ed H. Guppy, Library Assoc Record June 1902; rptd Chicago 1902.
Schurtleff, N. B. A decimal system for the arrangement and administration of libraries. 1856.
Petzholdt, J. Katechismus der Bibliothekenlehre. Leipzig 1856, 1871 (enlarged), ed A. Graesel Leipzig 1902 (as Handbuch der Bibliothekslehre).
Guild, R. A. The librarian's manual. 1858.
Edwards, E. Memoirs of libraries; together with a handbook of library economy. 2 vols 1859.
Elliot, J. A practical explanation of the method of issuing library books. 1870.
Dewey, M. A classification and subject index for cataloguing and arranging the books and pamphlets of a library. Amherst MA 1876 (anon), Boston 1885 (as Decimal classification and relative index for arranging, cataloguing and indexing libraries), Boston 1898, New York 1919, 1932 (rev and enlarged).
Transactions and proceedings of the [First International] Conference of librarians held in London 3–5 Oct 1877. 1878.
Hallett, C. H. Parish lending libraries: how to manage and keep them up. 1880.
Wheatley, H. B. How to catalogue a library. 1889.
Rogers, W. T. A manual of bibliography: introduction to the knowledge of books, library management and the art of cataloguing. 1891.
Slater, J. H. The library manual. 1892.
Hoyle, W. E. The Dewey decimal classification and the international catalogue of science. 1896.
Transactions and proceedings of the second International Library Conference held in London 13–16 July 1897. 1898.
Quinn, J. H. Manual of library cataloguing. 1899.
Cotgreave, A. Views and memoranda of public libraries. 1901.
Brown, J. D. Manual of library economy. 1903.
Roebuck, G. E. and W. B. Thorne. A primer of library practice for junior assistants. 1904.
Brown, J. D. Manual of practical bibliography. [1906.]
Thorne, W. B. The Library Assistants' Association: an outline of its development and work.
Sayers, W. C. B. An introduction to library classification: theoretical, historical and practical. 1918, 1950 (rev).
Dawe, G. Melvil Dewey 1851–1931. New York 1932.
Partridge, R. C. B. The history of the legal deposit of books throughout the British Empire. 1938.
Norris, D. M. A history of cataloguing and cataloguing methods 1100–1850. 1939.
Thornton, J. L. The chronology of librarianship. 1941.
Rider, F. Melvil Dewey. Chicago 1944.

Periodicals

Cannons, H. G. T. Bibliography of library economy: a classified index to the professional periodical literature. 1910, Chicago 1927.
Cole, G. W. Index to bibliographical papers. Chicago [1933].
Transactions and proceedings of the first [–8th] annual meeting of the Library Association of the United Kingdom 1878 [–85]. 7 vols 1879–90.
Monthly notes of the Library Association. 1880–3.
The library chronicle: a journal of librarianship and bibliography. Vols 1–5, 1884–8. Ed E. C. Thomas.
The library. Vol 1, 1889– . Quarterly; ed J. Y. Macalister.
The Library Assistants' Association: first annual report. 1 July 1896– .
The library assistant. No 1, Jan 1898– .
The library world. No 1, July 1898– .
The Library Association record. No 1, Jan 1899– . Monthly; ed H. Guppy, A. Esdaile.
The Library Association year book. 1899– . [PB]

2 Literary Relations with the Continent

This section, which is selective, is divided according to languages or groups of languages: Dutch and Flemish; French; German; Italian; Spanish and Portuguese; Scandinavian and Icelandic; Russian; and other Slavonic languages. Individual authors, English and foreign, are entered in separate alphabetical lists, linked by cross-references, under each language. Trns into English are within the scope of the section; see also under individual authors, below. Secondary works are confined to comparative studies and works essential to the recognition of an author in a foreign country.

Extra-European relations are not considered here. For publishing relations with the United States, see I. R. Brussel, Anglo-American first editions 1826–1900: east to west, 1935; Part 2: west to east 1786–1930, 1936. *For general studies see* M. E. de Meester, Oriental influences in the English literature of the nineteenth century, Heidelberg 1915; *and* J. Holloway, Widening horizons in English verse, 1966.

Annual lists may be found in Yearbook of Comparative and General Literature, Chapel Hill NC 1952– .

(1) GENERAL

Anthologies in translation

Herbert, W. Translations from the Italian, Spanish, Portuguese, German etc. 1806. Poetry.

Laura: or an anthology of sonnets (on the Petrarcan model) and elegiac quatorzains, English, Italian, Spanish, Portuguese, French and German. Ed C. Lofft 5 vols 1813–14.

Thorpe, B. Northern mythology. 3 vols 1851–2.

Half-hours with foreign authors. Tr G. L. 1861. Short stories and extracts from novels.

Waddington, S. The sonnets of Europe. 1886.

Ogden, A. Christmas stories from French and Spanish writers. 1893.

Garnett, R. Dante, Petrarch, Camõens: 124 sonnets translated. 1896.

General studies

Foreign Quarterly Review. 1827–46.

Foreign Review & Continental Miscellany. 1828–30.

Continental literature. Athenaeum 1869–1904. Yearly surveys; Dec nos until 1884, July nos thereafter.

Cosmopolis. 1896–8.

Brandes, G. Hovedstrømninger i det 19de aarhundredes litteratur. 6 vols Copenhagen 1872–90; tr as Main currents in 19th century literature, 6 vols 1901–5.

Ellis, H. The new spirit. 1890.

Archer, W. The theatrical 'world'. 5 vols 1894–8. An annual collection of review articles.

Merz, J. T. History of European thought in the nineteenth century. 4 vols Edinburgh 1896–1914.

Omond, T. S. The romantic triumph. 1900; C. E. Vaughan, The romantic revolt, 1907; G. Saintsbury, The later nineteenth century, 1907. In Periods of European literature, ed Saintsbury 12 vols Edinburgh 1897–1907.

Beers, H. A. A history of English romanticism in the nineteenth century. 1902.

Saintsbury, G. A history of criticism and literary taste in Europe. Vol 3, Edinburgh 1904.

Sanders, L. The Holland House circle. 1908.

Richter, H. Geschichte der englischen Romantik. 2 vols Halle 1911–16.

Van Tieghem, P. La littérature comparée. Paris 1931.

Ellis, H. Views and reviews. Vol 1, 1932.

Block, A. The English novel 1740–1850. 1939. A catalogue, including trns of foreign novels.

Neff, E. E. A revolution in European poetry 1660–1900. New York 1940.

Ullmann, S. Anglicism and anglophobia in continental literature. MP 37 1940.

Babits, M. Geschichte der europäischen Literatur. Vienna 1948.

Lovejoy, A. O. On the discrimination of romanticisms. In his Essays in the history of ideas, Baltimore 1948.

Van Tieghem, P. L'ère romantique: le romantisme dans la littérature européene. Paris 1948. With bibliographies.

Ernst, F. and K. Wais (ed). Forschungsprobleme der vergleichenden Literaturgeschichte. 2 vols Tübingen 1958.

Wais, K. An den Grenzen der Nationalliteraturen: vergleichende Aufsätze. Berlin 1958.

Lütkens, C. and W. Karbe. Das Bild vom Ausland: fremdsprachliche Lektüre an höheren Schulen in Deutschland, England and Frankreich. Munich 1959.

de Man, P. Structure intentionnelle de l'image romantique. Revue Internationale de Philosophie 14 1960.

Zagona, H. G. The legend of Salome and the principle of art for art's sake. Geneva 1960.

Dietrich, M. Europäische Dramaturgie im 19 Jahrhundert. Graz-Cologne 1961.

Peckham, M. Toward a theory of romanticism: a reconsideration. Stud in Romanticism 1 1961.

Remak, H. H. H. West European romanticism: definition and scope. In Comparative literature: method and perspective, ed N. P. Stallknecht and H. Frenz, Carbondale 1961.

McCutchion, D. Beast or angel? Romantic ambiguities in Goethe, Musset, Stendhal and Yeats. Jadavpur Jnl of Comparative Lit 1962.

Becker, G. J. Documents of modern literary realism. Princeton 1963.

Wellek, R. Concepts of criticism. New Haven CT 1963.

Beebe, M. Ivory towers and sacred founts: the artist as hero in fiction from Goethe to Joyce. New York 1964.

Schenk, H. The mind of the European romantics. 1966.
Grant, D. Realism. 1970 (Critical Idiom).
Knight, E. A theory of the classical novel. 1970.
Chadwick, C. Symbolism. 1971 (Critical Idiom).
Furst, L. R. and P. N. Skrine. Naturalism. 1971 (Critical Idiom).
Armstrong, J. The novel of adultery. 1976.
Mercier, M. Le roman féminin. 1976.
Calder, J. Heroes from Byron to Guevara. 1977.
Boyer, R. D. Realism in European theatre and drama 1870–1920. A bibliography. 1979.
Pritchett, V. S. The myth makers. Essays on European, Russian and South American novelists. 1979.
Miller, D. A. Narrative and its discontents. Problems of closure in the traditional novel. Princeton 1981.
Torgovnik, M. Closure in the novel. Princeton 1981.
Becker, G. J. Master European realists of the nineteenth century. New York 1982.
Tytler, G. Physiognomy in the European novel. Faces and fortunes. Princeton 1982.
Bell, M. The sentiment of reality, truth and feeling in the European novel. 1983.
Bann, S. The clothing of Clio: a study of the representation of history in nineteenth-century Britain and France. Cambridge 1984.
Coe, R. N. When the grass was taller. Autobiography and the experience of childhood. New Haven CT 1984.
Furst, L. R. Fictions of romantic irony in European narrative 1760–1857. 1985.
Olson, D. J. The city as a work of art: London, Paris, Vienna. New Haven CT 1986.
Cox, J. N. In the shadows of romance: romantic tragic drama in Germany, England and France. Athens OH 1987.
Mason, H. T. and W. Doyle. The impact of the French Revolution on European consciousness. 1989.
Bate, J. The politics of romantic Shakespearian criticism: Germany, England, France. European Romantic Rev 1 1990.
Porter, D. Haunted journeys: desire and transgression in European travel writing. 1991.
Erdman, D. V. (ed). The romantic movement: a selective and critical bibliography for 1987– . Westport CT 1988– .
Nelson, B. (ed). Naturalism in the European novel. New York and Oxford 1992.
Furst, L. R. Through the lens of the reader. Exploration of European narratives. 1993.

English authors

Arnold, Matthew

Arnold, M. The popular education of France; with notices of that of Holland and Switzerland. 1861.
Arnold, M. Schools and universities on the Continent. 1868.

Beckford, William

Beckford, W. Italy; with sketches of Spain and Portugal. 2 vols Paris 1834.
Chapman, G. Beckford. 1937.
William Beckford of Fonthill. Ed F. M. Mahmoud, Cairo 1960.

Byron, George Gordon

Axon, W. A. E. Byron's influence on European literature. In his Stray chapters on literature, folklore and archaeology, 1888.
Chiarini, G. Byron nella politica e nella letteratura della prima metà del secolo. Nuova Antologia 1–16 July 1891.
Maychrzak, F. Byron als Übersetzer. E. Studien 21–2 1895–6.
Storozhenko, N. J. Byrons Einfluss auf die europäische Literatur. In his Izoblasti Literatury, Moscow 1902.
Farinelli, A. Byron e il Byronismo. Bologna 1924.
Boyd, E. F. Byron's Don Juan: a critical study. New Brunswick NJ 1945.
Borst, W. A. Byron's first pilgrimage. New Haven CT 1948.

Shelley, Mary Wollstonecraft (with P. B. Shelley). History of a six weeks tour through a part of France, Switzerland, Germany and Holland, with letters descriptive of a sail round the lake of Geneva and of the glaciers of Chamouni. London 1817.
Wordsworth, Dorothy. The journal of a tour on the continent. 1820.

Others

Jacks, W. Burns in other tongues. Glasgow 1896.
Herford, C. H. The age of Wordsworth. 1897.
Baldensperger, F. La grande communion romantique de 1827: sous le signe de Scott. Revue de Littérature Comparée 7 1927.
Jabram-Desrivaux, L. Hardy européen. Point et Virgule July 1928.
Taylor, A. C. Carlyle et la pensée latine. Paris 1938.
Thalmann, L. Dickens in seinen Beziehungen zum Ausland. Zurich 1956.
Tristan, Flora. Promenades dans Londres. 1840.

(2) DUTCH AND FLEMISH

General studies

Bowring, J. and H. S. Van Dyk. Batavian anthology, or specimens of the Dutch poets etc. 1824.
Bowring, J. Sketch of the language and literature of Holland. 1829.
Delepierre, O. Old Flanders, or popular traditions and legends of Belgium. 1845.
Invloed der Engelsche taal–en letterkunde op de Nederlandsche. Noord en Zuid 9 1886.
Worp, J. A. Engelsche letterkunde op ons Tooneel. Tijdspiegel 1887.
Nederlandsche letteren bij Engelsche lezers. Noord en Zuid 11 1888.
Basse, M. Taal–en letteren. Amsterdam 1901. On G. Van de Linde and Ingoldsby's Legends.
Hoog, W. De. Studiën over de Nederlandsche en Engelsche taal – en letterkunde en haar wederzijdschen invloed. Vol 2, Dordrecht 1903.
Swaen, A. E. H. De wetenschappelijke beoefening van het Engels hier te lande. Groningen 1913.
Vries, T. De. Holland's influence on English language and literature. Chicago 1916.
Bithell, Jethro. Contemporary Flemish poetry. 1917.
Dekker, G. Die invloed van Keats en Shelley in Nederland gedurende die negentiende eeu. Groningen 1926.
Russell, J. A. English translations of Dutch novels. Gazette de Hollande 28 Oct 1931.
Downs, B. W. Anglo-Dutch literary relations 1867–1900. MLR 31 1936.
Russell, J. A. Dutch poetry and English: a study of the romantic revival. Amsterdam 1939.
Arents, P. De Vlaamse schrijvers in het Engels vertaald 1481–1949. Ghent [1950].
Oversteegen, J. J. Nederlandse literatuur in vertaling. Vrij Nederland 1 Mar 1958.
Schrickx, W. Betrekkingen van het Vlaamse geestesleven met de Engelse en Amerikaanse letteren. Levende Talen 1958.
Weevers, T. Poetry of the Netherlands in its European context 1170–1960. 1960. On Potgieter, Gezelle and English romanticism.
Russell, J. A. Dutch romantic poetry: the English influence. Bradford 1961.
Colmjon, G. De beweging van tachtig. Utrecht 1963. On the 1880 movement and England.
Michaël, H. (ed). Willem Kloos: zijn jeugd, zijn leven. The Hague 1965.
Berg, W. Van den. Rotterdam extra muros: de Literary Society. Negentiende Eeuw 20 1966.
Meijer, R. P. Literature of the Low Countries. Assen 1971; rev edn Cheltenham 1978.

Wolf, M. Albert Verwey and English romanticism: a comparative and critical study with original translations. The Hague 1978.
Spoor, H. Alexander Cohen in Londen en Den Haag. Maatstaf 31 1983.
Bunt, G. H. V. et al (ed). One hundred years of English studies in Dutch universities. Amsterdam 1987.
Schoneveld, C. W. Pioneering in the propagation of English letters: B. S. Nayler's teaching career in Holland 1820–1848. In Miscellanea Anglo-Belgica, ed C. W. Schoneveld et al, Leiden 1987.
Haley, K. H. D. The British and the Dutch: political and cultural relations through the ages. 1988.
Korpel, L. 'Truly and Entirely English, Yet Useful', or how Dutch translators between 1750 and 1820 view the English nature of their originals. In Something understood, ed B. Westeerweel and T. D'haen, Amsterdam 1990.
Korpel, L. Over het nut en de wijze der vertalingen. Nederlandse vertaalreflectie (1750–1820) in een Westeuropees kader, Amsterdam 1992.
Demoor, M. De Vlaamse literatuur op een blaadje gepresenteerd: Emiel de Laveleye en Paul Fredericq in The Athenaeum 1871–1904. Spiegel der Letteren 36 1994.
Gorp, H. Van. Historisch beschrijvend vertaalonderzoek. Enkele problemen vanuit een case study. In Letterlijkheid woordelijkheid, ed H. Bloemen et al, Antwerp 1995. On Gothic novels translated into Dutch.
Harskamp, J. Hel op aarde. Nederlandse reizigers en ballingen in Londen (1700–1900). Neerlandica Extra Muros 34 1996.

Individual authors

Bilderdijk, Willem

Wesseling, J. Bilderdijk en Engeland. Ghent 1949.
Meier, H. Pope's Essay on Man door Bilderdijk vertaald. Nieuwe Taalgids 76 1983.

Burns, Robert

Dijk, D. Van. Robert Burns en de Nederlandse letterkunde. Spektator 13 1983–4.

Byron, George Gordon

Popma, T. Byron en het Byronisme in de Nederlandsche letterkunde. Amsterdam 1928.
Schults, U. Het Byronisme in Nederland. Utrecht 1929.
Zonneveld, P. Van. Tassoos weeklacht. Een onbekende Byron-vertaling van Nicolaas Beets (1834). Jaarboek Maatschappij der Nederlandse Letteren 1984.
D'haen, T. The Dutch Byron: Byron in Dutch translation. In Centennial hauntings: Pope, Byron and Eliot in the Year 88, ed C. C. Barfoot and T. D'haen, Amsterdam 1990.
D'haen, T. De Nederlandse Byron. Literatuur 9 1992.

Carroll, Lewis

Matsier, N. Alice in Nederland: de vertaler, zijn schaamte en zijn voorgangers. Revisor 16 1989.
Matsier, N. Alice in Verbazië. Amsterdam 1996.

Coleridge, Samuel Taylor

Kuitert, R. Tweemaal Coleridge's 'Ancient Mariner' in het Nederlands. Nieuwe Taalgids 1958.

Conscience, Hendrik (1812–83)

De leeuw van Vlaenderen. Antwerp 1838; The lion of Flanders, 1855.
Hoe men schilder wordt. Antwerp 1843; Siska van Roosemael, Antwerp 1844; Wat eene moeder lyden kan, Antwerp 1844; Sketches from Flemish life [tr J. N. Trübner], 1846.
Graaf Hugo van Craenhove en zynen vriend Abulfaragus. Antwerp 1845; Houten Clara, Antwerp 1850; Tales of Old Flanders, 1855.
Het beulenkind. Antwerp 1846; The headman's son, 1861.
De loteling. Antwerp 1850; Baas Gansendonck, Antwerp 1850; Blinde Rosa, Antwerp 1850; De arme edelman, Antwerp 1851; Tales of Flemish life, tr B. Mayer, Edinburgh 1854.
Rikke-tikke-tak. Antwerp 1851; Tales and romances, 5 vols 1855.
De gierigaerd. Antwerp 1852; The miser, [1856].
De grootmoeder. Antwerp 1852; The good mother, Dublin 1852.
De boerenkryg. Antwerp 1853; Veva or the war of the peasants, 1855.
De plaeg der dorpen. Antwerp 1855; Het geluk van ryk te zyn, Antwerp 1855. The curse of the village, and the happiness of being rich, 1855. The curse of the village pbd separately 1855.
De geldduivel. Antwerp 1856; The demon of gold, [1857].
De jonge doctor. Antwerp 1860; Menschenbloed, Antwerp 1864; in Tales, 10 vols 1888–92.
Het yzeren graf. Antwerp 1860; The iron tomb, 1889.
Levenslust. Antwerp 1868; The lost glove, [1885].
See I. Simon, George Eliot and Conscience, Revue des Langues Vivantes 26 1960.

Couperus, Louis (1863–1923)

Eline Vere. 3 vols Amsterdam 1889; tr J. T. Grein, 1892.
Noodlot. Amsterdam 1890; Footsteps of fate, tr C. Bell, introd E. Gosse, 1891.
Extase. Amsterdam 1892; Ecstasy, tr A. Teixeira de Mattos and J. Gray, 1892.
Majesteit. Amsterdam 1893; Majesty, tr A. Teixeira de Mattos and E. Dowson, 1894.
Psyche. Amsterdam 1898; tr B. S. Berrington, 1908.
Russell, J. A. Couperus in English. Nieuwe Gids May 1927.
Kooij, J. G. Couperus en Engeland. Merlyn 2 1964.
Wellens, O. Couperus in de Engelse kritiek. Nieuwe Taalgids 73 1980.
Breugelmans, R. Louis Couperus in den vreemde: een lijst van zijn afzonderlijk verschenen vertalingen. Leiden 1989.

Daems, S. D.

Voor twee vaders. 1868; The double sacrifice, [1869].

Dickens, Charles

Finlay, I. F. Dickens's influence on Dutch literature. Dickensian 53 1957.
Luger, B. Dickens' populariteit in Nederland in de negentiende eeuw. Dutch Dickensian 8 1987.
Steijnen, K. Van. Dickens in Nederland. Dutch Dickensian 8 1987.
Zwaneveld, A. Dickens' entree in de Nederlandse letterkunde. Dutch Dickensian 9 1988.
Zwaneveld, A. Dickens en De Gids: Potgieter als literair-kritisch vertaler. Linguistica Antverpiensia 1990.
Luger, B. Dickens in the Netherlands. Dutch Dickensian 14 1993.

Eeden, Frederik van (1860–1932)

De kleine Johannes. Amsterdam 1885; Little Johannes, tr C. Bell, 1894.
Demoor, M. De kleine Johannes in Engeland. Nieuwe Taalgids 78 1985.
Demoor, M. Frederik van Eedens correspondentie met Edmund William Gosse. Mededelingen Frederik van Eeden Genootschap 30 [*s.d.*].
Fontijn, J. Biologisch utopisme: het darwinisme van Frederik van Eeden. Negentiende Eeuw 17 1993.

Eliot, George

Verheul, C. Ethisch realisme: de ontvangst van de romans van George Eliot in de periode 1860–1881. Voortgang 5 1984.

Gezelle, Guido (1830–99)

Decroos, J. Guido Gezelle en de Engelse letterkunde. Nieuwe Gids 43 1928.
Gaspar, R. Guido Gezelle en Engeland. Roeping 30 1954.
Mûelenaere, J. De. Rond Gezelles reizen naar Engeland. Gezelliana 11 1981–2.
Leeuw, B. B. De, et al (ed). De briefwisseling van Guido Gezelle met de Engelsen 1854–1899. 3 vols Ghent 1991.
Plas, M. van der. Mijnheer Gezelle. Biografie van een priester-dichter (1830–1899). Tielt/Baarn 1991.

Harris, Frank
Gijsen, M. Frank Harris en Maeterlinck. Nieuw Vlaams Tijdschrift Apr 1964.
Keats, John
Verkoren, L. De vertalingen van Keats' Hyperion door Mr W. W. Van Lennep. Neophilologus 26 1940–1.
Groot, H. B. De. Albert Verwey, Keats en Matthew Arnold. Nieuwe Taalgids 1968.
Lamb, Charles
Vat, D. J. Van der. Potgieter en Charles Lamb. Tijdschrift voor Taal en Letteren 1939.
Multatuli (E. Douwes Dekker, 1820–87)
Max Havelaar. 2 vols Amsterdam 1860; tr Baron A. Nahuijs, Edinburgh 1868; tr W. Siebenhaar with introd by D. H. Lawrence, 1927; tr R. Edwards, 1967.
Nahuijs, A. Multatuli in Engeland binnengeleid. Nederlandsche Spectator 7 Mar 1869.
Vanderauwera, R. Max Havelaar in English. Dutch Crossing 1980.
Vanderauwera, R. Texts and contexts of translation: a Dutch classic in English. Dispositio 7 1982.
Vanderauwera, R. Dutch novels translated into English: the transformation of a minority literature. Amsterdam 1985. On English translations of Max Havelaar.
Newman, John Henry
Couttenier, P. Gezelles onvoltooide vertaling van Newmans Dream of Gerontius. Gezelliana 1984.
Scott, Walter
Prins, J. W. Van Lennep en Scott. Vaderlandsche Letteroefeningen 1874.
Prinsen, J. De oude en de nieuwe historische roman in Nederland. Leiden 1919.
Vissink, H. Scott and his influence on Dutch literature. Zwolle 1922.
Drop, W. Verbeelding en historie: verschijningsvormen van de Nederlandse historische roman in de negentiende eeuw. Assen 1958.
Drop, W. De oudste Nederlandse vertalingen van Scott's romans. Nieuwe Taalgids 1959.
Tenter, P. Den. Scottomanie in Nederland: de Nederlandse vertalingen van Scott's romans tussen 1824 en 1834. Negentiende Eeuw 1984.
Shelley, Percy Bysshe
Kloos, W. Percy Bysshe Shelley in Nederland. Nieuwe Gids 1922.
Stutterheim, C. F. P. Perks Iris en Shelleys The Cloud. Nieuwe Taalgids 1936.
Baxter, B. M. Verwey's translations from Shelley's poetical works. Leiden 1963.
Naaijkens, T. De slag om Shelley: over de autonome vertaalopvattingen van Willem Kloos. In Vertalen historisch bezien, ed D. Delabastita and T. Hermans, The Hague 1995.
Wallis, A. S. C. (A. S. C. Opzoomer) (1857–1925)
In dagen van strijd. 3 vols Amsterdam 1877; In troubled times, tr E. J. Irving, 3 vols 1883, 1 vol 1885 (abridged).
Vorstengunst. 3 vols Haarlem 1883; Royal favour, tr E. J. Irving, 3 vols 1885, 1902.
Wilde, Oscar
Breugelmans, R. De weerklank van Wilde in Nederland en Vlaanderen 1880–1960. Studie Germanica Gandensia 3 1961.
Maas, N. (ed). Een pseudo-esthetische zeepbel. Nederlandse reacties op Oscar Wilde, deel 1: 1890–1897. Nijmegen 1987.
Maas, N. (ed). Nagloeiend vuurwerk. Nederlandse reacties op Oscar Wilde, deel 2: 1898–1913. Nijmegen 1987.
Wordsworth, William
Wevers, T. Het door Verwey beraamde boek over Wordsworth. Nieuwe Taalgids 1974.
Yeats, William Butler
Supheert, R. Yeats in Holland: the reception of the works of W. B. Yeats in the Netherlands before World War Two. Amsterdam 1995. [TH]

(3) FRENCH

In this section all French titles were pbd in Paris unless otherwise stated.

General studies

France

Croly, G. Paris in 1815. 2 pts 1817–21.
Morgan, Lady. France. 2 vols; La France, 2 vols London and Paris, 1817. Reply by W. Playfair, France as it is, not Lady Morgan's France, 2 vols 1819.
Genlis, Mme de. Memoirs of the Countess of Genlis, illustrative of the history of the eighteenth and nineteenth centuries. 8 vols London 1825–6.
Morgan, Lady. France in 1829–30. 2 vols 1830.
Trollope, F. Paris and the Parisians in 1835. 2 vols 1836.
Shelley, M. W. Lives of the most eminent literary and scientific men of France. (The Cabinet Cyclopedia vol 2). London 1838–9.
Pictures of the French. 1850. Trn of a collection of short stories by Balzac, Janin et al.
Gore, C. G. F. Greville: or a season in Paris. 1857.
Senior, N. W. Conversations with Thiers, Guizot and other distinguished persons during the Second Empire. 2 vols 1878.
Senior, N. W. Conversations with distinguished persons during the Second Empire. 2 vols 1880.
Hamerton, P. G. French and English. 1889.
Corelli, M. Wormwood: a drama of Paris. 1890.
du Maurier, G. Trilby. 1894.
The Yellow Book. 1894–7.
Conan-Doyle, A. The exploits of Brigadier Gerard. 1896.
Crackanthorpe, H. Vignettes. 1896.
The Pageant. 1896–7.
The Savoy. 1896.
Dowden, E. The French Revolution and English literature. 1897.
du Maurier, G. The Martian. 1897.
Saroléa, C. Le caractère anglais et le caractère français. Revue de Belgique Aug 1897.
Bodley, J. E. C. France. 1898.
Harland, H. Comedies and errors. 1898.
Sherard, R. H. Twenty years in Paris. 1905.
Cestre, C. La révolution française et les poètes anglais 1789–1809. Revue Bourguignonne 16 1906.
Gregory, A. The French Revolution and the English novel. New York 1915.
Moraud, M. La France de la Restauration d'après les visiteurs anglais. 1933.
Mailahn, W. Napoleon in der englischen Geschichtsschreibung von den Zeitgenossen bis zur Gegenwart. Berlin 1937.
Dechamps, J. Napoléon et ses admiratrices britanniques. In Studies in French presented to R. L. Graeme Ritchie, Cambridge 1949.
Ringenson, K. French guests in English literature. Studier i Modern Sprakvetenskap 17 1949.
Juden, B. and J. Riches. William Charles Macready et les comédiens anglais à Paris (1844–45). La Revue des Lettres Modernes 74–5 1963.
Campos, C. The view of France from Arnold to Bloomsbury. Oxford 1965. On Thackeray, Arnold, Pater, Swinburne, Meredith, Henry James, G. Moore et al.
Suddaby, E. and P. J. Yarrow. Lady Morgan in France. London 1971.
Yearbook of English studies: Anglo-French relations special number vol 15 MHRA 1985.
Simmons, C. A. Disease and dismemberment: two conservative metaphors for the French Revolution. Prose Studies 15 1992.

Cormick, M. Les grandes revues victoriennes et l'affaire Dreyfus. La Revue des Revues 17 1994.

Switzerland

Schirmer, G. Die Schweiz im Spiegel englischer und amerikanischer Literatur bis 1848. Zurich 1929.

Lunn, A. Switzerland and the English. 1944. On Wordsworth, Byron and Ruskin.

Lunn, A. Switzerland in English prose and poetry. 1947. An anthology.

Löhrer, H. Die Schweiz im Spiegel englischer Literatur 1849–75. Zurich 1952. On Arnold, Ruskin, Stephen et al.

Steffen, W. Die Schweiz im Spiegel englischer Literatur 1875–1900. Zurich 1953.

French and English literature

Galignani's Magazine and Paris Monthly Review. Paris 1822–3.

La France et la Grande Bretagne: des rapports littéraires etc. Revue Européenne Aug 1824.

Pichot, A. Voyage historique et littérature en Angleterre et en Ecosse. 3 vols 1825.

Bissot, L. A. Pichot: a romantic Prometheus. Oxford 1842.

The European library. 20 vols 1846–7. Trns of Thierry, Guizot, Mignet et al.

Chasles, V. E. P. Etudes sur la littérature et les mœurs de l'Angleterre au 19e siècle. 1850. On Scott, Byron, Keats, Shelley et al.

Ledru-Rollin (A. A. Ledru). De la décadence de l'Angleterre. 2 vols 1850; The decline of England, tr E. C., 2 vols 1850.

Forgues, E. D. Originaux et beaux esprits de l'Angleterre contemporaine. 2 vols 1860.

Curwen, H. Echoes from the French poets. 1870. Trns of Lamartine, Musset, Baudelaire, Gautier, Béranger et al.

Lang, A. Ballads and lyrics of old France. 1872.

Chasles, V. E. P. L'Angleterre littéraire. 1876.

Phillips, E. M. Chasles: critique et historien de la littérature anglaise. 1933.

Mendès, C. Recent French poets. GM Oct–Nov 1879. With trns of Coppée, Verlaine, Sully-Prudhomme, Mendès et al.

D'Heylli, G. La comédie française à Londres journal d'E. Got; journal de F. Sarcey. 1880.

Renard, G. L'influence de l'Angleterre sur la France depuis 1830. Nouvelle Revue 35 1885.

Henley, W. E. Views and reviews. 1890. On Dumas, Hugo, Banville, Balzac, Labiche, Champfleury.

Nordau, M. Entartung. 2 vols Berlin 1892; Degeneration, 1895; A. E. Hake, Regeneration: a reply to Nordau, 1895.

Barlow, G. French plays and English audiences. Contemporary Rev Aug 1893.

Delille, E. Some French writers. 1893. On Bourget, Loti, Baudelaire, Maupassant, Verlaine, Barrès.

Gray, J. Silverpoints. 1893. Trns of Baudelaire, Verlaine, Rimbaud, Mallarmé, Laforgue.

Vizetelly, H. Glances back through seventy years. 2 vols 1893.

Robertson, W. J. A century of French verse. 1895. With trns.

Saroléa, C. Le commerce des idées entre la France et l'Angleterre. Revue de Belgique Oct 1896.

Saroléa, C. L'influence de la culture française sur la culture anglaise. Revue Française d'Edimbourg 1 1897.

Potez, H. Le romantisme français et l'influence anglaise. La Quinzaine 1–16 Oct 1899.

Studies in European literature: the Taylorian lectures 1889–99. Oxford 1900. By Mallarmé, Pater, Dowden, W. M. Rossetti, Bourget, Ker et al.

Baldensperger, F. Le moine de Lewis dans la littérature française. Jnl of Comparative Lit 3 1903.

Gosse, E. French profiles. 1905.

Flowers of France: the romantic period etc. Tr J. Payne 2 vols 1906. Trns of Hugo, Musset, Lamartine et al.

Borgerhoff, J.-L. Le théâtre anglais à Paris sous la Restauration. 1913.

Maccunn, F. J. The contemporary English view of Napoleon. 1914.

Ellis, H. Affirmations. 1915.

Dechamps, J. Il y a cent ans: propos Stendhaliens. Revue des Etudes Napoléoniennes 19 1922.

de Nolva, R. Les sources anglaises de Leconte de Lisle. Mercure de France 1 July 1922. On the influence of Shelley and Byron.

Draper, F. W. M. The rise and fall of the French romantic drama, with special reference to the influence of Shakespeare, Scott and Byron. 1923.

Gosse, E. More books on the table. 1923.

Cazamian, M. L. Le roman et les idées en Angleterre. Publications de la Faculté des Lettres de Strasbourg 15, 73, 125 1923–54.

Baldensperger, F. La mouvement des idées dans l'émigration française 1789–1815. 2 vols 1924.

Frierson, W. C. L'influence du naturalisme français sur les romanciers anglais de 1885 à 1900. 1925.

Needham, H. A. Le développement de l'esthétique sociologique en France et en Angleterre aux xix siècle. 1926.

Reynaud, L. Le romantisme: ses origines anglo-germaniques. 1926. On Scott and Byron.

Evans, D. O. French romanticism and British reviewers. French Quart 9 1927.

Lockwood, H. D. Tools and the man: a comparative study of the French working man and English Chartists in the literature of 1830–48. New York 1927.

Devonshire, M. G. The English novel in France 1830–70. 1929. With bibliographies.

Clapton, G. T. Balzac, Baudelaire and Maturin. French Quart 12 1930.

Engel, C. E. Byron et Shelley en Suisse et en Savoie 1816. Chambéry 1930.

Jones, E. Les voyageurs français en Angleterre de 1815 à 1830. 1930.

Liljegren, S. B. Quelques romans anglais comme source partielle d'une religion moderne. In Mélanges Baldensperger vol 2, 1930.

Lehmann, K. Die Auffassung und Gestaltung des Napoleonproblems im englischen Drama. Erlangen 1931.

Moore, M. Shaw et la France. 1933.

Moraud, M. Le romantisme français en Angleterre de 1814 à 1848. 1933.

Ellis, H. From Rousseau to Proust. Boston 1935.

Walton, T. A French disciple of Morris: Jean Lahor. Revue de Littérature Comparée 15 1935.

Delattre, F. S. Butler et le Bergsonisme. Revue Anglo-américaine 13 1936.

Vat, D. G. van der. The fabulous opera: a study of continuity in French and English poetry of the nineteenth century. Groningen 1936.

Tronchon, H. Le jeune Quinet. 1937.

Hopkins, A. B. Mrs Gaskell in France 1849–90. PMLA 53 1938. With lists of trns and reviews.

Wais, K. Banville, Chateaubriand, Keats und Mallarmés faun. Zeitschrift für Französische Sprache und Literatur 62 1938.

Anderson, G. K. Marie de France and Arthur O'Shaughnessy: a study in Victorian adaptation. SP 36 1939.

Jones, K. La Revue Britannique: son histoire et son action littéraire 1825–40. 1939.

McCausland, S. W. Racine vu par les anglais de 1800 à nos jours. Revue de Littérature Comparée 19 1939.

Frierson, W. C. The English controversy over naturalism. In his English novel in transition 1885–1940, Norman OK 1942.

Morrissette, B. A. Early English and American critics of French symbolism. In Studies in honor of F. W. Shipley, St Louis 1942.

Baldensperger, F. English artistic prose and its debt to French writers. Modern Language Forum Dec 1944.
Bisson, L. A. Proust, Bergson and George Eliot. MLR 40 1945.
Lefèvre, J. L'Angleterre et la Belgique à travers les cinq derniers siècles. 1946.
Moraud, M. Le théâtre français à Londres sous la Restauration. French Rev 22 1948.
Salvan, J.-L. Le romantisme français et l'Angleterre victorienne. 1949.
Voisine, J. Corneille vu par les anglais de 1800 à nos jours. French Stud 3 1949.
Gilman, M. Revival and revolution in English and French romantic poetry. Yale French Stud 6 1950.
Goldgar, H. A. de. Axël, de Villiers de l'Isle Adam, et The shadowy waters de Yeats. Revue de Littérature Comparée 24 1950.
Häusermann, H. W. The Genevese background. 1952. On Shelley, Maria Edgeworth, Meredith, Conrad et al.
Simon, J. J.-E. Blanche et l'Angleterre. Revue de Littérature Comparée 26 1952.
Gilsoul, R. Les influences anglo-saxonnes sur les lettres françaises de Belgique de 1850 à 1880. Brussels 1953.
Robinson, J. K. A neglected phase of the aesthetic movement: English Parnassianism. PMLA 68 1953.
Dale, E. H. La poésie française en Angleterre 1850–90. 1954.
Jean, R. De Nerval et de quelques humoristes anglais. Revue de Littérature Comparée 29 1955.
Stewart, W. M. Poésie français, poésie anglaise. Actes de l'Académie Nationale de Bordeaux 4th ser 14 1955.
Kermode, F. Romantic image. 1957.
Prévost, J. Le dandysme en France 1817–39. Geneva 1957.
Guyard, M.-F. Barrès et les lettres anglaises. In Forschungsprobleme der vergleichenden Literaturgeschichte, 2 vols Tübingen 1958.
Leathers, V. British entertainers in France. Toronto 1959.
Souffrin, E. Gringoire [i.e. Banville] en Angleterre à l'époque victorienne. Revue de Littérature Comparée 33 1959.
Roche, A. Mireille chez les anglo-saxons. In Mirèio. Publications de la Faculté des Lettres de Montpellier 16 1960.
Ross Roy, G. A bibliography of French symbolism in English language publications to 1910. Revue de Littérature Comparée 34 1960.
Starkie, E. From Gautier to Eliot. 1960.
Barber, G. Galignani's and the publication of English books in France from 1800 to 1852. Library 5th ser 16 1961.
Heppenstall, R. The fourfold tradition. 1961.
Underwood, V. P. Rimbaud et les lettres anglo-saxonnes. Revue de Littérature Comparée 35 1961.
Reboul, P. Le mythe anglais dans la littérature française sous la Restauration. Lille 1962.
Duncan, B. The St James's theatre 1835–1957. 1964.
Chambers, R. La comédie au château: contribution à la poétique du théâtre. 1971.
Dibon, A.-M. Form and value in the French and English nineteenth-century novel. MLN 87 1973.
Mackworth, C. English interludes: Mallarmé, Verlaine, P. Valéry, Valery Larbaud in England 1860–1912. 1974.
Brooks, P. The melodramatic imagination. Balzac, Henry James, melodrama and the mode of excess. New Haven CT and London 1976.
Moers, E. Literary women: the great writers. 1976.
Sabin, M. English romanticism and the French tradition. Cambridge MA and London 1976.
Gille-Maisani, J.-C. Ecritures de poètes de Byron à Baudelaire. 1977.
Maxwell, R. City life and the novel: Hugo, Ainsworth, Dickens. Comparative Lit 30 1978.
Johnson, L. McKay. The metaphor of painting. Essays on Baudelaire, Ruskin, Proust and Pater. Ann Arbor MI 1980.
Tanner, T. Adultery and the novel. Contract and transgression. 1980.
Dougherty, S. B. Taine, James and Balzac: towards an aesthetic of romantic realism. The Henry James Rev 2 1980–1.
Winner, A. Characters in the twilight. Hardy, Zola and Chekhov. Charlottesville VA 1981.
Garber, F. The autonomy of self from Richardson to Huysmans. Princeton 1982.
Pilling, J. An introduction to fifty modern European poets. 1982.
Bowlby, R. Just looking: consumer culture in Dreiser, Gissing and Zola. 1985.
Peterson, C. L. The determined reader: gender and culture in the novel from Napoleon to Victoria. New Brunswick NJ 1986.
Sabiston, E. J. The prison of womanhood: four provincial heroines in nineteenth-century fiction. 1987.
Bermann, S. L. The sonnet over time: a study in the sonnets of Petrarch, Shakespeare and Baudelaire. Chapel Hill NC 1988.
Vest, J. M. The French face of Ophelia from Belleforest to Baudelaire. 1990.
Durey, J. F. Realism and narrative modality. The hero and heroine in Eliot, Tolstoy and Flaubert. 1993.
Yarrington, A. and K. Everest (eds). Reflections of revolution: images of romanticism. 1993.
Kelly, G. Women, writing and revolution 1790–1827. 1993.

French authors

For trns of English plays into French, see M. Horn-Monval, Répertoire bibliographique des traductions et adaptations françaises du théâtre étranger vol 5, 1963. *For selected articles on French authors from A to M in English periodicals, see* H. Talvart and J. Place, Bibliographie des auteurs modernes de langue française 1801–1927, 15 vols 1928– .

Balzac, Honoré de (1799–1850). *See also under De Quincey, James, G. Moore and Scott, cols 121, 123, 124, 125 below.*

Les chouans. 1829; The chouans, tr G. Saintsbury 1889.
Les contes drolatiques. 3 vols 1832–7; tr G. Sims 1874; tr R. Whittling 1896.
Histoire des treize. 2 vols 1834; The mystery of the rue Soly, tr Lady Knutsford 1894. An extract.
La recherche de l'absolu. 1834; Balthazar: or science and love, tr W. Robson 1859.
Le père Goriot. 1835; Daddy Goriot: or unrequited affection, 1860, 1878.
Histoire de la grandeur et de la décadence de César Birotteau. 2 vols 1838; History of the grandeur and downfall of Cesar Birotteau, tr J. H. Simpson 1860.
Scènes de la vie privée. Vol 1, 1842; The cat and battledore and other tales, tr P. Kent, 3 vols 1879.
Le cousin Pons. 1847; Poor relations: cousin Pons, tr P. Kent 1880.
Honoré de Balzac. Ed H. van Laun 1869, 1877, 1878, 1880, 1884. A selection, in French.
Correspondance 1819–50. 2 vols 1876; Correspondence, with a memoir by his sister, tr C. Lamb Kenney 2 vols 1878.
Public and private life of animals. 1877. Adaptations from Balzac, Janin, Musset, Sand et al by J. Thomson.
Balzac's novels in English. Tr K. P. Wormeley 12 vols 1886–91. A selection.
Shorter stories from Balzac. Tr W. Wilson and Count Stenbock 1890.
Comédie humaine. Ed G. Saintsbury 40 vols 1895–8.

▽

The style of Balzac and Thackeray. Dublin Univ Mag Dec 1864.
Walker, H. H. The Comédie humaine and its author. 1879. With trns of La bourse, Gaudissart II and Albert Savarus.
Garnand, H. J. The influence of Scott on the works of Balzac. New York 1926.
Badensperger, F. Orientations étrangères chez Balzac. Paris 1927.
Decker, C. R. Balzac's literary reputation in Victorian society. PMLA 47 1932.

Astre, G. A. Balzac et l'anglais mangeur d'opium. Revue de Littérature Comparée 15 1935. Balzac and De Quincey.
McNair, L. Balzac and Huxley. French Rev 12 1939.
Pacey, W. C. D. Balzac and Thackeray. MLR 36 1941.
Falconer, J. A. Balzac and Thackeray. ES 26 1945.
Maitre, R. Balzac, Thackeray et Charles de Bernard. Revue de Littérature Comparée 24 1950.
Mallison, V. Balzac and England. Revue des Langues Vivantes 16 1950.
Monod, S. La fortune de Balzac en Angleterre. Revue de Littérature Comparée 24 1950.
Benson, C. Yeats and Balzac's Louis Lambert. MP 49 1952.
Carey Taylor, A. and C. Dédéyan. Balzac et l'Angleterre. In Balzac: le livre du centenaire, 1952.
Hunt, H. J. The human comedy: first English reactions. In The French mind: G. Rudler, Oxford 1952.
Müller, G. Le père Goriot und Silas Marner. Archiv 189 1953.
Smith, S. R. B. Balzac et l'Angleterre. 1953.
Haggis, D. R. Clothilde de Lusignan, Ivanhoe and the development of Scott's influence on Balzac. French Stud 28 1974.
Haggis, D. R. Fiction and historical changes in La cousine Bette and the lesson of Walter Scott. Forum of Mod Lang Stud 10 1974.
Stowe, W. W. Balzac, James and the realist novel. Princeton 1983.
Stowe, W. W. Intelligibility and entertainment: Balzac and James. Comparative Lit 1983.
Armstrong, A. One of Balzac's sources for L'excommunié. French Stud Bull 37 1991.

Barbey D'Aurevilly (1808–89)

Berthier, P. Une vie 'en Byron': le cas Barbey D'Aurevilly. Romantisme 8 1974.

Baudelaire, Charles (1821–67). *See also under Coleridge, De Quincey, Hazlitt and Swinburne, cols 122, 122, 123, 126 below.*

Les fleurs du mal. 1857, 1861 (rev); Some translations from Baudelaire by H. C. [H. Curwen], 1894.
Petits poèmes en prose. 1869; Poems in prose, tr A. Symons 1905.
Les fleurs du mal, Petits poèmes en prose, Les paradis artificiels. Tr A. Symons 1925.
Saintsbury, G. In his Miscellaneous essays, 1892.
Turquet-Milnes, G. The influence of Baudelaire in France and England. 1913. On Swinburne, Wilde, Symons, Moore et al.
Symons, A. Baudelaire. 1920.
Lafourcade, G. Swinburne and Baudelaire. Revue Anglo-américaine 2 1924.
Clapton, G. T. Baudelaire et De Quincey. 1931.
Clapton, G. T. Carlyle and some early English critics of Baudelaire. In Miscellany of studies presented to L. E. Kastner, Cambridge 1932.
Ruff, M.-A. L'esprit du mal et l'esthétique Baudelairienne. 1955.
Gargano, J. W. James on Baudelaire. MLN 75 1960.
Matheny, M. H. Baudelaire's knowledge of English literature. Revue de Littérature Comparée 44 1970.
Bandy, W. T. Baudelaire, Busquet and English Glees. French Stud 29 1975.
Un mangeur d'opium avec le texte parallèle des Confessions of an English opium-eater et des suspiria de profundis de Thomas de Quincey. Ed M. Stauble-Lipman Wulf, Etudes Baudelairiennes 6–7 1976.
Gale, J. E. De Quincey, Baudelaire et Le Cygne. Nineteenth-Century French Stud 5 1977.
Clements, P. Strange flowers: some notes on the Baudelaire of Swinburne and Pater. MLR 76 1981.
Brunel, P. Baudelaire and Swinburne. Bérénice 7 1983.
Clements, P. Baudelaire and the English tradition. Princeton 1985.
Peyne, H. Baudelaire and English poets. Hommage Pichois 1985.
Howells, B. Héroisme, dandysme et la philosophie du costume: note sur Baudelaire et Carlyle. Revista di Letterature Moderne e Comparate 41 1988.

Chateaubriand, François René de (1768–1848)

Essai historique politique et moral sur les révolutions etc. London 1797; abridged London 1815; Historical, political and moral essay on revolutions, 1815 (trn of 1815 edn).
Atala. 1801; tr 1802, 1813, 1825, 1844; tr J. S. Harry 1867; tr 'Gerard' 1873 (in verse).
Le génie du christianisme. 5 vols 1802; The beauties of Christianity, tr F. Shoberl 3 vols 1813.
René. 1805; tr 1813.
Les martyrs. 3 vols 1809; The two martyrs, tr W. J. Walter 1819.
Itinéraire de Paris à Jérusalem. 3 vols 1811; Travels in Greece, Palestine, Egypt and Barbary, tr F. Shoberl 2 vols 1811.
De Buonaparte, des Bourbons etc. 1814; On Buonaparte and the Bourbons etc, tr 1814.
Recollections of Italy, England and America. 2 vols 1815. A selection from various essays pbd later in Oeuvres, 1826–31.
De la monarchie selon la Charte. London 1816; The monarchy according to the Charter, 1816.
Les Natchez. 1826; The Natchez, 3 vols 1827.
Les aventures du dernier Abencerage. 1826; Aben-Hamet, tr 1826; The last of the Abencerages, tr I. Hill 1835; The adventures of the last Abencerage, tr H. W. Carter 1870.
Essai sur la littérature anglaise etc. 1836; Sketches of English literature etc, 2 vols 1836.
Mémoires d'outre-tombe. 12 vols 1849–50; Memoirs of Chateaubriand, 1848; An autobiography, 4 vols 1849. Both incomplete.
Prescott, W. H. Chateaubriand's sketches of English literature. North Amer Rev Oct 1839.
Dempsey, M. A contribution to the study of the sources of the Génie du christianisme. 1928.
Roddier, H. Chateaubriand et la Revue d'Edimbourg. Revue de Littérature Comparée 11 1931.
Dechamps, J. Chateaubriand en Angleterre. 1934.
Reboul, P. Chateaubriand et les anglais. Revue de Littérature Comparée 33 1949.
Weil, A. Chateaubriand à l'étranger: ou le rayonnement du génie français. Information Littéraire 1949–50.
Kahn, E. Chateaubriand in England. Contemporary Rev Mar 1950.
Caddeau, P. Atala et le Voyage aux Amériques ont-ils vu le jour dans les Voyages du capitaine Cook? Revue de la Méditerranée 1961.
Le Hir, Y. Chateaubriand et Guizot, L'Essai sur la littérature anglaise et La Vie de Shakespeare. Revue des Sciences Humaines 38 1973.
Ballise, F. Les greniers de Chateaubriand à Londres. Actes et Travaux de l'Année 1973. Bulletin n.s. 17.
Maréchal-Trudel, M. Chateaubriand, Byron et Venise. Nizet 1978.
Clément, J. P. Chateaubriand et l'Angleterre. Europe 775–6 1993.

Comte, Isidore Auguste (1798–1857). *See also under Mill, col 124 below.*

Système de politique positive. 1824, 4 vols 1851–4; System of positive polity, tr J. H. Bridges, E. S. Beesly, R. Congreve, F. Harrison et al 4 vols 1875–7.
Cours de philosophie positive. 1830–42; The positive philosophy of Comte, tr and abridged by H. Martineau 2 vols 1853, 3 vols 1896.
Discours sur l'esprit positif. 1844; Preliminary discourse on the positive spirit etc, tr W. M. W. Call 1883; tr E. S. Beesly 1903.
Discours sur l'ensemble du positivisme. 1848; A general view of positivism, tr J. H. Bridges 1865.
Calendrier positiviste. 1849; The positivist calendar of 558 worthies of all ages and nations, ed F. Harrison 1894.
Catéchisme positiviste etc. 1852; The catechism of positivist religion, tr R. Congreve 1858.
Bibliothèque du prolétaire au 19e siècle. 1852; The positivist library of Auguste Comte, tr F. Harrison 1886.
Synthèse subjective: ou système universel des conceptions propres

à l'état normal de l'humanité. 1856; Religion of humanity etc, tr R. Congreve 1891.

▽

Lewes, G. H. Comte's philosophy of the sciences. 1853.
Spencer, H. Reasons for dissenting from the philosophy of M. Comte. 1864.
Mill, J. S. Comte and positivism. 1865. Reply by J. H. Bridges, The unity of Comte's life and doctrine, 1866.
Barton, F. B. An outline of the positive religion of humanity etc. 1867.
Bridges, J. H. Five discourses on positive religion. 1882.
Bridges, J. H. Comte: the successor of Aristotle and St Paul. 1883.
Caird, E. The social philosophy and religion of Comte. 1885.
Hutton, H. D. Comte's life and work. 1892.
The Positivist Review. Ed E. S. Beesly, later S. H. Swinny 1893–1923.
Roberty, E. de. Comte et Spencer. 1894.
Mill, J. S. Lettres inédites à Auguste Comte avec les réponses de Comte. Ed L. Lévy-Brühl 1899.
Whittaker, T. Comte and Mill. 1908.
Thomas, P. Shelley and Comte. Positivist Rev Jan 1911.
McAleer, E. C. Browning's Cleon and Comte. Comparative Lit 8 1956.

Constant, Benjamin (1767–1830)
De la justice politique. Traduction inédite de l'ouvrage de William Godwin. Enquiry concerning political justice and its influence on general virtue and happiness. Ed B. R. Pollin (Droit et Science Politique 5) Quebec 1972.
Courtney, C. P. Alexander Walker and Benjamin Constant: a note on the English translation of Adolphe. French Stud 29 1975.

Cousin, Victor (1792–1867)
Rapport sur l'état de l'instruction publique en Prusse. 1833; Report on the state of public instruction in Prussia, tr J. Austin 1834.
De l'instruction publique en Hollande. 1837; On the state of education in Holland etc, tr L. Horner 1838.
Du vrai, du beau et du bien etc. In his Cours de philosophie, 1841; Lectures on the true, the beautiful and the good, tr O. W. Wight 1854; The philosophy of the beautiful, tr J. C. Daniel 1848.
Cours de l'histoire de la philosophie moderne. 3 vols 1847; Course of the history of modern philosophy, tr O. W. Wight 2 vols Edinburgh 1852; Elements of psychology, tr C. S. Henry 1834. The part of the Cours dealing with Locke.
Justice et charité. 1848; Justice and charity, tr W. Hazlitt 1848.

▽

[Hamilton, W.] M. Cousin's Course of philosophy. Edinburgh Rev 50 1829.

Daudet, Alphonse (1840–97). *See also under Dickens, col 121 below.*
Le petit chose. 1868; My brother Jack. 1877.
Lettres de mon moulin. 1869; Letters from my mill, tr M. Carey 1880; tr F. H. Potter 1893.
Aventures prodigieuses de Tartarin de Tarascon. 1872; Prodigious adventures of Tartarin of Tarascon, tr 1887, 1887.
Fromont jeune et Risler aîné. 1874; tr E. Vizetelly 1880.
Les femmes d'artistes. 1874; Artists' wives, tr L. Ensor 1890.
Robert Helmont. 1874; tr L. Ensor 1888.
Jack. 1876; tr L. Ensor 1890.
Le nabab. 1877; The nabob, tr E. Clavequin 3 vols 1878.
Les rois en exil. 1879; Kings in exile, tr E. Clavequin 3 vols 1880; tr L. Ensor 1890.
Numa Roumestan. 1881; tr 1884.
L'évangéliste. 1883; Port salvation, tr C. H. Meltzer 2 vols 1883.
Sapho. 1884; tr 1886, 1886.
La Belle Nivernaise. 1886; tr R. Routledge 1887.
Souvenirs d'un homme de lettres. 1888; Recollections of a literary man, tr L. Ensor 1889.
Rose et Ninette. 1892; tr M. J. Serrano 1892.

▽

Sherard, R. H. Daudet. 1894.
Munro, W. A. Dickens et Daudet romanciers de l'enfant et des humbles. Toulouse 1908.
Delattre, F. Daudet et l'Angleterre. In his Dickens et la France, 1927.
Favreau, A. R. British criticism of Daudet 1872–97. PMLA 52 1937.

Dumas, Alexandre (1803–70). *See also under Scott, col 125 below.*
Dumas' historical library. 11 vols 1861. A selection.
The romances of Alexandre Dumas. 60 vols 1893–7.
Before this edn approximately 20 of Dumas' 120 works had been translated and often rptd. For a list, see R. W. Plummer, Dumas père: a bibliography of English translations, Dumasian 4–6 1957–9.

▽

Parigot, H. Le drame de Dumas. 1899. With chs on Shakespeare, Scott and Byron as sources.
Roberts, W. Dumas and Sue in English. Nineteenth Century Nov 1922.
Schwartz, H. S. The influence of Dumas on Wilde. French Rev 7 1933.
Morley, M. Monte-Christo at Drury Lane: a riot in two parts. Dumasian 4 1957.
Morley, M. Dumas plays in London. Dumasian 5 1958.

Dumas, Alexandre, ***fils*** (1824–95)
La dame aux camélias. 1848; The lady with the camelias, 1856.
La vie à vingt ans. 1850; Paris life at twenty, 1863.
Le régent Mustel. 1851; The resuscitated, tr G. de Croij 1877.
Le fils naturel. 1858; tr 1879.
Affaire Clémenceau: mémoire de l'accusé. 1866; Bella, tr H. L. Williams 1888.
La princesse de Bagdad. 1881; tr 1881.
Denise. 1885; tr 1885.
Francillon. 1887; tr 1887.

▽

Archer, W. Dumas and the English drama. Cosmopolis Feb 1896.

Flaubert, Gustave (1821–80). *See also under De Quincey, Eliot, James, Scott and Stevenson, cols 121–126 below.*
Madame Bovary. 1857; tr E. Marx-Aveling 1886; with introd by H. James 1902.
Salammbô. 1863; tr M. French Sheldon 1886; tr J. S. Chartres 1886.
L'éducation sentimentale. 1870; Sentimental education, tr D. F. Hannigan 2 vols 1898.
La tentation de Saint Antoine. 1874; The temptation of Saint Antony, tr D. F. Hannigan 1895.
Bouvard et Pécuchet. 1881; tr D. F. Hannigan 1896.

▽

Ferguson, W. D. The influence of Flaubert on George Moore. Philadelphia 1934.
Yvon, P. L'influence de Flaubert en Angleterre. Caen 1939.
Pacey, D. Flaubert and his Victorian critics. UTQ 16 1946.
Heywood, C. Flaubert, Miss Braddon and George Moore. Comparative Lit 12 1960.
Neale, M. Flaubert en Angleterre. Bordeaux 1966.
Rouxeville, A. The reception of Flaubert in Victorian England. Comparative Literary Stud 14 1977.
Gervais, D. Flaubert and Henry James. A study in contrasts. 1978.
Peterson, C. The heroine as reader in the nineteenth-century novel. Emma Bovary and Maggie Tulliver. Comparative Literary Stud 17 1980.
Williams, J. R. Emma Bovary and the Bride of Lammermoor. French Stud 20 1992.

Gaboriau, Emile (1835–73)
L'affaire Lerouge. 1866; The widow Lerouge, 1887.
Le dossier 113. 1867; File number 113, 1887.
Le crime d'Orcival. 1867; The mystery of Orcival, 1887.
Les esclaves de Paris. 2 vols 1868; The slaves of Paris, 1887, 1889.
Monsieur Lecoq. 1869; tr 1887, 1888.
La corde au cou. 1873; In deadly peril, tr G. Campbell 1888.

L'argent des autres. 1873; Other people's money, 1888.
Les amours d'une empoisonneuse. 1881; Marie de Brinvilliers, 1888.
Gautier, Théophile (1811–72). *See also under De Quincey and Swinburne, cols 122, 125 below.*
Mademoiselle de Maupin. 2 vols 1835–6; tr 1887.
Une larme du diable. 1839; The dead Leman and other tales from the French, ed A. Lang and P. Sylvester 1889.
Le roman de la momie. 1858; The romance of a mummy, tr M. Young 1886.
Une nuit de Cléopâtre. 1894; Cleopatra, 1896.
▽
Cockerham, H. Quatre voyages de Gautier en Angleterre. Quelques documents. Bulletin de la Société Théophile Gautier 2 1980.

Goncourt, Edmond de (1822–96) and Jules de (1830–70)
Collister, P. Marie Bashkirtseff in fiction: Edmond de Goncourt and Mrs Humphrey Ward. MP 82 1984.
Cirillo, N. R. A girl need never go wrong, or the female servant as ideological image in Germinie Lacerteux and Esther Waters. Comparative Literary Stud 28 1991.

Hugo, Victor-Marie (1802–85). *See also under Arnold, Byron, Hardy and Swinburne, cols 120, 121, 123, 126 below.*
Han d'Islande. 1823; Hans of Iceland, 1825, 1845; The demon dwarf, 1847; The outlaw of Iceland, tr G. Campbell 1885 etc.
Bug-Jargal. 1826; The slave king, 1833; The noble rival, 1845.
Cromwell. 1827; *see* A. C. Swinburne, Bothwell, 1874.
Le dernier jour d'un condamné. 1829; The last day of a condemned, tr 1840.
Hernani. 1830; tr 1830, 1832.
Notre-Dame de Paris. 1831; Notre-Dame, tr W. Hazlitt 3 vols 1833; E. Fitzball, Esmeralda: or the hunchback of Notre-Dame, 1844 (play).
Marion de Lorme. 1831; The King's edict, adapted by B. Fairclough, 1872.
Le roi s'amuse. 1832; tr H. T. Haley 1842; tr F. L. Slous 1843; *see* W. E. Burton, The court fool, 1885; *see* T. Taylor, The fool's revenge, 1869.
Lucrèce Borgia. 1833; tr W. T. Haley 1841; tr W. Young 1847 (in verse).
Claude Gueux. 1834; Capital punishment, tr D. Pyrke 1865.
Angelo, tyran de Padoue. 1835; Angelo, 1851; Angelo and the actress of Padua, adapted by G. H. Davidson, 1855; tr E. O. Coe 1880.
Ruy Blas. 1838; adapted by E. O'Rourke 1850; tr W. Alexander 1890; *see* J. Davidson, A queen's romance, 1904.
Les chants du crépuscule. 1841; Songs of twilight, tr G. W. M. Reynolds, Paris 1836.
Châtiments. Brussels 1852; *see* A. C. Swinburne, Dirae, 1873.
Napoléon le petit. Brussels 1852; Napoleon the little, 1852.
Les misérables. 5 vols 1862; tr F. C. L. Wraxall 3 vols 1862; tr C. E. Wilbour 2 vols 1887; tr I. F. Hapgood 5 vols 1897.
William Shakespeare. 1864; tr A. Baillot 1864.
Les travailleurs de la mer. 3 vols 1866; Toilers of the sea, tr W. M. Thomas 3 vols 1866; tr G. Campbell 1887.
L'homme qui rit. 1869; By order of the King, 3 vols 1870, 1 vol 1886; The laughing man, 1887; By the King's command, 1875.
Quatre-vingt treize. 1874; Ninety-three, tr F. L. Benedict 3 vols 1874; tr G. Campbell 1886.
L'art d'être grand-père. 1877; *see* A. C. Swinburne, A dark month, 1882.
Histoire d'un crime. 2 vols 1877–8; The history of the crime 4 vols 1877–8, 1 vol 1886; tr G. Campbell 1888.
Selections, chiefly lyrical etc. Ed H. L. Williams 1895.
▽
Stevenson, R. L. Hugo's romances. In his Familiar studies of men and books, 1882.
Swinburne, A. C. A study of Hugo. 1886.
Bowley, V. E. A. Notre-Dame and Les misérables on the English stage. French Quart 11 1929.
Schinz, A. Hugo, Napoléon III et Elizabeth Browning. Revue de Littérature Comparée 13 1933.
Thomas, J. H. L'Angleterre dans l'oeuvre d'Hugo. 1933.
Aubry, G. J. Hugo et Swinburne. Revue Bleue 7 Mar 1936. On their correspondence.
Hooker, K. W. The fortunes of Hugo in England. New York 1938. With list of articles on Hugo in English periodicals.
Rose, F. Tennyson and Hugo. Poetry Rev 30 1939.
Bowley, V. E. A. English versions of Hugo's plays. Adam International Rev 1952. With appendix listing trns.
Barrère, J.-B. Hugo et la Grande Bretagne. Revue de Littérature Comparée 28 1954.
Barineau, E. Les feuilles d'automne et les Mémoires de Byron. MP 55 1958.
Descotes, M. Victor Hugo et Waterloo: Archives Victor Hugo 10. Archives des Lettres Modernes 214 1984.
Victor Hugo et la Grande-Bretagne. Ed A. R. W. James. Liverpool 1986.

Huysmans, Joris Karl (1848–1907)
En route. 1895; tr with preface by C. Kegan Paul 1896.
La cathédrale. 1898; The cathedral, tr C. Bell 1898.
▽
Cevasco, C. J.-K. Huysmans and Aubrey Beardsley. Bulletin de la Société. J.-K. Huysmans 16 1978.

Joubert, Joseph (1734–1824)
Pensées, essais et maximes. 2 vols 1842; Pensées of Joubert, tr H. Attwell 1877; tr K. Lyttelton with preface by Mrs H. Ward 1898; tr G. H. Calvert 1903.
▽
Fairclough, G. T. A fugitive and gracious light. Lincoln NE 1961. On Joubert and Arnold.

De Kock, Charles Paul (1793–1871)
Sœur Anne. 4 vols 1825; Sister Anne, tr G. W. M. Reynolds 1840.
André le savoyard. 5 vols 1826; Andrew the savoyard, 1849.
Le barbier de Paris. 4 vols 1826; The barber of Paris, 1839.
Jean. 4 vols 1827; The modern Cymon, 2 vols 1833.

Lamartine, Alphonse de (1790–1869). *See also under Shelley, col 125 below.*
Méditations poétiques. 1820; Solitude and other poems, with translations from the Méditations poétiques by J. Forth, 1830.
Histoire des Girondins. 8 vols 1847; Pictures of the first French Revolution, 1850. A selection.
Les confidences. 2 vols 1849–51; Memoirs of my youth, The wanderer and his home, tr Lady Wilde 1849, 1851.
Christophe Colomb. 1853; The life and times of Columbus, 2 vols 1887.
Lombard, C. M. Portrait of Lamartine in the English periodical 1820–70. MLN 75 1960.
Lombard, C. M. Lamartine in America and England 1820–76: a check-list. BB 23 1961.

Lamennais, Hugues Félicité de (1782–1854)
Paroles d'un croyant. 1833; The words of a believer, 1834, 1845, 1858.
Le livre du peuple. 1838; The book of the people, tr J. H. Lorymer 1838.
De l'esclavage moderne. 1839; Modern slavery, tr W. J. Linton 1840.

Loti, Pierre (1850–1923)
Lerner, M. Pierre Loti and England. French Stud 29 1975.

Maeterlinck, Maurice (1862–1949)
La Princesse Maleine. Brussels 1889; L'intruse, Brussels 1890; Princess Maleine and the intruder, tr G. Harry and W. Wilson 1892.
Pelléas et Mélisande. Brussels 1892; Les aveugles, Brussels 1890; Pelleas and Melisander, and The sightless, tr L. Alma Tadema 1892.
Alladines et Palomides: Intérieur; La mort de Tintagiles. Brussels 1894; tr A. Sutro and W. Archer 1899.

Aglavaine et Sélysette. 1896; tr A. Sutro 1897.
Le trésor des humbles. 1896; The treasure of the humble, tr A. Sutro 1897.
La sagesse et la destinée. 1898; Wisdom and destiny, tr A. Sutro 1898.
La vie des abeilles. 1901; The life of the bee, tr A. Sutro 1901.
Monna Vanna. 1902; tr A. Sutro 1904.
L'oiseau bleu. 1909; The blue bird, tr A. Teixeira de Mattos 1909.

▽

Rabuse, G. J. M. Synges Verhältnis zur französischen Literatur und besonders zu Maeterlinck. Archiv 184 1938.
Halls, W. D. Some aspects of the relationship between Maeterlinck and Anglo-American literature. Annales de la Fondation Maeterlinck 1955. On Shakespeare, Carlyle and the Pre-Raphaelites.
Pouilliart, R. Maeterlinck et Carlyle. Revue de Littérature Comparée 38 1964.

Maistre, Joseph Marie de (1753–1811)
Holdsworth, F. de Maistre de l'Angleterre. 1935.
Stinglhamber, L. de Maistre, précurseur de Newman. Bulletin de l'Association Guillaume Budé 1944.

Mallarmé, Stéphane (1842–98). *See also under Keats, G. Moore, Verlaine, Wilde and Yeats, cols 123, 124, 118, 126 below.*
The National Observer. 1892–3.
Lhombreaud, R. S. Deux lettres de Mallarmé à Gosse. Revue de Littérature Comparée 25 1951.
Souffrin, E. Coup d'oeil sur la bibliothèque anglaise de Mallarmé. Revue de Littérature Comparée 32 1958.
Ryan, M. John Payne et Mallarmé. Revue de Littérature Comparée 32 1958.
Lhombreaud, R. S. Symons' renderings of Mallarmé. Princeton Univ Lib Chron 20 1959.
Austin, L. J. New light on Brennan and Mallarmé. Australian Jnl of Fr Stud 6 1969.
Austin, L. J. Mallarmé and the visual arts. French Nineteenth-Century Painting and Lit 1972.
Smith, H. J. The mirror of art: Mallarmé's Hérodiade and Tennyson's The Lady of Shalott. Romance Notes 16 1974.
Chapman, W. K. Symbolisme and its 'chief' agent in English: Mallarmé vis-à-vis Yeats. Romance Quart 37 1990.

Maupassant, Guy de (1850–93)
Une vie. 1883; A woman's life 1888; A woman's soul, tr H. Blanchamp 1902.
Yvette. 1885; tr A. G. with a preface by J. Conrad 1904.
Pierre et Jean. 1888; tr C. Bell 1890.
Sur l'eau. 1888; Afloat, tr L. Ensor 1889.
Boule du suif. 1897; tr 1899.

▽

Frierson, W. C. Realism in the 1890s and the Maupassant school in England. French Quart 10 1928; rptd in his English novel in transition, Norman OK 1942. Reply by G. J. Worth, The English Maupassant school of the 1890s: some reservations, MLN 72 1957.
Worth, G. J. Maupassant in Victorian England. In Literature and society, ed B. Slote, Lincoln NE 1964.
Terramorsi, B. Maupassant et James: les tours du fantastique. Europe 772–73 1993.

Mérimée, Prosper (1803–70)
Chronique du temps de Charles IX. 1829; A chronicle of the reign of Charles IX, tr A. R. Scoble 1853.
Colomba. 1840; tr A. R. Scoble 1853.
Carmen. 1845; tr 1887; tr E. H. Garrett 1896.
Histoire de don Pèdre I. 1848; The history of Peter the Cruel, 2 vols 1849.
Les faux Démétrius. 1853; Demetrius the imposter, tr A. R. Scoble 1853.
Lettres à une inconnue. 2 vols 1874; Letters to an incognita, 1874.

▽

Decreus, J. Opinions de Mérimée sur la Grande Bretagne et les anglais. Comparative Lit Stud 23–4 1946.
Healy, D. Mérimée et les anglais. 1946.
Bennett, B. and W. Little. Seven letters from Prosper Merimée to Mary Shelley. Comparative Lit 31 1979.

Michelet, Jules (1798–1874)
Histoire romaine: république. 1833; History of the Roman Republic, tr W. Hazlitt 1846.
Histoire de France. 15 vols 1833–65; The history of France [section on Middle Ages], tr W. K. Kelly 2 vols 1844–6; tr G. H. Smith 2 vols 1844–7.
Du prêtre, de la femme et de la famille. 1845; Priests, women and families, tr C. Cocks 1846; 1850.
Le peuple. 1846; The people, tr C. Cocks 1846.
Histoire de la revolution française. 7 vols 1847–53; A history of the French revolution, tr C. Cocks 2 vols 1847–8.
L'oiseau. 1856; The bird, tr A. E. 1868.
L'insecte. 1858; The insect, tr W. H. D. Adams 1875.
La sorcière. 1862; tr L. J. Trotter 1863.
La montagne. 1868; The mountain, tr W. H. D. Adams 1875.
La France devant l'Europe. Florence 1871; France before Europe, 1871.

Musset, Alfred de (1810–57)
Barberine. 1835; Fantasio, 1833; On ne badine pas avec l'amour, 1834; Il faut qu'une porte soit ouverte ou fermée, 1845; Comedies, tr S. L. Gwynn 1890.
Un caprice. 1848: A good little wife, tr 1850.

▽

Jamieson, P. Musset, De Quincey and Piranesi. MLN 71 1956.
Norden, P. A de Musset et l'Angleterre. Les Lettres Romanes 20 1966, 21 1967.
Malthus, C. Musset et Shakespeare: étude analytique de l'influence de Shakespeare sur le théâtre d'Alfred de Musset. Ed R. A. Barrell, American Univ Ser 2 62 1988.

Nodier, Jean Emmanuel Charles (1780–1844)
Promenade de Dieppe aux montagnes d'Ecosse. 1821; Promenade from Dieppe to the mountains of Scotland, Edinburgh 1822.

▽

Larat, J. Un voyageur romantique en Angleterre: Nodier. Anglo-French Rev Dec 1920.

Renan, Joseph Ernest (1823–90). *See also under Pater, col 124 below.*
Etudes d'histoire religieuse. 2 sers 1857, 1884; Studies in religious history, tr H. F. Gibbons 1893; tr 1886.
La poésie des races celtiques. In his Essais de morale et de critique, 1859; The poetry of the Celtic races, tr W. G. Hutchison 1892.
Histoire des origines du christianisme. 8 vols 1863–83; The life of Jesus [i.e. vol 1], 1864; abridged 1887; The apostles [i.e. vol 2], 1869; History of the origins of Christianity, 7 vols 1889–90.
Dialogues et fragments philosophiques. 1876; Philosophical dialogues and fragments, tr R. B. Mukharjî 1883.
Caliban. 1878; tr 1896.
Conférences d'Angleterre. 1880; Lectures on the influence of Rome on Christianity and the development of the Catholic Church, tr C. Beard 1880.
Souvenirs d'enfance et de jeunesse. 1883; Recollections of my youth, tr C. B. Pitman 1883.
Histoire du peuple d'Israël. 5 vols 1887–93; History of the people of Israel, 3 vols 1888–91.
L'avenir de la science. 1890; The future of science, tr A. D. Vandam and C. B. Pitman 1891.
Leaders of Christian and anti-Christian thought. Tr W. M. Thomson 1895. A selection of essays.

▽

Mott, L. F. Renan and Arnold. MLN 33 1918.
Tronchon, H. Renan et l'Angleterre. Revue de Littérature Comparée 7 1927.

Angell, J. W. Arnold's indebtedness to Renan's Essais de morale et de critique. Revue de Littérature Comparée 14 1934.
Smith, H. Renan versus an Anglo-Saxon publisher. Modern Languages Forum 27 1942.
Rivoallan, A. Un admirateur anglais de Renan: Arnold. Nouvelle Revue de Bretagne Sep 1952.
Harding, J. N. Wilde and Renan. Contemporary Rev May 1953.
Harding, J. N. Renan and Arnold: two saddened searchers. Hibbert Jnl 57 1959.
Gore, K. Ernest Renan's attitude to Great Britain. MLR 85 1990.

Rimbaud, Arthur (1854–91)

Underwood, V. P. Rimbaud et l'Angleterre. Nizet 1976.

Rostand, Edmond (1868–1918)

Armstrong, J. The semiotics of fin-de-siècle: Stalky and co. and Cyrano de Bergerac. Essays in Poetics 17 1992.

Rousseau, Jean-Jacques (1712–78). *See also under Byron, col 121 below.*

Emile, 1762; *see* R. L. Edgeworth, Practical education, 1798; Professional education, 1809; *see* H. Spencer, Education, intellectual, moral and physical, 1861.

▽

Schmidt, O. Rousseau und Byron: ein Beitrag zur vergleichenden Literaturgeschichte des Revolutionszeitalters. Oppeln 1890.
Allen, B. S. Godwin as a sentimentalist. PMLA 33 1918. On Godwin, Helvétius and Rousseau.
Gosse, E. Rousseau in England in the nineteenth century. In his Aspects and impressions, 1922.
Barzun, J. Shaw and Rousseau. In Shaw: a critical survey, ed L. Kronenberger 1954.
Voisine, J. Rousseau en Angleterre à l'époque romantique. 1956.

Saint-Simon, Henry de (1760–1825)

Nouveau christianisme. 1825; New Christianity, tr J. E. Smith 1834.

▽

Neff, E. E. Carlyle and Mill. New York 1924.
Murphy, E. M. Carlyle and the Saint-Simonians. SP 33 1936.
Shine, H. Carlyle and the Saint-Simonians: the concept of historical periodicity. Baltimore 1941.

Sainte-Beuve, Charles Augustin de (1804–69). *See also under Arnold, col 120 below.*

Causeries du lundi. 15 vols 1851–62; English portraits, 1875; ed G. Saintsbury 1885.
Essays on men and women. Ed W. Sharp 1890. A selection.

▽

Roth, G. Sainte-Beuve, Crabbe et le conte en vers. French Quart 3 1921.
Phillips, E. M. Sainte-Beuve and the Lake poets. French Quart 8 1926.
Phillips, E. M. Sainte-Beuve's criticism of English prose. French Quart 13 1931.
Combe, T. G. S. Sainte-Beuve poète et les poètes anglais. Bordeaux 1937.
Whitridge, A. Arnold and Sainte-Beuve. PMLA 53 1938.
Lehmann, A. G. Sainte-Beuve: critique de la littérature anglaise. Revue de Littérature Comparée 38 1954.
Phillips, E. M. Sainte-Beuve et l'Angleterre. In Mélanges offerts à Jean Bonnerot, 1954.

'Sand, George' (Aurore Dupin) (1804–76). *See also under Byron, col 121 below.*

Mauprat. 1837; tr V. Vaughan 1870.
Spiridion. 1839; tr 1842.
Consuelo. 8 vols 1843; tr 2 vols 1847; 1893.
Le compagnon du tour de France. 2 vols 1841; The journeyman joiner, tr F. G. Shaw, Dublin 1849.
La comtesse de Rudolstadt. 5 vols 1844; The countess of Rudolstadt, 1851; 1862; 1893.
Le meunier d'Angibault. 3 vols 1845; The miller of Angibault, 1853.
La mare au diable. 2 vols 1846; The haunted marsh, 1848; The enchanted lake, tr F. G. Shaw 1850; The devil's pool, 1861.
The works of George Sand. Tr M. M. Hays vols 1–6 1847.
Francois-le-Champi. Brussels 1848; Francis the waif, tr G. Masson 1888; tr J. M. Sedgwick 1895.
La petite Fadette. 2 vols 1849; Little Fadette, with introd by J. Mazzini, 1850.
Les maîtres sonneurs. 1853; The bagpipers, tr K. P. Wormeley, 1890.
Le Marquis de Villemer. 1861; The Marquis of Villemer, tr R. Keeler 1870.
Correspondance 1812–76. 6 vols 1882–4; Letters, selected and tr R. Ledos de Beaufort 3 vols 1886.

▽

Arnold, J. V. George Sand's Mauprat and Emily Brontë's Wuthering Heights. Revue de Littérature Comparée 46 1972.
Thomson, P. George Sand and English reviewers: the first twenty years. MLR 67 1972.
Thomson, P. George Sand and the Victorians: her influence and reputation in nineteenth-century England. 1977.
Blount, P. G. George Sand and the Victorians: Matthew Arnold as touchstone. George Sand Papers (1976) New York 1980.
Jurgrau, T. The linking of the Georges, Sand and Eliot: critical convention and reality. George Sand Papers (1976) New York 1980.
Corner, N. National chauvinism and male chauvinism: the British critics react to George Sand. George Sand Papers (1978) New York 1982.
Godwin-Jones, R. George Sand, Charlotte Brontë and the industrial novel. George Sand Papers (1978) New York 1982.
Jurgrau, T. George Sand's attitude towards the English. George Sand Papers (1978) New York 1982.

Sardou, Victorien (1831–1908)

Les pattes de mouche. 1860; A scrap of paper, adapted by J. P. Simpson 1861.
Les prés Saint-Gervais. 1862; The meadows of Saint-Gervais, tr J. R. Ware 1871.
Les ganaches. 1863; Progress, adapted by T. W. Robertson 1893.
Nos intimes! 1865; Friends or foes?, adapted by H. Wigan nd; Our friends, tr G. March 1879.
Ferande. 1870; tr 1883.
Dora. 1877; tr 1877; *see* B. C. Stephenson and C. Scott, Diplomacy, 1878.
Les bourgeois de Pont-Arcy (not pbd in France); The inhabitants of Pontarcy, 1878.
Fédora. 1908 (performed 1882); tr H. Merivale 1883; *see* H. L. Williams, Fedora: a novel, 1883.

▽

Raafat, Z. The literary indebtedness of Wilde's Salome to Sardou's Théodora. Revue de Littérature Comparée 40 1966.

Scribe, Augustin Eugène (Félix Augustin Debersey) (1796–1861)

This list does not include opera libretti and one-act farces based on Scribe.

Scribe and Varner. César: ou le chien du château. 1837; Caesar, the watchdog of the castle. 1886.
La muette de Portici. 1837; Masaniello, adapted by R. B. Brough 1857.
Le verre d'eau. 1840; The glass of water, adapted by W. E. Suter nd.
Scribe and E. Legouvé. Adrienne Lecouvreur. 1849; adapted by H. Herman 1850.
Giralda. 1850. An opera; tr Mrs Davidson 1850; adapted as a play by H. Welstead 1856.
Scribe and E. Legouvé. Bataille de dames. 1851; The ladies' battle, tr T. W. Robertson 1851; tr C. Reade 1851.
Scribe and E. Legouvé. Les doigts de fée. 1858; The world of fashion, tr J. Oxenford 1862.

▽

Stanton, S. S. Shaw's debt to Scribe. PMLA 76 1961.
Raafat, Z. Scribe's plays and their English versions in the nineteenth century. Revue de Littérature Comparée 45 1971.

Ségur, Comtesse de (1799–1874)
Fairy tales for little folks. Tr Mrs Chapman Coleman, 1869.
The inn of the guardian angel. Tr H. I. Adams, 1871.
Sophie's troubles. Tr P. P. S., 1889.
Sismondi, Jean Charles Léonard Simonde de (1773–1842)
Histoire des républiques italiennes du moyen âge. 8 vols Zurich 1807–9; Italian republics etc, 1832.
De la littérature du midi de l'Europe. 4 vols 1813; Historical view of the literature of the south of Europe, tr T. Roscoe 1823.
Nouveaux principes d'économie politique. 2 vols 1819; Political economy and the philosophy of government, 1847. A selection.
Sismondi and A. Renée. Histoire des français. 31 vols 1821–44; History of the crusades against the Albigenses etc, 1826; The battles of Cressy and Poitiers etc, 1831. 2 extracts.
Julia Severa: ou l'an 492. 3 vols 1822; tr 2 vols 1822.
Staël-Holstein, Germaine de (1766–1817)
De l'influence des passions sur le bonheur des individus et des nations. Lausanne 1796; A treatise on the influence of the passions upon the happiness of individuals and nations, 1798.
De la littérature considérée dans ses rapports avec les institutions sociales. 2 vols 1800; A treatise on ancient and modern literature, 2 vols 1803; The influence of literature upon society, 2 vols 1812.
Delphine. 4 vols Geneva 1802; tr 3 vols 1803.
Corinne. 2 vols 1807; Corinna, tr D. Lawler 5 vols 1807; tr I. Hill 1833.
De l'Allemagne. 3 vols 1810, London 1813; Germany, 3 vols 1813.
Réflexions sur le suicide. London and Stockholm 1813; Reflections on suicide, 1813.
An appeal to the nations of Europe against the continental system. 1813.
Considérations sur les principaux évènement de la révolution française. London 1818; Considerations on the principal events of the French Revolution, 1818.
Zulma et trois nouvelles: précédé d'un essai sur les fictions. 2 vols London 1813; tr 1813.
▽
Bertaut, J. Madame de Staël et l'Angleterre. Mercure de France 16 July 1917.
Whitford, R. C. Mme de Staël's literary reputation in England. Univ of Illinois Stud 4 1918.
Pange, V. de. Mme de Staël et le duc de Wellington. Correspondance inédite 1815–17. 1962.
Pange, V. de and N. King. La bibliothèque anglaise de Mme de Staël. Cahiers Staëliens 14 1972.
Pange, V. de. Le plus beau de toutes les fêtes. Mme de Staël et Elisabeth Hervey, duchesse de Devonshire, d'après leur correspondance inédite 1804–17. Klincksieck 1980.
'Stendhal' (Marie-Henri Beyle) (1783–1842). *See also under Browning, James, Scott and Thackeray, cols 121, 123, 125, 126 below.*
Rome, Naples et Florence en 1817. 1817; Rome, Naples and Florence in 1817, 1818.
Vie de Rossini. 2 vols 1824; Memoirs of Rossini, 1824.
New Monthly Magazine. 1825–9.
▽
Gunnell, D. Stendhal et l'Angleterre. 1909. With list of contributions to English periodicals.
Vigneron, R. Stendhal et Hazlitt. MP 35 1938.
Lafourcade, G. Stendhal et Arnold Bennett. Revue de Littérature Comparée 19 1939.
Imbert, H.-F. Stendhal et Tom Jones. Revue de Littérature Comparée 30 1956.
Dechamps, J. A propos d'un centenaire: Leigh Hunt et Stendhal. Stendhal Club 1 1959.
Del Litto, V. La vie intellectuelle de Stendhal: genèse et évolution de ses idées 1802–21. 1959.
Strauss, A. La fortune de Stendhal en Angleterre. 1966.
Alciatore, J.-C. Quelques remarques sur Stendhal et les héroïnes de Scott. Stendhal Club 8 1966.
Imbert, H. F. Conjectures sur l'origine scottienne du titre de 'Rouge et Noir'. Revue de Littérature Comparée 45 1971.
McWatters, K. G. Stendhal and England. Liverpool 1976.
Chroniques pour l'Angleterre: contributions à la presse britannique. Ed K. G. McWalters, tr R. Dénier. Grenoble 1980.
Chroniques pour l'Angleterre III. Ed K. G. McWalters. Grenoble 1983.
Sue, Marie Joseph Eugène (1804–57)
Arthur. 1839; tr 1846.
Jean Cavalier. 2 vols 1840; The Protestant leader, 3 vols 1849.
Le commandeur de Malte. 2 vols 1841; tr A. Doisy 1846.
Mathilde. 3 vols 1841; Matilda, 1846.
Le morne-au-diable (not pbd; performed in 1848); The female Bluebeard, 1845.
Paula Monti. 1842; tr 1845.
Thérèse Dunoyer. 2 vols 1842; tr 1845.
Les mystères de Paris. 5 vols 1842–3; tr J. D. Smith 1844; tr H. D. Williams 1869; etc.
Le juif errant. 10 vols 1844–5; performed as a play in France in 1849; The wandering Jew, 1844; tr D. M. Aird 1845; tr H. D. Mules 1846; tr H. D. Williams 3 vols 1868; *see* G. Landor, The wandering Jew, 1883 (dramatic adaptation).
Martin ou l'enfant trouvé. 1845; Martin the foundling, 1847.
▽
Roberts, W. Dumas and Sue in England. Nineteenth Century Nov 1922.
Taine, Hippolyte (1828–93). *See also under Carlyle and James, cols 121, 123 below.*
Histoire de la littérature anglaise. 4 vols 1863–4; History of English literature, tr H. van Laun 2 vols Edinburgh 1871.
Le positivisme anglais: étude sur Stuart Mill. 1864; English positivism: a study on Mill, tr T. D. Haye 1870.
Philosophie de l'art. 1865; The philosophy of art, tr J. Durand 1865.
De l'intelligence. 2 vols 1870; On intelligence, tr T. D. Haye 2 vols 1871.
Notes sur l'Angleterre. 1872; Notes on England, tr W. F. Rae 1872.
Carnets de voyage: notes sur la province 1863–5. 1897; Journeys through France, 1897.
▽
Murray, K. Taine und die englische Romantik. Munich 1914.
Roe, F. C. Taine et l'Angleterre. 1923.
Rivelaygue, J. Taine et la philosophie anglaise. Revue Philosophique de la France et de l'Etranger. 1988.
Tocqueville, Alexis de (1805–59). *See also under Mill, col 124 below.*
De la démocratie en Amérique. 4 vols 1835–40; Democracy in America, tr H. Reeve 4 vols 1835–40.
L'ancien régime et la Révolution. 1856; On the state of society in France before the Revolution of 1789 etc, tr H. Reeve 1856.
Correspondence and conversations with N. W. Senior. 2 vols 1872.
▽
Vallès, Jules (1832–85)
La rue à Londres. 1876–81.
▽
Beyer, R. La formule dans La rue à Londres. Les Amis de Jules Vallès 17 1993.
Disegni, S. Visions d'exil in Jules Vallès. Rhetorique, politique, imaginaire. Ed F. Martin 1993.
Verlaine, Paul (1844–96)
The Senate. 1895. Various poems and articles by Verlaine.
▽
Symons, A. Verlaine, Two Worlds Mar 1926.
Temple, R. Z. Verlaine and his English readers. Comparative Lit Newsletter 3 1945.
Starkie, E. Verlaine and Mallarmé at Oxford. Harlequin 1 1949.

Lhombreaud, R. A. Verlaine et ses amis d'Angleterre. Revue d'Histoire Littéraire de la France 53 1953.
Underwood, V. P. Verlaine et l'Angleterre. 1956.

Verne, Jules Gabriel (1828–1905)
Cinq semaines en ballon. 1863; Five weeks in a balloon, 1870.
De la terre à la lune. 1865; Autour de la lune, 1869; From the earth to the moon and a trip around it, tr L. Mercier 2 vols 1876.
Les anglais au pôle nord; Le désert de glace. 2 vols 1866; The English at the North Pole; The field of ice, 2 vols 1875–6.
Les enfants du capitaine Grant etc. 1868; A voyage around the world etc, 1876.
Vingt mille lieues sous les mers. 1869; Twenty thousand leagues under the seas, 1873, 1874 etc.
Le tour du monde en quatre-vingts jours. 1873; Around the world in eighty days, tr G. M. Towle 1874; tr H. Frith 1879 etc.
L'île mystérieuse. 1874; The mysterious island, tr W. H. G. Kingston 1875.
Le docteur Ox. 1874; Dr Ox's experiment etc, 1874.
Le Chancellor. 1875; The survivors of the Chancellor, tr E. Frewer 1875.
Michel Strogoff. 1875; tr W. H. G. Kingston 1876.
César Cascabel. 2 vols 1890; tr 1891.
L'ile à hélice. 1895; Floating island, tr W. J. Gordon Edinburgh 1896.

Vidocq, François Eugène (1775–1857)
Mémoires. 1828–9; tr H. T. R. 1828–9; *see* Vidocq: a melodrama, 1825.

Vigny, Alfred de (1797–1863). *See also under Byron, T. Moore and Scott, cols 121, 124, 125 below.*
Cinq-Mars. 1826; tr W. Hazlitt 1847.
Les consultations du docteur Noir. 1831–2; Servitude et grandeur militaires, 1835; Professional visits of le docteur Noir; Sealed orders. In Tales of the first French Revolution, 1849 (selection).
▽
Poems and romances of Vigny. Westminster Rev 29 1838.
Ascher, J. Vigny and Thomas Campbell. French Quart 4 1922.
Lebbin, E. Vignys Beziehungen zu England und zur englischen Literatur. Halle 1936.
Hope, W. G. The 'suffering humanitarian' theme in Shelley's Prometheus unbound and in certain poems of Vigny. French Rev 12 1939.
Bird, C. W. Vigny's Chatterton: a contribution to the study of its genesis and sources. Los Angeles 1941.
Whitridge, A. Vigny and Housman: a study in pessimism. American Scholar 10 1941.
Marshall, J. F. Vigny and W. C. Macready. PMLA 74 1959.
Vigny, les Pyrénées et l'Angleterre. Touzot 1979.

Volney, Comte (Constantin-François de Chasseboeuf) (1757–1820)
Les ruines. 1791; The ruins, 1795.
▽
Kellner, L. Shelley's Queen Mab und Volneys Les ruines. EStudien 22 1896.
Cameron, K. N. A major source of the Revolt of Islam. PMLA 56 1941.

Zola, Emile (1840–1903). *See also under C. Brontë, Dickens, James and G. Moore, cols 121, 122, 123, 124 below.*
Thérèse Raquin. 1867; tr E. A. Vizetelly 1886.
L'œuvre. 1871; His masterpiece?, 1886.
La Fortune des Rougon. 1871; The fortune of the Rougons, 1886.
La curée. 1872; The rush for the spoil, with a preface by George Moore, 1886.
Le ventre de Paris. 1873; Fat and thin, tr E. A. Vizetelly 1888.
La faute de l'abbé Mouret. 1875; Abbé Mouret's transgression, 1886.
Une page d'amour. 1876; A love episode, 1887.
L'assommoir. 1877; The assommoir, 1884; *see* C. Reade, Drink, 1879 (play).
Son excellence Eugène Rougon. 1879; His excellency E. Rougon, 1887.
L'attaque du moulin. 1880; The attack on the mill etc, with an essay by E. Gosse, 1892.
Nana. 1880; tr 1884.
Pot-Bouille. 1882; Piping hot! with a preface by George Moore, 1885.
Au bonheur des dames. 1883; The ladies' paradise, tr F. Belmont 3 vols 1883.
La joie de vivre. 1884; How jolly life is!, 1886.
Germinal. 1885; tr 1885.
La terre. 1887; The soil, 1888.
L'argent. 1887; Money, tr E. A. Vizetelly 1894.
Le rêve. 1889; The dream, tr E. E. Chase 1893.
La débâcle 1891; The downfall, tr E. A. Vizetelly 1892.
Le docteur Pascal. 1893; Doctor Pascal: or life and heredity, tr E. A. Vizetelly 1893.
▽
Pernicious literature: debate in the House of Commons, with opinions of the press. 1889 (Nat Vigilance Assoc pamphlet).
Ellis, H. Zola: the man and his work. Savoy 1 1896.
Vizetelly, E. A. With Zola in England. 1899.
Vizetelly, E. A. Zola: novelist and reformer. 1904.
Decker, C. R. Zola's literary reputation in England. PMLA 49 1934. With list of articles in English periodicals.
'Auriant'. Un disciple anglais de Zola: George Moore. Mercure de France 297 1940.
Haines, L. F. Reade, Mill and Zola. SP 40 1943.
Pryme, E. E. Zola's plays in England 1870–1900. French Stud 13 1959.
Burns, C. A. Zola in exile. Notes on an unpbd diary of 1878. French Stud 17 1963.
Hemmings, F. W. J. Zola par delà la Manche et l'Atlantique. Cahiers Naturalistes 23 1963.
Polet, J.-C. L'Angleterre et Zola. Cahiers Naturalistes 55 1981.
Curtis, S. Vizetelly and co. Poetry Nation Rev 32 1983.
Burns, C. Le voyage de Zola à Londres en 1893: 'Notes sur Londres': texte inédit d'Emile Zola. Cahiers Naturalistes 60 1986.
Burns, C. Echanges franco-britanniques (1): lettres inédites d'Emile Zola á Ernest Vizetelly (1891–93). Cultura Neolatina 62 1988.
Tilby, M. Emile Zola and his first English biographer. Laurels 59 1988.
Burns, C. Echanges franco-britanniques. Lettres d'Emile Zola à Ernest Vizetelly (1899–1902) et à Chatto et Windus (1897–1900). Cultura Neolatina 64 1990.
Morel, C. La fortune de Zola en Angleterre: les oeuvres illustrées. Cahiers Naturalistes 66 1992.

English authors

For a selective list of trns of English authors into French, see G. Lanson, Manuel bibliographiqe de la littérature française moderne 1500–1900, 1931, pt 4, section 2, ch 3. *For a comprehensive list of trns of plays, see* M. Horn-Monval, Répertoire bibliographique des traductions et adaptations françaises du théâtre étranger du XVe siècle à nos jours, vol 5 1962. *For a comprehensive list of trns of novels between 1830 and 1870, see Devonshire, col 104 above.*

Arnold, Matthew. *See also under Joubert, Renan and Sainte-Beuve, cols 112, 113, 115 above.*
A French Eton: or middle-class education and the State. 1864.
Essays in criticism. 2 sers 1865–88.
Mixed essays. 1879.
Irish essays. 1882.
▽
Furrer, P. Der Einfluss Sainte-Beuves auf die Kritik Arnolds. Wetzikon 1920.
Romer, V. L. Arnold and some French poets. Nineteenth Century June 1926.
Brown, E. K. The French reputation of Arnold. Stud in Eng (Toronto) 1931.
Sells, I. E. Arnold and France: the poet. Cambridge 1935.

Sells, I. E. Marguerite. MLR 38 1943.
Faverty, F. E. Arnold the ethnologist. Evanston 1951.
Mengers, M. Matters versus man. French Rev 28 1955. On Hugo, Arnold and Régnier.
Allott, K. Arnold's reading-lists in three early diaries. VS 2 1959.
Super, R. H. Documents in the Arnold–Sainte-Beuve relationship. MP 60 1963.
Harding, F. S. Arnold the critic and France. Geneva 1964.
Straumann, H. Arnold and the continental idea. In The English mind, ed H. S. Davies and G. Watson, Cambridge 1964.

Austen, Jane

King, N. J. Jane Austen in France. Nineteenth-Cent Fiction 8 1954.
Hellstrom, W. Francophobia in Emma. Stud in Eng Lit 1500–1900, 5 1965.

Bennett, Enoch Arnold. *See also under Stendhal, col 117 above.*

The old wives' tale. 1910.
Paris nights. 1913.
Journals vol 1. 1932.
▽
Evans, R. L. Bennett et la France. Modern Languages 21 1940.
Conacher, W. M. Bennett and the French realists. Queen's Quart 56 1949.

Brontë, Charlotte. *See also under G. Sand, col 115 above.*

Behdad, A. Visibility, secrecy and the novel: narrative power in Brontë and Zola. Literary Interpretation Theory 1 1990.

Brontë, Emily. *See under G. Sand, col 115 above.*

Browning, Robert and Elizabeth Barrett. *See also under Comte and Hugo, cols 108, 111 above.*

Mrs Browning in French. Academy 20 June 1903.
Minckwitz, M. J. Einige Beziehungen der englischen Dichterin E. Barrett-Browning zu Frankreich, insbesondere zur französischen Literatur. Zeitschrift für Französische Sprache und Literatur 30 1906.
Schmidt, K. Brownings Verhältnis zu Frankreich. Berlin 1909.
Hooreman, L. Promenades romaines: la rencontre inopinée de Stendhal et de Browning. Stendhal-Club 6 1964. On Ring and the book.

Burns, Robert

Angellier, A. Burns. Paris 1893.
Power, W. Burns's French interpreter. In Cahier Angellier, Paris 1927. On Angellier and Burns.
Sells, A. L. Leconte de Lisle and Burns. In Studies presented to R. L. Graeme Ritchie, Cambridge 1949.
Ross Roy, G. French translations of Burns. Revue de Littérature Comparée 37 1963.
Ross Roy, G. French critics of Burns. Revue de Littérature Comparée 38 1964.
Souffrin, E. Burns en France: ou l'image du poète laboureur. In Connaissance de l'étranger: mélanges offerts à la mémoire de J-M Carré, 1964.

Byron, George Gordon. *See also under Chateaubriand, Dumas père, Rousseau and G. Sand, cols 108, 110, 115 above.*

Vigny, A. de. Œuvres de Byron. Conservateur Littéraire 3 1820.
Hugo, V. Byron et ses rapports avec la littérature actuelle. Annales Romantiques 1827–8.
Pichot, A. Essai sur la vie, le caractère et le génie de Byron. 1830.
Guiccioli, T. Byron jugé par les témoins de sa vie. 1868; My recollections of Lord Byron and those of the eye-witnesses of his life, tr H. Jerningham 2 vols 1869.
[Cléron, L. de]. Les dernières années de Byron, par l'auteur de Robert Emmet. 1874.
Clark, W. J. Byron und die romantische Poesie in Frankreich. Leipzig 1901.
Estève, E. Byron et le romantisme français. 1907, 1929.
Estève, E. Le Byronisme de Leconte de Lisle. Revue de Littérature Comparée 5 1925.
Dargan, E. P. Byron's fame in France. Virginia Quart 2 1926.
Blanck, A. Floires et Blanceflor et l'épisode de Haïfée dans le Don Juan de Byron. In Mélanges Baldensperger vol 1, 1930.
Baker, A. T. Notes on Byron and Hugo. French Quart 14 1932.
Eggert, G. Byron and Napoleon. Leipzig 1933.
Straumann, H. Byron and Switzerland. Nottingham 1949.
Vandegans, A. Anatole France et Byron avant 1873. Revue de Littérature Comparée 23 1949.
Lowell, E. J. Byron and La nouvelle Héloïse: two parallel paradoxes. MLN 66 1951.
Mortier, R. La réaction d'un critique classique devant Byron. Revue des Langues Vivantes 17 1951.
Escarpit, R. Byron: un tempérament littéraire. 2 vols 1955–7. With comprehensive bibliography.
Escarpit, R. La traduction de Byron en français. Cahiers de l'Association Internationale des Etudes Françaises June 1956.
Souffrin, E. Le Byronisme de Banville. Revue de Littérature Comparée 37 1963.
Moçet, C. Lord Byron et George Sand: Le Corsaire, Lara et L'Usoque. In George Sand: collected essays, ed J. Glasgow, New York 1985.
Chotard, L. A propos du byronisme de Musset: la réception de Lord Byron a l'Académie Française. Revue de Littérature Comparée 64 1990.

Carlyle, Thomas. *See also under Baudelaire, Maeterlinck and Saint-Simon, cols 107, 112, 115 above.*

Voltaire. Foreign Rev 3 1829.
Diderot. Foreign Quart Rev 11 1833.
The French Revolution. 3 vols 1837.
▽
Taine, H. L'idéalisme anglais: étude sur Carlyle. 1864.
Taylor, A. C. Carlyle: sa première fortune littéraire en France 1825–65. 1929.

Coleridge, S. T.

Reed, A. Romantic metereology. The climates of Coleridge and Baudelaire. Hanover NH 1983.
Vlasopolos, A. The symbolic method of Coleridge, Baudelaire and Yeats. Detroit 1983.

De Quincey, Thomas. *See also under Balzac, Baudelaire and Musset, cols 105, 107, 114 above.*

Confessions of an English opium eater. 1822; L'anglais mangeur d'opium, tr A. de Musset 1828; Les paradis artificiels, tr C. Baudelaire 1860.
▽
Littlefield, W. Musset and the English opium eater. Bookman (New York) July 1902.
Clapton, G. T. Baudelaire et De Quincey. 1931.
Hughes, R. Vers la contrée de rêve: Balzac, Gautier et Baudelaire disciples de Quincey. Mercure de France 1 Aug 1939.
Dimof, P. Autour d'un projet de roman de Flaubert: La spirale. Revue d'Histoire Littéraire de la France 48 1948.

Dickens, Charles. *See also under Daudet, col 109 above.*

A tale of two cities. 1859.
▽
Delattre, F. Dickens et la France. 1927.
Atkins, S. P. A possible Dickens influence in Zola. MLQ 8 1947.
Flibbert, J. T. Dickens and the French. Debate over realism. Comparative Lit 23 1971.
Cupers, J.-L. Présence de la musique chez Dickens et Daudet: Le mystère d'Edwin Drood et La Petite Paroisse. Revue de Littérature Comparée 61 1987.

Eliot, George. *See also under Flaubert, col 110 above.*

Sealy, R. J. Brunetière, Montégut and George Eliot. MLR 66 1971.
Smalley, B. George Eliot and Flaubert: Pioneers of the modern novel. Athens OH 1974.
Durey, J. F. Intermodality in the novels of George Eliot, Leo Tolstoy and Gustave Flaubert. Revue de Littérature Comparée 66 1992.

Hardy, Thomas
The dynasts. 3 pts 1904–8.
▽
Cassidy, J. A. The original source of Hardy's Dynasts. PMLA 69 1954. On Hardy, Buchanan and Hugo.
Starr, W. Romain Rolland and Hardy. MLQ 17 1956.

Hazlitt, William. *See also under Hugo, Michelet, Stendhal and Vigny, cols 111, 114, 117, 120 above.*
Characteristics, in the manner of Rochefoucauld's Maxims. 1823.
Notes of journey through France and Italy. 1826.
The life of Napoleon Buonaparte. 4 vols 1830.
▽
Dechamps, J. Hazlitt et Napoléon. Revue des Etudes Napoléoniennes 45 1939.
Cohen, B. B. Hazlitt: Bonapartist critic of the Excursion. MLQ 10 1949.
Kempton, A. A painter's eye and a poet's perception: reflections on the art criticism of Hazlitt and Baudelaire. Franco British Stud 15 1993.

James, Henry. *See also under Balzac, Baudelaire and Flaubert, cols 106, 107, 110 above.*
The American. Boston 1877.
Madame de Mauves. 1879.
Portraits of places. 1883.
The reverberator. 1888.
The tragic muse. 1890.
Parisian sketches. 1898.
The ambassadors. 1903.
▽
Garnier, M.-R. James et la France. 1927.
Cestre, C. La France dans l'œuvre de James. Revue Anglo-américaine 10 1932.
Fay, E. G. James as a critic of French literature. French American Rev 2 1949.
McFarlane, I. D. A literary friendship: James and Bourget. Cambridge Jnl Oct 1950.
Fay, E. G. Balzac and James. French Rev Feb 1951.
Niess, R. J. James and Zola: a parallel. Revue de Littérature Comparée 30 1956.
Cargill, O. The first international novel. PMLA 73 1958. On James and Dumas.
Wegelin, C. The image of Europe in James. Dallas 1958.
Powers, L. H. James and Zola's roman expérimental. UTQ 30 1960.
Adams, P. G. James and his master Balzac. Revue de Littérature Comparée 35 1961. With a bibliography.
Dove, J. R. The alienated hero in Le rouge et le noir and the Princess Casamassima. In Studies in comparative literature, ed W. F. McNeir, Baton Rouge 1962.
Willett, M. Henry James' indebtedness to Balzac. Revue de Littérature Comparée 41 1967.
Frank, F. S. The two Taines of Henry James. Revue de Littérature Comparée 45 1971.
Grover, P. R. French literature and James's early criticism 1864–74. Forum of Mod Lang Stud 10 1974.
Gervais, D. James's reading of Madame Bovary. Cambridge Quart 7 1976.
Field, M. Nervous Anglo-Saxon apprehensions: Henry James and the French. French American Rev 5 1981.
Collister, P. A legendary hue: Henri Regnault and the fiction of Henry James and Mrs Humphrey Ward. Modern Language Review 87 (1992).

Keats, J.
Cohn, R. G. Keats and Mallarmé. Comparative Literary Stud 7 1970.

Bulwer Lytton, Edward
Richelieu. 1839.
The lady of Lyons. 1839.
Zanoni. vol 3 1842.
▽
Qualia, C. B. French dramatic sources of Lytton's Richelieu. PMLA 42 1927.

Meredith, George
Up to midnight. Graphic, London 1873; Boston 1913.
Beauchamp's career. 1874.
One of our conquerors. 1891.
Odes in contribution to the song of French history. 1898.
▽
Mackay, M. E. Meredith et la France. 1937.

Mill, John Stuart. *See also under Comte, Saint-Simon, Taine and Zola, cols 108, 115, 118, 119 above.*
Letters on the French Revolution of 1830. Ed F. E. Mineka, VS 1 1957.
Examiner. 1830–4. Various contributions on France by Mill.
Correspondance inédite avec Gustave d'Eichtal [the Saint-Simonian]. Ed E. d'Eichtal 1898.
Letters to Tocqueville. TLS 1–15 Sep 1950.
▽
Littré, E. Comte et Mill. Revue des Deux Mondes 15 Aug 1866.
Whittaker, T. Comte and Mill. 1908.
Mueller, I. Mill and French thought. Urbana 1956.

Moore, George. *See also under Baudelaire, Flaubert, Goncourt Frères and Zola, cols 107, 110, 111, 119 above.*
A modern lover. 1883.
Confessions of a young man. 1888.
▽
Jean-Aubry, G. Zola et George Moore. Nouvelles Littéraires 17 Jan 1925.
Chaikin, M. Balzac, Zola and Moore's A drama in muslin. Revue de Littérature Comparée 29 1955.
Chaikin, M. The composition of Moore's A modern lover. Comparative Lit 7 1955.
Chaikin, M. Moore's A mummer's wife and Zola. Revue de Littérature Comparée 31 1957.
Collet, G.-P. Moore et la France. Geneva 1957.
Noël, J. Moore et Mallarmé. Revue de Littérature Comparée 32 1958.
Brown, C. S. Balzac as a source of Moore's Sister Teresa. Comparative Lit 11 1959.
Furst, L. R. George Moore et Zola: une réevaluation. Cahiers Naturalistes 41 1971.
Seibert, M. A. George Moore and Paul Alexis: un cas de plagiat. Cultura Neolatina 62 1988.

Moore, Thomas
Baldensperger, F. Moore et Vigny. MLR 1 1906.
Thomas, A. B. Moore en France: la fortune des oeuvres de Moore dans la littérature française 1819–30. 1911.

Pater, Walter. *See also under Baudelaire, col 107 above.*
Renaissance Studies. 1873.
Imaginery portraits. 1887.
Gaston de Latour. 1889.
▽
Beyer, A. Paters Beziehungen zur französischen Literatur und Kultur. Halle 1931.
Rosenblatt, L. M. Marius l'épicurien de Pater et ses points de départ français. Revue de Littérature Comparée 15 1935. On Pater, Renan and J. Lemaître's Sérénus.
Rosenblatt, L. M. The genesis of Pater's Marius the Epicurean. Comparative Lit 14 1962.
Takeda, K. Romanticism by Pater and French literature in the romantic period. Hikaku Bungaku 1962.

Ruskin, John
Milsand, J. L'esthétique anglaise: étude sur Ruskin. 1864.
Audra, E. L'influence de Ruskin en France. Revue des Cours et Conférences Jan 1926.

Souza, S. de. L'influence de Ruskin sur Proust. Montpellier 1932.
Bisson, L. A. Proust and Ruskin reconsidered in the light of the Lettres à une amie. MLR 39 1944.
Delattre, F. Ruskin et Bergson. Oxford 1947.
Autret, J. L'influence de Ruskin sur Proust. Geneva 1955.
Carballo, J. R. Proust y la Biblia de Amiens. Insula Oct 1957.
Kolb, P. Proust et Ruskin: nouvelles perspectives. Cahiers de l'Association Internationale des Etudes Françaises 12 1960.
Autret, J. Ruskin and the French before Proust. Geneva 1965.

Scott, Walter. *See also under Balzac and Dumas père, cols 106, 110 above.*
Maigron, L. Le roman historique à l'époque romantique: essai sur l'influence de Scott. 1898.
François, E. Scott and Vigny. MLN 21 1906. On Quentin Durward and Cinq-Mars.
Devonshire, J. M. The 'decline' of Scott in France. French Quart 1 1919.
Garnand, H. J. The influence of Scott on the works of Balzac. New York 1926.
Smith, M. E. Une anglaise intellectuelle en France sous la Restauration: Mary Clarke. 1927.
Harland, R. W. Scott et le roman 'frénétique': leur fortune en France. 1928.
Lacroix, P. Soirées de Scott à Paris. 1929.
Dargan, E. P. Scott and the French romantics. PMLA 49 1934. With list of trns into French.
Genévrier, P. Scott, historien français. Tours 1935. On French material in Quentin Durward.
Cook, D. The Waverleys in French: Scott's authorship revealed in 1822. TLS 17 July 1937.
Latham, E. Dumas and Scott. In Notes et documents littéraires, Mercure de France 1 Jan 1938.
Sells, A. L. Leconte de Lisle and Scott. French Stud 1 1947.
Green, F. C. Scott's French correspondence. MLR 52 1957.
Rinsler, N. Nerval and Scott's Antiquary. Revue de Littérature Comparée 34 1960.
Haggis, D. R. Scott, Balzac and the historical novel as social and political analysis: Waverley and Les Chouans. MLR 68 1972.

Shelley, Percy Bysshe. *See also under Comte and Volney, cols 108, 119 above.*
de Nolva, R. Shelley et Lamartine. Nouvelle Revue d'Italie 25 Nov 1922.
Meyer, H. Rousseau und Shelley. Würzburg 1934.
Peyre, H. Shelley et la France: lyrisme anglais et lyrisme français au XIXe siècle. Cairo 1935. With full list of Shelley criticism in French.
Amiyakumar Sen. Shelley and the French Revolution. In his Studies in Shelley, Calcutta 1936.
Kapstein, I. J. Shelley and Cabanis. PMLA 52 1937.
Lebois, A. L'influence de Shelley sur Elémir Bourges. Revue de Littérature Comparée 22 1948.

Stevenson, Robert Louis. *See also under Hugo, col 111 above.*
An inland voyage. 1878.
Travels with a donkey in the Cévennes. 1879.
The treasure of a Franchard. In his Merry men and other tales and fables, 1887.
The wrecker. 1892.
▽
Saroléa, C. Stevenson et la France. Edinburgh [1893].
Carré, J.-M. Stevenson et la France. In Mélanges Baldensperger, vol 1 1930.
Fabre, F. Stevenson dans le Velay. Revue d'Auvergne 48 1932. With letters.
Maclean, C. La France dans l'œuvre de Stevenson. 1936.
Haggis, D. R. Light from R. L. Stevenson on a passage in Flaubert. N & Q 223 1978.

Swinburne, Algernon Charles. *See also under Baudelaire and Hugo, cols 107, 111 above.*
Chastelard. 1865.
Ode to France. 1870.
On the proclamation of the French Republic. In his Songs of two nations, 1875.
Poems and ballads: second series. 1878.
Rondeaux parisiens. 1917.
▽
Reul, P. de. Swinburne et la France: essai de littérature comparée. Brussels 1904.
Richter, L. Swinburnes Verhältnis zu Frankreich und Italien. Leipzig 1911.
Delattre, F. Swinburne et la France. Revue des Cours et Conférences 28 Feb 1926.
Delattre, F. Baudelaire et le jeune Swinburne 1861–7. In Mélanges Baldensperger, vol 1 1930.
Nicolson, H. Swinburne and Baudelaire. Oxford 1931.
Fontainas, A. Swinburne et les symbolistes. Yggdrasill 25 Apr 1937.
Souffrin, E. Swinburne et Les misérables. Revue de Littérature Comparée 34 1960.
Maxwell, C. Swinburne, Gautier and the Louvre hermaphrodite. N & Q 238 1993.

Symons, Arthur. *See also under Baudelaire, Mallarmé and Verlaine, cols 107, 113, 118 above.*
Poems. 1898.
The symbolist movement in literature. 1899.
Colour studies in Paris. 1918.
▽
Lhombreaud, R. Symons. 1963.
Leyris, P. Pour Arthur Symons. Mercure de France Jan 1964.

Tennyson, Alfred. *See also under Hugo and Mallarmé, cols 111, 113 above.*
Dejob, C. Les pauvres gens de Victor Hugo et Enoch Arden de Tennyson. Revue des Cours et Conférences 8 1900.
Bowden, M. Tennyson in France. Manchester 1930.
Pitollet, C. Les fleurs de James et celles de Tennyson. Revue de l'Enseignement des Langues Vivantes 56 1939.

Thackeray, William Makepeace. *See also under Balzac, col 106 above.*
The Paris sketch book. 2 vols 1840.
The history of the next French revolution. Punch Mar–Apr 1844.
▽
Walter, E. Entstehungsgeschichte von Thackerays Vanity fair. Palaestra 79 1908.
Donnelly, J. Stendhal and Thackeray: the source of Henry Esmond. Revue de Littérature Comparée 39 1965.

Wilde, Oscar.
Clive, H. P. Oscar Wilde's first meeting with Mallarmé. French Stud 24 1970.

Williams, Helen Maria
Sketches of the state of manners and opinions in the French republic towards the close of the eighteenth century. 1801.
The political and confidential correspondence of Louis XVI. 1803.
A narrative of events which have taken place in France from the landing of Napoleon Bonaparte till the restoration of Louis XVIII. 1815.
On the late persecution of protestants in the south of France. 1816.
Letters on events which have passed in France since the restoration in 1815. 1819.
▽
Woodward, L. D. Une anglaise amie de la révolution française: Hélène Maria Williams et ses amies. 1930.
Adams, M. R. Helen Maria Williams and the French Revolution. Wordsworth and Coleridge Stud in honour of G. M. Harper. 1939.

Wordsworth, William
Texte, J. Wordsworth et la poésie lakiste en France. In his Etudes de littérature européenne, 1898.

Wright, H. G. The reflection of Wordsworth's personality in his choice of French writers. MLR 42 1947.

Todd, F. M. Wordsworth, Helen Maria Williams et la France. MLR 43 1948. [PEB]

(4) GERMAN

Bibliographies

Morgan, B. Q. A critical bibliography of German literature in English translation 1481–1927. Madison WI 1922, New York 1965 (rev and enlarged).

Anglo-German literary bibliography 1933–70. Annually in JEGP 1935–71.

Schlösser, A. Die englische Literatur in Deutschland von 1895 bis 1934. Jena 1937.

Smith, A. H. and A. T. Hatto. A list of English, Scandinavian and German theses in the University of London. 1939.

Morgan, B. Q. and A. R. Hohlfeld (ed). German literature in British magazines 1750–1860. Madison WI 1949.

Price, L. M. English literature in Germany. Univ of Cal Pbns in Modern Philology 37 1953. On English literature in Germany from 16th century, with bibliography. *See also German trn* Price, Die Aufnahme englischer Literatur *under General Studies below for bibliography updated to 1960.*

Mönnig, R. Übersetzungen aus der deutschen Sprache 1948–64; no L, Deutschland und die Deutschen im englischsprachigen Schrifttum. Göttingen 1957– . 2nd rev edn as Translations from the German: English 1948–64, Göttingen 1968.

Goedeke, K. Grundriss zur Geschichte der deutschen Dichtung. Vol 4, 3rd rev edn, pts 1–4, Dresden 1910–16; pt 5, Berlin 1960. *See also* 2nd rev edn, vols 1–13, Düsseldorf and Dresden 1884–1953; vols 14–17 Berlin 1959–91, continuing; *also* Goedekes Grundriss zur Geschichte der deutschen Dichtung. Neue Folge. Fortführung von 1830 bis 1880. Vol 1, Berlin 1962; *and* Rambaldo, H. Index zu Goedeke. Nendeln 1975.

Smith, M. F. A selected bibliography of German literature in English translation 1956–1960. Metuchen NJ 1972. A second suppl to B. Q. Morgan *above*.

O'Neill, P. German literature in English translation: a select bibliography. Toronto 1981.

See also Oppel, Englisch-deutsche Literaturbeziehungen *under General studies below; and the annual* Bibliographie der deutschen Sprach- und Literaturwissenschaft: section IV, Beziehungen einzelner Völker (Regionen) zur deutschen Literatur; *and the annual bibliography in* Germanistik: section XVIII, Deutsche Literatur und angelsächsische Literaturen.

General studies

The Anti-Jacobin Review and Magazine. [Ed J. Gifford] 1798–1821.

Goede, C. A. G. A foreigner's opinion of England. 1802.

Holcroft, T. Memoirs. 1816.

Carlyle, T. State of German literature. Edinburgh Rev 46 1827.

Taylor, W. Historic survey of German poetry. 3 vols 1828–30. *See also* Carlyle's review in Edinburgh Rev 50 1831.

Carlyle, T. German playwrights. Foreign Rev 3 1829.

Carlyle, T. Richter's review of Madame de Staël's De l'Allemagne. Fraser's Mag Feb, May 1830.

Carlyle, T. German literature of the fourteenth and fifteenth centuries. Foreign Quart Rev 8 1831.

Carlyle, T. The Nibelungenlied. Westminster Rev 15 1831.

Carlyle, T. Lectures on German literature [May 1837]. Not pbd; *see* Spectator 6 May 1837 for concise report.

Mann, H. Report of an educational tour in Germany and parts of Great Britain and Ireland. 1846.

Gillies, R. P. Memoirs of a literary veteran. 1851.

'Eliot, George' (M. A. Evans). Three months in Weimar. 1855.

Carlyle, T. The history of Friedrich II of Prussia, called Frederick the Great. 6 vols 1858–65.

Lewes, G. H. Realism in art: recent German fiction. Westminster Rev 70 1858.

Mackay, R. W. The Tübingen school and its antecedents. 1863.

Deutsche Dichtungen in englischen Übersetzungen. Grenzboten 28 1869.

Henkel, W. The German influence on the poetry of England and America in the course of the 19th century. Eschwege 1869.

Eitner, K. Ein Engländer über deutsches Geistesleben im ersten Drittel dieses Jahrhunderts. Weimar 1871.

Arnold, M. Higher schools and universities in Germany. 1874.

Payne, J. Pestalozzi: influence of elementary education. 1875.

Payne, J. Froebel and the Kindergarten. 1876.

Payne, J. A visit to German schools. 1876.

Weddigen, F. H. O. Vermittler des deutschen Geistes in England und Nordamerika. Archiv 59 1878.

Weddigen, F. H. O. Geschichte der Einwirkungen der deutschen Literatur auf die Literaturen der übrigen europäischen Kulturvölker der Neuzeit. Leipzig 1882.

Paulsen, F. Die deutschen Universitäten. Berlin 1893; tr E. D. Perry, New York 1895; tr F. Tilly and W. W. Elwang 1906.

Herzfeld, G. William Taylor von Norwich: eine Studie über den Einfluss der neueren deutschen Litteratur in England. Halle 1897.

Stephen, L. The importance of German. In his Studies of a biographer, vol 2 1898.

Bradley, A. C. English poetry and German philosophy in the age of Wordsworth. Manchester 1900; rptd in his A miscellany, 1929.

Margraf, E. Der Einfluss der deutschen Literatur auf die englische am Ende des 18 und im ersten Drittel des 19 Jahrhunderts. Leipzig 1901.

Zeiger, T. Beiträge zur Geschichte des Einflusses der neueren deutschen Literatur auf die englische. Leipzig 1901.

Batt, M. Contributions to the history of English opinion of German literature. 1: Gillies and the Foreign Quarterly Review; 2: Gillies and Blackwood's Magazine. MLN 17–18 1902–3.

Herzfeld, G. Zur Geschichte der deutschen Literatur in England. Archiv 110 1903.

Eichler, A. John Hookham Frere. Vienna 1905.

Jaeck, E. G. Madame de Staël and the spread of German literature. New York 1915.

Whyte, J. Young Germany in its relations to Britain. New York 1917.

Sigmann, L. Die englische Literatur von 1800–50 im Urteil der zeitgenössischen deutschen Kritik. Heidelberg 1918.

Price, L. M. English–German literary influences: bibliography and survey. Univ of Cal Pbns in Modern Philology 9 1919–20.

Waddington, M. M. The development of British thought from 1820 to 1890 with special reference to German influences. Toronto 1919.

Block, M. The British and Foreign Review or European Quarterly Journal: ein Beitrag zur Geschichte der Aufnahme deutscher Literatur in England. Zurich 1921.

Egan, R. F. The genesis of the theory of 'art for art's sake' in Germany and in England. 2 vols Northampton MA 1921–4.

Schwaninger, C. Die Verdienste der Edinburgh Review um die Verbreitung deutscher Literatur in England 1802–29. Zurich 1921.

Ziehen, E. Philhelvetism. Die Neueren Sprachen Apr 1925.

Ernst, F. La tradition médiatrice de la Suisse aux xviiie et xixe siècles. Revue de Littérature Comparée 6 1926.

Purdie, E. German influence on the literary ballad in England during the Romantic revival. Pbns of Eng Goethe Soc n.s. 3 1926.

Stokoe, F. W. German influence in the English Romantic period 1788–1818, with special reference to Scott, Coleridge, Shelley and Byron. Cambridge 1926.

Schirmer, G. Die Schweiz im Spiegel englischer und amerikanischer Literatur bis 1848. Zurich 1929.
Stockley, V. German literature as known in England 1750–1830. 1929.
Engel, C. E. Byron et Shelley en Suisse et en Savoie (1816). Chambéry 1930.
Wellek, R. Immanuel Kant in England. Princeton 1931.
Price, L. M. The reception of English literature in Germany. Berkeley 1932.
Wenzel, P. Germany and the Germans as seen by English novelists of the 19th and 20th centuries. Bielefeld 1932.
Kornder, T. Der Deutsche im Spiegelbild der englischen Erzählungsliteratur des 19 Jahrhunderts. Erlangen 1934.
Willoughby, L. A. On some German affinities with the Oxford Movement. MLR 29 1934.
Carr, C. T. German grammars in England in the nineteenth century. MLR 30 1935.
Hathaway, L. German literature of the mid-nineteenth century in England and America as reflected in the journals of 1840–1914. Boston 1935.
Weber, C. A. Bristols Bedeutung für die englische Romantik und die deutsch-englischen Beziehungen. Halle 1935.
Stiven, A. B. Englands Einfluss auf den deutschen Wortschatz. Zeulenroda 1936.
Eastlake, A. E. The influence of English literature on the German novel and drama in the period from 1880 to 1900. 1937.
Frehn, P. Der Einfluss der englischen Literatur auf Deutschlands Musiker und Musik im 19 Jahrhundert. Düsseldorf 1937.
Funke, O. Die Schweiz und die englische Literatur. Berne 1937.
Weineck, K. Deutschland und der Deutsche im Spiegel der englischen erzählenden Literatur seit 1830. Halle 1938.
Schultz, F. Der Deutsche in der englischen Literatur vom Beginn der Romantik bis zum Ausbruch des Weltkrieges. Halle 1939.
Wagner, A. Goethe, Carlyle, Nietzsche and the German middle class. Monatshefte für Deutschen Unterricht 31 1939.
Taube, E. German influence on the English vocabulary in the nineteenth century. JEGP 39 1940.
Barzun, J. Darwin, Marx, Wagner: critique of a heritage. Boston 1941, 1958 (rev).
Metz, R. England und die deutsche Philosophie. Stuttgart 1941.
König, E. G. Ruskin und die Schweiz. Berne 1943.
Macphail, J. H. Blake and Switzerland. MLR 38 1943.
Atkins, S. Sir Herbert Croft and German literature. MLQ 5 1944.
Hewett-Thayer, H. W. Ferdinand Lassalle in the novels of Spielhagen and Meredith. Germanic Rev 19 1944.
Wildi, M. Der angelsächsische Roman und der Schweizer-Leser. Zurich 1944.
Hennig, J. Malvida von Meysenbug and England. Comparative Literary Stud 23–4 1946.
Lunn, A. Switzerland in English prose and poetry. 1947.
Schirmer, W. F. Der Einfluss der deutschen Literatur auf die englische im 19. Jahrhundert. Halle 1947.
Hennig, J. Irish–German literary relations: a survey. German Life & Letters 3 1950.
Schindler, J. Das Bild des Engländers in der Kunst-und Volksliteratur der deutschen Schweiz 1798–1848. Zurich 1950.
Graf, E. Die Aufnahme der englischen und amerikanischen Literatur in der deutschen Schweiz 1800–30. Zurich 1951.
Charles, R. A. French intermediaries in the transmission of German literature and culture to England 1750–1815. Unpbd diss, Pennsylvania State Univ 1952.
Löhrer, H. Die Schweiz im Spiegel englischer Literatur 1849–75. Zurich 1952.
Price, L. M. English literature in Germany. Berkeley 1953.
Steffen, W. Die Schweiz im Spiegel englischer Literatur 1875–1900. Zurich 1953.
Strout, A. L. Writers on German literature in Blackwood's Magazine. Library 9 1954.
Crispin, R. L. The currency and reception of German short prose fiction in England and America as reflected in the periodicals, 1790–1840. Unpbd diss, Pennsylvania State Univ 1955.
Hennig, J. Ireland's place in nineteenth-century German poetry. German Life & Letters 8 1955.
Koziol, H. Die Aufnahme deutscher Literaturwerke in England. Anglia 73 1955–6.
Oppel, H. Englische und deutsche Romantik: Gemeinsamkeiten und Unterschiede. Die Neueren Sprachen n.s. 5 1956.
Andrews, J. S. A few intermediaries of German literature in nineteenth-century Britain. N & Q 202 1957.
Shelley, P. A., A. O. Lewis jr and W. W. Betts jr (ed). Anglo-German and American-German crosscurrents. Chapel Hill NC 1957.
Forster, L. England und die deutsche Literatur. Deutsche Akademie für Sprache und Dichtung (Darmstadt) Jahrbuch 1958.
Haas, R. Übersetzungsprobleme im Feld deutsch-englischer Literaturbegegnung. Die Neueren Sprachen n. s. 7 1958.
Dockhorn, K. Der deutsche Historismus in England: ein Beitrag zur englischen Geistesgeschichte im 19. Jahrhundert. Göttingen and Baltimore 1959.
Mason, E. C. Deutsche und englische Romantik: eine Gegenüberstelling. Göttingen 1959.
Hofmann, C. Die Anglistik-Amerikanistik in der Deutschen Demokratischen Republik. Zeitschrift für Anglistik und Amerikanistik (East Berlin) 8 1960.
Hietsch, O. (ed). Österreich und die angelsächsische Welt. Vienna 1961.
Price, L. M. Die Aufnahme englischer Literatur in Deutschland 1500–1960. Berne and Munich 1961.
Siegmund-Schultze, D. Zur englandkundigen Literatur in Deutschland. Zeitschrift für Anglistik und Amerikanistik (East Berlin) 9 1961.
Straumann, H. Switzerland and the English-speaking world. In English studies today, ed G. A. Bonnard, Berne 1961.
Keiser, R. Die Aufnahme englischen Schrifttums in der Schweiz von 1830–60. Zurich 1962.
Oppel, H. Der Einfluss der englischen Literatur auf die deutsche. In Deutsche Philologie im Aufriss vol 3, ed W. Stammler, Berlin 1962.
Shelley, P. A. and A. O. Lewis (ed). Anglo-German and American-German crosscurrents II. Chapel Hill NC 1962.
Voisine, J. La Littérature anglaise en Allemagne au cours des siècles. Etudes Germaniques 18 1963.
Wilkinson, E. M. The inexpressible and the un-speakable: some Romantic attitudes to art and language. German Life & Letters 16 1963.
Byrne, M. St Clare. Charles Kean and the Meininger myth. Theatre Research 6 1964.
Enright, D. J. Aimez-vous Goethe?: an enquiry into English attitudes of non-liking towards German literature. Encounter Apr 1964.
Gronbech, V. Religious currents in the nineteenth century. Lawrence KS 1964. Mainly on German and English literature.
McFarland, G. F. Julius Charles Hare, Coleridge, De Quincey and German Romanticism. BJRL 47 1964.
Milburn, D. L. German drama in England, 1750–1850, with a list of German plays published and performed. Unpbd diss, Rice Univ 1964.
Straumann, H. Matthew Arnold and the continental idea. In The English mind, ed H. S. Davies and G. Watson, Cambridge 1964.
Byrne, M. St Clare. What we said about the Meiningers in 1881. E & S n.s. 18 1965.
Gray, R. English resistance to German literature from Coleridge to D. H. Lawrence. In The German tradition in literature, 1831–1945, Cambridge 1965.

Mönke, W. Das literarische Echo in Deutschland auf Friedrich Engels Werk Die Lage der arbeitenden Klasse in England. East Berlin 1965.

Wellek, R. Confrontations: studies in the intellectual and literary relations between Germany, England, and the United States during the nineteenth century. Princeton 1965.

Blumenthal, L. Geisweiler und Weimar: zur Rezeption deutscher Dichter in England um 1800. Jahrbuch der Deutschen Schillergesellschaft 11 1967.

Hanson, K. The Tauchnitz collection of British and American authors between 1841 and 1900. Yearbook of Comparative and General Lit 16 1967.

Wyatt, S. W. The English romantic novel and Austrian reaction. New York 1967.

Furst, L. R. Romanticism in historical perspective: the chronology of the romantic movements in England, France and Germany. Comparative Literary Stud 5 1968.

Hietsch, O. (ed). Österreich und die angelsächsische Welt II. Vienna and Stuttgart 1968.

Oppel, H. Englische und deutsche Romantik: Gemeinsamkeiten und Unterschiede. In Versdichtung der englischen Romantik, ed T. A. Riese and D. Riesner, Berlin 1968.

Gillies, A. A Hebridean in Goethe's Weimar: the Rev James Macdonald and the cultural relations between Scotland and Germany. Oxford and New York 1969.

Mews, S. Foreign literature in German magazines, 1870–1890. Yearbook of Comparative and General Lit 18 1969.

Mews, S. Sensationalism and sentimentality: minor Victorian prose writers in Germany. MLN 84 1969.

Oppel, H. Englisch-deutsche Literaturbeziehungen II: von der Romantik bis zur Gegenwart. Berlin 1971.

Thomas, L. H. C. Germany, German literature and mid-nineteenth-century British novelists. In Affinities: essays in German and English literature, ed R. W. Last, 1971.

Dischner, G. Ursprünge der Rheinromantik in England. Frankfurt am Main 1972.

Gilman, S. L. Very little Faust . . . Parodies of German drama on the mid-19th-century British stage. Arcadia 8 1973.

Bruford, W. H. Some early Cambridge links with German scholarship and literature, part 1. In Trivium: Erfahrung und Überlieferung, Festschrift für C. P. Magill, ed H. Siefken and A. Robinson, Cardiff 1974; part 2 in German Life & Letters 28 1974–5.

Boening, J. (ed). The reception of classical German literature in England 1760–1860: a documentary history from contemporary periodicals. New York and London 1977.

Ashton, R. The German idea: four English writers and the reception of German thought, 1800–1860. Cambridge 1980.

McCobb, E. A. More words for the Germans: Anglo-German relations in the nineteenth century. German Life & Letters 34 1980–1.

Klieneberger, H. R. The novel in England and Germany: a comparative study. 1981.

Rault, A. Die Spanier in Peru oder die Deutschen in England: englisches und deutsches Theater 1790–1810. Wissentschaftliche Zeitschrift der Ernst Moritz Arndt Universität Greifswald 32 1983.

Gish, T. G. and S. G. Frieden (ed). Deutsche Romantik and English romanticism. Munich 1984.

Pipkin, J. (ed). English and German romanticism: cross-currents and controversies. Heidelberg 1985.

Ashton, R. Little Germany: exile and asylum in Victorian England. Oxford and New York 1986.

Burwick, F. The haunted eye: perception and the grotesque in English and German romanticism. Heidelberg 1987.

Howard, M. Image and counter-image: German literature in early 19th century British magazines. In Space and boundaries of literature, ed R. Bauer, Munich 1990.

Blaicher, G. Das Deutschland Bild in der englischen Literatur. Darmstadt 1992.

Byrn, R. F. M. and K. G. Knight. Anglo-German studies. Leeds 1992.

Bachleitner, M. Der englische und französische Sozialroman des 19 Jahrhunderts und seine Rezeption in Deutschland. Amsterdam 1993.

Gassenmeier, M, J. Gurr, K. Kamolz and F.-E. Poitner (ed). The literary reception of British romanticism on the European continent. Essen 1996.

Anthologies in translation

Thompson, B. German theatre. 1800–1. Includes trns of Lessing, Goethe, Schiller and Kotzebue.

Taylor, W. Tales of yore. 1810. Includes trns of Wieland's Danischmend and Alxinger's Bliomberis.

Carlyle, T. German romance: specimens of its chief authors [Fouqué, Goethe, Hoffmann, Musäus, Richter]. 1827.

Austin, S. Fragments from German prose writers. New York 1841.

Crossthwaite, G. F. Stories from the German. 1842.

Romantic fiction: Chamisso, Fouqué, Tieck. 1843. Anon.

Oxenford, J. and C. A. Feiling. Tales from the German. 1844.

Mangan, J. C. Anthologica germanica. Dublin 1845.

Baskerville, A. The poetry of Germany. Leipzig and New York 1853.

Winkworth, C. Lyra germanica. 2 vols 1855–8.

Dulcken, H. W. The book of German songs from the 16th to the 19th century. 1856.

Garnett, R. Poems from the German. 1862.

Hedley, F. H. Masterpieces of German poetry, translated in the measure of the original. 1876.

Zimmern, H. amd A. (ed). Half hours with foreign novelists. 1880, 1884 (rev). Includes works by Auerbach, Freytag, Hackländer, Heyse, Keller, Marlitt, Sacher-Masoch, Spielhagen, Stifter.

Müller-Casenov, H. The humour of Germany; with an introduction and bibliographical index. 1892.

Francke, K. and W. G. Howard (ed). German classics of the nineteenth and twentieth centuries. New York 1913–15.

German authors

For more detailed bibliographies of German writers in their relation to England, see K. Goedeke, and for trns B. Q. Morgan, under Bibliographies above.

Arnim, Achim von (1781–1831)

Howie, M. D. Arnim and Scotland. MLR 17 1922.

Holt, R. F. Arnim and Sir Walter Scott. German Life & Letters 26 1973.

Büchner, Georg (1813–37)

Majut, R. Über literarische Beziehungen Büchners zu England. In Georg Büchner, ed W. Martens, Darmstadt 1965.

Keith-Smith, B. and K. Mills (ed). Büchner in Britain. Bristol 1987.

Droste-Hülshoff, Annette Freiin von (1797–1848)

Badt, B. Annette von Droste-Hülshoff, ihre dichterische Entwicklung und ihr Verhältnis zur englischen Literatur. Breslau 1909.

Nettenheim, J. Annette von Droste and die englische Romantik. Jahrbuch der Droste-Gesellschaft 1947.

Dees, H. Annette von Droste-Hülshoffs Dichtung in England und Amerika. Tübingen 1966.

Thomas, L. H. C. Die Judenbuche and English literature. MLR 64 1969.

Guthrie, J. Byron's influence on A. von Droste-Hülshoff's Lebt wohl. In Anglo-German studies, ed R. F. M. Byrn and K. G. Knight, Leeds 1992.

Eichendorff, Joseph Freiherr von (1788–1857)

Aus dem Leben eines Taugenichts. Berlin 1826; The happy-go-lucky, tr A. L. Wister 1889.

See Hanke, Spatiotemporal consciousness *under Novalis below.*

Feuerbach, Ludwig (1804–72)
Das Wesen des Christentums. Leipzig 1841; The essence of Christianity, tr 'George Eliot' 1854.
Fichte, Johann Gottlieb (1762–1814)
Sämmtliche Werke. 8 vols Berlin 1845–6.
Popular writings of Fichte, with a memoir. Tr W. Smith 2 vols 1848–9.
Fontane, Theodor (1819–98)
Wegmann, C. Fontane als Übersetzer englischer und schottischer Balladen. Münster 1910.
Rhyn, H. Die Balladendichtung Fontanes. Berne 1914.
Schoenemann, F. Fontane und England. PMLA 30 1915.
Shears, L. A. The influence of Walter Scott on the novels of Fontane. New York 1922.
Paul, A. Der Einfluss Scotts auf die epische Technik Fontanes. Breslau 1934.
Heynen, W. Vom Literaten Fontane in London. Preussische Jahrbücher 240 1936.
Stirk, S. D. England and the English in the letters of Fontane. Proc of the Leeds Philosophical Soc 4 1936.
Neuendorff, O. Fontanes Gang durch die englische Dichtung. Potsdam 1938.
Packer, W. A. Karl Stuart: a neglected phase in the development of Fontane's attitude toward England. Papers of the Michigan Acad of Science 38 1952.
Barlow, D. Fontane's English journeys. German Life & Letters 6 1953.
Andrews, J. S. The reception of Fontane in nineteenth-century Britain. MLR 52 1957.
Rowley, B. A. Fontane: a German novelist in the European tradition? German Life & Letters 15 1962.
Jolles, C. Zum Englandmotiv in Fontanes Erzählwerk. Fontane Blätter 1 1967.
Faucher, E. Fontane et Darwin. Etudies Germaniques 25 1970.
Jolles, C. Fontane und eine Episode aus Thackerays Vanity fair. Fontane Blätter 2 1970.
Turner, D. Fontane on Laurence Sterne. In Affinities, ed R. W. Last, 1971.
Jolles, C. Fontane's Studien über England. In Fontanes Realismus, ed H.-E. Teitge and J. Schobess, Berlin 1972.
Grieve, H. Fontane und Scott: die Waverley-Romane und Vor dem Sturm. Fontane Blätter 3 1974.
Eberhardt, W. Fontane und Thackeray. Heidelberg 1975.
See Klieneberger, The novel in England and Germany, *under General Studies above.*
Wittig Davis, G. A. Novel associations: Fontane and George Eliot within the context of nineteenth-century realism. New York 1983.
Bernd, C. A. Fontane's discovery of Britain. MLR 87 1992.
Chambers, H. Fontane's translation of The charge of the Light Brigade. In Anglo-German studies, ed R. F. M. Byrn and K. G. Knight, Hull 1992.
Sagarra, E. Fontane's Arabella Fitzpatrick, a mediator between Ireland and Germany? German Life & Letters 48 1995.
Fouqué, Friedrich Heinrich Karl, Baron de la Motte (1777–1843)
Undine. Berlin 1811; tr G. Soane 1818; tr T. Tracy 1841; tr E. Gosse 1896.
Aslaugas Ritter. Berlin 1813; Aslauga's knight, tr T. Carlyle 1827.
Sintram und seine Gefährten. Berlin 1814; Sintram and his companions, tr J. C. Hare 1820.
Numerous trns of these and other works by Fouqué throughout the century.
Freiligrath, Ferdinand (1810–76)
Weddigen, F. H. O. Freiligrath als Vermittler englischer und französischer Dichtung. Archiv 61 1879.
Roescher, F. A. Freiligraths Übersetzungen englischer Dichtungen. Giessen 1923.
Spink, G. W. Freiligrath als Verdeutscher der englischen Poesie. Berlin 1925.
Liddell, M. F. Freiligrath's debt to English poets. MLR 23 1928.
Spink, G. W. Freiligrath's Verbannungsjahre in London. Berlin 1932.
Freytag, Gustav (1816–95)
Soll und Haben. Leipzig 1854; Debtor and creditor, tr W. J. Stewart 1857; tr Malcolm 1858.
▽
Schwarz, O. Freytags Beziehungen zu Charles Dickens. Vienna 1911.
Freymond, R. Der Einfluss von Charles Dickens auf Freytag. Prager Deutsche Studien 19 1912.
Price, L. M. The attitude of Freytag and Julian Schmidt toward English literature (1848–1962). Hesperia (Göttingen) 7 1915.
Feilendorf, A. Walter Scotts Einfluss auf die historischen Romane Freytags. Vienna 1931.
Andrews, J. S. The impact on nineteenth-century Britain of Freytag's Soll und Haben. Proc of Leeds Philosophical Soc (Literary and Historical Section) 8 1959.
George, Stefan (1868–1933)
A selection from his works. Tr C. M. Scott 1910.
▽
Farrell, R. Georges Beziehungen zur englischen Dichtung. Berlin 1937.
Breugelmans, R. George und Oscar Wilde: a confrontation. Proc of Pacific Northwest Conference on Foreign Languages 15 1964.
Breugelmans, R. George and Oscar Wilde: part II of a confrontation – their aesthetic-religious views. Proc of Pacific Northwest Conference on Foreign Languages 17 1966.
Marx, O. George in seinen Übertragungen englischer Dichtung. Amsterdam 1969.
Goethe, Johann Wolfgang von (1749–1832)
For his influence in England, see J. M. Carré, Bibliographie de Goethe en Angleterre, Lyons 1920, *and* Goethe en Angleterre, Paris 1920; *and review by* A. E. Turner, MLR 16 1921; *also pbns of* Eng Goethe Soc 1886– .
Die Leiden des jungen Werthers. Leipzig 1774.
—
Long, O. W. English translations of Goethe's Werther. JEGP 14 1915.
Atkins, S. P. The testament of Werther in poetry and drama. Cambridge Mass 1949.
—
Wilhelm Meisters Lehrjahre. Berlin 1795–6.
Wilhelm Meisters Wanderjahre. Stuttgart 1829; William Meister's apprenticeship, tr T. Carlyle 1824.
—
Howe, S. Wilhelm Meister and his English kinsmen. New York 1930.
Gottbrath, K. Der Einfluss von Goethes Wilhelm Meister auf die englische Literatur. Munich 1937.
Hennig, J. Englandkunde im Wilhelm Meister. Goethe Jahrbuch 26 1964.
—
Faust. 2 pts Tübingen 1808–Stuttgart 1833.
The Urfaust *or original draft (1770–5) of the* First Part *was discovered by Erich Schmidt in 1887 in Dresden and pbd by him in the same year. There are 3 trns of the* Urfaust: (a) by R. McLintock, 1889 (unpbd ms); (b) by W. H. van der Smissen, *below;* (c) by D. M. Scott, *below. The first 35 English trns of* Faust *are discussed by L. Baumann, below. See also* B. Q. Morgan, Bibliography of German literature in English translation, *above. The following are the most noteworthy nineteenth-century English versions:*
Scenes from the Faust of Goethe. Tr P. B. Shelley [1822].
Faust pt 1. Tr A. Hayward 1833. Prose.
Faustus: a dramatic mystery. Tr J. Anster 2 pts 1835–64. A verse imitation.

Faust. Tr Anne Swanwick 2 pts 1849–78. Latest edn, with introd and bibliography by K. Breul, 1928. A popular verse trn.
Faust pt 1. Tr R. McLintock 1897. In original metres.

—

Carlyle, T. Faustus. New Edinburgh Rev 2 1822.
Carlyle, T. Goethe's Helena. Foreign Rev 1 1828.
Courtney, W. L. Faust on the English stage. Fortnightly Rev Jan 1886.
Heineman, W. Goethes Faust in England und Amerika: bibliographische Zusammenstellung. Berlin 1886.
McLintock, R. The five best English verse translations of Faust. Trans Manchester Goethe Soc 1894.
Tait, J. The literary influence of Goethe's Faust in England 1832–52. Trans Manchester Goethe Soc 1894.
Davidson, T. The philosophy of Goethe's Faust. Ed C. M. Bakewell, Boston 1906.
Baumann, L. Die englischen Übersetzungen von Goethes Faust. Halle 1907.
Robertson, J. G. Gillies and Goethe. MLR 4 1908.
Hauhart, W. F. The reception of Goethe's Faust in England in the first half of the nineteenth century. New York 1909.
Montgomery, M. The first English version of Faust part 1 and Dichtung und Wahrheit. Pbns of Eng Goethe Soc n.s. 3 1926.
Waterhouse, G. A unique translation of Goethe's Faust [Urfaust]. Discovery Sep 1927.
Nicholl, A. Faust on the English stage. In Das Buch des Goethe-Lessing Jahres, Brunswick 1929.
Bluhm, H. S. The reception of Goethe's Faust in England after the middle of the nineteenth century. JEGP 34 1935.
Metzger, L. Faust in England, 1800–1850. Unpbd diss, Columbia, Columbia Univ 1956.

—

Simmons, L. van T. Goethe's lyric poems in English translation prior to 1860. Madison WI 1918.
Fiedler, H. G. Goethe's lyric poems in English translation. MLR 18 1923.
Hinz, S. M. Goethe's lyric poems in English translation after 1860. Madison WI 1929.

—

Carlyle, T. Goethe. Foreign Rev 2 1828.
Carlyle, T. Goethe's works. Foreign Quart Rev 10 1832.
Carlyle, T. The death of Goethe. NM Mag 34 1832.

—

Müller, F. M. Goethe and Carlyle. Contemporary Rev June 1886.
Correspondence between Goethe and Carlyle. Ed C. E. Norton 1887.
Flügel, E. Der Briefwechsel zwischen Goethe und Carlyle. Grenzboten 46 1887.
Goethes und Carlyles Briefwechsel. Ed H. Oldenberg, Berlin 1887; ed G. Hecht, Dachau 1914.
Grimm, H. Goethe und Carlyle Briefwechsel. Deutsche Rundschau 4 1887.
Carr, M. Goethe in his connection with English literature. Pbns of Eng Goethe Soc 4 1890.
Boyesen, H. H. Goethe and Carlyle. In his Essays on German literature, 1892.
Carré, J. M. Goethe en Angleterre. Paris 1920.
Henriot, E. Goethe, Carlyle et Thackeray. L'Europe Nouvelle 15 Oct 1921.

—

Lewes, G. H. Life of Goethe. 1855.
Brandl, A. Die Aufnahme von Goethes Jugendwerken in England. Goethe-Jahrbuch 3 1882.
Brandl, A. Goethe und Byron. Österreiche Rundschau 1 1883.
Althaus, F. On the personal relations between Goethe and Byron. Pbns of Eng Goethe Soc 2 1888.
Hutton, R. H. Goethe and his influence. In his Literary essays, 1888.
Kaufmann, M. Goethe and modern thought. Scottish Rev no 18 1891.
Boyesen, H. H. The English estimate of Goethe. In his Essays on German literature, 1892.
Boyesen, H. H. Some English translations of Goethe. In his Essays on German literature, 1892.
Alford, R. G. Goethe's earliest critics in England. Pbns of Eng Goethe Soc 7 1893.
Mensch, R. A. J. Goethe and Wordsworth. Pbns of Eng Goethe Soc 7 1893.
Seely, J. M. Goethe reviewed after sixty years. 1894.
Sinzheimer, S. Goethe und Lord Byron: eine Darstellung der persönlichen und literarischen Verhältnisse mit Berücksichtigung des Faust und Manfred. Munich 1894.
Bernays, M. Beziehungen Goethes zu Walter Scott. Zur neueren Literaturgeschichte vol 1, Stuttgart 1895.
Brandl, A. Goethes Verhältnis zu Byron. Goethe-Jahrbuch 20 1899.
Heller, O. Goethe and Wordsworth. MLN 14 1899.
Oswald, E. Goethe in England and America: bibliography. Die Neueren Sprachen July 1899–1900; 1909 (separately).
Willoughby, L. A. An early English translation of Goethe's Tasso. MLR 9 1914.
Bode, W. Die Franzosen und Engländer in Goethes Leben und Urteil. Berlin 1915.
Lieder, F. W. C. Goethe in England and America. JEGP 16 1917.
Robertson, J. G. Goethe and Byron. Pbns of Eng Goethe Soc n.s. 2 1925.
Strich, F. Goethe und Byron. Die Horen 5 1929.
Norman, F. Goethe und das heutige England. Goethe-Jahrbuch 17 1931.
Bangs, A. R. Mephistophiles in England. PMLA 47 1932.
Böschenstein, H. Das literarische Goethebild der Gegenwart in England. Breslau 1932.
Boyd, J. Goethe's knowledge of English literature. Oxford 1932.
Brandl, A. Goethe und England. Fortschritte und Forschungen 31 1932.
Lovett, R. M. Goethe in English literature. Open Court Apr 1932.
Robertson, J. G. Goethe und England. Goethe-Jahrbuch 18 1932.
Vollrath, W. Goethe und Grossbritannien. Erlangen 1932.
Koch, J. Goethe und Byron. Archiv 88 1933.
Fairley, B. Goethe and Wordsworth. Pbns of Eng Goethe Soc n.s. 11 1934.
Henel, H. Ausländische Goethe-Kritik. Deutsche Vierteljahrsschrift für Literaturwissenschaft und Geistesgeschichte 12 1934.
Mennie, D. M. A note on Goethe as a translator of English prose (1830–2). MLR 30 1935.
Poeschel, C. and J. Rosenberg (ed). Goethe über England und die englische Literatur. Leipzig 1936.
Liljegren, S. B. The English source of Goethe's Gretchen tragedy. Lund 1937.
Hayens, K. C. Goethe and English letters. German Life & Letters 3 1939.
Strich, F. Goethe und die Weltliteratur. Berne 1946, 1957 (rev).
Vail, C. C. D. Shelley's translations from Goethe. Germanic Rev 23 1948.
Brie, F. Early English translations of Goethe's essays on Byron. MLR 44 1949.
Bruford, W. H. Goethe's reputation in England since 1832. In Essays on Goethe, ed W. Rose, 1949.
Bruford, W. H. Goethe and some Victorian humanists. Pbns of Eng Goethe Soc 18 1949.
Carré, J. M. L'Allemagne, la France et l'Angleterre en face de Goethe. Revue de Littérature Comparée 23 1949.
Lemke, V. J. English translations of some major works of Goethe. Virginia Univ Bull 6 1949.

Morgan, B. Q. Goethe in English. In Southwest Goethe Festival, ed J. Dallas, 1949.
Oppel, H. Wirkungen Goethes in England. Die lebenden Fremdsprachen 1 1949.
Robson-Scott, W. D. Goethe through English eyes. Contemporary Rev 176 1949.
Rose, W. Goethe's reputation in England during his lifetime. In Essays on Goethe, ed W. Rose, 1949.
Scott, D. F. S. Some English correspondents of Goethe. 1949.
Vail, C. C. D. Shelley's translations from Goethe's Faust. Symposium 3 1949.
Lewisohn, L. Goethe's poetry in the lands of English speech. In Goethe and the modern age, ed A. Bergstraesser, Chicago 1950.
Needler, G. H. Goethe and Scott. Toronto 1950.
Schneider, W. B. Goethe and English literature. In The Southern Illinois Goethe celebration, ed H. A. Hartwig, Carbondale IL 1950.
Spender, S. Goethe and the English mind. In Goethe and the modern age, ed A. Bergstraesser, Chicago 1950.
Hennig, J. The literary relations between Goethe and Thomas Hood. MLQ 12 1951.
Schirmer, W. F. Goethe und Byron: Forschungsprobleme der vergleichenden Literaturgeschichte. Tübingen 1951.
Wolff, E. B. On Goethe's reputation as a scientist in nineteenth-century England. German Life & Letters 6 1953.
Müller, J. Goethes Byrondenkmal. Zeitschrift für Anglistik und Amerikanistik 2 1954.
Willoughby, L. A. Goethe and the English language. German Life & Letters 10 1957.
Gray, R. D. Turner and Goethe's colour-theory. In his German studies presented to Walter H. Bruford, 1962.
Hennig, J. Goethes Schottlandkunde. Goethe-Jahrbuch 25 1963.
Hennig, J. Englandkunde im Wilhelm Meister. Goethe-Jahrbuch 26 1964.
Hennig, J. Goethe und die englisch-sprechende Welt. Goethe-Jahrbuch 28 1966.
Smith, C. J. Goethe's reaction to Byron as a poet and as a personality. Pbns of Eng Goethe Soc 36 1966.
Schier, R. D. The experience of the noumenal in Goethe and Wordsworth. Comparative Lit 25 1973.
Brown, J. K. Die Wahlverwandtschaften and the English novel of manners. Comparative Lit 28 1976.
Wesche, U. Goethe's Faust and Byron's Manfred: the curious transformation of a motif. Revue de Littérature Comparée 50 1976.
Phelps, L. R. Goethe's Faust and the young Shelley. In Wege der Worte: Festschrift für W. Fleischhauer, ed D. C. Riechel and C. W. Hoffmann, Bohlau 1978.
See Ashton, The German idea , *under General Studies above.*
DeLaura, D. J. Heroic egotism: Goethe and the fortunes of Bildung in Victorian England. In Goethe: one hundred and fifty years of continuing vitality, ed U. Goebel and W. T. Zyla, Lubbock TX 1984.
Creevy, P. The Victorian Goethe critics: notions of greatness and development. Victorian Institutes Jnl 13 1985.
Menhennet, A. Historical ambivalence in Goethe and Scott. New German Stud 13 1985.
Jeffers, T. Forms of misprision: the early and mid-Victorian reception of Goethe's Bildungsidee. UTQ 57 1988.
Zaumer, E. Goethe und die englische Literatur, pt 1. Moderne Sprachen 33 1989; pt 2 Moderne Sprachen 34 1990.
Stelzig, E. L. Memory, imagination and self-healing in the romantic crisis lyric: Trilogie der Leidenschaft and Resolution and independence. JEGP 90 1991.
Burwick, R. Goethe's Werther and Mary Shelley's Frankenstein. Wordsworth Circle 24 1993.

'Gotthelf, Jeremias' (Albert Bitzius) (1797–1854)

Uli der Knecht. Zurich 1841; Ulric the farm hand, tr J. Firth 1886, rev and ed J. Ruskin 1886.

▽

Waidson, H. M. Gotthelf's reception in Britain and America. MLR 43 1948. *See also his* Gotthelf: an introduction to the Swiss novelist, Oxford 1953.
Andrews, J. S. The reception of Gotthelf in British and American nineteenth-century periodicals. MLR 51 1956.
Parkinson, M. H. The rural novel: Gotthelf, Thomas Hardy, C. F. Ramuz. Berne 1984.

Grabbe, Christian Dietrich (1801–36)

Wiehr, J. The relations of Grabbe to Byron. JEGP 7 1908.

Grillparzer, Franz (1791–1872)

Sappho. Vienna 1818; tr J. Bramsen 1820; tr E. Frothingham, Boston 1876.
Medea. Vienna 1822; tr F. W. Thurstan and S. A. Wittman 1879.
König Ottokars Glück und Ende. Vienna 1825; Ottokar, tr T. Carlyle 1840 (selection).

Trns of Sappho, Der Traum ein Leben, *and* Weh'dem, der lügt, *were made by Archer Thompson Gurney before 1858, but never pbd.*

▽

Wyplel, L. Grillparzer und Byron. Euphorin 9–10 1902–3.
Fiedler, H. G. Notes on Meredith on Grillparzer's Ahnfrau. MLR 26 1931.
Morris, I. V. Grillparzer's impressions of the English. German Life & Letters 14 1960.
Burkhard, A. Grillparzer in England und Amerika. Vienna 1961.
Burkhard, A. Grillparzer in English translation. In Österreich und die angelsächsische Welt, ed O. Hietsch, Vienna 1961.
Kuhnelt, H. H. Grillparzer entdeckt England: englische Germanisten entdecken Grillparzer. Jahrbuch des Wiener Goethe Vereins 96 1992.

Grimm, Jakob (1778–1863) and Wilhelm (1786–1859)

Kinder- und Hausmärchen. Berlin 1812–22; German popular stories, tr 1823; Gammer Grethel, tr E. Taylor 1839; Household stories, tr 1853; Household tales, tr M. Hunt 1884.
Lang, A. The blue fairy book. 1889.

▽

Briggs, K. M. The influence of the brothers Grimm in England. In Grimm Gedenken, ed L. Denecke, Marburg 1963.
Brill, E. V. K. The correspondence between Jakob Grimm and Walter Scott. In Grimm Gedenken, ed L. Denecke, Marburg 1963.
Schoof, W. Englische und französische Beziehungen der Brüder Grimm. Wirkendes Wort 16 1966.
Wiley, R. Four unpublished letters of Jakob Grimm to John Mitchell Kemble. JEGP 67 1968.

Haeckel, Ernst (1834–1919)

Die Welträtsel. Bonn 1899; The riddle of the universe, tr J. McCabe 1900.

Hauptmann, Gerhart (1862–1946)

Voigt, F. A. Hauptmann und England. Germanisch-romanische Monatsschrift 25 1937.
Hutchins, W. J. and A. C. Weaver. Hauptmann in England: a bibliography. In Hauptmann: centenary lectures, ed K. Knight and F. Norman, 1964.

Hebbel, Friedrich (1813–63)

Reichart, W. A. Hebbel in Amerika und England: eine Bibliographie. Hebbel-Jahrbuch 1961.

Hegel, Georg Wilhelm Friedrich (1770–1831)

Phänomenologie des Geistes. Bamberg 1807; The phenomenology of mind, tr J. B. Baillie 1821, New York 1931 (rev).
Wissenschaft der Logik. 2 vols Nuremberg 1812–16; The logic of Hegel, tr W. Wallace 1874; Hegel's doctrine of formal logic, tr H. S. Macran, Oxford 1912.

Enzyklopädie der philosophischen Wissenschaften im Grundriss. Heidelberg 1817; Hegel's philosophy of the mind, tr W. Wallace, Oxford 1894.

Grundlinien der Philosophie des Rechts. Berlin 1821; Hegel's philosophy of right, tr S. W. Dyde 1896.

▽

Ritchie, D. G. Darwin and Hegel, with other philosophical studies. 1894.

Muirhead, J. H. How Hegel came to England. Mind 36 1927.

Mansell, D. jr. A note on Hegel and George Eliot. Victorian Newsletter 27 1965.

Slinn, W. Hegel and Browning. Stud in Browning 17 1989.

Heine, Heinrich (1797–1856)

Poems of Heine, complete. Tr E. A. Bowring 1858.

Das Buch der Lieder. Hamburg 1827; Book of songs, tr C. G. Leland 1864; tr T. Brooksbank 1904.

Poems and ballads. Tr T. Martin 1878, 1894 (3rd edn).

Poems. Tr K. Freiligrath-Kroeker 1887.

Prose writings. Ed Havelock Ellis 1887. Includes Reisebilder, The romantic school, Religion and philosophy, Confessions etc.

Reisebilder. Hamburg 1826 etc; Pictures of travel, tr C. G. Leland, Philadelphia 1855; Travel pictures, tr F. Storr 1887; Pictures of travel, tr R. D. Gillman 1907.

Lyrics and ballads. Tr F. Hellman, New York 1892, 1895.

Works. Tr C. G. Leland, T. Brookshank and M. Armour, 12 vols 1892–1905.

Poetical works. Tr J. Payne 1911.

▽

'Eliot, George' (M. A. Evans). German wit: Heine. Westminster Rev n.s. 9 1856.

Arnold, M. In his Essays in criticism. 1865.

Katscher, L. Englische Bücher über Heine und Schopenhauer. Magazin 90 1876.

Sharp, W. Life of Heine. 1888. With trns and criticism.

Winternitz, M. Heine in England. Zeit no 178 1900.

Melchior, F. Heines Verhältnis zu Lord Byron. Literarhistorische Forschungen no 27 1903.

Ochsenbein, W. Die Aufnahme Lord Byrons in Deutschland und sein Einfluss auf den jungen Heine. Berne 1905.

Hayens, K. Heine, Hazlitt and Mrs Jameson. MLR 17 1922.

Atkins, H. G. Heine. 1929. With bibliography, especially K. Kirby, Heine in English translation.

Hess, J. A. Heine's appraisal of John Bull. Modern Language Jnl 19 1934.

Black, G. A. James Thomson: his translations of Heine. MLR 31 1936.

Liptzin, S. Heine, blackguard and apostate: a study of the earliest English attitude towards him. PMLA 58 1943.

Liptzin, S. Heine and the early Victorians. Monatshefte für deutschen Unterricht 25 1943.

Liptzin, S. Heine, Hellenist and cultural pessimist: a late Victorian legend. PQ 22 1943.

Wormley, S. L. Heine in England. Chapel Hill NC 1943.

Haber, T. B. Heine and Housman. JEGP 43 1944.

Liptzin, S. Heine, the continuator of Goethe: a mid-Victorian legend. JEGP 43 1944.

Grasty, G. M. Heine's attitude toward the Anglo-Saxon nations. Unpbd diss. Duke Univ 1946.

Liptzin, S. The English legend of Heine. New York 1954.

Butler, E. M. Heine in England and Matthew Arnold. German Life & Letters 9 1955–6.

Marcuse, L. Heine in England. Aufbau (New York) 21 1955.

Weiss, G. Die Aufnahme Heines in Grossbritannien und den Vereinigten Staaten von Amerika, 1828–1856. Unpbd diss Mainz Univ 1955.

Weltmann, L. Heine und Hölderlin in England. Neue Deutsche Hefte 20 1955–6.

Polak, L. Heine in englischer Beleuchtung. Revue des Langues Vivantes 22 1956.

Liptzin, S. The English reception of Heine. Victorian Newsletter 11 1957.

Arnold, A. Heine in England and America: a bibliographical checklist. 1959.

Weiss, G. Heines Englandaufenthalt. Heine Jahrbuch 2 1963.

Johnston, O. W. Literary influence as provocation: Sir Walter Scott's impact on Heine and the young Germans. Scottish Literary Jnl 7 1980.

Krahe, P. Heine und Ruskin: Shakespeare-Bild und nationales Vorurteil. Heine Jahrbuch 19 1980.

Sammons, J. L. Heine and William Cobbett. Heine Jahrbuch 19 1980.

Perraudin, M. Heine, the German Byron. Colloquia Germanica 19 1986.

Prawer, S. S. Frankenstein's island: England and the English in the writings of Heine. Cambridge 1986.

Slattery, J. F. The German Byron. RMS 32 1988.

Winkler, M. Weltschmerz, europäisch: zur Ästhetik der Zerissenheit bei Heine und Byron. In Heinrich Heine und die Romantik, ed M. Winkler, Tübingen 1997.

Lauster, M. A cultural revolutionary: George Eliot's and Matthew Arnold's appreciation of Heinrich Heine. In Vormärzliteratur in europäischer Perspective II, ed M. Lauster and G. Oesterle, Bielefeld 1998.

Hoffmann, Ernst Theodor Amadeus (1776–1822)

Der goldene Topf. Bamberg 1814; The golden pot, tr T. Carlyle 1841.

Nachtstücke. Berlin 1817; Hoffmann's strange stories, Boston 1855; Weird tales, tr J. T. Bealby, New York 1885.

Die Serapionsbrüder. 4 vols Berlin 1819–21; Serapion brethren, tr A. Ewing 4 vols 1886–92.

▽

Scott, Walter. E. T. A. Hoffmann. 1827.

Gudde, E. Hoffmann's reception in England. PMLA 41 1926.

Koziol, H. Hoffmanns Die Elixiere des Teufels und M. G. Lewis The monk. Germanisch-romanische Monatsschrift 26 1938.

Zylstra, H. Hoffmann in England and America. Unpbd diss Harvard Univ 1940.

Ireland, K. R. Urban perspectives: fantasy and reality in Hoffmann and Dickens. Comparative Lit 30 1978.

Segebrecht, W. Hoffmann and English literature. In Deutsche Romantik and English romanticism, ed T. G. Gish and S. G. Frieden, Munich 1984.

Horstmann-Guthrie, U. Narrative technique and reader manipulation in Hoffmann's Elixiere and Hogg's Confessions. In Anglo-German studies, ed R. F. M. Byrn and K. G. Knight, Leeds 1992.

Mangold, H. 'Proper culture might have done great things': Hoffmann in der Kritik seiner britschen Zeitgenossen. Hoffmann Jahrbuch 1 1992–3.

Hölderlin, Friedrich (1770–1843)

Hamburger, M. Englische Hölderlin-Gedichte. Hölderlin Jahrbuch 13 1963–4.

Hamburger, M. Die Aufnahme Hölderlins in England. Hölderlin Jahrbuch 14 1964–5.

Burwick, F. L. Hölderlin and Arnold: Empedocles on Etna. Comparative Lit 17 1965.

Silz, W. Hölderlin and Wordsworth: bicentenary reflections. Germanic Rev 45 1970.

Stebner, G. Die Entdeckung Hölderlins für die englische Dichtung. Institut für Auslandsbeziehungen Stuttgart 20 1970.

Hamlin, C. The poetics of self-consciousness: Hölderlin's Hyperion and Wordsworth's Prelude. Genre 6 1973.

Klabes, G. Political reality and poetic mission: Hölderlin's and Shelley's heterocosm. In English and German romanticism, ed J. Pipkin, Heidelberg 1985.

Hofmannsthal, Hugo von (1874–1928)
Gilbert, M. E. Hofmannsthal and England. German Life & Letters 1 1937.
Howarth, H. Eliot and Hofmannsthal. South Atlantic Quart 59 1960. *See also his* Notes on some figures behind T. S. Eliot, 1965.
Hamburger, M. Hofmannsthals Bibliothek: ein Bericht. Euphorion 55 1961.
Koziol, H. Zu Thomas Otways Venice preserved und Hofmannsthals Das gerettete Venedig. In Österreich und die angelsächsische Welt, ed H. Hietsch, Vienna and Stuttgart 1961.
Hamburger, M. Hofmannsthal and England. In Hofmannsthal: studies in commemoration, ed F. Norman, 1963.
Pick, R. and A. C. Weaver. Hofmannsthal in England and America: a bibliography. In Hofmannsthal: studies in commemoration, ed F. Norman, 1963.
Klieneberger, H. R. Otway's Venice preserved and Hofmannsthal's Das gerettete Venedig. MLR 62 1967.
Lewis, H. B. Hofmannsthal and Browning. Comparative Lit 19 1967.
Goff, P. Hofmannsthal and Walter Pater. Comparative Literary Stud 7 1970.
Lewis, H. B. Hofmannsthal, Shelley, and Keats. German Life & Letters 27 1973–4.
Weiss, W. F. England, Hofmannsthal's insular mirage. Comparative Lit 25 1973.
Dill, H. J. Hofmannsthal and Keats. Germanic Rev 55 1980.
Howe, P. Hofmannsthal and Keats. In Hugo von Hofmannsthal: commemorative essays, ed W. E. Yuill and P. Howe, 1981.
Stillmark, A. Hofmannsthal and Oscar Wilde. In Hugo von Hofmannsthal: commemorative essays, ed W. E. Yuill and P. Howe, 1981.

Kant, Immanuel (1724–1804)
Kritik der reinen Vernunft. Riga 1781. Critique of pure reason, tr F. Haywood 1838; tr J. M. D. Meiklejohn 1856; tr F. M. Muller 1881; tr N. K. Smith 1929.
Kritik der praktischen Vernunft. Riga 1788; Critique of practical reason and other works on the theory of ethics, tr T. K. Abbott 1873, 1909 (6th edn).
Kritik der Urteilskraft. Berlin 1790; Critique of judgment, tr J. H. Bernard 1892; Critique of aesthetic judgment, tr J. C. Meredith, Oxford 1911.
▽
Mahaffy, J. P. and J. H. Bernard. Kant's critical philosophy for English readers. 1872.
Duncan, J. M. English translations of Kant's writings. Kantstudien 2 1906.
Schmitt-Wendel, K. Kants Einfluss auf die englische Ethik. Berlin 1912.
Wellek, R. Kant in England 1793–1838. Princeton 1931.

Keller, Gottfried (1819–90)
Romeo und Julia auf dem Dorfe. Brunswick 1856; A village Romeo and Juliet, tr H. T. and C. Porter 1897.
Kleider machen Leute. Stuttgart 1874; Clothes maketh man, tr K. F. Kroeker 1894. Includes The abused love-letters, Dietegen.
▽
Cunliffe, W. G. Keller the realist: a comparison with Samuel Butler. MLA Program 1967.
Klieneberger, H. R. Keller and George Eliot. New German Stud 5 1977. *See also his* The novel in England and Germany, *under General Studies above.*
Kolb, W. Die Rezeption Kellers im englischen Sprachraum bis 1920. Frankfurt am Main 1992.

Kleist, Heinrich von (1777–1811)
Michael Kohlhaas. Berlin 1810; Michael Kohlhaas, tr J. Oxenford 1844.
Die Heilige Cäcilie oder die Gewalt der Musik. Berlin 1810; St Cecilia: or the power of music, tr J. Oxenford 1844.
Prinz Friedrich von Homburg. Berlin 1821; Prince Friedrich von Homburg, tr F. Lloyd and W. Newton in Prussia's representative man, 1875.
▽
Peck, L. F. An adaptation of Kleist's Die Familie Schroffenstein. JEGP 44 1945. By M. G. Lewis.
Rennert, H. H. Affinities in romanticism: Kleist's essay Über das Marionettentheater and Keats's concept of negative capability. In Heinrich von Kleist studies, ed A. Ugrinsky et al, New York 1980.

Kotzebue, August (1761–1819)
For the many trns of Kotzebue's works, see B. Q. Morgan, under Bibliographies above.
Koeppel, F. Kotzebue in England. E Studien 13 1891.
Süpfle, T. Kotzebue in Frankreich und England. Zeitschrift für Vergleichende Literaturgeschichte 6 1892.
Sellier, W. Kotzebue in England. Leipzig 1901.
Thompson, L. F. Kotzebue: a survey of his progress in France and England. Paris 1928.
Gosch, M. Translators of Kotzebue in England. Monatshefte für Deutschen Unterricht 31 1939.
Lindsay, D. W. Kotzebue in Scotland 1792–1813. Pbns of Eng Goethe Soc 33 1963.
Jacob, H. Kotzebues Werke in Übersetzungen. In his Studien zur neueren Literatur, Berlin 1964.

Lewald, Fanny (1811–89)
Jolles, C. A feminist's impression of mid-Victorian Britain: Fanny Lewald's England und Schottland, Reisetagebuch. In Connections: essays in honour of E. Sagarra, ed P. Skrine, Stuttgart 1993.
Schutte Watt, H. Fanny Lewald und die deutsche Misere nach 1848 im Hinblick auf England. German Life & Letters 46 1993.
Skrine, P. Building bridges: Fanny Lewald, Margaret Fuller, and George Eliot. In Connections: essays in honour of E. Sagarra, ed P. Skrine, Stuttgart 1993.

Ludwig, Otto (1812–65)
Lohre, H. Ludwig und Charles Dickens. Archiv 124 1910.
Price, L. M. Ludwig's Zwischen Himmel und Erde and George Eliot's Adam Bede. In Dichtung und Deutung: Gedächtnisschrift für H. M. Wolff, ed K. S. Guthke, Berne 1961.
Thomas, L. H. C. Ludwig and Dickens. Hermathena (Dublin) 111 1971.

Nietzsche, Friedrich (1844–1900)
Complete works. Tr by several hands, ed O. Levy, 18 vols 1909–13. This edn based on Works, ed and tr A. Tille, T. Common et al, 6 vols New York 1896–9.
▽
Ellis, H. Friedrich Nietzsche. Savoy nos 2–4 1896.
Orage, A. R. Nietzsche: the Dionysian spirit of the age. 1905.
Foerster-Nietzsche, E. Nietzsche in France and England. Open Court 34 1920.
Petzold, G. von. Nietzsche in englisch-amerikanischer Beurteilung bis zum Ausgang des Weltkrieges. Anglia 53 1929.
Hultsch, P. Das Denken Nietzsches in seiner Bedeutung für England. Germanisch-romanische Monatsschrift 26 1938.
Reichert, H. and K. Schlechta. International Nietzsche bibliography. North Carolina Stud in Comparative Lit 29 1960.
KcKenny, J. L. Nietzsche and the Frankenstein creature. Dalhousie Rev 41 1961.
Furness, R. Nietzsche's views on the English and his concept of a European community. German Life & Letters 17 1964.
Sandvoss, E. Nietzsches Kritik an den Angelsachsen. Zeischrift für Religions- und Geistesgeschichte 17 1965.
Thatcher, D. S. Nietzsche in England, 1890–1914: the growth of a reputation. Toronto 1970.
Bridgwater, P. Nietzsche in Anglo-saxony: a study of Nietzsche's impact on English and American literature. Leicester 1972.
Thatcher, D. S. Nietzsche and Byron. Nietzsche Studien 3 1974.

'Novalis' (Friedrich Leopold, Freiherr von Hardenberg) (1772–1801)
His life, thoughts and works. Ed and tr M. J. Hope 1891.
Die Lehrlinge zu Sais. 1798, first pub Berlin 1802; The disciples at Sais and other fragments, tr F. V. M. T. and U. C. B. 1903. Includes Spiritual hymns, Thoughts on philosophy, love and religion, Flower pollen.
Hymnen an die Nacht. Berlin 1800; Hymns and thoughts on religion, tr W. Hastie 1888. Includes Hymns to night, Spiritual songs, Thoughts on religion.
Heinrich von Ofterdingen. Berlin 1802; Henry of Ofterdingen, Cambridge MA 1842.
▽
Carlyle, T. Novalis. Foreign Rev 4 1829.
Hanke, A. M. Spatiotemporal consciousness in English and German romanticism: a comparative study of Novalis, Blake, Wordsworth and Eichendorff. Berne 1981.

Raabe, Wilhelm (1831–1910)
Der Hungerpastor. 3 vols Berlin 1864; The hungerpastor, tr 'Arnold' 1885.
Abu Telfan oder die Heimkehr vom Mondgebirge. 3 vols Stuttgart 1868; Abu Telfan: or the return from the mountains of the moon, tr S. Delffs 3 vols 1882.
▽
Doernenburg, E. and N. Fehse. Raabe und Dickens. Magdeburg 1921.
Albaugh, K. The influence of W. M. Thackeray on Raabe. Unpbd diss, Stanford Univ 1941.
Brill, E. V. K. Raabe's reception in England. German Life & Letters 8 1955.
Andrews, J. S. Raabe's reception in England. N & Q 202 1957.
Hanson, W. P. New realities: common concerns in Raabe and Hardy. In Wilhelm Raabe: Studien zu seinem Leben und Werk, ed L. A. Lensing and H. W. Peter, Braunschweig 1981.
See Klieneberger, The novel in England and Germany *under General Studies above.*

Reuter, Fritz (1810–74)
Ut de Franzosentid. Wismar 1859; In the year '13: a tale of Mecklenburg life, tr C. L. Lewes, Leipzig 1867.
Ut mine Strombid. Wismar 1863; An old story of my farming-days, tr M. W. Macdowall, Leipzig 1878.
▽
Geist, H. Reuters literarische Beziehungen zu Charles Dickens. Erfurt 1913.
Andrews, J. S. The reception of Fritz Reuter in Victorian England. MLR 56 1961.

Richter, Johann Paul Friedrich ('Jean Paul') (1763–1825)
Leben des Quintus Fixlein. Bayreuth 1796; Quintus Fixlein, tr T. Carlyle 1864.
Blumen-, Frucht- und Dornenstücke: oder Ehestand, Tod und Hochzeit des Armenadvokaten Fr. St. Siebenkäs. Bayreuth 1796–7; Flower, fruit and thorn pieces: or the married life, death and wedding of Firmian Siebenkäs, tr E. H. Noel 1845.
Levana oder Erziehungslehre. Brunswick 1807; Levana: or the doctrine of education, tr A. H. 1848.
▽
Carlyle, T. Jean Paul Friedrich Richter. Edinburgh Rev 46 1830.
Carlyle, T. Jean Paul Friedrich Richter again. Foreign Rev 5 1830.
Schacht, F. E. Jean Paul im Lichte der englischen und amerikanischen Kritik des 19 Jahrhunderts. In Festgabe für Eduard Berend, ed H. W. Seiffert and B. Zeller, Weimar 1959.
Burwick, F. The dream-visions of Jean Paul and De Quincey. Comparative Lit 20 1968.

Schiller, Johann Christoph Friedrich von (1759–1805)
Works, historical and dramatic. Tr various hands 1846–9, 1897–1903.
Minor poems. Tr J. H. Merivale 1844.
Poems. Tr E. A. Bowring 1851.
Die Räuber. Stuttgart 1781; The robbers, tr H. G. Bohn in Works, 1846–9.
Don Carlos. Leipzig 1787; tr R. D. Boylan in Works, 1846–9.
Wallenstein. Tübingen 1800; tr S. T. Coleridge 1800 (omits Lager); tr J. A. W. Hunter 1885; tr T. Martin (Lager only), Blackwood's Mag Feb 1892.
Maria Stuart. Tübingen 1801; tr J. C. Mellish 1801.
Wilhelm Tell. Stuttgart 1804; tr S. Robinson 1825; tr T. Martin in Works, 1846–9.
J. S. Knowles. William Tell. 1856. Written 1825.
▽
Carlyle, T. Schiller's life and writings. London Mag 1823–4; 1825 (as The life of Schiller).
Carlyle, T. Schiller. Fraser's Mag Mar 1831.
Carlyle, T. Schiller, Goethe and Madame de Staël, and Goethe's portrait. Fraser's Mag May 1832.
Machule, P. Coleridges Wallensteinübersetzung. E Studien 31 1902.
Kipka, K. Schillers Maria Stuart im Auslande. Studien zur Vergleichenden Literaturgeschichte 5 1905.
Roscher, H. F. G. Die Wallensteinübersetzung von Samuel T. Coleridge. Leipzig 1905.
Rea, T. Schiller's dramas and poems in England. 1906.
Smith, H. Two English translations of Schiller's Wallenstein. MLR 9 1914.
Cooke, M. W. Schiller's Robbers in England. MLR 11 1915.
Willougby, L. A. English translation and adaptations of Schiller's Robbers. MLR 16 1921.
Willougby, L. A. Schiller's Kabale und Liebe in English translation. Pbns of Eng Goethe Soc n.s. 1 1924.
Ewen, F. The prestige of Schiller in England. New York 1932.
Willougby, L. A. Schiller in England and Germany. Pbns of Eng Goethe Soc 12 1935.
Dummer, E. H. Schiller in English. Monatschefte für Deutschen Unterricht 35 1943.
Wilkinson, E. M. Zur Sprache und Struktur der ästhetischen Briefe: Betrachtungen beim Abschluss einer mühevoll verfertigten Übersetzung ins Englische. Akzente 6 1959.
Witte, W. Schiller and Burns and other essays. Oxford 1959.
Pick, R. (ed). Schiller in England 1787–1960: a bibliography. 1961.
Witte, W. Das neue Schillerbild der britischen Germanistik. Jahrbuch der Schiller-Gesellschaft 5 1961.
Knepler, H. W. Schiller's Maria Stuart on the stage in England and America. In Anglo-German and American-German crosscurrents vol 2, ed P. A. Shelley and A. O. Lewis jr, Chapel Hill NC 1962.

Schlegel, August Wilhelm von (1767–1845)
Über dramatische Kunst und Literatur. 3 vols Heidelberg 1809–11; Lectures on dramatic art and literature, tr J. Black 1815; A. W. Schlegel's lectures on German literature from Gottsched to Goethe, taken down by G. Toynbee in 1833, ed H. G. Fiedler, Oxford 1944. Toynbee pbd a trn of his notes in 1838.
▽
Herzfeld, G. August Wilhelm von Schlegel in seinen Beziehungen zu englischen Dichtern und Kritikern. Archiv 138 1920.
Schnöckelborg, G. August Wilhelm Schlegels Einfluss auf William Hazlitt als Shakespeare-Kritiker. Münster 1931.
Schirmer, W. F. A. W. Schlegel und England. Jahrbuch der Shakespeare-Gesellschaft 75 1939.
Goslee, N. M. Plastic to picturesque: Schlegel's analogy and Keats's Hyperion poems. KSJ 10 1982.

Schlegel, Friedrich von (1772–1829)
Vorlesungen über die neuere Geschichte. Vienna 1811; A course of lectures on modern history, tr L. Purcell and R. H. Whitelock 1849.
Geschichte der alten und neueren Literatur. Vienna 1815; Lectures

on the history of literature ancient and modern, tr J. G. Lockhart, Edinburgh 1818.
Philosophie des Lebens. Vienna 1828; The philosophy of life and philosophy of language, tr A. J. W. Morrison 1847.
Philosphie der Geschichte. Vienna 1829; The philosophy of history, tr J. B. Robertson 1835.

Schnitzler, Arthur (1862–1931)
Anatol. Berlin 1893; Anatol: a sequence of dialogues paraphrased by Granville Barker, New York 1911.
Most of Schnitzler's works have been translated into English, and have for the greater part appeared in anthologies; see B. Q. Morgan under Bibliographies above.

Schopenhauer, Arthur (1788–1860)
Die Welt als Wille und Vorstellung. Leipzig 1818; The world as well and idea, tr R. B. Haldane and J. Kemp 4 vols 1883–6.
▽
Goodale, R. H. Schopenhauer and pessimism in nineteenth-century English literature. PMLA 47 1932.

Stifter, Adalbert (1805–68)
Rural life in Austria and Hungary. Tr M. Norman 1850. Includes My great-grandfather's notebook, Abdias the Jew, The Hochwald, Crazy castle, Maroshely, The village on the heath.
Pictures of life. Tr M. Howitt 1852. Includes Angela, The castle of fools, The village on the heath.
▽
Andrews, J. S. The reception of Stifter in nineteenth-century Britain. MLR 53 1958.
Reichart, W. A. and W. H. Grilk. Stifters Werk in Amerika und England: a bibliography. Adalbert-Stifter-Institut des Landes Österreich 9 1960. Suppl by E. Eisenmeier, ibid.
See Klieneberger, The novel in England and Germany *under General Studies above.*
Stillmark, A. Stifter and Wordsworth: observations on some affinities in creative imagination. In Adalbert Stifter heute, ed J. Lachinger et al, Linz 1985.

Storm, Theodor (1817–88)
Immensee. 1849, Berlin 1851; Immensee: or the old man's reverie, tr H. Clark, Münster 1863; Immen lake, tr M. Briton 1881.
▽
Andrews, J. S. Immensee and Victorian England. MLR 54 1959.

Strauss, David Friedrich (1808–74)
Das Leben Jesu. Tübingen 1835; The life of Jesus, tr 'George Eliot' 1846.
▽
Das Leben Jesu von Strauss in England und Frankreich. Blätter zur Kunde der Litteratur des Auslands 4 1839.

Sudermann, Hermann (1857–1928)
Frau Sorge. Berlin 1886; Dame Care, tr Bertha Overbeck, New York 1891.
Heimat. Stuttgart 1892; Magda tr C. E. A. Winslow, New York 1896.

Suttner, Bertha von (1843–1914)
Die Waffen nieder! Dresden 1889; Lay down your arms, tr T. Holmes 1892, 1906.

Tieck, Ludwig (1773–1853)
Phantasus. 3 vols Berlin 1812–16.
Tales from the Phantasus. Tr J. C. Hare, J. A. Froude et al 1845.
▽
Lüdeke, H. Tieck und das alte englische Theater. Frankfurt 1922.
Zeydel, E. H. Tieck and England. Princeton 1931.
Zeydel, E. H. Tieck as a translator of English. PMLA 51 1936.
Griggs, E. L. Tieck and Coleridge. JEGP 54 1955.
Corkhill, A. Tieck's William Lovell and Wilde's The picture of Dorian Gray. Archiv 224 1987.

Varnhagen von Ense, Karl August (1785–1858)
Carlyle, T. Varnhagen von Ense's Memoirs. Westminster Rev 32 1838.
Carlyle, T. Briefwechsel mit Varnhagen von Ense. Ed R. Preuss, Berlin 1892.
Fischer, W. Die Briefe R. Monckton Milnes an Varnhagen von Ense 1844–54. Heidelberg 1922.
The letters of Varnhagen von Ense to R. Monckton Milnes. Ed P. Glander, Heidelberg 1965.
Tarr, R. L. Some unpublished letters from Varnhagen von Ense to Carlyle. MLR 68 1973.

Wagner, Wilhelm Richard (1813–83)
Heydet, X. Wagner et Bernard Shaw. Revue de L'Enseignement des Langues Vivantes 1937.
Moser, M. Wagner in der englischen Literatur des 19 Jahrhunderts. Berne 1938.
Keller, H. Wagner in England. In Richard Wagner, Mittler zwischen Zeiten, ed G. Heldt, Salzburg 1990.

Werner, Zacharias (1768–1823)
Carlyle, T. Life and writings of Werner. Foreign Rev 1 1828.

Wyss, J. D. (1743–1818) and J. R. (1782–1830)
Der schweizerische Robinson. 2 vols Zurich 1812–13. Many trns in England and America.

Zedlitz, Joseph Christian, Freiherr von (1790–1862)
Totenkränze. Vienna 1828; Poems, tr L. Dick 1843.
▽
Spink, G. W. J. C. von Zedlitz and Byron. MLR 26 1931.

Zschokke, Heinrich (1771–1848)
Abällino der grosse Bandit. Frankfurt 1793 (as a novel), 1795 (as a play); Abaellino the great bandit, tr W. Dunlop, New York 1802; The bravo of Venice, tr M. G. Lewis 1805.

Among the more popular German writers of the century whose works have been widely read in English trn are: Bertha Behrens ('W. Heimburg'); W. Busch (Max und Moritz, 1865); F. W. Carové; Elizabeth, Queen of Roumania ('Carmen Sylva'); G. Ebers; Ernst Eckstein; F. Gerstäcker; Ida Hahn-Hahn; F. Hoffmann; H. Hoffmann (Struwelpeter, 1847); A. H. Lafontaine; G. von Moser; Klara Mundt ('Luise Mühlbach'); G. Nieritz; M. Nordau; Ida Pfeiffer; C. von Schmidt; Lola Kirschner ('Ossip Schubin'); K. A. Postl ('Charles Seasfield'); F. Spielhagen; Johann Spyri; J. Stinde (Die Familie Buchholz, 1884).

English authors

Arnold, Matthew
Preisinger, H. Arnold on Goethe. Trans Manchester Goethe Soc 1894.
White, H. C. Arnold and Goethe. PMLA 36 1921.
Orrick, J. B. Arnold and Goethe. Pbns of Eng Goethe Soc n.s. 4 1927.
Sells, I. E. Marguerite. MLR 38 1943.
Fischer, W. Arnold und Deutschland. Germanisch-romanische Monatshefte n.s. 4 1954.
Wright, C. D. How Arnold altered 'Goethe on Poetry'. VP 5 1967.
Wright, C. D. Arnold on Heine as 'continuator of Goethe'. SP 65 1968.
Allott, K. Conditional immortality: Arnold and Goethe. N & Q 217 1972.
Sheppard, R. Two liberals: a comparison of the humanism of Arnold and Wilhelm von Humboldt. German Life & Letters 24 1971.
Tesdorpf, I.-M. Die Auseinandersetzung Arnolds mit Heinrich Heine. Frankfurt am Main 1971.
Bruford, W. H. Some centenary reflections on Arnold's higher schools and universities in Germany. German Life & Letters 29 1975.
Simpson, J. Matthew Arnold and Goethe. 1979.
Barry, J. M. Goethe and Arnold's 1853 preface. Comparative Lit 32 1980.
Berlin, J. A. Arnold's response to Schelling: agreeing to disagree. ELN 17 1980.
De Laura, D. J. Arnold and Goethe: the one on the intellectual

throne. In Victorian literature and society: essays presented to Richard D. Altick, ed J. R. Kincaid and A. J. Kuhn, Columbus OH 1984.

Stone, D. D. Arnold, Nietzsche and the 'revaluation of values'. Nineteenth-Century Lit 43 1988.

Gossman, L. Philhellenism and antisemitism: Arnold and his German models. Comparative Lit 46 1994.

Austen, Jane

Butler, E. M. Mansfield Park and Kotzebue's Lovers' vows. MLR 28 1933.

Husbands, H. W. Mansfield Park and Lovers' vows: a reply. MLR 29 1934.

Fahnestock, M. L. The reception of Jane Austen in Germany: a miniaturist in the land of poets and philosophers. Unpbd diss, Indiana Univ 1982.

Zelicovici, D. The inefficacy of Lovers' vows. ELH 50 1983.

Conger, S. M. Reading Lovers' vows: Jane Austen's reflections on English sense and German sensibility. SP 85 1988.

Pedley, C. 'Terrific and unprincipled compositions': the reception of Lovers' vows and Mansfield Park. PQ 74 1995.

Bailey, Philip James

Black, J. A. Bailey's debt to Goethe's Faust. MLR 28 1933.

Beddoes, Thomas Lovell

Donner, H. W. Echoes of Beddosian rambles: Edgeworthstown to Zurich. SN 33 1961.

Donner, H. W. Beddoes to Leonhard Tobler: eight German letters. SN 35 1963.

Harrey, A. Death's jest-book and the German contribution. SN 39 1967.

Lundin, J. Beddoes at Göttingen. SN 43 1971.

Burwick, F. Beddoes and the 'Schweizerischer Republikaner'. SN 44 1972.

Borrow, George

Speck, W. A. Borrow and Goethe's Faust. PMLA 41 1926.

Grayburn, W. F. Borrow's German interests. In Anglo-German and American-German crosscurrents II, ed P. A. Shelley and A. O. Lewis, Chapel Hill NC 1962.

Brontë, Emily

Mackay, R. M. Irish heaths and German cliffs: a study of the foreign sources of Wuthering Heights. Brigham Young Univ Stud 7 1965.

Nicolai, R. R. Wuthering Heights: Emily Brontë's Kleistian novel. South Atlantic Bull 38 1973.

Hatch, R. B. Heathcliff's 'queer end' and Schopenhauer's denial of the will. Canadian Rev of Comparative Lit 1 1974.

Hoenselaars, A. J. Emily Brontë, Hamlet, and Wilhelm Meister. N & Q 237 1992.

Browning, Robert

Albrecht, R. Robert Brownings Verhältnis zu Deutschland. Munich 1912.

Phelps, W. L. Browning in Germany. MLN 28 1913.

Rhyme, O. P. Browning and Goethe. MLN 44 1929.

Buck, G. Das Nachleben Brownings in Kritik und Forschung. Germanisch-romanische Monatsschrift 21 1933.

Schneider, F. Browning's The ring and the book and Wassermann's Der Fall Maurizius. MLN 48 1933.

See Shaffer, Kubla Khan and The fall of Jerusalem *under Coleridge below*.

Heath, A. L. D. Phelps, Browning, Schopenhauer and music. Comparative Lit Stud 22 1985.

Ryals, C. de L. Browning's Christmas Eve and Schleiermacher's Die Weihnachtsfeier: a German source for the English poem. Stud in Browning 14 1986.

LeFew, P. A. A note on Browning and Schopenhauer. Stud in Browning 15 1988.

Kowal, M. An allusion to Goethe in Browning. N & Q 235 1990.

Bulwer-Lytton, Edward George Earle Lytton (1st Baron Lytton)

Schmidt, J. Bilder aus dem geistigen Leben unserer Zeit. Vol 1, Leipzig 1870.

Goldhan, A. H. Über die Einwirkung des Goetheschen Werther und Wilhelm Meister auf die Entwicklung Edward Bulwers. Leipzig 1895.

Liljegren, S. B. Bulwer-Lytton and Wertherism. In Essence and attitude in English romanticism, Uppsala and Leipzig 1945.

Zipser, R. A. Edward Bulwer-Lytton and Germany. Berne and Frankfurt am Main 1974.

Byron, George Gordon, Baron

Flaischlen, C. Lord Byron in Deutschland. Centralblatt für Bibliothekswesen 7–8 1890–1.

Ackermann, R. Lord Byron: sein Leben, seine Werke, sein Einfluss auf die deutsche Litteratur. Heidelberg 1901.

Eimer, M. Byron and Ch. D. Grabbe. Frankfurter Zeitung 15 Jan 1903.

Holzhausen, P. Lord Byron und seine deutschen Biographen. Beilage zur Allgemeinen Zeitung nos 174–5 1903.

Ochsenbein, W. Die Aufnahme Lord Byrons in Deutschland und sein Einfluss auf den jungen Heine. Berne 1905; rptd Hildesheim 1975.

Eimer, M. Byrons Beziehungen zur deutschen Kultur. Anglia 36 1912.

Leitzmann, A. Aus der Frühzeit der Byron-Eindeutschung: Knebel als Übersetzer Byrons. Viermonatsschrift der Goethe-Gesellschaft 4 1940.

Straumann, H. Byron and Switzerland. Nottingham 1949.

Korninger, S. Lord Byron und Nikolaus Lenau. Eng Miscellany (Rome) 3 1952.

Butler, E. M. Byron and Goethe. 1956.

de Beer, G. Meshes of the Byronic net in Switzerland. ES 43 1962.

Dowden, W. S. Byron through Austrian eyes. In Anglo-German and American-German crosscurrents II, ed P. A. Shelley and A. O. Lewis, Chapel Hill NC 1962.

Allentuck, M. Byron and Goethe: new unpublished references by H. G. Knight. PQ 52 1973.

Klapper, M. R. The German literary influence on Byron. Salzburg 1974.

Schowerling, R. Byron and German literary criticism: some remarks on the reception and influence of Byron and his Don Juan. In The Constance Byron Symposium, 1977, Salzburg 1977.

Hentschel, C. Byron and Germany: the shadow of Euphorion. In Byron's political and cultural influence in nineteenth-century Europe, ed P. G. Trueblood, 1981.

Sturzl, E. A. Byron and the poets of the Austrian Vormärz. Byron Jnl 9 1981.

Prochazka, M. 'The strangest nourishment for his hypochondriac humour': the expression of the subject in Byron's Manfred and Goethe's Faust. Philologica Pragensia 25 1982.

Sturzl, E. A. Byron and Grillparzer. In Lord Byron and his contemporaries, ed C. E. Robinson, Newark and London 1982.

Garber, F. Byron, Schlegel and the ironist's lucid contours. In English and German romanticism: cross-currents and controversies, ed J. Pipkin, Heidelberg 1985.

Blaicher, G. Wilhelm Müller and the political reception of Byron in nineteenth-century Germany. Archiv 223 1986.

Ritt, N. Byron and his contemporary reception in Vienna. In Festschrift für S. Korninger: a yearbook of studies in English language and literature 1985–6, ed O. Rauschbauer, Vienna 1986.

Soderholm, J. Byron, Nietzsche and the mystery of forgetting. Clio 23 1993–4.

Carlyle, Thomas. *See also under General Studies, cols 127–132, above.*

Streuli, W. Carlyle als Vermittler deutscher Literatur und deutschen Geistes. Zurich 1895.

Kräger, H. Carlyles Stellung zur deutschen Sprache und Literatur. Anglia 22 1899.
Küchler, F. Carlyle und Schiller. Leipzig 1902. *See also* Anglia 26 1903.
Pape, H. Jean Paul als Quelle von Carlyles Anschauung und Stil. Rostock 1904.
Baumgarten, O. Thomas Carlyle and Goethe. Tübingen 1906.
Vaughan, C. E. Carlyle and his German masters. E & S 1910.
Blankenagel, J. C. Carlyle as a critic of Grillparzer. PMLA 42 1927.
Harrold, C. F. Carlyle's interpretation of Kant. PQ 27 1928.
Storrs, M. The relation of Carlyle to Kant and Fichte. Bryn Mawr PA 1929.
Harrold, C. F. Carlyle and Novalis. SP 27 1930.
Lotter, K. Carlyle und die deutsche Romantik. Nuremberg 1932.
Harrold, C. F. Carlyle and German thought 1819–34. New Haven CT 1934.
Shine, H. Carlyle and the German philosophy problem during the year 1826–7. PMLA 50 1935.
Plagens, H. Carlyles Weg zu Goethe. Berlin 1938.
Brooks, R. A. E. (ed). Carlyle: journey to Germany, autumn 1848. New Haven CT1940.
Brie, F. Carlyle und Goethes Symbolum. Anglia 66 1942.
Fiedler, H. G. The friendship of Carlyle and Varnhagen von Ense. MLR 38 1943.
Kippenberg, A. Thomas Carlyles Weg zu Goethe. Bremen 1946.
Carr, C. T. Carlyle's translations from German. MLR 42 1947.
Shine, H. Carlyle's early writings and Herder's Ideen: the concept of history. In Booker Memorial studies, ed H. Shine, Chapel Hill NC 1950.
Cooper, B. A comparison of Quintus Fixlein and Sartor Resartus. Trans of Wisconsin Acad of Sciences, Arts & Letters 48 1959.
Metzger, L. Sartor Resartus: a Victorian Faust. Comparative Lit 13 1961.
Smeed, J. W. Carlyle's Jean Paul Übersetzungen. Deutsche Vierteljahresschrift 35 1961.
Plard, H. Le Sartor Resartus de Carlyle et Jean Paul. Etudes Germaniques 18 1963.
Smeed, J. W. Carlyle and Jean Paul Richter. Comparative Lit 16 1964.
Tennyson, G. B. Carlyle's earliest German translation. American N & Q 3 1964.
Krohn, M. Carlyle: Friedrich der Grosse Schlesien. Jahrbuch der Schlesischen Friedrich-Wilhelm-Universität zu Breslau 10 1965.
See Wellek, Confrontations *under General Studies above.*
La Valley, A. J. Carlyle and the idea of the modern: studies in Carlyle's prophetic literature and its relation to Blake, Nietzsche, Marx, and others. New Haven CT 1968.
Clubbe, J. John Carlyle in Germany and the genesis of Sartor Resartus. In Romantic and Victorian: studies in memory of William H. Marshall, ed W. P. Elledge and R. L. Hoffmann, Rutherford NJ 1971.
Tarr, R. L. and I. M. Campbell. Carlyle's early study of German, 1819–21. Illinois Quart 34 1971.
Casey, P. F. Carlyle as translator: Wilhelm Meisters Lehrjahre. Neuphilologische Mitteilungen 10 1975.
Moore, C. Carlyle and Goethe as scientist. In Carlyle and his contemporaries: essays in honour of Charles Richard Saunders, ed J. Clubbe, Durham NC 1976.
Carr, C. T. Carlyle, Goethe and the St Andrews chair of moral philosophy. German Life & Letters 31 1977.
Dibble, J. A. The Pythia's drunken song: Carlyle's Sartor Resartus and the style problem in German idealist philosophy. The Hague 1978.
See Ashton, The German idea *under General Studies above.*
Baker, L. C. R. Carlyle's secret debt to Schiller: the concept of Goethe's genius. Victorian Newsletter 61 1982.
Vijn, J. P. Carlyle and Jean Paul: their spiritual optics. Amsterdam 1982.
Block, E. Carlyle, Lockhart and the Germanic connection: the periodical context of Carlyle's early criticism. Victorian Periodicals Rev 16 1983.
Harding, A. J. Sterling, Carlyle, and German higher criticism: a reassessment. VS 26 1983.
Tennyson, G. B. Carlyle as mediator of German language and thought. In Thomas Carlyle 1981: papers given at the international Carlyle centenary symposium, ed H. W. Drescher, Frankfurt 1983.
Lloyd, T. 'High air-castles': Carlyle's reactions to Schiller's aesthetics. Victorian Institutes Jnl 12 1984.
Johnson, H. C. Goethe's influence on Carlyle. Stud in Eng Lang and Lit 26 1986.
Lloyd, T. Society and chaos: Schiller's impact on Carlyle's ideas about revolution. Clio 17 1987.
Lloyd, T. Towards natural supernaturalism: Carlyle's dyspepsia and the Germans. Kentucky Rev 11 1992.

Coleridge, Samuel Taylor

Ferrier, J. F. The plagiarisms of Coleridge. Blackwood's Mag Mar 1840.
Haney, J. L. The German influence on Coleridge. Philadelphia 1903.
Helmholtz, A. A. The indebtedness of Coleridge to A. W. Schlegel. Madison WI 1907.
Pizzo, E. Coleridge als Kritiker. Anglia 28 1916.
Richter, H. Die philosophische Weltanschauung von Coleridge und ihr Verhältnis zur deutschen Philosophie. Anglia 32 1920.
Dunstan, A. C. The German influence on Coleridge. MLR 17–18 1922–3. On Schiller, Goethe, Herder, Schlegel, Schelling.
Winkelmann, E. Coleridge und die Kantische Philosophie. Leipzig 1933.
Wolff, L. Coleridge et l'Allemagne. Revue Anglo-américaine 11 1933.
Willoughby, L. A. Coleridge and his German contemporaries. Pbns of Eng Goethe Soc n.s. 12 1935.
Lovejoy, A. O. Coleridge and Kant's two worlds. ELH 7 1940; rptd in his Essays in the history of ideas, Baltimore 1948.
Beach, J. W. Coleridge's borrowings from the German. ELH 9 1942.
Brinkley, R. F. Some unpublished Coleridge marginalia: Richter and Reimarus. JEGP 44 1945.
Benzinger, J. Organic unity: Leibniz to Coleridge. PMLA 66 1951. On Leibniz, Schlegel and Coleridge.
Stahl, E. L. Zur Theorie der Dichtung bei Coleridge im Hinblick auf Goethe. In Festschrift für Fritz Strich, Berne 1952.
Wells, G. A. Man and nature: an elucidation of Coleridge's rejection of Herder's thought. JEGP 51 1952.
Beyer, W. Coleridge's early knowledge of German. MP 52 1955.
Ashe, D. J. Coleridge, Byron and Schiller's Der Geisterseher. N & Q 201 1956.
Wilkinson, E. M. Coleridge's knowledge of German as seen in the early notebooks. In The notebooks of Samuel Taylor Coleridge vol 1, ed K. Coburn 1957.
Schrickx, W. Coleridge and Friedrich Heinrich Jacobi. Revue Belge de Philologie et d'Histoire 36 1958.
Wilkinson, E. M. Coleridge und Deutschland 1794–1804; zum ersten Band der Gesamtausgabe seiner Notebooks. In Forschungsprobleme der vergleichenden Literaturgeschichte ser 2, ed F. Ernst and K. Wais, Tübingen 1958.
Morgan, B. Q. What happened to Coleridge's Wallenstein? Mod Lang Jnl 43 1959.
Schrickx, W. Coleridge's marginalia in Kant's Metaphysische Anfangsgründe der Naturwissenschaft. Studia Germanica 1 1959.
Greiner, W. Deutsche Einflüsse auf die Dichtungstheorie von Coleridge. Die Neueren Sprachen Aug 1960.
Beyer, W. W. The enchanted forest. Oxford 1963.
McFarland, G. F. Julius Charles Hare: Coleridge, De Quincey and German literature. BJR 2 47 1964.

Orsini, G. N. G. Coleridge and Schlegel reconsidered. Comparative Lit 16 1964.
Orsini, G. N. G. Coleridge and German idealism: a study in the history of philosophy. Carbondale IL 1969.
Freedman, R. Eyesight and vision: forms of the imagination in Coleridge and Novalis. In The rarer action: essays in honour of F. Fergusson, ed A. Cheuse et al, New Brunswick NJ 1970.
Breitkreuz, H. Coleridge's German vocabulary. N & Q 218 1973.
Frank, F. S. Coleridge in Germany. Revue des Langues Vivantes 39 1973.
Mackinnon, D. M. Coleridge and Kant. In Coleridge's variety: bicentenary studies, ed J. Beer, Pittsburgh 1975.
Shaffer, E. S. Kubla Khan and The fall of Jerusalem. Cambridge 1975.
Wieden, F. Coleridge's assimilation of ideas from Schiller's early writings. In Analecta Helvetica et Germanica: eine Festschrift zu Ehren von H. Boeschenstein, ed A. Arnold et al, Bonn 1979.
See Ashton, The German idea *under General Studies above.*
Wheeler, K. Coleridge's friendship with Ludwig Tieck. In New approaches to Coleridge: biographical and critical essays, ed D. Sultana, 1981.
Nicholson, A. Kubla Khan: the influence of Bürger's Lenore. ES 64 1983.
Burwick, F. Coleridge, Schlegel and animal magnetism. In English and German romanticism: cross-currents and controversies, ed J. Pipkin, Heidelberg 1985.
Crick, J. Some editorial and stylistic observations on Coleridge's translation of Schiller's Wallenstein. Pbns of the Eng Goethe Soc n.s. 54 1985.
Jasper, D. (ed). The interpretation of belief: Coleridge, Schleiermacher and romanticism. 1986.
Crick, J. Coleridge's Wallenstein: two legends. MLR 83 1988.
Crisman, W. 'Thus far had the work been transcribed': Coleridge's use of Kant's pre-critical writings and the rhetoric of On the imagination. MLQ 52 1991.
Kaiser, D. A. The incarnated symbol: Coleridge, Hegel, Strauss, and the higher biblical criticism. European Romantic Rev 4 1994.
Reid, N. Coleridge and Schelling: the missing transcendental deduction. Stud in Romanticism 33 1994.

Davidson, John

Petzold, G. von. Davidson und sein geistiges Werden unter dem Einfluss Nietzsches. Leipzig 1928.

Dickens, Charles

Schmidt, J. Bilder aus dem geistigen Leben unserer Zeit. Vols 2, 4, Leipzig 1870–5.
Weizmann, L. Dickens und Daudet in deutscher Übersetzung. Berlin 1880.
Ludwig, O. Dickens und die deutsche Dorfgeschichte. In Schriften vol 6, Leipzig 1891.
Gummer, E. N. Dickens and Germany. MLR 33 1938.
Gummer, E. N. Dickens's works in Germany 1837–1937. New York 1940.
Hennig, J. Note on Dickens and Goethe. Comparative Lit Stud 23–4 1946.
Gibson, F. A. Dickens and Germany. The Dickensian 43 1947.
Thalmann, L. Charles Dickens in seinen Beziehungen zum Ausland. 1956.
Spilka, M. Dickens and Kafka: a mutual interpretation. Bloomington 1963.
Klieneberger, H. R. Dickens and W. Raabe. Oxford German Stud 1969. *See also his* The novel in England and Germany *under General Studies above.*
Reinhold, H. Die Helden und Heroinen der ersten Schaffensperiode von Dickens im Wandel der deutschen Kritik des 19 Jahrhunderts. In Grossbritannien und Deutschland: Festschrift für J. P. Bourke, ed O. Kuhn, Munich 1975.
Margalioth, D. Dickens contra Wagner. Univ of Hartford Stud in Lit 10 1982.
Bick, W. B. Czennia and S. Rohde-Gaur. Bibliographie der deutschen Übersetzungen der Romane von Dickens. Anglia 107 1989.
McInnes, E. O. 'Eine untergeordnete Meisterschaft': the critical reception of Dickens in Germany 1837–1870. Frankfurt am Main 1991.
Bick, W. Dickens' Oliver Twist: zur übersetzerischen Frührezeption der 'fremden' Grossstadtrealität. In Die literarische Übersetzung als Medium der Fremderfahrung, ed F. Lonker, Berlin 1992.

'Eliot, George' (Mary Ann Cross, b. Evans)

Conrad, H. George Eliot über die deutsche Literatur. Gegenwart 15 1886.
Pfeiffer, S. George Eliots Beziehungen zu Deutschland. Heidelberg 1925; rptd 1967.
Lusskey, A. E. George Eliot's The mill on the Floss and Storm's Immensee. Mod Lang Jnl 10 1926.
Simon-Baumann, L. George Eliot über Heinrich Heine. Anglia 55 1931.
Willey, B. George Eliot: Hennell, Strauss and Feuerbach. In his Nineteenth-century studies, 1949.
Müller-Schwefe, G. George Eliot als Übersetzerin. Die Neueren Sprachen 1956.
Casson, A. The mill on the Floss and Keller's Romeo und Julia auf dem Dorfe. MLN 75 1960.
Brebner, L. W. George Eliot and Marie von Ebner-Eschenbach: a comparative study. In Österreich und die angelsächsische Welt II, ed O. Hietsch, Vienna 1968.
Cunningham, V. George Eliot, Julian Fane, and Heine. N & Q 1971.
Wiebel, J. George Eliot's German readers. In George Eliot: the reception of her works and her personal standing during and after her lifetime. Unpbd PhD diss, Hamburg 1971.
Engel, M. T. J. The literary reputation of George Eliot in Germany, 1857–1970. Unpbd diss, Univ of Detroit 1974.
Stang, M. The German original of a George Eliot poem. N & Q 219 1974.
Witemeyer, H. George Eliot, Naumann, and the Nazarenes. VS 18 1974.
See Shaffer, Kubla Khan and The fall of Jerusalem, *under Coleridge above.*
Sullivan, W. J. George Eliot and Goethe's Faust. George Eliot Fellowship Rev 6 1975.
Argyle, G. German elements in the fiction of George Eliot, Gissing, and Meredith. Frankfurt am Main 1979.
See Ashton, The German idea, *under General Studies above.*
McCobb, E. A. Keller's influence on The mill on the Floss: a reassessment. German Life & Letters 33 1980.
McCobb, A. Kleist's Der Findling: the 'backbone' of George Eliot's Romola. Forum for Mod Lang Stud 16 1980.
Klieneberger, H. R. George Eliot and Gottfried Keller. In The novel in England and Germany: a comparative study, 1981.
McCobb, E. A. George Eliot's knowledge of German life and letters. Salzburg 1982.
Wiesenfarth, J. The Greeks, the Germans, and George Eliot. Browning Inst Stud 10 1982.
McCobb, E. A. The morality of musical genius: Schopenhauerian views in Daniel Deronda. Forum for Mod Lang Stud 19 1983.
See Wittig Davis, Novel associations, *under Theodor Fontane above.*
Diedrick, J. George Eliot's experiments in fiction: Brother Jacob and the German Novelle. Stud in Short Fiction 22 1984.
McCobb, E. A. Of women and doctors: Middlemarch and Wilhelmine von Hillern's Ein Arzt der Seele. Neophilologus 68 1984.
McCobb, E. A. Daniel Deronda as will and representation: George Eliot and Schopenhauer. MLR 80 1985.

Broek, A. G. van den, Adam Bede and Riehl's 'social-political-conservatism'. George Eliot Fellowship Rev 17 1986.
Hochberg, S. Onomastics and the German literary ancestry of Daniel Deronda's mother. ELN 28 1990.
Fraiman, S. The mill on the Floss, the critics and the Bildungsroman, PMLA 108 1993.
Röder-Bolton, G. German influences in The mill on the Floss. In Celtic and Germanic themes in European literature, ed N. Thomas, Lewiston NY 1994.
Shaffer, E. George Eliot and Goethe: 'hearing the grass grow'. Pbns of Eng Goethe Soc 66 1996–7.
Rignall, J. (ed), George Eliot and Europe. Aldershot 1997. Includes chapters on German connections.
Röder-Bolton, G. George Eliot and Goethe: an elective affinity. Amsterdam 1998.

Gissing, George Robert

Francis, F. J. Gissing and Schopenhauer. Nineteenth-Century Fiction 15 1961.
Young, A. C. (ed). The letters of Gissing to Eduard Bertz 1887–1903. London and New Brunswick NJ 1961.
See Argyle, German elements, *under George Eliot above.*
Argyle, G. Gissing's The whirlpool and Schopenhauer. Gissing Newsletter 17 1981.
Kropholler, P. F. New Grub Street in Germany. Gissing Newsletter 23 1987.
de Stasio, C. Ryecroft, Schopenhauer and Leopardi. Gissing Newsletter 24 1988.

Hardy, Thomas

Garwood, H. Thomas Hardy, an illustration of the philosophy of Schopenhauer. Philadelphia 1911.
Steinbach, A. Hardy und Schopenhauer. In Anglica, A. Brandl überreicht vol 2, Leipzig 1925.
Schaaf, R. The influence of Schopenhauer on the work of Hardy. Esch-sur-Alzette 1934.
Muchnic, H. Hardy and Thomas Mann. Northampton MA 1939.
Osawa, M. Hardy and the German men of letters. Stud in Eng Lit (Tokyo) 19 1939.
Weber, C. J. Hardy's copy of Schopenhauer. Colby Lib Quart 4 1947.
Ziegler, C. H. Hardy's critical and popular reception in Germany, 1873–1963. Unpbd diss, Vanderbilt Univ 1966.
Ziegler, C. H. Hardy's correspondence with German translators. ELT 11 1968.
Bachman, C. R. Communion and conflict in Hardy and Hauptmann: a contrast in artistic temperaments. Revue des Langues Vivantes 35 1969.
See Parkinson, The rural novel, *under Gotthelf above.*
Kelly, M. A. Schopenhauer's influence on Hardy's Jude the obscure. In Schopenhauer: new essays in honour of his 200th birthday, ed E. von der Luft, Lewiston NY 1988.
Gibson, J. Hardy: a borrowing from Schopenhauer. N & Q 235 1993.

Hopkins, Gerard Manley

Zinnhobler, R. Die Aufnahme des dichterischen Werkes von Hopkins im deutschen Sprachraum. Jahresbuch des Collegium Petrinum 1963–4.

Housman, Alfred Edward

Wysong, J. The influence of Heine on the poetry of Housman. Forum 4 1965.
Wipperfürth, H. Halbwegs zwischen Heine and Brecht: A. E. Housman in der Nachfolge Heines und der deutschen Spätromantik. Heine Jahrbuch 1995.

Keats, John

Green, D. B. Keats and Goethe. N & Q 195 1950.
Green, D. B. Keats and Schiller. MLN 66 1951.
de Mann, P. Keats and Hölderlin. Comparative Lit 8 1956.
Bonarius, G. Zum magischen Realismus bei Keats und Novalis. Giessen 1960.
Schier, R. Consciousness and the object: Keats's urn and Mörike's lamp. Canadian Rev of Comparative Lit 10 1983.
Klotz, K. H. Das Lichtmotiv bei Novalis und Keats. Seminar (Toronto) 30 1994.

Kingsley, Charles

Jacobsen, A. Kingsleys Beziehungen zu Deutschland. Heidelberg 1917.

Lewes, George Henry

See Ashton, The German idea, *under General Studies above.*
Pickett, T. H. Lewes's letters to K. A. Varnhagen von Ense. MLR 80 1985.

Meredith, George

Dick, E. Deutschland und die Deutschen bei Meredith. Germanisch-romanische Monatsschrift 6 1914.
Lees, J. Meredith's literary relations with Germany. MLR 12 1917.
Krusemeyer, M. Der Einfluss Goethes auf Meredith. EStudien 59 1925.
Brewer, E. V. The influence of Jean Paul Richter on Meredith's conception of the comic. JEGP 29 1930.
Downs, B. W. Meredith and Fontane. German Life & Letters 2 1938.
Petter, G. B. Meredith and his German critics. 1939.
Stone, J. Meredith and Goethe. UTQ 21 1952.
Green, D. B. Meredith's Austrian poets: a newly identified review essay with translations. MLR 54 1959.
Carsten, C. The influence of F. M. Müller's German love on Meredith's Modern love. ELN 10 1973.
Wilcox, R. Goethe's Einfluss auf Meredith. Frankfurt am Main 1974.
See Argyle, German elements, *under George Eliot above.*

Moore, George

Blisset, W. F. Moore and literary Wagnerism. Comparative Lit 13 1961.
Brooks, M. W. Moore, Schopenhauer, and the origin of The brook Kerith. ELT 12 1969.

Pater, Walter

Proesler, H. Pater und sein Verhältnis zur deutschen Literatur. Freiburg in Breisgau 1917.

Quincey, Thomas de

Christoph, F. Über den Einfluss Jean Paul Fr. Richters auf De Quincey. Hof 1899.
Dunn, W. A. De Quincey's relation to German literature and philosophy. Strasburg 1901.
Michelsen, P. De Quincey und Goethe. Euphorion 50 1956.
Michelsen, P. De Quincey und Schiller. German Life & Letters 9 1956.
Michelsen, P. De Quincey und die Kantische Philosophie. Revue de Littérature Comparée 33 1959.
Michelsen, P. De Quincey und Jean Paul. JEGP 61 1962.
Black, J. D. Confession, digression, gravitation: De Quincey's German connection. In Thomas De Quincey: bicentenary studies, ed R. L. Snyder, Norman OK 1985.
Groves, D. De Quincey, Schlegel and Victor Cousin. N & Q 235 1990.

Robinson, Henry Crabb

Sadler, T. (ed). Diary, reminiscences and correspondence. 1869.
Norman, F. Crabb Robinson and Goethe. Pbns of Eng Goethe Soc n.s. 4 1927.
Morley, E. J. Crabb Robinson in Germany 1800–5. Oxford 1929.
Schulte, E. Crabb Robinson, Goethe e l'Hyperion di Keats. Annali Instituto Universitario Orientale (Naples), Sezione Germanica 6 1963.
Marquardt, H. Crabb Robinson und seine deutschen Freunde. Vol 1, Göttingen 1964; vol 2, ed B. Reitemeyer, Göttingen 1967.
Koch, H. Crabb Robinson and Jean Paul Richter. Hesperus 29 1965.

Rossetti, Dante Gabriel

Willoughby, L. A. Rossetti and German literature. 1912.
Klinnert, A. Rossetti und Stefan George. Bonn 1933.

Scott, Sir Walter

Gillies, R. P. Recollections of Scott. 1837.

Schmidt, J. Bilder aus dem geistigen Leben unserer Zeit. Vol 1, Leipzig 1870.

Blumenhagen, K. Scott als Übersetzer. Rostock 1900.

Freyl, W. The influence of 'Gothic' literature on Scott. Rostock 1902.

Roesel, L. K. Die literarischen und persönlichen Beziehungen Scotts zu Goethe. Leipzig 1902.

Hohlfeld, A. R. Scott als Übersetzer. Studien zur Vergleichenden Literaturgeschichte 3 1903.

Korff, H. A. Scott und Alexis. Heidelberg 1907.

Kohler, H. F. Walladmor von W. Alexis. Marburg 1915. On the influence of Scott.

MacIntosh, W. Scott and Goethe: German influence on the writings of Scott. Glasgow 1924.

Koch, J. Scotts Beziehungen zu Deutschland. Germanisch-romanische Monatsschrift 15 1927.

Bachmann, F. W. Some German imitators of Scott. Chicago 1933.

Mennie, D. Scott's unpublished translations of German plays. MLR 33 1938.

Ochojski, P. M. Scott's continuous interest in Germany. Stud in Scottish Lit (Texas) 3 1966.

Ochojski, P. M. Waverley über alles: Scott's German reputation. In Scott bicentenary essays, ed A. Bell, New York 1973.

Steinecke, H. Wilhelm Meister oder Waverley? Zur Bedeutung Scotts für das deutsche Romanverständnis der frühen Restaurationszeit. In Teilnahme und Spiegelung, ed B. Allemann and E. Koppen, Berlin 1975.

Johnston, O. W. Literary influence as provocation: Scott's impact on Heine and the Young Germans. Scottish Lit Jnl 7 1980.

Whitmore, D. Scott's indebtedness to the German romantics. Wordsworth Circle 15 1984.

Kroeber, K. Frictional fiction: Scott in the light of von Clausewitz's On war. In English and German romanticism, ed J. Pipkin, Heidelberg 1985.

McInnes, E. Realism, history and the nation: the reception of the Waverley novels in Germany in the 19th century. New German Stud 16 1990–1.

Burwick, F. How to translate a Waverley novel: Scott, Willibald Alexis and De Quincey. Wordsworth Circle 25 1994.

Nemoianu, V. Absorbing modernization: the dilemmas of progress in the novels of Scott and in Faust II. In Interpreting Goethe's Faust today, ed J. K. Brown et al, Columbia SC 1994.

Bentin, W. The reception of Sir Walter Scott's novels in Germany and their influence upon German novelists and literary theory. In The literary reception of British romanticism on the European continent, ed M. Gassenmeier, Essen 1996.

Shelley, Mary

Conger, S. M. A German ancestor for Mary Shelley's monster: Kahlert, Schiller, and the buried treasure of Northanger Abbey. PQ 59 1980.

Shelley, Percy Bysshe

Imelmann, R. Shelleys Alastor und Goethe. Zeitschrift für vergleichende Literaturgeschichte 17 1909.

Liptzin, S. Shelley in Germany. New York 1924; rptd 1968.

Hess, A. Shelleys Lyrik in deutschen Übertragungen. Zurich 1949.

Steiner, F. Shelley and Goethe's Faust. Rivista di Letterature Moderne 4 1951.

Casto, R. C. Shelley as translator of Faust: the Prologue. RES 26 1975.

Klapper, M. R. The German literary influence on Shelley. Salzburg 1975.

Metscher, T. Shelley and Hölderlin. Gulliver 1 1976.

Ruge, E. The trumpet of a prophecy? Studien zur Rezeption Percy Bysshe Shelleys im Vormärz. Essen 1996.

Smith, Adam

Erämetsä, E. Adam Smith als Mittler englisch-deutscher Spracheinflüsse (The Wealth of Nations). Annalis Academiae Scientiarum Fennicae (Helsinki) ser B 1961.

Swinburne, Algernon Charles

Just, K. G. Die Rezeption Swinburnes in der deutschen Literatur der Jahrhundertwende. In Festschrift für Jost Trier, ed W. Foerste and K. H. Borck, Cologne 1964.

Sypher, F. J. jr. Swinburne and Wagner. VP 9 1971.

Tennyson, Alfred, Baron

Schmitt, K. Tennyson in Deutschland. Deutsches Museum 3 1853.

Asher, D. Lord Tennyson and Goethe. Pbns of Eng Goethe Soc 4 1890.

Meyer, W. Tennysons Jugendgedichte in deutscher Übersetzung. Münster 1914.

Jähne, A.-M. Tennyson in Deutschland. Marburg 1954.

Jordan, E. Tennyson's In memoriam – an echo of Goethe. N & Q 213 1968.

Kennedy, I. H. C. Tennyson's 'Bildungsgang': notes on his early reading. PQ 57 1978.

Cronin, R. Goethe, the apostles and Tennyson's supposed confessions. PQ 72 1993.

Thackeray, William Makepeace

Vulpius, W. Thackeray in Weimar. Century Mag 53 1897.

Kurrelmeyer, W. Thackeray and Friedrich von Heyde. MLN 48 1933.

Kohn-Bramstedt, E. Marriage and misalliance in Thackeray and Fontane. German Life & Letters 3 1939.

Schweighofer, K. Thackeray und die deutsche Literatur. Vienna 1949.

Mathison, J. K. The German sections of Vanity fair. Nineteenth-Century Fiction 18 1963.

Worth, G. J. More on the German sections of Vanity fair. Nineteenth-Century Fiction 19 1965.

Maxwell, J. C. Thackeray and Die Wahlverwandtschaften. N & Q 215 1970.

Oram, R. W. Thackeray's translations of German poetry and his Weimar commonplace book. N & Q 223 1978.

Vakhrushev, V. S. Germany in Thackeray's early works. Zeitschrift für Anglistik und Amerikanistik 29 1981.

Horstmann-Guthrie, U. The theme of loyalty in Henry Esmond and Vor dem Sturm. Jnl of European Stud 14 1984.

Prawer, S. S. Thackeray's Goethe: a 'secret history'. Pbns of the Eng Goethe Soc 62 1993.

Wilde, Oscar

Meyerfeld, M. Wilde in Deutschland. Das Literarische Echo 1 Jan 1903.

Sherard, R. H. Life of Wilde. 1911. With bibliography.

Defieber, R. Oscar Wilde: der Mann und sein Werk im Spiegel der deutschen Kritik und sein Einfluss auf die deutsche Literatur. Heidelberg 1934.

Oswald, V. A. Wilde, Stefan George, Heliogabalus. MLQ 10 1940.

Willoughby, L. A. Wilde and Goethe: the life of art and the art of life. Pbns of the Eng Goethe Soc 35 1965.

Kohlmayer, R. Oscar Wilde in Deutschland und Österreich. Tübingen 1996.

Wordsworth, William

Herzberg, M. J. Wordsworth and German literature. PMLA 40 1925.

Stallknecht, N. P. Wordsworth's Ode to duty and the Schöne Seele. PMLA 52 1937.

Hartmann, H. Wordsworth's Lapland night. RES 14 1938.

Willoughby, L. A. Wordsworth and Germany. In German studies presented to H. G. Fielder, Oxford 1938.

Todd, F. M. Wordsworth in Germany. MLR 47 1952.

Hirsch, E. D. jr. Wordsworth and Schelling: a typological study of Romanticism. New Haven CT 1960.

de Mann, P. The imagery of heaven and earth in Wordsworth and Hölderlin. MLA Program 1964.

Kliman, B. W. Wordsworth in a small German magazine. N & Q 210 1965.

Hartman, G. H. Wordsworth and Goethe in literary history. New Literary History 6 1975.

See Hanke, Spatiotemporal consciousness, *under Novalis above.*

Primeau, J. K. The influence of Gottfried August Bürger on the Lyrical ballads of Wordsworth: the supernatural vs the natural. Germanic Rev 58 1983.

Kelley, T. M. Wordsworth, Kant and the romantic sublime. PQ 63 1984. [JR]

(5) ITALIAN

Annual lists are pbd in Italian Studies (Leeds) *and in* Rivista di Letterature Moderne e Comparate (Florence).

General studies

For a full list of travel books see C. P. Brand, A bibliography of travel books describing Italy 1800–50, Ital Stud 11 1956. *Others, pbd in the second half of the century, can be found in* S. S. Lodovici, Bibliografia di viaggiatori stranieri in Italia nel secolo XIX, Rome 1938. *A comprehensive work is* R. S. Pine Coffin, Bibliography of English and American travellers to Italy, Florence 1974. *A full bibliography on the Risorgimento can be found in* H. W. Rudman, Italian nationalism and English letters, 1940.

Simonde de Sismondi, J. C. L. La littérature du midi de l'Europe. 4 vols Geneva 1818, tr T. Roscoe 1823. Historical view of the literature of the south of Europe.

Roscoe, T. The Italian novelists. Vol 4 1825.

Lardner, D. Eminent literary and scientific men of Italy, Spain and Portugal. Vol 2 1837. On Alfieri, Monti, Foscolo.

Merivale, L. A. I poeti italiani moderni. 1865. A selection, with bibliographical essays, including Alfieri, Monti, Foscolo, Manzoni, Leopardi.

Schuyler, E. Italian influences. New York 1901. On Landor, Dickens, E. B. Browning.

Wollaston, G. H. The Englishman in Italy. Oxford 1909.

Segrè, C. Lady Holland e i suoi ospiti italiani. In his Relazioni letterarie fra Italia e Inghilterra. Florence 1911.

Olivero, F. Saggi di letteratura inglese. Bari 1913. On Wordsworth, Coleridge, Hunt, Shelley, Keats and Italy.

Olivero, F. Studi su poeti e prosatori inglesi. Turin 1925. On Coleridge, Carlyle, Ruskin, Thompson, Morris and Italy.

King, R. W. Italian influence on English scholarship and literature during the romantic revival. MLR 20–1 1925–6.

Bräm, E. M. Die italienische Renaissance in dem englischen Geistesleben des 19 Jahrhunderts im besonders bei J. Ruskin. Zurich 1932. On Ruskin, Symonds, Lee.

Marshall, R. Italy in English literature 1755–1815. New York 1934.

Wicks, M. C. W. The Italian exiles in London 1816–48. Manchester 1937.

Rossi, J. I critici inglesi e americani del De Sanctis. Italica 15 1938.

Viglione, F. L'Italia nel pensiero degli scrittori inglesi. Milan 1947.

Bandy, W. T. Macaulay and his Italian translator. Italica 25 1948.

Branchi, E. C. Escursioni letterarie da Londra a Firenze: le fonti italiane della letteratura inglese. Santiago de Chile 1949.

Brand, C. P. Italians in England 1800–50; a bibliography of their publications. Ital Stud 15 1960.

Rebora, P. Interpretazioni anglo-italiane. Bari 1961.

Barrows, H. Convention and novelty in the romantic generation's experience of Italy. BNYPL June 1963.

Kroeber, K. The artifice of reality. Madison WI 1964. On Wordsworth, Foscolo, Keats, Leopardi.

Watson, G. The English Petrarchans: a critical bibliography of the Canzoniere. 1967 (Warburg Inst).

Brand, P. Romanticismo italiano e Romanticismo inglese. In Il Romanticismo: Atti del Sesto Congresso dell'Associazione Internazionale per gli studi di Lingua e Letteratura Italiana, Budapest 1968.

Anderson, P. J. M. Over the Alps. Reflections on travel and travel writing with special reference to the grand tours of Boswell, Beckford and Byron. 1969.

Macchioni-Jodi, R. Cecchi prosatore fra gli inglesi e La Ronda. Rassegna della Letteratura Italiana 86 1982.

Robertson, P. An experience of women: pattern and change in nineteenth-century Europe. Philadelphia 1982.

Cartago, G. Ricordi d'italiano. Osservazioni intorno alla lingua e italianismi nelle relazioni di viaggio degli inglesi in Italia. Bassano del Grappa 1990.

Cheyne, J. and L. Crisafulli Jones (ed). L'esilio romantico: forme di un conflitto. Bari 1990.

Cotsell, M. Creditable warriors: 1830–1876. 1990. On A. H. Clough, E. Barrett Browning, R. Browning.

Maynard, J. Victorian innocence abroad: the sexual and religious dialectics of an Englishman in Italy. Annals of Scholarship (Detroit) 7 1990. On A. H. Clough.

Thwaite, M. Elizabeth Gaskell and Italy. Gaskell Soc Jnl 4 1990.

DeCuir, A. Italy, England, and the female artist in George Eliot's Mr. Gilfil's Love Story. Stud in Short Fiction 29 1992.

Morrison, R. D. Hardy's pilgrimage poems of 1887 and the anxiety of influence. College Lang Assoc Jnl (Atlanta) 36 1992.

Tourn, G. Viaggiatori britannici alle valli valdesi (1753–1899). Rome 1994.

Italian authors

For a selected list of works pbd 1800–50 commenting on Italian authors, and a full list of anthologies of Italian literature pbd 1800–40, see C. P. Brand, Italy and the English Romantics, Cambridge 1957.

Alfieri, Vittorio (1749–1803)

Tragedie. Paris 1787–9; The tragedies of Alfieri, tr C. Lloyd 3 vols 1815. Contains Philip, Polinices, Antigone, Virginia, Agamemnon, Orestes, Rosamunda, Octavia, Timoleon, Merope, Mary Stuart, The conspiracy of the Pazzi, Don Garcia, Saul, Agis, Sophonisba, The first Brutus, Myrrha, The second Brutus.

▽

Byron, Lord. Marino Faliero. 1821.

Byron, Lord. The two Foscari. 1821.

Byron, Lord. Sardanapalus. 1821.

Swinburne, A. C. Marino Faliero. 1885.

Pudbres, A. Lord Byron, admirer and imitator of Alfieri. E Studien 33 1903.

Zanco, A. L'Alfierismo del Byron. Rivista Italiana del Dramma 5 1941.

Vincent, E. R. L'amore londinese di Vittorio Alfieri. Rassegna della Letteratura Italiana 61 1957.

Aratani, J. L'influenza di Alfieri sulle tragedie byroniane. Studi italici (Kyoto) 1971.

D'Agostini, C. Vittorio Alfieri a Londra (1768, 1770–1). Colloquium Helveticum 13 1991.

Boccaccio, Giovanni (1313–75). *See also under Rossetti and Symonds below.*

[Moore, T.] The spirit of Boccaccio's Decameron. 1812. *See* H. G. Wright, Moore as the author of The spirit of Boccaccio's Decameron, RES 23 1947.

Keats, J. Isabella: or the pot of basil. 1818.

Eliot, George (M. A. Evans). How Lisa loved the King. Boston 1869.

Wright, H. G. Boccaccio in England from Chaucer to Tennyson. 1957.

Viviani della Robbia, E. Shelley e il Boccaccio. Italica 36 1959.

Sturrock, J. Sigismonda and Ghismonda: Wordsworth and Scott on Dryden and Boccaccio. ES 63 1982.

Hill, A. G. Wordsworth, Boccaccio, and the pagan Gods of antiquity. RES 45 1994.

Carducci, Giosuè (1835–1907). *See also under Byron below.*

Poems. Tr with introductory essays by F. Sewall, 1893. A selection.

Ferretti, L. Carducci e la letteratura inglese. Milan 1927.

Scalia, S. E. Carducci et la critique anglo-saxonne. Revue de Littérature Comparée 15 1935.

Scalia, S. E. Carducci – his critics and translators in England and America 1881–1932. New York 1937.

Casti, Giovanni Battista (1721–1803)

Novelle. Paris 1801; The origin of Rome and of the Papacy, tr D. Whistlecraft 1861.

Gli animali parlanti. Paris 1802; The court of beasts, tr W. S. Rose 1816.

Li tre Giuli. Naples 1814; The tre Giuli, tr with a memoir of the author 1826.

▽

Fuess, C. M. Lord Byron as a satirist in verse. New York 1912.

Vassallo, P. G. Casti's Animali parlanti, the Italian epic and Don Juan: the poetry of politics. In Byron: poetry and politics, ed E. A. Sturzl and J. Hogg, Salzburg 1980.

Dante Alighieri (1265–1321). *See also under Browning, Byron, Coleridge, Hunt, Keats, Rossetti, Ruskin, Shelley, Tennyson below.*

Canzoniere. Tr C. Lyell 1845.

La divina commedia. Hell, purgatory and paradise, tr H. F. Cary 3 vols 1814, 1819, 1831, 1844, 1850, 1867, 1868, 1869, 1871, 1876, 1883, 1889, 1892, 1894, 1900; tr I. C. Wright 3 vols 1833–40; tr P. Bannerman, Edinburgh 1850; tr E. C. O'Donnell 1845; tr C. B. Cayley 4 vols 1851–55; tr F. Pollock 1854; tr H. W. Longfellow 3 vols 1867, 1886, 1890, 1891; tr D. Johnston 3 vols Bath 1867–8; tr J. I. Minchin 1885; tr F. K. H. Haselfoot 1887; tr C. E. Norton 3 vols 1891–2, 1899; tr A. J. Butler 1880–92. *For a full list see* C. F. Cunningham, The divine comedy in English: a critical bibliography 1782–1900, Edinburgh 1965.

▽

Church, R. W. Dante. Christian Remembrancer 11 1850.

Dobelli, A. Dante e Byron. Giornale Dantesco 6 1898.

Valgimigli, A. Il culto di Dante in Inghilterra. Giornale Dantesco 6 1898.

Toynbee, P. Dante in English literature from Chaucer to Cary 1380–1844. Vol 2 1909. An anthology.

Olivero, F. Dante e Coleridge. In Saggi di letteratura inglese, Bari 1913.

Galimberti, A. Dante nel pensiero inglese, Florence 1921.

Newman, F. M. The Francesca da Rimini episode in English literature. Cambridge MA 1942.

Friedrich, W. P. Dante's fame abroad 1350–1850. Rome 1950. With complete bibliography.

Doughty, O. Dante and the English Romantics. Eng Misc (Rome) 2 1951.

Gittings, R. Keats's debt to Dante. In his Mask of Keats. 1956.

Saly, J. Keats's answer to Dante: The fall of Hyperion. KSJ 14 1965.

Leggett, B. J. Dante, Byron, and Tennyson's Ulysses. Tennessee Stud in Lit 15 1970.

Montgomery, M. The reflective journey toward order: Dante, Wordsworth, Eliot and others. Athens GA 1973.

O'Malley, G. Dante, Shelley, and T. S. Eliot. In Romantic and modern: revaluations of literary tradition, ed G. Bornstein, Pittsburgh 1977.

Taylor, B. Byron's use of Dante in the Prophecy of Dante. KS J 28 1979.

Fontana, E. L. William Morris's Guenevere and Dante's Francesca: allusion as revision. EM 28–9 1979–80.

Ellis, S. Dante and English poetry: Shelley to T. S. Eliot. Cambridge 1983.

Bump, J. Influence and intertextuality: Hopkins and the school of Dante. JEGP 83 1984.

Cooksey, T. L. Dante's England, 1818: the contribution of Cary, Coleridge, and Foscolo to the British reception of Dante. Papers on Lang and Lit 20, Edwardsville IL 1984.

Parker, P. Dante and the dramatic monologue. Stanford Lit Rev 2 1985.

Boyle, R. S. J. Hopkins, Brutus, and Dante. VP 24 1986.

Crook, N. The even stranger ride of Morrowbie Jukes: Kipling and Dante again. Kipling Jnl 60 1986.

Cooksey, T. L. Dante Resartus: Byron, Novalis and the Carlylian poet as hero. Amer N & Q 14:2 1987.

Docherty, J. Dantean allusions in Wonderland. Jabberwocky: the Jnl of the Lewis Carroll Soc 19:1–2 1990.

Armstrong, T. Hardy's Dantean Purples. Thomas Hardy Jnl 7 1991.

Thompson, A. George Eliot, Dante, and moral choice in Felix Holt, The Radical. MLR 86 1991.

Cooksey, T. L. The central man of the world: the Victorian myth of Dante. Stud in Medievalism 4 1992.

Zuccato, E. S. T. Coleridge as a critic of Dante. Il Confronto Letterario 9:18 1992.

Foscolo, Ugo (1778–1827)

Ultime lettere di Jacopo Ortis. Milan 1802; Letters of Ortis, tr F. B. 1818.

Essays on Petrarch. 1821, 1823.

▽

Viglione, F. Foscolo in Inghilterra. Catania 1910.

Cortese, C. Foscolo e l'Inghilterra. Naples 1935.

Vincent, E. R. Byron, Hobhouse and Foscolo. Cambridge 1949, rptd New York 1972.

Vincent, E. R. Foscolo and John Allen: unpublished letters. Ital Stud 4 1949.

Wilkins, E. H. Samuel Carter Hall on Foscolo. Romantic Rev 41 1950.

Vincent, E. R. Foscolo: an Italian in Regency England. Cambridge 1953. With list of Foscolo's London pbns.

Limentani, U. Testimonianze inglesi sul Foscolo. Giornale Storico della Letteratura Italiana 3 1956.

Vincent, E. R. Overhearing Foscolo. Eng Misc (Rome) 7 1956.

Fasano, P. L' 'amicizia' Foscolo – Sterne e la traduzione didimea del Sentimental journey. Eng Misc (Rome) 14 1963.

Brand, C. P. Ugo Foscolo and the Edinburgh Review: unpublished letters to Francis Jeffrey. MLR 70 1975.

Toschi, L. 'To Callirhoe' ed altri inediti foscoliani. Rassegna della Letteratura Italiana 84 1980.

Toschi, L. Foscolo lettore di Sterne e altri 'sentimental travellers'. MLN 97 1982.

Varese, C. Foscolo, sternismo, tempo e persona. Ravenna 1982.

Matteo, S. Textual exile. The reader in Sterne and Foscolo. New York 1985.

Scotti, M. Inediti foscoliani, I: ancora del Foscolo, Lord Holland, l'abate Meneghelli, e i presunti autografi petrarcheschi. Rassegna della Letteratura Italiana 89 1985.

Illiano, A. From Gray's Elegy to Foscolo's Carme: highlighting the meditation and sublimation of the 'Sepulchral'. Symposium (Washington DC) 47 1993.

Costa, G. Ugo Foscolo's Europe: a journey from the sublime to Romantic humor. In The motif of the journey in nineteenth-century Italian literature, ed B. Magliocchetti and A. Verna, Gainesville FL 1994.

Goldoni, Carlo (1707–93)

La gelosia di Lindoro; Un curioso accidente. In New British theatre. Vols 1, 3 (as The word of honour; Love, honour and interest) c. 1860.

Un curioso accidente; Il burbero benefico; Il ventaglio; L'avaro fastoso. In The comedies of Carlo Goldoni, ed H. Zimmern 1892 (as A curious mishap; The beneficent bear; The fan; The spendthrift miser).

▽

Maddalena, E. Goldoni in Inghilterra e in America. Rivista d'Italia 15 Sep 1923.

De Petris, C. Lady Gregory, l'Italia e Goldoni. Il Veltro 34:5–6 1990.

Leopardi, Giacomo (1798–1827). *See also under Byron, Gissing, Keats, Shelley below.*

Operette morali. Milan 1826; Pensieri, Milan 1827; Essays and dialogues, tr C. Edwardes 1882; Essays, dialogues and thoughts, tr P. Maxwell 1893; tr J. Thomson ('B.V.') 1905.

Versi. Bologna 1824, Florence 1831; The poems of Leopardi, tr F. H. Cliffe 1893; tr J. M. Morrison 1900; tr T. Martin 1904.

▽

Marchesi, G. Leopardi e la poesia inglese. Iride 3 1899.

Bickersteth, G. L. Leopardi and Wordsworth. 1927.

Olivero, F. La letteratura inglese nei Pensieri di varia filosofia. In his Studi britannici, Turin 1931. Mainly on Byron.

Cotten, L. A. Leopardi and the City of dreadful night. SP 42 1945.

Rhodes, D. E. The composition of Mr Gladstone's essay on Leopardi. Ital Stud 8 1953.

Singh, H. A. E. Housman and Leopardi. Eng Misc (Rome) 13 1962.

Corrigan, B. The poetry of Leopardi in Victorian England 1837–78. Eng Misc (Rome) 14 1963.

Corrigan, B. Hardy and Leopardi: a study of affinity and contrast. Rivista di Letterature Moderne e Comparate 17 1964.

Enrico, H. Shipwreck in infinity: Leopardi, Coleridge, and Wordsworth on the imagination. In Proceedings: Pacific Northwest Conference on Foreign Languages, Victoria BC, 1970.

Dionisotti, C. Fortuna del Leopardi. In Essays in honour of John Humphreys Whitfield…, ed H. C. Davis, D. G. Rees, J. M. Hatwell and G. W. Slowey, 1975.

Lonardi, G. Leopardi, Browning e tre poesie di Montale. In Poetica e stile: saggi, ed L. Renzi, Padua 1976.

Casale, O. H. and A. C. Dooley. Leopardi, Arnold, and the Victorian sensibility. Comparative Lit Stud 17 1980.

Singh, G. S. Leopardi and Matthew Arnold: i miti e le delusioni dell'eredità romantica. Italianistica: Rivista di Letteratura Italiana 9 1980.

Mariani, A. Leopardi e Shelley: appunti per un'analisi contrastiva. Quaderni d'Italianistica (Toronto) 8 1987.

Singh, G. The fortune of Leopardi in 19th century England. Esperienze Letterarie: Rivista Trimestrale di Critica e Cultura (Naples) 13 1988.

Williams, P. Leopardi in the English-speaking world: a bibliography. Ital Stud 43 1988.

Johnson, T. Hardy, Leopardi and Tess of the d'Urbervilles. Thomas Hardy Jnl 9 1993.

Donati, C. Leopardi and The panoramic miscellany. Rassegna della Letteratura Italiana 92 1988.

Manzoni, Alessandro (1785–1873). *See also under Scott, col 167 below.*

I promessi sposi. 3 vols Milan 1825–6 (for 1827), 1840–2 (rev); The betrothed lovers, tr C. Swan 3 vols Pisa 1828; The betrothed, 1834, 1844, 1845 etc. 1845 alone based on Manzoni's text of 1840–2.

▽

Franzi, T. Promessi sposi giudicati dal primo traduttore inglese. Marzocco 25 Sep 1932.

Neri, N. La fortuna del Manzoni in Inghilterra. Atti della Accademia delle Scienze di Torino 74 1939.

Zentai, E. Confrontando Manzoni e W. Scott. In Il Romanticismo: Atti del Sesto Congresso dell'Associazione Internazionale per gli studi di Lingua e Letteratura Italiana, Budapest 1968.

Hempel, W. Manzoni und die Darstellung der Menschenmenge als erzähltechnisches Problem in den Promessi Sposi, bei Scott und in den historischen Romanen der französischer Romantik. Krefeld 1974.

Chandler, S. B. The motif of the journey in the eighteenth-century novel in Scott and Manzoni. Rivista di Studi Italiani 3 1985.

Erasmi, G. Lucy of Lammermoor and Lucia Mondella. In Perspectives on nineteenth-century Italian novels, ed G. Pugliese, Ottawa 1989.

Newton, R. and N. Lebowitz. Dickens, Manzoni, Zola, and James: the impossible romance. Columbia MO 1990.

Mazzini, Giuseppe (1805?–72). *See also under Swinburne below.*

King, H. E. H. The disciples. 1873.

Galimberti, A. Mazzini nel pensiero inglese. Nuova Antologia 1 July 1919.

Limentani, U. The ideas of Mazzini and Shaw on the function of art. Ital Stud 4 1949.

Daniels, E. A. Collaboration of Mazzini on an article in the Westminster Review. BNYPL Nov 1961.

Rivas, M. Mazzini et les écrivains anglais et americains de son temps. Studi Americani 18 1972.

Blakiston, N. Mazzini e l'Inghilterra. Il Veltro 17 1973.

Veyriras, P. Mazzini et la réhabilitation de George Sand en Angleterre (1837–1847). Confluents 1975.

Pulci, Luigi (1432–84). *See also under Hunt below.*

Morgante maggiore. Venice 1481; Canto 1, tr G. G. Byron 1822.

▽

Frere, J. H. The monks and the giants. Ed R. D. Waller, Manchester 1926.

Waters, L. The 'Desultory Rhyme' of Don Juan: Byron, Pulci, and the improvisatory style. ELH 45 1978.

Waters, L. Pulci and the poetry of Byron. Annali d'Italianistica 1 1983.

Cochran, P. Byron and Margutte. Byron Jnl 21 1993.

English authors

For a full list of secondary works on Italy and the English Romantics up to 1922, see C. Zacchetti, Shelley e Dante, Milan 1922.

Arnold, Matthew. *See also under Leopardi above.*

England and the Italian question. 1859.

▽

Bevington, M. M. Matthew Arnold's England and the Italian Question, Durham 1953.

Barksdale, R. K. Arnold and Tennyson on Etna. College Lang Assoc Jnl 2 1958.

Barrett Browning, Elizabeth

Casa Guidi windows. 1851.

▽

Pratesi, L. L'Italianità nei canti di E. B. Browning. Rocca San Casciano 1928.

Gilbert, S. From Patria to Matria: Elizabeth Barrett Browning's Risorgimento. PMLA 99 1984.

Phelps, D. 'At the Roadside of Humanity': Elizabeth Barrett Browning abroad. In Creditable warriors: 1830–1876, ed M. Cotsell 1990.

Browning, Robert. *See also under Leopardi above.*

Sordello. 1840.

King Victor and King Charles. In Bells and pomegranates vol 2, 1842.

Luria. 1846.

The ring and the book. 4 vols 1868.

Asolando. 1890.

▽

Nencioni, E. Robert Browning e l'Italia. Nuova Antologia 1 Jan 1890.

Clarke, H. A. Browning's Italy. New York 1907.

Corrigan, B. New documents on Browning's Roman murder case. SP 49 1952.

Guidi, A. I Browning e l'ambiente fiorentino. In L'otto-novecento, Florence 1957.

Bisignano, D. E. Nencioni e R. Browning. EM 14 1963.

Johnson, A. P. Sordello: Apollo, Bacchus, and the pattern of Italian history. VP 7 1969.

Guidi, A. Robert Browning e il Veneto. Filologia e Letteratura 16 1970.
Melchiori, B. Browning in Italy. In Robert Browning, ed I. Armstrong, Athens OH and London 1975.
Robertson, D. Browning on the Colle di Colma. Browning Soc Notes 5 1975. Including travel lit on Italy.
Alaya, F. The ring, the rescue, and the Risorgimento: reunifying the Brownings' Italy. Browning Inst Stud 6 1978.
Ross, M. Browning's art of perspective: 'The Englishman in Italy'. Eng Stud in Canada 7 1981.
Holloway, J. B. Death and the emperor in Dante, Browning, Dickinson and Stevens. Stud in Medievalism 2 1983.
Korg, J. Browning and Italy. Athens OH and London 1983.
Cervo, N. Chiarini's retort to Zanella: Browning's Italian critics. Browning Inst Stud 14 1986.
Brewer, W. D. 'In Heaven We Have the Real and True and Sure': the influence of Dante's Vita nuova on Browning's The ring and the book. Stud in Browning and His Circle 16 1988.
Ostermark Johansen, L. 'It's Art's Decline, My Son!' – John Ruskin and Robert Browning. Two Victorian views on the Italian Renaissance. Angles on the Eng Speaking World (Copenhagen) 5 1991.
Viscusi, R. 'The Englishman in Italy': free trade as a principle of aesthetics. In Critical essays on Robert Browning, ed M. E. Gibson, New York 1992.
Cook, E. The Italian journey: from James to Eliot to Browning. In The motif of the journey in nineteenth-century Italian literature, ed B. Magliocchetti and A. Verna, Gainesville FL, 1994.

Butler, Samuel

Alps and sanctuaries of Piedmont and the canton Ticino. 1881.

▽

Sella, A. Un inglese fervido amico dell'Italia: Samuel Butler. Novara 1916.
Gabrieli, V. Presentazione italiana di Butler. Civiltà Moderna 12 1940.
Vita-Finzi, C. Butler and Italy. Ital Stud 18 1963.
Angelo, G. A note on Samuel Butler in Sicily. EM 22 1971.
Bellorini, M. L'Italia di Samuel Butler. Jnl of Anglo-Ital Stud (Malta) 1 1991.

Byron, George Gordon, Baron. *See also under Alfieri, Casti, Dante, Foscolo, Leopardi and Pulci, above, and under Hunt and Shelley below.*

Childe Harold's pilgrimage. 3 vols 1812–18, 2 vols 1819.
Beppo: a Venetian story. 1818.
Don Juan. 8 vols 1819–24, 2 vols 1826.
The prophecy of Dante. 1821.

▽

Monti, G. G. Leopardi e Byron. In his Studi critici, Florence 1887. On Prisoner of Chillon and Dante's Ugolino.
Krause, F. Byrons Marino Faliero: ein Beitrag zur vergleichenden Literaturgeschichte. Breslau 1897.
With Byron in Italy. Being a selection of the poems and letters of Lord Byron. Which have to do with his life in Italy from 1816 to 1823. Selected and arranged by Anna Berneson McMahan, Chicago and Cambridge 1906.
Muoni, G. La leggenda del Byron in Italia. Milan 1907.
Simhart, M. Byrons Einfluss auf die italienische Literatur. Leipzig 1909.
Meneghetti, N. Lord Byron a Venezia. 1910
Zacchetti, C. Lord Byron e l'Italia. Palermo 1920.
'Stendhal' (M. H. Beyle). In his Mélanges de littérature vol 3, ed H. Martineau, Paris 1933.
Messinese, G. Byron and Italy. Tripoli 1937.
Niccolai, B. Bibliografia di studi inglesi in Italia: Byron. Bollettino di Studi Inglesi in Italia July 1937.
Quennell, P. C. Byron in Italy. 1941, rptd 1974.
Borst, W. A. Byron's first pilgrimage 1809–11. New Haven CT 1948.
Origo, I. The last attachment: the story of Byron and Teresa Guiccioli. 1949.
Guidi, A. Traduzioni e citazioni del Byron dai classici italiani. Annali Triestini 23 1953.
Wilson Knight, G. Byron: Christian virtues. 1953.
de Palacio, J. Byron traducteur et les influences italiennes. Rivista di Letterature Moderne e Comparate 1958.
Melchiori, G. Byron and Italy. Nottingham 1958.
Melchiori, G. L'Italia di Byron. Lettere Italiane 10 1958.
Poli, N. Echi di Byron in Carducci. Rivista di Letterature Moderne e Comparate 1958.
Lograsso, A. Byron traduttore del Pellico. Lettere Italiane 11 1959.
Blakiston, N. Byron, Shelley e Trelawny a Pisa. In Inghilterra e Toscana nell'Ottocento, Florence 1968.
Stringham, S. I due Foscari: from Byron's play to Verdi's opera. West Virginia Univ Philological Papers 17 1970.
Brilli, A. Byron e Leopardi: il riso dei morti. Studi Urbinati di Storia, Filosofia e Letteratura 45 1971.
Ogle, R. B. A Byron contradiction: some light on his Italian study. SiR 12 1973.
Churchill, K. J. Byron and Italy. Literary Half-Yearly 15:ii 1974.
King, M. Early Italian Romanticism and The Giaour. Byron Jnl 4 1976.
Melchiori, G. The influence of Byron's death on Italy, Byron Jnl 5 1977.
Smith, H. W. Byron and Silvio Pellico. Byron Jnl 7 1979.
Melchiori, G. Byron and Italy: catalyst of the Risorgimento. In Byron's political and cultural influence in nineteenth-century Europe, ed P. G. Trueblood, Atlantic Highlands NJ 1981.
Kennedy, R. F. Byron and Petrarch. Byron Jnl 11 1983.
Guiccioli, T. La vie de Lord Byron en Italie, ed E. A. Sturzl, Salzburg 1983.
Shilstone, F. W. Byron, Dante, and Don Juan's descent to English society. The Comparatist (Knoxville TN) 8 1984.
Vassallo, P. Byron: the Italian literary influence. New York 1984.
Ulmer, W. A. The Dantean politics of The Prisoner of Chillon. KSJ 35 1986.
Hinterhauser, H. Lord Byron in Calabrien. In Idee, Gestalt, Geschichte: Festschrift für Klaus von See, ed G. Weber, Odense 1988.
Sturzl, E. A. A love's eye view: Teresa Guiccioli's La vie de Lord Byron en Italie. Salzburg 1988.
Dawson, P. M. S. 'Thou Paradise of Exile': Byron, Shelley, and Italy. In L'esilio romantico: forme di un conflitto, ed J. Cheyne and L. Crisafulli Jones, Bari 1990.
Kernberger, K. Poet and persona, the two exiles in Byron's The prophecy of Dante. In L'esilio romantico: forme di un conflitto, ed J. Cheyne and L. Crisafulli Jones, Bari 1990.
Reiman, D. H. Byron in Italy: the return of Augustus. In Byron: Augustan and Romantic, ed A. Rutherford, New York 1990.
Spence, G. The lament of Tasso and poetic genius. Byron Jnl 18 1990.
Tinkler Villani, V. Byron's vision of Dante. In Centennial hauntings: Pope, Byron and Eliot in the year '88, ed C. C. Barfoot and T. D'haen, Atlanta 1990.
Webb, T. Byron as a man of the world. In L'esilio romantico: forme di un conflitto, ed J. Cheyne and L. Crisafulli Jones, Bari 1990.
Fisher, J. R. 'Here the Story Ends': Byron's Beppo, a broken Dante. Byron Jnl 21 1993.
Graziani, N. Byron e Teresa, l'amore italiano, Milan 1995.

Coleridge, Samuel Taylor. *See also under Dante, Leopardi above.*

Fisch, M. H. The Coleridges, Dr Prati and Vico. MP 41 1943.
Sells, A. L. Zanella, Coleridge and Shelley. Comparative Lit 2 1950.
Orsini, G. N. G. Coleridge e Croce: note di estetica e di critica della poesia. Rivista di Studi Crociani Ottobre–Dicembre 1964.
Sultana, D. Samuel Taylor Coleridge in Malta and Italy. New York 1969.

Whalley, G. Coleridge and Vico. In Giambattista Vico: an international symposium, ed G. Tagliacozzo and H. V. White, Baltimore 1969.
Greer, M. Coleridge and Dante: kinship in Xanadu. Univ of Dayton Rev 10 1974.
Darcy, C. P. Coleridge and the Italian artist, Migliarini. N & Q 221 1976.

Corelli, Marie (pseudonym of Mary Mackay)
Vendetta. 3 vols 1886.
A romance of two worlds. 1886.

Dickens, Charles
Pictures from Italy. 1846.
▽
Cannavò, F. D. Dickens e l'Italia. Rome 1918.
Marani Toro, I. Dickens e l'Italia. Rome 1925.
Piscopo, V. Dickens en Italie. Europe 488 1969.
Paroissien, D. H. Dickens' Pictures from Italy: stages of the work's development and Dickens' method of composition. EM 22 1971.
Piscopo, V. Dickens e l'Italia. Cultura e Scuola 10 1971.
Burgan, W. M. Little Dorrit in Italy. Nineteenth Cent Fiction 29 1975.
Curreli, M. Dickens, Gissing e la società italiana dell'Ottocento. Studi dell'Istituto Linguistico (Florence) 5 1982.
Thurin, S. S. Pictures from Italy: Pickwick and Podsnap abroad. Dickensian 83 1987.
Hollington, M. Dickens and Italy. Jnl of Anglo-Ital Stud (Malta) 1 1991.

Gissing, George R. *See also under Dickens above.*
By the Ionian sea: notes of a ramble in Southern Italy. 1901.
▽
Lloyd, M. Italy and the nostalgia of Gissing. Eng Misc (Rome) 2 1951.
Coustillas, P. A note on Gissing in Calabria. Gissing Newsletter 16 1980.
de Stasio, C. Ryecroft, Schopenhauer and Leopardi. Gissing Newsletter 24 1988.

Hunt, J. H. Leigh
The story of Rimini. 1816. From Dante.
Tasso, T. Gerusalemme liberata. Venice 1580; Jerusalem delivered, tr Hunt 1818.
Tasso, T. Aminta. Venice 1581; Amyntas: a tale of the woods, tr Hunt 1820.
Redi, F. Bacco in Toscana. Florence 1685. Bacchus in Tuscany: a dithyrambic poem, tr Hunt 1825.
Lord Byron and some of his contemporaries, with recollections of the author's life, and of his visit to Italy. 1828.
High and low life in Italy etc by J. J. Pidcock Raikes. Monthly Repository July 1837–Apr 1838.
A legend of Florence. 1840.
Stories from the Italian poets. 1846. With essays on Dante, Pulci, Boiardo, Ariosto, Tasso.
A jar of honey from Mount Hybla. 1858.
▽
Olivero, F. Leigh Hunt e i suoi studi sulla Divina Commedia. In his Saggi di letteratura inglese, Bari 1913.
Fischer, E. Hunt und die italienische Literatur. Trute 1936.
Short, C. The composition of Hunt's The story of Rimini. KSJ 21–2 1972–3.
Robinson, C. E. Leigh Hunt's dramatic success: a legend of Florence. In The life and times of Leigh Hunt, ed R. A. McCown, Iowa City 1985.
Hayden, J. O. Leigh Hunt's Story of Rimini: reloading the Romantic canon. Durham Univ Jnl 79 1987.

James, Henry
Roderick Hudson. Boston 1876.
The portrait of a lady. 3 vols 1881.
The Princess Casamassima. 3 vols 1886.
Italian hours. 1909.

Keats, John
Gay, H. N. John Keats e gli inglesi a Roma. Nuova Antologia 1 July 1912.
Benedetti, A. Correnti italiane nella poesia di Keats. Nuova Antologia 16 Feb 1921.
Hough, G. Tra Keats e Leopardi. Veltro 15 1971.
Robinson, J. Dante's Paradiso and Keats's 'Ode to a nightingale'. KSJ 25 1976.
Flick, A. J. Keats's first reading of Dante's Divine comedy. N & Q 223 1978.
Spiegelman, W. The 'Ode to a nightingale' and Paradiso XXIII. KSJ 33 1984.

Landor, Walter Savage
Imaginary conversations. 4 vols 1824–9; ed C. G. Crump 6 vols 1891 (with addns).
The Pentameron, and Pentalogia. 1837.
Andrea of Hungary; Giovanna of Naples; Fra Rupert. 2 vols 1839–40. A trilogy.
The Italics. 1848.
▽
Fornelli, G. Landor e l'Italia. Forlí 1931.
Elkin, F. Landor's studies of Italian life and literature. Philadelphia 1934.
Rezzano de Martini, M. C. Un admirador inglés de Boccaccio. In Giovanni Boccaccio, 1375–1975: Homenaje en el sexto centenario de su muerte, La Plata 1975.

Bulwer-Lytton, E. G. E. L.
The last days of Pompeii. 3 vols 1834.
Rienzi. 3 vols 1835.
Zanoni. 3 vols 1842.
▽
Lloyd, M. Bulwer-Lytton and the idealising principle. Eng Misc (Rome) 7 1956.

Meredith, George
Emilia in England. 3 vols 1864.
Vittoria. 3 vols 1867.
Huzzard, J. A. Meredith and the Risorgimento. Italica 35 1959.
Freimut, F. Politischen Geschehen und erzählerisches Gestalten: Das Risorgimento in englischer und italienischer Sicht bei Meredith und Fogazzaro. Arcadia 6 1971.

Rogers, Samuel
Italy: a poem. 2 pts 1822–8.
The Italian journals of Samuel Rogers, with an account of Rogers' life and travel in Italy in 1814–21. Ed J. R. Hale, 1956.
▽
Giddey, E. Samuel Rogers et son poème Italie. Geneva 1959.
Holcomb, A. M. Turner and Rogers' Italy revisited. SiR 27 1988.

Rossetti, Dante Gabriele
The early Italian poets from Ciullo d'Alcamo to Dante Alighieri. 1861 (rev as Dante and his circle 1874).
Dupré, H. Un italien d'Angleterre: le poète peintre Rossetti. Paris 1922.
Faggi, A. Rossetti. Il Marzocco 27 May 1928.
Waller, R. D. The Rossetti family. Manchester 1932.
Vincent, E. R. Gabriele Rossetti in England. Oxford 1936. On Rossetti's father.
Banerjee, R. D. K. Dante through the looking glass: Rossetti, Pound, and Eliot. Comparative Lit 24 1972.
Parry, G. An Englishman italianate: D. G. Rossetti's double life. Caliban 9 1973.
Gitter, E. G. Rossetti's translations of early Italian lyrics. VP 12 1974.
Magnier, M. La Maison de vie de Dante Gabriel Rossetti et l'Italie. Revue de Littérature Comparée 50 1976.

Cooksey, T. L. Rossetti's intelligenza nova: perception, poetry and vision in Dante at Verona. Victorian Newsletter 66 1984.
Goff, B. M. Dante's La vita nuova and two pre-raphaelite Beatrices. The Jnl of Pre-Raphaelite Stud 4 1984.
Bickley, P. and R. Hampson. 'Lips that have been kissed': Boccaccio, Verdi, Rossetti and The arrow of gold. L'Epoque Conradienne (Limoges) 1988.
Woodhouse, J. R. Conflitti e consolazione nell'esilio di Gabriele Rossetti. In L'esilio romantico: forme di un conflitto, ed J. Cheyne and L. Crisafulli Jones, Bari 1990. On Rossetti's father.
Zweig, R. 'Death in love': Rossetti and the Victorian journey back to Dante. In Sex and death in Victorian literature, ed R. Barreca, Bloomington IN 1990.
Cervo, N. A. Petrarch's Cervo and Cerva: the secret of D. G. Rossetti's 'The Stream's Secret'. VP 28 1990.

Ruskin, John

Stones of Venice. 3 vols 1851.
Ruskin's letters from Venice. Ed J. L. Bradley, New Haven CT 1955.
▽
Bidney, M. The 'Central Fiery Heart': Ruskin's remaking of Dante. Victorian Newsletter 48 1975.
Bidney, M. Ruskin, Dante, and the enigma of nature. TSLL 18 1976.
Titlebaum, R. John Ruskin and the Italian Renaissance. Eng Stud in Africa (Johannesburg) 19 1976.
Bidney, M. Dante retailored for the nineteenth century: his place in Ruskin's thought. Stud in Medievalism 1 1979.
Lutyens, M. Ruskin and Effie in Venice. In Studies in Ruskin, ed R. E. Rhodes and D. I. Janik, Athens OH 1982.
Della Terza, D. Ruskin e Venezia. Yearbook of Ital Stud (Florence) 5 1983.
Spear, J. L. Ruskin's Italy. Browning Inst Stud (New York) 12 1984.
Corradini, C. 'Lecturae Dantis' di John Ruskin. Studi Danteschi (Florence) 57 1985.
Bradley, A. Ruskin and Italy. Ann Arbor MI 1987.
Christmas story: John Ruskin's Venetian letters of 1876–1877. Ed V. A. Burd, Newark and London 1990.
Milbank, A. Ruskin and Dante: centrality and de-centering. BJRL 73 1991.

Scott, Walter

D'Ovidio, F. Appunti per un parallelo tra Manzoni e Scott. In his Discussioni Manzoniane, Città di Castello 1886.
Dotti, M. Delle derivazioni nei Promessi sposi di A. Manzoni dai romanzi di W. Scott. Pisa 1900.
Adiletta, P. Le fonti del Marco Visconti in alcuni romanzi storici di Walter Scott. Sarno 1905.
Agnoli, G. Gli albori del romanzo storico in Italia e i primi imitatori di Scott. Piacenza 1906.
Fassò, L. Intorno alla fortuna di Walter Scott in Italia. In Saggi e ricerche di storia letteraria, Milan 1947.
Gibboni, A. Parallelo tra Manzoni e Scott, ossia The fair maid of Perth e I promessi sposi. Campagna 1950.
Gell, W. Reminiscences of Sir Walter Scott's residence in Italy, 1832 ... Ed J. C. Corson, London, Edinburgh and Paris 1957.
Meiklejohn, M. F. M. Scott and Manzoni. Ital Stud 12 1957.
Bottoni, L. Scott e Manzoni nel 1821: tecniche descrittive e funzioni epistemologiche. Lingua e Stile 5 1970.
Jack, R. D. S. Scott and Italy. In Scott: bicentenary essays, ed A. Bell, New York 1973.
Ruggieri Punzo, F. Walter Scott in Italia 1821–1971. Bari 1975.
Ambrose, M. Walter Scott, Italian Opera and Romantic stage-setting. Ital Stud (Leeds) 36 1981.

Shelley, Mary

Rambles in Germany and Italy in 1840, 1842 and 1843. 2 vols 1844.

Shelley, Percy Bysshe. *See also under Boccaccio, Dante, Leopardi, Byron, Coleridge above.*

Epipsychidion. 1821.
Essays, letters from abroad. Ed M. Shelley, 2 vols 1850.
Letters and lyrics on Italy. Ed C. Cucchi, Naples 1934.
▽
Zanella, G. Shelley e Leopardi. Rome 1883; rptd in his Paralleli letterari, Verona 1885.
Olivero, F. Sull'Epipsychidion. In his Nuovi saggi di letteratura inglese, Turin 1919.
Bernheimer, L. Saggio di studi Shelleyani: Shelley in Italia. Piacenza 1920.
Raimondi, R. Shelley in Italia. Padua 1920.
Zacchetti, C. Shelley e Dante. Milan 1922.
Giartosio de Courten, M. L. Shelley e l'Italia. Milan 1923.
Mustacchia, N. Shelley e la sua fortuna in Italia. Catania 1925.
Bini, B. Shelley nel Risorgimento italiano. Fiume 1927.
Chirpelli, A. Leopardi e Shelley. Il Marzocco 17 July 1927.
Baker, C. Shelley's Ferrarese maniac. Eng Inst Essays. New York 1946.
Cline, C. L. Byron, Shelley and their Pisan circle. Cambridge MA 1952.
Neville, R. Shelley at work. Oxford 1956. On Dante.
de Palacio, J. Shelley et D'Annunzio: motifs rapportées ou influence créatrice? In Le romantisme anglo-américain: mélanges offerts à Louis Bonnerot, ed R. Asselineau et al, Paris 1971.
Kroeber, K. Experience as history: Shelley's Venice, Turner's Carthage. ELH 41 1974.
Wilson, M. Travellers' Venice: some images for Byron and Shelley. Univ of Toronto Quart 43 1974.
Webb, T. The violet in the crucible: Shelley and translation. Oxford 1976. Sections on Dante.
Milne, F. L. Shelley's The Cenci: the ice motif and the ninth circle of Dante's Hell. Tennessee Stud in Lit 22 1977.
Brown, R. E. The role of Dante in Epipsychidion. Comparative Lit 30 1978.
Folliot, K. Shelley's Italian sunset. Richmond VA, 1979.
Schulze, E. The Dantean quest in Epipsychidion. SiR 21 1982.
Fochi-Caturegli, A. Shelley interprete di Dante e Guido Cavalcanti. Italianistica: Rivista di Letteratura Italiana 14 1985.
Curreli, M. and A. L. Johnson (ed). Paradise of Exiles. Byron and Shelley in Pisa. Pisa 1988.
Schulze, E. Allegory against allegory: 'The Triumph of Life'. SiR 27 1988. On Dante and Petrarch.
Hartley, R. A. Shelley's copy of Dante. KSJ 39 1990.
Vassallo, P. From Petrarch to Dante: the discourse of disenchantment in Shelley's The triumph of life. Jnl of Anglo-Ital Stud (Malta) 1 1991.
Weinberg, A. M. Shelley's Italian experience. 1991.
Beatty, B. Repetition's music: The triumph of life. E & S 45 1992. On Dante.
Weinberg, A. M. Shelley's Italy: a paradise of exiles. Unisa Eng Stud (Pretoria) 30:1 1992.
Lindenberger, H. Shelley and Rossini in Italy – 1819. TWC 24:1 1993.

Swinburne, Algernon Charles

A song of Italy. 1867.
Siena. 1868.
Songs before sunrise. 1871.
▽
Galimberti, A. L'Aedo italiano. Palermo 1925.
Faggi, A. Swinburne aedo d'Italia. Il Marzocco, 16 May 1926.
Brown, C. S. More Swinburne–d'Annunzio parallels. PMLA 55 1940.
Le Bourgeois, J. Y. Swinburne and Mazzini: the origin of Swinburne's imperialism? Victorian Inst Jnl 2 1973.

Symonds, John Addington

Sketches in Italy and Greece. 1874. With trns of Petrarch and popular songs.
Renaissance in Italy. 7 vols 1875–86.

The sonnets of Michelangelo Buonarroti and Tommaso Campanella. Tr Symonds 1878.
Sketches and studies in Italy. 1879.
Italian byways. 1883.
The life of Benvenuto Cellini, newly translated. 1888.
Giovanni Boccaccio. 1895.
Gozzi, C. Memorie inutili. 3 vols Venice 1797; The memoirs of Count Carlo Gozzi, with essays by the translator, 2 vols 1890.
▽
Johnson, A. P. The Italian Renaissance and some Late Victorians. Victorian Newsletter 36 1969.
Dale, P. A. Beyond humanism: J. A. Symonds and the replotting of the Renaissance. CLIO: A Jnl of Lit, Hist, and the Philosophy of Hist (Fort Wayne) 17 1988.
Hodgens, R. M. Lewis and Symonds on Boiardo, Ariosto and Tasso. CSL: The Bull of the New York C. S. Lewis Soc 19:5 1988.

Tennyson, Lord Alfred

Raya, P. N. Italian influence on the poetry of Tennyson. Benares 1936.
Duncan, E. H. Tennyson's Ulysses and translations of Dante's Inferno: some conjectures. In Essays in memory of C. Burleson, ed T. G. Burton, Johnson City TN 1969.

Trollope, Frances

A visit to Italy. 1842.

Wordsworth, William. *See also under Boccaccio, Dante and Leopardi above.*

Memorials of a tour on the Continent. 1822.
▽
Shackford, M. H. Wordsworth's Italy. PMLA 38 1923.
Curry, K. Uncollected translations of Michelangelo by Wordsworth and Southey. RES 14 1938.
Vallese, T. Wordsworth in Italy. Symposium 6 1951.
Rossi, S. Wordsworth e l'Italia. Letterature Moderne 4 1953.
Rossiter Smith, H. Wordsworth and his Italian studies. N & Q June 1953.
Gatti-Taylor, H. The myth of the child in Wordsworth and Pascoli. Essays in Literature (Western Illinois Univ) 4 1977.
Wu, D. Tasso, Wordsworth, and the fragmentary drafts of 1788. N & Q 235 1990.
Hill, A. G. Wordsworth and Italy. Jnl of Anglo-Ital Stud (Malta) 1 1991.
King, F. Wordsworth's Italian Alps. In Imagining Romanticism: essays on English and Australian Romanticisms, ed D. Coleman and P. Otto, West Cornwall CT 1992. [CP]

(6) SPANISH AND PORTUGUESE

For a list of travel books describing the Peninsula, see R. Foulché-Delbosc, Bibliographie des voyages en Espagne et au Portugal, Paris 1896.

General studies

Lockhart, J. G. Ancient Spanish ballads, historical and romantic. Edinburgh 1822.
Bowring, J. Ancient poetry and romances of Spain. 1824. Góngora, Camões et al.
Kinsey, W. M. Portugal illustrated; in a series of letters. Embellished with a map, landscape, scenery, etc. 2nd edn 1829.
Adamson, J. Bibliotheca Lusitana. Newcastle 1836.
Hallanes, H. Introduction to the literature of Europe during the 15th, 16th and 17th centuries. 1837–9.
Adamson, J. Lusitania Ilustrata: Part I Sonnets, Newcastle 1842; Part II: Minstrelry, Newcastle 1846.
Kennedy, J. Modern poets and poetry of Spain. 1852. With trns of Valdés, Quintana, Martínez de la Rosa, Espronceda, Zorrilla et al.
Gibson, J. Y. The Cid ballads etc. 2 vols 1887.
Ford, J. D. M. English influence on Spanish literature in the early part of the 19th century. PMLA 16 1901.
Kelly, J. Fitzmaurice. The Relations between Spanish and English Literature. Liverpool 1910.
Somora, J. Cartas de Jovellanos y Lord Vassall Holland sobre la guerra de la Independencia 1808–1811. 2 vols Madrid 1911.
Buceta, E. El entusiasmo por España en algunos románticos ingleses. Revista de Filología Española 10 1923. On Southey, Scott, Wordsworth, Shelley, Byron, Landor.
García, C. Influencia de los escritores románticos ingleses en el romantismo español. Madrid, España y América II 1923.
Peers, E. A. Rivas and romanticism in Spain. Liverpool 1923.
Buceta, E. Traducciones inglesas de romances en el primer tercio del siglo XIX. Revue Hispanique 62 1924. Continued in Datos suplementarios acerca de las versiones de Lockhart, 68 1926. Continued in Datos suplementarios acerca de J. Bowring, Revista de Filología Española 20 1933.
Peers, E. A. Minor English influences on Spanish romanticism. Revue Hispanique 62 1924.
Buceta, E. El Don Carlos de Lord John Russell. Revista de Filología Española 13 1926.
Peers, E. A. The influence of Young and Gray in Spain. MLR 21 1926.
Walter, F. La littérature portugaise en Angleterre à l'époque romantique. Paris 1927. With full bibliography.
Buceta, E. Relaciones anglo-hispanas: apuntes preliminares para un estudio de las traducciones inglesas de romances en el primer tercio del siglo XIX. In Estudios eruditos in memoriam de Adolfo Bonilla y San Martin. Vol 2 Madrid 1930.
Paxeco, F. The intellectual relations between Portugal and Great Britain. Lisbon 1937.
Matthews, E. G. Studies in Spanish–English cultural and literary relations. New York 1938.
Ley, D. C. A Inglaterra e os escritores portugueses. Lisbon 1939.
Blecua, J. M. Mor de Fuentes y Lord Holland. Boletín del Seminario de Estudios de Literatura y Filología, Castilla 1940–1.
Umphrey, G. W. Spanish ballads in English. MLQ 6–7 1945–6.
Barker, J. W. Influencia de la literatura española en la literatura inglesa. Zaragoza 1946.
Macaulay, R. They went to Portugal. 1946. On Beckford, Southey, Byron, Borrow, Tennyson, Palgrave et al.
Pastor, A. Breve historia del hispanismo inglés. Arbor Apr 1948.
Weisinger, N. L. José Joaquín de Mora's indebtedness to Blake. Bull of Hispanic Stud 28 1951.
Lamb, N. J. Notes on some Portuguese 'emigrado' journals published in England. Bull of Hispanic Stud 30 1953.
Llorens, V. C. Liberales y románticos: una emigración española en Inglaterra 1823–34. Mexico City 1954.
Parreaux, A. Beckford et le Portugal en 1787. Bull des Etudes Portugaises 7 1954.
Hume, M. A. S. Spanish influence on English literature. 1955.
Benítez, R. Terence McMahon Hughes, hispanófilo y lusitanista irlandés del siglo XIX. Cuadernos Hispanoamericanos 117, Sep 1959.
O'Brien, R. Spanish plays in English translation. New York 1963.
Pujals, E. El romanticismo inglés. Orígenes, repercusión europea y relaciones con la literatura española. Santander 1969.
Ford, R. Letters to Gayangos. Ed R. Hitchcock, Exeter 1974.
Robertson, I. Los curiosos impertinentes. Viajeros ingleses por España 1760–1885. Madrid 1975.
Rudder, R. S. The literature of Spain in English translation, a bibliography. New York 1975.
Stern, I. Jane Austen and Júlio Dinis. Coloquio Letras 31 1976.
Núñez, D. El darwinismo en España. 1977.
Alas, G. El darwinismo. Ed F. García Sarriá, Exeter 1978.
Alberich, J. Bibliografía anglo-hispánica 1801–1850. Oxford 1978.
Machado de Sousa, M. L. D. Inês e D. Sebastião na literatura inglesa. Lisbon Editorial Vega 1980.

Spanish and Portuguese authors

For a full list of trns from the Spanish see R. U. Pane, English translations from the Spanish 1484–1943, New Brunswick NJ 1944. *In the following list the Spanish originals were all pbd in Madrid unless otherwise stated.*

Alas Leopoldo 'Clarín' (1852–1901)

Bull, W. E. Clarín's literary internationalism. Hispanic Rev 16 1948.

Coletes, A. De Ana Ozores a Serafina Gorgheggi: en torno a la impronta ánglica en las novelas mayores de Leopoldo Alas 'Clarín'. Boletin del Real Instituto de Estudis Asturianos 1995.

Coletes, A. Ironía y sátira anti-inglesa en la narrativa breve de Clarín: 'Snob', 'El Torso' y otros relatos. Bull of Hispanic Stud 73 1996.

Almeida Garrett José María (1799–1854)

Estorninho, C. Garrett and England: English reminiscences in the life and work of Almeida Garrett. Annual Report and Rev of the Historical Assoc, Portugal Branch, Twelfth Annual Report & Rev, Lisbon 1954; tr as Garrett e Inglaterra: Reminiscências inglesas na vida e obra de Almeida Garrett. Revista de Faculdade de Letras de Lisboa, 2a Série 21 no 1 1955.

Figuereido, F. de. Shakespeare e Garrett. Sao Paulo 1970.

Rodrigues Correia Raitt, Lia Noemia. Garrett and the English Muse. 1983.

Blanco White, J. M. (1775–1841)

'Leucadio Doblado' (J. M. Blanco White). Letters from Spain. 1822.

▽

Méndez Bejarano, M. Vida y obras de J. M. Blanco y Crespo (J. M. Blanco White). Madrid 1920.

Garnica, A. Blanco White, poeta inglés. Filología Moderna Madrid 1975–6.

Murphy, M. Blanco White: an anglicized Spaniard. History Today 28 no 1 1978.

Castañeda García, S. Costumbristas españoles en Inglaterra: observaciones sobre la obra de Blanco White, Valentín de Llanos y Telesforo de Trueba y Cossío. Actas del VII Congreso de la Asociación Internacional de Hispanistas, 1982.

Cuevas, M. A. Las ideas de Blanco White sobre Shakespeare. Anales de la Literatura Española (Alicante) 1 1982.

Calderón de la Barca, Pedro (1600–81)

Select plays of Calderón. Tr Norman MacColl 1888.

La dama duende; Nadie fíe su secreto. In Three comedies, [tr Lord Holland] 1807 (as The fairy lady; Keep your own secret).

Justina; La vida es sueño. The wonderful magician, tr J. H. 1848.

El príncipe constante; El secreto a vozes; El médico de su honra; Amar después de la muerte; El purgatorio de San Patricio; La vanda y la flor. In Dramas of Calderón, tr D. F. M'Carthy, 2 vols 1853 (as The constant prince; The secret in words; The physician of his own honour; Love after death; The purgatory of St Patrick; The scarf and the flower). With a list of previous trns in periodicals.

El pintor de su deshonra; Luis Pérez el Gallego; Las tres justicias en una; El alcalde de Zalamea; Guárdate de la agua mansa. In Six dramas of Calderón, tr E. FitzGerald 1853 (as The painter of his own dishonour; Keep your own secret; Gil Perez the Gallician; Three judgments at a blow; The mayor of Zalamea; Beware of smooth water).

Life's a dream; The great theatre of the world etc. Tr with an essay on Calderón by R. C. Trench 1856.

▽

Madariaga, S. de. Shelley and Calderón. 1920.

Gates, E. J. Shelley and Calderón. PQ 16 1937.

Camõens, Luis de (c. 1524–80)

Os Lusiadas. Lisbon 1572; The Lusiad [bks 1–4], tr E. Quillinan 1853.

Rhythmas. Lisbon 1595 etc; Poems from the Portuguese of Camõens, tr with remarks on Camõens by Viscount Strangford. 1803.

Adamson, J. Memoirs of the life and writings of Luis de Camõens, Newcastle 1810.

Adamson, J. Sonnets from the Portuguese of Luis de Camõens. Newcastle 1810.

Lardner, D. In his Eminent literary and scientific men of Italy, Spain and Portugal, vol 3 1957.

Estorninho, C. O culto de Camõens em Inglaterra. Arquivo de Bibliografia Portuguesa 10 1960.

Cervantes, Miguel de (1547–1616). *See also under Wordsworth, below.*

Cervantes y la literatura inglesa. Realidad 2 1947.

Eça de Queirós, J. M. (1845–1900)

Cartas de Inglaterra. Porto 1905.

▽

Sousa, A. G. de. William Shakespeare and Eça de Queirós. Portuguese Stud 1 1985.

Freeland, A. Eça de Queirós: consular correspondence from Newcastle. Portuguese Stud 2 1986.

Echegaray y Eizaguirre, José María (1832–1916)

El gran Galeoto. 1881; Locura ó santidad; 1877; The great Galeoto; Folly or saintliness, tr with introd by H. Lynch 1895.

El hijo de Don Juan. 1889; The son of Don Juan, tr with introd by J. Graham 1895.

Mariana. 1890; tr J. Graham 1892.

Espronceda, José (1808–42)

Churchman, P. H. Byron and Espronceda. Revue Hispanique 20 1920.

Pujals, E. Espronceda y Lord Byron. Consejo Superior de Investigaciones Científicas 1951 Anejos de Cuadenos de Literatura.

Llovens, V. El original inglés de una poesía de Espronceda. Nueva Revista de Filología Hispánica 5 1951.

Dale, B. Byron, Espronceda and the critics. Selecta 1 1980.

Fernán Caballero (Cecilia Bohl de Faber) (1796–1877)

La gaviota. 1849; The seagull, tr A. Bethell, 2 vols 1867.

Elia. 1850; La familia de Alvareda, 1856; The castle and the cottage in Spain, tr Lady Wallace 1861.

Cuadros de costumbres 1870; National pictures, 1882.

Palacio Valdés, Armando (1853–1916)

El cuarto poder. 1888; The fourth estate, tr R. Challice 1901.

La alegría del capitán Ribot, 1889; The joy of captain Ribot, tr M. C. Smith 1900.

La espuma. Barcelona 1890; Froth, tr C. Bell 1891.

El maestrante. 1893; The grandee, tr with introd by R. Challice 1894.

▽

O'Connor, D. J. Mrs. Humphrey Ward's Robert Elsmere (1888) and Palacio Valdés's La fe (1892). Romance Quart 37 1990.

Pardo Bazán, Emilia (1851–1921)

Ordóñez, E. J. Revising Realism: Pardo Bazán's Memorias de un solterón in the light of Galdós's Tristana and John Stuart Mill. In In the feminine mode: essays on Hispanic women writers, ed N. Valis and C. Maier, London and Toronto 1990.

Pérez Galdós, Benito (1843–1920). *See also under Dickens, below.*

Episodios nacionales. 1873–1910; Trafalgar, tr C. Bell 1884; Leon Roch, tr C. Bell, 2 vols 1886; The Court of Charles IV, tr C. Bell 1888.

Doña Perfecta. 1876; tr D. P. W. 1880; tr M. Wharton 1892; tr M. J. Serrano 1895.

Gloria. 1877; tr N. Wetherhell, 2 vols 1879.

Marianela. 1878; tr C. Bell 1883; tr M. Wharton 1893.

▽

MacDermott, D. Inglaterra y los ingleses en la obra de Peréz Galdós. Filología Moderna Madrid 21–2 1965–6.

Wright, C. C. Las aventuras de Pickwick: notes on Benito Pérez Galdós as translator of Dickens. Revista de Estudios Hispánicos 9 1984.

Tamayo y Baus, José (1829–98)

Alberich, J. El papel de Shakespeare en Un drama nuevo de Tamayo. Filología Moderna Madrid 10 1970.

Herzberger, D. K. Shakespeare and the creation of fiction in Tamayo y Baus's Un drama nuevo. Kentucky Romance Quart 32 1985.

Unamuno, Miguel de (1864–1936)

Clavería, C. Temas de Unamuno. Madrid 1953. On Unamuno and Carlyle.

Alberich, J. Temas ingleses en Unamuno y Baroja. Arbor Nov 1956.

Alberich, J. La literatura inglesa bajo tres símbolos unamunianos. Bull of Hispanic Stud 36 1959.

Blanco, M. G. Poetas ingleses en la obra de Unamuno. Bull of Hispanic Stud 36 1959.

Earle, P. G. Unamuno and English literature. New York 1960.

English authors

Borrow, George

The Zincali. 1841.

The Bible in Spain. 1843.

▽

Fréchet, R. Borrow: vagabond, polyglotte, agent biblique–écrivain. Paris 1956.

Byron, George Gordon

Childe Harold's pilgrimage. 1812.

Piñeyro, E. Un imitador de Byron: José Espronceda in Poetas famosos del siglo XX. Madrid 1883.

Churchman, P. H. Byron and Espronceda. Revue Hispanique 22 1909.

Churchman, P. H. Byron's experience in the Spanish Peninsula in 1809. Bull Hispanique 11 1909.

Churchman, P. H. The beginnings of Byronism in Spain. Revue Hispanique 23 1910. With critical list of trns.

Rycroft, W. S. Espronceda: la influencia de Byron. Boletín Bibliográfico (Lima) 2 1926.

Hendrix, W. S. Las Rimas de Béquer y la influencia de Byron. Boletín de la Real Academia de la Historia 98 1931.

Alfaro, M. Influencia que ejerció Lord Byron sobre los poetas españoles José de Espronceda y Gustavo Adolfo Bécquer. Ensayos Hispano-Ingleses. Homenaje a Walter Starkie. Barcelona, Janés 1948.

Samuels, D. G. Some Byronic influences in Spanish poetry 1870–80. Hispanic Rev 17 1949.

Pujals, E. Espronceda y Byron. Madrid 1951.

Ribbans, G. W. Bécquer, Byron y Dacarrete. Revista de Literatura 4 1953.

Sarmiento, E. A parallel between Byron and Fray Luis de León. RES 29 1953.

Pageard, R. and G. W. Ribbans. Heine and Byron in the Seminario Popular 1862–5. Bull of Hispanic Stud 33 1956.

Pujals, E. Lord Byron en España. Madrid 1982.

Shaw, D. L. Byron in Spain. Renaissance and Mod Stud 32 1989.

Ridenour, G. M. The Spanish Byron. SiR 30 1991.

Carlyle, Thomas

Hafter Monroe, Z. El diablo mundo in the light of Carlyle's Sartor Resartus. Revista Hispánica Moderna 37 1972–3.

Hafter Monroe, Z. Heroism in Alas and Carlyle's On heroes. MLN 95 1980.

Dickens, Charles

Burton, J. G. Galdós visto por un inglés y los ingleses vistos por Galdós. Revista de las Indias 17 1943.

Erickson, E. The influence of Dickens on the novels of Pérez Galdós. Hispania 19 1946.

Scott, Walter

The vision of Don Roderick. Edinburgh 1811.

▽

Churchman, P. H. and E. A. Peers. A survey of the influence of Scott in Spain. Revue Hispanique 55 1922. With a list of trns.

Peers, E. A. Studies in the influence of Scott in Spain. Revue Hispanique 58 1926.

González Palencia, A. Walter Scott y la censura gubernativa. Revista de la Biblioteca, Archivo y Museo del Ayuntamiento (Madrid) 4 1927.

Stoudemire, S. A. A note on Scott in Spain. In Romance studies presented to W. M. Day, Chapel Hill NC 1950.

Hafter, M. The Spanish version of Scott's Don Roderick. SiR 13 1974.

Shelley, Percy Bysshe

Mesquita, M. de. Um amigo português de Shelley. Revista de Historia (Coïmbre) 3 1914.

Madariga, Salvador de. Shelley and Calderón. Oxford 1920.

Hespelt, E. H. Shelley and Spain. PMLA 38 1923.

Gates, E. J. Shelley and Calderón. PQ 16 1937.

Southey, Robert

Letters written during a short residence in Spain and Portugal [with poems]. Bristol 1797.

Montalvo, G. O. de. Amadis of Gaul. c. 1500; tr with introd by Southey. 1803.

Moraes, F. de. Palmerín de Inglaterra. c. 1550; tr Southey, 4 vols 1807. *See* C. I. Patterson, The Keats–Hazlitt–Hunt copy of Palmerín of England in relation to Keats's poetry, JEGP 60 1961.

Poema del Cid. Chronicle of the Cid, tr with introd by Southey 1808.

Roderick: the last of the Goths. 1814.

▽

Pfandl, L. Southey und Spanien. Revue Hispanique 28 1913.

Buceta, E. Opiniones de Southey y de Coleridge acerca del Poema del Cid. Revista de Filología Espanola 9 1922.

Wordsworth William

The relations of Great Britain, Spain and Portugal to each other and to the common enemy. 1809. *See* Wordsworth's Tract on the Convention of Cintra etc, ed A. V. Dicey 1915.

▽

Sarmiento, E. Wordsworth and Don Quijote. Bull of Hispanic Stud 38 1961. [JJM]

(7) SCANDINAVIAN AND ICELANDIC

General studies

Scandinavia and Iceland

Bay, J. C. Denmark in English and American literature. Chicago 1915.

Burchardt, C. B. Norwegian life and literature: English accounts and views. Oxford 1920.

Afzelius, N. Sverige i ütlandsk och utlandet i svensk litteratur. Biblioteksbladet 1930.

Thesen, R. Synet på England i norsk litteratur 1830–1870. Syn og Segn 7 1935.

Downs, B. W. Anglo-Danish literary relations 1867–1900. MLR 39 1944.

Downs, B. W. Anglo-Norwegian literary relations 1867–1900. MLR 47 1952.

Matthews, G. Det viktorianska Englands syn på Finland. Finsk Tidskrift 160 1956.

Schiötz, E. H. Utlendingers reiser i Norge: En Bibliografi. 2 vols Oslo, Tromsø 1970–86.

Wawn, A. The Iceland journal of Henry Holland 1810. Hakluyt Soc 2nd ser 168 1987.

Wawn, A. The Anglo man. Þorleifur Repp, philology and nineteenth-century Britain. Studia Islandica 49. Reykjavik 1989.

Haraldur Sigurðsson (ed). Ísland i skrífum erlendra manna um þjóðlíf og náttúru landsins. Reykjavik 1991.

Townsend, J. A. B. The Viking Society: a centenary history. Saga-Book of the Viking Soc 23 1992.

Aho, G. 'Með Ísland á heilanum': Íslandsbækur breskra ferðalanga 1772 til 1897. Skírnir 167 1993.

Kidd, C. Teutonist ethnology and Scottish nationalist inhibition, 1780–1880. Scottish Historical Rev 74 1995.

Barton, H. A. Iter Scandinavicum. Scandinavian Stud 68 1996.

Sumarliði Ísleifsson. Ísland, framandi land. Reykjavik 1996.

Scandinavian and English literature

Jamieson, R., W. Scott and H. Weber. Illustrations of northern antiquities. Edinburgh 1814.

Stephens, G. Old popular ballads and songs of Sweden. Foreign Quart Rev 25 1840.

Wergeland, H. Den engelske lods: et digt. Christiania 1844.

[Charlton, E.] The literature and romance of northern Europe. Dublin Rev 33 1852.

[Charlton, E.] Scandinavian literature. Dublin Rev 32 1852.

Howitt, W. and M. The literature and romance of northern Europe. 2 vols 1852.

Brandes, G. Benjamin Disraeli. Copenhagen 1878; Lord Beaconsfield, tr G. Sturge 1880.

Gosse, E. Studies in the literature of northern Europe. 1875.

Metcalfe, F. The Englishman and the Scandinavian. 1880.

Stephens, G. Professor S. Bugge's Studies on northern mythology shortly examined. London and Copenhagen 1883.

Stephens, G. Handbook of the Old-Northern runic monuments of Scandinavia and England. London, Edinburgh and Cheapinghaven [Copenhagen] 1884.

Nicolaysen, S. E. Shelley og Wergeland. Nyt Tidsskrift 1893–4.

Boyesen, H. H. Essays on Scandinavian literature. 1895.

Brandes, G. Main currents in nineteenth-century literature. Vol 4, Naturalism in England. 1904.

Brandes, G. William Shakespeare 1895–6; tr W. Archer 1898.

Farley, F. E. Scandinavian influences in the English romantic movement. Cambridge MA 1903.

Wright, H. G. Studies in Anglo-Scandinavian literary relations. Bangor 1919. On Borrow, Kingsley, the Howitts, Strindberg et al.

Wright, H. G. Southey's relations with Finland and Scandinavia. MLR 27 1932.

Petersens, H.-A. and R. P. Gillies. Foreign Quart Rev och den svenska litteraturen. Samlaren 14 1933.

Barnes, T. Yeats, Synge, Ibsen and Strindberg. Scrutiny 5 1936.

Holst, O. Engelske oversaettelser af danske folkeviser. Danske Studier 17 1941. On Jamieson, Borrow, Morris.

Bull, F. The influence of Shakespeare on Wergeland, Ibsen and Bjørnson. Norseman 15 1957.

Eneberg, M. Charles Dickens i sin samtids Finland. Historiska och Litteraturhistoriska Studier (Helsinki) 35 1960.

Gosse, E. Correspondence with Scandinavian writers. Ed E. Bredsdorff, Copenhagen 1960.

Rudler, R. De første Shakespeareforestillinger i Norge. Edda 63 1963.

Nelson, W. W. Oscar Wilde och det Svenska nittitalet. Svensk Litteraturtidskrift 33 1964.

Bredsdorff, E. John Heath. In Scandinavian studies presented to Dr H. G. Leach, ed C. F. Bayerschmidt and E. J. Fris. Seattle 1965.

Greenway, J. The golden horns: mythic imagination and the nordic past. Athens GA 1977.

Dahl, P. and J. Mott. Georg Brandes. Orbis Litterarum, Suppl 5 1980.

Mjöberg, J. Romanticism and revival. In The northern world, ed D. Wilson, London 1980.

Shippey, T. A. Goths and Huns: the rediscovery of the northern cultures in the nineteenth century. In The medieval legacy, ed A. Haarder, Odense 1982.

Thwaite, Ann. Edmund Gosse: a literary landscape 1849–1928. 1984.

Pedersen, V. H. A mermaid translated: an analysis of some English versions of Hans Christian Andersen's Den lille havfrue. Dolphin 18 1990.

Simmons, C. A. Reversing the conquest. History and myth in nineteenth-century British literature. New Brunswick NJ and London 1990.

Ewbank, I.-S. The Tempest and after. ShS 43 1991.

Wawn, A. The cult of 'stalwart Frith-Thjof' in Victorian Britain. In Northern antiquity, ed Wawn, Enfield Lock 1994.

Nassaar, C. B. Hans Christian Andersen's The shadow and Wilde's The fisherman and his soul: a case of influence. Nineteenth-Cent Lit 50 1995.

Syndergaard, L. E. English translations of the Scandinavian medieval ballads. An analytical guide and bibliography. Turku 1995.

Wawn, A. George Stephens, Cheapinghaven and old northern antiquity. Stud in Medievalism 7 1995.

Old Icelandic

General

Bowring, J. Literature and literary societies in Iceland. Foreign Quart Rev 9 1832.

Busk, M. M. Scandinavian mythology and the nature of its allegory. Blackwood's Mag 38 1835.

Busk, M. M. Mythology of the north. Foreign Quart Rev 16 1836.

Percy, T. (rev I. A. Blackwell). Northern antiquities. 1847.

Thorpe, B. Northern mythology. 3 vols 1851–2.

Thorpe, B. Yule-tide stories. 1853.

Dufferin, Lord. Letters from high latitudes. 1857.

Jón Arnason (ed). Icelandic legends. Tr with introd by G. E. J. Powell and Eiríkr Magnússon. 2 ser 1864–6. Vol 1 rptd, Felinfach 1995 (Llanerch Publishers).

[Kennedy, P.] Icelandic legends. Dublin Univ Mag 64 1864.

[Clifford, C.]. Travels by Umbra. Edinburgh 1865.

[Anon.] Recent work on Icelandic literature. GM 1866.

[Kennedy, P.] The Old Norse mythology. Dublin Univ Mag 79 1872.

[Earle, J.] Icelandic illustrations of English. Quart Rev 139 1875.

Cole, G. R. F. Jón Jónsson's saga: the genuine autobiography of a modern Icelander. Fraser's Mag 95 1877.

Conybeare, C. A. Vansittart. The place of Iceland in the history of European literature. Oxford 1877.

[Metcalfe, F.] Old Norse mirror of men and manners. Quart Rev 143 1877.

Guðbrandur Vigfússon (ed). Sturlunga saga. 2 vols Oxford 1878.

G[osse], E. W. The Egils saga. Cornhill Mag 40 1879.

G[osse], E. W. The 'Eyrbyggja saga'. Cornhill Mag 41 1880.

Trollope, A. How the 'Mastiffs' went to Iceland. 1878.

Trollope, A. Iceland. Fortnightly Rev n.s. 24 1878.

Jón Stefánsson. Íslenzk áhrif á enskar bókmenntir. Tímarit hins Íslenzka Bókmentafjelags 11 1890.

Lang, A. The sagas. In Essays in little, 1891.

Ker, W. P. Epic and romance: essays on medieval literature. 1897.

Nordby, C. H. The influence of Old Norse literature upon English literature. New York 1901.

Herford, C. H. Northern myth in English poetry. BJRL 5 1918–20.

Allen, R. B. Old Icelandic sources in the English novel. Philadelphia 1933.

Litzenberg, K. The Victorians and the vikings. Univ of Michigan Contributions in Modern Philology 3, Ann Arbor MI 1947–8.

Cowan, E. J. Icelandic studies in eighteenth- and nineteenth-century Scotland. Studia Islandica 31. Reykjavik 1972.

Simpson, J. Eyrbyggja saga and nineteenth-century scholarship. In Proceedings of the First International Saga Conference, ed P. Foote 1973.

Wawn, A. Gunnlaugs saga ormstungu and the Theatre Royal, Edinburgh: melodrama, mineralogy and Sir George Mackenzie. Scandinavica 21 1982.

Young, M. History as myth: Charles Kingsley and Hereward the Wake. Stud in the Novel 17 1985.

McTurk, R. and A. Wawn (ed). Úr Dölum til Dala: Guðbrandur Vigfússon centenary essays. Leeds Texts and Monographs n.s. 11 1989.

Wawn, A. The spirit of 1892: sagas, saga-steads and Victorian philology. Saga-Book of the Viking Soc 23 1992.

Translations: Eddic and Skaldic poetry

Halldor Hermannsson. Bibliography of the Eddas. Islandica 13 1923.

[Ferguson, S.] Death-song of Regner Lodbrog. Blackwood's Mag 33 1833.

The prose or younger Edda. Tr G. W. Dasent, Stockholm 1842.

Head, E. Free translation from the Icelandic of the Edda: Helgakviða Hundingsbana. Fraser's Mag 72 1865.

The Edda of Saemund the learned, with a mythological index. Tr B. Thorpe 1866.

L[ang], A. 'The Gripis-Spa'. From the Elder Edda. Fraser's Mag 8 1874.

The Younger Edda: also called Snorri's Edda. Tr R. B. Anderson, Chicago and London 1880.

Corpvs Poeticvm Boreale. Ed and tr Gudbrand Vigfusson and F. York Powell, 2 vols Oxford 1883.

Translations: sagas

Fry, D. K. Norse sagas translated into English: a bibliography. New York 1980.

Acker, P. Norse sagas translated into English: a supplement. Scandinavian Stud 65 1993.

Friðþjófs saga. The saga of Frithiof the Bold, tr G. Stephens, Stockholm 1839; rptd Felinfach 1994 (Llanerch Publishers).

Snorri Sturluson. Heimskringla. The Heimskringla, tr with introd by S. Laing, 3 vols 1844; rev R. B. Anderson, 4 vols 1889.

Brennu-Njáls saga. The story of Burnt Njal, tr with introd by G. W. Dasent, 2 vols Edinburgh 1861.

Gísla saga. The story of Gisli the Outlaw, tr with introd by G. W. Dasent, Edinburgh 1866.

Víga-Glúms saga. The story of Viga-Glum, tr E. Head London and Edinburgh 1866.

Grettis saga. The story of Grettir the Strong, tr Eiríkr Magnússon and William Morris 1869.

Völsunga saga. The story of the Volsungs and Niblungs, tr Eiríkr Magnússon and William Morris 1870.

Orkneyinga saga. The Orkneyinga saga, tr with introd by Jón A. Hjaltalín and G. Goudie. Edinburgh 1873.

Coles, J. Summer travelling in Iceland. 1882. Þórðar saga hreðu, Bandamanna saga, Hrafnkels saga Freysgoða as appendices, tr Eiríkr Magnússon.

The saga library. Tr Eiríkr Magnússon and William Morris, 6 vols 1891–1905. Hávaðar saga Ísfirðings, Bandamanna saga, Hœnsa Þóris saga, Eyrbyggja saga, Heiðarvíga saga, Heimskringla.

Egils saga Skallagrímssonar. The story of Egil Skallagrimsson, tr W. C. Green 1893.

Ólafs saga Tryggvasonar. The saga of King Olaf Tryggwason, tr J. Sephton 1895.

Færeyinga saga. The tale of Thrond of Gate, tr F. York Powell 1896; rptd Felinfach 1995 (Llanerch Publishers).

Laxdæla saga. The Laxdale saga, tr M. Press 1899.

Sverris saga. The saga of King Sverri of Norway, tr with introd by J. Sephton 1899; rptd Felinfach 1994 (Llanerch Publishers).

Adaptations and independent works: prose

Allen, R. B. Old Icelandic sources in the English novel. Philadelphia 1933.

Bulwer Lytton, E. Harold: the last of the Saxon kings. 1848.

Kingsley, C. Hereward the Wake. 1866.

Ballantyne, R. M. Erling the Bold. 1869.

Ballantyne, R. M. The Norsemen in the west. 1872.

Hodgetts, J. F. The champion of Odin. 1885.

Oswald, E. J. The dragon of the north. 1888.

Haggard, H. Rider. Eric Brighteyes. 1891.

du Chaillu, P. Ivar the Viking. 1893.

Leighton, R. Olaf the Glorious. 1895.

Adaptations and independent works: verse

[Galt, J]. An extract from a Gothic poem. The Scots Mag 65 1803.

Sladden, Dilnot. The northmen. Canterbury 1834.

Zavarr [pseud]. The Viking; an epic. 1849.

Arnold, M. Balder dead. 1855

White, J. The Vikings. Oxford 1861.

Symington, A. J. Pen and pencil sketches of Faroe and Iceland. 1862. Poems in appendix.

Rowntree, G. Iceland. Cambridge 1875.

Buchanan, R. 'Balder the beautiful: a song of divine death' (1877). In Complete Poetic Works, 2 vols 1901.

L., H. Odin sagas and other poems. Manchester 1882.

Nugent, E. G. The rueing of Gudrun and other poems. 1884.

Leith, M. Original verses and translations. 1895.

Ferguson, R. M. The Viking's bride and other poems. Paisley 1896.

See also Herbert and Morris, below.

Individual authors

Baring-Gould, S. (1834–1924)

Iceland: its scenes and sagas. 1863.

Grettir the outlaw. 1890.

The Icelander's sword. 1894.

Early reminiscences. London and New York 1923.

Carlyle, Thomas (1795–1881)

On heroes, hero-worship and the heroic in history: Lecture 1. 1841.

The early kings of Norway. 1875.

▽

Cowan, E. J. The sage and the sagas: the brothers Carlyle and 'Early Kings'. Bibliothek 9 1979.

Fielding, K. J. Carlyle and Esaias Tegnér: an unpublished manuscript. Carlyle Newsletter 5 1984.

Bossche, C. V. Carlyle's Færeyinga saga translation. Carlyle Annual 10 1989.

Collingwood, W. G. (1854–1932)

Thorstein of the mere. 1895.

The bondwoman. 1896.

A pilgrimage to the saga-steads. Ulverston 1899. With Jón Stefánsson.

Haraldur Hannesson. Fegurð Íslands og fornir sögustaðir. Reykjavik 1988.

Dasent, Sir G. W. (1817–96)

Jest and earnest. 2 vols 1873.

The vikings of the Baltic [based on Jómsvíkinga saga]. 3 vols 1875.

▽

[Lawrence, H.] Old Iceland – the Burnt Njal. Brit Quart Rev 34 1861.

[Lowe, R.] The story of Burnt Njal. Edinburgh Rev 114 1861.

[Nicolson, A]. Burnt Njal. Macmillan's Mag 4 1861.

Quirk, R. Dasent, Morris and problems of translation. Saga-Book of the Viking Soc 14 1953–7.

Wawn, A. The assistance of Icelanders to George Webbe Dasent. Landsbókasafn Íslands: Árbók 1989, nýr flokkur 15 1991.

Wawn, A. The Victorians and the Vikings. George Webbe Dasent and Jómsvíkinga saga. In Proceedings of the Ninth Biennial Conference of the Br Assoc of Scandinavian Stud, ed J. Garton, Norwich 1992.

Herbert, William (1778–1847)

Select Icelandic poetry. 2 pts 1806.

Helga: a poem. 1815.

Hedin; or, The spectre of the tomb. A tale. 1820.

Attila, or The triumph of Christianity. 1838.

▽

Scott, W. Rev of Select Icelandic poetry. Edinburgh Rev 1806.

Kirby, W. F. William Herbert and his Scandinavian poetry. Saga-Book of the Viking Soc 7 1912.

Morris, William (1834–96)

The lovers of Gudrun. In his Earthly Paradise, 1869–70. Based on Laxdæla saga.

Three northern love stories. 1875. Trns of Gunnlaugs saga ormstungu, Friðþjófs saga, Víglundar saga. With Eiríkr Magnússon.
The story of Sigurd the Volsung and the fall of the Niblungs. 1876. Based on Völsunga saga.
Poems by the way. 1891.
The story of Kormak, the son of Ogmund. Ed G. J. Calder 1970.
▽
Litzenberg, K. William Morris and Scandinavian literature: a bibliographical essay. Scandinavian Studies 13 1933.
Litzenberg, K. The Elder Edda and Heimskringla in Morris's non-Norse poems. Scandinavian Stud 19 1935.
Litzenberg, K. Morris as a critic of Old Norse literature. Edda 40 1940.
Swannell, J. N. Morris as an interpreter of Old Norse. Saga-Book of the Viking Soc 15 1961.
Maurer, O. Morris and Laxdæla saga. TSLL 5 1964.
Ellison, R. C. 'The undying glory of dreams': William Morris and The Northland of Old, Victorian Poetry. Stratford upon Avon Stud 15 1972.
Harris, R. L. William Morris, Eiríkr Magnússon and Iceland: a survey of correspondence. VP 13 1975.
Aho, G. L. William Morris and Iceland. Kairos 1 1982.
Barribeau, J. L. William Morris and saga translation: 'The story of King Magnus, son of Erling'. In The Vikings, ed R. T. Farrell, Ithaca NY 1983.
Boos, F. Morris's radical revision of Laxdæla saga. VP 21 1983.
Cumming, M. The structure of Sigurd the Volsung. VP 21 1983.
MacCarthy, F. William Morris. 1994.
Aho, G. L. Introduction to Three Northern Love Stories 1875, rptd Bristol 1996 (Thoemmes Press).

Scott, Sir Walter (1771–1832)
Leider, P. R. Scott and Scandinavian literature. Smith College Stud in Mod Languages, Northampton MA 1920.
Batho, E. C. Sir Walter Scott and the sagas. MLR 24 1929.
Cowan, E. J. Icelandic studies in eighteenth and nineteenth-century Scotland. Studia Islandica 31. Reykjavik 1972.
Simpson, J. Scott and Old Norse literature. In Scott Bicentenary essays, ed A. Bell, Edinburgh 1973.
Tysdahl, B. J. Sir Walter Scott and the beginnings of Norwegian fiction, and a note on Ibsen's early plays. In Scott and his influence, ed D. Hewitt, Aberdeen 1983.
Wolf, K. and J. M. D'Arcy. Sir Walter Scott and Eyrbyggja saga. Stud in Scottish Lit 22 1987.
Wawn, A. Introduction to The pirate. Shetland Times Press, Kirkwall 1996.

Scandinavian authors

For a comprehensive list of trns from the Norwegian, see I. Fæhn and H. Haave, Norwegian literature in English translation since 1742, *in* E. Grönland, Norway in English, Oslo 1961. *For a full list of trns from the Danish, see* E. Bredsdorff, Danish literature in English translation, Copenhagen 1950. *For lists of trns from the Finnish and Swedish, see* S. Haltsonen, Suomalaista kaunokirjallisuutta vieroilla kielillä, Helsinki 1961 *and* E. Gustafson, A list of translations of Swedish literature into English, Stockholm 1962. *In the following list the Scandinavian originals were all pbd in Copenhagen unless otherwise stated.*

Andersen, Hans-Christian (1805–75)
Eventyr. 1834–72; A Danish story-book, tr C. Boner 1846; Wonderful stories for children, tr M. Howitt 1846; Stories and tales, tr H. W. Dulcken 1864; The shoes of fortune, tr C. Boner, with biographical sketch by K. R. H. Mackenzie, 1883; Fairy tales, tr H. L. Braekstad, introd by E. Gosse, 1900. There were over 50 English edns, listed in E. Bredsdorff, *above*.
▽
Bain, R. N. Hans-Christian Andersen. 1895. With a critical appendix on trns.
Drachmann, A. C. E. B. Browning and Hans Andersen. Edda 33 1933.
Bredsdorff, E. Hans Christian Andersen og England. Copenhagen 1954.

Asbjørnsen, Peter Christen (1812–85) and Jørgen Moe
Norske folkeeventyr. Christiania 1843–4; Norske huldreeventyr og folkesagn, 1845–8; Popular tales from the Norse, with introd by G. W. Dasent, Edinburgh 1859.
Norske folkeeventyr: ny samling. Christiania 1871; Tales from the fjeld, tr G. W. Dasent 1874.
▽
Mead, W. R. P. C. Asbjørnsen and his English correspondents. Norseman 10 1952.

Bjørnson, Bjørnstjerne (1832–1910)
The novels of Bjørnson. Ed E. Gosse, 13 vols 1895–1909.
Synnøve Solbakken. Christiania 1859; Love and life in Norway, tr A. Bethell 1870.
Arne. Bergen 1859; tr A. Plesner 1866.
Smaastykker. Bergen 1860; Brude-slaatten 1873; in Life by the fells and fjords, tr A. Plesner 1879.
De nygifte. 1865; The newly married couple, tr T. Soelfeldt 1868; tr S. and E. Hjerleid 1870.
En glad gut. 1868; Ovind; tr S. and E. Hjerleid 1869.
Fiskerjenten. 1868; The fishing girl, tr A. Plesner 1870.
En hanske. 1883; A gauntlet, tr H. Braekstad 1886; tr O. Edwards 1894.
▽
Brandes, G. Bjørnson och Ibsen. Stockholm 1882.
The later plays of Bjørnson. MacMillan's Mag Dec 1889.
Ibsen, H. Bjørnstjerne Bjørnson: a critical study, tr J. Muir 1899.

Bremer, Fredrika (1801–65)
Familien H. Stockholm 1830–1; The H . . . family, 1844.
Presidentens döttrar; Nina. Stockholm 1834, 1835; The president's daughters, and Nina, tr M. Howitt 3 vols 1843.
Grannarne. Stockholm 1837; The neighbours, tr M. Howitt 2 vols 1842.
Hemmet. Stockholm 1839; The home, tr M. Howitt 2 vols 1843.
Trälinnan. Stockholm 1840; The bondmaid, tr M. L. Putnam 1844.
Syskonlif. Stockholm 1848; Brothers and sisters, tr M. Howitt 3 vols 1848.
Hertha. Stockholm 1856; tr M. Howitt 1856.
Fader och dotter. Stockholm 1858; tr M. Howitt 1859.
Skizzer fra England i 1851. 1852; England in 1851, Boulogne 1853.
▽
Laing, S. Fredrika Bremer's novels. North Br Rev May 1844.
[anon.] Fredrika Bremer's Swedish novels. Dublin Rev 17 1844.
Gustafson, A. T. English influence in Fredrika Bremer. JEGP 28–30 1931–3.
Lundgreen, M. Sisters in the shadows: the link between Fredrika Bremer and Charlotte Brontë. Angles on the English-Speaking World 7 1993.

Goldschmidt, Meïr Aron (1819–87)
En jøde. 1845; The jew of Denmark, tr Mrs Bushby 1852; Jacob Bendixen, tr M. Howitt 3 vols 1852.
Hjemløs. 1837; Homeless: or a poet's inner life, translated by the author, 3 vols 1861.

Ibsen, Henrik (1828–1906). *See also under Byron, col 183, below.*
Kjærlighedens komedie. Christiania 1862; Love's comedy, tr with introd by C. H. Herford 1900.
Peer Gynt. 1867; tr W. and C. Archer 1892.
Brand. 1866; tr W. Wilson 1891.
De unges forbund. 1869; The league of youth, tr W. Archer 1890.
Kejser og Galilaeer. 1873; The emperor and the Galilean, tr C. Ray 1876.
Samfundets støtter. 1877; Gengangere, 1881; En folkefiende, 1882; The pillars of society and other plays [Ghosts; An enemy of society], tr W. Archer and E. Marx-Aveling, introd by H. Ellis, 1888.

Et dukkehjem. 1879; Nora: or a doll's house, tr with introd by H. F. Lord 1882.
Vildanden. 1884; The wild duck, tr F. E. Archer 1890.
Rosmersholm. 1886; tr L. N. Parker 1889.
Fruen fra Havet. 1888; The lady from the sea, tr E. Mark-Aveling, introd by E. Gosse, 1890.
Hedda Gabler. 1890; tr E. Gosse 1891.
Bygmester Solness. 1892; The master builder, tr E. Gosse and W. Archer 1893.
Lille Eyolf. 1894; Little Eyolf, tr W. Archer 1894.
▽
Archer, W. Ibsen and English criticism. Fortnightly Rev July 1889.
Courtney, W. L. Ibsen's social dramas. In his Studies at leisure, 1892.
Shaw, G. B. The quintessence of Ibsenism. 1893, 1915 (rev). Reply to Shaw's lectures by W. Archer, New Rev 5 1891.
Wicksteed, P. H. Four lectures on Ibsen. 1892.
Archer, W. The mausoleum of Ibsen. Fortnightly Rev July 1893.
Newman, E. The real Ibsen. Free Rev Oct 1893.
Boyesen, H. H. A commentary on the writings of Ibsen. 1894.
Filon, A. Ibsen à Londres: le drame de demain. Revue des Deux Mondes Nov 1895.
Russell, E. R. Ibsen on his merits. 1897.
Gosse, E. Ibsen. 1907.
Franc, M. A. Ibsen in England. Boston 1919.
Archer, C. William Archer. 1931. With bibliography.
Kröner, J. Die Technik des realistischen Dramas bei Ibsen und Galsworthy. Leipzig 1935.
Qvamme, B. Ibsen og det engelske teater. Edda 42 1942.
Koht, H. Shakespeare and Ibsen. JEGP 44 1945.
Arestad, S. Ibsen and Shakespeare: a study in influence. Scandinavian Stud 10 1946.
Burchardt, C. B. Ibsen and England. Norseman 5 1947.
Irvine, W. Shaw's criticism of Ibsen. South Atlantic Quart 46 1947.
Lamm, M. Ibsen och Shaw. Edda 47 1947.
James, H. In The scenic art, 1949. Two essays of 1897.
Setterquist, J. Ibsen and the beginnings of Anglo-Irish drama. Vol 1 J. M. Synge; vol 2 E. Martyn. Uppsala 1951–60.
Decker, C. R. Ibsen in England. In his Victorian conscience, New York 1952.
Edwards, H. Henry James and Ibsen. Amer Lit 24 1952.
Wade, A. Ibsen in translation. Drama 39 1955.
Adler, J. H. Ibsen, Shaw and Candida. JEGP 59 1960.
Gerould, D. C. Shaw's criticism of Ibsen. Comparative Lit 15 1963.
Gassner, J. Shaw on Ibsen and the drama of ideas. In his Ideas in the drama, New York 1964.
Stanley, R. Ibsen and his translator Archer. Meanjin 23 1964.
Tysdahl, B. J. Joyce and Ibsen. A study in literary influence. Oslo 1968.
Baylen, J. O. William Archer, Ibsen and late Victorian Britain. TSL 20 1975.
Tysdahl, B. J. Byron, Norway and Ibsen's Peer Gynt. ES 56 1975.
Ewbank, I.-S. Ibsen on the English stage. In Ibsen and the theatre: the dramatist in production, ed E. Durbach, New York 1980.
Davis, T. Ibsen's Victorian audience. Essays in Theatre 4 1985.
May, K. M. Ibsen and Shaw. New York 1985.
Powell, K. Wilde and Ibsen. ELT 28 1985.
Fisher, J. Going a-viking: Edward G. Craig's production of Ibsen's The Vikings. In Text and presentation, ed K. Hartigan, Lanham MD 1988.
Ewbank, I.-S. Shakespeare, Ibsen and Rome. In Shakespeare and cultural tradition, ed T. Kishi, Newark NJ and London 1994.
McFarlane, J. (ed). The Cambridge companion to Ibsen. Cambridge 1994.
Jan, S. William Archer's translations of Ibsen 1889–1908. Scandinavica 34 1995.
van Laan, T. Ibsen and Shakespeare. Scandinavian Stud 67 1995.

Kielland, Alexander (1849–1907)
Novelletter. 1879–80; Tales of two countries, tr W. Archer 1891; Norse tales and sketches, tr R. L. Cassie 1896.
Garman og Worse. 1880; tr W. Kettlewell 1884.
Skipper Worse. 1882; tr Earl of Ducie 1885.

Lie, Jonas (1833–1907)
Den fremsynte. 1870; The visionary, tr J. Muir 1893.
Kommandørens døttre. 1886; The commodore's daughters, tr H. L. Braekstad and G. Hughes 1892.
Trold. 2 vols 1891–2; Weird tales from northern seas, tr R. N. Bain 1893.
▽
Lyngstad, S. Jonas Lie. Boston 1977.

Oehlenschläger, Adam (1779–1850). *See also under Borrow, below.*
Haakon Jarl. 1805; tr 1840 (anon).
Palnatoke. 1809; tr J. Chapman 1855.
Axel og Valborg. 1810; tr R. M. Laing in his Hours in Norway, 1841.
Correggio. 1811; tr T. Martin 1854.
Vaulundurs saga. 1812; tr E. Kinnear in G. B. Depping, Wayland Smith, 1847.
Den lille hyrdedreng. 1818; The little shepherd boy, tr J. Heath 1827.
Nordens guder. 1819; The gods of the North, tr W. E. Frye 1845.
Aladdin. 1820; tr T. Martin 1857.
▽
Rose, E. A northern Hamlet [Oehlenschläger's Amleth]. Fraser's Mag May 1877.

Pontoppidan, Henrik (1857–1943)
Mimoser. 1886; The apothecary's daughters, tr G. Nielsen 1890.
Det forjættede land. 1891–5; Emmanuel: or Children of the soil; and The promised land, tr Mrs E. Lucas 1892, 1896.

Strindberg, August (1849–1912)
Fadren. 1887; The father, tr N. Ericksen 1899.
McCarthy, J. H. August Strindberg. Fortnightly Rev Sep 1892.
Gustafson, A. Some early English and American Strindberg criticism. In Scandinavian studies presented to George T. Flom, Urbana IL 1942.
Morgan, M. Strindberg and the English theatre. Mod Drama 7 1964.
Johnson, W. August Strindberg. Boston 1976.
Northam, J. Waiting for Prospero. In English drama: form and development, ed M. Axton and R. Williams, Cambridge 1977.
Tornquist, E. Strindberg and O'Neil. In Structures of influence: a comparative approach to August Strindberg, ed M. Johnson, Chapel Hill NC 1981.
Jacobs, B. Strindberg's Fadren (The Father) in English translation. Yearbook of Comparative and General Lit 35 1986.
Olsson, L. M. Strindberg's plays in English translation: a select bibliography. Swedish Book Rev 1986.
Sayers, W. Aweghost Strindberg in Finnegans Wake. James Joyce Quart 27 1990.
Wikander, M. H. Historical vision and dramatic historiography: Strindberg's Gustav III in the light of Shakespeare's Julius Caesar and Corneille's Cinna. Scandinavian Stud 62 1990.
Ewbank, I.-S. Richard III (c. 1591) and Gustav III (1902) and the drama of nationalism. In Literature and nationalism, ed V. Newey and A. Thompson, 1991.

Tegnér, Esaias (1782–1846)
[anon (A. Gillespie Smyth)] Frithioff: a Swedish poem. Blackwood's Mag 24 1828.
Stephens, G. Frithiof's saga, a Norwegian story. Stockholm 1839; facs reprint 1995. Translation of Esaias Tegnér's poem.
Benson, A. B. A list of the English translations of the Frithiofs saga. Germanic Rev 1 1926.

English authors

For a comprehensive list of trns into Norwegian, see R. Øksnevad, Det Britiske samvelde og Eire i norsk litteratur, Oslo 1949.

Borrow, George

Romantic ballads translated from the Danish [Kjæmpe viser, Oehlenschläger, Evald etc]. 1826.

The death of Balder [tr from J. Evald, Balders død, 1773]. 1889.

The gold horns [tr from A. Oehlenschläger, Guldhornene, 1803]. 1913.

▽

Wright, H. G. Borrow's translations from the Scandinavian languages. Edda 16 1921.

Hustvedt, S. B. Borrow and his Danish ballads. JEGP 22 1923.

Wright, H. G. Influence of George Borrow in Norway and Sweden. MLR 29 1934.

Williams, D. A. A world of his own: the double life of George Borrow. Oxford 1982.

Collie, M. and A. Fraser. George Borrow: a bibliographical study. Winchester 1984.

Byron, George Gordon

Holthausen, F. Skandinavische Byron-Übersetzungen. E Studien 25 1898.

Biller, G. Byron i den svenska litteraturen före Strindberg. Samlaren 33 1912.

Beck, R. Grímur Thomsen: a pioneer Byron student. JEGP 27 1928.

Beck, R. Gisli Brynjúlfsson: an Icelandic imitator of Childe Harold's prilgrimage. JEGP 28 1929.

Beck, R. Grímur Thomsen og Byron. Reykjavik 1937.

Sjöholm, S. Fröding och Byron. Edda 39 1939.

Skard, S. Byron i norsk litteratur. Edda 39 1939.

Farinelli, A. Byron e Ibsen. Milan 1944.

Simonsen, P. Om Hedda Gabler, Lille Eyolf og Lord Byron. Edda 62 1962. [AW]

(8) RUSSIAN

A. THE RECEPTION OF RUSSIAN LITERATURE AND CULTURE IN BRITAIN

Nineteenth-century studies of Russia

Lyall, R. The character of the Russians, and a detailed history of Moscow. London and Edinburgh 1823.

Landor, W. S. Imaginary conversations. Ed C. G. Crump 6 vols 1891–1901. (The 'Russian' conversations date originally from 1825–9.)

Morton, E. Travels in Russia, and a residence at St Petersburgh and Odessa in the years 1827 and 1829. 1830.

[Cobden, R.] Russia, by a Manchester manufacturer. Edinburgh 1836.

Paul, R. B. Journal of a tour to Moscow in the summer of 1836. 1836.

Venables, R. L. Domestic scenes in Russia; in a series of letters describing a year's residence in that country, chiefly in the interior. 1839; 1856 (2nd rev edn).

[Rigby, E., Lady Eastlake.] A residence on the shores of the Baltic, described in a series of letters by a lady. 2 vols 1841. Rptd as Letters from the shores of the Baltic, 1844, etc.

Kohl, J. G. Russia and the Russians, in 1842. 2 vols 1842.

Custine, A.-L.-L., marquis de. The Empire of the Czar; or, Observations on the social, political, and religious state and prospects of Russia, made during a journey through that Empire. Tr from Fr 3 vols 1843. Later known simply as Custine's Russia.

[Henningsen, C. F.] Revelations of Russia; or, The Emperor Nicholas and his Empire, in 1844, by one who has seen and describes. 2 vols 1844. This later became Revelations of Russia in 1846, by an English resident, 1846.

Golovin, I. G. Russia under the autocrat, Nicholas the First. 2 vols 1846.

[Anon.] Russia, the land of the Czar: a sketch historical, statistical and descriptive, of the Muscovite Empire, from 862 to 1854; to which is added an account of the war in the East, from the commencement of hostilities to the present date. Tr (from Ger) 1854.

Brooks, C. W. Shirley. The Russians of the south. 1854.

Golovin, I. G. The nations of Russia and Turkey and their destiny. 1854.

Lushington, F. Points of war. Cambridge and London 1854.

Oliphant, L. The Russian shores of the Black Sea in the autumn of 1852, with a voyage down the Volga and a tour through the country of the Don Cossacks. London and Edinburgh 1854.

Kelly, W. K. The history of Russia from the earliest period to the present time, compiled from the most authentic sources including the works of Karamsin, Tooke, and Ségur. 2 vols 1854–5.

Songs of the war, by the best writers. Ed, with original songs, J. H. Friswell '1855' [1854].

[Kolbe, E.] Recollections of Russia during thirty-three years' residence, by a German nobleman. Rev and tr (from Ger) L. Wraxall, Edinburgh 1855.

[McCoy, E.?] The Englishwoman in Russia: impressions of the society and manners of the Russians at home, by a lady ten years resident in that country. 1855.

Smith, Alexander, and the author of 'Balder' and 'The Roman' [S. Dobell]. Sonnets on the war. 1855.

Russell, W. H. The war: from the landing at Gallipoli to the death of Lord Raglan. 1855. The war: from the death of Lord Raglan to the evacuation of the Crimea; with additions and corrections. 1856. Together these became The British expedition to the Crimea, 1858 (rev edn); 1877 (new and rev edn).

Haxthausen, A., Freiherr von. The Russian Empire: its people, institutions, and resources. Tr (from Ger) R. Farie 2 vols 1856.

Milner, T. Russia: its rise and progress, tragedies and revolutions. 1856.

Sala, G. A. A journey due north; being notes of a residence in Russia in the summer of 1856. 1858.

Pearson, C. H. Russia, by a recent traveller: a series of letters. 1859.

Pepys, Lady C. A journey on a plank from Kiev to Eaux-Bonnes, 1859. 2 vols 1860.

Edwards, H. S. The Russians at home: unpolitical sketches. 1861.

Kinglake, A. W. The invasion of the Crimea: its origin, and an account of its progress down to the death of Lord Raglan. 8 vols Edinburgh and London 1863–87.

Grahame, F. R. [C. L. Johnstone.] The progress of science, art, and literature in Russia. 1865.

Ralston, W. R. S. The songs of the Russian people, as illustrative of Slavonic mythology and Russian social life. 1872; Russian folk-tales, 1873.

Joyneville, C. [C. L. Johnstone.] The life and times of Alexander I, Emperor of All the Russias. 3 vols 1875.

Wahl, O. W. The land of the Czar. 1875.

Wallace, D. M. Russia. 1877; many later edns.

[Novikova, O. A.; pseud 'O. K.'] Is Russia wrong? A series of letters by a Russian lady. Preface by J. A. Froude, 1878. Friends or foes? A sequel to 'Is Russia wrong?' By a Russian lady. 1878.

Stepniak, S. [S. M. Stepnyak-Kravchinsky.] Russia under the Tzars. Tr W. Westall 2 vols 1885; Career of a nihilist, 1889.

Stead, W. T. Truth about Russia. 1888.

Brandes, G. Impressions of Russia. Tr (from Danish) S. C. Eastman 1890.

Morfill, W. R. Russia. 1890.

Prelooker, J. Under the Czar and Queen Victoria: the experiences of a Russian reformer. 1896.

Kropotkin, P. A. Memoirs of a revolutionist. Preface by G. Brandes, 2 vols 1899.

Translations from Russian literature (in book form)

Dates given after Russian titles are those of first pbn; British pbn dates take no account of earlier American ones.

Karamzin, Nikolay Mikhaylovich (1766–1826).
(Bednaya Liza, 1792, Yuliya, 1794, et al;) Russian tales, tr A. A. Feldborg or J. B. Elrington (?), introd G. Sidney, 1803; rptd as Tales from the Russian, 1804.
Rossiyskaya antologiya: specimens of the Russian poets, with preliminary remarks and biographical notices. 1821. Rossiyskaya antologiya: specimens of the Russian poets, with introductory remarks; pt the second. 1823. Both ed and tr J. Bowring.
Poetical translations from the Russian language, tr W. H. Saunders 1826.
Bulgarin, Faddey Venediktovich (1789–1859)
(Ivan Vyzhigin. 1829;) Ivan Vejeeghen; or, Life in Russia, tr G. Ross 2 vols London and Edinburgh 1831.
Zagoskin, Mikhail Nikolayevich (1789–1852).
(Yuriy Miloslavskiy, ili Russkiye v 1612 godu. 1829;) The young Muscovite; or, The Poles in Russia, tr F. Chamier 3 vols 1833.
Lazhechnikov, Ivan Ivanovich (1792–1869).
(Basurman. 1838,) The heretic, tr T. B. Shaw 3 vols Edinburgh 1844.
Sollogub, Vladimir Aleksandrovich (1813–82)
(Tarantas. 1845;) The tarantas: travelling impressions of young Russia, tr F. von Rosenstrauch 1850.
Pushkin, Aleksandr Sergeyevich (1799–1837)
(Pikovaya dama. 1834;) The queen of spades, Edinburgh 1850, 1858 (with The captain's daughter); The queen of spades, and other stories; with a biography, tr and ed M. S. Edwards 1892.
(Kapitanskaya dochka. 1836;) The captain's daughter, Edinburgh 1857, 1858 (with The queen of spades), tr J. F. Hanstein 1859, tr J. Igelström and Mrs P. Easton 1883; The daughter of the commandant: a Russian romance, tr M. Milne-Home 1891.
(Povesti Belkina, 1831, et al;) Russian romance, tr Mrs J. B. Telfer 1875 (includes The captain's daughter, et al); The prose tales, tr T. Keane 1894.
(Yevgeniy Onegin. 1825–32;) Eugene Onéguine: a romance of Russian life, in verse, tr H. Spalding 1881.
[Verse] translations from Poushkin, in memory of the hundredth anniversary of the poet's birthday, tr C. E. Turner 1899.
Lermontov, Mikhail Yur'evich (1814–41).
(Geroy nashego vremeni. 1839–41;) Sketches of Russian life in the Caucasus, by a Russe, many years resident amongst the various mountain tribes, 1853; A hero of our own times, 1854; The hero of our days, tr T. Pulszky 1854; A hero of our time, tr R. I. Lipmann (Zubov) 1886; Lermontof's Modern hero, tr I. Nestor-Schnurmann, Cambridge 1899.
(Demon. 1829–41;) The demon: a poem, tr A. C. Stephen 1875; The demon of Lermontoff, tr F. Storr 1894.
Gogol', Nikolay Vasil'evich (in English usually Gogol, 1809–52)
(Pokhozhdeniya Chichikova, ili Mërtvyye dushi. 1842.) Home life in Russia, by a Russian noble. Revised by the editor of 'Revelations in Siberia', tr K. Lach-Szyrma 2 vols 1854;. Dead souls; or, Tchitchikoff's journeys, tr I. F. Hapgood 1887.
(Taras Bul'ba, 1835, et al;) Cossack tales, tr G. Tolstoy 1860; Taras Bulba; also St John's Eve, and other stories, tr I. F. Hapgood et al 1887.
(Revizor. 1836;) The inspector: a comedy, tr T. Hart-Davies 1892; The inspector-general (or 'Revizór': a Russian comedy), tr A. A. Sykes 1892.
Turgenev, Ivan Sergeyevich (1818–83)
(Zapiski okhotnika, 1847–52.) Mémoires d'un seigneur russe, tr (into Fr) E. Charrière, Paris 1854; Russian life in the interior; or, The experiences of a sportsman, tr (from Fr) and ed J. D. Meiklejohn, Edinburgh '1855' [1854]; Tales from the note-book of a sportsman, tr E. Richter 1895; A sportsman's sketches, tr C. Garnett 1895.
(Ottsy i deti, 1862.) Fathers and sons: a novel, tr E. Schuyler, New York distrib London 1867, rptd 1883; Fathers and children, tr C. Garnett, introd E. Garnett, 1895.
(Dym, 1867.) Smoke; or, Life at Baden: a novel, tr (from Fr) R. Crawley 2 vols 1868; Smoke: a Russian novel, tr (from Fr) W. F. West 1883; Smoke, tr C. Garnett, introd E. Garnett, 1896.
(Dvoryanskoye gnezdo, 1859.) Liza, tr W. R. S. Ralston 2 vols 1869; often rptd; A house of gentlefolk, tr C. Garnett, introd S. Stepniak, 1894.
(Nakanune, 1860.) On the eve: a tale, tr C. E. Turner 1871; On the eve, tr C. Garnett, introd E. Garnett, 1895.
(Nov', 1877.) Virgin soil, tr A. W. Dilke 1878, tr (from Fr) T. S. Perry 1883, tr C. Garnett, introd E. Garnett, 1896.
(Rudin, 1856.) Dimitri Roudine: a novel, tr (from Fr and Ger) 1883; Rudin, tr C. Garnett, introd S. Stepniak, 1894.
(Pervaya lyubov', 1860; et al.) First love, and Púnin and Babúrin, tr and introd S. Jerrold 1884.
(Mumu, 1854; Dnevnik lishnego cheloveka, 1850.) Mumu, and The diary of a superfluous man, tr H. Gersoni 1884; The diary of a superfluous man, etc, tr C. Garnett 1899.
(Neschastnaya, 1869; As'ya, 1858.) An unfortunate woman, and Ass'ya, tr H. Gersoni 1886; The unfortunate one: a novel, tr A. R. Thompson 1888; in The Jew, etc, tr C. Garnett, introd E. Garnett, 1899.
(Stikhotvoreniya v proze, 1882.) Poems in prose, tr (from Fr) Mrs T. S. Perry(?) 1887; Senilia: poems in prose, being meditations, sketches, etc, tr (from Ger and Danish) and introd S. J. MacMullan, Bristol and London 1890; Dream tales and prose poems, tr C. Garnett 1897.
(Veshniye vody, 1872.) Spring floods, tr E. Richter 1895; The torrents of spring, etc, tr C. Garnett 1897.
(Complete works; some given above.) The novels of Ivan Turgenev, tr C. Garnett 15 vols 1894–9. Vols 16–17 were pbd only in 1921.
Griboyedov, Aleksandr Sergeyevich (1795–1829)
(Gore ot uma (Woe from wit), 1831.) Gore ot ouma: a comedy, tr N. Benardaky, London and Edinburgh 1857.
Saltykov-Shchedrin, Mikhail Yevgrafovich (1826–89)
(Gubernskiye ocherki, 1856–7.) Tchinovnicks: sketches of provincial life, from the memoirs of the retired Conseiller de Cour Stchedrin (Saltikow), tr and ed F. Aston 1861.
Tolstoy, Lev Nikolayevich (1828–1910)
(Detstvo, 1852; Otrochestvo, 1854; Yunost', 1857.) Childhood and youth: a tale, tr M. von Meysenbug 1862; Childhood, boyhood, youth, tr I. F. Hapgood 1888; Boyhood, adolescence, and youth, tr C. Popoff 1890.
(Kazaki, 1863.) The cossacks: a tale of the Caucasus in 1852, tr E. Schuyler 2 vols 1878, tr N. H. Dole 1888; The cossacks, and other stories, 1887.
(V chëm moya vera? and Ispoved', 1884 (banned).) Christ's Christianity, 1885; What I believe, tr C. Popoff 1885; My religion, tr (from Fr) H. Smith 1889; How I came to believe, 1900.
(Voyna i mir, 1865–9.) War and peace, tr (from Fr) C. C. Bell 3 vols 1886, tr N. H. Dole 4 vols 1889.
(Anna Karenina, 1875–7.) Tr N. H. Dole 1886.
(Semeynoye schast'e, 1859; et al.) My husband and I, and other stories, 1887; Family happiness: a romance, tr N. H. Dole 1894.
(Utro pomeshchika, 1856; et al.) A Russian proprietor, and other stories, tr N. H. Dole 1887.
(Vlast' t'my, 1887.) The dominion of darkness: a drama in five acts, 1888.
(Smert' Ivana Il'icha, 1886; et al.) Ivan Ilyitch, and other stories, tr N. H. Dole 1889.
(Chem lyudi zhivy, 1882.) What men live by, tr N. H. Dole 1889.
(Gde lyubov', tam i Bog, 1885.) Where love is, there is God also, tr N. H. Dole 1889.
(Sevastopol'skiye rasskazy, 1855–6.) Sevastopol, tr I. F. Hapgood 1889.
(Kreytserova sonata, 1890.) The Kreutzer sonata, tr H. S. Edwards 1890, tr W. M. Thomson 1890, tr B. R. Tucker 1890.

(Plody prosveshcheniya, 1890.) The fruits of enlightenment: a comedy in four acts, tr E. J. Dillon, introd A. W. Pinero, 1891; The fruits of culture, tr G. Schumm 1891.

(Khozyain i rabotnik, 1895.) Master and man, tr A. H. Beaman 1895, tr S. Rapoport and J. C. Kenworthy 1895.

(Chto takoye iskusstvo? 1897–8.) What is art?, tr A. Maude 1898, tr C. Johnston 1898.

(Voskreseniye, 1899.) Resurrection, tr L. Maude 1900.

Krylov, Ivan Andreyevich (1768–1844).

(Basni, 9 bks, 1809–43.) Krilof and his fables, ed and tr W. R. S. Ralston 1869, 1871 (3rd enlarged edn); Krilof's original fables, tr J. H. Harrison 1883; A child's version of Aesop's fables, with a suppl containing fables by La Fontaine and Krilof, tr J. H. Stickney 1886.

Tolstoy, Aleksey Konstantinovich (1817–75)

(Smert' Ioanna Groznogo, 1866.) The death of Ivan the Terrible: a tragedy, tr I. H. Harrison 1869.

(Knyaz' serebryanyy, 1862.) Prince Serebrenni, tr M. Golitsyna 2 vols 1874; The terrible czar: a romance of the time of Ivan the Terrible, tr H. C. Filmore 2 vols 1892.

Dostoyevsky, Fëdor Mikhaylovich (1821–81)

(Zapiski iz Mërtvogo doma, 1860–2.) Buried alive; or, Ten years of penal servitude in Siberia, tr M. von Thilo 1881; Prison life in Siberia, tr (from Fr) H. S. Edwards 1887.

(Prestupleniye i nakazaniye, 1866.) Crime and punishment, tr (from Fr) 1886.

(Unizhënnyye i oskorblënnyye, 1861.) Injury and insult, tr F. Whishaw 1886.

(Selo Stepanchikovo i yego obitateli, 1859; Igrok, 1866.) The friend of the family, and The gambler, tr F. Whishaw 1887.

(Idiot, 1868.) The idiot, tr F. Whishaw 1887.

(Dyadyushkin son, 1859; Vechnyy muzh, 1870.) Uncle's dream, and The permanent husband, tr F. Whishaw 1888.

(Bednyye lyudi, 1846.) Poor folk, tr L. Milman, introd G. Moore, 1894.

Russian lyrics in English verse, tr C. T. Wilson 1887.

Rhymes from the Russian; being faithful translations of selections from the best Russian poets, tr J. Pollen 1891.

Tales from the Russian, tr M. S. Edwards(?) 1892. Pushkin, Lermontov, etc.

Korolenko, Vladimir Galaktionovich (1853–1921)

(Slepoy muzykant, 1886.) The blind musician, tr S. Stepniak and W. Westall 1890.

(Son Makara, 1885; Sokolinets, 1885; et al.) In Russian stories, 2 vols 1892: vol 1 Makár's dream, and other stories. vol 2 The Saghalien convict, and other stories.

Garshin, Vsevolod Mikhaylovich (1855–88)

(Trus, 1879; Krasnyy tsvetok, 1883; et al.) Stories from Garshin, tr E. L. Voynich, introd S. Stepniak, 1893.

Goncharov, Ivan Aleksandrovich (1812–91)

(Obyknovennaya istoriya, 1847.) A common story: a novel, tr C. Garnett 1894.

The humour of Russia, tr E. L. Voynich, introd S. Stepniak, 1895. (A coll of pieces, incl extracts from works by Gogol, Ostrovsky, Dostoyevsky, Saltykov-Shchedrin, etc.)

Ostrovsky, Aleksandr Nikolayevich (1823–86)

(Groza, 1860.) The storm, tr C. Garnett, introd E. Garnett, 1899.

Russian literature

Bibliographies

Griswold, W. M. A descriptive list of novels and tales dealing with life in Russia. Cambridge MA 1892.

Osborne, E. A. Early translations from the Russian. Bookman 82–4 1932–3.

Orel, H. The forgotten ambassadors: Russian fiction in Victorian England. Amer SEER 12 1953.

Line, M. B. A bibliography of Russian literature in English translation to 1900 (excluding periodicals). 1963. Integrated in M. B. Line, A. Ettlinger and J. M. Gladstone, Bibliography of Russian literature in English translation to 1945, Totowa NJ and London 1972.

Nerhood, H. W. To Russia and return: an annotated bibliography of travelers' English-language accounts from the ninth century to the present. Columbus OH 1968.

Cross, A. G. The Russian theme in English literature from the sixteenth century to 1980: an introductory survey and a bibliography. Oxford 1985.

Proffer, C. R., and R. Meyer. Nineteenth-century Russian literature in English: a bibliography of criticism and translations. Ann Arbor 1990.

General studies

Bowring, J. Politics and literature of Russia. Westminster Rev 1, Jan 1824.

Russian literature. Foreign Quart Rev 1, Nov 1827.

Europe in 1827. Part 4. Russia. In General Register for 1827, Edinburgh and London 1828.

Russian novels and novelists. Foreign Quart Rev 8, July 1831.

Russian poetry. Foreign Quart Rev 9, May 1832.

Russian novel writing. Foreign Quart Rev 21, Apr 1838.

Leeds, W. H. Russian fabulists, with specimens. Fraser's Mag 19, Sep 1839, and 25, Feb 1842.

Otto, Friedrich. The history of Russian literature, with a lexicon of Russian authors, tr G. Cox (from Ger), Oxford 1839.

Leeds, W. H. Russian literary biography, etc. Westminster Rev 36, July 1841.

Literary notices – Russia. Foreign and Colonial Quart Rev 3, Jan 1844.

Modern Russian literature. Eclectic Rev 9, Feb 1855.

Schuyler, E. Continental literature in 1869: Russia. Athenaeum 25 Dec 1869. Continental literature in 1872: Russia. Athenaeum 28 Dec 1872.

Ralston, W. R. S. Russian idylls. Contemp Rev 23, Apr 1874, and 27, Apr 1876. Russian revolutionary literature. Nineteenth Cent 1, May 1877.

Morfill, W. R. Russian literature. Westminster Rev 52, Oct 1877.

Turner, C. E. Studies in Russian literature. 1882. The modern novelists of Russia. 1890.

Panin, I. Lectures on Russian literature: Pushkin, Gogol, Turgenef, Tolstoy. New York and London 1889.

Mitchell, J. Characteristics of Russian literature. Temple Bar 89, June 1890.

Recent Russian literature. Rev of Revs 3 Apr 1891.

Wilson, H. S. Early Russian fiction. Dublin Rev Jan 1892.

Anglo-Russian Literary Society. Proc 1893–1916. Opening address by J. Pollen on 'Russian language and literature'. 1893.

Burton, R. G. An appreciation of Russian fictional literature. Westminster Rev 144, Nov 1895.

Sutherland, E. H. The drama in Russia. Theatre 26, Oct 1895.

Morfill, W. R. Russian literature during the last year. Cosmopolis 7, Aug 1897.

Volkonsky, S. M. Pictures of Russian history and Russian literature. Boston, New York and London 1897.

Bennett, A. Some younger reputations. Acad 17, Dec 1898.

Crawford, V. M. Studies in foreign literature. 1899.

Waliszewski, K. A history of Russian literature. 1900.

Carr, E. H. The romantic exiles: a nineteenth-century portrait gallery. 1933.

Decker, C. R. Victorian comment on Russian realism. PMLA 52, June 1937.

Decker, C. R. The aesthetic revolt against naturalism in Victorian criticism. PMLA 53, Sep 1938.

Marriott, J. A. R. Anglo-Russian relations, 1689–1943. 1944.
Woodham-Smith, C. B. The reason why. 1953.
Brewster, D. East–West passage: a study in literary relationships. 1954.
Tove, A. L. Konstantsiya Garnet – perevodchik i propagandist russkoy literatury. Russkaya literatura 1958 no 4.
Phelps, G. The early phases of British interest in Russian literature. SEER 36 1958, 38 1960. (Two related articles with the same title.)
Curran, E. M. The 'Foreign Quarterly Review' on Russian and Polish literature. SEER 40 1961–2.
Zhantiyeva, D. G. Esteticheskiye vzglyady angliyskikh pisateley kontsa XIX – nachala XX veka i russkaya klassicheskaya literatura. In Iz istorii literaturnykh svyazey XIX veka, Moscow 1962.
Alekseyev, M. P. William Ralston and Russian writers of the later nineteenth century. Oxford Slavonic Papers o.s. 11 1964.
Galton, D. The Anglo-Russian Literary Society. SEER 48 1970.
Cross, A. G. (ed). Russia under Western eyes, 1517–1825. 1971.
Orel, H. The Victorian view of Russian literature. Victorian Newsletter 51 spring 1977.
Literaturnoye nasledstvo, vol 91: Russko-angliyskiye literaturnyye svyazi (XVIII vek–pervaya polovina XIX veka). Ed V. R. Shcherbina, I. S. Zil'bershteyn et al from research by M. P. Alekseyev, Moscow 1982.
Atkinson, G. L. Some significant aspects of the reception of Russian literature in England in the middle of the nineteenth century (1840–1860). Unpbd PhD thesis, Victoria Univ of Wellington 1992.
Cross, A. G. Anglo-Russica: aspects of cultural relations between Great Britain and Russia in the eighteenth and early nineteenth centuries. Oxford and Providence RI 1993.
Alekseyev, M. P. and Yu. D. Levin. Vil'yam Rol'ston – propagandist russkoy literatury i fol'klora. St Petersburg 1994.

The novel

Gross, A. E. The Russian novel and the English novel. Chatauquan 37 1903.
Laughbaum, A. B. Some English novels (1855–1917) that deal with the Crimean War. Unpbd PhD thesis, Univ of Illinois 1948.
Orel, H. The first Russian novels in Victorian England. Nineteenth-Cent Fiction 9 1954. Victorians and the Russian novel: a bibliography. BB 21:3–4 Jan–Apr and May–Aug 1954. English critics and the Russian novel: 1850–1917. SEER 33, June 1955.
Phelps, G. The Russian novel in English fiction. 1956.
Davie, D. A. (ed and introd). Russian literature and modern English fiction: a collection of critical essays. Chicago and London 1965.
Wellek, R. The nineteenth-century Russian novel in English and American criticism. In The Russian novel from Pushkin to Pasternak, ed J. Garrard, New Haven CT 1983.

Poetry

Partridge, M. Slavonic themes in English poetry of the nineteenth century. SEER 41, June 1963.
Cross, A. G. Early English specimens of the Russian poets. Canadian-American Slavic Stud 9:4 winter 1975; rptd in his Anglo-Russica, 1993. 'O thou, great monarch of a pow'rful reign!' English bards and Russian Tsars. Oxford Slavonic Papers 15 1982; rptd in his Anglo-Russica, 1993.
Waddington, P. H. From 'The Russian Fugitive' to 'The Ballad of Bulgarie': episodes in English literary attitudes to Russia from Wordsworth to Swinburne. Oxford and Providence 1994. 'Theirs but to do and die': the poetry of the charge of the Light Brigade at Balaklava, 25 October 1854. Nottingham 1995.

Drama

Bratton, J. S. Theatre of war: the Crimea on the London stage, 1854–5. In Performance and politics in popular drama: aspects of popular entertainment in theatre, film and television, 1800–1976, ed D. Bradby, L. James and B. Sharratt, Cambridge 1980.

Russian authors

Dostoyevsky, F. M.

Ralston, W. R. S. Rev of 'Buried alive; or, Ten years of penal servitude in Siberia'. Acad 16 Apr 1881.
Wilson, H. S. The Russian novelist Dostoyevsky. Acad 12 Dec 1885.
A Russian novelist. Spectator 10 July 1886.
Lomas, J. Dostoyevsky and his work. Macmillan's Mag 55, Jan 1887.
Kaufmann, M. Two Russian realists. London Quart Rev 70, Apr 1888.
Morfill, W. R. 'Poor folk.' Acad 22 Sep 1894.
Neuschäffer, W. Dostojewskijs Einfluss auf den englischen Roman. Heidelberg 1935.
Muchnic, H. Dostoevsky's English reputation (1881–1936). Northampton MA 1939; rptd New York 1969.
Beebe, M. and C. Newton. Dostoevsky in English: a selected checklist of criticism and translations. Mod Fiction Stud 4 1958.
Terry, G. M. Dostoyevsky studies in Great Britain: a bibliographical survey. In New essays on Dostoyevsky, ed M. V. Jones and G. M. Terry, Cambridge 1983.

Gertsen (in English usually Herzen), **Aleksandr Ivanovich** (1812–70)

Ralston, W. R. S. Alexander Hertzen. Temple Bar 29, Apr 1870.
Partridge, M. Alexander Herzen and the English press. SEER 36, June 1958. Herzen, Ogarèv and the Free Russian Press in London. Anglo-Soviet Jnl 27:1 1966.

Gogol', N. V.

Watts, T. Rev of 'Home life in Russia'. Athenaeum 2 Dec 1854.
Russian literature. Dublin Univ Jnl 46, Sep 1855.
Turner, C. E. Nicholas Gógol. Br Quart Rev 47, Apr 1868.
Tilley, A. Gogol, the father of Russian realism. Nat Rev 23, July 1894.
Simmons, E. J. Gogol and English literature. MLR 26, Oct 1931.
Lefevre, C. A. Gogol's first century in England and America (1841–1941). Unpbd PhD thesis, Univ of Minnesota 1943. Gogol and Anglo-Russian literary relations during the Crimean War. Amer SEER 8:2 Apr 1949.
Proffer, C. R. 'Dead souls' in translation. SEEJ 8 1964.

Karamzin, N. M.

Cross, A. G. Karamzin and England. SEER 43 1964–5. Karamzin in English. Canadian-American Slavic Stud 3:4 1969.

Kol'tsov, Aleksey Vasil'evich (1809–42)

Ralston, W. R. S. A Russian poet. Fortnightly Rev 6, 15 Sep 1866.

Krylov, I. A.

Chambers's Jnl 23 Feb 1856.
Ralston, W. R. S. Krilof's fables. Saturday Rev 19 Oct 1867.
Cross, A. G. The English and Krylov. Oxford Slavonic Papers 16 1983; partially rptd (as The British and Krylov) in his Anglo-Russica, 1993.

Lermontov, M. Yu.

Russian literature – Michael Lermontoff. Story-Teller Sep 1843, pt 5.
Chorley, H. F. Rev of 'Sketches of Russian life in the Caucasus'. Athenaeum 22 Oct 1853.
Meysenbug, M. von, and A. I. Herzen. Russian literature: Michael Lermontoff. Nat Rev 11, July 1860.
Review of 'A hero of our time'. Athenaeum 26 June 1869.
Staley, A. E. Some translations from the Russian of Lermontoff. Blackwood's Mag 136, Aug 1884.
Shepherd, G. Impressions of Lermontov. Proc of the Anglo-Russian Lit Soc 13 1895.
Conover, H. F. Mikhail Iur'evich Lermontov: a bibliographical list in English. Washington DC 1938.

Heifetz, A. Lermontov in English: a list of works by and about the poet, 1814–1841–1941. New York 1942.
Chin Wen. From glaring cheat to daring feat: two episodes in the reception of M. Yu. Lermontov in Victorian England. New Zealand Slavonic Jnl 1980 no 2.

Nekrasov, Nikolay Alekseyevich (1821–77)

Turner, C. E. Nicholas Alexeitch Nekrasov. Fortnightly Rev 36, 1 Oct 1881.
Levin, Yu. D. Nekrasov v Anglii i Amerike. In N. A. Nekrasov, Nauchnyy byulleten' Leningradskogo universiteta 1947 nos 16–17.

Ostrovsky, A. N.

Ralston, W. R. S. The modern Russian drama: Ostrovsky's plays. Edinburgh Rev 128, July 1868.
Rogov, V. V. Ostrovsky v Anglii. In Literaturnoye nasledstvo 88: A. N. Ostrovsky. Novyye materialy i issledovaniya, bk 2 Moscow 1974.

Pushkin, A. S.

Shaw, T. B. Púshkin, the Russian poet. Blackwood's Mag 57–8 June–Aug 1845.
Jones, E. C. National literature: Russia. Labourer 3 1848.
Meysenbug, M. von, and A. I. Herzen. Russian literature and Alexander Pushkin. Nat Rev 7, Oct 1858.
Ralston, W. R. S. Rev of 'Eugene Onéguine'. Athenaeum 17 Sep 1881.
Morfill, W. R. Alexander Pushkin. Westminster Rev 63 1883.
Cross, S. H. Pouchkine en Angleterre. Revue de Littérature Comparée 17 1937.
Simmons, E. J. La littérature anglaise et Pouchkine. Revue de Littérature Comparée 17 1937.
Yarmolinsky, A. Pushkin in English: a list of works by and about Pushkin. New York 1937.
Simmons, E. J. English translations of 'Eugene Onegin'. SEER 17, July 1938.
Struve, G. Pushkin in early English criticism (1821–1838). Amer SEER 8:4 Dec 1949.

Saltykov-Shchedrin, M. Ye.

Turgenev, I. S. Rev of 'Istoriya odnogo goroda'. Acad 1 Mar 1871.
Foote, I. P. M. E. Saltykov-Shchedrin in English: a bibliography. Oxford Slavonic Papers 22 1989.

Tolstoy, L. N.

Rev of 'Childhood and youth'. Saturday Rev, 29 Mar 1862; rptd in Russian literature and modern English fiction, ed Davie 1965.
Rev of The cossacks. Examiner 12 Oct 1878.
Count L. N. Tolstoi and his works. Acad 22 Mar 1879.
Ralston, W. R. S. Count Leo Tolstoy's novels. Nineteenth Cent 5, Apr 1879.
Henley, W. E. Count Tolstoy's novels. Saturday Rev 1 Jan 1887.
Tolstoy's War and peace. Spectator 5 Feb 1887.
Wedgwood, J. Count Leo Tolstoy. Contemporary Rev 52, Aug 1887.
Count Tolstoy's life and works. Westminster Rev 130, Sep 1888.
Turner, C. E. Count Tolstoy as novelist and thinker. 1888.
Dillon, E. J. The 'Kreutzer sonata'. Universal Rev 6, Mar 1890.
Bers, S. A. Recollections of Count Leo Tolstoy, tr C. E. Turner 1893.
Sergeyenko, P. A. How Count Tolstoy lives and works. Tr I. F. Hapgood 1899.
Tolstoy's new novel ('Resurrection'). Acad 9 Sep 1899.
Garnett, E. Tolstoy and Turgenieff. Anglo-Saxon Rev 6, Sep 1900.
Massingham, H. W. The philosophy of a saint. Contemporary Rev 78, Dec 1900.
Wiener, L. Bibliography of works and articles on Tolstoy in English, German, and French. In Complete works of Count Tolstoy, tr and ed Wiener 1905, vol 24.
Yassukovitch, A. Tolstoi in English, 1878–1929: a list of works by and about Tolstoi available in the New York Public Library. New York 1929.
Holman, M. J. de K. The Purleigh colony: Tolstoyan togetherness in the late 1890s. In New essays on Tolstoy, ed M. V. Jones, Cambridge 1978.
Terry, G. M. Tolstoy studies in Great Britain: a bibliographical survey. In New essays on Tolstoy, ed M. V. Jones, Cambridge 1978.
Sendich, M. Tolstoy's War and peace in English: a bibliography of criticism (1879–1985). Russian Lang Jnl 41 1987.
Christian, R. F. The road to Yasnaya Polyana: some pilgrims from Britain and their reminiscences. SEER 66, Oct 1988.
Davie, D. A. Mr Tolstoy, I presume? The Russian novel through Victorian spectacles. In Slavic excursions: essays on Russian and Polish literature, ed Davie, Manchester 1990.

Turgenev, I. S.

Coleridge, J. D. Photographs from Russian life. Fraser's Mag 50, Aug 1854.
Dixon, E. S. Introd to 'The children of the Czar'. Household Words 3 Mar 1855.
Life in Russia. Eclectic Rev 9, Apr 1855.
Mohl, M. Peasant life in Russia. Nat Rev 8, Apr 1859.
Ralston, W. R. S. Russian literature – Turguenief's novels. North Br Rev 50, Mar 1869.
Turner, C. E. The works of Ivan Sérguevitch Tourgéneff. Br Quart Rev 50, Oct 1869.
Ralston, W. R. S. (?) Tourgueneff's recent works. Saturday Rev 16 Jan 1875.
Lavrov, P. L. 'Nov'', by Ivan Tourguénief. Athenaeum 17 Feb 1877.
Child, T. E. Ivan Turgenieff. Belgravia 33, Aug 1877.
Oliphant, M. Russia and nihilism in the novels of M. Tourgénief. Blackwood's Mag 127, May 1880.
Ralston, W. R. S. Ivan Turguenief. Saturday Rev 22 Oct 1881.
Turner, C. E. Tourgenieff's novels as interpreting the political movement in Russia. Macmillan's Mag 45, Apr 1882.
Ralston, W. R. S. Ivan Serguéyevitch Tourguénief. Athenaeum 15 Sep 1883.
Turguéneff: by one who knew him. Daily News 7 Sep 1883.
Kaufmann, M. Ivan Serguievitch Tourgenieff. London Quart and Holborn Rev 63, Oct 1884.
Garnett, E. Introds to C. Garnett's trns, vols 3–6, 12, 14–15; 1895–9.
Todhunter, M. Ivan Turgenev. Westminster Rev 146, Aug 1896.
Wells, H. G. The novel of types. Saturday Rev 4 Jan 1896.
[Bennett, A.] E. A. B. Ivan Turgenev: an enquiry. Acad 4 Nov 1899; rptd in Fame and fiction, 1901.
Ivan Turgenev. I. The controversialist. II. The artist. Literature 17 and 31 Mar 1900.
Harris, F. Ivan Turgénief: a snapshot. Contemporary Portraits 4th ser 1924.
Gettmann, R. A. Turgenev in England and America. Univ of Illinois Stud in Lang and Lit 27:2 1941; rptd Westport CT 1974.
Kain, R. M. The literary reputation of Turgenev in England and America, 1867–1906. Madison Quart 2 1942.
Kaun, A. Turgenev in England and America. JEGP 41 1942.
Bryner, C. Turgenev and the English-speaking world. In Three papers in Slavonic studies, presented at the 4th Intl Congress of Slavists, Vancouver 1958.
Davie, D. A. Turgenev in England, 1850–1950. In Studies in Russian and Polish literature in honour of Wacław Lednicki, ed Z. Folejewski et al, The Hague 1962.
Yachnin, R. and D. H. Stam. Turgenev in English: a checklist of works by and about him. New York 1962.
Turton, G. Turgenev and the context of English literature, 1850–1900. 1992.
Waddington, P. H. (ed). Ivan Turgenev and Britain. Oxford and Providence RI 1995.

Tyutchev, Fëdor Ivanovich (1803–73)

Lane, R. C. Bibliography: Tyutchev in English translation, 1873–1974. Jnl of European Stud 2 1975.

British authors

Arnold, Matthew

Count Leo Tolstoi. Fortnightly Rev 48, 1 Dec 1887; rptd in his Essays in criticism, 2nd ser, 1888.

Mainwaring, M. Arnold and Tolstoi. Nineteenth-Cent Fiction 6, Mar 1952.

Bidney, M. Zukovskij and Arnold: two mid-nineteenth-century versions of the Sohrab–Rustum episode. Forum for Mod Lang Stud 25, Jan 1989.

Blackmore, Richard Doddridge ('Melanter')

The bugle of the Black Sea; or, The British in the East. 1855.

Borrow, George

Targum; or, Metrical translations from thirty languages and dialects; and, The talisman, from the Russian of Alexander Pushkin, with other pieces. 1892 (originally 2 vols St Petersburg 1835).

Ives, H. George Borrow in Russia. Nat Rev Sep 1909.

Cross, A. G. George Borrow and Russia. MLR 64 1969; rptd in his Anglo-Russica, 1993.

Browning, Robert

Ivàn Ivànovitch. In Dramatic idyls, 1879.

▽

Alekseyev, M. P. Die Quellen zum Idyll 'Ivan Ivanovitsch' von Rob. Browning. Jahrbücher für Kultur und Geschichte der Slaven 5 1930. Zur Entstehungsgeschichte der 'Dramatic idyls' von Robert Browning. EStudien 66 1931.

Waddington, P. H. Browning and Russia. Baylor Browning Interests 28 Waco TX 1985.

Byron, George Gordon, Baron

Don Juan, cantos 6–11, 2 vols 1823.

▽

D'yakonova, N. Ya. Russkiy epizod v poeme Bayrona 'Don-Zhuan'. In Russko-yevropeyskiye literaturnyye svyazi, Moscow and Leningrad 1966.

Manning, C. A. Russian versions of 'Don Juan'. PMLA 38 1923.

Gissing, George

The crown of life. 1899.

▽

Phelps, G. Gissing, Turgenev, and Dostoyevsky. In Collected articles on George Gissing, ed P. Coustillas 1968.

Sloan, J. The literary affinity of Gissing and Dostoevsky: revising Dickens. ELT 32 1989.

Hardy, Thomas

Clifford, E. War and peace and The dynasts. MP 54, Aug 1956.

Lawrence, D. H. Thomas Hardy, Verga, and Tolstoy. Extract from his 'Study of Thomas Hardy', in Russian literature and modern English fiction, ed Davie 1965.

Zakharov, V. V. L. N. Tolstoy i Tomas Gardi: russkiye stseny v 'Dinastakh'. In Russko-yevropeyskiye literaturnyye svyazi, Moscow and Leningrad 1966.

James, Henry

His several essays on Turgenev, pbd in various places 1874–96, are conveniently collected in Henry James, Literary criticism: French writers; other European writers; the prefaces to the New York edition, ed L. Edel New York and Cambridge 1984. *See also* Daniel Deronda: a conversation, 1876, *in the companion vol,* Literary criticism: essays on literature; American writers; English writers, *also 1984.*

Kelley, C. P. The early development of Henry James. Univ of Illinois Stud in Lang and Lit 15, Feb–May 1930.

Lerner, D. The influence of Turgenev on Henry James. Slavonic Year-Book (SEER 20) 1941.

Auchincloss, L. Henry James and the Russian novelists. In Novelists on novelists, ed L. Kronenberger, Garden City NY 1962.

Hamilton, E. C. Henry James's 'The Princess Casamassima' and Ivan Turgenev's 'Virgin soil'. SAQ 61 summer 1962.

Mlikotin, A. M. Genre of the 'international novel' in the works of Turgenev and Henry James: a critical study. Los Angeles 1971.

Briggs, A. D. P. Alexander Pushkin: a possible influence on Henry James. Forum for Mod Lang Stud 8, Jan 1972.

Briggs, A. D. P. Someone else's sledge: further notes on Turgenev's Virgin soil and Henry James's The Princess Casamassima. Oxford Slavonic Papers 5 1972.

Peterson, D. E. The clement vision: poetic realism in Turgenev and James. Port Washington NY and London 1975.

Tedford, B. W. Of libraries and salmon-colored volumes: James's reading of Turgenev through 1873. Resources for Amer Lit Study 9 1979.

Kagan-Kans, E. Ivan Turgenev and Henry James: First love and Daisy Miller. In Amer Contributions to the 9th International Congress of Slavists, vol 2, Columbus OH 1983.

Moore, George

Turgueneff. Fortnightly Rev 49, 1 Feb 1888; rptd in Impressions and opinions, 1913. Preface to Dostoyevsky's Poor folk. 1894.

▽

Kennedy, E. Turgenev and George Moore's 'The untilled field'. ELT 18 1975.

Cave, R. A. Turgenev and Moore: A sportsman's sketches and The untilled field. In The way back: George Moore's The untilled field and The lake, ed R. Welch, Totowa NJ 1982.

Waddington, P. H. Turgenev and George Moore. In Some gleanings on Turgenev, New Zealand Slavonic Jnl 1983.

Rossetti, Dante Gabriel, and family

Waddington, P. H,. Russian interests of the Rossetti family, Pinehaven NZ 1998.

Rossetti, William Michael

Democratic sonnets. 2 vols 1907. The four 'Russian' sonnets date from 1881.

Arinshteyn (Arinstein) L. M. William Michael Rossetti's Democratic sonnets. VS 14, Mar 1971. With W. E. Fredeman.

Arinshteyn (Arinstein), L. M. Russkaya tema v 'Demokraticheskikh sonetakh' Uil'yama Rossetti. In Rossiya i zapad. Iz istorii literaturnykh otnosheniy, Leningrad 1973.

Scott, Walter

Struve, G. Walter Scott and Russia. SEER 11 1933.

Rozov, Z. Denis Davydov and Walter Scott. Slavonic Year-Book (SEER 19) 1939–40.

Struve, P. Russian friends and correspondents of Sir Walter Scott. Comparative Lit 2 1950.

Parker, W. M. Scott and Russian literature. Quart Rev 35 1967.

Christian, R. F. Sir Walter Scott, Russia and Tolstoy. Scottish Slavonic Rev 10 spring 1988.

Southey, Robert

The march to Moscow. 1813. Odes to His Royal Highness the Prince Regent, His Imperial Majesty the Emperor of Russia, and His Majesty the King of Prussia. 1814.

Stevenson, Robert Louis

Knowlton, E. C. A Russian influence on Stevenson. MP 14, Dec 1916.

Poddubnaya, R. N. and V. V. Pronenko. Otrazheniye tvorcheskogo opyta Dostoyevskogo v proze Stivensona. Filologicheskiye Nauki 1986 no 2.

Swinburne, Algernon Charles

Note of an English republican on the Muscovite crusade. 1876. Russia: an ode. Fortnightly Rev 55, 1 Aug 1890. The ballad of Bulgarie. 1893.

▽

Walker, R. Swinburne, Tolstoy and 'King Lear'. English 7 1949.

Burnett, T. A. J. Swinburne's 'The ballad of Bulgarie'. MLR 64, Apr 1969.

Tennyson, Alfred

The charge of the Light Brigade. Examiner, 9 Dec 1854.

Maud, and other poems. 1855.

Collins, W. 'Maud': Tennyson's point of war. Tennyson Research Bull 2, Nov 1974.

Bennett, J. R. The historical abuse of literature: Tennyson's 'Maud: a monodrama' and the Crimean War. Eng Stud 62, Jan 1981.

Shannon, E. F., Jr and C. Ricks. 'The charge of the Light Brigade': the creation of a poem. SB 38 1985.

O'Neill, J. N. Anthem for a doomed youth: an interdisciplinary study of Tennyson's 'Maud' and the Crimean War. Tennyson Research Bull 5, Nov 1990.

Waddington, P. H. Tennyson and Russia. Tennyson Soc Monographs 11, Lincoln 1987.

Thackeray, William Makepeace

The great Cossack epic of Demetrius Rigmarolovicz. Fraser's Mag 20, Dec 1839; rptd as The legend of St Sophia of Kioff: an epic poem, in twenty books, in his Miscellanies: prose and verse vol 1, 1855.

Trollope, Anthony

Trollope and Turgenieff. Literary World, 6 Oct 1883.

Waddington, P. H. Turgenev and Trollope: brief crossings of paths. AUMLA: Jnl of the Aust Univ Lang and Lit Assoc 42, Nov 1974.

Wilde, Oscar

Vera; or, The nihilists: a drama in four acts. 1880.

A fire at sea (tr from the Fr of Turgenev). Macmillan's Mag 54, May 1886.

A batch of novels: Russian novelists. Pall Mall Gazette, 2 May 1887.

▽

Abramovich, N. Ya. Religiya krasoty i stradaniya. O. Uayl'd i Dostoyevsky. St Petersburg 1909.

Pavlova, T. V. 'Vera, ili nigilisty' – 'russkaya' drama Oskara Uayl'da. Russkaya literatura 1986 no 3.

Stokes, J. Wilde on Dostoevsky. N & Q 225 1980.

Wordsworth, William

The Russian fugitive. In Yarrow revisited, and other poems, 1835.

▽

Coe, C. N. Wordsworth's 'The Russian fugitive'. MLN 64, Jan 1949.

B. THE RECEPTION OF BRITISH LITERATURE AND CULTURE IN RUSSIA

General works

Shavrov, M. Roman v Anglii. Russkiy vestnik, 1862 no 7.

Tsebrikova, M. K. Anglichanki romanistki. Otechestvennyye zapiski, 1871 nos 8, 9, 11.

Gerbel', N. V. Angliyskiye poety v biografiyakh i obraztsakh. St Petersburg 1875.

Korsh, V. F. and A. I. Kirpichnikov. Vseobshchaya istoriya literatury. 4 vols St Petersburg 1880–92. Vol 4 contains much about nineteenth-century Eng lit.

Pesni Anglii i Ameriki. Pesni, skazaniya, basni i pritchi. Moscow 1895.

Dikson, K. I. and A. V. Mez'er. Bibliograficheskiy ukazatel' perevodnoy belletristiki v svyazi s istoriyey literatury i kritikoy. St Petersburg 1897. Braginsky, D. A. Bibliograficheskiy ukazatel' perevodnoy belletristiki v russkikh zhurnalakh za pyat' let 1897g.–1901g. St Petersburg 1902. These two works rptd together London 1971.

Veselovsky, A. N. Zapadnoye vliyaniye v novoy russkoy literature. 4th enlarged edn Moscow 1910.

Vengerova, Z. A. Sobraniye sochineniy, 1: Angliyskiye pisateli XIX veka. St Petersburg 1913.

Salmon, A. L. British influences on Russian literature. Acad 88 1915.

Murray, M. Some English influences on Russian literature. Russian Rev 2:2 1919.

Simmons, E. J. English literature in Russia. HSNPL 13 1931. English literature and culture in Russia (1553–1840). Harvard Stud in Comparative Lit 12, Cambridge MA 1935; rptd New York 1964.

Harper, K. E. and B. A. Booth. Russian translations of nineteenth-century English fiction. Nineteenth-Cent Fiction 8:3 Dec 1953.

Kuleshov, V. I. Literaturnyye svyazi Rossii i zapadnoy Yevropy v XIX veke (pervaya polovina). Moscow 1965.

Foote, I. P. 'Otechestvennye zapiski' and English literature, 1868–84. Oxford Slavonic Papers 6 1973.

Yerofeyev, N. A. Tumannyy Al'bion. Angliya i anglichane glazami russkikh 1825–1853gg. Moscow 1982.

Simpson, M. S. The Russian gothic novel and its British antecedents. Columbus 1986.

English authors

Blake

Warner, N. O. Shaw, Tolstoy, and Blake's Russian reputation. Blake: An Illus Quart 17, winter 1983–4.

Brontës

Peterson, O. Semeystvo Bronte. St Petersburg 1895.

Browning

Regnard, A.-A. Rev of 'Dramatic idyls'. Vestnik Yevropy 1879 no 7.

Vengerova, Z. A. Robert Brauning i yego poeziya. Vestnik Yevropy 1893 no 9.

Bulwer Lytton

Bodyansky, O. Bul'ver. Biblioteka dlya chteniya 1836 no 16.

M., L. Eduard Bul'ver. Vestnik Yevropy 1885 nos 1, 7.

Burns

Ivanov, I. Robert Bërns. Russkaya mysl' 1896 no 7.

Levin, Yu. D. The Russian Burns: the reception of Robert Burns in pre-Revolutionary and Soviet times. Scottish Slavonic Rev 5 autumn 1985.

Byron

Veselovsky, A. N. Etyudy o bayronizme. In his Etyudy i kharakteristiki, Moscow 1907.

Veselovsky, A. N. Bayron. Moscow 1914.

Maslov, V. I. Nachal'nyy period bayronizma v Rossii. Kiev 1915.

Grossman, L. P. Russkiye bayronisty. In Bayron. Sbornik statey. Moscow 1924.

Brodsky, N. L. Bayron v russkoy literature. Literaturnyy kritik 1938 no 4.

D'yakonova, N. Ya. and V. E. Vatsuro. Byron and nineteenth-century Russian literature. In Byron's political and cultural influence in nineteenth-century Europe: a symposium, ed P. G. Trueblood, Atlantic Highlands, NJ 1981.

Armstrong, J. M. The true origins of the 'superfluous man'. Russian, Croatian and Serbian, Czech and Slovak, Polish Lit 12, Apr 1985.

Pronin, V. 'He held sway over our minds': for the 200th anniversary of the birth of George Gordon Byron. Soviet Lit 1988 no 1.

Carlyle

A., S. Tomas Karleyl'. Ocherk yego zhizni i proizvedeniy. Vestnik Yevropy 1881 nos 5–6.

Bulgakov, F. Tomas Karleyl'. Istoricheskiy vestnik 1881 no 3.

Coleridge

Gill, R. The 'Rime of the ancient mariner' and 'Crime and punishment': existential parables. Philosophy and Lit 5 fall 1981.

De Quincey

Alekseyev, M. P. F. M. Dostoyevsky i kniga de Kvinsi 'Confessions of an English opium-eater'. Uchënyye zapiski Vysshey shkoly Odessy 2 1922.

Dickens

Nabokov, V. Charles Dickens: a Russian appreciation. Dickensian 8, June–Aug 1912.

Russian correspondent, A. Dickens in Russia: a moral educator. TLS 7 Sep 1940.

Ivasheva, V. V. Dikkens v russkoy kritike XIX veka. Uchënyye zapiski Moskovskogo pedagogicheskogo instituta imeni V. I. Lenina 32, issue 6, Kaf. klass. fil. 1946.

Gilenson, B. Dickens in Russia. Dickensian 57, Jan 1961.

Fridlender, Yu. V., I. M. Katarsky and M. P. Alekseyev (ed). Charl'z Dikkens. Bibliografiya russkikh perevodov i kriticheskoy literatury na russkom yazyke, 1838–1960. Moscow 1962.
Katarsky, I. M. Dikkens v Rossii. Seredina XIX veka. Moscow 1966.
Gifford, H. Dickens in Russia: the initial phase. Forum for Mod Lang Stud 4, Jan 1968.
Anikst, A. Dickens in Russia. TLS 4 June 1970.

Eliot, George

Kovalevskaya, S. V. Vospominaniya o Dzhorzhe Elliote. Russkaya mysl' 1886 no 6.
Waddington, P. H. Turgenev and George Eliot: a literary friendship. MLR 66, Oct 1971.
Chapman, R. and E. Gottlieb. A Russian view of George Eliot. Nineteenth-Cent Fiction 33 1978.

Gaskell

Grossman, L. P. Dostoyevsky i chartistskiy roman ['Mary Barton']. Voprosy literatury 1959 no 4; tr (as Dostoevskii and the Chartist Novel) in Dostoevskii and Britain, ed Leatherbarrow 1995.
Johnson, C. A. Russian Gaskelliana. REL 7, July 1966.

Hardy

Weber, C. J. Russian translations of Hardy. Colby Lib Quart, 3rd ser 15, Aug 1954.
Foote, I. P. Thomas Hardy in Russian translation and criticism (to 1978). Thomas Hardy Yearbook 11 1984.

Maturin

Alekseyev, M. P. Charlz Robert Met'yurin i russkaya literatura. In his Angliyskaya literatura. Ocherki i issledovaniya, ed N. Ya. D'yakonova and Yu. D. Levin, Leningrad 1991.

Moore, Thomas

Alekseyev, M. P. Tomas Mur, yego russkiye sobesedniki i korrespondenty. In Mezhdunarodnyye svyazi russkoy literatury, ed Alekseyev, Moscow and Leningrad 1963.
Girivenko, A. N. Otrazheniye tvorchestva Tomasa Mura v russkoy literature pervoy treti XIX v. Izvestiya Akademii nauk SSSR (ser. lit. i yaz.) 43:66 Nov–Dec 1984. Lirika Tomasa Mura v Rossii vtoroy poloviny XIX veka. Izvestiya Akademii nauk SSSR (ser. lit. i yaz.) 46:3 May–June 1987. Tomas Mur v russkoy kritike serediny XIX v. Filologicheskiye nauki 1987 no 2. Poeziya Tomasa Mura v russkikh perevodakh pervoy poloviny XIX v. In Mezhliteraturnyye svyazi i problema realizma, ed I. V. Kireyeva, Gor'kiy 1988.

Rossetti, D. G.

Vengerova, Z. A. Dante Gabriel' Rosetti. In her Literaturnyye kharakteristiki, St Petersburg 1897.

Scott

Senkovsky, O. I. Val'ter Skott i yego podrazhateli. In his Sobraniye sochineniy, 9 vols 1858–9, vol 8.
N., N. Rossiyskiye Val'ter-Skotty. Delo 1878 no 11.
W., A. Sir Walter Scott in Russia: his influence as novelist and humanist. Glasgow Herald 27 Feb 1932.
Levin, Yu. D. Prizhiznennaya slava Val'tera Skotta v Rossii. Prilozheniye. Val'ter Skott v russkoy pechati, 1811–1833. In Epokha romantizma, Leningrad 1975.
West, J. Walter Scott and the style of Russian historical novels of the 1830s and 1840s. In Amer Contributions to the 8th International Congress of Slavists, vol 1: Linguistics and poetics, Columbus OH 1978.

Shelley, Mary

Freeborn, R. Frankenstein's last journey. Oxford Slavonic Papers 18 1985.

Shelley, P. B.

Tsebrikova, M. K. Shelli. Otechestvennyye zapiski 1873 nos 1, 5.
Chuyko, V. V. Shelli. Nablyudatel' 1892 no 10.

Stevenson

D'yakonova, N. Ya. Robert Louis Stevenson in Russia. Scottish Slavonic Rev 10 spring 1988.

Tennyson

Chuyko, V. Al'fred Tennison. Nablyudatel' 1892 no 12.
Girivenko, A. N. K istorii russkikh perevodov Al'freda Tennisona. Elegiya 'Umirayushchaya lebed''. Filologicheskiye nauki 1992 no 3.

Thackeray

Vvedensky, I. I. Vill'yam Tekkerey i yego romany. Otechestvennyye zapiski 1849 nos 5–6. 'Yarmarka tshcheslaviya.' Roman Vil'yama Tekkereya. Otechestvennyye zapiski 1851 no 7.
Zhizn' i sochineniya Tekkereya. Otechestvennyye zapiski 1855 no 1.
Troitsky, Yu. N. Tekkerey v russkoy kritike. Uchënyye zapiski Tul'skogo pedagogicheskogo instituta 1953, issue 4.

Trollope

Zotov, V. R. Predstaviteli sovremennogo realizma vo frantsuzskoy i angliyskoy literature. A. Dode i Trollop. Istoricheskiy vestnik 1885 no 1.

Russian authors

Belinsky, Vissarion Grigor'evich (1811–48)

Revs of Eng lit, pbd first in Molva, Otechestvennyye zapiski and elsewhere, collected in Sochineniya (12 vols, Moscow 1859–62), incl: the life and works of Walter Scott; Scott's Antiquary; Bulwer Lytton's Pilgrims of the Rhine; and Dickens's Oliver Twist.

▽

Alekseyev, M. P. Belinsky i Dikkens. In Venok Belinskomu, ed N. K. Piksanov, Moscow 1924.
Amirajibi, T. Angliyskiye pisateli v kritike Belinskogo. Trudy Tbilisskogo gosudarstvennogo instituta 63 1956.
Germanovich, B. I. Bayron v otsenke V. G. Belinskogo. Izvestiya Krymskogo pedagogicheskogo instituta imeni M. V. Frunze 28 Simferopol' 1957.
Germanovich, B. I. Dikkens v otsenke V. G. Belinskogo. Izvestiya Krymskogo pedagogicheskogo instituta imeni M. V. Frunze 28 Simferopol' 1957.

Botkin, Vasiliy Petrovich (1811–69)

Trn of writings by Carlyle, incl 'On heroes, hero-worship, and the heroic in history', and an essay on him. Sovremennik 1855 no 10, 1856 nos 1–2. Publichnyye chteniya Dikkensa v Parizhe. Moskovskiye vedomosti, 31 Jan 1863.

Chernyshevsky, Nikolay Gavrilovich (1828–89)

Rev of Thackeray's 'The Newcomes'. Sovremennik 1857 no 2.

▽

Seliverstov, M. L. Dikkens i Tekkerey v otsenke Chernyshevskogo. Frunze 1954.
Brojde, A.-M. Conflicting views of Chernyshevsky and Druzhinin on 'The Newcomes' by W. M. Thackeray. Scando-Slavica 20 1974.

Dostoyevsky, F. M.

Grossman, L. P. Genii Yevropy. In his Biblioteka Dostoyevskogo, Odessa 1919. (Dostoyevsky and Scott, Dickens, etc.)
Messac, R. Bulwer Lytton et Dostoïevski: de Paul Clifford à Raskolnikof. Revue de Littérature Comparée 6, Oct–Dec 1926.
Reizov, B. G. K voprosu o vliyanii Dikkensa na Dostoyevskogo. Yazyk i literatura 1930 no 5.
Katkov, G. Steerforth and Stavrogin: on the sources of The possessed. SEER 27, May 1949.
Futrell, M. H. Dostoevsky and Dickens. EM 7 1956; rptd in Dostoevskii and Britain, ed Leatherbarrow 1995.
Lary, N. M. Dostoevsky and Dickens: a study of literary influence. London and Boston 1973.
Klotz, K. Dostoevsky and The old curiosity shop. YULG 50 1976.
MacPike, L. Dickens and Dostoevsky: the technique of reverse influence. In The changing world of Charles Dickens, ed R. Giddings, Totowa NJ and London 1983.
Miller, R. F. Dostoevsky and the tale of terror. In The Russian novel from Pushkin to Pasternak, ed J. Garrard, New Haven CT 1983;

rptd in Dostoevskii and Britain, ed Leatherbarrow 1995. (Radcliffe, Maturin, etc.) The metaphysical novel and the evocation of anxiety: 'Melmoth the wanderer' and 'The brothers Karamazov', a case study. In Russianness: studies on a nation's identity, ed R. L. Belknap, Ann Arbor 1988.

Shapovalov, V. They came from 'Bleak House'. Dostoevsky Stud 9 1988.

Johae, A. Hallucination in 'Oliver Twist' and 'Crime and punishment'. New Comparison 9 spring 1990.

Terkla, D. Byron's underground Manfred. Comparatist 14, May 1990.

Leatherbarrow, W. J. (ed). Dostoevskii and Britain. Oxford and Providence RI 1995.

Druzhinin, Aleksandr Vasil'evich (1824–64)

Revs of Eng lit, pbd first in Biblioteka dlya chteniya, Sovremennik, Otechestvennyye zapiski and elsewhere, collected chiefly in vols 4–5 of Sochineniya (8 vols, St Petersburg 1865–7), incl: George Crabbe and his works; Walter Scott and his contemporaries; Ann Radcliffe's Romance of the forest; the poetry of Thomas Hood; Charlotte Brontë's novels; George Eliot's Romola; Bulwer Lytton's A strange story; Trollope's Orley Farm; Wilkie Collins's No name; Thackeray's The Newcomes, The adventures of Philip, comic poetry and lectures on The English humorists. There is much also on Eng lit in vol 6, Pis'ma inogorodnogo podpischika.

▽

Genereux, G. A. Alexander Druzhinin's writings on English literature. Unpub PhD thesis, UCLA 1968.

Gogol', N. V.

Gogol' i Dikkens. Pikvik i Chichikov. Istoricheskiy vestnik Oct 1915.

Bowen, C. M. Dead souls and Pickwick papers. Living Age 5 Aug 1916.

Futrell, M. H. Gogol and Dickens. SEER 34 1955–6.

Bryner, C. Gogol, Dickens, and the realistic novel. Slavic and East European Stud 8 1963.

Harper, K. E. Dickens and Gogol's Shinel'. In Amer Contributions to the 6th International Congress of Slavists, 2: Literary Contributions, The Hague 1968.

Fanger, D. Dickens and Gogol: energies of the word. In Veins of humor, ed H. Levin, Cambridge MA 1972.

Cox, G. The writer as a stand-up comic: a note on Gogol and Dickens. Ulbandus Rev 2:1 fall 1979.

Altshuller, M. The Walter Scott motifs in Nikolay Gogol''s story The lost letter. Oxford Slavonic Papers 22 1989.

Kornblatt, J. D. 'Bez skotov oboidemsia': Gogol' and Sir Walter Scott. In Issues in Russian literature before 1917: Selected papers of the 3rd world congress for Soviet and East European studies, ed J. D. Clayton, Columbus OH 1989.

Davis, S. B. From Scotland to Russia via France: Scott, Defauconpret and Gogol. Scottish Slavonic Rev 17 autumn 1991.

Korolenko, Vladimir Galaktionovich (1853–1921)

My first encounter with Dickens. In Russian literature and modern English fiction, ed Davie 1965.

Kozlov, Ivan Ivanovich (1779–1840)

Eyges, I. R. K perevodam Kozlova iz Bayrona. In Zven'ya 5, Moscow and Leningrad 1935.

Ober, K. H. and W. U. Kozlov's translations of two English Romantic poems. Germano-Slavica 6 1989. (C. Wolfe and T. Moore.)

Kyukhel'beker, Vil'gel'm Karlovich (1797–1846)

Levin, Yu. D. V. K. Kyukhel'beker o poezii Val'tera Skotta. Russkaya literatura 1964 no 2.

Levin, Yu. D. Kyukhel'beker and Crabbe. Oxford Slavonic Papers o.s. 12 1965.

Lermontov, M. Yu.

Bakhtin, N. N. Lermontov i Robert Bërns. Minuvshiye gody 1908 no 9.

Dashkevich, N. P. Motivy mirovoy poezii v tvorchestve Lermontova. In his Stat'i po novoy russkoy literature, Petrograd 1914; rptd Wiesbaden 1966.

Rozanov, M. N. Bayronicheskiye motivy v tvorchestve Lermontova. In Venok Lermontovu, Moscow 1914.

Neyman, B. V. 'Ispantsy' Lermontova i 'Ayvengo' Val'tera Skotta. Filologicheskiye zapiski 1915 nos 5–6.

Yakubovich, D. P. Lermontov i Val'ter Skott. Izvestiya AN SSSR, otd. obshch. nauk 1935 no 3.

Chërnyy, K. Lermontov i Bayron. In M. Yu. Lermontov, 1841–1941. Sbornik statey, Pyatigorsk 1941.

Nol'man, M. Lermontov i Bayron. In Zhizn' i tvorchestvo M. Yu. Lermontova, Moscow 1941.

Entwistle, W. J. The Byronism of Lermontov's 'A hero of our time'. Comparative Lit 1 1949.

Shaw, J. T. Byron and the Byronic tradition of the Romantic verse tale in Russian, and Lermontov's 'Mtsyri'. Indiana Slavic Stud 1 1956. Lermontov's 'Demon' and the Byronic oriental verse tale. Indiana Slavic Stud 2 1958.

Vatsuro, V. E. 'Irlandskiye melodii' Tomasa Mura v tvorchestve Lermontova. Russkaya literatura 1965 no 3.

Fëdorov, A. V. Lermontov i Bayron. In his Lermontov i literatura yego vremeni, Leningrad 1967.

Levin, Yu. D. Iz reministsentsiy angliyskoy literatury u Lermontova. Russkaya literatura 1975 no 2.

D'yakonova, N. Ya. Byron and Lermontov: notes on Pechorin's 'Journal'. In Lord Byron and his contemporaries: essays from the 6th International Byron Seminar, ed C. E. Robinson, Newark and London 1982.

D'yakonova, N. Ya. Byron and the evolution of Lermontov's poetry, 1814–1841. Renaissance and Mod Stud 32 1988.

Matyash, S. A. O yevropeyskom i russkom istochnikakh 'Borodina' Lermontova. Russkaya literatura 1992 no 3.

Maykov, Valerian Nikolayevich (1823–47)

Essays on Scott and on translations of Byron, in Kriticheskiye stat'i (1845–47), St Petersburg 1889.

Mikhaylov, Mikhail Larionovich (1829–65)

His work with Sovremennik incl a trn of Tennyson's 'Godiva' (1859 no 9); articles on George Eliot's Adam Bede and Mill on the Floss (1859 no 11, and 1860 no 9); and Yumor i poeziya v Anglii. Tomas Gud (Hood; 1861 nos 1, 8).

Nekrasov, N. A.

Yakovlev, N. V. Nekrasov i Barret-Brauning ('Plach detey'). Kniga i revolyutsiya 1921 no 2.

Levin, Yu. D. Nekrasov i angliyskiy poet Krabb. In Nekrasovskiy sbornik 2, Moscow and Leningrad 1956.

Ogarëv, Nikolay Platonovich (1813–77)

Chapman, H. M. Ogarëv in exile, 1856–1877. Unpbd PhD thesis, Victoria Univ of Wellington NZ 1998.

Polonsky, Leonid Aleksandrovich (1833–1913)

Articles in Vestnik Yevropy incl: Ocherki angliyskogo obshchestva v romane Trollopa (1870 nos 8 and 10); Zhenskiye tipy v romanakh Trollopa (1871 no 8); 'Skazki' Dikkensa (1873 nos 3 and 5); Sovremennyy roman v Anglii (1875 no 11).

Pushkin, A. S.

Spasovich, V. D. Bayronizm u Pushkina i Lermontova. Vilnius 1911.

Zhirmunsky, V. M. Bayron i Pushkin. Iz istorii romanticheskoy poemy. Leningrad 1924. (The 1978 edn of Bayron i Pushkin contains also Zhirmunsky's essay Pushkin i zapadnyye literatury.)

Yakovlev, N. V. Iz razyskaniy o literaturnykh istochnikakh v tvorchestve Pushkina. In Pushkin v mirovoy literature, Leningrad 1926. (Incl discussion of Wordsworth.)

Val'ter Skotta v 'Povestyakh Belkina'. In Pushkin i yego sovremenniki 37, Leningrad 1928.

Simmons, E. J. Pushkin's 'The avaricious knight' and Shenstone. MLN 45 1930.

Yakubovich, D. P. Iz zametok o Pushkine i Val'ter Skotte. In Pushkin i yego sovremenniki 38–9, Leningrad 1930.
Yakubovich, D. P. 'Kapitanskaya dochka' i romany Val'tera Skotta. In Pushkin. Vremennik Pushkinskoy komissii 4–5, Moscow and Leningrad 1939. Reministsentsii iz Val'ter Skotta v 'Povestyakh Belkina'. In Pushkin i yego sovremenniki 37, Leningrad 1928.
Gifford, H. Pushkin's 'Feast in time of plague' and its original. Amer SEER 8:4 Dec 1949. (J. Wilson.)
Davie, D. A. Pushkin, Walter Scott, and Mickiewicz. In his The heyday of Sir Walter Scott, 1961; rptd in his Slavic excursions: essays on Russian and Polish literature, Manchester 1990.
Vickery, W. N. Parallelizm v literaturnom razvitii Bayrona i Pushkina. In Amer Contributions to the 5th International Congress of Slavists, 2: Literary Contributions, The Hague 1963.
Greene, M. Pushkin and Sir Walter Scott. Forum for Mod Lang Stud 1 1965.
Gregg, R. A. Pushkin and Shenstone: the case reopened. Comparative Lit 17:2 spring 1965.
Raleigh, J. H. Scott and Pushkin. In From Smollett to James: studies in the novel and other essays, ed S. I. Mintz, A. Chandler and C. Mulvey, Charlottesville VA 1981.
Romanov, N. M. Evolyutsiya Pushkinskogo zamysla romana o Pelymove. Russkaya literatura 1981 no 4.
Bayley, J. Pushkin and Byron: a complex relationship. Byron Jnl 16 1988.
Dovgiy, O. L. Ob odnom istochnike 'Malen'kikh tragediy'. Dramaticheskaya stsena 'Khuan' Barri Kornuolla. Vestnik Moskovskogo universiteta, ser 9 (filologiya) no 6 Nov–Dec 1990.
Frazier, M. 'Kapitanskaia dochka' and the creativity of borrowing. SEEJ 37 winter 1993.

Ryleyev, Kondratiy Fëdorovich (1795–1826)

Shuvalov, S. V. Ryleyev i Bayron. Svitok 4, Moscow 1926.

Tolstoy, L. N.

Apostolov, N. N. Tolstoy and Dickens. In Family views of Tolstoy, tr and ed A. and L. Maude 1926.
Gusev, N. Dickens and Tolstoy. Dickensian 28 winter 1931–2.
Arthos, J. Ruskin and Tolstoi: The dignity of man. Dalhousie Rev 43 1963.
Buyniak, V. O. Leo Tolstoi and Charles Dickens. Slavic and East European Stud 9 1964.
Jones, W. G. George Eliot's Adam Bede and Tolstoy's conception of Anna Karenina. MLR 61 1966.
Buyniak, V. O. Leo Tolstoi and Matthew Arnold. Wascana Rev 3 1968.
Cain, T. Tolstoy's use of 'David Copperfield'. CritQ 15 autumn 1973.
Knowles, A. V. Some aspects of L. N. Tolstoy's visit to London in 1861: an examination of the evidence. SEER 56 1978.
Rogers, P. Lessons for fine ladies: Tolstoj and George Eliot's Felix Holt, the radical. SEEJ 29, winter 1985.
Rosenberg, B. Resurrection and Little Dorrit: Tolstoy and Dickens reconsidered. Stud in the Novel 17, spring 1985.
Crawford, T. Burns and Tolstoy. Scottish Lit Jnl 13, May 1986.
Rogers, P. Scrooge on the Neva: Dickens and Tolstoj's Death of Ivan Il'ic. Comparative Lit 40, summer 1988.
Rogers, P. A Tolstoyan reading of 'David Copperfield'. Comparative Lit 42, winter 1990.
Semczuk, A. Leo Tolstoy's early works and the novels of Dickens and Thackeray. Slavia orientalis 42, 1994.

Turgenev, I. S.

Colum, P. Maria Edgeworth and Ivan Turgenev. Br Rev 11:1 July 1915.
Gut'yar, N. M. Poyezdki I. S. Turgeneva v Angliyu. Trudy Kubanskogo pedagogicheskogo instituta 2–3, Krasnodar 1929.
Watson, G. Maria Edgeworth and Turgenev. In his edn of Castle Rackrent, 1964.
Simmons, J. S. G. Turgenev and Oxford. Oxoniensia 31 1966; rev version in Ivan Turgenev and Britain, ed Waddington 1995.
Kennedy, E. Genesis of a fiction: the Edgeworth–Turgenev relationship. ELN 6:4 June 1969.
Gutman, D. S. Turgenev i Bayron. In Tretiy mezhvuzovskiy Turgenevskiy sbornik, Orël 1971.
Freeborn, R. Turgenev at Ventnor. SEER 51 1973; rptd in Ivan Turgenev and Britain, ed Waddington 1995.
Zekulin, N. G. Turgenev in Scotland. SEER 54 1976.
Waddington, P. H. Turgenev and England. London and New York 1980.
Waddington, P. H. Turgenev and Maria Edgeworth: a contribution to the debate. In Some gleanings on Turgenev, New Zealand Slavonic Jnl 1983. Dickens, Pauline Viardot, Turgenev: a study in mutual admiration. New Zealand Slavonic Jnl no 1, 1974. Two authors of strange stories: Bulwer Lytton and Turgenev. New Zealand Slavonic Jnl 1992.
Zekulin, N. G. Turgenev and Anglo-Irish Writers. I: Maria Edgeworth. Canadian Slavonic Papers 25 1983.
Zekulin, N. G. Turgenev's 'Króket v Vindzore' ('Croquet at Windsor'). New Zealand Slavonic Jnl 1983; rptd in Ivan Turgenev and Britain, ed Waddington 1995.
Henry, P. and P. H. Waddington. Turgenev in Scotland. Slavica 23, Debrecen 1986.
Jones, W. G. (ed and contrib). Tolstoi and Britain. Oxford and Providence RI 1996.
Freeborn, R. Frankenstein and Bazarov. New Zealand Slavonic Jnl 1994.

Venevitinov, Dmitriy Vladimirovich (1805–27)

McMillin, A. B. Byron and Venevitinov. SEER 53 1975.

Zhukovsky, Vasiliy Andreyevich (1783–1852)

Reizov, B. G. V. A. Zhukovsky, perevodchik Val'tera Skotta. ('Ivanov vecher.') In Russko-yevropeyskiye literaturnyye svyazi, Moscow and Leningrad 1966.
Hewton, A. A comparison of Sir Walter Scott's 'The Eve of Saint John' and Zhukovsky's translation of the ballad. New Zealand Slavonic Jnl o.s. 11 1973.
Ober, K. H. and W. U. Zhukovskij's translation of 'The prisoner of Chillon'. SEEJ 17 1973. Zhukovskii and Southey's ballads: the translator as rival. TWC 5 1974. Two bards: Zhukovsky and Bowring. SEER 62:4 Oct 1984. [PHW]

(9) OTHER SLAVONIC LANGUAGES

General

Krasiński, V. Reflections on the importance of the Slavonic languages and literature in the present time, with remarks on the establishment of a Professor's chair at Oxford. 1844.
Ralston, W. R. S. Slavonic literature. Athenaeum 15 Oct 1870.
Naaké, J. T. (comp and tr). Slavonic fairy tales, collected and translated from the Russian, Polish, Servian, and Bohemian. 1874.
Morfill, W. R. Slavonic literature. 1883.
Curtin, J. (comp and tr). Myths and folk-tales of the Russians, Western Slavs, and Magyars. Boston and London 1890.
Coleman, A. P. John Bowring and the poetry of the Slavs, with a history of his writings on Slavonic poetry. Proc of the Amer Philosophical Soc 84, May 1941.
Sova, M. Sir John Bowring (1792–1872) and the Slavs. SEER 21, Nov 1943.
Simmons, J. S. G. Slavonic studies at Oxford. Vol I. The proposed chair at the Taylor Institution in 1844. Oxford Slavonic Papers o.s. 3 1952.
Partridge, M. Slavonic themes in English poetry of the nineteenth century. SEER 41, June 1963.
Lewanski, R. C. The literatures of the world in English translation: a bibliography. Vol 2: The Slavic literatures. New York 1971.
Tilney, P. V. R. Slavic folklore studies in nineteenth-century Britain. Canadian Slavonic Papers 18 1976.

Ukrainian

Ralston, W. R. S. Little-Russian poetry. Athenaeum 29 Aug 1874. Little-Russian historical poems. Saturday Rev 5 June 1875. Reviews of Les Chants historiques de l'Ukraine, tr A. Chodzko. Acad 18 Oct 1879; Athenaeum 8 Nov 1879.

Holubnychy, L. Mazepa in Byron's poem and in history. Ukrainian Quart 15 1959.

Manning, C. A. Mazepa in English literature. Ukrainian Quart 15 1959.

Zorivchak, R. An English writer–translator of Ukrainian literature. News from Ukraine 1989 no 37. (George Borrow.)

Shevchenko, Taras (1814–61)

Kisilewsky, V. J. Charles Dickens's publication on Taras Shevchenko seventy years ago. Ukrainian Quart 3 1946–7.

Bojko, J. Taras Shevchenko and West European literature. SEER 34 1955. (Burns.)

Velyhorsky, I. English echoes in the stories of Taras Shevchenko. Ukrainian Quart 12 1956.

Slavutych, Y. Shevchenko and Western European literature. Comparative Lit 10 1958.

Rudýcki, J. B. Burns and Shevchenko. Slavistica 35 1959.

Giergielewicz, M. Shevchenko and world literature. In U stolittya smerti Tarasa Shevchenka, Philadelphia 1962.

Kepes, G. Burns et Sevcsenko. In La littérature comparée en Europe orientale, ed I. Sötér et al, Budapest 1963.

Luckyj, G. S. N. Shevchenko and Blake. Harvard Ukrainian Stud 2:1 1978.

Zorivchak, R. Taras Shevchenko and British literature. News from Ukraine 1985 no 15.

Vovchok, Marko (Mariya Markovych; 1834–1907)

Zorivchak, R. Tvory Marka Vovchka v anhlomovnomu sviti. Vsesvit 1988 no 2.

Fed'kovich, Yuriy (1834–88)

Huts', H. Yuriy Fed'kovich i anhliys'ka literatura. Vsesvit 1984 no 8.

Drahomaniv (Dragomanov), Mykhaylo (1841–95)

Zorivchak, R. Mykhaylo Drahomaniv and English literature. Ukrainian Rev 39:4 winter 1991.

Franko, Ivan (1856–1916)

Rich, V. Ivan Franko and the English poets. Ukrainian Quart 22 1966.

Polish

Lipnicki, E. Byron im Befreiungskampfe der polnischen Nationalliteratur. Magazin 48 1877.

Byrons 'Don Juan' in polnischer Übersetzung. Magazin 51 1880.

Bełcikowski, A. Poland. A regular rev of Polish lit in the Athenaeum, each first Saturday in July or last Saturday in Dec, 1883–1900.

Zdiechowski, M. Byron i jego wiek. Studya Porównawczoliterackie, Cracow 1894–7.

Windakiewicz, S. Sir Walter Scott i Lord Byron w odniesieniu do polskiej poezyi romantycznej. Cracow 1914.

Krzyżanowski, J. Scott in Poland. SEER 12, July 1933.

Kühne, W. Alexander Bronikowski und Walter Scott. Zeitschrift für Slavische Philologie 13, 15 Dec 1936.

Brock, P. Joseph Cowen and the Polish exiles. SEER 32, Dec 1953.

Ordon, E. The reception of the Polish short story in English: reflections on a bibliography. Polish Rev 2 1957.

Zieliński, B. American and British literature in Poland. Polish Rev 4, 1959.

Curran, E. M. The 'Foreign Quarterly Review' on Russian and Polish literature. SEER 40 1961–2.

Taborski, B. Polish plays in English translation: a bibliography. Polish Rev 9 1964, 12 1967.

Górski, K. The reception of Shelley in Polish literature. In 'Gorski vijenac': a garland of essays offered to Professor Elizabeth Mary Hill, ed R. Auty, L. R. Lewitter and A. P. Vlasto, Cambridge 1970.

Zulawski, J. Byron's influence in Poland. Byron Jnl 2 1974. Byron and Poland: Byron and Polish Romantic revolt. In Byron's political and cultural influence in nineteenth-century Europe: a symposium, ed P. G. Trueblood, Atlantic Highlands NJ 1981.

Treugutt, S. Byron and Napoleon in Polish Romantic myth. In Lord Byron and his contemporaries: essays from the Sixth International Byron Seminar, ed C. E. Robinson, Newark NJ and London 1982.

Davies, N. 'The languor of so remote an interest': British attitudes to Poland, 1772–1832. Oxford Slavonic Papers 16 1983.

Koc, B. The knowledge of English in Poland during Conrad's youth. Conradian 8:1 winter 1983.

Malecka, A. Carlyle's reception in Poland at the end of the century. Carlyle Newsletter 9 spring 1988.

Taylor, N. Krystyn Lach-Szyrma: a Pole's impressions of nineteenth-century Scotland. Scottish Slavonic Rev 10 spring 1988.

Jedrzejewski, J. The Polish translations of Thomas Hardy. Thomas Hardy Jnl 7 1991.

Fredro, Aleksander (1793–1876)

Giergielewicz, M. Fredro's comedies in English. Polish Rev 14:4 1969 (and *see also* 15:1 1970).

Mickiewicz, Adam (1798–1855)

The books and the pilgrimage of the Polish nation, tr K. Lach-Szyrma 1833.

Konrad Vallenrod: an historical tale, from the Prussian and Lithuanian annals, tr H. Cattley 1841; Conrad Vallenrod: an historical poem, founded on events in the annals of Lithuania and Prussia, tr L. Jablonski 1841; Konrad Wallenrod: an historical tale, tr into Eng verse M. A. Biggs 1882; Conrad Vallenrod: an historical poem, tr M. H. Dziewicki, introd A. Bełcikowski, 1883.

Master Thaddeus; or, The last foray in Lithuania: an historical epic poem in twelve books, tr M. A. Biggs, introd W. R. Morfill, 1885.

Wojciechowski, K. 'Pan Tadeusz' Mickiewicza a romans Waltera Scotta. Cracow 1919.

Windakiewicz, S. The anglomania of Mickiewicz. SEER 8, June 1929.

Coleman, M. M. Mickiewicz in English, 1827–1955. Cambridge 1954.

Bugelski, B. R. (ed). Mickiewicz and the West: a symposium. Buffalo 1956.

Rose, W. J. Mickiewicz and Britain. In Mickiewicz in world literature: a symposium, ed W. Lednicki, Berkeley 1956.

Sand, G. Essay on the drama of fantasy: Goethe–Byron–Mickiewicz. In Adam Mickiewicz, 1798–1855: in commemoration of the centenary of his death, Zurich 1955.

Davie, D. Pushkin, Walter Scott, and Mickiewicz. In his The Heyday of Sir Walter Scott, 1961; rptd in Slavic excursions: essays on Russian and Polish literature, Manchester 1990. 'Pan Tadeusz' in English verse. In Mickiewicz in world literature: a symposium, ed W. Lednicki, Berkeley 1956; also in his Slavic excursions.

Słowacki, Juliusz (1809–49)

Erlich, V. 'Beniowski' and 'Don Juan': an attempt at a literary parallel. Symposium 1 1947.

Kraszewski, Józef Ignacy (1812–87)

The Jew, tr L. da Kowalewska, introd E. Gosse, 1893.

▽

Buyniak, V. O. George Eliot and Kraszewski – a literary connection? Selecta, Corvallis, 10 1989. In commemoration of Kraszewski's centennial: his Jermola and George Eliot's Silas Marner. In Essays for Yvonne Grabowski (1929–1989), ed J. McErlean, Toronto 1993.

Krasiński, Napoleon Aleksander Zygmunt (1812–59)
Mary Barton: an historical tale of Poland. 1846.
Gonta: an historical drama, in five acts. 1848.
▽
Lytton, E. R. Bulwer, Earl of. Orval; or, The fool of time. 1869. (Based on Krasiński's 'Nieboska komedia'.)
Kallenbach, J. (ed). Correspondance de Sigismond Krasiński et de Henry Reeve. Paris 1902.
Giergielewicz, M. Krasiński in the English-speaking world. Polish Rev 5:4 1960. Krasiński in the English-speaking world: a bibliographical review, in Zygmunt Krasiński, Romantic universalist: an international tribute, ed W. Lednicki, New York 1964.
Weintraub, W. Krasiński and Reeve. Polish Rev 5:2 1960. Krasiński and Reeve. In Zygmunt Krasiński, Romantic universalist, ed Lednicki, 1964.
Lednicki, W. (ed). Zygmunt Krasiński, Romantic universalist: an international tribute. New York 1964.
Krajewska, W. Zygmunta Krasińskiego recepcja literatury angielskiej. Kwartalnik neofilologiczny (Warsaw) 30:2 1983.

Norwid, Cyprian (1821–83)
Gömöri, George. The myth of Byron in Norwid's life and work. SEER 51, Apr 1973.
Zurowski, M. Hopkins, Mallarmé i Norwid. Poezja, Warsaw, 18:4–5 May 1983.
Halkiewicz-Sojak, G. Norwid o Epimenidesie i Byronie. Studia Norwidiana 5–6 1987–8.

Orzeszkowa, Eliza (1841–1910)
Welsh, D. J. Two talkative authors: Orzeszkowa and George Eliot. Polish Rev 10:1 1965.

Sienkiewicz, Henryk (1846–1916)
Trilogy With fire and sword, The deluge, and Pan Michael, tr J. Curtin, Boston and London 1890–3.
▽
Gerard, J. E. A Polish novelist – Henryk Sienkiewicz. Blackwood's Mag 145, Apr 1889.
Fiction. Saturday Rev 7 Dec 1895.
Gosse, E. W. Henry Sienkiewicz. Contemporary Rev 71, Apr 1897.
Crawford, V. M. Henryk Sienkiewicz. Month 92 1898.
Segel, H. B. Sienkiewicz's first translator, Jeremiah Curtin. Slavic Rev 24 1965.
Windle, K. Sienkiewicz abroad: early translations of a story by Henryk Sienkiewicz, with special reference to English, Russian and Spanish versions. In Polish colloquium, Univ of Melbourne, 19 Aug 1975: Proc, ed R. Sussex, Melbourne 1976.
Tye, R. The early reception of the novels of Henryk Sienkiewicz in England. Kwartalnik neofilologiczny 25 1978.

Hofmanowa, Klementyna
Lohrli, A. English versions of Dziennik Franciszki Krasińskiej. Papers of the Bibl Soc of America 76 1982.

Wendish
Stone, G. Morfill and the Sorbs. Oxford Slavonic Papers 4 1971.

Czech
Vočadlo, O. Anglie a Čechy. Lumir 17 1931.
Janeček, B. Bibliography of Czech literature in English translation. BB 16 1937–8.
Auty, R. Some unpublished translations from Czech by A. H. Wratislaw. In 'Gorski vijenac': a garland of essays, Cambridge 1970.
Pantučková, L. Thackeray in Czechoslovakia (with a glance at other Slavonic countries). Stud in the Novel 13 1981.
Naughton, J. D. Morfill and the Czechs. Oxford Slavonic Papers 17 1984.

Hanka, Václav (1791–1861)
Lyra Czecho-slovanská: Bohemian poems ancient and modern. Tr and introd A. H. Wratislaw 1849.
Manuscript of the Queen's court: a collection of old Bohemian lyrico-epic songs, with other ancient Bohemian poems. Tr into Eng verse A. H. Wratislaw 1852.

Mácha, Karel Hynek (1810–36)
Zdiechowski, M. Karl Hynek Mácha und Byrons Einfluss auf die tschechische Dichtkunst. Anzeiger der Akademie der Wissenschaften in Krakau, Cracow 1893. *See also* K. H. Mácha i Bayronizm czeski, Cracow 1893.
Wellek, R. Mácha and Byron. SEER 15 1937.

Slovak

Král', Janko (1822–76)
Apel, G. A Byronic hero in Slovak literature. SEER 34 1955–6.

Yugoslav
Petrović, I. Byron and the Jugoslavs. SEER 8, June 1929.
Stojanović, D. Anglo-Yugoslav cultural relations. Contemporary Rev, Feb 1940.
Klančar, A. J. Scott in Yugoslavia. SEER 27, Dec 1948.

Serbo-Croat
Low, D. H. The first link between English and Serbo-Croat literature. SEER 3, Dec 1924.
Fiedler, H. G. The first link between English and Serbo-Croat literature. SEER 6, Dec 1927.

Slovene
Klančar, A. J. Josip Jurčić (1844–81), the Slovene Scott. Amer SEER 5, May 1946.
Strojan, M. 'Parizina': dva prevoda. Primerjalna knjizevnost (Ljubljana) 7:1 1984.
Stanovnik, M. Slovenski prevodi Byronovih pesnitev v 19. stoletju. Primerjalna knjizevnost (Ljubljana) 13:2 1990.

Croatian
Filipović, R. Anglo-Croatian literary relations in the 19th century. SEER 32, Dec 1953.
Zivančević-Sekerus, I. Croatian writers in the Byronic mould. MLR 87 Jan 1992.

Serbian
Subotić, D. Serbian popular poetry in English literature. SEER 5–6, Mar and June 1927.
Servian popular poetry. London Mag Jan–Apr 1927.

Macedonian
Todorova-Janeshieva, L. Richard Morfill on the Miladinov brothers. Macedonian Rev 17:1 1987.

Bulgarian
Ralston, W. R. S. Bulgarian popular songs. Cornhill Mag 35, Feb 1877 [PHW].

3
Poetry

i. General works

Concentration here is on secondary material published during the period 1800–1920. Exceptions are the listing of anthologies containing poetry of the period, in sections C and D(2), and reference works in section E, which are brought up to the present.

A. HISTORIES AND SURVEYS

(1) GENERAL

Peacock, T. L. The four ages of poetry. 1820; ed H. F. B. Brett-Smith, Oxford 1921 (with Shelley's Defence of poetry).
Keble, J. Sacred poetry. Quart Rev 32 1825. Review of The star in the east; with other poems by J. Conder, 1824.
Keble, J. De poeticae vi medica. 2 vols Oxford 1844.
Griswold, R. W. The poets and poetry of England in the nineteenth century. Philadelphia 1845 (2nd edn), New York 1875 (rev and continued to the present time).
Howitt, W. Homes and haunts of the most eminent British poets. 2 vols 1847.
Moir, D. M. Sketches of the poetical literature of the past half-century in six lectures. Edinburgh 1851.
Cleveland, C. D. English literature of the nineteenth century. Philadelphia 1852, rev 1869.
Shairp, J. C. Studies in poetry and philosophy. Edinburgh 1868, 1887.
Brandes, G. M. C. Hovedstrømninger i det 19de aarhundredes litteratur. 6 vols Copenhagen 1872–90; tr 1901–5.
Hewlett, H. G. Poets of society. Contemporary Rev July 1872.
Brooke, S. A. Theology in the English poets. 1874.
Tomlinson, C. The sonnet: its origin, structure and place in poetry. 1874.
Smith, G. B. Poets and novelists. 1875.
Dennis, J. English lyrical poetry. In his Studies in English literature, 1876.
Gosse, E. A plea for certain exotic forms of verse. Cornhill Mag July 1877.
Dobson, A. Notes on some foreign forms of verse. In W. D. Adams, Latter-day lyrics, 1878.
du Prell, C. Psychologie der Lyrik. Leipzig 1880.
Shairp, J. C. Aspects of poetry. Oxford 1881.
Courthope, W. J. The liberal movement in English literature. 1885.
Sarrazin, G. Poètes modernes de l'Angleterre. Paris 1885.
Sonnenschein, E. A. Culture and science. Macmillan's Mag Nov 1885.
Scudder, V. D. Effect of the scientific temper in modern poetry. Andover Rev 8 1887.
Bourget, P. Science et poésie. Fortnightly Rev Apr 1888.
Lang, A. Letters on literature. 1889. 2 letters on vers de société.
Sarrazin, G. Renaissance de la poésie anglaise 1798–1889. Paris 1889.
Thomas, C. Poetry and science. Open Court 3 1889.
Werner, R. M. Lyrik und Lyriker: eine Untersuchung. Hamburg 1890.
Dewey, J. Poetry and philosophy. Andover Rev 16 1891.
Dixon, W. M. English poetry from Blake to Browning. 1894.
Swinburne, A. C. Social verse. In his Studies in prose and poetry, 1894.
Saintsbury, G. A history of nineteenth-century literature 1780–1895. 1896.
Blakeney, E. H. Poetry in the nineteenth century. [1899.] Rptd from Churchman.
Hyde, D. A literary history of Ireland from the earliest times to the present day. 1899, 1901, 1906, 1967.
Dowden, E. Puritan and Anglican: studies in literature. 1900.
Thomas, C. Have we still need of poetry? Forum 25 1900.
Gosse, E. English literature in the 19th century. In The nineteenth century: a review of progress, 1901.
Bradley, C. B. On the distinction between the art-epic and the folk epic. Univ of California Chron 8 1906.
Hull, E. A text book of Irish literature. 2 pts Dublin 1906–8.
Payne, W. M. The greater English poets of the nineteenth century. 1907.
Schelling, F. E. The English lyric. Boston 1907, London 1913.
Gingerich, S. F. Wordsworth, Tennyson and Browning: a study in human freedom. Ann Arbor MI 1911.
Hepple, N. Lyrical forms in England. Cambridge 1911.
Dixon, W. M. English epic and heroic poetry. 1912.
Henderson, T. F. The ballad in literature. Cambridge 1912.
Reed, E. B. English lyrical poetry: from its origins to the present time. New Haven CT 1912.
Rhys, E. Lyric poetry. 1913.
Forsythe, R. S. Modern imitations of the popular ballad. JEGP 13 1914.
Reschke, H. Die Spenserstanze im neunzehnten Jahrhundert. Heidelberg 1918.
Osmond, P. H. The mystical poets of the English Church. 1919.
Cazamian, L. L'évolution psychologique et la littérature en Angleterre 1660–1914. Paris 1920.

(2) THE ROMANTIC MOVEMENT

Talfourd, T. N. An attempt to estimate the poetical talent of the present age, including a sketch of the history of poetry and the

characters of Southey, Crabbe, Scott, Moore, Lord Byron, Campbell, Lamb, Coleridge and Wordsworth. 1815 (Pamphleteer vol 5).
Hunt, J. H. L. Lord Byron and some of his contemporaries. 1828.
von Goethe, J. W. Faust: zweiter Theil. Stuttgart 1833. Especially Act III, pbd separately 1827 as Helena: klassich-romantische Phantasmagorie. Euphorion, son of Faust and Helen, symbolises Byron.
Cunningham, A. Biographical and critical history of the last fifty years. Paris 1834 (prev pbd in Athenaeum 1833).
Heine, H. Die romantische Schule. Leipzig 1836.
Chasles, V. E. P. Vie et influence de Byron sur son époque. In Etudes sur la littérature et les moeurs de l'Angleterre au XIXe siècle. Paris 1850.
Dowden, E. Poetical feeling for nature. Contemporary Rev Aug 1866.
Shairp, J. C. On the poetic interpretation of nature. 1877.
Oliphant, M. O. The literary history of England in the end of the eighteenth and the beginning of the nineteenth century. 3 vols 1882.
de Laprade, V. Histoire du sentiment de la nature. Paris 1883.
Brandl, A. Samuel Taylor Coleridge und die englische Romantik. Berlin 1886; tr 1887.
Veitch, J. The feeling for nature in Scottish poetry. 2 vols Edinburgh 1887.
Biese, A. Die Entwickelung des Naturgefühls im Mittelalter und in der Neuzeit. Leipzig 1888.
Dowden, E. The French Revolution and English literature. 1897.
Herford, C. H. The age of Wordsworth. 1897.
Omond, T. S. The romantic triumph. 1897, Edinburgh 1900.
Hancock, A. E. The French Revolution and the English poets: a study in historical criticism. New York 1899.
Vaughan, C. E. The romantic revolt. Edinburgh 1900.
Beers, H. A. A history of English romanticism in the nineteenth century. New York 1901.
Cestre, C. La révolution française et les poètes anglais. Dijon 1906.
Machie, A. Natural knowledge in modern poetry. 1906.
Symons, A. The romantic movement in English poetry. 1909.
Courthope, W. J. History of English poetry, vol 6. 1910.
Richter, H. Geschichte der englischen Romantik. 2 vols Halle 1911–16.
Elton, O. A survey of English literature 1780–1830. 2 vols 1912.
Brooke, S. A. Naturalism in English poetry. 1920.

(3) VICTORIAN POETRY

Austin, A. The poetry of the period. 1870. On Tennyson, Browning, Swinburne, Arnold, Morris.
Forman, H. B. Our living poets: an essay in criticism. 1871.
Oliphant, M. O. and F. R. The Victorian age of English literature. 2 vols 1892.
Walker, H. The greater Victorian poets. 1895.
Walker, H. The age of Tennyson. 1897.
van Bever, A. and P. Léautaud. Poètes d'aujourd'hui 1880–1900: morceaux choisis, accompagnés de notices biographiques et d'un essai de bibliographie. Paris 1900 (3rd edn).
Smith, A. The main tendencies of Victorian poetry: studies in the thought and art of the greater poets. Birmingham 1907.
Brooke, S. A. A study of Clough, Arnold, Rossetti and Morris, with an introduction on the course of poetry from 1822 to 1852. 1908, 1910 (2nd edn).
Walker, H. The literature of the Victorian era. Cambridge 1910.
Kennedy, J. M. English literature 1880–1905. Berkeley Heights 1912.
Chesterton, G. K. The Victorian age in literature. 1913, 1966 (2nd edn).
Jackson, H. The eighteen-nineties. 1913, rptd 1964.
Elton, O. A survey of English literature 1830–80. 2 vols 1920.

B. ESSAYS AND STUDIES

(1) IDEALS AND POETIC THEORIES OF THE ROMANTIC SCHOOL

Wordsworth, W. Lyrical ballads. 1800, 1815 (with Essay supplementary to the Preface).
Bowles, W. L. Pope's poetical works. 10 vols 1806. Criticism of Pope's standards and methods prefixed.
Bowles, W. L. The invariable principles of poetry. 1819.
Bowles, W. L. Two letters to Lord Byron. 1821.
Coleridge, S. T. Biographia literaria. 2 vols 1817.
Coleridge, S. T. Anima poetae: from the unpublished notebooks. Ed E. H. Coleridge 1895.
Hazlitt, W. Lectures on the English poets. 1818.
Campbell, T. An essay on English poetry, prefixed to Specimens of the British poets. 7 vols 1819.
Byron, G. G., Baron. A letter to [John Murray]. 1821.
Byron, G. G., Baron. Observations upon Observations. 1821.
de Quincey, T. Letters to a young man whose education has been neglected. London Mag Mar 1823.
de Quincey, T. The Lake Poets: Wordsworth. Tait's Mag Feb 1839.
de Quincey, T. The Lake Poets: Southey, Wordsworth and Coleridge. Tait's Mag Aug 1839.
de Quincey, T. On Wordsworth's poetry. Tait's Mag Sep 1845.
de Quincey, T. Alexander Pope. North Br Rev 9 1848.
Heine, H. Zur Geschichte der neueren schönen Literatur in Deutschland. In Europe littéraire, Paris 1833; tr Ger 1833, 1836 (with addn of bk 3 entitled Die Romantische Schule); tr 1882.
Mill, J. S. Thoughts on poetry and its varieties. Monthly Repository n.s. Jan, Oct 1833.
Mill, J. S. Autobiography. 1873, 1874 (3rd edn). Ed H. Taylor.
Wilson, J. M. The enthusiast: a metrical tale with other pieces, and a preliminary chapter on poetry. Edinburgh 1834.
Taylor, H. Philip van Artevelde. 1834, 1846 (3rd edn). Preface.
Lofft, C. Ernest: or, political regenerations. 1839, 1868 (with preface on nature of poetry).
Hunt, J. H. L. Imagination and fancy: or selections from the English poets, with an essay in answer to the question What is poetry? 1844; ed A. S. Cook, Boston 1893.
Mackay, C. Egeria. 1850. Includes essay on poetry.
Lynch, T. T. On poetry. In Essays on some of the forms of literature, 1853.
Shairp, J. C. Aspects of poetry: being lectures delivered at Oxford. Oxford 1881.
Watts-Dunton, T. Essay on poetry. In Encyclopaedia Britannica, 1884 (9th edn).
Watts-Dunton, T. The sonnet. In Chambers' encyclopaedia, 1891.
Symond, J. A. The lyricism of the English romantic drama. In his In the key of blue, and other prose essays, 1893.
Texte, J. Keats et le néo-hellénisme dans la poésie anglaise. In Études de littérature européenne, Paris 1898.
Watts-Dunton, T. The renascence of wonder in English poetry. Introd to vol 3 of Chambers' cyclopaedia of English literature, ed D. Patrick, 1903.
Cowl, R. P. The theory of poetry in England: its development in doctrines and ideas from the sixteenth to the nineteenth century. 1914.
Watts-Dunton, T. Poetry and the renascence of wonder, with a preface by T. Hake. 1916. Based on earlier essays, which are rptd, with his contributions to Athenaeum 1876–1902 left unrevised at his death.

(2) POST-ROMANTIC IDEALS AND THEORIES OF POETRY: VICTORIAN AND LATER

Emerson, R. W. The poet. In his Essays ser 2, 1844.
Poe, E. A. The poet principle. Home Jnl (New York) 31 Aug 1850.
Rossetti, W. M. et al. The germ. 1850; ed T. B. Mosher 1898; 1901 (facs).
Ruskin, J. The Pre-Raphaelites. The Times 13 and 30 May 1851.
Ruskin, J. Pre-Raphaelitism. 1851.
Brimley, G. Poetry and criticism. In Essays, 1858.
Lewes, G. H. The inner life of art. 1865.
Buchanan, R. The fleshly school of poetry and other phenomena of the day. Contemporary Rev Oct 1871; 1872.
Forman, H. B. Pre-Raphaelite group. In his Our living poets, 1871.
Rossetti, D. G. The stealthy school of criticism. Athenaeum 16 Dec 1871.
Rossetti, D. G. The 'fleshly school' controversy. Tinsley's Mag 10 1872.
Dobell, S. T. The nature of poetry. In Thoughts on art, philosophy and religion, 1876.
Selkirk, J. B. Ethics and aesthetics of modern poetry. 1878.
Arnold, M. Wordsworth. Macmillan's Mag May, July 1879; rptd in his Essays in criticism ser 2, 1888.
Symonds, J. A. Matthew Arnold's selections from Wordsworth. Fortnightly Rev Nov 1879.
Arnold, M. The study of poetry. In English poets, ed T. H. Ward, vol 4 1880; rptd in his Essays in criticism ser 2, 1888.
Arnold, M. Byron. Macmillan's Mag Mar 1881; rptd in his Essays in criticism ser 2, 1888.
Whitman, W. The poetry of the future. North Amer Rev 132 1881.
Austin, A. Old and new canons of criticism in poetry. Contemporary Rev Dec 1881, Jan 1882.
Hamilton, W. The aesthetic movement in England. 1882.
Myers, F. W. H. Rossetti and the religion of beauty. In his Essays: modern, 1883.
Guyan, M.-J. L'esthétique du vers moderne. Revue Philosophique 17 1884.
Swinburne, A. C. Wordsworth and Byron. Nineteenth Cent Apr–May 1884.
Bain, A. On teaching English, with detailed examples and an inquiry into the definition of poetry. 1887.
Cook, A. S. (ed). The touchstones of poetry. San Francisco 1887.
Gurney, E. Tertium quid: chapters on various disputed questions. 2 vols 1887.
Davidson, J. W. The poetry of the future. New York 1888.
Everett, C. C. Poetry, comedy and duty. Boston and New York 1888.
Austin, A. On the position and prospects of poetry. Preface to 1889 edn of The human tragedy.
Henley, W. E. Views and reviews: essays in appreciation. 1890, 1902 (2nd edn).
Wilde, O. Intentions. 1891.
Stedman, E. C. The nature and elements of poetry. Boston and New York 1892.
Watts-Dunton, T. Tennyson as a Nature poet; Tennyson and the scientific movement. Nineteenth Cent May, Oct 1893.
Rossetti, W. M. (ed). Ruskin-Rossetti, Pre-Raphaelitism: papers 1854 to 1862. 1899.
Symons, A. The symbolist movement in literature. 1899.
Rossetti, W. M. (ed). The PRB journal. In Pre-Raphaelite diaries and titles, 1900.
Hunt, W. H. Pre-Raphaelitism and the Pre-Raphaelite brotherhood. 2 vols 1905–6, 1913 (2nd edn).
Hueffer, F. M. The Pre-Raphaelite brotherhood. [1907.]
Woodberry, G. E. The appreciation of literature. New York 1907.
Brooke, S. A. A study of Clough, Arnold, Rossetti and Morris, with an introduction on the course of poetry from 1822 to 1852. 1908.
Herford, C. H. A poetical view of the world. 1916.
Gosse, E. The future of English poetry. In Some diversions of a man of letters, 1919.
Grierson, H. J. C. Lord Byron, Arnold and Swinburne. 1920.

C. ANTHOLOGIES

Johnson, J. The Scots musical museum. 5 vols 1787–1803, 6 vols Edinburgh 1833; ed W. Stenhouse, D. Laing and C. K. Sharpe 4 vols Edinburgh 1853.
Thomson, G. Select collection of original Scottish airs, with select and characteristic verses by the most admired Scottish poets. 5 vols Edinburgh 1799–1818.
Burns, R. The Caledonian musical museum: being a collection of the best songs. 1801, 1821 (3rd edn).
The Nithsdale minstrel. Dumfries 1805.
The Caledonian musical repository: a choice of esteemed Scottish songs. 1806, Edinburgh 1809, 1811.
Cromek, R. H. Select Scottish songs ancient and modern. 2 vols 1810.
Cromek, R. H. Remains of Nithsdale and Galloway song. 1810, Paisley 1880.
Campbell, A. Albyn's anthology: or a select collection of the melodies and vocal poetry peculiar to Scotland and the Isles. 2 vols Edinburgh 1816–18.
[Hogg, James.] The poetic mirror: or the living bards of Britain. 1816, 1817 (2nd edn).
Motherwell, W. The harp of Renfrewshire. Paisley 1819, Glasgow 1820, Paisley 1872, 2nd ser Paisley 1873.
Struthers, J. The harp of Caledonia: a collection of songs, ancient and modern, chiefly Scottish. 3 vols Glasgow 1819–81.
Smith, R. A. The Scottish minstrel. 6 vols Edinburgh 1821–4.
Bullar, J. Selections from the British poets, commencing with Spenser and including the latest writers: with select criticisms from approved authors, and short biographical notices. Southampton and London 1822.
Aikin, J. The cabinet. Edinburgh 1824, 1825, 1831.
The British anthology, or poetical library 8 vols 1824–5.
Cunningham, A. The songs of Scotland, ancient and modern. 4 vols 1825.
Songs of the Edinburgh troop. Edinburgh 1825.
The living poets of England: specimens of the living British poets, with biographical and critical notices and an essay on English poetry. 2 vols Paris 1827.
Motherwell, W. Minstrelsy ancient and modern. Glasgow 1827, Paisley 1873.
Chambers, R. The Scottish songs. 2 vols 1829–32.
The laurel: fugitive poetry of the nineteenth century. 1830, 1841 (new edn). Rptd in The laurel and lyre: fugitive poetry of the nineteenth century, originally selected by the late Alaric A. Watts. New edn rev with addns, London and New York 1867.
The lyre: fugitive poetry of the nineteenth century. 1830, 1841 (new edn). Rptd in The laurel and lyre: fugitive poetry of the nineteenth century, originally selected by the late Alaric A. Watts. New edn rev with addns, London and New York 1867.
Whistle Binkie: a collection of songs for the social circle. Glasgow 1832–47 etc.
Chambers, R. A miscellany of popular Scottish songs. Edinburgh 1841.
A miscellany of popular Scottish poems. Edinburgh 1841.
O'Duffy, C. G. The ballad poetry of Ireland. Dublin 1843, 1845 (3rd edn), 1869 (40th edn) etc.
The spirit of the nation: ballads and songs by the writers of 'The Nation' with music. Dublin 1843, 1882 (3rd edn).
Hunt, L. Imagination and fancy: or selections from the English poets, illustrative of these first requisites of their art. 1844.

Hervey, T. K. The English helicon of the nineteenth century. 1845.
Ayrshire ballads and songs. 2 sers Ayr 1846, Edinburgh 1847.
Macmahon, T. The casket of Irish pearls: a selection of prose and verse from the best Irish writers. Dublin 1846.
Toovey, A. D. Biographical and critical notices of the British poets of the present century, with specimens of their poetry. 1848.
Thompson, H. Original ballads by living authors. 1850.
Kirkland, Caroline M. Garden walks with the poets. New York 1852, with alterations and addns London 1858.
Rogers, C. The modern Scottish minstrel. 6 vols Edinburgh 1856–7, 1870 (2nd edn) as The Scottish minstrel.
Williams, Mary. Pearls of poesy or anthology of British poets. Hamburg 1856.
Garden walks with the poets. 1858.
Burke, J. Gems from the Catholic poets, with a biographical and literary introduction. 1859.
'Giraldus' (W. Allingham). Nightingale Valley: a collection including a great number of the choicest lyrics and short poems in the English language. 1860.
Palgrave, F. T. The golden treasury of the best songs and lyrical poems in the English language. 1861, 1891 (enlarged); The golden treasury: second series, 1897.
Savile, B. W. Lyra sacra: being a collection of hymns ancient and modern, odes and fragments of sacred poetry. 1861.
[Inglis, R.] Gleanings from the English poets, Chaucer to Tennyson, with biographical notices of the authors. Edinburgh [1862], reissued under compiler's name [1881].
Grant, A. H. Half hours with our sacred poets. [1863.]
Bonar, A. R. The poets and poetry of Scotland from James I to the present time, with biographical sketches and critical remarks. Edinburgh 1864.
Wood, Emma C. Leaves from the poets' laurels. 1865, 1869.
Hunt, L. and S. A. Lee. The book of the sonnet. 2 vols Boston 1867.
Locker-Lampson, F. Lyra elegantarium: a collection of some of the best social and occasional verse by deceased English authors. 1867, rev and enlarged edn London, New York and Melbourne 1891.
Thornbury, G. W. Two centuries of song, or lyrics, madrigals and sonnets and other occasional verses of the English poets of the last two hundred years. 1867.
A[dams], W. H. D. The household treasury of English song: specimens of the English poets chronologically arranged, with biographical and explanatory notes. 1869.
Adams, W. H. D. The student's treasury of English song, containing choice selections from the principal poets of the present century: with biographical and critical notices. 1873.
Emerson, R. A. Parnassus. Boston 1875.
Wilson, J. G. The poets and poetry of Scotland. 2 vols 1876–7.
Murray, J. The prose and poetry of Ireland: a choice collection of literary gems. New York 1877.
Reade, C. and T. P. O'Connor. The cabinet of Irish literature. 4 vols 1879, 1893; rev K. Tynan Hinkson 1903.
Edwards, D. H. Modern Scottish poets. 16 vols Brechin 1880–97.
O'Sullivan, D. Popular songs and ballads of the Emerald Isle. New York 1880.
Ward, T. H. et al. The English poets. Vol 4, 1880.
Gosse, E. English odes. 1881. Spenser to Swinburne.
Waddington, S. English sonnets by living writers, with a note on the history of the sonnet. 1881.
Caine, T. H. Sonnets of three centuries: a selection. 1882.
[Linton, W. J.] Golden apples of Hesperus: poems not in the collections. Appledore 1882.
Linton, W. J. and R. H. Stoddard. Lyrics of the nineteenth century. 1884.
Sharp, W. Sonnets of this century. 1886.
Eyles, F. A. H. Popular poets of the period ... being ... biographical and critical sketches ... of poets of our own time and country with ... selections from their works. London and Brighton [1888], [1889].
Caine, W. R. H. Humorous poems of the century, with biographical notes. [1889.]
Palgrave, F. T. The treasury of sacred song. Oxford 1889.
Sharp, W. (ed). Great odes: English and American. [1890].
Bradshaw, J. An English anthology from Chaucer to the present time. 1891.
Douglas, G. Poems of the Scottish minor poets. 1891.
Miles, A. H. et al. The poets and the poetry of the century. 10 vols [1891–7], 1898, 12 vols 1905–7 (rearranged and expanded as The poets and the poetry of the nineteenth century). Selected from some 300 writers; introds by Miles et al.
Henley, W. E. Lyra heroica: a book of verse for boys. 1892.
Beeching, H. C. A paradise of English poetry. 2 vols 1893.
De Vere, A. The household poetry book. 1893.
Greig, J. Scots minstrelsie: a national monument of Scottish song. 6 vols Edinburgh 1893.
Leonard, R. M. The dog in British poetry. 1893.
Beeching, H. C. Lyra sacra: a book of religious verse. 1895, 1903.
Beeching, H. C. A book of Christmas verse. 1895, 1926 (2nd edn rev).
Henley, W. E. A London garland selected from 5 centuries of English verse. 1895.
Harris, afterwards Harris-Bickford, E. L. T. Poems from many pens: being a selection of the works of some present day poets. Camborne [1896].
Sharp, Elizabeth A. Lyra Celtica: an anthology of representative Celtic poetry. Edinburgh 1896.
Stedman, E. C. A Victorian anthology 1837–1895. Boston and New York 1896.
Henley, W. E. English lyrics: Chaucer to Poe. 1897.
Buckingham, E. M. The revival of English poetry in the nineteenth century: selections from Wordsworth, Coleridge, Shelley, Keats and Byron. 1898.
Lucas, E. V. The open road: a little book for wayfarers. 1899. Prose and verse.
Brooke, S. and T. W. Rolleston. A treasury of Irish poetry in the English tongue. 1900.
Quiller-Couch, A. T. The Oxford book of English verse 1250–1900. Oxford 1900.
Beeching, H. C. Lyra apostolica. 1901.
Archer, W. Poets of the younger generation. London and New York 1902.
Duff, M. E. G. The Victorian anthology. 1902.
[Mayle, S. C.] A garland of Christmas verse. 1903.
McCarthy, J. Irish literature. 10 vols Philadelphia 1904.
[Mayle, S. C.] A second garland of Christmas verse. 1905.
Stone, C. Sea songs and ballads 1400–1886. 1906.
Jerrold, W. The book of living poets. 1907.
Knight, W. A Victorian anthology. [1907.]
Cooke, J. The Dublin book of Irish verse 1728–1909. Dublin and London 1909.
Dixon, W. M. and H. J. C. Grierson. The English Parnassus: an anthology of longer poems (Chaucer to Omar Khayyám). Oxford 1909.
Leonard, R. M. The pageant of English poetry. 1909.
Dixon, W. M. The Edinburgh book of Scottish verse. Edinburgh 1910.
Douglas, G. The book of Scottish poetry. 1910.
Leonard, R. M. A book of light verse, fourteenth to nineteenth century. 1910.
Leonard, R. M. The book-lovers' anthology. 1911.
Graves, A. P. Welsh poetry old and new in English verse. 1912.
Quiller-Couch, A. T. The Oxford book of Victorian verse. Oxford 1912, 1948.

Colum, P. Broad-sheet ballads. Dublin [1913].
Jerrold, W. and R. M. Leonard. A century of parody and imitation. 1913.
Graves, A. P. The book of Irish poetry. Dublin [1914].
Gregory, P. Modern Anglo-Irish verse: an anthology selected from the work of living Irish poets. 1914.
Thompson, A. H. English Romantic poets. 6 vols Cambridge 1915–22.
Walker, Mrs H. A book of Victorian poetry and prose. Cambridge 1915.
Nicholson, D. H. S. and A. H. E. Lee. The Oxford book of English mystical verse, thirteenth to twentieth century. Oxford 1916.
Leonard, R. M. The poetry of peace. 1918.
Newbolt, H. An English anthology of prose and poetry, showing the main stream of English literature through six centuries. 1921.
Walters, L. Irish poets of today: an anthology. 1921.
Caldwell, T. The golden book of modern English poetry 1870–1920. 1922.
Colum, P. An anthology of Irish verse: the poetry of Ireland from mythological times to the present. New York 1922, [1948].
Brie, F. Englisches Lesebuch: neunzehntes Jahrhundert. Heidelberg 1923.
Tait, S. B. Chambers's garland of English verse. Edinburgh and London [1923].
Treble, H. A. English Romantic poems. Edinburgh [1923].
Buchan, J. The northern Muse. 1924.
Robinson, L. A golden treasury of Irish verse. 1925.
Crump, G. H. Poets of the romantic revival. 1927.
Lucas, E. V. The joy of life. 1927.
Williams, C. A book of Victorian narrative verse. Oxford 1927.
Wilson, J. D. The poetry of the age of Wordsworth: an anthology of the five major poets. Cambridge 1927.
Andrews, C. E. and M. O. Percival. Romantic poetry. 1928.
Collins, V. H. A book of Victorian verse, chiefly lyrical. 1928.
Milford, H. S. The Oxford book of Regency verse 1798–1837. Oxford 1928, 1935 (rev as The Oxford book of romantic verse), 1951 (as The Oxford book of English verse of the Romantic period).
Robinson, L. A. A little anthology of modern Irish verse. Dublin 1928.
Bernbaum, E. An anthology of romanticism. 5 vols New York 1929–33, 1948 (rev).
A garland of perennials. 1929.
Abdy, G. B. A Victorian pot-pourri of verses, known, unknown and forgotten. 1930.
Miller, G. M. The Victorian period. New York 1930.
Woods, G. B. Poetry of the Victorian period. Chicago 1930, 1955 (rev with J. H. Buckley).
Jiriczek, O. Victorianische Dichtung. Heidelberg 1931.
Powley, E. B. A hundred years of English poetry. Cambridge 1931.
A Scots garland: an anthology of Scottish vernacular verse. 1931.
Sitwell, E. The pleasures of poetry: a critical anthology. Second series: The romantic revival, 1931; Third series: The Victorian age, 1932.
Campbell, O. J., J. F. A. Pyre and B. Weaver. Poetry and criticism of the romantic movement. New York 1932.
Hayward, J. Nineteenth-century poetry: an anthology. 1932, 1950.
Miall, S. Poets at play: anthology of parodies and light verse. 1932.
A little book of Oxford Movement poetry. 1932.
Parrott, T. M. and W. Thorp. Poetry of the transition 1850–1914. New York 1932.
Stephens, J., E. L. Beck and R. H. Snow. English romantic poets. New York 1933.
Davidson, D. British poetry of the eighteen-nineties. New York [1937].
Henderson, W. Victorian street ballads. 1937.
Auden, W. H. The Oxford book of light verse. Oxford 1938, 1973.
Bowyer, J. W. and J. L. Brooks. The Victorian age. New York 1938, 1954 (rev).
Roberts, D. K. The century's poetry 1837–1937. 2 vols 1938, 1940, 4 vols 1942, 1945, 1950, 1956 (rev).
O'Lochlainn, C. Irish street ballads. Dublin 1939.
Cecil, Lord D. The Oxford book of Christian verse. Oxford 1940.
Bull, C. R. Regency poets. Melbourne 1941, 1957 (rev), 1959.
Brown, E. K. Victorian poetry. New York 1942, 1962 (with J. O. Bailey).
Grigson, G. The Romantics: an anthology of English prose and poetry. 1942, Cleveland OH 1962.
Booth, J. B. Seventy years of song. [1943.] Anthology of popular songs.
Greacen, R. Northern harvest: an anthology of Ulster writing. Belfast 1944.
Irvine, J. The flowering branch: an anthology of Irish poetry past and present. Belfast 1945.
Greacen, R. Irish harvest: an anthology of prose and poetry. Dublin 1946.
Hoagland, K. 1,000 years of Irish poetry: the Gaelic and Anglo-Irish poets from pagan times to the present. New York 1947.
Spender, S. A choice of English romantic poetry. New York 1947.
Garrity, D. New Irish poets. New York 1948.
Evans, M. R. An anthology of Victorian verse. 1949.
Aldington, R. The religion of beauty: selections from the aesthetes. 1950.
Auden, W. H. and N. H. Pearson. Tennyson to Yeats. New York 1950, London 1952, Harmondsworth 1977. Vol 5 of Poets of the English language.
Grigson, G. The Victorians. 1950.
Heath-Stubbs, J. and D. Wright. The forsaken garden: an anthology of poetry 1824–1909. 1950.
Taylor, G. Irish poets of the nineteenth century. 1951.
Blomberg, E. En bukett engelsk lyrik. Stockholm 1952.
Young, D. Scottish verse 1851–1951. 1952.
Messaien, P. Les romantiques anglais: text anglais et français. Paris 1955.
Noyes, R. English romantic poetry and prose. New York 1956.
Hugo, H. E. The romantic reader. New York 1957.
Pinto, V. de S. and A. E. Rodway. The common muse: an anthology of popular British ballad poetry, fifteenth to twentieth century. 1957.
Evans, A. A. Victorian poetry. 1958.
MacDonagh, D. and L. Robinson. The Oxford book of Irish verse XVIIth century–XXth century. Oxford 1958.
The preromantic and romantic poets. Paris 1958.
Carr, A. J. Victorian poetry: Clough to Kipling. New York 1959.
Houghton, W. E. and G. R. Stange. Victorian poetry and poetics. Boston 1959.
Bloom, H. English romantic poetry: an anthology. Garden City NY 1961, 2 vols 1963.
Frost, W. Romantic and Victorian poetry. 1961.
Francis Camilla, Sr. The Romantics and Victorians. New York [1961], [1966] (rev).
Abrams, M. H. The romantic period. In The Norton anthology of English literature vol 2, New York [1962].
Ford, G. H. The Victorian age. In The Norton anthology of English literature vol 2, New York [1962].
Parry, T. The Oxford book of Welsh verse. Oxford 1962.
Bebbington, W. G. The grooves of change: an anthology of Victorian poetry. 1963.
Hopkins, K. English poetry: a short history. Philadelphia 1963.
Marshall, W. H. The major English romantic poets: an anthology. New York 1963.
Creeger, G. R. and J. W. Reed. Selected prose and poetry of the romantic period. New York 1964.

Hayward, J. The Oxford book of nineteenth-century English verse. Oxford 1964.
Johnson, E. D. H. The world of the Victorians. New York 1964.
Martin, R. B. Victorian poetry: ten major poets. New York [1964].
Saul, G. Age of Yeats: the golden age of Irish literature. New York 1964.
Tosswill, T. D. Seven romantic poets. 1964.
Wright, D. Seven Victorian poets. 1964, 1969.
Brett, R. L. Poems of faith and doubt: the Victorian age. 1965.
Garrity, D. The Mentor book of Irish poetry: from A. E. to Yeats. New York 1965.
Stanford, D. Poets of the nineties: a biographical anthology. 1965.
Auden, W. H. Nineteenth century British minor poets. New York 1966.
Beckson, K. Aesthetes and decadents in the 1890s: an anthology of British poetry and prose. New York 1966.
McQueen, J. and T. Scotts. The Oxford book of Scottish verse. Oxford 1966.
Marshall, W. H. Victorian poets. 1966.
Merritt, J. D. The Pre-Raphaelite poem. New York 1966.
Perkins, D. English romantic writers. New York 1967.
Buckley, J. H. The Pre-Raphaelites. New York [1968].
Morgan, G. R. The world of Wales: an anthology of Anglo-Welsh poetry from the seventeenth to the twentieth century. Cardiff 1968.
Wright, D. The Penguin book of English Romantic verse. 1968.
Rafroidi, P. English Romantic poets. Paris [1969].
Tennyson, Sir C. B. L. and Hallam Tennyson. Victorian poetry 1830–1890. [1971.]
Bloom, H. and L. Trilling. Romantic poetry and prose. In J. F. Kermode and J. Hollander, Oxford anthology of English literature vol 2, 1973.
Stanford, D. Pre-Raphaelite writing: an anthology. London and Totowa NJ 1973.
Messenger, N. P. and J. R. Watson. Victorian poetry: 'The city of dreadful night' and other poems. London and Totowa NJ 1974.
Macbeth, G. The Penguin book of Victorian verse: a critical anthology. 1975.
Bold, A. The martial muse: seven centuries of war poetry. Exeter 1976.
Gray, D. and G. B. Tennyson. Victorian literature. 2 vols 1976.
Amis, K. New Oxford book of light verse. Oxford 1978.
Nott, S. Early Victorian printers' poetry. 1978.
Bergonzi, B. Poetry 1870–1914. 1980.
Richards, B. English verse 1830–1890. London and New York 1980.
Carr, S. The Batsford book of Romantic poetry. 1982.
Watson, J. R. Everyman's book of Victorian verse. 1982, 1987.
England, G. Words throo' t'shuttle ee: an anthology of industrial dialect verse from Victorian south and west Yorkshire. With a glossary by K. E. Smith. 1983.
Lyons, L. R. A book of Romantic verse. 1983.
Garlick, R. and R. Mathias. Anglo-Welsh poetry, 1480–1980. 1984, 1993 (up-dated to 1990).
Thwaite, A. Six centuries of verse. 1984.
Woodhead, C. Nineteenth and twentieth century verse: an anthology of sixteen poets. 1984.
Blaikie, T. Victorian love poetry. 1985.
Kinsella, T. The new Oxford book of Irish verse. Oxford 1986, 1989.
Maidment, B. The poorhouse fugitives: self-taught poets and poetry in Victorian Britain. Manchester 1987, 1992 (new edn).
Ricks, C. The new Oxford book of Victorian verse. 1987.
Tierney, F. M. and G. Clever. Nineteenth century narrative poetry. Ottawa 1988.
Grossman, J. and P. Dunhill. Nonsense and common sense: a child's book of Victorian verse. 1992.
Thomas, D. The Everyman book of Victorian verse: the post-romantics. 1992.
Gurney, S. British poetry of the nineteenth century. c. 1993.
Thomas, D. The Everyman book of Victorian verse: the Pre-Raphaelites to the nineties. 1993.
Shelley, E. The haunting muse: an anthology. St Leonards-on-sea 1994.
Masson, E. The Wordsworth book of love poetry. 1995.
Owen, M. Poetry 1380–1900, from Chaucer to Arnold and Hopkins. Tamworth 1995.

D. WOMEN'S POETRY

(1) GENERAL

Case, W. jr. Pictures of British female poesy. 1802. In verse.
Mitford, Mary Russell. Narrative poems on the female character, in the various relations of life. 1813, New York 1813.
Ward, Catharine G. [afterwards Mason]. Maid, wife and mother: or Women! a poem. 1819.
Ball, W. The crowning of the British living poetesses. 1827. In verse.
Michell, N. Living poets and poetesses: a biographical and critical poem. 1832, 1832 (2nd edn).
Cunningham, A. Biographical and critical history of the British literature of the last fifty years. Paris 1834.
D—, Emily. The Muse and poetess, a lesson from nature and other poems. 1835.
Fisher, Susan. A legend of the Puritans, or the influence of poetry and religion on the female character, with other poems. 1837.
Chorley, H. F. The authors of England: a series of medallion portraits. 1838, 1861.
Elwood, Mrs E. K. Memoirs of the literary ladies of England from the commencement of the last century. 2 vols 1843.
Costello, Louisa Stuart. Memoirs of eminent English women. 4 vols 1844.
Griswold, R. W. The poets and poetry of England in the nineteenth century. 1845, New York 1875 (rev edn).
Toovey, A. D. Biographical and critical notices of the British poets of the present century, with specimens of their poetry. 1848.
Moir, D. M. Sketches of the poetical literature of the past half-century in six lectures. Lecture vi pt 1. Edinburgh 1851.
Dreadnought, Deborah (pseud). The beauties of Bloomerism (with the special approbation of the board) by Deborah Dreadnought, secretary of the society for promoting the 'rights of women'. 1852. Verse satire.
Hale, Sarah Josepha Buell (pseud) [Caroline Matilda Kirkland]. Woman's record: or sketches of all distinguished women from the creation to 1854 a.d. in four eras with selections from female writers of every age. New York 1855.
Williams, Jane. The literary women of England: including a biographical epitome of all the most eminent to the year 1700, and sketches of the poetesses to the year 1850, with extracts from their works and critical remarks. 1861.
Hamilton, Janet. The uses and pleasures of poetry for the working classes. In Poems and essays, Glasgow 1863.
Kavanagh, Julia. English women of letters. 2 vols 1863.
Forman, H. B. Our living poets: an essay in criticism. 1871.
Brierley, Miss. Women-poets: being the inaugural address [of the Ladies' Debating Society, Birmingham], delivered by the President... on the 28th of October 1886, together with a report for the session for 1885–1886. 1886.
Black, Helen. Notable women authors of the day. Glasgow 1893, rptd Freeport NY 1972.
Lindsay, Lady Caroline B. E. The art of poetry with regard to women writers: a paper read at the literature meeting of the Women's International Congress... on Wednesday June 28th 1899. [1899?]

(2) ANTHOLOGIES

Women's verse is also represented (sometimes very sparingly) in many of the anthologies listed in C, above. Best coverage is given in Stedman, 1896.

Dyce, A. Specimens of British poetesses, selected and chronologically arranged. 1825, 1827.

Hale, Sarah Josepha Buell (pseud) [Caroline Matilda Kirkland]. The ladies wreath: a selection from the female poetic writers of England and America. Boston and New York 1837, 1839 (2nd edn).

Hunt, L. 'Specimens of British poetesses'. In Men, women and books: a selection of sketches, essays, and critical memoirs from his uncollected writings, vol 2 1847.

Bethune, G. W. The British female poets. Philadelphia 1848.

Rowton, F. The female poets of Great Britain, chronologically arranged, with copious selections and critical remarks. 1848, Philadelphia [1874] as Cyclopaedia of female poets, with addns.

Coppée, H. A gallery of distinguished English and American female poets. 1860.

Tytler, Sarah [Henrietta Keddie] and J. L. Watson (ed). The songstresses of Scotland. 2 vols 1871.

Robertson, E. R. English poetesses: a series of critical biographies with illustrative extracts. London, Paris and New York 1883.

Sharp, E. A. Women's voices: an anthology of the most characteristic poems by English, Scotch and Irish women. By Mrs William Sharp. 1887.

Sharp, E. A. Women poets of the Victorian era, edited with an introduction and notes by Mrs William Sharp. [1890.]

Miles, A. H. The poets and the poetry of the century. Vol 7 [1891], 1898.

Miles, A. H. The poets and poetry of the nineteenth century: Joanna Baillie to Jean Ingelow. Vol 8 [1907].

Miles, A. H. The poets and poetry of the nineteenth century: Christina G. Rossetti to Katharine Tynan. Vol 9 1907.

Sackville, Lady Margaret. A book of verse by living women. 1911.

Squire, J. C. A book of women's verse. 1921.

Teasdale, Sara. The answering voice: one hundred love lyrics by women. New York 1926.

Abdy, G. B. A Victorian pot-pourri of verses, known, unknown and forgotten. 1930.

Bax, C. and M. Stewart. The distaff muse: an anthology of poetry written by women. 1949.

Stanford, A. The women poets in English: an anthology. New York 1972.

Bernikow, L. The world split open: four centuries of women poets in England and America, 1552–1950. New York 1974, London 1979.

Kaplan, C. Salt and bitter and good: three centuries of English and American women poets. New York and London [1975].

Bogan, M. The women troubadours. New York 1976.

Barnstone, A. and W. B. A book of women poets from antiquity to now. New York 1978.

Cosman, C., J. Keefe and K. Weaver. The Penguin book of women poets. 1978, Harmondsworth 1979.

Scott, D. Bread and roses: an anthology of nineteenth and twentieth century poetry by women writers. 1982.

Kelly, A. A. Pillars of the house: an anthology of verse by Irish women from 1690 to the present. Dublin 1987.

Dugaw, D. Warrior women and popular balladry, 1650–1850. Cambridge 1989.

Pritchard, R. E. Englishwomen's poetry, Elizabethan to Victorian. Manchester 1990.

Kerrigan, C. An anthology of Scottish women poets. Edinburgh 1991. With Gaelic trns by M. Bateman.

Zundel, V. Faith in her words: six centuries of women's poetry. Oxford 1991.

Breen, J. Women Romantic poets 1785–1832. 1992, 1994 (new edn).

Breen, J. Victorian women poets 1830–1901: an anthology. 1994.

Hall, L. An anthology of poetry by women: tracing the tradition. 1994.

Reilly, C. Winged words: an anthology of Victorian women's poetry and verse. 1994.

Ashfield, A. Romantic women poets, 1770–1838: an anthology. Manchester and New York 1995; 2nd edn vol 1 Manchester 1997, vol 2 Manchester 1998.

Feldman, P. R. and T. M. Kelley (ed). Romantic women writers: voices and countervoices. Hanover NH and London 1995.

Leighton, A. and M. Reynolds. Victorian women poets: an anthology. Oxford and Cambridge MA 1995.

Armstrong, I. and J. Bristow. Nineteenth century women poets: an Oxford anthology. Oxford 1996. With C. Sharrock.

Higgonet, M. British women poets of the nineteenth century. 1996.

Feldman, P. R. British women poets of the Romantic era. Baltimore 1997.

Gurr, E. and C. de Piro. 19th and 20th century women poets. Oxford 1997.

Wu, D. Romantic women poets. Oxford 1998.

E. REFERENCE WORKS

This section lists bibliographies, encyclopaedias, dictionaries and guides concerned exclusively or in significant proportion with poetry and/or poets of the nineteenth century.

[Smibert, T.] Rhyming dictionary for the use of young poets, with an essay on English versification and explanatory observations on the selection and use of rhymes. [1856] (2nd edn).

Bellew, J. C. M. Poets' corner: a manual for students in English poetry: with biographical sketches of the authors. London and New York 1868, 1884 (new edn).

Carpenter, J. E. A handbook of poetry, being a clear and easy guide ... to the art of making English verse ... to which is added a new poetical anthology, and a concise dictionary of proper rhymes, etc. 1868.

O'Donoghue, D. J. The poets of Ireland: a biographical dictionary with bibliographical particulars. 3 vols 1892–3; new enlarged and rev edn 1901, 1912; rptd London and New York 1970.

Brewer, R. F. Orthometry: a treatise on the art of versification and the technicalities of poetry ... with a new and complete rhyming dictionary. 1893.

Granger, E. An index to poetry and recitations, etc. Chicago 1904; 3rd edn rev and enlarged ed H. H. Bessey [1940], Suppl 1938–44 New York 1945; 4th edn rev and enlarged, indexing anthologies pbd up to 31 Dec 1950, ed R. J. Dixon, New York 1957, as Granger's index; 10th edn rev as The Columbia index to poetry, indexing anthologies to June 1993, ed E. P. Hazen, New York 1994.

Hodgkins, L. M. A guide to the study of nineteenth-century authors. Boston 1904.

Dana, C. L. Poetry and the doctors: a catalogue of poetical works written by physicians. 1916.

Woods, G. B. English poetry and prose of the romantic movement. New York 1916 (with bibliography), 1929 (with supplementary bibliography).

Recorder (pseud) [J. Warren Owen?]. A bibliography of modern poetry, with notes on some contemporary poets. 1920.

Bernbaum, E. Guide through the romantic movement. New York 1930, 1949, 1954 (both rev and enlarged).

Templeman, W. D. et al. Victorian bibliography for 1932. MP 30 1933 (continued annually in MP until 1956); Bibliographies of studies in Victorian literature 1932–44, ed Templeman, Urbana IL 1945 (collected); Bibliographies of studies in Victorian literature 1945–54, ed A. Wright, Urbana IL 1956 (collected).

Jones, H. M. et al. Syllabus and bibliography of Victorian literature. 5 pts Ann Arbor MI 1934–5.

Ehrsam, T. G. and R. H. Deily. Bibliographies of twelve Victorian authors. New York 1936. Supplement by J. G. Fucilla, MP 37 1939. Lists books and articles on E. B. Browning, FitzGerald, D. G. and Christina Rossetti, Clough, Arnold, Tennyson, Morris, Stevenson, Swinburne, Hardy, Kipling.

Kunitz, S. J. and H. Haycraft. British authors of the nineteenth century. New York 1936. An encyclopaedia with brief bibliographies.

Graham, W. et al. The romantic movement: a current selective and critical bibliography for 1936. ELH 4 1937 (continued annually in ELH until 1949, in PQ 1950–64 and in ELN 1965–).

Batho, E. and B. Dobrée. The Victorians and after 1830–1914. 1938. Introductions to English literature vol 4, with critical bibliography.

Bruncken, H. Subject index to poetry: a guide for adult readers. Chicago 1940.

Raysor, T. M. et al. The English romantic poets: a review of research. New York 1950, 1956 (rev).

Faverty, F. E. et al. The Victorian poets: a guide to research. Cambridge MA 1956, 1968 (rev).

Houtchens, C. W. and L. H. The English romantic poets and essayists: a review of research and criticism. New York 1957, 1966 (rev).

Kuntz, J. M. and N. M. Martinez. Poetry explication: a checklist of interpretation since 1925 of British and American poems past and present. Boston 1962, 1980 (3rd edn).

Tobias, R. C. The year's work in Victorian poetry 1962. VP 1– 1963– . Continued annually.

Preminger, A. Encyclopedia of poetry and poetics. Princeton 1965. Enlarged edn 1975 as Princeton encyclopedia of poetry and poetics; new edn Princeton 1993 as A. Preminger and T. V. F. Brogan. The new Princeton encyclopedia of poetry and poetics.

Howard-Hill, T. H. Bibliography of British literary bibliographies. Oxford 1969, 1987 (2nd edn).

Spender, S. and D. Hall. The concise encyclopedia of English and American poets and poetry. London and New York 1963, London 1970 (2nd edn).

Marcan, P. Poetry themes: a bibliographical index to subject anthologies and related criticism in the English language: 1875–1975. 1977.

Reiman, D. H. English Romantic poetry, 1800–1835: a guide to information sources. Detroit [1979].

Rosenbaum, B. and P. White. Index of English literary manuscripts. Vol 4 1800–1900. London and New York 1982.

Kreissman, B. et al. Minor British poets 1789–1918, Parts 1–4, with suppls. Davis CA 1983–6. (A catalogue of the holdings of the Davis Collection, Univ of California. Pt 1: 1789–1839; pt 2: 1840–69; pt 3: 1870–99; pt 4: 1900–18.)

Stanford, D. E. British poets 1880–1914. Detroit 1983. Vol 19 of DLB.

Fredeman, W. E. and I. B. Nadel. Victorian poets before 1850. Detroit 1984. Vol 32 of DLB.

Smith, E. A dictionary of classical reference in English poetry. Cambridge 1984.

Brady, A. M. and B. Cleeves. A biographical dictionary of Irish writers. Co Westmeath 1985.

Fredeman, W. E. and I. B. Nadel. Victorian poets after 1850. Detroit 1985. Vol 35 of DLB.

Jackson, J. R. de J. Annals of English verse 1770–1835: a preliminary survey of the volumes published. London and New York 1985.

Williams, P. J. Literature of the Romantic period: a bibliography 1785–1837. Hawarden [1986].

Schlueter, P. and J. An encyclopedia of British women writers. New York and London 1988, London 1990.

Todd, J. British women writers: a critical reference guide. New York 1989, London 1989 as Dictionary of British women writers.

Turner, P. English literature 1832–1890 excluding the novel. Oxford 1989.

Alston, R. C. A checklist of women writers 1801–1900: fiction: verse: drama. 1990.

Greenfield, J. R. British Romantic poets 1789–1832. Detroit 1990. Vol 93 of DLB.

Greenfield, J. R. British Romantic poets 1789–1832. Second ser Detroit 1990. Vol 96 of DLB.

Aubrey, B. English Romantic poetry: an annotated bibliography. Pasadena CA 1991.

Davis, G. and B. A. Joyce. Poetry by women to 1900: a bibliography of American and British writers. 1991.

Johnson, C. R. Provincial poetry 1789–1839. British verse printed in the provinces: the Romantic background. Introd by R. Woof, Otley 1992.

Jackson, J. R. de J. Romantic poetry by women: a bibliography 1770–1835. Oxford and New York 1993.

Scott, R. A checklist of religious verse publications 1851–1860. History of the book – on demand series, 3. Oxford and Bristol 1993.

Shattock, J. The Oxford guide to British women writers. Oxford and New York 1993, 1994.

Reilly, C. W. Late Victorian poetry 1880–1899: an annotated biobibliography. 1994.

Martinez, N. and J. G. R. and E. Anderson. Guide to British poetry explication. Vol 3 Restoration — Romantics, New York 1995; vol 4 Victorian — contemporary, New York 1995.

Sutton, D. S. Location register of English literary manuscripts and letters: eighteenth and nineteenth centuries. 2 vols 1995.

Colman, A. U. Dictionary of nineteenth-century Irish women poets. Galway c. 1996.

ii. Early nineteenth-century poetry 1800–1835

Unless otherwise indicated, entries in this section have been compiled by J. R. de J. Jackson.

References

Rogers, C. (ed). The modern Scottish minstrel. 6 vols Edinburgh 1855–7. Cited as Rogers, *below*.

Miles, A. H. et al (ed). The poets and poetry of the century. 10 vols [1891–7], 12 vols 1905–7 (enlarged). Cited as Miles, *below*.

Numerals refer to vol nos in these edns; numerals in brackets to the enlarged edn of Miles. Further information about some poets may be found in J. Julian, A dictionary of hymnology, *1892, 1907 (rev).*

William A'Court, Baron Heytesbury 1779–1860

Montalto: a tragedy. 1821, 1840. Anon.

Catharine de Medicis: a tragedy. 1825.

Eliza Acton 1799–1859

Poems. Ipswich 1826, 1827.

The voice of the north. 1842.

Author of Modern cookery *(1845) and of* The English bread book *(1857).* *See col 2077.*

John Adamson 1787–1855

N. Luiz. Dona Ignez de Castro: a tragedy. Tr Adamson, Newcastle 1808.

Camoens. Sonnets from the Portuguese. Tr Adamson, Newcastle [1810].

R. W[harton?]. Cheviot: a poetical fragment. Ed [Adamson], Newcastle 1817.
The marriage of the Coquet and the Alwine. Ed [Adamson], Newcastle 1817. Anon.
Memoirs of the life and writings of ... Camoens. 2 vols 1820. Prose.
[M. Cockle.] Verses written at the house of Mr Henderson .... Ed Adamson, Newcastle 1823.
Lusitania illustrata .... Newcastle 1842, 1846. Prose and verse.
Reply of Camoens .... Newcastle 1845.
Sonnets. Newcastle 1845.
Ballads from the Portuguese. Tr J. A[damson] and R. C. C[oxe], Newcastle 1846.
Camoens. The Lusiad, bks I–V. Tr E. Quillinan and ed Adamson 1853.

John T. Agg, also 'Humphrey Hedgehog', 'Jeremiah Juvenal', 'Peter Pindar, jr' and 'Centinel' fl. 1804–34

The ghost of 'r—l stripes ...'. By 'Jeremiah Juvenal'. 1812 (3 edns).
Three r—l bloods ...: a poem. By 'Peter Pindar, jr'. 1812 (9 edns), 1814 (15th edn).
The r—l lover ...: a poem. By 'Peter Pindar, jr'. 1812 (12 edns), 1813 (4 edns).
The r—l sprain: an ode. By 'Humphrey Hedgehog'. 1812.
Turning out, or St S—'s in an uproar .... By 'Peter Pindar, jr'. 1812.
Rejected odes. Ed 'Humphrey Hedgehog'. 1813. Anon.
The r—l brood, or an illustrious hen and her pretty chickens: a poem. By 'Peter Pindar, jr'. 1813 (5 edns), 1814 (15th edn).
The r—l mystery ...: a poem. By 'Humphrey Hedgehog'. 1813 (6 edns).
The general-post bag, or news. By 'Humphrey Hedgehog'. 1814 (2 edns), 1815.
The London bazaar, or where to get cheap things: a humorous pindaric poem. By 'Humphrey Hedgehog'. [1816.]
Lord Byron's farewell to England, with other poems. 1816 (2 edns). Anon.
Lord Byron's pilgrimage to the holy land. London 1817 (2 edns, the 2nd as A pilgrimage to the holy land: a poem, by 'Lord Byron'); Philadelphia 1817. Anon.
The ocean harp: a poem in two cantos. 1819; Philadelphia 1819.
The r—l fowls ...: a poem. By the author of The r—l brood. 1820 (9 edns).
See also col 869.

Lucy Aikin 1781–1864

Collection
Memoirs, miscellanies and letters. Ed P. H. Le Breton 1864.

§1
Epistles on women, exemplifying their character and condition in various ages and nations. With miscellaneous poems. 1810; Boston 1810.
A. L. Barbauld. The works. Ed Aikin 2 vols 1825. Prose and verse.

§2
Correspondence of W. E. Channing and Aikin. Ed A. L. Le Breton 1874.
Edited numerous works for children and wrote memoirs of literary and historical figures. See also col 2078.

Sir Whitelaw Ainslie, also 'Caledonnicus' 1767–1837

Pizarro, or the Peruvian mother ...: a tragedy .... Edinburgh 1817.
Clemenza, or the Tuscan orphan: a tragic drama .... Bath 1822; London 1823.
Fitz-Raymond, or the rambler on the Rhine ... By 'Caledonnicus'. Edinburgh 1831. Anon.
Author of several medical pbns and descriptions of India.

David Anderson, mechanic, of Aberdeen fl. 1808–33

The Scottish village: a rural poem. Aberdeen 1808.
The martial achievements of Sir William Wallace: an historical play .... Aberdeen 1821.
Poems, chiefly in the Scottish dialect. Aberdeen 1826 (2 edns).
King Robert Bruce, or the battle of Bannockburn: an historical play. By the author of The Scottish village. 1833.

Edward Anderson, master of the brig 'Jemima' fl. 1792–1828

Poems, A description of a shepherd .... Workington [1792?].
The sailor: a poem .... Newcastle [1800?] (new edn); Leeds [1805?]; Newcastle 1806; Prescot 1807 (as The life of a sailor: a poem in three parts); 12th edn Prescot 1807; Leeds [c. 1810]; Hull 1828 ('12th edn'); Driffield 1878; Hull 1986.

Robert Anderson 1770–1833

Collections
The poetical works. 2 vols Carlisle 1820. With autobiography, essay on the peasantry of Cumberland, and Observations on the style and genius of the author by T. Sanderson.
Dialogues, poems, songs and ballads, by various writers, in the Westmoreland and Cumberland dialects. Ed A. Wheeler 1839. Includes 35 poems by Anderson.
The songs and ballads of Cumberland, to which are added dialect and other poems. Ed S. Gilpin, London and Carlisle 1866, 3 vols 1874 (rev). Includes poems by Anderson.
Cumberland ballads. Ed S. Gilpin 1866; London and Carlisle 1893.
Cumberland dialect: selections from the Cumberland ballads of Anderson. Ed G. Crowther, Carlisle 1904; Ulverston 1907.

§1
Poems on various subjects. Carlisle 1798.
Ballads in the Cumberland dialect. Carlisle 1805; Wigton 1808, 1815 (enlarged), 1823; Carlisle 1823, 1828 (ed T. Sanderson); Wigton 1834; Alnwick [1840?]; Wigton [1845?] (enlarged); Carlisle [1850?], 1864; Cockermouth 1870; Ulverston 1904 (centenary edn, ed T. Ellwood, as Anderson's Cumberland ballads and songs).

William Angus, A.M., of Glasgow fl. 1807–41

Juvenile pieces in prose and verse .... Glasgow 1815, 1831 (6th edn).
A selection of poetical and dramatic pieces .... Ed Angus, Glasgow 1813 (2nd edn), 1821.
Author of school-books.

John Anster 1793–1867

Ode to fancy, with other poems. Dublin 1813.
Lines on the death of the ... Princess Charlotte of Wales. Dublin 1818.
Poems with some translations from the German. Edinburgh 1819.
Faustus: a dramatic mystery, The bride of Corinth, The first Walpurgis night, translated from the German of Goethe. 1835. Faustus, i.e. Faust pt 1, has often been rptd, e.g. ed H. Morley 1883; 2 vols New York 1886–7, 1888; 1890; ed A. W. Ward, London 1907 (WC); 1985 (illustr H. Clarke). Extracts appeared anon in Blackwood's Mag June 1820.

Xeniola: poems, including translations from Schiller and 'De La Motte Fouqué' [Chamisso]. Dublin 1837.
Faustus: the second part, from the German of Goethe. 1864; ed H. Morley 1886 (with Marlowe's Faustus).
German literature at the close of the last century and the commencement of the present. In Lectures on literature and art delivered in Dublin, ser 2 1864.
Anster was a contributor, mainly on literary topics, to Blackwood's Mag *(1818–24),* Dublin Univ Mag *(1837–56) and* North Br Rev *(1847–55).*

Joseph Anstice 1808–36

Richard Coeur de Lion: a prize poem. Oxford [1828]. Anon.
Selections from the choric poetry of the Greek dramatic writers. Tr Anstice 1832.
Hymns. Bridgwater [1836].
Contributed hymns to The child's Christian year *(1841, 1842, 1844, 1849, 1864) and wrote on Roman history.*

Charles Bowker Ash b. 1781

Adbaston: a poem. Bath and London 1814.
The hermit of Hawkstone: a descriptive poem. Bath 1816.
A layman's epistle to a certain nobleman. 1824. Anon.
The poetical works. 2 vols 1831.

Joseph Aston 1762–1844

An heroic epistle, from the quadruple obelisk.... Manchester 1809. Anon.
The history of Johnny Shuttle and his cottage. [Manchester 1809.] Anon. Prose.
Retributive justice: a tragedy. [Manchester 1813] (priv ptd). Anon.
A family story: a comedy. [Manchester 1814] (priv ptd). Anon. Prose.
Conscience: a tragedy.... 1815; New York 1816.
Metrical records of Manchester.... 1822. Anon.
Plays, poetry and prose.... Manchester 1826.
Author of gazetteers and guides to Manchester and Lancashire.

Edwin Atherstone 1788–1872

Collections
Miles 2.
The dramatic works. Ed M. E. Atherstone 1888. Includes Pelopidas, Philip, and Love, poetry, philosophy and gout.

§1
The last days of Herculaneum, and Abradates and Panthea: poems. 1821.
A midsummer day's dream: a poem. 1824.
The fall of Nineveh: a poem. 2 vols 1828–30, 1847 (enlarged), 1854, 1868 (further enlarged).
The sea-kings in England: an historical romance. 3 vols Edinburgh 1830. Anon. Prose.
The handwriting on the wall: a story. 3 vols 1858. Prose.
Israel in Egypt: a poem. 1861.

James Atkinson 1780–1852

Rodolpho: a poetical romance. Edinburgh 1801.
Firdausi, A. H. Soohrab: a poem, freely translated. Tr Atkinson 1814, 1828.
The aubid: an eastern tale. 1819.
Foscolo, U. Ricciarda: a tragedy. Tr Atkinson, Calcutta 1823.
The city of palaces: a fragment, and other poems. Calcutta 1824.
Tassoni, A. La secchia rapita, or the rape of the bucket: an heroi-comical poem. Tr Atkinson 2 vols 1825, 1827.
Firdausi, A. H. The Shah Nameh.... Tr Atkinson 1832, 1886 (Chandos classics), 1892. Prose and verse.
Nizami, G. Laili and Majnun: a poem. Tr Atkinson 1832, 1836, 1894 (as The loves of Laili and Majnun); ed L. C. Byng 1905.
Author of several bks on the Near East and on medical topics.

E. L. Aveline fl. 1810–12

Simple ballads, intended for the amusement and instruction of children. 1810.
The mother's fables, in verse. Designed through the medium of amusement to correct some of the faults and follies of children. 1812 (anon), 1814, 1818, 1824, [1835], 1845 (attributed mistakenly to A. and J. Taylor), [1861?] (illustr W. Harvey).

Mary Bailey, formerly Walker fl. 1822–33

The months and other poems. London and Ballingdon 1822, 1833.
Palmyra: a poem. 1833 (2nd edn).
Reflections... upon the litany of the church of England. Ballingdon [1833]. Prose.
Musae sacrae: collection of hymns and sacred poetry. London and Ballingdon [1835]. Anon.

Thomas Bailey 1785–1856

What is life? And other poems. 1820.
The carnival of death: a poem. 1822.
Ireton: a poem. 1827.
My elbow chair. [Nottingham 183–?]
Recreations in retirement, by an old tradesman. 1836. Verse and prose.
The advent of charity and other poems. 1851.
Other prose pbns mainly on political and religious subjects and on local history.

Joanna Baillie 1762–1851

The BL and NLS house much miscellaneous ms material, including correspondence and reviews. Harvard also houses some alterations to plays.

Bibliography
Carhart, Margaret S. The life and work of Joanna Baillie, with a bibliography. New Haven CT and London 1923.

Collections and selections
The British theatre. Vol 24, ed E Inchbald, 1808.
The complete poetical works. Philadelphia 1832.
The dramatic and poetical works of Joanna Baillie. 1851, 1853.
Songs [with a memoir]. In The modern Scottish minstrel, ed Charles Rogers, vol 1 1855.
Selected poems. Ed W. Whyte, in The poets and the poetry of the century, vol 7 1893.

§1
Poems. 1790, 1994 (facs).
A series of plays: in which it is attempted to delineate the stronger passions of the mind. Each passion being the subject of a tragedy and a comedy. Vol 1 (Count Basil, The tryal, De Montfort), 1798, 1799, 1800, 1802, 1821; ed J. Wordsworth, London and New York 1990 (facs edn including Count Basil, The tryal and De Montfort).
Die Leidenschaften. Eine Reihe dramatischer Gemälde nach dem Englishen... von C. F. Cramer. Amsterdam and Leipzig 1806.
A series of plays: in which it is attempted to delineate the stronger passions of the mind. Each passion being the subject of a tragedy and a comedy. Vol 2 (The election, Ethwald, The second marriage) 1802 (2 edns), 1806, 1821.

A series of plays: in which it is attempted to delineate the stronger passions of the mind. Each passion being the subject of a tragedy and a comedy. Vol 3 (Orra, The dream, The siege, The beacon). 1804, 1805, 1812, 1821.
Epilogue to the theatrical representation [of Mary Berry's 'The fashionable friends'] at Strawberry-Hill. Written by Joanna Baillie, and spoken by the Hon Anne S. Damer, Nov 1800. [1804.]
Miscellaneous plays. 1804, 1805 (including Rayner, The country inn, Constantine Paleologus: or the last of the Caesars).
De Montfort; a tragedy in five acts .... [1807], 1808, 1809, [1816].
The family legend: a tragedy. Edinburgh 1810, London 1810, New York 1810.
The election. Philadelphia 1811.
Orra: a tragedy in five acts. New York 1812.
The siege: a comedy in five acts. New York 1812.
Metrical legends of exalted characters. 1821 (2 edns).
A collection of poems, chiefy manuscript, and from living authors. Ed for the benefit of a friend, by Joanna Baillie. 1823.
A lesson intended for the use of the Hampstead School. 1826.
The martyr: a drama in three acts. 1826.
The bride: a drama in three acts. 1828 (2 edns), Philadelphia 1828; tr Fr Paris 1830 (by Elisa Rivers, Countess de Molé or by C. F. A. Fayot).
A view of the general tenour of the New Testament regarding the nature and dignity of Jesus Christ; including a collection of the various passages in the Gospels, Acts of the Apostles, and the Epistles which relate to that subject. 1831, 1838.
Lines on the death of Sir Walter Scott. [1832.]
Dramas by Joanna Baillie. 3 vols 1836 (including Romerio, The alienated manor, Henriquez, The martyr, The separation, The stripling, The phantom, Enthusiasm, Witchcraft, The homicide, The bride, The match).
Epistles to Literati. Fraser's Mag 14 1836.
Fugitive verses. 1840, 1842.
Ahalya Baee: a poem[for private circulation]. 1849, Allahabad 1904.

Letters

Plarr, V. G. Sir Walter Scott and Joanna Baillie. Edinburgh Rev 216–17 1912–13.
Sutton, D. Joanna Baillie and Sir George Beaumont. N & Q 26 Feb 1938.
Unpublished letters of Joanna Baillie to a Dumfrieshire Laird. Ed Mrs W. H. O'Reilly, Trans of the Dumfrieshire and Galloway Natural History and Antiquarian Soc vol 17, Dumfries 1939.
Cunningham, W. R. Mrs Hemans at Mount Rydal. TLS 23 Oct 1943. (Letter from Joanna Baillie.)
Miller, F. Newspaper cuttings of some unpublished letters of Joanna Baillie.

§2

Remarks on the general tenour of the New Testament, regarding the nature and dignity of Jesus Christ: addressed to Mrs Joanna Baillie. [A reply to 'A view of the general tenour of the New Testament regarding the nature and dignity of Jesus Christ'.] 1851. Thomas Burgess was successively Bishop of Saint David's and of Salisbury.
Sadler, T. The Father seen in Christ: a sermon preached on the occasion of the death of Mrs Joanna Baillie. [1851.]
Dix, J. Lions: living and dead. 1852.
Gilfillan, G. In his Galleries of literary portraits vol 1, 1856.
Tytler, S. and J. L. Watson. Songstresses of Scotland. Vol 2, 1871.
Druskowitz, H. Drei Englishe Dichterinnen, etc [on Joanna Baillie, E. B. Browning and George Eliot]. 1885.
Pieszczek, R. Joanna Baillie; Ihr Leben, ihre Dramatischen Theorien und ihre Leidenschaftsspiele. Berlin 1910.
Badstuber, A. Joanna Baillie's Plays on the passions. Vienna 1911.
Meynell, A. In her Second person singular and other essays, 1921.
Carhart, M. S. The life and work of Joanna Baillie, with bibliography. New Haven CT and London 1923.
Nicoll, A. British drama. 1925.
Carswell, D. Sir Walter Scott; a four part study in biography [Scott, Hogg, Lockhart, Baillie]. 1930.
Grierson, H. The letters of Sir Walter Scott. 12 vols 1932–7.
Evans, B. Gothic drama from Walpole to Shelley. Berkeley 1947 (ch 11).
Norton, M. The plays of Joanna Baillie. RES 23 1947. [KM]

Marianne Baillie, Mrs Alexander 1795?–1831

Guy of Warwick: a legende, and other poems. Kingsbury 1817, 1818.
First impressions on a tour upon the Continent. 1819. Prose.
Lisbon in the years 1821, 1822 and 1823. 1824, 1825. Prose.
Trifles in verse. Ed [A. Baillie] 1825 (priv ptd).

Alexander Balfour 1767–1829

The genius of Caledonia .... Edinburgh 1798. Anon.
Contemplation, with other poems. Edinburgh and London 1820.
Characters omitted in Crabbe's parish register .... Edinburgh 1825.
Weeds and wildflowers ... with a memoir [by D. M. Moir]. Edinburgh, London and Dublin 1830. Prose and verse.
King Robert Bruce's breakfast, a traditionary story. Brechin 1835.
The old maid and widow, or the widow the best wife. Brechin 1835.
Author of several novels.

William Ball 1801–78

Nugae sacrae, or psalms and hymns and spiritual songs. 1825. Anon.
The crowning of the British poetesses. 1827. Anon.
Humanity, or the cause of the creatures advocated .. by the author of Nugae sacrae. 1828. Anon.
The transcript, also The memorial and other poems. [1853] (not pbd) (anon), 1855 (acknowledged).
The tribute: (the sequel). 1862.
Hymns or lyrics. Edinburgh 1864.
Notices of kindred and friends departed. Edinburgh 1865.
Salome's verse-book. Edinburgh 1866.
Verses composed since 1870, some elegiac, others occasional and miscellaneous. [London?] 1875, 2nd ser 1876, 3rd ser 1877 (not pbd).
Some other religious prose pbns.

William Ball fl. 1830–8

Creation: a poem. 1830.
Belshazzar's feast: a sacred lyrical drama. 1834.
Night watches: a poem. Naples 1834, 1835 (as Vigiliae, or night watches).
Freemen and slaves: an historical tragedy in five acts. 1838.

Anne Bannerman 1765–1829

Poems. Edinburgh and London 1800; Edinburgh 1807.
Tales of superstition and chivalry. 1802. Anon.

Richard Harris Barham, also 'Thomas Ingoldsby' 1788–1845

Collection

Favorite poems. New York 1891. With H. Carey.

§1

Verses spoken at St Paul's School. 1807.
Baldwin, or a miser's heir: a serio-comic tale, by an old bachelor. By ['G. H. E.']. 2 vols 1820. Anon. Prose.

The Ingoldsby legends, or mirth and marvels. By 'Thomas Ingoldsby'. 3 ser 1840, 1842, 1843 (2nd edn of ser 1); New York 1843 (3 edns); Philadelphia 1844; London 1847 (ser 3 ed [R. H. D. Barham], illustr G. Cruikshank, J. Leech and J. Tenniel); Philadelphia 1847, 1848; London 1848 (as collection), 1852; New York 1852; London 1855; New York 1856; Philadelphia 1856; London 1858, [1860]; New York [186-?]; Philadelphia 1860; London 1861, 1862, 1864; New York 1864; London 1865; New York 1865; London 1866 (Carmine edn); New York 1866; London 1867, 1868, 1869 (2 edns), 1870; New York 1870, 1872; London 1872, 1874, 1875; New York 1875; London 1876, 1877, 1878; New York 1878; Edinburgh and London 1879; London 1880; New York 1880, [188-?]; London 1881, 1882 (2 edns); New York '1884' [1885]; London 1885; Phildelphia 1885, 1886; London 1887 (2 edns), 1889 (6 edns), [1890], 1891, [1892]; ed E. A. Bond 1894, 1895, 1898 (illustr A. Rackham); New York [1899]; London and New York 1900; London 1901 (3 edns), 1903 (illustr H. Cole); ed J. B. Atlay 1903, 1904, 1905 (2 edns), 1906, 1907; New York and London 1907; London 1908 (2 edns); London and New York [1909]; Nottingham 1910; London 1911 (illustr H. G. Theaker); New York 1911; London 1912, ed J. Tanfield and G. Boas 1951. Selections: C. H. Ross's penny Ingoldsby [1875]; The smuggler's leap 1877, [1886]; The farce of Cathay, Shanghai 1870; The jackdaw of Rheims 1870, [1883]; Totteridge 1896; London [1912], 1913 (illustr C. Folkard), 1914 (illustr M. Travers), [1917]; Philadelphia [1919]; Tadworth 1976 (illustr L. Hemmant); The witch's frolic 1876, 1886, 1888; The lay of St Aloys (illustr E. M. Jessop) [1884]; The knight and the lady (illustr E. M. Jessop) [1886]; The lay of St Odille 1915; tr Ger by I. Schmidt, Leipzig [1897].

Some account of my cousin Nicholas. By 'Thomas Ingoldsby'. 3 vols Philadelphia 1835; 1841, 1 vol 1846; Buffalo, London and New York 1856. A novel rptd from Blackwood's Mag 1834.

The Ingoldsby lyrics, by 'Thomas Ingoldsby', edited by his son. 1881. Partly from The Ingoldsby legends, partly from other sources.

The Garrick Club: notices of one hundred and thirty-five of its former members. [New York?] 1896 (facs reprint, priv ptd).

§2

Barham, R. D. H. The life and letters of Barham. 2 vols 1870, 1 vol 1880.

Personal reminiscences by Barham, Harness and Hodder. Ed R. H. Stoddard, New York 1875.

Edward William Barnard 1791–1828

Poems, founded upon the poems of Meleager. 1817, 1818 (as Trifles, imitative of the chaster style of Meleager). Anon.

The protestant beadsman, or a series of biographical notices and hymns. 1822. Anon.

Fifty select poems of ... Flaminio imitated. Ed F. Wrangham, Chester 1829.

Bernard Barton 1784–1849

Collections

Selections from the poems and letters of Barton. Ed L. Barton 1849 (with memoir by E. FitzGerald); Philadelphia 1850 (as Memoir, letters and poems); London 1853 (as Poems and letters).

Miles 10 (11).

Selected poems. 1905.

A day in autumn, and Napoleon, and Verses on the death of Shelley. Ed D. H. Reiman, New York and London 1977 (facs reprint of 1820 and 1822).

Metrical effusions and The triumph of the Orwell and The convict's appeal. Ed D. H. Reiman, New York and London 1977 (facs reprint).

Poems by an amateur, 1818, and Poems 1820. Ed D. H. Reiman, New York and London 1977 (facs reprint).

§1

Metrical effusions. Woodbridge 1812.

Mr John Rogers and his opponents. By [B. B.]. [Ipswich 1813]. Anon.

The triumph of the Orwell. Woodbridge [1817.] Anon.

The convict's appeal. 1818. Anon.

Poems by an amateur. 1818. Anon.

A day in autumn: a poem. 1820.

Poems. 1820, 1821; Philadelphia 1821 (with addns); London 1822, 1825; Mountpleasant OH 1823; Augusta ME 1825; Boston 1826, 1832; Philadelphia 1844, 1848.

Napoleon and other poems. 1822, 1824 (as Minor poems).

Verses on the death of P. B. Shelley. 1822.

Ode to time. 1823.

Flowers. 1824.

Poetic vigils. 1824.

Devotional poems. 1825.

Devotional verses, founded on, and illustrative of, select texts of Scripture. 1826.

A missionary's memorial, or verses on the death of J. Lawson. 1826.

A widow's tale and other poems. 1827.

A new year's eve and other poems. 1828.

Bible letters for children [by L. Barton], with introductory verses by B. Barton. 1831, [1857?] (6th edn (as Bible stories)).

The missionary. [1833.]

The reliquary, with a prefatory appeal for poetry and poets. 1836. With L. Barton.

Triplets for the truth's sake. [1842?] Anon.

Household verses. 1845; Philadelphia 1846, 1849.

Sea-weeds, gathered at Aldborough. Woodbridge 1846 (priv ptd).

A memorial of J. J. Gurney. 1847; Philadelphia 1847.

A brief memorial of Major E. Moor FRS. Woodbridge 1848 (priv ptd).

Birthday verses at sixty-four. Woodbridge 1848.

Ichabod! Woodbridge 1848.

On the signs of the times. Woodbridge 1848 (priv ptd).

The gift of a friend. Philadelphia 1849; Buffalo NY [1870?].

The natural history of the Holy Land [by L. Barton], with poetical illustrations by B. Barton. [1856].

§2

Lucas, E. V. Bernard Barton and his friends. 1893.

Letters from B. Barton to Robert Southey. Ed C. Woodring, Cambridge MA 1950.

The literary correspondence of B. Barton. Ed J. E. Barcus, Philadelphia 1966.

Edited Fisher's Juvenile Scrap-Book *(1836, and with A. Strickland 1837 and 1839).*

R. C. Barton fl. 1816–20

Adelaide of Lorraine: a poetic narrative. By a gentleman in the country. 1816 (anon), 1818 (2 edns, acknowledged).

Rosalba: a tale of Sicily. 1819.

Chrysallina, or the butterfly's gala ... 1820.

Henrietta Battier, also 'Patt. Pindar' or 'Pat T. Pindar' 1751–1813

The protected fugitives: a collection of miscellaneous poems ... By a lady. Dublin 1791. Anon.

The Kirwanade, or poetical epistle ... By ['Patt. Pindar']. Dublin 1791 (nos 1 and 2). Anon.

The Gibbonade, or political reviewer ... By ['Patt. Pindar']. Dublin 1793–4 (nos 1–3). Anon.

Marriage ode royal, after the manner of Dryden. By ['Pat T. Pindar']. [Dublin?] 1795. Anon.
The lemon: a poem . . . in answer to . . . The orange . . . Dublin 1797. Anon.
An address to the subject of the projected union . . . By 'Patt. Pindar'. Dublin 1799.

Peter Bayley, also 'Giorgione di Castel Chiuso' 1778?–1823

Poems. 1803; Philadelphia 1804.
Idwal and other portions of a poem . . . . 1817, 1824 (as Idwal: a poem). Anon.
Sketches from St George's Fields. By 'Giorgione di Castel Chiuso'. 2 ser 1820–1.
A queen's appeal. 1820. Anon.
Orestes in Argos: a tragedy . . . . 1825 (2 edns, the 2nd in Dolby's British Theatre vol 12), [1826] (in Cumberland's British Theatre no 78), [1830?] (in Cumberland's British Theatre vol 12).

Nathaniel Thomas Haynes Bayly, also 'Q in the corner' 1797–1839

Collections
Songs, ballads and other poems. Ed H. B. Bayly 2 vols 1844, 1 vol 1857. With memoir.
Miles 9 (10).
Songs of the affections, selected by W. L. Hanchant. 1932.
Rough sketches of Bath, Epistles from Bath, Parliamentary letters, The dandies of the present. Ed D. H. Reiman, New York and London 1978 (facs reprint).

§1
Rough sketches of Bath, by 'Q in the corner'. Bath 1817 (2 edns), 1818; London 1819, 1820 (enlarged).
Epistles from Bath, or Q's letters to his Yorkshire relations, and miscellaneous poems by 'Q in the corner'. Bath 1817.
Parliamentary letters and other poems, by 'Q in the corner'. 1818, 1820.
The dandies of the present and the macaronies of the past: a rough sketch by 'Q in the corner'. Bath [1818?].
The tribute of a friend. Oxford 1819.
Mournful recollections. Oxford 1820.
Outlines of Edinburgh and other poems. 1822.
Erin and other poems. Dublin 1822.
Psychae, or songs on butterflies . . . in Latin rhyme. Tr [F. Wrangham], Malton 1828 (priv ptd).
Fifty lyrical ballads. Bath 1829 (priv ptd).
Musings and prosings. Boulogne 1833.
Flowers of loveliness, by various artists, with poetical illustrations by T. H. Bayly. 1837; London and New York 1837, [185-?].
Kindness in women: tales. 3 vols 1837; Calcutta 1838; 1 vol London 1862. Prose.
Weeds of witchery. 1837.
Songs and ballads. [1837?] anon, acknowledged ed [H. B. Bayly] 1844; Philadelphia 1844.
Also wrote numerous dramatic pieces, including the farce Perfection, *1836; a novel,* The Aylmers *3 vols 1827; collections of songs with music, e.g.* Songs of the days of chivalry, with music by T. H. Severn, *1831; single-sheet quarto issues of popular songs, e.g.* I'd be a butterfly.

Edward Dacres Baynes fl. 1818–47

Love and laudanum, or the sleeping dose: a farce. 1818. Prose.
Ovid. Epistles . . . . Vol 1. Tr Baynes 1818 (2 edns).
Childe Harold in the shades . . . . 1819. Anon.
Pastorals, Ruggiero, with other poems. 1819.
Annals of England: a poem. 1849.

Rev Thomas Beck, also 'Timothy Touch 'em' and 'Aliquis' fl. 1782–1821

Hymns calculated for . . . public . . . worship. Rochester 1782.
The cause of the dumb pleaded . . . . [1791?]
The missionary: a poem . . . . 1795.
The passions taught by truth: an allegorical poem. 1795.
The mission: a poem. 1796.
An elegy on the death of . . . Henry Hunter. 1802.
The age of frivolity: a poem. By 'Timothy Touch 'em'. 1806 (anon), 1807, 1809 (acknowledged).
An elegiac tribute to the memory of . . . John Newton . . . By the author of The age of frivolity. [1807?] Anon.
Poetic amusement . . . . [1809.]
Modern persecution: a poem in three cantos. By the author of The age of frivolity. 1811. Anon.
An elegy on the lamented death of . . . the Princess Charlotte. 1817.
Hymns for villagers . . . By 'Aliquis'. 1821. Anon.

John Belfour 1768–1842

Fables on subjects connected with literature. Imitated from the Spanish of de Yriarte [Iriarte]. 1804, 1806 (as Literary fables).
de Iriarte, T. Music: a didactic poem. Tr Belfour 1807.
Spanish heroism, or the battle of Roncesvalles: a metrical romance. 1809.
Odes in honour of . . . the prince regent . . . . 1812 (25 copies only).
Translated the Psalms and collected proverbs.

Henry Glassford Bell 1803–74

Poems. Edinburgh 1824.
Summer and winter hours. London and Edinburgh 1831.
Romances and minor poems. '1866' [1865].
Mary, Queen of Scots: a poem . . . . [1890]; Edinburgh and London [1907]; London and Glasgow 1910; London and Edinburgh 1911.
Editor, author of fiction, history, biography, reminiscences.

Elizabeth Ogilvy Benger 1778–1827

The female geniad: a poem, inscribed to Mrs Crespigny. 1791.
Poems on the abolition of the slave trade . . . . 1809. With J. Montgomery and J. Grahame.
Author also of novels and literary and historical memoirs.

Charles Frederick Bennett b. 1775

His memoirs and poetry. Holt 1817.
Donjon, prospect and reflection: a moral . . . poem. Canterbury 1834.

William Bennoch, later Bennet fl. 1822–40

The sabbath and other poems. Dumfries 1822.
Traits of Scottish life . . . . 3 vols 1830. Anon. Prose.
Songs of solitude. Glasgow 1831.
The prodigal son: a poem in three parts. 1836.
The chief of Glen-Orchay . . . . 1840. Anon.

Elizabeth Bentley 1767–1839

Genuine poetical compositions, on various subjects. Norwich 1791.
An ode on the glorious victory over the . . . fleets. Norwich [1805?].

Poems, being the genuine compositions .... Norwich, London and Cambridge 1821.
Miscellaneous poems, being the genuine compositions ... third volume. Norwich 1835.

James Beresford 1764–1840

The Aeneid of Virgil. Tr Beresford 1794.
The battle of Trafalgar .... [1805.]
The song of the sun ... from ... the Edda. 1805.
The cross and the crescent: an heroic metrical romance. 1824.
Author of religious prose and prose satire, including The miseries of human life *(1806).*

Lionel Thomas Berguer b. 1789

Alfieri, V. Philip, King of Spain. Tr Berguer 1809.
Stanzas, inscribed to Walter Scott, Esq. Edinburgh and London 1815.
Trifles in verse, including some experiments in Latin rhyme. Edinburgh and London 1817.
Stanzas to the queen, with other verses. 1820.
Edited The British essayists *(1823, 45 vols) and wrote on literature and politics.*

John Richard Best, later John Richard Digby Beste 1806–85

Cuma, the warrior-bard of Erin and other poems. 1829.
Satires and the beggar's coin: a poem. 1831, 1845 (as The beggar's coin, or love in Italy).
Author of a number of novels and memoirs and of some religious prose.

Mary Matilda Betham 1776–1852

Collections
The lay of Marie and Vignettes in verse. Ed D. H. Reiman, New York and London 1978 (facs reprint of 1816 and 1818).
Poems and elegies. Ed D. H. Reiman, New York and London 1978 (facs reprint of 1808 and 1797).

§1
Elegies and other smaller poems. Ipswich and London [1797].
Poems. 1808.
The lay of Marie: a poem. 1816; Poole 1996 (facs reprint).
Vignettes, in verse. 1818.
See also col 2083.

Elizabeth Beverley, Mrs R. fl. 1819–28

A poetical olio. 1819.
Entertaining and moral poems, on various subjects .... [1826?] (4 edns).
Entertaining moral poems, on a variety of subjects. 1826 (2nd edn).
The actress's ways and means .... [1820?], 1822 (4th edn), 1822 (6th edn), [1823?] (10th edn), 1823 (12th edn).
The book of variety .... 1823, 1824 (5th edn). Prose and verse.
A new dish of all sorts, containing original songs, poems .... 1824 (3rd edn).
The bee, containing letters ... to ... Poll Curious. 1827.
Useful subjects in prose and verse. 1828 (4th ed).
Reflections. 1829. Prose.
Pbd miscellaneous prose.

John Laurens Bicknell, the younger fl. 1820–4

The modern church: a satirical poem .... 1820.
Original miscellanies in prose and verse. London and Edinburgh 1820.
Psalms and hymns .... Ed [Bicknell] 1811.
Psalms selected for the service of the church. Ed Bicknell, Greenwich 1821, 1822.
The hour of trial: a tragedy. 1824.

John Bidlake 1755–1814

Elegy written on the author's revisiting the place of his former residence. 1788. Anon.
Elegy supposed to be written .... Plymouth 1790 (2nd edn).
Poems. Plymouth, London and Exeter 1794; London 1794.
The sea: a poem .... 1796.
The country parson: a poem. 1797.
Eugenio, or the precepts of Prudentius: a moral tale. 1799. Prose.
The summer's eve: a poem. 1800.
Virginia, or the fall of the decemvirs: a tragedy. 1800.
Youth: a poem. 1802.
The poetical works. 1804 (2nd ed).
The year: a poem. 1813.
Author of religious prose.

James Bird, of Yoxford 1788–1839

Collections
Three very interesting letters ... by Clare, Cowper and Bird. Great Totham 1837 (priv ptd).
Selections from the poems .... Ed (with memoir) by T. Harral [1840].

§1
Festival song. [1814.] Anon.
The vale of Slaughden: a poem in five cantos. Halesworth 1819; London 1819.
Machin, or the discovery of Madeira: a poem. 1821, 1831.
Cosmo, Duke of Tuscany: a tragedy .... 1822.
[B. Barton and W. Fletcher.] A short account of Leiston Abbey. With ... verses. Ed Bird 1823.
Poetical memoirs, The exile: a tale. 1823, 1824, 1833.
Dunwich: a tale of the splendid city, in four cantos. 1828.
Framlingham: a narrative of the castle, in four cantos. 1831.
The emigrant's tale: a poem ... and miscellaneous poems. 1833, 1835.
The smuggler's daughter: a drama. 1836 (2 edns).
Francis Abbott, the recluse of Niagara and Metropolitan sketches, 2nd ser. 1837.
Rhyming letter. 1837.

Mary Bishop, of Liverpool fl. 1812–13

Poetic tales and miscellanies. Liverpool and London 1812; London and Dublin 1813 (as St Oswald, and other poetic tales and miscellanies). Anon.

Joseph Blacket 1786–1810

Collections
Specimens of the poetry of ... Blacket, with an account of his life. Ed S. J. Pratt. 1809.
The remains of ... Blacket, consisting of poems .... Ed S. J. Pratt 2 vols 1811.

§1
The times: an ode .... 1809.

Anne Blanchard fl. 1822–3

Midnight reflections and other poems. 1822, 1823.

Rev Robert Bland 1779?–1825

Translations chiefly from the Greek anthology.... Tr [Bland and J. H. Merivale], London, Cambridge and Oxford 1806, 1813 (as Collections from the Greek anthology), 1833.
Edwy and Elgiva, and Sir Everard.... 1808, 1809.
The four slaves of Cythera: a romance. 1809.
Also wrote on classical prosody.

Robert Bloomfield 1766–1823

Bibliographies
Cranbrook, Earl of, and J. Hadfield. Some uncollected authors, 20: Bloomfield. BC 8 1959.

Collections
The poems of Bloomfield [i.e. The farmer's boy and rural tales]. Burlington NJ 1803, Wilmington DE 1803 (as The farmer's boy; Rural tales etc).
The poems of Bloomfield. 2 vols 1809. With prefaces by Bloomfield.
Collected poems. 2 vols 1817.
The poems of Bloomfield. New York 1821, 3 vols 1827, 1 vol 1831, 1835, Halifax 1847.
Poems by Bloomfield, The farmer's boy (illustrated). 1845.
The farmer's boy, and other poems. Philadelphia 1847.
Poetical works. Ed W. B. Rands [1855].
Poetical works. Illustr Birket Foster 1857, 1864.
The poetical works of Bloomfield and Henry Kirke White. 1871. Miles 1.
A selection of poems. Ed R. Gant 1947.

§1

The farmer's boy: a rural poem. Ed C. Lofft 1800 (3 edns), 1801, New York 1801, Philadelphia 1801, Leipzig 1801, Baltimore 1803, New York 1803 (5th Amer edn), Paris 1804, London 1827 (15th Br edn), Glasgow 1828, Boston 1877, Darlington 1898, London 1941; tr Latin 1801 (in part), 1804 (complete), Fr 1802.
Rural tales, ballads and songs. 1802, 1802, New York 1802, London 1803, Leipzig 1803, Paris 1804, London 1806, 1826 (10th edn).
Good tidings, or news from the farm: a poem. 1804.
Wild flowers: or pastoral and local poetry. 1806, Philadelphia 1806, London 1809, 1816, 1819, 1826.
Nature's music: consisting of extracts from several authors, in honour of the harp of Aeolus. 1808.
The banks of Wye: a poem. 1811, Philadelphia 1812, London 1813, 1823.
The history of little Davy's new hat. 1815, 1817, Paris 1818, London 1824; ed W. Bloomfield 1878; tr Fr 1818.
May day with the muses. 1822, 1822.
Hazelwood-hall: a village drama. 1823. In prose.
The remains of Bloomfield. [Ed J. Weston] 2 vols 1824.

Letters
Selections from the correspondence of Bloomfield. Ed W. H. Hart 1870.

§2

Views in Suffolk, Norfolk and Northamptonshire, illustrative of the works of Robert Bloomfield. 1806, 1818. With memoir by E. W. Brayley.
Hudson, W. H. A foot in England. 1909. Ch 24.
Fairchild, A. H. R. Robert Bloomfield. SP 16 1919.
Unwin, R. The rural muse. 1954. Ch 5.

Luke Booker 1762–1833

Poems on subjects sacred, moral and entertaining. Wolverhampton 1785.
The highlanders: a poem. Stourbridge [1787].
Miscellaneous poems. Stourbridge '1789' [1790]; London 1791, 1794.
Select psalms and hymns. Ed Booker, Dudley 1796 (2nd edn), 1813, 1823.
Malvern: a descriptive and historical poem. Dudley, London, Worcester, Birmingham, etc, 1798.
The hop-garden: a didactic poem. Newport, Salop and London [1799].
Calista, or a picture of modern life: a poem. 1803.
Poems, inscribed to... Lord Viscount Dudley.... 1803.
Tobias: a poem in three parts. 1804, 1805.
Millhouse, R. Blossoms... A selection of sonnets.... Ed Booker 1823 (2 edns).
Tributes to the dead, consisting of... epitaphs, many of them original. 1830. Verse and prose.
The champion of Cyrus: a drama in five acts. Dudley 1831.
The springs of Plynlimmon: a poem.... Wolverhampton 1834.
Author of religious and topographical prose.

Sir Alexander Boswell, also 'Simon Gray' 1775–1822

Collections
Frondes caducae. 7 vols [Auchinleck] 1816–18. Verse and prose (reprints).
The poetical works. Ed R. H. Smith, Glasgow 1871. With memoir. Rogers 2.

§1

Songs chiefly in the Scottish dialect. Edinburgh 1802, 1803. Anon.
The spirit of Tintoc: a ballad. Edinburgh 1803. Anon.
Epistle to the Edinburgh reviewers. Edinburgh 1803. Anon.
Edinburgh: or the ancient royalty, by 'Simon Gray'. Edinburgh 1810.
Sir Albion: a fragment. [Edinburgh? 1811]. Anon.
Clan-Alpin's vow: a fragment. Edinburgh 1811, 1817 (priv ptd).
The tyrant's fall: a poem on Waterloo. Auchinleck 1815.
Skeldon haughs, or the sow is flitted. Auchinleck 1816. Anon.
The woo-creel, or the bill o' Bashan. By [A. B.]. Auchinleck 1816. Anon.
Songs in the justiciary opera, by C– M– and B– I. C. C. Auchinleck 1816. With 'interpolations' by Boswell.
Song for the Harveian anniversary. Edinburgh 1816.
The election: a new song. [Edinburgh 1820?].
Elegiac ode to the memory of Dr Harvey. [Edinburgh 1821], 1824 (in A. Duncan, Tribute of regard to the memory of Sir H. Raeburn).

Jane Bourne, Mrs b. c. 1794

Northern reminiscences. Whitehaven 1832.
A companion to the Noah's ark, being conversations.... Swaffham 1833. Prose and verse.
Granny's history of England in rhyme. [1871].
Author of prose fiction for children.

Caroline Anne Bowles, later Southey 1786–1854

Collections of letters in the NLS (Blackwoods Coll), Houghton Lib, Harvard, Rochester Univ Lib. Ms notebook in BL.

Collections and selections
Gems selected from the poems of Caroline Bowles. Boston 1836.
Autumn flowers, and other poems. Boston and New York 1844, Boston 1845, Auburn 1848 (as The floral wreath of autumn flowers, by Mrs Southey) (4th edn).
Mrs Southey's (Caroline Bowles) poems. New York [1846?].
The select literary works, prose and verse, of Mrs Caroline Southey. Hartford CT 1851.
The poetical works of Caroline Bowles Southey. 1867.

Selection. In The poets and poetry of the century, ed A. H. Miles, enlarged edn 1905–7, vol 8, Joanna Baillie to Jean Ingelow.

§1

Ellen Fitzarthur: a metrical tale. 1820, 1822. Anon.

The widow's tale and other poems. 1822. Anon. Verse.
REVIEW: Blackwood's Mag 11, Mar 1822.

Solitary hours. Edinburgh 1826 (anon), 1839, New York 1846, 1847. Prose and verse.

Chapters on churchyards. 2 vols Edinburgh 1829 (anon), 1 vol 1841, New York 1842. First pbd in Blackwood's Edinburgh Mag Apr 1824–May 1829.

The cat's tail, being the history of Childe Merlin: a tale by the Baroness de Katzleben. Edinburgh 1831. Verse, illustr George Cruikshank.

Tales of the factories. 1833. Anon. Verse.

The birth-day: a poem in three parts, to which are added occasional verses. Edinburgh 1836, New York 1845, London 1849.
REVIEWS: Athenaeum 2 July 1836; Spectator 9, 23 July 1836; (John Wilson) Blackwood's Mag 41, Mar 1837.

The early called, the stoic, and the Lansbys of Lansby Hall. Philadelphia 1836. Only the first story by Bowles; first pbd in Blackwood's Mag 37, Jan–Feb 1835.

The smuggler. In The tale book, Konigsberg 1859.

Devereux Hall. In Tales from Blackwood vol 2 [1861], rptd from Blackwood's Mag 32, Oct 1832.

La petite Madelaine. In Tales from Blackwood vol 3, 1861, rptd from Blackwood's Mag 30, Aug 1831.

Harmless Johnny; or, the poor outcast of reason. Ed Dora Greenwell 1868.

The young greyhead; a tale of the ford. New York '1865' [1868]. First appeared in Blackwood's Mag 53, Feb 1843, rptd in Knickerbocker Jan 1848, misattributed to Thomas Miller, 1807–74.

Collaborative works

The life of the Rev Andrew Bell. 3 vols, the first vol by R. Southey ed Mrs Southey, 1844.

Robin Hood: a fragment, by the late Robert Southey and Caroline Southey, with other fragments and poems by R. S. and C. S. Edinburgh 1847.

Contributions to periodicals

See Gen Index of Blackwood's Mag *vols 1–50 (1855) for list of contributions by* 'C'.

To the author of 'The shepherd's calendar' [James Hogg]. Blackwood's Mag 15, June 1824. (By E.)

The seven temptations, by Mary Howitt. Blackwood's Mag 37, Apr 1835. Review.

Fanny Fairfield [in 3 pts]. Blackwood's Mag 39, Feb–Apr 1836. (By A.)

Letters

The correspondence of Robert Southey with Caroline Bowles. Ed E. Dowden, Dublin 1881.

The correspondence of Caroline Anne Bowles Southey to Mary Anne Watts Hughes. 99 letters ed in typescript by V. L. Schonert as Harvard PhD thesis 1957, from Houghton Lib at Harvard.

Misattributed works

All of the following are by Mrs Amelia Gillespie Smyth

Probation, and other tales. 1828.

Tales of the moors; or, rainy days in Ross-shire. 1828.

Olympia Morata, her times, life and writings. 1834.

Sundays at home; or, home happiness for young people. 1834.

Selwyn in search of a daughter, and other tales. 1835.

§2

Coleridge, H. N. Modern English poetesses. Quart Rev 66 1840.

Obits. Athenaeum 5 Aug 1854 (DNB attribs to T. K. Hervey); GM Sep 1854.

Robert Southey's second wife. Cornhill Mag 30, July–Dec 1874. Signed E. O. [Eleanor Orlebar].

R. G. [Richard Garnett]. In DNB (under Southey).

Bowles, C. A. In The feminist companion to literature in English, ed V. Blain, P. Clements and I. Grundy, 1990.

Courtney, J. In her Adventurous thirties, Oxford 1933.

Blain, V. Caroline Bowles Southey 1786–1854: the making of a woman writer. Aldershot 1998. [VB]

Sir John Bowring 1792–1872

Collections

Miles 10 (11).

God and other poems. Tr Bowring, ed M. S. L. Parr, Boston [1912]. Anon.

§1

Observations on the state of religion and literature in Spain. 1819.

Specimens of the Russian poets, with preliminary remarks and biographical notices. 1820, 1821; Boston 1822; 2 pts London 1821–3 (enlarged).

Matins and vespers, with hymns and occasional devotional pieces. 1823, 1824 (enlarged); Boston 1827; London 1841 ('altered and enlarged'); Boston 1844; London 1851; Boston 1853, 1854, 1861, 1868; London 1895.

Batavian anthology, or specimens of the Dutch poets, with remarks on the poetical literature and language of the Netherlands to the end of the seventeenth century. 1824. With H. S. Van Dyk.

Peter Schlemihl, from the German of 'La Motte Fouqué' [i.e. of Chamisso]. 1824 (illustr G. Cruikshank), 1861 (3rd edn), 1910 (illustr G. Browne); Philadelphia [1929] (illustr J. Gincano).

Ancient poetry and romances of Spain, selected and translated. 1824.

Hymns. 1825.

Servian popular poetry translated. 1827; ed B. L. Stanoyevich, Boston [1920] (as An anthology of Jugoslav poetry).

Specimens of the Polish poets, with notes and observations on the literature of Poland. 1827.

Sketch of the language and literature of Holland, being a sequal [*sic*] to his Batavian anthology. Amsterdam 1829; tr Du 1829. Rptd from Foreign Quart Rev 4 1829. Prose.

Brieven van John Bowring, geschreven op eene reize door Holland, Friesland en Groningen. Leeuwarden 1830. Partly tr from letters to the Morning Herald 1828, with sketch of Friesian literature tr from Foreign Quart Rev 3 1829. Prose.

Poetry of the Magyars, preceded by a sketch of the language and literature of Hungary and Transylvania. 1830. Verse and prose.

Cheskian anthology, being a history of the poetical literature of Bohemia with translated specimens. 1832. Prose and verse.

Minor morals for young people, illustrated in tales and travels, with engravings by G. Cruikshank and W. Heath. 3 pts London and Edinburgh 1834–9. Prose.

Manuscript of the queen's court: a collection of old Bohemian lyrics – epic songs, with other ancient Bohemian poems. Prague 1843.

The press, written for . . . the opening of the Barker steam press and other poetry. [Wortley 1846.]

The kingdom and people of Siam, with a narrative of a mission to that country in 1855. 2 vols 1857; New York 1975; ed D. K. Wyatt, Kuala Lumpur and London 1969 (reprint of 1857). Prose.

A visit to the Philippine Islands. 1859; tr Du 1861, Sp 1876. Prose.

Ode to the deity, translated from the Russian of [G. R.] Derzhavin. [1861.]

Translations from A. [i.e. S.] Petöfi, the Magyar poet. London and Hertford 1866.

Hwa tsien ki, the flowery scroll: a Chinese novel. 1868. Prose.

The oak: original tales and sketches. Ed C. Rogers [1869]. Prose.

A memorial volume of sacred poetry, to which is prefixed a memoir of the author by Lady Bowring. 1873.
Autobiographical recollections, with a brief memoir by L. B. Bowring. 1877. Prose.
Edited Westminster Rev *(1824–36), and Bentham's* Collected works *(1838–43), and pbd numerous works on public affairs.*

§2

Beer, R. Korrespondence J. Bowringa do Cech. Prague 1904.
Chudoba, F. Listy psané, J. Bowringovi ve vecech ceské, a slovanské, literatury. Prague 1912.
Filipovic, R. Bowring i Kopitar. Slavisticna. Revija (Ljubljana) vol 4 1951.
Bartle, G. F. An old radical and his brood. 1994.

Henry Boyd d. 1832

A translation of the Inferno of Dante Alighieri .... Tr Boyd 2 vols Dublin 1785.
Poems chiefly dramatic and lyric. Dublin 1793, 1796.
The divina commedia of Dante Alighieri .... Tr Boyd 3 vols 1802.
Monti, V. The penance of Hugo: a vision .... Tr Boyd 1805.
The woodman's tale after the manner of Spenser .... 1805, 1807.
Compositions ... from the divine poem of Dante Alighieri .... Tr Boyd 1807.
The triumphs of Petrarch .... Tr Boyd 1807; ed G. Biagi, Cambridge MA and London 1906; San Francisco 1927.
Contributed criticism to Milton Poetical works *1809 and 1826.*

Hugh Stuart Boyd 1781–1848

Luceria: a tragedy. 1806.
Select poems of Synesius and G. Nazianzen, to which are added some original poems. Tr Boyd 1814.
The Agamemnon of Aeschylus. Tr Boyd 1823.
Thoughts on an illustrious exile ... the prosecution of the protestants in 1815, with other poems. 1825.
[St Gregory.] Tributes to the dead in a series of ancient epitaphs. Tr Boyd 1826.
A Malvern tale, with other poems. 1827.
Also wrote on theological topics and translated selections from the church fathers.

Barbarina Brand née Ogle later Wilmot, Lady Dacre 1789–1819

The MS of Brand's play Ina *is held in the Larpent Coll, Huntington. MSS of 1838, including a sonnet to the Queen and trns from Italian poets are held by Lambeth Palace Lib, London, For other MSS holdings, see LR1 pp 275–6.*

Collection

Dramas, translations and occasional poems. 2 vols 1821, micros New York 1970 and Bethlehem PA 1995 (for Univ of California, Davis). The four dramas are: Gonzalvo de Cordova, Pedarias: a tragic drama, Ina: a tragedy (with original ending and cuts from stage version restored), and Xarifa: a tragic drama. The trns from Petrarch were rptd in Ugo Foscolo's Essays on Petrarch, 1823.

§1

Ina: a tragedy (stage version). 1815 (3 edns; 3rd is rptd from 2nd with new title page). Micro of 2nd edn New York 1966. Produced at Drury Lane by R. B. Sheridan 22 Apr 1815.
Frogs and bulls: a Lilliputian piece in three acts. 1838 (50 copies), micro Louisville KY 1973.

Translations

Le canzoni di Petrarca. [1815?] (priv ptd). With trns.
Due canzoni del Petrarca. Rome 1818 (priv ptd). With trns.
[Due canzoni del Petrarca.] Naples 1819 (priv ptd). With trns.
Traduzioni dall'italiano de Barbarina Lady Dacre. 1836 (priv ptd, 150 copies), micro Bethlehem PA 1994 (for Univ of California, Davis, with title Translations from the Italian).

Editions

[Sullivan, Arabella] (Brand's daughter). Recollections of a chaperon. Ed Lady Dacre. 3 vols 1833 (2 edns), 2 vols New York 1833, 1 vol 1849 (Bentley's Standard Novels no 114).
[Sullivan, Arabella.] Tales of the peerage and the peasantry. Ed Lady Dacre. 3 vols 1835 (2 edns), 2 vols New York 1835, 1 vol 1849 (Bentley's Standard Novels no 117), 1 vol [1859] (Parlour Lib vol 190).

§2

Obituary. Annual Register 1854.
Obituary. Athenaeum 20 May 1854.
Boase, F. In Modern English biography, vol 1, 1892.
Cooper, Thompson. DNB.
A family chronicle derived from notes and letters selected by Barbarina, the Hon Lady Grey [Brand's granddaughter]. Ed Gertrude Lyster 1908. Includes some verse fables and occasional verse not pbd before. [JW]

Matthew Bridges 1800–94

Jerusalem regained: a poem. 1825.
Protestant and catholic, with other poems. 1827 (new edn).
Babbicombe, or visions of memory, with other poems. 1842.
Hymns of the heart, for the use of catholics. [1848]; London and Dublin [1851].
The passion of Jesus. 1852.
Numerous, mainly religious, pbns in prose.

'Arthur Brooke'

See John Chalk Claris, below.

Brian Broughton 1767?–1838

Four picturesque views in North Wales .... 1798, 1801 (as Six picturesque views).
Copse-grove hill, or reflections in blank verse .... 1829.

Henry Brown fl. 1830–5

The mechanic's Saturday night ... By a mechanic. 1830. Anon.
Sunday: a poem in three cantos. 1835. Anon.
Also wrote on the cotton industry.

John Brown, of Great Yarmouth, also 'Mandanis' fl. 1806–21

Psyche, or the soul: a poem in seven cantos. 1818.
The stage: a poem. 1819, 1820.
Legitimacy: a poem, or Leonard and Louisa. 1820.
Patronage: a poem ... By 'Mandanis'. 1820.
Wrote on Scandinavian history and pbd other miscellaneous prose.

Mary Ann Brown or Browne, later Gray 1812–44

Mont Blanc and other poems. 1827.
Ada and other poems. 1828 (3 edns).
Repentance and other poems. 1829.
The coronal: original poems, sacred and miscellaneous. London and Liverpool 1833, 1835, London [1844].
The birth-day gift. London and Liverpool 1834, 1837.

Ignatia and other poems. London and Liverpool 1838.
Sacred poetry. 1840.
Sketches from the antique and other poems. Dublin 1844.
Author of a number of songs pbd with accompaniments.

John Bull, curate of Clipston fl. 1814–32

Poems and translations. 1814.
Devotional hymns . . . for public worship . . . 1827.
Also pbd sermons and religious works for the young.

Agnes Bulmer, formerly Collinson 1775–1836

§1

Thoughts on a future state, occasioned by the death of Mrs Rogers . . . Also an elegy. By a young lady. Birmingham 1795. Anon. With another 'young lady'.
Messiah's kingdom: a poem in twelve books. 1833; New York 1833.
Memoirs of Mrs Elizabeth Mortimer. 1836 (2 edns). Prose.
Scripture histories. 6 pts 1837–8. Prose.

§2

Collinson, A. R. Memoir of Mrs A. Bulmer . . . Mrs Bulmer's last poem . . . . 1837.
Select letters. Ed W. M. Bunting. 1842.

John Bulmer fl. 1821–35

Prichard, R. The vicar of Llandovery . . . . Tr Bulmer, Haverfordwest 1821; London 1830 (as Beauties of the vicar of Llandovery).
Hymns, original and select . . . . 1835.
Author of religious prose.

Sir James Bland Burges, after 1821 Sir James Lamb, also 'Alfred', 'Versus' 1752–1824

§1

Heroic epistle from Serjeant Bradshaw in the shades to John Dunning. 1780. Anon.
Considerations on the law of insolvency. 1783. Prose.
A letter to the Earl of Effingham. 1783. Prose.
Address to the country gentlemen of England. 1789. Prose.
Letters . . . on the Spanish aggression at Nootka 1790. Signed 'Verus'. Prose.
Narrative of the negociation between France and Spain in 1790. [1790?] Prose.
The birth and triumph of love. 1796, 1822, 1823; ed D. H. Reiman, New York and London 1978 (in Miscellaneous verse, with others, facs reprint).
Richard the First: a poem in eighteen books. 2 vols 1801 (anon); ed D. H. Reiman, New York and London 1977 (facs reprint, attributed).
The exodiad. 1807. By the authors of Calvary and Richard the First. With R. Cumberland.
Riches, or the wife and brother: a play. 1810 (2 edns); New York 1810; Philadelphia 1810; London 1814; ed 'D. G.' (George Daniel) 1826 (Cumberland's British Theatre vol 24), 1830, 1886 (in Dicks's Standard Plays no 717). Prose.
Songs, duets, etc. In Tricks upon travellers. 1810 (2 edns). Anon.
Dramas. 2 vols 1817.
The dragon knight: a poem in twelve cantos. 1818; ed D. H. Reiman, New York and London 1977 (facs reprint).
Reasons in favour of a new translation of the holy scriptures. 1819. Prose.
Burges, M. A. The progress of the pilgrim good-intent. Ed Burges 1814 (9th edn), 1822 (10th edn). Prose.
An enquiry into the procrastination attributed to the House of Lords. 1824. Prose.

§2

Selections from the letters and correspondence. Ed J. Hutton 1885.
His letters by 'Alfred' contributed to The Sun *were issued as vols in 1792 and 1793; he also wrote several political and legal works.*

William Burt 1778–1826

Carrington, N. T. Dartmoor: a descriptive poem . . . . Ed Burt, London and Devonport 1826; London 1826.
Christianity: a poem in three books . . . . Ed. T. S. Burt 1835 (with a memoir).
Author of works on politics and commerce.

Hans Busk, the elder 1772–1862

Fugitive pieces in verse. 1814.
The banquet, in three cantos. 1819 (anon), 1820 (acknowledged).
The dessert: a poem . . . By the author of The banquet. 1819 (anon), 1820 (acknowledged).
The vestriad: a poem. 1819, 1820.
The lay of life: a poem. 1834.
Hebrew lyrics. By an octogenarian. 1859. Anon.
Maiden hours and maiden wiles. [1869] (illustr 'Beaujolais'), [1872]. Anon.

George Gordon Byron, 6th Baron Byron 1788–1824

Manuscripts

The IELM, vol 4 pt 1 1982, contains an extensive listing of mss. Lord Byron. The complete poetical works, *ed McGann and Weller (see below), gives the locations of all poetry mss in the relevant sections of its notes.* Letters and journals of Lord Byron, *ed Marchand (see below), lists ms locations in each vol.* Lord Byron. The complete miscellaneous prose, *ed Nicholson (see below), also notes the locations of all mss.*

Manuscripts in photo-facsimile

Levine, A. and J. J. McGann (ed). Lord Byron, vol 1, Poems 1807–1818, in Manuscripts of the younger romantics 1986 reproduces the mss of Imitation of Martial VI 34, Manfred, Beppo, Mazeppa and Venice an ode, 4 lines from Oscar of Alva, and a galley-proof of Hints from Horace.
Levine, A. and J. J. McGann (ed). Lord Byron, vol 2, Don Juan cantos i–v, in Manuscripts of the younger romantics 1985 reproduces the rough mss of Don Juan cantos i–v.
Levine, A. and J. J. McGann (ed). Lord Byron, vol 3, Poems 1819–1822, in Manuscripts of the younger romantics 1988 reproduces the rough mss of To the Po, The prophecy of Dante, Stanzas ('Could love live for ever'), Morgante Maggiore, Francesca of Rimini, Marino Faliero, Werner, and Stanzas to a hindoo air.
Levine, A. and J. J. McGann (ed). Lord Byron, vol 4, Miscellaneous poems, in Manuscripts of the younger romantics 1988 reproduces the mss of The Edinburgh ladies' petition to Doctor Moyes, and his reply, Farewell! if ever fondest prayer, The corsair, The castled crag of Drachenfels from Childe Harold iii, Don Juan xiii, 6 pages from the Galignani edn of Don Juan i and ii, with Byron's annotations, and Byron's own annotated copy of Fugitive pieces.
Nicholson, A. (ed). Lord Byron, vol 5, Don Juan cantos vi–vii. Manuscripts of the younger romantics 1989 reproduces the rough mss of Don Juan cantos vi and vii, with facing transcripts.
Erdman, D. with the assistance of D. Worrall (ed). Lord Byron, vol 6, Childe Harold's pilgrimage; a critical, composite edition, in Manuscripts of the younger romantics 1991 reproduces much of the rough and fair-copy mss of Childe Harold cantos i–iv, with transcripts.

Burnett, T. A. J. (ed). Lord Byron, vol 7, Childe Harold's pilgrimage canto iii, in Manuscripts of the younger romantics 1988 reproduces the rough ms of Childe Harold iii, from the Scrope Davies papers, with facing selected transcript.
Nicholson, A. (ed). Lord Byron, vol 8, Don Juan cantos iii–iv, Manuscripts of the younger romantics 1992 reproduces the fair-copy mss of Don Juan cantos iii and iv, with facing transcripts.
Nicholson, A. (ed). Lord Byron, vol 9, Don Juan cantos x, xi, xii and xvii, Manuscripts of the younger romantics 1993 reproduces the rough mss of Don Juan cantos x, xi, xii, and the fragment of canto xvii, with facing transcripts.
Nicholson, A. (ed). Lord Byron, vol 10, Don Juan cantos xiv and xv, in Manuscripts of the younger romantics 1995 reproduces the rough mss of Don Juan cantos xiv and xv, with facing transcripts.
Giuliano, C. F. (ed). Lord Byron, vol 11, Don Juan canto viii, drafts of early stanzas of cantos iii and ix, in Manuscripts of the younger romantics 1997 reproduces the rough mss of Don Juan canto viii and of the Wellington stanzas from canto ix, plus the rough draft of Ode to Napoleon Bonaparte.
Cochran, P. (ed). Lord Byron, vol 13, The prisoner of Chillon and Don Juan canto ix, in Manuscripts of the younger romantics 1995 reproduces the rough mss of The prisoner of Chillon and Don Juan canto ix, with facing transcripts.

Manuscripts in transcription

Cameron, K. N. (ed). Shelley and his circle, 1773–1822, vol 4 1970. Contains transcript of the rough draft of Fare thee well and draft fragments of Oscar of Alva and of Greek song.
Reiman, D. H. (ed). Shelley and his circle, 1773–1822, vol 6 1973. Contains transcript of the mss of To E– N– Long, and On parting, and ms emendation of lines 884–5 of The bride of Abydos.
Reiman, D. H. (ed). Shelley and his circle, 1773–1822, vol 7 1986. Contains transcript by Doucet Devin Fischer and Ricki B. Herzfeld of the fair copy of Beppo, also of Mary Shelley's copy of To the Po, and Teresa Guiccioli's copy of Could love live for ever.
Reiman, D. H. (ed). Shelley and his circle, 1773–1822, vol 8 1986. Contains transcripts of 3 partial mss of Francesca of Rimini in the hand of Teresa Guiccioli, and 17 1820 marginalia and underlinings in an 1802 copy of Foscolo's Le ultime lettere di Jacopo Ortis, 15 not elsewhere reproduced.

Bibliographies and catalogues

Gerbel, N. V. O russkikh perevodakh iz Byrona. 5 vols St Petersburg 1864–7. At end of each vol.
Anderson, J. P. In R. Noel, Life of Lord Byron, 1890. Contains the fullest lists of musical settings and of magazine articles about Byron.
Flaischen, C. Lord Byron in Deutschland. Centralblatt für Bibliothekswesen 7 1890.
Parker, J. A. Bibliography of the works of Byron and Byroniana. In R. B. Wriothesley, Life of Byron, 1890.
Kölbing, E. Bibliographische Notizen. In The prisoner of Chillon and other poems, Weimar 1898. Also contains a list of vols of illustrations of Byron's works.
Ward, J. Collection of relics … relating to Lord Byron. Nottingham 1900.
Catalogue of the E. M. Kidd Collection. Nottingham 1903.
Lumbroso, A. Saggio di bibliografia Byroniana. In Il Generale Mengaldo, Lord Byron e l'Ode on the Star of the Legion of Honour, Rome 1903; rptd in Pagine Veneziane, Rome 1905.
Coleridge, E. H. A bibliography of the successive editions and translations of Lord Byron's poetical works. In Works of Lord Byron, Poetry vol 7, 1904. The best general bibliography of the poems.
Estève, E. Byron et le romantisme français. Paris 1907.
Churchman, P. H. The beginnings of Byronism in Spain. Revue Hispanique 23 1910. Lists Sp trns of Byron.
Morvay, G. Byron Magyarországon. In E. Koeppel, Byron forditótta Esty Jánosné, Budapest 1913.
Intze, O. Byroniana. [Birmingham 1914.]
Chew, S. C. Byron in England. New York 1924. The fullest list of Byroniana.
Griffith, R. H. and H. M. Jones. A descriptive catalogue of an exhibition of manuscripts and first editions of Lord Byron. Austin TX 1924.
Bibliographical catalogue of first editions, proof copies and manuscripts of books by Lord Byron exhibited at the fourth exhibition of the First Edition Club. 1925.
Wise, T. J. A Byron library. 1928 (priv ptd).
Choice selection … from the library of N. Egerton Leigh. Oxford 1929.
Elkin Mathews Ltd. Byron and Byroniana: a catalogue of books. 1930.
Wise, T. J. A bibliography of the writings in verse and prose of Lord Byron. 2 vols 1932–3 (priv ptd). The fullest discussion of the issues of the first edns. *See* J. Carter, TLS 27 Apr, 4 May 1933; *also* D. Cook, TLS 18 Sep 1937, and G. Pollard and J. Carter, TLS 16 Oct 1937.
Wamnes, A. B. The Astarte controversy. Madison WI 1930.
American Art Association. The library of the late Dr Roderick Terry. New York 1934.
Niccolai, B. Bibliografia di studi inglesi in Italia: Lord Byron. Bollettino di Studi Inglesi in Italia 6 1937.
Nottingham Corporation. The Roe–Byron Collection, Newstead Abbey. Nottingham 1937.
Pollard, H. G. Pirated collections of Byron. TLS 16 Oct 1937.
The romantic movement: a selective and critical bibliography. ELH 1937–49; PQ 1950–64; ELN 1965–79; New York 1980– (Garland).
Quintana, R. Byron 1788–1938: an exhibition at the Huntington Library. San Marino 1938.
Newton, A. E. Rare books. New York 1941.
C. J. Sawyer Ltd. Catalogue of rare books and manuscripts. 1946.
Steffan, T. G. Autograph letters and documents of the Byron circle at the library of the University of Texas. SE 1946. *See also* SP 43 1946 and MLQ 8 1947.
Pratt, W. W. Byron and his circle: calendar of manuscripts in the University of Texas Library. Austin TX 1948.
Chew, S. C. In English romantic poets: a review of research, ed T. M. Raysor, New York 1950, 1956 (rev).
Simkins, T., jun. The Byron collection in the rare book room of Duke University Library. Duke Univ Lib Notes 1951.
Bernbaum, E. (ed). Keats, Shelley, Byron and Hunt. A critical sketch of important books and articles concerning them published in 1940–1950. KSJ 1 1952.
Boyce, G. K. Modern literary manuscripts in the Morgan Library. PMLA 67 1952.
Pratt, W. W. Lord Byron and his circle: recent acquisitions. Univ of Texas Lib Chron 5 1956.
Hofman, A. Mss de J. J. Rousseau et de Byron à Prague. Philologica 9 1957.
Pratt, W. W. A decade of Byron scholarship 1946–1956: a selective survey. KSJ 7 1958.
Dwyer, J. T. Check list of primary sources for the Byron–Jeffrey relationship. N & Q July 1960.
Marchand, L. A. Recent Byron scholarship. In Essays in literary history presented to J. Milton French, ed R. Kirk and C. F. Main, New Brunswick NJ 1960.
Brown, T. J. English literary autographs xlii. BC 11 1962.
Jack, I. In his English literature 1815–1832. Oxford 1963.
Green, D. B. and E. G. Wilson. Keats, Shelley, Byron and their circles: a bibliography 1950–1962. Lincoln NE 1964.
Fogle, R. H. Romantic poets and prose writers. 1967.
Marshall, W. H. The Byron collection in memory of Meyer Davies jr. Univ of Pennsylvania Lib Chron 1967.

Schultz, H. C. English literary manuscripts in the Huntington Library. HLQ 31 1968.
Catalogue of books and manuscripts at the Keats–Shelley memorial house in Rome. 1969.
Elkins, A. C., jun. and I. J. Forstner. The romantic movement bibliography 1936–1970. 7 vols 1973.
British Council. Byron in Greece. 1974.
Burton, A and J. Murdoch. Byron: an exhibition. 1974.
Cooke, S. M. Byron commemoration, booklist. Nottingham 1974.
Reiman, D. H. and D. D. Fischer. Byron on the Continent. 1974.
Byron in the Gennadius Library. Athens 1975.
Leach, S. Lord Byron; a sesquicentennial exhibition catalogue. 1975.
Santucho, O. J. George Gordon Lord Byron: a comprehensive bibliography of secondary materials in English, 1807–1974, with a critical review of research by Clement Tyson Goode Jr. Metuchen NJ 1977.
Chernaik, J. and T. Burnett. The Byron and Shelley notebooks in the Scrope Davies find. RES n.s. 29, Feb 1978.
Hartley, R. A. Keats, Shelley, Byron, Hunt and their circles: a bibliography 1962–1974. Lincoln NE 1978.
Randolph, F. L. Studies for a Byron bibliography. 1979 – (incomplete).
Reiman, D. H. English romantic poetry, 1800–1835. A guide to information sources. New York 1979.
Hearn, R. B. et al. Byron criticism since 1952, a bibliography. 1980.
McGann, J. J. (introd). Lord Byron: a collection of 429 items. 1980.
Poe, C. M. Byron and Byroniana Collection at Northern Illinois University: a descriptive guide. DeKalb IL 1982.
Clubbe, J. George Gordon Lord Byron. In The English romantic poets, a review of research and criticism, ed Frank Jordan, 4th edn New York 1985. The fullest and most authoritative account pbd recently of all aspects of Byron.
Tsigakou, F.-M. Lord Byron in Greece. Athens 1987.
Kelsall, M. Byron at his bicentenary. Br Book News Sep 1988.
Burmeister, J. A collection of 300 items. 1990.
Hunter, P. D. Byron: the Harrow Collection. 1994.
Goode, C. T. George Gordon Lord Byron. A comprehensive annotated bibliography of secondary materials in English 1973–1994. Lanham MD 1997.

Concordances

Hagelman, W. and R. J. Barnes. A concordance to Don Juan. Ithaca NY 1967.
Dodson Young, I. A concordance to the poetry of Byron. Austin TX 1975.

Contemporary reviews

Hayden, J. O. The romantic reviewers 1802–1824. 1968.
Reiman, D. H. (ed). The romantics reviewed: contemporary reviews of British romantic writers, pt B: Byron and regency society poets, vols 1–5 1972.
Ward, W. S. Literary reviews in British periodicals, 1798–1826. 3 vols 1972–7.
Redpath, T. The young romantics and critical opinion 1807–1824. 1973.
Sullivan, A. British literary magazines, vol 2: the romantic age, 1789–1836. 1983.

Collections

Collections in English

The poetical works of Lord Byron.

2 vols Philadelphia 1813, 2 vols Boston 1814, 3 vols New York/Philadelphia 1815, 2 vols London 1815, 4 vols 1815 (twice), 4 vols London 1816, 3 vols Philadelphia 1816, 5 vols 1817, 1 vol New York/Philadelphia/Boston/Baltimore 1817, 8 vols London 1815–20, 6 vols Paris 1818, 6 vols Zwickau 1818–19, 13 vols Leipzig 1818–22, 3 vols London 1819, 6 vols Paris 1819, 7 vols Brussels 1819, 4 vols New York 1820, 5 vols London 1821, 5 vols Paris 1821, 16 vols Paris 1822–4 (with life by J. W. Lake), 4 vols London 1823, 12 vols Paris 1823, 12 vols Paris 1822–4 (with Life by Sir Cosmo Gordon), 8 vols Philaelphia 1824; 3 vols 1824 (the edition known as Knight and Lacey), 8 vols London 1823, 33 vols Zwickau 1824–38, 6 vols London 1825, 7 vols Paris 1825 (with life by Lake), 8 vols New York/Philadelphia 1825, 13 vols Paris 1826, 1 vol London 1826, 1 vol Paris 1826 (with life by Lake), 1 vol Frankfurt 1826, 6 vols London 1827, 1 vol Paris 1827 (with life by Lake), 1 vol Paris 1828, and facsimile of a letter from Lord Byron to the editor of Galignani's Messenger, 6 vols London 1829, 4 vols London 1829, 2 vols Philadelphia 1829 (three times), 1 vol Frankfurt 1829, 4 vols London 1830, 1 vol Paris 1830, 6 vols London 1831 (twice), 1 vol Paris 1831 (with life by Lake), 1 vol Philadelphia 1831 (with life by Lake), 8 vols Philadelphia 1831, 4 vols Paris 1832, The works of Lord Byron, with his letters and journals, and his life by Thomas Moore (poetry edited by John Wright) 17 vols 1832 vols 1–12, 1833 vols 13–17 (the earlier vols several times reprinted, inc 1835, 1837 and 1843, the life reprinted in 1 vol 1838, 6 vols 1851), 2 vols New York, 1833 (with life by F. Halleck), 1 vol Paris 1835 (with life by H. Lytton Bulwer), 4 vols Paris 1835, rpt 1840 (with life by J. Galt), 1 vol Paris 1835, 6 vols New York 1836–7 (with life by Moore), 1 vol London 1837 (twice), Frankfurt 1837, 1 vol Paris 1837 (with life by Galt), 1 vol London/Leipzig 1837 (three times), 7 vols Mannheim 1837, 1 vol 1838, 1 vol Paris 1839, Philadelphia 1839, 8 vols London 1839, 4 vols Paris 1840, 1841, 1 vol Paris 1842 with life by Bulwer, Tales, Poems and Dramas in 23 weekly parts, London 1842, 5 vols Leipzig 1842, 4 vols Philadelphia 1843 (with life by Moore), 1 vol London 1845, 1 vol Frankfurt 1846, Paris 1847, 1 vol Hartford CT 1847 (with life by Halleck), London 1848, 2 vols Edinburgh 1850 (with life by W. Anderson), 1 vol London 1850, 1 vol Philadelphia 1850, 1 vol London 1851 (with life by Bulwer), 1 vol Philadelphia 1851?? reprinted 1870 (with life by Allan Cunningham) [*see* TLS 14 June 1941], 1 vol Frankfurt 1852 (with life by Moore), 8 vols London 1853, 2 vols Philadelphia, 1853, 1854, 1 vol Boston 1854, 1 vol London (issued in parts 1854–5), 1 vol London 1854, 6 vols London 1855–6, 1 vol Edinburgh 1857 'with objectionable parts excluded', 1 vol New York 1857, 1 vol London 1857, 6 vols London 1857, 1 vol London 1859, reissued 1863, 1866, 1873, 1876 and 1883, Edinburgh 1859, 1 vol Philadelphia 1859, 1 vol Leipzig 1860, 3 vols Leipzig 1860, 1 vol Edinburgh 1861 (with life by A. Leighton), 10 vols Boston/New York/Cincinatti 1861 (with life by J. H. Lister), 1 vol Halifax 1863, 1 vol London 1863, 1865 (twice) 1866, 1867 1 vol, 1 vol Edinburgh 1868 (with life by A. Leighton), 1 vol London/New York 1868, 1 vol London 1869 (twice), Philadelphia 1869, New York 1869, 8 vols London 1870, 1 vol ed W. M. Rossetti, London 1870, Philadelphia 1870, ed Rossetti 1872, 1873, 1 vol ed W. B. Scott London 1874, 1 vol London 1874, 1 vol Boston 1874, London 1876, 1 vol London 1878, 1 vol Boston 1878, 1 vol ed Rossetti London 1878, 1 vol London 1881, 1 vol London/Edinburgh 1881, ed Rossetti and T. Seccombe 1882, 1 vol introd Scott London 1883 (twice), 3 vols London 1883, 12 vols London 1885, 1 vol New York c. 1886, 3 vols London 1886, 1 vol ed M. Blind, London 1886, 1887, 2 vols Edinburgh/Glasgow 1888, 1 vol New York 1889?, 1 vol introd Scott, London 1890, 1 vol new York c. 1890, 12 vols London 1891–2, 3 vols London 1892, 12 vols Philadelphia 1892, 1 vol Philadelphia 1895, 4 vols London/New York 1896, 1 vol London c. 1897, 1 vol Edinburgh 1897, 4 vols Philadelphia 1897, 1 vol London no date, 1 vol [?] New York no date, 1 vol New York no date, 1 vol London ed W. E. Henley (no more vols published). 13 vols London 1898–1904 (a new revised and enlarged edition: poetry, ed E. H. Coleridge 7 vols; Letters and journals, ed R. E. Prothero 6 vols), 1 vol London ed Coleridge 1905, 1 vol ed Page, Oxford 1904, rev J. D. Jump, Oxford 1960, 1 vol ed P. E. More, New York/Boston 1905, reprinted 1975 with introd R. F. Gleckner, 3 vols 1906, ed W. P. Trent 1910, ed Rossetti and Seccombe 1911, ed N. H. Dole, New York 1927.

Collected Poetry and Plays 1975–

Poems, ed P. E. More, introd R. F. Gleckner. 1975. Text rptd from 1905.

Lord Byron. The complete poetical works vol I ed J. J. McGann (1980).

Lord Byron. The complete poetical works vol II ed J. J. McGann (1980).

Lord Byron. The complete poetical works vol III ed J. J. McGann (1981).

Lord Byron. The complete poetical works vol IV ed J. J. McGann and B. Weller (1986, reissued with corrections 1992).

Lord Byron. The complete poetical works vol V ed J. J. McGann (1986, re-issued with corrections 1992).

Lord Byron. The complete poetical works vol VI ed J. J. McGann and B. Weller (1991).

Lord Byron. The complete poetical works vol VII ed J. J. McGann with a thematic index by C. B. Pearson (1993).

Collected Prose

Lord Byron. Selected prose. Ed P. Gunn 1972.

Lord Byron. The complete miscellaneous prose. Ed A. Nicholson 1991.

Translations of collections

French By 'A. E. de Chastopalli' (Amédée Pichot and Eusèbe de Salle) 10 vols Paris 1819–21, 5 vols 1820–2, 15 vols 1821–4, 8 vols 1822–5; Œuvres nouvelles 10 vols Paris 1824, 13 vols 1823–4, 20 vols 1827–31 (6th edn), 6 vols 1830, 1830–5, 1836, 1 vol 1837, 1842 (11th edn). By P. Paris 3 vols Paris 1827, 13 vols 1830–2, 1835. By B. Laroche 4 vols Paris 1836–7; 1 vol 1837, 1838, 4 vols 1840–1, 1 vol 1842, 4 vols 1847, 1850–1. By O. Hunter and P. Ramé 2 vols Paris 1841–2, 3 vols 1845. By L. Barré Paris 1856. By 'Daniel le Sueur' (J. Loiseau) 2 vols Paris 1891–2.

German By J. Körner, W. Reinhold, H. Döring, A. Schumann and C. K. Meissner 31 vols Zwickau 1821–8. By G. N. Bärmann, O. L. B. Wolff, K. L. Kannegiesser, A. Hungari, P. von Haugwitz, P. A. G. von Meyer and J. V. Adrian 12 vols Frankfurt 1830–1, 1837. By G. Pfizer 4 vols Stuttgart 1836–9, 1 vol 1851. By E. Ortlepp, F. Kottenkamp, H. Kurtz, – Duttenhofer, – Bardili and B. von Guseck 10 vols Stuttgart 1839, Pforzheim 1842, Stuttgart 1845, 1846, 12 vols Stuttgart 1856. By A. Böttger, 1 vol Leipzig 1840, 1841, 12 vols 1842, 1 vol 1844, 1845, 12 vols 1847, 1850, 8 vols 1854, 8 vols 1864, 1901. Ed O. Gildemeister 6 vols Berlin 1864, 1866, 1877, 1888. By A. Neidhart 8 vols Berlin 1865. By W. Schäffer, A. H. Janert, W. Gruezmacher, H. Stadelmann and A. Strodtmann 7 vols Hildeburghausen 1865–72. By A. Seubert 3 vols Leipzig [1874]. By A. Schröter 6 vols Stuttgart 1885–90. By H. Tuckermann 8 vols Stuttgart 1886. By E. Kölbing, Weimar 1896 (vols 1–2 only). Complete poetical works tr O. Gildemeister and A. Neidhart, A. Seubert et al, rev and ed S. Schmitz, 3 vols Munich 1977–8.

Italian By Carlo Rusconi 2 vols Padua 1842. By G. Gazzino, G. Nicolini, P. Isola, P. Rossi, A. Maffei, M. Mazzoni and P. G. B. Cereseto, Naples 1853. By G. de Stefano, Naples 1857. By P. Perrone, Naples 1886, 1891.

Modern Greek 3 vols Athens 1895 (anon).

Polish By B. M. Wolff, St Petersburg 1857 (vol 1 only, containing Childe Harold). By P. Chmielowski, Warsaw 1895.

Romanian Works, introd by D. Grigorescu and L.-M. Pop, Bucharest 1985. Works, 3 vols tr A. Covaci, P. Soloman, V. Teodorescu, S. Avadanci et al, Bucharest 1985–7.

Russian By N. V. Gerbel, M. Y. Lermontov, A. Pushkin, V. Jukovsky, K. Batiushkov, D. Minaev, I. Turgenev, L. Meya, P. Kozlov, I. Kozlov, N. Zorin et al 5 vols St Petersburg 1864–6, 4 vols 1874–7, 3 vols 1883–4. By P. I. Veinberg, St Petersburg 1876. By S. A. Vengerov (ed), V. Mazurkevitch, P. S. Kogan, S. A. Ilyin, A. M. Federov et al 2 vols St Petersburg 1904–5. Works, 3 vols tr O. Afonina, M. Kurginian and W. Levik, Moscow 1974.

Spanish Madrid 1880 (anon), 1898. By F. G. Pales 5 vols Madrid 1930–1.

Swedish By 'Talis Qualis' (C. W. A. Strandberg) 8 vols Stockholm 1854–6.

Ukrainian By K. Gumbert and A. Bogaevskoi, Kiev 1904.

Partial collections in English

Tales. 2 vols 1837, 1 vol Halifax 1845, London 1853, Leipzig 1857, London [1859] (as Eastern tales).

The corsair, Lara, Paris 1830; ed M. F. Sweetzer, Boston 1893. The Giaour, The bride of Abydos 1844, 1848. Beppo, Don Juan 2 vols 1853. The prisoner of Chillon, The siege of Corinth, ed J. G. C. Schuler, Halle 1886. The prisoner of Chillon, Mazeppa, The lament of Tasso, Oxford [1929].

Dramas. Paris 1832, 2 vols 1837, 1853.

Three poems not included in the works of Lord Byron [Lines to Lady [Jersey], The curse of Minerva, and The enigma (by Catherine Maria Fanshawe)], 1818; Suppressed poems [English bards, Ode to the land of the Gaul, A sketch, Windsor poetics], Paris 1818 (2nd edn); The works of Lord Byron [English bards, The curse of Minerva, Waltz etc], 'Philadelphia' 1820; The miscellaneous works [Werner, Heaven and earth, Morgante Maggiore, The age of bronze, The island, The vision of judgement, The deformed transformed], 2 vols 1824, 1830; Poems [Don Juan, Hours of idleness, English bards, Poems on his domestic circumstances], 1825; Don Juan (complete), English bards, Hours of idleness, The waltz, and all the other minor poems, 1826, 1827, 2 vols 1828, 1829; The miscellaneous poems [Hours of idleness, English bards, The curse of Minerva etc], 1829; Miscellanies, 3 vols 1837, 2 vols 1853.

Partial collections in translation

Albanian (The Giaour, The prisoner of Chillon and shorter poems) by D. Qirjazi, Tirana 1997.

Arabic By M. al-Siba'i, Cairo 1912; by A. M. al-Masiri and M. 'A. Zayd, Cairo 1964.

Armenian (Bride of Abydos, Parisina, Mazeppa) by H. Sevan, Yerevan 1971.

Chinese By Du Bingzheng, Shanghai 1964; by [?] Shanghai 1955. Three political satires (Vision of judgement, The Irish avatar, The age of bronze) by Qiu Congyi and Shao Xunmei, Shanghai 1981. (The Giaour, The corsair) by Li Jinxiu, Changsha 1988.

Czech (Corsair, Lara) by Cenek Ibl, Prague 1885.

Danish (Dramas and tales) by Edvard Lembcke 2 vols Copenhagen 1873; (Manfred, The prisoner of Chillon, Mazeppa) by Alfred Ipsen, Copenhagen [1888]; (Beppo, The vision of judgement) by Alfred Ipsen, Copenhagen 1891.

Dutch (Mazeppa, Parisina) by Nicholaas Beets (in his Gedichten), Haarlem 1837, 1848; (Poems) by J. J. L. Ten Kate, Leiden [c. 1870].

French (Childe Harold, cantos i–iv, Prisoner of Chillon, Corsair, Lara, Giaour, Lament of Tasso, Siege of Corinth), Bibliothèque Universelle (Geneva) 5–9 May 1817–Dec 1818; by D. Bonnefin 1844; (Corsair, Mazeppa) by Lucien Méchin, Paris 1848. (Manfred, Lara) by Hya du Pontavice de Heuseey, Paris 1856; (Prisoner of Chillon, Lara, Parisina, Poems) by H. Gomont, Nancy 1862; (Corsair, Lara, Siege of Corinth) by Paul Lorencin, Paris 1868; by A. Regnault, Paris 1874; (Two Foscari, Beppo) by Achille Morisseau, Paris 1881; (Corsair, Lara) Paris 1892; (The prisoner of Chillon, Childe Harold's pilgrimage iii) by P. Bensimon and R. Martin, Paris 1971.

German (Tales) by J. V. Adrian, Frankfurt 1820; (Prisoner of Chillon, Parisina) by Paul Graf con Haugwitz, Breslau 1821; (Manfred, Dream etc) by E. Köpke, Berlin 1835; (Bride of Abydos, Mazeppa) by W. Gerhard, Leipzig 1840; (Giaour, Hebrew melodies) by F. Friedmann, Leipzig 1854; (Cain, Mazeppa) by F. Friedmann, Leipzig 1855; (Manfred, Prisoner of Chillon, Hebrew melodies etc) by A. R. Nielo, Münster 1857; (Giaour, Prisoner of Chillon), Düsseldorf 1859 (anon); (Mazeppa, Corsair, Beppo) by W.

Schäffer, Leipzig 1864; (Manfred, Cain, Heaven and earth, Sardanapalus) by W. Gruezmacher, Hildburghausen 1870; (Bride of Abydos, Dream) by O. Riedel, Hamburg 1872; (Giaour, Bride of Abydos, Lara, Parisina) by A. Strodtmann, Hildburghausen 1872; (Prisoner of Chillon, Mazeppa), Leipzig [c.1875], (Prisoner of Chillon, Parisina) by O. Michaeli, Halle 1890; (Tales) by A. Neidhart, Halle [1903]; (Poems) by O. Gildemeister, Essen 1990; (Lord Byron: a reader) ed G. Veding, Frankfurt 1988, 1994 (3rd edn).

Greek (Prose) G. Polites, 3 vols Athens 1867–71; (The bride of Abydos, The curse of Minerva) by N. Mandrihardes, Athens 1937; (Poetical works) by M. Kessisis, Athens 1974.

Hungarian (Mazeppa, Dream, Poems) by Lázár Horváth, Budapest 1842; (Selected poems 1) by P. Davidhazi et al, Budapest 1975; (Selected poems 2) by E. Abrányi and G. Görgey, Budapest 1975.

Icelandic (Prisoner of Chillon etc) by Steingrímur Thorsteinson, Copenhagen 1866.

Italian (Prisoner of Chillon, Parisina, Siege of Corinth, Lara) by P. Isola, Turin 1827; (Corsair, Giaour) by P. Isola, Milan 1830; rptd together 2 vols Lugano 1832; (Bride of Abydos, Parisina, Corsair, Lara) by G. Nicolini, Milan 1834, 2 vols Milan 1837, 1842; (Poems) by G. Z. Finocchiaro, Palermo 1837; (Poems) by M. Mazzoni, Milan 1838; (Dramas) by P. de Virgilii, Brussels 1841; (Marino Faliero, Two Foscari) by P. G. B. Cereseto, Savona 1845; (Sardanapalus, Marino Faliero, Two Foscari) by A. Maffei, Florence 1862; (Tales and poems) Milan 1882 (anon); Childe Harold, Parisina, Beppo, Bride of Abydos) by G. Casella (in his Opere edite e postume vol 1), Florence 1884; (Cain, Parisina etc) by A. Maffei, Florence 1890, rptd 1968; (Parisina, Prisoner of Chillon) by A. Ricci, Florence [1924]; (Turkish tales) (with Cain) by G. Franci and R. Mangaroni, Pordenone 1988, rptd 1995 as Il Corsaro.

Japanese (Prisoner of Chillon etc) by T. Kimura, Tokyo 1918, by S. Okamoto, Tokyo 1936, by Yoshio Nakano and Kazuo Ogawa, Tokyo 1968; (The vision of judgement, Beppo) by I. Higashinaka, Kyoto 1984; (English bards and Scotch reviewers, Hints from Horace) by I. Higashinaka, Kyoto 1989.

Polish (Siege of Corinth, Corsair) by B[runo hr] K[iciński] in Poemata i powieści vol 1, Warsaw 1820; (Mazeppa) by H. Dembiński, (Giaour, Parisina etc) by W. Maleckiéj, Warsaw 1828, 1831; (Parisina, Calmar i Orla) by I. Szydlowski, Vilna 1834; (Giaour) by A. Mickiewicz, (Corsair) by A. E. Odyniec, Paris 1835, Wroclaw 1839; (Bride of Abydos) by A. E. Odyniec in Tlómaczenia vol 2, Leipzig 1838; (Corsair, Heaven and earth) by A. E. Odyniec in Tlómaczenia vol 3, Leipzig 1841; (Mazeppa) by A. E. Odyniec in Tlómaczenia vol 5, Vilna 1843; (Lament of Tasso, Werner, Bride of Abydos, Island) by A. Zawadzki, Warsaw 1846; (Manfred, Mazeppa, Siege of Corinth, Parisina, Prisoner of Chillon) by F. D. Morawski, Leszno 1853; (Parisina, Lara, Cain, Poems etc) by K. Kruzer (in his Przeklady i rymy wlasne vols 3–4), Warsaw 1876.

Portuguese (Childe Harold, Sardanapalus) by F. J. P. Guimarães (in Traducções Poeticas), Rio de Janeiro 1863.

Romanian (Prisoner of Chillon, Beppo, Lament of Tasso) by I. Eliad, Bucharest 1834; by V. Teodorescu, Bucharest 1961; (Poems) ed D. Grigorsecu, Bucharest 1983; (Poems) by V. Teodorescu, Bucharest 1983.

Russian (Dramas) by I. A. Bunin and N. A. Bruansky, St Petersburg 1922; Lyrika i Satira, ed M. N. Rosanova, Moscow 1935; Izbrannoe, tr Y. Kondrateva, Moscow 1951, rptd 1960; I. I. Kozlov, The translations from Byron, ed G. V. R. Barratt, Berne/Frankfurt 1972; (Childe Harold's pilgrimage, The corsair, The prisoner of Chillon) Perm 1988.

Spanish (Ode to Napoleon, Napoleon's farewell etc) Paris 1830 (anon); (Lara, Siege of Corinth, Parisina, Childe Harold, Mazeppa, Lament of Tasso, Beppo) by R. Canales, Barcelona [c. 1876]; (Parisina, Prisoner of Chillon, Lament of Tasso, Bride of Abydos) by A. Sellen, New York 1877; (Don Juan, Lament of Tasso) by J. A. R., Barcelona 1883; (Dramas) by J. A. Galiano, Madrid 1886; (The corsair, Lara, The siege of Corinth, Mazeppa) Madrid 1976, 9th reprint 1984; (Childe Harold, The corsair) Madrid 1983, rptd 1985, 1986, 1992, 1993; (The corsair, Lara) by M. Armino, Barcelona 1974.

Selections

Selections in English

The beauties of Byron. Ed T. Parry 1823, 1827.
Life and select poems. Ed C. Hulbert, Shrewsbury [1828].
Beauties of Byron. Ed B. F. French, Philadelphia 1828.
The beauties of Byron. Ed A. Howard [1829].
The beauties of Byron. Ed J. W. Lake, Paris 1829.
Select works of Lord Byron. 6 vols Frankfurt 1831–4.
Select works. 1833.
Select poetical works. Paris 1835, 1836.
Lord Byron's select works. Berlin 1837.
Select works. 1837.
The beauties of Byron. Ed A. Howard 1837.
The beauties of Byron and Burns. Hull 1837.
Byron's select works. Paris 1843.
A selection from Byron's poetical works. Ed C. Gräser, Marienwerder 1846.
Select poetical works. 1848.
Lord Byron's select works. Ed F. Breier, Oldenburg 1848.
Selections from the writings of Lord Byron by a clergyman [Whitwell Elwin]. 1854, [1874].
Poems. 1855.
Poems. [1859.]
The choice works. Halifax 1864.
A selection from the works of Lord Byron. Ed A. C. Swinburne 1866, [1885].
Songs. 1872.
Beautés de Byron. Ed A. Biard, Paris 1876.
Favourite poems by Lord Byron. Boston 1877.
The Byron birthday book. Ed J. Burrows 1879.
Poem. [1880.]
The beauties of Byron. Stuttgart [c. 1880].
The poetry of Byron, chosen and arranged by Matthew Arnold. 1881.
Gems from Byron. Ed H. R. Haweis 1886.
Poems carefully selected. 2 vols [1886].
Shorter poems by Burns, Byron and Campbell. Ed W. Murrison 1893, 1895.
Selections from Wordsworth, Byron, Shelley. Ed A. Ellis 1896.
Selections. Ed F. I. Carpenter, New York 1900, 1908.
Poems selected by C. Linklater Thomson. 1901.
Poems. Ed A. Symons [1904], [1927].
Songs. 1904.
Selected poetry. Ed J. W. Duff 1904.
Love poems of Byron. 1905.
With Byron in Italy: a selection of the poems and letters. Ed A. B. McMahon, Chicago 1906.
Poems selected by Charles Whibley. [1907.]
Byron's shorter poems. Ed R. H. Bowles 1907.
Selections from Byron. Ed S. M. Tucker [1907].
Love poems of Byron. 1911.
Byron and his poetry. Selections. Ed W. Dick 1913, rptd 1974, 1977.
Selected poems. 1913.
Selections. 1913.
Selected poems. [Ed W. Robertson 1913.]
Selections. Ed A. H. Thompson, Cambridge 1920.
Poems. Ed H. J. C. Grierson 1923.
Selections. Ed M. F. Dee [1926].
With Byron in love. Ed W. Littlefield, New York [1926].
An introduction to Byron. Ed G. N. Pocock [1927].
Selections. Ed W. R. Macklin 1927.

Selections. [1927.]
The shorter Byron. Ed E. Rhys 1927, [1928].
Selections. Ed H. Miles 1930.
Selections. Ed D. M. Walmsley 1931.
Selections. Ed J. G. Bullocke [1931].
Lyrical poems. Ed E. du Perron, Maastrict 1933.
The best of Byron. Ed R. A. Rice, New York 1933.
Don Juan and other satirical poems. Ed L. I. Bredvold 1935.
Childe Harold's pilgrimage and other romantic poems. Ed S. C. Chew 1936.
Satirical and critical poems. Ed J. Bennet, Cambridge 1937.
Poetry and prose. Introd by Quiller-Couch, ed D. N. Smith, Oxford 1940.
Byron. Ed D. Wellesley 1941, rptd 1976.
Poems. Ed G. Pocock 3 vols 1948, rev V. de S. Pinto 1963 (EL).
Byron for today. Ed R. Fuller 1948.
Selections from poetry, letters and journals. Ed P. C. Quennell 1950 (Nonesuch Lib).
Poems. Ed P. D. Dickinson 1950.
Poetry and letters. Ed E. E. Bostetter 1951, rev 1972.
Poetry. Ed L. A. Marchand 1951, rev 1967.
Byron poems. Ed A. S. B. Glover 1954, rptd 1985.
Selected verse and prose. Ed P. C. Quennell 1959.
Byronic thoughts. Ed P. C. Quennell 1960.
Byron's poetry. Ed V. de S. Pinto 1963.
Selections from poetry and prose. Ed I. Gregor and A. Rutherford 1963.
Selected poems of Byron. Ed R. Skelton 1964.
Selected poetry and prose of Byron. Ed W. H. Auden 1966.
Poetry and letters. Ed W. H. Marshall 1968.
The Byronic Byron. Ed G. Phelps 1971.
Lord Byron selections. Introd by R. M. Samarin, Moscow 1973 (in English).
A collection of Byron's verse. Introd by D. Dunn 1974.
Childe Harold's pilgrimage and other romantic poems. Ed J. D. Jump 1975.
Byron's Poetry. Ed F. D. McConnell 1978.
Byron: selected poems. Notes by I. Scott-Kilvert 1984.
Byron. Ed J. J. McGann. Oxford 1986 (Oxford Authors).
Lord Byron. Ed P. Porter 1989.
Selected poems. Ed S. Applebaum, New York 1993.
Byron poems. Ed P. Washington 1994.
Lord Byron: selected poems. Ed I. Hamilton 1994.
Byron: selected poetry and prose. Ed D. H. Low 1995.
Don Juan selections. 1996.
Lord Byron: selected poems. Ed S. J. Wolfson and P. J. Manning 1996.
Lord Byron. Ed J. Stabler 1997.
Lord Byron: selected poetry. Ed J. J. McGann, Oxford 1997.

Selections in translation

Arabic

Tr A. Al-Sàid, Cairo 1943; M. Al-Sibai, Cairo nd.

Armenian

Beauties of English poets. Venice 1852.
Lord Byron's Armenian exercises and poetry. Venice 1870, 1886.
Tr Alichan, Venice 1870.

Azeri

Tr B. Vahabzadä and A. Aslanov, Baku 1959.

Byelorrus

Tr Ja. Semjazon et al, Minsk 1963.
Lyrics. Tr R. Baradulin et al, Minsk 1989.

Bulgarian

Tr L. Ljubenov et al, Sofia 1968.
Slance na bezsannite. Tr G. Lenkov et al, Sofia 1989.

Chinese

Selections. Tr Zha Liang-zheng, Shanghai 1982.
Seventy poems. Tr Yang Deyu, Changsha 1981–6.
Selected longer poems. Tr Yuan Xiansheng, Beijing 1991.
Highlights. Tr Yang Deyu and Zha Liangzheng 1994.

Czech

Tr H. Zantovská, Prague 1959.

Estonian

Tr M. Nurme, Tallin 1957.

French

Choix de poésies de Byron, de W. Scott et de Th. Moore. 2 vols Geneva 1820.
Beautés de Lord Byron. Tr C. E. de Léonville, Paris 1825.
Les beautés de Lord Byron. Tr A. Pichot, Paris 1838.
Écrin poétique de littérature anglaise. Tr D. Bonnefin, Paris 1841.
Chefs d'oeuvre de Lord Byron. Tr Comte de Hautefeuille, Paris 1847.
Rough hewing of Lord Byron in French by Francis D'Autrey. 1869.
Chefs d'oeuvre de Lord Byron. Tr A. Regnault 2 vols Paris 1874.
Poems. Tr F. Guilhot and J.-L. Paul, Paris 1982.

Georgian

Darkness. Tr N. Toxadze in Pirveli'sxivi no 13, Tbilisi 1978.

German

Byrons Lieder. [Ed A. Friederick], Karlsruhe 1820.
Kleine Gedichte von Byron und Moore. [Ed C. von K.], Berlin 1829.
Lord Byrons Ausgewählte Dichtungen. Leipzig 1838.
Dichtungen von Lord Byron. Ed A. Rolein, Krefeld 1841.
Schönheiten aus Byrons Werken. Ed A. Böttger, Leipzig 1841.
Byron-Anthologie. Ed E. Hobein, Schwerin 1866.
Lord Byrons Lyrische Gedichte. Ed H. Stadelmann, Hildburghausen 1872.
Auswahl aus Byron. Ed J. Hengesbach [np] 1892.
Tr A. von Bernus, Heidelberg 1958.

Greek

Raizis, Byron. Athens 1994.

Hebrew

Tr Y. L. Gordon, St Petersburg 1844, rptd Warsaw 1904–5, Tel Aviv 1950, 1953; tr R. Grossman, Palestine 1942.
Cain, Heaven and earth, Manfred. Tr D. Frischmann, Tel Aviv 1954, rptd from Warsaw 1900; tr R. Avinoam (R. Grossman), Tel Aviv 1956; tr J Kochav, Tel Aviv 1971; tr S. Sandbank, Jerusalem/Tel Aviv 1972.

Hungarian

Manfred, Beppo, Mazeppa. Tr D. Kosztolányi, Budapest 1957.

Italian

A mii amici [by Pietro Isola]. [Novi c. 1870.]
Marino Faliero, Sardanapalus, The two Foscari. Tr D. Pettoello, Turin 1954.
Domestic pieces and other poems. Tr C. Dapino, ed C. Gorlier, Turin 1986.
Selected works. Ed T. Kemeny, Milan 1993.

Japanese

Tr T. Abe, Tokyo 1938; A. Tomoji, Tokyo 1954, rptd 1963; Y. Shin'ichi, Tokyo 1967; K. Ogawa, Tokyo 1969.
Poems. Tr K. Ogawa, Tokyo 1975.
Poems. Tr T. Abe, Tokyo 1977.

Kazakh

Tr G. Qajyrbekov, Alma-Ata 1960.

Kirghiz

Tr U. Abdykajymov, Z. Mamytbekov and O. Orozbaev, Frunze 1960.

Korean

Tr L. Seung-u, Seoul 1959.
Selected poems. Tr Tong-gyu Hwang, Seoul 1973.
So, we'll go no more a-roving. Tr K. Ki-t'ae, Seoul 1992.
Selections. Yanji, China 1993.

Lithuanian

Prisoner of Chillon, Manfred, Cain. Tr A. Churginas, Vilnius 1954, rptd 1958, 1962.

Moldovan

Tr I. Krecu and V. Teleuke, Lumima 1970.

Persian

Tr Shaja' al-din Shifa', Tehran 1955.

Polish

Childe Harold, Manfred, Cain. Tr J. Kasprowicz and J. Paskowsky, Warsaw 1954, rptd 1961.
Selections. Tr J. Kasprowicz et al, Wroclaw 1956, rptd 1964, 1966, 1967.
Selections. Tr A. Chodzko et al, Warsaw 1972, rptd 1974.
Selected poems. Wroclaw 1970.
Extracts. Tr A. Chodzko et al, Warsaw 1974.
Selected poems, Warsaw 1975.
Wybór dziet. Tr J. Kasprowicz et al 3 vols Warsaw 1986.

Portuguese

Byron no Brasil (trns in Portuguese with Brazilian imprints). O.C.d.c. Barbosa, Sao Paulo 1975.
Selections. Tr J. de Almeida Flor and S. Bianchi Ayres de Carvalho, Lisbon 1985.

Romanian

Tr St. Avadanei and Al. Pascu, Iasi 1972.

Russian

Vuibor iz sochineny. Ed M. Kachenovsky, Moscow 1821.
Selections. Moscow 1951.
Selections. Tr I. Bunin and G. Sengeli, Moscow 1959, rptd 1964, 1967.
Selections. Tr A. Blok et al, Moscow 1960.
Selected works. Ed Ju. Kondratev, Moscow 1973.
Selected works. Tr S. Il'in et al, ed O. Afonina, Moscow 1978.
Selected works. Tr and ed G. S. Usova et al. Moscow 1978, rptd 1980, 1987.
Selected works. Tr G. S. Usova et al, ed N. Lapidus, Minsk 1978.
Selected works. Tr in Evropy no 1, Moscow 1979.
Selected works. Ed R. M. Samarin, Moscow 1979.
Selected works. Tr I. Bunin, G. Sengeli, V. Ivanov et al, ed R. Usmanova, 4 vols Moscow 1981.
Selected works. Tr O. Afonina and R. Usmanova, Moscow 1981, rptd 1984, 1985.
Selected works. Tr A. Blok et al, Alma Ata 1982.
Selected works. Tr V. Levik et al, Moscow 1982, rptd 1985.
Selected works. Tr V. Ivanov et al, Moscow 1984, rptd 1985.
Selected works (1816–23). Tr I. Bunin et al, Moscow 1986.
Selected works. Tr V. Levik et al 2 vols Moscow 1987.
Selected works. Tr I. Bunin et al, Moscow 1987.
Lyrics. Tr V. Ivanov et al, Moscow 1988.
Don Juan (selections). Tr. A. N. Zverev, Moscow 1988.
Lyrics. Tr I. O. Shaitanov, Moscow 1988.
Selected lyrics. Tr A. Plesceev et al, Moscow 1988.
Poems. Tr V. Levik et al, Novosibirsk 1988.
Poems and tales. Tr L. Siffers et al, Kiev 1989.
Na pereput'ya bytya (On the crossroads of existence, Selected poems). Tr M. Bogoslovskaya et al, Moscow 1989.

Serbo-Croat

Tr D. Puvačič, Belgrade 1968.
Selected poems and plays. Tr D. Puvačič et al, Belgrade 1976.
Selections. Tr R. Kuic, Belgrade 1980.

Slovenian

Tr J. Menart, Ljubljana 1954.

Spanish

[Selections by various translators.] Barcelona [1922]; tr M. Alfaro, Madrid 1945.
Obras escogidas. Tr E. Villalva and J. A. Galiano, Buenos Aires 1951. Rptd from Madrid 1886 edn.
Selected poems. Tr J. M. M. Triana, Madrid 1985.
Poems of love and hate and a satire. Tr J. Valera, Palma, Majorca 1991.
Poems of love. Tr J. R. Blanca, Bilbao 1994.

Swedish

Works. Tr E. S. Bring, introd by E. H. Brag, Lund 1839.

Tadjik

Ruqhi ozod. Tr N. Raqhmatullo, Dushanbe 1988.

Ukrainian

Selections. Tr L. Siffers et al, Kiev 1977.
Poems. Tr in Vsevlt No 7, Kiev 1978.
Lyrics. Tr Dmytro Palamarchuk, Kiev 1982.

Uzbek

Selections. Tashkent 1974.
Selections. Tashkent 1975.

§1

In this section and the following the word 'proof' is used to indicate that the work is known to have been put in type, whether a copy is now extant or not. The word 'counterfeit' is used to indicate edns indistinguishable by normal methods of bibliographical description. Of Byron's earlier works many such were produced for commercial purposes before 1820.

Fugitive pieces. [Newark 1806] (anon) (priv ptd); ed H. Buxton Forman 1886 (facs); ed M. Kessel, New York 1933 (facs), rptd 1973.

Roe, H. C. The rare quarto edition of Lord Byron's Fugitive pieces described, with a note on the Pigot family. Nottingham 1919 (priv ptd).

Poems on various occasions. Newark 1807 (priv ptd). Contains 50 pieces of which 12 are new. Anon.

Hours of idleness: a series of poems, original and translated. Newark 1807 (one counterfeit of larger size – *see* Athenaeum 28 May 1898; T. M. B[lagg], Newark as a publishing town, Newark 1898, pp. 20–35; T. J. Wise, Bibliography vol 1 pp. 9–10), 1822, Glasgow 1825. Contains 39 pieces of which 12 are new.

REVIEWS: (John Higgs Hunt) Critical Rev Sep 1807; Satirist Oct 1807; (Henry Brougham) Edinburgh Rev 11 1808 (separately rptd 1820, 1820); NMM Feb 1819.

Ward, W. S. Byron's Hours of idleness and other than Scottish reviewers. MLN 59 1944.

Poems original and translated: second edition. Newark 1808. Contains 39 pieces of which 5 are new. One counterfeit (*see* Texas exhibition, 1924, pp. 93–7). Rptd as Hours of idleness, Paris 1819, London 1820 (4 edns), Paris 1820, 1822.

The British bards. [Newark 1808] (proof in BM). Largely incorporated in the next entry.

English bards and Scotch reviewers: a satire. [1809] (anon) (2 variants, 3 counterfeits), 1809 ('with considerable additions and alterations'), 1810 (8 counterfeits), 1810 (4th edn) (one counterfeit), Philadelphia 1811, London 1811 (4th edn) (6 counterfeits), Boston 1814, London 1816 ('with additions'), New York 1817, Paris 1818, 1819, Brussels 1819, Geneva 1820, London 1821, Paris 1821, London 1823, 1823, Glasgow 1824, 1825, London 1825, 1826, 1827, 1827, [c. 1830], Halifax 1834; ed J. Murray 1936 (Roxburghe Club) (facs of a copy with Byron's ms notes); tr Fr by Raoul (as Les poètes anglais et les auteurs de l'Edinburgh Review), Ghent 1821.

C[ampbell], J. D. et al. Athenaeum 5 May–7 July 1894.

Redgrave, G. R. The first four editions of English bards and Scotch reviewers. Library 2nd ser 1 1899.

König, C. Byrons English bards and Scotch reviewers Entstehung und Beziehungen zur zeitgenössischen Satire und Kritik. Berlin [1914].

Hints from Horace. 1811 (proof in BM). Extracts were pbd by R. C. Dallas in 1824 and by T. Moore in 1830; the full text was first pbd in the 6-vol edn of Works, 1831, vol 5 pp. 273–327.

Childe Harold's pilgrimage: a romaunt [cantos i–ii]. 1812 (7th–8th edns), 1815 (10th edn), Philadelphia 1816 (3rd Amer edn), London 1819 (11th edn).

Childe Harold's pilgrimage, canto the third. 1816 (3 issues), Boston 1817, Philadelphia 1817.

Childe Harold's pilgrimage, canto the fourth. 1818 (7 states – *see* W. H. McCarthy, The printing of canto iv of Childe Harold, YULG 1 1927), New York 1818, 1818, Philadelphia 1818 (with other poems).

Childe Harold's pilgrimage [cantos i–iv]. 2 vols 1819, Leipzig 1820, 1 vol London 1825, 2 vols Paris 1825, 1 vol London 1826, 1827, Paris 1827, 2 vols Brussels 1829, London [c. 1831], Nuremberg [1831], New York 1836, London 1837, Mannheim 1837, London 1839, 1841, 1842; ed A. Mommsen, Hamburg 1853, London 1853, Berlin 1885; ed F. Brockerhoff, Berlin 1854, London 1859, 1860, 1860, Leipzig 1862; ed W. Spalding [1866]; ed P. Weeg, Münster 1867, London 1869; ed W. Hiley 1877; ed J. Darmesteter, Paris 1882; ed A. Julien, Paris 1883; ed H. F. Tozer, Oxford 1885, 1907; ed W. J. Rolfe, Philadelphia 1886; ed M. Krummacher, Bielefeld 1886, 1891, 1893; ed H. G. Keene 1893; ed E. Chasles, Paris 1893; ed E. C. E. Owen [1897]; ed E. E. Morris 2 vols 1899; ed A. J. George, New York 1900; ed H. Bennett 1905; ed A. H. Thompson, Cambridge 1913; ed D. Frew 1918; [cantos iii–iv] ed B. J. Hayes [1932].

Selections: Glasgow [1882]; ed T. Morrison [1882], [1882]; ed E. D. A. Morshead 1893, 1894, [1900]; ed J. Downie [1901]; ed J. H. Fowler 1906; ed H. F. Tozer, Oxford 1907; ed J. C. Scrimgeour, Calcutta 1914; ed G. A. Sheldon 1933; ed J. H. Fowler 1958.

TRANSLATIONS: Albanian by S. Luarasi, Tirana 1974, 1977, rptd from 1956; Arabic by Z. Gabreal, Childe Harold iv stanzas 179–84, 1979?; Armenian by G. Alíshanian (canto iv only), Venice 1860, 1872, (canto iv only) by Alichan, Venice 1870; Bulgarian by N. Vranchev, Sofia 1925, by A. Podbrazachov, Sofia 1946, by D. Statkov, Sofia 1958; Byeloruss, introd by Y. Gaurauk, Minsk 1963; Chinese by Yuan Shui Pai, Chungking 1944, by Yang Xiling, Shanghai 1956–8, rptd 1990; Cz by Eliska Krásnohorská [i.e. Jindřiška Pechová], Prague 1890; Danish by A. Hansen, Copenhagen 1880; Fr [by Pauthier de Censay], Paris 1828, by P. A. Deguer, Paris 1828, by F. Ragon, Paris 1833, by E. Quiertant (canto i only), Paris 1852, by E. Quiertant (cantos i–iv), Paris 1861, by L. Davésiès de Pontès, 2 vols Paris 1862, 1870, by V. R. Jones, St Quentin 1862, by M. Ph. Alard, Dunkirk 1869, by H. Bellet, Paris 1881, by A. Julien, Paris 1883, by M. A. Elwall, Paris 1892, by D. Gibb, Paris 1892, by G. le Prévost, Paris 1910, by R. Martin, Paris 1949, rptd 1964; Ger by K. Baldamus, 3 vols Leipzig 1835, by J. C. von Zedlitz, Stuttgart 1836, by H. von Pommer Esche, Stralsund 1839, by C. D. (canto i only), Ansbach 1845, by A. Böttger, Leipzig 1846, by A. Büchner, Frankfurt 1853, 1855, by E. von Monbart, Cologne 1865, by A. H. Janert, Hildburghausen 1868, by F. Schmidt, Berlin 1869, by A. Seubert, 2 vols Leipzig 1871–6, by F. Dobbert, [Leipzig?] 1893; Greek by A. Paraschos, Athens 1867, rptd Athens/Constantinople 1881; Hungarian by J. Bickersteth, Geneva 1857; Ital by Michele Leoni (canto iv only), [np] 1819, by G. Gazzino, Genoa 1836, by M. Missirini (canto iv only), Milan 1848, by F. Armenio, Naples 1858, by G. Giovio (cantos i–ii only), Milan 1866, by P. Isola (canto iv only), Novi 1870, by A. Maffei (canto iv only), Florence 1872, 1874, 1897, by C. Faccioli, Florence 1873, by A. Ricci, 3 vols Florence [1924–8]; Jap (canto i stanzas 19–22, anon) [1905?], by B. Tsuchii 1924, by K. Ogawa 2 vols 1993, cantos i and iii ed T. Tabuki Kyushu 1992, 1994, by I. Higashinaka Kyoto 1994; Latin (part only, verse) by N. J. Brennan, Dublin 1894; Moldovan by V. Teleuke Kishinev 1985, rptd 1985; Norwegian by G. Uthang (cantos i and ii) 1995; Polish by M. B. Wolff, St Petersburg 1857, by Wiktor z Baworow, Lwow 1857, by F. Krauze, [np] 1865–71, by J. Kasprowicz, Warsaw 1895, by A. A. K[rajewski], Cracow 1896; Portuguese by F. J. Pinheiro Guimarães, Lisbon 1863; Rus by D. Minaev, Rosskoe Slovo, St Petersburg Jan, Mar, May, Oct 1864, by A. Kozlov, Rosskaya Mysl (Moscow) Jan–Feb, Nov 1890, by V. Fisher, Moscow 1912, by V. Levik, introd by A. A. Elistratova, Moscow 1973, by A. Blok, ed Ju Kondratsev, Irkutsk 1978, by V. Levin, Moscow 1985; Serbo-Croat by D. Andelinovic, Zagreb 1966, by L. Paljetak, Zagreb 1978; Slovak, Bratislava 1988; Sp 4 vols Paris 1829 (anon), by Antonio Ledesma (canto i only), Almeria 1884, Madrid 1983, rptd 1985, 1986, 1993; Swed by A. F. Skjoldebrand, Stockholm 1832.

REVIEWS: (F. Jeffrey) Edinburgh Rev 19 1812; (G. Ellis) Quart Rev 7 1812; O Investigador Portuguez em Ingleterra 6 Apr 1812; (F. Jeffrey) Edinburgh Rev 27 1816; (Sir Walter Scott) Quart Rev 16 1816; (John Wilson) Edinburgh Rev 30 1818; (Sir Walter Scott) Quart Rev 19 1818; (William Hazlitt) Yellow Dwarf 2 May 1818.

[Penn, Granville.] Lines to Harold. Stoke Park, Bucks [1812] (priv ptd); rptd in Original lines and translations, 1815; rptd as Addresses to Lord Byron on the publication of Childe Harold, Poetical Album ser 2 1829.

Hobhouse, J. C. Historical illustrations of the fourth canto of Childe Harold. 1818, 1818, New York 1818.

[Hodgson, F.] Childe Harold's monitor: or lines occasioned by the last canto of Childe Harold. 1818.

Kölbing, E. Zur Textüberlieferung von Byrons Childe Harold cantos i, ii. Leipzig 1896.

Maier, H. Enstehungsgeschichte von Byrons Childe Harold's pilgrimage, cantos i, ii. Berlin 1911.

Moll, O. E. E. Der Stil von Byrons Childe Harold's pilgrimage. Berlin 1911.

Dalgado, D. G. Childe Harold's pilgrimage to Portugal critically examined. Lisbon 1919.

Murray, J. Two passages in Childe Harold canto iv. TLS 25 Aug 1921.

Beck, R. Gisli Brynjúlfson: an Icelandic imitator of Childe Harold's pilgrimage. JEGP 28 1929.

[Gillies, R. P.] Childe Alarique: a poet's reverie, and other poems. 1813, Edinburgh 1814.

The Baron of Falconberg: or Childe Harold in prose by Mrs Bridget Bluemantle. 3 vols 1815.

The last canto of Childe Harold's pilgrimage, with notes by Lord Byron. 1818.

The soul's pilgrimage: a poem, written in reference to the sentiments of the noble author of Childe Harold's pilgrimage. Cambridge 1818.

Prodigious!!! or Childe Paddie in London. 3 vols 1818.

Childe Albert: or the misanthrope. Edinburgh 1819.

Harold the exile. 3 vols [1819]. *See* N & Q 13 Oct 1951.

Childe Harold in the shades: an infernal romaunt. 1819.

[Deacon, W. F.] The Childe's pilgrimage by Lord B. In Warreniana, 1824.

Bedford, J. H. Wanderings of Childe Harold. 3 vols 1825.

de Lamartine, Alphonse. Le dernier chant du pèlerinage d'Harold. Paris 1825 (4 edns); tr J. W. Lake, Paris 1826; another trn, 1827; another, Dublin 1848.

Verfèle, D. J. C. Les pèlerinages d'un Childe Harold parisien. Paris 1825.

Carry, A. Childe Harold aux ruines de Rome. Paris 1826.

The pilgrimage of Ormonde: or Childe Harold in the New World. Charleston 1831.

Driver, H. A. Harold de Burun. 1835.

B., J. The Childe Harold and the Excursion. [1842.]

Brynjúlfson, G. Faraldrð in Nor urfari, Copenhagen 1848; rptd in Lioðmoeli, Copenhagen 1891.

The curse of Minerva. 1812 (priv ptd) (anon), Philadelphia [=London?] 1815, Paris 1818, 1818, 1820, 1821. A slightly different text was first pbd in NMM Apr 1815, as The malediction of Minerva: or the Athenian marble market, and rptd under the original title by William Hone in the 8th edn of Poems on his domestic circumstances, 1816.

Waltz: an apostrophic hymn, by Horace Hornem esq. 1813, 1821, 1821, Paris 1821, London 1826.

The Giaour: a fragment of a Turkish tale. 1813, 1813 ('with some additions'), 1813 ('with considerable additions'), Boston 1813, Philadelphia 1813, London 1813 (5th edn) ('with considerable additions'), 1813 (6th edn), 1813 (7th edn) ('with some additions'), 1814 (9th–12th edns), 1815 (13th–14th edns), 1825, 1842, [1844]; tr Du by J. J. Ten Kate, Haarlem 1859; Fr by J. M. H. Bigeon, Paris 1828, by T. Carlier (in Voyages poétiques), Paris 1830, by L. Joliet, Paris 1833, by F. Le Bidau and A. Lejourdan, Marseilles 1860; Ger, Berlin 1819 (anon), by 'A. von Nordstern' [i.e. G. A. E. von Nostiz-Jänkendorf], Leipzig 1820, by A. Seubert, Leipzig [1874], by A. Strodtmann, Leipzig 1887; Greek by K. Lamprylos, Smyrna 1836, by K. Mandrikharis, Athens 1857, by A. K. Dosiou, Athens 1857, rptd 1873, [1898?]; Ital by Pellegrino Rossi, Genoa 1817, Milan 1818, by A. Maffei, Milan 1884; Polish by Ladislaus hr Ostrowski, Pulawy 1830, by A. Mickiewicz, Paris 1835, rptd Warsaw 1982, 1984, 1986, Wroclaw 1839, Zloczów [1896]; Rus by M. Kachenovsky, Vyestnik Evropui (Moscow) nos 15–17 1821, by N. R., Moscow 1822, by A. Coeikov, Novosti Literatur (St Petersburg) Sep–Oct 1826, by E. Mimel, St Petersburg 1862, by V. A. Petrov, St Petersburg 1873, 1874; Serbian by A. Popovič, Novisad 1860; Sp Paris 1828; Swed by 'Talis Qualis' [i.e. C. W. A. Strandberg], Stockholm 1855.

REVIEWS: (F. Jeffrey) Edinburgh Rev 21 1813; (G. Ellis) Quart Rev 10 1814.

Hoffmann, K. Üeber Lord Byrons The Giaour. Halle 1898.

Fischer, H. Der übertragene Giaour: eine geschmacksgeschichtliche Untersuchung. Die Neueren Sprachen Jan 1961.

The bride of Abydos: a Turkish tale. 1813 (2 issues), 1813 (2nd–5th edns), 1814 (6th–10th edns), Boston 1814, Philadelphia 1814, London 1818 (11th edn), [1844]; tr Bulgarian by N. D. Katrapov, Moscow 1850; Cz by J. V. Frič, Prague 1854; Danish by A. Schwartz, Copenhagen 1855; Du by J. van Lennep, Amsterdam 1826; Fr by L. Thiessé (as Zuleika et Selim), Paris 1816, by A. Clavareau, Ghent 1823; Ger by J. V. Adrian, Frankfurt 1819, by F. de Bailleul, Landau 1843, by O. Riedel, Hamburg 1872, by F. Kley, Halle 1884; Hungarian by Tercsi, Budapest 1885; Ital, Milan 1828 (anon), by A. Fava, Milan 1832, by G. Giovio, Milan 1854; Polish by Ladislaus hr Ostrowski, Warsaw 1818, by A. E. Odyniec, 1838; Rus by M. Kachenovsky, Vyestnik Evropui (Moscow) nos 18–20 1821, by Ivan Kozlov, St Petersburg 1826, 1831, by M. Politkovsky, Moscow 1859; Sp Paris 1828 (anon), by Joaquin Fiol, Palma, Majorca 1854; Swed [by C. W. A. Strandberg], Stockholm [1855].

REVIEWS: (F. Jeffrey) Edinburgh Rev 23 1814; (G. Ellis) Quart Rev 10 1814.

Dramatized: William Dimond, The bride of Abydos: a tragick play in three acts, 1818, New York 1818, London [1866]; W. O., The bride of Abydos: a tragedy in five acts, 1818. Parodied: The outlaw: a tale, by Erasmus, Edinburgh 1818. Adapted: [J. W. H. Payne], The unfortunate lovers: or the affecting history of Selim and Almena, a Turkish tale from the bride of Abydos, [c. 1821], New York 1822.

The corsair: a tale. 1814 (3 issues), 1814 (2nd–7th edns), New York 1814, Philadelphia 1814, Boston 1814, Baltimore 1814, London 1815 (8th–9th edns), 1818 (10th edn), 1825; ed J. W. Lake, Paris 1830, 1835, [1844], 1867; tr Armenian by Mirzayan, Tehran 1911; Chinese by Du Bingzheng, Shanghai 1949; Cz by C. Ibl, Prague 1885; Danish by H. Schou, Copenhagen 1855; Du by J. van den Bergh, Haarlem 1843; Fr by L. Thomas, Paris 1825, Paris 1952, by M. Laurencin, Paris 1979; Ger by F. L. von Tschirsky, Berlin 1816, by E. von Hohenhausen, Altona 1820, rptd 1992, by C. Pichler, Vienna 1820, by F. Friedmann, Leipzig 1852, by V. von Arentschild, Mainz 1872, by A. Seubert, Leipzig [1874]; Hungarian by Gésa Kacziány, Budapest 1892; Ital by L. C. Turin, 1819, Milan 1820, 1824 (anon), Leghorn 1833 (anon), by G. Nicolini, Milan 1842, by E. Migdonio, Florence 1842, by L. S. Honorati, Bologna 1870, by C. Rosnati, Pavia 1879; Jap by S. Okamoto, Tokyo 1952, by S. Ohta, Tokyo 1952; Polish by A. E. Odyniec, Wroclaw 1958; Rus by A. Boeikov, Novosti Literatur (St Petersburg) Oct–Nov 1825, by V. Olin, St Petersburg 1827; Slovak by J. Buza'ssy and Z. Hegedúshá, Bratislava 1983; Sp Paris 1827 (anon), Valençia 1832 (anon), by V. W. Querol and T. Llorente, Valencia 1863; Swed by 'Talis Qualis' [i.e. C. W. A. Strandberg], Stockholm 1868.

REVIEWS: (F. Jeffrey) Edinburgh Rev 23 1814; (G. Ellis) Quart Rev 11 1814.

Adapted or dramatized: [William Hone], Conrad the corsair: or the pirate's isle, adapted as a romance, 1817; G. Galzerani, Il corsaro: azione mimica, Milan 1826; E. F. C. Boulay-Paty and H. J. J. Lucas, Le corsaire, Paris 1830, 1901; G. Rossetti (senior), Il corsaro: scence melodrammatiche, [c. 1830]; Giacopo Ferretti, Il corsaro: melodramma romantico in due atti, Rome [1831]; G. Rossetti (senior), Medora e Corrado: cantata melodrammatica tratta dal Corsaro di Lord Byron, [c. 1832]; Uhde, H. Zur Poetik von Byrons Corsair, Leipzig 1907.

Ode to Napoleon Buonaparte. 1814 (anon), 1814 (anon) (2nd–9th edns), Boston 1814, New York 1814, Philadelphia 1814, London 1815 (11th edn), 1816 (12th edn), 1818 (13th edn); tr Fr by A. Guilbert London 1826; Georgian by I. Merabishvili 1996; Sp Paris 1830 (anon).

REVIEWS: (James Perry) Morning Chron 21 Apr 1814; (Leigh Hunt) Examiner 24 Apr 1814; (tr Fr A. Guilbert, 1826) Anti-Jacobin Rev May 1814.

Lara: a tale; Jacqueline: a tale. 1814 (anon, 2 issues; Jacqueline is by Samuel Rogers), 1814 (anon) (2nd–3rd edns), Boston 1814 (anon), London 1814 (4th edn, 1st separate and acknowledged edn), New York 1814, London 1817 (5th edn); tr Armenian by H. Sevan Yerevan 1974; Cz by C. Ibl, Prague 1885; Fr Avallon 1840 (anon) (priv ptd); Ger by J. V. Adrian (in Versmaase des Originals), Frankfurt 1819, by W. Schäffer and A. Strodtmann, Leipzig 1886; Ital by Girolamo, Count Bazoldo, Paris 1828, by A. Maffei, Milan 1882; Polish by J. Korsak, Vilna 1833; Portuguese by T. A. Craveiro, Rio de Janeiro 1837; Serbian by A. Popovič, Novisad 1860; Sp Paris 1828 (anon), by N. Plaza, Madrid 1922; Swed by 'Talis Qualis' [i.e. C. W. A. Strandberg], Stockholm 1869.

REVIEWS: (G. Ellis) Quart Rev 11 1814; (A. Dyce) Plagiarisms of Lord Byron, GM Feb 1818.

Hebrew melodies ancient and modern with appropriate symphonies and accompaniments by I. Braham and I. Nathan, the poetry written expressly for the work by Lord Byron. 2 pts [1815], 1 vol 1815 (poetry without the music; 2 issues), Boston 1815, New York 1815, Philadelphia 1815, London 1823, 1825, 1829 (with additions in Fugitive pieces and Reminiscences of Lord Byron by I. Nathan); ed T. Ashton 1972; ed F. Burwick and P. Douglass, Alabama 1988; tr Cz by Jaroslen Vrchlický and J. V. Sladek, Prague 1890; Danish by F. Andresen-Halmrast, Oslo 1889; Fr by J. A. Delérue (in Méandres), Rouen 1845; Ger by Franz Theremin, Berlin 1820, by J. E. Hilscher, Laibach 1833, by E. Nickles, Karlsruhe 1863, by H. Stadelmann, Memmingen 1866; Greek by M. Stratigopolous, Athens 1946; Hebrew by S. Mandelkern, Leipzig 1890, by Y. Orland, Jerusalem 1944, by S. Friedman, Tel Aviv 1983; Ital by P. P. Parzanese, Naples 1857, Ivrea 1855 (anon); Kazakh by G. Qajyrbekov, Alma Ata 1966; Rus by P. Kozlov, St Petersburg 1860; Sp by Tomás Aguiló (in La Fe), Palma Majorca

1844, rptd in his Obras en prosa y en versa, Palma, Majorca 1883; Swed by Theodor Lind, Helsingfors [1862]; Welsh (She walks in beauty only) by Wil Ifan (William Evans), music by M. L. Thomas, Swansea c. 1957, Yiddish by Nathan Horowitz, 1925, 1930.

REVIEWS: Christian Observer Aug 1815; Analectic Mag (Philadelphia) Dec 1815; (F. Jeffrey) Edinburgh Rev 27 1816.

Beutler, C. A. Über Lord Byrons Hebrew melodies. Leipzig 1912.

Slater, J. Byron's Hebrew melodies. SP 49 1952.

Morel, W. Zu Byrons Hebrew melodies. Anglia 73 1955.

The siege of Corinth: a poem; Parisina: a poem. 1816 (anon), 1816 (2nd–3rd edns) (anon), New York 1816, London 1818 (4th edn), 1824, 1826.

REVIEWS: Monthly Rev Feb 1816; Eclectic Rev Mar 1816; European Mag May 1816; Literary Panorama June 1816.

The siege of Corinth [alone]. 1824, Paris 1835, Lüneburg 1854, London 1879; ed J. G. C. Schuler, Halle 1886; ed K. Bandow, Bielefeld [c. 1890]; ed K. Kölbing, Berlin 1893; ed P. Hordern 1914; tr Armenian (extracts) by H. Sevan, Yerevan 1979; Du by J. Van Lennep, Amsterdam 1831; Fr by C. Mancel, Paris 1820, (extracts only) by F. de Reiffenberg in Poésies diverses, Paris 1825, by A. Giron, Brussels 1827; Ger by A. Wollheim, Hamburg [1817?], [by F. L. Breuer], Leipzig 1820, by G. E. Schumann, Hamburg 1827; Greek by O. S. Pylarinos, Athens 1855, by B. J. Lazanas, Athens 1995 (priv ptd); Ital by V. Padovan, Venice 1838; Portuguese by H. E. A. Couthino, 1839; Sp Madrid 1818, Paris 1826, by F. al Castellano 1828, Barcelona 1838, by F. Tarres, Barcelona 1957; Swed [by C. W. A. Strandberg], Stockholm [1854]. Dramatised by — Soumet and — Balochi, Le siège de Corinth: tragédie lyrique en cinq actes, Paris 1826.

Parisina [alone]. Tr Fr by A. Krafft, Paris 1900; Ger by J. V. Cirkel in his Gedichte, Münster 1826, by A. L. Frankel, Vienna 1836; Greek (extracts only) by L. Mavilis, Alexandria 1915; Ital, Milan 1821 (anon), by A. Maffei, Milan 1853, by C. Dall' Oro, Mantua 1854, by P. Pappalardo, Palermo 1855, by A. Canepa, Genoa 1864; Polish by I. Szydlowski, Vilna 1834; Rus by V. Verderevsky, St Petersburg 1827; Serbo-Croat by J. Menart, Ljubljana 1963; Sp Paris 1830 (anon), by H. de V[edia] in El seminario pintoresco (pp. 339, 349), Madrid 1841; Swed [by C. W. A. Strandberg], Stockholm [1854]; Welsh (extract only) Evening = Yr hwyr, music by J. H. Roberts, English words by Byron, tr Avalon (Owen Griffin Owen), Swansea 1930. Adapted in Parisina, poème imité de Lord Byron, Montpellier 1829. Dramatised by F. Romani as Parisina: dramma serio, Bologna 1836; as Parisina: melodramma, Venice 1838, Vercelli [c. 1840], Turin 1858; as Parisina: tragedia lirica, Milan 1841.

von Wurzbach, W. Lord Byrons Parisina und ihre Vorgaengerinnen. EStudien 25 1898.

Fare thee well! 18 Mar 1816 (52 lines; proof, Murray), [4 Apr 1816] (60 lines, priv ptd), 7 Apr 1816 (60 lines, priv ptd). First pbd in Champion 14 Apr 1816. A list of later appearances in newspapers is given in E. H. Coleridge, Works: poetry, vol 3 pp. 532–5.

A reply to fare thee well: lines addressed to Lord Byron. 1816, 1816.

Lady Byron's responsive fare thee well. 1816 (3 edns), 1825.

Lines addressed to Lady Byron. 1817. Attributed to Mrs Cockle.

Reply to Lord Byron's Fare thee well. 1817. Also attributed to Mrs Cockle.

Reply to fare thee well. Newcastle 1817.

A sketch from private life. 30 Mar 1816 (proof, Murray), [2 Apr 1816] (priv ptd). First pbd in Champion 14 Apr 1816.

A sketch from public life, and A farewell, by Tyro. 1816.

Lines on the departure of a great poet from his country. 1816. Attributed to C. Thomson.

[Poems on his domestic circumstances.] Fare thee well: a sketch from private life, Bristol 1816 (Barry & Son, 2 poems only), Dublin 1816 (W. Espy, 2 poems); Fare thee well: a sketch etc, Napoleon's farewell, On the star of the Legion of Honour and Ode from the French, 1816 (Sherwood Neely & Jones, 5 poems); An ode: on the star of the Legion of Honour, New York 1816 (the same 5 poems as the previous edn), tr Ital by A. Lumbroso, Rome 1903; Fare thee well: a sketch from private life, with other poems, 1816 (Rodwell & Martin, 6 poems); Fare thee well and other poems, Edinburgh 1816 (J. Robertson, 7 poems, 2 of which are not by Byron); Poems on his domestic circumstances, 1816 (William Hone, 20 edns, 7 poems, 2 of which are not by Byron; Adieu to Malta was added to the 6th Hone edn, its first appearance in print, and The curse of Minerva to the 8th edn; succeeding edns have the same title as Hone, except where noted); 1816 (Richard Edwards, 10 edns), 1816 (Effingham Wilson, 2nd edn), 1816 (J. Bumpus, 2 edns, prefatory matter by J. Nightingale); 1816 (J. Fairburn); Boston 1816 (J. Eliot, from Hone's 6th edn); Bristol 1816 (W. Sheppard, 2nd edn, 20 poems, of which 7 are not by Byron); Miscellaneous poems including those on his domestic circumstances, 1823 (S. Hodgson, 25 poems, of which 7 are not by Byron); 1824 (J. Bumpus, same title as previous edn, 25 poems of which 7 are not by Byron); Miscellaneous poems on his domestic and other circumstances, 1825 (William Cole, 29 poems, as in the 1824 edn, with 4 genuine poems added); tr Fr by A. Guilbert, 1826 (Ode from the French only).

Cook, D. Byron's Fare thee well. TLS 18 Sep 1937.

Pollard, H. G. Pirated collections of Byron. TLS 16 Oct 1937.

Poems. 1816 (John Murray, 2 issues), 1816 (2nd edn), Spelsbury, Oxon 1990 (facs). On the star of the Legion of Honour tr Ital by A. Lumbroso, Rome 1903.

The prisoner of Chillon and other poems. 1816 (2 issues), Lausanne 1818, 1822, London 1824, [1825?], Geneva 1830; ed T. Harvey, Paris 1846, Lausanne 1857, London 1865; ed R. S. Davies [1877]; ed F. Fischer, Berlin 1884; ed T. C. Cann, Florence 1885; ed H. Evans 1896; ed E. Kölbing, Weimar 1898; ed J. W. Cousins [1910]; ed G. B. Gifford, Lausanne [1939]; introd by D. Wakoski, San Francisco 1993; tr Abkhazian by M. Lašäria, Suxumi 1978; Albanian by Besa Myftiu in Nentori no 4 1988; Armenian by H. Toumanian, Tiflis 1896; Cz by A. Klásterský, Prague 1895, 1922, by H. Zantovska, Prague 1981; Danish by C. Thaarup, Copenhagen 1842; Du by K. L. Ledeganck in his Gedichten, Ghent 1856; Fr Vévey [c. 1870] (anon), Geneva 1892 (anon), by D. Lesuer, Lausanne 1954, by B. Bensimon and R. Martin, Paris 1971; Ger by G. Kreyenberg, Lausanne 1861, by M. von der Marwitz, Vévey [1865], by R. T., Berlin 1886, by J. G. Hagmann, Leipzig 1892, Lausanne 1954; Greek by A. Vlachos, Athens 1857, by C. A. Parmenides, 1865, by A. Yapintzakis, Athens 1990; Icelandic by Steingrimur Thorsteinson, Copenhagen 1866; Ital [np] 1830 (anon), by A. Maffei, Milan 1853, (Darkness only) by I. Turgenev, Peterburgskii Sbornik 1846, p. 501; Jap imitation by T. Kitamura 1889, by S. Okamoto, Tokyo 1952; Persian by Mas'ud Farzad and Javad Shaykh Al-islami, Tehran 1954; Polish by F. D. Morawski (in his Poematów), Leszno 1853, rptd separately Zloczów 1893; Rus by V. Zh[ukovsky], St Petersburg 1822, Moscow 1981, rptd 1984, 1985; Sp Paris 1830 (anon); Swed [by C. W. A. Strandberg], Stockholm [1854]; Turkish by G. Yener, Istanbul 1958. The Dream, originally pbd in this collection, was pbd separately 1849.

REVIEWS: (F. Jeffrey) Edinburgh Rev 27 1816; (Sir Walter Scott) Quart Rev 16 1816; Critical Rev Dec 1816; Eclectic Rev Mar 1817.

Monti, G. In his Studi critici, Florence 1887.

'van Amstel, A.' (J. C. Neuman). The true story of the prisoner of Chillon. Nineteenth Cent May 1900.

Monody on the death of the Right Honourable R. B. Sheridan. 1816 (anon) (2 issues), 1817, 1818.

The lament of Tasso. 1817, 1817 (2nd–5th edns), New York 1817, London 1818 (6th edn); tr Du by J. van Lennep, Amsterdam 1833; Fr by – Marvaud (in Huit Messéniennes), Paris 1824; Ital by M. Leoni, Pisa 1818, by P. M. (in Veglie di Torquato Tasso), Venice 1826, by G. Polidori (in La Magion del Terrore), 1843 (priv ptd), by

G. Godio, Turin 1873, by M. Roffi, Ferrara 1986.
REVIEWS: GM Aug 1817; Scots Mag Aug 1817; Blackwood's Mag Nov 1817.

Manfred: a dramatic poem. 1817 (3 issues), 1817 (2nd edn), Philadelphia 1817, New York 1817, 1817, London 1824, 1825, Brussels [c. 1830], London 1863 (as Manfred: a choral tragedy in 3 acts); ed G. Ferrando, Florence 1826; ed F. Carter 1829; ed Y. B. Kauvar and G. C. Sorenson, Rutherford NJ 1973; tr Armenian by H. Massehian, Paris 1922; Bohemian by J. Vrchlicky, Prague 1901; Bulgarian by N. Vranchev, Sofia 1926, by K. Khristov, Sofia 1938; Catalan by M. V. Balaña, Reus 1905; Chinese by Liu Rangyan, Shanghai 1955; Croatian by S. Mildtić, Zagreb 1894; Cz by J. V. Frič, Prague 1882, by M. Procházska 1991; Danish by P. F. Wulff, Copenhagen 1820, by E. Lembcke, Copenhagen 1843; Du by J. R. Steinmetz, Amsterdam 1857, by W. Gosler, Heusden 1882; Fr by the Comtesse de Lalaing, Brussels 1833, 1852, by F. Ponsard, Paris 1837, by E. Moreau, Paris 1887, by C. Trébla, Toulouse 1888, by F. Guilhot and J.-L. Paul, Montaigut-en-Combrailles 1985, unpbd trn by I. Famchon 1994; Ger by A. Wagner, Leipzig 1819, by T. Armin, Göttingen 1836, by 'Posgaru' (G. F. W. Suckow), Breslau 1839, by O. S. Seeman, Berlin 1843, Leipzig 1853 (anon), by H. von Koesen, Leipzig 1858, by L. Freytag, Berlin 1872, by A. Seubert, Leipzig [1874], (with music by Robert Schumann) Leipzig [c. 1880], by Thierry Preyer, Frankfurt 1883, by O. Gildemeister rptd from 1864,by (M. Stanke) Munich 1912 Frankfurt 1970, by H. O. Proskauer, Basle 1975, by J. E. Hilscher, Basle 1975; Greek by E. Green, Patras 1864, by T. A. Kamarados, Athens 1883, by A. M. Stratigopolous, Athens 1924, by L. Karanikola, Athens 1973; Hebrew by D. Frischmann, Warsaw 1900, rptd 1922; Hungarian by L. Horváth, Budapest 1842, by I. Kludik, Szolnok 1884, by E. Abrányi, Budapest 1891, 1897; Icelandic by Matthias Jochumsson, Copenhagen 1875; Ital by S. Pellico, Milan 1818, rptd 1859, by M. Mazzoni, Milan 1832, by A. Maffei, Florence 1870, ed G. Ferrando, Florence 1926, by C. Bene, Florence 1980 (Byron/Schumann version), by F. Buffoni, Milan 1984, by S. Gori, Milan 1994; Jap by T. Kitamura, 1891, by K. Ogawa, Tokyo 1960; Latvian by A. Johansons, Riga 1940; Polish by E. S. Bojanowski, Wroclaw 1835, by F. D. Morawski in Poematów, Leszno 1853, rptd separately Lwow [1885], by M. Chodźke, Paris [1859]; Romanian by T. M. Stoenescu, Bucharest 1896; Rus by O., Moskovski Vyestnik (Moscow) July 1825, by M. Vronchenko, St Petersburg 1828, by A. Borodin, Panteon (St Petersburg) Feb 1841, by D. Minaev, Russkoe Slovo (St Petersburg) Apr 1853, by E. Zarin, Biblioteca dlya Chteniya (St Petersburg) Aug 1858, by I. Bunin, Moscow 1912, by I. A. Bunin, Moscow 1977; Serbo-Croat by C. Mitelic, Zagreb 1894; Sp Paris 1830 (anon), by J. Galiano and F. de las Peñas, Madrid 1861, by A. R. Chaves, Madrid 1876.
REVIEWS: (F. Jeffrey) Edinburgh Rev 28 1817; Critical Rev June 1817; (John Wilson) Edinburgh Monthly Mag June 1817; Day & New Times 23 June 1817; Eclectic Rev July 1817; GM July 1817; Monthly Rev July 1817; (Goethe Kunst und Alterthum (Weimar) June 1820); rptd in Sämtliche Werke vol 37, Stuttgart 1907, pp. 184–7.

B., F. H. Manfred: an address to Lord Byron, with an opinion on some of his writings. 1817.

Düntzer, H. Goethes Faust in seiner Einheit und Ganzheit: über Byrons Manfred. Cologne 1836.

Rötscher, H. Manfred in ihren inneren Zusammenhange entwickelt. Berlin 1844, Bamberg 1884.

Lord Byron's Manfred at Drury Lane Theatre, by a dilettante behind the scenes. 1863.

Manfred: poem and drama, by the London hermit. Dublin Univ Mag Apr 1874.

Anton, H. S. Byrons Manfred. Erfurt 1875.

Kölbing, E. Zu Byrons Manfred. E Studien 22 1898.

Manfred: dramatische Dichtung von Lord Byron von einem Theologen. Oldenburg [1898].

Brandl, A. Goethes Verhältniss zur Byron. Goethe-Jahrbuch 20 1899.

Varnhagen, H. De rebus quibusdam compositionem Byronis dramatis quod Manfred inscribitur praecedentibus. Erlangen 1909.

Butterwick, J. C. A note on the first editions of Manfred. Book Collectors' Quart 3 1931.

Butler, M. H. An examination of Byron's revision of Manfred, act III. SP 60 1963.

Beppo: a Venetian story. 1818 (anon), 1818 (2nd–7th edns), Boston 1818, New York 1818, Paris 1821, London 1825.

Additional stanzas to the first, second and third editions of Beppo. [1818] (single sheet). These were first added to the 4th edn; the 5th edn was the first to bear Byron's name. Tr Danish by A. Ipsen, Copenhagen 1891; Du by J. van Lennep, Amsterdam 1834; Fr by S. Clogenson, Paris 1865, by A. Morisseau, Paris 1881, by J. Malaplate, Lausanne 1988; Ital by A. Brilli, Parma 1972; Rus by V. Lubich-Romanovich, Sine Otechestva (St Petersburg) Apr 1842, by D. Minaev, Sovremennik (St Petersburg) Aug 1863; Sp Paris 1829 (anon); Swed by 'Talis Qualis' (C. W. A. Strandberg), Stockholm [1854].
REVIEWS: (F. Jeffrey) Eclectic Rev n.s. 9 1818;Edinburgh Rev 29 1818; Monthly Rev Mar 1818.

A poetical epistle from Alma Mater to Lord Byron occasioned by lines in a tale called Beppo. Cambridge 1819.

Beppo in London: a metropolitan story. 1819.

Steffan, T. G. The Devil a bit of our Beppo. PQ 32 1953.

Mazeppa: a poem. 1819 (2 issues), Paris 1819, Boston 1819, Paris 1822, London 1824; ed H. M. Melford, Brunswick 1834; London [1854?]; tr Cz by A. Klásterský, Prague [c. 1895], 1922; Danish by C. Thaarup, Copenhagen 1842; Fr by J. Adolphe (in Manuel anglais), Paris 1830; Ger by T. Hell (Th. Winkler), Leipzig 1820, by E. Brauns, Göttingen 1836, by F. Friedmann, Leipzig 1855, by O. Gildemeister, Bremen 1858, by F. Freiligath, Stuttgart 1883; Greek by A. Vlachos, Athens 1858; Hungarian by Lázár Horváth, Budapest 1842, by D. Kosztolányi, Gyoma 1924; Ital by A. Arioti, Palermo 1847, by I. Virzi, Palermo 1876, by A. Maffei, Milan 1886, by L. Koch, Milan 1987; Polish by Michal Chodzkę, Halle 1860; Rus by M. Kachenovsky (in Vuibor iz sochineny Lorda Byrona), Moscow 1821, by A. Voeikov, Novosti Literatur (St Petersburg) Nov 1824, by Ya Grot, Sovremennik (St Petersburg) 9 1838, by I. Gogniev, Repertyar i Panteon (St Petersburg) Oct 1844, rptd Dramatichesky sbornik (St Petersburg) Apr 1860, by D. Michailovsky, Sovremennik (St Petersburg) May 1858; Sp Paris 1828 (anon), 1830, by J. M. R. Bárcena (in his Ultimas poesías líricas), Mexico City 1888, 1987; Swed [by C. W. A. Strandberg], Stockholm [1853]; Ukrainian by D. Zahul, 1933, by O. Veretenchenka, Demroum 1959. Adapted: Mazeppa travestied: a poem, 1820; H. M. Milner, Mazeppa: a romantic drama from Lord Byron's poem, [c. 1830], 1874; A. Cortesi, Mazeppa: ballo storico, Milan 1841; C. White, Mazeppa: an equestrian burlesque in two acts, New York [c. 1860].
REVIEWS: Blackwood's Mag July 1819; (W. Maginn) John Gilpin and Mazeppa, Blackwood's Mag July 1819; Monthly Rev July 1819; Eclectic Rev Aug 1819.

Englaender, D. Lord Byrons Mazeppa. Berlin 1897.

Holubnychy, L. Mazeppa in Byron's poem and in history. Ukrainian Quart 15 1959.

Don Juan [cantos i–ii]. 1819 (anon), 1819 (2 more edns), Paris 1819, Philadelphia 1819, London 1820 (3 edns), Paris 1821, London 1822, 1823; facs Spelsbury, Oxon 1992.

Don Juan: cantos iii, iv and v. 1821 (anon), 1821 (4 more edns), Paris 1821, New York 1821, London 1822 (rev) (5th edn).

Don Juan: cantos vi, vii and viii. 1823 (anon), 1823 (2 more edns), Paris 1823, Philadelphia 1823, London 1825.

Don Juan: cantos ix, x and xi. 1823 (anon), 1823, Paris 1823, Philadelphia 1823.

Don Juan: cantos xii, xiii and xiv. 1823 (anon), 1823 (2 more edns), Paris 1824, New York 1824.
Don Juan: cantos xv and xvi. 1824 (anon), 1824 (2 more edns), Paris 1824.
Dedication to Don Juan. 1833.
Don Juan [cantos i–v]. Illustr I. R. Cruikshank (pirate) 1821, 1822 (4 edns), 1823, 1823, 1824, [1826?]; [cantos v–xi], 1823; [cantos i–xvi], 2 vols 1826, 1826 (3 edns), 1827, 1827, 2 vols 1828, 1828, 1828, 1832, Nuremberg [1832], London 1833, 1834, 1835, 1836, 2 vols 1837, Mannheim 1838, London 1845, 1849, [c. 1850], Halifax 1857; ed E. H. Coleridge 1906; ed F. H. Ristine, New York 1927; ed L. I. Bredvold, New York 1935; ed P. C. Quennell 1949; ed T. G. Steffan and W. W. Pratt 4 vols Austin TX 1957 (variorum rev 1971); ed T. G. Steffan, E. Steffan and W. W. Pratt 1982; introd L. Kronenberger, New York 1984; ed B. Lee 1987 (cantos i–ii).
The beauties of Don Juan. 2 vols 1828.
TRANSLATIONS: Tr Arabic (abridged) by M. al-Siba'i, Cairo 1911; Armenian by L. Abrahamian, Moscow 1896, by H. Sevan, Yerevan 1988; Bulgarian by L. Lyubenov, Sofia 1986; Chinese by Zha Liang-zheng, Beijing 1980, by Zhu Weiji, rptd from 1956–8, Shanghai 1982; Cz by T. Vondrovic, Prague 1969; Danish by H. Schou (canto i only), Fredericia 1854, by H. Drachmann 2 vols Copenhagen 1880–1902; Fr by A[médée] P[ichot] 3 vols Paris 1827, by B. Laroche and J. Pribula 1836–7, rptd 1994, (cantos i–v) by A. Digeon, Paris 1854, rptd 1954, 2 vols Paris 1866, by P. Lehodey, Paris [1869], by A. Fauvel, Paris 1866, 1868, 1878; Ger (cantos i–iv) by A. von Marées, Essen 1839, by O. Gildemeister 2 vols Bremen 1845, by A. Böttger, Leipzig 1849, 1858, by W. Schäffer 2 vols Hildburgshausen 1867; Greek by K. Michailides, Athens 1870, by M. Kessisis 3 vols Athens 1981–7, (The isles of Greece only) canto iii by N. Pikkolou, Paris 1838, by K. Dosiou, Athens 1863; Hebrew (The isles of Greece only) canto iii by S. Tchernichovski, Palestine 1944; Hungarian by E. Abrányi, Budapest 1906, rptd 1964; Ital by A. Caccia, Turin 1853, by A. Sacchi, Milan 1865 (part as Aidea, Episodio di Don Glovanni), by V. Betteloni, Verona 1875, Milan 1880, by E. Casali, Milan 1876, cantos i–iv ed A. Brilli, tr V. Betteloni 1897, rptd 1982, by G. Dego, Milan 1972, by A. Alexis, Milan 1980, by S. Saglia, Brescia 1987, by Giovanelli, Milan 1991; Jap by F. Hayashi, Kyoto 1953, by K. Ogawa, Tokyo 1954, by K. Ogawa 2 vols 1993; Polish by Wiktor z Baworow (canto i only), Tarnopol 1863, (part of canto ii) by same, Cracow 1877, (canto iii) by same, Cracow 1877, (cantos ii–iv) by same, Tarnopol 1879, by E. Porebowicz, Warsaw 1885, 2 vols Warsaw 1922, by E. Porebowicz, Warsaw 1953, rptd 1959; Romanian by I. Eliade (cantos i–ii), Bucharest 1847; Rus by I. Jand, St Petersburg 1846, (cantos i–x) by V. Lubich-Romanovich 2 vols St Petersburg [1847], by N. A. Markevitch, Leipzig 1862, (cantos i–x) by D. Minaev, Sovremennik (St Petersburg) Jan–Oct 1865, by P. Kozlov, 2nd edn, ed P. Veinberg 2 vols St Petersburg 1889, by A. Kozlov 2 vols St Petersburg 1892, by T. Gnedic, Moscow/Leningrad 1959, rptd 1964, by A. Smirnova and N. Diakonova, Moscow 1964, by T. Gnedich, Moscow 1988, selections tr A. N. Zverev, Moscow 1988; Serbian by O. Glumchevik 2 vols Belgrade 1888; Serbo-Croat by O. Gluscevic, Belgrade 1957, by R. Kuic (cantos i–iv), Sarajevo 1982; Sp 2 vols Paris 1829 (anon), by F. Villalva 2 vols Madrid 1876, [1916], by J. A. R., Barcelona 1883, Madrid 1954, by A. Espina, Madrid 1966, rptd 1973, Barcelona 1993, by P. Ugalde, Madrid 1994; Swed (canto i only) Stockholm 1838 (anon), by C. W. A. Strandberg 2 vols Stockholm [1857–62]; Ukrainian by S. Golovanivskij, Kiev 1985.
REVIEWS: Monthly Rev July 1819, Aug 1821, July 1823, Oct 1823, Apr 1824; Literary Gazette 17–24 July 1819, 11–18 Aug 1821, 19 July 1823, 6 Sep 1823, 6 Dec 1823, 3 Apr 1824; Blackwood's Mag Aug 1819; Br Critic Aug 1819, Sep 1821; Br Rev Aug 1819, Dec 1821; NMM Aug 1819; Examiner 31 Oct 1819, 26 Aug 1821, 14, 21 Mar 1824; Don Juan unread [by William Maginn], Blackwood's Mag Nov 1819, Aug 1821, July 1823.
[Colton, C. C.]. Remarks, critical and moral, on the talents of Lord Byron and the tendencies of Don Juan. 1819.
[Hone, William?] Don John: or Don Juan unmasked. 1819 (3 edns).
Cottle, J. An expostulary epistle to Lord Byron. 1820.
[Stacy, J.]. A critique on the genius and writings of Lord Byron, with remarks on Don Juan. Norwich 1820.
Gordon. A tale: a poetical review of Don Juan. 1821.
[Lockhart, J. G.] A letter to Lord Byron by John Bull. 1821; ed R. L. Strout, Norman OK 1947. Also ascribed to John Black. *See* Athenaeum 7 Mar 1905.
von Goethe, J. W. Kunst und Alterthum 3 1821; rptd in Sämtliche Werke vol 37, Stuttgart 1907.
[Burgess, G.] Cato to Lord Byron on the immorality of his writings. 1824.
Thomas, J. W. An apology for Don Juan. 1824, 1825, 1850 ('to which is added a third canto'), 1855 (as Byron and the times: or an apology for Don Juan).
The morality of Don Juan, by the London hermit. Dublin Univ Mag May 1875.
de Bévotte, G. G. La légende de Don Juan: son évolution dans la littérature des origines au romantisme. Paris 1906.
Pfeiffer, A. Thomas Hopes Anastasius und Byrons Don Juan. Munich 1913.
Steffan, T. G. and W. W. Pratt. Don Juan. Austin TX 4 vols 1957 (variorum edn, rev 1971).
Childers, W. C. A note on the dedication of Don Juan. KSJ 12 1963.
Mortenson, R. Another continuation of Don Juan. Stud in Romanticism 2 1963.
Stavrou, C. N. Religion in Byron's Don Juan. Rice Univ Stud in Eng Lit 3 1963.

Continuations

[Hone, William?] Don Juan: canto the third. 1819.
Don Juan; with a biographical account of Lord Byron, canto iii. 1819.
A new canto. 1819.
Don Juan, canto xi. 1820.
Don Juan, canto iii. 1821.
[Thompson, W. G.?] A touch at an unpublished canto of Don Juan. Newcastle Mag Jan 1822.
[Clason, Isaac Star?] Don Juan: cantos ix, x and xi. Albany NY 1823.
Continuation of Don Juan: cantos xvii and xviii. Oxford 1825, 1825.
Don Juan: cantos xvii, xviii. 1825.
[Clason, Isaac Star]. Don Juan: cantos xvii–xviii. New York 1825.
Don Juan: canto xvii. Rambler July 1825.
Juan secundus: canto the first. 1825.
Don Giovanni: a poem in two cantos. Edinburgh 1825, 1825.
The seventeenth canto of Don Juan. 1829.
Don Juan: canto xvii. 1830.
[Clark, Charles?] Twenty suppressed stanzas of Don Juan in reference to Ireland. In Georgian revel-ations! or the most accomplished gentleman's midnight visit below stairs, Great Totham, Essex, 1838 (priv ptd); priv rptd separately as Some rejected stanzas of Don Juan, Great Totham 1845.
Baxter, G. R. Don Juan junior: a poem by Byron's ghost. 1839.
C[owley], W[illiam]. Don Juan reclaimed: or his peregrination continued from Lord Byron. 1840.
Morford, Henry. The rest of Don Juan. New York 1846.
[Daniel, H. J.?] Don Juan continued: canto xvii. 1849.
Wilberforce, E. and E. F. Blanchard. Don Juan: canto seventeenth. In Poems, 1857.
Wetton, H. W. The termination of the sixteenth canto of Lord Byron's Don Juan. 1864.
The new Don Juan: the introduction by Gerald Noel Byron, the last canto of the original Don Juan from the papers of the Countess

Guiccioli, by Lord Byron, never before published. [1880]. The whole book is by G. N. Byron.

Imitations and adaptations

Milner, H. M. The Italian Don Juan: or memoirs of the Devil. 1820.

Thornton, A. Don Juan, volume the first. 1821.

Thornton, A. Don Juan, volume the second: containing his life in London. 1822.

The Sultana: or a trip to Turkey, a melodrama in three acts, founded on Lord Byron's Don Juan. New York 1822.

Buckstone, J. B. Don Juan: a romantic drama in three acts. [1828], [1887].

Buckstone, J. B. A new Don Juan. 1828.

Letter to my grandmother's review. 1819 (proof, Murray). First pbd in Liberal no 1 [15 Oct 1822].

Ward, W. S. Lord Byron and my grandmother's review. MLN 64 1949.

Some observations upon an article in Blackwood's Magazine no xxiv, August 1819. [1820] (proof; no copy extant). First pbd in Works of Lord Byron vol 15, ed John Wright 1833.

Daghlian, P. B. Byron's Observations on an article in Blackwood's Magazine. RES 23 1947.

A letter to [John Murray] on the Rev W. L. Bowles' strictures on the life and writings of Pope. 1821 (2 issues), 1821 (2nd–3rd edns), Paris 1821; rptd 1974.

REVIEWS: (William Hazlitt) Blackwood's Mag May 1821; London Mag June 1821.

Campbell, T. Essay on English poetry. In Specimens of the British poets vol 1, 1819.

Bowles, W. L. Invariable principles of poetry in a letter addressed to T. Campbell. 1819.

[D'Israeli, I.]. [Review of Spence's Anecdotes]. Quart Rev 1820.

Bowles, W. L. A reply to the charges brought by the reviewer of Spence's Anecdotes. Pamphleteer 17 1820. *See* Bowles, *below*.

Gilchrist, O. G. Letter to the Rev W. L. Bowles. Stamford 1820.

Bowles, W. L. Observations on the poetical character of Pope. Pamphleteer 17–18 1820.

Bowles, W. L. Two letters to Lord Byron in answer to his Lordship's letter. 1821, 1821, 1822 (as Letters to Lord Byron on a question of poetical criticism).

MacDermot, M. A letter to the Rev W. L. Bowles in reply to his letter to T. Campbell, and to his two letters to Lord Byron. 1822.

A letter to Lord Byron protesting against the immolation of Gray, Cowper and Campbell at the shrine of Pope, by Fabius. 1823.

Bowles, W. L. A final appeal to the literary public relative to Pope. 1825.

Observations upon Observations: a second letter to John Murray esq on the Rev W. L. Bowles' strictures on the life and writings of Pope. 1821 (proof; no copy extant). First pbd in Works of Lord Byron vol 6, ed John Wright, 1832.

The Irish avatar. [1821] (priv ptd). The only copy known is in BM (Ashley Lib). *See* Athenaeum 26 June 1909. First pbd by Thomas Medwin in his Conversations of Lord Byron, 1824.

Marino Faliero, Doge of Venice: an historical tragedy in five acts, with notes; The prophecy of Dante: a poem. 1821 (2 issues), 1821 (2nd edn), 1823 (3rd edn); ed J. Hogg, Salzburg 1989.

REVIEWS: (F. Jeffrey) Edinburgh Rev 35 1821; (J. Wilson) Blackwood's Mag Apr 1821; Monthly Rev May 1821; (Leigh Hunt) Indicator 2 May 1821; Eclectic Rev June 1821; (R. Heber) Quart Rev 27 1822.

Marino Faliero [alone]. Paris 1821, Philadelphia 1821, 1821, London 1842; ed F. Brockerhoff, Berlin 1853; tr Danish by K. L. Rahbek, Copenhagen 1822; Ger by S. Hardt, Paderborn 1827, by C. Deahna, Bayreuth 1850, by Thierry Preyer, Frankfurt 1883, by A. Fitger, Oldenburgh [1886]; Ital by P. G. B. Cereseto, Savona 1845; Sp by M. Busquetz, Barcelona 1868.

Letter to R. W. Elliston on the injustice and illegality of his conduct in presenting Lord Byron's tragedy Marino Faliero. [1821.]

Marino Faliero: or the Doge of Venice: an interesting tale on which is founded the celebrated tragedy of Lord Byron. [c. 1822] (3 edns).

Kaiser, –. Byrons und Delavignes Marino Faliero. Düsseldorf 1870.

Krause, F. Byrons Marino Faliero: ein Beitrag zur vergleichenden Litteratur-geschichte. Breslau 1897.

[Dedication of Marino Faliero to Goethe.] Goethe-Jahrbuch 20 1899.

Schiff, H. Über Lord Byrons Marino Faliero und seine anderen geschichtlichen Dramen. Marburg 1910.

King, L. The influence of Shakespeare on Byron's Marino Faliero. Texas Univ Stud no 11 1931.

The prophecy of Dante [alone]. Paris 1821, Philadelphia 1821, London 1825; ed L. W. Potts 1879 (cantos i–ii); tr Fr by B. Laroche (in Oeuvres de Dante), Paris 1842, S. Rhéal 1846; Ital by L. da Ponte, New York 1821, by G. Giovio, Milan 1856, by M. Missirini, Milan 1858, by E. Roncaldier, Rome/Milan 1904; Sp by A. M. Vizcayno, Mexico City 1850.

Sardanapalus: a tragedy; The two Foscari: a tragedy; Cain: a mystery. 1821, Boston 1822, Spelsbury, Oxon 1990 (facs).

REVIEWS: (F. Jeffrey) Edinburgh Rev 36 1822; (Reginald Heber) Quart Rev 27 1822; Blackwood's Mag Feb 1822; Br Rev Mar 1822; Eclectic Rev May 1822; Examiner 2 June 1822; Portfolio (Philadelphia) Dec 1822.

Sardanapalus [alone]. Paris 1822, New York 1822, London 1823, [c. 1825], 1829, Arnsberg 1849, London [1853] (adapted for representation by Charles Kean), Manchester [1875] (adapted by Charles Clavert), ms edn J. R. Bartholomew, unpbd PhD thesis Univ of Texas 1964; tr Cz by Františec Krsek, Prague 1891; Danish by J. Ruesse, Copenhagen 1827; Du by H. Vinkeles, Amsterdam 1836; Fr by L. Alvin, Brussels 1834, by H. Becque, Paris 1867, by M. P. Berton, Paris 1882; Ger by E. Hertz, Posen 1854, by C. J. Arnold, Bremen 1854, by A. Böttger, Jena 1888, by J. Kainz, Berlin 1897, by O. Gildemeister, Zurich 1987; Ital, Milan 1884 (anon); Modern Greek by C. A. Parmenidos, Athens 1865; Polish by F. Krauze, Warsaw 1872; Rus by E. Zarin, Biblioteka dlya Chteniya (St Petersburg) Dec 1860, by O. N. Zhiuminoi, Artist (Moscow) Sep–Oct 1890; Sp Madrid 1847 (anon), (part only) by A. Bello (in his Obras completas vol 3), Santiago, Chile 1883; Swed by N. Arfvidsson, Stockholm 1864.

Nieschlag, H. Über Lord Byrons Sardanapalus. Halle 1900.

The two Foscari [alone]. Paris 1822, New York 1822; tr Danish by K. L. Rahbek, Copenhagen 1827; Fr by Escudier frères 1849, by A. Morisseau, Paris 1881; Greek by Th. Kamarados, Athens 1880; Ital by P. G. B. Cereseto, Savona 1845; Rus by E. Zarin, Biblioteka dlya Chteniya (St Petersburg) Nov 1861; Sp by M. Canete, Madrid 1846, by M. H. de Acosta, Barcelona 1868.

Cain [alone]. 1822 (6 edns), Paris 1822, New York 1822 London 1824; ed H. Grant 1830; 1832, Breslau 1840, London [1883]; ed B. Uhlmeyer, Nuremberg 1907; ed T. G. Steffan, Texas 1968; tr Chinese by Du Bingzhen, Shanghai 1950; Cz by J. Durdík, Prague 1871; Du by S. A. Kok, The Hague 1906; Esperanto by A. Kofman, Nuremberg 1896; Fr by F. D'Olivet, Paris 1823 (D'Olivet's version tr L. Redfield, New York 1923), by L. Fabulet, Paris 1923, facs Paris 1981, unpbd trn by I. Famchon 1994; Ger by G. Parthey, Berlin 1831, by F. Friedmann, Leipzig 1855, by A. Seubert, Leipzig [1874], by E. Blass, Berlin 1938, by G. O. Gildemeister and H. Koch, Frankfurt 1959; Greek by P. Georgoulis, Athens 1937, (parts) by H. N. de Villiers, Oxford 1925; Hebrew by D. Frichmann, Tel Aviv 1954 (rptd from Warsaw 1900); Hungarian by I. Gyory, [Budapest] 1895, by L. Mikes, Budapest 1898; Ital by A. Maffei, Milan 1852, by F. Milone, Florence 1949; Jap by K. Simada, Tokyo 1960; Polish by A. Pajgert, Lwow 1868; Portuguese by M. Bandeira, Rio de Janeiro 1961; Rus by E. Baruishev, St Petersburg 1881, by P. A. Kalenov, Moscow 1883, by I. Bunin, St Petersburg 1907; Sp by J. G., Madrid 1873; Yiddish by N. Horovitz, London 1925.

[Todd, H. J.] A remonstrance to Mr John Murray respecting a recent publication, by Oxoniensis. 1822.
A letter to Sir Walter Scott in answer to the remonstrance of Oxoniensis on the publication of Cain.
A vindication of the Paradise lost from the charge of exculpating Cain, by Phil-Milton. 1822.
Harness, W. The wrath of Cain. 1822.
Revolutionary causes; with a postscript containing strictures on Cain, by Britannicus. 1822.
A letter of expostulation to Lord Byron. 1822.
Uriel: a poetical address to Lord Byron. 1822, 1825.
Battine, W. Another Cain: a mystery. 1822.
Another Cain: a poem. 1822. Anon.
Adams, T. A scourge for Lord Byron: or Cain, a mystery unmasked. 1823.
Wilkinson, H. Cain: a poem containing an antidote to the impiety and blasphemy of Lord Byron's Cain. 1824.
von Goethe, J. W. Kunst und Alterthum 5 1824; rptd in his Sämtliche Werke vol 37, Stuttgart 1907, pp. 263–7.
A layman's epistle to a certain nobleman. 1824.
Remarks on Cain. [c. 1825] (priv ptd).
[Reade, J. E.] Cain the wanderer and other poems. 1830.
Monthly Mag May 1830; Fraser's Mag Apr 1831. Reviews of Harding Grant's edn.
Schaffner, A. Lord Byrons Cain und seine Quellen. Strasburg 1880.
Blumenthal, F. Lord Byron's mystery Cain and its relation to Milton's Paradise lost and Gessner's Death of Abel. Oldenburg 1891.
Graf, A. La poesia di Caino. Nuova Antologia 16 Mar, 1 Apr 1908.
Brooke, S. A. Byron's Cain. Hibbert Jnl 18 1919.

Heaven and earth. [1821] (proof; no copy extant), Paris 1823 (anon), London 1824 (anon), 1825, [c. 1825]. First pbd in Liberal no 2 1923; tr Danish by P. F. Wulff, Copenhagen 1827; Du by J. J. Abbink, Amsterdam 1837; Fr by A[médée] P[ichot] in Essai sur le génie et la caractère de Lord Byron, Paris 1824; Greek by G. S. Karadzas, Athens 1892; Ital by A. Maffei, Milan 1853.
REVIEWS: (J. Wilson) Blackwood's Mag Jan 1823; (F. Jeffrey) Edinburgh Rev 38 1823.
Mayn, G. Über Lord Byrons Heaven and earth. Breslau 1887.
Zuch, J. Thomas Moores The loves of the angels und Lord Byrons Heaven and earth: eine Parallele. Vienna 1905.

The vision of judgement. Paris 1822, London 1822 (with Southey's Vision of judgement, as The two visions), New York 1823, London 1824 (anon), 1825, [c. 1830] (anon), c. 1870; introd by M. le H. Redman, Cambridge 1926; ed E. M. Earl 1929; introd by R. Ellis Roberts 1932; ed F. B. Pinion 1958; ed L. Madden 1973 (facs); ed H. J. Donaghy, Idaho 1976; ed P. Cochran, unpbd PhD thesis Univ of Glasgow 1993. First pbd in Liberal no 1 1822, rptd with preface and errata in Liberal no 1 second issue, 1823. Tr Jap and ed I. Higashinaka, Kyoto 1984.
REVIEWS: Courier 16 Oct 1822; Literary Gazette 19 and 26 Oct, 2 Nov 1822.

The age of bronze: or carmen seculare et annus haud mirabilis. 1823 (anon), 1823 (2nd–3rd edns), Paris 1823, New York 1823, London 1824, 1825.
REVIEWS: Examiner 30 Mar 1823; Monthly Rev Apr 1823; Scots Mag Apr 1823; Literary Chron 5 Apr 1823; Literary Gazette 5 Apr 1823; Monthly Mag May 1823.

The island: or Christian and his comrades. 1823, 1823 (2nd–3rd edns), Paris 1823, New York 1823, London 1826, 1826; tr Ger [by F. L. Breuer], Leipzig 1827; Greek, by M. B. Raizis, Athens 1987; Ital by – Morrone, Naples 1840; Polish by A. Pajgert, Cracow 1859; Swed [by C. W. A. Strandberg], Stockholm [1856].
REVIEWS: Literary Chron 21 June 1823; Literary Gazette 21 June 1823; Monthly Rev July 1823; Atlantic Mag (New York) Apr 1826.
Lotze, C. Quellenstudien über Lord Byrons The island. Leipzig 1902.

Werner: a tragedy. 1823 (2 issues), Paris 1823, Philadelphia 1823; ed J. W. S. Howes, New York 1848, London 1865, 1866; tr Fr Paris 1844 (anon); Ger by G. Lotz, Hamburg 1823, by W. von Lüdemann, Zwickau 1825; Rus by Neizvustn, St Petersburg 1829.
REVIEWS: (W. Maginn) Blackwood's Mag Dec 1822; Scots Mag Dec 1822; European Mag Jan 1823; Eclectic Rev Feb 1823.
Stoehsel, C. Lord Byrons Trauerspiel Werner und seine Quelle. Erlangen 1891.
Gower, F. L. Did Byron write Werner? Nineteenth Cent Aug 1899.
Kluge, W. Lord Byrons Werner: eine dramentechnishce Untersuchung mit Quellenstudien. Leipzig 1913.
Motter, T. H. V. Byron's Werner re-estimated. In The Parrott presentation volume by pupils of Prof T. M. Parrott, Princeton 1935.

The deformed transformed: a drama. 1824 (2 variants), 1824 (2nd–3rd edns), Paris 1824, Philadelphia 1824, London [1883]; tr Hungarian by J. Eotvos, Budapest 1840, (Act 1 only) by M. Lukacs, Budapest 1849.
REVIEWS: London Mag Mar 1824; Monthly Mag Mar 1824; Scots Mag Mar 1824; Westminster Rev July 1824.
Varnhagen, H. Über Byrons dramatisches Bruchstück Der umgestaltete Missgestaltete. Erlangen 1905.

The parliamentary speeches of Lord Byron, printed from copies prepared by his Lordship for publication. 1824; tr Ital by V. Pepe 1992.
A political ode. 1880. I.e. An ode to the framers of the Frame Bill. First pbd in Morning Chron 2 Mar 1812.
A version of Ossian's address to the sun. Cambridge MA [1898] (priv ptd); rptd Atlantic Monthly Dec 1898.

Letters and journals

[Letter to the editor]. Galignani's Messenger (Paris) May 1819; facs rptd in Works (Galignani), Paris 1826, 1 vol edn.
[Part of journal for Sep 1816]. London Mag Mar 1820.
[Letter I]. Sir Charles Darell: or the vortex, by R. C. Dallas. 4 vols 1820. Vol 1 pp. 1–6 rptd in Dallas, Recollections, 1824, pp. 259–63.
[Letter on swimming the Hellespont]. Monthly Mag Apr 1821; rptd in Traveller 3 Apr 1821.
[Letter to E. D. Clarke]. The life and remains of E. D. Clarke, ed W. Otter, 1824, p. 627.
Correspondence of Lord Byron with a friend, including letters to his mother written from Portugal, Spain, Greece and the shores of the Mediterranean in 1809, 1810 and 1811. Ed R. C. Dallas [1824] (suppressed before pbn), 3 vols Paris 1825, 2 vols Philadelphia 1825; tr Fr Paris 1825, 1825.
[Letter to M. H. Beyle et al]. Conversations of Lord Byron at Pisa, by Thomas Medwin, 1824.
[Letter to Andreas Londos et al]. A narrative of Lord Byron's last journey to Greece, by Count Pietro Gamba, 1825.
[Letter to John Bowring]. Greece in 1823 and 1824, by L. F. C. Stanhope, 1825, p. 550.
[Letters to J. J. Coulmann]. Une visite à Byron à Gênes, suivie d'une lettre du noble Lord sur l'essai sur la vie et ses ouvrages de M. A[médée] P[ichot], by J. J. Coulmann, Paris 1826; tr Paul Pry, 1 Apr 1826.
[Letter to W. E. West]. Literary Souvenir 1827. Preface p. x.
[Letters to Thomas J. Dibdin]. Reminiscences of Thomas J. Dibdin, 1827, vol 2 pp. 65, 69–70.
[Letters to Leigh Hunt]. Lord Byron and some of his contemporaries, by Leigh Hunt, 1828.
[Letter to Isaac D'Israeli]. The literary character, by Isaac D'Israeli, 1828 (4th edn). Preface.
Letters and journals of Lord Byron, with notices of his life by Thomas Moore. 2 vols 1830, New York [1830], 1 vol Paris 1831, 3 vols London 1832, 1833, 1 vol 1837, 1847 (as The life of Lord Byron with his letters and journals), 1850, 1860 (as The life, letters and journals of Lord Byron), 1875; tr Fr by L. S. Belloc 5 vols Paris 1830.
REVIEWS: Athenaeum 25 Dec 1830, 1–8 Jan 1831; Edinburgh Rev

53 1831; Quart Rev 44 1831; Blackwood's Mag Feb–Mar 1831; Fraser's Mag Mar 1831.
[Letters to Hon Douglas Kinnaird]. Keepsake 1830, pp. 218–32.
[Letter to Henry Angelo]. Reminiscences of Henry Angelo vol 2, 1830, p. 132.
[Letter to John Galt]. The life of Lord Byron, by John Galt, 1830, pp. 179–80.
[Letter to Col Duffie]. Conversations on religion with Lord Byron by James Kennedy, 1830.
[Letters to Eugenius Roche]. London in a thousand years, with other poems, by Eugenius Roche, 1830, pp. 5–6.
[Letters to John Hunt]. Literary Guardian 5 Dec 1831–16 June 1832.
[Letters to the Earl of Blessington]. NMM July 1832.
[Letter to John Taylor]. Records of my life, by John Taylor, 1832, vol 2 p. 351.
Lord Byron. Discorso di Cesare Cantù; aggiuntevi alcune traduzioni ed un serie di lettere dello stesso Lord Byron ove si narrano i suoi viaggi in Italia e nella Grecia. Milan 1833; tr A. Kinloch as Lord Byron and his works: a biography and essay, 1883.
The works of Lord Byron in verse and prose, including his letters, journals etc. [Ed F. Halleck], New York 1833, Hartford CT, 1847.
[Letter to Sir James Mackintosh]. Life of the Rt Hon Sir James Mackintosh, 1835, vol 2 p. 268n.
[Letter to Col Wildman]. The Crayon miscellany no II: Abbotsford and Newstead Abbey, by Washington Irving, Philadelphia 1835, London 1835.
[Letter to Lady Byron]. Memoirs, journal and correspondence of Thomas Moore, ed Lord John Russell, vol 3, 1853, pp. 114, 115.
[Letters to E. J. Trelawny]. Recollections of the last days of Shelley and Byron, by E. J. Trelawny, 1858; ed J. E. Morpurgo 1952, New York 1961.
[Letters to J. Ridge]. N & Q 205, Nov 1860.
[Letters to Augusta Leigh]. Sharpe's London Mag July–Aug 1869.
[Letter on the separation]. Academy 9 Oct 1869.
[Letters to William Harness]. The literary life of the Rev William Harness, by A. G. L'Estrange, 1871.
[Letter to Mrs Parker]. Lord Byron: a biography, by Karl Elze, 1872, facs p. 1.
[Letter to Andrea Vacci]. Nuova Antologia (Florence) July 1874.
A facsimile of an interesting letter written by Lord Byron 15 Jan 1809. 1876.
Lord Byron: eine autobiographie nach Tagebüchern und Briefen, mit Einleitung und Erläuterungen von E. Engel. Berlin 1876, 1876.
[Letter to Francis Hodgson]. Memoirs of the Rev Francis Hodgson, by J. T. Hodgson, 2 vols 1878.
[Letters]. Catalogue of the collection of autograph letters formed by Alfred Morrison [1st ser], ed A. W. Thibaudeau, vol 1 1883 (priv ptd), pp. 142–51.
Letters written by Lord Byron during his residence at Missolonghi Jan–Apr 1824, to Mr Samuel Barff at Zante. Naples 1884 (priv ptd).
The letters and journals of Lord Byron, selected by Mathilde Blind. 1886.
[Letters to Mary Shelley]. The life and letters of Mary Wollstonecraft Shelley, by Mrs Julian Marshall, 2 vols 1889.
[Letters to Samuel Rogers]. Samuel Rogers and his contemporaries, by P. W. Clayden, 2 vols 1889.
[Letter to R. B. Hoppner]. Archivist Apr 1889.
[Letter to E. J. Dawkins]. Nineteenth Cent Nov 1891.
[Letter to C. J. Barry (28 May 1823)]. EStudien 17 1892.
[Letter to Rev R. Lowe]. Life and letters of Robert Lowe, Viscount Sherbrooke, by A. P. Martin, 1893, vol 1 p. 46.
[Letters]. The collection of letters formed by Alfred Morrison [2nd ser], vol 1 1893, pp. 446–78.
[Letter to Shelley (24 Apr 1822)]. EStudien 22 1895.
The works of Lord Byron. Vol 1: letters, 1804–13. Ed W. E. Henley 1897. No more vols pbd.
The works of Lord Byron: letters and journals. Ed R. E. Prothero [Baron Ernle] 6 vols 1898–1904.
Zehn Byroniana. Ed E. Kölbing, EStudien 25 1898.
[Letter to C. Barry]. Anglia Beiblatt Apr 1898.
[Letter to J. Ridge]. Newark Advertiser 4 May 1898.
[Letters to Elizabeth, Duchess of Devonshire]. The two Duchesses, by Vere Foster, 1898.
[Letters to John Murray]. Reference catalogue of British and foreign autographs and mss, ed T. J. Wise, Part vii, Byron, by John Murray, 1898. Facs.
[Letter to the Earl of Clare]. Daily Chron 19 Apr 1900.
The confessions of Lord Byron: a collection of his private opinions of men and matters. Ed W. A. L. Bettany, New York 1903, rptd 1973.
[Letters to George Steevens et al, ed C. K. Shorter]. Sphere 17 Sep 1904.
[Letters to Lady Byron]. Astarte, by Ralph Milbanke, Earl of Lovelace, 1905 (priv ptd).
[Letters]. Poems and letters of Lord Byron, ed from the original mss in the possession of W. K. Bixby by W. N. C. Carlton, Chicago 1912 (Soc of Dofobs) (priv ptd).
[Letters]. Byroniana und anderes aus dem englischen Seminar in Erlangen, Erlangen 1912.
[Letter to C. Barry]. Byroniana, by O. Intze, [Birmingham 1914].
[Letter to W. Baldwin]. Nation (New York) 18 Apr 1918.
[Letter to Hodgson (20 Jan 1811)]. Annual report of British School at Athens (1916–18), 22 1919, pp. 107–9. Facs.
[Letters to Augusta Leigh]. Astarte, 2nd edn with additional letters, ed Mary, Countess of Lovelace, 1921.
Lord Byron's correspondence, chiefly with Lady Melbourne, Mr Hobhouse, the Hon Douglas Kinnaird and P. B. Shelley. Ed J. Murray 2 vols 1922, rptd Philadelphia 1986.
[Letters to Mrs Stith]. Catherine Potter Stith and her meeting with Byron, by A. B. Benson, South Atlantic Quart 22 1923.
[Letters to Dallas, and to Hodgson]. A descriptive catalogue of an exhibition of manuscripts and first editions of Lord Byron, by R. H. Griffith and H. M. Jones, Austin TX 1924.
[Letters to Capt Hay and J. Webb, ed A. Koszul]. Revue Anglo-Américaine 2 1925.
[Letters to the Greek Committee]. Nineteenth Cent Sep 1926.
Lord Byron in his letters: selections by V. H. Collins. New York 1927, rptd 1973.
The Ravenna journal, mainly compiled at Ravenna in 1821. Ed Lord Ernle [R. E. Prothero] 1928 (First Editions Club) (priv ptd), rptd Norwood 1975.
[Letters to Lady Byron]. The life and letters of Lady Bryon, by E. C. Mayne, 1929.
The letters of George Gordon, Lord Byron, selected by R. G. Howarth. 1933, 1936, 1962 (EL).
[Letter to the Greek Committee]. Ed W. H. McCarthy, YULG 8 1934.
[Letters to Miss Mercer Elphinstone]. Cornhill Mag Apr 1934.
Three Byron letters. Ed C. O. Parsons, N & Q 26 May 1934.
[Letters to Lord Holland]. The home of the Hollands, by the Earl of Ilchester, [1937].
[Letters to Leigh Hunt]. My Leigh Hunt library, by L. A. Brewer, Iowa City 1938.
Nicolson, H. An account of a copy of Moore's life with additions by J. C. Hobhouse. Nineteenth Cent June 1939, rptd 1948.
To Lord Byron. Ed G. Paston and P. Quennell 1939.
Pratt, W. W. Byron at Southwell. Austin TX 1948, rptd New York 1973. 5 letters.
Origo, I. The last attachment. 1949, 1962. 139 Italian letters.
Borghese, M. L'appassionata di Byron. Milan 1949.
Marchand, L. A. Byron and Count Alborghetti. PMLA 64 1949. 9 letters.

Vincent, E. R. Byron, Hobhouse and Foscolo: new documents in the history of a collaboration. Cambridge 1949.
Quennell, P. C. Byron: a self portrait: letters and diaries. 2 vols 1950. 56 unpbd letters and 36 first pbd in full.
Cline, C. L. Byron, Shelley and their Pisan circle. Cambridge MA 1952. 29 letters.
Forster, H. B. Byron and Nicolas Karvellas. KSJ 2 1953.
Gates, P. G. A Leigh Hunt – Byron letter. KSJ 2 1953.
Selected letters. Ed J. Barzun, New York 1953. Tr Estonian, Riga 1953; Fr by R. Martin 1959; Ger by F. Borschel, Frankfurt 1960, by C. Gigon, Stuttgart 1963; Polish by Z. Kubiak, Warsaw 1960; Rus by Z. E. Alexandrova, Moscow 1963.
Bates, M. C. Two new letters of Keats and Byron. KSJ 3 1954.
Lovell, E. J. His very self and voice: collected conversations of Lord Byron. New York 1954.
Green, D. B. Three new Byron letters. KSJ 5 1956.
Marshall, W. H. A new letter from Byron to John Hunt. N & Q 202, Mar 1957.
de Beer, G. A Byron letter at St Petersburg. TLS 16 May 1958.
Jones, F. L. A Byron letter. N & Q 205, 10 June 1960.
Kendall, L. H., jun. An unpublished letter to Shelley. MLN 76 1961.
Lovell E. J., jun. Medwin's conversations of Lord Byron. 1966.
Lovell E. J., jun. Lady Blessington's conversations of Lord Byron. 1969.
Steffan, T. G. From Cambridge to Missolonghi: Byron's letters at the University of Texas. 1971.
Byron's letters and journals, vol 1: 1798–1810 In my hot youth. Ed L. A. Marchand 1973.
Byron's letters and journals, vol 2: 1810–1812 Famous in my time. Ed L. A. Marchand 1973.
Byron's letters and journals, vol 3: 1813–1814 Alas the love of women. Ed L. A. Marchand 1974.
Byron's letters and journals, vol 4: 1814–1815 Wedlock's the devil. Ed L. A. Marchand 1975.
Byron's letters and journals, vol 5: 1816–1817 So late into the night. Ed L. A. Marchand 1976.
Byron's letters and journals, vol 6: 1818–1819 The flesh is frail. Ed L. A. Marchand 1976.
Byron's letters and journals, vol 7: 1820 Between two worlds. Ed L. A. Marchand 1977.
Byron's letters and journals, vol 8: 1821 Born for opposition. Ed L. A. Marchand 1978.
Byron's letters and journals, vol 9: 1821–1822 In the wind's eye. Ed L. A. Marchand 1979.
Byron's letters and journals, vol 10: 1822–1823 A heart for every fate. Ed L. A. Marchand 1980.
Byron's letters and journals, vol 11: 1823–1824 For freedom's battle. Ed L. A. Marchand 1981.
Burnett, T. A. J. The rise and fall of a regency dandy, the life and times of Scrope Berdmore Davies. 1981.
Byron's letters and journals, index vol, The trouble of an index. Ed L. A. Marchand 1982.
Lord Byron selected letters and journals. Ed L. A. Marchand 1982; tr Bekarian, Yerevan 1988; Ger by T. Jacobson, Frankfurt 1985.
Byron's bulldog. The letters of John Cam Hobhouse to Lord Byron. Ed P. W. Graham, Columbus OH 1984.
Byron, a self-portrait: letters and diaries 1798 to 1824. Ed P. Quennell 1990.
The sayings of Lord Byron. Ed Stoddard Martin 1990.
Byron's letters and journals, suppl vol, What comes uppermost. Ed L. A. Marchand 1994.
The Clare Clairmont correspondence. Ed M. K. Stocking 2 vols Baltimore 1995.
George Gordon Lord Byron. Introd by D. Glen, Edinburgh 1995.
Cochran, P. 'Nobody has seen it' – Byron's first letter announcing Manfred. Byron Jnl 24 1996.

Translations of letters and journals

Armenian by A. Bekarian, Yerevan 1988; Bulgarian by J. Stefanova, Sofia 1985; Du by J. van Helmond, Amsterdam 1986; Estonian by A. Balodis Riga 1954; Fr by J. Delachaume, Paris 1911, Paris 1930, by R. Martin, Paris 1959, by J.-P. Richard and P. Bensimon, Paris 1987; Georgian, (Italian diaries) Tbilisi 1976; Ger by F. Burschell, Frankfurt 1960, by C. Gigon, Stuttgart 1963, ed C. Hentschel, tr A. Uthe-Spenker, Munich 1979; Hungarian by I. Bart, L. Horváth and I. Tótfalusi, Budapest 1978; Ital, Letters from Italy ed C. Béguin, tr D. Fink, Milan 1983, Italian letters tr E. Mazzarotto 1985, rptd 1989, by M. D'Amico, Turin 1989, Journals by M. Skey, Rome and Naples 1990; Polish by Z. Kubiak Warsaw, 1960; Rus by Z. E. Alexandrova, Moscow 1963; Serbo-Croat by N. Curcija-Prodanovic, Belgrade 1985; Slovenian by J. Menart 1975; Sp by C. Salazar, preface by J. Palas, nd; Swed, by G. Aman-Nilsson 1918.

Pieces first published in periodicals and in books by other writers

Stanzas to Jessy. Monthly Literary Recreations July 1807. With review of Wordsworth's Poems 1807.
Hobhouse, J. C. Imitations and translations from the ancient and modern classics. 1809. Pp. 185–230. 9 poems.
[Review of Gell's Geography of Ithaca]. Monthly Rev Aug 1811.
An ode to the framers of the Frame Bill. Morning Chron 2 Mar 1812; rptd separately as A political ode, 1880.
Stanzas on a lady weeping. Morning Chron 7 Mar 1812; rptd in Corsair, 1814 (2nd edn).
Address spoken at the opening of Drury Lane Theatre. Morning Chron 12 Oct 1812; rptd in Genuine rejected addresses, presented to the committee of management for Drury Lane Theatre, preceded by that written by Lord Byron, 1812.
REVIEW: (Leigh Hunt) Examiner 18 Oct 1812.
[Smith, James and Horace]. Rejected addresses: or the new theatrum poetarum. 1812.
A critique on the address spoken at the opening of the new Theatre Royal, Drury Lane. [1812.]
A sequel to the Rejected addresses or the theatrum poetarum minorum, by another author. 1813.
Parenthetical address by Dr Plagiary. Morning Chron 23 Oct 1812; rptd in Works vol 17, 1833 (Murray).
To Sarah, Countess of Jersey. Champion 31 July 1814; rptd in Three poems not included in Byron's works, 1818.
Elegiac stanzas on the death of Sir Peter Parker. Morning Chron 7 Oct 1814; rptd in Hebrew melodies, 1816.
'Bright be the place of thy soul'. Examiner 4 June 1815; rptd with music by I. Nathan, [1815], and in Poems, 1816.
Napoleon's farewell. Examiner 30 July 1815; rptd in Poems, 1816.
'We do not curse thee, Waterloo'. Morning Chron 15 Mar 1816; rptd in Poems, 1816.
On the star of the Legion of Honour. Examiner 7 Apr 1816; rptd in Poems, 1816.
[Translations from the Armenian: the epistle of the Corinthians to St Paul etc]. A grammar, Armenian and English, by Yarouthiun Augerean (Father Pascal Aucher). Venice 1819, 1832, 1873.
'Maid of Athens, ere we part'. In H. W. Williams, Travels in Italy, Greece and the Ionian Isles, Edinburgh 1820, vol 2, p. 290. *See* TLS 10 Dec 1931.
The vision of judgement; Letter to my grandmother's review; Epigrams on Lord Castlereagh. Liberal no 1, 15 Oct 1822.
Heaven and earth: a mystery; 'Aegle, beauty and poet'; translation from Martial; 'Why how now, Saucy Tom?'. Liberal no 2, 1 Jan 1823.
The blues: a literary eclogue. Liberal no 3, 26 Apr 1823.
Morgante Maggiore di Messer Luigi Pulci. Liberal no 4, 30 July 1823.
A critique on the Liberal. 1822.
The Illiberal! Verse and prose from the North. [1822.] Attributed to William Gifford by T. J. Wise.

Lord Byron, Leigh Hunt and the Liberal [selections from the Liberal]. Ed L. P. Pickering [1925].
Marshall, W. H. Byron, Shelley, Hunt and the Liberal. Philadelphia 1960.
'And dost thou ask the reason of my sadness?' Nicnac 25 Mar 1823.
Foscolo, Ugo. In his Essays on Petrarch, 1823, pp. 215–17.
Notizie estere. El Telegrafo Greco (Missolonghi) no 5, 17 Apr 1824; rptd Nineteenth Cent Sep 1926.
On this day I complete my 36th year. Morning Chron 29 Oct 1824.
Remember thee (1st edn only); Stanzas to the Po; The Irish Avatar. In T. Medwin, Conversations of Lord Byron at Pisa, 1824 (3 edns).
[Stanzas omitted from Childe Harold, canto ii]. In R. C. Dallas, Recollections of the life of Lord Byron, 1824.
Stanzas [on the death of the Duke of Dorset]. Edinburgh Annual Register for 1824, 1825. Pt 1 p. 265. *See* MLR 44 1949.
[Lines to Lady Blessington]. Annales Romantiques (Paris) 1827–8.
Verses written in compliance with a lady's request to contribute to her album. Casket 1829.
Lines on hearing that Lady Byron was ill. NMM Aug 1832; rptd with the next 2 entries in M. Gardiner, Countess of Blessington, Conversations of Lord Byron, 1834.
'Could love for ever'. NMM Oct 1832.
'But once I dared to lift my eyes'. NMM Mar 1833.
Question and answer. Fraser's Mag Jan 1833.
Newstead Abbey. In J. T. Hodgson, Memoir of the Rev Francis Hodgson vol 2, 1878, p. 187.
Last words on Greece. Murray's Mag Feb 1887.
'I watched thee when the foe was at our side'. Murray's Mag Feb 1887.
Farewell petition to J. C. H[obhouse]. Murray's Mag Mar 1887.
My boy Hobbie O! Murray's Mag Mar 1887.
The monk of Athos. In R. Noel, The life of Lord Byron, 1890, pp. 206–7.
[Epilogue on Wordsworth's Peter Bell]. Philadelphia Record 28 Dec 1891.
To the Hon Mrs George Lamb. In V. Foster, The two Duchesses, 1898, p. 374.
The King of the Humbugs. Good Words Aug–Sep 1904.
Magdalen; Harmodia. In R. Milbanke, Earl of Lovelace, Astarte, 1905 (priv ptd).
[Addn to English bards and Scotch reviewers]. TLS 30 Apr 1931.
Pratt, W. W. Byron at Southwell. Austin TX 1948.
Steffan, T. G. An early Byron manuscript in the Pierpont Morgan Library. SE 27 1948.
Pratt, W. W. An Italian notebook of Lord Byron. SE 28 1949.
Pratt, W. W. 'To these ladies': an unpublished poem by Byron. Ed W. Pafford, KSJ 1 1952.

Works incorrectly ascribed to Byron

The spurious continuations of Don Juan *are listed after the edns of that poem, above.*

A farrago libelli: a poem, chiefly imitated from the first satire of Juvenal. 1806. *See* B. Dobell, Eng Rev Aug 1915; S. C. Chew, MLN 31 1916.
Lord Byron's Farewell to England, with three other poems. 1816. Included in some later edns of Poems on his domestic circumstances. *See* Prothero, Prose works vol 3, p. 337. Ascribed to John T. Agg. *See* H. M. Jones, The author of two Byron Apocrypha, MLN 41 1926.
Reflections on shipboard by Lord Byron. 1816.
Lord Byron's Pilgrimage to the Holy Land. 1816, 1817 (2nd edn, without Byron's name). *See* Prothero vol 4, p. 19. Ascribed to John T. Agg. *See* H. M. Jones, MLN 41 1926.
Clarke, H. Lord Byron, the legal critics refuted: or an essay to prove from the arguments of Lord Byron's Counsel that Childe Harold and the Prisoner of Chillon are mercenary forgeries, and that Pilgrimage to the Holy Land is a genuine production. 1817.
Modern Greece. 1817. By Felicia Hemans.
Poems written by somebody. 1818.
Childe Harold's pilgrimage to the Dead Sea; Death on the pale horse; and other poems. 1818. *See* Prothero vol 4, p. 474.
The vampyre: a tale. 1819 (3 edns; first pbd in NMM Apr 1819); tr Fr by Amédée Pichot, Paris 1830; dramatised in Ger by L. Ritter, Brunswick 1822; tr Sp, Paris 1829. By J. W. Polidori. *See* Prothero vol 4, p. 286.
Anastasius: or memoirs of a Greek. 1819. By Thomas Hope.
Giuseppino: an Occidental story. 1821, 1821, Philadelphia 1822; Rptd in Arnaldo; Gaddo etc, 1836. By E. N. Shannon.
La mort de Napoléon: dithyrambe traduit de l'anglais de Lord Byron. Paris 1821 (7 edns).
Le cri d'Angleterre au tombeau de sa Reine: dithyrambe de Lord Byron traduit de l'anglais. Paris 1821.
Irner par Lord Byron. 2 vols Paris 1821.
The Duke of Mantua: a tragedy. 1823, 1833. By John Roby; included in The legendary and poetic remains of John Roby, 1854.
My wedding night: the obnoxious chapter in Lord Byron's memoirs. John Bull Mag July 1824.
The Count Arezzi. 1824. By Robert Eyres Landor.
Lettre de Lord Byron au Grand Turc. Paris 1824.
Arnaldo; Gaddo; and other unacknowledged poems by Lord Byron and some of his contemporaries. Ed 'Odoardo Volpi', Dublin 1836. By E. N. Shannon.
The inedited works of Lord Byron, now first published from his letters, journals and other manuscripts in the possession of his son Major Gordon Byron. 2 pts (all pbd), New York 1849. Some of this is a reprint of genuine originals already pbd.
Don Leon. [Pbd abroad before 1853? *See* N & Q 15 Jan 1853]; 1866, 1866; rptd 1934.
Leon to Annabella: an epistle after the manner of Ovid. Nd, 1865, 1866 (as The great secret revealed), Brussels 1875, Paris [c. 1900], New York 1922 (in Poetica erotica, ed T. R. Smith, vol 3).
The unpublished letters of Lord Byron, edited with a critical essay by H. S. Schultess-Young. 1872. Suppressed before pbn. The only letters in this book known to be authentic are those to Byron's mother, and these had been ptd previously.
The bride's confession. Paris 1916 (priv ptd).
Seventeen letters to an unknown lady 1811–17. Ed W. E. Peck, New York 1930. These letters derive from the Schultess-Young edn of 1872. Prothero, vol 6 p. 460, did not accept them as authentic.

Byron in poetry and fiction (to 1837)

[Lamb, Lady Caroline]. Glenarvon. 3 vols 1816 (3 edns), 1 vol [1865] (as The fatal passion); tr Fr, Paris 1819.
Olney, C. Glenarvon revisited. Univ of Kansas City Rev 22 1958.
[Barrett, Eaton Stannard]. Six weeks at Long's, by a late resident. 3 vols 1817.
Three weeks at Fladong's, by a late visitant. 1817.
[Peacock, Thomas Love]. Nightmare Abbey. 1818.
An account of Lord Byron's residence in the Island of Mitylene. 1818. *See* Prothero vol 4, p. 288; [F. W. Hasluck], Byron and Col Rooke, Saturday Rev 11 June 1921.
de Lamartine, Alphonse. L'homme: à Lord Byron. In his Méditations poétiques, Paris 1820; tr C. Hicks, Whitby 1837. Another Eng trn, 1843.
Delavigne, Casimir. Messénienne sur Lord Byron. Paris 1824, 1824; rptd in his Nouvelles Messéniennes, Paris 1824; tr Marseilles 1824.
de Vigny, Alfred. Sur la mort de Byron. La Muse Française (Paris) 15 June 1824.
Shelley, P. B. Julian and Maddalo. In his Posthumous poems, 1824.
Narrative of Lord Byron's voyage to Corsica and Sardinia by Capt Benson. 1824, Paris 1825.
Bedford, J. H. Wanderings of Childe Harold. 3 vols 1825.

[Shelley, Mary]. The last man. 3 vols 1826.
Taylor, John. Byronna the disappointed. [c. 1830.]
[Brydges, Sir S. E.] Modern aristocracy: or the bard's reception. Geneva 1831.
von Chamisso, A. Lord Byrons letzte Liebe (1827). Chios 1929.
Driver, H. A Harold de Burun: a semi-dramatic poem. 1835.
Laube, H. Lord Byron: eine Reisenovelle. Mannheim 1835.
[Shelley, Mary] Lodore. 3 vols 1835.
Mitford, J. The private life of Lord Byron: comprising his voluptuous amours, secret intrigues and close connection with various ladies of rank. [1836]; tr Fr, Paris 1837.
Magnien, Edouard. Mortel, ange ou démon. Paris 1836.
[Disraeli, Benjamin]. Venetia: or the poet's daughter. 3 vols 1837.
Hamilton, H. B. Inaugural essay on the portrayal of the life and character of Lord Byron in a novel entitled Venetia. Leipzig 1884.
Cipro, G. B. Lord Byron a Venezia. [Florence?] 1837. A play.

§2

Hobhouse, J. C. (Baron Broughton). A journey through Albania and other provinces of Turkey. 2 vols 1813, 1855 (as Travels in Albania). The substance of some letters written by an Englishman in Paris during the last reign of the Emperor Napoleon. 2 vols 1816, 1817, 1817. Letters addressed to Byron.
Hobhouse, J. C. Lord Byron's residence in Greece. Westminster Rev 2 1824.
Hobhouse, J. C. [Review of Dallas's Recollections and Medwin's Conversations]. Westminster Rev 3 1825.
Hobhouse, J. C. Italy: remarks made in several visits from 1816 to 1854. 2 vols 1859.
Hobhouse, J. C. Some account of a long life. 5 vols 1865 (priv ptd); rptd as Recollections of a long life, ed Lady Dorchester, 6 vols 1909–11.
REVIEW: Edinburgh Rev 133 1871.
Hobhouse, J. C. Contemporary account of the separation of Lord and Lady Byron, also of the destruction of Lord Byron's memoirs. 1870 (priv ptd); rptd in Recollections of a long life, 2nd edn vol 2.
Proofs of letters from John Cam Hobhouse to Lord Byron set up in type. (BL c.131 k2.)
[Irving, Washington]. Lord Byron. Analectic Mag (Philadelphia) July 1814; rptd in Poetical works of Lord Byron, Boston 1814.
[Irving, Washington]. An unwritten drama of Lord Byron. Gift for 1836 (New York) [1835]; ed T. O. Mabbott, Metuchen NJ 1925.
A catalogue of books the property of a nobleman [Byron] about to leave England, which will be sold by auction by [Robert H. Evans]. 5 Apr [1816].
A narrative of the circumstances which attended the separation of Lord and Lady Byron. 1816.
[Beyle, M. H.] Rome, Naples et Florence en 1817 par M. de Stendhal. Paris 1817; tr 1818.
[Beyle, M. H.] Lord Byron en Italie et en France. Revue de Paris Mar 1830; rptd in his Racine et Shakespeare, Paris 1854; tr as Reminiscences of Lord Byron in Italy, Mirror of Lit 17–24 Apr 1830.
Shelley, P. B. History of a six weeks' tour. 1817.
Hazlitt, W. In his Lectures on the English poets, 1818.
Hazlitt, W. In his Spirit of the age, 1825.
Hazlitt, W. Lord Byron. In The collected works of William Hazlitt, vol 4, London 1902.
Wiffen, J. H. The character and poetry of Lord Byron. NMM May 1819.
The radical triumvirate: or Infidel Paine, Lord Byron and Surgeon Lawrence colleaguing with the patriotic radicals to emancipate mankind from all laws, human and divine, by an Oxonian. 1820.
de Vigny, Alfred. Littérature anglaise: oeuvres complètes de Lord Byron. Le Conservateur Littéraire (Paris) Dec 1820.
Watts, A. A. Lord Byron's plagiarisms. Literary Gazette 24 Feb–31 Mar 1821.
[Watkins, John]. Memoirs of the life and writings of Lord Byron. 1822; tr Ger, Leipzig 1825.
Belloc, L. S. Lord Byron. Paris 1824.
Brydges, S. E. Letters on the character and poetical genius of Lord Byron. 1824.
Brydges, S. E. An impartial portrait of Lord Byron as a poet and a man. Paris 1825.
Dallas, R. C. Recollections of the life of Lord Byron 1808–14. 1824.
El Telegrafo Greco (Missolonghi) 24 Apr 1824.
Exposure of the mis-statements contained in Captain Medwin's pretended Conversations of Lord Byron. 1824.
Full particulars of the much lamented death of Lord Byron with a sketch of the life. 1824.
Gordon, Sir C. The life and genius of Lord Byron. 1824; rptd in Pamphleteer 24 1824.
Hugo, V. Sur George Gordon, Lord Byron. La Muse Française 15 June 1824.
Hugo, V. Lord Byron et ses rapports avec la littérature actuelle. Annales Romantiques (Paris) 1827–8.
Medwin, T. Journal of the conversations of Lord Byron at Pisa. 1824 (3 edns).
REVIEWS: Blackwood's Mag Nov 1824; GM Nov 1824.
Murray, J. Notes on Capt Medwin's Conversations of Lord Byron. 1824 (priv ptd); rptd in Works of Lord Byron (Murray), 1829.
Capt Medwin vindicated from the calumnies of the reviewers by Vindex. 1825.
Medwin, T. The angler in Wales. 2 vols 1834.
The particulars of the dispute between the late Lord Byron and Mr Southey. Edinburgh 1824.
Scott, W. The death of Lord Byron. Edinburgh Weekly Jnl 19 May 1824; rptd in his Miscellaneous prose works vol 1, Edinburgh 1841.
Simmons, J. W. An inquiry into the moral character of Lord Byron. New York 1824, London 1826.
Styles, J. Lord Byron's works viewed in connection with Christianity and the obligations of social life. 1824.
Blaquière, E. Narrative of a second visit to Greece, including facts connected with the last days of Lord Byron. 1825.
Byroniana: Bozzies and Piozzies. 1825.
Clinton, G. Memoirs of the life and writings of Lord Byron. 1825.
de Salvo, C. Lord Byron en Italie et en Grèce. Paris 1825.
Gamba, P. A narrative of Lord Byron's last journey to Greece. 1825.
[Kilgour, A.] Anecdotes of Lord Byron from authentic sources. 1825.
The life, writings, opinions and times of Lord Byron, including copious recollections of the lately destroyed memoirs by an English gentleman in the Greek Military Service. 3 vols 1825. Ascribed to Matthew Iley.
Parry, W. The last days of Lord Byron. 1825.
[Phillips, W.] A review of the character and writings of Lord Byron. Atlantic Monthly Oct 1825; rptd 1826. Also attributed to Andrews Norton.
Pichot, A. Essais sur Lord Byron. Paris 1825. For Byron's comments *see* J. J. Coulmann, Une visite à Byron à Gênes, Paris 1826.
Stanhope, L. F. C. Greece in 1823 and 1824, to which is added reminiscences of Lord Byron. 1825, Paris 1825.
Tricoupi, S. Funeral oration on Lord Byron, delivered at Missolonghi. 1825, 1836.
Albrizzi, I. T. In her Ritratti scritti, Pisa 1826.
Lake, W. J. The life of Lord Byron. Paris 1826, Frankfurt 1827. First pbd in Galignani's edn of the Works of Lord Byron, Paris 1822.
Catalogue of the library of the late Lord Byron, which will be sold at auction by R. H. Evans, 16 July 1827. Ed G. H. Doane, [Lincoln Nebraska] 1929 (priv ptd).
Hunt, J. H. L. Lord Byron and some of his contemporaries. 1828, 2 vols 1828.
REVIEWS: Quart Rev 37 1828; Athenaeum 2, 23, 30 Jan 1828.

Hunt, J. H. L. Autobiography. 3 vols 1850, 1 vol 1860 (rev); ed R. Ingpen 2 vols 1903.
Galt, J. The life of Lord Byron. 1830, [1908].
REVIEWS: Edinburgh Rev 52 1830; GM Sep 1830; Athenaeum 4 Sep 1830; Fraser's Mag Oct 1830.
Galt, J. Pot versus kettle. Fraser's Mag Dec 1830.
Galt, J. Prose and verse, humorous, satirical and sentimental. Ed R. H. Shepherd 1878. Contains rough notes for the Life.
Gordon, P. L. In his Personal memoirs or reminiscences, 2 vols 1830.
Kennedy, J. Conversations on religion with Lord Byron and others, held in Cephalonia a short time previous to his Lordship's death. 1830.
Moore, T. Letters and journals of Lord Byron, with notices of his life. 2 vols 1830, New York [1830], 1 vol Paris 1831, 3 vols 1832, 1833, 1 vol 1837, 1847, 1850, 6 vols 1851, 1 vol 1860, 1875; tr Fr, Paris 1830–1.
REVIEWS: Blackwood's Mag Feb–Mar 1830; (P. Mérimée) Le National (Paris) 7 Mar 1830; Athenaeum 25 Dec 1830, 1–8 Jan 1831; Edinburgh Rev 53 1831 (by T. B. Macaulay; rptd in his Critical and miscellaneous works vol 1, Philadelphia 1841); (J. G. Lockhart) Quart Rev 44 1831; Fraser's Mag Mar 1831; (C. W. Le Bas) Br Critic Apr 1831.
[Byron, Lady Isabella]. Remarks occasioned by Mr Moore's notices of Lord Byron's life. [1830] (priv ptd) (3 edns).
Campbell, T. [Lady Byron and Thomas Moore]. NMM Apr 1830.
Lord Byron vindicated and Mr Campbell answered. 1830.
Milligen, J. Memoirs of the affairs of Greece with various anecdotes of Lord Byron, and an account of his last illness and death. 1831.
Mazure, A. Étude morale sur Lord Byron. Revue Anglo-Française (Poitiers) 1 1833.
Browne, J. H. Voyage from Leghorn to Cephalonia with Lord Byron in 1823. Blackwood's Mag Jan 1834.
Browne, J. H. Narrative of a visit to Greece. Fraser's Mag Sep 1834.
Gardiner, M. (Countess of Blessington). Conversations of Lord Byron. 1834, 1893 (rev); tr Fr, Paris 1833. First pbd in NMM July 1832–Dec 1833.
Blümel, M. Die Unterhaltungen Lord Byrons mit der Gräfin Blessington als ein Beitrag zur Byronbiographie kritisch untersucht. Breslau 1900.
Gardiner, M. The idler in Italy. 3 vols 1839–40.
van Lennep, J. Vertalingen en Navolgingen in Poezy. Amsterdam 1834.
Conversations of an American with Lord Byron. NMM Oct–Nov 1835.
Irving, W. The Crayon miscellany, no 2 (Abbotsford and Newstead Abbey). Philadelphia 1835, London 1835.
Niccolini, G. Vita di Giorgio, Lord Byron. Milan 1835.
Mordani, F. La vita di Giorgio Lord Byron. Bologna 1839.
'Sand, George' (A. A. L. Dudevant). Essai sur le drame fantastique: Goethe, Byron, Mickiewicz. Revue des Deux Mondes 1 Dec 1839; rptd in Autour de la table, Paris 1862.
Thomsen, G. On Lord Byron. Copenhagen 1845.
von Düringsfeld, I. Byrons Frauen. Breslau 1845.
Villemain, A. F. In his Études de littératures anciennes et étrangères, Paris 1846.
Mazzini, G. Byron et Goethe. In his Scritti litterari d'un Italiano vivente, Lugano 1847; tr as Life and writings of Mazzini vol 6, 1891.
von Hohenhausen, E. Rousseau, Goethe, Byron. Cassel 1847.
Chasles, V. E. P. Vie et influence de Byron sur son époque. In Études sur la littérature et les moeurs de l'Angleterre au 19e siècle, Paris [1850].
Nisard, D. Lord Byron et la société anglaise. Revue des Deux Mondes 1 Nov 1850.
Kingsley, C. Thoughts on Shelley and Byron. Fraser's Mag Nov 1853; rptd in his Miscellanies vol 1, 1859.
Russell, Lord John. Memoirs, journal and correspondence of Thomas Moore. 6 vols 1853–6.
Hannay, J. In his Satire and satirists, 1854.
Ferguson, J. C. Lecture on the writings and genius of Byron. Carlisle 1856.
Rogers, S. Recollections of the table talk of Samuel Rogers. 1856.
Trelawny, E. J. Recollections of the last days of Shelley and Byron. 1858; ed E. Dowden 1906; ed J. E. Morpurgo 1952, New York 1961.
Trelawny, E. J. Records of Shelley, Byron and the author. 2 vols 1878, 1 vol 1887, 1905, rptd, ed D. Wright, 1973.
Trelawny, E. J. The relations of P. B. Shelley with his two wives and a comment on the character of Lord Byron. 1920 (priv ptd).
Trelawny, E. J. The relations of Lord Byron and Augusta Leigh. 1920 (priv ptd).
Mickiewicz, A. Goethe i Byron. Gazeta Codzienna (Warsaw) 29 Apr 1860; tr Fr in Mélanges posthumes vol 1, Paris 1872.
Mondot, A. Histoire de la vie et des écrits de Lord Byron. Paris 1860.
Finlay, G. In his History of the Greek revolution, 2 vols 1861.
Coulmann, J. J. In his Réminiscences, 3 vols Strasburg 1862–9.
Gronow, R. H. In his Reminiscences: being anecdotes of the camp, the court and the clubs, 1862.
von Treitschke, H. Lord Byron und der Radicalismus. Preussisches Jahrbuch, Berlin 1863; rptd in Historische und politische Aufsaetze, Leipzig 1865.
Gronow, R. H. Last recollections: being the fourth and final series. 1866.
Swinburne, A. C. Introduction to A selection from the works of Lord Byron, 1866; rptd in Essays and studies, 1875.
Guiccioli, Teresa, Countess of (Mme de Boissy). Lord Byron jugé par les témoins de sa vie. Paris 1868; tr 1869, New York 1869.
Austin, A. A vindication of Lord Byron. 1869.
Byron painted by his compeers: or all about Lord Byron from his marriage to his death as given in the various newspapers of his day. 1869.
[Fox, J.] Vindication of Lady Byron. Blackwood's Mag Oct 1869; rptd 1871.
[Hayward, A.] The Byron mystery. Quart Rev 127–8 1869–70. Letters of Lady Byron.
[Hayward, A.] In his Sketches of eminent statesmen and writers, 2 vols 1880.
[Lucas, S.] The Stowe–Byron controversy: a complete résumé of all that has been written and said on the subject. 1869.
Mackay, C. Medora Leigh: a history and an autobiography. 1869.
Martineau, H. In her Biographical sketches, 1869.
Stowe, H. B. The true story of Lady Byron's married life. Macmillan's Mag Sep 1869. Reply by A. Hayward, *below*.
Stowe, H. B. Lady Byron vindicated: a history of the Byron controversy. 1870. Reviewed by A. Hayward, *below*.
Elze, K. Lord Byron. Berlin 1870, 1881, 1886; tr 1872 (with addns).
Morley, J. Byron and the French Revolution. Fortnightly Rev Dec 1870; rptd in his Miscellanies vol 1, 1886.
L'Estrange, A. G. The literary life of the Rev William Harness. 1871.
Blaze de Bury, H. Lord Byron et le Byronisme. Revue des Deux Mondes 1 Oct 1872.
[Haussonville, Comtesse de]. La jeunesse de Lord Byron. Paris 1872.
[Haussonville, Comtesse de] Les dernières années de Lord Byron. Paris 1874.
Tribolati, F. Lord Byron a Pisa. Nuova Antologia July 1874; rptd in his Saggi critici e biografici, Pisa 1891.
Mackay, G. E. Lord Byron at the Armenian Convent. Venice 1876.
Lipnicki, E. Byron in Befreiungskampfe der polnischen Nationalliteratur. Magazin 48 1877.
Hodgson, J. T. Memoirs of the Rev Francis Hodgson. 2 vols 1878.
Torrens, W. M. Memoirs of William 2nd Viscount Melbourne. 1878.
Telles, A. Lord Byron em Portugal. Lisbon 1879.
Jebb, R. C. In his Modern Greece, 1880.

Nichol, J. Byron. 1880 (EML).
Ruskin, J. Fiction, fair and foul. Nineteenth Cent Sep 1880; rptd in his Works, ed E. T. Cook and A. D. O. Wedderburn, vol 34.
Arnold, Matthew. Preface to the poetry of Byron. 1881; rptd in Essays in criticism, 2nd ser, 1888.
'Rutherford, Mark' (W. H. White). Byron, Goethe and Mr Matthew Arnold. Contemporary Rev Aug 1881; rptd in Pages from a journal, 1901.
Edgecumbe, R. History of the Byron memorial. 1883.
Jeaffreson, J. C. The real Lord Byron. 1883.
REVIEWS: Quart Rev 156 1883 (by Abraham Hayward); Fortnightly Rev Apr 1883; Nineteenth Cent Aug 1883 (by J. A. Froude).
Jowett, B. Byron. [Oxford 1884] (priv ptd).
Swinburne, A. C. Wordsworth and Byron. Nineteenth Cent Apr–May 1884; rptd in his Miscellanies, 1886.
Weddigen, F. H. O. Lord Byrons Einfluss auf die europäische Literatur der Neuzeit. Hanover 1884, Leipzig 1901.
Dowden, E. In his Life of P. B. Shelley, 2 vols 1886.
'Gerard, William' (W. G. Smith). Byron re-studied in his dramas. 1886.
Jerningham, H. E. H. In his Reminiscences of an attaché, 1886.
[Milbanke, Ralph (Viscount Wentworth, later Earl of Lovelace)]. Lady Noel Byron and the Leighs: some authentic records of certain circumstances in the lives of Augusta Leigh and others that concerned Anne Isabella Lady Byron. 1887 (priv ptd).
Althaus, F. On the personal relations between Goethe and Byron. Pbns of Eng Goethe Soc 2 1888.
Arnold, M. In his Essays in criticism ser 2, 1888. Rptd from The poetry of Byron, 1881.
Axon, W. E. A. Byron's influence on European literature. In his Stray chapters on literature, folk-lores and archaeology, 1888.
Lombroso, C. L'uomo di genio. Turin 1888; tr 1891.
Megyery, A. Lord Byron. Budapest 1889.
Dallois, J. Études morales et littéraires à propos de Lord Byron. Paris 1890.
Noel, R. Life of Lord Byron. 1890.
Rabbé, F. Les maîtresses authentiques de Lord Byron. Paris 1890.
Westenholtz, F. Über Byrons historische Dramen. Stuttgart 1890.
Bancroft, G. History of the battle of Lake Erie and miscellaneous papers. New York 1891.
Chiarini, G. Lord Byron nella politica e nella letteratura della prima metà del secolo. Nuova Antologia 34 1891.
Ross, J. Byron at Pisa. Nineteenth Cent Nov 1891.
Smiles, S. A publisher and his friends: memoir and correspondence of the late John Murray. 2 vols 1891.
Lüder, A. Lord Byrons Urtheile über Italien. Dresden 1893.
Roe, J. C. Some obscure and disputed points in Byronic biography. Leipzig 1893.
Brandes, G. M. C. Shelley und Lord Byron: zwei literarische Charakterbilder. Leipzig 1894.
Hayman, H. Lord Byron and the Greek Patriots. Harper's Mag Feb 1894.
Hamann, A. The life and works of Lord Byron. Berlin 1895, 1910.
Maychrzak, F. Lord Byron als Übersetzer. Altenburg 1895.
Bleibtreu, K. Byron der Übermensch: sein Leben und sein Dichten. Jena [1896].
Carew Hazlitt, W. Four generations of a literary family. 2 vols 1897.
Donner, J. O. E. Lord Byrons Weltanschauung. Helsingfors 1897.
Dowden, E. The French Revolution and English literature. 1897.
Zdiechowski, M. Byron i jego wiek. In his Studya porównawczoliterachie, Cracow 1897.
Foster, V. The two Duchesses. 1898.
Graham, W. Last links with Byron, Shelley and Keats. 1898. *See* N & Q 27 Oct 1923.
Holthausen, F. Skandinavische Byron-Übersetzungen. EStudien 25 1898.
Kräger, H. Der Byronsche Heldentypus. Munich 1898.
Phillips, S. The poetry of Byron. Cornhill Mag Jan 1898.
Biondi, E. La figlia di Lord Byron. Faenza 1899.
Harnack, D. In his Essays und Studien, Brunswick 1899.
Holthausen, F. Tegnér und Byron. Archiv 101 1899.
Ackermann, R. Lord Byron: sein Leben, seine Werke, sein Einfluss auf die deutsche Literatur. Heidelberg 1901.
Clark, W. J. Byron und die romantische Poesie in Frankreich. Leipzig 1901.
Ritter, O. Byron and Chateaubriand. Archiv 109 1902.
Veselovsky, A. N. Byron. Moscow 1902.
Williams, E. E. The journal of Edward Ellerker Williams, companion of Shelley and Byron in 1821 and 1822. 1902.
Wylpel, L. Grillparzer und Byron. Euphorion 9–10 1902–3.
Bulloch, J. M. House of Gordon Gight. [1903] (New Spalding Club) (priv ptd).
Fuhrmann, L. Die Belesenheit des jungen Byron. Berlin 1903.
Hoops, J. Lord Byrons Leben und Dichten. Frankfurt 1903.
Köpel, E. Lord Byron. Berlin 1903; tr Hungarian, Budapest 1913.
Lumbroso, A. Il Generale Mengaldo, Lord Byron e l'Ode on the star of the Legion of Honour. Rome 1903; rptd in his Pagine Veneziane, Rome 1905.
Melchior, F. Heines Verhältnis zu Lord Byron. Berlin 1903.
Muoni, G. La fama del Byron e il Byronismo in Italia. Milan 1903.
Pudbres, A. Lord Byron, the admirer and imitator of Alfieri. EStudien 33 1903.
Coleridge, E. H. Lord Byron. Trans Royal Soc of Lit 25 1904.
Holzhausen, P. Bonaparte, Byron und die Briten. Frankfurt 1904.
Zabel, E. Byrons Kenntnis von Shakespeare und sein Urteil über ihn. Halle 1904.
Collins, J. C. The works of Lord Byron. In his Studies in poetry and criticism, 1905.
Leonard, W. E. Byron and Byronism in America. Boston 1905.
[Milbanke, Ralph (Viscount Wentworth, later Earl of Lovelace)]. Astarte: a fragment of truth concerning Lord Byron. 1905 (priv ptd); ed Mary, Countess of Lovelace 1921 (with additional letters).
Ochsenbein, W. Die Aufnahme Lord Byrons in Deutschland und sein Einfluss auf den jungen Heine. Berne 1905.
Prothero, R. E. (Baron Ernle). The Goddess of wisdom and Lady Caroline Lamb. Monthly Rev June 1905.
Wetz, W. Neuere Beiträge zur Byron-Biographie. Cologne 1905.
Murray, John [iv], E. H. Pember and R. E. Prothero. Lord Byron and his detractors. 1906 (Roxburghe Club) (priv ptd).
Calcano, J. Tres poetas pessimistas del siglo xix. Caracas 1907.
Eimer, M. Lord Byron und die Kunst. Strasburg 1907.
Estève, E. Byron et le romantisme français. Paris 1907, 1929.
Muoni, G. La leggenda del Byron in Italia. Milan 1907.
Muoni, G. Poesia notturna pre-romantica. Florence 1908.
Wiehr, J. The relations of Grabbe to Byron. JEGP 7 1908.
Churchman, P. H. Byron and Espronceda. Revue Hispanique (Paris) Mar 1909.
Churchman, P. H. Lord Byron's experiences in the Spanish Peninsula in 1809. Bulletin Hispanique (Bordeaux) Mar, June 1909.
Edgecumbe, R. Byron: the last phase. 1909.
Simhart, M. Lord Byrons Einfluss auf die italienische Literatur. Munich 1909.
Symons, A. In his Romantic movement in English poetry, 1909.
Austin, A. Byron and Wordsworth. In his Bridling of Pegasus, 1910.
Chesterton, G. K. In his Twelve types, 1910.
Churchman, P. H. The beginnings of Byronism in Spain. Revue Hispanique (Paris) Dec 1910.
Eimer, M. Die persönlichen Beziehungen zwischen Byron und den Shelleys. Heidelberg 1910.
Gribble, F. The love affairs of Lord Byron. 1910.
Lang, A. Byron and Mary Chaworth. Fortnightly Rev Aug 1910.

Meneghetti, N. Lord Byron a Venezia. Venice [1910].
Miller, B. Leigh Hunt's relations with Byron, Shelley and Keats. New York 1910.
Angeli, H. R. Shelley and his friends in Italy. 1911.
Brecknock, A. The pilgrim poet: Lord Byron of Newstead. 1911.
Polidori, J. W. The diary. Ed W. M. Rossetti 1911.
Dobosal, G. Lord Byron in Deutschland. Zwickau 1911.
Shaw, W. A. The authentic portraits of Lord Byron. Connoisseur July–Aug 1911.
Spasowicz, W. Byronism u Pushkina i Lermontova. Vilna 1911.
Byroniana und anderes aus dem englischen Seminar in Erlangen. Erlangen 1912.
Eimer, M. Byron und die Kosmos. Heidelberg 1912.
Fuess, C. M. Lord Byron as a satirist in verse. New York 1912.
Knott, J. The last illness of Lord Byron. St Paul MN 1912.
Mayne, E. C. Byron. 2 vols 1912, [1924].
Windakiewicz, S. Walter Scott i Lord Byron w odniesieniu do polskiej romantycznij. Cracow 1914.
Chew, S. C. The dramas of Lord Byron. Göttingen 1915.
Ward, J. and G. G. Napier. Lord Byron's lameness. Nottingham 1915 (priv ptd).
Hearn, L. Interpretations of literature. New York 1916.
Northup, C. S. Byron and Gray. MLN 32 1917.
Zacchetti, C. Lord Byron e l'Italia. Palermo 1919.
Fletcher, W. Lord Byron's illness and death as described in a letter to Augusta Leigh. Nottingham 1920 (priv ptd).
Prothero, R. E. (Baron Ernle). The end of the Byron mystery. Nineteenth Cent Aug 1921.
Chew, S. C. Byron in America. Amer Mercury 4 1924.
Chew, S. C. Byron in England: his fame and after-fame. 1924.
Estève, E. Le Byronisme de Leconte de Lisle. Revue de Littérature Comparée 5 1925.
Brecknock, A. Byron: a study of the poet in the light of new discoveries. [1926.]
Mayne, E. C. The life and letters of Anne Isabella, Lady Noel Byron. 1929.

Textual criticism

McGann, J. J. Editing Byron's poetry. Byron Jnl no 1 1973.
Lovell, E. J., jun. Review of Byron's letters and journals vols 1 and 2. KSJ 24 1975.
Rosen, C. Romantic documents. New York Rev of Bks 15 May 1975.
McGann, J. J. The correct text of Don Juan I 190–198. TLS 30 July 1976.
McGann, J. J. The Murray proofs of Don Juan I–II. Byron Jnl no 5 1977.
Bone, J. Drummond. Review of Byron's letters and journals vol 8. Byron Jnl no 7 1979.
Marchand, L. A. The manuscripts of Byron's letters. Literary Research Newsletter 1979.
Bone, J. Drummond. Review of The complete poetical works vol 2. Byron Jnl no 10 1982.
Kelsall, M. Review of The complete poetical works vol 1. Byron Jnl no 10 1982.
Stillinger, J. Review of The complete poetical works vol I. JEGP 81 1982.
Woodring, C. Review of The complete poetical works vol I. KSJ 31 1982.
Curran, S. Review of The complete poetical works vol 2. KSJ 32 1983.
McGann, J. J. A critique of modern textual criticism. 1983.
Manning, P. J. Review of The complete poetical works vol 3. Byron Jnl no 11 1983.
McGann, J. J. Shall these bones live? TEXT 1984.
Reiman, D. H. Review of The complete poetical works vols 1–3. Keats–Shelley Memorial Bulletin 34 1984.
McGann, J. J. (ed). Textual criticism and literary interpretation. 1985.
Kelsall, M. Review of The complete poetical works vol 4. Byron Jnl no 15 1987.
Reiman, D. H. Romantic texts and contexts. 1987.
Reiman, D. H. Review of The complete poetical works vols 4–5. Keats–Shelley Rev 3 1988.
St Clair, W. Review of The complete poetical works vol 5. Byron Jnl no 16 1988.
Ashton, T. L. Review of Manuscripts of the younger romantics vols 3 and 4. KSJ 38 1989.
St Clair, W. The temptations of a biographer. Byron Jnl no 17 1989.
Manning, P. J. Reading romantics: text and context. 1990.
McGann, J. J. and T. H. Howard-Hill. Literary pragmatists and the editorial horizon. In Devils and angels, ed P. Cohen, Charlottesville VA 1991.
Varadharajan, A. The problem of textual (ir)relevance in Byron's Don Juan. Pbns of the Bibl Soc of Canada, Spring 1991.
Bone, J. Drummond. Review of Lord Byron. The complete poetical works vol 6. Byron Jnl no 20 1992.
Newey, V. Byron manuscripts in photofacsimile. Byron Jnl no 20 1992.
Barton, A. Review of (inter alia) Lord Byron. The complete poetical works vol 7. New York Rev of Bks 10 June 1993.
Cochran, P. A note on the text of Manfred II ii. Byron Jnl no 22 1994.
Cochran, P. The transmission of the text of Byron's The vision of judgement. N & Q 239 Sep 1994.
Newey, V. Review of Lord Byron. The complete poetical works vol 7. Byron Jnl no 22 1994.
Reiman, D. H. Review of Lord Byron. The complete poetical works. Nineteenth Cent Lit 50, Sep 1995.
Cochran, P. Mary Shelley's fair copying of Don Juan. Keats–Shelley Rev 10, Spring 1996.
Leader, Z. Revision and romantic authorship. Oxford 1996.

Biographies (selected)

Marchand, L. A. Byron: a biography. 3 vols New York 1957.
Marshall, W. H. Byron, Shelley, Leigh Hunt and the Liberal. 1960.
Langley Moore, D. The late Lord Byron. 1961.
Marchand, L. A. Byron a portrait. 1970.
Grebanier, B. The uninhibited Byron: an account of his sexual confusion. 1971.
Brent, P. Lord Byron. 1974.
Langley Moore, D. Lord Byron: accounts rendered. 1974.
Elwin, M. Lord Byron's family. 1975.
Dangerfield, E. Byron and the romantics in Switzerland. 1978.
Clubbe, J. and E. Giddey. Byron et la Suisse. 1982.
Kent Thomas, G. Lord Byron's Iberian pilgrimage. 1983.
Crompton, L. Byron and Greek Love. Berkeley CA 1985.
Guiccioli, T. La vie de Lord Byron en Italie. Ed E. A. Stürzl 1985–7.
Boyes, M. Love without wings. 1988. About Elizabeth Pigot.
Boyes, M. Queen of a fantastic realm. 1988. About Mary Chaworth.
Cheetham, S. Byron in Europe. 1988.
Coote, S. Byron: the making of a myth. 1988.
Fleming, A. In search of Byron in England and Scotland: a guide book. 1988.
Johnson, A. and M. Curreli. The paradise of exiles: Byron and Shelley in Pisa. Salzburg 1988.
Massie, A. Byron's travels. 1988.
Page, N. A Byron chronology. 1988.
Richardson, J. Byron and some of his contemporaries. 1988.
Stürzl, E. A. Love's eye view: Teresa Guiccioli's La vie de Lord Byron en Italie. 1988.
Boyes, M. My amiable Mamma. 1991. About Mrs Byron.
Blumberg, J. Byron and the Shelleys. 1992.
Hart, C. (ed). Lives of the great romantics by their contemporaries, vol 2: Byron. 1996.

Soderholm, J. Fantasy, forgery and the Byron legend. 1996.
Grosskurth, P. Byron the flawed angel. 1997. [PC]

Jeremiah J. Callanan 1795–1829

Mss: of poems and prose pieces are held at the Royal Irish Acad Lib, Dublin.

Collections

The poems, with biographical introduction and notes. [1883.]

§1

The recluse of Inchidony, and other poems. 1830.
The poems. Cork 1847, Cork 1861 (new edn).

§2

Gems of the Cork poets, comprising the complete works of Callanan and others. Cork [1883].
MacCarthy, B. Jeremiah J. Callanan. Studies 35 1946.
Taylor, G. In his Irish poets of the nineteenth century, selected with introductions, 1951.

Dorothea Primrose Campbell c. 1794–1863

Poems. Inverness 1811; London 1816.
Harley Radington. 2 vols 1821. Prose.

Thomas Campbell 1777–1844

Manuscript holdings, mainly letters, are found in numerous libraries in Britain and the USA. Major collections are in the Huntington, Bodleian, Nat Lib of Scotland, Glasgow Univ, London Univ and Univ College London, BL, and Harvard. Campbell is not included in The Index of English literary manuscripts, *ed B. Rosenbaum and P. White, London and New York 1982.*

Bibliographies

Jordan, H. H. In English romantic poets and essayists: a review of research and criticism, ed C. W. and L. H. Houtchens, New York 1957, 1966 (rev). Campbell is not included in The English romantic poets: a review of research and criticism, ed F. Jordan, New York 1985.
Reiman, D. H. English romantic poetry, 1800–35: a guide to information sources. Detroit MI 1979. Highly selective.
Wellesley index to Victorian periodicals, 1824–1900, ed W. E. Houghton, Toronto 1966. Lists a no of Campbell's periodical contributions but is incomplete for New Monthly Mag.
See also Poole's Index to periodical literature, *6 vols New York 1938.*

Collections

Poems [contains Lochiel's warning, Hohenlinden], Edinburgh 1803;
Poetical works with biographical sketch by 'a gentleman of New York' (Washington Irving), 2 vols Albany NY 1810, 1 vol Baltimore 1810, Boston 1810, Portland ME1810, Philadelphia 1810, [1815], New York 1821, Paris 1822; in The Bouquet with works of Rogers and Collins, New York 1815; Miscellaneous poems, 1824; 'including Theodric' etc, New York 1825, Philadelphia 1826, 1827, 1828, 1835, 1845, 1847; 2 vols London 1828, 1830, 1832, 1833; in Beauties of the British poets, New York '1826' [1827]; in The living poets of England, Paris 1827; in British poets of the nineteenth century, Paris 1828; with Works of Rogers etc, Paris 1829, [1840?], Philadelphia 1830, 1836, 1848, 1859, Boston 1857; London 1835, 1836, 1837, 1838, 1839, 1840, 1843, 1846, 1849, [1851], nd; Edinburgh etc 1837, nd; illustr W. Harvey London 1840, 1846; illustr J. M. W. Turner 1837, 1843; Philadelphia 1842; ed W. A. Hill, illustr J. M. W. Turner London 1851, 1854, 1860; Boston 1851, 1854, 1856, 1863, 1866; London 1866; London and New York 1868, 1874, 1900; in In honorem, with others, 1856; in Favorite poems, Boston 1877, 1882; with Poetical works of Falconer, Boston 1854, 1878, 1880, 1882, nd; illustr W. Harvey, Hartford CT 1852; London and Edinburgh 1852; with G. Gilfillan's Literary portrait, New York 1852, 1857, 1859; with Biography and notes by Epes Sargent, Boston 1854, 1857, 1860; New York 1871; with Poetical works of Goldsmith and Beattie, 1853, 1855; with Goldsmith only, New York 1851, 1858; Boston 1854, 1857, 1860; London 1854, 1858, 1862; Philadelphia 1857; with Poetical works of Coleridge, Edinburgh [1859]; with works of Collins and Gray, 1860; illustr J. Gilbert 1862, nd, [1870?], [188-?], London and New York [1862], nd, [1894]; introd W. E. Aytoun, Boston 1857, 1864, 1877, 1882; London 1866, 1870, 1874, 1875, 1880; Boston 1866, 1874; New York nd, 1871, 1876, 1877; introd C. Rogers [1870]; 1873 (The Scottish minstrel); introd W. M. Rossetti, illustr T. Seccombe [1871], 1872, [1880]; in Favorite poems, Boston 1877; poems only [1878]; Chandos edn [1874], etc; Aldine edn, life by W. Allingham 1875, 1890, 1900, rptd 1972; Edinburgh and London nd, [1880], [1881], [1884], 1892; London 1878, [1880] 1881, 1887, 1894; New York 1885; ed J. Hogben 1885, 1886; ed A. H. Miles [1891], 1898, 1899, 1905; ed H. Morley 1892; ed. W. Murison 1893, 1895; ed W. Dent 1895; with Coleridge, etc, ed F. H. Sykes, Toronto 1895; with Coleridge, etc, ed W. Pakenham and J. Marshall Toronto [1895]; Selections, ed W. T. Webb 1902; ed L. C. Campbell, London and New York 1904; ed J. L. Robertson, Oxford 1907, 1908, rptd New York 1968.
REVIEWS: Literary Speculum 1, Jan 1822; Literary Gazette, 7 June 1828; Athenaeum, 28 May 1836; Quart Rev 57, Dec 1836; GM n.s. 3 vol 8, Oct 1837; Literary Gazette, 28 Oct 1837; Fraser's Mag 25, Mar 1842; Spectator 67, 10 Oct 1891.

§1

The wounded hussar. Glasgow 1799, Stirling [1800], Newcastle nd, Birmingham nd, London nd, [1850?], Belfast [1820?]. In Ancient and modern songs [1820?], [1850?]. A chapbook.
The pleasures of hope, with other poems. Edinburgh 1799, 1800; New York 1800, Glasgow 1800 (4th edn 'corrected and enlarged'), Edinburgh and London 1800, 1801; Edinburgh 1801, 1802, 1804 (7th edn); London 1800, 1801, 1803 (also designated 7th edn 'corrected and enlarged'), 1805, Dublin 1802, 1804, London and Edinburgh 1805 (8th edn); Edinburgh 1806, 1807 (both called 9th edn), New York 1800, 1800, Wilmington DE 1800 ('third American' edn); New York 1804; with Rogers's Pleasures of memory, London and Edinburgh 1805, Paris 1805, Philadelphia 1858; Cambridge MA 1807; Edinburgh 1807, 1808, 1810, 1811, 1813, 1815, 1821; London and Edinburgh 1815, 1816, Boston 1811, Belfast 1815, London 1815, 1816, 1819, 1821, 1822, 1825, 1826; illustr R. Westall 1820, 1821, 1822, 1825, 1826; Providence RI 1828; Belfast 1830; Paris 1824, 1825 (with trn by Albert Montémont); in The book of pleasures with S. Rogers and M. Akenside, Philadelphia 1843; in The book of pleasures with O. Goldsmith, New York 1851; with Gertrude of Wyoming, London and Edinburgh 1852, 1892; illustr B. Foster et al 1855, 1860, 1861, [1875]; [1869]; Philadelphia 1857; ed W. and R. Chambers, London and Edinburgh 1871; New York 1875; Boston 1877; ed L. J. Woodroffe, Dublin 1882; Berlin 1882. Tr Ger 1838, abridged 1879, with Medea, ed W. J. Blew 1887.
REVIEWS: Br Critic 14, July 1799; Monthly Mirror 8, July 1799; Monthly Rev 29, Aug 1799; Critical Rev 27, Oct 1799; Monthly Mag 8, Dec 1799; Poetical Register and Repository of Fugitive Poetry 3, 1803; Annual Register 44, 1803 (plus extracts in vols for 1799, 1801, 1802, 1809, 1824, 1825); Art Jnl n.s. 1, 1855.
The following bold and patriotic ode . . . Chester [c. 1800].
Loyal North Britons. Ed C. Orme 1803. Stanzas by Campbell.
Gertrude of Wyoming: a Pennsylvanian tale, and other poems. 1809, 1810, 1810, 1812, 1814, 1816, 1819, 1821, 1822, 1825, Oxford 1991 (facs); New York 1809, 1869; with W. L. Stone's History of Wyoming, New York and London 1841, 1844, 1849; Albany NY1864; New York 1856, 1858, 1869; London 1857, 1862, [1874]; ed. H. M. Fitzgibbon, Oxford 1889, 1891; Baden-Baden 1882 (with German trn).
REVIEWS: (F. Jeffrey) Edinburgh Rev 14, Apr 1809; Scots Mag 71,

Apr 1809; (W. Scott) Quart Rev 1, May 1809; Monthly Mirror n.s. 5, May 1809; Eclectic Rev 5 pt 1, June 1809; Monthly Rev 59, July 1809; London Rev 2, 1 Aug 1809; Antijacobin Rev and Mag 34, Sep 1809; Br Critic 34, Oct 1809.

Specimens of the British poets, with biographical and critical notes, and An essay on English poetry. 7 vols London and Edinburgh 1819; ed. P. Cunningham 1841, 1845, with notices and An essay only 1848; An essay, Boston 1819. Works of the British Poets, Philadelphia 1819–23, contains 6 of the lives by Campbell.
REVIEWS: Blackwood's Mag 4, Mar 1819; 5, May 1819; Br Critic 11, Apr 1819; Edinburgh Mag ns 4, Mar 1819; Edinburgh Rev 31, Mar 1819; Monthly Rev 90, Dec 1819; GM Mag 91 pt 1, Jan 1821, Apr 1821; NMM 63, Sep 1841; Westminster Rev 36, Oct 1841; Fraser's Mag 25, Mar 1842; GM n.s. 3, Dec 1848.

Theodric: a domestic tale, and other poems. 1824, New York 1825, Philadelphia 1825, Paris 1825.
REVIEWS: London Literary Gazette, 20 Nov 1824; Br Critic 22, Dec 1824; Blackwood's Mag 17, Jan, Apr 1825; Edinburgh Rev 41, Jan 1825; Westminster Rev 3, Jan 1825; Eclectic Rev 23, Feb 1825; US Literary Gazette, 1 Mar 1825; Quart Rev 31, Mar 1825.

Proposal on a metropolitan univ. in a letter to H. Brougham. The Times, 9 Feb 1825.
REVIEWS: London Mag n.s. 2, May 1825; Quart Rev 33, Dec 1825.

Two songs: the music by Mr J. Barnett, the nonsense by Mr T. Campbell. London Mag 15, May 1826.

Inaugural discourse on being installed Lord Rector of the University of Glasgow. Glasgow 1827, rptd in Inaugural addresses by Lord Rectors of the University of Glasgow, ed J. B. Hay 1839, 1848 (contains also Campbell's address of 12 Apr 1827 and his second inaugural address 5 Dec 1828), rptd in British eloquence of the nineteenth century, 1855.

Letters on the history of literature, addressed to the students at the University of Glasgow. Glasgow 1829. *See NMM*, Periodicals, *below.*)

Poland: a poem; Lines on the view from St Leonard's. 1831, 1831.
REVIEW: London Literary Gazette, 3 Sep 1831.

Letter to the Mohawk chief Ahyonwaeghs, commonly called John Brant. In W. W. Campbell, Annals of Tryon county, 1831. 1st pbd in NMM 4, 1821.

Address of the Literary Polish Association to the People of Great Britain. 1832. Tr Fr, Paris 1832.

The life of Mrs Siddons. 2 vols 1834, 1 vol New York 1834, London 1839, rptd New York 1972.
REVIEWS: Atlas 9, 6, 13 July 1834; Tait's Edinburgh Mag ns 1, Aug 1834; NMM 41, Aug 1834; Quart Rev 52, Aug 1834; Athenaeum, 5, 12 July 1834; Literary Gazette, 5 July 1834; Monthly Rev n.s. 2, Aug 1834; Mirror 24, 9, 30 Aug 1834; Blackwood's Mag 36, Aug, Sep 1834; GM new ser 3, vol 2, Oct 1834.

Epistle from Thomas Campbell, Esq to Horace Smith, from Algiers. Annual Register for 1835, 1836.

Letters from the south. 2 vols 1837, 1842 (as The journal of a residence in Algiers).
REVIEWS: Athenaeum, 11 Mar 1837; Tait's Edinburgh Mag 4, Apr 1837; NMM 50, May 1837; Monthly Rev n.s. 2, May 1837; Eclectic Rev n.s. 2, Oct 1837.

The dramatic works of William Shakespeare, with remarks on his life and writings by T. Campbell. 1838, 1843, 1848, 1859, New York and London 1863, 1866, rptd New York 1972. Tr Fr [1839], 1855.
REVIEW: Literary Gazette, 16 June 1838.

Cunningham, A. The life and land of Burns ... with contributions by Thomas Campbell. New York 1841.

The life of Petrarch. 2 vols 1841, 1842, 1843. 1 vol Philadelphia 1841; abridged in The sonnets, triumphs and other poems of Petrarch, 1859, 1875, 1879.
REVIEWS: Athenaeum, 15, 22 May 1841; Spectator, 22 May 1841; Literary Gazette, 19, 26 June 1841; GM new ser 3, vol 16, Aug 1841; Tait's Edinburgh Mag n.s. 8, Aug 1841; GM ns 4, vol 7, Aug 1859.

The pilgrim of Glencoe, and other poems. 1842.
REVIEWS: Literary Gazette, 5 Mar 1842; Spectator, 5 Mar 1842; Athenaeum, 12 Mar 1842; Monthly Rev new ser 1, Apr 1842; Eclectic Rev n.s. 11, June 1842.

Periodicals edited by Campbell

The New Monthly Magazine and Literary Journal. 1821–30. Major contributions include Lectures on poetry, 1 Jan 1821–17 Nov 1826; Suggestions respecting the plan of an university in London, 13 Apr 1825–14 June 1825; Letters to the students of Glasgow, 20 July 1827–23 Aug 1828; Letters from the south, Oct 1835–June 1836. Most others, except numerous poems, are identified in Wellesley 5 1989.

The Metropolitan: A Monthly Journal of Literature, Science, and the Fine Arts. 1831–2. Contributions include Poland: a poem, and Lines on the view from St Leonard's, June, July 1831.

The scenic annual for 1838.
REVIEW: GM new ser 3, vol 9, Jan 1838.

Letters, journals etc

Commonplace book of Thomas Campbell, c. 1820–40. 1843. Folger. Contains 131 pp. (many blank) of notes and extracts from Campbell's reading. His autograph and date 1843 pasted in.

Beattie, W. Life and letters of Thomas Campbell. 3 vols 1849, 1850, rptd New York 1973; 2 vols New York 1850, 1855, London 1860.
REVIEWS: Literary Gazette, 16 Dec 1848; Athenaeum, 23 Dec 1848; Tait's Edinburgh Mag n.s. 16, Jan 1849; Blackwood's Mag 65, Feb 1849; NMM 85, Feb 1849; GM new ser 3, vol 31, Feb 1849; North Br Rev 10, Feb 1849; Eclectic Rev n.s. 25, Mar 1849; Quart Rev 85, Dec 1849; Sharpe's London Mag 8 and 9, 1849; Amer Whig Rev n.s. 6, Oct 1850; Methodist Quart Rev 11, Jan 1851; New Englander 9, May 1851.

Two letters of Thomas Campbell the poet. NYPL Bull 10, Feb 1906. Anon.

Mumby, F. A. Letters of literary men. 2 vols 1906, New York 1906.

Seton, W. Three letters of Thomas Campbell. Nineteenth Cent 97, Jan 1925.

Duffy, C. and J. Glennon. Thomas Campbell: two letters. N & Q 194, July 1949.

Farr, K. D. The unstrung harp: an interpretative biography of T. Campbell, together with thirteen unpublished letters ... Unpbd MA thesis, Sonoma State Univ CA 1978.

Miller, M. R. Five recently found letters by Campbell. MLR 83, 2, Apr 1988.

Miller, M. R. Thomas Campbell and General Pepé. N & Q 243, June 1998.

Attributed works

Annals of Great Britain from the ascension of George III to the Peace of Amiens. 3 vols Edinburgh, Glasgow and London 1807. Pbd anon by Campbell, a work which he called in a letter to Lord Minto 30 Oct 1802 'little superior to compilation, and more connected with profit than reputation'.
REVIEWS: Monthly Rev 59, Aug 1809; Br Critic 36, Sep, Oct 1810.

Frederick the Great, his court and times, edited with an introduction by Thomas Campbell. 4 vols 1841–3, 2 vols 1842–3, 1844, 1845, Philadelphia 1842. Written anon by Frederick Shoberl. Campbell's introduction as 'sponsor' was only 13 pp.
REVIEWS: NMM 63, Dec 1841; 67, Jan 1843; Blackwood's Mag 51, Mar 1842; Edinburgh Rev 75, Apr 1842; Westminster Rev 38, July 1842.

History of our own times. 2 vols 1843, 1845. Shoberl again the author; Campbell may have written the preface.

Musical settings

Angel of life. Music by J. W. Callcott. [London] 1802.

The wounded hussar. Music by J. Hewitt. Philadelphia [1804 or 1805].

The beech-tree's petition. Music by R. Taylor. Philadelphia [1810–15].
Lord Ullin's daughter. Music by G. Hargreaves 1832, and by H. MacCunn. London and New York 1887, 1888.
Friend of the brave. Music by J. W. Calcott. Boston 1834.
Gertrude of Wyoming. Music by G. E. Hicks. 1846. Accompanied by G. Alexander's The fair maid of Wyoming: a tale...
Field flowers. In Three gems in one setting. Music by A. L. Bond. [1860].
The battle of the Baltic. Music by G. M. Hopkins. Bodleian MS Mus c 97. Music by C. V. Stanford. 1891.
Hohenlinden. Cantata by P. Pitt. London and New York 1899.
Reullura. Music by F. Koeller. 1896 (for MusD 1899). Bodleian 32720.
Ye mariners of England. Music by W. F. Kingdon. Exeter Coll Mus Bac 1899. Bodleian 32734. Music by C. L. Williams. London and New York 1901.
The nativity (cantata). Music by J Greig. (Nd). Bodleian 27066.
How delicious is the winning of a kiss at love's beginning. In Three songs for soprano and eight horns by P. E. Nelson, 1954.
Chamber music III. Includes Campbell. Music by W. Peterson. Nd.

§2

Many volumes of lives, letters and other reminiscences by and about Campbell's contemporaries contain references to him or judgements of him. See Byron, Carlyle, Coleridge, Crabbe, Hazlitt, Hunt, T. Moore, Peacock, S. Rogers, Scott, Shelley, Southey and Wordsworth.

Scots Mag 64, Jan 1802. Anon.
Grant, A. Letters from the mountains. 3 vols 1807 (3rd edn).
Memoir of Thomas Campbell. Monthly Mirror n.s. 5, May 1809.
Mr Campbell's first lecture on poetry. Examiner, 26 Apr 1812.
Irving, W. Biographical sketch of Thomas Campbell. Analectic Mag n.s. 5, Mar 1815.
Watkins, J. and F. Shoberl. Biographical dictionary of the living authors. 1816.
On the genius of Thomas Campbell. Scots Mag 82, Aug 1818.
Hazlitt, W. In his Lectures on the English poets, 1818.
Bowles, W. L. The invariable principles of poetry: in a letter to T. Campbell. Bath and London 1819.
Mr Campbell's lecture. GM 90 1, June 1820.
Hunt, L. Sketches of the living poets: Mr Campbell. Literary Gazette (Philadelphia) 1, 39, 29 Sep 1821. Also in L. Hunt's Literary criticism, ed L. H. and C. W. Houtchens 1956.
Blackwood's Edinburgh Mag 2–45, 1817–39. Contains numerous articles about or referring to Campbell, often derogatory. Many are by John Wilson and William Maginn.
Bowles, W. L. Letters to Mr T. Campbell as far as regards poetical criticism. Pamphleteer 20, 1822.
Bowles, W. L. Letters to Lord Byron... to which are added, the letter to Mr Campbell.... 1822.
MacDermot, M. Letter to the Rev. W. L. Bowles, in reply to his letter to Thomas Campbell. Pamphleteer 20, 1822.
[Hazlitt, W.]. The periodical press. Edinburgh Rev 38, May 1823.
Maginn, W. A running commentary on the Ritter bann. Blackwood's Mag 15, Apr 1824.
Mr Campbell's university. London Mag n.s. 2, 1 May 1825.
Mr Campbell's Last man. London Mag n.s. 1, Apr 1825.
London Univ. Quart Rev 33, Dec 1825.
Hazlitt, W. In his Spirit of the age, 1825.
The living poets of England. Vol 1 Paris 1827.
Memoir of Thomas Campbell. Mirror 14 (preface), 1829.
Lord Byron vindicated, and Mr Campbell answered. 1830.
Lockhart, J. G. and W. Maginn. Literary characters, no 2: the bard of hope. Fraser's Mag 1, June 1830.
Poland and Mr Campbell. Tatler 331, 24 Sep 1831.
A day in Kent. Fraser's Mag 3, Feb 1831.
Jerdan, W. National portrait gallery...with memoirs. Vol 3 1832.
Watts, W. A. Sketches of modern poets. In The literary souvenir, 1832.
Cunningham, A. Biographical and critical history of the British literature of the last fifty years. Paris 1834.
Sketches of the later English poets. Tait's Edinburgh Mag n.s. 1, July 1834.
Biographic sketches: Thomas Campbell. Chambers's Edinburgh Jnl 3, 5 July 1834.
Stewart, M. Memoir of the late Dugald Stewart. 1838.
Chorley, H. F. and A. Collas. The authors of England. 1838, 1861.
Grant, J. Portraits of public characters. Vol 2 1841.
Sanders, E. Review of Campbell's Lectures on [Greek] poetry. Boston 1841.
Chapters on English poetry. Tait's Edinburgh Mag n.s. 8, Oct 1841.
Obits: Athenaeum, 22 June 1844; Literary Gazette, 22 June 1844; Mirror, 22 June 1844; Illus London News, 6 July 1844; Athenaeum, 6, 13, 27 July 1844; NMM, Aug 1844; GM, Aug 1844; Fraser's Mag, Sep 1844; Annual Register (pbd 1845). *See also* Athenaeum, 25 Aug–1 Dec 1855 *for discussions of the monument and* Bentley's Misc, June 1845, *for poem by W. Beattie.*
Carruthers, R. Mornings with Thomas Campbell. Chambers's Edinburgh Jnl n.s. 3, 8, 15 Feb 1845.
Personal recollections of Thomas Campbell, esq. Dublin Univ Mag 25, May and June 1845.
Thomas Campbell: a literary retrospect by a middle-aged man. Bentley's Misc 18, June 1845.
Gilfillan, G. Galleries of literary portraits. Vol 1 Edinburgh 1845, 1856.
Literary and familiar reminiscences of Thomas Campbell, esq. NMM 74, 1845.
Alexander, G. The fair maid of Wyoming, to accompany G. E. Hicks' musical score. 1846.
Past and present condition of British poetry. Fraser's Mag 33, May 1846.
A graybeard's gossip about his literary acquaintance, no 5. NMM 80, July 1847.
Howitt, W. Homes and haunts of the most eminent British poets. Vol 2 1847, New York 1875.
Redding, C. Life and reminiscences of Thomas Campbell. NMM 77, July 1846–84, Dec 1848.
The poet Campbell. Dublin Univ Mag 33, Feb 1849.
Tuckerman, H. T. Thoughts on the poets. 1850.
Campbell and Washington Irving. International Monthly Mag 1, 19 Aug 1850.
Gillies, R. P. Memoirs of a literary veteran. Vol 3 1851.
Tuckerman, H. T. Thomas Campbell. Southern Literary Messenger 17, Apr 1851.
Jerdan, W. Autobiography. Vol 4 1853.
Tappan, H. P. Illustrious personages of the nineteenth century. New York 1853.
Tuckerman, H. T. Mental portraits; or studies of character. 1853, Boston 1857.
Redding, C. Campbell and the Literary Union. NMM 100, Jan 1854.
Patmore, P. G. My friends and acquaintance. 3 vols 1854, rptd in R. H. Stoddard (ed), Personal recollections of Lamb, Hazlitt, and others, 1875, New York 1875, 1878, 1887.
Thomson, K. Recollections of literary characters. Vol 2 1854.
Chambers, R. Biographical dictionary of eminent Scotsmen. New edn vol 5 Glasgow 1855.
Rogers, C. The Scottish minstrel. Edinburgh 1855, 1873.
Chambers, W. and R. Papers for the people, no 24. London and Edinburgh 1856.
Goodrich, S. G. Recollections of a lifetime. Vol 2 New York 1857.
Donaldson, T. L. Obituary: Mr Thomas Campbell. Art Jnl new ser 4, 10, 1858.
Redding, C. Fifty years' recollections. 3 vols 1858.
REVIEW: GM n.s. 4, 4, May 1858.

Redding, C. Literary reminiscences and memoirs of Thomas Campbell. 2 vols London 1860. 1st pbd as Life and reminiscences ... in New Monthly Mag, 1846–8.
REVIEWS: Athenaeum, 29 Oct 1859; Sat Rev 8, 19 Nov 1859; NMM 117, Dec 1859; N. Br Rev 32, May 1860.
Cronnelly, R. F. Irish family history ... to which is added a paper on the authorship of The exile of Erin. 2 vols Dublin 1864.
Jerdan, W. Men I have known. 1866.
Hall, S. C. and wife. Memories of the authors of the age: Thomas Campbell. Art Jnl n.s. 5, May 1866.
Lord Lyndhurst and Lord Brougham. Quart Rev 126, Jan 1869. On London Univ and Campbell.
Hall, S. C. Book of memories of great men and women of the age. 1871. Essentially a repetition of Hall and wife, *above*.
Hewlett, H. G. (ed). Henry Fothergill Chorley: autobiography, memoir, and letters. 1873.
Wilson, J. et al. Noctes Ambrosianae. New York 1875 (rev edn).
Mackay, C. Forty years' recollections. Vol 1 1877.
Recollections of Thomas Campbell and David M. Moir. Leisure Hour 27, 9 Mar 1878.
Rossetti, W. M. Lives of famous poets. 1878, rptd New York 1971.
Lyall, W. Thomas Campbell: a criticism. Canadian Monthly 14, 1879.
Oliphant, M. W. Literary history of England. 3 vols 1882, 2 vols New York 1883.
Carruthers, R. (ed). Chambers's cyclopedia of English literature. 8 vols New York 1885 (3rd edn).
Madden, R. R. Literary remains of the United Irishmen of 1798, with an essay on the authorship of The exile of Erin. Dublin 1887.
Univ of London. Quart Rev 164, Jan 1887; 191, Apr 1900. *See also* H. H. Bellot, University College London, 1826–1926, 1929.
Chambers, W. Literary celebrities. London and Edinburgh 1887.
Thomas Campbell. Temple Bar 85, Jan 1889.
Clayden, P. W. Rogers and his contemporaries. 2 vols 1889.
Rae, W. F. The bard of hope. Temple Bar 90, Sep 1890.
Ward, T. H. The English poets. Vol 4 1894.
Dixon, W. M. English poetry from Blake to Browning. 1894, 1896.
Courthope, W. J. History of English poetry. 6 vols London and New York 1895–1910. *See* The new Whigs and their influence on poetry and criticism, vol 6.
Saintsbury, G. E. B. English war-songs. In his Essays in English Literature 1780–1860, 2nd ser New York 1895.
Agnew, M. C. Lions in the twenties. Temple Bar 107, Jan 1896.
Hadden, J. C. Thomas Campbell. London and Edinburgh [1899].
English patriotic poetry. Quart Rev 192, Oct 1900.
Brandes, G. M. C. British spirit of freedom. In his Main currents in nineteenth-century literature. Vol 4 1901–6.
Funke, O. Campbell als dichter. Dissertation, Leipzig. Reichenbach, Germany 1902.
Campbell, L. Thomas Campbell, the poet. Monthly Rev 10, Feb 1903.
Symons, A. Thomas Campbell. Fortnightly Rev 82, 1 Sep 1904.
Saintsbury, G. E. B. History of English prosody. 3 vols 1906, 1910.
Allingham, H. and D. Radford (ed). William Allingham: a diary. 1907.
Coutts, J. History of the University of Glasgow. Glasgow 1909.
MacCunn, F. Sir Walter Scott's friends. Edinburgh 1909.
Symons, A. The romantic movement in English poetry. New York 1909.
Elton, O. Survey of English literature 1780–1830. 2 vols 1912.
Abercrombie, L. The war and the poets. Quart Rev 224, Oct 1915.
Saintsbury, G. E. B. Lesser poets 1790–1837. 1915.
MacFarlane, C. Reminiscences of a literary life. New York 1917.
Bayne, T. W. In DNB, Oxford 1917.
Floryan, J. Polish Rev 1, 1917. On Campbell and Poland.
Pierce, F. E. Currents and eddies in the English romantic generation. New Haven CT 1918.
Duffy, C. Thomas Campbell: a critical biography. Unpbd diss., Cornell Univ 1939.
Reiman, D. H. The Romantics reviewed: contemporary reviews. New York and London 1972. Only mentions Campbell except for 1 review of Theodric. [MRM]

George Canning 1770–1827

See also under Anti-Jacobin, *col 2935, below.*

Collections

Poetical works. [1823] (with biography); Glasgow 1825, London 1827; Paris 1827, 1828; London 1855.
The beauties of Canning. Ed A. Howard [1827].
A biographical memoir of Canning ... to which is added the whole of his ... poems. [Ed T. Forster,] Brussels 1827.
Speeches, with a memoir by R. Therry, 6 vols 1828, 1830, 1836, [1845]; tr Fr by H. de Janvry, Paris 1832.
The works. Ed A. Howard, New York 1829.
Select speeches. Ed R. Walsh, Philadelphia 1835, 1836, etc.
Poetical works. 1851 (in Cabinet ed of the British poets vol 4).
Selections from the Anti-Jacobin, together with some later poems. Ed L. Sanders 1904. With J. H. Frere, G. Ellis and others.

§1

Ulm and Trafalgar. 1806 (2 edns).
A letter to Earl Camden connected with the late duel. 1809 (2 edns). Prose.
Two letters to Earl Camden. 1809. Prose.
The doctor: a parody. In The man in the moon, 1820 (24 edns).
Satires, songs and odes on various subjects. 1821, 1824 (in P. Pindar, The works).
New morality. In The British satirist, Glasgow 1826.
The pilgrimage to Mecca. Warwick 1829; London 1831 (rptd in Translations of the Oxford Latin prize poems).
An anglo-sapphic ode ... to Robert Beverley. By a Can-tab. 1833.
Boyle, E. C. Memories and thoughts ... followed by a poem by G. Canning. 1886.
The knave of hearts. In Parodies of ballad criticism, ed W. K. Wimsatt, Los Angeles 1957 (Augustan Reprint Soc).
Canning, with J. Smith, R. Smith and J. H. Frere, edited the Microcosm, *by 'Gregory Griffin', in 40 nos, Eton (6 Nov 1786–30 July 1787), Windsor [1788], 2 vols Windsor [1790], [1809], London [1825], also in* British essayists *(vol 28, 1827). He contributed to Quart Rev. For his pbd dispatches and speeches, see* BLC.

§2

George Canning and his friends .... Ed J. Bagot 1909; New York 1909.
Hinde, W. George Canning. 1973.
The letter-journal ... 1793–1795. Ed P. Jupp 1991 (in Camden 4th ser vol 41).

Maria M. Cannon fl. 1824–5

Maria and St Flos: a poem, in a series of letters, to which is added, A search after happiness. Newbury, Trowbridge, Frome and Hungerford 1824; London 1825.

David Carey 1782–1824

The pleasures of nature .... 1803.
The reign of fancy: a poem. By [D. C.]. 1804.
Poems, chiefly amatory. 1807, 1809.
Craig Phadric, Visions of sensibility ... Inverness 1811.
Macbeth: a poem in six cantos. Ed J. Adam. 1817. Anon. By [J. Mann or Carey?].
Beauties of the modern poets .... Ed Carey 1820, 1821, 1826.

The lord of the desert . . . and other poems. 1821.
See also col 892.

Frederick Howard, 5th Earl of Carlisle 1748–1825

Collection

The manuscripts of the Earl of Carlisle. . . . 1897. Prose.

§1

Poems. . . . 1773 (3 edns); Dublin 1781; London 1807.
The father's revenge: a tragedy. 1783, 1800, 1812.
To Sir J. Reynolds on his late resignation. . . . 1790.
The step-mother: a tragedy. 1800, 1812.
The tragedies and poems. 1801.
Miscellanies. 1820. Prose and verse.
Author of letters on Ireland and on the stage.

Rebekah Carmichael, also Mrs Hay fl. 1790–1806

Collections and selections

Eighteenth-century women poets. Ed R. Lonsdale, Oxford 1990.

§1

Poems. Edinburgh 1790.
Extempore, on seeing Sir William Forbes's Funeral, a poem. Edinburgh 1806. [KM]

George Fullerton Carnegie 1799–1851

Golfiana, or niceties connected with the game of golf. Edinburgh 1833, 1842, 1843.
The destinies of Zohak, or the halls of Argenk: a poem. Edinburgh 1834.
Poems on various subjects. Edinburgh 1834.

Sir John Carr 1772–1832

The sea side hero: a drama in three acts. 1804. Prose.
Poems. 1809; ed D. H. Reiman, New York and London 1977 (facs reprint).
Author of travel literature.

Noel Thomas [Nicholas Toms] Carrington 1770–1830

Collection

The collected poems. . . . Ed H. E. Carrington 2 vols 1834; Devonport and London [1840?].

§1

The banks of Tamar: a poem. . . . Plymouth Dock 1820; London 1828.
Dartmoor: a descriptive poem. . . . Ed W. Burt, London and Devonport 1826; London 1826.
My native village and other poems. 1830.
Contributed to an often rptd guidebook to Teignmouth and Torquay (1829).

Henry Francis Cary 1772–1844

Collection

Works. 6 vols 1847–56. Prose and verse.

§1

An irregular ode to General Elliott. Birmingham [1788?].
Sonnets and odes. 1788.
Ode to General Kosciusko. 1797.
The inferno of Dante, with a translation in blank verse, notes and a life of the author. Tr Cary 2 vols 1805–6; New York 1931 (illustr W. Blake).
The vision, or Hell, Purgatory and Paradise of Dante, translated. Tr Cary 3 vols 1814, 1819, 1822; 2 vols Philadelphia 1822; 3 vols London 1831, 1 vol 1844, 1850; 2 vols 1866 (illustr G. Doré), 1869, [1871], 1876, 1889, 1892; ed P. Toynbee 1900–2, [1903], 1906; ed E. Gardner 1908 (EL); 1910 (illustr J. Flaxman with Botticelli drawings and the Italian text), 1928, [1930]; Florence [1930]; Geneva [1970] (as The divine comedy), 1994. Selection: Purgatorio and paradiso, Chicago [1883]; Dante's purgatorio, 1889; The inferno, ed M. Marqusee (illustr Doré), 1976.
The birds of Aristophanes, translated. Tr Cary 1824.
Pindar in English verse. Tr Cary 1833.
Lives of English poets, from Johnson to Kirke White. 1846, 1856. Rptd from London Mag Aug 1821–Dec 1824. Prose.
The early French poets: notices and translations. Ed H. Cary (H. F. C.'s son) 1846, 1856; ed T. E. Welby (without French texts) 1923; New York 1925; Port Washington NY [1970]. Rptd from London Mag Nov 1821–Apr 1824.

§2

Cary, H. Memoir of the Rev H. F. Cary . . . with his literary journal and letters. 2 vols 1847, 1848.
King, R. W. The translator of Dante. 1925.
Edited the poetical works of Pope, Cowper, Milton, Thomson and Young, and translated Herodotus.

W. Case, Jr, of Lynn fl. 1801–2

The minstrel youth: a lyrical romance. . . . 1801; Lynn 1802.
Pictures of British female poesy. Lynn 1802.

John Castillo 1792–1845

A specimen of the Bilsdale dialect. . . . Ed [J. Nelson], Northallerton [1831].
Awd Isaac, The steeple chase and other poems. Whitby 1843.
The bard of the dales, or poems . . . partly in the Yorkshire dialect. 1850; Stokesley 1858 (enlarged, with life).
Poems in the North Yorkshire dialect. Ed G. M. Tweddell, Stokesley 1878.

John Hobart Caunter 1794–1851

The cadet: a poem, to which is added Egbert and Amelia . . . By a late resident in the east. 2 vols 1814. Anon.
The island bride, in six cantos. 1830.
St Leon. 1835. Prose.
The fellow commoner. 3 vols 1836. Prose.
The poetry of the Pentateuch. 2 vols 1839. Prose.
The triumph of evil: a poem. 1845.
Author of biblical commentaries, lectures for children, sermons and descriptions of the East.

John Chaloner 1780–1862

Rome: a poem. London and Edinburgh 1821. Anon.
The vale of Chamouni: a poem. By the author of Rome. 1822. Anon.
Clara Chester: a poem. By the author of Rome and The vale of Chamouni. Edinburgh 1823. Anon.

Mason Chamberlin fl. 1800–18

Equanimity: a poem. 1800.
Harvest: a poem. 1800.
Ocean: a poem, in two parts. 1801.
The path of duty: a moral tale. . . . Blandford 1818. Prose.

Matthew James Chapman d. 1865

Barbadoes and other poems. 1833.
Jephtha's daughter: a dramatic poem. 1834.
The Greek pastoral poets. Tr Chapman 1836; Hendon 1853 (as Idylls of Theocritus, Bion and Moschus, Bohn Lib, with J. Banks), 1866, 1881.
Hebrew idyls and dramas. 1866.
Author of medical pbns.

John Clare 1793–1864

By far the largest collections of Clare mss are in Northampton Public Library and Peterborough Museum; see [D. Powell], Catalogue of the John Clare collection in the Northampton Public Library, Northampton 1964, *and* Margaret Grainger, A descriptive catalogue of the John Clare collection in Peterborough Museum and Art Gallery, Peterborough 1973. *For detailed accounts of other ms collections see* IELM 4 pt 1; *Barbara Rosenbaum's entry also includes details of periodical and magazine publication of Clare's poems, where appropriate and where known.*

Bibliographies

Blunden, E. and A. Porter. In John Clare: poems chiefly from manuscript, ed Blunden and Porter 1920.
Powell, D. A bibliography of the writings of John Clare. Unpbd Diploma in Librarianship thesis, London Univ 1953.
Crossan, G. In BB and Mag Notes 32, 1975, rptd with Addenda in Crossan, A relish for eternity, Salzburg 1976.
Dendurent, H. O. John Clare: a reference guide. Boston 1978.
Estermann, B. H. John Clare: an annotated primary and secondary bibliography. New York 1985.

Collections and selections

Cherry, J. L. Life and remains of John Clare. 1873.
Poems by John Clare. Ed A. Symons 1908.
John Clare: poems chiefly from manuscript. Ed E. Blunden and A. Porter 1920.
Madrigals and chronicles: newly found poems by John Clare. Ed E. Blunden 1924.
Poems. Ed J. W. Tibble 2 vols 1935.
Poems of John Clare's madness. Ed G. Grigson 1949.
Selected poems. Ed G. Grigson 1950 (ML).
Selected poems. Ed J. Reeves 1954.
Selected poems. Ed J. W. and A. Tibble 1965 (EL).
Later poems. Ed E. Robinson and G. Summerfield, Manchester 1964.
Selected poems and prose. Ed E. Robinson and G. Summerfield 1966, 1967 (new enlarged edn).
Selected poems. Ed E. Feinstein 1968.
John Clare. Ed E. Robinson and D. Powell, Oxford 1984 (Oxford Authors).
Later poems. Ed E. Robinson, D. Powell and M. Grainger 2 vols Oxford 1984.
Early poems. Ed E. Robinson, D. Powell and M. Grainger. 2 vols Oxford 1989.
Selected poetry. Ed G. Summerfield, Harmondsworth 1990.
Cottage tales. Ed E. Robinson, D. Powell and P. M. S. Dawson, Ashington 1993.

§1

Proposals for publishing a collection of trifles in verse. Market Deeping 1818.
Poems descriptive of rural life and scenery. Introd by J. Taylor, London and Stamford 1820 (3 edns), 1821. Significant textual variants in each edn.
REVIEWS: 1820: (O. Gilchrist) London Mag, Jan; New Times, Jan; Literary Chron, Jan; Northampton Mercury, Jan; Morning Post, Feb, Mar, May; NMM, Mar; Monthly Rev, Mar; Monthly Mag Mar; (J. Scott) London Mag, Mar; (J. Conder) Eclectic Rev, Apr; Lady's Monthly Museum, Apr; (O. Gilchrist) Quart Rev, May; Guardian, May; (J. G. Lockhart) Blackwood's Edinburgh Mag, June; Br Critic, June; Antijacobin Rev, June.
The village minstrel and other poems. Introd by J. Taylor 2 vols 1821, 1823.
REVIEWS: 1821: Br Critic, June; Literary Gazette, Oct; Literary Chron, Oct; GM, Oct; Monthly Mag, Nov; (J. Taylor) London Mag, Nov; European Mag, Nov; NMM, Nov; 1822: (J. Conder) Eclectic Rev, Jan.
The parish. Ed E. Robinson, Harmondsworth 1985. Written 1822–4; unpbd in Clare's lifetime.
The shepherd's calendar; with village stories, and other poems. 1827; ed E. Robinson and G. Summerfield 1964, 1993 (rev).
REVIEWS 1827: Literary Gazette, Mar; (J. Conder) Eclectic Rev, June; London Weekly Rev, June; Literary Chron Oct.
Proposals for publishing... The midsummer cushion. Helpstone 1832.
The midsummer cushion. Ed A. Tibble and R. K. R. Thornton, Ashington 1979, 1990 (rev). Written 1832; unpbd in Clare's lifetime.
The rural muse: poems. 1835.
Reviews 1835: Athenaeum, July; Literary Gazette, July; (J. Wilson, rptd with some alterations in his The recreations of Christopher North, 1864); Blackwood's Edinburgh Mag, July; NMM, Aug; Druids' Monthly Mag.
The rural muse. Ed R. K. R. Thornton, Ashington 1982.
For further details of reviews see Dendurent and Estermann, Bibliographies, *above; many are rptd in* Clare: the critical heritage, ed M. Storey 1973.

Letters, journals etc

Sketches in the life... written by himself. Ed E. Blunden 1931.
Prose. Ed J. W. and A. Tibble 1951.
Letters. Ed J. W. and A. Tibble 1951.
The journals, essays, and the journey from Essex. Ed A. Tibble, Manchester 1980.
John Clare's birds. Ed E. Robinson and R. Fitter, Oxford 1982.
Autobiographical writings. Ed E. Robinson. Oxford 1983.
The natural history prose writings. Ed M. Grainger, Oxford 1983.
Letters. Ed M. Storey, Oxford 1985.
Selected letters. Ed M. Storey, Oxford 1988, rptd 1990.

§2

Allen, W. Four letters to Lord Radstock on the poems of Clare. 1823.
De Quincey, T. In his literary reminiscences, Tait's Mag, Dec 1840.
Redding, C. Clare the poet. Eng Jnl, May 1841.
Hood, E. P. Clare, the peasant poet. In his Literature of labour, 1851.
Baker, A. E. Northamptonshire glossary. 2 vols 1854.
Watts, A. (ed), Men of the times. 1856.
Mitford, M. R. Recollections. Vol 1 1857.
Obituary. GM, July 1864.
Martin, F. W. Life of John Clare. 1865; ed E. Robinson and G. Summerfield 1965.
Hall, S. T. Bloomfield and Clare. In Biographical sketches, Burnley 1873.
Heath, R. Types of English agricultural life. In his The English peasant, 1893.
Thomas, E. Women, nature and poetry. In his Feminine influence on the English poets, 1910.
Thomas, E. John Clare. In his A literary pilgrim in England. 1917.
Tibble, J. W. and A. John Clare: a life. 1932, 1972 (rev).
Chapple, A. J. V. Some unpublished poetical manuscripts of Clare. YULG, 31 1956.
Robinson, E. and G. Summerfield. J. Taylor's editing of the Shepherd's calendar. RES 14, 1963.

Hooker, I. M. F. and N. Dermott Hunt. Some unpublished documents of the asylum period. Northamptonshire Past and Present 3, 1964.

Green, D. B. John Clare, John Savage and the Scientific Receptacle. REL 7, 1966.

Green, D. B. New letters of John Clare to Taylor and Hessey. SP 64, 1967.

Storey, M. Letters of John Clare. 1821. Revised datings, N & Qns 16, 1969.

Chilcott, T. John Taylor: a publisher and his circle. 1972.

Storey, M. Some previously unpublished letters from John Clare. RES 25, 1974.

Crossan, G. John Clare's poetry: an examination... of some recent editions. Stud in Romanticism 23, 1984.

Storey, M. 'Creeping into print': editing the letters of John Clare. In The theory and practice of text-editing, ed. I. Small and M. Walsh, Cambridge 1991.

Lucas, J. Revising Clare. In Romantic revisions, ed. R. Brinkley and K. Hanley, Cambridge 1993.

The John Clare Society Journal *is pbd annually (1982 on).* [MS]

John Chalk Claris, or 'Arthur Brooke' 1797?–1866

Collections

Thoughts and feelings and Retrospection, and Elegy on the death of Shelley. By J. C. Claris. Ed D. H. Reiman, New York and London 1977 (facs reprint).

Poems (1816)... Poems (1818), Durovernum. By J. C. Claris. Ed D. H. Reiman, New York and London 1978 (facs reprint).

§1

Poems. By 'Arthur Brooke'. Canterbury 1816 (priv ptd); London 1818.

Durovernum, with other poems. By 'Arthur Brooke'. 1818.

Thoughts and feelings. By 'Arthur Brooke'. 1820.

Elegy on the death of P. B. Shelley. By 'Arthur Brooke'. 1822.

Retrospection, with other poems. By 'Arthur Brooke'. 1822.

Ann Clarke fl. 1820–40

The Christian life a journey. Birmingham 1820 (3rd edn); London 1821, 1823 (7th edn). Prose.

The world an inn: an allegory. Birmingham 1820 (2nd ed); Bath 1830; London 1835 (6th edn). Prose.

Poems, moral and entertaining.... Northampton and London 1824; 2 vols London 1825.

The saviour's triumph and Satan's downfall, or captivity led captive: a tragical poem. Northampton and London 1824.

Poems: viz. dialogue between body and soul. [Southam 1840?]

Anne Clarke, of Shipston on Stour fl. 1808–14

Small literary patchwork... By a countrywoman. Shipston on Stour 1808; London and Shipston on Stour 1814. Anon.

William Branwhite Clarke 1798–1878

Pompeii: a poem. Ipswich 1819.

The river Derwent, part the first.... 1822.

Lays of leisure.... 1829.

The history and practice of psalmody. 1835. Prose.

Engaged in religious controversy, wrote sermons, and wrote on gold mining in Australia.

'Leigh Cliffe'

See George Jones, below.

Arthur Clifford 1778–1830

A poetical epistle to H. Clifford.... Edinburgh 1810.

A midnight meditation... at Tixall. [Edinburgh? 1813?] Anon.

Tixall poetry.... Ed Clifford, Edinburgh and London 1813.

Carmen seculare: an ode for the year 1814. 1814.

Clifford, or the battle of Towton: an historical tragedy.... Paris 1817.

Wrote on topography, genealogy and elementary Latin.

Ingram Cobbin 1777–1851

Philanthropy: a poem.... 1817.

The pilgrim's fate and other poems. 1818.

Scripture parables in verse.... 1818.

Georgiana, or anecdotes... with poetical effusions. Ed Cobbin 1820.

Malan, C. H. A. Hymns.... Tr [Cobbin] 1825.

Author of religious and educational works.

Elizabeth or Eliza Cobbold, Mrs John, formerly Knipe, also 'Carolina Petty Pasty' 1767–1824

Collection

Poems... with a memoir.... Ed [L. Jermyn], Ipswich 1825; Ipswich and London 1825.

§1

Poems on various subjects. By Eliza Knipe. Manchester 1783.

Six narrative poems. By Eliza Knipe. 1787.

The mince pye: an heroic epistle... By 'Carolina Petty Pasty'. 1800.

Cliff valentines, 1813. Ipswich 1813.

Cliff valentines, 1814. Ipswich 1814. Anon.

Ode on the victory of Waterloo. Ipswich, London, Bury St Edmunds and Colchester 1815.

Contributed to annuals and to Ipswich pbns.

Sir William Cockburn 1773–1858

Saint Peter's denial of Christ: a Seatonian prize poem. Cambridge 1802, 1808 (in Musae seatonianae vol 2).

Christ raising the daughter of Jairus: a Seatonian prize poem. Cambridge 1803, 1808 (in Musae seatonianae vol 2).

Author of religious and geological works.

Mary Cockle, Mrs E. fl. 1808–26

The fishes grand gala. A companion to the 'peacock at home'. 2 pts 1808; pt 1 only Philadelphia 1809.

Lines on the lamented death of Sir John Moore.... 1810.

Simple minstrelsy. 1812.

National triumphs. 1814.

Elegy to the memory of... Princess Charlotte. 1817 (4 edns).

An elegy on the death of... George the third. London and Edinburgh 1820; Newcastle 1820 (2 edns), 1839 (priv ptd).

Lines to a boy pursuing a butterfly. Newcastle 1826. Anon.

Wrote various shorter pieces and prose works for children.

William Coldwell fl. 1818–23

Fables and moral poems. Halifax 1818.

Hebrew harmonies and allusions. 1820.

[Hebrew title] The book of praises.... 1821.

William Cole, vicar of Broadchalk 1754–1812

To the feeling heart, exalted affection, or Sophia Pringle: a poem. Salisbury 1789.

The contradiction. 1796. Prose.
A loyal poetical gratulation . . . . 1799.

Hartley Coleridge 1796–1849

See also Samuel Taylor Coleridge, below.

Collections

Poems, with a memoir by his brother [Derwent Coleridge]. 2 vols 1851, 1851.
The poetical works of Bowles, Lamb and Hartley Coleridge. Ed W. Tirebuck 1887.
Miles 3.
Poems. Ed W. Bailey-Kempling, Ulverston 1903.
Poems. 1907.
Complete poetical works. Ed R. Colles [1908] (ML).
Poems. 1927.

§1

Poems. Vol 1 (all pbd) Leeds 1833, 1833 (as Poems, songs and sonnets).
Biographia borealis: or lives of distinguished northerns. Leeds 1833, London 1836 (as The worthies of Yorkshire and Lancashire); [ed D. Coleridge] 3 vols 1852 (as Lives of northern worthies); rptd Freeport NY 1973.
Lives of illustrious worthies of Yorkshire. Hull 1835. Part of the Biographia borealis, *above*, reissued with new title page.
The dramatic works of Massinger and Ford, with an introduction by H. Coleridge. 1840, 1848, 1851.
Essays and marginalia. [Ed D. Coleridge] 2 vols 1851; rptd Plainview NY 1973.
Ascham, R. The scholemaster, with memoir by H. Coleridge. 1884. Rptd from Biographia, *above*.
Essays on parties in poetry and on the character of Hamlet. Ed J. Drinkwater, Oxford 1925, New York 1925; rptd Norwood PA 1978.
New poems, including a selection from his published poetry. Ed E. L. Griggs 1942; rptd Westport CT 1972.
On the death of Mary Fleming. TLS 15 Mar 1947. Unpbd poem transcribed by A. S. Whitefield.
Hartley Coleridge poems. Ed A. Astbury, Warwick 1984.
Poems. 1833; introd by J. Wordsworth, Spelsbury 1990.

Letters

Letters of Hartley Coleridge. Ed G. E. and E. L. Griggs, Oxford 1936; rptd New York 1976.
Hartman, H. A letter of Hartley Coleridge. Colophon n.s. 3 1938.
Curry, K. A letter of Hartley Coleridge. RES 20 1944.
Griggs, E. L. Four letters of Hartley Coleridge. HLQ 9 1946.

§2

Horne, R. H. In his A new spirit of the age, 1844.
Bagehot, W. In his Literary studies, 1879.
Wilcox, J. Hartley Coleridge. Manchester Quart 17 1898.
Bradshaw, J. M. Material for a memoir of Hartley Coleridge. 1912.
Towle, E. A. A poet's children: Hartley and Sara Coleridge. 1912.
Turner, A. M. Wordsworth and Hartley Coleridge. JEGP 22 1923.
Williams, S. T. Hartley Coleridge as a critic of literature. Southern Atlantic Quart 23 1924.
Hall, W. C. Hartley Coleridge. Manchester Quart 51 1925.
Pomeroy, M. J. The poetry of Hartley Coleridge. Washington 1927.
Griggs, E. L. Hartley Coleridge: his life and work. 1929. With bibliography.
Griggs, E. L. Coleridge and his son. SP 27 1930.
Blunden, E. Coleridge the less. In his Votive tablets, 1931.
Griggs, E. L. Hartley Coleridge on his father. PMLA 46 1931.
Griggs, E. L. Hartley Coleridge's unpublished correspondence. London Mercury June 1931.
Hartman, H. Hartley Coleridge, poet's son and poet. 1931. With bibliography. Rptd New York 1971.
Rea, J. D. Hartley Coleridge and Wordsworth's Lucy. SP 28 1931.
Little, G. L. Hartley Coleridge, Wordsworth and Oxford. N & Q Sep 1959. [PL]

Samuel Taylor Coleridge 1772–1834

Manuscript materials

The most comprehensive guide to ms materials is Barbara Rosenbaum, Samuel Taylor Coleridge 1772–1834, *in* IELM *vol 4 pt I 1982. Further ms material is described, beyond the two subsections below, in Bibliographies and exhibition catalogues, below. It should be noted that descriptions of the holdings of some large collections – notably at NYPL and the Bodleian – have not been pbd and that many collections have been added to since the descriptions of them were pbd.*

Separate collections of Coleridge manuscripts

Patton, C. N. Important Coleridge and Wordsworth mss acquired by Yale. YULG 9 1934. *See* White (1897), *below*, on Norton Longman mss., *below*.
Brinkley, R. F. Some notes concerning Coleridge material at the Huntington. HLQ 8 1945. *See* Zall (1971), *below*.
Noyes, R. The Oscar L. Watkins Wordsworth–Coleridge Collection. Indiana Quart for Bookmen 1 1945.
Skeat, T. C. Note-books and marginalia of S. T. Coleridge. BM Quart 16 1952. Acquisition of the Ottery Collection.
Healey, G. H. The Cornell Wordsworth Collection: a catalogue of books and mss presented to the University by Mr Victor Emmanuel. Ithaca NY 1957. Includes Coleridge material.
Metzdorf, R. F. The Tinker Library. New Haven CT 1959. Includes Coleridge material.
The Indiana Wordsworth collection. Bloomington IN 1970. Includes Coleridge material in the Lilly Lib.
Kendall, L. H. Jr. A descriptive catalogue of the W. L. Lewis Collection. Fort Worth TX 1970. Includes Coleridge letters and inscribed books.
Stephens, F. The Coleridge Collection: a sample. Lib Chron of Univ of Texas n.s. 1 1970.
Siemens, R. The Wordsworth Collection: Dove Cottage papers facsimiles. Edmonton, Alberta 1971. Contains Coleridge material.
Zall, P. M. Coleridge in the Huntington Library (1794–1834). TWC 2 1971. Supplements Brinkley (1945), *above*.
Dendurent, H. O. The Coleridge Collection in the Victoria College Library, Toronto. TWC 5 1974.
Sultana, D. Coleridge's political papers in Malta. In New approaches to Coleridge: biographical and critical, ed Sultana, 1981.
Clubbe, J. The Peal Collection: an overview. Kentucky Rev 4 1982. *See also* the catalogue in the same issue by J. S. Gatton and J. Clubbe. Contains Coleridge material.
Clubbe, J. The W. Hugh Peal Collection at the University of Kentucky. TWC 15 1984.

Commentary on individual manuscripts and manuscript collections

Campbell, J. D. Illus London News 26 Dec 1891. On the BL Liber Aureus ms, containing Coleridge's schoolboy poems.
White, W. H. A description of the Wordsworth and Coleridge mss in the possession of Mr T. Norton Longman. 1897; facs Folcroft PA 1969. *See* Patton (1934), *above*.
Coleridge's poems. Ed J. D. Campbell and W. H. White 1899; facs Folcroft PA 1972; Norwood PA 1975; Philadelphia 1976. Type-facs of interleaved Poems 1796 proofs and other mss. (Cf Stephens (1974), *below*.)
Dobell, B. Coleridgiana. Athenaeum 9 Jan 1904. Describes John Taylor Coleridge's commonplace book, which includes transcripts of Coleridge poems, now at Univ of Pennsylvania.
Kaufman, P. The Reynolds-Hood commonplace book: a fresh appraisal. KSJ 10 1961. At Bristol Public Lib, containing Coleridge material.

King, F. H. Samuel Taylor Coleridge in Australian libraries: a checklist of pre-1900 holdings. Melbourne 1973.

Stephens, F. Cottle, Wise, and MS Ashley 408. PBSA 68 1974. On Cottle's indiscriminate combining of materials in a BL ms. (Cf Campbell and White (1899), *above*.)

Bibliographies and exhibition catalogues (primary material)

There is an amount of overlapping between this section and the previous one, which lists ms materials and library collections; also with §2, below, which lists bibliographies of secondary material and guides to research.

Anderson, J. P. Bibliography. In Hall Caine, Life of Samuel Taylor Coleridge, 1887. Includes books in the lib of the BM containing ms notes by Coleridge.

Campbell, J. D. Titles, prefaces, contents etc. In Poetical works of Coleridge, 1893, appendix K.

Shepherd, R. H. The bibliography of Coleridge, revised, corrected and enlarged by Colonel W. F. Prideaux. 1900. For Prideaux's critical views on Shepherd's work, *see* N & Q 9th ser vol 10, 18 Oct 1902; and for the Christabel controversy between Prideaux and T. Hutchinson, *see* N & Q 1902–3.

Coleman, E. H. Coleridge bibliography. N & Q 9th ser vol 10, 20 Sep 1902. Response to J. L. Haney, referring to earlier bibliographical materials in N & Q.

Haney, J. L. A bibliography of Samuel Taylor Coleridge. Philadelphia 1903; facs Folcroft PA 1969, Norwood PA 1977. Includes first comprehensive list of annotated and marked books (*see also* Marginalia, *below*).

Garnett, R. In his Coleridge, 1904.

Coleridge, E. H. Bibliography of the poetical works. In Complete poetical works, Oxford 1912, appendix 7; rptd many times.

Wise, T. J. A bibliography of the writings in prose and verse of Coleridge. 1913 (priv ptd); suppl: Coleridgiana, 1919; facs in 1 vol 1970; Norwood PA 1977.

Catalogue of a unique Coleridge collection. [1913] (with facs); rptd in Superb collected sets of the first edns of Milton, Coleridge, Swinburne, Wordsworth. New York 1914. Includes part of the Norton Longman Collection.

Wise, T. J. In his Ashley Library: catalogue of printed books, manuscripts and autograph letters collected by Wise, 11 vols 1922–36 (priv ptd); rptd 1971. Coleridge items chiefly in vols 1, 8, 10.

Wise, T. J. Two lake poets: a catalogue of printed books, and manuscript letters by Wordsworth and Coleridge collected by Wise. 1927 (priv ptd); facs 1965.

Dillon, A. E. The Coleridge Collection at the Manchester Reference Library. Lib Assoc Record 1 1931.

Coleridge centenary exhibition organized by the University of the South West of England. Exeter [1934]. [Introd initialled by Humphry House.]

Kennedy, V. W. and M. N. Barton. Coleridge: a selected bibliography. Baltimore 1935; facs New York 1969.

Coleridge: an excerpt from the general catalogue of printed books in the British Museum. 1947. The catalogue has of course been updated many times.

Samuel Taylor Coleridge 1772–1834: catalogue of an exhibition in the King's Library, 21 July–29 October 1972. 1972.

Collections

The successive collections of Coleridge's poems which appeared during his lifetime have been excluded from this category and are positioned under §1, below. Only nos B and D of the collections listed here have a shared title page, but nos A and C are often described as collected edns (e.g. in the National Union Catalogue). All four attempt to put Coleridge's writing as a whole into print in uniform format.

(A) Family edition. Ed D., H. N. and S. Coleridge 22 vols 1834–53; etc.

Though vols have separate title pages and are not numbered as part of a set, they were obviously conceived as a single unified project. William Pickering originally pbd every vol except for 4–5 (pbd by J. Murray) and 21–2 (pbd by E. Moxon). Moxon began to reprint titles as the project moved towards completion, specifically: Poems, *ed Derwent and Sara Coleridge 1852;* Dramatic works, *ed Derwent Coleridge 1852;* Lay sermons *and* Statesman's manual, *ed Derwent Coleridge 1852;* Aids to reflection, *ed Derwent Coleridge, 7th edn 1854;* The friend, *ed Derwent Coleridge 1863. Some bibliographical descriptions include in this collection only the 22 vols pbd by Pickering and others between 1834 and 1853; others include only the 15 vols pbd by Pickering alone between 1839 and 1853 – a sequence which is much more uniform in appearance.*

1–3. Poetical works. [Ed H. N. Coleridge] 3 vols 1834 and often rptd; Poems in 1 vol ed S. Coleridge, Pickering 1844 and 1848; Poems, ed D. and S. Coleridge, Moxon 1852; Dramatic works, ed D. Coleridge, Moxon 1852.

4–5. Table-talk. Ed H. N. Coleridge 2 vols 1835; 2nd edn 1836; etc.

6. Church and state; Lay sermons. Ed H. N. Coleridge (= 3rd edn) 1839.

7–8. Biographia literaria. Ed H. N and S. Coleridge (= 2nd edn) 2 vols 1847.

9–10. Aids to reflection. Ed H. N. Coleridge (= 4th edn) 2 vols 1839.

11–12. Notes and lectures on Shakespeare. Ed S. Coleridge 2 vols 1849.

13. Confessions of an inquiring spirit. Ed H. N. Coleridge 1840.

14–16. Essays on his times. Ed H. N. and S. Coleridge 3 vols 1850.

17–19. The friend. Ed H. N. Coleridge (= 4th edn) 3 vols 1850.

20. Notes, theological, political, and miscellaneous. Ed D. Coleridge 1853.

21–2. Notes on English divines. Ed D. Coleridge 2 vols 1853.

H. N. Coleridge also edited 4 vols of Literary remains in a larger format (1836–9) from which the 3 vols of Notes are in part drawn.

(B) Complete works, with an introductory essay upon his philosophical and theological opinions. Ed W. G. T. Shedd 7 vols New York 1853; rptd 1854, 1856, 1858, 1860 etc, up to 1884. Shedd's introd, Coleridge as a philosopher and theologian, rptd in his Literary essays, New York [1878].

1. Aids to reflectio; The statesman's manual. Ed H. N. Coleridge.
2. The friend. Ed H. N. Coleridge.
3. Biographia literaria. Ed H. N. Coleridge and S. Coleridge.
4. Notes and lectures upon Shakespeare etc. Ed S. Coleridge.
5. Literary remains; Confessions of an inquiring spirit. Ed H. N. Coleridge.
6. On the constitution of the church and state; Lay sermons. Ed H. N. Coleridge. Table-talk.
7. Poetical and dramatic works.

(C) Bohn Standard Library edition. 8 vols 1865–1911.

Bohn pbd a Select poetical works *in 1852, and Bell and Daldy a single-vol* Poems *in 1862 (Elzevir ser) and in 1864 (Chiswick ser). Bell and Daldy continued to publish Coleridge prose-titles from 1865 onwards in a uniform series which merged with Bohn's Standard Lib. The following vols are uniform in size and format, but do not carry a shared title page or vol numbers. The dates are those of first printing, after which several vols were rptd many times:*

1. The friend. 1865.
2. Biographia literaria; Lay sermons. [1866.]
3. Lectures and notes on Shakspere and other English poets. Ed T. Ashe 1883.
4. Table talk and Omniana. Ed T. Ashe 1884.
5. Aids to reflection; Confessions of an inquiring spirit. 1884.
6. Miscellanies, aesthetic and literary. Ed T. Ashe 1885.

7–8. Biographia epistolaris. Ed A. Turnbull 2 vols 1911.

(D) Collected works of Samuel Taylor Coleridge. Ed Kathleen Coburn. 16 multi-part vols 1969– .

The background and evolution of the edn are described in Coburn's In pursuit of Coleridge *(1977) and W. McGuire's* Bollingen *(1982). It does not include* Collected letters *(ed E. L. Griggs 6 vols 1956–71) or* Notebooks *(ed Coburn, Merton Christensen and A. J. Harding 5 double-vols 1957–). Editors of individual titles have replaced one another in the course of its preparation; Coburn and the associate editor, Bart Winer, have predeceased its completion;*

four titles (nos 8, 11, 15, 16) have yet to appear and no 12 has to be completed. Reviews of separate vols can be traced through YWES.

1. Lectures 1795: on politics and religion. Ed L. Patton and Peter Mann 1971.
2. The watchman. Ed L. Patton 1970.
3. Essays on his times. Ed. D. V. Erdman 3 vols 1978.
4. The friend. Ed B. E. Rooke 2 vols 1969.
5. Lectures 1808–1819: on literature. Ed R. A. Foakes 2 vols 1987.
6. Lay sermons. Ed R. J. White 1972.
7. Biographia literaria. Ed J. Engell and W. J. Bate 2 vols 1983.
8. Lectures 1818–1819: on the history of philosophy. Ed J. R. de J. Jackson.
9. Aids to reflection. Ed J. Beer 1993.
10. On the constitution of church and state. Ed J. Colmer 1976.
11. Shorter works and fragments. Ed H. J. Jackson and J. R. de J. Jackson 2 vols.
12. Marginalia. Ed G. Whalley and H. J. Jackson 5 vols 1980– .
13. Logic. Ed J. R. de J. Jackson 1981.
14. Table talk. Ed C. Woodring 2 vols 1990.
15. Opus maximum. Ed T. McFarland.
16. Poetical works. Ed J. C. C. Mays 3 vols.

Selections/collections of verse and of prose on literary subjects

Selections of essays and lectures of mainly non-literary (viz political and philosophical) subjects are included under Poems, essays and lectures, below; selections mainly of letters and marginalia are included under Letters, conversations, notebooks, marginalia; there is some overlap with edns of poems (e.g. Ancient mariner, Christabel and Kubla Khan*) listed in §1, below.*

The poetical works of Coleridge, Shelley and Keats. [Ed Cyrus Redding,] Paris 1829 etc; Philadelphia 1831 etc. The Coleridge sheets also issued separately in 1831 etc. A carefully edited and influential presentation.

Poetical works. [Ed H. N. Coleridge] 3 vols 1834. The last issued during Coleridge's lifetime, reissued (with slight changes) 1835, 1836, 1837, 1840, 1844. Cf §1, *below*, on earlier collections.

Poetical and dramatic works, with a life of the author. 1836; other edns 1837, 1838, 1844. Based on Poems 1797, augmented by poems from Lyrical ballads 1798 and the 2 Wallenstein trns.

The ancient mariner, and other poems. 1836 (Tilt's Miniature Classical Lib).

Works of Coleridge, prose and verse. Philadelphia 1840, 1843, 1845, 1847, 1849, 1852, 1863, 1884, etc.

The ancient mariner and other poems. Nuremberg [1841] (Campe's Pocket Classics).

Poetical works. Ed H. Hooker, Philadelphia 1842, 1844, 1846; New York 1851, 1853.

The ancient mariner and other poems. 1844 (Clarke's Cabinet ser).

Poems, with an introductory essay on his life and writings by H. T. Tuckerman. New York and Boston 1848.

Poetical works of Coleridge and Keats, with a memoir of each. 2 vols Boston 1852 etc; New York 1877 etc. (Riverside edn.)

Select poetical works. Ed H. G. Bohn 1852.

Poetical and dramatic works. Boston 1855, 1857, 1859, 1866.

The ancient mariner and other poems. Groombridge 1858.

Poetical works of T. Campbell and Coleridge. Edinburgh [1859].

Poems. 1862 (Bell & Daldy's Pocket Vols), 1864 (Elzevir ser); rptd 1881 etc.

Poetical and dramatic works, with a life of the author. Halifax 1864.

Christabel and the lyrical and imaginative poems of Coleridge. Ed A. C. Swinburne 1869; rptd 1873, 1882, etc.

Coleridge's Ancient mariner and other poems. 1872 (Chambers' English Classics).

Poetical works. Ed W. M. Rossetti [1872,] [1880] (Moxon's Popular Poets), 1892, 1912 (with dramatic writings).

Rime of the ancient mariner, and other poems. 1873 (Collins' School Classics).

Poetical works. Ed W. B. Scott 1874, [1880] (Excelsior ser), 1889 etc (Routledge's Pocket Lib).

Poetical works, with memoir. [1875] etc (Chandos Classics/Lansdowne Poets).

Favorite poems by Coleridge. Boston 1877. (illus; Vestpocket ser).

Poetical works, with life. Edinburgh and London [1881] (Landscape ser).

Poems, with a prefatory notice, biographical and critical, by J. Skipsey. 1884 etc (Canterbury Poets).

Table talk ... and the rime of the ancient mariner, Christabel, etc. 1884 (Morley's Universal Lib).

Poetical works. Ed T. Ashe 2 vols 1885 etc (Aldine).

The ancient mariner, Christabel, and miscellaneous poems. [Ed G. T. Bettany,] London and New York 1886 (Popular Lib of Literary Treasures).

Poems. 1888 (Chiswick ser).

Select poems. Ed H. G. Groser. In A. H. M. Miles, Poets and the poetry of the century vol 1, [1891] etc.

Selections from the prose writings. Ed H. A. Beers, New York 1893 etc (Readings for Students).

Passages from the prose and table talk of Coleridge. Ed W. H. Dirks [1894], 1905 (Camelot ser/The Scott Lib).

Select poems of Coleridge, Wordsworth etc. Ed F. H. Sykes, Toronto 1895.

[Select poems.] Ed W. Pakenham and J. Marshall, Toronto [1895].

The golden book of Coleridge. Ed S. A. Brooke 1895, 1906 (EL), etc.

Poems, chosen out of the works of Coleridge. Ed F. S. Ellis, Hammersmith 1896 (Kelmscott Press).

Four poets: poems from Wordsworth, Coleridge, Shelley and Keats. Ed O. J. F. Crawfurd 1897.

Poetry. Ed R. Garnett 1898 (ML). Reissued as Poems 1905 etc.

Ancient mariner, Kubla Khan and Christabel. Ed T. F. Huntington, New York 1898 etc (Macmillan's Pocket American and English Classics); ed Huntington and H. Y. Moffett, illustr A. G. Peck, New York 1936 (New Pocket Classics).

Selected poems. Ed A. Lang, illustr P. Wilson 1898 (Selections from the Poets).

Wordsworth, Coleridge and Keats: selections. Ed A. D. Innes 1901 (Blackwood's English Classics).

Select poems. Ed A. J. George, Boston 1897 etc. In chronological order.

[Poems.] Ed H. W. Mabie, New York [1902].

Christabel and The rime of the ancient mariner. Ed J. J. Burns, Chicago 1903 (Lakeside ser of English readings).

Christabel, Kubla Khan, Fancy in nubibus and Song from Zapolya. 1904. Designs by L. and E. Pissarro.

The poems and dramatic works. Ed W. Knight 1904 (Thin Paper Classics).

Christabel and other poems. Ed H. Bennett 1905 (Carlton classics).

Poems. Ed E. H. Coleridge 1905. Selection (Heinemann's Favourite Classics).

Poems. Ed E. Meynell [1905] etc (Red Letter Lib).

Poems. Ed A. Symons 1905.

Poems. Ed E. Dowden, illustr C. Pears, Edinburgh [1906] (Golden Poets).

Poems. Ed E. H. Coleridge, illustr G. Metcalfe [1907] etc.

Ancient mariner und Christabel. Ed A. Eichler, Vienna 1907.

Poems. Ed A. T. Quiller-Couch 1907 (WC).

Coleridge's literary criticism. Ed J. W. Mackail 1908; facs Folcroft PA 1974, Norwood PA 1976, Philadelphia 1978.

The ancient mariner and select poems. Ed H. M. Belchen 1908 (Scribner English Classics).

Lyrical poems. Ed A. T. Quiller-Couch, Oxford [1908] (Select English Classics).

The ancient mariner and Christabel. Oxford [1909] (Oxford Plain Texts).

Poetical works of Coleridge, Poe and Rossetti. [Ed G. Flower,] New York 1910.
Poems of nature and romance 1794–1807. Ed M. A. Keeling, Oxford 1910, 1923.
Golden hours with Coleridge. Illustr H. K. Elcock 1913 (Illus Pocket Classics).
Selected poems. Ed W. Robertson [1915] (King's Treasury ser).
Select poems. Ed S. G. Dunn 1916, 1918 (Indian Lib of English Poets).
Selections, from Coleridge. Ed L. R. Gibbs, Boston 1916.
Selections from the poems. Ed A. H. Thompson, Cambridge 1916 (English Romantic Poets ser).
Selected poems and dramas. Milan 1918.
Selected poems of Coleridge and Tennyson. Ed J. F. MacDonald, Toronto 1918.
The ancient mariner and other poems and prose. Ed W. B. Henderson 1920 (Kings Treasuries of Literature).
The poetry and prose of Coleridge, Lamb and Leigh Hunt; The Christ's Hospital anthology. Ed S. E. Winbolt 1920.
The rime of the ancient mariner and other poems. Ed L. Pound, Philadelphia [1920] (Lippincott's classics).
Coleridge's romantic poems. Ed H. A. Treble [1923] (Chambers' English Classics).
[Selected poems.] Ed H. Newbolt [1924] etc (Nelson's Poets).
Poetry and prose, with essays by Hazlitt, Jeffrey, De Quincey, Carlyle and others. Ed H. W. Garrod, Oxford 1925 etc.
Wordsworth and Coleridge. Ed G. Boas 1925; facs Folcroft PA 1977. A contrast.
Selected poems and prose. Ed R. B. Hales 1927 (Black's English Literature ser, Socrates Booklets).
[Select poems.] Ed H. Monro [1928] (Augustan Books of English Poetry).
Selections from the poems. Ed A. H. R. Ball [1931] (Selected English Classics).
[Prose and verse.] Ed B. I. and M. R. Evans 1931 (Methuen's English Classics).
The ancient mariner and other poems. Ed G. E. Hollingworth 1932 (Selected English Classics).
Rime of the ancient mariner, and other poems. Ed G. Guibillon, Paris 1933 (Les Classiques Pour Tous).
Select poetry and prose. Ed S. Potter 1933, 1950 (with some marginalia added), 1962 (Nonesuch).
The best of Coleridge. Ed E. L. Griggs, New York 1934, 1941, 1947 (Nelson English ser).
Poems and dramatic works. Ed W. Knight [1934].
Selected poems. [Ed S. Potter,] illustr S. Mrozewski 1935 (Nonesuch).
Ancient mariner and Gray's Elegy. [Ed P. T. Cresswell,] 2 pts 1936. Reissues Macmillan edns of 1896 and 1904, with new editorial matter.
Coleridge. Ed D. Wellesley 1942 (English Poets in Pictures ser).
Coleridge: vingt-cinq poèmes. Ed and tr G. d'Hangest, Paris 1945 (Collection Bilingue).
Poesie e prose. Ed M. Luzi, Milan [1949].
The portable Coleridge. Ed I. A. Richards, New York 1950, 1961, etc.
Poems. Ed G. Grigson 1951 (Crown Classics).
Selected poetry and prose. Ed E. W. Schneider, New York 1951; 2nd edn San Francisco 1971 (Rinehart edns).
Selected poetry and prose. Ed D. A. Stauffer, New York 1951 (Modern Lib edn).
Complete poems. Ed 'Morchard Bishop' (O. Stonor) 1954 (Macdonald Illus Classics).
Whalley, G. Coleridge and Sara Hutchinson and the Asra poems. 1955. Contains Sara's poems.
Selected poems. Ed R. C. Bald, New York 1956.
Selected poems and prose. Ed K. Raine 1957 etc (Pen).
William Wordsworth and Coleridge: selected critical essays. Ed T. M. Raysor, New York 1958 (Crofts Classics).
Selected poems. Ed R. Wilbur and G. R. Stange, New York 1959 (Laurel Poetry ser).
Selected poems. Ed J. Reeves 1959 (Poetry Bookshelf).
A Coleridge selection. Ed R. Wilson 1963 (Macmillan's English Classics).
Poems. Ed J. B. Beer 1963, 2nd edn 1974, 3rd edn 1993 (EL).
Coleridge. Ed B. Delvaille, Paris 1963 (Écrivains d'Hier et d'Aujourd'hui no 12).
Poems, selected. Ed G. Hough 1963 (Folio Soc).
Poetry and prose. Ed C. Baker, New York 1965 (Bantam Books).
Selected poems. Ed J. Colmer 1965 (New Oxford English ser).
Poems. Ed B. Deutsch, New York 1967 (Crowell Poets).
Selected poetry. Ed H. Bloom, New York 1972 (Signet Classics ser).
Coleridge at Nether Stowey. Ed U. Codrington 1972 (National Trust).
Coleridge's verse: a selection. Ed W. Empson and D. Pirie 1972, rptd Manchester 1989.
Imagination in Coleridge. Ed J. S. Hill 1978.
Samuel Taylor Coleridge. Ed H. J. Jackson 1985 (Oxford Authors ser).
Selected poems. Ed I. Hamilton 1993 (Bloomsbury Poetry Classics).
Samuel Taylor Coleridge. Ed H. J. Jackson 1994 (Oxford Poetry Lib).

§1

Individual works published in Coleridge's lifetime (including collaborations and translations, and translations into other languages)

Reviews are conveniently anthologised by J. R. de J. Jackson in Coleridge: the critical heritage *(1970) and* Coleridge: the critical heritage, vol 2 1834–1900 *(1991). See also* The Romantics reviewed: contemporary reviews of British Romantic writers, *ed D. Reiman, pt A 'The lake poets' (2 vols New York 1972); and* Romantic bards and British reviews: a selected edition of the contemporary reviews of the works of Wordsworth, Coleridge, Byron, Keats and Shelley *(1971).*

The fall of Robespierre: an historic drama. Cambridge 1794. Act 1 by Coleridge, acts 2–3 by Southey. Facs Oxford 1991.
A moral and political lecture delivered at Bristol. Bristol [1795]; expanded in Conciones, *below*; in Collected works: Lectures 1795.
The plot discovered. Bristol 1795; rptd in Conciones, *below*; in Collected works: Lectures 1795.
Conciones ad populum: or addresses to the people. [Bristol] 1795; facs Oxford 1992; in Collected works: Lectures 1795. For annotated copy at Harvard *see* C. C. Seronsy, Marginalia by Coleridge in three copies of his published works, SP 51 1954.
The plot discovered: or an address to the people, against ministerial treason. Bristol 1795; in Collected works: Lectures 1795.
An answer to A letter to Edward Long Fox MD. Bristol [1795]; rptd by R. A. Potts in A forgotten early prose work of S. T. Coleridge, Athenaeum 2 May 1908. Signed C. T. S. (for S. T. C.).
Lectures 1795: on politics and religion. Ed L. Patton and J. P. Mann 1971 (Collected works). Includes Conciones ad populum, The plot discovered, A moral and political lecture, etc.
Ode on the departing year. Bristol 1796.
Poems on various subjects. London and Bristol 1796 (ptd in Bristol); facs Oxford 1990. *See* June Starke, Effusion XV: a memory of pantisocracy, Turnbull Lib Record 11 1978, on a copy with a draft of the lines folded in.
[Sonnets from various authors.] [1796] (priv ptd); facs ed P. M. Zall, Glendale CA 1968. 4 sonnets and prefatory essay on the sonnet by Coleridge, 24 sonnets by Bowles, Lamb, Lloyd, Southey et al. Prefatory essay rptd variously in Poems 1797. For existing marked copies, *see* G. Whalley, Coleridge's Sheet of sonnets, 1796, TLS 23 Nov 1956; P. M. Zall, Coleridge and 'Sonnets from various authors', Cornell Lib Jnl 2 1967.
The watchman. 10 nos Bristol 1796. Advertised 'to be published every eighth day'; issued 1 Mar–13 May 1796. Prospectus rptd by J. D. Campbell, Athenaeum 9 Dec 1893. Coleridge's contributions

rptd in pt in Essays on his own times, ed S. Coleridge, 1850. *See* G. P. Winship, Coleridge bibliography, TLS 19 Mar 1925.

The watchman. Ed L. Patton 1970 (Collected works). For annotated copy at the University of Kansas, *see* W. P. Albrecht, An annotated copy of 'The watchman', TWC 9 1978.

Poems by S. T. Coleridge, second edition: to which are now added poems by Charles Lamb and Charles Lloyd. Bristol and London 1797 (ptd in Bristol). Includes much of Poems 1796, *above*, but substantially a new book. For the printer's copy prepared in part from proofs of Poems 1796, *see under* J. D. Campbell and W. H. White (1899) and F. Stephens (1974) in Manuscript materials, *above*. For an annotated copy, *see* W. E. Gibbs, Unpublished variants in S. T. Coleridge's poetry, MLN 46 1931.

Fears in solitude, written in 1798 during the alarm of an invasion; to which are added France: an ode and Frost at midnight. 1798; facs Oxford 1989. For an annotated copy, *see* B. I. Evans, Coleridge's copy of 'Fears in solitude', TLS 18 Apr 1935.

[1812] (another edn, perhaps rptd from Poetical Register 7 1812).

Lyrical ballads, with a few other poems [by W. Wordsworth and S. T. Coleridge]. [Bristol? and] London 1798 (ptd in Bristol); facs 1927 (English Replicas); Menston, Yorks 1971; Oxford 1990. Lewti cancelled in proof and Coleridge's Nightingale substituted. *See* D. F. Foxon, The printing of Lyrical ballads 1798, Library 5th ser 9 1954. *See also under* Wordsworth, *col 492*. For separate edns of the Ancient mariner, *see below*.

2 vols 1800 (with Coleridge's poem Love). For ms copy of this edn, *see under* C. H. Patton (1934) in Manuscript materials, *above*; Collected letters vol 1; G. L. Little, An important unpublished Wordsworth letter: December 18th, 1800, N & Q 204, Sep 1959; M. Peacock, Variants to the preface of Lyrical ballads, MLN 61 1946; F. A. Pottle, An important addition to Yale's Wordsworth–Coleridge collection, YULG 41 1966. *See also* RL II 703–4 for a copy annotated by Coleridge at Trinity College Cambridge (incompletely described here); J. W. Binns, The title-page epigraph of the Lyrical ballads, 1800, Library 6th ser 2 1980, on Jan Dousa the elder as source of Coleridge's Latin; G. Little, Coleridge's copy of Lyrical ballads 1800 and his connection with the Irving family, BC 33 1984, on an annotated copy of vol 1 at Victoria State Lib, Melbourne.

2 vols 1802 (with omission of Coleridge's Dungeon), 1805.

For separate edns of Lyrical ballads, see under Wordsworth, col 499. The most recent critical edns are ed R. L. Brett and A. R. Jones 1963 (text of 1798 with the additional 1800 poems and prefaces, with introd, notes and appendices); W. J. B. Owen, Oxford 1967 (text of 1798); D. Roper 1968 (text of 1805); J. Butler and K. Green, Ithaca NY 1992 (Cornell Wordsworth); M. Mason 1992 (based on 1805 text, Longman Annotated Texts ser).

The ancient mariner. The rime of the ancyent marinere. In Lyrical ballads 1798; The rime of the ancient mariner, in Lyrical ballads 1800 (extensively rev), 1802, 1805; in Sibylline leaves 1817 (with marginal gloss); in Poetical works 1828, 1829, 1834 (with minor successive revisions). See J. L. Lowes, The road to Xanadu, Boston 1927, 1930 (rev).

Edinburgh and London 1837 (illustr D. Scott), rptd 1883 etc; 1857 etc (illustr E. H. Wehnert, E. Duncan and B. Foster); 1863, New York 1875 (illustr J. N. Paton); Boston 1876 (illus); 1876 etc (illustr G. Doré); ed E. T. Stevens and D. Morris 1878 (Annotated Poems of English Authors); New York 1884 (illustr G. Doré), San Francisco 1952 (ed C. R. Wood, facs edn); ed W. Dent 1895 (Blackie's New English Classics); ed K. L. Bates, Boston [1889] (Students' Ser of English Classics); ed H. Bates 1896 etc (Longman's English Classics); Leeds [1896] (Pedley's Northern ser); [1896] (illustr W. Strang); ed A. J. George, Boston 1897 etc; ed L. R. Gibbs, Boston 1898 etc; ed J. P. Fruit, Boston 1899 (Cambridge Lit ser); East Aurora NY 1899 (illustr W. W. Denslow); 1899 (decorated by C. Ricketts); 1900 (illustr H. Cole); ed P. Edgar, New York 1900, 1901, Toronto 1902 (Morang's Educational ser); ed N. H. Pitman, Richmond VA 1901 (Johnson Ser of English Classics); ed C. R. Ashbee 1903; Edinburgh 1903; ed P. T. Creswell 1904, 1936 (Macmillan's English Classics); ed G. E. Woodberry, New York [1904] (Gateway ser); ed N. L. Frazer 1905 (Carmelite Classics); [1905]; ed R. M'William [1905] (Temple English Lit Ser for Schools); ed W. J. Alexander, Toronto 1905, 1905; 1906; 1906; ed P. Woodroffe, Edinburgh [1906] (English Masterpieces); ed M. A. Eaton, Boston 1906; ed A. Guthkelch 1907 (with early English ballads) (Bell's English Texts for Secondary Schools); ed J. W. Abernethy (with Christabel etc), New York 1907 (Merrill's English Texts); ed A. Eichler, Wiener Beiträge zur englischen Philologie 26 1907 (with Christabel); ed M. E. Kingsley and F. H. Palmer, Boston 1910 (Kingsley English Texts); 1910, 1926 (illustr W. Pogány); ed E. E. Garrigues, New York 1910 (Eclectic English Classics); ed M. A. Keeling, Oxford 1912; ed T. S. Sterling and J. W. Holme 1914; ed E. Smith 1914 (with Milton's sonnets); ed H. W. Bones, Chicago 1916 (Progressive School Classics); ed A. J. Hogan, Chicago 1922 (Loyola English Classics); [1927]; Yellow Springs OH 1927 (illustr G. Uhlmann); [1928] (illustr G. P. Micklewright) (Staple Inn ser); Bristol 1929 (also New York 1964) (illustr D. Jones; introd pbd separately ed D. Cleverdon 1972); ed O. Lowe, New York 1929 (Merrill's English Classics); ed A. T. Quiller-Couch, Oxford 1930; ed E. Blunden, New York 1931 (illustr H. Charles Tomlinson); 1937 (illustr E. Davies); New York 1938 (illustr G. Grant, Heritage Club ser); Mt Vernon NY 1939 (illustr P. McPharlin); Birmingham 1940 (illustr J. T. Dunning); 1943 (illustr M. Peake), rptd 1971, new edn 1978; 1944 (Corvinus Press); Edinburgh 1945 (illustr D. Grant); New York 1945 (illustr E. A. Wilson, Limited Edns Club); Larchmont NY 1946 (illustr H. A. Mueller); ed R. P. Warren, New York 1946; Christchurch 1952 (frontispiece by L. Bensemann); Victoria, Australia 1952 (illustr B. Tutt); ed V. W. Kennedy, Boston [1959]; ed R. A. Gettmann, San Francisco [1961]; Boston 1964 (illustr R. F. Bartlett); ed M. Gardner, 1965 (illustr G. Doré), rptd New York [1979]; New York 1966 (illustr H. Simon); ed R. C. Sharma, New Delhi 1967; New York 1969 (illustr C. Mozley); New York 1971 (illustr C. W. Hodges); 1972 (illustr E. Le Cain); 1976 (illustr P. Procktor); 1989 (illustr H. Emerson); ed M. Wallen, Barrytown NY 1993; 1994 (illustr G. Palmer) (Folio Soc). Also ptd variously with Kubla Khan, Christabel and other separate poems; *see* Collections, *above*, 1858, 1872, London and New York [1886], 1908, Oxford [1909], 1920, Philadelphia [1920], 1932, 1936, etc.

TRANSLATIONS

Du, Groningen 1896 (De oude Zeeman by G. B. Kuitert); Brussels and Maastricht 1931 (De Ballade van den oud matroos by A. Donker = N. A. Donkersloot); Ljouwert 1935 (De ballade fon d'ald-matroas, viz. Friesian, by A. R. Scholten).

Fr, Paris 1837 (Le vieux marin by J. A. X. Michiels, in prose, included in his Contes des montagnes, Paris 1858); 1877 (Le dit du vieux marin by A. Barbier, illustr G. Doré; illustr R. Cat, Paris 1969); Paris 1901 etc (La complainte du vieux marin by V. Larbaud); Paris 1920 (Le dit de l'ancien marinier by O. and G. Lavaud, illustr by A. Lhote); Paris 1921 (La ballade du vieux marin by A. Jarry, illustr A. Deslignères); Paris 1926 (La chanson du vieux marin by A. Barbeau); Caen 1929 (by P. Yvon, in his Trois poèmes); Paris 1930 (by P. Mélèse in his Les poètes Lakistes: Wordsworth, Coleridge); Paris 1939 (Le vieux marin by J.-A. Moisan, illustr N. Santon); Paris 1939 (Le dit du vieux marin, suivi de Christabel et de Koubla Khan, by H. Parisot), rev Paris 1947 (Collection romantique 1), Paris 1948 (illustr A. Masson); Paris 1945 (by G. d'Hangest in his Coleridge vingt-cinq poèmes); Paris? 1946 (La ballade du vieux marin by G. L. Mano, illustr M. Prassinas).

Ger, 1831 (Der alte Matrose by F. Freiligrath, inc in his Gedichte, Stuttgart and Tübingen 1838, rev 1839 etc); Heidelberg 1959 (Der alte Seemann by W. Breitweiser, with Kubla Khan); Frankfurt-on-Main 1963 (Der alte Seefahrer by H. Politzer).

Hebrew, New York 1910 (by A. Fleishman, with Kubla Khan).
Hungarian (Magyar), Gyoma 1921 (Ének a veñtengerészröl by S. Löring).
Ital, Milan 1889 (La leggenda del vecchio marinaro by E. Nencioni); Pisa 1889 (La rima del vecchio marinaro by E. Teza); 1913 (La ballata del vecchio marinaro by P. Ripari) (*see* C. Lutri, Poemetti e liriche, 1953); Florence [1947] (La ballata del vecchio marinaro by Mario Praza); Turin 1964 (La ballata del vecchio marinaro by B. Fenoglio).
Jap, 1905 (by N. Katagami, Rising Generation 13); 1905 (by N. Kishimoto in One hundred English marine poems); 1934 (by T. Saito).
Latin, np [1889] (Diomedea by O. A. Smith); Oxford 1906 (Carmen Coleridgianum quod senex nauta by R. Broughton).
Rus, St Petersburg 1893 (Starij morjak by A. Korinskij); 1930 (Sladkuv preklad stareho namornika by F. Chuduba).
'Morgan O'Doherty' (D. M. Moir), The rime of the auncient waggonere in four parts, Blackwood's Mag Feb 1819 (rptd in W. Maginn's Miscellanies, prose and verse, ed R. W. Montagu 2 vols 1885); The rime of the new-made baccalere: a parody, Oxford 1841, 1867.

Annual anthology. [Ed R. Southey] vol 2, Bristol [1800].

Wallenstein: a drama in two parts translated from the German of Frederic Schiller. 1800. The Piccolomini (5 acts) and The death of Wallenstein (5 acts). The one-act prelude, Wallensteins Lager, which made up Schiller's original trilogy, was not translated. For Coleridge's ms, *see* F. Freiligrath, Athenaeum 15 June, 31 Aug 1861 (*and* J. Gillman, note, 18 May 1861); Coleridge's Wallenstein-Uebersetzung, EStudien 31 1902 (collation of trn with Ger original); W. Grossman, The manuscript of Coleridge's Wallenstein, HLB 11 1957, rptd Euphorion 53 1959; J. Crick, Some editorial and stylistic observations on Coleridge's translation of Schiller's Wallenstein, Pbns of the English Goethe Soc 54 1984, and her Coleridge's Wallenstein: two legends, MLR 83 1988 (further discussion of texts and related problems).
Piccolomini (only) rptd New York 1805; both plays rptd in Coleridge's Poetical and dramatic works, 1836 etc (curiously, the only plays in this vol); Schiller's tragedies 1844 (Smith's Standard Lib), 1853 (Universal Lib), 1866; with revisions in Works of Schiller, historical and dramatic, ed H. G. Bohn 1846; in Complete works of Schiller, ed C. J. Hempel 1870; Dramatic works of Schiller 1889; ed N. H. Dole, Boston 1902; in an abridged version by William Poel entitled War, 1934.

Poems: third edition, 1803. Omits poems by Lamb and Lloyd; a fresh selection and arrangement supervised by Lamb.

The Friend: a literary, moral and political weekly paper, excluding personal and party politics and the events of the day. 28 nos Penrith 1809–10. Nos 1–27, with supernumerary no between 20 and 21, issued 1 June 1809–15 Mar 1810. Includes contributions by Wordsworth et al, but almost entirely Coleridge's composition. Rptd in Collected works.
1812. Reissue with supplementary matter. For annotated Rose copy, *see* J. Wordsworth, Some unpublished Coleridge marginalia, TLS 14 June 1957. Selection rptd as Three tales from Talmudic literature, New York 1964.
3 vols 1818. A new edn, carefully rev and with extensive addns. *See* E. L. Griggs, The Friend: 1809 and 1818 editions, MP 35 1938. For annotated Hughes copy, *see* F. H. Heinemann, Unknown Coleridge marginalia, N & Q 178, 29 June 1940; for Bristol Lib copy, J. Ross, The Friend, TLS 7 Feb 1948; for Harvard copy, C. C. Seronsy, Marginalia by Coleridge in three copies of his published works, SP 51 1954; P. Mann, Annotations by Coleridge in a copy of The Friend (1818), SB 26 1973 (T. F. Middleton's copy). Rptd Burlington VT 1831, in 1 vol.
3 vols 1837 (3rd edn), 1844 (4th edn). Ed H. N. Coleridge. With the author's last corrections, an appendix and a synoptical table of the contents of the work by H. N. Coleridge, 3 vols 1850 (also claiming to be 4th edn). *See* W. Baker, G. H. Lewes's annotations to Coleridge's The Friend (1837), Library 5th ser 31 1976.
Ed D. Coleridge 1863; rptd 1865 (Bohn's Lib) etc.
Ed B. E. Rooke 2 vols 1969 (Collected works). Reprints complete texts of 1809–10 and 1818.

Omniana: or horae otiosores. Ed R. Southey 2 vols 1812. Most of Coleridge's contributions were taken from notebooks and are identified in the contents by asterisks. Ed T. Ashe (Bohn's Lib) (with Table talk, *below*) and often rptd with addns from Allsop's Letters etc; ed as a whole, i.e. with Southey's contribution, by R. Gittings, Fontwell, Essex 1969 (Centaur Classics).

Remorse: a tragedy in five acts. 1813 (3 edns), 1884; 1st edn facs Oxford 1989; 2nd edn rptd New York 1813. Prologue by C. Lamb. For the first unpbd version, *see* Osorio (1873) *under* Poems and plays, *below*; *also* H. O. Dendurent, The texts and textual relationships of Coleridge's Osorio and Remorse (Evanston IL 1972), DAI 33:10 (Apr 1973) 5718A. For annotated copies, *see* C. G. Bouslog, Coleridge's marginalia in Sara Hutchinson's copy of Remorse, and C. Woodring, Two prompt copies of Coleridge's Remorse, both BNYPL 65 1961; J. D. Wilson, A note on Coleridge and the Quarterly Review, TWC 6 1975 (Edward Coleridge copy [now at Brandeis]).

Christabel; Kubla Khan: a vision; The pains of sleep. 1816 (3 edns); rptd Boston 1816; facs Oxford 1991. *See* J. A. Citron, Two unrecorded manuscripts of Christabel, TWC 13 1982 (at Bodleian and Boston Univ). For annotated copies, *see* Christabel, ed E. H. Coleridge 1907, *below* (Hinves copy); B. E. Rooke, An annotated copy of Coleridge's 'Christabel', Studia Germanica 15 1974 (Ramsgate copy).
Christabel. 1904 (illustr C. M. Watts), New York 1905, 1920; [1905] (Broadway Booklets); ed H. Bennett 1905; Christabel, illustrated facsimile of the manuscript and with textual and other notes, ed E. H. Coleridge 1907 (Royal Soc of Lit); 1908 (De la More Booklets); [1911] (Langham Booklets); ed T. Saito, Tokyo 1930.

TRANSLATIONS

Ital, Padua 1910 (Christabella by E. Teza).
Jap by Y. Tamatao, Muraski 1–2 1934–5.
Rus, Berlin 1923 (Kristabel by G. Ivanov).

Christabess, by S. T. Colebritche esq: a right woeful poem, translated from the doggerel by Sir Vinegar Sponge, 1816; 'Morgan O'Doherty' (D. M. Moir), Christabel: the introduction to part the third, Blackwood's Mag June 1819 (rptd in Maginn's Miscellanies, prose and verse, ed R. W. Montagu, 2 vols 1885); M. F. Tupper, Geraldine: a sequel to Coleridge's Christabel, 1838 (rptd in his Ballads for the times [1850], 1851, 1852, 1853); [J. Hogg], Isabelle, The poetic mirror, or The living bards of Britain, 1816; completed by E. Wahlert, New York 1909; completed by G. S. Connell, Cornwall NY 1926; D. B. Lyman, Christobel pts 3–4, suppl to College English Association Jnl 15 1953 (Coleridge's pts 1–2, applying the title Christobel to completed poem).

Kubla Khan. For the ms, *see* A. D. Snyder, Manuscript of Kubla Khan, TLS 2 Aug 1934; E. H. W. Meyerstein, A manuscript of Kubla Khan, TLS 12 Jan 1951 (the Crewe ms) (replies by B. R. Davies, 26 Jan 1951 and Meyerstein 9 Feb 1951); anon, Manuscript of Kubla Khan, TLS 16 Feb 1962; T. C. Skeat, Kubla Khan, BM Quart 26 1963 (on ms now in BM); H. Kelliher, The Kubla Khan manuscript and its first collector, BLJ 20 1994.

1905, Kubla Khan; a rhapsody for solo, chorus and orchestra, by S. Coleridge-Taylor; 1934 (illustr J. Vassos); New York 194? (illustr F. W. von Dachenhausen); completed by H. Sarason, Los Angeles 1956.

TRANSLATIONS

Fr, Paris 1939 (Koubla Khan, by H. Parisot), rptd Paris 1948.
Ger, by H. Hennecke, Neue Rundschau 49 1938 (rhymed metrical trn); by W. Breitweiser 1959 (with Ancient mariner).

The statesman's manual, or the Bible the best guide to political skill and foresight: a lay sermon addressed to the higher classes of society, with an appendix containing comments and essays connected with the study of the inspired writings. 1816. Referred to as first Lay sermon. Rptd separately Burlington VT 1832 and then with 2nd Lay sermon Burlington 1832; rptd with 2nd Lay sermon in On the constitution of the church and state, ed H. N. Coleridge 1839, 1852, etc; ed R. J. White in Political tracts of Wordsworth, Coleridge and Shelley, Cambridge 1953.

Lay sermons, ed R. J. White 1972 (Collected works) (with 2nd Lay sermon).

Biographia literaria: or biographical sketches of my literary life and opinions. 2 vols 1817; facs Menston, Yorks 1971; rptd New York 1817, 1834. For annotated copies, *see* N. F. D. Coleridge, Coleridge and Wordsworth, TLS 3 July 1948 (Derwent Coleridge's copy); B. R. Pollin, John Thelwall's marginalia in a copy of Coleridge's Biographia literaria, BNYPL 74 1970. For comment on the text, *see* D. N. Fogle, A compositional history of the Biographia literaria, SB 30 1977; E. C. Knowlton Jr, A Coleridge allusion to Angelica Catalani (1780–1849), N & Q 223, June 1978; N. Fruman, Review essay: aids to reflection on the new Biographia, SiR 24 1985; N. Fruman, Editing and annotating the Biographia literaria, in Coleridge's Biographia literaria, ed F. Burwick, Columbus OH 1989.

Ed H. N. Coleridge and Sara Coleridge 2 vols 1847 (with long introd and biographical suppl), New York 1848 (from 2nd London edn), 1852, 1853, 1858, 1872, 1881, 1882, 1884; 1866, 1870, 1876, 1884, 1889, 1891, 1894, etc (Bohn's Lib) (with 2 Lay sermons); chs 1, 3, 4, 14–22 ed A. J. George as Coleridge's principles of criticism, Boston 1897 (Heath's English Classics); ed A. Symons 1906, 1908, 1910, 1917, 1934, etc (EL); chs 1–4, 14–22 ed G. Sampson, with introd by A. T. Quiller-Couch, Cambridge 1920; ed J. C. Metcalf, New York 1926 (Modern Readers' ser); Englischer Besuch in Hamburg im Jahre 1798, ed K. Loewenfeld 1927 (German version of pts of Satyrane's letters, with plates).

Ed J. Shawcross 2 vols Oxford 1907 (with the aesthetic essays; text oscillates between 1817 and 1847).

Ed G. Watson 1956, 1960, 1965 (with addn) (EL). Excludes Satyrane's letters and the critique of Bertram; text of 1817. *See also* his Text of the biographia literaria, N & Q 199, June 1954.

Ed J. Engell and W. J. Bate 2 vols 1983 (Collected works).

Blessed are ye that sow beside all waters: a lay sermon addressed to the higher and middle classes on the existing distresses and discontents. 1817. Second Lay sermon. Rptd (with 1st Lay sermon) Burlington VT 1832. For marginalia, *see* M. J. Ryan, Coleridge and Anster: marginalia to the Lay sermons, Dublin Mag 2 1927.

Ed D. Coleridge 1852 (with Statesman's manual).

1866 (Bohn's Lib) (with Statesman's manual and Biographia literaria).

Ed R. J. White 1972 (Collected works) (with Statesman's manual).

A Hebrew dirge, chaunted in the Great Synagogue, St James's Place Aldgate on the day of the funeral of Her Royal Highness Princess Charlotte, by Hyman Hurwitz, with a translation in English verse by S. T. Coleridge esq. 1817; rptd Cincinnati 1962.

Sibylline leaves: a collection of poems. 1817. First collective edn, assembled in 1815 omitting contents of the 1816 Christabel vol. 18 poems rptd in Spirit of contemporary poetry vols 1 and 2, Boston MA 1827; rptd in full New York [1962] (Dolphin Masters). For annotated copies, *see* J. L. Lowes, The road to Xanadu, Boston 1927, rev 1930; N. van Patten, A presentation copy of Coleridge's Sibylline leaves, with manuscript notes, altered readings, and deletions by the author, Library 4th ser 17 1937; C. Woodring, A Coleridge miscellany, Columbia Lib Columns 24 1975 (Hood copy); M. L. Johnson, How rare is a 'unique annotated copy' of Coleridge's Sibylline leaves? A partial answer, with a variant of Lines on Donne, BNYPL 78 1975.

The raven, a Christmas tale. Illus [1848]; another edn, illustr E. Hallward, 1898.

The wanderings of Cain; tr Fr, Paris 1963 (Caïn errant by Paul Rozenberg, Passeport 2).

Zapolya: a Christmas tale in two parts; the prelude entitled The usurper's fortune and the sequel entitled The usurper's fate. 1817. For a corrected copy, *see* J. Drinkwater, A book for bookmen, 1926 (priv ptd).

[On method.] General introd to Encyclopaedia metropolitana, 1818 (also separate offprint, 1818). Rptd separately [1849], [1850], [1854] (3 edns); as Mental science, 1855, 1873, 1875 (with Whateley's Logic and rhetoric); ed A. D. Snyder 1934 (with ms fragments, detailed introd and notes; facs of this edn Folcroft PA 1973, Norwood PA 1976).

Remarks on the objections which have been urged against the principle of Sir Robert Peel's bill. [1818.] Rptd with The grounds of Sir Robert Peel's bill vindicated, as Two addresses on Robert Peel's bill (Apr 1818), ed E. Gosse, Hampstead 1913 (priv ptd).

The grounds of Sir Robert Peel's bill vindicated. 1818. Rptd in Two addresses, ed E. Gosse, Hampstead 1913 (priv ptd).

The tears of a grateful people: a Hebrew dirge and hymn, chaunted in the Great Synagogue, St James's Place Aldgate, on the day of the funeral of his late most gracious Majesty King George III of blessed memory, by Hyman Hurwitz, translated into English verse by a friend [Coleridge]. 1820.

Aids to reflection in the formation of a manly character, on the several grounds of prudence, morality and religion, illustrated by select passages from our elder divines, especially from Archbishop Leighton. 1825. Rptd Burlington VT 1829 (with essay and notes by J. Marsh); 1831, 1836. For annotated Harvard copy, *see* C. C. Seronsy, Marginalia by Coleridge in three copies of his published works, SP 51 1954.

Ed H. N. Coleridge 1839 (4th edn with author's last corrections), rptd Burlington VT 1840; also ed H. N. Coleridge 2 vols 1843 (5th edn, with essays by J. Marsh, J. H. Green and S. Coleridge and appendixes); also 1848.

Ed D. Coleridge (7th edn) 1854, 1859, 1861, 1866; ed T. Fenby, Liverpool 1873, 1874, 1877, 1883, Edinburgh 1896, 1900, 1915, London 1905 (New Universal Lib) (with copious index and trns of Greek and Latin quotations); ed H. N. Coleridge 1884 etc (Bohn's Lib) (with Confessions of an inquiring spirit etc).

Ed J. Beer 1993 (Collected works).

The poetical works, including the dramas of Wallenstein, Remorse and Zapolya. 3 vols 1828. *See* J. D. Campbell, Athenaeum 10, 31 Mar 1888; replies by T. Ashe 17 Mar and T. J. Cobden-Sanderson 7 Apr 1888.

3 vols 1829. Reset with a few additions. Guide text for Poetical works, ed J. D. Campbell 1893.

On the constitution of the Church and State according to the idea of each, with aids toward a right judgement on the late Catholic bill. 1830, 1830 (2nd edn).

Ed H. N. Coleridge 1839, 1852; rptd with the 2 Lay sermons in 1839 and after 1852; rptd New York 1853; ed J. Barrell 1972 (EL).

Ed J. Colmer 1976 (Collected works).

The devil's walk: a poem, edited with a biographical memoir and notes by Professor Porson [i.e. Coleridge and Southey]. Ed H. W. Montagu [1830], [1830] (with engravings on wood by Bonner and Slader after R. Cruickshank); 1830, 1830 (with names of Coleridge and Southey in place of Porson's on the title page). Rptd in R. Cruickshank, Facetiae, 2 vols 1831. Originally composed by Coleridge and Southey in 1799, ptd anon in Morning Post 6 Sep 1799 as The devil's thoughts; amplified by Southey in 1827 without Coleridge's collaboration.

On the Prometheus of Aeschylus: an essay, preparatory to a series of disquisitions respecting the Egyptian in connection with the sacredotal theology, and in contrast to the mysteries of ancient

Greece. Read May 18, 1825. Trans Royal Soc of Lit 2 pt 2 1834. Rptd priv in 1834, not in 1825 as stated by T. J. Wise in his Catalogue of the Ashley Library and elsewhere. Rptd in Literary remains vol 2, 1836; Notes and lectures upon Shakespeare, 1849; ed T. Ashe 1885 (in Miscellanies, aesthetic and literary); *see* G. Whalley, The publication of Coleridge's 'Prometheus' essay, N & Q 214, Feb 1969.

The poetical works. 3 vols 1834. In large part prepared and arranged by H. N. Coleridge, 66 uncollected pieces added to Poetical works 1829 with some rearrangement. Rptd 1835, 1836, 1840, 1844 (as Poetical and dramatic works). Guide text for Complete poetical works, ed E. H. Coleridge 2 vols 1912. The canon of Coleridge's poetical and dramatic works continued to be clarified and extended in the collective edns of S. Coleridge (1844), D. and S. Coleridge (1852), R. H. Shepherd (1877), J. D. Campbell (1893) and E. H. Coleridge (1912). *See* G. Whalley, Coleridge's poetical canon: selection and arrangement, REL 7 1966; D. Woolf, Sara Coleridge's marginalia, Coleridge Bull n.s. 2 1993.

Confessions of an inquiring spirit. Ed H. N. Coleridge 1840, 1849, 1853, 1863 (with some miscellaneous pieces and introd by J. H. Green); Boston 1841; ed H. N. Coleridge 1884 etc (Bohn's Lib) (with Aids to reflection, *above*), 1886 (with miscellaneous essays from Friend) (Cassell's Nat Lib); ed H. St J. Hart 1956 (with J. H. Green's introd) (Lib of Modern Religious Thought); facs of 1840 edn, Menston, Yorks 1971.

The poems. Ed Sara Coleridge 1844, 1848.

Hints towards the formation of a more comprehensive theory of life. Ed S. B. Watson 1848; rptd Philadelphia 1848; ed T. Ashe 1885 (in Miscellanies, aesthetic and literary); facs of 1848 London edn, Farnborough, Hants 1970.

Essays on his own times, forming a second series of the Friend. Ed Sara Coleridge 3 vols 1850; rptd New York 1971. Newspaper and periodical articles mostly from Watchman, Morning Post and Courier, and a number of topical and epigrammatic poems.

Essays on his times. Ed D. V. Erdman 3 vols 1978 (Collected works). Excludes Watchman and verse material collected in Poetical works 1912, but adds more attributed to Coleridge in the interim.

The poems: a new edition. Ed Derwent Coleridge and Sara Coleridge 1852 etc (in later edns associated with Dramatic works 1852, *below*); rptd New York 1854 etc, and Boston 1854 etc (with memoir by C. E. Norton); Leipzig 1860 (Tauchnitz edn with biographical memoir by F. Freiligrath); in Complete works, ed W. G. T. Shedd, New York 1853 etc; 3 vols Boston 1854; 1863 etc (with addns); 1870 (with introductory essay by Derwent Coleridge, and the 1798 text of the Ancient mariner and a few new poems in an appendix).

The dramatic works. Ed Derwent Coleridge 1852.

The poetical and dramatic works, founded on the author's latest edition of 1834. [Ed R. H. Shepherd] 4 vols London and Boston 1877, 1880 (with addns).

The poetical works. Ed J. D. Campbell 1893 etc (later edns Globe Lib). Text based on Poetical works 1829, *above*. The biographical introd was issued separately 1894 as Coleridge: a narrative of the events of his life; facs Highgate, London 1970.

The complete poetical works, including poems and versions of poems now published for the first time. Ed E. H. Coleridge 2 vols Oxford 1912, 1957, 1962, 1966 (later impressions with corrections); 1 vol Oxford 1912 (OSA) (omitting dramatic writings and bibliographical matter). Text based on Poetical works 1834, *above*.

(See also Letters, conversations, notebooks, Marginalia, etc, below.)

Poems, essays and lectures not published or not collected by Coleridge

The selections listed in individual works also contain previously unpbd poems, essays and unpbd lectures on literary subjects.

(A) Poems and plays

Osorio: a tragedy, as originally written in 1797. [Ed R. H. Shepherd 1873.] Early and unpbd version of Remorse collated with the pbd text. *See also* J. D. Campbell, Coleridge's 'Osorio' and 'Remorse', Athenaeum 5 Apr 1890.

Waugh, F. G. Lines by Coleridge. Athenaeum 28 Jan 1888. Replies by C. A. Ward 4 Feb; W. E. Mozley 11 Feb 1888.

Campbell, J. D. Unpublished verses by Coleridge. Athenaeum 15 Mar 1890. To Matilda Betham. Reply by E. B. de Betham 30 Aug 1890.

Campbell, J. D. A sonnet by Coleridge, original or translated? Athenaeum 29 Aug 1891.

Coleridge, E. H. Notes on Coleridge. Athenaeum 27 Jan 1894. Ms of Wanderings of Cain. *See* W. A. Ward, Athenaeum 20 Jan 1895.

Griggs, E. L. Diadestè, a fragment of an unpublished play by Samuel Taylor Coleridge. MP 34 1937.

Johnson, S. F. An uncollected early poem by Coleridge. BNYPL 61 1957.

Ober, W. U. Original versions of two Coleridge couplets. N & Q 202, Oct 1957. Epigrams on metres, tr from Schiller. Reply by K. Coburn, N & Q 203, May 1958.

Ober, W. U. 'Mohammed': the outline of a proposed poem by Coleridge and Southey. N & Q 203, Oct 1958. Ms in Sydney, Australia.

'Bishop, Morchard' (O. Stonor). Notes of two Coleridges. BNYPL 63 1959. A Latin tag and an unpbd couplet.

Erdman, D. V. Reliques of the contemporaries of William Upcott, emperor of autographs. BNYPL 64 1960. Includes punning ms by Coleridge.

Erdman, D. V. Lost poem found: the cooperative pursuit and recapture of an escaped Coleridge 'sonnet' of 72 lines. BNYPL 65 1961.

Braekman, W. L. An unpublished poem by Coleridge. N & Q 208, May 1963. [Mistaken] attribution from a BL ms.

Dunlap, R. Verses by Coleridge. PQ 42 1963. 6 unpbd lines.

Cox, J. S. and G. S. Cox. Samuel Taylor Coleridge and Mary Lamb: two recent discoveries. St Peter Port CI 1971. Verses in Weekly entertainer.

Braekman, W. L. An imitation by Samuel Taylor Coleridge of a medieval German love song. Neophilogus 56 1972. Version pbd in New Times.

Korn, F. An unreported poem by S. T. Coleridge. N & Q 226, Aug 1981. A printed version of 'The Teacher's Office', at Florida State Univ.

Little, G. and E. Hall. Coleridge's 'To the Rev W. L. Bowles': another version? RES n.s. 32 1981. Source in Bath Chron.

Kelliher, H. Thomas Wilkinson of Yanwath, friend of Wordsworth and Coleridge. BLJ 8 1982. Coleridge's ms version of lines by Wilkinson.

Morrison, A. Samuel Taylor Coleridge's Greek prize ode on the slave trade. In An infinite complexity: essays on romanticism, ed J. R. Watson, Edinburgh 1983. Greek text with discussion and trn.

McKusick, J. C. A new poem by Samuel Taylor Coleridge. MP 84 1987. Translation of the Song of Deborah, at NYPL.

Coleridge's 'Dejection': the earliest manuscripts and the earliest printings. Ed S. M. Parrish, Ithaca NY 1988. Contains facs.

Freeman, A. and T. Hofmann. The ghost of Coleridge's first effort: 'A monody on the death of Chatterton', Library 6th ser 11 1989. Heavy offsetting preserves earlier text in rogue copy.

Wu, D. 'Nina-Thoma': an addition to the Coleridge bibliography. N & Q 238, Dec 1993.

(B) Essays, reviews and discursive prose mainly on non-literary subjects

Hints towards the formulation of a more comprehensive theory of life. Ed S. B. Watson 1848, facs Farnborough, Hants 1970; Philadelphia 1848; ed T. Ashe 1885 (in Miscellanies, aesthetic and literary).

Ingleby, C. M. Coleridge's unpublished mss. N & Q 8, 9 July 1853, and 9, 27 May and 24 June 1854. Attacks J. H. Green as literary executor. *See also* Trans Royal Soc of Lit 9 1870.

Ward, C. A. Coleridge. Athenaeum 1 July 1893, 26 Oct 1895, 1 Feb 1896. Describes 2 vols of ms Opus maximum. Reply by L. E. Watson 23 Nov 1895.
Raysor, T. M. Unpublished fragments on aesthetics by S. T. Coleridge. SP 22 1925. From BL MS Egerton 2800.
Coleridge on logic and learning, with selections from the unpublished manuscripts. Ed A. D. Snyder, New Haven CT 1929; facs Folcroft PA 1973, Norwood PA 1976. Includes selections from philosophical notebooks.
The political thought of Coleridge. Ed R. J. White 1938; facs Folcroft PA 1970, London 1970.
Hellman, G. S. Coleridge on trial marriages: text of an unfinished essay. Saturday Rev of Lit 29 Aug 1942.
Patterson, C. I. The authenticity of Coleridge's Reviews of Gothic romances. JEGP 50 1951. Argues Coleridge was the author of only one of four reviews rptd by G. Greever (*see* Letters, Conversations, Notebooks, Marginalia, *below*, under 1926), namely The monk. But *see also* D. Roper, Coleridge and the 'Critical Review', MLR 55 1960.
Whalley, G. Coleridge on classical prosody: an unidentified review of 1797. RES n.s. 2 1951.
Political tracts of Wordsworth, Coleridge and Shelley. Ed R. J. White, Cambridge 1953.
Erdman, D. V. Coleridge on George Washington: newly discovered essays of 1800. BNYPL 61 1957.
Bostetter, E. E. Coleridge's manuscript essay On the passions. JHI 31 1970. On the ms at the BL.
Reid, S. W. The composition and revision of Coleridge's essay on Aeschylus' Prometheus. SB 24 1971. Adds to and corrects Whalley's account with reference to the ms at Duke Univ.
Haeger, J. H. Coleridge's 'bye blow': the composition and date of Theory of life. MP 74 1976.
Jackson, H. J. Coleridge on the King's Evil. SiR 16 1977. Draws on unpbd ms of scrofula essay at Victoria College Lib.
Jackson, H. J. Coleridge's 'Maxilian'. Comparative Lit 33 1981. On the text pbd in Blackwood's Mag Jan 1822.
Logic. Ed J. R. de J. Jackson 1981 (Collected works). Edited from the ms in its entirety for the first time (*see* Snyder (1929), *above*).
Nabholtz, J. R. The text of Coleridge's 'Essays on the principles of genial criticism'. MP 85 1987.
Of politics and society. Ed J. Morrow, in Coleridge's writings vol 1, ed J. Beer 1990.
Gamer, M. 'The most interesting novel in the English language': an unidentified addendum to Coleridge's review of Udolpho. TWC 24 1993. Letter pbd in Critical Rev Nov 1794.
Of humanity. Ed A. Taylor 1994, in Coleridge's writings vol 2, ed J. Beer 1994.

(C) Lectures and sermons

Collier, J. P. Coleridge's lectures on Shakespeare and Milton; Coleridge and his lectures; Manuscript of Coleridge's lectures in 1812; Coleridge and his lectures. N & Q 10, 22 July, 12 Aug 1854. Reply by J. M. G[utch] 5 Aug 1854. *See* W. J. Fitzpatrick, N & Q 12, 4 Aug 1855, with reports of lectures from the Dublin Correspondent.
Seven lectures on Shakespeare and Milton by the late S. T. Coleridge. Ed J. P. Collier 1856; facs New York 1968; New York 1975. Preface includes a defence against charges that the shorthand notes of Coleridge's lectures were a fabrication. *See* 'Detective' (A. E. Brae), Literary cookery, 1855.
Shakespeare, Ben Jonson, Beaumont and Fletcher: notes and lectures by S. T. Coleridge. Liverpool 1874, 1881; Edinburgh 1905.
Campbell, J. D. Coleridge's [literary] lectures in 1818. Athenaeum 16 Mar, 4 May 1889.
Campbell, J. D. Some [philosophical] lectures delivered by Coleridge in the winter of 1818–19. Athenaeum 26 Dec 1891, 2 Jan 1892.
Coleridge's essays and lectures on Shakespeare. [1907] etc (EL).
Coleridge's Shakespearean criticism. Ed T. M. Raysor 2 vols Cambridge MA and London 1930, rev 2 vols London 1960 (EL). An extension of the original edns of Notes and lectures on Shakespeare in above etc, with new material from ms etc.
Lectures and notes on Shakespeare and other dramatists. 1931 (WC).
Coleridge's miscellaneous criticism. Ed T. M. Raysor, Cambridge MA and London 1936. Lectures, marginalia and notes.
The philosophical lectures, hitherto unpublished. Ed K. Coburn 1949, 1950. The text, primarily based on a shorthand transcript taken at the lectures, is reconstructed by use of notebooks, marginalia and pbd works; with unpbd marginalia of Coleridge on Tennemann and Kant. *See* Coburn's S. T. Coleridge's philosophical lectures of 1818–19, RES 10 1934.
Colmer, J. A. An unpublished sermon by S. T. Coleridge. N & Q 203, Apr 1958. Among the Poole papers in the BL.
Coleridge's writings on Shakespeare. Ed T. Hawkes, New York 1959; rptd 1969 (Pen).
Foakes, R. A. (ed). Coleridge on Shakespeare: the text of the lectures of 1811–12. 1971.
Haven, R. Coleridge on Milton: a lost lecture. TWC 3 1972. A contemporary report pbd in Rifleman on 26 Jan 1812.
Fenner, T. L. 'The Traveller' reports on Coleridge's 1811 lectures. N & Q 219, Sep 1974.
Harding, A. J. Coleridge's college declamation, 1792. TWC 8 1977. Jesus College Cambridge ms, with a trn of the Latin.
Foakes, R. A. What did Coleridge say? John Payne Collier and the reports of the 1811–12 lectures. In Reading Coleridge: approaches and applications, ed W. B. Crawford, Ithaca NY 1979.
Foakes, R. A. (ed). Lectures 1808–1819: on literature. 2 vols 1987 (Collected works). Includes reports and supplementary records of the several series, on Shakespeare, other authors and general topics, freshly edited from original sources.
Foakes, R. A. (ed). Coleridge's criticism of Shakespeare: a selection. 1989.
The Romantics on Shakespeare. Ed J. Bate 1992 (Pen). Includes a full selection of Coleridge material.

Letters, conversation, notebooks, marginalia

It should be noted that the categories in this section overlap: Allsop might have been placed under Conversation, etc. There is also some overlap with previous sections (e.g. marginalia and extracts from letters are included in several selections of prose, above), and with later sections (e.g. Whalley 1969 in Section §2 below might have appeared here in category D).

(A) Letters

[Allsop, T.] Letters, conversations and recollections of Coleridge. 2 vols 1836, 1858, 1864 (omitting prefaces of 1st and 2nd edns).
Garnett, R. Letters from Coleridge to William Godwin. Macmillan's Mag 9 1864; rptd Littell's Living Age (Boston) 3rd ser 25 1864.
[Call, W. M.] Unpublished letters written by Coleridge. Westminster Rev 93 1870. Call was Dr Brabant's son-in-law.
Meteyard, E. A group of Englishmen (1795–1815): being records of the younger Wedgwoods and their friends. 1871. Includes Coleridge letters.
Paul, C. K. William Godwin: his friends and contemporaries. 2 vols 1876. Publishes Coleridge letters with surrounding discussion.
Unpublished letters to the Rev John Prior Estlin. Ed H. A. Bright, Trans Philobiblon Soc 15 1884; 1884 (priv ptd); facs Folcroft PA 1970, Norwood PA 1975.
Knight, W. G. Memorials of Coleorton: being letters from Coleridge, Wordsworth and his sister, Southey and Sir Walter Scott to Sir George and Lady Beaumont of Coleorton Leicestershire 1803–34. 2 vols Edinburgh 1887.
Sandford, Mrs H. Thomas Poole and his friends. 2 vols 1888. Contains letters and reminiscences.

Coleridge, E. H. and M. Stuart. Letters from the lake poets to Daniel Stuart. 1889 (priv ptd).

Smiles, S. A publisher and his friends: memoir and correspondence of the late John Murray. 2 vols 1891.

Letters. Ed E. H. Coleridge 2 vols 1895.

Linde, G. M. A letter of Coleridge's. Athenaeum 18 May 1895. Letter to Mary Evans Todd, 6 Apr 1808.

Gillman, A. W. The Gillmans of Highgate. 1895. Excerpts from letters and a memoir.

Oliphant, Mrs M. Annals of a publishing house: William Blackwood and his sons, their magazine and friends. 3 vols Edinburgh 1897–8.

Litchfield, R. B. Tom Wedgwood, the first photographer: an account of his life, his discovery, and his friendship with Coleridge, including the letters of Coleridge to the Wedgwoods. 1903.

Betham, E. A house of letters. [1905.] Includes letters to Matilda Betham.

Biographia epistolaris: being the biographical supplement of Biographia literaria, with additional letters etc. Ed A. Turnbull 2 vols 1911 (Bohn's Standard Lib).

Williams, O. Lamb's friend the census-taker. Life and letters of John Rickman. 1911. Publishes 7 Coleridge letters for the first time.

Axon, W. E. A. The thorny path of literature. Nation (New York) 21 Aug 1913; separately rptd London 1917. Letter to T. Curnick 9 Apr 1814.

Letters hitherto uncollected. Ed W. F. Prideaux 1913 (priv ptd); rptd in T. J. Wise, Bibliography (1970 edn).

Marriage. Ed T. J. Wise 1919 (priv ptd in 30 copies).

Watson, L. E. (née Gillman). Coleridge at Highgate. 1925; facs Folcroft PA 1970. Contains letters.

Greever, G. A Wiltshire parson and his friends: the correspondence of William Lisle Bowles, together with four hitherto unidentified reviews by Coleridge. Boston 1926. *See* C. I. Patterson (1951) and D. Roper (1960) *under* Essays, reviews and discursive prose not pbd by Coleridge, *above*, where the authenticity of the reviews is discussed further.

Rea, J. D. A letter of Coleridge [1824–5]. MLN 44 1929. On Aids to reflection.

Koszul, A. Coleridgiana. Revue Anglo-américaine 7 1930. 2 late letters and prospectuses.

Mabbott, T. O. Coleridge mss. N & Q 160, 2 May 1931. Undated letter to Lucius.

Birss, J. H. Coleridge mss. N & Q 161, 26 Dec 1931. Letter of 3 June 1823.

Unpublished letters, including certain letters republished from original sources. Ed E. L. Griggs 2 vols 1932.

Stewart, J. I. M. Some Coleridge letters. RES 10 1934. 6 letters 1818–34 to and from J. G. Lockhart.

Coleridge to a young clergyman. More Books 14 1939. To Rev J. Gillman, 9 Nov 1832.

Broughton, L. N. Some early nineteenth-century letters hitherto unpublished. In Nineteenth-century studies, ed H. Davis et al, Ithaca NY 1940; facs New York 1968. Letters by Coleridge, Wordsworth, Southey and Allsop.

Broughton, L. N. Some letters of the Wordsworth family, now first published, with a few unpublished letters of Coleridge and Southey and others. Ithaca NY 1942.

Letters of Coleridge, selected. Ed K. Raine 1950 (for 1952) (Grey Walls Letters ser); facs Folcroft PA 1969.

Joseph, M. K. Charles Aders ... with some unpublished letters ... by S. T. Coleridge. Auckland NZ 1953.

Renz, M. F. A Coleridge unpublished letter and some remarks concerning the poet's interest in the sound of words. N & Q 198, Apr 1953. To Mrs Lockhart, 26 July 1833.

Collected letters. Ed E. L. Griggs 6 vols Oxford 1956–71; vols 1 and 2 reissued with corrections in 1966.

Skeat, T. C. Letters of Charles and Mary Lamb and Coleridge. BM Quart 26 1962.

Martin, C. G. An unpublished Coleridge letter. N & Q 212, Jan 1967. To J. Cottle, Feb 1796, now at Austin TX.

Hasson, M. A. Coleridge's 'Letter to Peter Morris, M. D.' N & Q 217, Aug 1972. Ms in NLS.

Mann, P. Two autograph letters of S. T. Coleridge. RES n.s. 25 1974. To J. Cottle, Feb–Mar 1797, and G. Bartley, 16 Feb 1818, both in the Mildmay–White Collection.

Sheppard, C. D. W. A new Coleridge letter. N & Q 223, June 1978. To Rev J. Hughes?, 5 Sep 1823, in Leicester Univ Lib.

Stephens, F. C. An autograph letter of S. T. Coleridge. RES n.s. 33 1982. To J. H. B. Williams, early Sep 1832, now at Austin TX.

Gomme, A. Two letters from Coleridge to Mrs Montagu. TLS 11 Feb 1983. To the wife of Basil Montagu, Dec 1808 and Oct 1810, among the Acton Papers.

Nye, E. W. Coleridge and the Berkshire Chronicle: a new manuscript letter and 'A tale of terror'. PQ 64 1985.

Scharnhorst, G. Coleridge to T. J. Pettigrew: an unpublished letter. N & Q 232, Mar 1987. To Pettigrew c. 1819, from an auction catalogue.

Selected letters. Ed H. L. Jackson, Oxford 1987.

Nye, E. W. Coleridge and the publishers: twelve new manuscripts. MP 87 1989.

O'Leary, P. Sir James Mackintosh: the Whig Cicero. Aberdeen 1989. Quotes two unrecorded letters by Coleridge, both in private hands. Cf also Coleridge Bull 3 1990.

Hall, E. Samuel Rogers and an unpublished Coleridge letter. N & Q 235, Mar 1990. To Rogers, 7 Feb 1815.

Smith, L. S. Coleridge as Godfather: a corrected text of his 14 August 1828 letter to Richard Cattermole. N & Q 238, Dec 1993.

(B) Conversation

Specimens of the table-talk of the late Samuel Taylor Coleridge. Ed H. N. Coleridge 2 vols 1835, 1836 (corrected), 1851 etc; 1835 edn rptd New York 1835; ed H. Morley 1874, 1884 etc (with Ancient mariner, Christabel, Kubla Khan); ed T. Ashe in Table talk and Omniana, 1884 etc (Bohn's Standard Lib/The York Lib) (with additional table-talk from Allsop's Recollections and unpbd ms matter); ed H. Morley 1884 etc (Table-talk and Rime of the ancient mariner etc) (Morley's Universal Lib); ed J. P. Briscoe 1899 (The Bibelots); with Omniana and a note by C. Patmore 1917 (OSA); tr Jap by M. Okamoto, 1943.

[Willmott, R. A.] Conversations at Cambridge. 1836. Reports S. T. Coleridge at Trinity in June 1833.

[Methuen, T. A.] Retrospect of friendly communications with the poet Coleridge. Christian Observer 45, May 1845. Report of Coleridge's conversation in 1814–15; and letters.

Sterling, J. Essays and tales. Ed J. C. Hare 2 vols 1848. Reports of Coleridge's conversation in Aug–Sep 1827.

Robinson, H. C. Diary, reminiscences, and correspondence. Ed T. Sadler 3 vols 1869, 2 vols 1872. The first pbn of the most complete record of Coleridge's conversation outside Table-talk.

Young, J. C. A memoir of Charles Mayne Young 'tragedian'. 1871. Report of Coleridge's conversation at Godesberg in July 1828.

Browning, R. Sketch of a conversation between Coleridge and Kenyon. Academy 15 Aug 1885.

Robinson, H. C. Blake, Coleridge, Wordsworth, Lamb etc: being selections from the remains of Henry Crabb Robinson. Ed E. J. Morley, Manchester 1922.

Robinson, H. C. On books and their writers. Ed E. J. Morley 3 vols 1938.

Coleridge the talker: a series of contemporary descriptions and comments. Ed R. W. Armour and R. F. Howes. Ithaca NY 1940; rptd with addns New York 1969. *See also* Armour and Howes, Addenda to Coleridge the talker, Quart Jnl of Speech 32 1946.

Table talk. Ed C. Woodring 2 vols 1990 (Collected works). Edits 1835 collection afresh from ms, altering dates, and augmenting with other descriptions.

(C) Notebooks

Anima poetae, from the unpublished notebooks of Coleridge. Ed E. H. Coleridge 1895; facs Folcroft PA 1970.

Notizbuch aus den Jahren 1795–1798. Ed A. L. Brandl, Archiv 97 1896. Edn of Gutch memorandum book.

Latymer, Lord. A Coleridge notebook. TLS 11 Oct 1923. The 'clasped vellum' book. Reply by L. R. M. Strachan, 18 Oct 1923.

Coburn, K. Inquiring spirit: a new presentation of Coleridge from his published and unpublished prose writings. 1951. Includes excerpts from notebooks and marginalia, about one-third unpbd. Rptd New York 1968; rev edn Toronto 1979.

Coburn, K. (ed.) Notebooks. 5 double-vols 1957– (4 to date). Vol 4 ed with Merton Christensen and vol 5 is being ed A. J. Harding. Selections from vols 1–3 tr Ital, Bergamo 1991 (Diari 1794–1819 by E. Zuccato).

Kelliher, H. A stray notebook of miscellaneous writings by Coleridge. BLJ 14 1988. A notebook owned by Frances Sarah Bunyon.

Coleridge among the lakes and mountains: from his notebooks, letters and poems 1794–1804. Ed R. Hudson, 1991 (Folio Soc). Anthology, with contemporary illustrations.

(D) Marginalia

See also under Lectures and sermons, above.

J., G. [Mr Coleridge's marginalia.] Blackwood's Mag Nov 1819. Transcript, possibly by James Gillman, of Coleridge's letter written in Browne's Pseudodoxia epidemica addressed to Sara Hutchinson, Mar 1804. Coleridge may have helped prepare letter for pbn.

The literary remains. Ed H. N. Coleridge 4 vols 1836–9; rptd New York 1853, facs New York 1967; Hildesheim 1971. Vol 1 Uncollected poems, literary lectures, a few marginalia; vol 2 Lectures and notes on Shakespeare and other dramatists; vols 3–4 mostly marginalia, much theological. For H. N. Coleridge's editorial practice, *see* R. F. Brinkley, Coleridge transcribed, RES 24 1948, and P. Elmen, Editorial revisions of Coleridge's marginalia, MLN 67 1952.

Notes and lectures upon Shakespeare and some of the old poets and dramatists, with other literary remains. Ed Mrs H. N. Coleridge 2 vols 1849; rptd New York 1853. Rptd from Literary remains vols 1–2, *above*, with a few addns. Later edns variously entitled. Ed T. Ashe, Lectures and notes on Shakspere and other English poets, 1883 etc (Bohn's Lib), rptd Freeport NY 1972; Lectures and notes on Shakespeare etc, 19-? (New Universal Lib); 1930 (EL); Oxford 1931 (WC). Text chiefly follows Notes and lectures 1849, *above*, but with Collier's Seven lectures and lectures from Bristol newspapers. Rptd 1907 etc (EL) (as Coleridge's essays and lectures on Shakespeare and some other old poets and dramatists).

'Bonsall'. Coleridge's notes on Pepys's diary. N & Q 6, 4 Sep 1852.

Notes on English divines. Ed Derwent Coleridge 2 vols 1853, 1863. Marginalia rptd from Literary remains vols 3–4, *above*; intended, with the Notes and lectures upon Shakespeare, *above*, and Notes theological, political and miscellaneous, *below*, to form a fresh and comprehensive arrangement of the marginalia.

Notes theological, political and miscellaneous. Ed Derwent Coleridge 1853. Marginalia, about one-third from Literary remains, *above*, the rest unpbd.

G., J. M. [John Matthew Gutch]. Samuel Taylor Coleridge. N & Q 7, 19 Mar 1853. Marginalia on Parr's Spital sermon.

[Wyatt, M. D.] Coleridgiana. Athenaeum 24 Mar 1860. Marginalia on Wieland's Comische Erzählungen. *See also* L. L. Mackall, Coleridge marginalia on Wieland and Schiller, MLR 19 1924.

[Garnett, R.] Notes on Stillingfleet. Athenaeum 27 Mar 1875; Glasgow 1875 (priv ptd). Marginalia on Origines sacrae.

[Zimmern, H.] Coleridge marginalia. Blackwood's Mag Jan 1882; rptd Littel's Living Age 62 1882. Descriptive account, with quotations from marginalia, of books acquired by Wilson from J. H. Green's library, now the foundation for the unparalleled Coleridge collection in the BL.

Kant: Introduction to logic, and his Essay on the mistaken subtilty of the four figures. Tr T. K. Abbott, with notes by S. T. Coleridge, 1885; facs 1963 (Philosophical Lib), Bristol 1993.

Campbell, J. D. Coleridge on Cary's Dante. Athenaeum 7 Jan 1888. Marginalia in BL.

Campbell, J. D. Coleridge marginalia hitherto unpublished on Grew's Cosmologia sacra. Athenaeum 7 Apr 1888.

Campbell, J. D. Coleridge marginalia hitherto unpublished on Jahn's History of the Hebrew commonwealth. Athenaeum 23 June 1888.

Taylor, W. F. Critical annotations: being marginal notes inscribed in volumes formerly in the possession of Coleridge. Harrow 1889; facs Folcroft PA 1970, Norwood PA 1975. All in BL.

Brooke, W. T. Unpublished fragments of Coleridge and Lamb. Newbery House Mag 6 1892. Marginalia on Barclay's Argenis.

Young, H. S. Samuel Taylor Coleridge. Athenaeum 2 Sep 1893. Marginalia on Fulke Greville. Reply by J. D. Campbell, 9 Sep 1893.

Aitken, G. A. Coleridge on Gulliver's travels. Athenaeum 15 Aug 1896.

Mathewson, L. Coleridge's notes on comic literature: a find. Athenaeum 16 Jan 1897. Describes his copy of Raleigh's History of the world.

White, W. H. Coleridge on Spinoza. Athenaeum 22 May 1897. Marginalia on Paulus's edn of Spinoza.

Forman, H. B. Coleridge's notes on Flögel. Cosmopolis 9 1897, 10 1898. The vols were described anon, Athenaeum 26 Dec 1896.

Highham, C. Coleridge marginalia. N & Q 9th ser vol 4, 30 Dec 1899. On Swedenborg vols in the Swedenborg Soc, London.

Wheatley, H. B. Marginalia in Defoe's Robinson Crusoe. Hampstead Annual 5 1902. More accurate than Literary remains version. *See* Kligender, 1936, *below*.

Axon, W. E. A. Coleridge marginalia. N & Q 9th ser 12, 25 July 1903. Describes 2 edns of Browne's Religio medici and Nodier's Smarra.

Aynard, J. Notes inédites de Coleridge. Revue de Littérature Comparée 2 1922. On Schubert's Allgemeine Naturgeschichte, Richter's Museum and Geist, Schelling's Naturphilosophie, Steffens's Anthropologie.

Haney, J. L. The marginalia of Coleridge. In Schelling anniversary papers, ed J. L. Haney, New York 1923; facs New York 1967, Folcroft PA 1976. *See* Haney, A bibliography of Coleridge, 1903, *above*, ch 10 of which lists 341 titles of annotated and marked books, including works by Coleridge. *See also* Haney (1934) *under* Textual/bibiographical criticism, *below*.

Lehman, B. H. A paragraph deleted by Coleridge. MLN 39 1924.

Mackall, L. L. Coleridge marginalia on Wieland and Schiller. MLR 19 1924.

Drinkwater, J. The notes of Coleridge's in Milton's poems by Thomas Warton. London Mercury Sep 1926; rptd in his A book for bookmen, 1926 (priv ptd), with descriptions of a corrected Zapolya and 2 letters.

Raysor, T. M. Some marginalia on Shakespeare by Coleridge. PMLA 42 1927.

Nidecker, H. Notes marginales de Coleridge. Revue de Littérature Comparée 7–8, 10–13 1927–33. Notes on Kant, Schelling, Schubert, Hegel, Steffens, Oersted. All in BL.

Raysor, T. M. Coleridge marginalia. MLN 43 1928. On 4 annotated books in Dr Williams's library: Richter, Schelling, Steffens, with one note from Steffens's Anthropologie.

Snyder, A. D. Coleridge's reading of Mendelssohn's Morgenstunden and Jerusalem. JEGP 28 1929.

Ashley, A. J. Coleridge on Galt. TLS 25 Sep 1930. Marginalia on The provost.

Dike, E. B. Coleridge marginalia in Henry Brooke's The fool of quality. Huntington Lib Bull 2 1931; rptd separately Cambridge MA 1931.

Fletcher, E. G. Two Coleridge marginalia. N & Q 165, 30 Sep 1933. Swift's Gulliver, Howie's Biographia Scoticana.

Gibbs, W. E. Two unpublished notes by Coleridge. MLN 48 1933. Marginalia on Cowley and Mandeville's Bees.

Lindsay, J. I. Coleridge marginalia in a volume of Descartes. PMLA 49 1934.

Snyder, A. D. Coleridge marginalia in the Forster Library. N & Q 167, 24 Nov 1934. On Anderson's British poets.

Lindsay, J. I. Coleridge marginalia in Jacobi's Werke. MLN 50 1935.

Kligender, F. G. Coleridge on Robinson Crusoe. TLS 1 Feb 1936.

Potter, G. R. Unpublished marginalia in Coleridge's copy of Malthus's Essay on population. PMLA 51 1936. Reply by K. Curry 54 1939.

Evans, B. I. Coleridge on slang. TLS 29 May 1937. Marginalia on Marcus Aurelius's Conversations, tr J. Collier.

Patton, L. Coleridge and the soldier. TLS 21 Aug 1937. Marginalia on Stewart's Outlines for the British land forces.

Shearer, E. A. Wordsworth and Coleridge marginalia in a copy of Richard Payne Knight's Analytical inquiry. HLQ 1 1937. Reply by J. I. Lindsay, A note on the marginalia, ibid. *See also* J. H. Wagenblass, Coleridge in dubious battle, HLQ 13 1950. Includes Wordsworth marginalia.

Davies, D. Coleridge's marginalia in Mather's Magnalia. HLQ 2 1939.

Kurtz, B. P. Coleridge on Swedenborg, with unpublished marginalia on the Prodromus. In Essays and studies by members of the Department of English, University of California, Univ of California Pbns in English 14 1943.

Brinkley, R. F. Coleridge on John Petvin and John Locke. HLQ 8 1945.

Brinkley, R. F. Some unpublished Coleridge marginalia: Richter and Reimarus. JEGP 44 1945. Vol and marginalia described in Princeton Univ Lib Chron 5 1943.

Patton, L. Coleridge marginalia in the Duke University Library: Charles Tennyson Turner's Sonnets. Duke Univ Lib Notes 15 1945. Coleridge's notes not in his hand.

Finch, J. S. Charles Lamb's copy of The history of Philip de Commines with autograph notes by Lamb and Coleridge. Princeton Univ Lib Chron 9 1947.

Langford, G. John Barclay's Argenis: a seminal novel. Texas Univ Stud in English 26 1947. Quotes marginalia in BL in a more complete form than in Literary remains.

McElderry, B. R. Coleridge on Blake's Songs. MLQ 9 1948. Quasi-marginalia.

Patton, L. Coleridge's marginal comments on Bowles' The spirit of discovery. Duke Univ Lib Notes 19 1948. A ghost?

Brinkley, R. F. Coleridge's criticism of Jeremy Taylor. HLQ 13 1950.

Hough, G. Some Coleridge marginalia. MLN 66 1951. Hone's Apocryphal New Testament.

Wells, G. A. Coleridge and Goethe on scientific method in the light of some unpublished Coleridge marginalia in Heinroth's Anthropologie. German Life & Letters n.s. 1951.

Hardy, B. Coleridge's marginalia in Fuller's Pisgah-sight of Palestine. MLR 47 1952.

Seronsy, C. C. Coleridge marginalia in Lamb's copy of Daniel's Poetical works. HLB 7 1953.

Zall, P. M. A Coleridge inscription. TLS 22 May 1953. In Mary Lamb, Mrs Leicester's school.

Brinkley, R. F. (ed). Coleridge on the seventeenth century. Durham NC 1955; facs New York 1968. Chiefly reprints and fresh transcripts of marginalia in Literary remains; includes notebook material.

Seronsy, C. C. More Coleridge marginalia. SP 52 1955. On Petrarch, Aristophanes and Walker's rhyming dictionary.

Barnet, S. Coleridge on puns: a note to his Shakespeare criticism. JEGP 56 1957.

Barnet, S. Coleridge's marginalia in Stockdale's Shakespeare of 1784. HLB 12 1958.

Schrickx, W. Coleridge and F. H. Jacobi. Revue Belge de philologie et d'histoire 36 1958. Marginalia on Jacobi's Ueber die Lehre des Spinoza.

Davis, K. Unpublished Coleridge marginalia in a volume of John Donne's poetry. N & Q 208, May 1963. Charles Lamb's copy of Poems 1669, now owned by Mrs Weld Arnold.

Robinson, J. Coleridge's marginalia. N & Q 223, June 1978. On Scott's Minstrelsy of the Scottish border (2nd edn 1803) in the possession of Professor Donald Baker.

Marginalia. Ed G. Whalley, succeeded by H. J. Jackson. 5 vols 1980– (Collected works). 3 vols to date.

Coleridge's books and borrowings

See also under Manuscript materials and Bibliographies (Anderson, Haney etc), above; also Textual/bibliographical criticism, below (Lowes etc).

Baker, J. Books read by Coleridge and Southey, from the records of the Bristol Library. Chambers's Jnl 1 Feb 1890; rptd in his Literary and biographical studies 1908.

Kaufman, P. The reading of Southey and Coleridge: the record of their borrowings from the Bristol Library 1793–98. MP 21 1924. Corrects and expands Baker (1890), *above*.

Snyder, A. D. Books borrowed by Coleridge from the library of the University of Göttingen 1799. MP 25 1928.

Whalley, G. The Bristol Library borrowings of Southey and Coleridge 1793–8. Library 5th ser 4 1949. Corrects and expands Kaufman (1924), *above*.

[Whalley, G.] The dispersal of Coleridge's books. TLS 28 Oct 1949. Correction 9 Dec 1949.

[Whalley, G.] A library cormorant. Listener 52, 9 Sep 1954.

Kaufman, P. Coleridge's use of cathedral libraries. MLN 75 1960.

[Whalley, G.] Portrait of a bibliophile VII. BC 10 1961. On the dispersal and present location of Coleridge's books.

Shaver, C. L. and A. Shaver. Wordsworth's library: a catalogue. New York 1979. Appendix 2 lists books marked in the ms catalogue as belonging to Coleridge.

Mays, J. C. C. Coleridge's borrowings from Jesus College library, 1791–94. Trans of the Cambridge Bibl Soc 8 1985.

Coffman, R. J. Coleridge's library: a bibliography of books owned or read by Samuel Taylor Coleridge. Boston 1987. Ambitious but error-prone.

Pseudonymous works

Pseudonyms employed by Coleridge in his journalism are described in C. Woodring, Politics in the poetry of Coleridge, *Madison WI 1961, Appendix B.*

Attributed and spurious works

See also Textual/bibliographical criticism, below (e.g. Griggs 1954).

Wright, G. W. A sonnet by Coleridge. N & Q 152, 12 Feb 1927. To poverty, by Joseph Cottle.

Patton, L. The Coleridge canon. TLS 3 Sep 1938. Poems purloined by Coleridge for Watchman. Reply by B. R. Davis, 10 Sep 1938, mentions a Southey poem falsely ascribed to Coleridge.

Wasserman, E. R. Coleridge's 'metrical experiments'. MLN 55 1940, 63 1948. Coleridge's authorship questioned.

Maxwell, J. C. Coleridge: a false attribution. N & Q 208, May 1963. By James Hogg.

Beer, J. Who wrote 'The barberry-tree'? RES n.s. 37 1986. Beer suggests Coleridge while, in the same issue, Jonathan Wordsworth suggests William Wordsworth and J. C. C. Mays suggests an unidentified parodist.

'-iana' or imitations

Imitations, parodies and illustrations of particular works (poems) pbd in Coleridge's lifetime are included in Individual works, under §1, above.

Lloyd, C. Edmund Oliver. 2 vols Bristol 1798; facs Oxford 1990. Includes a fictional version of some events in Coleridge's life and in part responsible for Coleridge's quarrel with Lamb.

[Mant, Richard.] The simpliciad: a satirico-didactic poem, containing hints for the scholars of the new school. 1808; facs Oxford 1991. Dedicated to Wordsworth, Southey and Coleridge; parody of their writing, with parallels drawn in footnotes.

[Smith, Horace and James.] Rejected addresses: or a new theatrum poetarum. 1812; often rptd. Play-house musings is a parody of Coleridge.

Peacock, T. L. Melincourt. 3 vols 1817. Coleridge satirised as Moley Mystic.

Peacock, T. L. Nightmare Abbey. 1818. Coleridge satirised as Mr Flosky.

Peacock, T. L. Crotchet Castle. 1831. Coleridge satirised as Mr Skionar.

Ashton, H. William and Dorothy. 1938. A novel about the Wordsworths, the plot of which turns on Dorothy's love for Coleridge.

Trickett, R. The elders. 1966. Fictional exploration of Wordsworth–Coleridge relationship.

A portfolio of twenty drawings commemorating the bicentenary of the birth of Coleridge. Ed W. B. Crawford and R. S. Oden, Long Beach CA 1972. 10 California artists.

Coleridge's American disciples: the selected correspondence of James Marsh. Ed J. J. Duffy, Amherst MA 1973.

Bogdanov, M. The play of the ancient mariner. 1984.

Butler, D. The men who mastered time. 1986. 'Kubla Khan' reworked into a science-fiction context.

Kavanagh, P. J. Only by mistake: a novel. 1986. Coleridge allusions embedded in a Buchanesque plot.

Coleman, D. Jeffrey and Coleridge: four unpublished letters. TWC 18 1987. From Jeffrey to Coleridge.

Textual/bibliographical criticism

MacCarthy, D. F. Unnoted variations in the text of Coleridge. Athenaeum 28 July 1877. Reply by J. D. Campbell, 14 Mar 1885. 14 poems.

Caine, T. H. H. Notes on Coleridge. Athenaeum 11 July 1885. Dating of poems in periodicals.

Campbell, J. D. Coleridge's quotations. Athenaeum 20 Aug 1892. Reply by T. Bayne, 3 Sep 1892.

Ritter, O. Coleridgiana. EStudien 58 1924. Sources of some Coleridge poems, metrical experiments and epigrams, mostly from Ger.

Lowes, J. L. The road to Xanadu. Boston 1927, 1930 (2nd edn); rptd many times. A detailed use of notebook material and marginalia in the pursuit of Coleridge's sources which has had a profound effect on twentieth-century discussion and editing.

Haney, J. L. Coleridge the commentator. In Coleridge studies by several hands, ed E. Blunden and E. L. Griggs, 1934; facs New York 1960. *See also* Haney (1923) in Marginalia, *above*.

Bonjour, A. Coleridge's 'Hymn before sunrise': a study of facts and problems connected with the poem. Lausanne 1942; facs [Folcroft PA nd].

Gordon, I. A. The case-history of Coleridge's Monody on the death of Chatterton. RES 18 1942. With the text of the unedited second form.

Sparrow, J. Jortin and Coleridge. TLS 3 Apr 1943. A Coleridge poem tr from Jortin's Votum.

Brinkley, R. F. Coleridge transcribed. RES 24 1948. On H. N. Coleridge's editorial practice. Includes marginalia.

Coburn, K. Coleridge's quest for self-knowledge. Listener 42, 8 Sep 1949. On Coleridge notebooks.

Evans, B. I. Coleorton manuscripts of Resolution and independence and Ode to Dejection. MLR 46 1951.

Griggs, E. L. Samuel Taylor Coleridge and Thomas Pringle. Quart Bull of the South African Lib 6 1951.

Elmen, P. Editorial revisions of Coleridge's marginalia. MLN 67 1952. H. N. Coleridge's editorial practice.

Griggs, E. L. Notes concerning certain poems by Samuel Taylor Coleridge. MLN 69 1954.

Schulze, F. W. Wordsworthian and Coleridgian texts (1784–1822), mostly unidentified or displaced. Festschrift für Otto Ritter, ed G. Dietrich, Halle 1956.

Whalley, G. Coleridge's poetical canon: selection and arrangement. REL 7 1966.

Whalley, G. The harvest on the ground: Coleridge's marginalia. UTQ 38 1969.

Whalley, G. On reading Coleridge. In S. T. Coleridge, ed R. L. Brett, 1971.

Coburn, K. Editing the Coleridge notebooks. In Editing texts of the Romantic period, ed J. D. Baird, Toronto 1972.

Whalley, G. On editing Coleridge's marginalia. In Editing texts of the Romantic period, ed J. D. Baird, Toronto 1972.

Whalley, G. Lend your books to such a one. Charles Lamb Bull 10–11 1975. On Coleridge's marginal notes in Charles Lamb's books.

Coburn, K. In pursuit of Coleridge. 1977. Describes how she became involved with editing and the origins of the 'Collected Coleridge'.

Harding, A. J. James Marsh as editor of Coleridge. In Reading Coleridge: approaches and applications, ed W. B. Crawford, Ithaca NY 1979.

Jackson, H. J. Coleridge's collaborator, Joseph Henry Green. SiR 21 1982. Includes Green's role in editing.

McGuire, W. Bollingen: an adventure in collecting the past. Princeton 1982. Context in which pbn of The collected Coleridge was funded.

Whalley, G. Coleridge and the self-unravelling clue. In Editing polymaths: Erasmus to Russell, ed H. J. Jackson, Toronto 1983. On editing Coleridge's marginalia.

Modiano, R. Coleridge's marginalia. Text: Transactions of Society for Textual Scholarship 2 1985.

Woodring, C. Recording from Coleridge's voice. Text 3 1987. On the textual editing of conversation records.

Jackson, H. J. Writing in books and other marginal activities. UTQ 62 1992.

Mays, J. C. C. Reflections on having edited Coleridge's poems. In Romantic Revisions, ed R. Brinkley and K. Hanley, Cambridge 1992.

Stillinger, J. The multiple versions of Coleridge's poems: how many 'Mariners' did Coleridge write? SiR 31 1992.

Stillinger, J. Coleridge and textual instability: the multiple versions of the major poems. New York 1994.

Mays, J. C. C. Editing Coleridge in the historicised present. Text 8 1995.

§2

Bibliographies of criticism; concordances; biographies

(A) Bibliographies of secondary criticism; guides to research

Raysor, T. M. and R. Wellek. In English Romantic poets: a review of research, ed Raysor, New York 1950, 1956 (2nd edn); with M. F. Schultz in 3rd edn 1972, ed F. Jordan; superseded by M. F. Schultz in 4th edn 1985, also ed Jordan.

Hall, T. A check list of Coleridge criticism. BB 25 1968.

Haven, R., and J. and M. Adams. Samuel Taylor Coleridge: an annotated bibliography of criticism and scholarship – vol 1: 1793–1899. Boston 1976. Added to by Crawford, *below*.

Caskey, J. D. and M. D. Stapper. Samuel Taylor Coleridge: a selective bibliography of criticism 1935–1977. Westport CT 1978. Duplicates errors.

Reiman, D. H. English Romantic poetry, 1800–1835: a guide to information sources. Detroit 1979 (Gale Information Guide Lib ser). Ch 4 on Coleridge constitutes an intelligent selection.

Milton, M. L. T. The poetry of Samuel Taylor Coleridge: an annotated bibliography of criticism, 1935–1970. New York 1981.

Crawford, W. B. and E. S. Lauterbach, with A. M. Crawford. Samuel Taylor Coleridge: annotated bibliography of criticism and scholarship – vol 2: 1900–1939 (with additional entries for 1795–1899). Boston 1983. The most comprehensive to date.

(B) Concordances

Seely, G. W. Concordance to the poetical works of S. T. Coleridge. 1924.

Logan, Sister E. A concordance to the poetry of Samuel Taylor Coleridge. Saint-Mary-of-the-Woods IN 1940; facs Gloucester MA 1967.

(C) Biographies

This list excludes the classic accounts by Lamb, Hazlitt, De Quincey and other contemporaries (notably James Gillman and Joseph Cottle) and is also highly selective within the succeeding period.

Campbell, J. D. Coleridge: a narrative of the events of his life. 1894; ed L. Stephen 1896; facs Hampstead 1970. Biographical introd to his edn of Poetical works, 1893, which is in many ways still the most balanced account.

Chambers, E. K. Samuel Taylor Coleridge; a biographical study. Oxford 1938. Masterfully compressed but impatient with the subject's infirmities.

Hanson, L. The life of Samuel Taylor Coleridge, the early years. 1938. More sympathetic than Chambers, but the story only to 1800.

Deschamps, P. La formation de la pensée de Coleridge (1772–1804). Paris 1964 (Études anglaises 15). Intellectual biography in the French mode.

Bate, W. J. Coleridge. New York 1968. Efficient summary of the whole man and his interests.

Lefebure, M. The bondage of love: a life of Mrs Samuel Taylor Coleridge. 1986. Has influenced the approach to the husband. *See also* B. K. Mudge, Sara Coleridge: a Victorian daughter, her life and essays, New Haven CT 1989; and elsewhere on Hartley Coleridge.

Holmes, R. Coleridge: early visions. 1989; rptd 1990 etc (Pen). A portrait of Coleridge as person rather than intellectual, up to his departure for Malta. The first vol of a 2-vol set, which was warmly received. [JCCM]

Charles Collins fl. 1819–44

Comàla: a dramatic poem, versified ... After Ossian. Cambridge [1819?]. Anon.

Death on the pale horse ...: a poem. Cambridge [1819?]. Anon.

Juvenile blossoms. 1823.

Green leaves, or days of boyhood. 1844.

E. Colthurst fl. 1833–51

Emmanuel. Ed H. H. Beamish 1833. Anon.

Life: a poem. By the author of Emmanuel. Cork 1835. Anon.

Home. By the author of Emmanuel. Cork 1836. Anon. Prose.

Futurity. By the author of Emmanuel. Cork 1837. Anon. Prose and verse.

Futurity continued. By the author of Emmanuel. Cork 1838. Anon.

Loyalty: a poem. By the author of Futurity. Cork 1838. Anon.

The storm. By the author of Emmanuel. Liverpool and London 1840. Anon.

Irrelagh, or the last of the chiefs. 1849. Anon. Prose.

Love and loyalty. By the author of Irrelagh. 1851. Anon.

Charles Caleb Colton 1780?–1832

Hypocrisy: a satire in three books .... Bk 1 Tiverton 1812.

Napoleon: a poem .... [1812.]

Lines on the conflagration of Moscow. 1816, 1817 (as The conflagration of Moscow), 1822 (4th edn).

Lacon, or many things in few words. Vol 1 1820 (5 edns); New York 1820; London 1821 (7 edns); with vol 2 1822; New York 1821–2; London 1823 (16th–19th edns); New York 1823–4; Philadelphia 1824; London 1824–5; New York 1825; London 1826; Bridgeport 1828; Concord NH 1828; London 1829; New York 1832; London 1833; New York 1836; London 1837; New York 1845, 1849; London 1851; New York 1855, 1858, 1860; London 1865, 1866; New York 1866; London 1867; Philadelphia 1871.

Gray's elegy translated into Latin Ovidian verse. By the author of Lacon [Colton]. 1822.

Thoughts in rhyme. Ed M. Sherwill, Paris 1832.

Modern antiquity and other poems ... Ed [M. Sherwill] 1835.

Author of miscellaneous prose.

Josiah Conder, also 'J. C. O'Reid' 1789–1855

Collections

Miles 10 (11).

The associate minstrels and The star in the east. Ed D. H. Reiman, New York and London 1977 (facs reprint).

§1

The associate minstrels. Ed Conder 1810 (anon), 1813. By Conder and others.

Reviewers reviewed: including an enquiry into the moral and intellectual effects of habits of criticism, by 'J. C. O'Reid'. Oxford 1811. Anon. Prose.

Gloria in excelsis deo. 1812. Anon.

The star in the east, with other poems. 1824; London and Wellington, Salop [1824?].

The law of the sabbath, religious and political. 1830, 1852 (rev), 1853, 1900. Prose.

The congregational hymn-book. 1834, 1836, etc.

Illustrations of the Pilgrim's progress; with a sketch of the life and writings of Bunyan. [1836.] Life of Bunyan rptd in Pilgrim's progress, ed W. Mason, London and Paris 1838, etc. Prose.

The choir and the oratory, or praise and prayer. 1837.

The literary history of the New Testament. 1845, 1850. Anon. Prose.

The poet of the sanctuary: a centenary commemoration of Isaac Watts. 1851. Prose and verse.

Hymns of prayer, praise and devout meditation, prepared for publication by the author. Ed [E. R. Conder] 1856.

§2

Conder, E. R. Josiah Conder: a memoir. 1857.

Conder wrote and edited a number of other works on religious, political, geographical and literary subjects, and edited Eclectic Rev *(1814–36), and* Patriot *(1833–55).*

Mary Ann Cookson fl. 1829

Poems on various subjects ... Leith 1829 (3 edns).

Harriet, or Harriett, Cope fl. 1811–29

The triumphs of religion: a sacred poem .... 1811, 1819.

Suicide: a poem in four parts .... 1815.

Waterloo: a poem in two parts ... By the author of Triumphs of religion. [1822.] Anon.

A monody to the memory of Thomas Lord Erskine .... 1824.

The brazen serpent: a sacred poem in two parts .... 1827.
de Lamartine, A. The death of Socrates: a poem. Tr Cope 1829.

Louisa Stuart Costello 1799–1870

The soldier's orphan. 3 vols 1809. Prose.
The maid of the Cyprus isle and other poems. 1815 (2 edns).
Redwald: a tale of Mona and other poems. Brentford 1819.
Songs of a stranger. 1825.
Specimens of the early poetry of France, from the time of the troubadours and trouvères to the reign of Henri quatre. 1835, 1838, [1877] (with The book of French songs, tr J. Oxenford).
The queen's poisoner .... 3 vols 1841, 1848 (as Catherine de Medicis, or the Queen-Mother: a romance), 1853. Prose.
Gabrielle, or pictures of a reign: a historical novel. 3 vols [1843].
The rose garden of Persia. 1845, 1887, 1888, 1899; Boston [1899], 1900, 1902; London 1911, 1913, 1924. Trns from Persian poetry.
Clara Fane, or the contrasts of life. 3 vols 1848. Prose.
The lay of the stork: a poem. 1856.
Flowers from Persian poets. Tr Costello, New York [1901].
Also pbd books of travel and historical memoirs, mainly concerned with France.

Joseph Cottle, also 'Constantius' 1770–1853

§1

Poems, containing John the Baptist; Sir Malcolm and Alla: a tale; War: a fragment; with A monody to John Henderson, and a sketch of his character. Bristol 1795, London 1796.
Malvern hills: a poem. 1798, 1802 (3rd edn), 2 vols 1829 (with appendix of essays in prose).
Alfred: an epic poem. 1800, 2 vols 1804, Newburyport 1814, London 1816, 1 vol 1850. Rptd (1800 edn) New York 1979.
A new version of the Psalms of David. 1801, 1805.
John the Baptist: a poem. 1802. Rptd from Poems, 1795, *above*.
The fall of Cambria: a poem. 2 vols 1808, 1811. Rptd New York 1978 (introd by D. H. Reiman).
Messiah: a poem. 1815. Rptd New York 1978 (introd by D. H. Reiman).
An expostulatory epistle to Lord Byron. 1820.
Dartmoor, and other poems. 1823.
Hymns and sacred lyrics. 1828.
Early recollections, chiefly relating to the late Samuel Taylor Coleridge. 2 vols 1837, 1 vol 1847 (rev as Reminiscences of Coleridge and Southey), New York 1847, 1848. Rptd Highgate 1970.
Mr Cottle and the Quarterly Review. [Bristol 1839.] A 'second preface' to Early recollections, 1837, *above*.
Poems, containing John the Baptist, Malvern hills, An expostulatory epistle to Lord Byron, Dartmoor, and other poems. Introd by D. H. Reiman, New York 1978.
Cottle also edited, with Southey, the works of Thomas Chatterton, 1803, and pbd some theological prose.

§2

Mitford, M. R. Recollections of a literary life. Vol 3 1852.
Gibbs, W. E. Unpublished letters concerning Cottle's Coleridge. PMLA 49 1934.
Whalley, G. The Bristol Library borrowings of Southey and Coleridge 1793–8. Library 5th ser 4 1949. Appendix B: Borrowings by Joseph Cottle. [PL]

Peter L. Courtier b. 1776

Poems: consisting of elegies, sonnets, odes, canzonets .... 1795, 1796.
Revolutions: a poem in two books. 1796.
The warning voice. 1798. Anon.
Pleasures of solitude: a poem. 1800, 1802, 1804.
Poems. Vol 2 1805.
The lyre of love. Ed Courtier 2 vols 1806.

Edward Coxe, of Hampstead Heath fl. 1805–27

Miscellaneous poetry. Bath and London 1805.
The valentine: a poem on St Valentine's day .... 1810.
Goldsmith, O. History of England. Ed (with a continuation) Coxe, Derby 1827, 1828. Prose.

Thomas Crichton, also 'Senex' fl. 1804–21

The library: a poem. Paisley 1804. Anon (attribution uncertain).
Verses to the memory of Lord Nelson .... Paisley 1805. Anon.
Biographical sketches of the late A. Wilson. By 'Senex'. [Paisley 1819]. Anon. Prose.
Memoir of the life and character of ... J. Findlay. Paisley 1821. Prose.

Margaret Sarah Croker b. 1773

A monody on the lamented death of ... Princess Charlotte-Augusta .... 1817.
Nugae canorae. 1818, 1819.
The question, who is Anna? A tale. 3 vols 1818. Prose.
A tribute to the memory of Sir Samuel Romilly. 1818.
Monody on His late Royal Highness the Duke of Kent. 1820.

George Croly 1780–1860

Collection

The poetical works of the Rev George Croly. 2 vols 1830 (2 issues).
Paris in 1815, Lines on the death of ... Princess Charlotte .... Ed D. H. Reiman, New York and London 1977 (facs reprints).

§1

Paris in 1815: a poem. 1817 (anon), 1818 (acknowledged); 2nd pt (with other poems) 1821.
Lines on the death of ... Princess Charlotte. 1818.
The angel of the world: an Arabian tale; Sebastian: a Spanish tale, with other poems. 1820; New York 1844.
Catiline: a tragedy ... with other poems. 1822.
Gems principally from the antique, drawn by Richard Dagley, with illustrations in verse by George Croly. London and Edinburgh 1822.
Pride shall have a fall: a comedy. 1824 (6 edns). Anon. Prose.
May fair, in four cantos. 1827 (2 edns). Anon (authorship uncertain).
The beauties of the British poets, with a few introductory observations. Ed Croly 1828; Boston 1861.
Salathiel: a story of the past, the present and the future. 3 vols 1828 (2 edns, anon); 2 vols New York and Philadelphia 1828; London 1829; New York 1833; Cincinnati 1842; London 1842; New York 1843; Philadelphia 1843; 1 vol Cincinnati 1847; Philadelphia 1848, 1849, 1850; London 1855 (rev), 1856; Philadelphia 1856; Cincinnati 1858; London and New York 1858; London 1859, 1897; ed L. Wallace and I. K. F., New York and London 1901 (as Tarry thou till I come); Toronto 1901; tr Fr 1828, Ger Stuttgart 1829 (as Der ewige Jude). Prose.
Tales of the great St Bernard. 3 vols 1828 (anon), 1829 (anon), 2 vols New York 1829 (anon). Prose.
The modern Orlando. Cantos 1–7 (all pbd) 1846, 1848, 1855. Anon.
Marston, or the soldier and statesman. 3 vols 1846, 1 vol 1860 (3rd edn). Prose.

Scenes from scripture, with other poems. 1851.
Psalms and hymns for public worship. 1854. Partly original, partly compiled.
The book of Job, with a memoir by F. W. Croly. Edinburgh and London 1863.

§2

Herring, R. A few personal recollections of . . . Croly. 1861.
Croly also pbd numerous sermons and other theological works, e.g. The Apocalypse of St John: a new interpretation *(1827); historical and biographical works, e.g. on George IV (1830), and Burke (1840); edns of Jeremy Taylor and Joseph Butler and of Pope's and Byron's poems; and voluminous contributions to periodicals, including* Blackwood's Mag *and* Literary Gazette. *Four stories were rptd anon in* Tales from Blackwood *(vols 9–11, 1861).*

Thomas Kitson Cromwell 1792–1870

The school-boy, with other poems. 1816.
Honour, or arrivals from college: a comedy. 1820. Prose.
The druid: a tragedy . . . . 1832.
Author of sermons, topographical works and biographies.

Allan Cunningham 1784–1842

Collection

Poems and songs. Ed P. Cunningham 1847.

§1

Songs, chiefly in the rural language of Scotland. 1813.
Sir Marmaduke Maxwell: a dramatic poem . . . . 1822 (2 edns).
Traditional tales of the English and Scottish peasantry. 2 vols 1822, 1874, 1887. Prose.
The songs of Scotland, ancient and modern . . . . Ed Cunningham 4 vols 1825; New York 1975.
Paul Jones: a romance. 3 vols Edinburgh and London 1826; Philadelphia 1827; tr Ger by W. A. Lindau, Dresden and Leipzig 1842. Prose.
Sir Michael Scott: a romance. 3 vols 1828. Prose.
The anniversary, or poetry and prose for 1829. 1829.
The maid of Elvar: a poem . . . . 1832.
The works of Robert Burns . . . . Ed Cunningham 6 [8] vols 1834; 1 vol Leipzig 1835; 2 vols London [1840]; 1 vol London 1840, 1842, 1845, 1847, 1850.
The complete works of Robert Burns . . . . Ed Cunningham, London and Edinburgh 1835 (2 edns).
Lord Roldan: a romance. 3 vols 1836; New York 1836.

§2

Hogg, D. The life of . . . Cunningham. Dumfries and Glasgow 1875.
Editor of the Anniversary *(1829) and biographer.*

John William Cunningham 1780–1861

De Rancè: a poem. 1815 (2 edns); Elizabethtown NJ 1816; New York 1816; Middleboro MA 1857.
Morning thoughts in prose and verse on . . . St Matthew. By a country clergyman. 1824 (4 edns); Philadelphia 1825, 1831. Anon.
Morning thoughts . . . on . . . St Mark. 1828 (2 edns).
Author of numerous sermons and of other prose on church matters, notably The velvet cushion *(1814, anon).*

Mary Anne Curling b. c. 1796

Poetical pieces. Dover 1831; London 1831 (with some additional pieces).

Thomas Dale 1797–1870

The widow of the city of Nain and other poems. By an undergraduate of Cambridge. 1819 (anon, 2 edns), 1820, 1821 (2 edns, acknowledged), 1825 (8th edn), 1842 (with The outlaw of Taurus).
The outlaw of Taurus . . . . 1820 (2 edns), 1821, 1824.
Irad and Adah: a tale of the flood . . . . 1822 (2 edns), 1832.
The tragedies of Sophocles. Tr Dale 1824.
The poetical works. 1836.
Edited theological and literary texts, pbd sermons, and edited the Iris *(1830, 1831).*

John Darby, of Exeter fl. 1817–41

Three dialogues, with some gospel sonnets. Exeter 1817. Prose and verse.
Gospel poems, on different heads . . . . Exeter 1827.
An entire new work: summer evening's conversation . . . . Exeter 1829, 1831 (as Summer evening's conversation in the fields), 1832. Prose.
Gospel poems, never before seen in print . . . . Exeter 1834, 1835, 1841.
A dialogue between a watchman and the traveller . . . many excellent poems. Exeter 1837, 1839. Prose and verse.
A new work: gospel poems, also . . . an interesting dialogue . . . . Exeter 1841. Verse and prose.

George Darley, also 'Guy Penseval' 1795–1846

Collections

Miles.
Poems of the late G. Darley, a memorial volume printed for private circulation. Ed [R. and M. J. Livingstone], Liverpool and London [1850?].
Selections from the poems of G. Darley. Ed R. A. Streatfeild [1902?], 1904.
Complete poetical works. Ed R. Colles [1908] (ML).
The errors of ecstasie, Sylvia and Nepenthe. Ed D. H. Reiman, New York and London 1978 (facs reprints).
Poems, consisting of essays, lyric . . . Poems, moral and descriptive. Ed D. H. Reiman, New York and London 1978 (facs reprints).
Selected poems. Ed A. Ridler 1979.

§1

The errors of ecstasie: a dramatic poem, with other pieces. 1822.
Essays and sketches by the late R. Ayton, with a memoir [by Darley?]. 1825. Prose.
The labours of idleness, or seven nights entertainments, by 'Guy Penseval'. 1826, 1829 (as vol 2 of The new sketch book). Anon. Prose.
Sylvia, or the May queen: a lyrical drama. 1827; ed J. H. Ingram 1892.
The sorrows of hope. In The anniversary, ed A. Cunningham, 1829.
The new sketch book, by 'Geoffrey Crayon jun'. 2 vols 1829. Vol 2 consists of the unused sheets of Labours of idleness, *above*. Prose.
Familiar astronomy. 1830. Prose.
Nepenthe. 1835 (priv ptd); ed R. A. Streatfeild, 1897.
Syren songs. In The tribute, ed Lord Northampton, 1837.
Thomas à Becket: a dramatic chronicle. 1840.
The works of Beaumont and Fletcher, with an introduction by G. Darley. 2 vols 1840, 1851, 1862, 1866.
Ethelstan, or the battle of Brunanburh: a dramatic chronicle. 1841. Prose.

§2

Abbott, C. C. The life and letters of G. Darley, poet and critic. 1928. With bibliography.
Abbott, C. C. Further letters of G. Darley. Durham Univ Jnl 33 1940.
Darley contributed to London Mag *(Dec 1822–Mar 1825 including six letters*

to the dramatists of the day, signed 'John Lacy' and The characteristic of the present age of poetry *Apr 1824, and some lyrics and 'dramaticles'); to* Athenaeum *(1835–46, reviews and articles on literature and fine art, and some lyrics); to* Bentley's Misc *(1844, short stories and poems); and to* Illuminated Mag *(1844, short stories and poems). He also wrote mathematical bks.*

Mary Anne Davis fl. 1813–35

Fables in verse, from Aesop, La Fontaine and others. 1813, 1819, 1821 ('2nd edn'), 1822 ('2nd edn').
Tributary stanzas in memory of ... Bell. In J. Grant, A memoir of Miss F. A. Bell. 1827.
A selection from the parables of the New Testament ... in familiar verse. Frome 1836.

H. C. Deakin fl. 1829–31

Portraits of the dead .... 1829, 1831.
The deliverance of Switzerland: a dramatic poem. 1830, 1831.

Margaret Derenzy, formerly Graves d. 1829

Poems appropriate for a sick or a melancholy hour. Wellington, Salop and London [1824].
Parnassian geography, or the little ideal wanderer. Wellington, Salop and London [1824]. Anon.
A whisper to a newly-married pair, from a widowed wife. Wellington, Salop 1824 (2 edns), 1825, 1828; London 1832; Philadelphia 1832, 1833 (with 'Poems' and a biographical sketch); New York 1852; Calcutta 1886. Verse and prose.
The flowers of the forest. Wellington, Salop 1828. Anon.
The juvenile wreath. Wellington, Salop 1828, 1829. Anon.
The old Irish knight: a Milesian tale. 1828. Anon. Prose.
Nothing at all. 1835 (5th edn). Anon. Prose.

Thomas Dermody, also 'Marmaduke Myrtle' 1775–1802

Collections
The harp of Erin: containing the poetical works of the late T. Dermody. [Ed J. G. Raymond] 2 vols 1807.

§1
Poems. Dublin 1789; London 1800 (as Poems moral and descriptive).
Poems: consisting of essays, lyric, elegiac etc. Dublin 1792.
The rights of justice. [Dublin?] 1793. Prose (includes his Reform: a poem).
Poems on various subjects. 1802.
The histrionade, or theatric tribunal: a poem ... By 'Marmaduke Myrtle'. 1802. Anon.

§2
Raymond, J. G. The life of T. Dermody, interspersed with pieces of original poetry. 2 vols 1806.
Mabbott, T. O. Dermody: three letters. N & Q 26 May 1934.
Mabbott, T. O. Another letter. N & Q 7 Oct 1939.

Sir Aubrey De Vere, formerly Hunt 1788–1846

Collections
Miles 1.
Dramatic works. 2 vols 1858.

§1
Ode to the Duchess of Angoulême. 1815. Anon.
Julian the apostate: a dramatic poem. 1822, 1823, 1858 (with The Duke of Mercia, *below*), 1872.
The Duke of Mercia: an historical drama ... and other poems. 1823.
A song of faith, Devout exercises and sonnets. 1842, 1875 (as Sonnets: a new edition, with memoir by A. T. De Vere).
Mary Tudor: an historical drama. 1847, 1875, 1884 (with memoir by A. T. De Vere); adapted by K. A. Mellersh, Torquay [1914].
For criticism, see A. T. De Vere, col 605, below.

Thomas Frognall Dibdin 1776–1847

Poems. 1797.
Bibliography: a poem in six books. Bk 1 only. By [T. F. D.]. [1812.] Anon.
See also col 2685 below.

Eleanor Dickinson, Mrs Robert, formerly Blakey fl. 1824–30

The pleasures of piety, with other poems. London and Liverpool 1824.
The mamluk: a poem. 1830.

Charlotte Eliza Dixon, Mrs fl. 1814–30

The mount of olives, or the resurrection and ascension: a poem .... 1814, 1815.
'Bread cast upon the waters'. 1830.

Catherine Ann Dorset, Mrs Michael, formerly Turner 1750?–1817?

The peacock 'at home': a sequel to The butterfly's ball. By a lady. 1807, 1808; New York 1808; London and Edinburgh 1809; London [1810?], 1812 (26th edn); Philadelphia 1814; London 1815 (27th edn), 1817, 1822, 1824, 1831, 1834, 1838 ('20th edn'), 1841, 1844, 1849, 1851; ed C. Welsh 1883 (facs reprint); Greenock 1887 (illustr I. Paton). Anon.
The lion's masquerade. A sequel to The peacock 'at home'. By a lady. 1807, 1808; ed C. Welsh 1883 (facs reprint of 1807). Anon.
The lioness's rout, being a sequel to The butterfly's ball, The grasshopper's feast and The peacock 'at home'. By a lady. 1808. Anon.
Think before you speak, or the three wishes. By the author of The peacock 'at home'. 1809 (anon), 2nd edn [nd]; Philadelphia 1810 (2 edns), 1811, 1832; London 1900 (as The three wishes, attributed).
The peacock abroad, or visits returned. Greenwich 1812.
The peacock and parrot on their tour to discover the author of 'The peacock "at home"'. 1816.
See also col 1783.

Thomas Doubleday 1790–1870

Sixty-five sonnets, with prefatory remarks on the accordance of the sonnet with the powers of the English language. 1818. Anon.
The fisher's garland for 1821. Newcastle-on-Tyne 1821. Anon. With R. Roxby. Doubleday often contributed to this series until 1864. The series was partly collected in the Coquet-dale fishing songs, now first collected by a north country angler [i.e. Doubleday], 1852, and more fully in A collection of right merrie garlands for north country anglers, ed J. Crawhall, Newcastle-on-Tyne 1836, 1842, 1864.
The Italian wife: a tragedy. London and Edinburgh 1823. Anon.
Babington: a tragedy. Edinburgh and London 1825.
Dioclesian: a dramatic poem. 1829.
Caius Marius, the plebeian consul: a historical tragedy. 1836; London and Newcastle 1856.
The Coquet-dale fishing songs. Ed [Doubleday], Edinburgh and London 1852.

On mundane moral government, demonstrating its analogy with the system of material government. 1852. Prose.
The political life of Sir Robert Peel. 2 vols London and Edinburgh 1856. Prose.
The eve of St Mark: a romance of Venice. 2 vols London and Edinburgh 1857; 1 vol London 1864. Prose.
A letter to the Duke of Northumberland on the ancient Northumbrian music. London and Newcastle 1857. Prose.
The touchstone: a series of letters on social, literary and political subjects, originally published in the Newcastle Daily Chronicle under the signature of 'Britannicus'. London and Newcastle 1863. Prose.
Matter for materialists: a series of letters in vindication and extension of the principles regarding the nature of existence of Dr Berkeley. London and Newcastle 1870. Prose.
Doubleday also pbd several works on population and other political and social subjects.

David Douglas fl. 1823

The fall of Constantinople: a poem. 1823.
Visions of taste: a satire. 1823.

John Freeman Milward Dovaston 1782–1854

§1

Rhymes. 1805. Anon. [With O. G. Gilchrist and W. Gifford.]
Fitz-Gwarine: a ballad of the Welsh border.... Shrewsbury 1812; London and Shrewsbury 1816.
Poems, legendary, incidental and humorous.... Shrewsbury 1825 (3 edns).
The Cambrian and Salopian minstrel... By the poet 'Ferneat of the Breidden' and others. Shrewsbury [1823?]. Anon. With others.
The dove: scraps of poetry, selected.... Ed [Dovaston] [1823?].
Some account of the popular life... of T. Bewick. 1829. Prose.
Three popular lectures, one on natural history and two on national melody. Shrewsbury 1839. Prose.

§2

Bewick to Dovaston: letters 1824–1828. Ed G. Williams 1968.
Letters from Lambeth: the correspondence of the Reynolds family with... Dovaston 1808–1815. Ed J. Reynolds, Woodbridge 1981.

Harriet Downing, Mrs fl. 1816–52

Mary, or female friendship: a poem in twelve books. Bk 1 only. By a lady. 1816 (anon), 1816 (acknowledged).
The child of the tempest and other poems. 1821.
The bride of Sicily: a dramatic poem. 1830.
How Fanny teaches her children, and odds and ends.... 1836. Prose.
Satan in love: a dramatic poem. 1840.
Remembrances of a monthly nurse. 1852, [1862]. Prose.

John B. Drayton fl. 1813–21

Poems. 1813.
The early minstrel.... London and Edinburgh [1815?] (2nd edn).
Poetic sketches from Bunyan.... Ed T. Scott, Cheltenham 1821.

Henry Austen Driver fl. 1825–38

The Arabs: a tale in four cantos.... 1825.
Harold de Burun: a semi-dramatic poem.... 1835.
Byron and 'The abbey'. 1838. Prose.

Sir William Drummond 1770?–1828

The satires of Persius. Tr Drummond 1797, 1799, 1803, 1831 (as Persius).
Byblis: a tragedy. 1802.
Odin: a poem. Pt 1 1817.
Author of numerous contributions to classical scholarship.

William Hamilton Drummond 1778–1865

Hibernia: a poem. Belfast 1797. Anon.
The battle of Trafalgar: a heroic poem. Belfast and Dublin 1806; Charleston SC 1807.
Lucretius. The first book... of the nature of things. Tr Drummond, London and Edinburgh 1808.
The giants' causeway: a poem. Belfast and London 1811.
An elegiac ballad on the funeral of the Princess Charlotte. Dublin 1817. Anon.
Who are the happy: a poem.... Dublin 1818.
Clontarf: a poem. Dublin 1822. Anon.
Bruce's invasion of Ireland: a poem. Dublin 1826. Anon.
The pleasures of benevolence: a poem. 1835.
Contributed to Irish minstrelsy... with English poetical translations *(1831) and* Ancient Irish minstrelsy *(1852), and wrote on religion, the church, biography and animals' rights.*

P. J. Ducarel fl. 1805–36

Poems. 1805.
Poems, original and translated. 1807.
A paraphrase of the psalms.... 1833.
De Wyrhale: a tale of Dean forest in five cantos. 1836.

Robert Nugent Dunbar d. 1866

The lament of Britannia: a poem.... 1817.
Monody on the... death of Sir S. Romilly. 1818.
The cruise, or a prospect of the West Indian archipelago.... 1835.
The Caraguin: a tale of the Antilles. 1837.
Indian hours, or passion and poetry of the tropics. 1839.
The nuptials of Barcelona: a tale.... 1851 (2nd edn).
Illustrations of the beauties of tropical scenery. 1863 (anon), 1864 (acknowledged, as Beauties of tropical scenery, lyrical sketches and love-songs), 1866.

George Dyer 1755–1841

§1

An inquiry into the nature of subscription to the 39 Articles. [1789], 1792 (enlarged). Prose.
Poems. 1792.
The complaints of the poor people of England. 1793 (2 edns), 1798; Oxford 1990 (facs reprint). Anon. Prose.
Slavery and famine: punishments for sedition, or an account of the miseries and starvation at Botany Bay. 1794 (2 edns, the 2nd as Slavery... an account of New South Wales); ed G. Mackaness, Sydney 1947 (facs reprint); ed Mackaness, Dubbo 1979 (facs reprint). Prose.
A dissertation on the theory and practice of benevolence. 1795; rptd in Pamphleteer, vols 13–14 1818–19. Prose.
Memoirs of the life and writings of R. Robinson. 1796. Prose.
An English prologue and epilogue to... Ignoramus.... 1797.
The poet's fate: a poetical dialogue. 1797 (2 edns).
An address to the people of Great Britain on the doctrines of libels. 1799. Prose.
Odes. Ludlow 1800; ed D. H. Reiman, New York and London 1979 (facs reprint). With others.
Poems. 1801 (BL copy has cancelled title page and preface, 1800), 2

vols 1802; ed D. H. Reiman, New York and London 1978 (facs reprint of 1802).
Poetics, or a series of poems and disquisitions on poetry. 2 vols 1812. Verse and prose.
Four letters on the English constitution. 1812 (2 edns), 1817 (enlarged); rptd in Pamphleteer, vol 12 1818. Prose.
History of the university and colleges of Cambridge. 2 vols 1814. Prose.
To a lady requesting some verses .... [c. 1815.]
The privileges of the university and colleges of Cambridge. 2 vols 1824. Prose.
Academic unity. 1827. Prose.
Contributed to Analytical Rev, Critical Rev, Reflector *and* Monthly Mag.

Miss Edgar fl. 1810–24

Tranquillity: a poem, to which are added other original poems and translations from the Italian. Dundee, Edinburgh, Glasgow, Aberdeen and Montrose 1810; Edinburgh and London 1824.

James Edmeston 1791–1867

Poems. 1817.
The search and other poems. 1817.
Sacred lyrics .... [1st set] 1820, 1st and 2nd sets 1821, 3rd set 1822, collected 1823.
Anston park: a tale. 1821. Prose.
The cottage minstrel, or hymns .... 1821, 1836.
Patmos and other poems. 1824.
The woman of Shunem ... and other poems. 1829, 1830.
Fifty original hymns .... Northampton 1833.
Hymns for the chamber of sickness. [1844], [c. 1850].
Closet hymns and poems. [1846.]
Infant breathings, being hymns for the young. 1846, [1862].
Sacred poetry. 1848.

Rebecca Edridge fl. 1803–25

The lapse of time: a poem for the new year. Uxbridge and London 1803.
The scrinium: a collection of tales. 2 vols 1822. Prose.
The highest castle and the lowest cave. 3 vols 1825. Prose.

John Edwards b. c. 1772

All Saints' Church, Derby: a poem. Derby 1805.
The tour of the dove: a poem .... London and Derby 1821, [1825?].

Richard Edwards fl. 1813

The reviewers: a poem in accentuated verse. 1813.
Specimens of English accentuated verse .... 1813.
Specimens of English non-accentuated verse .... 1813.
Treatise on English prosody. 1813. Prose.

Anne Elfe fl. 1808–9

The lays of Caruth, bard of Dinham and other poems. 1808; ed J. E. Hardwick, Newport-on-Usk 1909.
Original poems. Chepstow, Monmouth, etc. 1809.

Charlotte Elliott 1789–1871

Selections

Selections from the poems of Charlotte Elliott, with a memoir by her sister E. B[abington]. [1873], reissued [1875].
REVIEWS: Br Quart Rev Jan 1874; Gospel Mag July 1874.
I wish you a happy new year: counsels and encouragements selected from Charlotte Elliott. [1877.] Mostly verse.
Miles 10 (11).
Words of hope and grace, with a biographical sketch. [1914.]

§1

The invalid's hymn book. Dublin 1834. Anon. 1841 (2nd edn revised and enlarged), 1854 (12th thousand rev, corrected and enlarged). (Includes Just as I am, with over a hundred other original hymns in later edn.)
Hours of sorrow: or, thoughts in verse chiefly adapted to seasons of sickness, depression and bereavement. 1836, 1856 (5th edn as Hours of sorrow cheered and comforted), 1869 (7th edn). Anon.
Morning and evening hymns for a week. Original. Brighton 1836. Anon. Frequently rptd, 37th thousand [c. 1865], [1906] as Hosannah: hymns for a week.
Thoughts in verse on sacred subjects and hymns. 1869, 1871 (2nd edn, with some miscellaneous poems, written in early years, and now first published).
Poetical leaflets. 16 nos. Religious Tract Soc [1873].
All I need: or the Christian's confidence [tract]. [1874.]
Leaves from the unpublished journals, letters and poems of Charlotte Elliott. [1874], [1878].
REVIEWS: Athenaeum 17 Oct 1874; Evangelical Mag n.s. 18, Dec 1874.
Charlotte Elliott also contributed to the Christian Remembrancer *pocket book, which she edited 1834–59, and to* Psalms and hymns, *ed H. V. Elliott, Brighton 1835.*

Attributed and spurious works

A keepsake for a young servant. 1841, 1847 (3rd edn).

§2

Obituary: Christian Observer Dec 1871.
Winslow, O. The king in his beauty: a tribute to the memory of Miss Charlotte Elliott. [1872.]
Just as I am. [1885.] With memorial sketch by H. L. L. [i.e. Jane Borthwick]. [RS]

Ebenezer Elliott 1781–1849

The major collection of Elliott's mss and letters is held in Sheffield City Libs. Other letters are in the Brotherton Lib in Leeds.

Bibliographies

Eaglestone, A. A., E. R. Seary and G. L. Phillips. Ebenezer Elliott: a commemorative brochure with bibliography. Sheffield 1949. Lists many fugitive pieces.
Brown, S. Ebenezer Elliott: the Corn Law rhymer. Leicester 1971. Provides a listing of both letters and secondary criticism.

Collections.

[Poetical works.] Vol 1: The splendid village, Corn Law rhymes and other poems, 1834; vol 2: The village patriarch, Love and other poems, 1834; vol 3: Kerhonah, The vernal walk, Win hill and other poems, 1835. Reissued as The poetical works of Ebenezer Elliott, 3 vols 1844.
The poetical works. Edinburgh 1840.
The poems. Ed R. W. Griswold, Philadelphia 1844, New York 1850. Includes poems not found in other edns.
The poetical works. Ed E. Elliott 2 vols 1876.

Selections

Miles 2.
Ward, T. H. In English poets vol 4, 1911. Preface by E. Dowden.
Ashraf, M. Introduction to working class literature in Great Britain. East Berlin 1978.
Maidment, B. E. The poorhouse fugitives. Manchester 1987.
Scheckner, P. An anthology of Chartist poetry. 1989.

§1

The vernal walk. Cambridge 1801, 1802. Anon.
The soldier and other poems, by Britannicus. Harlow 1810.
Night: a descriptive poem. 1818. Anon.
Peter Faultless to his brother Simon; Tales of night, in rhyme, and other poems, by the author of Night. Edinburgh 1820.
Love: a poem; The giaour: a satirical poem. 1823, 1823, 1831.
Scotch nationality: a vision. 1824, Sheffield 1875 (priv ptd).
The village patriarch: a poem. 1829, 1831.
Corn Law rhymes: the ranter. Sheffield 1830, 1831 (enlarged), 1831, 1904 (selection).
The splendid village: Corn Law rhymes, and other poems. 1833. Reissued 1834 as vol 1 of [Poetical works], *above*.
More verse and prose by the Cornlaw rhymer. 2 vols 1850. Contains review by Southey.

§2

Carlyle, T. Corn Law rhymes. Edinburgh Rev 55 1832; rptd in his Critical and miscellaneous essays, 1839.
Fox, W. J. The poor and their poetry. Monthly Repository 1832.
Wilson, J. Poetry of Ebenezer Elliott. Blackwood's Mag 1834; rptd in vol 6 of Works, Edinburgh 1856.
Prince, J. C. Ebenezer Elliott. Bradshaw's Jnl Sep 1842.
Fox, W. J. Lectures addressed chiefly to the working classes. 4 vols 1845.
Howitt, W. Memoir of Ebenezer Elliott. Howitt's Jnl 1847.
Howitt, W. Homes and haunts of the English poets. 1847.
Watkins, J. The life, poetry and letters of Ebenezer Elliott. 1850. Includes Autobiographical fragment which was partially rptd in People's Jnl 1850 and Athenaeum Jan 1850.
'Searle, January' [G. S. Phillips]. The life, character, and genius of Ebenezer Elliott. 1850, 1852.
Ebenezer Elliott. Tait's Edinburgh Mag Jan 1850.
Ebenezer Elliott, Household Words June 1850.
Ebenezer Elliott, the Corn Law rhymer. Eliza Cook's Jnl Sep 1850.
Literary Gazette Sep 1850.
Hood, E. P. Genius and industry. 1851.
Gilfillan, G. Literary portraits. 2 vols 1856.
Étienne, L. Les poètes des pauvres en Angleterre: 3, Ebenezer Elliott. Revue des Deux Mondes Sep 1856.
Hood, E. P. The peerage of poverty. [1881] (6th edn). [BM]

Mary Elliott, formerly Belson 1794?–1870

§1

The mice, and their picnic: a good moral tale. By a looking-glass maker. 1810, 1811, 1813. Anon.
Grateful tributes, or recollections of infancy. 1811, 1818; New York [nd]; London 1822, [1830?].
The baby's holiday, to which is added The white lily. 1812.
Simple truths in verse, for the amusement and instruction of children, at an early age. 1812, 1816, 1822, [1830?] (5th edn); New York [183-?]; London [1840?] (6th edn), [1845?].
My sister: a poem. Philadelphia 1816; New York [1830?].
Flowers of instruction, or familiar subjects in verse. 1820 (2 edns).
The progress of the quartern-loaf: a poem. [1820.]
The sunflower, or poetical truths, for young minds.... 1822, [1825?].
Innocent poetry, containing moral and religious truths for infant minds. 1823, [1825?].
Gems in the mine, or traits and habits of childhood, in verse. [1824]; Salem MA and Lancaster MA 1828.
The rose, containing original poems for young people. [1824], [1825?]; Birmingham 1899.
Poetic gift: containing Mrs Barbauld's hymns, in verse. New Haven CT [18—?]

§2

P. D. Jordan, The juvenilia...: a list. New York 1936.
Pbd numerous works of prose fiction for children.

Sir Charles Abraham Elton 1778–1853

Poems. 1804.
The remains of Hesiod the Ascraean. Tr Elton 1812, 1815, 1832, 1856 (Bohn's Classical Lib), 1894; selection 1873 (as The works of Hesiod, Callimachus and Theognis, with J. Banks and J. H. Frere).
Tales of romance, with other poems... including selections from Propertius. London, Bristol, Edinburgh and Dublin 1810; selections 1848 (as Elegies of Propertius), 1854.
Specimens of the classic poets.... Tr Elton 3 vols 1814; Philadelphia 1854, 1860, 1868.
The brothers: a monody... 1820.
Hesiod... Bion and Moschus.... Tr Elton 1832. With F. Fawkes and Viscount Royston.
Boyhood, with other poems and translations. London and Bristol 1835.
Some pbns on religious topics.

Lucy Emra c. 1806–c. 1835?

Scenes in the life and death of a missionary and other original poems. London and Bristol 1831, 1832 (as Heavenly themes: a selection of original poetry).
The types. 1836. Anon. Verse and prose.

Elizabeth or Eliza Bland Erskine, the Hon Mrs Esme Steuart, formerly Norton b. c. 1795

Isabel: a tale in two cantos and other poems. 1814.
Alcon Malanzore: a Moorish tale. Brussels 1815.
The charity sister: a tale. [New York 183-?]. Prose.
The martyr: a tragedy. 1848.
The gossip: a collection of tales, sketches. 3 vols 1852. Prose.
The lady of La Garaye. Cambridge 1862 (2 edns), Cambridge and London 1862 (2 edns), New York 1864, [1865?]; London 1866, New York 1866.

Thomas Erskine, Baron Erskine, also 'E' 1750–1823

Collections

A collection of essays on a variety of subjects, in prose and verse. Newark NJ 1797.
The poetical works... with a biographical memoir. 1823.

§1

The geranium. [c. 1795.] Anon.
Armata: a fragment. 1817 (4 edns). Anon.
The second part of Armata. 1817 (3 edns), 1818.
The farmer's vision. By 'E'. 1819, 1820. Anon.
The beauties of Erskine.... Ed A. Howard [1834?]. Prose and verse.
Substantial pbns on politics and law, listed in BLC.

Charles Wicksted Ethelston fl. 1803–30

The suicide, with other poems. 1803.
The unity of the church inculcated and enforced. Manchester 1814. Prose.
A pindaric ode to the genius of Britain. Manchester [1820?] (2 edns).

S. Evance, afterwards Mrs B. Hooper fl. 1808–18

Poems... selected from her earliest productions, to those of the present year. Ed [J. Clarke] 1808.

A poem occasioned by the cessation of public mourning for ... Princess Charlotte .... 1818.

James Everett, also 'William Cowper' 1784–1872

§1

An extraordinary chace, or the parson and the cat. By 'William Cowper'. Sheffield [1820?] (2nd edn), London 1831.

A subject's tribute in memory of George the Third. Sheffield 1820.

Elijah: tributary verses occasioned by the death of J. Benson. 1823 (2nd edn).

The Yorkshire hunt. By 'William Cowper'. London and Manchester 1830; London, Edinburgh, Glasgow and Dublin 1831. Anon.

Edwin, or Northumbria's royal fugitive restored .... 1831.

§2

Chew, R. J. Everett: a biography. 1875.

Author of sermons and memoirs and editor of Wesleyan pbns. He employed several pseudonyms.

Catherine Maria Fanshawe 1765–1834

Collections

The aenigma. 1818 (ptd as Byron's in Three poems not included in the works of Lord Byron).

A collection of poems from living authors. Ed J. Baillie 1823. Includes a few poems by Catherine Fanshawe ptd for the first time.

Memorials of Miss C. M. Fanshawe. [Ed W. Harness], Westminster (London) [1865] (priv ptd). Includes most of her poems.

Literary remains, with notes by W. Harness. 1876. Verse.

§1

Speech of the member for Odium. [1833.] Anon.

Charles Feist 1795–1856

Poetical effusions, comprising poems, ballads .... 1813.

Breathings of the woodland lyre. Newark 1815.

Elegiac lines on the death of ... Sophia Charlotte .... Halesworth 1818.

The wreath of solitude .... Newmarket [1818].

Thoughts in rhyme. By an East Anglian. London and Swaffham 1825, 1828. Anon.

Spring blossoms. Swaffham 1831 (3rd edn); London 1844. Prose.

Summer flowers from the garden of wisdom. 1833. Prose.

Useful rhymes for youth betimes! A poetical remembrancer of the sovereigns of England. 1837.

William Fernyhough fl. 1786–1814

Poems. Newcastle 1786.

Trentham park: a poem. Newcastle 1789.

Poems on various occasions. Newcastle 1814.

John Finlay 1782–1810

Wallace, or the vale of Ellerslie, with other poems. Glasgow, Edinburgh and London 1802 (anon); Glasgow 1804 (acknowledged), 1806.

Scottish historical and romantic ballads, chiefly ancient .... Ed Finlay, Edinburgh and Glasgow 1808.

Howard Fish fl. 1817–19

Amatory and other verses. 1817.

The wrongs of man: a satire .... 1819.

J. B. Fisher fl. 1808–18

Pathetic tales, poems. 1808.

Poems, pathetic, elegiac and romantic .... 1809.

Poetical rhapsodies. 1818.

James Fisher b. 1759

Poems on various subjects. Dumfries 1790.

A spring day .... Edinburgh 1803, 1806, 1808; New York 1813; Liverpool 1818, 1819; Edinburgh and London 1823 (7th edn). Prose.

An elegy on the death of David's psalms. Carlisle 1805.

A winter season ...: an essay on the good things in life. Edinburgh 1810; Liverpool 1815 (3rd edn); Edinburgh 1821 (5th edn); Northampton 1826 (6th edn). Prose.

Scripture riddles. Derby 1823, Northampton 1827 (3rd edn).

The Westminster assembly's shorter catechism, in verse. Derby 1824.

John Fisher 1774?–1846

The Valley of Llanherne and other pieces in verse. 1801.

Residence: two letters in verse. 1821. Anon.

The honeymoon. 1840.

Also pbd on church topics.

William Thomas Fitzgerald or Fitz-Gerald 1759–1829

Collection

The sturdy reformer, The tribute of an humble muse, Lines .... Ed D. H. Reiman, New York and London 1979 (facs reprints of 9 works).

§1

The sturdy reformer: a new song. 1792. Anon.

The tribute of an humble muse to an unfortunate captive queen. By W. T. F***g***d. 1793.

Lines on the murder of the queen of France .... 1794.

Nelson's triumph, or the battle of the Nile .... 1799.

Miscellaneous poems .... 1801.

The tears of Hibernia! Dispelled by the union .... 1802.

Britons never will be slaves!! [1803.] Single sheet.

Britons! To arms!! [1803] (4th edn). Single sheet.

Nelson's tomb: a poem .... 1805, [1806].

A tribute to the memory of H. Nelson. [1805.] Anon. Single sheet.

The battle of Salamanca. [1812.] Single sheet.

Poems for the anniversary of the literary fund. 1813. Anon. With Charles Symmons.

The tyrant's downfall .... 1814.

Wellington's triumph, or the battle of Waterloo. 1815, 1825 (as The battle of Waterloo).

An address for the anniversary of the literary fund. 1817.

An elegy on the death of the Princess Charlotte. 1817.

A poem for the anniversary of the literary fund. 1821.

The literary fund: anniversary poem. [1822.]

Alice Flowerdew, Mrs Daniel 1759–1830

Poems, on moral and religious subjects. London, Oxford and Norwich 1803, 1804; London 1811.

Eliza S. Francis fl. 1813–15

The rival roses, or wars of York and Lancaster: a metrical tale .... 2 vols 1813. Anon.

Sir Wilibert de Waverley, or the bridal eve: a poem. 1815.

Susan Fraser fl. 1809–11

Camilla de Florian and other poems. 1809 (2 edns), 1811 (as Poems).

John Hookham Frere 1769–1846

Collections

Aristophanes: a metrical version of The Acharnians, The knights and The birds. Malta [1839?] (priv ptd); London 1840; ed H. Morley 1886, 1909; selection: The knights. ed W. A. Landes, Studio City CA 1992. Included in many collections of Greek translations.
National poems. Ed R. Shepherd 1867.
Works in verse and prose. Ed W. E. and B. Frere 2 vols 1872, 3 vols 1873, 1874; London and New York 1874. Memoir by B. Frere.
Parodies and other burlesque pieces by Canning, Ellis and Frere. Ed H. Morley 1890 (Carisbrooke Lib).
Aristophanes: four plays. Ed W. W. Merry, Oxford [1907]. For other posthumous printings of single plays and groups, *see* BLC.

§1

The microcosm. Windsor 1786–7; 1809. *See under* Canning, *col 289, above*. Frere contributed 5 papers.
Ode on Aethelstan's victory. 1801 (in Ellis's Specimens of the early English poets).
Translations from the Cid. 1808 (in R. Southey, Chronicle of the Cid).
Prospectus and specimen of an intended national work by W. and R. Whistlecraft relating to King Arthur. Cantos 1–2 1817, 1818 (2 edns); Cantos 3–4 1818; The monks and the giants: prospectus and specimen. 1818, 1821 (4th edn), 1833; Bath 1842; ed R. D. Waller, Manchester, London and New York 1926; Oxford 1992 (facs reprint of 1818). Anon.
Fables for five years old. 1820; Malta 1830; Diss, Norfolk 1859. Anon.
Psalms, etc. 1835, [1839?]. Anon. A metrical paraphrase.
Aristophanes. The frogs. Tr Frere 1839.
Theognis restitutus, the personal history of the poet deduced from an analysis of his existing fragments: a hundred fragments in English metre. Malta 1842; London 1856 (Bohn's Lib, as The works of Theognis). Prose.
See also under Anti-Jacobin, *col 2935, below.*

§2

Festing, G. Frere and his friends. 1899.
von Eichler, A. Frere: sein Leben und seine Werke, sein Einflüss auf Byron. Vienna and Leipzig 1905.

Caroline Fry, later Wilson 1787–1846

A poetical catechism, or sacred poetry for the use of young persons. 1822 (2nd edn), 1826 (4th edn), 1857.
Serious poetry. 1822, 1823, 1826, 1833.
Death and other poems. 1823.
An autobiography. 1848; Philadelphia 1849; London 1850. Anon.
A number of religious pbns in prose.

Thomas Furlong 1794–1827

The misanthrope, with other poems. Dublin 1821 (2nd edn).
The doom of Derenzie: a poem. 1829.
Irish minstrelsy . . . with poetical translations. Ed James Hardiman 2 vols 1831.
Support under suffering, or letters to a young relative. [1855], 1871. Prose.

Edward Gandy fl. 1823–7

Lorenzo, the outcast son: a tragic drama . . . After Schiller. 1823.
Caswallon, king of Britain: a tragedy. 1826.
Moods and tenses. By one of us. 1827. Anon. Prose.

William Gardiner, master of Lydney Academy 1766–1825

Collection

Original poems, songs and essays . . . . Ed [M. A. Gardiner] 1854.

§1

The sultana, or the jealous queen: a tragedy. Gloucester and London 1806.
Poems on various occasions. 1813.
The voyage of Admiral George Carlton in search of loyalty: a poetic epistle. 1820.
Also wrote prose fiction for the young.

Catherine Grace Garnett, later Godwin 1798–1845

Collection

The poetical works . . . with a sketch of her life. Ed A. C. Wigan 1854.

§1

The night before the bridal: a Spanish tale; Sappho: a dramatic sketch and other poems. 1824.
The wanderer's legacy: a collection of poems on various subjects. 1829.
The reproving angel: a vision. 1835.
Author also of prose fiction.

Thomas Gent fl. 1805–28

Collection

Poetic sketches, Poems. Ed D. H. Reiman, New York and London 1978 (facs reprints of 1808 and 1828).

§1

Poetic sketches. Yarmouth 1805; London 1806, 1808.
Monody to the memory of . . . Sheridan. 1816.
Lines suggested by the death of the Princess Charlotte. 1817, 1818.
Poems. 1820, 1828.

John Gerrond b. 1765

Collection

The new poetical works of J. G., the Galloway poet. Dumfries 1848.

§1

Poems on several occasions . . . . Glasgow 1802.
The poetical and prose works . . . . Leith 1811, 1812, 1813, 1815.

William Gilbert 1760?–1825?

The hurricane: a theosophical and western eclogue, to which is subjoined A solitary effusion in a summer's evening. Bristol 1796; Oxford 1990 (facs reprint).

Octavius Graham Gilchrist 1779–1823

Rhymes. 1805. Anon.
The poems of Richard Corbet. Ed Gilchrist 1807 (4th edn).
A letter to W. Gifford . . . . 1811. Prose.
Editor of plays and critic of Elizabethan lit.

Robert Gilfillan 1798–1850

Collection

Rogers 3.

§1

Original songs. Edinburgh and Leith 1831; Edinburgh 1835 (enlarged as Songs), 1839 (as Poems and songs), 1851 (with memoir [by W. Anderson]).
Emmanuel's land. [Leith 1846?]

William Gillespie 1776–1825

The progress of refinement: an allegorical poem. Edinburgh and London 1805.
Consolation, with other poems. Edinburgh and London 1815.
The rebellion of Absalom: a discourse. Dumfries 1820 (2nd edn). Prose.

Thomas Gillet fl. 1817–32

The banks of Isis and other poems. Oxford 1817.
Fashion: a didactic sketch . . . . Oxford 1819.
Fashion, The emigrants and other poems. Oxford 1819.
The midland minstrel . . . . tales and local legends. Oxford and London 1822.
The juvenile wreath . . . poems, chiefly on subjects of natural history. Oxford 1832. Anon.

Robert Pearse Gillies 1788–1858

§1

Childe Alarique: a poet's reverie. Edinburgh 1813; Edinburgh and London 1814; Philadelphia 1815. Anon.
Wallace: a fragment. Edinburgh 1813. Anon.
Illustrations of a poetical character . . . . Edinburgh 1816. Anon.
Rinaldo, the visionary: a desultory poem. Edinburgh and London 1816.
Oswald: a metrical tale . . . . Edinburgh 1817. Anon.
Muellner, A. G. A. Guilt, or the anniversary: a tragedy. Tr [Gillies] Edinburgh 1819.
A winter night's dream: the seventh day. Edinburgh 1826.

§2

Memoirs of a literary veteran. 3 vols 1851.
Author of a number of works of prose fiction, and contributor to Ruminator *(1813). See col 917.*

Robert Gilmour, Captain fl. 1815–16

Lothaire: a romance in six cantos. 1815.
Tales in verse, with a vision of Morduth . . . by Douthal . . . . 1815 (2 edns).
The battle of Waterloo: a poem. 1816.

John Glanville, of St James's St fl. 1800–15

Poetical prolusions. 1800, 1811 (as Variety, or poetical prolusions).
Poems. By the author of Poetical prolusions. 1811.
Iberia, with an invocation to the patriots of Spain: a poem . . . . 1812.
The fair Persian: an eastern tale . . . . 1815. Anon.

William Glen 1789–1826

Collections

Rogers 3.
The poetical remains of William Glen (with memoir by C. Rogers). Edinburgh 1874.

§1

Poems, chiefly lyrical. Glasgow 1815.
Songs on the late battles. Glasgow 1815.
The lonely isle: a south-sea island tale. Glasgow 1816.
Heath flowers: being a collection of poems, chiefly lyrical, written in the Highlands. Glasgow 1817.
Reformiana: a poem. Glasgow 1817.
The star of Brunswick. Lanark 1818.
The Glasgow Whigs of eighteen hundred and twenty-one. Glasgow 1821.

Isaac Gompertz fl. 1813–25

The modern antique, or the muse in the costume of Queen Anne. 1813. Anon.
Time, or light and shade: a poem . . . . 1815.
Devon: a poem. Teignmouth 1825.

Rebecca Gooch fl. 1821–8

Original poems, on various subjects. Southwold, London, etc 1821; London, Norwich, etc 1828.

John Gordon fl. 1807–12

Poems. Edinburgh and London 1807; London 1812.

Edward Goulburn 1787–1868

The blueviad: a satyrical poem. 1805.
The Epwell hunt, or black collars in the rear . . . . Warwick [1807?]; Cheltenham [1835?]; Middle Hill 1840 (with M. B. Hawke), 1847; New York 1928 (as Hell for leather!); ed P. Morgan, Shipston-on-Stour 1984. Anon.
The pursuits of fashion: a satirical poem. 1810 (3 edns), 1812. Anon.
Frederick de Montford: a novel By the author of The pursuits of fashion. 3 vols 1811. Anon.

Lord Francis Leveson Gower, later Francis Egerton, Earl of Ellesmere 1800–57

Goethe and Schiller. Faust: a drama . . . and . . . Song of the bell. Tr [Gower] 1823, 2 vols 1825 (as Faust, with translations from the German).
Translations from the German . . . and original poems. 1824, 1830 (as Wallenstein's camp and original poems).
The mill: a Moravian tale. 1826. Anon.
Boyle farm: a poem . . . . 1827 (4 edns). Anon.
Hugo, V. Hernani. Tr [Gower] 1830; New York 1831 (as Dramatic scenes).
Dumas. A. and V. Hugo. Catherine of Cleves and Hernani: tragedies. Tr Gower 1832.
Beer, M. The paria: a tragedy. Tr [Gower] 1836.
Town and country. 1836. Anon.
Alfred: a drama. [1840?], [1871?] (as King Alfred). Anon.
Bluebeard, or dangerous curiosity and justifiable homicide: a tragedy. 1841, [1870?]. Anon.
The pilgrimage. Manchester 1841; London 1856 (as The pilgrimage and other poems). Anon.
Donna Charitea, Queen of Castille: a drama. 1843. Anon.
The eighteenth of November, 1852. 1853.
Contributed to Quart Rev, *wrote on European history, archeology, travel and war.*

Samuel Gower fl. 1821–41

Napoleon and other poems. 1821.
Poems and poetical translations. 1824.
A monopolygraph. London and Huddersfield 1841. Prose and verse.
A slight reminiscence of Cambridge. 1846. Prose.

Thomas Grady, also 'Phelim O'Shaughnessy' d. 1842

The vision: a poem. By an enemy to them all. Dublin 1798. Anon.
The West Briton: being a collection of poems . . . . Dublin 1800. Anon.

The barrister, with other poems. 1812. Anon.
No. l. Being the first letter of the country post bag .... Dublin 1815. Anon.
No. 2. Being the second letter of the country post bag .... Dublin 1815. Anon.
No. 3, or the nosegay ... the third letter of the country post bag. Dublin 1815, 1816. Anon.
The marauder: a poem in a series of consecutive epistles. By 'Phelim O'Shaughnessy'. Boulogne 1825. Anon.

John Graham, Rector of Tamlaght-ard, Derry

1776–1844

Historical poetry .... Londonderry 1823.
Derriana ... with historical poetry. Londonderry 1823; Dublin 1829 (as A history of the siege of Londonderry); Philadelphia and New York 1844; Toronto 1869, 1873. Prose and verse.
Poems, chiefly historical. Belfast 1829.
A history of Ireland .... Dublin 1839. Prose.
Michelburne, J. Ireland preserved .... Dublin 1841. Includes poetry by Graham.
Also contributed to the parochial survey of Ireland.

John Graham, of Wadham College 1813–45

Granada: a prize poem .... Oxford 1833.
A vision of fair spirits and other poems. 1834.
Geoffrey Rudel, or the pilgrim of love. 1836. Prose.

William Graham, of Carlisle fl. 1786–1821

The eclogues of Virgil. Tr Graham, Carlisle 1786.
Poetical pieces ... chiefly in the Scottish dialect. Carlisle 1821.

Rev James Grahame 1765–1811

Collections
The poems of James Grahame, John Logan and William Falconer [with lives of the authors]. Edinburgh 1823 (2 issues).
Poetical works [of H. K. White and J. Grahame]. Ed G. Gilfillan, Edinburgh 1856, [1878].
Poetical works of H. K. White and James Grahame. Ed C. C. Clarke, Edinburgh 1868; London [1878]. With life and notes.

§1

Poems in English, Scotch and Latin. Paisley 1794. Anon.
Rural calendar. Paisley 1797.
Wallace: a tragedy. Edinburgh 1799. Anon.
Mary Stewart, Queen of Scots: an historical drama. Edinburgh 1801. Anon.
The sabbath: a poem. Edinburgh 1804 (anon), 1805 (2 edns, adds Sabbath walks); New York 1805; Edinburgh 1806 (acknowledged), 1808, 1812; New York 1812; Edinburgh, Glasgow and London 1817; Edinburgh 1821; London 1825; Edinburgh 1827; London 1829; Paisley 1831; Edinburgh 1839; London 1851 (in Cabinet edn of British poets vol 3), 1857, [1863] (with G. Crabbe).
Biblical pictures. Edinburgh 1806.
The birds of Scotland, with other poems. Edinburgh 1806; Boston 1807; Philadelphia 1807 (omits Biblical pictures).
Thoughts on trial by jury in civil causes. Edinburgh 1806. Anon. Prose.
Poems. 2 vols London and Edinburgh 1807.
The siege of Copenhagen: a poem. 1808; Edinburgh 1808 (2 edns), 1840.
Africa delivered, or the slave trade abolished. In J. Montgomery, Poems on the abolition of the slave trade, 1809; Freeport NY 1971; ed D. H. Reiman, New York and London 1978 (facs reprint of 1809).
British Georgics. Edinburgh 1809, 1812; Edinburgh and London 1821 (as Rural poems ... or British Georgics).

§2

[Wilson, J.] Lines sacred to the memory of the Rev J. Grahame. Glasgow 1811.

Anne Grant of Laggan, formerly Macvicar

1755–1838

§1

Poems on various subjects. Edinburgh, London, etc 1803; London 1808 (as The highlanders and other poems); Edinburgh and London 1810; Philadelphia 1813.
Letters from the mountains ... By a lady. 3 vols 1806, 1807 (2 edns); 2 vols Boston 1809; London 1809; London and Edinburgh 1813; Boston 1819; 2 vols London 1845. Anon. Prose.
Memoirs of an American lady [C. Schuyler]. 2 vols 1808, 1809; Boston 1809; New York 1809; London 1817; New York 1836; 2 vols New York and Philadelphia 1846; Albany NY 1876; New York 1901, 1903, 1909.
Essays on the superstitions of the highlanders of Scotland. 2 vols 1811 (anon); New York 1813 (acknowledged). Prose.
Eighteen hundred and thirteen: a poem in two parts. Edinburgh and London 1814 (3 edns).
The touchstone, or the claims and privileges of true religion. 1842. Prose.

§2

Memoir and correspondence. Ed J. P. Grant 3 vols 1844, 1845.
Diary of Sir A. Johnston. Ed G. M. Paul, Edinburgh 1896. Contains letters by Grant.
Wrote songs that were set to music, and pbd some educational prose.

Johnson Grant 1773–1844

The pastoral care: a didactic poem .... 1808. Anon.
Arabia: a poem. Leeds 1811; London 1815 (2 edns).
The Joshuad: a poem. 1837 (priv ptd). Anon.
Occasional hymns, for the use of Kentish Town chapel. Ed Grant 1850 (3rd edn).
Author of sermons, memoirs, lectures and trns.

Sir Robert Grant 1779–1838

Collection
Miles 10 (11).

§1

Sacred poems. [Ed C. Grant, Lord Glenelg] 1839, 1844, 1868.
Grant contributed hymns to Christian Observer *(1806–15), and to* Psalms and hymns, *ed H. V. Elliott, 1835. His only separate pbns during his life were a few prose writings on the East India Company, e.g. a sketch of its history, 1813.*

Charles Gray 1782–1851

Address to the poor weavers: a poem. Cupar 1802.
Poems. Cupar and London 1811; Edinburgh and London 1814 (as Poems and songs).
Stray leaves from a forthcoming volume. [Valletta?] 1836.
Lays and lyrics. Edinburgh 1841; Edinburgh and London 1861.
A familiar epistle addressed to P. McLeod. Edinburgh 1845.
The ballads and songs of Ayrshire. Ed [Gray and J. Paterson] 2 ser 1846–7.

James Gray 1770–1830

§1

Cona, or the vale of Clwyd and other poems. 1814 (anon), 1816 (acknowledged).
The poems of Robert Fergusson .... Ed Gray, Edinburgh 1821.

§2

[Mowbray, J. T.] Sketch of the life of the Rev J. Gray. Edinburgh 1859.

John Boyd Greenshields fl. 1800–8

Selim and Zaida: an oriental poem, with other pieces. Edinburgh 1800; London 1802. Anon.
Home: a poem. Edinburgh 1806; Boston 1806; Edinburgh 1808. Anon.

William Greenwood, of Malton 1755–1811

The vale of Apperley and other poems. Malton 1822 (anon), 1823 (acknowledged).
Author also of memoirs.

George Nugent Temple Grenville, Baron Nugent 1788–1850

Portugal: a poem in two parts. 1812 (2 edns).
Wrote also on politics, geography and history.

William Parr Greswell 1765–1854

Memoirs and translations of Politianus [and others]. Manchester 1801, 1805. Prose.
The monastery of Saint Werburgh: a poem. Manchester 1823 (3 edns, priv ptd, the 2nd acknowledged).
Rodrigo: a Spanish legend. Manchester 1823. Anon (authorship uncertain).
Author of books on printing.

Richard Griffith fl. 1760–1804

Fables in verse, or present life under different forms. 1793. Anon.
The fête at Kensington-Gore .... 1800.
Kirk-leas: a descriptive poem, written in 1760. 1802.
Providence, or the two sparrows .... 1804.

James Grocott fl. 1819–30

Almedo: a poem. Liverpool 1819.
Reflection: a poem. Liverpool 1819.
The lay of the first minstrel: a poem. 1821.
The juvenile and other poems ... Manchester 1823.
Liverpool: a poem .... Liverpool 1830.

Henry Montague Grover 1791–1866

Anne Boleyn: a tragedy. 1826.
Socrates: a dramatic poem. 1828.
The history of the resurrection authenticated: a review of the four gospels on the resurrection. 1841. Prose.
Analogy and prophecy: keys of the church .... 1846. Prose.
A voice from Stonehenge. Pt 1 only 1847. Prose.
Changes of the poles and the Equator, considered as a source of error in the present construction of the maps and charts of the globe. 1848. Prose.
A catechism for sophs. 1848. Prose. A 'summary of scriptural doctrine'.
Soundings of antiquity: a new method of applying the astronomical evidences to the events of history, and an assignment of true dates to the epochs of the church. 1862. Prose.

John Gwilliam fl. 1811–45

The battle of Albuera: a poem .... 1811. Anon.
The battles of the Danube and Barrosa. 1811. Anon.
The delicious amour: a poem. 1812. By 'A Professor'.
The campaign: a poem .... 1813.
The mourning wreath .... 1813. Anon.
The bower of bliss, with other amatory poems .... 1814. Anon.
The exile of Elba: a poem, with The deliverance: an ode. 1814, 2 vols 1817 (as The imperial captive).
A cypress wreath for ... the Princess Charlotte .... Ed J. Coote 1817.
Rambles in the Isle of Wight .... 1843, 1844.
A peep at Windsor castle from Richmond Hill. [1844.]
Norris Castle, or recent tramps in the Isle of Wight. 1845.

Samuel Carter Hall 1800–89

§1

Lines written at Jerpoint Abbey. 1820 (2 edns), 1822, 1823, 1827. Anon.
The talents: a dramatic sketch. Cork 1820. Anon.
Ottava rima, to commemorate the king's ... entry into Dublin. Dublin 1821. Anon.
Poems. [1850?]
The trial of Sir Jasper: a temperance tale in verse. [1873], [1874].
An old story: a temperance tale in verse. [1875], [1876].
Words of warning, in verse and prose. [1877.]
After fifty years. [1880.] Single sheet.
Hereafter. [1880.]
My guardian angel. [1880?] Single sheet.
Rhymes in council: aphorisms versified. 1881.

§2

Retrospect of a long life: from 1815 to 1883. 2 vols 1883; New York 1883.
Prolific essayist and editor; *see col 2862, below.*

Thomas Hall, of Winchester fl. 1805–15

Poems on various subjects, written in the debtors' ward. Winchester [1805?], 1808; Oxford and London 1810; Hereford 1815.

Lawrence Hynes Halloran, also 'Philo-nauticus' 1766–1831

A collection of odes, poems and translations. Exeter [1790?].
An ode occasioned by the proposed visit of their majesties to ... Exeter. Exeter 1789.
Poems on various occasions. Exeter 1791. [With A. Geddes.]
The female volunteer, or the dawning of peace: a drama ... By 'Philo-nauticus'. 1801. Anon. Prose and verse.
Lachrymae Hibernicae, or the genius of Erin's complaint: a ballad .... 1801, 1807.
The battle of Trafalgar: a poem .... 1806.
Tributary stanzas ... to the memory of ... Dawson .... 1812.
Author also of sermons.

William Henry Halpin, also 'Peter Quince, the younger' fl. 1820–6

The Cheltenham mail bag, or letters from Gloucestershire ... Ed 'Peter Quince, the younger'. 1st ser 1820, 2nd ser 1826.
The glenfall, with other poems. Cheltenham 1820.

The Cheltenham anthology, comprising original poems and translations. Ed Halpin 1825.

Lady Anne Hamilton 1766–1846

§1

The epics of the ton, or the glories of the great world: a poem in two books.... 1807 (3 edns). Anon.

§2

A key to 'Epics of the ton'. Edinburgh 1883. Anon.

Author of works on English history and of memoirs.

Janet Hamilton, née Thomson 1795–1873

§1

Poems, and essays of a miscellaneous character on subjects of general interest. Glasgow 1863.

Poems of purpose and sketches in prose of Scottish peasant life and character in auld langsyne, sketches of local scenes and characters, with a glossary. Glasgow and Edinburgh 1865.

Poems and ballads, with introductory papers by the Rev George Gilfillan, and the Rev Alexander Wallace. Glasgow 1868, 1873.

Poems, essays and sketches etc. (Memorial vol) ed James Hamilton (with a portrait and facsimilies), Glasgow 1870, 1880, 1885.

Selected works by Janet Hamilton. Coatbridge 1984 (Monklands Lib).

§2

Sketch of the late Mrs Janet Hamilton; with addresses at her funeral and grave, by the Rev P. Cameron Black, and Rev Dr Alex Wallace, with a prefatory note by Rev George Gilfillan. Glasgow 1873.

Pictures in prose and verse; or, Personal recollections of the late Janet Hamilton, Langloan. Together with several unpublished poetic pieces. Ed John Young, Glasgow 1877.

Unveiling of the Janet Hamilton Memorial at Langloan, together with a report of the great public demonstration. Rptd from the Aidrie Advertiser 17 July 1880. [KM]

Sarah Hamilton c. 1769–1843

Sonnets, Tour to Matlock, Recollections of Scotland and other poems. By a resident of Sherwood Forest. 1825. Anon.

The art of war: a poem in six books... By Frederick II, King of Prussia. Tr Hamilton 1826.

The liberation of Joseph: a sacred dramatic poem in two parts, The beauties of vegetation, with digressive sketches of Norwich... in four cantos and other poems. 1827.

Alfred the Great: a drama in five acts. 1829. Anon.

The druid and the holy king: a lyrical poem. By a visitor of Royal Leamington Spa. Leamington 1838, 1840. Anon.

Thomas Hancock, MD 1783–1849

Elegy, supposed to be written on a field of battle.... 1818. Anon.

The law of mercy: a poetical essay.... 1819. Anon.

Author of medical and theological bks.

Thomas Edwards Hankinson 1805–43

Collection

Poems. Ed his brothers 1844, 1847, 1851, 1854, 1860.

§1

Venice: a poem.... Cambridge 1826. Anon.

The druids: a poem. Cambridge 1827.

Poems. Cambridge 1827.

David playing the harp before Saul: a Seatonian poem. Cambridge 1831.

The plague stayed: a Seatonian poem. Cambridge 1832.

St Paul at Philippi: a Seatonian poem. Cambridge 1833.

Jacob: a Seatonian poem. Cambridge 1834.

Ishmael: a Seatonian poem. Cambridge 1835.

Ethiopia stretching out her hands unto God: a Seatonian poem. Cambridge 1838.

The story of Constantine: a poem. 1838.

The ministry of angels. Cambridge 1840.

The call of Abraham: a Seatonian poem. Cambridge 1841.

The cross planted upon the Himalaya mountains: a Seatonian poem. Cambridge 1842.

§2

Sketch of the life... in a series of his own letters and unpublished poems. 2 vols Norwich 1861–2.

Author of sermons.

Joseph Hardaker fl. 1822–31

Poems, lyric and moral.... Bradford 1822.

The aeropteron, or steam-carriage: a poem. Keighley 1830.

The bridal of Tomar and other poems. Keighley 1831.

George Hardinge 1743–1816

Collection

The miscellaneous works in prose and verse. Ed J. Nichols 3 vols 1818.

§1

Rowley and Chatterton in the shades.... 1782; Ann Arbor MI 1979 (facs reprint); Los Angeles 1979; New York 1992. Anon.

The editor, the booksellers and the critic: an eclogue. 1800. Anon.

The filial tribute. 1807.

The Russian chiefs: an ode. 1813 (anon), 1814 (acknowledged).

Author of miscellaneous literary and biographical prose.

Thomas Harral d. 1853

A monody on the death of Mr J. Palmer.... 1798.

Claremont: a poem. 1818 (2nd edn).

Church and king and colour blue. [Ipswich 1819.] Anon (authorship uncertain). Single sheet.

The apotheosis of Pitt.... Bury 1822.

Selections from the poems of... J. Bird. Ed Harral [1840].

Author of topographical and historical bks.

Margaret Harries, later Mrs Cornwell Baron Wilson 1797–1846

Melancholy hours: a collection of miscellaneous poems. 1816.

Astarte: a Sicilian tale, with other poems. London and Edinburgh 1818 (2nd edn); London 1827 (4th edn); London and Edinburgh 1840.

Hours at home: a collection of miscellaneous poems. 1826, 1827.

The cypress wreath. 1828.

The maid of Switzerland: a romantic drama.... [1830?], 1888 (in Dicks's Standard Plays no 991). Prose.

The petticoat colonel...: a comic interlude.... 1831, 1835 (as Venus in arms, in Duncombe's British Theatre vol 26), 1838 (in Cumberland's Minor Theatre vol 14), 1888 (in Dicks's Standard Plays no 979). Prose.

Poems. 1831.

The naval forget me not, or songs of the ship. [1835?]

The life and correspondence of M. G. Lewis. 1839. Anon. Prose and verse.
Memoirs of Harriot, Duchess of St Albans. 2 vols 1839, 1840; Philadelphia 1840; London 1844, 1886, 1887. Prose.
Chronicles of life. 3 vols London and Bury 1840. Prose.
My native town! [Shrewsbury 1840?] Single sheet.
A volume of lyrics. London and Edinburgh 1840.
Popularity and the destinies of women. 2 vols 1842. Prose.
Our actresses. 2 vols 1844. Prose.
Edited various jnls for women.

William Henry Harrison 1795?–1878

The wreath of beauty, with other poems. 1816.
Montfort: a poem in three cantos. 1818.
Tales of a physician. 1829; 2nd ser 1831; 2 vols Philadelphia 1835. Prose.
The humourist: a companion for the Christmas fireside. 1830, 1831, 1832.
Christmas tales, historical and domestic. 1832, 1833, [1840?]. Prose.
Waldemar: a tale of the Thirty Years' War. 1833; Philadelphia 1834; London 1837. Prose.
A royal dream of the ninth of November. By the wooden spoon. 1837. Anon.
The tourist in Portugal. London and New York 1839. Prose.
The comet of many tales . . . . 1841. Prose.
Verses contributed to periodicals. 1859.
The cold water cure: a legend of long ago. 1864.
My holiday at Findon. 1866.
The merchant's daughter. [1867.] Anon.
Prologue and epilogue to the lord mayor's show . . . By [W. H. H.]. 1867. Anon.
The fossil bride: a legend of Folkestone and other verses. 1868.

Mary Kerr Hart, Mrs fl. 1830–2

Heath blossoms, or poems written in obscurity and seclusion . . . . Ballingdon, London, Ipswich, Bury, Hadleigh, Woodbridge and Edinburgh [1830?]; Southampton and London [1835?].
Enigmettes, or Flora's offering to the young. 1832.

William Nevile Hart fl. 1803–11

Good things, partly selected, partly original. London and Reading 1803. Prose.
The goodness of God: a poem . . . . 1806.
Pen and ink well employed. 1809.
An attempt to be useful. 1811. Prose.

Matthew Weld Hartstonge fl. 1812–25

Minstrelsy of Erin, or poems lyrical, pastoral and descriptive. Edinburgh 1812.
Marion of Drymnagh: a tale of Erin, in two cantos . . . . 1814.
Ode to desolation, with some other poems. 1815.
The eve of all-hallows, or Adelaide of Tyrconnel: a romance. 3 vols 1825. Prose.

Margaret Harvey 1768–1858

The lay of the minstrel's daughter: a poem in six cantos . . . . Newcastle 1814.
Raymond de Percy, or the tenant of the tomb: a romantic melodrama. Bishopswearmouth 1822. Verse and prose.

W. C. Harvey fl. 1817–18

The grave of hope: an elegy . . . . 1817.
Sensibility, The stranger and other poems. 1818.

Sibella Elizabeth Hatfield, afterwards Miles 1800–82

The wanderer of Scandinavia, or Sweden delivered, in five cantos, and other poems. 2 vols London and Truro 1826.
Moments of loneliness, or prose and poetic efforts on various subjects and occasions. London and Falmouth 1829.
Fruits of solitude, or prose and poetic compositions: consisting of sketches of natural and moral scenery, tales, essays, meditations . . . . London and Plymouth 1831.
Original Cornish ballads . . . . 1846.
Leisure evenings, or records of the past. Ed Hatfield [1860]. Prose and verse.
Hymns of thanksgiving for the recovery of the Prince of Wales. [1872.] Single sheet.
Wrote on the Te Deum, the factory question, and the Cornish peasantry; author of songs set to music.

Richard Hatt fl. 1810–18

The hermit, with other poems. 1810.
The poetical works . . . . 1814 (2nd edn), 1837.
Elegy. 1817 (4 edns, 4th edn as An epicedium . . . to the memory of . . . Princess Charlotte . . .), 1818.
Also wrote on law.

Hon Annabella Eliza Cassandra Hawke 1787–1818

The jackdaw 'at home'. 1808. Anon.
Babylon: a poem. 1810, 1811 (as Babylon and other poems).

Hon Martin Bladen Edward Hawke 1777–1839

Collections

The Epwell hunt . . . The Raby hunt. [Middle Hill 1840], 1847; New York 1928 (as Hell for leather!). With others.
Poems on hunting. Ed [C. J. Apperley], Pontefract 1842. With others.
The Badsworth hunt: Yorkshire songs. Ed W. Sheardown, Doncaster [1862] (2nd edn).

§1

Howell wood, or the Raby hunt . . . . Pontefract etc 1806. Anon.
Trafalgar, or Nelson's last triumph: a poem. [1806?]

Henry Thomas Heathcote fl. 1817–29

Lyrical pieces and other poems. 1817.
The exile, The knight and the enchanted sword and other poems. Brighton 1824.
Tiverton Castle . . .: an historical romantic play. Tiverton 1829. Prose.

Reginald Heber 1783–1826

Collections

The poetical works of Hemans, Heber and Pollok. Philadelphia 1834.
Poetical works. 1841; Philadelphia 1841; London 1842, 1845; Philadelphia 1847; New York [1850?]; London 1852 (with poems by F. Hemans and A. Radcliffe); Boston 1853, 1854; London 1854; ed M. A. De W. Howe, Philadelphia 1858, 1859; London 1869, 1870; Philadelphia 1870; London [1873?], [1874], [1878]. With poetical works of G. Herbert Edinburgh [1861]; London 1874, [1881]; New York 1885, 1890.

The poetical works of Crabbe, Heber and Pollok. Philadelphia 1856. Miles 10 (11).

From Greenland's icy mountains. Boston [1884?] (illustr T. Guilfoye and E. H. Garrett); Philadelphia [1884] (illustr F. B. Schell); Boston and New York 1885.

Poems and translations, hymns ... Ed D. H. Reiman, New York and London 1978 (facs reprints of 1812 and 1829).

§1

Palestine: a prize poem. Oxford 1803 (priv ptd), 1807; London 1809; Oxford 1810; London 1822 (with Gray's The bard); Philadelphia 1828 (with other poems), 1829; London 1843 (with other poems), 1865; tr Welsh 1822, Armenian 1830, Latin 1844. Set to music by W. Crotch, 1812; Oxford 1827 (as Palestine: a sacred oratorio); London [1880?], ed D. H. Reiman New York and London 1978 (facs rpt). First pbd in Poetical register for 1802, 1803.

A sense of honour: a prize essay. Oxford 1805, 1836.

Europe: lines on the present war. 1809 (2 edns).

Poems and translations. 1812, 1829; Liverpool 1841; Halifax 1857.

The whole works of Jeremy Taylor. Ed Heber 1822. With life.

Hymns, written and adapted to the weekly church service of the year. Ed [A. Heber] 1827 (3 edns); New York 1827; London 1828 (2 edns), 1832, 1834 (10th edn), 1842, 1849 (12th edn), 1867, 1870 (illus).

Select portions of psalms and hymns, with some compositions of a late distinguished prelate [i.e. Heber]. Welshpool 1827.

Narrative of a journey through India 1824–5. Ed [A. Heber] 2 vols 1828, 3 vols 1828 (2 edns); 2 vols Philadelphia 1828, 1829; 3 vols London 1829, 2 vols 1843, 1844, 1846, 1849, 1873; tr Sp 1860 (abridged). Selection, ed P. R. Krishnaswami 1923; ed M. A. Laird, Cambridge 1971.

Sermons preached in England. Ed [A. Heber] 1829 (2 edns).

Sermons preached in India. Ed [A. Heber] 1829.

A ballad. Chester [1830?].

Sermons on the lessons, the gospel or the epistle, for every Sunday in the year. 3 vols 1837, 2 vols 1838 (3rd edn).

The lay of the purple falcon: a metrical romance. By [R. Heber and R. Curzon, Baron Zouche]. 1847. Anon.

Blue-beard: a serio-comic oriental romance in one act. [1864], 1868, [1874]. Verse.

§2

[Heber, A.] The life ... with ... correspondence, unpublished poems .... 2 vols 1830; New York 1830.

The Heber letters 1783–1832. Ed R. H. Cholmondeley 1950. Includes 17 letters from Heber.

A number of sermons and charges were also pbd separately. Some hymns were first pbd in Christian Observer *(1811–16).*

Mary Ann Hedge fl. 1819–36

Original poems. 1820. Anon.

Juvenile poems. London and Colchester 1823 (3rd edn). Anon.

See also col 1804.

Felicia Dorothea Hemans, née Browne 1793–1835

Letters and mss are in Harvard, Huntington, BL, Bodleian, Liverpool Public Lib and Liverpool Record Office, National Libs of Scotland and Wales, Massachusetts Historical Assoc, Alexandra College Dublin, Boston Public Lib, Berg Collection (NYPL), Historical Soc of Pennsylvania, and McGill, Princeton, Edinburgh and Duke Univs. For private collections, see Leslie in §2, below.

Bibliographies

Boyle, A. An index to the annuals. Worcester 1967.

Jones, L. B. The New Monthly Magazine, 1821 to 1830. Unpbd Phd diss. Univ of Colorado 1970.

Jackson, J. R. de J. Romantic poetry by women. Oxford 1993.

See also §2, below.

Collections

Poetical works. 2 vols New York 1828 ('4th Amer edn').

Poetical works. 2 vols New Haven CT 1828, Philadelphia 1832. Expanded, '5th Amer edn'.

Poetical works of Hemans, Heber and Pollok. Philadelphia 1831 (rptd 1832, 1833, 1838).

Poetical works of Mrs Felicia Hemans. With critical preface, and memoir by D. M. Moir. Philadelphia 1835 (no preface), 1836 (rptd 1837, 1839, 1841, 1842, 1843, 1844, 1845, 1846, 1847, 1848, 1849, 1852, 1854, 1855, 1856, 1857, 1859, 1860, 1867); Boston 1848 (rptd 1849, 1850, 1851, 1852, 1853, 1855, 1856, 1857, 1858, 1859). With Hemans's notes. Edns may vary under this imprint.
REVIEWS: New York Rev Mar 1837; Amer Quart Rev June 1837; Christian Rev Sep 1837.

Works of Mrs Hemans. Ed (with memoir) by her sister [H. Hughes] 7 vols Edinburgh and London 1839[–57]; 7 vols Philadelphia 1840[–?] (with An essay by L. H. Sigourney). Blackwood edn.
REVIEW: Christian Observer 40 1840.

Complete works of Mrs Hemans. Ed her sister [H. Hughes] 2 vols New York and Philadelphia 1847; New York 1856. Appleton edn.

Poems of Felicia Hemans. Ed her sister [H. Hughes], Edinburgh 1849 etc; rptd as Poetical works of Felicia Hemans (with memoir by L. H. Sigourney), Boston 1853 (rptd 1858, 1860, 1861, 1864); New York 1853, 1868 (rptd 1873, 1874); Philadelphia [1860?]. Poems arranged chronologically.

Poetical works of Mrs Felicia Hemans. Ed and introd by W. M. Rossetti. London 1873 etc, Liverpool nd, New York 1902. Moxon edn.

Poetical works of Felicia Hemans. With preface. New York 1880, 1881. Amer Book Exchange edn.

Poetical works of Mrs F. Hemans with memoir. 1876, 1881. Gall & Inglis edn.

Poetical works of Mrs F. Hemans. Edinburgh [1876, 1881].

Poetical works, reprinted from the early editions. Edinburgh 1886, 1891.

Poetical works of Mrs Hemans. 1900, New York 1900. 'Albion' edn.

Poetical works of Mrs Hemans. Reprinted from early edns, with memoir, explanatory notes, etc. [Ed anon; rev by Charles Hemans.] nd. Warne 'Lansdowne' edn. Omits Siege of Valencia.

Poetical works of Felicia Dorothea Hemans. Oxford 1914. Lineated, indexed; lacks plays and Hemans's footnotes.

Poetical works of Mrs Hemans (with prefatory memoir, notes, etc). [1920?]. Eyre & Spottiswoode edn.

Poems, etc, by Felicia Hemans. Vols 64–70 of Romantic context: poetry. 128 vols. New York 1976–8 (facs; ed and introd by D. H. Reiman).

This list is not complete.

Selections

The league of the Alps; The siege of Valencia; The vespers of Palermo; and other poems [etc]. Ed A. Norton 2 vols [in 4 pts] Boston 1826–8.
REVIEWS: Amer Quart Rev Mar 1827, June 1837; United States Rev and Literary Gazette Mar 1827; (G. Bancroft) North Amer Rev Apr 1827; Christian Examiner Mar 1829.

Poems. Hartford CT 1827 ('3rd Amer edn').

Poetical works of Mrs Felicia Hemans, 2 vols New York 1828 (expanded 'fourth Amer edn').

Poetical works of Mrs Felicia Hemans. 2 vols Philadelphia 1832. Ash edn.

Short sketch of the life of Mrs Hemans; with remarks on her poetry; and extracts. 1835. J. Paul edn.
REVIEW: Athenaeum 28 Nov 1835.

Poetical remains of the late Mrs Hemans. With memoir by D. M. Moir. Edinburgh, London 1836 (First dated 1834).
REVIEWS: Literary Gazette 19 Mar 1836; Eclectic Rev July 1836; Dublin Rev 2, Dec 1836.
Early blossoms of spring, with a life of the authoress. 1840. Juvenile poems.
Songs of the affections and other poems. Liverpool 1842, Halifax 1860. Juvenile poems.
Sacred poems of Mrs Hemans; and the Hebrew melodies of Lord Byron. New York 1844.
Songs; Scenes and hymns of life; and other poems; from the last London edition by her sister. New York 1845.
Poems of Felicia Hemans. With an essay on her genius by H. T. Tuckerman. Ed R. Griswold, Philadelphia 1845 (rptd 1846, 1850); rev as Poetical works of Mrs Felicia Hemans, Boston 1852.
Records of woman, Songs of the affections and Songs and lyrics. Philadelphia 1853.
Poems. Edinburgh and London 1865.
Select poetical works. Leipzig 1865.
Poems by Mrs Hemans. 1873, 1880, 1885 (with illustrations), 1894, 1896. Routledge edn.
Extracts from the lyrical poems of Mrs Hemans, etc. 1875. Stewart's School Ser.
Favorite poems. Boston 1877.
Hemans' birthday book. Ed R. G. B., Edinburgh [1884].
Poems . . . selected for use in schools. [1887].
Dreams of heaven. New York 1891.
Selections from Mrs Hemans. 1911.
This list is not complete.

§1

Poems. Liverpool and London 1808.
REVIEWS: Annual Rev 7 1808; Poetical Register 7 1808; Monthly Rev 60, Nov 1809.
England and Spain: or valour and patriotism. 1808. Verse.
REVIEWS: Poetical Register 7 1808; Critical Rev Apr 1809; Br Critic Apr 1810.
The domestic affections, and other poems. 1812, 1843, 1844, Poole 1995.
The restoration of the works of art to Italy. Oxford and London 1816, London 1816 [expanded]. Verse.
REVIEWS: Champion June 1816; Augustan Rev July 1816; GM July 1816; Br Critic Sep 1816; Literary Panorama Sep 1816; Monthly Rev Mar 1817; Antijacobin Rev Sep 1817; Br Rev Jan 1820; Quart Rev Oct 1820; Ladies' Monthly Museum n.s. 13 1821.
Modern Greece: a poem. 1817, 1821. Anon.
REVIEWS: Br Lady's Mag July 1817; Blackwood's Edinburgh Mag Aug 1817; Br Rev Aug 1817; Monthly Rev Sep 1817; La Belle Assemblée Dec 1817; Literary and Political Examiner Apr 1818; Eclectic Rev Dec 1818; Fireside Mag Jan 1819.
Tales, and historic scenes, in verse. 1819, 1824; rptd and enlarged as Tales and historic scenes; and other poems, New York 1845, 1852, Edinburgh 1857.
REVIEWS: Br Critic July 1819; Edinburgh Monthly Rev Aug 1819; Fireside Mag Sep 1819; Literary Gazette 18 Sep 1819; NMM Oct 1819; Edinburgh Mag Nov 1819; Monthly Rev Dec 1819; Eclectic Rev Jan 1820; Monthly Mag Jan 1820; GM Mar 1820; Quart Rev Oct 1820; Ladies Monthly Museum n.s. 13 1821.
Wallace's invocation to Bruce: a poem. Edinburgh and London 1819.
REVIEW: Edinburgh Monthly Rev Nov 1819.
The sceptic: a poem. 1820, 1821 (with Stanzas to the memory of the late King).
REVIEWS: European Mag Jan 1820; Literary Gazette 22 Jan 1820; Literary Chron 11 Mar 1820; Br Critic Apr 1820; Edinburgh Monthly Rev Apr 1820; Antijacobin Rev May 1820; Christian's Pocket Mag May, June 1820; Br Rev June 1820; Quart Rev Oct 1820; Lonsdale Mag Dec 1820; Ladies' Monthly Museum n.s. 13 1821.
Stanzas to the memory of the late King. 1820; rptd with 2nd edn of The sceptic, 1821.
REVIEWS: Quart Rev Oct 1820; Ladies' Monthly Museum n.s. 13 1821.
Dartmoor: a poem which obtained the prize of fifty guineas proposed by the Royal Society of Literature. 1821.
REVIEWS: East Lothian Mag 1 1820; Literary Gazette 11 May 1822.
A selection of Welsh melodies. 1822. Power edn, music arranged by John Parry.
The siege of Valencia: a dramatick poem; The last Constantine, with other poems. 1823.
REVIEWS: Apollo Mag 1 1823; Br Rev 21 1823; Edinburgh Mag n.s. 13 1823; Literary Museum no 62 1823; New European Mag 3 1823; Literary Gazette 21 June 1823; Edinburgh Literary Gazette 25 June 1823; British Critic July 1823; Monthly Rev Oct 1823; NMM Nov 1823; Dublin Rev 2 Dec 1836.
The vespers of Palermo: a tragedy, in five acts. 1823, [Dicks' standard plays 155 nd], [1877?].
REVIEWS: Literary Museum no 87 1823; Mirror of the Stage 3 1823; Weekly Entertainer n.s. 8 1823; Monthly Rev Dec 1823; Literary Chron 20 Dec 1823; Edinburgh Literary Gazette 24 Dec 1823; NMM Jan 1824; Dublin Rev 2 Dec 1836.
The vespers of Palermo. Performed Covent Garden 12 Dec 1823, Edinburgh Theatre 5 Apr 1824.
REVIEWS: Examiner [Dec] 1823; The Times 13 Dec 1823; NMM Jan, Feb 1824.
The forest sanctuary, and other poems. 1825; Boston 1827, Edinburgh and London 1829 (enlarged), 1835; New York 1845; tr Ger 1871.
REVIEWS: (L. J. Park) Christian Examiner 3 1826; Inspector 1 1826; Lady's Mag n.s. 7 1826; Monthly Mag n.s. 1 1826; Panoramic Misc 1 1826; Spirit and Manners of the Age 1 1826; Ladies' Monthly Museum May 1826; Literary Gazette 6 May 1826; Literary Magnet June 1826; Monthly Mag or Br Register June 1826; Monthly Rev June 1826; NMM July 1826; Literary Chron 19 Aug 1826; Edinburgh Rev Oct 1829.
Hymns on the works of nature for the use of children. [Ed A. Norton], Boston 1827, London 1833; rptd as Hymns for childhood, Dublin and London 1834, 1839.
REVIEWS: Dublin Univ Mag 3 1834; Athenaeum 8 Feb 1834; Literary Gazette 15 Feb 1834; NMM Mar 1834; Eclectic Rev May 1834.
Records of woman, with other poems. Edinburgh, London, Boston and New York 1828, London 1830, 1834, 1837, 1850, Oxford 1991.
REVIEWS: Literary Gazette 10 May 1828; Monthly Rev June 1828; NMM July 1828; Ladies' Monthly Museum Feb, Apr 1829; Edinburgh Rev Oct 1829; Dublin Univ Mag Feb 1834; Dublin Rev Dec 1836.
Songs of the affections, with other poems. Edinburgh and London 1830, Philadelphia 1831 (rptd 1860, 1862, 1865, 1866, 1867, 1868, 1870, 1873, 1889), London 1835, Liverpool 1840, Manchester 1843, Boston 1845, Cincinnati 1850 (rptd 1854), London 1854.
REVIEWS: Literary Gazette 26 June 1830; Amer Quart Rev June 1837.
National lyrics, and songs for music. Dublin and London 1834, Philadelphia 1835, Dublin and London 1836.
REVIEWS: Literary Gazette 19 Apr 1834; Eclectic Rev May 1834; NMM May 1834.
Scenes and hymns of life, with other religious poems. Edinburgh and London 1834, Philadelphia 1834.
REVIEWS: Eclectic Rev Aug 1834; Athenaeum 2 Aug 1834; Literary Gazette 16 Aug 1834; Dublin Rev Dec 1836; Amer Quart Rev June 1837.
List of reprints and reviews, especially of later books, not complete.

Verse contributions to periodicals and to collaborative works

Edinburgh Annual Register (for 1815). 1818: Dirge of a highland chief, executed after the Rebellion [anon], 8 (cclvi–cclvii).

Blackwood's Edinburgh Magazine. 1818: On the death of the Princess Charlotte (Apr). 1819: The meeting of Wallace and Bruce on the banks of the Carron (Sep; later Wallace's invocation to Bruce). 1826: The heart's dirge (Aug). 1827: The homes of England (Apr); Song of emigration (July); The graves of the dead (Aug); The tomb of de Bruce (Oct); To the memory of Lord Charles Murray, Woman on the field of battle (Nov); The death-day of Körner (Dec). 1828: The broken lute (Mar); The bridal day (May); Nature's farewell (June); The message to the dead (Sep); The two voices (Oct); Tasso's coronation, The voice of the wind (Nov); The land of dreams, The Vaudois wife (Dec). 1829: The storm-painter in his dungeon (Feb); Songs of the affections (i The recall, ii The Indian with his dead child, iii The two homes) (Apr); Songs of the affections (iv The return, v The wish) (May); Songs of the affections (vi The soldier's death-bed, vii The charmed picture, viii The dreaming child) (June); Songs of the affections (ix The guerilla leader's vow, x Parting words, xi The summons) (July); The heart of Bruce in Melrose Abbey (Oct). 1830: Love and death (Jan); The lady of Provence (Feb); The requiem of genius (Mar); Triumphant music (Apr); Music in a room of sickness (June); We return no more (July); The shepherd poet of the Alps (Sep); To the mountain winds (Nov); The palmer, A thought of paradise, To a picture of the Madonna (Dec). 1831: Last song of Sappho, The penitent's return (Jan); Communings with thought, Flowers in a room of sickness, The necromancer, The sisters (Feb); The burial in the desert, The procession (Mar); Hymn of the mountain Christian (June); Dreams of heaven, To a butterfly near a tomb (Sep); The freed bird [rptd Feb 1832 with Latin version], Marguerite of France (Oct). 1832: The flower of the desert, Let us depart, The painter's last work, a scene, The swan and the skylark (Feb); A poet's dying hymn (Apr); The song of the gifted (May); Songs for music (i Oh, skylark, for thy wing, ii Let her depart, iii Where shall we make her grave, iv Summer song, v Ancient Norwegian war-song, vi The stream set free) (Aug); The English martyrs: a scene of the days of Queen Mary (Oct); The burial of the mighty [later The funeral day of Sir Walter Scott], The two monuments (Dec). 1833: Prayer of the lonely student, The traveller's evening song (Jan); The child reading the Bible (Feb); Female characters of Scripture: a series of sonnets (Invocation, The song of Miriam, Ruth, The vigil of Rizpah, The reply of the Shunamite woman) (Apr); Female characters of Scripture vii–xv (The Annunciation – Mary Magdalene bearing tidings of the Resurrection) (May); Hymns of life iii: Burial of a child in the forest (July); Hymns of life iv: Wood-walk and hymn, The water-lily (Aug); Hymns of life v: Easter-day in a mountain churchyard (Oct); Hymns of life vii: Flowers and music in a room of sickness, Songs of captivity (Introd, i The brother's dirge, ii The Alpine horn, iii Ye voices, iv I dream of all things free, v Far o'er the sea, vi The invocation, vii A song of hope) (Dec). 1834: Keene, or funeral lament of an Irish mother over her son, Scenes and hymns of life viii: Prisoner's evening service (Feb); The Indian's revenge (Apr); Thoughts and recollections (To a family Bible, On a remembered picture of Christ, Mountain sanctuaries, The lilies of the field, The birds of the air, The olive tree, Places of worship, A church in north Wales, Old church in an English park) (May); The English boy (July); Sonnets devotional and memorial i–ix: A prayer, The return to poetry, To Silvio Pellico, To the same, released, On reading Coleridge's Epitaph, written by himself, Hope of future communion with nature, Dreams of the dead (Dec). 1835: The Huguenot's farewell (Feb); Antique Greek lament (Mar); Despondency and aspiration: a lyric (May); Sabbath sonnet (July).

Kaleidoscope. [Liverpool] 1819: The meeting of Wallace and Bruce on the banks of the Carron (16 Nov).

Edinburgh Magazine. 1820: The Maremma: a tale [later The palace of the Maremma] (Nov).

Literary Gazette. 1822: The Cid's departure into exile [later Songs of the Cid I] (12 Oct); England's dead (19 Oct).

Belshazzar's feast. In A collection of poems, ed Joanna Baillie, 1823.

New Monthly Magazine. 1823: The farewell to the dead, Greek song: the bowl of liberty, Songs of the Cid I (The Cid's death-bed, a ballad) (Mar); Greek song: the voice of Scio, Songs of the Cid II and III, The voice of spring (Apr); The bird's release at the grave, Greek song: the shade of Theseus, Song for a Swiss festival on the anniversary of an ancient battle, The statue of a funeral genius (June); The wild huntsman, Valkiur song (July); The treasures of the deep [rptd in Poetical Album 1828], The sword of the tomb; a northern legend (Aug); Ancient song of a Greek exile [later Ancient Greek song of exile], Moorish bridal song, The isle of founts: an Indian tradition (Sep); Our lady's well (Oct); The release of Tasso (Nov); The lost Pleiad, The sleeper on Marathon (Dec). 1824: The hour of death (Jan); The child of the forests (Mar); Bring flowers (Apr); The conqueror's sleep, The messenger bird (June); The vassal's lament for the fallen tree (July); The cavern of the three Tells, Troubadour songs (The warrior crossed, They rear'd no trophy) (Aug); Troubadour song: the captive knight, And I too in Arcadia (Sep); The revelers (Oct); The bended bow, The crusader's return (Dec). 1825: Coeur de Lion at the bier of his father, Thekla's song: or the voice of a spirit (Jan); The Suliote mother (Mar); Greek funeral chant, The parting song [rptd in Poetical Album 1830] (Apr); Records of woman 1: Imelda, The stranger in Louisiana (May); The bard's prophecy, A voyager's dream of land (July); Records of woman 2: Costanza, The Sicilian captive (Aug); The hour of romance, The lady of the castle (Sep); Records of woman 3: The bride of the Greek isle (Oct); Bernardo del Caprio, The landing of the Pilgrim Fathers in New England (Nov); The graves of a household, Records of woman 4: The Indian city (Dec). 1826: Records of woman 5: The Switzer's wife (Jan); The effigies (Feb); The birds of passage, The vigil of arms (Mar); Records of woman 6: The American forest-girl (Apr); Records of woman 7: Gertrude, The sunbeam (May); The invocation (June); The Vaudois valleys (July); The burial of William the Conqueror, The mourner for the Barmecides (Aug); The departure [later The departed] (Sep); Records of woman 8: Joan of Arc in Rheims, Roman girl's song (Oct); The sound of the sea, The Spanish chapel (Nov); The Kaiser's feast (Dec). 1827: The last tree of the forest (Jan); Records of woman 10: Pauline (Feb); The deserted house, The parting ship (Mar); The graves of martyrs (Apr); Breathings of spring (May); The memorial pillar (June); The grave of a poetess, Records of woman 11: Edith (July); The antique sepulchre (Aug); The image in lava, The streams (Sep); Joanna [later Juana], The subterranean stream (Oct); Fairy favours, The meeting of the brothers (Dec). 1828: Haunted ground (Jan); The chamois hunter's love, Mozart's requiem (Apr); The dying improvisatore, Song (If thou hast crushed) (May); The beings of the mind (June); The lyre's complaint (Sep); The boon of memory (Oct); The coronation of Inez de Castro, No more (Dec). 1829: The fountain of oblivion, Thekla at her lover's grave (Jan); Sadness and mirth (Feb); The image of the dead [later The image in the heart] (Apr); The ruined house (June); The nightingale's death song (Sep); A thought of the future (Nov). 1830: The diver (Jan); Music in a room of sickness (June); A thought of paradise (Dec). 1831: Flowers in a room of sickness, The sisters (Feb); The haunted house (Mar); The prayer in the wilderness (Aug). 1832: To a flower brought from the field of Grütli (May); The home of love, To the blue anemone (Sep); Cathedral hymn (Dec). 1833: Repose of the Holy Family: a sonnet, The rising of the dead (May); Words for melodies (Dirge at sea, Sister! since I met thee last, Far away, Echo song, The lyre and flower, Pilgrim's evening song to the evening star, The lonely bird) (Dec). 1834: Songs of Spain (The Rio

Verde song, The Zegri maid, The last one, The bird of Ebro, Spanish evening hymn, Old Spanish battle song) (Jan); The rock of Cader-Idris: a legend of Wales, Songs for evening music (1–9) [see later Songs for summer hours] (Mar); The palace of the Maremma (May); Records of passing thought: a series of nine sonnets [later Records of the spring of 1834 i–ix] (Aug); Records of passing thought: a series of nine sonnets [x–xvii later Records of the spring of 1834 x–xvii; xviii uncollected] (Sep). 1835: Thoughts during sickness [7 sonnets] (Mar).

Literary Magnet. 1826: To the author of The excursion and the Lyrical ballads [later to the poet Wordsworth] (Apr). 1827: Angel visits, Evening song of the Tyrolese peasants, The penitent's offering, The wings of the dove (July–Dec).

Monthly Magazine or British Register. 1826: The traveller at the source of the Nile (July); Casabianca [rptd in Poetical Album 1830] (Aug); The adopted child (Sep); The Chevalier d'Assas [later The fall of d'Assas: a ballad of France] (Oct); The illuminated city (Nov); The Queen of Prussia's tomb (Dec). 1827: The palm tree (Jan); The spells of home (Feb); The things that change [uncollected] (Mar); Kindred hearts, The old warrior's grave [later Marshall Schwerin's grave] (May); The world in the open air (July); Our daily paths (Oct). 1828: The parting of summer (Feb); The dreamer (June); The King of Arragon's lament for his brother (July); The forsaken hearth (Sep).

Dublin University Magazine. 1833: Dying bird's prophecy; Mignon's song in remembrance of Italy (July). 1835: The poetry of the Psalms (June).

Athenaeum. 1833: Prologue, by Mrs Hemans, to the tragedy of 'Fiesco' (16 Feb); Song (Look on me with thy cloudless eyes) (16 Nov).

The above list is not complete. Hemans published regularly in verse annuals, including The Amulet *(1824, 1826, 1831–4)*, Bijou: *(1828–9)*, Cameo, Christmas Box *(1829)*, Forget-me-not *(1829, 1834–5)*, Friendship's Offering *(1827, 1829)*, Juvenile Forget-me-not *(1826–9, 1834–5)*, Juvenile Keepsake *(1829)*, Juvenile Souvenir *(1829)*, Keepsake *(1829)*, Literary Souvenir *(1825–30, 1833)*, New Year's Gift *(1829–30)*, Pledge of Friendship *(1827–8)*, Poetical Album *(1828, 1830)*, Remembrance *(1830–1), and* Winter's Wreath *(1828–32)*. *See Boyle, Bibliographies, above.*

Letters, journals, etc

Chorley, H. F. Memorials of Mrs Hemans. 2 vols 1836, New York 1836. Contains extracts of letters.

See also Hughes, Smith, in §2.

Translations, commentary

Translations from Camoens and other poets with original poetry. Oxford and London 1818.
REVIEWS: Quart Rev Oct 1820; Ladies' Monthly Museum n.s. 13 1821.

Italian lit: no 2, The Alcestis of Alfieri. Edinburgh Mag Dec 1820, rptd as Scenes from the Alcestis of Alfieri, NMM Feb 1834 [without choruses]; no 3, Il conte di Carmognola, a tragedy, by Alessandro Manzoni, Edinburgh Mag Feb 1821; no 4, Caius Gracchus, a tragedy, by Monti, Edinburgh Mag June 1821.

Patriotic effusions of the Italian poets. Edinburgh Mag June 1821; 4 rptd as Patriotic lays of Italy, NMM Apr 1834.

Passages translated from the 'Iphigenia' of Goethe. NMM May 1832.

German studies no 1. Scenes and passages from the 'Tasso' of Goethe. NMM Jan 1834.

On a lady who died at sea. Trn of Camoens. Athenaeum 9 Aug 1834. Rev and rptd from Translations from Camoens and other poets.

'iana', imitations, elegies

Jewsbury, M. J. Lays of leisure hours. 1829.

Jewsbury, M. J. The three histories. 1830, Boston 1831.

Landon, L. E. Stanzas on the death of Mrs Hemans. NMM July 1835.

Browning, E. B. Stanzas addressed to Miss Landon. NMM Sep 1835; rptd as Stanzas on the death of Mrs Hemans written in reference to Miss Landon's poem on the same subject, in The seraphim and other poems, 1838.

Wordsworth, W. Extempore effusion upon the death of James Hogg. 1837. (1835 Athenaeum version lacks stanza on Hemans.)

Landon, L. E. Felicia Hemans. Fisher's Drawing-Room Scrap Book, 1838, Leipzig 1838.

Thackeray, W. M. Mrs Perkins's ball ['Miss Bunion']. In The Christmas books of Mr M. A. Titmarsh, 1846.

Landor, W. S. The heroines of England. Examiner 2 June 1849. To the author of Festus: on the classick and romantick. Examiner 29 Dec 1849; rptd in Heroic idylls, 1863.

Singer, O. The landing of the Pilgrim Fathers, a cantata. Cincinnati 1876.

Thomas, A. G. and C. V. Stanford. The swan and the skylark: a cantata. 1894. Words by Hemans, Keats, Shelley.

Ritchie, A. T. Felicia felix. In her Blackstick papers, 1908.

Coward, N. The stately homes of England. In his Operette, 1938.

Bishop, E. Casabianca. In her North and south, Boston 1946.

Woods, R. L. Famous poems and the little-known stories behind them. New York 1961.

This list, especially of musical settings, is not complete.

§2

Selected works of criticism and biography

Remarks on Mrs Hemans's poems. Edinburgh Mag Nov 1819.

The living poets of England. Literary Magnet n.s. 1 Mar 1826.

[Bancroft, G.] Mrs Hemans's poems. North Amer Rev n.s. 30 Apr 1827.

[Jeffrey, F.] Felicia Hemans. Edinburgh Rev 50 1829; rptd in his Contributions to the Edinburgh Review, 1844.

[Jewsbury, M. J.] Felicia Hemans: Literary sketches no 1. Athenaeum 12 Feb 1831.

Biographical particulars of celebrated persons, lately deceased: Mrs Hemans. NMM June 1835.

Landon, L. E. On the character of Mrs Hemans's writings. NMM Aug 1835.

[Moir, D. M.] Obituary notice of Mrs Hemans. Blackwood's Edinburgh Mag July 1835.

Mrs Hemans. Western Monthly Mag Sep 1835.

Obituary – Mrs Hemans. GM July 1835.

Chorley, H. F. Memorials of Mrs Hemans. 2 vols. 1836, Philadelphia 1836. Portions in Athenaeum 13 June, 27 June, 11 July 1835.
REVIEWS: Literary Gazette 3 Sep 1836, Dublin Rev Dec 1836, New York Rev Mar 1837, Christian Rev Sep 1837.

Hervey, T. K. Life and writings of Mrs Hemans: Art xii, The vespers of Palermo, etc. Dublin Rev 2, Dec 1836.

Lawrence, Mrs [Rose D'Aguilar]. The last autumn at a favourite residence, with other poems: and Recollections of Mrs Hemans. Liverpool and London 1836.

Norton, A. The poetry of Mrs Hemans. Christian Examiner 3rd ser 1 1836.

Thatcher, B. B. The poetry of Mrs Hemans. Religious Souvenir, Philadelphia 1836.

[Butler, W. A.] The poetesses of our day. Dublin Univ Mag Aug 1837.

Genius and character of Mrs Hemans. Amer Monthly Mag Mar 1837.

Hall, S. C. Felicia Hemans. In The book of gems: poets and artists of Great Britain vol 3, 1838.

[Hughes (Owen), Harriett Mary Browne.] Memoir of the life and writings of Mrs Hemans. In vol 1 of The works of Mrs Hemans, Edinburgh 1839.
REVIEWS: Christian Examiner Jan 1840; Mrs. Hemans and the picturesque school, Fraser's Mag Feb 1840; Religious character of the poetry of Mrs Hemans, Christian Rev Mar 1840.

[Tuckerman, H. T.] In Southern Literary Messenger May–June 1841; rptd as Introd, Poems of Felicia Hemans, ed R. W. Griswold, New York 1853.

Elwood, A. K. Memoirs of the literary ladies of England. 1843.
Griswold, R. Poets and poetry of the nineteenth century. New York 1844, 1874.
Wilson, J. In his Noctes ambrosianae vol 1, 4 vols Edinburgh 1844.
Howitt, W. In Homes and haunts of the most eminent British poets vol 1, New York 1846.
Gilfillan, G. Female authors. no 1 – Mrs Hemans. Tait's Edinburgh Mag June 1847; rptd in Eclectic Mag July 1847, Littel's Living Age 14 1847, and in Second gallery of literary portraits, Edinburgh 1850.
Bethune, G. W. British female poets. 1848, Freeport NY 1972.
[Moir, D. M. and W. H. Smith.] Mrs Hemans. Blackwood's Edinburgh Mag Dec 1848; rptd in Eclectic Mag Feb 1849, Littell's Living Age Feb 1849.
Sainte-Beuve, C.-A. In his Causeries de lundi: portraits des femmes et portraits littéraires, 16 vols Paris [1850], vols 3, 11, 15, 16.
Moir, D. M. In his Sketches of the poetical literature of the past half-century, Edinburgh 1852.
Rowton, F. In his The female poets of Great Britain, Philadelphia 1853, Detroit 1981.
Williams, J. In her The literary women of England, 1861.
Dixon, W. H. Lady Morgan's memoirs, autobiography, diaries and correspondence. 1863 (2nd edn).
Correll, J. Felicia Hemans: her life and poems, Dublin 1865.
L'Estrange, A. G. Letters of Mary Russell Mitford. 3 vols 1st ser 1870.
Rossetti, W. M. Introd to Poetical works of Mrs Felicia Hemans. Ed W. M. Rossetti 1873 etc [Moxon etc], New York 1902; rptd as Felicia Dorothea Hemans, Lives of famous poets, 1878.
Blackburne [Casey], E. O. Illustrious Irishwomen. 2 vos 1877. Vol 1.
Felicia Dorothea Hemans: Celebrated authoresses and their works no xiii. Englishwoman's Domestic Mag Aug 1879.
Robinson, A. M. F. Felicia Hemans. In The English poets: selections with critical introds vol 1, ed T. H. Ward, 1880, New York 1907.
Graves, R. P. Life of Sir William Rowan Hamilton, vols 1–3. Dublin 1882.
Oliphant, M. In her The literary history of England, 1882, New York 1970.
Robertson, E. S. Mrs Hemans. In English poetesses: a series of critical biographies, 1883, ch 6.
Schipper, J. Neuenglische metrik, vol 2. Englische metrik in historischer und systematischer enwickelung dargestelt, 2 vols Bonn 1888.
Whately, E. W. Personal and family glimpses of remarkable people. 1889.
Walford, L. B. Twelve English authoresses. 1892.
Smith, N. In her Noble womanhood, 1898.
[Ardo.] Mrs Hemans: a literary progenitress of Rudyard Kipling. Acad and Lit 24 Oct 1903.
Miles, A. H. In his The poets and poetry of the nineteenth century vol 8, 1905.
Saintsbury, G. In A history of nineteenth century literature, New York 1909.
Symons, A. In The romantic movement in English poetry, 1909.
Nicholson, F. Correspondence between Mrs Hemans and Matthew Nicholson. Memoirs and Proc of the Manchester Literary and Philosophical Soc (no 9) 54 1910.
Ledderbogen, W. F. D. Felicia Dorothea Hemans' lyrik, eine stilkritik. Unpbd diss, Univ of Heidelberg 1913.
Werner, E. Die verstechnik der Felicia Hemans. Unpbd diss, Friedrich-Alexander-Univ, Erlangen-Nüremberg, Germany, 1913.
Williams, I. A. Wordsworth, Mrs Hemans, and Robert Perceval Graves. London Mercury 6, May–Oct 1922.
Rupprecht, W. K. Felicia Hemans und die englischen beziehungen sur deutschen literatur. Anglia 48 1924.
Duméril, E. Une femme poète au déclin du romantisme anglais: Felicia Hemans. Toulouse and Paris 1929.
Cunningham, W. R. Mrs Hemans at Rydal Mount. TLS 23 Oct 1943.
Leslie, M. I. Felicia Hemans: the basis of a biography. Unpbd diss, Univ of Dublin 1943.
Wilson, E. Felicia Hemans. Unpbd diss, Harvard Univ 1952.
Saintsbury, G. In A history of English prosody vol 3, New York 1961.
Kutrieh, M. G. Felicia Hemans. Popular British romantic women poets. Unpbd diss, Bowling Green State Univ KY 1974.
Reiman, D. H. Introd to Poems, England and Spain, Modern Greece, etc, by Felicia Hemans. In The romantic context: poetry, New York 1978, vols 64–70.
Trinder, P. W. Mrs Hemans. [Cardiff] 1984.
Clarke, N. Ambitious heights: writing, friendship, love – the Jewsbury sisters, Felicia Hemans, and Jane Welsh Carlyle. 1990.
Jones, N. R. Felicia Hemans. In DLB 2nd ser, vol 92, Detroit 1990.
Barker-Benfield, B. Hogg–Shelley papers of 1810–12. Bodleian Lib Record 14 Oct 1991.
Anderson, J. M. Beyond Calliope: epics by women poets of the romantic period. Unpbd diss, Boston College 1993.
Feldman, P. R. Felicia Hemans and the mythologizing of Blake's Death. Blake: An Illus Quart 27 (Winter 1993–4).
Sweet, N. The bowl of liberty: Felicia Hemans and the romantic Mediterranean. Unpbd diss, Univ of Michigan 1993.
Berliner, D. G. The female romantic imagination. Unpbd diss, Univ of Texas at Dallas, 194.
Albergotti, C. D. Byron, Hemans, and the reviewers, 1807–1835. Unpbd diss, Univ of South Carolina 1995.
Edgar, C. L. The negotiations of the romantic popular poet: a comparison of the careers of Felicia Hemans and Lord Byron. Unpbd diss, New York Univ 1996.
Taylor, B. D. Felicia Hemans: the making of a professional poet. Unpbd diss, Loughborough Univ 1998. [NLS]

John Abraham Heraud 1799–1887

§1

The legend of St Loy, with other poems. 1820, 1825.
Tottenham: a poem. 1820.
The descent into hell. 1830 (anon), 1835 (acknowledged and rev with addns).
A philosophical estimate of the controversy respecting the divine humanity. 1831. Prose.
A vision of hell: a poem. Glasgow [1831].
An oration on the death of S. T. Coleridge. 1834 (3 edns). Prose.
The judgement of the flood. 1834, 1857 (rev).
The substance of a lecture on poetic genius. 1837. Prose.
The Roman brother: a tragedy. 1840.
The life and times of Savonarola .... 1843. Anon. Prose.
Salvator, the poor man of Naples. 1845 (priv ptd).
Videna, or the mother's tragedy: a legend of early Britain. 1854.
Shakspere: his inner life .... 1865. Prose.
The wreck of the London: a lyrical ballad. 1866.
The in-gathering, Cimon and Pero: a chain of sonnets .... 1870.
The war of ideas: a poem. 1871.
Uxmal: an antique love story; Macée de Léodepart: an historical romance. 1877.
Edited Sunbeam *(1838–9) and* Monthly Mag *(1839–42), and contributed to* Quart Rev, Athenaeum, Fraser's Mag *and others.*

Hon William Herbert 1778–1847

Collections

Works. 3 vols 1842, suppl 1846.

§1

Musae Etonenses .... Ed [Herbert] 3 vols 1795; 2 vols Eton 1817; Eton and London [1856].

Rhenus. [Oxford 1797?]; tr Eng 1831 (in Translations of Oxford Latin prize poems by N. L. Torre).
Ossiani Darthula graece reddita. By [W. H.]. 1801.
Select Icelandic poetry, translated from the originals with notes. 2 pts 1804–6.
Translations from the German, Danish etc; to which is added miscellaneous poetry. 2 pts 1804–6, 2 vols 1806 (as Miscellaneous poetry).
Helga: a poem in seven cantos. 1815, 1820.
Hedin, or the spectre of the tomb: a tale from the Danish history. 1820.
Pia della Pietra. 1820.
The wierd wanderer of Jutland: a tragedy. 1821, 1822. Includes Julia Montalban: a tale.
The Guahiba: a tale. 1822.
Iris. York 1826. In Latin.
Attila, or the triumph of Christianity. 1838, 1841 (as Attila, King of the Huns).
Sylvae recentiores. 1845, 1846.
Herbert also pbd sermons, and bks and articles on education, the game laws, church reform and botanical subjects, contributing notes to edns of Gilbert White's Selborne.

William Hersee fl. 1809–29

Poems. 1809.
Poems rural and domestic. Chichester 1810, 1811; London 1822.
The fall of Badajoz: a poem. Chichester 1812.
The battle of Vittoria: a poem. 1813.
A specimen of poems. [1817?]

Thomas Kibble Hervey 1799–1859

Collection
The poems . . . with a memoir. By Mrs T. K. Hervey. Boston and Cambridge MA 1866.

§1
Australia, with other poems. 1824, 1825.
The poetical sketch-book . . . . 1829 (includes 3rd edn of Australia).
The devil's progress: a poem. By the editor of The Court Journal. 1830 (anon), 1830 (acknowledged), 1849.
Gems of modern sculpture. 1831. Anon.
Illustrations of modern sculpture. 1834 (pbd in pts 1832–4). Prose and verse.
Edited Amaranth *(1839),* Athenaeum *(1846–53),* Friendship's Offering *(1824) and other annuals.*

William Hett 1759–1833

Miscellanies. London, Boston, Lincs, and Stamford 1794. Prose.
Occasional poems. Salisbury and London 1794.
Discourses on several subjects and occasions. 2 vols 1818. Prose.
Miscellanies on various subjects in prose and verse. 1823.
The death of Absalom: a poem. Doncaster 1824.
Author also of sermons.

John Hicklin, of Nottingham fl. 1826–67

Leisure hours. Nottingham 1826. Prose and verse.
Literary recreations, in prose and verse. 1835.
The history of Nottingham Castle. 1836. Prose.
Robin Hood: a collection of poems, songs and ballads . . . . Ed Hicklin 1866, 1867.
Author of guidebooks.

Rev Brian Hill 1756–1831

Henry and Acasto: a moral tale. 1786 (3 edns), 1798, 1816.
Observations and remarks in a journey through Sicily and Calabria. 1792. Prose.
Author of sermons.

Isabel Hill 1800–42

The poet's child: a tragedy in five acts. 1820, 1821.
Zaphna, or the amulet: a poem. 1823.
The first of May, or a royal love-match: a petite comedy. 1829. Prose.
Holiday dreams, or light reading in poetry and prose. London and Edinburgh 1829.
Brother tragedians: a novel. 3 vols 1834.
Brian the probationer, or the red hand: a tragedy. 1842. With memoir by B. E. Hill.
Translated de Staël's Corinne *(1833) and Chateaubriand's* The last of the Abencerages *(1835).*

Elizabeth Hitchener 1782?–1822

§1
The fire-side bagatelle, containing enigmas on the chief towns of England and Wales. 1818.
The weald of Sussex: a poem. 1822.
Enigmas, historical and geographical. By a clergyman's daughter. 1834. Anon.

§2
Letters . . . to P. B. Shelley. Ed W. E. Peck, New York 1926; Folcroft PA 1977; Norwood PA 1978.

Sarah Hoare 1777–1856

A poem on the pleasures and advantages of botanical pursuits, with notes and other poems. By a friend to youth. Bristol 1825. Anon. Had appeared previously in P. Wakefield, An introduction to botany, in 1818 and 1819.
Poems on conchology and botany, with plates and notes. London and Bristol 1831.
Memoirs of Samuel Hoare. Ed F. R. Pryor 1911. With H. Hoare.

Francis Hodgson 1781–1852

Collections
Leaves of laurel, Childe Harold's monitor. Ed D. H. Reiman, New York and London 1978 (facs reprints).
Saeculomastix and Sacred leisure. Ed D. H. Reiman, New York and London 1978 (facs reprints).

§1
The satires of Juvenal. Tr Hodgson 1807.
Lady Jane Grey: a tale . . . with miscellaneous poems. 1809; ed D. H. Reiman, New York and London 1977 (facs reprint).
Sir Edgar: a tale in two cantos . . . 1810; ed D. H. Reiman, New York and London 1977 (facs reprint).
Leaves of laurel. 1813.
Bonaparte, L. Charlemagne, or the church delivered . . . . Tr Hodgson and S. Butler 1815; Philadelphia 1815.
Childe Harold's monitor, or lines occasioned by the last canto of Childe Harold . . . . 1818. Anon.
The friends: a poem in four books. 1818.
Saeculomastix, or the lash of the age we live in . . . . 1819. Anon.
Sacred leisure, or poems on religious subjects. 1820.
Excerpta e testamento veteri . . . Tr [Hodgson] 1828. Anon.

Mythologia versibus latinis accommodata. Tr Hodgson 1832, 1850. Anon.

Sacred lyrics . . . . Ed Hodgson 1842, 1850 (as Lyricorum sacrorum).

§2

Hodgson, J. T. Memoir . . . with numerous letters from . . . Byron and others. 2 vols 1878; Folcroft PA 1975; Philadelphia 1978.

John Hodgson 1779–1845

§1

Poems, written at Lanchester. Newcastle and London 1807.

The nativity of Jesus Christ . . . . Newcastle 1810.

Poetic trifles. Whelpington 1832.

§2

Raine, J. A memoir. 2 vols 1857–8.

Author of local histories, memoirs and sermons.

Francis Allen Hodson fl. 1807–17

The last sigh of the bard of Snowdon . . . . [1817.]

A monody on the death of the Princess Charlotte . . . . 1817.

James Hogg 1770–1835

Hogg mss are scattered, but significant collections are available at the Nat Lib of Scotland, at the Turnbull Lib, Wellington NZ, and at Yale.

Bibliographies

Hogg, W. D. The first editions of the writings of Hogg. Pbns Edinburgh Bibl Soc 12 1924.

Batho, E. C. In Ettrick shepherd, Cambridge 1927. Includes Hogg's contributions to periodicals etc, many unrptd.

Pierce, F. E. Hogg: the Ettrick shepherd. YULG 5 1931.

Batho, E. C. Notes on the bibliography of Hogg. Library 4th ser 16 1935.

Simpson, L. In Hogg: a critical study, 1962.

Mack, D. S. Hogg's prose: an annotational listing. Stirling 1985.

Hughes, G. H. Hogg's verse and drama: a chronological listing. Stirling 1990.

Anderson-Currie, S. Preliminary census of Hogg editions in North American libraries. Columbia SC 1993.

Collections

Poetical works. 4 vols Edinburgh 1822, New York 1825.

Tales and sketches. 6 vols Glasgow 1837, London 1852.

Poetical works. 5 vols Glasgow 1838–40, 1852.

Works. Ed T. Thomson 2 vols Glasgow 1865–6, 1869, 1872, 1973.

The Stirling/South Carolina research edition of the collected works of James Hogg. Edinburgh 1995– (to be completed in 31 vols: projected completion date 2010). Vols already published are listed under §1, *below*.

Selections

Poems, selected by Mrs Garden. Glasgow 1886, 1887.

Selected poems. Ed W. Whyte. In Poets and poetry of the century, ed A. H. Miles 1891.

Selected poems. Ed J. C. Hadden, Glasgow 1893; ed W. Wallace, London 1903.

Works, letters and manuscripts. Ed R. B. Adam, Buffalo 1930 (priv ptd).

Selected poems. Ed J. W. Oliver, Edinburgh 1940.

Selected poems. Ed D. S. Mack, Oxford 1970.

Memoir of the author's life and familiar anecdotes of Sir Walter Scott. Ed D. S. Mack, Edinburgh 1972.

Selected stories and sketches. Ed D. S. Mack, Edinburgh 1982; New York 1982.

Tales of love and mystery. Ed D. Groves, Edinburgh 1985.

A shepherd's delight. Ed. J. Steel, Edinburgh 1985.

Selected poems and songs. Ed. D. Groves, Edinburgh 1986.

§1

For reviews of individual works by Hogg, see the Hogg entries in W. S. Ward, Literary reviews in British periodicals 1798–1820, *New York 1972; and W. S. Ward,* Literary reviews in British periodicals 1821–6, *New York 1977. Early reviews are discussed in many vols of the Stirling/South Carolina ed of James Hogg, above.*

Scottish pastorals, poems, songs etc. Edinburgh 1801; ed E. Petrie, Stirling 1988.

The mountain bard: consisting of ballads and songs, founded on facts and legendary tales. Edinburgh 1807, 1807 (with the autobiographical Memoir of the life of James Hogg), 1821 (3rd edn 'greatly enlarged'), 1839 (with The forest minstrel, *below*), Glasgow 1840, New York [184?].

The shepherd's guide: being a practical treatise on the diseases of sheep. Edinburgh 1807.

The spy. 52 nos Edinburgh 1810–11. Ed and largely written by Hogg.

The forest minstrel: a selection of songs. 1810, Philadelphia 1816.

The Queen's wake: a legendary poem. Edinburgh 1813 (reissued as 2nd edn), 1814 (reissued 1815), Baltimore 1815, Boston 1815, Philadelphia 1815, New York 1818, Edinburgh 1819, 1819, 1842, [1867]; Selections, 1879.

The hunting of Badlewe: a dramatic tale. Edinburgh 1814.

A selection of German Hebrew melodies. [1815?].

The pilgrims of the sun: a poem. Edinburgh 1815, Philadelphia 1815, Philadelphia 1816.

The Ettricke garland: being two excellent new songs. Edinburgh 1815; ed D. S. Mack, Greenock 1971. One song by Hogg; the other by W. Scott.

The poetic mirror: or the living bards of Britain. 1816, 1817, Philadelphia 1816, Philadelphia 1817; ed T. E. Welby, London 1929; ed D. Groves [with additions] 1990.

Mador of the moor: a poem. Edinburgh 1816, Philadelphia 1816.

Dramatic tales. 2 vols Edinburgh 1817.

The long pack: a Northumbrian tale. Newcastle 1817, 1818, Glasgow [1840?], [1850?]; ed G. Richardson, Newcastle 1877 etc.

To the editor of the Glasgow Chronicle. Edinburgh, 1818. Pamphlet.

The Brownie of Bodsbeck and other tales. 2 vols Edinburgh 1818, New York 1818, Philadelphia 1833, Pittsburg 1833; ed G. Lewis, Selkirk 1903; ed D. S. Mack, Edinburgh 1976.

A border garland. Edinburgh [1819?], [1828?] (as The border garland).

The Jacobite relics of Scotland. 2 sers Edinburgh 1819–21, 1 vol Paisley 1874.

Winter evening tales. 2 vols Edinburgh 1820, 2 vols New York 1820 (S. Campbell); 2 vols New York 1820 (Kirk & Mercein); 2 vols Edinburgh 1821 (2nd edn); 2 vols New York [1830?]; 2 vols Philadelphia 1836.

The history of Duncan Campbell. Glasgow 1821, 1824.

The three perils of man, or war, women, and witchcraft: a border romance. 3 vols 1822, Glasgow 1837 (as The siege of Roxburgh, in Tales and sketches, *above*); ed D. Gifford, Edinburgh 1972, 1989.

The royal jubilee: a Scottish mask. Edinburgh 1822; ed V. Bold in Studies in Hogg and his World 5 1994.

The three perils of woman, or love, leasing and jealousy: a series of domestic Scottish tales. 3 vols 1823, New York 1823, London 1827; ed D. Groves, A. Hasler and D. S. Mack, Edinburgh 1995; tr Fr, 1825.

The private memoirs and confessions of a justified sinner, written by himself. 1824 (anon), 1828 (as The suicide's grave), 1837 (rptd with alterations as Confessions of a fanatic, in Tales and sketches, *above*, and other Victorian collections), 1895 (as The suicide's grave); ed T. E. Welby 1924; ed A. Gide 1947; ed J. Carey 1969; ed D. Gifford 1978; ed J. Wain 1983; ed D. Groves 1991; ed R. Lewis 1992; ed J. A. Cuddon, 1994; tr Jap 1987, Du 1989.

Queen Hynde: a poem, in six books. 1825.
Select and rare Scottish melodies. [1829].
The shepherd's calendar. 2 vols Edinburgh 1829, New York 1829; ed D. S. Mack, Edinburgh 1995.
Critical remarks on the psalms of David. Edinburgh 1830. With W. Tennant.
Songs by the Ettrick shepherd now first collected. Edinburgh 1831, New York 1832, 1855, [1912], Oxford 1989.
Altrive tales collected among the peasantry of Scotland, and from foreign adventurers. Vol 1 only pbd 1832, 1835.
A father's new year's gift. 1832.
A queer book. Edinburgh 1832; ed P. D. Garside, Edinburgh 1995.
A series of lay sermons on good principles and good breeding. 1834.
Familiar anecdotes of Sir Walter Scott. New York 1834, Glasgow 1834 (as The domestic manners and private life of Sir Walter Scott), Edinburgh 1882; ed J. E. H. Thomson, Stirling 1909; ed D. S. Mack, Edinburgh 1972.
The works of Robert Burns. 5 vols Glasgow 1834–6 etc (vol 5 contains Hogg's Memoir of Burns), 1847, 1848, 1851, 4 vols 1895. Ed with William Motherwell.
Tales of the wars of Montrose. 3 vols 1835, Philadelphia 1836; ed G. Hughes, Edinburgh 1996.
A tour in the Highlands in 1803: letters by Hogg to Scott. Paisley 1888, Edinburgh 1986.
Highland tours . . . in 1802, 1803 and 1804. Ed W. F. Laughlan, Hawick 1981.
Anecdotes of Sir Walter Scott. Ed D. S. Mack, Edinburgh 1983. A different work from Familiar anecdotes of Sir Walter Scott, *above*.

Contributions to periodicals and to collaborative works.
There are detailed listings in the bibliographies by G. H. Hughes *and* D. S. Mack, *above.*

§2

Biography

[Lockhart, J. G.] In Peter's letters to his kinsfolk, 1819.
Wordsworth, W. Extempore effusion on the death of the Ettrick shepherd. Athenaeum 30 Nov 1835.
Groves, D. James Hogg: The growth of a writer. Edinburgh 1988.

Textual and bibliographical criticism

Mack, D. S. James Hogg's Altrive tales: an 1835 reissue. The Bibliotheck 5, no 6, 1969.
Mack, D. S. The transmission of the text of Hogg's Brownie of Bodsbeck. The Bibliotheck 8, no 1–2, 1976.
Mack, D. S. Notes on editing James Hogg's 'Storms'. The Bibliotheck 12, no 6, 1985.
Mack, D. S. James Hogg's second thoughts on The three perils of man. Stud in Scottish Lit, 21 1986.
Groves, D. Beethoven and Scottish poetry. The Bibliotheck 15, no 2 1988.
Lodge, P. The bush aboon Traquair: The first version rediscovered. In Papers given at the second James Hogg Society conference (Edinburgh 1985), ed G. H. Hughes, Aberdeen, 1988.
Mack, D. S. Hogg, Blackwood, and The shepherd's calendar. In Papers given at the second James Hogg Society conference (Edinburgh 1985), ed G. H. Hughes, Aberdeen 1988.
Groves, D. Four unrecorded book reviews by the Ettrick shepherd, 1811–1812. Stud in Scottish Lit 25 1990.
Groves, D. James Hogg: Alterations to the bibliography. N & Q n.s. 37 1990.
Garside, P. Three perils in publishing: Hogg and the popular novel. Stud in Hogg and his World 2 1991.
Hughes, G. H. The evolution of Tales of the wars of Montrose, Stud in Hogg and his World 2 1991.
Scott, P. A checklist of James Hogg scholarship since 1960. Columbia SC 1992.
Mack, D. S. The Stirling/South Carolina edition of James Hogg: thoughts on editorial policy. Stud in Hogg and his World 4 1993.
Garside, P. Vision and revision: Hogg's ms poems in the Turnbull library. Stud in Hogg and his World 5 1994. [DM]

Thomas Hogg, of Truro 1777–1835

St Michael's Mount in Cornwall: a poem. Truro 1811.
The influence of the holy Bible: a poem. Truro [1817].
The fabulous history of . . . Cornwall. Truro and London 1827.
Wrote also on Cornish mineralogy and mathematical geology.

Margaret Holford, the younger, later Hodson 1778–1852

Elegiac ode, to the memory of lieut.-colonel Vassall. Bristol 1808, 1819 (in Memoir of the life of lieutenant-colonel Vassall).
Wallace, or the fight of Falkirk: a metrical romance. 1809 (anon), 1810 (acknowledged); Philadelphia 1810.
Poems. 1811.
Margaret of Anjou: a poem in ten cantos. 1816; Philadelphia and Boston 1816.
The past, etc. London and Bath 1819.
Warbeck of Wolfstein. 3 vols 1820, 1847; tr Fr by Collet, Paris 1821. Prose.
Italian stories. Tr Holford, London and Chiswick 1823.
Lines to the memory of . . . G. H. Walker . . . . [1832?]
Quintana, D. M. J. Lives of . . . Balboa and Pizarro. Tr Hodson, Edinburgh 1832.

John Holland 1794–1872

§1

Sheffield Park: a descriptive poem. Sheffield 1820, 1859.
The cottage of Pella: a tale of Palestine . . . . Sheffield 1821.
The village of Eyam: a poem . . . . Ed J. Wilson, Macclesfield 1821.
The hopes of matrimony: a poem. 1822, 1836.
Flowers from Sheffield Park . . . . London and Sheffield 1827.
The pleasures of sight: a poem. Sheffield 1829.
The bazaar, or money and the church . . . By a Christian poet. Sheffield [1830?]. Anon.
Hutton, M. Sheffield Manor and other poems. Ed Holland, Sheffield 1831.
Tyne banks: a poetical sketch . . . By a visitor in Newcastle. Newcastle 1832. Anon.
Cruciana . . . . Liverpool 1835. Prose.
Diurnal sonnets. Sheffield 1851.
A poet's gratulation. Sheffield [1851].
Montgomery, J. Sacred poems and hymns. Ed Holland, New York 1854.

§2

Hudson, W. The life of J. Holland of Sheffield Park. 1874.
Edited Sheffield Mercury, *and wrote on Sheffield manufactures, fossil fuel, Nottingham and Sheffield antiquities and topography.*

William Holloway fl. 1792–1812

Dovedall Hall, or the fortunate exiles: a novel, interspersed with . . . poetry. Waymouth 1792.
The fate of Glencoe: an historical ballad. Waymouth 1792.
The baron of Lauderbrooke: a tale. 1800. Prose.
The peasant's fate: a rural poem, with miscellaneous poems. 1802; Boston 1802; Baltimore 1803; Wilmington 1808; London 1821 (4th edn).
Scenes of youth, or rural recollections . . . . 1803.

The chimney-sweeper's complaint. By the author of The peasant's fate. 1806; Philadelphia 1807. Anon.
The minor minstrel, or poetical pieces.... 1808.
The country pastor, or rural philanthropist.... 1812.
Also wrote on natural history.

Thomas Hood 1799–1845

Manuscripts

Poems, plays, letters. BL Add mss.
Poems, Bristol Univ Lib.
Poems, prose. Avon County Ref Lib.

Bibliographies

The most thorough bibliography is C. Goodrich's unpbd Yale thesis, A bibliography of the works of Hood, *1934, commented on in the unpbd Harvard diss on Hood by A. Whitley, 1950.*
Gilmour, J. Some uncollected authors, VII: Hood. BC 4 1955.

Collections

Poems [serious]. 2 vols 1846, 1846, 1851 (4th edn), 1853 (6th edn), 1857 (9th edn), 1858, 1859, 17th edn 1864 etc.
REVIEW: Athenaeum 24 Jan 1846.
Poems of wit and humour [excluding those in Hood's Own]. 1847, 1849, 1851, 1856 (7th edn), 1860 (9th edn), 1863 (12th edn), 1866 (16th edn), [1872] (19th edn), 1875.
The choice works of Thomas Hood. 4 vols New York 1852, 1853, 1857.
Poetical works, with some account of the author. 4 vols Boston 1856, 1857.
Works comic and serious, in prose and verse. Ed with notes by his son [T. Hood jr]. 7 vols 1862–3.
REVIEW: Athenaeum 11 Apr 1863.
Works. Ed E. Sargent 3 vols New York 1862, 6 vols 1870.
The serious poems. Ed S. Lucas with preface by T. H. the younger [1867], 1870; 2 vols 1876 (with Comic poems, *below*), 1886; illustr H. G. Fell 1901.
The comic poems. Ed S. Lucas with preface by T. H. the younger [1867], 2 vols 1876 (with Serious poems), 1885.
Works. Ed his son and daughter [F. F. Broderip] 10 vols 1869–73 (illustr), 11 vols 1882–4.
Poetical works. Ed W. M. Rossetti, illustr G. Doré 2 sers [1871–5], [1880].
Choice works, in prose and verse: including the cream of the comic annuals. With a life of the author [by R. H. Shepherd]. 1876, 1906.

Selections

Humorous poems. Ed E. Sargent, Boston 1856.
Miscellaneous poems. Ed E. Sargent, Boston 1858, New York 1862.
Passages from the poems. Illustr Jr Etching Club 1858.
[Select poems.] Tr Ger 1859, Rus 1864.
Hood's gems. 1861.
Early poems and sketches. Ed his daughter 1869.
[Select poems.] Ed J. B. Payne, illustr G. Doré 1870, 1872, 1880.
Songs and etchings. 1871. 7 poems by Jonson, Hood, Shelley, C. Kingsley, S. Evans, Longfellow.
Poems. Glasgow [1889].
The poetical works of Hunt and Hood. 1889.
[Selections.] In Poets and poetry of the century, ed R. Garnett, vol 2, 1891.
Humorous poems. Ed A. Ainger 1893.
Poems. Ed A. Ainger 2 vols 1897.
Poems. Ed W. Jerrold, Oxford 1906, 1907, 1911, 1920, 1935 (WC).
Poems, selected by A. Ingram. 1906.
Poems chosen by A. T. Quiller-Couch. [1908].
Selections. 1928.
Poems. Ed C. Dyment 1948.
Selected poems. Ed J. Clubbe, Cambridge MA 1970.
Whimsicalities and warnings. Ed J. Ennis 1970.
Hood winked. 1982.
Selected poems. Ed J. Flint 1992.
Thomas Hood, poems comic and serious. Ed P. Thorogood, Bramber 1995.

§1

Odes and addresses to great people. 1825 (anon), 1825, 1826. In Burlesque plays and poems, 1885. With J. H. Reynolds.
Whims and oddities in prose and verse. 1st ser 1826, 1829 (4th edn); 2nd ser 1827, 1829 etc; new edn, ser 1 and 2, 1854, 1861, 1871 as Oddities in prose and verse, 1874.
National tales. 2 vols 1827; Philadelphia 1839.
The plea of the midsummer fairies, Hero and Leander, Lycus the centaur and other poems. 1827, Philadelphia 1827, New York 1844.
The Epping hunt. Illustr Cruikshank 1829, 1830, new edn 1837, 1889, New York 1928.
The dream of Eugene Aram the murderer. Gem 1829; illustr W. Harvey 1831, 1832; other edns 1868, 1902; tr Welsh 1853; Ger 1861.
REVIEW: Athenaeum 26 Nov 1831.
Tylney Hall: a novel. 3 vols 1834, rev 1840, 1857 (Railway Lib), [1878].
Hood's own: or laughter from year to year [illustr; contains Literary reminiscences]. 1839, 1855; 2nd ser, with preface by his son, 1861; [1882] (People's edn, both sers).
Up the Rhine. '1840' [1839], 1840, Frankfurt 1840, New York 1852.
REVIEW: Athenaeum 7 Dec 1839.
The loves of Sally Brown and Ben the carpenter. [1840?] A song, 4to, single sheet.
The song of the shirt. Punch Xmas 1843, New York 1865; tr Fr 1895.
Whimsicalities: a periodical gathering, with illustrations by Leech. 2 vols '1844' [1843], 1870 (enlarged), [1878].
REVIEWS: Athenaeum 30 Dec 1843 and 16 Apr 1870.
Lamia: a romance. In W. Jerdan, Autobiography vol 1, 1852. A poem, written c. 1827.
The headlong career and woful ending of precocious piggy. Ed F. F. Broderip, illustr T. H. jr '1859' [1858], [1880].
Fairy land: recreation for the rising generation, by the late Thomas and Jane Hood, their son and daughter etc. Ed F. F. Broderip 1861 (for 1860).
REVIEW: Athenaeum 8 Dec 1860.
Sonnet to his sister-in-law, Marianne Reynolds. Winchester 1936. Limited edn of 15.
Sonnet written in a volume of Shakespeare. KSJ 13 1964.
Hood's work was frequently rptd throughout the century, especially in America. Among the many additional reprints are those of Boston [c. 1860]; New York 1860; illustr Foster 1871, 1872; illustr Doré 1872; [1874], [1875]; [1878]; [1880]; 2 vols 1881; 1886; 1 vol [1887]; [1890]; ed J. Ashton [1891]; ed F. C. Burnand 1907. Separate edns of individual poems were also produced in Britain and America, including Miss Kilmansegg and her precious leg, *1870, [1871], 1904, and* The haunted house, *1896 (introd A. Dobson).*

Periodicals edited by Hood

Gem: a literary annual. 1829. Vol 1 only.
Comic Annual. 11 vols 1830–42. Literary contributions mainly by Hood. No vol issued 1840–1.
REVIEWS: Athenaeum 10 Dec 1831, 17 Dec 1831, 16 Nov 1833, 19 Jan 1839.
New Monthly Magazine. 1841–3.
Hood's Magazine. 1–3 1884–5.
The following contain contributions by Hood:
London Magazine. July 1821–July 1823. Ed John Taylor, with Hood as assistant and contributor.
Forget-me-not (in which 'Ruth' first appeared).
Friendship's Offering (in which 'I remember, I remember' first appeared).

Sporting, with literary contributions by Hood et al. Ed 'Nimrod' (C. J. Apperley) 1838.
Literary Souvenir.
Dublin Univ Mag.
The children in the wood. 1865. Preface by Hood.
See Wellesley vol 5, pp. 374–5.

Letters

Mabbott, T. O. Letters of Leigh Hunt, Hood and Allan Cunningham. N & Q 23 May 1931.
Letters of Hood from the Dilke papers in the British Museum. Ed L. Marchand, New Brunswick NJ 1945.
Whitley, A. Hood and Dickens: some new letters. HLQ 14 1951.
Parker, W. M. The stockbroker author. Quart Rev 290 1952. Includes excerpts from unpbd letters.
MS collections in the Columbia University libraries: a descriptive list. New York 1959.
Alexseev, M. P. (ed). In Niezdannye pisma inostrannykh pisateley 18–19 vekov 12 Leningradskikh rukopisnysh sobraniy, Moscow 1960.
Shuman, R. B. A whimsical letter of Hood. N & Q July 1963. Reply by P. F. Morgan, Oct 1963.
Morgan, P. F. Corrections in some letters of Hood. N & Q July 1963.
Morgan, P. F. (ed. Letters of Thomas Hood. Edinburgh 1973.

§2

Horne, R. H. In his A new spirit of the age vol 2, 1844.
Hall, Mrs S. C. A memory of Hood. Littell's Living Age 6 1845.
Gilfillan, G. In his A gallery of literary portraits vol 2, 1852.
Balmanno, Mrs M. Lamb and Hood. In her Pen and pencil, New York 1858.
[Broderip, F. F. and T. Hood jr.] Memorials of Hood collected by his daughter, with a preface and notes by his son. 2 vols 1860.
REVIEW: Athenaeum 7 July 1860.
Masson, D. Hood. Macmillan's Mag Aug 1860.
Thackeray, W. M. On a joke I once heard from the late T. Hood. In his Roundabout papers, 1863.
[Lawrance, H.?]. Recollections of Hood. Br Quart Rev 46 1867.
Cook, E. Poor Hood. In her Poetical works, 1870.
Cowden Clarke, C. On the comic writers of England, 15: Hood. GM Jan 1872.
Lowth, G. T. The Hood controversy on A poem reclaimed. Temple Bar Sep 1872.
Lucy, H. W. Hood: a biographical sketch. GM Jan 1875.
Cowden Clarke, C. and M. In their Recollections of writers, 1878.
Wainewright, T. G. In his Essays and criticisms, ed W. C. Hazlitt, 1880.
Elliot, A. Hood in Scotland. Dundee 1885.
Fields, J. T. In his Some noted princes, authors and statesmen in our time, ed J. Parton, New York 1885.
Mason, E. T. In his Personal traits of British authors vol 4, 1885.
Ashton, J. The true story of Eugene Aram. In Eighteenth-century waifs, 1887.
Henley, W. E. In his Views and reviews, 1890.
Dudley, T. U. Hood: punster, poet, preacher. Harper's Mag Apr 1891.
Saintsbury, G. In his Essays in English literature 1780–1860 ser 2, 1895.
Rolfe, W. J. Hood. Poet-Lore 8 1896.
Spielmann, M. H. Hood and Punch. Bookman (New York) Oct 1899.
Oswald, E. Hood und die soziale Tendenzdichtung seiner Zeit. Wiener Beiträge zur Englischen Philologie 19 1904.
Jerrold, W. Hood: his life and times. 1907.
Canby, H. S. Hood as a serious poet. Dial 45 1908.
More, P. E. Thomas Hood. National (New York) 26 Aug 1909; rptd in his Shelburne essays vol 7, New York 1910.
Shelley, H. C. Hood's homes and friends. In his Literary bypaths in old England, Cambridge MA 1909.
Olivero, F. Hood and Keats. MLN 28 1913.
Hudson, W. H. Hood: the man, the wit, and the poet. In his A quiet corner in a library, Chicago 1915.
Swann, J. H. The serious poems of Hood. Manchester Quart 51 1925.
Jerrold, W. Hood and Charles Lamb: the story of a friendship. 1930. Includes reprint of Literary reminiscences.
Clubbe, J. Victorian forerunner: the later career of Thomas Hood. Durham NC 1968.
Jeffrey, L. N. Thomas Hood. New York 1972 (Twayne's English Authors).

Samuel Hoole 1757–1839

Modern manners, in a series of familiar epistles. 1781, 1782 (as Modern manners, or the country cousins). Anon.
Aurelia, or the contest: an heroi-comic poem .... 1783. Anon.
Edward, or the curate: a poem. 1787.
Poems: consisting of modern manners .... 2 vols 1790.
Anecdotes representing the life of .... J. Hoole. 1803. Prose.
Poems on several occasions arising in real life. 1824.
Translated Leeuwenhoek and wrote on religion and navigation.

Caroline Horwood, later Baker fl. 1801–40

Trifles for children. 3 pts 1801–2. Prose.
The castle of Vivaldi ...: a novel. 1810, 1840. Prose.
The deserted boy, or cruel parents: a tale of truth .... Philadelphia 1817, 1825.
Original poetry for young minds. 1818 (2nd edn), 1819 ('2nd edn'), 1822, [1825], [1835] (6th edn).
Drawing-room tales ... by different authors. Ed Mrs Baker [1820?].
Little Emma and her father: a lesson for proud children. Philadelphia 1820, 1825.
Blue Beard, or the effects of female curiosity: in easy verse. 1821, 1823.
The brother and sister, or the advantages of good behaviour. Philadelphia 1825.

Miss E. Horwood fl. 1815–35

Instructive amusement for young minds, in original poetry. 1815.
Original poetry for little people. 1835, [1860?].

Mary Arnald Houghton fl. 1815–22

Emilia of Lindinau, or the field of Leipsic: a poem in four cantos. 1815 (2 edns); Baltimore 1816; Philadelphia 1816.
The mysteries of the forest. 3 vols 1822 (2nd edn). Prose.

W. House fl. 1821–8

Original hymns. 1821, 1828.

J. J. Howard fl. 1807–16

Ovid. The metamorphoses. Tr Howard 2 vols 1807.
Poems on different subjects. Ed M. Howard, Falmouth 1816.

Nathaniel Howard fl. 1804–30

Bickleigh Vale, with other poems. York and London 1804; Devonport 1856.
Dante Alighieri. The inferno. Tr Howard 1807.
On Persian poetry. Plymouth 1830. Prose.
Compiler of Latin and Greek vocabularies for schools.

Samuel Howell fl. 1820–7

The wandering minstrel: a collection of original poems.... 1820 (anon), 1827 (acknowledged).

Charles Hoyle fl. 1799–1830

The caldron, or follies of Cambridge: a satire. Winchester [1799]. Anon.
Moses viewing the promised land: a Seatonian prize poem. Cambridge 1804, 1808 (in Musae seatonianae vol 2).
Paul and Barnabas at Lystra.... Cambridge and London 1806.
Exodus: an epic poem.... 1807.
Three days at Killarney, with other poems. 1828. Anon.
The pilgrim of the Hebrides: a lay... By the author of Three days at Killarney. 1830. Anon.
Author of sermons.

John Clarke Hubbard d. 1805

Jacobinism: a poem. 1801 (anon, 2 edns, the 2nd acknowledged).
The triumphs of poesy: a poem. 1803.
Author of sermons.

Rev George Hughes 1788?–1830

Emmanuel!: a poem. By a graduate of Oxford. 1817. Anon.
Horae viaticae. 1818.
Madeline! A tale. 1818.
The last sigh of the Moor: a poem. 1820.
Poems. 1822.

John Hughes, also 'Old Tom of Oxford' 1790–1857

Herculaneum: carmen latinum, in theatro Sheldoniano recitatum. Oxford 1811.
Ode recited... on the visit of the Prince Regent and the foreign potentates. Oxford 1814.
The asses' skin memorandum book. 1820.
The new Christmas budget... By 'Old Tom of Oxford'. 1820.
The radical harmonist... the goose's apology: a Michaelmas ode. By 'Old Tom of Oxford'. 1820.
Solomon Logwood: a radical tale. By 'Old Tom of Oxford'. 1820 (4 edns).
Types of the times. By 'Old Tom of Oxford'. 1820.
Lays of past days.... 1850. Anon.
Artist and author of travel accounts.

John Hugman fl. 1808–36

The Halesworth dunciad: a satire on pedantry. Halesworth 1808. Anon.
Original poems... By a traveller. Brighton 1825; Clare 1825; Colchester 1825; Cambridge 1825 (2 edns), 1826; Halesworth 1827, 1828, 1829 (2 edns), 1830, 1832 (2 edns), 1833 (2 edns), 1834 (2 edns), 1835, 1836. Anon.

Anne Hunter, Mrs John, formerly Home 1742–1821

Collection

Rogers.

§1

Poems. 1802, 1803.
A new ballad entitled... The times. [1804?] (broadsheet).
The sports of the genii. 1804, 1816.
Some of her verse was pbd set to music.

John Hunter fl. 1798–1805

A tribute to the manes of unfortunate poets.... 1798, 1802, 1805 (as Poems).

Lydia Howard Huntley, later Mrs Charles Sigourney 1791–1865

Collections

Select poems. Philadelphia 1838 (3rd edn), 1841, 1842, 1843, 1844, 1845, 1847, 1848, 1849, 1850, 1852, 1854, 1856, 1857; selection New York 1846 (in G. C. de Rossi, The last supper).
The poetical works. Ed F. W. N. Bayley 1850; London and Edinburgh 1851; London 1852, 1854, 1857; Philadelphia [186-?]; London 1863.

§1

Moral pieces, in prose and verse. Hartford CT 1815.
Traits of the aborigines of America: a poem. Cambridge MA and Boston 1822.
Poems. By the author of Moral pieces. 1827 (anon); Boston, Hartford CT and New York 1827; Philadelphia 1834 (acknowledged), 1836; New York [1841]; Philadelphia 1842, 1846, 1849; New York 1851, 1853; Philadelphia 1854; New York 1860, 1875.
Lays from the west. Ed J. Belcher 1834.
Poetry for children. Hartford CT 1834 (anon), 1836 (attributed).
Sketches. Philadelphia 1834; Amherst MA 1839, 1840, 1842, 1844. Prose.
Lays of the heart, with Oriska and other poems. [1835?]
Simple tales for my own children, in poetry and prose. [1835?]
Zinzendorff and other poems. New York and Boston 1835, 1836; New York 1837.
Pretty poetry for little children. [1840?] With A. Sigourney and Mrs Baker.
Pocahontas and other poems. 1841; New York 1841, 1844, 1855, 1864.
Poems religious and elegiac. 1841.
Poetry for seamen. Boston 1845.
Scenes in my native land. 1845; Boston 1845; London 1848, 1852, [1902?]. Prose.
The coronal, or tales and pencilings in poetry and prose. London and Edinburgh 1848, 1850.
Illustrated poems. Philadelphia 1849, 1853, 1854, 1860, 1865; New York 1869.
Poems for the sea. Hartford CT 1850.
The western home and other poems. Philadelphia 1854.
Sayings of the little ones and poems for their mothers. Buffalo NY and New York 1855.
Gleanings. Hartford CT and New York 1860.
The man of Uz and other poems. Hartford CT 1862.

§2

Haight, G. S. Mrs Sigourney, the sweet singer of Hartford. 1930.
Edited annuals and educational books for children, and was frequently included in anthologies.

William Hurn 1754–1829

Heath-hill: a descriptive poem in four cantos. Colchester and London 1777.
The blessings of peace and the guilt of war: a lyric poem. 1784.
Psalms and hymns, the greater part original. Ipswich 1813; London 1824 (as Hymns and spiritual songs), 1833.
Also some religious pbns in prose.

Hyman Hurwitz 1770–1844

A Hebrew dirge.... Tr S. T. Coleridge 1817, 1820 (as The tears of a grateful people...) (4 edns).

The knell: an elegy on George the Third .... Tr W. Smith, Thurso 1827.
Wrote on the Hebrew language and translated Hebrew tales.

James Hyslop 1798–1827

Poems, with a sketch of his life and notes on his poems. Ed P. Mearns, Glasgow 1887.

Henry Ingram fl. 1815–44

The flower of Wye: a poem in six cantos. 1815.
Matilda, a tale of the crusades: a poem. London and Halifax 1830.
Zuleima: a tale of Persia, Cain, St Paul at Malta, with other poems .... Halifax and London 1844.

Samuel William Henry Ireland, also 'Anser Pen-drag-on', 'Cervantes', 'Charles Clifford', 'Flagellum', 'Paul Persius', 'Satiricus Sculptor' 1777–1835

Some of the attributions of pseudonymous works are doubtful.

§1

Miscellaneous papers and legal instruments under the hand and seal of William Shakespeare. Ed S. Ireland 1796.
An authentic account of the Shaksperian manuscripts. 1796. Prose.
The abbess: a romance. 4 vols 1799; 3 vols Baltimore 1801, 1802; London 1834; tr Sp 2 vols Madrid 1822, Barcelona 1836. Prose.
Vortigern: an historical tragedy; and Henry the Second: an historical drama, supposed to be written by the author of Vortigern. 2 pts 1799, 1832 (with facs of portions of the forged ms). Anon.
Rimualdo, or the castle of Badajos: a romance. 4 vols 1800. Prose.
Ballads in imitation of the antient. London and Bristol 1801.
Mutius Scaevola, or the Roman patriot: an historical drama. 1801.
A ballade, wrotten on the feastynge and merrimentes of Easter Maunday, laste paste. By 'Paul Persius', a learnedd clerke. 1802. Anon.
Rhapsodies. 1803.
The angler: a didactic poem. By 'Charles Clifford'. 1804. Anon.
The woman of feeling. 4 vols 1804. Prose.
The confessions of W. H. Ireland, containing the particulars of his fabrication of the Shakspeare manuscripts, together with anecdotes and opinions of many distinguished persons. 1805; ed R. G. White, New York 1874. Prose. An expansion of An authentic account, *above*.
Effusions of love from Chatelar to Mary, Queen of Scotland, interspersed with songs, sonnets and notes explanatory, by the translator. 1805, 1808. Anon.
Gondez the monk: a romance of the thirteenth century. 4 vols 1805. Prose.
All the blocks! Or an antidote to 'All the talents': a satirical poem. By 'Flagellum'. 1807, 1808. Anon.
The catholic: an historical romance. 3 vols 1807. Prose.
Stultifera navis, or the modern ship of fools. 1807; Philadelphia 1807. Anon.
The fisher boy: a poem. By 'H. C. Esq'. [1808.] Anon.
The sailor boy: a poem. By 'H. C. Esq'. 1809, 1815, 1822. Anon.
The cottage-girl: a poem. By 'H. C. Esq'. London, Bristol and Bath 1810. Anon.
Monody on the death of W. Cavendish. 1811. Anon.
Sketch of the character of the late Duke of Devonshire. 1811. Anon. With [W. Cavendish].
The death of Bonaparte. By 'Cervantes'. York 1812. Anon.
Neglected genius: a poem, illustrating the untimely and unfortunate fate of many British poets, containing imitations of their different styles. 1812.
The state doctors, or a tale of the times: a poem in four cantos. By 'Cervantes'. 1812. Anon.
Chalcographimania, or the portrait-collector and print-seller's chronicle: a humourous poem. By 'Satiricus Sculptor'. 1814. Anon.
Jack Junk, or the sailor's cruise on shore. 1814.
Scribbleomania, or the printer's devil's polichronicon. By 'Anser Pen-drag-on'. 1815. Anon.
Voltaire. The maid of Orleans. Tr [Ireland] 1822. Prose.
The life of Napoleon Bonaparte. 4 vols 1828. Prose.

§2

Grebanier, B. D. N. The great Shakespeare forgery ... 1966.
Ireland also pbd on European history and topography, and produced miscellaneous hackwork, some of which is listed in BL Cat.

James Jennings, of Huntspill fl. 1794–1828

Collection

'Zummerzetzhire' rhymes: a collection of poems. 1889 (2 edns), 1970. Contains poems by Jennings.

§1

The times: a satirical rhapsody. Pt 1 Bristol 1794.
Poems, consisting of The mysteries of Mendip, The magic ball .... 1810.
The prospects of Africa, with other poems. 1814.
Ornithologia, or the birds: a poem .... 1828, 1829.
The pleasures of ornithology: a poem. 1828.
Edited The family cyclopaedia *(1821), and wrote on language, phrenology, literary institutions and cooking.*

John Heneage Jesse 1815–1874

Mary Queen of Scots and other poems. 1829.
Tales of the dead and other poems. 1830.
Memoirs of the court of England during the reign of the Stuarts. 4 vols 1840, 3 vols 1855 (rev), 1857. Prose.
Memoirs of the court of England from the revolution in 1688 to the death of George the Second. 3 vols 1843. Prose.
George Selwyn and his contemporaries. 4 vols 1843–4, 1844, 1882; New York 1882; Boston [19—?]; London 1901; Boston 1902. Prose.
Memoirs of the pretenders and their adherents. 2 vols 1845, 1858, etc. Prose.
Literary and historical memorials of London. 2 vols 1847. Ser 2: London and its celebrities, 2 vols 1850. Both sers 3 vols London and Guildford 1871 (as London: its celebrated character and remarkable places); Boston 1901 (as Historical and literary memorials). Prose.
London: a fragmentary poem. 1847, 1871.
The maid of Albret, or the first love of Henry of Navarre. 1850.
Memoirs of King Richard the Third ... with an historical drama on the battle of Bosworth. 1862; New York 1894; London 1900, 1901; Boston 1902. Prose and verse.
Memoirs of the life and reign of George the Third. 3 vols 1867; 5 vols Boston 1902. Prose.
Memoirs of celebrated Etonians. 2 vols 1875, 1901; Boston 1902. Prose.
Author and editor of numerous histories and antiquarian works, including memoirs.

Mary Anne Jevons, Mrs Thomas 1795–1845

Poems for youth. By a family circle. Pt 1 Liverpool and London 1820; 2 vols (2 pts) London 1821, 1841. Anon. With others.

Sonnets and other poems, chiefly devotional. Liverpool and London 1845.
The syrens and other poems. [1879.]
Contributed to several annuals and edited The Sacred Offering *(1831–8).*

Rev W. R. Johnson fl. 1806–11

The history of England, in easy verse. 1806, 1810.
The history of Greece, in easy verse. 1807, 1811.
The history of Rome, in easy verse. 1808, 1811.
Goldsmith's grammar of geography, rendered into easy verse. 1809.

George Jones, also 'Leigh Cliffe' fl. 1819–36

Parga: a poem. 1819.
The protocol, or selections from the contents of a red box .... 'Ed' 'Leigh Cliffe' 1820 (2 edns).
Supreme bon ton and bon ton by profession: a novel. By the author of Parga. 3 vols 1820. Anon.
Temptation: a novel. By 'Leigh Cliffe'. 3 vols 1823.
Margaret Coryton. By 'Leigh Cliffe'. 3 vols 1829. Prose.
Anecdotal reminiscences of distinguished ... characters. By 'Leigh Cliffe'. 1830. Prose.
The sceptic and other poems. 1835.
The expatriated: a tale of modern Poland. 1836.
The pilgrim of Avon. By 'Leigh Cliffe'. London and Stratford-upon-Avon 1836; London and Stratford-upon-Avon 1890 (4th edn).

Jacob Jones fl. 1824–66

The fall of Constantinople: a poem .... 1824.
Longinus: a tragedy .... 1827 (2nd edn).
The stepmother: a tragedy .... 1829.
The Anglo-Polish harp, or songs for Poland. 1836.
Spartacus ...: a tragedy. 1837 (2 edns); Philadelphia and New York [1837?] (as The gladiator).
The cathedral bell: a tragedy. 1839.
Regulus ...: a tragedy. 1841.
A century of sonnets. 1866.

John Jones, servant b. 1774

The fable of the merchant, the slave and the lion .... 1824.
Attempts in verse .... Ed R. Southey 1831 (includes memoir).
Hints to servants, being a poetical ... version of ... Swift's ... Directions. 1843.

John Gale Jones 1769–1838

An invocation to E. Quin .... [1803], [1804].
Galerio and Nerissa, including ... poetic effusions .... 1804. Anon. Prose and verse.
Wrote also on whooping cough and engaged in political controversy.

Joseph Jones, perpetual curate of Repton 1782–1856

Poems. 1821.
Serious musings. 1822.
Moral hours: a poem. 1823.
The martyrs: a poem. 1824.
The closet lyre. London and Warrington 1832.
A lay for my country. Oxford '1733' [1833].
Osborne, or the country gentleman. Oxford 1833. Prose.
Rhymes. [1842.]
Sacred rhymes. London and Derby [1842].
Reppendune: a moral rhyme. Derby 1844.
The Christian triad, or faith, hope and charity: a sacred rhyme. London and Derby 1845.
Christianity and the Christian. London and Derby 1849. Prose and verse.
Cottage verse: a collection of hymns and spiritual songs. London and Derby [1852].
The imagination: a lecture. Derby and London 1852. Prose.
Pbd sermons, biblical commentary and other miscellaneous prose, and edited hymns and devotional works.

Mary Elizabeth Jones, formerly Pye d. 1834

Poems on several occasions. Stoke Park 1802.
Poems. 1826.

Thomas Jones fl. 1803–20

Poems ... and phantoms, or the Irishman in England: a farce. 1803. Verse and prose.
Confin'd in vain, or a double to do: a farce. 1805. Prose.
The sons, or family feuds: a tragic play .... 1809. Prose and verse.
Miscellanies, in prose and verse. 1820 (2 issues).

Lucy Joynes, of Nottingham d. 1851

Original poetry for infant and juvenile minds, in two parts. [1817?]; Wellington and London 1825 (3rd edn); London and Wellington 1833 (5th edn); London 1838 (6th edn).
Occasional and miscellaneous poems. Nottingham and London 1820.
Memoir of a pious child. 1829. Prose.
Mental pictures in verse, for infants. London and Nottingham 1832.
History and rhyme for young readers: the four English kings William, with notes. London and Nottingham 1834.

John Keats (1795–1821)

The largest collection of mss is in the Houghton Library at Harvard, although the Pierpont Morgan Library New York also has an important collection of literary mss. The principal English collection of poetical mss is at the BL. Summary account of mss given in The poems of John Keats, *ed J. Stillinger 1978, appendix V, and a fuller listing in* IELM. *See also* The manuscripts of the younger romantics: John Keats, *ed Stillinger 7 vols New York 1985–8, listed §2, below.*

Bibliographies and reference works

Johnson, R. U. Note on some volumes now in America once owned by Keats. Keats–Shelley Memorial Bull 2, 1913.
Williamson, G. C. The Keats letters, papers, and other relics forming the Dilke bequest in the Hampstead Public Library, 1914.
Baldwin, D. L., L. N. Broughton et al. A concordance of the poems of Keats. Washington DC 1917, Gloucester MA 1963.
Wise, T. J. A bibliography of the writings of John Keats. In The John Keats memorial volume, 1921.
Block, A. The book collector's vade mecum. 1932, 1938 (rev). Contains Keats checklist.
Perry, W. A bibliography of Keats. TLS, 13 Dec 1934.
MacGillivray, J. R. A bibliography and reference guide, with an essay on Keats' reputation. Toronto 1949.
Thorpe, C. D. In English romantic poets: a review of research, ed T. M. Raysor, New York 1950, 1956 (rev).
Keats–Shelley Jnl. 1952– . Contains annual bibliography. Bibliographies to June 1962 rptd in Keats, Shelley, Byron, Hunt and their circles: a bibliography, ed D. B. Green and E. G. Wilson, Lincoln NE 1964. Bibliographies from 1 July 1962 to 31 Dec 1974

rptd in Keats, Shelley, Byron, Hunt and their circles: a bibliography, ed R. A. Hartley, Lincoln NE 1978.

Rice, P. M. John Keats: a classified bibliography of critical writings on John Keats's poems 1947–1961. BB 24, 1965.

Catalog of books and manuscripts at the Keats–Shelley Memorial House in Rome. Boston 1969.

Owings, F. N. The Keats library: a descriptive catalogue. 1978.

Becker, M. J., R. J. Dilligan and T. K. Bender. A concordance to the poems of John Keats. New York 1981.

Hearn, R. B. et al. Keats criticism since 1954: a bibliography. Salzburg 1981.

Rhodes, J. W. Keats's major odes: an annotated bibliography of the criticism. Westport CT 1984.

Gee, C. M. and J. Knight. John Keats 1795–1821: a select booklist. 1985.

Pollard, D. A KWIC concordance of the letters of John Keats. Hove 1989.

Okada, A. Japanese scholarship on Keats. Keats–Shelley Jnl 39, 1990.

Collections

The poetical works of Coleridge, Shelley, and Keats. Paris 1829, Philadelphia 1831, 1832, Buffalo NY 1834, Philadelphia 1835, 1836, 1838, 1839, 1844, 1847, 1849, 1853, nd.

The poetical works of Howitt, Milman, and Keats. Philadelphia 1840, 1846, 1847, 1849, 1852.

Poetical works. 1840 (Smith's Standard Lib), 1841, 1844.

Poetical works. 1846, 1847, 1849, 1850, 1851, 1853.

Poetical works. New York 1846 (Lib of Choice Reading), 1848, 1850, 1855, 1857.

Poetical works. Memoir by R. M. Milnes (Lord Houghton). 1854, 1856, 1858, 1861, 1866, 1868, 1869 (rev), 1871, 1876; illustr G. Scharf 1854, 1862, 1866.

Poetical works. Life by J. R. Lowell. Boston, New York and Philadelphia 1854, Boston 1859 (British Poets), 1863, 1864, 1866, 1871.

Poetical works. Memoir by R. M. Milnes, Philadelphia 1855 'elegantly' illus.

Poetical works, reprinted from the early editions. London and New York [1868] (Chandos Classics), [1874?] (Lansdowne Poets). The first annotated edn. Reissued several times, usually without indication of date, sometimes by London publisher alone.

Poetical works. Memoir by W. M. Rossetti, illustr T. Seccombe. [1872] (Moxon's Popular Poets), [1880], 1888, [1878] (not illus).

Poetical works. Memoir and illustrations by W. B. Scott. [1873], 1894, 1880 (not illus) (Excelsior Ser), 1893 (Routledge's Poets for the People), 1894 (illus).

Poetical works. Memoir by J. R. Lowell. New York 1873, nd.

Poetical works, chronologically arranged. Memoir by Lord Houghton. 1876, 1883, 1886, 1890, 1891, 1892, 1899, 1901, 1906 (Aldine), 1914 (Bohn), Boston 1877, 1882, 1887, Toronto 1900.

Poetical works of Coleridge and Keats. Life by J. R. Lowell. Boston and New York 1878, [1888?].

Poetical works. New York 1880, 1881, 1885, 1891, nd.

Poetical works and other writings, now first brought together. Ed H. B. Forman 4 vols 1883, 1889 (rev) (Lib edn); Poetry and prose, 1890 (suppl vol).

Letters and poems. Ed J. G. Speed 3 vols New York 1883.

Poetical works. Ed F. T. Palgrave 1884 etc (Golden Treasury).

Poetical works. Ed W. T. Arnold 1884, 1884 (large-paper), 1888, 2 vols New York 1889. Basis of Globe edn 1907 etc.

Poetical works. Ed H. B. Forman 1884, 1885, 1889, 1895; illustr W. H. Low 1895, 1896, 1898, 1902, Philadelphia 1895, 3 vols 1891 (not illus), 2 vols New York 1895, 1 vol 1895.

Poetical works. Ed J. Hogben 1885, 1886, nd (Canterbury Poets).

Poetical works. Introd by A. Lang 1890?, [1911].

Poetical works. London and Sydney [1891?] (Newbery Classics).

Poems. Ed F. S. Ellis, Hammersmith 1894 (W. Morris's Kelmscott edn), 1974 (photo facs).

Poems. Ed G. Thorn Drury, introd by R. Bridges 2 vols 1896, London and New York 1896, 1905 (ML).

Poems. Ed A. Bates, Boston and London 1896 (Athenaeum Press Ser).

Poems. Illustr R. A. Bell, introd by W. Raleigh, London and New York 1897, 1898 (Endymion Ser).

Poems. Ed C. J. Holmes, decorated by Charles Ricketts 2 vols 1898.

Complete poetical works and letters. Ed H. E. Scudder, Boston and New York 1899, 1925 (without biographical introd) (Cambridge edn).

Poetical works. Ed H. B. Forman 'and Mrs Keats', New York [1900?]. Mrs Keats's precise identity is unclear.

Complete works. Ed H. B. Forman 5 vols Glasgow 1900–1, 1921–4, New York [1900–1].

Poetical works. 1901 etc, Oxford 1927 (rev) (WC).

Poems. New York 1902.

Poetical works. Ed W. S. Scott, London and New York 1902 (Hampstead edn), 1903; rev G. Sampson, New York 1903.

Poems. Introd by L. Binyon, notes by J. Masefield 1903 (Little Lib).

Poems. 1903 (Oxford miniature).

Poems. Ed G. Sampson 2 vols 1904 (Chiswick Quartos).

Poems. Ed E. de Selincourt 1905, 1906 (Methuen's Standard Lib), 1907 (rev), 1912, 1920, 1926, 1951, 1954, 1961, New York 1905, 1909, 1921.

Complete works. Ed N. H. Dole 4 vols London and Boston [1905–6] (Laurel edn).

Poetical works. Ed H. B. Forman, London and New York 1906 etc (OSA).

Poetical works. Ed G. Sampson 1906, Edinburgh 1906 (Edina edn).

Poems. 1906 (EL), 1944 (rev, with introd by G. Bullett).

Poems. Ilustr A. Burleigh [1911] (Burlington Lib).

Poetical works. Illustr A. A. Dixon, London and Glasgow [1912?].

Complete poetical works. Boston and New York 1912 (Autograph Poets), 1924 (Fireside poets).

Poems, arranged in chronological order with a preface by S. Colvin. 2 vols London and New York 1915, 1924, 1928.

Poetical works. Ed. L. Binyon, with essay by R. Bridges, illustr C. A. Shepperson 1916.

Complete poetry. Ed G. R. Elliott, New York 1927 (Mod Readers), 1929.

Poems and verses. Ed. J. M. Murry 2 vols 1930, decorated by M. Ayrton 1 vol 1948, New York 1949.

John Keats and Percy Bysshe Shelley: complete poetical works. New York 1932 (Mod Lib Giants), [1936?], London 1935.

Poems, with the Life and letters of Lord Houghton. 2 vols 1933 (Dent's Double Vols).

Complete poetical works. Ed H. B. Forman, introd by L. Bacon, New York 1934.

Complete poems and selected letters. Ed C. De Witt Thorpe, Garden City NY 1935.

Poetical works. Washington DC [1937].

Poetical works and other writings. Ed H. B. Forman, introd by J. Masefield 8 vols 1938–9 (Hampstead edn).

Poetical works and other writings. Ed H. B. Forman, rev M. B. Forman, memoir of George Keats by Naomi J. Kirk, New York 1938–9.

Poetical works. Ed H. W. Garrod, Oxford 1939, 1958 etc (rev with J. Jones).

Poetical works. Introd by J. Drinkwater, London and Glasgow 1942.

Complete poetry and selected prose. Ed H. E. Briggs, New York 1951 (Mod Lib).

Poetical works. Ed H. W. Garrod, Oxford 1956 (OSA), 1970.

Poems and selected letters. Ed C. Baker, New York 1962 (Bantam).

The poems. Ed M. Allott, Harlow 1970 (Longman Annotated Eng Poets).

The complete poems. Ed J. Barnard 1973, 1976 (Penguin Eng Poets).
The poems. Ed J. Stillinger, Cambridge MA and London 1978.
Complete poems. Ed J. Stillinger, Cambridge MA and London 1982.
The illustrated poetry. Memoir by R. M. Milnes, illustr G. Scharf 1984.

Selections

Selections from the British classics: Shelley and Keats. New York 1852 (Morrell's Standard Miniature Lib).
The Eve of St Agnes, and other poems. Illus, Boston 1876 (Vest-Pocket Ser).
Endymion, and other poems. 1887, 1892 (Cassell's Nat Lib).
Lines from Keats. Ed W. Ordway, Boston [1887]. Mostly two- or three-line quotations.
Odes and sonnets. Illustr W. H. Low, Philadelphia and London 1888.
Selections. Ed J. R. Tutin 1889, nd.
Selections. Ed H. G. Groser 1891 (Poets and Poetry of the Cent vol 2).
Roses of romance from the poems of John Keats. Ed E. H. Garrett, London and Cambridge MA 1892.
Poems. [1894?] (Masterpiece Lib).
The Keats birthday book. Comp by J. R. E. P., Edinburgh [1895].
Poems. [1895] (Penny Poets).
Odes, sonnets and lyrics. Ed C. H. O. Daniel, Oxford 1895.
Select poems: Goldsmith, Wordsworth, Scott, Keats, Shelley, Byron. Ed F. H. Sykes, Toronto 1896.
Odes. Ed A. C. Downer, Oxford 1897.
Four poets: poems from Wordsworth, Coleridge, Shelley, and Keats. Ed O. Crawfurd 1897.
Lyric poems. Ed E. Rhys 1897.
Endymion and the longer poems. Ed H. B. Forman 1898 (Temple Classics).
Ode on a Grecian urn and other poems. Boston 1898 (Riverside Lit Ser).
Ode on a Grecian urn, The eve of St Agnes and other poems. Boston 1898 (Riverside Lit Ser).
The revival of English poetry in the nineteenth century: selections from Wordsworth, Coleridge, Shelley, Keats and Byron. Introd by E. M. Buckingham, New York and Boston 1898.
Sonnets. Decorated borders and initials by C. Dean 1898.
Poems. Introd by J. Potter Briscoe 1900 (Bibelots).
Poems from Shelley and Keats. Ed S. C. Newsom, New York and London 1901 (Macmillan's Pocket Classics).
Wordsworth, Coleridge and Keats. Ed A. D. Innes 1901 (Blackwood's Eng Classics).
Poems of Keats and Coleridge. Ed C. Linklater Thomson 1901 (Black's Lit Ser).
Odes. Illustr R. A. Bell 1901, 1903.
The eve of St Agnes and other poems. Ed K. L. Bates 1902.
Isabella and The eve of St Agnes. Illustr R. A. Bell 1902.
Sonnets. Guildford 1902.
Select poems of Keats and Shelley. Ed E. H. Blakeney 1902 (Blackie's Eng Classics).
Odes. Edinburgh, London and Boston 1903.
Poems. Introd by A. Meynell 1903 (Red Letter Lib), New York 1903, 1904.
Sonnets. 1904.
Endymion and other poems. Introd by H. Morley 1905 (Cassell's Nat Lib).
Odes. 1905.
Odes, sonnets and La belle dame sans merci. 1906 (Wellwood).
Lamia, La belle dame sans merci etc. London and New York [1906] (Broadway Booklets).
The odes of John Keats (and Ballad, La belle dame sans merci). Edinburgh and London 1906 (Roses of Parnassus).
Realms of gold. 1906.
Poems. Ed A. Symons, Edinburgh [1907] (Golden Poets), Philadelphia 1907.
Poems from Shelley and Keats. Ed S. C. Newsom 1907 (Macmillan's Pocket Classics).
The seven golden odes. Portland ME 1907 (Bibelot).
Odes, sonnets and lyrics. Introd by E. C. Stedman, New York 1908.
The odes. 1908 (Oakleaf).
Odes and lyrics. Ed A. T. Quiller-Couch, Oxford 1908.
Keats's Isabella and The eve of St Agnes. Oxford [1909] (Oxford Plain Texts).
Selections from Byron, Wordsworth, Shelley, Keats, and Browning. Ed C. T. Copeland and H. M. Rideout 1909 (Gateway Ser)
Sonnets. [1909] (Langham).
Keats day by day. Ed C. M. Spender, designs by M. Tarrant 1910.
Odes. 1910 (Langham).
Shorter poems. 1910 (King's Treasury).
Shorter poems. 1910, [1911] (Smaller Classics).
Poems. Illustr E. J. Sullivan, London and Edinburgh [1910].
Sonnets. 1910.
Odes. Ed A. R. Weekes [1911] (University Tutorial Ser).
Poems. Ed P. Plowden, illustr E. A. Pike 1911.
Poems by Wordsworth, Coleridge, Shelley, and Keats. Ed J. Weber Linn, New York 1911.
Poems of Wordsworth, Shelley and Keats. Ed W. P. Trent and J. Erskine 1912, 1914.
Selected lyrics from Wordsworth, Keats and Shelley. Ed C. Swain Thomas, Boston 1913, 1934.
Days with the lyric poets: Keats, Burns, Longfellow. [1913].
Keats. Ed T. J. Cobden-Sanderson, Hammersmith 1914.
Selected poems. 1914 (Standard Eng Classics).
Selections. Ed A. H. Thompson, Cambridge 1915 (Eng Romantic Poets).
Odes, lyrics and sonnets. Ed M. (Robertson) Hills, Oxford 1916.
Poems of Keats: Endymion; the volume of 1820; and other poems. Ed W. T. Young, Cambridge 1917.
Selected poems. Introd by R. L. Blackwood, Melbourne [1920].
Poems. Ed R. Cobden-Sanderson, London and New York 1921 (commemorative edn).
Odes, sonnets and lyrics of John Keats. [Ed C. H. O. Daniel, rev T. B. Mosher] Portland ME 1922, 1924.
Poetry and prose, with essays by Charles Lamb, Leigh Hunt, Robert Bridges and others. Ed H. Ellershaw, Oxford 1922.
John Keats. Ed H. Newbolt, London and Edinburgh [1923].
Poems. Ed N. A. Crawford, Girard KS 1923.
Odes. Decorated by V. Gribble 1923.
Selections. London, Liverpool, Bournemouth and Boston 1923 (Medici Soc).
Selections from the poems of John Keats and Percy Bysshe Shelley. Ed R. Wilson, London and Toronto [1924] (King's Treasury).
Selections from Shelley and Keats. Ed M. H. Nicolson, New York and London 1924 (College Lib).
Eighteen poems. 1925 (Augustan Books).
Keats. Ed S. S. Sopwith 1925 (Companion Poets).
Shelley and Keats: selected poems. Ed G. Boas, London and Edinburgh 1925 (Teaching of Eng Ser).
Keats. Ed A. Noyes, notes by J. Duckworth 1925 (Helicon Poetry Ser).
John Keats. [1925] (Augustan Books).
Poems. Ed F. P. Bachman, New York 1926 (Eclectic Eng Classics).
Two odes. San Francisco 1926.
Odes. Bussum (Netherlands) 1927.
Odes. Birmingham 1927.
Selected poems. Ed H. M. Margoliouth 1927 (Socrates).
Selections. Ed B. Groom 1927, 1928 (with Lamia).
Hyperion, Isabella, The eve of St Agnes, Lamia. Ed G. E. Hollingworth 1928.

Select poems: Isabella, Hyperion, The eve of St Agnes, and Lamia. Ed J. H. Boardman, London and Glasgow 1928.
Lamia, Isabella, The eve of St Agnes, and other poems. Engravings by R. Gibbings, Waltham St Lawrence 1928 (Golden Cockerel).
Selected poems. Ed G. D. H. and M. I. Cole 1928 (Ormond).
Collected sonnets. Illustr J. Buckland Wright, Maastricht 1930.
Poems, with selections from his letters and from criticism. Ed C. W. Thomas, New York 1932.
Lamia, Isabella, The eve of St Agnes, selected odes. Ed G. E. Hollingworth and A. R. Weekes [1932].
Selections. 1932 (Little Treasury).
Selections: sonnets, odes and narrative poems. Ed L. C. Martin [1933] (Selected Eng Classics).
Selections. Ed J. Earnshaw 1934.
Odes. Ed B. I. Evans, Paris 1935.
Lamia, Hyperion, To autumn, To a nightingale, On a Grecian urn. Ed G. E. Hollingworth and A. R. Weekes [1936], 1943 (with Eve of St Agnes and Isabella).
Selected poems. 1937 (Zodiac Books).
The odes of Keats and Shelley. Mount Vernon NY 1937.
Regency poets: Byron, Shelley, Keats. Ed C. R. Bull, Melbourne 1941 (Australian School Anthologies).
Keats. 1941 (Eng Poets).
The eve of St Agnes, Isabella, Ode to autumn, Ode on a Grecian urn, Ode to a nightingale, Hyperion. Ed G. E. Hollingworth and A. R. Weekes 1942, 1943 (with Lamia).
A selection. Ed W. Fancutt 1943 (Kingsgate Pocket Poets).
Odes. 1944.
A critical edition of the early poems, with a philosophical supplement. Ed K. K. Carmichael. Nashville TN 1944.
Chosen poems. Ed N. T. Carrington 1947 (Brodie's).
John Keats. Ed R. Church 1948.
Selected poems. Ed G. H. Ford, New York 1950 (Crofts Classics).
Poems. Ed R. Vallance, introd by B. I. Evans, wood-engravings by D. Braby 1950.
Selected poems. Ed L. Whistler 1950 (Crown Classics).
Selected poetry and letters. Ed R. H. Fogle, New York 1951, 1969 (rev) (Rinehart).
Poetical works. London and Melbourne 1951.
A selection. Ed J. E. Morpurgo 1953 (Penguin).
Selected letters and poems. Ed J. H. Walsh 1954.
Poems and letters. Ed J. R. Caldwell, New York 1954.
Selected poems. Ed E. Blunden 1955.
Poems. Ed J. Mascarò, illustr L. Anglada, Palma de Mallorca 1955.
Selected poems and letters. Ed D. Bush, Boston 1959 (Riverside).
Poems. Ed D. Herbert 1963.
Selected poems. 1963 (Eng Poets).
Selected poems and letters. Ed R. Sharrock 1964.
Selected poems and letters of John Keats. Ed R. Gittings 1966.
Selected poetry. Ed P. de Man, New York and London 1966 (Signet).
A Keats selection. Ed N. Howlings 1966 (Eng Classics).
John Keats. 1969 (Longman's Poetry Lib).
A choice of Keats's verse. Introd by C. Day Lewis 1971 (Faber).
Keats at Wentworth Place: poems written December 1818 to September 1820. Introd by D. Hewlett 1971 (Keats House).
A selection from John Keats. Ed E. C. Pettet 1974.
Keats's sonnets. Ed T. Matsuura, Tokyo 1975.
Keats. Illustr P. Machin, Exeter 1985 (Webb & Bower).
Selected poems. Ed J. Barnard 1988 (Penguin Poetry Lib).
John Keats: an anthology. Norwich 1989 (Jarrold Eng Poets).
John Keats. Ed E. Cook, Oxford 1990 (Oxford Authors).
Lyric poems. New York and London 1991 (Dover Thrift Edns).
John Keats. Introd by G. Moore 1991 (Aurum Illus Poets).
Keats. 1993 (Bloomsbury Classics).
Poems: Keats. 1994 (EL Pocket Poets).
Keats. Ed E. Cook. Oxford 1994 (Oxford Poetry Lib).

§1

Poems. 1817, 1927 (photo facs), New York 1934 (photo facs), Spelsbury 1989 (photo facs).
Endymion: a poetic romance. 1818; illustr F. Joubert after E. J. Poynter 1873; illustr W. St John Harper, Cambridge MA [1888], Boston 1888; Rochelle NY 1902 (replica); ed H. C. Notcutt, Oxford 1927 (type facs); illustr J. Buckland-Wright 1947; ed T. Saito, Tokyo 1955; Spelsbury 1991 (photo facs).
Lamia, Isabella, The eve of St Agnes and other poems. 1820; ed M. Robertson, Oxford 1909 (type facs), 1909, 1920, 1922; London 1927 (photo facs), New York 1927, 1928; Famous editions of English poets, ed J. O. Beaty and J. W. Bowyer, New York 1931; (with The fall of Hyperion), ed D. G. Gillham 1969 (Collins Annotated), Plymouth 1988; Menston 1970 (photo facs); Spelsbury 1990 (photo facs).
Otho the great: a tragedy in five acts. 1883, 1967.
Lamia. Illustr W. H. Low, Philadelphia 1885, 1888, London 1888; 1906 (Cadogan); [1908?] (Verona).
Isabella. Illustr W. B. Macdougall 1898, Philadelphia 1898; [1905] (Broadway); illustr P. Henry 1906; illustr J. M. King, Edinburgh and London [1907], Philadelphia [1908?]; introd by A. Quiller-Couch, Oxford 1914.
The eve of St Agnes. Illustr E. H. Wehnert, New York 1856, 1859, 1866, London [1875] (Choice Ser); illustr C. O. Murray 1880; illustr E. H. Garrett, Troy NY 1885; Cambridge MA 1885 (Illuminated Missal Ser); with an appreciation by L. Hunt, River Forest IL 1896; Chicago 1900; illustr R. Savage 1900; 1902; Guildford and Philadelphia 1903 (Astolat Oakleaf Ser); 1904; [1905] (Broadway Booklets); [1908?] (Verona); 1910 (Oakleaf); notes by J. W. Hales, New York [1910]; 1910 (Arden); [1911]; 1914 (Gravure); illustr E. M. Craig 1928 (Helicon).
Ode to a nightingale. Ed T. J. Wise 1884; Reigate 1949.
Another version of Keats's Hyperion. [1857?]. Rptd by R. M. Milnes from his contribution to Miscellanies of the Philobiblon Soc 3, 1856–7 (1st pbn of The fall of Hyperion: a dream).
Hyperion: a fragment. Paris 1883; ed J. Hoops, Berlin 1899 (Englische Textbibliothek); Hyperion: a facsimile of Keats's autograph ms of The fall of Hyperion: a dream, ed E. de Selincourt, Oxford 1905; ed M. Robertson, Oxford 1914; 1945. Tr Du, 1888.
Hyperion: book I. Ed W. T. Arnold, Oxford 1877; ed J. S. Laurie, London 1877; 1877 (Allman's Eng classics).
Three essays by John Keats. Ed H. B. Forman 1889. A review of J. Hamilton Reynolds's 'Peter Bell' and two dramatic criticisms.
La belle dame sans merci. 1906; engravings by M. Renton, Solihull 1986.
John Keats: unpublished poem to his sister Fanny, April 1818. Introd by C. E. Hurd, Boston 1909.
The eve of St Mark. 1930.
Sonnet to Spenser. Philadelphia 1945.
To autumn. Ed S. King 1985.

Translations

The John Keats memorial volume, *1921 contains translations into Swedish, Arabic and Sanskrit.*

Czech

Obrys krásy. Prague 1977.

Danish

Hyperion. Tr K. Nielsen and E. Ditlevsen, Copenhagen 1949.
Breve. Tr T. S. Hausen, Copenhagen 1949. Letters.

Dutch

Ode on a Grecian urn. Rotterdam 1845. Eng and Du.
Dichterlijke verhalen: navolginen van F. Coppée, L. de Ronchaud, G. Eliot, J. Keats. Tr C. van Kempe Valk, Amsterdam 1888. Trn of Hyperion.
Hyperion. Tr W. W. van Lennep, Amsterdam 1927.

French

Poètes anglais contemporains: Robert Burns, John Keats, Elizabeth Browning, Robert Browning. Tr A. Buisson du Berger, Paris 1890. Trn of a passage from Endymion.

Poésies. Tr E. de Clermont-Tonnerre, Paris 1907, 1922. Eng and Fr.

Poèmes et poésies. Paris 1910 (Mercure de France).

Lettres à Fanny Brawne. Tr M. L. Des Garet, Paris 1912.

La veille de la Saint-Agnes. Tr E. de Clermont-Tonnerre, Abbeville 1913 (Les amis d'Edouard).

La correspondance inédite de John Keats. Tr L. Wolff, Paris 1928.

John Keats: poems. Ed F. Delattre, Paris 1946.

Lettres. Tr A. Bemberg, Paris 1949.

Tendre est la nuit: florilège des poèmes de John Keats. Tr P.-L. Matthey, Lausanne 1950.

Poèmes choisis. Notes by A. Laffay, Paris 1952.

La belle dame sans merci. Tr H. Parisot, Paris 1971.

Hypérion. Tr P. de Roux, Geneva 1989.

Seul dans la splendeur: John Keats. Tr R. Davreu, Paris 1990.

La vigile de la Sainte-Agnès. Tr A. Suied, Paris 1990.

Les odes; suivi de La belle dame sans merci. Tr A. Suied, Paris 1994.

German

Gothein, M. L. John Keats: Leben und Werke. 2 vols Halle 1897. With a trn of his poetical works.

Englische Dichter: Übersetzungen nach Percy B. Shelley, Thomas Moore, John Keats, Algernon Charles Swinburne und Anderen. Tr G. Freiligrath, Halle [1898].

Gedichte. Tr G. Etzel, Leipzig 1910.

Die Enrit des Auslandes in neuere Zeit. Ed H. Bethge, Leipzig [1910].

Perlen: englisher Dichtung in deutscher Fassung. Tr H. Behr, New York 1929. Six poems.

Sonette und Oden. Tr E. Jaime, Cologne 1946.

Bernus, A. von. Das irdische Paradies. Nuremberg 1947.

Hyperion: ein Fragment. Tr W. Schmiele, Darmstadt 1948.

Shelley and Keats: Oden und Hymnen. Tr U. Clemen, Munich 1949.

Gedichte und Briefe. Tr H. W. Häusermann, Zurich 1950.

Gedichte: Sankt Agnes-Abend. Hyperion. Tr A. von Bernus, Heidelberg 1958.

Gedichte. Tr H. Piontek, Wiesbaden 1960.

Gedichte zweisprachig. Tr H. Piontek, Munich 1984.

Hindi

Mahakavi Keats ka kavya-lok. Tr Yatendrakumar, Delhi 1958. Selected poems.

Hungarian

Három Költö. Antológia Byron, Shelley, Keats muveibol. [Budapest 1942].

Versei. Tr M. Babits, I. Bernáth et al, Budapest 1962.

Italian

Poemetti e odi di John Keats. Tr E. Sanfelice, Messina 1901.

Sonetti di John Keats. Tr E. Allodoli, Florence 1904.

Versioni da Thomas Gray, John Keats, Lord Byron, Percy Bysshe Shelley, Robert Browning. Tr T. Wiel, Venice 1906. Eng and Ital.

Iperione, Isabella, odi e sonnetti di John Keats. Tr E. Allodoli, Milan 1910.

Canti perfetti antologia di poeti inglese moderni. Tr L. Siciliani, Milan 1911.

Poemi. Tr F. Farffini, Naples 1911.

P. B. Shelley e J. Keats: liriche scelte. Introd by F. Olivero, Bologna 1919.

Iperione, odi e sonetti. Tr R. Piccoli, Florence [1925].

Lettere a Fanny Brawne. Tr G. Prampolini, Rome 1925.

Keats e Browning: poesie dall'inglese. Tr F. Gargaro, Milan 1937.

Porchi-Diano, F. Vita e poesia di Giovanni Keats. Con versioni e commenti di sonetti e di odi, testo inglese e illustrazioni. Milan 1938.

Keats. Tr F. Politi, Milan 1952. Selected poems.

Il sogno di Adamo. Sonetti e odi. Tr R. Mancini, Milan 1959.

Isabella, o il vaso di basilico. Tr P. Maffeo, Milan 1963.

La poesia di John Keats. Tr G. Baldini, Rome 1964.

Poesie: odi e sonnetti. Tr E. De Michelis, Rome 1973.

Japanese

Shokan-shū. Tr K. Sato, Tokyo 1952. Letters.

Keats shishū. Tr O. Mine, Tokyo 1964. Complete poetical works.

Keats shishū. Tr D. Yasuo, Tokyo 1965. Complete poetical works.

Keats shishū. Tr T. Einosuke, Tokyo 1967. Selections.

Lamia, Isabella, Sei Agnes no yomiya. Tr I. Nobuya, Tokyo 1967.

Keats no tegami. Tr M. Tōrn, Tokyo 1971. Letters.

Hyperion no botsuraku. Tr D. Yasuo, Tokyo 1973.

Keats zenshishū. Tr D. Yasuo, Tokyo 1973. Poems 1817.

Ramija. Tr D. Yasuo, Tokyo 1973. Poems 1820.

Keats shishū. Tr Takashima, Tokyo 1974.

Otto taitei. Tr T. Miyoko, Tokyo 1977. Otho the Great.

Shijin no tegami. Tr T. Einosuke, Tokyo 1977. Letters.

Latin

Keatsii Hyperionis libri I, II. Ed C. Merivale, Cambridge and London 1862. Eng with Latin trn.

Keatsii Hyperionis libri tres. Ed C. Merivale, Cambridge and London 1863.

Angellier, A. De Joh. Keatsii vita et carminibus. 1892. Trn of Ode on a Grecian urn and passages from Endymion, Hyperion, Lamia.

Norwegian

De Unge Døde. Tr N. Grieg, Oslo 1932. Three sonnets, La belle dame, Ode on a Grecian urn.

Polish

Ody. Tr S. Baliński 1951. Odes.

Poezje wybrane. Tr J. Żuławski, Warsaw 1962 (Biblioteka Poetow).

Romanian

Versuri. Tr A. Covaci, Bucharest 1968.

Scrisori. Tr C. and N. Melinescu, Bucharest 1974. Letters.

Russian

Poetical works. Moscow 1966. Eng text, Russian introd and notes.

Poeziji. Tr V. Mysyk, Kiev 1967.

Lirika. Tr V. Levik et al, Moscow 1979.

Serbo Croat

Izbor poezÿe: Bajron-Šeli-Kits. Tr I. Goran Kovačič, R. Kuič et al, Sarajevo 1954. Selected poems of Shelley, Byron and Keats.

Stihovi. Tr D. Andjelinovič, Belgrade 1959. Complete poetical works.

Spanish

Antología de líricos ingleses y angloamericanos. Madrid 1917 (Biblioteca Clásica vol 250).

Las cien mejores poesías (líricas) de la lengua inglesa. Tr F. Maristany, 1918.

Nuevos poemas. Tr R. A. Arrieta, Buenos Aires 1922.

Antología. Tr. R. A. Arrieta, Buenos Aires 1942.

Poesías. Madrid 1946 (Colección Adonais).

Poesías. Tr C. Miró, Madrid 1950.

Lines supposed to have been addressed to Fanny Browne [sic]. Buenos Aires 1958. Eng and Sp.

Poesía completa. Tr A. Sánchez, Barcelona 1974.

La oda a un ruiseñor. Tr J. Siles Artés, Murcia 1976.

Trece sonetos. Tr M. Jesús Velo and A. Amusco, Barcelona 1976.

Endimión. Tr P. L. Ugalde Ramo, Barcelona 1977.

Poesía completa. Tr A. Sánchez, Barcelona 1977.

Cartas. Tr M. Lucarda, Barcelona 1982.

Sonetos, odas y otros poemas. Tr J. María Martín Triana, Madrid 1982.

Isabel: o el test d'Alfàbrega. La vigília de Santa Agnès. Tr M. Villangómez Llobet, Barcelona 1984.

Poemes. Tr M. Manent, Barcelona 1985.

Contemporary reviews

Generous selection rptd in The Romantics reviewed, *ed D. H. Reiman 9 vols New York 1972.*

Poems, 1817. (J. H. Reynolds) Champion, 9 Mar 1817; Monthly Mag Apr 1817; (G. F. Mathew) European Mag, May 1817; (L. Hunt) Examiner, 1 June, 6, 13 July 1817; Eclectic Rev, Sep 1817; Scots Mag, Oct 1817.

Endymion, 1818. (J. W. Croker) Quart Rev 19, 1818; Literary Jnl and General Misc 17, 24 May 1818; Literary Chron, 18, 25 May 1818; Oxford Herald, 6 June 1818; Br Critic, June 1818; Champion, June 1818; (J. G. Lockhart) Blackwood's Mag, Aug 1818; Examiner, 11 Oct 1818; (P. G. Patmore) Baldwin's London Mag, Apr 1820; (F. Jeffrey on the Endymion and Lamia vols) Edinburgh Rev 34, Aug 1820; Scots Mag, Aug, Oct 1820.

Lamia, Isabella, The eve of St Agnes and other poems, 1820. Monthly Rev, July 1820; Literary Gazette, 1 July 1820; (C. Lamb) New Times, 19 July 1820; Literary Chron, 29 July 1820; Examiner, 30 July 1820; (L. Hunt) Indicator, 2, 9 Aug 1820; Guardian, 6 Aug 1820; Gold's London Mag, Aug 1820; Scots Mag, Aug, Oct 1820; Edinburgh Rev 34, Aug 1820; Kaleidoscope, 29 Aug 1820; (J. Scott) Baldwin's London Mag, Sep 1820; New Monthly Mag, Sep 1820; Br Critic, Sep 1820; Monthly Mag, Sep 1820; Eclectic Rev, Sep 1820.

Contributions to periodicals and collaborative works

Only first pbns are listed; poems were often rptd – see J. R. MacGillivray, Keats: A bibliography and reference guide, *1949 pp. 76–87.*

Examiner (ed L. Hunt). O Solitude! if I must with thee dwell, 5 May 1816; On first looking into Chapman's Homer, 1 Dec 1816; To Kosciusko, 16 Feb 1817; After dark vapours have oppress'd our plains, 23 Feb 1817; To Haydon, with a sonnet written on seeing the Elgin marbles, On seeing the Elgin marbles, 9 Mar 1817; This pleasant tale is like a little copse, 16 Mar 1817; [review of J. H. Reynolds, Peter Bell: a lyrical ballad], 25 Apr 1819; There is a joy in footing slow across a silent plain, 14 July 1822.

Champion. To Haydon, with a sonnet written on seeing the Elgin marbles, On seeing the Elgin marbles, 9 Mar 1817; On the sea, 17 Aug 1817; [dramatic reviews], 21, 28 Dec 1817, 4 Jan 1818. Review of 28 Dec perhaps by J. H. Reynolds; *see* L. M. Jones, Keats–Shelley Jnl 3 1954.

Yellow Dwarf. Hymn to Pan [from Endymion], 9 May 1818.

The literary pocket-book. Ed Leigh Hunt 1818. Four seasons fill the measure of the year, To Ailsa rock.

Annals of the Fine Arts. Ode to a nightingale, July 1819; Ode on a Grecian urn, Jan 1820.

Indicator (ed Leigh Hunt). La belle dame sans merci, 10 May 1820; A 'now', descriptive of a hot day (written with Leigh Hunt), and As Hermes once took to his feathers light, 28 June 1820; The cap and bells (pt only), 23 Aug 1820.

New Monthly Mag. On some skulls in Beauley Abbey, near Inverness (written with Charles Brown), Jan 1822; There is a joy in footing slow across a silent plain (pt only), Mar 1822.

The gem: a literary annual (ed Thomas Hood). On a Leander which Miss Reynolds, my kind friend, gave me, 1829.

London Literary Gazette. In drear-nighted December, 19 Sep 1829.

The comic annual, by Thomas Hood. To Mrs Reynolds' cat, 1830.

Western Messenger (Louisville KY). Ode to Apollo ('God of the golden bow'), June 1836; Not Aladdin magian, July 1836.

Plymouth, Devonport, and Stonehouse News. If by dull rhymes our English must be chain'd, 15 Oct 1836.

Ladies' Companion (New York). On fame ('Fame, like a wayward girl'), Hither, hither, love, 'Tis the 'witching time of night', Aug 1837.

Portsmouth and Devonport Weekly Jnl. To the Nile, 19 July 1838; Read me a lesson, muse, and speak it loud, 6 Sep; Staffa, 20 Sep; Bright star, 27 Sep; The day is gone, 4 Oct; To sleep, 11 Oct; Shed no tear, 18 Oct; Ah! woe is me, 25 Oct; On sitting down to read King Lear once again, 8 Nov; Lines on seeing a lock of Milton's hair, 15 Nov; Old Meg she was a gipsy, 22 Nov; In after time a sage of mickle lore, 4 July 1839.

Hood's Mag and Comic Misc. Time's sea hath been five years at its slow ebb, Sep 1844; Hush, hush! tread softly! Apr 1845.

Athenaeum. Of late two dainties were before me plac'd, 7 June 1873.

World (New York). Pensive they sit and roll their languid eyes, Give me your patience, sister, while I frame, 25 June 1877.

N & Q. Fill for me the brimming bowl, On peace, 4 Feb 1905.

TLS. Apollo to the Graces, You say you love, but with a voice, 16 Apr 1914.

The Times. On receiving a laurel crown from Leigh Hunt, To the ladies who saw me crown'd, 18 May 1914.

Letters, journals etc

Life, letters and literary remains. Ed R. M. Milnes 2 vols 1848. Many poems and letters first pbd here.

Letters to Fanny Brawne. Ed H. B. Forman, London and New York 1878, 1889 (rev and enlarged), New York 1878. Some copies with the London 1878 title page have the pagination of 1889, with a note in place of the 1889 preface.

Letters of John Keats to his family and friends. Ed S. Colvin, London and New York 1891, 1891, 1918 (rev), 1921, 1925, 1928. Letters to Fanny Brawne omitted.

Letters: complete revised edition. Ed H. B. Forman 1895.

Thoughts from Keats. Selected from his letters. Ed P. E. Gertrude Girdlestone 1898.

Letters to Fanny Brawne. New York 1901.

Letters. Ed N. H. Dole 1906.

Letters. Edinburgh 1908 (Holyrood Books). A selection.

Sayings from the letters of John Keats. Hull [1908].

Photographic reproduction of Keats's anatomical and physiological notebook presented to the Hampstead public library by Sir William Hale-White. 1925.

Letters to Fanny Brawne, with three poems and three additional letters. Introd by J. F. Otten, Maastricht 1931.

Keats's anatomical and physiological notebook printed from the holograph. Ed M. B. Forman, Oxford 1934.

The letters. Ed M. B. Forman 2 vols Oxford 1931, 1 vol 1935, 1947, 1952 (rev).

Letters. Introd by H. I'A. Fausset 1938 (Nelson Classics). Selection.

The Keats circle: letters and papers 1816–78. Ed H. E. Rollins 2 vols Cambridge MA 1948.

The letters: selected passages. Ed H. W. Häusermann, Berne 1949.

Selected letters. Ed L. Trilling, New York 1951.

Letters. Ed F. Page 1954 (WC).

Bates, M. C. Two new letters of Keats and Byron. Keats–Shelley Jnl 3, 1954.

More letters and poems of the Keats circle. Ed H. E. Rollins, Cambridge MA 1955.

The letters of Keats 1814–21. Ed H. E. Rollins 2 vols Cambridge MA 1958.

Letters. Ed S. Gardner 1965. Selection.

Letters of John Keats: a new selection. Ed R. Gittings 1970.

Love letters of John Keats. Ed O. E. Madden, Oxford 1993.

Unfinished poems concluded

Coward, E. F. King Stephen. New York 1912.

Price, C. Keats's finales: Hyperion and The eve of St Mark. 1922.

Regester, F. A. Medes. Keats's fragments and finales. 1936. Hyperion and Ode to Pan altered and with additions by Regester.

Questionable attributions

The poems of John Keats, *ed Stillinger 1978, appendix VI, publishes texts of questionable attributions and discusses their claims. This listing includes those pbd in periodicals or as books.*

New Monthly Mag. Love and folly, July 1822.

TLS. Sonnet to A. G. S., 27 Nov 1937.

Orion, and other anonymous and hitherto unpublished poems attributed to John Keats. Ed Bristol Williams, Webster Groves MO 1939.

§2

Textual matters

Exhaustive and up-to-date coverage of Keats's mss is provided by Stillinger, The texts of Keats's poems, *1974, and (ed)* The poems of John Keats, *1978 pp. 539–763.*

Jenks, E. Keats relics. Athenaeum, 1891.
Jenks, E. Keats relics and mss. Bookworm 4, 1891.
Relics of John Keats. Library ser 2 3, 1891.
Dilke, C. W. Keats's copy of the anatomy. Athenaeum, Jan 1893.
Kenyon, F. G. The new Keats MS. Athenaeum 29, Dec 1894.
Higginson, T. W. A Keats manuscript. Forum, June 1896.
Forman, H. B. Keats's manuscript of The cap and bells. Athenaeum, Jan 1902.
Grigor, J. Keats's 'Ode to a nightingale': the original MS. N & Q, 18 Apr 1903.
C. C. B. Keats's 'Ode to a nightingale': the original MS. N & Q, 9 May 1903.
Forman, H. B. Keats: some readings and notes. Athenaeum, Feb 1904.
To autumn. Century Mag, Nov 1904.
de Selincourt, E. Recently discovered Keats mss. N & Q, 4 Feb 1905.
Forman, H. B. Some Keats crumbs. Athenaeum July 1909.
Holman, T. B. Booksellers connected with Keats. N & Q, 31 May 1913.
Roberts, R. Fragments of a Keats manuscript. Keats–Shelley Memorial Bull 2, 1913.
de Selincourt, E. Keats: recent additions to our knowledge. TLS, 21 May 1914. 1st pbn of two 'laurel crown' sonnets.
Sargent, G. H. Keats treasures in America. Bookman's Jnl 3, 1921.
Stuart, H. A misprint in Keats. TLS, 26 May 1921.
Muirhead, J. F. The text of Keats. TLS, 9 July 1925.
Draper, W. A. A literary windfall. Amer Collector 5, 1927.
Gohdes, C. A note on the bibliography of Keats. MLN 43, 1929.
Mabbott, T. O. Arcturus and Keats: an early American publication of Keats's La belle dame sans merci. Amer Lit 2, 1931.
Stearns, B.-M. The first publication of two poems by Keats. TLS, 4 Aug 1932.
Pope, W. B. A book of Keats's. TLS, 6 Oct 1932.
Ridley, M. R. The text of Keats. TLS, 20 Oct 1932, 3 Nov, 10 Nov.
Ballman, A. B. On the revisions of Hyperion. MLN 47, 1932.
Forman, M. B. Letters of John Keats. Publisher's Weekly 124, 1933.
Page, F. The two Hyperions. TLS, 20 Nov 1937.
Thorpe, C. D. An unknown Keats manuscript. TLS, Aug 1938.
Clark, E. B. A manuscript of John Keats at Dumbarton Oaks. HLB 1, 1947.
Steele, M. A. E. The Woodhouse transcripts of the poems of Keats. HLB 3, 1949.
Whitley, A. The autograph of Keats's In drear nighted December. HLB 5, 1951.
Steele, M. A. E. Three early mss of Keats. Keats–Shelley Jnl 1, 1952.
Rollins, H. E. Unpublished autograph texts of Keats. HLB 6, 1952.
Stull, J. S. An early annotated edition of The eve of St Agnes. PBSA 46, 1952.
Jones, L. M. Keats's theatrical reviews in the Champion. Keats–Shelley Jnl 3, 1954.
Coles, W. A. The proof sheets of Keats's Lamia. HLB 8, 1954.
Roth, R. N. The Houghton-Crewe draft of Keats's Ode to a nightingale. PBSA 48, 1954.
Steele, M. A. E. A passport note attributed to Keats: a postscript. HLB 9, 1955.
Rollins, H. E. Benjamin Bailey's scrapbook. Keats–Shelley Jnl 6, 1957.
Jones, L. M. New letters, articles and poems by J. H. Reynolds. Keats–Shelley Jnl 6, 1957.
Stillinger, J. Keats's Grecian urn and the evidence of transcripts. PMLA 73, 1958.
Patterson, C. The Keats-Hazlitt-Hunt copy of Palmerin of England in relation to Keats's poetry. JEGP 60, 1961.
Stillinger, J. The text of The eve of St Agnes. SB 16, 1963.
Sperry, S. M., jr. Richard Woodhouse's interleaved and annotated copy of Keats's Poems, 1817. Literary Monographs 1, 1967.
Gittings, R. The odes of Keats, and their earliest known manuscripts. 1970.
Haworth, H. Keats's copy of Lamb's Specimens of English dramatic poets. BNYPL 74, 1970.
Stillinger, J. Review of Gittings, The odes of Keats. JEGP 71, 1972.
Anderson, N. Corrections to Amy Lowell's reading of Keats's marginalia. Keats–Shelley Jnl 23, 1974.
Stillinger, J. The texts of Keats's poems. Cambridge MA 1974.
Jones, L. M. The dating of the two Hyperions. SB 30, 1977.
Jackson, D. H. Line indentation in Stillinger's The poems of John Keats. SB 36, 1983.
Powell, M. K. Keats and his editor: the manuscript of Endymion. Library ser 6 6, 1984.
Stillinger, J. Stop-press corrections in Keats's Poems, 1817. PBSA 79, 1985.
Stillinger, J. (ed), The manuscripts of the younger romantics: John Keats. vol 1, Poems, 1817: a facsimile of Richard Woodhouse's annotated copy in the Huntington Library, New York 1985; vol 2, Endymion: a facsimile of the revised holograph manuscript, New York 1985; vol 3, Endymion, 1818: a facsimile of Richard Woodhouse's annotated copy in the Berg Collection, New York 1985; vol 4, Facsimiles of Richard Woodhouse's scrapbook materials in the Pierpont Morgan Library, New York 1985; vol 5, Manuscript poems in the British Library: facsimiles of the Hyperion holograph and George Keats's notebook of holographs and transcripts, New York 1988; vol 6, The Woodhouse poetry transcripts at Harvard: a facsimile of the W2 notebook, with description and contents of the W1 notebook, New York 1988; vol 7, The Charles Brown poetry transcripts at Harvard, New York 1988.
Lau, B. Further corrections to Amy Lowell's transcriptions of Keats's marginalia. Keats–Shelley Jnl 35, 1986.
Stillinger, J. The manuscripts of Keats's letters: an update. Keats–Shelley Jnl 36, 1987.
Morpurgo, J. E. The poet and Barabbas: Keats, his publishers and editors. In Literature and the art of creation, ed R. Welch and Suheil Badi Bushrui, Totowa NJ 1988.
Sato, T. A revaluation of Keats's 'Ode on indolence' with special attention to its stanzaic order. PQ 68, 1989.
Sato, T. The textual history of 'Ode on a Grecian urn' reexamined in terms of its first printed version in Annals of the fine arts. Univ of Saga Stud in Eng 18, 1990.
Sato, T. Some textual problems of 'Ode to a nightingale'. Eng and Eng–Amer Lit 25, 1990.
Stillinger, J. (ed). Poetry manuscripts at Harvard: John Keats. Essay by Helen Vendler. Cambridge MA 1990.

Pre-1920 criticism

Mathew, G. F. To a poetical friend. European Mag, Oct 1816.
Mathew, G. F. Art thou a poet? thou hast learn'd to feign. European Mag, Oct 1817.
Terrot, C. H. Common sense: a poem. 1819.
Woodhouse, R. From a correspondent. Sun, July 1820.
[Scott, J.]. The Mohock magazine. Baldwin's London Mag, Dec 1820.
Procter, B. W. (writing as 'L.'). Death of Mr John Keats. Baldwin's London Mag, Apr 1821.
G. V. D. On reading Lamia and other poems by John Keats. Gossip (Kentish Town), 19 May 1821.
M. M. On the neglect of genius. Imperial Mag, Dec 1821.

Clare, J. To the memory of John Keats. In his The village minstrel, 2 vols 1821.
Dalby, J. W. Remarks on the character and writings of the late John Keats, the poet. Arliss Pocket Mag, 1821.
Hazlitt, W. On living to one's self. In his Table talk, 1821.
Reynolds, J. H. The garden of Florence. 1821.
Shelley, P. B. Adonais. Pisa 1821, Cambridge 1829, Spelsbury 1992 (photo facs).
[Lockhart, J. G.]. Noctes Ambrosianae, I. Blackwood's Edinburgh Mag, Mar 1822.
[?Lockhart, J. G.]. Rhapsodies over a punch-bowl, I by Paddy from Cork. Blackwood's Edinburgh Mag, Mar 1822.
[Taylor, J.]. Necrological table for 1821. Baldwin's London Mag, June 1822.
Hunt, L. On Mr Shelley's new poem, Adonais. Examiner, 8 July 1822.
Maginn, W. Letter from a 'gentleman of the press' to Christopher North. Blackwood's Edinburgh Mag, July 1822.
H. D. Stanzas to the memory of Mr Keats, the poet. Imperial Mag 4, 1822.
Hazlitt, W. The periodical press. Edinburgh Rev, May 1823.
Hood, T. Sonnet written in Keats's Endymion. Baldwin's London Mag, May 1823.
Lockhart, J. G. and William Maginn. Letters of Timothy Tickler, VIII. Blackwood's Edinburgh Mag, Aug 1823.
Lockhart, J. G. and John Wilson. Noctes Ambrosianae, XII. Blackwood's Edinburgh Mag, Oct 1823.
Byron, George Gordon, 6th Baron. Don Juan: cantos IX, X, XI. 1823.
Hunt, L. Ultra-crepidarius. 1823.
Medwin, T. Journal of the conversations of Lord Byron. 1824.
W. Des persécutions littéraires. Globe (Paris), 23 June 1825.
Review of Adonais and Hellas. Revue Encyclopédique, Aug 1825.
Byron, George Gordon, 6th Baron. Anecdotes of Lord Byron. 1825.
Hazlitt, W. Mr Gifford. In his The spirit of the age, 1825.
Pichot, M. Amédée. Voyage historique et littéraire en Angleterre et en Ecosse. Paris 1825.
The plainspeaker. 2 vols 1826.
Ryan, R. Poetry and poets. 3 vols 1826.
Lockhart, J. G. Review of Hunt, Lord Byron and some of his contemporaries. Quart Rev, Mar 1828.
[Wilson, J.]. Review of Hunt, Lord Byron and some of his contemporaries. Blackwood's Edinburgh Mag, Mar 1828.
[Fairfield, S.] The young poets of Britain. Philadelphia Monthly Mag, 15 Sep 1828.
Bruce, W. Keats and Knowles. Philadelphia Album and Ladies' Literary Gazeteer, 15 Oct 1828.
Gorton, J. A general biographical dictionary. 2 vols 1828.
Hunt, L. The companion. 1828.
Landor, W. S. Imaginary conversations, vol 3. 1828.
Review of Tennyson, Poems chiefly lyrical. NMM, Mar 1831.
Pike, A. Sonnet to Keats. Enterpeiad, 1 Apr 1831.
Sketches of the British poets. Halifax Monthly Mag (Nova Scotia), 1 Aug 1831.
Procter, B. W. An elegy on the death of the poet Keats. Athenaeum, 10 March 1832.
Hunt, L. Poetical works. 1832. Cites examples of splendid imagery in Keats.
[Bulwer, E. L.]. Faults of recent poets. Poems by Alfred Tennyson. NMM, Jan 1833.
Croker, J. W. Review of Tennyson. Quart Rev, Apr 1833.
Hunt, L. The Eve of St Agnes. Leigh Hunt's London Jnl, 21 Jan 1835. Rptd in his Imagination and fancy, 1844.
Clark, J. F. Winander Lake and Mountains, and Ambleside Fall. Western Messenger, June 1836.
Hunt, L. In The book of gems, vol 3 1838.
Lockhart, J. G. Review of R. M. Milnes, Memorials of a residence. Quart Rev, June 1839.
[Aytoun, W. E.]. Chapters on English poetry: Moore, Keats, Crabbe, Campbell, and Rogers. Tait's Edinburgh Mag, Oct 1841.
Lowell, J. R. To the spirit of Keats. Arcturus, Dec 1841.
[Hayman, S.]. Keats and his poetry. Dublin Univ Mag, June 1843.
The genius of John Keats. Christian Remembrancer, Sep 1843.
Chambers, R. (ed). Cyclopaedia of English literature. 2 vols Edinburgh 1843.
Horne, R. H. A new spirit of the age. 1844.
Hunt, L. In his Imagination and fancy: or selections from the English poets, 1844.
Gilfillan, G. In his Gallery of literary portraits, Edinburgh 1845.
De Quincey, T. Notes on Gilfillan's 'Gallery of literary portraits'. Tait's Edinburgh Mag, Nov 1845–Apr 1846.
Howitt, W. Homes and haunts of the most eminent British poets. 1847.
Medwin, T. The life of Percy Bysshe Shelley. 2 vols 1847.
Dilke, C. W. Review of Milnes, Life of Keats. Athenaeum, 12 Aug 1848.
Moir, D. M. Sketches of the poetical literature of the past half-century. 1851.
Chichester, F. W. Poets and poetry of the nineteenth century. 1852.
Mitford, M. R. Recollections of a literary life. 1852.
De Quincey, T. Essays on the poets and other English writers. Boston 1853.
Bagehot, W. Percy Bysshe Shelley. Nat Rev, Oct 1856; rptd in his Collected works, ed N. St John-Stevas, Cambridge MA 1965.
Masson, D. The life and poetry of Keats. Macmillan's Mag, Nov 1860; rptd in his Wordsworth, Shelley, Keats and other essays, 1874.
Ruskin, J. Modern painters. 1860.
Masson, D. The life and poetry of Keats. Macmillan's Mag, Nov 1861.
Etienne, L. Le paganisme poétique en Angleterre. Revue des Deux Mondes, 15 May 1867.
Robinson, H. C. Diary, reminiscences, and correspondence. Ed T. Sadler 3 vols 1869.
Bewick, W. Life and letters. Ed T. Landseer 2 vols 1871.
Coleridge, S. Memoir and letters. New York 1874.
Lowell, J. R. In his Among my books: second series, Boston 1876.
Bouchier, J. Keats's 'Ode to a nightingale'. N & Q, 20 Oct 1877.
Swinburne, A. C. The 'Ode to a nightingale'. Athenaeum, 27 Jan 1877. Rptd in his Miscellanies, 1886.
Owen, F. M. John Keats: a study. 1880.
Arnold, M. Keats. In The English poets, ed T. H. Ward 4 vols 1880; rptd in his Essays in criticism: second series, 1888.
Milner, G. On some marginalia made by Dante G. Rossetti in a copy of Keats's poems. Manchester Quart, 1883.
Swinburne, A. C. In his Miscellanies, 1886 (*see Swinburne, 1877, above*).
De Vere, A. In his Essays chiefly on poetry, 1887.
Bridges, R. John Keats: a critical essay. 1895.
Hoops, J. Keats Jugend und Jugendgedichte. EStudien 11, 1895.
Saintsbury, G. A history of nineteenth-century literature. 1896.
Wenzel, G. Friedrich Hölderlin und John Keats. Magdeburg 1896.
Gothein, M. L. Keats: Leben und Werke. Halle 1897.
Read, W. A. Keats and Spenser. Heidelberg 1897.
Symons, A. John Keats. Monthly Rev, Oct 1901.
Bradley, A. C. John Keats. In Chambers's cyclopaedia of English literature, 1904.
More, P. E. In his Shelburne essays: fourth series, New York 1906.
Brooke, S. A. In his Studies in poetry, 1907.
Wilde, O. The English renaissance of art. In his Essays and letters, 1908.
Bradley, A. C. The letters of Keats. In his Oxford lectures on poetry, 1909.
Wolff, L. An essay on Keats's treatment of the heroic rhythm and blank verse. Paris 1909.
Saintsbury, G. History of English prosody. 3 vols 1910.
Starick, O. P. Die Belesenheit von John Keats und die Grundzuge seiner literarischen Kritik. Berlin 1910.

Wolff, L. John Keats: sa vie et son oeuvre. Paris 1910.
Hudson, W. H. Keats and his poetry. 1911.
Mackail, J. W. Lectures on poetry. 1911.
The Bookman memorial souvenir. Bookman (London), June 1912.
Spurgeon, C. Mysticism in English literature. 1913.
Hearn, L. Interpretations of literature. Ed J. Erskine 1915.
Powys, J. C. Visions and revisions: a book of literary devotions. 1915.
Thomas, E. Keats. London and New York [1916].
Babbitt, I. Rousseau and romanticism. 1919.
Rossetti, D. G. John Keats. Criticism and comments. 1919 (priv ptd by T. J. Wise). Five letters to H. B. Forman.

Biographies

Clarke, C. Cowden. Letter on John Keats, the poet. Morning Chron, 27 July 1821.
Hunt, L. On the suburbs of Genoa and the country about London. In his The literary examiner, 1823.
Procter, B. W. (writing as 'Iluscenor'). Recollections of books and their authors, no. 6: John Keats, the poet. Olio: or museum of entertainment, Jan–July 1828.
Hunt, L. Lord Byron and some of his contemporaries. 1828.
Hone, W. The every-day book and table book. 1830–1.
Clarke, C. Cowden. In his The riches of Chaucer, 1 1835.
Brown, C. A. In his Shakespeare's autobiographical poems, 1838.
Brown, C. A. Walks in the north during the summer of 1818. Plymouth and Devonport Weekly Jnl, 1, 8, 15, 22 Oct 1840.
Dendy, W. C. The philosophy of mystery. 1841.
Severn, J. Sonnet by the late John Keats. Union Mag, Feb 1846.
Milnes, R. M. Life, letters and literary remains of Keats. 2 vols 1848, New York 1848, 1 vol London 1867; ed R. Lynd 1927 (EL); Oxford 1931 (WC).
Hunt, L. In his Autobiography, with reminiscences of friends and contemporaries, 3 vols 1850; ed E. Blunden, Oxford 1928 (WC); ed J. E. Morpurgo 1948.
Clarke, C. Cowden. Letter. Examiner, 9 July 1853.
Taylor, T. In his Life of Benjamin Robert Haydon, from his autobiography and journals, 3 vols 1853.
Clarke, C. Cowden. Recollections of Keats. Atlantic Monthly, Jan 1861; GM, Feb 1874 (rev).
Severn, J. On the vicissitudes of Keats's fame. Atlantic Monthly, Apr 1863.
J. H. C. Chatterton. N & Q, 24 Aug 1872.
Haydon, B. R. In his Correspondence and table talk, 2 vols 1876.
Haydon, B. R. Diary. Ed W. B. Pope 5 vols Cambridge MA 1960–3.
Procter, B. W. An autobiographical fragment and biographical notes, 1877.
Clarke, C. Cowden. and M. Cowden Clarke. In their Recollections of writers, 1878; introd by R. Gittings, Fontwell 1969 (photo facs).
Forman, H. B. Severn and Keats. Athenaeum, 23, 30 Aug 1879.
Richardson, B. W. An Esculapian poet – John Keats. In his Asclepiad, 1884; rptd in his Disciples of Aesculapius, 1900.
Colvin, S. Keats. 1887 (EML).
Rossetti, W. M. Life of Keats. 1887.
Sharp, W. In his Life and letters of Joseph Severn, 1892.
Graham, W. Keats and Severn. New Rev, May 1894; rptd in his Last links with Byron, Shelley and Keats, 1898.
Colvin, S. A morning's walk in a Hampstead garden. Monthly Rev, Mar 1903; rptd in The John Keats memorial volume, 1921.
Miller, B. Leigh Hunt's relations with Byron, Shelley and Keats. New York 1910.
Colvin, S. Keats and his friends: unpublished poems and letters. TLS, 16 April 1914.
Colvin, S. Keats: his life and poetry, his friends, critics and after-fame. 1917, 1918, 1920.
Blunden, E. Shelley and Keats as they struck their contemporaries. 1925.
Dilke, C. W. Memoir. In Endymion, introd by H. Clement Notcutt, 1927.
Brown, C. A. Life of John Keats. Ed D. H. Bodurtha and W. B. Pope 1937.
Brown, C. A. Some letters and miscellanea of Charles Brown, the friend of Keats and Thomas Richards. Ed M. B. Forman 1937.
Hewlett, D. Adonais: a life of John Keats. 1937.
Bate, W. J. John Keats. Cambridge MA and Oxford 1963.
Ward, A. John Keats: the making of a poet. London and New York 1963.
Brown, C. A. Letters. Ed J. Stillinger. Cambridge MA 1966.
Gittings, R. John Keats. 1968, 1971 (Pen).
Stillinger, J. Another early biographical sketch of 'young Keats'. ELN 18, 1981.
Pinion, F. B. A Keats chronology. 1992.
Motion, A. Keats. 1997.

The Keats–Shelley Jnl *and* The Keats–Shelley Rev *(formerly* The Keats–Shelley Memorial Bull*) are published annually.* [DW]

John Keble 1792–1866

On translation from dead languages: a prize essay. Oxford 1812. Prose.
The Christian year: thoughts in verse for the Sundays and holydays throughout the year. 2 vols Oxford 1827 (2 edns, anon); New York [1827?]; Philadelphia 1827; Oxford 1828, 1829, 1832, 1833, 1834; Philadelphia 1834, 1835; Oxford 1835, 1836, 1837, 1839, 1840; Philadelphia 1840; Oxford and London 1841 (2 edns); Philadelphia 1842; Oxford 1843, 1844 (2 edns), 1845 (3 edns), 1846 (2 edns); Philadelphia 1847; Oxford 1847, 1848; Philadelphia 1848; Oxford 1849 (3 edns); New York 1850; Oxford 1850 (4 edns); Philadelphia 1850, 1851; Oxford 1852 (2 edns); New York 1853; Oxford 1853, 1854; Philadelphia 1854; Oxford 1856; Philadelphia 1856, 1857; Oxford 1857 (2 edns), 1858 (4 edns); New York 1858; Oxford 1859 (5 edns), 1860 (5 edns); Philadelphia 1860; Oxford 1861 (4 edns), 1862 (2 edns); New York 1862; Oxford 1863; Philadelphia 1863; Oxford 1864 (3 edns); Philadelphia 1864; Oxford 1865 (3 edns); Boston 1865; New York 1866; Oxford 1866 (3 edns); Boston 1867; Philadelphia 1867; Oxford 1868 (2 edns, one a facs of 1827), 1869; Boston 1869; Philadelphia [1869?], 1870; New York 1872; London 1873; New York 1873; Oxford 1873 (5 edns); London [1874] (abridged), [1874] (with memoir by W. Temple); 1875 (2 edns, one illustr F. Overbeck); New York 1875; London 1876, 1877, '1878' [1877] (facs of original draft, with collation of the variations between draft and the pbd edns), 1878, 1879 (2 edns), 1880 (5 edns), 1881, 1882 (2 edns), 1883 (2 edns, one with memoir and portrait), 1884 (2 edns, one The Canterbury Poets), [1885]; New York 1885; ed A. H. Grant, London [1886]; ed 'Pilgrim' (J. Hogg), London 1886 (with Collects, and a series of meditations and exhortations selected from the works of H. P. Liddon); London 1887 (3 edns, one ed H. Morley); New York 1887; London [1889]; New York 1890, 1891; London 1891, 1892, 1893 (2 edns, one illus, including a portrait), 1894, 1895 (2 edns, one with introd and notes by W. Lock and 5 designs by R. Anning Bell), 1896 (authorised edn); New York 1896; London 1897 (2 edns, one a 2-vol facs of 1st edn with preface by Bishop of Rochester and a list of alterations made by the author in the text of later edns); London 1898 (2 edns, one ed W. Lock); New York 1898; London 1900, 1901; New York 1902; London 1903 (Unit Lib), [1903] (Red Letter Lib); Guildford 1904; New York 1905; London [1906]; Chicago [1907]; London [1907], 1909; ed J. C. Sharp, London [1914]; Oxford 1914 (WC and one with Lyra innocentium and other poems and the sermon National apostasy); Detroit 1975; London 1977; Detroit 1990; New York 1991. Numerous undated edns have appeared, many of the hymns have been rptd separately and there has been a large number of vols composed of selections from The Christian year.
National apostasy considered in a sermon. Oxford 1833, 1847 (in Sermons, academical and occasional), 1914 (in The Christian year,

Lyra innocentium, and other poems etc); ed R. J. E. Boggis, Torquay [1931]; London 1931; Abingdon 1983.
Ode for the Encaenia at Oxford. 1834 (anon), 1869 (in Miscellaneous poems).
Tracts for the times. Nos 4, 13, 40, 52, 54, 57, 60, 1834; no 89, 1841.
Lyra apostolica. 1836, 1837, 1838, 1843, 1864. 46 poems signed. With J. E. Bowden and others.
Primitive tradition recognized in Holy Scripture: a sermon. 1836, 1837 (2 edns, one with postscript and Tract 78 as appendix).
The psalter, or psalms of David in English verse. 1839 (anon), 1840 (anon), 1869, 1904, 1906.
The case of Catholic subscription to the XXXIX articles. 1841 (priv ptd), 1865 (with Tract 90 by J. H. Newman), 1866.
Praelectiones poeticae. 1844.
Lyra innocentium: thoughts in verse on Christian children. Oxford 1846 (anon, 3 edns); New York 1846; Oxford 1847, 1851, 1854, 1867, 1870, 1884; ed W. Lock, London 1899; illustr B. Handler, London 1903, [1906], 1914 (with The Christian year and other poems and the sermon National apostasy).
Sermons, academical and occasional. Oxford 1847, 1848.
On eucharistical adoration. Oxford 1857, 1859, 1867.
Sermons, occasional and parochial. Oxford and London 1867; Oxford 1868.
Miscellaneous poems. Ed [G. Moberly], Oxford and London 1869 (2 edns); New York 1869; Oxford 1870. Contains Ode for the Encaenia, the poems contributed to the Lyra apostolica, selections from The Christian year and Lyra innocentium, and Remains.
Village sermons on the baptismal service. Ed [E. B. Pusey], Oxford '1869' [1868]; London 1869.
Letters of spiritual counsel and guidance. Ed R. F. Wilson 1870, 1875 (enlarged); ed B. W. Randolph 1904.
Sermons for the Christian year [with an 'Advertisement' by E. B. P., i.e. E. B. Pusey]. 11 vols Oxford 1875–80.
Occasional papers and reviews. Ed E. B. Pusey, Oxford 1877. Includes Life of Sir Walter Scott; Sacred poetry; Unpublished papers of Bishop Warburton; Copleston's Praelectiones academicae; Miller's Bampton lectures, etc.
Studia sacra. Ed J. P. N. [J. P. Norris] 1877.
Keble's lectures on poetry 1832–41. Tr from Latin by E. K. Francis, 2 vols Oxford 1912.
The Christian year, Lyra innocentium and other poems, together with National apostasy. 1914.

§2

Shairp, J. C. Keble: an essay on the author of The Christian year. Edinburgh 1866, 1868 (in Studies in poetry and philosophy).
Coleridge, J. T. A memoir of Keble. Oxford 1869, 2 vols Oxford 1869 (with corrections and addns), New York 1869 (with corrections and addns), Oxford 1870 (with corrections and addns), Oxford 1874, New York 1875 (with corrections and addns), Oxford 1880, New York 1977.
Yonge, C. M. Musings over The Christian year and Lyra innocentium, together with a few gleanings of recollections of Keble, gathered by several friends. 1871, 1898.
Lock, W. Keble: a biography. 1893. Appendix 2 contains complete list of Keble's pbd works.
Wood, E. F. L. (Earl of Halifax). John Keble. 1909, 1932.
See also J. R. Griffin, John Keble, saint of Anglicanism. *Macon GA 1987*
[JRdeJJ and DL]

Rann Kennedy 1772–1851

Selections

Kennedy, C. R. Poems original and translated. 1857 (2nd edn). Contains 2 poems by R. Kennedy.
Kennedy, B. H. Between whiles, or wayside amusements of a working life. London and Cambridge 1877. Contains 2 poems by R. Kennedy.

§1

A poem on the death of … the Princess Charlotte. 1817 (2 edns).
A tribute in verse to … George Canning …. London and Birmingham 1827.
Britain's genius: a mask on occasion of the marriage of Victoria …. 1840.
Edited a prayer book and a psalter, edited Byron and translated Virgil.

William Kennedy 1799–1871

§1

Fitful fancies. Edinburgh and London 1827.
The arrow and the rose, with other poems. 1830.
An only son: a narrative. 1831 (anon); Boston 1832, 1862.
The siege of Antwerp: a historical play. 1838.
Texas: the rise … of the republic. 2 vols 1841 (2 edns); Fort Worth TX 1925; selection: Texas, its geography. New York and Boston 1844. Prose.

§2

Marshall, J. J. Life of W. Kennedy …. Dungannon 1920.
Edited The Continental Annual *(1832).*

Mary Kentish, Mrs fl. 1819–21

Poems on various subjects. 1819; Liverpool, London and Edinburgh 1821.
The two friends, or the dying fawn: a tale. [1820?] Prose.
How to be happy, or the cottage of content. New Haven CT 1827; London [1840?]. Prose.
The maid of the village, or the farmer's daughter of the woodlands. 1835, 1838, 1847. Prose.

John Kenyon 1784–1856

Rhymed plea for tolerance. 1833 (3 issues, anon), 1839 (acknowledged) (rev with addns).
Poems, for the most part occasional. 1838.
A day at Tivoli, with other verses. 1848, 1849.

Charlotte King

See Charlotte Dacre, col 899.

Harriet Rebecca King fl. 1823–52

Poems. Salisbury and London 1823; Salisbury 1824.
Oakdale cottage, or the Christmas holidays. 1829. Prose.
Nuneham Park, or the summer holidays: a sequel. 1831. Prose.
Metrical exercises upon scripture texts, and miscellaneous poems. 1834 (2 edns).
Thoughts in verse upon scripture texts. 2 vols 1842–6.
Nursery hymns upon the creed, the Lord's prayer. 1843.
Catechetical readings in the Pentateuch. 1852. Prose.

Sophia King, later Fortnum b. c. 1782

Trifles of Helicon. 1798. With Charlotte King.
Waldorf, or the dangers of philosophy. 2 vols 1798; New York 1974 (facs reprint). Prose.
Cordelia, or a romance of real life. 1799; tr Fr (as Cordelia, ou faiblesse excusable) by P. Chanin, Paris 1800. Prose.

The fatal secret, or unknown warrior ... with legendary poems. 1801. Prose and verse.
The victim of friendship: a German romance. 1801. Prose.
Poems, legendary, pathetic and descriptive. 1804.
The adventures of Victor Allen. 2 vols 1805. Prose.

William King, of Edmonton fl. 1833–5

The parricide: a play. London and Tottenham 1833.
Scraps of poesy. Tottenham [1835]. With W. S. Finch.

Ann Cuthbert Knight, later Fleming d. 1860

Home: a poem. Edinburgh and London 1815.
A year in Canada and other poems. Edinburgh and London 1816.

Henry Gally Knight 1786–1846

Iberia's crisis: a fragment of an epic poem. 1809. Anon.
Noradin, or the lamps of fate: a dramatic poem. 1809. Anon.
Phrosyne: a Grecian tale in two cantos. 1814 (anon), 1817 (with Alashtar: an Arabian tale; acknowledged).
Ilderim: a Syrian tale in four cantos. 1816; Philadelphia 1816. Anon.
Eastern sketches, in verse. 1819 (2 edns), 1830.
Hannibal in Bithynia: a play. 1839 (3 edns).
Edited Miniature *1804–5, 1806, and wrote also on architecture, travel, politics, foreign policy and the Catholic question.*

Walter Laidlaw 1780–1845

Poems chiefly on Jedburgh and vicinity, with a selection from his prose writings and a biographical sketch. Ed Sir G. B. Douglas, Kelso [1901].
Recollections of Sir Walter Scott: 1802–1804. Ed J. Sinton, Hawick 1905.

Robert Eyres Landor 1781–1869

Collection

Selections from his poetry and prose, with an introduction biographical and critical by E. Partridge. 1927. Also pbd in 2 pts: Selections from Robert Landor; Robert Eyres Landor: a biographical and critical sketch.

§1

An essay on the character and doctrines of Socrates. Oxford 1802. Anon.
The dun cow: an hyper-satirical dialogue. 1808. (Anon?)
Guy's porridge pot. 1808 (anon), 1809 (with The dun cow roasted whole).
The Count Arezzi: a tragedy. 1824. Anon.
The impious feast: a poem in ten books. 1828.
The Earl of Brecon: a tragedy, Faith's fraud: a tragedy, The ferryman: a drama. 1841.
The fawn of Sertorius. 2 vols 1846. Anon. Prose.
The fountain of Arethusa. 2 vols 1848. Prose.

§2

Partridge, E. H. Robert Eyres Landor: a biographical and critical sketch. 1927; Freeport NY [1970].

Hon Elizabeth Susan Law, or Abbot, later Lady Colchester 1799–1883

Goldsmith, O. Il villaggio abbandonato (The deserted village). Tr Ital 1825, 1832.
Thérèse de Villarejo: roman espagnol. By E*******. [1826?] (not pbd). Prose.
Goldsmith, O. Il viaggiatore (The traveller). Tr Ital 1832.
Miscellaneous poems, dedicated to J. Jekyll, Esq. By E. S. L. 1832 (not pbd), 1849 (by E. S. C.).
Giustina, a Spanish tale of real life: a poem in three cantos. By E. S. L. 1833 (not pbd).
Views in London ... sketched from a window in the 'palais de la verité', and extracts from an album. Dedicated to Sophia, Countess of Darlington. By an amateur. Chiswick 1833 (not pbd). Anon.
Poems by Lady Colchester. [1835?] (not pbd).
Home reminiscences. By E. S. C. 1861 (not pbd).
Charles, Lord Colchester. Memoranda of my life. Ed [E. S. L.] 1869. Prose.
Algernon Graham, Earl of Kingsbury. 1872. Prose.
Fitz-Edward. 1875. Prose.
Days before the flood: a tale. By E. C. S. 1884. Prose.

C. F. Lawler ('Peter Pindar') fl. 1804–21

Attributions are tentative.

Collections

The works of 'Peter Pindar'. 4 vols 1816, 1823, 1824, 1830; selection: ed P. M. Zall, Bath and Columbia SC 1972.

§1

The elegant sharper, or the science of villainy display'd. 1804. Anon.
R—l sprain, or a kick from Yar—h to Wa—s. By 'Peter Pindar'. [1812.]
A scourge for stripes ... By 'Peter Pindar'. 1812.
The eldest chick of the r—l brood. By 'Peter Pindar'. [1813?] (3 edns).
R—l disaster, or dangers of a q—n. By 'Peter Pindar'. 1813.
R—l quarrels, or curtain lectures. By 'Peter Pindar'. 1813 (4 edns).
The lamentations of the porter-vat. By 'Peter Pindar'. [1814] (2 edns).
Lilliputian navy!! The r—t's fleet, or John Bull at the Serpentine. By 'Peter Pindar'. [1814] (7 edns).
Midnight dreams, or prophetic visions of the r—l brood. By 'Peter Pindar'. 1814 (2 edns).
More kings! A poem. By 'Peter Pindar'. 1814 (2 edns), 1815.
The P—e's jubilee, or r—l revels! By 'Peter Pindar'. [1814.]
Physic and delusion! Or Jezebel and the doctors. By 'Peter Pindar'. [1814.]
The regent and the king, or a trip from Hartwell to Dover. By 'Peter Pindar'. 1814 (3 edns).
The r—l runaway, or c—tte and coachee!! By 'Peter Pindar'. [1814] (5 edns).
The r—l showman, or the r—t's gala. By 'Peter Pindar'. 1814.
Royalty fog-bound, or the perils of a night. By 'Peter Pindar'. 1814 (6 edns), 1815.
The r—t's fair, or grand galante-show!! By 'Peter Pindar'. [1814] (2 edns).
The temple knock'd down, or r—l auction. By 'Peter Pindar'. [1814.]
Bonaparte in Paris! Or the flight of the Bourbons! By 'Peter Pindar'. [1815.]
The cork rump, or queen and maids of honour. By 'Peter Pindar'. 1815.
The fat knight and the petition, or cits in the dumps! By 'Peter Pindar'. 1815.
The German sausages, or the devil to pay at congress! By 'Peter Pindar'. 1815 (2 edns).
The groans of the quartern loaf: a poem. By 'Peter Pindar'. [1815] (3 edns).
Love at head-quarters, or a week at Brussels ... By the author of The royal sprain. 1815. Anon.

R—l loggerheads, or the congress of state tinkers. By 'Peter Pindar'. [1815.]
R—l robbery!! The crown jewels, or diamond cut diamond. By 'Peter Pindar'. 1815.
Salms for a r—l duke, or doleful lamentations. By 'Peter Pindar'. 1815 (2 edns).
The bench in an uproar... By 'Peter Pindar'. 1816.
Fair! Fat! and forty... By 'Peter Pindar'. 1816.
A peep behind the curtain, or the battle royal. By 'Peter Pindar'. 1816 (2 edns).
The r—l marriage, or Miss Lump and the grenadier. By 'Peter Pindar'. [1816] (4 edns).
Royal rantipoles, or the humours of Brighton... By 'Peter Pindar'. 1816.
Royalty bewitched... By 'Peter Pindar'. 1816.
The r—t's bomb!... By 'Peter Pindar'. 1816.
State secrets disclosed!!... By 'Peter Pindar'. [1816?]
Stripes for sinecurists, or a scourge for st—e paupers. By 'Peter Pindar'. [1816?]
Wedding! and bedding!... By 'Peter Pindar'. [1816?] (2 edns).
Who wears the breeches?... By 'Peter Pindar'. [1816.]
Wooing!! and cooing!!... By 'Peter Pindar'. 1816 (4 edns).
Bubbles of treason, or state trials at large. By 'Peter Pindar'. 1817.
Choice cabinet pictures... By 'Peter Pindar'. 1817.
The contest of legs, or diplomatics in China. By 'Peter Pindar'. 1817.
A new form of prayer for 1817. By 'Peter Pindar'. 1817.
R—l chickens in the shell. By 'Peter Pindar'. 1817.
The r—l cruise! Or half seas over. By 'Peter Pindar'. [1817.]
Shots at the regent!!! Royalty beset. By 'Peter Pindar'. 1817.
The Bath pump room. By 'Peter Pindar'. 1818.
The disappointed duke, or the admiral and the heiress. By 'Peter Pindar'. [1818.]
Hunting for the heir!!! The r—l h-mb-gs. By 'Peter Pindar'. 1818.
Who can get an heir!! By 'Peter Pindar'. 1818.
The ambassador at court. By 'Peter Pindar'. 1819.
Peter Pindar's ghost!! Or poetic epistles from the other world. By 'Peter Pindar'. 1821.

Sir James Henry Lawrence 1773–1840

The virgin of the sun: a play. By A. von Kotzebue. Tr from Ger 1799. Prose.
Das Paradies der Liebe. 2 vols Munich [1800?], [1918], 1923; tr Eng by the author, 4 vols London 1811 (as The empire of the Nairs, or the rights of women) (2 edns), 1813, 1824; tr Fr by the author, 4 vols Paris 1814 (as L'empire des Nairs). Prose.
Love: an allegory. 1802.
A picture of Verdun, or the English detained in France. By a détenu. 2 vols 1810. Anon. Prose.
Dramatic emancipation, or strictures on the state of the theatres. 1813. Prose.
The Englishman at Verdun, or the prisoner of peace: a drama. 1813. Prose and verse.
The Etonian out of bounds. 2 vols 1828; 3 vols Paris and London 1828; 2 vols London 1834. Prose and verse.
Wrote also on religion, literary property, and British and foreign codes of honour.

Rose Lawrence, formerly D'Aguilar fl. 1799–1829

Gortz of Berlingen with the iron hand. By Goethe. Tr [Lawrence] Liverpool [1799]. Anon. Prose.
The works of S. Gessner. Tr [Lawrence] Liverpool 1802. Anon. Prose.
The last autumn at a favourite residence with other poems. By a lady. 1828; London and Liverpool 1829 (acknowledged), 1836.
Edited collections of verse for children.

John Lawson 1787–1825

The maniac and other poems. 1810; Philadelphia 1811; London 1821; Calcutta 1826.
Orient harping: a desultory poem. Calcutta 1818; London 1820; London and Chiswick 1821; Calcutta 1822.
Woman, a poem: female influence. Calcutta 1820; London 1821 (as Woman in India part 1).
A missionary hymn book. Calcutta 1821.
An elegy to the memory of... Martyn. 1823.
The lost spirit: a poem. Calcutta 1823; London 1825.

Alicia Lefanu, the younger fl. 1804–26

Lucy Osmond. New York 1804. Anon. Prose.
The flowers, or the sylphid queen, a fairy tale in verse. 1809.
Rosara's chain, or the choice of life: a poem. 1812, 1815 (3rd edn), 1823.
Strathallan. 4 vols 1816 (2 edns), 1817; tr Fr by H. de J***, 5 vols Paris 1818. Prose.
Helen Monteagle. 3 vols 1818. Prose.
Leolin Abbey. 3 vols 1819. Prose.
Don Juan de las sierras, or el empecinado. 3 vols 1823. Prose.
Tales of a tourist. 4 vols 1823. Prose.
Memoirs of the life and writings of Mrs Frances Sheridan. 1824. Prose.
Henry the Fourth of France. 4 vols 1826. Prose.

Charles Leftley, the younger 1770–1797

See William Linley, below.

Charles Valentine Le Grice 1773–1858

§1

An imitation of Horace's first epistle. Cambridge 1793; Penzance 1824; Truro 1850.
The Tineum... The icead.... Cambridge 1794. Prose and verse.
A prize declamation... on Richard Cromwell,... and a speech to prove that the reign of Anne has been improperly called the Augustan age of English genius. Cambridge 1795. Prose.
Analysis of Paley's principles of moral and political philosophy. Cambridge 1795, 1796 (enlarged); London 1799, 1802, 1811, 1820, 1822. Prose.
A general theorem for a [Trinity] College declamation, with copious notes by 'Gronovius' [i.e. Le Grice]. Cambridge 1796, [1835].
Daphnis and Chloe: a pastoral novel, now first selectly translated. Penzance 1803. Anon. Prose.
The petition of an old uninhabited house in Penzance to its master in town. Penzance 1811, 1823, 1858. Anon.
College reminiscences of Mr Coleridge, reprinted from the GM December 1834, by desire. Penzance [1842]. Also rptd in J. Cottle, Reminiscences of Coleridge and Southey, 1847; Highgate 1970 (reprint). Prose.

§2

Blunden, E. Coleridge's fellow Grecian. 1956.
Pbd a number of sermons from 1802 to 1814, and various poems as broadsheets from 1832 to 1855; the BL has gathered them in a vol.

Chandos Leigh, first baron Leigh 1791–1850

The island of love: a dream. 1812.
Trifles light as air. 1813 (2 edns).
Juvenile poems. 1815 (priv ptd), [1817]. Anon.
An epistle to Emma. [1816.]
Fragments of essays. 1816. Anon. Prose.
Verses. [Stoneleigh 1816] (priv ptd); London 1818 (as Poems).

Dedicatory stanzas to Mary, also an ode on the death of the Princess Charlotte. Warwick 1818.
The view and other poems. Warwick 1819; London 1819, 1820, 1822.
Sylva: poems on several occasions. London and Edinburgh 1823.
Second letter to a friend in town and other poems. 1824.
A third letter to a friend in town. Warwick 1825.
Epistles to a friend in town, Golconda's fête and other poems. 1826, 1828, 1831.
Poems now first collected. 1829, 1839.
Fourth epistle to a friend in town. Warwick and Leamington 1830.
The spirit of the age. Warwick 1832 (priv ptd).
Fifth epistle to a friend in town. 1835.
Poland. Warwick 1836.
Poems. Leamington 1840 (priv ptd). Anon.
A vision, allegorical. 1840. Anon.
Supplementary verses. Warwick 1841, 1843.
Thoughts at Whitsuntide and other poems. 1842.
Walks in the country. 1844.
Minor poems. Leamington 1850.
Also wrote political tracts and an abridgement of Butler's Analogy of religion.

Elizabeth Anne Le Noir, Mrs Jean Baptiste, formerly Smart 1754–1841

Village anecdotes, or the journal of a year, from Sophia to Edward, with original poems. 3 vols 1804; Reading and London [1807?]. Prose and verse.
Clara de Montfier: a moral tale, with original poems. Ed C. Burney and C. Munter 3 vols Reading and London 1808; Reading 1819 (as The maid of la Vendée). Prose and verse.
Miscellaneous poems. 2 vols Reading 1825–6.

Eliza Lucy Leonard fl. 1815–27

The ruby ring, or transformations. 1815, 1816.
The miller and his golden dream. Wellington and London 1822; Wellington 1827.

Stewart or Stuart Lewis 1756?–1818

Fair Helen of Kirkconnel: a tragical poem. Edinburgh 1796; Dumfries 1817 (3rd edn).
The African slave with other poems. Edinburgh 1816.

William Lewis, painter fl. 1817–18

The bard's lament: a vision. 1817, 1818.

John Leyden 1775–1811

Collections
Rogers 2.
Poetical remains. Ed R. Heber 1819. With memoir by J. Morton.
Poems and ballads. Kelso 1858; London 1875. With memoir by W. Scott and suppl by R. White.
Poetical works. London and Edinburgh 1875. With memoir by T. Brown.
Journal of a tour in the highlands . . . in 1800. Ed (with bibliography) J. Sinton, Edinburgh and London 1903.
Journal of a tour to Gilsland and the Cumberland lakes. Ed J. Sinton, Hawick 1906.
An Anglo-Indian poet. Ed P. Seshadri, Madras 1912.

§1

A historical and philosophical sketch of the discoveries and settlements of the Europeans in northern and western Africa. Edinburgh and London 1799 (anon); London 1799 (acknowledged); 2 vols Edinburgh 1817 (enlarged as Historical account of discoveries and travels in Africa); London 1818; tr Ger Bremen 1802, Fr Paris 1804, 1817, 1821.
The complaynt of Scotland, written in 1548; with a preliminary dissertation and glossary. Ed Leyden, Edinburgh 1801.
Scotish descriptive poems, with some illustrations of Scotish literary antiquities. Ed Leyden, Edinburgh 1803. Includes his Biographical sketch of John Wilson, which was rptd 1852, with the text of Wilson's Clyde: a poem.
Scenes of infancy: descriptive of Teviotdale. Edinburgh 1803, 1811; Jedburgh 1844; Kelso 1875 (with memoir by W. M. Tulloch).

§2

Morton, J. Memoirs of the life and writings. 1822.
Reith, J. Life of Dr John Leyden. 1923.
Leyden contributed to M. G. Lewis, Tales of wonder *(1801), and assisted Scott with the earlier vols of* Minstrelsy of the Scottish border *(1802). He was an authority on several oriental languages, publishing treatises and trns.*

Wilbrahim Liardet fl. 1806–7

The case of the hypochondriac explained. 1806.
Fifty of Aesop's fables rendered into verse. 1806.
The hypochondriack: a sentimental poem. 1807.

Isabella Lickbarrow fl. 1814–18

Poetical effusions. Kendal and London 1814; Oxford and New York 1994 (facs reprint).
A lament upon the death of Her Royal Highness the Princess Charlotte, and Alfred: a vision. Liverpool 1818.

I. S. or J. S. Anna Liddiard, Mrs William fl. 1810–19

Poems. Dublin 1810.
The Sgelaighe, or a tale of old, with a second edition of poems. Bath and London 1811.
Kenilworth and Farley Castle with other poems. Dublin 1813; Dublin and London 1815 (as Kenilworth: a mask).
Mont St Jean: a poem . . . Theodore and Laura: a tale . . . . London and Dublin 1816. With W. Liddiard.
Mount Leinster, or the prospect: a poem. 1819. Anon.

William Liddiard 1773–1841

The life-boat, or Dillon O'Dwire: a poem. Dublin 1815.
Mont St Jean: a poem . . . Theodore and Laura: a tale . . . . London and Dublin 1816. With I. S. Anna Liddiard.
The legend of Einsidlin: a tale of Switzerland, with poetical sketches of Swiss scenery. 1829.
A three months' tour in Switzerland and France. 1832. Prose and verse.
Retrospection . . . The lord of the valley . . . and other poems. 1841.

William Linley 1771–1835

Forbidden apartments: a tale. 2 vols 1800.
The adventures of Ralph Reybridge. 4 vols 1809. Prose.
Sonnets, odes, and other poems . . . By Charles Leftley. Ed Linley 1814, 1816.
An address to . . . Lord Byron . . . Sonnets and odes, elegies, ballads and sketches. 1819. With F. H. B. and C. Leftley.
Primarily a composer.

William Lipscomb fl. 1754–1842

Beneficial effects of inoculation. 1772, 1793 (as Verses on the beneficial effect of inoculation); Oxford 1807; London 1810. Anon.
Poems: to which are added translations of select Italian sonnets. Oxford and York 1784.
The pardoner's tale from Chaucer. 1792.
The Canterbury tales of Chaucer completed in a modern version. 3 vols Oxford 1795. Anon. With J. Ogle.
Poems and translations. 1830. Anon.

'Cynthia Little', pseudonym fl. 1829–31

A review of the first masquerade at the royal gardens, Brighton. 1829.
The mess-room, or Cupid fra Diavolo: a humorous poem. 1831.

Charles Lloyd 1775–1839

§1

Poems on various subjects. Carlisle 1795.
Poems on the death of Priscilla Farmer, by her grandson. 1796.
Poems by S. T. Coleridge: second edition; to which are now added poems by Charles Lamb and Charles Lloyd. Bristol 1797. 28 poems by Lloyd.
Blank verse, by Charles Lloyd and Charles Lamb. 1798.
Edmund Oliver. 2 vols Bristol 1798. A novel. Rptd in 1 vol with introd by J. Wordsworth, Oxford 1990.
A letter to the Anti-Jacobin reviewers. Birmingham 1799. On Edmund Oliver.
Lines suggested by the fast appointed on Wednesday, February 27, 1799. Birmingham 1799.
The tragedies of Vittorio Alfieri, translated. 3 vols 1815.
Nugae canorae: poems – third edition, with additions. 1819. Mainly new poems. Rptd with introd by D. H. Reiman, New York 1977.
Isabel: a tale. 2 vols 1820. Prose.
Desultory thoughts in London; Titus and Gisippus, with other poems. 1821. Rptd with introd by D. H. Reiman, New York 1977.
Memoirs of the life and writings of Vittorio Alfieri. 1821.
Poetical essays on the character of Pope as a poet and moralist, and on the language and objects most fit for poetry. 1821.
The Duke d'Ormond: a tragedy; and Beritola: a tale. 1822. Verse.
Poems. 1823.
Poems on various subjects, Blank verse, Poetical essays on the character of Pope, Poems. Introd by D. H. Reiman, New York 1978.

Letters

The Lloyd–Manning letters. Ed F. L. Beaty, Bloomington IN 1957.

§2

[Southey, R.] Alfieri's life and writings. Quart Rev 14 1816.
Conway, M. D. English lakes and their genii. Harper's New Monthly Mag 62 1881.
[Lamb, C.] Nugae canorae: poems by Charles Lloyd. Examiner 24–5 Oct 1819; rptd in his Works, ed T. Hutchinson, vol 1, 1908.
De Quincey, T. Reminiscences of Charles Lloyd. Tait's Mag 7 1840; rptd in his Collected writings, ed D. Masson, vol 2, Edinburgh 1889.
Lucas, E. V. Charles Lamb and the Lloyds. 1898.
Hunt, H. C. Note on Lloyd. TLS 20 Feb 1937.
Zall, P. M. Hazlitt's 'romantic acquaintance': Wordsworth and Lloyd. MLN 71 1956.
Smith, H. R. Lloyd: the friend of the Lake poets. N & Q Dec 1956, Oct 1957. [PL]

Mary Ann Lloyd fl. 1820–31

A manual, consisting of a defence of the Bible... in prose and verse. 1820.
Lines on the passions. Addressed to a young gentleman.... 1823.
'Think of Jesus': a poem written for Good Friday in the year of our Lord 1823. [1823.]
The funds and more companies, with technical phrases on stock, or flippancies of the times: in rhyme. 1823 (2 edns), [1825].
Various briefer pbns (broadsheets, 2 pp. issues), some of which have been collected as a vol of 'Poems' by the BL.

Richard Llwyd 1752–1835

Collection

The poetical works of... the bard of Snowdon. [1837.]

§1

Beaumaris Bay: a poem.... Chester and London [1800] (anon), 1832 (acknowledged).
Gayton wake, or Mary Dod: a poem. Chester and London 1804.
Poems, tales, odes, sonnets, translations. 2 vols Chester and London 1804.

Samuel Lover 1797–1868

See col 951.

Robert Lowth 1762?–1822

Billesdon Coplow. Melton Mowbray 1800 (anon); London 1800 (2 edns); Prescot [1800]; London 1804, 1831 (acknowledged), 1833; London, Derby and Stamford 1845; London 1854.
Select psalms in verse. Ed with W. H. Aston 1811.

Charles Lucas 1769–1854

The old serpentine temple of the druids. Bath 1795; Marlborough 1801 (as A descriptive account... of the... temple of the druids). Anon.
The castle of St Donats, or the history of Jack Smith. 3 vols 1798 (anon); Baltimore [1800?] (attributed); tr Fr Tours [1894].
The infernal Quixote: a tale of the day. 4 vols 1801; Dublin 1801. Prose.
The Abissinian reformer, or the Bible and the sabre. 3 vols 1808. Prose.
Joseph: a religious poem. 2 vols 1810.
Poems on various subjects. Tewkesbury 1810.
Gwelygordd, or the child of sin. 3 vols 1820. Anon. Prose.
Pbns on theology and the church.

Henry Luttrell 1765?–1851

Lines written at Ampthill Park in the autumn of 1818. 1819. Anon.
Advice to Julia: a letter in rhyme. 1820 (2 edns) (anon), 1822 (as Letters to Julia, in rhyme, to which are added lines written at Ampthill-Park; acknowledged).
Crockford-House: a rhapsody in two cantos, A rhymer in Rome. 1827. Anon.

Henry Francis Lyte 1793–1847

Collection

The poetical works. Ed with a biographical sketch by J. Appleyard 1907.

Selection

Miles 10 (11).

§1

Observations on the scriptures suited to the present juncture: in a sermon preached at St Mary's Chapel, Penzance, Nov 28 1819. 1820.

Tales in verse illustrative of the several petitions of the Lord's prayer. 1826, 1829.

Without God in the world: a sermon preached in the chapel at Saltram, Oct 19 1823 etc. 1826.

Poems chiefly religious. 1833, 1841 (1 poem added), 1845.
REVIEW: Athenaeum 17 May 1834.

The spirit of the psalms: or the psalms of David adapted to Christian worship. 1834, 1836 (4th edn corrected and enlarged), [1864] reprint of 3rd edn).

Silex scintillans etc, by Henry Vaughan. 1847, Boston 1856, London 1858, 1883. With memoir by Lyte.

Remains, with a prefatory memoir by A. M. M. H. [daughter Mrs Hogg]. 1850.
REVIEW: Christian Remembrancer 43, Jan 1851.

Miscellaneous poems. 1868, 1875. Reprint of Poems chiefly religious, 1845, *above*, with 24 poems added, including Abide with me.
REVIEW: Br Quart Rev 49, Jan 1869.

Abide with me: with 15 illustrations and a memorial sketch by H. L. L. [i.e. Jane Borthwick]. [1883.]

§2

Skinner, B. G. Henry Francis Lyte. Exeter 1974. Includes selection of poems in appendix. [RS]

Elizabeth Wright Macauley 1785?–1837

Macauley's literary amusements. Ed Macauley, Newcastle 1809.

A pamphlet on the difficulties and dangers of a theatrical life. Dublin 1810. Includes The birth of friendship. Prose and verse.

Marmion: a melodrama. After W. Scott. Cork 1811 (2nd edn).

Effusions of fancy: consisting of The birth of friendship, The birth of affection and The birth of sensibility. 1812 (2 edns, the 2nd as Poetical effusions).

Theatric revolution, or plain truth addressed to common sense. 1819. Prose.

Three questions to the public. 1820. Prose.

Tales of the drama. Chiswick and London 1822; Exeter 1833; Boston 1834; Hartford CT 1847, 1848, 1852, 1855. Prose.

Mary Stuart. London and Edinburgh 1823 (3 edns).

Autobiographical memoirs. 1834, 1835. Prose.

John MacCreery, or McCreery 1768–1832

The press: a poem. Published as a specimen of typography. Pt 1 Liverpool 1803; pt 2 Liverpool 1827; London 1828 (2 pts together).

William Mackenzie 1772–1852

The sorrows of seduction . . . with other poems. 1805 (anon), 1806, 1810, 1817 (acknowledged).

The academy, or a picture of youth. 1808. Anon.

The Swiss patriots, with other poems. 1817.

John Macker or Macken, also 'Ismael Fitzadam' 1784?–1823

Minstrel stolen moments, or shreds of fancy. Dublin 1814. Anon.

The hart of the desert . . . with other pieces in verse. By 'Ismael Fitzadam'. 1818.

Lays on land. By 'Ismael Fitzadam'. 1821.

William Maclaren or M'Laren 1772–1832

Address delivered at the celebration of the birth of Burns. 1815. Prose.

Emma, or the cruel father: a poetical tale. Paisley 1817.

Isabella, or the robbers: a poetical tale. Paisley 1827; London 1828; Aberdeen 1830; Edinburgh 1831.

Mary Anne M'Mullan, or McMullan, Mrs W. fl. 1816–53

The crescent: a national poem to commemorate the glorious victory at Algiers. 1816.

The naiad's wreath. 1816.

The wanderings of a goldfinch, or characteristic sketches in the nineteenth century. 1816. Prose.

Britain, or fragments of poetical aberration. 1818.

Lines from the land of streams: a miscellany. By the author of The crescent. 1841. Anon. Verse and prose.

Dioramic sketches, ancient and modern. 1853. Anon.

Mary Macqueen, Mrs Storie 1786–1854

Collections and selections

Andrew Crawfurd's collection of ballads and songs. Vol 1, ed Emily Lyle, Aberdeen 1975 (Scottish Text Soc).

An anthology of Scottish women poets. Ed C. Kerrigan, Edinburgh 1991. [KM]

Ann McTaggart, Mrs c. 1753–1834

Theodora: a tragedy, Villario: a play, and Hortensia: a tragedy. London, Edinburgh and Dublin 1814–15 (anon, in The New British Theatre); London 1832 (as Plays: Theodora, Hortensia, Villario, and A search after perfection; acknowledged).

Constantia: a tragedy in five acts, and Valville, or the prejudices of past times: a drama in five acts. 1824.

Memoirs of a gentlewoman of the old school. By a lady. 2 vols 1830. Anon. Prose.

Plays: Valville, or the prejudices of past times, Theodora, Hortensia, A search after perfection, and Constantia. 1832.

Mrs Maddocks fl. 1820–9

Scripture female portraits in verse: for the instruction of youth. 1820.

The female missionary advocate: a poem. 1827 (anon), 1830.

Cottage similes, or poems on domestic occurrences, designed for those in humble life. By the author of The female missionary advocate. Ed [E. Henderson] 1829. Anon.

Richard Manley d. c. 1834

Miscellaneous pieces in verse, moral and religious. Southmolton 1830.

Summer musings, in verse. Southmolton 1831.

The poetical remains. Southmolton 1835.

Richard Mant 1776–1848

Collections

Miles 10 (11).

Verses to the memory of Joseph Warton, Poems, The slave . . . . Ed D. H. Reiman, New York and London 1978 (facs reprints).

§1

Verses to the memory of Joseph Warton. Oxford 1800.

The poetical works of the late Thomas Warton. Ed with a memoir by Mant, 2 vols Oxford 1802 (5 edns).

The country curate. Oxford 1804.
The fate of Switzerland. Oxford [c. 1805]. Anon.
Poems. Oxford and London 1806.
The slave. Oxford 1806, 1807 (as The slave and other poetical pieces).
The simpliciad: a satirico-didactic poem. 1808 (anon); Oxford 1991 (facs reprint, attributed).
The book of psalms, in an English metrical version. Oxford and London 1824.
The holydays of the church, with metrical sketches. 2 vols 1828–31.
The gospel miracles, in a series of poetical sketches. 1832.
Christmas carols, with an introductory account of the Christmas carol. Ed Mant 1833.
The happiness of the blessed ... musings on the church. 1833 (2 edns); Philadelphia 1833; London 1835, 1837, 1841, 1847; New York 1847, 1848; London 1854, 1870. Prose and verse.
The British months: a poem. 2 vols 1835.
Ancient hymns from the Roman breviary. Tr Mant 1837, 1871. Includes original hymns by Mant.
The sun-dial of Armoy: a poem. Dublin 1847 (in English and Latin).
The matin bell, or the church's call to daily prayer. Oxford 1848.
The youthful Christian soldier, with spiritual songs and hymns. Dublin 1848. Prose and verse.

§2

Berens, E. A memoir of the life. 1849.
Mant, W. B. Memoirs. Dublin 1857.
Mant also pbd numerous sermons and other religious prose works, including a History of the Church of Ireland, *2 vols 1840.*

John Marshall 1757–1825

The village pedagogue ... By a country schoolmaster. Newcastle 1810, 1817.
Shireleb, or hymns, doctrinal and devotional. 1828.
The druid's talisman: a legend of the peak, with other poems. 1845.

William Barrett Marshall fl. 1823–36

Tears for pity. 1823, 1824.
Also wrote on medical education and on New Zealand.

George Martin, of Glasgow fl. 1811–24

Night: a poem. Glasgow 1811. Anon.
Revelation: a poem. Glasgow 1824.

Thomas Martin, Wesleyan minister 1780–1866

The manger, or the birth of Christ: a poem. 1816.
A Sunday school hymn book. Bristol 1821.
The stranger at home: a poem. Devonport 1824.
The centenary: a commemorative poem ... events in the history of methodism. 1839.
Also pbd sermons.

Martin Kedgwin Masters fl. 1807–11

The progress of love: a poem. 1807; Boston 1808; London 1811.
Lost and found: a comedy. 1811; New York 1811. Prose.

Charles Masterton fl. 1811–32

The seducer: a tragedy, in five acts. 1811.
Amyntor and Adelaide, or a tale of life. 1816.
The stern resolve: a tragedy. 1823, 1837.
Bentivoglio: a tragedy. 1824.
The wreck: a dramatic romance. 1824.
Blighted love: a dramatic romance. 1832.

John Matthews 1755–1826

Eloisa en dishabillè. By a lounger. 1780, 1801, [1810?] (by a 'Greek professor'), [1815?], 1819 (by 'Prof Porson'), 1822. Anon.
Ode to Cloacina upon the most fashionable model. 1782. Anon.
A sketch from the landscape: a didactic poem addressed to R. P. Knight. 1794.
Fables from Lafontaine in English verse. 1820. Anon.

Thomas Maude, of the Middle Temple 1801–65

Speculum: a Byronic satire on some recent residents of the city of Durham. [Durham 1819?], 1969 (reprint).
A legend of Ravenswood and other poems. 1823.
Monody on the death of Lord Byron. 1824.
The village grammar-school and other poems. London and Edinburgh 1824.
The memorial. 1827.
The traveller's lay: a poem. 1830.
The school boy: a poem. 1836, 1837.
Also wrote on education and on the Mosaic cosmogony, and pbd a sermon.

Samuel Maxey fl. 1803–8

J. P. Claris de Florian. Estelle: a pastoral romance. Tr Maxey 1803. Prose.
J. P. Claris de Florian. Ruth: a sacred eclogue and Tobit: a poem. Tr Maxey 1805.
The victory of Trafalgar: a naval ode .... 1805, 1808.

John Mayne 1759–1836

Rogers.
English, Scots and Irishmen: a patriotic address. 1803 (2 edns). Broadsheet.
Glasgow: a poem. 1803.
The siller gun: a poem .... Gloucester and London 1808; London and Edinburgh 1836.

John Herman Merivale 1779–1844

Collection

Poems original and translated. 2 vols 1838, 3 vols 1844 (corrected); ed D. H. Reiman, New York and London 1978 (facs reprint of 1838).

§1

Translations chiefly from the Greek anthology, with tales and miscellaneous poems. London, Cambridge and Oxford 1806; London 1813 (as Collections from the Greek anthology), 1833; 1848 (as The Greek anthology). With R. Bland. Anon.
The minstrel, or the progress of genius ... book the third [J. Beattie's poem continued]. 1808.
Ode on the deliverance of Europe. 1814.
Orlando in Roncesvalles: a poem. 1814; ed D. H. Reiman, New York and London 1978 (facs reprint).
The two first cantos of Richardetto, from the original of N. Forteguerri. 1820. Anon.
The minor poems of Schiller. Tr Merivale 1844.
Schiller. Das Lied von der Glocke: the song of the bell. Tr Merivale, London, Edinburgh and Leipzig 1856; London 1869.
Leaves from the diary of a literary amateur. Ed E. H. A. Koch, Hampstead 1911. Prose.
Merivale contributed to Quart Rev, NMM and GM. His pbns on legal subjects are not listed here.

William Henry Merle fl. 1828–50

Constanca: a poem. 1828.
Odds and ends, in verse and prose. 1831 (illustr Cruikshank).
Glenlonely, or the daemon friend. 3 vols 1837. Anon. Prose.
Melton de Mowbray, or the banker's son. 3 vols 1838. Anon. Prose.
Bathurst, or church, and state and county as they were. 3 vols 1850. Anon. Prose.

Nicholas Michell 1807–80

§1

The siege of Constantinople, in three cantos. 1831.
Living poets and poetesses: a biographical and critical poem. 1832 (2 edns).
An essay on woman, in three parts. 1833 (2 edns).
The Saxon's daughter: a tale of the crusades, in six cantos. 1835.
The fatalist, or the fortunes of Godolphin. By an essayist on the passions. 3 vols 1840; 2 vols in 1 Philadelphia 1840. Anon. Prose.
The traduced: an historical romance. 3 vols 1842; New York 1843. Prose.
The eventful epoch, or the fortunes of Archer Clive. 3 vols 1846. Prose.
Ruins of many lands: a descriptive poem. 1849, 1850, 1854 (4th edn), 1872, 1875.
The burial of Wellington: an elegiac and tributary poem. 1852.
Spirits of the past: an historical poem. 1853.
The poetry of creation. 1856, 1871, 1876 (4th edn).
Pleasure: a poem. 1859, 1871, 1876.
The wreck of the homeward bound, or the boat of mercy. 1862 (2 edns).
The Shakespeare festival, or the birth of the world's poet: an ode. London and Falmouth 1864.
Sibyl of Cornwall: a poetical tale, The land's end, St Michael's Mount and other poems. 1869, 1871, 1876.
The immortals, or glimpses of paradise: a poem. 1870, 1871, 1876.
Famous women and heroes: a poem. 1871, 1876 (3rd edn).
London in light and darkness, with the author's minor poems. 1871, 1876.
The heart's great rulers: a poem. 1874.
Nature and life, including the miscellaneous poems. 1874 (in Lansdowne poets), 1878.

§2

Men of the west. Pt 4 Plymouth 1877. Anon.

Robert Millhouse 1788–1839

Collections

Sketches of obscure poets, with specimens of their writings. 1833. Anon.
The sonnets and songs . . . with a biographical sketch. Ed J. P. Briscoe, Nottingham 1881.

§1

Vicissitude: a poem in four books. Ed J. Millhouse, Nottingham and London [1821].
Blossoms . . . a selection of sonnets . . . . Ed L. Booker 1823 (2 edns).
The song of the patriot, sonnets and songs. Ed J. Millhouse 1826.
Sherwood Forest and other poems. 1827.
The destinies of man. London and Nottingham 2 pts 1832–4.

§2

Stapleton, A. In the footsteps of Robert Millhouse. [Nottingham] 1908.

Richard Alfred Milliken 1767–1815

Poetical fragments . . . with a memoir of his life. Ed [H. K.], London, Edinburgh and Dublin 1823.

§1

The river's-side: a poem. Cork 1807.
The groves of blarney, to which are added the dream of Napoleon . . . . Waterford [1830?]; London [1840?]; [Dublin 1860?]. Anon.

John Mitford, vicar of Benhall 1781–1859

§1

The crusades. [1804?]
Agnes, the Indian captive . . . with other poems. 1811.
A letter to R. Heber esq . . . on Mr Weber's edition of Ford. 1812. Prose.
Sacred specimens selected from the early English poets, with prefatory verses. Ed Mitford 1827.
Lines suggested by a fatal shipwreck. 1855; Woodbridge 1856.
Cursory notes on various passages in the text of Beaumont and Fletcher, as edited by A. Dyce. 1856. Prose.
Miscellaneous poems. 1858.
The Rev John Mitford on cricket. Ed F. S. Ashley-Cooper, Nottingham 1921. Writings rptd from GM. Prose.
The poems of Thomas Gray . . . . Ed Mitford 1814, 2 vols 1816 (as The works of Thomas Gray).

§2

Houstoun, M. C. Letters and reminiscences. 1891.
Mitford edited GM (1834–50), contributing frequently to it, and edited numerous edns of the English poets (with memoirs), chiefly in the Aldine Ser (1830–9).

John Mitford, journalist 1782–1831

The military adventures of Johnny Newcome . . . . 1815.
The poems of a British sailor. 1818.
The adventures of Johnny Newcome in the navy . . . . 1819 (2 edns), 1823, 1904.
A peep into W—r Castle. 1820 (9 edns), 1820 (as The suppressed poem: a peep into W—r Castle). Anon.
My cousin in the army, or Johnny Newcome on the peace establishment: a poem. By a staff officer. 1822, 1825. Anon.
The amours and intrigues of Queen Caroline . . . . 1828.
The private life of Lord Byron, comprising his voluptuous amours. [1836?]; tr Fr by M. F. 2 vols Paris 1837. Prose.
Ed Quizzical Gazette *(1831)*.

H. W. Montagu fl. 1828–33

Montmorency: a tragic drama . . . with some minor poems. Ed H***** 1828. Prose and verse.
Porson [S. T. Coleridge and R. Southey]. The devil's walk: a poem. Ed Montagu 1830; London, Edinburgh, Glasgow and Dublin 1830 (acknowledged).
Monsieur Mallet, or my daughter's letter . . . . 1830 (illustr R. Cruikshank), 1831 (in Facetiae vol 2).
Lives of the twelve, or the modern Caesars. Vol 1 only 1832. Prose.
The campaigns of Wellington. 1833. Prose.

James Montgomery 1771–1854

Mss correspondence is held in the Sheffield City Museum and Sheffield Archives.

Bibliographies

Tallent-Bateman, C. T. James Montgomery: a literary estimate [with bibliography]. Papers of Manchester Lit Club 15 1889. Bibliography ptd in Reports and proceedings.

Collections

The poetical works. 2 vols 1820.

The poetical works. 4 vols 1828.

The poetical works of Rogers, Campbell, James Montgomery, Lamb and Kirke White. Paris 1829.

The poetical works, collected by himself. 4 vols 1841, 1 vol 1850, 1851 (2nd edn), Philadelphia 1853, 4 vols 1855, 1858, Edinburgh [1870], London 1873, [1878] (Chandos Poets), 1 vol [1879] (Lansdowne Poets), [1881] (Landscape edn).

Poetical works. Ed (with memoir) R. W. Griswold 2 vols Philadelphia 1845, Boston 1853.

The poetical works. Ed (with memoir) R. Carruthers 5 vols in 2 Boston 1858 (reprint of 4-vol edn with original hymns of 1853), London 1860.

Poems: to which is added a memoir of the author. 1861.

Selections

The British poets of the nineteenth century. Paris 1828.

The poetical keepsake: containing the best poems of the following authors: Montgomery et al. 1847.

Poems, selected by R. A. Willmott, illustrated by Birket Foster. 1860.

Favourite hymns for the closet or sick-chamber, by Cowper, Montgomery et al. Edinburgh 1880 (6th edn).

§1

The history of a church and a warming-pan. 1793; rptd for priv circulation 1871.

Prison amusements, and other trifles: principally written during nine months of confinement in the castle of York, by Paul Positive. 1797.

The whisperer: or tales and speculations by Gabriel Silvertongue. 1798. Prose and verse.

The loss of the locks: a Siberian tale. 1800. Poem. No copy extant? Rptd in J. Holland and J. Everett, Memoirs of J. Montgomery vol 1, 1854. Pbd in Iris 1799.

The ocean. 1805. Poem. No copy extant? Pbd in Iris 1805.

The wanderer of Switzerland, and other poems. Sheffield 1806, 1806, London 1806, Boston 1807, Edinburgh 1808 (4th edn), Morristown NJ 1811, Edinburgh 1815 (7th edn), London 1832 (11th edn), 1841 (13th edn).
REVIEWS: Eclectic Rev 2, May 1806; Edinburgh Rev 9, Jan 1807; Quart Rev 6, Dec 1811.

Poems on the abolition of the slave trade. Illustr R. Smirke 1809. With J. Grahame and E. Benger. Montgomery's The West Indies: a poem in four parts, was pbd separately in 1809, and also in 1814 as The abolition of the slave trade.

The West Indies and other poems. 1810, 1810 (3rd edn), New Brunswick NJ 1811, London 1828 (7th edn).
REVIEWS: Eclectic Rev 12, Sep 1810; Quart Rev 6, Dec 1811; NMM 2, Oct 1814.

The world before the flood: a poem in ten cantos, with other occasional pieces. 1813, New York 1814, London 1823 (6th edn), 1826 (7th edn).
REVIEWS: Eclectic Rev 19, May 1814; Baptist Mag 6, July 1814.

Verses to the memory of Richard Reynolds. 1816, 1817 (3rd edn).
REVIEW: Monthly Rev 82, Feb 1817.

The state lottery, a dream. By Samuel Roberts. 1817. Includes poem Thoughts on wheels.
REVIEW: Monthly Rev 85, Feb 1818.

Greenland, and other poems. 1819, 1819, New York 1819, London 1825.
REVIEWS: Eclectic Rev 30, Sep 1819; Monthly Rev 91, Jan 1820.

Abdallah and Labat. In Abdallah: or the Arabian martyr, a Christian drama, by Thomas Foster Barham, 1821.

Polyhymnia: or select airs of celebrated foreign composers, adapted to English words by James Montgomery. 1822. Pbd in London Mag 5, June 1822.

Songs of Zion: being imitations of psalms. 1822, Boston 1823, London 1828 (3rd edn).

The chimney-sweeper's friend, and climbing-boy's album. Ed Montgomery 1824. 2 poems by Montgomery.

Prose, by a poet. 2 vols 1824, Philadelphia 1824. 1 poem in each vol. Anon.

The Christian psalmist: or hymns selected and original, with an introductory essay. Glasgow 1825, 1826 (4th edn), London [1862] (10th edn).
REVIEW: (With Christian poet, *below*) Blackwood's Mag 24, Dec 1828.

The Christian poet, or selections in verse on sacred subjects: with an introductory essay. Glasgow 1827, 1828 (3rd edn).
REVIEW: Blackwood's Mag 24, Dec 1828.

The pelican island, and other poems. 1827, Philadelphia 1827, London 1828 (2nd edn).
REVIEW: (With Poetical Works 1820) Blackwood's Mag 22, Oct 1827.

Lectures on poetry and general literature delivered at the Royal Institution in 1830 and 1831. 1833, New York 1838, London 1846.
REVIEW: Athenaeum 293, 8 June 1833.

Verses in commemoration of the Rev James Hervey of Weston-Favell – written expressly for the Hervey jubilee. Northampton 1833.

A poet's portfolio: or minor poems: in three books. 1835, 1836 (2nd edn).
REVIEWS: Eclectic Rev 61, May 1835; Edinburgh Rev 61, July 1835.

Eminent literary and scientific men of Italy, Spain etc. 3 vols 1835–7. Part of D. Lardner, The cabinet cyclopaedia; Ariosto, Dante and Tasso by Montgomery.

Hymns for the opening of Christ Church, Newark on Trent, 1837. 1837.

A hymn for the Wesleyan centenary. 1839. Single sheet 12°.

Our Saviour's miracles: six original sketches in verse. Bristol 1840.

The West Indian planter. Derby [c. 1840]. Single poem.

Poems on the loss and re-building of St Mary's Church, Cardiff, by Wordsworth, Montgomery, etc. Cardiff 1842.

Liturgy and hymns for the use of the protestant church of the United Brethren: a new and revised edition. 1849. Rev and contributed to by Montgomery.

Original hymns for public, private and social devotion. 1853; ed J. Holland, New York 1854 (as Sacred poems and hymns).
REVIEW: Wesleyan Methodist Mag 84, Mar 1853.

Also minor prose writings, a few poems issued in single-sheet or pam form, and many hymns contributed to collections ed W. B. Collyer 1812, T. Cotterill 1819, and others. Montgomery was editor and proprietor of Sheffield Iris *1794–1825. See also* Wellesley *vol 5 1989.*

§2

Holland, J. and J. Everett. Memoirs of Montgomery. 7 vols 1854–6; abridged by H. C. Knight, Boston 1857 (as Life of Montgomery).

Holbrook, A. S. The life and work of Montgomery. London Quart 179 1954.

Kay, J. A. The poetry and hymns of Montgomery. London Quart 179 1954.

Obituaries: Athenaeum 6 May 1854; The Times 8 May 1854. [RS]

Mrs Maria Henrietta Montolieu fl. 1798–1823

Abbé de Lille. The gardens: a poem. Tr Montolieu (anon) 1798, 1805 (tr acknowledged).

The enchanted plants: fables in verse. . . . 1800 (anon), 1801 (acknowledged), 1803; New York 1803; Philadelphia 1826 (with Langhorne's Fables of flora); Cincinnati 1850.

The festival of the rose, with other poems. 1802.

The enchanted plants, and Festival of the rose, with other poems. 1812 ('3rd edn'), 1822.

Gethsemene: a poem founded on The messiah of Klopstock. 1823.

Dugald Moore 1805–41

Collection

Rogers.

§1

The African: a tale, and other poems. Glasgow 1829, 1830.
Scenes from the flood, The tenth plague . . . . Glasgow and Edinburgh 1830.
The bridal night, The first poet, and other poems. Glasgow 1831.
The bard of the north . . . . Glasgow 1833.
The hour of retribution, with other poems. Glasgow 1835.
The devoted one and other poems. Glasgow 1839.

Thomas Moore 1779–1852

Reading University Library is the repository for Moore mss previously owned by Longman. Rice University TX is the repository for most of his letters. See also Location register of English literary manuscripts and letters: 18th and 19th centuries, *1995*.

Bibliographies

Power, J. A catalogue of vocal music by Moore and Sir John Stevenson. 1814, 1815.
Muir, P. H. Moore's Irish melodies 1808–34. Colophon 15, 1933.
MacManus, M. J. A bibliographical hand-list of the first editions of Moore. Dublin 1934.
Jordan, H. H. In English romantic poets and essayists: a review of research, ed C. W. and L. H. Houtchens, New York 1957, 1966 (rev).

Collections

Works. 6 vols Paris 1819, 1827, 7 vols London 1820, 1823, 1827, 4 vols 1821, 6 vols New York 1825, 1 vol Leipzig 1826, 1833, 1840, Paris 1827, 1829, nd; 2 vols Philadelphia 1829 ('fifth edn'), Paris 1835, 1 vol Philadelphia 1836, 1839, 1845; The poetical works, collected by himself, 10 vols London 1840–1, 1853, 1 vol Paris 1841, 1842 ('collected and arranged by himself'), 3 vols London 1841 ('collected by the author'), 5 vols Leipzig 1842, 1 vol London 1844, 1845, 1850, 1853, 1855, 1860, 1865, New York 1850, 1867, Boston 1854, 1856; ed F. J. Child 6 vols Boston 1856, 1871, [1880]; 1 vol Philadelphia 1856, 1858, London 1859, 1863 [1881], Edinburgh [1859], 1863, [1870], [1881], London and Edinburgh 1874; ed W. M. Rossetti, illustr T. Seccombe, London [1870], [1872], [1880], [1881]; Glasgow [1870]; memoir by D. Herbert, Edinburgh 1872, 1887, Brooklyn NY 1872; London 1883 and at least 8 more edns nd before 1900, New York 1884, 1887; memoir by N. A. Dole 2 vols London [1895]; ed A. D. Godley, London 1910, 1924, rptd New York 1979; ed W. M. Rossetti, London 1911. Tr Ger, 1843.
[Extensive selections]. Melodies, songs, sacred songs and national airs. New York 1819, 1821; Selected poetical works, Paris 1847; Songs, ballads and sacred songs, London 1849; Melodies, national airs, miscellaneous poems, Boston 1857; 130 of Moore's songs and Irish melodies, London [1859]; Irish melodies, Lalla Rookh, National airs etc, [1867]; Prose and verse, humorous, satirical and sentimental, ed R. H. Shepherd 1878; Poetical works, ed J. Dorrian 1888; ed J. R. Tutin [1892]; ed C. L. Falkiner 1903; Lyrics and satires, ed S. O'Faolain, Dublin 1929; Life and poems, ed B. Clifford, London, Cork and Belfast 1984; Political writings, ed B. Clifford, Belfast 1993. Tr Fr 1820 (with Byron and Scott), 1829, 1841; Ital 1836 (2nd edn), 1870.

§1

Odes of Anacreon, translated into English verse, with notes. 1800, 2 vols 1802, 1803, 1804, 1805, 1806, 1810, 1815, 1820 (10th edn), 1 vol Dublin 1803, Philadelphia 1804, London 1826, Paris 1835 (with Greek), London [1871].
The poetical works of the late Thomas Little esq. 1801, 1802, 1803, 1804, 1804, 1805, 1806 (8th edn), 1808, 1810, 1812, 1814, 1819 (14th edn), 1822, 1833 (16th edn), Dublin 1804, 1810, 1817, New York 1804, Philadelphia 1804; London 1825, 1828, 1838, 1990 (facs of 1801 edn).
Moore sometimes composed or adapted music for his own lyrical poems. Some early examples are: O lady fair! a ballad for three voices, 1802, 1802, [1804]; When time who steals our years away: a ballad, 1802; Good night, a ballad, 1803; Songs and glees, 1805; A Canadian boat song, arranged for three voices, 1805. *He also collaborated with Michael Kelly to compose* The gypsy prince: a comic opera in thee acts, *1801, of which little more than the music survives.*
Epistles, odes and other poems. 1806, 2 vols 1807, 1810, 1814, 1817, 1822, 1 vol Philadelphia 1806 (2nd edn).
REVIEW: (F. Jeffrey) Edinburgh Rev 8, 1806.
The works of Sallust, translated into English by the late Arthur Murphy. 1807. With life of Sallust by Moore.
Corruption and Intolerance: two poems with notes, addressed to an Englishman by an Irishman. 1808, 1809.
A selection of Irish melodies, with symphonies and accompaniments by Sir John Stevenson and characteristic words by Moore. 10 pts and suppl 1808 (pts 1–2), 1810, 1811, 1813, 1815, 1818, 1821, 1824, 1834 (pt 10 and suppl). Stevenson was the composer for the first seven parts only (to 1818). For further details *see* P. H. Muir, Colophon 15 1933. The Irish melodies were not authorised for pbn without musical accompaniment until 1821; *see below*.
The sceptic: a philosophical satire, by the author of Corruption and intolerance. 1809.
A letter to the Roman Catholics of Dublin. 1810, Dublin 1810 (2nd edn); rptd in Veto controversy, ed B. Clifford, Belfast 1985.
A melologue upon national music. London and Dublin 1811.
MP, or the blue-stocking: a comic opera in three acts, by Anacreon Moore. 1811, New York 1812.
Spirit of Boccaccio's Decameron, translated, selected, connected and versified, from the Italian. 1812. Perhaps by Moore.
Intercepted letters: or the two penny post bag, by Thomas Brown the younger. 1813 (at least 11 edns), 1814, 1818 (16th edn), Philadelphia 1813.
Lines on the death of — [R. B. Sheridan] from the Morning Chronicle of August 5 1816. 1816.
Sacred songs. No 1, 1816; no 2, 1824.
Lalla Rookh: an oriental romance. 1817 (6 edns), 1818 (at least 3 edns), 1823, 1826 (13th edn), 1829 (15th edn), 1832, 1838, 1842 (20th edn), Philadelphia 1817, 1826, 1839, 1856, New York 1817, 1818, 1824, 1834, 1844, 1849, 1851, 1860, 1868, [1874], [1884], [1888], 1890, [1891], Boston 1828, 1885, 1887, [1892], 1899, Paris 1835; illustr R. Westall 1840, 1842, 1844; illustr eminent artists 1846, 1851, 1853, 1856; 1850, 1854, 1859, 1859, 1860, 1884, 1891, 1912, Dublin 1861, nd; illustr J. Tenniel, London 1861, New York 1867; Chicago [1900], New York and Toronto 1930, rptd Rockville MD 1992. Tr (complete or separate stories) Ital 1818, 1838, 1872, 1886, 1874, Fr 1820 (2 versions), 1887, [1888], Ger 1823, 1825, 1844 (with music by R. Schumann), [1846], 1859, 1878, 1879, [1892, 1901], [1877] (as an opera by J. Rodenberg), 1881, Polish 1826 (prose), 1838–43, 1852, Swedish 1829, Du 1834, Sp 1836, Danish 1878, Telugu 1920.
REVIEW: (F. Jeffrey) Edinburgh Rev 57, 1817.
The Fudge family in Paris, edited by Thomas Brown the younger. 1818 (at least 9 edns), New York 1818, Philadelphia 1818.
REVIEW: (W. Hazlitt) Yellow Dwarf 25 Apr 1818, rptd in Works, ed P. P. Howe 1930–4 vol 7.
National airs. 6 nos 1818–27.
Tom Crib's memorial to congress, with preface, notes and appendix, by one of the fancy. 1819 (4 edns), New York 1819.
Irish melodies, and A melologue upon national music. Dublin 1820 (unauthorised edn without music).
Irish melodies, with an appendix containing the original advertisements and the prefatory letter on music. 1821 (1st authorised edn of words only), 1822 (at least 3 edns), 1825 (6th edn), 1827 (8th

edn), 1832 (10th edn), 1824 (with National airs), 1846 (with other poems), 1849; illustr D. Maclise 1853, [1858], 1866; 1854, 1856, 1859, [1874], 1887, 1904, 1908, Dublin 1833 (with other poems), [1846], London 1859, 1862, [1879] (with National airs), Philadelphia 1821, 1850, 1866, 1873, Brussels 1822 (with National airs), Paris 1823, 1843, Pisa [1823] (with National airs), New York [1844], 1874. Tr Swedish 1825, 1858, Latin 1835, 1856–9, Irish 1842, Fr 1869, 1879 (selection), Ger [1874], 1884; Sp 1875 (2nd edn), Ital 1880.

REVIEWS: Quart Rev 28, 1822; (J. G. Lockhart) Blackwood's Mag 4, 1818.

The loves of the angels: a poem. 1823 (4 edns), 1823 (5th edn as The loves of the angels: an eastern romance); rev text and notes to make 'machinery and allusions entirely Mahometan' 1824, 1826, Philadelphia 1823, Paris 1823, 1823, 1843, New York [1844]. Tr Fr 1823 (2 edns, 1 prose), 1830, 1837, Du 1835, Swedish 1843, 1864, Ital 1873, 1882 (prose), 1886, 1898.

REVIEWS: (J. Wilson) Blackwood's Mag 13 1823; (W. Hazlitt) Edinburgh Rev 38, 1823.

Fables for the holy alliance; Rhymes on the road, by Thomas Brown the younger. 1823.

Memoirs of Captain Rock, the celebrated Irish chieftain, with some account of his ancestors, written by himself. 1824 (at least 5 edns), Paris 1824, New York 1978. Tr Fr, 1829.

REVIEW: (S. Smith) Edinburgh Rev 81, 1824.

Memoirs of the life of the Right Honourable Richard Brinsley Sheridan. 1825, 1825, 2 vols 1825, 1826, 1827 (new preface), 1 vol Philadelphia 1825, 2 vols Paris 1825, 1 vol London 1835, 2 vols New York 1853, 1858, Chicago and St Louis 1882, London 1958, 1968 (reprint of 1858 edn). Tr Fr, 1826.

REVIEW: (F. Jeffrey) Edinburgh Rev 89, 1826.

Evenings in Greece: first [second] evening (with music). 1826, New York 1844. Tr Ger, 1846.

The epicurean: a tale. 1827 (4 edns), 1828, 1864, Philadelphia 1827, Paris 1827, 1828, 1832, 1835, Boston 1831, New York and Boston 1841, New York 1844, 1862; illustr J. M. W. Turner London 1839 (with Alciphron); Chicago 1890, London 1899. Tr Fr 1827 (2 versions), [1861], 1865 (verse by T. Gauthier, illustr G. Doré), Ger 1828, Sp 1832, Danish 1844; Ital 1852 (adaptation by S. Torelli).

REVIEWS: (J. Wilson) Blackwood's Mag 22, 1827; (T. L. Peacock) Westminster Rev 8, 1827.

Odes upon cash, corn, Catholics and other matters, selected from the columns of the Times journal. 1828, Philadelphia 1828, Paris 1829.

Letters and journals of Lord Byron, with notices of his life. 2 vols 1830, 1831, 1833, 1920, St Clair Shores MI 1972 (reprint of 1920 edn). Tr Fr 1830.

REVIEW: (T. B. Macaulay) Edinburgh Rev 27, 1830.

The life and death of Lord Edward Fitzgerald. 2 vols 1831, 1 vol Paris 1831, 1835; ed M. MacDermott, London 1897; abridged as The life and times etc, Dublin 1909 (Irish Lib).

REVIEW: (R. Southey) Quart Rev 46, 1831.

The summer fete: a poem with songs [and music]. 1831, Paris 1832, 1833, Philadelphia 1833.

Travels of an Irish gentleman in search of a religion, with notes and illustrations by the editor of Captain Rock's memoirs. 2 vols 1833, 1 vol Paris 1833, Baltimore and Pittsburgh [186?]. Tr Fr 1833, 1834, 1835, 1836, 1841, Ger 1834, Ital 1850.

The Fudges in England: being a sequel to The Fudge family in Paris, by Thomas Brown the younger. 1835, 1835, Paris 1835, 1835.

The history of Ireland. 4 vols 1835–46 (in D. Lardner, The cabinet cyclopaedia), Paris 1835–46, 2 vols Philadelphia 1843–6. Tr Fr 1835 (2 versions), 1836, Ger 1846.

REVIEW: W. M. Thackeray. See Contributions to the Morning Chronicle, ed G. N. Ray 1955.

Alciphron: a poem. Illustr J. M. W. Turner 1839, Paris 1840.

Letters, diaries etc

Memoirs, journal and correspondence of Moore. Ed Lord John Russell 8 vols 1853–6; abridged by Russell 1860.

Notes from the letters of Moore to his music publisher, James Power (the publication of which were suppressed in London). Ed T. C. Croker, New York [1854].

'Thomas Moore' anecdotes: being anecdotes, bon-mots and epigrams from the journal. Ed W. Harrison 1899 (2nd edn).

Tom Moore's diary: a selection. Ed J. B. Priestley, Cambridge 1925.

Letters of Moore. Ed W. S. Dowden 2 vols Oxford 1964.

Journal 1818–41. Ed P. C. Quennell, New York 1964. Selection.

Journal 1818–47. Ed W. S. Dowden, B. G. Bartholomew and J. L. Linsley 6 vols Newark NJ and London 1983–92.

§2

Hazlitt, W. In his The spirit of the age, 1825.

Burke, J. A life of Moore. Dublin 1852.

Vallat, G. Étude sur la vie et les oeuvres de Moore. Paris 1886.

Stockmann, A. Moore: der irische Freiheitssänger. Freiburg 1910.

Thomas, A. B. Moore en France 1819–30. Paris 1911.

Wright, H. G. Moore as the author of Spirit of Boccaccio's Decameron. RES 23, 1947.

Schneider, E. Tom Moore and the Edinburgh review of Christabel: Jeffrey, Hazlitt, Tom Moore. PMLA 70, 1955. Attributes review to Moore.

Jordan, H. H. Moore and the review of Christabel. MP 54, 1956. Against attribution to Moore.

Schneider, E. Tom Moore and the Edinburgh review of Christabel. PMLA 77, 1962.

Dowden, W. S. Moore and the review of Christabel. MP 60, 1962. Against attribution to Moore.

Coburn, K. Who killed Christabel? TLS, 20 May 1965. Attributes review to Moore.

Eldridge, H. G. The American republication of Thomas Moore's Epistles, odes and other poems. PBSA 62, 1968.

Pearsall, R. B. Chronological annotations to 250 letters of Thomas Moore. PBSA 63, 1969.

Jordan, H. H. Bolt upright: the life of Thomas Moore. 2 vols Salzburg 1975. [JLL and BGB]

Sydney Owenson, Lady Morgan

See Owenson, col 967.

William Motherwell 1797–1835

Collections

Miles.

Rogers.

The poetical works. Boston 1843, 1847; ed J. M'Conechy, Glasgow 1847, 1849; Boston 1851, 1853, 1859, 1860; London 1860; New York [186-?]; Boston 1863, 1864; Glasgow 1865; Boston 1866; New York 1879; Paisley 1881; New York 1885.

§1

The harp of Renfrewshire: a collection of songs and other poetical pieces .... Ed Motherwell, Paisley 1819; Glasgow 1820, 1821 (as Beauties of the Scottish poets); Paisley 1872–3 (with second ser).

Renfrewshire characters and scenery: a poem in three hundred and sixty-five cantos. By 'Isaac Brown'. Only one canto pbd Paisley 1824, 1881. Anon.

Minstrelsy ancient and modern .... Ed Motherwell, Glasgow 1827, [1829?]; 2 vols Boston 1846; modified by C. Mackay, London 1861 (as The legendary and romantic ballads of Scotland); London 1864 (as Early Scottish ballads); 1 vol Paisley 1873.

M'Alpie, J. Certain curious poems. Ed Motherwell, Paisley 1828.

Poems, narrative and lyrical. Glasgow 1832; Boston 1841, 1844; London 1846; Boston 1846, 1847, 1851.
Scottish proverbs, collected and arranged by Andrew Henderson. Ed Motherwell, Edinburgh 1832; Edinburgh and Glasgow 1876.
The works of Robert Burns. Ed Motherwell (with 'the Ettrick Shepherd' [James Hogg]) 5 vols London, Glasgow and Edinburgh 1838–41.
The laird of Logan, or anecdotes and tales . . . . Glasgow 1841. Prose.
Posthumous poems. Boston 1851.

John Moultrie 1799–1874

Collections

Poems; with memoir by Prebendary [Derwent] Coleridge. 2 vols 1876.

§1

Poems. 1837, 1852 (3rd edn).
The dream of life, lays of the English Church and other poems. 1843.
Saint Mary, the virgin and the wife. 1850, 1850, 1856. Poem.
The black fence: a lay of modern Rome. 1850, 1851 (4th edn).
Psalms and hymns. 1851, 1860. Compiled by Moultrie and including about 20 of his hymns.
The song of the Rugby church-builders. [1851].
A pentecostal ode. 1852.
The poetical remains of William Sidney Walker, with a memoir [by Moultrie]. 1852.
Sermons. 1852.
Altars, hearths and graves. 1854. Poems.
Moultrie also contributed poems to Etonian *1820–1, and to* Knight's Quart Mag *1823–4.*

Cornelius Neale 1789–1823

§1

Mustapha: a tragedy. London and Weybridge 1814. Anon.
Lyrical dramas, with domestic hours: a miscellany of odes and songs. 1819 (2 edns).

§2

Jowett, W. Memoir of the Rev C. Neale to which are added his remains. 1834, 1835, 1842.

Henry Neele 1798–1828

Collection

The literary remains. 1829; New York and Philadelphia 1829. Prose and verse.

§1

Odes and other poems. 1816, 1817, 1821.
Poems, dramatic and miscellaneous. 1823, 2 vols 1827.
England. 3 vols 1828, 1872. Prose.
The romance of history: England. 3 vols 1828 (2 edns); 2 vols Philadelphia 1828; 3 vols London 1829, 1831, 1833, 1839 (as Romances of history), [1872] (illustr T. Landseer); London and New York [1875]; London [188-?], 1889. Prose.
Lectures on English poetry. 1829, 1830, 1839. Prose.
The tales. Hamilton NY 1830. Prose.

John Nicholson 1790–1843

Collection

Poems by John Nicholson, the Airedale poet, with a sketch of his life and writings by J. James. London and Bradford 1844; ed W. Dearden, London and Bingley 1859 ('4th edn', enlarged); ed A. Holroyd, Bingley 1876; ed W. G. Hird, London and Bradford 1876 (as The poetical works).

§1

The siege of Bradford in 1642: a dramatic poem. Bradford 1821, 1831.
Airedale in ancient times, Elwood and Elvina, The poacher, and other poems. London and Bradford 1825 (2 edns).
Lines on the grand musical festival . . . . Bradford 1825.
Lines on the present state of the country. Bradford 1826 (3 edns).
The Airedale poet's walk through Knaresbrough. Knaresbrough 1826.
The lyre of Ebor . . . and other poems. London and Bradford 1827.
The Yorkshire poet's journey to London. London and Leeds 1828 (2nd edn).
The vale of Ilkley, and The poet's sick-bed. Bradford 1831.
England's lament for the loss of her constitution: a poem. Bradford 1850.

William Nicholson, the peddlar poet 1782?–1849

Collections

Rogers 3.
Poetical works, with a memoir by M. M'L. Harper. Castle-Douglas 1878 (3rd edn); Dalbeattie 1897 (4th edn).

§1

Tales in verse and miscellaneous poems. Edinburgh 1814, 1828 (with memoir by J. Macdiarmid).

Thomas Noble fl. 1801–32

The dawn of peace: an ode . . . . 1801.
Practical perspective, exemplified on landscapes. 1805, 1809. Prose.
Academic letters: epistles from youths at school to their friends and parents. 1808. Prose.
Blackheath: a poem, Lumena, or the ancient British battle. 1808.
Poems. Liverpool and London 1821.
Julia, or pre-existent spirits . . . with . . . smaller poems . . . . Derby [1828].
Edited The Voice of the Country *(1832 etc), and a dictionary and topographical works.*

Mrs Offley, of Dorchester fl. 1820

The assize ball, or Lucy of the moor. 1820; Dorchester and London 1820 (2 edns). Anon.

Adelaide D. O'Keeffe 1776–1855?

Original poems, calculated to improve the mind of youth and allure it to virtue. By Adelaide. Pt 1 and pt 2 1808; pt 1 only Philadelphia 1810, pt 2 1821. Anon.
Patriarchal times, or the land of Canaan: a figurate history. 2 vols 1811, 1820 (3rd edn); New York 1822; London 1826; Philadelphia 1828, [1848]. Prose.
Zenobia, queen of Palmyra: a narrative. 1814, 1824. Anon.
Dudley. 3 vols 1817, 1819; tr Fr by M. H. Montolieu (as Dudley et Claudy) 5 vols Paris 1824. Prose.
National characters exhibited in forty geographical poems . . . . Lymington and London 1818.
A trip to the coast, or poems descriptive of various interesting objects on the sea-shore. 1819.
Poems for young children. [1848.]
The broken sword, or a soldier's honour. 1854. Prose.
Contributed to J. and A. Taylor's Original poems for infant minds *(1804, etc).* *See also col 467, below.*

Shirley Palmer d. 1860?

The Swiss exile: a poem. Lichfield 1804; London 1807.
Edited London Medical Repository *and* New Medical and Physical Jnl, *and wrote on medical topics.*

Andrew Park, also 'James Wilson' of Paisley 1807–63

Collections
Rogers.
The poetical works. 1854.

§1
A vision of mankind and miscellaneous poems. Glasgow 1833.
The bridegroom and the bride, with miscellaneous poems. Glasgow 1834.
Blindness, or the second sense restored and lost: a poem. 1839.
Watty and Meg. By 'J. Wilson'. Kilmarnock [1840?].
The queen's welcome to Edinburgh. Edinburgh [1842]. Broadsheet.
The royal visit. Glasgow 1842.
Songs. Glasgow 1842, 1848.
The mariners: an opera, and songs for all seasons. 1843.
Silent love: a poem. By 'J. Wilson'. Paisley 1843, 1845 (4th edn); Glasgow 1846; London 1851.
Miscellaneous poems. [1844?] Anon.
The squire's daughter: a tragedy. 1846.
The book of poetical apophthegms. Ed Park 1852 (2nd edn).
Beauty: a poem. 1853.
To the memory of Burns: centenary ode. Glasgow 1859 (2nd edn).
The world, past, present and future, and other poems. Glasgow 1862.

Richard Parkinson 1797–1858

§1
The ascent of Elijah . . . . London and Cambridge 1830.
Poems sacred and miscellaneous. 1832; London and Manchester 1845.
The old church clock. 1843; London and Manchester 1844 (3rd edn); Manchester 1880 (5th edn, with memoir by J. Evans). Prose.
Byrom, J. The private journal and literary remains. Ed Parkinson 4 vols 1854–7.

§2
Evans, J. Canon Parkinson. Manchester 1878.
Author of numerous sermons, editor of memoirs.

William Parsons fl. 1785–1807

Elegy written at Florence. Geneva 1785 (priv ptd).
Odes. Rome 1786 (priv ptd). Anon.
A poetical tour in the years 1784, 1785, and 1786 . . . . 1787. Anon.
An ode to a boy at Eton, with three sonnets and one epigram. 1796.
Fidelity, or love at first sight: a tale . . . . 1798 (priv ptd).
Travelling recreations. 2 vols 1807. Prose.
Oakwood in Sussex. Chelsea 1811. Anon.
Contributed to The Florence miscellany *(1785).*

Samuel Pattison fl. 1790–1802

Original poems, chiefly on divine subjects . . . . Manchester [1790?]; London 1801 (as Original poems chiefly on sublime subjects).
Original poems, moral and satirical. 1792.
The Christian in the holy of holies, or the grateful effusions of a believer. Bristol 1793.
The golden lamp yet burning! A poem . . . . Bristol 1799 (2nd edn).
The feeling mother: a tender story . . . . [1802.]

David William Paynter 1791–1823

The history and adventures of Godfrey Ranger. 3 vols Manchester 1813. Prose.
Eurypilus, king of Sicily: a tragedy . . . . Manchester 1817.
The muse in idleness. Manchester 1819.
King Stephen, or the battle of Lincoln: an historical tragedy . . . . Manchester 1822.
The wife of Florence: a tragedy . . . . Manchester 1823.
Contributed to J. Watson, The spirit of the doctor *(1820).*

Ann Pearson, Mrs Fenwick fl. 1816–34

The grateful remembrance, in letters of advice to an absent niece, on different subjects. Hexham 1816. Prose and verse.
Miscellaneous pieces. Hexham 1834. Verse and prose.

William Peebles 1753–1826

Sermons on various subjects, to which are subjoined hymns. Edinburgh 1794.
The crisis, or the progress of revolutionary principles . . . By a clergyman of Scotland. Edinburgh and London 1803 (anon), 1804 (acknowledged).
Poems, consisting chiefly of odes and elegies. Glasgow 1810. Anon.
Burnomania: the celebrity of . . . Burns considered . . . Epistles in verse. Edinburgh 1811. Anon.

Charles Peers fl. 1805–24

Christ's lamentation over Jerusalem: a Seatonian prize poem. Cambridge 1805, 1808 (in Musae Seatonianae vol 2).
The siege of Jerusalem . . . . 1823, 1824.

John Fitzgerald Pennie 1782–1848

The royal minstrel, or the witcheries of Endor: an epic poem. Dorchester 1817; London 1819.
Ethelwolf, or the Danish pirates: a tragedy. 1821, 1828. Prose and verse.
The garland of wild roses . . . . 1822.
The harp of Parnassus, including several original pieces. Ed Pennie 1822.
Rogvald: an epic poem. 1823.
Corfe Castle, or Keneswitha. 1824. Anon. Prose.
Scenes in Palestine, or dramatic sketches from the Bible. 1825, 1827.
The tale of a modern genius. 3 vols 1827. Anon. Prose.
Britain's historical drama: a series of national tragedies. 2 pts 1832 and 1839. Verse and prose.
The Judith play. Ed W. D. Filliter 1908.

Elizabeth Steel Perkins, Mrs fl. 1834–9

The botanical and horticultural meeting, or Flora's and Pomona's fête: a poem, in humble imitation of The butterfly's ball . . . By a lady. Birmingham 1834 (anon); London 1834, 1835 (4th edn); Brighton 1838 (as Flora and Pomona's fête; authorship acknowledged); London and Tamworth [1854] (as Flora and Pomona's fête).
The elements of botany. 1837. Prose.
Flora's fancy fête, or floral characteristics: a poem . . . a sequel. Brighton [1839].
Also active as an illustrator of botanical books.

Alexander Peterkin, the elder, also 'Anti-harmonicus' 1780–1846

Britannia's tears: a vision. 1800.
A poetical epistle to J*** T*** ... By 'Anti-harmonicus'. Edinburgh 1807. Anon.
A review of the life and works of Robert Burns. Ed Peterkin, Edinburgh 1815; New York 1824 (as The life and works). Prose.
Also wrote on ecclesiastical law, the Scottish church, and Scottish topography.

C. Philippart, Mrs John fl. 1813–14

La puebla's tree. [1813.] Broadsheet.
Muscovy: a poem, in four cantos, with notes, historical and military .... London and Edinburgh 1813; London, Edinburgh and Dublin 1814.
Victoria. [1813.]

Charles Phillips 1787?–1859

The consolations of Erin: an eulogy. 1811 (3 edns).
The loves of Celestine and St Aubert. 2 vols 1811 (2nd edn).
The emerald isle: a poem. 1812 (3 edns), 1813; New York 1813; Middlebury VT 1815; Philadelphia 1816; London 1818 (3 edns).
A garland for the grave of R. B. Sheridan. 1816.
An elegy on the death of ... Princess Charlotte .... Newcastle 1817.
The lament of the emerald isle. 1817 (2 edns), 1818 (5 edns).
Author of memoirs and numerous speeches (listed in BLC); also wrote on Napoleon and on capital punishment.

S. H. Piercy fl. 1810–17

Elegy occasioned by the ... death of ... Princess Amelia. 1810.
Elegy on the ... death of ... Princess Charlotte .... 1817.

Edward Trapp Pilgrim fl. 1785–1837

Poetical trifles .... 1785, 1813.
Hymns, written chiefly on the divine attributes of the deity. Exeter 1828, 1837 (3rd edn).
Poetical scraps on various subjects, serious and comic. Exeter 1837.
Author of pamphlets for missionary socs.

Robert Pollok 1798–1827

Collections

The poetical works of Hemans, Heber and Pollok. Philadelphia 1834.
The poetical works of Crabbe, Heber and Pollok. Philadelphia 1843, 1856.
Miles 10 (11).

§1

Helen of the glen: a tale for youth. Glasgow 1824 (4 edns); Boston 1825; New York 1827; Boston 1829; Glasgow 1829, 1830; Boston 1834, 1841; New York 1841; Boston 1842, 1843; New York 1843, 1844, 1845, 1850, 1851; London and Edinburgh 1870; New York 1872; Richmond VA [1900]. Prose.
Ralph Gemmell: a tale. Edinburgh 1825 (anon); Boston 1827 (as The banks of the Irvine: a Scottish tale); Edinburgh 1829 (acknowledged); Edinburgh and Glasgow 1829; New York 1842, 1845, 1850; Richmond VA 1871; New York 1873. Prose.
The course of time: a poem in ten books. 2 vols Edinburgh and London 1827 (2 edns); Amherst MA 1828; Boston and New York 1828; Edinburgh 1828 (5 edns); Exeter MA 1828; New York 1828; Philadelphia 1828; Boston 1829; Edinburgh 1829; Philadelphia 1829; Boston 1830; Philadelphia and Raleigh NC 1830; Watervliet 1830; Boston 1831; New York 1831 (3 edns); Edinburgh and London 1832; New York 1832; Boston 1833; Edinburgh 1833; New York 1833 (2 edns); Rochester NY 1833; Boston 1834; Concord NH 1834; Philadelphia 1834; New York 1835; Wheeling VA 1835; Concord NH 1836; Edinburgh and London 1836; Exeter MA 1836; Philadelphia 1836; Edinburgh 1838; Pittsburgh 1838; Boston 1839; London 1839; Boston 1840; Edinburgh and London 1840; Hartford CT 1841; Portland ME 1841, 1842; Boston 1842; Cincinnati 1842; Boston 1843; Philadelphia 1843; Edinburgh and London 1844; New York and Philadelphia 1844; Portland ME 1844; Cincinnati [1846?]; Edinburgh and London 1846; Hartford CT 1846; Philadelphia 1846; Portland ME 1846; Fitchburg MA 1847; Hartford CT 1847; New York 1847; Portland ME 1847; Hartford CT 1848; New York 1848; Cincinnati 1849; Hartford CT 1849; New York 1849; London and Edinburgh 1849; Philadelphia 1849; New York 1850 (2 edns); Philadelphia 1850; Boston 1851; Edinburgh and London 1851; New York 1851, 1852; Boston 1852; Cincinnati 1852; Philadelphia 1852; Boston 1853; Hartford CT 1853; New York 1853; Edinburgh and London 1854; New York 1854, 1856 (3 edns); Philadelphia 1856; Edinburgh and London 1857 (illustr edn); Edinburgh 1858; Edinburgh and London 1859; Edinburgh 1860; Edinburgh and London 1863; Philadelphia 1864; New York 1867; Edinburgh and London 1868; New York 1868; Edinburgh and London 1869; London 1869; Philadelphia 1870; New York 1871; Edinburgh 1872; New York and Chicago 1873, 1875; Philadelphia 1882; New York 1883, 1884; Washington 1884; Edinburgh and London [1898] (illustr B. Foster); tr Ger by W. Hey, Hamburg 1830 (as Der Lauf der Zeit). A number of undated US edns appeared, mainly in New York.
The persecuted family. Edinburgh 1828 (with memoir), 1829; Boston 1829; New York 1829; Richmond VA 1829; Boston 1830; New York 1841; Boston 1843; New York 1843, 1845, 1850; Richmond VA 1870; New York 1873; Edinburgh 1881. Prose.
Tales of the covenanters [i.e. Helen of the glen, Ralph Gemmell, The persecuted family]. Edinburgh 1833; Glasgow and Edinburgh 1836; New York 1842 (as Tales of the Scottish covenanters), 1843, 1844; New York and Pittsburgh 1844; New York 1845, 1848; Edinburgh 1850; New York 1850, 1851, 1853; Edinburgh 1859; ed A. Thomson 1895; Kilmarnock [1928]. Prose.

Eleanor Anne Porden, later Franklin 1797?–1825

§1

The veils, or the triumph of constancy: a poem in six books. 1815.
The arctic expeditions: a poem. 1818.
Ode addressed to .... Viscount Belgrave on his marriage ... 1819.
Charity: a second contribution in aid of the Bedford Free School. 1821. Anon.
Ode on the coronation of ... George the Fourth. 1821.
Coeur de Lion, or the third crusade: a poem in sixteen books. 2 vols 1822.

§2

Gell, E. M. John Franklin's bride: E. A. Porden. 1930.

B. E. Pote fl. 1826–41

Abbassah: an Arabian tale .... 1826. Anon.
The assassins of the paradise: an oriental tale .... 1831.
Also wrote on biblical subjects.

Ethelinda Margaretta Potts, Mrs Cuthbert fl. 1814–35

Moonshine. 1814.
A visit to Bonaparte in Plymouth-Sound, with another piece descriptive of Stoke. Dock and Plymouth 1815.

Moonshine... containing sketches in England and Wales. 1832 ('2nd edn'), 1833 (2nd edn).
Moonshine... containing miscellaneous trifles. 1832 ('2nd edn'), 1833 (2nd edn).
Moonshine... containing unconnected trifles and appendix. 1835.
To my grandchildren. [1835?] Prose.

Thomas Jeffrey Llewelyn Prichard d. 1875 or 1876

Mariette Mouline, The death of Glyndower.... 1823.
Welsh minstrelsy: containing The land beneath the sea, with various other poems. 1824, 1825.
The adventures and vagaries of Twm Shon Catti... interspersed with poems. Aberystwyth 1828; Cowbridge [1839]; Cardiff [1870?]; Ferndale [1870] (in Welsh); Llanidloes 1872 (in Welsh), 1873; London [1900?] (as The comical adventures of Twm Shon Catty); Llanerch 1991.
The Cambrian wreath.... Ed Prichard, Aberystwyth 1828, 1860.
The heroines of Welsh history. London, Bristol and Swansea 1854. Prose.
Author of guidebooks to Wales; some of his works also appeared in Welsh.

Thomas Pringle 1789–1834

Collections
The poetical works of Pringle, with a sketch of his life by L. Ritchie. 1838, 1839.
Rogers 3.
Afar in the desert and other South African poems, with a memoir. Ed J. Noble 1881.
Afar in the desert and Evening rambles. Cape Town 1910.
Thomas Pringle: his life, times and poems. Ed W. Hay, Cape Town 1912.
Some poems. 1916.
African sketches: Thomas Pringle in South Africa. Cape Town 1970.
African poems. Ed E. Pereira and M. Chapman, Durban 1989.

§1
The institute: a heroic poem. Edinburgh 1811. Anon. With R. Story.
The autumnal excursion, or sketches in Teviotdale, with other poems. Edinburgh 1819.
Some account of the present state of the English settlers in Albany. 1824; Cape Town 1955. Prose.
[African sketches.] In G. Thompson, Travels and adventures in southern Africa, 2 vols 1827 (rptd from South African Jnl), 1 vol 1834.
Ephemerides, or occasional poems, written in Scotland and South Africa. 1828.
Glen-Lynden: a tale of Teviotdale. 1828. Prose.
Remarks on the demoralizing effects of slavery. 1828. Anon. Prose.
The history of Mary Prince, a West Indian slave, with a supplement by the editor [Pringle]. 1831 (3 edns). Anon. Prose.
African sketches. 1834; tr Ger Stuttgart 1836; selection Edinburgh [1902] (as South African sketches).
Narrative of a residence in South Africa, with biographical sketch by J. Conder. 1834 (as pt 2 of African sketches), 1835, 1840, 1851; ed W. Hay, Cape Town 1924 (selected, as The Pringle school reader), 1966; London 1986 (reprint of 1834); tr Ger 1835, Du Gronigen 1837. Prose.
McLeod, A. L. Two letters of Pringle. N & Q Jan 1961.

§2
Conder, J. A biographical sketch. 1835.
Meiring, J. M. Thomas Pringle: his life and times. Cape Town and Amsterdam 1968.
Doyle, J. R. Thomas Pringle. New York [1972].
Pringle also pbd miscellaneous prose and edited periodicals in Britain and South Africa, including Edinburgh Monthly Mag *(1817) and* Constable's Edinburgh Mag *(1817–18).*

Bryan Waller Procter, 'Barry Cornwall' 1787–1874

Collections
The poetical works of 'Barry Cornwall'. 3 vols 1822, [1823?], 1872, 1882.
The poetical works of Milman, 'Barry Cornwall' [et al]. Paris 1829.
The songs and miscellaneous poems. [New York 1844.]
Miles 2.
A Sicilian story and Mirandola. Ed D. H. Reiman, New York and London 1977 (facs reprints of 1820 and 1821).
Dramatic scenes and Marcian Colonna. Ed D. H. Reiman, New York and London 1978 (facs reprints of 1819 and 1820).

§1
Dramatic scenes and other poems. By 'Barry Cornwall'. 1819, 1820, 1821, 1857 (enlarged, and illustr Birket Foster, Tenniel et al); Boston 1857; New York 1857.
A Sicilian story, with Diego de Montilla and other poems. By 'Barry Cornwall'. 1820 (2 edns), 1821; New York [1821?]; Boston 1827.
Marcian Colonna: an Italian tale, with three dramatic scenes, and other poems. By 'Barry Cornwall'. 1820, 1821; Philadelphia 1821.
Mirandola: a tragedy. By 'Barry Cornwall'. 1821 (3 edns); Philadelphia 1821.
The flood of Thessaly, The girl of Provence, and other poems. By 'Barry Cornwall'. 1823; New York 1978 (facs reprint of 1823).
Effigies poeticae, or the portraits of the British poets. 2 vols 1824 (2 edns, the 1st anon). Prose.
English songs and other small poems. By 'Barry Cornwall'. 1832, 1844; Boston 1844; London 1846, 1851 (enlarged); Boston 1851; London 1856, 1870, 1880, 1882.
Willis, N. P. Melanie and other poems. Ed [Procter] 1835.
The life of Edmund Kean. By 'Barry Cornwall'. 2 vols 1835; New York 1835, 1847. Tr Ger 1836. Prose.
The works of Ben Jonson, with a memoir by 'Barry Cornwall'. 1838.
The works of W. Shakspere, with a memoir and essay on his genius by 'Barry Cornwall'. 3 vols 1843, 2 vols 1853, 1857–9, 3 vols 1875–80, [c. 1900].
Essays and tales in prose. 2 vols Boston 1853.
Selections from Robert Browning. Ed Procter and J. Forster 1863.
Charles Lamb: a memoir. By 'Barry Cornwall'. 1866; Boston 1866; London 1869, 1870 (rptd in Complete correspondence of Lamb), 1879 (rptd in Essays of Elia, with a memoir of Lamb); Boston 1892. Prose.
Procter: an autobiographical fragment. Ed C. Patmore 1877; Boston 1877; ed R. W. Armour 1936 (selected, as The literary recollections of 'Barry Cornwall').
Procter made numerous contributions to periodicals, including Literary Gazette, London Mag *and* Edinburgh Rev.

§2
Armour, R. W. 'Barry Cornwall': a biography. 1935.

Marianne Prowse, Mrs Isaac S. d. 1850

Poems. By Mrs I. S. Prowse. Torquay and London 1830.

George Pryme 1781–1868

§1
Poematia: numismatibus annuis dignata.... [Cambridge 1802.]
Ode graeca praemio dignata.... Cambridge 1804.
The conquest of Canaan: a Seatonian prize poem. Cambridge 1810.
Ode to Trinity College, Cambridge. 1812. Anon.

Memoir of the life of D. Sykes. Wakefield 1834. Prose.
Jephthah and other poems. London and Cambridge 1838.

§2

Autobiographic recollections. Ed A. Bayne, Cambridge 1870.
The Pryme letters.... Hull 1983 (in Malet Lambert local history originals vol 14).
Also wrote on political economy.

Sara Leigh Pyke, also 'Serena' fl. 1795–1832

Israel: a juvenile poem. By 'Serena'. Bath, London and Taunton 1795. Anon.
The triumph of messiah. Exeter, London, Bristol, Bath, Axminster and Plymouth 1812.
Eighty village poems. Taunton 1832.

Catharine Quigley fl. 1813–19

Poems. Dublin 1813.
The microscope, or village flies, in three cantos; with other poems.... Monaghan 1819.

Edward Quillinan 1791–1851

Collections

Poems, with a memoir by W. Johnston. 1853, Ambleside 1891.
Consolation, Elegiac verses, Monthermer, The sacrifice of Isabel, Wood cuts and verses, Carmina Brugensiana. Introd by D. H. Reiman, New York 1978.

§1

Ball-room votaries. 1810, 1810. Verse.
Dunluce Castle: a poem. Lee Priory, Kent 1814 (priv ptd).
Stanzas. Lee Priory 1814 (priv ptd).
Consolation: a poem. Lee Priory 1815 (priv ptd).
Monthermer: a poem. 1815.
The sacrifice of Isabel: a poem. 1816, New York 1816.
Verses, addressed to Lady Brydges, in memory of her son Edward William George Brydges. 1816.
Elegiac verses, addressed to a lady. Lee Priory 1817 (priv ptd).
Miscellaneous poems. Lee Priory 1820 (priv ptd).
Wood cuts and verses, edited with a preface by E. Quillinan. Lee Priory 1820 (priv ptd).
The retort courteous. 1821. Reply to T. Hamilton's attack on Dunluce Castle in Blackwood's Mag.
Carmina Brugesiana: domestic poems. Geneva 1822 (priv ptd).
The King: the lay of 'a papist'. [1829.]
The conspirators. 3 vols '1841' [1840]. A novel.
The rangers of Connaught. In The Edinburgh tales, ed Mrs C. I. Johnstone, vol 1 Edinburgh 1845; also in J. L. Tieck, The elves, New York 1864.
The Lusiad [of Camões] books 1–5, translated. Ed J. Adamson 1853.

Letters

The correspondence of Henry Crabb Robinson with the Wordsworth circle. Ed E. J. Morley 2 vols Oxford 1927. Includes about 70 letters from Quillinan, and a reprint from Blackwood's Mag Apr 1843 of his article defending Wordsworth against Landor.

§2

Quillinan, D. Journal of a few months' residence in Portugal. 2 vols 1847. [PL]

Thomas Quin fl. 1817–27

The city of refuge: a poem.... 1817, 1824, 1827.
Author of Latin textbooks for schools.

Thomas Raffles 1788–1863

Memoirs of the life and ministry of T. Spencer... with a poem. Liverpool 1813 (2 edns), 1817 (4th edn), 1820; London 1827; Philadelphia 1831, 1836.
Poems by three friends. 1813, 1815 (as Poems); ed D. H. Reiman, New York and London 1978 (facs reprint of 1813). Anon. With J. B. Brown and J. H. Wiffen.
Klopstock. The Messiah. Tr Raffles 3 vols 1814.
Letters during a tour. Liverpool 1818; New York 1818; Liverpool 1819, 1820, 1827, 1832. Prose.
Cowper's rose bushes. Ed [J. F.], Newcastle 1829.
Editor, author of sermons, hymn collector, and contributor to The Investigator *(1820–4).*

Thomas Ragg 1808–81

The incarnation and other poems.... 1833 (2nd edn).
The deity: a poem.... Ed I. Taylor 1834 (2 edns).
The martyr of Verulam and other poems. 1834, 1835.
Sketches from life, Lyrics from the pentateuch and other poems. 1837, 1842.
Heber, Records of the poor, Lays from the prophets and other poems. 1840, 1841.
The lyre of Zion: a selection of poems. Ed Ragg 1841.
Scenes and sketches from life and nature, Edgbaston and other poems. 1847, 1850.
Collected hymns and wrote on religion and science, including Creation's testimony to its God *(13 edns 1855–77).*

John Rannie fl. 1789–1806

Poems. 1789; Aberdeen and London 1791; Aberdeen 1791.
Pastorals. Perth [1790?] (2nd edn).
The highland lassie, or a trip from the north: a musical drama. 1803.
Musical dramas, with select poems and ballads. [1806?]
Some of his verse was pbd with musical settings.

William Read 1795?–1866

The hill of caves, in two cantos, with other poems. London and Belfast 1818.
Rouge et noir... Versailles and other poems. 1821 (2 edns), 1830. Anon.
Sketches from Dover Castle, Julian and Francesca, Rouge et noir and other poems. 1859.

John Edmund Reade 1800–70

Collection

The poetical works. 2 vols 1852, 4 vols 1857, 2 vols 1860, 3 vols 1865.

§1

The broken heart and other poems. 1825.
Sibyl leaves, to which is added A vision of eternity. 1827.
Cain the wanderer, A vision of heaven, Darkness and other poems. 1829. Anon.
The revolt of the angels...: an epic drama. 1830.
Italy: a poem. 1838, 1845.
Catiline, or the Roman conspiracy: an historical drama. 1839.
The deluge: a drama. 1839.
The drama of a life. London and Bath 1840.
A record of the pyramids: a drama. 1842.
Sacred poems from subjects in the Old Testament. 1843.
Prose from the south. 2 vols 1846, 1847, 1849.
Revelations of life and other poems. 1849.
Man in paradise: a poem, with lyrical poems. 1856.

The light of other days. 3 vols 1858. Prose.
Wait and hope. 3 vols 1859. Prose.
Saturday Sterne. 3 vols 1862. Prose.
The laureate wreath and other poems. 1863.
Memnon and other poems. 1868.

Cyrus Redding 1785–1870

Mount Edgecumbe: a poem. 1811, 1812.
Gabrielle: a tale of the Swiss mountains. 1829.
Also wrote novels, recollections, literary memoirs, topographical works and bks on wine.

Sophia Reeve, Mrs fl. 1807–28

The mysterious wanderer: a novel. 3 vols 1807.
The flowers at court. 1809.
Holiday annals, interspersed with tales and poetical pieces for young people. Norwich, London and Gainsborough [1820?].
Stanmore, or the monk and the merchant's widow. 3 vols 1824. Prose.
Christmas trifles, consisting principally of geographical charades, valentines, and poetical pieces for young persons. Norwich, London and Derby 1826; London and Norwich 1827.
Cuthbert: a novel. 3 vols 1828. Anon.

Sarah Renou fl. 1815–38

Village conversations, or the vicar's fireside. 2 vols London and Bristol 1815–16 (anon), 3 vols 1817 (acknowledged); 3 vols London and Bristol 1822. Prose.
The temple of truth: a poem in five cantos. London and Bristol 1818; Edinburgh and London 1821; London and Bristol 1822.
The Ionian, or woman in the nineteenth century. 3 vols 1824. Prose.
Delineations physical, intellectual and moral, exemplifying the philosophy of Christianity. 1838. Prose.

John Hamilton Reynolds, also 'John Hamilton' and 'W. W.' 1796–1852

Collections

Poetry and prose. Ed G. L. Marsh, Oxford and London 1928. A selection, with detailed biographical introd.
Selected prose. Ed L. M. Jones, Cambridge MA and London 1966. With bibliography.
Peter Bell, Benjamin the waggoner and The fancy. Ed D. H. Reiman, New York and London 1977 (facs reprints).
The Eden of imagination, Safie, The naiad. Ed D. H. Reiman, New York and London 1978 (facs reprints).
The garden of Florence, The press, Odes and addresses. Ed D. H. Reiman, New York and London 1978 (facs reprints).

§1

Leaves of laurel . . . odes, for the vacant laureateship. Ed 'Q. Q.' and 'W. W.' 1813. Anon.
Safie: an eastern tale. 1814.
The Eden of imagination: a poem. 1814.
An ode. 1815. Anon.
The naiad: a tale, with other poems. 1816. Anon.
Peter Bell: a lyrical ballad. 1819 (3 edns). Anon (signed 'W. W.'); an anticipatory parody of Wordsworth's poem.
Benjamin the waggoner, a ryghte merrie and conceitede tale in verse: a fragment. 1819. Anon. A further burlesque of Wordsworth, possibly by Reynolds.
The battered tar, or the waggoner's companion . . . with sonnets. [1820?]
The fancy: a selection from the poetical remains of the late Peter Corcoran, of Gray's Inn, student-at-law, with a brief memoir of his life. 1820; ed J. Masefield [1905].
The garden of Florence and other poems. By 'John Hamilton'. 1821.
The press, or literary chit-chat: a satire. 1822. Anon.
Odes and addresses to great people. 1825 (2 edns), 1826. Anon. With T. Hood.
Confounded foreigners: a farce in one act. [1838] (in The Acting National Drama vol 3). Prose.

§2

The letters. Ed L. M. Jones. Lincoln NE [1973].
Reynolds contributed to many periodicals, notably Champion *(1815–17) and* London Mag *(1820–4), and wrote* One, two, three, four, five . . . a musical entertainment *(1819).*

George Ambrose Rhodes, also 'W. Shakspeare' fl. 1806–30

Dion: a tragedy, and miscellaneous poetry. 1806, 1820. Prose and verse.
The gentleman: a satire . . . with other poems. 1818, 1819. Anon.
The fifth of November, or the gunpowder plot: an historical play. By 'W. Shakspeare'. 1830.

Thomas Rhodes, of Coventry fl. 1808–24

The patriot queen, or female heroism: a tragedy. Coventry 1808.
Marriage no jest: a comedy . . .. Coventry 1809. Prose.
The speaking cat: a satirical poem. Coventry 1809.
Poetical miscellanies. Coventry [1810?].
The disappointed miller: a farce. Coventry [1824]. Prose.

Rebecca Ribbans 1794?–1821

Lavenham church: a poem. Ed [F. Ribbans], Ipswich, Hadleigh, Sudbury, Ballingdon, Bury, Thetford, London and Lavenham 1822.
Effusions of genius. Ipswich, London, Bury and Cambridge 1829.

Catherine Eliza Richardson, Mrs Gilbert G. 1777–1853

Poems. Edinburgh and London 1828 (2 edns); Edinburgh, London and Dumfries 1829.
Poems . . . second series. London and Edinburgh 1834.

Charlotte Richardson, Mrs 1775–1825

Poems written on different occasions. Ed C. Cappe, York and London 1806 (2 edns); Philadelphia 1806.
Poems, chiefly composed during the pressure of severe illness. Vol 2 (vol 1 being Poems written on different occasions, 1806) York and London 1809.
To my Bible: a poem. [1810?] Single sheet.

Charlotte Caroline Richardson, Mrs John 1796–1854

Waterloo: a poem on the late victory . . . to which is added Truth: a vision. [1815.]
Isaac and Rebecca. 1817.
Harvest: a poem in two parts, with other poetical pieces. London and Whitby 1818.
The soldier's child, or virtue triumphant: a novel. 2 vols 1821.
Ludolph, or the light of nature: a poem. London and Whitby 1823.

Sarah Richardson, Mrs Joseph d. 1824

Richardson, J. Literary relics. Ed S. Richardson 1807.
Original poems, intended for the use of young persons. 1808.
Ethelred: a legendary tragic drama. [1809?], [1810?].
Gertrude: a tragic drama in five acts. [1810?]
The exile of Poland. Tr Richardson 1819. Anon. Prose.
Abridged history of the Bible, in verse. 5 pts of 16 (all pbd?) 1820–2.

Anne Ritson, Mrs fl. 1809–25

A poetical picture of America . . . interspersed with anecdotes . . . By a lady. 1809. Anon.
Classical enigmas, adapted to every month in the year . . . By a lady. 1811, 1815. Anon.
The poetical chain, consisting of miscellaneous poems, moral, sentimental and descriptive . . . . 1811.
Exercises for the memory: an entire new set of improving enigmas . . . . 1813, 1814, 1818 ('2nd edn').
Spring flowers, or easy lessons for young children. 1821; New York 1825. Prose and verse.

Rev William Robb fl. 1793–1822

Two didactic essays on human happiness . . . . 1793.
The patriotic wolves: a fable. Edinburgh 1793 (3rd edn, anon); Edinburgh and London 1793 (4th edn, acknowledged).
Poems illustrative of the genius . . . of Christianity . . . . Edinburgh and London 1809.
A monody in prospect of death . . . London and Edinburgh 1822 (3rd edn); Edinburgh, London and St Andrews 1822 (5th edn).

Emma Roberts 1794?–1841

Almegro: a poem in five cantos. 1819.
Memoirs of the rival houses of York and Lancaster. 2 vols 1827. Prose.
Oriental scenes, dramatic sketches and tales, with other poems. Calcutta 1830; London 1832.
Scenes and characteristics of Hindostan, with sketches of Anglo-Indian society. 3 vols 1835; 2 vols Philadelphia 1836; 2 vols London 1837. Prose.
Views in India, China and on the shores of the Red Sea . . . with descriptions. 1835; tr Ger by J. E. Stahlschmidt [1835]. Prose accompanying pictures by others.
The East India voyager, or ten minutes advice to the outward bound. 1839. Prose.
Notes of an overland journey through France and Egypt to Bombay. 1841. Prose.
Hindostan, its landscapes, palaces, temples, tombs. 2 vols [1845–7]. Prose.
Edited the poems of L. E. Landon (1839) and wrote books on cooking.

Samuel Roberts 1763–1848

Collection
Autobiography and select remains. 1849. Prose and verse.

§1

The chimney sweeper's boy: a poem. Sheffield and London 1807. Anon.
Tales of the poor, or infant suffering. Sheffield 1813; New York 1821; London and Sheffield 1829. Anon. Verse and prose.
The blind man and his son. 1816. Anon.
The state lottery: a dream . . . also Thoughts on wheels: a poem. 1817. With J. Montgomery.
Mary, Queen of Scots and [M. Roberts]. The royal exile. Ed S. Roberts 1822.
The negro's friend, or the Sheffield anti-slavery album. Sheffield 1826. Anon. With others.
Yorkshire tales and poems. London and Sheffield 1839 (2nd edn). Prose and verse.
Also wrote in prose on the Poor Laws, on Sabbatarianism, on the plight of Jews and gypsies, on war, on chimney sweeping and on Milton.

Ellen Robinson, Mrs fl. 1811–21

Poem, written on the death of the Rev Thos. Spencer . . . . Liverpool 1811, 1812, 1823.
Poems on different subjects. Liverpool 1814.
The power, wisdom and goodness of God displayed . . . : a poem. Liverpool 1816.
A tribute . . . to the memory of a beloved son. Liverpool [1821?] (2 edns).

John Roby 1793–1850

Collection
The legendary and poetical remains . . . with a sketch of his literary life. Ed [E. R. Roby] 1854.

§1

Jokeby: a burlesque on Rokeby . . . By an amateur of fashion. London, Edinburgh and Dublin 1813 (9 edns); Boston and New York 1813. Anon.
The lay of the poor fiddler . . . . 1814. Anon.
Sir Bertram: a poem . . . . 1815, 1817.
Lorenzo, or the tale of redemption! 1820 (2nd and 3rd edns).
The Duke of Mantua: a tragedy. 1823 (2 edns), 1824 (4th edn). Anon.
The history of the borough and parish of Tamworth. 1826. With H. W. Roby.
Traditions of Lancashire. (Second ser) 4 vols 1829–31, 1841 (as Popular traditions of England first series), 1843; London and Edinburgh 1867; London and Manchester 1872; London and Edinburgh 1879; London and New York 1882; London 1892; Manchester [1906]; London 1911 (as Lancashire legends); London and New York 1928–30; London 1931. Prose.
Seven weeks in Belgium, Switzerland, Lombardy. 2 vols 1838. Prose.
The three sisters, or past, present and future. Edinburgh 1854. Prose.

J. Hamilton Roche fl. 1810–30

A Suffolk tale, or the perfidious guardian. 2 vols 1810. Prose.
Salamanca: a poem. 1812.
Russia: a heroic poem. 1813, 1814.
The sudburiad, or poems from the cottage. [1813.]
France: a heroic poem. [1814.]
Wahlstadd place, or secrets from . . . St James's. [1815?] Anon.
Cathoeridea, or poems from Paris. Paris 1820.
Odes to the death, on the late royal visitations. Paris 1820.
Les amours des muses, or poems from Finistère. Brest [1826?].
Waterloo: a heroic poem. Brussels 1830.

Thomas Rodd, the elder, also 'Philobiblos' 1763–1822

The Theriad: an heroi-comic poem . . . By a young gentleman. Utopia [London] '1790' [1789]. Anon.
Le Fèvre, P. F. A. Zuma: a tragedy . . . . Tr Rodd 1800.
[G. Perez de Hita.] Ancient ballads from the civil wars of Granada . . . . Tr Rodd 1801, 1803.
G. Perez de Hita. Las guerras civiles, or the civil wars of Granada . . . . Tr Rodd vol 1 1801, 1803 (as The civil wars of Granada).

An elegy, on his grace Francis, the late Duke of Bedford. 1802.
The battle of Copenhagen: a poem. [1806?]
Elegiac stanzas on ... C. J. Fox. 1806. Anon.
Turpin. History of Charles the Great and Orlando ... with the most celebrated ancient Spanish ballads .... Tr Rodd 1812, 1821 (as Ancient Spanish ballads).
Sonnets, amatory, descriptive .... 1814.
Romance de la memorable victoria ... que tuovo ... Don Juan de Austria. Tr Rodd [1815?]. Anon. Prose.
A defence of the veracity of Moses. By 'Philobiblos'. 1820. Anon. Prose.
Bookseller and editor of correspondence.

Alexander Rodger 1784–1846

Collection
Rogers 3.

§1

Scotch poetry: consisting of songs, odes, anthems and epigrams. 1821.
Peter Cornclips: a tale of real life, with other poems. Glasgow 1827.
Poems and songs, humorous and satirical. Glasgow and Greenock 1838; ed R. Ford, Paisley and London 1897; London 1901.
Whistle Binkie, or the piper of the party. 2nd ser ed Rodger, Glasgow 1839, 3rd ser 1841, 4th ser 1842, 5th ser 1843, [collected] 1846, 1853, 1878, 1890 (enlarged). Songs by various authors.
Stray leaves from the portfolios of Alisander the seer, Andrew Whaup and Humphrey Henkeckle. Glasgow 1842 (2 edns). Verse and prose.

Samuel Rogers 1763–1855

Collections
The poetical works of Rogers, Campbell [et al]. Paris 1829 (2 issues).
The poetical works. Philadelphia 1830, 1831, 1836, 1839, 1841, 1843, 1845, 1848, 1849, 1850, 1852, 1854, 1855, 1856, 1859, 1865.
Italy, The pleasures of memory, Human life, and other poems. [1845] (in Standard Poets vol 7).
Poetical works. 1848, 1856, 1869 (illustr J. M. W. Turner and T. Stothard); ed E. Bell 1875 (Aldine).
The complete poetical works. Ed E. Sargent, Boston 1854, 1860.

§1

The choice: a poem. [1774.]
An ode to superstition, with some other poems. 1786. Anon.
The pleasures of memory: a poem in two parts. 1792 (4 edns) (anon), 1793, 1794 (illustr T. Stothard); Boston 1795; London 1795, 1796 (2 edns), 1798, 1799, 1801, 1802; Dublin 1802 (anon); London 1803; Dublin 1804 (anon); Paris 1805; Wilmington 1805 (with Pains of memory by R. Merry); London 1806; New York 1808 (with Pains of memory); London 1810; Belfast 1815; Paris and London 1818; New York and Richmond VA 1820 (with Pains of memory); London 1828 (in British poets of the nineteenth century); Belfast 1830; Philadelphia 1836 (in The book of pleasures, with The pleasures of imagination by M. Akenside and The pleasures of hope by T. Campbell), 1839 (in The book of pleasures); Philadelphia 1841 (in The poems of the pleasures); New York 1851; Philadelphia 1858, 1865; London [1865]; Philadelphia 1870; London [1875]; Boston 1877; rptd Oxford 1989; tr Fr by M. Albert-Montemont, Paris 1825, Ger 1836.
An epistle to a friend, with other poems. By the author of The pleasures of memory. 1798 (2 edns).
Verses written in Westminster Abbey after the funeral of Charles James Fox. [1806.] Anon.
The voyage of Columbus: a poem. 1810 (anon), [1812].
Miscellaneous poems. 1812. Anon. With E. C. Knight et al.
Poems. 1812; Philadelphia and New York 1813; London 1814, 1816, 1820, 1822, 1827, [1833], 1834 (illustr J. M. W. Turner and T. Stothard), 2 vols 1834, 2 vols 1836, 1838 (illustr Turner and Stothard), 1839, 1840, 1842; Philadelphia 1843, 1844; London 2 vols 1845, 1846; Philadelphia 1846; London 1849, 1851; New York 1851, London 1852, 1853; New York 1853; London 1854, ed S. Sharpe (illustr Turner and Stothard), 1860; London and New York 1890 (in Routledge's Pocket Lib).
Jacqueline: a poem. 1814 (anon, 2 edns) (pbd with Byron's Lara).
Human life: a poem. 1819 (3 edns); Philadelphia 1819; Cambridge MA 1820; tr Ital by N. Paciotti, Turin 1820.
Italy: a poem, pt 1. 1822 (anon), 1823 (2 edns, acknowledged in the 2nd); Philadelphia 1823; pt 2 London 1828, 1830 (both pts illustr Turner and Stothard), 1836, 1838, 1839, 1840; Paris 1840; London 1842, 1844, 1848, 1852, 1854, 1859, 1886, 1890.
Recollections of the table-talk of Samuel Rogers, with a memoir [by A. Dyce]. 1856 (3 edns); New York 1856 (2 edns); New Southgate 1887; ed 'Morchard Bishop' (O. Stonor), London 1952.
Recollections. [Ed W. Sharpe] 1859 (2 edns); Boston 1859.
Reminiscences and table-talk ... collected by G. H. Powell. 1903.
Italian journal. Ed J. R. Hale 1956; tr Ger 1986.
Samuel Rogers and William Gilpin: their friendship and correspondence. Ed C. P. Barbier 1959.

Matthew Rolleston 1788?–1817

The anti-corsican: a poem in three cantos .... Exeter and London 1805. Anon.
Moses ... conducting the children of Israel ...: a prize poem. 1810 (in Oxford prize poems). Anon.
Mahomet: a prize poem .... 1810 (in Oxford prize poems). Anon.

Mary Rolls, Mrs Henry fl. 1815–36

Sacred sketches from scripture history. 1815.
Moscow: a poem. 1816.
A poetical address to Lord Byron. 1816.
The home of love: a poem. London, Oxford, Cambridge, Liverpool, Coventry and Warwick 1817.
Legends of the north, or the feudal Christmas: a poem. 1825.
Lines addressed to the members of the Royal National Institution. [1825?] Single sheet.

James Rondeau fl. 1817–35

Leopold's loss, or England's tears o'er the urn of ... Princess Charlotte Augusta: a monody. 1817.
Humorous recitations in verse ... 1820, 1822 (as Recitations ... in verse).
Anti-negro emancipation: an appeal to Mr Wilberforce. 1824. Anon. Prose.
Elements of truth, or the missionary assistant. 1835. Prose.

Jane Elizabeth Roscoe, later Hornblower 1797–1853

Poems. By one of the authors of Poems for youth by a family circle. 1820, 1821. Anon. With others.
Memoir of the Rev Benjamin Goodier. Liverpool 1825. Anon. Prose.
Poems. 1843.
Vara, or the child of adoption. New York 1854, 1858. Anon. Prose.
Nellie of Truro. By the author of Vara. 1856; New York 1856, 1857; London [1876]. Anon. Prose.
The Julia. By the author of Vara. New York 1859. Anon. Prose.

Robert Roscoe 1789–1850

Chevy Chase: a poem, founded on the ancient ballad. 1813 (authorship uncertain), 1820. Anon.
Fitchett, J. King Alfred: a poem. Ed Roscoe 6 vols 1841–2.

William Roscoe 1753–1831

Collections

The poetical works. Liverpool 1853; London 1857 (as 1st collected edn).
William Roscoe of Liverpool. Ed G. Chandler 1953. Contains biography and poetical works.

§1

Mount Pleasant: a descriptive poem. Warrington 1777. Anon.
The wrongs of Africa: a poem. 2 pts 1787–8. Anon.
The wrongs of Almoona, or the African's revenge. By a friend to all mankind. Liverpool 1788. Anon (authorship uncertain).
Ode to the people of France ... after Petrarch. Liverpool 1789. Anon (authorship uncertain).
The life, death and wonderful achievements of Edmund Burke: a new ballad. 1792, [1800?]. Anon. Single sheet.
The life of Lorenzo de Medici. 2 vols Liverpool 1795; London 1796, 1797; 4 vols Basil 1799; London 1800, 1806, 1825, 3 vols 1825 (in English historians); Heidelberg 1825–6; London 1836; New York 1842; Philadelphia 1842; London 1846 (3 edns, one with memoir by W. Hazlitt), 1847, 1851, 1862, 1863, 1865, 1875, 1877, 1881; ed W. Hazlitt 1883, 1889, 1891, 1895, 1898, 1906. Tr Fr by F. Thurot, Paris [1799]; Ger Berlin 1797, Vienna 1817; Greek by X. Parmenidou, Athens 1858; Ital by G. Mecherini, Pisa 1816. Prose.
Tansillo, L. The nurse: a poem. Tr Roscoe, Liverpool and London 1798, 1800; Dublin 1800; New York 1800; Liverpool 1804.
The life and pontificate of Leo the Tenth. 4 vols Liverpool 1805; 6 vols London 1806, 4 vols 1827, 1828; Heidelberg 1828; London 1842, 2 vols 1846 (2 edns); ed W. Hazlitt 1846; London 1853, 1868, 1883. Tr Ger by H. P. K. Henke, Leipzig 1806–8, and by A. F. G. Glaser, Vienna 1818; Ital by L. Bossi, Milan 1816–17.
The butterfly's ball and the grasshopper's feast. [1807], [1810?] (with The peacock at home, by [C. A. Dorset]), 1822, 1824, [1830], 1831; numerous edns with The peacock at home (20th edn 1838); Derby [1840?]; London [1854?], 1855; ed C. Welsh 1883 (facs reprint); New York [1967] (illustr D. Bolognese); London 1973 (illustr A. Aldridge); New York 1975.
Lines written ... on parting with his library. [Liverpool 1816.]
Poems for youth, by a family circle. Pt 1. ed M. A. Jevons 1820. With others. Pt 2 1821.
The dingle: a poem. [1860?] (illustr S. T. d'E.).
Publications on law and politics, editions, memoirs.

§2

Roscoe, H. The life. 2 vols 1833.
Traill, T. S. Memoir. Liverpool 1853.

William Stanley Roscoe 1782–1843

Poems. 1834.
The vale of the cross. Philadelphia [1835?].

William Stewart Rose 1775–1843

A naval history of the late war. Vol 1 (all pbd) 1802. Prose.
de Herberay, N. Amadis de Gaul, freely translated from the first part of the French version. Tr Rose 1803.
Le Grand. Partenopex de Blois, freely translated. Tr Rose, London and Edinburgh 1807.
The crusade of St Lewis and King Edward the martyr. 1810. Ballads.
Casti, G. B. The court and parliament of beasts, freely translated [or rather adapted] from the Animali parlanti: a poem. 1816, 1819.
Letters from the north of Italy, addressed to H. Hallam. 2 vols 1819. Anon. Prose.
Berni, F. The Orlando innamorato. Tr Rose, Edinburgh and London 1823. Abridged, prose, with passages in verse.
Ariosto, L. Orlando furioso. Tr Rose 8 vols 1823–31, 2 vols 1858 (with brief memoir by C. Townsend), 1864, 1907–10, etc; Indianapolis MO [1968].
Thoughts and recollections. 1825. Anon. Prose.
Apology addressed to the travellers' club, or anecdotes of monkeys. 1825. Anon (attribution uncertain). Prose.
A letter to H. Hallam ... on the conduct of the catholic priesthood. 1826. Prose.
To the Right Honourable J. H. Frere. Brighton [1834]. Verse.
Rhymes. Brighton 1837 (priv ptd).
Rufus, or the red king: a romance. 3 vols [1838]. Anon. Prose.
Some verses to Byron (1818) were first ptd in Works of Byron: letters, *ed R. E. Prothero, vol 4 1900, pp. 212–14.*

Sir William Rough d. 1838

Lorenzino de Medici and other poems. 1797.
The conspiracy of Gowrie: a tragedy 1800. Anon (authorship uncertain).
Lines on the death of ... Sir Ralph Abercromby. By the author of The conspiracy of Gowrie. 1801. Anon (authorship uncertain).
Wilkes, J. Letters. Ed [Rough] 4 vols 1804, 1805.
Two epistles out of Wales .... 1808.
Poems, miscellaneous and fugitive .... 1816.
Lines addressed to W. Wordsworth. Colombo 1835. Anon. With B. Bailey.

Frances Arabella Rowden d. c. 1840

A poetical introduction to the study of botany. 1801, 1812, 1818.
The pleasures of friendship: a poem in two parts. 1810, 1811, 1818.
A Christian wreath for the pagan deities. 1820. Prose.
A biographical sketch of the most distinguished writers. 1821. Prose.

Henry Rowe, rector of Ringshall d. 1819

Poems. 2 vols 1796.
The montem: a musical entertainment. 1808.
Fables in verse. 1810.

Charlotte Rowles fl. 1829–35

Nadaber: a tradition, with other poems. 1829. With Martha Rowles.
Eastern scenes in early ages. London, Wrexham and Yeovil 1835.

Martha Rowles

See Charlotte Rowles, above.

Elizabeth Rowse, Mrs fl. 1802–33

A grammatical game, in rhyme. By a lady. London, Bath and Cambridge 1802. Anon.
Outlines of English history, in verse. 1808, 1811; Clapham and London 1833.

Robert Roxby 1767?–1846

The lay of the reedwater minstrel .... Newcastle 1809 (anon), 1832 (acknowledged).

Stanzas to Miss J*** H******. Newcastle 1837; 1849 (in Stray leaves of northern history and tradition).
Poems. Newcastle 1842.
The auld fisher's invitation to his friend. Newcastle 1844. Anon.
Edited The Fisher's Garland *(1821–45).*

Richard Ryan 1796–1849

Biographica Hibernica. 2 vols 1819–21, 1821, 1821–2. Prose.
Eight ballads on the fictions of the ancient Irish, and other poems. 1822.
Poems on sacred subjects. 1824.
Dramatic table-talk. 3 vols 1825. Anon. Prose.
Poetry and poets...: a collection of anecdotes. Ed Ryan 3 vols 1826.
Everybody's husband: a comic drama. 1831 (in Cumberland's Minor Theatre vol 34), [1875?] (in Lacy's Acting Edn vol 92). Prose.
Quite at home: a comic entertainment. 1836 (in Cumberland's British Theatre vol 35). Prose.
Also translated French drama and edited plays.

Maria Grace Saffery, Mrs John 1772–1858

Cheyt Sing: a poem... inscribed... to... Charles James Fox... By a young lady of fifteen. London, Newbury and Salisbury 1790. Anon.
Shoveller, J. Memoirs of... J. Horsey... added an elegy by Mrs Saffery. Portsea 1803.
Poems on sacred subjects. London and Edinburgh 1834.

John Humphrey St Aubyn, also 'L. Bouverie' fl. 1821–38

Mazza: a tale in three cantos. 1821.
Phantoms: a poem in two parts.... 1823.
Robert d'Artois, or the heron vow. 3 vols 1835. Anon. Prose.
The elopement, or the deadly struggle. By 'L. Bouverie'. 3 vols 1838. Prose.

James Sansom fl. 1795–1814

Oppression, or the abuse of power.... 1795.
True greatness, or tributary stanzas to... Nelson.... 1806. Anon.
Greenwich: a poem descriptive and historical. 1808, 1809.
Carmen triumphale, for the year 1814. 1814.

Martha Savory, later Mrs Yeardley 1781–1851

§1
Inspiration: a poetical essay. 1805.
Poetical tales, founded on facts. 1808, 1813 (as Pathetic tales, founded on facts).
Life's vicissitudes, or winter's tears: original poems... containing The mausoleum... and various fugitive pieces. 1809.
An original wreath of forget-me-not presented to those who love to reflect on heavenly things. London and York 1829.
True tales from foreign lands, in verse designed for the young. London and York [1835].
Eastern customs. London and York 1842. Prose. With J. Yeardley.
Poetical sketches of scripture characters. 1848.

§2
Extracts from the letters of J. and M. Yeardley. Lindfield 1835.

James Sayers 1748–1823

The foundling chapel brawl: a non-heroic ballad. 2 pts 1804–5. Anon.
All the talents' garland, or a few rockets let off at a celebrated ministry. 1807 (3 edns, the 3rd as All the talents' garland including Elijah's mantle and other poems). Anon.
Elijah's mantle: a poem. 1807 (6 edns). Anon.
The uti possidetis and status quo: a political satire. 1807. Anon.
Hints to J. Nollekens... on his modelling a bust of Lord G******le. 1808. Anon.
Also a caricaturist.

John Scafe fl. 1815–20

Poems in four parts. Alnwick 1815. Anon.
Poems. 2 vols Newcastle 1818.
King Coal's levee, or geological etiquette.... Alnwick 1818, 1819; London 1819, 1820. Anon.
The genius and other poems. Newcastle 1819.
Court news, or the peers of King Coal.... 1820. Anon.
A geological primer in verse, with a poetical geognosy. 1820.

Martha Ann Sellon fl. 1811–14

The Caledonian comet elucidated. 1811. Anon.
Individuality, or the causes of reciprocal misapprehension, in six books. 1814.

David Service, also 'Dr Sigma' fl. 1802–22

The Caledonian herd boy: a rural poem. Yarmouth 1802.
An elegy on the death of Mr Swanton, painter. Yarmouth [1802].
Crispin, or the apprentice boy: a poem. Yarmouth 1804.
The wild harp's murmurs, or rustic strains. Yarmouth and London [1806].
A voyage and travels in the regions of the brain... and Dumbarton Castle, a sonnet. Yarmouth 1808. Prose and verse.
A tour in pursuit of ideas, a picturesque view of all the Yarmouth public-houses: a poem. By 'Dr Sigma'. Yarmouth 1822. Anon.

James Service, of Chatton fl. 1822–61

The wandering knight of Dunstanborough Castle and miscellaneous poems. Alnwick 1822.
Metrical legends of Northumberland.... Alnwick 1834.
The pilgrim of John Bunyan, paraphrased in verse. Glasgow 1861.

Mary Sewell, née Wright 1797–1884

Ms letters in Norfolk Record Office, Norwich.

Collections
Mrs Sewell's poems and ballads. With memoir by E. Boyd-Bayly. 2 vols [1886], another edn [1886].
Popular stories and ballads by Mrs Sewell. In Household Tracts for the People. Sold individually and including Saved from the sea, The housewife's lament, Hedgerow teachings, The neighbours, Conscience makes the coward, Think before you marry, The little shoes, Almost wrecked, The lord will provide, There's help at hand, The old man's story, Sister's love or Lost in the bush.

§1
Walks with Mamma 'in words of one syllable'. c. 1822–32.
Homely ballads for the working man's fireside. 1858. Containing ballads also sold individually: Faith, hope and charity, The funeral bell, The miller's wife, Abel Howard and his family, The thieves' ladder, The guilty conscience; or, Hell begun, The poor little boy, The common, The working woman's appeal, Mrs Godliman, A religious woman, The young English gentleman, The primrose gatherers, Boy going to service, The drunkard's

wife, The young nurse girl, The bad manager, Sixty years ago.

The children of summerbrook. 1859, [1861] 3rd edn. Contains verses also sold separately in 3 vols as Village children at home; Village children at school; The happy school fellows.

The lady's dilemma. [1859.] Poem.

The lost child: a ballad of English life. [1865] (3rd edn), [1866?] (6th edn). Rptd with The romance of Mallee Scrub, New York 1866.

Mother's last words: a ballad for boys. 1860, [1861] (2nd edn), [1865], [1870]. At least 24 edns.

Isabel Gray: or, the mistress didn't know. 1861, [1870]. Poem.

Our father's care: a ballad. [1861], [1861] (3rd edn), [1870] (44th edn).

Stories in verse for the street and lane: being the second series of 'Homely ballads for the working man's fireside'. 1861. Contains ballads sold individually: The chaffinch's nest, Widow Haye; or, Gossiping neighbours, Miriam, The boy and the rooks, The lady's dilemma, The drunkards, A sad story, The London attic (another story), The green hill side, The traveller and the farmer, The little schismatics; or, Irreligion, Marriage as it may be, The bad servant, A ghost story, Crazed, The two noblemen.

Patience Hart's first experience in service. 1862 (2nd edn); nd (5th edn). Rev edn pbd posthumously. Novel.

An appeal to Englishwomen. [1863.] Anti-slavery polemic.

Homely ballads and stories in verse. (In 18 nos.) [1864], [1870]. Contains verses in Homely ballads for the working man's fireside, Stories in verse for street and lane, Isabel Gray, and The lady's dilemma.

The little forester and his friends. A ballad of the olden time. [1866.] Re-telling in verse of Mrs Sherwood's The little woodman and his dog Caesar.

The rose of Cheriton. A ballad. [1867?], [1870] (2nd edn, an abridgement), reissued [1870].

Poor Betsy Rayner: or The power of kindness. nd. Ballad.

Ballads for children. [1868.] Includes Mother's last words and Our father's care and The children of Summerbrook.

Church ballads. [1868.]

Church ballads. 2nd series: On the festivals. [1869.]

Isabel Gray: or the mistress didn't know, and Katie, the young nurse girl. [1870.]

Pictures and ballads of London life. [1870.]

Davie Blake the sailor! 1875 (2nd edn). Includes prose piece The sailor on shore.

Mother's last words and other ballads. [1876.]

The martyr's tree. [1880.] Verse.

A vision of the night. [1882.] Verse.

The suffering poor. [1883.] Verse.

Sixpenny charity. [1884?] Prose.

Thy poor brother: letters to a friend on helping the poor. [1886] (3rd edn).

§2

Mrs Bayly. The life and letters of Mrs Sewell. 1889. (Includes 76-page 'autobiography' by Sewell.)

The home life and letters of Mrs Ellis, by her nieces. 1893. (Mrs Sewell and Mrs Ellis were sisters-in-law.)

See also the memoir by E. B. Bayly in Mrs. Sewell's poems and ballads, *under collections, above.* [HT-M and AG]

Mary Sewell of Chertsey, Mrs George fl. 1803–9

Poems. Chertsey, London, Bath, Canterbury and Uxbridge 1803; Egham and Chertsey, London, Bath, Canterbury and Uxbridge 1803.

Poems. 2 vols Egham and Chertsey, London, Canterbury, Bath and Uxbridge 1805 (vol 1 being the 2nd edn of Poems 1803).

Trafalgar: a poem to the memory of Lord Nelson . . . Chertsey and London 1806.

Poems and essays. Vol 3 (a sequel to Poems 1805) Chertsey, London, Canterbury, Bath, Uxbridge and Egham 1809.

Richard Scrafton Sharpe fl. 1799–1852

The Margate new guide. . . . 1799. Anon.

Theodore, or the gamester's progress: a poetic tale. 1799, 1802, 1824. Anon.

Parodies on Gay, to which is added The battle of the busts . . . . [1800?] Anon.

Matilda, or the Welch cottage: a poetic tale. 1801. Anon.

Old friends in a new dress, or familiar fables in verse . . . . 1807, 1809, 1820, 1826, 1837. Anon (authorship uncertain).

Mirth for midsummer . . .: a collection of parlour poetry . . . . 1823, 1825 (as Smiles for all seasons, or mirth for midsummer). Anon.

Cottage poetry. 1829. Anon.

The Westons, or scenes in a village, consisting of cottage prose and cottage poetry. [1852] (2nd edn).

The children's poem, Dame Wiggins of Lee, *is traditionally ascribed to Sharpe.*

L. O. Shaw fl. 1814–36

Poems and dramatic pieces. 2 vols Burnley 1814–15.

The duel: a satirical poem with other poems. Blackburn 1815; Haslingdon, London and Manchester [1836] (as The duel, The battle of Waterloo and other poems).

The reformers: a satirical poem. Burnley 1817.

Percy Bysshe Shelley 1792–1822

Mss of most of Shelley's verse and prose of 1817–22 have survived and are scattered in public and private collections throughout the UK and America. The principal collections are located in: (1) Bodleian: 22 notebooks and boxes, including substantial parts in Shelley's or Mary Shelley's hand of Laon and Cythna, Rosalind and Helen, Julian and Maddalo, Prometheus unbound, Peter Bell III, Swellfoot, Sensitive plant, Epipsychidion, Witch of Atlas, Adonais, Hellas, Charles I, Triumph of life, *trns from Euripides, Goethe and Calderón,* Speculations on morals and metaphysics, Coliseum, On manners of the antients, Essay on Christianity, Defence of poetry. *Most of this material is now pbd in facs, with transcripts, notes and commentary, as the Garland series* Bodleian Shelley mss. *Individual items in this series, pbd from 1986 (23 in all when complete), are listed below under §1. Microfilms of the Bodleian collection are at Duke Univ. (2) Huntington: 3 notebooks including drafts of* Mask of anarchy, Vision of the sea, Cyprian, Una favola: *3 poems in Mary Shelley's hand, and* Hellas *in E. Williams's hand. For facs with transcripts, notes and commentary, see the Garland series* Mss of the younger romantics: Shelley, vols 3, 4 and 6 *under §1, below. (3) Houghton Lib, Harvard Univ: a fair-copy notebook, and 7 poems. For facs with transcripts, notes and commentary, see* Mss of the younger romantics: Shelley, vol 5, *under §1, below. (4) Pforzheimer Lib, now in the NYPL: the Esdaile notebook of early poems, some 20 other poems and fragments including the press copy of* Athanase, *and* A philosophical view of reform. *The Esdaile notebook is pbd in facs with transcript, notes and commentary as* Mss of the younger romantics: Shelley, vol i, *listed under §1, below. (5) BL:* Masque of anarchy *(Wise ms), the 'Scrope Davies Notebook' (on long-term loan from Barclay's Bank; contains fair copies of* Hymn to intellectual beauty, Mont Blanc, *and 2 otherwise unknown sonnets), and 12 minor poems and fragments; transcripts at Duke Univ. (6) Pierpont Morgan Lib:* Julian and Maddalo, *and 4 other poems. (7) Lib of Congress:* Mask of anarchy *(Hunt ms) and minor prose. (8) Eton College Lib: 6 poems and fragments.*

The letters are also widely scattered. Collections of more than 20 letters are located in the Bodleian, Pforzheimer Lib, BL and Huntington. The 8th Baron Abinger's large collection of material relating to Shelley and his circle is now on long-term loan to the Bodleian. Microfilms of this collection (as made in

1948–52) are in the Bodleian and at Duke Univ (a later, somewhat differently ordered microfilm is in the Pforzheimer); see Library Notes *(Duke Univ)* 27 1953, *or* Bodleian ms Shelley adds. d. 11, *for detailed contents. The Ingpen papers, including transcripts and photostats, are at the Univ of California, Berkeley; the Dowden papers, also including transcripts, and the ms of his* Life of Shelley, *are at Trinity College Dublin.*

Bibliographies

Forman, H. The Shelley library, pt 1: Shelley's own books, pamphlets and broadsides; posthumous separate issues; and posthumous books wholly or mainly by him. 1886 (Shelley Soc); rptd New York 1975, 1982. No pt 2 pbd.

Anderson, J. In W. Sharp, Life of Shelley, 1887.

Ellis, F. An alphabetical table of contents to Shelley's poetical works. 1888 (Shelley Soc); rptd New York 1975.

Ellis, F. A lexical concordance to the poetical works of Shelley. 1892 (also in 2 vols); Tokyo 1963 (with appendix by T. Saito).

[Welch, C.] Hand-list of mss, letters, printed books and personal relics of Shelley and his circle, exhibited in the Guildhall library. 1893.

Bulletin of the Keats–Shelley Memorial, Rome. No 1, ed R. Rodd and H. Gay, Rome 1910, London 1961; no 2, Rome 1913; no 3, ed D. Hewlett 1950, 1952. Ser in annual progress from no 3 to no 36 1985, then pbd as Keats–Shelley Review, ser in annual progress from no 1 1986. *See* C. Sheraw, Bibliographical index to The Keats–Shelley Memorial Bulletin, I–XX, 1910–1969, Taunton 1984.

[Kooistra, J.] Shelley bibliography 1908–22. ES 4 1922. Addns by L. Verkoren, 5 1923, 20 1938.

Granniss, R. A descriptive catalogue of the first editions in book form of the writings of Shelley. New York 1923 (priv ptd); rptd Norwood PA 1976, Philadelphia 1977. With 30 plates.

Liptzin, S. Shelley in Germany. New York 1924.

Wise, T. A Shelley library. 1924 (priv ptd); rptd New York 1982. Vol 5 of The Ashley library: a catalogue of printed books, manuscripts and autograph letters. *See also* vols 1 (1922) and 11 (1936).

de Ricci, S. A bibliography of Shelley's letters, published and unpublished. Paris 1927 (priv ptd).

[Griffith, R.] An account of an exhibition of books and manuscripts of Shelley, something of their literary history, their present condition and their provenance. [Austin TX] 1935.

Peyre, H. Shelley et la France. Paris 1935.

White, N. The unextinguished hearth: Shelley and his contemporary critics. Durham NC 1938, 1968.

White, W. Fifteen years of Shelley scholarship: a bibliography 1923–38. ES 21 1939 (with addns by W. White and L. Verkoren).

Rogers, N. The Shelley-Rolls gift to the Bodleian. TLS 27 July–10 Aug 1949.

Weaver, B. In English romantic poets: a review of research and criticism, ed T. Raysor, New York 1950, 1956 (2nd rev edn); ch on Shelley by B. Weaver and D. Reiman, New York 1972 (3rd rev edn); by S. Curran, New York 1985 (4th rev edn).

White, W. Shelley scholarship 1939–50. ES 32 1951 (with addns by L. Verkoren).

The Keats–Shelley Journal New York 1952– . Contains annual bibliography. *See also* Keats, Shelley, Byron, Hunt and their circles: a bibliography: July 1 1950–June 30 1962, ed D. Green and D. Wilson, Lincoln NE 1964; and Keats, Shelley, Byron, Hunt, and their circles: a bibliography: July 1, 1962–Dec 31, 1974, ed R. Hartley, Lincoln NE 1978. Cross-indexed cumulated reprints of the KSJ bibliographies.

Bernbaum, E. Keats, Shelley, Byron, Hunt: a critical sketch of important books and articles 1940–53: a critical survey. KSJ 3 1954.

Taylor, C. The early collected editions of Shelley's poems: a study in the history and transmission of the printed text. New Haven CT 1958.

Cameron, K. and D. Reiman (ed). The Carl H. Pforzheimer library: Shelley and his circle 1773–1822. 8 vols [4 further vols projected] Cambridge MA 1961, 1971, 1973, 1985– . Catalogue, full texts and commentary.

Gilenson, B. Shelley in Russian. Soviet Lit 3 1963.

Massey, I. The first edition of Shelley's Poetical works 1939: some manuscript sources. KSJ 16 1967.

Ring, J. Catalogue of books and manuscripts at the Keats–Shelley memorial house in Rome. 1969.

Reiman, D. (ed). The romantics reviewed: contemporary reviews of British romantic writers. Pt C vols 1–2 1972.

Redpath, T. The younger romantics and critical opinion, 1807–1824: poetry of Byron, Shelley, and Keats as seen by their contemporary critics. 1973.

Pollin, B. (ed). Music for Shelley's poetry: an annotated bibliography of musical settings of Shelley's poetry. New York 1975. Suppls 1982, 1992.

Shelley: the critical heritage. Ed J. Barcus 1975.

Dunbar, C. A bibliography of Shelley studies: 1823–1950. 1976.

Ward, W. Literary reviews in British periodicals 1821–1826: a bibliography with a supplementary list of general (non-review) articles on literary subjects. New York 1977.

Tokoo, T. Index to the contents of Shelley's notebooks and other literary manuscripts mainly in the Bodleian library. Humanities: Bull of the Faculty of Letters, Kyoto Prefectural Univ 34 1982.

Shaaban, B. Shelley in the Chartist press. Keats–Shelley Memorial Bull 34 1983.

Tokoo, T. The contents of Shelley's notebooks in the Bodleian library. Humanities: Bull of the Faculty of Letters, Kyoto Prefectural Univ 36 1984.

Barker-Benfield, B. Shelley's Bodleian visits. BLR 12 1987.

Engelberg, K. The making of the Shelley myth: an annotated bibliography of criticism of Percy Bysshe Shelley 1822–1860. 1988.

Barker-Benfield, B. Shelley's guitar: an exhibition of manuscripts, first editions and relics, to mark the bicentenary of the birth of Percy Bysshe Shelley. Oxford 1992 (with plates).

Woof, R. Shelley: an ineffectual angel? [Grasmere] 1992 Exhibition catalogue.

Harata, H. A bibliography of Shelley studies in Japan. KSJ 42 1993.

Ishikawa, S. Shelley studies in Japan: with a bibliography. KSJ 42 1993.

Fraistat, N. Illegitimate Shelley: radical piracy and the textual edition as cultural performance. PMLA 109 1994.

Collections

Miscellaneous and posthumous poems. Vol 1 (all pbd) 1826. Benbow's unauthorised edn; selections from this were reissued as Miscellaneous poems, 1826.

The poetical works of Coleridge, Shelley and Keats. Paris 1829, Philadelphia 1831 etc. Galignani's edn, with memoir by C. Redding.

The works of Shelley, with his life. 2 vols 1834. Ascham's unauthorised edn; selections from this were reissued as Posthumous poems, 1834.

The poetical works. Ed M. Shelley 4 vols 1839 (with preface and notes; prints Queen Mab with omissions), 1 vol 1840 (rev with added postscript) (engraved title page dated 1839; adds Swellfoot, Peter Bell III, and Queen Mab complete), 1 vol 1841 (omits Queen Mab), 4 vols 1846, 1 vol Philadelphia 1846, 3 vols London 1847, 1 vol Philadelphia 1847, 1 vol London 1847 (with Essays, letters . . . fragments etc), 1 vol London 1850, 1 vol Philadelphia 1851, 3 vols London 1853, 1 vol London 1853, 1 vol London 1854, 1 vol London 1854 (with Essays, letters . . . fragments etc), 3 vols Boston 1855, 1 vol London 1856, 3 vols London 1857, 2 vols Boston 1857 (with memoir by J. Lowell), 1 vol London 1862, 3 vols London 1866, 3 vols London 1869, 1 vol London 1869, 1 vol Philadelphia [1884],

3 vols Boston 1889, 1 vol London, New York and Melbourne 1889 (including Essays, letters . . . fragments etc).
Essays, letters from abroad, translations and fragments. Ed M. Shelley 2 vols 1840, New York 1840, Philadelphia 1840, 1 vol London 1845, 2 vols 1852, 1856.
The poetical works. Ed G. Cunningham, illustr on steel by G. Standfast, 1844.
The poetical works. Ed G. Foster, Philadelphia 1845, New York 1850.
The works. Ed M. Shelley 1847, 1854. Comprises Poetical works, *above*, and Essays, letters from abroad, with separate pagination.
The poetical works: including various additional pieces from manuscript and other sources, the text carefully revised, with notes and a memoir by W. Rossetti. 2 vols 1870, 1 vol [1870] (unannotated edn), 3 vols 1878 (rev), 1 vol [1878] (unannotated edn), 3 vols 1881, 1 vol New York [1885], London 1887, 3 vols 1894, 1897, 1 vol 1911, [1951], New York [1953].
The poetical works, now first given from the author's original editions with some hitherto inedited pieces, with memoir by Leigh Hunt. [Ed R. Shepherd] 3 vols [1872–5] (vol 3, and a 4th vol containing the prose, were entitled The works of Shelley), 3 vols 1888, 2 vols 1902, 1912.
The poetical works. Ed W. B. Scott [1874] (with memoir), [1880], 1889, 1895.
The poetical works. [1874.]
The poetical works. Ed H. Forman 4 vols 1876–7, 1882 (with notes by M. Shelley), 2 vols 1882 (without notes), 1886, 1892, 5 vols 1892 (Aldine).
The prose works. Ed H. Forman 4 vols 1880.
The works in verse and prose. Ed H. Forman 8 vols 1880. Comprises The poetical works 1876–7 and The prose works, *above*.
Poetical works. 1888, 1897.
The prose works. Ed R. Shepherd 2 vols 1888, 1902, 1912.
Poetical works. Ed E. Dowden 1890, New York 1893 etc.
The complete poetical works. Ed G. Woodberry 4 vols Boston 1892, London 1893 (Centenary edn, with memoir, textual notes, and 'contemporary records'), 1 vol Boston 1901 (Cambridge Poets ser), 1949, ed and rev N. Ford, New York 1975.
The poetical works, overseen by F. Ellis and printed by William Morris at the Kelmscott Press. 3 vols [1894–5] (priv ptd).
Poems. [Decorated by C. Ricketts] 3 vols 1901–2 (priv ptd).
Poetical works. 1902.
Shelley: poetical works. Ed T. Hutchinson, Oxford 1904, reset 1905 [Oxford Standard Authors], 1907 etc, New York 1933 (introd by B. Kurtz), reset Oxford 1934 (without introd), 1945 etc, corrected by G. Matthews 1970.
The complete works. Ed N. Doyle 8 vols 1904–6.
The poems. Introd by C. Locock 4 vols 1906–9.
The poetical works. Ed A. Koszul 2 vols [1907], 1 vol 1934, 2 vols (with rev introd) 1953 (Everyman).
Poetical works. Introd by R. Garnett [1911].
The poems. Ed C. Locock with introd by A. Clutton-Brock 2 vols 1911.
The lyrical [dramatic, narrative] poems and translations, arranged in chronological order. Ed C. Herford 4 vols 1918–27.
The complete works. Ed R. Ingpen and W. Peck 10 vols 1926–30 (Julian edn); rptd New York 1965.
The complete poetical works of Keats and Shelley. New York 1932, London 1935.
Shelley's prose: or the trumpet of a prophecy. Ed D. Clark, Albuquerque 1954 rev 2nd edn 1966, rptd 1988.
The complete poetical works of Percy Bysshe Shelley. Vol 1 [of 4, only 2 pbd]: 1802–13, ed N. Rogers, Oxford 1972.
The complete poetical works of Percy Bysshe Shelley. Vol 2 [of 4, only 2 pbd]: 1814–17, ed N. Rogers, Oxford 1975.
The poems of Shelley: volume one [of 3]. Ed K. Everest and G. Matthews 1989 (Longman's Annotated English Poets).
The prose works of Percy Bysshe Shelley. Vol 1 [of 2]. Ed E. Murray, Oxford 1993.
Shelley's poetical works were tr Ger 1840–4, 1866, Ital 1858, 1878, 1902, 1911, 1917, 1925, Fr 1885–7, Rus 1893–5, 1937, 1963, Romanian 1957. The prose works were tr Rus 1895–9, Fr 1903, Ital [1917].

Selections

Miscellaneous poems. 1826. Selected from Miscellaneous and posthumous poems, 1826 (Benbow's edn).
The beauties of Shelley, consisting of miscellaneous selections from his poetical works, the entire poems of Adonais and Alastor and a revised edition of Queen Mab free from all objectionable passages with a biographical preface. 1830 (S. Hunt's edn), 1832 (Lumley's edn), 1856.
The beauties of Shelley, consisting of Rosalind and Helen, Posthumous and miscellaneous poems, Revolt of Islam, Queen Mab and Prometheus unbound. 1836 (Ascham's edn).
The works of Shelley, comprising Queen Mab, The revolt of Islam, The Cenci &c &c &c [with preface]. 1836. Daly's edn, based on Ascham's Works, 1834; reissued as Poetical works of Shelley complete, 1837, 1839.
Einige Dichtungen. Tr F. Prössel, Leipzig 1841.
The minor poems. 1846, 1859.
Queen Mab and other poems. 1846, 1859.
Queen Mab and other poems. Halifax 1865.
A selection from the poems. Ed M. Blind, Leipzig [1872], 1920 (Tauchnitz).
Poems selected from Shelley. Ed R. Garnett 1880.
Poems. Ed S. Brooke 1880.
The lyrics and minor poems, with a prefatory notice by J. Skipsey. 1885, New York 1885.
Essays and letters. Ed E. Rhys 1886, [1905]; rptd Freeport NY 1971.
Poems and sonnets. Ed 'Charles Alfred Seymour' (T. Wise), Philadelphia [i.e. London] 1887 (priv ptd).
The banquet of Plato, and other pieces. Ed H. Morley 1887, 1905.
Prometheus unbound, with Adonais [etc]. Ed H. Morley 1888, 1905, 1906.
The sensitive plant. Ed S. Silvagni, Prato 1888.
The skylark and Adonais, with other poems. Ed J. Abernethy, New York [1890].
A defense of poetry. Ed A. Cook, Boston 1891.
The lyric poems. Ed E. Rhys [1895].
Select poems. Ed W. Alexander, Boston 1898.
Poems: narrative, elegiac and visionary. [Ed H. Forman] 1899, 1901, 1904 (Temple Classics).
The sensitive plant. [Ed E. Rhys], illustr L. Housman, 1899 (priv ptd).
Poems from Shelley and Keats. Ed S. Newsom, New York 1900, 1907, 1922.
Poems of Shelley, selected and arranged for use in schools by E. Speight. 1901.
Poems. Ed W. Raleigh, illustr R. Bell, 1902, 1907; facs reprint 1979.
Poems. Ed A. Meynell 1903, 1923.
Thoughts from Shelley. [Selected by V. Neale] 1903.
A defence of poetry etc. Ed M. Shelley, Indianapolis [1904] (priv ptd). Rptd from Essays, letters from abroad, 1845.
With Shelley in Italy: a selection of the poems and letters. Ed A. McMahan, Chicago 1905, London 1907. With 64 photographs.
Poems of Shelley. Ed H. Bennett 1907, 1924.
Shelley selected. Ed J. Collins [1907], [1915].
Selected poems. Ed G. Clarke, New York [1907], London [1910].
Select poems. Ed G. Woodberry, Boston 1908.
The banquet of Plato translated by Shelley. Ed B. Rogers 1908 (priv ptd).
Shelley's literary and philosophical criticism. Ed J. Shawcross 1909; rptd Folcroft PA 1969, 1977, Norwood PA 1978.

Shelley's Defence of poetry; Browning's Essay on Shelley. Ed L. Winstanley, Boston 1911.
Nature poems by Shelley. Illustr W. Hyde 1911.
The sensitive plant. Ed E. Gosse, illustr R. Robinson, 1911, Philadelphia [1911.]
Selected poems. [1911.]
Shelley [prose and verse selections]. Ed R. Ingpen [1912].
Selected poems. Oxford 1913, 1921 (WC).
Selections from the poems. Ed A. Thompson, Cambridge 1915, 1919, 1920.
Selected prose works. Ed H. Salt 1915, [1922].
Peacock's Four ages of poetry; Shelley's Defence of poetry; Browning's Essay on Shelley. Ed H. Brett-Smith, Oxford 1921, 1923 (2 issues, one abridged; the abridgement only rptd 1953); Norwood PA 1977 (reprint of 1921).
[Poésies choisies.] Tr A. Koszul, Paris 1922, 1927, 1930, 1943.
Poems: an anthology in commemoration of the poet's death. Ed T. Cobden-Sanderson 1922.
Odes, poèmes et fragments lyriques choisis. Ed and tr A. Fontaines, Paris 1923.
Selected poems. Ed G. Roth, Paris 1923.
Shelley. Ed H. Newbolt, Edinburgh [1923], 1954.
Select poems and prose. Ed R. Ackermann, Frankfurt 1924 (with glossary).
Shelley and Keats, contrasted by G. Boas. [1925].
Poems. Ed O. Campbell 1925.
Poems. Ed N. Crawford, Girard KS [1925].
Shelley. [Ed E. Thompson 1925] (Augustan Books ser).
Poems, selected by A. Symons. 1926.
Selections from Shelley. Ed E. Blakeney 1926.
Oeuvres choisies: texte anglais et traduction en vers par M. Castelain. 3 vols Paris 1929–35.
Poetry and prose, with essays by Browning, Bagehot, Swinburne, and reminiscences by others. Ed A. Hughes, Oxford 1931; rptd 1973, New York 1980.
The best of Shelley. Ed N. White, New York 1932.
Selections from the poems. Ed V. de S. Pinto [1932].
Songs: a collection of lyrics and sonnets completed from the minor fragments. Ed C. Bostlemann and W. Peck, Morristown NJ 1937.
Shelley. Ed D. Wellesley 1941.
The reader's Shelley: selections. Ed C. Grabo and M. Freeman, New York [1942].
Selected poems, essays and letters. Ed E. Barnard, New York 1944.
Selected poems. Ed L. Untermeyer, New York 1944 (priv ptd).
Shelley in Italy: an anthology. Ed J. Lehmann 1947.
A defence of poetry. Ed E. Blunden, Tokyo 1948; ed F. B. Pinion [1955].
The Shelley companion. Ed H. Stenning 1948.
Poems. Ed J. Heath-Stubbs 1948.
Poems. Ed R. Church, illustr J. Buckland-Wright, 1949, rptd 1973 (Folio Soc).
Shelley's poetical works. Ed 'Morchard Bishop' (O. Stonor) 1949.
Selected poetry and prose. Ed C. Baker, New York 1951 (Modern Lib).
Shelley: selected poetry, prose and letters. Ed A. Glover 1951 (Nonesuch Lib).
Selected poems. Ed E. Blunden 1954.
Selected poetry and prose. Ed K. Cameron, New York 1956.
A selection. Ed I. Quigly 1956 (Pelican); rptd as Shelley: poems, Harmondsworth 1985 (Pen Poetry Lib).
Selected poems. Ed F. Jones, New York [1956].
Odes of Keats and Shelley. New York 1957 (priv ptd).
Poems and lyrics. New York 1957 (priv ptd).
Selections from Shelley's poetry. Ed F. Pinion 1958.
Poetry and prose. Ed I. Neupokoevna, Moscow 1959.
Selected poems. Ed J. Holloway 1960.
Poèmes: traduction, préface et notes par M. Cazamian. [Paris 1960.]
Selections from Shelley's poetry and prose. Ed D. Welland 1961.
Selected poems and prose. Ed G. Matthews, Oxford 1964.
Choix de textes, suite iconographique et commentaire, étude par Stephen Spender [etc]. Paris 1964.
Selected poetry and prose. Ed H. Bloom, New York 1966.
Shelley's critical prose. Ed B. McElderry, Lincoln NE 1967.
Selected poems. Ed E. Chinol, Milan 1968.
Pesme. [Tr] R. Kuic, Belgrade 1969. In Serbo-Croat.
Adonais e altre poesie. Tr R. Sanesi, Milan 1970; rptd 1981.
Mám v duši more. [Tr] I. Mojik, Bratislava 1970. In Cz.
Poesia. Ed G. Sardelli, Milan 1970.
Political writings, including A defence of poetry. Ed R. Duerksen, New York 1970.
Selected poetry. Ed N. Rogers 1970.
Shelley: Alastor, Prometheus unbound, Adonais, and other poems. Ed P. Butter 1970 [Collins Annotated Student Texts].
A choice of Shelley's verse. Ed S. Spender 1971.
Poems. Selected by K. Raine, Harmondsworth 1973; rptd Harmondsworth 1978 (Poet to Poet).
Versei. Trans M. Babits et al, Budapest 1973. In Hungarian.
Poems. Ed S. Spender, illustr by R. Smith, New York 1974.
Adonais, Hymn to intellectual beauty, To a skylark; Prometeo (atto primo). Tr C. Grasso, Rome 1975.
Lines and fragments. Illustr A. Clements and ptd by M. McCord, Belfast 1977 (priv ptd).
Shelley: selected poems. Ed T. Webb 1977 [Everyman's Univ Lib].
Shelley's poetry and prose. Ed D. Reiman and S. Powers, New York 1977 corrected edn 1982.
Zastrozzi, a romance and St Irvyne; or, the rosicrucian: a romance. Introd by F. Frank, New York 1977.
Poesie. Ed R. Quadrelli, Milan 1980.
Shelley on love: an anthology. Ed R. Holmes 1983.
Prince Athanase and The triumph of life. Ed N. Wright, Wellington NZ 1985.
Zastrozzi and St Irvyne. Ed S. Behrendt, Oxford 1986 (WCp).
Shelley. Comp and illustr P. Machin, Topsfield, MA 1987.
Shelley's revolutionary year: Shelley's political poems and the essay A philosophical view of reform. Ed P. Foot 1990.
Percy Bysshe Shelley. Ed P. Porter 1991 [The Illustr Poets].
Shelley: selected poetry and prose. Ed A. Macrae 1991 [Routledge English Texts].
Shelley's poetry: Julian and Maddalo, Hellas, and other poems [in Jap]. Ed and tr N. Takahashi, Tokyo 1992.
Shelley: Opere. Tr Francesco Rognoni, Turin 1995. In Italian, with parallel English text, and annotation in Italian.
Shelley: poems and prose. Ed T. Webb 1995. With a selection of criticism and linking commentary by G. Donaldson.

§1

For contemporary and early reviews, and obituaries, see the following under Bibliographies, *above: N. White,* Unextinguished hearth; *Barcus,* Critical heritage; *Engelberg,* Making of the Shelley myth; *Dunbar,* Bibliography of Shelley studies; *Redpath,* Younger romantics and critical opinion; *Reiman,* Romantics reviewed; *Ward,* Literary reviews in British periodicals.

Zastrozzi: a romance by P. B. S. 1810, 1839; ed P. Hartnoll 1955 (priv ptd); ed E. Chesser 1965.
Original poetry by Victor and Cazire [P. B. and Elizabeth Shelley]. Worthing 1810; ed R. Garnett 1898; ed S. Looker in his Shelley, Trelawny and Henley, Worthing 1950 (photo facs); Folcroft PA 1974 (reprint of 1898).
Posthumous fragments of Margaret Nicholson: being poems found amongst the papers of that noted female who attempted the life of the king in 1786. Ed John Fitzvictor [P. B. Shelley], Oxford 1810; ed H. Forman [1877] (priv ptd).
St Irvyne or the Rosicrucian: a romance, by a gentleman of the University of Oxford. 1811 (reissue dated 1822), 1840.

The necessity of atheism [anon, by T. Hogg and Shelley]. Worthing [1811], London 1906; ed S. Looker in his Shelley, Trelawny and Henley, Worthing 1950 (photo facs); ed E. Chesser 1965; tr Rus 1973.

A poetical essay on the existing state of things, by a gentleman of the University of Oxford. [1811]. No known copy.

An address to the Irish people. Dublin 1812; ed T. Wise 1886, 1890 (Shelley Soc), 1890; New York 1975 (reprint of 1890).

Proposals for an association of those philanthropists, who convinced of the inadequacy of the moral and political state of Ireland to produce benefits which are nevertheless attainable, are willing to unite to accomplish its regeneration. Dublin [1812].

Declaration of rights. [Dublin 1812]; rptd in Republican 24 Sep 1819; Miscellanies of the Philobiblon Soc 12 1868–9; Fortnightly Rev 15, Jan 1871; Fifty major documents of the nineteenth century, ed L. Snyder, Princeton 1955. Two copies of this anon broadside are in the Public Record Office, and one in the Huntington.

The Devil's walk: a ballad. [Barnstaple? 1812]; rptd by W. Rossetti, Fortnightly Rev 15, Jan 1871. Pbd as anon broadside; one copy in Public Record Office, one at Univ of Texas.

A letter to Lord Ellenborough. [1812] (priv ptd) (one known copy, in Bodleian); [ed J. Wheeler] 1883; ed T. Wise 1887, 1894 (Shelley Soc); tr Rus 1973.

A vindication of natural diet: being one in a series of notes to Queen Mab, a philosophical poem. 1813; [ed H. Salt and W. Axon] 1884 (Shelley Soc), 1886, 1922; Folcroft PA (reprint of 1884); New York 1975 (reprint of 1886); Philadelphia 1978 (reprint of 1884).

Queen Mab: a philosophical poem, with notes. 1813 (priv ptd). Numerous unauthorised edns 1821–57, including 1821 (Clark's edn, some copies bowdlerised), 1821 (Benbow's edn, with false New York imprint), 1822 (Carlile's edn, some copies without the notes), 1823, 1826, 1829 (Brooks's edn), 1830 (S. Hunt's bowdlerised edn), New York 1831, London 1847 (Watson's edn); introd by J. Wordsworth, Spelsbury 1990 (facs; Revolution and romanticism 1789–1834); tr Ger [1897], Jap 1972.

A refutation of deism, in a dialogue. 1814 (anon); rptd in Theological Inquirer Mar–Apr 1815; 1890.

[Review of] Hogg's Memoirs of Prince Haimatoff. Critical Rev 6 1814 (anon); ed T. Wise 1886, 1886 (rev) (Shelley Soc); New York 1975 (reprint of 1886); rptd in Memoirs of Prince Haimatoff, ed S. Scott, 1952 (Folio Soc).

Alastor: or the spirit of solitude, and other poems. 1816; ed H. Forman 1876 (priv ptd); ed B. Dobell 1885, 1887 (Shelley Soc); New York 1975 (reprint of 1885); tr Fr 1884, 1895, 1991 (with preface), Du [1906], 1909 (Frisian, 1918), Ger 1909, 1960, Ital 1923.

A proposal for putting reform to the vote throughout the kingdom, by the Hermit of Marlow. 1817; ed H. Forman 1887 (facs of holograph ms) (Shelley Soc); New York 1975 (reprint of 1887).

An address to the people on the death of Princess Charlotte, by the Hermit of Marlow. [1817], [1843?] ('facsimile reprint' but no copy known of supposed 1817 edn; ptd from ms?), Edinburgh 1883 (priv ptd).

Remarks on 'Mandeville' and Mr Godwin, by E. K. ['Elfin Knight', i.e. Shelley]. Examiner 28 Dec 1817; rptd by Medwin, Athenaeum 27 Oct 1832.

History of a six weeks' tour through a part of France, Switzerland, Germany, and Holland: with letters descriptive of a sail round the lake of Geneva, and of the glaciers of Chamouni [by Shelley and M. Shelley]. 1817 [anon; reissued 1829]; ed C. Elton 1894 (abridged); introd by J. Wordsworth, Spelsbury 1989, rptd 1991 (facs; in Revolution and romanticism, 1789–1834).

Laon and Cythna, or the revolution in the golden city: a vision of the nineteenth century in the stanza of Spenser. 1818. Suppressed, rev and reissued as The revolt of Islam: a poem in twelve cantos, 1818 (a few copies dated 1817; reissued 1829).

Rosalind and Helen: a modern eclogue; with other poems. 1819; ed H. Forman 1876 (priv ptd); ed H. Forman 1888 (Shelley Soc); New York 1975 (reprint of 1888).

The Cenci: a tragedy in five acts. 1819 (ptd in Italy), 1821, 1827 (Benbow's unauthorised edn); ed A. and H. Forman 1886 (Shelley Soc); New York 1903 (priv ptd); ed G. Woodberry, Boston 1909 (with bibliography); Leipzig 1916 (Tauchnitz), 1922, London [1928]; ed. A. Hicks and R. Clark, Caldwell ID 1945 (a stage version); ed R. Duerksen, Indianapolis 1970; New York 1970 (reprint of 1886); New York 1975 (reprint of 1886); introd by J. Wordsworth, Oxford 1991 (facs; in Revolution and romanticism, 1789–1834); tr Ger 1837, 1904, 1907, 1924, Ital 1844, 1892, 1898, 1912, 1931, Rus 1864, 1899, Fr 1883 (preface by A. Swinburne), 1990, Polish 1912, Cz 1922, 1960, Jap 1955, Armenian 1977.

Prometheus unbound: a lyrical drama in four acts, with other poems. 1820; ed V. Scudder, Boston [1892], London [1892]; ed G. Dickinson 1898, 1904 (priv ptd), New York 1904 (priv ptd); ed R. Ackermann, Heidelberg 1908; ed A. Hughes, Oxford 1910, 1957; ed G. Fernando, Florence 1922 (notes in Ital); Oxford 1923 (plain text); ed L. Zillman, Seattle 1959 (variorum edn, with bibliography); New York [1960]; ed N. Basu, Calcutta 1961; ed L. Zillman, 1968 (Shelley's Prometheus unbound: the text and the drafts); tr Ger 1876, 1887, Fr 1884, 1912, 1942, Danish 1892, Ital 1892, 1892, 1894, 1901, 1904, 1922, 1925, 1946, Norwegian 1892, 1951, Arabic 1947, Serbo-Croat 1952, Hebrew 1953, Jap 1957, Hungarian 1961, Georgian 1962, Bengali 1975.

Oedipus tyrannus or Swellfoot the tyrant: a tragedy in two acts, translated from the original Doric. 1820 (anon; edn suppressed); ed H. Forman [1876], [1884]; tr Polish 1912.

Epipsychidion: verses addressed to the noble and unfortunate Lady Emilia V— now imprisoned in the convent of —. 1821 (anon, withdrawn); ed H. Forman 1876 (priv ptd); ed R. Potts 1887 (Shelley Soc) (introd by S. Brooke); 1921, Montagnola 1923; Menston, Yorks 1971 (facs of 1821 and of Bodleian ms Shelley d. 1); New York 1975 (reprint of 1887); tr Ital 1893, 1928, Ger 1900, Jap 1923, Polish [1924].

Adonais: an elegy on the death of John Keats, author of Endymion, Hyperion etc. Pisa 1821, Cambridge 1829; [ed H. Forman 1877] (priv ptd); ed T. Wise 1886, 1887 (rev) (Shelley Soc); ed W. Rossetti, Oxford 1890; ed W. Rossetti, rev A. Prickard, 1903, 1904 (facs); ed A. Weekes [1910]; San Francisco 1922 (facs, priv ptd); ed S. Policardi, Milan 1925 (notes in Ital); ed N. Douglas 1927 (photo facs); ed C. Sawyer 1936; ed F. Pinion [1955]; New York 1975 (reprint of 1886); ed A. Knerr, New York 1984 (a critical edn); [New York 1990] (priv ptd); introd by J. Wordsworth, Spelsbury 1992 (facs; in Revolution and romanticism, 1789–1834); tr Ital 1830, 1899, 1925, 1948, 1956, Ger 1900, 1910, Frisian 1916, Sp 1936, 1944, 1947, 1954, Danish 1950.

Hellas: a lyrical drama. 1822; ed T. Wise 1886, 1887 (Shelley Soc); New York 1970 (reprint of 1886); New York 1975 (reprint of 1886); tr Ital 1855, Fr 1884, 1906.

Poetical pieces by the late Percy Bysshe Shelley: containing Prometheus unmasked, a lyrical drama, with other poems; Hellas: a lyrical drama; The Cenci: a tragedy in five acts; Rosalind and Helen: with other poems. 1823. A reissue of the 1st edns (2nd edn of Cenci) with a new title page; some copies omit Hellas.

Posthumous poems. [Ed M. Shelley] 1824 [suppressed]; ed I. Massey, Montreal 1969 (Mary Shelley's fair-copy book, Bodleian ms Shelley adds. d. 9, collated with the holographs and the printed texts); introd by J. Wordsworth, Spelsbury 1991 (facs; in Romanticism and revolution, 1789–1834).

The masque of anarchy: a poem now first published, with a preface by L. Hunt. 1832, 1842; ed H. Forman 1887 (Shelley Soc) (photo facs of the holograph ('Wise') ms, entitled The mask of anarchy); ed T. Wise 1892 (facs of 1832) (Shelley Soc); foreword by D. Gould 1970, 1973 (2nd edn); New York 1975 (reprint of 1887); New York 1975 (reprint of 1892); introd by J. Wordsworth, Spelsbury 1990 (facs of 1832; in Romanticism and revolution, 1789–1834).

The Shelley papers: memoir by T. Medwin and original poems and papers by Shelley. 1833, 1844. Original material rptd from Athenaeum 28 July, 11, 25 Aug, 1–29 Sep, 20–7 Oct, 10–24 Nov, 8 Dec (by T. Kelsall) 1832, 20 Apr 1833; adds one spurious poem.

Essays, letters from abroad, translations and fragments. Ed M. Shelley 2 vols 1840, Philadelphia 1840, London 1841, 1 vol 1845, 2 vols 1852, 1856. First pbn of A defence of poetry; *see under* Collections, *above*.

Shelley memorials, from authentic sources; to which is added An essay on Christianity. Ed Lady Shelley [and R. Garnett] 1859, 1859, Boston 1859, London 1862 ('2nd edn'), 1875 ('3rd edn'); St Clair Shores MI 1970.

Relics of Shelley. Ed R. Garnett 1862.

The daemon of the world: the first part as published in 1816 with Alastor; the second part deciphered and now printed from his manuscript revision and interpolations in the newly discovered copy of Queen Mab. Ed H. Forman 1876 (priv ptd).

To the Nile; and Shelley fragments. St James's Mag Mar 1876. Pt of Essay on Christianity.

Notes on sculptures in Rome and Florence together with a Lucianic fragment and a criticism on Peacock's poem Rhododaphne. Ed H. Forman 1879 (priv ptd) (from ms).

[Fragment of a satire on satire.] Ed E. Dowden in his Correspondence of Robert Southey with Caroline Bowles, 1881.

The wandering jew [or The victim of the eternal avenger]. Ed B. Dobell 1887 (Shelley Soc); New York 1975 (reprint of 1887). Text conflated from extracts in Edinburgh Literary Jnl 20, 27 June, 4 July, 26 Dec 1829 and from text 'in a complete state' in Fraser's Mag July 1831.

An examination of the Shelley manuscripts in the Bodleian Library, by C. Locock. Oxford 1903; rptd Norwood PA 1975. New and corrected texts.

Shelley's prose in the Bodleian manuscripts. Ed A. Koszul, Oxford 1910.

Note books of Shelley, from the originals in the library of W. K. Bixby [now in Huntington], deciphered, transcribed and edited, with a full commentary, by H. Buxton Forman. 3 vols Boston 1911 (priv ptd). *See below*, Mss of the younger romantics vol 4, ed M. Quinn, 1990.

A philosophical view of reform. Ed T. Rolleston, Oxford 1920; ed W. Peck 1930 (priv ptd); ed R. White in his Political tracts of Wordsworth, Coleridge and Shelley, Cambridge 1953, rptd Folcroft PA 1974, Norwood PA 1977.

New fragments by Shelley. Ed E. Gosse, TLS 24 Feb 1921. Verses from mss now at Eton College.

Inédits italiens de Shelley. [Ed] A. Koszul, Revue de Littérature Comparée 2 1922.

[Prose fragment on the resettlement of the Jews.] Ed T. Saito in The Shelley memorial volume by members of the English Club, Imperial University of Tokyo, Tokyo 1923. With photo facs of ms, which was probably destroyed in 1945–6.

The celandine. Ed W. Peck, Boston Herald 21 Dec 1925; ed E. Blakeney, Winchester 1927 (priv ptd).

An unpublished ballad by Shelley ['Young parson Richards']. Ed W. Peck, PQ 5 1926; ed Peck, Iowa City 1926 (priv ptd).

The Shelley notebook in the Harvard Library. Ed G. Woodberry, Cambridge MA 1929 (photo facs); rptd Folcroft PA 1969. *See below*, The Harvard Shelley poetic manuscripts, ed D. Reiman 1991; *and compare* G. Woodberry, Notes on the manuscript volume of Shelley's poems in the library of Harvard College, Cambridge MA 1889; autograph ascriptions corrected by M. Kessel, TLS 5 Sep 1936.

On the vegetable system of diet. Ed R. Ingpen 1929 (priv ptd); rptd in his Verse and prose from the manuscripts of Shelley, 1934, *below*; 1940, 1947.

Plato's Banquet translated from the Greek: a discourse on the manners of the antient Greeks relative to the subject of love; also A preface to the Banquet. Ed R. Ingpen 1931 (priv ptd) (from ms). *See* Shelley's translations from Plato, *below*.

Verse and prose from the manuscripts of Shelley. Ed J. Shelley-Rolls and R. Ingpen 1934 (priv ptd); rptd Folcroft PA 1974, Philadelphia 1977.

Sadak the wanderer: an unknown Shelley poem. Ed D. Cook, TLS 16 May 1936. Rptd from Keepsake 1828.

A Shelley letter. Ed E. Blakeney, Winchester 1936 (priv ptd). Verse letter to Fergus Graham.

[Verses from Claire Clairmont's jnl]. In N. White, Shelley vol 2, New York 1940; ed L. Robertson, MLR 47 1953.

[Translation from Aristotle, Ethics IX viii]. In Shelley at Oxford, ed W. Scott, 1944 (priv ptd).

Unpublished fragments by Shelley and Mary. Ed F. Jones, SP 45 1948. On miracles and the game laws.

Shelley's translations from Plato: a critical edition. Ed J. Notopoulos in his Platonism of Shelley: a study of Platonism and the poetic mind, Durham NC 1949, rptd New York 1969. Includes unpbd material.

Music at Marlow: an unpublished holograph note by Shelley. Ed N. Rogers, Keats–Shelley Memorial Bull 5 1953.

[A midsummer night's dream poem.] Ed N. Rogers in his Shelley at work, Oxford 1956, 1967 (rev).

[Italian version of Ode to liberty.] Ed N. Rogers in his Shelley at work, Oxford 1956, 1967 (rev).

[An incitement to Satan.] Ed G. Matthews, Stand 5 1960. A poem.

[The pursued and the pursuer.] Ed G. Matthews, Stand 5 1960. A poem.

Time: an unpublished sequel. Ed I. Massey, SiR 2 1962.

The Esdaile notebook: a volume of early poems. Ed K. Cameron, New York 1964, London 1964 (rev); ed N. Rogers as The Esdaile poems, Oxford 1966.

Brew, C. A new Shelley text: Essay on miracles and Christian doctrine. Keats–Shelley Memorial Bull 28 1977.

Chernaik, J. and T. Burnett. The Byron and Shelley notebooks in the Scrope Davies find. RES 29 1978.

Dawson P. Shelley and the improvvisatore Sgricci: an unpublished review. Ed Keats–Shelley Memorial Bull 32 1981.

The Esdaile notebook: a facsimile of the holograph notebook in the Carl H. Pforzheimer library. Ed D. Reiman 1985 (Mss of the younger romantics: Shelley, vol 1).

Hellas: a lyrical drama: a facsimile of the press-copy transcript by Edward E. Williams, with Shelley's corrections, together with other poems by Shelley in the Henry E. Huntington library. Ed D. Reiman 1985 (Mss of the younger romantics: Shelley, vol 3).

The mask of anarchy: facsimile of the intermediate fair-copy holograph in the Ashley Collection, the British Library, the press-copy transcription by Mary W. Shelley . . . in the Library of Congress, proofs of the first edition, 1832 . . . in the Luther A. Brewer Collection, University of Iowa, and a holograph addition to Leigh Hunt's preface in the Ashley Collection, the British Library. Ed D. Reiman 1985 (Mss of the younger romantics: Shelley, vol 2).

Peter Bell the Third: a facsimile of the press-copy transcript . . . and The triumph of life: a facsimile of Shelley's holograph draft. Ed D. Reiman 1986 (Bodleian Shelley mss, vol 1).

Bodleian MS. Shelley adds. d. 7. Ed I. Massey 1987 (Bodleian Shelley mss, vol 2).

Bodleian MS. Shelley e. 4. Ed P. Dawson 1987 (Bodleian Shelley mss, vol 3).

Bodleian MS. Shelley d. 1, including drafts of Speculations on morals and metaphysics, A defence of poetry, Ode to Naples, The witch of Atlas, Epipsychidion, and Mary Wollstonecraft Shelley's The fields of fancy/Mathilda. Ed E. Murray. Parts i and ii [i.e. 2 vols] 1988 (Bodleian Shelley mss, vol 4).

Bodleian MS. Shelley d. 3. Ed T. Tokoo 1988 (Bodleian Shelley mss, vol 8).

Shelley's last notebook. Bodleian MSS. Shelley adds. e. 15, adds. e. 20 and adds. c. 4 folios 212–45. Ed D. and H. Reiman 1990 (Bodleian Shelley mss, vol 7).

The mask of anarchy draft notebook: a facsimile of Huntington MS. HM 2177, including drafts of The mask of anarchy, A vision of the sea. Ed M. Quinn 1990 (Mss of the younger romantics: Shelley, vol 4).

The Julian and Maddalo draft notebook, Bodleian MS. Shelley adds. e. 11, including drafts for Julian and Maddalo, Prometheus unbound, Stanzas written in dejection . . . near Naples, A future state, On love, A discourse on the manners of the antient Greeks relative to the subject of love, as well as other fragments of poems and prose. Ed S. Jones 1990 (Bodleian Shelley mss xv).

The Charles the First draft notebook: a facsimile of Bodleian MS. Shelley adds. e. 17, including drafts of Charles the First, Buona notte, The boat on the Serchio, Written on hearing the news of the death of Napoleon, The zucca, Song (a widowed bird), To the moon (Art thou pale), Sonnet to Byron; together with Mary Shelley's fair-copy transcript of Orpheus, her research notes for Valperga, and miscellaneous fragments of verse and prose. Ed N. Crook 1991 (Bodleian Shelley mss, vol 12).

The Harvard Shelley poetic manuscripts. Facsimiles of the two Harvard Shelley fair-copy notebooks donated by Edward A. Silsbee and manuscripts of Shelley's poetry bequeathed by George E. Woodberry (MS. Eng 258.2, MS. Eng 258.3 and MS. Eng 822), together with leaves earlier removed from MS 258.2 and now in the Bodleian Library and the Pierpont Morgan Library. Ed D. Reiman 1991 (Mss of the younger romantics: Shelley, vol 5).

The Prometheus unbound notebooks. A facsimile of Bodleian MSS. Shelley e. 1, e. 2, and e. 3, including fair copies of Prometheus unbound, Ode to heaven, Misery. A fragment, and a draft translation of Plato's Ion together with fragments and prose writings. Ed N. Fraistat 1991 (Bodleian Shelley mss, vol 9).

Drafts for Laon and Cythna: Bodleian MSS. Shelley adds. e. 14 and adds. e. 19. Ed T. Tokoo 1992 (Bodleian Shelley mss, vol 13).

Shelley's Pisan winter notebook (1820–1821): Bodleian MS. Shelley adds. e. 8. Ed C. Adamson 1992 (Bodleian Shelley mss, vol 6).

The Geneva notebook of Percy Bysshe Shelley: Bodleian MS. Shelley adds. e. 16 and MS. Shelley adds. c. 4, folios 63, 65, and 72. Ed M. Erkelenz 1992 (Bodleian Shelley mss, vol 11).

Shelley's devils notebook: Bodleian MS. Shelley adds. d. 9. Ed P. Dawson and T. Webb 1993 (Bodleian Shelley mss, vol 14).

Shelley's 1819–1821 Huntington notebook. A facsimile of Huntington MS. HM 2176 including drafts of Prometheus unbound, Ode to the west wind, The sensitive plant, Fragment of a satire on satire, Una favola, together with minor poems and fragments. Ed M. Quinn 1994 (Mss of the younger romantics: Shelley, vol 6).

The Defence of poetry fair copies: a facsimile of Bodleian MSS. Shelley e. 6 and adds. d. 8. Ed M. O'Neill 1994 (Bodleian Shelley mss, vol 20).

The Hellas notebook: Bodleian MS. Shelley adds. e. 7. Ed M. Neth and D. Reiman 1994 (Bodleian Shelley mss, vol 16).

Drafts for Loan and Cythna, Cantos v–xii: Bodleian MS Shelley adds. e. 10. Ed S. Jones 1994 (Bodleian Shelley mss, vol 13).

The Homeric Hymns and Prometheus Drafts Notebook: Bodleian MS. Shelley adds. e. 12. Ed N. Goslee 1994 (Bodleian Shelley mss, vol 18).

The Witch of Atlas Notebook: Bodleian MS. Shelley adds. e. 6. Ed C. Adamson 1994 (Bodleian Shelley mss, vol 5).

Miscellaneous Poetry, Prose, and Translation from Bodleian MS Shelley adds. c. 4. Ed E. Murray 1995 (Bodleian Shelley mss, vol 21).

Shelley's 1821–2 Huntington Notebook (HM 2111). Ed M. Quinn 1996 (Mss of the younger romantics, vol 7).

The Faust Translation Notebook: Bodleian MS Shelley adds. e. 18. Ed N. Crook and T. Webb 1996 (Bodleian Shelley mss, vol 19).

Additional Materials in the Hand of Mary Shelley: MSS Shelley adds. c. 5 and adds. d. 6. Ed A. Weinberg. Parts i and ii [i.e. 2 vols] 1997 (Bodleian Shelley mss, vol 22).

Fair-copy Holographs of Shelley's Poems in British and American Libraries. Ed D. Reiman and M. O'Neill 1997 (Mss of the younger romantics, vol 8).

Letters, diaries, marginalia etc.

For first pbn and present location of individual letters, see F. Jones (ed), Letters, *1964, below, vol 2 pp. 452–6.*

Prose works. Ed H. Forman 4 vols 1880. The first collected edn of the letters.

The correspondence of Robert Southey with Caroline Bowles; together with his correspondence with Shelley. Ed E. Dowden 1881.

Shelley and Mary. Ed Lady Jane and Sir Percy F. Shelley 3 (or 4) vols [1882] (priv ptd).

Select letters. Ed R. Garnett 1882.

Letters to Robert Southey and other correspondents. Ed T. Wise 1886 (priv ptd).

Essays and letters. Ed E. Rhys 1886.

Letters from Harriet Shelley to Catherine Nugent. 1889 (priv ptd).

Letters to Jane Clairmont. Ed T. Wise 1889 (priv ptd); rptd Norwood PA 1978.

Letters to Elizabeth Hitchener. Ed T. Wise 2 vols 1890 (priv ptd); ed B. Dobell 1908.

Letters to William Godwin. Ed T. Wise 2 vols 1891 (priv ptd).

The best letters. Ed S. Hughson, Chicago 1892.

Letters to Leigh Hunt. Ed T. Wise 2 vols 1894 (priv ptd).

Letters to T. J. Hogg. Ed T. Wise with notes by W. Rossetti and H. Forman 1897 (priv ptd).

Journal of Edward Ellerker Williams, companion of Shelley and Byron in 1821 and 1822. Ed R. Garnett 1902; rptd Norwood PA 1978.

Letters. Ed R. Ingpen 2 vols 1909, 1912 (adds 5 letters), 1914 (rev) (Bohn's Lib).

Polidori, J. The diary, 1816. Ed W. Rossetti 1911.

Shelley's letter to Ollier 16 Aug 1818. EStudien 51 1918.

Letters of Elizabeth Hitchener to Percy Bysshe Shelley. Ed W. Peck 1926; rptd Folcroft PA 1977, Norwood PA 1978.

The Shelley correspondence in the Bodleian Library. Ed R. Hill, Oxford 1926; rptd New York 1976, 1982. Contains detailed lists of mss, letters and relics.

Complete works: correspondence. Ed R. Ingpen 1926. Vols 8–10 of the Julian edn.

Letters, selected by R. Johnson. 1929.

Shelley's lost letters to Harriet. Ed L. Hotson 1930; rptd Freeport NY 1972, Folcroft PA 1974, Norwood PA 1977, New York 1982.

The journal of Harriet Grove for 1809–10. Ed R. Garnett 1932 (priv ptd).

After Shelley. The letters of T. J. Hogg to Jane Williams. Ed S. Norman, Oxford 1934; rptd Norwood PA 1977.

Lettere dall'Italia sull'Italia. Ed C. Zacchetti, Naples 1934.

The letters of Mary Wollstonecraft Shelley. Ed F. Jones 2 vols Norman OK 1944.

Mary Shelley's journal. Ed F. Jones, Norman OK 1947.

New Shelley letters. Ed W. Scott 1948; rptd Westport CT 1979. The letters are rptd from Scott's The Athenians, 1943 (priv ptd; rptd Folcroft PA 1973), Harriet and Mary, 1944 (priv ptd; rptd Folcroft PA 1974, Norwood PA 1978), Shelley at Oxford (priv ptd; rptd Folcroft PA 1974).

Mayor, A. A suspected Shelley letter [16 Dec 1816]. Library 5th ser 4 1949. Reply by T. Ehrsam, 5 1950.

Maria Gisborne and Edward E. Williams, Shelley's friends: their journals and letters. Ed F. Jones, Norman OK 1951.

Letters. Ed F. Jones 2 vols Oxford 1964. First complete edn.

Jones, F. Shelley's letter of 23 June 1811 to Hogg. Keats–Shelley Memorial Bull 15 1964.

Maxwell, J. A Shelley letter: an unrecorded printing. N & Q 209 May 1964.

The journals of Claire Clairmont. Ed M. Stocking, Cambridge MA 1968.

Kendall Jr, L. On the date of a Shelley letter to Hogg. KSJ 19 1970.

Rogers, N. An unpublished Shelley letter. Keats–Shelley Memorial Bull 24 1973. Verse letter to E. Graham.

Robinson, C. The Shelleys to Leigh Hunt: a new letter of 5 April 1821. Keats–Shelley Memorial Bull 31 1980.

Stocking, D. and M. Stocking. New Shelley letters in a John Gisborne notebook. Keats–Shelley Memorial Bull 31 1980.

Robinson, C. Shelley to the editor of the Morning Chronicle: a second new letter of 5 April 1821. Keats–Shelley Memorial Bull 32 1981.

Robinson, C. Shelley to Byron in 1814: a new letter. KSJ 35 1986.

The journals of Mary Shelley. Ed P. Feldman and D. Scott-Kilvert 2 vols Oxford 1987 (includes numerous entries by Shelley); rptd in 1 vol, Baltimore 1995.

Hartley, R. Shelley's copy of Dante. KSJ 39 1990.

Barker-Benfield, B. Hogg–Shelley papers of 1810–12. BLR 14 1991.

Hawkins, D. A newly discovered Shelley diary. Contemporary Rev 261 1992.

Hawkins, D. Shelley's first love: the love story of Percy Bysshe Shelley and Harriet Grove. Hamden CT 1992. Includes text of Shelley's pocketbook diary for 1810.

The Clairmont correspondence: letters of Claire Clairmont, Charles Clairmont and Fanny Imlay Godwin. Ed M. Stocking 2 vols Baltimore MD 1995.

§2
Textual/Bibliographical studies

Blind, M. Shelley. Westminster Rev n.s. 38 1870.

Swinburne, A. Notes on the text of Shelley. In his Essays and studies, 1875.

Shelley Society note-book, part I. 1888.

Shelley Society papers, part I. 1888. 9 articles.

Shelley Society papers, part II. 1891. 10 articles.

Zupitza, J. Zu einigen kleineren Gedichten Shelleys. Archiv 94 1895.

Zupitza, J. and J. Schick. Zu Shelley's Prometheus unbound. Archiv 102 1899.

Forman, H. Shelley's stanza-numbering in the Ode to Naples. Athenaeum 22 Apr 1905. A new ms.

Vaughan, P. Early Shelley pamphlets. 1905; rptd New York 1982.

Peck, W. Shelley's autograph corrections of the Daemon of the world. TLS 23 June 1921.

Jones, F. The revision of Laon and Cythna. JEGP 33 1933.

Ballman, A. The dating of Shelley's prose fragments On life, On love, The punishment of death. ELH 2 1935.

Verkoren, L. A study of Shelley's Defence of poetry: its origin, textual history, sources and significance. Amsterdam 1937; rptd Folcroft PA 1969, New York 1970, New York 1982.

Clark, D. The date and source of Shelley's A vindication of natural diet. SP 36 1939.

White, N. Probable dates of composition of Shelley's Letter to Maria Gisborne and Ode to a skylark. SP 36 1939.

Notopoulos, J. The dating of Shelley's fragment The moral teachings of Jesus Christ. MLR 35 1940.

Glasheen, F. and A. The publication of The wandering jew. MLR 38 1943.

Notopoulos, J. The dating of Shelley's prose. PMLA 58 1943.

Nitchie, E. Variant readings in three of Shelley's poems. MLN 59 1944. On To Stella; Methought I was a billow; On Keats.

Clark, D. The dates and sources of Shelley's metaphysical, moral and religious essays. SE 28 1949.

Brown, T. English literary autographs I. BC 1 1952. Shelley's handwriting.

Glasheen, A. Shelley's first published review of Mandeville. MLN 59 1954.

Rogers, N. Four missing pages from the Shelley notebook in the Harvard College Library. KSJ 3 1954.

Rogers, N. Shelley at work: a critical inquiry. Oxford 1956, 1968 (rev).

Steadman, J. Errors concerning the publication date [11 Jan 1818] of Ozymandias. N & Q 201 1956.

Massey, I. Music, when soft voices die: text and meaning. JEGP 59 1960.

Matthews, G. A new text of Shelley's scene for Tasso. Keats–Shelley Memorial Bull 11 1960.

Matthews, G. The triumph of life: a new text. SN 32 1960.

Matthews, G. The triumph of life apocrypha. TLS 5 Aug 1960.

Shelley and Dante: an essay in textual criticism. Ed J. de Palacio, Revue de Littérature Comparée 35 1961. New text of Shelley's trn of Dante's Convito.

Matthews, G. Shelley and Jane Williams. RES n.s. 12 1961.

Rogers, N. Shelley and the visual arts. Keats–Shelley Memorial Bull 12 1961.

Shelley traducteur de Dante: le chant xxviii du Purgatoire. Ed J. de Palacio, Revue de Littérature Comparée 36 1962. Commentary in French.

Matthews, G. Julian and Maddalo: the draft and the meaning. SN 34 1963.

Norman, S. Shelley bequest. BLR 7 1963.

Boas, L. Shelley: three unpublished lines. N & Q 209 1964.

Rees, J. 'But for such faith': a Shelley crux. RES n.s. 15 1964. On Mont Blanc; *see also* J. Kinnaird, N & Q 213 1968.

Reiman, D. Shelley's The triumph of life: a critical study based on a text newly edited from the Bodleian manuscript. Urbana IL 1965; rptd New York 1979.

Rogers, N. Shelley's spelling: theory and practice. Keats–Shelley Memorial Bull 16 1965.

Hunter, P. Textual differences in the drafts of Una favola. SiR 6 1966.

New texts of Shelley's Plato. Ed J. Notopoulos, KSJ 15 1966.

Raben, J. Shelley's Invocation to Misery: an expanded text. JEGP 65 1966.

Rogers, N. The punctuation of Shelley's syntax. Keats–Shelley Memorial Bull 17 1966.

Bateson, F. Exhumations v. Shelley on Wordsworth: two unpublished stanzas from Peter Bell the Third. Essays in Criticism 17 1967.

Raben, J. Shelley's The boat on the Serchio: the evidence of the manuscript. PQ 46 1967.

Woodings, R. A devil of a nut to crack: Shelley's Charles the First. SN 40 1968.

Woodings, R. Shelley's widow bird. RES n.s. 19 1968.

Chernaik, J. Shelley's 'To Constantia'. TLS 6 Feb 1969.

Matthews, G. Shelley's lyrics. In The morality of art, ed D. Jefferson, 1969.

Murray, E. Mont Blanc's unfurled veil. KSJ 18 1969.

Chernaik, J. Textual emendations for three poems by Shelley. KSJ 19 1970.

Curran, S. Shelley's emendations to the Hymn to intellectual beauty. ELN 7 1970.

Curran, S. Shelley's satiric fragment on a heavenly feast: a corrected text. N & Q 215 1970.

McTaggart, W. England in 1819: church, state and poverty. 1970.

Webb, T. Shelley's Hymn to Venus: a new text. RES 21 1970.

Andrews, S. Shelley, Medwin, and The wandering jew. KSJ 20 1971.

Brew, C. Shelley and Mary in 1817: a critical study of the text and poetical evolution of the dedication of The revolt of Islam, based on a new examination of the manuscripts and including hitherto unpublished material. 1971.

Chernaik, J. The lyrics of Shelley. 1972. Includes new texts of 26 poems.
Curran, S. and J. Wittreich Jr. The dating of Shelley's On the devil, and devils. KSJ 21–2 1972–3.
Collins, J. Harry Buxton Forman and his Shelley reprints. BC 23 1974.
Delisle, F. A study of Shelley's A defense of poetry: a textual and critical evaluation. 2 vols Salzburg 1974.
Casto, R. Shelley as translator of Faust: the prologue. RES 26 1975.
de Palacio, J. Shelley traducteur de soi-même. Revue des Sciences Humaines n.s. no 158 1975.
Hood, S. Note 381. Shelley's The Cenci. BC 24 1975. Notes a variant of the 1st edn.
Klapper, R. The German literary influence on Shelley. Salzburg 1975. Includes transcript of Shelley's prose trn of Faust.
Murray, E. Gnashing and wailing in Prometheus unbound. KSJ 24 1975.
Webb, T. The violet in the crucible: Shelley and translation. Oxford 1976.
Burnett, T. The Scrope Davies papers, a progress report. Manuscript 29 1977.
Murray, E. Annotated manuscript corrections of Shelley's prose essays. KSJ 26 1977.
Rogers, N. The Scrope Davies Shelley find. Keats–Shelley Memorial Bull 28 1977.
Matthews, G. Whose little footsteps? Three Shelley pieces re-addressed. In D. Reiman et al (ed), The evidence of the imagination: studies of interactions between life and art in English romantic literature. New York 1978.
Murray, E. Shelley's contributions to Mary's Frankenstein. Keats–Shelley Memorial Bull 29 1978.
Murray, E. The trial of Mr Perry, Lord Eldon, and Shelley's Address to the Irish. SiR 17 1978.
Robinson, C. Roots to rocks in Shelley's Alastor. Amer N & Q 22 4 1979.
Dawson, P. The unacknowledged legislator: Shelley and politics. Oxford 1980. Includes a chronology of the prose.
Bennett, B. and A. Fredman. A note on the dating of Shelley's The triumph of life. KSJ 32 1981.
Bodleian Shelley mss re-examined: a re-edited text of some of Shelley's prose works in the Bodleian mss. (i) [Speculations on metaphysics and morals]. Ed T. Tokoo, Humanities: Bull of the Faculty of Letters, Kyoto Prefectural Univ 33 1981.
Burnett, T. The rise and fall of a regency dandy: the life and times of Scrope Berdmore Davies. 1981. [On the provenance of Mont Blanc, Hymn to intellectual beauty, and 2 sonnets newly discovered in the Scrope Davies find.]
Reiman, D. The Norton Shelley. KSJ 30 1981.
Adamson, C. The watermarks of ms Shelley adds. e. 6 and ms Shelley adds. e. 8 and the dating of their texts. Keats–Shelley Memorial Bull 33 1982.
Bodleian Shelley mss re-examined: a re-edited text of some of Shelley's prose works in the Bodleian mss. (ii) [On Christianity]. Ed T. Tokoo, Humanities: Bull of the Faculty of Letters, Kyoto Prefectural Univ 35 1983.
Murray, E. Shelley's Notes on sculptures: the provenance and authority of the text. KSJ 32 1983.
Robinson, C. Percy Bysshe Shelley, Charles Ollier, and William Blackwood: the contexts of nineteenth-century publishing. In Shelley revalued: essays from the Gregynog conference, ed K. Everest, Leicester 1983.
Webb, T. The avalanche of ages: Shelley's Defence of atheism and Prometheus unbound. Keats–Shelley Memorial Bull 35 1984.
Goslee, N. Shelley at play: a study of sketch and text in the Prometheus notebooks. HLQ 48 1985.
Murray, E. The dating and composition of Shelley's The assassins. KSJ 34 1985.
Burling, W. New light on Shelley's lines to —. KSJ 35 1986.
Quinn, M. Leigh Hunt's presentation copy of Shelley's Alastor volume. KSJ 35 1986.
Crook, N. Shelley's earliest poem? N & Q 232 1987. On Verses on a cat.
Shelley's fragment of A satire upon satire: a complete transcription of the text with commentary. Ed S. Jones. KSJ 37 1988.
Reiman, D. Romantic texts and contexts. Columbia SC 1988.
Erkelenz, M. Shelley's draft of Mont Blanc and the conflict of faith. RES 40 1989.
Glickman, S. Roberts as editor: Shelley's Adonais and Alastor. Canadian Poetry 25 1989.
Maxwell, C. Shelley's Medusa: the sixth stanza. N & Q 234 1989.
Murray, E. A suspect title-page of Shelley's History of a six weeks' tour. PBSA 83 1989.
Brinkley, R. Documenting revision: Shelley's Lake Geneva diary and the dialogue with Byron in History of a six weeks' tour. KSJ 39 1990.
Athanase. Ed K. Everest, Keats–Shelley Rev 7 1992.
The boat on the Serchio. Ed N. Crook, Keats–Shelley Rev 7 1992.
Brinkley, R. Spaces between words: writing Mont Blanc. In Romantic revisions, ed R. Brinkley and K. Hanley, Cambridge 1992.
Brinkley, R. and K. Hanley (ed). Romantic revisions. Cambridge 1992.
Everest, K. Ozymandias: the text in time. In Percy Bysshe Shelley: bicentenary essays, ed K. Everest for the Eng Assoc (E & S 45), Cambridge 1992.
Tokoo, T. Shelley's text. Eigo Seinen 138 1992 (in Jap).
To-morrow. Ed C. Adamson, Keats–Shelley Rev 7 1992.
Goslee, N. Dispersoning Emily: drafting as plot in Epipsychidion. KSJ 42 1993.
Hogle, J. Shelley's texts and the premises of criticism. KSJ 42 1993.
Jones, S. Love, the Universe: a fragment in context. KSJ 42 1993.
Reiman, D. Textual authorities for Shelley. KSJ 42 1993.
Tokoo, T. The composition of Epipsychidion: some manuscript evidence. KSJ42 1993.

Criticism to 1920

Hazlitt, W. On paradox and common-place. In his Table talk vol 1, 1821.
Hazlitt, W. On the philosophy and poetry of Shelley. London Mag & Theatrical Inquisitor Feb 1821.
Hunt, L. Lord Byron and some of his contemporaries. 1828, 2 vols 1828 (rev), 3 vols Paris 1828.
Hunt, L. Autobiography. 3 vols 1850; ed J. Morpurgo 1949.
Browning, R. In Letters of Shelley, 1852. The letters were forged and the edn suppressed. Browning's introd ed W. Harden 1888 (Shelley Soc); ed R. Garnett 1903, rptd Norwood PA 1977; 1908, rptd Philadelphia 1977; Boston 1911; ed H. Brett-Smith, Oxford 1921, 1923.
Bagehot, W. In Estimates of some Englishmen and Scotchmen, 1858; rptd in Literary studies vol 1, ed R. Hutton, 1879, and in Collected works vol 1, ed N. St John-Stevas, 1965.
Arnold, M. In his Essays in criticism: second series, 1888.
Salt, H. Shelley: a monograph. 1888, 1892; rev and rptd as Shelley: poet and pioneer, 1896.
Shaw, G. Shaming the devil about Shelley. [1892.] In his Pen portraits and reviews, 1932.
Yeats, W. The philosophy of Shelley's poetry, [1900.] In his Ideas of good and evil, 1903; rptd in his Essays and introductions, 1961.
Bradley, A. Shelley's view of poetry. [1904.] In his Oxford lectures on poetry, 1909.
Droop, A. Die Belesenheit Shelleys nach den direkten Zeugnissen und den bisherigen Forschungen. Weimar 1906.
Clutton-Brock, A. Shelley: the man and the poet. 1910, 1923 (rev).
Brailsford, H. Shelley, Godwin and their circle. [1913], Oxford 1951 (rev).

Santayana, G. Shelley: or the poetic value of revolutionary principles. In his Winds of doctrine, 1913; rptd in his Essays in literary criticism, ed I. Singer, New York 1956.
de Madariaga, S. In his Shelley and Calderón and other essays, 1920.

Biographical studies

Medwin, T. Journal of the conversations of Lord Byron, noted during a residence with his Lordship at Pisa in the years 1821 and 1822. 1824 (3 edns), Paris 1824, New York 1824, 2 vols 1825, 1 vol Baltimore 1825, London 1832; ed E. Lovell, Princeton 1966.
Medwin, T. Life of Percy Bysshe Shelley. 2 vols 1847; ed H. Forman, Oxford 1913 ('from a copy copiously amended and extended by the author'); rptd St Clair Shores MI 1971, Folcroft PA 1973.
Smith, H. A graybeard's gossip about his literary acquaintances. NMM Oct, Nov 1847.
Hogg, T. Life of Shelley. 2 vols 1858 [ms of 2 further vols is lost]; ed E. Dowden 1906.
Peacock, T. Memoirs of Shelley. Fraser's Mag June 1858, Jan, Mar 1860, Mar 1862; ed H. Brett-Smith, Oxford 1909; rptd in his Works vol 8, ed H. Brett-Smith and C. Jones, 1934.
Trelawny, E. Recollections of the last days of Shelley and Byron. 1858, Boston 1858; ed E. Dowden 1906, Oxford 1923, 1931; ed J. Morpurgo 1952 (Folio Soc) ('with additions from contemporary sources'); rev as Records of Shelley, Byron and the author, 2 vols 1878, 1 vol 1887, [1905]; ed D. Wright 1973 (Pen Eng Lib).
Hunt, T. Shelley, by one who knew him. Atlantic Monthly Feb 1863; rptd in E. Blunden, Shelley and Keats as they struck their contemporaries, 1925, rptd Philadelphia 1977.
MacCarthy, D. Shelley's early life, from original sources. 1872; rptd Folcroft PA 1976.
Paul, C. In his William Godwin: his friends and contemporaries, 2 vols 1876.
Dowden, E. Life of Shelley. 2 vols 1886, 1 vol 1896 (rev and abridged); ed H. Read 1951.
Rossetti, W. Memoir of Shelley, with new preface. 1886, 1886 (Shelley Soc), 1971, 1975. Originally prefixed to Poetical works, ed W. Rossetti, 1870, 1878 (rev).
Elton, C. An account of Shelley's visits to France, Switzerland and Savoy in the years 1814 and 1816. 1894.
Koszul, A. La jeunesse de Shelley. Paris 1910.
Trelawny, E. Letters. Ed H. Forman 1910.
Angeli, H. Shelley and his friends in Italy. 1911; rptd New York 1982.
Garnett, R. Letters about Shelley interchanged by three friends [E. Dowden, R. Garnett, W. Rossetti]. 1917; rptd New York 1971, Folcroft PA 1973.
Ingpen, R. Shelley in England: new facts and letters from the Shelley–Whitton papers. 1917.
Maurois, A. Ariel: ou la vie de Shelley. Paris 1923; Eng trn by E. D'Arcy, 1924 etc.
Peck, W. Shelley: his life and work. 2 vols 1927; rptd Folcroft PA 1973.
White, N. Shelley. 2 vols New York 1940 (rptd New York 1972), 2 vols London 1947 (rev); abridged as Portrait of Shelley, New York 1945.
Blunden, E. Shelley: a life story. 1946; rptd Folcroft PA 1973.
Cameron, K. The young Shelley: genesis of a radical. New York 1950; rptd New York 1973.
Cameron, K., F. Jones and N. White. An examination of the Shelley legend. Philadelphia 1951.
Cline, C. Shelley, Byron and their Pisan circle. Cambridge MA 1952.
Norman, S. Flight of the skylark: the development of Shelley's reputation. Norman OK 1954.
King-Hele, D. Shelley: his thought and work. 1960, 1971 (2nd edn, rev), 1984 (3rd edn, rev).
Boas, L. Harriet Shelley: five long years. Oxford 1962; rptd Westport CT 1979.
Buxton, J. Byron and Shelley: the history of a friendship. 1968.
Fuller, J. Shelley: a biography. 1968.
Reiman, D. Percy Bysshe Shelley. New York 1969, 1989 (rev).
Matthews, G. Shelley. 1970 [British Council Writers and their Work].
Cameron, K. Shelley: the golden years. Cambridge MA 1974.
Holmes, R. Shelley: the pursuit. 1974; tr Fr 1990.
Tomalin, C. Shelley and his world. 1980 [rev edn (Pen) 1992].
Rees, J. Shelley's Jane Williams. 1985.
Crook, N. and D. Guiton. Shelley's venomed melody. Cambridge 1986.
O'Neill, M. Percy Bysshe Shelley: a literary life. 1989.
St Clair, W. The Godwins and the Shelleys. 1989.
Blumberg, J. Byron and the Shelleys: the story of a friendship. 1992.
Gittings, R. Claire Clairmont and the Shelleys 1798–1879. Oxford 1992. [KE]

Charles Doyne Sillery 1807–37

Vallery, or the citadel of the lake .... 2 vols Edinburgh, London, Glasgow and Dublin 1829.
An essay on the creation of the universe. Edinburgh 1830. Prose.
A discourse on the sufferings of our saviour. Edinburgh 1833; London [1837] (as The man of sorrows, with a biographical notice).
Eldred of Erin: a poem .... Edinburgh 1833 (2nd edn).
The royal mariner. 1834.

Edward Smedley 1788–1836

Collection

Poems ... with a selection from his correspondence and a memoir of his life. 1837.

§1

A few verses, English and Latin. 1812. Anon.
The death of Saul and Jonathan: a poem. 1814 (2 edns).
Jephtha: a poem. 1814 (2 edns); London and Cambridge 1816.
Jonah: a poem. 1815.
Farewell to Harold. [1816.] Prose.
Prescience, or the secret of divination: a poem. 1816.
Religio christiani: a churchman's answer .... Cambridge 1818. Anon.
Religio clerici: a churchman's epistle. 1818 (2 edns), 1819, 1821 (as Religio clerici: two epistles). Anon.
A churchman's second epistle .... 1819. Anon.
The parson's choice of town or country .... 1821. Anon.
Lux renata: a protestant's epistle .... 1827. Anon.
The marriage in Cana: a poem. 1828.
Saul at Endor: a dramatic sketch. 1829.
Edited Br Critic, Quart Theological Rev *(1827–43) and the* Encyclopaedia Metropolitana; *wrote on French and Venetian history and on the occult.*

Charles Smith 1749?–1824

The Mosiad, or Israel delivered .... 1815.
Poems. 1815.

Elizabeth Smith 1776–1806

§1

Fragments, in prose and verse. By a young lady, lately deceased. Ed H. M. Bowdler, Bath, London and Edinburgh 1808 (anon) (5 edns); Dublin 1808; Bath, London and Edinburgh 1809 (2 edns), 2 vols 1809 (attributed), 2 vols 1810 (variant also issued of vol 2 as Memoirs of F. and M. Klopstock); Boston 1810; 2 vols Bath, London and Edinburgh 1811–12; Burlington NJ 1811; 2 vols London 1818, 2 vols 1824.

The Book of Job.... Tr Smith, ed F. Randolph, Bath 1810 (2 edns). Prose.

§2

Balfour, C. L. A sketch of E. Smith. 1854.

Elizabeth Smith, of Worcestershire fl. 1829–34

Poems on Malvern and other subjects. Worcester and London 1829, 1834.

Englesfield Smith fl. 1797–1809

The scaith of France, or the death of St Just... 1797, 1810.
The poetical works.... 1802, 1822.
Legendary tales. 1807.
Rudigar the Dane: a legendary tale. 1809; Edinburgh 1815.

George Charles Smith 1782–1863

The fisherman's Saturday. [1815?]
The poor sea boy. [1815.]
A father's tears over the corpse of his beloved son.... 1819, [1822?].
The prose and poetical works.... 1819, 1824. A collection of pams.
The gale abated. [1820?]
The harp suspended by the rivers of Babylon, or songs in the desert. [1820?]
Select pieces on storms. 1820.
The sailors' hymn book.... Ed Smith 1822.
The open air preaching hymn book. 1830.
The sailor's chronometer and compass melody, or... hymns and... songs. 1831.

Numerous prose pbns in support of benevolent socs for seamen and on other local public issues, and tracts for children.

Horatio (Horace) Smith, also 'Paul Chatfield' 1779–1849 and James Smith 1775–1839

Collections

Memoirs, letters and comic miscellanies in prose and verse. By James Smith. Ed H. Smith 2 vols 1840, 1841; Philadelphia 1841.
The poetical works of H. Smith. 2 vols 1846, 1851; New York 1857; Boston 1858, 1859.
Poems. By Horace Smith. 1889.
Rejected addresses and Horace in London. Ed D. H. Reiman, New York and London 1977 (facs reprints of 1812 and 1813).

§1

Rejected addresses, or the new theatrum poetarum. By H. and J. Smith. 1812 (8 edns) (anon), 1813 (7 edns); New York 1813; London 1815, 1817, 1821; Philadelphia 1828; London 1833 ('carefully revised'), 1839; Boston 1840, 1841; London 1841, 1847; Boston 1848, 1851; London 1851 (attributed), 1852, 1855 (2 edns); Boston 1860; ed E. Sargent, New York 1860 (with memoirs); London 1865; New York and Boston 1866; London 1869; New York 1871; London 1873, [1875?] (in Murray's People's Classics); New York 1876; London 1879, [1880], 1885, 1888 (Routledge's Pocket Lib); ed P. Fitzgerald 1890; Philadelphia 1890; London 1894; ed A. D. Godley, London 1904; London and New York 1907; ed A. Boyle, London 1929 (with bibliography).
Horace in London, consisting of imitations of the first two books of the odes of Horace. By [H. and J. Smith]. 1813 (3 edns); Boston, New York and Cambridge MA 1813; London 1815. Anon. Rptd from Monthly Mirror.
Amarynthus, the nympholept: a pastoral drama... By [H. Smith]. 1821 (anon); ed D. H. Reiman, New York and London 1977 (facs reprint of 1821, attributed).
The tin trumpet, or heads and tales... to which are added poetical selections. By 'Paul Chatfield'. Ed J. Saunders 2 vols 1836; Philadelphia 1836; New York 1859; London 1869, 1870, 1875.

For the novels etc of Horace Smith alone, see col 1077, below.

Thomas Charlton Smith fl. 1817–24

Rude rhymes. Dublin 1817.
Bay leaves. Edinburgh and London 1824.

Joseph Snow fl. 1813–57

Modern accomplishments. 1813. Anon. Prose.
Misanthropy and other poems. 1819.
The hour of trial! A few stanzas hastily written. 1820.
Minor poems. 1828.
Forms of prayers... also poems.... 1831.
Sketches and minor poems. 1831.
Prayers... with original poems.... 1835.
Light in darkness, or sermons in stones: churchyard thoughts in verse. 1845, 1847 (as Lyra memorialis), 1857 (2 edns).

Eleanor Snowden fl. 1829–31

The maid of Scio: a tale of modern Greece, in six cantos. Dover 1829; London 1832.
The Moorish queen, A record of Pompeii, and other poems. London and Dover 1831.

William Sotheby 1757–1833

§1

Poems: consisting of a tour through parts of north and south Wales.... Bath 1790; London 1794 (as A tour through parts of Wales, sonnets, odes).
Wieland. Oberon: a poem. Tr Sotheby 2 vols 1798, 1805 (illustr H. Fuseli), 1826.
The battle of the Nile: a poem. 1799.
Virgil. The Georgics. Tr Sotheby 1800; Middletown CT and New York 1808; London 1815, 1827 (in a hexaglot edn), 2 vols 1830 (as The eclogues... The Georgics... The Aeneid; with Wrangham and Dryden); New York 1848.
The siege of Cuzco: a tragedy.... 1800.
The Cambrian hero...: an historical tragedy. Egham 1800. Anon (attribution doubtful).
A poetical epistle to Sir George Beaumont. 1801.
Julian and Agnes, or the monks of great St Bernard: a tragedy. 1801, 1814 (as The confession).
Oberon, or Huon de Bordeaux: a mask, and Orestes. Bristol and London 1802.
Orestes: a tragedy. Bristol and London 1802.
Saul: a poem in two parts. 1807; Boston 1808.
Constance de Castile: a poem. 1810; Boston 1812.
A song of triumph. 1814.
Tragedies. 1814. Includes The death of Darnley, Ivan, Zamorin and Zama, The confession, Orestes.
Ellen, or the confession: a tragedy. 1816.
Ivan: a tragedy. 1816.
Farewell to Italy, and occasional poems. 1818.
Poems. 1825.
Italy and other poems. 1828 (2 edns).
Homer. The first book of the Iliad [and 2 other] specimens of a new version of Homer. Tr Sotheby 1830.
Homer. The Iliad. Tr Sotheby 2 vols 1831.
Homer. The Odyssey. Tr Sotheby 2 vols 1834.

Lines suggested by the third meeting of the British Association, with a short memoir of his life. 1834.

Robert Southey 1774–1843

The main collections of Southey mss are in BL, Bodleian, Huntington, Fitz Park Museum Keswick and Nat Lib of Wales. For location of mss of some individual works see §1, below.

Bibliographies

Haller, W. Appendix A, Works of Robert Southey. In his The early life of Robert Southey, New York 1917.

Zeitlin, J. Southey's contributions to the Critical Review. N & Q, Feb–May 1918.

Havens, R. D. Southey's contributions to the Foreign Review. RES 8, 1932.

Curry, K. Uncollected translations of Michaelangelo by Wordsworth and Southey. RES 14, 1938.

Curry, K. Southey's contributions to the Annual Review. Bull of Bibliography 16, 1939.

Curry, K. The contributors to the Annual Anthology. PBSA 42, 1948.

Shine, H. and H. C. The Quarterly Review under Gifford. Chapel Hill NC 1949. Identifies Southey's articles 1809–24. *But see* K. Curry and R. Dedmon 1975, *below*.

Curry, K. Two new works of Robert Southey. SB 5, 1953.

Curry, K. In The English romantic poets and essayists: a review of research and criticism, ed C. W. and L. H. Houtchens, New York 1957, 1966 (rev).

Barber, G. Poems by Robert Southey, 1797. Bodleian Lib Record 6, 1960. *See* S. Nowell-Smith, Book Collector 11, 1962.

Curry, K. The published letters of Robert Southey: a checklist. BNYPL, Mar 1967.

Raimond, J. Robert Southey: l'homme et son temps. Paris 1968.

George, D. Two manuscript poems by Southey and Wordsworth. N & Q, 18 1971.

Volz, R. and J. Rieger. The Rochester Southey collection. Wordsworth Circle 5, 1974.

Curry, K. Southey. 1975.

Curry, K. and R. Dedmon. Southey's contributions to the Quarterly Review. Wordsworth Circle 6 1975.

Bernhardt-Kabisch, E. Robert Southey. Boston 1977.

Curry, K. Robert Southey: a reference guide. Boston 1977.

Curry, K. Robert Southey's contributions to the Monthly Magazine and the Athenaeum. Wordsworth Circle 11, 1980.

Priestley, M. A. The Southey collection in the Fitz Park Museum, Keswick, Cumbria. Wordsworth Circle 11, 1980.

Wellens, O. Robert Southey, critical reviewer: some new attributions. Wordsworth Circle 11, 1980.

Collections

The minor poems. 3 vols 1815, 1823. A reprint of Poems, 1797–9 and Metrical tales, 1805, *below*.

The poetical works, complete in one volume. Paris 1829, [1830?]. Includes poems not found in other collections.

Selections from the poems. [Ed I. Moxon] 1831, 1833 (as The beauties of the poems).

Selections from the prose works. [Ed I. Moxon] 1832, 1833 (as The beauties of the prose works).

The poetical works of Robert Southey, collected by himself. 10 vols 1837–8, New York 1839. Each vol has a separate preface by Southey. Frequently rptd in whole or in part and dated 1844–59 or nd; 1 vol-edns New York 1842, Philadelphia 1846, New York 1848, London 1850, New York 1851, 1853, 1856, London 1863, 1873, 1884.

[Southey's poems]. Vol 1, Joan of Arc and Madoc: epic poems; vol 2, The curse of Kehama and Ballads and metrical tales; vol 3, Thalaba the destroyer and minor poems. [1854?]

Joan of Arc, and minor poems. Illustr J. Gilbert 1854. Rptd as Joan of Arc, ballads, lyrics and minor poems, New York 1857, [1870?], London 1881; rptd as Minor poems, ballads and Joan of Arc, 1858.

Poetical works, with a memoir of the author [by H. T. Tuckerman]. 10 vols Boston 1860, 1864, 5 vols [1884].

Selections from the poems. Ed S. R. Thompson 1888.

Poems, chosen and arranged by E. Dowden. 1895.

Poems, containing Thalaba, The curse of Kehama, Roderick, Madoc, A tale of Paraguay and selected minor poems. Ed M. H. Fitzgerald 1909.

Select prose. Ed J. Zeitlin, New York 1916.

Angielscy 'poeci jezior'. Tr S. Kryński, Wroclaw 1963. Southey selection pp. 375–416.

A choice of Robert Southey's verse. Ed. G. Grigson 1970.

The contributions of Robert Southey to the Morning Post. Ed K. Curry, University AL 1984.

§1

The fall of Robespierre: an historic drama. Cambridge 1794, Oxford 1991. Coleridge wrote act 1, Southey acts 2 and 3.
REVIEW: (anon) Critical Rev, Nov 1794.

Poems: containing The retrospect, odes, elegies, sonnets etc by Robert Lovell and Southey. Bath 1795.

Joan of Arc: an epic poem. Bristol 1796, 2 vols Bristol 1798 (rev), 1 vol Boston 1798, 2 vols 1806 (rev), 1812 (rev), 1817, 1 vol 1853, Oxford 1993. Ms in BL.
REVIEWS: (J. Aikin) Monthly Rev, Apr 1796; (anon) Critical Rev, June 1796.

Poems. Bristol 1797 (for 1796), 1797 (rev), Boston 1799; vol 2 Bristol 1799; 2 vols 1800, 1801, 1806–8, Oxford 1989.
REVIEW: (J. Aikin), Monthly Rev, Mar 1797.

Letters written during a short residence in Spain and Portugal, with some account of Spanish and Portugueze poetry. Bristol 1797, 1799, 2 vols 1808 (enlarged as Letters written during a journey in Spain, and a short residence in Portugal).

On the French revolution, by Mr Necker, translated from the French. 2 vols 1797. Vol 2 by Southey.

The annual anthology. 2 vols Bristol 1799–1800. Anon, ed and partly written by Southey.

Thalaba the destroyer. 2 vols 1801, 1809, Boston 1812, London 1814, 1821, 1 vol 1846, 1853, 1856, 1860, Oxford 1991; tr Ger, 1837 (in part). Ms in BL and Nat Lib of Wales.
REVIEWS: (F. Jeffrey) Edinburgh Rev, Oct 1802; (W. Taylor) Critical Rev, Dec 1803.

Amadis of Gaul, by Vasco Lobeira. 4 vols 1803, 3 vols 1872. Tr Southey.
REVIEW: (W. Scott) Edinburgh Rev, Oct 1803.

The works of Thomas Chatterton. 3 vols 1803. Ed J. Cottle and Southey.

Madoc: a poem, in two parts. 1805, 2 vols Boston 1806, London 1807, 1812, 1815, 1825, 1 vol 1853. Ms of early draft in BL. Full texts in Fitz Park Museum Keswick.
REVIEWS: (J. Ferrier) Monthly Rev, Oct 1805; (anon) Eclectic Rev, Dec 1805.

Metrical tales and other poems. 1805, Boston 1811. Poems rptd from Annual Anthology 1799–1800.
REVIEW: (W. Taylor) Annual Rev 4, 1806.

Letters from England, by Don Manuel Alvarez Espriella, translated from the Spanish. 3 vols 1807 (anon), 2 vols Boston 1807 (anon), 3 vols 1808 (anon), 2 vols New York 1808 (anon), 3 vols 1814, 2 vols Philadelphia 1818, New York 1836; ed J. Simmons 1951; tr Fr 1817; Ger 1818. Selected passages as Mr Rowlandson's England, ed. J. Steel, Woodbridge 1985. Ms in Chetham's Lib Manchester.
REVIEW: (F. Jeffrey) Edinburgh Rev, Jan 1808; (C. L. Moody) Monthly Rev, Apr 1808.

Palmerin of England, by Francisco de Moraes. 4 vols 1807. Tr A.

Munday 1581 from the Fr version, extensively corrected by Southey from the original.

Specimens of the later English poets, with preliminary notices, by Southey [and G. C. Bedford]. 3 vols 1807.

REVIEW: (anon) Universal Mag, July 1807.

The remains of Henry Kirke White: with an account of his life. 2 vols 1807, 1811 (5th edn 'corrected'), Philadelphia 1811, London 1813, New York 1815, London 1816, 1819, 1821; vol 3 1822. The contents of vol 3 were included in the 10th and later edns, 2 vols 1823, 1 vol 1825 etc. Ed R. T. Beckwith, Oxford 1985.

Chronicle of the Cid, from the Spanish. 1808, 1846, Lowell MA 1846, London 1868, 1883; ed R. Markham, New York 1883; ed V. S. Pritchett, New York 1958.

REVIEW: (J. Foster) Eclectic Rev, Mar 1809.

The geographical, natural and civil history of Chili, translated from the original Italian of the Abbé Don J. Ignatius Molina. Middletown CT 1808, London 1809. The 2nd edn annotated by Southey.

Memoria sobre a litteratura portugueza, traduzida do inglez. [Hamburg 1809]. Tr from Quart Rev 1, 1809.

The curse of Kehama. 1810, 2 vols New York 1811, London 1812, 1818, 1 vol 1853; ed H. Morley 1886. Mss in BL, Bodleian and Univ of Rochester Lib NY.

REVIEWS: (anon) Critical Rev, Mar 1811; (J. Foster) Eclectic Rev, Mar–Apr 1811.

History of Brazil. Pt 1 1810, 1822; pt 2 1817; pt 3 1819; tr Portuguese 1862, 1948–54, 1981.

REVIEWS: (anon) Eclectic Rev, Sep 1810; (J. Lowe) Monthly Rev, Dec 1812.

The history of Europe [in Edinburgh Annual Register for 1808–11]. Vols 1–4 Edinburgh 1810–13. Anon.

Omniana: or horae otiosores. 2 vols 1812. Anon; 45 contributions by Coleridge, 201 by Southey.

The origin, nature and object of the new system of education. 1812. Anon.

An exposure of the misrepresentations and calumnies in Mr Marsh's review of Sir George Barlow's administration at Madras, by the relations of Sir George Barlow. 1813. Anon.

The life of Nelson. 2 vols 1813, New York 1813, London 1814 (rev), 1825, 1 vol 1830 (rev) etc (at least 30 edns by 1900); ed G. A. R. Callender 1922; ed H. Newbolt 1925; ed E. R. H. Harvey 1953; ed K. Fenwick 1956; ed C. Oman 1962 (EL), ed. R. D. Madison, Annapolis MD 1990.

REVIEWS: (anon) Critical Rev, July 1813; (anon) Br Critic, Oct 1813.

Roderick: the last of the Goths. 1814, 2 vols 1815, 1815, 1 vol Philadelphia 1815, 2 vols 1816, 1818, 1826, 1 vol 1891; tr Fr 1820, 1821, Du 1823–4. Ms (as Pelayo) in Victoria and Albert Museum.

REVIEWS: (G. C. Bedford) Quart Rev, Apr 1815; (J. T. Coleridge) Br Critic, Apr 1815.

Odes to His Royal Highness the Prince Regent, His Imperial Majesty the Emperor of Russia and His Majesty the King of Prussia. 1814.

Carmen triumphale, for the commencement of the year 1814. Rptd with the Odes, *above*, 1821.

A summary of the life of Arthur Duke of Wellington, from the period of his first achievements in India to his invasion of France and the decisive battle of Waterloo. Dublin 1816. Anon; rptd from Quart Rev 13, 1815. Copy in Nat Lib of Ireland.

The poet's pilgrimage to Waterloo. 1816 (12 large-paper copies also issued), 1816, New York 1816, Boston 1816.

REVIEW: (J. Conder) Eclectic Rev, Aug 1816.

The lay of the laureate: carmen nuptiale. 1816. On the marriage of the Princess Charlotte. Mss in Fitz Park Museum Keswick.

REVIEWS: (F. Jeffrey) Edinburgh Rev, June 1816; (W. Hazlitt) Examiner, 7–14 July 1816.

Wat Tyler: a dramatic poem. 1817 (many pirated edns), Newcastle [1820?], London [1820?], [1825?], Newcastle [1830?], London [1835?], Boston 1850, Oxford 1989. Ms in Fitz Park Museum Keswick.

REVIEW: (W. Hazlitt) Examiner, 9 Mar 1817. *See also* anon The changeling: a poem in two cantos addressed to a laureat. 1817.

A letter to William Smith esq MP. 1817 (4 edns). On the Wat Tyler controversy.

REVIEW: (W. Hazlitt) Examiner, 4, 11, 18 May 1817.

The byrth, lyf and actes of King Arthur, with an introduction and notes. 2 vols 1817.

The life of Wesley, and the rise and progress of Methodism. 2 vols 1820, 1820, New York 1820; ed C. C. Southey 1846 (embodying notes by Coleridge and Remarks on Wesley by A. Knox), New York 1847, London 1858, 1 vol 1864; ed J. A. Atkinson 1889; ed M. H. Fitzgerald 2 vols Oxford 1925; abridged by A. Reynolds 1903; tr Ger 1828.

REVIEW: (J. G. Lockhart) Blackwood's Mag, Feb 1824; *see also* R. Watson, Observations on Southey's Life of Wesley, 1820.

A vision of judgement. 1821, 1822 (as The two visions: or Byron v. Southey: containing The vision of judgement by Dr Southey LL D; also another Vision of judgement, by Lord Byron), New York 1823 (with Byron's travesty), London 1824 (with Byron). Both poems ed E. M. Earl 1929; ed R. E. Roberts, Harrow Weald 1932. Ms in BL.

REVIEW: (anon) Monthly Rev, June 1821. *See also* G. G. Byron, The vision of judgment, Liberal 1, 1822.

The expedition of Orsua and the crimes of Aguirre. 1821, Philadelphia 1821. Rptd slightly rev from Edinburgh Annual Register vol 3 pt 2.

Life of John Duke of Marlborough. 1822. Anon; abridged from Quart Rev 23, 1820.

History of the Peninsular War. Vol 1 1823, vol 2 1827, vol 3 1832; rptd 6 vols, vols 1–4 1828, vols 5–6 1837. Ms in Fitz Park Museum Keswick.

REVIEWS: (anon) Literary Gazette, 14–21 Dec 1822; (G. Procter and J. W. Croker) Quart Rev, Apr 1823.

The book of the church. 2 vols 1824, 1824, 1825, Boston 1825, 1 vol 1837, 1841, 1848, 1859, 1869 (with notes from Vindiciae ecclesiae anglicanae, *below*), [1885].

A tale of Paraguay. 1825, Boston 1827, London 1828. Mss in BL and Fitz Park Museum Keswick.

REVIEW: (anon) Eclectic Rev, Oct 1825.

Vindiciae ecclesiae anglicanae: letters to Charles Butler esq, comprising Essays on the Romish religion and vindicating the Book of the church. 1826.

All for love; and The pilgrim to Compostella. 1829, Paris 1829. Mss in Fitz Park Museum Keswick.

Sir Thomas More: or colloquies on the progress and prospects of society. 2 vols 1829, 1831, 1 vol 1887.

REVIEWS: (T. B. Macaulay) Edinburgh Rev, Jan 1830; (anon) Fraser's Mag June 1830.

The pilgrim's progress: with a life of John Bunyan. 1830, Boston 1832, New York 1837, London 1839, 1844, New York 1846, London 1847, 1881.

REVIEW: (Sir W. Scott) Quart Rev, Oct 1830.

The devil's walk: a poem by Professor Porson. 1830, 1830, 1830 (as by Coleridge and Southey), 1830. By Coleridge and Southey. Originally ptd as The devil's thoughts, Morning Post, 6 Sep 1799 and expanded by Southey alone in 1827.

Select works of the British poets, from Chaucer to Jonson, with biographical sketches. 1831.

Attempts in verse by John Jones, an old servant, with some account of the writer, written by himself, and an introductory essay on the lives and works of our uneducated poets by Robert Southey. 1831, 1836 (as Lives of uneducated poets); [Southey's essay] ed J. S. Childers, Oxford 1925 (as The lives and works of the uneducated poets).

REVIEWS: (J. G. Lockhart) Quart Rev, Jan 1831; (T. H. Lister) Edinburgh Rev, Sep 1831.

Essays, moral and political, now first collected. 2 vols 1832.

Lives of the British admirals, with an introductory view of the naval history of England. Vol 1 1833, Philadelphia 1835 (as The early naval history of England), London 1839; vol 2 1833; vol 3 1834, 1848; vol 4 1837; vol 5 1840 (continued by R. Bell); ed D. Hannay 1 vol 1895 (as English seamen), 1 vol 1904.

Letter to John Murray esq 'touching' Lord Nugent, in reply to a letter from his Lordship, touching an article in the Quarterly Review, by the author of that article. 1833. Anon.

The doctor. Vols 1–2 1834, 1835; vol 3 1834; vol 4 1837; vol 5 1838 (all anon); vols 6–7 ed J. W. Warter 1847. Vols 1–3 rptd in 2 vols New York 1836, 1860; vols 1–7 ed J. W. Warter 1 vol 1848, 1849, 1853, 1856, New York 1856, London 1862, 1864, 1865, New York 1872; abridged by R. B. Johnson [1898], (by M. H. Fitzgerald 1930). Ms in Chetham's Lib Manchester.

REVIEW: (J. G. Lockhart) Quart Rev, Mar 1834.

Horae lyricae: poems by Isaac Watts, with a memoir of the author. 1834, 1837, Boston 1854.

The works of William Cowper, with a life of the author. 15 vols 1835–7, 8 vols 1853–5. Life of Cowper rptd Boston 1 vol 1858.

REVIEW: (H. Merivale) Edinburgh Rev, July 1836.

The life of the Rev Andrew Bell, comprising the history of the rise and progress of the system of mutual tuition. 3 vols 1844. Southey wrote vol 1, C. C. Southey vols 2–3.

Select biographies: Cromwell and Bunyan. 1844. Cromwell rptd from Quart Rev 25, 1821, Bunyan from Pilgrim's progress, 1830. Cromwell rptd New York 1854, 1868.

Oliver Newman: a New-England tale (unfinished): with other poetical remains. [Ed H. Hill] 1845. Ms in Fitz Park Museum Keswick.

Robin Hood: a fragment by the late Robert Southey and Caroline Southey, with other fragments and poems. Edinburgh 1847.

Southey's common place book. Ed J. W. Warter 4 ser 1849–50. Ser 1, Choice passages, 1849, 1850; ser 2, Special collections, 1849, 1850; ser 3, Analytical readings, 1850; ser 4, Original memoranda, 1850. Ser 1–2, New York 2 vols 1849–50, 2 vols 1860; ser 1–4 4 vols 1876. Mss in Hispanic Soc of New York Lib.

Review of Churchill's poems by the late Mr Southey. [1852] (priv ptd). Rptd from Annual Rev, 1804, rptd in Poetical works of Charles Churchill, ed W. Tooke, Boston 1854.

Journal of a tour in the Netherlands in the autumn of 1815. 1902, Boston 1902; ed W. R. Nicoll 1903; tr Du, 1946.

Journal of a tour in Scotland in 1819. Ed C. H. Herford 1929.

Journals of a residence in Portugal 1800–1, and a visit to France 1838. Ed A. Cabral, Oxford 1960.

Letters

Robberds, J. W. In his Memoir of the life and writings of the late William Taylor, 2 vols 1843.

Southey, C. C. The life and correspondence of the late Robert Southey. 6 vols 1849–50, 1 vol New York [1850], 1851, 1855.

Selections from the letters of Robert Southey. Ed J. W. Warter 4 vols 1856.

Forster, J. In his Walter Savage Landor: a biography, 2 vols 1869.

The correspondence of Robert Southey with Caroline Bowles: to which are added correspondence with Shelley, and Southey's dreams. Ed E. Dowden, Dublin 1881.

Memorials of Coleorton: being letters from Coleridge, Wordsworth and his sister, Southey and Sir Walter Scott, to Sir George and Lady Beaumont 1803–34. Ed W. Knight 2 vols Edinburgh 1887.

Robert Southey: the story of his life written in his letters. Ed J. Dennis, Boston 1887, London 1894.

Letters from the Lake Poets to Daniel Stuart, editor of the Morning Post and the Courier 1800–38. 1889 (priv ptd). Comp M. Stuart, ed E. H. Coleridge. Southey's letters pp. 387–434; poems contributed to Morning Post by Southey pp. 437–48.

Williams, O. Lamb's friend the census-taker: life and letters of John Rickman. 1911. Mss in Huntington.

Letters of Robert Southey: a selection. Ed M. H. Fitzgerald, Oxford 1912 (WC).

Letters by Robert Southey to Sir John Taylor Coleridge. Ed. W. Brackman, Studia Germanica Gandensia 6, 1964.

New letters of Robert Southey. Ed K. Curry 2 vols New York 1965. *For fuller list, see* K. Curry, The published letters of Robert Southey: a checklist, BNYPL, Mar 1967; *also*

Conder, E. R. Josiah Conder: a memoir. 1857.

Martin, C. G. Robert Southey: two unpublished letters [to Tom Southey]. N & Q, Aug 1967.

Martin, C. G. Robert Southey: an unpublished letter [to William Coxe]. N & Q 17, 1970.

Reed, M. L. New letters of Wordsworth and Southey [to Lord Holland]. Princeton Univ Lib Chron 32, 1971.

Llorens, V. Blanco White and Robert Southey: fragments of a correspondence. Stud in Romanticism 11, 1972.

Antippas, A. P. Four new Southey letters [to Joseph Cottle, John May and Thomas Clarkson]. Wordsworth Circle 5, 1974.

Mann, P. Two unpublished letters of Robert Southey [to Anna Seward and John Major]. N & Q 22, 1975.

Horsfall, N. Four unpublished letters of Robert Southey [to Peter Elmsley]. N & Q 22, 1975.

Letters of Robert Southey to John May, 1797 to 1838. Ed. C. Ramos, Austin TX 1976.

Albrecht, W. P. A letter from Southey to Maria Gowen Brooks. ELN 15, 1978.

Southey contributed to Flagellant 1795 (*no 5 contains his attack on flogging*), Monthly Mag 1796–1800, Critical Rev 1798–1803, Morning Post 1798–9 (*poems*), Annual Rev 1802–8, Athenaeum 1807–9, Quart Rev 1809–39, Foreign Rev 1828–30. *For contributions to annuals see* Literary Souvenir 1826–8, Amulet 1829, Anniversary 1829, Keepsake 1829.

§2

Coleridge, S. T. In his Biographia literaria, 2 vols 1817.

Hazlitt, W. In his Political essays with sketches of public characters, 1819.

Tilbrook, S. Historical and critical remarks upon the modern hexametrists, and upon Mr Southey's Vision of judgement. 1822.

Landor, W. S. Southey and Porson. In his Imaginary conversations, vol 1 1824; The works of W. S. Landor, 2 vols 1846 (Southey and Porson, Southey and Landor).

Benbow, W. A scourge for the Laureate, in reply to his infamous letter abusive of Lord Byron. [1825?].

Wilson, John. The female characters in our modern poetry. 1, Kailyal. In The curse of Kehama. 2, Oneiza. In Thalaba, Blackwood's Mag 37, May, July 1835.

Cottle, J. In his Early recollections, 2 vols 1837, 1 vol 1847 (rev as Reminiscences of Coleridge and Southey).

Lockhart, J. G. In his Life of Sir Walter Scott, 7 vols Edinburgh 1837–8.

De Quincey, T. In his Lake reminiscences from 1807 to 1830, no 4: Wordsworth and Southey. Tait's Mag 6, 1839; rptd in De Quincey's Works, ed D. Masson vol 2 Edinburgh 1889, and in Reminiscences of the English Lake poets, ed J. E. Jordan 1961 (EL), ed. D. Wright, Harmondsworth 1970.

Catalogue of the valuable library of the late Robert Southey esq. [1844], 1974 (in Sale catalogues of libraries of eminent persons, ed A. N. L. Munby vol 9. Introd by R. Park and E. M. Wilson).

Landor, W. S. To the Rev C. Cuthbert Southey [on his father's character and public services]. Fraser's Mag, Dec 1850, rptd in Works, ed T. E. Welby vol 12 1931.

Thackeray, W. M. In his Four Georges, 1861. *See under* George III.

Jerdan, W. In his Men I have known, 1866.

Robinson, H. C. In his Diary, reminiscences and correspondence, ed T. Sadler 3 vols 1869, 2 vols Boston 1869, London 1872. Cf Correspondence with the Wordsworth circle, ed E. J. Morley 2 vols Oxford 1927 and On books and their writers, ed E. J. Morley 3 vols 1938.
Dowden, E. Southey. 1874 (EML).
Dennis, J. In his Studies in English literature, 1876.
Carlyle, T. In his Reminiscences, vol 2 1881.
Taylor, H. In his Autobiography, vol 1 1885 ch 17.
Smiles, S. In his A publisher and his friends: memoir of the late John Murray, with an account of the origin and progress of the house 1768–1843, 2 vols 1891.
Dowden, E. The early revolutionary group. In his French Revolution and English literature, 1895.
Saintsbury, G. In his Essays in English literature, ser 2 1895. Essay on Southey rptd in his Collected essays and papers, vol 1 1923.
Stephen, L. Southey's letters. In his Studies of a biographer, vol 4 1902.
Schmidt, J. Robert Southey: sein Naturgefühl in seinen Dichtungen. Leipzig 1904.
Grannis, R. S. An American friend of Southey (Maria Gowen Brooks). 1913.
Pfandl, L. Southey und Spanien. Revue Hispanique 28, 1913.
Lounsbury, T. R. Southey as poet and historian. Yale Rev new ser 4, 1915.
Haller, W. The early life of Robert Southey 1774–1803. New York 1917.
Beer, M. In his History of British socialism, vol 1 1919.
Simmons, J. Southey. 1945.
Carnall, G. Robert Southey and his age. Oxford 1960.
Many reviews of Southey's publications are rptd in L. Madden, Robert Southey: the critical heritage, *1972.* [GC]

Sara Spence, Mrs George fl. 1795–1821

Poems and miscellaneous pieces. Bury St Edmunds and London 1795.
Poems and a meditation. Colchester and London 1821.

Mrs Walter Spencer, formerly Jackson fl. 1781–1812

Poetical trifles, or miscellaneous poems on various subjects. 1781.
Commemorative feelings, or miscellaneous poems, interspersed with sketches in prose .... 1812.
Miscellaneous poems. Windsor 1812.

William Robert Spencer 1769–1834

Collection
Miles 9 (10).

§1
Bürger, G. A. Leonora. Tr Spencer 1796; Dublin 1799 (with trns by others); London 1809.
Beth-Gêlert, or the grave of the greyhound. Oxford 1800; York [c. 1815]. Anon.
Urania, or the illuminé: a comedy. 1802. Anon. Prose and verse.
The year of sorrow. 1804.
Poems. 1811, 1835 (enlarged, with memoir).
Miscellaneous poems. Windsor 1812.
Wife, children and friends. Boston, Lincs [1830?]. Anon.

John Stagg 1770–1823

Miscellaneous poems. Carlisle 1790, 1804; Workington 1805; Wigton 1807, 1808.
The minstrel of the north, or Cumbrian legends: a poetical miscellany .... 1810; Manchester 1816, 1817.
The magazine of the muses: a selection of poems .... Ed Stagg, Manchester 1814, 1815.
The Cumbrian minstrel .... 2 vols Manchester 1821.
Legendary, gothic and romantic tales, in verse ... By a northern minstrel. Shrewsbury 1825. Anon.

Charles Edward Stewart 1749–1819

A collection of trifles in verse. Sudbury 1797.
Critical trifles, in a familiar epistle .... Sudbury 1797.
Extract from The regicide: an heroic poem .... 1801.
The arguments in verse of The Foxiad: an historical poem .... Sudbury and London 1803. Anon.
Charles's small-clothes: a national ode. By the author of The Foxiad. Sudbury 1808. Anon.
Last trifles in verse. Sudbury 1812.
The aliad: an heroic epistle to Clootz redivivus. 1815. Anon.
The political works in verse .... 1816.
Author of sermons and political prose.

John Stewart b. 1745

Britons united, or Britannia roused .... 1800.
The pleasures of love: a poem. 1806 (2 edns).
The resurrection: a poem. 1808.
Genevieve, or the spirit of the drave .... 1810.
Alhagranza: a Moorish metrical romance. London and Cork 1816.

Thomas Stewart, of Naples fl. 1828–45

An epistle from Abelard to Eloise. 1828.
Retirement: a poem. 1829.
Elegy on the convent of the grotto at Amalfi. Palermo 1830 (priv ptd). Anon.
Napoleon's dying soliloquy, and other poems. 1834.
The Constantiniad: a poem, books i to vi. Bk 1 only 1845.

Mary R. Stockdale, later Sterndale b. c. 1769?

Berquin, A. The family book, or children's journal ... interspersed with poetical pieces. Tr Stockdale 1798, 1799.
The effusions of the heart: poems .... 1798.
Lombard, V. The school for children ... interspersed with poetical pieces. Ed Stockdale 1800.
The panorama of youth. 2 vols 1807; Edinburgh 1811; Philadelphia 1816. Prose.
The mirror of the mind: poems .... 1810, 1817.
The Christian poet's lament over the Christian statesman: an elegy on ... Perceval. 1812.
The widow and her orphan family: an elegy. 1812.
The mother and child: a poem. 1818.
A plume for Sir Samuel Romilly, or the offering of the fatherless: an elegy. 1818.
A shroud for Sir Samuel Romilly: an elegy. 1818.
A wreath for the urn: an elegy on ... Princess Charlotte ... with other poems. 1818.
The life of a boy. 2 vols 1821. Anon. Prose.
The wedding ring: a funereal offering. 1821.
Vignettes of Derbyshire. 1824. Anon. Prose.

Robert Story 1795–1860

Collections
The poetical works. 1857.
The lyrical and other minor poems of Story, with a sketch of his life and writings by J. James. London and Bradford 1861.

§1
The harvest: a poem. 1816; Berwick 1818.
Craven blossoms .... Skipton 1826.
The magic fountain, with other poems. 1829.
The isles are awake. 1834.
The outlaw: a drama. 1839.
Love and literature: being the reminiscences, literary opinions and fugitive pieces of a poet in humble life. London and Keighley 1842.
Songs and lyrical poems. Liverpool [1845?], 1849 (3rd edn, as Songs and poems).
Guthrum the Dane: a tale of the heptarchy. 1852, 1853.
The third Napoleon: an ode. 1854, 1855 (enlarged). Anon.
The Alloway [Burns] centenary festival: an ode. 1859.
Contributed to the Burns centenary poems *(1859)*.

Agnes Strickland 1796–1874

§1
Worcester field, or the cavalier: a poem in four cantos, with historical notes. [1826].
The seven ages of woman, and other poems. 1827.
Demetrius: a tale of modern Greece in three cantos, with other poems. 1833.
Historic scenes and poetic fancies. 1850.
Floral sketches, fables and other poems. [1836], [1861.]

§2
Strickland, J. M. The life of A. Strickland. Edinburgh 1887.
Contributed to Poems *by the Rev J. S. Mitford (1830). See also col 2199.*

Charles Strong 1784?–1864

§1
Specimens of sonnets from ... Italian poets .... Tr Strong 1827.
Sonnets. By the author of 'Specimens'. Torquay 1829; London 1835, 1862 (with 15 additional sonnets by 'C. L.'). Anon.

§2
The sonnets of Strong. Blackwood's Mag Nov 1835.

John Struthers 1776–1853

Collection
The poetical works ... with autobiography. 2 vols London, Edinburgh and Dublin 1850.

§1
Poems on various subjects. Glasgow 1801.
The peasant's death ... and other poems. Glasgow 1806.
The poor man's sabbath .... Glasgow [1806? (2nd edn); Edinburgh 1808; Boston 1813; Glasgow 1832, 1839.
The winter day, with other poems. Glasgow 1811.
Poems, moral and religious. 2 vols Glasgow 1814.
The plough and other poems. Glasgow 1818.
The harp of Caledonia: a collection of songs .... Ed Struthers, 3 vols Glasgow 1819; Edinburgh 1821.
The British minstrel: a selection of ballads .... Ed Struthers, 2 vols Glasgow 1821, 1822.
Dychment: a poem. Glasgow 1836.
Also wrote on the history of Scotland and on the national church.

Charles Swan d. 1838

The counterfeit saints ... with other poems. 1819 (2 edns).
Retribution: a poem .... 1820 (2 edns).
The heir of Foiz ... and other poems .... 1822, 1823 (as Gaston, or the heir of Foiz).
Author of trns, of sermons, and of a travel memoir.

Edmund Lewis Lenthal Swift or Swifte 1777–1875

Anacreon in Dublin .... 1814 (3 edns). Anon.
Waterloo, and other poems. 1815.
Juvenal. Tenth and thirteenth satires. Tr Swift 1818.
Translator of Homer and writer on Irish history and the church.

Caroline Symmons fl. 1789–1803

The Sicilian captive: a tragedy. 1800 (priv ptd). Anon.
The raising of Jaïrus' daughter: a poem ... with a few poetical productions .... London, Cambridge and York 1804. With F. Wrangham.
The cottage of the Var. 1809. Prose.
Poems. 1812. With Charles Symmons.

Charles Symmons 1749–1826

Inez: a tragedy. 1796. Anon.
Genius: an ode. [1801.]
Milton. The prose works, with a life of the author. Ed Symmons 1806, 1810 (the Life excerpted separately), 1822.
Poems. 1812. With Caroline Symmons.
Poems for the anniversary of the literary fund 1813. 1813. Anon. [With C. T. Fitzgerald.]
Virgil. Sixth book of the Aeneis. Tr [Symmons] 1814.
Virgil. The Aeneis. Tr Symmons 1817; Chiswick 1820.
The literary fund: anniversary poem 1822. 1822.
Shakspeare. The dramatic works and poems. Ed Symmons and S. W. Singer, Chiswick [1826] (the Life of Shakspeare only).
Author of sermons; contributed to Lines written at Jerpoint Abbey *(1823–7).*

Anne Tallant fl. 1834–5

Octavia Elphinstone: a Manx story, and Lois: a drama, founded on a legend in the noble family of —. 2 vols 1834, 1835. Prose and verse.

Robert Tannahill 1774–1810

Collections
Seventeen favourite songs ... by Burns and Tannahill .... Glasgow [1815?].
The poetical works. New edn Glasgow 1825, 1836; London [1870] (enlarged).
The songs, ballads and fragments ... with a sketch of his life. Ed A. Laing, Brechin 1833, [1840?].
The works of ... Tannahill. [1835?]; ed P. A. Ramsay, London and Edinburgh 1838; London 1850, 1853, 1859, [1860?].
The poems and songs of Tannahill [with memoir of Tannahill and R. A. Smith]. Ed P. A. Ramsey, Glasgow 1838.
The poetical works of Tannahill. Belfast 1844; London [1870].
Rogers 2.
The songs of Tannahill, complete. Glasgow 1859.
The select songs of Burns and Tannahill. Glasgow [1883] (in A strange life).
The poems and songs of Tannahill. Ed D. Semple, Paisley 1874 (Centenary edn), 1900.
The poems and songs and correspondence of Tannahill. Ed D. Semple, Paisley 1876.
Miles 2.
The songs and poems of Tannahill [with memoir by A. Reekie]. Paisley 1911. Includes some musical settings.
Robert Tannahill. Ed I. Livingston, Paisley 1977 (in Renfrewshire men of letters ser vol 1).

§1

The soldier's return: a Scots pastoral, in two acts. Paisley 1807 (2 edns, the 2nd as The soldier's return: a Scottish interlude, in two acts, with other poems and songs, chiefly in the Scottish dialect), 1822; ed J. J. Lamb 1873.

Poems and songs, chiefly in the Scottish dialect. 1815; Glasgow 1815; London and Edinburgh 1815; 2 vols London 1817; New York 1819, 1820, 1821; Glasgow 1825.

§2

The life of the Renfrewshire bard. Paisley 1815. Anon.

Contributed to Poetical Mag *vol 2 (1808) and to collections of songs with music.*

The Taylors of Ongar, Rev Isaac Taylor, Mrs Ann Taylor née Martin, Ann Taylor later Gilbert, Jane Taylor, Isaac Taylor jr, later of Stanford Rivers, Jefferys Taylor

The Taylors of Ongar (so called to distinguish them from the Taylors of Norwich) wrote, between 1803 and 1853, more than 70 bks for children, and for young people. They wrote both collectively and individually, and often illustrated their works with engravings of their own designs. A full list of pbd drawings and engravings by the Taylor family are in C. D. Stewart, The Taylors of Ongar *(see Bibliographies, below).*

Manuscripts

Principal repositories are the Suffolk Record Office, Bury St Edmunds, and the Guildhall, Lavenham, Suffolk; Nottinghamshire Archives; Colchester and Essex Museum; The Osborne Collection of Early Children's Books, Toronto, Canada. Ann Taylor Gilbert's Commonplace book *is in the Alexander Turnbull Lib, Wellington, New Zealand; her* Album *is in the Osborne Collection, Toronto.*

Bibliographies

Harris, G. E. Contributions towards a bibliography of the Taylors of Ongar and Stanford Rivers. 1965.

Stewart, C. D. The Taylors of Ongar: an analytical bio-bibliography. 2 vols New York 1975.

Immel, A. Addenda to Stewart, The Taylors of Ongar: The new cries of London. PBSA 82 1988.

Collections and selections

Hymns for infant schools, partly original and partly selected from Hymns for infant minds ... by Mrs Gilbert. 1827. Comprises 13 hymns from Hymns for infant minds (4th edn 1811); 14 hymns from Original hymns for Sunday schools (4th edn 1816); 9 original hymns by Ann Taylor Gilbert.

The family pen. Memorials, biographical and literary, of the Taylor family of Ongar. Ed Rev Isaac Taylor 2 vols 1867. First English collection of Taylor works. Includes a new and rev edn of Memoirs and poetical remains of ... Jane Taylor, 1825; selections from the works of all the Taylors except Mrs Ann; some unpbd material, and a biographical essay by the editor.

The poetical works of Ann and Jane Taylor. Illustr B. Foster, engr Dalziel and J. Cooper, nd [c. 1877]. First English collected edn of the poetical works of Ann and Jane, comprising Hymns for infant minds, Original poems and Rhymes for the nursery, from texts of Good-Aim ser 1876.

Tales, essays and poems by Jane and Ann Taylor. Ed G. A. Oliver, Boston 1884. Comprises 35 poems from Original poems; Display; 26 pieces from The contributions of Q. Q., 3 poems from Jane's Poetical remains; 1 poem from Essays in rhyme; and a biographical sketch by the editor.

The 'Original poems' and others by Ann and Jane Taylor and Adelaide O'Keefe. Ed E. V. Lucas, illustr F. D. Bedford, nd [1903], [1905], New York [1905], London 1925. Centenary issue. Comprises The wedding among the flowers; selections from Original poems, Rhymes for the nursery and Aesop in rhyme; and a biographical and critical introd by the editor.

Old fashioned stories and poems. Ed E. M. Tappan [1907] (The Children's Hour 6). Includes 12 selections from Original poems, Rhymes for the nursery and The contributions of Q. Q.

Ann and Jane Taylor. Ed M. MacLeod, illustr F. D. Bedford and H. C. Appleton, [1914] (The Children's Poets). 67 poems from Original poems (Lucas edn).

Taylor, Ann and Jane. Original poems for infant minds ... and Rhymes for the nursery (Classics of Children's Literature 1621–1932). Preface by C. D. Stewart, New York 1976. (photo facs of 1st edns).

See also Collections and selections under Rev Isaac Taylor and Jane Taylor, below.

Collaborative works

The new cries of London. [Pt I]: 1803, 1804, 1806, 1813 (rev). Pt II: 1808 (no copies located), 1812 [Pts I and II combined], '1823' [1824]. Supposedly a revision of an earlier work (never identified). Pbd anonymously, but the joint work of Ann, Jane, Isaac jr and, perhaps, Rev Isaac Taylor. Some illustr Taylors.

Original poems, for infant minds. By several young persons. 2 vols 1804–5, 1805–6 (2nd edn rev), 1805–6 (3rd edn), Philadelphia 1806, London 1806–8 (4th edn rev), Philadelphia 1807, Boston 1808 (1 vol), Newbury 1808, London 1808–11 (7th edn rev), Philadelphia 1809 (illus edn), London 1812–35 (8th–31st edns); Boston, Philadelphia, New York etc 1813–50 (17 edns); London 1835–6 (new edn, rev authors); 1836–9 (2 edns); 1839–41 (2 edns, new and rev); New York 1851 (includes Poetical remains of Jane); Philadelphia, New York and Boston 1853–69 (10 edns); London 1854 (new edn, rev Isaac jr and son); 1856–66 (4 edns); 1865 (1st one-vol edn, 1st English illus edn by Henry Anelay and G. P. Nicholls); 1 vol 1868 (Virtue's New Gift Books ser: Illustr Contemporary Artists); 1 vol Philadelphia 1869 (Illustr Contemporary Amer Artists); London nd [c. 1874, c. 1875 and c. 1882] (Authors' Complete edn, 2 vols in 1); [1876] (Beeton's Good-Aim ser, 1); [c. 1877], New York 1879, London 1881. Some illustr Taylors. Tr Du, Ger, Rus.

REVIEWS: Imperial Rev Aug 1804; Guardian of Education Jan 1805; Eclectic Rev May, Dec 1805; Critical Rev Nov 1805; Br Critic Apr 1806; Monthly Rev July 1806.

By Ann Taylor (49 poems), Jane Taylor (43 poems), Rev Isaac and Isaac Taylor jr (6 poems), Adelaide O'Keeffe (33 poems), and Bernard Barton (1 poem). The work soon became (erroneously) accepted as the work of Ann and Jane Taylor alone.

Many selections pbd in England, USA and elsewhere, including The English Van Alphen, Amsterdam 1852; Little Ann and other poems, illustr Kate Greenaway, 1883; Sundry rhymes from the days of our grandmothers, illustr G. W. Edwards, 1888; Meddlesome Matty, introd by E. Sitwell, illustr A. Wyndham Payne, 1925. Many printings of individual poems including My Mother (10 English edns 1807–73, 10 US edns 1816–80, a jigsaw puzzle and broadsides), Little Ann and her mamma (illustr J. D. Watson and Kronheim) nd (c. 1871); Greedy Dick 1903, Dirty Jack [1912]; The vulgar little lady (illustr R. Marshall and E. Evans) 1913. My Mother set to music c. 1805 by Thomas Attwood (and later by T. James and others); and made into jigsaw puzzles (1811, c. 1870).

See also Collections and selections above.

Rural scenes; or, a peep into the country for good children. 1805, '1805' (1806, 2nd issue), 1806 (rev and enlarged), 1806, 1810, 1814 (rev and enlarged 'for children') [1818], New York 1823 (rev), London [1826] (rev), nd [c. 1845] (new edn, illustr John Gilbert and others), Philadelphia 1845 ('first Amer edn'), London 1848 (8th edn), 1853 (new edn, no known copies), 1863 (no known copies), 1865 ('10th edn', 'rev and improved' and 'for youth)' 1876 (no known copies), 1879 (no known copies). Some illustr Taylors. Supposedly a revision of an earlier work (never identified). Pbd anonymously, but the joint work of Ann, Jane and Isaac jr, with some contributions by Rev Isaac. Cooperstown NY 1824 (selection).

REVIEW: Eclectic Rev Dec 1805.

City scenes: or, a peep into London for good children. 1806 (no known copies), 1809 (2 edns), Philadelphia 1809, London 1814 (rev and enlarged 'for children'; includes 2nd type printing of Blake's Holy Thursday), 1818 (rev and enlarged; 3 edns), 1823 (rev), 1828 (rev and enlarged; pbd plain and coloured; 2 edns), nd [c. 1845] (rev and enlarged, illustr John Gilbert and Folkard, pbd plain and coloured), 1879 (Little Ladders to Learning, no known copies). Supposedly a revision of an earlier work (never identified). Pbd as 'By the author of Rural scenes', but the work of Ann, Jane and Isaac jr. Some illustr Taylors.

REVIEW: Literary Panorama Dec 1809.

Rhymes for the nursery. 1806, 1807 (2nd edn rev), 1809–12 (4 edns), 1813 (7th edn rev), Hartford CT 1813 (from 2nd English edn), London 1814–35 (20 edns), 1836–43 (new edn, rev, 4 edns). nd [c. 1845] (1st illus edn by John Gilbert, rev, pbd plain and coloured), Philadelphia 1849–60 (4 edns from 1845 English edn), London 1850–4 (new edn, rev, 3 edns), 1857–[63] (new rev and enlarged, 3 edns), 1859 (from 1845 edn), 1876–7 (Beeton's Good-Aim ser. 22, 2 edns), 1872 (no known copies), 1878 (rev), 1881 (as 1845 but illustr W. Small, Dalziel and others), 1886 (no known copies). Some illustr Taylors. Tr Ger 1848. Pbd as 'By the authors of Original poems', but the work of Ann (40 poems) and Jane (42 poems) alone. (Includes Jane's most famous poem The star ['Twinkle, twinkle little star'].) Many selections, both in England and USA, some with different titles (The little field daisy, The snowdrop, etc.) *See also* Collections and selections, *above*.

REVIEWS: Critical Rev Aug 1806; Monthly Mirror Oct 1806.

Limed twigs, to catch young birds. 1808, Philadelphia 1811 (from 1st English edn), London 1811–c. 1847 (8 edns), Philadelphia 1849 (rev for schools, illustr A. C. Howland, 2 edns), New York 1852 (with some Rhymes for the nursery), London 1880 (no known copies), 1881 (illustr G. Browne). (Progressive reading lessons in dialogue form.) Pbd as 'By the authors of Original poems etc', but the work of Ann and Jane alone. Some illustr Taylors.

REVIEW: Juvenile Rev 1817.

Signor Topsy-Turvey's wonderful magic lantern; or, The world turned upside down. 1810, Philadelphia 1811 (no known copies), 1814 (as The world turn'd upside down, in 2 pts, with 16 of original 24 poems, illustr J. Yeager), Northampton MA 1979 (priv ptd selection of 8 poems as The world turned upside down, illustr T. L. J. Cotsen). Some illustr Taylors. Supposedly a revision, with new poems, of an earlier work (never identified). Pbd as By the author of 'My Mother' and other poems, but the 24 poems the work of Ann, Jane and Rev Isaac Taylor.

The associate minstrels. Ed Josiah Conder 1810, 1810 (2nd issue, enlarged), 1813 (2nd edn, rev). Pbd anonymously; the 52 poems comprise 20 by the Taylors (Ann 10, Jane 9, Rev Isaac 1); 32 by Josiah Conder, his father and future wife, and Jacob Strutt. Illustr Taylors.

REVIEW: Eclectic Rev Aug 1810.

Hymns for infant minds. 1810, 1810 (2nd edn, rev), Boston nd [1810], 1810 (2nd Amer edn, illus), London 1810 (3rd edn, no known copies), 1811 (4th edn, rev), Boston, New York, New Haven CT etc 1811–30 (34 edns), London 1812–c. 1842 (30 edns), New York nd [c. 1830], Worcester MA 1831 (Amer schools edn with analyses by H. J. Howland), New York, New Haven CT etc 1840–9 (3 edns), London 1844 (35th edn, new edn rev and enlarged by Ann Taylor Gilbert, frontispiece by Josiah Gilbert), 1845–62 (11 edns), New York 1857 (as 'By Jane Taylor', illustr A. C. Howland), London 1868 (47th edn, first large format edn), nd [c. 1870], [1876] (Beeton's Good-Aim ser, 21), 1876 (first English illus edn, selected, rev and illustr J. Gilbert; includes hymns from other Taylor pbns and some unpbd hymns by Ann Taylor Gilbert), 1876 (2nd English illus edn, rev), 1877, 1878 and 1885 (Routledge Poetry Ser of Shilling Juveniles), 1886 (authorised edn, as 1876). Pbd as 'By the authors of Original poems and Rhymes for the nursery'. Of the 70 hymns, 32 were by Ann, 30 by Jane, 5 by Isaac jr. Many selected edns both in England and USA, some with different titles (Good child's little hymn book, etc.) Some illustr Taylors. Tr Rus 1831.

REVIEWS: Eclectic Mag Oct 1810, Literary Panorama Oct 1810.

The mother's fables. Designed ... to correct ... the faults and follies of children. 1812, 1814 (with new sub-title), 1818 (illus edn), 1818 (without illus), 1824 ('4th edn'), 1835 (new edn), 1842 (no known copies), [1861] (new edn 'By E. L. Aveline', illustr William Harvey and Dalziel). Supposedly a revision and improvement of an earlier work (never identified). Advertised as 'By the authors of Original poems etc', it was the work of Ann, Jane, probably Isaac jr and, perhaps, Jefferys. Despite the attribution of the 1861 edn to E. L. Aveline, the text of Pt 1 remains unchanged from previous edns. Some illustr Taylors.

REVIEW: Juvenile Rev 1817.

Original hymns for Sunday schools. 1812, 1814 (3rd edn), 1816 (4th edn, rev), Boston 1820 (1st Amer edn from 4th English edn, unsigned illus), Hartford CT, Philadelphia 1820 (4 edns), London 1822–35 (3 stereotype edns), c. 1858 (9th edn, no known copies). Pbd as 'By the authors of Hymns for infant minds etc', the 36 hymns were the joint work of Ann and Jane Taylor. Tr Rus 1831.

REVIEW: Eclectic Rev Jan 1813.

Correspondence between a mother and her daughter at school. 1817, 1817–29 (7 edns), New York 1818, Boston 1827 (as Familiar letters between ...), London 1855 (no known copies). Tr Du 1822. By Mrs Ann and Jane Taylor.

REVIEWS: GM July 1817; Literary Panorama Aug 1817; Monthly Rev Oct 1817.

Incidents of childhood. 1821. Often ascribed to several members of the Taylor family; *see* §1 under Isaac Taylor jr, *below*.

The linnet's life. 1822. 12 poems illus. Pbd anon, probably the joint work of Ann, Jane, Rev Isaac and, possibly, Isaac jr. Illustr Taylors.

c.1804–10 Isaac Taylor jr made drawings for a book by the Taylor family, Bible stories large and small, *but no pbd records exist under this title.*

Contributions to books

Ann Taylor Gilbert's Album (1813–1936). Photo-facs of ms New York 1978. Poems, prose, watercolours, drawings.

§2

The family pen. Memorials, biographical and literary, of the Taylor family, of Ongar. Ed Rev (Canon) Isaac Taylor. 2 vols 1867.

Galton, Sir Francis. Hereditary genius: an inquiry into its laws and consequences. 1869.

Balfour, Clara Lucas. Women worth emulating. 1877.

A dictionary of hymnology. Ed John Julian 1892, 1925 (rev).

Taylor, Henry. An annotated catalogue of books written by the Taylors of Ongar, with notes on their careers as artists from 1750–1895. Typescript for priv circ 1895.

The 'Original poems' and others by Ann and Jane Taylor and Adelaide O'Keeffe. Ed E. V. Lucas, illustr F. D. Bedford, nd [1903].

Armitage, D. M. The Taylors of Ongar. Cambridge 1939.

Stewart, C. D. The umbelliferous trio; the literary, moral and educational contributions to literature of Ann, Jane and Jefferys Taylor. Unpbd MA thesis, Univ of Toronto 1968.

Stewart, C. D. The Taylors of Ongar: an analytical bio-bibliography. 2 vols New York 1975.

Articles in periodicals include Christian Pocket Mag *Nov 1820;* Christian Remembrancer *55 1868;* Aunt Judy's Mag *Christmas 1875* (Ann and Jane Taylor *by Mrs Ewing);* Quiver *3rd ser 15, 1880 (by Eliza Clarke);* Essex Rev *7 1898 (by J. Ewing Ritchie);* Daily News 5 Feb 1926 *(by Robert Lynd);*

The Sunday Times *7 Mar 1926 (by Edmund Gosse)*; Essex County Standard *12 Jan 1968* (Jane and Ann Taylor as engravers, *by J. Bensusen-Butt*).
See also under each Taylor author of individual works, below [CDS].

Rev Isaac Taylor 1759–1829

Three unpbd sketch books (c. 1787), unpbd drawings, sketches and letters at Suffolk Record Office, Bury St Edmunds. Educational mss on geography, geometry and mechanics at Colchester and Essex Museums. Some unpbd poems and letters in the Osborne Collection, Toronto.

Collections and selections

Scenes all the world over. 2 vols '1821' [1822]. Comprises 5th edn Scenes in Europe, 2nd edns of Scenes in Asia, Africa and America. Sold plain and coloured. Illustr Taylors.

Scenes in Africa and America, for the amusement and instruction of little tarry-at-home travellers. [1829] (new edn). Based on texts of Scenes in Africa 4th edn, Scenes in America 2nd edn, with some textual changes. Sold plain and coloured. Illustr Taylors.

Scenes in Europe and Asia, for the amusement and instruction of little tarry-at-home travellers. [1827] (new edn, 1st thus), nd [c. 1830] (new edn, enlarged). Based on texts of 4th edn Scenes in Europe, 2nd edn Scenes in Asia, with some excisions and addns. Sold plain and coloured. Illustr Taylors.

Scenes in foreign lands. 1841, nd [c. 1844], 1851 (no known copies). New edn of Scenes in Europe, Asia, Africa and America, re-written and updated. Sold plain and coloured. Illustr Taylors.

§1

Twelve addresses to youth, on moral and religious subjects. [1811]. Advertised in 1845, 'on board sheets', no known copies.

The child's birthday. 1811, 1815 (rev). Moral tales. Illustr Taylors.
REVIEW: Evangelical Mag Oct 1811.

Self-cultivation recommended; or, hints to a youth leaving school. 1817, 1817 (2nd edn), 1818, Boston 1820 (from 3rd London edn), London 1820 (4th edn), 1825 (5th edn), Ithaca NY 1842 ('1st Amer edn' from 3rd London edn), 1842 (3rd Amer edn from 11th London edn). No known copies of 11th edn. Illustr Taylors. Tr Du 1825, Fr 1825.
REVIEWS: Evangelical Mag Mar, May 1818.

Scenes in Europe, for the amusement and instruction of little tarry-at-home travellers. 1818, 1819 (rev), 1820 (rev), 1821 (4th edn, rev), 1821, Philadelphia 1822 (1st Amer edn from 3rd London), London 1823 (6th edn), Philadelphia 1824, London 1825, Philadelphia 1825, London 1825 (8th edn), Philadelphia 1832 (4th Amer edn). Sold plain and coloured. Illustr Taylors. Tr Du 1827. The 1st of the popular 'Scenes' ser (unnumbered) pbd by Harris. For 2nd–7th vols in the ser (Asia, Africa, Amer, England, British wealth, Commerce), *see below*.
REVIEWS: GM Apr 1818; Evangelical Mag May 1818.

Advice to the teens; or practical helps towards the formation of one's own character. 1818, 1818 (2nd edn), Boston 1820 (from 2nd London edn), London 1820 (3rd edn), 1825 (4th edn), 1835 (no known copies), Boston 1838. Illustr Taylors. Tr Du 1825, 1832. Ch 6 'The private study' rptd in vol 2 of The family pen 1867.

Scenes in Asia, for the amusement and instruction of little tarry-at-home travellers. 1819, 1821 (2nd edn, rev), 1822, New York 1826 (from 2nd London edn), London 1826 (4th edn), Hartford CT 1829, 1830, Albany NY 1843, 1850. Sold plain and coloured. Illustr Taylors. Tr Du 1831 (from 5th London edn). No known copies of 5th edn.
REVIEW: GM Aug 1819.

Character essential to success in life: addressed to those who are approaching manhood. 1820, Boston 1820 (1st and 2nd Amer edns), London 1820 (2nd edn), Canandaigua NY 1821, Hamilton NY 1824, London 1824 (3rd edn), Hartford CT 1836, 1837 (as Youth's own book, 2 edns), New York 1844 (as Advice to young men on character). Some illustr Taylors.
REVIEWS: Monthly Rev Mar 1821; Evangelical Mag Apr 1821.

Scenes in Africa, for the amusement and instruction of little tarry-at-home travellers. 1820, 1821 (2nd edn, rev), 1821 (new issue), 1824 (4th edn), 1826 (5th edn), New York 1827. Sold plain and coloured. Illustr Taylors. Tr Du 1828.

Picturesque piety: or scripture truths illustrated by forty-eight engravings and an original poem to each. 2 vols 1821, Boston 1821 (1 vol). Some illustr Taylors.
REVIEW: Evangelical Rev May 1821.

Scenes in America, for the amusement and instruction of little tarry-at-home travellers. 1821, 1822 (2nd edn, rev), 1824 (3rd edn), Hartford CT 1824, 1825, 1828–30, London [1828] (4th edn), Hartford CT 1840, Rochester NY 1840, 1841, Hartford CT 1848, New York 1968 (photo facs of 1st edn with new preface). Sold plain and coloured. Illustr Taylors. Tr Du 1829 (from 5th London edn).

Scenes in England, for the amusement and instruction of little tarry-at-home travellers. 1822, 1823 (2nd edn, rev), nd [1826] (3rd edn, rev), nd [1830] (4th edn, rev). Sold plain and coloured. Illustr Taylors.

Scenes of British wealth, in produce, manufactures, and commerce, for the amusement and instruction of little tarry-at-home travellers. 1823, 1823, 1825 (2nd edn), Hartford CT 1826 (as Scenes of wealth), [1832] (new edn), 1836 (re-written and including Scenes of commerce, *below*). Sold plain and coloured. Illustr Taylors.

Beginnings of biography. Being the lives of one hundred persons eminent in British story. 2 vols 1824, 1824 (2 vols in 1), 1824 (2nd edn). Advertised in 1827, 1845, 1853 as Beginnings of British biography. No known copies. Illustr Taylors.

Bunyan explained to a child; being pictures and poems, founded upon The pilgrim's progress. 2 vols 1824–5, 1825 (2nd edn, i.e. a new issue). Illustr Taylors.
REVIEWS: Evangelical Mag Aug 1824, Mar 1825.

A book of martyrs, for the young. 1826, 1826, 1826 (2nd edn).
REVIEW: Evangelical Mag June 1826.

Beginnings of European biography. 3 vols 1827–8. Illustr Taylors.

The balance of criminality; or, mental error compared with immoral conduct, addressed to young doubters. 1828.
REVIEWS: Evangelical Mag Mar 1828; Eclectic Rev Apr 1828.

The biography of a brown loaf. 1829. Illustr Taylors.

The mine (A nutshell of knowledge). 1829, New York 1829, London 1830 (Little Lib 1, 2nd edn with 1 new engr), 1831, 1832 (4th edn, rev), 1834 (5th edn), Boston 1834 (Peter Parley's Little Lib, 7), New York 1835, 1837 (Sunday School and Youth Lib, 80), Philadelphia 1841, London 1845 (6th edn with addns and corrections by Jane Loudon), Philadelphia 1854, and 1861. Some illustr Taylors. The 1st vol in Harris's 'Little Lib' ser (unnumbered except in advertisements). Rev Isaac and Jefferys Taylor wrote 5 of the 18 vols in the ser: The mine, The ship, The forest, The farm, The ocean. Tr Fr 1835.

Scenes of commerce, by land and sea; or, 'where does it come from?' answered. For the amusement and instruction of little tarry-at-home travellers. [1830], 1836 (new edn, re-written and including Scenes of British wealth, *above*), 1839 (3rd edn, rev with addns), 1845, 1851 (no known copies). Some illustr Taylors.

The ship. 1830 (Little Lib [2]), 1831 (2nd edn, rev and enlarged probably by Jefferys Taylor), 1833 (3rd edn), New York 1835 (Peter Parley's Little Lib, 3, from 2nd English edn), London 1835 (4th edn, re-written with additional illus), Philadelphia 1841, London nd [c. 1845] (rev and corrected by Matthew Henry Barker with 4 new engrs by A. Le Petit after W. H. Prior), 1846 (no known copies), Philadelphia 1854. Some illustr Taylors.

The child's life of Christ; interspersed with original poetry. 1832. Illustr Taylors.
REVIEW: Evangelical Mag Dec 1832.

The glory of Zion, *a sermon, 1807, was attributed to Rev Isaac in a bio-*

graphical dictionary of 1816. (L attributes to Isaac Taylor of Calne; O attributes to Rev Isaac's father, Isaac.)

Collaborative works

For Rev Isaac's contributions to Original poems *(1804–5),* The associate minstrels *(1810),* Signor Topsy-Turvey's wonderful magic lantern *(1810), and* The linnet's life *(1822), see The Taylors of Ongar, Collaborative works, above.*

Original hymns . . . by various authors. Ed J. Leifchild. 1842. 8 hymns.

The family pen. Ed. I. Taylor. 2 vols 1867. Vol 2 The goose: a poem.

Ann Taylor Gilbert's Album [1813–1936] photofacs. New York 1978. Watercolour and 3 poems.

Contributions to periodicals

The minor's pocket book. 1807, 1808, 1810, 1812, 1813, 1814, 1829. Verse solutions to Charades, enigmas, rebuses and other poems and verses, signed T. [CDS]

Mrs Ann Taylor, née Martin 1757–1830

Some unpbd letters at Suffolk Record Office, Bury St Edmunds and in the Osborne Collection, Toronto. Contributions to Ann Taylor Gilbert's Album *also in the Osborne Collection.*

§1

Maternal solicitude for a daughter's best interests. 1814, 1814 (2nd edn, corrected), 1814 (3rd edn, corrected), 1815 (4th edn), New York 1816 (from 2nd London edn), London 1816, Philadelphia 1816 (from 5th London edn), London 1817, 1818 (7th and 8th edns), 1820, 1822, 1824, 1825 (12th edn), 1830 ('12th edn'), nd [1853] (rev and enlarged by Clara Lucas Balfour). Tr Fr nd [c. 1823–6].
REVIEWS: Evangelical Mag Feb 1814, Literary Panorama Feb 1814, GM Jan 1816.

Practical hints to young females, on the duties of a wife, a mother, and a mistress of a family. 1815, 1815 (2nd–5th edns), Boston 1816 (from 3rd London edn), London 1816 (6th and 7th edns), 1818 (8th and 9th edns), Boston 1820, London 1822 (10th and 11th edns), 1826 (12th edn), Boston 1826, London 1830 (13th edn), Boston 1837 (as The wife at home), London 1848 (as Hints on the duties of a wife).
REVIEWS: GM Jan 1815, Eclectic Rev July 1815, Evangelical Mag July 1815, Monthly Rev July 1815.

The present of a mistress to a young servant: consisting of friendly advice and real histories. 1816, Philadelphia 1816, London 1816 (2nd–4th edns), 1819 (5th and 6th edns), 1822 (8th edn), 1830 (10th edn), 1832 ('10th edn'), 1835 (11th edn), 1851 (new edn, re-written by Emma Roberts). Some illustr Taylors.

Reciprocal duties of parents and children. 1818, 1818, 1819, Philadelphia 1819, London 1820, Boston 1825 (adds 2 extracts from pbns of Mrs Ann Taylor and Jane Taylor), 1827.
REVIEWS: Eclectic Rev Apr 1819, Monthly Rev Nov 1819, GM Dec suppl 1819.

The family mansion. A tale. 1819, 1820 (2nd–4th edns), Philadelphia 1820 (3 edns), London 1827 (5th edn), 1830 ('5th edn').
REVIEWS: NMM Feb 1820, Eclectic Rev Apr 1820.

Retrospection: a tale. 1821, 1822, Boston 1822, Philadelphia 1822, 1823 (3rd and 4th edns), 1830 ('4th edn').
REVIEWS: GM Nov 1821, Eclectic Rev Mar 1822, Monthly Rev Apr 1822.

The itinerary of a traveller in the wilderness; addressed to those who are performing the same journey. (Moral essays.) 1825 (3 edns), New York 1825, Boston 1825.
REVIEWS: Evangelical Mag May 1825, GM June 1825, Eclectic Rev July 1825.

The hymn 'Calvary' signed 'Anne' in Youth's Mag *1812, was ascribed to Mrs Ann Taylor some 50 years later. Two poems, 'On the death of a wasp' and 'The golden day', by [Mrs] Ann Taylor were inscribed in her daughter Ann's ms album, later pbd as Ann Taylor Gilbert's* Album. *New York 1978.*

Collaborative works

For Correspondence between a mother and her daughter at school, *by Mrs Ann Taylor and Jane Taylor, see The Taylors of Ongar, Collaborative works, above.* [CDS]

Ann Taylor, later Gilbert 1782–1866

Some 200 letters at Nottinghamshire Archives; miscellaneous poems and letters and her Album *in the Osborne Collection, Toronto;* Commonplace book *at Alexander Turnbull Lib, New Zealand.*

§1

The wedding among the flowers. '1808' [1809]. Pbd as 'By one of the authors of Original poems etc'. Rptd in Original poems, ed E. V. Lucas [1903]. Illustr Taylors. Unpbd corrections by author for 2nd edn in BL.
REVIEW: Literary Panorama May 1809.

Hymns for infant schools, partly original and partly selected. 1827, 1828 (stereotyped edn), 1830. 9 new hymns by Ann Taylor Gilbert, with selections from Hymns for infant minds (from text of 4th edn 1811) and Original hymns for Sunday schools (from text of 4th edn, 1816). 6th edn 1852 advertised but no known copies. Tr Rus 1831.
REVIEW: Evangelical Mag Feb 1828.

Original anniversary hymns [for] Sunday schools. 1827.
REVIEW: Eclectic Rev Mar 1828.

The convalescent. 12 letters on recovery from sickness. 1839. 2nd edn 1840 advertised but no known copies.
REVIEWS: Evangelical Mag June 1839; Eclectic Rev Nov 1839.

Seven blessings for little children. 1844, 1846 (2nd edn). (Poems on the Beatitudes.) 1858 edn advertised but no known copies.
REVIEW: Scottish Congregational Mag Sep 1844.

A biographical sketch of the Rev Joseph Gilbert. 1853.
REVIEW: Eclectic Rev Sep 1853.

Autobiography and other memorials of Mrs Gilbert (formerly Ann Taylor). Ed Josiah Gilbert 2 vols 1874, 1876 (2nd edn), 1878 (3rd, 1st 1-vol edn), 1879, 1888 (5th edn). Illustr Taylors.
REVIEW: Nation 13 May 1875.

Collaborative works

For Ann's contributions to The new cries of London *(1803),* Original poems *(1804–5),* Rural scenes *(1805),* City scenes *(1806),* Rhymes for the nursery *(1806),* Limed twigs *(1808),* Signor Topsy-Turvey's wonderful magic lantern *(1810),* The associate minstrels *(1810),* Hymns for infant minds *(1810),* The mother's fables *(1812),* Original hymns for Sunday schools *(1812),* The linnet's life *(1822), see The Taylors of Ongar, Collaborative works, above.*

Contributions to books

The associate minstrels. Ed Josiah Conder 1810. 10 poems.

Taylor, Mrs Ann. Maternal solicitude. 1814. Advertisement by a mother.

The chimney-sweeper's friend. J. Montgomery, comp, illustr Cruikshank. 1824. The stolen child.

The Amulet. 1826. The life of man.

Poetic gleanings, from modern writers. Ed A. Waspe Knight. 1827. To a sister on her birthday (rev).

Hymns to be sung at the opening of the new Nether Chapel, Sheffield. 1828. 2 hymns.

The missionary: or Christian's new year gift. Ed W. Ellis, illustr G. Baxter [1833]. 2 poems.

The bow in the cloud; or the negro's memorial. Ed M. A. Rawson. 1834. 3 poems.

Sketches from a youthful circle. New edn [1835]. Preface.

The congregational hymn book. [1836.] 1 hymn, 'Thou who didst for Peter's faith'.

Letters on . . . Dr Knight's lecture on . . . intemperance. 1836. Letter I. By a Rustic Rambler.

Original hymns... by various authors. Ed John Leifchild 1842. 101 hymns.
[Gilbert, Caroline.] A child's walk through the year. 1858. Preface.
The family pen. Ed Canon Isaac Taylor 2 vols 1867. Poem 'Lines addressed to her brother Isaac'.
Autobiography and other memorials of Mrs Gilbert. Ed Josiah Gilbert 2 vols 1874. Poems, verses and prose writings.

Contributions to periodicals

The Minor's Pocket Book. 1799, 1800, 1803, 1804, 1805, 1806, 1809, 1810, 1811, 1813, 1814, 1828. Verse solutions to enigmas, charades, rebuses and other poems signed 'A', 'Anna', 'Clara', 'Emmeline', 'Eugenia', 'Juvenilia', 'Maria'.
The Eclectic Review. 1812–15. Reviews of Self-control, by Mary Brunton (June 1812); Tales of fashionable life, by Maria Edgeworth (Oct 1812); Christian morals, by Hannah More (June 1813); Popular essays, by Elizabeth Hamilton (July 1814); Memoirs of Mrs Harriet Newell (Dec 1815).
The Sheffield Iris. 8 Nov 1836. Letter from a Rustic Rambler rptd in Letters on Dr Knight's lecture, 1836.
London University College Magazine. [1848.] Poem 'Song of the tea kettle' (later rptd in Autobiography, 1874).
The Sunday School Magazine. 1848. Sixty years ago (recollections of country Sundays and the Sunday school started by Rev Isaac Taylor in 1790).

Published letters, diaries, notebooks

Gilbert, Ann. Autobiography, and other memorials. 2 vols 1874. Letters passim.
Ann Taylor Gilbert's Album [1813–1936]. Introd and biographical notes by C. D. Stewart, photo facs New York 1978. [CDS]

Jane Taylor 1783–1824

Unpbd letters, poems and drawings at Suffolk Record Office, Bury St Edmunds and at the Guildhall, London. A few letters in the Osborne Collection, Toronto. The ms of her first attempt at a novel now missing (Osborne holds a photographed copy). A transcription pbd in BC 26 Spring 1977.

Collections and selections

Memoirs and poetical remains of the late Jane Taylor, with extracts from her correspondence. 2 vols 1825. Illustr Taylors. *See* full entry under Isaac Taylor jr, *below*.
Scenes of early life, Boston 1831. 10 pieces from The contributions of Q. Q.
Bible thoughts for the young. Illustr Abel Bowen, Boston 1831. 12 pieces from The contributions of Q. Q.
The writings of Jane Taylor. 5 vols Boston 1832. First collected edn. Contains Memoirs, correspondence and poetical remains; The contributions of Q. Q.; Display; Essays in rhyme; Correspondence between a mother and her daughter at school; Original poems ('by the Taylor family').
The pleasures of taste, and other stories. Ed Sarah J. Hale, Boston 1839 (The School Lib Jnl ser, 2). 35 pieces from The contributions of Q. Q.; 7 letters from Correspondence between a mother and her daughter at school.
Waste not, want not, and other stories by Maria Edgeworth, Jane Taylor and Mrs Barbauld. Ed with introd and notes by Michael V. O'Shea, Boston [1901] (Heath's Home and School Classics, 20). 'The discontented pendulum' and 'The philosopher's scales' from The contributions of Q. Q.
Jane Taylor, prose and poetry. Ed with introd by Florence V. Barry 1925 (Oxford Misc ser). 15 letters from rev edn of Memoirs and correspondence in The family pen; 17 poems from 4th edn Original poems; 4 poems from 1845 edn of Rhymes for the nursery; 14 extracts from Display; 7 poems from Essays in rhyme; 12 pieces from The contributions of Q. Q.
See also The Taylors of Ongar, Collections and selections, above.

§1

Display. A tale for young people. 1815, 1815 (2nd edn corrected), Boston 1815, London 1815 (3rd edn), 1816 (4th and 5th edns), 1817–20 (6th–9th edns), 1823 (10th and 11th edns), Boston nd [1828] (as Elizabeth Palmer), London 1829 (12th edn), 1832 (13th edn), 1840 (14th edn), 1848 (no known copies); nd [c. 1865], nd [c. 1873] (new edn). Tr Fr 1823 (as Elizabeth et Emilie).
REVIEWS: Literary Panorama June 1815, Br Critic July 1815, Eclectic Rev July 1815, Critical Rev Aug 1815, Evangelical Mag Oct 1815, GM Mar 1816, Monthly Rev Mar 1816.
Essays in rhyme, on morals and manners. 1816, Boston 1816, London 1816 (2nd edn corrected), 1817, 1820 (4th edn corrected), 1825 (5th edn), 1830 ('4th edn'), Boston 1832 (from 4th London edn), 1840 ('5th edn'). Edns of 1839, 1855, 1860, 1863 recorded, but no known copies.
REVIEWS: Eclectic Rev July 1816; Evangelical Mag Nov 1816; GM Nov 1816; Monthly Rev Apr 1817.
The poem 'The studious mechanic' included in Poetic gems, nd [c. 1840].
The poem 'Recreation', from 4th edn 1820, illustr Charles Edward Brock and pbd in Sphere 24 Nov 1924 as 'Scandal in the Duke of Brunswick's days: Recreation'.
The contributions of Q. Q. to a periodical work [Youth's Mag]: with some pieces not before published. 2 vols 1824, 1826 (2nd edn), New York 1826, 1827, London 1829–31 (4th–6th edns), 1834 (7th edn), Boston 1835 (from 5th London edn), London 1838 (new edn, 1st 1-vol edn), 1840 (new edn), 1845 (10th edn), New York 1847, 1850 (1st illus edn by Alfred Cornelius Howland), London 1851 (11th edn), 1855 (12th edn), 1866 (13th edn, rev preface), New York 1882 (as A day's pleasure, illustr Howland). Preface to 1st edn and rev preface to 1866 edn by Isaac Taylor jr. Many printings of individual pieces from Q. Q. including Francis' dream, New York nd [c. 1827]; I can do without it, Philadelphia nd [1830]; Busy idleness, New York 1832; A day's pleasure etc, New York 1833; Lucy's wishes, New York 1836; The discontented pendulum, nd [c. 1855]; How it strikes a stranger, nd [c. 1882].
REVIEWS: Eclectic Rev Nov 1824, Evangelical Mag Jan 1825, GM Dec 1826.

Collaborative works

For Jane's contributions to The new cries of London *(1803)*, Original poems *(1804–5)*, Rural scenes *(1805)*, City scenes *(1806)*, Rhymes for the nursery *(1806)*, Limed twigs *(1808)*, Signor Topsy-Turvey's wonderful magic lantern *(1810)*, Hymns for infant minds *(1810)*, The associate minstrels *(1810)*, The mother's fables *(1812)*, Original hymns for Sunday schools *(1812)*, Correspondence between a mother and her daughter *(1817)*, The linnet's life *(1822)*, *see The Taylors of Ongar, Collaborative works, above.*

Contributions to books

The associate minstrels. Ed Josiah Conder 1810. 10 poems.
Ann Taylor Gilbert's Album [1813–1936]. Photo facs New York 1978. A watercolour, a pencil drawing and a poem.
Taylor, Jefferys. Harry's holiday. 1818. Preface.
Chisman, Sarah. A mother's journal, during the last illness of her daughter. 1820. Preface.
Taylor, Isaac [jr]. Memoirs and poetical remains... of Jane Taylor. 2 vols 1825. Prev unpbd poems and correspondence.
Gilbert, Ann Taylor. Autobiography and other memorials. 2 vols 1874. Prev unpbd poem.

Contributions to periodicals

The Minor's Pocket Book, 1804, 1807, 1809, 1810, 1811, 1812, 1813, 1814. Verse solutions to enigmas, charades, and other poems and verses signed 'Eliza', 'J.' and 'J.T.'.
The Youth's Magazine. 1816, 1817–22, 1824. Stories and prose pieces under pseud Q. Q., later collected (with 1 exception) in The contri-

butions of Q. Q. to a periodical work, 2 vols 1824. 1 piece, 'Personal religion', pbd separately [c. 1868] in Hodder & Stoughton's Tracts for Today ser.

The Sheffield Iris. 21 Jan 1816 (a poem 'To Ami. In reply'), 16 July 1816 ('The squire's pew', a poem 1st pbd in Essays in rhyme, 1816).

Letters

Extracts from correspondence. In vol 2 of Isaac Taylor [jr], Memoirs and poetical remains . . . of the late Jane Taylor, 2 vols 1825. New, rev and enlarged edn. In vol 1 of The family pen, 2 vols 1867.

§2

Taylor, Isaac [jr]. Memoirs . . . of the late Jane Taylor. Vol 1 of Memoirs and poetical remains . . ., 2 vols 1825.

Annual biography and obituary for the year 1827.

Elwood, Anne K. Memoirs of the literary ladies of England. 2 vols 1843.

Knights, Helen C. Jane Taylor: her life and letters. 1880.

Walford, L. B. Four biographies from 'Blackwood'. Edinburgh 1888.

Roberts, R. Ellis. 'Another Jane'. New Statesman 1 May 1926.

Kirkman, M. C. 'A half-forgotten singer'. English Churchman and St James's Chron Suppl 5005, 1 Dec 1938.

'Another Jane' [transcription with notes of ms The adventures of Don Floris in Spain, and Cecilia]. BC 26 Spring 1977. Original ms now missing, photographed copy held by Osborne Collection, Toronto.

Kestner, J. Everyone knows her rhyme, but who remembers Jane? Smithsonian 14, 7, 1983. Illus. [CDS]

Isaac Taylor jr, later of Stanford Rivers 1787–1865

Unpbd letters, a diary (1793–1836), sketch book, many drawings and engravings and portrait silhouettes at Suffolk Record Office, Bury St Edmunds. Several drawings in Ann Taylor Gilbert's Album *in the Osborne Collection, Toronto.*

§1

Incidents of childhood. 1821, 1822. Pbd anonymously; claimed by Isaac jr. 2 of these stories rptd in The family pen 1867, 1 ascribed to Jemima (Taylor) Herbert. Illustr Taylors.
REVIEW: Eclectic Rev Dec 1821.

Elements of thought; or first lessons in the knowledge of the mind. 1822, 1824, 1833 (new edn), 1834–46 (6 edns), New York 1851 (no known copies), 1851 (2nd Amer edn from 9th London edn), London 1853 (10th edn), 1857 (new edn, re-written as The world of mind), New York 1858 (as The world of mind), London 1866 (11th edn), 1870 (12th edn), 1881 (13th edn).
REVIEWS: Monthly Rev July 1822, GM Aug 1825, Athenaeum Feb 1858 (World of mind).

Memoirs and poetical remains of the late Jane Taylor: with extracts from her correspondence. 2 vols 1825, 2 vols 1826, Boston 1826 (1 vol), Philadelphia 1827 (1 vol), 1828 (2 vols), Lowell MA 1829 (2 vols), London 1831 (new edn, 1 vol), Boston 1832 (1 vol), 1833 (1 vol), London 1841 (4th edn, 1 vol), 1845 (no known copies), 1867 (rev edn as Memoirs and correspondence of Jane Taylor in The family pen, vol 1). Illustr Taylors.
REVIEWS: Monthly Rev Jan 1826; Evangelical Mag Jan 1826; Eclectic Rev Feb 1826; Christian Examiner 3 and 6, 1826; Christian Monthly Spectator 8 1826; US Rev and Literary Gazette 1 1827.

Individual works after 1825 (first editions only)

The history of the transmission of ancient books to modern times. 1827.

The process of historical proof. 1828.

Herodotus, tr from the Greek . . . with . . . notes. 1829.

A new model of Christian missions. 1829.

The natural history of enthusiasm. 1829.

The temple of Melekartha. 3 vols 1831. A novel.

Saturday evening. 1832.

Fanaticism. 1833.

Spiritual despotism. 1835.

Physical theory of another life. 1836.

Home education. 1838.

Ancient Christianity and the doctrine of the Oxford Tracts for the Times. 2 vols 1839.

Man responsible for his dispositions, opinions and conduct. 1840.

Four lectures on spiritual Christianity. 1841.

Two letters on the Scottish church. 1843.

Loyola and Jesuitism in its rudiments. 1849.

Wesley and Methodism. 1851.

The restoration of belief. 3 pts. 1852–5.

The world of mind. 1857. A rewriting of Elements of thought, 1822.

Logic in theology. 1859.

Ultimate civilization. 1860.

The spirit of Hebrew poetry. 1861.

Lectures delivered before the Young Men's Christian Association in Exeter Hall, from November 1861 to February 1862.

Considerations on the Pentateuch. 1863.

Collaborative works

For Isaac jr's contributions to The new cries of London *(1803)*, Original poems *(1804–5)*, Rural scenes *(1805)*, City scenes *(1806)*, Signor Topsy-Turvey's wonderful magic lantern *(1810)*, Hymns for infant minds *(1810)*, The mother's fables *(1812)*, Original hymns for Sunday schools *(1812)*, The linnet's life *(1822)*, *see The Taylors of Ongar, Collaborative works, above.*

Contributions to books and periodicals

The minor's pocket book. 1803 (poem 'Consumption' signed 'Imus'), 1807 (verse Charade I signed 'I.T.').

Ann Taylor Gilbert's Album [1813–1936]. Photo facs New York 1978.

The Eclectic Review. Mar, Apr, May 1819. Review of Mme de Staël's Considerations sur . . . la Révolution Française, Jan 1820; review of Washington Irving's Sketchbook of Geoffrey Crayon, gent. Other unsigned reviews July 1817, May 1818, Oct 1818, May 1820, Jan 1821.

Taylor, Jane. The contributions of Q. Q. to a periodical work. 2 vols 1824. Preface.

Memoirs and poetical remains . . . of the late Jane Taylor. 2 vols 1825. Preface.

Contributions to books and periodicals

Isaac of Stanford Rivers contributed to a number of books, including The Imperial dictionary of universal biography *[18—?] (11 entries); Jonathan Edwards,* An inquiry into . . . freedom of will, *1831 (introd);* The missionary, *1833 ('A Sunshine prospect'); Thomas Ragg,* The deity, *1834 (introd); Blaise Pascal,* Thoughts on religion and philosophy, *1838 (introd); Gustavus Pfizer,* Life of Luther, *tr J. S. Williams 1840 (introd); Mrs Henry van Hagen,* Evenings in the land of Uz, *1843 (introd); William Nevins,* Thoughts on Popery, *1843 (rev);* Josephus, *tr Robert Traill 1847 (ed); Jefferys Taylor,* The family bible *1853 (preface);* The Jewish war of Flavius Josephus, *new tr by Robert Traill 1862 (ed with notes); Jane Taylor,* The contributions of Q. Q. *13th edn 1866 (new preface).*
His main contributions to periodicals were for Eclectic Rev; North Br Rev *and* Edinburgh Rev. *See* Wellesley *vol 5; see also* Good Words *1864 (Personal recollections).*

§2

Obituaries: Illus London News 12 Aug 1865; GM Sep 1865.

Fraser, James. The literary life of Isaac Taylor. In Macmillan's Mag Oct 1865.

Isaac Taylor. Leisure Hour 6 Apr 1867 (3 pts).

Taylor, Henry. The historian of enthusiasm. In James Stephen, Essays in ecclesiastical biography vol 2, 1868 (rptd with corrections and addns from Edinburgh Rev 143).

Gilbert, Josiah. Isaac Taylor. Expositor 3rd ser 2, Aug 1885. [CDS]

Jefferys Taylor 1792–1853

Unpbd poems, letters and sketches at Suffolk Record Office, Bury St Edmunds. Contributions to Ann Taylor Gilbert's Album *in the Osborne Collection, Toronto.*

§1

Harry's holiday; or the doings of one who had nothing to do. Preface by Jane Taylor. 1818, 1819, 1822, [1851] (new edn, rev, The Favourite Lib vol 7), nd [c. 1856] (reprint of Favourite Lib edn pbd with 2 other works in Tales for Boys ser), 1862 (advertised as Favourite Lib ser 11, Tales for Boys 4; no known copies), 1880 (no known copies). Some illustr Taylors.

Aesop in rhyme, with some originals ... [and] an engraving to each fable. 1820, 1823 (2nd edn, corrected); New Haven CT 1824 (a selection as Fables in rhyme); Boston nd [c. 1826], London 1828, 1834 (no known copies), 1844 (4th edn), 1846 (no known copies), nd [c. 1857] (5th edn). Some illustr Taylors. 4 of the original fables rptd in Appendix IV of E. V. Lucas edn of Original poems [1905].
REVIEWS: Eclectic Rev Aug 1821; GM Nov 1821; Monthly Rev Mar 1822.

Ralph Richards, the miser. (A tale.) 1821. Rptd in The family pen, 1867. Illustr Taylors.

Tales and dialogues, in prose and verse. 1822 (no known copies), 1822 (2nd edn), 1825 (new edn). The narrative poem 'The tolling bell' rptd in The family pen, 1867. Illustr Taylors.

The little historians: a new chronicle of the affairs of England ... in Church and State. 3 vols 1824. Illustr Taylors.
REVIEW: GM May 1824.

Parlour commentaries on the Constitution and laws of England. '1825' (1826). Illustr Taylors.

Old English sayings newly expounded, in prose and verse. 1827. Illustr Taylors.

The barn and the steeple. 1828. Argument between the Dissenting and Established Churches.
REVIEW: Eclectic Rev May 1828.

The forest; or, rambles in the woodland. 1831 (Little Lib [3]), 1832 (2nd edn, enlarged with additional illustrations), New York 1832, London 1835 (3rd edn). Some illustr Taylors.

The farm: a new account of rural toils and produce. 1832 (Little Lib [8]), 1834, Boston 1834 (Peter Parley's Little Lib 5, rev), New York 1834 (new frontispiece), 1837, Philadelphia 1841, 1854. Some illustr Taylors.

A new description of the earth; considered chiefly as a residence for man. 1832, nd [c. 1840]. Illustr Taylors.

A month in London; or, some of its modern wonders described. 1832. Sold plain and coloured.

The ocean: a description of wonders and important products of the sea. 1833 (Little Lib [12]), New York nd [c. 1833–4], London 1835 (enlarged and with additional illustrations). Pbd anonymously, but poem at end signed Jefferys Taylor, and 2nd edn of The forest (1832) attributes to Jefferys a work called Wonders of the ocean.

The young islanders. A tale of the last century. 1842, New York 1842 (with additional illustrations), London 1844 (new edn), 1848 (no known copies), 1849 (new edn), New York 1854 (sub-titled The school-boy Crusoes), London nd [1855] (Run and Read Lib [54], sub-titled And what came of their adventures; A 'Yellow-back'), Boston 1861–3 (3 edns), Philadelphia 1876, New York 1881, nd [c. 1884–9] (titled Boy Crusoes) (a Robinsonnade).
REVIEW: Eclectic Rev May 1842.

Cottage traditions: or the peasant's tale of ancestry. 1842, 1843 (with title The peasant's tale; bound with James Strickland's Edward Evelyn, but separately paginated), 1848 (with title The peasant's tale; bound with Edward Evelyn, but normal pagination through both titles).

Incidents of the Apostolic age in Britain. [A tale.] 1844.

A glance at the globe, and at the worlds around us. 1848, nd [c. 1857].

The family bible newly opened; with Uncle Goodwin's account of it. 1853. Preface by Isaac Taylor of Stanford Rivers. Frontispiece engr by Mason Jackson after Sir John Gilbert.
REVIEW: Eclectic Rev May 1853.

Jefferys may be the author of the 6 poems signed 'Edward Lambe' in the 1806 Minor's pocket book.

Contributions to books

Three poems and 5 drawings from his sketchbook in Ann Taylor Gilbert's ms Album, *photo facs edn New York 1978.* [CDS]

Emily Taylor 1795–1872

The vision of Las Casas and other poems. 1825. 1845.

Poetical illustrations of passages of scripture. Wellington, Salop and London 1826.

Sabbath recreations, or select poetry of a religious kind ... with original pieces. Ed Taylor, London and Wellington, Salop 1829 (2 edns); Boston 1829; London 1835; Boston 1839.

Lays for the sabbath: a collection of religious poetry. Ed Taylor, Boston 1846, 1850, 1860.

Flowers and fruit gathered by loving hands from old English gardens. Ed Taylor 1864.

Wrote numerous prose works for children.

George Taylor, of the Bank of England fl. 1805–21

An elegy on the ... death of ... Nelson .... 1805.

The tears of the muses on the death of Fox .... Snowhill [1806].

The flower of Brunswick: an elegy. 1817.

The mental claims of the sexes, with other poems. 1821.

John Taylor 1757–1832

§1

Verses on various occasions. 1795. Anon.

Monsieur Tonson: a tale. Glasgow [1796], [1798?] (in Poetry, original and selected); London 1810 (anon, as Monsieur Tonson: a new version), 1813; Philadelphia [1820?]; London 1823, 1830 (2 edns, illustr Cruikshank), 1831, [1850?].

Frank Hayman: a tale. 1798. Single sheet.

The Caledonian comet. 1810. Anon.

Poems on several occasions .... Edinburgh 1811.

Poems on various subjects. 2 vols 1827.

Plays and dramas, original and translated from the Greek and Italian. Worcester 1830 (priv ptd).

§2

Records of my life. 2 vols 1832; New York 1833; ed R. H. Stoddard, London [c. 1874] (selections from).

William Taylor 1765–1836

Lessing, G. E. Nathan the wise: a dramatic poem .... Tr Taylor, Norwich 1791; London 1805 (printed in Norwich 1791); Leipzig and New York 1868 (in Collection of German Authors vol 9); ed H. Morley 1886.

Goethe. Iphigenia in Tauris. Tr Taylor, Norwich 1793; Berlin 1794.

Author of memoirs, an edn of Sayers, a history of German poetry (3 vols 1828–30), a book on English synonyms, and of individual poems pbd in jnls.

Laura Sophia Temple 1763–after 1820

Poems. 1805.

Lyric and other poems. London and Bristol 1808.

The siege of Zaragoza and other poems. 1812.

James Templeman fl. 1808–10

Alcander and Lavinia: a metrical romance.... 1808, 1809 (anon, as The mysterious shreik, or Alcander and Lavinia), 1810.
Gilbert, or the young carrier: an amatory rural poem. 1808, 1809 (2 pts, the 2nd as Gilbert, or true love rewarded ...). Anon.
Metrical tales and romances, in verse.... 1809.

William Tennant 1784–1848

Collections
Miles 2.
The comic poems. Ed A. Scott and M. Lindsay, Edinburgh 1989.

§1

Anster fair: a poem in six cantos. Edinburgh 1812 (anon), 1814 (other poems added); Baltimore 1815; Boston 1815; Edinburgh 1815, 1816 (attributed); Edinburgh and London 1821, 1838 (with memoir), 1871; Edinburgh 1877.
Elegy on trottin' Nanny. Cupar 1814. Anon.
The dominie's disaster and other poems. Cupar 1816. Anon.
The thane of Fife: a poem in six cantos. Edinburgh 1822.
Cardinal Beaton: a drama in five acts. Edinburgh 1823.
John Baliol: an historical drama. Edinburgh 1825.
Papistry storm'd, or the dingin' down o' the cathedral: ane poem in sax sangs. By M. W. T. Edinburgh 1827; ed J. Thomson, Glasgow 1905.
Critical remarks on the psalms of David. Edinburgh 1830; London 1836. Rptd from Edinburgh Literary Jnl. With J. Hogg.
Hebrew dramas, founded on incidents of Bible-history. Edinburgh 1845.

§2

Conolly, M. F. Memoir of the life and writings. [1861.]
Also wrote on Chaldaic and Syriac grammar and edited the poems of A. Ramsay.

Charles Hughes Terrot 1790–1872

Hezekiah and Sennacherib: a poem. Cambridge 1816.
Common sense: a poem. Edinburgh and London 1819. Anon.
Author of a number of sermons and other ecclesiastical prose.

John Thelwall, also 'John Beaufort' and 'Sylvanus Theophrastus' 1764–1834

Collection
The politics of English jacobinism: writings. Ed G. Claeys, Univ Park PA [1995?].

§1

Orlando and Almeyda: a legendary tale. 1787.
Poems on various subjects. 2 vols 1787.
A speech in rhyme. 1788.
Ode to science. 1791.
The peripatetic. By 'Sylvanus Theophrastus'. 3 vols 1793. Anon. Prose.
John Gilpin's ghost, or the warning voice of King Chanticleer: an historical ballad ... dedicated to the treason-hunters of Oakham. 1795.
Poems written in close confinement in the Tower and Newgate upon a charge of treason. 1795.
The daughter of adoption: a tale of modern times. By 'John Beaufort'. 4 vols 1801. Anon. Prose.
Poems chiefly written in retirement – The fairy of the lake: a dramatic romance; Effusions of relative and social feeling; and specimens of The hope of Albion, or Edwin of Northumbria: an epic poem; with memoir of the life of the author and notes and illustrations of runic mythology. Hereford 1801 (2 edns), 1802, [1805?]; Oxford 1989 (reprint of 1801).
The black bowl, Feb 3 1208, or tears of Eboracum: an old monkish legend. York 1802.
The trident of Albion: an epic effusion. Liverpool 1805.
A monody occasioned by the death of the Right Hon C. J. Fox. 1806 (anon), 1806 (as Monody on ... Fox, authorship acknowledged).
Ode addressed to the energies of Britain in behalf of the Spanish patriots. 1808.
The poetical recreations of the Champion and his literary correspondents, with a selection of essays, literary and critical which have appeared in the Champion newspaper. Ed Thelwall 1822. Includes poems by the Lambs.
Thelwall to Hardy. TLS 19 June 1953. Extracts from correspondence.
Thelwall also pbd many miscellaneous lectures and tracts, mainly on elocution and political subjects. He was editor of Biographical & Imperial Mag *(1789–92),* Champion *(1818–21) and* Monthly Mag *(1824).*

§2

Mrs Thelwall. The life. 1837.

William Thom, of Inverury 1789–1848

Collections
Rogers 3.
Miles 3.
Aberdeen awa' rhymes. 1916. By Thom, W. Anderson and others.

§1

Envy at arms! Or caloric.... Edinburgh 1805 (2 edns). Anon (authorship uncertain).
Rhymes and recollections of a hand loom weaver. London and Aberdeen 1844; London 1845 (enlarged), 1847; ed W. Skinner, Paisley 1880.

§2

Kennedy, J. P. Some passages in the life of W. Thom. 1846.
Bruce, R. W. Thom, the Inverurie poet: a new look. Aberdeen 1970.

William Gill Thompson 1796–1844

The coral wreath, or the spell-bound knight, with other poems. Newcastle 1821.
Erminia: a poem. 1821.
An address delivered in the loyal Northumbrian social society. Newcastle 1822.
Lines on the death of Lord Byron. Newcastle 1824.
A poetical address, delivered at the ... Burns club Jan. 26 1824. Newcastle 1824.
The Tyne fisher's farewell to his favourite stream. Newcastle 1824; London 1836, 1842. Anon.
A poetical address delivered at the ... Burns club Jan. 31 1825. Newcastle 1825.
Sketches in the picture gallery of Newcastle. Newcastle 1827.
Sketches in prose. Newcastle 1829.
The widow's son of Nain and other poems. Newcastle 1829.
Love in the country, or the vengeful miller: a rustic drama. Newcastle 1831. Prose.
The outcast of the storm: a poem. Newcastle 1831.
A tribute to the memory of ... J. Losh. Newcastle 1833.
Editor of Fisher's Garland *(1822, 1831, 1834, 1838–40).*

James Thomson, of Kenleith 1763–1832

Poems in the Scottish dialect. Edinburgh 1801; Leith 1819; ed R. B. Langwill, London 1894.
To the memory of ... T. Craig. Edinburgh 1814.

Poems chiefly in the Scottish dialect, on raising and selling the dead. Leith 1821.

Romaine Joseph Thorn fl. 1793–1820

Clito and Delia: a poem. 1793.
Retirement: a poem. Bristol 1793.
Bristolia: a poem . . . . [1794.]
Howe triumphant! or the glorious first of June: an heroic poem. Bristol [1794].
Christmas: a poem. Bristol 1795.
Lodon and Miranda . . . . Bristol and London 1799.
Poems, very considerably enlarged . . . . Cork 1808.
The rhyme bag, or poetical depot . . . . Cork 1817.
Lorenzo: a tale. Bristol [1820].
The mad gallop, or a trip to Devizes . . . . Bristol [nd] (2nd edn).

Edward Thurlow, afterwards Hovell-Thurlow, 2nd Baron Thurlow 1781–1829

Collections

Select poems. Brussels 1816; Chiswick 1821 (priv ptd).
The sonnets of Edward Lord Thurlow. Brussels 1819 (priv ptd).
Poems on several occasions, An appendix . . . . Ed D. H. Reiman, New York and London 1978 (facs reprint of 1813).

§1

Sidney, Sir Philip. The defence of poesy. Ed Thurlow, with 5 original sonnets 1810.
Verses prefixed to The defence of poesy, the induction to an heroic poem, also verses dedicated to the Prince Regent. 1812. Anon.
Hermilda in Palestine . . . with other poems. 1812. Anon.
Poems on several occasions. 1813 (2 edns, the 2nd enlarged), 1822 ('2nd edn').
An appendix to Poems on several occasions: being a continuation of the Sylva. 1813.
Ariadne: a poem. 1814, 1822.
Carmen britannicum, or the song of Britain, written in honour of his Royal Highness George Augustus Frederick Prince Regent. 1814.
The doge's daughter . . . . 1814.
Moonlight; The doge's daughter; Ariadne; Carmen britannicum, or the song of Britain; Angelica, or the rape of Proteus. 1814.
Moonlight: a poem, with several copies of verses. 1814. A different collection.
Angelica, or the rape of Proteus: a poem. 1822.
Arcite and Palamon. After Chaucer. 1822 (2 edns, the 2nd as The knight's tale and The flower and the leaf).
The odes of Anacreon. Tr Thurlow 1822.
The flower and the leaf: after . . . Chaucer. 1825.

Mary Tighe, formerly Blachford 1772–1810

Collection

Keats and M. Tighe: the poems of M. Tighe. Ed E. V. Weller, New York 1928.

§1

Psyche, or the legend of love. 1805 (anon), 1811 (as Psyche, with other poems, authorship acknowledged, 2 edns), 1812; Philadelphia 1812; London 1816, 1843, 1844, 1853 (in trn of Apuleius by H. Gurney), 1876, 1889; ed D. Reiman, New York 1978 (facs reprint of 1805); Oxford 1992 (facs reprint of 1811).

§2

Mary: a series of reflections during twenty years. [Ed W. Tighe], Dublin 1811 (priv ptd). Verse and prose.
Henchy, P. The works of Mary Tighe: published and unpublished. Bibl Soc of Ireland Pbns 6 no 6 Dublin 1957.

William Tighe fl. 1802–12

The plants: a poem . . . . Cantos 1 and 2 London and Dublin 1808; cantos 3 and 4 London 1811, 4 cantos together 1812.

James G. Todd b. 1798

Poems and songs. Stirling and London 1818; Aberdeen 1826.
Strila, or the palace of strife . . . . Edinburgh and Cupar 1823, 1824 (with memoir).

William Edward Pretyman Tomline fl. 1804–7

Poema (ode graeca . . . graecia hodierna) . . . . Cambridge 1804.
Poema (ode graeca . . . in obitum . . . ducis d'Enghien). Cambridge 1805.
A speech on the character of . . . W. Pitt. Cambridge 1806 (2 edns); London 1807. Prose.

Charlotte Elizabeth Tonna, née Browne, formerly Phelan, also 'Charlotte Elizabeth' 1790–1846

Collections

The works of 'Charlotte Elizabeth'. Ed H. B. Stowe 3 vols New York 1844–5, 2 vols 1846–7 (5th edn), 1848, 1849 (7th edn), 1850, 1852.
Posthumous and other poems. By 'Charlotte Elizabeth'. 1846; New York 1847.
The minor poems of 'Charlotte Elizabeth'. Dublin [1848].

§1

The shepherd boy and the deluge. By 'Charlotte Elizabeth'. 1823.
Osric: a missionary tale, with The garden and other poems. By 'Charlotte Elizabeth'. Dublin, London, Edinburgh, Glasgow and Bristol [1825?]; London 1826; New York 1845 (4th edn), 1846, 1847, 1848, 1849, 1850, 1851, 1854.
Izram: a Mexican tale, and other poems. By 'Charlotte Elizabeth'. 1826; New York 1845, 1846, 1847, 1849, 1850, 1851, 1854.
A visit to St George's chapel. [1827].
Personal recollections. By 'Charlotte Elizabeth'. 1841, 1847 (3rd edn). Prose.
The convent bell and other poems. By 'Charlotte Elizabeth'. New York 1845, 1846.

§2

Balfour, C. L. A sketch of 'Charlotte Elizabeth'. 1854.
See also col 1413.

Thomas Tovey fl. 1803–18

Things as they were . . .: a poem. Gloucester 1803.
Cheltea: a descriptive poem . . . . Cheltenham and Stroud 1818.
An earnest address to all ranks of people. Cheltenham and Stroud 1828. Prose.

George Townsend 1788–1857

Poems. London and Cambridge 1810.
Armageddon: a poem . . . . Ely 1814 (anon); London 1815 (acknowledged), 1817.
Illustrations of the 'Pilgrim's progress' . . . from designs by T. Stothard, with descriptive sonnets by G. Townsend. 1840.
Flowers from the garden of the church, or the collects . . . versified. By a Durham theological student [G. T.]. 1854 (2 edns). Anon.
Sermons and other prose pbns on church topics.

Chauncy Hare Townshend 1798–1868

Jerusalem: a poem. [Cambridge] 1817, 1820; London 1828 (in Cambridge prize poems), 1859.
Poems. 1821.
The weaver's boy: a tale, and other poems. 1825 (2nd edn).
The reigning vice: a satirical essay.... 1827. Anon.
Philosophy in the fens, or talk on the times: a poem. By 'T. Greatly' [Townshend]. 1851. Anon.
Sermons in sonnets... with other poems. 1851, 1857.
The burning of the Amazon: a ballad-poem. 1852.
The three gates. 1859, 1861.
Also wrote on mesmerism and on Scottish topography.

Joseph Train 1779–1852

§1
The poetical reveries of.... 1806.
Strains of the mountain muse. Edinburgh 1814.

§2
Fitzhugh, R. T. The Train manuscript. Chapel Hill NC 1943 (in Robert Burns: his associates and contemporaries).

William Tremenheere fl. 1789–1821

Homer. The Iliad... Book I. Tr Tremenheere 1792.
An ode written upon the death and victory of Lord Viscount Nelson. 1805. Anon.
Verses on the victory of Trafalgar and the death and funeral of... Nelson. [1806.]
Author of numerous sermons 1789–1821.

Melesina Trench, formerly Chenevix, Mrs Richard 1768–1827

Collection
The remains. Ed [R. C. Trench] 1860, 1862, [1864]. Prose.

§1
Campaspe: an historical tale, and other poems. Southampton 1815. Anon.
Ellen: a ballad, founded on a recent fact, and other poems.... Bath 1815. Anon.
Laura's dream, or the moonlanders. 1816. Anon.
Aubrey, in five cantos. Southampton 1818. Anon.
A monody on the death of Mr Grattan. 1820.
Author of a book on education, of a jnl of a visit to Germany and contributor to the Leadbeater papers *(1862).*

Henry Tresham 1749?–1814

The sea-sick minstrel, or maritime sorrows. 1796. Anon.
Rome at the close of the eighteenth century!!!.... 1799.
Britannicus to Buonaparte: an heroic epistle.... 1803.
Recreation at Ramsgate: poetical effusions.... Ramsgate 1805.
A tributary lay to the memory of... Lansdowne. 1810.
The British gallery of pictures. 1818, 1820. With W. Y. Ottley.

Thomas Trotter, MD 1760–1832

Collection
The farmer's boy... The snow-storm. By Bloomfield, Trotter and others. Wilmington DE 1803.

§1
Suspiria oceani: a monody on the death of... Earl Howe.... 1800.
The noble foundling...: a tragedy.... 1812.
Sea weeds: poems written... during a naval life. Newcastle, London and Edinburgh 1829.
Also wrote on medical and maritime subjects in prose.

Elizabeth Tuck fl. 1821–3

The juvenile poetical moralist. Frome 1821.
Vallis vale and other poems. London, Bath and Frome 1823. Anon.

Elizabeth Turner c. 1774–1846

Collections
Cautionary stories, containing The daisy and cowslip. 1825 (anon); ed E. V. Lucas 1897 (as Mrs Turner's cautionary stories), 1898, 1902.
Short poems for young children. By the author of The pink. 1859.
Grandmamma's book of rhymes for children. Ed G. K. Chesterton 1927 (illustr M. R. Cooper).

§1
The daisy, or cautionary stories in verse. 1807; Philadelphia 1808; London 1810, 1812, 1814, 1816 (6th edn), 1823 (10th edn), [1840] (25th edn), [1842?] (26th edn); New York [1851]; London [1860?] (27th edn), 1885 (30th edn), [1885?] (31st edn), [1887?], 1899; Birmingham 1899; New York [1900]; London 1910 (illustr R. A. Hobson).
The cowslip, or more cautionary tales in verse. 1811, 1812; Philadelphia 1813; London 1814, 1815, 1817, 1820 (7th edn), 1822, 1824, 1825, [184–?], [1842] (22nd edn); New York 1851; London [1865?] (25th edn), [1885]; Birmingham 1899. Anon.
The pink: a flower in the juvenile garland, consisting of short poems. 1823, [1835?]. With M. Howitt.
The blue-bell, or tales and fables. Derby 1838.
The crocus. 1844. Anon.

Horace Twiss, also 'Horatius' 1787–1849

St Stephen's chapel: a satirical poem. By 'Horatius'. 1807. Anon.
Farewell address, spoken by Mrs Siddons. [1812.]
Posthumous parodies and other pieces.... 1814. Anon.
The Carib chief: a tragedy.... 1819 (3 edns); New York 1820.
Author of political and legal works.

James Usher, of Whitechapel fl. 1823–33

A new version of the psalms... Tr Usher 1823, 1827.
The dirge of Fauntleroy. [1824?] (2 edns).
A version of the messiah.... [1824] (in Hymns and religious poetry).
The odes of Anacreon. Tr Usher 1833.
Buonaparté, The royal exchange, Odes of Horace. 1842.

Anna Jane Vardill, later Niven 1781–1852

Poems and translations, from the minor Greek poets and others; written chiefly between the ages of ten and sixteen. By a lady. 1809 (2 edns), 1816. Anon.
The pleasures of human life: a poem. 1812.

David Vedder 1790–1854

Collections
Rogers.
Poems, lyrics and sketches. Ed G. Gilfillan, Kirkwall [1878].

§1
The covenanters' communion and other poems.... Edinburgh 1828.
Memoir of Sir W. Scott. Dundee 1832. Prose.

Orcadian sketches: legendary and lyrical pieces. Edinburgh and Dundee 1832.
Poems, legendary, lyrical and descriptive. Edinburgh 1842.
The pictorial giftbook, or lays and lithography.... Edinburgh 1848.
The story of Reynard the fox. Tr Vedder [1852] (illustr G. Canton), [1856], 1857.

Charles Verral fl. 1810–15

The pleasures of possession.... 1810.
Poems, including Servius Tullius.... [1815?].

John Vincent, curate of Constantine fl. 1809–12

Fowling: a poem (in five books).... 1808 (anon); Edinburgh 1812 (authorship acknowledged).
Also pbd a sermon in 1812.

Josiah Walker d. 1831

Monody on the death of John Thurlow Esq. Norwich 1782. Anon.
An ode... to... society... universal good-will. Norwich 1785.
The defence of order: a poem. Edinburgh 1803 (3 edns).
Poems by Burns.... Ed Walker 2 vols Edinburgh 1811.

William Sidney Walker 1795–1846

Collections

The poetical remains... with a memoir. Ed J. Moultrie, London and Rugby 1852.
Gustavus Vasa and The heroes of Waterloo. Ed D. H. Reiman, New York and London 1977 (facs reprints of 1813 and 1815).

§1

Gustavus Vasa and other poems. 1813 (2 edns).
The heroes of Waterloo: an ode. 1815.
The appeal of Poland: an ode. Cambridge 1816.
Poems from the Danish.... Tr Walker, Philadelphia 1816.
Shakespeare. Senarii graeci, praemio Porsoniano dignati. Tr Walker [scenes tr into Latin], [Cambridge] 1818.
Shakespeare's versification and its apparent irregularities explained. Ed [W. N. Lettsom] 1854. Prose.
A critical examination of the text of Shakespeare. Ed [W. N. Lettsom] 3 vols 1860. Prose.
Also edited Latin verse.

Catharine or Catherine George Ward, later Mason b. 1787

Poems. Edinburgh 1805; Coventry and London 1812.
Tales of the glen. London and Windsor 1813.
The Dandy family, or the pleasures of a ball night. 1815.
A tributary poem on the death of... Princess Charlotte. [1817.]
Maid, wife and mother, or women! A poem.... 1819.
Miscellaneous poems. 1820.
Author also of numerous novels.

Charlotte Wardle fl. 1814

St Aelian's, or the cursing well: a poem. 1814.
Norway: a poem (with Danish tr by N. H. Jaeger). London and Christiania [1814].

Mary Ann Wassell fl. 1815–59

The rivals, or the general investigation. 1815 (2 edns); Cheltenham 1859 (5th edn).

George Watson, later Watson-Taylor, also 'Sir J. Cheakill' d. 1841

England preserved: an historical play.... 1795 (2 edns), 1802, 1811 (in The Modern Theatre vol 8).
The old hag in a red cloak: a romance.... 1801, 1802 (in The school for satire). Anon.
Equanimity in death: a poem. 1813.
The cross-Bath guide.... Ed 'Sir J. Cheakill'. 1815. Anon.
The profligate: a comedy. 1820. Anon. Prose.
Poems written in English... By Charles, Duke of Orleans. Ed [Watson]. 1827.
Pieces of poetry, with two dramas. 2 vols Chiswick 1830. Anon. Verse and prose.

William Watt, of Islington 1793–1859

Comus and Cupid. Glasgow 1835; London 1844, 1860 (as Poems and songs).
Remarks on shooting... in familiar verse. London and Manchester 1835; London 1839.
The cosset lamb, Enigma, My home in the forest wide.... 1847.

Alaric Alexander Watts 1797–1864

§1

Poetical sketches, with stanzas for music. 1822 (priv ptd).
Poetical sketches, The profession, The broken heart... with stanzas for music and other poems. 1823, 1824 (3rd edn), 1828, 1843.
Scenes of life and shades of character. 2 vols 1831. With others. Prose.
Lyrics of the heart. 1851; New York 1852; Philadelphia 1853; Rugeley [1855?] (a selection, The sister of charity).

§2

Watts, A. Alfred. Alaric Watts: a narrative of his life. 2 vols 1864, 1884.
Also a few minor prose writings and numerous contributions to periodicals. Watts edited the following periodicals and annuals: Leeds Intelligencer *(1822–5);* Manchester Courier *(1825–6);* Literary Souvenir *(1825–35);* Cabinet of British Art *(1835–8) (continuation of* Souvenir, *above);* Poetical Album *(1825) and (1828–9);* United Services Gazette *(1833–47);* Men of the time *(1856).*

Susanna or Susannah Watts 1768–1842

Collection

Hymns and poems... with a few recollections of her life. Leicester 1842.

§1

Dodsley, R. Chinese maxims, translated from The oeconomy of human life into heroic verse, in seven parts. Tr Watts, Leicester 1784.
de' Medici, Lorenzo. Original poems and translations, particularly Ambra. Tr chiefly by Watts. London and Leicester 1802.
A walk through Leicester, being a guide.... 1804 (anon); Leicester 1820; Leicester and Brussels 1967 (attributed). Prose.
Elegy on the death of the Princess Charlotte Augusta of Wales. Leicester [1817?].
The selector. Ed Watts 1823.
The insects in council, addressed to entomologists, with other poems. London and Leicester 1828; London 1835.
The animals' friend... to inculcate kindness.... 1833. Prose.

Lewis Way 1772–1840

Poems. Stansted 1822 (priv ptd). Anon.
The withered chaplet from Villa Franca. [n.p. 1822.] Anon.

Palingenesia: the world to come. Paris and London 1824. Anon.
Author of memoirs, sermons and other religious pbns.

Cornelius Webbe, or Webb 1790?–1850?

§1

Sonnets, amatory, incidental and descriptive, with other poems. 1820 (priv ptd).

Summer, An invocation to sleep, Fairy revels and Songs and sonnets. 1821.

The posthumous papers, facetious and fanciful, of a person lately about town. 1828; New York 1828. Anon. (Dramatised in 182-? as Two eyes between two.) Prose.

Lyric leaves. 1832.

Glances at life in city and suburb. 1st ser 1836; ser 2, 1845; 1848 (both ser). Prose.

The man about town. 2 vols 1838; Philadelphia 1839; London 1841, 1857 (vol 2 as The absent man). Prose.

§2

Green, D. B. Four letters of Webbe. N & Q Jan 1958.

Margaretta Wedderburn fl. 1811–18

Mary Queen of Scots: an historical poem, with other miscellaneous pieces. Edinburgh, London and Glasgow 1811; London 1818.

George Weguelin b. 1766

The eccentric. 1829.

An olympic romance, entitled the whim of the brain . . . . 1830.

The poetical works . . . . 3rd ser 1832.

Charles Jeremiah Wells, also 'H. L. Howard' 1799?–1879

Collection

Miles 3.

§1

Dramas adapted for the representation of juvenile persons. By 'H. Howard'. 1820.

Joseph and his brethren: a dramatic poem. By 'H. L. Howard'. 1823, 1824; ed A. C. Swinburne 1876; London and New York 1908 (WC), [1913], 1918.

A dramatic scene. Ed H. B. Forman. In Literary anecdotes of the nineteenth century, ed W. R. Nicoll and T. J. Wise, vol 1 1895. Written c. 1876; intended for insertion in Joseph and his brethren, *above*.

Stories after nature. 1822 (anon); ed W. J. Linton 1891 (attributed). Prose.

§2

Forman, H. B. Concerning the friend who sent Keats some roses. [Boston 1913] (in Bibliophile Soc Twelfth year book).

Harriet West, Mrs John, formerly Atkinson 1789–1839

§1

Sacred poems for Sundays and holidays, throughout the year. 1833 (2 edns).

§2

West, J. Memoir of Mrs J. West. London and Blandford 1840; London 1842, 1866 (4th edn).

Thomas Whitby fl. 1819–20

The priory of Birkenhead: a tale. 1819.

Retrospection: a rural poem. 1820.

Samuel Whitchurch, of Bath fl. 1785–1816

A monody to the memory of Admiral Hyde Parker . . . . 1785.

The negro convert: a poem . . . . Bath 1785.

Elegy on the death of Mr Thomas Tuppen . . . . 1795.

Hispaniola: a poem . . . . Bath 1804.

Epistle to Mr Joseph Lancaster on . . . education. Bath and London [1810].

My mother. Southwark [1810]. Single sheet.

David Dreadnought, the reformed English sailor. Pt 1 Bath 1812, 1813 (complete in 4 pts as David Dreadnought, or nautic tales and adventures); London 1815.

The Sunday-school: a poem. 1816.

Henry Kirke White 1785–1806

Collections

The remains of Henry Kirke White, with an account of his life by R. Southey. 2 vols London, Cambridge and Nottingham 1807; London 1808 (2 edns), 1810, 1811; Philadelphia 1811; Boston 1813; London 1813; Boston 1815; New York 1815; London 1816, 1819; New York 1820; London 1821, Boston 1822; London 1822 (vol 3); Boston 1823; 2 vols London 1823 (contents of previous vol 3 included), 1 vol 1824, 1825, 4 vols 1825; Glasgow 1825, 1827, 1828; London 1828, 1830, 1831, 1834, 1836; Glasgow 1837, 1838; Cambridge 1839; Glasgow 1844; London 1850, 1855, 1913.

The beauties of White. Ed A. Howard [1823]; Boston 1826, 1827; Philadelphia 1829; Boston and Hartford CT [1830]; London, Glasgow and Dublin [1830?]; Hartford CT 1831, 1833, 1836.

Poetical remains; the prose remains. 2 vols 1824, 1831, 1848.

The poetical works and remains. 1824, 1837, 1840; Philadelphia 1844; London 1850, 1851, 1852, 1853, 1854, 1855; Edinburgh [1855]; New York 1855; Philadelphia 1855; New York 1856; New York and London 1857; London 1858, 1860; London and New York 1861; London 1864; London and New York 1867; New York 1869; Boston 1873; New York 1881, 1883, 1900.

The poetical remains. 1824, 1825, 1826, 1851 (in Cabinet edn).

The life and remains. 1825; London and Edinburgh 1825; London 1826, 1827, 1834, 1835, 1841, 1845, 1848, 1850; London and Edinburgh 1851; London 1852, [1870].

The complete works. Boston 1829; New York [1830?]; Boston 1831, 1837; New York 1849.

The poetical works of Rogers, Kirke White [et al]. Paris 1829.

The poetical works, with a memoir by Sir H. Nicolas. 1830 (Aldine edn vol 6), 1836, 1838 (Standard Lib), 1840, 1841, 1853; Boston and Cambridge MA 1854; Boston, New York and Philadelphia 1854; London 1857, 1859; Boston 1859; London 1860; Boston 1864, 1865; London 1866, [1867] (illustr B. Foster); Boston 1871; London [1871], 1898, 1907.

The works. 1835; Philadelphia 1842, 1844, 1846, 1848; London 1848; New York 1849; London 1850; New York 1851, 1853; Philadelphia 1856.

Memoir and poetical remains of Kirke White, also Melancholy hours. Ed J. Todd, Philadelphia 1844; Boston 1850, 1851, 1853, 1854; Boston, New York and Philadelphia 1854; Boston and New York 1855; Boston 1859, 1860, 1861; New York 1869.

Poems. New York 1851.

The poetical and prose works. Edinburgh [1855?]; Edinburgh and London [1881].

The life . . . with selections. 1856 (in Lib of Christian Biography vol 10).

The poetical works of Kirke White and James Grahame. Ed G. Gilfillan, Edinburgh 1855, 1856; New York 1856; Edinburgh 1868; London [1878] (Cassell's Lib).
The poetical works of Robert Bloomfield and Kirke White. 1871.
The poetical works. Ed H. K. Swann [1897?] (in The Canterbury Poets).
Miles 10 (11).
The poetical works of I. Watts and H. K. White. 2 vols Boston [1880].
Poems, letters and prose fragments. Ed J. Drinkwater [1907] (ML); London and New York [1922?].
Poems, hymns and prose writings. Ed R. T. Beckwith, Oxford 1985.

§1

Clifton Grove: a sketch in verse, with other poems. 1803.
[Uncollected poems and prose, ed T. O. Mabbott.] N & Q 7 Sep 1940, 13 Jan 1945, 15 June, 2 Nov 1946, 4 Sep 1948.
Mabbott, T. O. Letters of Kirke White. N & Q 16 Nov 1946.

John Whitehouse 1756?–1824

Poems, consisting chiefly of original pieces .... 1787.
Odes moral and descriptive .... 1794.
An elegiac ode to the memory of ... Reynolds .... 1792.
Stolberg, F. L. Hymn to the earth. Tr Whitehouse 1800.
Hymn of thanksgiving .... 1814.
Panegyric of Samuel Whitbread. Northampton 1816.
Tribute of affection to the memory of Mrs ... Whitehouse. 1819.

William S. Wickenden, 'The bard of the forest' 1797–c. 1867

The rustic's lay and other poems. Gloucester 1817.
Count Glarus of Switzerland, interspersed with ... poetry. Gloucester and London [1819].
Poems. By 'the bard of the forest'. Cambridge 1823 (anon); Sherborne 1827 (acknowledged); London 1859 (5th edn).
Poems and tales with an autobiographical sketch of his early life. 1851.
Prose and poetry. By 'the bard of the forest'. Cambridge 1852.
Author of numerous works of fiction.

Jeremiah Holmes Wiffen 1792–1836

Collection

The brothers [J. H. and B. B. Wiffen]: memoirs and miscellanies. Ed S. R. Pattison 1880, [1896] (in Monthly Tract Soc, n.s. 364).

§1

Poems by three friends. 1813 (anon), 1815 (as Poems, acknowledged). With T. Raffles and J. B. Brown.
Aonian hours and other poems. London and Newport 1819; London 1820.
Julia Alpinula, with other poems. 1820 (2 edns).
The works of Garcilasso de la Vega. Tr Wiffen 1823. With critical and historical essay on Spanish poetry.
Tasso. Jerusalem delivered, book the fourth .... Tr Wiffen 1821, 2 vols 1824–5 (completed, with a life of the author), 3 vols 1826, 2 vols 1830, 1846; 1 vol New York 1846; London 1854; New York 1858; London 1872. Life of Tasso pbd separately, New York 1859.
The echo of antiquity: the past and the future. 1826.
Verses written on the alameda at Ampthill Park. 1827 (priv ptd).
Letters of W. Thompson ... with tributary verses. 1828.
Historical memoirs of the first race of ancestry whence the house of Russell had its origin. 2 vols 1833. Prose.
Verses written at ... Woburn Abbey. By [J. H. W.]. 1836 (priv ptd). Anon.

Joseph Wilde fl. 1810–14

The hospital: a poem .... Norwich [1810].
Infancy: a poem .... Norwich 1814.

Miss Williams, of Glanravon fl. 1815–16

Dependance: a poem. [1815?]
Fashion: a poem. 1816.

Taliesin Williams, called Taliesin ab Iolo Morganwg 1787–1847

Cardiff Castle: a poem .... Merthyr Tydfil 1827.
Gwent and Dyfed royal eisteddfod ... The Welsh ode .... Tr A. Bruce, London and Cardiff 1835.
The doom of Colyn Dolphyn: a poem. London and Merthyr Tydfil 1837.
Pbns also in Welsh.

Barbarina Wilmot

See Barbarina Brand, above.

Charles Wolfe 1791–1823

Collections

Remains of the late Rev Charles Wolfe. Ed J. A. Russell 2 vols Dublin and London 1825; 1 vol London 1826 (2 edns), 1827; Hartford CT 1828; London 1829, 1832, 1836, 1842, 1847. Poems and sermons, with memoir.
Sermons of the late Rev Charles Wolfe [with memoir by G. J. Davies]. 1883. Rptd from Remains, *above*.
Poems. 1903, 1909. With memoir by C. L. Falkiner and ms facs of The burial of Sir John Moore.

§1

The burial of Sir John Moore. Newry Telegraph 19 Apr 1817.
The burial of Sir John Moore; with other poems [and a memoir]. 1825.

Elizabeth Wolferstan, Mrs Samuel Pipe 1763–1845

The enchanted flute, with other poems, and Fables from La Fontaine. 1822, 1823.
Eugenia: a poem, in four cantos. 1824.
Ovid. The fable of Phaeton. Tr [Wolferstan] 1828.
Fairy tales in verse. Lichfield 1829; London and Lichfield 1830, 1833.
On reading Lady Flora Hastings' poems. [1840?] Anon (attribution uncertain).
Golden rules. 1841.
Old stories versified. 1842.

George Woodley 1786–1846

Mount Edgcumbe: a descriptive poem, The shipwreck: a naval eclogue. By [G. W.]. Dock 1804. Anon.
The church yard and other poems. 1808.
Britain's bulwarks, or the British seaman: a poem. Plymouth 1811.
Portugal delivered: a poem .... London and Plymouth 1812.
Redemption: a poem in twenty books. 2 vols Truro 1816.
Cornubia: a poem in five cantos .... London and Truro 1819.
Published miscellaneous prose works.

William Wordsworth 1770–1850

Mss of works by Wordsworth and his family are chiefly held at the Wordsworth Lib, Grasmere, where there are approximately 90 per cent of all known Wordsworth and Wordsworth family papers. As yet there is no complete and accurate catalogue of the Grasmere papers, but in the early 1960s incomplete facs sets of major Grasmere mss held at that time were deposited in the Bodleian and the lib of the Univ of Alberta, and later at Cornell Univ Lib. See R. Siemens, The Wordsworth collection: a catalogue. Dove Cottage papers facsimiles of the University of Alberta, *below.*

In Britain, important items are held at the BL (many items of correspondence and several poetic mss, including one of 'Peter Bell', with other materials); see T. J. Wise, Two lake poets: a catalogue of printed books, manuscripts, and autograph letters by William Wordsworth and Samuel Taylor Coleridge, *below, for full details of items in the Ashley Lib, now in the BL. Some major items are kept at several colleges of Cambridge Univ, and the location of others will be described in the relevant forthcoming vol of* IELM.

In the US, the libs at Amherst, Cornell, and Indiana Univs have important collections: see the catalogues by Patton, Healey, Noyes and Curtis, below. There are significant holdings at the Houghton Lib, Harvard (including mss of 'Ode, January 18, 1816', 'Lines left upon a seat in a yew-tree', 'The female vagrant', 'She dwelt among the untrodden ways', 'London, 1802', 'Intimations of immortality'; revisions in a copy of Yarrow revisited, and other poems; *and c. 100 letters); the Beinecke Rare Book Lib, Yale (including mss or drafts of 'Lines written near Richmond', 'Intimations of immortality', 'The blind highland boy'; a corrected copy of* Lyrical ballads, *1800; proofs of* To the Freeholders of Westmorland, *and various letters); Wellesley College (including a ms of* An evening walk, *revised copies of* Descriptive sketches, *and* The poetical works, 1832, *proofs of 'Laodamia', and c. 60 letters); the Pierpont Morgan Lib, New York (the Coleorton Papers of Sir George Beaumont, including a commonplace book with poems by Wordsworth and some letters); Princeton (including 37 letters, 18 mss, and an interleaved copy of* The poetical works, 1828; *and the Huntington Lib (c. 178 items, including literary mss and letters to Edward Moxon, Francis Wrangham, and others). The Library of Congress National Union Catalog of Manuscript Collections (1959–93) contains listings of other Wordsworth items in American institutions.*

Facs (photo) reproductions are available as follows: in all vols of The Cornell Wordsworth Edition, 1975– , *the complete mss relevant to the reading texts printed are reproduced; BL Additional MS 47864 is reproduced in* The manuscript of William Wordsworth's poems, in two volumes (1807), a facsimile, 1984, *introd by W. H. Kelliher; the earliest seven letters printed in* The love letters of William and Mary Wordsworth *are reproduced in* My dearest love: letters of William and Mary Wordsworth, 1810 *(Ambleside 1981).*

Bibliographies and reference works

Catalogue of the varied and valuable historical, poetical, theological and miscellaneous library of the late venerated poet-laureate. Preston [1859]; rptd in Trans Wordsworth Soc no 6 [1884?].

Tutin, J. R. The Wordsworth dictionary of persons and places. Hull 1891; rptd New York 1967, 1968.

Tutin, J. R. An index to the animal and vegetable kingdoms of Wordsworth. Hull 1892.

White, W. H. A description of the Wordsworth and Coleridge manuscripts in the possession of Mr T. Norton Longman. 1897.

Cooper, L. A concordance to the poems of William Wordsworth. 1911; rptd New York 1965; Temecula CA 1992, 1996.

Wise, T. J. A bibliography of the writings in prose and verse of William Wordsworth. 1916 (priv ptd); rptd Folkestone 1971.

Wise, T. J. Two lake poets: a catalogue of printed books, manuscripts, and autograph letters by William Wordsworth and Samuel Taylor Coleridge. 1927 (priv ptd); rptd 1965.

Munby, A. N. L. Wordsworth and Coleridge. Early appreciation in the north. TLS 22 Aug 1936.

Patton, C. H. The Amherst Wordsworth Collection: a descriptive bibliography. Amherst MA 1936.

Logan, J. V. Wordsworthian criticism: a guide and bibliography. Columbus OH 1947; rptd 1961; New York 1974. Secondary material only.

Bernbaum, E. In Guide through the romantic movement, New York 1949 (2nd edn).

Gordan, J. D. Wordsworth 1770–1850: an exhibition. BNYPL 1950; New York 1950. Catalogue of centennial exhibition in NYPL.

Coe, C. N. Wordsworth and the literature of travel: a bibliography. N & Q 197, 27 Sep, 11 Oct 1952.

Bernbaum, E. and J. V. Logan. In English romantic poets: a review of research, ed T. H. Raysor, New York 1956 (rev).

Healey, G. H. The Cornell Wordsworth Collection: a catalogue of books and manuscripts presented to the university by Mr Victor Emmanuel Cornell, 1919. Ithaca NY 1957. The most authoritative bibl account of books pbd during Wordsworth's lifetime, and related materials.

Barnes, J. C. A bibliography of Wordsworth in American periodicals through 1825. PBSA 52 1958.

Maxwell, J. C. Wordsworth in the Supplement to the Cambridge bibliography of English literature. N & Q 203, Feb 1958.

Henley, E. F. and D. H. Stam. Wordsworthian criticism 1945–1959: an annotated bibliography. New York 1960, 1965 (rev to 1964). Secondary material only.

Henley, E. F. A check list of Masters' theses in the United States on Wordsworth. Charlottesville VA 1962.

Woof, R. S. Wordsworth's poetry and Stuart's newspapers: 1797–1803. SB 15 1962.

Reed, M. L. Wordsworth: the chronology of the early years, 1770–1799. Cambridge MA 1967.

Swayze, W. E. Early Wordsworthian biography: books and articles containing material on the life and character of William Wordsworth that appeared before the publication of the official Memoirs by Christopher Wordsworth in 1851. BNYPL 54, Apr 1969.

Siemens, R. The Wordsworth collection: a catalogue. Dove Cottage papers facs of the University of Alberta. Edmonton 1971.

Bauer, N. S. Wordsworth and the early anthologies. Library 5th ser 27 1972.

Bernbaum, E., J. V. Logan, jun., and F. T. Swetnam, jun. In English romantic poets: a review of research and criticism, ed F. Jordan, New York 1972 (3rd edn); ed K. Kroeber, New York 1985 (4th edn rev).

Curtis, J. R. Wordsworth in the Lilly Library: a description of letters and manuscripts. TWC 3 1972.

Ward, W. S. In Literary reviews in British periodicals 1798–1820: a bibliography, with a supplementary list of general (non-review) articles on literary subjects. 2 vols New York 1972.

Butler, J. A. Wordsworth in Philadelphia Area Libraries, 1787–1850. TWC 4 1973.

Stam, D. H. Wordsworthian criticism 1964–1973: an annotated bibliography. New York 1974. Secondary material only.

Bauer, N. S. Early burlesques and parodies of Wordsworth. JEGP 74 1975.

Bauer, N. S. Romantic poetry and the unstamped political press, 1830–1836. SiR 14 1975.

Reed, M. L. Wordsworth: the chronology of the middle years, 1800–1815. Cambridge MA 1975.

Bauer, N. S. William Wordsworth: a reference guide to British criticism, 1793–1899. Boston 1978. Secondary material only.

Bauer, N. S. Wordsworth's poems in contemporary periodicals. Victorian Periodical Newsletter 11 June 1978.

Hill, A. G. Wordsworth and his American friends. BRH 81 1978.

Noyes, R. The Indiana Wordsworth Collection: a catalogue. Boston 1978.

Shaver, C. L. and A. C.. Wordsworth's library: a catalogue including a list of books housed by Wordsworth for Coleridge from c. 1810 to c. 1830. New York 1979.

Gatton, J. S. et al. Catalog of the Peal Exhibition [Oct 1982]. Kentucky Rev 4 1982 (special issue).

Bennett, J. R. The comparative criticism of Blake and Wordsworth: a bibliography. TWC 14 1983.

McCracken, D. Wordsworth and the lake district: a guide to the poems and their places. Oxford 1984.

Pinion, F. B. A Wordsworth companion: survey and assessment. 1984.

Jones, M. and K. Kroeber. Wordsworth scholarship and criticism, 1973–1984: an annotated bibliography, with selected criticism, 1809–1972. New York 1985. Secondary material only.

McFahern, P. and T. F. Beckwith. A complete concordance to the Lyrical ballads of Samuel Taylor Coleridge and William Wordsworth, 1798 and 1800 edns. New York 1987.

Pinion, F. B. A Wordsworth chronology. Basingstoke 1988.

Crosby, D. K. Wordsworth's Excursion: an annnotated bibliography of criticism. BB 48 1991.

Wu, D. Wordsworth's reading 1770–1799. Cambridge 1993.

Hanley, K. An annotated critical bibliography of William Wordsworth. 1995. Primary and secondary works.

Wu, D. Wordsworth's reading 1800–1815. Cambridge 1996.

Collected works

Poems by William Wordsworth: including Lyrical ballads, and the miscellaneous pieces of the author, with additional poems, a new preface and a supplementary essay. 2 vols 1815; Oxford 1989 (facs). In 1820 a leaf was issued in River Duddon for use as the title page of a third vol, to be made up from River Duddon, Peter Bell, Waggoner, and Thanksgiving ode.

The miscellaneous poems of William Wordsworth. 4 vols 1820.

The poetical works of William Wordsworth. 4 vols Boston 1824. First Amer collected edn, based on 'the latest English edn' (1820), but containing Excursion.

The poetical works of William Wordsworth. 5 vols 1827.

The poetical works of William Wordsworth, complete in one volume. Paris 1828 (pirated).

The poetical works of William Wordsworth: a new edition. 4 vols 1832.

The poetical works of William Wordsworth: the first complete American, from the last London edition. New Haven CT 1836.

The poetical works of William Wordsworth: new edition. 6 vols 1836 [vols 1–2], 1837 [vols 3–6], 1840 (with variations), 1841, 1843; New York 1841; 7 vols, rev 1846, rev 1849. Some leaves included in vol 5 1840 were also ptd separately as Appendix [1840], independently distributed and paginated as a supplement to 1840. Poems, chiefly of early and late years was issued in 1842, with an alternative title page, to form vol 7.

The complete poetical works of William Wordsworth; together with a description of the country of the lakes in the north of England, now published with his works. Ed H. Reed, Philadelphia, Boston and Pittsburgh 1837; reissued 1839, frequently rptd.

Poems, chiefly of early and late years; including the Borderers, a tragedy, by William Wordsworth. 1842. Contains alternative title page, presenting the book as vol 7 of The poetical works 1836–7 and reprints.

The poems of William Wordsworth, DCL, poet laureate: a new edition. 1845; rev 1847, 1849. Prelude and other additions added after 1850, frequently rptd.

The poetical works of William Wordsworth, DCL, poet laureate: a new edition. 6 vols 1849 [vols 1–2], 1850 [vols 3–6].

The poetical works of William Wordsworth: a new edition. Boston 1850.

The poetical works of William Wordsworth. Boston 1854, 1880. With unsigned memoir attributed to J. R. Lowell.

The poetical works of William Wordsworth. 6 vols 1857, 1864, 1865, 1869, 1870 (Centenary edn), 1874, 1881, 1882. Includes Fenwick notes.

The poetical works of William Wordsworth. Ed W. M. Rossetti 1870, 1871. Based on 1-vol edn of 1845, with Prelude.

The poetical works of William Wordsworth. Ed W. Knight 11 vols Edinburgh 1882–9. Last 3 vols are Knight's Life.

The complete poetical works of William Wordsworth. Ed J. Morley with introd 1888. Frequently rptd as Globe edn. As machine-readable data, www.columbia.edu, New York 1993. The Recluse ['Home at Grasmere'] first pbd here and in separate edn of 1888.

The poetical works of William Wordsworth. Ed E. Dowden 7 vols 1892–3 (Aldine).

The poetical works of William Wordsworth. Ed T. Hutchinson with introd and notes, London 1895; 5 vols London 1895. Basis of OSA edn, frequently rptd; rev edn, ed E. de Selincourt 1904, 1936; with introd and notes by G. McL. Harper, New York 1933.

The poetical works of William Wordsworth. Ed W. Knight 8 vols 1896. Same editor's 1882–9 edn heavily rev (Eversley).

The complete poetical works of William Wordsworth. Ed A. J. George, Boston and New York 1904 (Cambridge edn). With Recluse. Rev edn, ed P. D. Sheats, Boston 1982.

The poems of William Wordsworth. Ed N. C. Smith 3 vols 1908.

The poetical works of William Wordsworth, edited from the manuscripts, with textual and critical notes. Ed E. de Selincourt and H. Darbishire 5 vols Oxford 1940–9; rev edn 1952–9.

Wordsworth's poems. Ed P. Wayne 3 vols 1955 (EL).

The Cornell Wordsworth edn. Ed S. Parrish (general), M. L. Reed (associate), J. Butler (assistant), J. Curtis (coordinating for the collective vols) and M. H. Abrams, G. Hartman, and J. Wordsworth (advisory), Hassocks and Brighton 1975–81; Ithaca NY 1975– . 18 of a projected complete edn of 22 vols with index. See Selections and §1, *below*, for the separate vols.

William Wordsworth: the poems. Ed J. O. Hayden 2 vols Harmondsworth 1977; rptd New Haven CT 1981.

Prose works

The prose works of William Wordsworth, for the first time collected, with additions from unpublished manuscripts. Ed A. B. Grosart 3 vols 1876.

The prose works of William Wordsworth. Ed W. Knight 2 vols 1896 (Eversley).

The prose works of William Wordsworth. Ed W. J. B. Owen and J. Worthington Smyser 3 vols Oxford 1974.

Selections

Selections from the poems of William Wordsworth, esq. chiefly for the use of schools and young persons. Ed J. Hine 1831; new edn 1834. *See* H. Taylor, Rev of Poetical works (1832) and Selections from the poems of William Wordsworth (1834), Quart Rev 52 Nov 1834.

Juvenile poems for young children. Boston 1833.

The sonnets of William Wordsworth. 1838.

Poems from the poetical works of William Wordsworth. New York 1841; Philadelphia 1842; republished 1843, rptd frequently.

Select pieces from the poems of William Wordsworth. 1843, pbd by Burns. Newly set edn pbd by Moxon 1847, rptd 1854.

Poems by William Wordsworth; with an introductory essay on his life and writings. New York and Boston 1849. Essay by H. T. Tuckerman.

The earlier poems of William Wordsworth. 1857.

Pastoral poems of William Wordsworth. 1858. Frequently rptd.

Select poems. 1858, c. 1862. With life.

Passages from 'The excursion'. Illustr A. Fraser 1859.

Poems of William Wordsworth. Ed R. A. Willmott, illustr B. Foster, J. Wolf and J. Gilbert 1859, 1866.

Poems for the young. Illustr J. Macuhirter and J. Pettie 1863, 1866, 1870.

The select poetical works of William Wordsworth. 2 vols Leipzig 1864.

A selection from the works of William Wordsworth. Ed F. T. Palgrave 1865 (Moxon's Miniature Poets).
Selections from the poetical works of William Wordsworth. Ed H. H. Turner 1874 (English School Classics).
Poems of Wordsworth. Ed M. Arnold 1879. Rptd frequently. Illustr E. H. Garrett, New York [1892].
Poems of Wordsworth, selected from the best editions. 2 vols 1880. Pbd by W. Kent rptd 1885 in Cassell's Miniature Poets.
Selections from William Wordsworth. New York and Cincinnati 1883.
The sonnets of William Wordsworth. 1884. Essay by R. C. Trench.
Poems of Wordsworth. Selected and prepared for use in schools and classes, in Hudson's text-book of poetry. Selection I Boston 1884, selection II 1889.
Selections from Wordsworth by William Knight and other members of the Wordsworth Society. Ed W. Knight et al. 1888; New York 1889.
Early poems. 1889.
Select poems of William Wordsworth. Ed W. J. Rolfe, New York 1889. With engravings.
Selections from Wordsworth. Notes by A. J. George, Boston 1889.
Pastorals, lyrics, and sonnets, from the poetic works of William Wordsworth. Boston and New York 1890.
Select poems. [c. 1890] (The Penny Poets 32).
A selection from the sonnets of William Wordsworth. Illustr A. Parsons, New York 1891.
Wordsworth for the young. Ed C. M. St John Boston [1891]. Illus.
Wordsworth's prefaces and essays on poetry. Ed A. J. George, Boston 1892.
Lyrics and sonnets of Wordsworth. Ed C. K. Shorter 1892.
Selections from Wordsworth. Ed J. H. Dillard, New York 1892 (English Classic Ser 90).
Selected poems from Wordsworth. 1892 (Cassell's Nat Lib).
Evening voluntaries by William Wordsworth. Illustr W. G. Beal, Boston 1893.
Wordsworth for the young. Notes by J. C. Wright [1893].
Prose writings of Wordsworth. Ed W. Knight [1893].
Poems dedicated to national independence and liberty. Introd S. A. Brooke. 1897.
Selections from Wordsworth. Ed W. T. Webb 1897.
Selections from the poets: Wordsworth. Ed A. Lang, illustr A. Parsons 1897.
Poems by William Wordsworth. Ed E. Dowden, Boston and London 1898.
Selections from the poems of William Wordsworth. Ed W. H. Venable, New York 1898 (Eclectic English Classics).
The sonnets of William Wordsworth. 1899.
Selections from the poetry of William Wordsworth. Ed E. E. Speight 1899 (New English Ser).
Selections from the poems of William Wordsworth. Ed N. C. Smith 1901.
Selected poems of William Wordsworth. Ed J. Seabury, New York [1902].
Poems from Wordsworth. Ed and illustr T. S. Moore [c. 1902].
A selection of the shorter poems of Wordsworth. Ed E. Fulton 1903 (Macmillan's Pocket American and English Classics).
Poems by William Wordsworth. Introd by A. Meynell 1903.
Poems of Wordsworth. Ed W. Knight, from 2 separate publishers, [1904]; London and New York 1904.
Selections from Wordsworth. With Lowell's essay and notes by H. B. Cotterill 1904.
Wordsworth's literary criticism. Ed N. C. Smith, Oxford 1905.
Poems. Ed S. Brooke, illustr E. H. New 1907.
The shorter poems of William Wordsworth. London and New York [1907]; rptd frequently (EL).
The longer poems of William Wordsworth. London and New York 1908; rptd frequently (EL).
The poems of William Wordsworth. Ed N. C. Smith 1908.
Wordsworth. Ed E. Hallam Moorhouse 1911 (The Regent Lib).
The patriotic poetry of William Wordsworth. Introd by A. H. D. Acland, Oxford 1915.
The happy warrior and other poems by William Wordsworth. 1915.
Wordsworth's shorter poems. Illustr H. K. Elcock [c. 1916].
Select poems. Ed S. G. Dunn 1918.
Poems of William Wordsworth. Ed C. L. Thomson, Cambridge 1920.
Wordsworth: poetry and prose. Oxford 1921; rptd 1924, 1928.
Selected poems of William Wordsworth. Ed S. F. Gingerich, Boston [c. 1923] (Riverside College Classics).
William Wordsworth. 1924 (Nelson's Poets).
The Grasmere Wordsworth. Ed J. Hawke 1925.
A selection of shorter poems. Ed G. D. H. and M. I. Cole 1928.
William Wordsworth. [1928] (The Augustan Books of English Poetry, Second Series, No 19).
Selected poems of William Wordsworth. 1929.
Selections from Wordsworth. Ed P. Wayne [1932].
Wordsworth: representative poems. Ed A. Beatty, New York 1937.
Poems: lyrics and sonnets. New York [1946].
A Wordsworth anthology. Selected by L. Housman, New York 1946.
Wordsworth. Selected by N. Nicholson [1949].
The critical opinions of William Wordsworth. Ed M. L. Peacock jun, Baltimore 1950. Classified extracts, mainly from Wordsworth's prose criticism, letters and reported conversations.
Wordsworth. Rev edn selected by W. E. Williams, Harmondsworth [1950].
Selected poetry. Ed M. Van Doren, New York [1950] (Modern Lib).
Poetry and prose. Ed W. M. Merchant 1955 (Reynard Lib).
The poetry of Wordsworth. Stereo sound cassette read by C. Hardwicke, CDL 51026/SWC1026, 1955.
Wordsworth and Coleridge: selected critical essays. Ed T. M. Raysor, New York 1958.
Selected poems. Ed R. Sharrock 1958.
Selected poems. Ed H. M. Margoliouth 1959.
A Wordsworth selection. Ed E. Batho 1962.
Home at Grasmere: extracts from the journal of Dorothy Wordsworth (written between 1800 and 1803) and from the poems of William Wordsworth. Ed C. Clark, Harmondsworth 1960; rptd 1978.
Selected poetry and prose. Ed J. Butt, Oxford 1964.
The poetry of Wordsworth. Ed T. Crehan 1965.
Literary criticism. Ed P. M. Zall, Lincoln NE 1966 (Regents Critics).
Selected poetry and prose. Ed G. H. Hartman, New York 1970; rptd 1980.
Literary criticism. Ed W. J. B. Owen 1974.
William Wordsworth. Ed S. Gill, Oxford 1984 (Oxford Authors).
William Wordsworth: the Pedlar; Tintern Abbey; the two-part Prelude. Ed J. Wordsworth, Cambridge 1985.
William Wordsworth: the Ruined cottage; the Brothers; Michael. Ed J. Wordsworth, Cambridge 1985.
The tuft of primroses, with other late poems for The recluse. Ed J. F. Kishel, Ithaca NY 1986 (Cornell Wordsworth).
Selected prose. Ed J. O. Hayden, Harmondsworth 1988.
Selected poetry and prose. Ed P. Hobsbaum 1989.
Shorter poems, 1807–1820. Ed C. H. Ketcham, Ithaca NY 1990 (Cornell Wordsworth).
Selected poetry. Ed N. Roe 1992 (Pen Poetry Lib).
The Fenwick notes. Ed J. R. Curtis 1993.
Selected poems. New York 1993.
Poetical works. 1994 (Wordsworth Poetry Lib).
William Wordsworth. Ed S. Gill and D. Wu, Oxford 1994 (Oxford Poetry Lib).
Selected poems. 1994 (Bloomsbury Poetry Classics).

Selected poems. Ed D. W. Davies 1994 (EL).
Early poems and fragments, 1785–1797. Ed C. Landon and J. Curtis, Ithaca NY 1997. (Cornell Wordsworth.)
Translations of Chaucer and Virgil. Ed. B. E. Graves, Ithaca NY 1998. (Cornell Wordsworth.)

§1

An evening walk: an epistle, in verse; addressed to a young lady; from the lakes of the north of England, by W. Wordsworth BA of St John's Cambridge. 1793; ed J. Averill, Ithaca NY 1984 (Cornell Wordsworth), with all versions prior to final 1845, especially that of 1794; Oxford 1989 (facs).

Descriptive sketches in verse, taken during a pedestrian tour of the Italian, Grison, Swiss, and Savoyard Alps, by W. Wordsworth BA of St John's Cambridge. 1793; ed E. Birdsall, assisted by P. M. Zall, Ithaca NY 1984 (Cornell Wordsworth), with facing texts of 1793 and 1836 edns.
REVIEWS: T. Holcroft, Rev of Descriptive sketches and Rev of An evening walk, Monthly Rev n.s. 12, Oct 1793.

Lyrical ballads, with a few other poems. 1798 (2 issues, the first with imprint 'Bristol: printed by Biggs and Cottle, for T. N. Longman, Paternoster-Row, London'; the second with imprint 'London: printed for J. & A. Arch, Gracechurch-Street'; *see* R. W. Daniel, The publication of Lyrical ballads, MLR 33 1938. For details of variants in individual copies, *see* Healey, *above*, items 3–4); ed E. Dowden 1890, 1891, 1898; ed T. Hutchinson 1898, 1907, 1910, 1920; introd by G. Sampson 1903; ed H. Littledale 1911, rptd several times; Noel Douglas Replicas 1926 (facs); ed F. W. Schulze, Halle 1952; ed W. J. B. Owen, Oxford 1967, 2nd edn 1969, text of the 1800 Preface collated with 1802; Menston, York 1971 (facs); Oxford 1993 (facs).
REVIEWS: R. Southey, Rev of Lyrical ballads (1798), Critical Rev n.s. 24, Oct 1798; C. Burney, Rev of Lyrical ballads (1798), Monthly Rev n.s. 29, June 1799.

Lyrical ballads, with other poems, in two volumes, by W. Wordsworth. 1800, ptd in Bristol; ed R. L. Brett and A. R. Jones 1963, text of 1798 with the additional 1800 poems and prefaces, including 1802 variants; rev 2nd edn 1965, 1991, as machine-readable data Charlottesville VA 1993; ed J. Butler and K. Green as Lyrical ballads, and other poems, 1797–1800, Ithaca NY 1993 (Cornell Wordsworth); 2 vols in one, ed J. Wordsworth, Spelsbury 1997. For the many variants in individual copies, *see* E. L. McAdam, The publication of Lyrical ballads 1800, YULG 8 1933; J. E. Wells, Lyrical ballads 1800: cancel leaves, PMLA 53 1938; Healey, *above*, items 6–11.

Lyrical ballads, with pastoral and other poems, in two volumes, by W. Wordsworth. 1802; rev 1805 (new edn called 4th on title pages); ed G. Sampson as The lyrical ballads 1798–1805, 1903, rptd several times; ed D. Roper 1968, 2nd edn 1976 [1805]; ed M. Mason as Wordsworth and Coleridge: annotated lyrical ballads, 1992 [1805].

Lyrical ballads, with other poems: in two volumes, by W. Wordsworth. Philadelphia 1802 (2 issues; *see* Healey, *above*, items 14–15). Mostly a reprint of 1798–1800.

Poems, in two volumes, by William Wordsworth, author of Lyrical ballads. 1807 (for variants in individual copies, *see* Healey, *above*, item 19); ed T. Hutchinson 1897; ed H. Darbishire, Oxford 1914, 1952 (rev); ed J. Curtis as Poems in two volumes, and other poems, 1800–1807, Ithaca NY 1983 (Cornell Wordsworth); ed A. R. Jones, Atlantic Highlands NJ 1987. See Lord Byron, Rev of Poems (1807), Monthly Lit Recreations 3 July 1807; F. Jeffrey, Edinburgh Rev 11 Oct 1807; J. Montgomery, Eclectic Rev 4 Jan 1808.

Concerning the relations of Great Britain, Spain and Portugal to each other, and to the common enemy, at this crisis: and specifically as affected by the Convention of Cintra: the whole brought to the test of those principles, by which alone the independence and freedom of nations can be preserved or recovered. 1809 (for variants and authentic ms corrections in individual copies, *see* Healey, *above*, item 22; early paragraphs appeared in Courier 27 Dec 1808 and 13 Jan 1809, with variant titles over the signature 'G.'); ed A. V. Dicey, Oxford 1915 ('with two letters ... written in the year 1811'); ed R. J. White, in Political tracts of Wordsworth, Coleridge and Shelley, Cambridge 1953 (with omissions). *See* H. C. Robinson, Rev of Concerning ... the Convention of Cintra, London Rev 2 Nov 1809.

The excursion, being a portion of The recluse: a poem, by William Wordsworth. 1814 (facs Oxford 1991); 2nd edn 1820; 1844. For variants in individual copies, *see* Healey, *above*, item 24. Rptd as a vol of Poetical works, 1827, 1832, 1836–7, 1849–50 and reissues. Extra copies of the vol concerned were usually ptd and issued separately with appropriate title pages at each issue of Poetical works (*see* W. J. B. Owen, Library 5th ser 12 1957) and at other dates, e.g. 1847, Boston 1849. Numerous late 19th and early 20th-century printings of the whole or parts, e.g. The deserted cottage, illustr B. Foster, J. Wolf, J. Gilbert, London and New York 1859; Wordsworth's excursion: the wanderer, ed H. H. Turner [c. 1880]; The excursion: book 1, The wanderer, New York 1889; 1904 (Temple Classics); ed E. E. Reynolds 1935. For various versions of material from bk 1, *see* J. Wordsworth, The music of humanity: a critical study of Wordsworth's Ruined cottage incorporating texts from a manuscript of 1799–1800, 1969; The ruined cottage and The pedlar by William Wordsworth, ed J. Butler, Ithaca NY 1979 (Cornell Wordsworth); The pedlar with other poems, ed J. Wordsworth, Cambridge 1985; The ruined cottage with other poems, ed J. Wordsworth, Cambridge 1985.
REVIEWS: W. Hazlitt, Character of Mr Wordsworth's new poem, The excursion, Examiner 347, 21, 28 Aug, 2 Oct 1814; C. Lamb and W. Gifford, Rev of The excursion, Quart Rev 12 Oct 1814; F. Jeffrey, Edinburgh Rev 24 Nov 1814.

The brothers. New York 1815.

The white doe of Rylstone: or the fate of the Nortons, a poem by William Wordsworth. 1815 (with The force of prayer: or the founding of Bolton priory); 1859; ed M. T. Quinn 1889; ed W. Knight, Oxford 1891; ed A. P. Comparetti, Ithaca NY 1940; ed K. Dugas, Ithaca NY 1988 (Cornell Wordsworth).
REVIEWS: [F. Jeffrey], The white doe of Rylstone, Edinburgh Rev 25 1815; J. Wilson, Essays on the lake school of poetry, no 1: Wordsworth's White doe of Rylstone, Blackwood's Mag 3 July 1818.

The little maid and the gentleman; or, we are seven, embellished with engravings. York [c. 1815–Jan 1841]. Unauthorised chapbook.

Original poetry: sonnet addressed in a letter (and published by the poet's permission) to B. R. Haydon, painter, by Wordsworth. A single leaf, rptd from Champion 31 Mar 1816, with the sonnet High is our calling. Only one copy known (*see* Healey, *above*, item 37).

Thanksgiving ode, January 18, 1816, with other short pieces, chiefly referring to recent public events, by William Wordsworth. 1816. Includes various odes and sonnets later collected in the group Poems dedicated to national independence and liberty, and some other poems.

A letter to a friend of Robert Burns, occasioned by an intended republication of the account of the life of Burns, by Dr Currie; and of the selection made by him from his letters, by William Wordsworth. 1816.

To the freeholders of Westmorland. Kendal 1818. Broadsheet dated 28 Feb 1818; part of the text of Two addresses, with variants.

Two addresses to the freeholders of Westmorland. Kendal 1818. Previously pbd in Kendal Chron 14 Feb 1818, in Carlisle Patriot 7 Mar 1818, and in broadsheet, *above*.

Deception exposed, or an antidote for the poison of the Westmorland yeoman's address. [Kendal?] 1818.

Peter Bell: a tale in verse, by William Wordsworth. 1819 (facs Oxford 1992); 1819 (2nd edn). Contains also Sonnets suggested by Mr W. Westall's views of the caves &c in Yorkshire, previously pbd in Blackwood's Mag Jan 1819; later collected in the group Miscellaneous sonnets. Ed J. E. Jordan, Ithaca NY 1985 (Cornell Wordsworth).

The waggoner: a poem, to which are added sonnets, by William Wordsworth. 1819. Contains 12 sonnets later collected in the group Miscellaneous sonnets. Ed P. F. Betz, Ithaca NY 1981 (Cornell Wordsworth).

Lament of Mary Queen of Scots on the eve of a new year. Lee Priory 1820.

The river Duddon: a series of sonnets; Vaudracour and Julia; and other poems, to which is annexed A topographical description of the country of the lakes in the north of England, by William Wordsworth. 1820; illustr R. S. Chattock 1884. Also includes Dion, Artegal and Elidure, The prioress's tale, and about 30 shorter poems.

Lyrical ballads, with other poems, by W. Wordsworth. 1820. A reissue of sheets of Lyrical ballads 1800, vol 2 (or, in some copies, of Lyrical ballads 1805, vol 2) with a misleading title page. *See* J. E. Wells, Wordsworth's Lyrical ballads 1820, PQ 17 1938.

A description of the scenery of the lakes in the north of England: third edition (now first published separately) with additions, and illustrative remarks upon the scenery of the Alps, by William Wordsworth. 1822 (facs Oxford 1991), 1823 ('fourth' edn), 1835, Kendal 1835 ('fifth' edn, rev and enlarged as A guide through the district of the lakes in the north of England); ed E. de Selincourt 1906, rptd several times; ed W. M. Merchant, illustr J. Piper 1951, Bloomington IN 1952, rptd New York 1968; ed P. Bicknell as The illustrated Wordsworth's guide to the lakes, Exeter 1984; nd Malvern (facs); as A complete guide to the lakes . . . with Mr Wordsworth's description of the scenery of the country 1842, Kendal 1842; 1843, 1846; Kendal, Liverpool and Manchester 1843, 1846. Edns later than 1835 (except that in the Amer edn of Poetical works, 1837) contain addns by 'the Rev Professor [Adam] Sedgwick' (1842, 1843, 1846, 1853, 1859).

Ecclesiastical sketches by William Wordsworth. 1822; ed A. F. Potts, New Haven CT 1922 (as The ecclesiastical sonnets).

Memorials of a tour on the Continent 1820, by William Wordsworth. 1822.

Epitaph. 1835. Priv ptd version of Written after the death of Charles Lamb. Unique copy, BM Ashley 5139; rptd Ithaca NY 1904. A longer version without title 1836; *see* Healey, *above*, item 95 ['To the dear memory of a frail good man'] 1836 (for private circulation); F. M. Todd, Wordsworth's monody on Lamb: another copy [in Turnbull Lib, Wellington, NZ], MLR 50 1955.

Yarrow revisited, and other poems, by William Wordsworth. 1835; Boston and New York 1835; London 1836 (2nd edn); Boston 1836; 1839 (3rd edn [as 5th vol for 1832 Poetical works, reissued with new title page]).

The little maid and the gentleman. Philadelphia 1836. Unauthorised chapbook.

Sergeant Talfourd's copy-right bill. 1838.

Petition to the House of Commons on the copyright; appendix . . . session (1839). [Rptd as] petition of Wm Wordsworth, esq., in T. N. Talfourd, Three speeches . . . for an extension of copyright, 1840.

England in 1840! [1840?]. Collection of 8 of Wordsworth's political sonnets, of uncertain occasion; no imprint. *See* Healey, *above*, item 112.

We are seven. [Alnwick? 1840]. Unauthorised chapbook containing We are seven and another poem, not Wordsworth's; no imprint. *See* H. Hughes, Two Wordsworthian chapbooks, MP 25 1928.

Poems, chiefly of early and late years; including The borderers, a tragedy. 1842. For multiple versions of works included, *see* The Salisbury Plain poems,ed S. Gill, Ithaca NY 1975 (Cornell Wordsworth); The borderers, ed R. Osborn, Ithaca NY 1982 (Cornell Wordsworth).

'When Severn's sweeping flood' (published to be sold at the Cardiff bazaar in aid of St Mary's church). 1842; rptd in Poems on the loss and re-building of St Mary's church, Cardiff, by William Wordsworth, James Montgomery, Thomas William Booker, John Dix, Cardiff 1842.

Grace Darling. Carlisle [1843] (priv ptd); Newcastle [1843].

Sacred to the memory of Robert Southey. 1843; 1844 (new edn).

To the Queen. Kendal 1846 (priv ptd). Forgery, presumably by T. J. Wise; true date of issue c. 1889. *See* J. Carter and G. Pollard, Enquiry into the nature of certain nineteenth-century pamphlets, 1934, pp. 355–6.

Verses composed at the request of Jane Wallas Penfold, by William Wordsworth esq, poet laureate. [1843.] Unique copy, BM Ashley 5140. Contains Fair lady! can I sing of flowers. Also in Jane Wallas Penfold, Madeira flowers, fruits, and ferns [etc], 1845.

Kendal and Windermere railway: two letters re-printed from the Morning Post, revised with additions. Kendal 1845. Priv ptd, followed by London issue with imprints of Whittaker and Moxon as well as the Kendal imprint, with slight variants; *see* J. E. Wells, Wordsworth and railways in 1844–5, MLQ 6 1945. Earlier, variant versions in Morning Post 16 Oct, 11, 20 Dec 1844.

Ode performed in the Senate-House, Cambridge, on the sixth of July MDCCCXLVII, at the first commencement after the installation of His Royal Highness the Prince Albert Chancellor of the University. Cambridge 1847. 4 leaves ptd by Univ Press; another issue 'Metcalfe and Palmer, printers, Cambridge' of 8 leaves, with further information on title page; another, London, 4 leaves, with frontispiece of Prince Albert, gilt borders etc; another, London 1849, with the music of Thomas Attwood Walmisley, iv + 52 pp.

The prelude, or growth of a poet's mind; an autobiographical poem, by William Wordsworth. 1850, Oxford 1993 (facs); New York and Philadelphia 1850; 1851 (2nd edn); with notes by A. J. George, Boston 1888; 1896 (Temple Classics); ed B. Worsfold 1904, London and Boston 1907; Hammersmith 1915; selections ed B. Groom 1924; ed E. de Selincourt, Oxford 1926, 1932, 1957 (rev H. Darbishire 1959); bks I, II, and parts of V and XII, ed H. Darbishire, Oxford 1928; Extracts . . ., with other poems, ed G. Mallaby, Cambridge 1932; text of 1805, ed E. de Selincourt, Oxford 1933, rev S. Gill; text of 1850, ed E. E. Reynolds 1932; with a selection from the shorter poems etc, ed C. Baker, New York [1954]; multiple texts, ed J. C. Maxwell, Harmondsworth 1971, rptd New Haven CT 1981; in Norton anthology of English literature, 3rd edn vol 2, ed M. H. Abrams, New York 1974, first pbn of the 2-part Prelude of 1798–9, ed S. Gill and J. Wordsworth; The prelude, 1798–99, ed S. Parrish, Ithaca NY 1977 (Cornell Wordsworth); The prelude 1799, 1805, 1850, ed J. Wordsworth, M. H. Abrams and S. Gill (Norton), New York and London 1979; The fourteen-book prelude, ed W. J. B. Owen, Ithaca NY 1985 (Cornell Wordsworth); The two-part prelude, ed J. Wordsworth, Cambridge 1985; The thirteen-book prelude, ed M. L. Reed, Ithaca 1991 (Cornell Wordsworth); The prelude, 1798, 1799, 1805, 1850, ed J. Wordsworth, Harmondsworth 1995 (Pen). The five-book prelude, ed D. Wu, Oxford 1997.

REVIEWS: Examiner no 2217 27 July 1850; Spectator 23 3 Aug 1850; Christian Remembrancer n.s. 20 Oct 1850; Prospective Rev 7 1851.

Autobiographical memoranda dictated by William Wordsworth, P. L., at Rydal Mount, November, 1847 [Essay upon epitaphs, I]. In Christopher Wordsworth's Memoirs of William Wordsworth, 2 vols 1851.

A letter to the Bishop of L[l]andaff on the extraordinary avowal of his political principles contained in the appendix to his late sermon: by a republican [1793] [Substantial ms fragment in an unreliable text]; The country churchyard, and critical examination of ancient epitaphs, and Celebrated epitaphs considered (Essays upon epitaphs, II and III); Isabella Fenwick's notes to the poems, editorially rearranged and with alterations. All first pbd, together with various letters and extracts, in Grosart's edn of Prose works 1876.

The recluse ['Home at Grasmere']. London and New York 1888, 1891; pbd simultaneously in Complete poetical works of William Wordsworth, the Globe edn, ed and with introd by J. Morley, London and New York 1888; ed B. Darlington, Hassocks and Ithaca NY 1977 (Cornell Wordsworth).

Various first printings of prose works in The prose works of William Wordsworth, ed W. Knight 2 vols 1896 (Eversley).

Preface to The borderers [1797?]. Ms first pbd by E. de Selincourt, Nineteenth Cent Nov 1926; rptd in de Selincourt, Oxford lectures on poetry, Oxford 1934, and in Poetical works, ed de Selincourt, vol 1. None of these versions is wholly accurate.

Essay on morals [1798?]. Ms fragment first pbd in full by G. L. Little, REL 2 1961.

Early contributions to periodicals, anthologies etc

Lifetime. *Cited with slight corrections and additions from the catalogue in Healey, above, for later items. For Wordsworth's many contributions to* The Morning Post, *commending 14 Dec 1797, and to* The Courier, *commencing 7 Apr 1800, see Woof on the poems in Stuart's Newspapers, above, for detailed listings.*

European Mag and London Rev 11 1787. On seeing Miss Helen Maria Williams weep at a tale of distress. Signed 'Axiologus'; attributed to Wordsworth.

The Morning Chronicle 21 Aug 1795. La naissance de l'amour, tr Wordsworth.

Wrangham, F. Poems 1795. Issued probably 1798; reissued and rev probably 1802. La naissance de l'amour, tr Wordsworth.

The Morning Post and Gazetteer 2 Apr 1800. The mad mother.

The charms of melody, or siren medley, no 94. Dublin c. 1801. Lucy Gray, We are seven.

The Port Folio 1 Philadelphia 1801. Simon Lee, The last of the flock, The thorn, Anecdote for fathers, Ellen Irwin, Strange fits of passion, The waterfall and the eglantine, Lucy Gray, Andrew Jones.

The beauties of modern literature, in prose and verse. Richmond VA 1802. The pet lamb.

The Port Folio 3 Philadelphia 1803. The fountain, A whirl-blast from behind the hill.

Melmoth, S. (ed). Beauties of British poetry. Huddersfield 1803 (2nd edn). Ptd and sold by Brook and Lancashire, also by T. Hurst, Crosby and co, London. Goody Blake and Harry Gill.

The Port Folio 4 Philadelphia 1804. The oak and the broom. Written in Germany, on one of the coldest days of the century.

The anti-Gallican; or standard of British loyalty, religion, and liberty; including a collection of the principal papers, tracts, speeches, poems, and songs, that have been published on the threatened invasion: together with many original pieces on the same subject. 1804. Anticipation.

The poetical register, and repository of fugitive poetry for 1803. 1805 (2nd edn). Anticipation.

Duppa, R. The life and literary works of Michel Angelo Buonarotti. 1806. Yes! hope may with my strong desire keep pace; 1807 (new edn), with additional Wordsworth verses; also includes No mortal object did these eyes behold and The prayers I make will then be sweet indeed; 1816 (new edn).

The Parnassian garland; or, beauties of modern poetry: consisting of upwards of two hundred pieces, selected from the works of the most distinguished poets of the present age, with introductory lines to each article. Designed for the use of schools and the admirers of poetry in general. 1807. The wandering Jew.

The Balance and Columbian Repository 4 New York 1807. Alice Fell.

Murray, L. Introduction to the English reader: or, a selection of pieces in prose and poetry; calculated to improve the younger classes of learners in reading, and to imbue their minds with the love of virtue. With rules and observations for assisting children to read with propriety. Philadelphia 1809; rptd 1838. The pet lamb.

Wordsworth made many contributions to The Friend *10 Aug 1809–22 Feb 1810. See Healey above #466 for a detailed listing.*

'Introduction' in J. Wilkinson's Select views in Cumberland, Westmorland, and Lancashire, 1810; reissued 1817 and 1821. The 1st edn of the [Guide to the lakes]; 2nd edn in The river Duddon 1820, pp. 213–321.

The Examiner 28 Jan 1816. How clear, how keen, how marvellously bright.

The Examiner 11 Feb 1816. While not a leaf seems faded, while the fields.

The Examiner 31 Mar 1816. To B. R. Haydon.

Annals of the fine arts, for 1817. 1818. Upon the sight of a beautiful picture, To B. R. Haydon.

Kendal Chron 31 Jan 1818. Advertisement; to the editor. Letter to the editor over the signature 'A friend to consistency'.

Kendal Chron 21 Feb 1818. To the editor of the Chronicle. 2 letters to the editor, over the signature 'A friend to truth'; rptd by J. E. Wells, PMLA 55 1940.

Kendal Chron 14 Mar 1818. To the editor of the Chronicle. Letter to the editor, over the signature 'A friend to truth'.

Blackwood's Mag 14 Jan 1819. Pure element of waters! Whereso'er, Was the aim frustrated by force or guile, At early dawn, or when the warmer air.

Westmorland Gazette 31 Dec 1819. To the editor of the Westmorland Gazette. Over the signature 'An enemy to detraction'.

Baillie, J. (ed). A collection of poems chiefly manuscript, and from living authors. 1823. Not love, not war, nor the tumultuous swell, A volant tribe of bards on earth are found.

Scott, E. (ed). Specimens of British poetry: chiefly selected from authors of high celebrity, and interspersed with original writings. Edinburgh 1823. September 1819.

The Wesleyan-Methodist Mag for the year 1824 (an abridged edn, containing selections from the larger work), being a continuation of The Arminian or Methodist Mag 3 3rd ser 1824. Inscription in a hermit's cell.

Knox, V. Elegant extracts, or useful and entertaining passages, from the best English authors and translations; principally designed for use of young persons. New edn prepared by J. G. Percival, Boston 1826. Numerous pieces.

Whitelaw, A. (ed). The casquet of literary gems. 2 vols Glasgow and London 1827, 1833. The Italian itinerant, To a highland girl, The seven sisters, She dwelt among the untrodden ways, The world is too much with us, The fountain, The three cottage girls, Glen Almain, Earth has not anything to show more fair, Where lies the land to which yon ship must go?

Croly, G. (ed). The beauties of the British poets, with a few introductory observations. 1828; rptd Boston 1849. Several selections.

Johnstone, J. Specimens of the lyrical, descriptive, and narrative poets of Great Britain, from Chaucer to the present day: with a preliminary sketch of the history of early English poetry, and biographical and critical notices. Edinburgh 1828.

The casket, a miscellany, consisting of unpublished poems. 1829. The peat stack (Untouched through all severity of cold).

[Dix, D. L. (ed).] The garland of Flora. London and Boston 1829. Brief passages from Wordsworth.

[Reynolds, F. M. (ed).] The Keepsake MDCCCXXIX. [1829.] The country girl (The gleaner), The triad, The wishing gate, A gravestone upon the floor of Worcester cathedral, A tradition of Darley dale.

The casket: or youth's pocket library. Boston 1830 (3rd edn). To a skylark (Ethereal minstrel!).
The laurel: fugitive poetry of the XIX century. 1830. The wishing gate, To a highland girl.
The New Monthly Mag and Literary Jnl (original papers) 33, July 1831. To B. R. Haydon, on seeing his picture of Napoleon Buonaparte on the island of St Helena.
Pierpoint, J. (ed). The American first class book; or, exercises in reading and recitation: selected principally from modern authors of Great Britain and America; and designed for the use of the highest class in publick and private schools. Boston 1831. Many pieces.
The Penny Mag of the Soc for the Diffusion of Useful Knowledge. 1832. I grieved for Buonaparté, with a vain; Fidelity.
Philological museum. 2 vols Cambridge 1832. Various pieces including trn of part of the first bk of the Aeneid.
The Penny Mag of the Soc for the Diffusion of Useful Knowledge. 1833. To my sister, Lines composed above Tintern Abbey.
Greenbank's Periodical Lib 2 Philadelphia 1833. 14 poems by Wordsworth.
Dyce, A. (ed). Specimens of English sonnets. 1833. Numerous examples.
The naturalist's poetical companion; with notes. London and Leeds 1833. To the cuckoo, Fidelity, To the small celandine, The skylark, The green linnet.
Watts, A. A. (ed). The literary souvenir. 1833. On Sir Walter Scott's quitting Abbotsford for Naples.
The bard: a selection of poetry. London and York 1834. To a skylark (Ethereal minstrel), Composed upon Westminster Bridge, The swan (Dion).
Newcastle Jnl 5 Dec 1835. Extempore effusion upon the death of James Hogg.
The Athenaeum 12 Dec 1835. Extempore effusion, upon reading, in the Newcastle Journal, the notice of the death of the poet, James Hogg.
Housman, R. F. (ed). A collection of English sonnets. 1835. Numerous examples.
The Gentleman's Mag n.s. 5, Jan 1836. Extempore effusion upon the death of James Hogg.
Westmorland Gazette and Kendal Advertiser 16 Apr 1836. [Speech on laying the foundation stone of the new school in the village of Bowness, Windermere.]
Lord Northampton. The tribute: a collection of miscellaneous unpublished poems, by various authors. 1837. Stanzas (A night thought).
Frost, J. (ed). Select works of the British poets, in a chronological series from Falconer to Sir Walter Scott. With biographical and critical notices. Designed as a continuation of Dr Aikin's British poets. Philadelphia 1838. Numerous poems.
Hall, S. C. The book of gems: the modern poets and artists of Great Britain. 1838. Several poems.
Bunbury, Sir H. (ed). The correspondence of Sir Thomas Hanmer... with a memoir of his life, to which are added, other relicks of a gentleman's family. 1838. Letter to C. J. Fox, 14 Jan 1801.
The lily, a holiday present, with steel embellishments. New York [c. 1839]. The cottage girl (The gleaner).
Tait's Edinburgh Mag 6 Sep 1839. George and Sarah Green.
The poetic wreath: consisting of select passages from the works of English poets, from Chaucer to Wordsworth. Alphabetically arranged. Philadelphia 1839. Numerous examples.
Selections from the British poets. 2 vols New York 1840–1. Numerous poems.
The Quart Rev 69, Dec 1841. Sonnets upon the punishment of death.
Horne, R. H. (ed). The poems of Geoffrey Chaucer, modernized. 1841. The cuckoo and the nightingale, extract from Troilus and Cressida.
The New World, a weekly journal of popular lit, science, music, and the arts. Containing the latest works by distinguished authors, sermons by eminent divines, original and selected tales and poetry, etc, etc. Jan–July 1842. To the clouds, Suggested by a picture of a bird of paradise, Maternal grief, Guilt and sorrow, Chaucer and Windsor [erroneously attributed to Wordsworth].
Book of the poets; the modern poets of the nineteenth century. 1842. Numerous poems.
Hall, S. C. Gems of the modern poets, with bibliographical notices. Philadelphia 1842. Numerous poems.
Contributions of William Wordsworth to the revival of Catholic truths. 1842. Numerous extracts and several poems.
Rio, Alexis François. La petite chouannerie ou histoire d'un collège breton sous l'empire. Paris 1842. The eagle and the dove.
Griswold, R. W. (ed). The poetry of love. Boston 1844. She was a phantom of delight, She dwelt among the untrodden ways.
Griswold, R. W. (ed). The poetry of love, from the most celebrated authors, with several original pieces. Philadelphia 1844. She dwelt among the untrodden ways, Look at the fate of summer flowers, Let other bards of angels sing, As often as I murmur here.
[Albin, A. (ed).] A token of friendship. New York [c. 1845]. Conversation with a friend (The fountain).
Griswold, R. W. (ed). Poets and poetry of England in the nineteenth century. Philadelphia 1845. Numerous poems.
Spencer farm, with some account of its owners. Sudbury 1845. Preface by Wordsworth.
Harvey, T. The poetical reader; a selection from the eminent poets of the last period of English literature, with a preliminary essay, biographical introductions, and notes in French and German, for the use of young people of both nations. Geneva and Paris 1846.
M'Kim, J. M. Voices of the true-hearted. Philadelphia 1846. Several poems.
The Home Jnl 2 Oct 1847. A sad and lovely face, with upturn'd eyes.
The Glasgow University album for 1847. Glasgow 1847. On the banks of a rocky stream.
Lunt, Mrs J. S. F. (ed). Forget-me-not; or the Philipena. Lowell MA 1847. A pen – to register; a key –, 'Beloved Vale!' I said, 'when shall I con'.
Griffith, M. L. (ed). Literary extracts, in prose and verse: with a few original pieces. Bath 1848. Final stanzas of Hymn for the boatmen as they approach the castle of Heidelberg.
Evenings at Derley Manor. Pencillings and sketches of the English poets and their favourite scenes. 1849. Virtue (Excursion, bk 4 1062–77).
Griswold, R. W. (ed). The sacred poets of England and America, for three centuries. Illus with steel engravings, New York and Philadelphia 1849.
Scrymgeour, D. The poetry and poets of Britain, from Chaucer to Tennyson, with biographical sketches, and a rapid view of the characteristic attributes of each. Preceded by an introductory essay on the origin and progress of English poetical literature. Edinburgh 1850. Several poems.

Letters, journals etc

Memorials of Coleorton: being letters from Coleridge, Wordsworth and his sister, Southey and Sir Walter Scott to Sir George and Lady Beaumont of Coleorton, Leicestershire, 1803 to 1834. Ed W. A. Knight 2 vols Edinburgh 1887.
Letters from the lake poets, Coleridge, Wordsworth, Southey, to Daniel Stuart, editor of the Morning Post and the Courier 1800–38. 1889 (priv ptd).
Unpublished letters of Wordsworth and Coleridge. Athenaeum 8 Dec 1894.
Poems and extracts chosen by William Wordsworth for an album presented to Lady Mary Lowther, Christmas, 1819. Printed literally from the original album with facsimiles. 1905.

The letters of the Wordsworth family from 1787 to 1855. Ed W. Knight 3 vols 1907.

The law of copyright. 1916 (priv ptd). Originally a letter to Morning Post 23 Apr 1838.

The correspondence of Henry Crabb Robinson with the Wordsworth circle (1808–1866). Ed E. J. Morley 2 vols Oxford 1927.

Wordsworth & Reed: the poet's correspondence with his American editor 1836–1850, and Henry Reed's account of his reception at Rydal Mount, London, and elsewhere in 1854. Ed L. N. Broughton, Ithaca NY 1933.

The letters of William and Dorothy Wordsworth. Ed E. de Selincourt 6 vols Oxford 1935–9; 2nd edn, general ed A. G. Hill, 8 vols 1967–93 as follows: 1. The early years 1787–1805, rev C. L. Shaver, 1967; 2. The middle years pt 1: 1806–11, rev M. Moorman, 1969; 3. The middle years pt 2: 1812–20, rev M. Moorman and A. G. Hill, 1970; 4. The later years pt 1: 1821–28, rev A. G. Hill, 1978; 5. The later years pt 2: 1829–34, rev A. G. Hill, 1979; 6. The later years pt 3: 1835–39, rev A. G. Hill, 1982; 7. The later years pt 4: 1840–53, rev A. G. Hill, 1988; 8. A suppl of new letters, rev A. G. Hill, 1993. Standard edn.

Henry Crabb Robinson on books and their writers. Ed E. J. Morley 3 vols 1938.

Some letters of the Wordsworth family, now first published, with a few unpublished letters of Coleridge and Southey and others. Ed L. N. Broughton, Ithaca NY 1941.

Wordsworth's pocket notebook. Ed G. H. Healey, Ithaca NY 1942.

The letters of Wordsworth, selected. Ed P. Wayne, Oxford 1954 (WC).

The letters of Sara Hutchinson from 1800 to 1835. Ed K. Coburn, Toronto and London 1954.

Owen, W. J. B. Letters of Longman & co. to Wordsworth, 1814–36. Library 9 1954.

Letters of Mary Wordsworth 1800–55. Ed M. E. Burton, Oxford 1958.

The early Wordsworthian milieu: a notebook of Christopher Wordsworth with a few entries by William Wordsworth. Ed Z. S. Fink, Oxford 1958.

Jordan, J. E. De Quincey to Wordsworth: a biography of a relationship with the letters of Thomas De Quincey to the Wordsworth family. Berkeley CA 1962.

The letters of John Wordsworth. Ed C. H. Ketcham, Oxford and Ithaca NY 1969.

The love letters of William and Mary Wordsworth. Ed B. Darlington, Ithaca NY 1981; London 1982.

Letters of William Wordsworth: a new selection. Ed A. G. Hill, Oxford and New York 1984; rptd 1990.

Averill, J. H. A fragment of a late Wordsworth notebook (1835). MP 78 1990. A half-page of drafts for poems on Burns and James Hogg.

See also entries for Dorothy Wordsworth (col 2207) and Dora Wordsworth (col 2306).

Translations

Appendix in The poetical works, *1840 contains the three poems,* While from the purpling east, To May, *and* The somnambulist, *tr John Wordsworth, the poet's son, into Latin.*

Il Trifoglio: ovvero scherzi metrici d'un'Inglese, non pubblicati, ma presentati a quei pochi amici, cui piiacque 'meas esse putare nugas'. 2nd edn 1839. To a skylark (in Ital).

Linwood, W. Anthologia Oxoniensis. 1846 She dwelt among the untrodden ways, My heart leaps up, 'Tis sung in ancient minstrelsy, Not seldom, cloth'd in safron vest (in both Eng and Latin).

Sabrinae Corolla in Hortulis Regiae Scholae Salopiensis Contexuerunt Tres Viri Floribus Legendis. 1850. Lines in a lady's album (Small service is true service while it lasts), Milton (in both Eng and Latin).

Quelques poèmes de William Wordsworth. Tr E. Legouis, Paris 1896.

Two poems in Dutch. *See* Healey, *above*, item 452.

§2

See the critical apparatuses, transcriptions and appendices in the Cornell Wordsworth edn for the fullest accounts of specific textual issues, variants and mss.

Dowden, E. The text of Wordsworth's poems. Contemporary Rev 33 Nov 1878; rptd with minor changes in Transcripts and studies, 1888.

Wordsworth, J. The music of humanity: a critical study of Wordsworth's Ruined cottage incorporating texts from a manuscript of 1799–1800. 1969.

Hayden, J. O. Substantive errors in the standard edition of Wordsworth's poetry. Library 29 1974.

Parrish, S. Foreword to the Cornell Wordsworth edition. In The Salisbury plain poems of William Wordsworth, ed S. Gill, Hassocks 1975.

Parrish, S. The worst of Wordsworth. TWC 7 1976.

Gill, S. Wordsworth's poems: the question of text. RES 34 1983. Rev in Romantic revisions, ed R. Brinkley and K. Hanley, Cambridge 1992.

Parrish, S. The editor as archaeologist. Kentucky Rev 4 1983.

Stillinger, J. Textual primitivism and the editing of Wordsworth. SiR 28 1989.

Gill, S. Copyright and the publishing of Wordsworth, 1850–1900. In Literature in the marketplace, ed J. Jordan and R. Patten, Cambridge 1995.

Pre-1920 criticism

[Jeffrey, F.] Rev of Southey's Thalaba. Edinburgh Rev 1 Oct 1802.

[Jeffrey, F.] Rev of Crabbe's Poems. Edinburgh Rev 12 Apr 1808; rptd with additions in Contributions to the Edinburgh Rev, 4 vols 1844.

Byron, G. G. English bards and Scotch reviewers. 1809.

[Jeffrey, F.] Rev of Cromek's Reliques of Robert Burns. Edinburgh Rev 13 Jan 1809; rptd in Contributions to the Edinburgh Rev, 4 vols 1844.

Wilson, J. and A. Blair. Letter to the Editor. Friend no 17, 14 Dec 1809.

[Scott, Sir W.] Of the living poets of Great Britain. Edinburgh Annual Register 1–2 1810.

[Jeffrey, F.] Rev of The dramatic works of John Ford. Edinburgh Rev 18 Aug 1811; rptd in Contributions to the Edinburgh Rev, 4 vols 1844.

[Jeffrey, F.] Rev of Wilson's The isle of palms. Edinburgh Rev 20 Nov 1812.

[Jeffrey, F.] Rev of Rejected addresses. Edinburgh Rev 20, Nov 1812; rptd in Contributions to the Edinburgh Rev, 4 vols 1844.

Hunt, L. Preface and notes. In The feast of the poets, with notes and other pieces in verse, by the editor of the Examiner, 1814.

[Jeffrey, F.] Rev of Wilson's City of the plague. Edinburgh Rev 26, June 1816.

[Jeffrey, F.] Rev of Byron's Childe Harolde's pilgrimage: canto the third and The prisoner of Chillon. Edinburgh Rev 27 Dec 1816; rptd in Contributions to the Edinburgh Rev, 4 vols 1844.

Coleridge, S. T. In his Biographia literaria; or biographical sketches of my literary life and opinions, 2 vols 1817.

Wilson, J. Observations on Mr Wordsworth's letter relative to a new edition of Burns' works. Blackwood's Mag June 1817.

Wilson, J. Vindication of Mr Wordsworth's letter to Mr Gray, on a new edition of Burns. Blackwood's Mag Oct 1817.

Wilson, J. Letter occasioned by N's vindication of Mr Wordsworth in last number. Blackwood's Mag Nov 1817.

Hazlitt, W. In his Lectures on the English poets, 1818.

Hazlitt, W. My first acquaintance with poets. Liberal 3 Apr 1823.

Landor, W. S. Southey and Porson. London Mag 8 July 1823; rptd in

Imaginary conversations of literary men and statesmen, 2 vols 1824; 1826 (2nd edn).
Hazlitt, W. Mr Wordsworth. In The spirit of the age: or contemporary portraits, 1825.
Wilson, J. Sacred poetry. Blackwood's Mag 24, Dec 1828.
Townsend, C. H. An essay on the theory and the writings of Wordsworth. Blackwood's Mag 26, pt 1 Sep 1829; pt 2 Oct 1829; pt 3 Nov 1829; pt 4 Dec 1829.
Mill, J. S. The two kinds of poetry. Monthly Repository n.s. 7, Oct 1833; rptd with variations in Thoughts on poetry and its varieties in Dissertations and Discussions 1859.
De Quincey, T. Lake reminiscences. Tait's Mag n.s. 6, Jan, Feb, Apr 1839.
De Quincey, T. William Wordsworth and Robert Southey. Tait's Mag n.s. 6, July 1839.
De Quincey, T. Recollections of Grasmere. Tait's Mag n.s. 6 Sep 1839.
De Quincey, T. On Wordsworth's poetry. Tait's Mag n.s. 12, Sep 1845; rptd with Postscript in Sketches: critical and biographic, 1857.
Anon. Religious character of Wordsworth's poetry. Christian Observer n.s. no 150, June 1850.
Ruskin, J. Modern painters vol 3, 1856. Especially ch 17, The moral of landscape.
Arnold, M. On translating Homer, last words: a lecture given at Oxford. 1862.
De Quincey, T. In his Recollections of the lakes and lake poets, Coleridge, Wordsworth and Southey, Edinburgh 1863.
Bagehot, W. Wordsworth, Tennyson, and Browning; or, pure, ornate, and grotesque art in English poetry. Nat Rev n.s. no 1, Nov 1864.
Clough, A. H. Rev of The works of William Wordsworth. North Amer Rev 100, Apr 1865.
Clough, A. H. Lecture on the poetry of Wordsworth. In his Poems and prose remains, 1869.
Graves, R. P. Recollections of Wordsworth and the lake country. In his Afternoon lectures on literature and art, Dublin 1869.
Brooke, S. A. Theology in the English poets: Cowper, Coleridge, Wordsworth and Burns. 1874.
Pater, W. Wordsworth. Fortnightly Rev Apr 1874; rptd in his Appreciations, 1889.
Lowell, J. R. Wordsworth. In Among my books, ser 2, Boston 1876.
Stephen, L. Wordsworth's ethics. Cornhill Mag 34, Aug 1876; rptd and expanded in Hours in a library: third ser, 1879.
Hutton, R. H. The weak side of Wordsworth. Spectator 55, 27 May 1882; rptd in A Victorian spectator: uncollected writings of R. H. Hutton, ed R. H. Tener and M. Woodfield, Bedminster 1989.
Rawnsley, H. D. Reminiscences of Wordsworth among the peasantry of Westmorland. In The transactions of the Wordsworth Society, ed W. Knight, 1882; rptd in Lake country sketches, Glasgow 1903; ed G. Tillotson 1969.
Courthope, W. J. Wordsworth's theory of poetry. Nat Rev 4 Dec 1884; rev in The liberal movement in English literature, 1885.
Swinburne, A. C. Wordsworth and Byron. Nineteenth Cent 15, Apr 1884, May 1884; rptd in Miscellanies, 1886.
Minto, W. Wordsworth's great failure. Nineteenth Cent 26, Sep 1889.
Bussière, G. and E. Legouis. Le général Michel Beaupuy. Paris 1891.
Reynolds, M. The treatment of nature in English poetry between Pope and Wordsworth. Chicago 1896.
Dowden, E. The French revolution and English literature. 1897.
Palgrave, F. T. The landscape of Wordsworth. In his Landscape in poetry from Homer to Tennyson, London and New York 1897.
Stephen, L. Wordsworth's youth. Nat Rev 28 Feb 1897.
White, W. H. An examination of the charge of apostasy against Wordsworth. London and New York 1898; rptd 1976.
Yarnall, E. Wordsworth and the Coleridges, with other memories literary and political. New York and London 1899.
Raleigh, W. Wordsworth. 1903.
Cestre, C. La révolution française et les poètes anglais. Paris 1906.
Cooper, L. A glance at Wordworth's reading. MLN 22 1907; rev in his Methods and aims in the study of literature, Boston 1915; in Cornell Stud in Eng 31 1940.
Cooper, L. Some Wordsworthian similes. JEGP 6 1907; rptd in his Aristotelian papers, Ithaca NY 1939.
Eagleston, A. J. Wordsworth, Coleridge and the spy. Nineteenth Cent 63, Aug 1908. Rptd in Coleridge: studies by several hands, ed E. Blunden and E. L. Griggs, 1934.
Lienemann, K. Die Belesenheit von Wordsworth. Berlin 1908.
Bradley, A. C. English poetry and German philosophy in the age of Wordsworth. Manchester 1909.
Bradley, A. C. In his Oxford lectures on poetry, 1909.
Cooper, L. The 'forest hermit' in Coleridge and Wordsworth. MLN 24 1909.
More, P. E. In his Shelburne essays: seventh series, Boston 1910.
Robertson, E. S. Wordsworthshire. 1911.
Rice, R. Wordsworth's mind. Bloomington IN 1913.
Stork, C. W. The influence of the popular ballad on Wordsworth and Coleridge. PMLA 29 1914.
Strunk, W. Some related poems of Wordsworth and Coleridge. MLN 29 1914.
de Selincourt, E. In his English poets and the national ideal, Oxford 1915.
Dicey, A. V. The statesmanship of Wordsworth. Oxford 1917.
Greenbie, M. L. B. Wordsworth's theory of poetic diction. New Haven CT 1917; rptd New York 1977.
Cooper, L. The making and use of a verbal concordance. Sewanee Rev 27 1919.

Biographies

Wordsworth, C. Memoirs of William Wordsworth. 2 vols 1851.
Knight, W. A. The life of William Wordsworth. 3 vols Edinburgh 1889.
Legouis, E. La jeunesse de William Wordsworth, 1770–1798. Paris 1896; tr J. W. Matthews as The early life of William Wordsworth, 1770–1798, 1897; rptd with new material 1921, 1932; reissued with introd by N. Roe, 1988.
Harper, G. M. William Wordsworth, his life, works and influence. 2 vols 1916; rev and abridged (with additions) in 1 vol 1929.
Harper, G. M. Wordsworth's French daughter. Princeton 1921.
Legouis, E. William Wordsworth and Annette Vallon. 1922; rptd 1992; rev edn Hamden CT 1967.
Meyer, G. W. Wordsworth's formative years. Univ of Michigan Pbns Lang and Lit 20, Michigan and London 1943.
Moorman, M. William Wordsworth, a biography: the early years, 1770–1803. Oxford 1957; rptd with corrections 1967, 1969. Standard.
Moorman, M. William Wordsworth, a biography: the later years, 1803–1850. Oxford 1965. Standard.
Byatt, A. S. Wordsworth and Coleridge in their time. 1970; rptd as Unruly times: Wordsworth and Coleridge in their time, 1989.
Chard, L. F. Dissenting republican: Wordsworth's early life and thought in their political context. The Hague 1972.
Field, B. Barron Field's memoirs of Wordsworth. Ed G. Little, Sydney 1975.
Roe, N. Wordsworth and Coleridge: the radical years. Oxford 1988.
Gill, S. William Wordsworth: a life. Oxford 1989. Standard.
Swaab, P. (ed). Wordsworth. Lives of the great romantics by their contemporaries 3, 1996.
Johnston, K. R. The hidden Wordsworth: poet, lover, rebel spy. New York 1998.
The Wordsworth Circle (TWC), *1970– , contains essays, reviews and surveys of Wordsworth scholarship.* [KH]

Francis Wrangham 1769–1842

Collections

Sermons practical and occasional; dissertations, translations, including new versions of Virgil's Bucolica and of Milton's Defensio secunda; Seaton poems etc. 3 vols 1816.

§1

Reform: a farce modernised from Aristophanes by S. Foote jr. 1792. Anon (authorship uncertain).
The destruction of Babylon. 1795; [Cambridge 1808?]; London 1817 (in Cambridge prize poems).
The restoration of the Jews: a poem. Cambridge 1795, 1808.
Ad Bruntonam e Granta exituram hendecasyllabi. Cambridge 1799 (in J. H. Smyth ed Poemata). Single sheet.
The holy land: a poem. [Cambridge 1800.]
Poems. '1795' [c. 1802] (priv ptd), 1803.
Thirteen practical sermons: founded upon Doddridge's Rise and progress of religion in the soul [with 2 more sermons]. 1800, 1802.
The raising of Jaïrus' daughter: a poem. 1804.
A dissertation on the best means of civilizing the subjects of the British Empire in India, and of diffusing the light of the Christian religion throughout the eastern world. 1805. Prose.
A poem on the restoration of learning in the East. Cambridge, London and Oxford 1805, 1830 (as The restoration of learning in the East).
A volunteer song. York [1805?]; London [1805?] (as Trafalgar: a song).
The sufferings of the primitive martyrs. Cambridge 1812.
Joseph made known to his brethren. Cambridge 1812.
Plutarch's lives. Tr Wrangham. 1813 (2nd edn), 1816, 1826. Prose.
Poetical sketches of Scarborough. 1813 (2 edns) (illustr J. Green, T. Rowlandson); Driffield 1893. Anon. By Wrangham and others.
Poems. [1814?] (priv ptd).
Virgil. Bucolics. Tr Wrangham, Scarborough 1815; London 1816, 1830 (rev, with trns of other works by Virgil by other authors in Valpy's Classical Lib vol 8); New York 1848.
Humble contributions to a British Plutarch. 1816.
Scraps. 1816. Prose and verse.
A few sonnets attempted from Petrarch in early life. Tr [Wrangham], Ickham 1817 (priv ptd).
The pleiad: or a series of abridgements of seven distinguished writers, in opposition to the pernicious doctrines of deism. 7 pts 1820; 1 vol Edinburgh and London 1828; Philadelphia 1830.
Specimens of a version of Horace's first four books of odes, attempted in octosyllabic verse. 1820. From bk 3 only (priv ptd).
Hendecasyllabi. 1821. Anon.
The lyrics of Horace: being the first four books of his odes. Tr Wrangham, York and London 1821; Chester [1822?].
Scarborough Castle: a poem. Scarborough 1823.
Sertum Cantabrigiense, or the Cambridge garland. Malton 1824.
The poet's favourite tree. Scarborough 1826 (in J. Cole ed, The antiquarian trio).
Bayly, T. H. Psychae, or songs on butterflies ... attempted in Latin rhyme. Tr Wrangham, Malton 1828 (priv ptd).
Fifty select poems of ... Flaminio imitated ... By E. W. Barnard. Ed Wrangham, Chester 1829.
The quadrupeds' feast. Chester [1830?] (priv ptd). Anon.
Homerics ... attempted. Tr Wrangham, Chester 1834 (priv ptd). Trns of Odyssey 5 and Iliad 3.
Epithalamia tria Mariana etc. Tr Wrangham, Chester 1837. Trns from George Buchanan and others.
Bailey, J. Comicorum graecorum fragmenta. Tr Wrangham 1840.
A few epigrams attempted in Latin translation by an old pen nearly worn to its stump. [Chester 1842.]

§2

Sadler, M. T. H. Archdeacon Francis Wrangham .... 1937. A bibliography.

Edited and translated works by other authors and pbd many sermons and some other short works on religious topics.

Frances Wright, Mme D'Arusmont 1795–1852

Altorf: a tragedy .... Philadelphia 1819; London 1822.
Numerous prose pbns on politics and society and some prose fiction.

Murdo Young fl. 1817–38

The shades of Waterloo! A vision, in verse. 1817 (4 edns).
Antonia: a poem .... 1818.
Wallace: an historical tragedy. 1837, 1838.
Edited the Sun, *and wrote on shorthand.*

iii. Mid-nineteenth-century poetry 1835–1870

References

Rogers, C. (ed). The modern Scottish minstrel. 6 vols Edinburgh 1855–7. Cited as Rogers, *below*.
Miles, A. H. et al (ed). The poets and poetry of the century. 10 vols 1905–7 (enlarged). Cited as Miles, *below*.
Numerals refer to vol nos in these edns; numerals in brackets to the enlarged edn of Miles. Further information about some poets may be found in J. Julian, A dictionary of hymnology, *1892, 1907 (rev).*

Sarah Flower Adams, Sarah Fuller Adams née Flower 1805–48

Bibliographies

Stephenson, H. W. The author of Nearer, my God, to thee. 1922. Includes list of her contributions to periodicals and of references to her.

Selections

Garnett, R. (ed). In A. H. Miles, The poets and poetry of the century, enlarged edn 1905–7, vol 8, Joanna Baillie to Jean Ingelow.
Hymns and anthems. Ed W. J. Fox 1841, 4th edn 1858, 5th edn 1867. Contains 13 pieces by Adams, including Nearer, my God, to thee (rptd separately Boston 1876, London [1884], New York 1887, [1904]; edited in facs priv ptd J. Julian, London 1911).

§1

Vivia perpetua: a dramatic poem in five acts. 1841, 1893 (priv ptd, with hymns, and memoir by E. F. Bridell-Fox).
Poems by Elizabeth Barrett. Westminster Rev 42, Dec 1844.
The flock at the fountain. 1845, 1874 (rev edn Sunday-School Assoc). A catechism and hymns for children.
The royal progress, in seven cantos, a legend of the Isle of Wight. In The Illuminated Mag, ed W. J. Linton, 1845.
Uncollected poems. In W. J. Fox, Lectures addressed chiefly to the working classes 4, 1849.
A summer recollection: a poem. In M. D. Conway, The centenary history of the South Place Society, 1894, appendix 2.
See Stephenson for listing of contributions under S. Y. (poems, essays, stories) to the Monthly Repository *1834–6.*

§2

Obit. Westminster Rev 50 1849.
Taylor, Emily. In her Memories of some contemporary poets with selections from their writings, 1868.
Garnett, R. In Miles 8.

R. G. [Richard Garnett]. In DNB.
Julian, J. A dictionary of hymnology. 1892, 1907 (rev).
Bridell-Fox, E. F. [Memoir] in Vivia perpetua. 1893.
Julian, J. Original autograph ms [in facs] of Nearer, my God, to thee, with biographical, critical and historical notes. 1911.
Whitaker, R. Nearer, my God, to thee. Unity 21 Feb 1938.
Adams, S. F. The feminist companion to literature in English. Ed V. Blain, P. Clements and I. Grundy 1990. [VB]

Thomas Aird 1802–76

Collections

Poetical works. 1848, 1856, 1878 (5th edn, with memoir by J. Wallace).
Foster, B. F. Summer scenes: a series of photographs from some of his choicest water-colour drawings, with selections from the poems of Aird etc. 1867.

§1

Murtzoufle: a tragedy in three acts; with other poems. 1826.
Religious characteristics. Edinburgh 1827. Didactic essays.
The captive of Fez: a poem in five cantos. Edinburgh 1830.
Othuriel and other poems. 1839.
The old bachelor in the Old Scottish village. Edinburgh 1845, 1857 (rev and enlarged). Essays and sketches.
Poetical works of D. M. Moir. 2 vols 1852. Ed Aird, with memoir.
For two articles by Aird, see Wellesley, *p. 788.*

§2

Gilfillan, G. In his Galleries of literary portraits vol 1, Edinburgh 1856.

William Alexander 1824–1911

Selections

Selected poems of W. Alexander and C. F. Alexander. Ed A. P. Graves 1930.

§1

Popular lectures and general reading: a lecture. 1862.
Victor Hugo as poet. In The afternoon lectures on English literature ser 2, 1864.
Specimens poetical and critical. 1867 (priv ptd).
Matthew Arnold's poetry. In The afternoon lectures on English literature ser 4, 1867.
Specimen of a translation of Virgil: Aeneid bk 1, 1–181. 1869.
St Augustine's holiday and other poems. 1886.
Tenebrae. [1896.] Verses.
Poems of C. F. Humphreys. 1896. Ed Alexander, with preface.
The findings of the book and other poems. 1900. Includes St Augustine's holiday, *above*, etc.
The soldier's prayer (Is war the only thing that has no good in it?). [1900.]
Alexander also wrote and edited a number of theological works.

§2

Garrod, H. B. The poems of Alexander. Academy 15 Jan 1887.
Julian.
Primate Alexander, Archbishop of Armagh: a memoir. Ed E. Alexander 1913.

Henry Alford 1810–71

Bibliographies

Life, journals and letters, edited by his widow. 1873, 1874 (3rd edn).

Collections

The school of the heart and other poems. 2 vols Cambridge 1835.
Poetical works. 2 vols 1845, 1851 (as Select poetical works, with several pieces not before published), Boston 1853 (with 12 previously unpbd poems), 1865 (enlarged), 1868 (enlarged).

§1

Poems and poetical fragments. Cambridge 1833. Anon.
Chapters on the poets of ancient Greece. 1841.
The Abbot of Muchelnaye: sonnets. 1841, 1925.
Psalms and hymns adapted to the Sundays and holydays throughout the year; to which are added some occasional hymns. 1844.
Prose hymns, chiefly from Scripture, printed for chanting. 1844.
Memorial of the Rev Henry Alford: consisting of extracts from his correspondence, six selected sermons and a memoir by his eldest son. Ed J. Alford 1854.
English descriptive poetry: a lecture. In Evening recreations, ed J. H. Gurney, 1856.
The Odyssey of Homer in hendecasyllabic verse, bks 1–12. 1861.
A plea for the Queen's English: stray notes on speaking and spelling. 1864 (for 1863), New York [1864], 1870 (rev and enlarged), 1888 (7th edn). First pbd as The Queen's English, the first 3 words being omitted by mistake.
The year of praise: being hymns, with tunes, for the Sundays and holydays of the year. Ed H. Alford 1867.
Works of John Donne. 1870. Ed H. Alford, with memoir.
The Riviera: pen and pencil sketches from Cannes to Genoa. 1870.
Alford also pbd numerous sermons and other religious works and edited Contemporary Rev *Jan 1866–Mar 1870. See* Wellesley *p. 789.*

Letters and papers

Letters from abroad. 1865, 1865.
Life, journals and letters. Ed F. Alford 1873, 1874 (3rd edn).

§2

Moon, G. W. A defence of the Queen's English: in reply to A plea for the Queen's English, by the Dean of Canterbury. 1863.
The poems of Alford. Eclectic Rev 123 1866.
Garbett, E. L. God's view of our Babylon shown in slaying Alford. [1885.]
Miles, A. H. In Miles 10 (11).
Davidson, J. In Julian.
Hare, A. J. C. In his Biographical sketches, 1895.

William Allingham 1824–89

The largest collection of ms material – primarily letters to Allingham but also containing some of his letters and mss – is held by the Univ of Illinois, Urbana. Letters are also found in BL (including correspondence with Macmillans), HRHRC, NLS, NYPL (Berg Collection), Pierpont Morgan Lib, Princeton (correspondence with the Brownings), Queen's Univ of Belfast (letters to Henry Sutton), Tennyson Research Centre, Lincoln (correspondence with the Tennysons), Yale (correspondence with A. H. Clough).

Bibliographies

Kropf, H. Allingham und seine Dichtung. Biel 1928. Includes a list of articles on, and references to, Allingham.
O'Hegarty, P. S. A bibliography of William Allingham. Dublin Mag 22 1945; Dublin 1945 (priv ptd).
In W. E. Fredeman, Pre-Raphaelitism: a biblio-critical study, Cambridge MA 1965.
Warner, A. William Allingham: a bibliographical survey. Irish Booklore 1976.
Husni, S. William Allingham: an annotated bibliography. [Beirut 1984.] Includes lists of periodical contributions and secondary sources.
Samuels Lasner, M. William Allingham: a bibliographical study. Philadelphia 1993. Details of first and later edns and variants; rev from articles pbd in BC 1990.

Collections

[Works.] 6 vols 1887–90 (also various later issues, edns and impressions). Comprises: Blackberries, Irish songs and poems, Laurence

Bloomfield in Ireland, Flower pieces and other poems, Life and phantasy, Thought and word, and Ashby manor.

Miles 5.

Sixteen poems. Selected by William Butler Yeats. Dundrum 1905 (Dun Emer Press); rptd (facs) Shannon 1971.

Poems. Selected and arranged by Helen Allingham. 1912. Gold Treasury ser.

Poems. Ed with an introd by J. Hewitt. Dublin 1967.

§1

Poems. 1850.

Day and night songs. 1854.

Peace and war: an ode. 1854. First pbd in Daily News 20 Feb 1854, not rptd in later vols.

The music master: a love story, and two series of day and night songs. 1855, 1860 (2nd issue, as Day and night songs and the music master, a love poem). Illustr Arthur Hughes, John E. Millais and D. G. Rossetti. Some of the poems were first ptd in Household Words etc.

The poetical works of Edgar Allan Poe and Richard H. Dana. 1857. Anon ed and with introd by Allingham.

Nightingale valley: a collection, including a great number of the choicest lyrics and short poems in the English language, edited by 'Giraldus'. '1860' [1859], 1862 (2nd issue, with Allingham's name on title page, subtitle altered to: a collection of choice lyrics and short poems from the time of Shakespeare to the present day).

Poems: first American edition. Boston 1861. Text altered significantly from Poems 1850, *above*, 20 poems added.

Laurence Bloomfield in Ireland: a modern poem. 1864, 1869 (2nd issue, adds a preface, subtitle altered to: or the new landlord), 1888 (2nd edn, rev, adds dedication to Samuel Ferguson, subtitle altered to: or rich and poor in Ireland). An early version appeared in Fraser's Mag Nov 1862–Nov 1863.

The ballad book: a selection of the choicest British ballads. Ed Allingham. 1864. (several later impressions). Gold Treasury ser; Cambridge MA 1865 (several later impressions).

Fifty modern poems. 1865.

In fairyland: a series of pictures from the elf-world by Richard Doyle, with a poem by William Allingham. '1870' [1869], New York 1870, London 1873 (2nd issue). Illustr Richard Doyle.

Ye dirty old man (dirty Dick): a legend of Bishopsgate, from Household Words conducted by Charles Dickens. [1870 or later.] Anon. Poem, first pbd in Household Words 8 Jan 1853, used in advertisement book by London liquor merchant; another printing from perhaps as early as 1855 recorded.

Rambles by 'Patricius Walker'. 1873, 1893 (as vols 1–2 of Varieties in prose). Essays on England and Ireland.

The poetical works of Thomas Campbell: memoir by W. Allingham. 1875, 1890.

Songs, ballads and stories. 1877, Boston 1877. Selections from previous vols, rev and rearranged.

A question. [c. 1876–8.] Broadside. Anonymous poem on the Eastern Question.

Evil May-day &c. [1882], [1883] (2nd issue, with Longman imprint on pasted-in slip). An argumentative poem on the relation of religion to dogma and science.

Ashby Manor: a play in two acts. [1882], [1883] (2nd issue, with Longman imprint on pasted-in slip); rptd in Thought and word 1890, *below*.

The fairies. [1883.] Illustr E. Gertrude Thomson, 1912 (as Up the airy mountain). Rptd from Poems 1850, *above*. Set to music by Arnold Bax 1907.

Blackberries picked off many bushes, by 'D. Pollex and others', put in a basket by W. Allingham. 1884, 1890 (2nd issue). Poems by Allingham.

Day and night songs. 1884. Bears little relation to 1854 vol of same name; rptd in Flower pieces and other poems, *below*.

Hopgood & Co: a new and original serio-comic piece, in one act. [Guildford?] 1885 (priv ptd). Rptd in vol 3 of Varieties in prose, *below*.

At Stratford-on-Avon. [Guildford? 1886] (priv ptd). Bifolium. Poem on Shakespeare first pbd in Macmillan's Mag Mar 1864.

Flower pieces. [Guildford? 1886] (priv ptd). Trial version of poems forming opening section of Flower pieces and other poems, *below*; some first pbd in Poems 1850, *above*, others in Flowers and months in Athenaeum Feb 1886.

Rhymes for the young folk. [1887.] Illustr Helen Allingham, Harry Furniss, Kate Greenaway and Caroline Paterson, New York [1915], London 1930 (as Robin red breast and other verses).

Irish songs and poems. 1887, 1890 (2nd issue), 1901.

Flower pieces and other poems. 1888, 1893 (3rd issue). Illustr D. G. Rossetti. Includes The music master, Day and night songs, *above*.

Life and phantasy. 1889, 1893 (2nd issue). Illustr Arthur Hughes and John E. Millais.

Thought and word, and Ashby Manor: a play in two acts. 1890. Includes four stage designs by Helen Allingham.

Varieties in prose. 3 vols 1893. Vols 1–2 contain Rambles, vol 3 contains Irish sketches, Hopgood & Co, and Essays on modern prophets, Painter and critic, Poetry, Disraeli's monument to Byron, Some curiosities of criticism, and Baudelaire.

By the way: verses, fragments and notes, arranged by Helen Allingham. 1912.

Letters and papers

William Allingham: a diary. Ed H. Allingham and D. Radford 1907, rptd Fontwell Surrey 1967 (with introd by G. Grigson), rptd 1985 (Penguin Lives and Letters ser, with introd by J. J. Norwich); 1990 (Folio Soc, introd by J. J. Norwich, adds illus from contemporary photographs.

Letters to William Allingham. Ed H. Allingham and E. Baumer Williams 1911. Includes letters from Allingham, principally to Ralph Waldo Emerson, Leigh Hunt and Arthur Hughes.

Letters from William Allingham to Robert and Elizabeth Barrett Browning. [1913?] (priv ptd).

Cameron, K. W. Allingham and Emerson: some new evidence. Emerson Soc Quart no 6 1957. 5 letters to Ralph Waldo Emerson.

Allingham also edited Fraser's Mag 1874–9.

§2

[Rossetti, W. M.] Poetry and the drama. Critic 15 Oct 1850. Rev of Poems 1850.

[Patmore, C.] Allingham's Poems. Palladium Nov 1850.

[Patmore, C.] Rev of Day and night songs. Critic 1 Apr 1854.

[Patmore, C.] Rev of The music master, 1855. In New poets, Edinburgh Rev Oct 1856.

[Rossetti, W. M.]. Poetry and the drama. Critic 1 Apr 1857. Rev of The Music master.

Monkhouse, C. Allingham's new poems. Acad 3 Feb 1883. Rev of Evil May-day &c. and Ashby Manor.

Tynan, K. The poetry of William Allingham. Irish Fireside 30 Oct 1886.

Yeats, W. B. The poet of Ballyshannon. Providence Sunday Journal 22 Sep 1888; rptd in Yeats, Letters to the New Island, 1934.

Letters of D. G. Rossetti to Allingham 1845–70. Ed G. B. Hill 1897. Many originally appeared in Atlantic Monthly July–Aug 1896.

Yeats, W. B. In Miles 5.

Johnson, L. In A treasury of Irish poetry in the English tongue, ed S. A. Brooke and T. W. Rolleston, 1900.

Graves, A. P. William Allingham. Trans Royal Soc of Lit 32 1913.

Kropf, H. Allingham und seine Dichtung. Biel 1928.

Howe, M. L. Notes on the Allingham canon. PQ 12 1933.

Donaghy, J. L. William Allingham. Dublin Mag 22 1945.

Browne, J. N. Poetry in Ulster. In Arts in Ulster, ed S. H. Bell, 1951.
White, H. O. An Allingham pamphlet. TLS 17 Aug 1956. On Flower pieces, *above*.
Warner, A. William Allingham. Lewisburg PA 1975.
Husni, S. Incorrect references to William Allingham. N & Q 228 Aug 1983.
Boyd, T. W. A regular illustrated book: William Allingham and his pre-Raphaelite friends make The music master. Publishing History 37 1995. [MSL]

Matthew Arnold 1822–88

The most complete guide to Arnold mss is in IELM, *vol 4 pt 1 1982. A checklist of prose mss appears in* Complete prose works, *ed Super 1960–77, vol 12. Many papers are held at Balliol College, Oxford and in the Tinker Collection at Yale. A range of Arnoldiana is in the Brotherton Collection at Univ of Leeds. An extensive collection of originals and photographs has been assembled at the Alderman Lib, Univ of Virginia.*

Bibliographies etc

Smart, T. B. The bibliography of Arnold. 1892, 1904 (rev and expanded in Works vol 15). Correction by W. F. Prideaux, N & Q 16 Apr 1892.
Ehrsam, T. G., R. H. Deily and R. M. Smith. In their Bibliographies of twelve Victorian authors, New York 1936. Addn by J. G. Fucilla, MP 37 1940.
Parrish, S. M. A concordance to the poems of Arnold. Ithaca NY 1959.
Faverty, F. E. Matthew Arnold. In his The Victorian poets: a guide to research, 1968.
DeLaura, D. J. Matthew Arnold. In his Victorian prose: a guide to research. New York 1973.
Tollers, V. L. A bibliography of Arnold 1932–1970. Univ Park PA 1974.
Machann, C. The essential Matthew Arnold. Oxford 1993. Bibliography of secondary works.

Collections and selections

Poems: a new and complete edition. Boston 1856.
Essays in criticism [first series]. Boston 1865, 1866 etc. Includes On translating Homer, A French Eton.
Poems. 2 vols 1869.
Poems: new and complete edition. 2 vols 1877, New York 1878 (rev), London 1881 (new edn), New York 1883.
Selected poems. 1878, 1878, 1880 etc, New York 1878. Chosen by Arnold.
Passages from the prose writings. 1880; ed W. E. Buckler, New York 1963. Chosen by Arnold.
The Arnold birthday book, arranged by his daughter Eleanor Arnold. 1883. From his poems.
Poems. 3 vols 1885, 1888, 1895 (Lib edn).
Reports on elementary schools 1852–82. Ed F. Sandford 1889; ed F. S. Marvin 1908.
Poetical works. 1890, 1891 etc.
Poems. Ed G. C. Macaulay 1896.
Selected poems. Ed W. T. Stead 1896.
The strayed reveller, Empedocles on Etna and other poems. Ed W. Sharp 1896.
Poetical works, with introduction by N. H. Dole. New York 1897.
Selections from the prose writings. Ed L. E. Gates, New York 1897.
Poems. Ed A. C. Benson 1900.
Poems, narrative, elegiac, and lyrical. Ed H. B. Forman 1902.
Works. 15 vols 1903–4 (Deluxe edn). Includes Letters, ed G. W. E. Russell.
Selected poems. Ed A. Waugh 1905.
Essays literary and critical. Ed G. K. Chesterton 1906.
Poems prior to 1864. Ed L. Magnus 1906.
Poems 1849–64. Oxford 1906 (WC) (introd by A. T. Quiller-Couch).
Critical essays. Ed H. Bennett 1907.
Poems 1840–66. Ed R. A. Scott-James 1908 (EL).
Poems 1840–67. Ed H. S. M[ilford], Oxford 1909 (introd by A. T. Quiller-Couch); ed G. St Quintin, Oxford 1926; with addns as Poetical works, Oxford 1942, 1945 (OSA). Complete text in chronological arrangement with variant readings.
Essays in criticism: third series. Ed E. J. O'Brien, Boston 1910.
Thoughts on education chosen from the writings of Arnold. Ed L. Huxley 1912.
Essays, including Essays in criticism 1865, On translating Homer, with F. W. Newman's reply and five other essays now for the first time collected. Oxford 1914 (OSA).
Arnold as dramatic critic: a reprint of articles signed 'An old playgoer' contributed by him to the Pall Mall Gazette. Ed C. K. Shorter 1903 (priv ptd); as Letters of an old playgoer, ed B. Matthews, New York 1919.
Poems. Ed H. Newbolt 1923.
Selected essays. Ed H. G. Rawlinson 1924.
Selections from Arnold's poetry. Ed R. E. C. Houghton 1924.
Selections from Arnold's prose. Ed D. C. Somervell 1924.
Prose selections. Ed E. T. Campagnac 1928.
Selected poems. Ed H. Alsop 1931.
Poetry and prose, with W. Watson's poem and essays by L. Johnson and H. W. Garrod. Ed E. K. Chambers, Oxford 1939.
Matthew Arnold: an introduction and a selection. Ed C. Dyment 1948.
The portable Arnold. Ed L. Trilling, New York 1949.
Poetical works. Ed C. B. Tinker and H. F. Lowry, Oxford 1950 (OSA). Arnold's arrangement.
Five uncollected essays. Ed K. Allott, Liverpool 1953.
Arnold: a selection of his poems. Ed K. Allott 1954.
Poetry and prose. Ed J. Bryson 1954 (Reynard Lib).
Essays, letters and reviews. Ed F. Neiman, Cambridge MA 1960.
Complete prose works. Ed R. H. Super, Ann Arbor MI 1960–77. 11 vols; does not include correspondence. 1 On the classical tradition, 1960; 2 Democratic education, 1962; 3 Lectures and essays in criticism, 1962; 4 Schools and universities on the Continent, 1964; 5 Culture and anarchy, 1965; 6 Dissent and dogma, 1968; 7 God and the Bible, 1970; 8 Essays religious and mixed, 1972; 9 English literature and Irish politics, 1973; 10 Philistinism in England and America, 1974; 11 The last word, 1977. Cited as Super, *below*.
Selected essays. Ed N. Annan, Oxford 1964.
An Arnold verse selection. Ed D. Grant 1964.
Selected poems and prose. Ed F. W. Watt, Oxford 1964.
Poems. Ed K. Allott 1965 (Longmans Annotated Eng Poets); 2nd edn 1979 (rev M. Allott).
An Arnold prose selection. Ed J. D. Jump 1965.
Essays on English literature. Ed F. W. Bateson 1965.
Culture and the State. Ed P. Nash, New York 1966.
Matthew Arnold and the education of the new order. Ed P. Smith and G. Summerfield 1969.
Selected prose. Ed P. J. Keating 1971.
Matthew Arnold on education. Ed G. Sutherland, Harmondsworth 1973 (Pen).
Selected poems and prose. Ed M. Allott 1978 (EL); new edn 1993.
Matthew Arnold. Ed M. Allott and R. H. Super 1986 (Oxford Authors).
Matthew Arnold. Ed H. Bloom, New York 1987.
Selected poems. Ed T. Peltason, Oxford 1994 (Oxford Classics).
Selected poems. Ed K. Silver, Manchester 1994.

§1

Alaric at Rome: a prize poem. Rugby 1840; ed (with other poems) C. K. Shorter 1894; ed T. J. Wise 1893 (priv ptd); ed (with other poems) R. Garnett 1896.

Cromwell: a prize poem. Oxford 1843; rptd 1863, 1891 and in Oxford prize poems, Oxford 1846.

The strayed reveller and other poems, by A. 1849.

Empedocles on Etna and other poems, by A. 1852, 1896. *See* L. Bonnerot, Empédocle sur l'Etna: étude critique et traduction, Paris 1947.

Poems: a new edition. 1853 (with critical preface), 1854 (rev), 1857 (rev).

Poems: second series. 1855.

Merope: a tragedy. 1858; ed J. C. Collins (with R. Whitelaw's trn of Sophocles' Electra), Oxford 1906, 1917 (rev).

Oratio anniversaria in memoriam publicorum benefactorum academiae Oxoniensis ex instituto N. domini Crewe. 1858.

England and the Italian question. 1859; ed M. M. Bevington, Durham NC 1953 (with F. Stephen's reply). In Super vol 1.

The popular education of France, with notices of that of Holland and Switzerland. 1861. In Super vol 2. Previously issued in Education Commission reports 1860 (confidential), 1861.

On translating Homer: three lectures, 1861; On translating Homer: last words, 1862. New York 1883 (both texts, with On the study of Celtic literature), London 1896 (Popular edn); ed W. H. D. Rouse 1905. In Super vol 1.

The twice-revised code. 1862. Originally appeared in Fraser's Mag 55, Mar 1862. In Super vol 2.

Oratio anniversaria in memoriam publicorum benefactorum academiae Oxoniensis ex instituto N. domini Crewe. 1862.

Heinrich Heine: reprint from the Cornhill Magazine, August 1863. Philadelphia 1863.

A French Eton: or middle class education and the State. 1864, 1892 (with Schools and universities in France). Originally appeared in Macmillan's Mag 8–10 (Sep 1863–May 1864). In Super vol 2.

Essays in criticism, first series. 1865, 1869, 1875, New York 1883, London 1884, Leipzig 1887; ed G. K. Chesterton 1906 (EL); ed W. Raleigh 1912; ed C. A. Miles and L. Smith, Oxford 1918; ed T. M. Hoctor, Ann Arbor MI 1958; ed K. Allott 1964 (EL); tr Sp 1894. Original articles appeared as: Maurice de Guérin, Fraser's Mag 57, Jan 1863; The bishop and the philosopher, Macmillan's Mag 7, Jan 1863; Eugénie de Guérin, Cornhill Mag 7, June 1863; Heinrich Heine, Cornhill Mag 8, Aug 1863; Marcus Aurelius, Victoria Mag 2, Nov 1863; A word more about Spinoza, Macmillan's Mag 9, Dec 1863; Joubert, Nat Rev 18, Jan 1864; Pagan and mediaeval religious sentiment, Cornhill Mag 9, Apr 1864; The literary influence of academies, Cornhill Mag 10, Aug 1864; The functions of criticism at the present time, Nat Rev 1 (n.s.), Nov 1864; added in 1875: A Persian passion play, Cornhill Mag 24, Dec 1871. In Super vol 3.

On the study of Celtic literature. 1867, New York 1883 (with On translating Homer), London 1891 (Popular edn); ed E. Rhys 1910 (EL) (with other essays by Arnold and review by Strangford); ed A. Nutt 1910. Original articles appeared in 4 pts in Cornhill Mag 13–14, Mar–July 1866. In Super vol 3.

New poems. 1867, Boston 1867, London 1868.

Schools and universities on the Continent. 1868. Previously issued in Schools Inquiry Commission report. Partly rptd in his Higher schools and universities in Germany, 1874, 1882, and in A French Eton, to which is added Schools and universities in France, 1892. In Super vol 4.

Culture and anarchy: an essay in political and social criticism. 1869, 1875, 1882, New York 1883 (with Friendship's garland), London 1889 (Popular edn); ed J. D. Wilson, Cambridge 1932; ed I. Gregor 1971; ed S. Collini, Cambridge 1993; ed S. Lipman, New Haven CT 1994. Original articles appeared in 6 pts in Cornhill Mag 16–18, July 1867–Aug 1868. In Super vol 5.

St Paul and Protestantism; with an introduction on Puritanism and the Church of England. 1870, 1870, 1875, New York 1883 (with Last essays on church and religion), London 1887 (Popular edn). Original articles appeared in 3 pts in Cornhill Mag 20–1, Oct 1869–Feb 1870. [Added in 1887: A comment on Christmas, Contemporary Rev 47, Apr 1885.] In Super vol 6 [11].

Friendship's garland: being the conversations, letters and opinions of the late Arminius Baron von Thunder-ten-Tronckh collected and edited with a dedicatory letter to Adolescens Leo Esq of the Daily Telegraph. 1871, New York 1883 (with Culture and anarchy), London 1897, 1903 (Popular edn). Original articles appeared in Pall Mall Gazette as: My countrymen, 13 Feb 1866; An explanation, 20 Mar 1866; 'Geist', 21 July 1866; Democracy, 4 Aug 1866; An aggrieved friend, 7 Aug 1866; 'Ce dogue', 15 Aug 1866; Stein plus Hardenberg, 19 Nov 1866; Von Thunder-ten-Tronckh on compulsory education, 20, 22 Apr 1867; The deceased wife's sister, 8 June 1869; England's position, 9 Aug 1870; The great heart of England, 21 Nov 1870; Audi alteram partem, 25 Nov 1870; A sad story, 29 Nov 1870. In Super vol 5.

A Bible-reading for schools: the great prophecy of Israel's restoration (Isaiah chs 40–66) arranged and edited for young learners. 1872, 1889 etc.

Literature and dogma: an essay towards a better apprehension of the Bible. 1873 (3 edns), New York 1873, Boston 1873, London 1874 ('fourth edn'), 1876 ('fifth edn'), New York 1876, 1877, 1883, London 1883, 1903 (Popular edns); 1910 (Nelson's Shilling Lib); tr Fr 1876. Original articles appeared in 2 pts in Cornhill Mag 24, July, Oct 1871. In Super vol 6.

Isaiah 40–66, with the shorter prophecies allied to it, arranged and edited with notes. 1875.

God and the Bible: a review of objections to Literature and dogma. 1875, Boston 1876, New York 1879, 1883, London 1884 (Popular edn). Original articles appeared in 8 pts in Contemporary Rev 24–6, Oct 1874–Sep 1875. In Super vol 7.

Last essays on church and religion. 1877, New York 1883 (with St Paul and Protestantism), London 1903 (Popular edn). Original articles appeared as: Bishop Butler and the zeit-geist, Contemporary Rev 27, Feb–Mar 1876; The Church of England, Macmillan's Mag 33, Apr 1876; A last word on the Burials Bill, Macmillan's Mag 34, July 1876; A psychological parallel, Contemporary Rev 28, Nov 1876. In Super vol 8.

The six chief lives from Johnson's Lives of the poets, with Macaulay's Life of Johnson edited with a preface. 1878 etc, 1886 (4th edn with notes), 1889. Preface also appeared as Johnson's Lives, Macmillan's Mag 38, June 1878. In Super vol 8.

Mixed essays. 1879, 1880, New York 1880, 1883 (with Irish essays), London 1903 (Popular edn). Original articles appeared as: A French critic on Milton, Quart Rev 143, Jan 1877; Falkland, Nineteenth Cent 1, Mar 1877; A French critic on Goethe, Quart Rev 145, Jan 1878; Equality, Fortnightly Rev 29, Mar 1878; Irish Catholicism and British liberalism, Fortnightly Rev 30, July 1878; Porro unum est necessarium, Fortnightly Rev 30, Nov 1878. Added in 1880: George Sand, Fortnightly Rev 27, June 1877; A guide to English literature, Nineteenth Cent 2, Dec 1877. In Super vol 8.

Poems of Wordsworth chosen and edited. 1879, 1879 (with addns), 1880 etc. Preface also published as: Wordsworth, Macmillan's Mag 40, July 1879. In Super vol 9.

On the study of poetry: general introduction; Thomas Gray: critical introduction; John Keats: critical introduction. In English poets, ed T. H. Ward, 1880; rptd in Essays in criticism: second series, 1888.

Letters, speeches and tracts on Irish affairs by E. Burke, collected and arranged. 1881.

Poetry of Byron, chosen and arranged. 1881, 1890 etc. Preface appeared as: Byron, Macmillan's Mag 43, Mar 1881. In Super vol 9.

Irish essays and others. 1882, New York 1883 (with Mixed essays), London 1891 (Popular edn). Articles first appeared as: Ecce, convertimur as gentes, Fortnightly Rev 31, Feb 1879; A speech at Eton, Cornhill Mag 39, May 1879; The French play in London,

Nineteenth Cent 6, Aug 1879; Copyright, Fortnightly Rev 33, Mar 1880; The future of liberalism, Nineteenth Cent 8, July 1880; The incompatibles, Nineteenth Cent 9, Apr–June 1881; Irish grammar schools, Fortnightly Rev 36, Aug 1881. In Super vol 9.

Isaiah of Jerusalem in the authorised English version, with an introduction, corrections and notes. 1883. Preface also appeared as: Isaiah of Jerusalem, Nineteenth Cent 13, Apr–May 1883. In Super vol 10.

Discourses in America. 1885, New York 1889; ed F. R. Tomlinson, New York 1924. Original articles appeared as: Literature and science, Nineteenth Cent 12, Aug 1882; Numbers, Nineteenth Cent 15, Apr 1884; Emerson, Macmillan's Mag 50, May 1884. In Super vol 10.

Education department: special report on certain points connected with elementary education in Germany, Switzerland and France. 1886, 1888 (with new prefatory note). In Super vol 11.

General Grant: an estimate. Boston 1887; ed J. Y. Simon, Carbondale IL 1966 (with Mark Twain's rejoinder). Rptd from Murray's Mag Jan–Feb 1887.

Schools. In The reign of Queen Victoria, ed T. H. Ward, 1887.

Essays in criticism: second series. 1888 (posthumous edn with prefatory note by Lord Coleridge), 1889 etc, Leipzig 1892; ed S. R. Littlewood 1938; ed K. Allott 1964 (EL). Articles first appeared as: Amiel, Macmillan's Mag 56, Sep 1887; Count Leo Tolstoi, Fortnightly Rev 48, Dec 1887; Shelley, Nineteenth Cent 23, Jan 1888; Milton, Century Mag 36, May 1888. In Super vols 9–12.

Civilization in the United States: first and last impressions of America. Boston 1888; tr Fr 1902. Original articles appeared as: A word about America, Nineteenth Cent 9, May 1882; A word more about America, Nineteenth Cent 17, Feb 1885; General Grant, Murray's Mag 1, Jan–Feb 1887; Civilization in the United States, Nineteenth Cent 23, Apr 1888. In Super vols 10–12.

For contemporary reviews of individual works, see §2, below.

Contributions to periodicals

The following items were not reprinted by Arnold.

The 'principle of examination'. Daily News 25 Mar 1862. In Super vol 1.

The code out of danger. London Rev 4, 10 May 1862. In Super vol 2.

Ordnance maps. London Rev 5, 6 Dec 1862. In Super vol 2.

Tractatus theologico-politicus. London Rev 5, 27 Dec 1862. In Super vol 2.

Dante and Beatrice. Fraser's Mag 67, Jan 1863. In Super vol 2.

Dr Stanley's lectures on the Jewish church. Macmillan's Mag 7, Feb 1863. In Super vol 2.

Mr Walter and schoolmasters' certificates. London Rev 6, 11 Apr 1863. In Super vol 2.

Education and the State. Pall Mall Gazette 11, 22 Dec 1865. In Super vol 4.

The Mansion-house meeting. Pall Mall Gazette 17 Jan 1866. In Super vol 4.

The Eisteddfod. Pall Mall Gazette 5 Sep 1866. In Super vol 3.

Theodore Parker. Pall Mall Gazette 24 Aug 1867. In Super vol 5.

German and English universities. Pall Mall Gazette 5 May 1868. In Super vol 4.

A new history of Greece. Pall Mall Gazette 12 Oct 1868. In Super vol 5.

On the modern element in literature. Macmillan's Mag 19, Feb 1869. In Super vol 1.

A recantation and apology. Pall Mall Gazette 2 Aug 1869. In Super vol 5.

Obermann. Academy 1, 9 Oct 1869. In Super vol 5.

Melancholy if true. Pall Mall Gazette 13 Oct 1869. In Super vol 5.

Sainte-Beuve. Academy 1, 13 Nov 1869. In Super vol 5.

A first requisite for church reform. Pall Mall Gazette 30 May 1870. In Super vol 6.

Endowments. Pall Mall Gazette 12 Nov 1870. In Super vol 6.

A few words about the Education Act. Educational Rev 1, Jan 1871. In Super vol 7.

Curtius's History of Greece. Pall Mall Gazette 28 Apr 1871; also 4 June 1872; 22 July 1872; 25 Mar 1876. In Super vol 5.

A French Elijah. Pall Mall Gazette 24 Nov 1871. In Super vol 7.

Renan's Réforme intellectuelle et morale de la France. Academy 3, 15 Feb 1872. In Super vol 7.

Savings banks in schools. Pall Mall Gazette 22 Nov 1873. In Super vol 7.

A speech at Westminster. Macmillan's Mag 29, Feb 1874. In Super vol 7.

Roman Catholics and the State. Pall Mall Gazette 8 Apr 1875. In Super vol 7.

A Deptford poet. Pall Mall Gazette 25 June 1875. In Super vol 7.

The Irish university question. The Times 31 July 1879. In Super vol 9.

Joseph de Maistre on Russia. Quart Rev 148, Oct 1879. In Super vol 9.

Cost of elementary schools. The Times 20 Oct 1879. In Super vol 9.

A Genevese judge. Pall Mall Gazette 13 July 1881. In Super vol 9.

An Eton boy. Fortnightly Rev 37, June 1882. In Super vol 10.

A septuagenarian poet. St James's Gazette 2 June 1882. In Super vol 10.

A Liverpool address. Nineteenth Cent 12, Nov 1882. In Super vol 10.

A French worthy. Pall Mall Gazette 8 Nov 1882. In Super vol 10.

At the princess's. Pall Mall Gazette 6 Dec 1882. In Super vol 10.

An old playgoer at the play. Pall Mall Gazette 30 Mar 1883. In Super vol 10.

An old playgoer on 'Impulse'. Pall Mall Gazette 25 May 1883. In Super vol 10.

An old playgoer at the Lyceum. Pall Mall Gazette 30 May 1883. In Super vol 10.

Address to the Wordsworth Society. Macmillan's Mag 48, June 1883. In Super vol 10.

George Sand. Pall Mall Gazette 12 Aug 1884. In Super vol 11.

Hamlet once more. Pall Mall Gazette 23 Oct 1884. In Super vol 11.

A lay sermon by Mr Matthew Arnold. Pall Mall Gazette 1 Dec 1884. In Super vol 11.

The nadir of liberalism. Nineteenth Cent 19, May 1886. In Super vol 12.

The political crisis. The Times 22 May 1886. In Super vol 12.

Common schools abroad. Century Mag 32, Oct 1886. In Super vol 12.

Thirty-five years of school inspecting. Pall Mall Gazette 13 Nov 1886. In Super vol 12.

The zenith of conservatism. Nineteenth Cent 21, Jan 1887. In Super vol 12.

A 'friend of God'. Nineteenth Cent 21, Apr 1887. In Super vol 12.

Up to Easter. Nineteenth Cent 21, Apr 1887. In Super vol 12.

From Easter to August. Nineteenth Cent 22, Sep 1887. In Super vol 12.

Disestablishment in Wales. National Rev 11, Mar 1888. In Super vol 12.

Letters and papers

The letters of Matthew Arnold, *ed Cecil Lang, 6 vols, Vol 1 1996, vol 2 (1860–65) 1997, Vol 3 (1866–70) 1998; Charlottesville VA 1996–.*

Galton, A. H. Some letters of Arnold. Cent Guild Hobby Horse Apr 1890; rptd in his Two essays upon Arnold, 1897.

On Home Rule for Ireland: two letters to The Times. 1891 (priv ptd). With prefatory notes by T. B. Smart.

Russell, G. W. E. Letters of Arnold 1848–88. 2 vols 1895, New York 1895, 2 vols in 1 New York 1900, 2 vols London 1901 (with new notes); in Works, 1904, vols 13–15.

Arnold's notebooks, with a preface by [Eleanor Arnold] Wodehouse. 1902; ed by H. F. Lowry, K. Young and W. H. Dunn 1952; Arnold's diaries: the unpublished items transcribed and edited by W. B. Guthrie, Ann Arbor MI 1959.

Letters from Arnold to John Churton Collins. 1910 (priv ptd).
Gosse, E. Arnold and Swinburne. TLS 12 Aug 1920. 6 letters.
Powell, A. F. Sainte-Beuve and Arnold: an unpublished letter. French Quart 3 1921.
Whitridge, A. [J. H.] Newman and Arnold. TLS 10 Mar 1921; addn, 31 Mar 1921. Rptd in his Unpublished letters of Arnold, *below*.
Drinkwater, J. Some letters from Arnold to Robert Browning. Cornhill Mag Dec 1923; rptd in his Book for bookmen, 1926.
Koszul, A. Une lettre inédite de Matthew Arnold. Revue de Littérature Comparée 3 1923. To Edouard Reuss.
Whitridge, A. Unpublished letters of Arnold. New Haven CT 1923.
Houghton, R. E. C. Letter of Arnold. TLS 19 May 1932. To Mr Hill, 5 Nov 1852.
Lowry, H. F. The letters of Arnold to Arthur Hugh Clough. Oxford 1932. Correction by J. C. Maxwell, N & Q 198, Oct 1953; addn by K. Allott, N & Q 201, June 1956.
Motter, T. H. V. A new Arnold letter and an old Swinburne quarrel. TLS 31 Aug 1933.
Motter, T. H. V. A check list of Arnold's letters. SP 31 1934.
Gordon, I. A. Three new letters of Arnold. MLN 56 1941. To R. D. Adams of Sydney.
Armytage, W. H. G. Arnold and a liberal minister 1880–5. RES 23 1947. Letters to A. J. Mundella.
Armytage, W. H. G. Arnold and Richard Cobden in 1864: some recently discovered letters. RES 25 1949.
Armytage, W. H. G. Arnold and W. E. Gladstone: some new letters. UTQ 18 1949.
Armytage, W. H. G. Arnold and T. H. Huxley: some new letters 1870–80. RES n.s. 4 1953.
Allott, K. Arnold: two unpublished letters. N & Q 200, Aug 1955. To W. H. Lucas.
Armytage, W. H. G. Arnold and a reviewer. RES n.s. 6 1955. Letter to N. MacColl.
Lowe, R. L. Arnold and Percy William Bunting: some new letters 1884–87. SB 7 1955.
Lowe, R. L. Two Arnold letters. MP 52 1955. To Thomas Arnold and Sidney Colvin.
Buckler, W. E. Arnold's books: toward a publishing diary. Geneva 1958. Letters to publishers.
Brooks, R. L. Arnold and his contemporaries: a check list of unpublished and published letters. SP 56 1959; addn, 63 1966.
Neiman, F. 'My dear Sumner': three letters from Arnold. Victorian Newsletter 17 1960.
Brooks, R. L. Arnold's correspondence. MP 59 1962. Unpbd letters housed in USA.
DeLaura, D. J. Four Arnold letters. TSLL 4 1962.
Mattheisen, P. F. and A. C. Young. Some letters of Arnold. Victorian Newsletter 24 1963. To E. Gosse.
Monteiro, G. Arnold and John Hay: three unpublished letters. N & Q 208 Dec 1963.
DeLaura, D. J. Three Arnold letters. Lib Chron 7 1964.
Mattheisen, P. F. and A. C. Young. An unpublished Arnold letter. Amer N & Q Jan 1964. To G. W. Smalley.
DeLaura, D. J. Eight more Arnold letters. Lib Chron 8 1965.
DeLaura, D. J. Arnold and the American 'literary class': unpublished correspondence and some further reasons. BNYPL Apr 1966.
Mattheisen, P. F. and A. C. Young. Arnold in America 1884. N & Q 211, Feb 1966.
Gordon, J. B. Arnold and the Elcho family. N & Q 212 Oct 1967.
Williamson, E. Arnold's letters to George Stacey Gibson. Victorian Newsletter 31 1967.
Davis, A. K. Arnold's letters: a descriptive checklist. Charlottesville VA 1968.
Allott, K. An allusion to Pope in an early unpublished Arnold letter. VP 7 1969.
Baylen, J. O. Arnold and the Pall Mall Gazette: some unpublished letters, 1884–1887. South Atlantic Quart 68 1969.
McCarthy, P. Mrs Matthew Arnold: some considerations and some letters. HLB 17 1969.
Cameron, K. W. Arnold at home: an English criticism of his letters to Emerson. Amer Transcendental Quart 5 1970.
Peterson, W. S. G. W. E. Russell and the editing of Arnold's Letters. Victorian Newsletter 37 1970.
Godshalk, W. L. Arnold to Hamilton Mabie: an unrecorded letter. N & Q 216 July 1971.
Horn, V. E. Arnold: a letter redated. N & Q 216 July 1971.
McCarthy, P. Mrs Matthew Arnold. TSLL 12 1971.
Rawson, C. J. Arnold to Henry Reeve: an unpublished letter. N & Q 216 July 1971.
Williamson, E. L. Words from Westminster Abbey: Arnold and Arthur Stanley. SEL 11 1971.
Winnifrith, T. J. Arnold and Clough. N & Q 216 July 1971.
Rea, E. E. Arnold on education: unpublished letters to Harriet Martineau. YES 2 1972.
Tener, R. H. A new Arnold letter. N & Q 218 July 1973.
Trevor, M. The Arnolds: Thomas Arnold and his family. New York 1973.
Montiero, G. Addendum to Davis' Matthew Arnold's letters. PBSA 68 1974.
Pady, D. S. Arnold to Thomas Brower Peacock. N & Q 219 Dec 1974.
Allott, K. and M. Arnold the poet. In Matthew Arnold: writers and their backgound, ed K. Allott, 1975.
Ridley, H. Arnold to Henry Montagu Butler: two new letters. Arnoldian 3 1975.
Carrive, L. Lettre inédite de Matthew Arnold à Felix Pecaut. EA 24 1976.
Dietrich, M. A Goethe quotation in a letter of Arnold. N & Q 221 Sep 1976.
Tollers, V. Arnold's unpublished letters to Manning, Wilson, and Millais. Arnoldian 3 1976.
McNally, J. An Arnold letter of December 22, 1867. Arnoldian 4 1977.
Lowe, R. L. An exchange of letters from Frederic Mayer Bird and Arnold. MP 75 1978.
Godshalk, W. L. An unrecorded letter from Arnold to William Parsons Atkinson. ELN 17 1979.
Livingston, J. C. A note from Arnold to Wilfrid Ward. Arnoldian 6 1979.
Demoor, M. Arnold to Lady Eastlake: a new Arnold letter. N & Q 226 Oct 1981.
Waller, J. Of poets and rivers: five letters of Arnold to George Stovin Venables. Browning Inst Stud 9 1981.
Middlebro, T. Arnold as helper: letter to a young teacher. N & Q 230 1985.
Stedman, J. Some unpublished letters of Arnold to Richard D'Oyly Carte. Arnoldian 14 1986.
Bell, B. Ten letters from Mrs Matthew Arnold to George Smith. Arnoldian 15 1988.
Fullerton, C. W. Matthew Arnold: two new letters. N & Q 233 Sep 1988.
Machann, C. Two new letters on Arnold and English Protestantism in 1869. Victorian Newsletter 74 1988.
Machann, C. and F. D. Burt. The literary and critical career of Arnold: thirteen new letters. MP 87 1989.
Powell, J. and T. Langford. An unnoticed letter of condolence from Arnold to Bertram Wodehouse Currie. Nineteenth Cent Prose 16 1989.
Lang, C. An Arnold family album. Arnoldian 15 1989–90.
Machann, C. Arnold and education: nine new letters. VP 28 1990.
Brooks, R. L. Arnold's lost Pawsey's London diary, 1886. Manuscripts 44 1992.

I have a letter from Major Pond: an unpublished letter from Arnold to James Burton Pond. Nineteenth Cent Prose 20 1993.
Machann, C. Selected letters of Arnold. Basingstoke 1993.
Baker, W. Arnold and the Eastern question: an unpublished letter to George Howard. N & Q 240 1995.
Baker, W. Arnold's burnt hand: an unpublished early letter. N & Q 240 1995.

§2

The standard bibliography of secondary sources to 1974 is Tollers (see Bibliographies, above) and more recent sources can be found in Machann (see Bibliographies, above). Annual bibliographies for Arnold appear in The Arnoldian *(1981–8),* YWES, *in the summer issue of* VS, *and occasionally in* VP. *A large number of contemporary reviews are rptd in the 2 vols of the Critical Heritage ser, the first of which includes an extensive bibliography:* Matthew Arnold: the poetry, *ed C. Dawson, 1973; and* Matthew Arnold: prose writings, *ed C. Dawson and J. Pfordresher, 1979.*

Criticism to 1920

Aytoun, W. The strayed reveller. Blackwood's Mag 66 1849.
[Kingsley, C.] The strayed reveller. Fraser's Mag 29 1849.
Rossetti, W. M. The strayed reveller and other poems. Germ Feb 1850; 1901 (facs), New York 1965 (facs).
Boyle, G. D. Empedocles on Etna. North Br Rev 9 1853.
[Clough, A. H.] Recent English poetry. North Amer Rev 77 1853; rptd in his Poems and prose remains, 1869.
[Lewes, G. H.] Schools of poetry: Arnold's poems. Leader 26 Nov, 3 Dec 1853.
[Coleridge, J. D.] Arnold's poems. Christian Remembrancer n.s. 27 1854.
[Froude, J. A.] Arnold's poems. Westminster Rev 61 1854; rptd in his Essays in literature and history, [1906] (EL).
[Shairp, J. C.] Arnold's poems. North British Rev 21 1854.
['Eliot, George'.] Arnold's poems. Westminster Rev 64 1855.
[Swinburne, A. C.] Modern Hellenism. Undergraduate Papers (Oxford) 1 Dec 1857. On Arnold's inaugural lecture.
[Connington, J.] Merope. Fraser's Mag 57 1858.
Newman, F. W. Homeric translation in theory and practice: a reply to Arnold. 1861.
Spedding, J. Arnold on translating Homer. Fraser's Mag June 1861, June 1862; rptd in his Reviews and discussions, 1879.
[Stephen, J. F.] On translating Homer. Saturday Rev 27 July 1861.
Maurice, F. D. Spinoza and Professor Arnold. Spectator 3 Jan 1863.
[Stephen, J. F.] Arnold and his countrymen. Saturday Rev 3 Dec 1864.
Wright, I. C. A letter to the dean of Canterbury on the Homeric lectures of Arnold. 1864.
[Hutton, R. H.] Essays in criticism. Spectator 25 Feb 1865.
[James, H.] Arnold's Essays in criticism. North Amer Rev 101 1865; rptd in his Views and reviews, Boston 1908.
Dallas, E. S. In his The gay science, 1866.
[Stephen, J. F.] Arnold and the middle classes. Saturday Rev 10 Feb 1866.
Strangford [Smythe, P. E.]. Arnold on Celtic literature. Pall Mall Gazette 19 Mar 1866.
Giffen, R. Celtic literature. Fortnightly Rev 1 July 1867.
Harrison, F. Culture: a dialogue. Fortnightly Rev Nov 1867; rptd in his Choice of books, 1886.
Sidgwick, H. The prophet of culture. Macmillan's Mag Aug 1867; rptd in Eclectic Mag Oct 1867 and in his Miscellaneous essays and addresses, 1904.
[Stephen, L.] New poems. Saturday Rev 7 Sep 1867.
[Swinburne, A. C.] Mr Arnold's New poems. Fortnightly Rev Oct 1867; rptd in his Essays and studies, 1875.
Ascher, I. G. New poems. St James's Mag 21 1868.
Bagehot, W. Arnold and the universities. Fortnightly Rev 3 June 1868.
Browning, O. Arnold and education. Quart Rev 125 1868.
Farrar, F. W. Schools and universities on the Continent. Fortnightly Rev 9 1868.
Forman, H. B. Criticisms on contemporaries. Tinsley's Mag Sep 1868.
Austin, A. The poetry of the period. Temple Bar 28 1869.
[Anon.] Review of St Paul and Protestantism. Br Quart Rev 52 1870.
[Simcox, E.] Review of St Paul and Protestantism. Academy 13 Aug 1870.
Forman, H. B. In his Our living poets, 1871.
[Hutton, R. H.] Review of Friendship's garland. Spectator 8 July 1871.
Oliphant, M. Review of Friendship's garland. Blackwood's Mag 109 1871.
[Shairp, J. C.] In his Culture and religion, 1871.
[Hutton, R. H.] Poetry of Arnold. Br Quart Rev 55 1872.
[Anon.] Review of Literature and dogma. Saturday Rev 1 Mar 1873.
Dunn, H. Facts, not fairy-tales: brief notes on Mr Arnold's Literature and dogma. 1873.
Newman, F. W. Literature and dogma. Fraser's Mag July 1873.
Tulloch, J. Amateur theology. Blackwood's Mag 113 1873.
[Anon.] The Bible as interpreted by Arnold. Westminster Rev 45 1874.
Courthope, W. J. Modern culture. Quart Rev 137 1874.
Hewlett, H. G. Poems of Arnold. Contemporary Rev 24 1874.
Réville, A. Review of God and the Bible. Academy 18 Dec 1875.
Bradley, F. H. In his Ethical studies, 1876.
Mallock, W. H. The new republic: or culture, faith and philosophy in an English country house. Belgravia June–Dec 1876; 1877, 1878; ed J. M. Patrick, Gainesville FL 1950.
Saintsbury, G. Modern English prose. Fortnightly Rev 19 1876.
Stedman, E. C. In his Victorian poets, 1876.
Bayne, T. Our modern poets. St James's Mag 31 1877.
[Hutton, R. H.] The poetic place of Arnold. Spectator 20 July 1878.
Pattison, M. Review of Mixed essays. Academy 17 May 1879.
Symonds, J. A. Arnold's selections from Wordsworth. Fortnightly Rev 32, Nov 1879; rptd as Is poetry at bottom a criticism of life? in his Essays speculative and suggestive, 1890.
Huxley, T. H. In his Science and culture, 1880.
[Henley, W. E.] Review of Poetry of Byron. Athenaeum 25 June 1881.
White, W. H. Byron, Goethe and Mr. Arnold. Contemporary Rev Aug 1881; rptd Appleton's Jnl Oct 1881 and in his Pages from a journal with other papers, 1900.
Lang, A. Matthew Arnold. Cent Mag 23 1882.
[Whitman, W.] Our eminent visitors. Critic (New York) 17 Nov 1883.
[James, H.] Matthew Arnold. Eng Illus Mag Jan 1884; rptd in his Literary reviews and essays, New York 1957.
[Swinburne, A. C.] Wordsworth and Byron. Nineteenth Cent Apr–May 1884; rptd in his Miscellanies, 1886.
Galton, A. H. In his Urbana scripta, 1885.
[Jacobs, J.] Review of Discourses in America. Athenaeum 27 June 1885.
[Hutton, R. H.] Newman and Arnold. Contemporary Rev 49 1886.
Alexander, W. Matthew Arnold: poem. Spectator 28 Apr 1888.
Arnold, E. To Matthew Arnold. Pall Mall Gazette 17 Apr 1888.
[Arnold, T.] Matthew Arnold (by one who knew him well). Manchester Guardian 18 May 1888.
Austin, A. Arnold on the loves of the poets. Nat Rev Jan 1888.
Austin, A. Matthew Arnold. Nat Rev May 1888.
Binyon, L. Matthew Arnold's poetry. Temple Bar 84 1888.
Burroughs, J. Arnold's criticism. Century Mag 36 1888.
Dawson, W. J. Death of Arnold. Spectator 21 Apr 1888.
Derry and Raphoe, W. Matthew Arnold. Spectator 28 Apr 1888.
[Jacobs, J.] Matthew Arnold. Athenaeum 21 Apr 1888.
Le Gallienne, R. Matthew Arnold: poem. Academy 21 Apr 1888.
Lund, T. W. M. Matthew Arnold: the message and meaning of a life. 1888.

Matthew Arnold: poem. Punch 28 Apr 1888.
Meredith, G. E. The source of Arnold's power. Church Rev 52 1888.
Morley, J. [tribute to Arnold] Hansard, 27 Apr 1888.
Morris, M. Matthew Arnold. Quart Rev Oct 1888.
Myers, F. W. H. Matthew Arnold. Fortnightly Rev 1 May 1888.
Norton, C. E. Matthew Arnold. Proc of the Amer Acad of Arts and Sciences 15 1888.
[Obituary] Academy 21 Apr 1888.
[Obituary] Pall Mall Gazette 16 Apr 1888; also 17 Apr 1888.
[Obituary] Saturday Rev 21 Apr 1888.
[Obituary] The Times 17 Apr 1888.
Prothero, R. Poetry of Arnold. Edinburgh Rev 168 1888.
Roosevelt, T. Some recent criticism of America. Murray's Mag Sep 1888; rptd in Eclectic Mag Nov 1888.
Traill, H. D. Matthew Arnold. Contemporary Rev 53 1888.
Watson, R. A. Gospels of yesterday: Drummond, Spencer, Arnold. 1888.
Coleridge, J. D. Arnold's poetry. New Rev June 1889.
Coleridge, J. D. Arnold's prose. New Rev Aug 1889.
[Coleridge, J. D.] Matthew Arnold. New Rev 1 1889.
Dawson, W. J. Matthew Arnold. Great Thoughts 3 1889.
Robertson, J. M. Science in criticism. In his Essays towards a critical method, 1889.
Grant-Duff, M. E. Matthew Arnold's writings. Murray's Mag 7 1890.
[Henley, W. E.] Arnold's writings. Murray's Mag Mar 1890; Kingston-on-Thames 1890 (priv ptd); rptd in his Out of the past, 1903.
[Henley, W. E.] In his Views and reviews, 1890. Rptd with addns from Athenaeum 22 Aug 1885.
Minto, W. Arnold's meliorism. Scottish Art Rev 1 1890.
Watson, W. In Laleham churchyard: poem. Spectator 30 Aug 1890.
[Coleridge, J. D.] Matthew Arnold. The Times 2 Nov 1891.
[Jacobs, J.] In his George Eliot, Matthew Arnold, Browning, etc., 1891.
[Johnson, L.] Poetical works of Arnold. Academy 10 Jan 1891.
Kirk, J. F. In his A supplement to Allibone's critical dictionary, 1891.
Robertson, J. M. In his Modern humanists: sociological studies of Carlyle, Mill, Emerson, Arnold, Ruskin and Spencer, 1891.
Roget, F. F. Matthew Arnold. The Ladder 1 1891.
Sharp, A. In her Victorian poets, 1891.
Birrell, A. In his Res judicatae, 1892.
Housman, A. E. Introductory lecture, University College, London. 1892 (priv ptd), 1933 (priv ptd), Cambridge 1937; rptd in his Selected prose, *below*.
Inwright, H. M. Is Arnold's poetry consoling? Spectator 16 July 1892.
[Hutton, R. H.] Arnold's popularity. Spectator 25 Mar 1893.
Innes, A. D. In his Seers and singers, 1893.
Stephen, L. Matthew Arnold. Nat Rev Dec 1893; rptd in Eclectic Mag Mar 1894, in Living Age 13 Jan 1894, and in his Studies of a biographer, 1898.
Birrell, A. Essays about men, women, and books. 1894.
Bradfield, T. The ethical tendency of Arnold's poetry. Westminster Rev 142 1894.
Smart, T. B. In his Essays about men, women, and books, 1894.
Austin, A. Arnold in his letters. Nat Rev Oct 1895.
Dowden, E. Matthew Arnold's letters. Saturday Rev 7 Dec 1895.
Flexner, A. Arnold's poetry from an ethical standpoint. International Jnl of Ethics 5 1895.
Gladstone, W. E. Bishop Butler and his censors: Mr Arnold. Nineteenth Cent Dec 1895.
Morley, J. Matthew Arnold. Nineteenth Cent Dec 1895.
Saintsbury, G. In his Corrected impressions, 1895.
Walker, H. In his The greater Victorian poets, 1895.
Carr, V. In his In the Dorian mode, 1896.
Harrison, F. Matthew Arnold. Nineteenth Cent Mar 1896; rptd in Living Age 9 May 1896 and in his Tennyson, Ruskin, Mill and other literary estimates, 1899.
Hudson, W. H. In his Studies in interpretation: Keats, Clough, Arnold, New York 1896.
Farrar, F. W. In his Men I have known, New York 1897.
Fitch, J. G. Thomas and Matthew Arnold, and their influence on English education. New York 1897.
Fruman, J. Victoria's poets. Spectator 3 Apr 1897.
Macarthur, H. In his Realism and romance, Edinburgh 1897.
Palgrave, F. T. The landscape of Browning, Arnold, Barnes and Charles Tennyson. In his Landscape in poetry, 1897.
Crozier, J. B. In his My inner life, 1898.
Dixon, W. M. In his The republic of letters, 1898.
Oakeshott, B. N. Arnold as a political and social critic. Westminster Rev 149 1898.
'P'. Reputations reconsidered: Arnold. Academy 15 Jan 1898.
Gates, L. E. In his Three studies in literature, New York 1899.
Saintsbury, G. Matthew Arnold. Edinburgh 1899.
Gates, L. E. The return to conventional life. Critic (New York) Mar 1900; rptd in his Studies and appreciations, New York 1900.
Brownell, W. C. Matthew Arnold. Scribner's Mag July 1901; rptd with addns in his Victorian prose masters, New York 1901.
Churton Collins, J. In his Ephemera critica, 1901.
Garnett, R. In his Essays of an ex-librarian, 1901.
Lewisohn, L. A study of Arnold. Sewanee Rev 9–10 1901–2.
Chesterton, G. K. Matthew Arnold. Bookman (New York) Oct 1902.
Grierson, F. Blunders of Arnold. Westminster Rev Mar 1902.
Mustard, W. P. Homeric echoes in Balder dead. In Studies in honor of Basil L. Gildersleeve, Baltimore 1902.
Paul, H. W. Matthew Arnold. 1902 (EML).
Watts-Dunton, T. Matthew Arnold. In Chambers Encyclopedia (10th edn) 1902–3.
Robertson, J. M. De mortuis: Matthew Arnold [1888]. In his Criticisms: second faggot, 1903.
Thomas, E. In his Oxford, 1903.
Chesterton, G. K. The atmosphere of Arnold. Bookman (New York) Apr 1904.
Dawson, W. H. Arnold and his relation to the thought of our time. New York 1904.
Russell, G. W. E. Matthew Arnold. 1904.
Schrag, A. Arnold, poet and critic. Basle 1904.
Sibbald, W. A. Arnold as a popular poet. Macmillan's Mag 89 1904.
Nevinson, H. W. In his Books and personalities, 1905.
Rice, R. Arnold and Joubert. Reader Mag (Indianapolis) Nov 1905.
Warren, T. H. Matthew Arnold. Quart Rev 202 1905; rptd in his Essays of poets and poetry, 1909.
Mackie, A. Arnold as naturalist: Arnold's birds. In his Nature knowledge in modern poets, 1906.
Starbird, R. S. The ethnological in Arnold. Bull Washington Univ Assoc 4 1906.
Boas, F. S. Some poems of Arnold. Trans Royal Soc of Lit n.s. 29 1909; rptd in his From Richardson to Pinero, 1936.
Garrod, H. W. The theology of Arnold. Oxford & Cambridge Rev no 6 1909; rptd in Living Age 5 Feb 1910.
More, P. E. Criticism. In his Shelburne essays, 7th ser New York 1910.
Harris, F. Talks with Arnold. Academy 28 Jan 1911.
Sharp, W. On Arnold. In his Papers critical and reminiscent, 1912. Rptd from his edn of Arnold's poems.
Mobbs, R. Étude comparée des jugements de Mme Humphry Ward, de M. Arnold et W. Pater sur le Journal intime de H.-F. Amiel. Geneva 1913.
Bendz, E. P. The influence of Pater and Arnold in the prose-writings of Oscar Wilde. Gothenburg 1914.
Chesterton, G. K. In his The Victorian age in literature, 1914.
Kelso, A. P. Arnold on continental life and literature. Oxford 1914.
Strachey, G. L. A Victorian critic. New Statesman 1 Aug 1914; rptd in his Characters and commentaries, 1933.
Powys, J. C. In his Visions and revisions, New York 1915.

Raleigh, W. A. An introduction to Arnold's Essays in criticism. 1916; rptd in his Some authors, Oxford 1923.
Sherman, S. P. Arnold: how to know him. Indianapolis 1917.
Goldmark, R. I. The Hellenism of Arnold. In her Studies in the influence of the classics on English literature, New York 1918.
Malleson, J. P. The most eloquent voice of the nineteenth century. Spectator 26 Oct 1918.
Quiller-Couch, A. T. In his Studies in literature, Cambridge 1918. Rptd from edn of Arnold's poems (WC).
Courtney, J. E. In her Freethinkers of the nineteenth century, 1920.
Grierson, H. J. C. Lord Byron: Arnold and Swinburne. PBA 9 1920; rptd in his Background of English literature, 1925.
Eliot, T. S. The second order mind. Dial Dec 1920.

Bibliographical and textual criticism

Mainwaring, M. Notes toward a Matthew Arnold bibliography. MP 49 1952.
Buckler, W. E. An American edition of Arnold's Poems. PMLA 69 1954. Correction by J. C. Maxwell, ibid. Edn of New York 1878 rev Arnold.
Townsend, F. G. A neglected edition of Arnold's St Paul and Protestantism. RES n.s. 5 1954.
Super, R. H. Arnold's Oxford lectures on poetry. MLN 70 1955.
Ullmann, S. O. A. A 'new' version of Arnold's Essay on Wordsworth. N & Q 200 Dec 1955.
Super, R. H. The authenticity of the first edition of Arnold's Alaric at Rome (1840). HLQ 19 1956.
Neiman, F. Some newly attributed contributions of Arnold to the Pall Mall Gazette. MP 55 1958.
Metzdorf, R. F. The Tinker library. New Haven CT 1959.
Neiman, F. Arnold's review of the Lettres et opuscules inédits by Joseph de Maistre. MLN 74 1959.
Super, R. H. Arnold's notebooks and Arnold bibliography. MP 56 CT 1959.
Brooks, R. L. A septuagenarian poet: an addition to the Arnold bibliography. MP 57 1960.
Brooks, R. L. Arnold and the Pall Mall Gazette. MP 58 1961.
Brooks, R. L. A neglected edition [Boston 1856] of Arnold's poetry and a bibliographical correction. PBSA 55 1961.
Brooks, R. L. An unrecorded American edition [New York 1878] of the Selected poems of Arnold. Library 5th ser 16 1961.
Coulling, S. M. B. Arnold and the Daily Telegraph. RES 12 1961.
Housman, A. E. Appendix. In his Selected prose, ed J. Carter, Cambridge 1961. 3 pages from an unpbd paper of c. 1891.
Super, R. H. The first publication of Thyrsis. N & Q 205 June 1961.
Brooks, R. L. A Deptford poet: an addition and a correction to the Arnold bibliography. PQ 41 1962.
Brooks, R. L. The publication of Arnold's early volumes of poetry. Victorian Newsletter 22 1962.
Brooks, R. L. Some unaccomplished projects of Arnold. SB 16 1963.
Osbourne, D. G. Arnold 1843–9: a study of the Yale manuscript. Ann Arbor MI 1963.
Brooks, R. L. Arnold and Ticknor & Fields. Amer Lit 35 1964.
Brooks, R. L. The Story manuscript of Arnold's New Rome. PBSA 58 1964.
Super, R. H. American piracies of Arnold. Amer Lit 38 1966.
Brooks, R. L. Arnold's Joseph de Maistre on Russia. HLQ 30 1967.
Super, R. H. American piracies of Arnold. Amer Lit 38 1967.
Schulz, H. C. English literary manuscripts in the Huntington Library. HLQ 31 1968.
Godshalk, W. L. Autograph fragments of two Arnold poems. PMLA 85 1970.
Lefcowitz, A. B. Some additions to Arnold's library. PBSA 65 1971.
Coulling, S. M. B. Matthew Arnold and his critics: a study of Arnold's controversies. Athens OH 1975.
Ullmann, S. O. A. Editing Yale's Tinker: an interim report. Arnoldian 3 1975.
Wynne, M. G. The manuscript of Arnold's George Sand. Arnoldian 3 1975.
Farrell, J. P. The Arnold of the Complete prose works. Arnoldian 5 1977.
Coulling, S. M. B. Arnold, 1845–1974: a review of criticism and research. Br Stud Monitor 8 1978.
Houghton, W. E. Victorian periodical literature and the articulate classes. VS 22 1979.
Marks, P. The Charivari: American style. Arnoldian 7 1980.
Savory, G. J. The Charivari: British style. Arnoldian 7 1980.
Fleissner, R. F. Arnold's Shakespeare textually revised. Arnoldian 8 1981.
Brake, L. Literary criticism and the Victorian periodicals. YES 16 1986.
Kaplan, F. Arnold in the Oxford Authors series. Arnoldian 15 1987–8.
Davis, C. B. Juvenilia: two possible Arnold poems. VP 26 1988.
Savory, G. J. Arnold and Arnoldiana in Vanity Fair. VP 26 1988.
Ullman, S. O. A. The Yale manuscript. Ann Arbor MI 1988.
Nadel, I. B. Textual criticism and non-fictional prose: the case of Arnold. UTQ 58 1989.
Super, R. H. Arnold's Literature and dogma, the Cornhill Magazine, and censorship. N & Q 234 June 1989.
Edwards, S. O. Revision in the religious prose of Arnold. In Victorian authors: revisions, motivations and modes, ed J. Kennedy, Athens OH 1991.
Kaplan, F. The discourses of journalism. In Pater in the 1990s, ed L. Brake and I. Small, Greensboro NC 1991.
Brooks, R. L. Then comes the whistling clown: publishing the uncollected poetic drafts and fragments. BC 43 1994.
Coulling, S. M. B. The manuscript of Culture and its enemies. Nineteenth Cent Prose 21 1994.

Biographies

Saintsbury, G. Matthew Arnold. Edinburgh 1899.
Paul, H. W. Matthew Arnold. 1902 (EML).
Russell, G. W. E. Matthew Arnold. 1904.
'Kingsmill, Hugh'. Matthew Arnold. 1928.
Trilling, L. Matthew Arnold. New York 1939, 1949, 1955 (rev).
Bonnerot, L. Matthew Arnold, poète: essai de bibliographie psychologique. Paris 1947.
Brown, E. K. Arnold: a study in conflict. Chicago 1948.
Jump, J. D. Matthew Arnold. 1955.
Bush, D. Matthew Arnold. 1971.
Honan, P. Matthew Arnold: a life. 1981.
Murray, N. A life of Matthew Arnold. 1996. [BB]

William Edmondstoune Aytoun, 'T. Percy Jones' 1813–65

Collections

Miles 4, 9 (10).
Poems. Ed F. Page, Oxford 1921.
Stories and verse. Ed W. L. Renwick, Edinburgh 1964 (Scottish Reprints no 2). Contains The Glenmutchkin railway, How I stood for the Dreepdaily burghs, The emerald stud, How we got possession of the Tuilleries, Firmilian, and Bon Gaultier ballads.

§1

Poland, Homer and other poems. 1832. Anon.
The life and times of Richard the First, King of England. 1840.
Our Zion: or Presbyterian popery, by ane of that ilk. Edinburgh 1840. Anon. Tract written in opposition to the veto act.
The elder's warning. Edinburgh Evening Post and Scottish Standard 1843.

The book of ballads, edited by 'Bon Gaultier'. 1845, 1849 (enlarged), 1903 (16th edn). With T. Martin.

Lays of the Scottish cavaliers and other poems. 1849, 1849 (adds appendix on Macaulay, also issued separately), New York 1852, 1853, London 1853, 1856, New York 1858, London 1863, 1865, 1866, 1870, 1877, 1881, 1886, 1888, 1889, 1890, 1893, 1896, 1897, 1900, 1901. Lays often rptd separately, numerous selections also rptd for school use.

The Napoleon ballad, edited by 'Bon Gaultier'. New York 1852. With T. Martin.

Firmilian, or the student of Badajoz: a spasmodic tragedy by 'T. Percy Jones'. Edinburgh 1854, New York 1855.

Bothwell: a poem in six parts. Edinburgh 1855, 1856, Boston 1856, Edinburgh 1858 (3rd edn rev).

The Glenmutchkin railway. 1858. A short story rptd from Blackwood's Mag in Tales from Blackwood vol 1 1858, [1868], [1907] (in The Glenmutchkin railway and other humorous Scots stories).

The ballads of Scotland. Ed Aytoun 2 vols Edinburgh 1858, 1859 (rev and enlarged), 1870 (4th edn rev and enlarged).

Poems and ballads of Goethe. 1859, 1860 (rev and enlarged), 1877. Tr Aytoun with T. Martin. Many poems first ptd in Blackwood's Mag.

Inaugural address. Edinburgh 1861. On rhetoric and the art of public speaking.

Norman Sinclair: a novel. 3 vols 1861.

Nuptial ode on the marriage of the Prince of Wales. 1863.

The burial march of Dundee and the island of the Scots. Ed W. K. Leask 1897.

Endymion: or a family party of Olympus. In Ixion in heaven and Endymion: Disraeli's skit and Aytoun's burlesque, ed E. Partridge 1927. Written in 1842.

Aytoun also contributed extensively to Blackwood's Mag; *see* Wellesley 5 1989.

§2

Martin, T. Memoir of Aytoun. 1867. The appendix contains several sketches and essays by Aytoun which are inaccessible elsewhere, and reprints the Nuptial ode on the marriage of the Prince of Wales.

Masson, R. Pollok and Aytoun. Edinburgh 1898.

Bell, M. In Miles 4. *See* also Miles 9 (10).

TLS 25 Aug 1921.

Frykman, Eric. W. E. Aytoun pioneer professor of English at Edinburgh. Gothenburg 1963.

Weinstein, Mark. William E. Aytoun and the Spasmodic Controversy. 1968.

Westwater, M. The spasmodic career of Sydney Dobell. 1992. [MW]

Philip James Bailey 1816–1902

Selections

Miles 4.

§1

Festus: a poem. 1839, 1845 (with addns and a selection of press notices), Boston 1845, 1847, 1848, 1849, 1850, 1852, London 1852, Boston 1853, London 1854, 1860, 1864 (7th edn, enlarged), New York 1864, 1865, London 1866, New York 1867, London 1877 (10th edn), 1884, 1889 (with long preface); tr Fr [1890] (excerpts). Selections from Festus 1893. By 1889 the bulk of Angel world, Mystic and Universal hymn, *below*, had been included in Festus. In 1884 'A student' issued The beauties of Festus, with a descriptive index.

The angel world and other poems. 1850, Boston 1850.

The mystic and other poems. 1855, Boston 1856, 1858.

The age: a colloquial satire [and other poems]. 1858. A verse trialogue between author, critic and friend.

The international policy of the great powers. 1861.

Universal hymn. 1867.

Nottingham castle: an ode. 1878.

Causa britannica: a poem in Latin hexameters with English paraphrase. Ilfracombe 1883.

Letters and papers

Selections from the letters of Philip James Bailey. Ed M. Peckham, Princeton Univ Lib Chron 7 1946.

§2

Bagehot, W. 'Festus'. Prospective Review 80, Oct 1847.

Powell, T. In his Living authors of England, New York 1849, London 1851.

Gilfillan, G. In his A second gallery of literary portraits, 1850.

Brown, J. H. In Miles 4.

Nicoll, W. R. and T. J. Wise. In Literary anecdotes of the nineteenth century vol 2, 1896.

Obituary. Athenaeum 13 Sep 1902.

Gosse, E. Philip James Bailey. Fortnightly Rev Nov 1902; rptd in his Portraits and sketches, 1912.

Ward, J. Bailey: personal recollections. Nottingham 1905 (priv ptd).

McKillop, A. D. A Victorian Faust. PMLA 40 1925. On Festus.

Goldschmidt, E. Der Gedankegehalt von Baileys Festus. EStudien 117 1932.

Black, G. A. Bailey's debt to Goethe's Faust in his Festus. MLR 28 1933.

Peckham, M. A Bailey collection. Princeton Univ Lib Chron 7 1946.

Peckham, M. American editions of Festus: a preliminary survey. Princeton Univ Lib Chron 8 1947.

Fairchild, H. N. Wild bells in Bailey's Festus? MLN 54 1949.

Peckham, M. English editions of Bailey's Festus. PBSA 44 1950.

Birley, R. In his Sunk without trace, 1962.

Westwater, M. In her Spasmodic career of Sydney Dobell, 1992. [MW]

William Barnes 1801–86

MSS located in Berg Collection, NYPL; Princeton Univ Lib; Folger Lib, Univ of Wisconsin; Univ of British Columbia. See also LR.

Bibliographies

Baxter, L. In her The life of William Barnes, poet and philologist, 1887.

In A dictionary of English authors: biographical and bibliographical, ed R. F. A. Sharp, 1904, rptd Detroit 1978.

Hearl, T. W. In his William Barnes, 1801–1886, the schoolmaster: a study of education in the life and work of the Dorset poet. Dorchester 1966.

Chedzoy, A. In his William Barnes: a life of the Dorset poet, Stanbridge, Wimborne 1985.

A catalogue of works by and about William Barnes (1801–1886) in Dorchester Reference Library. Ed J. C. Ward, Dorchester 1986.

In Love poems and letters, ed C. H. Lindgren, Dorchester 1986.

See also Wellesley 5 1989.

Collections

A fadge of Barnes. Being the pieces, in prose and verse contributed by William Barnes, the Dorset poet, to The Hawk, 1867. To which are added two previously unpublished letters from Barnes to James Allen. Ed J. S. Cox, Beaminster 1956.

The poems of William Barnes. Ed B. Jones 2 vols Arundel 1962, Fontwell, Sussex 1963.

One hundred poems. Blanford Forum 1971 (essay by E. M. Forster).

Selections

A selection from unpublished poems. Winterborne Monkton 1870.

In Miles 8.

Poems in the Dorset dialect. By the late William Barnes. Dorchester 1906.
Selected poems of William Barnes. Chosen and edited with a preface and glossarial notes by Thomas Hardy. Oxford 1908, London 1908, '1921' [1922], 1933.
A selection from Poems of rural life in the Dorset dialect. Ed Barnes's son (W. M. Barnes) 1909.
In The English Poets, ed T. H. Ward, 5 1918.
Twenty poems in common English by William Barnes. Ed J. Drinkwater, Oxford 1925.
In The Romantics: an anthology, ed G. Grigson, 1942.
Poems grave & gay. Ed G. Dugdale, Dorchester 1949, 1972, Weymouth 1978 (new edn ed A. Chedzoy).
Selected poems of William Barnes 1801–1886. Ed with introd by G. Grigson 1950, Cambridge MA 1950.
In Seven Victorian poets, ed D. Wright, 1964, New York 1966, 1973.
Ten Dorset poems. Kettering 1970.
William Barnes: a selection of his poems. Ed R. Nye, Oxford 1972.
Poems in the Dorset dialect. Oxford 1980 (foresay D. M. Daniell).
Poems from William Barnes. Ed W. Partridge, Sutton Mandeville, Salisbury 1981 (preface M. Franklin).
William Barnes, the Dorset poet. Introd and selected by C. Wrigley. Stanbridge, Wimborne 1984, rptd 1988, rptd 1990.
Dorset poems: William Barnes. Tr P. Tennant with introd by P. Levi 1989 (engravings by Barnes, Folio Soc).
Selected poems. Ed A. Motion 1994
Collected prose works. 6 vols 1996.

§1

Poetical pieces. Dorchester 1820.
Orra: a Lapland tale. (Woodcuts engraved by Barnes.) Dorchester 1822.
Etymological dictionary. Shaftesbury and London 1829.
The solution of the problem to tri-sect the arc of a circle. [Dorchester?] 1832 (no known copy extant).
A catechism of government in general, and of England in particular. Shaftesbury 1833.
The mnemonic manual. 1833 (no copy now exists).
A few words on the advantages of a more common adoption of the mathematics as a branch of education or subject of study. 1834.
A mathematical investigation of the principle of hanging doors, gates, swing bridges and other heavy bodies. Dorchester 1835.
A corrective concordance or imposition book. Dorchester 1839.
An arithmetical and commercial dictionary. 1840.
An investigation of the laws of case in language, exhibited in a system of natural cases. Dorchester 1840.
A pronouncing dictionary of geographical names. 1841.
The elements of English grammar, with a set of questions and exercises. Dorchester 1842.
The elements of linear perspective and the projection of shadows with sixteen diagrams cut in wood by the author. 1842.
Sabbath lays: six sacred songs. Music by F. W. Smith. 1844.
Exercises in practical science. Dorchester 1844.
Poems of rural life in the Dorset dialect: with a dissertation and glossary. 1844, 1847, 1848 (2 edns with dissertation and glossary enlarged), 1862 (3 edns without dissertation), 1866 (4 edns without dissertation and glossary).
REVIEW: North Br Rev Nov 1859.
Poems, partly of rural life, in national English. 1846.
Outlines of geography and ethography for youth. Dorchester 1847.
Humilis Domus: some thoughts on the abodes, life, and social condition of the poor, especially in Dorsetshire. [Dorchester?] 1849 (priv ptd). Rptd from Poole and Dorset Herald.
Se gefylsta (The helper), an Anglo-Saxon delectus. 1849, 1866 (2 edns).
A philological grammar grounded upon English, and formed from a comparison of more than sixty languages. 1854.
Notes on ancient Britain and the Britons. 1858.
Views of labour and gold. 1859.
The Song of Solomon in the Dorset dialect. 1859 (priv ptd).
Hwomely rhymes. A second collection of poems in the Dorset dialect. 1859, 1863 (2 edns as Poems of rural life in the Dorset dialect. Second collection).
REVIEW: North Br Rev Nov 1859.
Poems of rural life in the Dorset dialect. Third collection. 1862, 1869 (2 edns), 1870 (illus), 1887, 1905.
REVIEW: Chambers's Jnl 2 May 1863.
Tiw; or a view of the roots and stems of the English as a Teutonic tongue. '1862' [1861].
A grammar and glossary of the Dorset dialect, with the history, outspreadings and bearings of south-western English. 1863, Berlin 1863, London 1864, 1886 (rev).
A guide to Dorchester and its neighbourhood. Dorchester [1864?], [1881] (rev), 1887 (rev edn).
Poems in the Dorset dialect. Boston 1864, Oxford 1980.
Poems of rural life in common English. 1868, Boston 1869.
REVIEW: Chambers's Jnl 1 Aug 1868.
Rural poems. Boston 1869 (illustr W. Homer and H. Billings).
Early England and the Saxon English; with some notes on the father-stock of the Saxon-English, the Frisians. 1869.
Dorset grammar and glossary. [1870?]
An outline of English speech-craft. 1878.
Poems of rural life in the Dorset dialect. (First–third collections). 1879, 1887, 1888, 1893, 1898, 1902, 1905.
REVIEW: New Quart Mag Oct 1879.
An outline of rede-craft (logic), with English wording. 1880.
Ruth, a short drama from the Bible. With a dissertation on the law of the Goel-ha-dom. Dorchester [1881].
A glossary of the Dorset dialect, with a grammar of its word shapening and wording. Dorchester 1886, St Sampson, Guernsey 1970 (2nd edn, facs of 1886 edn).
REVIEW: Acad 27 Mar 1886.
Some Dorset folklore. St Peter Port, Channel Islands 1969. Rptd from Hone's Year Book 1832.
Folklore. Dorchester 1996.

Contributions to periodicals and anthologies

Dorset County Chron. 6 Dec 1827–73.
Gentleman's Mag. June 1830–Feb 1849.
Hone's Year Book. 1832.
Leisure Hour. Dorset folk and Dorset. Jan–May 1883.
Retrospective Rev. 1853–4.
For contributions to Fraser's Mag *and* Macmillan's Mag, *see* Wellesley 5 *1989.*
Reader. Sep 1863–July 1864.
Ladies' Treasury. 1863–7.
Archaeological Jnl. Ancient Dorset, June 1865.
'Farm labourer', and employment of women and children in agriculture. Royal Commission Blue Book, appendix, pt 2, to Second Report. 1869.
British Archaeological Assoc Jnl. On the origin of the hundred and tithing of English law, Mar 1872.

Letters

In Love poems and letters, ed C. H. Lindgren, Dorchester 1986.

Introductions

Additions from various sources and notes to a glossary, with some pieces of verse, of the old dialect of the English colony in the Baronies of Forth and Bargy, by Jacob Poole. 1867. Ed and introd by Barnes.

§2

Patmore, C. Macmillan's Mag June 1862.
Chambers's Jnl 2 May 1863.

A simple singer. Chambers's Jnl 1 Aug 1868.
Doyle, Sir F. H. C. Provincial poetry. In his Lectures delivered before the University of Oxford, 1868. 1869.
Obituaries: The Times 9 Oct 1886, Spectator 16 Oct 1886, Acad 23 Oct 1886, New York Times 30 Oct, 4 Nov 1886.
Hardy, T. Athenaeum 16 Oct 1886. Rptd in L. Johnson, The art of Thomas Hardy, 1894, 1923.
Patmore, C. Fortnightly Rev 1 Nov 1886, rptd in his Religio poetæ, 1893.
Palgrave, F. T. Nat Rev Feb 1887.
Baxter, L. The life of William Barnes. 1887.
Wallis, C. J. GM 1888.
DNB 22 Suppl 1901. (T. S.).
Hardy, T. Louis Napoleon and the poet Barnes. Insert in F. H. Cheetham, Louis Napoleon and the genesis of the second empire, 1909.
Coffin, A. C. Trans Yorkshire Dialect Soc Dec 1916.
Woodberry, G. E. In his Literary memoirs of the nineteenth century, New York 1921.
Jacobs, W. D. William Barnes linguist. Albuquerque 1952.
Dugdale, G. William Barnes of Dorset. 1953.
Levy, W. T. William Barnes: the man and the poems. Dorchester 1960.
Hearl, T. W. William Barnes, 1801–1886, the schoolmaster. Dorset 1966.
Millgate, M. In his Thomas Hardy: a biography, Oxford 1982.
Parins, J. W. William Barnes. Boston 1984.
Chedzoy, A. William Barnes: a life of the Dorset poet. Stanbridge, Wimborne 1985.
Keen, L. William Barnes. The Somerset engravings 1989
Jennings, R. Lofty aims and lowly duties: three Victorian schoolmasters. Sheffield 1994.
Phillips, A. The rebirth of England and English: the vision of William Barnes. Hockwold-cum-Wilton 1997. [DA]

Thomas Lovell Beddoes 1803–49

Mss: a few poems and letters in Bodleian; 2 poems in draft and a few letters, BL Add Mss; Scaroni, or the mysterious cave: a romantic fiction *(1818). Godalming, Charterhouse Lib.*

Bibliography

Donner, H. W. In Works, Oxford 1935.

Collections

Poems posthumous and collected. 2 vols 1851. Vol 1 includes memoir by T. F. Kelsall; vol 2 Death's jest-book, 1850; in 1 vol without Jest-book as Poems by the late Thomas Lovell Beddoes, author of Death's jest-book, with a memoir, 1851.
REVIEW: in Spectator 13 Sep 1851.
Poetical works. Ed E. Gosse 2 vols 1890. Memoir rptd in Gosse, Critical kit-kats, 1896.
Poems. Ed R. Colles 1907 (ML).
Complete works. Ed E. Gosse 2 vols 1928, 1 vol 1928 (75 copies).
An anthology. Ed F. L. Lucas, Cambridge 1932. Introd rptd in Lucas, Studies French and English, 1934.
Works. Ed H. W. Donner, Oxford 1935.
Plays and poems. Ed H. W. Donner 1950 (ML).

Selections

Selected poems. Ed J. Higgens, Manchester 1876.
Miles 3.
Lyrics from Thomas Lovell Beddoes. Portland ME 1899 [The Bibelot vol 5 no 3].
Resurrection songs. Chislehurst Gothic Soc [c. 1992].

§1

For single poems etc, see bibliography in Works, *1935, above.*

The improvisatore, in three fyttes, with other poems. Oxford 1821.
REVIEW: Monthly Rev June 1821.
The brides' tragedy. 1822, facs reprint Oxford 1993.
REVIEWS: Edinburgh Rev 38 1823; Monthly Rev Jan 1823; London Mag Feb 1823, Dec 1823, May 1824; Album May 1823; GM Oct 1823; Blackwood's Mag Dec 1823.
Antistraussianischer [Grauss-] Gruss an einen Herrn Antistes von Struthio Camelus. [Zurich 1839, 1839.]
Death's jest-book: or the fool's tragedy. 1850. Anon.
REVIEW: Spectator 6 July 1850; Examiner 20 July 1850; Blackwood's Mag Oct 1856.
Two German poems. Studia Neophilologica 37 1965.

Letters

Letters. Ed E. Gosse 1894.
Todd, A. C. Beddoes and his guardian. TLS 10 Oct 1952. 2 unpbd letters.
Donner, H. W. Echoes of Beddoesian rambles: Edgeworthstown to Zürich. Studia Neophilologica 33 1961. 2 unpbd letters.
Beddoes to Leonhard Tobler: 8 German letters. Studia Neophilologica 35 1963.

§2

Monthly Rev June 1821. Review of Improvisatore.
Procter, B. W. London Mag Feb 1823, Mar 1824; Edinburgh Rev 38 1823. Reviews of Brides' tragedy.
Procter, B. W. An autobiographical fragment. 1877.
Monthly Rev Jan 1823; Album May 1823; GM Oct 1823; G. Darley, London Mag Dec 1823, May 1824; J. Wilson, Blackwood's Mag Dec 1823. Reviews of Brides' tragedy.
Bayerisches Volksblatt 29 March 1832 (report of speech for Poland); 16 June 1832 (speech for freedom); 24 July, 30 Aug 1832 (deportation).
Der Freisinnige 9 July 1832. Report of speech for freedom.
Nürnberger Correspondent 25, 30 July 1832. Deportation.
Volksbote 23 Jan 1838 (performance of Henry IV); 7 Dec 1838 (Booing Soc); 3 May 1839 (Strauss feud).
Scherr, I. T. Beobachtungen, Bestrebungen und Schicksale. Vols 3, 4, St Gall 1840.
Illuminated Mag May 1844.
Spectator 6 July 1850 (review of Death's jest-book); 13 Sep 1851 (review of Poems posthumous and collected).
Forster, J. Examiner 20 July 1850, 27 Sep 1851, rptd in Littell's Living Age 15 Nov, Eclectic Mag Dec 1851.
Bristol Mirror 23 Dec 1854.
Blackwood's Mag Oct 1856.
Kelsall, T. F. Fortnightly Rev July 1872.
Collins, M. A poet not laureate. Dublin Univ Mag Nov 1879.
Gosse, E. Athenaeum 20 Oct 1883.
Gosse, E. TLS 11 Mar 1909.
Symons, A. Acad 15 Aug 1891; rptd in his Figures of several centuries, 1916.
Crosse, A. Temple Bar Mar 1894.
Hannigan, D. F. Westminster Rev 149 1898.
Miller, B. Sewanee Rev 11 1903.
Strachey, L. The last Elizabethan. New Quart Mag 1 1907; rptd in his Books and characters, 1922.
Wooster, H. D. Bibliophile Mar 1909.
Feller, A. Thomas Lovell Beddoes. Marburg 1914.
Snow, R. H. Beddoes: eccentric and poet. New York 1928.
Blunden, E. Beddoes and his contemporaries. TLS 13 Dec 1928; rptd in his Votive tablets, 1931.
Church, R. Beddoes: the last of the alchemists. Spectator 9 Feb 1929.
Bayley, A. R. TLS 16 May 1929. Letter from Bourne to Beddoes.
Lindsay, J. TLS 16 May 1929. Letter from Kelsall to Browning.
Donner, H. W. The Browning box: or the life and works of Beddoes as reflected in letters by his friends and admirers. Oxford 1935.
Donner, H. W. Beddoes: the making of a poet. Oxford 1935.
Wagner, G. Horizon 19 1949.

Nomachi, S. Stud in Eng Lit (Tokyo) 26 1949.
Coxe, L. O. Beddoes: the mask of parody. Hudson Rev 6 1953.
Todd, A. C. The mother of Beddoes. Studia Neophilologica 29 1957.
Hoyt, C. A. Themes and imagery in the poetry of Beddoes. Studia Neophilologica 35 1963.
Nickerson, C. C. Beddoes' readings in Bodley. Studia Neophilologica 36 1964.
Harrex, A. Death's jest-book and the German contribution. Studia Neophilologica 39 1967.
Thompson, J. R. Thomas Lovell Beddoes. Boston 1985.

Charles Dent Bell 1819–98

Selections

Miles 10 (11).

§1

Blanche Neville: a record of married life. By the author of 'Faith in earnest'. 1853. A novel.
The miners' sons: Martin Luther and Henry Martyn. 1853.
The Bible in England. 1854.
Time redeemed: or the past recalled. [1875.]
Voices from the lakes and other poems. 1877 (for 1876).
The four seasons at the lakes. 1878. Poems.
Henry Martyn. 1880, New York 1881. A biography.
Songs in the twilight. 1881.
Hymns for the church and the chamber. 1882 (for 1881).
The hymnal companion to the Book of Common Prayer. With an appendix ... Ed Rev C. D. Bell 1884.
Songs in many keys. 1884.
Verses for Christmas and the New Year. No iv 1885.
Gleanings from a tour in Palestine and the East. 1887, 1889.
A winter on the Nile in Egypt and in Nubia. 1888.
Reminiscences of a boyhood in the early part of the century. 1889. Anon.
Poems old and new. 1893. A selection from earlier vols, with new poems.
The Church of England hymnal. Ed Bell, H. E. Fox and A. H. Mann 1894.
Diana's looking-glass and other poems. 1894.
Some of our English poets. 1895. Essays on Gray, Goldsmith, Cowper, Scott, Coleridge and Wordsworth.
Tales told by the fireside. 1896. 7 short stories.
Bell also pbd sermons and devotional works.

§2

Julian.
Miles, A. H. in Miles 10 (11).

William Cox Bennett 1820–95

Selections

Miles 5.

§1

[A collection of poems, printed on single sheets.] [184-?] (priv ptd, no title page).
My sonnets. Greenwich 1843 (priv ptd). Anon.
Songs, ballads etc. Greenwich 1845. Anon.
Poems. 1850.
REVIEWS: Athenaeum 18 Jan 1851; Literary Gazette 25 Jan 1851.
The triumph for Salamis: a lyrical ballad. Greenwich [1850?] (priv ptd).
Verdicts. 1852.
Endowed parish schools and high church vicars. Roan's school: past, present and future. Three letters to the parishioners of Greenwich. Greenwich [1853].
War songs. 1855.
REVIEW: Athenaeum 13 Oct 1855.
Queen Eleanor's vengeance and other poems. 1857 (for 1856).
REVIEW: Athenaeum 3 Jan 1857.
Songs by a song-writer: first hundred. '1859' [1858]; as Songs of a song-writer (enlarged) 1876.
REVIEWS: Spectator 1 Jan 1859 (brief notice); Athenaeum 9 Apr 1859, 14 Oct 1876; Chambers's Jnl 9 Apr 1859; Br Quart Rev July 1859; Saturday Rev 16 Sep 1876 (brief notice).
Baby May and other poems on infants. 1859, 3rd thousand 1861, 1865 as 8 poems from Baby May, 1875 as Baby May, home poems and ballads (includes Pt 1, The worn wedding-ring and other home poems, *below*, and Narrative poems and ballads).
The worn wedding-ring and other poems. 1861.
REVIEWS: Athenaeum 12 Jan 1861; Spectator 12 Jan 1861 (brief notice).
Poems. 1862, New York 1862.
Shall we have a national ballad history for the English people: an appeal to the poets of England and America. 1866. (Became preface to Proposals of 1868, *below*.)
Our glory-roll and other national poems. [1867.]
REVIEWS: Athenaeum 2 Feb 1867; Br Quart Rev Apr 1867.
Proposals for and contributions to a ballad history of England and the states sprung from her. 1868. Includes several ballads by Bennett. The preface originally pbd 1866 as Shall we have a national ballad history for the English people? Rptd as Contributions to a ballad history [1879].
REVIEW: Athenaeum 17 July 1869.
Songs for sailors. 1872, 1873.
REVIEW: Athenaeum 21 Dec 1872.
Narrative poems and ballads. 1875. Pt 2 of W. C. Bennett's Poems. See Baby May, *above*, for Pt 1.
Prometheus the fire-giver: an attempted restoration of the lost first part of the Promethean trilogy of Aeschylus. 1877. Anon.
Sea songs. 1878.
REVIEW: Athenaeum 24 Aug 1878.
Songs for soldiers. [1879.] Issued in nos 1–3.
The lark: songs, ballads and recitations. [1885.] Originally pbd as The lark: songs, ballads and poems for the people, in periodical of the same name at Greenwich [1883–4].
Goschen's gospel. 1886. Broadside rptd from Liberal Home Ruler.
New Irish Melodies. 1886. Broadside rptd from Liberal Home Ruler.
'Locksley Hall'. An appeal from 'Locksley Hall sixty years after' to 'Locksley Hall'. 1887. Rptd from Liberal Home Ruler.
Bennett pbd articles and poems in People's Jnl *and* Howitt's Jnl. *His poems also appeared in* Athenaeum, Belgravia, Bentley's Misc, Eclectic Rev *and* Nat Mag. *See* Wellesley 5 1989.

Edition

The consecutive narrative series of reading books, by C. Morell, edited by J. R. Morell, to which also is added a selection of the best English poetry, edited by W. C. Bennett (in Book 5). [1870]; reissued separately as The school book of poetry [1872].

Attributed or spurious work

Anti-Maud, by a poet of the people. 1855, 1856 (2nd edn, enlarged).

§2

Obit: The Times 8 Mar 1895; Athenaeum 9 Mar 1895.
In Miles 5. [RS]

Alexander Bethune 1804–43

Collections

Tales of the Scottish peasantry, by A. and J. Bethune, with biography of the authors by J. Ingram. 1884. Includes Tales and sketches and Scottish peasant's fireside, *below*.

§1

Tales and sketches of the Scottish peasantry. Edinburgh 1838. With J. Bethune.
Lectures on practical economy. 1839. With J. Bethune.
Poems by the late J. Bethune, with a sketch of the author's life by his brother. Edinburgh 1840, 1841.
A Scottish peasant's fireside: a series of tales and sketches. Edinburgh 1843.

Letters and papers

Memoirs of Alexander Bethune. Ed W. H. MacCrombie, Aberdeen 1845. Includes selections from his correspondence and literary remains.

§2

Bethune, J. The Bethunes: or the Fifeshire foresters. [1863.] In verse, with explanatory notes.

Edward Henry Bickersteth 1825–1906

Selections

Miles 10 (12).

§1

The two brothers. 1845 (anon), 1871 (enlarged as The two brothers, and other poems), 1872, New York 1875.
Poems and songs. 1848.
Poems. Cambridge 1849.
Nineveh: a poem. 1851.
Ezekiel: a Seatonian prize poem. 1854.
Psalms and hymns, based on the Christian psalmody of the late Rev E. Edward Bickersteth, compiled anew by E. H. Bickersteth. [1858], [1860], [c. 1865] (6th edn).
The Tower of London, Caubul, Caesar's invasion of Britain. In A complete collection of the English poems which have obtained the Chancellor's Gold Medal vol 1, Cambridge 1859.
Winged words: a collection of some of his poems made by the author. [1861.]
Yesterday, to-day and for ever: a poem in twelve books. 1866, 1867, 1869, New York 1869, London 1885 (17th edn).
The annotated hymnal companion to the Book of Common Prayer. 1870, 1871 (4 edns), 1880 (rev and enlarged), 1906, 1914.
The two brothers and other poems. 1871, 1872.
Ode on the national thanksgiving for the recovery of the Prince of Wales. 1872.
The shadow of the rock and other poems. Ed Bickersteth 1873. Selected from various authors.
Milton's Paradise lost. In The St James lectures: companions for the devout life, ed J. E. Kempe 1875, 1877.
Songs in the house of pilgrimage. Hampstead [1880?].
From year to year: poems and hymns for all the Sundays and holy days of the Church. '1884' [1883], 1896 (3rd edn, rev and enlarged). Contains Peace, perfect peace.
Bickersteth also pbd many sermons and other religious writings.

§2

In Miles 10 (12).
Julian.
Obit: The Times 17 May 1906.
Aglionby, F. K. The life of Bickersteth. 1907.

John Stanyan Bigg 1828–65

§1

The sea-king: a metrical romance in six cantos with notes historical and illustrative. 1848.
Night and the soul: a dramatic poem. 1854.
REVIEW: Athenaeum 1409, 28 Oct 1834.
[Burns centenary poem.] In Burns centenary poems, ed G. Anderson and J. Finley, Glasgow 1859.
Alfred Staunton: a novel. 1860 (for 1859).
Shifting scenes and other poems. 1862.

§2

Gilfillan, G. In his A third gallery of portraits, Edinburgh 1854.

John Stuart Blackie 1809–95

Mss: poems, commonplace books, letters, autobiography, lectures, essays in NLS.

Selections

Rogers, C. In his Modern Scottish minstrel vol 4, Edinburgh 1855.
Miles 4.
Selected poems. Ed A. S. Walker 1896.

§1

[Goethe's] Faust [pt 1], translated into English verse, with notes and preliminary remarks. 1834.
The water cure in Scotland. Five letters. Aberdeen 1849.
The lyrical dramas of Aeschylus translated into English verse. 2 vols 1850, 1 vol 1906, 1911 (EL).
On the living language of the Greeks, and its utility to the classical scholar. An introductory lecture delivered in the University of Edinburgh. Edinburgh 1853.
Lays and legends of ancient Greece, with other poems. Edinburgh 1857, 1880.
Songs. 1857.
On beauty: three discourses delivered in the University of Edinburgh, with an exposition of the doctrine of the beautiful according to Plato. Edinburgh 1858.
Lyrical poems. Edinburgh 1860.
The Gaelic language: its classical affinities and distinctive character. Edinburgh 1864. A lecture.
Homer and the Iliad. 4 vols Edinburgh 1866. A trn in ballad metre with notes.
On forms of government: a historical review and estimate of the growth of the principal types of political organism in Europe. 1867.
Musa burschicosa: a book of songs for students and university men. Edinburgh 1869.
War songs of the Germans. Edinburgh 1870.
Four phases of morals: Socrates, Aristotle, Christianity, Utilitarianism. Edinburgh 1871.
Lays of the Highlands and islands. 1871, 1872.
On self culture, intellectual, physical and moral: a vade mecum for young men and students. Edinburgh 1874, [1873].
The language and literature of the Scottish Highlands. Edinburgh 1876.
Songs of religion and life. Edinburgh 1876 (for 1875).
The natural history of atheism. 1877.
The wise men of Greece, in a series of dramatic dialogues. 1877.
Altavona: fact and fiction from my life in the Highlands. Edinburgh 1882, 1882.
The wisdom of Goethe. Edinburgh 1883. A critical estimate with Blackie's trns from Goethe's prose and verse.
Essays civil and moral by Francis Bacon; with an introduction by Prof J. S. Blackie. [1886.]
Messis vitae: gleanings of song from a happy life. 1886.
Life of Robert Burns. 1888.
Scottish song: its wealth, wisdom and significance. Edinburgh 1889. Essays.
A song of heroes. 1890.
Christianity and the ideal of humanity in old times and new. Edinburgh 1893.

Blackie also pbd much prose, mainly lectures, on educational, philological, political and religious matters, and also pbd school-books. He contributed to Blackwood's Mag, North Br Rev *etc; see* Wellesley *pp. 812–13.*

Letters and papers

The day-book of Blackie, selected and transcribed from the mss by A. S. Walker. 1901.

Letters to his wife, with a few earlier ones to his parents. Ed A. S. Walker 1909.

Notes of a life. Ed A. S. Walker 1910. Letters and part of an unfinished autobiography.

§2

Whyte, W. In Miles 4.

Stoddart, A. M. Blackie: a biography. 2 vols 1895.

Kennedy, H. A. Professor Blackie, his sayings and doings. 1895.

Samuel Laman Blanchard 1804–45

Mss: letters, BL Add Mss; Hereford, County Record Office.

Collections

Sketches from life: with memoir by E. Bulwer Lytton. 3 vols 1843, 1846, 2 vols New York 1846. Collected essays.

Poetical works. Ed B. Jerrold 1876. With memoir.

Miles 3.

§1

Lyric offerings. 1828.

Life and literary remains of L. E. L[andon]. 2 vols 1841.

George Cruikshank's omnibus. Ed Blanchard 1842.

The cemetery at Kensal Green: the grounds and monuments with a memoir of . . . the late Duke of Sussex. [1843?]

Literary remains of E. L. Johnson. 1844 (priv ptd).

A memoir of W. H. Ainsworth. In Works of W. H. Ainsworth vol 1, 1850, 1853, 1857, 1884.

Corporation characters: forming a select portrait gallery of civic celebrities. Illus. 1855. Prose.

Finden's gallery of modern art: a series of engravings with original descriptive tales by L. Blanchard et al. 2 vols [1859].

Blanchard also contributed to Ainsworth's Mag, *the* Monthly Mag *(of which he was acting editor in 1831), and the* NMM. *In 1832 he edited the daily* True Sun, *and in 1836 he moved to edit the* Constitutional, *and the* Court Jnl *in the following year. From 1837–9 he edited the* Courier, *a liberal evening paper. When its change of ownership led to a political change of sympathy he resigned. From 1841 he was also a contributor to the* Examiner. *See* Wellesley, *5, pp. 79–80.*

§2

Thackeray, W. M. A brother of the press on the history of a literary man, Laman Blanchard, and the chances of the literary profession. Fraser's Mag Mar 1846; rptd in Works, ed A. T. Ritchie, vol 13, 1899.

Japp, A. H. In Miles 3.

Mathilde Blind 1841–96

Collections and selections

A selection from the poems of Mathilde Blind. Ed A. Symons 1897.

The poetical works of Mathilde Blind. Ed Arthur Symons, with a memoir by Richard Garnett. 1900.
REVIEW: Athenaeum 3 Dec 1898.

Selection. Ed R. Garnett in A. H. Miles (ed), The poets and poetry of the century, enlarged edn 1905–7, vol 9, Christina G. Rossetti to Katharine Tynan.

§1

Poems (by Claude Lake). 1867.

Shelley. A lecture. 1870. Pam.

The prophecy of St Oran and other poems. 1881, 1882.
REVIEWS: Westminster Rev n.s. 60 1881; Acad 20, 16 July 1881.

George Eliot (in Eminent Women ser). 1883, 1888 (new edn); Boston 1883, 1904 (new edn with supplementary chs by F. Waldo and G. A. Turkington).
REVIEW: Spectator 56, 28 Apr 1883; Acad 23, 28 Apr 1883.

Tarantella. A prose romance. 2 vols. 1885 [1884], Boston 1885, London 1886.
REVIEW: Spectator 58, 28 Feb 1885.

The heather on fire: a tale of the highland clearances. [In verse.] 1886.
REVIEW: Acad 30, 7 Aug 1886.

Madame Roland (in Eminent Women ser). 1886, Boston 1886, 1888, 1892.
REVIEW: Acad 30, 21 Aug 1886.

Shelley's view of nature contrasted with Darwin's. 1886 (priv ptd 25 copies).

The ascent of man. 1889, 1890 (with introd by A. R. Wallace), 1899.
REVIEWS: Acad 35, 15 June 1889; Spectator 84, 30 June 1900.

Dramas in miniature. 1891.
REVIEWS: Acad 40, 12 Dec 1891; Athenaeum 21 May 1892.

Songs and sonnets. 1893.
REVIEWS: Acad 44, 5 Aug 1893; Athenaeum 30 Sep 1893.

Birds of passage. Songs of the orient and occident. 1895, '1896' [1895].
REVIEWS: Athenaeum 27 July 1895; Acad 48, 12 Oct 1895.

Shakespeare sonnets. 1902.

Contributions to periodicals

Shelley. Works ed W. M. Rossetti. Westminster Rev n.s. 38 July 1870. Essay. Authorship claimed in Athenaeum 10 Feb 1872.

Lilja [Icelandic poem]. Review of edn by E. Magnusson. Dark Blue 1 1871.

The song of the Willi. Dark Blue 1 1871. Poem.

A month at the Achensee [in the Tyrol]. Dark Blue 4 1872.

Maxims and reflections; from the German of Goethe. Fraser's Mag 93 n.s. 13 Mar 1876. Rev of trn.

Mary Wollstonecraft. New Quart Mag 10 July 1878.

The tale of Tristam and Iseult. Nat Rev 2 Feb 1884.

Personal recollections of Mazzini. Fortnightly Rev n.s. 49, May 1891.

Editions, translations, introductions

A selection from the poems of Percy Bysshe Shelley (with memoir). 1872.

D. F. Strauss, The old faith and the new. Trn. 1873, New York 1873 (rev and with Amer version of author's prefatory postscript).

The poetical works of Lord Byron [with introductory notice]. 2 vols 1886.

The letters and journals of Lord Byron [selected, with introd]. 1886, New York [19–?].

The journal of Marie Bashkirsteff [with introd]. 1890.
REVIEWS: Spectator 64, 14 June 1890; Acad 38, 5 July 1890.

A study of Marie Bashkirsteff. In C. A. A. Theuriet, Jules Bastien-Lepage and his art, 1892.

§2

Robertson, E. S. In his English poetesses, 1883.

Obits: Acad 50, 5 Dec 1896; Athenaeum 5 Dec 1896.

R. G. [Richard Garnett]. In DNB.

Blind, M. The feminist companion to literature in English. Ed V. Blain, P. Clements and I. Grundy. 1990. [VB]

Horatius Bonar 1808–89

Mss: Letters on church affairs and editorial work to J. J. Bonar 1830–73 are held in the NLS.

Bibliographies

Horatius Bonar DD: a memorial. 1889.

Collections

Miles 10 (11).

Hymns: selected and arranged by his son H. N. Bonar, with a brief history of some of the hymns. 1904, 1908 (slight emendations and 1 previously unpbd piece).

The land of light and other hymns of faith and hope. [1912.]

Selections

Songs of the dawn: selections from the poems of Horatius Bonar, Charlotte Murray and others. [1887.]

§1

Songs for the wilderness. 1843–4, 1850 (3rd edn).

The night of weeping: or words for the suffering family of God. 1845, 3rd thousand 1846. Prose.

Hymns original and selected. 1846.

The morning of joy: being a sequel to the Night of weeping. 1850. Prose.

Hymns of faith and hope. 1st ser 1857–75, 2nd ser 1861–75, 3rd ser 1867–72, 1909 (selection).
REVIEWS: Literary Churchman 5 Sep 1857; Br Quart Rev 45, Jan 1867.

Words of peace and welcome. 1860. Prose.

Family sermons. 1863.

The nun: or, convent life. [1869.]

The song of the new creation and other pieces. 1872.

My old letters. 1877, new edn in 2 vols 1879. In verse.

Hymns of the nativity, and other pieces. 1879.

Communion hymns. 1881.

Verses for Christmas and the New Year. 1885. With L. A. Bennett. Bk 2 by Bonar.

Songs of love and joy: poems. [1888].

'Crowned with light': a poem. 1889.

'Until the day break' and other hymns and poems left behind. Ed H. N. Bonar 1890.

Contributions to periodicals and collaborative work

Garnered grain. 1889. With L. A. Bennett.

Bonar contributed to North Br Rev *and* Sunday at Home. *He edited the* Presbyterian Rev *for some of the period 1831–48;* Border Watch *1844–8;* Quart Jnl of Prophecy *1848–73;* Christian Treasury *1859–79. See* Wellesley 5 *1989.*

Editions and introductions

The Bible hymn-book. Edinburgh 1845.

The new Jerusalem: a hymn of the olden time. Edinburgh 1852.

Lays of the holy land from ancient and modern poets. 1858.

Introduction to Hymns and thoughts in verse by E. A. W. [1864.]

Lyra consolationis: or hymns for the day of sorrow and weariness. 1866.

Words old and new: or gems from the Christian authorship of all ages. 1866. Prose.

Introduction to The song of songs by B. S. Clarke. 1881.

Bonar also pbd sermons, tracts and travel bks, and wrote introds to many prose works of a broadly religious nature.

§2

Obit: The Times 1 Aug 1889.

Horatius Bonar DD: a memorial. 1889. Includes autobiographical fragment, first and last sermons, bibliographical data and an unpbd poem.

Gibb, G. L. Horatius Bonar and his hymns. Edinburgh 1989. [RS]

Thomas Edward Brown 1830–97

Mss located in Bryn Mawr College PA; Manx Museum Lib; Pierpont Morgan Lib, New York. See also LR.

Bibliographies

Mozley, J. R. Poems of Thomas Edward Brown. Quart Rev Apr 1898, rptd Living Age 10 Sep 1898.

Simpson, S. G. In Thomas Edward Brown the Manx poet: an appreciation. London and Felling-on-Tyne 1906, New York 1906.

Radcliffe, W. In Thomas Edward Brown: a memorial volume, Cambridge 1930.

Cubbon, W. Thomas Edward Brown, the Manx poet, 1830–1897. A bibliography. Douglas, Isle of Man 1934. Rptd in his A bibliographical account of works relating to the Isle of Man vol 2, Oxford 1939.

Nowell-Smith, S. T. E. Brown. BC Autumn 1962.

See also Wellesley 5 *1989.*

Collections

Collected poems of T. E. Brown. Ed H. F. Brown, H. G. Dakyns and W. E. Henley, with introd by W. E. Henley, 1900, 1901, 1909, 1920, 1927, 1976 (reprint of 1900).
REVIEWS: Acad 29 Sep 1900; Bookman Nov 1900; Dial Jan 1901.

Poems of Thomas Edward Brown. Ed with introd by H. F. Brown and H. G. Dawkins 1908, 1919.

Poems of Thomas Edward Brown. Introductory memoir by A. Quiller-Couch. 2 vols Liverpool 1952 (reprint of Collected poems 1900 without introd by Henley).
REVIEW: TLS 6 June 1952.

Selections

In The poets and the poetry of the century, ed A. H. Miles, vol 5 1891–97.

In The English poets, ed T. H. Ward, vol 5, 1918.

Twenty-three poems. 1931 (Augustan Books of Poetry).

§1

The students' guide to the school of 'Litterae Fictitiae', commonly called novel-literature. Oxford 1855 (2 edns). With H. E. Tweed?

Betsy Lee. A fo'c'sle yarn. Cockermouth 1873 (anon), London 1873 (anon), New York 1873 (anon).

Christmas rose. Cockermouth 1873.

The library. A sermon preached in Clifton College Chapel, Sunday, Nov 2 1873. Clifton 1873.

Chalse a Killey: to Chalse in Heaven. Ramsey, Isle of Man [1875?].

The doctor, by the author of 'Betsy Lee'. Douglas, Isle of Man 1876.

Captain Tom and Captain Hugh; a Manx story in verse. Douglas, Isle of Man 1878.

Old John. Douglas, Isle of Man [1880?]. Pam.
REVIEW: Isle of Man Times 8 Jan 1881.

Tommy big-eyes. By the author of 'Betsy Lee'. 1880.

Fo'c'sle yarns, including Betsy Lee, and other poems. 1881, 1889 (2nd edn).
REVIEWS: Acad 30 Apr 1881; Athenaeum 7 May 1881; Scots Observer 15 June 1889.

The doctor, and other poems. 1887. In 1891 unsold sheets were sold as Kitty of the Sherragh Vane and The doctor.

The Manx witch, and other poems. 1889, New York 1889.
REVIEWS: Scots Observer 26 Oct 1889; Acad 4 Jan 1890; Athenaeum 25 Jan 1890.

Old John, and other poems. 1893, New York 1893.
REVIEWS: Nat Observer 15 Apr 1893; Acad 27 May 1893; Dial 16 July 1893; Sylvia's Jnl July 1893; Athenaeum 16 Sep 1893.

Manx idioms: a lecture. Douglas, Isle of Man 1897.

Contributions to periodicals, introductions and collaborative works

Chambers's encyclopaedia. 1888–92 edn, 1901 edn. Isle of Man.

Scots Observer. 10 Aug 1889–6 Sep 1890.

National Observer. 6 Dec 1890–14 Oct 1893.

Ramsey Courier. Rights of way in the Isle of Man, 19 Nov 1892, 24 Dec 1893.

For contributions to Contemporary Rev *and* New Rev *see* Wellesley 5 1989.
Introd to E. Rydings, Manx tales, Manchester 1895.
Preface. Manx ballads and music, ed A. W. Moore, Douglas, Isle of Man 1896.

Letters

Letters of T. E. Brown. Ed S. T. Irwin 1900 (3 edns), New York 1900, Liverpool 1952 (4th edn).
New letters from T. E. Brown. Mannin May 1917.

§2

A literary gossip. Literary Opinion Oct 1891.
Modern men. The author of Fo'cs'le yarns. Nat Observer 28 May 1892.
Canton, W. Bookman May 1897.
Obits and notes on death: The Times 1 Nov 1897; Wetminster Gazette 1 Nov 1897; Guardian 3 Nov 1897; Literature 6 Nov 1897; Spectator 6 Nov 1897; Isle of Man Times 6 Nov 1897; Caine, H., Isle of Man Times 6 Nov 1897; Sitwell, E., Isle of Man Times 6 Nov 1897; Acad 6 Nov, 13 Nov 1897; Dialect poetry. Spectator 13 Nov 1897; New York Times 27 Nov 1897; Henley, W. E., New Rev Dec 1897; Storr, W., New Rev Dec 1897.
Canton, W. Good Words Mar 1898.
Mozley, J. R. Quart Rev Apr 1898.
Shimmin, F. M. Primitive Methodist Quart Oct 1898.
White, I. M. Scots Mag May 1899.
Hughes-Green, S. H. W. Fortnightly Rev Nov 1900.
Henley, W. E. Pall Mall Mag Nov 1900.
Annalist [Charles Whibley]. Blackwood's Mag Nov 1901, rptd in his Musings without method, Edinburgh and London 1902.
Seacombe, T. DNB 1901.
Harris, A. M. Parents' Rev June 1901.
Mozley, J. R. Temple Bar Aug 1901.
News Notes. Bookman Nov 1901.
Strachan, L. R. M. EStudien 34 (3), 1904.
The Cryptian (Gloucester) Apr 1903.
Simpson, S. G. Thomas Edward Brown the Manx poet. London and Felling-on-Tyne 1906, New York 1906.
Morrison, S. and A. M. Williams. T. E. Brown calendar. Peel, Isle of Man 1913.
Gift of T. E. Brown portraits. Mannin May 1914.
Sharp, T. The Homer of the Isle of Man. Poetry Rev June 1914.
T. E. Brown memorial. Mannin May 1915.
Rydings, E. T. E. Brown. Mannin May 1917.
Cubbon, W. T. T. E. Brown the patriot. Douglas, Isle of Man 1917.
Tarver, J. C. Nineteenth Cent Dec 1920.
Spender, C. The poetry of T. E. Brown. Contemporary Rev Mar 1925.
Thomas Edward Brown: a memorial volume, 1830–1897. Cambridge 1930.
Norris, S. Two men of Manxland. Hall Caine, novelist. T. E. Brown, poet. Douglas, Isle of Man 1947.
Manxman on the modern side. TLS 6 June 1952.
Tobias, R. C. T. E. Brown. Boston 1978 (Twayne English Authors ser).
Sutton, M. K. How listeners shape stories: a model for readers in Brown's Fo'c'sle yarns. Jnl of Narrative Technique Spring 1986.
Sutton, M. K. Earning authority: the narrator's task in T. E. Brown's third Fo'c'sle yarn. TSLL Spring 1988.
Sutton, M. K. Mutiny among the listeners in Brown's first (uncensored) Fo'c'sle yarns. VP Autumn 1988.
Sutton, M. K. The drama of storytelling in T. E. Brown's Manx yarns. Newark DE 1991.
Shimmin, N. L. In The 1890s: an encyclopedia of British literature, art, and culture, ed G. A. Cevasco, New York 1993.
DLB vol 35. Detroit 1995. [DA]

Elizabeth Barrett Browning 1806–61

Some noteworthy collections of letters and ms material relating to Barrett Browning are in the Armstrong Browning Lib of Baylor Univ, the Berg Collection and Rare Book Division of the NYPL, the libs of Wellesley College, Yale, Harvard and Texas Univs and Scripps College (Claremont CA), as well as in the BL, the Bodleian, the Pierpont Morgan Lib, the Huntington and the Fitzwilliam and Victoria and Albert museums. Detailed information on mss may be found in P. Kelley and B. A. Coley (comps), The Browning collections: a reconstruction, *Winfield KS 1984, and in* IELM *vol 4, London and New York 1982.*

Bibliographies and reference works

Primary materials

Slater, J. H. Elizabeth Barrett Browning. In Early editions, 1894.
[Forman, H. B.] Elizabeth Barrett Browning and her scarcer books. In Literary anecdotes of the nineteenth century, ed W. R. Nicoll and T. J. Wise, vol 2 1896; rptd priv 1896.
Wise, T. J. A bibliography of the writings in prose and verse of Elizabeth Barrett Browning. 1918, rptd 1970. Suppl by G. B. Taplin, PBSA 44 1950; rptd in his Life of Elizabeth Barrett Browning, 1957.
Wise, T. J. In A catalogue of the library of the late John Henry Wrenn vol 1, Austin TX 1920.
Ehrsam, T. G., R. H. Deily and R. M. Smith. Elizabeth Barrett Browning. In Bibliographies of twelve Victorian authors, New York 1936.
Greer, C. L. Browning and America. Chapel Hill NC 1952. Lists items in nineteenth-century American anthologies.
Barnes, W. A bibliography of Elizabeth Barrett Browning. Austin and Waco TX 1967. Includes forgeries and fugitives, reprints, first periodical or other pbn of works later collected; the standard bibliography.
Kimball, J. C. Browning realia and its significance: a documentation of the museum items in the Armstrong Browning Library. Unpbd MA thesis, Baylor Univ 1972.
East, S. K. C. Browning music: a descriptive catalog of the music in the Armstrong Browning Library: 1972. Waco TX 1973.
Hudson, G. W. Elizabeth Barrett Browning concordance. Detroit 1973.

Secondary materials

Monti, G. Elisabetta Barrett Browning. Emporium 3, May 1896. Lists trns, in Ital.
Brooks, A. E. Browningiana in Baylor University. Waco TX 1921.
Russell, F. T. One word more on Browning. Stanford CA 1927. Lists Ger stud.
Armstrong, A. J. and T. Sone. A bibliography of foreign Browningiana. In Browning the world over, Waco TX 1932.
Ehrsam, T. G., R. H. Deily and R. M. Smith. Elizabeth Barrett Browning. In Bibliographies of twelve Victorian authors, New York 1936. Suppl by J. G. Fucilla, MP 37 1939; rptd in Bibliographies of studies in Victorian literature 1932–44, ed W. D. Templeman, Urbana IL 1945 and 1945–54, ed . Wright, Urbana IL 1956.
Forster, M. and W. M. Zappe. Robert Browning bibliography. Halle 1939. Lists Ger stud.
Caskey, E. P. Contemporary criticism of Elizabeth Barrett and Elizabeth Barrett Browning. Unpbd MA thesis, Baylor Univ 1948.
Broughton, L. N., C. S. Northup and R. B. Pearsall. In Robert Browning: a bibliography, Ithaca NY 1953. Rev by W. D. Templeman, Browning Newsletter 2 1969.
Jannattoni, L. Elizabeth Barrett Browning, con un saggio di bibliografia italiana. Florence 1953. Lists stud and trns, in Ital.
Terhune, A. McK. Elizabeth Barrett Browning. In The Victorian poets: a guide to research, ed F. E. Faverty, Cambridge MA 1956. Rev by M. Timko, Cambridge MA 1968.

Bisignano, D. J. The Brownings and their Italian critics. Unpbd PhD diss, New York Univ 1964. Lists Ital stud and trns.

Buckley, J. H. Elizabeth Barrett Browning. In Victorian poets and prose writers, ed O. B. Hardison jun, New York 1966 (Goldentree Bibliographies).

Radley, V. L. Elizabeth Barrett Browning. New York 1972. Contains annotated bibliography.

Tennison, J. E. Elizabeth Barrett Browning: an index to the NCBEL. Browning Newsletter 8 1972.

Peterson, W. and R. C. Keenan. R. and E. B. Browning: annotated bibliography for 1971. Browning Inst Stud 1 1973. Updated annually; continued in Victorian Lit and Culture. Indexed by E. N. Shapiro and W. S. Peterson, Cumulative index 1973–82, Browning Inst Stud 11 1983.

Peterson, W. S. Robert and Elizabeth Barrett Browning: an annotated bibliography 1951–70. New York 1974.

Mukoyama, Y. Browning study in Japan. PhD diss, Baylor Univ 1976; rptd Tokyo 1977. Expands Armstrong and Sone 1932, *above*. Lists stud and trns in Jap.

Magill, F. N. Elizabeth Barrett Browning. In Magill's bibliography of literary criticism, Englewood Cliffs NJ 1979.

Yoder, L. Elizabeth Barrett Browning. In Research guide to biography and criticism, ed W. Beacham, vol 1 Washington 1985.

Reynolds, M. Aurora Leigh by Elizabeth Barrett Browning. Athens OH 1992. Includes detailed bibliography.

Donaldson, S. Elizabeth Barrett Browning: an annotated bibliography of commentary and criticism 1826–1990. Boston 1993.

Collections

For a list of edns and reprints, see W. Barnes, A bibliography of Elizabeth Barrett Browning, *Austin and Waco TX 1967, pts A and E.*

Poems. New edition. 2 vols 1850 (includes some poems from The seraphim, Prometheus bound, and Poems (1844)); rev 3rd edn 2 vols 1853; rev and expanded 4th edn 3 vols 1856 (later called 'Last London edition corrected by the author'); 5th edn 3 vols 1862; and many more edns and rpts.

Prometheus bound and other poems. New York and Boston 1851 (Amer publishers pirated numerous edns under this title in her lifetime and after); introd by A. Meynell 1896.

Poems. Introd by H. T. Tuckerman, New York and Boston 1853 (numerous reprints).

Aurora Leigh and other poems. New York 1861 (numerous reprints).

Works of Mrs Browning. Ed R. Browning 5 vols New York 1863–4; Poems, preface by R. Browning, 1887.

Poetical works. New York 1871 (numerous reprints).

Earlier poems of Elizabeth Barrett Browning 1826–33. Ed R. H. Shepherd 1878.

Poetical works from 1826 to 1844. Ed J. H. Ingram 1887.

Poetical works. Ed F. G. Kenyon, London and New York 1897.

Complete poetical works. Ed H. W. Preston, Boston and New York 1900 (Cambridge edn); rptd with introd by R. M. Adams, Boston 1974.

Complete works. Ed C. Porter and H. A. Clarke 6 vols New York 1900; rptd 1901, 1903, 1973.

Poetical works. Ed A. Birrell 1903.

Poetical works. Introd by W. T. Dobson, Edinburgh 1903.

Poetical works. London and New York 1904 (Oxford Complete edn), rptd as WC 1912.

Complete poetical works. Introd by L. Whiting 2 vols New York 1918.

Selections

For a list of reprints, see W. Barnes, A bibliography of Elizabeth Barrett Browning, *Austin and Waco TX 1967, pt E.*

Poems of the intellect and the affections. Philadelphia 1865.

A selection. Ser 1 and 2, ed R. Browning 1866, Leipzig (Tauchnitz) 1872, and many reprints; new edn introd by R. Browning, London and New York 1884.

Poems of childhood. New York 1867; rptd (adding 2 poems) as Poems of memory and hope, New York 1872.

Mrs Browning's birthday book. Ed R. H. Stoddard, New York 1882.

Selected poems. New York 1887.

Romances, lyrics and sonnets from the poetic works. Boston and New York 1888.

From queens' gardens. Selected poems. Ed R. Porter, Troy NY 1889.

Mrs Browning birthday book. Preface by C. Mackeson 1889.

Poems, with a memoir. London and New York 1893.

Brownings for the young. Ed F. G. Kenyon, London and New York 1896.

Selected poems. New York 1898.

Beautiful thoughts from Robert and Elizabeth Browning. Arranged by M. Shipp, New York 1900.

Poems of Robert and Elizabeth Barrett Browning. Ed C. L. Thomson 1901.

Love poems of Elizabeth Barrett Browning. London and New York 1902.

Poems. Ed H. W. Mabie, New York 1902.

Poems. Introd by A. Meynell 1903.

A selection from Mrs Browning's poems. Ed H. E. Hersey, New York and London 1903.

Florence in the poetry of the Brownings. Introd by A. B. McMahan, Chicago 1904.

Mrs Browning birthday book. Introd by C. W. Vick, London and New York 1904.

Selected poems. Introd by E. Lee, Boston 1904.

Select poems by Robert Browning and Elizabeth Barrett Browning. Ed E. F. Lowd and M. C. Craig, New York and Boston 1907.

Love poems from the works of Robert Browning and Elizabeth Barrett Browning. Selected by E. Harris, Chicago and New York 1909.

From day to day with the Brownings. Comp by W. and F. Rice, New York 1911.

Thoughts from Mrs Browning. Ed A. Bachelor, Boston 1912.

An E. B. Browning birthday book. 1914.

Selections from the Brownings. Ed H. O'B. Boas 1933.

Two poets, a dog, and a boy: a selection of verse. Ed F. T. Russell, Philadelphia and London 1933.

Best known poems of Elizabeth and Robert Browning. Garden City NY 1942.

Love poems of Elizabeth Barrett Browning and Robert Browning. Introd by L. Untermeyer, New Brunswick NJ 1946.

Poetry of the Brownings. Comp by C. Bax 1947.

Poems. Ed S. J. Looker 1948.

The Brownings: letters and poetry. Introd by C. Ricks, Garden City NY 1970.

Aurora Leigh and other poems. Introd by C. Kaplan 1978.

Selected poems. Introd by M. Hicks, Manchester 1983.

Selected poems. Introd by M. Forster, London and Baltimore 1988.

Sonnets from the Portuguese and other poems. Mineola NY 1992.

Elizabeth Barrett Browning. Ed P. Porter, London and New York 1992.

Selected poetry and prose. Ed M. B. Raymond and M. R. Sullivan, Durham NC 1993.

§1

For a list of Barrett Browning's poems first pbd in periodicals and annuals, see W. Barnes, A bibliography of Elizabeth Barrett Browning, *Austin and Waco TX 1967, pt C. Reviews of Barrett Browning's works are rptd chronologically in vols of* The Brownings' correspondence, *ed P. Kelley, R. Hudson and S. Lewis, Winfield KS 1984– . Reviews and criticism for 1826–1990 are excerpted in S. Donaldson,* Elizabeth Barrett Browning: an annotated bibliography, *Boston 1993.*

The battle of Marathon. 1820 (priv ptd); ed H. B. Forman 1891 (facs).

Essay on mind, with other poems. 1826 (anon).

Prometheus bound, and miscellaneous poems. 1833.
The seraphim, and other poems. 1838.
'He giveth His beloved sleep' [originally titled 'The sleep']. In The seraphim, *above*; Boston c. 1880, 1882; New York 1882, 1902; 1897, 1907.
'The virgin Mary to the child Jesus'. In The seraphim, *above*; ed W. A. Muhlenberg, New York 1868 and 1870 (as 'The true Mary').
'Queen Annelida and false Arcite'. In The poems of Geoffrey Chaucer modernized, ed R. H. Horne 1841.
Poems. 2 vols 1844, New York '1845' [1844] (as A drama of exile: and other poems).
'The cry of the children'. In Poems, 1844, *above*; New York 1908; N & Q 24 Dec 1949. Tr Rus 1864; Fr 1887, 1912; Ital 1952.
'Lady Geraldine's courtship'. In Poems, 1844, *above*; often rptd separately.
'Rhyme of the Duchess May'. In Poems, 1844, *above*; 1873, London and Edinburgh 1907, Philadelphia 1908.
'The romaunt of the page'. In Poems, 1844, *above*; London and Glasgow c. 1910. Tr Ital 1906.
A new spirit of the age. 2 vols 1844. With R. H. Horne (essays on Carlyle and Tennyson). Barrett Browning's pt of Carlyle essay rptd; *see* Nicoll and Wise 1896, *under* Bibliographies, primary, *above*.
'The runaway slave at Pilgrim's Point'. In Poems, 1850 (*see* Collections, *above*); 1888 printing is a forgery by T. J. Wise.
Sonnets [or] Sonnets from the Portuguese. In Poems, 1850 (*see* Collections, *above*); often rptd separately. Earliest independent edn Boston 1886. A famous edn dated Reading 1847 is a forgery by T. J. Wise. Var edn, ed F. Ratchford, New York 1950; introd by A. Mayor, Utrecht 1957 (type-facs); ed W. S. Peterson, Barre MA 1977 (facs); ed M. W. Dow, Troy NY 1980. Many trns, including Fr (1903, L. Morel; 1905, F. Henry; 1944, A. Maurois); Ger (1908, R. M. Rilke, rptd many times); Ital (1902 and 1907, T. V. de Dominicis); Polish; Du; Hungarian; Sp; Rus.
'Stanzas – a fragment' (stanzas 2 and 5 of 'Human life's mystery'). In Poems, 1850 (*see* Collections, *above*); ed T. J. Wise 1918; Stanford CA 1942, 1943; ed P. Kelley and R. Hudson, Browning Inst Stud 7 1979.
Casa Guidi windows. 1851; ed A. M. F. Robinson 1901; introd by W. A. Sim, Florence 1926; ed J. Markus, New York 1977.
'A song for the ragged schools of London'. In Two poems (here titled 'A plea for the ragged schools of London'; the other is by Robert Browning), 1854; ed R. Browning 1862; ed N. Barker, London and Berkeley CA 1983.
Aurora Leigh. London '1857' [1856] (rptd 3 times), rev 1859 ('4th edn'); New York and Boston '1857' [1856]. Rptd numerous times throughout the century, including Leipzig 1872 (Tauchnitz); preface by A. C. Swinburne 1898; ed H. B. Forman 1899 (Temple Classics); introd by E. W. Rinder 1899; ed C. Porter and H. A. Clarke 1902; introd by C. Kaplan 1978 (facs); introd by G. B. Taplin, Chicago 1979 (facs); ed M. Reynolds, Athens OH 1992, New York 1996 (Norton Critical); ed K. McSweeney 1993 (WCp); ed J. and J. B. Holloway 1996 (Pen). Tr Fr 1887 (in part), 1890 (prose); Ital 1908.
Poems before congress. 1860, New York 1860 (as Napoleon III and other poems).
Last poems. Ed R. Browning 1862; introd by T. Tilton, New York 1862.
'Bianca among the nightingales'. In Last poems, *above*; tr Ital 1906.
'Lord Walter's wife'. In Last poems, *above*; Wausau WI 1899.
'A musical instrument'. In Last Poems, *above*; New Preston CT 1924.
'My Kate'. In Last poems, *above*; 1911.
The Greek Christian poets and the English poets. 1863, New York 1889. First pbd as Some account of the Greek Christian poets, and The book of the poets, Athenaeum 1842.
'Psyche apocalypté'. With R. H. Horne (a projected lyrical drama). St James's Mag Feb 1876, 1876 (separately). Autograph ms pbd in vol 2 of Hitherto unpublished poems and stories, *below*.
The enchantress and other poems. 1913; rptd in New poems, *below*, and in vol 2 of Hitherto unpublished poems and stories, *below*.
'Epistle to a canary'. Ed E. Gosse 1913; rptd in New poems, *below*.
'Leila, a tale'. 1913; rptd in New poems, *below*.
'The maiden's death'. Cornhill Mag Dec 1913; rptd in New Poems, *below*, and in vol 2 of Hitherto unpublished poems and stories, *below*.
'A true dream'. In Enchantress, *above*; New York 1914; rptd in New poems, *below*.
New poems by Robert and Elizabeth Barrett Browning. Ed F. G. Kenyon 1914. Only 5 are by Barrett Browning.
Hitherto unpublished poems and stories, with an 'inedited' [*sic*] autobiography. Ed H. B. Forman, 2 vols Boston 1914.
The poets' enchiridion [and other poems]. Ed H. B. Forman, Boston 1914; rptd in vol 2 of Hitherto unpublished poems and stories, *above*. Full version of 'The poets' enchiridion' only, ed H. Harrod, SE 26 1947 (early version here called 'The development of genius').
'The poet's record'. In Anthony Munday, ed E. Conway, New York 1927 (priv ptd).
'A ring'. TLS 21 June 1947.
'Stanzas, excited by some reflections on the present state of Greece'. Ed G. Taplin, N & Q 10 June 1950.
'Kings'. Ed B. P. McCarthy, N & Q 15 Sep 1951; in Diary by E. B. B., *below*.
'The sorrows of the muses'. Ed W. Barnes, Books at Iowa 4 1966 (with facs page).
Fragment of 'An essay on woman'. Ed K. Moser, Stud in Browning 12 1984.

Diary, autobiographical writings and marginalia

Glimpses into my own life and literary character. *See* vol 1 of Hitherto unpublished poems and stories, *above*; rptd as one of Two autobiographical essays, ed W. S. Peterson, Browning Inst Stud 2 1974.
Marginalia by E. B. B.: Milton's prose works. Ed C. R. H. T., Turnbull Lib Rec July 1940.
Elizabeth Barrett's commentary on Shelley: some marginalia. Ed J. Thorpe, MLN 66, Nov 1951.
Diary by E. B. B.: the unpublished diary of Elizabeth Barrett Barrett 1831–32. Ed P. Kelley and R. Hudson, Athens OH 1969. Rptd as The Barretts at Hope End, ed E. Berridge, 1974.
My own character. One of Two autobiographical essays, ed W. S. Peterson, Browning Inst Stud 2 1974.

Collected letters

Letters to and from both Brownings are pbd in The Brownings' correspondence, *ed P. Kelley, R. Hudson and S. Lewis, Winfield KS 1984– . (14 vols as of 1999, to Dec 1847). A full list is in* The Brownings' correspondence: a checklist, *ed P. Kelley and R. Hudson, Arkansas City KS and New York 1978, and 5 suppls in Browning Inst Stud (1978–82).*
Barrett Browning also wrote joint letters with Robert, which may be found in edns of his letters: Armstrong (1923), Hood (1933), DeVane and Knickerbocker (1950), McAleer (1951).
Letters addressed to Richard Hengist Horne. Ed S. R. Townshend Mayer 2 vols 1877. Also pbd as vol 1 of Letters and essays of Elizabeth Barrett Browning, ed R. H. Stoddard, New York 1877, which was also titled Life, letters, and essays of Elizabeth Barrett Browning.
The letters of Elizabeth Barrett Browning. Ed F. G. Kenyon 2 vols London and New York 1897 (4-vol typescript from which these letters were selected is in the BL). Selected as Elizabeth Barrett Browning in her letters, ed P. Lubbock, 1906.
The letters of Robert Browning and Elizabeth Barrett Barrett 1845–46. Ed [R. W. B. Browning] 2 vols London and New York

1899, numerous reprints; ed E. Kintner, 2 vols Cambridge MA 1969; also ed V. E. Stack, London 1969, and as How do I love thee? The love-letters of Robert Browning and Elizabeth Barrett, New York 1969, rptd 1987; ed and selected by D. Karlin as Robert Browning and Elizabeth Barrett: the courtship correspondence, New York and Oxford 1989.

Letters to Robert Browning and other correspondents. Ed T. J. Wise 1916 (priv ptd).

Letters to her sister 1846–59 [to Henrietta Cook]. Ed L. Huxley 1929. Also pbd in Cornhill Mag 66, May and June, and 67, July and Aug 1929.

Letters addressed to Mrs. Gaskell by celebrated contemporaries. Ed R. D. Waller, BJRL 19, Jan 1935.

Twenty-two unpublished letters of Elizabeth Barrett Browning and Robert Browning addressed to Henrietta and Arabella Moulton-Barrett. New York 1935. Rptd as Addressed to Wimpole Street, ed W. R. Benét, Woman's Home Companion Sep–Dec 1935, and Argosy 19, Feb–Apr 1936. Rptd as From Robert and Elizabeth Browning, a further selection, 1936.

Letters from Elizabeth Barrett to B. R. Haydon. Ed M. H. Shackford, New York 1939; ed W. B. Pope as Invisible friends: the correspondence of Elizabeth Barrett Barrett and Benjamin Robert Haydon 1842–45, Cambridge MA 1972.

New letters to Isa Blagden. Ed E. C. McAleer, PMLA 66, Sep 1951.

Unpublished letters of Thomas De Quincey and Elizabeth Barrett Browning. Ed S. Musgrove, Auckland Univ College Bull 44 1954.

Elizabeth Barrett to Miss Mitford. Ed B. Miller, London and New Haven CT 1954; as Letters to Mary Russell Mitford, Waco TX, Winfield KS and Wellesley MA 1983; selections pbd as Women of letters, ed M. B. Raymond and M. R. Sullivan, Boston 1987.

Elizabeth Barrett to Mr [Hugh Stuart] Boyd. Ed B. P. McCarthy, London and New Haven CT 1955.

Pasquale Villari and the Brownings. Ed E. C. McAleer, Boston Public Lib Quart 9 1957.

Letters of the Brownings to George Barrett. Ed P. Landis with R. E. Freeman, Urbana IL 1958.

British and American literary letters in Scandinavian public collections. Ed N. E. Enkvist, Acta Academiae Aboensis Humanitora 27 1964.

Browning to his American friends: letters between the Brownings, the Storys, and James Russell Lowell 1841–90. Ed G. R. Hudson, New York 1965.

Brownings and Tennysons: letters to Alfred, Emily, and Hallam Tennyson 1852–89. Ed T. J. Collins, Waco TX 1971.

Ruskin and the Brownings: twenty-five unpublished letters. Ed D. J. DeLaura, BJRL 54 1972.

Elizabeth Barrett Browning's letters to Mrs David Ogilvy 1849–61. Ed P. N. Heydon and P. Kelley, New York 1973.

Elizabeth Barrett Browning and her brother Alfred. Ed R. Hudson, Browning Inst Stud 2 1974.

The Brownings and Mrs Kinney. Ed R. A. Bosco, Browning Inst Stud 4 1976.

Translations

A number of lyric trns are collected in Last poems *(1862) and* Hitherto unpublished poems and stories *(1914), both above. See also Barnes, under Bibliographies, primary, above, for a full list at the end of the Index of textual variants.*

Prometheus bound, translated from the Greek of Æschylus. 1833; retranslated 1850; ed W. R. Agard, New York 1950; Ithaca NY 1952; ed W. A. Landis, Studio City CA 1992.

Æschylus' Soliloquy [erroneously attributed to Robert Browning]. 1913 (rptd several times in discussions of authorship; *see* S. Donaldson, Elizabeth Barrett Browning: an annotated bibliography, Boston 1993).

§2

Reviews and criticism for 1826–1990 are excerpted in S. Donaldson, Elizabeth Barrett Browning: an annotated bibliography, *Boston 1993. Annual bibliographies of Browning criticism appear in two periodicals devoted to study of the Brownings:* Browning Inst Stud, *now* Victorian Lit and Culture *(indexed by E. N. Shapiro and W. S. Peterson 1973–82, vol 11 1983), 1973–; and* Browning Newsletter, *now* Stud in Browning *(semi-annual 1969–82, annual 1983–). See also* Victorian Poetry, Guide to the Year's Work *1974–79, and 1983–; and* Victorian Studies, Victorian bibliography: Brownings 1958–. *The section below focuses mainly on textual matters.*

The IELM section on the Brownings lists descriptions and catalogues of mss and other materials in repositories.

Slater, J. H. E. B. Browning. In Early editions, 1894.

Sotheby, Wilkinson and Hodge. Browning collections. 1913. Rptd (facs) J. Woolford (ed) in Sale catalogues, ed A. N. L. Munby, vol 6 1972. *See also* B. Coley and P. Kelley, Lot 931: a reconstruction, Waco TX 1981, expanded to full 1913 catalogue as The Browning collections: a reconstruction, P. Kelley and B. A. Coley (comps), Waco TX, New York, London and Winfield KS 1984.

Palmer, G. H. Catalogue of early and rare editions of English poetry [at Wellesley College]. Boston 1923.

Catalogue of the papers of Lt-Col Harry Peyton Moulton-Barrett deceased. 1937; rptd P. Kelley (ed), Browning Inst Stud 5 1977.

[French, H. D.] Elizabeth Barrett Browning: an exhibition commemorating the Sonnets from the Portuguese. Friends of the Wellesley Coll Lib 8 1950.

Johnson, R. C. and G. T. Tanselle. The Haldeman-Julius Little Blue Books as a bibliographical problem. PBSA 64 1970.

Christie, Manson & Woods. Books and manuscripts from the library of Arthur A. Houghton Jnr. 1979. *See also* J. Klingman, A catalogue of Elizabeth Barrett Browning and Robert Browning manuscript materials and books, Waco TX 1979.

Kelley, P. and R. Hudson. Elusive Browningiana: a list of unlocated manuscripts, marginalia and annotated works. Browning Inst Stud 7 1979.

Forster, M. Elizabeth Barrett Browning: a biography. London and New York 1988.

Duval, S. Robert Browning and Elizabeth Barrett Browning: first editions from the Victorian collection. Provo UT 1989. [SD]

Robert Browning 1812–89

Major collections of mss, letters, books belonging to Browning, etc, are at the Armstrong Browning Lib, Baylor Univ, Texas; Balliol College, Oxford; BL; Brighton Area Lib; Harvard Univ; the Huntington; NYPL (Berg Collection); Pierpont Morgan Lib; Princeton Univ (Taylor Collection); Univ of Texas, Austin; Victoria and Albert Museum; Wellesley College; Yale Univ. Full list of holdings in Kelley and Coley, The Browning collections *(see below). See also* IELM *vol 4 pt 1 1982.*

Bibliographies etc

For surveys of contributions to Browning scholarship and criticism, lists, and descriptions of lib holdings or acquisitions, see: Annual bibliography in VS; LITHR [Lit Information and Retrieval] Database; Armstrong Browning Lib Newsletter; Browning Newsletter; MLA (SPIRS) Database; Stud in Browning and his Circle; SEL; Victorian Newsletter; Victorian Lit and Culture *(formerly* Browning Inst Stud*)*; VP; YWES.

Furnivall, F. J. Bibliography of Browning from 1833 to 1881. Browning Soc Papers 1 1881–4.

Orr, A. A handbook to the works of Browning. 1885. Discusses the whole canon in classified groups, as authorised and partly supervised by Browning; subsequent edns (1886, 1887, 1890 etc) incorporate suggestions and revisions by Browning.

Porter, C. and H. A. Clarke. A Browning reference list. Poet-Lore Oct–Nov 1889.

Cooke, G. W. A guide book to the poetic and dramatic works of Browning. Boston 1891. Still useful.
Berdoe, E. The Browning cyclopaedia: a guide to the study of the works of Browning, with copious notes and references on all difficult passages. 1892, 1897 (rev). Not always reliable, but useful.
Molineux, M. A. Phrase book from the poetic and dramatic works. Boston 1896. Contains also an index of significant words.
Wise, T. J. A complete bibliography of Browning. 1897. First pbd as Materials for a bibliography of Browning in W. R. Nicholl and Wise, Literary anecdotes of the nineteenth century vol 1, 1895.
Kenyon, Sir F. G. Cornhill Mag Aug 1913; New York Times 27 Apr 1913, 3 May 1913. On the Browning sale.
Brooks, A. E. Browningiana in Baylor University. Baylor Bull 24 1921. Bibliography of criticism.
Broughton, L. N. and B. F. Stelter. A concordance to the poems of Browning. 1924, rptd New York 1970.
Wise, T. J. A Browning library. 1929.
Sone, T. A bibliography of Browning. Tokyo 1931.
Armstrong, A. J. Browning the world over. Waco TX 1933. Includes extensive bibliography of foreign Browningiana.
DeVane, W. C. A Browning handbook. Ithaca NY 1935, New York 1955 (rev). The standard handbook.
Forster, M. and W. Zappe. Browning bibliographie. Halle 1939.
Marchand, L. The Symington Collection. Jnl of the Rutgers Univ Lib Dec 1948.
Raymond, W. O. Browning studies in England and America 1910–49. In The infinite moment, Toronto 1950.
Moore, W. L. C. The Baylor University collection of the musical settings of the poetry of Browning. Unpbd MA diss, Baylor Univ 1951 (MA diss).
Moore, S. Special features of the Browning Library. Texas Lib Jnl 28 1952. On the Armstrong Browning Lib.
Broughton, L. N., C. S. Northup and R. B. Pearsall. Browning: a bibliography 1830–1950. Ithaca NY 1953. Rptd New York 1970. Includes sections on Browning's writings; reference works; biography and criticism; verse criticism, appreciation, and parody; a calendar of letters; musical settings to Browning's poems.
Lauterbach, E. S. Victorian manuscripts at the Huntington Library. Victorian Newsletter 4 1953.
Faverty, F. E. (ed). The Victorian poets: a guide to research. Cambridge MA 1956. Section on Browning by W. C. DeVane. 2nd edn 1968: section on Browning by P. Honan.
Gordan, J. D. New in the Berg Collection: 1952–1956. BNYPL 61 1957.
DeVane, W. C. A guide to research materials on the major Victorians (pt II): Browning. Victorian Newsletter 13 1958.
Todd, W. B. (ed). Thomas J. Wise: centenary studies. Austin TX 1959. Includes Todd's textual collation of Wise's introd to A Browning library 1929.
A Browning exhibit in the treasure room. Boston Pub Lib Quart 11 1959.
A[rmstrong], M[ary]. Some recent additions to the art collection in the Armstrong Browning Library. Waco TX 1961.
Barnes, W. The Browning collection. LCUT 7 1963.
Haslam, G. E. (ed). Wise after the event etc. Manchester 1964. Catalogue of material relating to T. J. Wise.
Litzinger, B. and K. L. Knickerbocker. In Browning critics, Lexington KY 1965. Includes bibliography 1951–65.
Barnes, W. Catalogue of the Browning collection: the University of Texas. 1966 (Univ of Texas Bibl Ser).
Catalogue of the celebrated collection of Sir Maurice Pariser, of Manchester, of the notorious nineteenth century pamphlets and other Wiseiana [Sotheby]. Dec 1967. Includes Browning forgeries by Wise.
Baker, R. Collection: the University of Texas at Austin. Browning Newsletter 1 1968. Browning items since 1963.
Schulz, H. C. English literary mss in the Huntington Library. HLQ 31 1968.
A literary gift for the college library. Independent-Jnl (San Rafael) Mar 1969. Donation of 150-vol Browning collection.
Armstrong Browning Library 1959–1969. Armstrong Browning Lib Newsletter 7 1969.
Luedecke, M. A. A bibliography of the Brownings: 1965–1968. Browning Newsletter 2 1969.
Raymond, W. O. General collection of items in the University of Toronto Library. Browning Newsletter 3 1969.
Templeman, W. D. Additions to a bibliography of the Brownings 1929–1930. Browning Newsletter 2 1969.
Ewing, D. C. The Browning collection of the Pierpont Morgan Lib. Browning Newsletter 3 1969.
Carson, J. C. A collection of books from the Brownings' personal libraries. Unpbd MA thesis, Baylor Univ 1970.
Hart, N. I. The Browning collection of the Henry E. Huntington Library. Browning Newsletter 4 1970.
East, S. C. K. List of the musical settings in the Armstrong Browning Library omitted from the Browning Newsletter Bibliography. Browning Newsletter 7 1971. *See also* East 1973, *below*.
French, H. D. The Browning collection of the Wellesley College library. Browning Newsletter 6 1971.
Jack, I. Browning. In English poetry: select bibliographical guides, ed A. E. Dyson, 1971.
Shorter, M. D. Browning: an index to the NCBEL. Browning Newsletter 6 1971.
Szladits, L. L. New in the Berg Collection: 1965–1969. BNYPL 75 1971.
Crowell, N. B. A reader's guide to Browning. Albuquerque 1972.
Johnson, R. C. and T. Tanselle. Addenda to the bibliographies of . . . the Brownings etc. PBSA 66 1972.
Kimball, J. C. Browning realia and its significance: a documentation of the museum items in the Armstrong Browning Library. Unpbd MA thesis, Baylor Univ 1972.
Munich, A. The Yale Browning collection: the Beinecke Library. Browning Newsletter 8 1972.
Tobias, R. C. The Fannie Barrett Browning collection at the University of Texas. Browning Newsletter 8 1972.
Woolford, J. (ed). The Browning collections (Sotheby catalogue 1913). In Sale catalogues of the libraries of eminent persons, vol 6: Poets and men of letters, 1972. Facs of 1913 Sotheby catalogue.
Brown, M. The Shelley collection. Casa Magni, Lerici, Italy. Browning Soc Notes 3 1973.
East, S. K. C. Browning music: a descriptive catalog of the music related to Browning and Elizabeth Barrett Browning in the Armstrong Browning Library. Waco TX 1973.
Herring, J. 1913 Sotheby sale catalogue – list of books. Stud in Browning and his Circle 1 1973.
Peterson, W. S. et al. Annual bibliography in Browning Inst Stud. 1973–90. Continues Browning Newsletter – Peterson. Continues under new title Victorian Lit and Culture 1991– . No bibliography in vol 21 1993.
A reprint of the [1913] Dobell Browning catalogue. Browning Inst Stud 2 1974.
Peterson, W. S. Browning and Elizabeth Barrett Browning: an annotated bibliography 1951–70. New York 1974. Format modelled on Browning, Northup, Pearsall 1953, *above*.
Gordan, J. D. and L. L. Szladits. Joint lives: Elizabeth Barrett and Robert Browning: a selection of works from the Henry W. and Albert A. Berg Collection of English and American literature. New York 1975.
Kelley, P. and R. Hudson. Elusive Browningiana: a list of unlocated manuscripts, marginalia, and annotated works. Browning Inst Stud 7 1979.
Kelley, P. and R. Hudson. Supplement no 2 to The Brownings' correspondence: a checklist. Browning Inst Stud 7 1979.

Klingman, J. Baylor Browning collection adds Houghton materials. Stud in Browning and his Circle 7 1979.

Hermann, F. Sotheby's: portrait of an auction house. 1980. *See* ch 9 for the Browning 1913 sale.

Kelley, P. and B. Coley. The paintings, sculpture and drawings of Robert Wiedemann Barrett Browning (1849–1912): a catalogue raisonné. Stud in Browning and his Circle 10 1982.

Kelley, P. and B. Coley. The Browning collections: a reconstruction. Winfield KS 1984. Contents: the Brownings' lib; first works; presentation vols; mss of Elizabeth Barrett Browning; mss of Robert Browning; likenesses of Elizabeth Barrett Browning; likenesses of Robert Browning; works of art, household and personal effects; works of Robert Browning, sen; works of Robert Wiedemann Barrett Browning; other associated mss and documents; other associated vols; appendices: Christie's Moulton-Barrett catalogue, notes on Pen's estate, calendar of meaningful dates, buyers from Browning collections [Sotheby's 1913]; Browning collections [Sotheby's 1913] (lots keyed to Reconstruction entries), summary of collections.

Meredith, M. Meeting the Brownings. Waco TX 1986. Exhibition catalogue.

Coley, B. A. 'Done into doggerel'. Stud in Browning and his Circle 15 1987. Browning books acquired by the Armstrong Browning Lib.

Duval, S. Robert Browning and Elizabeth Barrett Browning, first editions. Provo UT 1989.

Drew, P. An annotated critical bibliography of Browning. 1990.

Shroyer, R. J. and T. J. Collins. A concordance to the poems and plays of Browning. New York 1996. Computer-generated concordance based on the Yale edn.

For additions to the collections at the Armstrong Browning Lib, see Armstrong Browning Lib Newsletter, *passim.*

Publications acknowledged or authorised by Browning Collections

Poems. 2 vols 1849. 'A new edition' on title page (Bells and pomegranates was the 'first edition': hence omission of Strafford and Sordello, though Paracelsus was also not pbd in Bells and pomegranates). Extensively rev American edn Boston 1849, 1850, 1856, 1859, 1863, 1864, 1865, 1866, 1867, 1869, 1871, 1874, 1876, 1879, 1880, 1881, 1882 (3 reprints), 1883, 1884, 1885, 1886 (4 reprints), 1887 (2 reprints) (vol 1 includes Landor's sonnet to Browning). Vol 1: Paracelsus; Pippa passes; King Victor and King Charles; Colombe's birthday. Vol 2: A blot in the 'scutcheon; The return of the Druses; Luria; A soul's tragedy; Dramatic romances and lyrics (contents as Dramatic lyrics and Dramatic romances and lyrics, omitting Claret and tokay, and section 2 of Home-thoughts, from abroad: running-title Dramatic lyrics): Cavalier tunes, My last duchess, Count Gismond, Incident of the French camp, Soliloquy of the Spanish cloister, In a gondola, Artemis prologuizes, Waring, Rudel to the lady of Tripoli, Cristina, Madhouse cells I [Johannes Agricola in meditation] and II [Porphyria's lover], Through the Metidja to Abd-el-Kadr, The pied piper, 'How they brought the good news from Ghent to Aix', Pictor ignotus, The Italian in England, The Englishman in Italy, The lost leader, The lost mistress, Home-thoughts, from abroad, Home-thoughts, from the sea, The bishop orders his tomb at St Praxed's church, Garden-fancies I [The flower's name] and II [Sibrandus Schafnaburgensis], The laboratory, The confessional, The flight of the duchess, Earth's immortalities, Song ['Nay, but you who do not love her'], The boy and the angel, Meeting at night, Parting at morning, Saul, Time's revenges, The glove.

REVIEWS: Atlas 13 Jan 1849; Literary Gazette 3 Mar 1849; English Rev June 1849; [Edmunds, C.] Eclectic Rev Aug 1849; [Powell, T.] Literary World (New York) Sep 1849; [Forster, J.] Examiner 8 Sep 1849; Graham's Mag Dec 1849; [Whipple, E. P.] Graham's Mag Dec 1849; Albion 1 Dec 1849; Literary World (New York) 8 Dec 1849; American Whig Rev Apr 1850; Brownson's Quart Rev Apr 1850; C. C. S[mith] Christian Examiner and Religious Misc May 1850; [J. Weiss] Massachusetts Quart Rev June 1850; [Simms, W. G.] Southern Quart Rev Sep 1850; [H., C. W. D.] Monthly Religious Mag Dec 1850; Guardian 12 Mar 1851; Christian Remembrancer Apr 1851.

Poetical works. 3 vols 1863. Not pbd in America. 'Third Edition' on title page. Vol 1: Lyrics; Romances; Men, and women (reclassifies poems from Dramatic lyrics (DL), Dramatic romances and lyrics (DRL), and Men, and women (M&W)). Lyrics: Cavalier tunes I–III [DL]; The lost leader [DRL]; 'How they brought the good news from Ghent to Aix' [DRL]; Through the Metidja to Abd-el-Kadr [DL]; Nationality in drinks [Claret, Tokay, Beer (Nelson) ('Here's to Nelson's memory!'; DRL]; Garden-fancies I [The flower's name] [DRL], Garden fancies II [Sibrandus Schafnaburgensis] [DRL], Garden fancies III [Soliloquy of the Spanish cloister] [DRL]; The laboratory [DRL]; The confessional [DRL]; Cristina [DL]; The lost mistress [DRL]; Earth's immortalities [DRL]; Meeting at night [DRL]; Parting at morning [DRL]; Song ['Nay, but you who do not love her', DRL]; A woman's last word [M&W]; Evelyn Hope [M&W]; Love among the ruins [M&W]; A lover's quarrel [M&W]; Up at a villa – down in the city [M&W]; A toccata of Galuppi's [M&W]; Old pictures in Florence [M&W]; De gustibus – [M&W]; Home-thoughts, from abroad [DRL]; Home-thoughts, from the sea [DRL]; Saul [DRL, M&W]; My star [M&W]; By the fire-side [M&W]; Any wife to any husband [M&W]; Two in the Campagna [M&W]; Misconceptions [M&W]; A serenade at the villa [M&W]; One way of love [M&W]; Another way of love [M&W]; A pretty woman [M&W]; Respectability [M&W]; Love in a life [M&W]; Life in a love [M&W]; In three days [M&W]; In a year [M&W]; Women and roses [M&W]; Before [M&W]; After [M&W]; The Guardian-angel – a picture at Fano [M&W]; Memorabilia [M&W]; Popularity [M&W]; Master Hugues of Saxe-Gotha [M&W]. Romances: Incident of the French camp [DL]; The patriot – an old story [M&W]; My last duchess – Ferrara [DL]; Count Gismond – Aix en Provence [DL]; The boy and the angel [DRL]; Instans tyrannus [M&W]; Mesmerism [M&W]; The glove [DRL]; Time's revenges [DRL]; The Italian in England [DRL]; The Englishman in Italy – Piano di Sorrento [DRL]; In a gondola [DL]; Waring [DL]; The twins [M&W]; A light woman [M&W]; The last ride together [M&W]; The pied piper of Hamelin, a child's story [DL]; The flight of the duchess [DRL]; A grammarian's funeral [M&W]; Johannes Agricola in meditation [DL]; The heretic's tragedy [M&W]; Holy-cross day [M&W]; Protus [M&W]; The statue and the bust [M&W]; Porphyria's lover [DL]; Childe Roland to the dark tower came [M&W]. Men, and women: 'Transcendentalism: a poem in twelve books' [M&W]; How it strikes a contemporary [M&W]; Artemis prologuizes [DL]; An epistle containing the strange medical experience of Karshish, the Arab physician [M&W]; Pictor ignotus [DRL]; Fra Lippo Lippi [M&W]; Andrea del Sarto [M&W]; The bishop orders his tomb at St Praxed's church [DRL]; Bishop Blougram's apology [M&W]; Cleon [M&W]; Rudel to the lady of Tripoli [DL]; One word more [M&W]. Vol 2: Tragedies and other plays: Pippa passes; King Victor and King Charles; The return of the Druses; A blot in the 'scutcheon; Colombe's birthday; Luria; A soul's tragedy; In a balcony; Strafford. Vol 3: Paracelsus; Christmas-eve and Easter-day; Sordello.

REVIEWS: Reader May 1863; Guardian 15 July, 5 Aug, 9 Dec 1863; Weldon's Register Aug 1863; [Donne, W. B.] Saturday Rev 15 Aug 1863; London Rev 19 Sep 1863; Critic Oct 1863; [Hutton, R. H.] Nat Rev Oct 1863; [Conway, M. D.] Victoria Mag Feb 1864; [Marzials, Sir F. T.] London Quart Rev Apr 1864.

Poetical works. 3 vols 1865. Not pbd in America. 'Fourth edition' on title page. Format and pagination identical with preceding but many minor revisions.

Poetical works. 6 vols 1868. Not pbd in America. Edns of 1870 and

1875 have identical format and pagination but contain variant readings. Vol 1: Pauline; Paracelsus; Strafford. Vol 2: Sordello; Pippa passes. Vol 3: King Victor and King Charles; Dramatic lyrics [as 1863 Lyrics, with Soliloquy of the Spanish cloister as an independent poem following Garden-fancies I–II]; The return of the Druses. Vol 4: A blot in the 'scutcheon; Colombe's birthday; Dramatic romances [as 1863 Romances, with Johannes Agricola in meditation removed to Men and women]. Vol 5: A soul's tragedy; Luria; Christmas-eve and Easter-day; Men and women [as 1863, with Johannes Agricola in meditation incorporated between An epistle and Pictor ignotus]. Vol 6: In a balcony; Dramatis personae.

REVIEWS: Guardian 5 Aug 1868; Sat Rev 15 Aug 1868; [Wilkins, A. S.] Free Churchman and Christian Spectator Oct 1868; [Hood, E. P.] Eclectic & Congregational Rev Dec 1868; [Stirling, J. H.] North Br Rev Dec 1868.

Poetical works. 4 vols Leipzig 1872 (vols 1–2), 1884 (vols 3–4). Tauchnitz edn.

Poetic and dramatic works of Browning. Ed G. W. Cooke 6 vols Boston 1887, 1888. Riverside edn. Further issues 1889 (enlarged), 1892, 1894 (enlarged). Vol 1: Pauline; Paracelsus; Strafford; Sordello; Pippa passes; King Victor and King Charles. Vol 2: Dramatic lyrics; The return of the Druses; A blot in the 'scutcheon; Colombe's birthday; Dramatic romances; A soul's tragedy; Luria. Vol 3: The ring and the book. Vol 4: Christmas-eve and Easter-day; Men and women; In a balcony; Dramatis personae; Balaustion's adventure; Prince Hohenstiel-Schwangau; Fifine at the fair. Vol 5: Red cotton night-cap country; Aristophanes' apology; The inn album; Pacchiarotto and how he worked in distemper and other poems. Vol 6: The Agamemnon of Aeschylus; La Saisiaz; The two poets of Croisic; Dramatic idyls; Jocoseria; Ferishtah's fancies; Parleyings with certain people of importance in their day. Asolando added in 1889.

Poetical works. 16 vols 1888–9. The final collected edn supervised by Browning. Vols 1–10 reissued as edn was being ptd with some variant readings. Asolando added in 1894 as vol 17, with biographical and historical notes by E. Berdoe. Vol 1: Pauline; Sordello. Vol 2: Paracelsus; Strafford. Vol 3: Pippa passes; King Victor and King Charles; The return of the Druses; A soul's tragedy. Vol 4: A blot in the 'scutcheon; Colombe's birthday; Men and women. Vol 5: Dramatic romances; Christmas-eve and Easter-day. Vol 6: Dramatic lyrics; Luria. Vol 7: In a balcony; Dramatis personae. Vol 8: The ring and the book [bks 1–4]. Vol 9: The ring and the book [bks 5–8]. Vol 10: The ring and the book [bks 9–12]. Vol 11: Balaustion's adventure; Prince Hohenstiel-Schwangau; Fifine at the fair. Vol 12: Red cotton night-cap country; The inn album. Vol 13: Aristophanes' apology; The Agamemnon of Aeschylus. Vol 14: Pacchiarotto and how he worked in distemper with other poems; La Saisiaz; The two poets of Croisic. Vol 15: Dramatic idyls 1st ser; Dramatic idyls 2nd ser; Jocoseria. Vol 16: Ferishtah's fancies; Parleyings with certain people of importance in their day. Vol 17 [added 1894]: Asolando; Biographical and historical notes to the poems [by E. Berdoe].

Complete poetic and dramatic works. Boston 1895. Cambridge edn, with apparatus by B. Cooke and H. E. S[cudder]. Includes some previously uncollected poems.

Poetical works. Ed A. Birrell 2 vols 1896. Often rptd and sometimes rev; issued until 1928 or later in both London and New York.

Complete works. Ed C. Porter and H. A. Clarke, preface by W. L. Phelps, richly illus, 14 vols New York 1898. Florentine edn; sold under many bindings and imprints bearing diverse names for 20 years.

Poetical works. 1904 etc. An edn begun by Grant Richards and continued in WC, Oxford edn etc; as Poetical works complete from 1833 to 1868 and shorter poems thereafter, Oxford 1941.

Poems and plays. 2 vols 1906 (EL); vol 3 1911; vol 4 1940; ed J. Bryson 1954.

Works. Ed F. G. Kenyon 10 vols 1912. Centenary edn.

Complete poetical works, with additional poems first published in 1914. Ed A. Birrell and F. G. Kenyon 1915. Globe edn.

Complete works. Ed J. H. Finley 6 vols 1926.

The poems and plays. Ed S. Commins, New York 1934 (Mod Lib).

Complete works. Gen ed R. A. King jun, succeeded by J. W. Herring; executive ed A. C. Dooley. Athens OH 1969– Ohio Univ Press edn. Vol 1 1969: Pauline; Sonnet ['Eyes, calm beside thee, (Lady could'st thou know!)']; Paracelsus. Vol 2 1970: Strafford; Sordello. Vol 3 1971: Pippa passes; King Victor and King Charles; essay on Chatterton; Dramatic lyrics; The return of the Druses. Vol 4 1973: A blot in the 'scutcheon; Colombe's birthday; Dramatic romances and lyrics; Luria. Vol 5 1981: A soul's tragedy; Christmas-eve and Easter-day; essay on Shelley; Men and women, vol 1. Vol 6: Men and women, vol 2; Ben Karshook's wisdom; Eurydice to Orpheus; Dramatis personae; Deaf and dumb, reissued with corrections 1996. Vol 7 1986: The ring and the book, bks i–iv. Vol 8 1988: The ring and the book, bks v–viii. Vol 9 1989: The ring and the book, bks ix–xii. Vol 13 1995: The inn album; Pacchiarotto and how he worked in distemper, with other poems. Forthcoming: vol 10 (Balaustion's adventure; Prince Hohenstiel-Schwangau); vol 11 (Fifine at the fair; Red cotton night-cap country); vol 12 (Aristophanes' apology); vol 14 (The Agamemnon of Aeschylus; La Saisiaz; The two poets of Croisic); vol 15 (Dramatic idyls; Dramatic idyls, second series; Jocoseria); vol 16 (Ferishtah's fancies; Parleyings with certain people of importance); vol 17 (Asolando; Lyrics pbd 1882–1889; unpbd and uncollected poems; Thomas Wentworth, Earl of Strafford [by John Forster with Browning's help]; addenda; general index).

Poetical works 1833–1864. Ed I. Jack, Oxford 1970.

Stange, G. R. The poetical works of Robert Browning. Boston 1974. Rev edn of 1895 Cambridge edn, excluding dramatic works.

Poetical works. Gen ed I. Jack, succeeded by M. Meredith 1981– (Oxford Eng Texts). Vol 1 1981: Pauline; Paracelsus; uncollected and unpbd poems to 1840. Vol 2 1981: Strafford; Sordello. Vol 3 1988: Pippa passes; King Victor and King Charles; Dramatic lyrics; The return of the Druses; A blot in the 'scutcheon; Colombe's birthday. Vol 4 1991: Dramatic romances and lyrics; Luria; A soul's tragedy; Christmas-eve and Easter-day; Essay on Shelley; Fugitives omitted from vol 1; trn of sonnet by Giambattista Zappi ['And who is he that, sculptured in huge stone']. Further vols projected of complete edn.

Poems. Ed J. Pettigrew and T. J. Collins 2 vols London and Yale 1981. Vol 1: poems pbd in vol or collections by Browning to 1871 (Prince Hohenstiel-Schwangau), including Pippa passes but excluding other plays. Vol 2: remainder of pbd poems except The ring and the book and trn of Agamemnon; uncollected and unpbd poems; essay on Shelley. With The ring and the book, ed R. Altick.

Poems. Ed J. Woolford and D. R. Karlin 1991– (Longman Annotated Eng Poets). Vol 1 (1826–40) and vol 2 (1841–6) 1991. Further vols (with J. P. Phelan) projected of complete edn except plays written for stage. Vol 2 includes Essay on Chatterton.

Smaller collections and selections

For further selections, see L. N. Broughton et al, Bibliography, *Ithaca NY 1953. For Amer selections pbd during Browning's lifetime, see L. Greer,* Browning and America, *Chapel Hill NC 1952, appendix F.*

Bells and pomegranates. 1846. Bound copies of eight numbers: Pippa passes; King Victor and King Charles; Dramatic lyrics; The return of the Druses; A blot in the 'scutcheon; Colombe's birthday; Dramatic romances and lyrics; Luria and A soul's tragedy. *See* separate entries.

Selections from the poetical works of Browning. [Ed John Forster and B. W. Procter, who are responsible for titles of extracts from longer poems and plays, and provide plot-summaries to introduce extracts from plays; but variants by Browning.] 1863. [1] Dramatic lyrics: Cavalier tunes; My last duchess; Incident of the French camp; Soliloquy of the Spanish cloister; The pied piper of Hamelin; How they brought the good news from Ghent to Aix; The Italian in England; The lost leader; The bishop orders his tomb at St Praxed's church; Garden-fancies; The laboratory; The confessional; The flight of the duchess; Earth's immortalities; The boy and the angel; Meeting at night; Parting at morning; The glove. [2] Paracelsus: Paracelsus aspires and is warned [I 306–483]; Paracelsus parts from his friends [I 700–832]; At Basil, after fourteen years [III 1–131]; The second parting [III 981–1057]; The friends meet again [IV 604–93]; In the hospital of Salzburg [V 338–449]; Lesson of the life of Paracelsus [V 806–907]. [3] Sordello: Childhood of Sordello [I 373–663]. [4] Dramas: Strafford: The popular party expect the arrival in England of Wentworth [I 1–266]; Pippa passes pt I (Morning); King Victor and King Charles [I 145–409]; The return of the Druses [V 1–372]; A blot in the 'scutcheon [I iii 1–241]; Colombe's birthday [I 1–131, IV 94–397]; Luria [I 132–61, 290–331, III 159–229, IV 165–327]; Christmas-eve and Easter-day [Christmas-eve 1–186, 781–895, 524–95]; [5] Men and women: Love among the ruins, Evelyn Hope, Up at a villa – down in the city, A toccata of Galuppi's, An epistle of Karshish, Instans tyrannus, How it strikes a contemporary, The statue and the bust, Bishop Blougram's apology, In a year, Andrea del Sarto, Saul, In a balcony, De gustibus –, Protus, Two in the Campagna, Holy-cross day, The guardian-angel, Cleon.

Sordello, Strafford, Christmas-eve and Easter-day. Boston 1864, 1880, 1883–4.

A selection from the works of Browning. 1865 (Moxon's Miniature Poets). Includes brief preface and contains some variant readings. My star; A face; The lost mistress; Song from Pippa passes ['You'll love me yet']; Youth and art; Love in a life; Life in a love; Dîs aliter visum; Cristina; Song from Pippa passes ['Give her but a least excuse to love me!']; Song from A blot in the 'scutcheon ['There's a woman like a dew-drop']; Song ['Nay, but you who do not love her']; By the fire-side; Song from James Lee ['Ah, Love, but a day']; Misconceptions; From James Lee ['Is all our fire of shipwreck wood']; From the same ['The swallow has set her six young on the rail']; From the same ['I leaned on the turf']; A lovers' quarrel; A woman's last word; From James Lee ['Oh, good gigantic smile']; Any wife to any husband; The worst of it; A pretty woman; A light woman; A serenade at the villa; The last ride together; Claret; Tokay; Song [One way of love]; Rudel to the lady of Tripoli; Time's revenges; Waring; The Englishman in Italy; In a gondola; Home-thoughts, from abroad; Home-thoughts, from the sea; Romance from Paracelsus [IV 450–552]; Song from the same [V 417–45]; Romance from Pippa passes ['A King lived long ago']; Song from the same ['The year's at the spring']; Memorabilia; Popularity; Pictor ignotus; The patriot; Master Hugues of Saxe-Gotha; A grammarian's funeral; Abt Vogler; Artemis prologuizes; Porphyria's lover; Childe Roland to the dark tower came; Caliban upon Setebos; Rabbi ben Ezra; Epitaph in the catacombs [Easter-day 275–88]; May and death; The common lot [Christmas-eve 1211–27]; Apparent failure; Euridice to Orpheus; Prospice; Michelagnolo [Easter-day 796–807]; Adapted from One word more [3–201].

Lyrics of life, with illustrations by S. Eytinge. Boston 1866, 1869, 1871. Important Amer selection: many reprints.

Lyrics of life, bound with Longfellow, Household poems, and Tennyson, Song for all seasons, with collective title Companion poets. Boston 1867, 1869, 1871.

Poetical works of Browning. Pbd in 19 monthly numbers as suppl to timetable in the Official guide of the Chicago and Alton Railroad. 1872. Unfinished; projected as complete edn but finishing with Two in the Campagna from Dramatic lyrics (as reclassified in 1863).

Selections from the poetical works of Browning. 1872. Includes dedication to Tennyson and preface. After pbd as Second ser 1880, rptd 1884 as First ser with some variants. Amer edn New York 1884. My star; A face; My last duchess; Song from Pippa passes ['Give her but a least excuse to love me']; Cristina; Count Gismond; Song ['Nay, but you who do not love her']; A serenade at the villa; Youth and art; The flight of the duchess; Song from Pippa passes ['The year's at the spring']; 'How they brought the good news from Ghent to Aix'; Song from Paracelsus [IV 190–205]; Through the Metidja to Abd-el-Kadr; Incident of the French camp; The lost leader; In a gondola; A lovers' quarrel; Earth's immortalities; The last ride together; Mesmerism; By the fire-side; Any wife to any husband; In a year; Song from James Lee ['Oh good gigantic smile o' the old brown earth']; A woman's last word; Meeting at night; Parting at morning; Women and roses; Misconceptions; A pretty woman; A light woman; Love in a life; Life in a love; The laboratory; Gold hair; The statue and the bust; Love among the ruins; Time's revenges; Waring; Home-thoughts, from abroad; The Italian in England; The Englishman in Italy; Up at a villa – down in the city; Pictor ignotus; Fra Lippo Lippi; Andrea del Sarto; The bishop orders his tomb at St Praxed's church; A toccata of Galuppi's; How it strikes a contemporary; Protus; Master Hugues of Saxe-Gotha; Abt Vogler; Two in the Campagna; De gustibus–; The guardian-angel; Evelyn Hope; Memorabilia; Apparent failure; Prospice; Childe Roland to the dark tower came; A grammarian's funeral; Cleon; Instans tyrannus; An epistle of Karshish; Caliban upon Setebos; Saul; Rabbi ben Ezra; Epilogue [to Dramatis personae].

Favorite poems by Browning, Boston 1877. Many reprints.

Selections from the poetical works of Browning. Second series. 1880. Rptd 1884 with some variants. Amer edn New York 1884. A wall; Apparitions; Natural magic; Magical nature; Garden-fancies I–II; In three days; The lost mistress; One way of love; Rudel to the lady of Tripoli; Numpholeptos; Appearances; The worst of it; Too late; Bifurcation; A likeness; May and death; A forgiveness; Cenciaja; Porphyria's lover; Filippo Baldinucci on the privilege of burial; Soliloquy of the Spanish cloister; The heretic's tragedy; Holy-cross day; Amphibian; St Martin's summer; James Lee's wife; Respectability; Dîs aliter visum; Confessions; The householder; Tray; Cavalier-tunes I–III; Before; After; Hervé Riel; In a balcony; Old pictures in Florence; Bishop Blougram's apology; Mr Sludge 'the medium'; The boy and the angel; A death in the desert; Fears and scruples; Artemis prologuizes; Pheidippides; The patriot; Popularity; Pisgah-sights 1–3; At the Mermaid; House; Shop; A tale [The two poets of Croisic 1293–1400].

A selection for the use of schools. Ed F. Ahn, Berlin 1882; Lyrical and dramatic poems, ed E. T. Mason, New York 1883; Selections, ed R. G. White, New York 1883; A Browning calendar, Chicago 1886 (first of many edns); Bits from Browning, ed Mrs N. V. Walker, Boston 1886.

Men and women and Sordello. Boston 1883, 1885, 1886.

Christmas-eve and Easter-day, and other poems, with an introductory essay on Browning's theory concerning personal immortality. Ed H. E. Hersey and W. J. Rolfe 1887.

Lyrics, idyls and romances from the poetic and dramatic works of Robert Browning. Boston 1887, 1888, 1890.

Bits of burnished gold from Browning. Ed R. Porter, New York 1888; Good and true thoughts from Browning, ed A. Cross, New York 1888; The Browning reciter, ed A. H. Miles 1889 ('tenth thousand'); Shorter poems, ed N. Bögholm, New York 1890; Browning year book, ed C. M. Tyths, New York 1892; Fifine at the fair, and other poems, ed J. Morrison, Edinburgh 1892; The Browning primer, ed F. J. Furnivall, New York 1893; A blot, and other dramas, ed F. Rindler 1896; The Brownings for the young, ed F. G. Kenyon 1896; Dramatic romances and other poems, ed E. Dixon 1897; Poems, ed O. Browning 1897; Poems, ed R. Garnett, illustr Byam Shaw 1897; Saul and other poems, ed E. H. Turpin, New York 1898; The best of Browning, ed J. Mudge and W. V. Kelley, New York 1898; The lyric poems, ed E. Rhys 1898; Shorter poems, ed F. T. Baker 1899; Earlier monologues, ed H. B. Forman 1900; Select poems, ed E. H. Blakeney 1900; Selections, ed W. Hall Griffin 1902; Browning's poems, ed A. D. Innes 1903; A blot, and other plays, ed A. Bates, Boston 1904; Florence in the poetry of the Brownings, ed A. B. McKahan, Chicago 1904 (lavishly ptd and illus); Select poems, ed A. B. George, Boston 1905; Selections, ed R. M. Lovett, Boston 1906; Selections, ed C. W. French, Chicago 1907; Selections, ed J. C. Saul, Toronto 1907; Lyrical poems, ed A. T. Quiller-Couch, Oxford 1908; Poems, ed A. Birrell, Edinburgh 1908; Selections, ed R. D. Stocker 1908; Selections, ed R. A. S. Rankin, Glasgow 1909; Shorter poems, ed J. W. Cunliffe, New York 1909; A selection, ed W. T. Young, Cambridge 1911; Poems, ed C. W. Hodell 1911; Selections, ed E. F. Hoernle, illustr A. Ross, Edinburgh 1911; Introd to Browning, ed E. B. Halleck, New York 1912; Rabbi ben Ezra and other poems, illustr B. Partridge 1914; A Browning anthology, ed F. A. Forbes, Oxford 1917; Browning for the trenches 1918 (Boston Browning Soc) (distributed free to US soldiers; sold as the Victory edn 1919); Poems and plays, ed H. E. Joyce, New York 1922; Browning, humanist, ed E. Compton-Rickett 1924; Select poems, ed R. Ishikawa, Tokyo 1925.

Tennyson and Browning contrasted. Ed G. Boas 1925; Shorter poems, ed F. T. Baker and N. Y. Moffett, New York 1927; Selected poems, ed L. E. Robinson, Philadelphia 1930; The best of Browning, ed C. J. Weber, Fairfield ME 1930; Poems, ed B. R. Redman, New York 1932; Selections, ed H. Boaz 1933.

Two poets, a dog and a boy. Ed F. T. P. Russell, illus C. Odell, Philadelphia 1933.

Selected poems. Ed W. T. Hutchins and J. R. Reed 1937.

Poetry and prose, with appreciations by Landor, Bagehot, Swinburne, Henry James, Saintsbury and F. L. Lucas. Ed H. Milford, Oxford 1941.

The best of Browning. Ed W. H. Rogers, New York 1942; Selections, ed W. Fancutt 1944; Selected poems, ed W. C. DeVane, New York 1949; Poetry and prose, ed S. Nowell-Smith 1950; Thirty poems, ed W. S. Mackie 1950; Selected poems, ed K. L. Knickerbocker, New York 1951; Browning: a selection, ed W. E. Williams 1954; Selected poetry, ed J. Reeves 1954; Poems, ed D. Smalley, Boston 1956; ed H. Gregory, New York 1956; ed W. Reed, New York 1960; ed R. Wilbur, New York 1960; ed E. Shanks 1961; ed R. Sprague 1964; ed G. M. Ridenour, New York 1966; ed K. Allott 1967; ed E. Lucie-Smith 1967; The Brownings: letters and poetry, ed C. Ricks, New York 1970; ed J. Korg, New York 1971; ed C. Day Lewis, New York 1971; ed D. R. Karlin 1989; ed M. Meredith 1989; ed A. Day 1991.

The plays of Robert Browning. Ed T. J. Collins and R. J. Shroyer. New York 1988.

§1

Individual volumes and single poems

Pauline: a fragment of a confession. 1833. Anon; omitted from Poems 1849, Poetical works 1863; Included with apologetic preface from 1868; ed T. J. Wise 1886; ed N. H. Wallis 1931 (comparing states of the text).

REVIEWS: Literary Gazette 23 Mar 1833; [Fox, W. J.] Monthly Repository Apr 1833; [Cunningham, A.] Athenaeum 6 Apr 1833; Atlas 14 Apr 1833; Court Jnl 11 May 1833; [Johnstone, C.] Tait's Edinburgh Mag Aug 1833; [Maginn, W.] Fraser's Mag Dec 1833.

Paracelsus. 1835. Untitled preface, 5 pts (I Paracelsus aspires; II Paracelsus attains; III Paracelsus; IV Paracelsus aspires; V Paracelsus attains) and Note [biographical extract with annotations by Browning]. Ed G. Lowes Dickinson 1899 (Temple Classics); ed M. L. Lee and K. B. Locock 1909; ed C. P. Denison, New York 1911.

REVIEWS: Colburn's New Monthly Mag 1835; Spectator 15 Aug 1835; Atlas 16 Aug 1835; Weekly Dispatch 16 Aug 1835; Athenaeum 22 Aug 1835; [Forster, J.] Examiner 6 Sep 1835; Metropolitan Mag Oct 1835; [Fox, W. J.] Monthly Repository Nov 1835; [Johnstone, C.] Tait's Edinburgh Mag Nov 1835; Leigh Hunt's London Jnl 21 Nov 1835; [Heraud, J.], Fraser's Mag Mar 1836; [Forster, J.] Evidences of a new genius for dramatic poetry, NMM Mar 1836; [Ord, J. W.] Metropolitan Jnl 16 Apr, 23 Apr 1836; Monthly Mag Sep 1842; [Emerson, R. W. or M. Fuller] Dial Apr 1843 (first Amer rev); [Gurney, A. T.] Theologian June 1845.

The king: 'A king lived long ago'. Monthly Repository Nov 1835. Signed 'Z'. Later incorporated as Pippa's song in pt III of Pippa passes, 1841.

Johannes Agricola. Monthly Repository Jan 1836 (with Porphyria, *below*). Signed 'Z'. In Dramatic lyrics untitled section I of Madhouse cells; in 1849 subtitled Johannes Agricola in meditation; from 1863 collective title dropped and title became Johannes Agricola in meditation.

Porphyria. Monthly Repository Jan 1836. In Dramatic lyrics untitled section II of Madhouse cells; in 1849 subtitled Porphyria's lover; from 1863 collective title dropped and title became Porphyria's lover.

Lines: Still ailing, wind? Monthly Repository May 1836. Signed 'Z'. Later incorporated in section vi of James Lee (Dramatis personae 1864).

Strafford: an historical tragedy. In 5 acts. Produced at Covent Garden Theatre. 1837, 1882 (for North London Collegiate School); ed E. H. Hickey 1884; ed A. Wilson 1901; ed H. B. George, Oxford 1908; 1929 (playbook).

REVIEWS: Bell's Life in London and Sporting Chron May 1837; Metropolitan Mag May 1837; New Monthly Belle Assemblée May 1837; [Jerrold, D.] Constitutional 2 May 1837; Morning Chron 2 May 1837; Morning Post 2 May 1837; Sun 2 May 1837; The Times 2 May 1837; [Fox, W. J.] True Sun 2 May 1837; [Conan] Morning Herald 4 May 1837; [Darley, G.] Athenaeum 6 May 1837; Literary Gazette 6 May 1837; Parthenon 6 May 1837; Spectator 6 May 1837; Atlas 7 May 1837; [Forster, J.] Examiner 7 May 1837, 14 May 1837; John Bull 7 May 1837; Weekly Dispatch 7 May 1837; Casket 13 May 1837; Court Jnl 27 May 1837; GM June 1837; New Monthly Belle Assemblée June 1837; [Forster, J.] New Monthly Mag and Humorist June 1837; [Merivale, H.] Edinburgh Rev July 1837; Dramatic Spectator 30 Sep 1837.

Sordello. 1840. 6 books. Ed H. Buxton Forman 1902; ed A. J. Whyte 1913; ed J. C. Berkey, unpbd diss, Univ of Pennsylvania 1965; ed M. Peckham, New York 1977.

REVIEWS: Spectator 14 Mar 1840; Bell's Life in London 15 Mar 1840; Atlas 28 Mar 1840; Metropolitan Mag Apr 1840; New Monthly Belle Assemblée Apr 1840; [Irvine, G.] Dublin Rev May 1840; [Lewes, G. H.] Monthly Chron May 1840; Monthly Rev May 1840; [Hervey, T. K.] Athenaeum 30 May 1840.

Pippa passes: a drama. 1841. Untitled prologue and 4 pts (I Morning; II Noon; III Evening; IV Night). In verse and prose. No I of Bells and pomegranates, *above* ser title of Browning's poems and plays, pbd 1841–6. Tr Ger 1919. Includes Advertisement explaining purpose of ser (prose). Often rptd, e.g. illustr L. L. Brooke 1898; illustr M. Armstrong, New York 1903; ed A. Symons 1906; ed A. L. Irvine 1924; ed E. A. Parker 1927.

REVIEWS: Spectator 17 Apr 1841; Metropolitan Mag May 1841; Monthly Rev May 1841; Atlas 1 May 1841; [Johnstone, C.] Tait's Edinburgh Mag June 1841; Morning Herald 10 July 1841; [J. Forster] Examiner 2 Oct 1841; [Hervey, T. K.] Athenaeum 11 Dec 1841; People's Jnl 18 July 1846.

King Victor and King Charles; a tragedy. 1842. In 2 pts, each divided into 2 sections (First Year 1730: King Victor Pt I; King Victor Pt II. Second Year 1731: King Charles Pt I; King Charles Pt II). In verse. No II of Bells and pomegranates, *above*. Not produced on stage. REVIEWS: Spectator 5 Mar 1842; [Forster, J.] Examiner 2 Apr 1842; [Hemans] Athenaeum 30 Apr 1842; Metropolitan Mag June 1842; Atlas July 1842.

The serenade. 1842. In British Institution catalogue to accompany Maclise's painting of that name. Enlarged as In a gondola in Dramatic lyrics.

Dramatic lyrics. 1842. No III of Bells and pomegranates, *above*. Includes prose Advertisement about dramatic principle of poems, in subsequent edns ptd as note to Cavalier tunes. Cavalier tunes (I. Marching along; II Give a rouse; III My wife Gertrude); Italy and France (I Italy; II France); Camp and cloister (I Camp (Fr); II Cloister (Sp)); In a gondola; Artemis prologuizes; Waring; Queen-worship (I Rudel and the lady of Tripoli; II Cristina); Madhouse cells (I and II); Through the Metidja to Abd-el-Kadr; The pied piper of Hamelin. From 1849 My wife Gertrude was titled Boot and saddle; Italy and France became separate poems with the titles My last duchess and Count Gismond; the sections of Camp and cloister became Incident of the French camp and Soliloquy of the Spanish cloister: Soliloquy of the Spanish cloister became Garden fancies III in 1863, but later detached; the sections of Queen-worship became separate poems, with one minor change of title: Rudel to the lady of Tripoli. Ed T. J. Wise 1896; Ed J. O. Beatty and J. W. Bowyer, New York 1931 (facs).
REVIEWS: Atlas Nov 1842; [Forster, J.] Examiner 26 Nov 1842; Spectator 10 Dec 1842; Morning Herald 20 Dec 1842; Atlas Feb 1843; Metropolitan Mag Feb 1843; [Hervey, T. K.] Athenaeum Apr 1843; Monthly Mag Apr 1843.

The return of the Druses; a tragedy. 1843. In 5 acts. Verse. No IV of Bells and pomegranates, *above*. Not produced on stage. Ed C. Porter, Boston 1902 (stage version).
REVIEWS: Spectator 4 Feb 1843; Athenaeum 1 July 1843; [Horne, R. H.] Foreign and Colonial Quart Jan 1844.

A blot in the 'scutcheon; a tragedy. 1843. In 3 acts. Verse. Produced at Theatre Royal, Drury Lane. No V of Bells and pomegranates, *above*. In bound copies of Bells and pomegranates 1846, the words 'Second edition' appear on the title page of most copies but the text is rptd rather than revised. Other edns 1892, 1916, 1923, and in play anthologies. Ed T. F. Wilson 1972. DAI.
REVIEWS: Weekly Chron 12 Feb 1843; Morning Chron 13 Feb 1843; Morning Post 13 Feb 1843; The Times 13 Feb 1843; Athenaeum 18 Feb 1843; Atlas 18 Feb 1843; [J. Forster] Examiner 18 Feb 1843; John Bull 18 Feb 1843; Literary Gazette and Jnl of Belle Lettres 18 Feb 1843; Spectator 18 Feb 1843; Era 19 Feb 1843; Weekly Chron 19 Feb 1843; New Monthly Belle Assemblée Mar 1843; Pathfinder 1 Apr 1843; [Lewes, G. H.] Westminster Rev May 1843; New Quart Rev Oct 1846.

Colombe's birthday; a play. 1844. In 5 acts. Verse. No VI of Bells and pomegranates, *above*. Produced at Haymarket Theatre 1853.
REVIEWS: [Forster, J.] Examiner 22 June 1844; [Horne, R. H.] New Quart Rev Oct 1844; Athenaeum 19 Oct 1844.

Claret and tokay. Hood's Mag June 1844. Omitted from Poems 1849; in Poetical works 1863 incorporated as sections I and II of Nationality in drinks.

The laboratory. Hood's Mag June 1844. Included as section I of France and Spain in Dramatic romances and lyrics 1845.

Garden fancies. [I The flower's name; II Sibrandus Schafnaburgensis]. Hood's Mag July 1844. Included in Dramatic romances and lyrics 1845.

The boy and the angel. Hood's Mag Aug 1844. Included in Dramatic romances and lyrics 1845.

The tomb at St Praxed's. Hood's Mag Mar 1845. Included in Dramatic romances and lyrics 1845. From 1849 titled The Bishop orders his tomb at St Praxed's church.

The flight of the duchess. Part the first. Hood's Mag Apr 1845. Lines 1–215. Completed in Dramatic romances and lyrics 1845.

Dramatic romances and lyrics. 1845. No VII of Bells and pomegranates, *above*. How they brought the good news from Ghent to Aix; Pictor ignotus; Italy in England; England in Italy; The lost leader; The lost mistress; Home-thoughts, from abroad (I 'Oh, to be in England'; II 'Here's to Nelson's memory'; III 'Nobly Cape Saint Vincent to the north-west died away'); The tomb at St Praxed's; Garden fancies (I The flower's name; II Sibrandus Schafnaburgensis); France and Spain (I The laboratory; II Spain – the confessional); The flight of the Duchess; Earth's immortalities (I 'See, as the prettiest graves will do in time'; II 'So the year's done with!'); Song ('Nay, but you, who do not love her'); The boy and the angel; Night and morning (I Night; II Morning); Claret and tokay; Saul; Time's revenges; The glove. For poems previously pbd in Hood's Mag, *see* preceding entries. From 1849 Italy in England became The Italian in England, and England in Italy became The Englishman in Italy. From 1849 Home-thoughts, from abroad consisted only of 'Oh, to be in England'. 'Here's to Nelson's memory' omitted 1849; from 1863 became section III of Nationality in drinks ['Beer']. From 1849 'Nobly Cape Saint Vincent' became separate poem with title Home-thoughts, from the sea. From 1849 France and Spain became two separate poems, The laboratory and The confessional. From 1849 Night and morning became separate poems (though always ptd together) with titles Meeting at night and Parting at morning. From 1863 Claret and tokay became pts I and II of Nationality in drinks. Saul consists of lines 1–190 with note 'End of pt the first'; the completed poem with different metrical layout was later included in Men, and Women 1855. The only known recording of Browning's voice includes his attempt to recite 'How they brought the good news from Ghent to Aix', broken off at the beginning of the 2nd stanza. Rptd 1897; illustr C. Ricketts 1899; illustr E. F. Brickdale, New York 1909.
REVIEWS: [Forster, J.] Examiner 15 Nov 1845; [Jerrold, D.] Douglas Jerrold's Shilling Mag Dec 1845; Critic 27 Dec 1845; [Toulmin, C.] New Monthly Belle Assemblée Jan 1846; New Quart Rev Jan 1846; Oxford and Cambridge Rev Jan 1846; [Chorley, H. F.] Athenaeum 17 Jan 1846; Britannia 14 Mar 1846; Christian Remembrancer Apr 1846; Fraser's Mag June 1846.

Luria [and] A soul's tragedy. 1846. No VIII of Bells and pomegranates, *above*. Includes Luria; a tragedy (in 5 acts; verse); explanatory note on title of Bells and pomegranates (prose); A soul's tragedy (in two pts: I verse; II prose).
REVIEWS: [Fuller, M.] New York Daily Tribune 1 Apr, 10 July 1846; [Forster, J.] Examiner 25 Apr 1846; NMM and Humorist May 1846; [Jerrold, D.] Douglas Jerrold's Shilling Mag June 1846; [Toulmin, C.] New Monthly Belle Assemblée June 1846; Westminster Rev June 1846; Hood's Mag Aug 1846; New Quart Rev Oct 1846.

Christmas-eve and Easter-day. Consists of two separate poems, Christmas-eve and Easter-day. 1850, 1900, 1907; ed O. Smeaton 1918; H. T. Krynicky, unpbd diss, Univ of Pennsylvania 1972.
REVIEWS: Amer Whig Rev Apr 1850; [Marston, J. W.] Athenaeum 6 Apr 1850; Spectator 6 Apr 1850; Literary Gazette 13 Apr 1850; Critic 15 Apr 1850; [Lewes, G. H.] Leader 27 Apr 1850; [Forster, J.] Examiner May 1850; [Rossetti, W. M.] Germ May 1850; [Hutton, R. H.] Prospective Rev May 1850; Atlas 18 May 1850; NMM and Humorist June 1850; English Rev Sep 1850; [MacDonald, G.] Monthly Christian Spectator May 1853; Atlantic Monthly May 1864.

The twins. In pam Two poems (with Elizabeth Barrett Browning's A plea for the ragged schools of London). 1854. The pam was for sale at a charity bazaar organised by Elizabeth Barrett Browning's sister Arabella. Later included in Men, and women 1855.

Men, and women. 2 vols 1855, 1 vol Boston 1855, London 1856, 1863, 1864, 1866, 1867, 1869, 1874, 1879, 1881, 1883 [with introductory note by Browning]; ed H. B. Forman 1899; 2 vols Westminster 1899; illustr H. Osprovat 1903; ed B. Worsfold 1904; 1908; Oxford 1910; ed G. E. Hadow, Oxford 1911, 1920 (facs); Garden City NY 1961; ed F. B. Pinion 1963; ed P. Turner 1972; ed J. W. Harper 1975. Vol I: Love among the ruins; A lover's quarrel; Evelyn Hope; Up at a villa – down in the city; A woman's last word; Fra Lippo Lippi; A toccata of Galuppi's; By the fire-side; Any wife to any husband; An epistle of Karshish the Arab physician; Mesmerism; A serenade at the villa; My star; Instans tyrannus; A pretty woman; 'Childe Roland to the dark tower came'; Respectability; A light woman; The statue and the bust; Love in a life; Life in a love; How it strikes a contemporary; The last ride together; The patriot; Master Hugues of Saxe-Gotha; Bishop Blougram's apology; Memorabilia. Vol 2: Andrea del Sarto; Before; After; In three days; In a year; Old pictures in Florence; In a balcony; Saul; 'De gustibus –'; Women and roses; Protus; Holy-cross day; The guardian angel; Cleon; The twins; Popularity; The heretic's tragedy; Two in the Campagna; A grammarian's funeral; One way of love; Another way of love; 'Transcendentalism: a poem in twelve books'; Misconceptions; One word more. From 1868 title became Men and women. From 1863 contents became 'Transcendentalism'; How it strikes a contemporary; Artemis prologuizes [DL]; An epistle; Pictor Ignotus [DRL]; Fra Lippo Lippi; Andrea del Sarto; The bishop orders his tomb [DRL]; Bishop Blougram's apology; Cleon; Rudel to the lady of Tripoli [DL]; One word more. From 1868 Johannes Agricola in meditation [DL] was inserted after An epistle. For distribution of other poems, *see* Poetical works 1863. From 1863 In a balcony became a separate poem. A supposed 1855 separate issue of The statue and the bust was a T. J. Wise forgery.

REVIEWS: [Chorley, H. F.] Athenaeum 17 Nov 1855; Saturday Rev 24 Nov 1855; Albion Dec 1855; Putnam's Mag Dec 1855; Southern Literary Messenger Dec 1855; Atlas 1 Dec 1855; Critic 1 Dec 1855; [Forster, J.] Examiner 1 Dec 1855; Leader 1 Dec 1855, cont 8 Dec 1855; Literary Gazette 1 Dec 1855; Spectator 22 Dec 1855; [Morris, W.] Oxford & Cambridge Mag 1 1856; Bentley's Misc Jan 1856; [Masson, D.] British Quart Rev Jan 1856; Christian Examiner and Literary Misc Jan 1856; [Brimley, G. and T. C. C.] Fraser's Mag Jan 1856; New Quart Rev Jan 1856; [Simpson, R.], Rambler Jan 1856; [Eliot, George] Westminster Rev Jan 1856; Guardian 9 Jan 1856; [Oliphant, M.] Blackwood's Mag Feb 1856; Crayon Feb 1856; Irish Quart Rev Mar 1856; Christian Remembrancer Apr 1856, Oct 1857; Putnam's Monthly Mag Apr 1856; Dublin Univ Mag June 1856; McNicoll, T. London Quart Rev 6 July 1856; [Thomson, J. (B. V.)] Jersey Independent 20 Feb 1862.

Ben Karshook's wisdom. Keepsake 1856. Not collected by Browning.

May and death. Keepsake 1857. Later included in Dramatis personae 1864.

Untitled. 'Only the prism's obstruction shows aright'. 8 lines. In Poetical works 1868 with title Deaf and dumb: a group by Woolner; as addition to Dramatis personae, placed after May and death. Ms in letter to Thomas Woolner 24 Apr 1862. Intended to accompany Woolner's sculpture of that name, but not ptd in exhibition catalogue.

Dramatis personae. 1864. Amer edn Boston 1864, 1871, 1874, 1878, 1882. 2nd edn 1864 contains revisions. Ed M. Edwardes 1906 (Temple Classics); illustr E. F. Brickdale 1909; 1910; ed J. O. Beatty and J. W. Bowyer, New York 1931 (facs); ed D. L. Powell, unpbd diss. Univ of Pennsylvania 1968; ed F. B. Pinion 1969; James Lee (I At the window; II By the fire-side; III In the doorway; IV Along the beach; V On the cliff; VI Under the cliff; VII Among the rocks; VIII Beside the drawing-board; IX On deck); Gold hair; The worst of it; Dîs aliter visum; Too late; Abt Vogler; Rabbi ben Ezra; A death in the desert; Caliban upon Setebos; Confessions; May and death; Prospice; Youth and art; A face; A likeness; Mr Sludge 'the medium'; Apparent failure; Epilogue (First speaker: 'On the first of the Feast of Feasts'; Second speaker: 'Gone now! All gone across the dark so far'; Third speaker: 'Witless alike of will and way divine'). From 1868 James Lee became James Lee's wife, and the following sections were renamed: I James Lee's wife speaks at the window; VI Reading a book, under the cliff. For additional poems in Poetical works 1868, *see* preceding and following items. A supposed 1864 separate issue of Gold hair was a T. J. Wise forgery.

REVIEWS (1ST EDN): [Conway, M. D.] Morning Star 2 June 1864; [Massey, G.] Athenaeum 4 June 1864; Examiner 4 June 1864; Reader 4 June 1864; Sat Rev 18 June 1864; [Hutton, R. H.] Spectator 18 June 1864; London Rev 25 June 1864; Br Quart Rev July 1864; [Hood, E. P.] Eclectic & Congregational Rev July 1864; Englishwoman's Domestic Mag July 1864; B[ell], R. St James's Mag July 1864; [Conway, M. D.] Victoria Mag 1 July 1864; Guardian 20 July 1864; [Weiss, J.] Atlantic Monthly Nov 1864; Boston Rev Nov 1864; Christian Examiner Nov 1864; Godey's Mag Dec 1864. (2nd edn): Eclectic and Congregational Rev Oct 1864; [Stigand, W.] Edinburgh Rev Oct 1864; [Weiss, J.] Atlantic Monthly Nov 1864; Boston Rev Nov 1864; Christian Examiner and Religious Misc Nov 1864; [Irwin, T. C.] Dublin Univ Mag Nov 1864; [Bagehot, W.] Nat Rev Nov 1864, rptd in Literary studies, ed R. H. Hutton, 2 vols 1879; G. Christian Spectator Jan 1865; Wedmore, Sir T. F. NMM 1865.

Euridice to Orpheus: a picture by Leighton. Royal Acad exhibition catalogue 1864 (ptd as prose). From 1868 included in Dramatis personae, placed after Prospice.

Gold hair: a legend of Pornic. Atlantic Monthly May 1864. Pbd from advance proofs as part of agreement for Amer edn.

Prospice. Atlantic Monthly June 1864. Pbd from advance proofs as part of agreement for Amer edn.

Under the cliff [from James Lee] Atlantic Monthly June 1864. Pbd from advance proofs as part of agreement for Amer edn.

The ring and the book: in four vols. Vols 1–2 1868, vols 3–4 1869; 2 vols Boston 1869, 1870, 1872, 1873, 1877, 1882, 1883, 1886; '2 vols in 1' Boston 1883, 1885, 1886; 4 vols 1872 ('second edn'), 3 vols 1889; ed C. Porter and H. A. Clarke 1898; illus 1898; ed F. M. Padelford, Boston 1899; ed J. Buchan 1908; ed C. W. Hodell 1911 (EL); ed E. Dowden 1912; New York 1912; London 1919; ed M. J. Moses, New York 1929; ed A. K. Cook, Oxford 1940; ed W. Sypher, New York 1961; ed R. Altick 1971; tr Ger 1927. Vol 1: I The ring and the book; II Half-Rome; III Other half-Rome. Vol 2: IV Tertium Quid; V Count Guido Franceschini; VI Giuseppe Caponsacchi. Vol 3: VII Pompilia; VIII Dominus Hyacinthus de Archangelis; IX Juris Doctor Johannes-Baptista Bottinius. Vol 4: X The Pope; XI Guido; XII The book and the Ring.

REVIEWS OF VOL 1: St James's Mag Dec 1868; Daily Telegraph 4 Dec 1868; London Rev 5 Dec 1868, rptd Every Saturday 2 Jan 1869, Eclectic Mag Feb 1869; [Hutton, R. H.] Spectator 12 Dec 1868; Buchanan, R. W. Athenaeum 26 Dec 1868, rptd in Master spirits 1873; Sat Rev 26 Dec 1868; Br Quart Rev Jan 1869; Fortnightly Rev Jan 1869; [Symonds, J. A.] Macmillan's Mag Jan 1869; B[agehot?], W. Tinsley's Mag Jan 1869; [Wise, J. R.] Westminster Rev 1 Jan 1869; Press and St James's Chron 30 Jan 1869; Monthly Religious Mag July 1869.

REVIEWS OF VOL 1 OF AMER EDN: [Stedman, E. C.] Round Table 9 Jan 1869; [Conway, M. D.] Atlantic Monthly Feb 1869; [Dennett, J. R.] Nation 18 Feb 1869; Eclectic Mag Mar 1869; Harper's New Monthly Mag Mar 1869; Putnam's Mag Mar 1869.

REVIEWS OF VOLS 1–2: St James's Mag Jan 1869; Illus London News 16 Jan 1869; Guardian 20 Jan 1869; [Hutton, R. H.] Spectator 30 Jan 1869; [Greenwood, F.] Cornhill Mag Feb 1869; Chambers's Jnl 24 July 1869.

REVIEW OF VOL 2 OF AMER EDN: Eclectic Mag May 1869.

REVIEWS OF VOLS 2–4: Buchanan, R. W. Athenaeum 20 Mar 1869, rptd New Eclectic Mag May 1869 and in Master Spirits 1873; [Wise, J. R.] Westminster Rev 1 Apr 1869.

REVIEWS OF VOLS 3–4: [Hutton, R. H.] Spectator 13 Mar 1869; Guardian 24 Mar 1869; Illus London News 27 Mar 1869.
REVIEWS OF VOLS 1–4: Christian Watchman and Reflector 28 Jan 1869; Conway, M. D. Atlantic Monthly Feb 1869; [Dennett J. R.] Nation 18 Feb 1869; Eclectic Mag Mar, May 1869; [Morley, J.] Fortnightly Rev Mar 1869; Harper's Mag Mar, May 1869; Morning Star 15 Mar 1869; Putnam's Monthly Mag Mar, June 1869; Scotsman 26 Mar 1869; Collins, M. Br Quart Rev Apr 1869; [Mozley, J. R.] Macmillan's Mag Apr 1869; [Mozley, J. R.] Quart Rev Apr 1869; Saturday Rev 3 Apr 1869; Examiner and London Rev 17 Apr 1869; [Chadwick, J. W.] Christian Examiner May 1869; Eclectic Mag May 1869; [Leighton, B.] The Times 11 June 1869; [Doherty, J.] Dublin Rev July 1869; [Fane, J. H. C.] Edinburgh Rev July 1869; [Forman, H. B.] London Quart Rev July 1869, as Browning and the epic of psychology 1869, and in Our living poets 1871; [Cutler, E. J.] North Amer Rev July 1869; Every Saturday 14 Aug 1869; [Simpson, R.] North Br Rev Oct 1869; [Skelton, Sir J.] Fraser's Mag Nov 1869; Month Dec 1869; Browne, W. H. New Eclectic Mag Dec 1869; H[asell], E. St Paul's Mag Dec 1870, Jan 1871, rptd Eclectic Mag Mar–Apr 1871, Living Age 14 Jan, 28 Mar 1871; Thomson, J. (B. V.) GM Dec 1881.

Helen's tower. 1870. Sonnet priv ptd in vol of same name with other tributes to Lady Dufferin. Ms dated 26 Apr 1870. Pbd Pall Mall Gazette 28 Dec 1883. Not collected by Browning.

Balaustion's adventure, including a transcript from Euripides. 1871, Boston 1871, London 1872 ('second edn': contains revisions), 1881; ed E. A. Parker 1928. The 'transcript from Euripides' is a version of his Alkestis.
REVIEWS: [Williams] Athenaeum 12 Aug 1871; Examiner 12 Aug 1871; Spectator 30 Sep 1871; Colvin, Sir S. Fortnightly Rev Oct 1871; The Times 6 Oct 1871; [Oliphant, M.] Edinburgh Rev Jan 1872; Forman, H. B. London Quart Rev Jan 1872; Preston, M. J. Southern Rev Jan 1872; Hasell, E. J. St Paul's Mag June, July 1873.

Hervé Riel. Cornhill Mag Mar 1871. Later included in Pacchiarotto [etc] 1876. For Amer edn, *see* Fifine at the fair and other poems, *below*.
REVIEWS: Echo 15 Feb 1871; Daily News 28 Feb 1871.

Prince Hohenstiel-Schwangau, saviour of society. 1871. For Amer edn, *see* Fifine at the fair and other poems, *below*. Ed A. C. Dooley, unpbd diss, Northwestern Univ 1971.
REVIEWS: [Williams] Athenaeum 23 Dec 1871; Examiner 23 Dec 1871; Spectator 30 Dec 1871; Literary World 5 Jan 1872; The Times 2 Jan 1873.

Fifine at the fair. 1872. Includes Prologue: Amphibian, and Epilogue: The householder.
REVIEWS: Shepherd, R. H. Echo 6 June 1872; [Williams] Athenaeum 8 June 1872; Examiner July 1872; Colvin, Sir S. Fortnightly Rev July 1872; [Thompson, J. R.] Evening Post (Chicago) 5 July 1872; Sat Rev 17 Aug 1872; [Wise, J. R.] Westminster Rev 1 Oct 1872; Everett, C. C. Old and New Nov 1872; The Times 2 Jan 1873; [Orr, A.] Temple Bar Feb 1873.

Fifine at the fair and other poems. Boston 1872, 1883. Includes Prince Hohenstiel-Schwangau and Hervé Riel.

Red cotton night-cap country: or turf and towers. 1873, Boston 1873.
REVIEWS: [MacColl, N.] Athenaeum 10 May 1873; Orr, A. Contemporary Rev June 1873; [Howells, W. D] Atlantic Monthly July 1873; Simcox, E. J. Fortnightly Rev July 1873.

Aristophanes' apology, including a transcript from Euripides: being the last adventure of Balaustion. 1875, Boston 1875. The 'transcript from Euripides' is a trn of his Herakles.
REVIEWS: [Williams] Athenaeum 17 Apr 1875; Gosse, E. W. Examiner 24 Apr 1875; [Oliphant, M.] Blackwood's Mag July 1875; [Forman, H. B.] London Quart Rev July 1875; Scudder, H. D. Atlantic Monthly Oct 1875; The Times 4 Oct 1875; Symons, J. A. Acad 27 Nov 1875.

The inn album. New York Times 14, 21, 28 Nov 1875; London 1875, Boston 1876.
REVIEWS: [Symonds, J. A.] Acad 27 Nov 1875; [Williams] Athenaeum 27 Nov 1875; Examiner 11 Dec 1875; [Stevenson, R. L.] Vanity Fair 11 Dec 1875; James, H. Nation 20 Jan 1876; Bradley, A. C. Macmillan's Mag Feb 1876; Howells, W. D. Atlantic Monthly Mar 1876; [Rossetti, W. M.] Macmillan's Mag Mar 1876; [Furnivall, F. J.] N & Q 25 Mar 1876; Taylor, B. International Rev May–June 1876.

Pacchiarotto and how he worked in distemper; with other poems. 1876, Boston 1877. Includes Prologue ('O the old wall here! How I could pass'); Of Pacchiarotto, and how he worked in distemper; At the 'Mermaid'; House; Shop; Pisgah-sights, I and II; Fears and scruples; Natural magic; Magical nature; Bifurcation; Numpholeptos; Appearances; St Martin's summer; Hervé Riel; A forgiveness; Cenciaja; Filippo Baldinucci on the privilege of burial; Epilogue ('The poets pour us wine –').
REVIEWS: Austin, A. Examiner 10 June 1876, Examiner 12 Aug 1876. (Austin's response to Browning's attack in Of Pacchiarotto, and the jnl's comment); [Williams] Athenaeum 22 July 1876; Dowden, E. Acad 12 Aug 1876; Saturday Rev 12 Aug 1876; Spectator 26 Aug 1876; Guardian 27 Sep 1876; Scudder, H. E. Atlantic Monthly Dec 1876.

The Agamemnon of Aeschylus. Verse trn. Includes untitled prose preface. 1877. No separate Amer pbn.
REVIEWS: Athenaeum 27 Oct 1877; Symons, J. A. Acad 3 Nov 1877; Swinburne, A. C. Athenaeum 10 Nov 1877; Spectator 10 Nov 1877; Saturday Rev 17 Nov 1877; Guardian 21 Nov 1877; N & Q 23 Mar 1878; [Fleeming-Jenkin, H. C.] Edinburgh Rev Apr 1878; London Quart Rev Apr 1878.

La Saisiaz [and] The two poets of Croisic. 1878. Two separate poems pbd in 1 vol. Includes untitled prologue ('Good, to forgive!') and epilogue ('What a pretty tale you told me'). Ed T. P. Trammell, unpbd diss, Ohio Univ 1969.
REVIEWS: [Watts, W. T.] Athenaeum 25 May 1878; Simcox, G. A. Acad 1 June 1878; Saturday Rev 15 June 1878; Guardian 4 Dec 1878.

Dramatic idyls. 1879, 1882 ('second edn'). Includes Martin Relph; Pheidippides; Halbert and Hob; Ivàn Ivànovitch; Tray; Ned Bratts. Ed (with 2nd ser) E. L. Wolfe, unpbd diss, Univ of Pennsylvania 1969.
REVIEWS: Orr, A. Contemporary Rev May 1879; Wedmore, F. Acad 10 May 1879; [Watts, W. T.] Athenaeum 10 May 1879; Spectator 31 May 1879; Saturday Rev 21 June 1879; Allen, G. Fortnightly Rev July 1879; N & Q 2 Aug 1879.

Dramatic idyls: second series. 1880. Includes untitled prologue ('"You are sick, that's sure" – they say'); Echetlos; Clive; Muléykeh; Pietro of Abano; Doctor —; Pan and Luna; untitled epilogue ('"Touch him ne'er so lightly", into song he broke'). Pietro of Abano includes note with version of trn of quatrain attributed to Abano: *see* 1845.
REVIEWS: The Times 10 Apr 1880; [Watts, W. T.] Athenaeum 10 July 1880; Pall Mall Gazette 26 July 1880; Saturday Rev 21 Aug 1880; B., A. L. O. Spectator 21 Aug 1880; N & Q 28 Aug 1880; Guardian 22 Sep 1880; Br Quart Rev 1 Oct 1880.

Agamemnon, La Saisiaz and Dramatic idyls. Boston 1882, 1883.

Untitled ['Thus I wrote in London, musing on my betters']. 10 lines. First pbd Century Mag Nov 1882. Addition to 'Touch him ne'er so lightly' (*see* Dramatic idyls: second series). Not collected by Browning.

Balaustion's adventure, Aristophanes' apology, Pacchiarotto and other poems. Boston 1883, 1885, 1886.

Jocoseria. 1883, Boston 1883, London 1883 ('second edn'), 1884 ('third edn'). Ed R. E. Reid, unpbd diss, Ohio Univ 1968. Includes Wanting is – what?; Donald; Solomon and Balkis; Cristina and Monaldeschi; Mary Wollstonecraft and Fuseli; Adam, Lilith and Eve; Ixion; Jochanan Hakkadosh; Never the time and the place; Pambo. Jochanan Hakkadosh includes prose note on Rabbinical source of poem followed by 3 untitled sonnets: I ('Moses the meek was thirty cubits high'); II ('And this same fact has met with

unbelief!'); III ('Og's thigh-bone – if ye deem its measure strange').
REVIEWS: Acad 17 Feb 1883; The Times 8 Mar 1883; [Hutton, R. H.] Spectator 17 Mar 1883; [Watts-Dunton, W. T.] Athenaeum 24 Mar 1883; Saturday Rev 24 Mar 1883; Symons, J. A. Acad 31 Mar 1883; Lathrop, G. P. Atlantic Monthly June 1883; Shepherd, R. H. GM June 1883; Harper's Mag Aug 1883; Fortnightly Rev 1 Nov 1883.

Dramas. Boston 1883, 1885, 1886.

Fifine at the fair, Red cotton night-cap country, and the Inn album [also contains Prince Hohenstiel-Schwangau, saviour of society and Hervé Riel]. Boston 1883, 1885.

Goldoni. Pall Mall Gazette 8 Dec 1883. Sonnet. Ms dated 27 Nov 1883. Not collected by Browning.

Agamemnon, La Saisiaz, Dramatic idyls, and Jocoseria. Boston 1884, 1885, 1886.

Dramatis personae, Dramatic romances and lyrics, Strafford etc. Boston 1884, 1886.

Ferishtah's fancies. 1884, Boston 1885, 1886, London 1885 (2nd edn), 1885 (3rd edn). Includes Prologue ('Pray, Reader, have you eaten ortolans'); 1 The eagle; 2 The melon-seller; 3 Shah Abbas; 4 The family; 5 The sun; 6 Mihrab Shah; 7 A camel-driver; 8 Two camels; 9 Cherries; 10 Plot-culture; 11 A pillar at Sebzevah; 12 A beanstripe, also apple-eating; Epilogue ('Oh, Love – no, Love! All the noise below, Love'). Each numbered poem is followed by an untitled lyric: [1] 'Round us the wild creatures, overhead the trees'; [2] 'Wish no word unspoken, want no look away!'; [3] 'You groped your way across my room i' the dear dark dead of night'; [4] 'Man I am and man would be, Love – merest man and nothing more'; [5] 'Fire is in the flint: true, once a spark escapes'; [6] 'So, the head aches and the limbs are faint!' [7] 'When I vexed you and you chid me'; [8] 'Once I saw a chemist take a pinch of powder'; [9] 'Verse-making was least of my virtues: I viewed with despair'; [10] 'Not with my Soul, Love! – bid no Soul like mine'; [11] 'Ask not one least word of praise!' [12] '"Why from the world" Ferishtah smiled "should thanks"'.
REVIEWS: [Watts-Dunton, W. T.] Athenaeum 6 Dec 1884; Saturday Rev 6 Dec 1884; Spectator 6 Dec 1884; Beeching, H. C. Acad 13 Dec 1884; Critic 13 Dec 1884; Daily Telegraph 21 Feb 1885; Woodberry, G. E. Atlantic Monthly Apr 1885; [Forman, H. B.] London Quart Rev Jan 1886.

Untitled sonnet ['Sighed Rawdon Brown: "Yes, I'm departing, Toni!"']. Cent Mag Feb 1884. Ms dated 28 Nov 1883. Not collected by Browning.

The names. In Shakspearean show book (for a charity bazaar) and Pall Mall Gazette, both 29 May 1884. Sonnet. Ms dated 12 Mar 1884. Not collected by Browning.

The founder of the feast. World 16 Apr 1884. 15 lines. Ms dated 5 Apr 1884. Revised by Browning after pbn to make it a sonnet but not collected by him.

Why I am a Liberal. In Why I am a Liberal, being definitions by the best minds of the Liberal party, ed Andrew Reid, 1885. Sonnet.

Duty. Present Day Apr 1886. 12 lines. Not collected by Browning and not included in any subsequent edn. Rptd with commentary by M. Mason in TLS 27 Apr 1984.

Spring song ['Dance, yellows and whites and reds']. In The new Amphion: the book of the Edinburgh Univ Union Fancy Fair, 1886. Subsequently incorporated without title as concluding lines of Parleying With Gerard de Lairesse.

Parleyings with certain people of importance in their day, to wit: Bernard de Mandeville, Daniel Bartoli, Christopher Smart, George Bubb Dodington, Francis Furini, Gerard de Lairesse, and Charles Avison; introduced by a dialogue between Apollo and the Fates; concluded by another between John Fust and his friends. 1887, Boston 1887. Ed D. W. St John, unpbd diss, Ohio Univ 1976. Contents as indicated in title with slight variations: Apollo and the Fates – a prologue; the 'parleyings' numbered: I With Bernard de Mandeville; II With Daniel Bartoli [etc]; Fust and his friends – an epilogue. With Charles Avison concludes with song in honour of Pym ('Fife, trump, drum, sound! and singers then') and musical score of Avison's Grand March.
REVIEWS: Saturday Rev 1 Jan 1887; [Watts-Dunton, T.] Pall Mall Gazette 28 Jan 1887; [Hutton, R. H.] Spectator 5 Feb 1887; Garrod, H. B. Acad 12 Feb 1887; Athenaeum 19 Feb 1887; [Oliphant, M.] Blackwood's Mag Mar 1887; Westminster Rev Apr 1887; Woodberry, G. E. Atlantic Monthly May 1887.

Untitled ['Fifty years' flight! Wherein should he rejoice']. 4 lines. Pall Mall Gazette Jan 1888. Composed for Jubilee window in St Margaret's Church, Westminster (window destroyed in World War II). Ms dated 18 Dec 1887. Not collected by Browning.

The isle's enchantress [on F. Moscheles' painting]. Pall Mall Gazette 26 Mar 1889.

Untitled ['And as I wandered by the happy shores']. First pbd in F. Moscheles, Fragments of an autobiography, with his note explaining that it was a 'Variation of a description by Moscheles for The isle's enchantress': *see* preceding entry.

To Edward FitzGerald. Athenaeum 13 July 1889.

Phonograph recording by Browning of first 5 lines of 'How they brought the good news from Ghent to Aix', with his apology for being unable to go on. 7 Apr 1889 (BBC sound archive).

Lines for the tomb of L. L. Thaxter. Poet-Lore Aug 1889.

Asolando: fancies and facts. 1890 [postdated for 1889], 1890, 1893 (10th edn), Boston 1890. Silently annotated 1894; tr Ital 1938. Includes Prologue ('The poet's age is sad: for why?'); Rosny; Dubiety; Now; Humility; Poetics; Summum bonum; A pearl, a girl; Speculative; White witchcraft; Bad dreams I; Bad dreams II; Bad dreams III; Bad dreams IV; Inapprehensiveness; Which?; The Cardinal and the dog; The Pope and the net; The bean-feast; Muckle-mouth Meg; Arcades ambo; The lady and the painter; Ponte dell' Angelo, Venice; Beatrice Signorini; Flute-music, with an accompaniment; 'Imperante Augusto natus est –'; Development; Rephan; Reverie; Epilogue ('At the midnight in the silence of the sleep-time'). The Cardinal and the dog written 1842.
REVIEWS: Spectator 25 Jan 1889; Saturday Rev 14 Dec 1889; Critic 21 Dec 1889; [Oliphant, M.] Blackwood's Mag Jan 1890; Symons, A. Acad 11 Jan 1890; Athenaeum 18 Jan 1890; Phelps, W. L. New Englander and Yale Rev Mar 1890; Harper's Mag Apr 1890; London Quart Rev Apr 1890; Prideaux, W. F. N & Q 3 May 1890.

Prose works, including introductions and prefaces

Letters of Percy Bysshe Shelley. 1852. Introd [anon]. All but one of the letters were discovered to be spurious and the vol withdrawn soon after pbn. Browning's piece is generally referred to as the Essay on Shelley. Rptd by F. J Furnivall for both the Browning Soc (1881) and the Shelley Soc (1888); Bibelot 1902; Warwick 1903; ed R. Garnett 1903; ed J. C. Thompson, Hull 1908; ed L. Winstanley, Boston 1911 (with Shelley, Defence of poetry); ed H. F. B. Brett-Smith, Oxford 1921 (with Shelley, Defence; Peacock, Four ages of poetry).

Dedication and Advertisement. Prefacing Elizabeth Barrett Browning, Last poems, 1862.

Advertisement. Preface to Elizabeth Barrett Browning, The Greek Christian poets and the English poets, 1863.

Note on Elizabeth Barrett Browning. In A selection of the poetry of Elizabeth Barrett Browning, 1866. Another note in her Poems, 1887, contradicting her biographer J. H. Ingram. *See* Athenaeum 31 Jan 1891.

Introductory note. In Morte dell' uxorcida Guido Franceschini decapitato, ed Sir J. Simeon, 1870. Referring to Simeon's recent death.

Introduction to the Divine order and other sermons, by Thomas Jones. 1884.

Prefatory note. In Elizabeth Barrett Browning, Poems, 1887. Biographical information on Elizabeth Barrett Browning and Barrett family, prompted by erroneous statements in recent memoir of Elizabeth Barrett Browning by J. H. Ingram.

Publications not acknowledged by Browning and fugitives (impromptu verse recorded by other persons, contributions to albums, occasional verse in letters, etc)

The dance of death. 1826?. Early poem, possibly from lost collection Incondita. Transcribed and attributed to Browning by his friend Sarah Flower (later Sarah Flower Adams), in her letter to W. J. Fox of 31 May 1827. First pbd Cornhill Mag 36 1914.

The first-born of Egypt. Ibid.

Untitled ['Oh, faithless fair!']. 1833?. 8 lines. First pbd in Michelmore catalogue 21, item 66 [c. 1935].

Impromptu on hearing a sermon by the Rev T. R– pronounced 'heavy'. Epigram (2 lines) on Thomas Ready. Ms in letter to W. J. Fox conjecturally dated 28 Mar 1833. First pbd Orr, Life and letters, 1891.

Cockney anthology – a specimen. I On Andrea del Sarto's Jupiter & Leda [10 lines]; II On the deleterious effects of tea [4 lines]. Ms dated 6 Feb 1834. Contribution to album belonging to 'Anna', unidentified. First pbd Poems, ed Pettigrew and Collins, 1981. Another version of II in ms dated 11 June 1883 with title: Classicality applied to tea-dealing: a fancy inspired by Westbourne Grove.

Sonnet ['Eyes, calm beside thee, (Lady could'st thou know!)']. Monthly Repository Oct 1834. Signed 'Z'. Not collected by Browning.

Untitled ['Words we might else have been compelled to say']. 1837. Epitaph for James Dow and his family, on tombstone in burial-ground of St Mary's Church, Barnsley, Yorks. 20 lines. Browning's ms not extant. First correctly identified and pbd by E. G. Bayford in N & Q 193, June 1948. A different version (possibly an earlier draft) from transcript by Browning's sister Sarianna pbd Cornhill Mag Feb 1914 with conjectural title and date Lines in memory of his parents (1866).

A forest thought ['In far Esthonian solitudes']. 4 Nov 1837. Browning's ms (if any) not extant: inscribed in album of William and Anne Dow on occasion of son's Christening. First pbd Country Life 17 1905.

Untitled ['I will strain my eyes to blindness']. 37 lines. To Helen Faucit (Lady Martin), written in her album and dated 4 Mar 1843. First pbd complete Poetical works ed Jack et al.

Untitled ['Reader, Robert Browning wishes']. 8 lines. Ms contribution to album belonging to Mary Talfourd, dated 6 May 1845. First pbd with commentary by R. S. Kennedy in Browning Soc Notes 23 1996.

Untitled ['And sinners were we to the extreme hour']. Trn of lines by Dante. 5 lines. In letter to Elizabeth Barrett of 21 Dec 1845. First pbd Letters of Browning and Elizabeth Barrett Browning, 1899.

Untitled ['Studying my ciphers, with the compass']. Trn of quatrain attributed to Pietro of Abano. In letter to Elizabeth Barrett Browning of 8 Feb 1846 but written earlier. First pbd Letters of Browning and Elizabeth Barrett Browning, ed Browning, 1899. Another version in note in Pietro of Abano (Dramatic idyls: second series 1880); another in letter to F. J. Furnivall 21 Oct 1881.

Untitled ['Where's Luigi Pulci, that one don't the man see?']. Impromptu trn of epigram by Lorenzo de' Medici. In letter to Elizabeth Barrett Browning of 8 Feb 1846. First pbd Letters of Browning and Elizabeth Barrett Browning, ed Browning, 1899.

Untitled ['Be it your unerring rule']. Trn of epigram by Goethe. 4 lines. In letter to Elizabeth Barrett of 8 Apr 1846, written out as prose. First pbd Letters of Browning and Elizabeth Barrett Browning, ed Browning, 1899.

Untitled ['Could I, heart-broken, reach his place of birth']. Epigram on Correggio. In letter to Anna Jameson conjecturally dated 5 May 1846. First pbd Sotheby's catalogue 10 Dec 1913.

The Moses of Michael Angelo. Ms dated 27 Sep 1850. Trn of sonnet by Giambattista Felice Zappi. First pbd Cornhill Mag Sep 1914.

Untitled ['How much upon a level']. 4 lines. Unpbd. Recorded by Elizabeth Barrett Browning in letter to Arabella Moulton-Barrett 30 Apr 1853.

Study of a hand, by Lionard. 1857. Sent, with Barrett Browning's My heart and I, to Marguerite Power for pbn in Keepsake, but not pbd there. Later incorporated in James Lee in Dramatis personae.

Untitled ['Oh, my Isa! Ah, my Annette!']. 3 lines in a letter to Isa Blagden [1 Aug 1857]. Pbd in Dearest Isa, ed E. McAleer, 1951.

Untitled ['An Angel from his Paradise drove Adam']. 2 lines reworking lines by Walter Savage Landor. Ms accompanying letter to Kate Field dated 21 Aug 1859. First pbd as Landor's in 1900; first attributed to Browning in Poems, ed Pettigrew and Collins, 1981.

Untitled ['Dear Miss Unger']. 6 lines. Verse skit. First pbd in A catalogue... collected since the printing of the first catalogue in 1886 by the late Frederick Locker Lampson 1900. Ms not extant; recorded as having been inserted in Locker-Lampson's copy of Christmas-eve and Easter-day but probably not contemporary with pbn (1850); conjecturally after Browning's return to live in London 1861.

Very original poem, written with even a greater endeavour than ordinary after intelligibility, and hitherto only pbd on the first leaf of the author's son's account-book. 4 lines. First pbd N & Q 211, Sep 1966. Ms dated 8 Mar 1864. An unpbd ms dated 10 Aug 1884 has title Economic precept written more than twenty years ago in the first account-book possessed by my son; it has some variant readings. Undated fair copy bears title Written in a child's account-book by Robert Browning.

Terse verse ['Hail, ye hills and heaths of Ecclefechan!']. 8 lines. Rhyming skit on birthplace of Thomas Carlyle and Jane Welsh Carlyle. First pbd by Hallam Tennyson in Tennyson: a memoir 1897 from undated ms conjecturally dated Dec 1865.

On being defied to express in a hexameter: 'You ought to sit on the safety-valve'. 10 lines in Latin. First pbd Cornhill Mag 37 1914. Ms dated 22 Feb 1866. Another undated ms exists titled Plane te valvam; it lacks the last line.

Untitled ['Don't play with sharp tools, these are edge 'uns']. 2 lines. Impromptu rhyme (2nd line: 'My Ned Jones!'). No ms. Recorded in diary of William Allingham for 21 Apr 1867, pbd 1907.

Untitled ['And now in turn see Swinburne bent']. 7 lines. No ms. First pbd R. Secor, Stud in Browning and his Circle 2 1974 from record by Violet Hunt from papers of William Allingham referring to meeting with Browning on 8 Feb 1868.

Untitled ['Twas Goethe taught us all']. 4 lines. Skit on pronunciation of 'metamorphosis'. First pbd Athenaeum 11 Jan 1896. Ms in letter to F. T. Palgrave of 1 Apr 1869.

Untitled ['Dear Hosmer; or still dearer Hatty']. 29 lines. Round-robin invitation. Ms not extant. First pbd C. Carr, Harriet Hosmer: letters and memories, 1912, from Hosmer's transcript dated 5 Sep 1869.

Untitled ['F. Then, what do you say to the poem of Mizpah? / An out-and-out masterpiece – that's what it is, Pa!']. First pbd New poems, ed F. G. Kenyon, 1914, with title Dialogue between father and daughter. Ms not extant. Dated here to 1870 on conjecture that 'Mizpah' is transcription error for 'Rizpah', title of poem by Tennyson pbd 1870.

The dogma triumphant: epigram on the voluntary imprisonment of the Pope as proving his infallibility. 4 lines. First pbd New poems, ed Kenyon, 1914, from ms signed 'Italia' now lost. Probable date from subject-matter Winter 1870–1.

Untitled ['The gift is small, / The love is all']. First pbd B. Miller, Browning: a portrait, 1952. In letter of 31 Mar 1871 to daughter of Lady Ashburton accompanying a gift.

Mettle and metal. Epigram ('Ay, Trochu, in Paris which Prussians environ'). 4 lines. First pbd W. Irvine and P. Honan, The book, the ring and the poet, 1974. Ms dated 30 Apr 1871.

Untitled ['In Dickens, sure, philosophy was lacking']. 4 lines. Epigram after reading Forster's biography. First pbd The book of the spiritual life, 1905 (by Lady Dilke [E. F. G. Pattison], ed Sir C. Dilke). Ms in letter to Mrs Emily Pattison of 27 Dec 1871.

Untitled ['He gazed and gazed and gazed and gazed, / Amazed, amazed, amazed, amazed']. Impromptu on painting of naked Venus. Recorded and first pbd by Laura Troubridge in Memories and reflections, 1925. Date c. 1872 from Troubridge's age at time of anecdote.

Untitled. Trn from Aeschylus' Agamemnon, lines 750–9. 25 Oct 1874. Unpbd.

Untitled ['A prig, Sir, is Coventry Patmore!']. 4 lines. Unpbd. In letter to George Murray Smith 12 Mar 1875.

Untitled ['Wagner gave six concerts: five']. 4 lines. First pbd Amer Art Assoc catalogue 16 Dec 1929 from ms dated 21 May 1877, now lost.

Replies to challenges to rhyme. 6 items: 'If ever you meet a rhinoceros' (4 lines); 'Hang your kickshaws and your made-dishes' (3 lines); 'You may at Pekin as at Poggibonsi' (2 lines); 'Ah, massa, such a fiery oss' (4 lines); 'Venus, sea froth's child' (4 lines); '"Horns make the buck" cried rash Burdett' (4 lines). First pbd together New poems, ed F. G. Kenyon, 1914. First item pbd Hallam Tennyson, Alfred Lord Tennyson: a memoir, 1897. Date c. 1878 by reference to item 5, which alludes to marriage of Hannah de Rothschild.

Untitled ['We don't want to fight']. 4 lines. Epigram on Disraeli. First pbd Mary Gladstone (Mrs Drew): her diaries and letters, ed Lucy Masterman, 1930. Impromptu recorded by Mary Gladstone on 4 Apr 1878.

Untitled ['Oh Love, Love']. 18 lines. Trn of pt of chorus from Euripides' Hippolytus. Pbd with acknowledgement J. P. Mahaffy, Euripides, 1879. Mahaffy dates receipt of Browning's lines 18 Dec 1878.

Untitled ['The blind man to the maiden said']. 20 lines. Trn of verses by Wilhelmine von Hillern. Pbd with acknowledgement to 'a friend' by Clara Bell in her trn of von Hillern's romance The hour will come, 1879. Browning's ms not extant.

The delivery to the secular arm: a scene during the existence of the Spanish Inquisition at Antwerp 1570. 5 lines. First pbd New poems, ed Kenyon, 1914. Trn of lines by Calderón intended as motto for painting by Browning's son Pen (executed: *see* The Browning collections, ed Kelley and Coley, 1984, K21). Two mss dated 28 July 1880; the other is entitled 'A scene in the building of the inquisitors at Antwerp'.

Gerousios oinos. First pbd Cornhill Mag Apr 1914. 48 lines. In proofs of Jocoseria but withdrawn from vol before pbn. Ms not extant; date probably 1882.

Untitled ['And to these Rhodians she, the sharp-eyed one']. 12 lines. First pbd New poems, ed F. G. Kenyon, 1914. Epigram on current court case based on trn from Pindar. Ms dated 10 Jan 1884 (for 1883); another ms in letter to J. D. Williams 10 Mar 1883.

K. de K. Bronson ['Pray, do I write your name the proper way?']. 4 lines. First pbd (photograph of ms) The Browning collections, ed Kelley and Coley, 1984. Ms dated 4 Nov 1883.

Untitled ['All sorts of singers have this common vice']. 4 lines. Pall Mall Gazette 13 Dec 1883 with inaccurate report of origin. Impromptu trn from Horace in album belonging to Felix Moscheles. Dated by Moscheles 10 July 1883. Not collected by Browning. Another version beginning 'In the whole tribe of singers is this vice' in letter to Frederick Lehmann 29 Dec 1884; first pbd Baylor Browning Interests 24 1975.

Untitled ['The air one breathes with Smith may be the sharper: / But save me from Scirocco's heat in Harper!']. First pbd Letters of Browning, ed. T. L. Hood, 1933. Ms in letter to F. J. Furnivall 17 Feb 1884.

Untitled ['Be the next three months a game at Tennis – / Of which I am the ball – at the end comes Venice!']. First pbd in More than friend: the letters of Browning to Katharine de Kay Bronson, ed M. Meredith, Waco TX and Winfield KS 1985. In letter of 13 Apr 1884.

Untitled limerick ['There was a sky-painter at Folkestone']. First pbd Learned lady: letters from Browning to Mrs Thomas FitzGerald, ed E. C. McAleer, 1966. Ms of letter dated 26 Apr 1884.

Untitled ['All we can dream of loveliness within'. First pbd Mrs C. J. Bloomfield-Moore, Lippincott's Mag May 1890. Concluding 4 lines of sonnet composed Christmas 1884 with set rhymes and subject ('Keely's discovery'). Lines 1–10 of sonnet not given; ms not extant.

Untitled ['Thou, whom these eyes saw never, – say friends true']. 7 lines. Poet-Lore Aug 1889. Epitaph for tomb of Levi Lincoln Thatcher. Not collected by Browning. Two mss dated 19 Apr 1885.

Untitled ['Her advent was not hailed with shouts']. 4 lines. First pbd Marie and Squire Bancroft, The Bancrofts: recollections of sixty years, 1909. Impromptu welcome for Marie Bancroft at dinner, recorded by her husband on menu card. No ms. Conjectural date of occasion 29 June 1885.

Last poem ['I dined at Natorp's yester-eve']. 4 lines. First pbd Poems, ed Pettigrew and Collins, 1981. Ms in undated letter to unidentified friend accepting invitation to dinner; conjectural date between 1879 and 1887.

Untitled ['Oh Love, I bring no posies']. 5 lines. Facs pbd The Browning collections, ed Kelley and Coley, 1984, who date it c. 1885.

Epps. First pbd Cornhill Mag Oct 1913. Ms dated 6 Jan 1886.

Untitled ['Yellow and pale as ripened corn']. 4 lines. First pbd by Ernest Rhys, Sir Frederic Leighton, 1895. Motto for a painting by Leighton. Ms undated; Leighton's painting dated 1887.

Untitled ['Bancroft, the message-bearing wire']. 4 lines. First pbd by Mrs C. L. Bloomfield-Moore, Lippincott's Mag May 1890. Lines composed for a birthday telegram sent 3 Oct 1887.

Margaret E. Keep. Magari. 8 lines, dated 13 Dec 1887, with the note 'Improvised by Robert Browning'. Unpbd.

Untitled ['Horns to bulls, gave nature']. 8 lines. First pbd Anderson Galleries catalogue 8 Apr 1936. Trn from Anacreontic verse; ms with original Greek sent to Felix Moscheles 30 July 1888.

Untitled ['Hail to the man who upward strives']. 8 lines. In Letters of Felix Mendelssohn to Ignaz and Charlotte Moscheles, tr and ed Felix Moscheles, 1888. Trn of 2 quatrains by Karl Klingemann written for separate birthday celebrations (1832, 1844) in honour of Ignaz Moscheles. Not collected by Browning.

The isle's enchantress. Pall Mall Gazette 26 Mar 1889. 5 lines. Motto for a painting by Felix Moscheles. Pbd by Moscheles and not collected by Browning.

Untitled ['And as I wandered by the happy shores']. 5 lines. First pbd Felix Moscheles, Fragments of an autobiography, 1899. Early version of motto for Moscheles' painting, replaced by preceding item.

Untitled ['What seems a soul where Love's outside the porch']. 30 July 1889. Italian trn entered in album. Facs in M. S. Porter, Recollections of Louisa May Alcott, John Greenleaf Whittier, and Robert Browning, Boston 1893.

Untitled ['Is Loredano proved the worst of vipers']. 2 lines in a letter to K. de K. Bronson, 5 Nov 1889. Pbd in More than friend, ed Meredith.

Untitled ['Here I'm gazing, wide awake, / Robert Browning, no mistake!']. First pbd W. M. Rossetti, Mag of Art Apr 1890. Ms written below pencil sketch by G. D. Giles dated 24 Nov 1889.

Inscription on an ancient sundial at Newquay, Cornwall. Trn of Latin inscription. First pbd Daily Telegraph 28 Feb 1997. Written c. 1889.

Prose works not acknowledged

Some strictures on a late article in the Trifler. Trifler Feb 1835. Humorous essay on debt contributed to mag pbd in Browning's circle. Rptd J. Maynard, Browning's youth, 1977.

Thomas Wentworth, Earl of Strafford. In Lives of eminent British statesmen vol 2 (Biography section of the Cabinet Cyclopaedia), 1836. By John Forster, with anonymous help from Browning. The extent of Browning's contribution seems to have been considerable but cannot be precisely identified.

Untitled ['The causes of the failure of undoubtedly the finest actor of the day']. Ms draft of unfinished article on William Charles Macready. First pbd William Baker, Browning Soc Notes 8 1978. Date probably shortly after production of A blot in the 'scutcheon, 1843.

Conjectures and researches concerning the love madness and imprisonment of Torquato Tasso. By Richard Henry Wilde. 1842. Anonymous review in Foreign Quart Rev 39, July 1842. Generally referred to as Essay on Chatterton; Thomas Chatterton's career is real subject after opening remarks on Tasso. Not acknowledged or collected by Browning. Ed with critical introd by D. Smalley 1948.

Untitled. Note on Wordsworth, probably addressed to R. H. Horne c. 1843, suggesting an epigraph for his essay on Wordsworth in A new spirit of the age. First pbd Poems, ed Woolford and Karlin, 1991, vol 1.

Untitled ['Tizian's way of painting']. Trn for William Page c. 1854.

Notes in correction. Attached to Notes on a case of clairvoyance by J. T. Knowles. Pbd as Knowles's letter to the editor, Spectator 30 Jan 1869.

Title unknown. Trn from the Latin of Charles II's grant of arms to Col W. Carelose. Dated 21 July 1882. 8 pages. Extracts in Sotheby's sale catalogue 25 Feb 1918. Current whereabouts unknown.

Untitled. Prose. Notes on Dryope, possibly for his son's bronze statue on the subject, 1883. Unpbd.

Undated items: poetry (from The Browning collections, ed Kelley and Coley, 1984)

Untitled ['Sipping grog one day at sea']. 14 lines. First pbd Poems, ed Pettigrew and Collins, 1981, from undated ms draft of unfinished poem.

Dictated by the Spirit of Shelley to Sophia ['When spots of interest we view']. 14 lines. Lines 1–7 first pbd Amer Art Assoc catalogue 18 Jan 1935. Ms not extant; date unknown.

Untitled ['He a recreant; in me a true knight thou dubs't, and / "On its own bottom let every tub stand".]' First pbd Browning memorials (Dobell catalogue), 1913. Undated; ms not extant.

Untitled ['He for his volume meant / To get some emolument.' First pbd Browning memorials (Dobell catalogue) 1913. Undated; ms not extant.

Untitled ['He said – and stopped the lyre together with the heavenly voice']. 4 lines. Unpbd. Trn from Apollonius.

The power of beauty. 8 lines. Trn from Anacreon. First pbd Catalogue for sale 4249 (the H. B. Smith Collection) of the Amer Art Assoc – Anderson Galleries, rptd Poems, ed Pettigrew and Collins, 1981. Undated; ms not extant.

Iliad. Bk viii. 202–31. 'She, thus having spoken, departed, the swift-footed Iris'. 30 lines. Browning's trn. Unpbd.

Untitled ['Imposthume – costume – I have lost you M'M']. Browning memorials 1913, item 478.

Untitled ['O the terror of the death song of Urgandea']. 6 lines, with Browning's comment '(nonsense – for the metre's sake –'). Unpbd.

Untitled ['Without their ensigns, axe & fasces']. Unpbd.

Undated items: prose (from The Browning collections, ed Kelley and Coley, 1984)

Augustus Caesar. Suggested topic for painting by Browning's son. Unpbd.

Ion. Suggested topic for painting by Browning's son. Unpbd.

Pan and Pheidippides. Suggested topic for painting by Browning's son. Unpbd.

The witch of Atlas. Suggested topic for painting by Browning's son. Unpbd.

Attributed and spurious works

The following items refer to poems previously thought to be by Browning but now known to be by Elizabeth Barrett Browning.

Untitled ['I am an old and solitary man']. First pbd with title 'Aeschylus' soliloquy' Cornhill Mag Nov 1913; rptd New poems, ed Kenyon, 1914 and successive edns include Pettigrew and Collins 1981; ed Woolford and Karlin in Browning Soc Notes 1978; error based on existence of ms in Browning's hand, now known to be a transcript of ms by Elizabeth Barrett Browning.

Translations from the Anacreontea. 10 trns. First pbd Poems, ed Pettigrew and Collins, 1981. Now known to be by Elizabeth Barrett Browning.

Untitled ['She was fifteen – had great eyes']. First pbd Poems, ed Pettigrew and Collins, 1981. Now known to be by Elizabeth Barrett Browning.

The following items are of doubtful authorship.

Lines on Zermatt churchyard. The Times 30 Aug 1866. Attributed to Browning N & Q 28 Sep 1867.

Untitled ['Go forth o song amid the banks of morning']. 3 lines on verso of ms by Elizabeth Barrett Browning dated 1844. Unpbd.

Untitled ['Hath man's censorious baseness gone about']. 10 lines. In letter to R. H. Horne conjecturally dated 1844. First pbd Anderson Galleries catalogue 15 Mar 1920. Ms not extant.

To my critics. Examiner 5 Aug 1876. 28 lines on controversy with Alfred Austin.

Untitled ['Footfall through this tanglewood']. Ms (unsigned and undated) not extant. 5 stanzas of varying length, nd. Anderson Galleries catalogue 10 Nov 1924.

Letters and accounts, Letters and autobiographical documents

Separate pbn of individual letters included in vols 1–14 of The Brownings' correspondence, *ed P. Kelley et al (i.e. to 1846), not listed. Biographies which include letters (e.g. Orr 1891) not separately listed.*

General collections

Wise, T. J. (ed). Letters from Browning to T. J. Wise and other correspondents. 1912. (priv ptd). First major collection.

Hood, T. L. (ed). Letters of Browning collected by Thomas J. Wise. 1933.

DeVane, W. C. and K. L. Knickerbocker (ed). New letters of Browning. 1950.

Kelley, P. and R. Hudson (ed; from vol 9 Kelley and S. Lewis). The Brownings' correspondence. 1984–. Vol 1 (1809–26) 1984; vol 2 (1827–31) 1984; vol 3 (1832–7) 1985; vol 4 (1838–40) 1986; vol 5 (1841–May 1842) 1987; vol 6 (June 1842–Mar 1843) 1988; vol 7 (Apr–Sep 1843) 1989; vol 8 (Oct 1843–May 1844) 1990; vol 9 (June–Dec 1844) 1991; vol 10 (Jan–June 1845) 1992; vol 11 (July 1845–Jan 1846) 1993; vol 12 (Feb–Apr 1846) 1994; vol 13 (May–Sep 1846) 1995; vol 14 (Sep 1846–Dec 1847). Comprehensive edn of letters from Browning and Elizabeth Barrett Browning, with some letters to them. Vols 1 and 2 contain no letters by Browning. In progress.

Special collections

Hunt, J. H. L. In The correspondence of Leigh Hunt, 1862.

Mr Browning on his critics. Pall Mall Gazette 19 Feb 1887. Letter from Browning.

Murray, A. Portrait as Beatrice Cenci, with critical notice containing four letters from Browning, 1891.

Collingwood, W. G. Life and work of John Ruskin. 1893. One letter from Browning.

Browning's Lost leader. Dial 1 Mar 1894. One letter from Browning.
Wise, T. J. Letters from Browning to various correspondents. 2 vols 1895. First of a ser of pams ed Wise, each containing a few letters.
Philip Gilbert Hamerton: An autobiography [etc]. Boston 1896.
Palgrave, F. T. A letter by Browning [1 Apr 1869]. Athenaeum 11 Jan 1896.
Browning, R. B. (ed). Letters of Browning and Elizabeth Barrett Browning. 2 vols 1899. The 'courtship' correspondence.
Rossetti, W. M. Ruskin, Rossetti, Pre-Raphaelite papers. 1899. 7 letters.
Whiting, L. Kate Field: a record. Boston 1899.
James, H. William Wetmore Story and his friends. 2 vols 1903.
Knight, W. A. Retrospects; first series. 1904. 17 letters.
Kenyon, F. G. Robert Browning and Alfred Domett. New York 1906. Chiefly letters.
Rolfe, W. J. An unpublished Browning letter. Nation 17 Feb 1910.
Allingham, H. P. and F. B. Williams (ed). Letters to William Allingham. 1911.
Wise, T. J. Letters from Robert Browning to T. J. Wise and other correspondents. 1912.
Lucas, E. V. Browning: a castigation and a sculptor's jest. Methuen's Annual 1914. Prints letter of 21 Jan 1863.
Phelps, W. L. Two unpublished letters of Browning. MLN Nov 1914.
Wise, T. J. (ed). The death of Elizabeth Barrett Browning by Robert Browning. 1916.
Phillipps, L. M. and B. Christian (ed). Some Hawarden letters 1878–1913, written to Mrs Drew (Mary Gladstone). 1917. 2 letters.
Scott, L. C. Life and letters of C. P. Cranch. 1917. 1 letter.
Shorter, C. (ed). The Browning Society by Browning: being letters from Browning to James Dyke Campbell. [1917] (priv ptd). 9 letters.
Shorter, C. (ed). Letters to my son by Browning. [1917.] (priv ptd). 4 letters.
Wise, T. J. (ed). Critical comments on Algernon Charles Swinburne and D. G. Rossetti. 1919.
— Edward FitzGerald and Elizabeth Barrett Browning by Robert Browning. 1919.
— The last hours of Elizabeth Barrett Browning by Robert Browning. 1913.
— Letters from Le Croisic by Robert Browning. 1919.
— Reflections on the Franco-Prussian War July–Oct 1870 by Robert Browning. 1919.
— Some records of Walter Savage Landor by Robert Browning. 1919.
— An opinion on the writings of Alfred Lord Tennyson with a statement regarding his changed views regarding Percy Bysshe Shelley by Robert Browning. 1920.
Thomas, W. (ed). Deux lettres inédites de Browning à Joseph Milsand. Revue Germanique Oct 1923. With Fr trn.
Brewer, L. A. (ed). Some Lamb and Browning letters to Leigh Hunt. 1924. (priv ptd). 1 letter from Browning to Hunt dated 3 Oct 1856.
Drinkwater, J. A book for bookmen. 1926. Includes letters from Matthew Arnold to Browning.
Murray, Alma. Ten letters of Browning concerning Miss Alma Murray – Mrs Alfred Forman. Edinburgh 1929 (for private circulation; only 30 copies; 5 letters previously pbd).
Faucit, H., Lady Martin. Letters to Browning. Baylor Bull July 1931.
Martin, Sir T. Letters to Browning. Baylor Bull July 1931.
Nightingale, F. A letter to Browning. Baylor Bull July 1931.
Phelps, W. L. Browning's unwillingness to leave biographical material [includes 2 letters by Browning]. Scribner's Mag Apr 1933.
Armstrong, A. J. (ed). Intimate glimpses from Browning's letter file. Baylor Bull Sep 1934 (Baylor Browning Interests, 8th ser). Letters to Browning from various correspondents.
Benét, W. R. (ed). Twenty-two unpublished letters of Elizabeth Barrett Browning and Browning addressed to Henrietta and Arabella Moulton-Barrett. 1935. Previously appeared serially in Woman's Home Companion Sep–Dec 1935. Pbd serially in England in Argosy Feb–Apr 1936; book pbd 1936 with title From Robert & Elizabeth Browning: a further selection of the Barrett–Browning family correspondence.
Donner, H. W. (ed). The Browning box, or the life and works of Thomas Lovell Beddoes as reflected in letters by his friends and admirers. 1935. Includes 29 letters from Browning.
Hopkins, F. M. A noteworthy discovery: 24 A. L. S. of Browning and E. B. B. written soon after their marriage. Publishers' Weekly 13 Apr 1935.
Rhys, E. Letters from limbo. 1936. 1 letter from Browning to Rhys dated 16 July 1886.
Curle, R. Browning and Julia Wedgwood: a broken friendship as revealed in their letters. New York 1937.
Thorpe, Dorothea, Lady Charnwood. Call back yesterday: a book of old letters with some memories. 1937.
Brewer, L. A. My Leigh Hunt library. 1938. Includes 2 letters from Browning to Hunt.
Armour, A. W. Notables and autographs. New York 1939. 1 letter of 9 May 1876 by Browning to Mrs Inwood Jones.
Phelps, W. L. Browning to Macready. TLS 28 Jan 1939. Includes 5 letters by Browning.
Armytage, W. H. G. (ed). Some new letters of Browning 1871–1889. MLQ 12 1951. Excerpts from letters to Maria Theresa Mundella.
McAleer, E. C. (ed). Dearest Isa: Browning's letters to Isabella Blagden [1850–72]. 1951. Supersedes Letters of Browning to Miss Isa Blagden, ed A. J. Armstrong, [1923].
Armytage, W. H. G. (ed). Browning and Mrs Pattison: some unpublished Browning letters [1867–76]. Univ of Toronto Quart 21 1952. Appendices list Amer edns, his poems in Amer anthologies, etc.
McLachlan, H. J. A Browning letter. TLS 8 Feb 1952. Quotes letter to V. D. Davis 30 Dec 1881.
Purves, J. New letters of Browning. TLS 6 June 1952. Prints letter to Reuben Browning 13 Oct 1860.
Lowe, R. L. (ed). Browning to Percy William Bunting: an unpbd letter. N & Q 201 1956. Letter dated 3 Mar 1885.
McAleer, E. C. (ed). Pasquale Villari and the Brownings. Boston Public Lib Quart 9 1957. 3 letters dated 26 Mar 1859; 29 Aug [1859]; 28 May 1862.
Adrian, A. A. The Browning–Rossetti friendship: some unpublished letters. PMLA 73 1958. 9 letters from Rossetti to the Brownings.
Landis, P. and R. E. Freeman (ed). Letters of the Brownings to George Barrett [1838–89]. Urbana IL 1958.
A letter from Browning to John Ruskin. Baylor Browning Interests 17 1958. Letter dated 1 Feb 1856.
Provisional catalogue of exhibits in the Tennyson room at the Usher Art Gallery. Lincoln 1959[?]. 3 letters from Browning to Tennyson.
Bevington, M. M. (ed). Three letters of Browning to the Editor of the Pall Mall Gazette. MLN 75 1960. Letters dated 12 Apr 1868; 6 Feb 1870; 16 Mar 1870.
Brown, T. J. English literary autographs, 35: Elizabeth Barrett Browning 1808–1861, and Browning 1812–1889. BC 9 1960.
Dougherty, C. T. (ed). Browning letters in the Vatican library. Manuscripta 4 1960. 1 letter from Browning to H. F. Chorley 11 Aug 1853.
Kelley, P. Browning and George Smith. Quart Rev 299 1961. Excerpts from letters.
Sanders, S. A supplementary calendar of letters. Baylor Browning Interests 18 1961.
Dougherty, C. T. (ed). Three Browning letters to his son. Manuscripta 6 1962. Letters dated 22 July 1887; 23 Feb 1889; 8 Aug 1889.
Kendall, L. H., jun (ed). A new Browning letter. N & Q 207 1962. Letter to George Barnett Smith 24 Dec 1884.
Sanders, C. R. Lost and unpublished Carlyle–Browning correspondence. JEGP 62 1963.

Enkvist, N. E. British and American literary letters in Scandinavian public collections. Acta Academiae Aboensis Humaniora 27 1964. Prints letter from Browning and Elizabeth Barrett Browning to Mary Boyle 3 Dec 1848.

Hudson, G. R. (ed). Browning to his American friends: letters between the Brownings, the Storys and James Russell Lowell 1841–1890. New York 1965.

Ricks, C. (ed). Two letters by Browning. TLS 3 June 1965. Letter to Tennyson 2 July 1863; to Lady Tennyson 21 July 1889.

Smalley, D. Joseph Arnould and Robert Browning: new letters (1842–50) and a verse epistle. PMLA 80 1965.

DeLaura, D. J. (ed). A Browning letter: the occasion of Mrs Browning's A curse for a nation. VP 4 1966. Letter to Paulo E. Giudici 7 Apr 1863.

McAleer, E. C. (ed). Learned lady: letters from Browning to Mrs Thomas FitzGerald 1876–1889. 1966.

Smith, J. H. (ed). Browning to Lady Colvile: an unpublished letter. N & Q 211, Feb 1966. Letter dated 9 Dec 1868.

Kintner, E. (ed). The letters of Browning and Elizabeth Barrett Browning 1845–1846. 2 vols 1969.

Metzdorf, R. F. A checklist of manuscripts in the library of Arthur A. Houghton. New York 1969. 26 letters.

Raymond, W. O. Holographs of Browning letters in the University of Toronto library. Browning Newsletter 3 1969.

Stack, V. E. (ed). The love-letters of Browning and Elizabeth Barrett. 1969. Selections.

Baly, E. Mystery of a letter from Browning. Daily Telegraph 8 June 1970. On a letter from Browning to Agnes Zimmermann dated 26 Apr 1875. Replies 16 June and 30 June.

Dowell, D. F. (ed). A hitherto unpublished letter from Browning to James Thomas Fields. Browning Newsletter 4 1970. Letter dated 12 July 1868.

Hart, N. I. A second supplement to A calendar of letters. Browning Newsletter 4 1970. Letters in Huntington Lib and Scripps College Lib.

Peckham, M. (ed). A Browning letter on The inn album. Browning Newsletter 5 1970. Letter to C. E. Appleton conjecturally dated 17 Jan 1886.

Collins, T. J. (ed). The Brownings to the Tennysons: letters from Browning and Elizabeth Barrett Browning to Alfred, Emily, and Hallam Tennyson 1852–1889. Baylor Browning Interests 22 1971.

Herring, J. W. (ed). A Browning letter to Mr Pfeiffer. Browning Newsletter 7 1971. Letter dated 16 Dec 1886.

Taplin, G. B. (ed). The Brownings and the Reverend William Ware. Browning Newsletter 7 1971. 1 letter from Browning and Elizabeth Barrett Browning 28 Oct 1848.

DeLaura, D. J. (ed). Ruskin and the Brownings: twenty-five unpublished letters. BJRL 54 1972. 2 letters by Browning.

A Browning letter and Sonnets from the Portuguese. [No ed.] Browning Soc Notes 3 1973. Letter to Mary Schlesinger Talbot 12 Dec 1887.

Kelly, R. (ed). Daniel Home, Mr Sludge, and a forgotten Browning letter. Stud in Browning and his Circle 1 1973.

Wingate, B. A note on a Browning letter. Stud in Browning and his Circle 1 1973. First complete printing of letter to W. Hamlet Smith 10 Feb 1887.

George, D. (ed). Four new Browning letters: Browning to the Rev James Graham of Much Cowarne. Stud in Browning and his Circle 2 1974. Letters of 6 and 26 Apr 1888, 28 Jan and 8 May 1889.

Hart, N. I. (ed). A Browning letter on the poetical works of 1863. N & Q 219, June 1974. Letter to the Rev Walter G. Wilkinson 21 May 1864.

Sanders, C. R. The Carlyle–Browning correspondence and relationship. BJRL 57 1974 and 1975. In 2 pts.

Scheuerle, W. H. (ed). An unpublished Browning letter to Mary Baring. Stud in Browning and his Circle 2 1974. Letter dated 31 Mar 1871.

Whitla, W, Letters of Browning and his sister to the Snellgroves. Browning Soc Notes 4 1974.

Litzinger, B. (ed). The letters of Browning to Frederick and Nina Lehmann 1863–1889. Baylor Browning Interests 24 1975.

Waddington, P. (ed). Two unpublished letters of Browning to Pauline Viardot-Garcia. ELN 13 1975. Letters dated 21 Jan and 2 Feb 1871.

Collins, T. J. and W. J. Pickering (ed). Letters from Browning to the Rev. J. D. Williams 1874–1889. Browning Inst Stud 4 1976.

Kelley, P. and R. Hudson. The Brownings' correspondence: a checklist. Winfield KS and New York 1978. A comprehensive listing, including Appendix: the Brownings' travels. Suppls in Browning Inst Stud.

Kelley, P. and R. Hudson. The Brownings' correspondence: supplement no 1 to the Checklist. Browning Inst Stud 6 1978.

Peterson, W. S. Some reflections on editing the Brownings' correspondence. Browning Soc Notes 8 1978.

Turner, W. C. (ed). The poet Browning and his kinsfolk by his cousin Cyrus Mason. Unpbd diss, Tulane Univ 1978.

Peterson, W. S. (ed). Browning's trumpeter: the correspondence of Browning and Frederick J. Furnivall 1872–1889. 1979.

Crowder, A. B. Robert Browning to George Smith: a letter. Stud in Browning and his Circle 8 1980.

Kelley, P. and R. Hudson. The Brownings' correspondence: supplement no 4 to the Checklist. Browning Inst Stud 9 1981.

Kelley, P. and R. Hudson. Editing the Brownings' correspondence: an editorial manual. Browning Inst Stud 9 1981.

Scharnhorst, G. An uncollected letter from Robert Browning to Edward Chapman. Stud in Browning and his Circle 9 1981.

Thompson, N. S. (ed). A new Browning letter. N & Q 226, Oct 1981. Letter to Giuseppe Chiarini dated 17 Dec 1874.

Wedgwood, B. The mysterious disappearance of the Browning–Wedgwood letters. Browning Soc Notes 11 1981.

Collins, T. J. (ed). Three additional letters from Browning to the Tennysons. Tennyson Research Bull Nov 1982.

Jack, I. (ed). Browning on Sordello and Men and women: unpublished letters to James T. Fields. HLQ 45 1982.

Kelley, P. and R. Hudson. The Brownings' correspondence: supplement to the checklist [no 5]. Browning Inst Stud 10 1982.

Meredith, M. (ed). More than friend: the letters of Browning to Katharine de Kay Bronson. Waco TX and Winfield KS 1985.

Campbell, J. J. (ed). Two unpublished Browning letters. N & Q 232, Mar 1987. Letters to B. M. Ball.

Lasner, M. S. Browning's first letter to Rossetti: a discovery. Browning Inst Stud 15 1987. Referring to Rossetti's identification of Browning as author of Pauline.

Karlin, D. (ed). Browning and Elizabeth Barrett: the courtship correspondence 1845–1846: a selection. 1990.

§2

Bibliographical and textual studies

Poet-Lore Aug–Sep 1892. Some Browning first edns (includes a letter by Browning).

Kingsland, W. G. Forster's Life of Strafford – Is it Forster's or Browning's? Poet-Lore Nov 1894.

Critic 2 Jan 1897. Expiration of copyright on four of Browning's poems.

Literary Digest 29 July 1899. A poem which was mistaken for Browning's (entitled Sometime, somewhere).

Machen, Minnie G. The Bible in Browning. New York 1903.

Hudson, C. M. He himself with his human hair in Christmas-eve. N & Q 12 Mar 1904.

Poet-Lore Winter 1904. A miniature wrongly attributed to Browning.

Nation 17 Jan 1907. Variations in a proof copy of Men and women. (There is only one article.)

Hodell, C. W. The old yellow book. Washington 1908. Facs and trns of the primary source for The ring.
Stuart, D. R. An error in Balaustion's adventure. MLN Nov 1908.
Baker, H. T. Dates of The ring and the book. Nation 13 Jan 1910.
Smith, C. C. John Forster. Proc of the Massachusetts Historical Soc Mar 1911. On Browning's connection with the Life of Strafford.
Dobell, B. Browning memorials. c. 1913.
Dial 16 Jan 1913. Mistakes of Browning's biographers.
Athenaeum 29 Mar 1913. Discovery of a second copy of the Old yellow book.
Brockington, R. C. Browning's answers to questions concerning some of his poems. Cornhill Mag Mar 1914.
Fellowship 15 June 1914. The first publisher of Paracelsus.
H[utchins], H. C. A bibliographical study of Browning's Paracelsus. Gazette of the Grolier Club Nov 1922, May 1923.
Reneau, Mary D. First edition of Pauline. Baylor Bull July 1931.
Corkey, E. A Browning misprint [in the love letters]. TLS 16 Nov 1935.
Malloch, A. Browning's copy of Linacre's Latin grammar. Proc of the Charaka Club 1935.
Partington, W. Forging ahead. New York 1939. Includes discussion of T. J. Wise's Browning forgeries.
Cundiff, P. A. The dating of Browning's conception of the plan of The ring and the book. SP July 1941.
D., A. E. Browning selections. N & Q 182, 6 June 1942.
Shackford, M. H. The authorship of Aeschylus' soliloquy. TLS 21 Mar 1942. Reply by G. D. Hobson 11 Apr. *See* section on misattributed poems, *above*.
D., A. E. Browning: uncollected sonnets. N & Q 184, 16 Jan 1943. Helen's tower; Goldoni; The names; The founder of the feast.
D., A. E. Browning: an uncollected translation. N & Q 184, 30 Jan 1943. 'The blind man to the maiden said'.
D., A. E. Browning: album verses. N & Q 184, 13 Feb 1943. 'Thus I wrote in London, musing on my betters'.
D., A. E. Browning: uncollected poems. N & Q 184, 24 Apr 1943.
N & Q 187, 29 July 1944. On a poem attributed to Browning. *See also* Philips, M., 4 Feb 1950.
King, R. A. Account book. In Browning's Finances from his own account book, Waco TX 1947.
Weber, C. J. Much ado about Browning. Colby Lib Quart 1951. William James's copy of Men and women.
Greer, L. Browning and America. Chapel Hill NC 1952.
Archibald, R. C. Musical settings of Browning's poetry and drama. N & Q 199, June 1954.
Cole, S. Counterfeit. 1955. Includes discussion of T. J. Wise's Browning forgeries.
Reynolds, H. Case of the Shelley poem [Memorabilia]. Christian Science Monitor 17 Sep 1956. On early draft entitled Incident in a life.
Szladits, L. L. Browning's French night-cap. BNYPL 61 1957. On revs to Red cotton night-cap country.
Altick, R. D. Memo to the next annotator of Browning. VP 1 1963.
Schmidtchen, P. W. Browning's copy of 'Aristotle'. Hobbies 68 1963.
Huebenthal, J. The dating of Browning's Love among the ruins, Women and roses, and Childe Roland. VP 4 1966.
Honan, P. The texts of fifteen fugitives by Browning. VP 5 1967. All previously pbd.
Jack, I. '1848' edition of Browning's poems. Browning Newsletter 2 1969. *See also* 3 1969 and 8 1972.
King, R. A., jun. A new last edition of Browning's Poetry. Browning Newsletter 3 1969.
McNally, J. Revision of Home-thoughts, from the sea. Browning Newsletter 2 1969.
Peterson, W. S. A re-examination of Browning's prose Life of Strafford. Browning Newsletter 3 1969.
Kelley, P. and R. Hudson. A note on Browning variants. N & Q 215, Jan 1970. On a revision in Parleyings with certain people of importance in their day.
Johnson, R. C. and T. Tanselle. The Haldeman–Julius 'little blue books' as a bibliographical problem. PBSA 64 1970. On cheap Amer reprints.
Allen, F. C. A critical edition of Browning's 'Bishop Blougram's apology'. DAI 1971. Pbd Salzburg 1976.
Hancher, M. Browning and the Poetical works of 1888–89. Browning Newsletter 6 1971.
Abbot, C. Revisions in the 'second edition' of A blot in the 'scutcheon. Browning Newsletter 8 1972.
Agost, L. L. The annotations in Fannie Barrett Browning's copy of the May 1913 Sotheby auction catalogue. Browning Newsletter 9 1972.
Kincaid, A. N. and P. W. M. Blayney. A book of Browning's and his 'Essay on Chatterton'. Browning Soc Notes 2 1972.
King, R. A., jun. Corrections and new emendations in the Ohio Browning edition. Browning Newsletter 8 1972.
Maynard, J. Browning's Sicilian pastoral. HLB 20 1972. On an early draft version of Love among the ruins.
Peterson, W. S. and F. L. Stanley. The J. S. Mill marginalia in Browning's Pauline: a history and transcription. PBSA 66 1972.
Pettigrew, J. S. Date correction of Browning letter to Charles D. Browning. Browning Newsletter 9 1972.
Kelley, P. and W. S. Peterson. Browning's final revisions. Stud in Browning and his Circle 1 1973.
Markus, J. Browning's 'Andrea' letter at Wellesley College: a correction of DeVane's Handbook. Stud in Browning and his Circle 1 1973.
Peckham, M. Lessons to be learned from the Ohio Browning edition. Stud in Browning and his Circle 1 1973.
Pettigrew, J. Baylor's 1848 Poems. Browning Newsletter 8 1973.
Burr, M. A. Browning's note to Forster. VP 12 1974.
Carpenter, A. Browning's experiences and the dating of 'Mr Sludge, "the medium"'. Stud in Browning and his Circle 2 1974.
Connes, G. Browningiana. Études anglaises 27 1974.
Loucks, J. F. 'Popularity' and a forgotten Browning letter. Stud in Browning and his Circle 2 1974.
Machann, C. The Wise–Wrenn copy of Browning's Helen's tower. PBSA 68 1974. Another T. J. Wise forgery.
Maynard, J. Browning Juvenilium [*sic*]? TLS 23 Mar 1974.
Meredith, M. Browning and the Book Collector. Browning's first editions and publishers. Browning Soc Notes 4 1974.
Monteiro, G. The legitimising of Pauline. Stud in Browning and his Circle 2 1974. About the 1868 edn.
Poston, L. Browning rearranges Browning. Stud in Browning and his Circle 2 1974.
Peterson, W. S. The proofs of Browning's Men and women. Stud in Browning and his Circle 3 1975.
Loucks, J. F. The dating of Browning's Here's to Nelson's memory. Stud in Browning and his Circle 4 1976.
Maynard, J. The dating of Browning's Lines to the memory of James Dow: a mythling and some small facts. VP 14 1976.
Vann, J. D. Three uncollected reviews of Pippa passes. Stud in Browning and his Circle 4 1976.
Barnes, W. Two Robert Brownings: the edition of 1863. In The warden's meeting: a tribute to John Sparrow, ed E. Davies, J. J. Bent and E. D. Rhodes, Oxford 1977.
Busby, B. S. A note to the editor of Thomas Wentworth, Earl of Strafford. Stud in Browning and his Circle 5 1977.
Crowder, A. B. Stages in the composition of The inn album. Browning Inst Stud 5 1977.
Dooley, A. C. Further notes on Men and women proofs. Stud in Browning and his Circle 5 1977.
Dooley, A. C. The textual significance of Browning's 1865 Poetical works. PBSA 71 1977.

Peckham, M. Thoughts on editing Sordello. Stud in Browning and his Circle 5 1977.

Ryskamp, C. Literature association books 1800–1950. Princeton Univ Lib Chron 38 1977. Browning's copy of Shelley's Miscellaneous poems.

Hogg, J. Robert Browning and the Victorian theatre: volume 2: acting versions of Strafford, A blot in the 'scutcheon and Colombe's birthday. Salzburg 1978.

Pettigrew, J. For 'flute' read 'lute': or, notes on the 'notes' on Sordello in the Ohio edition. Library 33 1978.

Browning, V. [E. Baly]. My Browning family album. 1979.

Darling, M. E. Notes on Browning's Gold Hair and Apparent failure. Stud in Browning and his Circle 7 1979. Suggests redating Apparent failure to 1856.

Dooley, A. C. Browning's Poetical works of 1888–89. Stud in Browning and his Circle 7 1979. With descriptive appendix by P. Bateman.

Ference, M. L. The library of Browning and Elizabeth Barrett Browning: a preliminary study. 1979. DAI.

Meredith, M. Browning and the prince of publishers. Browning Inst Stud 7 1979.

Busby, B. S. The life of Strafford: Browning's apprenticeship in biography. Stud in Browning and his Circle 8 1980.

Crowder, A. B. Robert Browning and his new publisher. Stud in Browning and his Circle 10 1982.

Vann, J. D. The Atlas and Browning's Dramatic lyrics. Stud in Browning and his Circle 10 1982.

Barker, N. and J. Collins. A sequel to An enquiry into the nature of certain nineteenth century pamphlets by John Carter and Graham Pollard. The forgeries of H. Buxton Forman and T. J. Wise re-examined. 1983.

Desiderata for Browning scholarship. Stud in Browning and his Circle 11 1983.

Korg, J. A definitive edition of Browning's poems. Charlottesville VA 1983. Review.

Baker, W. S. G. Robert Browning's Iliad: an unnoted copy. Stud in Browning and his Circle 12 1984.

Desiderata for Browning scholarship. Stud in Browning and his Circle 12 1984.

Mason, M. A new Browning poem ['Duty']. TLS 27 Apr 1984.

Meidl, A. A. Strafford manuscript in the Lord Chamberlain's Records Office. Browning Inst Stud 12 1984.

Meredith, M. Learning's crabbed text: a reconsideration of the 1868 edition of Browning's Poetical works. Stud in Browning and his Circle 13 1985.

Baly, E. The poet's last residence: 29 de Vere Gardens: unpublished Browning correspondence. Browning Soc Notes 16 1986–7.

Bornstein, G. The arrangement of Browning's Dramatic lyrics (1842). In Poems in their place: the intertextuality and order of poetic collections, ed N. Freistat, Chapel Hill NC 1986.

Bornstein, G. Poetic remaking: the art of Browning, Yeats, and Pound. 1988. Includes discussion of Browning's arrangement of Dramatic lyrics.

Burt, F. D. Browning's Pied piper of Hamelin: a child's story and The cardinal and the dog: considering the poet's early interest in drama and art. Stud in Browning and his Circle 16 1988.

Crowder, A. B. Browning: a decisive reviser. Browning Soc Notes 18 1988–9.

Thomas, C. F. Art and architecture in the poetry of Browning: an illustrated compendium of sources. 1988.

Woolford, J. Browning the revisionary. 1988. Includes discussion of Browning's rearrangement of his poems.

Crowder, A. B. Browning and how he worked in good temper: a study of the revisions of Pacchiarotto. Browning Inst Stud 17 1989.

Duval, S. The importance of collecting presentation and inscribed copies: an example from the Browning books in Brigham Young University's Victorian College. In The best for the patron: proceedings of the research forum, academic library section, Mountain Plains Library Association. Ed R. J. Olsen and B. H. Hall. Emporia KS 1990.

Plasa, C. A. The economy of revision: Keats, Browning and T. S. Eliot. Unpbd diss, 1990.

Jack, I. Elizabeth Barrett and Browning's 'Dramatic romances and lyrics'. In Browning e Venezia, ed S. Perosa, Florence 1991.

Dooley, A. C. Author and printer in Victorian England. 1992.

Hudson, G. R. Robert Browning's literary life. Austin TX 1992.

Millgate, M. Testamentary acts: Browning, Tennyson, James, Hardy. Oxford 1992.

Samuels, M. L. Collecting Elizabeth Barrett and Robert Browning. Gazette of the Grolier Club 44 1992.

Kennedy, R. S. An unpublished epigram by Browning ['Reader, Browning wishes']. Browning Soc Notes 23 1996.

Woolford, J. and D. R. Karlin. Robert Browning. 1996. *See* ch 1.

Reviews and studies

The following includes all reviews to 1869; selected thereafter. See also Browning: the critical heritage, *ed B. Litzinger and D. Smalley, 1970. Many reviews excerpted.*

Chasles, P. De l'art dramatique et du théâtre actuel en Angleterre. Revue des Deux Mondes Apr 1840.

[Horne, R. H.] Church of England Quart Rev Oct 1842. Overview of existing acknowledged works.

Gentleman's Mag Aug 1843. Rev of Bells and pomegranates nos 1–4.

Horne, R. H. Robert Browning and J. W. Marston. In A new spirit of the age, 1844.

B[risted], C. A. English poetry and poets of the present day. Knickerbocker Mag June 1845.

[Horne, R. H.] New Quart Rev Apr 1845. Overview of plays.

Lowell, J. R. In Conversations on some of the old poets, Cambridge MA 1845.

[Warburton, B. E. G.] English Rev Dec 1845. Rev of Paracelsus and other poems 1835–45.

Chorley, H. F. Pippa passes, Colombe's birthday etc. People's Jnl 18 July, 22 Aug 1846.

Eclectic Rev Apr 1846. Rev of Bells and pomegranates nos 1–7.

Fuller, M. Browning's poems. In her Papers on literature and art, New York 1846. Rptd from review of Luria etc.

Forgues, E. D. Poètes et romanciers de la Grande Bretagne: Browning. Revue des Deux Mondes 15 Aug 1847.

[Lewes, G. H.] Browning and the poetry of the age. Br Quart Rev Nov 1847.

Athenaeum 27 Nov 1848; Literary Gazette 2 Dec 1848; Theatrical Times 2 Dec 1848; Era 3 Dec 1848; Weekly Dispatch 3 Dec 1848; [Forster, J.] Examiner 9 Dec 1848. Revs of a production of A blot in the 'scutcheon.

Lowell, J. R. North Amer Rev Apr 1848. Rev of Paracelsus, Sordello, Bells and pomegranates.

Simms, G. W. Graham's Mag Sep 1848; Sharpe's London Mag Nov 1848, continued Dec 1848. Revs of Bells and pomegranates.

Browning's poems: Paracelsus, Sordello and plays. Church of England Quart Rev 12 1849.

Powell, T. In Living authors of England, New York 1849. This work had a deleterious effect on Browning's reputation in America.

Christian Remembrancer Apr 1851. Rev of Poems 1849 and Christmas-eve and Easter-day.

[Kingsley, C.] Fraser's Mag Feb 1851; Amer Whig Rev Dec 1851. Revs of Sordello, Paracelsus and Poems 1849; and of Poems 1850 by Elizabeth Barrett Browning.

Milsand, J. Revue des Deux Mondes 15 Aug 1851. Rev of Poems 1849, Christmas-eve and Easter-day.

Moir, D. M. Browning: Paracelsus, Sordello, Bells and pomegran-

ates. In Sketches of the poetical literature of the past half century, 1851.
Powell, T. In Pictures of the living authors of Great Britain, 1851.
Athenaeum 21 Feb 1852; Literary Gazette 21 Feb 1852; Spectator 21 Feb 1852; [Palgrave, F. T.] Literary Gazette 28 Feb 1852 (letter raising doubts about the authenticity of the letters); Guardian 3 Mar 1852; Athenaeum 6 Mar 1852; Critic 15 Mar 1852; [Lewes, G. H.] Westminster Rev Apr 1852. Revs of Letters of Shelley.
Mitford, M. R. Married poets: Elizabeth Barrett Browning and Robert Browning. In her Recollections of a literary life, 1852.
Chamber's Edinburgh Jnl 16 July 1853. General study.
Daily News 26 Apr 1853; Morning Post 26 Apr 1853; The Times 26 Apr 1853; Morning Herald 27 Apr 1853; Athenaeum 30 Apr 1853; Atlas 30 Apr 1853; Court Jnl 30 Apr 1853; [Forster, J.] Examiner 30 Apr 1853; Illus London News 30 Apr 1853; John Bull 30 Apr 1853; Literary Gazette and Jnl of Science and Art 30 Apr 1853; Spectator 30 Apr 1853. Revs of production of Colombe's birthday.
Gannon, N. J. In Essay on the characteristic errors of our most distinguished living poets, Dublin 1853.
Jameson, A. In her Commonplace book of thoughts, memories and fancies, 1854.
New York Observer 7 Sep 1854.
[Curtis, G. W. ?] Putnam's Mag Apr 1856; Russell's Mag Dec 1857. Overviews.
Milsand, J. La poésie expressive et dramatique en Angleterre. Revue Contemporaine Sep 1856.
Ruskin, J. In Modern painters vol 4, 1856.
LeVert, O. W. In her Souvenirs of travel vol 2, Mobile 1857.
H. N & Q Dec 1858. The first of many queries about How they brought the good news.
Forgues, E. D. In Originaux et beaux esprits d'Angleterre contemporaine, Paris 1860.
Taylor, B. The Brownings. In At home and abroad: a sketchbook, second ser, New York 1860.
[Curtis, G. W.] Harper's New Monthly Mag Sep 1861, Mar 1864, Jan 1869, Nov 1871, Oct 1888, Mar 1890. Overviews from 'The editor's easy chair'.
Massey, G. The poems and plays of Browning. North Br Rev May 1861.
Townsend, C. H. In Three gates in verse, 2nd edn 1861.
Exon. Historical basis of How they brought the good news. N & Q 1 Feb 1862; Rossetti, W. M. N & Q 25 Feb 1862; B., N. N & Q 8 Aug 1868; Bouchier, J. N & Q 23 May 1868; Amery, A. N & Q 21 Oct 1871.
Bathos. N & Q Apr 1863. Political squib (source and subject of The lost leader).
Chambers's Jnl 7 Feb 1863. Overview.
[Donne, W. B.] Saturday Rev Feb 1863; Critic Mar 1863; London Rev 21 Mar 1863; [Hood, E. P.] Eclectic & Congregational Rev May 1863; [Marzials, Sir F. T.] London Quart Rev July 1863. Revs of Selections 1863.
Reeve, L. In Portraits of men of eminence in literature, science, and art vol 1, 1863.
Shirley [Skelton, Sir J.] Fraser's Mag Feb 1863; [Hutton, R. H.] Spectator 5 Sep 1863. Overviews.
Chamber's Repository Mar 1864; Christian Watchman and Reflector 21 Apr 1864. Overviews.
Cobbe, F. P. In her Italics: brief notes on politics, people, and places, 1864.
E. [Ellis, R.] Monthly Religious Mag Apr 1864; [Weiss, J.] Atlantic Monthly May 1864; [Everett, C. C.] Christian Examiner July 1864. Reviews of Sordello etc.
Everett, C. C. Christian Examiner and Religious Misc July 1864. Overview.
Examiner 15 Oct 1864; London Rev 15 Oct 1864; Massey, G. Reader 26 Nov 1864; Saturday Rev 7 Jan 1865. Replies to the Edinburgh Rev's review of Dramatis personae.
Reader Feb 1864; Peterson's Mag Nov 1864. Advance notices of Dramatis personae.
Spiritual Mag July 1864. Browning on spiritualism. Sep 1864. Sonnet by Daniel Home ['Mr Sludge'] on Browning.
Metcalf, W. J. Public Opinion 25 Nov 1865; Harding, M., Public Opinion 2 Dec 1865; C., R. G. Public Opinion 9 Dec 1865; also Public Opinion 16, 23 and 30 Dec 1865. Debate on the rival merits of Browning and Tennyson.
Reader 14 Oct 1865; N & Q 21 Oct 1865; Public Opinion 21 Oct 1865; [Lewes, G. H.] Fortnightly Rev 1 Dec 1865. Revs of Selections 1865.
The Times 11 Jan 1865; [Massey, G.] Quart Rev July 1865; [Greenwell, W. J.] Marlburian Mar 1866; [D., V. P. V.] Marlburian 6 Nov 1867. Overviews.
Craik, G. L. Manual of English literature. 1867. Overview.
Addis, J. N & Q 6 July 1867; Lydiard. N & Q 20 July 1867. On The boy and the angel.
[Alford, H.] Contemporary Rev Jan–Feb 1867; Eclectic Mag Mar–Apr 1867 (same essay).
Dowden, E. Fraser's Mag Oct 1867. Defence of Sordello.
Nencioni, E. Nuova Antologia July 1867. Rev of 1863 Poetical works and Dramatis personae.
Nettleship, J. T. Essays on Browning's poetry. 1868, 1890 (enlarged as Essays and thoughts). The first full-scale book on Browning.
[Austin, A.] Temple Bar June 1869; rptd in The poetry of the period, 1870. This essay particularly angered Browning, who lampooned Austin in Of Pacchiarotto.
Cornhill Mag Feb 1869; Browne, W. H. Southern Mag Dec 1869. Overviews.
Dowden, E. Mr Tennyson and Mr Browning. 1869. Comparison of the two poets.
Forman, H. B. London Quart Rev July 1869. Reissued separately as Robert Browning and the epic of psychology, 1869; reviewed in Our living poets, 1871.
Smiles, S. In Brief biographies, Boston 1869.
Hodgson, S. H. In Theory of practice, 1870.
James Russell Lowell and Robert Browning. New England Quart Jan 1870.
Étienne, E. Revue des Deux Mondes 1 Feb 1871. Overview.
Hawthorne, N. In Passages from English notebooks, Boston 1871.
Hutton, R. H. In Essays, theological and literary, 1871.
Shepherd, R. H. St James's Mag Aug 1871. On 'Mr Browning's first poem [Pauline]'.
Forster, J. In Life of Charles Dickens, 1872–4. Prints a letter of Dickens praising A blot in the 'scutcheon.
Hume, D. D. In Incidents in my life, 2nd ser, New York 1872. By the 'medium' satirised in Mr Sludge 'the medium', offering his own account of their relations.
Taylor, B. Atlantic Monthly Jan 1872. Appraisal and parody.
Austin, A. In Memoir to poems by the late Isa Blagden, 1873. A friend of Browning's friend Blagden, Austin was an enemy of Browning's.
Bouchier, J. N & Q 13 Dec 1873. On the original of The lost leader. Many responses.
Buchanan, R. W. In Master-spirits, 1873. Revised from his review of The ring and the book.
Devey, J. In Comparative estimate of modern English poets, 1873.
Foxall, S. N & Q 28 Feb 1874. How they brought the good news. *See also* Addis, J. 11 Apr 1874; C., T. W. 23 May 1874; and Storr, F. 4 July 1874.
Orr, S. Contemporary Rev May 1874. Overview.
Stedman, E. C. In Victorian poets, Boston 1875.
Swinburne, A. C. In Essays and studies, 1875; also his Works of George Chapman: poems and minor translations, 1875.
D., F. N & Q 22 July 1876. The pied piper of Hamelin. *See also* Moth 26 Aug 1876.
[Furnivall, F. J.] N & Q 25 Mar 1876. The inn album.

Rossetti, W. M. Macmillan's Mag Mar 1876; Dowden, E. Contemp Rev July 1877. Overviews.

L., F. N & Q 12 May 1877. On the original of How it strikes a contemporary.

Gigadibs. N & Q 7 July 1877. Sordello (Who was 'my English eyebright'?).

S., R. N & Q 8 Sep 1877. Christmas-eve. *See also* F. M. J. 6 Oct 1877.

Morley, H. Nineteenth Cent Feb 1878. Rev of Pacchiarotto, Agamemnon.

Saturday Rev 7 Jan 1881, 7 Jan 1882; Acad 9 July, 5 Nov, 3 Dec 1881, 11 May 1882; Critic 22 Oct 1881; Cambridge Rev 9 Nov 1881; Literary World (Boston) 3 Dec 1881, 25 Feb, 11 Mar 1882; Pall Mall Gazette 22 Dec 1881; Furnivall, F. J. Literary World 11 Mar 1882. Notices of newly founded Browning Socs in London, Cambridge, Boston, Dublin, Cornell etc.

Furnivall, F. J. (ed). The [London] Browning Society's papers. 13 pts 1881–91. Usually bound into 3 vols. Includes the following articles: [Pt I] Browning, Essay on Shelley; Carson, T. W., Sample of the end-changed, fresh, and left-out lines in Paracelsus; Furnivall, F. J., A bibliography of Robert Browning 1833–1881 and trial-list of criticisms and notices of Browning's works; Furnivall, F. J., Changed rymes [*sic*] and fresh lines in Sordello; Kirkman, J., Introductory address at the inaugural meeting of the Browning Society. [Pt 2] Additions to the Bibliography; Kirkman, J., Introductory address to the Browning Society; Nettleship, J. T., On Browning's Fifine at the fair and classification of Browning's works; Orr, A., Classification of Browning's poems; Radford, E. W., The Moorish front to the Duomo in Luria and the original of Ned Bratts; Sharpe, J., Analysis and summary of Fifine at the fair; Sharpe, J., On Pietro of Abano and the leading ideas of Dramatic idyls, 2nd ser; Thomson, J., Notes on the genius of Browning. [Pt 3] Beale, D., The religious teaching of Browning; Bury, J., Browning's philosophy; Corson, H., The idea of personality as embodied in Browning's poetry; Johnson, E., Conscience and art in Browning; Johnson, E., On Bishop Blougram's apology; Marx, E., An account of Abbé Vogler. [Pt 4] Bulkeley, H. J., James Lee's wife; Nettleship, J. T., Browning's intuition; Revell, W. F., Browning's poems on God and immortality as bearing on his life here; Turnbull, Mrs, Abt Vogler; West, E. D., One aspect of Browning's villains; Westcott, B. F., On some points in Browning's view of life. [Pt 5] Morison, J. A. C., On Caliban upon Setebos; Raleigh, W. A., On some prominent points in Browning's teaching; Turnbull, Mrs, On In a Balcony. [Pt 7] Berdoe, E., Browning as a scientific poet; Johnson, E., On Mr Sludge, 'the medium'; Symons, A., Is Browning dramatic? [Pt 8] Bulkeley, H. J., The reasonable rhythm of some of Mr Browning's poems; Bury, J. T., On Aristophanes' apology; Fleming, A., On Andrea del Sarto; Herford, C. H., On Prince Hohenstiel-Schwangau; Nettleship, J. T., The development of Browning's genius in capacity as poet or maker; Outram, L. S., Columbe's birthday, act IV, on the avowal of Valence; Pearson, S., On Browning as a landscape painter. [Pt 9] Furnivall, F. J., A grammatical analysis of O lyric love; Glazebrook, Mrs, On A death in the desert; Ormerod, H., Some notes on Browning's poems referring to music; Symons, A., Some notes on Parleyings; Todhunter, J., Strafford at the Strand Theatre. [Pt 10] Barnett, P. A., On Browning's Jews and Shakespeare's Jew; Berdoe, E., On Browning's estimate of life; Ormerod, H., On Abt Vogler; Revell, W. J., On Browning's view of life; Stoddart, A. M., On Saul; Whitehead, C. M., On Browning as a teacher of the nineteenth century. [Pt 11] Berdoe, E., On Paracelsus; Glazebrook, Mrs., Numpholeptos and Browning's women; Graham, J. J. G., The wife-love and friend-love of Robert Browning; Ireland, A., A toccata of Galuppi's; King, J., Prince Hohenstiel-Schwangau; Oldham, J. B., On the difficulties in Browning's poems; Ormerod, H., Andrea del Sarto and Abt Vogler; Robertson, W., On La Saisiaz. [Pt 12] Alexander, W. J., On an analysis of Sordello; Furnivall, F. J., On Robert Browning's ancestors; Ireland, A., On Browning's treatment of parenthood; Revell, W. F., On the value of Browning's work; Rossetti, W. M., On Taurello Salinguerra; Sagar, B., On the line-numbering in The ring and the book. [Pt 13] Ireland, A., On Browning's Cristina and Monaldeschi; Moulton, R. G., On Balaustion's adventure; Oldham, J. B., On Browning's dramatic method; Revell, W. F., On the value of Browning's work; Stefansson, J., How Browning strikes a Scandinavian. Also includes reports of meetings, Browning notes and queries, and occasional reprints of early reviews.

Furnivall, F. J. Acad 31 Dec 1881. On Ben Karshook's wisdom and Mill's notes on Pauline.

Gosse, E. W. Cent Illus Monthly Mag. On Browning's early poetry.

Literary World (Boston) 27 Aug 1881. On Browning's attitude to periodical publication, with a letter from him.

Stevenson, R. L. In Virginibus Puerisque, 1881. Opinion of The ring and the book on p. 43.

Lewis, M. A. Macmillan's Mag July 1882.

Literary World (Boston) 25 Feb, 11 Mar, 22 Apr, 2 Dec 1882.

N & Q 13 May 1882. Rev of 2nd vol of Browning Soc papers.

Punch 22 July 1882.

Symons, A. J. Wesleyan Methodist Mag Dec 1882. Browning as a religious poet.

Christian Register 31 May 1883; Critic 17 Mar 1883. Revs of Selections ed R. G. White.

Courthorpe, W. J. Nat Rev June 1883; Pall Mall Gazette June 1883. Noting misprints in Jocoseria.

Cooke, G. W. Jnl of Speculative Philosophy July 1885. Overview.

Faucit, H. S. In her On some of Shakespeare's female characters, 1885. By the actress who performed in many of the original stagings of Browning's plays.

Ferrar, M. N & Q 28 Mar 1885. A mistake in Ferishtah?

Tennyson, A. Tiresias and other poems. 1885. Dedicated to Browning.

Chicago Tribune 9 Feb 1886. On the 'healthy craze' for Browning.

Corson, H. Introduction to the study of Robert Browning's poetry. Boston 1886, 2nd edn 1888, 3rd edn 1889.

G., G. G. N & Q 7 Aug 1886. How they brought the good news. *See also* Brierley, H., 23 Oct 1886.

Symons, A. An introduction to the study of Browning. 1886 (including a reprint of discarded prefaces to some of Mr Browning's works), 1906 (enlarged). Reviewed by W. Pater, Guardian 9 Nov 1887, rptd in Essays from the Guardian, 1896.

Cohen, M. M. The Jewish Messenger Mar 1887. Study of Jochanan Hakkadosh.

Dowden, E. Fortnightly Rev June 1887. Overview.

Fotheringham, J. Studies in the poetry of Robert Browning 1887.

Kingsland, W. G. Robert Browning: chief poet of the age 1887.

O'Connell, R. N & Q 8 Jan 1887. The statue and the bust. *See also* Furnivall, F. J., 15 Jan 1887.

Trollope, T. A. In What I remember, 1887.

Wilde, O. Pall Mall Gazette 17 Feb 1887.

Amer N & Q 26 May 1888. Halbert and Hob.

Amer N & Q 2 June 1888. Mr Sludge, the medium.

Amer N & Q 16 June 1888. Caliban upon Setebos.

Amer N & Q 16 June, 30 June, 14 July 1888. The ring and the book.

Amer N & Q 30 June 1888. Bishop Blougram's apology.

Amer N & Q 7 July 1888. The lost leader.

Amer N & Q 15 Dec 1888. Childe Roland.

Atlantic Monthly Sep 1888.

Dowden, E. In Transcripts and studies, 1888. On Sordello.

Fay, H. W. Acad 16 June 1888. On Browning's 'distressing blunder' over the meaning of the word 'twat' in Pippa passes.

Pall Mall Gazette 9 July 1888. Browning and periodicals. Browning's reply 9 July 1888.

Pater, W. H. In The renaissance, 3rd edn 1888.
Shelley Society. Notebook 1888.
Alexander, W. J. An introduction to the poetry of Robert Browning. Boston 1889.
Amer N & Q 27 Apr 1889. The ring and the book.
Amer N & Q 11 May 1889. Balaustion's adventure.
Amer N & Q 1 June 1889. A gallic view of Browning.
Lennox, A. M. C. Amer N & Q 23 Feb 1889. The flight of the duchess.
Lennox, A. M. C. Amer N & Q 16 Nov 1889. On attribution to Browning of 'In Venice! This night'.
Lennox, A. M. C., Amer N & Q 28 Dec 1889. Browning in 1861.
Morison Campbell, J. Sordello: an outline analysis of Mr Browning's poem. 1889.
Obituaries and general estimates. Pall Mall Gazette 13 Dec, 16 Dec 1889; New York Evening Post 13 Dec 1889; The Times 13 Dec 1889; Saturday Rev 14 Dec 1889; [Hutton, R. H.] Spectator 14 Dec 1889; Pall Mall Budget 19 Dec 1889; Harry, G. L'independence Belge 20 Dec 1889; Nettleship, J. T. Acad 21 Dec 1889; [Jacobs, J.] Athenaeum 21 Dec 1889; Brooke, S. A. Contemporary Rev Jan 1890; Pall Mall Gazette 1 Jan 1890; Conway, M. D. Nation 9 Jan 1890; Woodberry, G. E. Atlantic Monthly Feb 1890; Phelps, W. L. New Englander and Yale Rev Mar 1890; James, H. Speaker 4 Jan 1891.
Poet-Lore, Boston 1889–1915. Jnl originally devoted principally to Browning: subsequently more general.
R., A. R. N & Q 30 Nov 1889. Queries on Dîs aliter visum, The worst of it, The bishop orders his tomb. *See also* Marshall, E. H., 21 Dec 1889.
Symons, J. A. Fortnightly Rev 1 Jan 1889. Elizabethan and Victorian poetry. Many refs to Browning.
Westminster Abbey. Order of service for funeral 31 Dec 1889.
Wright, W. A. Athenaeum 20 July 1889; Critic 20 Aug 1889; Nation 8 Aug 1889; Tyrell, R. Y. Fortnightly Rev Aug 1889. On Browning's 'To Edward FitzGerald'.
Amer N & Q 18 Jan, 15 Mar 1890. Sordello.
Berdoe, E. Browning's message to his time, 1890; Nettleship, J. T. Robert Browning: essays and thoughts, 1890; Jones, Sir H. Browning as a philosophical and religious teacher, New York 1891.
Bouchier, J. N & Q 19 July 1890. Caliban upon Setebos.
[Davidson, W. T.] London Quart Rev Jan 1890. Rev of Complete works.
Gosse, E. W. Robert Browning: personalia. Boston and New York 1890.
Hutton, R. H. Good Words 1890.
Poet-Lore 2 1890. On the Chicago railway edn.
Rossetti, W. M. Mag of Art May–July 1890. On portraits of Browning.
Wilde, O. Nineteenth Cent July 1890.
Bouchier, J., N & Q 29 Aug 1891. Browning: a lyric to spring. *See also* Sagar, B. and C. C. F., 17 Oct 1891.
Dewey, J. Andover Rev Aug 1891.
James, H. Speaker 4 Jan 1891.
N & Q 14 Mar 1891. The lost leader. *See also* Black, W. G., W. C. B. and F. C. C., 28 Mar 1891; and Black, W. G., 10 Oct 1891.
Orr, A. Athenaeum 25 July 1891. Browning's relations with Arnold.
Prideaux, W. F. N & Q 11 July 1891. Domett and Browning. *See also* St Swithin, 15 Aug 1891; and Prideaux, W. J., 14 Nov 1891.
Amer N & Q 12 Mar, 26 Mar, 9 Apr 1892. General queries.
Critic 9 Jan 1892; Saturday Rev 26 Nov 1892; Clarke, H. A. Poet-Lore May 1893; N & Q 11 Feb 1893, Nov 1894; Spectator 15 Apr 1893. Revs of Life of Strafford.
Duffy, Sir C. G. Contemporary Rev Jan 1892. Carlyle on Browning.
James, H. The private life. Atlantic Monthly Apr 1892. Clare Vawdrey is a portrait of Browning.
Morison, J. Of Fifine at the fair etc. 1892.
Prideaux, W. F. N & Q 12 Mar 1892. Boot and saddle. *See also* Coleman, E. H., 16 Apr 1892; Pickford, J., 2 July 1892; Bouchier, J., 23 July 1892.
Revell, W. F. Browning's criticism of life. New York 1892.
Ritchie, Lady (Annie Thackeray). Records of Tennyson, Ruskin and Browning. 1892. Reminiscences by the addressee of Red cotton night-cap country.
Bayne, T. N & Q 30 Dec 1893. Metre of Too late.
Collingwood, W. G. In Life and work of John Ruskin, 1893.
Hutton, R. H. In The footsteps of the poets, 1893.
Milsand, J. In Littérature anglaise et philosophie, Paris 1893. By a close friend of Browning's.
Shaw, M. W. N & Q 3 Feb 1894. Browning or Southey. *See also* Pickford, J., 7 Apr 1894; and Shaw, M. W., 1 Apr 1894.
X., S. N & Q 10 Mar 1894. Swinburne on Browning.
St Swithin. N & Q 24 Mar 1894. The pied piper of Hamelin.
Berdoe, E. (ed) Browning studies. Selected reprints from Browning Soc papers, 1895.
Spence, R. M. N & Q 11 May 1895. Fifine at the fair.
Spence, R. M. N & Q 1 June 1895. Parallel passages in Browning and E. B. B.
Spence, R. M. N & Q 21 Sep 1895. Misprint in The ring and the book.
Thornton, R. H. N & Q 28 Sep 1895. Literary parallels in Browning. *See also* B., C. C., 9 Nov 1895.
Bayne, T. N & Q 19 Dec 1896. Sordello.
Hill, A. et al. Notes to the pocket volume of selections from the poems of Robert Browning. 1896.
MacColl, M. Contemporary Rev June 1896. Reminiscences.
J., J. A. N & Q 12 Sep 1896. Childe Roland. *See also* B., C. C. A. Mayall and E. A. C., 3 Oct 1896.
Marshall, G. N & Q 19 Dec 1896. Pauline.
Thornton, R. H. N & Q 18 Jan 1896. Master Hugues of Saxe-Gotha.
Beatty, A. Browning's verse-form: its organic character. New York 1897.
Boston Browning Soc papers. 1897.
Platt, J. N & Q 30 Oct 1897. How they brought the good news from Ghent to Aix.
Pope, G. U. St John in the desert; an introduction and notes to Browning's A death in the desert. 1897.
Spence, R. M. N & Q 18 Sep, 6 Nov 1897. Prince Hohenstiel-Schwangau.
Spence, R. M. N & Q 16 Oct 1897. The ring and the book, x, 1375–80. *See also* Mount, C. B. and E. Thomas, 20 Nov 1897; Spence, C. C. B. and E. Marshall, 8 Jan 1898; and Spence, R. M. and T. S. Omond, 26 Feb 1897.
Fotheringham, J. Studies of the mind and art of Robert Browning. 1898.
Hutton, R. H. Lutheran Church Rev 17 1898. Browning's theology.
Omond, T. S. N & Q 26 Nov 1898. Pacchiarotto.
Platt, J. N & Q 7 May 1898. Accented words in Muleykéh.
Moscheles, F. In Fragments of an autobiography, 1899. Reminiscences.
Saintsbury, G. In Corrected impressions: essays on Victorian writers, New York 1899.
Spence, R. M. N & Q 14 Oct 1899. La saisiaz.
Spence, R. M. N & Q 11 Nov 1899. A persistent misprint in Parleying with Gerard de Lairesse.
Spence, R. M. N & Q 23 Dec 1899. Luria. *See also* Bayne, T. and C. C. B., 20 Jan 1900.
Spence, R. M. N & Q 30 Dec 1899. Meeting at night and Parting at morning.
Whiting, L. In her Kate Field: a record, Boston 1899 and her Study of Elizabeth Barrett Browning, Boston 1899.
Bronson, K. C de K. Cent Mag Apr 1900; Cornhill Mag Feb 1902. By a close friend of Browning's later years.

Ford, C. L., N & Q 3 Mar 1900. Respectability (a possible indebtedness to Seneca).
F., G. S. N & Q 10 Mar 1900. Paracelsus.
Griffin, W. H. Monthly Rev Nov 1900. On The ring and the book, with a trn of a source document.
Martin, Sir T. In Helena Faucit [Lady Martin], 1900. Reminiscences by the husband of Browning's close friend.
Porter, C. and H. A. Clarke. Browning study programmes. New York 1900.
Santayana, G. In Interpretations of poetry and religion, New York 1900. Includes a famous essay comparing Browning and Whitman, 'The poetry of barbarism'.
Simpson, P., N & Q 22 June 1900. Hoti in Howell and Browning.
Spence, R. M. N & Q 17 Feb 1900. Parleyings with Christopher Smart, vi: an intended emendation.
Chesterton, G. K. and J. E. H. Williams. Bookman (New York) Jan 1901.
Gosse, E. W. In DNB, 1901.
Kenyon, J. B. In Loiterings in old fields: literary sketches. New York 1901. Reminiscences by this old friend of Browning and Elizabeth Barrett Browning.
Mayall, A., N & Q 12 Oct 1901. Dîs Aliter Visum.
Munroe, J. (ed). Furnivall, a volume of personal records. 1901.
Pigou, A. C. Robert Browning as a religious teacher. 1901.
Brooke, S. A. The poetry of Robert Browning 1902.
K., L. N & Q 18 Jan 1902. Epilogue to Asolando. *See also* Eames, J. B. and St Swithin, 1 Mar 1902; and Omond, T. S., 5 Apr 1902.
K., L. N & Q 25 Oct 1902. Browning and Ruskin.
Stephen, Sir L. In Encyclopaedia Britannica, 1902.
Chesterton, G. K. Robert Browning. 1903. A biography, but memorable for its chs of literary analysis.
James, H. In William Wetmore Storey and his friends, Edinburgh 1903.
Layton, E. M. N & Q 28 Feb 1903. Green and yellow in Sordello.
Phelps, W. L. Independent 5 Mar, 11 June 1903. Browning and Maeterlinck.
Acad and Lit 23 Jan 1904; review of Essay on Shelley.
Conway, M. D. In Autobiography: memoirs and experiences, Boston 1904; Knight, W. A. In Retrospects 1904. Important reminiscences, letters and documents.
Furnivall, F. J. Pippa passes ii 59. N & Q 25 June 1904. *See also* S., H. K. St J. 23 July 1904; and Ford, C. L. and Krueger, G., 3 Sep 1904.
Griffin, W. H. Contemporary Rev Jan, Mar 1905. On Browning's early friends.
Herford, C. H. Robert Browning. 1905.
Marzials, Sir F. T. Browning. 1905.
Tamm. The Robert Browning settlement. Dagny 1905.
Watkin, R. G. Robert Browning and the English Pre-Raphaelites. Breslau 1905.
Duff, D. An exposition of Browning's 'Sordello' with historical and other notes. 1906.
Herlet, B. Robert Brownings Übersetzung des Agamemnon von Aeschylus. Erlangen 1906.
Hutton, R. H. In Brief literary criticisms, ed E. M. Roscoe, 1906.
Man of Kent. Identification of Kentish Sir Byng in Cavalier tunes. N & Q 22 Sep 1906.
Rossetti, W. M. In Some reminiscences, New York 1906.
Allingham, W. In Diary, ed H. D. Allingham and D. Radford, 1907. Important reminiscences.
Bayne, T. N & Q 14 Dec 1907. Wordsworth and Browning. *See also* C. C. B. and C. L. Ford, 11 Jan 1908; Breslar, M. L. R. and T. Bayne, 1 Feb 1908; 28 Mar 1908.
Bagehot, W. In Estimations in criticism, 1908.
Corson, H. Cornell Era 8 Feb 1908. Reminiscences.
Curry, S. S. Browning and the dramatic monologue. Boston 1908.
Statham, H. H. The wild harangue of Vimmercato in Sordello bk V. N & Q 18 Jan 1908.
Crawford, A. W. Methodist Rev Jan–Feb 1909. Rabbi ben Ezra and Fitzgerald's Rubaiyát.
Gosse, E. W. In Representative biographies of English men of letters, ed C. T. Copeland and F. W. Cheney, New York 1909.
Hornbrook, F. B. The ring and the book. Boston 1909.
James, H. In Italian hours, 1909.
Mayhew, A. L. Miramoline (in Sordello). N & Q 16 Jan 1909.
Phelps, W. L. MLN June 1909.
Berger, P. Revue de Synthèse Historique 1910.
Garnett, R. and E. Garnett. In their Life of W. J. Fox, 1910. On an early friend and mentor of Browning.
Griffin, W. H. and H. C. Minchin. Life of Robert Browning, New York 1910.
Whiting, L. In her Louise Chandler Moulton, New York 1910.
Breslar, M. L. R. N & Q 21 Oct 1911. Kingsley and Browning.
Furnivall, F. J. In A volume of personal record, 1911.
Whiting, L. The Brownings: their life and art. Boston 1911.
Hosmer, H. In Harriet Hosmer, letters and memories, ed C. Carr, New York 1912. Hosmer was a one-time friend of Browning's.
James, H. Trans of the Royal Soc Lit 7 May 1912; Literary Digest 1 June 1912, 12 Sep 1912. On The ring, and James's proposed rewriting of it.
Knight, W. A. (ed). The Robert Browning centenary celebration at Westminster Abbey. 1912.
Lubbock, P. Quart Rev Oct 1912.
Macready, W. C. In Diaries 1833–51, ed W. Toynbee, 1912. Macready produced Browning's staged plays in the 1830s and 1840s.
Minchin, H. C. Fortnightly Rev 1 May 1912. Browning and Wordsworth.
New York Browning Society. Addresses commemorating the birth of Robert Browning. New York 1912.
Nichol, Sir W. R. Bookman (London) May 1912. Browning's father.
Phillips, M. A. Cornhill Mag May 1912. Browning and Mill.
Pomeroy, S. G. In her Little-known sisters of well-known men, Boston 1912. On Browning's sister Sarianna.
Singleton, A. H. Publications of the English Goethe Society. 1912. Browning and Goethe.
Ward, W. P. In Life and times of Cardinal Wiseman, 1912. On Bishop Blougram.
Young, F. Saturday Rev 11 May 1912. Browning and James.
Berger, P. Revue de Synthèse Historique Oct 1913.
Chesterton, G. K. In Victorian age in literature, New York 1913.
Lowell, J. R. In The round table, Boston 1913.
Phelps, W. L. Cent Mag Jan 1913. Browning's son's reminiscences.
Phelps, W. L. Browning in Germany. MLN Jan 1913.
Treves, Sir F. The country of 'The ring and the book'. 1913.
Ward, W. H. Independent 30 Oct 1913. On Aeschylus' soliloquy.
Whiting, L. The Brownings, their life and art. Boston 1913.
Whitney, C. E. Musical Monitor and World Oct 1913; Burk, J. N., Harvard Musical Rev Oct 1915; Harris, C. A., Calcutta Rev Apr 1916; Phelps, W. L., North Amer Rev Oct 1917. Browning as a musician.
Athenaeum 19 Dec 1914; Walker, H., Bookman (London) Feb 1915; Dial 1 Apr 1915; Burton, R., Bellman 3 Apr 1915; Contemporary Rev May 1915; Firkins, O. W., Nation 24 June 1915. Revs of New poems, ed Kenyon, 1914.
Lucas, E. V. In A wanderer in Venice, 1914. Browning and Wagner.
Carlyle, A. Cornhill Mag May 1915. Letters between Browning and Carlyle.
de Selincourt, E. in English poets and the national ideal, 1915.
Phelps, W. L. Robert Browning: how to know him. Indianapolis 1915, London 1916.
Phelps, W. L. MLN Jan 1916. Browning in France.
Symons, J. A. North Amer Rev Oct 1916. Reminiscences.
Goewey, J. M. Descriptive catalogue of the Goewey collection of Browning pictures. San Francisco 1917.

James, H. In The middle years, New York 1917.
Meade, C. J. N & Q Dec 1917. Browning: motto from Hanmer. *See also* S., W. B. Jan 1918 identifying the motto of Colombe's birthday.
Pater, W. H. In Essays from the Guardian, 1918.
C., A. K. N & Q Feb 1918. The ring and the book.
Birrell, A. In Frederick Locker-Lampson, a character-sketch, 1920. Includes letters from Browning's sister.
Cook, A. K. A commentary upon Browning's The ring and the book. Oxford 1920, New York 1966.
Elton, O. In Survey of English literature (1830–1880), New York 1920.
Pound, E. In Instigations, New York 1920. On Browning's Gr trns.
Swisher, W. S. Psychoanalytic Rev Apr 1920. Freudian interpretation of Pauline.
Wise, T. J. (ed). Letters to his son Robert Wiedemann Barrett Browning and his daughter-in-law Fanny Browning by Robert Browning. 1920.

Biographies

Orr, A. Life and letters of Browning. 1891. By a friend of Browning's: still valuable.
Miller, B. Robert Browning: a portrait. 1952. Brilliant and controversial.
Maynard, J. Browning's youth. 1977. The best for the period it treats. [JW, DK, JP]

James Drummond Burns 1823–64

Selections

Miles 10 (12).

§1

The vision of prophecy and other poems. Edinburgh 1854, 1858. 2nd edn reissued 1865.
The heavenly Jerusalem: or glimpses within the gates. 2 vols Edinburgh 1856, 1865. Essays, with 2 poems.
The evening hymn. 1857, 1880. A collection of hymns and prayers.

§2

Reminiscences of the late J. D. Burns from the Weekly Review of 17 December 1864. [1864.]
Hamilton, J. Memoir and remains of the Rev James D. Burns. 1869. Includes hymns and other verse.
Grosart, A. B. In Miles 10 (12).
Mearns, J. In Julian.

Wathen Mark Wilks Call 1817–90

Selections

Miles 4.

§1

Lyra hellenica. Cambridge 1842. Metrical trn of the Prometheus of Aeschylus and some of the Homeric hymns. With an appendix of original poems.
Reverberations. 1849, 1875 (rev, with A chapter from my autobiography), 1876 (2nd edn). Poems.
Golden histories. 1871. Poems.
REVIEWS: Westminster Rev Jan 1872; Saturday Rev 17 Feb 1872.
Final causes: a refutation. 1891. Contains a reprint of A chapter from my autobiography.
Call also contributed anon to the Westminster Rev. *His criticism includes articles on George Eliot, Carlyle and Kant.*

§2

The poems of Call. Westminster Rev 97 1872.
Obit: Athenaeum 30 Aug 1890.
Japp, A. H. In Miles 4.
Conway, M. D. Religion and progress interpreted by the life and last work of Call. Monist 2 1892. A full-length study.

George Douglas Campbell, 8th Duke of Argyll

1823–1900

Address delivered to the members of the Glasgow Athenaeum, on 21 January 1851. In The importance of literature to men of business, 1852.
The reign of law. 1866, New York 1869, 5th and cheaper edn 1870.
Primeval man. 1869. Essay.
The unity of nature. 1884.
Scotland as it was and as it is. 2 vols Edinburgh 1887.
The Highland nurse: a tale. New York [1891], London [1892].
The burdens of belief and other poems. 1894.
Poems. Edinburgh 1898.
Campbell was a prolific writer on economics, theology and popular science; see Wellesley *5 1989 and col 2517.*

Letters and papers

George Douglas, eighth Duke of Argyll: autobiography and memoirs. Ed Dowager Duchess of Argyll 1906.

Edward Caswall 1814–78

Mss: poems, letters, diaries 1846–7 (including poems), Birmingham Oratory Lib.

§1

A new art teaching how to be plucked: being a treatise after the fashion of Aristotle, writ for the use of students in the universities; to which is added fragments from the examination papers, by Scriblerus Redivivus. Oxford 1835, 1835 (2nd edn), 1874 (12th edn), new edn London 1893.
Pluck examination papers for candidates at Oxford and Cambridge in 1836, by Scriblerus Redivivus. Oxford 1836, 1836.
Morals from the churchyard, in a series of cheerful fables. 1837.
Sketches of young ladies, in which these interesting members of the animal kingdom are classified according to their several instincts, habits and general characteristics, by Quiz. 1837, 1838 (6th edn), [1869] (with Sketches of young couples, and young gentlemen by Dickens); tr Sp 1842.
Lyra catholica: containing all the breviary and missal hymns, with others from various sources. Tr Caswall 1849, 1851, 1884, New York 1851, 1884.
A Catholic hymn book for schools and private use. [1850?] [Selected from Lyra catholica.]
The masque of Mary and other poems. 1858, [1887].
L'incoronata: a tale of May. Birmingham 1860.
A May pageant and other poems. '1865' [1864], 1873 (with every line reduced by two syllables, as The tale of Tintern), [1907].
Hymns and poems, original and translated. 1872, 1873 (2nd edn); ed E. Bellasis 1908.
Caswall, who became a Roman Catholic in 1847, also wrote and translated devotional works.

§2

Julian.

Elizabeth Charles, née Rundle 1828–96

Bibliography

List of books written by Mrs Rundle Charles. In Our seven homes: autobiographical reminiscences, 1896.

Selections

Selections from the writings of the author of The Schönberg-Cotta family, by a friend. 1877. Prose.

Thoughts and characters: selections from the writings of the author of The Schönberg-Cotta family, by a friend. [1884.]

Comfort and counsel for every day from the writings of Elizabeth Rundle Charles by two of her friends. 1898. Prose and verse. Birthday book presentation.

§1

Poetry

The three wakings: with hymns and songs. 1859. Anon.

The women of the Gospels, The three wakings and other verses. 1868. New edn of above with addns.

Songs of many seasons. 1882.

Songs old and new. Collected edn 1887; enlarged edn of Women of the Gospels; rptd 1894, 1896.

Prose

Rest in Christ, or the crucifix and the cross. 1848, 1869 (2nd edn).

Tales and sketches of Christian life in different lands and ages. 1850.

The two vocations: or the sisters of mercy at home. A tale. 1853, 1858 (2nd edn).

What the Christians at Hamburg are doing: or, the poor ye have always with you. 1853.

Mary, the handmaid of the Lord. 1854.

The cripple of Antioch, and other scenes from Christian life in early times. 1856.

The song without words: leaves from a very old book. 1856.

The voice of Christian life in song: or, hymns and hymn-writers of many lands and ages. 1858, 1865 (2nd edn), 5th edn rev and enlarged as Te deum laudamus: Christian life in song. The song and the singers. 1897.

The black ship with other allegories and parables. 1861.

Wanderings over bible lands and seas. 1862.

The martyrs of Spain and the liberators of Holland: memoirs of the sisters Dolores and Constanza Cazalla. 1862.

Chronicles of the Schönberg-Cotta family. 1864, 2 vols Leipzig 1867, London 1872, 1885, [1903], [1910], [1914].
REVIEW: Literary Churchman 16 Jan 1864.

Sketches of Christian life in England in the olden time. 1864.
REVIEW: Athenaeum 9 Dec 1893.

Diary of Mrs Kitty Trevelyan: a story of the times of Whitefield and the Wesleys. 1865, New York 1865.

Winifred Bertram and the world she lived in. 1866, 1868, 1884.
REVIEW: Victoria Mag 8, Dec 1866.

The Draytons and the Davenants: a story of the civil wars. 1867.
REVIEW: Br Quart Rev 45, Jan 1867; Victoria Mag 8, Feb 1867.

On both sides of the sea: a story of the Commonwealth and the Restoration. 1868.

Diary of Brother Bartholomew with other tales and sketches of Christian life in different lands and ages. 1870. Extracts from the diary of Brother Bartholomew, a monk of the abbey of Marienthal, in the Odenwald in the 12th century. First separate issue [1910].

The victory of the vanquished: a tale of the first century. 1871.
REVIEW: Br Quart Rev 53, Jan 1878.

The cottage by the cathedral and other parables. 1872.

Against the stream: the story of an heroic age in England. 3 vols 1873, 1 vol [1882].
REVIEW: Br Quart Rev 58, Oct 1873.

The Bertram family. 1876, 1882.
REVIEW: Br Quart Rev 64, Oct 1876.

Conquering and to conquer: a story of Rome in the days of St Jerome. 1876, [1882].

Lapsed, but not lost: a story of Roman Carthage. 1877.
REVIEWS: Br Quart Rev Apr 1878; Saturday Rev 15 Apr 1882.

Joan the maid: deliverer of England and France. A story of the fifteenth century. 1879, [1894].

Sketches of the women of Christendom: dedicated to the women of India. 1880.

The raven and the angels: with other stories and parables. 1883.

An old story of Bethlehem: one link in the great pedigree. [1884.]

Three martyrs of the nineteenth century: studies from the lives of Livingstone, Gordon and Patteson. 1885.

The true vine. 1885.

The great prayer of Christendom: thoughts on the Lord's Prayer. 1886.

'By thy cross and passion': thoughts on the words spoken around and on the cross. 1887.

Martyrs and saints of the first twelve centuries: studies from the lives of the black letter saints of the English calendar. 1887.
REVIEW: Saturday Rev 22 Oct 1887.

'By the coming of the Holy Ghost': thoughts for Whitsuntide. 1888.

'By thy glorious resurrection and ascension': Easter thoughts. 1888.

The beatitudes: thoughts for all saints' days. 1889.

'By the mystery of thy holy incarnation'. [1890.]

Within the veil: studies in the epistle to the Hebrews. [1891.] Our life: an education and a sacrifice 1898 (an excerpt from Within the veil).

The book of the unveiling: studies in the Revelation of St John the Divine. 1892.

Lady Augusta Stanley. Reminiscences. 1892.

Early Christian missions of Ireland, Scotland and England. 1893.

Attila and his conquerors: a story of the days of St Patrick and St Leo the Great. [1894.]

Ecce ancilla domine: Mary the mother of our Lord. Studies in the Christian ideal of womanhood. 1894.

Ecce homo, ecce rex: pages from the story of the moral conquests of Christianity. 1895.

Our seven homes: autobiographical reminiscences. 1896.

Contributions to periodicals

Hannah More. Good Words 15, 699, 774, 845.

Translations, introductions etc.

Neander, Augustus Light in the dark places: or, memorials of Christian life in the Middle Ages. 1850.

Watchwords for the warfare of life: from Doctor Martin Luther. 1869.

Introduction to Maria A. West, The romance of missions or, inside views of life and labor, in the land of Ararat. [1876.]

Introduction to J. Williamson, Pilgrim-lays for the homeward bound and words of counsel and comfort in sunshine and shade, 1881.

Attributed or spurious works

Rest in Christ: or the crucifix and the cross. 1848. 16° pam. [On attractions of the Roman Catholic Church.]

§2

Obit: The Times 30 Mar 1896. [RS]

Arthur Hugh Clough 1819–61

The main Clough archive (poetry, prose and correspondence) is in the Bodleian; the diaries and other mss are at Balliol, and there are also collections in the Norton and Lowell papers, Houghton Lib, Harvard, and in the Turnbull Lib, Wellington NZ.

Bibliographies

Ehrsam, T. G., R. H. Deily and R. M. Smith. In Bibliographies of twelve Victorian authors, New York 1936, rptd 1968; suppl by J. G. Fucilla, MP 37 1939.

Terhune, A. M. In Victorian poets: a guide to research, ed F. E. Faverty, Cambridge MA 1957, 1967 (rev M. Timko).

Houghton, W. E. The prose works of Clough: a checklist and calendar, with some unpublished passages. BNYPL 64 1960; rev in Gollin, Houghton and Timko, *below*.

Timko, M. In Innocent Victorian: the satiric poetry of Arthur Hugh Clough, Athens OH 1966.

Gollin, R. M., W. E. Houghton and M. Timko. Clough: a descriptive catalogue. BNYPL 70 Nov 1966 and 71 Jan and Mar 1967; rev as Arthur Hugh Clough: a descriptive catalogue: poetry, prose, biography and criticism, New York [1967]. Contains unpbd verse, extensive primary lists and full secondary bibliography to 1964, with annotations.

Greenberger, E. B. Clough's undergraduate essays. In Arthur Hugh Clough: the growth of a poet's mind, Cambridge MA 1970.

Scott, P. G. Some uncollected authors 47: Arthur Hugh Clough. BC 23 1974; rev and expanded as The early editions of Arthur Hugh Clough, New York 1977.

Collections

Poems. 1862 (memoir by F. T. Palgrave), Boston 1862 (memoir by C. E. Norton), Boston 1870.
REVIEWS: [R. H. Hutton,] Spectator 12 July 1862; [H. F. Chorley,] Athenaeum 26 July 1862; Sat Rev 26 July 1862; D. Masson, Macmillan's Mag 6, Aug 1862; Parthenon 2 Aug 1862; [J. R. Findlay,] Scotsman 29 Aug 1862; [G. H. Lewes,] Cornhill Mag 6, Sep 1862; [W. Bagehot,] Nat Rev 13, Oct 1862 (rptd in Literary Studies, 1879, and Collected works, ed N. St John Stevas, vol 2 1965); North Amer Rev 95, Oct 1862; Church and State Rev 1, Oct and Dec 1862; [W. L. Collins,] Blackwood's Mag 92, Nov 1862; [W. Y. Sellar,] North Br Rev 37, Nov 1862; Br Controversialist, n.s. 9 1863; [R. W. Church,] Christian Remembrancer 45, Jan 1863; Boston Rev 3, Mar 1863.

Poems. 2nd edn 1863 (memoir by Palgrave, texts slightly rev, with additional poems), [1906] (ML).
REVIEW: [R. H. Hutton,] Spectator 10 Oct 1863.

Letters and remains. [Ed Mrs Clough] 1865 (priv ptd). Includes Dipsychus and unpbd poems.
REVIEWS: [J. A. Symonds,] Cornhill Mag 14, Oct 1866; [William Allingham,] Fraser's Mag 74, Oct 1866; [W. H. Smith,] Macmillan's Mag 15, Dec 1866; [C. E. Norton,] North Amer Rev 105, Oct 1867.

Poems and prose remains. Ed Mrs Clough [and J. A. Symonds]. 2 vols 1869 (with memoir by Mrs Clough); rptd St Clair Shores MI [1969].
REVIEWS: Athenaeum 15 Aug 1869; [R. H. Hutton,] Spectator 11 Sep 1869 (rptd in Essays; theological and literary 1871 and Literary essays 1892); Sat Rev 18 Sep 1869; [M. Collins?,] Br Quart Rev 50, Oct 1869; [Henry Sidgwick,] Westminster Rev 92, Oct 1869; (rptd in Miscellaneous essays and addresses, 1904); Guardian 6 Oct 1869; H. de B. Hollings, Academy 9 Oct 1869; Every Sat 16 Oct 1869; Once a Week 16 Oct 1869; John Dowden, Contemporary Rev 12, Dec 1869; Table-talk, Putnam's Mag 4, Dec 1869.

Poems. 1871 (with memoir by Mrs Clough), 1874, 1877, 1878, 1879, 1880, 1882; reset 1883, 1885.

Poems. 1888, 1890, 1892, 1895, 1898, 1903, 1909.

Prose remains. 1888.

Poems. Ed H. S. Milford 1910. The first scholarly collation of variant texts.

Poems (var title Poetical works). New York 1911.

Poems. 1913 (with memoir by C. Whibley), 1920.

Poems. Ed H. F. Lowry, A. L. P. Norrington and F. L. Mulhauser, Oxford 1951. Main text (pp. 1–296) rptd with introd by Norrington 1968 (OSA), 1986.
REVIEW: R. M. Gollin, MP 60 1962.

Selected prose works. Ed. B. B. Trawick, Tuscaloosa AL 1964.
REVIEW: K. Allott, N & Q 210 1965.

Poems (second edn rev and expanded). Ed F. L. Mulhauser, trns ed J. Turner, 1974 (Oxford English Texts). The definitive edn with much additional mss material.

Selections

The Bothie and other poems. Ed E. Rhys (Canterbury Poets) [1884], 1896.

The love story of a young man; or 'The Bothie of Tober-na-vuolich', and other poems. (Penny Poets xxix) [1892]; (Penny Poets in Sixpenny Volumes, no 2) [1892].

Selections from the poems. Ed. Mrs Clough (Golden Treasury) 1894, 1894, 1904, 1909 etc.

Poems. (Oxford Plain Texts) Oxford 1912, 1914, 1915.

Selected poems. Ed F. H. Langman, Canberra 1964.

Selection. Ed J. Purkis (Longmans English Series), Harlow 1967.

A choice of Clough's verse. Ed M. Thorpe 1969.

Selected poems. Ed S. Chew (Fyfield Books), Manchester 1987.

Selected poems. Ed J. McCue (Pen), 1991.

Selected poems. Ed J. P. Phelan (Longmans Annotated Texts), Harlow and New York 1995.

§1

The close of the eighteenth century: a prize poem (anon). Rugby 1835.

The longest day: a poem, written ... June 1836. [Rugby? 1840–8]; *see* Harris, 1967, and Scott, The title-page of Clough's The longest day, 1971, *under Textual and bibliographical studies, below*.

A consideration of objections against the Retrenchment Association. Oxford 1847.

The Bothie of Toper-na-fuosich: a long-vacation pastoral. Oxford 1848, Cambridge MA 1849; reissued with rev, in Poems, London 1862; ed and annotated by P. Scott, St Lucia, Queensland 1967.
REVIEWS: Spectator 2 Dec 1848; [C. Kingsley,] Fraser's Mag 39, Jan 1849; R. W. Emerson, Mass Quart Rev 2, Mar 1849 (rptd in his Uncollected writings, New York 1912); C. A. Bristed, Literary World 4, June 1849; Literary Gazette 18 Aug 1849; W. M. Rossetti, Germ 1, Jan 1850; [W. Whewell,] English hexameters, North Br Rev 19, May 1853; [R. H. Hutton,] Mr. Clough's long-vacation pastoral, Spectator 12 July 1862.

Ambarvalia. (with poems by T. Burbidge) 1849; Clough's section separately bound as Poems [1849], [1850?], [1852?].
REVIEWS: Spectator 20 Jan 1849; Athenaeum 10 Feb 1849; Guardian 28 Mar 1849; Literary Gazette 21 Apr 1849; [J. Conington?,] Fraser's Mag 39, May 1849; Rambler 4, July 1849; [T. H. Gill,] Prospective Rev 6, Jan 1850; English Rev 13, Mar 1850.

Specimen pages of Plutarch's lives. Boston 1855.

Plutarch's lives: the translation called Dryden's corrected from the Greek and revised. 5 vols Boston 1859, 1861, 1863, 1864, 1865, 1868, 1871, 1872, 1874, 1875, 1878, 1881, 1882, 1885, 1888, 1891, 1895, 1899, 1902, 1905, 1907, 1909, 1910; separate London issue 5 vols 1859; also as Plutarch's lives of illustrious men, 1 vol Boston 1876, 1880 etc; in Plutarch's lives and writings, 10 vols Boston 1909 (Book Lover's edn); ed E. Rhys 3 vols 1910 etc (EL); 1 vol New York 1932 etc (Mod Lib); 1 vol Chicago 1952 etc (Great Books of Western World); selection New York 1909; selection ed E. Fuller, 2 vols New York 1959, 1969 (Laurel Classics).
REVIEWS: Athenaeum 24 Sep 1859; North Amer Rev 89, Oct 1859; The Times 12 Dec 1859; [F. L. Lushington,] Nat Rev 10, Apr 1860; [W. B. Donne,] Westminster Rev 73, Apr 1860.

Greek history from Themistocles to Alexander in a series of lives from Plutarch. 1860; new ed, 1866, 1868.

Contributions to periodicals etc

See R. M. Gollin et al, Descriptive catalogue, *above, pts 1 and 2, for itemized lists.*

[25 poems and 13 prose pieces.] Rugby Mag 2 vols 1835–7.

A stray valentine. Youth's Literary Messenger 2, Philadelphia 1838.

Verses written in a diary. Youth's Literary Messenger 2, Philadelphia 1838.

He sate, no stiller stands a rock. In T. Burbidge, Poems longer and shorter, 1838; *see* S. Nowell-Smith, TLS 8 Mar 1974.

[77 brief biographies.] In Dictionary of Greek and Roman biography and myth, ed W. Smith 3 vols 1844–9.
I give thee joy. Balance 30 Jan 1846.
Letter to the editor, Political economy, The militia, Expensive living, A few practical hints, Spirit of trade. Balance 23 and 30 Jan, 6 and 13 Feb, 6 and 20 Mar 1846. Signed 'M. A. O.'
Differ to agree. Balance 13 Feb 1846.
Illustrations of Latin lyrical metres. Classical Museum 4 1847. *See* G. Tillotson, TLS 18 June 1954.
[2 letters to the editor.] Spectator 6 and 20 Nov 1847. Signed 'Alpha'.
Letter. In Testimonials in favour of Mr. Francis R. Sandford [Edinburgh 1852]. *See* R. M. Gollin, N & Q 203 1958.
Letter. In Testimonials in favour of Mr. Bonamy Price [Edinburgh 1852].
Letter. In Oxford University Commission: report of her Majesty's Commissioners appointed to inquire into the state, discipline, studies and revenues of the University and colleges of Oxford, Cmnd [1482], Parliamentary Papers Session 1852, vol 22, 1852.
Last words: Napoleon and Wellington. Fraser's Mag 46, Feb 1853.
Oxford University Commission. North Amer Rev 76, Apr 1853.
As ships, becalmed. In Thalatta: a book for the seaside, ed S. Longfellow and T. W. Higginson, Boston 1853.
Recent English poetry. North Amer Rev 77, July 1853.
Recent social theories. North Amer Rev 77, July 1853.
Upon the water in a boat. Putnam's Mag 2, July 1853.
In vain I seem to call. Putnam's Mag 2, July 1853.
Letters of Paripedemus, 1 and 2. Putnam's Mag 2, July and Aug 1853.
My dear sir, here is a chapter. Putnam's Mag 2, Aug 1853.
Considerations on some recent social theories. Westminster Rev 60, Oct 1853.
Contemporary literature of America [collab]. Westminster Rev 60, Oct 1853.
Peschiera. Putnam's Mag 3, May 1854.
The struggle. Crayon 2, Aug 1855. *See* F. G. Townsend, PMLA 67 1952.
Amours de Voyage. Atlantic Monthly 1, Feb–May 1858; rev in Poems 1862; ed and annotated by P. Scott, St Lucia, Queensland 1974.
Poems and ballads of Goethe. Fraser's Mag 59, June 1859.

Letters, journals etc

See also Letters and remains, 1865; Poems and prose remains, 1869, *above; the Rugby jnls remain unpbd.*
Letters of Matthew Arnold to Arthur Hugh Clough. Ed H. F. Lowry, Oxford 1932; rptd Oxford 1968, Folcroft PA 1969.
Emerson–Clough letters. Ed H. F. Lowry and R. L. Rusk, Cleveland OH 1934, New York 1968, Folcroft PA 1977; rptd in Correspondence of Emerson and Carlyle, ed J. Slater, New York 1957, and in Correspondence, ed Mulhauser 1957, *below*.
K. Allott. An Arnold–Clough letter. N & Q 201 1956.
Correspondence. Ed F. L. Mulhauser, 2 vols Oxford 1957. Vol 2 contains 'Appendix C: Catalogue of all known letters'.
Green, D. B. Clough and the Parkers. N & Q 208 1963. Two letters to J. W. Parker, enclosing poem 'Last words'.
Peattie, R. W. William Michael Rossetti. TLS 30 July 1964. Letter from Clough.
New Zealand letters of Thomas Arnold the younger, with . . . letters of Arthur Hugh Clough 1847–51. Ed J. Bertram, Wellington NZ 1966.
Stubbs, J. K. An unpublished letter of A. H. Clough. N & Q 212 1967.
Winnifrith, T. J. Matthew Arnold and Clough. N & Q 216 1971. Clough letter of Aug 1850.
Leach, S. J. Two new letters from Arthur Hugh Clough. N & Q 221 1976. To R. M. Milnes.
Tener, R. H. Clough to Bagehot: a new letter. N & Q 222 1977.
Oxford diaries. Ed A. Kenny, Oxford 1989.

§2

Biographies

See Poems and prose remains, 1869, *above*.
Levy, G. Arthur Hugh Clough: 1819–1861. 1938.
Johari, G. P. Arthur Hugh Clough at Oriel and University Hall. PMLA 66 1951.
Chorley, K. Arthur Hugh Clough: the uncommitted mind. 1962.
Veyriras, P. Arthur Hugh Clough (1819–1861). Paris 1964.
Biswas, R. K. Arthur Hugh Clough: towards a reconsideration. Oxford 1972. The fullest modern biography.

Textual and bibliographical studies

Jervey, C. (comp). Inscriptions on the tablets and gravestones in St Michael's Church and Churchyard, Charleston, South Carolina. Ed C. Jervey, Columbia SC 1906. Prints epitaph for G. A. Clough. *See also* Garrod, Polhemus *and* Savory, *below*.
Garrod, H. W. In his Poetry and the criticism of life, Cambridge MA 1931. Prints epitaph; *see* Jervey, *above*.
Ms of 'Say not' at Sotheby's. N & Q 181 1941.
Mulhauser, F. L. Clough's 'Love and Reason'. MP 42 1945.
Norrington, A. L. P. 'Say not, the struggle nought availeth'. In Essays mainly on the nineteenth century presented to Sir Humphrey Milford, Oxford 1948.
Robertson, D. A., Jr. Clough's 'Say not' in ms. N & Q 196 1951.
Townsend, F. G. Clough's The struggle: the text, title, and date of publication. PMLA 67 1952.
Gift of manuscripts of poetical works of A. H. Clough. BLR 4 1953.
Tillotson, G. New verses by Arthur Hugh Clough. TLS 18 June 1954.
Bertram, J. The ending of Clough's Dipsychus. RES n.s. 7 1956.
Polhemus, G. W. A Clough epitaph. N & Q 204 1959. *See* Jervey, *above*.
Gollin, R. M. The 1951 edition of Clough's poems: a critical re-examination. MP 60 1962.
Borrie, M. A. F. Three poems of Arthur Hugh Clough. BM Quart 27 1963. Bethesda, a sequel; The latest decalogue; and O stream, descending.
Barish, E. A new Clough manuscript. RES n.s. 15 1964. Solvitur acris hiems.
Nowell-Smith, S. Contemporary collectors 41: the Ewelme collection. BC 14 1965.
Randall, D. A. Variant bindings of Clough's poems. BC 14 1965.
Harris, W. The curious provenience of Clough's 'The longest day'. N & Q 212 1967.
Scott, P. G. The text and structure of Clough's 'Latest decalogue'. N & Q 212 1967.
Barish, E. Salsette and Elephanta: an unpublished poem by Clough. RES n.s. 20 1969.
Bertram, J. An unpublished poem by Clough. N & Q 214 1969. On the marriage of the professor of astronomy.
Barish, E. Clough's The judgement of Brutus: a newly found poem. VP 8 1970.
Barish, E. [Greenberger]. Appendix B: new poetry and prose. In Arthur Hugh Clough: the growth of a poet's mind, Cambridge MA 1970.
Scott, P. G. Clough's The Bothie of Toper-na-fuosich. BC 19 1970. Bindings.
Scott, P. G. Further notes on Clough bindings. BC 19 1970.
Scott, P. G. The publication of Clough's Ambarvalia poems. BC 19 1970.
Muirhead, A. Clough's The Bothie of Toper-na-fuosich. BC 20 1971.
Scott, P. G. A second edition of the Rugby Magazine, no 1. BC 20 1971.
Sparrow, J. Clough's The Bothie of Toper-na-fuosich. BC 20 1971.
Wynn, Marjorie G. The Clough bindings. BC 20 1971.
Scott, P. G. The title-page of Clough's The longest day. Library 5th ser 25 1971.
Scott, P. G. An unlisted Clough poem. N & Q 216 1971. Breaking-up.

Leedham-Green, E. S. Four unpublished translations by Arthur Hugh Clough. RES n.s. 23 1972.

Mulhauser, F. L. The manuscript of 'Dipsychus continued'. N & Q 217 1972.

Scott, P. G. A. H. Clough's poems (1862): the English and American editions. HLB 20 1972.

Rutland, R. B. The genesis of Clough's Bothie. VP 11 1973.

Nowell-Smith, S. An unascribed Clough poem. TLS 8 Mar 1974. He sate, no stiller.

McGrane, P. S. Unpublished poetic fragments and manuscripts. VP 14 1976. Additions to Poems, ed Mulhauser 1974.

Savory, J. An epitaph poem by Arthur Hugh Clough. VP 14 1976. *See* Jervey, *above*.

Oliver, H. The Shore Smith family library: Arthur Hugh Clough and Florence Nightingale. BC 28 1979.

Scott, P. G. The editorial problem in Clough's Adam and Eve. Browning Institute Stud 9 1981.

Burnett, A. A Clough poem – by Macaulay. N & Q 235 1990. A woman fair and stately.

Phelan, J. P. The textual evolution of Clough's Dipsychus and the Spirit. RES 46 1995.

Landmark Works of Criticism

See also Clough: the critical heritage, ed M. Thorpe, 1972.

Powell, T. Burbidge and Clough. In Living authors of England, New York 1849.

[Hutton, R. H. and T. Hughes.] Clough – in memoriam. Spectator 23 Nov 1861.

Arnold, M. In On translating Homer, 1861; in Complete prose works, ed R. H. Super, vol 1, Ann Arbor MI 1960.

Arnold, M. Thyrsis. Every Sat 10 Mar 1866; Macmillan's Mag 13, Apr 1866; New Poems 1867.

[Lowell, J. R.] Swinburne's tragedies. North Amer Rev 102, Apr 1866; rptd in My study windows, 1871.

[Norton, C. E.] Clough. North Amer Rev 105, Oct 1867.

[Symonds, J. A.] Arthur Hugh Clough. Fortnightly Rev 10, Dec 1868; rptd in Last and first, ed A. Morell, New York 1919.

[Mozley, J. R.] Modern English poets. Quart Rev 126, Apr 1869.

Shairp, J. C. Balliol Scholars 1840–1843. Macmillan's Mag 27, Mar 1873; rptd in Glen Dessaray and other poems, ed F. T. Palgrave, 1888.

[Brown, J. B.] Scepticism and modern poetry. Blackwood's Mag 115, Feb 1874; rev in 'J. B. Selkirk', Ethics and aesthetics of modern poetry, 1878.

Lyttelton, A. T. The poetry of doubt. Church Quart Rev 6, Apr 1878; rptd in Modern poets of faith, doubt and paganism, 1904.

[Hutton, R. H.] The unpopularity of Clough. Spectator 25 Nov 1882; rptd in Brief literary criticisms, ed E. M. Roscoe, 1906.

Waddington, S. Arthur Hugh Clough: a monograph. 1883.

[Hutton, R. H.] Amiel and Clough. Spectator 9 Jan 1886; rptd in Brief literary criticisms, 1906.

Patmore, C. Clough. St James Gazette 10 Aug 1888; rptd in Principle in art, 1889.

Swinburne, A. C. Social verse. Forum 12 1891; rptd in Complete works, ed E. Gosse and T. J. Wise, vol 15, 1926.

Hudson, W. H. In Studies in interpretation, 1896.

Robertson, J. M. In New essays toward a critical method, 1897. Reply, Academy 2 Oct 1897; response by E. Forster, Academy 23 Oct 1897.

Arnold, T. Clough: a sketch. Nineteenth Century 93, Jan 1898.

Brooke, S. A. In Four Victorian poets, 1908.

Huth, A. O. Über Clough's the Bothie of Toper-na-fuosich. Leipzig 1911.

Lutonsky, P. Clough. Vienna 1912.

Guyot, E. Essai sur la formation philosophique du poète Clough. Paris 1913.

Anon. Arthur Hugh Clough. Contemporary Rev 105, Feb 1914.

Osborne, J. I. Arthur Hugh Clough. 1919, New York 1920.

Shackford, M. H. The Clough centenary: his Dipsychus. Sewanee Rev 27 1919; rev in Studies of certain nineteenth-century poets, Natick MA 1946.

Houghton, W. E. The poetry of Clough: an essay in revaluation. New Haven CT 1963. The landmark study in Clough's modern reappraisal. [PS]

Sara Coleridge 1802–52

See also S. T. Coleridge, col 297, above. Sara Coleridge's ms essays, diaries and a number of letters are housed at the HRHRC, Austin TX.

Selections

Miles 7 (8).

§1

Account of the Abipones, translated from the Latin of M. Dobrizhöffer. 3 vols 1822.

The right joyous and pleasant history of the feats, gests and prowesses of the Chevalier Bayard, translated from the French. 2 vols 1825, 1 vol [1906].

Pretty lessons in verse for good children. 1834, 1835, 1839, 1845, 1853, 1875, 1927.

Phantasmion. 1837 (anon), 2 vols New York 1839; ed Lord Coleridge, London 1874, Boston 1874. A fairy tale with lyrics.

On rationalism. In S. T. Coleridge, Aids to reflection vol 2, 1843.

January brings the snow. New York 1986, London 1989, New York 1989 (juvenile edns).

For two reviews by Sara Coleridge, see Wellesley *vol 5 1989.*

§2

[Coleridge, H. N.] Quart Rev 66 1840. Long review of Sara Coleridge, Caroline Bowles, Elizabeth Barrett et al.

Memoir and letters of Sara Coleridge. Ed E. Coleridge 2 vols 1873, 1875 (4th edn abridged), 1 vol New York 1874, rptd 1973.

Garnett, R. In Miles 7 (8).

Towle, E. A. A poet's children: Hartley and Sara Coleridge. 1912.

Wilson, M. In his These were Muses, 1924.

Sara Coleridge and Henry Reed. Ed L. N. Broughton, Ithaca NY 1937. Includes Reed's memoir of Sara Coleridge and her letters to Reed.

Griggs, E. L. Coleridge fille: a biography of Sara Coleridge. Oxford 1940, rptd Folcroft PA 1973, Norwood PA 1976, Philadelphia 1977.

Woolf, V. In her Death of the moth and other essays, 1942.

Raymond, M. B. A letter from Sara Coleridge. TWC 15 1984.

Mudge, B. K. Sara Coleridge: a Victorian daughter. New Haven CT 1989. With a textual appendix: the essays of Sara Coleridge.

Woolf, D. Sara Coleridge's marginalia. Coleridge Bull n.s. 2 Autumn 1993. [PL]

John Conington 1825–69

The victory of suffering: a prize poem. 1842.

The Agamemnon, with a translation into English verse and notes. 1848, 1907.

The Choephoroe translated into English with notes. 1857.

The poetry of Pope. In Oxford essays, 1858.

The works of Virgil, with a commentary. 3 vols 1858. Many selections and abridgements followed.

The University of Oxford and the Greek Chair. Oxford 1863.

The odes and Carmen saeculare of Horace, translated. 1863, 1903 (with Latin text).

The Aeneid of Virgil, translated. 1866.

The style of Lucretius and Catullus as compared with that of the Augustan poets: a lecture. 1867.

The satires, epistles and Art of poetry of Horace, translated into English verse. 1870, 1904 (with Latin text).

The satires of A. Persius Flaccus, with a translation and commentary. Oxford 1872.

Miscellaneous writings. Ed J. A. Symonds with a memoir by H. J. S. Smith 2 vols 1872. Includes King Lear, Hamlet, The English translators of Virgil, Six lectures on Latin literature, The poems of Virgil translated into English prose, Fables of Babrius etc.
The poems of Virgil, translated. 1882. Rptd from Miscellaneous writings, *above*.
See also Wellesley *vol 5 1989*.

Eliza Cook 1812–89

Collections

Poems. 4 vols 1846–53.
Poems. 3 vols [1848?], vol 1 5th edn 1848; vol 2 3rd edn 1848, vol 3 1848.
REVIEW: Literary Gazette 17 Feb 1849.
Poetical works. Philadelphia 1853.
Poems. A new edn in 1 vol 1859, reissued 1864.
Auswahl englischer Gedichte der Eliza Cook, aus dem Englischen in's Deutsche übertragen von Hermann Simon. Leipzig 1865.
Poetical works. 1870, New York [1882], [1905], [1920]. A complete edn (Chandos Classics).
Poetical works. [1874?], New York [1874?].

Selections

Poems: selected and edited by the author. 1861.
Miles 7 (8).
Selections from the poems of Mrs Hemans and the patriotic poems of Eliza Cook. [1895?] Masterpiece Lib 38.

§1

Lays of a wild harp: a collection of metrical pieces. 1835.
Melaia and other poems. 1838, 1840 (with addns from Lays of a wild harp).
REVIEW: NMM Nov 1839.
Poems: second series. 1845.
Eliza Cook's journal. May 1849–54. A weekly periodical ed and partly written by Eliza Cook. Many of her poems first pbd here, as well as the aphorisms collected in Diamond dust.
I'm afloat. [1850?] Songs.
The Englishman: two songs. [1850?]
Songs of the haymakers: Standard bearer and In this old chair my father sat. [1850?]
Mother be proud of your boy in blue. [1860?] Songs.
Songs of the haymakers: gipsy's tent. [1860?]
Jottings from my journal. 1860. Short essays, several rptd from Eliza Cook's journal.
New echoes, and other poems. 1864.
REVIEWS: Athenaeum 10 Dec 1864; Saturday Rev 10 Dec 1864; Reader 11 Feb 1865.
Diamond dust. 1865. A collection of aphorisms, mostly original.
REVIEWS: Athenaeum 30 Dec 1865; Reader 30 Dec 1865.
Cook's poems appeared also in Catholic World, Metropolitan Mag, NMM, Once a Week, *and* Weekly Dispatch. *Her journalism was pbd in* Eclectic Mag *and* Nat Mag.

§2

In Notable women of our own times, [1883?].
Obit: The Times 26 Sep 1889; Athenaeum 28 Sep 1889. [RS]

Thomas Cooper, 'Adam Hornbook' 1805–92

Mss: Notebook *(including poems) 184–, papers, letters, Lincolnshire Archives Office.* The purgatory of suicides, *Lincoln Central Lib.*

Bibliographies

List of published works in R. J. Conklin, Cooper the Chartist, Manilla 1935.

Collections

Poetical works. 1877, 1886.

§1

The Wesleyan chiefs and other poems. 1833.
Wise Saws and modern instances. 2 vols 1845, 1 vol 1874 (enlarged as Old-fashioned stories). Short stories and sketches.
The purgatory of suicides: a prison-rhyme in ten books. 1845, 1847, 1853 (3rd edn).
The Baron's yule feast: a Christmas-rhyme. 1846.
The land for the labourers, and the fraternity of nations: a scheme for a new industrial system, published in Paris, and intended for proposal to the National Assembly. [1848.] Ed Cooper.
The life and character of Henry Hetherington. 1849. Abridged from Cooper's éloge by G. J. Holyoake.
The plain speaker. 1849. Ed Cooper.
Captain Cobler, or the Lincolnshire rebellion: an historical romance of the reign of Henry VIII. 1850.
Cooper's journal: or unfetterd thinker and plain speaker for truth, freedom and progress. [1850], facs reprint New York 1970.
Eight letters to the young men of the working-classes. 1851. Rptd from Plain Speaker. Advice on the art of living.
Alderman Ralph: or the history of the borough of Willowacre, by Adam Hornbook. 2 vols 1853.
The family feud: a tale by Adam Hornbook. 1855.
The bridge of history over the gulf of time: a popular view of the historical evidence for the truth of Christianity. 1871, 1880, 1892.
The life of Thomas Cooper, written by himself. 1872, 1873 (4th edn), facs reprint, intro J. Saville, Leicester 1971.
Plain pulpit talk. 1872, 1874 3rd thousand; The atonement and other discourses: being a second series of Plain pulpit talk, 1880.
The paradise of martyrs: a faith rhyme, part first, in five books. 1873. No further pts pbd.
Evolution, the stone book and the Mosaic record of creation. 1878.
Thoughts at fourscore and earlier: a medley. 1885. Includes the Letters to the young working men.
Cooper also edited and contributed to numerous Chartist and other jnls including Chartist Pioneer *(ed)*, Douglas Jerrold's Shilling Mag, English Chartist, Howitt's Jnl, Leicester Mercury, Lloyd's Illustrated Weekly, Midland Counties Illuminator *(ed)*, Northern Tribune and Reasoner. *He also pbd theological works and sermons.*

§2

Holyoake, G. J. Cooper delineated as convert and controversialist. [1861.]
Cazamian, L. Kingsley et Cooper: étude sur une source d'Alton Locke. Paris 1903.
Conklin, R. J. Cooper the Chartist. Manilla 1935, 1936.
Hobman, D. L. Cooper, Chartist and poet. Contemporary Rev Oct 1948.

William Davies 1829/30–97

§1

Songs of a wayfarer. 1869.
The shepherd's garden. 1873. Poems.
The pilgrimage of the Tiber from its mouth to its source, with some account of its tributaries. 1873.
A fine old English gentleman, exemplified in the life and character of Lord Collingwood: a biographical study. 1875.
Dante Alighieri and his works. 1888.
Letters of James Smetham; memoir by W. Davies. 1891. Ed with S. Smetham et al.
The literary works of James Smetham. 1893. Ed Davies.
Davies contributed to Fortnightly Rev, Quarterly Rev *and* Temple Bar.
See Wellesley *vol 5, pp. 208–9. See also* Wellesley *vol 5 1989.*

§2

Obit: The Times 12 May 1897; Athenaeum 15 May 1897.

Thomas Osborne Davis 1814–45

Mss: Notebooks, poems, songs and prose pieces, Dublin, Royal Irish Acad Lib.

Collections

The poems, now first collected, with notes and historical illustrations. Dublin 1846, New York 1854, new edn ed J. Mitchel 1868.
Prose writings. Ed T. Rolleston [1889].
Selections from his prose and poetry. Ed T. Rolleston [1910?], London and Leipzig 1914.

§1

An address read before the historical society, Dublin, on the 26th June 1840. 1840.
The speeches of the Right Honourable John Philpot Curran. Ed Davis 1843, 1845 (with memoir); 1855, 1861 (2nd edn).
The spirit of the nation. Ballads and songs by the writers of The Nation. Dublin 1845.
The life of the Right Hon J. P. Curran. Dublin 1846, [1846?] (7th edn).
Literary and historical essays. Ed C. G. Duffy, Dublin 1846.
Letters of a Protestant, on repeal. Dublin 1847.
Poems. Ed J. Mitchel, New York 1868.
Essay on Irish songs. 1869.
The patriot parliament of 1689, with its statutes, votes and proceedings. Ed C. G. Duffy. Dublin and New York 1893.
National and other poems. Dublin 1907.
Essays, literary and historical. Dundalk 1914 (Centenary edn). With preface and notes by D. O'Donoghue and an essay by J. Mitchel.
Essays and poems, with a centenary memoir. Dublin 1945.
Songs, ballads and poems. Dublin 1945.

§2

The poems of Davis. Irish Quart Rev 5 1852.
Davis the thinker and teacher: the essence of his writings in prose and poetry. Ed A. Griffith, Dublin 1914.
Duffy, C. G. Davis: the memoirs of an Irish patriot 1840–6. 1890.
Duffy, C. G. Short life of Davis 1840–6. 1895.
Schiller, J. Davis: ein irischer Freiheitssänger. Vienna 1915. With bibliography.
Ahern, J. L. Thomas Davis and his circle, etc. Waterford 1945.
Yeats, W. B. Tribute to Thomas Davis. Cork 1947, 1965.
Gwynn, D. Denny Lane and Thomas Davis. Studies 38 1949.
Gwynn, D. John E. Pigot and Thomas Davis. Studies 38 1949.

Aubrey Thomas de Vere 1814–1902

Bibliographies

Winckler, P. and W. Stone. De Vere: a bibliography. Victorian Newsletter 10 1956.

Collections

Poetical works. 6 vols 1884–98. Vol 2 rptd London and New York 1895, vols 4–6 rptd London and New York 1897–8.
De Vere's poems: a selection. Ed J. Dennis 1890.
Selections from the poems. Ed G. Woodberry, New York and London 1894.
Poems from the works of de Vere. Ed M. Domvile 1904.

§1

A song of faith, devout exercises and sonnets. 1842.
The Waldenses, or the fall of Rora: a lyrical sketch, with other poems. Oxford and London 1842.
The search after Proserpine, Recollections of Greece and other poems. Oxford and London 1843.
Mary Tudor, an historical drama, The lamentation of Ireland and other poems. 1847, new edn 1884. Ed de Vere.
English misrule and Irish misdeeds: four letters from Ireland addressed to an English Member of Parliament. 1848, 2nd edn 1848; reissued New York and London 1970.
Picturesque sketches of Greece and Turkey. 2 vols 1850, Philadelphia 1850.
Poems. 1855.
May carols: or ancilla domini. 1857, New York 1866 (as May carols, or The month of Mary), London 1870 (with addns), 1881 (with addns).
Julian, the apostate, and The Duke of Mercia. 1858. Drama.
Select specimens of the English poets. Ed de Vere 1858.
The sisters, Inisfail and other poems. London and Dublin 1861.
Inisfail: a lyrical chronicle of Ireland. Dublin 1863.
Hymns and sacred poems. London, Dublin and Derby 1864.
The month of Mary. 1864. A selection from May carols, *above*.
The infant bridal and other poems. 1864, new and enlarged edn [1876].
Thoughts on St Gertrude. London and Dublin [1864–5].
The Church settlement of Ireland: or Hibernia pacanda. London and Dublin 1866, 1866.
The Church Establishment in Ireland, illustrated exclusively by Protestant authorities. London and Dublin 1867.
Ireland's church property, and the right use of it. London and Dublin 1867.
The life of S. Aloysius Gonzaga. Ed E. H. Thompson [1867].
Pleas for secularization. London and Dublin 1867.
Reply to certain strictures by Myles O'Reilly Esq. London and Dublin 1868.
Ireland's Church question: five essays. 1868. Collects The Church settlement of Ireland; The Church Establishment in Ireland; Ireland's church property; Pleas for secularization; Reply to certain strictures by Myles O'Reilly Esq, *above*.
Irish odes and other poems. New York 1869.
The legends of Saint Patrick. London and Dublin 1872, London 1889, 1905.
Alexander the Great: a dramatic poem. London and Dublin 1874.
Sonnets . . . a new edn with memoir by A. T. de Vere. 1875.
St Thomas of Canterbury: a dramatic poem. 1876.
Antar and Zara: an eastern romance; Inisfail and other poems meditative and lyrical. 1877.
The fall of Rora, The search after Proserpine and other poems meditative and lyrical. 1877.
Proteus and Amadeus: a correspondence [with W. S. Blunt]. Ed A. T. de Vere 1878.
Legends of the Saxon saints. 1879, 1893.
The children of Lir: an Irish legend. [New York] [1881].
Constitutional and unconstitutional political action. Limerick 1881.
The foray of Queen Maeve, and other legends of Ireland's heroic age. 1882.
Ireland and proportional representation. Dublin and London 1885.
Essays, chiefly on poetry. 2 vols London and New York 1887.
Legends and records of the Church and the Empire. 1887.
Saint Peter's chains, or Rome and the Italian revolution: a series of sonnets. London and New York [1888].
Essays, chiefly literary and ethical. 1889, London and New York 1889.
The household poetry book: an anthology of English speaking poets from Chaucer to Faber. Ed de Vere 1893.
Medieval records and sonnets. 1893.
Religious problems of the nineteenth century: essays. Ed J. Wenham 1893.
The search after Proserpine and other poems. 1896.
Recollections. London and New York 1897.

§2

Taylor, H. In his Notes from books, 1849.
[Dixon, W.] The poetry of the de Veres. Quart Rev 183 1896; rptd in his In the republic of letters, 1898.

Towle, E. Recollections of de Vere. Sewanee Rev 7 1899.
Woodberry, G. De Vere on poetry. In his Makers of literature, New York 1900.
Ward, Wilfred P. Aubrey de Vere: a memoir based on his unpublished diaries and correspondence. 1904.
Pijpers, T. A. Aubrey de Vere as a man of letters. Utrecht [1941].

Sydney Thompson Dobell, 'Sydney Yendys' 1824–74

Collections

Poems: author's edition. Boston 1860. England in time of war, Sonnets on the war, other poems, Roman, Balder.
Poetical works, with introductory notice and memoir by J. Nichol. 2 vols 1875.
Poems, selected. Canterbury edn. 1887.
Miles 5.
Home in war time: poems selected. Ed W. G. Hutchinson 1900.

§1

The Roman: a dramatic poem by Sydney Yendys. 1850, 1852.
Balder: part the first. 1853, 1854 (adds preface). Pt 2 never completed; fragments are ptd in Thoughts on art, philosophy and religion, *below*.
Sonnets on the war. 1855. With Alexander Smith.
England in time of war. 1856. Poems.
Love, to a little girl. 1863. In verse.
Of parliamentary reform: a letter to a politician. 1865.
America. [1869.] 2 sonnets written in 1855.
Thoughts on art, philosophy and religion. Ed J. Nichol 1876. Selected from unpbd works of Dobell.
Home in war time. 1900.

Letters and papers

Life and letters. Ed E. J[olly] 2 vols 1878.

§2

The Roman. Athenaeum 13 Apr 1850, 14 Jan 1854.
Balder. Fraser's Mag July 1854.
'Jones, T. P.' (W. E. Aytoun). Firmilian, or the student of Badajoz: a spasmodic tragedy. Edinburgh 1854. Ridicules Dobell and the Spasmodic School of poetry.
Gilfillan, G. In his A third gallery of literary portraits, Edinburgh 1854.
Oliphant, M. Modern light literature. Blackwood's Edinburgh Mag 79, Feb 1856.
Patmore, C. New poets. Edinburgh Rev 104, Oct 1856.
Eliot, G. Belles lettres. Westminster Rev 10 n.s. Oct 1860.
Buchanan, R. Sydney Dobell. Temple Bar 56, May 1879.
Buchanan, R. W. In his A look around literature, 1887.
Garnett, R. In Miles 5.
Sackville, Lady M. and E. Dobell. Dobell, nature poet. Poetry Rev 35 1944.
Thale, J. Dobell's Roman: the poet's experience and his work. Amer Imago 12 1955.
Preyer, R. Dobell and the Victorian epic. UTQ 30 1961.
Donnelly, D. Philistine taste in Victorian poetry. VP 1978.
Pittock, M. Dobell, Balder and post Romanticism. EIC 42, 1992.
Westwater, M. The spasmodic career of Sydney Dobell. 1992.
Dobell's works were widely reviewed during his lifetime. See Westwater, *above, pp. 160–1.* [MW]

Alfred Domett 1811–87

Mss: diaries, BL Add Mss.

Selections

Miles 4.

§1

Poems. 1833
Venice. 1839. A poem.
Narrative of the Wairoan massacre. 1843.
Petition to the House of Commons for the recall of Governor Fitzroy. 1845.
Ranolf and Amohia: a South-Sea day dream. 1872, 2 vols 1883 (rev as A dream of two lives). A poem.
Flotsam and jetsam: rhymes old and new. 1877.
It was the calm and silent night: a Christmas hymn. New York 1884.

Letters and papers

Diary 1872–85. Ed E. A. Horsman 1953.
Canadian journal: being an extract from a journal of a tour in Canada, the United States and Jamaica, 1833–5. Ed E. A. Horsman and L. R. Benson, London, Ontario 1955.

§2

Gisborne, W. In his New Zealand rulers and statesmen, 1840–85, 1886.
Miles 4.
Robert Browning and Domett. Ed F. G. Kenyon 1906. Letters from Browning to Domett.

Sir Francis Hastings Charles Doyle 1810–88

Mss: letters, BL Add Miss; letters (including poems) 1840, Edinburgh, NLS.

Selections

Miles 4.

§1

Miscellaneous verses. 1834, 1840, 1841 (2nd edn).
The two destinies: a poem. 1844.
Oedipus, King of Thebes. 1849. Tr from the Oedipus tyrannus of Sophocles into English verse.
The vision of Er, the Pamphylian. [1850?] A poem.
The Duke's funeral: a poem. [1852.]
The return of the guards and other poems. 1866, 1883.
Lectures delivered before the University of Oxford 1868. 1869. Includes Inaugural lecture, Provincial poetry, and Dr Newman's Dream of Gerontius.
Ode for music, to be sung in the Sheldonian theatre, Oxford. [Oxford 1870.]
Lectures on poetry delivered at Oxford: second series. 1877. Includes lectures on Wordsworth, Scott and Shakespeare, with 14 original poems.
Robin Hood's bay: an ode. 1878.
To the memory of General Gordon. [1885.] A poem.
The Yorkshire heiress, a comedy [1885?]
Reminiscences and opinions 1813–85. 1886, New York 1887. An autobiography.
Senilia. 1888 (priv ptd). A poem.
Racecourse and hunting field: the Doncaster St Leger by Doyle; and Melton in 1830, probably by B. Osbourne. Ed S. J. Looker 1931.
For two brief articles, see Wellesley *vol 5, 1989.*

§2

Japp, A. H. In Miles 4.

Lady Helen Selina Dufferin Blackwood, Baroness Dufferin, later Hay, Countess of Gifford, née Sheridan 1807–67

§1

The Irish emigrant etc. [1840?] (anon), [1850?]. Songs.
Terence's farewell etc. [1840] (anon), [1855?]. Songs.
Finesse. 1863 (anon). Play.

Lispings from low latitudes, or, extracts from the journal of the Hon Impulsia Gushington [ed Lord Dufferin]. 1863 (anon).
Songs, poems and verses. With a memoir by her son, Marquess of Dufferin and Ava. 1894.
To my dear son on his 21st birthday. Helen's Tower, Clandeboye. 1861 (priv ptd). Poem.

§2

Beaver, A. The beautiful Sheridans. Longman's Mag 45, Nov 1904.
DNB (under Sheridan).

Rowland Eyles Egerton-Warburton 1804–91

Mss: poems 1844–71, letters, Chester, Cheshire Central Records Office
Poems. Chester 1833.
Hunting songs, ballads etc. 1834, 1846 (enlarged), 1859 (rev and enlarged as Hunting songs and miscellaneous verses), 1860, 1873 (enlarged), 1877; ed H. E. Maxwell, Liverpool 1912, London 1925. 11th edn ptd in G. Fergusson, The green collars: the Tarporley hunt club and Cheshire hunting history, 1993.
The Hawkstone bow-meeting. 1835.
Cheshire chivalry by the author of the 'Woore Country'. 1838. Verses describing a hunt.
Rhymes on the rules of the Cheshire bowmen. Northwich [1840?].
Three hunting songs. Chester 1855.
Four new songs. 1859.
Documents and letters relating to the cattle plague in the years 1747–9. Manchester 1866.
The return of the guards and other poems. 1866, 1883.
Epigrams and humorous verses by Rambling Richard. 1867.
Lectures delivered before the University of Oxford, 1868. Oxford 1869. [On poetry.]
A looking-glass for landlords. 1875. In verse.
Lectures on poetry, delivered at Oxford, 2nd series. 1877.
Poems, epigrams and sonnets. 1877.
Songs and verses on sporting subjects. 1879.
Twenty-two sonnets, with illustrations. 1883.
Reminiscences and opinions, 1813–85. 1886.

John Ellerton 1826–93

Selection
Miles 10 (12).

§1

Hymns for schools and Bible classes. Brighton 1859.
Church hymns. Ed with W. W. How 1871.
Notes and illustrations of Church hymns. 1881.
Hymns, original and translated. 1888.
Ellerton also pbd sermons and devotional works.

§2

Julian.
Miles, A. H. In Miles 10 (12).
Housman, H. Ellerton: being a collection of his writings on hymnology together with a sketch of his life and works. 1896.

Henry Ellison 1811–80

Selection
Miles 10 (11).

§1

Madmoments: or first verseattempts by a bornnatural. Malta 1833, 2 vols 1839. [Title and other errors corrected.]
[Man and nature in their poetical relations. 2 vols 1838?] The only evidence for this vol is a mention in the prefatory remarks of the following.
Touches on the harp of nature. 1839.
The poetry of real life. First series 1844, 1844 edn improved, 1851.
Stones from the old quarry: or moods of mind, by Henry Browne. 1875. Mainly sonnets.

§2

Brown, J. Henry Vaughan. In Horae subsecivae ser 1, Edinburgh 1882.
Grosart, A. B. In Miles 10 (11).

Anne Evans 1820–70

Elstey; settled for life. [1860]. Parlour Lib vol 201.
Poems and music, with a memorial preface by A. T. Ritchie. 1880.

Sebastian Evans 1830–1909

Selections
Miles 5.

§1

Sonnets on the death of the Duke of Wellington. Cambridge 1852.
Rhymes read in the Queen's drawing room at Aston Hall 25 Jan 1859, in memory of the birth of Robert Burns. [1859.]
Brother Fabian's manuscripts and other poems. 1865. Facs reprint 1984.
Politics and Protestantism. Birmingham 1868. [An address.]
Songs and etchings. 1871. 7 poems by B. Jonson, T. Hood, P. B. Shelley, C. Kingsley, S. Evans and H. W. Longfellow.
In the studio: a decade of poems. 1875.
John Baptist Spagnoll of Mantua, Carmelite, to John Crestoni, of Piacenza, Carmelite, then going away for a time to Monte Calestano. Englished, with an introduction, by S. Evans. 1844 (priv ptd).
In quest of the Holy Graal: an introduction to the study of the legend. 1898.
The high history of the Holy Graal. 1898, 1903, [1910]. Rptd Cambridge 1969. Tr Evans.
To the memory of W. M. Thackeray: a poem. 1899. Appended to Thackeray's writings in Nat Standard and Constitutional.
The upper ten. 1891 [by S. and F. Evans, adapted from Le monde où l'on s'ennuie by E. Pailleron]; 2nd edn 1901 as Lady Chillingham's houseparty: or Margery's romance. An English version of Le monde où l'on s'ennuie by E. Pailleron, tr with F. B. Goldney. [Drama.]
Geoffrey of Monmouth. Tr Evans 1904 (Temple Classics), rev 1963 by C. W. Dunn.
Galfridus: histories of the Kings of Britain. Tr Evans 1912.
Evans pbd other trns and political tracts; see also Wellesley *vol 5 1989. He edited the* Birmingham Daily Gazette, *1867–70, and the* People *for a period during the 1870s.*

§2

Knight, J. In Miles 5.

Frederick William Faber 1814–63

Mss: poems 1837–40, letters, Lambeth Palace Lib; poems and letters, BL Add Mss.

Collections
Poems. 1856, 1857 (3rd edn), [1886]; tr Ger 1870 (with long biographical and critical introd).
Ausgewählte englische Gedichte von Dr Friedrich Wilhelm Faber. Ed W. Bottmann, Regensburg 1859. Poems in Eng with notes in Ger.
Hymns selected from F. W. Faber. Ed H. L. Blunt, Northampton MA 1867.

Hymns selected from Faber by R. P. Smith. 1874, 1885, 1905.
Heavenly promises: a selection of devotional poetry from the writings of Faber, George Herbert, John Keble etc. 1898.
Characteristics from the writings of Father Faber. Ed J. Fitzpatrick 1903.
Selected poetry of Father Faber. Ed J. Fitzpatrick 1907.
Works, prose and verse. 11 vols 1914.

§1

The knights of St John. Oxford 1836. Newdigate prize poem.
The Cherwell water-lily and other poems. 1840.
The Styrian lake and other poems. 1842, [1907].
The rosary of Our Lord Jesus Christ. [1843], 1858.
Sir Lancelot: a poem. 1844, 1857; tr Ger 1859.
The rosary and other poems. 1845.
Hymns. Derby 1848, 1849 (enlarged as Jesus and Mary: or Catholic hymns), 1852 (enlarged), 1854 (enlarged as The oratory hymn book), 1861 (complete edn with 150 hymns).
Ethel's book: or tales of the angels. 1858, Baltimore 1867, 1887, 1901, New York [1907]. Stories for children.
The first Christmas: the infant Jesus. 1889. Verses.
Faber also pbd numerous sermons and religious tracts, as well as contributing nine lives to The lives of the English saints, *1844–5.*

Letters and papers

Bowden, J. E. The life and letters of F. W. Faber. 1869, [1888].
Addington, R. Faber poet and priest: selected letters 1833–63. Cowbridge, Glamorgan 1974.

§2

Faber, F. A. A brief sketch of the early life of the late F. W. Faber. 1869, 1901 (rev).
Hall-Patch, W. Father Faber. 1914.
Plus, R. Frédéric William Faber. Études 108 1931.
Faber, G. C. In his Oxford apostles, 1933.
Blunt, H. F. A forgotten masterpiece: Faber's Sir Lancelot. Catholic World 157 1943.
Cassidy, J. F. The life of Father Faber. 1946.

Julian Henry Charles Fane, 'Neville Temple' 1827–70

§1

Monody on the death of Adelaide the Queen Dowager. [Cambridge 1850]; rptd in A complete collection of the English poems which have obtained the Chancellor's Gold Medal vol 1, 1859.
Poems. 1852, 1852 (enlarged).
Poems by Heinrich Heine, translated. 1854.
Julian Fane, ad matrem 1849–57. [1857] (priv ptd).
Tannhäuser: or the battle of the bards, by Neville Temple [Fane] and Edward Trevor [E. R. B. Lytton]. 1861, Mobile 1863.

§2

Obit: The Times 21 Apr 1870.
Lytton, E. R. B. Julian Fane: a memoir. 1871.

Sir Samuel Ferguson 1810–86

Mss: poems, Belfast Lib and Soc for Promoting Knowledge.

Collections

Poems of Sir Samuel Ferguson. Ed A. P. Graves 1918.
Selected poems, with life and notes. Dublin 1931.
The poems. Ed P. Colum, Dublin 1963.

§1

The Cromlech on Howth: a poem [1861]. [1864].
Lays of the western Gael, and other poems. 1865; ed A. Williams, Dublin 1888.
Congal: a poem in five books. Dublin 1872, 1907. Introd by Lady Ferguson.
Leabhar Breac. Dublin 1872–6. Lithographic reproduction of the Irish ms, with preface by Ferguson.
Deirdre. Dublin 1880.
Poems. Dublin 1880.
Shakespearean breviates: an adjustment [in verse] of twenty four of the longer plays of Shakespeare to convenient reading limits. Dublin 1882.
The forgoing of the anchor: a poem. 1883.
Hibernian nights' entertainments. 3 vols Dublin 1887. Rptd from Dublin Univ Mag.
Ogham inscriptions in Ireland, Wales and Scotland. Edinburgh and Dublin 1887.
Remains of St Patrick: the Confessio and Epistle to Coroticus, translated into English blank verse. Dublin 1888.
Lays of the Red Branch. Dublin 1897. Introd by Lady Ferguson.
Poems. Dublin [1918]. Introd by A. Graves.
Aideen's grave. Dublin [1925].

§2

[Stokes, M.] Obituary. Blackwood's Mag Nov 1886.
O'Hagan, J. The poetry of Ferguson. Dublin 1887.
Williams, A. In his Studies in folk-song and poular poetry, Boston 1894.
Ferguson, M. (Lady Ferguson). Ferguson in the Ireland of his day. 2 vols Edinburgh and London 1896. A biography.

Edward FitzGerald 1809–83

The main collections of FitzGerald mss are in Trinity College Cambridge and in Cambridge UL.

Bibliographies

Prideaux, W. F. Notes for a bibliography of Edward FitzGerald. 1901. List of separate pbns to 1900 and of contributions to books and periodicals, with notes.
Potter, A. G. A bibliography of the Rubáiyát of Omar Khayyám together with kindred matter in prose and verse pertaining thereto. Boston 1923, 1929.
Ehrsam, T. G. and R. H. Deily. In their Bibliographies of twelve Victorian authors, New York 1936; suppl by J. G. Fucilla, MP 37, 1939.
Terhune, A. M. The life of Edward FitzGerald. 1947. Contains important bibliographical appendices.
Terhune, A. M. Edward FitzGerald. In The Victorian poets: a guide to research, ed. F. E. Faverty, Cambridge MA 1956.
Terhune, A. M. Edward FitzGerald. In A guide to research materials of the major Victorian poets, pt l. Victorian Newsletter 12, 1957.
Rubáiyát of Omar Khayyám: a catalogue of various editions, offered for sale [by] B. Quaritch. 1959.
Timko, M. Edward FitzGerald. In The Victorian poets: a guide to research (rev), ed. F. E. Faverty, Cambridge MA 1968.
Jewitt, I. B. H. Edward FitzGerald. Boston 1977.
Trivedi, H. Colonial transactions: English literature and India. Manchester 1995.

Collections (including letters)

Works, reprinted from the original impressions, with some corrections derived from his own annotated copies. 2 vols New York 1887.
Letters and literary remains. Ed W. A. Wright 3 vols 1889.
Letters. Ed W. A. Wright 2 vols 1894.
Letters to Fanny Kemble 1871–83. Ed W. A. Wright 1895.
Miscellanies. Ed W. A. Wright 1900.
More letters. Ed W. A. Wright 1901.
The variorum and definitive edition of the poetical and prose writings of Edward FitzGerald including a complete bibliography

and interesting personal and literary notes. Ed G. Bentham 7 vols New York 1902; preface by E. Gosse, rptd 1967.

Letters and literary remains. Ed W. A. Wright 7 vols 1902–3. Absorbs collections of letters made by Wright, *above*.

Miscellanies. [Ed H. Morley] 1904.

FitzGerald and 'Posh': 'herring merchants', including a number of letters from FitzGerald to Joseph Fletcher or 'Posh' not hitherto published. Ed J. Blyth 1908.

Some new letters of Edward FitzGerald to Bernard Barton, with a foreword by Viscount Grey. Ed F. R. Barton 1923, New York 1924 (as Edward FitzGerald and Bernard Barton).

Letters to Bernard Quaritch 1853–83. Ed C. Q. Wrentmore 1926.

A FitzGerald friendship: letters from Edward FitzGerald to William Bodham Donne. Ed N. C. Hannay and C. B. Johnson 1932.

Thackeray, W. M. Letters and private papers. Ed G. N. Ray 4 vols Cambridge MA 1945–6. Vol 1 contains The FitzGerald album.

Letters of Edward FitzGerald. Ed J. M. Cohen 1960.

Selected works. Ed J. Richardson 1962 (Reynard Lib).

FitzGerald to his friends: selected letters. Ed A. Hayter 1979.

The letters of Edward FitzGerald. Ed A. M. Terhune and A. B. Terhune. 4 vols Princeton NJ 1980.

Day, A. Edward FitzGerald to the Tennysons: three letters. N & Q 29, 1982.

Trela, D. J. FitzGerald to Carlyle to Fitzgerald: two unpublished letters. N & Q 31, 1984.

A letter from Woodbridge to [A. Biddell]. Ipswich 1994.

§1

Memoir of Bernard Barton. In Selections from the poems and letters of Bernard Barton, ed L. Barton 1849, Philadelphia 1850, London 1853.

Euphranor: a dialogue on youth. 1851, 1855 (rev), [1882] (rev, priv ptd, as Euphranor: a May-Day conversation at Cambridge, ''Tis forty years since'); ed F. Chapman 1906 (from 1851 text).

REVIEWS: (J. Spedding) Examiner, 8 Feb 1851; (E. B. Cowell) Westminster Rev, Apr 1851.

Polonius: a collection of wise saws and modern instances. 1852, 1854; ed S. S. Allen 1905.

Six dramas of Calderón freely translated. 1853, 1854; ed H. Oelsner 1903, [1928] (EL).

REVIEW: (anon) Literary Gazette, 27 Aug 1853; (anon) Athenaeum, 10 Sep 1853; (W. B. Donne) Fraser's Mag, Mar 1857.

Salámán and Absál: an allegory translated from the Persian of Jámí. 1856 (anon), 1871 (rev, priv ptd), 1879 (rev, with 4th edn of the Rubáiyát, *below*), Leigh-on-Sea 1946; ed. A. J. Arberry London 1956.

REVIEW: (anon) Athenaeum, 2 Aug 1856.

Rubáiyát of Omar Khayyám, the astronomer-poet of Persia, translated into English verse. 1859 (anon), 1868 (rev, anon), 1872 (rev, anon), 1879 (rev, anon, with the Salámán and Absál of Jámí, *above*); ed N. H. Dole 2 vols Boston 1896 (includes Fr and Ger versions, with voluminous critical material), 1898 (enlarged, adding Ital and Danish versions); ed T. Williams, Philadelphia 1898 (text of lst and 4th edns), rptd 1991; ed H. M. Batson and E. D. Ross 1900; ed R. Arnot, New York 1901 (as The Sufistic quatrains of Omar Khayyám in definitive form; includes trns by E. H. Whinfield and J. B. Nicholas); ed F. Henry, Paris 1903 (text of 4th edn with Fr trn); ed. E. F. Thompson, priv ptd, Worcester MA 1907 (text of 1st edn with Persian text); ed E. Heron-Allen 1908 (text of 2nd edn); ed R. A. Nicholson 1909 (text of 1st edn); ed F. H. Evans 1914 (var text); ed E. Rhys [1928] (EL, text of 1st and 2nd edns with Six plays of Calderón, *above*); rptd (photo facs) from lst edn New York 1934; ed C. Ganz and E. D. Ross 1938 (with unpbd trn into 'monkish Latin' by FitzGerald); ed G. F. Maine 1947 (text of 1st, 2nd and '5th' edns with variants); 1953 (with Euphranor, and Salámán and Absál, *above*), rptd 1988; ed A. J. Arberry 1959 (as The romance of the Rubáiyát: text of 1st edn with introd, notes and bibliography); ed C. J. Weber, Waterville ME 1959 (critical text with bibliography); *for earliest Fr trn, see* F. Henry, 1903, *above*; Latin 1893, Greek 1902, Welsh Romani 1902, Sp 1904, Hebrew 1905, Ger 1907, Welsh 1907, Irish 1909, Ital [1910], Jap 1910, Yiddish 1911, Arabic 1912, Swedish 1912, Polish 1921, Cz 1922, Afrikaans [1924], Gujerati 1927, Tamil 1928, Sanskrit 1929, Kannada 1930, Hindi 1931, Malay [1935], Portuguese 1935, Hungarian 1941, Dutch 1944, Swahili 1952, Nepali 1957, Galician 1965, Esperanto 1980.

REVIEWS: (anon) Literary Gazette, 1 Oct 1859; (C. E. Norton) North Amer Rev 109, 1869; (T. W. Hinchcliffe) Fraser's Mag, June 1870.

Tutin, J. R. A concordance to FitzGerald's translation of the Rubáiyát. 1900.

The mighty magician and Such stuff as dreams are made of: two plays translated from Calderón. 1865 (priv ptd). Such stuff as dreams, ed. W. A. Landes, Studio City CA 1992 (as Life a dream).

Agamemnon: a tragedy taken from Aeschylus. [1869] (priv ptd), London 1876.

Readings in Crabbe. Tales of the Hall. [1879] (priv ptd), 1882, 1883 (with enlarged introd).

The downfall and death of King Oedipus: a drama in two parts, chiefly taken from the Oedipus Tyrannus and Colonæus of Sophocles. 2 pts 1880–1 (priv ptd).

The two Generals: I, Lucius Aemilius Paullus; II, Sir Charles Napier. nd. 2 poems, priv ptd.

Occasional verses. 1891 (priv ptd).

Eight dramas of Calderón, freely translated. 1906. Consists of Six dramas, 1853, and The mighty magician and Such stuff as dreams, 1865, *above*.

Dictionary of Madame de Sévigné. Ed M. E. FitzGerald 2 vols 1914.

A FitzGerald medley. Ed C. Ganz 1933.

For contributions to books and periodicals. see W. F. Prideaux, Notes for a bibliography of FitzGerald, *pp. 57–72, above.*

§2

For personal memoirs of FitzGerald, see W. F. Prideaux, *pp. 72–4, above.*

Groome, F. H. Two Suffolk friends. 1895. FitzGerald and Archdeacon Groome.

Nicoll, W. R. and T. J. Wise. Literary anecdotes of the nineteenth century. 2 vols 1895–6. Vol 2 includes An old commonplace book of Edward FitzGerald's.

Heron-Allen, E. Some sidelights upon FitzGerald's poem The rubáiyát of Omar Khayyám. 1898.

Ritchie, A. T. Biographical introduction to vol 9 of The works of William Makepeace Thackeray, 13 vols 1898. Contains preface 'concerning Mr FitzGerald's collection of drawings and letters, 1829–1850'. *See* G. N. Ray 1945–6, *above.*

Jackson, H. FitzGerald and Omar Khayyám: an essay and a bibliography. 1899.

More, P. E. In his Shelburne essays, ser 2 New York 1899.

Glyde, J. The life of FitzGerald, with an introduction by E. Clodd. 1900.

Bjerregaard, C. H. A. Sufi interpretations of the quatrains of Omar Khayyám and FitzGerald. New York 1902.

Wright, T. The life of Edward FitzGerald. 2 vols 1904.

Benson, A. C. Edward FitzGerald. 1905 (EML).

Benn, A. W. Rationalism in politics and literature. In his The history of rationalism in the nineteenth century, 2 vols 1906.

Dutt, W. H. In his Some literary associations of East Anglia, [1907]. The homes and haunts of FitzGerald.

Edward FitzGerald 1809–1909: centenary celebrations souvenir. Ipswich 1909.

The book of the Omar Khayyám Club 1892–1910. 1910 (priv ptd).

Adams, M. Omar's interpreter: a new life of Edward FitzGerald. 1909, 1911 (rev).

Bailey, J. In his Poets and poetry, Oxford 1911.

Adams, M. In the footsteps of Borrow and FitzGerald. 1913.

Nicholson, R. A. Omar Khayyám: some facts and fallacies. Aberdeen Univ Rev 1, 1914.
Browning, R. Edward FitzGerald and Elizabeth Barrett Browning. 1919 (priv ptd). 3 letters from Browning to his son.
Terhune, A. M. The life of Edward FitzGerald. 1947.
Martin, R. B. With friends possessed: a life of Edward FitzGerald. 1985. [GC]

Charles Robert Forrester 1803–50

Selections
Miles 9 (10).

§1
Castle Baynard: or the days of John, by Hall Willis. 1824.
Absurdities in prose and verse, written and illustrated by Alfred Crowquill. 1827. Illustr A. H. Forrester.
Eccentric tales from the German of W. F. von Kosewitz. 1827. Kosewitz is Forrester.
Sir Roland: a romance of the twelfth century, by Hall Willis. 4 vols 1827.
The battle of the 'annuals': a fragment. 1835. Anon.
The Lord Mayor's fool or maxims of Kit Largosse, collected and digested by G[abriel] G[rindlaye] [pseud]. 1840.
Phantasmagoria of fun, edited and illustrated by Alfred Crowquill. 2 vols 1843. Illustr A. H. Forrester.

§2
Obit: GM May 1850.
Miles, A. H. In Miles 9 (10).

Thomas Hornblower Gill 1819–1906

Selections
Miles 10 (11).

§1
The fortunes of faith: or Church and State. 1841. Verse.
Songs of the revolution. 1848.
The anniversaries: poems in commemoration of great men and great events. Cambridge 1858.
The papal drama: a historical essay. 1866.
The golden chain of praise: hymns. [1868], 1894 (greatly enlarged); tr Sp, [1917].
Luther's birthday: hymns. 1883.
The triumph of Christ: memorials of Franklin Howorth. 1883.
Richard Serjeant: a biographical sketch. 1885.
Elegy in memory of Wilfred Austin Gill. (Grove Park) [1900].

§2
Julian, J. and W. G. Horder. In Julian.
Horder, W. G. In Miles 9 (10).

Dora Greenwell 1821–82

Collections
Poems: selected with biographical introduction by William Dorling. 1889 (Canterbury Poets).
REVIEW: Saturday Rev 9 Mar 1889.
Miles 7 (8).
Selected poems. Ed C. L. Maynard 1906.
Selections from the prose of Dora Greenwell. Ed W. G. Hanson 1950 (with biographical introd).

§1
Poems. 1848, rptd 1904.
REVIEWS: Spectator 24 June 1848; Athenaeum 23 Sep 1848; Literary Gazette 14 Oct 1848.
Stories that might be true, with other poems. 1850.
REVIEW: Literary Gazette 25 Jan 1851.
A present heaven. Letters to a friend. Edinburgh 1855, 1867 (rev as The covenant of life and peace: addressed to a friend). Letters on the Gospel.
The patience of hope. Edinburgh 1860, Boston 1863 (8th edn with preface by J. G. Whittier). A treatise on the spiritual life.
Poems. Edinburgh 1861, 1867 (omits some earlier poems and adds later ones).
REVIEWS: Victoria Mag 9, Aug 1867; Br Quart Rev Oct 1867; Athenaeum 2 May 1868.
Two friends. 1862, 1867; ed C. L. Maynard [1926], 1952. Essays on the spiritual life.
Home thoughts and home scenes, in original poems by J. Ingelow, D. Greenwell et al. 1865. 10 poems by Greenwell.
Essays. 1866. Includes Our single women, Hardened in good, Prayer, Popular religious literature, Christianos ad Leones.
REVIEWS: Br Quart Rev 45, Jan 1867; Victoria Mag 8, Jan 1867.
Lacordaire. Edinburgh 1867. Biography.
REVIEW: Athenaeum 18 July 1868.
On the education of the imbecile. 1869. Rptd from North Br Rev Sep 1868 and ed for Royal Albert Idiot Asylum, Lancaster.
Carmina Crucis. 1869; ed C. L. Maynard 1906. Verse.
REVIEWS: Spectator 26 June 1869; Victoria Mag 13, July 1869.
Colloquia crucis: a sequel to Two friends. 1871.
REVIEW: Br Quart Rev 58, July 1873.
John Woolman. 1871. A biographical sketch.
Songs of salvation. 1873, rptd as Everlasting love and other songs of salvation [1906].
The soul's legend. 1873. Verse.
Liber humanitatis: a series of essays on various aspects of spiritual and social life. 1875.
REVIEWS: Saturday Rev 14 Aug 1875; Victoria Mag 27, May 1876.
Camera obscura. 1876. Verse.
REVIEW: Athenaeum 12 Aug 1876.
A basket of summer fruit: dedicated to the American Evangelists who lately visited England. 1877. Essays.
The power of prayer. [1910.] With T. P. Forsyth. 'Prayer as will' by Greenwell.

Editions, etc.
Harmless Johnny: or the poor outcast of reason, by Caroline Bowles. Ed Greenwell 1868 for the Royal Albert Idiot Asylum, Lancaster.
A poor boy: abridged from the French of the Countess de Gasparin for the Royal Albert Idiot Asylum. 1868.
The wow o'Rivven: or the idiot's home, by George MacDonald. Ed Greenwell 1868.
Benjie of Millden: by the author of 'Bygone days in our village'. Ed Greenwell 1869 for the Royal Albert Idiot Asylum. 1869.
Greenwell also pbd in several periodicals. See Wellesley vol 5 1989. *Her poems appeared in* Good Words, Cornhill Mag, GM, St Paul's, Sunday Mag.

§2
Dorling, W. Memoirs of Dora Greenwell. [1885.]
Maynard, C. L. Dora Greenwell: a prophet for our own times on the battleground of our faith. [1926.]
Bett, H. Dora Greenwell. 1950. [RS]

Thomas Gordon Hake 1809–95

Mss: poems and letters, BL Add Mss.

Selections
Miles 4.
Poems, selected with prefatory note by A. Meynell. 1894.

§1

Poetic lucubrations: containing the Misanthrope and other effusions. 1828.
The piromides: a tragedy. 1839.
A treatise on varicose capillaries. 1839.
Vates: or the philosophy of madness. 4 pts 1840.
Poems, consisting of the Deity; Cenci; Antinelli; and the Evening star. To which is added a Polish hymn [1852.]
The world's epitaph: a poem. 1866 (priv ptd).
On vital force. 1867.
Madeline, with other poems and parables. 1871. Partly rptd from World's epitaph, *above*.
Parables and tales. 1872; ed T. Hake 1917.
New symbols. 1876. Poems.
Legends of the morrow. 1879. In verse.
Maiden ecstasy. 1880. Poems.
The serpent play: a divine pastoral, in 5 acts and in verse. 1883.
On the powers of the alphabet, 1 A tonic scale of alphabetic sounds. 1883. Only pt 1 pbd.
The new day: sonnets. Ed W. G. Hodgson 1890. With a portrait of Hake by D. G. Rossetti and long critical preface.
Memoirs of eighty years. 1892.

§2

Rossetti, D. G. Dr Hake's poems. Fortnightly Rev Apr 1873; rptd in Rossetti, Collected works vol 2, 1886 etc.
Bayne, T. In Miles 4.
Rossetti, W. M. In his Memoir of D. G. Rossetti, prefixed to D. G. Rossetti's family letters, 2 vols 1895.
Symons, A. In his Studies in two literatures, 1897.
Watts-Dunton, T. In his Old familiar faces, 1916.

Sir John Hanmer, afterwards Baron Hanmer 1809–81

§1

Proteus and other poems. 1832 (priv ptd), 1833 (2nd edn).
Poems on various subjects. 1836 (priv ptd).
Fra Cipolla and other poems. 1839.
Sonnets. 1840.
A memorial of the parish and family of Hanmer in Flintshire. 1876 (priv ptd). With an appendix of sonnets and epigrams.

§2

Obit: The Times 11, 15 Mar 1881.

Robert Stephen Hawker 1803–75

Mss: poems (1824–55), Worcester College, Oxford; poems (including Quest of sangraal*), letters and thought books, Bodleian; letters, BL Add Mss.*

Bibliographies

Wallis, A (ed). Poetical works. 1899.
Woolf, C. Some uncollected authors 39: Hawker of Morwenstow. BC 14 1965.
See also Bibliography of British literary bibliographies [BBLB].

Collections

Poetical works. Ed J. G. Godwin 1879.
Poetical works edited from the original mss and annotated copies, together with a prefatory notice and bibliography. Ed A. Wallis 1899.
Miles 3.
Twenty poems. Ed J. Drinkwater, Oxford 1925.
A selection of Hawker's Cornish ballads on local topics. Ed F. C. Hamlyn, Truro [1928].
Hawker of Morwenstow. The Augustan books of poetry series. [1932.]
Selected poems. Ed C. Woolf. 1975.

§1

Tendrils, by Reuben. Cheltenham 1821.
[The song of the western men.] A song on the imprisonment of the Bishop of Bristol, 1688. [c. 1826.]
Pompeii: a prize poem. Oxford 1827; rptd in Oxford English prize poems, 1828.
Down with the church. [Launceston 1831.] Signed 'A man'. Electioneering song.
Records of the western shore: first series. Oxford 1832, Camelford, Cornwall 1868. Poems.
Poems. Stratton, Cornwall 1836. Contains 3rd edn of Pompeii, 2nd edn of Records of the western shore ser 1, and 1st edn of Records of the western shore ser 2.
Minster church and The confirmation day August 1836. 1836 (priv ptd). Poems.
A welcome to the Prince Albert submitted to the Queen on the approach of Her Majesty's marriage. Oxford 1840. In verse.
Ecclesia: a volume of poems. Oxford 1840. Includes one poem – 'The wreck' – by his wife, C. E. H.
The baptism of the peasant and the prince. 1842.
The poor man and his parish church. Plymouth 1843, 1843 (2nd edn). Poems.
Reeds shaken with the wind. 1843. Poems.
Reeds shaken with the wind: second cluster. Derby 1844.
Echoes from old Cornwall. 1846. Poems.
A voice from the place of S. Morwenna. 1849.
A letter to a friend containing some matters relating to the church. By a Cornish vicar. 1857. Poems.
Aishah – Shechinah [a poem signed 'Breachan']. [Morwenstow 1860.]
King Arthur's was-hael [signed Ben-Tamar]. [Morwenstow] 1860.
The quest of the sangraal: chant the first. Exeter 1864 (priv ptd).
St Nectan's Kieve etc. 1868.
The Cornish ballads and other poems. Oxford 1869 (including 2nd edn of The quest of the sangraal), Oxford 1884; ed C. E. Byles [with additional poems] 1904. Facs reprint of 1869, introd K. J. Walter and T. A. H. Delmar, New York 1994.
The carol of the Pruss [signed R. S. H.]. Morwenstow 1870.
Footprints of former men in far Cornwall. 1870; ed C. E. Byles [1903], 1948. Prose sketches with some verses.
Aurora. [Printed for W. M[askell] for private circulation.] 1873.
A canticle for Christmas, 1874. [Morwenstow] 1874.
Prose works. Ed J. G. Godwin, Edinburgh 1893. A new edn of Footprints of former men in far Cornwall, with addns.
Hawker also issued a number of sermons and single poems as leaflets.

Letters and papers

Stones broken from the rocks: extracts from note-books. Ed E. R. Appleton and C. E. Byles, Oxford 1922.

§2

Gould, S. B. The vicar of Morwenstow. 1875, 1876 (rev), new edn 1899.
Lee, F. G. Memorials of Hawker. 1876.
Noble, J. A. In Miles 3.
Noble, J. A. In his Sonnet in England and other essays, 1893.
Byles, C. E. Life and letters of Hawker. 1905.
Burrows, M. F. Hawker: a study of his thought and poetry. Oxford 1926.
Hawker of Morwenstow. TLS 20 Dec 1934.
Rowse, A. L. Hawker of Morwenstow: a belated medieval. E & S new ser 12 1959.
Brendan, P. Hawker of Morwenstow: portrait of a Victorian eccentric. Foreword by J. Fowles. 1975.

Richard Henry (or Hengist) Horne 1803–84

Mss: a few poems, plays, letters, BL Add Mss.

Bibliographies
Shumaker, E. J. A concise bibliography of the complete works of Horne. Granville OH 1943.

Selections
Miles 2.

§1
Exposition of the false medium and barriers excluding men of genius from the public. 1833. Anon.
Zara, or the black death. A poem of the sea. By the author of Naufragus. 1833.
The spirit of peers and people: a nation tragi-comedy. 1834.
Introduction to characteristics, by W. Hazlitt. 1837. Introd by Horne.
Cosmo de'Medici: an historical tragedy. 1837, 1875 (with added poems). In verse.
The death of Marlowe: a tragedy in one act. 1837, 1870 (5th edn). Chiefly in verse; rptd in Works of Marlow, ed A. H. Bullen, vol 3 1885.
The life of Van Amburgh the brute tamer, with anecdotes of his pupils, by Ephraim Watts. [1838.]
Gregory VII: a tragedy in one act. 1840, 1849 (3rd edn). In verse, includes an essay on tragic influence.
The history of Napoleon. 2 vols 1840, 1841, New York 1852, 1 vol 1879.
Poems of Chaucer, modernized. 1841. By various writers. Horne contributed the introd and 3 tales.
Orion: an epic poem in three books. 1843 (3 edns), Melbourne 1854 (adds preface), London 1872 (9th and definitive edn); ed E. Partridge 1928 (with introd on Horne's life and work).
A new spirit of the age. Ed [and largely written by] Horne 2 vols 1844, 1 vol 1844; ed W. Jerrold, Oxford 1907 (WC).
Ballad romances. 1846.
The good-natured bear: a story for children of all ages. 1846, 1856, [1878].
Memoirs of a London doll, written by herself. Ed 'Mrs Fairstar' 1846, Boston 1852, London 1855, New York 1922 (introd by C. W. Hart), London 1923.
Judas Iscariot: a miracle play, with other poems. 1848; rptd in Bible tragedies, [1891].
The poor artist: or seven eye-sights and one object. 1850, 1871 (adds preliminary essay on varieties of vision in man).
Memoir of the Emperor Napoleon. [1850?]
The dreamer and the worker: a story of the present time. 2 vols 1851.
The complete works of Shakespeare. Ed Horne [1857].
Australian facts and prospects, to which is prefixed the author's Australian autobiography. 1859.
Prometheus the fire bringer: a drama in verse. Edinburgh 1864, Melbourne 1866.
The two Georges: a dialogue of the dead. Melbourne [1865?]. In verse.
The south-sea sisters: a lyric masque. Melbourne [1866]. With trns into Fr and Ger verse.
Galatea secunda: an odaic cantata. Melbourne 1867 (priv ptd).
Was Hamlet mad? being a series of critiques on the acting of the late W. Montgomery. Written in Melbourne in 1867. Ed R. H. H. [1871].
Parting legacy of R. H. Horne to Australia (John Ferncliff: an Australian narrative poem). Melbourne [1868]. A prospectus.
The great peace-maker: a sub-marine dialogue. 1871 (priv ptd), 1872. Poem, rptd from Household Words.
Ode to the Mikado of Japan. 1873.
Psyche apocalypté a lyric drama. 1876. Drafts and correspondences between Horne and his co-author E. B. Browning, with connecting narrative by Horne, all rptd from St James's Mag and United Empire Rev for Feb 1876.
The Countess von Labnoff, or the three lovers. [From the New Quart] [1877].
Letters of Elizabeth Barrett Browning addressed to R. H. Horne. Ed S. R. T. Mayer 2 vols 1877. Connecting narrative by Horne.
The history of duelling in all countries, translated from the French of Coustard de Massi, with introductions and concluding chapter by 'Sir L. O'Trigger'. [1880.]
Laura Dibalzo; or the patriot martyrs. A tragedy. 1880.
King Nihil's round table: or the regicide's symposium. 1881. A dramatic scene.
Sir Featherbright, an apologue [in verse]. n.p. [1881?].
Bible tragedies: John the Baptist, or the valour of the soul; Rahman, the apocryphal book of Job's wife; Judas Iscariot, a mystery [1881.] In prose and verse.
Soliloquium fratris Rogeri Baconis. 1882 (priv ptd). In verse, rptd from Fraser's Mag.
The last words of Cleanthes: a poem. [1883.] Rptd from Longman's Mag.
Sithron the star-stricken, translated from an ancient Arabic manuscript by Salem ben Uzäir. 1883. Written in Eng by Horne.
King Penguin: a legend of the South Sea Isles. Ed F. M. Fox, New York 1925.
Horne edited Monthly Repository of Theology & General Lit *July 1836–June 1837. See also* Wellesley 5 *1989.*

§2
Poe, E. A. R. H. Horne. Graham's Mag (Philadelphia) Mar 1844; rptd in Works, ed C. F. Richardson, vol 6, New York 1902.
Powell, T. In his Pictures of the living authors of Britain, 1851. Chiefly on Gregory VII and Orion.
Forman, H. B. In his Our living poets, 1871.
Forman, H. B. In Miles 2.
Forman, H. B. In his Literary anecdotes of the nineteenth century, ed W. R. Nicoll and T. J. Wise, vol 1, 1895.
Gosse, E. In his Portraits and sketches, 1912.
Dickens, C. Notes and comments on certain writings by R. H. Horne. 1920 (priv ptd). 6 letters from Dickens to Horne.
Letters from A. C. Swinburne to Horne. 1920 (priv ptd).
Mabbott, T. O. Changes in the text of Horne's Orion. N & Q 1928.
Partridge, E. In his Literary sessions, 1932.
Shackford, M. E. B. Browning, Horne: two studies. Wellesley MA 1935.
Mineka, F. E. The dissidence of dissent: the Monthly Repository 1806–38. Chapel Hill NC 1944.
DeVane, W. C. and K. L. Knickerbocker (ed). New letters of Robert Browning. New Haven CT 1950. Includes letter to Horne and several references to him.
Fielding, K. J. Dickens and Horne. English 9 1952.
Pearl, C. Always morning: the life of Richard Henry 'Orion' Horne. Melbourne 1960.
Blainey, Ann. The farthing poet: a biography of R. H. Horne, 1802–84, a lesser literary lion. 1968.

William Walsham How 1823–97

Selections
Miles 10 (12).

§1
Psalms and hymns, compiled by T. B. Morrell and How. 1854, [1860], [1864], [1872].
Hymns [1886].
A supplement to Psalms and hymns. [1867.]
Poems: enlarged edition. [1886.]
Was lost and is found: a tale of the London mission of 1874. [1886.] In verse.
Public worship. [1894.] In verse.
A sermon in a children's ward in a hospital. 1896. In verse.
A souvenir of the late Bishop Walsham How. [1898]. A poem, To a mother on the death of her boy.

How was one of the compilers of Church hymns, *1871, and pbd many sermons and tracts: see also* Wellesley 5 1989.

§2

Miles, A. H. In Miles 10 (12).
How, F. D. How: a memoir. 1898.
How, F. D. Lighter moments: from the notebooks of Bishop W. How. 1900.
How, F. D. How: first Bishop of Wakefield. 1909.
Julian.

John Dawson Hull c. 1800–86

§1

The reverie and other poems. Belfast 1833.
Hymns and spiritual songs. 1844, rev enlarged edn 1860 as Hymns and spiritual songs for all hours.
The lake and other poems. [1846.] Anon.
Hymns for all hours. Bath [1850].
Lays of many years. [1854.]
The rural parsonage, the river and other poems: by a clergyman. 1857.
The song of a pilgrim, Home and other poems. 1873.
A chaplet for the church: original Christian melodies. [1881.]
Poems. Ed Rev R. Wilton 1889. Prev unpbd poems.
Hull also pbd theological works. [RS]

Cecil Frances Humphreys, afterwards Alexander 1818–95

For British holdings of letters see LR 1, p. 10.

Collections

Poems. Ed W. Alexander 1896, rptd London and New York 1897.

Selections

Selected poems of William Alexander and Cecil Frances Alexander. Ed A. P. Graves 1930.

§1

Most of the following works were issued under the initials C. F. H. or (after 1850) C. F. A.

Verses written on the accession of Her Majesty the Queen. 1837.
Verses for holy seasons; with questions for examination. 1846 (2 edns). Preface by W. F. Hook. 1849 (3rd edn), rptd for 1st Amer edn Philadelphia 1852, with subtitle 'or, a Christian year for youth'. Other edns London 1858, 1869, 1888.
The Baron's little daughter and other tales in prose and verse. ed Rev W. Gresley 1848, [1850?] (2nd edn), 1888 (6th edn).
Hymns for little children. 1848, Philadelphia [1850] (preface by J. Keble), London 1850 (4th edn), 1857 (14th edn), 1866 (268th thousand), New York 1872 (rptd from 278th thousand), London 1878 (546th thousand), 1884 (62nd edn), 1901 (702nd thousand), 1903 (illustr J. and E. Drew). Over 100 edns by 1935. Individual hymns have been anthologised regularly, notably 'All things bright and beautiful', 'Once in royal David's city', and 'There is a green hill far away'.
The lord of the forest and his vassals: an allegory. 1848.
Moral songs. 1849, [c. 1850] (2nd edn), 1855, 1867 (9th edn), 1873, '1880' [1879], 1882 (14th edn).
Narrative hymns for village schools. 1853, 1857, 1859 (5th edn), 1864 (8th edn), 1867 (10th edn, bound with her Hymns descriptive and devotional), 1872 (12th edn), 1875 (13th edn), 1878 (14th edn), 1894 (16th edn).
Poems on subjects in the Old Testament. Part I, Genesis–Exodus. 2 vols 1854, 1871 (2nd edn). Part II 1857. Parts I and II 1871, 1888. 'The burial of Moses' rptd separately, Boston 1890, illustr A. S. Cox.
Hymns descriptive and devotional: for the use of schools. 1858 (2 issues), 1867 (bound with her Narrative hymns for village schools), 1880, 1903.
The legend of the golden prayers and other poems. 1859.
 REVIEW: (J. S. Bigg) Dublin Univ Mag 54, Sep 1859.
Short points for daily meditation. 1879 (anon).
Easy questions on the life of Our Lord. 1891.

Collaborative works

Irish lake poetry. Dublin Univ Mag 52, Oct 1858 (with W. Alexander).
Some account of the parish church of St Colmanell, Aloghill by A. T. Lee; with an original poem by C. F. A. [1867.]

Edition and translation

The Sunday book of poetry. Selected and arranged by C. F. A. 1864 (2 edns), Cambridge MA 1865, Boston 1869, London 1872, London and New York 1892.
Quireach phádruig: or St Patrick's breastplate. 1902. Mrs Alexander's trn and the Irish text.

§2

Obit: The Times 14, 19 Oct 1895.
Alexander, W. (her husband). Preface to her Poems, 1896.
Wallace, V. Mrs Alexander: a life of the hymn-writer Cecil Frances Alexander, 1818–1895. Dublin 1995. [JW]

John William Inchbold 1830–88

§1

Annus amoris. 1876.

§2

Obit: Athenaeum 4 Feb 1888.

Jean Ingelow, 'Orris' 1820–97

Letters and literary mss are held at the Huntington.

Collections

Poetical works. Boston 1880, New York [188?], Troy NY [1887], Boston 1894.
Poetical works. 1898, 1902. Rptd from Poems, 2 vols 1893, and Poems: third ser, 1888.

Selections

Lyrical and other poems. 1886, 1895 (4th edn).
Miles 7 (8).
Poems, selected and arranged by A. Lang. Pocket edn 1908.
Poems, with an introduction by A. Meynell. 1908.
Poems. [1912.]
Poems. Oxford 1913.
Stedman, E. A. Jean Ingelow 1820–97. 1935 (priv ptd). A memoir and some poems.

§1

A rhyming chronicle of incidents and feelings. Ed E. Harston 1850. Anon.
 REVIEW: Athenaeum 1169, 23 Mar 1850.
Allerton and Dreux: or the war of opinion. 2 vols 1851. Anon.
Tales of Orris. Bath [1860], rptd with one exception in Stories told to a child, 1865, *below*. Rptd from Youth's Mag.
One story by two authors: or a tale without a moral, by J. I. and F. M. L. 1862. Rptd from Monthly Packet with additions. [With Frances Levett.]
Poems. 1863. 23rd edn 1880, [1906] (Muses' Lib), 1908.
 REVIEWS: Athenaeum 1805, 25 July 1863; Reader 2, 25 July 1863; Victoria Mag 1, Sep 1863; Br Quart Rev 38, Oct 1863; Saturday Rev 16, 19 Dec 1863; Spectator 37, 6 Feb 1864. 12th edn 1866 reviewed in Athenaeum 2037, 10 Nov 1866; Spectator 39, 10 Nov 1866; Br Quart Rev 45, Jan 1867.

Studies for stories. 2 vols 1864, 1 vol Boston 1865. Anon.
REVIEWS: in Saturday Rev 18, 17 Dec 1864; Literary Churchman 11, 25 Feb 1865; Atlantic Monthly 15, Mar 1865; Br Quart Rev 41, Apr 1865.
Home thoughts and home scenes: in original poems by J. Ingelow, D. Greenwell, etc. 1865. 2 poems by Ingelow.
Stories told to a child. 1865, 10th thousand 1867, [1891].
The grandmother's shoe. 1867. Stories told to a child, vol 1.
The golden opportunity. 1867. Stories told to a child, vol 2.
The suspicious jackdaw, and The life of Mr John Smith. 1867. Stories told to a child, [vol 3].
The Moorish gold, and The one-eyed servant. 1867. Stories told to a child, vol 4.
Little Rie and the rosebuds, and Can and could. 1867. Stories told to a child, vol 5.
Deborah's book, and The lonely rock. 1867. Stories told to a child, vol 6.
The minnows with silver tails, and Two ways of telling a story. 1867. Stories told to a child, vol 7.
The wild duck-shooter, and I have a right. 1867. Stories told to a child, vol 8.
A story of doom and other poems. 1867, 1868 (3rd edn). 6 edns by 1880, some called Poems: second series. 6th thousand 1874, 6th edn 1877.
REVIEW: Athenaeum 2069, 22 Jan 1867.
A sister's bye-hours. 1868. Anon. Stories.
Mopsa the fairy. 1869, Boston MA 1869. Everyman edn [1912], 1964. A long fairy story.
REVIEW: Athenaeum 2171, 5 June 1869.
The little wonder-horn. A new series of Stories told to a child. 1872, 1877. 12 of the 14 stories rptd in The little wonder-box, 6 vols, 32°, 1887.
REVIEW: Athenaeum 2355, 14 Dec 1872.
Off the Skelligs. 4 vols 1872, 1879, 1906 (5th edn).
REVIEWS: Athenaeum 2355, 14 Dec 1872; Spectator 46, 4 Jan 1873; Br Quart Rev 58, July 1873; Saturday Rev 36, 12 July 1873.
Fated to be free. 3 vols 1875, new edn 1876, 1900. Rptd from Good Words.
One hundred holy songs, carols and sacred ballads, original and suitable for music. 1878. Anon.
Sarah de Berenger: a novel. 1879, 3 vols 1880, 1886.
REVIEW: Saturday Rev 62, 16 Oct 1886.
Poems. 2 vols 1880, New York 1880, London 1893. Vol 1 rptd from 23rd edn of Poems (1863) with 1 additional poem; vol 2 rptd from 6th edn of A story of doom and other poems, with addns.
Don John: a story. 3 vols 1881, Boston MA 1881.
REVIEWS: Athenaeum 2818, 29 Oct 1881; Spectator 54, 3 Dec 1881; Saturday Rev 54, 9 Sep 1882.
The high tide on the coast of Lincolnshire 1571. Boston MA 1883, Boston, Lincolnshire 1972. First pbd in Poems (1863).
Poems: third series. 1885, Boston MA 1885 as Poems of the old days and the new, 1888.
REVIEWS: Athenaeum 3006, 6 June 1885; Br Quart Rev 82, July 1885; Saturday Rev 60, 29 Aug 1885.
John Jerome, his thoughts and ways; a book without beginning. 1886.
Very young and Quite another story. 1890.
REVIEW: Athenaeum 3296, 27 Dec 1890.
A motto changed. 1893 (as Christmas no of Good Words), New York 1894.
The old man's prayer. Manchester [1895]. Verse drama.
Laura Richmond. 1901. First pbd in A sister's bye-hours.
The black polyanthus, and Widow Maclean. 1903. First pbd in A sister's bye-hours.
Ingelow contributed to Good Words, Fraser's Mag, NMM, Harper's, Longman's Mag, St Paul's *and the* Youth's Mag. *See* Wellesley *vol* 5.

§2

Forman, H. B. Our living poets. 1871.
Robertson, E. S. English poetesses. 1883.
Obit: The Times 21 July 1897; Athenaeum 24 July 1897.
Some recollections of Jean Ingelow and her early friends. 1901, Port Washington NY and London 1972.
Peters, M. Jean Ingelow, Victorian poetess. Ipswich 1972.
Ingelow's work was popular in America, and there were separate reprints of many individual poems and stories. [RS]

John Kells Ingram 1823–1907

Bibliographies

Lyster, T. Bibliography of the writings of John Kells Ingram, 1823–1907, with a brief chronology. Dublin 1909.

§1

Who fears to speak of ninety-eight? Nation (Dublin) 1 Apr 1843; rptd in The spirit of the Nation, 1843, and in his Sonnets and other poems, 1900, *below*.
On the 'Opus majus' of Roger Bacon. From the Nat Hist Rev and Quart Jnl Science. Dublin 1858.
Considerations on the state of Ireland: an address. Dublin 1863, 1864 (2nd edn).
Shakespeare. 1863. Lecture.
Tennyson's works. 1863. Lecture.
A comparison between the English and Irish poor law, with respect to the conditions of relief. [Dublin 1864.]
Sonnets and other poems. 1900.

§2

Falkiner, C. L. Memoir of John Kells Ingram, LL. D. Dublin 1907.

William Josiah Irons 1812–83

Selections

Miles 10 (12).
Rhymes, after Horace: six verse translations. Edinburgh 1982 (priv ptd).

§1

Hymn for advent: Dies irae [of Thomas de Celano] translated [as Day of wrath! o day of mourning!]. [1854.]
The words of the hymns in the appendix of the Brompton metrical psalter. [Compiled by W. J. Irons] 1861.
The idea of a national church. 1862. Replies to 'Essays and reviews'.
Hymns for use in church. 1866.
Analysis of human responsibility. [1869.]
Christianity as taught by St Paul. Oxford 1870.
Psalms and hymns for the church. [1875], 1883.
Irons also pbd many sermons and theological tracts.

§2

Obit: The Times 20 June 1883.
Miles, A. H. In Miles 10 (12).
Julian.

William Johnson, later Cory 1823–92

Mss: poems, plays, notebooks, journals, letters etc, Eton College Lib.

Bibliography

Mackenzie, F. C. Cory: a biography. 1950. Includes a list of Cory's works.
See also Bibliography of British literary Bibliographies. *ed.* T. H. *Howard-Hill, Oxford 1987.*

Collections

Ionica. 1891. A reprint of Ionica (1858) and Ionica II, with 85 additional poems and biographical introd and notes by A. C. Benson.

Miles 5.

§1

Ionica. 1858 (anon), 1891, 1905 (3rd edn with biographical introd and notes by A. C. Kan).

Plato, written 1843. In A complete collection of the English poems which have obtained the Chancellor's Gold Medal at the University of Cambridge vol 1, Cambridge 1859.

Eton reform. 2 vols 1861.

On the education of the reasoning faculties. In Essays on a liberal education, ed F. W. Farrar, 1867.

Nuces: exercises on the syntax of the public school Latin primer. 3 vols 1867–70, 1873.

Early modern Europe. Cambridge 1869.

Lucretilis: an introduction to the art of writing Latin lyric verses. 2 vols Eton 1871, new edn Eton 1884, limited edn Cambridge 1851 [75 copies].

Iophon: an introduction to the art of writing Greek iambic verses. 1873.

Ionica II. 1877 (priv ptd). Anon.

A guide to modern English history [1815–35]. 2 vols 1880–2.

Hints for Eton masters. 1898.

Letters and papers

Extracts from the letters and journals, selected and arranged by F. W. Cornish. Oxford 1897 (priv ptd).

§2

Nicoll, W. R. and T. J. Wise. In their Literary anecdotes of the nineteenth century vol 2, 1896.

Paul, H. Stray leaves. 1906. With personal reminiscences.

Notes of the table talk of Cory. In Gathered leaves from the prose of Mary E. Coleridge, ed E. Sichel 1910.

Brett, R. B. Ionicus. 1923. A biography and appreciation, including letters and extracts from Ionica and Lucretilis.

Madan, G. William Cory. Cornhill Mag Aug 1928.

Cory, P. In search of a grandfather. Blackwood's Mag Oct 1946.

Mackenzie, F. C. Cory: a biography. 1950. With unpbd poems.

Ebenezer Jones 1820–60

Selections

Miles 5.

§1

Studies of sensation and event: poems. 1843; ed R. H. Shepherd 1879 (with memorial notices by S. Jones and W. J. Linton). Includes additional poems in appendix.

REVIEWS: Spectator 16, 2 Dec 1843; Spectator 13 Sep 1879.

The land monopoly: the suffering and demoralization caused by it; and the justice and expediency of its abolition. 1849.

§2

Shepherd, R. H. In his Forgotten books worth remembering, 1878. A series of monographs: No 1 Studies of sensation and event.

Watts, T. Athenaeum 21–8 Sep, 12 Oct 1878.

Linton, W. J. In Miles 5.

Rees, T. H. Ebenezer Jones, the neglected poet 1820–1860. [1909.] [RS]

Ernest Charles Jones 1819–68

Selections

Miles 4.

Ernest Jones, Chartist: selections from writings and speeches, with introduction and notes by J. Saville. 1952.

§1

Infantine effusions. Hamburg 1830.

The student of Padua: a domestic tragedy. 1836. A play in verse.

The wood-spirit: a novel. 2 vols 1841, 1855.

My life: a poem. 1846. Introd signed 'Percy-Vere'.

The maid of Warsaw, or the tyrant Czar: a tale of the last Polish revolution. 1854.

The lass and the lady, or love's ladder: a tale of thrilling interest. 1855. Completed by T. Frost. Pbd in parts.

Woman's wrongs: a series of tales. 1855.

The battle-day, and other poems. 1855.

The songs of the lower classes: a song of Cromwell's time. 1856.

Songs of democracy. 1856. Song of the day labourers, A song of resurrection, The marriage feast, Song of the factory slave. Pbd separately as flysheets.

The Emperor's vigil, and the waves and the war. 1856.

The revolt of Hindustan, or the new world: a poem. 1857.

Corayda, a tale of faith and chivalry, and other poems. 1860.

Democracy: a debate between Professor Blackie and the late E. Jones. 1885.

Jones also pbd lectures on social and political subjects.

§2

Obit: The Times 27, 29 Jan, 31 Mar 1868.

Leary, F. The life of Ernest Jones. 1887.

Miles, A. H. In Miles 4.

Robert Dwyer Joyce 1830–83

Ballads, romances and songs. Dublin 1861.

A much admired song called the Drian-naun Don. Dublin [1865?] Anon.

Legends of the wars in Ireland. Boston 1868.

Ballads of Irish chivalry: songs and poems. Complete edn. Boston MA 1872; ed P. Joyce London 1908.

Deirdrè. Boston 1876, Dublin 1877.

Blanid. Boston and Cambridge MA 1879.

Russell, M. Robert Dwyer Joyce. Irish Monthly Jan 1878.

Frances Anne Kemble, afterwards Butler, then Kemble 1809–93

Manuscripts

The ms of Kemble's play An English tragedy *is held in the Library of Congress, together with some of her letters. Over 100 letters, some undated (c. 1830–70), others dated 1877–9, are held at the Univ of Illinois, Urbana. Other letters are held by Columbia Univ Lib (micro New York 1984), Folger, the Berg Collection of NYPL, the Cairns Collection of Univ of Wisconsin-Madison, Boston Public Lib, Massachusetts Historical Soc, New York Historical Soc, Historical Soc of Pennsylvania, and the Lib and Historical Soc of Stockbridge MA. The BL holds the ms of* Francis the First *together with an autobiographical volume and ms copies of her 1844 Poems. See also LR 2, pp. 534–6.*

Collections

Plays by Frances Anne Kemble. 1863. Contains An English tragedy: a play in five acts (also micro New York 1968); Mary Stuart, tr from the Ger of Schiller (also micro New York 1970); Mademoiselle de Belle Isle, tr from the Fr of Alexandre Dumas (also micro New York 1966). Micro Ann Arbor MI [1970] (except for last title), and BL 1974.

Fanny Kemble: the American journals. Ed E. Mavor 1990. Comprises Journal of Frances Anne Kemble, 1835, and Journal of a residence on a Georgian plantation in 1838–1839, 1863.

Selections

Miles 7 (8).

§1

Francis the first: an historical drama. 1832 (8 edns), micros New York 1968 (from 8th edn), Cambridge MA 1976, and Bethlehem PA 1995 (for Univ of California, Davis); New York and Philadelphia 1832, micro Louisville KY [1965?]; 1833 (10th edn). Acting version, with title Francis the first: a tragedy in five acts, London, New York and Philadelphia 1832, 6th Amer edn of this version 'with other poetical pieces' and memoir 1833, micro Cambridge MA [19 ?].

REVIEWS: Athenaeum 17 Mar 1832; (H. H. Milman) Quart Rev 47, Mar 1832.

Journal by Frances Anne Butler. 2 vols 1835, micro Ann Arbor MI 1960; 2 vols Philadelphia 1835, micros Chicago 1970, New Haven CT 1975; rptd New York [1970] as The journal of Frances Anne Butler, better known as Fanny Kemble, micro New York [19 ?]; 1 vol Brussels 1835 (as Journal of a residence in America). The journal has also been rptd as Fanny Kemble: journal of a young actress, ed M. Gough, New York 1990, with complete proper names added from a copy in the Columbia Univ Lib.

REVIEWS: Southern Literary Messenger 1, 1834–5; Niles' Weekly Register 48 1835; Athenaeum 30 May 1835; [E. G. E. Bulwer-Lytton] Edinburgh Rev 61, July 1835; (J. W. Croker) Quart Rev 54, July 1835; Fraser's Mag 12, Sep 1835.

The star of Seville: a drama in five acts. By Mrs Butler (late Miss Kemble). 1837 (2 edns), New York 1837. Micros New York 1965, Ann Arbor MI 1978.

REVIEW: Athenaeum 15 Apr 1837.

Poems. By Frances Anne Butler (late Fanny Kemble). Philadelphia 1844, London, Edinburgh and Dublin 1844 (contents arranged differently).

REVIEWS: Athenaeum 3 Aug 1844; (J. G. Lockhart) Quart Rev 75, Mar 1845.

A year of consolation. By Mrs Butler (late Fanny Kemble). 2 vols in 1 New York 1847, micro Ann Arbor MI [1970?]; 2 vols London 1847, micro Woodbridge CT 1975; 2 vols in 1 Hartford CT 1851.

REVIEWS: Athenaeum 1 and 8 May 1847; (Abraham Hayward) Edinburgh Rev 86, July 1847; (Richard Ford) Quart Rev 81 Sep 1847.

Answer of Frances Anne Butler to the libel of Pierce Butler praying a divorce. n.p. 1848.

Poems. Boston 1859 (mostly new), micro Atlanta GA 1991. London '1866' [1865].

Journal of a residence on a Georgian plantation in 1838–1839. 1863, New York 1863, micros Louisville KY [1960?], Ann Arbor MI 1967, Chicago 1970, Woodbridge CT 1975, New York [19 ?], Washington [19 ?] (Library of Congress). 1863 edn rptd London and New York 1961 (ed and introd by J. A. Scott) and Athens GA 1984. New York reissue 1864 rptd Chicago 1969 (preface by J.-L. Brindamour). New edn Savannah GA 1992. Also pbd in Principles and privilege: two women's lives on a Georgia plantation, Ann Arbor MI 1994 (with Journal of Fanny Butler Leigh). Selections, Claremont CA 1951 (ed J. A. Foster). Play by Anne O'Connell based on text, video Northbrook IL and Atlanta GA 1981. Extracts on slavery were rptd in the nineteenth century by emancipation groups – e.g. by Isa Craig as The essence of slavery, Ladies' London Emancipation Soc Tract no 2 1863 – and as The views of Judge Woodward and Bishop Hopkins on negro slavery in the South, [Philadelphia?] 1863, micros Louisville KY 1962 and Sanford NC [1980].

For contemporary responses to the Journal, *see M. E. Lombard,* Contemporary opinions of Mrs Kemble's Journal of a residence on a Georgian plantation, *Georgia Historical Soc Quart, Dec 1950.*

Record of a girlhood. By Frances Anne Kemble. 3 vols 1878, 1879 (2nd edn), (3rd edn, rev), 1 vol New York 1879 (2 edns, as Records of a girlhood; micro New Haven CT 1975), other US edns 1883, 1884. Rptd in part from Kemble's Old woman's gossip, Atlantic Monthly 36–9 1875–7. Extracts rptd as Fanny Kemble's ride on the Liverpool and Manchester railway, [New York 1939] (priv ptd, limited edn).

REVIEWS: Theatre 1 Dec 1878; (Abraham Hayward) Quart Rev 154, July 1882.

Records of later life. 3 vols 1882 (2 edns); 1 vol New York 1882, micros New Haven CT 1976, Washington 1978 (LC); 1883 (2nd edn).

REVIEWS: Atlantic Monthly 50 1882; Littell's Living Age 154 1882; Athenaeum 8 July 1882; (George Archdale) Temple Bar 66, Oct 1882.

Notes upon some of Shakespeare's plays. 1882, micros Ann Arbor MI [196 ?], Washington [19 ?] (LC), facs New York 1972. Introd pbd Cornhill Mag 8, Dec 1863 as On the stage, and rptd New York 1926, ed and introd by G. Arliss (Pbns of the Dramatic Museum of Columbia Univ, 5th ser, Papers on acting III).

Poems. 1883, micro Washington 1985 (LC). Some from 1844 vol, many from 1859 vol, 25 new poems and 5 trns from Fr.

REVIEW: Critic 4 1884.

Adventures of John Timothy Homespun in Switzerland: stolen from the French of Tartarin de Tarascon. 1889. Play imitating Daudet's Tartarin sur les Alpes.

Far away and long ago. 1889, New York 1889 (Leisure Hour ser no 225); micros Ann Arbor MI 1978, Woodbridge CT [197-?].

REVIEWS: Nation 49 1889; Athenaeum 8 June 1889.

Further records 1848–1883: a series of letters forming a sequel to Record of a girlhood and Records of later life. 2 vols 1890, 2 vols New York 1891, rptd 1972 (2 vols in 1); micros New Haven CT 1976, Washington [19 ?] (LC).

REVIEW: Atlantic Monthly 67 1891.

Kemble's letters and extracts from her jnls have appeared in Fanny, the American Kemble: her journals and unpublished letters, *ed with annotations by Fanny Kemble Wister (her great-granddaughter), Tallahassie GA 1972, and in* The terrific Kemble, *ed Eleanor Ransome, Hamilton, Ontario 1978.*

Contributions to periodicals

A mother's memories. Pittsfield Sun 8 Feb 1849.

Some notes on Shakespeare. Atlantic Monthly 1860.

Lady Macbeth. Macmillan's Mag 17, Feb 1868. Signed Fanny Kemble.

Salvini's Othello. Temple Bar 71, July 1884. Signed Fanny Kemble.

The rose lily: a Yankee yarn. Temple Bar 82, Jan 1888.

For Kemble's contributions to Bentley's Misc *and* NMM, *see* Wellesley *vol 5 1989.*

Translation

The Christmas tree, and other tales: adapted from the German by Frances Kemble. '1856' [1855].

Imitations

My conscience! Fanny Thimble Cutler's journal of a residence in America, whilst performing a profitable theatrical engagement: beating the nonsensical Fanny Kemble journal all hollow. Philadelphia 1835.

Fanny Kemble in America: or journal of an actress with remarks on the state of society in America and England. By an English lady four years resident in the United States. Boston 1835.

In her biography, Fanny Kemble *(Chapel Hill NC 1933), L. S. Driver argues that both imitations were written by Kemble herself in response to unfavourable reviews.*

§2

Obit: New York Sun 17 Jan 1893; Pall Mall Gazette 17 and 21 Jan 1893; Philadelphia Times 17 Jan 1893; New York Times 18 Jan 1893; London Daily Mail 20 Jan 1893 (by Kemble's publisher George Bentley).

Coleman, J. Fanny Kemble. Theatre 33, Mar 1893.

James, Henry. Essays in London and elsewhere. New York 1893.

Lee, H. Frances Anne Kemble. Atlantic Monthly 71 1893.

MacMahon, E. Fanny Kemble. Littell's Living Age 197 1893.
Ritchie, Anne Thackeray. Chapters from some unwritten memoirs – Mrs Kemble. Macmillan's Mag 68, July 1893.
Todd, C. B. Fanny Kemble at Lenox. Lippincott's Monthly Mag 52 1893.
Upson, A. J. Fanny Kemble in America, and Fanny Kemble's suddenness, Critic 22 1893.
Beard, N. Some recollections of yesterday. Temple Bar 102, July 1894.
Driver, L. S. Fanny Kemble. Chapel Hill NC 1933.
Wright, C. Fanny Kemble. 1972.
Marshall, D. Fanny Kemble. 1977.
Furnas, J. C. Fanny Kemble. New York 1982. [JW]

Charles Rann Kennedy 1808–67

Classical education reformed. 1837.
Translation of selected speeches of Demosthenes, with notes. 1841.
Ode on the birth of the Prince. 1842. On Albert Edward, Prince of Wales.
Poems, original and translated. 1843, 1857 (rearranged and enlarged). Includes 2 poems by Rev R. Kennedy.
The Olynthiac and other public creations of Demosthenes. 1848. Tr with notes by Kennedy. Frequently rptd.
Works of Virgil. Tr R. and C. R. Kennedy 2 vols 1849.
A letter to the Lord Chancellor on the subject of circuit leagues. 1850.
Specimens of Greek and Latin verse, chiefly translation. 1853. English verse tr into Greek and Latin.
Francis Beaumont: a tragedy. Birmingham [1860?]. In verse.
The works of Virgil. 1861.
Hannibal: a poem. [1866.]
Kennedy also wrote on classical and legal subjects.

Letitia Elizabeth Landon, afterwards Maclean, 'L. E. L.' 1802–38

Collections

The poetical works. 3 vols 1827.
The poetical works. [1830?] Containing The Venetian bracelet and other poems.
The miscellaneous poetical works. 1835.
Works. 2 vols Philadelphia 1838, 1847.
Poetical works. 4 vols 1839.
Poetical works, with a memoir of the author. 2 vols 1850, 1853, 1855, 1867.
Complete works. 2 vols Boston 1856.
Poetical works. Ed W. B. Scott [1873], [1880].
Miles 7 (8).

§1

The fate of Adelaide: a Swiss romantic tale, and other poems. 1821.
The improvisatrice and other poems. 1824, 1825 (6th edn), 1831.
The troubadour, catalogue of pictures and historical sketches. 1825 (3 edns), 1827.
The golden violet, with its tales of romance and chivalry, and other poems. 1827.
The Venetian bracelet, the lost Pleiad, a history of the lyre and other poems. 1828.
Romance and reality. 3 vols 1831, 1 vol 1856 (with memoir). A novel.
Francesca Carrara. 3 vols 1834. A novel.
The vow of the peacock, and other poems. 1835.
Traits and trials of early life. 1836, 1844. Tales with poems interspersed.
Ethel Churchill: or the two brides. 3 vols 1837, 1847. A novel.
A birthday tribute, addressed to the Princess Alexandrina Victoria. [1837.] In verse.
Duty and inclination: a novel, edited by Miss Landon. 3 vols 1838.
Floers of loveliness. 1838, [1854]. Poems, with Lady Blessington and T. H. Bayly.
The Easter gift: a religious offering. [1838.]
The Zenana, and minor poems of Letitia Elizabeth Landon; with a memoir by Emma Roberts. 1839.
Lady Anne Granard: or keeping up appearances. 3 vols 1842, 1 vol 1847. A novel.
The gift of friendship, with contributions by Letitia Elizabeth Landon [1877.]
Landon also edited or contributed to various annuals, scrapbooks etc, as well as writing numerous articles and reviews for W. Jerdan's Literary Gazette *from c. 1820.*

Letters and papers

Blanchard, S. L. Life and literary remains of Letitia Elizabeth Landon 2 vols 1841. Vol 2 consists of unpbd works by Landon.

§2

S[heppard], S. Characteristics of the genius and writings of Letitia Elizabeth Landon 1841.
Elwood, A. K. In her Memoirs of the literary ladies of England vol 2, 1843.
Hall, S. C. and A. M. Memories of authors: Miss Landon. Atlantic Monthly Mar 1865.
Robertson, E. S. In his English poetesses, 1883.
Bates, W. In his Maclise portrait-gallery of illustrious literary characters, 1883.
Bell, M. In Miles 7 (8).
Lefèvre-Deumier, J. In his Célébrités anglaises: essais et études biographiques et littéraires, Paris 1895.
Enfield, D. E. Laetitia Elizabeth Landon: a mystery of the thirties. 1928.

Edward Lear 1812–88

The mss of Lear's diaries are in the Houghton Lib, Harvard. The letters to Chichester Fortescue (Lord Carlingford) are in the Somerset Record Office.

Bibliographies

Field, W. B. O. Edward Lear on my shelves. Munich 1933 (priv ptd).
Noakes, V. Edward Lear 1812–1888. 1985, New York 1986. Royal Academy of Arts exhibition catalogue.

Collections

The Lear omnibus, filled up by R. L. Mégroz: (the first rearrangement of Edward Lear's nonsense). 1938, [1945].
Edward Lear's nonsense omnibus, with all the original pictures, verses and stories . . . Introd E. Strachey, London and New York 1943, Harmondsworth 1986.
The complete nonsense of Edward Lear. Ed H. Jackson 1947.

Selections

A nonsense birthday book: compiled from 'The book of nonsense' and 'More nonsense'. London and New York [1893].
Edward Lear's journals: a selection. Ed H. Van Thal 1952.
The birds of Edward Lear: a selection of the 12 finest bird plates of the artist. Ed A. Thorpe 1975 (limited edn).
A book of bosh: lyrics and prose. Chosen by B. Alderson. Harmondsworth 1975.
For lovers of birds; For lovers of cats; For lovers of flowers & gardens; For lovers of food & drink. Compiled by V. Noakes and C. Lewsen. 4 vols 1978.
A book of learned nonsense: a centenary anthology of writings & sketches. Ed P. Haining 1987.
Edward Lear in the Levant: travels in Albania, Greece and Turkey in Europe 1848–1849. Ed S. Hyman 1988.
Edward Lear, the Corfu years: a chronicle presented through his letters and journals. Ed P. Sherrard, Athens and Dedham 1988.

§1

Views in Rome and its environs: drawn from nature and on stone. 1841.

A book of nonsense. 2 vols 1846, 1 vol [1855], 1861 ('with many new pictures and verses'), 1870 (coloured edn), 1909 (miniature edn). First pbd under the pseudonym 'Derry Down Derry'. See J. G. Schiller, Nonsensus: cross-referencing Edward Lear's original 116 limericks with eight holograph mss and comparing them to printed texts from the 1846, 1855 and 1861 versions . . . Stroud 1988.

Illustrated excursions in Italy. 2 vols 1846.

Journals of a landscape painter in Albania, etc. 1851, 1965 (as Edward Lear in Greece), 1988 (as Journals of a landscape painter in Greece and Albania).

Journals of a landscape painter in southern Calabria, etc. 1852, 1964 (as Edward Lear in southern Italy).

Views in the seven Ionian islands. 1863, Oldham 1979 (facs edn of 1000 copies).

Journal of a landscape painter in Corsica. 1870, 1966 (as Edward Lear in Corsica).

Nonsense songs, stories, botany and alphabets. 1871.

More nonsense, pictures, rhymes, botany, etc. 1872.

Laughable lyrics: a fourth book of nonsense poems, songs, botany, music, etc. 1877.

Poems by Alfred, Lord Tennyson, illustrated by Edward Lear. London and New York 1889.

Nonsense songs and stories. 9th rev edn London and New York 1894, London 1984 (facs edn). Selections from the earlier books of nonsense with additional material.

Queery Leary nonsense: a Lear nonsense book. Ed Lady Strachey 1911.

Edward Lear's ABC. [1914.]

Facsimile of a nonsense alphabet drawn and written by Edward Lear. 1926. Edn limited to 1000 copies.

Lear in Sicily: twenty line drawings by Edward Lear illustrating a tour made in May–July 1847 . . . . Ed G. Proby 1938.

Edward Lear's Indian journal: watercolours and extracts from the diary of Edward Lear (1873–1875). Ed R. Murphy 1953.

Teapots and quails and other new nonsenses. Ed A. Davidson and P. Hofer 1953.

ABC: first publication of this Lear alphabet penned and illustrated by Edward Lear, himself. New York and London 1965.

Rhymes of nonsense: an alphabet. 1968. Edn limited to 500 copies.

Ye long nite in ye wonderfull bedde: a bread-and-butter letter with reservations? Cambridge [1971].

Lear in the original: drawings and limericks by Edward Lear for his Book of nonsense, now first pbd in facs together with other unpbd nonsense drawings. Ed H. W. Liebert, New York and London 1975.

Bosh and nonsense. 1982 (reproduced from 2 sketchbooks for Ada Duncan).

The tragical life and death of Caius Marius esquire . . . New York 1983 (reproduced in an edn of 100 copies from an original ms).

Many of the items contained in Lear's books of nonsense have been and continue to be pbd separately or in various combinations both with Lear's own illustrations and with others. Translations, painting books and other ephemera are not listed. Lear's major natural history art-work includes Illustrations of the family of psittacidae or parrots *(1832),* Gleanings from the menagerie and aviary at Knowsley Hall *(1846), and* Tortoises, terrapins and turtles *(1872 with J. de C. Sowerby).*

Letters

Letters of Edward Lear to Chichester Fortescue, Lord Carlingford, and Frances Countess Waldegrave. Ed Lady Strachey 1907.

Later letters of Edward Lear to Chichester Fortescue (Lord Carlingford), Frances Countess Waldegrave and others. Ed Lady Strachey 1911.

Lear's Corfu: an anthology drawn from the painter's letters and prefaced by Lawrence Durrell. Corfu 1965.

A letter from Edward Lear to R. W. Raper. Edinburgh 1969 (35 copies).

Edward Lear: selected letters. Ed V. Noakes, Oxford 1988.

§2

Davidson, A. Edward Lear: landscape painter and nonsense poet (1812–1888). 1938, rptd 1968.

Noakes, V. Edward Lear: the life of a wanderer. 1968, 1979 (rev), 1985.

Byrom, T. Nonsense and wonder: the poems and cartoons of Edward Lear. New York 1977.

Caboni, A. Nonsense: Edward Lear e la tradizione del nonsense inglese. Roma 1988.

Levi, P. Edward Lear: a biography. 1995. [EH]

Robert Leighton 1822–69

Selections

Miles 5.

Rogers, C. Modern Scottish minstrels. 1870.

§1

Rimes and poems: by Robin. Glasgow [1850?].

Poems by Robin. 1855.

[Burns centenary poem.] In Burns centenary poems, ed G. Anderson and J. Finlay, Glasgow 1859.

Rhymes and poems. 1861, 1861.

Poems. Liverpool 1866, 1869.

Scotch words, and the bapteesement o' the bairn. 1869 (3 edns), New York 1869, London 1870, New York 1873. With biography.

Reuben and other poems. 1875.

Records and other poems. 1880. Reuben and Records together constitute Leighton's collected works.

§2

Miles, A. H. In Miles 5.

William James Linton 1812–98

Collections

Prose and verse: written and published in the course of fifty years 1836–86. 20 vols [1886]. A collection made by Linton and presented to the BM.

Poems and translations. 1889.

Miles 4.

§1

Modern slavery, by Robert de la Mennais. Tr from the French by Linton 1840.

The life of Thomas Paine. By the editor of 'The National'. 1840.

Bob Thin or the poorhouse fugitive. 1845 (priv ptd). A satire.

The lovers' stratagem and other tales. 1849.

The people's land and an easy way to recover it. By the editor of 'The National'. 1850. Letters on Ireland.

The plaint of freedom. To the memory of Milton. Newcastle-upon-Tyne 1852.

Help for Poland. [1854.]

The ferns of the English lake country. 1865.

Claribel and other poems. 1865. Claribel is a dramatic poem in 2 acts.

Ireland for the Irish: rhymes and reasons against landlordism. New York 1867.

The flower and the star, and other stories for children. Boston 1868, London [1892].

The religion of organization. Boston 1869. An essay, rptd from Boston Radical.

The house that Tweed built. 1871. Anon. A political lampoon in verse.

The Paris commune. In answer to the calumnies of the New York Tribune. Boston 1871. Rptd from The Radical.
Pot-pouri. New York 1875. Parodies of E. A. Poe.
Famine: a masque. Hamden CT 1875, [1887].
The American odyssey: adventures of Ulysses: exposed in modest hudibrastic measure by Abel Reid and A. N. Broome. Washington 1876. Reid and Broome are pseudonymous for Linton.
Poetry of America: 1878. Selections from 100 American poets from 1776–1876, with some Negro melodies.
James Watson: a memoir. Hamden CT 1879 (priv ptd), Manchester 1880.
Reminiscences of Eben Jones. In Jones's Studies of sensation and event, 1879.
Voices of the dead. [1879?] A letter to the editor of Nineteenth Cent.
Cetewayo and Dean Stanley. [1880.] Anon.
Golden apples of Hesperus: poems not in the collections. New Haven CT 1882. Ed Linton.
Wind-falls, two hundred and odd. [1882.] Quotations ed Linton.
Rare poems of the sixteenth and seventeenth centuries. New Haven CT 1882 (priv ptd in edn of 5 copies), London 1883. Partly a reprint of Golden apples of Hesperus, *above*.
English verse. 5 vols New York 1883, London 1884. Ed Linton and R. H. Stoddard.
Love-lore. Hamden CT 1887 (priv ptd), 1895 (adds other poems).
Catoninetales: a domestic epic by Hattie Brown. Ed [actually written by] Linton 1891. Parodies.
The flower and the star, and other stories for children. [1891.]
Wells, C. J. Stories after nature, with a preface by Linton. 1891.
Heliconundrums. Hamden CT 1892 (priv ptd).
Broadway ballads, collected for the centennial commemoration of the republic, by Abel Reid. [Hamden CT 1893.]
European republicans: recollections of Mazzini and friends. 1893.
Life of J. G. Whittier. 1893.
A Christmas carol. [Hamden CT? 1893.]
Times and seasons. [Hamden CT 1893.]
Of a mollusc. [Hamden CT 1895.]
Ultima verba. 1895 (priv ptd).
Memories. 1895.
Darwin's probabilities. Hamden CT 1896. A review of The descent of man.
Linton also edited English Republic, Illuminated Mag *and* National.

§2

Kitton, F. G. W. J. Linton. Eng Illustr Mag April 1891.
Bullen, A. H. In Miles 4.
Obit: The Times 3 Jan 1898; Athenaeum 8, 15 Jan 1898.
Layard, G. S. In his Life of Mrs Lynn Linton, 1901.
Hopson, W. F. Side lights on Linton 1812–97. PBSA 27 1933.
Smith, F. B. Radical artisan: William James Linton, 1812–97. Manchester 1973.

Frederick Locker-Lampson 1821–95

Mss: collections in Harvard, Houghton Lib; Huntington. Letters to Tennysons, Lincoln, Tennyson Research Centre.

Bibliographies

See Bibliography of British literary bibliographies, ed T. H. Howard-Hill, Oxford 1987.
Livingston, F. V. Bookman's Jnl May, July–Sep 1924. Detailed account of all edns of Locker-Lampson's works.

Selections

A selection from the works of Frederick Locker. 1865, 1868. Includes 20 unpbd pieces, the rest rev.
Miles 5.

§1

London lyrics. 1857, 1862 (with alterations and omissions, adds 20 new poems), 1868 (priv ptd as Poems) (adds 6 poems, omits others), 1870 (adds 6 poems), 1872 (adds 10 poems), 1874 (adds 8 poems), 1876 (final revision, adds 6 poems), 1882 (as London rhymes; omits much, but adds 9 poems), New York 1883 (pirated as Poems), 1884 (authorised edn, as Poems, and differing slightly from 1876 edn); ed A. D. Godley 1903 (from 1857 edn); ed A. Dobson 1904 (definitive edn).
Lyra elegantiarum. 1867 (suppressed), 1867 (rev), 1891 (rev and enlarged, with C. Kernahan). A collection of English vers de société and vers d'occasion, ed Locker.
Patchwork. 1879 (priv ptd), 1879. A commonplace book, with 5 poems by Locker-Lampson, 3 of which are new.
The Rowfant library. 1886. A catalogue. An appendix, with preface by A. Birell and memorial verses by A. Dobson, A. Lang, Lord Crewe and W. S. Blunt pbd separately 1900.
My confidences: an autobiographical sketch addressed to my descendents. Ed A. Birrell 1896, 1908.

§2

Dobson, A. In Miles 5.
Swinburne, A. C. In his Studies in prose and poetry, 1894.
Birell, A. Locker-Lampson: a character sketch. 1920.
Locker-Lampson, O. Locker-Lampson, with some unpublished sketches and poems. Scribner's Mag Apr 1921.
Locker-Lampson, O. Recollections of Locker-Lampson. Cornhill Mag Jan–Feb 1921.
Kernahan, C. Austin Dobson and Lyra elegantiarum. London Quart Rev 1922; Living Age 4 Mar 1922.
Dunbar, J. R. Some letters of Joaquin Miller to Locker. MLQ 11 1950. 10 letters.
Flanagan, J. T. Dr Holmes selects American verse. JEGP 51 1952. Rejected suggestions for Lyra elegantiarum.
Bates, M. C. That delightful man. HLB 13 1959.
Ketton-Cremer, R. W. Locker-Lampson's Lyra elegantiarum, 1867. BC 8 1959.

Capel Lofft 1806–73

The Whigs: their prospects and policy. 1835.
Self-formation: or the history of an individual mind. By a fellow of a college. 2 vols 1837, 1 vol Boston 1896. Anon. A mental autobiography.
Ernest, or political regeneration: a poem. 1839 (anon), 1868 (as Ernest: the rule of right, adds a long preface on the nature of poetry, and much revision). A long poem on the history of Chartism.
REVIEW: [Millman, H. H.] Quart Rev 65 1840.
New Testament: suggestions for reformation of Greek text on principles of logical criticism, by 'R. E. Storer'. 1868.

Thomas Toke Lynch 1818–71

Bibliography

Gatherings from notes of discourses by the late Thomas Toke Lynch (1852–1871). 1885. Contains list of Lynch's writings.

Selections

The rivulet birthday book, compiled chiefly from The rivulet and Theophilus Trinal by M. Theobald. [1891].
Selections from The rivulet. Manchester [1910].
Miles 10 (11).

§1

Thoughts on day: a Christian address. 1844 (anon), 1856 (adds a morning and an evening hymn), 1872 (3rd edn).

Memorials of Theophilus Trinal, student. 1850, 1853, 1869 (enlarged), 1882. 54 poems in 1st edn, 81 in 3rd edn.
REVIEWS: Athenaeum 1199, 19 Oct 1850; Spectator 23, 19 Oct 1850.
Wrong charged and right pleaded: a letter to the editor of the Christian Witness and British Banner occasioned by an editorial passage respecting 'the Glasgow case'. 1850.
An address delivered at Blagrove's Rooms, Mortimer Street, London, at a social meeting of the members and friends of the Church assembling for worship there. 1851.
Essays on some of the forms of literature. 1853.
Lectures in aid of self improvement, addressed to young men and others. 1853, 1856 (2nd edn).
The rivulet: a contribution to sacred song. 1855, 1856, 1868 (enlarged), 1883 (5th edn).
REVIEWS: Literary Churchman 2, 9 Feb 1856; Br Quart Rev 23, Apr 1856; Literary Churchman 2, 20 Sep 1856 (2nd edn).
The ethics of quotation: with a preliminary letter to the secretaries of the Congregational union, by Silent Long. 1856. With Songs controversial, *below*, this pam constitutes Lynch's reply to the attack made on Rivulet, *above*, in Br Banner.
Songs controversial, by Silent Long. 1856. 15 pieces addressed to the editor of Br Banner, attacking his reviews of The rivulet.
Among transgressors: a theological tract. 1860.
An old question and answer: a sermon preached at the assembly room, 3 Gower Street North, on Sunday morning, 30 September 1860. [1860.]
The twofold promise: a sermon preached at the assembly room, 3 Gower Street North, on Sunday morning, 7 October 1860. [1860.]
A group of six sermons. 1869.
The Mornington lecture: Thursday evening addresses. 1870.
REVIEWS: Spectator 43, 26 Mar 1870; Br Quart Rev 51, Apr 1870.
Sermons for my curates. 1871. Ed Samuel Cox.
REVIEWS: Br Quart Rev 54, Oct 1871; Spectator 7 Sep 1872.
Letters to the Scattered and other papers. 1872. First pbd in Christian Spectator.
REVIEW: Spectator 12 Oct 1872.
Lynch pbd poems and articles in the Christian Spectator.

§2

Most of this material, which is selected, concerns the controversy over the supposed pantheism of The rivulet.
Campbell, J. Nonconformist theology. [1856.] 'On the pernicious errors of Mr Lynch's Rivulet'.
Grant, B. What is negative theology? [1856.]
Grant, B. 'What's it all about?' 1856.
James, J. A. The rivulet controversy. 1856.
Little, J. The controversy – what results? 1856.
Binney, T. Who is right and who wrong? 1857.
White, W. Memoir of Thomas T. Lynch. 1874. Includes a list of Lynch's writings.
Horder, W. G. In Miles 10 (11). [RS]

Denis Florence MacCarthy 1817–82

§1

The book of Irish ballads. Ed D. F. MacCarthy 1846, London and Dublin 1846, 1853, 1861, 1869 (rev and enlarged), 1874 (rev and enlarged).
The poets and dramatists of Ireland. Dublin 1846. With contribution by MacCarthy.
Ballads, poems and lyrics, original and translated. Dublin 1850, [1860?].
The bell-founder and other poems. London and Dublin 1857.
Under glimpses and other poems. 1857.
Irish legends and lyrics, with poems of the imagination and fancy. Dublin 1858.
The poets and poetry of Ireland. New York 1868. With contribution by MacCarthy.
Shelley's early life from original sources. [1872.]
The centenary of Moore, May 28th, 1879; an ode. 1880 (priv ptd).
Poems. Dublin 1882, 1884 (2nd edn).
Poems. Dublin 1931.
MacCarthy also translated the works of Calderón into verse dramas, collected in 1853.

§2

The poems of MacCarthy. Dublin Rev 28 1850.
The poems of MacCarthy. Irish Quart Rev 7 1858.
Taylor, G. Notes towards an anthology. Bell 3 1942.

Charles Mackay 1814–89

Mss: poems, autobiographical writings, essays, unpbd novel, handbook for poets and versifiers, personal papers etc, Perth Museum and Art Gallery archives.

Collections

Selected poems. In Modern Scottish minstrel, ed C. Rogers, vol 6, 1857. With memoir by F. Bennoch.
Poetical works. 1857, New York 1857, 1868, 1877 [Chandos Classics].
Collected songs. 1859 (for 1858). Includes 100 songs pbd for first time.
Poetical works. 1876. With introd rptd from Egeria and other poems.
Selected poems and songs. 1888. Introd of short criticisms by D. Jerrold, G. Combe and A. B. Reach, with a long anon review rptd from St James's Mag.
Miles 4.

§1

Songs and poems. 1834.
A history of London from its foundation by the Romans to the accession of Queen Victoria. 1838.
The hope of the world and other poems. 1840.
The Thames and its tributaries, or rambles among the rivers. 2 vols 1840.
Longbeard, Lord of London: a romance. 3 vols 1841, 1850 (as Longbeard: or the revolt of the Saxons).
Memoirs of extraordinary popular delusions and the madness of crowds. 3 vols 1841, Philadelphia 1850, 2 vols London 1852 etc; 2 vols New York 1856; ed B. M. Barch, Boston 1932, selections 1973.
The salamandrine or love and immortality. 1842, Glasgow 1845, Edinburgh 1845, 1853, 1856. (3 issues.)
Legends of the isles and other poems. Edinburgh 1845, 1857 (as Legends of the isles and Highland gatherings). Some of the poems rptd 1856 as Ballads and lyrical poems.
Voices from the crowd, and other poems. 1846, 1846 (3rd edn), 1857 (5th edn rev). Rptd from Daily News.
The scenery and poetry of the English lakes. 1846, 1852.
Education of the people, and the necessity for the establishment of a national system. Glasgow 1846, 1852.
Life and times of Sir Robert Peel from the date of his final retirement to his premature death. 1846, 1851. Vol 4 of the Life and times of Sir Robert Peel, carried to vol 3 by C. Taylor.
Voices from the mountains. 1847, 1857.
[Poem.] In G. Cruickshank, The bottle, [1847].
Town lyrics and other poems. 1848.
[Poem.] In G. Cruickshank, The drunkard's children, 1848.
The world as it is. 3 vols 1849–53. With W. C. Taylor. A system of modern geography.
Egeria: or the spirit of nature; and other poems. 1850. With an introductory essay on poetry.
The life-boat. [1850.] A song.
Far, far upon the sea. [1850?], [1860?].

Cheer, boys, cheer. [1850?]
Tubal-Cain. [1850?]; ed L. A. Sloa, Chicago [1916].
Longbeard. 1850 [Railway Lib].
The Mormons: or latter-day saints. 1851, 1852, 1853, 1857.
The reason why. Manchester [1852]. An anti-Corn Law ballad.
Songs for music. 1856.
The lump of gold, and other poems. 1856, 1861.
Ballads and lyrical poems. 1856, 1859.
The joy-bell and the requiem. In In honorem: songs of the brave, 1856.
Under green leaves. 1857.
The home affections pourtrayed [*sic*] by the poets. 1858.
Life and liberty in America. 2 vols 1859, New York 1859.
A man's heart: a poem. 1860.
The whisky-demon. 1860, Edinburgh 1860.
Original songs for the rifle volunteers, by S. Lover, C. Mackay and T. Miller. 1861.
The history of the United States of America by W. H. Bartlett. With a continuation . . . by Charles Mackay. 2 vols 1861, 1867.
The gouty philosopher. 1862, 1864 (2nd edn). Essays.
Studies from the antique and sketches from nature. 1864, 1867 (2nd edn). Verse.
Street tramways for London. 1868.
The souls of the children. Ramsgate 1869.
Under the blue sky. 1871. Papers rptd from All the Year Round, Robin Goodfellow etc.
Baron Gimbrosh, DPhil and sometime Governor of Barataria. 1872.
Lost beauties of the English language: an appeal to authors. 1874.
Forty years' recollections of life, literature and public affairs from 1830 to 1870. 2 vols 1877.
Gideon Brown: a true story of the covenant. 1877. Ed Mackay.
The Gaelic etymology of the languages of western Europe. 1877.
The Liberal Party: its present position and future work. 1880.
Luck: and what came of it. 3 vols 1881. A novel.
The poetry and humour of the Scottish language. Paisley 1882. In part rptd from Blackwood's Mag.
Interludes and undertones: or music at twilight. 1884 ('for 1883').
New light on some obscure words and phrases in the works of Shakespeare and his contemporaries. 1884.
A glossary of obscure words and phrases in the works of Shakespeare and his contemporaries. 1884, 1887.
The founders of the American republic. Edinburgh 1885.
Through the long day. Memorials of a literary life. 2 vols 1887.
The strange experience of Mr Rameses. 2 vols 1887. Anon.
A dictionary of Lowland Scotch. Edinburgh 1888 (priv ptd), London 1888. With an appendix of Scottish proverbs.
Gossamer and snowdrift: posthumous poems. Ed E. Mackay 1890.
Mackay also edited anthologies and periodicals, was The Times *correspondent in American Civil War and contributed extensively to* Blackwood's Mag; *see* Wellesley *vol 5, 1989.*

§2

Powell, T. In his Pictures of the living songs of Britain, 1851.
Miles, A. H. In Miles 4.
Wykoff, G. S. England's forgotton Civil War correspondent. South Atlantic Quart 1927.

James Clarence Mangan 1803–49

Bibliographies

O'Hegarty, P. A bibliography of Mangan. Dublin 1941. Rptd from Dublin Mag.

Collections

Poems, original and translated: being a selection from his contributions to Irish periodicals. [Dublin] 1852. Christmas supplement to Nation 25 Dec 1852.
Poems, with a biographical introduction. Ed J. Mitchel, New York 1859, 1870.
Essays in prose and verse. Ed C. P. Meehan, Dublin 1884.
Irish and other poems, with a selection from his translations. Dublin 1886.
Irish poetic gems, from Mangan, Moore and Griffin. Dublin 1887.
Selected poems. Ed L. Guiney 1897.
Poems. Ed D. O'Donoghue, Dublin 1903. Centenary edn. Introd by J. Mitchel.
Prose writings. Ed D. O'Donoghue, Dublin 1904. With essay by Lionel Johnson.
Dark Rosaleen [etc]. Dublin [1923].
Poems. Dublin 1931.

§1

Anthologia germanica: a series of translations from the most popular of the German poets. 2 vols Dublin 1845.
The poets and poetry of Munster. Dublin 1849 (trns from Irish with Irish texts, ed J. O'Daly), 1850; London and Dublin 1851 (3rd edn); ser 2 Dublin 1860, 189-? (Irish texts rev by W. Hennessey and ed C. Meehan).
Romances and ballads of Ireland. Ed H. Ellis, Dublin 1850. With contributions by Mangan.
The tribes of Ireland: a satire by Aenghus O'Daly. Dublin 1852. Irish texts with poetical trn by Mangan.
Autobiography. Ed J. Kilroy, Dublin 1968.

§2

Ingram, J. James Clarence Mangan. Dublin Univ Mag 90 1877.
Fragment of an unpublished autobiography. Irish Monthly Nov 1882.
MacColl, J. The life of Mangan. Dublin [1887].
O'Donoghue, D. The life and writings of Mangan. Edinburgh 1897, Chicago 1897.
Graves, A. James Clarence Mangan. Cornhill Mag Mar 1898.

Sir Theodore Martin, 'Bon Gaultier' 1816–1909

§1

Disputation between the body and soul. Edinburgh 1838. Poem, signed T. M., with other poems by Martin signed E. N., Martinus Scriblerus and I. G.
Dante and Beatrice. [1845?] Essay on 'Vita Nuova'.
The book of ballads, edited by 'Bon Gaultier'. 1845, [1849] (with new ballads), 1857 (5th edn), 1866 (9th edn), 1903 (16th edn). By Martin and W. E. Aytoun.
Hertz, King René's daughter. 1850, 1864 (2nd edn), 3rd edn in Madonna Pia, *below*. Trn.
Öhlenschläger, Correggio: a tragedy, with notes. 1854. Trn.
Madonna Pia: a tragedy and three other dramas [King Renée's daughter; The camp of Wallenstein; The gladiator of Ravenna]. 1855 (priv ptd), 1860, Edinburgh 1894.
Öhlenschläger, Aladdin: or the wonderful lamp. 1857, 1863. Trn.
Goethe, Poems and ballads. 1859, 1860 (rev and enlarged), 1877, 1907. Tr with W. E. Aytoun.
The odes of Horace translated into English verse. 1860, 1861.
The poems of Catullus translated into English verse. 1861, 1875.
Dante, The Vita nuova. 1862, 1864, 1871, 1893 (3rd edn). Trn.
Poems, original and translated. 1863 (priv ptd).
Goethe, Faust pt 1. 1865, 1866, 1877; Pts 1–2 1870, 1954. Trn.
Memoir of W. E. Aytoun. 1867, 1868.
Horace. 1870. An account of his life and works.
The odes, epodes and satires of Horace. 1870, 1870 (3rd edn), 1881. Trn.
Schiller, Complete works, ed C. J. Hempel vol 1. William Tell tr Martin. 1870, rptd New York 1951.
Essays on the drama. 2 vols 1874–89.

The life of his Royal Highness the Prince Consort. 5 vols 1875–80; tr Fr 1883.
Heine, Poems and ballads. 1878, 1894, 1907. Trn.
Horace, Works, translated into English verse, with life and notes. 2 vols Edinburgh 1881.
A life of Lord Lyndhurst. 1883, 1884.
Sketch of the life of Princess Alice. 1885.
'Halm, F.', The gladiator of Ravenna. 1885. Trn.
Shakespeare or Bacon? Edinburgh 1888.
Schiller, The song of the bell and other translations. Edinburgh 1889.
Virgil, The Aeneid books 1–6. Edinburgh 1896. Trn.
Helena Faucit (Lady Martin). Edinburgh 1900, 1900.
Queen Victoria as I knew her. 1902 (priv ptd), 1908.
Leopardi, Poems. 1904. Trn.
Monographs: Garrick, Macready, Rachel and Baron Stockmar. 1906.
Martin pbd several addresses etc. See also Wellesley *vol 5, p. 1002.*

§2

Theodore Martin. Dublin Univ Mag 90 1877.
Whyte, W. In Miles 9 (10). Under Aytoun-Martin, 'Bon Gaultier'.
Obit: Blackwood's Mag Sep 1909.
Parsons, C. O. The friendship of Martin and William Harrison Ainsworth. N & Q 23 June 1934.

Gerald Massey 1828–1907

Collections

Complete poetical works. Boston 1857, 1861. With biographical sketch by S. Smiles.
My lyrical life: poems old and new. 2 vols 1889.
Miles 5.

§1

Poems and chansons. Tring 1848.
Voices of freedom and lyrics of love. 1850.
The ballad of Babe Christabel, with other lyrical poems. 1854, 1854 (4th edn enlarged), 1855.
Craigcrook Castle. 1856, 1856. 7 poems forming one narrative poem.
Robert Burns: a centenary song and other lyrics. 1859, 1859.
Havelock's march and other poems. 1861. Poems on the Indian Mutiny.
Shakespeare's sonnets never before interpreted. 1866, 1872 (priv ptd) (re-written as The secret drama of Shakespeare's sonnets), 1882. Re-written and greatly enlarged from an article in Quart Rev.
In memory of John William Spencer, Earl Brownlow. [1869] (priv ptd).
A tale of eternity and other poems. 1870.
Concerning spiritualism. 1871. Subsequently withdrawn by Massey.
Carmen nuptiale. [1880?] (priv ptd).
A book of the beginnings. 2 vols 1881. Theories of the origins of myths and mysteries. Extracts rptd 1881.
The natural genesis. 2 vols 1883. Pt 2 of A book of the beginnings.
Ancient Egypt the light of the world. 2 vols 1907.
Massey also priv ptd a number of lectures on his theories. See also Wellesley, *vol 5.*

§2

Dixon, H. Athenaeum 4 Feb 1854. A review of Babe Christabel.
Miles, A. H. In Miles 5.
Collins, J. C. In his Studies in poetry and criticism, 1905.
Milne, J. A silent singer. Book Monthly July 1905.
Milne, J. Poet and thinker. Book Monthly Sep 1907.
Wright, D. Gerald Massey. Open Court Aug 1924.
Evans, B. I. In his English poetry in the later nineteenth century, 1933, 1966 (rev).

Thomas Miller 1807–74

Mss: letters, BL Add Mss.

Bibliography

In The poets and poetry of Scotland vol 2, 1877. Ed J. G. Wilson.

§1

Songs of the sea nymphs. 1832.
A day in the woods: a connected series of tales and poems. 1836.
Beauties of the country. 1837.
Royston Gower: or the days of King John. 3 vols 1838, [1874]. An historical romance.
Lady Jane Grey: an historical romance. 3 vols 1840, 2 vols Philadelphia 1840.
Poems. 1841.
Summer morning. A poem. 1841.
Godfrey Malvern, or the life of an author. 1843, 2 vols 1844, 1857.
Poetical works of J. Beattie and W. Collins, with memoirs of their lives and writings, by Miller. 1846.
The mysteries of London. Third series by T. Miller. 1846.
The poetical language of flowers: or the pilgrim of love. 1847, New York 1848, 1855.
The babes in the wood: a new version of the old ballad. 1850.
Original poems for my children. 2 sers 1850, 1852.
Our old town. 1857. Facs reprint in Golden memories, Gainsborough 1993.
Birds, bees and blossoms: original poems for children. [1857], [1858], [1864], [1869].
Langley-on-the-lea: or love and duty. 1860.
Original songs for the rifle volunteers. 1861. With S. Lover and C. Mackay.
Songs of the seasons for my children. 1865.
My father's garden. 1867. Fiction.
Miller also pbd children's books, botanical guides and historical works.

William Miller 1810–72

Mss: poems and songs, Glasgow, Univ Lib; poems, songs, letters, Glasgow, Mitchell Lib.
Songs for the nursery. Ed Miller 1844.
Scottish nursery songs and other poems. Glasgow 1863.
Willie Winkie and other song and poems. Ed R. Ford, Paisley 1902.

Richard Monckton Milnes, 1st Baron Houghton 1809–85

Mss: plays, poems and letters, Cambridge, Trinity College; also collections of papers in Humanities Research Centre, Univ of Texas, Austin, and Harvard, Houghton Lib.

Collections

The poems of Richard Monckton Milnes, author of Memorial of a tour in Greece. 1838.
Memorials of many scenes: poems, legendary and historical. 2 vols 1844. Selected from Memorials of a tour in Greece, Memorials of a residence on the Continent, and Poetry for the people, with some new poems.
Selections from the poetical works. 1863.
A selection from the works of Lord Houghton. 1867, 1868. Poems.
Poetical works. 2 vols 1876. Includes songs pbd as fly-sheets and not mentioned separately below.
Miles 4.

§1

The influence of Homer. Cambridge 1829. A prize essay.
Memorials of a tour in some parts of Greece, chiefly poetical. 1834, new edn 1844 as Memorials of many scenes.

Memorials of a residence on the Continent, and historical poems. 1838.
Poems of many years. 1838 (priv ptd), 1840 (for general circulation), 1846.
Poetry for the people, and other poems. 1840.
One tract more, by a layman. 1841. In support of the Anglo-Catholic movement.
Palm leaves. 1844. Poems written during and about a tour in the East.
Poems, legendary and historical. 1844.
The life, letters and literary remains of John Keats. 2 vols 1848; ed R. Lynd 1927 (EL), Oxford 1931 (WC). Also pbd, in an abridged form, with Keats's poetical works, 1854 etc.
As I wandered by the brookside. Songs. [1850?]
Miscellanies of the Philobiblon Society. 15 vols 1853–84. Ed Milnes, with numerous contributions by him.
Good night and good morning: a ballad. 1859.
On the present social results of classical education. In Essays on a liberal education, ed F. W. Farrar 1867.
Monographs: personal and social. 1873.
Milnes also wrote on contemporary political and social subjects; see also Wellesley, *vol 5 1989.*

Letters and papers

Reid, T. W. The life, letters and friendships of Milnes. 2 vols 1890.
Fischer, W. Die Briefe Milnes. Heidelberg 1922.

§2

Gibbs, H. J. In Miles 4.
Pope-Hennessy, J. Monckton Milnes at Cambridge. Cornhill Mag 163 1947.
Pope-Hennessy, J. Monckton Milnes. 2 vols 1950–2.
Wilson, E. G. Edward Moxon and the first two editions of Milne's biography of Keats. HLB 5 1951.
Clive, J. Some more or less eminent Victorians. VS 2 1958.

Robert Montgomery 1807–55

Bibliographies

GM Mar 1856.

Collections

Poetical works. 3 vols Glasgow 1839.
Poetical works. 6 vols 1839–40, 1841–3; ed J. W. Twycross 1853.

Selections

Selections from the poetical works. 1836, 1837.
Religion and poetry: being selections spiritual and moral from the poetical works. With an introductory essay by Archer Gurney. [Ed S. J. H.] 1847.
Lyra Christiana: poems on Christianity and the church, original and selected. 1851. Selected by Montgomery.
Christian poetry for school and family use. A selection suitable for Sunday reading and recitation. Ed E. Farr [1854].

§1

Poetical trifles, by a youth. Bath 1825. Anon.
The stage-coach: a poem. 1827.
The age reviewed: a satire in two parts. 1827, 1828 (rev and corrected).
The omnipresence of the Deity: a poem. 1828, 1828 (2nd edn rev and enlarged), 1828 (7th edn), as vol 3 of Poetical works, Glasgow 1839.
REVIEWS: Blackwood's Mag 23, May 1828; Eclectic Rev 47, May 1828; Edinburgh Rev 51, Apr 1830; Literary Churchman 1, 30 June 1855.
The puffiad: a satire. 1828. Anon.
A universal prayer: Death: A vision of Heaven: and A vision of Hell. 1828, 1829 3rd edn with addns (4th edn), 1846.
REVIEW: Blackwood's Mag 26, Aug 1829.
Satan: a poem. 1830, Glasgow 1839 (5th edn as vol 1 of Poetical works), Glasgow 1841 (8th edn as Satan or intellect without God), London 1842 (10th edn).
REVIEWS: Fraser's Mag 1, Feb 1830; Eclectic Rev 51, Mar 1830; Edinburgh Rev 51, Apr 1830; Westminster Rev 12, Apr 1830.
Oxford: a poem. Oxford 1831, 1835 (4th edn, with recollections of Shelley), 1843 (6th edn).
REVIEW: Fraser's Mag 3, Apr 1831.
The Messiah: a poem in six books. 1832, 1836 (5th edn), 1842 (8th edn).
REVIEW: Spectator 5, 9 June 1832.
Woman, the angel of life: a poem. 1833, 1833 (2nd edn, Introductory lines moved to appendix), Glasgow 1839 (as vol 2 of Poetical works), 1841 (5th edn).
REVIEW: Athenaeum 291, 25 May 1833.
Ellesmere lake; the Pistyll Rhaiadr; and the vale of Clwyd. 1836. Poems.
Sacred gift: a series of meditations upon scripture subjects. [1842.] Verse. Rptd as Sacred meditations and moral themes in verse [1847] (3rd edn).
Luther: a poem. 1842, 1842, 1845, 1852 (6th edn rev and enlarged).
REVIEWS: Athenaeum 753, 2 Apr 1842; Spectator 15, 2 Apr 1842; Fraser's Mag 25, June 1842; Eclectic Rev 76, Aug 1842.
Scarborough: a poetic glance. 1846.
The Christian life: a manual of sacred verse. 1849, 1850 (3rd edn rev), [1855] (7th edn).
REVIEWS: Athenaeum 1104, 23 Dec 1848; Spectator 22, 6 Jan 1849; Literary Gazette 1682, 14 Apr 1849.
Forty lines on Wellington. [1852.]
The hero's funeral: a poem. 1852, 1853 (2nd edn). On the Duke of Wellington.
REVIEW: Church of England Quart Rev 34, July 1853.
The sanctuary: a companion in verse for the English prayer book. 1855.
REVIEWS: Literary Churchman 1, 30 June 1855; Rambler 4 n.s. Aug 1855.
Montgomery also pbd numerous sermons and theological works.

§2

Obit: The Times 6 Dec 1855; GM Mar 1856.
Maginn, W. In A gallery of illustrious literary characters, ed W. Bates, [1873].
Hopkins, K. Reflections on Satan Montgomery. TSLL 4 1962. [RS]

Edward Moxon 1801–58

Mss: letters, Dove Cottage and Wordsworth Museum, Grasmere.

§1

The prospect and other poems. 1826.
Christmas: a poem. 1829.
Sonnets. 2 pts 1830–5 (priv ptd), 1837 (priv ptd), 1843 (priv ptd), Boston 1848, 1871.
REVIEWS: Athenaeum 13 Apr 1833; Quarterly Rev 59, 1837.
Charles Lamb. [1835].
Moxon edited Englishman's Mag *Aug–Oct 1831.*

§2

Lamb, C. Athenaeum 13 Apr 1833; rptd in his Works, ed E. V. Lucas, vol 1, 1903. On Sonnets.
[Croker, J. W.] Quart Rev 59 1837. A contemptuous review of the Sonnets.
White, N. I. Literature and the law of libel. SP 22 1925. On Moxon's trial for blasphemous libel in 1841.
Merriam, H. G. Moxon: publisher of poets. New York 1939.
Wilson, E. G. Moxon and the first two editions of Milnes's biography of Keats. HLB 5 1951.

Arthur Joseph Munby 1828–1910

§1

Benoni: poems. 1852.
Elegiacs. In Burns centenary poems, 1859.
Verses new and old. 1865.
A memorial of Joseph Munby of Clifton Holme. [1875.]
Dorothy: a country story in elegiac verse. Ed Munby 1857, 1880.
Vulgar verses by 'Jones Brown'. [1890.]
Faithful servants: epitaphs and obituaries. 1891. Ed Munby.
Vestigia retrorsum: poems. 1891.
Susan: a poem by the author of 'Dorothy'. 1893.
Ann Morgan's love: a pedestrian poem. 1896.
Poems, chiefly lyric and elegiac. 1901.
Relicta: verses. 1909.

§2

Marston, P. B. A realistic poet. Atlantic Monthly Apr 1882.
Master and servant. GM Jan 1892.
Bayne, T. The poetry of Munby. GM Nov 1904.
Hudson, D. Munby: man of two worlds: the life and diaries of Arthur Joseph Munby 1828–1910. 1972.

Joseph John Murphy 1827–94

§1

Sonnets and other poems, chiefly religious. 1890.
Murphy also wrote several prose works on religious matters.

§2

Grosart, A. B. In Miles 10 (11).

John Mason Neale 1818–66

Mss: poems, hymns, diaries, etc, Lambeth Palace Lib.

Selections

Selections from the writings. 1884, new edn 1887.
Collected hymns, sequences and carols. Ed M. S. Lawson 1914.

§1

The fisherman's song: Speed the plough!; Work over. [1840.]
The history of the pews. 1841; suppl 1842.
Agnes de Tracy: a tale of the times of St Thomas of Canterbury. 1843, [1906].
Hymns for children in accordance with the catechism. Cambridge 1843, 2 pts 1844–5 (rev), 3 sers 1848 (rev and corrected).
Hymns for the sick. 1843, 1849, 1868 (4th edn), [1906].
Songs and ballads for the people. 1842, 1843, 1844, 1845.
Hymns for the young: a second series of hymns for children. Cambridge 1843, 1860.
The loosing of the Euphratean angels. A Seatonian poem. Cambridge 1845.
A mirror of faith: lays and legends of the Church in England. [1845.]
The triumphs of the cross: tales and sketches of Christian heroism. [1845], 2nd ser 1846.
Annals of virgin saints. 1846.
A history of the Holy Eastern Church. 5 vols 1847–73.
Songs and ballads for manufacturers. 1846, 1850 (2nd edn).
The unseen world. 1847, 1853.
Duchenier: or the revolt of La Vendée. 1848.
Edom: a Seatonian prize poem. Cambridge 1849.
Hymni ecclesiae, a breviariis quibusdam et missalibus Gallicanis, Germanis, Hispanis, Lusitanis desumpti. 1851.
Mediaeval hymns and sequences. 1851, 1863 (with addns and corrections).
The hymnal noted. 2 pts 1852–4, 1863 (2nd edn rev and greatly enlarged), 1870 (5th edn). Mainly tr Neale.
A short commentary on The hymnal noted, from ancient sources. 1852.
Mammon. Seatonian prize poem. Cambridge 1852.
Sequentiae ex missalibus Germicis, Anglicis, Gallicis, aliisque medii aevi collectae. 1852.
Carols for Christmas tide. 1853.
Carols for Easter tide. [1854.]
The Egyptian wanderers: a story for children. 1854.
Judith: a Seatonian poem. Cambridge 1856.
Sinai: a Seatonian prize poem. Cambridge 1857.
Theodora Phranza: or the fall of Constantinople. 1857; ed E. Rhys [1913] (EL).
Egypt: a Seatonian prize poem. Cambridge 1858.
The disciples at Emmaus: a Seatonian prize poem. Cambridge 1859.
The rhythm of Bernard de Morlaix on the celestial country. 1859, 1866 (7th edn), new edn 1914.
Ruth: a Seatonian poem. Cambridge 1860.
A commentary on the Psalms. 1860. With R. F. Littledale.
The daughters of Pola. [1861.]
Hymns of the Eastern Church. 1862, 1866 (3rd edn), 1882 (4th edn, with addns), 1918.
King Josiah: a Seatonian poem. Cambridge 1862.
The seven churches of Asia. A Seatonian prize poem. Cambridge 1863.
Christ was born on Christmas Day: a carol. 1864.
Seatonian poems. Cambridge 1864.
The celestial country. 1865. Trn of a portion of Bernard de Morlaix, De contemptu mundi; a metrical trn of the Vexilla regis of Fortunatus and of the Cantemus cuncti of Gotteschalcus.
Hymns, chiefly mediaeval, on the joys and glories of paradise. 1865, 1866 (2nd edn).
Hymn for use during the cattle plague. 1866.
Sequences, hymns and other ecclesiastical verses. [1866.]
The invalid's hymn book, being a selection of hymns appropriate to the sick room, original or translated. [1866.]
Hymns suitable for invalids, preface by R. F. Littledale. 1866. Duplicate of preceding, with new title page.
Original sequences, hymns and other ecclesiastical verses. 1873.
A dissolution of the religious houses AD 1536; The curse of the abbeys. [1886.] 2 historical poems.
Good King Wenceslas: a carol. Birmingham 1895. With introd by W. Morris.
Neale also pbd many sermons, commentaries, historical novels for children, trns etc.

Letters and papers

Letters. Ed M. S. Lawson 1910.

§2

Moultrie, G. Dr Neale. [1866.]
St Margaret's Mag 1–4 1887–95. A memoir in half-yearly pts, with a full account of Neale's life and writings.
Julian.
Towle, E. A. John Mason Neale DD: a memoir. 1906. With a list of his writings.
Obit: Guardian 15 Aug 1866 [by R. F. Littledale].
Lough, A. G. The influence of Neale. 1962.

Charles Neaves, Lord Neaves 1800–76

Songs and verses, social and scientific. Edinburgh 1868, 1868 (2nd edn), 1869 (3rd edn), 1875.
On fiction as a means of popular teaching. A lecture. Edinburgh 1869.
A glance at some of the principles of comparative philology. Edinburgh 1870.
The Greek anthology. 1870, 1874. An account, with specimens in English.

A lecture on cheap and accessible pleasures. With a comparative sketch of the poetry of Burns and Wordsworth. Edinburgh 1872.
Some helps to the study of Scoto-Celtic philology. Edinburgh 1872.
Neaves also pbd numerous didactic works and contributed to Blackwood's Mag *etc; see also* Wellesley *vol 5 1989.*

Francis William Newman 1805–97

§1

Lectures on logic, or on the science of evidence generally. Oxford 1838.
The difficulties of elementary geometry. 1841.
History of the Hebrew monarchy. 1847.
The soul: her sorrows and her aspirations. 1849. Prose.
A collection of poetry for the practice of elocution. 1850.
Phases of faith. 1850, [1853 2nd edn, 1860 6th edn]; 1907, rptd Leicester 1970, introd by U. C. Knoepflmacher. Prose.
Regal Rome. An introduction to Roman history. 1852. Prose.
The odes of Horace translated into rhymed metres, with introduction and notes. 1853.
The Iliad of Homer faithfully translated. 1856.
Theism, doctrinal and practical. 1858; 1873 (rev as Hebrew theism: the common basis of Judaism, Christianity and Mohammedism), 1873. Prose and verse.
Homeric translations in theory and practice. 1861. A reply to Arnold; rptd in Essays by Matthew Arnold, Oxford 1914.
Hiawatha rendered into Latin. 1862.
A handbook of modern Arabic. 1866.
Translations of English poetry into Latin verse. 1868.
The cure of the great social evils. 1869.
Miscellanies: chiefly addresses. 3 vols 1869–89.
Anthropomorphism. A comment . . . on some poetry sent him by a lady. Ramsgate 1870.
Europe of the near future. 1871.
A dictionary of modern Arabic. 2 vols 1871.
On the historical depravation of Christianity. 1873.
The two theisms. 1874.
Ancient sacrifice. 1874.
Religion not history. 1877.
Libyan vocabulary. 1882.
Comments on the text of Aeschylus. 1884.
Rebilius Cruso. 1884. Robinson Crusoe in Latin.
Life after death? 1886, 1887.
Kabai vocabulary. 1887.
Reminiscences of two exiles and two wars. 1888.
Contributions chiefly to the early history of the late Cardinal Newman. 1891, 1891 (2nd edn).
Hebrew Jesus: his true creed. Nottingham 1895.
Newman also pbd numerous lectures and educational works. See also Wellesley *vol 5 1989.*

§2

Arnold, M. On translating Homer. 1861.
Arnold, M. On translating Homer: last words. 1862.
Gribble, F. Francis W. Newman. Fortnightly Rev July 1905.
Harrison, F. In his Collected essays vol 4, 1908.
Sieveking, I. G. Memoir and letters of Francis W. Newman. 1909.
Robbins, W. The Newman brothers. 1966.

Robert Nicoll 1814–37

§1

Poems and lyrics. Edinburgh 1835, 1842 (enlarged, with memoir by C. I. Johnstone), Glasgow 1852, Paisley 1877, 1914.
Marion Wilson: a tale of the persecuting tomes. In C. I. Johnstone, The Edinburgh tales vol 2, Edinburgh 1846.

§2

Kingsley, C. Robert Nicoll. North Br Rev Nov 1851.
Smiles, S. The life and work of Nicoll. Good Words 16 1875.
Drummond, P. R. The life of Nicoll, with some hitherto uncollected pieces. 1884.

Caroline Elizabeth Sarah Norton, née Sheridan and afterwards Lady Stirling-Maxwell 1808–77

Strathclyde Regional Arhives, Glasgow, holds over 450 letters from Norton to her second husband Sir William Stirling-Maxwell, plus poems and drawings. For other British holdings of letters – whose recipients include Mary Shelley, E. L. Bulwer-Lytton, Elizabeth Gaskell, Thomas Lawrence, Benjamin Disraeli, Lockhart, John Delane and various political figures, see LR 2, pp. 708–11.

Bibliographies

Jasper, D. E. Caroline Norton: her writings. BB 53 1990.

Selections

Miles 7 (8).
Selected writings of Caroline Norton. Facs, introd by J. O. Hoge and J. Marcus. Delmar NY 1978.

§1

The dandies' rout. [1820?]
The sorrows of Rosalie: a tale with other poems. 1829 (anon). Dedicated to Lord Holland. 4th edn with additional poems 1829. Bound with The undying one and other poems, New York and Boston 1854.
The undying one and other poems. 1830 (2 edns) dedicated to the Duchess of Clarence, new edn 1853. Bound with The sorrows of Rosalie, New York and Boston 1854.
REVIEWS: (William Maginn) Fraser's Mag 2, Sep 1830; Edinburgh Rev 53, June 1831.
Poems. Boston 1833 (collected contributions to annuals), rptd with a notice of the author by Rufus W. Griswold, Philadelphia 1846 and [1857?], New York 1875 (bound with L. H. H. Sigourney, Poems).
The wife and woman's reward. 3 vols 1835 (anon), 2 vols New York 1835. A woman's reward rptd New York 1846.
A voice from the factories. In serious verse. 1836 (anon). Dedicated to the Right Honourable Lord Ashley, rptd in [William Dodd], The labouring classes of England . . . in a series of letters. By an Englishman, Boston 1847. Rptd Oxford and New York 1994 (facs).
Observations on the natural claim of the mother to the custody of her infant children, as affected by the common law right of the father: illustrated by cases of peculiar hardship. 1837.
The separation of mother and child by the law of Custody of Infants, considered. 1838 (anon); micros New Haven CT [1980] and Woodbridge CT [1986?].
A letter to the Right Reverend the Lord Bishop of Exeter on the custody of infants. 1839; micro Woodbridge CT [1986?].
A plain letter to the Lord Chancellor on the Infant Custody bill . . . By Pearce Stevenson, esq. 1839, rptd New York 1922, introd Frank Altschul; micros Woodbridge CT [1980?] and BL 1987.
The dream, and other poems. 1840 (dedicated to the Duchess of Sutherland), New York 1841, other edns 1841, 1846, 1847.
REVIEWS: (Hartley Coleridge) Quart Rev 66, Sep 1840; (R. H. Horne) A new spirit of the age vol 2, 1844.
Lines. 1840. On Queen Victoria.
The child of the islands: a poem. 1845 (dedicated to Richard Brinsley Sheridan), New York and Baltimore 1846, London 1846 (2nd edn), New York 1849, New York and Boston 1855. On the Prince of Wales.
REVIEWS: (Abraham Hayward) Edinburgh Rev 82, July 1845; (J. G. Lockhart) Quart Rev 76, June 1845.
Aunt Carry's ballads for children: Adventures of a wood sprite, The story of Blanche and Brutikin. 1847.

Letters to the mob, by Libertas. 1848. Rptd from Morning Chron.
Tales and sketches: in prose and verse. 1850. Bound with Camille Dufour Crosland, Toil and trial.
Stuart of Dunleath: a story of modern times. Dedicated to the Queen of Holland. 3 vols 1851, 1 vol New York 1851, 2 vols Leipzig 1851 with subtitle, a story of the present time, other 1 vol edns 1853, 1856, [1860] (Parlour Lib no 90), [1873].
Altamont: or the charity sister. New York 1852.
English laws for women in the nineteenth century. 1854 (priv ptd), rptd Westport CT 1981, Chicago 1982 (introd by J. Huddleston); micros Wooster OH 1974, New Haven CT 1975, Woodbridge CT [1986?], BL 1987 and Cambridge MA [19 ?]; tr Ger 1855.
A letter to the Queen on Lord Chancellor Cranworth's marriage and divorce bill. 1855 (3 edns, 3rd edn bound with her English laws for women), 1857 (4th edn); micros BL 1987, Woodbridge CT [1987?] and Cambridge MA [19 ?].
A review of the divorce bill of 1856, with propositions for an amendment of the laws affecting married persons. 1857; micro BL 1987.
The lady of La Garaye. Cambridge '1862' [1861], 1862, 1863, 1871, 1875, 1881, 1893. 1863 edn rptd 1866, New York [1864] and 1866. Poem.
REVIEW: (Abraham Hayward) Edinburgh Rev 115, Jan 1862.
Lost and saved. 3 vols 1863 (4 edns, rptd Delmar NY [1988?], facs), 2 vols Leipzig 1863, another 3-vol edn [1864], 1 vol Amer edns Philadelphia 1863, 1864, [187-?].
REVIEW: (J. McCarthy) Westminster Rev n.s. 26, July 1864.
Old Sir Douglas. 3 vols '1868' [1867], 1 vol Boston [186-?] and Philadelphia 1867, 2 vols Leipzig 1867 (micro Washington 1985, LC), 3 vols London 1868 (micro Cambridge MA [1970]), 1 vol London and New York 1872, 1 vol London 1877. First pbd in Macmillan's Mag Jan 1866–Oct 1867.
Taxation, by an irresponsible taxpayer. [187-?]
Norton's many songs, some based on her poems, are listed in J. G. Perkins, The life of Mrs Norton, *1909, rptd 1910.*

Contributions to periodicals

For Caroline Norton's contributions to the NMM, Edinburgh Rev, Macmillan's Mag, Dublin Univ Mag, *see* Wellesley *vol 5 1989.*

Collaborative works

The English bijou almanack for 1836–41: poetically illustrated by L. E. L., S. Lover, the Hon Mrs Norton, Miss Mitford. Partly rptd as Albert Schloss's bijou almanack, 1839–43, introd by Ian Bain, 1969.
Lowe, Richard T. A history of the fishes of Madeira ... with original figures from nature of all the species by the Hon C. E. L. Norton and M. Young. 1843.
The centenary festival: verses on Robert Burns. First pbd in the Daily Scotsman. Rptd in The Burns Centenary poems, 1859.
Crippled Jane, in Home thoughts and home scenes: in original poems by Jean Ingelow, Dora Greenwell, Mrs Tom Taylor, the Hon Mrs Norton, Amelia B. Edwards, Jennett Humphreys and the author of John Halifax, Gentleman. 1865, Boston [1865?].

Letters

Letters etc dated from June 1836 to July 1841. [1841?] (priv ptd); micro BL 1987. Bound with The separation of mother and child ...
Coolidge, B. Some unrecorded letters of Caroline Norton in the Altschul Collection of the Yale University Library. By Bertha Coolidge. Boston 1934 (priv ptd, 75 copies); micro Princeton 1983.
Macnaghten, A. I. Some letters of Caroline Norton. N & Q 8, 22 Jan, 5 Feb, 5 Mar 1949.
The letters of Caroline Norton to Lord Melbourne. Ed James O. Hoge and Clarke Olney. Columbus OH 1974.

Editions and preface

Mrs Norton's story book, compiled for the amusement of her children. To which are added instructions for the proper application of the stories. 1830 (2 edns).
[Melville, Elizabeth.] A residence at Sierra Leone ... By a lady. Ed Norton 1849.
Stapleton, Miss. The pastor of Silverdale and other poems. With a prefatory note by the Hon Mrs Norton. 1867 (2 edns), [1873] (4th edn).
Fisher's drawing-room scrapbook: being a selection of the most favourite subjects from the drawing-room scrapbooks. Ed Norton and Charles Mackay [185-?].
The rose of Jericho. Ed Norton. 1870. Tr from Fr by Caroline Norton's mother Caroline Sheridan.
Norton contributed to and sometimes edited the following annuals: Keepsake, *vols 1–30, 1828–57;* Court Mag and Belle Assemblée, *vols 1–9, 1832–6, and vols 10–11, 1837 (as* Court Mag and Monthly Critic); Fisher's Drawing-room Scrapbook, *1846–8;* Schloss's English Bijou Almanac, *1841. She also contributed to the* English Annual, *vol 1 1834 and vol 2 1835.*

§2

Living literary characters (no II): the Honourable Mrs Norton. NMM 31 Feb 1831.
Obit: Pictorial World, 25 July 1877. Temple Bar 52, Jan 1878.
Arnold, A. The Hon Mrs Norton and married women. Fraser's Mag n.s. 17, Apr 1878.
In DNB. Garnett, Richard.
Perkins, J. G. The life of Mrs Norton. 1909, rptd 1910.
Acland, A. S. Caroline Norton. New York 1948.
Chedzoy, A. A scandalous woman: the story of Caroline Norton. 1992. [JW]

Eliza Ann Harris Ogilvy 1822–1912

§1

A book of Highland minstrelsy. 1846, 1848, new edn 1860.
Traditions of Tuscany, in verse. 1851.
Poems of ten years (1846–55). 1856.
Elizabeth Barrett Browning's letters to Mrs David Ogilvy, 1849–1861, with recollections by Mrs Ogilvy. Ed P. N. Haydon and P. Kelley, New York 1973, London 1974.

John Walker Ord 1811–53

§1

The wandering bard and other poems. Edinburgh 1833. Anon.
England: a historical poem. 2 vols 1834–5.
Remarks on the sympathetic connection existing between the body and the mind especially during disease. 1836.
The bard and minor poems. Collected and ed John Lodge 1841.
Rural sketches and poems chiefly relating to Cleveland. 1845, 1850.
The history and antiquities of Cleveland. 1846, facs reprint Stockton-on-Tees 1972.
Roseberry Topping. A poem by T. Pierson. Ed Ord 1847.
Prince Oswy: a legend of Rosebury. 1868. In verse.

§2

Whellan, T. In his York and the North Riding vol 2, 1859.

George Outram 1805–56

§1

Legal lyrics: and metrical illustrations of the Scotch forms of process. 1851 (priv ptd), 1871 (priv ptd); ed H. G. Bell, Edinburgh 1874 as Lyrics legal and miscellaneous; ed J. H. Stoddard, Edinburgh 1887 as Legal and other lyrics, 1916 (with addns).

§2

White, W. In Miles 9 (10). With selections.
Outram edited the Glasgow Herald *from May 1837 until his death.*

Henry Nutcombe Oxenham 1829–83

§1

The sentence of Kaires and other poems. Oxford 1854, 1867, 1871 (3rd edn, as Poems).
Recollections of Ober-Ammeragau in 1871. 1871, 1880.
Memoir of Lieutenant R. de Lisle RN. 1886.
Oxenham pbd or translated a number of controversial and devotional works from the Roman Catholic standpoint. See also Wellesley *vol 5, p. 1038.*

§2

The Rev Henry N. Oxenham. Saturday Rev 31 March 1887.
Oakley, J. Recollections of an old friend [signed Vicesimus]. Rptd, with corrections and additions, from the Manchester Guardian, Manchester 1888.

Francis Turner Palgrave 1824–97

Mss: poems, Golden treasury, *journal, letters, etc, BL Add Mss; letters to Tennysons, Lincoln, Tennyson Research Centre. There are also collections of mss at the Humanities Research Centre, Univ of Texas, Austin, and Univ of Virginia Lib, Charlottesville.*

Bibliography
See Bibliography of British Literary bibliographies, ed. T. H. Howard-Hill, Oxford 1987.

Selections
Miles 5.
Selected poems. Ed B. L. Pearce 1985.

§1

Idyls and songs. 1848–54.
Preciosa: a tale. 1852.
Essay on the first century of Italian engraving. In F. T. Kugler, Handbook of painting, 1855.
The passionate pilgrim: or Eros and Anteros by Henry J. Thurston [i.e. Palgrave]. 1858; introd by R. B. Johnson 1926.
The golden treasury. Cambridge and London 1861, New York 1861, 9th thousand Cambridge and London 1862, 1878, 1884, 1891 (rev and enlarged), 1896 etc; second ser 1897. Often rptd.
Handbook to the fine art collections in the International Exhibition. 1862, 2nd edn rev and completed 1862.
Poems by Arthur Hugh Clough. With a memoir by Palgrave. 1862, 1863.
Essays on art. Cambridge 1866, New York 1867.
Original hymns. 1867, 1868 (enlarged), 1870 (3rd edn).
The five days' entertainments at Wentworth Grange. 1868.
Gems of English art of the century. 1869.
Lyrical poems. 1871.
A Lyme garland. Lyme [1874].
The children's treasury of English song. 2 pts 1875, 1876 (as The children's treasury of lyrical song).
The visions of England. 1880 (priv ptd), 1881 (for general circulation), 1886, 1889, 1891.
The captive child. Carisbrooke Castle 8 Sep 1650. [1880?] A poem.
The life of Jesus Christ illustrated from the Italian painters. 1885.
Ode for the twentieth of June 1887. [1887] Oxford 1887 (as Ode for the twenty-first of June 1887).
The treasury of sacred song. Oxford 1889, 1906.
Amenophis and other poems sacred and secular. 1892. Includes all the earlier poems Palgrave wished to preserve, as well as some new poems.
Prothalamion. [1893] (priv ptd).
Landscape in poetry, from Homer to Tennyson. 1897.
[Miscellaneous essays.] 4 vols [1847–97]. Presented to BM.
Palgrave also pbd numerous edns and selections of the poets. See also Wellesley *vol 5 1989.*

§2

Wedmore, T. F. Palgrave as an art critic. Colburn's New Monthly Mag May 1866.
Bayliss, W. The Professor of Poetry at Oxford and the witness of art. 1888.
Gibbs, J. H. In Miles 5.
Horder, W. G. In Julian.
Chamber, E. K. Acad 14 Jan 1893. Review of Amenophis.
Palgrave, G. F. Palgrave: his journals and memories of his life. 1899.
Evans, B. I. Tennyson and the origins of the Golden treasury. TLS 8 Dec 1932.
Horne, C. J. Palgrave's Golden treasury. ES 2 1949.
Owens, R. J. Palgrave's marginalia on Landor's works. N & Q 206, June 1961.
Lewis, N. Palgrave and his Golden treasury. Listener 4 Jan 1962.

Coventry Kersey Dighton Patmore 1823–96

Major mss holdings: Princeton and the Boston College Lib both contain collections of Patmore's letters: in addition, Princeton has holograph notes in Patmore's hand and working drafts of several of his articles; Boston College has the partial ms of his 'Autobiography' and a notebook of 'Poetry together with original notes on scientific subjects by Patmore', together with photocopies of his extant literary mss. The original ms of The unknown Eros *is in the BL; the ms* The rod, the root, and the flower *in the Nottingham Univ Lib; the only extant ms of* The angel in the house, *together with Shane Leslie's variorum edn, which he presented to Alice Meynell in 1893, is in the Grantham Lib, Sussex.*

Bibliographies
Courage in politics and other essays 1885–96, now first collected. Ed F. Page 1921. With bibliography of Patmore's prose contributions to periodicals.
Martin, R. B. Patmore. Princeton Univ Lib Chron 14 1952. On Patmore letters etc at Princeton.
Stevenson, L. In Victorian poets: a guide to research, ed F. E. Faverty, Cambridge MA 1956, 1968 (rev).
Reid, J. C. The mind and art of Patmore. 1957. The fullest account of Patmore's life and art, Reid's study also contains a full bibliography (pp. 330–46) of his pbd poems and prose writings, together with a detailed chronological listing of his extensive contributions to periodicals, drawn in large part from Page, *above*. Reid's checklist also contains a comprehensive catalogue of secondary material on Patmore, including a number of contemporary reviews, but missing out the devastatingly dismissive, doggerel review of The angel in the house, ptd as prose, parodying Patmore's poetic style, that appeared in Athenaeum 20 Jan 1955, of which the following sample is characteristic:

> The gentle reader we apprise
> that this new 'Angel in the House' Contains a
> tale not very wise About a person and a spouse.
> The author, gentle as a lamb, Has managèd his
> rhymes to fit, And, haply, fancies he has writ
> Another 'In Memoriam'.

Dictionary of Literary Biography 35 (A. W. Heidemann)

Collections
Poems. 4 vols [1879]. Vol 1: Amelia, Tamerton Church-tower etc; vol 2: The angel in the house; vol 3: The victories of love; vol 4: The unknown Eros (42 odes).
Florilegium amantis. Ed R. Garnett [1879], 1888. Selected poems.
Poems: collective edition. 2 vols 1886, 1886, 1887 (3rd edn) (with selections from the poems of Henry Patmore), 1890 (4th edn), 1894 (5th edn), 1897 (6th edn) etc.
The poetry of pathos and delight from the works of Patmore. 1896. Passages selected by Alice Meynell.
Works: new Uniform edition. 5 vols 1897, 1907.

The angel in the house, together with the Victories of love. Ed A. Meynell [1905].
Poems. Ed B. Champneys 1906, 1909, 1915, 1921, 1928.
Poèmes. Tr P. Claudel, Paris 1912. With an introd by V. Larbaud.
Selected poems. Ed D. Patmore 1931. With introd and bibliography.
Selected verses. 1934.
Mystical poems of nuptial love: The wedding sermon, The unknown Eros and other odes. Ed T. Connolly, Boston 1938.
A selection of poems. Ed D. Patmore 1948.
Poems. Ed F. Page, Oxford 1949 (OSA).

§1

Poems. 1844.
Tamerton church-tower and other poems. 1853 (Pickering), 1854 (Parker) (rev).
The angel in the house: the betrothal. 1854, Boston 1856. Anon.
[The angel in the house]: the espousals. 1856, Boston 1856. Anon.
The angel in the house. Bks i–ii The betrothal, The espousals. 2 vols in 1 1854–6 (Parker), 1858 (2nd edn, Parker), 1860 (3rd edn?, Parker), 2 vols 1863 (vol 1 a reissue in a Macmillan case of Parker's sheets and title page, dated 1860 and certified 3rd edn; vol 2 contains The angel in the house pt 2 bks i–ii: Faithful for ever and The victories of love, the first combined reprint of the 2 vols, *below*, with title poem and 7 selections from Tamerton church-tower, *above*), 1863 (Macmillan reprint without certificate of edn), 1866 (4th edn; rev in 1 vol), [1878] (5th edn, Bell, pt 1 only), 1885 (6th edn), 1887 (Cassell's Nat Lib no 70), 1888 (with other poems), 1892, 1896, 1898, 1905, 1920 etc.
Faithful for ever. 1860, Boston 1861, London 1866.
The children's garland from the best poets. 1862 (for 1861) (Golden Treasury); illustr J. Lawson 1873 etc. Anthology selected and arranged by Patmore.
The victories of love. Macmillan's Mag Sep–Nov 1861; Boston 1862, 1863 (Macmillan), 1878 (4th edn) (Bell), 1888 (rev with Faithful for ever) (Cassell's Nat Lib no 122).
Odes: not published. [1868.] Anon; rptd T. Connolly, Boston 1936. Reid, *above*, identifies another priv ptd edn entitled Nine odes, 1870.
The unknown Eros and other odes. 1877 (odes i–xxxi) (anon), 1878 (odes i–xlvi) (signed), 1890 (3rd edn, rev).
Bryan Waller Procter [Barry Cornwall]: an autobiographical fragment and biographical notes, with personal sketches of contemporaries, unpublished lyrics and letters of literary friends. 1877. Ed Patmore.
Amelia. 1878 (priv ptd black letter edn).
Amelia. Tamerton church-tower etc; with prefatory study on English metrical law. 1878.
Saint Bernard on the love of God. Tr M. C. and C. Patmore 1881, 1884.
How I managed and improved my estate. 1886. Rptd from St James's Gazette.
Hastings, Lewes, Rye and the Sussex marshes. 1887.
Principle in art. 1889, 1890 (2nd edn), 1898 (rev and rearranged). Rptd from St James's Gazette.
Religio poetae. 1893, 1898 (rev and rearranged). Rptd from Fortnightly Rev, Edinburgh Rev etc.
The rod, the root and the flower. 1895, 1907 (2nd edn, rev), 1923; ed D. Patmore 1950.
The wedding sermon. [1911.]
Principle in art and other essays. 1912.
Principle in art, Religio poetae and other essays. 1913.
Courage in politics. *See* Bibliographies, *above*.
Seven unpublished poems to Alice Meynell. 1922 (priv ptd).
Essay on English metrical law: a critical edition with a commentary by M. A. Roth. Washington 1961.

Letters

Further letters of Gerard Manley Hopkins, including his correspondence with Patmore. Ed C. C. Abbott, Oxford 1938, 1956 (rev and enlarged). With nearly 30 letters from Patmore to Hopkins.
Patmore, D. Patmore and Robert Bridges: some letters. Fortnightly Rev Mar 1948.
Patmore, D. Three poets discuss new verse forms: the correspondence of Hopkins, Bridges and Patmore. Month Aug 1951.

§2

De Vere, A. The angel in the house. Edinburgh Rev 107 1858; rptd in his Essays chiefly literary and ethical, 1889.
Brimley, G. The angel in the house. In his Essays, 1858, 1882 (3rd edn).
Forman, H. B. In his Our living poets, 1871. Patmore is included among the Pre-Raphaelite group.
Garnett, R. In Poets and poetry of the century, ed A. H. Miles 10 vols 1891–7.
Nicoll, W. R. and T. J. Wise. The angel in the house: Emily Augusta Patmore. In their Literary anecdotes of the nineteenth century vol 2, 1896.
Meynell, A. Patmore's odes. In her Rhythm of life and other essays, 1896.
Garvin, L. Patmore: the praise of the odes. Fortnightly Rev Feb 1897.
Symons, A. In his Studies in two literatures, 1897, 1924 (vol 8 of Collected works).
Champneys, B. Memoirs and correspondence of Patmore. 2 vols 1900, 1901.
Gosse, E. Patmore. 1905. Incorporates Gosse's earlier writings on Patmore in Contemporary Rev and North Amer Rev.
Trobridge, G. Patmore and Swedenborg. Westminster Rev 165 1906.
Lubbock, P. Quart Rev 208 1908.
Brégy, K. In his Poet's chantry, 1912. From 2 articles in Catholic World Mar–Apr 1910.
Johnson, L. Patmore's genius. In his Post liminium: essays and critical papers, ed T. Whittemore, 1912.
Page, F. A neglected great poem: Patmore's Tamerton church-tower. Catholic World July 1912.
Freeman, J. Patmore and Francis Thompson. In his Moderns: essays in literary criticism, 1916.
Symons, A. In his Figures of several centuries, 1916.
Page, F. Patmore's Unknown Eros. Catholic World Sep 1917.
Wheaton, L. Emily Honoria Patmore and Patmore's poetry. Dublin Rev 163 1918.
Burdett, O. The idea of Patmore. Oxford 1921.
Page, F. Patmore: points of view. Catholic World June 1921.
Meynell, A. In her Second person singular and other essays, Oxford 1922.
Burdett, O. Centenary of Patmore. Dublin Rev 173 1923.
Freeman, J. Quart Rev 240 1923.
Gosse, E. The laureate of wedded love. In his More books on the table, 1923.
Freeman, J. In his English portraits and essays, 1924.
Weinig, Sister M. A. Coventry Patmore. Boston 1981 (Twayne ser).
Crook, J. Mordaunt. Coventry Patmore and the aesthetics of architecture. PBA 76 (1990): 171–201. [WEF]

Sir Joseph Noel Paton 1821–1901

Selections

Miles 5.

§1

Poems by a painter. 1861. Anon.
Spindrift. Edinburgh 1867. Poems.
A Christmas carol. New York [1907].

§2

Miles 5.

Emily Jane Pfeiffer née Davis 1827–90

Selections
Japp, A. H. (ed). In Miles 8.

§1

The Holly branch; an album for 1843. 1843. By Emily Davis.
Valisneria; or, a midsummer night's dream. A tale. 1857.
Margaret; or, the motherless. [A poem.] 1861.
REVIEW: Athenaeum 21 Dec 1861.
Gerard's monument and other poems. 1873, 1878 (enlarged).
REVIEW: Westminster Rev n.s. 53 1878.
Poems. 1876, 1878.
REVIEWS: Spectator 49, 22 Jan 1876; Westminster Rev n.s. 49 1876.
Glan-Alarch: his silence and song. 1877.
REVIEWS: Spectator 50, 14 Apr 1877; Westminster Rev n.s. 52 1877.
Quarterman's grace and other poems. 1879.
REVIEWS: Acad 17, 15 Mar 1879; Spectator 52, 24 May 1879.
Sonnets and songs. 1880, [1886] (rev and enlarged)
REVIEWS: Acad 31, 29 Jan 1887; Spectator 60, 12 Feb 1887.
The Wynnes of Wynhavod: a drama of modern life. [In verse.] 1881.
Under the aspens: lyrical and dramatic. '1882' [1881].
REVIEWS: Acad 20, 3 Dec 1881; Spectator 55, 14 Jan 1882; Westminster Rev n.s. 61 1882; Athenaeum 21 Jan 1882 (with The Wynnes of Wynhavod).
The rhyme of the lady of the rock; and how it grew. [Prose and verse.] 1884, 1885 (2nd edn).
REVIEW: Acad 25, 19 Apr 1884.
Flying leaves from east and west. 1885. Prose.
REVIEW: Acad 28, 19 Dec 1885.
Women and work: an essay. Boston 1887, London '1888' [1887].
REVIEWS: Spectator 61, 11 Feb 1888; Athenaeum 25 Feb 1888; Acad 33, 3 Mar 1888.
Flowers of the night. 1889
REVIEW: Acad 35, 29 June 1889.

Contributions to periodicals
Madonna Dunya. Contemporary Rev 31 1878.
Studies from the antique. Contemporary Rev 35 1876.
The tyranny of fashion. Cornhill Mag 38 o.s. July 1878.
The pillar of praise. Contemporary Rev 38 1880.
Woman's claim. Contemporary Rev 39, Feb 1881.
The suffrage for women. Contemporary Rev 47 Mar 1885.
The posthumous critics of a dead poet, and deathless poetry. The Jnl of Pre-Raphaelite and Aesthetic Stud 1, 2 1988 (originally intended for pbn in Contemporary Rev July 1883).

§2

Robertson, E. S. In his English poetesses, 1883.
Obits: Acad 1 Feb 1890; Athenaeum 1 Feb 1890.
Japp, A. H. In Miles 8.
Emily Pfeiffer. Western Mail 8 Oct 1895.
R. G. [Richard Garnett]. In DNB.
Pfeiffer, E. N. The feminist companion to literature in English, ed V. Blain, P. Clements and I. Grundy, 1990. [VB]

Edward Hayes Plumptre 1821–91

Selections
Miles 10 (12).

§1

Lazarus and other poems. 1864, 1884 (4th edn).
The tragedies of Sophocles. 2 vols 1865, 1 vol 1867 (rev), 1902. Trn with biography.
Master and scholar. 1866, New York 1866, 1884. Poems.
The tragedies of Aeschylus. 2 vols 1868, 1 vol 1891. Trn with biography, and appendix of rhymed choral odes.
The Divina commedia of Dante Alighieri. Samples of a new translation 1883.
Things new and old. [1884.] Poems.
The Commedia and Conzoniere of Dante: a new translation with notes and biographical introduction. 2 vols 1886–7.
The life of Thomas Ken, Bishop of Bath and Wells. 2 vols 1888, 1890.
Life of Dante. Ed A. J. Butler 1900, 1903.
Plumptre also pbd many sermons and other theological works, and contributed a few articles on Dante to Quart Rev *and* Contemporary Rev; *see also* Wellesley *vol 5, p. 1050.*

§2

C[otton], J. S. Dean Plumptre. Acad 7 Feb 1891.
Obit: The Times 12 Feb 1891.
Horder, W. G. In Miles 10 (12).
Julian.

Winthrop Mackworth Praed 1802–39

Mss: letters, poems, journal etc, Eton College Lib.

Collections
The poetical works, now first collected by R. W. Griswold. New York 1844.
Lillian and other poems, now first collected [by R. W. Griswold]. New York 1852, 1853 (as Poetical works), 1854, 1856, 1857, new and enlarged edn New York 1860.
Poetical works. Ed W. A. Whitmore 2 vols New York[?] 1859–60.
Poems, with a memoir by Derwent Coleridge. 2 vols 1864, 1864, rev and enlarged edn New York 1865, London 1869, 1874, New York 1885. The authorised and standard edn.
Political and occasional poems. Ed G. Young 1888. Supplements Coleridge edn, *above*.

Selections
Charades. New York 1752 (for 1852).
Lillian, and other poems, with biographical introduction by R. Griswold. New York 1852.
A selection from the works. Ed G. Young 1866, [1885].
Poems. Ed F. Cooper 1886 [The Canterbury Poets].
Essays, collected and arranged by G. Young. 1887 (Morley's Univ Lib).
Select poems. Ed A. D. Godley 1909.
Poems. Ed F. Greenslet, Boston 1909.
Selected poems. Ed K. Allott 1953 (ML).

§1

Carmen graecum numismate annuo dignatum 1822 (Pyramides Aegyptiacae). [Cambridge 1822.]
Epigrammata numismate annuo dignata 1822 (Nugae seria ducunt in mala). [Cambridge 1822.]
Carmen graecum numismate annuo dignatum 1823. In obitum T. F. Middleton, Episcopi Calcuttensis, [Cambridge 1823].
Lillian: a fairy tale. 1823. Verse.
Australasia: a poem which obtained the Chancellor's Medal. Cambridge 1823.
Athens: a poem which obtained the Chancellor's Medal. Cambridge 1824. Rptd with the preceding in Cambridge prize poems, 1828 (4th edn).
Epigrammata numismate annuo dignata 1824 (Scribimus indocti doctique). [Cambridge 1824.]
The ascent of Elijah: a poem. Seatonian prize poem. Cambridge 1831.
Intercepted letters about the Infirmary Bazaar. Nd. 4 leaflets of 4 pp. each, in verse and ptd on light green paper.
Speech in committee on the Reform Bill, on moving an amendment. 1832.
Trash dedicated without respect to J. Halse esq MP. Penzance 1833.
Political poems. 1835 (priv ptd).

I remember, I remember. [1840?]
Every-day characters. 1896. First pbd in NMM 1828–32 and in Literary Souvenir 1831.
Letters of Praed. Etoniana 1 July 1941–28 Dec 1943. 67 letters dating from Praed's Eton days.

Contributions to periodicals

The Etonian. 2 vols 1821. Ed and largely written by Praed and W. Blunt, Oct 1820–Aug 1821.
Knight's Quarterly Magazine. 1823–4.
The Brazen Head. 1826. 4 nos only; written and ed by Praed, C. Knight and J. B. B. St Leger.
Praed also contributed to Morning Chron *1823–5,* Albion *1830–2,* Morning Post *1832–4,* The Times *and other papers, and to* Literary Souvenir, *ed A. A. Watts 1825 and other poetical annuals.*

§2

Saintsbury, G. In his Essays in English literature 1780–1860, 1890.
Kraupa, M. Praed: sein Leben und seine Werke. Vienna 1910.
Previté-Orton, C. W. In his Political satire in English poetry, Cambridge 1910.
Hudson, D. A poet in Parliament. The life of Winthrop Mackworth Praed, 1802–39. 1939.
Hudson, D. W. M. Praed. N & Q 3 Jan 1942. Addns to his biography.
Allott, K. The text of Praed's poems. N & Q Mar 1953.
Paden, W. D. Twenty new poems attributed to Tennyson, Praed and Landor: pt 1. VS 4 1961.

John Critchley Prince 1808–66

A considerable collection of Prince's letters and his commonplace book are to be found in Manchester Central Reference Lib. The mss of several poems and letters between Prince and various publishers and printers are also to be found there, and have been catalogued by B. E. Maidment in A descriptive catalogue of records relating to John Critchley Prince in the possession of Abel Heywood and Co. *(1975).*

Collections

Poetical works. Ed R. A. D. Lithgow 2 vols 1880.

Selections

The festive wreath. Ed J. B. Rogerson, Manchester [1842].
Select pieces in prose and poetry originally contributed to the Ashton Times by J. C. Prince and others. Manchester 1850.
The poets and poetry of Blackburn. Ed G. Hull, Blackburn 1902.
The poorhouse fugitives. Ed B. E. Maidment, Manchester 1987.

§1

Hours with the Muses. [1841], 1841 (enlarged), 1842 (enlarged), 1847 (enlarged), Hyde [1857] (6th edn with new preface).
Dreams and realities in verse and prose. Ashton-under-Lyne 1847, 1849, 1850.
The poetic rosary. Manchester 1850, 1851.
Autumn leaves: original poems. Hyde 1856, Manchester 1865 (with addns).
Miscellaneous poems. Manchester [1861].

Contributions to periodicals

Prince edited Shephard's Quart Mag. *He contributed poems to* The Herald of the Future, The Fleet Papers, Bradshaw's Jnl, Howitt's Jnl, Jerrold's Mag, *and many other jnls. Substantial prose contributions to* Bradshaw's Jnl *include Rambles of a rhymester (1842) and Random readings of the poets (1842–3).*

§2

Review of Hours with the Muses. Odd Fellows' Mag 1841.
Review of Hours with the Muses. Bradshaw's Jnl 1842.
'Young Manchester' [D. Buxton]. The neglect of literary men. Manchester Courier 1846.
Procter, R. W. Literary reminiscences and gleanings. Manchester 1860.
The Prince of provincial poets. Ben Brierley's Jnl 1871.
Ossoli, M. F. In his Art, literature and the drama, 1874.
Lithgow, R. A. D. The life of Prince. 1880.
Bowker, J. John Critchley Prince. Ben Brierley's Jnl 1881.
Hood, E. P. In his The peerage of poverty [1881].
Miles 10.
Whittaker, G. H. The reed-maker poet. [1936.] [BM]

Adelaide Anne Procter, 'Mary Berwick' 1825–64

Correspondence in Reading Univ lib; Correspondence and poems, Univ of Iowa; Letters, Girton Coll Lib [to Bessie Rayner Parkes].

Collections

Ausgewählte Gedichte nach dem Englischen herausgegeben von C. Schlüter und H. Brinckmann. Cologne [1867].
The poems. (Author's edition) Boston 1870; re-issued 1881.
Complete works, with introductions by C. Dickens. 1905. With unpbd poem.
Legends and lyrics together with A chaplet of verses, with introduction by C. Dickens. [1905] (ML), Oxford 1914 (OSA).

Selections

Miles 7 (8).
The lost chord and other poems. Bavaria [1892].
Poems of Adelaide Procter. Edinburgh and London, 1907.
Poems. Selected from 'Legends and Lyrics'. [1910] (Langham Booklets).
Selected poems. 1911.

§1

Legends and lyrics. Vol 1 1858, 1860 (4th edn). Vol 2 1861, 1866 (with addns and introd by C. Dickens). Frequently rptd, both separately and together, 1895 (with addns), 1906 (EL) (omits introd by Dickens). Most of the poems first appeared in Household Words as the work of 'Mary Berwick' initially, and many were later rptd separately. She also published in Good Words.
REVIEWS: Vol 1: Athenaeum 1597, 5 June 1858; Spectator 31, 26 June 1858; Nat Mag 4, Nov 1858; Saturday Rev 7, 5 Feb 1859. Vol 2: Athenaeum 1731, 29 Dec 1860; Spectator 34, 12 Jan 1861. New edn: Athenaeum 1989, 9 Dec 1865; Victoria Mag 6, Jan 1866.
A chaplet of verses. 1862, 1868 (3rd edn).
REVIEW: Athenaeum, 1807, 4 June 1862.
The Victoria regia. Ed A. A. Procter 1861. Contains one poem by Procter.
REVIEWS: Spectator 34, 14 Dec 1861; Sat Rev 12, 21 Dec 1861; Athenaeum 1785, 11 Jan 1862.
The angel's story. [1881]; rptd as The angel's story and other poems, 1908.

§2

Obit: Atlantic Monthly 16, Dec 1865 [by Dickens].
Robertson, E. S. In his English poetesses, 1883.
Janku, F. A. A. Procter: ihr Leben und ihre Werke. Vienna 1912.
Maison, M. Queen Victoria's favourite poet. Listener 29 Apr 1965. [RS]

William Brighty Rands 1823–82

Selections

Miles 5.
Lilliput lyrics. Ed R. B. Johnson, London and New York '1899' [1898].

§1

Robert Bloomfield: a sketch of his life and writings. [1855.]
Chain of lilies and other poems. 1857.

Tangled talk: an essayist's holiday, by 'Thomas Talker'. 1864.
Lilliput levee: poems of childhood, child-fancy and child-like moods, with the addition of several new poems. 1864, 1867, 1868 (enlarged). Poems.
Views and opinions by 'Matthew Browne'. 1866.
Chaucer's England, by 'Matthew Browne'. 2 vols 1869.
Lilliput lectures. 1871; ed R. B. Johnson 1897. Poems.
Lilliput revels. New York 1871, by the author of Lilliput levee; ed R. B. Johnson 1905. Poems.
Lilliput legends. By the author of Lilliput levée. 1872. Poems.
Rands also pbd fairy tales, essays etc under his own name and under several pseudonyms. For his extensive contributions to Contemporary Rev *(1868–80) etc, see* Wellesley *vol 5, pp. 644–5.*

§2

Japp, A. H. In Miles 5.

William Caldwell Roscoe 1823–59

Collections

Poems and essays. Ed R. H. Hutton 2 vols 1860 (with memoir).
Poems. Ed E. M. Roscoe 1891.
Miles, A. H. In The poets and the poetry of the century [1891–97] vol 5. Also in The poets and the poetry of the nineteenth century 1905–07 vol 5.

§1

Eliduc, Counte of Yoeloc. 1846. Drama.
Violenzia: a tragedy. 1851. Anon. Drama.
Roscoe's poems were first pbd in book form in the collections.
For Roscoe's contributions to Nat Rev *and* Prospective Rev, *see* Wellesley 5 *1989. Roscoe was one of the editors of* Prospective Rev *(1852–5).*

§2

William Caldwell Roscoe's poetry. Nat Rev 11 1860.
William Caldwell Roscoe. Dublin Univ Mag 57 1861.
Le Gallienne, R. In Miles 5. [GW]

Christina Georgina Rossetti 1830–94

Major mss holdings: (see Holograph poems and their locations in Crump, variorum edn vol 1 below). The bulk of C. G. R.'s ms poems are contained in 17 small notebooks: 9 in Bodleian (1845–56), 7 in BL (1842–5, 1856–66) and 1 in family collection (1859–60). Other holograph notebooks are located in BL (Sing-song *and* Il rosseggiar dell' oriente), *Huntington* (Maude: prose and verse), *Texas Univ* (A pageant and other poems), *and King's College, Canterbury* (Verses). *All these collections contain lesser groups of mss, as do the univ libs of Brown, Duke, Harvard, Princeton (open, Troxell and Taylor collections), British Columbia, Kansas, and Yale, the Berg Collection (NYPL), the Iowa State Dept of History and Archives, the History Soc of Pennsylvania, and a few private collections. The largest collection of C. G. R.'s family letters is in the Angeli-Dennis Papers at the Univ of British Columbia.*

Bibliographies and reference works

Anderson, J. P. Appended to M. Bell, Christina Rossetti, 1898.
Ehrsam, T. G., R. H. Deily and R. M. Smith. In their Bibliographies of twelve Victorian authors, New York 1936. Suppl by J. G. Fucilla, MP 37 1939.
Jones, H. M. The Pre-Raphaelites. In Victorian poets: a guide to research, ed F. E. Faverty, Cambridge 1956, 1968 (new ch in 2nd edn by W. E. Fredeman).
Packer, L. M. Selective bibliography. In her Christina Rossetti, 1963.
Fredeman, W. E. In his Pre-Raphaelitism: a bibliographical study, Cambridge MA 1965 (section 44).
Crump, R. W. Christina Rossetti: a reference guide. Boston 1976. A chronological survey of writings about C. G. R., including reviews, from 1862–1973.
The Bible and the poetry of Christina Rossetti: a concordance. Comp by Nilda Jiménez 1979.
(de Groot, H.) In Dictionary of literary biography vol 35, 1985.

Collections

Poetical works. Ed W. M. Rossetti 1904 etc (with memoir).
The complete poems of Christina Rossetti: a variorum edition. Ed R. W. Crump 3 vols 1979–90. *See* McGann, *§2, below.*

Selections

Redeeming the time: daily musing from the works of Christina Rossetti, 1903.
Goblin market, prince's progress and other poems. 1913 (World's Classics).
Poems of Christina Rossetti. Selected and with introd by: W. M. Rossetti 1904 (Golden Treasury); Alice Meynell [1910]; C. B. Burke [nd]; W. de la Mare 1930; R. Ironside 1953; K. Jarvis 1956; N. Lewis 1959 (Pocket Poets); M. Zaturenska 1970; E. Jennings 1970; C. H. Sisson 1984; P. Porter 1986 (Great English Poets); I. Hamilton 1992 (Bloomsbury Poetry Classics); R. Van de Weyer 1996 (Fount Classics, subtitled Feasts and fasts); J. Marsh 1996 (Everyman Poets).
Doves and pomegranates: poems for young readers. Selected by D. Powell, introd N. Lewis 1969.
Poems and prose. Ed J. Marsh 1994.

§1

Christina Rossetti's fugitive writings appeared in a wide range of jnls and anthologies, which form a vital part of her publishing history. Because most of the poems, some of which were embedded in Commonplace *and other prose works, were rptd during her lifetime and all are included in Crump's variorum edn (above), only single and double titles or total number are cited; unrptd prose materials, however, are identified. The list is compiled from Anderson's bibliography in M. Bell and Crump's notes.*
Periodicals: Aikin's Year 1852–4 (W. M. R. identifies jnl as ed Mary Howitt, but unlocated; one poem, Behold I stand at the door and knock); Argosy 1866–75 (1 story, 7 poems, including If, illustr F. Sandys); Atalanta 1890 (1 poem, Yea, I have a goodly heritage); Athenaeum 1848–90 (8 poems); Bouquet Culled from Marylebone Gardens 1851–2 (2 poems in Italian and a prose work, Corrispondenze famigliare, signed 'Calta'; see Eng trn below); Century Feb 1884 (unrptd article, Dante, the poet illustrated out of the poem); Century Guild Hobby Horse 1887–9 (3 poems); Churchman's Shilling Mag 1867 (3 stories, 1 unrptd article, Dante, an English classic); Crayon 1856 (1 story); Dawn of day 1882, 1893 (True in the main: 2 sketches and 2 poems rptd from Verses 1893); Dublin Univ Mag 1878 (1 poem, Yet a little while); Germ 1850 (7 poems signed 'Ellen Alleyn'); Literary Opinion 1892 (3 poems and 1 unrptd essay, The house of Dante Gabriel Rosetti); Macmillan's Mag 1861–83 (23 poems); Mag of Art 1890–4 (2 poems: An echo from Willowwood, illustr C. Ricketts; The way of the world, illustr W. Britten); New and Old: for Seed-time and Harvest (1 poem, A helpmeet for him and A harmony on First Corinthians, unrptd); Once a Week 1859 (1 poem, Maude Clare); Our Paper 1855 (1 poem, The dead bride, rptd from Verses 1847); Scribner's Mag (*see* Century) 1872–3 (3 poems); Shilling Mag (1 poem, Amor Mundi, illustr F. Sandys); Victoria Mag 1864 (1 poem, The eleventh hour).
Anthologies and other sources: Marshall's Ladies' Daily Remembrancer 1850 (2 poems: Charades, New enigmas); Beautiful poetry 1853 (1 poem, Death's chill); Pictorial calendar of the seasons etc, ed Mary Howitt 1854 (1 poem, The rose); Midsummer flowers. For the young 1854 (1 poem, The trees' counselling); Düsseldorf artists' album, ed Mary Howitt 1854 (1 poem, A summer evening, rptd in Goblin market as Twilight calm); Memoirs of Mallet du Pan, tr W. M. Rossetti and B. H. Paul 1855 (partly C. G. R.'s trn); Imperial dictionary of biography, ed J. F.

Waller et al 1857–63 (33 unrptd articles, including a major one on Petrarch); Poems: an offering to Lancashire etc, ed Isa Craig 1863 (1 poem, A royal princess); A welcome: original contributions in poetry and prose 1863 (1 poem, Dream love); Lyra Eucharistica, 1863, 1864 (2nd edn), Lyra Messianica, 1864, 1865 (2nd edn), Lyra Mystica, 1865, ed O. Shipley (13 poems); A round of days described in original poems by some of our most celebrated poets, and in pictures by eminent artists 1866 (2 poems: An English drawing-room, rptd 1875 as Enrica, 1865; By the sea; both poems rptd in F. Walker et al, Picture poesies: poems chiefly by living authors and drawings, 1874; Lyra Anglicana, collected and arranged by R. H. Haynes 1867 (1 poem, The love of Christ which passeth knowledge, rptd from Goblin market); Lyrics of light and life, ed F. G. Lee 1875, 1878 (2nd edn) (1 poem, A rose plant in Jericho); Translations, literal and free, of the dying Hadrian's address to his soul, Bath 1876 (1 poem, with Italian trn, Soul rudderless, unbraced, rptd New poems as Hadrian's death-song translated); A masque of poets, Boston 1878 (1 poem, Husband and wife); The children's hymn book, comp by Mrs Carey Brock 1881 (1 poem, Thou art the same and thy years shall not fail); Sonnets of three centuries, ed T. Hall Caine 1882 (1 sonnet, Today's burden); Dante Gabriel Rossetti: his family letters with a memoir, ed W. M. Rossetti 2 vols 1895 (3 poems, including The chinaman and The P. R. B.); The family letters of C. G. R., ed W. M. R. 1908 (1 poem: So I began my walk of life; no stop).

Verses by Christina Rossetti, dedicated to her mother. 1847 (priv ptd by G. Polidori); ed J. D. Symon 1906 (Eragny Press). Contains poem To my mother on the anniversary of her birth, 27 April 1842, originally pbd as a single sheet by G. Polidori [1842], her earliest ptd poem.

Goblin market and other poems, with two designs by D. G. R. 1862, 1865; illustr L. Housman 1893; rptd with introd by G. Greer 1975; tr Ital by T. P. Rossetti, Florence 1867.

The prince's progress and other poems, with 2 designs by D. G. R. 1866; rptd with Goblin market as Poems, Boston 1866.

Outlines for illuminating: Consider. New York 1866 (single sheet).

Commonplace and other short stories. 1870; subtitled A tale of to-day; and other stories, Boston 1870.

Sing-song: a nursery rhyme book, with 120 illustrations by A. Hughes. 1872, Boston 1872, 1878, 1893 (new and enlarged edn with 5 additional poems), Toronto 1981 (facs 1st edn).

Annus Domini: a prayer for each day of the year, founded on a text of Holy Scripture. 1874, Boston [nd].

Speaking likenesses, with pictures thereof by A. Hughes. 1874, Boston 1874.

Goblin market, The prince's progress and other poems: new edition with four designs by Dante Gabriel Rosetti. 1875, Boston 1876, 1882 (as Poems), London 1879, 1884, 1888. With 37 new poems. *See* Poems 1890, *below*.

Seek and find: a double series of short studies of the Benedicite. 1879.

A pageant and other poems. 1881.

Called to be saints: the Minor Festivals devotionally studied. 1881. With 13 poems.

Letter and spirit: notes on the Commandments. 1883.

Time flies: a reading diary. 1885. With 130 poems.

Poems: new and enlarged edition, with four designs by Dante Gabriel Rosetti. 1890, 1890, 1891, 1892, 1894, 1895, 1896. A reprint of Goblin market etc 1875, together with A pageant 1881, and 13 new poems.

The face of the deep: a devotional commentary on the Apocalypse. 1892. Prose with over 200 poems and verse fragments, many rptd in Reflected lights, ed W. Jay, 1900.

Verses reprinted from Called to be saints, Time flies and The face of the deep. 1893. With some alterations and addns. Rptd with introd by W. K. L. C.

New poems, hitherto unpublished and uncollected. Ed W. M. Rossetti 1896.

The Rossetti birthday book. Ed Olivia Rossetti [Agresti] 1896.

Maude: a story for girls. Ed with a prefatory note by W. M. Rossetti 1897; subtitled Prose and verse by Christina Georgina Rosetti; 1850, Chicago 1897; ed with introd by R. W. Crump. Hamden CT 1976; ed E. Showalter London 1993.

Familiar correspondence newly translated from the Italian of Christina G. Rossetti. Stanford Dingley 1962. Trn of an 8-pt fictional 'Corrispondenza famigliare' between two young ladies, one Italian – Angela-Maria de' Ruggieri – the other English – Emma Ward – and 2 short poems by C. G. R. written in Italian under the sobriquet 'Calta' that appeared in the first 3 collections of The Bouquet, Culled from Marylebone Gardens, ptd for private circulation 1852. The anon ed suggests that the letters may have been written as exercises for C. G. R.'s Italian pupils and that other letters 'would have followed but for the early decease of the magazine and the withering of the Bouquet', but no mention is made of the date the magazine ceased publication. Waterloo Directory of Victorian Periodicals identifies 7 collections 1851–5. The phrase 'Da continuarsi', which concludes each of the 8 letters, raises the question whether (a) one or more later instalments may appear in subsequent vols (4–7), or (b) the balance of the fragmentary epistle-narrative may still exist in manuscript. Letter 7 contains the poem Love in a mist (Purporea rosa); letter 8 The roses which you have from me (Questa rosa ch'io done).

Crump, R. Eighteen moments' monuments: Christina Rossetti's bouts-rimés sonnets in the Troxell collection. Princeton Univ Lib Chron 33 1972; also pbd separately ed R. S. Fraser.

de Groot, H. B. Christina Rossetti's A nightmare: a fragment completed. RES n.s. 24 1973.

Letters

Bell, M. In his Christina Rossetti, 1898, *below*.

Ruskin: Rossetti: Pre-Raphaelitism. Ed W. M. Rossetti 1899.

Rossetti papers 1862–70. Ed W. M. Rossetti 1903.

Family letters of Christina Rossetti. Ed W. M. Rossetti 1908.

Curti, M. E. A letter of Christina Georgina Rossetti. MLN 51 1936.

Troxell, J. C. Three Rossettis: unpublished letters to and from Dante Gabriel, Christina, William. Cambridge MA 1937.

Packer, L. M. Christina Rossetti and Alice Boyd of Penkill Castle. TLS 26 June 1959.

Packer, L. M. Christina Rossetti's correspondence with her nephew: some unpublished letters. N & Q 204 Dec 1959.

Putt, S. G. Christina Rossetti, almsgiver. English 13 1961.

Packer, L. M. The Rossetti–Macmillan letters: some 133 unpublished letters written to Alexander Macmillan, F. S. Ellis and others by Dante Gabriel, Christina and William Michael Rossetti 1861–89. Berkeley 1963. *See also* her F. S. Ellis and the Rossettis: a publishing venture and misadventure, Western Humanities Rev 16 1962.

Cline, C. L. (ed). The owl and the Rossettis: letters of Charles A. Howell and Dante Gabriel, Christina, and William Michael Rossetti. University Park PA 1978. Texts of only 2 letters by C. G. R. plus a summary of 1 other.

Harrison, A. H. Eighteen early letters by Christina Rossetti. In Kent, *below*. A discursive examination of the context and content of 18 C. G. R. letters in the Troxell collection (Princeton), dating 1845–54 which W. M. R., having sold the copyright to Mackenzie Bell (*see* §2 *below*), was unable to include in his edn of her Family letters (*see above*).

Christina Rossetti in the Maser collection . . . including a group of Christina's letters. Bryn Mawr Coll Lib 1991. 32 letters to various correspondents plus another 11 to Amelia Heimann and her daughter Golde.

The letters of Christina Rossetti. Ed Anthony H. Harrison. A 4-vol edn in progress. Vol 1 1842–73, Charlottesville VA 1997.

§2

The first wave in the critical revaluation of C. G. R. occurred at the time of the centenary of her birth in 1930, followed in the 1960s by the interest generated by Lona Mosk Packer's biography and her edn of C. G. R.'s letters to Macmillan (see above). The past 2 decades have witnessed a major revival of critical interest in the life and works of Christina Rossetti. Recent studies are subsumed under 3 headings: (1) collections of critical essays; (2) biographies; and (3) critical studies.

Forman, H. B. In his Our living poets, 1871.
Symons, A. In Poets and poetry of the century, ed A. H. Miles, 10 vols 1891–7.
Law, A. The poetry of Christina Rossetti. Westminster Rev 143 1895.
Nash, J. J. G. A memorial sermon for the late Christina Rossetti. 1895.
Noble, J. A. The burden of Christina Rossetti. In his Impressions and memories, 1895.
Procter, E. A. A brief memoir of Christina Rossetti. 1895.
Watts-Dunton, T. Reminiscences of Christina Rossetti. Nineteenth Cent Feb 1895.
Benson, A. C. In his Essays, 1896.
Gosse, E. In his Critical kit-kats, 1896.
Symons, A. In his Studies in two literatures, 1897.
Bell, M. Christina Rossetti: a biographical and critical study. 1898.
Westcott, B. F. An appreciation of the late Christina Rossetti. 1899.
Cary, E. L. The Rossettis: Dante Gabriel and Christina. New York 1900.
More, P. E. In his Shelburne essays: third series, New York 1905.
Breme, M. I. Christina Rossetti und der Einfluss der Bibel auf ihre Dichtung. Münster 1907.
Hueffer, F. M. [Ford]. Christina Rossetti and Pre-Raphaelite love. In his Memories and impressions, 1911.
Sharp, W. Some memories of Christina Rossetti. In his Papers critical and reminiscent, ed Mrs W. Sharp, 1912. Rptd from Atlantic Monthly June 1895.
Venkatesan, N. K. Christina Rossetti. Madras 1914.
Mason, E. Two Christian poets, Christina Rossetti and Paul Verlaine. In his A book of preferences, 1915.
Watts-Dunton, T. In his Old familiar faces, 1916.
de Wilde, J. F. Christina Rossetti: poet and woman. Nijkerk 1923.
de la Mare, W. Christina Rossetti. Trans Royal Soc of Lit 6 1926.

Centenary and later studies

Collections of critical essays

Kent, D. A. (ed). The achievement of Christina Rossetti. Ithaca NY 1987.
Charles, E. K. (ed). Christina Rossetti: critical perspectives. 1988.
Harrison, A. H. (ed). Centennial of Christina Rossetti. Double no of VP 32, 3–4, Morgantown WV 1994.

Critical studies

McGann, J. J. Christina Rossetti's poems: a new edition and a revaluation. VS 1980, rptd in his The beauty of inflections: literary investigations in historical method and theory, Oxford 1985.
McGann, J. J. The poetry of Christina Rossetti. In The Pre-Raphaelite poets, ed Harold Bloom, New York 1986 (Modern Critical Views). A condensed synoptic 2-pt essay rptd from VS 1980, and Cannons, ed R. von Hollberg, Chicago 1983.
Rosenblum, D. Christina Rossetti: the poetry of endurance. Carbondale IL 1986.
Harrison, A. H. Christina Rossetti in context. 1988.
Mayberry, K. J. Christina Rossetti and the poetry of discovery. 1989.

Biographies

Packer, L. M. Christina Rossetti. Berkeley 1963.
Battiscombe, G. Christina Rossetti: a divided life. 1981.
Jones, K. Learning not to be first: the life of Christina Rossetti. 1991.
Jurlaro, F. Christina Rossetti: the true story. 1991.
Thomas, F. Christina Rossetti. 1992, 1994.
Marsh, J. Christina Rossetti: a literary biography. 1994. [WEF]

Dante Gabriel Rossetti 1828–82

Major mss holdings: Ashmolean, Bodleian and Worcester College libs (Oxford), BL, Brotherton (Leeds), Durham Univ Lib, Fitzwilliam Museum (Cambridge), Lady Lever Art Gallery (Port Sunlight), Manx Museum (Douglas, Isle of Man), Univ College London, NLS, Victoria and Albert Museum, Arizona State Univ, Berg Collection (NYPL), Delaware Art Museum (Wilmington DE), Duke Univ (see Baum and Fisher, below), Harvard, HRHRC, Huntington, Univ of Kansas, Library of Congress, Pierpont Morgan Lib, Princeton, Yale, Univ of British Columbia.

Special projects

McGann, Jerome. Dante Gabriel Rossetti: A hypermedia research archive of the complete writings and pictures. To be pbd as an online work (with some adjunct CD-ROM components) by Univ of Michigan Press in 4 instalments, the first scheduled to appear in 1998–9. The archive will contain all of D. G. R.'s critical and creative writings and pictures in every documentary state (all mss and all authorised ptd texts as well as all salient scholarly texts, plus full colour digital facs of the pictures and textual materials); plus a corpus of essential contemporary materials (W. M. Rossetti's pbd work on his brother, as well as the key works of Marillier, F. G. Stephens, Pater, Swinburne, and others); plus full-scale original notes and critical commentaries by the editor on all these materials. The whole is hyperlinked and electronically organised for full (and indexed) computer search and analysis. (Note by J. McGann.)

Bibliographies

The fullest bibliography of Rossetti ever attempted is J. B. Gregory's unpbd diss, Univ of London 1931.

Anderson, J. P. Appended to J. Knight, Life of Rossetti, 1887.
Rossetti, W. M. Bibliography of the works of Rossetti. 1905. Rptd from Bibliographer 1–2 1902–3. Addns by W. F. Prideaux, Bibliographer 2 1903.
Rossetti, W. M. Rossetti: classified lists of his writings with the dates. 1906 (priv ptd).
Vaughan, C. E. Bibliographies of Swinburne, Morris, Rossetti. Oxford 1914 (Eng Assoc pam).
Ehrsam, T. G., R. H. Deily and R. M. Smith. In their Bibliographies of twelve Victorian authors, New York 1936. Suppl by J. G. Fucilla, MP 37 1939.
Jones, H. M. The Pre-Raphaelites. In Victorian poets, ed F. E. Faverty, Cambridge MA 1956; ed W. E. Fredeman Cambridge MA 1968 (rev).
Fredeman, W. E. In his Pre-Raphaelitism: a bibliocritical study, Cambridge MA 1965 (sections 22–34).
Fennell, F. L. Dante Gabriel Rossetti: an annotated bibliography. New York 1982. Secondary material.
Barker, N. and J. Collins. A sequel to An enquiry into the nature of certain nineteenth century pamphlets. 1983. Updates An enquiry by J. Carter and G. Pollard 1934.
(Boos, F.) In Dictionary of literary biography vol 35, 1985.

Collections and selections

Collected works. Ed W. M. Rossetti 2 vols 1886, 1887 etc. Vol 1 contains Poems (essentially the 1881 text) and literary prose, vol 2 trns and miscellaneous prose, including art notices.
Poetical works. Ed W. M. Rossetti 1891 etc. Same as vol 1 of Collected works, *above*, without the prose.
Poems of Rossetti, with illustrations from his own pictures and designs. Ed W. M. Rossetti 2 vols 1904; 1908 (Pocket edn). First authorised restoration of Nuptial sleep to House of life; several poems added.

Works. Ed W. M. Rossetti 1911. The standard edn.
Poems and translations. Introd by E. G. Gardner 1912 (Everyman).
Rossetti. 1912 (Royal Lib).
Poems and translations 1850–70. Oxford 1913 (OSA); Oxford 1914 (WC). 1914.
Selections from Rossetti and Morris. Ed H. M. Burton 1929.
Dante Gabriel Rossetti. Introd by John Buchan [nd].
Rossetti: an anthology. Ed F. L. Lucas, Cambridge 1933.
Poems, ballads and sonnets. Ed P. F. Baum, New York 1937.
Poems. Ed L. I. Howarth 1950.
Poems. Introd by O. Doughty. 1957 (Everyman).
The essential Rossetti. Selected by J. Hollander 1989.
Selected poems and translations. Ed C. Warner 1991.

§1

The first pbd poem, My sister's sleep, *was intercalated in an article by* Elizabeth Youatt *in* La Belle assemblée Sep 1848 *(see Bentley, below). The sonnet* This is the Blesed Mary, pre-elect, *appeared in the catalogue of the Free Exhibition, 1849.* The blessed damozel, Hand and soul, *and 11 other pieces, mostly sonnets, were pbd in the 4 nos of* Germ, Jan–Apr 1850. Sister Helen *appeared in the English edn of the* Düsseldorf artists' album, ed M. Howitt, Leipzig 1854; The burden of Nineveh, *the 2nd version of* The blessed damozel, *and* The staff and the scrip *were included in* Oxford and Cambridge Mag nos 8 and 11–12, 1856, *rptd with many changes in* Crayon 1858 *and* New Path [Blessed damozel *only*] 1863; *3 sonnets on pictures first appeared in* W. M. Rossetti and A. C. Swinburne, Notes on the Royal Academy exhibition, 1868 (pt 2). *Rossetti also contributed substantial portions to* A. Gilchrist, Life of Blake, 1863, *reviews of* T. G. Hake *to* Academy 1871, 1873, *and several poems and prose works to* Athenaeum, Century, Critic, Fortnightly Rev, N & Q, Spectator *etc. Poems first appearing in miscellaneous vols are:* Sudden light, *in* Poems: an offering to Lancashire, ed Isa Craig 1863; Lost days, *in* A welcome: original contributions in verse and prose, 1863; Autumn song (MS), *in* Specimens from a cycle of English songs and lyrics, the music by E. Dannreuther (priv ptd programme of the musicale 18 June 1877); Raleigh's cell in the Tower, *in* Sonnets of three centuries, ed T. Hall Caine 1882; On certain Elizabethan revivals, *in* T. Hall Caine, Recollections of Rossetti, 1882. *Several poems by Rossetti first appeared in vol 2 of* Family letters with a memoir, ed W. M. Rossetti 1895, *below (detailed in* W. M. Rossetti's Bibliography, *above). For* Sister Helen (1857) *and* Verses (1881), *the first a suspected, the second a confirmed* T. J. Wise *forgery, see* J. Carter and H. G. Pollard, An enquiry into the nature of certain nineteenth-century pamphlets, 1934, *and* Barker and Collins, *above.*

Sir Hugh the Heron: a legendary tale in four parts, by Gabriel Rossetti Junior. 1843 (priv ptd by G. Polidori).
The early Italian poets from Ciullo d'Alcamo to Dante Alighieri (1100–1200–1300) in the original metres, together with Dante's Vita nuova. 1861, 1874 (rev and rearranged as Dante and his circle). Often rptd; ed S. Pucell with foreword by J. Wain, Berkeley 1981.
Of life, love, and death: sixteen sonnets. Fortnightly Rev Mar 1869.
Hand and soul. 1869 (priv ptd).
Poems. 1870 (4 edns), 1871, 1872, Leipzig 1873 (Tauchnitz, rev with memoir by F. Hueffer). First appearance of House of life. 2 private printings (1869, 1870) preceded this vol. For the history of the pbn of Poems 1870 and clarification of the several 'trial books', *see* J. C. Troxell (in Colophon), R. N. Keane and Roger Lewis, *below.*
The stealthy school of criticism. Athenaeum 16 Dec 1871. A reply to Buchanan, *below.*
Poems. A new edition. 1881. A revision of Poems 1870, with 4 new poems and 3 trns, omitting House of life and 3 other sonnets.
Ballads and sonnets. 1881, 1881, 1882, Leipzig 1882 (Tauchnitz, with expanded memoir by F. Hueffer). House of life expanded to 101 sonnets, Nuptial sleep dropped.
Rossetti, W. M. Some scraps of verse and prose by Rossetti. Pall Mall Mag Dec 1898; New York 1898. All but 2 of these scraps appear in Works 1911, *above.*
Lenore, by G. Bürger. Ed W. M. Rossetti 1900. Tr Rossetti.
Henry the leper [by Hartmann von Aue], paraphrased by Rossetti. Ed W. P. Trent 2 vols Boston 1905.
The house of life: a sonnet sequence. Ed P. F. Baum, Cambridge MA 1928.
Rossetti: an analytical list of manuscripts in the Duke University Library, with hitherto unpublished verse and prose. Ed P. F. Baum, Durham NC 1931.
Howe, M. L. Some unpublished stanzas by Rossetti. MLN 48 1933. On Border song.
The blessed damozel: the unpublished manuscript, texts and collation. Ed P. F. Baum, Chapel Hill NC 1937.
Rossetti's Sister Helen. Ed J. C. Troxell, New Haven CT 1939.
Jan Van Hunks. Ed J. R. Wahl, New York 1952. 2 earlier edns ed T. Watts-Dunton (1912), and M. Bell (1929).
The Kelmscott love sonnets. Ed J. R. Wahl, Cape Town 1954. From House of life mss in Bodleian.
Fisher, B. J., (ed). Rossetti's 'William and Marie': hints of the future. ELN 9, Dec 1971 (first printing of text of the poem, reproduced from ms at Duke).

American editions and collections

In 1870, Rossetti's authorised American publisher, Roberts Brothers of Boston, issued 2 edns of Poems: *250 copies from the English sheets with a new title page and binding, and a reset reprint from the 1st edn; Roberts also pbd a stereotype reprint of* Ballads and sonnets *in 1881; a 2-vol companion set of* Ballads and sonnets *and* Poems: a new edition *in 1882, with contents rearranged; a stereotype reprint of* W. M. Rossetti's *2-vol edn of the* Collected works; *and a single-vol 'Author's edition' of* Complete poems *in 1887. Capitalising on D. G. R.'s death, 2 identical unauthorised and adulterated edns of* Poems *were issued in 1883 by Lathrop in Boston and Alden in New York. Some time after 1886, Crowell of New York issued a 1 vol stereotype edn of the Lathrop–Alden text, adding W. M. R.'s 1886 preface and notes, 34 stray poems and 15 versicles and fragments, and indices of poems and first lines, unique features that appear in no other edn of Rossetti's works.*

Reviews

For a selected listing of reviews of Rossetti's vols pbd during his lifetime, see section 29 in Fredeman, *above. Rossetti's paranoic aversion to reviews and the controversy surrounding his manipulation of the press reception of his* Poems 1870 *underscore the need for a more complete account of the reviews of this vol. 25 reviews have been located, 14 of which, appearing in major British, American and continental periodicals, are signed:* P. P. Alexander, Edinburgh Courant; Sidney Colvin, Pall Mall Gazette (21 Apr); J. R. Dennett, North Amer Rev (Oct); H. Buxton Forman, Tinsley's Mag (Mar); T. G. Hake, NMM (June); Joseph Knight, *3 reviews:* Globe (20 Apr), Sunday Times (1 May), *and* Graphic (14 May); J. W. Marston, Athenaeum (1 May); William Morris, Academy, (14 May); A. Pichot, Revue Britannique (June); W. J. Stillman, Putnam's New Monthly (July); A. C. Swinburne, Fortnightly Rev (May); Frederick Wedmore, St James's Mag (Apr). *The authorship of another 11 have been identified, though the reviews are unsigned:* [Alfred Austin] Standard (26 May); [Sidney Colvin] Westminster Rev (Jan 1871); [W. J. Courthope] Quarterly Rev (Jan 1872); [W. D. Howells] Atlantic Monthly (July); [R. H. Hutton] Spectator (11 June); [J. R. Lowell] Nation (New York) (14 July); [M. Oliphant] Blackwood's Mag (Aug); [F. T. Palgrave?] Saturday Rev (14 May); [W. Brighty Rands] Contemporary Rev (June); [John Skelton] Fraser's Mag, n.s. 1 (May). *The most notorious review was by* Robert Buchanan, Contemporary Rev (Oct 1871), *pbd under the pseudonym Thomas Maitland and expanded in 1872 into the pam* The fleshly school of poetry and other phenomena of the day. *14 unsigned reviews are known, 7 each in Britain and America:* Broadway (Oct); Guardian (5 Oct); John Bull (7 May); Literary World; New Eclectic Mag (July); North Br Rev (July); Westminster Rev (1 July); Harper's Mag (Aug); Lippincott's Mag (Sep); New Englander (Oct);

Old and New (July); Western Lakeside Monthly (Nov); Catholic World; Evening Post (New York).

Letters

Letters appearing in memoirs etc are not detailed.

[Horne, H. P.] Rossetti: some extracts from his letters to Frederick Shields. Century Guild Hobby Horse Apr 1889. Letters rptd in Life and letters of Shields, ed E. Mills 1912.

Prinsep, V. C. A collector's correspondence. Art Jnl Aug 1892. Rossetti's letters to F. Leyland.

Dante Gabriel Rossetti: his family letters, with a memoir. Ed W. M. Rossetti 2 vols 1895. 317 letters in vol 2.

Letters of Rossetti to William Allingham 1854–70. Ed G. B. Hill 1897. Rptd from Atlantic Monthly May–Aug 1896. Expurgated passages restored by M. L. Howe, MLN 39 1934.

Ruskin; Rossetti; Pre-Raphaelitism: papers 1854–62. Ed W. M. Rossetti 1899.

Some early correspondence of Rossetti. In Pre-Raphaelite diaries and letters, ed W. M. Rossetti, 1900.

Rossetti papers 1862–70. Ed W. M. Rossetti 1903.

Letters addressed to A. C. Swinburne by Ruskin, Morris, Burne-Jones and Rossetti. 1919 (priv ptd by T. J. Wise).

John Keats: criticism and comment. 1919 (priv ptd by T. J. Wise). 5 letters from Rossetti to H. B. Forman.

A romance of literature. 1919 (priv ptd by T. J. Wise). Reciprocal letters from Swinburne and Rossetti relating to exhumation of Rossetti's poems.

Letters from Rossetti to Swinburne regarding the attacks made upon the latter by Mortimer Collins and upon both by Robert Buchanan. 1921 (priv ptd by T. J. Wise).

Whistler and his circle: letters and documents. 1927. Bookseller's cat, with summaries of D. G. R.'s correspondence with his solicitor James Anderson Rose, now in Library of Congress.

Letters of Rossetti to his publisher F. S. Ellis. Ed O. Doughty 1928.

Purves, J. Letters of Rossetti to Alice Boyd. Fortnightly Rev May 1928.

Compton-Rickett, A. Portraits and personalities. 1937. 9 letters rptd from TLS 16 Oct 1919.

Three Rossettis: unpublished letters to and from Dante Gabriel, Christina, William. Ed J. C. Troxell, Cambridge MA 1937.

Rossetti's letters to Fanny Cornforth. Ed P. F. Baum, Baltimore 1940.

Meyerstein, E. H. W. Rossetti on Patmore's Odes (1868). TLS 28 Apr 1950. Unpbd letter from Rossetti to Patmore.

Adrian, A. A. The Browning–Rossetti friendship: some unpublished letters. PMLA 73 1958.

[Baum, P. F.] Rossetti to George Eliot. Duke Univ Lib Notes no 34 1959. Unpbd letter from Rossetti.

Sambrook, A. J. Rossetti and R. W. Dixon. Études Anglaises 14 1961. Pair of letters exchanged between Rossetti and Dixon, both unpbd.

The Rossetti–Macmillan letters: some 133 unpublished letters written to Alexander Macmillan, F. S. Ellis and others, by Dante Gabriel, Christina and William Michael Rossetti 1861–89. Ed L. M. Packer, Berkeley 1963.

Briggs, R. C. H. Letters to Janey. Jnl of William Morris Soc 1 1964. Excerpts from Rossetti's letters in BM.

Packer, L. M. Maria Francesca to Dante Gabriel Rossetti: some unpublished letters. PMLA Dec 1964.

Letters of Dante Gabriel Rossetti. Ed O. Doughty and J. R. Wahl 4 vols Oxford 1965–7.

LeBourgeois, J. A Rossetti–Morris letter. N & Q 216, July 1971.

Grylls, R. Glynn (Lady Mander). Rossetti and Browning (11 letters in Troxell collection, Princeton). In Fraser, *below*.

Minnick, T. A new Rossetti letter. Blake Newsletter 5 1972.

Macmillan, C. B. Catalogue of Dante Gabriel Rossetti's letters at Univ of Texas at Austin. 1975. (Unpbd PhD diss 1975.)

Bryson, J. (ed in assoc with J. C. Troxell). Dante Gabriel Rossetti and Jane Morris: their correspondence. Oxford 1976.

Boos, F. Two unpublished letters of Dante Gabriel Rossetti. Jnl of William Morris Soc 3 1978.

Cline, C. L. (ed). The owl and the Rossettis: letters of Charles A. Howell and Dante Gabriel, Christina, and William Michael Rossetti. University Park PA 1978.

Cline, C. L. Dante Gabriel Rossetti's 'last' letter. LCUT 9 1978.

Fennell, F. L. (ed). The Rossetti–Leyland letters: the correspondence of an artist and his patron. Athens OH 1978.

Fredeman, W. E. 'Fundamental brainwork': the correspondence between Dante Gabriel Rossetti and Thomas Hall Caine. AUMLA 52 1979.

Lasner, M. S. Browning's first letter to Rossetti: a discovery. Browning Inst Stud 15 1987.

Gardner, J. H. Letters of Dante Gabriel Rossetti in the W. Hugh Peel collection. Kentucky Rev 10 1990.

Peattie, R. W. Selected letters of William Michael Rossetti. University Park. PA 1990. 22 letters to D. G. R.

Boyd, T. Suggested dates for some of D. G. R.'s letters of 1854. N & Q 236, Sep 1991.

The correspondence of Dante Gabriel Rossetti. Ed W. E. Fredeman. A multi-volume edn in progress. Vols 1–2 The formative years: Charlotte Street to Cheyne Walk: 1835–1862, Cambridge 1997.

§2

Forman, H. B. In his Our living poets, 1871.

Buchanan, R. In his Fleshly school of poetry and other phenomena of the day, 1872. Expanded from article by 'Thomas Maitland' in Contemporary Rev Oct 1871.

Swinburne, A. C. In his Essays and studies, 1875. Rptd from Fortnightly Rev May 1870.

Stedman, E. C. In his Victorian poets, 1876.

Caine, T. H. Recollections of Rossetti. 1882, 1908 (rev in My story), 1928 (rev).

Placci, C. Rossetti. Florence 1882.

Sharp, W. Rossetti and pictorialism in verse. Portfolio 13 1882.

Sharp, W. Rossetti: a record and a study. 1882.

Tirebuck, W. E. Rossetti: his work and influence. 1882.

Myers, F. W. H. Rossetti and the religion of beauty. In his Essays: modern, 1883.

Watts-Dunton, T. The truth about Rossetti. Nineteenth Cent Mar 1883.

Sarrazin, G. In his Poètes modernes de l'Angleterre, Paris 1885.

Swinburne, L. J. Rossetti and the Pre-Raphaelites. New Haven CT 1885. Rptd from New Englander & Yale Rev n.s. 8 1885.

Knight, J. Life of Rossetti. 1887.

Nicholson, P. W. Rossetti: poet and painter. Edinburgh 1887.

Pater, W. In his Appreciations, 1889. Rptd from The English poets vol 4, ed T. H. Ward, 1880.

Patmore, C. Rossetti as a poet. In his Principle in art, 1889.

Rossetti, W. M. Rossetti as designer and writer. 1889.

Caine, T. H. In Poets and poetry of the century, ed A. H. Miles, 10 vols 1891–7.

Hardinge, W. A note on the Louvre sonnets of Rossetti. Temple Bar Mar 1891.

Scott, W. B. Autobiographical notes. Ed W. Minto 2 vols 1892.

[Skelton, J.] Mainly about Rossetti. In his Table talk of Shirley, 1894.

Stephens, F. G. Rossetti. 1894.

Wood, E. Rossetti and the Pre-Raphaelite movement. 1894.

Kingsland, W. Rossetti's Jenny: with extracts from an hitherto unpublished version of the poem. Poet-Lore Jan 1895.

Marillier, H. C. Rossetti: an illustrated memorial of his art and life. 1899, 1904 (abridged and rev).

Cary, E. The Rossettis: Dante Gabriel and Christina. New York 1900.

Hueffer, F. M. [Ford]. Rossetti: a critical essay on his art. 1902.

Spens, J. The ethical significance of Rossetti's poetry. International Jnl of Ethics 12 1902.
Benson, A. C. Rossetti. 1904 (EML).
Dunn, H. T. Recollections of Rossetti and his circle. 1904.
Hunt, W. H. Pre-Raphaelitism and the Pre-Raphaelite Brotherhood. 2 vols 1905, 1913 (2nd edn, rev M. E. Holman Hunt).
Waldschmidt, W. Rossetti der Maler und der Dichter: die Anfänge der Präraphaelitischen Bewegung in England. Jena and Leipzig 1905.
Singer, H. Rossetti. 1906.
Brooke, S. A. A study of Clough, Arnold, Rossetti and Morris. 1908.
Rutter, F. Rossetti: painter and man of letters. 1908.
Horn, K. Zur Entstehungsgeschichte von Rossettis Dichtungen. Bernau 1909.
Routh, J. Parallels in Coleridge, Keats and Rossetti. MLN 25 1910.
Symons, A. Dante Gabriel Rossetti. [1910.] In the Int Art ser, simultaneously pbd in Fr and Ger. Symons's Studies in strange souls (1929) is a comparative study of Rossetti and Swinburne; he also pbd several shorter essays on Rossetti.
Bassalik-de Vries, J. William Blake in his relation to Rossetti. Basle 1911.
Ulmer, H. Rossettis Verstechnik. Bayreuth 1911.
Butterworth, W. Rossetti in relation to Dante. 1912.
Sharp, W. Rossetti in prose and verse. In his Papers critical and reminiscent, ed Mrs W. Sharp, 1912. Rptd from Nat Rev Mar 1887.
Suddard, M. The house of life. In her Keats, Shelley and Shakespeare, Cambridge 1912.
Willoughby, L. Rossetti and German literature. 1912.
Boas, Mrs F. S. Rossetti and his poetry. 1914.
Taglialatela, E. Rossetti: studio e versione. Rome 1914.
Villard, L. The influence of Keats on Tennyson and Rossetti. Saint-Étienne 1914.
Wagschal, F. E. B. Brownings Sonnets from the Portuguese und Rossettis House of life. Zeitschrift für Französischen und Englischen Unterricht 13 1914.
Watts-Dunton, T. In his Old familiar faces, 1916. Reprints of 4 articles from Athenaeum 1882–98.
Schücking, L. Rossettis Persönlichkeit. EStudien 51 1917.
Tisdel, F. M. Rossetti's House of life. MP 15 1917.
Venkatesan, N. K. Rossetti: the Pre-Raphaelite poet-painter. Madras 1918.
McKillop, A. D. Festus and The blessed damozel. MLN 34 1919.
Trombly, A. E. Rossetti the poet: an appreciation. Austin 1920.
Trombly, A. A translation of Rossetti's. MLN 42 1927. On The leaf, trn not from Leopardi but from Arnault.
Ghose, S. N. Dante Gabriel Rossetti and contemporary criticism (1849–82). Dijon 1929.
Wallerstein, R. The Bancroft manuscripts of Rossetti's sonnets, with the texts of two hitherto unpublished sonnets. MLN 44 1929.
Howe, M. L. Some unpublished stanzas by Dante Gabriel Rossetti. MLN 48 1933. Border song, first ptd in N & Q and not in Works, ed W. M. Rossetti. Includes text.
Sanford, J. A. The Morgan library manuscript of Rossetti's The blessed damozel. SP 35 1938.
Troxell, J. C. The trial books of Dante Gabriel Rossetti. Colophon 3 1938. Rptd in Fraser, *below*.
Baum, P. F. The Bancroft manuscripts of Dante Gabriel Rossetti. MP 39 1941. A general description of the manuscript holdings in Delaware Art Museum (see Wallerstein, *above*).
Doughty, O. Dante Gabriel Rossetti: a Victorian romantic. Oxford 1949, 1960 (rev). The standard biography.
Metzdorf, R. F. The full text of Rossetti's sonnet on Sordello. HLB 7 1953.
Fredeman, W. E. Prelude to the last decade: Dante Gabriel Rossetti in the summer of 1872. Manchester 1971. Rpt from BJRL. Contains new biographical material based on 150 letters from various correspondents relating to Rossetti's breakdown and attempted suicide following attacks by Buchanan and others on Poems 1870.
Surtees, V. Dante Gabriel Rossetti: a catalogue raisonné. 2 vols Oxford 1971. Excerpts from numerous letters to and from Rossetti, letters and diaries by other writers and artists, and ptd sources treating Rossetti.
Keane, R. D. G. Rossetti's Poems 1870: a study in craftsmanship. In Fraser, *below*.
Fraser, R. (ed). Essays on the Rossettis. Princeton 1972.
Sussman, H. Rossetti's changing style: the revisions of My sister's sleep. Victorian Newsletter 1972.
Fredeman, W. E. Rossetti's The blessed damozel: a problem in literary history and textual criticism. In English Studies Today 5 1973.
Peterson, Carl A. The Pierpont Morgan manuscript of Rossetti's The blessed damozel: dating, authenticity, significance. PBSA 67 1973.
Bentley, D. M. R. The Belle Assemblée version of My sister's sleep. VP 12 1974. The 1st printing of the poem, embedded in an article by Elizabeth Youatt.
Fredeman, W. E. The P. R. B. Journal: William Michael Rossetti's diary of the Pre-Raphaelite Brotherhood 1849–53 together with other Pre-Raphaelite documents. Oxford 1975.
Boos, F. S. The poetry of Dante G. Rossetti: a critical reading and a source study. The Hague 1976.
Nowell-Smith, S. and C. Cox. Rossetti's Early Italian poets. BC 25 1976.
Lewis, R. C. The making of Rossetti's Ballads and sonnets. In Fredeman 1982, *below*.
Fredeman, W. E. (ed). Centennial essays on Rossetti. VP 20 1982.
Lewis, R. C. Dante Gabriel Rossetti. In his Thomas J. Wise and the Trial Book Fallacy, 1995. Revises and augments earlier articles on Thomas J. Wise and the trial books of Rossetti's Poems (Jnl of Pre-Raphaelite Stud 2 1989) and on the text of Rossetti's Autumn song (BC 39 1990). [WEF]

Lady John Scott, Lady John Douglas Scott, or Lady John Douglas-Montague Scott, or Alicia Ann(e) Scott; Alicia Ann(e) Spottiswood 1810–1900

The NLS is the principal repository of mss and ephemera of Lady John Scott, including a large collection of her songs.

Bibliographies

V. Blair, P. Clements ad I. Grundy (ed). Feminist companion to literature in English. London 1990.

§1

Songs and verses. Ed with a memoir by Margaret Warrender, Edinburgh 1904, 1911.
Thirty songs by Lady John Scott, with accompaniments by Alfred Moffat. Ed Donald Ross, Edinburgh 1910.

§2

The burial of Lady John Scott, authoress of 'Annie Laurie', 16 March 1900. [Containing a poem signed G. G. N., i.e. George G. Napier, and a facs letter of Lady John Scott on her share in 'Annie Laurie'.] Glasgow 1900.
Alston, J. C. Westruther 'Auld' Kirk (16 March 1900), A poem inspired by the burial of Lady John Scott Spottiswood at Westruther 'Auld' Kirk. 1901. (With a note by Walter Lockie. Rptd from the Berwickshire News 8 Oct 1901.)
Walker, William. About some 'auld sangs', with particular reference to the songs of Alicia Anne Scott. 1912.
Irving, Joseph G. Annie Laurie. The Romantic story of the song and its heroine, (illustrations including portrait). Dumfries 1948.
Elliot, William W. Annie Laurie: the story of its composition (by Lady John Scott after the original version by William Douglas of Fingland). Ilfracombe 1954. [KM]

William Bell Scott 1811–90

Bibliographies and reference works

Fredeman, W. E. Scott in his Pre-Raphaelitism: a bibliocritical study. 1965.
Knight, Joseph. In Miles 4.
Dictionary of literary biography 32 1984 (W. E. Fredeman).

§1

Hades: or the transit and The progress of mind. 1838, Edinburgh 1838. 2 poems.
The year of the world: a philosophical poem. 1846, Edinburgh 1846.
Memoir of David Scott. 1850.
Poems. 1854.
Albert Dürer: his life and works. 1869.
Poems: ballads, studies from nature, sonnets etc. 1875.
The little masters: Altdorfer, Beham [etc]. 1879.
A poet's harvest home: being one hundred short poems. 1882, 1893 (with An aftermath of twenty short poems).
Scott also pbd a number of collections of works of art, and edited Byron, Coleridge, Mrs Inchbold, Keats, Miss Landon, Scott, Shakespeare and Shelley. See also Wellesley *vol 5, 1989.*

Journals and letters

Autobiographical notes on the life of William Bell Scott and notices of his artistic and poetic circle of friends 1830–82. Ed W. Minto 2 vols 1892.
Fredeman, W. E. A Pre-Raphaelite gazette: the Penkill letters of Arthur Hughes to William Bell Scott and Alice Boyd 1886–97. 1967.
Fredeman, W. E. Prelude to the last decade: Dante Gabriel Rossetti in the summer of 1872. 1971.
Fredeman, W. E. The letters of Pictor Ignotus: William Bell Scott's correspondence with Alice Boyd, 1859–84. 1976.

§2

Forman, H. B. In his Our living poets, 1871.
William Bell Scott, poet and painter. London Quart Rev 1875.
Rossetti, W. M. Scott and modern British poetry. Macmillan's Mag Mar 1875.
Obit: Athenaeum 29 Nov 1890.
Horne, H. P. Scott: poet, painter and critic. Century Guild Hobby Horse 1891.
Broers, B. C. In her Mysticism and the Neo-Romanticists, 1923.
Evans, B. I. In his English poetry in the later nineteenth century, 1933, 1966 (rev).
Fredeman, W. E. Review of Lona Parker's Christina Rossetti. VS 1964.
Black, D. J. Hermits and termits ... together with biographical notices in Robert ... David ... and William Bell Scott. 1972.
Trevelyan, R. Enter Scotus. In his A Pre-Raphaelite circle, 1978.
[WEF]

Louisa Catherine Shore 1824–95

Collections

Poems by A[rabella] and L[ouisa Shore]. 1897.
Poems, with a memoir by A. Shore and an appreciation by F. Harrison. 1897.

§1

War lyrics. 1855, 1855 (enlarged). With Arabella Shore.
Gemma of the isles: a lyrical drama, and other poems by A. and L. 1859. With A. Shore.
Hannibal: a drama [in verse]. 2 pts 1861; ed A. Shore 1898.
Fra Dolcino and other poems. By A. and L., authors of 'War lyrics'. 1870. With A. Shore.
Elegies and memorials, by A. and L., authors of 'Gemma of the isles'. 1890, 1894. With A. Shore.
The citizenship of women socially considered. Rptd, with a few alterations, from 'The Westminster Review' of July 1874. [1895.]

Elizabeth Siddal 1829–62

Poems and drawings of Elizabeth Siddal. Ed R. C. Lewis and M. S. Lasner, Wolfville Nova Scotia 1978.
He & she & angels three: three poems. Limited edn of 100. 1979.

§2

Marsh, J. The legend of Elizabeth Siddal. 1989.

Menella Bute Smedley 1819–77

Selections

Miles 7 (8).

§1

Lays and ballads from English history. By S. M. [1845], a new edn [1856].
The maiden aunt. [1845?], [1849]. By S. M. Tales, rptd from Sharpe's Mag.
A very woman. By S. M. In Seven tales by seven authors, ed F. E. Smedley, 1849, 1860, 1867.
The use of sunshine: a Christmas narrative. By S. M. 1852. Prose.
Nina: a tale for the twilight. By S. M. 1853. Prose.
The story of Queen Isabel and other verses. 1863.
Twice lost. By the author of Queen Isabel. 1863, 1866. Prose.
Linnet's trial. By the author of Twice lost. [1864.]
A mere story. By the author of Twice lost. 1865.
Poems. 1868.
Poems written for a child, by two friends. 1868, 1869, [1895]. With Mrs E. A. Hart.
Child-world. By the authors of Poems written for a child. 1869. With Mrs E. A. Hart.
Child-nature. By one of the authors of Child-world. 1869.
Other folks' lives. 1869. Prose.
Linnet's trial. 1871. Prose.
Two dramatic poems. 1874. Blind love and Cyril, with shorter pieces.
Boarding-out and pauper schools especially for girls. Being a reprint of the principal reports on pauper education. In the Blue-book for 1873–4, ed M. B. Smedley 1875.
See also Wellesley *vol 5, p. 719.*

§2

Forman, H. B. In his Our living poets, 1871.
Robertson, E. S. In his English poetesses, 1883.
Japp, A. H. In Miles 7 (8).

James Smetham 1821–89

Mss: notebooks, including poems, 1846–54 and undated, BL Add mss.

Collections

Literary works. Ed W. Davies 1893.

§1

Essay on Blake, from the London Quarterly Review. In A. Gilchrist, Life of William Blake vol 2, 1880.
Letters, with an introductory memoir. Ed S. Smetham and W. Davies 1891, 1892. 9 poems printed in appendix, some for the first time.
Smetham contributed to the London Quart Rev. See Wellesley *vol 5, p. 719.*

§2

Beardmore, W. G. Smetham: painter, poet, essayist. [1906.]
Casteras, S. P. James Smetham: artist, author, Pre-Raphaelite associate. Aldershot 1995.

Alexander Smith 1830–67

Collections

Miles 5.

Poems. Boston 1853.

A life drama and other poems. Boston 1858.

A life drama, City poems etc. Ed R. E. D. Sketchley [1901].

Poetical works. Ed W. Sinclair, Edinburgh 1909.

Dreamthorp. Selections. Madison NJ 1935.

Christmas. A selection from Dreamthorp. New York 193-? (priv ptd).

§1

Poems. 1853, Boston 1853, London 1854 (3rd edn), Boston 1854, London 1856, Boston 1857.

Sonnets on the war. 1855. With S. Dobell.

City poems. Cambridge 1857, Boston 1857.

A life drama and other poems. Boston 1858, 1859.

Edwin of Deira. Cambridge 1861, Boston 1861, Cambridge 1862 (2nd edn).

Testimonials in favour of Mr Alexander Smith. 1862.

Dreamthorp: a book of essays written in the country. Edinburgh 1863, Boston 1864, Edinburgh 1881; ed J. Hogben London 1906; ed H. Walker and F. A. Cavenagh 1914; ed H. Walker, Oxford 1914 (WC) (with selection from Last leaves), New York 1934, 1950.

Divine emblems. Intro to poetry of John Bunyan. 1864.

A summer in Skye. 1865, 2 vols Edinburgh 1865, 1 vol Boston 1885; ed L. M. Watt Edinburgh [1907] (with unpbd letter); ed W. F. Gray, Edinburgh 1912; ed W. F. Laughlan 1995.

The poetical works of Robert Burns. Ed Smith 1865. (Globe edn 1868.)

Alfred Hagart's household. Boston 1865, 2 vols London 1866. A tale.

Miss Oona McQuarrie: a sequel to Alfred Hagart's household. [1866], Boston 1866.

Last leaves: sketches and criticisms. Ed P. P. Alexander, Edinburgh 1868 (with memoir).

Smith also wrote for J. W. S. Howe, Golden leaves from the American poets *(1866). See also* Wellesley *vol 5 1989.*

§2

Kingsley, C. Smith and Alexander Pope. Fraser's Mag Oct 1853.

Aytoun, E. W. Firmilian: or the student of Badajoz. [1854.] Parodies Smith's poems.

Gilfillan, G. In his Galleries of literary portraits vol 1, Edinburgh 1856.

Brisbane, T. The early years of Alexander Smith, poet and essayist. 1869.

Japp, A. H. In Miles 5.

Looker, S. J. Alexander Smith. Poetry Rev May–June 1921.

Grimsditch, H. B. Smith: poet and essayist. London Mercury July 1925.

Alexander Smith. TLS 25 Dec 1930.

Reilly, J. J. Some Victorian reputations. Catholic World Apr 1937.

Garrod, H. W. Matthew Arnold's 1853 preface. RES 17 1941.

Murphy, R. Smith on the art of the essay. In If by your art: testament to Percival Hunt, Pittsburgh 1948.

Westwater, M. in The spasmodic career of Sydney Dobell. 1992.

[MW]

Walter Chalmers Smith 1824–1908

Collections

Miles 10 (12).

Selections from the poems. Glasgow 1893.

Poetical works. 1902.

§1

The Bishop's walk and the Bishop's times. By 'Orwell'. 1860. Verse.

Hymns of Christ and the Christian life. 1867.

Olrig Grange. Ed 'Hermann Künst', Glasgow 1872, 1888. Verse.

Borland Hall. By the author of Olrig Grange. 1874. Verse.

Hilda among the broken gods. By the author of Olrig Grange. Glasgow 1878, 1882 (3rd edn). Verse.

Raban: or life splinters. Glasgow 1881 [for 1880]. Verse.

North country folk. Glasgow 1883, 1888. Verse.

Kildrostan: a dramatic poem. Glasgow 1884.

Thoughts and fancies for Sunday evenings. Glasgow 1887.

A heretic and other poems. Glasgow 1891 [for 1890].

Nicolson, A. Verses. With memoir by Smith. 1893.

Smith also pbd a Life of Thomas Chalmers *(1884), lectures and sermons. He contributed articles to the* Nat Br Rev. *See* Wellesley *vol 5 1989.*

§2

Saintsbury, G. Smith's North-Country folk. Acad 23 1882.

The poems of Smith. Scottish Rev 1 1883.

Horder, W. G. In Miles 10 (12).

Edward George Geoffrey Smith Stanley, 14th Earl of Derby 1799–1869

§1

Syracuse. In Translations of the Oxford and Cambridge prize poems, 1833. A trn of Stanley's Latin poem.

Translations of poems, ancient and modern. 1862 (priv ptd), 1868 (3rd edn). Trns of poems in Greek, Latin, Fr, Ital and Ger.

The Iliad of Homer rendered into English blank verse. 2 vols 1864; 1865 (5th edn); ed F. M. Stawell [1910] (EL).

Many of Lord Derby's speeches were also pbd.

Papers

Journal of a tour in America 1824–5. 1930 (priv ptd).

§2

Henkel, W. Ilias und Odyssee und ihre Übersetzer in England von Chapman bis auf Lord Derby. Leipzig 1867.

Kebbel, T. E. Life of the Earl of Derby KG. 1890. With ch on Derby as man of letters.

Saintsbury, G. The Earl of Derby. 1892. With ch on his literary work.

Thomas Tod Stoddart 1810–80

Mss: notebooks (1825–80), poems, play, articles, etc, in NLS.

§1

The death-wake or lunacy: a necromaunt in three chimeras. Edinburgh 1831; ed A. Lang 1895. In verse.

The art of angling as practised in Scotland. Edinburgh 1835, 1836.

Angling reminiscences. Edinburgh 1837, London 1887.

Angling songs. 1839, Edinburgh 1889, with a memoir by A. M. Stoddart.

Songs and poems in three parts. Edinburgh and Kelso 1839.

Abel Massinger, or the aëronaut: a romance. Edinburgh 1846.

The angler's companion to the rivers and lochs of Scotland. Edinburgh 1847, 1853, 1892; ed H. Maxwell 1923.

An angler's rambles and angling songs. Edinburgh 1866, 1889 (with memoir by A. M. Stoddart).

Rambles by Tweed. In H. C. Pennell, Fishing gossip, 1866.

Song of the seasons and other poems. Edinburgh 1873, Kelso 1881 (with autobiographical sketch).

The crown jewel. [1898?] Drama in verse.

§2

Wilson, J. G. In his Poets and poetry of Scotland vol 2, 1876.

Stoddart, Scottish angler. Chambers' Jnl 12 Mar 1881.

Lang, A. Stoddart: a Scottish romanticist of 1830. In his Adventures among books, 1905.

Lady Emmeline Charlotte Elizabeth Stuart-Wortley 1806–55

Poems. 1833.
London at night and other poems. 1834.
The knight and the enchantress, with other poems. 1835.
Travelling sketches in rhyme. 1835.
The village churchyard and other poems. 1835.
The visionary: a fragment, with other poems. 2 pts 1836–9.
Fragments and fancies. 1837.
Hours at Naples and other poems. 1837.
Impressions of Italy and other poems. 1837.
Lays of leisure hours. 2 vols 1838.
Queen Berengaria's courtesy and other poems. 3 vols 1838.
Sonnets, written chiefly during a tour . . . 1839.
Eva, or the error: a play. 1840.
Jairah: a dramatic mystery, and other poems. 1840.
Alphonzo Algarves: a play. 1841. Prose.
Angiolina del' Albano, or truth and treachery: a play. 1841.
Lillia-Bianca: a tale of Italy. 1841.
The maiden of Moscow: a poem in twenty-one cantos. 1842.
Adelaida, or letters . . . to which are added poems. 1843. Prose and verse.
Moonshine: a comedy. 1843, [1885] (in Dicks' Standard Plays no 668). Prose.
Ernest Mountjoy: a comedietta. 1844. Prose.
Honour to labour: a lay of 1851. [1851.]
On the approaching close of the great exhibition and other poems. 1851.
Travels in the United States during 1849 and 1850. 3 vols 1851 New York 1851.
The Great Exhibition: honour to labour – a lay of 1851. [1851.]
The slave and other poems. 1853.
[Sketches of travel in America]. 1853. In prose.
A visit to Portugal and Madeira. 1854.
The sweet south. 2 vols 1856 (priv ptd). Prose.
Stuart-Worley edited Keepsake *in 1840 and wrote accounts of travel in America and in Portugal.*

§2

[Coleridge, H. N.] Quart Rev 66 1840. A long review.
Bethune, G. W. In his British female poets, 1848.
Lady E. Stuart-Wortley's travels in America. Littell's Living Age 29 1851.
Obituary GM Feb 1856.

Henry Septimus Sutton 1825–1901

Selections

Miles 10 (12).
Fragments of verse. [1916.]
A Sutton treasury. Manchester 1899, London 1909.

§1

The evangel of love. [1847.]
Clifton grove garland. Nottingham 1848.
Poems. Nottingham 1848.
Quinquenergia: or proposals for a new practical theology. 1854. Introd in verse. Also contains Rose's diary [poems], priv ptd separately [Glasgow 1889?], and 1899, *below*.
Poems. Glasgow 1886.
Rose's diary and other poems. Manchester 1899.

§2

Horder, W. G. In Miles 10 (12).
Davis, V. D. In Julian.
Obits: Manchester Guardian 3 May 1901; The Times 6 May 1901.

Charles Swain 1801–74

Ms of Poems, 1848–50 and undated, Manchester Central Lib.

Collections

Poems. Ed C. C. Smith, Boston 1857 (with a short life).
Selections compiled by his third daughter [Clara Swain Dickins]. 1906.

§1

Metrical essays on subjects of history and imagination. 1827, 1828.
Beauties of the mind: a poetical sketch with lays historical and romantic. 1831. Title poem recast and enlarged in The mind and other poems, *below*.
The mind and other poems. 1832, 1832, 1841, 1870 (5th edn), 1873.
Dryburgh Abbey, the burial place of Sir Walter Scott: a vision, forming a poetical catalogue of all the principal characters in the Waverley novels. 1832, Boston 1833, 1868 (with other poems).
Memoir of Henry Liverseege. 1835, 1864.
Cabinet of poetry and romance: female portraits from the writings of Byron and Scott. 1845.
Rhymes for childhood. 1846.
Dramatic chapters, poems and songs. 1847, 1850.
English melodies. 1849.
Letters of Laura d'Auverne. 1853. Poems.
Art and fashion, with other sketches, songs and poems. 1863.
Songs and ballads. 1867, 1868 (2nd edn), 1877 (5th edn).
Swain also contributed regularly to the annuals, especially Forget-me-not.

§2

Obit: Free Lance, Manchester, 2 Oct 1874. In verse.

Sir Henry Taylor 1800–86

Mss of Autobiography, *letters and poems in BL. Diaries, journals, notebooks, poems and letters in Bodleian.*

Collections

Poetical works. 3 vols '1864' [1863]. Plays and poems.
Works. 5 vols 1877–8.
Miles 3.

§1

Isaac Comnenus. 1827, 1845 (adds Edwin the fair), 1852, 1875. Verse tragedy.
Philip van Artevelde: a dramatic romance. 2 vols 1834, 1 vol 1844 (3rd edn), 1846, 1852 (6th edn), 1872; tr Ger 1852.
REVIEW: Quart Rev 51 1834.
The statesman. 1836; ed H. J. Laski, Cambridge 1927; ed L. Silberman 1957.
Edwin the fair: an historical drama. 1842; rptd in Isaac Comnenus, 1845, *above*. In verse.
The eve of the conquest and other poems. 1847, 1852 (3rd edn); rptd in A Sicilian summer, 1875, *below*.
Notes from life in six essays. 1847, 1848, Boston 1853 (7 essays), London 1854. Prose.
Notes from books in four essays. 1849. Chiefly from Quart Rev; 2 essays on Wordsworth.
The virgin widow: a play. 1850, 1875 (as A Sicilian summer). Chiefly in verse.
St Clement's Eve: a play. 1862. In verse.
Crime considered. 1869. A letter to Gladstone on the criminal code.
A Sicilian summer: with The eve of the conquest and minor poems. 1875.
Autobiography 1800 to 1844 (1844 to 1875). 1874, 1877 (priv ptd), 2 vols 1885 2nd edn.
Taylor also wrote for London Mag *(c. 1823) and for* Quart Rev, Fraser's Mag *and* Nineteenth Cent; *see also* Wellesley *vol 5 1989.*

Letters

Correspondence. Ed E. Dowden 1888.

§2

Some remarks on the preface to Philip van Artevelde. 1835.

Horne, R. H. In his A new spirit of the age vol 2, 1844.

Powell, T. In his Pictures of the living authors of Britain, 1851.

Forman, H. B. In his Our living poets, 1871.

Bilderbeck, J. B. Taylor and his drama of Philip van Artevelde. 1877.

De Vere, A. In his Essays chiefly on poetry vols 1–2, 1887. 5 papers on Taylor.

Japp, A. H. In Miles 3.

Knanth, R. Taylors Leben und Werke. Strasbourg 1913.

Taylor, U. Guests and memories. 1924. Chiefly on Taylor's later life and friendships.

Abercrombie, L. In The eighteen-sixties, ed J. Drinkwater, 1932 (Royal Soc of Lit).

Alfred, 1st Baron Tennyson 1809–92

Tennyson's notebooks are in Trinity College, Cambridge (those inherited by his son Hallam) and at Harvard (those inherited by the children of his son Lionel). The Tennyson Research Centre at Lincoln holds a ms of In memoriam, *together with a large number of revised proofs and the biggest single collection of letters from and to Tennyson. Other poetical mss are widely scattered. In the 1830s his poems circulated in ms among his friends; hence such transcriptions as the Heath ms in the Fitzwilliam Museum, Cambridge. The most complete census of Tennyson's poetical mss yet prepared is to be found in a facs edn of the mss* The Tennyson archive, ed C. Ricks and A. Day, 31 vols New York and London 1987–93. *The Harvard mss are described and indexed in* E. F. Shannon, jr, and W. H. Bond, Literary manuscripts of Alfred Tennyson in the Harvard College Library, HLB 10 1956. *The Trinity College mss are described and indexed in detail in* J. C. Yearwood, jr, A catalogue of the Tennyson manuscripts at Trinity College, Cambridge, unpbd PhD thesis, Univ of Texas at Austin 1977; hbk reprint University Microfilms International JXK80-21537.

Bibliographies etc

Brightwell, D. B. A concordance to the entire works of Tennyson. 1869 (pbd by Moxon without Tennyson's sanction or knowledge); 1870 (rev); *see also* Wise, The Ashley Library vol 7, *below* p. 132.

[Langley, S.] A concordance to the works of Tennyson. Strahan 1870.

[Shepherd, R. H.] A bibliography of the works of Tennyson. 1896, rptd New York 1970.

L[ivingston], L. S. A bibliography of the first editions in book form of Tennyson. New York 1901; suppl [1903?].

Thomson, J. C. Apocryphal poems of Tennyson. 1905.

Thomson, J. C. A bibliography of the writings of Tennyson. Wimbledon 1905.

W[ise], T. J. A bibliography of the writings of Tennyson. 2 vols 1908 (priv ptd). Advance proofs had circulated discreetly since c. 1900 and had been used by both Livingston, and Thomson, *above*. Harvard has a set with the pts in a different order; the rev proofs of vol 1 were ptd in 1907. Wise and the bibliographers who relied upon him are now known to include many forged edns; Shepherd, *above*, though incomplete, includes only one forgery (Idylls of the hearth), which may have been inserted by his posthumous editor. Wise may still be trusted on such matters as collected edns and contents of authentic edns. Rptd in 1 vol facs 1967.

Baker, A. E. A concordance to the poetical and dramatic works of Tennyson. 1914, New York 1966; suppl, 1931 (The devil and the lady).

Baker, A. E. A Tennyson dictionary. [1916].

Wise, T. J. The Ashley Library: a catalogue, vol 7. 1925 (priv ptd). A few Tennyson items in vols 8–10.

Ehrsam, T. G., R. H. Deily and R. M. Smith. In their Bibliographies of twelve Victorian authors, New York 1936, rptd 1968; suppl by J. G. Fucilla, MP 37 1939.

Baum, P. F. In The Victorian poets: a guide to research, ed F. E. Faverty, Cambridge MA 1956, 1968 (rev).

Wyllie, J. C. (ed). The Tennyson collection presented to the University of Virginia. Charlottesville [1961]. *See* W. D. Paden, Library 5th ser 18 1965.

Collins, R. L. Tennyson's original issue of poems, reviews, etc. 1842–1886: a compilation by Henry Van Dyke. Princeton Chron 24 1962.

Tennyson, C. and C. Fall. Alfred Tennyson: an annotated bibliography. Athens GA 1967.

Campbell, N. (ed). Tennyson in Lincoln: a catalogue of the collections in the research centre. 2 vols Lincoln 1971, 1973.

Revell, P. and S. Allsobrook. A catalogue of the Tennyson collection in the library of University College, Cardiff. Cardiff 1972.

Beetz, K. H. Tennyson: a bibliography, 1827–1982. Metuchen NJ and London 1984.

Shaw, M. and C. U. Snaith. An annotated critical bibliography of Alfred, Lord Tennyson. Hemel Hempstead and New York 1989.

Collections

Collected edns began to appear in 1870; see Wise, Bibliography, *above. The canonical text appears in the* Eversley edn, ed Hallam Tennyson with annotations by the poet, 9 vols 1907–8, 1 vol 1913; Amer Eversley edn 6 vols New York 1908.

Among the numerous other collected edns pbd since 1902, the outstanding one is The poems of Tennyson, ed C. Ricks, Harlow 1969; 2nd edn in 3 vols 1987.

Selections

Among the numerous edns of selections may be mentioned W. H. Auden (ed), Tennyson: an introduction and selection, New York 1944, 1946; R. W. Hill (ed), Tennyson's poetry, New York 1972; C. Ricks (ed), Tennyson: a selected edition, Harlow 1989; A. Day (ed), Alfred Lord Tennyson: selected poems, 1991.

§1

Tennyson required 2 successive proofs for Poems, chiefly lyrical, 1830, *and later more;* Poems, 1842, *and* The princess, 1847, *were often rev, largely on proofs. He had* In memoriam, 1850, *ptd in a preliminary version or 'Trial' edn and distributed copies to friends, to be recalled or destroyed; incompletely rev, the setting of type was unexpectedly used in several early edns, with successive corrections and revisions by the poet. After 1855 he again commonly used unpbd preliminary versions or 'Trial' edns, each ptd in a few copies and lent to advisers for eventual recall or destruction; single examples survive, used by the poet in revision and later given to trusted friends. The gradual discovery of these practices encouraged forgers to provide numerous 'priv ptd edns' for the rare book market. See* J. Carter and G. Pollard, An enquiry into the nature of certain nineteenth century pamphlets, 1934, 1983 (2nd edn, ed N. Barker and J. Collins); W. Partington, Forging ahead, New York 1939 (rev edn T. J. Wise in the original cloth, 1946); W. B. Todd (ed), T. J. Wise centenary studies, Austin 1959; J. Carter and G. Pollard, The forgeries of Tennyson's plays, Oxford 1967; N. Barker and J. Collins, A sequel to an enquiry into the nature of certain nineteenth century pamphlets, 1983; W. E. Fredeman, The story of a lie: a sequel to a sequel, Rev 7 1985.

A first edn here is a vol, offered with the author's consent to the general public, of which a significant portion of the contents had not appeared earlier. This excludes periodical pbns, unpbd preliminary versions or 'Trial' edns, priv ptd edns, copyright edns, and such intermediate pbns as collected edns prior to the final canonical edn. An edn with music or illustrations which was offered to the public preceding pbn of the text in a vol counts as a first edn, as well as (by default) a separate priv ptd pam or leaflet of a poem not rptd in the series of firsts. Edns neither first nor in a sequence of revisions are omitted. Known unpbd preliminary versions or 'Trial' edns, authentic priv ptd edns, and copy-

right edns are noted within the entries; proofs and similar objects, piracies and forgeries are listed where their omission might allow confusion.

Poems by two brothers. Ptd Louth 1827; ed Hallam Tennyson 1893 (adds 4 poems by Alfred from the ms and Timbuctoo). With Charles Tennyson; Frederick contributed 4 poems. For 2 additional poems by Alfred in the ms (from copies of 1893), *see* C. Ricks, VP 3 1965.

Prolusiones academicae. Cambridge 1829. Includes Timbuctoo; priv distributed offprint of Timbuctoo, Cambridge 1829.

Poems, chiefly lyrical. 1830. (Partly rptd and rev in 1842; *see below*.
REVIEWS: (W. J. Fox) Westminster Rev 14 1831; (L. Hunt) Tatler 24, 26 Feb 1831; (A. H. Hallam) Englishman's Mag Aug 1831; ('Christopher North', J. Wilson) Blackwood's Mag Feb–May 1832. On Fox, *see* W. D. Paden, Tennyson and the reviewers 1829–35, Stud in Eng (Univ of Kansas Pbns, Humanistic ser 4) 1940; and on North, *see* A. L. Strout, RES 14 1938.

Poems. 1833 (for 1832). Partly rptd and rev in 1842; *see below*.
REVIEWS: (W. Jordan) Literary Gazette 8 Dec 1832; (R. Bell?) Atlas 16 Dec 1832; (W. J. Fox) Monthly Repository Jan 1833; (E. Bulwer?) NMM Jan 1833; (J. Forster?) True Sun 19 Jan 1833; (J. W. Croker) Quart Rev 49 1833; (J. S. Mill) London Rev 1 1835.

The lover's tale [withdrawn from Poems, 1833]. 1833 (for 1832) (priv circulated edn of c. 8 copies), [1868] (Trial, rev), 1879 (rev). Piracy by R. H. Shepherd [1870], 1875. Forgery of first piracy '1870' [c. 1890].

[Early poems, suppressed in 1842. Ed J. D. Campbell] 1862; ed J. C. Thomson (with Timbuctoo and The lover's tale of 1833) in The Avon Booklet vol 1 nos 3–6 1903 and as Suppressed poems 1830–62, Warwick 1904, 1910.

Poems. 2 vols 1842, 1843, 1845, 1846, 1 vol 1848, 1850, 1851, 1853 (some edns rev with addns); partly illustr Millais, Holman Hunt and Rossetti 1857; ed J. C. Collins 1900 (with suppressed poems); ed A. M. D. Hughes, Oxford 1914 (with suppressed poems).

Reviews: (J. Forster) Examiner 28 May 1842; (F. Gardner?) Christian Remembrancer July 1842; Tait's Mag Aug 1842; (F. H. Chorley) Athenaeum 6 Aug 1842; Morning Post 9 Aug 1842; Weekly Dispatch 21 Aug 1842; (J. Sterling) Quart Rev 70 1842; Cambridge Univ Mag Oct 1842; (R. M. Milnes) Westminster Rev 38 1842; (L. Hunt) Church of England Quart Rev 12 1842; (J. J.) Christian Teacher Oct 1842; (W. Jerdan) Literary Gazette 19 Nov 1842; (W. A. Case?) London Univ Mag Dec 1842; (J. Spedding) Edinburgh Rev 77 1843.

The princess. 1847, 1850 (rev), 1851 (rev), 1853 (rev); illus Maclise 1860; ed J. C. Collins 1902 (with In memoriam and Maud).

In memoriam. 1850 (3 edns), 1851, 1851, 1855, 1856 etc. Within the sequence occasional revision (*see* headnote); additional poem in 4th edn, another inserted in 1870. Preceded by Trial edn [1850]. Poem ed Collins (with variants) 1902; ed S. Shatto and M. Shaw (with full collation of mss), Oxford 1982.

Ode on the death of the Duke of Wellington. 1852, 1853 (rev).

Maud and other poems. 1855, 1855, 1856 (rev), 1857, 1858, 1859 (rev) etc. Within the sequence occasional revision. Preceded by Trial edn [1855] and by The charge of the Light Brigade, 1855 (priv ptd) (1,000 copies for soldiers in the Crimea). Maud ed Collins (with variants) 1902; Maud: a definitive edition ed S. Shatto (with full collation of mss) 1986.

[Stanzas on the marriage of the Princess Royal: 'God bless our prince and bride!']. [1858] (priv ptd for court use). One example known; stanzas pbd in Hallam Tennyson, Memoir, 1897.

Idylls of the king. 1859, 1859 etc. Preceded by Trial edns called Enid and Nimuë: the true and the false (1857), and The true and the false: four idylls of the king (1859). Enlarged edns 1862, 1869 (for 1870), 1873, 1889. *See below:* The holy grail; Gareth and Lynette; the last idyll pbd in Tiresias and other poems, 1885. Edn of 1862 preceded by Dedication [1862] (priv ptd) (perhaps a proof of central fold in preliminary gathering of 1862 edn possibly sent to Windsor, in contrast to his later practice of submitting poems in ms); edn of 1873 (in Library edn vols 5 and 6) preceded by To the Queen, for court use [1873] (priv ptd) single fold, gilt edges (and proofs? with second, outer fold bearing title page and imprint, smaller pages, no gilt 1873). One version of Enid and Nimuë (1857) pbd without authorisation, Guildford 1902. *See also* J. Pfordresher (ed) A variorum edition of Tennyson's Idylls of the king (with collation of mss), New York and London 1973.

Ode written expressly for the opening of the International Exhibition, composed by William Sterndale Bennett Op. 40. 1862. Score for soprano, contralto, tenor, bass and piano or organ, here accorded priority to the vocal parts. BM copy bears on last page, which advertises Bennett's compositions, the date 20 Feb 1862; pages of music undated [plate no C. H & Co 3405]; cover dated 1 May 1862, when the Exhibition formally opened. Pbd as Ode sung at the opening of the international exhibition in Library edn vol 3 1872.

A welcome to HRH the Princess of Wales from the Poet Laureate. Owen Jones, Illuminator. Day & Son Lithographers to the Queen. 1863. Preceded by priv ptd edn for the court [1863] (4 states). Pbd as A welcome to Alexandra in Enoch Arden 1864.

Enoch Arden and other poems. 1864 etc; forgery of title page as Idylls of the hearth 1864; illustr A. Hughes 1866.

A selection from the work of Tennyson. 1865 (Moxon's Miniature Poets), 1870. Includes 5 unpbd poems and 2 versions of poems not pbd elsewhere etc; *see* Wise, Bibliography, *above*, vol 1, pp. 180–1.

The holy grail and other poems. 1870 (for 1869). Preceded by Trial edn The birth of Arthur [1868]. Also preceded by The victim, Canford Manor 1867 (priv ptd) (folio; proofs in 8vo).

The window or the songs of the wrens: words written for music by Tennyson, the music by Arthur Sullivan. 1871 (for 1870). Preceded by The window: or the loves of the wrens, Canford Manor 1867 (priv ptd); piracy by R. H. Shepherd '1867' (for 1870).

Gareth and Lynette. 1872. Preceded by Trial edn Gareth and Lineth [1872].

A welcome to Marie Alexandrovna. [1874] (priv ptd for court use) (4to; in some proofs the spelling Alexandrowna). Pbd Cabinet edn vol 4 1874. Forgery (8vo) '1874' (for c. 1897).

Queen Mary. 1875, 1875.

Harold. 1877 (for 1876).

Ballads and other poems. 1880. Preceded by Trial edn 1880.

Hands all round, a national song: the music arranged and edited by C. Villiers Stanford. [1882].

The cup and the falcon. 1884. Preceded by Trial edn 1882.

Becket. 1884, 1893 (acting edn).

Tiresias and other poems. 1885. Preceded by Trial edn 1885 and by Early spring 1883 (copyright edn); To HRH Princess Beatrice 1885 (priv ptd for court use) (4to, gilt edges; proofs? on different paper, larger pages, not gilt).

Gordon boys' morning and evening hymns: the words edited by Lord Tennyson, the music by Lady Tennyson, edited by Dr Bridge. 1885.

An ode written for the opening of the Colonial and Indian Exhibition 1886 by Alfred Lord Tennyson set to music by Arthur Sullivan for solo, chorus and orchestra. Vocal score, the orchestral music reduced to a piano score; nd, BM copy received 2 June 1886.

Locksley Hall sixty years after. 1886. Preceded by Trial edn 1886 and by unpbd preliminary version of The promise of May 1883.

Carmen saeculare: an ode for the Jubilee of Her Majesty Queen Victoria written by Alfred Lord Tennyson and set to music by C. Villiers Stanford Op. 26: pianoforte arrangement by the composer. [1887]. Final page of music dated Feb 1887 [plate no 7432]; title page and cover undated. Probably followed (in Apr) by offprint from Macmillan's Mag – perhaps for court use [1887] (priv ptd). Rptd with title On the jubilee of Queen Victoria in Demeter and other poems, 1889.

Demeter and other poems. 1889. Preceded by Trial edn Demeter 1889 and by The throstle, 1889 (copyright edn).

The foresters. 1892, 1892. Preceded by Trial edn [1881?].

The death of Oenone, Akbar's dream and other poems. 1892. Preceded by Trial edn 1892 and by The silent voices 1892 (copyright edn). Edn of The silent voices with music by J. F. Bridge 1892. Vol includes Riflemen form!, previously pbd [in earlier version] only in newspapers of 1859; an early version pbd without authorisation as Rifle clubs, New York 1899.

Tennyson's patriotic poems. 1914. Includes A call to arms [also called Arm, arm, arm! – 'Oh, where is he, the simple fool'], previously pbd anon in newspapers of 1852; ed C. Ricks MP 62 1964.

The devil and the lady. Ed C. Tennyson 1930, Bloomington 1964 (facs).

Unpublished early poems. Ed C. Tennyson 1931, Bloomington 1964 (facs, with The devil and the lady, *above*). Preceded by C. Tennyson, Tennyson's unpublished poems, Nineteenth Century Mar–June 1931.

Tennyson, C. Tennyson papers I–IV. Cornhill Mag Mar–June 1936.

Hallam Tennyson, Materials for life of A. T., 1896 (priv ptd), *his* 1897 Memoir, *the annotations in the* Eversley edns *and his memoir in the one-vol* Eversley edn, *1913, all contain poems not pbd elsewhere.* The Christ of Ammergau, *which Tennyson dictated extempore to Knowles in 1870, was pbd from Knowles's papers,* Twentieth Cent Jan 1955. *All unpbd poems are collected by* Ricks *in his* The poems of Tennyson, 2nd edn in 3 vols Harlow 1987.

For further reviews of Tennyson's pbd vols, see E. F. Shannon, jr, Tennyson and the reviewers 1827–51, Cambridge MA 1952, *and his* The critical reception of Maud, PMLA 68 1953; J. O. Eidson, Tennyson in America: his reputation and influence from 1827 to 1858, Athens GA 1943. *For later reviews, see* J. D. Jump (ed), Tennyson: the critical heritage, 1967, *and* I. Armstrong (ed), Victorian scrutinies: reviews of poetry 1830–1870, 1972.

Contributions to periodicals etc

Timbuctoo. Cambridge Chron and Jnl 10 July 1829.

Anacreontics. Pbd Oct 1830 in The Gem for 1831.

A fragment [Where is the giant of the sun]. Pbd Oct 1830 in The Gem for 1831.

No more. Pbd Oct 1830 in The Gem for 1831.

Sonnet [Check every outflash, every ruder sally]. Englishman's Mag Aug 1831; rptd Oct 1832 in Friendship's Offering for 1833.

Sonnet [Me my own fate to lasting sorrow doometh]. Pbd Oct 1831 in Friendship's Offering for 1832.

Sonnet [There are three things which fill my heart with sighs]. Pbd Oct 1831 in Yorkshire Literary Annual for 1832.

St Agnes's eve. Pbd Nov 1836 in The Keepsake for 1837.

Oh! that 'twere possible. The Tribute (ed Lord Northampton) Sep 1837.

The new Timon, and the poets [Part I]. Punch 28 Feb 1846.

Literary squabbles. Punch 7 Mar 1846.

To —, after reading a life and letters. The Examiner 24 Mar 1849.

Lines [Here often, when a child, I lay reclined]. Manchester Athenaeum Album 1850.

Come not, when I am dead. Pbd Nov–Dec 1850 in The Keepsake for 1851.

Stanzas [What time I wasted youthful hours]. Pbd Nov–Dec 1850 in The Keepsake for 1851.

To W. C. Macready. The Times 3 Mar 1851.

The penny-wise. Morning Chron 24 Jan 1852.

Britons, guard your own. The Examiner 31 Jan 1852.

For the penny-wise. Fraser's Mag Feb 1852.

Hands all round! [1852]. The Examiner 7 Feb 1852.

The third of February, 1852. The Examiner 7 Feb 1852.

Suggested by reading an article in a newspaper. The Examiner 14 Feb 1852.

The charge of the light brigade. The Examiner 9 Dec 1854.

Riflemen form! The Times 9 May 1859.

The grandmother. Once a Week 16 July 1859.

Sea dreams. Macmillan's Mag Jan 1860.

Tithonus. Cornhill Mag Feb 1860.

Ode sung at the opening of the international exhibition. The Times 24 Apr, 14 July 1862; Fraser's Mag June 1862.

A welcome to Alexandra. The Times 10 Mar 1863.

Hendecasyllabics. Cornhill Mag Dec 1863.

Milton: alcaics. Cornhill Mag Dec 1863.

On translations of Homer. Cornhill Mag Dec 1863.

Specimen of a translation of the Iliad in blank verse. Cornhill Mag Dec 1863.

Long as the heart beats life within her breast. Court Jnl 19 Mar 1864.

The victim. Good Words 1 Jan 1868.

The spiteful letter. Once a Week 4 Jan 1868.

Wages. Macmillan's Mag Feb 1868.

1865–1866. Every Sat (US) 22 Feb 1868; Good Words Mar 1868.

Lucretius. Macmillan's Mag May 1868; Every Sat (US) 2 May 1868.

Thine early rising well repaid thee. The Marlburian 20 Sep 1871.

The last tournament. Contemporary Rev Dec 1871.

England and America in 1782. New York Ledger 6 Jan 1872.

A welcome to Her Royal Highness Marie Alexandrovna, Duchess of Edinburgh. The Times 7 Mar 1874.

Prefatory sonnet to the Nineteenth Century. Nineteenth Cent Mar 1877.

Montenegro. Nineteenth Cent May 1877.

To Victor Hugo. Nineteenth Cent June 1877.

Achilles over the trench. Nineteenth Cent Aug 1877.

The revenge. Nineteenth Cent Mar 1878.

Dedicatory poems to the Princess Alice. Nineteenth Cent Apr 1879.

The defence of Lucknow. Nineteenth Cent Apr 1879.

Prefatory poem to my brother's sonnets. In Charles Tennyson Turner, Collected sonnets, 1880.

Child-songs. St Nicholas (New York) Feb 1880.

De profundis. Nineteenth Cent May 1880.

Despair. Nineteenth Cent Nov 1881.

The charge of the heavy brigade at Balaclava. Macmillan's Mag Mar 1882.

To Virgil. Nineteenth Cent Sep 1882.

Frater ave atque vale. Nineteenth Century Mar 1883.

Early spring [1883]. Youth's Companion (Boston) 13 Dec 1883.

Helen's tower. Good Words Jan 1884.

Compromise. St James' Gazette 29 Oct 1884

Freedom. Macmillan's Mag Dec 1884.

The fleet. The Times 23 Apr 1885.

Epitaph on General Gordon. The Times 7 May 1885.

To H. R. H. Princess Beatrice. The Times 23 July 1885.

Vastness. Macmillan's Mag Nov 1885.

On the jubilee of Queen Victoria [Carmen saeculare]. Macmillan's Mag Apr 1887.

In memoriam. W. G. Ward. The Athenaeum 11 May 1889.

The throstle. New Rev Oct 1889.

Because she bore the iron name. Daily News 27 Jan 1890.

To sleep! to sleep! the long bright day is done. New Rev Mar 1891.

Take, lady, what your loyal nurses give. The Times 27 June 1891.

The death of the Duke of Clarence and Avondale. Nineteenth Cent Feb 1892.

Letters

Letters of literary men vol 2. Ed F. A. Mumby 1906.

Tennyson and William Kirby: unpublished correspondence. Ed L. Pierce, Toronto 1929.

Ellmann, M. J. Unpublished letters of Tennyson 1833–6. MLN 65 1950.

Lang, C. Y. and E. F. Shannon, jr (ed). The letters of Alfred Lord Tennyson. 3 vols Oxford 1982, 1987, 1990.

§2

Biographies

Tennyson, H. Alfred Lord Tennyson: a memoir. 2 vols 1897.
Tennyson, C. Alfred Tennyson. 1949.
Martin, R. B. Tennyson: the unquiet heart. Oxford 1980.

Textual/bibliographical material

[Shepherd, R. H.] Tennysoniana. 1866, 1879 (rev).
Blair, D. An unacknowledged poem of Tennyson's? (in Good Words Feb 1868, signed T.). N & Q 2 Oct 1869. Reply by G. A. Schrumpf 23 Oct 1869: a trn of Flyttfoglarne by E. J. Stagnelius.
Shepherd, R. H. The lovers' tale: a supplementary chapter to Tennysoniana. 1870 (priv ptd).
Blair, D. Tennysoniana. N & Q 8 June 1872.
Wallis, A. A Tennyson forgery. N & Q 23 Feb 1884. On a clumsy forgery of first edn of In memoriam.
Shepherd, R. H. The genesis of Maud. North Amer Rev Oct 1884. Prints passages later cancelled from proofs of second edn of the poem.
Jones, R. The growth of the Idylls of the king. Philadelphia 1895.
Illustrated catalogue of rare Tennyson items. H. Sotheran [1902].
Description of a collection of holograph mss poems by Tennyson in the possession of B. Quaritch. 1914.
Reid, F. The Moxon Tennyson in Illustrators of the Sixties [1928].
Wise, T. J. An apocryphal Tennyson poem. TLS 27 Mar 1930; also Kempling, W. Bailey and A. Rogers, TLS 3 Apr 1930.
Tennyson manuscripts. TLS 17 July 1930.
Troxell, G. M. Tennyson emergent: sale of autograph manuscripts. Sat Rev of Lit (New York) 16 Aug 1930.
Pollard, G. Tennyson's A welcome, 1863. TLS 15 Feb and 15 Mar 1934.
Wise, T. J. Tennyson's A welcome, 1863. TLS 8 Mar 1934.
Adkins, N. F. Tennyson's Charge of the heavy brigade: a bibliographical note. N & Q 15 Sep 1934; also N & Q 13 Oct 1934.
Ratchford, F. E. An exhibition of manuscripts and printed books at the University of Texas, Oct 1–30, 1942: Alfred Lord Tennyson, 1809–1892. Austin 1942.
Motter, T. H. Vail. The writings of Arthur Hallam. New York and London 1943.
Memorabilia. N & Q 27 Feb 1943. On suppressed poems of Tennyson.
Shannon, E. F., jr. The proofs of Gareth and Lynette in the Widener collection. PBSA 41 1947.
T., C. B. Gabriel Wells. YULG 21 1947. On ms of Merlin and Vivien.
Donahue, M. J. Tennyson: two unpublished epigrams. N & Q 27 Nov 1948.
Donahue, M. J. The revision of Tennyson's Sir Galahad. PQ 28 1949.
Donahue, M. J. Tennyson's Hail, briton! and Tithon in the Heath manuscript. PMLA 64 1949.
Ellmann, M. J. Tennyson: revision of In memoriam, section 85. MLN 65 1950.
Gwynn, F. L. Tennyson's Tithon, Tears, Idle tears, and Tithonus. PMLA 67 1952.
Paden, W. D. A note on the variants of In memoriam and Lucretius. Library 5th ser 8 1953.
Buckler, W. E. Tennyson's Lucretius bowdlerised? RES n.s. 5 1954.
Grandsen, K. W. Some uncatalogued mss of Tennyson. BC 4 1955. In Palgrave bequest to BM.
Gordan, J. D. New in the Berg collection: 1952–1956. BNYPL 61 1957.
Tennyson, C. The Idylls of the king. Twentieth Cent 161 1957.
B., A. C. Extant copies of Tennyson's Timbuctoo. BC 7 1958.
Elliott, P. L., jr. Another manuscript version of To the Queen. N & Q Feb 1958.
Hartman, J. E. The manuscripts of Tennyson's Gareth and Lynette. HLB 13 1959.
Marshall, G. O. Textual changes in a presentation copy of Tennyson's Poems (1833). Lib Chron of the Univ of Texas 6 no 3 1959.
Nowell-Smith, S. Tennyson's In memoriam 1850. BC 9 1960.
Shannon, E. F., jr. The history of a poem: Tennyson's Ode on the death of the Duke of Wellington. SB 13 1960.
Paden, W. D. Twenty new poems attributed to Tennyson, Praed, and Landor. VS 4 nos 3 and 4 1961.
Nowell-Smith, S. Tennyson, A. C. and F. Poems by two brothers, 1827. BC 11 1962.
Ricks, C. The variants of In memoriam. Library 5th ser 18 1963.
Ricks, C. Tennyson's Hail, briton! and Tithon: some corrections. RES n.s. 15, Feb 1964.
Ricks, C. Tennyson's Rifle clubs!!! RES n.s. 15, Nov 1964.
Paden, W. D. Tennyson's The lover's tale, R. H. Shepherd and T. J. Wise. SB 18 1965.
Ricks, C. A note on Tennyson's Ode on the death of the Duke of Wellington. SB 18 1965.
Ricks, C. Tennyson's Lucretius. Library 5th ser 20 1965.
Ryals, C. de L. A nonexistent variant in Tennyson's Poems, chiefly lyrical, 1830. BC 14 1965.
Hardie, W. The light brigade. TLS 3 June 1965.
Ricks, C. Tennyson: Armageddon into Timbuctoo. MLR 61 1966.
Ricks, C. Tennyson's method of composition. Proc of the Br Acad 52 1966.
Short, C. Tennyson and The lover's tale. PMLA 82 1967.
Hall, P. E. Tennyson's Idylls of the king and The holy grail. BC 17 1968.
Nowell-Smith, S. Tennyson's In memoriam 1850. BC 17 1968.
Alfred Tennyson flies to the moon – a hitherto unpublished poem. Listener 81 1969.
Nishimae, Y. The Tennyson manuscripts at Trinity College, Cambridge. Hiroshima Stud in Eng Lang and Lit. 16 nos 1 and 2 1969.
Nowell-Smith, S. Tennyson's Tiresias, 1885. Library 5th ser 24 1969.
Ricks, C. The Tennyson manuscripts. TLS 21 Aug 1969.
Fredeman, W. E. The bibliographical significance of a publisher's archive: the Macmillan papers. SB 23 1970.
Motter, T. H. Vail. Tennyson's lines to Adelaide Kemble. TLS 16 July 1970.
Adicks, R. The garden trees: a collaboration between Tennyson and Hallam. Tennyson Research Bull 1 no 5 1971.
Niermeier, S. F. C. The problem of the In memoriam manuscripts. HLB 19 1971.
Scott, P. G. Tennyson and the Macmillan papers. Tennyson Research Bull 1 no 5 1971.
Landow, G. P. The page proofs of ll. 1–132 of the 1842 version of The miller's daughter. Tennyson Research Bull 2 no 1 1972.
Scott, P. G. The proof of Tennyson's Achilles over the trench. Tennyson Research Bull 2 no 1 1972.
Allentuck, M. New light on Rossetti and the Moxon Tennyson. Apollo 97 1973.
Pfordresher, J. A bibliographic history of Alfred Tennyson's Idylls of the king. SB 26 1973.
Sendry, J. The In memoriam manuscripts: some solutions to the problem. HLB 21 1973.
Sendry, J. Tennyson's 'butcher's books' as aids to composition. VP 11 1973.
Sinclair, D. The first pirated edition of Tennyson's Poems. BC 22 1973.
Tyree, D. W. A bibliographical item on The charge of the light brigade. Tennyson Research Bull 2 no 2 1973.
Ricks, C. The Lincoln ms from The coming of Arthur. Tennyson Research Bull 2 no 2 1973.
Ricks, C. Query on poem from Trinity notebook. N & Q June 1973.
Cox, J. T. A new date for Wiseian forgery: Tennyson's 'trial' issue of Becket (1879). PBSA 68 1974.
Sendry, J. The In memoriam manuscripts: additional evidence. HLB 22 1974.

Staines, D. The prose drafts of Tennyson's Idylls of the king. HLB 22 1974.
Stevenson, C. B. An early version of Sweet and low. Tennyson Research Bull 2 no 3 1974.
Tennyson, C. and C. Ricks. Tennyson's Mablethorpe. Tennyson Research Bull 2 no 3 1974.
Wiebe, M. G. The maid of Astolat: a trial printing of Tennyson's Elaine and Guinevere idylls. BC 23 1974.
Goslee, D. F. The stages in Tennyson's composition of Balin and Balan. HLQ 38 1975.
Hagen, J. S. Tennyson's revision of the last stanza of Audley court. Costerus 4 1975.
Goslee, D. F. Three stages of Tennyson's Tiresias. JEGP 75 1976.
Pfordresher, J. Yet another idylls manuscript. Tennyson Research Bull 2 no 5 1976.
Schuck, T. R. Christopher Rick's Tennyson and the laureate's publication history. N & Q Feb 1976.
Gaskell, P. From writer to reader: studies in editorial method. 1978. Includes discussion of revision of Oenone.
Shatto, S. Tennyson's library. BC 27 1978.
Shatto, S. Tennyson's revisions of In memoriam. VP 16 1978.
Shatto, S. The first written sections of In memoriam. N & Q June 1978.
Sendry, J. In memoriam: the minor manuscripts. HLB 27 1979.
Shannon, E. F., jr. and C. Ricks. A further history of Tennyson's Ode on the death of the Duke of Wellington: the manuscript at Trinity College and the galley proof at Lincoln. SB 32 1979.
Day, A. Two unrecorded stages in the revision of Tennyson's Oenone for Poems, 1842. Library 6th ser 2 1980.
Martin, R. B. An unpublished early poem by Alfred Tennyson. Tennyson Research Bull 3 no 4 1980.
Shatto, S. Tennyson's In memoriam: section 123 in the manuscripts. Library 6th ser 2 1980.
Shaw, M. The opening section of In memoriam: first and second thoughts. N & Q Dec 1980.
Day, A. The Lincoln manuscript fragment of Tennyson's The passing of Arthur. Library 6th ser 3 1981.
Day, A. Notable acquisitions by the Tennyson Research Centre: Tennyson's annotated copy of William Trollope's Pentalogia graeca and an unlisted ms poem. Tennyson Research Bull 3 no 5 1981.
Day, A. A Tennyson discovery. TLS 11 Dec 1981. Prints hitherto unknown poem.
Paden, W. D. Tennyson's The new Timon, R. H. Shepherd, and Harry Buxton Forman. SB 34 1981.
Shannon, E. F., jr. The publication of Tennyson's Lucretius. SB 34 1981.
Trapp, J. B. Mantua's Tennyson manuscript. TLS 18 Sep 1981.
Day, A. and P. G. Scott. Tennyson's Ode on the death of the Duke of Wellington: addenda to Shannon and Ricks. SB 35 1982.
Pollard, A. Three Horace translations by Tennyson. Tennyson Research Bull 4 no 1 1982.
Rosenberg, J. D. The mistaken point of In memoriam, section LXXII. Tennyson Research Bull 4 no 1 1982.
Collins, R. L. Tennyson manuscripts at the University of Rochester. Tennyson Research Bull 4 no 3 1984.
Collins, R. L. The texts of The vicar of Shiplake. Tennyson Research Bull 4 no 3 1984.
Ricks, C. Spedding's annotations of the Trinity ms of In memoriam. Tennyson Research Bull 4 no 3 1984.
Sturman, C. Annotations by Tennyson in a newly discovered copy of Poems, chiefly lyrical. Tennyson Research Bull 4 no 3 1984.
Ricks, C. The baby boy: an unpublished version. Tennyson Research Bull 4 no 4 1985.
Shannon, E. F., jr. and C. Ricks. The charge of the light brigade: the creation of a poem. SB 38 1985.
Belcher, M. A forgotten poem by Tennyson? Tennyson Research Bull 5 no 2 1988.
Scott, P. Tennyson's Maud and its American publishers: a relationship reconsidered. PBSA 83 1989.
Bailey, L. G. An early version of stanza three, The fleet. Tennyson Research Bull 5 no 4 1990.
Fredeman, W. E. Tennyson and his bibliographers. Rev 12 1990.
Hood, J. W. A note on revisions to Tennyson's The sea-fairies. Tennyson Research Bull 5 no 5 1991.
Kolb, J. Two Tennyson variants: The roses on the terrace and The eagle. Tennyson Reseach Bull 5 no 5 1991.
Shatto, S. The textual genesis of Maud. In Victorian authors and their works: revision, motivations and modes, ed J. Kennedy, Athens OH 1991.
Smith, W. S. Two early Tennyson fragments and their classical models. Tennyson Research Bull 5 no 5 1991.

Landmark works of criticism

[Fox, W. J.] Westminster Rev 14 1831. On Poems, chiefly lyrical.
[Hunt, L.] Tatler 24, 26 Feb 1831. On Poems, chiefly lyrical.
[Hallam, A. H.] Englishman's Mag Aug 1831. On Poems, chiefly lyrical.
[Wilson, J.] ('Christopher North'). Blackwood's Mag May 1832. On Poems, chiefly lyrical. *See* A. L. Strout, 'Christopher North' on Tennyson, RES 14 1938.
[Croker, J. W.] Quart Rev 49 1833. On Poems 1833.
[Mill, J. S.] London Rev 1 1835. On Poems 1833.
M[ilnes], R. M. (Baron Houghton). Westminster Rev 38 1842. On Poems 1842.
Horne, R. H. [and E. Barrett]. In Horne, A new spirit of the age, 1844. For E. B.'s contributions, *see* E. B. Browning, Tennyson: notes and comments, 1919 (priv ptd).
Gilfillan, G. Alfred Tennyson. Tait's Mag Apr 1847; rptd in his A second gallery of literary portraits, 1850.
[Kingsley, C.] Tennyson. Fraser's Mag Sep 1850. On In memoriam.
Mann, R. J. Tennyson's Maud vindicated: an explanatory essay. [1855].
[Gladstone, W. E.] Tennyson's poems. Quart Rev 106 1859. On Idylls of the king.
Gatty, A. The poetical character illustrated from the works of Tennyson. 1860.
Arnold, M. In his On translating Homer: last words, 1862. On Tennyson's style.
Robertson, F. W. An analysis of In memoriam. 1862.
Dowden, E. Mr Tennyson and Mr Browning. In his Afternoon lectures on English literature, 1863.
Bagehot, W. Wordsworth, Tennyson and Browning: or pure, ornate and grotesque art in English poetry. Nat Rev Nov 1864; rptd in his Literary studies, ed R. H. Hutton 1879.
Cheetham, S. The Arthurian legends in Tennyson. Contemporary Rev Apr 1868.
Jebb, R. C. On Mr Tennyson's Lucretius. Macmillan's Mag June 1868.
Tainsh, E. C. A study of the works of Tennyson. 1868, 1869 (rev), 1893 (rev).
[Austin, A.] The poetry of the period: Mr Tennyson. Temple Bar May 1869; rptd in his Poetry of the period, 1870.
Alford, H. The Idylls of the king. Contemporary Rev Jan 1870.
[Oliphant, M.] The epic of Arthur. Edinburgh Rev 131 1870.
Hutton, R. H. Tennyson. Macmillan's Mag Dec 1872; rptd in his Literary essays, 1888.
Gatty, A. A key to Tennyson's In memoriam. 1881, 1882 (rev), 1885 (with a few comments by Tennyson).
Swinburne, A. C. Tennyson and Musset. Fortnightly Rev 1 Feb 1881; rptd in his Miscellanies, 1886.
Myers, F. W. H. Tennyson as a prophet. Nineteenth Cent Mar 1889.
Van Dyke, H. The poetry of Tennyson. New York 1889, 1891 (rev), 1898 (rev).

Waugh, A. Alfred Lord Tennyson. 1892, 1893 (rev), 1894 (rev).
Swinburne, A. C. Threnody. Nineteenth Century Jan 1893.
Symonds, J. A. Recollections of Tennyson: an evening at Thomas Woolner's. Cent Mag 46 1893.
Adams, F. New Rev 10 1894; rptd in his Essays in modernity, 1899.
Brooke, S. A. Tennyson: his art and relation to modern life. 1894, 1900.
Saintsbury, G. In his Corrected impressions, 1895.
Bradley, A. C. A commentary on In memoriam. 1901, 1902 (rev), 1930 (rev).
Lang, A. Alfred Tennyson. 1901.
Bradley, A. C. The reaction against Tennyson (1914). In his A miscellany, 1929.
Lounsbury, T. R. The life and times of Tennyson: 1809–1850. New Haven CT 1915. [AD]

Charles Tennyson, afterwards Turner 1808–79

Mss of letters, diaries 1856–76, sonnets and personal papers in Tennyson Research Centre, Lincoln. Ms of Poems by two brothers *in Trinity College Lib, Cambridge.*

Selections

Collected sonnets, old and new. 1880, 1898. With preface by Hallam Tennyson, and introd by J. Spedding, rptd from Nineteenth Cent.
Miles 4.
Charles Tennyson. [1931.]
A hundred sonnets . . . selected and with an introd by John Betjeman and Sir Charles Tennyson. 1960.
The collected sonnets. Ed F. B. Pinion and M. Pinion 1988.

§1

Poems by two brothers. 1827, 1893 (with addns). With Alfred and Frederick Tennyson. *See also col 677, above.*
Sonnets and fugitive pieces. Cambridge 1830.
Sonnets 1864.
Small tableaux. 1868.
Sonnets, lyrics and translations. 1873.

§2

S[hepherd], R. H. Tennysoniana: notes bibliographical and critical on early poems of Alfred and Charles Tennyson. 1866–[75].
Japp, A. H. In Miles 4.
Jelinek, K. A. A. Charles Tennyson-Turners Leben und Werke. Leipzig 1909.
Nicholson, H. Tennyson's two brothers. Cambridge 1947.
Tennyson, C. The Vicar of Grasby. English 8 1950.

Frederick Tennyson 1807–98

Mss letters in Tennyson Research Centre, Lincoln; Ms of Poems by two brothers *in Trinity College Lib, Cambridge; various mss in Lilly Lib, Indiana Univ. See* VS *suppl 7, Dec 1963, pp. 57–76, for listing.*

Selections

Miles 4.
Shorter poems. Ed C. B. L. Tennyson 1913. Contains 11 previously unpbd poems.

§1

Poems by two brothers. 1827, 1893 (with addns). With Alfred and Charles Tennyson. *See also col 677, above.*
ΑΙΓΥΠΤΟΣ: carmen Graecum numismate annuo dignatum et in curia Cantabrigiensi recitatum comitiis maximis AD MDCCCXXVIII. In Prolusiones academicae, Cambridge 1828.
Days and hours. 1854.
Veritas. Revelation of mysteries. Biblical, historical and social, by means of the Median and Persian laws. By H. Melville. Ed F. Tennyson and A. Tuder 1874.
Aeson. [18 ?]. Anon.
Apollo. [18 ?]. Anon. Rptd in The isles of Greece, *below*.
King Athamas. [18 ?]. Anon.
Kleis; Alcaeus. [18 ?]. Anon. Rptd in The isles of Greece, *below*.
Psyche. [18 ?]. Anon.
Pygmalion. [18 ?]. Anon.
Sappho. [18 ?]. Anon. Rptd in The isles of Greece, *below*.
Ariadne. [1887]. Anon. Rptd in Daphne and other poems, *below*.
The four travellers. [1887?]. Anon.
Atlantis. [1888.] Anon. Rptd in Daphne and other poems, *below*.
Daphne. [1888.] Anon. Rptd in Daphne and other poems, *below*.
Hesperides. [1888.] Anon. Rptd in Daphne and other poems, *below*.
Niobe. [1888.] Anon.
Songs of joy. [1888.] Anon.
The isles of Greece; Sappho and Alcaeus. 1890.
Daphne and other poems. 1891.
Poems of the day and year. 1895.

§2

Frederick Tennyson's poems. Fraser's Mag June 1854.
Japp, A. H. In Miles 4.
Rawnsley, H. D. Memories of the Tennysons. Glasgow 1912.
Letters to Frederick Tennyson. Ed H. J. Schonfield 1930.
Nicolson, H. Tennyson's two brothers. Cambridge 1947.
Fall, C. An index of the letters from papers of Frederick Tennyson. SE 36 1957.

George Walter Thornbury 1828–76

Selections

Miles 5.

§1

Lays and legends: or ballads of the new world. 1851.
The monarchs of the main: or adventures of the buccaneers. 3 vols 1855, 1 vol 1858.
Art and nature at home and abroad. 2 vols 1856. Travel notes.
Shakspere's England: or sketches of our social history in the reign of Elizabeth. 2 vols 1856.
Songs of the Cavaliers and Roundheads, Jacobite ballads etc. 1857.
Every man his own trumpeter. 3 vols 1858. Prose.
Life in Spain, past and present. 2 vols 1859.
Turkish life and character. 2 vols 1860.
British artists from Hogarth to Turner. 2 vols '1861' [1860].
Cross country. 1861. Prose.
Ice bound. 1861. Prose.
The life of J. M. W. Turner. 2 vols '1862' [1861], 1 vol 1877 (rev and mostly re-written).
True as steel. 3 vols 1863. A novel.
Wildfire. 3 vols 1864. A novel.
Haunted London. 1865, [1879].
Tales for the marines. 2 vols [1865].
Greatheart. 1866. A novel.
Two centuries of song. 1867, New York 1867. Anthology with notes.
The fables of La Fontaine, translated into English verse. [1867], Ware 1984.
The Vicar's courtship. 3 vols 1869. A novel.
Old stories re-told. 1870.
A tour round England. 2 vols 1870.
Criss-cross journeys. 2 vols 1873.
Old and new London. A narrative of its history, its people, its places. 6 vols 1873–8 etc. Vols 1–2 by Thornbury.
Historical and legendary ballads and songs. '1876' [1875].
Thornbury pbd many collections of tales, topographical works, trns etc. He was associated with Dickens in Household Words *and* All the Year

Round. *He also pbd articles in* Dublin Univ Mag *and* Temple Bar. *See* Wellesley *vol 5, p. 776.*

§2

The writings of Thornbury. Dublin Univ Mag 50 1859.
Kent, C. George Walter Thornbury. Athenaeum 17 June 1876.
Ingram, J. H. In Miles 5.

Richard Chenevix Trench 1807–86

Collections

Poems, collected and arranged anew. Cambridge 1865, 2 vols London 1885 (as Poems).
Miles 4.
In time of war: poems. 1900. Preface by F. W. H. Myers.
Sonnets. Ed A. J. Romilly, Bristol [1901].
Sonnets and elegiacs. '1910' [1909].

§1

The story of Justin Martyr and other poems. 1835, 1836, 1857 (4th edn), 1862 (5th edn).
Sabbation, Honor Neale and other poems. 1838.
Poems. [1841] (priv ptd). Anon.
Notes on the parables of our Lord. 1841, 1844, 1845, 1864, 1882, 1886; ed A. S. Palmer 1906.
Genoveva: a poem. 1842.
Poems from eastern sources: the steadfast prince and other poems. 1842, 1851 (enlarged).
Elegiac poems. 1843. Anon.
The fitness of Holy Scripture for unfolding the spiritual life of men. 1845.
Notes on the miracles of our Lord. 1846, 1847, 1856, 1858, 1872, 1886.
Sacred poems for mourners. Ed P Maurice, introd by Trench 1846.
Sacred Latin poetry, chiefly lyrical. 1849, 1864 (2nd edn), corrected and improved. An anthology.
On the study of words: five lectures. 1851, 1852 (2nd edn rev and enlarged), New York 1852, London 1856, 1859, 1872, 1886; ed A. S. Palmer 1904, 1927 (EL). There are many Eng and Amer reprints.
Poems from eastern sources: Genoveva and other poems. 1851, 1851 (2nd edn).
On the lessons in proverbs: five lectures. 1853; ed A. S. Palmer 1905 (with bibliography of proverbs).
Synonyms of the New Testament. Cambridge 1854, 1855 (3rd edn rev), Cambridge 1860 (5th edn).
English past and present: five lectures. 1855, New York 1860; rev A. L. Mayhew 1889; ed A. S. Palmer 1905.
On teaching by words. 1855.
Alma and other poems. 1855.
Poems. New York 1856.
On some deficiencies in our English dictionaries. 1857, 1860 (rev and enlarged).
A select glossary of English words, used formerly in senses different from their present. 1859, 1859, 1865 (3rd edn rev and improved), 1873; ed A. S. Palmer 1906.
The history of the English sonnet. 1863.
Gustavus Adolphus: social aspects of the Thirty Years' War. 1865, 1887 (3rd edn enlarged).
Studies in the Gospels. 1867.
A household book of English poetry. 1868, rev 1870. An anthology.
Plutarch: his life, his Lives and his morals. 1873. 4 lectures.
Lectures on medieval church history. 1877, 1879 (2nd edn rev).
Brief thoughts and meditations on some passages in Holy Scripture. 1884.
Trench also pbd numerous theological tracts and sermons.

Letters

Trench: letters and memorials. Ed M. Trench 2 vols 1888.

§2

Myers, F. W. H. Archbishop Trench's poems. Nineteenth Cent Oct 1877.
De Vere, A. Archbishop Trench's poems. Nineteenth Cent June 1888.
Silvester, J. Archbishop Trench: a sketch of his life and character. [1891.]
Gibbs, H. J. In Miles 4.
Julian.
Pritchett, V. S. Books in general. New Statesman 16 Oct 1943. Discusses On the study of words.

Martin Farquhar Tupper 1810–89

Mss: correspondence with Gladstone, BL Add Ms; letters and literary mss, Huntington.

Collections

Complete poetical works. Hartford CT 1850; Complete prose works, Hartford CT 1850.
Complete poetical works. New York [c. 1855].

Selections

Cithara: a selection from the lyrics. 1863.
A selection from the works. Moxon's Miniature Poets. 1866, reissued [1886].
Select miscellaneous poems. [1874], Edinburgh and London [1881].

§1

Sacra poesis. 1832.
A voice from the cloister, by a young collegian. [1835/6?].
Geraldine: a sequel to Coleridge's Christabel, with other poems. 1838.
REVIEWS: Spectator 11, 17 Nov 1838; Blackwood's Mag 44, Dec 1838; Athenaeum 579, 1 Dec 1838.
An ode on the coronation of her majesty Queen Victoria, June 28, 1838. 1838.
Proverbial philosophy: a book of thoughts and arguments, originally treated. 1838, 2nd ser 1842; 1867 (new edn 1st and 2nd ser); 3rd ser 1867; [1871] in 4 ser, now first complete, including 50th edn of the two 1st ser, reissued [1881]; New York 1876. Authorised edn. Frequently rptd throughout the century.
REVIEWS: Athenaeum 547, 21 Apr 1838, 806, 8 Apr 1843 (2nd ser); Literary Gazette 1819, 29 Nov 1851 (of 21st thousand and Fr edn); Athenaeum 1418, 30 Dec 1854; Literary Gazette 2027, 24 Nov 1855; Spectator 40, 12 Jan 1867 (3rd ser); Athenaeum 2065, 25 May 1867; Saturday Rev 33, 13 Jan 1872 (4 ser complete).
Philosophie Proverbiale: traduit en Français d'après la dixième édition par George Métivier. 1851.
A modern pyramid to commemorate a septuagint of worthies. 1839. A sonnet and an essay on each of 70 famous men.
St Martha's near Guildford, Surrey. [Guildford?] 1841. Not pbd.
The crock of gold: a rural novel. 1844, new edn 1849.
REVIEW: Spectator 17, 10 Feb 1844.
A thousand lines now first offered to the world we live in. 1845.
Hactenus. 1848.
REVIEW: Literary Gazette 1641, 1 July 1848.
The loving ballad to Brother Jonathan. [1848.] Broadsheet.
Ballads for the times (now first collected). 1850, 1851 (enlarged and rev), 1852 (rev).
Farley Heath: a record of its Roman remains and other antiquities; also a poem and a tale. Guildford 1850.
King Alfred's poems turned into English metres. 1850.
Half a dozen no-popery ballads. [1851.]
A hymn for all nations. 1851; tr 30 languages 1851.
REVIEW: Literary Gazette 1791, 17 May 1851.
A dirge for Wellington. 1852.
REVIEWS: Athenaeum 1300, 25 Sep 1852; Literary Gazette 1862, 25 Sep 1852.
Things to come: a prophetic ode. 1852.

Half a dozen ballads for Australian emigrants. 1853.
A batch of war ballads. 1854.
REVIEWS: Literary Gazette 1939, 18 Mar 1854; Athenaeum 1393, 8 July 1854.
A dozen ballads for the times about Church abuses: reprinted, with additions, from the Daily News. 1854.
A dozen ballads for the times about white slavery. 1854.
REVIEW: Literary Gazette 1938, 11 Mar 1854.
Lyrics of the heart and mind. 1855, 1855 (as Lyrics. A new edition).
REVIEWS: Spectator 28, 20 Jan 1855; Athenaeum 1434, 21 Apr 1855; Saturday Rev 2, 9 Aug 1856.
A missionary ballad. [1855?]
Alfred: a patriotic play. Westminster 1858 (priv ptd).
Stephan Langton. 2 vols [1858], 1863 (as Stephan Langton: or the days of King John), 1880, 1923.
REVIEWS: Saturday Rev 7, 15 Jan 1859; Reader 2, 10 Oct 1863.
Some verse and prose about national rifle-clubs. 1859.
Three hundred sonnets. 1860.
REVIEWS: Athenaeum 1697, 5 May 1860; Saturday Rev 10, 4 Aug 1860.
Plan of the ritualistic campaign. [1865?] (priv ptd), 1868 (as The anti-ritualistic satire).
Raleigh: his life and his death; a historical play in five acts. 1866. Verse drama.
REVIEW: Saturday Rev 21, 24 Feb 1866.
Our Canadian dominion: half a dozen ballads about a King for Canada. 1868.
REVIEW: Spectator 41, 1 Aug 1868.
Twenty-one Protestant ballads published in the Rock. 1868.
REVIEW: Spectator 41, 1 Aug 1868.
A creed, etcetera. 1870.
REVIEW: Athenaeum 2236, 3 Sep 1870.
Fifty of the Protestant ballads and 'the anti-ritualistic directorium'. 1874.
Washington: a drama in five acts. New York 1876. Verse drama.
Three five-act plays and twelve dramatic scenes, suitable for private theatricals or drawing-room recitation. 1882.
My life as an author. 1886. Autobiography.
REVIEWS: Athenaeum 3055, 15 May 1886; Saturday Rev 62, 3 July 1886.
Jubilate! an offering in 1887. [1887.] For Queen Victoria.
Tupper was also a prolific prose writer. See Wellesley *vol 5 1989.*

Translations

T. Sullivan's La bannière sur le char de la victoire. [1866.]
J. Sullivan's Élégie sur la mort de Lord Palmerston. 1866.

§2

Obits: The Times 30 Nov 1889; Saturday Rev 7 Dec 1889.
Drinkwater, J. In The eighteen-eighties, ed W. de la Mare, 1930 (Royal Soc of Lit).
Hudson, D. Martin Tupper: his rise and fall. 1949. [RS]

Thomas Wade 1805–75

Mss: Plays, BL Add mss; ms of unpbd trn of Dante's Inferno *(executed 1845–6), Macauley Collection, Univ of PA.*

Selections

Miles 3.
The contention of death and love, Helena and Fifty sonnets. In Literary anecdotes of the nineteenth century, ed W. R. Nicoll and T. J. Wise, vol 1 1895.

§1

Tasso and the sisters: poems. 1825.
Woman's love, or the triumph of patience: a drama. 1829. In prose and verse.
The phrenologists: a farce. 1830. In prose.
The Jew of Arragon: a tragedy. 1830. In verse.
Mundi et cordis de rebus sempiternis et temporariis: carmina. 1835. Lyrics and sonnets in Eng.
The contention of death and love. 1837.
Helena: a poem. 1837.
Prothanasia and other poems. 1839.
What does Hamlet mean? a lecture. Jersey [1840?].
Wade edited Bell's Weekly Messenger *c. 1838, and later* The Br Press, *Jersey, and later* Wade's London Rev, *Oct 1844–Jan 1846.*

§2

Forman, H. B. In Miles 3.
Forman, H. B. Wade: the poet and his surroundings. In Literary anecdotes of the nineteenth century, ed W. R. Nicoll and T. J. Wise, vol 1 1895. Includes unpbd poems.
West, S. G. An aspiring English translator of Os Lusíados: Thomas Wade, poet and dramatist, 1805–1875. Lisbon 1973.

Edward Walsh 1805–50

Reliques of Irish Jacobite poetry. Ed J. Daly with English metrical versions by Walsh, Dublin 1844, 1866.
Irish popular songs. With English metrical translations by Walsh. Dublin 1847.

Anna Laetitia Waring, 'ALW' 1823–1910

Selections

Miles 10 (11).

§1

Hymns and meditations, by A. L. W. 1850, 1850, 1852, 1854, 1855, 1856, 1858, 1860, Philadelphia 1860 (with selections from several authors), London 1863, Boston 1863, 1870, New York 1871, London 1878 (13th edn), [1883], [1889], 1911. Most of the edns contain some addns.
Additional hymns. 1858.
Days of remembrance: a memorial calendar (compiled by ALW). 1886.

§2

Obit: The Times 24 May 1910.
Horder, W. G. In Miles 10 (11).
Crawford, G. A. In Julian.
Talbot, M. S. In remembrance of Anna Laetitia Waring. 1911. Contains additional hymns and other previously unpbd verses. [RS]

Edwin Waugh 1817–90

Mss: articles, poems, songs, travel notes, draft letters 1846–66, Rochdale Area Central Lib; diary 1847–51 and letters, Manchester Central Lib.

Collections

Poesies from a country garden. 2 pts Manchester 1866.
Samples of Lancashire wares. [1879.] Includes selections from Waugh.
The chimney corner. 1879; ed G. Milner [1892]. Prose sketches, mostly in the Lancashire dialect.
Complete works. 11 vols 1881–9.
Fireside tales. [1885.]
Besom Ben stories. Ed G. Milner [1892].
Tufts of heather from the Lancashire moors. Ed G. Milner 2 sers [1892].
Rambles in the Lake Country and other travel sketches. Ed G. Milner 2 sers [1893].

§1

A ramble from Bury to Rochdale: containing a Lancashire dialogue and Jone o'Jeffrey's Tale. 1853, Manchester 1855.

Sketches of Lancashire life and localities. Manchester 1855, Manchester 1869 (3rd edn); ed G. Milner 2 pts [1892].

Come whoam to thy childer an' me. [Manchester? 1856]. Verse.

What ails thee, my son Robin? Manchester [1856]. Verse.

Chirrup. Manchester [1858]. A song.

Poems and Lancashire songs. 1859, 1870 (3rd edn, with addns), 1876 (4th edn, with addns).

Over sands to the lakes. Manchester 1860.

The Birtle carter's tale about Owd Bodle. Manchester 1861, 1865 (as Owd Bodle).

The goblin's grave: revised from Lancashire sketches. Manchester 1861, 1865.

Rambles in the Lake Country and its borders. Manchester 1861, 1864.

Lancashire songs. Manchester [1863], 1865, [1892] (6th edn).

Fourteen days in Scotland. Manchester [1864].

Tufts of heather from the Lancashire moors: The barrel organ; The dead man's dinner; Tattlin Matty. Manchester [1864], 1866 (4th edn).

Besom Ben. Manchester 1865, [1892].

Prince's Theatre, Manchester: the grand comic Christmas pantomime, for 1866 and 1867, or Robin Hood and ye merrie men of Sherwood. [1866.] Verse.

Ben an' th' bantam: a sequel to Besom Ben. Manchester 1866.

The birthplace of Tim Bobbin in the parish of Flixton. Manchester [1867].

Home-life of the Lancashire factory folk during the cotton famine. Manchester 1867.

Th' owd blanket: a sequel to Ben an' th' bantam. Manchester [1867].

Tufts of heather from the Northern moors. Manchester 1867.

Dules gate: or a frisk through a Lancashire clough. Manchester [1868]. Prose.

Sneck-bant, or th' owd tow-bar. Manchester [1868]. Prose.

Yeth-bobs an' scaplins, or Tufts of heather and chips of rock. A sequel to Sneck-bant. Manchester [1868]. Prose.

Irish sketches. Manchester [1869]. Prose.

Johnny o'Wobbler's an' th' two-wheeled dragon: a velocipede story. Manchester [1869]. Prose.

An old nest. Manchester [1869]. Prose.

Snowed-up, or the white house on the moor top. Manchester [1869]. Prose.

Craig Dhu, or my lodging by the sea. Manchester [1870?]. Prose.

A striking story; and The swallowed sixpence (Lancashire sketches). [1871], [1878] as The nomination: a striking story...

Rambles and reveries. 1872. Poems.

Lancashire anecdotes, No 2 Owd Buzzart. Manchester [1872].

Jannock, or the bold trencherman. Manchester [1873]. A tale.

The old coal man: a sketch. Manchester [1873].

Old cronies, or wassail in a country inn. Manchester [1875].

The hermit cobbler. Manchester [1878].

Around the Yule-log: a series of fireside tales. [1879]. Prose.

In the Lake Country. Manchester 1880.

Poems and songs. Oldham 1889, 2nd ser Liverpool 1889; ed G. Milner [1893] (with an introductory essay on the dialect of Lancashire as a vehicle for poetry); ed C Hayes, Manchester 1992, as Poems and songs of old Lancashire.

§2

Waugh's Besom Ben stories. Saturday Rev 6 May 1882.

Lamb, R. Obituary. Leisure Hour 39 1890.

Obits: Athenaeum 10 May 1890; Temple Bar Oct 1890.

Watson, W. Lancashire laureate. Nat Rev June 1890.

Newbiggin, T. Lancashire characters and places. Manchester 1891.

Espinasse, F. Manchester memories: Waugh. In his Literary recollections and sketches, 1893.

Joyce, P. Democratic subjects: the self and the social in nineteenth century England. Cambridge 1994. On Waugh and John Bright.

Thomas Westwood 1814–88

Selections

Miles 4.

§1

Poems. 1840.
REVIEWS: Spectator 13, 2 May 1840; Athenaeum 673, 19 Sep 1840.

Beads from a rosary. 1843.

The burden of the bell and other lyrics. 1850.
REVIEWS: Athenaeum 1191, 24 Aug 1850; Literary Gazette 21 Sep 1850.

Berries and blossoms: a verse-book for young people. 1855.
REVIEWS: Athenaeum 1428, 10 Mar 1855; NMM 104, June 1855.

Foxglove bells: a book of sonnets. Brussels and London 1856.
REVIEWS: Literary Gazette 2040, 24 Feb 1856; Athenaeum 1490, 17 May 1856.

A new bibliotheca piscatoria: or general catalogue of angling and fishing literature. 1861; rev T. Westwood and T. Satchell 1883.
REVIEWS: Athenaeum 2888, 3 Mar 1883; Saturday Rev 57, 22 Dec 1883.

The chronicle of the Compleat angler of Isaac Walton and Charles Cotton: being a bibliographical record. 1864. The essay on Lamb rptd in E. V. Lucas, Life of Charles Lamb vol 2, 1905.
REVIEW: Athenaeum 1922, 27 Aug 1864.

A stream in Arden – Hey for coquet! A lay of the sea. In H. C. Pennell, Fishing gossip, 1866. Poems.

The sword of kingship: a legend of the Mort d'Arthure. 1866 (priv ptd).

The quest of the sancgreall, The sword of kingship and other poems. 1868.
REVIEW: Athenaeum 2109, 28 Mar 1868.

Gathered in the gloaming. 1881 (priv ptd), 1885.

The secrets of angling, by J. D.: a reprint, with introduction by Thomas Westwood. 1883.

In memoriam Isaak Walton, obiit 15th December 1683. [1884.] 12 sonnets and an epilogue.

Letters

A literary friendship: letters to Lady Alwyne Compton. 1914. With preface by Lady Compton and a memoir by Rosa Westwood.

For Westwood's contributions to periodicals, see Wellesley vol 5 1989.

§2

Obit: Athenaeum 24 Mar 1888.

Watkins, M. G. Obituary. Acad 31 Mar 1888.

Miles, A. H. In Miles 4. [RS]

Charles Whitehead 1804–62

Mss: plays, letters, business papers, BL Add Mss.

Collections

The solitary and other poems. With The cavalier, a play. 1849.

Miles 3.

§1

The solitary: a poem. 1831.

The autobiography of Jack Ketch. 1834, 1836. Prose burlesque.

The lives and exploits of English highwaymen, pirates and robbers. 2 vols 1834.

The cavalier: a drama. 1836. In verse.
Victoria Victrix. 1838. A poem.
Richard Savage. 3 vols 1842; ed H. Orrinsmith 1896, 1903. Prose romance based partly on Dr Johnson's Life of Savage.
The Earl of Essex. 3 vols 1843.
Smiles and tears. 3 vols 1847.
Whitehead also made numerous contributions to periodicals, particularly Bentley's Misc *(1837–51), and pbd a revision (1846) of Grimaldi's memoirs as originally ed Dickens (1838). See* Wellesley *vol 5, p. 831.*

§2
Bell, H. T. M. A forgotten genius: Whitehead. 1884.
Bell, H. T. M. In Miles 3.
Crump, J. Whitehead: his life and work. Dickensian 48 1952.
Fielding, K. J. Whitehead and Charles Dickens. RES n.s. 3 1952.

Jane Francesca Elgee, Lady Wilde 1821–96

§1
Jacta alea est. Nation (Dublin) 29 July 1848; rptd as appendix in H. Wyndham, Speranza: a biography of Lady Wilde, 1951.
Ugo Bassi: a tale of the Italian Revolution. 1857. Verse.
Poems by Speranza. Dublin 1864, Glasgow [1871], Dublin [1907].
The American Irish. Dublin [187-?]. A pam; rptd as an appendix in H. Wyndham, Speranza: a biography of Lady Wilde, 1951.
Driftwood from Scandinavia. 1884. Prose.
Ancient legends, mystic charms and superstitions of Ireland. 2 vols 1887, 1888; rptd Galway 1971.
Ancient cures, charms and usages of Ireland. 1890.
Notes on men, women and books. 1891. Essays.
Social studies. 1893.
Essays and stories. 1907, Boston 1909, 1910.

§2
Lambert, E. Mad with much heart: a life of the parents of Oscar Wilde. 1967.
Lady Wilde also translated works from the Fr and Ger for The Parlour Lib.

Isaac Williams 1802–65

Mss: poems, autobiography, letters, prose, Lambeth Palace Lib.

Bibliography
In O. W. Jones, Isaac Williams and his circle, 1971.

Collections
The poetical works. 6 vols 1874–5.
Selections from the writings. 1890.

§1
Ars geologica poema. Oxford [1823]. Anon.
Lyra apostolica. 1836, 1864 (13th edn); ed H. S. Holland and H. C. Beeching 1899. Williams contributed 9 poems.
The cathedral: or the Catholic and Apostolic Church of England. 1838, 1839, 1841, 1857, 1859 (8th edn), 1874 (10th edn); ed W. Benham 1889. Verse.
Thoughts in past years. By the author of The cathedral. 1838, New York 1841, 1848, 1852 (6th edn enlarged). Poems.
Hymns translated from the Parisian breviary. By the author of The cathedral. 1839.
Ancient hymns for children. 1842, 1848. Selected from Hymns translated, *above.*
The baptistery: or the way of eternal life. 2 vols Oxford 1842–4, 1 vol 1846, 1852, 1858. Verse.
Hymns on the catechism. By I. W. 1843, 1843 (2nd edn), 1866 (5th edn).
Some meditations and prayers selected from the way of eternal life, in order to illustrate and explain the pictures by Boetius a Bolswert, or the same work. 1845. Trn from Latin of A. Sucquet.
Sacred verses with pictures. 2 pts 1845, 1846.
The altar: or meditations in verse on the great Christian sacrifice. 1847 (anon), 1849.
The Christian scholar. By the author of The cathedral. Oxford 1849, 1854. Verse.
The seven days, or the old and new creation. 1850. Verse.
The Christian seasons. 1854. Verse.
Female characters of Holy Scripture. 1859. Sermons.
The poetical works. Vol 1 The cathedral 1874. Vol 2 The baptistery 1874. Vol 3 Hymns for the Parisian breviary 1874. Vol 4 The Christian scholar 1874. Vol 5 Thoughts on past years 1875. Vol 6 The seven days, or the old and new creation 1875.
Williams pbd a number of sermons, religious tracts and 'harmonies' of the Gospels. He wrote nos 80, 86–7 of Tracts for the times.

Papers
Autobiography. Ed G. Prevost 1892, 1893 (3rd edn).

§2
Griswold, R. W. In his Sacred poets of England and America, 1859.
Miller, J. In his Singers and songs of the Church, 1869 (2nd edn).
Williams and the Oxford Movement. Church Quart Rev 34 1892.
Overton, J. H. In Julian.
Jones, O. W. Isaac Williams and his circle. 1971.

Alexander Wilson d. 1852

The songs of the Wilsons: with a memoir of the family and several additional songs never before published. Ed J Harland 1865, 1866, [1873]. Poems by M. T. and A. Wilson.

John Mackay Wilson 1804–35

A glance at Hinduism: a poem . . . . Berwick on Tweed 1824.
Navarin: a poem. 1828.
The enthusiast: a metrical tale . . . Edinburgh and Berwick on Tweed 1834.
Numerous edns were pbd of his Historical . . . tales of the borders of Scotland *(1834).* [JR de JJ]

Richard Wilton 1827–1903

Selections
Miles 10 (12).

§1
Wood-notes and church-bells. 1873.
Lyrics: sylvan and sacred. 1878.
Sungleams: rondeaux and sonnets. [1882.]
Morine, G. Poems. 1888. Preface by Wilton.
Benedicite and other poems. [1889.]
Hull, J. D. Poems. 1889. Ed Wilton.
Historic Londesborough. [1895?].
Lyra pastoralis: songs of nature, church and home. 1902.
Wilton also assisted A. B. Grosart in translating into Eng verse the sacred Latin poems of George Herbert and Richard Crashaw.

§2
Miles, A. H. In Miles 10 (12).
Young, M. B. Richard Wilton: a forgotten Victorian. 1967.

David Wingate 1828–92

Mss: Correspondence with Blackwood's Mag *1862–86, NLS.*

Selections
Select poems and essays. Glasgow 1890.

§1

Poems and songs. Edinburgh 1862, 1863.
Annie Weir and other poems. Edinburgh 1866.
Liby Neil: a poem. 1879.
Poems and songs. 1883. Different from 1862, *above*.

§2

[Oliphant, M.] David Wingate. Blackwood's Mag July 1862.
Wilson, J. G. In his Poets and poetry of Scotland vol 2, 1877.
Wingate contributed to Blackwood's Mag. *See also* Wellesley *vol 5, p. 849*.

Catherine Winkworth 1827–78

Selections

A selection of hymns from the Lyra germanica. 1859.
Lyra germanica. [1905?] (ML). A collected edn.
Miles 12.

§1

Lyra germanica: hymns for the Sundays and chief festivals of the Christian year. 1855, New York 1856, London 1859, 1862, 1901. Trns from Ger.
REVIEWS: Spectator 28, 22 Aug 1855; Athenaeum 1455, 15 Sep 1855; Literary Gazette 2017, 15, 22 Sep 1855.
Lyra germanica: second series; The Christian life. 1858, 1865 (6th edn).
REVIEWS: Literary Churchman 4, 16 July 1858; Athenaeum 2089, 9 Nov 1867.
Lyra germanica: translated from the German. New edn 1875. 1st and 2nd ser combined.
The chorale book for England. 1863, 1865 with suppl. Trns of Ger hymns.
Life of Amelia Wilhelmina Sieveking, from the German. Ed with the author's sanction 1863.
REVIEW: Reader 1, 16 May 1863.
Veni sancti spiritus. New York 1865. Latin and Eng.
Life of pastor Fliedner of Kaiserswerth. Tr from the Ger (with the author's sanction) 1867.
REVIEW: Athenaeum 2089, 9 Nov 1867; Spectator 41, 11 Apr 1868.
Christian singers of Germany. 1869. Prose account. Pbd in 3 pts in Sunday Library for Household Reading, Apr, May, June.
REVIEW: Br Quart Rev 50, Oct 1869.
Prayers from the collection of the late Baron Bunsen, part 1 for the family, part 2 prayers and meditations for private use. Selected and ed Winkworth 1871.
REVIEW: Br Quart Rev 55, Jan 1872.

§2

Shaen, M. J. Memorials of two sisters: Susanna and Catherine Winkworth. Ed their niece, Margaret J. Shaen, 1908.
Leaver, R. A. Catherine Winkworth: the influence of her translations on English hymnody. St Louis MO 1978. Contains a complete listing of her hymn trns (ch 6). [RS]

Susanna Winkworth 1820–84

Selections

Selections from the Life and sermons of the Reverend Doctor John Tauler. Boston 1878.

§1

The life and letters of Barthold George Niebuhr and selections from his minor writings. Edited and translated by Susanna Winkworth with essays on his character and influence by the chevalier Bunsen and professors Brandis and Loebell. 3 vols 1851–2, 1852 (2nd edn).
REVIEWS: Athenaeum 1313, 25 Dec 1852; Br Quart Rev 19, Jan 1854.
Theologia Germanica: which setteth forth many fair lineaments of divine truth, and saith very lofty and lovely things touching a perfect life. Edited by Doctor Pfeiffer from the only complete manuscript yet known. Translated from the German by Susanna Winkworth, with a preface by the reverend Charles Kingsley. 1854. Further issues: Golden treasury 1874, new edn 1893, reissued 1966. Revised to accord with the modern Ger version of Joseph Bernhart 1950.
REVIEWS: Literary Gazette 1954, 1 July 1854; Athenaeum 1403, 16 Sep 1854; Br Quart Rev 21, Apr 1855.
The life of Luther in forty-eight historical engravings by Gustav Koenig. With explanations by Archdeacon Hare: continued by Susanna Winkworth. 1855.
REVIEW: Christian Reformer, n.s. 12, Feb 1856.
Signs of the times: letters to Ernst Moritz Arndt on the dangers to religious liberty in the present state of the world. By Christian Charles Josias Bunsen. Tr from the Ger. 1856.
REVIEW: Br Quart Rev 24, July 1856.
The history and life of the reverend doctor John Tauler of Strasbourg: with twenty-five of his sermons. Translated from the German, with additional notices of Tauler's life and times, and a preface by the reverend Charles Kingsley. 1857, reissued 1905.
REVIEWS: Spectator 30, 17 Jan 1857; Br Quart Rev 25, Apr 1857.
German love: from the papers of an alien. Translated with the sanction of the author [G. E. M.]. 1858.
REVIEWS: Literary Gazette 2137, 2 Jan 1858; Athenaeum 1579, 30 Jan 1858; Br Quart Rev 65, Apr 1877.
God in history, or the progress of man's faith in the moral order of the world by Christian Charles Josias Bunsen. Tr from the German. 3 vols 1868–70.
REVIEW: Athenaeum 2110, 4 Apr 1868.

Contributions to periodicals

See Wellesley *vol 5 1989*.
Miss Cobbe's 'Broken Lights'. Victoria Mag 3, July 1864.

Editions

Letters and memorials of Catherine Winkworth. Priv ptd. Clifton 1883; 2nd vol (with M. J. Shaen) Clifton 1886.

§2

Obit: Athenaeum 6 Dec 1884.
Shaen, M. J. Memorials of two sisters: Susanna and Catherine Winkworth. 1908.
Skrine, P. Susanna and Catherine Winkworth: Clifton, Manchester and the German connection. Hymn Soc Occasional Papers, 2nd ser no 2, June 1992. [RS]

Thomas Woolner 1825–92

Selections

Miles 5.

§1

My beautiful lady. Ptd in Germ Jan 1850, and separately in expanded form 1863, 1864, 1866 (3rd edn illustr). Verse.
Pygmalion. 1881. Verse.
REVIEW: (A. Meynell) Art Jnl 34 1882.
Silenus. 1884. Verse.
Tiresias. 1886. Verse.
REVIEW: (H. B. Garrod) Acad 29 May 1886.
Poems; Nelly Dale; Children. 1887.
My beautiful lady; Nelly Dale. 1893 (vol 82 of Cassell's Nat Lib). Verse.

§2
Forman, H. B. In his Our living poets, 1871.
Tupper, J. L. Thomas Woolner. Portfolio 2 1871.
Stephens, F. G. Thomas Woolner. Art Jnl 46 1894.
Le Gallienne, R. In Miles 5.
Woolner, A. Thomas Woolner, sculptor and poet: his life in letters. 1917.
Evans, B. I. In his English poetry in the later nineteenth century, 1933.
Woolner: My beautiful lady. BLR 3 1950.
Ormond, L. Tennyson and Thomas Woolner. Lincoln 1981.

Christopher Wordsworth 1807–85

§1
The Druids: Chancellor's Medal poem. Cambridge 1827, 1828, 1859 (in Cambridge prize poems).
Iphigenia in Aulide – carmen latinum. Cambridge [1827]. Prize poem.
The invasion of Russia by Napoleon Buonaparte: a poem which obtained the Chancellor's Medal. Cambridge 1828, 1859 (in Cambridge prize poems).
Hannibal, translated from the Latin ode. In University of Oxford translations of the Oxford and Cambridge prize poems, 1833.
Ode at Cambridge on 7 July 1835 after the installation of the Chancellor of the University. 1835.
Athens and Attica. 1836, 1855 (3rd edn rev). Prose.
Greece: pictorial, descriptive and historical. 1839, Paris 1841. Tr Fr 1844, rev 1853.
Diary in France. 1845, 1846.
Memoirs of William Wordsworth. 2 vols 1851, 2 vols Boston 1851.
The inspiration of the Bible: five lectures. 1861.
The interpretation of the Bible: five lectures. 1861.
The holy year: or hymns for Sundays, holy days and other occasions throughout the year. Ed W. H. Monk 1862, 1864, 1865.
Journal of a tour in Italy. 2 vols 1863.
Additional hymns for the holy year. Oxford 1864.
Thoughts on English hymnology, or preface to Holy year. 1865.
Church history up to AD 451. 4 vols 1881–3.
Wordsworth also pbd a Commentary *on the whole Bible, numerous sermons, religious tracts, translations etc. He wrote a preface to* Ballads from English history *[1864].*

§2
Overton, J. H. and E. Wordsworth. Christopher Wordsworth, Bishop of Lincoln. 1888, new and cheaper edn 1890.
Overton, J. H. In Julian.
Strudwick, V. Christopher Wordsworth: Bishop of Lincoln 1869–1885. Lincoln 1987.

iv. Late nineteenth-century poetry 1870–1900

References
Miles, A. H. et al (ed). The poets and poetry of the century. 10 vols [1891–7], 12 vols 1905–7 (enlarged). Referred to as Miles throughout.
Numerals refer to vol nos in these edns; numerals in brackets to the enlarged edn of Miles. Further information about some of the poets may be found in J. Julian, a dictionary of hymnology, 1892, 1907 (rev).

Alexander Anderson 1845–1909

§1
A song of labour and other poems. Dundee 1873.
The two angels, and other poems, with an introductory sketch by G. Gilfillan. 1875.
Songs of the rail. 1878, 1878 (2nd edn).
Ballads and sonnets. 1879. Partly rptd from A song of labour and Two angels, *above*, with many new poems.
Later poems of Anderson, Surface man. Ed A. Brown, Glasgow 1912 (with biographical sketch).

§2
Cuthbertson, D. The life-history of Alexander Anderson. Inveresk [1929] (priv ptd).
Evans, B. I. In his English poetry in the later nineteenth century, 1933, 1966 (rev).

Sir Edwin Arnold 1832–1904

Collections
Arnold birthday book. Ed K. L. and C. Arnold 1885. From The works of Arnold, with new poems.
Poems, national and non-oriental, with some new pieces, selected from The works of Arnold. 1888.
Poetical works. 8 vols 1888.
Oriental poems. Ed J. M. Watkins 1904.
Indian poems and Indian idylls. 1915.
The Arnold poetry reader: selections, with memoir and notes by E. L. Arnold. [1920.]

§1
The feast of Belshazzar: a prize poem. Oxford 1852.
Poems, narrative and lyrical. Oxford 1853.
Griselda: a tragedy, and other poems. 1856.
The wreck of the Northern Belle: a poem. Hastings 1857.
Hitopadesa ... with a vocabulary in Sanskrit, English and Murathi, together with a partial translation. Ed Arnold, Bombay 1859.
Education in India: a letter from the ex-principal of an Indian government college to his appointed successor. 1860.
The book of good counsels: from the Sanskrit of the 'Hitopadesa'. 1861.
The Marquis of Dalhousie's administration of British India. 2 vols 1862–5.
Political poems by Victor Hugo and Garibaldi. Done into English by an Oxford graduate (E[dwin] A[rnold]). 1868. (Rptd from the Morning Star, with a preface by G. J. Holyoake.)
The poets of Greece. 1869.
Hero and Leander. From the Greek of Musaeus. [1873.]
The Indian song of songs. From the Sanskrit ... with other oriental poems. (Translated into English verse.) 1875.
A simple transliteral grammar of the Turkish language. Compiled from various sources. With dialogues and vocabulary. 1877.
The light of Asia, or the great renunciation – Mahâbhinishkramana. Being the life and teaching of Gautama ... as told in verse by an Indian Buddhist. 1879, 1885 (28th edn), 1889 (new edn), Leipzig 1891 (copyright edn), London 1925; ed E. D. Ross, New York 1926.
Poems. Boston 1880.
Indian poetry. 1881.
Pearls of the faith: or Islam's rosary. 1883, 1887 (4th edn).
The secret of death, from the Sanskrit with some collected poems. 1885.
The song celestial. A translation of the Bhagavad-gita. 1885, 1897 (8th edn), Bajendra 1989, New York and London 1993.
India revisited. 1886. Rptd with addns from Daily Telegraph.
Death – and afterwards. 1887, New York 1897. Rptd with suppl from Fortnightly Rev Aug 1885.

Lotus and jewel, containing In an Indian temple, A casket of gems, A queen's revenge, with other poems. 1887.
With Sa'di in the garden: or the book of love. Tr from the Persian. 1888.
In my lady's praise: being poems, old and new, written in the honour of Fanny, Lady Arnold, and now collected for her memory. 1889.
The light of the world, or the great consummation: a poem. 1891, 1891 (4th edn), 1909 (Pocket edn); tr Du, Amsterdam 1892.
Seas and lands. 1891, 1892 (new edn). Rptd from Daily Telegraph. Letters.
Japonica. 1892. Rptd from Scribner's Mag. Essays.
Potiphar's wife and other poems. 1892.
Adzuma, or the Japanese wife: a play in four acts. 1893.
Aspects of life, etc. Birmingham [1893]. Birmingham and Midland Inst presidential addresses 1893.
Wandering words. 1894. Rptd from Daily Telegraph etc.
The tenth muse and other poems. 1895.
East and West. 1896. Rptd from Daily Telegraph etc.
Victoria, Queen and Empress: the sixty years. 1896. Rptd from Daily Telegraph.
Golden pages. Kimpaku. Being a birthday book edited and arranged by Lady T. Arnold, with twelve poems upon the months by Sir Edwin Arnold. 1899.
The Gulistan. Being the rose-garden of Shaikh Sa'di. Trn in prose and verse. 1899.
The Queen's justice: a true story of Indian village life. 1899.
The voyage of Ithobal: a poem. 1901, Toronto 1901.
The birth of wine: an unpublished poem. Saturday Rev of Lit 30 Sep 1933.

§2

Bell, M. Arnold. In Miles 5.
Obit: Times 26 Mar 1904.
Evans, B. I. In his English poetry in the later nineteenth century, 1933, 1966 (rev).
Arnold and Walt Whitman. N & Q 21 Aug 1948. An 1889 letter from Arnold to Whitman.
Hendrick, G. Whitman and Arnold. Western Humanities Rev 14 1960.
Pieris, W. E. Edwin Arnold: a brief account of his life and contribution to Buddhism. Kendy 1970.

Alfred Austin 1835–1913

Bibliographies

Crowell, N. B. In his Austin: Victorian, Albuquerque 1953.

Selections

Days of the year: a poetic calendar from the works of Austin. Ed W. Sharp 1886.
English lyrics. Ed W. Watson 1890.
Love poems of Alfred Austin. 1912.

§1

Randolph: a poem in two cantos. 1855, 1877 (recast as Leszco the bastard: a tale of Polish grief).
Five years of it: a novel. 2 vols 1858.
A note of admiration, addressed to the editor of The Saturday Review. 1861.
The season: a satire. 1861, 1861 (rev with preface), 1869 (rev).
The human tragedy: a poem. 1862 (withdrawn), 1876 (rev), 1889 (rev), 1889 (rev with preface On the position and prospects of poetry), 1891 (omits preface).
An artist's proof: a novel. 3 vols 1864.
Won by a head: a novel. 3 vols 1866.
A vindication of Lord Byron. 1869. Reply to Mrs Stowe.
The poetry of the period. 1870. Rptd from Temple Bar.
The golden age: a satire in verse. 1871.
Interludes. 1872.
Isa Blagden. Poems, with memoir by Austin. 1873.
Madonna's child. 1873. Incorporated as Act 2 in The human tragedy, 1876, 1895.
Rome or death! a poem. 1873. Forms Act 3 of The human tragedy, 1876.
The tower of babel: a poetical drama. 1874, 1890.
Savonarola: a tragedy. 1881, 1891. In verse.
Soliloquies in song. 1882.
At the gate of the convent, and other poems. 1885.
Prince Lucifer. 1887, 1887 (adds essay The end and limits of objective poetry), 1891 (omits essay).
Love's widowhood, and other poems. 1889.
Lyrical poems. 1891.
Narrative poems. 1891. In the heart of the forest, At the gate of the convent, Love's widowhood etc and new poems.
Fortunatus the pessimist: a dramatic poem. 1892.
A betrothal. May 3rd 1893. [1893.] On the engagement of George, Duke of York, to Princess Victoria Mary.
The garden that I love. 2 ser 1894–1907. In the form of a diary.
In Veronica's garden. 1895. In the form of a diary.
England's darling. 1896, 1901 (5th edn) (as Alfred the Great, England's darling).
The conversion of Winckelmann, and other poems. 1897.
Victoria: June 20 1837, June 20 1897. 1897.
Lamia's winter quarters. 1898, 1907. A story.
Songs of England. 1898, 1900, 1900, 1900 (all enlarged).
The spotless king. 1899. In A. Bowker, Alfred the Great, 1899.
Spring and autumn in Ireland. 1900. Rptd from Blackwood's Mag.
Polyphemus. 1901.
A tale of true love, and other poems. 1902.
Haunts of ancient peace. 1902, 1908. A story.
Flodden field: a tragedy. 1903.
Victoria the wise. [1903.]
The poet's diary, edited by Lamia. 1904.
The door of humility: a poem. 1906, 1907.
Sacred and profane love, and other poems. 1908.
The bridling of Pegasus. 1910. 9 essays on poetry and poets.
Autobiography of Alfred Austin, poet laureate, 1835–1910. 2 vols 1911.
Austin also pbd some political and controversial pams. He was the proprietor and editor of Nat Rev *for 10 years from 1883. He contributed widely to periodicals – see* Wellesley *vol 5, pp. 36–7. He was appointed poet laureate in 1896.*

§2

Whyte, W. Austin. In Miles 6.
O., J. Austin. Athenaeum 7 June 1913.
Sherman, S. P. The complacent Toryism of Austin. In his On contemporary literature, New York 1917.
Welby, T. E. Austin. Bookman (London) Dec 1930.
Evans, B. I. In his English poetry in the later nineteenth century, 1933, 1966 (rev).
May, J. L. A neglected poet. Dublin Rev 402 1937.
Crowell, N. B. Austin: Victorian. Albuquerque 1953.
The Banjo-Byron. TLS 13 Nov 1953. *See also* V. G. Miller, 27 Nov 1953.
Murray, C. C. Austin. TLS 20 Nov 1953.

John Evelyn Barlas, 'Evelyn Douglas' 1860–1914

Bibliographies

Lowe, D. In his Barlas: sweet singer and Socialist, Cupar, Fife 1915.
Salt, H. S. In his edn of Selections, 1925, *below*.

Selections

Selections. Ed H. S. Salt 1925.
Yewleaf and lotus petal. Sonnets. Berkeley Heights NJ 1935 (priv pbd).

§1
Poems lyrical and dramatic. 1884.
The queen of the hid isle: an allegory of life and art. Love's perversity, or Eros and Anteros. A drama. 1885.
Punchinello and his wife Judith: a tragedy. Chelmsford 1886. In verse.
Phantasmagoria: dream fugues. Chelmsford 1887.
Bird-notes. Chelmsford 1887.
Holy of holies: confession of an anarchist. Chelmsford 1887. Anon.
Love sonnets. Chelmsford 1889.
Selections from Songs of a bayadere and Songs of a troubadour. Dundee 1893 (priv ptd).

§2
Lowe, D. Barlas: sweet singer and Socialist. Cupar, Fife 1915.

George Barlow 1847–1913

Collections
A sextet of singers, or songs of six. [1896.]
Poetical works. 11 vols 1902–14.
Selected poems. 1921. With note by C. W., bibliography and short life.

§1
A life's love. [1873], new edn 1882. Sonnets.
An English madonna, by James Hinton. 1874.
Under the dawn. 1875.
The gospel of humanity: or the connection between spiritualism and modern thought. 1876.
The marriage before death, and other poems. 1878.
Through death to life. 1878.
The two marriages: a drama in three acts. 1878.
Love-songs. 1880.
Time's whisperings: sonnets and songs. 1880.
Song-bloom. 1881.
Song-spray. 1882.
An actor's reminiscences, and other poems. 1883.
Love's offering, by James Hinton. 1883.
Poems real and ideal. 1884.
Loved beyond words. 1885.
The pageant of life: an epic poem in five books. 1888, new edn 1910.
From dawn to sunset. 1890.
A lost mother. 1892.
The crucifixion of man: a narrative poem. 1893, 2nd edn 1895.
Jesus of Nazareth. [1896]. Tragedy in prose and verse.
Woman regained. A novel of artistic life. [1896.]
The daughters of Minerva. A novel of social life. [1898.]
To the women of England, and other poems. 1901.
A coronation poem. 1902.
Vox clamantis: sonnets and poems. 1904.
The higher love. A plea for a noble conception of human love. 1905. Rptd from Contemporary Rev.
The triumph of woman. 1907. Essay.
A man's vengeance, and other poems. 1908.
The genius of Dickens. [1909.] Rptd from Contemporary Rev.
Songs of England awaking. 1909, 1910 (2nd edn).

§2
Miles, A. H. Barlow. In Miles 8 (7).
Bennett, E. T. The poetical work of Barlow: a study. 1903.

Jane Barlow 1857–1917

§1
Bog-land studies. '1892' [1891], 1893 (enlarged), 1894.
Irish idylls. 1892, New York 1893, London 1894, 1897, 1898 (8th edn), 1984.
Kerrigan's quality. 1894.
The battle of the frogs and mice, rendered into English. 1894.
The end of Elfintown. 1894.
Maureen's fairing and other stories. 1895, New York 1895.
Strangers at Lisconnel: a second series of Irish idylls. 1895, New York 1895, London 1984.
Mrs Martin's company and other stories. 1896.
A creel of Irish stories. 1897, New York 1898.
From the east unto the west. 1898, 1905. Tales.
From the land of the shamrock. 1900, New York 1900.
Ghost-bereft, with other stories and studies in verse. 1901.
At the back of beyond. New York 1902.
The founding of fortunes. 1902, New York 1902, London 1906.
By beach and bog-land: some Irish stories, etc. 1905.
Irish neighbours. 1907. Tales.
The mockers, and other verses. 1908.
Irish ways. 1909.
Flaws: a novel. 1911.
Mac's adventures. 1911.
Doings and dealings. 1913. Novel.
Between doubting and daring: verses. Oxford 1916.
In Mio's youth: a novel. 1917.

§2
MacArthur, J. Jane Barlow. Critic 24 1894.
Tynan, K. Jane Barlow. Catholic World 69 1899.
Tynan, K. Jane Barlow. Living Age 295 1917.

Charlotte Alington Barnard, 'Claribel' 1830–69

§1
Fireside thoughts, ballads, etc., etc. by Claribel. 1865.
Verses and songs. [1870] (priv ptd).
Thoughts, verses and songs. By Claribel. 1877.

§2
Smith, Phyllis Mary, assisted by Margaret Godsmark. The story of Claribel: Charlotte Alington Barnard. Lincoln 1965.
Barnard was a prolific writer of songs – usually both lyrics and music – and pbd many of these individually as song sheets, in England and the USA. Most are included in her pbd collections.

Aubrey Vincent Beardsley 1872–98

Beardsley's original drawings are scattered among many libraries and museums. The principal collections are at the Victoria and Albert Museum, London; Princeton (the Gallatin Collection); and the Fogg Art Museum, Harvard. Letters will be found in quantity at Princeton, Harvard (Houghton Lib), Bodleian, the Clark Lib (UCLA), and HRHRC, Austin TX. The ms of Under the hill *is in the Rosenbach. A number of drawings and other items remain in private collections in Europe, Britain and the USA.*

Bibliographies and catalogues of drawings
Vallance, A. Iconography in A book of fifty drawings, 1897, *below*. Expanded in R. Ross, Aubrey Beardsley, 1909.
Gallatin, A. E. List of drawings by Aubrey Beardsley. New York 1900.
Gallatin, A. E. Aubrey Beardsley's drawings: a catalogue and a list of criticisms. New York 1903. A 4-page Addendum 1904 lists more items.
Gallatin, A. E. Aubrey Beardsley: catalogue of drawings and bibliography. New York 1945, (facs) Mamaroneck NY 1980.
Gallatin, A. E. and A. D. Wainwright. The Gallatin Beardsley collection in the Princeton University Library: a catalogue. Princeton 1952. First pbd Princeton Univ Lib Chron 1949–51.
Additions to the Beardsley collection. Princeton Univ Lib Chron Winter 1958.

Reade, B. and F. Dickinson. Aubrey Beardsley exhibition at the Victoria and Albert Museum. 1966. *See below under* Exhibition and sale catalogues.
Salerno, N. Aubrey Beardsley: an annotated secondary bibliography. In Reconsidering Aubrey Beardsley, ed R. Langenfeld, Ann Arbor MI 1989.
Samuels Lasner, M. A selective checklist of the published work of Aubrey Beardsley. Boston 1995. Includes section on forgeries.
Samuels Lasner, M. An index to The yellow book: a checklist and index. 1998.
Samuels Lasner, M. A supplement to A selective checklist of the published work of Aubrey Beardsley, in The death of Pierrot: a Beardsley miscellany, in §2 below. Ed S. Halliwell and M. Sturgis. Bicester, Oxon 1998.
Appendices in J. H. Desmarais, The Beardsley industry. §2 below. Lists of contemporary criticism and exhibitions of drawings, includes items not in Salerno, above.
Zatlin, L. Aubrey Beardsley: a catalogue raisonné. New Haven CT 2000 [forthcoming]. Lists all known drawings.

Exhibition and sale catalogues

Drawings by Aubrey Beardsley. Carfax & Co [Oct 1904].
Exposition des dessins d'Aubrey Beardsley, 1872–1898. Paris Galeries Shirleys Feb 1907. Introd by H. C. Pollitt and extract from R. Ross's eulogy in Volpone.
Catalogue of an exhibition of drawings by Aubrey Beardsley. Baillie Gallery Aug and Sep 1909.
Birnbaum, M. Aubrey Vincent Beardsley. New York Berlin Photographic Company 1911. Served as 'Catalogue of the first American exhibition of the original work of Aubrey Beardsley': subsequent venues at Art Institute of Chicago Dec 1911 and Buffalo Fine Arts Academy/Albright Art Gallery Jan 1912 have different versions of catalogue.
Catalogue of the Beardsley–Garrido–Goff exhibition. Brighton Public Art Galleries Dec 1914–Jan 1915. Introd by H. D. Roberts.
Forty-three original drawings by Aubrey Beardsley: the collection of F. H. Evans of London. New York Anderson Galleries 20 Mar 1919.
An exhibition of original drawings by Aubrey Beardsley. With a foreword by J. Pennell. Philadelphia Rosenbach Galleries May 1919.
Aubrey Beardsley: loan exhibition of original drawings. New York Galleries of E. Gimpel and Wildenstein Apr–May 1920. Introd by A. E. Gallatin.
Catalogue: loan exhibition of drawings by Aubrey Beardsley (1872–1898). National Gallery Millbank Nov 1923–Mar 1924. Introd and entries by R. A. Walker.
Catalogue of an exhibition of original drawings by Aubrey Beardsley. [New York] Brooklyn Museum Dec 1923–Jan 1924. Introd by J. Pennell.
The John Lane collection of original drawings by Aubrey Beardsley. New York Anderson Galleries 22 Nov 1926.
Catalogue no 165: books from the library of John Lane, publisher. Dulau and Co [1929]. Includes many Beardsley items.
Catalogue no 170: the choice & remarkably extensive Aubrey Beardsley collection. Frank Hollings 1931.
Aubrey Beardsley: exhibition of drawings & books. New York Grolier Club Mar–Apr 1945.
Quarto 8: Aubrey Beardsley. Some items from the collection of R. A. Walker. Bishop's Stortford May 1950 (Elkin Mathews).
A study in yellow: the Yellow Book artists. Univ of Kansas Museum of Art, Lawrence KS 1962. Introd by K. L. Mix. Many Beardsley items.
Reade, B. and F. Dickinson. Aubrey Beardsley exhibition at the Victoria and Albert Museum. 1966. Catalogues also issued for versions of the exhibition held in New York 1967, Japan 1983, Munich 1984, Rome 1985 and Milan 1985.
Catalogue no 44: Aubrey Beardsley. J. Stephan Lawrence Rare Books, Chicago [1979].
Catalogue no 60: Aubrey Beardsley. Warrack & Perkins Church Enstone [1985].
The artists of the Yellow Book & the circle of Oscar Wilde. Clarendon and Parkin Galleries Oct–Nov 1983. Includes many Beardsley items.
Stetz, M. D. and M. Samuels Lasner. England in the 1890s: literary publishing at the Bodley Head. Washington 1990. Includes many Beardsley items.
Stetz, M. D. and M. Samuels Lasner. The Yellow Book: a centenary exhibition. Harvard 1994. Includes many Beardsley items.
Catalogue no 18: Wilde, Beardsley, and the eighteen-nineties, the collection of Giles Gordon. With a foreword and afterword by P. Ackroyd. Gekoski Summer 1994.
Beautiful decadence. Tokyo Isetan Museum of Art 6–30 Nov 1997. Exhibibtion later held at two other venues in Japan. Primarily Beardsley items.
Aubrey Beardsley: a centenary tribute. Tokyo 1998. Exhibition catalogue, rpts 1 drawing for the first time.

Collections of drawings

All the works contained in Fifty drawings by Aubrey Beardsley: selected from the collection of H. S. Nichols. *New York 1920 (ptd for subscribers only), are forgeries.*
[Poe, Edgar Allan.] [The works of Edgar Allan Poe. Newly collected and edited, with a memoir, critical introductions, and notes by E. C. Stedman and G. E. Woodberry.] [Chicago 1894–5.] 4 drawings in portfolio issued to accompany set. Rptd Chicago 1901 (with explanatory text), Indianapolis 1926 (priv ptd) (with 15 forgeries).
A book of fifty drawings. With an iconography by A. Vallance. 1897. 50 drawings (front cover design, publisher's device by Beardsley).
Six drawings illustrating Théophile Gautier's romance Mademoiselle de Maupin. 1898. 6 drawings.
A second book of fifty drawings. 1899. 50 drawings (front cover design, publisher's device by Beardsley).
The early work of Aubrey Beardsley. With a prefatory note by H. C. Marillier. 1899. 179 drawings (front cover and title page designs, spine ornament, publisher's device by Beardsley), 1912 (2nd edn) [1911] (plates rearranged and redistributed in conjunction with '1912' edn of The later work; adds reproduction of cover of Le morte darthur), 1920 (3rd edn). Rptd (in altered form) 2 different edns New York 1967.
The later work of Aubrey Beardsley. '1901' [1900]. 173 drawings, plus reproduction of cover of Le morte darthur (front cover and title page designs, spine ornament, publisher's device by Beardsley). Introd (anon) by J. Lane, 1912 (2nd edn) [1911] (contents rearranged and redistributed in conjunction with 1912 edn of The early work), 1920 (3rd edn), [1930] (4th edn) (slight changes). Rptd (in altered form) 2 different edns New York 1967.
Drawings for The sixth satire of Juvenal. 1903. 3 drawings. Probably issued by L. Smithers; the date may be fictitious.
An issue of five drawings illustrative of Juvenal and Lucian. 1906. 5 drawings, all rptd in special issue of The uncollected work (4 of the drawings later appeared in priv ptd portfolio dated 1915).
A portfolio of Aubrey Beardsley's drawings illustrating 'Salome' by Oscar Wilde. [1906.] 17 illus (16 from 1907 edn, plus Salome on Settle; front cover device from 1st edn 1894 on front cover).
Nineteen early drawings by Aubrey Beardsley: from the collection of Mr Harold Hartley. With an introd by Georges Derry [pseud of R. A. Walker]. [London?] 1919 (priv ptd). 19 illus to Book ii of Virgil's Aeneid.
Derry, Georges [pseud of R. A. Walker]. An Aubrey Beardsley scrap book. With illus to Ibsen's 'Ghosts'. 1920. 1 drawing.
Walker, R. A. Some unknown drawings of Aubrey Beardsley: collected and annotated by R. A. Walker (Georges Derry). 1923. 13

drawings, also reproduces painting A caprice, and facs of letters. Also contains works by others.

Reproductions of eleven designs omitted from the first edition of Le morte darthur illustr Aubrey Beardsley and pbd in 1893. With a foreword by A. Vallance and a note on the omitted designs by R. A. Walker. 1927. 14 drawings. Generally known as the 'Morte darthur portfolio' and issued in conjunction with 3rd edn of Le morte darthur.

The uncollected work of Aubrey Beardsley. With an introd by C. Lewis Hind. [1925.] 154 drawings, facsimiles of letters, etc. (Front cover design, spine ornament and title page design by Beardsley; includes some forgeries.)

Walker, R. A. The best of Beardsley. [1948.], [1956?], 1983, New York 1983. 134 drawings (front cover design adapted from cover for Volpone).

The collected drawings of Aubrey Beardsley. With an appreciation by Arthur Symons. Ed B. S. Harris, New York [1967]. 79 drawings, pages from books, book covers, etc. (Also includes 49 forgeries.)

Reade, B. Beardsley. Introd by J. Rothenstein [1967], New York 1967 (under title Aubrey Beardsley, rptd New York [1974?]), Woodbridge 1987 (rev with minor changes and without Rothenstein's introd). 503 drawings, posters, pages from books, book covers, etc.

Beardsley's illustrations for Le morte darthur: reproduced in facs from the Dent edition of 1893–94. Arranged by Edmund V. Gillon, Jr. New York [1972].

Clark, K. The best of Aubrey Beardsley. New York [1978], London 1979. 66 drawings.

Wilson, S. Beardsley. Oxford [1976], new edn Oxford [1983] (rev text and more illus), Tokyo 1985 (Japanese trn). 54 drawings, pages from books, book covers, etc.

Reed, A. Aubrey Beardsley. Leicester 1991.

Aubrey Beardsley: sixty selected drawings. With an essay by B. Elliott. 1995.

Principal works illustrated by Beardsley

Smith, Sydney and R. Brinsley Sheridan. Bon-mots of Sydney Smith and R. Brinsley Sheridan: Edited by Walter Jerrold. With grotesques by Aubrey Beardsley. 1893. 74 grotesques, title page design and front cover ornament – subsequently used for further vols in Bon-mots ser: Bon-mots of Charles Lamb and Douglas Jerrold, 1893 (adds 29 new designs, reprints 39 from first vol); Bon-mots of Samuel Foote and Theodore Hook, 1894 (adds 25 new designs, reprints 41 from earlier vols).

Malory, Sir Thomas. The birth, life, and acts of King Arthur, of his noble knights of the Round Table . . . With an introd by Prof Rhys, and original designs by Aubrey Beardsley. 1893–4. Pbd in 12 pts then in 2 vols, special issue in 3 vols; facs of 2-vol version pbd Woodbridge 1985; 2nd edn 1 vol 1909 (adds 10 chapter headings), facs pbd New York 1990; 3rd edn 1 vol 1927 (adds 1 chapter heading and sketch, includes notes by A. Vallance and R. A. Walker), facs pbd New York 1985; New York 1972, 1988.

Egerton, George [pseud of Mary Chavelita Dunne]. Keynotes. 1893. Front cover design (also adapted for title page) and key monogram by Beardsley. The clothbound issue formed the first vol in the Keynotes ser (33 vols 1893–7); Beardsley provided front cover/title page designs for a further 21 vols in ser pbd 1894–6 (also key monograms for at least 17), reproduced in 1896 advertising booklet Keynotes series of novels and short stories, 21 designs by Aubrey Beardsley (front cover/title page design by the artist) and in 20 miniature posters, drawn by Aubrey Beardsley, representing the title designs of the 'Keynotes Series'. Boston [c. 1896].

Davidson, J. Plays: being An unhistorical pastoral, A romantic farce, Bruce: a chronicle play, Smith: a tragic farce, and Scaramouch in Naxos: a pantomime. 1894. Frontispiece and title page vignette (repeated on front cover) by Beardsley.

Wilde, Oscar. Salome: a tragedy in one act. Tr from the French of Oscar Wilde. Pictured by Aubrey Beardsley. 1894. 13 illus and front and back cover ornaments, San Francisco 1896, London 1904 (adds 3 drawings for total of 16), '1907' [1906] (16 illus, text rev; includes note by R. Ross and programmes for first English production and for Strauss's opera), rptd 1912; Boston 1906 (13 illus from 1894 edn); Boston 1907 (16 illus), facs pbd Boston [1964?] and 1989; Paris 1907 (16 illus); Leipzig [1907] (16 illus), rptd 1919, 1924, 1959; '1912' [1911] (16 illus); Boston 1912 (15 illus); Warsaw 1914 (16 illus, Polish trn by Leona Choromanskiego); Hanover 1918 (16 illus, Ger trn by Paul Steegemann); Hanover 1919 (16 illus, Ger trn by Curt Moreck); London 1920 (16 illus, includes note by R. Ross and programmes for first English production and for Strauss's opera), rptd 1927 and 1930; Boston 1920 (16 illus, Fr text); Salome and other stories: illustr Aubrey Beardsley [after 1920?] (9 illus); Paris 1920 (16 illus, Fr text); [Tokyo 1929] (16 illus, text in Eng and Jap, tr Arakawa Kinnosuko); New York 1930 (16 illus); New York [1930?]; New York [1931] (16 expurgated illus), rptd [1931?]; Cleveland OH [1931?] (16 illus), rptd Grand Rapids MI 1969; Tokyo 1938 (16 illus, Jap trn by Konosuke Hinatsu, possibly a pseud), rptd 1954; London 1938 (16 illus, introd by H. Jackson, pbd by Limited Editions Club with companion vol containing Fr text illustr André Derain); Stockholm 1946 (16 illus, Swed trn); New York [1947?] (16 illus); Socking[?], Germany 1949 (15 illus, Fr text); Garden City NY [1950?]; London 1957 (18 illus, 17 from 1907 portfolio – substituting unexpurgated version of Enter Herodias – and J'ai baisé ta bouche Jokanaan: Salomé with the head of John the Baptist, trn and introd by R. A. Walker); Tokyo 1958 (16 illus, Jap trn by Tsuneari Fukuda), rptd 1959; Paris [1966] (16 illus); New York [1967] (20 illus, 17 from 1907 portfolio, plus front and back cover ornaments from 1894 edn and J'ai baisé ta bouche Jokanaan: Salomé with the head of John the Baptist, text and illus an amalgam from various edns, includes note by R. Ross); Barcelona 1979 (tr Sp); Jerusalem 1981 (Hebrew trn); [1989] (13 illus, introd by Steven Berkoff, in part facs 1907, ed with note by R. Ross).

Grahame, K. Pagan papers. 1894. Title page design by Beardsley.

Yeats, W. B. The land of heart's desire. 1894, Chicago 1894 (frontispiece only). Design for title page (also used for front cover) by Beardsley also appeared on a series of programmes for the play.

The Yellow Book: an illustrated quarterly. 1894–5. Beardsley served as art editor for the first 4 vols, Apr 1894–Jan 1895; these vols contain 20 illus (2 signed with pseuds Philip Broughton and Albert Foschter), cover designs and title pages. (Back cover and spine of vol 5 Apr 1895 also by Beardsley, used by mistake after he was dismissed from editorship.) Beardsley also provided designs (most repeated as title pages) for the magazine's prospectuses and posters.

Lucian. Lucian's true history: translated by Francis Hickes. Illustr W. Strang, J. B. Clark and Aubrey Beardsley. With an introd by C. Whibley. 1894 (priv ptd). 2 illus by Beardsley. Special issue of 54 copies has additional illustration, variant version of A snare of vintage, rptd in special issue of The uncollected work, 1902.

Davidson, John. A full and true account of the wonderful mission of Earl Lavender . . . . 1895. Frontispiece by Beardsley.

Ruding, W. An evil motherhood: an impressionist novel. 1896. Frontispiece by Beardsley. Earliest issue has Black coffee (intended for The Yellow Book) bound in; later issues substitute Portrait of the author.

The Savoy. 1896. 8 nos, collected 1896 in 3 vols (with front cover and spine designs by Beardsley). 30 illustrations, front cover designs, title and contents pages and publisher's device by Beardsley, also 1 illustration ptd on separate Christmas card in no 1. The mag pbd Beardsley's poems The three musicians and The ballad of a barber, trn of Catullus's Carmen ci, and ch i–iv of Under the hill, all rptd in Under the hill and other essays in prose and verse. Beardsley designed the front cover, publisher's device and initial A for the mag's prospectus Nov 1895 (issued in 2 forms, Pierrot and John Bull); also a poster advertising the collected issue in 3 vols Nov 1896 (adapted from front cover design for no 8).

Pope, Alexander. The rape of the lock. 1896 (8 illustrations, frontispiece and front cover design by Beardsley); 2nd 'Bijou' edn '1897' [1896] (adds reproductions of front cover for 1896 edn and of new front cover design); 3rd edn '1902' [1901] (8 illus and frontispiece from 1896 edn), rptd 1916; Leipzig 1908 (8 illus, frontispiece and front cover design from 1896 edn, Ger trn by Rudolf A. Schröder); New York 1968 (facs of 1896 edn).

Dowson, Ernest. Verses. 1896. Front cover design by Beardsley.

Aristophanes. The Lysistrata. 1896. 8 illus by Beardsley (anon trn by Samuel Smith); [Vienna] 1905 (priv ptd, some copies add a forgery); [Germany] 1905 (priv ptd); 1927 (adds the forgery Adoration of the penis; the imprint 'Beardsley Press' is assuredly fictitious); Paris 1921 (priv ptd, includes introd by George Frederick Lees); New York 1967 (facs of 1896 edn), New York 1968 (adds illus by Athenian artists, text tr Jack Brussel); [1973]. In c. 1929 a set of collotype plates were ptd to accompany an unpbd introd by R. A. Walker.

Dowson, E. The Pierrot of the minute: a dramatic phantasy in one act. With a frontispiece, initial letter, vignette, and cul-de-lampe by Aubrey Beardsley. 1897, Munich 1921 (Ger tr by Johannes von Guenther).

Jonson, B. Ben Jonson his Volpone: or the foxe. A new edition. With a critical essay on the author by Vincent O'Sullivan and a frontispiece, five initial letters, and a cover design illustrative and decorative by Aubrey Beardsley. Together with an eulogy of the artist by Robert Ross. 1898 [text ed anon by Ernest Dowson, the prospectus [July 1898] reproduces frontispiece and incorporates notes about the book by Beardsley]; Berlin 1910 (Ger tr by M. Mauthner); Potsdam '1927' [1926?] (Ger adaptation by Stefan Zweig); New York 1928 (S. Zweig's adaptation trn into Eng by Ruth Langner).

Beardsley executed a number of other commissions for book and catalogue covers, title pages, posters, etc, from publishers, principally J. M. Dent, John Lane and Leonard Smithers, but also William Heinemann and T. Fisher Unwin. He also pbd many drawings in periodicals – such as Past and present, The Studio, Pall Mall Budget, Pall Mall Gazette, *and* The Poster *– and on occasion produced designs for invitation cards and book plates. Details will be found in Reade and Dickinson's catalogue of the 1966 Victoria and Albert Museum exhibition, in Gallatin's several lists, and in M. Samuels Lasner's* A selective checklist of the published work of Aubrey Beardsley, *all cited in Bibliographies and catalogues of drawings, above.*

Literary works

The valiant. Past and present: the magazine of the Brighton Grammar School X June 1885. Poem. Rptd in S. Weintraub, Beardsley, *below*.

Two to one. Brighton Society 11 June 1887. Rptd in Matthew Strugis, A new poem by Aubrey Beardsley, Keynotes vol II, no 8 1996. Poem.

A ride on an omnibus. Brighton Soc 9 July 1887. Poem.

A very free (library) reading with apologies to W. S. Gilbert. Brighton Soc 14 Apr 1888. Poem. Attributed to Beardsley but probably not by him.

The story of a confession album. Tit-Bits 17, 4 Jan 1890. Unsigned story. Rptd in L. Zatlin, The story of a confession album: the precursor of Aubrey Beardsley's fascination with triangles, in Transforming genres: new approaches to British fiction of the 1890s, ed N. L. Manos and M.-J. Rochelson, New York 1994.

Letter to the editor. Daily Chron 2 Mar 1894. [Reply to criticism of his frontispiece for John Davidson, Plays.] Rptd in Letters of Aubrey Beardsley.

Letter to the editor. Daily Chron 17 Apr 1894. [Regarding portrait of Mrs Patrick Campbell pbd in vol 1 of The Yellow Book.] Rptd in A. E. Gallatin, Catalogue of drawings and bibliography, and in Letters of Aubrey Beardsley.

Letter to the editor. Pall Mall Budget 1336, 3 May 1894. [Defending title page design for vol 1 of The Yellow Book.] Rptd in Letters of Aubrey Beardsley.

The art of the hoarding. New Rev 11 July 1894. Beardsley's contribution forms pt 3 of The art of the hoarding (other parts by Jules Chérêt and Dudley Hardy), illus with 2 works by the artist. Text rptd in A. E. Gallatin, Catalogue of drawings and bibliography, and in R. A. Walker, A Beardsley miscellany.

Under the hill and other essays in prose and verse: with illus. 1904 (contains Under the hill (expurgated version of The story of Venus and Tannhäuser), The three musicians, The ballad of a barber, and trn of Catullus's Carmen ci, all rptd from The Savoy; also 2 letters to the press and Table talk of Aubrey Beardsley (17 drawings and front cover design – adapted from original cover for Salome – by Beardsley), New York 1977 (facs, with introd by E. Lucie-Smith); London 1913, 1921, 1928, 1930, Leipzig 1905 (frontispiece by Beardsley, Ger trn by R. A. Schröder of Under the hill, The three musicians, The ballad of a barber, and Catullus's Carmen ci), rptd 1909, Frankfurt 1965 (Schröder's Ger trn of Under the hill alone with 5 Beardsley drawings); Paris 1908 (Fr trn by A. J. H. Cornette of Under the hill, The three musicians, The ballad of a barber, Catullus's Carmen ci, and Table talk of Aubrey Beardsley with 13 drawings, introd by J.-E. Blanche); Girard KS [c. 1931] (Little Blue Books ser no 1643, Under the hill only).

The story of Venus and Tannhäuser . . . . 1907 (priv ptd, first 'complete' text of unfinished Under the hill using its original title (an expurgated version appeared in The Savoy and in Under the hill and other essays in prose and verse)); Munich 1909 (Ger trn); Munich 1920 (Ger trn by Curt Moreck, adds 7 drawings); Hanover [1920] (Ger trn by P. Templin, includes continuation of story and epilogue by F. Blei); Berlin [1920] (Ger trn); [Paris? c. 1920?]; New York 1927 (priv ptd, with 16 drawings by B. R. Elliott); [Berlin? 1930] (priv ptd, adds 9 drawings by Beardsley); Paris 1959 (text of 1927 edn 'completed' by J. Glassco, frontispiece and title page designs for The story of Venus and Tannhäuser, 6 drawings from The Savoy, and 2 other related works by Beardsley), rptd London 1966 and New York 1959 and 1967 (also Du trn Amsterdam 1971); Paris 1963 (Fr trn by O. Colonna, 6 Beardsley drawings); Buenos Aires [1967] (Portuguese trn and introd by M. Toledo); New York [1967] (frontispiece and title page designs for The story of Venus and Tannhäuser, plus 80 Beardsley drawings, cover designs, etc, introd by P. J. Gillette); Wiesbaden [1967] (illustr N. Kaspar); Munich [1968] (Ger trn by J. Wilkat, includes 28 letters to Smithers, illus with 73 Beardsley drawings); London 1974 (ed with introd by R. Oresko, 13 Beardsley drawings, text based on 1907 edn, with two passages in ch 7 interpolated from The Savoy); London [1985] (frontispiece and title page designs for The story of Venus and Tannhäuser, plus 46 drawings, cover designs, etc, by Beardsley, also forgery Adoration of the penis).

Kresby a verse: prelozil Jarmil Krecar. Bradac 1916. Czech trn of The ballad of a barber, The three musicians, and Beardsley's version of Catullus's Carmen ci (also has 6 drawings).

The ballad of a barber. [Regensburg] 1919 (priv ptd). Poem rptd with the accompanying 2 drawings from The Savoy.

A Beardsley miscellany: selected and edited by R. A. Walker. 1949. Includes The art of the hoarding, a variant text of The story of Venus and Tannhäuser (one page of ms reproduced), and facs of ms of The ballad of a barber, of the prospectus for Volpone, and of the previously unpublished poem The ivory piece (also 12 drawings).

Reconsidering Aubrey Beardsley. Ed R. Langenfeld 1989, *see below under* §2, includes poem The ivory piece and prose The celestial love.

Letters and papers

Last letters of Aubrey Beardsley. With an introductory note by the Rev John Gray. 1904, Folcroft PA 1973 (facs); tr Ger. Leipzig 1910. 162 letters (plus 4 telegrams) to André Raffalovich, with 14 other letters (3 to John Gray); includes account of the artist's funeral, possibly written by Mabel Beardsley.

Briefe: Kalendernotizen und die vier zeichnungen zu E. A. Poe von Aubrey Beardsley. Munich 1908. 4 illus to Edgar Allan Poe and 181 letters to Smithers, tr F. Waerndorfer. Introd by F. Blei; includes some 'notes' purportedly written by Beardsley in a notebook.

King, A. W. An Aubrey Beardsley lecture. With an introd and notes by R. A. Walker and some unpbd letters and drawings. 1924. 16 letters (some in facs) to A. W. King, and 14 drawings; main text a talk about Beardsley by King.

Letters from Aubrey Beardsley to Leonard Smithers. Ed with introd and notes by R. A. Walker 1937. 186 letters to Smithers, plus 1 to Ernest Dowson and 1 to J. H. Ashworth.

Ross, M. (ed). Friend of friends: Robert Ross. 1952. Includes 12 letters from Beardsley.

Walker, R. A. Letters of Aubrey Beardsley. Princeton Univ Lib Chron Spring 1955. 60 letters.

A letter to Smithers. With a note by P. Gannon. Edinburgh 1963. Letter to Leonard Smithers, 18 Sep 1897.

The letters of Aubrey Beardsley. Ed H. Maas, J. L. Duncan and W. G. Good, Rutherford NJ [1970], London 1970, Deddington 1990. 631 letters (7 with sketches reproduced) and 3 drawings. Collects all previously pbd letters and adds many new ones.

Aubrey Beardsley: poems. Introd and notes by M. Sturgis. [Edinburgh] 1998 (priv ptd for the Eigteen Nineties Society). Collects 16 poems by Beardsley (also illus with drawings and facs of mss).

In black and white: the literary remains of Aubrey Beardsley. Ed S. Calloway and D. Colvin. 1998.

§2

Nicholas Salerno's annotated secondary bibliography in Reconsidering Aubrey Beardsley, *ed R. Langenfeld, lists more than 1,500 items encompassing books, articles, dissertations, catalogues and reviews. What follows is a selection of the important biographies and early criticism (virtually all of which reproduce Beardsley's work).*

Pennell, J. A new illustrator: Aubrey Beardsley. The Studio 1, Apr 1893. Issue of mag has 9 drawings and front cover design (also used for poster) by Beardsley.

What the 'Yellow Book' is to be: some meditations with its editors. Sketch 5, 11 Apr 1894. Interview with Beardsley and Henry Harland.

A new master of art: Mr Aubrey Beardsley. To-day 12 May 1894. Interview.

Pennell, J. In his Pen drawing and pen draughtsmen: their work and their methods. A study of the art to-day with technical suggestions. 1894.

An apostle of the grotesque. Sketch 9, 10 Apr 1895. Interview.

Hiatt, C. In his Picture posters: a short history of the illustrated placard, 1895.

Pennell, J. In his Modern illustration, 1895.

In Posters in miniature, introd by E. Penfield; New York 1896, introd by P. Pollard.

Lawrence, A. H. Mr Aubrey Beardsley and his work. Idler 11, Mar 1897. Interview, in part probably written by Beardsley.

Beerbohm, M. Aubrey Beardsley. Idler 13, May 1898. Rptd in his A variety of things, 1928.

L[awler], W[illiam]. Aubrey Beardsley. London Year Book 1898.

Vallance, A. The invention of Aubrey Beardsley. Mag of Art May 1898.

W[hite], G[leeson]. Aubrey Beardsley in memoriam. Studio 13, 14 May 1898.

Cochran, C. B. Aubrey Beardsley at school. The Poster: an illustrated monthly chronicle 1 Aug–Sep 1898.

Symons, A. Aubrey Beardsley. 1898; 1905 (rev and enlarged edn) (includes facs of ms of Beardsley's version of Catullus's Carmen ci, large paper edn has 2 additional drawings by Beardsley); Paris 1906 (Fr trn of 1905 edn by J. Cohen and E. and L. Thomas). Reset edn 1948, rptd 1966, 1967 and 1971. The 1905 text was also used for introd to The art of Aubrey Beardsley, New York [1918] (Mod Lib ser) (many later printings). Based on article pbd in Fortnightly Rev May 1898.

Gallatin, A. E. Aubrey Beardsley as a designer of bookplates. 1902. Also pbd in Reader Dec 1902.

[Lane, J.] Aubrey Beardsley and The Yellow Book. 1903. Contains texts of 2 letters from Beardsley previously rptd in Under the hill and other essays in prose and verse.

Gallatin, A. E. In his Whistler's art dicta and other essays, 1904.

Ross, R. Aubrey Beardsley. With 16 full-page illus and a revised iconography by A. Vallance. 1909, 2nd edn 1921. Text first appeared as the eulogy in Volpone (iconography rev from A book of fifty drawings).

Derry, Georges [R. A. Walker]. The book-plates of Aubrey Beardsley. The Bookplate Booklet 1 Oct 1919.

Pennell, J. Aubrey Beardsley and other men of the nineties. Philadelphia 1924 (priv ptd).

Macfall, [C.] H. Aubrey Beardsley: the clown, the harlequin, the pierrot of his age. New York 1927; 2nd edn as Aubrey Beardsley: the man and his work, London [1928] (special issue of 100 copies has drawings and facs of letter not in ordinary issue) facs edns pbd Folcroft PA 1971, Freeport NY 1972, Norwood PA 1976 and Philadelphia 1977.

Rothenstein, W. In his Men and memories: recollections of William Rothenstein, 1872–1900, 1931. Includes letter and extracts from 2 letters to Rothenstein, all rptd in Letters of Aubrey Beardsley, also facs of ms of The three musicians.

Evans, B. Ifor. In his English poetry in the later nineteenth century, 1933, 1966 (rev).

May, J. Lewis. In his John Lane and the nineties, 1936. Includes extracts from letters to G. F. Scotson-Clark and John Lane; full texts ptd in Letters of Aubrey Beardsley.

Walker, R. A. Le morte darthur with Beardsley illus: a bibliographical essay. Bedford 1945. Expanded from Bibliographical notes on 'Le morte d'Arthur', TLS 31 Mar 1945.

Pierrot of the minute. TLS 19 Mar 1949.

Walker, R. A. How to detect Beardsley forgeries. Bedford 1950. Appendix contains list of spurious works.

Townsend, J. B. The Yellow Book. Princeton Univ Lib Chron Winter 1955. Documents regarding Beardsley's dismissal as art editor of the mag.

Mix, K. L. A study in yellow: the Yellow book and its contributors. Lawrence KS 1960.

Reade, B. Aubrey Beardsley. 1966. Victoria and Albert Museum picture book.

Lavers, A. Aubrey Beardsley, man of letters. In Romantic mythologies, ed Ian Fletcher, 1967.

Weintraub, S. Beardsley: a biography. New York 1967, London 1967, Harmondsworth 1972 (rev Pen edn); Aubrey Beardsley: imp of the perverse, Univ Park PA 1976 (rewritten edn with much new material, virtually a different book). Ger trn of 1967 edn by C. Spiel, Munich 1968.

Brophy, B. Black and white: a portrait of Aubrey Beardsley. 1968, New York 1969.

Easton, M. Aubrey and the dying lady: a Beardsley riddle. 1972, Boston 1972. Contains previously unpbd documents.

Brophy, B. Beardsley and his world. 1976, New York 1976.

Gray, J. Aubrey Beardsley: an obituary memoir. Tr from the Fr. Edinburgh 1980 (priv ptd). Rptd from La Revue Blanche 1898.

Benkovitz, M. J. Aubrey Beardsley: an account of his life. New York 1981, London 1981. Includes previously unpbd documents.

Meulenkamp, Wim G. J. M. Aubrey Beardsley, John Lane en Leonard Smithers: een tekenaar en zijn uitgevers. Antiek XVII/3 Oct 1982.

March, D. D'Albert s'expose: Aubrey Beardsley's drawings for Mademoiselle de Maupin. New York 1985 (priv ptd).

Flint, R. C. Aubrey Beardsley and Punch. Southeastern College Art Conference Rev 11 Spring 1986.

Fletcher, I. Aubrey Beardsley. Boston 1987. Twayne's English Authors ser.

March, D. Priapusa: Mancure & Fardeuse. Or the reine des ribauds in the land of the queen of love. New York 1988 (priv ptd). Study of The story of Venus and Tannhäuser.

Reade, B. Beardsley re-mounted. 1989. Rptd in Reconsidering Aubrey Beardsley, ed R. Langenfeld, *below*.

Langenfeld, R. (ed). Reconsidering Aubrey Beardsley: with an annotated secondary bibliography by Nicholas Salerno. Foreword by S. Wilson. Ann Arbor MI 1989. Includes extract from juvenile poem A ride on an omnibus and two unfinished works, The ivory piece (poem) and The celestial love (prose) in I. Fletcher's essay Inventions for the left hand: Beardsley in verse and prose.

Zatlin, L. G. Aubrey Beardsley and Victorian sexual politics. Oxford 1990.

Snodgrass, C. Aubrey Beardsley: dandy of the grotesque. New York 1995.

Sturgis, M. Aubrey Beardsley: a biography 1998, New York 1999.

Zatlin, L. Beardsley, Japonisme, and the perversion of the Victorian ideal. Cambridge 1998.

Calloway, S. Aubrey Beardsley. 1998.

Desmarais, J. H., The Beardsley industry: the critical reception in England and France 1893–1914. 1998.

Halliwell S. and M. Sturgis (ed). The death of Pierrot: a Beardsley miscellany. Bicester, Oxon 1998. Includes suppl to Samuels Lasner, Bibliographies *above*. [MSL]

Henry Charles Beeching 1859–1919

Bibliographies

Stephen, G. A. Bibliography of Beeching. Norwich Public Lib Readers' Guide 7 1919.

§1

Mensae secundae. Verses written in Balliol College. Oxford 1879. By Beeching, J. W. Mackail and J. B. B. Nichols.

Love in idleness. 1883 (anon), 1891 (with addns and omissions, as Love's looking glass). By Beeching, J. W. Mackail and J. B. B. Nichols.

A paradise of English poetry. 2 vols 1893; new edn 1896. Ed Beeching.

A book of Christmas verse. 1895; 1926 (2nd edn rev). Ed Beeching.

In a garden and other poems. 1895.

Lyra sacra. A book of religious verse, selected and arranged by H. C. Beeching. 1895; 1903 (2nd edn).

The poems of Henry Vaughan, Silurist. Ed E. K. Chambers, with introd by Beeching. 2 vols 1896.

St Augustine at Ostia: Oxford sacred poem. 1896.

Pages from a private diary. 1898 (anon), 1903 (by Urbanus Sylvan). Rptd from Cornhill Mag with alterations.

In memoriam . . . with analysis and notes by Beeching. 1899, 1923.

Conferences on books and men. 1900. By the author of Pages from a private diary.

A selection from the poetry of S. Daniel and M. Drayton. With introd and notes by Rev H. C. Beeching. 1899.

Lyra apostolica. 1901. Ed Beeching.

Two lectures introductory to the study of poetry. Cambridge 1901.

Religio laici: a series of studies addressed to laymen. 1902.

The sonnets of Shakespeare. Introd and notes by H. C. Beeching. Boston and London 1904.

Provincial letters and other papers. 1906. Anon.

Poems of Herrick. [1907.] Ed Beeching.

The religion of Shakespeare. The sonnets. 1907.

William Shakespeare: player, playmaker and poet. 1908.

Francis Atterbury. 1909.

In re Shakespeare. London and New York 1909.

Blake's religious lyrics. 1912.

Shakespeare and the English ideal. Norwich 1916. A lecture.

The character of Shakespeare. [1917.] Br Acad annual Shakespeare lecture.

Beeching also pbd numerous sermons and lectures, edited Milton's poems, several devotional series, and four of Shakespeare's plays (Julius Caesar, Merchant of Venice, Coriolanus, Macbeth).

§2

Archer, W. In his Poets of the younger generation, 1902.

Greenwood, G. G. In re Shakespeare: Beeching versus Greenwood – rejoinder on behalf of the defendant. 1909.

Lee, S. Norwich Public Lib Readers' Guide 7 1919.

Huxley, L. Obituary. Cornhill Mag Apr 1919.

Henry Thomas Mackenzie Bell 1856–1930

Collections

Collected poems. 1901.

Poems. 1909.

Selected poems. 1921.

§1

The keeping of the vow and other verses. 1879.

Verses of varied life. 1882.

Old year leaves: being old verses revived. 1883, 1886.

A forgotten genius, Charles Whitehead: a critical monograph. 1884; new edn 1894.

Spring's immortality and other poems. 1893, 1895, 1896.

Pictures of travel and other poems. 1898.

Christina Rossetti: a biographical and critical study. 1898.

The taking of the flag and other recitations. 1900. Introd by J. J. Nesbitt.

Poetical tributes to the memory of her most gracious majesty, Queen Victoria. Ed C. F. Forshaw, with foreword by Bell, 1901.

'John Clifford': a poem. [1908.]

School recitations. Poems by Mackenzie Bell. Ed C. Lockington. 1908.

The heart's summer and other poems. London and New York [1913].

Holy quietude and other poems. London and New York [1913].

Lyrics of consolation. London and New York [1913].

Poetical pictures of the Great War. 4 sers 1917.

Half hours with representative novelists of the nineteenth century. 3 vols 1927.

Bell also edited some Pre-Raphaelites and contributed to Miles.

§2

Smythe, A. E. The balance of life: a biographical sketch of the life and work of the poet and literary critic, Henry Thomas Mackenzie Bell. [1955].

Arthur Christopher Benson 1862–1925

See col 2313.

Louisa Sarah Bevington, afterwards Guggenberger 1845–95?

Selections

Miles 8.

§1
Key-notes by Arbor Leigh. 1876, 1879 (under her own name).
Common sense country. [188-?]
Poems, lyrics and sonnets. 1882.
The why I ams: Why I am a communist by W. Morris; Why I am an expropriationist by L. S. Bevington. 1894.
Chiefly a dialogue: concerning some difficulties of a dunce. [? 1895].
Liberty lyrics. 1895.
Anarchism and violence. 1896. Essay.
Bevington contributed articles to Fortnightly Rev, Modern Rev *and* Nineteenth Cent. *See* Wellesley *vol* 5 *1989*.

Robert Laurence Binyon 1869–1943

Collections
Laurence Binyon. [32 poems.] [1926.] Augustan Books of Modern Poetry.
A Binyon anthology. 1927.
Collected poems. 2 vols 1931.

§1
Four poems. In Primavera: poems by Binyon, S. Phillips, M. Ghose and A. S. Cripps. Oxford 1890; 1890 (2nd edn).
Persephone. The Newdigate poem. 1890.
Lyric poems. 1894.
Carvalhos. [c. 1895.]
Poems. Oxford 1895.
London visions. 1896 (bk 1), 1896 (12 poems, of which 5 rptd from Pall Mall Gazette and Poems 1895, *above*), 1899 (bk 2), 1908 (collected edn, rptd from Poems 1895, and from Porphyrion and other poems, *below*, adding new poems).
The praise of life: poems. 1896.
The supper: a lyrical scene. 1897 (priv ptd).
Porphyrion and other poems. 1898.
Western Flanders: a medley of things seen, considered and imagined. 1899.
Odes. 1901, 1913 (rearranged and rev).
The death of Adam and other poems. [1903], 1904.
Dream come true. London and New York 1905.
Penthesilea: a poem. 1905.
Paris and Œnone. 1906. A tragedy in one act.
Attila: a tragedy in four acts. 1907.
England and other poems. 1909.
Auguries. 1913.
The winnowing-fan: poems on the Great War. 1914.
Bombastes in the shades: a play in one act. 1915. In Oxford Pamphlets 1914–15.
The anvil. 1916.
The cause: poems of war. Boston and New York 1917, 1917.
For the fallen, and other poems. [1917.] Selected from The winnowing-fan, *above*.
The new world: poems. 1918.
English poetry in its relation to painting and the other arts. 1918 (Br Acad).
Poetry and modern life. 1918.
The four years: war poems collected and newly augmented. 1919.
Six poems on Bruges. 1919. With 6 colour prints by F. Brangwyn.
The secret: sixty poems. 1920.
The English ode. Trans Royal Soc of Lit 2 1922.
Arthur: a tragedy. 1923. In verse.
Ayuli: a play in three acts and an epilogue. Oxford 1923.
The golden treasury of modern lyrics. 1924. Ed Binyon.
The sirens: an ode. 1924, 1925.
Little poems from the Japanese, rendered into English verse. Leeds 1925 (priv ptd).
Tradition and re-action in modern poetry. 1926 (Eng Assoc).
The wonder night. London and New York 1927.
Boadicea: a play in eight scenes. 1927.
Sophro the wise: a play for children. 1927, [1937].
The idols: an ode. 1928.
Three short plays: Godstow nunnery, Love in the desert, Memnon. 1930. In verse.
Landscape in English art and poetry. Tokyo 1930, 1931.
Akbar. 1932, 1939.
Koya San. Four poems from Japan. 1932.
The Inferno of Dante, translated into English verse. 1933.
Three poems. Derby 1934.
The case of Christopher Smart. 1934 (Eng Assoc).
The young king. A play. Canterbury 1934, 1935.
The English romantic revival in art and poetry: a reconsideration. 1935 (Rickman Godlee lecture).
Brief candles. 1938. A play.
The Purgatorio of Dante, translated into English triple rhyme. 1938.
Note on Milton's imagery and rhythm. In Seventeenth-century studies presented to Sir H. Grierson, Oxford 1938.
Art and freedom. Oxford 1939 (Romanes lecture).
The north star and other poems. 1941.
The ruins. Horizon 6 1942. Early versions of poems included in The burning of the leaves.
The Paradiso of Dante, translated into English triple rhyme. 1943.
British Museum diversion: a play for puppets. Horizon 10 1944.
The burning of the leaves and other poems. Ed C. M. Binyon 1944.
The madness of Merlin. Ed G. Bottomley 1947.
Binyon also pbd several works on English and oriental art, and edited the works of Blake, Keats, Swinburne and Tennyson. His trn of Dante's Divine comedy *was pbd in* Dante: the selected works, *ed P. Milano, 1972*.

§2
Streatfield, R. A. Two poets of the new century, Stephen Phillips and Binyon: a critical appreciation. 1901.
Archer, W. In his Poets of the younger generation, 1902.
William, H. H. Binyon and his contemporaries. In his Modern English writers, 1918.
Maynard, T. In his Our best poets: English and American, 1924.
Twitchett, E. G. The poetry of Binyon. London Mercury Sep 1930.
Thouless, P. Binyon and John Masefield. In her Modern poetic drama, Oxford 1934.
Southworth, J. G. Binyon. Sewanee Rev 43 1935; rptd in his Sowing the spring, 1940.
Edwardian poets. TLS 20 Mar 1953.
Sayers, D. L. Binyon's death. TLS 27 Mar 1953.

Wilfrid Scawen Blunt 1840–1922

Bibliographies
Reinehr, Sr M. J. In The writings of Blunt: an introduction and study, Milwaukee 1941.

Collections
The poetry of Blunt, selected and arranged by W. E. Henley and G. Wyndham. 1898.
Love poems. Ed F. Chapman, London and New York 1902.
Poetical works. 2 vols 1914.
Poems. Selected by F. Dell. 1923.

§1
Sonnets and songs by Proteus. 1875.
Proteus and Amadeus: a correspondence. Ed A. de Vere 1878. Between Blunt and W. Meynell on religion and philosophy.
The love sonnets of Proteus. 1880, 1885 (4th edn), 1904.
The future of Islam. 1882. Essays rptd from Fortnightly Rev.

The wind and the whirlwind. 1883. Poem on Britain in Egypt.
Ideas about India. 1885.
In vinculis. 1889.
A new pilgrimage and other poems. 1889.
The celebrated romance and other poems. 1889.
The celebrated romance of the stealing of the mare. 1892, 1930. Tr from Arabic by A. Blunt, done into verse by Blunt.
Esther, a young man's tragedy, love lyrics and Natalia's resurrection. 1892, Boston 1895 (as Esther and The love sonnets of Proteus).
The love lyrics and songs of Proteus. 1892 (Kelmscott Press). Rptd from 1875 and 1880 edns, *above*, but in full texts with additional sonnets.
Griselda, a society novel in rhymed verse. 1893.
Satan absolved, a Victorian mystery: a poem. London and New York 1899.
Muallakāt: the seven golden odes of pagan Arabia. 1903. Done into English verse.
Fand of the fair cheek. A three-act tragedy in rhymed verse. Written for the Irish Nat Theatre Soc. 1904 (priv ptd).
Atrocities of justice under British rule in Egypt. 1906, 1907 (with new preface).
The bride of the Nile: a political extravaganza in three acts of rhymed verse. 1907 (priv ptd).
Francis Thompson. [1907.] Rptd from Acad.
The secret history of the English occupation of Egypt: being a personal narrative of events. 1907, 1907 (with special appendices), New York 1922, Farnborough, Hants 1969.
India under Ripon: a private diary. 1909.
Gordon of Khartoum: being a personal narrative of events in continuation of The secret history, *above*. 1911.
The land war in Ireland. 1912.
My diaries: being a personal narrative of events 1888–1914. 2 vols 1919–20, 1922 (with preface by Lady Gregory).
Blunt also wrote several works on travel and politics.

§2

Le Gallienne, R. Blunt. In Miles 6.
'Ouida' (M. L. de la Ramée). In his Critical studies, 1900.
Schuster, G. N. In his Catholic spirit in modern English literature, New York 1922.
Cunninghame Graham, R. B. Blunt. Eng Rev Dec 1922.
Symons, A. In his The Café Royale, 1923.
Lytton, N. S. In his The English country gentleman, 1925. Later reworked as Wilfred Scawen Blunt: a memoir by his grandson, 1961.
MacCarthy, D. In his Portraits, 1931.
Evans, B. I. In his English poetry in the later nineteenth century, 1933, 1966 (rev).
Forster, E. M. In his Abinger harvest, 1936.
Leslie, S. In his Men were different, 1937.
MacCarthy, D. Shooting with Blunt. London Mercury May 1937.
Finch, E. Blunt 1840–1922. 1938.
Blunt's band. TLS 24 Aug 1940.
Reinehr, Sr M. J. The writings of Blunt: an introduction and study. Milwaukee 1940.
White, W. A. E. Housman on Blunt and Kipling. N & Q 29 Nov 1941.
Croft-Cooke, R. Squire of Crabbet Park. Listener 25 Sep 1947. *See* S. Cockerell, 2 and 16 Oct 1947, and R. Croft-Cooke, 9 Oct 1947.
Cockerell, S. Blunt's burial. TLS 28 May 1954.
Deux lettres inédites de Blunt à Gobineau. Revue de Littérature Comparée 30 1956.
Adams, W. S. In his Edwardian portraits, 1957.
Faulkner, P. (ed). Jane Morris to Wilfred Scawen Blunt: the letters . . . together with extracts from Blunt's diaries. 1986.

Francis William Bourdillon 1852–1921

§1

Among the flowers and other poems. 1878.
Aucassin and Nicolette: a love story. 1887 (tr with Old French text, introd, notes and bibliography), 1897 (rev), 1908, 1911, 1913 (trn only, rev and freer), 1947, 1970.
Young maids and old China. 1888, [1889], [1892].
Where lilies live and waters wind away. [1889.]
Ailes d'alouette. 2 sers Oxford 1890–1902 (priv ptd).
A lost god. 1891.
Love lies bleeding. 1891. Anon.
Love in a mist. 1892. Anon.
Sursam corda: poems. 1893.
Chryseis. 1894. Anon.
Nephelé. 1896. A tale.
Minuscula: lyrics of nature, art and love. 1897.
Through the gateway. 1900, [1902] (priv ptd).
The early editions of the Roman de la rose. 1906 (Bibl Soc).
Preludes and romances. 1908.
Ode in defence of the Matterhorn against the proposed railway to its summit. [1910.]
Verses by V. London and Oxford 1910.
Moth-wings and other poems. 1913. Selected from Ailes d'alouette, *above*, with addns.
Christmas roses for nineteen hundred and fourteen. 1914.
Easter lilies for nineteen hundred and fifteen. [1915.]
Russia re-born: poems. 1917.
Gerard and Isabel. 1921. A romance.

§2

Obit: The Times 14 Jan 1921.

Robert Seymour Bridges 1844–1930

Mss: The most important collection of Bridges's letters and papers is found in the Bodleian. Other important collections of his letters include the Univ of Reading and the archives of the Royal College of Physicians. Although most of Bridges's letters to Gerard Manley Hopkins were destroyed by Bridges, his letters to members of Hopkins's family, written between 1889–1929, are also in the Bodleian, most of them unpbd; there are also other letters.

Bibliographies

[Daniel, C. H. O.] Notes on a bibliography of Bridges. Oxford Mag 19 June 1895.
Chaundy, L. and E. H. M. Cox. Bibliographies of modern authors, no 1: Bridges. 1921. Primary materials.
Madan, F. Bibliography of the Daniel Press. In Memorials of C. H. O. Daniel, 1921. Primary materials.
Manly, J. M. and E. Rickert. Robert Bridges. In Contemporary British literature: bibliographies and study outlines, New York 1921, 1928 (updated). Primary materials.
Boutell, H. S. English first editions: Bridges, a bibliographical check-list. Publishers' Weekly 24 May 1930. Primary materials.
McKay, G. L. A bibliography of Bridges. New York 1933, 1966. Primary materials.
Nowell-Smith, S. Check-list of the works of Bridges. Book-collector's Quart 16 1934. Primary materials.
Ritz, J. G. In Bridges and Gerard Hopkins 1863–89: a literary friendship. Oxford 1960.
Kable, W. S. The Ewelme Collection of Bridges: a catalogue. Columbia SC 1967. Primary materials.
(Anderson, E. A.) Robert Seymour Bridges (1844–1930). In English poetry, 1900–1950: a guide to information sources, Detroit 1982. Primary and secondary materials.
Fike, F. Robert Seymour Bridges: a bibliography of secondary sources, 1874–1981. BB 41 1984.

Hamilton, L. T. Robert Bridges: an annotated bibliography, 1873–1988. Newark NJ 1991. Primary and secondary materials.

Collected works

Poetical works of Robert Bridges. 6 vols 1898–1905. Vol 1, 1898: Prometheus, Eros and Psyche, Growth of love; vol 2, 1899: Shorter poems (bks 1–5), New poems; vol 3, 1901: Nero, pt 1 and Achilles in Scyros; vol 4, 1902: Palicio and the return of Ulysses; vol 5, 1902: The christian captives and The humours of the court; vol 6, 1905: The feast of Bacchus and Nero, pt 2. Rptd Oxford 1929–33, Chicago 1970 (microfiche), Cambridge MA 1978 (microfiche). Individual vols are listed in §1, *below*.

Poetical works of Robert Bridges excluding the eight dramas. Oxford 1912, rptd 1913, 1914; 1936 (OSA, enlarged; updates 1912 by adding all poems written after 1913 except Testament of beauty); New York 1975 and 1978; Oxford 1953 (with Testament of beauty), rptd 1959, 1964, 1971.
REVIEWS: Bookman (London) 43 1912; Abercrombie, L., Manchester Guardian 19 Nov 1912; Contemporary Rev 104 1913; Nation 96 1913; Bailey, J., Quart Rev 219 1913; De la Mare, W., Saturday Westminster Gazette 30 Aug 1913; Jack, P. M., New York Times 28 June 1936.

Poems. Oxford 1943, rptd 1948, 1961.

Robert Bridges. [1943] (selection of poems).

Robert Bridges: poetry and prose. Ed J. Sparrow, Oxford 1955 (with appreciations by G. M. Hopkins et al).

Robert Bridges: selected poems. Ed D. E. Stanford, Cheadle, Cheshire 1974.

§1

Poems. 1873; 2nd ser 1879 (anon); 3rd ser 1880, Oxford 1884 (H. Daniel) (anon); Shorter poems, 1890 (4 bks in 1 vol), bk 5 Oxford 1893 (H. Daniel), 1894 (rev), 1896 (rev); ed M. M. Bridges, Oxford 1931 (enlarged).
REVIEWS: Lang, A., Acad 5 1874; Acad 15 1879; Acad 19 1881 (review of 3rd ser).

Carmen elegiacum. 1876, 1877 (rev).

The growth of love. 1876, Oxford 1889 (H. Daniel) (rev and enlarged), 1890, Portland ME 1894 (alleged pirated reprint of 1890, rptd 1913).
REVIEW: Spectator 59 1876

Prometheus the firegiver. Oxford 1883 (H. Daniel), 1884 (rev).
REVIEWS: Mackail, J. W., Acad 26 1884; Patmore, C., St James's Gazette 10 1885; Athenaeum 85 1885.

Nero: an historical tragedy. Pt 1 1885; pt 2 [1894].

Eros and Psyche. 1885, 1894 (rev).
REVIEWS: Patmore, C., St James's Gazette 11 1885; Spectator 59 1886 (review of Nero and Eros and Psyche).

On the elements of Milton's blank verse in Paradise lost. 1887 (priv ptd); rptd in Milton's Paradise lost Book I, ed Rev H. C. Beeching, Oxford 1887. See Editions, *below*.

The humours of the court. G. Bell [London 1888] (rptd 1893).

The feast of Bacchus. Oxford 1889 (H. Daniel), 1894 (rev).

On the prosody of Paradise regained and Samson Agonistes. Oxford 1889.

Plays. 1890. No 2, Palicio; no 3, The return of Ulysses; no 4, The Christian captives; no 5, Achilles in Scyros (corrected reprint 1892, rptd 1913); with Nero, pts 1–2, Humours of the court, and Feast of Bacchus, as Eight plays, 1894.

Eden: an oratorio. London and New York 1891 (with music by C. V. Stanford).

Founder's day: a secular ode on the ninth jubilee of Eton College. [Oxford 1893], rptd 1900.

The humours of the court and other poems. London and Boston 1893 (includes bk 5 of Shorter poems).

Milton's prosody: an examination of the rules of the blank verse in Milton's later poems, with an account of the versification of Samson Agonistes. Oxford 1893, 1894, 1901 (enlarged), 1921 (with further addns).

Invocation to music: an ode in honour of Henry Purcell. London and New York 1895 (with music by C. H. H. Parry), 1896 (rev as Ode for the bicentenary commemoration of Henry Purcell, with other poems and a preface on the musical setting of poetry). Ode rptd in Later poems, 1912, *below*; other poems in New poems in Poetical works, *above*, 1899.
REVIEWS OF 1896 EDN: Athenaeum 108 1896; Watson, H. B. M., Bookman (London) 10 1896; Spectator 76 1896.

John Keats: a critical essay. 1895 (priv ptd); rptd in Poems of John Keats, ed G. T. Drury, 1896, *below*; and in Poetical works of John Keats, ed L. Binyon, [1916] (rev); *see* Editions, *below*.

Professorship of poetry. Oxford 1895. Pam.

Chants for the psalter. [Oxford 1897] (title page reads Yattendon 4–part chants).

Christmas day, 1897. Oxford [1897] (priv ptd). Poem.

A song of darkness and light. 1898 (with music by C. H. H. Parry); rptd as A hymn of nature in Later poems, 1912, *below*.

The poetical works of Robert Bridges, vol 1. London and Oxford 1898 (Oxford edn rpts Smith, Elder edn).
REVIEWS: Acad 53 1898; Acad 55 1898; Bookman (London) 15 1898; Spectator 1 1898.

The poetical works of Robert Bridges, vol 2. London and Oxford 1899.

Shorter poems, bk 5. 1899 (new edn of 1890); rptd 1910, 1913, 1914.
REVIEWS: Acad 56 1899; Spectator 82 1899; Gosse, E., Independent 52 1900.

The poetical works of Robert Bridges, vol 3. 1901.
REVIEWS: Symons, A., Monthly Rev 4 1901; Athenaeum 119 1902.

A practical discourse on hymn-singing. Oxford 1901.

The poetical works of Robert Bridges, vols 4 and 5. 1902.
REVIEWS: Acad 62 1902; MacDonell, A., Bookman (London) 21 1902; Newbolt, H., Monthly Rev 6 1902.

Now in wintry delights. Oxford 1903; rptd in Poems in classical prosody, 1912, *below*.
REVIEW: TLS 10 Apr 1903.

Peace ode written on the conclusion of the three years' war. Oxford 1903; rptd in Later poems and in Poems in classical prosody, 1912, *below*.

Demeter: a masque. Oxford 1905 (2 edns; one containing lyrics and full score by W. H. Hadow, the other with lyrics and only incidental music); rptd in Poetical works, 1912, *above*.
REVIEWS: Acad 68 1905; Athenaeum 126 1905 (rptd in Littell's Living Age 246 1905); Saturday Rev 100 1905; TLS 16 June 1905.

The poetical works of Robert Bridges, vol 6. 1905.

Theobaldus stampensis. Oxford 1907. One-act play.

Eton memorial ode. London and New York [1908] (with music by C. H. H. Parry); rptd in Later poems, 1912, *below*.

Poems. 1909.

About hymns. Chilswell 1911.

Sonnet XLIV of Michelangelo Buonarroti, translated for Andrew Lang. 1912 (priv ptd).

Later poems and Poems in classical prosody. In Poetical works, Oxford 1912, *above*.

Hell and hate. TLS 24 Sep 1914.

Poems written in the year MCMXIII. Chelsea 1914 (priv ptd); rptd in October and other poems, 1920, *below*.

Ode on the tercentenary of the commemoration of Shakespeare. 1916 (priv ptd); rptd in Shakespeare's England, Oxford 1916 and TLS 6 July 1916.

The chivalry of the sea: naval ode. 1916 (with music by C. H. H. Parry); rptd in October and other poems, 1920, *below*.

An address to the Swindon branch of the Workers' Educational Association. Oxford 1916, rptd in Collected essays; see Letters and papers, *below*.

Ibant obscuri: an experiment in the classical hexameter. Oxford 1916.
REVIEWS: Nation 105 1917; TLS 8 Mar 1917.
Lord Kitchener. 1916 (priv ptd).
The necessity of poetry. Oxford 1918. Pam.
Britannia victrix. Oxford 1918; rptd in The Times 25 Nov 1918; rptd 1919 and in New verse, 1925, *below*.
October and other poems with occasional verses on the war. 1920, rptd 1922, 1929.
REVIEWS: Bickley, F., Bookman (London) 58 1920; M[urray], J. M., Athenaeum 9 Apr 1920; Gorman, H., New York Times 29 Aug 1920.
Dedication speech made at the unveiling of a war memorial at the Newbury Grammar School on 12 July 1921. A broadsheet.
Poor poll. 1923 (priv ptd); rptd in New verse, 1925, *below*.
The tapestry. 1925 (priv ptd). Rptd in part from October and other poems, 1920, *above*, and rptd in part in New verse, 1925, *below*.
New verse written in 1921 with the other poems of that year and a few earlier pieces. Oxford 1925, 1926 (rev).
REVIEWS: Shanks, E., Saturday Rev 140 1925; TLS 17 Dec 1925.
The influence of the audience. New York 1926 (priv ptd). Rptd from Works of William Shakespeare, Stratford-on-Avon 1907; rptd in Collected essays, papers etc, 1927.
Henry Bradley: a memoir. Oxford 1926; rptd in Collected papers of H. Bradley, Oxford 1928, and in Three friends, 1932.
The testament of beauty: a poem in four books. 5 pts [1927–9] (priv ptd), 1 vol Oxford 1929 (limited issue); Oxford 1929 (standard issue); New York 1929, 1st American issue; Oxford 1930 (corrected reprint); the poem went through 9 impressions from 1929–30. Rptd 1934, 1938, 1940 and 1944.
REVIEWS: Bridges issues a poem on his 85th birthday, New York Times 24 Oct 1929; C[lerke], A. M., Oxford Mag 48 1929–30; Church, R., Bookman (London) 77 1929; Henderson, W. B. D., Yale Rev 19 1929–30; New Statesman 34 1929; Porter, A., Spectator 143 1929; Read, H., Review of The testament of beauty, and Poetical works of Robert Bridges, 6 vols, Nation and Athenaeum 46 1929; Saturday Rev of Lit 6 1929; TLS 24 Oct 1929; Twitchett, E. G., London Mercury Dec 1929; Welby, T. E., Saturday Rev 148 1929; Wood, H. G., Central Lit Mag 29 1929–30; de Selincourt, E., Hibbert Jnl 28 1930 and in Oxford lectures on poetry, Oxford 1934; Magnus, L., Cornhill Mag May 1930, rptd Trans Royal Soc Lit 10 1931.
Poetry: the first of the broadcast national lectures. Cambridge 1929.
On receiving trivia from the author. Stanford Dingley, Berks 1930 (priv ptd).
The shorter poems of Robert Bridges. Oxford 1931; rptd 1946, Westport CT 1979.
REVIEWS: Scovell, E. J., New Statesman and Nation 2 1931; TLS 25 June 1931; Walton, E. L., New York Times 23 Aug 1931; Winters, Y. Hound and Horn 5 1931–2; Z[abel], M. D., Poetry 39 1931–2.
Verses written for Mrs Daniel. Oxford 1932 (introd by G. S. Gordon).
REVIEW: TLS 4 Aug 1932.
Three friends: memoirs of Digby Mackworth Dolben, Richard Watson Dixon, Henry Bradley. Oxford 1932, 1938.
REVIEW: TLS 17 Nov 1932.
On hearing of the death of Theodore Watts-Dunton. Winchester 1940.
Four collects. Stanford Dingley, Berks 1947.

Contributions to periodicals

Bridges's periodical contributions are extensive. For a full list of his contributions to periodicals, Soc for Pure English tracts etc, see McKay, and Hamilton, under Bibliographies, above.
A holy war. The Times 3 Sep 1914.
Waste in hotels. The Times 9 Sep 1914.
Mr Bridges on football. The Times 19 Nov 1914.
Fight for right. TLS 6 Apr 1916.
Treatment of prisoners. The Times 19 July 1916.
Perse School, Cambridge. Times Education Suppl 7 Dec 1916.
The freedom of the seas. The Times 7 Feb 1917.
20,000,000,000! The Times 8 Feb 1917.
Books for hospitals. The Times 23 May 1918.
Our prisoners of war in Germany. The Times 4 Nov 1918.
Reconciliation: Oxford letter to German intellectuals. The Times 18 Oct 1920.
The poet laureate on reconciliation. The Times 27 Oct 1920.
Poems unpublished or difficult to obtain. Ed W. M. Whitehill, Boston 1924.
To the donors of the clavichord. [Oxford 1924 (priv ptd)], rptd The Times 11 Nov 1924.
Mr Bridges's thanks. The Times 11 Nov 1924.
Broadcast English. The Times 6 Jan 1928.
An aerodome near Oxford. The Times 5 Nov 1929.
A national theatre. The Times 26 Nov 1929.

Letters and papers

Collected essays, papers etc. 30 pts Oxford 1927–36. Pt 1, 1927: Influence of audience on Shakespeare's drama; 2–3, 1928: Humdrum and harum-scarum, poetic diction; 4, 1929: Critical introduction to Keats; 5, 1930: George Darley; 6–7, 1931: Poems of Mary Coleridge, Lord de Tabley's poems; 8–10, 1932: Dantë in English literature, Poems of Emily Brontë, Dryden on Milton; 11–15, 1933: Studies in poetry, Springs of Helicon, Wordsworth and Kipling, Wordbooks, Letter on English prosody; 16–20, 1934: The Bible, Bunyan's Pilgrim's progress, Sir Thomas Browne, George Santayana, The glamour of grammar; 21–6, 1935: The musical setting of poetry, Some principles of hymn-singing, About hymns, English chanting, Chanting, Psalms noted in speech rhythm; 27–30, 1936: An address to the Swindon WEA, The necessity of poetry, Poetry, An account of the casualty department. Pts 5–30 ed M. M. Bridges.
The message of one of England's greatest poets to a printer. Ed G. W. Jones [1931].
Smith, L. P. Robert Bridges: recollections. Society for Pure English 35 1931. 3 letters.
Men and memories: recollections of William Rothenstein. 3 vols New York 1932–9. 12 letters.
The pursuit of poetry: a book of letters about poetry written by English poets, 1550–1930. Ed D. Flower, London 1939. 1 letter.
Correspondence of Bridges and Henry Bradley 1900–23. Oxford 1940.
Patmore, D. Coventry Patmore and Robert Bridges: some letters. Fortnightly Rev 169 1948.
Patmore, D. Three poets discuss new verse forms. Month n.s. 6 1951. 3 letters.
XXI letters: a correspondence between Robert Bridges and R. C. Trevelyan on new verse and The testament of beauty. Stanford Dingley, Berks 1955, rptd 1957, 1973, 1974, 1975, 1976.
Green, D. B. A new letter of Bridges to Coventry Patmore. MP 55 1958.
Stanford, D. E. Robert Bridges and Samuel Butler on Shakespeare's sonnets: an exchange of letters. SQ 22 1971.
Stanford, D. E. Robert Bridges on his poems and plays: unpublished letters by Robert Bridges to Samuel Butler. PQ 50 1971.
The correspondence of Robert Bridges and W. B. Yeats. Ed R. J. Finneran 1977.
The selected letters of Robert Bridges. Ed D. E. Stanford 2 vols Newark NJ 1983.

Editions, prefaces and introductions

Bridges edited Hymns in four parts, *vol 1, Oxford 1895;* Hymns in four parts, *vol 2, Oxford 1897;* Hymns in four parts, *Oxford 1897 (combines vols 1 and 2);* Hymns in four parts, *vol 3. Oxford 1898;* Hymns in four parts, *vol 4, Oxford 1899;* Hymns in four parts, *Oxford 1899 (4 previous vols com-*

bined); The small hymn-book, *London and Oxford 1899 (lyrics to* The Yattendon hymnal, *rptd 1914, 1920)*; Hymns: The Yattendon hymnal, *ed Bridges and H. E. Wooldridge 1899*; Last poems of R. W. Dixon, *Oxford 1905, rptd 1909*; The poems of D. M. Dolben, with memoir, *Oxford 1911, 1915 (rev)*; *Society for Pure English [tracts], Oxford 1913–29*; The spirit of man, *1916*; Poems of G. M. Hopkins, *Oxford 1918, 1930, 1948, rptd 1967*; The Chilswell book of English poetry, *1924 rptd 1926*; Selections from the letters of W. Raleigh, *1928 (introd by Bridges)*; The collected papers of H. Bradley, with a memoir, *Oxford 1928*.

On the elements of Milton's blank verse in Paradise lost. In Milton's Paradise lost, Book I, ed Rev H. C. Beeching, Oxford 1887.

Gerard Manley Hopkins. In The poets and poetry of the century, ed Alfred H. Miles, 10 vols 1893, vol 8 Robert Bridges and contemporary poets.

Odes, sonnets and lyrics of John Keats. Oxford 1895; rptd Portland ME 1922.

Poems of John Keats. Ed G. T. Drury 2 vols London and New York 1896.

On the influence of the audience. In The works of William Shakespeare, ed A. H. Bullen 10 vols Stratford-on-Avon 1907.

The star fields, and other poems, by Willoughby Weaving. Oxford 1916.

The historic names of the streets and lanes of Oxford, by H. E. Salter. Oxford 1921.

The British Legion album. Comp by E. L. Deighton. 1922.

Keats: poetry and prose. Ed Henry Ellershaw, Oxford 1922; rptd 1928, 1948.

§2

Lang, A. Vol II. Of modern English poetry. In his Letters on literature, 1889, rptd 1893.

Warren, T. H. In Poets and poetry of the century, ed A. H. Miles, vol 8 1893, rptd London and New York 1896.

Dowden, E. In his New studies in literature, 1894, rpt 1895.

Warren, T. H. Bridges, poet laureate: a lecture. Oxford 1913.

Young, F. and E. B. Bridges: a critical study. 1914, rptd 1970.

Squire, J. C. Bridges's lyrical poems. London Mercury Apr 1920.

Quinn, J. Complete catalogue of the library of John Quinn. 2 vols New York 1924.

Jackson, H. Robert Bridges, George Moore, Bernard Shaw, and printing. Fleuron 4 1928.

Obits: Publishers' Weekly 117 1930; College notes, Pelican Record 19 (1930); The Times 22 Apr 1930; St. Bartholomew's Hospital Jnl 37 1930; Denniston, J. G. The Times 28 Apr 1930; Week-End Rev 1 1930; Elton, O. Pelican Record 19 1930; MacCarthy, D. Life & Letters 4 1930; Parker, S. E. The Times 3 May 1930; P[into], V. de S[ola] Wessex 1 1930; Commonweal 12 1930; Spectator 144 1930; New York Times 22 Apr, 23 Apr 1930; Mercure de France 220 1930; Shepard, O. American Bookman Apr–May 1930; Waugh, A. Bridges, Fortnightly Rev June 1930.

Smith, L. P. Soc for Pure English tract no 35 1931. Includes E. Daryush on Bridges's work on the English language.

Nowell-Smith, S. H. Bibliography of Robert Bridges. TLS 28 Dec 1933.

Wilkinson, C. H. Bibliography of Robert Bridges. TLS 28 Dec 1933.

Trevanian, M. (pseud). Bridges: Shorter poems (1890). Bibl N & Q 2, 7 Oct 1936.

Nowell-Smith, S. H. Bridges: poems, 1873. Bibl N & Q 2, 8 Feb 1937.

Jackson, H. Robert Bridges. In his The printing of books, New York 1939, rptd 1970.

Guerard, A. The dates of some of Bridges's lyrics. MLN 55 1940.

M., D. Bridges: poems, 1873. Bibl N & Q 2, 11 June 1941.

Adams, C. M. Robert Bridges's first edition. American N & Q 1, 3 June 1941.

Tindall, W. Y. The Robert Bridges Collection. Columbia Univ Quart 33 1942.

Nowell-Smith, S. Bridges's classical prosody: new verse and variants. TLS 28 Aug 1943.

Nowell-Smith, S. The phonotypes of Robert Bridges. Alphabet and Image 5 1947.

Marchand, L. A. The Symington Collection. Jnl of the Rutgers Univ Lib 12 1948.

Nowell-Smith, S. A poet in Walton Street. In Essays mainly on the nineteenth century, ed G. F. J. Cumberlege, London, New York and Toronto 1948.

Martin, R. B. Coventry Patmore. Princeton Univ Lib Chron 14 1952.

Nowell-Smith, S. Bridges, Hopkins and Dr Daniel. TLS 13 Dec 1957.

Nowell-Smith, S. Housman inscriptions. TLS 6 Nov 1959.

Nowell-Smith, S. Bridges's debt to Hopkins. TLS 12 May 1961.

Ritz, J.-G. Bridges's debt to Hopkins. TLS 30 June 1961.

Tillotson, G. Bridges's debt to Hopkins. TLS 30 June 1961.

Gardner, W. H. Bridges's debt to Hopkins. TLS 18 Aug 1961.

Mackenzie, N. Bridges's debt to Hopkins. TLS 1 Sep 1961.

Nowell-Smith, S. Bibliographical Notes and Queries: Note 189, Mosher and Bridges. BC 11 1962.

Van Trump, J. D. and A. P. Ziegler, Jr. Thomas Bird Mosher: publisher and pirate. BC 11 1962.

Morison, S. Robert Bridges. In his John Fell, the university press and the Fell types, Oxford 1967.

White, N. and T. Dunne. A Hopkins discovery. Library 24 1969.

Barker, N. The printer and the poet. Cambridge 1970.

Barker, N. Stanley Morison. Cambridge 1972.

Godman, P. Robert Bridges on English quantitative verse: an unpublished letter. N & Q 224 1979.

Philips, C. L. Robert Bridges: a biography. Oxford 1992. [LTH]

Oliver Madox Brown 1855–74

See col 1473.

Robert Williams Buchanan 1841–1901

Bibliographies

Jay, H. In her Buchanan, 1903.

Collections

Poems. Boston 1866, 1868 (3rd edn).

Poetical works. 3 vols 1874.

Selected poems. 1882.

A poet's sketch book: selections from the prose writings of Buchanan. 1883.

Poetical works. 1884, 2 vols 1901 (enlarged as Complete poetical works).

The Buchanan ballads, old and new. 1892. Vol 1 in Buchanan's Poems for the people, selected from his ballad books with addns.

§1

Storm-beaten, or Christmas Eve at the 'Old Anchor' inn. 1862. With C. Gibbon.

Undertones. 1863, 1865 (2nd edn, enlarged and rev).

Idyls and legends of Inverburn. 1865.

The old ballads of Denmark. [1865.]

London poems. 1866; London and New York 1867; new edn 1883.

Ballad stories of the affections. [1866], 1867, 1869. Adopted into English verse from Scandinavian.

Wayside poesies: original poems of the country life. 1867. Ed Buchanan.

North coast and other poems. '1868', [1867].

David Gray and other essays, chiefly on poetry. 1868.

The life and adventures of J. J. Audubon, from material supplied by his wife. 1868, 1869. Ed Buchanan.

The book of Orm: a prelude to the epic. 1870.

Napoleon fallen: a lyrical drama. 1871, 1871 (2nd edn).

The drama of kings. 1871.
The land of Lorne, including The cruise of the 'Tern' to the Outer Hebrides. 2 vols 1871, 1883 (as The Hebrid Isles).
The fleshly school of poetry and other phenomena of the day. 1872. Rptd from Contemporary Rev.
Saint Abe and his seven lovers. 1872, Toronto 1872, as Saint Abe and his seven wives, London 1896 (with bibl note on the poem).
White rose and red: a love story, by the author of Saint Abe. 1873. Verse.
Master-spirits. 1873. Essays.
The shadow of the sword: a romance. 3 vols 1876, 3 vols 1883 (adds preface), 1908 (St Martin's Lib), Liverpool 1919. A novel.
Balder the beautiful: a song of divine death. 1877.
A child of nature: a romance. 3 vols 1881.
God and the man: a romance. 3 vols 1881, new edn '1894' [1895].
Foxglove Manor: a novel. 3 vols 1881, 1884, 1885.
The martyrdom of Madeline: a novel. 3 vols 1882.
Ballads of life, love and humour. 1882.
Love me for ever: a romance. 1883.
Annan water: a romance. 3 vols 1883.
The new Abelard: a romance. 3 vols 1884.
The master of the mine: a novel. 2 vols 1885.
Malt: a story of a caravan. 1885.
Stormy waters: a story of to-day. 3 vols 1885.
The earthquake; or six days and a sabbath. 1885.
That winter night; or love's victory. Bristol 1886, 1887 (rev and enlarged). Novel.
A look round literature. 1887. Essays.
The city of dream: an epic poem. 1888.
The heir of Linne: a novel. 2 vols 1888, Toronto 1888.
On descending into hell: a letter to the Home Secretary concerning the proposed suppression of literature. 1889.
The moment after: a tale of the unseen. 1890.
Come, live with me and be my love: a novel. 2 vols 1891.
The coming terror and other essays and letters. 1891, 2nd edn 1891, [1896] (cheap edn). Includes On descending into hell.
The outcast: a rhyme for the time. 1891.
The piper of Hamelin: a fantastic opera in two acts. 1893.
The Wandering Jew: a Christmas carol. 1893, 2nd edn 1893.
Woman and the man: a story. 2 vols 1893.
Red and white heather. North country tales and ballads. 1894.
Rachel Dene: a tale of the Deepdale mills. 2 vols 1894.
The charlatan: a novel. 2 vols 1895, 1910 (popular edn). With H. Murray.
Lady Kilpatrick: a novel. 1895.
Diana's hunting: a novel. 1895.
A marriage by capture: a romance of to-day. 1896.
Effie Hetherington: a novel. 1896.
The devil's case: a bank holiday interlude. [1896.] A poem.
The ballad of Mary the Mother: a Christmas carol. 1897. Includes other poems.
The Rev Annabel Lee: a tale of to-morrow. 1898.
Father Anthony: a romance of to-day. 1898, popular edn [1911], 1920 (new edn).
The new Rome: poems and ballads of our Empire. [1899.]
Andromeda: an idyll of the great river. 1900.
The ballad of Judas Iscariot. 1904, 1982.
The strange adventures of Miss Brown. A farcical play in three acts. London and New York [1921]. With C. Marlowe (Harriott Jay).
Sweet Nancy: a comedy in three acts. 1914. Founded on Rhoda Broughton's novel, Nancy.

§2

Rossetti, D. G. The stealthy school of criticism. Athenaeum 16 Dec 1871. Reply to Buchanan's attack.
Smith, G. B. In his Poets and novelists, 1875.
Stedman, E. C. Latter-day British poets. Scribner's Mag Feb 1875.
Walkley, A. B. In his Playhouse impressions, 1892.
Noble, J. A. Buchanan. In Miles 6.
Obit: Athenaeum 15 June 1901.
Murray, H. Buchanan: a critical appreciation. 1901.
Walker, A. S. Buchanan, the poet of modern revolt: an introduction to his poetry. 1901.
Jay, H. Robert Buchanan: some account of his life, his life's work and his literary friendships. 1903.
Symons, A. In his Studies in verse and prose, 1904.
Hearn, L. In his Appreciation of poetry, ed J. Erskine, New York 1916.
Buchanan also wrote prefaces to collections by Longfellow (1868) and the Hon Roden Berkeley Wriothesley Noel (1892).

Arthur Henry Bullen 1857–1920

See col 2680.

Charles Stuart Calverley, earlier Blayds 1831–84

Mss: poems and translations, Christ's College Lib, Cambridge.

Bibliographies

In his Complete works, 1901.
King, H. D. A descriptive catalogue of the Calverley material in the Toronto University Library. N & Q Oct–Dec 1954.

Collections

Complete works, with a biographical notice by W. J. Sendall. 1901, 1913, 1920.
Verses, translations and fly leaves. 1904.
Verses and translations. Ed O. Seaman 1905.
The English poems. Ed H. D. Spear, Leicester 1974.

§1

Parthenesis ruinae, carmen Latinum, cancellarii praemio donatum. Oxford 1851.
Poema Latinum numismate annus dignitatum et in curia cantabrigiensis recitatem comitiis maximis. Cambridge 1853.
Verses and translations. 1862, 1865 (3rd edn rev), 1871 (4th edn rev), 11th edn Cambridge 1886, 17th edn 1902.
Translations into English and Latin. Cambridge 1866, 1885 (rev).
Theocritus translated into English verse. Cambridge 1869, 1883 (rev); Cambridge MA, Boston and New York 1906.
Fly leaves. Cambridge 1872, 1873 (5th edn), 8th thousand 1881, 1885 (as Verses and fly leaves), 1903 (cheap edn).
The literary remains of Calverley, with a memoir by W. J. Sendall. 1885, 1885 (2nd edn).
The idylls of Theocritus and the eclogues of Virgil, translated into English verse. 1904.
The eclogues of Virgil, translated into English verse. Ed M. Hadas, New York 1960.

§2

Whyte, W. Calverley. In Miles 9 (10).
Thompson, F. Calverley. Acad 13 July 1901; rptd in his Literary criticism, ed T. L. Connolly, New York 1948.
Babington, P. L. Browning and Calverley, or poem and parody: an elucidation. 1925.
Ince, R. B. Calverley and some Cambridge wits of the nineteenth century. 1929.
A Cambridge poet. Spectator 9 Jan 1932. *See* A. Waugh, 16 Jan and reply 23 Jan 1932.
Evans, B. I. In his English poetry and the later nineteenth century, 1933, 1966 (rev).
Preston, A. W. Calverley of Cambridge. Queen's Quart 54 1947.
R., V. Calverley: myrtle and tamarisk. N & Q 15 Mar 1952.
King, H. D. Calverley and Jean Ingelow. N & Q 30 Aug 1952.

King, H. D. Calverley. N & Q 22 Nov 1952.
King, H. D. Words in the poems of Calverley. N & Q Aug 1953.

William Canton 1845–1926

Collections

[Nineteen poems.] [1925.] Augustan Books of Modern Poetry.
Poems. Ed G. D. Canton 1927. With bibl sketch.

§1

A lost epic and other poems. 1887.
The invisible playmate: a story of the unseen. 1894; pbd with W. V., *below*, 1897; 1912 (EL).
W. V. her book and various verses. 1896, 1897 (pbd with The invisible playmate).
A child's book of saints. 1898, 1906 (EL), London and New York 1960.
In memory of W. V. 1901, 1912 (EL).
The comrades: poems, old and new. 1902.
A history of the British and Foreign Bible Society. 5 vols 1904–10.
Canton also wrote several works on the Bible and the Bible Soc, and other works for children, including a collection of fairy tales.

§2

Noble, J. A. Canton. In Miles 8 (7).
de M., S. The poetry of Canton. Contemporary Rev May 1927.

Edward Carpenter 1844–1929

See col 2330.

'Lewis Carroll' 1832–98

See col 1492.

Mary Elizabeth Coleridge 1861–1907

Collections

Poems. Ed H. Newbolt '1908' [1907], 1927 (8th edn).
Gathered leaves from the prose of Mary E. Coleridge, with a memoir by E. Sichel. 1910. Includes 6 unpbd poems; Appendix A consists of Notes on the table talk of William Cory.
The collected poems. Ed T. Whistler 1954.

§1

The seven sleepers of Ephesus. 1893. A novel.
Fancy's following. Oxford 1896. Pbd under pseudonym Ἄνοδος.
The king with two faces. London and New York 1897, 1908 (cheap edn). An historical romance.
Fancy's guerdon, by Anodos. 1897. Rptd partly from Fancy's following, *above*, with addns.
The garland of new poetry. 1899. 12 poems by Anodos.
Non sequitur. 1900. Essays.
The fiery dawn. 1901. A novel.
The shadow on the wall. 1904. A romance.
The lady on the drawingroom floor. 1906. A novel.
Holman Hunt. London and New York [1908].
Coleridge also wrote a preface to the Last poems of Richard Watson Dixon, *ed R. Bridges, 1905.*

§2

De la Mare, W. M. E. Coleridge: an appreciation. [1907]. Rptd from the Guardian.
Binyon, L. In The English poets, ed T. H. Ward, vol 5, 1918.
Bridges, R. In his Collected essays vol 5, 1931. Rptd from Cornhill Mag.
Evans, B. I. In his English poetry in the later nineteenth century, 1933, 1966 (rev).
Reilly, J. J. In praise of Mary Coleridge. In his Of books and men, 1942.
Cecil, E. Mary Coleridge. Spectator 12 Nov 1943.
Chitty, J. E. Charlotte Yonge and Mary Coleridge, TLS 25 Mar 1944. *See also* F. Algar and G. Battiscombe, TLS 8 Apr and J. E. Chitty, 22 Apr 1944.
White, B. Mary Coleridge: an appreciation. E & S 31 1945.

William John Courthope 1842–1917

See col 2335.

Thomas William Hodgson Crosland 1865–1924

Collections

Collected poems. 1917.
Last poems. 1928.

§1

The pink book: being verses good, bad and indifferent. Brighton 1894.
Literary parables. 1898.
Fifty fables. 1899. Prose.
Other people's wings. 1899. Parodies and verses.
The absent-minded mule and other occasional verses. 1899.
The finer spirit and other poems. 1900.
Pleasant odes. 1900.
An Englishman's love letters. 1901. Parody.
English songs and ballads. 1902, 1927 (new and rev edn).
Outlook odes. 1902.
The unspeakable Scot. 1902. A satire.
The unspeakable Crosland. Being a Scot's reply [by Crosland]. [1902.]
The egregious English. 1903, 1925. First pbd under pseud 'Angus McNeill'.
The five notions. 1903. Parody of Kipling's The five nations.
Lovely woman. 1903. A satire.
Red rose: a poem. 1903, 1905.
A looking-glass for Mr Chamberlain. [1904.]
The truth about Japan. 1904.
The lord of creation. 1904, 1925 (with appreciation by H. Savage).
Wisdom for the holidays. 1905. A satire.
The suburbans. 1905. A satire.
The wild Irishman. 1905. A satire.
The wicked life. 1905. A satire.
The country life. 1906. A satire.
The beautiful teetotaller. 1907. A satire.
Who goes racing? 1907. A satire.
Little stories. [1907.]
Taffy was a Welshman. 1912. A satire.
The first stone. 1912. Satire on Wilde's De profundis.
Sonnets. 1912, 1915.
A chant of affection and other war verses. 1915.
Find the angels; The showman; A legend of the war. 1915. Parody of Machen.
The soul of a crown prince. [1916.]
War poems by X. 1916.
The English sonnet. 1917.
The fine old Hebrew gentleman. [1922.] A satire.
Pop goes the weasel. 1924. Sequel to The unspeakable Scot.
The rogue. 1926. A satirical novel.
Crosland also wrote for children, and edited The best poetry *(1903) and* The collector's library *(2 vols 1903).*

§2

Brown, W. S. The life and genius of Crosland. 1928.

Henry Harry Cust, Henry John Cockayne Cust
1861–1917

Mss located in Princeton Univ Lib.

Bibliographies
See Wellesley *vol 5 1989.*

Selections
Occasional poems. Chosen by N. C. and R. S. (E. M. E. Cust and Sir R. Storrs), Jerusalem 1918.
REVIEW: New York Times 7 Dec 1919.

§1
The Small Holdings Bill. Debate in the House of Commons on the second reading. Grantham [1891].

Contributions to periodicals
Cust edited the Pall Mall Gazette *1892–96. For the* Nat Rev *and the* New Rev, *see* Wellesley *vol 5 1989.*
North Amer Rev. Feb 1900; July 1902.

Introductions and prefaces
Introd to Machiavelli's The art of war and Florentine history. Tudor translations vols 39 and 40, 1905.
The Henley Memorial: an account of the inaugural ceremony in St Paul's Cathedral July 11th 1907. 1908. Speech.
Preface to G. de Wesselitsky, Russia and democracy: the German canker in Russia, 1915.

§2
Obits. Daily Telegraph 3 Mar 1917, The Times 3 Mar 1917.
Whibley, C. Musings without method. Blackwood's Mag Apr 1917.
Scott, J. W. R. In The story of the Pall Mall Gazette, 1950.
Scott, J. W. R. In The life and death of a newspaper (Pall Mall Gazette), 1952.
Guillaume, A. In William Ernest Henley et son groupe: néo-romantisme et impérialisme à fin du XIX siècle, Paris 1973.
Egremont, E. In The cousins: the friendship, opinions and activities of Wilfrid Scawen Blunt and George Wyndham, 1977.
Lambert, A. In Unquiet souls, New York 1984.
Abdy, J. and C. Gere. In The souls, 1984.
Ridley J. and C. Percy (eds). The letters of Arthur Balfour and Lady Elcho 1885–1917. 1992. [DA]

John Davidson 1857–1909

Bibliographies
Stonehill, C. A. and H. W. In their Bibliographies of modern authors: second ser, 1925.
Townsend, J. B. The quest for Davidson. Princeton Univ Lib Chron 13 1952. *See also* David and Arthur Symons, 15 1954.
Lester, J. A., jr. Davidson: a Grub Street bibliography. Charlottesville VA 1958.

Collections
Selected poems. 1905.
John Davidson [seventeen poems]. 1925. Augustan Books of Modern Poetry.
Poems and ballads. Ed R. Macleod [1959].
A selection of his poems. Ed M. Lindsay, preface by T. S. Eliot, with an essay by H. McDiarmid 1961.
Poems. Ed A. Turnbull 2 vols Edinburgh and London 1973.
Three poets of the Rhymers' Club. Ed D. Stanford, Cheadle 1974. (Poems by Davidson, Dowson and Johnson.)
Selected poems and prose of John Davidson, ed J. Sloan. 1995.

§1
Diabolus amans: a dramatic poem. Glasgow 1885.
The north wall. Glasgow 1885. A novel.
Bruce. Glasgow 1886. A verse play.
Smith: a tragedy. Glasgow 1888.
Plays. Greenock 1889 (An unhistorical pastoral, A romantic farce, Scaramouch in Naxos), 1894 (adds Bruce and Smith, frontispiece by A. Beardsley).
Perfervid: the career of Ninian Jamieson. 1890.
In a music hall, and other poems. 1891.
The great men and a practical novelist. 1891. Collection of tales.
Laura Ruthven's widowhood: a novel. 1892. With C. J. Wills.
Persian letters. 2 vols 1892, [1923]. Trn of Montesquieu.
Fleet Street eclogues. 2 sers London and New York 1893–6.
Sentences and paragraphs. 1893. Essays and epigrams.
Ballads and songs. London and Boston 1894, 1895 (4th edn).
A random itinerary. London and Boston 1894. Play.
Baptist lake: a novel. 1894.
A full and true account of the wonderful mission of Earl Lavender. 1895. A satirical novel.
St George's day: a Fleet Street eclogue. New York 1895. Included in Fleet Street eclogues ser 2, *above.*
Miss Armstrong's and other circumstances. 1896. A collection of tales.
For the crown. 1896. Trn of Coppée.
The pilgrimage of Strongsoul and other stories. 1896.
New ballads. London and New York '1897' [1896].
Godfrida. 1898. A dramatic work.
The last ballad and other poems. London and New York 1899.
A ballad of a nun. New York [c. 1900]; London and New York 1905 as The ballad of a nun.
Self's the man: a tragi-comedy. 1901.
The testament of a vivisector. 1901.
The testament of a man forbid. 1901.
The testament of an empire-builder. 1902.
A rosary. 1903. Miscellaneous prose and verse.
The knight of the maypole. 1903. A comedy in prose and verse.
The testament of a Prime Minister. 1904.
A queen's romance. 1904. Trn of Hugo, Ruy Blas.
The theatrocrat: a tragic play of church and state. 1905.
Holiday and other poems, with a note on poetry. 1906.
God and Mammon. Pt 1 The triumph of Mammon, 1907; pt 2 Mammon and his message, 1908.
The testament of John Davidson. 1908.
Fleet Street and other poems. 1909.
The man forbid, and other essays. Boston 1910.

§2
Thompson, F. A thesis in verse. Daily Chron 29 June 1901. Review of The testament of a vivisector, rptd in his Literary criticisms, ed T. L. Connolly, New York 1948.
Miles, A. H. In Miles 8.
Archer, W. In his Poets of the younger generation, 1902.
Jackson, H. In his Eighteen nineties, 1913.
Fineman, H. Davidson: a study of the relation of his ideas to his poetry. Philadelphia 1916.
Johnson, L. In his Reviews and critical papers, ed R. Shafer, 1921.
von Petzold, G. Davidson und sein geitiges Werden unter dem Einfluss Nietzsches. Leipzig 1928.
Bett, H. In his Studies in literature, 1929.
Evans, B. I. In his English poetry in the later nineteenth century, 1933, 1966 (rev).
Thouless, P. In his Modern poetic drama, Oxford 1934.
Lock, D. R. Davidson and the poetry of the 'nineties. London Quart 161 1936.
Weygandt, C. Henley, Stevenson and Davidson. In his Time of Yeats, New York 1937.
Applejoy, P. A view of Davidson against a 'nineties background. Catholic World Feb 1942.

Turner, P. Davidson: the novels of a poet. Cambridge Jnl 5 1952.
Lester, J. A., jr. Two notes on Davidson. N & Q Mar 1954.
Macleod, R. D. Davidson: a study in personality. 1957.
Lester, J. A., jr. Prose-poetry transmutation in the poetry of Davidson. MP 1958.
Townsend, J. B. Davidson: poet of Armageddon. New Haven CT 1961.
Reijnders, K. Tweemaal: non in een landschap. Forum der Letteren 3 1962.

Richard Watson Dixon 1833–1900

Bibliograpies

Nowell-Smith, S. Some uncollected authors, 29: Dixon. BC 10 1961.

Collections

Poems: a selection, with a memoir by R. Bridges. 1909.
The collected poems. Ed S. M. C. Johnson and T. K. Bender, New York c. 1989.

§1

The Sicilian vespers, a prize poem. Birmingham [1852]. (King Edward's School, Birmingham) photostat.
The close of the tenth century of the Christian era. Oxford 1858. Prize essay.
Christ's company and other poems. 1861, facs reproduction 1978.
St John in Patmos. Oxford [1863]. Prize poem.
Historical odes and other poems. 1864.
Essay on the maintenance of the Church of England as an established church. 1874.
The life of James Dixon, DD. 1874.
The history of the Church of England from the abolition of the Roman jurisdiction. 6 vols 1878–1902. Memoir of Dixon by H. Gee, vol 5 1900.
Mano: or a poetical history of the time of the close of the tenth century: concerning the adventures of a Norman knight: which fell part in Normandy, part in Italy. In four books. 1883, 1891 (rev). A narrative poem.
Odes and eclogues. Oxford 1884 (priv ptd).
Lyrical poems. Oxford 1887 (priv ptd).
The story of Eudocia and her brothers. Oxford 1888 (priv ptd). With preface on five-beat couplet verse.
Songs and odes. Ed R. Bridges 1896.
Mackail, J. W. The life of William Morris. Vol 1 1899. Dixon contributed reminiscences.
The last poems of Dixon. Ed R. Bridges 1905. With preface by Mary Coleridge.

Letters

The correspondence of Gerard Manley Hopkins and Dixon. Ed C. C. Abbott, Oxford 1935.

§2

Miles, A. H. Dixon. In Miles 5.
Coleridge, Mary. The last hermit of Warksworth. In her Non sequitur, 1900.
Lahey, G. F. In his Gerard Manley Hopkins, 1930.
Bridges, R. Three friends: memoirs of Dolben, Dixon and Bradley. Oxford 1932.
Evans, B. I. In his Engish poetry in the later nineteenth century, 1933, 1966 (rev).
Kent, M. Dixon. Bookman (London) May 1933.
Hanson, W. G. Gerard Manley Hopkins and Dixon. London Quart 169 1944.
Sambrook, J. A poet hidden: the life of Dixon. 1962.
Soden, G. A poet hidden. TLS 30 Mar 1962.

Austin Dobson 1840–1921

See col 2337.

Digby Mackworth Dolben 1848–67

Mss: notebook and poems, Northants Record Office, Northampton.

Collections

Poems. Ed R. Bridges 1911 (with memoir and letters), 1915 (rev and enlarged). Memoir rptd in Three friends: memoirs of Dolben, Dixon and Bradley, Oxford 1932.
Uncollected poems. Ed M. Cohen, Reading 1973.
Poems and letters of Digby Mackworth Dolben 1848–1867. Ed M. Cohen, Avebury 1981.

§1

Sonnet. 1982.

§2

Evans, B. I. In his English poetry in the later nineteenth century, 1933, 1966 (rev).
Watkin, Dom A. Dolben and the Catholic Church: some fresh evidence. Dublin Rev 225 1951.

Charles Montagu Doughty 1843–1926

§1

On the Jöstedal-Brai glaciers in Norway. 1866. A geological paper.
Documents épigraphiques recueillis dans le nord de l'Arabie. Paris 1884. Introd by E. Renan.
Travels in Arabia deserta. 2 vols Cambridge 1888, London 1921 (new preface and introd by T. E. Lawrence), 1926. Abridged as Wanderings, *below.*
Under arms. 1900.
The dawn in Britain. 6 vols 1906; ed B. Fairley 1935 (selected passages); 1943.
Adam cast forth. 1908. Sacred drama in 5 songs.
Wanderings in Arabia. Ed E. Garnett 2 vols 1908, 1923, 1939. Abridgement of Travels in Arabia deserta, *above.*
The cliffs. 1909. A verse play.
The clouds. 1912. Poetic drama.
The titans. 1916.
Mansoul: or the riddle of the world. 1920, 1923 (rev).
Hogarth's Arabia. 1922 (priv ptd). Rptd from Observer.
Passages from Arabia deserta. Ed E. Garnett 1931, 1956 (Pen).

§2

Burton, R. Acad 28 July 1888. On Arabia deserta.
Edinburgh Rev 207 1908. On Wanderings in Arabia and The dawn in Britain.
Doughty. TLS 11 Feb 1926.
Armstrong, M. The works of Doughty. Fortnightly Rev Jan 1926.
Freeman, J. Doughty. Bookman (London) Mar 1926, London Mercury Aug 1926.
Hogarth, D. G. The life of Doughty. 1928.
Taylor, W. Doughty's English. Society for Pure English 1939.
Holloway, J. Poetry and plain language: the verse of Doughty. EIC 4 1954.
Rope, H. E. G. A note on Doughty's Dawn in Britain. Nine 4 1956.
Bishop, J. The heroic ideal in Doughty's Arabia deserta. MLQ 21 1960.
Assad, T. J. Three Victorian travellers: Burton, Blunt, Doughty. 1964.

Lord Alfred Douglas 1870–1945

Bibliographies

Braybrooke, P. In his Douglas: his life and work, 1931.

Collections

Collected poems. 1919.
Lord Alfred Douglas. [Select poems.] 1926. Augustan Books of Modern Poetry.
Collected satires. 1926.
Complete poems, including the light verse. 1928.

§1

Salome. London and Boston 1894, 1904; London and New York 1906, 1912, 1927; London 1938. Trn from Wilde's Fr.
Poems (Poèmes). Paris 1896. In Fr and Eng.
Perkin Warbeck and some other poems. 1897.
Tails with a twist. By the Belgian hare. 1898; 1979 (new edn).
The city of the soul. 1899; 3rd edn London and New York 1911.
The Duke of Berwick. 1899, 1925.
The placid pug and other rhymes. By the Belgian hare. 1906.
The Pongo papers and The Duke of Berwick. 1907. Rhymes in Pongo papers rptd from Vanity Fair.
Poems. Bruges 1908. (Contains Poems 1896 and City of the soul.)
Sonnets. 1909, 1935, 1943 (with addns).
'The rhyme of F double E'. Boulogne-sur-Mer [1914].
Oscar Wilde and myself. 1914, [1919].
To a certain judge. [1915.] Sonnet.
The Rossiad. Galashiels [1916?]; 4th edn 1921. A lampoon.
Eve and the serpent. Galashiels [1917].
Fashionable intelligence about the 'Morning Post'. [1918.]
In excelsis. 1924. Sonnet sequence.
Nine poems. 1926 (priv ptd).
Two loves, and other poems. Maastricht 1928, East Lansing MI c. 1990.
The autobiography of Douglas. 1929.
The true history of Shakespeare's sonnets. 1933.
Lyrics. 1935.
Poèmes. Tr F. d'Avilla, Paris 1937.
Without apology. 1938.
Oscar Wilde: a summing up. Ed D. Hudson 1940.
The principles of poetry: an address delivered before the Royal Society of Literature. 1943.
From the nineties: some translations of Baudelaire and Verlaine. Edinburgh 1982. (By Douglas and others).
Douglas also wrote (with F. Harris) a preface to The life and confessions of O. Wilde *(1925), and a preface to the poems of Marie Stopes (1944). He edited* The Spirit Lamp, *in Oxford 1892–3.*

§2

Brown, W. S. Douglas: the man and the poet. 1918.
Braybrooke, P. Douglas: his life and work. 1931.
Sherard, R. H. A letter from Douglas on André Gide's lies about himself and Oscar Wilde. In his Si le grain ne meurt, Calvi, Corsica 1933.
Obit: Douglas: a poet of distinction. The Times 21 Mar 1945.
Freeman, W. The life of Lord Alfred Douglas. 1948.
Benkovitz, M. J. Notes toward a chapter of biography: Douglas and Roland Firbank. BNYPL Mar 1963.
Cooke, R. C. Bosie: the story of Lord Alfred Douglas, his friends and enemies. 1963.
Hyde, M. (ed). Bernard Shaw and Alfred Douglas, a correspondence. 1982, 1989.

Edward Dowden 1843–1913

See col 2340.

Ernest Christopher Dowson 1867–1900

Bibliographies

Harrison, H. G. In V. Plarr, Dowson 1888–1897, 1914.
Stonehill, C. A. and H. W. In their Bibliographies of modern authors ser 2, 1925.
Three decadent poets: Ernest Dowson, John Gray and Lionel Johnson: an annotated bibliography. Ed G. A. Cevasco. New York 1990.

Collections

Longaker, M. In his Dowson, Philadelphia 1944.
Poems, with a memoir by A. Symons. Portland ME 1902, 1905.
Poems and prose. New York 1919, 1932. With memoirs by A. Symons.
Complete poems. New York 1928.
The poetical works. Ed D. Flower 1934, 1950 (Cassell's Pocket Lib), 1967. Includes 40 unpbd poems.
Poems. 1946. Includes Verses, Decorations and The Pierrot of the minute.
Poems. Ed M. Longaker, Philadelphia [1962].
Three poets of the Rhymers' Club. Ed D. Stanford, Cheadle 1974. (Poems by Dowson, Davidson and Johnson.)

§1

The book of the Rhymers' Club. 1892. Contains 6 poems by Dowson; The second book 1894 contains 6 more poems.
A comedy of masks: a novel. 3 vols 1893, 1896. With A. Moore.
Couperus, Majesty. 1894. With A. Texeira de Mattos. Trn.
Dilemmas: stories and studies in sentiment. 1895, Leipzig 1903 (tr into Ger); selections in Dilemmas: the diary of a successful man, 1990, Lewes 1992.
Zola, La terre. 2 vols 1895 (priv ptd). Trn.
Balzac, La fille aux yeux d'or. 1896, 1928. Trn.
Verses. 1896; reissue 1965. With Decorations 1899, 1994.
The Pierrot of the minute: a dramatic phantasy in one act. 1897, 1923 (Grolier Club).
Laclos, Les liaisons dangereuses. 2 vols 1898 (priv ptd), 1940. Trn.
Memoirs of Cardinal Dubois. 2 vols 1899. Trn.
Voltaire, La pucelle. 2 vols 1899. Trn.
Adrian Rome. 1899. With A. Moore. A tale.
Decorations: in verse and prose. 1899.
de Goncourt, E. The confidantes of a king: the mistresses of Louis XV. 2 vols London and Edinburgh 1907. Trn.
The story of beauty and the beast. 1908. Trn.
Stories. Ed M. Longaker, Philadelphia 1947; London 1949.
Letters of Ernest Dowson. Ed D. Flower and H. Maas. 1967.
New letters. Ed D. Flower, Andoversford 1984.

§2

Obit: Sherard, R. H. Author May 1900.
Jepson, E. The real Dowson. Acad Nov 1907.
Plarr, V. Dowson 1888–1897: reminiscences, unpublished letters and marginalia. 1914.
Huxley, A. Dowson. In The English poets, ed T. H. Ward, vol 5, 1918.
Plarr, M. Cynara: the story of Dowson and Adelaide: a novel. 1933.
Wright, E. C. Eight poems by Dowson. BM Quart 12 1938.
'Gawsworth, John' (T. I. F. Armstrong). The Dowson legend. Essays by Divers Hands n.s. 17 1939.
Marshall, L. B. A note on Dowson. RES n.s. 3 1952. With text of poem Beata solitudo.
Fletcher, I. Some unpublished letters of Dowson to Herbert Horne. N & Q 207, Mar 1962.
Munro, J. M. A previously unpublished letter from Dowson to Arthur Symons. Études Anglaises 17 1964.
Dakin, L. Ernest Dowson: the swan of Lee. Montreal 1972.

George du Maurier 1834–96

See col 1517.

'Violet Fane', Mary Montgomerie Lamb, later Singleton, later Lady Currie 1843–1905

Collections

Collected verses. 1880.
Poems. 2 vols 1892. With critical introd.
Collected essays. 1902.

§1

From dawn to noon: poems. 1872.
Denzil Place: a story in verse. 1875.
The queen of the fairies (a village story), and other poems. 1876.
Anthony Babington. 1877. Play in prose and verse.
Edwin and Angelina papers. 1878. Essays by 'V' rptd from the World.
Sophy: or the adventures of a savage. 3 vols 1881.
Thro' love and war. 3 vols 1886.
The story of Helen Davenant. 3 vols 1889.
Autumn songs. 1889.
De Valois, M. Memoirs. 1892. Trn.
Under cross and crescent: poems. 1896.
Betwixt two seas: poems and ballads written at Constantinople and Therapia. 1900.
Two moods of a man, with other papers and short stories. 1901.

§2

Japp, A. H. Mary M. Singleton. In Miles 7 (9).
Obit: The Times 16 Oct 1905.

'Marianne Farningham', Mary Ann Hearn, 'Eva Hope' 1834–1909

Bibliographies

List of publications for James Clarke in Marianne Farningham, A working woman's life. 1907.
Appendix in S. B. Black, A Farningham childhood, Darenth Valley Pbns 1988.

Selections

The story of the years: a text book and diary with verses by Marianne Farningham selected by her father. 1880.
Songs of joy and faith. 1909.

§1

Poetry

Lays and lyrics of the blessed life: consisting of Light from the cross and other poems. 1860, 5th edn [1866].
REVIEW: Baptist Messenger 28, Mar 1861.
Morning and evening hymns for a week. 1863.
REVIEW: Baptist Messenger 68, July 1864.
Poems. 1866.
REVIEW: Baptist Messenger 89, Apr 1866.
Leaves from Elim. [1873.]
REVIEW: Evangelical Mag 16 n.s. Nov 1873.
Songs of sunshine. 1878.
REVIEW: Br Quart Rev 69, Apr 1879.
Souvenir of the Queen's Jubilee. 1887.
Harvest gleanings and gathered fragments. 1903.
REVIEW: Christian World 47, 10 Dec 1903.
Lyrics of the soul. 1908.
REVIEW: Christian World 52, 10 Dec 1908.

Prose

Echoes from Darenth Vale: tales and truths, in prose and verse. 1858 [under own name, Marianne Hearn].
Life sketches, and Echoes from the valley. 1861. 1st ser 1861; 2nd ser 1868; 3rd ser 1871.
REVIEW: Baptist Messenger 41, Apr 1862.
Chats by the sea. 1868.
Girlhood. 1869, 4th edn (10th thousand) 1869, (25th thousand) new and rev edn 1895.
Home life. [1869.]
REVIEW: Athenaeum 2185, 11 Sep 1869.
Little tales for little readers. [1869.]
Boyhood. [1870.]
The cathedral's shadow. 1871.
Sunday schools of the future. 1871.
Under the shadow: a daily text book for all in sorrow and suffering, compiled by one of themselves. With an introd by Marianne Farningham. [1871.]
A round of stories for Christmas circles. 1872 (with Emma Jane Worboise and Maggie Symington). 'Listening for the bells' and 'Out of the depths'.
Brothers and sisters. 1873.
Dell's new year. '1875' [1874].
Sunday afternoons with Jesus. 1874.
The summer and autumn of life. 1876. Prose and verse.
What of the night?: a temperance tale of the times. 1876.
Will you take it?: the history of a young women's class. To which is added a paper on young women's classes in the provinces, read at the Sunday school union conference in May 1877. [1877.]
The children's holidays: out-of-door stories for the little ones. 1878.
Homely talks about homely things. 1886.
Nineteen hundred?: a forecast and a story. 1892.
A story of fifty years: a souvenir of the ministerial jubilee of the Reverend John Turland Brown, College Street Chapel, Northampton. 1893.
In evening lights. 1897. Religious essays.
A window in Paris: a romance of the days of the Franco-German war. 1898.
Women and their saviour: thoughts of a minute for a month of mornings. 1904.
Women and their work: wives and daughters of the old testament. [1906.]
A working woman's life: an autobiography. 1907.

Writing as 'Eva Hope'

Grace Darling, the heroine of the Farne islands: her life and its lessons. 1875. anon.
Livingstone, great missionary traveller. 1875. anon.
Our Queen: life and times of Victoria, Queen of Great Britain and Ireland, Empress of India, etc. By the author of Grace Darling. [1882]; new edn [1897]. Jointly written with her niece.
New world heroes. Lincoln and Garfield: the life story of two self-made men, whom the people made presidents. [1884]; new edn [1892]. *See* Heroes of the great republic, *below*.
Life of General Gordon. [1885.]
Queens of literature of the Victorian era. 1886. (Chs on Mary Somerville, Harriet Martineau, Elizabeth Barrett Browning, Charlotte Brontë, George Eliot, Felicia Hemans.)
Stanley and Africa. [1890.]
Heroes of the great republic: lives of General Grant, General Lee, Abraham Lincoln, President Garfield, Lloyd Garrison. [1892.]
Spurgeon: the people's preacher. [1892.]

Edited by 'Eva Hope'

Poetical works of Henry Wadsworth Longfellow: with a prefatory notice, biographical and critical. 1884.
Poetical works of John Greenleaf Whittier (selected): with a prefatory notice, biographical and critical. 1885.
Poetical works of William Cowper: with a prefatory notice, biographical and critical. 1885.

Farningham was a regular contributor, in prose and verse, to the Christian World *from its inception in 1857 to her death. She also contributed regularly to the* Sunday School Times, *which she edited from 1885. Her poetry appeared in a number of other periodicals, including the* Baptist

Messenger, British Herald, Gospel Herald, *the* Treasury *and the Northampton daily press.*

§2

Obit: The Times 17 Mar 1909; Christian World 18 Mar 1909.
Glandwr-Morgan, W. Marianne Farningham in her Welsh home. [1909], 3rd edn Birmingham [1925].
Black, S. B. A Farningham childhood. Darenth Valley Pbns 1988. [RS]

'Michael Field', Katharine Harris Bradley 1846–1913 and Edith Emma Cooper 1862–1914

Bibliographies

Sturgeon, M. In her Michael Field, 1922.
Treby, I. C. (ed). The Michael Field catalogue: a book of lists, being lists of sources of manuscripts, published works, portraits and other materials. 1998.

Selections

Selections. Ed T. Sturge Moore 1923.

§1

The new Minnesinger and other poems, by Arran Leigh. 1875.
Bellerophon and other poems, by Arran and Isla Leigh. 1881.
Callirrhoë, Fair Rosamund. [1884], 1897 (Fair Rosamund ptd separately). Plays.
The father's tragedy, William Rufus, Loyalty or love. [1885.] Plays.
Brutus Ultor: a play in verse. [1886.]
Canute the great, The cup of water. [1887.] Plays.
Long ago. 1889. Based on fragments of Sappho.
The tragic Mary. 1890. Play.
Stephania: a trialogue. 1892.
Sight and song. 1892.
Underneath the bough: a book of verses. 1893, 1893 (rev and reduced edn), Portland ME 1898 (adds new poems and restores some deleted from 2nd edn).
A question of memory: a play in four acts. 1893.
Attila, my Attila: a play in verse. 1896.
The world at auction: a drama in verse. 1898.
Noontime branches. Oxford 1899 (priv ptd). Play.
Anna Ruina: a drama in verse. 1899.
The race of leaves. 1901. Play.
Julia Domna: a drama in verse. 1903.
Borgia: a period play. 1905.
Queen Mariamne: a play. 1908.
Wild honey from various thyme: poems. 1908.
The tragedy of pardon, Diane. 1911. Plays.
The accuser, Tristran de Léonois, A messiah. 1911. 3 plays.
Poems of adoration. 1912.
Mystic trees. 1913.
Dedicated: an early work of Michael Field. 1914.
Whym Chow, flame of love. 1914 (priv ptd).
Deirdre; A question of memory; Ras Byzance. 1918. Plays.
In the name of time: a tragedy. 1919.
The wattlefold: unpublished poems. Ed E. C. Fortey, Oxford 1930.
Works and days: extracts from the journals of Field. Ed T. and D. C. Sturge Moore 1934.

§2

Johnson, L. Michael Field. In Miles 8 (9).
Sturgeon, M. In her Studies of contemporary poets, 1920 (rev).
Sturgeon, M. Michael Field. 1922.
Symons, A. Michael Field. Forum 69 1923.
Smith, L. P. Michael Field. Dial 78 1925; rptd in his Reperusals and recollections, 1936.
Boas, F. S. Two unpublished poems by Field. London Mercury July 1925.
Evans, B. I. In his English poetry in the later nineteenth century, 1933, 1966 (rev).
Alexander, C. In his Catholic literary revival, Milwaukee 1935.
Around my shelves. Poetry Rev 41 1950. With unpbd poem. [VB]

Norman Rowland Gale 1862–1942

Bibliography

In A. Hayes and R. le Gallienne. N. Gale. Rugby [1894?].

Collections

A Norman Gale treasury. Ed A. Broadbent, Manchester 1905.
Country lyrics, selected from A country muse and Orchard songs. [1913].
Collected poems. 1914.

§1

Unleavened bread. 1885. By Aura.
Primulas and pansies: simple verses, by the author of Unleavened bread. Boston 1886.
Marsh marigolds. Rugby 1888. By the author of Primulas and pansies.
Anemones: a collection of simple songs from Unleavened bread, Primulas and pansies, Marsh marigolds, with fresh flowers from the author's garden. Rugby 1889. Anon.
Cricket song and other trifling verses. Rugby 1890. Anon.
Saga and song: being a ballad made of the Regina Elizabeth etc. Rugby 1890. Anon.
Thistledown: a set of six essays by Rusticus and a friend of his. Rugby 1890. Anon.
Gorillas. Rugby [1891]. Anon.
The candid cuckoo. Old Bilton 1891.
A June romance. Rugby 1892 (priv ptd), 1894.
Here be the blue and white violets. Rugby nd.
A country muse. 2 sers 1892–3, 1894, 1895.
A Cotswold village. Rugby 1893 (priv ptd; subsequently pbd in Orchard songs).
Orchard songs. 1893.
A verdant county. In A. Hayes, A fellowship in song, 1893.
Cricket songs. 1894.
On two strings. Rugby 1894 (priv ptd). With R. K. Leather.
Holly and mistletoe: a book of Christmas verse. Anon. [By E. Nesbit, N. Gale and R. Le Gallienne.] [1895].
Songs for little people. 1896.
The light side of cricket: stories, sketches and verses. Ed V. Christian 1898. (By N. Gale, W. P. Ridge, E. Philpotts.)
Barty's star. [1903.]
More cricket songs. 1905.
A book of quatrains. Rugby [1909].
Song in September. 1912.
Solitude. 1913.
Curly heads and long legs: stories and verses. [1914]. By E. Vredenburg, N. Gale and others.
A merry-go-round of song. 1919.
Verse in bloom. [1924.]
A flight of fancies. [1926.]
Messrs Bat and Ball. 1930.
Close of play. Rugby 1936.
Brackenham Church. Oxford 1938 (priv ptd).
Unpigeonholed. Bexhill-on-Sea [c. 1940] (priv ptd).

§2

Tomson, G. R. A. Country muse. Acad 3 Sep 1892.
Noble, J. A. Gale. In Miles 8 (7).

Richard Garnett 1835–1906

See col 2343.

Sir William Schwenck Gilbert 1836–1911

See col 2038.

Sir Edmund Gosse 1849–1928

See col 2345.

Alfred Perceval Graves 1846–1932

Songs of Killarney. 1873, 2nd edn 1877.
Irish songs and ballads. Manchester 1880.
Father O'Flynn and other Irish lyrics. 1889.
Songs of Irish wit and humour. 1884. Ed Graves.
The Irish song book. 1894, 1895 (2nd edn). Ed Graves.
The Irish poems of Graves. 2 vols Dublin and London 1908.
Father O'Flynn and Ould Doctor Mack. 1908.
The Irish fairy book. [1909], 1938.
Welsh poetry, old and new, in English verse. 1912.
Irish literary and musical studies. 1913.
The book of Irish poetry. [1914.] Ed Graves.
The reciter's treasury of Irish verse and prose, compiled and edited by Graves and G. Pertwee. [1915.]
Anglo-Irish literature. In A. W. Ward and A. R. Walker, Cambridge history of eng lit vol 14, 1916.
A Celtic psaltery: being mainly renderings in English verse from Irish and Welsh poetry. 1917.
Poems of Sir Samuel Ferguson. Dublin [1918]. Ed Graves.
Songs of the Gael. Dublin [1925].
English verse translations of the Welsh poems of Ceiriog Hughes. Wrexham 1926.
Irish Doric in song and story. 1926.
The Celtic song book: being representative folk songs of the six Celtic nations, chosen by Graves. 1928.
The progenitors, or our first parents, a morality: an Old Irish religious poem done into English verse. Oxford 1929.
To return to all that: an autobiography. 1930. With bibliography.

David Gray 1838–61

Mss: poems and letters, NLS.

Collections

The luggie and other poems, with a memoir by J. Hedderwick and a prefatory notice by R. M. Milnes. Cambridge 1862.
Poems, with a memoir of his life. Boston 1864.
The poetical works. A new and enlarged edn. Ed H. G. Bell 1874.
Miles 6.

§1

In the shadows: a poem in sonnets. Portland ME 1900 (The Bibelot, vol 6), London 1920.

§2

Gray. Cornhill Mag 1863.
Buchanan, R. W. In his David Gray and other essays, 1868.
Noble, J. A. Gray. Miles 6.
Russell, G. W. E. In his Selected essays, 1914.
Evans, B. I. In his English poetry in the later nineteenth century, 1933, 1966 (rev).
Gray: born 1838. TLS 29 Jan 1938.
Tusiani, J. Gray and Sergio Corazzina: a parallel. Eng Misc (Rome) 9 1958.
Stuart, A. V. David Gray: the poet of The luggie. A centenary booklet. Kirkintilloch 1961.
Stuart, A. V. Gray 1838–1861: a study of ms material and poetry. Poetry Rev 54 1963.

John Gray 1866–1934

Bibliographies

Three decadent poets: Ernest Dowson, John Gray and Lionel Johnson: an annotated bibliography. Ed. G. A. Cevasco. New York 1990.

Collections and selections

The selected prose of John Gray. Ed. J. H. McCormack. Greensboro NC 1992.
The poems of John Gray. Ed. I. Fletcher. 1988.

§1

Silverpoints. 1893.
The blue calendar. 3 pts 1895–7 (priv ptd). Carols.
Spiritual poems, chiefly done out of several languages. 1896.
Ad matrem: poems. London and Edinburgh 1904.
The long road. Oxford 1926.
Sound: a poem. 1926 (priv ptd).
Poems. 1931.
Park: a fantastic story. 1932.
Gray also pbd trns from Bourget, Couperus, Goethe and Nietzsche, edns of Campion, Constable, Drayton and Sidney, devotional works and anthologies.

Letters

A friendship of the nineties: letters between John Gray and Pierre Louys. Ed A. W. Campbell. Tr S. Robinson. Edinburgh 1984.

§2

Obit: The Times 19 June 1934.
Around my shelves. Poetry Rev 41 1950. Contains an unpbd poem.
Sewell, B. (ed). Two friends: Gray and André Raffalovich. Aylesford 1963. *See* TLS 31 May, 17 June 1963.
Sewell, B. In the Dorian mode: a life of John Gray. 1866–1834. Padstow 1983.

Alexander Balloch Grosart 1835–99

See col 2691.

Philip Gilbert Hamerton 1834–94

See col 2353.

Thomas Hardy 1840–1928

See col 1560.

Frances Ridley Havergal 1836–79

Mss: correspondence and papers are held at the Hereford and Worcester Record Office. Notebook of poems and correspondence are at Birmingham Univ Lib.

Bibliographies

List of works by the late Frances Ridley Havergal. [1880–81?]
Appendix in Janet Grierson, Frances Ridley Havergal: Worcestershire hymnwriter, 1979.

Collections

Poetical works. 2 vols 1884.
REVIEW: Saturday Rev 18 Apr 1885.
Poetical works. (1 vol Lib edn) [188–?].

Selections

The Frances Ridley Havergal service of song. Sidmouth [1880]. Poetical and musical extracts.
Life chords. 1880. Comprising 'Zenith', 'Loyal responses' and other poems.
Miss Havergal's daily text book. A manual of prayer and praise con-

taining a portion of scripture and verses for every day in the year. 1881.
Swiss letters and Alpine poems. Ed her sister, J. Miriam Crane, [1881].
Threefold praise and other pieces. Sydney, Brisbane and Melbourne [1881], [1888].
Messages for life's journey. Ed and arranged by Jane Peck [1882?], 10th thousand 1883. Prose and verse.
Footprints and 'Living songs'. Ed the Rev Charles Bullock [1883].
Life echoes: with a few selected pieces by William Henry Havergal. 1883.
Ivy leaves. Selections from the poems of Frances Ridley Havergal. With an introd by Frances A. Shaw. 1884.
Songs of the master's love. [1885.]
Coming to the King. Hymns by Frances Ridley Havergal and others. [1886.]
Fern fronds. Texts and verses for morning and evening. obl 16° [1886.]
Fulness of joy. [1886.]
Grasses. Texts and verses for morning and evening. obl 16° [1886].
Rose petals. Texts and verse for morning and evening. obl 16° [1886].
Seaweeds. Texts and verses for morning and evening. obl 16° [1886].
Silver streams. [1886.]
Streamlets of song for the young. Collected by her sister [J. Miriam Crane] 1887. Includes list of life and works.
Bells across the snow. [1890.]
Winging Heavenward. Scripture texts and poems for a month. Selected by Cecilia Havergal. [1890.] 8 poems.
A service of suffering, or leaves from the biography of Mrs Croad … with extracts from her writings. Also poems by the late Miss F. R. Havergal, and other friends …. [1892] (2nd edn).
Mottoes for the months. [1893.]
Red letter days. A register of anniversaries and birthdays. [1893.]
Forget me nots of promise. [1895.]
Gems from Havergal. Poetry selected by Frances A. Shaw. [1912.]
Gems from Havergal. Prose selected by Beatrice Havergal Shaw. [1912.]
Darlow, T. H. Frances Ridley Havergal. A Saint of God. A new memoir. With a selection of extracts from her prose and verse. 1927.
The Havergal–Murray daily text book, with scripture texts and selected verses from Frances Ridley Havergal and Charlotte Murray. [1927.]

§1
Poetry

The ministry of song. 1869, [1871] (2nd edn), 1872 (3rd edn), New York 1872, London 1874 (5th edn), 68th thousand 1882.
REVIEW: Baptist Messenger Nov 1869.
Under the surface. 1874, 1876 (3rd edn), rptd 1910.
REVIEW: Br Quart Rev 60, July 1874.
Loyal responses, or daily melodies for the king's minstrels. 1878, 20th thousand 1879.
Life mosaic: the ministry of song and under the surface. 1879.
REVIEW: Athenaeum 1 Mar 1879.
Songs of peace and joy. Music by Charles H. Purdey. Words selected from The ministry of song and Under the surface. 1879.
Under his shadow. The last poems of Frances Ridley Havergal. 1879, 50th thousand 1882.

Prose

Bruey: a little worker for Christ. 1873 (2nd edn).
REVIEW: Gospel Mag July 1873.
The approaching mission services. By a lady. Ed Rev A. W. Thorold [1874].
Little pillows; or, good-night thoughts for the little ones. 1875, 108th thousand 1882, [1929] as A book of good-night thoughts.
Morning bells; or waking thoughts for the little ones. 1875.
My king, or daily thoughts for the king's children. 1877.
Royal Beauty; or evening thoughts for the king's guests. 1877, 1880 (ch 19 as Most blessed forever and other extracts).
Morning commandments; or morning thoughts for the king's servants. 1877.
The royal invitation, or daily thoughts on coming to Christ. 1878, 25th thousand 1879.
Kept for the master's use. 40th thousand 1879; 50th thousand 1880; rptd as Meet for the master's use [1942].
Morning stars; or names of Christ for his little ones. 1879.
Echoes from the word for the Christian year. [1880], 9th thousand [1882]. First appeared as monthly papers for Day of Days during 1879. Also pbd in Home Words.
All things. 1880. (From an address to the YWCA at Plymouth 1878.)
'Him with whom we have to do'. A Bible motto for 1880. [1880.]
Ben Brightboots, and other true stories, hymns and music. [1882.]
My Bible study: for the Sundays of the year. [1882.]
Specimen-glasses for the king's minstrels. [1882.] Papers on hymns and hymn writers.
Starlight through the shadows, and other gleams from the king's word. [1882.]
The four happy days. 1883. Tale and hymns.
Life echoes, with a few selected pieces by W. H. Havergal. 1883.
Royal gems and wayside chimes for the months of the year. [1884.]
Holiday work. Paisley [1886]. Essay.

Contributions to periodicals and collaborative work

Songs of grace and glory, for private, family and public worship: hymnal treasures of the church of Christ, from the sixth to the nineteenth century. 1871, 28th thousand 1873. With Charles B. Snepp. (Havergal's name does not appear on the title page; her assistance is documented in her letters, and acknowledged in Snepp's preface.)
Lilies and shamrocks. 2 poems and letters. 4th thousand [1883]. With C. W. Ashby.
Havergal's work appeared in Children's Hour, Christian Standard, Church of England Mag, Day of Days, Good Words, Home Words, Our Own Fireside, *and* Sunday School World.

Letters

Swiss letters and Alpine poems. Ed her sister, J. Miriam Crane, [1881].
Letters by the late Frances Ridley Havergal. Ed her sister, M. V. G. H., 1885.
REVIEW: Athenaeum 21 Nov 1885.
Treasure trove. Extracts from unpbd letters and Bible notes. [1886.] Comp by Frances A. Shaw [niece].

§2
Biographies

Memorials of Frances Ridley Havergal. By her sister, M. V. G. H., 1881, 117th thousand 1882, 250th thousand [1885].
Grierson, J. Frances Ridley Havergal: Worcestershire hymnwriter. 1979. [RS]

Alfred Hayes 1857–1936

§1

The last crusade and other poems. Birmingham 1887.
Welcome to the queen. Birmingham 1887.
David Westren. Birmingham '1888' [1887].
The march of man and other poems. 1891.
A fellowship in song: Hayes, Richard Le Gallienne, Norman Gale. 3 pts Rugby 1893.
The vale of Arden and other poems. '1895' [1894], Birmingham 1897.
The cup of quietness. 1911.
Simon de Montfort: an historical drama in five acts. 1918.
Boris Goduno, by Pushkin, rendered into English verse. [1918.]

The Mayflower. 1920. With W. E. Sterling.
Czar Feodor Ioanovich, by Tolstoi, rendered into English verse. 1924.
The death of Ivan the terrible, by Tolstoi, rendered into English verse. 1926.

§2

Noble, J. A. Hayes. In Miles 8 (7).

William Ernest Henley 1849–1903

Mss: The main holdings are Yale and Pierpont Morgan Lib. Other mss located in Archives of William Heinemann, London; Berg Collection, NYPL; Brown Univ RI; Harvard; Huntington; HRHRC, Austin TX; California State Univ, Hayward; Columbia Univ; Duke Univ; Indiana Univ; Lib of Congress; Musée Rodin, Paris; Nat Lib of Ireland; New York Univ Lib; Osterreichsches Staatsarchiv, Vienna; Pennsylvania State Univ; Princeton; Rochester Univ; Southern Illinois Univ at Carbondale; Stanford Univ; Univ of British Columbia; Univ of Illinois at Urbana-Champaign; Univ of Iowa Libraries (Iowa City); Univ of Kentucky; Univ of Virginia. See also LR.

Bibliographies

The Bookworm. Bibliographical. Acad 18 July 1903, 22 Aug 1903, 19 Mar 1904.
Hutchinson, W. G. A Henley bibliography. Acad 25 July 1903.
Chesterton, G. K. W. E. Henley. Eng Illus Mag Aug 1903.
Ewing, J. C. Letter. Acad 1 Aug 1903.
Cornford, L. C. In Henley, 1913.
Williamson, K. In Henley, 1930.
In Nineteenth century readers' guide to periodical literature 1890–1899, ed H. G. Cushing and A. V. Morris, New York 1944.
Buckley, J. H. In Henley, Princeton 1945.
Sadleir, M. William Ernest Henley. BC Summer 1956.
Buckley, J. H. In Victorian poets and prose writers, New York 1966.
Flora, J. M. In Henley, 1970.
Guillaume, A. In Henley, Paris 1973.
A Bookman's catalogue: the Norman Colbeck collection. Vancouver 1987.
See also Wellesley *vol 5* 1989.

Collections

The works of W. E. Henley. 7 vols 1908, New York 1908, London 1920, 5 vols London 1921, 5 vols New York 1921, London 1926, New York 1970, Temecula CA 1992.
REVIEWS: Outlook 27 June 1908; Athenaeum 25 July 1908; Bookman Aug 1908; Spectator 8 Aug 1908; Athenaeum 28 Nov 1908; Bookman Dec 1908; Dial 16 Dec 1908; TLS 24 Feb 1921; Bookman Mar 1921; TLS 17 Mar 1921; Morning Post 22 Apr 1921.

Selections

In Ballades and rondeaus, chants royal, sestinas, villanelles, &c, ed G. White, London and Newcastle-on-Tyne 1887, New York 1888, 1892, 1893, 1897, London 1900, 1905, 1909.
In Songs and poems of the sea, ed Mrs William Sharp, 1888.
In Miles 8.
The Bibelot. In hospital, July 1901; London voluntaries: rhymes and rhythms, Aug 1901; Lyrics Sep 1903; Ballades Oct 1904.
In hospital: rhymes and rhythms. Portland ME 1903, 1908 (2nd edn), 1921 (3rd edn).
In Traveller's joy, compiled by W. G. Waters, 1906. Poems.
In A vers de société anthology, collected by C. Wells, New York 1907.
Echoes of life and death: forty-seven lyrics. Portland ME 1908, 1916 (2nd edn).
Rhymes and rhythms and Arabian nights entertainments. Portland ME 1909.
London voluntaries and other poems. Portland ME 1910.
Verses. Chicago 1910 (priv ptd).
Lyrics of joy. Chicago 1911.
In The flag of England, ed J. Fawside, 1914.
In England, my England: a war anthology, ed G. Goodchild, 1914 (dedicated to memory of Henley).
In Pro patria: a book of patriotic verse, ed W. J. Halliday, London and Toronto 1915.
In Pro patria et rege: poems on war, ed Prof Knight, 1915 (1st ser), 1915 (2nd ser).
In Our glorious heritage: a book of patriotic verse for boys and girls, ed C. S. Evans, 1918.
In The English poets, ed T. H. Ward, vol 5 1918.
In The book of poetry, ed E. Markham, vol 3 New York 1926–7.
In Poetry of the nineties, ed C. E. Andrews and M. O. Percival, New York 1926.
In Victorian verse, ed V. H. Collins, Oxford 1928.
W. E. Henley. 1931 (Augustan Books of Modern Poetry).
Lyrics of François Villon. Tr by Henley and others. Croton Falls NY 1933.
In Fin de siècle: a selection of late 19th century literature and art, ed N. Wallis, note by H. Jackson, 1947.
In Poetry 1870 to 1914, ed B. Bergonzi, 1980 (Longman English ser).
In British poetry and prose 1870–1905, ed I. Fletcher, Oxford 1987.
In The new Oxford book of Victorian verse, ed C. Ricks, Oxford 1987.
In hospital, two poem sequences 100 years apart by Cicely Herbert and W. E. Henley. 1992.

§1

A book of verses. 1888, 1889 (2nd edn), New York 1889 (2nd edn), London 1891 (3rd edn), New York 1891 (3rd edn), London 1893 (4th edn), New York 1893 (4th edn), London 1897 (5th edn), 1908 (6th edn), 1908 (Works), New York 1908 (Works), London 1912 (7th edn), 1920 (Works), 1921 (Works), New York 1921 (Works), London 1926 (Works), New York 1970 (Works), Temecula CA 1992 (Works).
REVIEWS: Edinburgh Evening Dispatch (3rd edn) 26 May 1888; Spectator 26 May 1888; Scotsman 28 May 1888; Merry England June 1888; Pall Mall Gazette 11 June 1888; Glasgow Herald 21 June 1888; Scottish Leader 21 June 1888; Acad 23 June 1888 (rptd Literary Opinion 1 July 1888); Saturday Rev 23 June 1888; Longman's Mag July 1888; Critic 7 July 1888; Fortnightly Rev 1 Aug 1888; Athenaeum 25 Aug 1888; St James's Gazette 12 Sep 1888; Harper's New Monthly Mag Nov 1888; New Princeton Rev Nov 1888; Scots Observer 24 Nov 1888; Woman's World Dec 1888; Nation 26 Dec 1888; New York Times 23 June 1889.
Prologue to Beau Austin. 3 Nov 1890. Broadside.
Views and reviews: essays in appreciation: literature. 1890, New York 1890, London 1892 (2nd edn), New York 1893, 1897, 1902, 1906, London 1908 (Works), New York 1908, London 1913 (3rd edn), 1920 (Works), 1921 (Works), New York 1921 (Works), London 1926, New York 1970 (Works), Temecula CA 1992 (Works).
REVIEWS: Scots Observer 12 July 1890; Tablet 19 July 1890; Nation 24 July 1890; Catholic World Aug 1890; Critic 16 Aug 1890; Spectator 30 Aug 1890; Dial Oct 1890; Harper's New Monthly Mag Oct 1890; Athenaeum 11 Oct 1890; Lamp Feb 1903.
The song of the sword and other verses. 1892, New York 1892, London 1908 (Works), New York 1908 (Works), London 1920 (Works), 1921 (Works), New York 1921 (Works), London 1926 (Works), New York 1970 (Works), Temecula CA 1992 (Works).
REVIEWS: Nat Observer 14 May 1892; Saturday Rev 14 May 1892; Spectator 21 May 1892; Weekly Register 21 May 1892; Cambridge Observer 24 May 1892; Bookman June 1892; Fortnightly Rev Aug 1892; Critic 6 Aug 1892; Dial 16 Sep 1892; GM Nov 1892; Literary World 1 July 1902.
Three plays: Deacon Brodie; Beau Austin; Admiral Guinea. 1892, New York 1892. With Robert Louis Stevenson.
REVIEWS: GM Nov 1892; Bookman Jan 1893.
London voluntaries: the song of the sword and other verses (2nd edn of Song of the sword rev). 1893, 1903 (2nd edn rev), 1908

(Works), New York 1908 (Works), London 1912 (3rd edn), 1920 (Works), 1921 (Works), New York 1921 (Works), London 1926 (Works), New York 1970 (Works), Temecula CA 1992 (Works).
REVIEWS: Atlantic Monthly July 1894; Great Thoughts Dec 1900.

Two days. 1894. Poem, broadside.

The plays of W. E. Henley and R. L. Stevenson: Deacon Brodie; Beau Austin; Admiral Guinea; Robert Macaire. 1896, 1907, 1908 (Works), New York 1908 (Works), London 1920 (Works), 1921 (Works), New York 1921 (Works), London 1926 (Works), New York 1970 (Works), Temecula CA 1992 (Works). Rptd in the various edns of Stevenson's Works.

The poetry of Robert Burns. Ed Henley and T. F. Henderson 4 vols Edinburgh 1896–7, London 1896–7, 1901 (4 vols in 1), Edinburgh 1901, 1905, New York 1905 (edn de luxe), London 1927 (in The complete writings of Robert Burns, ed F. H. Allen, introd by J. Buchan, 10 vols), New York 1970 (reprint of 1896–7 edn).
REVIEWS: Speaker 25 Apr 1896; Spectator 13 June 1896; Glasgow Evening News 21 Aug 1896; Black and White 29 Aug 1896; Speaker 30 Oct 1896; Acad 6 Mar 1897; Athenaeum 6 Mar 1897; Blackwood's Mag Apr 1897; Daily Chron 23 Apr 1897; Spectator 5 June 1897; Acad 25 Sep 1897; Daily Chron 27 Sep 1897; Scotsman 27 Sep 1897; Westminster Gazette 27 Sep 1897; Pall Mall Gazette 28 Sep 1897; Br Weekly 30 Sep 1897; Acad 2 Oct 1897; Athenaeum 2 Oct 1897; Saturday Rev 2 Oct 1897; Acad 9 Oct 1897; Speaker 16 Oct 1897; Bookman Nov 1897; Literature 6 Nov 1897; Macmillan's Mag Jan 1898; Acad 15 Jan 1898; Spectator 15 Jan 1898; Edinburgh Evening News 26 Jan 1898; Scotsman 26 Jan 1898; Scots Mag 21 Mar 1898.

The complete poetical works of Robert Burns. Ed Henley and T. F. Henderson, Cambridge edn, 1 vol Boston and New York 1897, 1900, 1905, 1912, 6 vols 1926, Boston 1969, 1970, 1982.

Prologue to 'Admiral Guinea'. 1897.

Burns: life, genius, achievement: an essay. 1898. Rptd from The poetry of Burns, ed Henley and T. F. Henderson 1898, 1908 (Works), New York 1908 (Works), London 1920 (Works), 1921 (Works), New York 1921 (Works), London 1926 (Works), New York 1970 (Works), 1974, Temecula CA 1992 (Works).
REVIEW: Literary World 4 Feb 1898.

Poems. 1898 (3 edns: some 1st edn copies dated 1897), New York 1898 (3 edns), London 1900 (4th edn), New York 1900 (4th edn), London 1901 (5th edn), New York 1901 (5th edn), London 1903 (6th impression), New York 1903 (6th impression), London 1904 (7th impression), New York 1904 (7th impression), London 1905 (8th impression), New York 1905 (8th impression), London 1906 (9th impression), New York 1906 (9th impression), London 1907 (10th impression), New York 1907 (10th impression), 1908 (Works), New York 1908 (Works), London 1909 (11th impression), New York 1909 (11th impression), London 1910 (12th impression), New York 1910 (12th impression), London 1912 (13th impression), New York 1912 (13th impression), London 1913 (14th impression), New York 1913 (14th impression), London 1916 (15th & 16th impressions), New York 1916 (15th & 16th impressions), London 1917 (17th impression), New York 1917 (17th & 18th impressions), London 1917 (18th edn), 1919, New York 1919 (19th impression), London 1920 (Works), London 1921 (Works), New York 1921 (Works), 1922 (20th impression), 1926 (21st impression), London 1926 (Works), New York 1970 (Works), Temecula CA 1992 (Works), Oxford and New York 1993 (1st edn rptd).
REVIEWS: Echo 29 Jan 1898, 12 Feb 1898; Daily Telegraph 16 Feb 1898; Morning Post 17 Feb 1898; Outlook 26 Feb 1898; Acad 5 Mar 1898, rptd in W. Archer's Study and stage, 1899; Spectator 12 Mar 1898; Bookman Mar 1898; Literature 26 Mar 1898; New York Times 26 Mar 1898; Literary World 22 Apr 1898; Bookman (USA) May 1898; Dial 16 May 1898; Harper's Monthly Mag Nov 1898; Nation 24 Nov 1898.

Hawthorn and lavender: songs and madrigals. 1899 (13 pp.), [Aug] 1901 (16 pp.). First pbd North Amer Rev Nov 1899–Sep 1901: pbd as Hawthorn and lavender, with other verses (112 pp.) 1901, 1901 (10 copies), London and New York 1901, New York 1905, London 1906 (3rd edn), London 1908 (Works), New York 1908 (Works), London 1910 (4th edn), 1920 (Works), 1921 (Works), New York 1921 (Works), London 1926 (Works), New York 1970 (Works), Temecula CA 1992 (Works).
REVIEWS: Pall Mall Gazette 22 Nov 1901; Outlook 23 Nov 1901; Literary World 29 Nov 1901; Bookman Dec 1901; Acad 14 Dec 1901; Athenaeum 21 Dec 1901; Literature 28 Dec 1901; TLS 4 Jan 1902; New York Times 11 Jan 1902; Nation 23 Jan 1902; Literary Digest 1 Feb 1902; Critic Mar 1902; Independent 6 Mar 1902; Spectator 22 Mar 1902; Daily Mail 4 Apr 1902; Dial 1 May 1902.

For England's sake: verses and songs in time of war. 1900, 1908 (Works), New York 1908 (Works), London 1920 (Works), 1921 (Works), New York 1921 (Works), London 1926 (Works), New York 1970 (Works), Temecula CA 1992 (Works).
REVIEWS: St James's Gazette 31 July 1900; Outlook 4 Aug 1900; Saturday Rev 4 Aug 1900; Spectator 18 Aug 1900; Literary World 2 Nov 1900; Cryptian Dec 1915.

In memoriam Reginae delectissimae Victoriae. Worthing 1901 (folio); rptd Morning Post 2 Feb 1901; rptd in Poetical tributes to the memory of Her Most Gracious Majesty Queen Victoria, ed C. F. Forshaw, 1901; and in The passing of Victoria. The poets' tribute, ed J. A. Hammerton, 1901, 1908 (Works), New York 1908 (Works), London 1920 (Works), London 1921 (Works), New York 1921 (Works), London 1926 (Works), New York 1970 (Works), Temecula CA 1992 (Works).

Views and reviews: essays in appreciation. II. art. 1902, New York 1902, London 1908 (Works), New York 1908 (Works), London 1920 (Works), 1921 (Works), New York 1921 (Works), London 1926 (Works), New York 1970 (Works), Temecula CA 1992 (Works).
REVIEWS: Morning Post 8 May 1902; Acad 10 May 1902; Pall Mall Gazette 16 May 1902; TLS 25 June 1902; Literary World 4 July 1902; New York Times 11 Oct 1902; Book Buyer (The Lamp) Feb–July 1903; Dial 16 Mar 1903.

A song of speed. 1903, New York 1903, London 1908 (Works), New York 1908 (Works), London 1920 (Works), 1921 (Works), New York 1921 (Works), London 1926 (Works), New York 1970 (Works), Temecula CA 1992 (Works). First pbd in World's Work Apr 1903. Poem.
REVIEWS: Acad 28 Mar 1903; Literary World 3 July 1903.

A king in Babylon. New York 1933. Poem.

Parker, W. M. W. E. Henley: twenty-five new poems: a centenary discovery. Poetry Rev June–July 1949.

Collaborative works

Deacon Brodie or the double life: a melodrama. 1880 (priv ptd), 1888 (rev edn), first pbd in Three plays: Deacon Brodie; Beau Austin; Admiral Guinea, 1892, New York 1892. Pbd separately 1897, 1908 (Works). In English and American drama of the nineteenth century ser, New York 1966 (micro-opaque). First performance 21 Dec 1882 in Bradford. With R. L. Stevenson.
REVIEWS: People 21 Jan 1883; Glasgow Evening News 26 June 1883; New York Times 6 May 1887; Montreal Gazette 27 Sep 1887; Morning News (Chicago) 2 Nov 1887; Athenaeum 20 Feb 1897.

Admiral Guinea: a melodrama in four acts. Edinburgh. 1884 (priv ptd). First pbd in Three plays: Deacon Brodie; Beau Austin; Admiral Guinea, 1892, New York 1892. Pbd separately 1897, 1908 (Works). Rptd in English and American drama of the nineteenth century ser, New York 1966 (micro-opaque). First performance 29 Nov 1897 in London. With R. L. Stevenson.
REVIEWS: Daily Chron 30 Nov 1897; Daily Mail 30 Nov 1897; Daily News 30 Nov 1897; Daily Telegraph 30 Nov 1897; Morning Post 30 Nov 1897; Pall Mall Gazette 30 Nov 1897; The Times 30 Nov 1897; Athenaeum 4 Dec 1897.

Beau Austin: a play in four acts. Edinburgh 1884 (priv ptd). First published in Three plays: Deacon Brodie; Beau Austin; Admiral Guinea, 1892, New York 1892. Pbd separately 1897, 1908 (Works). Rptd in English and American drama of the nineteenth century ser, New York 1966 (micro-opaque). First performance 17 Nov 1890 in London. With R. L. Stevenson.

REVIEWS: Athenaeum 8 Nov 1890; Spectator 8 Nov 1890; Tablet 8 Nov 1890; World 12 Nov 1890; Fortnightly Rev Dec 1890; Theatre Dec 1890; Athenaeum 6 Mar 1897.

Macaire: a melodramatic farce in three acts. Edinburgh 1885 (priv ptd), Chicago 1895 (Chap-Book 1 and 15 June 1895), London 1897, 1908 (Works). Rptd in English and American drama of the nineteenth century ser, New York 1966 (micro-opaque). First performance 4 Nov 1900 in London. With R. L. Stevenson.

REVIEWS: Theatre July 1895; Acad 26 Mar 1898.

Pictures at play or dialogues of the galleries by two art-critics. (Anon.) London and New York 1888 (illustr H. Furniss), rptd New York 1970. With A. Lang.

A book of English prose, character and incident, 1387–1649. 1894, Philadelphia 1894, London 1905. Co-edited with C. Whibley.

Macaire: a melodramatic farce in three acts. Chap-Book 1 and 15 June 1895. With R. L. Stevenson.

The poetry of Wilfrid Blunt. 1898. Co-edited with G. Wyndham.

London types (quatorzains). Text to illustr W. Nicholson. 1898, New York 1898, London (Works 1908, etc).

Slang and its analogues past and present. 7 vols, 1890–1904. Rptd 3 vols Millwood NY 1965, 8 vols 1966, 1 vol New Hyde Park NY 1966, 1 vol New York 1970 (introd by T. M. Bernstein), 3 vols Millwood NY 1986, 2 vols Ware 1987. With John S. Farmer. (Henley co-editor from vol 2.)

The collected poems of T. E. Brown. Introd by Henley 1900, 1901, 1909, 1920, Douglas, Isle of Man 1976 (reprint of 1900 edn). Co-edited with H. F. Brown and H. G. Dakyns.

A dictionary of slang and colloquial English (abridged from Slang and its analogues). London and New York 1905, 1912. With J. S. Farmer.

Contributions to periodicals, encyclopaedias and anthologies

Henley edited London: The Conservative Weekly Journal of Politics, Finance, Society and the Arts *from early 1878 to 5 Apr 1879,* The Mag of Art *from 1 Nov 1881 to Aug 1886,* The Scots Observer *(which became* The National Observer*) from Dec 1888 to 24 Mar 1894, and* The New Rev *from Jan 1895 to Dec 1897.*

Period. Bohemian ballads (8 poems). 18 Dec 1869–26 Feb 1870.

Cornhill Mag. July 1875–Sep 1893.

Macmillan's Mag. Notes on the Forth. Oct 1875. Poem.

Good Words. Boat songs. 1875.

Encyclopaedia Britannica, 9th edn, 1875–89. Caricature; Christobel de Castillejo; Beatrice Cenci; Alain Chartier; Pierre Boscobel de Chastleard; André-Marie de Chenier; Philip Dormer Chesterfield, fourth Earl of Stanhope; Hernan, or Hernando Cortes; James Fenimore Cooper.

St James's Mag. On the beach. Jan and Mar 1876. Poem.

London. 3 Feb 1877–1 Feb 1879, including the series A gallery of fair women and Living novelists.

Saturday Rev. 6 Oct 1877–11 June 1887.

Illus Sporting and Dramatic News. Ballade of actresses. 12 Oct 1878.

Vanity Fair. The Comédie Française. 7 June 1879.

Manchester Guardian: The Comédie Française in London, 7 July 1879; Sarah Bernhardt, 31 May 1880.

Acad. 16 Mar 1878–5 Jan 1884.

Pall Mall Gazette. 8 July 1879–9 July 1894.

Athenaeum. 1 Nov 1879–17 Nov 1888.

Belgravia Annual. Joe Symonds. Christmas 1879. Poem.

Univ Mag. Contemporary portraits: Alphonse Legros. Feb 1880.

Teacher. Review of The egoist (Meredith). 14 Feb 1880.

Theatre. A corporation of actors. 1 Nov 1880.

In The English poets, ed T. H. Ward, 1880: vol 1 Samuel Butler; vol 2 Robert Henryson; vol 3 John Byrom; vol 4 Charles Kingsley.

Art Journal. Apr 1881–Jan 1888.

Our Times. May 1881.

Ballade Rachel (in Fr). In The garland of Rachel, ed E. Gosse, Oxford 1881.

Mag of Art. Feb 1882–Oct 1886.

Overland Mail. Louis Stevenson's new books, 3 Nov 1882.

Belgravia Mag. Roundel. Mar 1883.

Living Age. Salvini. 24 May 1884.

The Critic. London letter. 27 Feb 1886–4 Feb 1888; Notes, 3 Apr 1886.

State. Mrs Kendal, 17 Apr 1886; George Meredith's Works, 17 Apr 1886.

Longman's Mag. At the sign of the ship (1st section). Aug 1886.

Hospital sketches. In Voluntaries for an east London hospital, ed H. B. Donkin, 1887; 2nd edn as The story of an east London hospital 1904; rptd (rev) in his A book of verses, 1888.

Universal Rev. In passing, 6 July 1888. Poem.

Chambers's Encyclopaedia. Dumas (father and son); Victor-Marie Hugo. 1888–92 edn, 1901 edn, 1923 edn.

In Poets at play, ed F. Langbridge, 1888.

Scots Observer. 22 Dec 1888–1 Nov 1890.

Nat Observer. 13 Dec 1890–17 Mar 1894.

Programme of Beau Austin. Theatre Royal, Haymarket, London 3 Nov 1890.

In The child set in the midst: by modern poets, ed W. Meynell, 1892.

New Rev. Two Days. Nov 1895; In Memoriam: T. E. Brown, Dec 1897. Poems.

Pageant. Song (O have you blessed, behind the stars). 1896.

Black and White. The end of it. Christmas No 1896. Poem.

McClure's Mag. To R. T. H. B.. Nov 1897; The way of life, Oct 1901. Poems.

Tobacco poems. In Lyra nicotiana: poems and verses concerning tobacco, ed W. G. Hutchinson, 1898.

In London in song, ed W. Whitten, [1898].

Outlook. 5 Feb–29 Oct 1898.

Cornish Mag. Home, Dearie, Home. 1 Nov 1898. Poem.

Pall Mall Mag. July 1899–Jan 1903.

North Amer Rev. Nov 1899–Sep 1901.

Sphere. 17 Feb 1900–29 Mar 1902.

A note on Bunyan. The literary year-book and bookman's directory 1900.

The Old Nurse. In The dual land, 1900. Poem.

Daily Mail. Unidentified book reviews 1897–8; In Memoriam (G. W. Steevens), 22 Jan 1900, poem; rptd in The works of George Warrington Steevens, vol 1; Concerning ballads, 26 Dec 1902.

Thrush. The way of it. Jan 1901; rptd McClure's Mag Oct 1901. Poem.

To a girl singing. In The May book compiled by Mrs Aria in aid of Charing Cross Hospital, 1901.

Country Life. 'Bare, ruined quires'. 6 Dec 1902. Poem.

T. P.'s Weekly. Cameos from the classics: the poetry of W. E. Henley. 24 July 1903.

For contributions to Nat Rev, see Wellesley *vol 5 1989.*

Letters

In E. A. Sharp, William Sharp (Fiona Macleod): a memoir, 1910, 2 vols 1912.

In H. R. Haggard, The days of my life, 2 vols 1926.

Hallam, J. H. Some early letters and verses of W. E. Henley. Blackwood's Mag Sep 1943.

Payen-Payne, V. Some letters of William Ernest Henley. 1933.

Connell, J. (J. H. Robertson). Unpublished letters. Nat and Eng Rev May 1951, June 1951. To Henley from H. James, L. Stephen, Meredith, Hardy et al. Letters now at Pierpont Morgan Lib.

In M. Ross, Robert Ross: friend of friends, 1952.

In E. H. Cohen, The Henley–Stevenson quarrel, Gainsville FL 1974.
In The collected letters of Joseph Conrad, ed. F. R. Karl and L. Davies, 4 vols Cambridge 1983–90.
Glines, E. 'My dear Miss Page' and 'Demon Harry': some early letters of William Ernest Henley. HLQ Autumn 1986.
In The letters of Rudyard Kipling, ed. T. Pinney. 1990–7.
In The letters of Robert Louis Stevenson, ed B. A. Booth and E. Mehew, 8 vols 1994–5; selected letters, ed. E. Mehew 1997.
In The life and letters of George Wyndham. ed J. W. Mackail and G. Wyndham. nd.
Atkinson, D. A. P. ed. Selected letters of W. E. Henley. Aldershot 1999.

Translations, editions and introductions

Jean-François Millet: twenty etchings and woodcuts. 1881. Biographical notes by Henley.
The 'Graphic gallery' of Shakespeare's heroines: a guide to an exhibition. 1888.
The Graphic gallery of Shakespeare's heroines. Stories by Henley (folio), 1888, Boston 1888.
Preface to Memorial catalogue of the French and Dutch loan collection. Edinburgh 1888.
Catalogue of a loan collection of pictures by the great French and Dutch romanticists of this century. Apr 1889 (withdrawn because of its severe criticism), May 1889.
A century of artists. Glasgow 1889. Historical and biographical notes by Henley.
Introd to Sir Henry Raeburn: a selection from his portraits. Edinburgh 1890.
Modern men from the Scots Observer. 1890. Ed Henley?
Twenty modern men from the National Observer. 1891. Ed Henley?
Lyra Heroica. A book of verse for boys. Ed Henley, New York 1891, London 1892, 1892, 1893 (3rd edn), New York 1896, 1898, 1899, London 1901, New York 1903, 1907, 1915, 1918, London 1920, 1921 (Golden Treasury ser), New York 1922, London 1924, New York 1925, 1926 (Prize Lib edn), 1927, 1930, London 1933, New York 1934, London 1940, New York 1942, 1970, Miami 1975. School edns: 1892, 1896, 1899, 1900 (additional notes by W. W. Greg and L. C. Cornford), 1903 (additional notes . . .), 1906 (additional notes . . .), 1908 (additional notes . . .), 1912 (additional notes . . .).
Collection Cottier. Ed Henley, Paris, New York and Edinburgh 1892 (in Eng and Fr).
Tudor translations. Henley as general ed 1st ser, 44 vols 1892–1909; New York 1896–9 (16 vols).
English classics. Henley as general ed, 5 vols 1894–6, Chicago 1894–6.
A London garland. Selected from five centuries of English verse by W. E. Henley. London and New York 1895, New York 1896.
The works of Lord Byron. Ed Henley (1 vol only pubd) 1897, New York 1897.
English lyrics: Chaucer to Pope 1340–1809. Ed Henley 1897, Philadelphia 1897, 1898, 1900, 1905.
Introd. In C. de Thierry, Imperialism, 1898.
The works of Tobias Smollett. Ed and introd by Henley 12 vols Westminster 1899–1901.
Memoir, in Things seen, vol 1 of The works of George Warrington Steevens, 7 vols Edinburgh and London 1900–2, Indianapolis 1900.
The works of Shakespeare. Ed Henley, completed by W. Raleigh (vols 8–10), the Edinburgh folio edn, 10 vols 1901–4.
The works of Shakespeare. Ed Henley, 20 vols 1904 (including Ellen Terry extra illus edn).
Greatest short stories, ed S. Cody, selected by Henley, Dobbs Ferry NY 1902, New York 1950 (re-edited edn).
Essay, The complete works of Henry Fielding, Drury Lane edn, ed A. R. Waller and A. Glover, 16 vols New York 1902, London 1903, 1967.
Introd to The collected works of William Hazlitt, 13 vols 1902–4.
Introd to vol 9, Reprinted pieces. In The complete works of Charles Dickens, ed F. G. Kitton, 1903–8.
Introd to vol 32, Othello. In The complete works of William Shakespeare, ed S. Lee, 40 vols 1908.
Lyrics of François Villon. Done into English by Algernon Charles Swinburne, Dante Gabrielle Rossetti, William Ernest Henley, John Payne, and Léonie Adams. Introd by L. Adams. Croton Falls NY 1933.
In The ballads and lyrics of François Villon. Mount Vernon NY 1940.
The lyrical poems of François Villon: in the original French and in the English versions. New York 1979 (in slipcase).

§2

Lang, A. At the sign of the ship. Longman's Mag Jan 1889.
Runciman, J. Weatherley's latest success. Hawk 18 Feb 1890.
Runciman, J. King Plagiarism and his court. Fortnightly Rev Mar 1890.
Nutt, A. Athenaeum 8 Mar 1890.
Runciman, J. Charges of plagiarism. Athenaeum 29 Mar 1890.
Black and White 8 Aug 1891.
Whibley, C. Literary Opinion Nov 1891, rptd Bookman (USA) Nov 1895.
Symons, A. Fortnightly Rev Aug 1892.
'Spy' cartoon. Vanity Fair 26 Nov 1892.
Parker, G. Lippincott's Monthly Mag July 1893.
Quiller Couch, A. T. Reviews and reminders. English Illus Mag Sep 1893.
Keeble, S. E. Great Thoughts and Christian Graphic 9 Sep 1893.
Symons, A. The decadent movement in literature. Harper's New Monthly Mag Nov 1893.
Blackburn, V. The Sketch 2 May 1894.
Cust, H. C. Pall Mall Gazette 21 Dec 1894; rptd Pall Mall Budget 27 Dec 1894.
In the witness-box. Sunday Times 23 Dec 1894.
Watson, H. B. M. Bookman Oct 1895; rptd Bookman (USA) Nov 1895.
Frederic, H. New York Times 5 Apr 1896.
Discoveries in Burns. Black and White 6 Mar 1897.
Symons, A. In his Studies in two literatures, 1897.
Chambers, E. K. Bookman July 1897.
Notes and news. Acad 18 Sep 1897.
An Academy of letters. Acad 6 Nov 1897.
Notes and news. Acad 4, 11 Dec 1897.
The London of the writers. Acad 1 Jan 1898.
The passing hour. Black and White 22 Jan 1898.
Notes and news. Acad 25 June 1898.
Rothenstein, W. In his English portraits, 1898.
Shorter, C. K. In my library. English Illus Mag Aug 1898.
Portrait [by Rothenstein]. Critic Dec 1898.
Literary week. Acad 22 July 1899, 25 Nov 1899, 24 Feb 1900, 23 June 1900.
Japp, A. H. Robert Burns and Mr W. E. Henley's heavy weight on him. 1899.
The literary world. St James's Gazette 5 Aug 1899.
Authors and publishers. Literature 2 Sep 1899.
'England, my England'. Acad 16 Dec 1899.
In The literary year-book and bookman's directory, 1899.
Greg, W. W. and L. C. Cornford. Notes and elucidations to Henley's Lyra Heroica. 1900.
Ruse, E. Helps to the study of Lyra Heroica, by W. E. Henley. 1900.
C. K. S. Literary letter. Sphere 14 July 1900.
Sanders, L. Literary portraits: W. E. Henley. Literature 11 May 1901.
Henley and Burns; or, the critic censured. Ed J. D. Ross, Edinburgh 1901, rptd Port Washington NY 1970.
Henley–Stevenson quarrel. Daily News 22 Nov 1901, Acad 23 Nov 1901, Pall Mall Gazette 23 Nov 1901, Referee 24 Nov 1901, The Sun 25 Nov 1901, What the world says. World 27 Nov 1901, Literature

30 Nov 1901, 'Rosy' biographies. New York Times 30 Nov 1901, St James's Gazette 30 Nov 1901, Literary leprosy. Saturday Rev 30 Nov 1901, London letter. New York Times 14 Dec 1901, Acad 14 Dec 1901, Literary Digest 14 Dec 1901, Literary quarrels. Morning Post 16 Dec 1901, Does the end justify the means? The Referee 22 Dec 1901, Brenton, E. C. New York Times 28 Dec 1901, Literary Digest 4 Jan 1902.

Mr Henley and the actor-manager. Outlook 7 Dec 1901.

Newbolt, H. Memories and portraits. Monthly Rev Jan 1902.

Archer, W. Mr Henley and his new poem. World's Work Apr 1903.

Obits and notices: Daily Mail 13 July 1903, Daily News 13 July 1903, New York Times 13 July 1903, St James's Gazette 13 July 1903, The Times 13 July 1903, Masterman, C. F. G. Daily News 14 July 1903, Pall Mall Gazette 14 July 1903, Daily Mail 15 July 1903, Daily News 15 July 1903, Woking Observer and Weybridge Chron 15 July 1903, Dial 16 July 1903, Literary World 17 July 1903, Whibley, C. TLS 17 July 1903, T. P.'s Weekly 17 July 1903, Westminster Budget 17 July 1903, Thompson, F. Acad 18 July 1903 (rptd in his A renegade poet and other essays, 1910), Watson, H. B. M. Athenaeum 18 July 1903, Gloucester Jnl 18 July 1903, Graphic 18 July 1903, Illus London News 18 July 1903, Kelly, J. F. Outlook 18 July 1903, Queen 18 July 1903, Spectator 18 July 1903, St James's Gazette 18 July 1903, Colvin, S. Letter, TLS 24 July 1903, T. P.'s Weekly 24 July 1903, Athenaeum 25 July 1903, Literary Digest 25 July 1903, Hind, C. L. Acad 1 Aug 1903, Leroi, P. L'Art Aug 1903, Blackburn, V. Fortnightly Rev Aug 1903, Bookman (USA) Aug 1903, Critic Aug 1903, Reid, T. W. Nineteenth Cent Aug 1903, T. P.'s Weekly 14 Aug 1903, Kitton, F. G. Acad 15 Aug 1903, Literary Digest 22 Aug 1903, Gilman, L. Independent 27 Aug 1903, Archer, W. Letter Acad 29 Aug 1903, Acad 29 Aug 1903, Blackshaw, R. Critic Sep 1903, Archer, W. Pall Mall Mag Sep 1903, Boynton, H. W. Atlantic Monthly Sep 1903, Lamp Sep 1903, Mag of Art Sep 1903, Bailey, J. C. Monthly Rev Sep 1903, Low, S. Nineteenth Cent Sep 1903 (rptd Living Age 17 Oct 1903), Nutt, A. Acad 5 Sep 1903, T. P.'s Weekly 25 Sep 1903, Bookman, Oct 1903, rptd Bookman (USA) Nov 1903, T. P.'s Weekly 6 Nov 1903.

Mr Henley and R. L. S. T. P.'s Weekly 25 Dec 1903.

Catalogue of the library of the late W. E. Henley, Esq. Mar 1904.

Bronner, M. William Ernest Henley the innovator. Poet-Lore Winter 1904.

Watson, H. B. M. Mr Henley and the National Observer. T. P.'s Weekly 27 Jan 1905.

Watt, F. Henley as editor. Outlook 11 Mar 1905.

Shields, R. A blurred memory of childhood. Cornhill Mag Aug 1905.

Watts, F. The portraits of the Henleys. Art Jnl Feb 1906.

Elton, O. In his Frederick York Powell: a life, 2 vols Oxford 1906.

The Henley Memorial: an account of the inaugural ceremony in St Paul's Cathedral July 11th, 1907. 1908.

Chesterton, G. K. W. E. Henley. Poet. Bibliophile Mar 1908.

Henley the critic and other matters. Bookman Dec 1908.

Chandler, B. P. Stevenson and Henley. Putnam's Mag Dec 1909.

Murdoch, W. G. B. In his memories of Swinburne: with other essays, Edinburgh 1910, [Folcroft PA] 1975.

Price, W. J. Encyclopaedia Britannica, 11th edn 1910–11.

Sellars, Mrs W. Y. Some recollections. Cornhill Mag Dec 1910.

Henderson, T. F. In DNB Suppl 1901–11.

Cornford, L. C. William Ernest Henley. 1913, Boston and New York 1913, rptd New York 1972, New York 1982.

Flewker, H. N. W. E. Henley: early recollections. Individualist Jan–Feb 1916.

Hind, C. L. In his introd to S. Phillips, Christ in Hades, 1918.

Neff, M. North Amer Rev Apr 1920.

Stephens, H. William Ernest Henley as a contemporary and an editor. London Mercury Feb 1926.

Williamson, K. W. E. Henley: a memoir. 1930, rptd Brooklyn NY 1974, 1982.

Roudin, M. B. The unpublished poems of In hospital by William Ernest Henley. Bull of the Inst of History of Medicine 4 1936.

Connell, J. (J. H. Robertson). In W. E. Henley, 1949, rptd Port Washington NY 1972.

Flora, J. M. William Ernest Henley. New York 1970 (Twayne English Authors ser).

Cohen, E. H. The text of Apparition: a purview of the Henley–Stevenson friendship. Stud in Scottish Lit 11 1973.

Cohen, E. H. Two anticipations of Henley's Invictus. HLQ Feb 1974.

Cohen, E. H. A 'lost' Henley poem. PBSA Second Quarter 1974.

Cohen, E. H. Uncollected early poems by William Ernest Henley. BNYPL Spring 1976.

Cohen, E. H. An early sonnet-portrait by Henley. VP Autumn 1976.

ORE Number 28: special issue on W. E. Henley (1849–1903). 1982 (priv ptd).

Greiman, L. R. William Ernest Henley and the Magazine of Art. Victorian Periodicals Rev Summer 1983.

In DLB vol 19 Detroit 1983.

Anson, J. S. W. E. Henley's Hospital outlines: rejections and revisions. VP Autumn 1984.

Cohen, E. H. The evolution of Henley's In hospital. In Victorian authors and their works: revision motivation and methods, ed J. Kennedy, Athens OH 1991.

Cohen, E. H. Ennui: an uncollected Hospital poem by W. E. Henley. Durham Univ Jnl Jan 1995. [DA]

Emily Henrietta Hickey 1845–1924

Selections

Miles 8 (9).

Selections. In E. M. Dinnis, Emily Hickey: poet, essayist, pilgrim: a memoir, [1927].

§1

A sculptor and other poems. 1881.

Browning, R. Strafford, with notes by Hickey. 1884.

Verse-tales, lyrics and translations. 1889.

Michael Villiers, idealist: and other poems. 1891.

Noel, R. B. W. Livingstone in Africa, with preface by Hickey. 1895.

Poems. 1896.

Ancilla domini: thoughts in verse on the life of the Blessed Virgin Mary. [1898] (priv ptd).

The poetry of the Hon Roden Noel. 1901 (priv ptd). With J. A. Symonds.

St Patrick's breastplate. [1901.] Prose trns by W. Stokes, with metrical rendering by C. F. Humphreys and E. H. Hickey.

Our Lady of May and other poems. 1902.

Havelock the Dane: an old English romance rendered into later English. 1902.

Thoughts for creedless women. [1906.]

Our Catholic heritage in English literature. 1910.

Later poems. 1913.

Devotional poems. 1922.

Jesukin and other Christmastide poems. 1924.

§2

Miles, A. H. Hickey. In Miles 8 (9).

Dinnis, E. M. Emily Hickey: poet, essayist, pilgrim: a memoir. [1927.]

Edmond Gore Alexander Holmes 1850–1936

Selections

Sonnets and poems, selected and arranged by T. J. Cobden-Sanderson. 1920, 1936.

§1

Poems. 1876.

Poems: second series. 1879.

The silence of love. '1899' [1898], 1901.
What is poetry? 1900.
Walt Whitman's poetry: a study and a selection. London and New York 1902.
The triumph of love. London and New York 1903. Sonnets.
The creed of my heart and other poems. 1912, 1919 (2nd edn).
Sonnets to the universe. 1918.
In quest of an ideal: an autobiography. [1920.]
Holmes also wrote on education and philosophy.

Gerard Manley Hopkins 1844–89

Manuscripts

Major collections in Campion Hall, Oxford (listed in Journals and papers, *ed H. House, below, Appendix 4, and in the Bodleian (on deposit from Lord Bridges). Revised fair copies of* Harry Ploughman *and* Tom's garland *in BL; of* Spring, In the valley of the Elwy, Morning, midday and evening sacrifice *and four early poems in HRHRC, Austin TX; of* Andromeda *(entitled* The Catholic Church Andromeda*) in the Robert Taylor Collection, Princeton; and of other individual poems in the Archives of the Irish Province of the Soc of Jesus, Dublin, the College of the Holy Cross, Worcester MA and Harvard. D. M. Dolben's transcripts of two early poems are in the Northants Record Office; and six undergraduate essays from the Notebook DII (four unpbd) are at Balliol College. Full list of mss given in* IELM, *compiled by Barbara Rosenbaum, vol 4 (pt 2) 1990 pp. 275–327. Marginalia in printed books and mss listed on pp. 326–7.*

Abbott, C. C. G. M. Hopkins: a letter and drafts of early poems. Durham Univ Jnl 32 1939–40.
Blakiston, J. M. G. An unpublished Hopkins letter. TLS 25 Sep 1948. Contains A fragment of anything you like, Il Mystico and A windy day in summer.
Bischoff, D. A. The manuscripts of Hopkins. Thought 26 1952.
MacKenzie, N. H. The lost autograph of The wreck of the Deutschland and its first readers. Hopkins Quart 3 1976.
Early poetic manuscripts and note-books of Hopkins, in facsimile. Ed N. H. MacKenzie, New York 1989.
Higgins, L. A new catalogue of the Hopkins (mss) Collection at Campion Hall, Oxford. Hopkins Quart 18 1991.

Bibliographies

Weyand, N. A chronological bibliography. In his Immortal diamond, New York 1949.
Charney, M. A bibliographical study of Hopkins criticism 1918–49. Thought 25 1950.
Patricia, Sr M. Forty years of criticism: a chronological check list of criticism of the works of Hopkins 1909–49. BB 20 1950.
Pick, J. In The Victorian poets: a guide to research, ed F. E. Faverty, Cambridge MA 1956, 1968 (rev).
McChesney, D. A Hopkins commentary . . . on the main poems 1876–89. 1968.
A concordance of the poetry in English of Hopkins. Ed A. Borrello, Metuchen NJ 1969.
Cohen, E. H. Works and criticism of Hopkins: a comprehensive bibliography. Washington 1969.
A concordance to the English poetry of Hopkins, compiled by R. J. Dilligan and T. K. Bender. Madison WI 1970.
Mariani, P. L. A commentary on the complete poems of Hopkins. New York 1970.
Seelhammer, R. Hopkins collected at Gonzaga. Chicago 1970.
Dunne, T. Hopkins: a comprehensive bibliography. Oxford 1976.
A concordance to the sermons of Hopkins, compiled by W. Foltz and T. K. Bender. New York 1989.

Collections

Poems. Ed R. Bridges, Oxford 1918.
REVIEWS: Clutton-Brock, Arthur, TLS Jan 1919; Maynard, T., New Witness Jan 1919; Guiney, L. I., Month Mar 1919; Shanks, E., New Statesman Mar 1919; Bliss, Fr G., Tablet Apr 1919; Murry, J. M., Athenaeum 6 June 1919, rptd in his Aspects of literature, 1920; Lappin, H. A., Catholic World July 1919; Barraud, Fr C., Month Aug 1919; Russell, M., Irish Monthly Aug 1919; Page, F,. Dublin Rev 167 1920; Sapir, E., Poetry 18 1921.
Poems: second edition, with additional poems. Ed C. Williams, Oxford 1930; ed W. H. Gardner, Oxford 1948 (3rd edn rev and enlarged); ed Gardner and N. H. Mackenzie, Oxford 1967 (4th edn rev and enlarged); rptd with corrections 1970 (Oxford Paperbacks).
Sermons and devotional writings of Hopkins. Ed C. Devlin, Oxford 1959.
Poems (Oxford Authors). Ed C. Phillips, Oxford 1986.
Poetical works. Ed N. H. MacKenzie, Oxford 1990.

Selections

Selections from the notebooks. Ed T. Weiss, New York 1945.
Selected poems. Ed J. Reeves 1953.
A Hopkins reader. Ed J. Pick 1953. Prose and verse.
A selection of poems and prose. Ed W. H. Gardner 1953 (Pen), 1966 (rev and enlarged).
Selected poems chosen by F. Meynell. 1954 (Nonesuch).
Selected poems and prose. Ed G. Storey, Oxford 1967.
All my eyes see; the visual word of Hopkins (contains many of his drawings). Ed R. K. R. Thornton, Sunderland 1975.
Selected prose. Ed G. Roberts, Oxford 1980.

Translations of Hopkins

Fr trns by E. Roditi (4 poems) and G. Landier (selected letters), Mesures *(Paris) Jan 1935;* Poems and prose, *Paris 1957, and* The wreck of the Deutschland, *Paris 1964, both tr P. Leyris; tr Ger by M. Brauns,* Der Dichtr Hopkins, *1946; I. Behn, 1948; W. and U. Clemen,* Hopkins: Gedichte, Schriften, Briefe, *1954; tr Ital by A. Guidi (*The wreck of the Deutschland and The loss of the Eurydice*), 1947, 1948, 1952; tr Hungarian, B. Inecs (3 poems),* Az angol irodalun Kincseshaza, *ed G. Halász [1942]; 4 poems in* Angol Köttak antológiája, *ed M. Vajda 1960; Sp, Fr and Ital trns of some poems in J. M. G. Mora,* Hopkinsiana, *Huatabampo, Mexico 1954.*

§1

For single poems, trns and extracts from his journal, priv ptd or in miscellanies, see N. Weyand, Chronological bibliography, *above.*
Winter with the Gulf Stream. Once a Week 14 Feb 1863.
Barnfloor and winepress. Union Rev 3 1865.
Songs from Shakespeare in Latin: 'Full fathom five thy father lies'. Irish Monthly Nov 1886; 'Come unto these yellow sands', Feb 1887.
In Poets and poetry of the century, ed A. H. Miles, vol 8 [1893]. Includes texts and extracts of 11 poems, with introd by R. Bridges.
Lyra sacra. Ed H. C. Beeching 1895. Includes 5 poems.
Rosa mystica. Irish Monthly May 1898.
Carmina Mariana. Ed O. Shipley 1902. Includes 2 poems.
The spirit of man. Ed R. Bridges 1916. Includes texts and extracts of 6 poems.
A vision of the mermaids: facsimile edition of full text dated Christmas 1862. Oxford 1929.
Early poems and extracts from the notebooks and papers. [Ed H. House] Criterion 15 1935.
Jesu dulcis memoria. Month Oct 1947. Trn by Hopkins.
St Thecla (an unpublished poem). Studies 45 1956.

Letters and papers

Letters of Hopkins to Robert Bridges; Correspondence of Hopkins and Richard Watson Dixon. Ed C. C. Abbott 2 vols Oxford 1935.
A curious halo. Nature 16 Nov 1882; Shadow-beams in the east at sunset, 15 Nov 1883; The remarkable sunsets, 3 Jan 1884. Letters on unusual sunsets, rptd in Correspondence of Hopkins and Dixon, *above.*
Arnold, T. A manual of English literature. 1885 (5th edn). Includes a

notice of R. W. Dixon by Hopkins, rptd in Correspondence of Hopkins and Dixon, *above*.

Further letters of Hopkins. Ed C. C. Abbott, Oxford 1938, 1956 (rev and enlarged). Letters to and from Coventry Patmore et al.

Note-books and papers of Hopkins. Ed H. House, Oxford 1937; 2nd edn rev and enlarged in 2 vols as:

Journals and papers of Hopkins. Ed H. House, completed by G. Storey, Oxford 1959. Includes appendices on his drawings (J. Piper), music (J. E. Stevens), and philological notes (A. Ward).

Unpublished journal of Hopkins [extracts from 1866–8]. Month Dec 1950.

Storey, G. (ed). Six new letters of Hopkins [to his father and Katharine Tynan]. Month May 1958.

Thomas, A. Hopkins the Jesuit: the years of training. 1969. Contains unpbd jnl.

Seven uncollected and four new letters of Hopkins (to the Bishop of Liverpool, Nature, Dr Michael F. Cox, Dr Muncke, Everard Hopkins, William Butterfield and W. A. Comyn Macfarlane). Hopkins Research Bull 1971–5.

Unpublished lecture, 'On Duty' (Dublin Note-book p. 32). Hopkins Research Bull 1976, pp. 3–6.

Selected letters. Ed C. Phillips, Oxford 1990.

§2

Bridges, R. The poets and the poetry of the century. 1893.

Macleod, Fr J. The diary of a devoted student of nature. Letters and Notices Apr 1906.

Brégy, K. Hopkins. Catholic World Jan 1909; rptd in her Poet's chantry, 1912.

Keating, J. Impressions of Fr Hopkins. Month July–Sep 1909.

Kilner, J. The poetry of Hopkins. Poetry Sep 1914; rptd in her Circus and other essays, New York 1921.

Unsigned review of The spirit of man. New York Times Rev of Books Mar 1916.

Young, E. Brett. The poetry of G. Hopkins. Today Jan 1918.

Harting, E. M. Hopkins and Digby Dolben. Month Apr 1919.

'Plures'. Hopkins: his character. Dublin Rev 167 1920.

For contemporary and later criticism, see Gerard Manley Hopkins: the critical heritage, *ed G. Roberts, 1987.*

Biographies

Martin, R. B. Hopkins: a very private life. 1991.

White, N. Hopkins: a literary biography. Oxford 1992. [GS]

Nora Hopper, later Chesson 1871–1906

Ballads in prose. 1894.

Under quicken boughs. 1896.

Songs of the morning. 1900.

Aquamarines. 1902.

Mildred and her mills, and other poems. [1903].

The bell and the arrow: an English love story. 1905.

Selected poems. 5 vols 1906.

Father Felix's chronicles. '1907' [1906]. A novel.

Alfred Edward Housman 1859–1936

The Library of Congress Washington DC has the substantial remains of the ms notebooks Housman used for composing, correcting and polishing from c. 1890, together with a number of fair copies. The library of Trinity College Cambridge has the ms printer's copy (lacking no XXXV) of A Shropshire lad, *and the Fitzwilliam Museum has the ms copy of* Last poems *from which the printer's copy was typed, lacking nos III, XV, XVII, XVIII and XXI. The Lilly collection of Indiana Univ includes mss, letters, juvenilia, light verse and some fair copies. The BL has a number of fair copies and Housman's diary for 1888-90 and some diary material for 1891 and 1898. There are significant numbers of Housman's letters at the BL, the Library of Congress and the libraries of Harvard Univ, Univ of Illinois, Indiana Univ (Lilly Library), Trinity College Cambridge, University College London. Colby College Waterville ME possesses Carl J. Weber's collection of more than 60 edns of* A Shropshire lad.

Bibliographies etc

Gow, A. S. F. List of Housman's writings. In his Housman: a sketch, Cambridge 1936.

Hyder, C. K. A. A concordance to the poems of Housman. Lawrence KS 1940, rptd Gloucester MA 1966.

Ehrsam, T. G. A bibliography of Housman. Boston 1941.

Stallman, R. W. Annotated bibliography of Housman: a critical study. PMLA 60, 1945.

Carter, J. and J. Sparrow. Housman: an annotated handlist. 1952. Rptd from Library 4th ser 21, 1940.

Takeuchi, Y. The exhaustive concordance to the poems of A. E. Housman. Tokyo 1971.

Carter, J. and J. Sparrow. A. E. Housman: a bibliography. 1982. 2nd edn of Housman, 1952, *above*, rev and substantially enlarged by W. White.

Collections and selections

Collected poems. Ed J. Carter 1939, New York 1940, London 1953 (14th impr corrected), 1960 (rev with note on text by J. Carter), New York 1965 (ed J. Carter), London 1971 (declared by W. White 1982 to be 'an error-free printing').

Collected poems. Ed J. Sparrow 1956 (Pen), 1961, 1995.

Selected poems. New York (Edns for the Armed Services). Lib of Congress gives 1940 as the date of its 2 copies; W. White 1982 conjectures 1942.

Complete poems. Ed T. B. Haber, introd by B. Davenport, New York 1959 (Centennial edn). W. White (1982) states that after at least 3 printings this edn was withdrawn as unauthorised and that since the 1960s the Amer edn has followed that pbd London by Cape.

Selected prose. Ed J. Carter, Cambridge 1961, 1962 (corrected).

Collected poems and selected prose. Ed with introd and notes by C. Ricks 1988, 1989 (Pen).

Unkind to unicorns: comic verse of A. E. Housman. Ed J. Roy Birch, illustr D. Harris, Cambridge 1995.

The poems of A. E. Housman. Ed A. Burnett. Oxford 1997.

§1

Introductory lecture delivered in University College London. Cambridge 1892 (priv ptd), 1933 (priv ptd with 1 correction), 1937. Tr Greek, Oxford 1938 (V. Turner).

A Shropshire lad. 1896, New York 1897, London 1898 (1st Grant Richards edn), 1900 (3rd Grant Richards edn, described by Housman in a letter to Richards of 12 Oct 1902 as 'almost exactly correct'), 1908 (8 colour illustrations by W. Hyde), New York 1922 (authorised U.S. edn), London 1940 (wood-engravings by A. M. Parker), ed C. J. Weber, Waterville ME 1946 (with bibliography) (Jubilee edn), London, 1994 (facs of 1896 edn) (Woodstock Bks). Many other edns in England and USA. Poems. Tr Latin, Oxford 1929 (C. Asquith), Welsh, Denbigh 1939 (J. T. Jones), Danish, Copenhagen 1944 (P. P. M. Pedersen, incl 24 lyrics from A Shropshire lad and Last poems).

REVIEWS: (Ward, T. H.) The Times, 27 Mar 1896; (Bland, H.) New Age, 16 Apr 1896; (Nicoll, W. R.) Br Weekly, 23 Apr 1896; (Gale, N) Acad 11 July 1896; (Guiney, L. I.) Chap-Book (Chicago), 1 Feb 1897; (Archer, W.) Fortnightly Rev 64, 1 Aug 1898; Acad, 8 Oct 1898, Athenaeum 8 Oct 1898; Lit, 29 Oct 1898; Sat Rev (London), 5 Nov 1898.

Last poems. 1922, New York 1922 (set from uncorrected Eng proof; has original setting of pp. 55, 79 and the correct punctuation p. 52), New York 1924, London 1928 (Richards Press, reset and rptd), Chipping Campden 1929, New York 1931 (11th printing). Many other edns.

REVIEWS: TLS, 19 Oct 1922; (Gosse, E.) Sunday Times, 22 Oct 1922; (Squire, J. C.) London Mercury 7, Nov 1922; (Williams-Ellis, A.) Spectator 4, Nov 1922; (Freeman, J.) Bookman (London) 63, Dec 1922; (Priestley, J. B.) London Mercury 7, Dec 1922; (Benét, W. R.) Bookman (New York) 57, Mar 1923; (Firkins, O.W.) Yale Rev 12, July 1923; (Sapir, E.) Dial 75, Aug 1923; (Lucas, F. L.) New Statesman and Nation, 20 Oct 1923.

Fragment of a Greek tragedy. Amherst MA 1925 (priv ptd, 92 copies). 1st pbd Bromsgrovian 2, 8 June 1883, rptd Univ College Gazette 1897; Cornhill Mag, Apr 1901; Trinity Mag 2, Feb 1921. Parody.

Preface to Nine essays by Arthur Platt. Cambridge 1927.

The name and nature of poetry. Cambridge 1933, New York 1933; rptd Cambridge 1937, 1939, 1945, New York 1936, 1939, 1989 (with 'other selected prose'). (Leslie Stephen Lecture, Univ of Cambridge. Tr Sp Mexico City [1945] (O. G. Barreda); Ital, Pistoia 1958 (R. Anzilotti; appendix to his La poesía di A. E. Housman).

Three poems: the parallelogram, the amphisbaena, the crocodile. Univ College London 1935 (priv ptd, 55 copies); ed W. White, Los Angeles 1941; 1st pbd respectively Union Mag of Univ College London 1, Dec. 1904; 2, June 1906; 5, Mar 1911.

More poems. Ed L. Housman 1936. New York 1936 (text not identical with London edn).

Memorial suppl to Bromsgrovian. Bromsgrove 1936 (Nov). Contains some early verse not hitherto rptd.

Additional poems. In L. Housman, A. E. H.: some poems, some letters and a personal memoir, 1937. Nos 1–18 of the 'additional poems' rptd in Collected poems, 1939, *above*.

Alfred Edward Housman: recollections. New York 1937. Text as Memorial suppl 1936 (*above*) with addns and corrections.

A morning with the Royal Family. Los Angeles 1941 (illus), London 1955 (priv ptd by Cape). 1st pbd Bromsgrovian 1, 15 Feb 1882; 1, 29 Mar 1882. Prose.

The manuscript poems of A. E. Housman. Ed from Housman's note-books by T. B. Haber. London and Minneapolis MN 1955.

The confines of criticism. Cambridge 1969. Complete text, with notes by J. Carter, of Housman's 1911 Cambridge inaugural lecture. 1st pbd, slightly incomplete, TLS, 9 May 1968. Title is not Housman's.

Contributions to periodicals

The death of Socrates. Bromsgrove, Droitwich and Redditch Weekly Messenger, 8 Aug 1874, rptd with commentary in W. White, The death of Socrates: Housman's first published poem, PMLA 68, 1953.

Sir Walter Raleigh (1873) In W. White, Un poème inédit de Housman: Sir Walter Raleigh, Etudes Anglaises 6, 1953.

Such few other poems as Housman published in periodicals were rptd in his various collections, except for those in Ye Rounde Table *(Oxford), 1878 (see Haber, 1967, §2).*

Letters

Housman, L. In his A. E. H.: some poems, some letters and a personal memoir, 1937.

Martin, H. With letters from Housman. Yale Rev 26, 1936.

Richards, G. In his Housman 1897–1936, Oxford 1941.

Letters from Housman to E. H. Blakeney. Winchester 1941 (priv ptd by Blakeney, 18 copies).

White, W. More Housman letters. Mark Twain Quart 5, 1943.

Clemens, C. Some unpublished Housman letters. Poet Lore 57, 1947.

White, W. Fifteen unpublished letters by Housman. Dalhousie Rev 29, 1950.

White, W. Published letters of A. E. Housman: a survey. BB 22, 1957.

Thirty Housman letters to Witter Bynner. Ed T. B. Haber, New York 1957.

White, W. A. E. Housman to Joseph Ishill: five unpublished letters. Berkeley Heights NJ 1959 (priv ptd).

Haber, T. B. Three unreported letters of Housman. PBSA 57, 1963.

Maas, H. The letters of A. E. Housman. 1971.

Fifteen letters from Housman to Walter Ashburner. Ed. A. Bell, Edinburgh 1976

Attributed work

Two cities. Hampstead 1904. Prose.

This item not listed by W. White 1982, nor by BL catalogue. It appears in National Union Catalogue, *thus:* '[Alfred Edward Housman] Two cities. Printed and published for the author at the Asphodel Press, XVIII Well Walk, Hampstead, the twelfth day of June 1904. 16pp.' *The 2 cities are Edessa and Merv. W. White in* Two problems *in* A. E. Housman bibliography, PBSA 45, 1951, *referred to* Two cities, *which he described as being of 14 pp. with 2 woodcuts, as 'an example of the 1st problem' (i.e. 'the inclusion of spurious [...] items'). White added 'This prose tale has appeared at least twice in catalogues, under the name of A. E. Housman, but there is absolutely no other evidence that he is the author [...] I should therefore be interested to receive evidence to support its authenticity.' No evidence was forthcoming in PBSA for 1952–4; none of White's subsequent contributions to PBSA, 1954–66, refer to the matter.*

Imitations (parodies)

Hugh Kingsmill. The table of truth. 1933. Contains (pp. 116–17) 'Two poems: after A. E. Housman' (the 1st of which was in Housman's view the best parody of him) and 'In a charabanc (Robert Browning's version of A. E. Housman's 'Bredon Hill')'.

Terence Beersay (pseud.) A Shropshire lag. 1936 (99 copies). 7 parodies of Housman.

Stephen L. Robertson (pseud.) The Shropshire racket. 1937 (illustr T. Derrick). 20 parodies of Housman.

§2

Sorley, C. In The letters of Charles Sorley, Cambridge 1919. Paper, c. 1913 on A Shropshire lad.

Flecker, J. E. The new poetry and Mr Housman's Shropshire lad. In his Collected prose, 1922. Unfinished (pre-1915), essay.

Jackson, H. The poetry of A. E. Housman. Today 5 1919.

Monro, H. Section 1, pt 3, Some contemporary poets, 1920.

Symons, K. E. Memories of A. E. H. Edwardian 17, Sep 1936. More memories of A. E. H. Ibid 17, Dec 1936. Recollections by Housman's sister.

Tillotson, G. The publication of Housman's comic poems English 1, 1937, rptd in his Essays in criticism and research, Cambridge 1942.

Clemens, C. An evening with A. E. Housman. Webster Groves MO 1937.

Gow, A. S. F. A. E. Housman: a sketch. Cambridge 1936.

Housman, L. A. E. H.: Some poems, some letters and a personal memoir. 1937. New York 1938 (as My brother, A. E. Housman).

Withers, P. A buried life: personal recollections of A. E. Housman. 1940.

Richards, G. Housman 1897–1936. Oxford 1941.

A Shropshire lad bibliography. TLS, 30 Mar 1946.

White, W. A Shropshire lad in process: the textual evolution of some A. E. Housman poems. Library 5th ser 9, 1954.

Sparrow, J. Review of Haber, The manuscript poems of A. E. Housman (1955), TLS, 29 Apr 1955.

Carter, J. The Housman mss in the Library of Congress. Bk Collector 4, 1955.

Carter, J. The text of Housman's poems. TLS, 15 June 1956.

Carter, J. Housman's contributions to an Oxford magazine. Bk Collector 6, 1957.

Watson, G. L. A. E. Housman: a divided life. 1957.

Haber, T. B. The making of A Shropshire lad: a manuscript variorum. Seattle and London 1960.

Haber, T. B. Housman's notebooks and his posthumous poetry. Iowa Eng Yearbook 8, 1963.

Haber, T. B. Three unreported letters of Housman. PBSA 57, 1963.

Haber, T. B. A. E. Housman. New York 1967. Reprints some of Housman's contributions to Ye Rounde Table (1878).
Housman, L. A. E. Housman's De amicitia. Encounter, 29 Oct 1967. Annotated by J. Carter.
Pugh, J. Bromsgrove and the Housmans. Bromsgrove 1974. Prints the poem Iona.
Graves, R. P. A. E. Housman: the scholar-poet. Oxford 1979.
Page, N. A. E. Housman: a critical biography. 1983.
Gardner, P. (ed). A. E. Housman: the critical heritage. 1992.
Much of interest and value is to be found in the various issues of the Housman Soc Jnl (1974 on). [PG]

Laurence Housman 1865–1959

Bibliographies

Housman, L. Book list. In his Back words and fore words, 1945.

Collections

Selected poems. 1908.
Little plays of St Francis. 3 vols 1935. Complete edn.
Collected poems. 1937.
The golden sovereign. 1937. Collection of plays.
Happy and glorious: a dramatic biography. 1945. Selection of Queen Victoria plays.
Back words and fore words: an author's year-book 1893–1945: a selection in chronological order from the plays, poems and prose writings. 1945.

§1

A farm in fairyland. 1894.
The house of joy. [1895.] Fairy tales.
Green arras. 1895. Poems.
All-fellows: seven legends of lower redemption, with insets in verse. 1896.
God and their makers. 1897.
The field of clover. 1898. Tales.
Spikenard: a book of devotional love-poems. 1898.
The story of the seven young goslings. [1899.]
Rue. 1899. Poems.
The little land, with songs from its four rivers. 1899.
An Englishwoman's love-letters. 1900.
The love concealed. 1928.
Four plays of St Clare. 1934.
Victoria Regina: a dramatic biography. 1934.
The unexpected years. 1937, New York [1936]. Autobiography.
A. E. H.: some poems, some letters and a personal memoir. 1937.
Hop-o'-me-heart: a grown-up fairy tale. Flansham 1938.
What next? Provocative tales of faith and morals. 1938.
The preparation of peace. 1940.
Gracious majesty. 1941.
Palestine plays. 1942.
Samuel the king-maker: a play in four acts. 1944.
Cynthia. 1947. Poems.
Strange ends and discoveries: tales of this world and the next. 1948.
Old Testament plays. 1950.
The family honour: a comedy in four acts. 1950.
The kind and the foolish: short tales of myth, magic and miracle. 1952.
Housman pbd more plays, dramatic dialogues, poems, fairy tales etc. See also under A. E. Housman, col 753 above.

§2

Archer, W. In his Poets of the younger generation, 1902.

Douglas Hyde 1860–1949

Bibliographies

O'Hegarty, P. A bibliography of Dr Douglas Hyde. Dublin 1939.

§1

Beside the fire: a collection of Irish Gaelic folk stories. 1890, Dublin 1978. Ed Hyde.
The love songs of Connacht. London and Dublin 1893, 1895, Dundrum 1904, Dublin 1963, Shannon 1969, Dublin 1987. Tr and ed Hyde.
The revival of Irish literature: addresses by Hyde and others. 1894.
The last three centuries of Gaelic literature. Dublin 1894.
The three sorrows of story-telling and Ballads of St Columkille. 1895.
The story of early Gaelic literature. 1895.
A literary history of Ireland from the earliest times to the present day. 1899, New York 1899, London 1903, 1906, 1967 (new edn).
The poorhouse. Dublin 1900. With Lady Gregory.
The twisting of the rope, translated from Irish by Lady Gregory. Dublin nd.
Irish poetry: an essay in Irish with translation in English. Dublin 1902.
Songs ascribed to [Anthony] Raftery. 1903, Shannon 1973. Collected and tr Hyde.
The religious songs of Connacht. 2 vols Dublin 1906, facs 1972. Ed Hyde.
Beside the fire: a collection of Irish Gaelic folk stories. 1910.
Legends of saints and sinners, collected and translated by Hyde. [1916.]
Mayo stories told by Thomas Casey, collected, edited and translated by Hyde. Dublin 1939.
Poems from the Irish. Dublin 1963. Introd by M. Gibbon.
Poets and dreamers. 1974. Includes 9 plays by Hyde.

§2

Cary, E. Hyde, a Gaelic poet and dreamer. Lamp 28 1904.
Coffey, D. Douglas Hyde. Dublin 1917.
Weygandt, C. Hyde and his Songs of Connacht. In his Tuesdays at ten, Philadelphia 1928.
Coffey, D. Hyde, president of Ireland. Dublin 1938.
Madden, R. Hyde, saviour of Gaelic Ireland. Catholic World 1938.
Stewart, H. Hyde: the first president of Eire. Dalhousie Rev 18 1938.
Lennon, M. Douglas Hyde. Bell 16 1951.

Selwyn Image 1849–1930

Collections

Image's letters were pbd 1932; he has also pbd lectures and introds.

§1

Poems and carols. 1894; rptd with Diversi Colores, by Herbert Horne, Oxford and New York 1994.
New poems. 1908.
[Collected] poems. Ed A. H. Mackmurdo 1932.
A literary history of Ireland. 1967, 1980.
Language, love and lyrics, essays and lectures. Ed B. O'Conaire, Dublin 1986.
Selected plays. Ed G. W. and J. E. Dunleavy, Gerrards Cross 1991.

§2

Miles, A. H. Image. In Miles 10 (12).
Obit: The Times 22 Aug 1930.

Lionel Pigot Johnson 1867–1902

Bibliographies

Three decadent poets: Ernest Dowson, John Gray and Lionel Johnson: an annotated bibliography. Ed G. A. Cevasco. New York 1990.

Collections

Twenty-one poems, selected by W. B. Yeats. Dundrum 1904, 1908 (enlarged by T. B. Mosher).

Selections from the poems, including some now collected for the first time, with a prefatory memoir [by C. K. Shorter]. 1908.
Post liminium: essays and critical papers. Ed T. Whittemore 1911.
Some poems, selected with an introduction by L. I. Guiney. 1912.
Poetical works, with an introduction by Ezra Pound. 1915.
The religious poems, selected by G. F. Engelbach, with a preface by W. Meynell. 1916.
A new selection from the poems, compiled by H. V. Marrot. 1927.
[Select poems.] 1931 (Augustan Books of Modern Poetry).
Selected poems. 1934.
The complete poems. Ed I. Fletcher 1953. More than 50 uncollected poems.
In Three poets of the Rhymers' Club, ed D. Stanford, Cheadle 1974.

§1

Sir Walter Raleigh in the Tower: a prize poem. Chester [1885].
The fools of Shakespeare: an essay. In Noctes Shakesperianae, Winchester College Shakspere Soc 1887.
The book of the Rhymers' Club. 1892. Contains 6 poems by Johnson; Second book, 1894 contains 6 more.
The Gordon riots. [1893] (Catholic Truth Soc lecture).
Bits of old Chelsea. 1894. Etchings by W. W. Burgess, descriptions by Johnson and R. Le Gallienne.
The poems of Mr Bridges: a brief and general consideration. In R. S. Bridges, The growth of love, 1894.
The art of Thomas Hardy. 1894 (with bibliography by J. Lane), 1923 (with ch on Hardy's poetry by J. E. Barton).
Poems. 1895; facs reprint Oxford 1993.
Ireland with other poems. 1897.
James Clarence Mangen. In A treasury of Irish poetry, ed S. A. Brooke and T. W. Rolleston, 1900. Not the same as review from Post liminium, in Mangan's prose writings.
Poetry and Ireland: [2] essays by W. B. Yeats and Johnson. Dundrum 1908. Preliminary note by E. C. Yeats (?) is on Johnson.
Four poems or Christmas songs wherein is set forth the birth of our holy and blessed Redeemer. Cleveland 1917.
Some Winchester letters. London and New York 1919.
Reviews and critical papers. Ed R. Shafer 1921.
Ysleta: two poems. 1929.
Matthew Arnold: poetry and prose, with Sir William Watson's poem and essays by Johnson and H. W. Garrod. Ed E. K. Chambers, Oxford 1940.
Seven new poems. Ed I. Fletcher, Poetry Rev 41 1950.
Fifteen new poems. Poetry Rev 43 1952.
Some letters to Richard Le Gallienne. Edinburgh 1979.
Selected letters. Ed M. Pittock, Edinburgh 1988.

§2

Obit: Athenaeum 18 Oct 1902.
Guiney, L. I. Obituary. Atlantic Monthly Dec 1902.
Waugh, A. In his Tradition and change, 1919.
TLS 7 July 1921.
Tynan, K. In her Memories, 1924.
Weygandt, C. In his Tuesdays at ten, Philadelphia 1928.
Pinto, V. de S. Johnson: an appreciation. Wessex 2 1932.
Evans, B. I. In his English poetry in the later nineteenth century, 1933, 1966 (rev).
Welby, T. E. Johnson. In his Second impressions, 1933.
Shacksnovis, A. A poem by Johnson. TLS 15 Feb 1936.
Patrick, A. W. Johnson (1867–1902): poète et critique. Paris 1939.
Pick, J. Divergent disciples of Water Pater. Thought 23 1948.
Feldman, A. B. The art of Johnson. Poet-Lore 57 1953.
Palmer, H. Johnson. Spectator 17 Apr 1953.
Alexander, C. In his Catholic literary revival, Milwaukee 1955.
Fletcher, I. Johnson's The dark angel. In Interpretations: essays on twelve English poets, ed J. Wain, 1955.
Brophy, L. Laureate of the cross. Irish Digest Feb 1962.
Charlesworth, B. The gray world of Johnson. Carrell (Miami) 4 1963.
Fletcher, I. Amendments and additions to The complete poems of Lionel Johnson, 1953. Victorian Newsletter 33 1968.

Ellen Johnston 'The Factory Girl' 1835–73

§1

Autobiography, poems and songs. Glasgow 1861, 1867 (2nd edn rev).

Harriet Eleanor Hamilton King 1840–1920

Selections

Miles 7 (9).

§1

Aspromonte and other poems. 1869, 1871 (2nd edn).
The disciples. 1873, 1877 (3rd edn) 1889 (11th edn).
A book of dreams. 1883.
Ballads of the north and other poems. 1889.
The prophecy of Westminster and other poems: in honour of Henry Edward, Cardinal Manning. 1895.
The hours of passion. 1902.
Letters and recollections of Mazzini. Ed G. M. Trevelyan 1912.

§2

Robertson, E. S. In his English poetesses, 1883.
Hickey, E. H. Hamilton King. In Miles 7 (9).
Hickey, E. H. Two Catholic poetesses. Dublin Rev Jan 1921.

Rudyard Kipling 1865–1936

See col 1604.

Andrew Lang 1844–1912

See col 2362.

William Larminie 1849–1900

§1

Glanuluala and other poems. 1889.
Fand and other poems. Dublin 1892.
West Irish folk-tales and romances. 1893, 1898, [1972]. Collected and tr Larminie.
Legends as material for literature. In J. Eglinton et al, Literary ideals in Ireland, [1899].

§2

'Eglinton, John' (W. K. Magee). William Larminie. Dublin Mag 19 1944.
O'Meara, J. William Larminie 1849–1900. Studies 36 1947.

Francis Burdett Thomas Coutts-Nevill, 5th Baron Latymer 1852–1923

Selections

Selected poems. 1923.

§1

The girls of England: a battle call. [1882.]
The training of the instinct of love, with a preface by E. Thring. 1885.
Two heirs presumptive: a tale. 1894.
Poems. London and New York 1896. Includes An essay in a brief model.
The Alhambra and other poems. London and New York 1898.
The revelation of St Love the Divine: a poem. London and New York 1898.
The mystery of godliness. London and New York 1900.

The nut brown maid. 1901. New version of the old ballad.
The poet's charter, or the book of Job. London and New York 1903.
Musa verticordia. London and New York 1905.
The song of songs: a lyrical folk-play of the ancient Hebrews arranged in VII scenes. London and New York 1906.
The heresy of Job. London and New York 1907. With Blake's engravings.
The romance of King Arthur. London and New York 1907. Uther Pendragon: a poem, Merlin: a play, Launcelot du Lake: a drama, The death of Launcelot: a poem.
Egypt and other poems. London and New York 1912.
Psyche: a poem. London and New York 1912.
A ballad of the war. 1915. Rptd from English Rev June 1915.
The royal marines. 1915.
Ventures in thought. London and New York 1915. Essays.
Icarian flights: translations (in verse) of some of the Odes of Horace. London and New York 1920. With W. H. Pollock.
The spacious times, and others. London and New York 1920. Poems.
Well. 1922. A Yorkshire village, with F. Redmayne.
Latymer also ed Flowers of Parnassus. *27 vols 1900–6.*

§2

Archer, W. In his Poets of the younger generation, 1902.
Obit. The Times 9 June 1923.

Emily Lawless 1845–1913

Collections

The poems of Emily Lawless. Ed P. Fallon, Dublin 1965.

§1

A Chelsea householder. 3 vols 1882, New York 1883. Novel.
A millionaire's cousin. 1885. Novel.
Hurrish: a study. 1886, Edinburgh and London 1887, 1902, London 1902, [1913]; facs London and New York 1979, Belfast 1992. Novel.
Major Lawrence, FLS. 3 vols 1887, 1888. Novel.
Ireland, with additions by A. Bronson. 1887, New York 1888 (as The story of Ireland), 1908, London 1912 (rev and enlarged).
Plain Frances Mowbray and other tales. 1889.
With Essex in Ireland: being extracts from a diary kept in Ireland during the year 1599 by Mr Henry Harvey. New York 1890, London 1902; facs London and New York 1979. An historical novel, with contribution by E. Lawless.
Grania: the story of an island. 1892, 1892 (2 vols), New York 1892; facs London and New York 1979.
Maelcho: a sixteenth-century narrative. 2 vols 1894, 1902; facs London and New York 1979.
Atlantic rhymes and rhythms. By E. L. 1898 (priv ptd), rptd in With the wild geese, *below.*
Traits and confidences. 1898; facs London and New York 1979. Stories and sketches.
A garden diary: September 1899–September 1900. 1901.
With the wild geese. 1902. Introd by S. Brooke.
Maria Edgeworth. 1904, New York 1904 (EML).
The book of Gilly: four months out of a life. 1906. A novel.
The point of view: some talks and disputations. 1909 (priv ptd).
The race of Castlebar: a narrative. 1913. With Shan F. Bullock.
The inalienable heritage, and other poems. 1914.

Eugene Jacob Lee-Hamilton 1845–1907

Bibliographies

Lyon, H. T. A publishing history of the writings of Lee-Hamilton. PBSA 51 1957.

Selections

Dramatic sonnets, poems and ballads: selections from the poems. Ed W. Sharp [1903] (Canterbury Poets).

§1

Poems and transcripts. 1878.
Gods, saints and men. 1880.
The new Medusa and other poems. 1884.
Apollo and Marsyas and other poems. 1884.
Imaginary sonnets. 1888.
The fountain of youth: a fantastic tragedy in five acts. 1891. Verse.
Sonnets of the wingless hours. 1894.
The inferno of Dante. 1898. Trn.
Forest notes. 1899. With Mrs Lee-Hamilton.
The lord of the dark red star: being the story of the supernatural influences in the life of an Italian despot of the thirteenth century. London and Newcastle-on-Tyne. 1903. Fiction.
The romance of the fountain. 1905. Fiction.
Mimma bella, with a preface by A. E. Lee-Hamilton. Portland ME 1908, London 1909.

§2

Symonds, J. A. Lee-Hamilton. In Miles 8 (7).
Obit: The Times 11 Sep 1907.
Evans, B. I. In his English poetry in the later nineteenth century, 1933, 1966 (rev).
[Weber, C. J.] From Florence to Colby by way of Kansas. Colby Lib Quart 3 1954.
MacBeth, G. Lee-Hamilton and the romantic agony. Crit Q 4 1962.
Pantazzi, S. Lee-Hamilton. PBSA 57 1963.

Edward Cracroft Lefroy 1855–91

Bibliographies

Smith, T. D'A. Some uncollected authors 30: Lefroy. BC 10 1961.

Selections

Lefroy: his life and poems. Ed W. A. Gill, with critical estimate of sonnets by J. A. Symonds, 1897. Selected poems and 30 new sonnets.

§1

Undergraduate Oxford. Oxford 1878. Rptd from Oxford & Cambridge Undergraduates' Jnl 1876–7.
Cutisus and galingale: a series of sonnets. Blackheath [1883].
Echoes from Theocritus: a cycle of sonnets. Blackheath [1883], London 1885, 1922 (with introd by J. A. Symonds).
Sketches and studies, and other sonnets. By the author of Echoes from Theocritus. Blackheath [1884].
Lefroy also pbd sermons and addresses.

§2

Miles, A. H. Lefroy. In Miles 8 (7).

Richard Le Gallienne 1866–1947

See col 1622.

Amy Levy 1861–89

Mss: Some letters at Colby College Lib, ME; others priv owned.

Bibliographies

See M. New below.

Collections

New, M. (ed). The complete novels and selected writings of Amy Levy, 1861–89. [Reprints selected poems and from periodicals, short fiction and essays. Includes Chronology of selected writings.] Gainesville FL 1993.

§1

Xantippe and other verse. Cambridge, 1881.
REVIEW: Acad 20, 10 Sep 1881.

A minor poet. 1884, 1891 (2nd edn with portrait and additional poems rptd from Xantippe and other verse), Boston 1901.
REVIEW: Acad 26, 5 July 1884.
Reuben Sachs. A sketch. 1888, London and New York 1888, 1889, New York 1979 (AMS Press); tr Ger (by Eleanor Marx) 1889, Gr 1896.
REVIEWS: Athenaeum 26 Jan 1889; Spectator 62, 16 Feb 1889.
The romance of a shop. 1888, Boston 1889.
REVIEW: Athenaeum 27 Oct 1888.
Miss Meredith: a tale. 1889. First serialised in Br Weekly Apr–June 1889. Montreal nd.
REVIEW: Athenaeum 14 Dec 1889.
A London plane-tree and other verse. 1889, New York 1890, 1891.
REVIEWS: Athenaeum 14 Dec 1889; Acad 37, 1 Feb 1890.
The unhappy princess. An extravaganza for little people. In Fairy plays for home performance no 21, [1894, etc].
A ballad of religion and marriage. [c. 1915] (priv ptd, 12 copies).

Contributions to periodicals

Listed below are items not included in Wellesley.
Euphemia: a sketch. Victoria Mag 36 Aug–Sep 1880.
Newnham College. Alexandra Mar 1881.
James Thomson [B. V.]: a minor poet. Cambridge Rev Feb 1883.
The diary of a plain girl. London Soc 44 1883.
Olga's Valentina, London Soc 45 1884.
Sokratics in the Strand. Cambridge Rev Feb 1884.
In the Black Forest. London Soc 46 1884.
In holiday humour. London Soc 46 1884.
In retreat. London Soc 46 1884.
Easter-tide at Tunbridge Wells. London Soc 47 1885.
Revenge. London Soc 47 1885.
Another morning in Florence. London Soc 48 1886.
Out of the world. London Soc 48 1886.
The Ghetto at Florence. Jewish Chron Mar 1886.
The Jew in fiction. Jewish Chron June 1886.
Jewish humour. Jewish Chron Aug 1886.
Lost and won. Lawn-Tennis Aug 1886.
Middle-class Jewish women of to-day. Jewish Chron Sep 1886.
A meadowshire romance (in four parts). Lawn-Tennis Aug–Sep 1886.
Jewish children. Jewish Chron Nov 1886.
At Prato. Time 19 1888.
The poetry of Christina Rossetti. Woman's World 1 1888.
The recent telepathic occurrence at the British Museum. Woman's World 1 1888.
Women and club life. Woman's World 1 1888.
Cohen of Trinity. GM 266 1889.
Eldorado at Islington. Woman's World 2 1889.
Addenbrooke. Belgravia Mar 1889.
Wise in her generation. Woman's World 3 1890.

Translations

The shepherd (from Goethe). Cambridge Rev June 1880.
From Grillparzer's Sappho. Cambridge Rev Feb 1882.
From Heine (My heart, my heart is heavy). Cambridge Rev Apr 1882.
Peres, J. B. Historic and other doubts; or, the non-existence of Napoleon proved. [1885.] (By Lily.)
Jehudah Halevi (extracts from the Ger of Geiger) and one poem from Heinrich Heine. In Kate, Lady Magnus, Jewish portraits, 1888.

§2

Chambers, E. K. Poetry and pessimism. Westminster Rev 138 1892.
Lask, Beth Zion. In Trans of the Jewish Historical Soc of England 11 1928.
Wagenknecht, Edward. In Daughters of the Covenant: portraits of six Jewish women, Amherst 1983 (Univ of Massachusetts Press).
Obits: Jewish Chron 13 Sep 1889; Acad 36, 21 Sep 1889; Woman's World 3 1890 (by Oscar Wilde).
New, M. 1993. *See above*. [VB]

Caroline Blanche Elizabeth, Lady Lindsay

1844–1912

Selections

Selected poems. 1907.

§1

Runa: a sketch. [c. 1875.] Drama.
A weak plot: a comedietta. [c. 1875.]
Lisa's love. Moxon's selected novelettes no 5. [1880.]
Some recollections of Miss Margaret Gillies. [1887.] Rptd from Temple Bar Oct 1887.
Caroline. 1888. Novel.
About robins: songs, facts and legends, collected and illustrated by Lady Lindsay. [1889.]
Lyrics and other poems. 1890, 1890 (2nd edn).
Bertha's earl. 3 vols 1891. Novel.
The philosopher's window and other stories. 1892.
A string of beads: verse for children. Edinburgh and London 1892.
A tangled web. 2 vols 1892, 1 vol 1893. Novel.
Dora's defiance. Philadelphia 1894.
The king's last vigil and other poems. 1894, 1895 (2nd edn).
Forget-me-not: a play. [c. 1895.]
Three girls: a comedietta. 1895.
The flower-seller and other poems. 1896.
Original plays by B. L. nd [c. 1896] (priv ptd). Collects Runa, A weak plot, Forget-me-not and Three girls.
The Christmas of the sorrowful. [1898], 7th thousand [1898]. Poems.
The apostle of the Ardennes. 1899. Poems.
The art of poetry with regard to women writers: a paper read at the literature meeting of the Women's International Congress ... on Wednesday, June 28th 1899. [1899.]
For England. [1900.] Poems.
Kitty's garland. 1900. Poems.
The prayer of St Scholastica, and other poems. 1900, 1901 (3rd edn), Boston 1901.
A Christmas posy of carols, songs and other pieces. 1902.
From a Venetian balcony, and other poems of Venice and the near lands. 1903.
Godfrey's quest: a fantastic poem. 1905.
Lays and lyrics. Venice 1907.
Poems of love and death. 1907.
From a Venetian calle. 1908. Poems.
Within hospital walls. 1910. Poems.
Lindsay contributed articles to New Rev. *See* Wellesley *vol 5 1989*.

Sir Alfred Comyns Lyall 1835–1911

§1

Asiatic studies, religious and social. 1882, 2 vols 1899 (one essay omitted, essay on history and fable added), selections 1907.
Warren Hastings: a biography. 1889.
Verses written in India. 1889, 1896 (4th edn), [1907] (6th edn rev and enlarged as Poems).
The rise of the British dominion in India. 1893, 1910 (5th edn corrected and enlarged), New York 1963.
Tennyson. 1902 (EML).
The life of the Marquis of Dufferin and Ava. 2 vols 1905, 1909 (Nelson's Shilling Lib).
Some aspects of Asiatic history. 1910.
Studies in literature and history. Ed J. O. Miller 1915.

§2

Miles, A. H. Lyall. In Miles 5.
Prothero, G. W. Commemorative address. 1912. In Commemorative addresses of the academic committee, 1912 (Royal Soc of Lit).
Ubert, C. P. Lyall. PBA 5 1912.
Durand, H. M. The life of the Right Hon Sir Alfred Comyns Lyall. Edinburgh 1913.

Edward Robert Bulwer Lytton, 1st Earl of Lytton, 'Owen Meredith' 1831–91

Mss: poems, commonplace book, letters, dramatic works and autobiography, Herts County Record Office, Hertford.

Bibliographies

Harlan, A. B. In his Owen Meredith: a critical biography, New York 1946.

Collections

Poetical works. 2 vols 1867.
Poems. 2 vols Boston 1869.
Poems, selected and rev by the author. Copyright edn. 2 vols Leipzig 1869.
The imperial bouquet of pretty flowers. Ed E. N. A. Chick, Calcutta 1877. Selection of poems and public speeches in India, with critique on his poetry rptd from Pioneer.
Poems, selected by M. Betham-Edwards. 1890.
Selected poems, with an introd by Lady [B.] Balfour. 1894.

§1

Poems and ballads of Schiller. Tr Lytton 1844.
Leila, or the seige of Granada, and Calderon the courtier. 1853.
Clytemnestra, The Earl's return, The artist and other poems. 1855.
The wanderer. 1857, 1893 (rev, adds preface, discards pseud).
Lucile. 1860, 1893 (3rd edn, adds preface). A novel in verse.
Tannhäuser: or the battle of the bards, by Neville Temple and Edward Trevor. 1861, 1861 (3rd edn). Really by Julian Fane and Lytton.
Serbski pesme or national songs of Servia. 1861; ed G. H. Powell 1917. Free versions of Serbian songs and ballads.
The ring of Amasis, from the papers of a German physician (Dr N—). 2 vols 1863, 1890 (shortened and recast in form of a novel).
Chronicles and characters. 2 vols 1868. 'An attempt at a poetic history of the education of man'.
Orval: or the fool of time and other imitations and paraphrases. 1869. Founded on the Infernal comedy by Krazinski. Many Serbski pesme rptd.
Julian Fane: a memoir. 1871.
Memoir of Edward Lord Lytton. In Speeches of Edward Lord Lytton, 1874.
Fables in song. 2 vols Edinburgh 1874, Toronto 1874; tr Fr, Paris 1891.
King Poppy: a story without an end. 1875 (priv ptd), 1892 (rev). Anon. A narrative poem.
The life, letters and literary remains of Edward Bulwer, Lord Lytton. 2 vols 1883. On his novelist father.
Glenaveril, or the metamorphoses: a poem in six books. 2 vols 1885; tr Fr, Paris 1888.
Baldine and other tales. 2 vols 1886. Tr from the Ger of K. E. Elder.
After paradise: or legends of exile with other poems. 1887.
The ring of Amasis: a romance. 1890.
Marah. 1892. Preface by E. L. [Edith Lady Lytton].
The poem of Queen Victoria. Tr from Fr, Paris 1892.
A strange story. London and New York [c. 1895].

Letters

Personal and literary letters. Ed Lady B. Balfour 2 vols 1906.
Letters of Owen Meredith to Robert and Elizabeth Barrett Browning. Ed A. B. and J. L. Harlan, Waco TX 1937.
Letters of Edward Bulwer-Lytton, Baron Lytton, to Richard Bentley 1829–73, and of his son Lord Lytton to George Bentley 1873–87. BLR 2 1948.

§2

Obit: The Times 25–6 Nov 1891.
'Owen Meredith'. Athenaeum 28 Jan 1893.
Whyte, W. Robert Earl of Lytton. In Miles 5.
Balfour, Lady B. The history of Lord Lytton's Indian administration 1876–80. 1899.
Sadleir, M. Bulwer and his wife: a panorama 1803–36. 1931.
Strachey, G. L. The first Earl of Lytton. Independent Rev Mar 1907. Review of Personal and literary letters, rptd in his Characters and commentaries, 1933.
Lytton, Earl of. The poetry of Owen Meredith. In The eighteen-eighties, ed W. de la Mare, Cambridge 1930.
Evans, B. I. In his English poetry in the later nineteenth century, 1933, 1966 (rev).
Harlan, A. B. Not by Elizabeth Barrett Browning. PMLA 57 1942.
Harlan, A. B. Owen Meredith: a critical biography. New York 1946.

William Hurrell Mallock 1849–1923

See col 1629.

Philip Bourke Marston 1850–87

Mss: letters to D. G. Rossetti in Bodleian.

Bibliographies and reference works

Fredeman, W. E. In his Pre-Raphaelitism: a bibliocritical study, 1965.
The English poets, ed T. W. Ward, vol 5 1918 (J. Drinkwater).
Miles 8 (C. Kernahan).
Dictionary of literary biography 35, 1985 (Kelly, L. D.).

Collections and selections

Song-tide: poems and lyrics of Love's joy and sorrow. Ed W. Sharp, with memoir, 1888.
Collected poems, with biographical sketch by L. C. Moulton. 1892, Boston 1892.

§1

Song-tide and other poems. 1871, 1874, Boston 1881.
All in all: poems and sonnets. 1875.
Wind-voices. 1883, Boston 1883.
For a song's sake and other stories. Ed W. Sharp, with memoir, 1887, rptd in Song-tide, 1888.
Garden secrets. Ed L. C. Moulton, Boston 1887.
A last harvest: lyrics and sonnets from the book of love, with biographical sketch by L. C. Moulton. 1891.

§2

Swinburne, A. C. Fortnightly Rev Jan 1891.
Le Gallienne, Richard. In his Retrospective reviews vol 1, 1896.
Kernahan, C. In his Celebrities, 1923.
Osborne, C. C. Philip Bourke Marston. 1926 (priv ptd).
Evans, B. I. In his English poetry in the later nineteenth century, 1933, 1966 (rev). [WEF]

Herman Charles Merivale 1839–1906

See col 2051.

Alice Christina Gertrude Meynell, née Thompson 1847–1922

Mss located in Bryn Mawr College, PA; Dartmouth College, NH; Univ of Notre Dame, IN; HRHRC, Austin TX; Boston Athenaeum; Boston College Lib;

Colby College Lib, ME; Houghton Lib, Harvard; Princeton; Lib of Congress; Southern Illinois Univ Lib at Carbondale; Berg Collection, NYPL; Univ of Chicago Lib. See also LR.

Bibliographies

Nevinson, H. W. Alice Meynell. Eng Illus Mag Oct 1903.
Bibliographies of modern authors. Alice Meynell. London Mercury Apr 1920.
Stonehill, C. A. and H. W. In their Bibliographies of modern authors ser 2, 1925, Folcroft PA 1978, Norwood PA 1978.
Tuell, A. K. Mrs Meynell and her literary generation. New York [1925].
In Nineteenth century readers' guide to periodical literature 1890–1899, ed H. G. Cushing and A. V. Morris, 2 vols New York 1944.
Alice Meynell, 1847–1922. Catalogue of the centenary exhibition of books, manuscripts, letters and portraits, etc. 1947.
Odes of Coventry Patmore. Ed with bibliography by J. Merrell, [Sunbury-on-Thames] 1971 (facs of 1865 edn).
See also Wellesley *vol 5 1989.*

Collections

The poems of Alice Meynell. (Complete edn) 1923, New York 1923, 1924, Toronto 1923, New York 1925, 1927, London 1940 (ed F. Page), 1947, 1951, Westport CT 1979 (reprint of 1940 edn).
The poems of Alice Meynell, 1847–1923. 1947 (Centenary edn), Westminster MD 1955.

Selections

In The poets and the poetry of the century, ed A. H. Miles, 8 1891.
Ten poems, 1913–1915. Selected by F. Meynell 1915 (50 copies).
In Shorter lyrics of the twentieth century, 1900–1922, ed W. H. Davies, 1922.
In Childhood in verse and prose, ed S. Miles, Oxford 1923.
Alice Meynell. [1926] (Augustan Books of Modern Poetry).
Selected essays. 1926 (Essays of to-day and yesterday), New York 1926 (Essays of to-day and yesterday).
In The book of poetry, ed E. Markham, New York, vol 8, 1926–7.
Selected poems and prose. Ed A. A. Cook 1928.
Wayfaring. 1929 (Travellers' Lib). Essays.
Selected poems of Alice Meynell. Ed W. M[eynell] 1930, New York 1931.
Alice Meynell: prose and poetry. Centenary volume. Ed F. P[age], V. M[eynell], O. S[owerby] and F. M[eynell], introd V. Sackville-West 1947, Freeport NY 1970.
Essays. Ed F. Meynell, Westminster MD 1947.
Selected poems of Alice Meynell; newly chosen from Collected poems 1923, Preludes 1875. 1965.
The wares of Autolycus: selected literary essays of Alice Meynell. Chosen and introd by P. M. Fraser 1965.
In British poetry and prose 1870–1905, ed I. Fletcher, Oxford 1987.
In The new Oxford book of Victorian verse, ed C. Ricks, Oxford 1987.
In Victorian women poets: an anthology, ed A. Leighton and M. Reynolds, 1995.

§1

Preludes. By A. C. Thompson. With illustrations and ornaments by Elizabeth Thompson. 1875.
REVIEW: Irish Monthly 1876.
The poor sisters of Nazareth. An illustrated record of life at Nazareth House, Hammersmith. 1889.
REVIEW: Catholic World Feb 1890.
Poems. 1893 (2 edns), 1893 (50 large paper copies), 1896, Boston 1896, London 1898 (6th edn), 1900, Boston 1900, London 1903, 1911, 1917, 1921 (enlarged edn), 1922, Boston 1922, London 1927, 1944.
REVIEWS: Nat Observer 24 Dec 1892; Tablet 21 Jan 1893 (rptd in Francis Thompson's Literary criticisms, ed T. L. Connelly, New York 1948); Bookman Feb 1893; Literary World 24 Feb 1893; Spectator 11 Mar 1893; Sylvia's Jnl Mar 1893; Athenaeum 22 Apr 1893; Dial 1 Apr 1896.
The rhythm of life, and other essays. 1893 (also 1 edn of 550 copies), 1896, Boston 1896, London and New York 1905 (9th edn), London 1928 (priv ptd), Westport CT 1929 (priv ptd), Freeport NY 1970.
REVIEWS: Nat Observer 24 Dec 1892; Bookman Feb 1893; Literary World 24 Feb 1893; Spectator 11 Mar 1893; Sylvia's Jnl Mar 1893; Athenaeum 22 Apr 1893; National Rev Aug 1896; Dial 1 Nov 1896.
Unto us a Son is born. [c. 1895.] Poem.
The colour of life, and other essays on things seen and heard. 1896 (4 edns), Chicago 1896 (4 edns), London 1897 (5th edn), New York 1897 (5th & 6th edns), London 1900, 1901 (8th edn), 1904, New York 1904, London and New York 1905, London 1906 (9th edn), New York 1906 (9th edn), Freeport NY 1973.
REVIEWS: Bookman July 1896; Nat Rev Aug 1896; Spectator 29 Aug 1896; Literary World 18 Sep 1896; Athenaeum 3 Oct 1896.
Other poems. 1896 (priv ptd), New York 1896 (priv ptd).
The children. New York 1896, 1897 (3 edns), 1911, New York 1911. Essays.
REVIEWS: Woman 10 June 1896; Tablet 22 Aug 1896; Bookman Dec 1896; Woman 9 Dec 1896; Acad 12 Dec 1896; Literary World 1 Jan 1897; Spectator 30 Jan 1897; Bookman (USA) Feb 1897; Fortnightly Rev Feb 1897; Speaker 6 Mar 1897; Chap-Book 1 Apr 1897; Athenaeum 24 Apr 1897; Dial 1 June 1897; Critic 7 Aug 1897.
London impressions: etchings and pictures in photogravure by W. Hyde and essays by A. Meynell. 1898 (folio).
The spirit of place, and other essays. London and New York 1899, Boston 1899, London and New York 1905.
REVIEWS: Acad 14 Jan 1899; Athenaeum 14 Jan 1899; Bookman Feb 1899; Outlook 4 Feb 1899; Literary World 17 Feb 1899; Bookman [USA] Apr 1899; Dial 16 June 1899; New York Times 19 Aug 1899.
John Ruskin. 1900, New York 1900, Edinburgh 1901, Folcroft PA 1972.
REVIEWS: Acad 2 June 1900; Literature 2 June 1900; Literary World 6 July 1900; New York Times 7 July 1900; Dial 16 Oct 1900.
Later poems. 1902.
REVIEWS: Outlook 7 Dec 1901; Bookman Feb 1902; Literary World 7 Feb 1902; Athenaeum 15 Feb 1902; TLS 7 Mar 1902; Monthly Rev Apr 1902; Dial 1 May 1902.
Children of the old masters. 1903 (with plates), 1903 (plates).
Ceres' runaway and other essays. 1909 (3 edns), New York 1910, London 1919, 1960, Freeport NY 1967.
REVIEWS: Athenaeum 16 Oct 1909; Morning Post 16 Dec 1909; New York Times 25 Dec 1909; Dial 1 Feb 1910.
Mary, the Mother of Jesus: an essay. 1912 (illustr R. A. Bell), 1923 (illustr R. A. Bell), [1925] (illustr R. A. Bell).
REVIEW: Bookman Dec 1912.
Childhood. 1913. New York 1913. Essays.
REVIEW: New York Times 11 Jan 1914.
Collected poems of Alice Meynell. 1913, New York 1913, 1914, 1915, London 1919, 1923, 1923 (limited edn), New York 1923, Toronto 1923.
REVIEWS: Poetry 14 May 1913; Athenaeum 24 May 1913; TLS 29 May 1913; Pall Mall Gazette 30 May 1913; Bookman July 1913; New York Times 13 July 1913; New York Times 30 Nov 1913; Bookman Apr 1923.
Essays. 1914, New York 1914, 1916, London 1918, 1919, 1922, 1923, New York 1924, London 1925, 1930, 1937, 1947 (centenary edn), Westminster MD 1947, Westport CT 1970.
REVIEWS: TLS 2 July 1914; Athenaeum 4 July 1914; Dial 1 Oct 1914.
The shepherdess, and other verses. [1914.] Later poems (with 2 omissions).
Poems on the war. Ed C. Shorter 1915 (20 copies priv ptd).
A father of women and other poems. 1917.
REVIEWS: TLS 27 Sep 1917; Bookman Oct 1917; Guardian 8 Oct

1917; Land and Water 11 Oct 1917; Spectator 16 Mar 1918; Dial 25 Apr 1918.

Hearts of controversy. [1917], New York 1917, London 1918, New York 1918, 1920, Freeport NY 1968. Essays.

REVIEWS: TLS 25 Oct 1917; Sphere 8 Dec 1917; Bookman Jan 1918; Dial 28 Mar 1918; Egoist Apr 1918; North Amer Rev Apr 1918; New York Times 12 May 1918.

The second person singular, and other essays. 1921, 1921 (2 impressions), 1922, Freeport NY 1968.

REVIEWS: TLS 19 Jan 1922; Bookman Feb 1922.

The last poems of Alice Meynell. 1923.

REVIEWS: TLS 1 Mar 1923; Bookman Apr 1923; Dublin Rev Apr 1923.

At night. Americus GA 1978 (55 copies).

Contributions to periodicals, collaborative works and anthologies

Alice Meynell, together with her husband Wilfrid, worked on the Weekly Register *from 1881 to 1898 and on* Merry England. *She was a prolific contributor of poems and essays to leading jnls.*

Tablet. Contributions from 19 Feb 1876.

Irish Monthly. Future poetry, Feb 1877.

Spectator. Vintages and vintagers of Tuscany, 12 Oct 1878.

Tinsley's Mag. Young art at the Royal Academy, July 1881; A retrospect of pictures, Aug 1882.

Mag of Art. Dec 1878–Apr 1901.

Pen. Sonnet, 22 May 1880; The modern poet, 26 June 1880; Dante Gabriel Rossetti, 30 July 1880.

Weekly Register. 1880–98.

Good Words. A ramble round Arundel, with an artist's holiday sketches, Aug 1881.

Art Jnl. Mar 1882–Dec 1890.

C. H. Boughton, 1883; J. L. E. Messonier, 1883. In Some modern artists and their work, ed W. Meynell, 1883.

St Nicholas. Elizabeth Butler, Jan 1883.

Merry England. Oct 1883–Mar 1895.

Century Mag. How Edwin Drood was illustrated, Feb 1884.

In Songs and poems of the sea, ed Mrs William Sharp, 1888.

Scots Observer. 2 Feb 1889–27 Dec 1890.

In Women's voices: an anthology of the most characteristic poems by English, Scotch and Irish women, ed Mrs W. Sharp, 1887.

Nat Observer. 10 Jan 1891–13 Jan 1894.

Art Jnl Annual. William Holman Hunt, Christmas 1893. With Archdeacon Farrar.

Pall Mall Gazette. Alice Meynell contributed a weekly article in the series The wares of Autolycus, every Friday from 2 June 1893 until 25 Mar 1896, then every Wednesday until 28 Dec 1898 when the series ceased. She remained a contributor until 20 June 1905, her contributions including art reviews.

Saturday Rev. Cradle-song at twilight, 6 July 1895; The fugitive, 2 Feb 1912. Poems.

Illus London News. Review of Meredith's The amazing marriage, 14 Dec 1895.

Album. A series of articles on childhood from 4 Mar 1895–2 Dec 1895; rptd as Childhood 1913.

Bookman (USA). Aug 1896–Apr 1899.

Woman. My faith and my work, 12 Aug 1896.

Bookman. Nov 1896–Dec 1912.

Athenaeum. 12 Dec 1896–30 May 1914.

Acad. 12 Dec 1896–26 June 1897.

Monthly Rev. Dec 1900–Oct 1904.

Atlantic Monthly. Jan 1903–Nov 1922.

Speaker. 7 Oct 1903–23 Jan 1904.

Daily Mail. The best women's book of the year. Review of Mrs Le Bailly's Other poems. 16 Dec 1903.

Harper's Monthly. The trick of education, Feb 1904.

Daily Chron. Nov 1904–Dec 1916.

Venture. To any householder, 1903; Customs of publicity, 1905.

Wayfarer's love: contributions from living poets. Ed the Duchess of Sutherland 1904.

North Amer Rev. The English women-humorists, June 1905; Length of days (poem), Mar 1915.

Outlook. 14 Jan 1905–10 Nov 1906.

Daily News. 11 May 1905; Pessimism in fiction, 18 June 1912.

Dublin Rev. Jan 1906–Jan 1923.

Living Age. 10 Mar 1906–13 Nov 1909.

Harper's Bazar. Hand, June 1907; Lines, June 1907. Poems.

Catholic World. Father Tabb, Feb 1910.

Fortnightly Rev. Christ in the universe, Oct 1911; Two questions, Mar 1916. Poems.

Home Progress. Lady of the lambs, Sep 1912. Poem.

Literary Digest. 18 Jan 1913–19 Aug 1922.

Poetry. Maternity, Mar 1913. Poem.

Current Opinion. After a parting, Dec 1913; Thrush before dawn, Dec 1914. Poems.

Little Rev. The garden, Mar 1914. Poem.

In Pro patria et rege: poems on war, ed Prof Knight, 1915 (1st ser).

The New York Times Current History. The heroic language, Mar 1915; In honour of America, Sep 1918. Poems.

A Miscellany: an occasional mag. Unto us a Son is given, Christmas 1915. Poem.

Poetry Rev. Stephen Phillips, Jan 1916.

Sphere. Intimations of mortality from recollections of early childhood, 12 Apr 1919. Poem.

Observer. Review of L. Binyon's The four years, 20 June 1919.

London Mercury. Nov 1919–Nov 1922.

Time and Tide. Evelina, 14 May 1920.

Letters

In E. Meynell, The life of Francis Meynell, 1913 (2 impressions), 1916 (new edn), 1918.

Odes of Coventry Patmore. Ed with bibliography by J. Merrell, [Sunbury-on-Thames] 1971 (facs of 1865 edn and with unpbd letter from A. Meynell to O. Burdett).

Editions, introductions, collaborative works and translations

Dickens memento, with introd by Francis Phillimore [Alice Meynell], and Hints to Dickens' collectors by John F. Dexter. 2 pts 1885.

Barbé, D. Lourdes, yesterday, to-day, and tomorrow. Tr Meynell 1893.

The poems of Thomas Gordon Hake. Selected with a prefatory note by A. Meynell 1894, Chicago 1894, New York 1971.

Poetry of pathos and delight from the works of Coventry Patmore. Ed Meynell 1896, New York 1896.

Introd to Prometheus bound and other poems of Elizabeth Barrett Browning. 1896.

The flower of the mind. Ed Meynell 1897, 1898, 1899, 1904, 1907 (3rd edn), St Louis 1907, New York 1910, 1925.

Introd to The confessions of Saint Augustine. Tr E. B. Pusey, ed T. Scott, 1900, 1909, Boston 1909, New York 1910.

Preface to Petrarch, Love's crucifix: nine sonnets and a canzone, tr A. Tobin 1902 (illustr G. Robertson).

Introd to The Madonna, the text translated from the Italian of Adolfo Venturi, 1902.

Introd to Red Letter Lib poetry series: Tennyson (1903); Wordsworth (1903); Elizabeth Barrett Browning (1903); Robert Browning (1903); Keats (1903); Shelley (1903); Tennyson's In memoriam (1904); Coleridge (1904); A seventeenth century anthology ([1904]), Boston 1904, London 1930; Herrick (1905); Cowper (1905), Boston and New York 1910; Arnold (1906); Christina Rossetti (1906, 1907, 1910, Boston 1907); Jean Ingelow ([1908]); Blake (1911).

Introd to The Work of John S. Sargent, R. A. 3 vols 1903 (plates and 2 portfolios), 1927 (also includes introd by J. B. Manson).
Introd to L'œuvre de John S. Sargent, Paris 1904 (150 copies).
Preface to A little child's wreath, ed E. R. Chapman, 1904.
Introd to The Gospel of the Childhood of Our Lord Jesus Christ, tr H. C. Greene, New York 1904.
Introd to C. Patmore, The angel in the house together with The victories of love, 1905 (Muses Lib).
A selection from the verses of John B. Tabb made by A. Meynell. [1906], New York 1906, Boston 1907, London 1907 (2nd edn), Boston 1910.
Introd to vol 7, The taming of the shrew. In The complete works of William Shakespeare, ed S. Lee, Renaissance edn, 40 vols New York 1907.
Bazin, R. The nun. Tr Meynell 1908.
Introd to C. M. Yonge, The heir of Redclyffe Hall, [1909] (EL).
Introd to A. Cashmore, The mount of vision: a book of mystic verse, 1910.
Introd to J. Ruskin, The seven lamps of architecture, 1910.
Selections from Samuel Johnson. 1911 (Regent Lib), Folcroft PA 1911, Chicago 1913, Norwood PA 1977. With G. K. Chesterton.
Introd to E. B. Browning, The art of scansion, 1916 (priv ptd).
Watson, H. C. Selected essays and reviews. Also his last letter from the front. Ed Meynell, Bedford 1919.
Catalogue of the library of Coventry Patmore. 1921.
The school of poetry. An anthology chosen for young readers. [1923], New York 1924, [1936].

§2

Patmore, C. Fortnightly Rev Dec 1892.
Mullins, Mrs R. Sylvia's Journal Oct 1893.
Patmore, C. Saturday Rev 13 June 1896.
Chambers, E. K. Bookman Aug 1896.
Beerbohm, M. Tomorrow Sep 1896.
Alder, I. B. Englishman Apr 1897.
English Illus Mag Sep 1897. Interview.
Tooley, S. A. Humanitarian Apr 1898.
Hinkson, K. T. Book Buyer Apr 1899.
C. K. S. Literary letter. Sphere 22 Sep 1900.
Reilly, T. B. Catholic World July 1901.
Archer, W. In his Poets of the younger generation, 1902; rptd 1970.
Nevinson, H. W. Critic Oct 1903.
Alica. The household. Daily News 11 May 1905.
Gosse, E. W. In his Coventry Patmore, 1905.
Brégy, K. Catholic World Jan 1911.
J. P. C. Francis Thompson: a few words on the new edition. Pall Mall Gazette 10 Apr 1913.
Harper's Weekly 4 July 1913. Portrait.
Hinkson, K. T. Catholic World Aug 1913.
Meynell, E. In his The life of Francis Thompson, 1913 (2 impressions), 1916 (new edn), 1918.
Jones, Ll. Little Rev Apr 1914.
Royal Society of Literature. Address of reception to Mrs Alice Meynell by Henry Newbolt. Oxford 1915.
Ford, Mrs S. G. Bookman Oct 1915; rptd Living Age Feb 1916.
Gilman, L. Chastity triumphant. North American Rev Apr 1918.
Maynard, T. America 6 July 1918.
Obits and notices: New York Times 28 Nov 1922; The Times 28 Nov 1922; The Times 30 Nov 1922; Spectator 2 Dec 1922; Tablet 2 Dec 1922; Literary Digest 23 Dec 1922; Chesterton, G. K., Dublin Rev Jan/Mar 1923; rptd Dublin Rev Autumn 1947; Moorhouse, E. H., Fortnightly Rev Jan 1923; Noyes, A., Bookman Jan 1923; Squire, J. C., London Mercury Jan 1923; Garvin, J. L., Living Age 13 Jan 1923; Matthewman, S., Literary Digest 20 Jan 1923; Matthewman, S., Atlantic Monthly Feb 1923; Maynard, T., Freeman 7 Feb 1923; Monroe, H., Poetry Feb 1923; Lynd, S., Daily News 26 Feb 1923; Marks, J., North Amer Rev Mar 1923; Repplier, A., Catholic World Mar 1923; Bone, F., London Quart and Holborn Rev Apr 1923; Squire, J. C., Dublin Rev Apr 1923; Tuell, A. K., Atlantic Monthly Apr 1923; Tuell, A. K., Sewanee Rev Apr 1923; Berry, G., Scribner's Mag May 1923.
Clark, C. T. Alice Meynell, a tribute. San Francisco 1923 [50 copies].
Meynell, E. The letters of George Meredith to Alice Meynell with annotations thereto, 1896–1907. 1923, Norwood PA 1927, Folcroft PA 1971, 1976.
Tuell, A. K. Mrs Meynell and her literary generation. New York [1925].
Meynell, V. Alice Meynell: a memoir. 1929, New York 1929, 1948, 1971.
Page, F. DNB 1922–30.
Tynan, K. Commonweal 8 Jan 1931.
Michalik, K. Alice Meynell: her life and her works. Cracow 1934.
Alice Meynell centenary tribute, 1847–1923; a symposium opening an exhibition of Alice Meynell manuscripts, letters, first and rare editions. Ed T. L. Connolly, Boston 1947; Alice Meynell Exhibition, TLS 18 Oct 1947.
Meynell, V. A personal note. Dublin Rev Autumn 1947.
Meynell, V. In Francis Thompson and Wilfrid Meynell: a memoir, 1952.
Schlack, B. A. The 'poetess of poets': Alice Meynell rediscovered. Women's Stud 7 1980.
Badeni, J. The slender tree: a life of Alice Meynell. Padstow 1981.
In DLB vol 19 1983. [DA]

Cosmo Monkhouse, William Cosmo Monkhouse 1840–1901

Mss: located in Berg Collection, NYPL; Colby College Lib; Harvard; Huntington Lib; Pierpont Morgan Lib; Princeton; Univ of British Columbia Lib. See also LR.

Bibliographies

In R. F. Sharp, A dictionary of English authors: biographical and bibliographical, 1904, rptd Detroit 1978.
In Nineteenth century readers' guide to periodical literature 1890–1899, ed H. G. Cushing and A. V. Morris, 2 vols New York 1944.
See also Wellesley *vol 5* 1989.

Selections

In Ballades and rondeaus, chants royal, sestinas, villanelles, &c., ed G. White, London and Newcastle-on-Tyne 1887, New York 1888, 1892, 1893, 1897, London 1900, 1905, 1909.
In The poets and the poetry of the century, ed A. H. Miles, 6 1891–97.
Lyrics. The Bibelot 6 (3) 1900, Portland ME 1900.

§1

A dream of idleness, and other poems. 1865.
A question of honour. 3 vols 1868. Novel.
Joseph Mallord Turner. 1879, [1929] (Great Artists ser).
Corn and poppies. 1890, 1890. Poems.
REVIEWS: Scots Observer 14 June 1890; Acad 28 June 1890; Athenaeum 9 Aug 1890.
Life of Leigh Hunt. 1893 (Great Writers ser).
REVIEWS: Acad 13 May 1893; Athenaeum 10 June 1893; Spectator 30 Sep 1893.
The Christ upon the hill. A ballad. Etched by W. Strang. 1895.
REVIEW: Athenaeum 25 Jan 1896.
In the National Gallery. 1895, [1900?].
To Our Sovereign Lady Queen Victoria. June 22, 1897. [1897.] Poems.
British contemporary artists. 1899, New York 1899, 1901.
REVIEW: New York Times 16 Dec 1899.
Pasiteles the elder, and other poems. 1901 (preface A. Dobson).
Nonsense rhymes. [1902] (illustr G. K. Chesterton).

Contributions to periodicals, collaborative works and anthologies

Acad. 24 Jan 1880–15 Oct 1887.
Art Jnl. Apr 1881–Feb 1901.
Mag of Art. Jan 1882–July 1900.
Portfolio. July 1884–Dec 1892.
Scots Observer. 20 Apr–16 Nov 1889.
Blackwood's Mag. Under the oak and True lover, 8 Feb 1890. Poems.
Critic. O love, no skill can move thy will, 6 Sep 1890. Poem.
Spectator. Secret and On one not beautiful, 11 Oct 1890. Poems.
Scribners Mag. Dec 1894–19 Dec 1897.
Art Jnl Easter Annual. 1897–1901.
Parents' Rev. Art in education, Sep 1898.
Art Jnl Jubilee. 1899.
DNB. Monkhouse contributed 137 articles to the DNB, among them those on Landseer, Millais, Reynolds and Turner: *see* G. Fenwick, The contributors' index to the National Dictionary of Biography 1885–1901, Winchester 1989.
For contributions to Nat Rev-II *and* St Paul's Mag, *see* Wellesley *vol* 5 *1989*.

Editions, introductions, etc

Masterpieces of English art. 1869 (illus). Text by Monkhouse.
A few words about Hogarth. In The works of W[illiam] H[ogarth], 2 vols 1872.
Pictures by W. Etty. With descriptions and a biographical sketch of the painter by W[illiam] C[osmo] M[onkhouse]. 1874.
Pictures by Sir C. Eastlake. With a sketch of the artist by W[illiam] C[osmo] M[onkhouse]. 1875 (folio).
The works of J. H. Foley, RA Sculptor. With notes by W. C. M[onkhouse]. 1875 (folio).
The studies of Sir Edwin Landseer. With a history of his art-life by W. C. M[onkhouse]. [1877] (folio).
The Turner Gallery. Descriptive text by W. C. M[onkhouse], 3 vols [1878] (folio), 1 vol New York 1879.
Pictures of Sir Edwin Landseer. A new series with descriptions by W. C. M[onkhouse]. [1877.]
The works of Sir Edwin Landseer. With a history of his art-life by W[illiam] C[osmo] M[onkhouse]. [1879 (folio), 1880 (folio)], Alton 1990 (facs of 1879 edn, ed J. Batty).
Preface. In The life and works of Joseph Wright, ARA, ed W. Bemrose, 1885.
The National Gallery. The Pre-Raphaelites. 1887.
Heaton, Mrs C. A concise history of painting. Rev edn by Monkhouse 1888, 1917.
The earlier English water-colour painters, etc. 1890 (folio), 1890, 1897 (folio, 2nd edn).
Introd to the Exhibition illustrative of the French revival of etching, 1891.
In The child set in the midst: by modern poets, ed W. Meynell, 1892.
Historical catalogue of the collection of water-colour drawings by deceased artists. Ed and introd by Monkhouse 1894.
Introd to R. Mills, Catalogue of blue and white oriental porcelain exhibited in 1895, 1895.
Introd to Catalogue of coloured Chinese porcelain exhibited in 1896, 1896.
Introd to the Exhibition of drawings in water colour by A. W. Hunt, 1897.
Introd to the Exhibition of drawings and studies by Sir Edward Burne-Jones, Bart, 1899.

§2

Obits: The Times 22 July 1901; A[dams], W. A. W. Acad 27 July 1901; Lee, Sir S. Athenaeum 27 July 1901; Bond, R. W. Letter, Acad 3 Aug 1901.
Dobson, A. DNB. 1901–11.
Gosse, E. W. Art Jnl Mar 1902.
Buckley, J. H. In William Ernest Henley: a study in the 'counter-decadence' of the nineties, Princeton 1945, rptd New York 1971.
Connell, J. (J. H. Robertson). In W. E. Henley, 1949, rptd Port Washington NY 1972. [DA]

Sir Lewis Morris 1833–1907

Collections

Poetical works. 3 vols 1882, 1907 (rev and enlarged). Songs unsung, 1883, and Songs of Britain (4th edn) sometimes vols 4 and 5 of 1st edn of Poetical works.
Works. 1890, 10th thousand 1894, 16th thousand 1907.
Selections. 1897.
Poems. [1904.] Authorised selection.

§1

Songs of two worlds: by a new writer. 3 ser 1871–5, 1878.
The epic of Hades: by the author of Songs of two worlds. 1876 (bk 2 only), 1877 (bks 1–2), 1877 (complete), 1903.
Gwen: a drama in monologue. '1879' [1878], 1880 (3rd edn).
The ode of life: by the author of Epic of Hades. 1880.
Songs unsung. 1883.
Gycia: a tragedy. 1886. Mostly verse.
Songs of Britain. 1887, 1887 (2nd edn).
A vision of saints. 1890, 1892.
Odatis: an old love-tale: a poem. [1892.]
Love and sleep and other poems. [1893.]
Ode on the marriage of HRH the Duke of York and HSH Princess Victoria Mary of Teck. 1893.
Meliora: a poem. 1894.
Songs without notes. 1894, 1895 (2nd edn).
Idylls and lyrics. 1896.
The diamond jubilee: an ode. 1897. Rptd from The Times.
Harvest-tide. 1901.
The life and death of Leo the Armenian (Emperor of Rome): a tragedy. 1904.
The new rambler: from desk to platform. 1905. Essays.

§2

Rees, J. R. Morris. In Miles 5.
Obits: The Times 13 Nov, 24 Dec 1907; Athenaeum 16 Nov 1907.
Evans, B. I. In his English poetry in the later nineteenth century, 1933, 1966 (rev).
B., E. M. Lewis Morris. Nat Rev Feb 1934.

William Morris 1834–96

The three main collections of Morris mss are at the BL, the Huntington and the Pierpont Morgan Libs. The largest, in the BL, is described in R. Flower, The Morris manuscripts, BM Quart *14 1940. Two later catalogues detail both public and accessible private ms collections:* K. L. Goodwin, A preliminary handlist of manuscripts and documents of Morris, 1983 (Morris Soc), *and R. Pearson, in* IELM vol 4 no 3 1993. *Several collections of Morris mss and printed materials are available on microfilm:* Britain's literary heritage: Morris. Reading 1985–90. Pt 1 Literary manuscripts of Morris from the British Library. 9 reels. 1985; pt 2 Literary manuscripts of Morris from the Huntington Library, San Marino CA. 6 reels. 1987; pt 3 Archives of the Socialist League, 1884–1891. Minutes and Papers of the Council of the League from the Nettlau Archive at the International Institute of Social History, Amsterdam. 37 reels. 1988–9; pt 4 Art, book design and literary papers from Kelmscott Manor, the Society of Antiquaries of London and the BL Department of Printed Books. 5 reels. 1990.

Bibliographies

Forman, H. B. The books of Morris described, with some account of his doings in literature and in the allied crafts. 1897, New York 1969 (photo facs).

Scott, T. [J. H. Isaacs] A bibliography of the works of Morris. 1897. Essentially the same as that appended to A. Vallance, Art of Morris, 1897.

A note by Morris on his aims in founding the Kelmscott Press; together with a short description of the press by S. C. Cockerell and an annotated list of the books printed thereat. Hammersmith 1898 (Kelmscott Press); rptd in H. H. Sparling, The Kelmscott Press and Morris, master-craftsman, 1924, Folkstone 1975, 1988 (photo facs).

Vaughan, C. E. In Bibliographies of Swinburne, Morris, Rossetti. Oxford 1914 (Eng Assoc).

[Winship, G. P.] A chronological list of books printed at the Kelmscott Press: with illustrative material from a collection made by Morris and H. C. Marillier, now in the library of Marsden J. Perry of Providence RI. Boston 1928 (Grolier Club).

Ohtsuki, K. List of new contributions, home and foreign, to the W. Morris bibliography in his year. Tokyo 1934.

Litzenberg, K. Morris and Scandinavian literature: bibliographical essay. Scandinavian Stud 13 1935.

Ehrsam, T. G., R. H. Deily and R. M. Smith. In Bibliographies of twelve Victorian authors, New York 1936; suppl by J. G. Fucilla, MP 37 1939.

Jones, H. M. The Pre-Raphaelites. In Victorian poets, ed F. E. Faverty, Cambridge MA 1956; ed W. E. Fredeman 1968 (2nd edn, rev).

William Morris Gallery and Brangwyn Gift. Catalogue of the Morris Collection. 1958, 1969 (rev).

Briggs, R. C. H. Handlist of the public addresses of Morris to be found in generally accessible publications. 1961 (Morris Soc).

Fredeman, W. E. Morris and his circle: selective bibliography of publications 1960–2, 1963–5. Jnl of William Morris Soc 1–2 1964–6. A continuing bibliography including the Pre-Raphaelites. Continued biennially by D. and S. Latham as Morris: an annotated bibliography. In Jnl of William Morris Soc 5 1983 for 1978–80 etc. First pbd in the Summer issue, currently in the Spring.

Haslam, G. E. Wise after the event: a catalogue of books, pamphlets, manuscripts and letters relating to Wise. Manchester 1964; also a later version: Sotheby and Co: a catalogue of the celebrated collection of Wiseianna formed by Sir Maurice Pariser. Manchester 4–5 Dec 1967. An exhibition and a sale catalogue with details of the Pariser collection. Materials relating mainly to the Wise–Forman productions.

Fredeman, W. E. In Pre-Raphaelitism: a bibliocritical study, Cambridge MA 1965 (section 43).

LeMire, E. D. A calendar of Morris's platform career, and A bibliographical checklist of Morris's speeches and lectures. 1969. Appended to The unpublished lectures of Morris, *see* Collections and selections, *below*.

Briggs, R. C. H. The work of Morris: an exhibition arranged by the Morris Society. 1972. Catalogue of an exhibition of printed and ms materials.

Pollard, H. G. A catalogue of books and pamphlets from the library of Maurice Buxton Forman. 1973. A Quaritch sale catalogue with details of H. B. Forman's Morris books, his holograph notes concerning them, with running commentary by Pollard.

Needham, P. Morris and the art of the book. With essays by Needham, J. Dunlap and J. Dreyfus. New York 1976. Exhibition catalogue of Morris books and mss in the Pierpont Morgan Lib.

LeMire, E. D. The Socialist League leaflets and manifestoes: an annotated checklist. The International Rev of Social History 22 1977.

In fine print: Morris as book-designer. 1977. William Morris Gallery exhibition catalogue.

Bacon, A. K. Some additions to E. D. LeMire's calendar and bibliography of Morris's speaking career. N & Q 223, Aug 1978.

Pearson, M. Morris, 1834–1896: aspects of his life and work. Toronto 1978. Exhibition catalogue.

Bensusan, G. Twenty years of the Journal. Jnl William Morris Soc 4 Winter 1981. Reprints the contents list of the first 20 years.

Walsdorf, J. J. Morris in private press and limited editions: a descriptive bibliography of books by and about Morris, 1891–1981. Phoenix AZ [1983?].

Morris: the Sanford and Helen Berger collection. Foreword by J. D. Hart and J. Elliot, preface by S. Berger, Berkeley 1984. Exhibition catalogue.

Peterson, W. S. A bibliography of the Kelmscott Press. Oxford 1984, 1985 (rev).

Aho, G. Morris: a reference guide. Boston 1985. Secondary materials.

Felsenstein, F. Morris and the Brotherton Collection. Univ of Leeds Rev vol 28 1985.

Schulte, E. Morris in Italian today. Jnl William Morris Soc 7 Spring 1987. Lists trns of Morris's works into Italian 1963–85.

The Estelle Doheny Collection from The Edward Laurence Doheny Memorial Library, St John's Seminary, Camarillo CA. Pt 4: printed books and mss concerning Morris and his circle. New York 1989. A Christie's sale catalogue of rare Morris books and mss.

Albert, S. D. My work is the embodiment of dreams: Morris, Burne-Jones and Pre-Raphaelite influences on book design. In Pocket cathedrals: Pre-Raphaelite book illustration, ed P. Casteras, New Haven CT 1991. Catalogue of an exhibition at Yale Univ.

In self-respect and decent comfort: an exhibition of books and mss from the collection of Sanford and Helen Berger, marking the 100th anniversary of the Kelmscott Press. Palo Alto CA 1991. Catalogue of an exhibition at Stanford Univ.

Latham, D. and S. An annotated critical bibliography of Morris. London and New York 1991. Mainly secondary materials.

Clayson, J., and E. and R. Frow. Monopoly: or how labour is robbed; a bibliographical note. Jnl Morris Soc 9 Spring 1992.

Pye, J. W. A bibliography of American editions of Morris published by Roberts Brothers, Boston, 1867–1898. Brockton MA 1993. Descriptive bibliography.

Collections and selections

The two sides of the river / Hapless love / and The first foray of Aristomenes . . . Not for sale. '1876' [Mar 1890]. A false date on an unauthorised pam, *see* N. Barker and J. Collins, A sequel to An enquiry, §2, *below*. The two sides of the river appeared first in Fortnightly Rev Oct 1868 and is rptd in Poems by the way, 1891; Hapless love was pbd in Good Words Apr 1869 and The first foray of Aristomenes in Athenaeum 13 May 1876; neither of the last 2 was rptd during Morris's lifetime. Rptd (introd T. B. Mosher) Portland ME Sep 1899 (The Bibelot vol 5 no 9), rptd (ed and introd T. B. Mosher) 1899 (reprints from Bibelot no 6).

A selection from the poems of Morris. Ed F. Hueffer, Leipzig 1886 (Tauchnitz).

Atalanta's race and other tales from The earthly paradise. Ed O. F. Adams, assisted by W. G. Rolfe, Boston 1888. A school anthology.

Morris: poet, artist, socialist: a selection from his writings together with a sketch of the man. Ed F. W. Lee (with letters from Morris quoted), New York 1891.

Morris to R. Buchanan. Ed H. B. Forman, in Poets and poetry of the century, ed A. H. Miles 1891, 1896 (rev). Anthology.

The legend of St George and the dragon, by Sir Edward Burne-Jones, R. A. [with verses selected from poems of Morris to accompany Burne-Jones's paintings]. 1895 (T. McLean Galleries).

The defence of Guenevere: a book of lyrics. Portland ME 1896 (Mosher). Anthology selected from several Morris books.

Architecture and history, and Westminster Abbey. [Ed S. C. Cockerell assisted by R. Proctor] Sep 1900 (Golden type octavo), rptd Dec 1900. 2 papers written for the Soc for the Protection of Ancient Buildings. The first was first pbd as Paper read by Mr Morris in The Seventh Annual Report of the Soc 1884; as

Medieval and modern craftsmanship in The Architect 13 Sep 1884; rptd The Clarion Oct 1884; as The medieval and the modern craftsman in Merry England Oct 1884; as Paper read at the seventh annual meeting of the SPAB 1 July 1884 in Morris: artist, writer, socialist vol 1, *see below*. Tr Du [1903]. The second was first pbd as Concerning Westminster Abbey, *see* §1 *below*; rptd in Morris: artist, writer, socialist vol 1, *see below*.

Pre-Raphaelite ballads. Decorated by H. M. O'Kane [Helen Margaret Clarke Conwell], New York 1900 (A. Wessels Co).

Art and its producers, and The arts and crafts today: two addresses delivered before the National Association for the Advancement of art . . . [Ed S. C. Cockerell assisted by R. Proctor] [June] 1901 (Golden type octavo); tr Ital 1963. Each lecture was first pbd in the Trans of the National Assoc for the Advancement of Art, Liverpool 1888 (1st lecture); London 1890 (2nd lecture). Both rptd in Collected works of Morris vol 22, *see* Collections and selections *below*.

Architecture, industry and wealth: Collected papers of Morris. [Ed S. C. Cockerell and R. Proctor] 1902 (Golden type quarto); 1902 (ordinary edn); New York 1978 (photo facs, Connoisseurship, criticism and art history in the nineteenth century); tr Ital 1963.

Five Arthurian poems. Decorative initials and borders by H. M. O'Kane [Mrs Clarke Conwell], New Rochelle NY 1902 (Elston Press). Includes The defence of Guenevere, King Arthur's tomb, Sir Galahad: a Christmas mystery, The chapel in Lyoness, and A good knight in prison.

Hopes and fears for art [and] Signs of change. [Ed S. C. Cockerell and R. Proctor] 1902 (Golden type quarto); rptd Hopes and fears 1914, Signs of change 1915 (Collected works vols 22, 23); introd P. Faulkner, Bristol 1994 (Collected works vols 22, 23, photo facs, Thoemmes Morris Lib).

Some notes on early woodcut books with a chapter on illuminated mss. Decorated initials and borders by H. M. O'Kane [Mrs Clarke Conwell], New York 1902 (The Elston Press). Some notes . . . was first pbd as The woodcuts of Gothic books in Jnl of the Soc of Arts 2 Feb 1892, rptd The Architect 26 Feb 1892; in Jnl of Decorative Art 12 1892. The chapter on illuminated mss was first pbd as Some notes on the illuminated books of the middle ages in The Mag of Art 17, Jan 1904. Both are rptd in Morris: artist, writer, socialist vol 1, *see below*.

The story of the unknown church and other tales. Portland ME Mar 1902 (The Bibelot, vol 8 no 3, bound in with Lindenborg pool and A dream); rptd 1902 (reprints from The Bibelot 11, bound in with Lindenborg pool and A dream); rptd 1902 (Brocade Ser 34, bound in with Lindenborg pool and A dream); Wimbledon 1904 (Avon Booklet vol 2 no 8, bound in with Lindenborg pool); 1905 (J. Finch, title story only); tr Ital 1988. The 3 stories were first pbd in The Oxford and Cambridge Mag Jan, Sep, Mar 1856, respectively, and they are rptd in The hollow land and other contributions to The Oxford and Cambridge Mag, *see below*.

The hollow land and other contributions to The Oxford and Cambridge Mag. [Ed S. C. Cockerell and R. Proctor] 1903 (Golden type octavo). Morris's contributions to The Oxford and Cambridge Mag were also pbd in an edn of 2 vols: vol 1 The world of romance, being contributions to The Oxford and Cambridge Mag; vol 2 Gertha's lovers and other stories, 1906 (Avon Booklets); tr Ger 1986; introd on the Morris attributions E. D. LeMire Bristol 1996 (Golden type octavo photo facs Thoemmes Morris Lib).

Golden wings: a prose romance and a poem. New York and Boston 1904 (H. M. Caldwell Co).

The poems of Morris. Ed P. R. Colwell, New York 1904 (T. R. Crowell & Co).

Kunst en maatchappii. Lezingen van Morris. Introd N. Polak, tr M. Hugenholz-Zeeven, Rotterdam [1905]. Five Morris lectures and essays on the arts and crafts.

Early romances of Morris in prose and verse. Introd A. Noyes 1907 (EL); rev P. Faulkner 1963 (2nd edn EL).

The collected works of Morris. Ed with introds by May Morris, 24 vols 1910–15, New York 1966 (photo facs); Bristol 1992 (photo facs Thoemmes Morris Lib). Introds to the 24 vols pbd separately, preface J. Dunlap, 2 vols New York 1973 (photo facs).

Atalanta's race, and The proud king. Ed with introd and notes [by J. W. Mackail] for use by schools and colleges 1912 (Longman's Class Books of English Lit), rptd 1920, 1921, 1922. First pbd in The earthly paradise vol, *see* §1 *below*.

The defence of Guenevere, The life and death of Jason, and other poems. Oxford 1914 (WC).

The pilgrims of hope, and Chants for Socialists. [Sep] 1915 (Longman's Pocket Lib). This vol includes, besides the two title poems, May Day [1892] and May Day 1894, both first pbd in Justice.

Six poems selected from the early writings of Morris. Cleveland OH 1915 (Clerk's Private Press).

Prose and poetry 1856–70. Oxford 1920 (OSA).

Atalanta's race and two other tales from The earthly paradise. Ed A. Quiller-Couch [1922] (King's Treasuries of Lit).

Poems of Morris. Ed N. A. Crawford, Girard KS [1923] (Little Blue Book no 492).

Thirteenth century prose tales by Morris. Preface by C. J. Finger, ed E. Haldeman-Julius, Girard KS [1923] (Ten Cent Pocket Series no 352).

William Morris, selected by H. Newbolt. 1923.

Selections from the prose works of Morris. Ed A. H. R. Ball, Cambridge 1931.

Stories in prose, stories in verse, shorter poems, lectures, and essays: centenary edition. Ed G. D. H. Cole 1934 (Centenary edn, Nonesuch).

Morris: artist, writer, socialist. Ed May Morris, 2 vols Oxford 1936, New York 1966. A suppl to The collected works, *above*.

On art and Socialism: essays and lectures. Ed H. Jackson 1947.

Selected writings. Ed W. Gaunt 1948.

Selections. Ed U. I. Shvedor, Moscow 1959 (introd in Rus, lectures in Eng).

Selected writings and designs. Ed A. Briggs 1962 (Pen), 1977. With a suppl on Morris as designer by G. Shankland.

Three works of Morris. Ed A. L. Morton 1968. Including News from nowhere (1890), The pilgrims of hope ('1886' [1900?]) and The dream of John Ball (1888).

The unpublished lectures of Morris. Ed E. D. LeMire, Detroit and Toronto 1969. 10 lectures from mss in the BL.

The ideal book: essays and lectures on the arts of the book. Ed W. S. Peterson, London and Berkeley 1982; tr Ger 1986. Collects 8 Morris essays and lectures and 4 interviews.

The juvenilia of Morris: with a checklist and unpublished early poems. Ed F. S. Boos, New York 1983 (Morris Soc).

Political writings. Ed A. L. Morton 1984.

Opere. Ed M. M. Elia, Rome 1985. Anthology, in Ital, of Morris's prose fiction, poetry and political writing.

Morris by himself: designs and writings. Ed G. Naylor 1988.

Selected poems. Ed P. Faulkner, Manchester 1992.

Art and society: lectures and essays by Morris. Medford MA 1993. Selected from Hopes and fears for art, and Signs of change.

Morris: news from nowhere and other writings. Ed C. Wilmer, Harmondsworth 1993 (Pen).

Political writings, contributions to Justice and Commonweal, 1883–90. Ed N. Salmon, Bristol 1994 (Thoemmes Morris Lib).

Journalism: contributions to Commonweal 1885–90. Ed N. Salmon, Bristol 1996 (Thoemmes Morris Lib). Together with Political writings (1994), *above*, this vol completes the Morris contributions to Justice and Commonweal.

The sweet days die, poems by Morris. Introd P. Todd. 1996.

§1

Morris's contributions to periodicals are detailed in the bibliographies of Forman and Scott (see Bibliographies, *above) which cover the four jnls with which Morris was most intimately associated:* (1) The Oxford and Cambridge Mag (Jan–Dec 1856). *After the first number, edited by Morris, this jnl was edited by W. Fulford, but Morris was its financial mainstay and its principal contributor. With the exception of* Winter weather, *all of Morris's poems were rptd in* The defence of Guinevere, 1858; *his tales, essays and poems in* The hollow land and other contributions to the Oxford and Cambridge Magazine *and in* Collected works; (2) Justice; (3) The Commonweal, *which Morris edited from its beginning,* vols 1–6, Feb 1885, through 1890, (4) The Architect, *where many of Morris's lectures were first printed.*

By current count, some 17 Morris publications are proved or suspected forgeries, piracies, or sophistications, produced by the industry of T. J. Wise in collaboration with Morris's bibliographer, H. B. Forman. These unauthorised publications, though using genuine Morris texts, are fabricated rarities, with false dates either stated or implied in the publications themselves or in Forman's The books of Morris described *(see* Bibliographies, *above). They are listed here, with annotations and references, in the chronological sequence according to the dates of publication designed for them by their creators.*

The Oxford and Cambridge Magazine. No 1 ed Morris, nos 2–12 ed W. Fulford, Oxford Jan–Dec 1856; New York 1972 (photo facs).

Sir Galahad: a Christmas mystery. '1858' [1890?]. A forgery, i.e. a later fabrication (the date, not the text, is false) intended to be accepted as a rare first edn. *See* J. Carter and H. G. Pollard, An enquiry into the nature of certain nineteenth-century pamphlets, in §2, *below*. Rptd New Rochelle NY 1902 (Elston Press); Chicago [1904] (Blue Sky Press); Englewood NJ 1915 (Hillside Press). First pbd in The defence of Guenevere and other poems, *see below*.

The defence of Guenevere and other poems. 1858; 1875 (ordinary edn, new set); Boston 1875 (2nd issue, ordinary edn, imported English sheets); 1883 (ordinary edn), rptd 1889; 1892 (Kelmscott Press, rev); 1896 (ordinary edn, The poetical works of William Morris); London and New York 1900 (new set, 'Reprinted from the Kelmscott Press edition, as revised by the author'), rptd 1903; illustr J. M. King 1904 (Bodley Head); ed R. Steele 1904 (The King's Poets); 1905 ('Cheap edn', Longman); Philadelphia [1906] (G. W. Jacobs); ed R. Steele 1907 (King's Classics no 25); 1908 ('Best edn', Longman); 1909 ('Cheap edn', Longman); 1910 (Collected works vol 1, bound in with The hollow land and other contributions to the Oxford and Cambridge Mag); introd J. Drinkwater [1912] (The Muses' Lib); as The early poems of Morris, illustr F. Harrison, 1914 (Blackie & Son); 1915 (new impression, 'reprinted from the Kelmscott Press edition, as revised by the author'); 1916 (Longman's Pocket Lib); ed M. Lourie, New York 1981 (Garland).

The life and death of Jason: a poem. 1867; Boston 1867 (new set); Boston 1867 (2nd edn, i.e. 2nd issue, 1st edn); '1868' [1867] (2nd edn rev, ordinary edn); 1868 (2nd edn, rev), rptd 1869, 1870 (5th edn); Boston 1871 (ptd using English plates); 1872 (6th edn); Boston 1877; 1877 (7th edn); 1882 (8th edn, rev); Boston 1889 (9th edn); Boston 1893 (ptd using English plates); 1895 (Kelmscott Press); 1896 (Longman's reissue, ordinary edn); 1897 (9th edn, The poetical works of Morris); New York 1900 (Longman's re-issue of 'Author's edn' copies); 1902 (10th impression, The poetical works of Morris); New York 1903 ('Author's edn'); 1907 (11th impression); 1907 (Longman's Pocket Lib); New York 1909 ('Author's edn'); 1910 (Collected works vol 2); ed J. Drinkwater. [1910] (Muses Lib); introd by E. Rhys [1911] (EL); 1912 (Collins Illustr Pocket Classics); ed E. Maxwell, Oxford 1914 (Clarendon, rptd from The defence of Guenevere . . . and other poems, *see* Collections and selections, *above*); 1914 (Longman's Pocket Lib); as The life and death of Jason: a metrical romance, decorated by M. Armfield, [1915] (Headley Bros), rptd New York 1917 (Dodd Mead & Co); ed E. Maxwell, Oxford 1919 (Clarendon, rptd from The defence of Guenevere . . . and other poems, *see* Collections and selections, *above*); 1926 (Longman's Pocket Lib); introd by E. Rhys [1927] (EL).

The earthly paradise: a poem. 3 (or 4) vols 1868–70. Vol 1, later called pts 1 & 2, (Mar–Aug) 1868; vol 1, pts 1 & 2, Boston 1868 ('Author's edition' from imported Eng sheets); vol 1, later called pts 1 & 2 1868 (2nd edn); 1868 (3rd edn); vol 1 pts 1 & 2 Boston 1868 ('Author's edition', re-set 'from Eng 3rd edition'), rptd 1868; 1869 (4th edn); vols 1 & 2, separate pts 1 & 2. 1870 (5th edn); vol 2, or 3, pt 3, 1870 (1st edn, 2nd vol of 3 vols, 3rd vol of 4 vols); vol 2 pt 3 Boston 1870 ('Author's edn' from imported Eng sheets); vol 2 Boston 1870 ('Author's edn', new set), rptd 1870; vol 2, or 3, pt 3, 1870 (2nd edn, i.e. 2nd issue); rptd 1870 (3rd edn); vol 2 pt 3 Boston 1870 ('Author's edn'); vol 3, or 4, pt 4, 1870 (completes both the 3-vol and 4-vol Eng ordinary, later 'Library' edn), rptd 1870 (2nd edn), 1871 (3rd edn); vol 3 pt 4 Boston 1871 ('Author's edn', imported Eng sheets, completes Boston imported edn in 3 vols); Boston 1871 ('Author's edn' re-set, completes US setting in 3 vols), rptd 3 vols Boston 1871 (2 versions, '16mo' and 'Cheap edn'); vols 1 & 2, 2 pts, 1871 (6th edn); 10 pts 1872 ('Popular edn'); 3 vols Boston 1874 ('6-quire edn'); 3 vols Boston 1878 ('Author's edn', '6-Quire'); vols 1 & 2, 2 pts, 1880 (8th edn); 3 vols Boston 1884 ('Author's edn', '16mo edn'); 5 pts 1886 (complete set made by combining sheets of the 10-pt 'Popular edn'); 3 vols Boston 1888 ('Cheap edn'); in 1 vol 1890 ('Cheap edn', rev); 3 vols, pts 1 & 2 in 1 vol, Boston 1891 (9th edn, pts 3 & 4 in 2 vols 7th edn); 3 vols Boston 1893 ('Author's edn' rptd US setting); in 1 vol 1895 ('Cheap edn'), rptd 1896; 4 vols 1896; 8 vols 1896–7 (Kelmscott Press); vols 1 & 2 1896–7 (10th edn, for Longman as part of The poetical works of Morris, and the Lib edn in 4 vols, incorporating the revisions made for the 1-vol edn in 1890 and used also with the Kelmscott Press edn of 1896–7); vol 3 pt 3 1896 (8th edn for 'Lib edn' in 4 vols, incorporating the revisions of 1890); vol 4 pt 4 1897 ('Lib edn', incorporating the revisions of 1890); in 1 vol 1898 ('Cheap edn'), rptd 1900; vol 1 of 4 vols 1902 (11th impression 'Lib edn'); pt 2 of 10 pts 1902 ('Popular edn'); vol 3 of 4 vols 1902 ('Lib edn'); in 1 vol 1902 ('Cheap edn'); vol 2 of 4 vols 1903 (11th edn, 'Lib edn'); pt 2 of 10 1903 ('Popular edn'); pt 3 of 10 1903 ('Popular edn'); pt 7 of 10 1904 ('Popular edn'); vol 4 of 4 vols 1904 (9th edn, 'Lib edn'); pt 2 of 10 1904 ('Popular edn'); Introd J. W. Mackail. 4 vols or 12 pts London and New York 1905 (same sheets 4 vols called 'Silver Lib' only in London); in 1 vol 1905 ('Cheap edn'); in 1 vol 1907 (New impression); in 1 vol 1910 (New impression); vols 1 & 2 of 4 vols 1910 (Collected works vols 3–4); vols 3 & 4 of 4 vols 1911 (Collected works vols 5–6); vol 1 of 3 vols 1911 (The Muses Lib, never completed?); vol 1 of 4 vols 1912 ('Lib edn'); vol 3 of 4-vols 1912 ('Lib edn'); pt 2 of 12. 1913 (sheets from 'Silver Lib' edn); vol 2 of 4 vols 1914 ('Lib edn'); in 1 vol 1918 ('Cheap edn'), rptd 1923.

The lovers of Gudrun: a poem. Boston 1870. Excerpt from pt 3 of The earthly paradise, made up of 'Author's edn' sheets with pagination as in the original edn.

Love is enough: or the freeing of Pharamond: a morality. '1873' [1872]; Boston 1873 (from imported Eng sheets); Boston 1873 ('Author's edn', 'Popular edn' new set in US); 1873 (2nd edn); 1873 (3rd edn); 1889 (3rd edn); 1896 (new edn, 'The poetical works of Morris', bound in with Poems by the way); '1897' [1898] (Kelmscott Press); 1911 (Collected works vol 9, bound in with Poems by the way).

England and the Turks. The Daily News 26 Oct 1876. Rptd in Morris: artist, writer, socialist, *see* Collections and selections, *above*.

The story of Sigurd the Volsung and the fall of the Niblungs. '1877' [1876]; Boston '1877' [1876] (from imported Eng sheets); 1877 (2nd edn); Boston 1879 (re-set US edn); 1880 (3rd edn); Boston 1881; Boston 1887 (4th edn); 1887 (4th edn re-set); Boston 1891 (5th edn); 1893 (5th edn); Boston 1896 (5th edn); London and New York 1896 (5th edn, The poetical works of Morris); illustr E. Burne-Jones

1898 (Kelmscott Press); 1898 (ordinary edn); New York 1900 (US ordinary edn); London and New York 1901 (7th impression, The poetical works of Morris in London; new impression in New York); New York 1903 (US ordinary edn); 1904 (New impression The poetical works of Morris); New York 1906 (US ordinary edn); 1910 (ordinary edn); 1911 (Collected works vol 12); New York 1914 (new impression); as Morris's Sigurd the Volsung, book 1, an edn with variant readings and annotations, ed S. C. Blersch, unpbd diss, Ohio Univ 1975; introd J. Ennis, Bristol 1994 (Collected works vol 12 photo facs Thoemmes Morris Lib).

Society for the Protection of Ancient Buildings: Principles [by Morris]. 1877, 1896, 1899 etc; tr Fr (all issues). Single folio broadsheet in 3 pts: list of Committee members, Principles, and list of local correspondents, rptd at intervals down to the present, the text of the Principles remaining the same in all rpts.

Unjust war: to the working-men of England. May 1877 (anon). A single sheet handbill and placard ptd on one side and signed 'A Lover of Justice'; rptd in Morris: artist, writer, socialist, *see* Collections and selections, *above*.

Wake, London lads! [Jan 1878]. A single sheet octavo handbill for a lyric to be sung to the tune of The Hardy Norseman's Home of Yore, at a meeting of The Eastern Question Association.

The decorative arts, their relation to modern life and progress: an address delivered before the Trades' Guild of Learning. London and Boston [Feb 1878] (Boston impression from English stereos). First pbd as The decorative arts, The Architect 8 Dec 1878; rptd as The lesser arts in Hopes and fears for art, *below*.

Address delivered in the Town Hall, Birmingham 19th February 1879. Birmingham [1879] (Birmingham Soc of Arts and School of Design). First pbd untitled The Birmingham Daily Post 20 Feb 1879; rptd 1882 as The art of the people in Hopes and fears for art, *below*; as The art of the people: an address delivered before the Birmingham Society of Arts, Chicago 1902 (R. F. Seymour); as The art of the people, Riverside CT 1914 (F. C. Bursch).

Labour and pleasure versus labour and sorrow: an address ... in the Town Hall, Birmingham, 19th February [1880]. Birmingham 1880; rptd as The beauty of life in Hopes and fears for art, *below*.

Speech ... at a meeting of the Kyrle Society ... January 27 1881. Feb 1881. A single sheet fol broadside off-printed on one side in 3 cols from The Women's Union Jnl Feb 1881; rptd in Morris: artist, writer, socialist, *see* Collections and selections, *above*.

Address delivered ... in the Burslem Town Hall, Oct 13 1881. Burslem 1881 (The Wedgwood Institute: reports of the Schools of Science & Art for the year 1880–81). First pbd as The conditions and prospects of art, The Architect 29 Oct, 5 Nov 1881. Rptd as Art and the beauty of the earth in Hopes and fears for art, *below*; as Art and the beauty of the earth, a lecture delivered by Morris at the Burslem Town Hall ... [ed S. C. Cockerell] '1898' [1899] (Golden type octavo), rptd 1899. Tr Ger 1986.

Hopes and fears for art: five lectures delivered in Birmingham, London and Nottingham 1878–1881. [Feb] 1882 (ordinary edn); Boston 1882 (US setting from advance Eng sheets); 1882 (2nd edn); Boston 1882 (US ordinary edn); 1883 (3rd edn); 1889 (4th edn); 1896 (4th edn reissued with Longman imprint); Boston 1897 (US ordinary edn); 1898 (5th edn); New York 1901 (US ordinary edn); [ed S. C. Cockerell and R. Proctor] 1902 (Golden type quarto, bound in with Signs of change); 1903 (6th edn); New York 1905 (US ordinary edn), rptd 1908; 1914 (Collected works vol 22, bound in with Lectures on art and industry); 1919 (Longman's Pocket Lib); Dayton OH 1970 (ordinary edn microfiche by National Cash Register); New Haven CT 1972 (ordinary edn microfilm, no 801, reel 59 of American Architectural Books); introd P. Faulkner, Bristol 1994 (Collected works vol 22 photo facs Thoemmes Morris Lib); tr Ital 1963. The decorative arts, first published as a pam in 1878 (*see above*) here is retitled The lesser arts; The address delivered in ... Birmingham (*see above*) here appears as The art of the people; Labour and pleasure versus labour and sorrow (*see above*) is here as The beauty of life; Making the best of it previously appeared as Hints on house decoration, The Architect 18, 25 Dec 1880; The prospects of architecture in civilization is first published here.

The history of pattern designing, and The lesser arts of life. In Lectures on art delivered in support of the Society for the Protection of Ancient Buildings, preface by J. T. Micklethwaite, [Feb] 1882. The history of pattern designing was first pbd as Morris on Egyptian, Greek and Roman art, The Architect 19 Apr 1879; The lesser arts of life was first pbd here. Both rptd in Architecture, industry and wealth, *see* Collections and selections, *above*.

The progress of decorative art in England [an address]. As Mr Morris on art matters, The Manchester Guardian 21 Oct 1882; rptd as Mr Morris on English decorative art, The Architect, 28 Oct 1882; rptd from The Manchester Guardian as Mr Morris on art matters, 1961 (Morris Soc).

Art, wealth and riches. The Manchester Quart 2 1883, with a 4° pam off-print Manchester 1883; rptd in Architecture, industry and wealth, *see* Collections and selections *above*. Tr Du 1903, Ital 1963.

Chants for Socialists. No 1 The day is coming [1884]; [No 2] The voice of toil: All for the cause. Two chants for Socialists [1884]. Rptd from Justice. The date is implied by Forman's positioning of this entry in The books of Morris described (*see* Bibliographies, *above*), but this pam was fabricated at a later date (*see* N. Barker and J. Collins, A sequel to An enquiry, §2, *below*); [No 3] Chants for Socialists 1885 (6 poems, some copies have a red wrapper added by Forman (*see* H. G. Pollard, A catalogue of books in Bibliographies, *above*). All 6 rptd from Justice and The Commonweal); [No 4] Chants for Socialists 1885 (the previous 6 poems plus Down among the dead men, rptd from Commonweal); 1915 (Collected works vol 24, bound in with The pilgrims of hope and Scenes from the fall of Troy); 1915 (Longman's Pocket Lib, bound in with The pilgrims of hope). Tr Ger 1909.

Art and socialism: the aims and ideals of the English socialists of today, a lecture delivered (January 23rd, 1884) before the Secular Soc of Leicester ... Leek 1884 (Leek Bijou Reprints no 7); Leek 1884 (2nd edn, Leek Bijou Reprints no 7); Leek 1884 (2nd edn [3rd impression, 1st edn] Leek Bijou Reprints no 7); in Architecture, industry and wealth, ed S. C. Cockerell and R. Proctor 1902; 1915 (Collected works vol 23). Tr Du 1903, Ital 1963.

The God of the poor. '1884' [1890?]. The date 1884 is implied by Forman's positioning of this entry in The books of Morris described (*see* Bibliographies, *above*). An unauthorised pam with a false date implied. See N. Barker and J. Collins, A sequel to An enquiry, *below*, §2. First pbd Fortnightly Review 1 Aug 1868; rptd in Poems by the way, *below*.

Mural decoration. With J. H. Middleton. In Encyclopaedia Britannica vol 17 1884 (9th edn). Rptd in Morris: artist, writer, socialist, vol 1, *see* Collections and selections, *above*.

A review of European society, with an exposition and vindication of the principles of social democracy, by J. Sketchley. Introd by Morris, 1884.

A summary of the principles of socialism written for the Democratic Federation by H. M. Hyndman and Morris. 1884 (Modern Press), rptd 1884 (Modern Press), rptd 1896 (W. Reeves).

Textile fabrics: a lecture delivered in the lecture room of the [International Health] Exhibition, July 11th 1884. Pam.

The Commonweal. Vols 1–6 ed Morris, 1885–90. Monthly from Feb 1885, weekly from 1 May 1886, 16 pp. folio each issue, with 4 pp. suppl Apr–Sep 1885. Morris's contributions rptd in Political writings: contributions to Justice and Commonweal, ed N. Salmon, Bristol 1994 (Thoemmes Morris Lib) and in Journalism: contributions to Commonweal 1885–90, ed N. Salmon Bristol 1996 (Thoemmes Morris Lib), *see* Collections and selections, *above*.

The Socialist League: Hammersmith Branch [manifesto, by Morris]. Hammersmith [1885] (anon). A single sheet octavo leaflet ptd one side only.

Useful work versus useless toil. 1885 (Socialist Platform no 2, ser ed Morris and E. B. Bax); 1886 (Socialist Platform no 2); 1888, rptd in Signs of change (*see* Collections and selections, *above*); 1890 ('Freedom' Lib); 1893 (Hammersmith Socialist Soc); 1898 ('Torch' Lib); 1907 ('Freedom' Lib); Chicago [1909?] (Pocket Lib of Socialism no 48); Sydney 1919; [1977] (photo facs); 1986 (1st edn photo facs Communist Party of Britain Marxist-Leninist).

The manifesto of the Socialist League [signed by The Council of the S. L., drafted by Morris and E. B. Bax]. 1885; 1885 (2nd edn rev, and annotated by Morris and E. B. Bax). An authentic pam which may sometimes be found with an added wrapper created and described by H. B. Forman (*see* N. Barker and J. Collins, A sequel to An enquiry, §2, *below*). First pbd Today Jan 1885.

Socialists at play . . . prologue spoken at the entertainment of the Socialist League; South Place Institute, July 11, 1885. Octavo pam rptd from Commonweal July 1885. A forged 1st edn. (*See* N. Barker and J. Collins, A sequel to an enquiry, *below*, §2).

For whom shall we vote? addressed to the working-men electors of Great Britain. Nov 1885 (by Morris, but signed and dated by the Council of the Socialist League). Octavo pam.

The labour question from the Socialist standpoint. In The claims of labour, ed J. Oliphant, Edinburgh 1886, and as an off printed pam, Edinburgh 1886 (The Claims of Labour Lectures no 5); thereafter rptd as True and false society 1888 (The Socialist Platform no. 6); Hammersmith 1893 (Hammersmith Socialist Soc); 1915 (Collected works vol 23); tr Du 1898.

The pilgrims of hope. Introd by H. B. Forman, '1886' [1900?]. An unauthorised pam with a false date implied. *See* N. Barker and J. Collins, A sequel to An enquiry, §2, *below*. First pbd in 13 irregularly issued instalments in The Commonweal Mar 1885–July 1886, ending with a note 'To be concluded'. Rptd [Preface by T. B. Mosher] Portland ME 1901 (reprints from Priv Ptd Books no 8); 1915 (Collected works vol 24, bound in with Chants for Socialists and Scenes from the fall of Troy); 1915 (Longmans Pocket Lib, bound in with Chants for Socialists); tr Ital 1983.

A short account of the Commune of Paris. With E. B. Bax and V. Dave. [Apr] 1886 (The Socialist Platform no 4).

Socialism. Norwich 1886 (a Daylight Supplement). A single folio sheet offprinted in 4 cols each side. First pbd in [Norwich] Daylight, 13 Mar 1886; rptd in Morris: artist, writer, socialist, *see* Collections and selections, *above*.

What Socialists want. 1886 (anon) (Socialist League Leaflets no 11). A single demy octavo sheet ptd on both sides, rptd 1888.

Socialism: the end and the means. A lecture pbd in [Norwich] Daylight 16 Oct 1886, and as a broadsheet, Norwich [Oct] 1886. A single folio sheet offprinted in 4 cols on both sides.

The aims of art. 1887 (pam, Office of The Commonweal). First pbd in The Artist 8, Sep, Oct, Nov 1887; rptd in Signs of change, *see below*.

All for the cause: a song for Socialists. 1887. Words by Morris, music by E. B. Bax. A single folio sheet folded to form 4 pp. 4to leaflet. First pbd Justice, ptd as a poem in Two chants for Socialists, *see above*, and rptd in Poems by the way, *see below*.

Appeal for the preservation of Inglesham Church. Society for the Protection of Ancient Buildings. [June 1887] (anon). A single sheet octavo leaflet ptd on only one side. 1898 (2nd edn), a single sheet folded to form 2 octavo leaves ptd on pp. 1 & 4 only, with notes at the end. Rptd in Morris: artist, writer, socialist vol 1, *see* Collections and selections, *above*.

On the external coverings of roofs. Society for the Protection of Ancient Buildings. [1887] (anon). S. C. Cockerell's copy, in the BL, is thus dated in his hand. Rptd in Architecture, industry and wealth, *see* Collections and selections, *above*.

Alfred Linnell, killed in Trafalgar Square, November 20 1887: a death song. Sold for the benefit of Linnell's orphans, with a memorial design by Walter Crane. [1887]; rptd as a poem in Morris: artist, writer, socialist vol 1, *see* Collections and selections, *above*.

The tables turned: or Nupkins awakened, a Socialist interlude. 1887 (Office of The Commonweal); rptd in Morris: artist, writer, socialist vol 2, *see* Collections and selections, *above*.

The principles of Socialism made plain; and objections, methods and quack remedies for poverty considered, by F. Fairman. With preface by Morris, 1888.

The Socialist platform written by several hands for the Socialist League, together with the Manifesto and Chants for Socialists by Morris. '1888', '1890' (enlarged to include Monopoly) [1900?]. Though projected by Morris and E. Belfort Bax in their prefatory note to The Socialist Platform no 1, the combined vol of the Platform was only realised in unauthorised wrappers created by H. B. Forman. *See* N. Barker and J. Collins, Sequel to An enquiry, §2, *below*.

A dream of John Ball and A King's lesson. Frontispiece E. Burne-Jones [Mar] 1888. For A King's lesson, *see* separate entry, *below*. A dream of John Ball was first pbd in Commonweal 13 Nov 1886–22 Jan 1887; rptd 1889 ('Cheap edn', without frontispiece); 1890 (3rd edn, without frontispiece); 1892 (4th edn, without frontispiece); frontispiece E. Burne-Jones, 1892 (Kelmscott Press); 1895 (5th edn, without frontispiece); 1896 (5th edn 2nd issue, without frontispiece); as The dream of John Ball: being an idyl in prose (without A King's lesson), East Aurora NY 1898 (The Roycroft Shop); as A dream of John Ball and A King's lesson, 1898 (6th edn, without frontispiece); 1900 (7th edn, without frontispiece); as A dream of John Ball: being an idyl in prose [with A King's lesson], Portland ME 1902 (Old World Ser 28); frontispiece re-cut by R. Catterson-Smith, 1903 (new edn); 1907 (Pocket Lib); as A dream of John Ball: being an idyl in prose [with A King's lesson], Portland ME 1908 (Old World Ser 28); 1910 (ordinary edn, with frontispiece); 1910 (Pocket Lib); New York [191-?] (Miniature Lib); 1912 (Collected works vol 16); 1912 (ordinary edn, with frontispiece); 1912 (Pocket Lib), rptd 1913, 1915, 1918, 1920; (without A King's lesson) ed E. Haldeman-Julius, Girard KS [1920?] (Ten Cent Pocket Ser no 37); 1924 (Pocket Lib), rptd 1928; Berlin 1958 (Seven Seas); New York [197-?] (Oriole Chapbooks); 1987 (Journeyman Press, ordinary edn); tr Du 1898, Ger 1904, Ital 1980.

Signs of change: seven lectures delivered on various occasions. 1888 (ordinary edn); 1896 (new edn, 2nd impression, ordinary edn, Longman's imprint); [ed S. C. Cockerell and R. Proctor] 1902 (Golden type quarto, bound in with Hopes and fears for art); 1903 (new impression, ordinary edn); 1913 (new impression, ordinary edn); 1915 (Collected works vol 23, bound in with Lectures on Socialism); introd P. Faulkner, Bristol 1994 (Collected Works vol 23 photo facs Thoemmes Morris Lib); tr Ger 1902. Several of the lectures collected here were first pbd elsewhere: Useful work versus useless toil and The aims of art first appeared as pam pbd by the Socialist League in 1885 and 1887 respectively (*see above*). Three appeared first in Commonweal: How we live and how we might live (4, 11, 18, 25 June, 2 July 1887); Whigs, democrats and socialists (26 June, 3 July 1886); Feudal England (20, 27 Aug, 3, 10 Sep 1887). The hopes of civilisation and The dawn of a new epoch were first pbd here.

A tale of the house of the Wolfings and all the kindreds of the Mark, written in prose and verse. Includes a 16-line poem pbd first on this title page. '1889' [Dec 1888] (ordinary edn); frontispiece portrait by Hollyer, Boston 1890 (1st impression US setting); 1890 (2nd edn); Boston 1890 ('Cheap edn', 2nd impression US ordinary edn); Boston 1890 ('Cheap edn', 3rd impression US ordinary edn); Boston 1890 ('Cheap edn', 4th impression US ordinary setting, omits frontispiece); Boston 1892 ('Cheap edn', 5th impression ordinary US setting); 1896 (2nd edn, i.e. 2nd issue, with

Longman's imprint); New York 1900 (6th impression, US edn); [ed S. C. Cockerell and R. Proctor] 1901 (Golden type quarto); 1904 (3rd impression, ordinary edn); New York 1906 (7th impression, US ordinary edn); 1909 (4th impression, ordinary edn); 1912 (Collected works vol 14); 1913 (Longman's Pocket Lib); New York 1914 (imported Eng sheets from the Eng 4th impression, ordinary edn); 1979 (Prose romances of Morris, ordinary edn, photo facs).

Society for the Protection of Ancient Buildings: The twelfth annual report of the Soc: report of the Committee and paper read by Mr Morris. July 1889; rptd as Address at the twelfth annual meeting, 3 July 1889, in Morris: artist, writer, socialist vol 1, *see* Collections and selections, *above*.

Glass, painted or stained. In Chambers Encyclopaedia vol 5 1890 (new edn); rptd in Morris; artist, writer, socialist vol 1, *see* Collections and selections, *above*.

The roots of the mountains wherein is told somewhat of the lives of the men of Burgdale, their friends, their neighbours, their foemen and their fellows in arms. Includes an original poem of 14 lines on the title page, which was published in advance as a leaflet advertising the book. '1890' [Nov 1889] ('Superior' and ordinary edns); 1896 (1st edn, 2nd issue, Longman's imprint); 1900 (2nd edn, i.e. 2nd impression ordinary edn); [ed S. C. Cockerell and R. Proctor] '1901' [Jan 1902] (Golden type quarto); 1906 (2nd edn, 3rd impression, ordinary edn); 1912 (Collected works vol 15); in 2 vols 1913 (Longman's 'Pocket Library'); 1913 (4th impression, 1st edn); 1979 (Prose romances of Morris, photo facs).

Monopoly: or how labour is robbed. 1890 (The Socialist Platform no 7), rptd 1891; [c. 1891] ('Freedom' Lib); Hammersmith 1893 (Hammersmith Socialist Soc); New York 1896 (Commonwealth Lib no 28); [1898] (The 'Torch' Lib); 1915 (Collected works vol 23); tr Du nd, Cz nd. First pbd in Commonweal, 7, 14, 21 Dec 1889.

News from nowhere, or an epoch of rest: being some chapters from a utopian romance. Boston 1890 ('author's edn', 1st edn text from Commonweal without Morris's revisions); [Mar] 1891 (ordinary edn, 1st Eng, rev); New York 1891 (US ordinary edn, Unsettled Questions no 3); [Apr] 1891 (2nd edn); [June] 1891 (2nd edn); Boston [July] 1891 ('Author's edn', US ordinary edn); [Mar] 1892 (3rd edn); New York [Nov] 1892 (US ordinary edn); frontispiece by C. M. Gere, '1892' [1893] (Kelmscott Press); Boston 1894 ('Author's edn', US ordinary edn); 1895 (4th edn, ordinary edn); 1896 (4th edn, Longman's imprint), rptd 1897; Boston 1898 ('Author's edn', US ordinary edn); 1899 (6th impression); New York 1901 ('Author's edn', new impression); 1902 (7th edn); New York 1903 ('Author's edn', new impression); 1905 (8th edn); New York 1906 ('Author's edn'); 1907 (9th impression); 1908 (10th impression); London and New York 1910 (11th impression, Eng ordinary edn); New York 1910 ('Author's edn', new impression, US ordinary edn); 1912 (Longman's Pocket Lib); 1912 (Collected works vol 16, bound in with A dream of John Ball and A King's lesson); 1913 ('new impression', Longman's Pocket Lib); New York 1913 ('Author's edn', new impression); 1914 (Longman's Pocket Lib); Chicago [1917]; 1918 (Longman's Pocket Lib), rptd 1919, 1920, 1924; New York 1926; 1934 (Longman's Swan Lib no 14), rptd [1936], 1940; ed. J. R. Redmond 1970; as Morris's News from nowhere: a critical and annotated edn, ed M. R. Liberman, unpbd diss Univ of Nebraska 1971 (3 versions of the novel compared: the Commonweal version, the 1st edn, and the Kelmscott edn); ed. K. Kumar, Cambridge 1995; tr Ital 1895, 1992, Du 1898, Fr 1902, Polish 1902, Rus [1906], Cz 1926, Sp 1928, Swed 1978. First pbd in 39 weekly instalments in Commonweal 6, 11 Jan–4 Oct 1890.

The legend of the briar rose: a series of pictures painted by E. Burne-Jones. With 4 quatrains by Morris. 1890, rptd in Poems by the way, *see below*.

Statement of principles of the Hammersmith Socialist Society. Dec 1890, rptd 1893. Anon.

The Socialist ideal of art. '1891' [1900? after 1893]. The imprint of this pam is fictitious. See N. Barker and J. Collins, A sequel to An enquiry, *see* §2, *below*. The text was first pbd in New Rev Jan 1891; New York '1892' [1891] bound in with O. Wilde, The soul of man under socialism, and W. C. Owen, The coming solidarity; East Aurora NY 1898.

The story of the glittering plain which has been also called the land of living men or the acre of the undying. [May] 1891 (Kelmscott Press); 1891 ('Popular edn', ordinary edn); Boston 1891 (Kelmscott Press edn photo facs); Boston 1892 ('Popular edn' US setting, ordinary edn); 1902 (English 'Popular edn' 2nd issue); illustr W. Crane, 1894 (2nd Kelmscott Press edn); Boston 1896 ('Popular edn', 2nd issue US ordinary edn); Boston 1896 ('Popular edn', 3rd issue US ordinary edn); 1898 (new edn, 2nd impression ordinary edn); New York 1900 (USA 'Popular edn', 2nd impression); 1904 (new edn, ordinary edn); [unsigned introd J. W. Mackail] 1905 (Longman's Class Books of Eng Lit); New York 1905 ('Popular edn', US ordinary edn); [introd Mackail] 1906 (Longman's Class Books of Eng Lit), rptd 1908, 1912; 1912 (Collected works vol 14, bound in with The house of the Wolfings); 1913 (Longman's Pocket Lib, new edn); London and New York 1914 (Eng 'Popular edn'); 1979 ('Popular edn' photo facs); as The glittering plain: or the land of the living men, illustr W. Crane, 1987 (2nd Kelmscott Press edn, photo facs, Prose romances of Morris); introd N. Talbot, Bristol 1996 (photo facs from Collected works vol 14, here bound in with Child Christopher and Goldilind the fair, Thoemmes Morris Lib); tr Ger 1985. First pbd as The glittering plain: or the land of the living men, in Eng Illustr Mag 7 in 4 instalments, June–Sep 1890.

Poems by the way. 1891 (Kelmscott Press); 1891 (Chiswick Press, ordinary edn); Boston 1892 (US setting); 1892 (2nd edn, ordinary edn); 1896 (2nd edn, 2nd issue Longman's imprint); Boston 1896 (US ordinary edn); 1899 (2nd edn, ordinary edn); New York 1900 (remaining Roberts stock with Longman's imprint); 1910 (new edn, Longman's Pocket Lib); 1911 (Collected works vol 9, bound in with Love is enough); introd D. Latham, Bristol 1994 (photo facs of Collected works vol 9, Thoemmes Morris Lib).

Address on the collection of paintings of the English Pre-Raphaelite school. Birmingham 1891; rptd in Morris: artist, writer, socialist, *see* Collections and selections, *above*.

A King's lesson. Ed and ptd by J. Leatham, Aberdeen 1891 (Penny Pam Ser); London and Aberdeen 1901 (2nd edn, J. Leatham, London distributor: W. Reeves); London and Peterhead 1902 (3rd edn, Leek Bijou Reprints no 1, The Sentinel Press, Peterhead, London distributor: The Twentieth Century Press); London and Peterhead [1904?] (4th edn, J. Leatham at the Sentinel Office); Cottingham [1914?] (5th edn, J. Leatham); Turriff [post-1916] (6th edn, J. Leatham, The Deveron Press). In J. Leatham's publications of A King's lesson and Under an elm-tree (*see below*) each successive edn is entirely re-set. A King's lesson was first pbd as An old story retold, in Commonweal 18 Sep 1888, then as A King's lesson bound in with The dream of John Ball in 1888, *see above*.

Under an elm-tree: or thoughts in the country-side. Ed and ptd by J. Leatham, Aberdeen 1891 (Penny Pam Ser, some copies could have an unauthorised pale green printed wrapper of which 50 were created by H. B. Forman, *see* N. Barker and J. Collins, A sequel to An enquiry, §2 *below*); Aberdeen 1891 (2nd edn); foreword by H. Burke, Hammersmith [1893?] (new edn, The Liberty Press); Peterhead 1902 (3rd edn 'cum privilegio auctoris', Leek Bijou Reprints no 2, London distrbutor: The Twentieth Century Press); foreword by J. Leatham, Westerton-of-Clerkhill, Peterhead [1907?] (4th edn, The Clerkhill Press); afterword W. B. Yeats, extract from The happiest of poets, Portland ME Apr 1912 (The Bibelot vol 18 no 4). First pbd in Commonweal July 1889.

The nature of Gothic: a chapter of the Stones of Venice by John Ruskin. Preface by Morris. Feb 1892 (Kelmscott Press); New York 1977 (photo facs).

The reward of labour: a dialogue. [Dec 1892] (Hammersmith Socialist Lib no 1) First pbd Commonweal 21, 28 May 1887.
Manifesto of English Socialists [with H. M. Hyndman and G. B. Shaw]. [May] 1893 (anon).
Concerning Westminster Abbey. The Society for the Protection of Ancient Buildings. [June] 1893 (anon). This pam sometimes has a wrapper fabricated by H. B. Forman, *see* N. Barker and J. Collins, A sequel to An enquiry, §2, *below*. Text rptd in Architecture and history, and Westminster Abbey, *see* Collections and selections, *above*.
Medieval lore. Ed R. Steele, preface by Morris, [July] 1893; ed I. Gollancz 1895 (Medieval Lib); 1905 (A. Loring); 1907 (Chatto); New York 1966 (photo facs). Morris's preface rptd in Morris: artist, writer, socialist vol 1, *see* Collections and selections, *above*.
Utopia by Sir Thomas More. Foreword by Morris [Sep] 1893 (Kelmscott Press). Morris's foreword rptd in Morris: artist, writer, socialist vol 1, *see* Collections and selections, *above*.
Arts and crafts essays by members of the Arts and Crafts Exhibition Society. Ed with a preface and 3 essays by Morris: Textiles, Printing (with Emery Walker), Of dyeing as an art [July] 1893, rptd 1899, 1903; introd P. Faulkner, Bristol 1996 (1st edn photo facs Thoemmes Morris Lib). Morris's contributions are rptd in Morris: artist, writer, socialist, *see* Collections and selections, *above*.
Gothic architecture: a lecture for the Arts and Crafts Exhibition Society. [Oct] 1893 (Kelmscott Press), rptd in Morris: artist, writer, socialist, *see* Collections and selections, *above*.
Socialism: its growth and outcome. With E. B. Bax. New York and London 1893; rptd 1896 (2nd edn Social Science Ser); rptd 1908 (3rd edn); Chicago 1909; New York 1984 (photo facs). First pbd as Socialism from the root up, in Commonweal at irregular intervals 15 May 1886–19 May 1888.
Help for the miners: the deeper meaning of the struggle. 10 Nov 1893 (a single sheet octavo ptd on both sides as an offprint from Daily Chron); rptd in Morris: artist, writer, socialist vol 2, *see* Collections and selections, *above*.
Address at the distribution of prizes to students of the Birmingham Municipal School of Art. Birmingham [July] 1894; [ed S. C. Cockerell] 1898 (Golden type octavo); 1915 (Collected works vol 22); in Fourteen addresses delivered to students of the Birmingham Municipal School of Art, Birmingham 1924.
The wood beyond the world. Frontispiece designed by E. Burne-Jones, [Oct] 1894 (Kelmscott Press); '1895' [1894] photo facs of Burne-Jones frontispiece; Boston 1895 (re-set); 1900 (re-issue); New York 1902 (2nd impression, US setting); 1904; rptd 1911; 1913 (Longman's Pocket Lib); 1913 (Collected works vol 17, bound in with Three Old French romances and Child Christopher); New York 1972 (Kelmscott Press Photo facs); 1979 (The prose romances of Morris, ordinary edn, photo facs); ed T. Shippey, Oxford 1980; tr Ger 1984.
Why I am a Communist. Bound in with L. S. Bevington's Why I am an expropriationist. 1894 (The why I ams, 2nd ser). First pbd Liberty Feb 1894. Rptd in Morris: artist, writer, socialist vol 2, *see* Collections and selections, *above*.
Good King Wenceslas: a carol, by Dr Neale. Illustr A. J. Gaskin, introd Morris, Birmingham 1895. Introd rptd in Morris: artist, writer, socialist vol 1, *see* Collections and selections, *above*.
Child Christopher and Goldilind the Fair. 2 vols [Sep] 1895 (Kelmscott Press); [unsigned preface by T. B. Mosher] Portland ME 1900 (Miscellaneous Ser no 12); 1913 (Collected works vol 17, bound in with The wood beyond the world and Three Old French romances); ed R. Matthews, Van Nuys CA 1977 (Newcastle, Forgotten Fantasy Classics); introd N. Talbot, Bristol 1996 (from Collected works vol 17, photo facs Thoemmes Morris Lib). Morris's version of Havelock the Dane.
Gossip about an old house on the upper Thames. Birmingham 'Nov 1895' [1900?]. A fabricated pam made, except for preliminaries and postlims of leaves excised from the mag Quest Nov 1895. *See* N. Barker and J. Collins, A sequel to An enquiry, §2 *below*. First pbd Quest Nov 1895; rptd, illustr photo facs C. M. Gere and E. H. New, Flushing NY 1901 (J. E. Hill) and in Morris: artist, writer, socialist vol 1, *see* Collections and selections, *above*.
The well at the world's end: a tale. Illustr E. Burne-Jones, 1896 (Kelmscott Press); 2 vols 1896 (Longman's ordinary edn), rptd 1903, 1910; 2 vols 1913 (Collected works vols 18, 19); 2 vols 1913 (Longman's Pocket Lib); Introd by L. Carter 2 vols 1970, 1971; 2 vols 1979 (ordinary edn photo facs, The prose romances of Morris); tr Ger 1986.
How I became a Socialist, by Morris; with some account of his connection with the Social-Democratic Federation by H. M. Hyndman. Oct 1896. Rptd from Justice July 1894, May Day 1895 and 1896. Some copies have an unauthorised wrapper created by H. B. Forman, *see* H. G. Pollard, A catalogue, in Bibliographies, *above*.
The water of the wondrous isles. [July] 1897 (Kelmscott Press); New York and London [Oct] 1897 (set and ptd in Boston for both USA and Britain, Longman's ordinary edn), rptd 1902, 1909; 1913 (Collected works vol 20); 2 vols 1914 (Longman's Pocket Lib); 1979 (ordinary edn, photo facs The prose romances of Morris); introd N. Talbot, Bristol 1994 (Collected works vol 20 photo facs Thoemmes Morris Lib).
Some German woodcuts of the fifteenth century. Ed S. C. Cockerell '1897' [Jan 1898] (Kelmscott Press). Rpts as an introd part of Morris's article On the aesthetic qualities of the woodcut books of Ulm and Augsburg in the fifteenth century, first pbd in Bibliographica vol 1 no 4 1895.
The sundering flood. '1897' [Feb 1898] (Kelmscott Press); New York and London 1898 (set and ptd in Boston for both USA and Britain, Longman's ordinary edn); rptd 1910; 2 vols '1914' [Dec 1913] (Longman's Pocket Lib); 1914 (Collected works vol 21, bound in with Four unfinished romances); 1979 (ordinary edn, photofacs The prose romances of Morris).
The hollow land: a tale. 2 pts, Portland ME July, Aug 1897 (The Bibelot vol 3 nos 1, 2); [unsigned introd by T. B. Mosher] Portland ME 1897 (reprints from Bibelot 2); [unsigned introd by T. B. Mosher] Portland ME 1900 (Brocade Ser 22); [unsigned introd by T. B. Mosher] Portland ME 1903 (Brocade Ser 22); Hingham MA 1905 (F. Goudy, The Village Press); [unsigned introd by T. B. Mosher] Portland ME 1908 (Brocade Ser 22); tr Ital 1988. First pbd in 2 pts The Oxford and Cambridge Mag Sep, Oct 1856; rptd in The hollow land and other contributions to The Oxford and Cambridge Mag, *see* Collections and Selections, *above*.
Browning's 'Men and women'; a review. Portland ME [Mar] 1898 (The Bibelot vol 4 no 3). First pbd The Oxford and Cambridge Mag Mar 1856. Rptd in The hollow land and other contributions to The Oxford and Cambridge Mag, *see* Collections and selections, *above*.
A note by Morris on his aims in founding the Kelmscott Press, together with a short description of the press by S. C. Cockerell and an annotated list of the books printed thereat. [Mar] 1898 (Kelmscott Press); rptd in H. H. Sparling, The Kelmscott Press and Morris, master-craftsman, 1898, *see* Bibliographies, *above*; rptd as Aims in founding the Kelmscott Press, 1985 (Cadenza).
Gertha's lovers: a tale. [Unsigned introd by T. B. Mosher], in 2 pts, Portland ME Jan, Feb 1899 (The Bibelot vol 5 nos 1, 2), rptd 1899 (reprints from Bibelot 5), rptd 1902 (Brocade Ser 32), rptd 1905. First pbd in 2 pts The Oxford and Cambridge Mag July, Aug 1856; rptd in The hollow land and other contributions to The Oxford and Cambridge Mag, *see* Collections and selections, *above*.
The ideal book: an address. New York 1899, rptd 1909; in Zeitschrift für Bücherfreunde band 5 1900; in The art and craft of printing, New Rochelle NY 1902; '1908' [1907]; rptd 1957. Lecture delivered

in 1893 and first pbd in Trans Biblio Soc vol 1 1893. Rptd in Morris: artist, writer, socialist vol 1 and in The ideal book: essays and lectures on the arts of the book, *see* Collections and selections, *above*.

Some hints on pattern designing. [Ed S. C. Cockerell and R. Proctor] 1899 (Golden type octavo). A lecture first pbd in 2 pts The Architect 17, 24 Dec 1881. Rptd 1914 (Collected works vol 22, bound in with Hopes and fears for art, *see* Collection and selections, *above*).

Golden wings: a tale. Portland ME Apr 1900 (The Bibelot vol 6 no 4); rptd Sep 1900 (reprints from Bibelot 8, bound in with Svend and his brethren, *below*), rptd 1902; 1905 (J. Finch & Co); Portland ME 1906 (Brocade Ser 33). First pbd The Oxford and Cambridge Mag Dec 1856; rptd in The hollow land and other contributions to The Oxford and Cambridge Mag, *see* Collections and selections, *above*.

Svend and his brethren: a tale. Portland ME Sep 1900 (The Bibelot vol 6 no 9), rptd 1900 (reprints from Bibelot 8, bound in with Golden wings); Aiken SC 1901; Portland ME 1902 (Brocade Ser 33, bound in with Golden wings); 1905 (J. Finch & Co); Portland ME 1906 (Brocade Ser 33, bound in with Golden wings); Englewood NJ 1906. First pbd The Oxford and Cambridge Mag Aug 1856; rptd in The hollow land and other contributions to the Oxford and Cambridge Mag, *see* Collections and selections, *above*.

The churches of north France No 1. Portland ME Mar 1901 (The Bibelot vol 7 no 3); rptd 1901 (reprints from Bibelot 9, bound in with Death the avenger and death the friend); as Some great churches in France: three essays by Morris and W. Pater [unsigned foreword by T. B. Mosher], Portland ME 1903 (Brocade Ser 39, bound in with 2 essays by Pater), rptd 1905, 1912. The Morris essay was first pbd as The churches of north France No 1 – in the shadow of Amiens, The Oxford and Cambridge Mag Feb 1856; rptd in The hollow land and other contributions to The Oxford and Cambridge Mag, *see* Collections and selections, *above*.

The art and craft of printing. New Rochelle NY 1902; as Printing: an essay, with E. Walker, binding design by B. Goudy, Hingham MA 1903. First pbd as Printing in Arts and crafts essays by members of the Arts and Crafts Exhibition Society, *see above*; rptd in Morris: artist, writer, socialist vol 1, *see* Collections and selections, *above*.

The doom of King Acrisius. New York 1902 (R. H. Russell & Son, companion vol to Pygmalion and the image, *see below*). First pbd in The earthly paradise vol 1, *see above*.

A dream. Portland ME July 1902 (The Bibelot vol 8 no 7); Wimbledon May 1904 (Avon Booklet vol 2 no 11); 1905; tr Ital 1988. First pbd in The Oxford and Cambridge Mag Mar 1856; rptd in The hollow land and other contributions to The Oxford and Cambridge Mag, *see* Collections and selections, *above*.

In praise of my lady. St Charles IL 1902 (Morris Press). First pbd in The defence of Guenevere and other poems, *see above*.

Pygmalion and the image. New York 1902 (companion vol to The doom of King Acrisius, *see above*). First pbd in The earthly paradise vol 1, *see above*.

Communism. Ed G. B. S. [George Bernard Shaw] 1903 (Fabian Tract no 113), rptd 1907, 1923; 1915 (Collected works vol 23, bound in with Signs of change); in The Socialist Leader, 4, 11, 18 Jan 1969.

The man born to be king. Ed with introd and notes [by J. W. Mackail] for use by schools and colleges. 1905 (Longman's Class Books of Eng Lit); rptd 1906, Jan & Apr 1911, 1912; tr Ger 1933. First pbd in The earthly paradise vol 1, *see above*.

A factory as it might be. Preface by J. Leatham, 1907 (Social Democratic Federation). First pbd in 3 pts Justice: pt 1 as A factory as it might be, pts 2 & 3 as Work in a factory as it might be, 17, 31 May, 28 June 1884. Rptd in Morris: artist, writer, socialist vol 2, *see* Collections and selections, *above*.

Journals of travels in Iceland 1871, 1873. 1911 (Collected works vol 8); introd J. Morris 1969 (Collected works vol 8 photo facs), rptd 1995.

The revolt of Ghent. Ed J. Leatham, Huddersfield, London and Manchester [1911] (omits the 7th instalment of the original). First pbd in Commonweal in 8 weekly instalments, 7 July–18 Aug 1888. Lecture first delivered 29 Jan 1888.

Summer dawn. Illustr L. A. Govey. 1911 (Feather Weights). First pbd in The defence of Guenevere and other poems, *see above*.

Two red roses across the moon. Illustr L. A. Govey, 1911 (Feather Weights). First pbd in The defence of Guenevere and other poems, *see above*.

Sir Peter Harpdon's end: a tragedy. Ed and introd [T. B. Mosher], critical estimate by J. Drinkwater, 2 pts, Portland ME July, Aug 1914 (The Bibelot vol 20 nos 7, 8). Scene 4, excised from the first pbd version in The defence of Guenevere and other poems (*see above*), is here restored, using the text as ptd in the introd to the Collected works version, vol 1 1910, *see* Collections and selections, *above*.

Waddington, S. Sonnets by Morris. Athenaeum 24 Oct 1914. Identifies 2 Morris sonnets pbd unsigned in Atlantic Monthly Feb, Mar 1870.

Morris, M. Sonnets by Morris. Athenaeum 7 Nov 1914. Confirms, by reference to the mss, that the 2 sonnets attributed to Morris by Waddington, *above*, are indeed by Morris.

Scenes from the fall of Troy and other poems and fragments. [Jan] 1915 (Collected works vol 24, *see* Collections and selections, *above*).

The wanderers: being the prologue to The earthly paradise. Ed with an introd and notes [by J. W. Mackail] for use by schools and colleges. 1923 (Longman's Class Books of Eng Lit).

Some thoughts on the ornamented mss of the middle ages [from an unpbd ms in the Huntington Lib]. Introd M. B. Cary, jr, New York 1934 (Press of the Woolly Whale); rptd in The ideal book: essays and lectures in the arts of the book, *see* Collections and selections, *above*.

Morris and his Praise of wine. Los Angeles 1958 (priv ptd). With transcript of Morris's poem, and of an unpbd sonnet written after 1867. The title poem is included in Morris: artist, writer, socialist, *see* Collections and selections, *above*.

Mr Morris on art matters. 1961. Lecture delivered in 1882 as The progress of decorative art in England, rptd from Manchester Guardian 21 Oct 1882 (Morris Soc); also pbd as Mr Morris on English decorative art, The Architect 28 Oct 1882.

Ellison, R. C. An unpublished poem by Morris. English 15 1964.

DeLaura, D. J. An unpublished poem of Morris. MP 62 1965.

An unpublished lecture of Morris: 'How shall we live then?' Ed P. Meier, in The International Review of Social History [Amsterdam] 16 1971 (also an offprint therefrom).

The story of Cupid and Psyche . . . with wood engravings designed by E. Burne-Jones and mostly engraved by Morris, with an introd by A. R. Dufty. 1974.

Goodwin, K. Unpublished lyrics of Morris. In YES 5 1975. Several lyrics here are taken from draft mss in the BL. Ed. R. Pearson. Silence and pity: an unpublished fair copy. In Jnl Morris Soc 9 Spring 1991. A revised version, here with a title, of one of the lyrics previously pbd in draft form by K. Goodwin in Unpublished lyrics of Morris, *see above*.

The expedition of 'The Ark'. Ed J.-M. Baïssus. Jnl Morris Soc 3 1977. Log of a journey up the Thames to Kelmscott Manor, from BL Add MS 45407.

A book of verse: a facsimile of a ms written in 1870. Introd J. I. Whalley, 1980.

Morris's Socialist diary. Ed F. Boos, Iowa City IA 1981 (priv ptd, with notes by F. Boos); 1981 (The History Workshop no 13); ed F. Boos, New York and London 1984.

A variorium edition of the omitted prologue and tales of Morris's Earthly paradise. Ed D. Latham, unpbd diss, York Univ, Toronto 1981. Prints text of 1st prologue, The story of Dorothea, The story of Orpheus and Eurydice, The wooing of Swanhild, and The story of Aristomenes.

The novel on blue paper. Ed P. Fitzgerald 1982 (Journeyman Chapbook 6).

How we live and how we might live. With a modern assessment. 1990 (Socialist Party of Great Britain); tr Ger 1993. First pbd in Commonweal, 4, 11, 18, 25 June, 2 July 1887; in Signs of change, 1888 (ordinary edn, Reeves & Turner); [ed S. C. Cockerell and R. Proctor] 1902 (Golden type quarto); 1915 (Collected works vol 23, bound in with Lectures on art and industry).

The widow's house by the great water. Ed. H. Timo, Iowa City IA 1990 (Morris Soc).

Translations

Grettis Saga: the story of Grettir the strong. Tr from Icelandic by Morris and E. Magnússon. 1869; London and New York 1900 (2nd edn & 'New edn'); [ed S. C. Cockerell and R. Proctor] 1901 (Golden type quarto); 1911 (Collected works vol 7, bound in with The story of the Völsungs and Niblungs); 1980 (photo facs).

Völsunga Saga: the story of the Völsungs and Niblungs with certain songs from the Elder Edda. Tr from Icelandic by E. Magnússon and Morris. 1870, rptd 1879; ed H. H. Sparling, London and New York 1888 (Camelot Ser); [ed S. C. Cockerell and R. Proctor]. 1901 (Golden type quarto, bound in with Three northern love stories and other tales); 1911 (Collected works vol 7, bound in with Grettis Saga: the story of Grettir the strong); introd R. Gutman. New York and London 1962; 1980 (photo facs).

Three northern love stories and other tales. Tr from Icelandic by Morris and E. Magnússon. 1875. The story of Gunnlaug the worm-tongue and Raven the Skald first pbd Fortnightly Rev Jan 1869; The story of Frithiof the bold in 2 pts in Dark Blue Mar–Apr 1871. The remaining 4 tales – Viglund the fair, Hogni and Hedinn, Roi the fool, and Thorstein staff-smitten – appear here for the first time. Rptd Apr 1901 ('Popular edn' new set); [ed S. C. Cockerell and R. Proctor] Nov 1901 (Golden type quarto, bound in with Völsunga Saga); 1911 (Collected works vol 10, bound in with The tale of Beowulf); intro by G. Aho, Bristol 1996 (photo facs from Collected works vol 10).

The Aeneids of Virgil done into English verse. '1876' [1875]; Boston '1876' [1875] (imported English sheets); 1876 (2nd edn); Boston 1876 ('Author's edn', re-set 'from the London 2nd edn'); 1889 (2nd edn); Boston 1896 ('Author's edn', 'from the London 2nd edn'); 1896 (The poetical works of Morris), rptd 1900 (The poetical works of Morris); New York 1900 ('Author's edn', from the 2nd London edn'); [ed S. C. Cockerell and R. Proctor] 1902 (Golden type quarto); 1910 ('New impression', 'Author's edn', 'from the 2nd London edn'); 1911 (Collected works vol 11).

The Odyssey of Homer done into English verse by Morris. 2 vols Apr, Nov 1887; complete in 1 vol 1887; 1897 (Longman's 'Popular edn', Poetical works of Morris); [ed S. C. Cockerell and R. Proctor] 1901 (Golden type quarto); 1904 (Longman's 'Popular edn', Poetical works of Morris);1912 (Collected works vol 13).

The story of Gunnlaug the worm-tongue and Raven the Skald. Even as Ari Thorgilson the learned, the priest, hath told it who was the man of all Iceland most learned in tales of the land's inhabiting and in lore of time agone. Tr from Icelandic by Morris and E. Magnússon. '1891' [1890] (priv ptd). Text first pbd The Fortnightly Rev Jan 1869.

The Saga library. 5 vols 1891–5 [vol 6, index and notes to Heimskringla by Magnússon 1905]. Tr from Icelandic by Morris and Magnússon. Vol 1 The story of Howard the Halt, The story of the banded men, The story of Hen Thorir, 1891, 1891 (2nd impression, 1st edn), 1894 (3rd impression); vol 2 The story of the Ere-Dwellers (Eyrbyggja Saga) with the story of the Heath-Slayings (Heiðarviga Saga) as appendix, 1892, 1892 (2nd impression), 1906 (3rd impression); Saga Lib vols 3–5, The stories of the kings of Norway called the Round World (Heimskringla), by Snorri Sturluson, vols 1–3 1893–5.

The order of chivalry. Tr from French by W. Caxton. Ed with memoranda concerning the two pieces here reprinted, by F. S. Ellis. Bound in with L'Ordene de Chevalerie, with verse tr Morris. Hammersmith 'Feb' [Apr] 1893 (Kelmscott Press); 1913 (Collected works vol 17, bound in with The wood beyond the world, Child Christopher, and Old French romances). The order of chivalry is from a 13th-century Catalans original by Ramon Llull, Llibre d'orde de cavalayleria. The poem L'Orden de Chevalerie is from a 13th-century original reprinted in Fabliaux et contes, Paris 1808.

The tale of King Florus and the Fair Jehane. Tr from Old French by Morris. [Dec] 1893 (Kelmscott Press); introd J. Jacobs, in Old French romances 1896 (G. Allen); introd J. Jacobs, Portland ME [Sep] 1898 (Brocade Ser 11), rptd [Nov] 1898, 1904, 1915.

Of the friendship of Amis and Amile. Done out of ancient French by Morris [Apr] 1894 (Kelmscott Press); introd J. Jacobs. In Old French romances 1896 (G. Allen); as The story of Amis and Amilie, foreword by T. B. Mosher, Portland ME [Aug] 1896 (Brocade Ser 3), rptd Dec 1896, 1897, 1898, 1899, 1909.

The tale of the Emperor Coustans and of Over Sea. Done out of ancient French into English by Morris. [Sep] 1894 (Kelmscott Press); introd J. Jacobs in Old French romances.1896 (G. Allen); introd J. Jacobs, Portland ME 1899 (Brocade Ser 13), rptd 1900, 1912.

Old French romances. Done into English by Morris. With introd by J. Jacobs. [Reprints the 4 old French tales pbd as 3 vols, *above*.] [May] 1896 (G. Allen, ordinary edn); 1913 (Collected works vol 17, bound in with Child Christopher and The wood beyond the world); 1914 (ordinary edn).

The tale of Beowulf, sometime King of the folk of the Weder Geats. Done out of the Old English tongue by Morris and A. J. Wyatt. [Feb] 1895 (Kelmscott Press); 1898 (new edn, Longman's ordinary edn, The poetical works of Morris), rptd 1904, 1910; 1911 (Collected works vol 10, bound in with Three northern love stories).

The history of over-sea. Tr from Old French by Morris. Portland ME [June] 1899 (Brocade Ser 14), rptd 1900; done into English out of the Ancient French, decorations by L. Rhead, New York 1902; Portand ME 1909 (Brocade Ser 14). First pbd 1894 (Kelmscott Press, bound in with The tale of the Emperor Coustans), and in Old French romances, *see above*.

The saga of Hen Thorir. Tr from Icelandic by Morris and E. Magnússon. Design and borders by A. E. Goetting. Cincinnati 1903. First pbd in Saga Library vol 1.

The story of Frithiof the Bold. Tr from Icelandic by Morris and E. Magnússon. Portland ME Jan, Feb 1908. First pbd in Dark Blue Mar, Apr 1871; rptd in Three northern love stories, *see above*.

Kormak's saga: the story of Kormak son of Ogmund. Ed G. Calder. Tr Morris and E. Magnússon. 1963 (Morris Soc). From a ms in the Pierpont Morgan Lib.

Letters

Letters on socialism. 1894 (priv ptd by T. J. Wise). 4 letters to Rev G. Bainton; rptd in The collected letters of Morris, *see below*.

[Letter to P. Webb re Kelmscott Press presentation copies, dated 27 Aug 1894]. 1903 (100 copies priv ptd for Webb's presentation of his Kelmscott Press books to Trinity College, Cambridge); rptd in Walsdorf, Morris in private press and limited editions, *see* Bibliographies, *above*.

Hubbard, E. This then is a Morris book. East Aurora NY 1907 (with 7 letters to R. Thomson, dated 20 June, 24 July 1884; 1, 15 Jan, 6 Apr, 23 July 1885; 25 Feb 1886).

[Morris to J. Leatham, 21 Apr 1893]. Pbd in The Gateway (Turriff) 29 July 1942.

Letters of Morris to his family and friends. Ed P. Henderson 1950.

Unpublished letters of Morris. Ed R. P. Arnot 1951 (Labour Monthly Pam no 6). Letters to J. L. Mahon and Rev. J. Glasse.

Stokes, E. E., jr. Morris letters at Texas. Jnl Morris Soc 1, 1963.
Arnot, R. P. Morris, the man and the myth. Including letters of Morris to J. L. Mahon and Dr J. Glasse. 1964. Includes 30 unpbd letters to Mahon.
Stokes, E. E. Morris to Louisa Baldwin: more letters at Texas. Jnl Morris Soc 2 1968. 12 letters.
Le Bourgeois, J. Y. Morris to G. B. Shaw. Durham Univ Jnl vol 34 1973. 13 letters.
Harris, R. L. Morris, E. Magnússon and Iceland: a survey of unpublished correspondence. VP 13 Fall–Winter 1975.
Landow, G. P. Morris to Swinburne [27 Apr 1882]. Jnl Morris Soc vol 4 Winter 1979.
Collected letters of Morris. Ed N. Kelvin in 4 vols, 5 pts, Princeton and London 1984–96. Vol 1 (1841–80) 1984; vol 2 pt A (1881–4), pt B (1885–8) 1987; vol 3 (1889–92) 1995; vol 4 (1893–6) 1996.
Four letters from Morris. Ed P. Stansky, San Francisco 1984.
Faulkner, P. Morris and the Working Men's College. Jnl Morris Soc 8 1989. 5 letters to the College.
See also E. P. Thompson, *§2, below.*

§2

Representative reviews of Morris's major works are rptd in Morris: the critical heritage, ed P. Faulkner, 1973. *The reviews cited here, selected from those that do not appear in Faulkner, also respond to the original edns. Apart from the reviews and contemporary criticism, the secondary sources listed below are limited, with few exceptions, to those concerned with the texts of Morris's publications, their language, their revisions, their printing and other aspects of their transmission.*

The William Morris Society, *founded in 1956, with branches in the USA and Canada, publishes both a quarterly* Newsletter *and, twice yearly,* The Jnl of the William Morris Soc (1961–). *Its headquarters at Kelmscott House, 26 Upper Mall, Hammersmith, houses a collection of Morris books, papers and memorabilia. Significant collections of Morris materials, including Morris and Company products as well as books and papers, are located at* The William Morris Gallery, Walthamstow, *and at* The Victoria and Albert Museum.

New mag [review of the 1st no of The Oxford and Cambridge Mag]. Spectator 19 Jan 1856 (anon).
[Review of the 1st and 2nd nos of The Oxford and Cambridge Mag]. John Bull 16 Feb 1856 (anon).
Sanders, T. C. Undergraduate Lit [review of The Oxford and Cambridge Mag]. Saturday Rev 28 Feb 1857.
Shirley, [J. S.] A raid among the rhymers [review of Defence of Guenevere]. Fraser's Mag 61, June 1860.
[Review of The life and death of Jason]. Athenaeum 15, June 1867 (anon).
[Review of Earthly paradise vol 1]. Athenaeum 30, May 1868 (anon).
James, H. [Review of Earthly paradise vol 1]. North Amer Rev 107, July 1869.
Criticisms on contemporaries: Morris. Tinsley's Mag 3, Oct 1869 (anon).
Austin, A. In Poetry of the period, 1870.
[Review of Grettis Saga]. Saturday Rev 29 Jan 1870 (anon).
Forman, H. B. In Our living poets, 1871.
[Review of Love is enough]. Athenaeum 23 Nov 1872 (anon).
Fraser, G. Love is enough. Dark Blue 4, Jan 1873. Review.
[Review of Love is enough]. Spectator 11, Jan 1873 (anon).
Howells, W. D. [Review of Love is enough]. Atlantic Monthly 31, Mar 1873.
[Review of Love is enough]. London Quart Rev 1873 (anon).
Swinburne, A. C. In Essays and studies, 1875.
Watts, T. [Review of Sigurd the Volsung]. Athenaeum 9 Dec 1876.
Morley, H. [Review of Sigurd the Volsung]. Nineteenth Century 2, Nov 1877.
The decoration of houses. Art Jnl (New York) 4, Apr 1878 (anon). Review of The decorative arts.
[Review of Some hints on house decoration]. American Architect and Building News 8 Jan 1881.
Hamilton, W. In his Aesthetic movement in England, 1882.
Poets and politics. Spectator 10 Oct 1885 (anon). Review of Chants for Socialists.
Shaw, G. B. Mr Morris on the Aims of art. Pall Mall Gazette 3 July 1886. Review of Morris's The aims of art.
Lang, A. Morris's Odyssey. Macmillan's Mag 56, June 1887.
The Aristophanes of Farringdon Road: a Socialist interlude. Pall Mall Gazette 17 Oct 1887. Review of the 1st-night performance of The tables turned: or Nupkins awakened.
Ballantyne, A. Wardour-Street English. Longman's Mag 12, Oct 1888. Review of Morris's Odyssey trn.
[Review of The dream of John Ball and A King's lesson]. Athenaeum 22 Dec 1888 (anon).
[Review of The dream of John Ball and A King's lesson]. Westminster Rev 130, July 1888 (anon).
[Review of Signs of change]. Westminster Rev 130, July 1888 (anon).
Elton, C. [Review of Roots of the mountains]. Academy 21 Dec 1889.
Pater, W. Aesthetic poetry. In Appreciations, 1889.
Wilde, O. Mr Morris's last book. Pall Mall Gazette 2 Mar 1889. Review of The house of the Wolfings.
Bellamy, E. News from nowhere: Morris's idea of the good time coming. New Nation 14 Feb 1891. Review.
Mallock, W. H. The individualist ideal: a reply. New Rev 4, Feb 1891. Responds to Morris's The socialist ideal of art, *see* §1, *above.*
[Review of News from nowhere]. The Week [Toronto] 27 Mar 1891.
Payne, W. M. The glittering plain. Dial 5 Dec 1891. Review.
The glittering plain. Westminster Rev 138, July 1892 (anon). Review.
The laureateship. Spectator 15 Oct 1892 (anon).
Moulton, L. C. Three English poets. Arena 6 June 1892.
[Review of Poems by the way]. Saturday Rev 6 Feb 1892 (anon).
[Review of Poems by the way]. Athenaeum 12 Mar 1892 (anon).
The question of the laureateship. Bookman 3, Nov 1892 (anon).
Kingsland, W. G. A poet's politics: Morris in unpublished letters on Socialism. In Poet Lore vol 7 nos 10 & 11 1895. Review of the T. J. Wise edn of Morris's Letters on Socialism, *see* §1, *above.*
Blatchford, R. A radical tribute to Morris. Clarion 10 Oct 1896. Obituary.
Carpenter, E. Morris. Freedom 10 Dec 1896. Obituary.
Cunningham-Graham, R. B. With the great north-west wind. Saturday Rev 10 Oct 1896. Obituary.
Le Gallienne, R. Morris. Star 7 Oct 1896. Obituary.
Magnússon, E. Morris. Cambridge Rev 26 Nov 1896. Obituary.
Oelsner, H. [Review of Old French romances]. Academy 2 May 1896.
Shaw, G. B. Morris as actor and dramatist. Saturday Rev 10 Oct 1896.
Symons, A. Atlantic Monthly Dec 1896.
Crane, W. Morris. Scribner's Mag 22, July 1897.
Ellis, F. S. The life work of Morris. Jnl Soc of Arts 27 May 1897.
[Review of Water of the wondrous isles]. Academy 30 Oct 1897 (anon).
Block, L. J. Morris's last romances. Dial 16 May 1898. The water of the wondrous isles and The sundering flood.
Morris's last romance. Saturday Rev 26 Mar 1898 (anon review of The sundering flood).
Proctor, R. Sir Galahad. Athenaeum 22 Jan 1898. Questions the authenticity of this pam.
Abbott, L. D. Morris's Commonweal. New England Mag n.s. 20, June 1899.
Leatham, J. William Morris: master of many crafts. Peterhead 1899.
Mackail, J. W. The life of Morris. 2 vols 1899. The standard biography.
H., R. [Review of Art and the beauty of the earth]. Ethical World 26 Aug 1899.
W., E. [E. Wood]. [Review of Architecture, industry and wealth]. Fabian News 12 Dec 1902.

Collected essays of Morris. The Builder 20 Dec 1902 (anon). Review of Architecture, industry and wealth, *see* Collections and selections, *above*.

Yeats, W. B. The happiest of the poets. In Ideas of good and evil, 1903. Rptd from Fortnightly Rev Mar 1903.

[Burne-Jones, G.] Memorials of Burne-Jones. 2 vols 1904.

Brooke, S. A. A study of Clough, Arnold, Rossetti and Morris. 1908.

Jackson, H. Morris: craftsman-Socialist. 1908; 1926 (rev with 4 new chs).

Noyes, A. Morris. 1908 (EML).

Crane, W. Morris to Whistler: papers and addresses on arts and crafts and the Commonweal. 1911.

[Marillier, H. C.] Brief sketch of the Morris movement. 1911.

Cole, G. D. H. Morris. The Blue Book vol 1 no 5 1913. Review of The Collected works.

Waddington, S. Sonnets by Morris. Athenaeum 24 Oct 1914. Attributes 2 unsigned sonnets ptd in Atlantic Monthly Feb & Mar 1870 to Morris.

Morris, M. Sonnets by Morris. Athenaeum 7 Nov 1914. Agrees with Waddington, *see above*. The 2 sonnets, Rhyme slayeth shame and May grown a-cold, are rptd in Collected works vol 24, *see* Collections and selections, *above*.

H. K., St J. S. Morris: Sigurd the Volsung. N & Q 2 Dec 1916.

Rogers, P. Morris's Summer dawn. TLS 21 June 1928.

Eddison, E. R. Some principles of translation. In Egil's Saga, Cambridge 1930.

Carter, J. and H. G. Pollard. An enquiry into the nature of certain nineteenth-century pamphlets. 1934. Sir Galahad proved a forgery and The two sides of the river / Hapless love / The first foray of Aristomenes suspected of being another unauthorised publication with a false date. Ed N. Barker and J. Collins 1983 (2nd edn, rev). Revision incorporates the post-1934 research of Carter and Pollard.

Litzenberg, K. Morris and the reviews: a study in the fame of a poet. RES 12, Oct 1936.

Litzenberg, K. The diction of Morris. In Arkiv för Nordisk Filologi 53 1937.

Thompson, E. P. William Morris: romantic to revolutionary. 1955, 1977 (rev). Political biography.

Briggs, R. C. H. She and he. Jnl Morris Soc 1 Winter 1962.

Pariser, M. P. TLS 23 July 1964. Survey of Buxton Forman's letters to T. J. Wise, referring to their forged pam The two sides of the river / Hapless love / The first foray of Aristomenes. Rptd in N. Barker and J. Collins, A sequel to An enquiry, *see below*.

Dunlap, J. R. The book that never was. New York 1971.

Collins, J. H. B. Forman and Morris: a preliminary enquiry. The Book Collector 21 Winter 1972.

Dunlap, J. R. The road to Kelmscott: Morris and the book arts before the founding of the Kelmscott Press. Unpbd diss, Columbia Univ, New York 1972.

Simpson, J. M. Eyrbyggia Saga and nineteenth-century scholarship. In Proceedings of the First International Saga Conference, Univ of Edinburgh, ed P. Foote et al 1973 (Viking Soc).

Schofield, J. The defence of Guenevere and contemporary critics. Jnl Morris Soc 3 Spring 1974.

Gardner, D. L. An 'idle singer' and his audience: a study of Morris's poetic reputation in England, 1858–1900. The Hague 1975.

Goodwin, K. L. An unpublished tale from The earthly paradise. VP 13 Fall-Winter 1975.

MacDonald, J. A. The revision of News from nowhere. Jnl Morris Soc, Summer 1976.

In fine print, Morris as book designer. Walthamstow 1977 (anon). William Morris Gallery exhibition catalogue.

Thompson, S. O. American book design and Morris. New York and London 1977.

Blersch, S. C. The craft of revision: Morris and Sigurd the Volsung. In After summer seed, ed J. Hollow, New York and London 1978 (Morris Soc).

Buckley, C. Morris and his critics. Jnl Morris Soc, Winter 1978.

Fisher, B. F., jr. Morris's What all men long for and what none shall have: restorations and reconsiderations. Lib Chron 43 1978.

Gallasch, L. The use of compounds and archaic diction in the works of Morris. Berne 1979 (European Univ Stud, vol 60 ser 14).

Latham, D. Morris's misunderstood revision of 'Guenevere'. N & Q 224, Aug 1979.

Tilling, P. M. Morris's translation of Beowulf: studies in his vocabulary. In Studies in English literature, ed Tilling, Coleraine 1981.

Talbot, N. On editing Morris. In Australasian Victorian Studies Association: Conference Papers. Christchurch NZ 1982.

Barker, N. and J. Collins. A sequel to An enquiry . . . : the forgeries of H. Buxton Forman and T. J. Wise re-examined. 1983. 15 Morris titles are added to the list of those found to be deliberately deceptive.

Boos, F. Victorian responses to Earthly paradise tales. Jnl Morris Soc 5 Winter 1983–4.

Bacon, A. Morris's lectures and the question of audience: a study of the versions of Art and labour. YULG 58, Apr 1984.

Carter, S. The book becomes, the making of a fine edition. Cambridge 1984.

Irving, H. Morris and the contemporary Socialist press. Jnl Morris Soc 6 Winter 1984–5.

Kelvin, N. Editing the letters of Morris. In City University of New York English Forum vol 1, 1985.

Kirchhoff, F. Morris's anti-books: the Kelmscott Press and the late prose romances. In Forms of the fantastic, ed. J. Hokenson and H Pearce, Westport CT 1986.

Liberman, M. R. Major textual changes in Morris's News from nowhere. Nineteenth-Century Lit 41, Dec 1986.

Peterson, W. S. The Kelmscott Press: a history of Morris's typographical adventure. Oxford 1986.

Ellison, R. Iceland obituaries of Morris. Jnl Morris Soc 8 Autumn 1988.

Dreyfus, J. Morris and the printed book: a reconsideration of his views on type and book design in the light of later computer-aided techniques. 1989 (Morris Soc).

Kelvin, N. Patterns in time: the decorative and the narrative in the works of Morris. In Nineteenth-century lives, ed L. S. Lockridge, J. Maynard and D. D. Stone, Cambridge MA 1989.

Kirchhoff, F. Revision and the Pre-Raphaelite text. In Victorian authors and their works, ed J. Kennedy, Athens OH 1991.

Pearson, R. The novel on blue paper: an additional page. Jnl Morris Soc 9 Autumn 1991.

Collins, J. The two forgers: a biography of Harry Buxton Forman and Thomas James Wise. Aldershot 1992.

Londraville, J. M. Morris's editing of 'So many stories written here'. Jnl Morris Soc 10 Autumn 1992.

McGann, J. 'A thing to mind': the materialist aesthetic of Morris. HLQ 55 Winter 1992.

Salmon, N. The revision of A dream of John Ball. Jnl Morris Soc 10 Autumn 1993.

LeMire, E. D. Morris in America: a publishing history from archives. The Book Collector 43 1994. [EDL]

Robert Fuller Murray 1863–94

The scarlet gown: being verses by a St Andrew's man. 1891, 1909 (with additional poems, with introd by A. Lang); ed J. H. Baxter 1932.

Robert F. Murray: his poems, with a memoir by A. Lang. 1894.

Ernest James Myers 1844–1921

Collections

Gathered poems. 1904.
[Selected poems.] [1931] (Augustan Books of Poetry).

§1

A Greek idyll. Oxford 1865. (Gainsford prize.)
The Puritans. 1869. One-act verse play.
Poems. 1877.
The defence of Rome and other poems. 1880.
Aeschylus: an essay. 1880. In Hellenica, ed E. Abbott, 1880.
The Iliad of Homer done into English prose. 1883, 1914 (rev edn), extracts 1935. With A. Lang and W. Leaf.
The judgment of Prometheus and other poems. 1886.
Lord Althorp: a biography. 1890.
Myers also wrote an English prose version of the Odes of Pindar *(1874) and an introd to Milton's prose works (1883).*

§2

Miles, A. H. Myers. In Miles 8 (7).
Obit: The Times 28 Nov 1921.

Frederic William Henry Myers 1843–1901

Collections

Collected poems, with autobiographical and critical fragments. Ed E. Myers 1921.

§1

[Burns centenary poem.] In The Burns centenary poems, ed G. Anderson and J. Finlay, 1859.
The distress in Lancashire: Chancellor's medal poem. Cambridge 1863.
Saint Paul. 1867; New York 1868 (2nd edn); London 1870, (3rd edn) (with 4 additional poems) as Poems; London and New York 1905 (4th edn), 1906 [1914] ed O. Smeaton; 1916 ed J. Watson.
Books to read: a lecture in Dublin Apr 22 1868. Cambridge 1868.
Greek oracles. In Hellenica, ed E. Abbott, 1880.
Wordsworth. 1881 (EML).
The renewal of youth and other poems. 1882.
Essays classical: essays modern. 2 vols 1883; 1921 as Essays classical and modern.
Phantasms of the living. 1886, Gainsville FL. Facs 1970. With E. Gurney and F. Podmore.
Science and a future life, with other essays. 1893.
Human personality and its survival of bodily death. 2 vols 1903, New York 1904, London 1919 (abridged), New York 1954 new edn.
Fragments of prose and poetry. Ed E. Myers 1904.
Saint John the Baptist. [1927.]
Fragments of an inner life: an autobiographical sketch. 1961.

§2

Morshead, E. D. A. The renewal of youth, and other poems. Acad 18 Nov 1882.
Anderson, M. B. Myers. Dial 4 1884.
Symonds, J. A. Myers. In Miles 8 (7).
Mallock, W. H. The gospel of Myers. Nineteenth Cent Apr 1903.
Muirhead, J. H. The survival of the soul: Human personality and its survival of bodily death. Contemporary Rev July 1903.
Sidgwick, A. The posthumous works of Myers. Independent Rev 5 1904.
Benson, A. C. In his Leaves of the tree: studies in biography, 1911.
Lodge, O. J. In his Conviction of survival, 1930.
The road to immortality: being a description of the after life purporting to be communicated by the late F. W. H. Myers through Geraldine Cummins. 1932, 1935 (as Beyond human personality).
Evans, B. I. In his English poetry in the later nineteenth century, 1933, 1966 (rev).
MacArthur, J. S. Believer in the future life. Hibbert Jnl 41 1943.
MacArthur, J. S. Nineteenth-century prophet on France. Church Quart Rev 138 1944.

Constance Caroline Woodhill Naden 1858–89

Collections

Selections from the philosophy and poetical works. Ed Emily and Edith Hughes, introd G. M. McCrie 1893.
The complete poetical works, with an explanatory foreword by R. Lewins. 1894.
Miles 8.

§1

Songs and sonnets of springtime. 1881.
What is religion? A vindication of free thought by C. N., annotated by R. Lewins. 1883.
A modern apostle, The elixir of life and other poems. 1887.
Induction and deduction: a historical and critical sketch of successive philosophical conceptions respecting the relations between inductive and deductive thought, and other essays. Ed R. Lewins (with a memoir by M. M. Daniell) 1890.
Further reliques of Constance Naden: being essays and tracts for our times. Ed G. M. McCrie 1891.

§2

Hughes, W. R. Constance Naden: a memoir. 1890.
Brewer, E. C. Constance Naden and Hylo-idealism: a critical study. Annotated by R. Lewins. 1891.
Dale, R. W. Constance Naden. Contemporary Rev Apr 1891; rptd in Further reliques, 1891.
Garnett, R. In Miles 8.

Edith Nesbit 1858–1924

Mss: Fabian papers at Nuffield College include letters about Nesbit's involvement with the Fabian Soc. Letters to her agents are in the Berg Collection, NYPL. Letters to the Soc of Authors are in the BL, and to H. G. Wells in the Wells Papers at the Univ Lib of Illinois at Urbana-Champaign. Parts of her correspondence with her publishers are in the Macmillan Papers at the BL and in the John Lane Papers in the HRHRC, Austin TX. Jocelyn Nixon's private archive contains several ms notebooks of poems (some extracted from periodicals), and some correspondence. The Doris Langley Moore archive contains transcripts of many letters from Nesbit.

Bibliographies

Moore, D. L. E. Nesbit, a biography: 1933. A list of her writings is included at the end.
Streatfield, N. Magic and the magician. 1958. Contains a brief list of writings. This list was expanded for the Bodley Head monograph 1960.
Goodacre, S. His bibliography included at the end of A woman of passion: the life of E. Nesbit, by J. Briggs, 1987.

§1

Lays and legends. 1886.
The lily and the cross. 1887, New York 1887.
The star of Bethlehem. 1887, New York 1887.
The better part, and other poems. 1888.
The message of the dove. 1888, New York 1888.
Landscape and song. 1888, New York 1888.
Leaves of life. London and New York 1888.
Carols and sea songs. 1889, New York 1889.
Songs of two seasons. Illustr J. McIntyre 1890.
The voyage of Columbus, a narrative in verse. 1892.
Sweet lavender (verses). 1892, New York 1892.

Lays and legends. 2nd ser (verses) 1892.
Grim tales. 1893.
Something wrong. 1893.
The Marden mystery. Chicago 1894.
Pussy tales. 1895.
Doggy tales. 1895.
Rose leaves. 1895.
A pomander of verse. 1895, Chicago 1895.
As happy as a king. 1896.
In homespun. 1896, Boston 1896. Vol 22 in the Keynote ser.
The children's Shakespeare, no 1532. Ed E. Vredenburg 1897; Philadelphia 1900. Reissued in 1910 as Children's stories from Shakespeare, and in 6 vols as The Gem Shakespeare Library [1914?]. For details, *see* 1910, *below.*
Royal children of English history. 1897.
Songs of love and empire. 1898.
Pussy and doggy tales. 1899, New York 1900. A combined edn of the two 1895 vols, with new material.
The story of the treasure seekers, being the adventures of the Bastable family in search of a fortune. Illustr G. Browne (15) and L. Baumer (2) 1899, New York 1899. Rptd often, then reissued both separately and as 1st pt of The complete story of the Bastable family, 1929, with later reprintings; reset with original illustrations 1958; new edn with illustrations by C. Leslie 1958 (Pen); pbd together with The would-be-goods, illustr S. Einzig, with introd by N. Streatfield, 1966 (Nonesuch Cygnet).
The secret of Kyriels. 1899, Philadelphia 1899.
The book of dragons, illustrated by H. R. Millar, with decorations by H. Granville Fell. London and New York 1900, rptd 1901.
Nine unlikely tales for children. Illustr H. R. Millar (8), C. Shepperson (20), frontispiece by M. Bowley, 1901, New York 1901. Rptd often up to 1928, then taken over by Ernest Benn, and further rptd.
The would-be-goods, being the further adventures of the treasure seekers. Illustr A. H. Buckland (17) and J. Hassell (2) 1901, New York 1901. Often rptd; reset with the original illustrations 1958; new edn, illustr C. Leslie, 1958 (Pen); pbd with The treasure seekers, illustr S. Einzig, with introd by N. Streatfield, 1966 (Nonsuch Cygnet).
To wish you every joy. 1901.
Thirteen ways home. 1901.
The revolt of the toys, and what comes of quarrelling. 1902, New York 1902.
Five children and it. Illustr H. R. Millar 1902, New York 1905. Often rptd. Reset with the original illustrations 1957; new edn with the original illustrations 1959 (Pen).
The red house. Illustr A. L. Kellar 1902, New York 1902. Several reprints.
The rainbow queen, and other stories. 1903.
Playtime stories. 1903.
The literary sense. 1903, New York 1903.
The phoenix and the carpet. Illustr H. R. Millar 1904, New York 1904. Often rptd. Facs of 1st edn 1956; new edn with the original illustrations 1959 (Pen).
The new treasure seekers. Illustr G. Browne (31) and L. Baumer (2) 1904, New York 1904. Often rptd. Reset with illustrations by C. W. Hodges 1949; new edn with original illustrations 1958 (Pen).
The story of the five rebellious dolls. 1904, New York 1904.
Pug Peter and other stories for boys and girls. Leeds and London 1905. Anon.
Oswald Bastable and others. Illustr C. E. Brock (7) and H. R. Millar (13) 1905.
The rainbow and the rose. London, New York and Bombay 1905.
The story of the amulet. Illustr H. R. Millar 1906, New York 1906. Often rptd; reset with the original illustrations 1957; new edn with original illustrations 1959 (Pen).
The railway children. Illustr C. E. Brock 1906, New York 1906. Often rptd; new edn 1948; new edn with original illustrations 1960 (Pen); new edn, illustr P. Kay, 1989.
The incomplete amorist. Illustr C. F. Underwood 1906, New York 1906.
Man and maid. 1906.
The enchanted castle. Illustr H. R. Millar 1907, New York 1907. Often rptd; facs of 1st edn 1957; reset edn, illustr L. Lamb, 1957.
Twenty beautiful stories from Shakespeare . . . retold by E. N. Ed E. T. Roe, Chicago 1907, rptd 1926.
The old nursery stories. 1908. No. 1 of The Children's Bookcase ser (later books in the series were by other authors).
The house of Arden, a story for children. Illustr H. R. Millar 1908, New York 1909. Often rptd; reset edn, illustr D. E. Walduck, 1949.
Jesus in London, a poem. 1908.
Ballads and lyrics of socialism 1883 to 1908. 1908 (pbd for the Fabian Soc).
Harding's luck. Illustr H. R. Millar 1909, New York 1910. Several reprints; reset edn, illustr D. E. Walduck, 1949.
These little ones. Illustr S. Pryse 1909.
Cinderella, a play with twelve songs to popular airs. 1909.
Daphne in Fitzroy Street. 1909, New York 1909 (as The house with no address), rptd London 1914 with the revised title.
Garden poems. London and Glasgow 1909.
The magic city. Illustr H. R. Millar 1910. Further reprints.
Children's stories from Shakespeare, with When Shakespeare was a boy by Dr F. J. Furnivall. 1910, Philadelphia 1912. A reissue of the 1897 vol with new title and illustrations; rptd in The Gem Shakespeare Lib 6 vols [1914?].
Fear. 1911.
The wonderful garden, or the three C's. Illustr H. R. Millar 1911. Further rptd.
Ballads and verses of the spiritual life. 1911.
Dormant. 1911, New York 1912 (as Rose Royal).
The magic world. Illustr H. R. Millar (21) and S. Pryse (3), London and New York 1912; 1924 (2nd impression); further rptd.
Our new story book. 1913, New York 1913.
Wet magic. Illustr H. R. Millar 1913; further reprints.
Wings and the child, or the building of magic cities. 1913, New York 1913.
The incredible honeymoon. New York 1916, London 1921.
The New World Literary Series, book two. Ed H. C. Wylde, London and Glasgow 1921.
The lark. 1922.
Many voices. 1922.
To the adventurous. 1923.
Five of us, and Madeleine. 1925, New York 1926; 2nd impression London 1926; further rptd.
The Bastable children. Preface by C. Morley, New York 1925. A reprint of the 3 Bastable books. Often rptd. English edn pbd under the title Complete history of the Bastable family, with illustrations by G. Brown, L. Baumer, A. H. Buckland and J. Hassall, 1928.

Undated works

Fading light. Illustr A. Warne Browne and W. Hagelberg, London and New York.
May-time and play-time. London and New York.
Miss Mischief. London and New York c. 1891.
Off to fairyland. London and New York.
Fairies. London. A shaped book.
Sunnylands. London and New York.
Bright eyes. London and New York. A book in the shape of a butterfly.
Songs of the cornfield. London. A book in the shape of a straw hat and sickle.

Books edited or arranged by E. Nesbit

Spring songs and sketches; Summer songs and sketches; Autumn songs and sketches; Winter songs and sketches. A series of illustrated books of verses, selected and arranged by E. N. and R. Ellice Mack. London and New York 1886. A similar series of books – for Morning, Noon, Eventide and Night – was pbd in 1887.

River sketches. Words selected and written by E. N. London and New York 1887.

Winter snow; In the spring time; The time of roses; Autumn leaves. A series of books, with contents selected and arranged by E. N. London and New York 1888.

Lilies and heartsease; Daisy days; Falling leaves. A similar series of books, ed E. N. and R. E. Mack, London and New York 1888.

By land and sea. Poems selected by E. N., London and New York 1888.

The life of happy children. By C. Brooke, A. Hoatson and E. Bland. Selected and arranged by E. N., London and New York 1889.

Songs of Scotland. Selected by E. N., illustr H. Bellingham Smith, G. E. Corner and G. Gorsky, 1890.

The girl's own birthday book. Selected and arranged by E. N. 1894.

Poets' whispers, a birthday book. Quotations selected and arranged by E. N. 1895.

Collaborative works

The prophet's mantle. In collaboration with Hubert Bland, under the pseud 'Fabian Bland'. 1885, Chicago 1889.

Easter-tide. By E. N. and C. Brooke. 1888, New York 1888.

All round the year. By E. N. and C. Brooke. 1888.

The lilies round the cross. 1889, New York 1889. With Helen J. Wood.

Life's sunny side. 1890, New York 1890. Poems by E. N. and others.

Told by the fireside. 1890. Short stories by E. N. and others.

Twice four. 1891. Short stories by E. N. and others.

Story upon story, and every word true. 1892. By E. N. and others.

Contributions to the following books of verse and prose, pbd 1893: Flowers I bring and songs I sing; Our friends and all about them; Listen long and listen well; Sunny tales for snowy days; Told by the sunbeams and me; What really happened; We've tales to tell.

Contributions to 15 of the Nister's Holiday Annuals between 1893 and 1915.

Contributions to the following books of verse and prose, pbd 1894: Hours in many lands; Tales that are true for brown eyes and blue; Tales to delight from morning till night; Fur and feathers, tales for all weathers; All but one, told by the flowers; Lads and lasses.

A graven image. 1894. Short stories by E. N. and O. Barron.

The butler in Bohemia. 1894. Short stories, written in collaboration with O. Barron.

Contributions to the following books of verse and prose, pbd 1895: Tick tock, tales of the clock; Stories in a shell; Treasures from storyland; Friends in fable, a book of animal stories; Rosy cheeks and golden ringlets.

Dulcie's lantern, and other stories. 1895. By E. N. and others.

Holly and mistletoe, a book of Christmas verse. 1895. With Norman Gale and Richard le Gallienne.

Once upon a time, the favourite nursery tales [retold by E. N. and others]. London and New York 1897. Much of this material was included in later Nister editions – e.g. Little red riding hood and other nursery tales (undated) and Favourite fairy tales (1912), where E. N. is named as one of several authors.

Dinna forget. London 1897, New York 1898. Poems by E. N. and others.

Tales told in the twilight. London and New York 1897. Very short stories by E. N. and others.

Dog tales, and other tales. By E. N. and others. Ed E. Vredenburg 1898.

A book of dogs, being a discourse on them, with many tales and wonders. Gathered by E. N. London and New York 1898.

Contributions to Father Tuck's Annual. 1900.

Cat tales. London and New York 1904. With Rosamund Bland.

Days of delight. Ed E. Vredenburg 1910 (71 pp.). In Father Tuck's Golden Gift ser. There are possibly 19 vols in the series. Only a few have Nesbit contributions. Father Tuck's Welcome Gift ser may also date from this time – *see* undated section, *below.*

Children's stories from English history. Told by E. N. and Doris Ashley. 1910. Rptd material from Royal children of English history, 1897; reissued 1914.

My sea-side-story book. By E. N. with G. Manville Fenn. London and New York 1911.

Favourite fairy tales. Retold by E. N. and others. 1911.

Battle songs. Chosen by E. N. 1914.

Essays. By Hubert Bland. Ed 'E. Nesbit Bland'. 1914.

Undated collaborative works

Sunny hours. In Father Tuck's Welcome Gift ser, no 401. There were 6 vols in this series, some of which may have had E. N. contributions. The numbering suggests a date before 1910 (see Golden Gift ser under that year, *above*).

My farmyard story book. By E. N. and others. London and New York.

Stories for all times. By E. N. and others. London and New York.

Hallowe'en house. By Mrs Molesworth, E. N. and others. London and New York.

Round the hearth. By E. N. and others. Ed and arranged by Robert Ellice Mack.

Merry playtimes, a picture book for boys and girls. By E. N. and others. London and New York.

Our own story book. By E. N. and others. London and New York.

Merry companions. By E. N. and others. London and New York.

In picture land, a book of pictures and stories for little ones. By E. N. and others. London and New York.

Blue eyes and cherry pies. By E. N. and others. London and New York.

The beautiful world, and other poems. By E. N. and others. London and New York.

Contributions to periodicals

E. Nesbit was a prolific contributor to periodicals of all descriptions. Her first contribution was a 'set of verses with a moral tag' in The Sunday Mag *in 1874 (not yet precisely identified). The first positively identified contribution was a set of verses 'A Year Ago' in* Good Words *Dec 1876. The following lists the more important of the rest of her huge output:*

Argosy. Over 30 contributions 1877–97.

Atalanta. At least 8 contributions 1891–8.

Black and White. 4 chs from children's books 1899–1907.

Daily Chron. Weekly articles for children Apr–July 1910.

Girls Own Paper. My school days, Oct 1896–Sep 1897.

Home Chimes. Short stories 1887–9.

Illus London News. Chs from children's books 1896–1901.

London Mag. Chs from children's books 1903–6.

Longman's Mag. 4 adult short stories and poems 1890–1.

Neolith, an experimental mag, pbd quarterly under the direction of E. N., Graily Hewitt, F. Ernest Jackson and Spencer Pryse. 4 issues only pbd (3 with Nesbit stories). 1907–8.

Pall Mall Mag. Chs from children's books 1893–5.

Sketch. Adult short stories and poems 1893–5.

Strand Mag. July 1899–Aug 1913. Large sections of many of her most important children's books, from The book of dragons to Wet magic (111 contributions in all).

Weekly Dispatch. Numerous contributions Jan 1882–Mar 1892. In the middle years a poem and/or a short story appeared virtually every week.

§2

Obit: The Kentish Express 10 May 1924.

Moore, D. Langley. E. Nesbit, a biography. 1933, 1936, 1951, rev edn Philadelphia and New York 1966, London 1967.

Magic and the magician: E. Nesbit and her children's books. London and New York 1958.
Bell, A. E. Nesbit. 1960, New York 1964, rev London 1968.
Briggs, J. A woman of passion, the life of E. Nesbit 1858–1924. London and New York 1987, rev edn Harmondsworth 1989 (Pen).
Nesbit was the subject of a BBC TV play by Ken Taylor in 1973 in the series The Edwardians. *A version of the series was pbd in book form:* The Edwardians, *by P. Brent, 1972 (see pp. 147–67).* [SHG]

Sir Henry John Newbolt 1862–1938

Collections

Collected poems 1897–1907. [1910], [1918].
Prose and poetry, selected by the author. London and Toronto [1920].
Selected poems. Ed J. Betjeman 1940.
Selected poems. Ed P. Dickinson c. 1981.

§1

A fair death. [1881.] Anon.
Taken from the enemy: a novel. 1892, 1911 (new edn).
Mordred: a tragedy. 1895. Verse.
Admirals all and other verses. 1897 etc, New York 1898, London [1904] (21st edn).
The island race. 1898, 1902 (5th edn); facs Oxford 1995. Poems.
The sailing of the long ships and other poems. 1902.
The year of Trafalgar: being an account of the battle and of the events which led up to it, with a collection of the poems and ballads written thereupon between 1805 and 1905. 1905.
The old country: a romance. 1906, 1929.
Clifton Chapel and other school poems. 1908.
Songs of memory and hope. 1909.
The new June. 1909, [1929]. Fiction.
The Twymans: a tale of youth. Edinburgh 1911.
Poems new and old. 1912, 1919 (2nd edn).
Drake's drum and other songs of the sea. [1914.]
Aladore. Edinburgh 1914. Fiction.
The book of the blue sea. 1914. Prose.
The story of the Oxfordshire and Buckingham light infantry, the old 43rd and 52nd regiments. [1915.]
The war and the nations. 1915. Rptd from Fortnightly Rev.
The book of the thin red line. 1915.
Tales of the Great War. 1916.
A new study of English poetry. 1917, 1919.
The book of the happy warrior. 1917. Prose.
St George's day and other poems. 1918.
Submarine and anti-submarine. 1918. Prose.
The book of the long trail. 1919. Prose.
Poetry and time. [1919] (Warton lecture).
The book of good hunting. 1920. Prose.
A naval history of the war 1914–18. 5 vols 1920–31.
The book of the Grenvilles. 1921.
Days to remember. 1923. On the European war, with J. Buchan.
Studies green and gray. 1926. Criticism.
The linnet's nest. [1927], New York 1927. Poetry.
The building of Britain. [1927.] On paintings in St Stephen's Hall, Westminster.
The idea of an English association. 1928 (English Assoc).
A child is born. 1931. Poetry.
My world as in my time: memoirs ... 1862–1932. 1932. Prose.
A perpetual memory and other poems, with brief memoirs by W. de la Mare and F. Furse. 1939.
The later life and letters of Newbolt. Ed M. Newbolt 1942. Vol 2 of My world as in my time.
Newbolt also edited and contributed to the Teaching of English ser, 1925–32. He produced teaching anthologies, including New paths on Helicon *[1927], and edited the* Monthly Rev *1900–7, vols 1–16.*

§2

Archer, W. In his Poets of the younger generation, 1902.
Bridges, R. Newbolt. In Miles 7.
Kernahan, C. In his Six famous living poets, 1922.
Palmer, H. Watson and Newbolt. In his Post-Victorian poetry, 1938.
The lyrics of Newbolt. The Times 23 Apr 1938.
Betjeman, J. Newbolt after a hundred years. Listener 28 June 1962.
Chitty, S. Playing the game: a biography of Sir Henry Newbolt. 1997.

'Moira O'Neill', Nesta Higginson, later Skrine c. 1870–?

§1

An Easter vacation. 1893, New York 1894. Novel.
The elf-errant. 1895, 1902. A tale.
Songs of the glens of Antrim. Edinburgh and London 1900, New York 1910, 1922 (with More songs of the glens of Antrim, *below*).
More songs of the glens of Antrim. 1921, New York 1922 (with Songs of the glens of Antrim, *above*).
From two points of view. Edinburgh and London 1924. Prose.
Collected poems. Edinburgh and London 1933.

§2

Nesta Higginson ('Moira O'Neill'). Book Buyer 11 1895.
A school of Irish poetry. Edinburgh Rev 209 1909.

Arthur William Edgar O'Shaughnessy 1844–81

Mss: collection in Duke Univ Lib, Durham NC. Poems 1865–9 in NLS.

Bibliographies and references

The English poets, ed T. H. Ward, vol 5 1880 (E. Gosse).
Garnett, R. In Miles 8.
Fredeman, W. E. In his Pre-Raphaelitism: a bibliocritical study, 1965.
Fredeman, J. C. In DLB vol 35, 1985.

Collections and selections

O'Shaughnessy: his life and work, with selections from his poems. Ed L. C. Moulton 1894.
Lyrics. Bibelot (Portland ME) 16 1910.
Poems. Ed W. Percy, New Haven CT 1923.

§1

An epic of women, and other poems. 1870; facs London and New York 1978.
Lays of France. Founded on the lays of Marie. '1872' [1871], 1874.
Music and moonlight: poems and songs. 1874; facs London and New York 1977.
Toyland. 1875. With E. O'Shaughnessy.
Songs of a worker. Ed A. Deacon 1881; facs London and New York 1978.
Lyrics. Bibelot (Portland ME) 16 1910.

§2

Forman, H. B. In his Our living poets, 1871.
Hamilton, Walter. In his The aesthetic movement in England. 1882.
Le Gallienne. R. In his Retrospective reviews vol 1, 1896.
A pathetic love episode in a poet's life: being letters [from Helen Snee] to Arthur O'Shaughnessy; also a letter from him containing A dissertation on love. [1916.]
Broers, B. C. O'Shaughnessy. In her Mysticism and the neo-romantics, 1923.
Brönner, O. Das Leben Arthur O'Shaughnessy's. 1933.

Evans, B. Ifor. In his English poetry in the later nineteenth century, 1933, 1966 (rev).
Anderson, G. K. Marie de France and Arthur O'Shaughnessy: a study in Victorian adaptation. SP 36 1939.
Paden, W. D. Arthur O'Shaughnessy: the ancestry of a Victorian poet. BJRL 46 1964. [WEF]

John Payne 1842–1916

Bibliographies and reference works

Garnett, R. P. In Miles 8.
Fredeman, W. E. In his Pre-Raphaelitism: a bibliocritical study 1965.
Willerton, C. W. In DLB vol 35 1985.
See also Wright and Williams, below.

Collections and selections

The poetical works. 2 vols 1902 (priv ptd).
Selections from the poetry of Payne, made by T. and L. Robinson. New York 1906.

§1

The masque of shadows and other poems. 1870.
Intaglios: sonnets, etc. 1871.
Songs of life and death. 1872.
Lautrec. 1878.
New poems. 1880.
The descent of the dove: being a supplement to The poetical works. 1902 (priv ptd).
Vigil and vision. 1903; suppl, 12 Sonnets de combat, 1903 (priv ptd).
Songs of consolation: new poems. 1904. Includes Descent of the dove, *above.*
Hamid the luckless and other tales in verse. 1904. Rptd from Flowers from Syrian gardens (Poetical works, vol 1), with Hamid the luckless in place of The scavenger of Baghdad.
Sir Winfrith and other poems. Olney 1905.
Verses for the Newton–Cowper centenary. [1907.]
The quatrains of Ibn Et-Tefrid. 1908 (priv ptd), 1909 (with omissions); ed T. Wright 1921.
Carol and cadence: new poems MDCCCCII–VII. 1908 (priv ptd).
Flower o' the thorn. 1909 (priv ptd).
Humoristica. 3 ser 1909–[10] (priv ptd).
The way of the winepress, etc. Olney 1920.
Nature and her lover and other poems. Ed T. Wright, Olney 1922. Rptd from Carol and cadence, *above.*
The autobiography of Payne, with preface and annotations by T. Wright. Olney 1926.
Payne also translated Villon, 1878; The book of a thousand and one nights, *1882–4;* Tales from the Arabic, *1884–5;* Decameron, *1886;* Matteo Bandello, *1890;* Omar Kheyyam of Nisha Pour, *1898;* Shemseddin Mohammed Hafiz, *1901;* Tales from the Arabian Nights, *1906;* Flowers of France, *1906, 1907, 1913, 1914;* Heine, *1911.*

§2

Forman, H. B. In his Our living poets, 1871.
Wright, T. The life of John Payne. 1919.
Williams, C. R. McGregor. John Payne. Paris 1926.
Evans, B. Ifor. In his English poetry in the later nineteenth century, 1933, 1966 (rev).
Lhombréaud, R. Une lettre inédite de Mallarmé en anglais. Revue de Littérature Comparée 26 1952.
Ryan, M. Payne et Mallarmé: une longue amitié. Revue de Littérature Comparée 32 1958. [WEF]

Stephen Phillips 1864–1915

See col 2053.

Victor Gustave Plarr 1863–1929

Collections

Collected poems. Ed I. Fletcher 1974.

§1

Scenes from the Alcestis of Euripides. [1886] (priv ptd).
The book of the Rhymers' Club. 1892 (contains 6 pieces by Plarr), 1894 (bk 2, contains 6 more poems).
In the Dorian mood: verses. 1896.
Nine poems. In The garland of new poetry by various writers, '1899' [1898].
Literary etiquette. 1903. Prose.
The tragedy of Asgard. 1905.
Ernest Dowson 1888–97: reminiscences, unpublished letters and marginalia. 1914.
Plarr's Lives of the Fellows of the Royal College of Surgeons of England. Rev D'A. Power, W. G. Spencer and G. E. Gask 2 vols 1930. Includes memoir of Plarr.
Plarr also translated Zola's Nana *(1894), and revised the 14th edn of* Men and women of our time *(1895).*

Sir Frederick Pollock 1845–1947

§1

Leading cases done into English, by an apprentice of Lincoln's Inn. 1876 (2nd edn), 1892 as Leading cases done into English and other diversions.
Spinoza: his life and philosophy. 1880.
Essays in jurisprudence and ethics. 1882.
An introduction to the history of the science of politics. 1890.
Oxford lectures and other discourses. 1890. Prose.
Outside the law: diversions partly serious. 1927. Prose and verse.
For my grandson: remembrances of an ancient Victorian. 1933.
Holmes–Pollock letters: the correspondence of Mr Justice Holmes and Pollock 1874–1932. Ed M. de W. Howe 2 vols Cambridge 1942.
Pollock also wrote on legal subjects.

§2

Wright, R. A. W. In memoriam Pollock. In his Legal essays and addresses, 1940.
Shientag, B. L. Pollock: legal scholar and teacher. In his Moulders of legal thought, 1943.

Sir Arthur Quiller-Couch 1863–1944

See col 1677.

Ernest Radford 1853–?

Translations from Heine and other verses. 1882.
Measured steps. 1884.
Syllabus of a course of 12 lectures upon the method of art study. '1885–6'. [1885].
Poems of Walter Savage Landor. 1889. Ed Radford.
Chambers twain. 1890.
The book of the Rhymers' Club. 1892 (contains 5 pieces by Radford), 1894 (bk 2, with 8 more pieces).
Old and new: a collection of poems. 1895.
Dante Gabriel Rossetti. [1905.]
A collection of poems. 1906.
Johnson and the literary club. [1907.]
Songs in the whirlwind. 1918. With A. Radford.

Sir Walter Raleigh 1861–1922

See col 2385.

Hardwick Drummond Rawnsley 1850–1920

§1

A book of Bristol sonnets. 1877.
The miners' rescue, Troedyrhin colliery, Rhondda Vale, Glamorganshire, Apr 20 1877: a poem. 1877.
Sonnets at the English lakes. 1881, 1882 (2nd edn).
Sonnets round the coast. 1887.
Poems, ballads and bucolics. 1890.
Notes for the Nile, together with a metrical rendering of the hymns of ancient Egypt and of the precepts of Ptah-Hotep: the oldest book in the world. Leipzig and London 1892.
The undoing of De Harcla: a ballad of Cumberland. 1892.
Valete, Tennyson and other memorial poems. Glasgow 1893.
Idylls and lyrics of the Nile. 1894.
Ballads of brave deeds, with a frontispiece and preface by G. F. Watts. 1896.
Sonnets in Switzerland and Italy. 1899.
Ballads of the war. 1900, 1901 (new edn).
Memories of the Tennysons. Glasgow 1900, 1912 (2nd edn).
A sonnet chronicle 1900–6. Glasgow 1906.
Poems at home and abroad. Glasgow 1909.
The European war 1914–15: poems. [1915.]
Rawnsley also pbd 12 books on the English lake country, all but the first in Glasgow: A coach drive, *Keswick 1890;* Literary associations, *1894;* Life and nature, *1899;* Ruskin, *1901;* A rambler's notebook, *1902;* Lake country sketches, *1903;* Months at the lake, *1906;* Wordsworth, Tennyson, *1906;* Round the lake country, *1909;* By fell and dale, *1911;* Chapters, *1913;* Past and present, *1916. He also pbd sermons, biographies etc.*

§2

Noble, J. A. Rawnsley. In Miles 8 (7).
Rawnsley, E. F. Canon Rawnsley: an account of his life. Glasgow 1923.

James Rhoades 1841–1923

Collections

Collected poems. Ed L. N. P[arker] 1925.

§1

The prince of Wales at the tomb of Washington. Rugby 1861.
The death of the Prince Consort. 1862. Prize poem.
Poems. 1870.
Timoleon: a dramatic poem. 1875.
The Georgics of Virgil, translated into English verse. 1881.
Dux Redux, or a forest tangle: a comedy. 1887.
The Aeneid of Virgil books 1–6, translated into English verse. 1893.
Teresa (a tragedy in one act) and other poems. 1893.
The little flowers of St Francis of Assisi, rendered into English verse. 1904, Oxford 1925 (WC).
Out of the silence. '1907' [1906].
The Aeneid of Virgil, translated into English verse. 1907.
The training of the imagination. 1908. Prose.
O soul of mine! 1912.
The city of the five gates. 1913.
Words by the wayside. 1915.
The poems of Virgil, translated into English verse. Oxford 1921 (WC).

§2

Layard, G. S. Rhoades (1841–1923). Bookman (London) May 1923.

James Logie Robertson 1846–1922

§1

Poems. Dundee 1878.
Orellana and other poems. Edinburgh 1881.
Our holiday among the hills. Edinburgh 1882. With Janet L. Robertson.
Horace in homespun, by Hugh Haliburton. Edinburgh 1886, 1925 (signed, adding new poems and memoir by Janet L. Robertson).
The white angel of the Polly Ann and other stories. Edinburgh 1886.
'For puir auld Scotland's sake', by Hugh Haliburton. Edinburgh 1887. Essays.
In Scottish fields, by Hugh Haliburton. Edinburgh 1890. Essays.
Ochil idylls and other poems, by Hugh Haliburton. 1891.
A history of English literature for secondary schools. Edinburgh 1894.
Furth in field, by Hugh Haliburton. 1894. Essays.
Outlines of English literature for young scholars. Edinburgh 1897.
Excursions in prose and verse. Edinburgh 1905.
Nature in books: a literary introduction to natural science. 1914.
Petition to the Deil and other war verses. Paisley 1917.
Robertson also edited Burns's letters and poems, and various English poets, including Campbell, Chaucer, Scott and Thomson. He produced educational textbooks and contributed prefaces to literary works, including Thackeray's Virginians.

§2

Robertson, J. L. In J. L. Robertson, Horace in homespun, Edinburgh 1925.
Smellie, P. James Logie Robertson, the poet of the Ochils ... A lecture delivered to the Rymour Club, Edinburgh. [Perth?] 1938. Rptd from Perthshire Advertiser 23 July 1938.

Agnes Mary Frances Robinson, later Darmesteter, later Duclaux 1857–1944

Collections

Lyrics selected from the works. 1891.
Collected poems, lyrical and narrative, with a preface. 1902.

§1

A handful of honeysuckle. 1878.
The crowned Hippolytus of Euripides, translated with new poems. 1881.
Arden: a novel. 2 vols 1883, New York 1883.
Emily Brontë. 1883.
The new Arcadia and other poems. 1884.
An Italian garden: a book of songs. 1886, Portland ME 1897, 1908, tr Fr 1888.
Margaret of Angoulême. 1886, Boston 1887; tr Fr 1900.
The witching time: tales for the year's end. Ed Henry Norman 1887.
Songs, ballads and a garden play. 1888.
Poésies, traduites de l'anglais par J. Darmesteter. 1888.
The end of the Middle Ages: essays and questions in history. '1889' [1888].
Lyrics, selected from the works of A. M. F. Robinson. 1890.
Retrospect and other poems. 1890, Boston 1893.
Marguerites du temps passé. Paris 1892; tr Eng 1898.
Froissart. Paris 1894; tr Eng 1895.
The life of Ernest Renan. 1897, Boston 1897; tr Fr 1898.
Grands écrivains d'outre-manche: les Brontës–Thackeray–les Brownings–Rossetti. Paris [1901].
The fields of France. Little essays in desscriptive sociology. 1903.
The return to nature: songs and symbols. 1904.
The French procession: a pageant of great writers. 1909.
The French ideal. Pascal, Fénélon and other essays. 1911.
A short history of France from Caeser's invasion to the battle of Waterloo. 1918.
Twentieth century French writers: reviews and reminiscences. [1919], New York 1920.
Victor Hugo. 1921.
La pensée de Robert Browning. 1922.

Images and meditations: poems. 1923.
Marie Lenéru: a reminiscence. 1924.
The life of Racine. 1925.
Portrait of Pascal. 1927.

Translations

Euripides. The crowned Hippolytus. With new poems by A. M. F. Robinson. 1881.
Darmesteter, James. ES 1896.

Editions and introductions

Margaret [D'Angoulême]. The fortunate lovers. Tr Arthur Machen, ed Robinson, 1887.
Darmesteter, James. Critique et politique. Introd by Robinson 1895.
Darmesteter, James. Nouvelles études anglaises. 1896.
Barrett Browning, Elizabeth. Casa guidi windows. Introd by Robinson 1901.
De Sévigné, M. Mme de Sévigné: textes. Selected and with notes by Robinson. 1914.
Browning, Robert. Poèmes de Robert Browning. Tr P. Alfassa and G. de Voisins, introd by Robinson 1922.
Lenéru, Marie. La maison sur le roc, pièce en trois actes. Preface by Robinson. 1927.
De Sévigné, M. Letters from the Marchioness de Sévigné to her daughter. Introd by Robinson 1927.
Renan, H. Souvenirs et impressions. Introd by Robinson 1930.

§2

Robertson, E. S. In his English poetesses, 1883.
Watson, W. Lyrics selected from the works of A. Mary F. Robinson (Madame Darmesteter). Acad 21 Feb 1891.
Symons, A. A. M. F. Darmesteter. In Miles 8 (7).
Lynch, H. A. Mary F. Robinson. Fortnightly Rev Feb 1902.
Mary Duclaux et Maurice Barrès: lettres échangées. [Paris] 1959.
Marandon, S. Qui fut Mary Robinson? Les Langues Modernes 54 1960. [MD]

James Rennell Rodd, 1st Baron Rennell 1858–1941

§1

Newdigate prize poem: Raleigh. Oxford [1880].
Songs in the south. 1881.
Rose leaf and apple leaf. Introd by O. Wilde, Philadelphia 1882, London 1906.
Poems in many lands. 1883, 1886.
Feda with other poems, chiefly lyrical. 1886.
The unknown madonna and other poems. 1888.
Sir Walter Raleigh. 1889. Prose.
The violet crown and songs of England. 1891, 1913 (with new poems).
Ballads of the fleet and other poems. London and New York 1897, 1901 (with additional pieces).
Myrtle and oak. Boston and Chicago 1902.
Love, worship and death: some renderings from the Greek anthology. 1916, 1919 (new and enlarged edn).
Social and diplomatic memories. 3 ser 1922–5. Prose.
Trentaremi and other moods. 1923.
Diplomacy. 1929. Prose.
The essence of poetry. In T. W. Rock, Reading: a vice or virtue, 1929.
War poems with some others. 1940.
Lord Rennell also pbd books on Frederick, Crown Prince and Emperor, modern Greece, Greece of the Middle Ages, Homer's Ithaca, Rome, and several pams and introds.

§2

Williams, F. H. The poems of Rennell Rodd. American 5 1882.
Miles, A. H. Rennell Rodd. In Miles 8 (7).

Thomas William Hazen Rolleston 1857–1920

§1

Walt Whitman. 1883.
Prose writings of Thomas Davis. [1889], 1914. Ed Rolleston.
Deirdre: the feis ceoil prize cantata. Dublin [1897], Edinburgh [1897].
A treasury of Irish poetry in the English tongue. 1900, New York 1900, London 1910, 1923, 1932. Ed Rolleston with S. A. Brooke.
Imagination and art in Gaelic literature; being notes on some recent translations from the Gaelic. [1900.]
Parallel paths: a study in biology, ethics and art. 1908.
Sea spray: verses and translations. Dublin 1909.
The high deeds of Finn, and other bardic romances of ancient Ireland. Introd by S. Brooke 1910, New York 1911.
Myths and legends of the Celtic race. 1911, New York 1911.
Ireland and Poland: a comparison. 1917, New York 1917.
Ireland's vanishing opportunity. Dublin 1919.
Three love tales after Richard Wagner: Tannhaüser, Lohengrin, Parsifol. 1920. Verse.
Whitman and Rolleston: a correspondence. Ed H. Frenze, Dublin 1951.

§2

Rolleston, C. Portrait of an Irishman: a biographical sketch. 1939.

'A. E.' or 'AE', George William Russell 1867–1935

Mss: Most of AE's mss and letters are in the Nat Lib of Ireland, Dublin, the Lilly Lib of Indiana Univ and at Colby College, Waterville ME and Yale Univ. There are notebooks in the County Museum Armagh and the Congressional Lib Washington. Letters and rare pams are at Harvard and in the Berg Collection, NYPL.

Bibliographies

[MacManus, M. J.] Bibliography of AE, George Russell. Dublin Mag Jan 1930. Addns, Oct 1935.
Kindilien, C. The Russell collection at Colby College: a check list. Colby Lib Quart ser 4 1955.
Denson, A. Printed writings by George W. Russell (AE): a bibliography. Evanston IL 1961. Contributions by P. Colum, M. Bonn and T. Bodkin.

Collections

Collected poems. 1913, 1913, 1914, New York 1915 (in part), London 1917, 1919 (enlarged), 1920, 1926 (enlarged), 1927, 1928, 1930 (in part), 1931 (in part), 1935 (enlarged).
Selected poems. 1935, New York 1935, London 1951, New York 1951.

§1

To the fellows of the Theosophical Society. Dublin 1894. A letter.
Homeward: songs by the way. Dublin 1894, 1895, London 1896, 1901, London and New York 1908, Portland ME 1895 (enlarged), 1895, 1904, 1904.
The future of Ireland and the awakening of the fires. [Dublin 1897]. Rptd from Irish Theosophist.
Ideals in Ireland: priest or hero? Dublin [1897].
The earth breath and other poems. London and New York 1897, 1906, New York 1906.
Cooperative credit. Dublin [1898], 1898 (in I. A. O. S. Annual report for 1898); tr Irish 1899.
An artist of Gaelic Ireland. [Dublin 1902, 1902, 1902]. Rptd from Freeman's Jnl. Rptd in Jack Yeats, Catalogue of sketches of life in the west of Ireland. nd.
The nuts of knowledge: lyrical poems, old and new. Dundrum 1903.
Deirdre: a drama in three acts. Dublin 1903 (rptd from All-Ireland, rev, and from Irish Homestead), 1907, 1922.
The divine vision and other poems. 1904, New York 1904.

Controversy in Ireland: an appeal to Irish journalists. Dublin [1904]. Two articles rptd from Dana and Leader.
The mask of Apollo, and other stories. Dublin [1905], London [1905].
Some Irish essays. 1906.
By still waters: lyrical poems old and new. Dundrum 1906.
Ireland and tariff reform, by 'Libra'. Dublin [1909].
The hero in man. [1909], 1910, Bombay [1945]. Prose.
The building up of a rural civilisation. Dublin 1910. An address.
The renewal of youth. 1911. Prose.
Cooperation and nationality: a guide for rural reformers from this to the next generation. Dublin 1912, New York 1913, Chicago and New York 1940; tr Finnish 1912.
The rural community: an address to the American commission of agricultural inquiry. Dublin 1913.
To the masters of Dublin: an open letter. [Dublin 1913.] Rptd from Irish Times 7 Oct 1913; rptd in 1,000 years of Irish prose, ed V. Mercier and D. H. Greene, New York 1952, 1961.
The tragedy of labour in Dublin. [London 1913.] Rptd from The Times 13 Nov 1913.
The Dublin strike. 1913, Dublin [1913]. A speech; rptd in 1,000 years of Irish prose, ed V. Mercier and D. H. Greene, New York 1952, 1961.
Oxford university and the co-operative movement. Oxford 1914.
Ireland, agriculture and the war. Dublin 1915.
Gods of war, with other poems. Dublin 1915 (priv ptd).
Imaginations and reveries. 1915, Dublin 1915, New York 1916, London 1921, Dublin 1921, London 1925, New York 1932.
Talks with an Irish farmer. Jan–Sep 1916 (Irish Homestead leaflets nos 1–12).
The national being: some thoughts on an Irish polity, Dublin 1916, 1918, 1918, Madras 1923, London 1925, New York 1930.
Templecrone: a record of co-operative effort. Dublin [1917]. Rptd from Irish Homestead.
Salutation: a poem on the Irish rebellion of 1916. 1917 (priv ptd).
Thoughts for a convention: memorandum on the state of Ireland. 1917, 1917, Dublin 1917, 1917, 1918, London 1918.
Conscription for Ireland: a warning to England. Dublin [1918]. Rptd from a letter pbd in Manchester Guardian 11 May 1918.
The candle of vision. 1918, 1918, 1919, 1919, 1919, New York 1919, London 1920, 1927, 1931.
Literary imagination. Dublin [1919]. Rptd from Irish Homestead.
Michael. Dublin 1919 (priv ptd).
A plea for justice, being a demand for a public enquiry into the attacks on co-operative societies in Ireland. Dublin [1920], Dublin [1921], (with addns).
The economics of Ireland and the policy of the British government. New York 1920, 1920, 1921.
Thoughts for British co-operators: being a further demand for a public enquiry into the attacks on co-operative societies in Ireland. Dublin [1921].
The inner and the outer Ireland. Dublin 1921, 1921, London 1921. Rptd from Pearson's Mag. Tr Fr [1921]; Sp [1922].
Ireland and the Empire at the court of conscience. Dublin 1921. Rptd from Manchester Guardian.
Ireland, past and future. 1922.
The interpreters. 1922, New York 1923.
The national being. Madras 1923.
Voices of the stones. 1925, New York 1925, London 1931.
Midsummer Eve. New York 1928.
Dark weeping; with designs by P. Nash. 1929, 1929 (no 19 of Ariel poems).
Enchantment, and other poems. New York 1930.
Vale, and other poems. 1931, New York 1931, 1931, London 1931.
Song and its fountains. 1932, New York 1932.
Verses for friends. Dublin 1932 (priv ptd).
The avatars: a futurist fantasy. 1933, New York 1933.
The house of the Tirans, and other poems. 1934, New York 1934.
The living torch: AE. Ed M. Gibbon 1937, New York 1938. Mainly articles and reviews rptd from Irish Statesman.
A golden standard for literature. Norton MA 1939. Rptd from Living Torch, *above*.

Letters

Some passages from the letters of AE to W. B. Yeats. Dublin 1936.
AE's letters to Minanlabain. Ed L. Porter, New York 1937. Letters to the editor and her husband, written 1930–5.
Letters from AE. Ed A. Denson [1961]. Foreword by M. Gibbon.

Contributions to books

Literary ideals in Ireland, by J. Eglinton, W. B. Yeats and G. Russell. 1899. With essays by Russell.
Ideals in Ireland. Ed Lady Gregory 1901, New York 1901. With essay by Russell.
New songs. London and Dublin 1904, 1904, [1904], [1904]. Poems by P. Colum, E. Gore Booth et al; selection and preface by Russell.
Lyrics, by 'Seumas O'Sullivan' [J. S. Starkey]. Portland ME 1910. Selection and preface by Russell.
The United Irishwomen: their place, work and ideals. Dublin 1911, 1911. With essay by Russell.
Rural reconstruction in Ireland, by L. Smith-Gordon and C. Staples. 1917. Preface by Russell.
Essays, Irish and American, by J. B. Yeats. Dublin 1918. An appreciation by Russell.
Secret springs of Dublin song. Ed S. Mitchell, Dublin 1918. Poem entitled Y—s by Russell.
The coming of Cuchulain, by S. J. O'Grady. Dublin and London 1919. Introd by Russell.
An Irish commune, by E. T. Craig. Dublin [1920]. Introd by Russell.
The government of Ireland, by Mrs J. R. Green. 1921. Foreword by Russell.
Mors et vita [poems], by Shan F. Bullock. 1923. Foreword by Russell.
Guilds and co-operatives in Italy, by O. Por. 1923. Introd by Russell.
Island blood, by F. R. Higgins. 1925. Foreword by Russell.
Anglo-Irish literature, by H. Law. 1926. Foreword by Russell.
Living India, by S. Zimand. Dublin 1928. Introd by Russell.
Agin the governments: memories and adventures, by F. Fletcher-Vane. 1929. Foreword by Russell.
Standish James O'Grady: the man and the writer, by H. O'Grady. Dublin 1929. A tribute by Russell; includes 8 poems by Russell wrongly attributed to O'Grady.
Collected poems, by K. Hinkson [Tynan]. 1930. Foreword by Russell.
First hymn to Levin and other poems by 'Hugh MacDiarmid' [C. M. Grieve]. 1931. Introd by Russell.
The wild bird's nest: poems translated from the Irish, by 'Frank O'Connor' [Michael O'Donovan]. Dundrum 1932. With essay by Russell.
Twenty-five lyrics, by 'Seumas O'Sullivan' [J. S. Starkey]. Flansham, Sussex 1933. Introd by Russell.
Selected poems, by Oliver St J. Gogarty. New York [1933], London 1938 (as Others to adorn). Foreword by Russell.
The valley of the bells and other poems, by I. Haugh. Oxford 1933. Introd by Russell.
Land under England, by J. O'Neill. 1935. Foreword by Russell.

§2

Ford, J. AE, the neo-Celtic mystic. Poet-Lore 16 1905.
Weygandt, C. AE, the Irish Emerson. Sewanee Rev 15 1907.
A school of Irish poetry. Edinburgh Rev 209 1909. On Yeats, M. O'Neill and Colum.
Boyd, E. AE – mystic and economist. North Amer Rev 202 1915.
Figgis, D. AE – George W. Russell: a study of a man and of a nation. Dublin 1916.
Boyd, E. In his Appreciation and depreciations, Dublin 1918.

Colum, P. AE, poet, painter and economist. New Republic 15 1918.
Garnier, C. George Russell, AE: poète du sommeil, avec fragments de lettres inédites. Études Anglaises 3 1939.
Curran, C. P. George Russell. Studies 24 1935.
Finlay, T. AE: in memoriam. Dublin Mag 10 1935.

William Sharp 1855–1905

See col 1627.

Dora Sigerson, later Shorter 1866–1918

Collections

Collected poems. 1907, New York 1907. Introd by G. Meredith.
[Twenty-one poems.] [1926] (Augustan Books of Modern Poetry).

§1

Verses. 1893.
The fairy changeling and other poems. London and New York 1898.
My lady's slipper and other verses. 1898, New York 1899.
Ballads and poems. 1899.
The father confessor: stories of death and danger. 1900.
The woman who went to Hell and other ballads and lyrics. [1902], New York [1902].
As the sparks fly upward: poems and ballads. [1904.]
The country-house party. 1905 (2nd edn). Novel.
The story and song of Black Roderick. 1906, New York 1906. Novel.
Through wintry terrors. 1907. Novel.
The troubadour and other poems. 1910.
New poems. Dublin 1912, 1921 (3rd edn).
Madge Linsey and other poems. Dublin 1913.
Do-well and do-little: a fairy tale. [1913.]
Love of Ireland: poems and ballads. Dublin 1914, London 1916, Dublin 1916 (with Poems of the Irish rebellion, 1916).
Comfort the women: a prayer in time of war. [1915] (priv ptd).
An old proverb: 'it will be all the same in a thousand years'. [London] 1916 (priv ptd).
The sad years [and other poems]. 1918, New York 1918, 1918 (priv ptd). Introd by K. Tynan.
A legend of Glendalough and other ballads. Dublin and London 1919.
Sixteen dead men and other poems of Easter week. New York 1919.
A dull day in London and other sketches. [1920]. Prefatory note by Thomas Hardy.
The tricolour: poems of the Irish revolution. Dublin 1922; ed D. Barry, Cork 1976 (enlarged).

§2

Colum, P. The poetry of Dora Sigerson Shorter. Bookman (New York) 1919.
In memoriam Dora Sigerson 1918–23. 1923 (priv ptd). Poems by various writers.

George Sigerson 1839–1925

§1

The poets and poetry of Munster: a selection of Irish songs, – with metrical translations. By Erionnach. Dublin 1860 (2nd ser).
Modern Ireland: its vital questions, secret societies ... by an Ulsterman. 1868, 1869 (2nd edn).
History of the land tenures and land classes of Ireland, with an account of the various secret agrarian confederacies. London and Dublin 1871.
Political prisoners at home and abroad. 1890.
Irish literature: its origin, environment and influence. In The revival of Irish literature: addresses by Sir C. G. Duffy, Dr G. Sigerson and Dr D. Hyde, 1894.
Bards of the Gael and Gall: examples of the poetic literature of Erinn, done into English after the metres and modes of the Gael. 1897, 1907 (rev and enlarged), New York 1907, Dublin 1925 (with memorial preface by D. Hyde).
The saga of King Lir. A sorrow of story. Dublin and London 1913.
The last independent parliament of Ireland. Dublin 1918.
Sedulius: the Easter song. Dublin 1922. Tr Sigerson.
Songs and poems. Dublin 1927. Introd by P. Colum.

§2

Garnier, C. George Sigerson 1925. Revue Anglo-américaine 3 1925.
Colum, P. An Irish poet-scholar. Commonweal 6 1927.

George Augustus Simcox 1841–1905

§1

Prometheus unbound: a tragedy. 1867.
Poems and romances. 1869.
Recollections of a rambler. 1874.
Simcox also pbd a history of Latin literature and edited the Greek Testament, Demosthenes, Juvenal and Thucydides.

§2

Miles, A. H. Simcox. In Miles 8 (7).
Haber, T. B. The poetic antecedents of Housman's Hell gate. PQ 31 1952. *See* J. Sparrow, PQ 33 1954.

Joseph Skipsey 1832–1903

Collections

Songs and lyrics, collected and revised. 1892.
Selected poems. Ed B. Bunting, Sunderland 1976.

§1

Poems, songs and ballads. London and Newcastle 1862.
The collier lad and other lyrics. 1864 (priv ptd).
Poems. 1871.
A book of miscellaneous lyrics. Bedlington 1878, 1881 (rev as A book of lyrics, including Songs, ballads and chants).
Carols from the coal-fields and other songs and ballads. 1886. With biographical note by R. S. Watson.
Skipsey also edited 6 vols of The Canterbury Poets.

§2

Watts[-Dunton], T. Skipsey's Miscellaneous lyrics. Athenaeum 16 Nov 1878.
Lewin, W. Songs and lyrics. Acad 20 Apr 1892.
Watson, R. S. Skipsey: his life and work. [1908.]
Runciman, J. F. Skipsey: poet of the Northumbrian pits. Living Age 262 1909.
Miles, A. H. Skipsey. In Miles 5.
Evans, B. I. In his English poetry in the later nineteenth century, 1933, 1966 (rev).

Douglas Brooke Wheelton Sladen 1856–1933

§1

Frithjof and Ingebjorg and other poems. 1882.
Australian lyrics. Melbourne 1883, 2nd edn rev London 1885.
A poetry of exiles and other poems. [1884], 1885 (rev).
A summer Christmas and a sonnet upon the S. S. Ballaarat. London and New York [1884].
In Cornwall and across the sea, with poems written in Devonshire. 1885.
Edward the Black Prince: an epic drama. [1887].
A ballad for the tercentenary of the Spanish Armada. Penzance [1888].

Lestee the loyalist: a romance of the founding of Canada. Tokyo 1890.
Gordon, A. L. The life and best poems of the poet of Australia. 1934 (Westminster Abbey memorial vol).
Sladen also pbd novels, biographies, books of travel and Twenty years of my life, *1915, and* My long life: anecdotes and adventures, *1939.*

G. W. Steevens, George Warrington Steevens

1869–1900

Mss: located in Berg Collection, NYPL; King's College Lib, Cambridge; National Lib of Scotland.

Bibliographies

See Wellesley *vol 5 1989.*

Collections and selections

The works of George Warrington Steevens. Ed G. S. Street 7 vols Edinburgh and London 1900–2 (memorial edn with memoir by W. E. Henley in vol 1).
Chapters from 'In India'. 1927 (Readers of Today ser).

§1

Naval policy: with some account of the warships of the principal powers. 1896, New York 1896.
REVIEWS: Athenaeum 24 Oct 1896; Literary World 20 Nov 1896; Spectator 28 Nov 1896; Speaker 13 Feb 1897.
Monologues of the dead. Edinburgh and London 1896, 1902.
REVIEWS: Acad 26 Sep 1896, 30 Jan 1897; Literary World 4 Apr 1902.
The land of the dollar. Edinburgh 1897 (3 edns), New York 1897, 1898, 1900 (4th & 5th edns), Freeport NY 1971.
REVIEWS: Br Weekly 28 Jan 1897; Acad 6 Feb 1897; Athenaeum 6 Feb 1897; New York Times 13 Feb 1897; Spectator 13 Feb 1897; Literary World 26 Feb 1897; Blackwood's Mag Apr 1897; Living Age May 1897; Chap-Book 1 Aug 1897; Bookman (USA) Sep 1897; Dial 1 Oct 1897; Nation 28 Oct 1897; New York Times 30 Oct 1897.
With the conquering Turk: confessions of a Bashi-Bazouk. Edinburgh and London 1897, New York 1897, 1901.
REVIEWS: Athenaeum 20 Nov 1897; Literary World 24 Dec 1897; Literature 25 Dec 1897; Westminster Rev Feb 1898; New York Times 9 Apr 1898; Chap-Book 1 May 1898; Nation 19 May 1898; Dial 1 July 1898.
The downfall of Mahadism. 1898.
Egypt in 1898. Edinburgh 1898, New York 1898, 1899.
REVIEWS: Acad 11 June 1898; Literature 11 June 1898; New York Times 3 Sep 1898; Speaker 17 Sep 1898; Nation 29 Sep 1898; Dial 1 Oct 1898; Spectator 15 Oct 1898; Literary World 21 Oct 1898.
With Kitchener to Khartoum. Edinburgh and London 1898 (15 edns), New York 1898, Toronto 1898, Edinburgh and London 1899, New York 1899, 1900, 1908, London [1909], New York 1911, 1915, London [1919] (school edn with ch on Egypt), Glasgow and London [1925?] (school edn), London 1987, 1990.
REVIEWS: Acad 8 Oct 1898; Literature 8 Oct 1898; Spectator 15 Oct 1898; Speaker 29 Oct 1898; Bookman Nov 1898; Dial 16 Feb 1899; New York Times 25 Feb 1899; Nation 22 June 1899.
The tragedy of Dreyfus. 1899, New York 1899.
REVIEWS: Acad 23 Sep 1899; Athenaeum 30 Sep 1899; Bookman Oct 1899; New York Times 21 Oct 1899; Spectator suppl 4 Nov 1899; Nation 23 Nov 1899; Harper's Mag suppl 30 Dec 1899.
In India. Edinburgh and London 1899 (3 edns), 1899 (Nelson Lib of Notable Books), New York 1899, London 1900, 1901, New York 1905, [1910], 1927, Delhi 1984 (as India of yesteryears), Cambridge 1992 (as In the India of the Raj).
REVIEWS: Speaker 4 Feb 1899; Spectator 4 Feb 1899; Athenaeum 7 Oct 1899; Literary World 13 Oct 1899; Outlook 14 Oct 1899; Acad 11 Nov 1899; Nation 14 Dec 1899; Critic Feb 1900.
From Capetown to Ladysmith. An unfinished record of the South African war. Ed V. Blackburn, Edinburgh and London 1900 (2 edns), Leipzig 1900 (Tauchnitz), New York 1900, Toronto [1900], New York 1969.
REVIEWS: Acad 3 Mar 1900; Athenaeum 3 Mar 1900; Literature 3 Mar 1900; The Times 8 Mar 1900; Literary World 9 Mar 1900; Dial 1 Apr 1900; Amer Historical Rev Oct 1900; Spectator 9 Feb 1901.
Glimpses of three nations. Ed V. Blackburn, New York 1900, Edinburgh 1901.
REVIEWS: Dial 16 Feb 1901; Athenaeum 25 May 1901; Acad 1 June 1901; Literature 1 June 1901; Spectator suppl 2 Nov 1901.
Things seen. Ed G. S. Street, memoir by W. E. Henley, Edinburgh and London 1900, Indianapolis 1900, Toledo OH 1902.
REVIEWS: Spectator 23 June 1900; Athenaeum 30 June 1900; Acad 7 July 1900; New York Times 25 May 1901.
Chicago. New York 1907 (Historic Landmarks of America).
Denver. New York 1907 (Historic Landmarks of America).

Contributions to periodicals and collaborative works

Steevens, sometime Fellow of Pembroke College, Oxford, was editor of the Cambridge Observer, *1893, on the staff of the* Pall Mall Gazette, *1893–95, and the* Daily Mail *from 1896. During the siege of Ladysmith he was editor of the* Ladysmith Lyre *from 27 Nov 1899 until his death.*
Nat Observer. 2 May 1891–26 Aug 1893.
Daily Mail. June 1897–8 Dec 1903. Rptd as Foreign affairs, in Politics in 1896, ed F. Whelen, 1897.
Living Age. New humanitarianism, 12 Mar 1898.
Scribner's Mag. Installation of Lord Curzon as Viceroy of India, May 1899.
McClure's Mag. Scenes and actors in the Dreyfus case, Oct 1899.
Harper's Mag. France as affected by the Dreyfus case, Oct 1899.
Windsor Mag. England's free hand on the Nile, Feb 1901.

§2

Acad 4 Dec 1897.
Notes and news. Acad 25 Dec 1897.
(Note re his unfinished novel John King.) Literature 7 Oct 1899.
Chronicle and comment. Bookman (USA) Nov 1899.
Obits: St James's Gazette 20 Jan 1900; New York Times 21 Jan 1900; Daily Mail 22 Jan 1900; The Times 22 Jan 1900; Natal Mercury 22 Jan 1900; St. James's Gazette 22 Jan 1900; Lee, S. Letter, Daily Mail 23 Jan 1900; Natal Witness 23 Jan 1900; Politics and persons, St James's Gazette 25 Jan 1900; The literary world, Acad 27 Jan 1900; Literary gossip, Athenaeum 27 Jan 1900; (Photo and short note), Graphic 27 Jan 1900; Personal (photo), Illustr London News 27 Jan 1900; Literature 27 Jan 1900; Natal Witness 27 Jan 1900; Outlook 27 Jan 1900; News of the week, Spectator 27 Jan 1900; The Sphere 27 Jan 1900.
The siege of Ladysmith. St James's Gazette 29 Jan 1900.
Authors and publishers. Literature 10 Feb 1900.
Abrahams, B. A. City of London School Mag Mar 1900.
Chronicle and comment. Bookman (USA) Mar 1900.
The lounger. Critic Mar 1900.
Many inventions. Illus London News 14 Apr 1900. Photo.
The literary world. Acad 3 Mar 1900, 23 June 1900.
Chronicle and comment. Bookman (USA) June 1900.
Letter re memorial to G. W. S. The Times 2 July 1900.
G. W. Steevens. Literary World 6 July 1900.
Sphere. 4 Aug 1900. Photo.
Lee, S. In DNB (vol 22 suppl) 1901.
The literary week. Acad 3 May 1902.
Browning, O. In his Memories of sixty years, 1910.
Bullard, F. L. In his Famous war correspondents, 1914.
Stearn, R. T. Steevens and the message of Empire. Jnl of Imperial and Commonwealth History Jan 1989. [DA]

James Kenneth Stephen 1859–92

Mss: poems and letters, King's College Lib, Cambridge.

Collections

Select poems. [1926] (Augustan Books of Modern Poetry).

§1

Lapsus calami. By J. K. S. Cambridge 1891, London 1891 (3rd edn, with omissions and addns), Cambridge 1928.
Quo musa tendis? Cambridge 1891.
Lapsus calami and other verses, with introd by H. Stephen. 1896.
Stephen also pbd books on international law and a defence of compulsory Greek.

§2

Miles, A. H. Stephen. In Miles 9 (10).
J. K. S. Acad 19 Aug 1905.
Benson, A. C. In his Leaves of the tree: studies in biography, 1911.
Evans, B. I. In his English poetry in the later nineteenth century, 1933, 1966 (rev).
Master of light verse: in memory of J. K. S. TLS 31 Jan 1941.

Robert Louis Stevenson 1850–94

See col 1688.

Algernon Charles Swinburne 1837–1909

Major collections include those in the BL (the Ashley Collection, formed by T. J. Wise), Leeds Univ (the Brotherton Collection), Georgetown Univ and Syracuse Univ (the Edith S. and John S. Mayfield Collection), the NYPL (the Berg Collection), Univ of Texas (the Wrenn Collection and others), Rutgers Univ (the Symington Collection), the Pierpont Morgan Lib, the Huntington, the Univ of Michigan (the Kerr Collection), and others. Swinburne's mss are indexed in LR and IELM. The Catalogue of the Ashley Manuscripts, *by T. A. J. Burnett 1998, is to appear in 1999; see too the* Index to manuscripts in the British Library, (Cambridge 1984–).

Bibliographies and reference works

Because of the forgeries created by T. J. Wise and H. B. Forman, Wise's bibliographic work must be used with caution. See the investigations under §2 below; W. E. Fredeman includes an invaluable 'Master list of indicted works' in The story of a lie: a sequel to A sequel, Rev (Univ of Virginia) 7, 1985.

Shepherd, R. H. The bibliography of Swinburne: a bibliographic list in chronological order of the published writings in verse and prose of Algernon Charles Swinburne (1857–1883). [1884,] [rev 1887.]
Wise, T. J. A bibliographical list of the scarcer works and uncollected writings of Algernon Charles Swinburne. Literary anecdotes of the nineteenth century: contributions towards a literary history of the period. Ed W. R. Nicoll and T. J. Wise. Vol 2 1896, ptd separately 1897.
Thomson, J. C. Bibliographical list of the writings of Algernon Charles Swinburne. Wimbledon 1905 (priv ptd).
Writings of Swinburne: little known facts of the poet's bibliography. Boston Evening Transcript 21 Apr 1909. Based on work by the American collector L. H. Chubbuck.
O'Brien, E. J. A bibliography of the works of Algernon Charles Swinburne. In A pilgrimage of pleasure, essays and studies, Boston 1913.
Vaughan, C. E. Bibliographies of Swinburne, Morris and Rossetti. The Eng. Assoc Dec 1914. Pamphlet 29.
Gosse, E. A catalogue of the works of Algernon Charles Swinburne in the library of Mr. Edmund Gosse. 1919 (priv ptd).
Wise, T. J. A bibliography of the writings in prose and verse of Algernon Charles Swinburne. 2 vols 1919–20 (priv ptd), 1927 (rev) vol 20 of Complete works, Bonchurch edn (includes Swinburne's contributions to periodicals), 1966.
Livingston, F. V. Swinburne's proof sheets and American first editions: bibliographical data relating to a few of the publications of Algernon Charles Swinburne with notes on the priority of certain claimants to the distinction of 'editio princeps'. Cambridge MA 1920 (priv ptd).
A catalogue of first editions of the works of Algernon Charles Swinburne in the library of Edward K. Butler. Boston 1921 (priv ptd).
Wise, T. J. Privately printed works of Swinburne. Bookman's Jnl 5 Aug 1921.
Wise, T. J. The Ashley library, a catalogue of printed books, manuscripts and autograph letters, collected by Thomas James Wise. Vols 6–10, 1925–30 (priv ptd).
Wise, T. J. A Swinburne library: a catalogue of printed books, manuscripts, and autograph letters by Algernon Charles Swinburne. 1925 (priv ptd).
Hyder, C. K. Swinburne's literary career and fame. Durham NC 1933.
Ehrsam, T. G., R. H. Deily and R. M. Smith. In their Bibliographies of twelve Victorian authors, New York 1936. Suppl by J. G. Fucilla, MP 37 1939.
Marchand, L. The Symington Collection at Rutgers. Victorian Newsletter Apr 1952.
Hyder, C. K. Algernon Charles Swinburne. In Victorian poets: a review of research, ed F. E. Faverty, Cambridge MA 1956, 1968 (rev).
Todd, W. B. Swinburne manuscripts at Texas. Texas Quart 2 1959.
Atalanta in Calydon by Algernon Charles Swinburne: an exhibition. Brooklyn New York 1965. Based on the Kerr Collection, now at the Univ of Michigan.
Fredeman, W. E. In his Pre-Raphaelitism: a bibliocritical study, Cambridge MA 1965.
Beetz, K. H. Algernon Charles Swinburne: a bibliography of secondary works, 1861–1980. Metuchen NJ 1982. *See also* T. L. Meyers, Literary Research Newsletter 8 Spring 1983.
Rooksby, R. Algernon Swinburne. Book and Magazine Collector 158, May 1997. Private Press editions.
An annual review of Swinburne studies appears in the Guide to the year's work in Victorian poetry in the autumn issue of VP.

Collections and selections

Selections. Ed R. H. Stoddard, New York 1884.
REVIEWS: Literary World 20 Sep 1884; Payne, W. M., Dial 5, Oct 1884; Critic (New York) 1 Nov 1884; Nation (New York) 18 Dec 1884.
Selections from the poetical works. 1887, 1889 (3rd edn), New York [1890?], London 1892, 1896 (6th edn), 1900 (8th edn), 1905, 1908 (12th edn), 1910, 1913, 1915, 1916 (20th impression), 1917. The selections were augmented in the 14th, 17th and 20th impressions. The 18th added a preface by T. Watts-Dunton and the 20th a supplemental note by him.
REVIEWS: Athenaeum 4 June 1887; Nation (New York) 4 Aug 1887; Morshead, E. D. A., Acad 3 Sep 1887; Critic (New York) 1 Oct 1887; Literary Weekly 1 Oct 1887; Literary World (Boston) 1 Oct 1887); Payne, W. M., Dial 8, Dec 1887.
Lyrical poems. Ed W. Sharp, Leipzig 1901 (Tauchnitz).
Dead love and other inedited pieces. Portland ME 1901.
The poems of Algernon Charles Swinburne. 6 vols (with Atalanta and Erechtheus) 1904, 1904, New York 1904, London 1909, 1910, 1912 (adds Cleopatra), 1917, 1919–20, New York 1972 (facs). The important dedicatory epistle in Hyder (ed), Swinburne replies, 1966, *below*.
REVIEWS: Literary World n.s. 69, 17 June 1904; Athenaeum 18 June 1904; Independent 58, 22 June 1904; Thompson, F., Acad 66, 25 June 1904; N & Q 10th ser 1, 25 June 1904; Blackwood's Mag 176,

July 1904; Douglas, J., Bookman July 1904; Saturday Rev 98, 2 July 1904; TLS 8 July 1904; Spectator 93, 16 July 1904; Living Age 242, 13 Aug 1904; Athenaeum 17 Aug 1904; Literary Digest 29, 20 Aug 1904; Athenaeum 27 Aug 1904; Critic (New York) 45, Sep 1904; GM Sep 1904; Davray, H. D., Mercure de France 51, Sep 1904; Elton, O., Speaker n.s. 10, 10 Sep 1904; and n.s. 11, 18 Feb 1905; N & Q 10th ser 2, 17 Sep 1904; Saturday Rev 98, 17 Sep 1904; Literary World n.s. 70, 23 Sep 1904; Douglas, J., Bookman 26 Sep 1904; Eclectic Mag of Foreign Lit 143, Oct 1904; Davray, H. D., Mercure de France 52, Dec 1904; Acad 67, 24 Dec 1904; Saturday Rev 93, 31 Dec 1904; Rhys, E., Fortnightly Rev 83, Jan 1905; Davray, H. D., Mercure de France 53, Feb 1905; Payne, W. M., Dial 38, 1 Mar 1905; Nation (New York) 80, 13 Apr 1905; Outlook 80, 10 June 1905; Boynton, H. W., Critic (New York) 47, July 1905; Greenslet, F., Atlantic Monthly 96, Sep 1905.

The tragedies of Algernon Charles Swinburne. 5 vols 1905, 1906, New York 1906, London 1909.

REVIEWS: TLS 30 June 1905; N & Q 10th ser 4, 8 July 1905, 4, 18 Nov 1905, 4, 16 Dec 1905, 5, 10 Feb 1906; Saturday Rev 100, 8 July 1905; Murray, G., Speaker n.s. 12, 16 Sep 1905; Davray, H. D., Mercure de France 58, 15 Nov 1905; Bailey, J., TLS 2 Feb 1906; Saturday Rev 101, 24 Feb 1906; Nation (New York) 82, 10 May 1906; Dial 40, 16 May 1906; Hellman, G. S., New York Times (Saturday Rev) 19 May 1906; Noyes, A., Bookman 30 May 1906; Outlook 83, 23 June 1906.

Selected poems. Ed W. M. Payne, Boston 1905.

Anactoria and other lyrical poems. New York 1906.

Poems. Ed A. Beatty, New York 1906.

Selected dramas. Ed A. Beatty, New York 1909.

Félise: a book of lyrics. Portland ME 1909.

Poems and tragedies. 2 vols Philadelphia [1910], Toronto 1910.

Swinburne calendar for the year 1913. 1912.

Golden pine edition. 5 vols 1917, 1918 plus A study of Shakespeare (1918) and William Blake (1925).

Springtide of life: poems of childhood. Ed E. Gosse 1918. Illustr A. Rackham.

Poems. Ed E. Rhys, New York 1919 (Mod Lib).

Selections. Ed E. Gosse and T. J. Wise 1919, 1920, New York 1920, London 1923, 1925, 1926.

Poems and ballads (2nd and 3rd ser). Portland ME 1902, 1921.

Collected poetical works. 2 vols 1924, New York [1924], London 1927.

Complete works (Bonchurch edn). Ed E. Gosse and T. J. Wise 20 vols 1925–7, New York 1968 (facs). Vol 1 includes Early poems. The standard edn but incomplete and inaccurate.

Poems and ballads. Ed G. S. Viereck, Girard KS 1925. Selections.

Selections. Ed W. O. Raymond, New York 1925.

Golden book of Swinburne's lyrics. Ed E. H. Blakeney 1927.

Selections. Ed H. M. Burton 1927.

Selected poems. Ed H. Wolfe 1928. Illustr H. Clarke.

The best of Swinburne. Ed C. K. Hyder and L. Chase, New York 1937.

Selected poems. Ed L. Binyon, Oxford 1940 (WC), 1995.

Poems and prose. Ed R. Church 1940 (EL).

Laus veneris and other lyrics. Mt Vernon New York [1942].

Selected poems. Ed H. Treece 1948.

Selected poems. Ed H. Hare 1950.

Selected poems. Ed E. Shanks 1950.

A Swinburne anthology: verse, drama, prose, criticism. Ed K. Foss 1955.

A selection. Ed E. Sitwell 1960.

Poems. Ed B. Dobrée 1961.

Swinburne replies: notes on poems and reviews; under the microscope; dedicatory epistle. Ed C. K. Hyder, Syracuse NY 1966.

Selected poetry and prose. Ed J. D. Rosenberg, New York 1968 (Modern Lib).

Poems and ballads; Atalanta in Calydon. Ed M. Peckham, Indianapolis 1970. Omits some poems.

Swinburne as critic. Ed C. K. Hyder 1972.

A choice of Swinburne's verse. Ed R. Nye 1973.

Selected poems. Ed L. M. Findlay, Manchester 1982.

Arthurian poets: Algernon Charles Swinburne. Ed J. P. Carley 1990.

Poèmes choisies. Ed P. Aquien. Paris 1990.

Apologie de Sade: réunion de textes stupéfiants jamais traduits ou écrits directement en français tous rassemblés pour la première fois savoir Charenton en 1810, Frank Fane, Will Drew et Phil Crewe, La flagellation de Charlie Collingwood, Félicien Cossu, Ernest Clouët, La fille du policeman, lettres à Richard Monckton Milnes, lettres à divers, etc. Le tout enrichi de documents d'époque et publié pour la délectation des membres de la Société du Roman Philosophique; se trouve à la chaumière dolmance sur la plage d'Étretât et dans l'arrière-boutique de tous les mauvais libraires de France et d'Angleterre. En dépôt aux éditions à l'écart à Reims. Imprimé l'an de grâce 1992 pour célébrer le bicentenaire de la comédie en un acte du citoyen Sade Le Suborneur. Reims 1992.

Algernon Charles Swinburne. Ed C. Maxwell 1997 (EL).

§1

The standard (but not necessarily accurate) account of edns is that by Wise in vol 20 of the Bonchurch edn; Lafourcade's edn of Atalanta in Calydon *(1930) includes apparently independent data on some titles. Additional notes come from the letter-books of Chatto and Windus, Swinburne's publisher, at the Univ of Reading. A no of unpbd or uncollected works or fragments by Swinburne appear in the vols of* The catalogue of the Ashley library, *Wise's bibliographies of Swinburne, and Lafourcade's* La jeunesse de Swinburne, 2 vols Paris 1928; *one poem, 'Stances à Collette' appears in* The Swinburne letters, ed C. Y. Lang, vol 4, pp. 126–7.

The Queen-Mother; Rosamond: two plays. 1860, 1860 (for 1865, Moxon's issue), 1866 (Hotten's issue of Moxon), New York 1866, Boston 1866, 1866, London 1868, 1908, Woodbridge CT 1975 (microfilm of Boston 1866), Chicago 1978 (microfiche of 1860), New York 1967 (microcard of 1860).

REVIEWS: Spectator 12 Jan 1861; Athenaeum 4 May 1861; Skelton, J., Fraser's Mag 71, June 1865; Nation (New York) 2, 1 May 1866; Eclectic Mag of Foreign Lit n.s. 3 June 1866; Nat Quart Rev 13 June 1866; New Englander 25 July 1866; London Quart Rev 31, Jan 1869; Baynes, T. S., Edinburgh Rev 134, July 1871; Colles, R., GM n.s. 68, Mar 1902.

Dead love. 1864 priv ptd (a forgery, 1890, itself counterfeited in 1904). Portland ME 1901. Rptd in A pilgrimage of pleasure, Boston 1913, and in Bonchurch edn vol 17.

O Virgin Mother of gentle days and nights. [1865.] A lithograph sheet.

Atalanta in Calydon. 1865, 1865, 1866, Boston 1866, London 1868, Boston 1868, London 1875, New York 1877, London 1879, 1882, 1883, New York 1884 (in anthology), London 1885, 1889, 1892, 1893, 1894 (Kelmscott), 1896, Portland ME 1897, London 1898, 1899, 1901, Leipzig 1901, Portland ME 1902, London 1905, 1906, 1907, Portland ME 1907, London 1909, 1911, 1912, Portland ME 1912, London 1913, 1917; ed M. C. Weir, Ann Arbor MI 1922; London 1923; ed J. H. Blackie, 1930; Oxford 1930 (facs of 1865); ed J. H. Haldane, London 1949, 1963, New York 1967 (microcard of Boston 1866), ed M. Peckham, Indianapolis 1970, Chicago 1970 (microfiche of 1865); tr Ger 1878, 1902, Fr (in Jeune Belgique, vol 12 [1912–13]), Polish 1907, Swed 1912, Ital 1922, 1928, Jap 1988.

*Wise (Bonchurch edn, vol 20) lists one other edn: 1910. Lafourcade (*Swinburne's Atalanta in Calydon, 1930*) says 21 edns (about 14,000 copies) issued by the publisher by 1917. Chatto and Windus letter-books (Reading Univ) indicate other edns: 1907, 1894.*

REVIEWS: Athenaeum 1 Apr 1865; N & Q 3rd ser 7, 1 Apr 1865; London Rev 10, 8 Apr 1865; Spectator 38, 15 Apr 1865; Reader 5, 22 Apr 1865; Morning Herald 27 Apr 1865; Saturday Rev 19, 6 May 1865; Warren, J. Leicester, Fortnightly Rev 1, 15 May 1865; Skelton, J., Fraser's Mag 71, June 1865; The Times 6 June 1865; Lord

Houghton, Edinburgh Rev 122, July 1865; Examiner 15 July 1865; Tablet 12 Aug 1865; Christian Examiner 79, Nov 1865; Round Table 1, 4 Nov 1865; Norton, C. E., Nation (New York) 1, 9 Nov 1865; Albion 11 Nov 1865; Sunday Times 31 Dec 1865; Harper's Monthly Mag 32, Jan 1866; Lowell, J. R., North Amer Rev 102, Apr 1866; Westminster Rev 87, Apr 1867; Étienne, L., Revue des Deux Mondes 69, 15 May 1867; Christian Remembrancer n.s. 55, Jan 1868; London Quart Rev 31, Jan 1869; De Bow's Rev n.s. 6 Mar 1869; Cantab 1 Apr 1873.

Chastelard. 1865, 1866 (Hotten's re-issue), New York 1866, London 1868, New York 1869, London 1878, 1894, Leipzig 1908, London 1910, New York 1967 (microcard of 1865), Chicago 1978 (microfiche of 1865). tr Ger 1873, Fr 1910, Du 1946.

Wise (Bonchurch edn, vol 20) lists other edns: 1893, 1909. Lafourcade (Swinburne's Atalanta in Calydon, 1930) *says 5 edns only issued by the publisher by 1909.*

REVIEWS: Reader 6, 2 Dec 1865; Spectator 38, 2 Dec 1865; London Rev 11, 9 Dec 1865; Athenaeum 46, 23 Dec 1865; Round Table 3, 13 Jan 1866; James, H., Nation (New York) 2, 18 Jan 1866; Urban, S., GM 220, Mar 1866; Lowell, J. R., North Amer Rev 102, Apr 1866; Lord Houghton, Fortnightly Rev 4, 15 Apr 1866; Pall Mall Gazette 27 Apr 1866; Saturday Rev 21, 26 May 1866; Westminster Rev 86, July 1866; Morley, H., Examiner 22 Sep 1866; Westminster Rev 87, Apr 1867; London Quart Rev 29 Jan 1868; London Quart Rev 31, Jan 1869; Baynes, T. S., Edinburgh Rev 134, July 1871; Cantab 1 Apr 1873.

Cleopatra. 1866 priv ptd, (a probable forgery, 1888, from Cornhill Mag Sep 1866); rptd in 1899 Laus veneris: poems and ballads, Portland ME 1912 (vol 6 of Poems 1904), Leeds 1924.

Laus veneris. 1866 priv ptd, (a forgery, 1890). Portland ME 1900, (2 edns), New York 1906, Portland ME 1906, Yellow Springs OH 1929, London 1948 (illustr J. Buckland-Wright); tr Fr 1895, Ital 1907, 1920.

[The historical and imaginative literature of England.] In Report of the anniversary, Royal Literary Fund, 1866. Rptd in E. V. Lucas, David Williams, founder of the Royal Literary Fund, 1920. Also in T. L. Meyers, Swinburne's speech to the Royal Literary Fund, May 2, 1866, MP 86 1988.

Poems and ballads. 1866, 1866 (Hotten's issue), 1866, New York 1866 (US edns often entitled Laus veneris and other poems and ballads), New York 1867, London 1868, New York 1868, 1869, 1870, London 1871, New York 1871, London 1873 (5th edn), 1878, New York 1876, 1878, 1880, London 1881, New York 1881, 1882, London 1883, 1884, New York 1884, London 1885, New York 1886, London 1887, New York 1887, London 1889, 1890, 1891, 1892, 1893, 1894, 1896, 1897, New York 1897, London 1898, 1899, Portland ME 1899, London 1900, 1902, 1903, Portland ME 1904, London 1906, New York 1906, London 1907, 1908, 1909, 1912, 1917, 1919, Indianapolis 1970 (selections ed M. Peckham), Chicago 1970 (microfiche of 1866); tr Fr 1891.

Wise (Bonchurch edn, vol 20) lists other edns: 1873 (6th edn; a new edn), 1875, 1875, 1876, 1877, 1878, 1878, 1880, 1882, 1883, 1888, 1893, 1894, 1901, 1904, 1905, 1909, 1910, 1910, 1914 and 1916. Chatto and Windus letter-books (Reading Univ) indicate other edns: 1888, 1901, 1901. Lafourcade (Swinburne's Atalanta in Calydon, 1930) *says 45 edns (about 30,000 copies) issued by the publisher by 1917.*

REVIEWS: Rossetti, W. M., Swinburne's Poems and ballads: a criticism, 1866; Morning Star, 23 July 1866, 6 Aug 1866; Reader 7, 28 July 1866; London Rev 13, 4 Aug 1866; Morley, J., Saturday Rev 22, 4 Aug 1866, rptd Eclectic Mag of Foreign Lit 67, Nov 1866; Tablet 11 Aug 1866; Buchanan, R., Athenaeum 4, 18 Aug 1866; Fun 18 Aug 1866; Pall Mall Gazette 20 Aug 1866; Illus London News 25 Aug 1866; Living Age 90, 8 Sep 1866; Morley, H., Examiner 22 Sep 1866; Spectator 39, 22 Sep 1866; Lord Houghton, Examiner 6 Oct 1866; Skelton, J., Fraser's Mag 74, Nov 1866; White, R. G., Galaxy 2, 1 Dec 1866; Schuyler, E., Nation (New York) 3, 6 Dec 1866; Round Table 4, 8 Dec 1866; Eclectic Rev n.s. 11 Dec 1866; Nat Quart Rev 14 Dec 1866; Thomson, J., Nat Reformer 23 Dec 1866; Taylor, J. B., North Amer Rev 104, Jan 1867; Crescent Monthly Feb 1867; Westminster Rev 87 Apr 1867; Gildersleeve, B. L., Southern Rev 1 Apr 1867; Étienne, L., Revue des Deux Mondes 69, 15 May 1867; Davidson, T., Radical 3 Jan 1868; London Quart Rev 31, Jan 1869; Baynes, T. S., Edinburgh Rev 134, July 1871; Cantab 1 Apr 1873.

Notes on poems and reviews. 1866, 1866; ed C. K. Hyder, Syracuse NY 1966.

REVIEWS: Examiner 27 Oct 1866; Pall Mall Gazette 2 Nov 1866; Athenaeum 3 Nov 1866, rptd Living Age 1 Dec 1866; London Rev 13, 3 Nov 1866; Spectator 39, 3 Nov 1866; Fun 17 Nov 1866; Saturday Rev 22, 17 Nov 1866; Living Age 91, 15 Dec 1866, rptd London Rev 13 Jan 1869; Westminster Rev 87, Apr 1867; London Quart Rev 31, Jan 1869; Baynes, T. S., Edinburgh Rev 134, July 1871.

An appeal to England against the execution of the condemned fenians. Manchester 1867. A broadside; the pam is forged (1890).

Dolores. 1867. priv ptd (a forgery, 1895?), 1916; tr Latin 1906, Swed 1917.

A song of Italy. 1867, Boston 1867, London 1868, Portland ME 1904, Chicago 1978 (microfiche of 1867).

REVIEWS: Athenaeum 6 Apr 1867; Examiner 13 Apr 1867; Pall Mall Gazette 13 Apr 1867; Spectator 40, 13 Apr 1867; Saturday Rev 23, 20 Apr 1867; Purnell, T., Every Saturday 3, 4 May 1867; Norton, C. E., North Amer Rev 105, July 1867; Westminster Rev 88, July 1867; Contemporary Rev 5 July 1867; Round Table 6, 6 July 1867; London Quart Rev 31, Jan 1869.

William Blake. 1868 (for 1867), 1868, 1906 (with new preface), New York 1906, 1967 (facs); ed H. J. Luke, Lincoln NE 1970; Chicago 1976 (microfiche of 2nd edn 1868), New York 1980 (facs).

REVIEWS: Athenaeum 4 Jan 1868; Conway, M. D., Fortnightly Rev n.s. 3, 1 Feb 1868; [Green, J. R.] Sat Rev 1 Feb 1868; Examiner 8 Feb 1868; Imperial Rev [8(?) Feb 1868] (no copies known; *see* Round Table 22 Feb 1868); Spectator 41, 14 Mar 1868; Westminster Rev 89, Apr 1868; Broadway Annual 1868, London Quart Rev 31, Jan 1869; TLS 5, 10 Aug 1906; Athenaeum 11 Aug 1906; Symons, A., Saturday Rev 102, 25 Aug 1906; Dial 41, 1 Dec 1906; Current Lit 42, Feb 1907; Outlook 85, 2 Mar 1907.

Siena. 1868 (6[?] copies; counterfeited 1889), Philadelphia 1868, Portland ME 1910; tr Ital 1890.

REVIEW: Amer Quart Church Rev 20 Oct 1868.

[Remarks on American literature and culture.] Jnl of the Anthropological Soc of London 6 1868. Also in T. L. Meyers, Whitman and Swinburne: further evidence, Walt Whitman Quart 14 Summer 1996.

Ode on the Proclamation of the French Republic, Sep 4, 1870. 1870, Chicago 1978 (microfiche).

REVIEWS: Athenaeum 17 Sep 1870; Examiner 24 Sep 1870; Graphic 2, 24 Sep 1870; Saturday Rev 30, 24 Sep 1870; London Quart Rev 35, Jan 1871.

Songs before sunrise. 1871, 1871, Boston 1871, London 1874, 1875, 1880, 1883, 1888, 1892, 1896, 1899, Portland ME 1901, London 1903, 1909, 1909, New York 1909, London 1911, 1915, Chicago 1978 (microfiche of 1871); tr Fr 1909.

Wise (Bonchurch edn, vol 20) lists other edns: 1877, 1895, 1908. Lafourcade (Swinburne's Atalanta in Calydon, 1930) *says 13 edns (about 6,500 copies) issued by the publisher by 1917.*

REVIEWS: Athenaeum 14 Jan 1871; Examiner 14 Jan 1871; Saturday Rev 31, 14 Jan 1871; Hüffer, F., Acad 2, 15 Jan 1871; Graphic 3, 28 Jan 1871; Amos, S., Fortnightly Rev 15, 1 Feb 1871; Literary World (Boston), 1 Mar 1871; Westminster Rev n.s. 39, Apr 1871; Tinsley's Mag 8 June 1871; Baynes, T. S., Edinburgh Rev 134, July 1871; Hayward, A., Quart Rev Jan 1872.

Bothwell, Act one [an early version]. 1871 (priv ptd).

Under the microscope. 1872, Portland ME 1899; ed C. K. Hyder,

Syracuse NY 1966; Chicago 1978 (microfiche of 1872), New York 1986 (facs).
REVIEWS: Examiner 6 July 1872; Maitland, T. [R. W. Buchanan], St Pauls Mag 11 Aug 1872.
Bothwell. 1874, 1874, 2 vols 1875, 1882, 1901, New York 1968 (microfiche of 1874).
Wise (Bonchurch edn, vol 20) lists another edn: 1900; tr Ger 1897.
REVIEWS: Athenaeum 23 May 1874; Examiner 30 May 1874; Saturday Rev 37, 6 June 1874; Spectator 47, 6 June 1874; Saintsbury, G., Acad 5, 13 June 1874; Belgravia 23, June 1874; London Quart Rev 42, July 1874; Temple Bar 41, July 1874; Westminster Rev n.s. 46, July 1874; Lord Houghton, Fortnightly Rev 22, 1 July 1874; Nichol, J., Glasgow Herald 9 July 1874; Morley, J., Macmillan's Mag 30 Oct 1874; Catholic World 20 Dec 1874.
The devil's due. 1875, (a forgery, 1897), New York 1986 (facs).
George Chapman: a critical essay. 1875, Chicago 1970 (microfiche), New York 1972 (facs), Folcroft PA 1972 (facs), Norwood PA 1976 (facs), Philadelphia 1977 (facs).
REVIEWS: Gosse, E., Examiner 20 Feb 1875; Spectator 48, 20 Mar 1875; Westminster Rev n.s. 47, Apr 1875; Symonds, J. A., Acad 7, 1 May 1875.
Songs of two nations. 1875, 1893, Chicago 1970 (microfiche of 1875).
REVIEWS: Gosse, E., Examiner 27 Mar 1875; Acad 7, 10 Apr 1875.
Auguste Vacquerie. Paris 1875 (tr from Examiner 6 Nov 1875).
Essays and studies. 1875, 1876, 1888, 1897, 1901, 1911, Chicago 1970 (microfiche of 1875), Plainview NY 1973 (facs), Freeport NY 1973 (facs of 1888).
Wise (Bonchurch edn, vol 20) lists other edns: 1887, 1896.
REVIEWS: Athenaeum 22 May 1875; Amer Bibliopolist 7 June 1875; Gosse, E., Examiner 12 June 1875; Pall Mall Gazette 23 June 1875; Westminster Rev n.s. 48, July 1875; Saintsbury, G., Acad 8, 3 July 1875; Spectator 48, 3 July 1875; Saturday Rev 40, 10 July 1875; James, H., Nation (New York) 21, 29 July 1875; Scribner's Monthly 10 Aug 1875; British Quart 62, Oct 1875; Benton, J., Appleton's Jnl 14, 13 Nov 1875; Quart Rev 141, Apr 1876; North Amer Rev 123, July 1876.
Note of an English republican on the Muscovite crusade. 1876, Cambridge 1987 (microfiche).
REVIEWS: Acad 10, 23 Dec 1876; Athenaeum 23 Dec 1876; Spectator 49, 23 Dec 1876; Pall Mall Gazette 2 Feb 1877.
Erechtheus. 1876, 1876, 1881, 1894, 1917; ed M. C. Weir 1922; New York 1967 (microcard of 1876), Chicago 1978 (microfiche of 1876); tr Danish 1877.
Wise (Bonchurch edn, vol 19) lists other edns: 1887, 1896, 1901, 1911.
REVIEWS: Athenaeum 1 Jan 1876; Spectator 49, 1 Jan 1876; World 5 Jan 1876; Symonds, J. A., Acad 9, 8 Jan 1876; Gosse, E., Examiner 8 Jan 1876; Saturday Rev 41, 8 Jan 1876; Pall Mall Gazette 15 Jan 1876; Br Quart Rev 63, Apr 1876; London Quart Rev 46, Apr 1876; Westminster Rev n.s. 49, Apr 1876; Scribner's Monthly 12 May 1876; Edinburgh Rev 144, July 1876; International Rev 3 Aug 1876; Blackwood's Mag Oct 1879.
Lesbia Brandon. 1877 (galleys); ed R. Hughes 1952 (2 impressions); ed E. Wilson New York 1962; ed E. Wilson New York 1963; Westport CT 1978 (facs of New York 1962); tr Fr 1987; Sp nd; Ital 1981, 1991 (of 1952 edn). *See* controversy in TLS 10–17, 31 Oct, 7, 28 Nov 1952; the letter of 31 Oct (by C. Y. Lang) details problems with the Hughes edn. *See also* J. S. Mayfield, Two leaves of Swinburne's ms of 'Lesbia Brandon', The Courier, Spring 1967 (rptd with corrected transcription in Mayfield, Swinburneiana, [Bethesda MD] 1974); R. Rooksby, Swinburne's Reginald, N & Q n.s. 38, Sep 1991 (early fragment of Lesbia Brandon); M. Sherry, Swinburne at Princeton, Jnl Rutgers Univ Lib 55, Dec 1993 (S. Solomon's illustrations). New edn in preparation.
A note on Charlotte Brontë. 1877, 1877, 1894, New York 1970 (facs of 1894), Folcroft PA 1973 (facs), New Haven CT 1976 (microfilm of 1877), 1977 (microfiche of 1877).
REVIEWS: Athenaeum 1 Sep 1877; Examiner 1 Sep 1877; Spectator 50, 1 Sep 1877; Dowden, E., Acad 12, 8 Sep 1877; World, 19 Sep 1877; Br Quart Rev 66, Oct 1877; Contemporary Rev 30 Oct 1877; The Times 2 Nov 1877; Perry, T. S., Atlantic Monthly 41, June 1878.
Poems and ballads: second series. 1878, 1878, New York 1878 (including Tristram and Iseult), 1880, London 1882, 1884, New York 1885[?], 1886[?], London 1887, New York 1887, London 1889, 1891, 1893, 1895, 1897, 1899, 1901, 1902, Portland ME 1902, London 1908, 1912, 1917, Chicago 1970 (microfiche of 1878); tr Fr 1902.
*Wise (Bonchurch edn, vol 20) lists other edns: 1880, 1886, 1900, 1902, 1910, 1915, 1916. Chatto and Windus letter-books (Reading Univ) indicate other edns: 1903 (or 1904), 1905. Lafourcade (*Swinburne's Atalanta in Calydon, *1930) says 20 edns (about 11,000 copies) issued by the publisher by 1917.*
REVIEWS: Pall Mall Gazette 5 July 1878; [Watts-Dunton, T.] Athenaeum 6 July 1878; Examiner 6 July 1878; Saintsbury, G., Acad 14, 13 July 1878; Nation (New York) 27, 18 July 1878; Saturday Rev 46, 20 July 1878; Literary World (Boston) 1 Aug 1878; North Amer Rev 127, Sep–Oct 1878; Br Quart Rev 68, Oct 1878; Westminster Rev n.s. 54, Oct 1878; Appleton's Jnl n.s. 5 Oct 1878; Smith, G. B., International Rev 5 Oct 1878; N & Q 5th ser 10, 26 Oct 1878; Contemporary Rev 34, Jan 1879; Edinburgh Rev 171, Apr 1890.
Charles Collingwood's flogging. The Pearl no 3 Sep 1879, ii, 77–83. Rptd in I. Gibson, The English vice, 1978.
An election. [1879 or 1880.] A lithographed leaflet.
Frank Fane: a ballad. The Pearl no 11 May 1880. Rptd in I. Gibson, The English vice, 1978.
A study of Shakespeare. 1880, 1880, New York 1880, 1887, London 1895 (3rd edn rev), 1902, 1909, New York 1965 (facs), Chicago 1978 (microfiche of 1880).
Wise (Bonchurch edn, vol 20) lists another edn: 1908.
REVIEWS: Dowden, E., Acad 17, 3 Jan 1880; Examiner 10 Jan 1880; [Watts-Dunton, T.] Athenaeum 31 Jan 1880; Saturday Rev 49, 31 Jan 1880; Br Quart Rev 71, Apr 1880; Westminster Rev 113, Apr 1880; N & Q 6th ser 1, 1 May 1880; Spectator 53, 3 July 1880.
Songs of the springtides. 1880, New York [1882?], London 1891 (3rd edn), 1902 (4th edn), Portland ME 1906 (Thalassius and On the cliffs only), Chicago 1978 (microfiche of 1880).
Wise (Bonchurch edn, vol 20) lists another edn: 1880.
REVIEWS: Examiner, 15 May 1880; Saintsbury, G., Acad 17, 22 May 1880; [Watts-Dunton, T.] Athenaeum 22 May 1880; N & Q 6th ser 1, 22 May 1880; Saturday Rev 49, 29 May 1880; GM 246, June 1880; Nation (New York) 30, 17 June 1880; Br Quart Rev 72, July 1880; Westminster Rev 114, July 1880; Dial 1 July 1880; Lowell, R., Literary World 11, 17 July 1880; Congdon, C. T., North Amer Rev 131, Aug 1880; Sharp, W., Mod Thought 1 Aug 1880; Nineteenth Cent 8 Aug 1880; Scribner's Monthly 20 Oct 1880.
Specimens of modern poets: the heptalogia or seven against sense: a cap with seven bells. 1880, Portland ME 1898, Chicago 1978 (microfiche of 1880), New York 1986 (facs). Anon.
REVIEW: Nichol, J., Glasgow Herald 24 Mar 1881.
Studies in song. 1880, New York 1880, 1887, London 1896, 1907, Chicago 1978 (microfiche of 1880).
REVIEWS: Dial 1 Jan 1881; Dowden, E., Acad 19, 8 Jan 1881; [Watts-Dunton, T.] Athenaeum 15 Jan 1881; Congregationalist 10 Feb 1881; Nation (New York) 32, 10 Feb 1881; American, 12 Feb 1881; Literary World 12, 26 Feb 1881; Spectator 54, 5 Mar 1881; Br Quart Rev 73, Apr 1881; Westminster Rev 115, Apr 1881.
Euthanatos: M. T. 23rd Jan 1881. Printed leaflet.
Mary Stuart: a tragedy. 1881, New York 1881, 1887, London 1899 (2nd edn); ed W. M. Payne, Boston 1906; Leipzig 1908, London 1910, New York 1967 (microcard of 1881), Chicago 1970 (microcard of 1881), nd (microcard of Boston 1906).
Wise (Bonchurch edn, vol 20) lists other edns: 1898, 1909.
REVIEWS: Daily Chron 24 Nov 1881; Glasgow Herald 24 Nov 1881; Leeds Mercury 24 Nov 1881; Saturday Rev 52, 3 Dec 1881;

Athenaeum 10 Dec 1881; Morshead, E. D. A., Acad 20, 10 Dec 1881; Athenaeum, 17 Dec 1881; Critic (New York) 1, 17 Dec 1881; Pall Mall Gazette 17 Dec 1881; Br Quart Rev 75, Jan 1882; Literary World 13, 14 Jan 1882; Simcox, G. A., Fortnightly Rev n.s. 31, 1 Feb 1882; Dial 2 Feb 1882; Nation (New York) 34, 27 Apr 1882; Westminster Rev 118, July 1882; Bayne, T., Fraser's Mag n.s. 26 Oct 1882; Lippincott's Monthly Mag 32, Nov 1883.

Tristram of Lyonesse and other poems. 1882, 1882, 1884, 1892, 1896, 1899, 1903, Portland ME 1904, London 1909, 1915, Chicago 1970 (microfiche of 1882).

REVIEWS: [Watts-Dunton, T.] Athenaeum 22 July 1882; Pall Mall Gazette 29 July 1882; Saturday Rev 54, 29 July 1882; Symonds, J. A., Acad 22, 5 Aug 1882; Critic (New York) 2, 12 Aug 1882; Spectator 55, 12 Aug 1882; Urban, S., GM 253, Sep 1882; Literary World 13, 9 Sep 1882; Br Quart Rev 76, Oct 1882; Westminster Rev 118, Oct 1882; American 1 Nov 1882; Dial 3 Mar 1883.

A century of roundels. 1883, 1883, New York 1883, 1885[?], 1886, 1887, London 1892, 1909, Chicago 1978 (microfiche of 1883).

REVIEWS: The Times 6 June 1883; [Watts-Dunton, T.] Athenaeum 16 June 1883; Noble, J. A., Acad 23, 23 June 1883; Br Quart Rev 78, July 1883; Pall Mall Gazette 5 July 1883; Literary World 14, 14 July 1883; Amer 6, 28 July 1883; Spectator 56, 28 July 1883; Schovelin, T. A., Dial 4 Aug 1883; Ker, W. P., Contemporary Rev 44, Sep 1883; Scottish Rev 2 Sep 1883; Le Livre 4, 10 Oct 1883; Critic (New York) 3, 13 Oct 1883.

In the album of Adah Menken Dolorida. [1883] (priv ptd), (pirated, 1887). Swinburne's, despite his and others' denials (e.g. T. Watts-Dunton, The Times 21 May 1909).

A midsummer holiday and other poems. 1884, 1884, New York 1884, London 1889, Chicago 1978 (microfiche of 1884).

REVIEWS: The Times 12 Nov 1884; [Watts-Dunton, T.] Athenaeum 22 Nov 1884; Pall Mall Gazette 22 Nov 1884; Saturday Rev 58, 29 Nov 1884; Spectator 57, 29 Nov 1884; GM 257, Dec 1884; Morshead, E. D. A., Acad 26, 6 Dec 1884; Br Quart Rev 81, Jan 1885; Ker, W. P., Contemporary Rev 47, Jan 1885; Book Buyer n.s. 2 Feb 1885; Woodberry, G. E., Atlantic Monthly 55, Apr 1885; Dial 6 June 1885; London Quart Rev 65, Jan 1886.

Marino Faliero. 1885, 1907, New York 1967 (microcard of 1885).

REVIEWS: The Times 14 May 1885; Robertson, E., Acad 27, 13 June 1885; [Watts-Dunton, T.] Athenaeum 13 June 1885; Br Quart Rev 82, July 1885; Book Buyer n.s. 2 July 1885; Ker, W. P., Contemporary Rev 48, Aug 1885; Dial 6 Jan 1886.

A study of Victor Hugo. 1886, New York 1886 (Victor Hugo), London 1909, Port Washington NY [1970] (facs), Folcroft PA 1976 (facs), Norwood PA 1978 (facs), Philadelphia 1978 (facs).

REVIEWS: Nation (New York) 42, 25 Feb 1886; Pall Mall Gazette 27 Feb 1886; Dial 6 Mar 1886; The Times, 6 Mar 1886; [Watts-Dunton, T.] Athenaeum 13 Mar 1886; Morshead, E. D. A., Acad 29, 27 Mar 1886; Huss, H. C. O., MLN 1 Apr 1886; Literary World (Boston) 17, 3 Apr 1886; Critic (Boston) n.s. 5, 17 Apr 1886; Urban, S., GM 261, July 1886.

Miscellanies. 1886, New York 1886, London 1895, 1911, Chicago 1970 (microfiche of 1911), New York [197–?] (microfiche).

REVIEWS: Pall Mall Gazette 7 June 1886; [Watts-Dunton, T.] Athenaeum 19 June 1886; Literary World n.s. 33, 25 June 1886; Saturday Rev 62, 17 July 1886; N & Q 7th ser 2, 24 July 1886; Spectator 59, 18 Sep 1886; Anderson, M. B., Dial 7 Nov 1886.

The commonweal: a song for unionists. 1886 [probably a piracy, 1889].

A word for the Navy. 1886 (priv ptd), 1887 (Redway edn), 1896 (Popular edn). (Also 1887, forged, 1887–91.)

The question. 1887 (a forgery, 1887–91).

The jubilee. 1887 (a forgery, 1887–91).

Gathered songs. 1887. priv ptd (a forgery, 1887–91).

Locrine. 1887, New York Times 17 Nov 1887, New York Evening Sun 17 Nov 1887, New York 1887, 1888, [1892?], London 1896, New York 1967 (microcard of New York 1887[?]), Chicago 1978 (microfiche of 1887).

REVIEWS: Pall Mall Gazette 18 Nov 1887; The Times 18 Nov 1887; Shepherd, R. H., GM 263, Dec 1887; Saturday Rev 64, 3 Dec 1887; Garrod, H. B., Acad 32, 10 Dec 1887; [Watts-Dunton, T.] Athenaeum 24 Dec 1887; Spectator 61, 7 Jan 1888; Payne, W. M., Dial 8 Feb 1888; Literary World (Boston) 19, 18 Feb 1888; Westminster Rev 129, Mar 1888; Nation (New York) 46, 17 May 1888; Critic (New York) 13, 17 Nov 1888; Public Opinion 14, 10 Dec 1892; Acad 56, 25 Mar 1899 (review of performance).

Unpublished verses. [1888] (priv ptd; a piracy), New York 1903 (Some unpublished verses to a mistress).

The ballad of dead man's bay. 1889. priv ptd (a piracy, possibly a forgery, 1891).

The bride's tragedy. 1889. Priv ptd (a piracy, possibly a forgery, 1889–96), New York 1967 (microcard).

The brothers. 1889, (a forgery 1892–6).

A logical ballad of home rule. St James's Gazette 2 Mar 1889 (rptd in Bonchurch vol 20 p. 497).

Poems and ballads: third series. 1889, 1889, New York 1889, London 1892, 1895, 1897, 1899, 1902 (7th edn), Portland ME 1902, London 1903, 1908, 1910, 1913 (11th impression), Chicago 1970 (microfiche of 1889).

Wise (Bonchurch edn, vol 20) lists other edns: 1901, 1912, 1916. Lafourcade (Swinburne's Atalanta in Calydon, 1930) *says 12 edns (about 7,500 copies) issued by the publisher by 1917.*

REVIEWS: The Times 10 Apr 1889; Saturday Rev 67, 20 Apr 1889; Cotterell, G., Acad 35, 27 Apr 1889; Public Opinion 7, 27 Apr 1889; Scots Observer 1, 27 Apr 1889; [Watts-Dunton, T.] Athenaeum 25 May 1889; Spectator 62, 1 June 1889; Wilde, O., Pall Mall Gazette 27 June 1889; GM 267, July 1889; Literary World (Boston) 20, 6 July 1889; Book Buyer n.s. 6 Sep 1889; Payne, W. M., Dial 10 Sep 1889; Critic (New York) 15, 16 Nov 1889; Nation (New York) 49, 26 Dec 1889; Edinburgh Rev 171, Apr 1890.

A study of Ben Jonson. 1889, New York 1889, 1890, 1968 (facs); ed H. B. Norland, Lincoln NE 1969; Chicago 1978 (microfiche of 1889).

REVIEWS: The Times 12 Nov 1889; Davidson, J., Acad 36, 23 Nov 1889; Critic (New York) 16, 1 Mar 1890; Nation (New York) 50, 6 Mar 1890; Literary World (Boston) 21, 15 Mar 1890; Dial 10 Apr 1890; Schelling, F. E., MLN 5 June 1890.

A sequence of sonnets on the death of Robert Browning. 1890 (priv ptd), (pirated 1891).

Russia: an ode. [1890.] Claimed by Wise as a separate pbn, but only a proof for the periodical pbn.

The sisters: a tragedy. 1892, New York 1892, 1979 (microcard of 1892).

REVIEWS: The Times 12 May 1892; Saturday Rev 73, 21 May 1892; Nat Observer 8, 28 May 1892; Bookman 2 June 1892; Walford, L. B., Critic (New York) 20, 4 June 1892; Literary Digest 5, 18 June 1892; Cotterell, G., Acad 42, 2 July 1892; [Watts-Dunton, T.] Athenaeum 2 July 1892; Spectator 69, 2 July 1892; Literary World (Boston) 23, 16 July 1892; GM 273, Aug 1892; Sharp, W., Pagan Rev 15 Aug 1892; Payne, W. M., Dial 13, 16 Sep 1892; Public Opinion 14, 26 Nov 1892; Critic (New York) 21 Dec 1892.

Music: an ode. 1892.

The ballad of Bulgarie. 1893 (priv ptd, pirated). Included in C. Y. Lang, New writings, Syracuse NY 1964; correct text in T. A. J. Burnett. Swinburne's The ballad of Bulgarie, MLR Apr 1969.

Grace Darling. 1893 (priv ptd; possibly an intended piracy, then authorised).

Astrophel and other poems. 1894, 1894, New York 1894, Chicago 1978 (microfiche of 1894).

REVIEWS: The Times 26 Apr 1894; Saturday Rev 77, 5 May 1894; Quiller-Couch, A. T., Speaker 9, 5 May 1894; Literary World n.s. 49, 18 May 1894; Morshead, E. D. A., Acad 45, 26 May 1894; GM 276, June 1894; [Watts-Dunton, T.] Athenaeum 2 June 1894; Bookman 6 June 1894; Henley, W. E., Pall Mall Gazette 13 June

1894, rptd Critic (New York) 21 July 1894; Critic (New York) 21 July 1894; Spectator 72, 16 June 1894; Book Buyer n.s. 11 July 1894; Poet Lore 6, June–July 1894; Critic (New York) 25, 21 July 1894.

Studies in prose and poetry. 1894, 1897, 1907 (3rd impression), 1915, Freeport NY 1972 (facs).

Wise (Bonchurch edn, vol 20) lists another edn: 1906 (3rd edn).

REVIEWS: The Times 6 Nov 1894; Saturday Rev 78, 17 Nov 1894; Bookman 7 Dec 1894; Literary World n.s. 50, 21 Dec 1894; [Watts-Dunton, T.] Athenaeum 22 Dec 1894; Hankin, St. J., Acad 46, 29 Dec 1894; GM 278, Jan 1895; Nat Observer 13, 2 Mar 1895; Coupe, C., Dublin Rev 116, Apr 1895.

The tale of Balen. 1896, New York 1896.

REVIEWS: The Times 28 May 1896; Literary World n.s. 53, 5 June 1896; The Guardian 51, 10 June 1896; D'Esterre-Keeling, E., Acad 49, 13 June 1896; Book Buyer n.s. 13 June 1896; [Watts-Dunton, T.] Athenaeum 20 June 1896; GM 281, July 1896; Bookman (New York) 3 July 1896; Lang, A., Cosmopolis 3 July 1896; Critic (New York) 29, 4 July 1896; Macdonell, A., Bookman 10 July 1896; Saturday Rev 82, 15 Aug 1896; Payne, W. M., Dial 21, 1 Sep 1896; Atlantic Monthly 78, Oct 1896; Nation (New York) 63, 8 Oct 1896.

Robert Burns. Edinburgh 1896 (priv ptd; pirated; false place of pbn).

A channel passage 1855. 1899.

Rosamund, Queen of the Lombards. 1899, New York 1899, London 1900, New York 1967 (microcard of New York 1899), Chicago 1970 (microfiche of New York 1899), nd (microcard of 1899).

REVIEWS: [Watts-Dunton, T.] Athenaeum 28 Oct 1899; Literature 5, 4 Nov 1899; Speaker n.s. 1, 4 Nov 1899; Literary World (Boston) n.s. 60, 10 Nov 1899; Acad 57, 11 Nov 1899; Saturday Rev 88, 11 Nov 1899; Literary Digest 19, 16 Dec 1899; Macdonell, A., Bookman 17 Dec 1899; Independent 51, 21 Dec 1899; GM 288, Jan 1900; Poet Lore 12, Jan–Mar 1900; Sewanee Rev 8 Jan 1900; Bookman (New York) 10 Jan 1900; Payne, W. M., Dial 28, 16 Jan 1900; Brownell, W. C., Book Buyer n.s. 20 Feb 1900; Thomas, E. M., Critic (New York) 36, Feb 1900; Spectator 84, 3 Feb 1900; Nation (New York) 70, 10 May 1900.

A year's letters. Portland ME 1901, as Love's cross-currents, London 1905, 1905, 1905, New York 1905, Leipzig 1905; ed E. Wilson, New York 1962; New York 1963; ed M. Zaturenska, New York 1964; ed F. J. Sypher, New York 1974; ed F. J. Sypher, also New York 1976; Westport CT 1978 (facs of New York 1962). First pbd 1877 as 'A year's letters,' by Mrs Horace Manners, The Tatler 25 Aug–29 Dec 1877. 1905 and 1964 edns lack 1877 prefatory letter but include dedication; tr Fr 1976, 1990 (2nd edn); Ital 1983.

Wise (Bonchurch edn, vol 19) lists another edn: 1906.

REVIEWS: TLS 14 July 1905; Acad 69, 15 July 1905; New York Times (Saturday Rev) 15 July 1905; Outlook 80, 29 July 1905; Spectator 95, 29 July 1905; Punch 129, 2 Aug 1905; Athenaeum 5 Aug 1905; Saturday Rev 100, 5 Aug 1905; Gaines, C. H. Harper's Weekly 49, 12 Aug 1905; Nation (New York) 81, 17 Aug 1905; Barry, W. Bookman 28 Aug 1905; Contemporary Rev 88 Sep 1905; Payne, W. M., Dial 39, 1 Sep 1905; Independent 59, 7 Sep 1905; Literary Digest 31, 30 Sep 1905; Dunbar, Olivia Howard, Critic (New York) 47, Nov 1905; Rev of Revs 32, Dec 1905; Moss, M., Atlantic Monthly 97, Jan 1906.

Percy Bysshe Shelley. Philadelphia 1903. Also in Chambers's Cyclopaedia of Eng Lit 1903.

A channel passage and other poems. 1904, 1904, 1904.

REVIEWS: TLS 2 Sep 1904; Literary World n.s. 70, 16 Sep 1904; Thompson, F., Acad 67, 17 Sep 1904; Saturday Rev 98, 17 Sep 1904; Spectator 93, 17 Sep 1904; Athenaeum 8 Oct 1904; Rhys, E., Bookman 27 Oct 1904; Davray, H. D., Mercure de France 52, Nov 1904; Monthly Rev 17 Nov 1904; Agresti, A., Italia Moderna 3rd ser 2, Dec 1904; Meyerfeld, M., Das Literarische Echo 7, 1 Jan 1905.

The Duke of Gandia. 1908, New York 1908, nd (microcard of New York 1908).

REVIEWS: Nation (New York) 86, 9 Apr 1908; Acad 74, 18 Apr 1908; Athenaeum 18 Apr 1908; New York Times (Saturday Rev) 18 Apr 1908; Saturday Rev 105, 25 Apr 1908; Bookman 34, May 1908; Davray, H. D., Mercure de France 73, 1 May 1908; Living Age 257, 2 May 1908; Outlook 89, 30 May 1908; Spectator 101, 4 July 1908; Payne, W. M., Dial 45, 1 Aug 1908; T. P.'s Weekly 12, 2 Sep 1908; Henry, A. S., Book News Monthly 27 Jan 1909.

The age of Shakespeare. 1908, New York 1908, London 1909, New York 1965 (facs).

REVIEWS: TLS 24 Sep 1908; Dowden, E., Nation 3, 26 Sep 1908; Cooper, F. T., Forum 40, Oct 1908; Saturday Rev 106, 3 Oct 1908; Spectator 101, 3 Oct 1908; Dithmar, E. A., New York Times (Saturday Rev) 13, 31 Oct 1908; Nation (New York) 87, 5 Nov 1908; Athenaeum 28 Nov 1908; Schuyler, M., Bookman (New York) 28 Nov 1908; Current Lit 45, Dec 1908; Independent 65, 3 Dec 1908; Literary Digest 37, 5 Dec 1908; Brocklehurst, J. H., Papers of the Manchester Literary Club 35 1909; Dial 46, 16 Jan 1909.

Shakespeare, written in 1905 and now first published. 1909, Folcroft PA 1974 (facs), Norwood PA 1975 (facs), Philadelphia 1978 (facs). Used as introd to the Oxford edn of Shakespeare, ed W. J. Craig, 1911.

REVIEWS: Athenaeum 11 Sep 1909; Nation (New York) 28 Oct 1909.

Three plays of Shakespeare. 1909, New York 1909, Chicago 1976 (microfiche of New York 1909).

REVIEWS: Athenaeum 27 Feb 1909; Amer Monthly Rev of Revs 39, June 1909; Independent 67, 8 July 1909; Fuller, E., Bookman (New York) 29 Aug 1909.

Lord Soulis. 1909 (priv ptd).

In the twilight. 1909 (priv ptd).

To W. T. W. D. 1909 (priv ptd).

Lord Scales. 1909 (priv ptd).

M. Prudhomme at the international exhibition. 1909 (priv ptd).

Of liberty and loyalty. 1909 (priv ptd). Rptd in Ode to Mazzini; the saviour of society; liberty and loyalty, Boston 1913.

The saviour of society. 1909 (priv ptd). Rptd in Ode to Mazzini; the saviour of society; liberty and loyalty, Boston 1913.

The marriage of Monna Lisa. 1909 (priv ptd).

The portrait. 1909 (priv ptd).

The chronicle of Queen Fredegonde. 1909 (priv ptd).

Burd Margaret. 1909 (priv ptd).

The worm of Spindlestonheugh. 1909 (priv ptd).

Border ballads. 1909 (priv ptd).

Ode to Mazzini. 1909 (priv ptd). Rptd in Ode to Mazzini; the saviour of society; liberty and loyalty, Boston 1913; tr Ital 1946. Missing lines in Ode to Mazzini restored in Posthumous poems (1917).

The ballad of truthful Charles and other poems. 1910 (priv ptd).

A criminal case. 1910 (priv ptd).

The ballade of Villon and Fat Madge. 1910 (priv ptd).

A record of friendship. 1910 (priv ptd). Added material in T. J. Wise, A Swinburne library, p. 197.

Blest and The centenary of Shelley. 1912 (priv ptd).

Border ballads. Boston 1912 (priv ptd).

Les fleurs du mal and other studies. 1913 (priv ptd), New York 1985 (facs).

The cannibal catechism. 1913 (priv ptd).

Charles Dickens. Ed T. Watts-Dunton. 1913, Norwood PA 1978 (facs). First pbd in periodical form in 1902.

REVIEWS: TLS 25 July 1902; Saturday Rev 26 July 1902; Literary Digest 16 Aug 1902; Harper's Weekly 6 Sep 1902; Chesterton, G. K., Nation 29 Mar 1913; Athenaeum, 8 Mar 1913; Bookman 44 May 1913; de Wyzewa, T., Revue des deux mondes 15 May 1913; T. P.'s Weekly, 23 May 1913.

Ode to Mazzini; the saviour of society; liberty and loyalty. Boston 1913. Missing lines in Ode to Mazzini restored in Posthumous poems (1917).

A pilgrimage of pleasure, essays and studies. Boston 1913.

Mr Whistler's lecture on art. [Boston 1913] (unbound facs of ms).
Sappho. Saturday Rev 21 Feb 1914.
A study of Victor Hugo's Les misérables. 1914 (priv ptd). The 1st and 5th essays are not by Swinburne.
Aeolus. [1914] (priv ptd).
Pericles and other studies. 1914 (priv ptd).
Thomas Nabbes. 1914 (priv ptd).
Christopher Marlowe in relation to Greene, Peele and Lodge. 1914 (priv ptd).
Théophile. 1915 (priv ptd).
Lady Maisie's bairn and other poems. 1915 (priv ptd).
Félicien Cossu. 1915 (priv ptd). Included in New Writings, ed Lang, *below*.
Two unpublished papers by A. C. Swinburne. Fortnightly Rev n.s. 99, May 1916. Prints Christopher Marlowe in relation to Greene, Peele and Lodge, and Thomas Nabbes (*see above*). The Marlowe essay also in North Amer Rev May 1916.
Ernest Clouët. 1916 (priv ptd). Included in New Writings, ed Lang, *below*.
A vision of bags. 1916 (priv ptd).
Poems from Villon and other fragments. 1916 (priv ptd).
The death of Sir John Franklin. 1916 (priv ptd).
The triumph of Gloriana. 1916 (priv ptd).
Poetical fragments. 1916 (priv ptd).
Seale, E. J. A literary discovery: unpublished lines by Swinburne on Robert Buchanan's 'Mangy Muse'. The Star 19 Mar 1917.
Wearieswa': a ballad. 1917 (priv ptd).
Posthumous poems. Ed E. Gosse and T. J. Wise 1917, New York 1918.
REVIEWS: TLS 21 June 1917; Spectator 23 June 1917; Athenaeum July 1917; Contemporary Rev 111, July 1917; Bailey, J., Quart Rev 228, July 1917; Binyon, L., Bookman 52, Aug 1917; Tynan, K., Studies Dec 1917; Chew, S., MLN Apr 1918; Aiken, C., Dial 63, 18 July 1918; Colum, P., New Republic 24 Aug 1918.
Rondeaux parisiens. 1917 (priv ptd). Included in New Writings, ed Lang, *below*.
The character and opinions of Dr Johnson. 1918 (priv ptd), [New York] 1985 (priv ptd) (facs, including ms).
The Italian mother and other poems. 1918 (priv ptd).
The ride from Milan and other poems. 1918 (priv ptd).
The two knights and other poems. 1918 (priv ptd).
A lay of lilies and other poems. 1918 (priv ptd).
Queen Yseult. 1918 (priv ptd).
Undergraduate sonnets. 1918 (priv ptd).
Lancelot, The death of Rudel and other poems. 1918 (priv ptd).
Contemporaries of Shakespeare. Ed E. Gosse and T. J. Wise 1919.
REVIEW: Spectator 27 Sep 1919.
The queen's tragedy. 1919 (priv ptd).
French lyrics hitherto unpublished. 1919 (priv ptd).
William the ranter on William the canter. New York Times 9 Feb 1919, Sunday Times 2 Mar 1919. Rptd in Bonchurch vol 20, p. 536.
Two new poems. London Mercury 4 Nov 1920. Neither was new.
Ballads of the English border. Ed W. A. MacInnes 1925, Ann Arbor MI 1971 (facs), Folcroft PA 1974 (facs).
REVIEWS: Read, H., Nation and Athenaeum 1 May 1926; TLS 15 July 1926.
Two unpublished manuscripts: De monumentis epilaphiisque mortuorum and Limits of experience, written during his college years at Oxford [1857–8]. San Francisco 1927.
Swinburne's Hyperion and other poems. Ed G. Lafourcade 1927.
Hughes, R. Greek verses of Swinburne hitherto unpublished in England. Nineteenth Cent and After 1937. Verses from Le tombeau de Théophile Gautier (1873) actually ptd and translated in W. R. Rutland, Swinburne: a nineteenth century Hellene, Oxford 1931.
What is thought that is not free. Stanza ptd in G. Lafourcade, Swinburne vindicated, London Mercury and Bookman 37, Feb 1938.
Two scenes from a tragedy by Algernon Charles Swinburne. Ed E. H. W. Meyerstein, London Mercury and Bookman 37, Feb 1938.
Swinburne on Keats. Book Club of California Quart Newsletter 8 Mar 1941. Facs ms of a fragment from an essay.
Lucretia Borgia: the chronicle of Tebaldeo Tebaldei. Ed R. Hughes 1942.
Changes of aspect and Short notes. Ed C. K. Hyder, PMLA 58 Mar 1943.
Columbus, with a note by J. S. Mayfield. Jacksonville FL 1944 (priv ptd), Bethesda MD 1991 (microform).
An old saying, with a foreword by Robert Graves. Washington DC 1945 (priv ptd). From the ms of the poem in Astrophel and other poems.
Hughes, R. Unpublished Swinburne. Life and Letters Today 56, Jan 1948.
Lang, C. Y. Swinburne on Keats: a fragment of an essay. MLN Mar 1949. [1866?]
Pasiphaë. Ed R. Hughes 1950.
A roundel of retreat. [Washington DC 1950] (priv ptd). The imprint, an obvious jest, reads: London, Charles Ottley, Landon & Co, 1950.
Christmas antiphonies: in church. [New York] 1950. Christmas card of George Arents including ms facs of poem in Songs before sunrise.
Christmas antiphonies: beyond church. [New York] 1951. Christmas card of George Arents including ms facs of poem in Songs before sunrise.
Charenton in 1810. In Appendix to James Pope-Hennessy, Monckton Milnes: the flight of youth 1851–1885, 1955. A later ms is edited in New Writings, ed Lang, *below*.
Henry, A. W. A reconstructed Swinburne ballad. HLB 12, Autumn 1958. Corrects and completes Duriesdyke with Lady Maisie's bairn.
Will Drew and Phil Crewe and Frank Fane by a great English literary figure. [Ed J. S. Mayfield, Bethesda MD 1962] (priv ptd).
Le prince prolétaire. Bethesda MD 1963 (priv ptd).
The influence of the Roman censorship on the morals of the people. Brooklyn New York 1964 (priv ptd).
New writings by Swinburne. Ed C. Y. Lang, Syracuse NY 1964.
The ballad of Bulgarie. In T. A. J. Burnett, Swinburne's The ballad of Bulgarie, MLR Apr 1969 (corrected text).
On the duties of an university towards the nation. Introd by W. P. Tolley. The Courier Fall 1969. Rptd in Mayfield, Swinburneiana, *below*, with a bibl note.
Duriesdyke and other ballads. In The literary ballad, ed A. H. Ehrenpreis, Columbia SC 1970.
Shelley. Worcester MA 1973. Rptd in Shelley: a poem by Swinburne, KSJ 24 1975.
Shelley, Temple of Janus, Song (O Love, sole winged Power). Transcribed in appendix to T. L. Meyers, Swinburne and Shelley, unpbd diss, Univ of Chicago 1973.
Hide-and-seek. 1975. Poem.
The unhappy revenge, The laws of Corinth, The loyal servant, Laugh and lie down. In E. P. Schuldt, Four early unpublished plays of Algernon Charles Swinburne, unpbd diss, Reading Univ 1976.
On the source of false impressions, De scriptoribus antiquis, De vita henrici viii. In E. P. Schuldt, Three unpublished Balliol essays of A. C. Swinburne, RES 27 Nov 1976.
The statue of John Brute. Toronto 1978 (priv ptd). Prose fragment.
Charles Collingwood's flogging, Frank Fane: a ballad. Appendix C in I. Gibson, The English vice: beating, sex, and shame in Victorian England and after, 1978.
Milton. Williamsburg VA 1987 (priv ptd). Rptd in T. L. Meyers, Two

poems by Swinburne: Milton and On the effect of Wagner's music, VP 31 Summer 1993.

Balliol college essays and notes, 1860 [notes on Roman and feudal law, on Charlemagne, crusades, on Saint Louis, Joinville, Hallam's middle ages: notes]. In A. Harrison, Swinburne's medievalism: a study in Victorian love poetry, Baton Rouge LA 1988.

On political and speculative liberty. In R. Rooksby, A short note on the Swinburne manuscripts at Worcester College, Oxford, Victorians Inst Jnl 18 1990.

Three unpublished poems by Algernon Charles Swinburne [King Ban, The white hind, By the sea-side]. In The whole music of passion: new essays on Swinburne, ed R. Rooksby and N. Shrimpton, 1993.

On the effect of Wagner's music. In T. L. Meyers, Two poems by Swinburne: Milton and On the effect of Wagner's music, VP 31 Summer 1993.

A nine days' wonder, 1745. Introd by R. Rooksby, Victorians Inst Jnl 24 1996.

Contributions to periodicals and collaborative works

A list of Swinburne's contributions to periodical lit appears in vol 20 of the Bonchurch edn.

William Congreve. In The imperial dictionary, ed J. F. Waller, 1857.

Undergraduate papers. Oxford 1858; ed F. J. Sypher, Delmar NY 1974 (facs). The early English dramatists and The monomaniac's tragedy (rptd in New writings, ed Lang, *above*); Queen Yseult (rptd 1918 [priv] and in Bonchurch edn vol 1); Modern Hellenism (convincingly ascribed to Swinburne); Church imperialism (rptd in Lafourcade, La jeunesse de Swinburne vol 2).

Pilgrimage of pleasure. In Mary Gordon, Children of the chapel, 1864, 1875, 1910; ed R. Lougy, Athens OH 1982. Rptd in A pilgrimage of pleasure, essays and studies, Boston 1913.
REVIEWS: Spectator 8 Oct 1910; Dial 1 Nov 1913.

Notes on the Royal Academy exhibition, 1868. Part II. 1868, [New York] 1976 (facs).
REVIEW: London Quart Rev 31, Jan 1869.

Le tombeau de Théophile Gautier. Paris 1873. Six poems, in English, French, Latin and Greek.

William Congreve. In Encyclopaedia Britannica, 1877.

John Keats. In Encyclopaedia Britannica, 1882.

Walter Savage Landor. In Encyclopaedia Britannica, 1882.

Christopher Marlowe. In Encyclopaedia Britannica, 1883.

Mary Queen of Scots. In Encyclopaedia Britannica, 1883.

The story of Catherine by A. Owen [A. C. Ogle]. 1885. See T. L. Meyers, Swinburne reshapes his grand passion: a version by 'Ashford Owen'. VP 31, Spring 1993.

The Whippingham papers: a collection of contributions in prose and verse, chiefly by the author of the 'romance of chastisement'. [Dec 1887] (priv ptd), 1995. Three works only are Swinburne's: Arthur's flogging, Reginald's flogging, A boy's first flogging at Birchminster.

Cyril Tourneur. In Encyclopaedia Britannica, 1888.

Victor Hugo. In Encyclopaedia Britannica, 1902.

Percy Bysshe Shelley. Philadelphia 1903. Also in Chambers's Cyclopaedia of English literature, 1903.

Laird of Waristoun. In B. F. Fisher IV, Rossetti and Swinburne in tandem: 'The laird of Waristoun', VP 11, Autumn 1973.

Letters

The standard edn is The Swinburne letters, ed C. Y. Lang, 6 vols New Haven CT 1959–62, *which incorporates previously ptd letters, including those in earlier collections (except Lang omits letter XLVIII (dated 1869) in vol 18 of Bonchurch).*

Letters to T. J. Wise, 1909; Letters on Chapman, 1909; Letters to J. C. Collins, 1910; Letters on Morris, Omar Khayyám etc, 1910; Letters to A. H. Bullen, 1910; Letters to Purnell and others, 1910; Letters concerning Poe, 1910; Letters to Gosse, 5 ser 1910–11; Letters to Stedman, 1912; Letters to Burton and others, 1912; Letters to Henry Taylor, 1912; Letters to Locker-Lampson and others, 1912; Letters to the press, 1912; Letters to Lytton, 1913; Letters to Locker, 1913; Letters to Mallarmé, 1913; Letters to Morley, 1914; Letters to Dowden, 1914; Letters to Milnes and others, 1915; Letters to Lady Trevelyan, 1916; Letters to Nichol, 1917; Letters to Hugo, 1917. All priv ptd.

The boyhood of Swinburne. Ed Mrs D. Leith 1917.

The letters of Swinburne. Ed T. Hake and A. Compton-Rickett 1918.

The letters of Swinburne. Ed E. Gosse and T. J. Wise 2 vols 1918. Rptd, rev and enlarged in vol 18 of Bonchurch edn.

A romance of literature. 1919; Letters to Horne, 1920; Autobiographical notes, 1920. All priv ptd.

Supplementary vols of Swinburne's correspondence, in preparation by T. L. Meyers, will print some 500 letters not included in The Swinburne letters, *including:*

Burne-Jones, G. Memorials of Edward Burne-Jones. 2 vols 1904. Letter by Swinburne, vol 1, p. 234.

Collected works of William Morris. Ed M. Morris 24 vols. 1910–15. Letters of 12 Feb 1889 (vol 14, p. 27), 21 Nov 1883 (vol 19, pp. 19–20).

Wright, H. G. Unpublished letters from Theodore Watts-Dunton to Swinburne. RES Apr 1934.

Peters, R. L. The crowns of Apollo: Swinburne's principles of literature and art. Detroit 1965. Letter to J. A. Symonds 1 Feb 1876, pp. 168–9.

Seronsy, C. C. An autograph letter by Swinburne on Daniel and Drummond of Hawthornden. N & Q 210, Aug 1965.

Fredeman, W. E. A Preraphaelite gazette: the Penkil letters of Arthur Hughes to William Bell Scott and Alice Boyd, 1886–89. BJRL 50 1967. Letter of 3 Mar 1891.

Baylen, J. O. Swinburne and the Pall Mall Gazette. Research Stud 36, Dec 1968. Letter of 28 Jan 1886.

Fuller, J. O. Swinburne: a critical biography. 1968. Includes Swinburne's letter of 13 Mar 1905 and letters from Mary Gordon Leith.

LeBourgeois, J. Y. Some unpublished letters of Swinburne. N & Q 217, July 1972.

Fisher, B. F. IV. Some Swinburne letters. Lib Chron 38 Spring 1972.

Byars, J. A. Eight unpublished letters from A. C. Swinburne. N & Q 218, Mar 1973.

Landow, G. P. Swinburne to W. J. Linton and J. W. Inchbold: two new letters. MLR 68, Apr 1973.

Meyers, T. L. Swinburne: four more letters. N & Q 219, June 1974.

Sypher, F. J. 'My dear Ulrica . . .': Swinburne's earliest letter. Quart Jnl of the Lib of Congress 31, Apr 1974.

Baker, W. A. C. Swinburne to Herbert Spencer, 12 Mar 1881: an unpublished letter. N & Q 220, Oct 1975.

Sypher, F. J. New letters by Swinburne. HLB 24, Jan 1976.

Meyers, T. L. Two Swinburne letters. N & Q 221, Feb 1976.

Meyers, T. L. Further Swinburne letters. N & Q 224, Aug 1979, 225, June 1980.

Birchfield, J. D. New light on the Swinburne–Leith correspondence. The Kentucky Rev 1 Spring 1980.

Atkinson, F. G. Some unpublished Swinburne letters. N & Q 225, June 1980.

Bawcutt, N. W. A new Swinburne letter. N & Q 227, Aug 1982.

Rooksby, R. Swinburne and Rossetti: three unpublished letters. N & Q 232, Dec 1987.

Lang, C. Y. An Arnold family album. The Arnoldian 15 (Special Issue 1989–90). Letter of 9 Oct 1867.

Introductions

A selection from the works of Lord Byron. 1866.
REVIEWS: Athenaeum 17 Mar 1866; The Spectator 39, 31 Mar 1866; Westminster Rev 86, July 1866; London Quart Rev 31, Jan 1869.

Christabel and the lyrical and imaginative poems of S. T. Coleridge. 1869, New York 1869, London 1873, 1875, 1878, 1882.
REVIEWS: Athenaeum 21 Aug 1869; Forman, H. B., Contemporary Rev 13 Feb 1870.

The works of George Chapman, poems and minor translations. 1875, Chicago 1970 (microfiche).

Shelley, P. B. Les Cenci. Paris 1883. Introd in French to Tola Dorian's trn.

Wells, C. Joseph and his brethren. 1876, 1908 (WC).
REVIEWS: Athenaeum 5 Feb 1876; Westminster Rev n.s. 49, Apr 1876; Scribner's Mag 12 June 1876.

Thomas Middleton. Ed Havelock Ellis 1887, 1904, St Clair Shores MI 1969.

Robert Herrick. Ed Alfred Pollard 2 vols 1891.

Shelley, P. B. Epipsychidion. Ed R. A. Potts, introd by S. A. Brook, 1887. An extract from E & S (1875).

Browning, E. B. Aurora Leigh. 1898.
REVIEW: Literary World n.s. 58, 16 Dec 1898.

Shakespeare, W. Pericles. 1907. Introd in vol 13 of Harrap edn of Shakespeare, ed Sydney Lee.

Reade, C. The cloister and the hearth. 1908 (EL), 1927.

Attributed works

Reviews in the Spectator 1862 of works by Sir H. Taylor, C. Rossetti, A. H. Clough and R. Garnett, attributed to Swinburne in S. C. Chew, Swinburne's contributions to 'the Spectator' in 1862, MLN 35, Feb 1920, and repeated in Chew's Swinburne [Boston 1929], have been disproven; *see* W. D. Paden, Swinburne, the Spectator in 1862, and Walter Bagehot, in Six studies in nineteenth-century English literature and thought, 1962, *below*. Of 5 reviews of Hugo attributed to Swinburne by Gosse (Bonchurch edn, vol 19), only the middle 3 (21 June, 26 July, 16 Aug) are by Swinburne (*see* R. H. Tener, Swinburne as reviewer, TLS 25 Dec 1959).

Review of R. Buchanan, David Gray and other poems (1868). Pall Mall Gazette 21 Feb 1868. Attributed in C. Murray, D. G. Rossetti, A. C. Swinburne and R. W. Buchanan: the fleshly school revisited. BJRL 65 1982.

Index Expurgatorius of Martial. 1868. Attributed as 'problematic' by P. Mendes. Clandestine erotic fiction. Aldershot 1993.

Infelicia, by Adah Isaacs Menken. 1868. None of the poems are by Swinburne.

Cythera's Hymnal. 1870. Attributed as 'problematic' by P. Mendes, Clandestine erotic fiction. 1993.

Hints on flogging, shewing how to enjoy it in perfection, in a letter to a lady from Allan Bummingham. In The Whippingham papers, *above*. Attributed in I. Gibson, The English vice, [1978]. Spurious.

Harlequin, Prince Cherrytop. 1879. Attributed as problematic by P. Mendes, Clandestine erotic fiction. 1993.

God save the queen (obscene parody). The Pearl 18, Dec 1880, attributed unconvincingly by P. Mendes, Clandestine erotic fiction 1993.

Flossie: a venus of fifteen by one who knew this charming goddess and worshipped at her shrine. 1897. This and all later editions. Spurious. See P. Mendes, Clandestine erotic fiction. Aldershot 1993.

The Arab chief: a ballad. 1912 (priv ptd). Juvenilia. 1912 (priv ptd). (*See* correspondence in The Times, 5, 11, 12, 14, 15, 16 Apr 1913.) Spurious (by Sir A. C. Sterling).

There was a young lady of Tottenham. Limerick quoted in [Julian Osgood Field,] More uncensored recollections, New York 1926, p. 206.

Larsen, T. Swinburne on Middleton. TLS 17 June 1939. *See* F. Page, TLS 8 July 1939 and K. Muir, TLS 24 Feb 1945; Muir effectively deflates these claimed marginalia.

A letter by Swinburne on Kate Greenaway. Jacksonville FL 1944 (priv ptd). A forgery.

Say, is it day, is it dusk, in thy bower. In Appendix to James Pope-Hennessy, Monckton Milnes: The flight of youth. 1851–1885, 1955. A draft of D. G. Rossetti's Song of the bower.

The Shelley flower. Amer Book Prices Current 1951–2. Ms described.

Oscar Wilde. In Victorian verse: a critical anthology, ed George Macbeth, Harmondsworth 1987. Plausible, but evidence is wanting.

§2

Obituaries

The Times 12 Apr 1909; Muret, M., Jnl des Débats 12 Apr 1909; TLS 15 Apr 1909; More, P. E., Nation (New York) 15 Apr 1909; Literary World 15 Apr 1909; Independent 15 Apr 1909; Puaux, R., Temps 16 Apr 1909; Douglas, J., Athenaeum 17 Apr 1909; Spectator 17 Apr 1909; Acad 17 Apr 1909; Nation 17 Apr 1909; Saturday Rev 17 Apr 1909; Outlook 17, 24 Apr 1909; Brand, W. F., Illustrierte Zeitung 22 Apr 1909; Independent 22 Apr 1909; Literary Digest 24 Apr 1909; Burton, R., Bellman 24 Apr 1909; Gaines, C. H., Harper's Weekly 24 Apr 1909; Harper's Weekly 24 Apr 1909; Outlook 24 Apr 1909; de Barral, O., Revue Hebdomadaire 24 Apr 1909; Foote, G. W., Freethinker, 18, 25 Apr 1909; The Dickensian 5, May 1909; Nicoll, W. R., Contemporary Rev 95, May 1909; Eng Rev 2, May 1909; Rev of Revs and World's Work (New York) 39, May 1909; Seccombe, T., Readers' Rev 2, May 1909; Chasse, C., Mercure de France 79, May 1909; Dial 1 May 1909; Literary Digest 8 May 1909; Living Age 29 May 1909; The Bookman 36, June 1909; contributions by E. W. Gosse, W. M. Rossetti, W. Crane, I. Zangwill, A. S. Kok, G. B. Shaw, J. Todhunter, R. W. Gilder and G. M. C. Brandes; Rhys, E., Nineteenth Cent and After 65, June 1909; Gosse, E., Fortnightly Rev 91, June 1909, tr Mercure de France 80, July 1909; Current Lit 46, June 1909; Macdonald F., The Queen's Quart 17, July 1909; Ofterning, M., Hochland 7, July 1909; Kellett, E. E., London Quart Rev 112, July 1909; Westminster Rev 172, July 1909; Chautauquan 55, July 1909; Weygandt, C., Book News Monthly 27, July 1909; Price, W. J. Sewanee Rev 17, Oct 1909.

Criticism and biographies

Rossetti, W. M. Swinburne's Poems and ballads: a criticism. 1866.

Maitland, T. [R. W. Buchanan]. The fleshly school of poetry. Contemporary Rev 18, Oct 1871. Rptd in The fleshly school of poetry and other phenomena of the day, 1872, New York 1986.

Gosse, E. Swinburne's unpublished writings. Fortnightly Rev 102, Aug 1914.

Gosse, E. The life of Algernon Charles Swinburne. 1917. Rev as vol 19 of the Bonchurch edn.

Latham, F. L. The Newdigate of 1858, and Swinburne's poem on the death of Sir John Franklin. TLS 19 July, 16 Aug 1917. *See* further correspondence from E. Gosse, M. Leith and G. Lafourcade, TLS 26 July, 2 Aug, 6 Sep 1917, 9 Feb 1928.

Gosse, E. The first draft of Swinburne's 'Anactoria'. MLR 14 July 1919. Rptd in Aspects and impressions, 1922.

Watts-Dunton, C. Swinburne, Watts-Dunton, and the new volume of Swinburne selections. Athenaeum 12 Dec 1919.

Chew, S. C. Swinburne's contributions to 'the Spectator' in 1862. MLN 35, Feb 1920. Notes textual changes in several poems collected in Poems and ballads (1866); the speculative attributions of reviews other than of Les misérables, repeated in Chew's Swinburne (Boston 1929), have been disproven (*see* Tener and Paden, *below*).

Rummons, C. The ballad imitations of Swinburne. Poet Lore 33 1922.

Ratchford, F. E. Swinburne at work. Sewanee Rev 31, July 1923. On The sailing of the swallow, Tristram of lyonesse and other mss.

Ratchford, F. E. The first draft of Swinburne's 'Hertha'. MLN 29, Jan 1924.

Lafourcade, G. Atalanta in Calydon: le manuscrit, les sources. Revue Anglo-Américaine (Paris) 3, Oct, Dec 1925.
Lafourcade, G. La jeunesse de Swinburne. 2 vols Paris 1928. Contains works not elsewhere ptd.
Praz, Mario. Il manoscritto dell' 'Atalanta in Calydon'. La Cultura 8, July 1929.
Lafourcade, G. Introduction. Swinburne's Atalanta in Calydon: a facsimile of the first edition. Oxford 1930.
Duffy, J. O. G. The first American 'Atalanta'. TLS 5 Feb 1931.
Symons, A. Notes on two manuscripts. Eng Rev 54, May 1932. On mss of Cleopatra, Chastelard, Atalanta in Calydon.
Hyder, C. K. Swinburne and the popular ballad. PMLA 49 Mar 1934.
Carter, J. and G. Pollard. An enquiry into the nature of certain nineteenth-century pamphlets. 1934 (2nd edn, with an epilogue, ed N. Barker and J. Collins 1983.)
Partington, W. Forging ahead: the true story of the upward progress of Thomas James Wise. New York 1939. Rev as Thomas J. Wise in the original cloth, 1947.
Ratchford, F. E. Letters of Thomas J. Wise to John Henry Wrenn: a further enquiry into the guilt of certain nineteenth-century forgers. 1944.
Certain nineteenth century forgeries: an exhibition of books and letters at the University of Texas, June 1–Sep 30, 1946. Described by F. E. Ratchford.
Mayfield, J. S. These many years by Algernon Charles Swinburne. Washington DC 1947 (facs of Rondel, Poems and ballads 1866).
Carter, J. and G. Pollard. The firm of Charles Otterly, Landon & Co.: footnote to An enquiry. 1948.
A Swinburne manuscript. TLS 4 Sep 1948. Ave atque vale.
Mayfield, J. S. Swinburne's Unpublished erotic verses to a mistress. Amateur Book Collector 2 Apr 1952. Rptd in his Swinburneiana, *below*, with a further note on the falsely described Unpublished verses 1866 and a subsequent 1903 printing.
Lang, C. Y. The first chorus of Swinburne's Atalanta. YULG 27, Jan 1953.
Marchand, L. A. The Watts-Dunton letter books. Jnl of the Rutgers Univ Lib 1953.
Baum, P. F. A Swinburne manuscript. Lib Notes 27, Apr 1953. On The queen's pleasance, Tristram of Lyonesse.
Mayfield, J. S. Swinburne's Boo. Eng Misc: A Symposium of History, Literature and the Arts 4 1953. Rptd in his Swinburneiana, *below*, with a bibliographical note. On the composition of The triumph of time.
Lang, C. Y. Some Swinburne manuscripts. Jnl of the Rutgers Univ Lib 18, Dec 1954.
Lang, C. Y. A manuscript, a mare's-nest and a mystery. YULG 31 1957. On A leave-taking.
Baum, P. F. The Fitzwilliam manuscript of Swinburne's Atalanta, verses 1038–1204. MLR Apr 1959.
Bissell, E. E. Gosse, Wise and Swinburne. BC Autumn 1959. Corrects text of 'The cup of God's wrath' in Posthumous poems.
Lang, C. Y. Swinburne's lost love. PMLA 74, Mar 1959.
Paden, W. D. Footnote to a footnote. TLS 23 Oct 1959. On the printing of A word for the Navy; *see* correspondence from A. R. Redway and J. C. Troxell, TLS 20 Nov, 4 Dec 1959.
Tener, R. H. Swinburne as reviewer. TLS 25 Dec 1959. Identification of only 3 reviews as Swinburne's in the Spectator 1862; *see* Chew, *above*.
Todd, W. B. (ed). Thomas J. Wise: centenary studies. Austin 1959. Includes G. Pollard, The case of The devil's due, and W. B. Todd, A handlist of Thomas J. Wise.
Todd, W. B. Swinburne manuscripts at Texas. Texas Quart 2 Autumn 1959.
Paden, W. D. Swinburne, the Spectator in 1862, and Walter Bagehot. In Six studies in nineteenth-century English literature and thought, ed H. Orel and G. J. Worth, Lawrence KS 1962. Disproves attributions of reviews other than 3 of Les misérables; *see* Chew and Tener, *above*.
Mayfield, J. S. A note for Swinburne collectors. The Courier July 1962. Rptd in his Swinburneiana, *below*. Notes a missing comma in A channel passage and other poems.
Lang, C. Y. Atalanta in manuscript. YULG July 1962.
Ehrenpreis, A. H. Swinburne's edition of popular ballads. PMLA 78, Dec 1963.
Nowell-Smith, S. Swinburne's The queen-mother [and] [*sic*] Rosamond. BC 13 Autumn 1964.
Bratcher, J. T. and L. H. Kendall jr. Two further footnotes to 'An enquiry'. TSLL 8 Spring 1965.
Powell, E. G. The manuscript of Swinburne's 'Off shore'. Lib Chron of the Univ of Texas 8 1966.
Dahl, C. The composition of Swinburne's trilogy on Mary Queen of Scots. TStL 12 1967.
Gullible, R. An enquiry into An enquiry. BC 16, Summer 1967. Review article.
Mayfield, J. S. Two leaves of Swinburne's manuscript of 'Lesbia Brandon'. The Courier Spring 1967. Rptd with corrected transcription in his Swinburneiana, *below*.
Mayfield, J. S. A rare find. Amer BC 6 Mar 1967. Account of Mayfield's finding of 2 pp. of Lesbia Brandon.
Mayfield, J. S. Swinburne's 'Autumn in Cornwall'. The Courier. Spring 1968. Rptd in his Swinburneiana, *below*.
Peters, R. L. A. C. Swinburne's 'Hymn to Proserpine': the work sheets. PMLA 83, Oct 1968.
Greenberg, R. A. Swinburne's Heptalogia improved. SB 21 1969.
Bratcher, J. T. and L. H. Kendall jr. A suppressed critique of Wise's Swinburne transactions: addendum to 'An enquiry'. Austin TX [1970].
Carter, J., and G. Pollard. Gorfin's stock; working paper no 4. Oxford 1970.
Mayfield, J. S. At Sotheby's on Tuesday. Manuscripts 23:2 Spring 1971. Rptd in his Swinburneiana, *below*. On the ms of The young Tamlane.
Paul, K. and W. H. McClain. Stefan George's Swinburne translations. MLN Oct 1971. On trns from Poems and ballads.
Peattie, R. W. William Michael Rossetti and the defense of Swinburne's Poems and ballads. HLB 19, Oct 1971.
Fisher, B. F. IV. Swinburne's Tristram of Lyonesse in process. TSLL 14 Fall 1972.
Mayfield, J. S. Swinburne's Atalanta in Calydon: the Oxford facsimile. BC 21 Winter 1972. Rptd in his Swinburneiana, *below*. On the 1st edn of Atalanta in Calydon.
Peattie, R. W. Swinburne and his publishers. HLQ Nov 1972.
Garner, S. Harold Frederic and Swinburne's Locrine: a matter of clubs, copyrights, and character. Amer Lit 45, 1973, pp. 285–92. On the printing of Locrine in the New York Times.
Sypher, F. S. jr. Victoria's lapse from virtue: a lost leaf from Swinburne's La soeur de la reine. HLB 21, Oct 1973.
Workman, G. La soeur de la reine and related Victorian romances by Swinburne. HLB 21, Oct 1973.
Henderson, P. Swinburne: the portrait of a poet. 1974.
Mayfield, J. S. One hundred copies? In his Swinburneiana, *below*. On the number of copies of the 1st edn of Atalanta in Calydon.
Mayfield, J. S. Swinburneiana: a gallimaufry of bits and pieces about Algernon Charles Swinburne. [Bethesda MD] 1974 (priv ptd).
Mayfield, J. S. Swinburne in miniature. The Courier Summer 1974. On Shelley.
Monteiro, G. The first printing of Swinburne's 'Two [*sic*] brothers'. N & Q 219, Dec 1974.
Todd, W. B. Suppressed commentaries on the Wiseian forgeries: addendum to An enquiry. Austin TX 1974.
Forbes, J. Two flagellation poems by Swinburne. N & Q 220, Oct 1975.

Sypher, F. J. A year's letters. TLS 2 Apr 1976. Corrections to the scholarly edn.

Paley, M. D. John Camden Hotten, A. C. Swinburne, and the Blake facsimiles of 1868. BNYPL 79 Spring 1976.

Mayfield, J. S. A. C. Swinburne's Atalanta in Calydon. N & Q 222, Oct 1977.

Mayfield, J. S. A Swinburne collector in Calydon. The Quart Jnl of the Lib of Congress 37 Winter 1980.

Swinburne, A. C. At Eleusis. In British literary manuscripts, ser II, from 1800 to 1914, ed V. Klinkenborg et al, New York 1981.

Stamberg, S. The man who <loved> liked Swinburne. In Every night at five: Susan Stamberg's 'All Things Considered' book. New York 1982. Interview (1980) with J. S. Mayfield on collecting 101 copies of Atalanta in Calydon.

Barker, N. and J. Collins. A sequel to An enquiry into the nature of certain nineteenth century pamphlets by John Carter and Graham Pollard: the forgeries of H. Buxton Forman and T. J. Wise re-examined. 1983, 1992 (2nd edn).

Fredeman, W. E. The story of a lie: a sequel to A sequel. Rev (Univ of Virginia) 7 (1985). Includes an invaluable 'Master list of indicted works.'

Rooksby, R. The Swinburne collection at Balliol. Victorians Inst Jnl 17 1989.

Rooksby, R. A short note on the Swinburne manuscripts at Worcester College, Oxford. Victorians Inst Jnl 18 1990.

Rooksby, R. Algernon Charles Swinburne. Book and Magazine Collector 80, Nov 1990.

Freeman, A. Butler, Swinburne and Wise. BC 40, Summer 1991. On edns of A word for the Navy.

Rooksby, R. Swinburne's Reginald. N & Q 236, Sep 1991. Early fragment of Lesbia Brandon.

Collins, J. The two forgers: a biography of Harry Buxton Forman and Thomas James Wise. Newcastle DE 1992.

Burnett, T. A. J. Swinburne at work: the first page of Anactoria. In The whole music of passion: new essays on Swinburne, ed R. Rooksby and N. Shrimpton, 1993.

Meyers, T. L. Swinburne's copyright: gone missing. VP 31 Summer 1993. *See also* T. L. Meyers, Found: Swinburne's copyright, VP 33, Spring 1995.

Jones, J. A date and source for Swinburne's The statue of John Brute. N & Q 239, Sep 1994.

Rooksby, R. Swinburne's revision of the 'Prelude' to Tristram of Lyonesse. N & Q 240, June 1995.

Rooksby, R. 'Regret': a Swinburne revision. VP 34 Spring 1996.

Meyers, T. L. Swinburne and Whitman: further evidence. Walt Whitman Quart 14 Summer 1996. Unpublished remarks, correspondence and squibs (on J. A. Symonds).

Rooksby, R. A. C. Swinburne's 'A nine days' wonder'. Victorians Institute Jnl 24 1996.

Rooksby, R. Anthologizing Algernon: the problem of Swinburne's later poetry. ELT 40, Sep 1997.

Rooksby, R. A. C. Swinburne: a poet's life. Aldershot 1997. [TLM]

Arthur Symons 1865–1945

Princeton, the principal repository of holographs, typescripts and correspondence by or relating to Symons, has 29 boxes of such material. Other important holdings are at Arizona, BL, Columbia, Folger Lib, Harvard, Iowa, Leeds, NYPL, Northwestern, Queens (Canada) and HRHRC. For other holdings see LR.

Bibliographies

Stern, C. S. Arthur Symons: an annotated bibliography of writings about him. ELT 17:2, 1974.

Beckson, K., I. Fletcher, L. Markert and J. Stokes. Arthur Symons: a bibliography. Greensboro NC 1990. A primary bibliography.

Collections and selections

Poems. 2 vols 1902 [Dec 1901], New York 1902. Omissions in both volumes.

Lyrics. Portland ME 1903 (100 copies). Rptd from Bibelot (Portland ME), Apr 1903.

Poésies. Bruges 1907. With an essay by the translator and editor, Louis Thomas. Other trns by P. Verlaine, S. Merrill and Edouard Thomas.

Collected works. 9 vols. 1924, New York 1973. Incomplete.

Holdsworth, R. V. (ed). Arthur Symons: poetry and prose. Cheadle 1974.

Beckson, K. (ed). Selected works of Arthur Symons. 16 vols Tokyo 1997.

§1

An introduction to the study of Browning. London and New York 1886, 1887 (rev and enlarged).

Days and nights. London and New York 1889, rptd with omissions in Collected works, vol 1, *above*. Poems.

Silhouettes. 1892, 1896 (rev and enlarged), Portland ME 1906 (some poems restored from the edn of Poems, 1902, *above*), rptd with omissions in Collected works, vol 1, *above*. Poems.

London nights. 1895, New York 1896, London 1897 (rev with preface), rptd in Collected works, vol 1, *above*. Poems.

Amoris victima. 71 pp. 1897, New York 1897, rptd in Collected works, vol 1, *above*. Poems.

Studies in two literatures. 1897, rptd with omissions in Collected works, vol 8, *above*.

Aubrey Beardsley. 32 pp. 1898, (preface and essay with Beardsley drawings), 1905 (Beardsley drawings increased). Essay included in Studies in seven arts, Collected works, vol 9, *above*. Tr Fr, Paris 1906 (by J. Cohen, Edouard and Louis Thomas).

The symbolist movement in literature. 1899 [1900], 1908 (Huysmans essay rev), New York 1908, 1919 (rev and enlarged), rptd in Studies in two literatures, Collected works, vol 8, *above*, as Impressions and notes: French writers (essays added from various pbns and trns from Mallarmé and Verlaine). In 1958 R. Ellmann edited a new edn (New York) with an influential introduction.

Images of good and evil. 1899 [1900], rptd in Collected works, vol 2, *above*. Poems.

The loom of dreams. 43 pp. 1901 (12 copies priv ptd), rptd in Poems, vol 2, and in Collected works, vol 2, *above*. Poems.

Plays, acting and music. 1903, New York 1903, London 1909 (rev and enlarged), New York 1909, London 1928 (much omitted from the 1909 edn and considerably rev and enlarged). Criticism.

Cities. 1903, London and New York 1903. Travel.

Studies in prose and verse. 1904, New York 1904. Reprints several essays from Studies in two literatures, *above*. Most of the essays tr into French as Portraits anglais, Paris 1907.

Spiritual adventures. 1905, New York 1905, rptd in Collected works, vol 5, *above*. Stories.

A book of twenty songs. 34 pp. 1905, rptd in The fool of the world, *below*.

The fool of the world and other poems. 1906, New York 1907, rptd in Collected works, vol 2, *above*.

Studies in seven arts. 1906, New York 1906 [1907], 1925 (enlarged), rptd (with the addn of the 1905 preface on Aubrey Beardsley, *above*) in Collected works, vol 9, *above*. Prose.

Great acting in English. 13 pp. 1907 (priv ptd), rptd in 1909 edn of Plays, acting and music, *above*. 1st ptd in a different version in Monthly Rev, June 1907.

William Blake. 1907, New York 1907, rptd, without the preface and contemporary sources, in Collected works, vol 4, *above*.

Cities of Italy. 1907, 1907 (2nd edn; essays on Rome and Venice enlarged versions of those in Cities, *above*). Travel.

London: a book of aspects. 54 pp. Minneapolis MN 1908 (12 copies priv ptd), rptd in Cities and sea-coasts and islands, *below*. Prose.
Dante Gabriel Rossetti. 60 pp. Washington DC 1909, Paris (in Fr) 1909, Berlin (in Ger) 1909, London 1910.
The romantic movement in English poetry. 1909, New York 1909.
For Api. 30 pp. 1913 (priv ptd), rptd in Collected works, vol 3, *above*. Poems.
Songs for Api. 14 pp. 1913 (priv ptd), rptd in Collected works, vol 3, *above*.
Knave of hearts 1894–1908. 1913, New York and London 1913, rptd in Collected works, vol 3, *above*. Poems.
Figures of several centuries. 1916, New York 1916. Prose.
Tragedies. 1916. The harvesters, The death of Agrippina, Cleopatra in Judaea. The harvesters rptd in Tragedies, Collected works, vol 6, and the other 2 in Tragedies, vol 7, *above*.
Tristran and Iseult. 1917, New York 1917. Rptd in Tragedies, Collected works, vol 6, *above*.
Cities and sea-coasts and islands. Glasgow and Sydney 1918, New York 1919. Includes London: a book of aspects, *above*. Travel.
Colour studies in Paris. 1918, New York 1918 (illus). Prose.
Studies in the Elizabethan drama. New York 1919, London 1920. Includes essays on Elizabethan dramatists in Studies in two literatures, *above*.
The toy cart. Dublin and London 1919. Rptd in Cesare Borgia . . ., *below*, and Collected works, vol 7, *above*. Play.
Lesbia and other poems. New York 1920, rptd in Collected works, vol 3, *above*.
Cesare Borgia, Iseult of Brittany, The toy cart. New York 1920. Plays.
Charles Baudelaire: a study. London 1920, New York 1921.
Love's cruelty. 80 pp. 1923, New York 1924, rptd in Collected works, vol 2, *above*. Poems.
Dramatis personae. Indianapolis IN 1923, London 1925 (corrected). Prose.
The Café Royal and other essays. 1923 [1924].
Michel Eyquem Seigneur de Montaigne. 6 unnumbered pp. Chicago 1925 (50 copies). 1st ptd Bookman's Jnl, Dec 1923, the 1st 3 paragraphs omitted.
Studies in modern painters. 88 pp. New York 1925.
Notes on Joseph Conrad with some unpublished letters. 38 pp. 1925 [1926].
Parisian nights: a book of essays. 49 pp. 1926.
Eleonora Dusa. 1926, New York 1927. Portions rptd from Plays, acting and music, *above*; Studies in seven arts, *above*; and Café Royal and other essays, *above*.
A study of Thomas Hardy. 70 pp. 1927 [1928].
Studies in strange souls. 83 pp. 1929. On Rossetti and Swinburne.
Mes souvenirs. 41 pp. Chapelle-Réanville (France) 1929. In Eng.
From Toulouse-Lautrec to Rodin with some personal impressions. 1929, New York 1930.
Confessions: a study in pathology. 88 pp. New York 1930. Autobiography.
A study of Oscar Wilde. 88 pp. 1930.
Jezebel mort and other poems. 1931.
Wanderings. London and Toronto 1931. Travel.
A study in Walter Pater. 112 pp. 1932.
Amoris victimia [error for victima]. 22pp. 1940 (priv ptd). Poems and prose.
Lhombreaud, R. Documents and detection (with some unpbd documents of Arthur Symons), News Letter of the Br Council no. 6, 1953. Includes The music hall and A proposal for the utilisation of war. Poem and essay.
Johnson, A. Arthur Symons' The life and adventures of Lucy Newcome: preface and text. ELT 28:4 1985. Unpbd story.
Johnson, A. An episode in the life of Jenny Lane. ELT 29:4, 1986. Unpbd story.
Ware, T. (ed). Arthur Symons's reviews of Bliss Carman. Canadian Poetry 37 1995. 4 previously pbd reviews in the Athenaeum 1894–7.

Translations

Zola. L'assommoir. 1894 (included in Zola's works), 1928 (separately, with introd).
Verhaeren. The dawn. 1898, 1916 (in Verhaeren's plays).
d'Annunzio. The child of pleasure. 1898. Only the verse tr by Symons.
d'Annunzio. The dead city. 1900.
d'Annunzio. Gioconda. 1901.
d'Annunzio. Francesca da Rimini. 1902.
Dumas fils. The lady of the camellias. 1902.
Baudelaire. Poems in prose. 60pp. 1905. Included in Les fleurs du mal, *below*.
von Hofmannsthal. Electra: a tragedy in one act. New York 1908.
Casanova. Memoirs. 1922. Vol 12, chs 7 and 8 tr Symons.
From Catullus, chiefly concerning Lesbia. 1924. Poems in Latin and Eng.
Villiers de l'Isle-Adam. Claire lenoir. New York 1925.
Villiers de l'Isle-Adam. Queen Ysabeau. Chicago 1925.
Baudelaire. Les fleurs du mal, Petits poèmes en prose, Les paradis artificiels. 1925.
Baudelaire. The letters of Charles Baudelaire to his mother. 1927, New York 1927 (as Letters of Charles Baudelaire).
Pignata. The adventures of Giuseppe Pignata. 1930.
L'amour de moy. 1934. A 15th-cent song. Tr Symons.
Louÿs, The woman and the puppet. 1935, New York 1936.
Mallarmé. Poésies. Ed B. Morris, Edinburgh 1986.

Contributions to periodicals

Symons published over 1350 articles and revs. For a full listing see K. Beckson et al, Arthur Symons: a bibliography, *above*.

Contributions to collaborative works

Symons edited edns and anthologies, frequently with introds, of Eng, Amer and Continental poets and prose writers; he also contributed his own poems and prose to various anthologies. For a full listing of the 85 vols see K. Beckson et al, Arthur Symons: a bibliography, *above*.

Letters and memoirs

Fletcher, I. Symons and Beardsley. TLS, 18 Aug 1966. Unpbd letter on their 1st meeting.
Beckson, K. and J. M. Munro. Letters from Arthur Symons to James Joyce: 1904–1932. James Joyce Quart 4, 1967. 14 unpbd letters to Joyce, Grant Richards and Elkin Mathews.
Beckson, K. (ed). The memoirs of Arthur Symons: life and art in the 1890s. University Park PA 1977. Rptd and unpbd memoirs.
Beckson, K. Arthur Symons on John Millington Synge: a previously unpublished memoir. Eire-Ireland: a jnl of Irish stud 21:4, 1986.
Morris, B. Reassessing Arthur Symons's relationship with Lady Gregory. Yeats: an annual of critical and textual stud 5, 1987. 3 unpbd letters to Lady Gregory.
Morris, B. Arthur Symons' letters to W. B. Yeats: 1891–1902. Ibid. 12 unpbd letters.
Beckson, K. and J. M. Munro (eds). Arthur Symons: selected letters, 1880–1935. London and Iowa City 1989. 3 letters to Joyce rptd from Beckson and Munro, Letters from Symons to Joyce, *above*, and 8 letters to Yeats rptd from Morris, Symons letters to Yeats, *above*.
Beckson, K. Arthur Symons's Iseult Gonne: a previously unpbd memoir. Yeats annual 7, 1990.
Ware, T. Two unpublished letters from Arthur Symons to Bliss Carman. ELN 28:3, 1991.

§2

Pater, W. An introduction to the study of Browning. Guardian, 9 Nov 1887. Rptd in Essays from the Guardian, 1901. Review.

Pater, W. A poet with something to say. Pall Mall Gazette, 23 Mar 1889. Review of Days and nights.
Gray, J. M. Days and nights. Acad 20 Apr 1889. Review.
Pinkerton, P. Silhouettes. Ibid, 15 Oct 1892. Review.
LeGallienne, R. Latest Paris fashions. Daily Chron, 26 Oct 1892. Rptd as Arthur Symons: Silhouettes, Oct 1892, in Retrospective reviews, vol 1, London and New York 1896. Review of Silhouettes.
Archer, W. Three poets of the younger generation. London Quart Rev, Oct 1893. The Symons ch enlarged in Poets of the younger generation, London and New York 1902.
Verlaine, P. Deux poètes anglais. Revue Encyclopédique, July 1895. Review of London nights. In Fr.
Yeats, W. B. That subtle shade. Bookman, Aug 1895. Rptd in Uncollected prose, ed J. P. Frayne vol 1 New York 1970. Review of London nights.
Pah! Pall Mall Gazette, 2 Sep 1895. Review of London nights.
Merrill, S. Arthur Symons. L'aube (Geneva) Jan 1897. In Fr.
Yeats, W. B. Mr Arthur Symons' new book. Bookman, Apr 1897. Rptd in Uncollected prose, ed J. P. Frayne and C. Johnson vol 2 New York 1975. Review of Amoris victima.
Studies in two literatures. Athenaeum, 16 Oct 1897. Review.
Twose, G. M. R. Aubrey Beardsley in perspective. Dial (Chicago), 16 June 1899. Review.
Thompson, F. And yet – he is a master. Acad, 2 June 1900. Review of Symons's tr of d'Annunzio's The dead city.
Poems. Athenaeum, 18 Jan 1902. Review.
Beerbohm, M. An aesthetic book. Sat Rev, 19 Sep 1903. Rptd in Around theatres, 1924. Review of Plays, acting and music.
Huneker, J. G. About Arthur Symons and his new book. Lamp (New York), June 1904. Review of The symbolist movement in literature.
More, P. E. Shelburne essays. lst ser. London and New York 1905. Review of 1902 edn of Poems.
Thompson, F. Studies in prose and verse. Acad 7 Jan 1905. Rptd in Literary criticisms, ed T. L. Connolly, New York 1948.
Thompson, F. Review of Poems of Ernest Dowson with memoir by Arthur Symons. 1905. Unpbd until its appearance in his Literary criticisms, ed T. L. Connolly, New York 1948.
Norman, G. Arthur Symons – poet, critic, playwright. Theatre Mag (New York), Mar 1905.
Beerbohm, M. Between two halls. Sat Rev, 14 Apr 1906. Review of The fool of the world.
Ruyters, A. La critique d'Arthur Symons. Antée (Brussels), Apr 1907. Review of Portraits anglais. In Fr.
McCarthy, D. An aesthetic traveller. Albany Rev, May 1907. Review of Cities of Italy.
Merrill, S. L'oeuvre poétique d'Arthur Symons. Antée (Brussels), June 1907. In Fr.
Murdoch, W. G. Blaikie. The work of Arthur Symons: an appreciation. Edinburgh 1907.
Hutton, E. Genius loc. Bookman, Mar 1908. Review of Cities of Italy.
Symbolism in literature. Bookman, June 1908. Review of 1908 edn of The symbolist movement in literature.
Gribble, F. The pose of Mr Arthur Symons. Fortnightly Rev, July 1908.
Runciman, J. F. The romantic movement in English poetry. Sat Rev, 25 Sep 1909. Review.
de la Mare, W. The spirit of romance. Bookman, Dec 1909. Review of The romantic movement in Eng poetry.
Bickley, F. The art of criticism. Bookman, Mar 1910. Review of 1909 edn of Plays, acting and music.
Harris, F. Contemporary Portraits, 3rd ser. New York 1910. A chapter on Symons pbd in 1920.
Le Gallienne, R. A vivisectionist of literature. In his attitudes and avowals with some retrospective reviews. 1910. Review of The romantic movement in Eng poetry.
Murdoch, W. G. Blaikie. The renaissance of the nineties. 1911.
Bagshaw, W. Arthur Symons. Manchester Quart 31, 1912.
Jackson, H. The eighteen nineties. 1913.
Thomas, E. Arthur Symons' poems. Bookman, Feb 1914. Review of Knave of hearts.
Urban, W. M. Arthur Symons and impressionism. Atlantic Monthly, Sep 1914.
Pinkerton, P. Plays by Arthur Symons. TLS, 14 Sep 1916. Review of tragedies.
Waugh, A. Through pity and terror. Outlook, 23 Sep 1916. Rptd as Tragedies of Mr Arthur Symons in Tradition and change, 1919. Review.
Mr Symons's essays. TLS, 21 Dec 1916. Review of Figures of several centuries.
Waugh, A. The poet as critic. Outlook, 30 Dec 1916. Rptd as Mr Arthur Symons' criticism in Tradition and change, 1919. Review of Figures of several centuries.
Roberts, R. Ellis. New gods and old. Bookman, Mar 1917. Review of Figures of several centuries.
Roberts, R. Ellis. The visible world. Bookman, Nov 1918. Review of Cities and seacoasts and islands.
Colum, P. Symons the interpreter. New Republic, 13 Aug 1919. Review of 1919 edn of The symbolist movement in literature and Cities and seacoasts and islands.
Lewisohn, L. The problem of modern poetry. Bookman, Jan 1919.
Eliot, T. L. The perfect critic. In his The sacred wood: essays on poetry and criticism, 1920.
Muddiman, B. The men of the nineties. 1920.
Huneker, J. Steeplejack. New York 1920–1.
Mason, E. Baudelaire. Bookman, Apr 1921. Review of Charles Baudelaire: a study.
Jones, H. M. Arthur Symons and the Puritans. Doubledealer (New Orleans), Oct 1921.
Gorman, H. S. A revenant of the nineties. In his The procession of masks, Boston 1923.
Welby, T. Earle. The works of Arthur Symons. Sat Rev, 24 May 1924. Review of 4 vols of Collected works.
Welby, T. Earle. Arthur Symons: a critical study. 1925.
Burdett, O. The Beardsley period. 1925.
Lhombreaud, R. Arthur Symons: a critical biography. 1963, Philadelphia 1964.
Beckson, K. Arthur Symons: a life. Oxford and New York 1987.
Beckson, K. London in the 1890s: a cultural history. 1993. [KB]

Francis Thompson 1859–1907

The largest collection of Thompson mss, notebooks, letters and works is in the Burns Library Boston College Boston MA. There is an important collection in the Harris Library Preston Lancs. There are also minor collections at the Lilly Library Indiana University and Ushaw College Durham and in the Meynell family library, Sussex.

Bibliographies

Stonehill, C. A. and H. W. In their Bibliographies of modern authors, ser 2 1925.
In Thompson, Poetical works, Oxford 1937 (OSA).
Connolly, T. L. In Poems of Thompson, New York 1941.
Connolly, T. L. In Literary criticisms of Thompson, ed Connolly, New York 1948.
Connolly, T. L. In his The real Robert Louis Stevenson and other critical essays, New York 1959.
Reid, J. C. In his Thompson: man and poet, 1959.
Pope, M. P. A critical bibliography of works by and about Thompson. New York 1959, rptd from BNYPL 1958–9.
Danchin, P. In his Thompson: la vie et l'oeuvre d'un poète, Paris 1959.

Collections and selections

The child set in the midst. Ed W. Meynell 1892. Contains 4 poems by Thompson.

Selected poems. Ed W. Meynell 1908.

Eyes of youth: a book of verse. Ed W. Meynell 1910. Foreword by G. K. Chesterton. Contains 4 poems by Thompson.

A renegade poet and other essays. Boston 1910. Introd by E. J. O'Brien.

Poems. Portland ME 1911. Includes A word on Thompson by A. Symons, foreword by T. B. Mosher.

Works. Ed W. Meynell 3 vols 1913 (vols 1–2 poetry, vol 3 prose); 3 vols in 1 Westminster MD 1949.

Collected poetry. 1913.

Uncollected verses. 1917 (priv ptd).

Complete poetical works. [c. 1920] (Mod Lib) New York nd.

Essays of today and yesterday: Thompson. 1927. Introd by W. Meynell.

Youthful verses. Preston 1928 (priv ptd).

Selected poems and prose. 1929.

Selected poems. New York 1930 (rev).

Poems. Ed T. L. Connolly, New York 1932, 1941 (rev).

Selected poems. 1934 (rev).

Poetical works. Oxford 1937 (OSA), rptd 1955.

Selected poems. Ed P. Beard 1938.

Poems. 1946. Collected edn with a bibliography of 1st printings to 1913.

Literary criticisms newly discovered and collected. Ed T. L. Connolly, New York 1948.

The man has wings: new poems and plays. Ed. T. L. Connolly, New York 1957.

Poèmes choisis. Ed and tr P. Danchin, Paris 1962.

The poems of Thompson: a new edition. Ed B. M. Boardman c. 2000.

§1

The 3 vols of poetry pbd during Thompson's lifetime are listed here to distinguish them from the errors of subsequent edns and collections as listed above. See note below. For single essays, poems and trns into Fr, Norwegian, Irish, Cz and Hebrew, and separate printings of The hound of heaven, *see M. P. Pope,* Bibliographies, *above; and for essays, T. L. Connolly,* Bibliographies, *above. It should be noted that none of these bibliographical sources is complete and that in particular many of the essays remain uncollected.*

The life and labours of Saint John Baptist de la Salle. 1891, rptd 1911 (preface by W. Meynell).

Poems. 1893.

Sister songs: an offering to two sisters. 1895; also priv ptd as Songs wing to wing: an offering to two sisters, 1895.

New poems. 1897.

Victorian ode. 1897 (priv ptd).

Health and holiness. 1905. Introd by G. Tyrell.

Ode to the English martyrs. 1906 (priv ptd).

Shelley. 1909. Introd by G. Wyndham.

Saint Ignatius Loyola. Ed J. H. Pollen 1901 (preface by W. Meynell), rptd 1951 (introd by H. Kelly).

Sir Leslie Stephen as a biographer. 1915 (priv ptd). Bibliography and chronology by C. Shorter.

The mistress of vision. Sussex 1918 (preface by V. McNabb, commentary by J. O'Connor), rptd Aylesford 1966 (introd by J. Jerome, essay by H. Williamson).

Little Jesus [1897]; 1920 (priv ptd).

The hound of heaven: a sequence of paintings by R. H. Ives Gammell, based on the poem, with interpretations by B. M. Boardman, Boston MA 1994.

All edns and collections pbd after Thompson's death repeat the errors found mainly but not exclusively in Works, 1913. The forthcoming new edn, Boardman, listed above, sets out to provide accurate texts based on original mss.

Letters

The letters of Francis Thompson. Ed J. E. Walsh, New York 1969.

§2

Tynan, K. A new and great poet. Illus London News, Dec 1893.

Patmore, C. Mr Thompson: a new poet. Fortnightly Rev, Jan 1894.

Symons, A. Francis Thompson's poems. Athenaeum, 3 Feb 1894.

'A. T. Q. C.' [A. Quiller-Couch] A literary causerie: Thompson's New poems. Speaker, May 1897.

Symons, A. Thompson's New poems. Athenaeum, 12 June 1897.

Lucas, E. V. Thompson's cricket verses. Cornhill Mag, July 1908, rptd in his One day and another, 1909.

Meynell, A. Some memories of Thompson. Dublin Rev 142, 1908.

De Lattre, F. Le poète Thompson. Paris 1909, rptd from Revue Germanique 5, 1909; also in his De Byron à Thompson: essais de littérature anglaise, Paris 1913.

Tynan, K. Thompson. Fortnightly Rev, Feb 1910.

Cock, A. A. Thompson. Dublin Rev 159 1911.

Beacock, G. A. Thompson. Borna (Leipzig,) 1912.

O'Conor, J. F. X. A study of Thompson's Hound of heaven. New York 1912.

Armstrong, M. D. The poetry of Thompson. Forum 50, 1913.

Lewis, C. M. Thompson. Yale Rev, Oct 1914.

Jackson, H. In his The eighteen nineties, 1913.

Harrison, A. The poetry of Thompson. Eng Rev 15, 1913.

Figgis, D. Thompson. Contemporary Rev, Oct 1913, rptd in his Byeways of study, Dublin 1918.

Meynell, E. The life of Francis Thompson. 1913, 1926 (5th edn rev and condensed).

Meynell, E. The notebooks of Thompson. Dublin Rev, Jan 1917, rptd in Living Age 294, 1917.

Allen, H. A. The poet of the return to God. Catholic World, June 1918.

Moore, T. V. The hound of heaven. Psychoanalytic Rev 5, 1918.

Walsh, J. E. Strange harp strange symphony: the life of Francis Thompson. 1968.

Boardman, B. M. Between heaven and Charing Cross: the life of Francis Thompson. New Haven and London 1988. [BMB]

James Thomson, 'B.V.' 1834–82

Mss: The Bodleian holds Bertram Dobell's extensive collection of mss relating to Thomson, containing holographs of most of the poetry with the exception of The city of dreadful night, *prose 'phantasies', trns from Heine and Leopardi, notebooks, diaries in London, Colorado and the Basque Country, letters by and to him, other writings and memoranda. The Pierpont Morgan Lib, New York, has a complete (but for one verse) ms of* The city of dreadful night *as brought to America by G. W. Flaws after Thomson's death. The BL contains early drafts for 15 of the 22 sections of* The city of dreadful night, *with corrected proofs of* Sunday up the river, *and 3 notebooks containing* Weddah *and* Om-el-Bonain, In the room *and verse and prose fragments. A holograph of the* Six sonnets to Joseph and Alice Barnes *is in the Bradlaugh Collection at the Bishopsgate Inst. The Alderman Lib, Univ of Virginia, holds 2 letters to George Eliot and a letter to the editor of Acad. Four letters to Philip Bourke Marston are in the Louise Chandler Moulton Papers at the Lib of Congress. The run of* Cope's Tobacco Plant *held by Glasgow Univ Lib has corrections to Thomson articles apparently in Thomson's hand (N & Q 228, Aug 1983).*

Bibliographies

Dobell, B. and J. M. Wheeler. In The city of dreadful night, Portland ME 1892.

Walker, I. B. In her Thomson: a critical study, Ithaca NY 1950. Secondary.

Vachot, C. In his James Thomson, Paris 1964 [in Fr]. Primary and secondary.

Schaefer, W. D. In his James Thomson ('B.V.'): beyond 'The city'. Berkeley and Los Angeles 1965. Primary and secondary.

Prose and poetry selections

The story of a famous old Jewish firm and other pieces in prose and rime. 1883 (priv ptd).

Shelley: a poem; with other writings relating to Shelley, by the late James Thomson (B.V.); to which is added an essay on the poetry of William Blake by the same author. 1884 (priv ptd). Preface by B. Dobell.

Selections from original contributions of Thomson to Cope's Tobacco Plant. Introd by W. Lewin, Liverpool 1889. Excerpts from journalistic essays and criticism; with cartoon showing contemporary figures as illustration to mock heroic 'Pilgrimage to Saint Nicotine' poem excerpt.

Poems, essays and fragments. Ed with preface by J. M. Robinson 1892. Frontispiece portrait photograph 1860.

The speedy extinction of evil and misery: selected prose of James Thomson ('B.V.'). Ed W. D. Schaeffer, Berkeley CA and Los Angeles 1967.

§1

Poems

The pilgrimage to Saint Nicotine. Liverpool 1878.

The city of dreadful night and other poems. 1880.

REVIEWS: Athenaeum 1 May 1880; George Saintsbury, Acad 12 June 1880; Westminster Rev July 1880; George Simcox, Fortnightly Rev 1 July 1880; Philip Bourke Marston, Modern Thought May 1881.

The title poem first appeared in Nat Reformer *in 22 Mar, 12 and 26 Apr, and 27 May 1874, and was reviewed in* Acad *6 June 1874 and* Spectator *20 June 1874.*

Vane's story, Weddah and Om-el-Bonain and other poems. 1881 [for 1880].

REVIEWS: Westminster Rev Jan 1881; Acad 5 Feb 1881.

Address at the opening of the new hall of the Leicester Secular Society, Sunday 6th March 1881, delivered by Mrs Theodore Wright. [1881.]

A voice from the Nile and other poems. 1884. With memoir by B. Dobell. Bound in are quotes from 2 reviews of Essays and phantasies, Westminster Rev Apr 1884.

The city of dreadful night and other poems. 1888 (2nd edn).

The city of dreadful night. Portland ME 1892. Introd by E. Cavazza.

Poetical works. Ed with memoir by B. Dobell 2 vols 1895.

The city of dreadful night and other poems. 'Cheap edition'. Introd by B. D. [Bertram Dobell] 1899.

The city of dreadful night and other poems. Portland ME 1909.

The city of dreadful night and other poems. Introd by B. D. [Bertram Dobell] 1910.

The city of dreadful night and other poems. Introd by B. Dobell 1919.

The city of dreadful night and other poems. 1922.

The city of dreadful night. Yellow Springs OH 1926 (edn of 500).

Poems of James Thomson ('B.V.'). Ed G. H. Gerould, New York 1927.

The city of dreadful night and other poems. Introd by E. Blunden 1932.

The city of dreadful night and other poems. Preface by H. S. Salt, 1932.

Poems and some letters of James Thomson, edited, with a biographical and critical introduction and textual notes, by Anne Ridler. 1963. Gives mss dates of composition and cites variants in notes. Reissued as Poems and some letters of James Thomson, edited, with a biographical and critical introduction and textual notes, by Anne Ridler, Carbondale 1963 (Centaur edn).

The city of dreadful night. Introd by E. Morgan, Edinburgh 1994.

Prose

A commission of inquiry on royalty etc. 1876 (with A bible lesson on monarchy). Anti-royalist satire.

The story of a famous old Jewish firm. 1876. Secularist satire.

The devil in the Church of England and The one thing. 1876. Secularist satire.

The story of a famous old Jewish firm etc. In Leek Bijou Freethought Reprints no 6 1881.

Essays and phantasies. 1881. Literary and cultural criticism and fiction. (Bound in are extended quotes from reviews of The city of dreadful night and Vane's story.)

REVIEWS: Acad 21 May 1881; Spectator 22 Oct 1881.

Satires and profanities. Ed G. W. Foote 1884. (Frontispiece portrait photo 1881.) Secularist satire. 1890 (New edn).

Biographical and critical studies. Ed B. Dobell 1896. Literary criticism.

A lady of sorrow. Portland ME 1901. Fiction. In Essays and phantasies and Schaefer 1967, *above*.

A lady of sorrow. Portland ME 1913 (2nd edn).

Thomson on George Meredith. 1909 (50 copies priv ptd).

Walt Whitman: the man and the poet. Ed and introd by B. Dobell 1910; facs 1970, New York 1971.

Contributions to periodicals

Thomson contributed prose and poetry regularly to periodicals 1858–82, notably to Tait's Edinburgh Mag *1858–9,* Nat Reformer *1860–75,* Secularist *1876–77, and* Cope's Tobacco Plant *1875–80. Listed in Schaefer, Bibliographies, above. Add to prose contributions:*The United Kingdom anti-papal league, Nat Reformer *2 May 1875. Besides 'B.V.' other pseudonymns used were 'Crepusculus' (in* Tait's*), 'Bysshe Vanolis', 'X.', 'J.S.T.', 'T.J', 'J.T.', and 'Sigvat'.*

Translations by Thomson

Essays, dialogues and thoughts of Giacomo Leopardi. With memoir of Leopardi. Introd by and ed B. Dobell. [1905.] Leonard 1993, *see §2 below*, cites significant differences between Dobell's edited versions and two trns pbd in Thomson's lifetime.

Novalis, F. Hymns to night, in Novalis and the poets of pessimism, ed S. Reynolds, Norwich 1995. Also in P. N. Rev 20 no 6 1994 with ms note by T. Leonard.

Pbd trns from the Ger of Goethe and Heine; the Fr of Baudelaire, Béranger, Bousquet, Courier, Gautier and Renan; and the Ital of Colletta and Leopardi, are listed in Schaefer (see Bibliographies, above). Heine trns are in The city of dreadful night *1880,* Vane's story *1881 [for 1880],* Satires and profanities *1884,* Poems, essays and fragments *1892, and* Poetical works *1895. Goethe is in 1881 and 1895; Béranger in 1895.*

Translations of Thomson

Esperanto. La urba de terura rokto, Auld, W. Aabyhaj Denmark 1977.

German. Nachstadt: und andere lichtscheue schriften. Horstmann, Univ of Zurich 1992.

§2

Marston, P. B. In English poets, ed T. H. Ward, vol 4 1880.

Obits: (P. B. Marston) Athenaeum June 1882; Secular Rev 17 June 1882.

Flaws, G. G. James Thomson, a study. In Secular Rev 24 June, 1 July 1882.

Foote, G. W. James Thomson the man. Progress Apr 1884.

Foote, G. W. James Thomson the poet. Progress June 1884.

Mccall, W. A Nirvana trilogy. 1886.

Salt, H. S. The life of Thomson. 1889, 1898, 1914 (rev edn). The rev edn reduces from 335 to 169 pp., 144 pp. of Salt's literary criticism reduced to 23 pp. Salt's notes for the 1st edn, containing letters from and notes of interviews with people who knew Thomson, and Salt's transcription of a 23-verse occasional poem no longer extant, have been acquired from the Rationalist Press Assoc by the Bodleian.

Noel, R. In Poets and poetry of the century, ed A. H. Miles, vol 5 [1892].

Dobell, B. The laureate of pessimism. 1910; facs reprint Port Washington NY 1970.

Harris, F. James Thomson, an unknown immortal. In Contemporary portraits, 2nd ser New York 1919.
Leonard, T. Places of the mind: the life and work of James Thomson ('B.V'). 1993. (Portrait photographs 1860, 1869, 1881.) [TL]

John Todhunter 1839–1916

Alcestis. New York 1874, London '1879' [1878].
Laurella and other poems. 1876.
A study of Shelley. 1880.
Forest songs, and other poems. 1881.
The true tragedy of Rienzi, tribune of Rome. 1881. Prose and verse.
Helena in Troas. 1886.
Notes on Shelley's unfinished poem 'The triumph of life'. 1887 (priv ptd).
The banshee and other poems. 1888, Dublin 1891.
A Sicilian idyll: a pastoral play. 1890, 1891. Verse.
How dreams come true: a dramatic sketch in two scenes. [1890] (priv ptd).
The legend of Stauffenberg: a dramatic cantata. Dublin 1890. Words by Todhunter, music by J. Culwick.
The poison flower, a phantasy in three scenes. Suggested by Hawthorne's 'Rappacini's daughter'. 1891. Subsequently pbd in Isolt of Ireland, *below*.
The black cat: a play in three acts. 1895.
Life of Patrick Sarsfield, Earl of Lucan; with a short narrative of the principal events of the Jacobite war in Ireland. 1895.
Three Irish bardic tales: being metrical versions of the three tales known as the three sorrows of storytelling. 1896.
Ye minutes of ye CLXXVIIth meeting of ye Sette of odd volumes, extracted from ye diary of Samuel Pepys. [1896] (priv ptd).
An essay upon essays, written by command of his oddship brother Francis Elgar and read before the sette of odd volumes Jan 4 1895. 1896 (priv ptd).
A riverside walk: an easy-going essay by a peripatetic philosopher. 1898 (priv ptd).
An essay in search of a subject, written by command of his oddship brother Silvanus Thompson magentiser and read before the sette of odd volume May 31st 1904. 1904 (priv ptd).
Sounds and sweet airs. '1905' [1904].
Heine's Book of songs. Oxford 1907. Tr Todhunter.
From the land of dreams: Irish poems. Dublin and London 1918. Introd by T. Rolleston.
Essays. 1920. Foreword by S. J. O'Grady.
Goethe's Faust, first part. Oxford 1924. Tr Todhunter.
Isolt of Ireland: a legend in a prologue and three acts; and The poison flower. 1927. Blank verse plays.
Trivium amoris; and The wooing of Artemis. London and Toronto 1927.
Selected poems. Ed D. Todhunter and A. Graves 1929. With biographical sketch by T. Rolleston.

Henry Duff Traill 1842–1912

See col 2397.

Frederic Herbert Trench 1865–1923

Collections
Collected works. Ed H. Williams 3 vols 1924.
Selected poems. Ed H. Williams 1924.

§1

Deirdre wed, and other poems. '1901' [1900].
New poems: Apollo and the seaman, The queen of Gothland, Stanzas to Tolstoy and other lyrics. 1907, New York 1908.
All that matters: a play. [1911.]
Lyrics and narrative poems. [1911.]
Ode from Italy in time of war: night on Mottarone. Florence 1915 (priv ptd).
Poems, with fables in prose. 2 vols 1918.
Napoleon: a play. 1919, 1919 (2nd edn).

§2

Clarke, A. The poetry of Trench. London Mercury 10 1924.
George, R. The poetry of Mr Trench. Contemporary Rev July 1924.
Chevalley, A. Trench, poète anglais: notice sur sa vie et ses oeuvres. Paris 1925.

Katharine Tynan, later Hinkson 1861–1931

Mss: diaries 1889–1926, 1915, Univ College Lib, Dublin. Correspondence John Rylands Univ Lib, Manchester.

Collections
Twenty one poems, selected by W. B. Yeats. Dundrum 1907.
The flower of peace: a collection of the devotional poetry of Katharine Tynan. 1914.
Collected poems. 1930.
[Twenty-four poems.] [1931] (Augustan Books of Modern Poetry.)
Poems of Katharine Tynan. Dublin 1963. Introd by M. Gibbon.

§1

Verse
Louise de la Vallière and other poems. 1885.
Shamrocks. 1887.
Ballads and lyrics. 1891.
Irish love-songs, selected by Katharine Tynan. 1892.
Cuckoo songs. 1894.
Miracle plays: our Lord's coming and childhood. 1895.
The wind in the trees: a book of country verse. 1898.
Poems. 1901.
Innocencies: a book of verse. London and Dublin 1905.
A little book of xxiv carols. Portland ME 1907, 1916.
The rhymed life of St Patrick. 1907.
Experiences. 1908.
Lauds. 1909.
New poems. 1911.
Irish poems. 1913.
The wild harp: a selection from Irish poetry by Katharine Tynan. 1913.
Flower of youth: poems in war-time. 1915.
The holy war. 1916.
Late songs. 1917.
Herb o' grace: poems in war-time. 1918.
Even song. Oxford 1922.

Prose
The land I love best. 1890.
A nun, her friends and her order: being a sketch of the life of Mother Xaviera Fallon. 1891.
An isle in the water. 1895, 1904. Stories.
The land of mist and mountain. [1895.] Stories.
The way of a maid. 1895.
A lover's breast-knot. 1896.
Oh, what a plague is love! 1896, 1904.
Led by a dream, and other stories. 1899.
The dear Irish girl. 1899.
The handsome Brandons: a story for girls. 1899, Chicago 1900.
A daughter of the fields. 1900, [1910].
The adventures of Carlo. 1900, [1932].
Three fair maids, or the Burkes of Barrymore, etc. '1901' [1900], 1909.
A union of hearts. [1901.]
That sweet enemy. 1901, [1908].

A girl of Galway. '1902' [1901], [1914].
The queen's page: a story of the days of Charles I of England. [c. 1902].
A king's woman: being the narrative of Miss Penelope Fayle, now Mistress Frobisher, concerning the late troublous times in Ireland. 1902.
Love of sisters. 1902.
A red, red rose. 1903.
The handsome Quaker, and other stories. 1903.
The honourable Molly. 1903, [1907].
Judy's lovers. 1904.
Julia. 1904, [1912].
The French wife. 1904.
A daughter of kings. 1905, 1909.
Dick Pentreath. 1905.
Fortune's favourite. 1905.
Luck of the Fairfaxes: a story for girls. [1905.]
A book of memory: the birthday book of the blessed dead. [1906.]
A little book for John O'Mahoney's friends. 1906 (priv ptd), Portland ME 1909.
A little book for Mary Gill's friends. Petersfield 1906.
A little book of courtesies. 1906.
For Maisie: a love story. 1906.
The adventures of Alicia. 1906.
The story of Bawn. 1906.
The yellow domino and other stories. 1906.
Her ladyship. 1907.
The story of our Lord, for children. Dublin 1907, 1923.
Mary Gray. 1908, 1911.
Men and maids. Dublin 1908.
The house of the crickets. 1908.
The lost angel and other stories. 1908.
Cousins and others. [1909.]
Her mother's daughter. 1909.
Ireland. 1909, 1927 (2nd edn).
Kitty Aubrey. 1909.
Peggy the daughter. 1909, 1912.
Betty Carew. 1910.
Freda. 1910.
The house of the secret. 1910.
The story of Cecilia. 1911.
The story of Clarice. 1911.
Heart o' gold, or the little princess: a story for girls. [1912.]
Honey, my honey. 1912.
Princess Katharine. 1912.
Rose of the garden. 1912.
A midsummer rose. 1913.
Mrs Pratt of Paradise farm. 1913.
Twenty-five years: reminiscences. 1913, New York [1913].
The daughter of the manor. '1914' [1913].
A little radiant girl. 1914, London and Glasgow 1937.
A shameful inheritance. 1914.
Lover's meeting. London and Melbourne [1914].
Men, not angels, and other tales told to girls. [1914.]
Molly, my heart's delight. 1914.
Countrymen all. London and Dublin 1915.
The house of the foxes. 1915.
The squire's sweetheart. 1915.
Margery Dawe. '1916' [1915], [1934].
John a dreams. 1916.
Lord Edward [Fitzgerald]: a study in romance. 1916.
The middle years. 1916, Boston 1917.
The web of Fraulein. 1916.
The west wind. 1916.
Kit. 1917.
Kitty at school and college. Dublin [1917?].
Miss Mary. 1917.
The rattlesnake. 1917.
Book of Irish history. Dublin and Belfast 1918.
Miss Gascoigne. 1918.
My love's but a lassie. 1918.
Love of brothers. 1919.
The man from Australia [1919], [1931].
The years of the shadow. 1919, Boston 1919.
Denys the dreamer. 1920.
The house. [1920.]
Sally victrix. [1921.]
The second wife, together with A July rose. 1921.
Bitha's wonderful year, etc. [1921.]
A mad marriage. [1922.]
The house on the bogs. 1922.
The wandering years. 1922.
White ladies. 1922.
Mary Beaudesert. VS 1923.
Pat, the adventurer. London and Melbourne 1923.
They loved greatly. 1923.
The golden rose. 1924.
The house of doom. 1924.
Memories. 1924.
Wives. [1924.]
Dear Lady Bountiful. 1925.
Life in the occupied area. [1925] (priv ptd).
Miss Phipps. London and Melbourne 1925.
The briar bush maid. London and Melbourne 1926.
The heiress of Wyke. London and Melbourne 1926.
The infatuation of Peter. [1926.]
The moated grange. [1926], rptd as The night of terror [1932].
Haroun of London. [1927.]
The face in the picture. London and Melbourne 1927.
The wild adventure. London and Melbourne 1927.
Castle perilous. London and Melbourne 1928.
Lover of women. [1928.]
The house in the forest. London and Melbourne 1928.
A fine gentleman. London and Melbourne 1929.
The most charming family. London and Melbourne 1929.
The rich man. [1929.]
The river. 1929, [1934].
Denise the daughter. London and Melbourne 1930.
Grayson's girl. 1930, London and Dublin [1952].
The admirable Simmons. London and Melbourne 1930.
The playground. London and Melbourne 1930.
A lonely maid. London and Melbourne 1931.
Della's orchard. London and Melbourne 1931.
Philippa's lover. London and Melbourne 1931.
The forbidden way. [1931.]
The other man. London and Melbourne 1932.
The pitiful lady. London and Melbourne 1932.
An international marriage. London and Melbourne 1933.
Connor's wood. 1933.
A lad was born. 1934, [1945] (abridged).
The house of dreams. London and Melbourne 1934.
The summer aeroplane. 1975.

§2

The poems of Katharine Tynan. Irish Monthly Dec 1884.
Bregy, K. The poetry of Katharine Tynan Hinkson. Catholic World 97 1913.
Alspach, R. The poetry of Katharine Tynan Hinkson. Ireland Amer Rev 4 1940.
Hinkson, P. Katharine Tynan. Irish Lib Bull 2 1941.
Yeats, W. B. Letters to Katharine Tynan. Ed R. McHugh, Dublin [1953].
Tynan, K. Letters 1884–5. Apex 1 1973.

Arthur Edward Waite 1857–1942

Collections

Collected poems. 2 vols 1914.
The open vision: a selection from the poems. Eton 1959.

§1

A lyric of the fairy land and other poems. 1879, 1888 (Canterbury Poets).
Israfel: letters, visions and poems. 1886, 1894.
A soul's comedy. 1887.
Elfin music. 1888.
Lucasta: parables and poems. 1894.
A book of mystery and vision. 1902.
Strange houses of sleep. 1906.
The book of the holy grail. 1921. Poems.
The holy grail: its legends and symbolism. 1933.
Shadows of life and thought: a retrospective review in the form of memoirs. 1938.
Waite also wrote on alchemy, freemasonry, the Rosicrucians etc. He edited The Unknown World, *Aug 1894–Jan 1895.*

Frederick William Orde Ward 1843–1922

Collections

Selected poems. Ed C. O. O. Ward and R. Markland 1924.

§1

The cry of the woman-child. 1886. By Frederick Harald Williams, pseud for his first 6 books.
Women must weep. 1888.
'Twixt kiss and lip, or under the sword. 1890, 1890 (3rd edn).
Confessions of a poet. 1894.
Matin bells and scarlet and gold. 1897.
English roses. 1899.
New century hymns for the Christian year. [1901.]
The prisoner of love. 1904.
The last crusade: patriotic poems. [1917.]
Songs for sufferers, from a sick-room. [1917.]
Ward also pbd theological works and a paper on Shelley.

§2

Miles, A. H. Ward. In Miles 12.
TLS 18 Dec 1924. Review of Selected poems.

John Byrne Leicester Warren, 3rd Baron de Tabley 1835–95

Mss: poems and correspondence with Robert Browning, John Rylands Univ Lib, Manchester.

Collections

Poems, dramatic and lyrical. 2 ser 1893–5.
Collected poems. 1903.
Select poems. Ed J. Drinkwater 1924.

§1

Poems: by G. F. Preston [pseud]. 1859. With G. Fortescue.
Ballads and metrical sketches. By George F. Preston. 1860.
The threshold of Atrides. By George F. Preston. 1861.
Glimpses of antiquity. By George F. Preston. 1862.
Praeterita. By William Lancaster [pseud]. Cambridge and London 1863.
An essay on Greek federal coinage. 1863.
On some coins of Lycia under the Rhodian domination, and of the Lycian league. 1863.
Eclogues and monodramas. 1864.
Studies in verse. 1865.
Philoctetes: a metrical drama. 1866.
Orestes: Orestes: a metrical drama. 1867.
A screw loose: a novel. 1868.
Ropes of sand: a novel. 1869.
Rehearsals: a book of verses. London and Bungay 1870.
Searching the net: a book of verses. 1873.
The soldier of fortune: a tragedy in five acts. 1876. Verse.
A guide to the study of book plates. 1880.
A new year's greeting. Oxford 1893.
The flora of Cheshire. Ed S. Moore 1899. Includes letters and memoir by M. G. Duff.
Orpheus in Thrace and other poems. Ed E., Lady Leighton-Warren 1901.
Warren wrote introds and prefaces to a number of literary texts.

§2

Le Gallienne, R. The poetry of Lord de Tabley. Nineteenth Cent May 1893.
Miles, A. H. Lord de Tabley. In Miles 6.
Monkhouse, C. Poems dramatic and lyrical, by Lord de Tabley. Acad 6 Apr 1895.
Watts[-Dunton], T. Lord de Tabley. Athenaeum 30 Nov 1895; rptd in his Old familiar faces, 1916.
Gosse, E. Lord de Tabley: a portrait. Contemporary Rev Jan 1896; rptd in his Critical kit-kats, 1896.
Walker, H. Warren. 1903.
Hearn, L. In his Life and literature, New York 1917.
Bridges, R. Lord de Tabley's poems. In his Collected essays vol 7, Oxford 1931.

Sir Thomas Herbert Warren 1853–1930

§1

By Severn sea and other poems. Oxford 1897, 1898.

§2

Magnus, L. Warren of Magdalen. 1932.

Rosamund Marriott Watson, 'Graham R. Tomson', née Rosamund Ball, later Armytage, later Tomson 1860–1911

Mss located in the Berg Collection, NYPL; Bodleian; Dorset County Museum; HRHRC, Austin TX; Harvard; Smith College MA.

Bibliographies

In Nineteenth century readers' guide to periodical literature 1890–1899, ed H. G. Cushing and A. V. Morris 2 vols New York 1944.
See also Wellesley *vol 5 1989.*

Collections

The poems of Rosamund Marriott Watson. Introd by H. B. M. Watson 1912, New York 1912.
REVIEWS: The Times 26 Sep 1912; Pall Mall Gazette 27 Sep 1912; Bookman Nov 1912; Poetry Dec 1912; Dial 1 Feb 1913.

Selections

In Ballades and rondeaus, chants royal, sestinas, villanelles, &c, ed G. White, London and Newcastle-on-Tyne 1887, New York 1888, 1892, 1893, 1897, London 1900, 1905, 1909.
Lyrics by Rosamund Marriott Watson. Bibelot Oct 1904.
In Poets and poetry of the century, ed A. H. Miles, vol 8 1891–7. 2nd edn as The poets and the poetry of the nineteenth century, vol 9 1907.
Lyrics from the heart of the garden and The road to spring. Bibelot 17 1911.
On the downs. In The book of Sussex, ed C. F. Cook, Hove 1914. Poem.

In A soldier's book of love poems, ed G. Locker-Lampson, 1917.
In Poetry of the nineties, ed C. E. Andrews and M. O. Percival, New York 1926.
In The book of poetry, ed E. Markham, New York 1926–7, vol 9.
In The Yellow Book: a selection, ed N. Denny, 1949. Poems.
In Winged words: an anthology of Victorian women's poetry and verse, ed C. Reilly, 1994.
In Victorian women poets: an anthology, ed A. Leighton and M. Reynolds, 1995.

§1

Tares. 1884, Portland ME 1898, 1906. Poems.
REVIEW: Acad 21 Mar 1885.
The bird-bride: a volume of ballads and sonnets. 1889.
REVIEWS: Scots Observer 4 May 1889; Literary World 24 May 1889; Woman's World June 1889.
A summer night, and other poems. 1891, 1895, Chicago 1895.
REVIEWS: Literary Opinion Dec 1891; Acad 9 Jan 1892; Literary World 15 Jan 1892; Speaker 16 Jan 1892; Dial Apr 1896.
Vespertilia, and other verses. 1895, Chicago 1895.
REVIEWS: Acad 30 Nov 1895; Speaker 4 Jan 1896; Literary World 14 Feb 1896; Athenaeum 4 Apr 1896.
The art of the house. 1897, New York 1897, London 1900.
REVIEWS: Acad 13 Feb 1897; Speaker 10 Apr 1897; Athenaeum 3 July 1897.
Old books, fresh flowers. Gouverneur NY 1899 (priv circulation).
An island rose. 1900.
The patchwork quilt. 1900, New York 1900?, London and New York 1987.
After sunset. 1903, London and New York 1904. Poems.
REVIEWS: Acad 7 Nov 1903; New York Times 26 Dec 1903.
The heart of the garden. 1905, 1906, Philadelphia 1906, London 1907. Poems.
REVIEW: Bookman Apr 1906.
The H. G. Wells calendar. 1911, 1915 (2nd impression).

Contributions to periodicals, collaborative works and anthologies

Watson edited Sylvia's Jnl *from Jan 1893 to Apr 1894. She also contributed to the Wares of Autolycus column in the* Pall Mall Gazette. *From 1904 to 1911 she was a poetry reviewer for* Athenaeum. *She also contributed to the* Illus London News.

Scribner's Mag. June 1887–Nov 1911. Poems.
Longman's Mag. July 1887–Nov 1892. Poems.
Ballade of Nicolete. In Aucassin and Nicolete done into English by Andrew Lang, 1887, 1896, Portland ME 1896, London 1897, 1898, 1900 (40 copies as The song-story of Aucassin and Nicolete done into English by Andrew Lang), 1904, 1905 (illus), 1913. Also in Aucassin and Nicolete, Girard KS 1923.
Ballade of Nicolete. In Aucassin & Nicolete: being a love story translated out of the ancient French by Andrew Lang, East Aurora NY 1899 (1st verse only unsigned).
Harper's Mag. Aug 1887–Aug 1909. Poems.
Ballads of the north countrie. Introd and notes by Graham R. Tomson 1888, New York 1888, London 1895.
Border ballads. Introd and notes by Graham R. Tomson 1888 (Canterbury Poets ser).
In Ballads of books, ed A. Lang, 1888.
Art Jnl. Apr 1888–Aug 1888. Poems.
Woman's World. Nov 1888–Sep 1890.
Scots Observer. 2 Jan 1889–24 May 1890.
Universal Rev 15 Jan 1889–15 June 1890. Poems.
Scottish Art Rev. Feb 1889–Oct 1889.
Selections from the Greek anthology. Ed Graham R. Tompson 1889, New York 1889.
Art Rev. Jan 1890–Dec 1890.
Spectator. Asphidel, 8 Feb 1890. Poem.
Living Age. 25 Oct 1890–23 Dec 1911. Poems.
For contributions to Macmillan's Mag, *see* Wellesley *vol 5 1989*.
Atlantic Monthly. Sep 1890–Sep 1894. Poems.
National Observer. 13 Dec 1890–28 Oct 1893.
Atlanta. A new year fantasy, Jan 1891; Lavender and pansies, Jan 1891. Poems.
Independent (New York). 19 Nov 1891–13 Oct 1910.
The Critic. After sunset, 13 Feb 1892. Poem.
Concerning cats: a book of poems by many authors. Selected by Graham R. Tomson 1892, New York 1892.
Nation. Farm on the links, 31 Mar 1892. Poem.
Art Jnl. The hunting of Rothiemuir, Apr 1892. Poem.
Century Mag. Gloria mundi, July 1892. Poem.
Cosmopolitan. Sheep bells, July 1892; Ghosts, Sep 1892. Poems.
In The child set in the midst: by modern poets, ed W. Meynell, 1892.
Acad. 3 Sep 1892–2 June 1894.
Speaker. 8 Oct 1892–30 Sep 1893.
Lippincott's Monthly. Armistice, June 1893. Poem.
Black and White. The nameless bird, Christmas Number 1893. Poem with O. Crawfurd.
The Yellow Book. Jan 1895–Apr 1897. Poems.
Pall Mall Mag. Mar 1895–Feb 1909.
In A London garland, ed W. E. Henley, 1895. Poem.
Pearson's Mag. Between the lights, Apr 1896. Poem.
Athenaeum. 4 Apr 1896–29 Apr 1911. Reviews and poems.
The Pageant. A song of songs, 1897. Poem.
Once upon a time, the favourite nursery tales retold by R. M. Watson and others. 1897.
Omar Khayyam. In In praise of Omar: an address before the Omar Khayyam club, ed J. Hay, Portland ME 1898 (925 copies). Poem.
Omar Khayyam. In The Rubaiyat of Omar Khayyam, the astronomer poet of Persia, rendered into English verse, ed T. Williams, Philadelphia 1898.
In London in song, ed W. Whitten, [1898].
New Liberal Rev. May 1901–Jan 1902. Poems.
Outlook. Green pavilions, 10 Aug 1901. Rptd from Pall Mall Mag Aug 1901. Poem.
T. P.'s Weekly. A song of London, 20 Feb 1903.
Harmsworth's London Mag. The child alone, Mar 1907. Poem.
Current Literature. Launch of the leaves, Oct 1907. Poem.
Omar Khayyam. In E. Fitzgerald, Omar Khayyam: the Rubaiyat, Philadelphia 1908. Poem.
Mother Goose, complete rhymes and jingles. With 240 illustrations by Gordon Browne, R. Marriott Watson, L. L. Weedon and others. New York nd.
Hampton's Mag. Garden of memory, Feb 1911. Poem.
Literary Digest. All Souls' Day, 12 Oct 1912; Scythe song, 12 Oct 1912. Poems.
Introd to Great thoughts from H. G. Wells, New York 1912.

§2

Eliot, M. The Critic 25 Oct 1890.
Literary gossip. Literary Opinion Nov 1891.
Portrait. The Chap-Book 15 June 1896.
Archer, W. In his Poets of the younger generation, 1902, rptd 1970.
Obits: The Times 2 Jan 1912, Athenaeum 6 Jan 1912.
N & Q 4 Jan 1936. Biographical information.
Connell, J. (J. H. Robertson). In his W. E. Henley, 1949, rptd Port Washington NY 1972.
Mix, K. L. In her A study in yellow: The Yellow Book and its contributors, Lawrence KS 1960.
Millgate, M. Thomas Hardy and Rosamund Tomson. N & Q 218, July 1973.
In The collected letters of Thomas Hardy, ed R. L. Purdy and M. Millgate, Oxford 1978–88.

Hughes, L. K. In The 1890s: an encyclopedia of British literature, art, and culture, ed G. A. Cevasco, 1993.

Hughes, L. K. Myth and marriage in poems by 'Graham R. Tomson' (Rosamund M. Watson). VP Summer 1994. Rptd in Leighton A. ed. Victorian women poets: a critical reader. Oxford 1996. [DA]

Sir William Watson 1858–1935

Autograph letters and mss of Watson are in the Bodleian

Bibliographies

Watson, W. In his Heralds of the dawn, 1912.

Swayze, W. E. The Watson collection. YULG 27 1952.

Woolf, C. Some uncollected authors 12: Watson. BC 5 1956. *See also* N. Colbeck, BC 6 1957, W. E. Swayze, BC 6 1957.

Collections

Collected poems. 1898, 3rd edn London and New York 1899.

Selected poems. '1903' [1902], 2nd edn London and New York 1903.

[Collected] poems. Ed J. A. Spender 2 vols 1905.

A hundred poems selected from various volumes. 1922.

Poems selected with notes by the author. 1928.

The poems of Sir William Watson 1878–1935. 1936.

I was an English poet: poems selected by Lady Watson. Ashville 1941.

§1

The prince's quest and other poems. 1880, 1892.

Epigrams of art, life and nature. Liverpool 1884. With note on epigrams.

Wordsworth's grave and other poems. 1890, 1892 (as Poems, adds 26 poems), Portland ME 1898, with Lachrymae musarum, *below*, London 1904.

Lachrymae musarum. 1892 (priv ptd), 1892 (adds poems), Portland ME 1898, with Wordsworth's grave. Verses on the death of Tennyson.

Shelley's centenary. 1892 (priv ptd).

The eloping angels: a caprice. 1893.

Excursions in criticism: being some prose recreations of a rhymer. [1893.]

Odes and other poems. 1894.

The father of the forest and other poems. 1895 (priv ptd), London and Chicago 1895.

Ode for the centenary of the death of Burns. 1895.

The purple east: a series of sonnets on England's desertion of Armenia. 1896; tr Ital, Padova 1896.

The lost Eden. 1897.

The year of shame, with an introduction by the Bishop of Hereford. London and New York 1897.

The hope of the world and other poems. '1898' [1897], 1898 (2nd edn).

Two sonnets and an epigram. 1901.

New poems. Greenfield MA and London 1902, New York 1909.

Ode on the day of the coronation of King Edward VII. London and New York 1902.

For England: poems written during estrangement. '1904' [1903].

Sable and purple with other poems. 1910.

The heralds of the dawn. London and Cambridge MA 1912. A play.

The muse in exile. 1913. With address on the poet's place in the scheme of life.

The man who saw and other poems arising out of the war. 1917.

Retrogression and other poems. '1917' [1916].

Pencraft: a plea for the older ways. '1917' [1916]. Prose.

The superhuman antagonists and other poems. 1919.

Ireland arisen. 1921.

Ireland unfreed. 1921.

Poems brief and new. 1925.

Watson edited an anthology of love poetry, Lyric love *(1892), and the poems of Alfred Austin (1890).*

§2

Noble, J. A. Watson. In Miles 8 (7).

Archer, W. In his Poets of the younger generation, 1902.

Yeats, W. B. Scholar poet. In his Letters to the new island, ed H. Reynolds, Cambridge MA 1934.

Watson: a distinguished poet. The Times 14 Aug 1935. Leader and obituary.

Nichols, W. B. The chord of iron: an elegy of Watson. 1935.

Scott-James, R. A. Editorial notes. London Mercury Sep 1935.

Nelson, J. G. Sir William Watson. New York [1966].

Wilson, J. M. I was an English poet: a critical biography of Sir William Watson (1858–1936). 1981.

Theodore Watts-Dunton 1836–1914

See col 2399.

(Julia) Augusta Webster, née Davies 1837–94

Selections

Selections from the verse of Augusta Webster. 1893.
REVIEW: Athenaeum, 26 Aug 1893.

Ed. Mackenzie Bell in A. H. Miles, The poets and poetry of the century, enlarged edn 1905–7, vol 8.

§1

Blanche Lisle, and other poems (by Cecil Home). 1860.

Lesley's guardians (by Cecil Home). 3 vols 1864.
REVIEW: Athenaeum 30 July 1864.

Lilian Gray: a poem (by Cecil Home). 1864.
REVIEW: Athenaeum 24 Dec 1864.

Dramatic studies. 1866.
REVIEWS: Westminster Rev n.s. 30 1866; Athenaeum 11 Aug 1866; Saturday Rev 9 Feb 1867.

A woman sold, and other poems. 1867.
REVIEWS: Westminster Rev n.s. 31 1867; Athenaeum 4 May 1867.

Portraits. 1870 (and reprint), London and New York 1893 (enlarged). Poems.
REVIEWS: Westminster Rev n.s. 37 1870; Spectator 43, 16 Apr 1870; Athenaeum 26 Aug 1893 (with selections); Acad 44, 2 Sep 1893; Spectator 71, 18 Nov 1893.

The auspicious day. 1872. Verse drama.
REVIEWS: Westminster Rev n.s. 42 1872; Athenaeum 12 Oct 1872.

Yu-Pe-Ya's lute. A Chinese tale in English verse. 1874.
REVIEWS: Westminster Rev n.s. 45 1874; Athenaeum 11 Apr 1874.

Parliamentary franchise for women rate-payers. [1878] Rptd from the Examiner.

A housewife's opinions. '1879' [1878]. First appeared in the London Examiner. Essays.
REVIEW: Athenaeum 4 Jan 1879.

Disguises. A drama. 1879.
REVIEWS: Spectator 53, 31 Jan 1880; Acad 17, 3 Apr 1880.

A book of rhyme. 1881.
REVIEWS: Westminster Rev n.s. 60 1881; Athenaeum 20 Aug 1881; Spectator 55, 29 July 1882.

In a day. A drama. 1882, 1893.
REVIEWS: Athenaeum 23 Dec 1882; Acad 22, 30 Dec 1882.

Daffodil and the Croaxaxicans: a romance of history. 1884. A story for children.
REVIEW: Athenaeum 13 Dec 1884.

The sentence. A drama. 1887.
REVIEWS: Acad 32, 19 Nov 1887; Athenaeum 8 Sep 1888.

Mother and daughter. An uncompleted sonnet-sequence. With an introductory note by W. M. Rossetti. To which are added 7, her only other, sonnets. London and New York 1895.
REVIEW: Athenaeum 14 Sep 1895.

Contributions to periodicals
The Brissons [rocks in Cornwall] (by Cecil Home). Macmillan's Mag 5, Nov 1861.
Webster was the regular poetry reviewer for the Athenaeum *during the 1880s and 1890s, and wrote for the* Examiner *in the 1870s.*

Translations
The Prometheus Bound of Aeschylus. 1866.
REVIEW: Westminster Rev n.s. 30 1866.
The Medea of Euripides. 1868.
REVIEW: Westminster Rev n.s. 33 1868.

§2
Forman, H. B. In Our living poets, 1871.
Robertson, E. S. In his English poetesses, 1883.
Obit: Athenaeum 15 Sep 1894.
Augusta Webster. Memorial poem by A. H. Japp. Acad 46, 15 Sep 1894.
E. L. [Elizabeth Lee]. In DNB.
Webster, A. In The feminist companion to literature in English, eds V. Blain, P. Clements and I. Grundy, 1990. [VB]

Oscar Wilde 1854–1900

See col 2060.

James Chapman Woods

A child of the people and other poems. 1879.
Old and rare books: an elementary lecture. 1885.
A pageant of poets and other poems. 1931.
Woods also pbd guide-books, travel books etc.

Margaret Louisa Woods 1856–1945

See col 1725.

Theodore Wratislaw 1871–1933

Collections
Selected poems. Ed J. Gawsworth 1935. With biographical note.

§1
Love's memorial. Rugby 1892. Anon.
Some verses: by the author of Love's memorial. Rugby 1892.
Caprices: poems. 1893; facs with Orchids 1896; London and New York 1984, Oxford 1994.
The pity of love: a tragedy. 1895. Verse.
Orchids: poems. 1896.
Algernon Charles Swinburne: a study. 1900.
Love in a mist, or, a woman's wooing, adapted as a comedietta by Mrs F. Ward. Worcester [1903].
Two ballads transcribed from the French of Master François Villon. Rugby 1933.
Oscar Wilde: a memoir. Ed K. Beckson 1979.
Three nineties studies: W. B. Yeats, John Gray, Aubrey Beardsley. Edinburgh 1980.

§2
Ellis, S. M. A poet of the nineties: Wratislaw. In his Mainly Victorian, [1925].
Around my shelves. Poetry Rev 41 1950. Contains unpbd epitaph.

4
The Novel

i. General works

(1) BIBLIOGRAPHIES ETC

Wedgwood, F. J. Contemporary records: fiction 1–10. Contemporary Rev July 1883–Dec 1886.
Nield, J. A guide to the best historical novels and tales. 1902, 1904, 1911, 1929.
Chandler, F. W. In his Literature of roguery, 2 vols London, Boston and New York 1907, 2 vols New York 1958.
Faxon, F. W. Literary annuals and gift books: a bibliography 1823–1903. Boston 1912, Pinner 1973. Private Libraries Association.
Baker, E. A. and J. Packman. A guide to the best fiction in English. 1913, 1932 (rev and enlarged), 1967.
Sadleir, M. Excursions in Victorian bibliography. 1922.
Parrish, M. L. In his Victorian lady novelists, 1933, rptd 1969. On George Eliot, Mrs Gaskell, the Brontës.
Ehrsam, T. G. and R. H. Deily. Bibliographies of twelve Victorian authors. New York 1936. Includes Kipling, Hardy, R. L. Stevenson; suppl by J. G. Fucilla, MP 37 1939.
Blakey, D. The Minerva Press 1790–1820. 1939.
Block, A. The English novel 1740–1850: a catalogue. 1939, 1961 (rev). Includes prose romances, short stories and trns of foreign fiction.
Summers, M. A Gothic bibliography. [1941.]
Queen, E. The detective short story: a bibliography. Boston 1942, New York 1969.
Henkin, L. J. Problems and digressions in the Victorian novel 1860–1900. BB 18–20 1943–50.
Templeman, W. D. (ed). Bibliographies of studies in Victorian literature for the thirteen years 1932–44. Urbana IL 1945.
Carter, J. and M. Sadleir. Victorian fiction. Cambridge 1947. Exhibition catalogue. *See also* Victorian fiction, Princeton 1947. A Princeton exhibition.
Bleiler, E. F. Checklist of fantastic literature. Chicago 1948.
Rouse, H. B. A selective and critical bibliography of studies in prose fiction. JEGP 49–52 1950–2.
Sadleir, M. XIX century fiction: a bibliographical record. 2 vols 1951.
Leclaire, L. A general analytical bibliography of the regional novelists of the British Isles 1800–1950. Paris 1954.
Cook, D. E. and I. S. Monro. Short story index. New York 1955; suppl 1950–4, New York 1956.
Wright, A. (ed). Bibliographies of studies in Victorian literature for the ten years 1945–54. Urbana IL 1956.
Roger, D. Fantastic novels: a check-list. Perth 1957.
Altick, R. D. and W. R. Matthews, Guide to doctoral dissertations in Victorian literature 1886–1958. Urbana IL 1960.
Henderson, J. The Gothic novel in Wales 1790–1820, with a checklist of novels connected with Wales. Nat Lib of Wales Jnl 1960.
Stevenson, L. In his English novel: a panorama, 1961.
Maison, M. In her Search your soul, Eustace: a survey of the religious novel in the Victorian age, 1961.
Stevenson, L. (ed). Victorian fiction: a guide to research. Cambridge MA 1964.
James, L. In his Fiction for the working man 1830–50, 1963, Harmondsworth 1974.
Ray, G. N. Nineteenth-century English fiction. Los Angeles 1964. A lecture.
Carter, J. Victorian detective fiction: a catalogue of the collection made by Dorothy Glover and Graham Greene. 1966.
Boyle, A. An index to the annuals 1820–1850. Worcester 1967.
Slack, R. C. (ed). Bibliographies of studies in Victorian literature for the ten years 1955–64. Urbana, Chicago and London 1967.
Hagen, O. A. In Who done it? A guide to detective, mystery and suspense fiction, 1969. Contains a comprehensive bibliography of mystery fiction 1841–1967.
Howard-Hill, T. H. Bibliography of British literary bibliographies. Oxford 1969, 1987 (rev).
Altick, R. D. and A. Wright. Selective bibliography for the study of English and American literature. New York 1971, 1975.
Clarke, I. F. The tale of the future: an annotated bibliography of those satires, ideal states, imaginary wars and invasions . . . that have been published in the United Kingdom between 1644 and 1970. 1971, 1972 (2nd edn), 1978 (3rd edn).
Gupta, B. K. India in English fiction 1800–1970. An annotated bibliography. Metuchen NJ 1973.
The 1890s. A literary exhibition. Sep 4–21 1973. Compiled by G. Krishnamurti. 1973.
The archives of British publishers on microfilm. lst and 2nd series. Bishop's Stortford 1974–5 (Chadwyck Healey).
Dyson, A. E. (ed). The English novel: select bibliographical guide. 1974.
Havlice, P. P. Index to literary biography. 2 vols Metuchen NJ 1975; suppl 2 vols 1983.
Jefferson, M. Victorian social fiction. An exhibition catalogue and list of other significant works. 1975.
James, L. (ed). In Print and the people 1819–51, 1976 (pbd in the US as English popular literature), Harmondsworth 1978.
McLean, R. In Joseph Cundall, a Victorian publisher. Notes on his life and a checklist of his books, Pinner 1976 (Private Libs Assoc).
Brown, P. A. H. Modern British and American private presses (1850–1965). Catalogue of holdings of the British Library. 1977.
Dowling, L. C. Aestheticism and decadence: a selective annotated bibliography. New York 1977.

Ingram, A. Index to the archives of Richard Bentley and son 1829–1898. Cambridge 1977.
Ford, G. H. (ed). Victorian fiction: a second guide to research. New York 1978.
Furlong, G. The archives of Routledge and Kegan Paul Ltd (1853–1973) publishers. A handlist. 1978.
Hasan, M. Nineteenth century English literary works, a bibliography of rare books available in India. Delhi 1978.
Storey, R. and L. Madden, Primary sources for Victorian studies: a guide to the location and use of unpublished materials. Chichester 1978.
Harris, W. V. British short fiction in the nineteenth century. A literary and bibliographic guide. Detroit 1979.
Hubin, A. J. Bibliography of crime fiction 1749–1975. San Diego 1979.
Morbey, C. C. F. In Charles Knight, an appreciation and bibliography of the work of a great Victorian publisher. Birmingham 1979.
Sargent, L. T. British and American Utopian literature 1516–1975. An annotated bibliography. Boston 1979.
Schlobin, R. C. The literature of fantasy. A comprehensive, annotated bibliography of modern fantasy fiction. New York and London 1979. Begins with Sara Coleridge.
Currey, L. W. and D. G. Hartwell. Science fiction and fantasy authors: a bibliography of first printings of their fiction and selected nonfiction. Boston 1980.
Harris, M. A. A checklist of the 'Three Decker' Collection in the Fisher Library, University of Sydney. Sydney 1980.
Thomas, S. (ed). Index to fiction in Time (1879–91, Murray's Magazine (1887–91) and the Quarto (1868–98). Victorian Fiction Research Guide 4. St Lucia, Queensland 1980.
Ellis, E. E. The British Museum in fiction. A checklist. Buffalo NY 1981.
Freeman, R. E. (ed). Bibliographies of studies in Victorian literature for the ten years 1965–1974. New York 1981.
Grimes, J. and D. Daims. Novels in English by women 1891–1920. A preliminary checklist. New York and London 1981.
Thomas, S. (ed). Indexes to fiction in Tinsley's Magazine, later The Novel Review 1867–1892. Victorian Fiction Research Guide 7. St Lucia, Queensland 1981.
Versteeg, M., S. Thomas and J. Huddleston. Index to fiction in The Lady's Realm. Victorian Fiction Research Guide 5. St Lucia, Queensland 1981.
Wolff, R. L. and K. F. Bruner. Nineteenth-century fiction. A bibliographical catalogue based on the collection of Robert Lee Wolff. 5 vols New York and London 1981–6.
Daims, D. and J. Grimes. Toward a feminist tradition. An annotated bibliography of novels in English by women 1891–1920. New York and London 1920.
Rosenbaum, B. et al (ed). Index of English literary manuscripts. Vol 4: 1800–1900. Pt 1 Arnold–Gissing. London and New York 1982; Pt 2 Hardy–Lamb, London and New York 1982; Pt 3 Landor–Patmore, London and New York 1993.
Schlobin, R. C. Urania's daughters: a checklist of women science fiction writers 1692–1982. Mercer Island WA 1983.
Thomas, S. (ed). Index to fiction in the Pall Mall Magazine 1893–1914. Victorian Fiction Research Guide 9. St Lucia, Queensland 1983.
Breen, J. L. Novel verdicts: a guide to courtroom fiction. 1984.
Carpenter, K. In Desert isles and pirate islands: the island theme in nineteenth-century English juvenile fiction: a survey and bibliography. Frankfurt am Main 1984.
Cross, N. (comp). Archives of the Royal Literary Fund 1790–1918. 1984. World Microfilms 124 reels.
Frank, F. S. Guide to the Gothic. An annotated bibliography of criticism. 1984.
Peterson, W. S. A bibliography of the Kelmscott Press. Oxford 1984.
Robinson, D. Women novelists 1891–1920. An index to biographical and autobiographical sources. 1984.
Thomas, S. (ed). Indexes to fiction in the Harmondsworth Magazine, later the London Magazine 1898–1915. Victorian Fiction Research Guide 10. St Lucia, Queensland 1984.
Albert, W. Detective and mystery fiction. An international bibliography of secondary sources. Madison IA 1985.
Huff, C. British women's diaries: a descriptive bibliography of selected nineteenth-century women's manuscript diaries. New York 1985.
Morgan, J. Victorian literature at St Deiniol's Library, a bibliography of poetry, plays and fiction 1837–1901. [Hawarden] 1985?
Menendez, A. The road to Rome: an annotated bibliography. 1986. Contains a list of novels depicting conversion to Rome.
Felmingham, M. The illustrated gift book 1880–1930, with a checklist of 2500 titles. Aldershot 1987.
Stewart, K. A. Scottish women writers to 1987, a select guide and bibliography. [Glasgow] 1987.
Thomas, S. Indexes to fiction in Cassell's Family Magazine, later Cassell's Magazine 1874–1910. Victorian Fiction Research Guide 12. St Lucia, Queensland 1987.
Edwards, P. D., I. G. Sibley, and M. Versteeg (ed). Indexes to fiction in Belgravia 1867–1899. Victorian Fiction Research Guide 14. St Lucia, Queensland 1988.
Hartman, D. K. and J. Drost. Themes and settings in fiction, a bibliography of bibliographies. New York and London 1988.
Murphy, M. C. Women writers and Australia, a bibliography of fiction nineteenth century to 1987. Parkville, Univ of Melbourne, 1988.
Todd, W. B. and A. Bowden. Tauchnitz international editions in English 1841–1955: a bibliographical history. New York 1988.
Bell, P. Victorian women: an index to biographies and memoirs. Edinburgh 1989.
Berrian, B. F. and A. Broek. Bibliography of women writers from the Caribbean 1831–1986. Washington 1989.
Carter, M. L. (ed). The vampire in literature: a critical bibliography. Ann Arbor MI 1989.
Davis, G. and B. A. Joyce. Personal writings by women to 1900, a bibliography of American and British writers. 1989.
Mazzeno, L. W. The Victorian novel: an annotated bibliography. 1989.
Thomas, S. Chambers's Journal 1854–1910. Indexes to Fiction. Victorian Fiction Research Guide 17. St Lucia, Queensland 1989.
Alston, R. C. A checklist of women writers 1801–1900. 1990.
Kirkpatrick, R. J. Bullies, beaks and flannelled fools: an annotated bibliography of boys' school fiction, 1742–1990. 1990.
Adelaide, D. Bibliography of Australian women's literature 1795–1990: a listing of fiction, poetry, drama and non-fiction. Port Melbourne, Australia 1991.
Hill, L. A new checklist of English-language fiction relating to Malaysia, Singapore and Brunei. [Hull] 1991.
Tobias, R. C. (ed). Bibliographies of studies in Victorian literature for the ten years 1975–1984. New York 1991.
Eliot, S. A measure of popularity: public library holdings of twenty-four popular authors 1883–1912. Bristol 1992.
Ruddick, N. British science fiction. A chronology, 1478–1990. 1992.
Weedon, A. Summary statistics for George Bell and Sons and the Bohn Libraries, 1865–1920. Bristol 1992.
Mendes, P. Clandestine erotic fiction in English 1800–1930. A bibliographical study. Aldershot 1993.
Topp, C. W. Victorian yellowbacks and paperbacks, 1849–1905. 1. George Routledge. Denver 1993.
Baldwin, D. and G. L. Morris. The short story in English. Britain and North America. An annotated bibliography. 1994.

Cox, S. B. Blood; a vampyric bibliography. Reading 1994.
Thesing, W. B. and B. Lewis (ed). Indexes to fiction in The Idler 1892–1911. St Lucia, Queensland 1994.
Murphy, R. C. The Wars of the Roses in fiction, an annotated bibliography 1440–1994. 1995.
Mazzeno, L. W. The British novel 1680–1832, an annotated bibliography. 1997.

(2) HISTORIES AND STUDIES

Barbauld, A. L. The British novelists: with an essay and prefaces, biographical and critical. 50 vols 1810.
Taylor, H. Novels of fashionable life. Quart Rev 48 1832.
Smith, W. H. The novel and the drama: some advice to an author. Blackwood's Mag June 1845.
Patmore, C. K. D. Popular serial literature. North Br Rev 7 1847.
Smith, I. G. Recent works of fiction. North Br Rev 15 1851.
Oliphant, M. O. Modern novelists – great and small. Blackwood's Mag May 1855.
Sensation novels. Blackwood's Mag May 1962.
Novels. Blackwood's Mag Aug 1863, Sep 1867.
New novels. Blackwood's Mag Sep 1880.
Recent novels. Blackwood's Mag Mar 1882.
Three young novelists. Blackwood's Mag Sep 1884. On F. M. Crawford, 'F. Anstey', J. F. Fargus.
Novels. Blackwood's Mag Dec 1886. On Children of Gibeon, Princess Casamassima, Sir Percival, A bachelor's blunder.
Stephen, J. F. The relation of novels to life. In Cambridge essays contributed by members of the University, 1855.
Sellar, W. Y. Religious novels. North Br Rev 26 1856.
Jeaffreson, J. C. Novels and novelists. 2 vols 1858.
Mansel, H. L. Sensation novels. Quart Rev 113 1863.
Smith, A. Novels and novelists of the day. North Br Rev 38 1863.
Senior, N. W. Essays on fiction. 1864. On Scott, Lytton, Thackeray.
Arnold, T. Recent novel writing. Macmillan's Mag Jan 1866.
Japp, A. H. Children and children's books. Contemporary Rev May 1869.
Mozley, A. On fiction as an educator. Blackwood's Mag Oct 1870.
Pollock, J. Novels of their times, I. Macmillan's Mag Aug–Sep 1872.
Brandes, G. Hovedstrømninger i det 19 aarhundredes litteratur. Copenhagen 1875; tr 6 vols 1901–2.
Shand, A. I. Recent Scotch novels. Edinburgh Rev 143 1876.
The new Scottish novelists. Edinburgh Rev 184 1896.
Watt, J. C. Great novelists: Scott, Thackeray, Dickens, Lytton. Edinburgh 1880.
Lanier, W. S. The English novel. New York 1883.
Ritchie, A. E. A book of sibyls: Mrs Barbauld, Mrs Opie, Miss Edgeworth, Miss Austen. 1883.
Blackstick papers. 1908.
Besant, W. The art of fiction. 1884. Reply by James 1888, *below*.
Hillebrand, K. About old and new novels. Contemporary Rev Mar 1884.
Hope, Eva. Queens of literature of the Victorian era. 1886.
Morris, M. W. Some thoughts about novels. Macmillan's Mag Mar 1887.
Candour in English fiction. Macmillan's Mag Feb 1890.
James, H. The art of fiction. In his Partial portraits, 1888; rptd in his House of fiction, ed L. Edel, 1957.
The new novel. In his Notes on novelists, 1914; rptd in James and H. G. Wells, ed L. Edel and G. N. Ray, 1958.
Saintsbury, G. Names in fiction. Macmillan's Mag Dec 1888.
The present state of the English novel. In his Miscellaneous essays, 1892
The historical novel. Macmillan's Mag Aug–Oct 1894; rptd in his Essays, 1895.
A history of nineteenth-century literature. 1896.
Novels of university life. Macmillan's Mag March 1898.
The English novel. 1913.
Hitchman, F. Penny fiction. Quart Rev 171 1890.
Howells, W. D. Criticism and fiction. London and New York 1891; ed C. and R. Kirk, [New York] 1959.
MacColl, M. Morality in fiction. Contemporary Rev Aug 1891.
Hamilton, C. J. Women writers: their works and ways. 2 ser 1892–3.
Walford, L. B. Twelve English authoresses. 1892.
Wedgwood, F. J. Fiction and faith. Contemporary Rev Aug 1892.
Black, H. C. Notable women authors of the day. Glasgow 1893; rptd 1906, 1974.
Crawford, F. M. The novel. 1893.
Gosse, E. Questions at issue. 1893. Includes The tyranny of the novel, The limits of realism in fiction.
Edwards, A. A. B. The art of the novelist. Contemporary Rev Aug 1894.
Lyall, A. C. Novels of adventure and manners. Quart Rev 179 1894; rptd in his Studies in literature and history, 1915.
Mayer, Gertrude Townsend. Women of letters. 2 vols 1894.
Minto, W. The literature of the Georgian era. 1894. Includes novelists from Mrs Radcliffe to Bulwer-Lytton.
My first book. Ed J. K. Jerome 1894. Essays by Besant, Payn, Russell, Allen, Hall Caine, Ballantyne, Kipling, Stevenson, Marie Corelli and other novelists.
On the art of writing fiction. [1894.] Essays by Baring-Gould, 'Lanoe Falconer', L. T. Meade et al.
Bridges, R. Novels that everybody read. In his Suppressed chapters and other bookishness, New York 1895.
Harrison, F. Studies in early Victorian literature. 1895. On Disraeli, Thackeray, Dickens, C. Brontë, C. Kingsley, Trollope, George Eliot.
Lilly, W. S. Four English humourists of the nineteenth century. 1895. On Dickens, Thackeray, George Eliot, Carlyle.
Noble, J. A. The fiction of sexuality. Contemporary Rev Apr 1895.
Douglas, G. The Blackwood group. 1897.
Gregg, H. C. The Indian Mutiny in fiction. Blackwood's Mag Feb 1897.
Early Victorian fiction. Blackwood's Mag May 1897.
The medical woman in fiction. Blackwood's Mag July 1898.
Murray, D. C. My contemporaries in fiction. 1897. Dickens to George Moore.
Traill, H. D. The new fiction. 1897. Rptd essays, mainly on 19th-century fiction.
Women novelists of Queen Victoria's reign. 1897. Appreciations by A. Sergeant, C. M. Yonge et al.
Scudder, V. D. Social ideals in English letters. Boston and New York 1898, 1923 (enlarged).
Cross, W. L. The development of the English novel. New York 1899.
Lyall, A. C. The Anglo-Indian novelist. Edinburgh Rev 190 1899; rptd in his Asiatic studies, 1907.
Oliphant, J. Victorian novelists. 1899.
Gwynn, S. L. Some recent novels of manners. Edinburgh Rev 192 1900.
Beers, H. A. A history of English romanticism in the nineteenth century. New York 1901, London 1902.
Brownell, W. C. Victorian prose masters. New York 1902.
Machen, A. Hieroglyphics. 1902, 1960.
Möbius, H. The Gothic romance. Leipzig 1902.
Die englischen Rosenkreuzerromane und ihre Vorlaüfer, während des 18 und 19 Jahrhunderts. Hamburg 1911.
Cazamian, L. Le roman social en Angleterre 1830–50. Paris 1904, 1935, London 1973 (tr with a foreword by M. Fido). On Dickens, Disraeli, Mrs Gaskell, Charles Kingsley.
L'influence de la science 1860–90. Strasburg 1923.
L'anti-intellectualisme et l'esthéticisme 1880–1900. Paris 1935.
Les doctrines d'action et l'aventure 1880–1914. Paris 1955.

Courtney, W. L. The feminine note in fiction. 1904.
Dawson, W. J. Makers of English Fiction. 1905.
Stevenson, R. L. Essays in the art of writing. 1905.
'Melville, Lewis' (L. S. Benjamin). Victorian novelists. 1906.
Baker, E. A. History in fiction. 2 vols 1907, London and New York 1914 (rev as A guide to historical fiction), New York 1969.
The history of the English novel. 9 vols 1924–38 (vols 5–9).
Chandler, F. W. The literature of roguery. 2 vols Boston 1907.
Courtney, W. P. The secrets of our national literature. 1908. Anon and pseudonymous fiction.
Jackson, H. Great English novelists. [1908.]
The eighteen-nineties: a review of art and ideas at the close of the nineteenth century. 1913.
Canby, H. S. The short story in English. New York 1909.
Zeidler, K. J. Beckford, Hope und Morier als Vertreter des orientalischen Romans. Leipzig 1909.
Dibelius, W. Englische Romankunst. 2 vols Berlin 1910.
Phelps, W. L. Essays on modern novelists. New York 1910.
The advance of the English novel. New York 1916.
Williams, H. Two centuries of the English novel. 1911.
Modern English writers. 1918, 1925 (rev).
Johnson, R. B. Famous reviews. 1914.
The women novelists. 1918.
Novelists on novels. 1928.
Gregory, A. The French Revolution and the English novel. New York and London 1915.
Waugh, A. Fiction in the nineteenth century. In his Reticence in literature and other papers, 1915.
Tradition and change. 1919.
Hearn, L. Interpretations of literature. 2 vols 1916. 2 chs in vol 1 on English fiction in the 19th century.
Scarborough, D. The supernatural in modern English fiction. 1917.
Whiteford, R. N. Motives in English fiction. New York and London 1918.
Phillips, W. C. Dickens, Reade and Collins – sensation novelists: a study in the conditions and theories of novel writing in Victorian England. New York 1919, rptd 1968.
Russell, F. T. Satire in the Victorian novel. New York 1920.
Bald, M. Woman writers of the nineteenth century. Cambridge 1923.
Cruse, A. The Englishman and his books in the early nineteenth century. 1930.
Ford, F. M. The English novel. 1930.
Gibson, B. H. History from 1800–32 of English criticism of prose fiction. Urbana IL 1931.
Leavis, Q. D. Fiction and the reading public. 1932, 1965, Harmondsworth 1979.
Lovett, R. M. and H. S. Hughes. The history of the novel in England. Boston 1932.
Watt, W. W. Shilling shockers of the Gothic school: a study of chapbook Gothic romances. Cambridge MA 1932.
Edgar, P. The art of the novel. New York 1933.
Cruse, A. The Victorians and their books. 1935, 1936, 1962, 1968. (Pbd in US as The Victorians and their reading.)
Kunitz, S. J. and H. Haycraft (ed). British authors of the nineteenth century. New York 1936.
Shepperson, A. B. The novel in motley: a history of the burlesque novel in English. Cambridge MA 1936.
Fox, R. The novel and the people. 1937, 1944, New York 1945, London 1948.
Utter, R. O. and G. B. Needham. Pamela's daughters. New York 1937, 1972.
Summers, M. The Gothic quest. 1938.
Marriott, J. English history in English fiction. London and Glasgow 1940.
Bentley, P. The English regional novel. 1941.
Taylor, J. T. Early opposition to the English novel: the popular reaction from 1760 to 1830. New York 1943.
Wagenknecht, E. Cavalcade of the English novel 1850–1919. New York 1943, 1954 (rev).
Hinkley, L. L. Ladies of literature. New York 1946.
McCullough, B. Representative English novelists. New York 1946.
Stebbins, L. P. A Victorian album: some lady novelists of the period. 1946.
McCarthy, B. A. The later women novelists 1744–1818. Cork 1947.
Parkinson, C. L. Portsmouth Point: the British navy in fiction. Liverpool 1948.
Drummond, A. L. The churches in English fiction. Leicester 1950.
Walbank, F. A. Queens of the circulating library. 1950.
Church, R. The growth of the English novel. 1951, 1961.
Neill, S. D. A short history of the English novel. 1951.
Allen, W. The English novel; a short critical history. 1954, Harmondsworth 1958, 1960 etc.
Altick, R. D. The English common reader: a social history of the mass reading public, 1800–1900. Chicago 1957, 1963.
Dalziel, M. Popular fiction a hundred years ago. 1957.
Proctor, M. R. The English university novel. Berkeley CA 1957.
Varma, D. P. The Gothic flame. 1957, New York 1966.
Stevenson, W. B. Detective fiction. Cambridge 1958.
Flanagan, T. The Irish novelists 1800–50. New York 1959.
Stang, R. The theory of the novel in England 1850–70. 1959.
Rosenberg, E. From Shylock to Svengali: Jewish criminal and paragon in the English novel 1795–1895. Stanford CA 1960, London 1961.
Stevenson, L. English novel: a panorama. 1960.
Maison, M. Search your soul, Eustace; a survey of the religious novel in the Victorian age. 1961.
Freeman, W. Dictionary of fictional characters. 2 vols 1963, 1967, 1973 (rev by F. Urquhart).
James, L. Fiction for the working man, 1830–1850: a study of the literature produced for the working classes in early Victorian urban England. 1963, Harmondsworth 1974.
Carrier, E. J. Fiction in public libraries 1876–1900. New York 1965.
Graham, K. English criticism of the novel 1865–1900. Oxford 1965.
Karl, F. R. An age of fiction: the nineteenth-century British novel. New York 1965.
Marcus, S. The other Victorians: a study of sexuality and pornography in mid-nineteenth-century England. 1966, 1969.
Chew, S. C. and R. D. Altick. The nineteenth century and after, 1789–1939. In A literary history of England vol 4, ed A. C. Baugh, New York 1967.
Hagen, O. A. Who done it? A guide to detective, mystery and suspense fiction. 1969.
Colby, V. The singular anomaly. Women novelists of the nineteenth century. New York 1970.
Griest, G. L. Mudie's circulating library and the Victorian novel. Newton Abbot 1970.
Harvey, J. R. Victorian novelists and their illustrators. 1970.
Pollard, A. (ed). The Victorians. 1969, 1970 etc (Sphere History of literature in the English language vol 6).
Keating, P. J. The working classes in Victorian fiction. 1971, 1979.
Kettle, A. (ed). The nineteenth century novel, critical essays and documents. 1972, 1981 (rev).
Altick, R. D. Victorian people and ideas: a companion for the modern reader of Victorian literature. New York [1973], London 1974.
Hardison, O. B. (ed). The British novel: Scott through Hardy. Northbrook IL 1973.
Vicinus, M. The industrial muse: a study of nineteenth century British working class literature. 1974.
Attenborough, J. A living memory: Hodder and Stoughton publishers, 1868–1975. 1975.

Barnes, M. Best detective fiction: a guide from Godwin to the present. 1975.
Cunningham, V. Everywhere spoken against: dissent in the Victorian novel. Oxford 1975.
Kovacevic, I. Fact into fiction: English literature and the industrial scene 1750–1850. Leicester 1975.
Rance, N. The historical novel and popular politics in nineteenth century England. 1975.
Singh, B. A survey of Anglo-Indian fiction. 1975.
Street, B. V. The savage in literature: representations of 'primitive' society in English fiction 1858–1920. 1975.
Cadogan, M. and P. Craig. You're a brick, Angela!: a new look at girls' fiction from 1839–1975. 1976.
Ousby, I. Bloodhounds of heaven: the detective in English fiction from Godwin to Doyle. Cambridge MA 1976.
Sutherland, J. Victorian novelists and publishers. 1976.
Newburg, V. E. Popular literature: a history and guide. 1977.
Wolff, R. L. Gains and losses: novels of faith and doubt in Victorian England. 1977.
Hogan, R. (ed). Dictionary of Irish literature. 1978, 2 vols Westport CT 1996 (rev).
Sutherland, J. Fiction and the fiction industry. 1978.
Olmsted, J. C. (ed). A Victorian art of fiction: essays on the novel in British periodicals, 1830–1850. 1979.
Punter, D. The literature of terror. A history of Gothic fictions from 1765 to the present day. 1979.
Wilson, H. W. and D. L. Hoeveler. English prose and criticism in the nineteenth century. A guide to information sources. Detroit 1979.
Cronin, J. The Anglo-Irish novel. The nineteenth century. Belfast and New York 1980.
Gretton, T. Murders and moralities: English catchpenny prints, 1800–1860. 1980.
Harris, L. L. et al. Nineteenth century literature criticism: excerpts from criticism of the works of novelists, poets, playwrights, etc ... 1800–1900. Detroit 1981– .
Mussel, K. Women's Gothic and romantic fiction: a reference guide. Westport CT 1981.
Quigley, I. The heirs of Tom Brown: the English school story. 1982.
Bleiler, E. F. The guide to supernatural fiction ... 1750–1960. New York 1983.
Nadel, I. B. and W. E. Fredeman (ed). Victorian novelists after 1885. DLB vol 18, Detroit 1983.
Nadel, I. B. and W. E. Fredeman (ed). Victorian novelists before 1885. DLB vol 21, Detroit 1983.
Royle, T. The Macmillan companion to Scottish literature. 1983.
Terry, R. C. Victorian popular fiction 1860–1880. 1983.
Cross, Nigel (comp). Archives of the Royal Literary Fund 1790–1918. 1984. World Microfilms 124 reels.
Engel, E. and M. King. The Victorian novel before Victoria. 1984.
Brown, J. P. A reader's guide to the nineteenth century English novel. New York 1985.
Cross, Nigel. The common writer: life in nineteenth century Grub Street. Cambridge 1985.
Eigner, E. M. and G. Worth (ed). Victorian criticism of the novel. Cambridge 1985.
Staley, T. F. (ed). British novelists 1890–1929: modernists. DLB vol 36, Detroit 1985.
Staley, T. F. (ed). British novelists 1890–1929: traditionalists. DLB vol 34, Detroit 1985.
Vann, J. D. Victorian novels in serial. New York 1985.
Wheeler, M. English fiction of the Victorian period 1830–1890. 1985.
Barnes, M. Murder in print. A guide to two centuries of crime fiction. 1986.
Donaldson, W. Popular literature in Victorian Scotland: language, fiction and the press. Aberdeen 1986.
Gilmour, R. The novel in the Victorian age: a modern introduction. 1986.
Nathan, R. B. Nineteenth century women writers of the English-speaking world. New York 1986.
Flint, K. (ed). The Victorian novelist: social problems and social change. 1987.
Muresianu, S. A. The history of the Victorian Christmas book. New York 1987.
Thesing, W. B. (ed). Victorian prose writers after 1867. DLB vol 57, Detroit 1987.
Thesing, W. B. (ed). Victorian prose writers before 1867. DLB vol 55, Detroit 1987.
Benstock, B. and T. F. Staley (ed). British mystery writers 1860–1919. DLB vol 70, Detroit 1988.
Schlueter, P. and J. Schleuter (ed). An encyclopaedia of British women writers. New York 1988.
Sutherland, J. The Longman companion to Victorian fiction. 1988.
Keating, P. The haunted study: a social history of the English novel 1875–1914. 1989.
Todd, J. (ed). British women writers. A critical reference guide. New York 1989.
Blain, V., P. Clements and I. Grundy. The feminist companion to literature in English. Women writers from the Middle Ages to the present. 1990.
Horsman, A. The Victorian novel. Oxford History of English Literature vol 13, Oxford 1990.
Altick, R. D. The presence of the present: topics of the day in the Victorian novel. Columbus OH 1991.
Anderson, P. J. and J. Rose (ed). British literary publishing houses, 1820–1880. Detroit 1991.
Greenfield, J. R. (ed). British romantic prose writers 1789–1832. First series. DLB vol 107, Detroit 1991.
Greenfield, J. R. (ed). British romantic prose writers 1789–1832. Second series. DLB vol 110, Detroit 1991.
Hughes, L. K. and M. Lund. The Victorian serial. 1991.
Turner, A. K. Victorian criticism of American writers; a guide to British criticism of American writers ... 1824–1900. San Bernardino CA 1991.
Dooley, A. Author and printer in Victorian England. 1992.
Eliot, S. A measure of popularity: public library holdings of twenty-four popular authors 1883–1912. Bristol 1992.
Mudge, B. K. (ed). British romantic novelists 1789–1832. DLB vol 116, Detroit 1992.
Propas, S. W. Victorian studies: a research guide. New York 1992.
Shattock, J. The Oxford guide to British women writers. Oxford 1993, 1994 (rev).
Trotter, D. The English novel in history 1895–1920. 1993.
Eliot, S. Some patterns and trends in British publishing 1800–1919. 1994.
Flint, K. The woman reader 1837–1914. Oxford 1994.
Murphy, P. T. Toward a working-class canon: literary criticism in British working class periodicals 1816–1858. Columbus OH 1994.
Serafin, S. (ed). Nineteenth century British literary biographers. DLB vol 144, Detroit 1994.
Thesing, W. B. (ed). British short fiction writers 1880–1914: the realist tradition. DLB vol 135, Detroit 1994.
Zaidman, L. M. (ed). British children's writers 1880–1914. DLB vol 141, Detroit 1994.
Johnson, G. M. (ed). Late Victorian and Edwardian British novelists. First series. DLB vol 153, Detroit 1995.
Kelley, G. and E. Applegate (ed). British reform writers 1789–1832. DLB vol 158, Detroit 1995.
Naufftus, W. F. (ed). British short fiction writers 1880–1914: the romantic tradition. DLB vol 156, Detroit 1995.
Serafin, S. (ed). Late nineteenth and early twentieth century British literary biographers. DLB vol 149, Detroit 1995.

Sutherland, J. Victorian fiction, writers, publishers, readers. Basingstoke 1995.
Brothers, B. and J. Gergits (ed). British travel writers 1837–1875. DLB vol 166, Detroit 1996.
Erickson, L. The economy of literary form: English literature and the industrialisation of publishing, 1800–1850. 1996.
Greenfield, J. R. (ed). British short fiction writers 1800–1880. DLB vol 159, Detroit 1996.
Khorana, M. (ed). British children's writers 1800–1880. DLB vol 163, Detroit 1996.
Nelson, C. C. British women fiction writers of the 1890s. New York 1996.

ii. The early nineteenth-century novel 1800–1835

This section has been restricted, with few exceptions, to writers born between 1760 and 1800.

John Agg, 'Humphrey Hedgehog', 'Jeremiah Juvenal', 'Peter Pindar Jun.'

§1

The dawn of liberty on the continent of Europe: or the struggle of the Spanish patriots for the emancipation of their country. Bristol 1808.
Mac Dermot, or the Irish chieftain: a romance intended as a companion to the Scottish chiefs. 3 vols 1810.
The royal sufferer, or intrigues at the close of the eighteenth century: a fashionable novel interspersed with anecdotes connected with the British Court. 3 vols 1810.
Edwy and Elgiva: an historical romance of the tenth century. 4 vols 1811.
The ghost of 'r—l stripes', by Jeremiah Juvenal. London 1812, 1812 (3rd edn), 1812 (5th edn). Poem.
Three r—l bloods: a poem by Peter Pindar jun. 1812, 1812 (3rd edn), 1812 (4th edn), 1812 (5th edn), 1812 (7th edn), 1812 (8th edn), 1812 (9th edn), 1813 (12th edn), 1813 (13th edn), 1814 (15th edn).
The r—l lover, or a d-ke defeated: a poem by Peter Pindar. 1812, 1812 (10th edn), 1812 (11th edn), 1813 (15th edn, with addns), 1813 (16th edn).
The r—l sprain: an ode by Humphrey Hedgehog. 1812.
Turning out, or St S—'s in an uproar: a poem by Peter Pindar jun. 1812.
The r—l mystery, or the secrets of an illustrious family: a poem by Humphrey Hedgehog. [1813?] (4th edn), 1813 (6th edn).
Rejected odes, or poetical hops, steps and jumps of a dozen popular bards for the obtainment of the situation of poet laureate: with a preface shewing how they came into the hands of the editor, Humphrey Hedgehog. 1813.
The secret memoirs of an illustrious princess, or the royal sufferer, interspersed with singular anecdotes of those personages connected with the court of Alb: a political, amatory and fashionable work. 3 vols 1813.
The general post-bag, or news! foreign and domestic: to which is added La bagatelle. By Humphrey Hedgehog esq. 1814, 1814, 1815 (with addns). Poems.
A month in town: a satirical novel by Humphrey Hedgehog esq. 3 vols 1814, 1815, 1816 (corrected with a new preface).
A month at Brussels: a satirical novel. 3 vols 1815.
The London bazaar, or where to get cheap things: a humorous pindaric poem by Humphrey Hedgehog esq. [1816.]
Eighteen hundred and fifteen: a satirical novel by Humphrey Hedgehog esq. 3 vols 1816.
Lord Byron's farewell to England: with three other poems. 1816, 1816, Philadelphia 1816.
The secret memoirs of a prince: or a peep behind the scenes. 1816.
Lord Byron's pilgrimage to the Holy Land: a poem. '1817' [1816], 1817 (as A pilgrimage to the Holy Land), Philadelphia 1817.
The pavilion, or a month in Brighton: a satirical novel by Humphrey Hedgehog esq. 3 vols 1817.
The ocean harp: a poem in two cantos with some smaller pieces. Philadelphia 1819.
History of Congress: exhibiting a classification of the proceedings of the Senate and the House of Representatives. Philadelphia 1834 and 1843.
Proceedings of the Convention of the Commonwealth of Pennsylvania, to propose amendments to the Constitution. 14 vols Harrisburg PA 1837–8; tr Ger [also Harrisburg] 1837–9.

Attributed or spurious works

The elegant sharper: or the science of villainy display'd. By Peter Pindar jun. 1804. Also attributed to C. F. Lawler.
The r—l brood, or an illustrious hen and her pretty chickens: a poem by Peter Pindar jun. 1813, 1813 (3rd edn), 1813 (4th edn), 1813 (5th edn), 1813 (9th edn), 1813 (11th edn), 1813 (13th edn), 1814 (15th edn). Also attributed to C. F. Lawler.
The r—l fowls, or the old black cock's attempt to crow over his illustrious mate: a poem by the author of The r—l brood. 1820, 1820, 1820, 1820, 1820, 1820 (6th edn), 1820 (9th edn), 1820 (10th edn).
The old black cock and his dunghill advisers in jeopardy: the palace that Jack built, by the author of The r—l fowls. 1820 (6 edns). Verse satire.

Agg also edited two periodical works, Town talk, *[1811], and* The Busy body, *1816–18.*

For a listing of reviews and notices of Agg's works, see Ward (1972), and (of his poetry) J. R. de J. Jackson, Annals of English verse *(1985).* [PG]

Jane Austen 1775–1817

Principal repositories of ms materials are the Bodleian (Volume the first), *the BL* (Volume the second, Volume the third, *and 2 draft chs of* Persuasion), *the Pierpont Morgan Lib, New York* (Lady Susan, *the 1st six leaves of* The Watsons *and over 50 letters), and King's College, Cambridge* (Sanditon). *Other significant holdings are in Fitzwilliam Museum, and Univ Lib, Cambridge; Winchester City Museum; and Bibliotheca Bodmeriana, Cologny-Genève. For general listing of surviving mss, see* IELM vol 4 pt 1 1982. *Detailed information about the locations of ms letters can be found in Modert and Le Faye's edns (see below, §1). Articles about ms holdings in individual collections are included in §2.*

Bibliographies and reference works

Keynes, Sir G. Jane Austen: a bibliography. 1929; rptd New York 1968, Folcroft PA 1969, Norwood PA 1976.
Apperson, G. L. A Jane Austen dictionary. 1932; rptd New York 1968, Folcroft PA 1973, Norwood PA 1976.
Chapman, R. W. Jane Austen: a critical bibliography. Oxford 1953, 1955 (2nd edn); rptd 1969.
Pinion, F. B. A Jane Austen companion: a critical survey and reference book. London 1973.
Roth, B. and J. C. Weinsheimer. An annotated bibliography of Jane Austen studies, 1952–1972. Charlottesville VA 1973.
De Rose, P. and S. W. McGuire. A concordance to the works of Jane Austen. New York 1982.
Gilson, D. J. A bibliography of Jane Austen. Oxford 1982 (Soho Bibliographies ser), rptd Winchester 1997 (with new introd and corrections).
Roth, B. An annotated bibliography of Jane Austen studies, 1973–1983. Charlottesville VA 1985.

Grey, J. D. The Jane Austen handbook. 1986.
Gilson, D. J. and J. D. Grey. Jane Austen's juvenilia and Lady Susan: an annotated bibliography. In Jane Austen's beginnings: the juvenilia and Lady Susan, ed J. D. Grey, Ann Arbor MI 1989.
Roth, B. An annotated bibliography of Jane Austen studies, 1984–1994. Athens OH 1996.

Collections

Novels by Miss Jane Austen. 5 vols (vol 1 Sense and sensibility, with a memoir by Henry Austen dated 5 Oct 1832; vol 2 Pride and prejudice; vol 3 Emma; vol 4 Mansfield Park; vol 5 Northanger Abbey, and Persuasion), 1833, 1856, 1866; 2 vols Philadelphia 1838; Steventon edn, 6 vols (vol 6 the 1871 Memoir) London 1882, 1886; Routledge sixpenny novels, 1884; ed R. B. Johnson 10 vols 1892, 1898; 12 vols Boston 1892; Winchester edn, 10 vols London 1898; Temple edn, 10 vols 1899; Hampshire edn, ed R. B. Johnson 6 vols 1902; Old manor house edn, ed R. B. Johnson 10 vols New York 1906; ed R. B. Johnson 10 vols London 1908–9; 6 vols 1922; Adelphi edn, 7 vols 1923; Oxford edn, ed R. W. Chapman 5 vols Oxford 1923, 1926 (2nd edn), 1933 (3rd edn), etc (with alterations to notes by M. Lascelles in reprintings 1965–6), 6 vols (vol 6 Minor works) 1954 etc, 1988, 1994 (ET); Georgian edn, 5 vols London 1927; 7 vols 1933–4; Chawton edn, 6 vols 1948; Folio Jane Austen, 6 vols 1975; ed D. J. Gilson and L. Ross 19 vols 1994 (Novels, Letters, and Memoir; facs of original edns).

§1

Volume the first. Ed R. W. Chapman, Oxford 1933; rptd with new preface by B. C. Southam 1984.
Volume the second. Ed G. K. Chesterton 1922 (as Love and freindship and other early works); ed B. C. Southam, Oxford 1963; tr Ital 1979 (as Amore & amicizia e altri romanzi).
Love and freindship and other early works. Ed G. Killalea 1978. Mostly items from Volume the second.
Love and freindship. Ed J. McMaster, Edmonton 1995.
The history of England, by a partial, prejudiced and ignorant historian. 1962, Toronto 1966, Kettering [1977]; ed D. Le Faye London 1993 (ms facs); ed J. Fergus, Edmonton 1995. From Volume the second.
Volume the third. Ed R. W. Chapman, Oxford 1951.
The 3 ms notebooks contain transcripts of virtually all the juvenilia c. 1787–93, entered and corrected until c. 1809.
The juvenilia of Jane Austen and Charlotte Brontë. Ed F. Beer 1986 (Pen). Selection.
Catharine and other writings. Ed M. A. Doody and D. Murray, Oxford 1993 (WCp). Collection of juvenilia, verse and ms fragments.
Sir Charles Grandison: or the happy man. Ed B. Southam (as Jane Austen's 'Sir Charles Grandison'), Oxford 1980, Burford 1981 (with ms facs). Ms adaptation of S. Richardson's novel, in 5 acts, probably begun c. 1791–2 and completed c. 1800.
Charades written a hundred years ago by Jane Austen and her family. [Ed M. A. Austen-Leigh?] [1895]; rptd Folcroft PA 1972. 3 of the 22 by Jane Austen.
Lady Susan. Ed J. E. Austen-Leigh 1871 (in Memoir (*see below*)); New York 1882 (with The Watsons); ed R. W. Chapman, Oxford 1925, London 1984 (new preface by B. C. Southam); ed R. B. Johnson 1931; ed R. B. Johnson 1934 (with The Watsons and Sanditon); ed J. Bailey 1939 (with The Watsons); ed Q. D. Leavis 1958 (with Sense and sensibility and The Watsons); ed M. Drabble 1974 (with The Watsons and Sanditon); ed J. Davie (with Northanger Abbey, The Watsons and Sanditon), Oxford 1980, with introd by T. Castle 1990 (WCp); ed A. W. Litz, New York and London 1989 (ms facs, with facs of 1925 ptd edn); tr Danish 1945, Ger 1964, Fr 1980, Sp 1984. Probably composed c. 1794–5, fair copy by the author c. 1805.
The Watsons. Ed J. E. Austen-Leigh 1871 (in Memoir); ed A. B. Walkley 1923; ed R. W. Chapman, Oxford 1927, London 1985 (new preface by B. C. Southam); ed R. B. Johnson 1934 (with Lady Susan and Sanditon); ed J. Bailey 1939 (with Lady Susan); ed Q. D. Leavis 1958 (with Sense and sensibility and Lady Susan); ed M. Drabble 1974 (with Lady Susan and Sanditon); ed J. Davie (with Northanger Abbey, Lady Susan and Sanditon), Oxford 1980, with introd by T. Castle 1990 (WCp); tr Fr 1980. Fragment of c. 17,500 words, probably written c. 1803–5.
Minor works. Ed R. W. Chapman 1954, 1963 (rev), 1969 (rev B. C. Southam); tr Fr 1984 (as Juvenilia et autres textes). Vol 6 of Works 1954; collected edn of juvenilia, early works, verse and the ms fragments.
Sense and sensibility: a novel, by a lady. 3 vols 1811, 1813 (corrected), Bentley's Standard Novels 23 1833 (rptd 1837, 1846, 1853, 1854), 2 vols Philadelphia 1833, 2 vols London 1844, 1 vol Philadelphia 1845, London 1849, 1851 (with Pride and prejudice), New York 1856, 1857 (with Persuasion), Boston 1863 (with Persuasion), Leipzig 1864 (Tauchnitz), London 1870, 1870, New York 1880, London [1883], 1886, [1887]; ed A. Dobson 1896; ed J. Jacobs 1899; ed R. B. Johnson [1906] (EL); [1908], 1908, 1908; ed Lord D. Cecil 1931 (WC); ed P. Quennell 1933; ed R. Church 1958; ed Q. D. Leavis 1958 (with Lady Susan and The Watsons); ed I. Watt, New York 1961; ed M. Lascelles, London 1962 (EL), with introd by P. Conrad 1978; ed T. Tanner 1969 (Pen); ed J. Kinsley and C. Lamont 1970 (Oxford Eng Novels); ed W. A. Craik 1972 (Pan Classics); ed M. Drabble 1989 (Virago Classics); ed J. Kinsley, with introd by M. A. Doody, Oxford 1991 (WCp); ed R. Ballaster 1995 (Pen); tr Fr 1815, 1828, 1945, 1948, 1948, Danish 1855–6, Du 1922, 1971, Cz 1932, 1986, Polish 1934, 1977, Sp 1942, 1946, Portuguese 1943, 1944, 1961, Ital 1945, 1951, 1957, 1961, 1961, Turkish 1946–8, 1969, Finnish 1952, Jap 1952, Bengali 1953, Serbo-Croat 1959, Swed 1959, Ger 1972, 1982, 1984, Romanian 1972, Hungarian 1986.
REVIEWS: Br Critic 39 1812; Critical Rev 4th ser 1 1812.
Pride and prejudice: a novel. 3 vols 1813, 1813, 2 vols 1817, Philadelphia 1832 (as Elizabeth Bennet), Bentley's Standard Novels 30 London 1833 (rptd 1836, 1839, 1846, 1853, 1854), 2 vols 1844, 1 vol Philadelphia 1845, Boston 1848, London 1849, 1851 (with Sense and sensibility), New York 1855, 1857 (with Northanger Abbey), Boston 1864 (with Northanger Abbey), London 1870, 1870, Leipzig 1870 (Tauchnitz), London [1877], New York 1880, London [1883], [1885], [1887]; ed G. Saintsbury 1894; ed A. Dobson 1895; ed E. V. Lucas 1900; ed W. K. Leask [1900]; ed R. B. Johnson [1906] (EL); 1907, [1907], 1908, 1908; ed K. M. Metcalfe 1912; ed W. D. Howells, New York [1918]; ed R. W. Chapman, London 1929 (WC); ed E. Bowen 1948; ed V. S. Pritchett 1952; ed M. Schorer, Boston 1956; ed R. Church, London 1957; Moscow 1961; ed B. A. Booth, New York 1963; ed M. Lascelles, London 1963 (EL), with introd by P. Conrad 1978; ed D. J. Gray, New York 1966 (Norton Critical edns); ed B. Brophy, London 1967 (rptd Pan Classics 1971); ed F. W. Bradbrook and J. Kinsley 1970 (Oxford Eng Novels), with introd by I. Armstrong 1990 (WCp); ed T. Tanner 1972 (Pen); ed J. Grey, New York 1982; ed M. Drabble London 1989 (Virago Classics); ed P. Norris 1993; ed V. Jones 1996 (Pen); tr Fr 1822, 1822, 1932, 1945, 1946, 1946, 1947, 1948, 1954, Ger 1830, 1939, 1948, 1948, 1951, 1965, 1976, 1977, Swed 1920, 1953, 1968, Finnish 1922, 1947, Sp 1924, 1943, 1944, 1945, 1946, 1946, 1956, 1956, 1959, 1963, 1967, 1970, 1970, 1973, 1973, Danish 1928–30, 1952, Norwegian 1930, 1947, 1973, Ital 1932, 1934, 1945, 1950, 1952, 1952, 1956, 1957, 1958, 1958, 1959, 1959, 1966, 1967, 1968, 1974, 1975, Portuguese 1941, 1943, 1949, 1956, 1970, 1975, Cz 1946, 1949, 1967, 1968, Du 1946, 1964, 1969, Greek 1950, Jap 1950, 1960, 1968, 1969, Thai 1950, Turkish 1950, 1968, 1972, Hebrew 1952, Bengali 1953, Serbo-Croat 1953, 1964, Icelandic 1956, Polish 1956, Tamil 1957, Chinese 1958, 1961, 1964, Hungarian 1958, Korean 1958, Persian 1958, Rus 1967, Romanian 1969, Arabic 1970.
REVIEWS: Br Critic 41 1813; Critical Rev 4th ser 3 1813; New Rev or Monthly Analysis of General Lit 1 1813.
Mansfield Park: a novel. 3 vols 1814, 1816 (corrected), 2 vols

Philadelphia 1832, Bentley's Standard Novels 27 London 1833 (rptd 1837, 1847, 1853, 1854), 1 vol Philadelphia 1845, Belfast 1846, London 1851, 1857, New York 1857, Boston 1863, Leipzig 1867 (Tauchnitz), London 1870, 1870, [1875], [1876], 1881, New York 1881, London [1883], 1885, [1889], [1895]; ed A. Dobson 1897; ed R. B. Johnson [1906] (EL); 1908, 1909, 1912, [1924]; ed M. Lascelles 1929 (WC); ed G. B. Stern 1953; ed Q. D. Leavis 1957; ed R. Church 1959; ed M. Lascelles 1963 (EL), with introd by P. Conrad 1978; ed R. A. Brower, Boston 1965; ed T. Tanner, London 1966 (Pen); ed J. Kinsley and J. Lucas 1970 (Oxford Eng Novels), with introd by M. Butler 1990 (WCp); ed M. Dickens and W. A. Craik 1972 (Pan Classics); ed M. Drabble 1989 (Virago Classics); ed P. Norris 1993; ed K. Sutherland 1996 (Pen); ed C. L. Johnson, New York 1997 (Norton Critical edn); tr Fr 1816, 1945, 1981, Portuguese 1942, Sp 1943, 1954, Finnish 1954, Serbo-Croat 1956, Ital 1961, 1962, 1965, Ger 1968, 1989, Hungarian 1968, Turkish 1968, Danish 1974, Du 1984.

Emma: a novel. 3 vols '1816' [Dec 1815], Philadelphia 1816 (3 vols in 2), Bentley's Standard Novels 25 London 1833 (rptd 1836, 1841, 1851, 1854), 2 vols Philadelphia 1833, 1 vol 1845, London 1849, 1857, New York 1857, Boston 1863, London 1870, 1870, [1877], Leipzig 1877 (Tauchnitz), New York 1881, London 1881, [1883]; ed A. Dobson 1896; ed J. Jacobs 1898; ed R. B Johnson [1906] (EL); ed E. V. Lucas 1907 (WC); 1909, 1909, [1909], 1921; ed C. Van Doren, New York 1928; ed M. Dickens, London 1947; ed G. B. Stern 1953; ed L. Trilling, Boston 1957; ed R. Church, London 1962; ed M. Lascelles 1964 (EL), with introd by P. Conrad 1980; ed R. Blythe 1966 (Pen); ed A. Calder-Marshall 1969 (rptdPan Classics 1971); ed R. D. Spector, New York 1969; ed J. Kinsley and D. Lodge, London 1971 (Oxford Eng Novels), with introd by T. Castle 1995 (WCp); ed S. M. Parrish, New York 1972 (Norton Critical edns); ed M. Drabble London 1989 (Virago Classics); ed F. Stafford 1996 (Pen); tr Fr 1816, 1933, 1945, 1946, Ital 1932, 1945, 1951 (M. Praz), 1953, 1954, 1959, 1963, 1969, Cz 1934, 1982, Sp 1945, 1971, 1972, Du 1949, Finnish 1950, Serbo-Croat 1954, Swed 1956, Chinese 1958, 1963, Danish 1958, Ger 1961, 1965, 1980, Arabic 1963, Polish 1963, Portuguese 1963, Turkish 1963, Tamil 1966, Hungarian 1969, Romanian 1977. REVIEWS: Augustan Rev 2 1816; Br Critic n.s. 6 1816; Br Lady's Mag 4 1816; Champion 31 Mar 1816; GM 86 1816; Literary Panorama n.s. 6 1817; Monthly Rev n.s. 80 1816; Quart Rev 14 1815 (W. Scott).

Northanger Abbey and Persuasion: with a biographical notice of the author [by Henry Austen]. 4 vols '1818' [Dec 1817], Bentley's Standard Novels 28 1833 (rptd 1837, 1848, 1854), 1 vol 1850, 1857, 1870, 1870, Leipzig 1871 (Tauchnitz), London [1877], 1881, [1883]; ed A. Dobson 1897; ed R. B. Johnson [1906]; ed M. Lascelles 1962 (EL); ed J. Davie and J. Kinsley 1971 (Oxford Eng Novels). REVIEWS: Br Critic n.s. 9 1818; Edinburgh Mag n.s. 2 1818; GM 88 1818; Quart Rev 24 1821 (R. Whately).

Northanger Abbey. 2 vols Philadelphia 1833, 1 vol 1845, New York 1857 (with Pride and prejudice), Boston 1864 (with Pride and prejudice), New York 1881, London 1895; ed E. V. Lucas 1901; ed K. M. Metcalfe, Oxford 1923; ed M. Sadleir, London 1930 (WC); ed R. F. Patterson [1932]; ed R. West 1932; 1943 (Pen); ed R. Church 1960; ed M. Elwin 1961; ed O. Manning 1968 (rptd Pan Classics 1971); ed A. H. Ehrenpreis 1972 (Pen); ed J. Davie, Oxford 1980 (with Lady Susan, The Watsons and Sanditon), with introd by T. Castle 1990 (WCp); ed M. Drabble, London 1989 (Virago Classics); ed E. Mahoney 1994; ed M. Butler 1995 (Pen); tr Fr 1824, 1899, 1980, Sp 1921, 1945, 1945, 1945, 1953, 1957, Portuguese 1943, 1956, 1963, Ger 1948, Jap 1950, Finnish 1953, Du 1956, Ital 1959, 1961, Serbo-Croat 1959, Danish 1975, Polish 1975, Romanian 1976, Cz 1983.

Persuasion. 2 vols Philadelphia 1832, 1 vol 1845, New York 1857 (with Sense and sensibility), Boston 1863 (with Sense and sensibility), London 1909, 1928; ed F. Reid 1930 (WC); 1943 (Pen); ed E. Blunden 1944; ed A. Thirkell 1946; ed D. Daiches, New York 1958; ed R. Church, London 1961; ed M. Elwin 1961; ed D. W. Harding 1965 (with Memoir) (Pen); ed A. Wright, Boston 1965; ed W. A. Craik, London 1969 (rptd Pan Classics 1971); ed J. Davie 1971, with introd by C. Rawson, Oxford 1990 (WCp); ed M. Drabble, London 1989 (Virago Classics); ed P. Rogers 1994; ed P. M. Spacks, New York 1994 (Norton Critical edns); tr Fr 1821, 1882, 1945, 1980, Ger 1822, 1948, 1966, 1971, Swed 1836, 1954, Sp 1919, 1941, 1945, 1945, 1947, 1958, Jap 1942, 1968, 1969, Ital 1945, 1961, 1962, Finnish 1951, Du 1953, Portuguese 1954, 1955, 1971, Serbo-Croat 1957, 1976, Polish 1962, Cz 1968, 1972, Danish 1975.

Two chapters of Persuasion. Ed R. W. Chapman, Oxford 1926 (with ms facs; rptd Folcroft PA 1976; facs); London 1985 (as The manuscript chapters of Persuasion; with new preface by B. C. Southam). Ch 10 first ptd in 1871 Memoir.

Plan of a novel according to hints from various quarters. Ed J. E. Austen-Leigh 1871 (in Memoir (*see below*), altered and reduced); ed R. W. Chapman, Oxford 1926 (rptd Folcroft PA 1972; facs). 1926 edn includes Jane Austen's transcript of opinions of Mansfield Park and Emma, and notes on dates of composition and profits from several of the novels.

Sanditon. Ed J. E. Austen-Leigh 1871 (in Memoir (*see below*), extracts amounting to one-sixth); ed R. W. Chapman, Oxford 1925 (with facs); ed R. B. Johnson, London 1934 (with Lady Susan and The Watsons); ed M. Drabble 1974 (with Lady Susan and The Watsons); ed B. C. Southam 1975 (ms facs); ed J. Davie (with Northanger Abbey, Lady Susan and The Watsons), Oxford 1980, with introd by T. Castle 1990 (WCp); ed P. Washington 1996 (with other stories) (EL). Unfinished draft, c. 24,000 words, untitled, written 17 Jan–18 Mar 1817.

Three evening prayers. Ed W. M. Roth, San Francisco 1940.

Shorter works. Ed R. Church 1963, 1975. Selection.

Letters

Letters of Jane Austen. Ed Lord E. Brabourne 2 vols 1884; rptd 1994 (ed L. Ross, introd by D. J. Gilson).

Five letters from Jane Austen to her niece Fanny Knight, printed in facsimile. Oxford 1924; rptd Folcroft PA 1974.

The letters of Jane Austen. Ed R. B. Johnson 1925, New York 1926, London 1926. Selection.

Jane Austen's letters to her sister Cassandra and others. Ed R. W. Chapman 2 vols Oxford 1932, New York 1935; 1 vol London 1952 (2nd edn), 1959 (corrected), 1979 (corrected).

Jane Austen: letters 1796–1817. Ed R. W. Chapman 1955, New York 1955, London 1956; introd by M. Butler, Oxford 1985 (as Selected letters).

Five letters from Jane Austen to her sister Cassandra, 1813. Ed F. P. Lock, with introd by D. J. Gilson, Brisbane 1981.

Jane Austen's manuscript letters in facsimile: reproductions of every known letter, fragment and autograph copy with an annotated list of all known letters. Ed J. Modert, Carbondale and Edwardsville IL 1990.

Jane Austen's letters. Ed D. Le Faye, Oxford and New York 1995, 1996. Significantly rev 3rd edn of R. W. Chapman's edn of Jane Austen's letters to her sister Cassandra and others, 1952, *above*.

Austeniana

Hubback, C. A. The younger sister: a novel. 3 vols 1850. Written by a niece of Austen.

Lang, A. Old friends: essays in epistolary parody. London and New York 1890, 1892, 1893.

Brinton, S. B. Old friends and new faces: an imaginary sequel to the novels of Jane Austen. [1913].

Barrington, E. (pseud). 'The ladies!': a shining constellation of wit and beauty. Boston 1922 (rptd New York 1971), London 1923, 1927. Attributed to L. A. Beck (Bodleian) or E. L. M. Beck (BL).

Oulton, L. The Watsons: a fragment by Jane Austen, concluded. [1923], [1923] ('2nd edn', possibly only a reprint), New York 1923.

Brown, E. and F. The Watsons, by Jane Austen: completed in accordance with her intentions. 1928.

Brown, F. Margaret Dashwood: or interference. 1929. Written by a great-grand-niece of Austen.

Brown, F. Susan Price: or resolution. 1930.

Cobbett, A. Somehow lengthened . . . : a development of Sanditon. 1932.

Smith, N. R. Jane Fairfax. 1940.

Bonavia-Hunt, D. A. Pemberley shades. 1949, New York 1949; rptd Folcroft PA 1977.

Coates, J. The Watsons: Jane Austen's fragment continued and completed. 1958, New York 1958; rptd Westport CT 1973.

Drabble, M. A summer bird-cage. 1963, 1967, 1976, 1982. Modern rendering of Pride and prejudice.

[Dobbs, M.] Sanditon, by Jane Austen and another lady. Boston 1975, London 1975, 1976, Bergenfield NJ 1976. Appeared in condensed form in Redbook Feb 1975 and Woman's Jnl (London) May 1975. Dobbs discusses her completion of the work in J. Hall, Sanditon's 'other lady', Woman's Jnl (London) Aug 1975.

The Watsons, [by] Jane Austen and another. 1977, 1978.

Karr, P. A. Lady Susan: based on the unfinished novel by Jane Austen. New York 1980, London 1984, Bath 1984.

Gillespie, J. Ladysmead. New York 1982, London 1982. Contains characters from Mansfield Park.

Grey, C. The journal of Miss Jane Fairfax. 1983. Retelling of Emma from the perspective of Jane Fairfax.

Lefroy, A. A. Jane Austen's Sanditon: a continuation by her niece, together with Reminiscences of Aunt Jane. Ed M. G. Marshall, Chicago 1983. *See also* D. Le Faye, Sanditon: Jane Austen's manuscript and her niece's continuation, RES 38 1987.

Aiken, J. Mansfield revisited: a novel. 1984, Bath 1986, London 1986.

Aiken, J. Jane Fairfax. 1990. Retelling of Emma with Jane Fairfax as the central character.

Barrett, J. Presumption. New York 1993, London 1994. A sequel to Pride and prejudice.

Tennant, E. Pemberley: a sequel to Pride and prejudice. 1993, 1994, 1995.

Gillespie, J. Uninvited guests. 1994. Relates to characters from Northanger Abbey.

Tennant, E. An unequal marriage. 1994. A sequel to Pride and prejudice.

Aiken, J. Emma Watson: The Watsons completed. 1996.

Aylmer, J. Darcy's story: from Pride and prejudice. 1996.

'Barrett, J.' The third sister [continuation of Sense and sensibility]. 1996.

Billington, R. Perfect happiness: the sequel to Jane Austen's Emma. 1996.

Tennant, E. Elinor and Marianne. 1996.

Tennant, E. Emma in love. 1996.

Commentaries on fictional continuations of Austen's works can be found in A. W. Morton, The inimitable Jane, *in* Detection: how to prove authorship and fraud in literature and documents, New York 1978; *and* H. Ganner-Rauth, To be continued? Sequels and continuations of nineteenth-century novels and novel fragments, Eng Stud 64 1983.

§2

Obituaries

Hampshire Chron and Courier 21 July 1817; Hampshire Telegraph and Sussex Chron 21 and 28 July 1817; Courier 22 July 1817; Salisbury and Winchester Jnl 26 July 1817; Kentish Gazette 5 Aug 1817; Star 8 Aug 1817; London Chron 9–11 Aug 1817; GM Aug 1817; Monthly Mag Sep 1817; NMM Sep 1817.

Pre-1920 landmark criticism

Also see Jane Austen: the critical heritage, ed B. C. Southam, 2 vols 1968–87.

Mitford, M. R. Letter to Sir W. Elford, 20 Dec 1814. Rptd in Critical heritage, ed Southam, vol 1.

Robinson, H. C. Diary entries for 12 Jan 1819; 1 Feb 1819; 20 Apr 1822; 13, 22 Sep 1839; and 23 Sep 1842. Rptd in Critical heritage, ed Southam, vol 1.

Scott, Sir W. Letter to J. Baillie, 10 Feb 1822. Rptd in Critical heritage, ed Southam, vol 1.

Retrospective Rev 7 1823. In an unsigned review of a new edn of R. Paltock's anonymous eighteenth-century novel, The life and adventures of Peter Wilkins, 1823.

Blackwood's Mag June 1824. In an unsigned review of S. Ferrier's The inheritance, 1824.

Scott, Sir W. Jnl entries for 14, 28 Mar 1826; and 18 Sep 1827. Rptd in Critical heritage, ed Southam, vol 1.

[Lister, T. H.] Edinburgh Rev 51 1830. In an unsigned review of C. Gore's Women as they are, 1830 (2nd edn).

Cunningham, A. Biographical and critical history of the literature of the last fifty years: British novels and romances. Athenaeum 16 Nov 1833.

Coleridge, Sara. Letter to E. Trevenen, Aug 1834. Rptd partially in Critical heritage, ed Southam, vol 1.

Macready, W. C. Diary entries for 15 Feb 1834; and 8–10 July 1836. Rptd in Critical heritage, ed Southam, vol 1.

Mackintosh, Sir J. In Memoirs of Sir James Mackintosh, ed R. J. Mackintosh, 2 vols 1835, vol 2.

Newman, Cardinal J. H. Letter to H. Mozley, 10 Jan 1837. Rptd in Critical heritage, ed Southam, vol 1.

Longfellow, H. W. Jnl entry for 23 May 1839. Rptd in Critical heritage, ed Southam, vol 1.

Browning, E. B. Letter to M. R. Mitford, 6 July 1843. In Elizabeth Barrett to Miss Mitford: the unpublished letters of E. B. Browning to M. R. Mitford, ed B. Miller 1954.

Elwood, A. K. In her Memoirs of literary ladies of England, 1843.

Macaulay, T. B. The diary and letters of Madame D'Arblay. Edinburgh Rev 76 1843.

Carlyle, T. Jnl entry for 7 Mar 1845. Quoted in G. E. Fasnacht, Acton on books and reading, TLS 6 May 1955.

Lewes, G. H. The novels of the past season. New Quart Rev 6 1846.

Lewes, G. H. Recent novels: French and English. Fraser's Mag Dec 1847.

Brontë, C. Letters to G. H. Lewes, 12 and 18 Jan 1848; and to W. S. Williams, 12 Apr 1850. Rptd in T. Winnifrith, The Brontës and their background, 1973.

[Lewes, G. H.] The Leader, 22 Nov 1851. In an unsigned review of the anonymous novel, The fair Carew: or husbands and wives, 1851.

Lewes, G. H. The lady novelists. Westminster Rev 58 1852.

Jacox, F. Female novelists, no 1 – Miss Austen. NMM May 1852. Rptd in Critical heritage, ed Southam, vol 1.

[Eliot, G?] The progress of fiction as an art. Westminster Rev 60 1853.

Kirk, J. F. Thackeray as a novelist. North Amer Rev July 1853. Rptd in Critical heritage, ed Southam, vol 1.

Lewes, G. H. The novels of Jane Austen. Blackwood's Mag July 1859.

Masson, D. In his British novelists and their styles, Boston 1859.

Pollock, Sir W. F. British novelists – Richardson, Miss Austen, Scott. Fraser's Mag Jan 1860.

Kavanagh, J. In her English women of letters: biographical sketches, Leipzig 1862, 2 vols London 1863.

Dallas, E. S. The Times 26 June 1866. In an unsigned review of G. Eliot's Felix Holt, 1866.

Miss Austen. Englishwoman's Domestic Mag 3rd ser 2 1866. Rptd in part in Critical heritage, ed Southam, vol 1.

Pollock, J. Jane Austen. Saint Pauls Mag Mar 1870. Rptd in Critical heritage, ed Southam, vol 1. R. W. Chapman considers that this article might have been written by Anthony Trollope, then editor of the periodical; but Southam notes the piece does not match Trollope's known views. Wellesley identifies article as by J. Pollock.

Oliphant, M. Miss Austen and Miss Mitford. Blackwood's Mag Mar 1870.

Simpson, R. North Br Rev 52 1870. An unsigned review of J. E. Austen-Leigh's Memoir (*see under* Biographies, *below*).

Smith, G. Jane Austen. Nation (New York) 10 1870.

Trollope, A. In his On English prose fiction as a rational amusement. Ptd in Four lectures, ed M. L. Parrish, 1938. A lecture delivered in Edinburgh, 28 Jan 1870.

Forsyth, W. In his Novels and novelists of the eighteenth century, 1871, New York 1871.

Hutton, R. H. Miss Austen's posthumous pieces. Spectator 22 July 1871.

Thackeray, A. I. (later Ritchie). Jane Austen. Cornhill Mag 34 1871. Rptd in her Toilers and spinsters, 1874; rev in her Book of sybils, 1883.

'Tytler, Sarah'. [H. Keddie]. Jane Austen and her works. [1880], 1884, Folcroft PA 1976.

Oliphant, M. In her Literary history of England, 3 vols 1882, vol 3. Extracts rptd in Jane Austen – Northanger Abbey and Persuasion: a casebook, ed B. C. Southam 1976.

James, H. Letter to G. Pellew, 23 June 1883. Rptd in Critical heritage, ed Southam, vol 2.

Lefroy, F. C. Is it just?, and A bundle of letters. Temple Bar Feb 1883. By a grand-niece of Austen. Wellesley gives E. C. W. Grindon as the author of the 2nd article.

Pellew, G. Jane Austen's novels. Boston 1883, Folcroft PA 1973, Norwood PA 1976.

W., M. A. [Ward, Mrs Humphry]. Style and Miss Austen. Macmillan's Mag Dec 1884.

Stephen, Sir L. DNB. 1885.

Lang, A. In his Letters to dead authors, 1886, New York 1889, London 1892.

Cone, H. G. and J. L. Glider. In their Pen-portraits of literary women by themselves and others, 2 vols New York [1887].

Adams, O. F. Chapters from Jane Austen. Boston 1888.

Moore, G. Turgueneff. Fortnightly Rev Feb 1888.

Dodge, R. E. N. The note of provinciality in Miss Austen's novels. Harvard Monthly June 1889.

Fawcett, M. In her Some eminent women of our time: short biographical sketches, 1889.

Malden, S. F. Jane Austen. 1889 (Eminent Women ser), Boston 1889, Norwood PA 1976.

Smith, G. Life of Jane Austen. 1890 (Great Writers ser), Port Washington NY 1972, Folcroft PA 1973.

Clymer, W. B. S. A note on Jane Austen. Scribner's Mag Feb 1891. Rptd in Critical heritage, ed Southam, vol 2.

Howells, W. D. In his Criticism and fiction, New York 1891. Rptd in Critical heritage, ed Southam, vol 2.

Repplier, A. Three famous old maids. Lippincott's Monthly Mag 47 1891. Rptd in her Essays in miniature, New York 1892, London 1893; the volume was rptd in New York, 1970.

Pollock, W. H. A note of plagiarism. Nat Rev Mar 1892.

Garrett, E. The domestic novel as represented by Jane Austen. Atalanta Nov 1893.

Quiller-Couch, A. T. Our incomparable Jane. Speaker 7 1893.

Raleigh, Sir W. The English novel. London and New York 1894.

Jack, A. A. Essays on the novel as illustrated by Scott and Miss Austen. London and New York 1897, Port Washington NY 1969.

Pollock, W. H. Jane Austen: her contemporaries and herself, an essay in criticism. 1899, New York 1970, Folcroft PA 1972, Norwood PA 1976.

Howells, W. D. Jane Austen's Elizabeth Bennet; Jane Austen's Anne Elliot and other heroines; Jane Austen's Emma Woodhouse, Marianne Dashwood and Fanny Price. Harper's Bazaar 33 1900. Rptd in his Heroines of fiction, 2 vols New York 1901, vol 1; also in W. D. Howells as critic, ed E. H. Cady, 1973.

Bonnell, H. H. Charlotte Brontë, George Eliot, Jane Austen. New York 1902.

Robertson, J. M. Criticisms 1 1902. Rptd in Critical heritage, ed Southam, vol 2. Written c. 1890.

Gosse, E. In his English literature: an illustrated record, 4 vols London and New York 1903, vol 4 (From the age of Johnson to the age of Tennyson).

Twain, M. Letters from W. D. Howells of 1 May 1903, and to Howells of 18 Jan 1909. In Mark Twain–Howell's letters, ed H. N. Smith and W. M. Gibson, 2 vols Cambridge MA 1960, vol 2.

James, H. The lesson of Balzac. Atlantic Monthly 96 1905. Rptd in his Question of our speech, New York 1905; also in The house of fiction: essays on the novel by Henry James, ed L. Edel, 1957.

Mitton, G. E. Jane Austen and her times. 1905, 1906, 1917, Port Washington NY 1970.

Phelps, W. L. Introduction to Jane Austen's novels. 1906.

Burton, R. In his Masters of the English novel, New York 1909.

Helm, W. H. Jane Austen and her country-house comedy. 1909, New York 1973.

Dibelius, W. In his Englische romankunst, 2 vols Berlin 1910.

Bradley, A. C. Jane Austen: a lecture. E & S 2 1911. Rptd in his Miscellany, 1929; and partially in Critical heritage, ed Southam, vol 2.

Fitzgerald, P. Jane Austen: a criticism and appreciation. 1912, Norwood PA 1976.

Sackville, M. Jane Austen. 1912.

Butterworth, S. Persuasion. N & Q 11th ser 7 1913. Notes an error in W. and R. A. Austen-Leigh's Life and letters, 1913, with regard to rewriting of chs 10 and 11 of Persuasion: that the authors omit to mention that the reference is to the 2nd vol.

Cornish, F. W. Jane Austen. 1913 (Eng Men of Letters ser), 1914, 1926, Freeport NY 1971.

Woolf, V. TLS 8 May 1913. In an unsigned review of W. and R. A. Austen-Leigh's Life and letters, 1913, and S. G. Brinton's Old friends and new faces, [1913] (continuations of the novels).

Bassi, E. Medaglioni letterari: la vita e le opere di Jane Austen e George Eliot. Rome 1914.

Rague, K. and P. Jane Austen. Paris 1914 (Les grands écrivains étrangers ser). Includes list of Fr trns.

Villard, L. Jane Austen: sa vie et son oeuvre. Paris 1915; tr Eng 1924 (in part).

Chesterton, G. K. The evolution of Emma. New Witness 10 1917. Rptd in his Uses of diversity: a book of essays, 1920.

Farrer, R. Jane Austen, obi. July 18, 1817. Quart Rev 228 1917.

Johnson, R. B. In his Women novelists, [1918], Freeport NY 1967, St Clair Shores MI 1971, New York 1972.

Summers, M. Jane Austen: an appreciation. Trans Royal Soc of Lit 2nd ser 36 1918. Rptd in his Essays in petto, 1928.

Moore, G. In his Avowals, 1919.

Textual and bibliographical criticism

Smiles, S. A publisher and his friends: memoir and correspondence of the late John Murray. 2 vols 1891. In vol 1: a history of the publication of Emma, and Scott's review; in vol 2: references to Northanger Abbey and Persuasion.

Verrall, A. W. On the printing of Jane Austen's novels. Cambridge Observer 15 Nov 1892.

Haney, J. L. Northanger Abbey. MLN 16 1901. Identifies authorship of the 'Northanger novels', citing contemporary reviews.

Aravamuthan, T. G. Pride and prejudice: calendar mistake. N & Q 11th ser 2 1910. Queries datings of letters in Pride and prejudice.

Dodds, M. H. Novels in Northanger Abbey. N & Q 11th ser 6 1912.

A., G. E. P. Jane Austen's Persuasion. N & Q 12th ser 1 1916.

Summers, M. Northanger Abbey: 'horrid' romances. N & Q 12th ser 2 1916.

McKillop, A. D. Jane Austen's Gothic titles. N & Q 12th ser 9 1921.

Keynes, Sir G. The text of Mansfield Park. TLS 30 Aug 1923. Identifies textual differences between the 1st and 2nd edns.

Marsh, E. Some notes on Miss Austen's novels. London Mercury 10 1924.

Hopkins, A. B. Jane Austen's Love and freindship: a study in literary relations. SAQ 24 1925.

Sampson, J. Jane Austen's Sanditon. TLS 16 Apr 1925. A correction supported in TLS by 'N. W. H.', 30 Apr 1925, and R. W. Chapman, 14 May 1925.

Chapman, R. W. A Jane Austen collection. TLS 14 Jan 1926. A description of mss by or relating to Austen.

Flower, R. The first draft of Jane Austen's Persuasion. BM Quart 1 1926–7.

Brown, E. C. The date of The Watsons. Spectator 11 June 1927.

Sadleir, M. The Northanger novels: a footnote to Jane Austen. Edinburgh Rev 246 1927. Ptd in an expanded form as Pamphlet 68 of the Eng Assoc.

A., G. E. P. Jane Austen's Love and freindship and other early works. N & Q 156 1929.

Chapman, R. W. Jane Austen and her publishers. London Mercury 22 1930.

Bell, H. I. Letters of Jane Austen. BM Quart 5 1930–1.

Leavis, Q. D. In her Fiction and the reading public, 1932.

Bell, H. I. A deposit of Jane Austen manuscripts. BM Quart 11 1936–7.

Chapman, R. W. Jane Austen's text: authoritative manuscript corrections. TLS 13 Feb 1937.

Chapman, R. W. Jane Austen, poet. TLS 17 June 1939. Reproduction and text of an autograph ms of Austen's poem I've a pain in my head.

Chapman, R. W. A Jane Austen title. TLS 28 Oct 1939. On Austen's adoption of the title of Pride and prejudice after the pbn of M. Holford's novel First impressions, 1801.

Sadleir, M. Austen, Jane: the first collected edition. Bibliographical N & Q vol 2 no 2, May 1939. On Bentley's 1833 collected edn of her novels.

Hogan, C. B. [Bibl notes: Austen, Jane (1775–1817)]. PBSA 34 1940. Description of 1st Amer edn of Emma, Philadelphia 1816.

Tompkins, J. M. S. Elinor and Marianne: a note on Jane Austen. RES 16 1940.

Leavis, Q. D. A critical theory of Jane Austen's writings. Scrutiny 10 1941–2, and 12 1944–5; rptd in A selection from Scrutiny, ed F. R. Leavis 2 vols Cambridge 1968, vol 2.

Chapman, R. W. Emma. TLS, 20 Nov 1948. Suggests The Watsons as preliminary sketch of Emma.

Chapman, R. W. Jane Austen: facts and problems. Oxford 1948, 1950 (corrected), 1961, 1963, 1970.

Robertson, M. The last novels of Jane Austen. Boston Public Lib Quart 1 1949.

Emden, C. S. Northanger Abbey redated? N & Q 195 1950.

Hogan, C. B. Jane Austen and her early public. RES n.s. 1 1950.

Chapman, R. W. Volume the third. TLS 8 June 1951. Identifies minor error in Volume the third, ed R. W. Chapman Oxford 1951.

Rhydderch, D. Mr Cadell and Jane Austen. TLS 4 May 1951.

Suddaby, E. A sentence in Pride and prejudice. TLS 11 Apr 1952. On disputed phrase, 'to have anger', which has its precedent in S. Richardson's Clarissa.

King, N. J. Jane Austen in France. Nineteenth Cent Fiction 8 1953–4.

McKillop, A. D. Critical realism in Northanger Abbey. In From Jane Austen to Joseph Conrad: essays collected in memory of J. T. Hillhouse, ed R. C. Rathburn and M. Steinmann, jr, Minneapolis 1958. Includes discussion of possible date of composition of Northanger Abbey.

Southam, B. C. Additions and corrections to the Index of characters in the Oxford Jane Austen. N & Q 203 1958. Supplemental information to Appendices of Chapman's edns of Austen's collected works.

Harkness, B. Bibliography and the novelistic fallacy. SB 12 1959. On importance of retaining original vol divisions.

Derry, W. Jane Austen. TLS 29 Dec 1961. Seven notes on the novels and letters. *See also* correspondence in TLS: by B. C. Southam, 19 Jan 1962; and R. Gathorne-Hardy, 26 Jan 1962.

Litz, A. W. The chronology of Mansfield Park. N & Q 206 1961.

Southam, B. C. The text of Sanditon. N & Q 206 1961. About difference between the ms copy (held at King's College, Cambridge) and Chapman's 1925 edn, and printing errors in vol 6 (Minor works) of the Oxford Jane Austen, 1954.

Lloyd, J. D. K. Jane Austen. TLS 2 Feb 1962. Suggested emendation for Mansfield Park.

Southam, B. C. Interpolations to Jane Austen's Volume the third. N & Q 207 1962.

Southam, B. C. The manuscript of Jane Austen's Volume the first. Library 5th ser 17 1962.

Southam, B. C. Mrs Leavis and Miss Austen: the critical theory reconsidered. Nineteenth Cent Fiction 17 1962–3.

Southam, B. C. Northanger Abbey. TLS 12 Oct 1962.

Southam, B. C. A note on Jane Austen's Volume the first. N & Q 207 1962. About misprints in Chapman's 1933 and 1954 edns.

Kaser, D. (ed). In his Cost book of Carey & Lea 1825–1838, Philadelphia and London 1963. Details of pbn costs of early Amer edns of Austen's works.

Southam, B. C. Jane Austen's juvenilia: the question of completeness. N & Q 209 1964.

Southam, B. C. Jane Austen's literary manuscripts: a study of the novelist's development through the surviving papers. 1964 (Oxford Eng Monographs).

Jenkins, E. Extracts from The Morning Chronicle. In The Jane Austen Soc: Report for the Year 1964, Alton [1965].

Lascelles, M. Mansfield Park. TLS 21 Oct 1965. Further correspondence in TLS: M. Curtis 28 Oct 1965; S. Pigrome 4 Nov 1965; and H. C. Stevens 11 Nov 1965.

Nash, R. The time scheme for Pride and prejudice. ELN 4 1966–7.

Bartlett, L. C. and W. R. Sherwood. Jane Austen: Emma, 1815. In The English novel, ed Bartlett and Sherwood, Philadelphia 1967. Excerpts from 6 nineteenth-century accounts of Emma and 5 pieces of Austen's correspondence regarding the pbn of Emma.

Gilson, D. J. The first American editions of Jane Austen. BC 16 1967.

Andrews, P. B. S. The date of Pride and prejudice. N & Q 213 1968.

Brogan, H. Mansfield Park. TLS 19 Dec 1968. *See also* further correspondence in TLS: B. C. Southam 2 Jan 1969; M. Kirkham and H. Brogan 9 Jan 1969; and M. Lascelles 30 Jan 1969.

Butler, M. Unfavourable review. TLS 29 Feb 1968.

Emden, C. S. The composition of Northanger Abbey. RES n.s. 19 1968.

Gilson, D. J. The early American editions of Jane Austen. BC 18 1969.

Mansell, D., jr. The date of Jane Austen's revision of Northanger Abbey. ELN 7 1969–70.

Lock, F. P. Jane Austen: some non-literary manuscripts in the Fitzwilliam Museum and the University Library, Cambridge. Trans Cambridge Bibl Soc 5 1970.

Gilson, D. J. The early American editions of Jane Austen. BC 20 1971. Suppl to 1969 article.

Hodge, J. A. Jane Austen and the publishers. Cornhill Mag 1071 1972. Rptd (as Jane Austen and her publishers) in Jane Austen: bicentenary essays, ed J. Halperin, Cambridge 1975.

Gullans, C. B. Mansfield Park and Dr Johnson. Nineteenth Cent Fiction 27 1972–3. Suggests a punctuational solution for a textual crux on a Johnsonian model.

Jackel, D. Jane Austen and 'thorough novel slang'. N & Q 218 1973. Identifies sources for phrase 'vortex of dissipation'.

Lock, F. P. A Jane Austen quotation identified. N & Q 218 1973.

Cahoon, H. Jane Austen, 1775–1817. In Autograph letters and manuscripts (vol 1 of Major acquisitions of the Pierpont Morgan Lib), New York 1974. Describes the library's ms of Lady Susan.

Gilson, D. J. Serial publication of Jane Austen in French. BC 23 1974.

Barr, J. and H. Kelliher. Jane Austen, 1775–1817: catalogue of an exhibition held in the King's Library, British Library, reference division, 9 Dec 1975 to 29 Feb 1976. 1975.

Beinlich, U. 16 Dezember: 200, Geburtstag der englischen Schriftstellerin Jane Austen. Bibliographische Kalenderblätter der Berliner Stadtbibliothek vol 17 no 12 1975. Chronology of main events of Austen's life and list of modern East Ger edns, trns and stud.

Cahoon, H. Jane Austen: letters and manuscripts in the Pierpont Morgan Library. New York 1975.

Chard, L. F., II. Jane Austen and the obituaries: the names of Northanger Abbey. Stud in the Novel 7 1975.

Greene, D. New verses by Jane Austen. Nineteenth Cent Fiction 30 1975–6.

Jane Austen Soc. Jane Austen bicentenary, 1775–1975: loan exhibition, Jane Austen's house, Chawton, 2nd July–31st August. Alton [1975].

Wright, A. Jane Austen abroad. In Jane Austen: bicentenary essays, ed J. Halperin, Cambridge 1975.

Southam, B. C. Sanditon: the seventh novel. In Jane Austen's achievement: papers delivered at the Jane Austen bicentennial conference at the University of Alberta, ed J. McMaster, New York 1976.

Crum, M. Austen, Jane (1775–1817). In English and American autographs in the Bodmeriana: catalogue, Cologny-Genève 1977 (Bibliotheca Bodmeriana catalogues 4).

Luijters, G. Jane Austen. The Hague 1977 (Isis-reeks 7). Includes annotated bibliography of Du trns.

BL Jnl 4 1978. On recently acquired ms of Volume the second in BL.

Gilson, D. J. Jane Austen and James Stainer Clarke. BC 27 1978. On discovery of Regent librarian's copy of 1st edn of Northanger Abbey and Persuasion.

Butler, M. Disregarded designs: Jane Austen's sense of the novel. In The Jane Austen Soc: Report for the Year 1978, Alton [1979].

Craddock, P. The almanac of Sense and sensibility. N & Q 222 1979.

Lock, F. P. The geology of Sense and sensibility. YES 9 1979.

Ram, A. Jane Austen's appeal to Indian readers. Indian Scholar no 2 July 1980. Includes bibliography of Indian edns of Austen's work.

Tanselle, G. T. Jane Austen, Emma 1816: a cancel? BC 29 1980.

Gilson, D. J. Face value. Antiquarian Bk Monthly Rev 8 1981. On fake 1st edns of Sense and sensibility, Pride and prejudice, and Mansfield Park.

Klinkenborg, V., H. Cahoon and C. Ryskamp. Jane Austen, 1775–1817. In British literary manuscripts: series II, from 1800–1914, New York 1981. Includes complete checklist of Austen mss in Pierpont Morgan Lib, also reproducing and describing pages from autograph ms of Lady Susan and of a letter dated 21 May 1801.

Gilson, D. J. Jane Austen's verses. BC 33 1984. Notes whereabouts of Austen mss and differences between mss and pbd texts.

Aiken, J. How might Jane Austen have revised Northanger Abbey? Persuasions 7 1985.

Epstein, J. L. Jane Austen's juvenilia and the female epistolary tradition. Papers on Lang and Lit 21 1985.

Kilroy, G. J. F. Mansfield Park in two volumes. English: The Jnl of the Eng Assoc 34 1985.

Smith, E. Spanish translations of Northanger Abbey. Persuasions 7 1985.

Burrows, J. F. The reciprocities of style: literary criticism and literary statistics. E & S 39 1986.

Burrows, J. F. Computation into criticism: a study of Jane Austen's novels and an experiment in method. Oxford 1987.

Garside, P. D. Jane Austen and subscription fiction. Br Jnl for 18th-Cent Stud 10 1987.

Gilson, D. J. Jane Austen's handwriting. BC 36 1987.

Le Faye, D. Jane Austen verses. TLS 20 Feb 1987.

Litz, A. W. Jane Austen: the juvenilia. Persuasions 9 1987.

Milligan, I. A missing word in Sense and sensibility?. N & Q 232 1987.

Brattin, J. J. The misdated express in Pride and prejudice. Pbns of the Missouri Philological Assoc 13 1988.

Le Faye, D. Jane Austen's verses and Lord Stanhope's disappointment. BC 37 1988.

Pickrel, P. The Watsons and the other Jane Austen. ELH 55 1988.

Marshall, M. G. Jane Austen's manuscripts of the juvenilia and Lady Susan: a history and description. In Jane Austen's beginnings: the juvenilia and Lady Susan, ed J. D. Grey, Ann Arbor MI 1989.

Robbins, S. P. Jane Austen's epistolary fiction. In Jane Austen's beginnings: the juvenilia and Lady Susan, ed J. D. Grey, Ann Arbor MI 1989.

Derry, S. Jane Austen's reference to Hannah More in Catharine. N & Q 235 1990. Discusses details of composition of Catharine: or the bower.

Erickson, L. The economy of novel reading: Jane Austen and the circulating library. Stud in Eng Lit 30 1990.

Fergus, J. Jane Austen. Basingstoke and London 1991 (Macmillan Literary Lives ser). Surveys conditions of authorship and relations with publishers in Austen's time.

Gilson, D. J. A cancel in Jane Austen's Emma 1816. BC 40 1991.

Le Faye, D. Jane Austen: new biographical comments. N & Q 237 1992. On Bentley's 1833 edn of Austen's novels; it reproduces H. Austen's letter to Bentley.

Noll-Wiemann, R. Jane Austen's fragmente. Anglia (Tübingen) 110 1992.

Axelrad, A. M. Jane Austen's Susan restored. Persuasions 15 1993.

Harding, D. W. The supposed letter form of Sense and sensibility. N & Q 238 1993.

Vick, R. Jane Austen and Lord Howard. N & Q 239 1994.

Sacco, T. L. A transcription and analysis of Jane Austen's last work, Sanditon. Lewiston and Lampeter 1995.

Biographies

Austen, H. Biographical notice. Ptd in Jane Austen, Northanger Abbey and Persuasion, 4 vols 1818. Rptd, with slight alterations, as Memoir of Miss Austen, prefacing Bentley's edn of Sense and sensibility, 1833; original version rptd in Critical heritage, ed Southam, vol 1.

Austen, C. M. C. My aunt Jane Austen: a memoir. Alton 1952; rptd 1953, 1957. Written in 1867.

Austen-Leigh, J. E. A memoir of Jane Austen. '1870' [Dec 1869], 1871 (2nd edn, with Lady Susan and fragments of two other tales), 1872 (3rd edn), 1879 (4th edn), 1883 (5th edn), 1886 (6th edn), Boston 1892 (as Lady Susan, The Watsons), London 1898 (rptd 1901, 1904), 1906; ed R. W. Chapman, Oxford 1926 (text of 1871, omitting extracts from juvenilia, minor works and fragments; rptd 1951; 1987 with new intro by F. Weldon); ed D. W. Harding 1965 (1871 text, omitting extracts, etc, with Persuasion) (Pen); introd F. Weldon London 1989 (Folio Soc); ed L. Ross, with introd by D. J. Gilson, 1994 (1870 text).

Adams, O. F. The story of Jane Austen's life. Chicago 1891, Boston '1897' [1896] (2nd edn rev; rptd Norwood PA 1976).

Hill, C. Jane Austen: her homes and her friends. London and New York 1902, 1923, Norwood PA 1976; ed L. Ross, introd by D. J. Gilson, London 1994. Quotes from family mss previously unknown.

Hubback, J. H. and E. C. In their Jane Austen's sailor brothers, being the adventures of Sir Francis Austen, G. C. B., Admiral of the Fleet, and Rear-Admiral Charles Austen, London and New York 1906, Norwood PA 1976.

Austen-Leigh, M. A. In her James Edward Austen-Leigh: a memoir, 1911.

Austen-Leigh, W. and R. A. Jane Austen: her life and letters, a family record. 1913, New York 1913, 1965.
Austen-Leigh, M. A. Personal aspects of Jane Austen. 1920, Folcroft PA 1974.
Johnson, R. B. Jane Austen: her life, her work, her family, and her critics. London, Toronto and New York 1930.
Jenkins, E. Jane Austen: a biography. 1938, 1948, New York 1949, London 1958, New York 1959, 1960, 1969, London 1972, 1973.
Lascelles, M. Jane Austen and her art. Oxford 1939, 1941 (corrected), London 1963, 1995.
Austen-Leigh, R. A. Austen papers 1704–1856. 1942 (priv ptd); ed L. Ross, introd by D. J. Gilson, 1994. With addns and corrections to Memoir and Life and letters, 1913.
Hodge, J. A. The double life of Jane Austen. 1972, New York 1972 (as Only a novel: the double life of Jane Austen).
Cecil, Lord D. A portrait of Jane Austen. 1978, New York 1979.
Tucker, G. H. A goodly heritage: a history of Jane Austen's family. Manchester 1983.
Halperin, J. The life of Jane Austen. Baltimore 1984, Brighton 1984; tr Fr 1992.
Honan, P. Jane Austen: her life. 1987.
Le Faye, D. Jane Austen: a family record. 1989, Boston 1989. Substantial revision and enlargement of W. and R. A. Austen-Leigh's Life and letters, 1913, *above*.
Tucker, G. H. Jane Austen the woman: some biographical insights. 1994, New York 1994.
Nokes, D. Jane Austen: a life. 1997.
Tomalin, C. Jane Austen: a life. 1997.
The Jane Austen Soc has produced annual reports from May 1940, which have been further re-issued as collected reports on a periodic basis. Persuasions: The Jane Austen Soc Jnl of North America *began publication on 16 Dec 1979.* [PG and AM]

John Banim 1798–1842 and Michael Banim 1796–1874

The pseudonym 'the O'Hara family' was used for work in which both brothers collaborated but which was mostly planned, written or extensively revised by John Banim.

Bibliographies

Sadleir, M. In his XIX century fiction: a bibliographical record, 2 vols 1951.

§1

The Celt's paradise, in four duans by John Banim. 1821, 1821, New York 1869. A poem.
Damon and Pythias: a tragedy in five acts by John Banim. 1821, 1821, New York 1821, [1825?] (in J. Duncombe, British Theatre vol 61), Baltimore 1826, Philadelphia 1826, 1829, Baltimore 1832, Philadelphia 1837, Philadelphia and New York 1845, Boston [1846?], New York [185–?], New York 1860, London 1860, 1865 (in British Theatre vol 3), New York [187–?], [1883] (in J. Dicks, Standard plays). By J. Banim; R. L. Sheil had a small share in this play.
A letter to the committee appointed to appropriate a fund for a national testimonial commemorative of His Majesty's first visit to Ireland. Dublin 1822. By J. Banim.
Revelations of the dead-alive. 1824 (anon), 1845 (as London and its eccentricities in the year 2023: or revelations of the dead-alive, by the author of Boyne Water). Essays by J. Banim.
Tales by the O'Hara family [ser 1] containing Crohoore of the bill-hook; The Fetches; and John Doe. 3 vols 1825; ser 2 comprising The Nowlans and Peter of the castle, 3 vols 1826, 1827, 1831, Belfast 1846; ed R. L. Wolff, New York and London 1978 (both ser).
REVIEWS: (ser 1) GM 95 1825, Lady's Mag 6 1825, Monthly Mag 59 1825; (ser 2) Dublin and London Mag 2 1826, Literary Chron 1826.
Ser 1–2 (as vols 1, 7 and 11 of the Parlour novelist) 3 vols London and Belfast 1846.
Peter of the castle and The Nowlans. 3 vols 1833; Peter tr Fr 1829, Ger 1834; Nowlans tr Ger 1835.
The Nowlans. 3 vols '1834' [1833], 1838, 1846, 1 vol 1853; introd by K. Casey, Belfast 1992.
Crohoore of the bill-hook and The Fetches. 1838, 1848, New York 1865, 1875; Crohoore tr Ger 1828, Fr 1829.
John Doe. 1842, 1853.
The Peep o'day: or John Doe and Crohoore of the bill-hook. Ed M. Banim, London [1862], Dublin 1865, New York 1865, London 1870, New York 1875, London 1876, New York 1896.
The Peep o'day: or Captain John Doe, the last of the guerillas. New York 1877, 1897.
Peter of the castle and The Fetches. Ed M. Banim 1866, Dublin 1866, New York 1867, 1896.
The Boyne Water: a tale by the O'Hara family. 3 vols 1826, 1836; ed M. Banim, Dublin 1865, 1 vol New York 1866, 1869, 1875, 1880; ed B. Escarbelt, Lille 1976; ed R. L. Wolff, New York and London 1978; tr Fr 1829.
REVIEWS: Dublin and London Mag 2 1826; GM 96 1826; NMM 18 1826.
The Anglo-Irish of the nineteenth century: a novel. 3 vols 1828, 1 vol Dublin 1865 (as Lord Clangore). By J. Banim. Ed R. L. Wolff, New York and London 1978; tr Fr 1829.
The Croppy: a tale of 1798 by the authors of the O'Hara tales etc. 3 vols 1828, 2 vols Philadelphia 1839, 1 vol Dublin 1865, New York 1865, 1896; ed R. L. Wolff, New York and London 1978; tr Fr 4 vols 1832.
The denounced by the authors of Tales of the O'Hara family. Contains The last baron of Crana and The Conformists. 3 vols 1830, 2 vols New York 1830, 1 vol New York 1865; ed M. Banim, Dublin 1866, New York 1896; ed R. L. Wolff, New York and London 1979.
The smuggler: a tale by the authors of Tales of the O'Hara family. 3 vols 1831, 2 vols New York 1832, 1 vol 1833, 1849, 1856.
Chaunt of the cholera: songs for Ireland by the authors of the O'Hara tales etc. 1831.
The ghost-hunter and his family, by the O'Hara family. 1833, Philadelphia 1833, 1852, 1863, New York 1869, [1870] (as Joe Wilson's ghost), [1913]; ed R. L. Wolff, New York and London 1978; tr Fr 2 vols 1833.
REVIEW: Tait's Edinburgh Mag 2 1835.
The Mayor of Wind-gap and Canvassing, by the O'Hara family. 3 vols 1835, New York 1835, Paris 1835, 1 vol Philadelphia 1835; ed M. Banim, Dublin 1865, New York 1865, 1885. Canvassing is by Miss Martin of Ballynahinch; ed R. L. Wolff, New York and London 1979.
REVIEW: Westminster Rev 22, Apr 1835.
The bit o' writin' and other tales by the O'Hara family. 3 vols 1838, 2 vols Philadelphia 1838; ed M. Banim, Dublin 1865, 1 vol New York 1866, 1869, [1885]; ed R. L. Wolff, New York and London 1979.
Father Connell: a novel by the O'Hara family. 3 vols 1842, New York 1842, 3 vols London 1847, 1 vol 1849, Dublin 1858 (with introd and notes), New York 1869, 1896.
REVIEW: Tait's Edinburgh Mag 9 1842.
The loaded dice, by John Banim. In The omnibus of modern romance, New York 1844.
Clough Fion by M. Banim. Dublin Univ Mag Sep 1852, New York 1869, 1896.
The town of the cascades, by M. Banim. 2 vols 1864, 1 vol 1866.
Irish tales, by M. Banim. 1866.
John Banim also wrote the following plays: The prodigal: a tragedy *(all trace lost)*; Turgesius; The moorish wife; Sylla *(adapted from M. Jouy)*; The sergeant's wife; *and the novel,* The dwarf bride, *1829–31 (ms lost).* Crohoore of the bill-hook *was dramatised by W. Mitchell, Newcastle-on-Tyne 1828.*

§2

[Lister, T. H.] Novels descriptive of Irish life. Edinburgh Rev 52 1831.

Griffin, D. The life of Gerald Griffin. 1843. Chs 7–8.

Horne, R. H. In his A new spirit of the age vol 2, 1844.

Irish Quart Rev 4–6 1854–6. Papers on John Banim.

Murray, P. J. The life of John Banim the Irish novelist with extracts from his correspondence, also other selections from his poems. 1857, New York and Montreal 1884; ed R. L. Wolff, New York and London 1978.

Steger, M. A. John Banim: ein Nachahmer Walter Scotts. Erlandgen 1935.

Flanagan, T. In his Irish novelists 1800–50, Berkeley CA 1959. Chs 11–12.

McCormack, W. J. A ms letter from Michael Banim. Hermathena 1974. [CC]

Richard Harris Barham 1788–1845

See col 228.

Eaton Stannard Barrett 1786–1820

Bibliographies

Summers, M. In his A Gothic bibliography, [1941].

Block, A. In his The English novel 1740–1850, 1961.

§1

The rising sun: a serio-comic satiric romance by Cervantes Hogg, FSM. 2 vols 1807, 1807, 3 vols 1807 (3rd edn), 1807, 1809.

The second Titan war against heaven; or, the talents buried under Portland Isle. A satirical poem. 1807.

All the talents: a satirical poem in three dialogues by Polypus. 1807 (at least 19 edns in 1807). The 17th and subsequent edns were published as All the talents … to which is added, a pastoral epilogue), New York 1979 (facs, with The second Titan war and The talents run mad).

REVIEWS: Antijacobin Rev Apr 1807, Monthly Rev Apr 1807.

All the talents: a satirical poem. Dialogue the fourth by Polypus. 1807.

REVIEW: Monthly Rev July 1807.

All the talents' garland, including Elijah's mantle and other poems. 1807, 1807.

REVIEWS: Monthly Rev July 1807; Br Critic Aug 1808.

All the talents: a satirical poem in four dialogues. 1808.

The comet. 1808, 1808, 1808 (5th edn).

REVIEW: Br Critic Oct 1809.

The Miss-led general: a serio-comic, satiric, mock-heroic romance. 1808, 1808.

The setting sun: or Devil amongst the placement [and] a parody on the Beggar's opera, by Cervantes Hogg. 3 vols 1809.

The tarantula: or the dance of fools. 2 vols 1809.

Woman: a poem. 1810, 1818, 1818, 1819, 1822, 1841, ed D. Reiman, New York 1979 (facs).

REVIEWS: Monthly Rev Aug 1810; Br Critic Oct 1810; Quart Rev Apr 1818.

The metropolis: or a cure for gaming interspersed with anecdotes of living characters in high life by Cervantes Hogg. 3 vols 1811.

The heroine: or adventures of a fair romance reader. 3 vols 1813, 1814 (rev and sub-titled Adventures of Cherubina), 1815, 2 vols Philadelphia 1815, 3 vols London 1816, 2 vols Boston 1816, Baltimore 1832, 1 vol Richmond VA 1835; ed W. Raleigh 1909; ed M. Sadleir 1927, New York 1928.

REVIEW: Monthly Rev Mar 1814.

My wife! what wife? a comedy in three acts. 1815.

REVIEW: The Examiner July 1815.

The talents run mad: or eighteen hundred and sixteen, a satirical poem. 1816.

Six weeks at Long's, by a late resident. 3 vols 1817, 1817, 1817. This book has also been attributed to William Jerdan and Michael Nugent; Jerdan claims authorship in his Autobiography 2 vols 1852.

All the talents in Ireland! a satirical poem; with notes by Scrutator *was printed by J. J. Stockdale, the publisher of the other* Talents *poems, in 1807 and has sometimes been attributed to Barrett. There were also at least two other works inspired by* All the talents, *including* All the blocks! or, an antidote to all the talents by Flagellum *(1807), and* The late session of the house of c-m-s, to which are added the tears of victory and a word to the author of 'The talents run mad' by An Englishman *(1816).* Amatory poems with translations and imitations from ancient amatory authors, *ed I. M. M. (1805) and* The thespiad *(1810) have been attributed to Barrett, as have two anonymous novels,* The hero; or the adventures of a night, *and* The black castle; or the spectre of the forest. An historical romance. And the fate of Isabella *[1810?]. Barrett may have contributed the dedicatory sonnet to the anonymous vol* Henry Schultze … with other poems *(1821), and he probably published review articles in various mags. The* Quarterly*'s review of William Hazlitt's* Lectures on the English poets *(July 1818) has been attributed to Barrett and William Gifford.*

§2

Mendenhall, J. C. Univ of Pennsylvania General Mag 30 1927. Barrett's letters to his bookseller.

McKillop, A. D. MLN 53 1938. On The hero; or the adventures of a night, incorrectly attributed to Barrett. [PP]

Thomas Haynes Bayly 1797–1839

See col 231.

Amelia Beauclerc

Bibliographies

Summers, M. In his A Gothic bibliography, [1941].

§1

Eva of Cambria, or the fugitive daughter: a novel by Emma de Lisle. 3 vols 1811. Wrongly attributed by its publisher to Emma de Lisle, the pseudonym of Emma Parker (*see below*).

Ora and Juliet, or influence of first principles: a novel by the author of Eva of Cambria. 4 vols 1811.

The castle of Tariffa, or the self-banished man: a novel. 4 vols 1812.

Alinda, or the child of mystery: a novel. 4 vols 1812.

Montreithe, or the peer of Scotland: a novel. 4 vols 1814. Anon.

Husband hunters!!! a novel. 4 vols 1816.

The deserter: a novel. 4 vols 1817.

Disorder and order: a novel. 3 vols 1820. [PG]

Anna Maria Bennett c. 1750–1808

§1

Anna: or memoirs of a Welch heiress, interspersed with anecdotes of a nabob. 4 vols 1785 (anon), 2 vols Dublin 1785, 4 vols London 1786, 2 vols Dublin 1786, 4 vols London 1796, 2 vols London and Dublin 1804, 1 vol London 1854; tr Fr 1788.

Juvenile indescretions: a novel by the author of Anna, or the Welch heiress. 5 vols 1786, 2 vols Dublin 1786, 5 vols London 1805; tr Fr 1788.

Agnes de Courci: a domestic tale. 4 vols Bath 1789, 2 vols Dublin 1789, 4 vols London 1797; tr Fr 1806.

Ellen, Countess of Castle Howel: a novel. 4 vols 1794, 2 vols Dublin 1794, 4 vols London 1805; tr Fr 1822.

The beggar girl and her benefactors: a novel. 7 vols 1797, 3 vols Dublin 1797, 1798, 5 vols London 1799, 5 vols 1813; tr Fr 1798.
Vicissitudes abroad: or the ghost of my father: a novel. 6 vols 1806.

Attributed and spurious works

De Valcourt. 2 vols 1800 (anon), 1 vol Dublin 1800, Philadelphia 1801. Attributed to A. M. Bennett by Block and National Union Catalogue and on title page of Dublin and Philadelphia edns. However, De Valcourt also attributed to Eliza Lake on title page of The wheel of fortune (1806).
Faith and fiction: or shining lights in a dark generation, a novel by Elizabeth Bennett. 5 vols 1816; tr Fr 1816.
Emily: or the wife's first error; and Beauty and ugliness: or the father's prayer and the mother's prophecy. Two tales by Elizabeth Bennett. 4 vols 1819; tr Fr 1820.

BL attributes these novels to A. M. Bennett, while Blakey, Summers and Bibliothèque Nationale have Elizabeth Bennet(t). A. M. Bennett died in 1808, but DNB *asserts this novel was pbd posthumously, citing* R. Watt's Bibliotheca Britannica *(1824). BL also adopts* DNB*'s erroneous form of name, Agnes Maria Bennett.*

Henry Bennet et Julie Johnson, ou les esquirses des coeur, roman traduit de l'anglais. 3 vols Paris 1794. Bibliothèque Nationale attributes this to A. M. Bennett, though notes it has also been attributed to Jean Raithby.

For a listing of reviews and notices of A. M. Bennett's works, see Ward (1979, 1972).

§2

Lewes, C. L. In his Memoirs vol 4, 1805.
Fuller, J. F. A curious genealogical medley. In Miscellanea genealogica et heraldica, 1913. On A. M. Bennett and her relations. [CF]

William Bennet, 'Lee Gibbons' 1796–1879

§1

The cavalier: a romance by Lee Gibbons, student of law. 3 vols 1821, 2 vols Philadelphia 1822; tr Ger 1822.
Malpas, or le poursuivant d'amour: a romance. 3 vols 1822; tr Ger 1824, Fr 1825.
The king of the peak: a romance. 3 vols 1823, 1 vol 1883.
Owain goch: a tale of the revolution. 3 vols 1827. [PG]

Marguerite, Countess of Blessington, née Power 1789–1949

Bibliographies

Sadleir, M. In his XIX century fiction: a bibliographical record, 2 vols 1951.

§1

Sketches and fragments. 1822, 1823. Anon.
The magic lantern: or sketches of scenes in the metropolis, by the author of Sketches and fragments. 1822, 1823.
Journal of a tour through the Netherlands to Paris in 1821 by the author of Sketches and fragments etc. 1822.
Rambles in Waltham Forest: a stranger's contribution to the triennial sale for the benefit of the Wanstead Lying-in charity. 1827. Verse, illustr C. M. H.
The repealers: a novel. 3 vols 1833, 1833 (as Grace Cassidy: or the repealers).
Conversations of Lord Byron with the Countess of Blessington. 1834, 1850, Boston 1859 (as A journal of conversations with Lord Byron) (with a memoir of the author), London 1893; tr Fr 1933. Serialised in NMM 1832–3.
The two friends: a novel. 3 vols 1835.
The confessions of an elderly gentleman. Illustr E. T. Parris 1836, 1847; tr Ger 1837.
The victims of society. 3 vols 1837, Paris 1837.
The works of Lady Blessington. 2 vols Philadelphia 1838. For contents, *see* Sadleir, *above*.
The confessions of an elderly lady. Illustr E. T. Parris 1838.
The governess. 2 vols 1839, Paris 1840.
The idler in Italy. 2 vols 1839, 3 vols 1839, Paris and Philadelphia 1839.
Desultory thoughts and reflections. 1839, 1839, New York and Paris 1839.
The belle of a season. Illustr A. E. Chalon 1840. Verse.
The idler in France. 2 vols 1841, Paris 1841.
The lottery of life. 3 vols 1842, Paris 1842, London 1844, [1857]. Tales.
Meredith. 3 vols 1843.
Strathern, or life at home and abroad: a story of the present day. 4 vols 1845.
The memoirs of a femme de chambre: a novel. 3 vols 1846, Leipzig 1846, Philadelphia [1850] (as Ella Stratford: or the orphan child).
Marmaduke Herbert, or the fatal error: a novel, founded in fact. 3 vols 1847, 2 vols Leipzig 1847.
Country quarters: a novel, with a memoir ... by Miss [M. A.] Power. 3 vols 1850, 2 vols Leipzig 1850, 1 vol London 1852 (2nd edn).

Lady Blessington edited various gift books and was for many years editor and principal contributor to The Book of Beauty *and* Keepsake. *She also edited* Lionel Deerhurst: or fashionable life under the Regency, *by Barbara Hemphill (3 vols 1846).*

§2

Madden, R. R. The literary life and correspondence of the Countess of Blessington. 3 vols 1855.
Maginn, W. In his A gallery of illustrious literary characters, 1873.
The Blessington papers. In Collection of autograph letters formed by A. Morrison ser 2, 1895. Chiefly letters written to Lady Blessington.
Sadleir, M. Blessington–D'Orsay. 1933, 1947.
Rosa, M. W. The silver fork school: novels of fashion preceding Vanity Fair. New York 1936, ch 8.

Caroline Anne Bowles, later Southey 1786–1854

See col 236.

Anna Eliza Bray, née Kempe, first married name Stothard 1790–1883

Bibliographies

Wolff, R. L. In his Nineteenth-century fiction: a bibliographical catalogue, 5 vols New York and London 1981–6.

Collections

Novels and romances. 10 vols 1845–6, 12 vols 1884 (rev).

§1

Letters written during a tour through Normandy, Britanny and other parts of France in 1818; with engravings after drawings by C. Stothard. 1820.
Memoirs, including original journals, letters, papers and antiquarian tracts of the late C. A. Stothard; and some account of a journey in the Netherlands. 1823.
De Foix: or sketches of the manners and customs of the fourteenth century, an historical romance. 3 vols 1826, 1833, 1 vol 1846 (rev), 1884 (rev).
The white hoods: an historical romance. 3 vols 1828, 1833, 1 vol 1845 (rev), 1884 (rev); tr Fr 1828, Ger 1835.
The Protestant: a tale of the reign of Queen Mary, by the author of De Foix, The white hoods etc. 3 vols 1828, 2 vols New York 1829, 3 vols London 1833, 1 vol 1884 (rev).
Fitz of Fitz-ford: a legend of Devon. 3 vols 1830, 1 vol 1845 (rev), 1884 (rev).

The Talba, or Moor of Portugal: a romance. 3 vols 1830, 2 vols New York 1831, 1 vol London 1845 (rev), 1884 (rev).
Warleigh, or the fatal oak: a legend of Devon. 3 vols 1834, 1 vol 1845 (rev, as Warleigh: an historical romance).
A description of the part of Devonshire bordering on the Tamar and the Tavy in a series of letters to Robert Southey esq. 3 vols 1836, 1838 (as Traditions, legends, superstitions and sketches of Devonshire), 1844 (as Legends, superstitions and sketches of Devonshire), 2 vols London and Plymouth 1879 as The borders of the Tamar and the Tavy.
Trelawny of Trelawne, or the prophecy: a legend of Cornwall. 3 vols 1837, 1845, 1 vol 1884 (rev).
Trials of the heart. 3 vols 1839, 2 vols Philadelphia 1839, 1 vol London 1845 (rev), 1884 (rev).
The mountains and lakes of Switzerland; with descriptive sketches of other parts of the continent. 3 vols 1841.
Henry de Pomeroy, or the eve of St John: a legend of Cornwall and Devon. 3 vols 1842, 1 vol 1846 (with The white rose: a domestic tale), 1884 (rev); tr Ger 1846.
Courtenay of Walreddon: a romance of the west. 3 vols 1844, 1 vol 1846 (rev), 1884 (rev).
Trials of domestic life. 3 vols 1848, 1849 (as A father's curse and a daughter's sacrifice), 1 vol 1884 (rev).
The life of Thomas Stothard; with personal reminiscences. 1851.
A peep at the pixies: or legends of the west, with illustrations by H. K. Browne ['Phiz']. 1854.
Handel: his life, personal and professional, with thoughts on sacred music. London and Bungay 1857.
The good St Louis and his times. 1870.
The revolt of the Protestants of the Cevennes; with some account of the Huguenots in the seventeenth century. 1870.
Hartland Forest: a legend of North Devon. 1871, 1884 (rev).
Roseteague: or the heir of Treville Crewse. 2 vols 1874.
Joan of Arc and the times of Charles VII, King of France. 1874.
Silver linings: or light and shade. 1880.
Autobiography of Anna Eliza Bray [to 1843]. Ed J. A. Kempe 1884.
Mrs Bray edited the Poetical remains *of her husband, Rev E. A. Bray, and* A selection from sermons, *2 vols 1860; also M. M. Colling,* Fables and other pieces in verse, *1831, and A. J. Kempe,* The monumental effigies of Great Britain, *1817–32.*

§2

Boase, G. C. Anna Eliza Bray and her writings. Lib Chron 1 1884.
Hamer, L. Folklore and history studies in early nineteenth-century England: Jane Porter and Anna Eliza Bray. The Folklore Historian 10 1993. [AM]

James Norris Brewer fl. 1796–1829

Bibliographies

Summers, M. In his A Gothic bibliography, [1941].

§1

The mansion house: a novel written by a young gentleman. 2 vols 1796.
A winter's tale. 4 vols 1799, 1811.
Mountville Castle: a village story. 3 vols 1808.
Secrets made public: a novel. 4 vols 1808.
An old family legend, or one husband and two marriages: a romance. 4 vols 1811.
Sir Ferdinand of England: a romance. 4 vols 1813. Summers dates 1802, with 2nd edn 1813, but no other evidence of an earlier edn has been discovered.
Sir Gilbert Easterling: a story supposed to have been written by himself about the year 1598. 4 vols 1813.
The Fitzwalters, barons of Chesterton: or ancient times in England. 4 vols 1829.

Attributed works

The witch of Ravesworth: a romance. 2 vols 1808. Attributed by DNB and Summers to J. N. Brewer, though the title page has George Brewer as author.

Other works

J. N. Brewer also contributed to numerous topographical works, including Beauties of England and Wales, *18 vols 1801–18, and* wrote Some thoughts on the present state of the English peasantry, *a pam on the Poor Laws, in 1807.*

For a listing of reviews and notices of Brewer's works, see Ward (1979, 1972). [PG]

Mary Brunton, née Balfour 1778–1818

Bibliographies

Block, A. In his The English novel 1740–1850, 1961.

Collections

Works. 7 vols Edinburgh 1820.

§1

Self control. 3 vols Edinburgh 1811, 1811, 1811, 2 vols Philadelphia 1811, New York 1811, London 1815 (4th edn), 1 vol 1832 (Standard Novels), Edinburgh 1839, London 1844 (Standard Novels), Aberdeen 1847, New York 1848 (Lib of Select Novels), London 1849, 1850 (Railway Lib), New York 1974 (facs); introd by S. Maitland, London 1986; tr Fr 1829 (as Laure de Montreville ou l'empire sur soi-même).
REVIEWS: Scots Mag Mar 1811; Monthly Rev Aug 1811; Br Critic Sep 1811; Critical Rev Oct 1811.
Discipline. 3 vols Edinburgh 1814, London 1815, 2 vols Boston 1815, Philadelphia 1815, London and Edinburgh 1832 (to which is prefixed a memoir of 1819 of the life and writings of the author, including extracts from her correspondence [by her husband Alexander Brunton]), Philadelphia 1834, London 1837, 1844 (Standard Novels), 1849, 1852 (Parlour Lib); introd by F. Weldon, London 1986.
REVIEWS: Scots Mag Feb 1815, Br Critic Dec 1815, Monthly Rev Dec 1815.
Emmeline; with some other pieces to which is prefixed a memoir of her life including some extracts from her correspondence [by her husband Alexander Brunton]. Edinburgh 1819, 1820 (2nd edn), New York 1819; ed C. Franklin, London 1992 (facs); tr Fr 4 vols 1830.
REVIEWS: Edinburgh Mag May, June 1819, Br Critic Feb 1820.

§2

Self-control. Glasgow, Mar–Apr 1811. (Two-part epitome of the novel.)
E. E. 'Remarks on the character and writings of the late Mrs Brunton . . .' Edinburgh Mag, Jan 1819.
Elwood, Anne Katharine Curteis. In her Memoirs of the literary ladies of Great Britain vol 2, 1843, New York 1973 (facs).
E. A. D. R. Mary Brunton, and her one talent. [1869], 1885.
Blain, Clements and Grundy (ed). The feminist companion to literature in English. 1990. [PP]

Sir Samuel Egerton Brydges 1762–1837

See col 2083.

Sarah Harriet Burney 1772–1844

§1

Clarentine: a novel. 3 vols 1796 (anon), 2 vols Dublin 1797 ('by Mrs Bennet'), 3 vols London 1816, 2 vols Philadelphia 1818; tr Fr 1816, 1819.

Geraldine Fauconberg, by the author of Clarentine. 3 vols 1808, 1812, 2 vols Philadelphia 1817; tr Fr 1825.

Traits of nature. 5 vols 1812, 4 vols 1812, 2 vols Philadelphia 1812, 4 vols London 1813; tr Fr 1819 (as Le jeune Cleveland: ou traits de nature).

Tales of fancy. Vol 1 (The shipwreck) 1816, Boston 1816; tr Fr 1816, Ger 1821. Vols 2–3 (Country neighbours: or the secret) 1820, 2 vols New York 1820; tr Fr 1820. As 3 vols, 1816–21, 1820.

The romance of private life. 3 vols 1839, 2 vols Philadelphia 1840 (as The renunciation: a romance of private life).

S. H. Burney also translated Paul and Virginia, *from the Fr of J. H. Bernadin de Saint Pierre, and edited Henry Mackenzie's* Man of feeling, *both as series vols for the publisher Tegg. She is not the author of* Seraphina: or a winter in town, *3 vols 1809, or of* Lindamira: or an old maid in search of a husband, *3 vols 1810, both of which appeared under the name of Caroline Burney.*

For a listing of reviews and notices of S. H. Burney's works, see Ward (1972).

§2

Clark, L. J. From manuscript to print: the use of physical evidence in an edition of correspondence. In An index of civilisation: studies of printing and publishing history in honour of Keith Maslen, ed R. Harvey et al, Clayton, Victoria, Australia 1993.

Letters of Sarah Harriet Burney. Ed L. J. Clark, Athens GA 1996. [PG]

Lady Charlotte Susan Maria Bury, née Campbell

1775–1861

Bibliographies

Sadleir, M. In his XIX century fiction: a bibliographical record, 2 vols 1951.

Block, A. In his The English novel 1740–1850, 1961.

§1

Poems on several occasions, by a lady. Edinburgh 1797. Anon.

Self indulgence: a tale of the nineteenth century. 2 vols Edinburgh 1812, Boston 1812, Philadelphia 1812.

Conduct is fate. 3 vols Edindurgh 1822. Anon.

REVIEWS: Edinburgh Mag Apr 1822, Monthly Rev June 1822.

Suspirium sanctorum, or holy breathings: a series of prayers. 1826, 2 vols 1830. Anon.

'Alla giornata': or to the day. 3 vols 1826. Anon.

REVIEW: Monthly Rev Oct 1826.

Flirtation: a novel. 3 vols 1827 (anon), 1828, 1828 (3rd edn), 2 vols New York 1820, London 1834 (Colburn's Modern Novelists), 1 vol Paris 1836.

The exclusives. 3 vols 1830, 2 vols New York 1830.

Journal of the heart. 1830; ser 2, 1835.

The separation. 3 vols 1830, 2 vols New York 1830.

The three great sanctuaries of Tuscany: Valombrosa, Camaldoli, Laverna, a poem illustrated by E. Bury. 1833.

The disinherited; and the Ensnared. 3 vols 1834, 1 vol Paris 1837.

The devoted. 3 vols 1836, 1 vol Paris 1836, 1837.

The divorced. 2 vols 1837, 1 vol 1858, Paris 1837, Philadelphia 1858.

Love. 3 vols 1837, 2 vols Philadelphia 1838, 1 vol London and New York 1860.

Diary illustrative of the times of George the Fourth interspersed with original letters from the late Queen Caroline and from other distinguished persons. 2 vols 1838 (anon), 4 vols 1838 (expanded, vols 3–4 ed J. Galt; BL copy contains suppressed pages), Philadelphia 1838–9, 4 vols in 2 Paris 1838–9, 2 vols 1896 (as The Court of England under George the Fourth); ed A. F. Steuart 2 vols 1908 (as The diary of a lady in waiting).

REVIEWS: Quart Rev Jan 1838, Edinburgh Rev Apr 1838.

The history of a flirt, related by herself. 3 vols 1840, 185–? (Parlour Lib). Anon.

Family records: or the two sisters. 3 vols 1841. 1 vol Philadelphia 1841, Paris 1841.

The manœuvring mother. 3 vols 1842, 1 vol 1858.

The wilfulness of woman. 3 vols 1844, New York 1846.

The roses. 3 vols 1853.

The lady of fashion. 3 vols 1856.

The two baronets: a novel of fashionable life. London and New York 1864.

Bury also edited Mrs C. F. Gore, Memoirs of a peeress: or the days of Fox, *1837, and Caroline Lucy,* Lady Scott, A marriage in high life, *1828, 1857; tr Fr 1832, Ger 1837.*

§2

Lady Charlotte Bury. NMM Mar 1837.

'Charles Yellowplush, esq' [W. M. Thackeray]. Skimmings from the diary of George IV. Fraser's Mag Mar 1838.

Obit: GM May 1861.

Prucher, A. Figure europée del primo '800 nel Diary di Lady Bury. Florence 1961.

Todd, Janet (ed). Dictionary of British women writers 1660–1800. 1985. [PP]

Miss Byron, 'A Modern Antique' fl. 1808–16

§1

The English-woman: a novel. By Miss Byron. 5 vols 1808, 1812.

Celia in search of a husband. By a modern antique. 2 vols 1809, 1809, 1809.

Hours of affluence, and days of indigence: a novel. By Miss Byron. 4 vols 1809.

The alderman and the peer; or the ancient castle and modern villa. 3 vols 1810. Blakey and Summers have The modern villa and ancient castle: or the peer and the alderman.

The Englishman: a novel. 6 vols 1812.

The English exposé: or men and women 'abroad' and 'at home'. By a modern antique. 4 vols 1814.

The bachelor's journal: inscribed (without permission) to the girls of England. Edited by Miss Byron. 2 vols 1815.

The spinster's journal. By A modern antique. 3 vols 1816.

Attributed or spurious works

Zameo: or the white warrior! An operatic romance. By Medora Gordon Byron, a minor. To which is prefixed a memoir of Miss Byron. nd.

Duncombe's edition of The British theatre. Vol 15 1834, Zameo: a melodrama [1840?].

This work by Mrs Jane Briancourt includes a 'memoir' with the first edn, a jeu d'esprit representing the pseudonymous author as a natural daughter of Lord Byron. BL catalogues separately from Miss Byron, but the latter is sometimes wrongly attributed the forenames 'Medora Gordon'. It seems likely, though not certain, that Miss Byron and 'A modern antique' are the same author.

For a listing of reviews and notices, see Ward (1972). [CF]

David Carey 1782–1824

§1

The pleasures of nature: or, the charms of rural life: with other poems. 1803.

The reign of fancy: a poem. 1804.

Secrets of the castle: or the adventures of Charles D'Almaine. 2 vols 1806.

Poems, chiefly amatory. 1807, 1809.

Criag Phadric, visions of sensibility, with legendary tales, and occasional pieces. Inverness 1811. Poems.

Beauties of the modern poets: being selections from the works of the most popular authors of the present day. 1820, 1821, 1826.

Lochiel: or the field of Culloden. 3 vols 1820 (anon); tr Fr 1822.

A legend of Argyle: or 'tis a hundred years since. 3 vols 1821. Anon.
The lord of the desert: sketches of scenery, foreign and domestic: odes and other poems. 1821.
Life in Paris: comprising the rambles, sprees and amours of Dick Wildfire, of Corinthian celebrity, and his bang-up companions, Squire Jenkins and Captain O'Shuffleton. 1822, 1828, 2 vols New Orleans 1837.
Frederick Moreland. 2 vols 1824.

Attributed or spurious works.
Picturesque scenes: or a guide to the Highlands. 1811. Attributed to Carey by DNB and Summers, but no evidence of a work with this title discovered.
Macbeth: a poem in six cantos. 1817. Also attributed to James Mann; with notes by J. Adam.
Hardenbrass and Haverill, or the secret of the castle: a novel. 4 vols 1817.
Reft Rob, or the witch of Scot-muir: a Scottish tale. 1817, 1834 (as The nuptial doom: or the witch of Scots-muir).
The history of Julius Fitz-John. 3 vols 1818.
Normanburn: or, the history of a Yorkshire family: a novel. 4 vols 1819.
The above sequence of four novels has been associated with Carey, and more commonly with James Athearn Jones, though their true authorship remains uncertain.

Carey also edited the Inverness Jnl *and wrote for several London periodicals. See also col 290.* [PG]

William Carleton 1794–1869

Bibliographies
Sadleir, M. In his XIX century fiction: a bibliographical record, 2 vols 1951.
Hayley, B. A bibliography of the writings of William Carleton. Gerrards Cross 1985.

Selections
Popular tales and legends of the Irish peasantry [by Carleton, Denis O'Donoho, Mrs S. C. Hall etc]. Illustr S. Lover, Dublin 1834. Contains 2 stories by Carleton.
The battle of the factions and other tales of Ireland. Philadelphia 1845.
Characteristic sketches of Ireland and the Irish [by Carleton, Lover and Mrs Hall]. Dublin 1842, 1845, Halifax 1846, 1849, 1852 (as Tales and stories of Ireland). Contains 5 tales by Carleton.
Alley Sheridan and other stories. Dublin 1857. Serialised in Nat Mag 1857.
The poor scholar; Frank Martin and the fairies; The country dancing master and other Irish tales. 1869.
Works. New York 1882.
Amusing Irish tales. Ser 1, London and Glasgow 1889; ser 2, 1890.
Stories from Carleton. Ed W. B. Yeats [1889], New York 1889.
Stories from Carleton. Ed T. Hopkins [1905].
Carleton's stories of Irish life. Ed D. Figgis, Dublin 1919, New York 1920.
Tubber Derg or the red well; Party fight and funeral; Dandy Kehoe's christening and other Irish tales. nd.
Inside the margins: a Carleton reader. Ed T. Hurson, Belfast 1992.

§1
Father Butler; The Lough Dearg pilgrim: being sketches of Irish manners. Dublin 1829, Philadelphia 1835, London and Dublin 1839. Anon; first pbd in Christian Examiner 1828 and Church of Ireland Mag respectively.
Traits and stories of the Irish peasantry. Illustr W. H. Brooke. Ser 1, 2 vols Dublin 1830, 1832, 1834, 1835; ser 2, 3 vols Dublin 1833, 1834; ser 1–2, 5 vols Dublin 1836; in monthly parts illustr Phiz et al 1842; with autobiographical introd 2 vols 1843; illustr Phiz 5 vols 1853, 2 vols 1856, 1 vol 1860 (as Irish life and character); illustr W. Harvey et al 2 vols 1864, 1 vol 1872, 1875, 2 vols 1876, 1 vol 1877, 2 vols 1881 (with author's last corrections), 10 pts New York 1886, 1 vol 1893; ed D. J. O'Donoghue 4 vols 1896; ed F. A. Niccolls, Boston 1911; tr Ger 1837, Fr 1861 (3 tales).
Tales of Ireland. Illustr W. H. Brooke, Dublin and London 1834, 1848. First pbd in Christian Examiner 1831.
Fardorougha the miser: or the convicts of Lisnamona. Dublin, London and Edinburgh 1839, Dublin 1846, London 1848 (with introd), 1857, 1871 etc. First pbd in Dublin Univ Mag 1837–8; tr Irish 1933.
The fawn of Spring-vale; The clarionet and other tales. 3 vols Dublin and London 1841; reissued as Jane Sinclair or the fawn of Spring-vale etc, 3 vols Dublin and London 1843; and as The clarionet; The dead boxer; and Barney Branagan, 1850.
Art Maguire: or the broken pledge. Dublin 1845, Dublin and London 1847.
Parra Sastha: or the history of Paddy Go-Easy and his wife Nancy. Dublin 1845, 1846.
Rody the rover: or the Ribbonman. Dublin 1845, Philadelphia [186–?].
Valentine M'Clutchy, the Irish agent: or chronicles of the Castle Cumber property. 3 vols Dublin 1845, illustr Phiz 1 vol Dublin 1847, 1859, London 1860; tr Fr 1845 (serialised in L'Univers).
Tales and sketches illustrating the character, usages, traditions, sports and pastimes of the Irish peasantry. Dublin 1845; illustr Phiz 1846, 1849, 1851, 1855 (as Irish life and character). Some of these stories were rptd from the Irish Penny Jnl.
Denis O'Shaughnessy going to Maynooth. Illustr W. H. Brooke 1845. First pbd in Traits and stories ser 2, 1833.
The black prophet: a tale of Irish famine. Belfast and London 1847; illustr W. Harvey, London and Belfast 1847, 1862; ed D. J. O'Donoghue, illustr J. B. Yeats 1899; tr Irish 1940. First pbd in Dublin Univ Mag 1846.
The emigrants of Ahadarra: a tale of Irish life. 1848, 1857, 1871.
The Irishman at home: characteristic sketches of the Irish peasantry. Dublin 1849. First pbd in part in the Dublin Penny Jnl.
The tithe proctor: a novel, being a tale of the Tithe Rebellion in Ireland. 1849, 1857.
Red Hall: or the baronet's daughter. 3 vols 1852, 1 vol Dublin 1853, 3 vols 1854, 1 vol Dublin 1858 (as The black baronet: or the Chronicles of Ballytrain), 1875.
The Squanders of Castle Squander. 2 vols 1852, 1 vol 1876. First pbd in Illustr London Mag 1851–2.
Willy Reilly and his dear Cooleen Bawn: a tale founded upon fact. 3 vols 1855, 1 vol Dublin 1857, Philadelphia 1883, London 1896; ed E. A. Baker 1904, Dublin 1909.
The evil eye, or the black spectre: a romance. Illustr E. Fitzpatrick, Dublin 1860, 1864.
Redmond Count O'Hanlon, the Irish rapparee: an historical tale. Dublin 1862. First pbd in Hibernian Mag 1861.
The double prophecy: or trials of the heart. 2 vols London and Dublin 1862. Serialised in Hibernian Mag and Irish Amer 1861.
The silver acre and other tales. 1862. Serialised in Illustr London Mag 1853–4 (illustr Phiz).
The fair of Emyvale, and the Master and scholar. 1870. Serialised in Illustr London Mag July–Sep 1853 (illustr Phiz).
The red haired man's wife. Dublin and London 1889. Serialised in Carlow College Mag 1870.
The life of William Carleton: being his autobiography and letters ... [continued] by D. J. O'Donoghue. 2 vols 1896; ed P. Kavanagh 1968.
The courtship of Phelim O'Toole. Ed A. Cronin 1962. First pbd in Traits and stories ser 2, 1833.
King Richard McRoyal: or the dream of an antiquarian. Ed L. Bradley, Armagh 1983.

According to O'Donoghue, above, vol 2 pp. 309 and 344, Carleton left the ms of a 3-vol novel, Anne Cosgrave: or the chronicles of Silver Burn, *which seems never to have been pbd.*

§2

Our portrait gallery, 15: Carleton. Dublin Univ Mag Jan 1841.
Davis, T. O. Nation (London) 12 July 1845; rptd in his Essays literary and historical, 1914.
Murray, P. A. Edinburgh Rev 196 1852.
Shaw, R. Carleton's country. Dublin and Cork 1930.
McHugh, R. Carleton: a portrait of the artist as propagandist. Stud 27 1938.
Kiely, B. Poor scholar: a study of the works and days of Carleton. 1947.
Flanagan, T. In his Irish novelists 1800–50, New York 1959. Chs 16–18.
Bell, S. H. Carleton and his neighbours. Ulster Folklife no 7 1961.
Morrison, R. A note on Carleton. Universities Rev 31 1965.
Boué, A. William Carleton: romancier irlandais. Paris 1978.
Wolff, R. L. William Carleton, Irish peasant, novelist: a preface to his fiction. New York 1980.
Hayley, B. Carleton's traits and stories and the 19th century Anglo-Irish tradition. Gerrards Cross 1983.
Sullivan, E. A. William Carleton. Boston 1983.

Frederick Chamier 1796–1870

§1

The life of a sailor, by a Captain in the Navy. 3 vols 1832, 2 vols Philadelphia 1833, London 1850, 1856, [1873?]. Pbd in part in Metropolitan Mag 1831.
The unfortunate man. 3 vols 1835, 2 vols New York 1835.
Ben Brace, the last of Nelson's Agamemnons. 3 vols 1836, 2 vols Philadelphia 1836, 1 vol 1839 (rev), 1840, 1856 etc.
The Arethusa: a naval story. 3 vols 1837, 1 vol 1860 (as The saucy Arethusa), 1867 etc.
Walsingham, the gamester. 3 vols 1837, 1 vol Philadelphia 1838.
Jack Adams the mutineer. 3 vols 1838, 1 vol 1861 (subtitled The mutiny of the Bounty).
The spitfire: a tale of the sea. 3 vols 1840, 2 vols Philadelphia 1840, 1 vol [1860].
Tom Bowling: a tale of the sea. 3 vols 1841, 1 vol 1883 etc.
Passion and principle: a novel. Ed F. Chamier 3 vols 1842.
The perils of beauty. 3 vols 1843.
Ben Bradshawe, the man without a head: a novel. 3 vols 1843, 1 vol 1859. Anon. Attributed to Chamier.
The mysterious man: a novel by the author of Ben Bradshawe. 3 vols 1844. Attributed to Chamier.
Count Königsmark: an historical romance. 3 vols 1845.
Jack Malcolm's log. 3 vols 1846.
A review of the French revolution of 1848. 2 vols 1849, 1852 (as France and the French).
My travels: or an unsentimental journey through France, Switzerland and Italy. 3 vols 1855.
Chamier revised W. James, Naval history of Great Britain *and continued it with an account of the Burmese war and the battle of Navarino, 6 vols 1837. He also translated Zagoskin,* Young Muscovite, or the Poles in Russia: a novel, *3 vols 1834, 2 vols New York 1834.*

§2

Soane, J. Memoirs of Mr and Mrs J. Soane, Miss Soane and Captain Chamier from 1800 to 1835. [1835?] (priv ptd).
Memoir of Chamier. NMM Apr 1838.
The Times 2 Nov 1870.
Danilewicz, M. L. Chamier's anecdotes of Russia [pbd in NMM 1829–30]. Slavonic & East European Rev 40 1961.

Mary Charlton fl. 1794–1824

Bibliographies

Blakey, D. In her Minerva Press, 1939.
Summers, M. In his A Gothic bibliography, [1941].

§1

The Parisian: or genuine anecdotes of distinguished and noble characters. 2 vols 1794. Anon.
Andronica, or the fugitive bride: a novel. 2 vols 1797; tr Fr 1799.
Phedora: or the forest of Minski. 4 vols 1798; tr Fr 1799.
Ammorvin and Zallida: a novel. 2 vols 1798. Anon.
Rosella, or modern occurrences: a novel. 4 vols 1799, 2 vols Dublin 1800.
The pirate of Naples: a novel. 3 vols 1801; tr Fr 1801.
The wife and the mistress: a novel. 4 vols 1802, 1803.
The homicide: a novel taken from the Comedie di Goldoni. 2 vols 1805, 1813 (as Rosaura di Viralva: or the homicide); tr Fr 1817 (as Rosaura de Viralva).
Pathetic poetry for youth. 1811, 1815.
Grandeur and meanness, or domestic persecution: a novel. 3 vols 1824.
Past events: an historical novel of the eighteenth century. 3 vols 1824 (anon), 1830 (as Past events, or the treacherous guide: a romance).
Mary Charlton also translated The reprobate, *2 vols 1802, and* The rake and the misanthrope, *2 vols 1804, both from the Ger of Augustus La Fontaine; and* The philosophic kidnapper, *3 vols 1803, from the Fr.*
For a listing of reviews and notices of Charlton's works, see Ward (1979, 1972, 1977). [PG]

Richard Cobbold 1797–1877

Bibliographies

Sadleir, M. In his XIX century fiction: a bibliographical record, 2 vols 1951.

§1

Original, serious and religious poetry. Ipswich 1827.
Valentine verses: or lines of truth, love and virtue, with illustrations [by Cobbold]. Ipswich 1827.
The spirit of the litany of the Church of England. Eye 1833. Poem.
Men and women. 1843. Anon.
The history of Margaret Catchpole, a Suffolk girl, with illustrations [by Cobbold]. 3 vols 1845, 2 vols 1845, 1 vol 1847, 1852, [1856], [1858] (enlarged), [1878]; ed C. Shorter, Oxford 1907 (WC), 1930. Dramatised by E. Stirling, 1858.
Mary Ann Wellington: the soldier's daughter, wife and widow. [With illustrations by Cobbold.] 3 vols 1846, 1 vol 1853 ('improved'), [1875].
The bottle, or Cruikshank illustrated: a poem . . . . 1847.
Zenon, the Martyr: a record of the piety, patience, and persecution of the early Christian nobles. 3 vols 1847, 1855, [1874].
The young man's home, or the penitent returned: a narrative of the present day. 1848.
The character of woman: a lecture delivered April 1848. Diss nd.
Freston Tower: or the early days of Cardinal Wolsey. [With illustrations by Cobbold.] 3 vols 1850, 1 vol 1856, [1880], 1913.
Courtland: a novel, by the daughter of Mary Ann Wellington. 3 vols 1852.
John H. Steggall: a real history of a Suffolk man, narrated by himself, edited by the author of Margaret Catchpole. 1857, 1859, nd (in picture boards, as The Suffolk gipsy).
Geoffrey Gambado: or a simple remedy for hypochondriacism and melancholy splenetic humours. [1865] (priv ptd).
The biography of a Victorian village: Richard Cobbold's account of Wortham, Suffolk 1860. Ed R. Fletcher 1977. From original ms vols in the Suffolk Record Office.

Cobbold left a novel in ms, Jack Rattler: or the horrors of transportation, *now in the Sadleir Collection. He also pbd sermons and devotional works.*

Harriet Corp

§1

An antidote to the miseries of human life, in the history of widow Placid, and her daughter Rachel. 1807 (anon), 1808, 1808, 1808, New York 1808, London 1809, New Haven CT 1809, London 1810, 1812, 1814, 1817, 1824, Philadelphia 1831, New York 1846, London [1871].

Talents improved: or the philanthropist. [1807?], 1837 (3rd edn), 1837. Also attributed to James Beresford.

A sequel to the antidote to the miseries of human life: containing a further account of Mrs Placid and her daughter Rachel. 1809, 1809, New York 1810, London 1811, 1814, 1820.

Cottage sketches: or active retirement. 2 vols 1812, 1813, Boston 1813.

Familiar scenes, histories, and reflections. 1814, 1821.

Coelebs deceived. 2 vols 1817, Philadelphia 1817.

Tales characteristic, descriptive and allegorical. 1829.

Travellers in search of truth. 1849.

For a listing of reviews and notices of Corp's works see Ward (1972). [PG]

George Croly 1780–1860

See col 326.

Allan Cunningham 1784–1842

§1

Songs, chiefly in the rural language of Scotland. 1813.

Sir Marmaduke Maxwell: a dramatic poem; The mermaid of Galloway; The legend of Richard Faulder; and twenty Scottish songs. 1822, 1822. The mermaid of Galloway rptd [1845?].
REVIEWS: Br Critic n.s. 17 1822; Eclectic Rev n.s. 18 1822; London Mag 6 1822; Monthly Rev 2nd ser 97 1822.

Traditional tales of the English and Scottish peasantry. 2 vols 1822, 1 vol 1874; ed H. Morley 1887.
REVIEW: Monthly Rev 2nd ser 99 1822.

The songs of Scotland, ancient and modern, with introduction and notes. 4 vols 1825.
REVIEWS: Edinburgh Rev 47 1828; Monthly Rev 3rd ser 1 1826.

Paul Jones: a romance. 3 vols Edinburgh 1826, Philadelphia 1827; tr Ger 5 vols 1842.
REVIEWS: Literary Chron nos 395–6, Dec 1826; Literary Gazette no 516 1826.

Sir Michael Scott: a romance. 3 vols '1828' [1827].
REVIEWS: [De Quincey, T.?] Edinburgh Saturday Post 22 Dec 1827; London Mag 21 1827.

Lives of the most eminent British painters, sculptors and architects. 6 vols 1829–33, 1830–7, 3 vols New York 1831, 5 vols New York 1844 etc; ed W. Sharp 1886 (selection), [1893]; ed R. Davies and C. A. Hunt 1908 (selection).

Some account of the life and works of Sir Walter Scott. Boston 1832.

The Maid of Elvar: a poem in twelve parts. 1832.
REVIEWS: [Wilson, J.] Blackwood's Mag June 1832; Fraser's Mag 5 1832.

The cabinet gallery of pictures, selected from the collections of art, public and private, which adorn Great Britain, with biographical and critical descriptions. 2 vols 1833–4, 1836.

Biographical and critical history of the British literature of the last fifty years. Paris 1834.

Lord Roldan: a romance. 3 vols 1836, 2 vols New York 1836.

The life and correspondence of Robert Burns. 1836.

The life and land of Burns with contributions by T. Campbell [and] an essay by T. Carlyle. New York 1841.

The life of Sir David Wilkie. Ed P. Cunningham 3 vols 1843.

Poems and songs. Ed P. Cunningham 1847, 1875.

Select songs. In C. Rogers, The modern Scottish minstrel vol 3, 1856.

Haunted ships. In Supernatural tales, ed Gary Grant, 1974.

Cunningham contributed the majority of material, including at least 25 original songs, to R. H. Cromek's Remains of Nithsdale and Galloway song, *1810. He also contributed a tale,* Gowden Gibbie, *to A. Picken's* Club book, *1831, and wrote memoirs of Burns, Byron and Thomson for his edns of their works. He edited M. Pilkington,* General dictionary of painters, *1840, and* The anniversary *1829. He contributed 12 papers of Recollections to* Blackwood's Mag *Nov 1819–Jan 1821, and was a frequent contributor to the* London Mag *1820–5.*

§2

Gilfillan, G. In his Galleries of literary portraits vol 1, Edinburgh 1856.

Hall, S. C. Allan Cunningham. Art Jnl 18 1866.

Maginn, W. In his A gallery of illustrious literary characters, ed W. Bates, 1873.

Hogg, D. The life of Cunningham, with selections from his works and correspondence. Dumfries 1875.

Fairley, J. A. Allan Cunningham. Hawick Archaeological Soc, 1907.

Miller, F. Allan Cunningham's contributions to Cromek's Remains of Nithsdale and Galloway song. Rptd from Trans of the Dumfriesshire and Galloway Natural History and Antiquarian Soc 12 Nov 1920 [1923].

Allan Cunningham. TLS 31 Oct 1942.

Sikes, H. M. Hazlitt, the London Magazine and the 'anonymous reviewer' [of Cunningham's Sir Marmaduke Maxwell]. BNYPL Mar 1961.

Read, D. M. Cromek, Cunningham, and Remains of Nithsdale and Galloway song: a case of literary duplicity. SB 40 1987.

Groves, D. Allan Cunningham and the Edinburgh Saturday Post. RES n.s. 41 1990. [PG]

T. J. Horsley Curties

§1

Ethelwina, or the house of Fitz-Auburne: a romance of former times, by T. J. Horsley. 3 vols 1799; tr Fr 1802.

Ancient records, or the Abbey of Saint Oswythe: a romance. 4 vols 1801, 1832; tr Fr 1813.

The Scottish legend, or the isle of Saint Clothair: a romance. 4 vols 1802.

The watch tower, or the sons of Ulthona: an historic romance. 5 vols 1803–4.

St Botolph's Priory, or the sable mask: an historic romance. 5 vols 1806.

The monk of Udolpho: a romance. 4 vols 1807; foreword by D. P. Varma, with introd by M. M. Tarr, New York 1977 (facs).

Attributed or spurious works

The ruins of the Abbey of Fitz-Martin. In New gleaner, or entertainment for the fireside 2 1810. This story, bearing the signature 'Curtis', is an amalgamation and distillation of Ancient records and The monk of Udolpho.

For a listing of reviews and notices of Curties's works, see Ward (1972). [PG]

Ann Curtis, née Kemble, later Hatton ('Ann of Swansea') 1764–1838

§1

Poems on miscellaneous subjects: by Ann Curtis, sister of Mrs Siddons. 1783.

The songs of Tammany; or the Indian chief: a serious opera. By Ann

Julia Hatton. New York 1794, rptd New York 1931 in the Tarrytown Mag of History.
Cambrian pictures: or every one has errors. By Ann of Swansea. 3 vols 1810, 1813.
Poetic trifles. Waterford 1811.
Sicilian mysteries, or the fortress Del Vechii: a romance. 5 vols 1812.
Conviction: or she is innocent! A novel. 5 vols 1814.
Secret avengers, or the rock of Glotzden: a romance. 4 vols 1815.
Chronicles of an illustrious house; or the peer, the lawyer, and the hunchback: a novel. 5 vols 1816.
Gonzalo de Baldivia, or a widow's vow: a romantic legend. 4 vols 1817.
Secrets in every mansion, or the surgeon's memorandum-book: a Scottish record. 5 vols 1818.
Cesario Rosalba, or the oath of vengeance: a romance. 5 vols 1819.
Lovers and friends, or modern attachments: a novel. 5 vols 1821.
Guilty or not guilty: or a lesson for husbands. 5 vols 1822.
Woman's a riddle: a romantic tale. 4 vols 1824.
Deeds of the olden time: a romance. 5 vols 1826.
Uncle Peregrine's heiress: a novel. 5 vols 1828.
Gerald Fitzgerald: an Irish tale. 5 vols 1831.
For a listing of reviews and notices of Ann Curtis's works, see Ward, 1972, 1977.

§2

Fitzgerald, Percy. The Kembles. 1871.
Bromham, Ivor J. 'Ann of Swansea' (Ann Julia Hatton: 1764–1838). In Glamorgan Historian 7, ed S. Williams, Cowbridge 1971. [CF]

Catherine Cuthbertson

§1

Romance of the Pyrenees. 4 vols 1803, (anon) 1807 (3rd edn), Amherst NH 1809, London 1812, 1822, 1 vol 1840, 1844.
Santo Sebastiano or the young protector: a novel. 5 vols 1806, 1809, Philadelphia 1813, London 1814, 1820, Boston 1832, London 1 vol 1847 (illus).
Forest of Montalbano: a novel. 4 vols 1810, Philadelphia 1812; tr Fr 1813.
Adelaide or the countercharm: a novel. 5 vols 1813.
Rosabella or a mother's marriage: a novel. 5 vols 1817, 1818.
The hut and the castle: a romance. 4 vols London and Edinburgh 1823.
Sir Ethelbert or the dissolution of monasteries: a romance. 3 vols 1830.
For a listing of reviews and notices of Cuthbertson's works, see Ward (1972, 1977). [CF]

Charlotte Dacre, afterwards Byrne 1782–c. 1841

§1

The confessions of the nun of St Omer: a tale by Rosa Matilda. 3 vols 1805.
Hours of solitude: a collection of original poems by Charlotte Dacre, better known by the name of Rosa Matilda. 2 vols 1805.
Zofloya, or the Moor: a romance of the fifteenth century by Charlotte Dacre, better known as Rosa Matilda. 3 vols 1806; ed M. Summers 1928; tr Fr 4 vols 1812.
The libertine, by Charlotte Dacre, better known as Rosa Matilda. 4 vols 1807, 1807; tr Fr 3 vols 1816.
The passions, by Rosa Matilda. 4 vols 1811.
George the Fourth: a poem by the author of Hours of solitude [and] lyrics designed for various melodies. 1822.

§2

Summers, M. Byron's 'lovely Rosa'. In his Essays in petto, 1928.

Robert Charles Dallas 1754–1824

Collection

Miscellaneous writings: consisting of poems, Lucretia, a tragedy, and moral essays; with a vocabulary of the passions; in which their sources are pointed out; their regular currents traced; and their deviations delineated. 1797, The miscellaneous works and novels of R. C. Dallas . . . A new edition 7 vols 1813.

§1

Percival, or nature vindicated: a novel. 4 vols 1801, 1802.
Elements of self-knowledge: an anatomical display of the human frame and an enquiry into the genuine nature of the passions, compiled, arranged and partly written by R. C. Dallas. 1802, 1805 (rev).
The history of the Maroons, from their origin to the establishment of their chief tribe at Sierra Leone. 2 vols 1803; tr Ger 1805.
Aubrey: a novel. 4 vols 1804.
The Morlands: tales illustrative of the simple and surprising. 4 vols 1805.
The knights: tales illustrative of the marvellous. 3 vols 1808.
Not at home: a dramatic entertainment. 1809, New York 1811.
The new conspiracy against the Jesuits detected and briefly exposed. 1815, as The Jesuits from the writings of Dallas 1846; tr Fr 1817, Ger 1820, Ital, 1835.
A letter to Charles Butler esq relative to the new conspiracy against the Jesuits. 1817.
Juvenile attempts at English and Greek verse. 1818.
Ode to the Duke of Wellington, and other poems. 1819.
Sir Francis Darrell, or the vortex: a novel. 4 vols 1820.
Adrastus: a tragedy; Amabel or the Cornish lovers; and other poems. 1823, introd by D. H. Reiman, New York 1977.
Recollections of the life of Lord Byron from the year 1808 to the end of 1814. Ed A. R. C. Dallas 1824, London and Philadelphia 1825; tr Fr 1825.

Attributed works

Felix Alvarez: or manners in Spain containing descriptive accounts of some of the prominent events of the late Peninsular War; interspersed with poetry original and from the Spanish. 3 vols 1818, 2 vols New York 1818.
NSTC and National Union Catalogue attribute this work to Alexander Robert Charles Dallas (1791–1869), son of R. C. D., who also edited his father's Recollections of the life of Lord Byron, *which was published posthumously. Dallas also edited some of Byron's letters (1824 and 1825) and made a number of trns from the Fr, including* The siege of Rochelle: or the Christian heroine, *by Madame de Genlis, 3 vols 1808; and* Annals of the French Revolution *by Bertrand de Moleville, 9 vols 1800.*
For a listing of reviews and notices of R. C. Dallas's works, see Ward (1972, 1977). [CF]

Selina Davenport née Wheler 1779–after 1856

Bibliography

Summers, M. In his A Gothic bibliography, [1941].

§1

The sons of the viscount and the daughters of the Earl: a novel depicting recent scenes in fashionable life by a lady. 4 vols 1813.
The hypocrite, or the modern Janus: a novel. 5 vols 1814.
Donald Monteith, the handsomest man of the age: a novel. 5 vols 1815, 4 vols 1832.
The original of the miniature: a novel. 4 vols 1816.
Leap Year, or woman's privilege: a novel. 5 vols 1817.
An angel's form and a devil's heart: a novel. 4 vols 1818.
Preference: a novel. 2 vols 1824.
Italian vengeance and English forbearance: a romance. 3 vols 1828.
The Queen's page: a romance. 3 vols 1831.

The unchanged: a novel. 3 vols 1832.
Personation: a novel. 3 vols 1834. [PG]

Isaac D'israeli 1766–1848

See col 2139.

Emily Eden 1797–1869

§1

Portraits of the princes and people of India. 1844.
The semi-detached house. Ed Lady T. Lewis 1859 (anon), 1860, Boston 1860, London 1872; ed A. Eden 1928; illustr S. Suba, Boston 1948.
The semi-attached couple, by the author of The semi-detached house. 2 vols 1860, Boston 1861, London 1865; ed J. Gore 1927, 1934; ed A. Eden, illustr S. Suba, Boston 1947; illustr D. Braby 1955.
'Up the country': letters written to her sister from the upper provinces of India. 2 vols 1866, 1867; ed E. Thompson 1930.
Letters from India. Ed E. Eden 2 vols 1872.
Letters. Ed V. Dickinson 1919.

§2

Dunbar, J. Golden interlude: the Edens in India. 1955.

Maria Edgeworth 1768–1849

The principal repositories of mss and correspondence by or relating to Maria Edgeworth are in the Bodleian and the Nat Lib of Ireland, Dublin, with significant additional material in the BL; Cambridge Univ Lib; the Fitzwilliam Museum, Cambridge; King's College, Cambridge; and the NLS, Edinburgh. For details of the whereabouts of other mss, consult LR (19th century).

Bibliographies

Slade, B. C. Maria Edgeworth 1767–1849: a bibliographical tribute. 1937.

Collections

[Works.] 13 vols Boston etc 1822–5, 20 vols in 10 New York 1835–6 (Harper's Stenotype Lib).
REVIEW: US Literary Gazette 1 1825.
Tales and miscellaneous pieces. 14 vols 1825.
Tales and novels. 18 vols 1832–3, 1848, 10 vols 1857, 1874, 1893, 12 vols 1893.
Classic tales (a selection), with a biographical sketch by G. A. Oliver. Boston 1883.
Tales. Ed A. Dobson 1903. Children's stories.
Tales that never die. Ed C. Welsh, with introd by C. E. Norton, New York 1908.
Selections from the works. Ed G. Griffin, with introd by M. C. Seton, Dublin [1919].
The works of Maria Edgeworth. 12 vols. General eds M. Butler, W. J. McCormack and M. Myers 1999– .

§1

Almost all new London edns (including collected edns) pbd in Edgeworth's lifetime have considerable revisions and corrections; see especially Belinda, Patronage, *below. Only complete works are listed here; numerous edns of single stories, as well as selections, have been omitted. With the exception of* Harrington and Ormond, *Fr trns of the books or excerpts therefrom up to 1821 were pbd in the periodical* Bibliothèque Britannique *(from 1816,* Bibliothèque Universelle*), Geneva.*

Letters for literary ladies, to which is added An essay on the noble science of self-justification. 1795 (anon), 1799 (signed), 1799, 1805, Georgetown 1810, London 1814, New York 1974, London 1993.
The parent's assistant: or stories for children. 3 vols 1796 (anon; contains The little dog Trusty, The orange man, Tarlton, Lazy Lawrence, The false key, The purple jar, The bracelets, Mademoiselle Panache, The birthday present, Old Poz, The mimic), 2 vols 1796 (adds The barring out), Dublin 1798, 6 vols 1800 (signed; adds 8 new stories and omits 3 transferred to Early lessons), illustr 1800, Cork 1800 (vol 1 of London edn only), Drogheda 1802 (selected), London 1804, 3 vols Georgetown 1809, London 1810, Boston [181–?], 6 vols 1813, 3 vols Boston 1813, Boston, Philadelphia and New York [1814], 7 vols London 1815–27, 1 vol Edinburgh 1817 [tr Fr], 6 vols 1817, 2 vols New York 1820–7, 6 vols 1822, 1824, 2 vols Geneva [1826?], 6 vols Paris 1827, 3 vols Dublin 1829, London 1831, 4 vols Paris 1832–3, 3 vols 1836, 1 vol 1837, Philadelphia and New York 1847, London 1848, Philadelphia 1853, 2 vols London 1853, 1 vol 1854, 1855 (illus), 1856, 1857, 1858, 1859, [1860?] (illus), 1864, Philadelphia 1867 (illus), [1885] (Excelsior ser), Philadelphia nd; ed A. T. Ritchie 1897. One or more stories often rptd and combined with stories from her other books in England and USA; tr Fr, nd but pre–1817, Paris 1820, Geneva 1827, Paris 1833, 1837, 1838, 1840; one or more stories often rptd and combined with stories from her other books in France and Germany; tr Irish (Forgive and forget, with Rosanna; *see* Popular Tales, *below*) 1833 (Ulster Gaelic Soc).
A letter to the Rt Hon the Earl of Charlemant on the Tellograph and on the Defence of Ireland. Dublin 1797. By R. L. Edgeworth with ME's assistance.
Practical education. 2 vols 1798, 3 vols 1801, 2 vols New York 1801, London 1808, 1811 (as Essays on practical education), 1815, Providence and Boston 1815, Boston 1823, 3 vols London 1827, New York 1835; ed J. Wordsworth 1996; tr Fr 1800, 1801, Ger 1803. With her father R. L. Edgeworth.
REVIEW: [Pictet, C.] Bibliothèque Britannique 12 1799. Critical comments by translators following twelfth and final extract.
Castle Rackrent, an Hibernian tale: taken from facts, and from the manners of the Irish squires, before the year 1782. 1800, 1800, Dublin 1800 (all anon), London 1801 (signed), Dublin 1801, 1802 (3rd edn), Newbern NC [c. 1802] (no known copy), London 1804, 1810, Boston 1814, London 1815, 1828, Paris 1841, Glasgow 1870 (5th edn), London 1921, 1953, Oxford 1964, Ware 1994; ed Henry Morley 1886 (Morley's Universal Lib); ed A. T. Ritchie 1895; ed B. Mathews 1910 (EL) (all 3 with Absentee, *below*), 1921; ed A. N. Jeffares, Edinburgh 1953; ed G. Watson, Oxford 1964, 1969, 1980; ed C. Ó. Marcaigh with introd by P. Murray, Dublin 1971; ed M. Butler, London 1992; tr Ger 1802, 1982, Fr 1813, 1933, Romanian 1980, Cz 1982.
REVIEWS: Monthly Rev May 1800; Br Critic Nov 1800.
[Early lessons.] Harry and Lucy, part i: being the first part of Early lessons, by the author of The parent's assistant. 1801 (by R. L. Edgeworth and Mrs Honora Edgeworth; substantially a reprint of Practical education: or the history of Harry and Lucy, vol 2 (anon), ptd but never (?) pbd 1780); pt ii, 1801 (by R. L. Edgeworth); Rosamond, pt i, 1801 (containing The purple jar from Parent's assistant and 2 other stories); pt ii, 1801 (3 stories); pt iii, 1801 (The rabbit); Frank, pts i–iv, 1801; The little dog Trusty, The orange man, and The cherry orchard: being the tenth part of Early lessons [first 2 stories from Parent's assistant], 1801–2 (2 issues); [complete work] 10 vols 1803 (no known copies of pts i, ii, iv–vi), 7 vols Philadelphia 1804–8, 3 vols 1809, 10 vols 1809, 2 vols 1813, 6? vols Boston 1813, 2 vols 1814, 1815, 1 vol 1815, 17 London edns to 1848, 3 vols Paris 1836, 1853, 4 vols 1855, 1856 (illus); ed L. Valentine 1875; several Amer edns of separate sections of work; tr Ger 1801, Fr 1803, 1817, 1823, 1826, 1829–34, 1832, 1833, 1838, Brussels 1829, Du 1810 (Rosamond), Ital 1830, 1846.
Moral tales for young people (including Mademoiselle Panache transferred from Parent's assistant). 5 vols 1801, 3 vols 1802, Paris 1804, London 1806, 1809 (5th edn), 5 vols Philadelphia 1810, 3 vols Georgetown 1811, London 1813, 1817, New York 1818, 1819, 2 vols

Paris 1820, 3 vols London 1821, 2 vols 1826, Paris 1827, London 1830, 3 vols 1833, Paris 1834, London 1836, 1839, 1 vol 1846, Philadelphia 1846, London 1856, London and New York 1859, London 1863, 1865, 1875 (Lily ser), 1875, 1881, 1892, 1895 (Blaikie's School and Home Lib); ed L. Valentine 1874; tr Fr 1804, 1813, 1837, 1840, 1842 (one story), Ger nd. Tales often rptd singly and in selections, sometimes combined with stories from Parent's assistant, both in France and USA.

Belinda. 3 vols 1801, 2 vols Dublin 1801, 3 vols London 1802, 2 vols Dublin 1802; ed A. L. Barbauld 1810 (British Novelist ser) (with Modern Griselda, *below*; major alterations in latter part of story), 3 vols 1811, 2 vols Boston and New York 1814, London 1820 (British Novelist ser) (with Modern Griselda), 3 vols 1821, 2 vols Paris 1842, London [1884], 1 vol 1896, 1986; ed A. T. Ritchie 1896 (illus); ed E. Ni Chuilleanain 1993; ed U. Kirkpatrick 1994; tr Fr 1802, Ger 1803.
REVIEW: Monthly Rev Apr 1802.

The mental thermometer. 1801 (Juvenile Lib, vol 2) (signed), 1815 (Irish Farmers' Jnl 15–22 July) (anon), 1825 (in Friendship's Offering) (signed).

Essay on Irish bulls. 1802, 1803, Philadelphia 1803, New York 1803 (2 edns), London 1808, 1815, 1823 (5th edn). Essay on Irish humour; with R. L. Edgeworth.

Popular tales. 3 vols 1804, 2 vols Philadelphia 1804, 3 vols London 1805, 1807, 1811, 2 vols Poughkeepsie 1813, 3 vols London 1814, 1817, 2 vols Philadelphia 1819, Boston 1823, 3 vols London 1823, Paris 1837, Philadelphia and New York 1848, London 1850, 1856, Baltimore 1870, London [1874] (Lily ser), [1875], London and New York [1878?], London [1881] (Ruby ser), [1884], 1892, 2 vols Frankfurt nd (Preface by R. L. Edgeworth); ed A. T. Ritchie London 1895; tr Ger 1807, Fr 1813 (selection), 1814, 1823, 1835, 1840 (2 edns), 1848, Bengali (Encyclopaedia Bengalensis) 1849 (Lame Jervas). Tales often translated and rptd singly and in selections.
REVIEW: [Jeffrey, F.] Edinburgh Rev 4 1804.

The modern Griselda: a tale. 1805, 1805 (2nd edn corrected); ed A. L. Barbauld 1810 (British Novelist ser) (with Belinda), Georgetown 1810, London 1813, 1819, 1820 (British Novelist ser) (with Belinda), Paris 1843; tr Fr 1813.

Leonora. 2 vols 1806, New York 1806, London 1815; tr Fr 1807, Ger 1809.
REVIEW: [Jeffrey, F.] Edinburgh Rev 8 1806.

Review of the Stranger in Ireland: or a tour in the southern and western parts of that country in the year 1805 by J. Carr esq. Edinburgh Rev 10 1807 (anon); 1992 (in M. Butler ed Rackrent and Ennui).

Essays on professional education, by R. L. (and Maria) Edgeworth. 1809, 1812.

Tales of fashionable life. Vols 1–3 (Ennui, Almeria, Madame de Fleury, The dun, Manoeuvring), 1809 (3 edns), 2 vols Georgetown 1809, 3 vols Boston 1810, 5 vols London 1812, 6 vols 1812, 1812, 3 vols 1813, 1 vol Paris 1813, 3 vols London 1815, 1824; tr Fr 1811. Vols 4–6 (Vivian, Emilie de Coulanges, The absentee) 1812 (3 edns), Boston 1812, London 1814, 1818, 6 vols in 2 Philadelphia 1822–3, London 1824, 6 vols in 3 Paris 1831, 1856; tr Fr 1813, Swed 1837 (Vivian). Numerous selections and edns of single tales.
REVIEWS: Analectic Mag 1 1813. Vols 1–3: Christian Observer 8 1809; [Jeffrey, F.] Edinburgh Rev 14 1809; [Stephen, H. J. and W. Gifford] Quart Rev 2 1809. Vols 4–6: Christian Observer 11 1812; [Foster, J.] Eclectic Rev 8 1812; [Jeffrey, F.] Edinburgh Rev 20 1812; [Croker, J. W.] Quart Rev 7 1812.

Notes and a preface by Maria Edgeworth to Cottage dialogues among the Irish peasantry, by Mary Leadbeater. 1811, Philadelphia 1811. Irish and later edns omit Maria Edgeworth's preface and notes.

The absentee. New York 1812, 2 vols in 1 Washington 1812; ed N. Demurova, Moscow 1972; ed W. J. McCormack and K. Walker, Oxford 1988.

Patronage. 4 vols 1814, 1814, 1814, 3 vols Philadelphia 1814, 4 vols London 1815 (in the 1825 collected edn, *above*, there were substantial alterations, including rewriting of the last vol), 2 vols Paris 1841 (with Comic dramas, *below*), London [1884], 1 vol 1986; tr Fr 1816.
REVIEWS: [Smith, S.] Edinburgh Rev 22 1814; [Ward, J., later first Earl of Dudley] Quart Rev 10 1814.

Continuation of Early lessons. 2 vols 1814, 1815, Boston 1815, London 1816, 10 edns to 1845. From 1821 pbd as vols 3–4 of Early lessons, *above*; tr Fr 1839–44. Continuation of Harry and Lucy, Frank Rosamond, the first with R. L. Edgeworth.

On French oaths. Irish Farmers' Jnl 1–8 July 1815 (anon), Amulet or Christian & Literary Remembrancer 1827 (signed).

Readings on poetry. 1816, 1816, New York 1816, Boston 1816. With R. L. Edgeworth; preface and last ch by Maria Edgeworth.

Comic dramas, in three acts. 1817, 1817, Philadelphia 1817, Boston 1817, 2 vols Paris 1841 (with Patronage). Love and law, The two guardians, The rose, the thistle and the shamrock; The two guardians omitted from collected edns of 1825, 1832–3.
REVIEWS: Monthly Rev 83 1817; Quart Rev 17 1817.

Harrington; a tale; and Ormond: a tale. 3 vols 1817, 1817, New York 1817, Philadelphia 1817, 1 vol Paris 1841, London 1884; ed A. T. Ritchie 1895; ed A. H. Johnson 1900 (Gresham's Lib of Standard Authors); tr Fr 1817. Also the two works issued as follows: Harrington, 3 vols New York 1817, tr Fr 1817; Ormond, 1895, [1900], 1904, Shannon 1972, 2 vols London 1978, 1 vol Gloucester 1990, Belfast 1992.
REVIEWS: Blackwood's Mag 1 1817; [Jeffrey, F.] Edinburgh Rev 28 1817.

A review and analysis of the Théorie des peines et des Récompenses, par Monsieur J. Bentham; redigée en Français d'après des manuscrits par Monsieur E. Dumont. Philanthropist 7 1819 (1st instalment), Enquirer 1 1822 (1st–2nd instalments) (anon; incomplete; complete ms in Bibliothèque Publique et Universitaire, Geneva).

Memoirs of Richard Lovell Edgeworth esq. 2 vols 1820, 1821, 1 vol 1844 (abridged), Shannon 1969; ed B. L. Tollemache 1896 (selection). Vol 1 by R. L. Edgeworth, vol 2 by Maria Edgeworth.
REVIEWS: [Jeffrey, F.] Edinburgh Rev 34 1820; London Mag 1 1820; [Croker, J. W.] Quart Rev 23 1820.

Rosamond: a sequel to Early lessons. 2 vols 1821, Philadelphia 1821, London 1822, 1830, 1 vol Paris 1836, London 1842 (Bodley), 2 vols 1842, 1 vol Paris 1846, London 1850, 1856, 1856, [1917] (retold in easy words by A. Pitt-Kethley), 2 vols Boston nd; tr Ger 1827, Fr 1839–44, Ital 1846.

Frank: a sequel to Frank in Early lessons. 3 vols 1822, 2 vols New York 1822, Cambridge MA 1822, 3 vols London 1825, 6 London edns to 1848, New York 1834, 1 vol Paris 1835, 1836, Baltimore 1836, New York 1836, London 1844, 1846, 3 vols 1854 (7th edn), 1856, 1856, 1862, Edinburgh 1866 (with other tales), 1887; tr Ger 1827, Fr 1831, Ital 1839.

Harry and Lucy concluded: being the last part of Early lessons. 4 vols 1825, Boston 1825, London 1827 (2nd edn corrected), 1 vol Paris 1836, 3 vols London 1837 (3rd edn revised and corrected), 1840, 1846, 1 vol Paris 1846, 3 vols London 1853, 1 vol 1856, 1866; tr Fr 1826.
REVIEW: Monthly Rev 109 1826.

Thoughts on bores. Janus (Edinburgh) 1826. Anon; first acknowledged in collected edn 1832–3, vol 17.

Little plays for children: The grinding organ; Dumb Andy; The dame school holiday. 1827, Philadelphia 1827, New York 1827, London 1834. Vol 7 of Parent's assistant.

Garry Owen: or the snow-woman. 1829 (The Christmas box, ed C. Croker), Salem MA 1829, 1832 (with Poor Bob the chimney sweeper, 1829?; no known copy?), Paris 1835 (Poor Bob), 1844 (Garry Owen), Edinburgh 1848 (Garry Owen), 1849 (Poor Bob) (both in Chambers' Lib for Young People); tr Fr 1835.

Helen: a tale. 3 vols 1834, 1834, 1 vol Boston 1834, 2 vols New York and Boston 1834, 2 vols Philadelphia 1834, 1 vol Paris 1834, 1837, London 1838 (Bentley's Standard Novelists), Paris 1846, London 1846, 1870, 1877, 1879, 1880, 1883, [1884], 2 vols 1924, 1 vol 1987; ed A. T. Ritchie 1896; tr Fr 1834, Ger 1834, Swed 1836–7, Danish 1870. REVIEWS: [Peabody, Rev W. B. O.] North Amer Rev 39 1834; [Lockhart, J. G.] Quart Rev 51 1834.

Orlandino. Edinburgh 1848 (Chambers' Lib for Young People), Boston 1848, Paris 1849, Edinburgh 1853 (with 3 stories by other hands), 2 vols London 1864 (Entertaining Lib for the Young), London and Edinburgh 1869 (Chambers' Lib for Young People), [19??].

The most unfortunate day of my life: being a hitherto unpublished story, together with the Purple jar and other stories. 1931.

Letters and papers

Many unpbd letters are now in the Nat Lib of Ireland, Dublin. Letters to Swiss correspondents are in the Bibliothèque Publique et Universitaire, Geneva.

Memoirs of Mrs Inchbald, including her familiar correspondence. Ed J. Boaden 2 vols 1833.

Davy, J. Fragmentary remains of Sir Humphry Davy. 1858.

A memoir of Maria Edgeworth, with a selection from her letters by the late Mrs [Frances] Edgeworth. 3 vols 1867 (priv ptd).

Constable, T. Archibald Constable and his literary correspondents. 3 vols Edinburgh 1873.

Le Breton, A. L. A memoir of Mrs Barbauld, including letters and notices of her family and friends. 1874.

Graves, R. P. Life of Sir W. R. Hamilton, including selections from his poems, correspondence and miscellaneous writings. 3 vols Dublin 1882–3.

Hare, A. J. C. The life and letters of Maria Edgeworth. 2 vols 1894, rptd Freeport NY 1971.

Lettres intimes du Maria Edgeworth pendant ses voyages en Belgique, en France, en Suisse et en Angleterre en 1802, 1802 et 1821. Tr Mlle P. G., Paris 1896.

Hill, C. Some unpublished letters of Maria Edgeworth. Hampstead Annual 1897.

Correspondence of Ricardo with Maria Edgeworth. Economic Jnl 17 1907.

Grey, R. Maria Edgeworth and Etienne Dumont. Dublin Rev 145 1909.

Law, H. W. and I. The book of the Beresford Hopes. 1925 (priv ptd).

Butler, H. J. and H. E. (ed). The black book of Edgeworthstown and other Edgeworth memories 1585–1817. 1927.

Butler, H. J. and H. E. Some unpublished letters: Sir Walter Scott and Maria Edgeworth. MLR 23 1928.

Partington, W. (ed). The private letter-books of Sir Walter Scott. 1930.

Chosen letters. Ed F. V. Barry 1931. Includes 8 unpbd letters.

Partington, W. (ed). Sir Walter's post-bag. 1932.

Waller, R. D. Letters addressed to Mrs Gaskell by celebrated contemporaries. BJR Lib 19 1935.

Romilly, S. H. Romilly–Edgeworth letters 1813–18. 1936.

Romilly, S. H. The lost letters of Maria Edgeworth. Quart Rev 268 1937.

Hone, J. The Moores of Moore Hall. 1939. Includes some of her letters to the Moore family.

Tour in Connemara, and the Martins of Ballinahinch. Ed H. E. Butler 1950.

Häusermann, H. W. The Genevese background. 1952. First pbn of a number of her letters preserved in or near Geneva.

Scott, W. S. Letters of Maria Edgeworth and Anna Letitia Barbauld selected from the Lushington papers. Illus 1953.

Butler, R. F. Maria Edgeworth and Sir Walter Scott: unpublished letters 1823. RES n.s. 9 1958.

Donner, H. W. Echoes of Beddoesian rambles. Studia Neophilologica 33 1961. Includes some of her letters about Thomas Lovell Beddoes.

Colvin, C. Two unpublished mss by Maria Edgeworth. REL 8 1967.

Hurst, M. Maria Edgeworth and the public scene. 1969.

Colvin, C. Letters from England, 1813–44. 1971.

Macdonald, E. E. The education of the heart. The correspondence of Rachel Mordecai Lazarus and Maria Edgeworth. 1977.

Colvin, C. Maria Edgeworth in France and Switzerland. Selections from the Edgeworth family letters. 1979.

Peters, J. G. An unpublished letter from Maria Edgeworth to Eliza Fletcher. ELN 30 1993.

Attributed or spurious works

'Mrs Edgeworth'. Fictitious author(s) were often linked to Maria Edgeworth and her family, where no association appears to exist. Spurious publications below were troublesome to Maria Edgeworth and her relatives. See Bent's Monthly Literary Advertiser 1810.

Adelaide; or, the chateau de St Pierre. A tale of the sixteenth century. 1806.

The wife; or, a model for women. 3 vols 1810; tr Fr 1813.

Fatherless Fanny; or, the memoirs of a little mendicant, and her benefactors. A modern novel. 4 vols 1811, 1819?, Manchester 1819, 1820 [illus], [? 1841], London 1867, Derby nd; tr Fr 1812.

La mère intrigante. Paris 1812.

Conseils a mon fils. [? 1813].

The ballad singer; or, memoirs of the Bristol family. A novel. 4 vols 1814.

Forster. Paris 1821.

Glenfell, ou les Macdonalds et les Campbells, histoire écossaise du 19e siècle, suivi de Murad le malheureux. Paris 1822.

§2

Pictet, M.-A. In his Voyage de trois mois en Angleterre, en Ecosse et en Irlande. Geneva [1802].

Seward, A. Memoirs of the life of Dr Darwin. 1804.

Wakefield, E. An account of Ireland, statistical and political. 2 vols 1812.

Memoir of Maria Edgeworth. Boston Monthly Mag 1 1826 [with portrait].

[Lockhart, J. G.] In his Memoirs of the life of Sir Walter Scott. 7 vols Edinburgh 1837–8, 10 vols Edinburgh 1839.

Didactic fiction. Christian Remembrancer 3 1842.

Maria Edgeworth at Edgeworthstown. Eclectic Museum 1 1843.

Maria Edgeworth. Bentley's Misc 24 1848.

Hall, Mrs S. C. Edgeworthstown: memories of Maria Edgeworth. Art Jnl 1 1849, 28 1866.

Maria Edgeworth. Dublin Univ Mag 33 1849.

Maria Edgeworth. Irish Quart Rev 1 1851.

[Hayward, A.] Miss Edgeworth – her life and writings. Edinburgh Rev 126 1867; rptd in his Biographical and critical essays, 5 vols 1858–74.

Miss Edgeworth's life and letters. Sharpe's London Mag 36 1869.

Hillard, G. S. Life, letters and journals of George Ticknor. 1876.

Oliver, G. A. A study of Maria Edgeworth, with notices of her father and friends. Boston 1882.

Miss Edgeworth's novels. The Literary World (Boston) 13 July 1882.

Maria Edgeworth. The Literary World (Boston) Dec 1882.

Ritchie, A. T. A book of sybils. 1883.

Zimmern, H. Maria Edgeworth. 1883.

Two women of letters. [Edgeworth and Miss Mitford]. Atlantic Monthly 51 1883.

Miss Edgeworth's novels. Saturday Rev 61 1886.

[Purcell, E.] Life and letters of Maria Edgeworth. Acad 46 1894.

Macaulay, James. Maria Edgeworth. Leisure Hour 44 1895.

Saintsbury, George. Maria Edgeworth. Macmillan's Mag 72 1895.

The novels of Maria Edgeworth. Quart Rev 182 1895.

Maria Edgeworth. Temple Bar 105 1895.
A glimpse of Maria Edgeworth. Argosy 62 1896.
Krans, H. S. Irish life in Irish fiction. New York 1903.
Lawless, E. Maria Edgeworth. 1904 (EML).
Ward, W. Moral fiction a hundred years ago. Dublin Rev 144 1909.
Grey, R. Heavy fathers. Fortnightly Rev July 1909.
Hill, C. Maria Edgeworth and her circle in the days of Buonaparte and Bourbon. 1910.
Patterson, A. The Edgeworths: a study of later eighteenth century education. 1914.
Colum, P. Maria Edgeworth and Ivan Turgenev. Br Rev 11 1915.
Michael, E. F. Die irischen Romane von Maria Edgeworth. Dresden 1918.
Colvin, C. Maria Edgeworth's literary manuscripts in the Bodleian Library. BLR 8 1970.
Colvin, C. [with M. Butler]. A revised date of birth for Maria Edgeworth. N & Q Sep 1971.
Butler, M. Maria Edgeworth: a literary biography. 1972.
McCormack, W. J. and K. Walker (ed). The absentee. 1988. Contains Edgeworth's notes for Essay on the genius and style of Edmund Burke 1805–7, and a textual note on alterations to text between 1812 and 1832.
McCormack, W. J. The tedium of history; an approach to Maria Edgeworth's Patronage (1814). In Ideology and the historian, ed Ciaran Brady, Dublin 1991.
See also Amer Monthly Mag *3: 193; (S. C. Hall and Mrs S. C. Hall)* Art Jnl *18: 345; (J. Foster)* Eclectic Rev *12: 879. 16: 979;* Englishwoman's Domestic Mag *13: 28. 25: 43;* Godey's Lady's Book *76: 161; (A. Repplier)* Lippincott's Mag *47: 390;* Littell's Living Age *59: 290;* London Mag *14: 49; (Goldwin Smith)* Nation *36: 322, (A. V. Dicey) 63: 162, (J. W. Chadwick) 60: 129; (W. Phillips)* North Amer Rev *6: 153, (E. Everett) 17: 383; Selections from* Edinburgh Rev *2: 464, and appendix;* Sharpe's London Mag *50: 326;* Southern Literary Messenger *15: 578, 3: 465, 532;* Spectator *57: 285, 73: 811; (C. H. Dall)* Unitarian Rev *19: 333.* [JD]

Pierce Egan 1772–1849

See col 2141.

Eliza Fenwick 1766?–1840

Bibliography

Block, A. In his The English novel 1740–1850, 1961.
Frank, F. S. In his The first gothics: a critical guide to the gothic novel. New York 1987.
Grundy, Isobel. In her edn of Secresy, Peterborough, Ontario 1994.

§1

Secresy, or, the ruin on the rock, by a woman. 2 vols 1795, Boston 1795, Philadelphia 1795, New York 1974 (facs), introd by J. Todd 1 vol 1989; ed I. Grundy, Peterborough, Ontario 1994.
REVIEWS: Analytical Rev July 1795; Monthly Rev Sep 1795; Br Critic Nov 1795.
The life of Carlo, the famous dog of Drury Lane theatre. With his portrait and other copper plates. 1804.
REVIEW: Critical Rev Jan 1805.
Mary and her cat. 1804. There are no known complete copies of this book.
Presents for good girls. [1804.]
Presents for good boys. 1805.
A visit to the juvenile library, or knowledge proved to be the source of happiness. 1805, New York 1977 (facs).
The class book; or three hundred and sixty-five reading lessons adapted to the use of schools. By Rev David Blair. 1806, 1807, 1836, 1858 (13th edn).
Infantine stories. Composed progressively, in words of one, two & three syllables. 1810, 1815.
Lessons for children; or rudiments of good manners, morals and humanity. nd, 1811 (2nd edn), 1813; tr Fr 1820.
Rays from the rainbow. Being an easy method for perfecting children in the first principles of grammar, without the smallest trouble to the instructor. 1812 (2nd edn).

Letters

The fate of the Fenwicks, letters to Mary Hays (1798–1828). Ed A. F. Wedd 1927.
In a letter pbd in The fate of the Fenwicks, *Fenwick stated that she pbd* The class book *under the pseud of the Rev David Blair. She may have also pbd other anthologies and children's books under that or another pseud for Benjamin Tabart's Juvenile Lib.*

§2

A biographical dictionary of the living authors of Great Britain and Ireland. 1816, Detroit 1966 (facs).
Todd, Janet (ed). Dictionary of British women writers 1660–1800. 1985.
Grundy, Isabel. In her edition of Secresy, Peterborough, Ontario 1994. [PP]

Susan Edmonstone Ferrier 1782–1854

Bibliographies

Leclaire, L. In his A general analytical bibliography of the regional novelists of the British Isles 1800–1950, Paris 1954.
Cullinan, Mary. In her Susan Ferrier, Boston 1984.

Collections

Ferrier's Marriage, Inheritance, Destiny. London and New York nd.
Miss Ferrier's novels. 2 vols London and New York 1873–4.
Miss Ferrier's novels. 6 vols London and Edinburgh 1881–2.
Miss Ferrier's novels. 6 vols Boston 1893.
Novels. Ed R. B. Johnson, illustr N. Erichsen 6 vols 1894.
Works. Ed Lady M. Sackville 4 vols 1928. Vol 4 consists of Doyle's Memoir, *below.*

§1

Marriage: a novel. 3 vols 1818 (anon), London and Edinburgh 1819, 1819, 2 vols Edinburgh 1826, 1 vol London 1831 (Standard Novels), 1841 (rev), 1847 (Parlour Lib), 1856 (rev and corrected), New York 1860 (Lib of Select Novels), London [1873], [1878], New York 1882, 2 vols Boston 1893; ed Earl of Iddesleigh (with biographical preface by A. Goodrich-Freer) 2 vols London 1902; ed R. B. Johnson 1 vol 1928 (EL); 1953, New York and London 1971, Bampton, Oxfordshire 1984, New York and London 1986; tr Fr 4 vols 1825 (different translations).
REVIEWS: Blackwood's Mag June 1818; Br Critic July 1818.
The inheritance. 3 vols 1824, 1825, 1831, 1 vol 1831 (Standard Novels), 2 vols Philadelphia 1831, 1 vol London 1841, 1841 (rev), 1841 (Standard Novels), 1847 (Parlour Lib), 1853, 1857 (rev and corrected), [1873], [1878], 2 vols Boston 1893; ed Earl of Iddesleigh (with biographical preface by A. Goodrich-Freer) 2 vols London 1903; 1 vol Bampton, Oxfordshire 1984; tr Fr 5 vols 1824, Swed (as Arfgodset) 3 vols in 7 Stockholm 1836.
REVIEWS: Blackwood's Mag June 1824, Br Critic Nov 1824.
Destiny: or the chief's daughter. 3 vols 1831, London and Edinburgh 1831, 1 vol London 1831 (Standard Novels), 1841 (rev), 1852, 1856 (rev and corrected), [1873], [1878], 2 vols Boston 1893; tr Swed (as Odet, eller testamentet) 3 vols in 7 Stockholm 1836.
REVIEW: Monthly Rev May 1831.

§2

Gore, C. Review of Women as they are. Edinburgh Rev July 1830.
Lockhart, J. G. Noctes ambrosianae 58. Blackwood's Mag Sep 1831.
[Moir, G.] Susan Ferrier's novels. Edinburgh Rev 74, 1842.
Miss Ferrier's novels. Temple Bar Oct 1878.

Hamilton, C. J. In her Women writers ser 1, 1892. Ch 14.
Douglas, G. In his Blackwood group, [1897].
Memoir and correspondence of Susan Ferrier 1782–1854. Ed J. A. Doyle 1898, 1929.
Gwynn, S. Miss Ferrier. Macmillan's Mag Apr 1899.
Johnson, R. B. In his Women novelists, [1918].
Grant, A. Susan Ferrier of Edinburgh: a biography. Denver 1957.
Parker, W. M. Susan Ferrier and John Galt. 1965.
Blain, Clements and Grundy (ed). The feminist companion to literature in English. 1990. [PP]

James Baillie Fraser 1783–1856

Bibliographies

Sadleir, M. In his XIX century fiction: a bibliographical record, 2 vols 1951.

§1

Journal of a tour through part of the Himālā mountains and to the sources of Jumna and Ganges. 1820.
Narrative of a journey into Khorasan 1821–2 including accounts of countries NE of Persia. 1825.
Travels and adventures in the Persian provinces on the southern banks of the Caspian Sea. With notices on the geology and commerce of Persia. 1826.
The Kuzzilbash: a tale of Khorasan. 3 vols 1828. Anon.
The Persian adventurer: being the sequel of the Kuzzilbash. 3 vols 1830.
The Highland smugglers, by the author of Adventures of a Kuzzilbash. 3 vols 1832.
Tales of the Caravanserai: the Khan's tale. 1833, Philadelphia 1833, London 1850.
An historical and descriptive account of Persia including descriptions of Afghanistan and Beloochistan. 1834, New York 1836, 1842, London 1843.
Narrative of the residence of the Persian princes in London in 1835 and 1836, with an account of their journey from Persia and subsequent adventures. 2 vols 1838, 1838.
A winter's journey (Tâtar) from Constantinople to Tehran, with travels through various parts of Persia, etc. 2 vols 1838.
Travels in Koordistan, Mesopotamia, etc . . . . 2 vols 1840.
Mesopotamia and Assyria from the earliest ages to the present time . . . . Edinburgh and London 1842, New York 1842, 1845, Edinburgh 1846.
Alle Neemroo, the Buchtiaree adventurer: a tale of Louristan. 3 vols 1842.
The dark falcon: a tale of the Attruck. 4 vols 1844.
Military memoir of Lieut-Col James Skinner . . . and several personages in the service of the native powers in India. 2 vols 1851.
Fraser was a regular contributor to Blackwood's Mag *1829–38.*

§2

Archer, M. and T. Falk. India revealed: the art and adventures of James and William Fraser 1802–35. 1989.

John Galt 1779–1839

NLS contains many letters, and Galt's mss of The howdie, The last of the lairds, *and* Ringan Gilhaize. *Other mss (largely unpbd) are in National Archives of Canada, Ottawa; Archives of Ontario, Toronto; Public Record Office; Scottish Record Office; and the Public Record Office of Northern Ireland, Belfast. The mss poems once in the James Watt Library, Greenock, are missing. Minor holdings of letters and mss are in BL, Bodleian, Derbyshire County Lib, Harvard, HRHRC, and in the libs of the univ of Toronto, Edinburgh and Guelph (Ontario). Harriet Pigott collected ms material for* A life of Galt *in 1838, now in Bodleian. For other holdings, see N. M. Whistler's unpbd 1992 Univ of Cambridge PhD dissertation* John Galt and the New World.

Bibliographies

Lumsden, H. The bibliography of John Galt. Records of Glasgow Bibl Soc 9 1931.
Booth, B. A. A bibliography of John Galt. BB 16 1936.
Gordon, I. A. John Galt: the life of a writer. Edinburgh 1972.
Whistler, N. M. John Galt and the New World. Unpbd PhD diss, Univ of Cambridge 1992.
The fullest bibliography is in Whistler. An updated bibliography is in preparation by T. Sauer, Univ of Guelph. The national union catalogue for pre-1956 imprints contains much additional information, especially about Amer edns.

Collections

Colls of Galt's works contain only a very small proportion of his literary output. Galt used many publishers, but one, William Blackwood, kept control of Galt's best-known fictions against Galt's wishes, making a proper contemporary col of his works unfeasible.
Blackwood's standard novels. Ed D. M. Moir, 4 vols 1841–3. Vol 1 Annals of the parish, The Ayrshire legatees; vol 2 The provost, The steam-boat, The omen; vol 3 Sir Andrew Wylie; vol 4 The entail. Regularly rptd (*see* M. Sadleir, Nineteenth century fiction, vol 2); rptd in 4 vols 1907.
Works. Ed D. S. Meldrum and S. R. Crockett, illustr J. Wallace, 8 vols Edinburgh and Boston 1895. This edn re-edited by D. S. Meldrum and W. Roughead with the addition of Ringan Gilhaize, 10 vols Edinburgh 1936.

§1

For contemporary reviews of individual works, see I. A. Gordon, 1972; William S. Ward, Literary reviews in British periodicals 1798–1820 A bibliography, *2 vols New York and London 1972, and* Literary Reviews in British periodicals 1821–1826 A bibliography, *New York and London 1977 (Ward lists 126 reviews of Galt's works); and F. H. Lyell,* A study of the novels of John Galt, *1942. The earliest available reviews of most works are included in the list that follows, along with a few especially important reviews, and reviews not in Ward or Lyell.*

The posthumous 1841–3 Blackwood edn determined the text of many of the major Galt fictions. Most readers were unaware that the editor D. M. Moir had silently introduced numerous deviations from the original texts as proofed by Galt. Until comparatively recently all edns of single works presented only texts altered by Moir. The collected edns continue to do so. Moir's interference reached its limit, while Galt was absent in Canada, in a bowdlerised and reshaped The last of the lairds, *1826: see I. A. Gordon's* Plastic surgery on a nineteenth century novel . . . *in* Library, *Sep 1977. The first Galt novels to be rptd as Galt proofed them were Ringan Gilhaize, ed G. Douglas 1899, and* The entail, *ed J. Ayscough, Oxford 1913. Annals of the parish, ed J. Kinsley, Oxford 1967, initiated a new series of Galt titles (5 ed I. A. Gordon 1970–85), all faithful to the original printings, and with full textual notes. Ringan Gilhaize was edited, with textual notes, by P. J. Wilson 1984.*

The battle of Largs: a Gothic poem with several miscellaneous pieces. 1804. Anon (8 reviews for Largs listed in Ward).
Voyages and travels in the years 1809, 1810 and 1811: containing statistical, commercial and miscellaneous observations on Gibraltar, Sardinia, Sicily, Malta, Serigo and Turkey. 1812. Quarto.
REVIEWS: GM Feb, Mar, June 1812.
Cursory reflections on political and commercial topics as connected with the Regent's accession to royal authority. 1812, 1812. 99-page pam.
The tragedies of Maddalen, Agamemnon, Lady Macbeth, Antonia and Clytemnestra. 1812, 1812.
REVIEWS: Brit Critic May 1814; Quart Rev Apr 1814.
The life and administration of Cardinal Wolsey. 1812, 1817, Edinburgh 1824; ed W. Hazlitt 1846. Quarto.
REVIEW: Quart Rev Sep 1812.
Letters from the Levant: containing views of the state of society, manners, opinions and commerce in Greece and several of the principal islands of the archipelago. 1813.
REVIEW: Br Critic Jan 1814.

Lives of the British admirals: containing also a new and accurate naval history, from the earliest periods. By Dr John Campbell. Continued to the year 1779 by Dr Berkenhout. 8 vols, commencing 1812. The original editor of this new edn was Henry Redhead Yorke. Galt contributed the anon lives of Anson, Hawke and Byron to vol 6, ed W. Stevenson 1814.

The original and rejected theatre (later The new British theatre), edited by John Galt. 4 vols 1814–15. This periodical contains 10 of Galt's dramas, all anon. Vol 1 (1814) includes The prophetess, The word of honour, The witness (performed and printed at Edinburgh in 1818 as The appeal, *see below*), The masquerade, and The watch-house (written in collaboration with his brother Thomas). The mermaid is in Vol 2 (1814), and vol 3 of the same year holds The sorceress, Orpheus, The apostate (part of which was rptd in The Knickerbocker in July 1838 as The Atlantines), and Love, honour, and interest. Vol 4 (1815) has Hector, and The Savoyard: a drama.

King Edward III: an historical drama. 1815. Anon. Copy in Huntington.

The Majolo: a tale. 1815. Anon. A second vol was added, and the work was rptd in 1816, *see below*.

The life and studies of Benjamin West, esq President of the Royal Academy of London, prior to his arrival in England; compiled from materials furnished by himself. 1816, Philadelphia 1816, 1817, London 1817, 1820. A 2nd vol or part was pbd in 1820, *see below*. 1816 vol abridged Boston 1831, 1832 (as The progress of genius: or authentic memoirs of the early life of West). Facs edn, including both parts, ed N. Wright, Gainesville FL 1960.
REVIEW: Critical Rev May 1816.

The crusade: a poem. 1816. Anon.

The Majolo: a tale. 2 vols 1816. Galt added his name, and another vol, to The Majolo of 1815.
REVIEW: Eclectic Rev Jan 1816.

The appeal: a tragedy in three acts: as performed at the Theatre-Royal, Edinburgh. 1818. Anon. The play is Galt's The witness of 1814, with a prologue by J. G. Lockhart, and epilogue by Sir Walter Scott.
REVIEW: Monthly Mag Apr 1818.

The rocking-horse: or true things and sham things: intended for the amusement and instruction of children, by 'Robin Goodfellow'. [1819?] (no known copies), New York 1825 (copy in UCLA lib).

The history of Gog and Magog, the champions of London: containing an account of the origin of many things relative to the city. A tale. By 'Robin Goodfellow'. 1819, facs edn 1985, of 1819 copy in the Osborne and Lillian H. Smith cols, Toronto Public Lib.

Glenfell: or Macdonalds and Campbells. An Edinburgh tale of the nineteenth century. 1820. Anon. Fiction; tr Fr 1823.

The wandering Jew: or the travels and observations of Hareach the prolonged . . . By the 'Rev T. Clark'. 1820, [1820] (second edn, rev as The travels and observations of Hareach, the wandering Jew . . .).

An abridgement of the most popular modern voyages and travels . . . By the 'Rev T. Clark'. 4 vols 1820. Vols sold separately. Vol 1 Europe; vol 2 Asia; vol 3 Africa; vol 4 America. For example, a fuller title for vol 2 is Popular voyages and travels: comprising the tour of Asia . . . with introductory remarks on the character and manners of various Asiatic nations.

All the voyages round the world . . . By 'Captain Samuel Prior'. 1820, 1821, New York 1843.

The life, studies, and works of Benjamin West, esq President of the Royal Academy of London, composed from materials furnished by himself. 2 vols London and Edinburgh 1820, 1960. Vol 1 is as pbd in 1816; vol 2, headed Part 2, is The life and works of Benjamin West, esq President of the Royal Academy of London, subsequent to his arrival in this country; composed from materials furnished by himself.

The earthquake: a tale. 3 vols Edinburgh 1820 (anon), 2 vols New York 1821.
REVIEW: Blackwood's Mag Jan 1821.

Andrew of Padua, the improvisatore: a tale from the Italian of the Abbate Furbo. And The vindictive father, from the Spanish of Leandra of Valladerras. 1820. Anon. Copy in Guelph Public Lib.

A description of Death on the pale horse; also a catalogue of pictures, representing a series of events connected with the life and death of our Saviour: painted by B. West . . . . 1820. Signed J. G. Copy in Boston Athenaeum.

Pictures, historical and biographical, drawn from English, Scottish and Irish history. 2 vols 1821, 1824.

Annals of the parish: or the chronicle of Dalmailing during the ministry of the Rev Micah Balwhidder. Written by himself. Edinburgh 1821 (anon), Philadelphia 1821, Edinburgh 1822, 1841 (with the Ayrshire legatees, *below*), 1844 etc; ed J. I. Watson (with The Ayrshire legatees), Glasgow 1877; ed S. R. Crockett 1895; ed A. Ainger 1895; ed G. S. Gordon 1908; ed J. MacInnes [1908]; abridged G. C. Pringle (as The minister of Dalmailing) 1909; ed G. B. Macdonald 1910 (EL); illustr H. W. Kerr 1910, 1928; ed W. M. Parker 1952; ed J. Kinsley, Oxford 1967; ed J. Kinsley and I. A. Gordon, Oxford 1986 (WC); tr Fr 3 vols 1824. Dramatised for television by H. MacMillan, BBC Scotland Oct–Nov 1981 (dir J. Hunter, prod T. Cotter); Audio-cassette edn, Audio visual lib services, Falkirk 1982.
REVIEWS: Blackwood's Mag May 1821 (several reviews were rptd by Moir in an appendix to Annals, 1841).

The Ayrshire legatees: or the Pringle family. Edinburgh 1821 (anon), Edinburgh 1823 (with The gathering of the West, *below*), New York 1823, Edinburgh 1841 (with Annals, *above*, and a memoir by Δ [D. M. Moir]), 1844 etc; ed J. I. Watson (with Annals, *above*), Glasgow 1877; ed A. Ainger (with Annals) 1895, 1896, 1903; ed G. B. Macdonald 1910; abridged Glasgow [1922]; ed F. Beaumont [1930]. First pbd in Blackwood's Mag June 1820–Feb 1821, rptd in Portfolio (Philadelphia) 1821–2.
REVIEW: John Bull July 1821.

The national spelling-book . . ., revised and improved by the 'Rev T. Clark'. 1821, 1823.

The national reader: consisting of early lessons in history, geography, biography, natural history, mythology . . . by the 'Rev T. Clark'. 1821, 1821, 1823.

Sir Andrew Wylie, of that ilk. 3 vols Edinburgh 1822, 1822, 2 vols New York 1822, London 1841, 1850, 1854, 1868 etc, 2 vols Boston 1895. Fiction.

The Provost. Edinburgh 1822 (anon), 1822, New York 1822, Edinburgh 1842 (with The steam-boat and The omen), 1850, 1869, 2 vols Boston 1896; illustr J. M. Aitken 1913; 1968; ed I. A. Gordon, Oxford 1973; ed I. A. Gordon, Oxford 1982 (WC); tr Fr 3 vols 1824 (with Annals). Fiction.
REVIEW: Quarterly Rev Jan 1822.

The steam-boat. Edinburgh 1822 (anon), New York 1823; Edinburgh 1842 (with The provost and The omen), 1850, 1869 etc; tr Ger 1826. First pbd in Blackwood's Mag Feb–Sep 1821.

The gathering of the West: or We've come to see the King. Edinburgh 1823 (anon, with The Ayrshire legatees); ed B. A. Booth, Baltimore 1939, rptd New York 1979. First pbd in Blackwood's Mag Sep 1822, and pbd in 1822 in pam form (same setting, different pagination). Fiction.

The English primer; or child's first book . . . by the 'Rev T. Clark'. [1822]; tr Fr, date unknown.

The English mother's first catechism for her children: containing those things most necessary to be known at an early age. Illustrated by one hundred engravings. By the 'Rev T. Clark'. Intended as a sequel to The English primer. 1822, 1824; tr Fr, date unknown.

New general school atlas . . . by the 'Rev T. Clark'. [1822?].

A new series of maps . . . by the 'Rev T. Clark'. [1822?].

The universal traveller, containing the popular features and contents of the best standard modern travels, in the four quarters of the world. By 'Samuel Prior'. 1822.

The entail: or the lairds of Grippy. 3 vols Edinburgh '1823' [1822] (anon), New York 1823, London 1842, 1850, 2 vols Boston 1896; ed J. Ayscough, Oxford 1913 (WC); ed I. A. Gordon, Oxford 1984 (WC); tr Ger 1823. Fiction.
REVIEW: Literary Gazette Dec 1822.

Ringan Gilhaize: or the covenanters. 3 vols Edinburgh 1823 (anon), 2 vols New York 1823, Glasgow [1870]; ed G. Douglas 1899, 1902; ed P. Wilson, Edinburgh 1984. Fiction.
REVIEW: Literary Chron May 1823.

Modern geography and history . . . by the 'Rev T. Clark'. 1823.

The spaewife: a tale of the Scottish chronicles. 3 vols Edinburgh 1823 (anon), 2 vols Philadelphia 1824, 1 vol [1880?]. Fiction.
REVIEW: Edinburgh Literary Gazette Mar 1824.

The bachelor's wife: a selection of curious and interesting extracts. Edinburgh 1824.

Rothelan: a romance of the English histories. 3 vols Edinburgh 1824 (anon), 2 vols New York 1825; tr Ger 1826, 1826, 1827.
REVIEW: Examiner Nov 1824.

The omen. Edinburgh '1826' [1825] (anon); rptd 1842 (with The provost and The steam-boat), New York 1844 (in The omnibus of modern romance), 1850, 1869. Fiction.
REVIEWS: Literary Gazette Feb 1826; Blackwood's Mag (by Sir Walter Scott) July 1826.

The last of the lairds: or the life and opinions of Malachi Mailings esq of Auldbiggings. Edinburgh 1826 (anon), New York 1827; illustr H. W. Kerr 1926. The final chapters were written by D. M. Moir. Ed I. A. Gordon (from Galt's ms in NLS), Edinburgh and London 1976 (replacing Moir's altered text). Fiction.
REVIEW: Literary Chron Dec 1826.

To shareholders of the Canada Co. 1829. Pam.

Lawrie Todd: or the settlers in the woods. 3 vols 1830, 1830, 2 vols New York 1830, 1832, etc; ed G. Thorburn 1845, 1849 (rev), [1880?]; Melbourne [1890?]. Autobiography (G. Thorburn's) and fiction.

Southennan. 3 vols 1830, 2 vols New York 1830. Fiction.

The life of Lord Byron. 1830, 1830, Dublin 1830, New York and Philadelphia 1830, 1831, 1832, New York 1835, 1841, 1845, [1908]; tr Fr 1836.
REVIEW: Literary Gazette Aug 1830.

Bogle Corbet: or the emigrants. 3 vols 1831; ed E. Waterston, Toronto 1977. Fiction.
REVIEW: Literary Gazette Apr 1831.

The lives of the players. 2 vols 1831, Boston 1831, 1 vol 1886.
REVIEW: NMM Aug 1831.

The member: an autobiography, by 'Archibald Jobbry'. 1832, '1833' [1832] (with The radical, *below*, as The reform); ed I. A. Gordon, Edinburgh and London 1975, Edinburgh 1985. Fiction.
REVIEW: The Athenaeum Jan 1832.

Stanley Buxton: or the schoolfellows. 3 vols 1832, 2 vols Philadelphia 1833, Boston 1833. Fiction.
REVIEW: NMM May 1832.

The radical: an autobiography, by 'Nathan Butt!'. 1832, '1833' [1832] (with The member, *above*, as The reform). Fiction.

The Canadas as they at present commend themselves to the enterprise of emigrants, colonists and capitalists, compiled and condensed from original documents furnished by John Galt, by Andrew Picken. 1832, 1836.

The stolen child: a tale of the town. 1833, Philadelphia 1833.

Eben Erskine: or the traveller. 3 vols 1833, 2 vols Philadelphia 1933. Fiction.

The Ouranoulogos: or the celestial volume. Edinburgh and London 1833. Plate by J. Martin, illustrating Galt's story The deluge. Royal quarto.

Autobiography. 2 vols Edinburgh 1833, Boston 1834, Philadelphia 1834.

Poems. 1833.

Stories of the study. 3 vols 1833.

The literary life and miscellanies. 3 vols 1834.

Efforts. By an invalid. Greenock 1835, London 1835. Poems.

A contribution to the Greenock calamity fund. Greenock 1835. Poems.

Scotland delivered. Irvine, Ayrshire 1837 (anon). Poem. Attributed to Galt on the basis of internal evidence by H. B. Timothy, *see below*.

The demon of destiny and other poems. Greenock 1839.

The howdie and other tales. Ed W. Roughead, Edinburgh 1923.

A rich man and other stories. Ed W. Roughead 1925.

Poems. Ed G. H. Needler 1954.

The collected poems of John Galt, 1779–1839. Ed H. B. Timothy, 2 vols: vol 1 [London, Ontario?] 1969 (reprints pbd poems); vol 2 [Regina, Saskatchewan?] 1982.

Selected short stories. Ed I. A. Gordon, Edinburgh 1978.

Contributions to periodicals

Galt edited or helped to edit several newspapers and mags, and wrote hundreds of contributions in many genres for numerous jnls (for a list of his pseudonyms etc, see Whistler, Bibliographies, *above). His most frequent appearances were in* NMM *(1814–32),* Blackwood's Mag *(1819–36),* Fraser's Mag *(1830–7) and* Tait's Edinburgh Mag *(1832–6), many indexed in* Wellesley 5. *For items prior to Wellesley's starting-point, and for appearances in* Monthly Mag *(1812–34), and occasional contributions to* Philosophical Mag, GM *and* Literary Souvenir, *see Whistler, and index in I. A. Gordon, 1972. Whistler vol 2, section 2, pp. 1–31, identifies many contributions not described in Lumsden, Booth, or the list of Galt's works in Gordon. Whistler vol 3 reproduces (mainly in facs) 23 of Galt's pre-1809 publications, and nearly 70 of his periodical publications on 'New World' matters.*

Collaborative works

Galt wrote part of the biography of John Wilson prefixed to Scottish descriptive poems, 1803. He collaborated with Henry Redhead Yorke on The lives of the British admirals, *1814; with his brother Thomas on the play* The watch-house, *1814; and with Benjamin West on the creation of Galt's biography of West, 1816 and 1820. Galt contributed a biographical sketch to J. F. W. Herschel's edn of William Spence's* Mathematical essays, *1819. He collaborated with other authors in works pbd by J. Souter and Sir Richard Phillips; with Grant Thorburn, whose autobiography forms the first part of* Lawrie Todd, *1830; and with various other writers for* Blackwood's Mag. *Five stories are in A. Picken's* The club book, *3 vols 1831, all rptd in W. Hazlitt's* Romanticist and novelist's library, *1841; for Galt's collaboration with J. Martin on* The Ouranoulogos, *1833, see Gordon and Whistler,* Bibliographies, *above. Galt includes a story by his son Alexander in* Stories of the study, *1833 (The black pirate).*

Letters

Most of Galt's correspondence, of which many hundred letters are extant, is unpbd. A preliminary catalogue of his letters, and a checklist of his correspondents, is in Whistler. Some of his letters were printed in his autobiographies, and in D. M. Moir's Biographical memoir *of 1841; those to Lady Blessington in* R. R. Madden's Literary life and correspondence of the Countess of Blessington, *1855, and in A. Morrison's* The Blessington papers, *1895. An edn of the letters is planned, under the editorship of N. M. Whistler.*

Translations, editions, introductions, prefaces and commendatory verses

Galt's plays The word of honour, *1814, and* Love, honour and interest, *1814, are translated and adapted from the Italian of C. Goldoni;* Andrew of Padua, *1820, is translated and adapted from the Italian of Abbate Furbo, and its companion-piece* The vindictive father *is from the Spanish of Leandra of Valladerras. Galt edited many plays for his* Rejected or New British Theatre *1814–15; several works for J. Souter and Sir Richard Phillips; vols 3 and 4 of Lady Charlotte Bury's* A diary illustrative of the life and times of George the Fourth, *1838; Harriet Pigott's 3-vol* Records of real life in the palace and the cottage, *1839 (which is introduced by a sketch of Galt's character and works by Lady Charlotte Bury, see copy in Thomas Fisher Lib, Univ of Toronto). The 1824 Oliver and Boyd edn of the works of Henry Mackenzie is introduced by Galt's* Critical dissertation on Mackenzie's tales. *Galt wrote prefaces to Pigott and Bury, and a preface to Blackwood's 1822 edn of A. Graydon's* Memoirs of a life, chiefly passed in Pennsylvania..., *1811. Galt's* Triumphal glee... sung after drinking the health of his Royal Highness the Prince Regent... *broadsheet, 1815 (copy in Aberdeen Univ Lib), is one of several commendatory verses and songs, some with music, pbd by Galt.*

Attributed works

Galt published over 90 vols, used more than 20 publishers, and more than 20 pseudonyms (or initials) to indicate or conceal his authorship. Every serious student of Galt's work has added to his bibliography, and no bibliography of Galt is likely to be definitive. Galt's own later eds of his works are often a useful source of information (see Lawrie Todd, *3rd edn). Because he was so playful about claiming, hiding, or sharing his authorship, works are sometimes ascribed to Galt that should not be (for example* Pen Owen, *1851 New York edn, and* The life of George the Third, *1820), and other authors have garnered praise for work that is, or may be, by Galt (see Whistler,* Bibliographies, *above). Galt viewed his literary activities as secondary, and foresaw that his colonising activities would provide a subject for literature. Part of D. D. C. Chambers's group of poems* Van Egmond: studies for a lost portrait (Northward Jnl 54 1990) *is a recent example of literature about Galt as nation-builder.*

§2

Mr Galt's novels. Literary Gazette June 1822.
Note on Galt. Blackwood's Mag June 1822.
Secondary Scottish novels. Edinburgh Rev Oct 1822.
Moir, D. M. Essay on Galt. Edinburgh Literary Gazette May 1829.
Review of Autobiography. Johnstone's Edinburgh Mag (with a general assessment of Galt's work) Oct 1833.
Genius of Galt. Monthly Mag Jan 1834.
Hazlitt, W. 'Advertisement' to 3rd edn of Life of Wolsey. 1846.
Maginn, W. In A gallery of illustrious literary characters, 1873.
Gilray, T. John Galt. Encyclopaedia Britannica 1879.
John Galt. In Dublin Univ Mag 84 1879.
Millar, J. H. The novels of John Galt. Blackwood's Mag June 1896.
Douglas, G. John Galt. In The Blackwood group, Edinburgh and London 1897.
Oliphant, M. William Blackwood and his sons. 1897.
Millar, J. H. A literary history of Scotland. 1903.
Gordon, R. K. John Galt. Toronto 1920.

Biographies

Moir, D. M. Biographical memoir of John Galt. Edinburgh 1841.
Aberdein, J. W. John Galt. Oxford 1936.
Gordon, I. A. John Galt: the life of a writer. Edinburgh 1972.
Scott, P. H. John Galt. Edinburgh 1985. [NW]

John Gamble 1770–1831

Sketches of history, politics and manners, taken in Dublin and the North of Ireland in the autumn of 1810. 1811, 1826.
A view of society and manners in the North of Ireland, in the summer and autumn of 1812. 1813.
Sarsfield, or wanderings of youth: an Irish tale. 3 vols 1814.
Howard. 2 vols 1815.
Northern Irish tales. 2 vols 1818.
Views of society and manners in the North of Ireland, in a series of letters written in the year 1818. 1819.
Charlton, or scenes in the North of Ireland: a tale. 3 vols 1823, 1827 (as Charlton: or scenes in Ireland).

For a listing of reviews and notices of Gamble's works, see Ward (1972, 1977). [PG]

Thomas Gaspey 1788–1871

The mystery, or forty years ago: a novel. 3 vols 1820 (anon), New York 1820; tr Fr 4 vols 1821.
Calthorpe, or fallen fortunes: a novel. 3 vols 1821, 2 vols Philadelphia 1821; tr Fr 1821, Ger 1823.
Takings, or the life of a collegian: a poem. Illustr R. Dagley 1821.
The Lollards: a tale founded on the persecutions which marked the early part of the fifteenth century. 3 vols 1822, 1 vol 1843 (rev), [1859]; tr Ger 1822.
Other times: or the monks of Leadenhall. 3 vols 1823, 1 vol [1858]; tr Ger 1827.
The witch-finder, or the wisdom of our ancestors: a romance. 3 vols 1824, 1 vol [1858].
History of George Godfrey, written by himself. 3 vols 1828 (anon).
The self-condemned: a romance, by the author of The Lollards. 3 vols 1836, 1 vol New York 1836, London 1838.
'Many coloured life': or tales of woe and touches of mirth, by the author of The Lollards etc. 1842.
The life and times of the good Lord Cobham. 2 vols 1843, 1844.
The pictorial history of France and of the French people. 2 vols 1843, 1 vol 1850. With G. M. Bussey.
The dream of human life, by the author of The Lollards. 2 vols [1849–52].
The history of Smithfield. 1852.
The political life of Wellington. [1853] (vol 3 of The life and times of the... Duke of Wellington, ed W. F. Williams).
The history of England from the reign of George the Third. 4 vols 1852–4 (vols 5–8 of The history of England, ed D. Hume), London and New York 1855–9 (as The history of England under the reign of George III, George IV, William IV and Queen Victoria [to 1852]; continued to 1859 by H. Tyrrell).

Attributed and spurious works

Richmond: or scenes in the life of a Bow Street officer, drawn up from his private memoranda. 3 vols 1827 (anon), 2 vols 1827, with introd by E. F. Bleiler 1 vol New York 1976. Also attributed to T. S. Surr.
Glory: a tale of morals drawn from history. Illustr J. Absolon. 1844. Attributed to George Gaspey. In A. Block, The English novel 1740–1850, 1961 (rev).

The following works are attributed by a variety of sources to Thomas Gaspey, but according to the DNB *these are by his son, Thomas W. Gaspey. This latter wrote books about the Rhine and Heidelberg, as well as numerous philological works. Thomas W. Gaspey also died in 1871 which perhaps explains some of the confusion that surrounds both father and son. Perhaps a clue to the authorship of these disputed texts can be found in the fact that whereas Thomas W. Gaspey was a PhD from Heidelberg, his father was a journalist and novelist.*

Laurence Stark: a family picture. Translated [from J. J. Engel] by Gaspey. Heidelberg 1843.
Family devotions, for every morning and evening throughout the year: translated from Sturm und Tiede by T. W. Gaspey and H. Schirges, by Thomas Gaspey. [1848?]
Heidelberg and its castle: a souvenir, dedicated to its English visitors. Darmstadt [185–?].
Tallis's illustrated scripture history for the improvement of youth: by the editor of Sturm's family devotions. 2 vols [1850?], London and New York 1851, 1 vol London [1852].
Gaspey's British conversations: social, commercial, historical, literary, etc. Heidelberg 1861.
Englisches konversations-grammatik zum schul- und privatunterricht. Heidelberg 1876, 1883, 1893, 1901, 1911, 1920, 1923, 1928, 1932, 1938, 1942. [AM]

Robert Pearse, or Pierce Gillies 1788–1858

§1

Childe Alarique: a poet's reverie. Edinburgh 1813 (anon), London and Edinburgh 1814 (with other poems), Philadelphia 1815.

Wallace: a fragment. Edinburgh 1813. Anon. Poem.

The confessions of Sir Henry Longueville: a novel. 2 vols Edinburgh 1814. Anon.

Illustrations of a poetical character, in four tales: with other poems. Edinburgh 1816 (anon), 1816 (enlarged).

Rinaldo, the visionary: a desultory poem. Edinburgh 1816. Anon.

Oswald: a metrical tale, illustrative of poetical character. Edinburgh 1817. Anon.

Tales of a voyager to the Arctic Ocean. 3 vols 1826 (anon), 2 vols Philadelphia 1827, 3 vols London 1834; tr Ger 1827.

Tales of a voyager to the Arctic Ocean: second series. 3 vols 1829, 1834.

Basil Barrington and his friends. 3 vols 1830.

Ranulph de Rohais: a romance of the twelfth century. 3 vols 1830.

Thurlston tales. 3 vols 1835, 2 vols Philadelphia 1835.

Recollections of Sir Walter Scott Bart. 1837.

Palmario: or the merchant of Genoa. 3 vols 1839.

Memoirs of a literary veteran: including sketches and anecdotes of the most distinguished literary characters from 1794 to 1849. 3 vols 1851.

Translations

Guilt, or the anniversary: a tragedy, from the German [of A. G. A. Muellner]. Edinburgh 1819. From Muellner's Die Schuld. Play.

The devil's elixir: from the German of E. T. A. Hoffmann. 2 vols Edinburgh 1824. From Hoffmann's Die Elixiere des Teufels.

German stories: selected from the works of Hoffmann, De la Motte Fouqué, Pichler, Kruse, and others. 3 vols Edinburgh 1826.

A winter night's dream: the seventh day. Edinburgh 1826. Poem. Loosely translated from the Swed of J. H. Akenthal.

Gillies also contributed to S. E. Brydges's The ruminator: containg a series of moral, critical and sentimental essays, *1813, and was the reputed author of* Extempore to Walter Scott, Esq, on the publication of the new edition of the bridal of Triermain *[1819]. He also edited the* Foreign Quart Rev, *from its foundation in 1827, and was a frequent contributor to* Blackwood's Mag, Fraser's Mag, *and other periodicals between 1824 and 1840.*

For a listing of reviews and notices of Gillies's works, see Ward (1972, 1977).

§2

Groves, D. Robert Gillies and A winter night's dream. N & Q 238, Dec 1993. [PG]

William Nugent Glascock 1787?–1847

Bibliographies

Sadleir, M. In his XIX century fiction: a bibliographical record, 2 vols 1951.

§1

The naval-sketch book: or the service afloat and ashore, with characteristic reminiscences, fragments and opinions, by an officer of rank. Ser 1 2 vols 1826, 1826, 1831; ser 2 2 vols 1834, 1835, 1 vol Philadelphia 1835, 2 vols London 1836, 1843. Ser 2 by the author of Tales of a tar.

Sailors and saints: or matrimonial manœuvres. 3 vols 1829, 1829, 2 vols New York 1829, 3 vols London 1834.

Tales of a tar, with characteristic anecdotes. 1830.

The naval service: or officers' manual for every grade in His Majesty's ships. 2 vols 1836, 1 vol 1838, 1848 (rev); ed J. Allen with ch on the steam engine by R. Roughton 1854, 1859; tr Fr 1840.

Land sharks and sea gulls. Illustr G. Cruikshank 3 vols 1838, Philadelphia 1838, London [1859], 1 vol [1860]. [AM]

George Robert Gleig, Reverend and later Chaplain-General 1796–1888

Ms fragment of Gleig's autobiography in Nat Lib os Scotland.

Bibliographies

Wolff, R. L. In his Nineteenth-century fiction: a bibliographical catalogue, 5 vols New York and London 1981–6.

§1

Narrative of the campaigns at Washington and New Orleans 1814–15. 1821 (anon), Philadelphia 1821, London 1826, 1827 (rev), 1836 (rev), 1847, 1861, 1879, 1886; tr Ger 1832.

The subaltern. Edinburgh and London 1825 (anon), New York 1825, Edinburgh 1826, London 1826, Edinburgh and London 1828, 1845, London 1845, 1852, 1855, Edinburgh 1872 (rev), London and Edinburgh 1872, Edinburgh 1900, London, New York and Toronto 1915; tr Sp 1830. Serialised in Blackwood's Mag Mar–Sep 1825.

Sermons doctrinal and practical for plain people. 1829, 1830.

The Chelsea Pensioners. 3 vols 1829, 1833, 1834, 1 vol 1840, 1841, [1870]; tr Ger 1830.

The country curate. 2 vols 1830, New York 1830, 1 vol London 1834, 1846 (rev), London and New York 1856. Chs 1–9 serialised in Blackwood's Mag Nov 1825–May 1826.

The life of Major-General Sir Thomas Munro, Bart. and KCB, late governor of Madras. 3 vols 1830, 2 vols 1831, 1 vol 1849 (rev), 1861 (rev).

The history of the Bible. 1830, 2 vols 1830–1, New York 1831, [1832?], 1833, 1835, 1836, 1838, 1839, [184–], 1842, 1844, 1846, 1857, 1859; ed S. Stall, Philadelphia, London and Toronto 1915 (as Gleig's wonderful book concerning the most wonderful book in the world).

The history of the British Empire in India. 4 vols 1830–5.

Lives of the most eminent British military commanders. 3 vols 1831–2, 1831–49, 1834, 2 vols New York 1835.

A subaltern in America: comprising his narrative of the campaigns of the British army at Baltimore, Washington, etc. during the late war. Philadelphia and Baltimore 1833. This is possibly a pirated edn, which only appeared in the US. 21 chs appeared in Blackwood's Mag Mar–Sep 1827.

Allan Breck. A novel. 3 vols 1834, 2 vols Philadelphia 1835.

The chronicles of Waltham. 3 vols 1835, 1 vol 1835, 1861, 3 vols 1865 (as Waltham: or chronicles of a country village).

The family history of England: with pictorial illustrations. 3 vols 1836–42, 1852, 1854, 1872 (rev), 1879.

The hussar. 2 vols 1837, 1837, [1837], 1 vol Cincinnati 1838, 2 vols London 1844, 1 vol Philadelphia and London 1847, [1857].

Chelsea Hospital and its traditions. 3 vols 1838, 1 vol 1839.

Germany, Bohemia and Hungary: visited in 1837. 3 vols 1839.

The life of Oliver Cromwell. Sandbornton NH 1840.

Memoirs of the life of the Right Hon Warren Hastings, first Governor-General of Bengal. 3 vols 1841.

A memoir of the late Major General Craufurd, with an account of his funeral. 1842, 1871 (as The funeral of General Craufurd). Rptd from the Gem.

The veterans of Chelsea Hospital. 3 vols 1842, 1844, 1 vol London and New York 1857; tr Ger 1850.

The light dragoon. 2 vols 1844, 1850, 1 vol 1851, 1853, 1856.

A sketch of the military history of Great Britain. 1845.

Things old and new: being a sequel to the Chronicles of Waltham. 1845 (2nd edn).

Sale's brigade in Afghanistan: with an account of the seizure and defence of Jellalabad. 1846, 1851, 1861, 1879.

The story of the battle of Waterloo. 1847, New York 1847, London 1848, New York 1855, 1875, London 1907.

The life of Robert, first Lord Clive. 1848, 1861, 1869, 1907.

The Leipsic campaign. 1852, 2 vols 1852 (as The battle of Leipzig), 1 vol 1856.

The Duke of Wellington. 1853.

India and its army. 1857. Rptd from Edinburgh Rev 1857.
Essays biographical, historical and miscellaneous, contributed chiefly to the Edinburgh and Quarterly Reviews. 2 vols 1858.
History of the life of Arthur, Duke of Wellington: from the French of M. Brialmont. 4 vols 1858–60, 1 vol (as The life of Arthur, [first] Duke of Wellington) 1862, 1864, 1865, 1871 (rev), 1873 (rev), New York 1899, London and New York 1903, 1909, 1927 (as The life of the Duke of Wellington).
The Harrises: being an extract from the commonplace-book of Alexander Smith the Elder. 3 vols 1870 (anon), 1 vol 1889 (as With the Harrises seventy years ago: by the author of The subaltern).
The life of Sir Walter Scott. Edinburgh 1871. Rptd from Quart Rev.
The history of the reign of George III to the battle of Waterloo. 1873.
The great problem: can it be solved? 1876.
Personal reminiscences of the first Duke of Wellington. Ed M. E. Gleig, Edinburgh and London 1904, New York 1904.

Attributed and spurious works
The stranger's grave. 1823, Boston 1824, Exeter 1828, London 1845. Previously attributed to De Quincey, but more probably by Gleig.
Saratoga: a tale of revolution. 2 vols 1824. Also attributed to Eliza Lanesford (Foster) Cushing.
Tales of a voyager to the Arctic ocean. 3 vols 1826, 2 vols 1827, 3 vols 1829, 6 vols 1834 (including 3 vols from a second ser). More correctly attributed to Robert Pierce Gillies.
The subaltern's log book including anecdotes of well known military characters. 2 vols 1828, New York 1829.
Gleig supervised and contributed to Gleig's school series, *58 vols 1850–[75]. He also edited* The only daughter, *3 vols 1838, and* Self-devotion: or the history of Katherine Randolph, *1842, by [Harriette Campbell];* Leaves from the journal of a subaltern during the campaign in the Punjaub, Sep 1848 to Mar 1849, *1849; and* The soldier's manual of devotion *[1862]. He wrote supplementary text for a number of works, including C. Werner,* Carl Werner's Jerusalem, Bethlehem and the Holy Places: with descriptive letterpress by G. R. Gleig, *1865; and* A glimpse of Oriental nature: pictures with verses by a lady, with a Preface by G. R. Gleig, *1865. He pbd sermons and devotional works and engaged in controversies on military and church matters.*

§2
Siborne, W. History of the war in France and Belgium, with remarks on G. R. Gleig's Story of Waterloo. 1848.
Macaulay, T. B. Warren Hastings. 1856. With review of Gleig's Life of Hastings.
Maginn, W. In his A gallery of illustrious literary characters, ed W. Bates [1873]. Rptd from Fraser's Mag.
Hamley, E. B. Death of Mr Gleig. Blackwood's Mag Aug 1888.
Symonds, B. The stranger's grave: laying a De Quinceyan ghost. In CLB 83, July 1993. Concerning the claims of authorship of De Quincey and Gleig. [AM]

Catherine Grace Frances Gore, née Moody

1799–1861

Manuscripts
Letters in Bentley Collection, BL.
Also biographical notice with letter, 1860, BL.

Bibliographies
Sadleir, M. In his XIX century fiction: a bibliographical record, 2 vols 1951.
Woolf, R. L. in his Nineteenth-century fiction: a bibliographical catalogue, 5 vols New York and London 1981–6.

§1
The two broken hearts: a tale. 1823 (anon). Poem.
Theresa Marchmont, or the maid of honour: a tale. 1824, rptd in vol 1 of Edinburgh tales, ed. J. Stone, 1845.
The bond: a dramatic poem. 1824.
A good night's rest: or two in the morning: a farce, in 1 act. [1825], (pbd in Duncombe's British theatre), [1883].
Richelieu: or the broken heart: an historical tale. 1826. Attributed to Gore.
The lettre de cachet: a tale; The reign of terror. 1827 (anon); rptd in Romances of real life, 1829.
The abbey of Laach. In Tales of all nations, 1827.
Hungarian tales, by the author of The lettre de cachet. 3 vols 1829. Selection rptd in Edinburgh tales, 1845.
Romances of real life, by the author of Hungarian tales. 3 vols 1829, 1 vol 1859.
Women as they are: or The manners of the day. 3 vols 1830, 2 vols 1833. Anon.
REVIEW: [Lister, T. H.] Edinburgh Rev 51 1830.
The historical traveller, comprising narratives connected with the most curious epochs of European history and with the phenomena of European countries. 2 vols 1831, 1833.
Pin-money: a novel, by the authoress of The manners of the day. 3 vols 1831, 1854, [1876], 2 vols Philadelphia 1834.
REVIEW: Westminster Rev 15 1831.
The Tuileries: a tale, by the authoress of Hungarian tales and Romances of real life. 3 vols 1831, 2 vols New York 1831, 1 vol London 1841 (as The soldier of Lyons: a tale of the Tuileries).
Mothers and daughters: a tale of the year 1830. 3 vols 1831, 1 vol 1831, 1834, 1849. Anon.
REVIEW: Westminster Rev 14 1831.
The opera: a novel, by the authoress of Mothers and daughters. 3 vols 1832.
The fair of Mayfair. 3 vols 1832, 2 vols Philadelphia 1834 (as The miseries of marriage: or the fair of Mayfair). Anon.
REVIEW: Westminster Rev 17 1832.
The sketch book of fashion, by the authoress of Mothers and daughters. 3 vols 1833.
Polish tales, by the authoress of Hungarian tales. 3 vols 1833.
The Hamiltons: or the new era, by the authoress of Mothers and daughters. 3 vols 1834, 1 vol 1850 (sub-titled Official life in 1830), 2 vols Leipzig 1858.
The King's seal: a comedy. 1835 (with Kenny James) (pbd in Webster's Acting National Drama).
The diary of a désennuyée. 2 vols 1836 (anon).
Mrs Armytage: or female domination, by the authoress of Mothers and daughters. 3 vols 1836, 1 vol Brussels 1836, London [1848], 1863.
King O'Neil: or the Irish Brigade. A comedy in two acts. 1837 (pbd in Webster's Acting National Drama).
The maid of Croissey: or Theresa's vow. A drama in two acts. 1837 (pbd in Webster's Acting National Drama), [1880].
Memoirs of a peeress: or the days of Fox. 'Ed Lady Charlotte Bury' 3 vols 1837, 2 vols Philadelphia 1837, Paris 1837, 1 vol 1859 (rev).
Stokeshill Place: or the man of business, by the authoress of Mrs Armytage, Mothers and daughters, etc. 3 vols 1837.
The heir of Selwood: or three epochs of a life, by the authoress of Mothers and daughters, Mrs Armytage, Stokeshill Place, etc. 3 vols 1838, 2 vols Philadelphia 1838, 1 vol London 1855.
The rose fancier's manual. 1838.
Mary Raymond and other tales. 3 vols 1838, 2 vols Philadelphia 1838.
The woman of the world, by the authoress of the Diary of a désennuyée. 3 vols 1838, 1 vol [1861].
The Cabinet Minister, by the authoress of Mothers and daughters, Mrs Armytage, Heir of Selwood. 3 vols 1839, 3 vols Paris 1839, 2 vols Philadelphia 1839.
The courtier of the days of Charles II, with other tales, by the authoress of Mrs Armytage. 3 vols 1839, 2 vols New York 1839, 1 vol Paris 1839, London 1847, 1860.

Dacre of the South: or the olden time, a drama (in 5 acts and in verse). 1840.

The dowager: or the new school for scandal. 3 vols 1840, 2 vols Philadelphia 1841, 1 vol 1854, [1876].

Preferment: or My uncle the Earl, by the authoress of Mrs Armytage. 3 vols 1840, 1 vol 1857.

The abbey and other tales. 2 vols Philadelphia 1840.

Greville: or a season in Paris, by the authoress of Mrs Armytage, The peeress, etc. 3 vols 1841, 3 vols 1844, [1847] (as Greville: or Paris in 1840), 1 vol [1858], 1 vol Paris 1841.

Cecil, or the adventures of a coxcomb: a novel. Anon 3 vols 1841, 1 vol 1845, 1860.

REVIEW: [Hayward, A.] Edinburgh Rev 73 1841.

Cecil a peer: a sequel to Cecil or the adventures of a coxcomb, by the same author. 3 vols 1841, 1842 (as Ormington: or Cecil, a peer, with a word from the author), 2 vols Philadelphia 1842.

Paris in 1841. 1842 (with engravings after T. Allom), 1849 (as Paris and its environs), ed T. Forester (based on the work by C. G. F. Gore), 1959 (same).

The man of fortune and other tales, by the authoress of Mrs Armitage [sic], Stokeshill Place, etc. 3 vols [1842], 2 vols Philadelphia 1842.

The ambassador's wife. 3 vols 1842, 1 vol 1863.

The money-lender. 3 vols 1843, 1 vol New York (as Abednego the money-lender) 1843, London 1854.

Modern chivalry: or a new Orlando furioso. (anon, signed G. F. G.) Illustr George Cruikshank. (originally pbd in Ainsworth's Mag). 2 vols 1843, New York 1844.

The banker's wife, or court and city: a novel, by the authoress of Mothers and daughters, Mrs Armytage, etc. 3 vols 1843, 1 vol 1859.

Agathonia, a romance. 1844. Anon.

Marrying for money. In Omnibus of modern romance, New York 1844.

The birthright and other tales, by the authoress of The Banker's wife, The man of fortune, etc. 3 vols 1844.

Quid pro quo: or the day of the dupes. The prize comedy. [1844], [1886].

REVIEW: [G. H. Lewes] Westminster Rev 42 1844.

The popular member, The wheel of fortune [etc], by the authoress of Mothers and daughters, The banker's wife, etc. 3 vols 1844.

Self, by the author of Cecil. 3 vols 1845, 1856 (sub-titled The narrow, narrow world).

The story of a royal favourite. 3 vols 1845, 1 vol 1862 and 1863 (as The royal favourite).

The snow storm: a Christmas story. Illustr George Cruikshank [1845], Boston 1848, London [c. 1850] (with The inundation and New Year's day), [1895].

Peers and parvenus: a novel. 3 vols 1846, 1859.

New Year's day: a winter's tale. Illustr George Cruikshank. [1846], [c. 1850 with The snow storm and The inundation), [1854] (as The lost son: a winter's tale).

Men of capital. 3 vols 1846, 1 vol 1857.

The débutante: or the London season, by the authoress of Mothers and daughters, Peers and parvenus, etc. 3 vols 1846, 1 vol 1861.

Sketches of English character. (Originally Sketches of modern character, in NMM.) 2 vols 1846, 1 vol 1852, 1856 (rev).

Castles in the air: a novel. 3 vols 1847, 1 vol Leipzig 1856, London 1856, 1857.

Temptation and atonement, and other tales. (Many originally in NMM). 3 vols 1847, [1848], 1 vol [1859].

The inundation, or pardon and peace: a Christmas story. Illustr George Cruikshank [1847], [c. 1850 with The snow storm and New Year's day], Boston (nd).

The diamond and the pearl: a novel. 3 vols 1848, 1849, [1859] (rev).

Adventures in Borneo. 1849.

The Dean's daughter: or the days we live in, by the authoress of Mothers and daughters, Mrs Armytage, The banker's wife, etc. 3 vols 1853, 2 vols 1853, 2 vols Leipzig 1853, 1 vol New York 1853, 1883.

Progress and prejudice. 3 vols 1854, 2 vols Leipzig 1854, 1 vol New York 1854.

Transmutation: or the Lord and the lout, by N or M. 1854.

Mammon: or the hardships of an heiress. 3 vols 1855, 1856, 2 vols Leipzig 1855.

A life's lessons: a novel, by the authoress of Mammon, Mothers and daughters, etc. 3 vols 1856, 2 vols Leipzig 1857.

The two aristocracies: a novel. 3 vols 1857, 2 vols Leipzig 1857.

Heckington: a novel. 3 vols 1858, 2 vols 1858, 2 vols Leipzig 1858, 1 vol London 1864.

The bride of Zante and other tales. 1861. (Originally in Romances of real life, 1829).

Parodies

Bede, Cuthbert. Mammon's marriage, by Mrs Bore, the authoress of Mammon and salmon, Mothers and grandmothers and Peers and peris. The Shilling book of beauty [1856].

[Thackeray, William.] Lords and liveries, by the authoress of Dukes and Déjeuners, Hearts and diamonds, Marchionesses and milliners, etc. etc., (Punch's Prize Novelists), Punch 12–26 June 1847.

Catherine Gore contributed to Tales of all nations, *1827,* Heath's Picturesque Annual, *1832,* The tale book *1859, the* NMM, *1835–46,* Blackwood's Edinburgh Mag *1843–4,* Bentley's Misc, *the* Dublin Univ Mag, Tait's Edinburgh Mag, *and* Ainsworth's Mag, *1843. She edited* Fascination and other tales, *3 vols 1842, 1 vol [1862]. She also edited the following trns: Salvoisy,* The Queen's champion *(pbd in* Webster's Acting National Drama, *from the French); Joseph Xavier Boniface,* Picciola; or captivity captive, *2 vols 1837 (from the Fr); Charles de Bernard,* The lover and the husband etc, *3 vols 1841;* The peeress, *3 vols [1841?] (cf. J. Roby,* Popular traditions of England, *1st series, 1841); Andreas Nicolai de St Aubain,* Modern French life, *3 vols 1842 (tales from the Fr); and T. C. Heiberg,* The Queen of Denmark, *3 vols 1846 (from the Danish).*

§2

[Thackeray, William]. Modern novelists and recent novels. NMM 38 1833.

Memoir of Mrs Gore. NMM 49 1837.

Novels of fashionable life. Dublin Univ Mag 12 1838.

Horne, R. H. (ed). A new spirit of the age. 2 vols 1844, vol 1.

[Russell, C. W.] Our lady novelists. Dublin Rev 23 1847.

[Jacox, Francis.] Female novelists no. 2: Mrs Gore. NMM 95 1852.

[Lewes, G. H.] The lady novelists. Westminster Rev 58 n.s. 2, 1852.

[Oliphant, Margaret]. Modern novelists – great and small. Blackwood's Edinburgh Mag 77 1855.

Oliphant, Margaret. Annals of a publishing house: William Blackwood and his sons. 2 vols Edinburgh 1897.

Rosa, M. W. The Silver-Fork School: Novels of fashion preceding Vanity Fair. New York 1936.

Obits: Athenaeum 9, 16, 23 Feb 1861; GM n.s. 10 1861. [HK]

Thomas Colley Grattan 1792–1864

Bibliographies

Sadleir, M. In his XIX century fiction: a bibliographical record, 2 vols 1951.

Wolff, R. L. In his Nineteenth-century fiction: a bibliographical catalogue, 5 vols New York and London 1981–6.

§1

Philibert: a poetical romance. 1819, Paris 1822. 6 cantos with notes.

High-ways and by-ways: or tales of the roadside, picked up in the

French provinces by a walking gentleman. 3 ser 1823–7 (anon). Ser 1 (The father's curse, La Vilaine tête, The birth of Henry IV, and The exile of the Landes) 1823, 2 vols 1823, 1823–4, Boston 1824, London 1824, 1824; ser 2 (Caribert, The priest and the garde-du-corps, The vouée au blanc) 3 vols 1825, Paris 1825, 2 vols Philadelphia 1825, 1827 3 vols London 1827, [1834]; ser 3 (The cagot's hut, Seeing is not believing, The conscript's bride) 3 vols 1827, 1833. Series rptd 3 vols Boston 1840, 1 vol London 1847; ser 1–2 rptd 2 vols London and Belfast 1847–8; ser 2–3 rptd 6 vols London 1831; ser 1–2 tr Ger 1824–5, Fr 1825.

The history of Switzerland, from the conquests of Caesar to the abdication of Buonaparte. 1825 (anon), New York 1913 (with History of Netherlands, *below*). An abridgement of Planta, History of the Helvetic confederacy.

Ben Nazir, the Saracen: a tragedy. 1827.

Traits of travel: or tales of men and cities. 3 vols 1829, 2 vols New York 1829, Boston 1829; tr Ger 1830.

The heiress of Bruges: a tale of the year sixteen hundred. 4 vols 1830, 3 vols Brussels 1830, London 1831, 2 vols New York 1834, 3 vols London 1834, 1 vol 1834, 1847, 1853, 1856; tr Fr 1831, Cz 1926.

The history of the Netherlands. 1830, Philadelphia 1831, London 1833, Philadelphia 1835, London 1838, New York 1843, 1855, Philadelphia 1881, New York 1899 (as Holland: the history of the Netherlands [continued] by J. Hawthorne), 1901, [1901], [1904], Philadelphia 1907 (as Holland and Belgium, ed W. H. Claflin; Switzerland, ed C. Dandliker, rev E. J. Benton), New York 1909, Chicago [1910], New York 1913, 1916, 1928, 1932 etc.

Jacqueline of Holland: a historical tale. 3 vols 1831, 2 vols New York 1831, 1 vol London 1843 (rev), 1857, [1884].

Legends of the Rhine and of the Low Countries. 3 vols 1832, 2 vols Philadelphia 1833, 1 vol Frankfurt am Main 1836 (with Planché, Lays and legends of the Rhine), Philadelphia 1843, Frankfurt am Main 1847, London 1849, 1854.

Tales. 1832.

Agnes de Mansfeldt: a historical tale. 3 vols 1835, 1835, 1836, 1 vol Brussels 1836, Philadelphia 1836, Brussels 1846, London 1847, 1847, 1851.

The sleeping partners: a sketch of hard frost. In Chairolas, ed E. G. E. L. Bulwer-Lytton, Philadelphia 1836.

The boundary question revised, and Dr Franklin's red line shown to be the right one, by a British subject. New York 1843; rptd in his Civilized America, 1859, *below*.

Julie Corryeur: a romance of the Alps. Philadelphia 1843.

The master passion and other tales and sketches. 2 vols 1845.

A chance medley of light matter. New York 1845.

The Cagot's hut; and The conscript's bride. 1852. First pbd in Highways and by-ways ser 3.

Reminiscences of Hannah More. In Homes and haunts of the wise and good, Philadelphia 1854.

The forfeit hand and other tales. 1857. First pbd in Legends of the Rhine.

The curse of the black lady and other tales. 1857. First pbd in Legends of the Rhine.

Civilized America. 2 vols 1859, 1859.

England and the disrupted states of America. 1861, 1861, 1862.

Beaten paths and those who trod them. 2 vols 1862. Reminiscences.

Observations of a British consul 1839–46. In American social history as recorded, ed A. Nevins, New York 1923.

Grattan contributed regularly to the Edinburgh Rev *and* Westminster Rev *as well as to* NMM. *He began his own periodical,* The Paris Monthly Rev of Br Lit, *Jan 1822–Apr 1823, and wrote* My acquaintance with the late Edmund Kean *for the* NMM *39 1833. He was the British correspondent for* The Times *in 1834 during the Brussels riots, which indirectly led to his appointment as British Consul at Massachusetts. Grattan also translated numerous works of modern French poets into Eng.* [AM]

Sarah Green

Bibliographies

Blakey, D. In her Minerva Press, 1939.

Summers, M. In his A Gothic bibliography, [1941].

§1

Charles Henly: or the fugitive restored. 2 vols 1790. Anon.

Mental improvement for a young lady on her entrance into the world, addressed to a favourite niece. 1793, 1794, 1796. Anon.

A letter to the publisher of Brothers's prophecies. 1795.

Court intrigue, or the victim of constancy: an historical romance. 2 vols 1799.

The private history of the Court of England. 2 vols 1808, 1808 (corrected). Anon.

Tankerville family. 3 vols 1808.

Tales of the manor. 2 vols 1809.

The festival of St Jago: a Spanish romance. 2 vols 1810.

The reformist!!! a serio-comic political novel. 2 vols 1810, 1816 (as Percival Ellingford: or the reformist).

Romance readers and romance writers: a satirical novel. 3 vols 1810. Prefaced by a critical literary retrospection, partly rptd in R. B. Johnson, Novelists on novels, 1928.

The royal exile, or victims of human passions: an historical romance of the sixteenth century. 4 vols 1810, 1811.

Good men of modern date: a satirical tale. 3 vols 1811, 2 vols Philadelphia 1813.

Deception: a fashionable novel. 3 vols 1813.

The Carthusian friar, or the mysteries of Montanville: a posthumous romance. 4 vols 1814.

The fugitive: or family incidents. 3 vols 1814.

Who is the bridegroom? or nuptial discoveries: a novel. 3 vols 1822.

Gretna Green marriages, or the nieces: a novel. 3 vols 1823.

Scotch novel reading, or modern quackery: a novel really founded on facts, by a Cockney. 3 vols 1824.

Parents and wives, or inconsistency and mistakes: a novel. 3 vols 1825.

Sarah Green also translated Raphael: or peaceful life, *from the Ger of A. Lafontaine, 2 vols 1812.*

For a listing of reviews and notices of Green's works, see Ward (1979, 1972, 1977). [PG]

Elizabeth Caroline Grey, née Duncan 1798–1869

Bibliography

Summers, M. In his A Gothic bibliography, [1941].

§1

De Lisle: or the sensitive man. 3 vols 1828 (anon), 2 vols New York 1828.

The trials of life. 3 vols 1829, micro Cambridge MA 1977. 2 vols Philadelphia and New York 1829.

The way of the world. 3 vols 1831.

Alice Seymour: a tale. 1831 (anon), 1845 (new edn).

Hyacinthe: or the contrast. 1835 (anon), Philadelphia 1845, 1845 (new edn).

The duke: a novel. 3 vols 1839. 2 vols Philadelphia 1840, as The duke and the cousin, micro New York 1991, new edn 1 vol Philadelphia 1847, new edn 1 vol 1856 (Routledge's Railway Lib).
REVIEW: Athenaeum 5 Oct 1839.

The young prima donna: a romance of the opera. 3 vols 1840, 2 vols in 1 Philadelphia 1840 (micro Cambridge MA [1977?]), new edn 1 vol London 1854 (Routledge's Railway Lib), new 1 vol edns Philadelphia [1867] and London 1877.
REVIEW: Athenaeum 8 Aug 1840.

The little wife; and The baronet's daughters. 3 vols 1841, micro New York 1991. New 1-vol edn of The little wife London 1852

(Routledge's Railway Lib). New edn of The baronet's daughters [Philadelphia?] [187-?].
REVIEW: Athenaeum 3 July 1841.
Vileroy or the horrors of Zindorf Castle: a romance of chivalry. 1842, rptd 1844 (micro Bethlehem PA 1992 for Univ of California, Davis), 1850 (new edn).
The belle of the family or the jointure: a novel. 3 vols 1843, 1 vol Philadelphia [1843?], new edn 1 vol London 1857, Philadelphia 1857.
REVIEW: Athenaeum 21 Oct 1843.
The dream of a life: a romance. 1843, rptd 1852, micro New York 1991.
The gambler's wife: a novel. 3 vols 1844, 2nd edn 3 vols 1845, 1 vol New York 1845, also in 4-vol ser Selected Novels, bound with 3 other novels (by Frederika Bremer, Charles Lever and E. L. Bulwer-Lytton). Other 1-vol edns New York 1847, London 1853 and 1860, New York 1860, London [188–?], New York [1884] (Seaside Lib no 285), micros Cambridge MA 1980 and Washington [19–?] (LC).
The old dower house: a tale of bygone days. 3 vols 1844, 1 vol Philadelphia 1844, new edn 1 vol London 1857.
REVIEW: Athenaeum 16 Mar 1844.
The bosom friend: a novel. 3 vols 1845, 1 vol New York 1845, also in 4-vol ser Selected Novels, bound with 3 other texts including Catherine Gore's Self. New edn 1 vol 1858, rptd [1865], micro Cambridge MA [1978], 1 vol New York 1862.
REVIEW: Athenaeum 9 Aug 1845.
Sybil Lennard: a novel. 3 vols 1846, 1 vol New York 1848, with subtitle A record of woman's life. New edn 1 vol 1854 (Parlour Lib). New edn 1 vol 1885.
REVIEW: Athenaeum 27 June 1846.
The ordeal by touch: a prize romance for which one hundred pounds were paid. 1847. First pbd as serial in Lloyd's Weekly Misc 1846.
The iron-mask: a romance. [1847.] First pbd as serial in Lloyd's Weekly Misc 1846–7.
Daughters. 3 vols 1847, micro Bethlehem PA 1992 (for Univ of California, Davis). New edn 1 vol [1861] (Parlour Lib), new edn [1884] as The daughters.
REVIEW: Athenaeum 17 July 1847.
The assassins of the cavern: a romance. 1848.
Aline: an old friend's story. 3 vols 1848, 1 vol New York 1848.
REVIEW: Athenaeum 24 June 1848.
The rectory guest: a novel. 3 vols 1849, 1 vol New York 1849, as Magdalen and Marcia: or the rectory guest. New edn 1 vol 1858, 1 vol 1885 with The opera singer's wife.
REVIEW: Athenaeum 21 July 1849.
Claude Duval, the dashing highwayman: a tale of the road. [1850.]
The gambler's wife: or murder will out. [1850.] First pbd in 17 penny nos.
An old country house. 3 vols 1850 (micro Cambridge MA 1979), 1 vol New York 1850, new edn 1 vol London 1859 (Routledge's Railway Lib).
Gentleman Jack: or life on the road. 1852. First pbd in penny nos.
The gipsy's daughter: a tale. 2 vols 1852, 1 vol New York 1852, 1 vol Philadelphia [185–?].
Mary Seaham: a novel. 3 vols 1852, 1 vol Philadelphia 1852, new 1-vol edns 1865 (micro Cambridge MA 1979) and 1884.
REVIEW: Athenaeum 10 July 1852.
Paul Clifford or hurrah for the road: a romance of old times. 1853. Condensed version pbd c. 1870 as Paul's perils.
The young husband. 3 vols 1854. 1 vol New York 1854, New edn 1 vol 1861 (Parlour Lib).
Sybil's little daughter: a sequel to The gipsy's daughter. 3 vols 1854.
Cousin Harry: a novel. 3 vols 1858. 3 vols in 1 Philadelphia [1860?] and New York nd.
Two hearts: a tale. 1858.
The little beauty: a tale. 3 vols 1860, 3 vols in 1 Philadelphia 1860 and New York [1860].
The opera singer's wife. 1861. New edn 1 vol 1885 with The rectory guest.
One of the family or the ladies: a novel. 2 vols 1861.
REVIEW: Athenaeum 27 Apr 1861.
The autobiography of Frank, the happiest little dog that ever lived. 1861, new edn [1882].
Passages in the life of a fast young lady. 3 vols 1862, 1 vol Philadelphia [1862], as The flirt, or passages in the life of a fashionable young lady, rptd Philadelphia 1884 (Seaside Lib vol 83 no 1688), micro Cambridge MA 1977.
Good society: or contrasts of character. 3 vols 1863 (micro Cambridge MA 1979), 1 vol New York 1863, also bound with Lion-hearted [1865?].
Lion-hearted: a novel. 2 vols 1864, rptd 1864, 1 vol New York [1865?] bound with Good society. [JW]

Basil Hall 1788–1844

See col 2144.

Elizabeth Hamilton 1758–1816

§1

Translation of the letters of a Hindoo Rajah, with a preliminary dissertation on the history of the Hindoos. 2 vols 1796, Dublin 1797, London 1801, 1811 (5th edn), Boston 1819. Essays in fictional form.
REVIEWS: Critical Rev July 1796; Br Critic Sep 1796; Analytical Rev Oct 1796; Monthly Rev Oct 1796; Scots Mag Jan 1797. Excerpts in Scots Mag Feb 1797.
Memoirs of modern philosophers: a novel. 3 vols Bath 1800, 2 vols Dublin 1800, 3 vols Bath and London 1800, 1801, 1804, New York 1974 (facs), London 1992 (facs), 1994 (facs); tr Fr 4 vols 1802 (as Bridgetina: ou les philosophes modernes).
REVIEW: Monthly Rev Apr 1801.
Letters on education. Bath 1801, Dublin 1801; 2nd vol added and retitled Letters on the elementary principles of education, Bath 1801, 1802, 1803, Alexandria VA 1803, London 1803, Philadelphia 1804, London 1808, 1810 (5th edn, rev and augmented), 1818 (6th edn), 1837, Boston 1825; tr Fr 2 vols 1804, Ger (as Briefe über erziehung) Jena 1832.
REVIEWS: Critical Rev Feb, Nov 1802; Br Critic Mar, Nov 1802; Monthly Rev Aug, Sep 1802.
Memoirs of the life of Agrippina, the wife of Germanicus. 3 vols Bath 1804, London 1804, 2 vols 1811.
REVIEWS: Scots Mag Dec 1804; Br Critic July 1805; Critical Rev Feb 1806.
Letters addressed to the daughter of a nobleman on the formation of the religious and the moral principle. 2 vols 1806, 1806, 1814, Salem MA 1821, New York 1974 (facs).
REVIEW: Br Critic Apr 1807.
The cottagers of Glenburnie. Edinburgh 1808, 1808, New York 1808, Edinburgh 1810 (4th edn), 1810 (5th edn), Philadelphia 1812, Edinburgh 1815 (6th edn), Belfast c. 1820, Edinburgh 1822 (7th edn), Glasgow 1826 (abridged; pbd with Idleness and industry as Tales from the cottage), Edinburgh 1828 (8th edn), London 1837, 1839, Dublin c. 1840, London 1841, 1845 (pbd with The two sisters; or life's changes), 1850, Edinburgh 1851 (with memoir); ed J. L. Watson, Halifax 1857, London and Edinburgh 1859, [1872], Glasgow [188–?], Edinburgh 1885, 1887 (The Girl's Own Lib), New York 1974 (facs).
REVIEWS: Edinburgh Rev July 1808; Br Critic Aug 1808; Scots Mag Sep 1808; Critical Rev Dec 1808.

Exercises in religious knowledge. Edinburgh 1809, 1810.
REVIEWS: Scots Mag May 1809; Br Critic Oct 1809.
A series of popular essays illustrative of principles connected with the improvement of the understanding, the imagination and the heart. 2 vols Edinburgh and London 1813, 1815 (2nd edn), Boston 1817.
REVIEWS: GM Aug 1813; Critical Rev Mar 1814.
Hints addressed to patrons and directors of schools: to which are subjoined examples of questions calculated to excite and exercise the minds of the young. 1815.
Examples of questions calculated to excite and exercise the infant mind (appendix of Hints addressed to patrons . . .). 1815, Salem MA 1829.
According to Benger's Memoirs, *Hamilton's first published writing was an anonymous contribution to the* Lounger *in 1785.*

§2

Obits: Scots Mag Aug 1816; GM Aug 1816.
E. [Maria Edgeworth?] Character and writings of Mrs. Elizabeth Hamilton. GM Supplement 1816.
Benger, E. O. Memoirs of Mrs Elizabeth Hamilton with selections from her correspondence and unpublished writings. 1818.
REVIEWS: GM May 1818; Scots Mag June 1818; Br Critic July 1818.
Elwood, Anne Katharine Curteis. In her Memoirs of the literary ladies of Great Britain vol 2, 1843, New York 1973 (facs).
Keddie, Henrietta. In her The songstresses of Scotland, 2 vols 1871.
Todd, Janet (ed). Dictionary of British women writers 1660–1800. 1985. [PP]

Thomas Hamilton 1789–1842

Bibliographies

Sadleir, M. In his XIX century fiction: a bibliographical record, 2 vols 1951.

§1

The youth and manhood of Cyril Thornton. 3 vols Edinburgh and London 1827 (anon), Boston 1827, 2 vols New York 1827, 3 vols Edinburgh and London 1829, 2 vols New York 1831, 1 vol Edinburgh 1842, 1856, 1868, 1880 (as Cyril Thornton: his youth and manhood); ed and introd by M. Lindsay, Aberdeen 1990.
REVIEW: [Wilson, J.] Blackwood's Mag July 1827.
Annals of the Peninsular campaigns 1808–14. 3 vols Edinburgh and London 1829, Philadelphia 1831; rev F. Hardman 1849.
Men and manners in America. 2 vols Edinburgh 1833, Philadelphia 1833, Edinburgh 1834, 1 vol 1843 (augmented); tr Fr 1834, Ger 1834.
Hamilton contributed freely to Blackwood's Mag *1826–38.*

§2

Douglas, G. In his Blackwood group, 1897. [PG]

Anne Raikes Harding 1781–1858

Correction: a novel. 3 vols 1818, 1819. Anon.
Decision: a tale. 3 vols 1819, 2 vols New York 1819.
The refugees: an Irish tale. 3 vols 1822.
Realities, not a novel: a tale from real life. 4 vols 1825.
Dissipation: a tale of simple life. 4 vols 1827.
Experience: a tale for all ages. 4 vols 1828.
An epitome of universal history, from the earliest periods to the revolutions of 1848: together with historical charts and an extensive chronological table on the system of Grey's Memoria Technica. 1848.

Attributed works

Jessy Allan, the lame girl: a story founded on facts. Edinburgh 1823 etc. Actually by Grace Kennedy.
Willoughby. 2 vols 1826. Attributed to A. R. Harding in Summers, who distinguishes it from Willoughby, or reformation (1823), itself sometimes wrongly attributed to Grace Kennedy. No copy of a Willoughby (1826) has been discovered.
For a listing of reviews and notices of Harding's works, see Ward (1972, 1977). [PG]

Jane Harvey b. 1776

§1

A sentimental tour through Newcastle: by a young lady. Newcastle-upon-Tyne 1794.
Poems on various subjects. Newcastle-upon-Tyne 1797.
Warkfield Castle: a tale. 3 vols 1802.
The castle of Tynemouth: a tale. 2 vols 1806, Newcastle-upon-Tyne 1830.
The governor of Belleville: a tale. 4 vols 1808.
Ethelia: a novel. 3 vols 1810, 1814.
Memoirs of an author. 3 vols Gainsborough 1812, 1814 as Auberry Stanhope: or memoirs of an author.
Records of a noble family. 4 vols London and Gainsborough 1814.
Brougham Castle: a novel. 2 vols 1816.
Any thing but what you expect. 3 vols Derby 1819.
The friends: or the history of Harcourt and Powlett. Derby [1820?].
Singularity: a novel. 3 vols 1822.
Mountalyth: a tale. 3 vols 1823.
The ambassador's secretary: a tale. 4 vols 1828.
Fugitive pieces. Newcastle-upon-Tyne 1841. In verse.
Harvey also wrote hymns and moral poems for children, sometimes anonymously.

Contributions to collaborative works

A real treasure for the pious mind, compiled by a lady of Connecticut. From the collections and writings of the Countess of Huntington, Mrs Rowe, Miss Harvey, Mr Perin, and Mr Smith. Hartford CT 1797, 1799.

Attributed or spurious works

Minerva Castle: a tale. 3 vols 1802. Blakey, Summers and Block record this but no copy appears to exist.
Ceraline. 4 vols 1821. Summers and Block have attributed a novel of this title to Harvey but no copy appears to exist.
For a listing of reviews and notices of J. Harvey's works, see Ward (1972, 1977). [CF]

Laetitia-Matilda Hawkins 1759–1835

§1

Letters on the female mind, its powers and pursuits: addressed to Miss H. M. Williams, with particular reference to her letters from France. 2 vols 1793.
The countess and Gertrude: or modes of discipline. 4 vols 1811, 1812.
REVIEWS: Br Critic 39 1812; Critical Rev 4th ser 2 1812; Antijacobin Rev 45 1813.
Rosanne: or a father's labours lost. 3 vols 1814.
Sermonets addressed to those who have not yet acquired, or who may have lost, the inclination to apply the power of attention to compositions of a higher kind. 1814. Written jointly with her brother, Henry.
Heraline: or opposite proceedings. 4 vols 1821, 1821.
Anecdotes, biographical sketches and memoirs, collected by Laetitia-Matilda Hawkins. 1822.
Devotional exercises, extracted from Bishop Patrick's Christian sacrifice: adapted to the present time. 1823.
Memoirs, anecdotes, facts and opinions [continuation of Anecdotes, biographical sketches and memoirs]. 2 vols 1824; ed F. H. Skrine 1926 (selection, as Gossip about Dr Johnson and others).
Annaline: or motive-hunting. 3 vols 1824.

Hawkins also translated Siegwart: a monastic tale, *from the Ger of J. M. Miller, 3 vols 1806.*

For a listing of other reviews and notices of Hawkins's works, see Ward (1972, 1977). [PG and PP]

C. D. Haynes, afterwards Mrs Golland

Bibliographies

Summers, M. In his A Gothic bibliography, [1941].

§1

The castle of le blanc. 21 pts 1816–19. Serialised in the Lady's Mag, but apparently not pbd separately.

The foundling of Devonshire, or who is she? a novel. 5 vols 1818.

Augustus & Adeline, or, the monk of St Barnardine: a romance. 4 vols 1819.

Eleanor, or the spectre of St Michael's: a romantic tale. 5 vols 1821; tr Fr 1824.

The ruins of Ruthvale Abbey: a novel. 4 vols 1827.

The maid of Padua, or past times: a Venetian tale. 4 vols 1835.

The witch of Aysgarth. 3 vols 1841. [PG]

Elizabeth Helme d. 1810

Bibliographies

Blakey, D. In her Minerva Press, 1939.

Summers, M. In his A Gothic bibliography, [1941].

§1

Louisa: or the cottage on the moor. 2 vols 1787 (anon), 1787 (new edn corrected, with addns), 1787, 1787, 1787, Dublin 1787, Paris 1787, Leipzig 1789, Wilmington DE 1795 (as The history of Louisa the lovely orphan), Boston 1798, New York 1800, London 1801 (7th edn), 1840 (in pts), 1 vol 1840; tr Fr 1787, Ger 1789, Rus 1790, Sp 1823.

Clara and Emmeline: or the maternal benediction: a novel. 2 vols 1788; tr Fr 1788.

Duncan and Peggy: a Scottish tale. 2 vols 1794, 1815.

The farmer of Inglewood Forest: a novel. 4 vols 1796, 2 vols Cork 1801, 4 vols London 1811, 1 vol Newcastle-upon-Tyne 1822 ('6th edn'), 1 vol London and Bristol 1824 ('7th edn'), 4 vols London 1827 ('4th edn'), 1841, 1842, 1878; tr Fr 4 vols 1818.

Instructive rambles in London and the adjacent villages. 2 vols 1798, 1 vol Philadelphia 1799, 2 vols London 1800, 1 vol 1800, 1803, 1806, 1808, 1811, 1812, New York 1814, London 1818, 1825.

Albert: or the wilds of Strathnavern. 4 vols 1799, 2 vols Dublin 1800, 4 vols London 1821.

St Margaret's cave, or the nun's story: an ancient legend. 4 vols 1801, 1819; with introd by D. P. Varma 4 vols New York 1977 (facs); tr Fr 1803, Ger 1803.

Maternal instruction: or family conversations on moral and entertaining subjects. 2 vols 1802, 1 vol New York 1804, London 1807, 1810, 1815, 1818.

St Clair of the Isles, or the outlaws of Barra: a Scottish tradition. 4 vols 1803, 1824 (3rd edn), 1 vol 1825, 1837, 1840, 1841, 1844, 1867, [1889]; tr Fr 1808, Ger 1811.

The pilgrim of the cross, or the chronicles of Christabelle de Mowbray: an ancient legend. 4 vols Brentford 1805; tr Fr 1807.

The history of England related in familiar conversations by a father to his children. 2 vols 1805, 1806, 1818 (5th edn); tr Fr 1823.

The history of Scotland related in familiar conversations by a father to his children. 2 vols Brentford 1806.

The fruits of reflection: or moral remembrances on various subjects. 2 vols Brentford 1809.

Magdalen, or the penitent of Godstow: an historical novel. 3 vols Brentford 1812, Boston 1813.

Modern times, or the age we live in: a posthumous novel. 3 vols Brentford 1814, 1817.

A preparatory exercise on the road leading to the land of learning, by easy paths and short stages. Brentford 1816.

Attributed works

James Manners, little John and their little dog Bluff. 1799, 1801, Philadelphia 1801, London 1807, 1813, 1818. By her daughter Elisabeth Helme, Jr.

Elizabeth Helme pbd an abridgement of Plutarch's Lives, *1795, trns of* Cortez, *1799,* Columbus, *1800 and* Pizarro, *1800, from the Ger of J. H. Campe, and of* Travels from the Cape of Good Hope, *1790, from the Fr of F. Le Vaillant; she also translated* St Alma: a novel, *1791, from the French of J. C. Gorgy.*

For a listing of reviews and notices of Helme's works, see Ward (1979, 1972). [PG]

William Browne Hockley 1792–1860

Pandurang Hari: or memoirs of a Hindoo. 3 vols 1826 (anon), 2 vols 1873 (with introd by H. B. E. Frere), 1 vol 1877, 1898; tr Ger 1828. Written by Cyrus Redding from Hockley's notes.

The Zenana: or a Nuwab's leisure hours, by the author of Pandurang Hari. 3 vols 1827; ed Lord Stanley of Alderley 2 vols 1874 (as Tales of the Zenana: or a Nuwab's leisure hours); tr Ger 1827.

The English in India. 3 vols 1828, 2 vols 1835. A novel.

The Vizier's son: or the adventures of a mogul. 3 vols 1831.

The memoirs of a Brahmin: or the fatal jewels. 3 vols 1843.

§2

Singh, B. Meadows Taylor and other predecessors of Kipling. In his A survey of Anglo-Indian fiction, Oxford 1934.

Misra, Udayon. Hockley and the Imperial attitude. In his The Raj in fiction, New Delhi 1987. [PG]

Barbara Hofland 1770–1844

See Barbara Hoole, below.

James Hogg 1770–1835

See col 363.

James Hook 1772–1828

Pen Owen. 3 vols Edinburgh 1822 (anon), 2 vols New York 1822, 1 vol London 1842, 1850, 1869; tr Fr 1823.

REVIEWS: [J. Wilson] Blackwood's Mag 11, June 1822; New Edinburgh Rev 3 1822.

Percy Mallory. 3 vols Edinburgh 1824, 2 vols Philadelphia 1824; tr Fr 1824.

REVIEW: [H. Thomson] Blackwood's Mag 15, Jan 1824.

James Hook also pbd pams and sermons.

For a listing of shorter reviews and notices of Hook's two novels, see Ward (1977). [PG]

Theodore Edward Hook 1788–1841

Mss of Hook's correspondence to J. W. Croker, consisting of 116 letters from 1820 to 12 Aug 1841, are held at the Univ of Chicago Lib, and mss of letters and printed miscellany are held at Univ of Illinois at Urbana.

Bibliographies

Sadleir, M. In his XIX century fiction: a bibliographical record, 2 vols 1951.

Wolff, R. L. In his Nineteenth-century fiction: a bibliographical catalogue, 5 vols 1981–6.

Collections

Ausgewählte Romane, aus dem Englischen von E. A. Moriarty und J. Seybt. 16 pts Leipzig 1842–3.

Choice humorous works, with a new life of the author, portraits by Maclise and D'Orsay, caricatures and facsimiles. [1873], [1879], [1883], 1902.

Bon-mots of Samuel Foote and Thoedore Hook. Ed W. Jerrold 1894.

§1

The soldier's return: or what can beauty do? a comic opera. 1805 (anon), Philadelphia 1807.

Catch him who can: a musical farce. 1806, 1829.

The invisible girl: a piece in one act. 1806, 1807, [182–?], 1826, [1840].

Tekeli, or the siege of Montgatz: a melodrama in three acts. 1806, 1807, New York 1807, London 1808, New York 1815, [182–?], Philadelphia 1823, New York and Philadelphia 1825, London 1829, [1832], New York [1842], London [1855].

The fortress: a melo-drama, from the French. 1807, Philadelphia 1808.

Music-mad: a dramatic sketch. 1808, New York 1812, Boston 1812.

The man of sorrow, by Alfred Allendale [pseud]. 3 vols 1808, 1842, 1 vol (as Ned Musgrave: or the most unfortunate man in the world) 1842, 1853, 1854, New York 1854, Philadelphia nd.

Killing no murder: a farce in two acts. 1809 (2nd edn, together with a preface and the scene suppressed by the Lord Chamberlain), 1809, 1809, 1809, New York 1809, London 1810, 1811, 1817; ed G. Daniel 1833; [183–?], Calcutta [18–?].

Safe and sound: an opera in three acts. 1809, New York 1810.

Darkness visible: a farce. 1811, 1811, New York 1812, London 1817.

The trial by jury: a comic piece in two acts. 1811, New York 1811.

Facts illustrative of the treatment of Napolean Buonaparte in Saint Helena. 1819 (anon), 1819, 1910 (in C. K. Shorter, Napoleon in his own defence); tr Fr 1819.

Exchange no robbery, or the diamond ring: a comedy, by Richard Jones [pseud]. 1820, 1820, [1825], 1829; ed G. Daniel 1887.

Tentamen: or an essay towards the history of Whittington, some time Lord Mayor of London, by Vicesimus Blinkinsop [pseud]. 1820, 1821. A satire on Sir Matthew Wood, the partisan of Queen Caroline.

Sayings and doings: a series of sketches from life. 3 ser 1824–8 (anon). Ser 1 (Danvers, The friend of the family, Merton, and Martha the gypsy) 3 vols 1824, 1824, 2 vols Philadelphia 1824, 1 vol Andover [183–?], London 1836, 1872; ser 2 (The Sutherlands, The man of many friends, Doubts and fears, and Passion and principle) 3 vols 1825, 2 vols Philadelphia 1825, 1 vol London 1838 (rev), 1872; ser 3 (Cousin William, and Gervase Skinner) 3 vols 1828, 2 vols Philadelphia 1828, 3 vols London 1834, 1 vol Paris 1836, London 1839. Ser 1–3, 6 vols Philadelphia 1824–8, 3 vols London 1836.

Passion and principle. [18–?], London and New York [187–?], London [1872]. Sayings and doings.

A day at the inn: an interlude in one act. [183–?], [1883] (with The gentleman in black).

Gervase Skinner: or the sin of economy. [1830], New York 1857 (as Gervase Skinner: penny wise and pound foolish), London and New York [1872] (with Danvers), [1872] (vol 5 of Theodore Hook's novels). Taken from the Sayings and doings ser.

Maxwell: a story of the middle ranks. 3 vols 1830, 2 vols New York 1831, 1 vol London 1834, 1839, 1840, 1849, 1854 (rev), 1860, [1872], [1878].

The life of General the Right Hon Sir David Baird, Bart. 2 vols 1832.

Love and pride. 3 vols 1833, 2 vols Philadelphia 1834, 1 vol London 1842 (as The widow and the Marquess: or love and pride), 1868, London and New York [1872], [1873], London [18–?].

The parson's daughter. 3 vols 1833, 1833, 2 vols Philadelphia 1833, 1 vol London 1835 (rev and corrected), 1847, 1851, 1852 (rev), London and New York 1867, London 1872, 3 vols [1873], 1933.

Cousin William: a tale. New York 1835, 1837 (with The man of many friends), 2 vols Hartford, S. Andrus 1846, London and New York (as Cousin William: or the fatal attachment) [187–?], [1872], [1873]. Taken from the Sayings and doings ser.

Magpie Castle and other tales. Philadelphia 1835.

The man of many friends: a tale. New York 1835, [1872] (with The friend of the family). Taken from the Sayings and doings ser.

Captain Gray. Ed E. G. E. L. Bulwer-Lytton, Philadelphia 1836.

Gilbert Gurney. 3 vols 1836, 1836, 2 vols Philadelphia 1836, 1 vol Paris 1836, London 1841, Philadelphia 1845, London 1850, 1857, [1871], 3 vols [1872–3], 1 vol [187–?]; tr Fr 1861. Serialised in NMM 1834–5.

Jack Brag. 3 vols 1837, 1837, 1 vol Paris 1837, Philadelphia 1837, London 1839 (rev), 1847, 1850, Edinburgh and Dublin 1855, London [1863], London and New York 1872, London [1879], 1884, [18–?] (rev).

Gurney married: a sequel to Gilbert Gurney. 3 vols 1838, 1839, 1 vol Paris 1839, 2 vols Philadelphia 1839, 1 vol London 1842, [1860], [1863], [1863], London and New York [1872], London [187–?]. Serialised in NMM 1837–8.

Births, deaths and marriages. 3 vols 1839, 2 vols Philadelphia 1839, 1 vol Paris 1839, London 1842 (as All in the wrong: or births, deaths and marriages), [1857], [1863] (as All in the wrong), [1872].

Merton: or 'there's many a slip 'twixt the cup and the lip'. [1840], Philadelphia 1844, London and New York [1872], [1873]; tr Fr 1828. Taken from Sayings and Doings ser.

Precepts and practice. Illustr Phiz 3 vols 1840, 1 vol Paris 1840, 1857, [1863]. A collection of pieces first pbd in NMM.

Fathers and sons: a novel. 3 vols 1842, 2 vols Philadelphia 1842, 1 vol Paris 1847, London 1847, [1860], 1872. Serialised in NMM 1840–1.

Peregrine Bunce, or settled at last: a novel. 3 vols 1842, 1 vol Philadelphia 1844, London 1857, 1858, London and New York [1873], London nd (part of ser entitled 'Hook's novels').

The Ramsbottom letters. 1872, [1873], [1874] (with additional material as The Ramsbottom papers, complete and unabridged).

Snowdon: a novel. New York 1875.

Hook also edited Reminiscences of Michael Kelly, *1826; J. A. Bernard,* The French stage and the French people, *2 vols 1841; and* Adventures of an actor, *1842, as well as the following novels: A. Dumas,* Pascal Bruno, *1837; J. T. J. Hewlett,* Peter Priggins, *3 vols 1841;* The Parish clerk, *3 vols 1841; and H. M. G. Smythies,* Cousin Geoffrey: the old bachelor, *3 vols 1840. He was editor of* Arcadian *1819–20, of* John Bull *from 1820 to 1841, and of* NMM *and* Humourist *from vol 49 to 62. He also supervised the publication of* The blue book: or kalendar of literature, science and art for 1830, *[1829]. Portraits of Hook appeared in Disraeli's* Coningsby *and Thackeray's* Vanity Fair.

§2

Maginn, W. Blackwood's Mag March 1824. Review of Sayings and doings.

Lockhart, J. G. Blackwood's Mag Feb 1825. Review of Sayings and doings.

Memoir. NMM Oct 1841. With portrait.

Theodore Edward Hook. Fraser's Mag Nov 1841.

[Lockhart, J. G.] Peregrine Bunce. Quart Rev 72 1843.

Horne, R. H. In his A new spirit of the age vol 2, 1844.

Theodore Edward Hook. Chambers's Jnl 7 Feb 1846.

A graybeard's gossip about his literary acquaintance no 6. NMM Aug 1847.

Barham, R. H. D. The life and remains of Hook. 2 vols 1849, 1850, 1853 (rev and corrected), 1877 (rev), 1883.

[Lockhart, J. G.] Hook: a sketch. 1852 (3 edns), 1853.

Hall, A. M. and S. C. Memories of authors: Hook and his friends. Atlantic Monthly Apr 1865.

Maginn, W. In his A gallery of illustrious literary characters, ed W. Bates, [1873].

Saintsbury, G. Theodore Hook. Macmillan's Mag Nov 1893.

Hook, satirist and novelist. Temple Bar Nov 1894.
Saintsbury, G. Three humorists. Hook, Barham, Maginn. Macmillan's Mag Dec 1895; rptd in his Collected essays vol 2, 1923.
St Cyres, S. H. N. Theodore Hook. Cornhill Mag Jan 1904.
Brightfield, M. F. Hook and his novels. Cambridge MA 1928.
Repplier, A. The laugh that failed. Atlantic Monthly Aug 1936.
Hoaxer and wit: Hook. TLS 23 Aug 1941.
Shuman, R. B. Structure and style in the novels of Hook. N & Q Aug 1958.
Shuman, R. B. Hook as a legal critic. N & Q Aug 1958. [AM]

Barbara Hoole, afterwards Hofland, née Wreaks

1770–1844

§1

Poems. Sheffield [1805].
La fête de la rose; or, the dramatic flowers. 1809.
The history of an officer's widow, and her young family. 1809 (anon), 1814, Philadelphia 1815, London 1834.
Tales, in verse, for the use of children. Knaresborough 1810.
Little dramas for young people on subjects taken from English history. 1810.
The daughter-in-law. 1812, 1829, 1853.
A season at Harrogate; in a series of poetical epistles, from Benjamin Blunderhead esquire to his mother. Knaresborough 1812, Harrogate 1838 (rev).
The history of a clergyman's widow and her young family. 1812 (anon), 1825, [1866].
The son of a genius: a tale for the use of youth. 1812, New York 1814, London 1816, New York 1818, London 1819, 1821, 1822, 1827 (rev), 1832, 1841 etc; tr Fr 1817.
Says she to her neighbour, What? by an old-fashioned Englishman. 4 vols 1812.
The sisters; a dramatic tale. 1813, 1814, 1828, 1866.
Patience and perseverance: or the modern Griselda, by the author of Says she to her neighbour, What? 4 vols 1813.
The panorama of Europe: or a new game of geography. 1813, 1824, 1828, 1840 etc.
Iwanowna: or the maid of Moscow. 1813, 2 vols 1816. Anon.
The young northern traveller 1813, tr Fr, 1825, 1829 'New edn'.
A visit to London: or Emily and her friends. 4 vols 1814.
Ellen the teacher. 2 vols 1814, 1819, 1836, 1886.
The merchant's widow and her family. 1814 (anon), 1823 (as The history of a merchant's widow and her young family), 1826, 1857, 1868; tr Fr 1831.
A father as he should be: a novel. 4 vols 1815.
The affectionate brothers: a tale. 2 vols 1816, 1829, [1835?], 1863.
Matilda; or the Barbadoes girl: a tale. 1816 (anon), 1819, [1825?] (5th edn), 1866.
The blind farmer and his children. 1816, 1819, [1830?] (6th edn), New York 1831.
The good grandmother, and her offspring: a tale. 1817, 1828, 1850.
The funeral: a monody to the memory of Princess Charlotte. Sheffield [1817].
A descriptive account of the mansions and gardens of White Knights; with twenty-three engravings from pictures by T. C. Hofland. [1819] (priv ptd).
A letter of an English woman. 1820.
Tales of the Priory. 4 vols 1820.
Alicia and her aunt; or, think before you speak. 1822, 1841 (rev).
Theodore, or the Crusaders: a tale for youth. (1821), 1823, 1824, etc.
Tales of the manor. 4 vols 1822.
Adelaide, or the intrepid daughter: a tale. 1823 (anon), 1825 (3rd edn), 1830 (4th edn).
The daughter of a genius: a tale for youth. 1823, 1823, 1848, etc.
Integrity: a tale. 1823, Philadelphia 1828, London 1836, 1840, 1868, 1871.
Decision: a tale. 1824, New York 1825, etc.
Patience: a tale. 1824, 1838.
Alfred Campbell, the young pilgrim: containing travels in Egypt and the Holy Land. 1825, 1841.
Moderation: a tale. 1825, 1826, Boston [1860?].
Reflection: a tale. 1826, 1838, 1868.
The young pilgrim, or Alfred Campbell's return to the East. 1826, 1840, 1841.
William and his Uncle Ben. A tale. 1826, [1865].
River scenery, by Turner and Girtin, with descriptions by Mo Hoflaud. 1827.
Self-denial. A tale. 1827, 1830, 1830, 1835, etc.
Katherine: a tale. 4 vols 1828.
Africa described in its ancient and present state. 1828, 1834.
Tales of Clairmont Castle. 1828, snd ser nd, Philadelphia nd.
The young cadet; or Henry Delamere's voyage to India. [1828?], 1832, 1836.
Beatrice, a tale founded on facts. 3 vols 1829.
The young Crusoe, or the shipwrecked boy. 1829, 1836[?], 1866, 1882, 1894.
The stolen boy. A story founded on facts. [1830?], Cincinnati 1844; tr Ger 1842.
Poetical illustrations of the various scenes represented in Mr Linton's Sketches in Italy. 1832.
Richmond and the surrounding scenery. Illustr J. D. Harding et al 1832.
Elizabeth and her three beggar boys. [1833?], New York 1838.
Rich boys and poor boys; and other tales. [1832?], 1840.
The American juvenile keepsake. Ed Mrs Hofland, New York 1834.
The captives in India: a tale; and A widow and a will. 3 vols 1834, Washington 1835.
Description of the house and museum on the north side of Lincoln's Inn Field. 1835 (priv ptd).
Fortitude: a tale. 1835, 1838.
Humility: a tale. 1837, 1868.
Energy: a tale. 1838, Boston 1844.
The illustrated alphabet, with poetry. 1839.
Farewell tales. 1840, Boston 1847.
The Czarina: an historical romance of the Court of Russia. 3 vols 1842, New York 1842.
The godmother's tales. 1842.
The King's son: a romance of English history. 3 vols 1843.
Emily's reward: or, the holiday trip to Paris. 1844.
Hildebrand: or, the days of Queen Elizabeth. 3 vols 1844.
The unloved one: a domestic story. 3 vols 1844, New York 1844, 1 vol 1860.
Daniel Dennison; and the Cumberland statesman. 3 vols 1846, 1848, New York 1847, etc.
Popular description of Sir John Soane's house, museum and library. Ed A. T. Bolton, Oxford 1919.

§2

Ramsay, T. The life and literary remains of Barbara Hofland. 1849.
L'Estrange, A. G. K. In his Friendships of Mary Russell Mitford, 1882.
Butts, D. Mistress of our tears. A literary and bibliographical study of Barbara Hofland. Aldershot 1992. [DB]

Thomas Hope 1770–1831

§1

Observations on the plans and elevations designed by James Wyatt, architect, for Downing College. Cambridge 1804.
Household furniture and interior decoration. 1807, 1937, 1946.

Costume of the ancients. 2 vols 1809, 1812 (enlarged), 1841, 1875, New York [1962] (as Costumes of the Greeks and Romans); tr Fr 1828.
Designs of modern costumes. 1812, [1973].
Anastasius: or memoirs of a Greek, written at the close of the eighteenth century. 3 vols 1819 (anon), 1820, 1820, 2 vols New York 1820, 3 vols London 1827 (4th edn), 2 vols 1831, Paris 1831, New York 1831, 1832, London 1836, New York 1847, 1856, 1873; tr Fr 1820, 1844, Ger 1821.
REVIEWS: [S. Smith] Edinburgh Rev 35 1821; [W. Gifford] Quart Rev 24 1821.
An essay on the origin and prospects of man. 3 vols 1831.
An historical essay on architecture. 2 vols 1835, 1835, 1840; tr Fr 1839, Ital 1840; index by E. Cresy, 1836.

§2

Zeidler, K. J. Beckford, Hope and Morier als Vertreter des orientalischen Romans. Leipzig 1909.
Baumgarten, S. Le crépuscule néo-classique: Hope. Paris 1958.
Moussa-Mahmoud, F. Orientals in picaresque (Hope, Morier, Meadows Taylor). Cairo Stud in Eng 1962. [PG]

Edward Howard 1792?–1841

Bibliographies

Sadleir, M. In his Excursions in Victorian bibliography, 1922.
Sadleir, M. In his XIX century fiction: a bibliographical record, 2 vols 1951.
In both works, Howard is wrongly identified as the Hon Edward Granville Howard.

§1

Rattlin the reefer, edited by the author of Peter Simple. Illustr A. Hervieu 3 vols 1836, 1836, 1 vol Paris 1836, 3 vols 1837, 1 vol Leipzig 1837, London 1838, 1850 etc; ed W. L. Courtney, illustr E. F. Wheeler, London and Boston 1897, 1903; ed G. Pocock 1930 (EL); tr Fr 1837, Ger 1837. The first 58 chs were serialised in Metropolitan Mag Sep 1834–Feb 1836. Dramatised by J. T. Haines, 1836.
The old Commodore, by the author of Rattlin the reefer. 3 vols 1837, 1 vol 1837, Paris 1837, London 1855; tr Fr 1838, Ger 1838.
Outward bound: or a merchant's adventures. 3 vols 1838, 2 vols Philadelphia 1838, 1 vol 1860, 1875; tr Fr 1838, Ger 1838. Serialised in Metropolitan Mag 1836–7.
Memoirs of Admiral Sir Sidney Smith, KCB, etc. 2 vols 1839; tr Ger 1840.
Jack ashore. 3 vols 1840, 1 vol Paris 1840, London 1848 etc; tr Fr 1840 Ger 1844.
Sir Henry Morgan the buccaneer. 3 vols 1842, 1 vol Paris 1842, New York 1847, London 1857 etc; tr Ger 1844.
Howard was sub-editor, and from 1837 to 1839(?) editor, of Metropolitan Mag. *He contributed stories and sketches to it and to* NMM *etc.*

§2

Marryat, F. Metropolitan Mag Aug 1836. On the pbn of Rattlin the reefer.
Memoir of Edward Howard, with portrait by Osgood. NMM Dec 1838.
Obits: Athenaeum 8 Jan 1842; Annual Register 1842.
Bentley, G. N & Q 22 June, 20 July 1889, 19 Nov, 17 Dec 1892. On the authorship of Rattlin the reefer.

Mary Howitt née Botham 1799–1888

See col 2156.

William Howitt 1792–1879

See col 2157.

Catherine Hutton 1756–1846

See col 2164.

Mrs Isaacs

Bibliographies

Summers, M. In his A Gothic bibliography, [1941].
Block, A. The English novel 1740–1850. 1961.

§1

Ariel: or the invisible monitor. 4 vols 1801. Anon.
Glenmore Abbey, or the lady of the rock: a novel. 3 vols 1805.
Ella St Laurence, or the village of Selwood and its inhabitants: a novel. 4 vols 1809.
The wanderings of fancy: consisting of miscellaneous pieces in prose and verse. 1812.
The wood nymph: a novel. 3 vols [1813].
Tales of to-day. 3 vols 1816; tr Fr, Paris 1817. Contains The heiress of Riversdale, Juliet, and The sisters.
Earl Osric: or the legend of Rosamond. 4 vols 1820. [EH]

Frances Jacson or Jackson 1754–1842

§1

Plain sense: a novel. 3 vols 1795 (anon), 1796, 2 vols Dublin 1796, 3 vols London 1799, 2 vols Philadelphia 1799.
Disobedience: a novel. 4 vols 1797.
Things by their right names: a novel. 2 vols 1812, Boston 1812, London 1814.
Rhoda: a novel. 3 vols 1816, 1816, 2 vols Boston, New York and Philadelphia 1816.
Isabella: a novel. 3 vols 1823, 2 vols Boston 1823.

§2

Percy, J. An unrecognised novelist: Frances Jacson (1754–1842). BLJ 23 1997. Attributes through biographical evidence the above novels to Jacson, rather than to Alethea Brereton Lewis (*see below*). [PG]

George Payne Rainsford James 1799–1860

Bibliographies

Sadleir, M. In his XIX century fiction: a bibliographical record, 2 vols 1951.

Collections

Works, revised and corrected by the author, with an introductory preface. 21 vols 1844–9.
Novels and tales. 43 vols [c. 1860].

§1

The ruined city: a poem. 1828 (priv ptd), 1829 (with Adra, or the Peruvians).
Adra, or the Peruvians: the ruined city etc. 1829.
Richelieu: a tale of France. 3 vols 1829, 1831, 1 vol 1839, 1856, 1874, 2 vols New York 1895; ed R. Dircks 1909 (EL).
Darnley: or the field of the cloth of gold. 3 vols 1830, 1 vol 1836, 1850, 1853, 1874.
De l'Orme, by the author of Richelieu and Darnley. 3 vols 1830, 1 vol 1836, 1837 (rev), 1854, 1856.
The history of chivalry. 1830, New York 1839, London 1857.
Philip Augustus: or the brothers in arms, by the author of Darnley, De l'Orme etc. 3 vols 1831, 1 vol 1837, 1850, 1851, 1854.
Memoirs of great commanders. 3 vols 1832, 2 vols Boston 1835; illustr Phiz [or rather E. Corbould] 1858.
Henry Masterton: or the adventures of a young cavalier, by the author of Richelieu, Darnley etc. 3 vols 1832, 1837, 1 vol Leipzig 1840, London 1851.

The string of pearls, by the author of Darnley etc. 2 vols 1832, 1 vol 1849. Tales.
France in the lives of her great men: the history of Charlemagne. 1832, New York 1845, London 1847 (2nd edn, as The history of Charlemagne, with a sketch of the history of France).
Delaware, or the ruined family: a tale. 3 vols Edinburgh 1833, 1 vol 1848 (as Thirty years since: or the ruined family), [1855], 1865.
Mary of Burgundy: or the revolt of Ghent, by the author of Darnley. 3 vols 1833, 2 vols 1837, 3 vols 1844, 1 vol 1850, 1854, 1877.
The life and adventures of John Marston Hall, by the author of Darnley. 3 vols 1834, 1 vol 1851.
The gipsy: a tale, by the author of Richelieu. 3 vols 1835, 1 vol 1850, 1854, 2 vols New York 1855, 1 vol 1879.
On the educational institutions of Germany. 1835.
My aunt Pontypool. 3 vols 1835, 1 vol 1857.
One in a thousand: or the days of Henry Quatre, by the author of The gipsy. 3 vols 1835, 2 vols New York 1836, 1 vol London 1845, 1850.
The desultory man, by the author of Richelieu. 3 vols 1836.
A history of the life of Edward the Black Prince and of various events connected therewith .... 2 vols 1836.
Attila: a romance, by the author of The gipsy. 3 vols 1837, 2 vols New York 1837, 3 vols 1845, 1 vol 1853, [1879].
Memoirs of celebrated women. 2 vols 1837, Philadelphia 1839. Ed James.
The life and times of Louis the Fourteenth. 4 vols 1838, 2 vols 1851, 1 vol 1874, 2 vols 1890–1.
The robber: a tale by the author of Richelieu. 3 vols 1838, 1 vol 1850, 2 vols New York 1855.
Henry of Guise: or the states of Blois. 3 vols 1839, 2 vols New York 1840, 1 vol 1854.
A brief history of the United States boundary question, drawn up from official papers. 1839.
The Huguenot: a tale of the French Protestants, by the author of The gipsy. 3 vols 1839, 1 vol 1853, 1865, [1881].
A book of the passions. With sixteen engravings. 1839, Paris 1939.
Charles Tyrrell: or the bitter blood. 2 vols 1839, New York 1839, 1 vol London 1852, 1865.
Blanche of Navarre: a play. 1839, New York 1839.
The gentleman of the old school: a tale. 3 vols 1839, 1 vol 1852.
The King's highway: a novel. 3 vols 1840, 2 vols New York 1840, 3 vols London 1844, 1 vol 1851, 1854, New York 1880.
The man at arms, or Henri de Cerons: a romance. 1840, 2 vols New York 1840, 1 vol 1842, 1844, 1857, New York 1879.
Corse de Leon, or the brigand: a romance. 3 vols 1841, 1 vol 1851, 1882.
Letters illustrative of the reign of William III from 1696 to 1708 now first published. 3 vols 1841. Ed James.
Bertrand de la Croix: or the siege of Rhodes. 1841. First pbd in The club book 1831; rptd in Eva St Clair and other tales, 1843.
The ancient régime: a tale. 3 vols 1841, 1 vol 1850 (as Castelnau).
The Jacquerie, or the lady and the page: an historical romance. 3 vols 1841, 1 vol Paris 1842, London 1852.
Some remarks on the Corn Laws, with suggestions for an alteration in the sliding scale. 1841.
Morley Ernstein: or the tenants of the heart. 3 vols 1842, 1 vol Brussels 1842, 3 vols London 1843, 1 vol 1850, 1853, tr Swed, 1844.
A history of the life of Richard Cœur de Lion, King of England. 4 vols 1842–9, 2 vols 1854.
The commissioner: or de lunatico inquirendo. Illustr Phiz 1843 (anon), Dublin 1843.
Forest days: a romance of old times. 3 vols 1843, 1 vol 1852; abridged 1911; tr Hungarian 1873.
The false heir. 3 vols 1843, 1 vol 1853.
Eva St Clair and other collected tales. 2 vols 1843, 1 vol 1855.
Agincourt: a romance. 3 vols 1844, 1 vol Leipzig 1844, New York 1844, London 1852.
Arabella Stuart: a romance from English history. 3 vols 1844, 1 vol 1853.
Rose d'Albret, or troublous times: a romance. 3 vols 1844, 1 vol 1856.
Arrah Neil: or times of old. 3 vols 1845, 1 vol 1853, 1887.
The smuggler: a tale. 3 vols 1845, 1 vol Paris 1845, London 1851, New York 1880, London 1887, 1908.
The step mother: or evil doings. 1845 (priv ptd), 3 vols 1846, 1 vol 1855.
Heidelberg: a romance. 3 vols 1846, 1 vol Paris 1846, Leipzig 1846, London 1852.
The life of Henry the Fourth, King of France and Navarre. 3 vols 1847, 2 vols New York 1847.
The castle of Ehrenstein, its lords spiritual and temporal, its inhabitants earthly and unearthly. 3 vols 1847, 1 vol New York 1847, 3 vols London 1849, 1 vol 1854, New York 1879. Chs 1–6 ptd in Novel Times 1845; chs 1–13 illustr Phiz in Ainsworth's Mag 1845.
A whim, and its consequences. 3 vols 1847 (anon), 1850, 1 vol 1853.
The convict: a tale. 3 vols 1847, 1 vol New York 1847, 3 vols London 1849, 1 vol 1851, 1854, 1890.
Russell: a tale of the reign of Charles II. 3 vols 1847, New York 1847, London 1849, 1 vol 1854.
Beauchamp: or the error. 3 vols 1848. Serialised in NMM 1845–6.
Margaret Graham: a tale founded on facts. 2 vols 1848, 1 vol 1857, New York 1878 (sub-titled The reverses of fortune). Serialised in NMM 1847.
The last of the fairies. Illustr J. Gilbert [1848], 1863, New York 1879.
Sir Theodore Broughton: or laurel water. 3 vols 1848, 1 vol 1853.
Camaralzaman: a fairy drama. 1848.
Gowrie: or the King's plot. 1848 (as vol 17 of the Collected works), 1851.
An investigation of the circumstances attending the murder of John, Earl of Gowrie and Alexander Ruthven. 1849.
Rizzio: or scenes in Europe during the sixteenth century, by W. H. Ireland. 3 vols 1849. Ed James.
Dark scenes of history. 3 vols 1849, 1 vol 1852.
The fight of the fiddlers: a serio-comic verity. Illustr H. K. Browne 1849. First pbd in Eva St Clair and other collected tales, 1843.
The forgery: or best intentions. 3 vols 1849, 1849, 1 vol 1853.
John Jones's tales for little John Joneses. 2 vols 1849.
The woodman: a romance of the times of Richard III. 3 vols 1849, 1849, 1 vol 1857.
The old oak chest: a tale of domestic life. 3 vols 1850, 1 vol New York 1880.
Henry Smeaton: a Jacobite story of the reign of George the First. 3 vols 1851.
The fate: a tale of stirring times. 3 vols 1851.
Remorse and other tales. New York 1852.
Revenge: a novel. 3 vols 1852, 1 vol Philadelphia 1860 (as The man in black).
Adrian, or the clouds of the mind: a romance. 2 vols 1852, 1 vol New York 1852. With M. B. Field.
Pequinillo: a tale. 3 vols 1852, 1 vol New York 1852.
The bride of Landeck. New York 1858. First pbd in Harper's NMM June–Nov 1852.
Agnes Sorel: an historical romance. 3 vols 1853, 1 vol New York 1853, 1884, 1889.
A life of vicissitudes: a story of revolutionary times. New York 1852, 3 vols 1853 (as The vicissitudes of a life: a novel).
An oration on the character and services of the late Duke of Wellington. Boston 1853.
Ticonderoga, or the Black Eagle: a tale of times not long past. 3 vols 1854, 1 vol New York 1854, London 1859 (as The Black Eagle: or Ticonderoga).
Prince Life: a story for my boy. 1856.

The old dominion, or the Southampton massacre: a novel. New York 1856, 3 vols London 1856, 1 vol 1858.

Leonora d'Orco: a historical romance. 3 vols 1857, 1 vol 1858; tr Fr 1858.

Lord Montagu's page: a historical romance. 3 vols 1858, 1 vol Philadelphia 1858.

The cavalier: an historical novel. Philadelphia 1859, 2 vols 1864 (as Bernard Marsh: a novel).

James contributed to Seven tales by seven authors, *ed F. E. Smedley, 1849, 1860, and wrote lives of eminent foreign statesmen for vols 2–5 of* Lardner's cabinet cyclopaedia, *1836, 2 vols Philadelphia 1836.*

§2

The novels of James. Dublin Univ Mag Mar 1842.

Horne, R. H. In his A new spirit of the age vol 1, 1844.

Recollections of James. Bentley's Misc Feb 1861.

Frost, W. A. The novels and short stories of James. N & Q 26 Aug 1916. Annotated list.

Ellis, S. M. The solitary horseman: or the life and adventures of James. 1927. With bibliography.

Duffy, C. Letter from G. P. R. J. to B. Taylor. N & Q 19 June 1943.

Maria Jane Jewsbury, later Fletcher 1800–33

Manuscripts

Mss of Jewsbury's letters of 1818 and 1827–32 to her family are held in the John Rylands Univ Lib of Manchester. Mss of her letters to William and Dora Wordsworth (1825–32) are held in the Dove Cottage Papers (Wordsworth Trust, Grasmere): they include her satirical newspaper co-written with Dora Wordsworth in 1825, the Kent's Bank Mercury. *The Spencer Lib of the Univ of Kansas holds two letters of 1829 and 1830 to Caroline Bowles; Duke Univ Lib holds a letter from Jewsbury to the Rev Thomas Raffles, plus clippings of her poems, an engraving and obituary. For other British holdings of mss see LR I, 516.*

Selections

Maria Jane Jewsbury: occasional papers. Selected with a memoir by E. Gillett 1932.

§1

Phantasmagoria: or sketches of life and literature. 2 vols Leeds 1825 (anon). Dedicated to William Wordsworth. Some prose pieces rptd in Maria Jane Jewsbury: occasional papers, 1932.

Letters to the young. 1828, Boston 1829 as Letters of Maria Jane Jewsbury addressed to her young friends (bound with Legh Richmond's Advice to his daughters) (micro New Haven CT 1975), London 1829 (2nd edn), 1832 (3rd edn), Boston 1834, Boston, Philadelphia and New York 1835, rptd Philadelphia 1863, 1837 (4th edn), Philadelphia [1851] as Light for the young.

Lays of leisure hours. 1829. Dedicated to Felicia Hemans.

The three histories: the history of an enthusiast, the history of a nonchalant, the history of a realist. 1830, Boston 1831, 1832 (2nd edn), Philadelphia 1834, Derby 1838 (3rd edn).
REVIEWS: Literary Gazette 24 Apr 1830; Athenaeum 1 May 1830; NMM 30 1830; Edinburgh Jnl 8 May 1830.

Contributions to periodicals

Curiosity and scandal. Coventry Herald, Spring 1818. Rptd in Maria Jane Jewsbury: occasional papers, 1932.

Jewsbury contributed to the Manchester Gazette *from 1821. Over 70 contributions to 13 annuals listed in A. Boyle,* An index to the Annuals, *vol 1 1967; some of these rptd in* Lays of leisure hours, *1829, and in* Maria Jane Jewsbury: occasional papers, *1932. Contributions to the* Athenaeum *1830–1 listed in M. C. Fryckstedt,* The hidden rill: the life and career of Maria Jane Jewsbury, II. BJRL 67 1984–5. *Jewsbury's contributions for 1832 cannot be identified with certainty, but N. Clarke attributes to her four articles titled* On modern female cultivation *(4, 11, 25 Feb and 11 Aug), plus a review of Mrs John Sandford's* Woman in her social and domestic character, *5 May. See Clarke's* Ambitious heights: writing, friendship, love – the Jewsbury sisters, Felicia Hemans and Jane Welsh Carlyle, *1990. Jewsbury's journal of her voyage to and experience in India, plus her poem sequence,* Oceanides, *were pbd in the* Athenaeum *between Dec 1832 and Dec 1833*

Letters and journals

There is no edn of Jewsbury's letters, but selections and extracts have been pbd in Maria Jane Jewsbury: occasional papers, *1932, and in N. Clarke,* Ambitious heights, *1990, as well as in the following:*

Chorley, H. F. Memorials of Mrs Hemans, with illustrations of her literary character from her private correspondence. 2 vols 1836.

Fryckstedt, M. C. The hidden rill: the life and career of Maria Jane Jewsbury. BJRL 66 1983–4 and 67 1984–5.

Extracts from Jewsbury's journal of her voyage to and residence in India, 1832–3, were pbd in F. Espinasse, Lancashire worthies, *2nd ser 1877, rptd from the* Athenaeum.

§2

Mrs Fletcher. Athenaeum 21 June 1834 (anon). Obituary.

Ellis, Sarah Stickney. Mrs Fletcher, late Miss Jewsbury. Christian Keepsake 1838.

Chorley, H. F. Review of Zoe (novel by Jewsbury's sister Geraldine). Athenaeum 1 Feb 1845.

Williams, Jane. The literary women of England. 1861.

See also texts listed under Letters and journals, above. [JW]

Christian Isobel Johnstone 1781–1857

The Saxon and the Gael: or the northern metropolis, including a view of the Lowland and Highland character. 4 vols London and Edinburgh 1814. Anon.

Clan-Albin: a national tale. 4 vols London, Edinburgh and Dublin 1815 (anon), 1815, 3 vols Philadelphia 1815, 1 vol London 1853 (as Clan Albyn).

The wars of the Jews, as related by Josephus adapted to the capacities of young persons. 1823, 1824, Boston 1826, London 1832 (4th edn), New York and Boston 1853 (as Stories from the history of the Jews). Adapted from Flavius Josephus, De bello Judaico.

The cook and housewife's manual, containing the most approved modern receipts for making soups, gravies, sauces, by Margaret Dods. Edinburgh 1826 (11 edns by 1862).

The students: or biography of Grecian philosophers. [1827.]

Elizabeth de Bruce. 3 vols Edinburgh and London 1827, 2 vols New York 1827; tr Ger 1827.

Diversions of Hollycot: or the mother's art of thinking. 1828, New York 1829, Edinburgh 1845 (3rd edn), London and Edinburgh 1876.

Scenes of industry displayed in the bee-hive and the ant-hill. [1829?], 1830.

Lives and voyages of Drake, Cavendish and Dampier: including an introductory view of the earlier discoveries in the South Sea and the history of the buccaneers. Edinburgh 1831, New York 1832, 1836, Edinburgh 1837, New York 1839, 1842, 1844, Edinburgh 1846, New York 1846, 1900.

Nights of the round table: or stories of Aunt Jane and her friends. 2 ser Edinburgh 1832, 1 vol Philadelphia 1845, Edinburgh [1847].

True tales of the Irish peasantry, as related by themselves, selected from the Report of the Poor-Law Commissioners. [1836?], Edinburgh 1836 (2nd edn).

Rational reading lessons. Edinburgh 1842.

The Edinburgh tales. 3 vols Edinburgh 1845–6. Ed Mrs Johnstone. Includes tales by Mrs Johnstone first pbd in Inverness Courier, Edinburgh Weekly Chron and Johnstone's Edinburgh Mag, later merged with Tait's Mag, which she and her husband owned and edited.

Mrs Johnstone also edited the Poems of Robert Nicoll, *1842.* [PG]

George Jones, 'Leigh Cliffe'

§1

Parga: a poem. 1819. Anon.
The protocol: or selections from the contents of a red box found in the neighbourhood of St James's Square. 1820, 1820.
Supreme bon ton, and bon ton by profession: a novel. 3 vols 1820.
The knights of Ritzberg: a romance. 3 vols 1822.
Temptation: a novel. 3 vols 1823.
Margaret Coryton. 3 vols 1829.
Anecdotal reminiscences of distinguished literary and political characters. 1830.
The sceptic: and other poems. 1835.
The expatriated: a tale of modern Poland. 1836. Verse fiction.
The pilgrim of Avon. 1836, 1890 (4th edn). Poem.
For a listing of reviews and notices of Jones's works, see Ward (1972, 1977).
[PG]

Hannah Maria Jones, later Lowndes 1796?–1854

Bibliographies
Summers, M. In his A Gothic bibliography, [1941].

§1

Gretna Green, or the elopement of Miss D– with a gallant son of Mars: founded on recent facts. 1821 (anon), 1823, 1836.
The British officer, or love and honour: a tale. 1821. Chapbook.
The forged note, or Julian and Marianne: a moral tale founded on recent facts. 1824.
The gamblers, or the treacherous friend: a moral tale founded on recent facts. 1824, 1825 (as The victim of fashion: or a treacherous friend), 1836, [c. 1870].
The wedding ring, or married and single: a domestic tale. 1824, 4 vols 1824.
Rosaline Woodbridge, or the midnight visit: a romantic tale. 1827, 3 vols 1827, 1 vol 1854.
The strangers of the glen, or the travellers benighted: a tale of mystery. 1827.
Horatio in search of a wife. Leeds 1828–30 (in pts), 1830. Written jointly with Anna M. Morgan.
Emily Moreland: or the maid of the valley. 1829, 3 vols 1829, 1 vol 1836, [1839], [1852?].
The Scottish chieftains: or the perils of love and war. 1831, 1854, 1856 (in 59 pts).
The gipsy mother: or the miseries of enforced marriage. [1833], [1835?], [1836], [1840], 1854.
Village scandal, or the gossip's tale: a picture of real life. 1835.
The gipsey girl, or the heir of Hazell Dell: a romantic tale. 1836, [1842], London and New York [1845?], London and New York [1865?].
The child of mystery, or the cottager's daughter: a tale of fashionable life. 1837, [1857?].
The pride of the village, or the farmer's daughters: a domestic story. 1837, [1870?] (as part of a series entitled Ladies of England novelist).
The outlaw's bride, or the heir of Glenshannon: a romantic tale. 1838.
The gipsey chief, or the haunted oak: a tale of other days. [1840], [1840], 1850, [1870?].
The love token, or the mistress and her guardian: a domestic story. [1844?]
The peasant girl: a domestic story. 1844 (serialised in Lloyd's Entertaining Jnl, 30 Mar–21Dec), 1845.
Family faults: or a mother's errors. 1845, 1854.
The ruined cottage, or the farmer's maid: a romance of real life. 1847–8 (in 78 pts).
The shipwreck'd stranger. 1848 (in pts).
The trials of love, or woman's reward: a romance of real life. 1848–9 (in pts), [1853].
Katharine Beresford, or the shades and sunshine of a woman's life: a romantic story. 1850, 1852, [1854].
The curate's daughters, or the twin roses of Arundale: a domestic story. [1853] (in 31 pts).

Attributed or spurious works.
Jane Shore, or the goldsmith's wife. 1839, [1850?].
Rose of England: or the adventures of a prince. 1841, 1852–3 (in pts).
Both works are also attributed to Mrs Mary E. Bennett.

Hannah Maria Jones's works were issued in a variety of forms, usually first appearing in parts, these being re-issued in collected form, and (in the earlier years) sometimes reprinted to produce multi-vol versions: re-issues of the single-vol form, with often undated title pages, were common. [PG]

Isabella Kelly, later Hedgeland

c. 1758–c. 1857

Bibliographies
Summers, M. In his A Gothic bibliography, [1941].

§1

Madeline, or the castle of Montgomery. 3 vols 1794. Anon.
A collection of poems and fables. London and Edinburgh 1794.
The Abbey of Saint Asalph: a novel by the author of Madeline. 3 vols 1795, introd by D. P. Varma, New York 1977.
The ruins of Avondale Priory: a novel by Mrs Kelly. 3 vols 1796.
Joscelina, or the rewards of benevolence: a novel. 2 vols 1797; tr Fr 1799.
Eva: a novel. 3 vols 1799; tr Fr 1803.
Ruthinglenne, or the critical moment: a novel. 3 vols 1801; tr Fr 1818.
The baron's daughter: a Gothic romance. 4 vols 1802.
Poems. 1802, 1805, Chelsea 1807, as Poems and fables on several occasions.
A modern incident in domestic life. 2 vols Brentford 1803.
The secret: a novel. 4 vols Brentford 1805.
Literary information consisting of anecdotes, explanations and derivations. 1811.
Jane de Dunstanville, or characters as they are: a novel. 4 vols 1813, 1819.

Attributed and spurious works
The matron of Erin: a national tale. 3 vols London and Dublin 1816.
The fatalists, or records of 1814 and 1815: a novel. 5 vols 1821.
Both these novels are attributed by Summers to a Mrs Kelly of Ireland.

For a listing of reviews and notices of I. Kelly's works, see Ward (1979, 1972).
[CF]

Mary Ann Kelty 1789–1873

The favourite of nature: a tale. 3 vols 1821 (anon), 1821, 1822, 1 vol 1840; tr Fr 1823.
Osmond: a tale. 3 vols 1822, 1823; tr Ger 1822, Fr 1824.
Trials: a tale. 3 vols 1824, 2 vols Philadelphia 1824; tr Fr 1824.
The story of Isabel. 3 vols 1826.
Times of trial: being a brief narrative of the progress of the Reformation and of the sufferings of some of the reformers. 1830.
Biography for young ladies. 1839.
Mamma and Mary: discoursing upon good and evil, in six dialogues. 1840, [1840?] (2nd edn).
Gentle Gertrude: a tale for youth. 1843.
Visiting my relations and its results: a series of small episodes in the life of a recluse. 1851, 1852, 1853.
Alice Rivers: or passages in the life of a young lady. 2 vols 1852.
Reminiscences of thought and feeling. 1852, New York 1853.
Life by the fireside. 1853.

Waters of comfort: a small volume of devotional poetry of a practical character. 1856.
The solace of a solitaire: a record of facts and feelings. 1869.
M. A. Kelty also wrote a large number of pietistic works, including an account of the early Quakers, several devotional diaries, and other religious and philosophical reflections.
For a listing of reviews and notices of Kelty's early novels, see Ward (1977).
[PG]

Grace Kennedy 1782–1825

Collected works

The works of Grace Kennedy (with A short account of the author). 6 vols Edinburgh 1827; tr Ger 1835–6, 1844.

§1

The decision: or religion must be all, or is nothing. Edinburgh 1821 (anon), 1822 (2nd edn, enlarged), 1822 (3rd edn), 1822 (4th edn), Boston 1823, Albany NY 1824, Edinburgh 1824 (6th edn), 1825 (7th edn), Philadelphia 1826, 1827 (8th edn), New York 1827, Princeton 1827, New York 1829, Edinburgh 1831, Brussels 1836, Edinburgh 1838 (10th edn), New York 1852, 1854; tr Fr 1828.
Profession is not principle: or the name of Christian is not Christianity. Edinburgh 1822, 1822 (2nd edn), Boston 1824, Edinburgh 1824 (3rd edn), 1825 (4th edn), Trenton NJ 1826, Edinburgh 1828 (5th edn), Exeter NH 1828, New York 1829, Edinburgh 1833 (6th edn), New York 1845, Edinburgh [1856] (8th edn).
Father Clement: a Roman Catholic story. Edinburgh 1823, 1824 (2nd edn), 1825 (3rd edn), 1825 (4th edn), Philadelphia [1825], Edinburgh 1826 (5th edn), Boston and New York 1827, New York 1827, Edinburgh 1828 (6th edn), New York 1829, Edinburgh 1831 (7th edn), 1834 (8th edn), Newark NH 1834, Edinburgh 1838 (9th edn), 1842 (10th edn), Philadelphia 1843, 1847, New York 1845, 1848, Philadelphia [1850], Newark 1851, New York 1853, 1856, Edinburgh 1858 (12th edn), 1861 (13th edn), London [1870], [1876]; tr Fr 1825 etc, Ger 1826, Ital 1859, Sp [187–?].
Jessy Allan, the lame girl: a story founded on facts. Edinburgh 1823, 1823 (3rd edn), Salem MA 1824, Hartford CT 1827, Edinburgh 1828 (6th edn), 1831 (7th edn), 1840 (14th edn), New York 1850; tr Fr 1829.
Andrew Campbell's visit to his Irish cousins. Edinburgh 1824, 1829 (3rd edn), New York 1829.
Anna Ross: a story for children. Edinburgh 1824, 1826 (3rd edn), New York 1826, Philadelphia [1827], New York 1828, Edinburgh 1829 (4th edn), Oxford NY 1832, Edinburgh 1833 (5th edn), New York 1835, Edinburgh 1838 (6th edn), 1848 (9th edn), 1854 (11th edn), 1856 (12th edn), New York 1860, Edinburgh 1861 (as Anna Ross: the orphan of Waterloo), [1875], London [1875], New York 1877, 1881, London [1883?]; tr Fr 1826 etc, Ger 1833.
Dunallan, or know what you judge: a story. 3 vols Edinburgh 1825, 1825 (2nd edn), 1826 (3rd edn), 2 vols Boston 1827, New York 1828, Exeter NH 1828, Edinburgh 1829, 1834, 1 vol 1841 (6th edn), Philadelphia [1848?], 1871, Boston and Cleveland OH 1859, London [1875?], [1876], [1877], New York 1883; tr Fr 1828.
Philip Colville: or a Covenanter's story. Edinburgh 1825, New York 1829, [1850?], [1869]; tr Ger 1836.

Attributed or spurious works

Caroline Ormsby: or the real Lucilla. 1810, 1812. Anon.
The acceptance, by the author of Caroline Ormsby. 3 vols 1810.
The decision: a novel. 3 vols 1811.
Willoughby, or reformation: the influence of religious principles. 2 vols 1823.
Evidently the work of another author, these novels are attributed to Kennedy in some catalogues as a result of both having written a work titled The decision. *Also sometimes incorrectly attributed to Kennedy is* Florence, or the aspirant: a novel, *3 vols 1829.*
For a listing of reviews and notices of Kennedy's works, see Ward (1977).
[PG]

James Sheridan Knowles 1784–1862

See col 1970.

Lady Caroline Lamb, née Ponsonby 1785–1828

§1

Glenarvon. 3 vols 1816 (anon), 1816 (rev and with an authorial preface, plates and music), 1816, 2 vols Philadelphia 1816, 3 vols London 1817, 1 vol [1865] (as The fatal passion), [1866], 1972 (facs edn with introd by J. L. Ruff); tr Fr 1819, 1824.
Verses from Glenarvon; to which is prefixed the original introduction not published with the early editions of that work. 1819.
A new canto. 1819.
Gordon: a tale. 1821.
Graham Hamilton. 2 vols 1822, 1 vol Philadelphia 1822, 2 vols London 1823, 1 vol 1882.
Ada Reis: a tale. 3 vols 1823, 2 vols Paris 1824.

Contributions to collaborative works

Fugitive pieces and reminiscences of Lord Byron with some original poetry, letters and recollections of Lady Caroline Lamb. Ed I. Nathan 1829.

§2

Mayer, S. R. T. Lady Caroline Lamb. Temple Bar June 1878.
Green, A. J. Did Byron write the poem to Lady Caroline Lamb? PQ 7 1928.
Jenkins, E. Lady Caroline Lamb. 1932, rev 1972.
Clubbe, John. Glenarvon revised and revisited. TWC 10 1979. On the changes made for the 2nd edn.
For a listing of reviews and notices of C. Lamb's works, see Ward (1979, 1972).
[CF]

Francis Lathom 1777–1832

Bibliography

Summers, M. In his A Gothic bibliography, [1941].

§1

The Castle of Ollada. 2 vols 1795 (anon), 1831.
All in a bustle: a comedy by the author of The Castle of Ollada. Norwich 1795, 1800.
The midnight bell: a German story founded on incidents in real life. 3 vols 1798 (anon), Cork 1798, 2 vols Dublin 1798, 3 vols (in 1) Philadelphia 1799, 3 vols London 1825; ed D. P. Varma 1968; with introd by L. Jenkins [c. 1989]; tr Fr 1798, Ger 1800.
Men and manners: a novel. 4 vols 1799, Dublin 1799, 1800.
Orlando and Seraphina, or the funeral pile: an heroic drama. [1800.] Based on Tasso, Gerusalemme liberata.
Mystery: a novel. 2 vols 1800, 1 vol Dublin 1800.
The dash of the day: a comedy. Norwich 1800, 1800, 1800, Dublin ('3rd edn') 1801.
Holiday time, or the school boy's frolic: a farce. Norwich 1800.
Curiosity: a comedy. 1801. Adapted from the Fr of Madame de Genlis.
The wife of a million: a comedy. Norwich [1802?].
Astonishment!!! a romance of a century ago. 2 vols 1802, 3 vols 1821.
Very strange but very true! or the history of an old man's young wife: a novel. 4 vols 1803.
Erestina: a tale from the French. 2 vols 1803, 1 vol Norwich [1807?].
The impenetrable secret, find it out! a novel. 2 vols 1805, 1831.
The mysterious freebooter, or the days of Queen Bess: a romance. 4 vols 1806, 1829 (3rd edn), 1 vol 1844.

Human beings: a novel. 3 vols 1807.
The fatal vow, or St Michael's Monastery: a romance. 2 vols 1807.
The unknown, or the northern gallery: a romance. 3 vols 1808, 4 vols 1826; tr Fr 1810.
London, or truth without treason: a novel. 4 vols 1809.
The romance of the Hebrides: or wonders never cease! 3 vols 1809.
Italian mysteries, or more secrets than one: a romance. 3 vols 1820; tr Fr 1823.
The one-pound note and other tales. 2 vols 1820.
Puzzled and pleased: or the two old soldiers and other tales. 3 vols 1822.
Live and learn, or the first John Brown, his friends, enemies and acquaintance, in town and country: a novel. 4 vols 1823.
The Polish bandit: or who is my bride? and other tales. 3 vols 1824.
Young John Bull, or born abroad and bred at home: a novel. 3 vols 1828.
Fashionable mysteries: or the rival duchesses and other tales. 3 vols 1829.
Mystic events, or the vision of the tapestry: a romantic legend of the days of Anne Boleyn. 4 vols 1830.
Lathom also translated The castle of the Tuileries, *2 vols 1803, from the Fr of P. J. A. Roussel.*
For a listing of reviews and notices of Lathom's works, see Ward (1979, 1972). [PG]

Thomas Pike Lathy

Bibliographies

Summers, M. In his A Gothic bibliography, [1941].

§1

Reparation, or the school for libertines: a dramatic piece in three acts. Boston 1800.
Usurpation, or the inflexible uncle: a novel. 3 vols 1805.
The paraclete: a novel. 5 vols 1805.
The invisible enemy, or the mines of Wielitska: a Polish legendary romance. 4 vols 1806.
Gabriel Forrester, or the deserted son: a novel. 4 vols [1807].
Love, hatred and revenge: a Swiss romance. 3 vols 1809.
The angler: a poem in ten cantos, with proper instructions in the art, rules to choose fishing rods, lines, hooks [etc] by Piscator. 1819, 1820, 1822, 1841. Almost entirely plagiarised from The anglers, by Thomas Scott of Ipswich, 1758.
Memoirs of the Court of Louis XIV, comprising biography and anecdotes of the most celebrated characters of that period styled the Augustan era of France. 3 vols 1819, 1820.
For a listing of reviews and notices of Lathy's works, see Ward (1972). [PG]

Sir Thomas Dick Lauder 1784–1848

Lochandhu: a tale of the eighteenth century. Ed C. M. Montgomery 3 vols Edinburgh 1825 (anon), 1 vol Elgin 1877, 1891; tr Fr 1828.
The Wolfe of Badenoch: a historical romance of the fourteenth century. 3 vols Edinburgh 1827, 1827, 1 vol Elgin 1863, London 1870, 1886, 1892, Stirling 1930 ('6th edn'); tr Ger 1827, Fr 1828.
An account of the great floods of August 1829 in the province of Moray and adjoining districts. Edinburgh 1830, 1830; ed G. Gordon, Elgin 1873.
Highland rambles, and long legends to shorten the way. 2 vols Edinburgh 1837, London 1880.
Legendary tales of the Highlands: a sequel to Highland rambles. 3 vols 1841, 1 vol 1880 (as Highland legends), 1881 (as Tales of the Highlands), 1890 (as Highland legends).
The Edinburgh tales. Ed C. I. Johnstone 3 vols 1845–6. Lauder contributed The story of Farquharson of Inverey to vol 1, and Donald Lamont, the Braemar drover, to vol 3.
Memorial of the royal progress in Scotland. Edinburgh 1843.
Directions for taking and curing herrings; and for curing cod, ling, tusk and hake, with Gaelic translations by A. Macgregor. Edinburgh 1846, Dublin 1846.
The mill of Dalveney [chiefly drawn from an account of the great floods etc]. 1872.
Lauder edited Sir U. Price, Essays on the picturesque, *1842, to which he contributed an essay* On the origin of taste, *and Gilpin's* Forest scenery, *1834. With Thomas Brown and William Rhind he issued the* Miscellany of natural history, *2 vols 1833–4. He also pbd some topographical works.*
[PG]

Harriet Lee 1757–1851

Bibliography

Summers, M. In his A Gothic bibliography, [1941].

§1

The errors of innocence. 5 vols 1786, 2 vols Dublin 1786; tr Fr 1788.
The new peerage, or our eyes may deceive us: a comedy. 1787, 1787 (2nd edn), Dublin 1788.
Clara Lennox: or the distressed widow. 2 vols 1797; tr Fr 1798.
Canterbury tales. 5 vols 1797–1805 (vol 1 1797, vol 2 1798, vol 3 1799, vol 4 1801, vol 5 1805), 1797–9 (vols 1–3), 1799–1800 (vols 1–3) (2nd edn), 2 vols 1831, 1832 (rev and with new preface), Philadelphia 1833, 1837, 1842, New York 1857, 3 vols New York 1865, 1 vol with introd by Harriett Gilbert 1989. In 1st edn Harriet Lee's name appears alone on title page of vols 1, 4–5; not at all on vol 2; jointly with Sophia Lee's on vol 3. Sophia Lee wrote only the introd to vol 1; vol 2 and part of vol 3, comprising The two Emilys and Pembroke. Vol 3 was rptd separately Dublin 1799 as The officer's tale and clergyman's tale; Kruitzner: or the German's tale from vol 4 was often rptd separately; 1822, 5th edn 1823, New York 1823, New York and Philadelphia 1823; tr Fr 1824. The latter was dramatised by Byron in 1822 as Werner, and dramatised by Lee herself as The three strangers in 1826.
The mysterious marriage, or the heirship of Roselva: a play in three acts. 1798, Dublin 1798.
Constantia de Valmont: a novel. Philadelphia 1799.
Arundel: a novel. Philadelphia 1800.
For a listing of reviews and notices of H. Lee's works, see Ward (1979, 1972).

§2

Obit: Bristol Jnl 9 Aug 1851.
Mrs Harriet Lee. Littell's Living Age 31 1851.
See also Todd and Shattock under Histories and studies, above. [CF]

Sophia Lee 1750–1824

Bibliographies

Summers, M. In his A Gothic bibliography, [1941].

§1

The chapter of accidents: a comedy. 1780, 1780 with prologue by G. Colman, 1781, Dublin 1781, London 1782, 1792, 1796, Bell's British Theatre vol 34 1797, rptd in English Comedy (ed R. Steele and C. Cibber) 1810, rptd in The Modern Theatre (ed Mrs Inchbald) vol 9 1811, rptd in The London Theatre (ed T. Dibdin) vol 21 1815, Chiswick 1816, rptd in The New English Drama (ed T. H. Oxberry) vol 18 1818, 1823, rptd in The London Stage vol 2 1824, 1832, rptd and illustr in The British Drama vol 9 1864, rptd in Dicks Standard plays no 257 [1883?]; tr Ger 1782, 1788. Based on Diderot, Père de famille.
The recess: or a tale of other times. 3 vols 1783–5, 2 vols Dublin [1785?], 3 vols London 1786, 2 vols Dublin 1786, 3 vols corrected London 1787, 2 vols Dublin [1790?], 2 vols Dublin 1791, 3 vols corrected London 1792, Portsea [1800?], London 1804, 3 vols 1821, 3

vols [1825?], 1 vol 1826, foreword by J. M. S. Tompkins and introd by D. P. Varma, New York 1972; tr Fr 1787, Portuguese, 1806.
A hermit's tale: a poem, recorded by his own hand, and found in his cell, by the author of The recess. 1787 (anon), 1787 (2nd edn), Dublin 1787.
Almeyda, Queen of Granada: a tragedy. 1796, 1796, 1796, Dublin 1796. Partly from Shirley, The Cardinal.
Canterbury tales. 5 vols 1797–1805. Mainly by Harriet Lee. Sophia contributed 2 tales, The young lady's tale: the two Emilys (vol 2 1798) and The clergyman's tale (vol 3 1799) and the introd to vol 1 1797.
The life of a lover, in a series of letters. 6 vols 1804; tr Fr 5 vols 1808 (as Savinia Rivers).

Translations

Sophia Lee translated Varbeck, *one of the Nouvelle historiques 1774–84 by François Thomas Marie de Baculard, as* Warbeck: a pathetic tale, *2 vols 1786.*

Attributed or spurious works

Ormond: or the debauchee. By Sophia Lee. 3 vols 1810. Authorship dubious.

For a listing of reviews and notices of S. Lee's works, see Ward (1979, 1972).
[CF]

Alicia Lefanu ('The Younger') c. 1795–c. 1826

Bibliographies

Summers, M. In his A Gothic bibliography, [1941].

§1

The flowers, or the sylphid queen: a fairy tale in verse. 1809.
Rosara's chain, or the choice of life: a poem. 1812, 1815 (3rd edn), 1823.
Strathallan. 4 vols 1816, 1816, 1817; tr Fr 1818.
Helen Monteagle. 3 vols 1818.
Leolin Abbey: a novel. 3 vols 1819; tr Fr 1824.
Tales of a tourist: containing The outlaw and Fashionable connexions. 3 vols 1823.
Don Juan de las Sierras, or El Empecinado: a romance. 3 vols 1823.
Memoirs of the life and writings of Mrs Frances Sheridan. 1824.
Henry the Fourth of France: a romance. 1826.

Attributed works

The India voyage. 2 vols 1804. Attributed to Alicia Lefanu, the younger, by Block and Summers (see under Bibliographies, *above*), but actually by her mother, Elizabeth Lefanu.

For a listing of reviews and notices of Lefanu's works, see Ward (1972, 1977).
[PG]

Alethea Brereton Lewis, 'Eugenia de Acton' 1749–1827

§1

Vicissitudes in genteel life. 4 vols Stafford 1794. Anon.
The microcosm. 5 vols 1801.
Essays on the art of being happy: addressed to a young mother. 2 vols 1803.
A tale without a title: give it what you please. 3 vols 1804.
The nuns of the desert: or the woodland witches. 2 vols 1805.
The discarded daughter: a novel. 4 vols 1810.

For 5 novels previously attributed in catalogues to Lewis, see Frances Jacson, above. [PG]

Matthew Gregory Lewis 1775–1818

The original autograph ms of The monk *is in the Wisbech and Fenland Museum, Wisbech, Cambridgeshire. The Larpent Collection in the Huntington contains ms versions of several of Lewis's dramatic works, including* The harper's daughter: or love and ambition *(Huntington MS LA 1377). For a listing of other mss, including Lewis's correspondence, see L. F. Peck,* A life of Lewis, *1961.*

Bibliographies

Summers, M. In his A Gothic bibliography, [1941].
McNutt, D. J. In his The eighteenth-century Gothic novel: an annotated bibliography of criticism and selected texts, New York 1975.
Frank, F. S. In his Gothic fiction: a master list of twentieth century criticism and research, Westport CT 1988. Secondary material.

§1

The effusions of sensibility: an unfinished burlesque novel [1791]. In Mrs Baron-Wilson, Life and correspondence of Lewis vol 2, 1839.
The monk: a romance. 3 vols 1796, 1796, 2 vols Dublin 1796, Waterford '1796' (watermarked 1818), 3 vols London 1797, 2 vols Dublin 1797, 3 vols 1798 (as Ambrosio, or the monk: a romance), 2 vols Boston 1799, 3 vols London 1800, 2 vols Dublin 1800, New York 1802, 3 vols Paris 1807, 2 vols Dublin 1808, 3 vols London 1815, 1822, New York 1822, 1830, London 1830, 1832, 1 vol Paris 1832, New York 1845, London 1846, [1859], Philadelphia [1884]; ed R. F. Stalham 3 vols London 1906, 1924; ed E. A. Baker 1907; ed L. F. Peck, New York 1952, 1959; ed H. Anderson, London 1973, 1980 (WCp); ed D. P. Varma 1984; tr Fr 1797 etc, 1931, Ger 1797, Sp 1822, 1978. Dramatised by J. Boaden as Aurelio and Miranda, 1798, 1798, 1799; adapted and abridged as The castle of Lindenberg: or the history of Raymond and Agnes 1798 etc; and as Raymond and Agnes: or the bleeding nun of the Castle of Lindenberg, 1820, New York 1821, London 1823, New York 1828, London 1841; dramatised under that title, 1829, [1877?]. Dramatised in Fr 1798 etc; tr Fr (abridged) [1884?] (as Le Moine incestueux).
REVIEWS: Analytical Rev 24 1796; Br Critic 7 1796; [Coleridge, S. T.] Critical Rev 2nd ser 19 1797; European Mag 31 1797; Monthly Rev n.s. 23 1797.
Village virtues: a dramatic satire. 1796.
REVIEWS: Analytical Rev 24 1796; Monthly Rev n.s. 21 1796; Critical Rev 2nd ser 19 1797.
Alonzo the brave and fair Imogene: a ballad. Glasgow [1797?] (anon) (also as part of Poetry original and selected vol 2), London [1810?], [1820?], [1830?].
The minister: a tragedy translated from the German of Schiller. 1797, 1798, Dublin 1798.
REVIEWS: Br Critic 10 1797; Critical Rev 2nd ser 25 1797; Monthly Mirror 3 1797.
The castle spectre: a drama. 1798 (8 edns), Boston [1798], Dublin 1798, Cork 1799, Dublin 1799, Salem MA 1799, Philadelphia 1801, London 1803 (10th edn), 1803 (11th edn), New York 1808, London 1818, 1819, [1824], [1827?], [1840?], [1850], 1864; Oxford 1992 (facs of 1st edn, with introd by J. Wordsworth); ed J. N. Cox, in his Seven Gothic dramas 1789–1825, Athens OH 1992; tr Fr 1807.
REVIEWS: Monthly Mirror 4 1797, 5 1798; Analytical Rev 28 1798; Br Critic 11 1798; Critical Rev 2nd ser 22 1798; European Mag 33 1798; Monthly Rev n.s. 26 1798.
Osric the lion: a poem. Glasgow [1798?] (also as part of Poetry original and selected vol 4).
Rolla, or the Peruvian hero: a tragedy translated from the German of Kotzebue [trn of Die Spanier in Peru]. 1799, 1799 (2nd edn), 1799 (4th edn), 1799 (6th edn).
REVIEW: Monthly Mirror 11 1801.
Tales of terror. Kelso 1799 (re-issued as An apology for tales of terror). Includes 4 ballads by Lewis with others by W. Scott (its instigator) and Southey.
The love of gain: a poem imitated from Juvenal. 1799 (3 edns). With Latin text.
REVIEWS: Analytical Rev n.s. 1 1799; Br Critic 13 1799; Critical Rev 2nd ser 1799.
Crazy Jane: a ballad. London [1800?], Nottingham [1800?], Boston

and New York [1799–1800?], Waterford [1830?], Manchester [1835?].

The East Indian: a comedy. 1800, 1800 (2nd edn), 1800 (4th edn), Dublin 1800 (as Rivers: or the East Indian), New York 1800. Adapted as an opera 1818, 1886.
REVIEWS: Br Critic 15 1800; Monthly Rev n.s. 32 1800.

Tales of wonder, written and collected by M. G. Lewis. 2 vols '1801' [1800], Dublin 1801, New York 1801, 1 vol London 1801 (2nd edn, abridged), Dublin 1805, Vienna 1805, London 1816, 1817, 1836, [1869]. With contributions by Scott and Southey.
REVIEWS: Br Critic 16 1800; Antijacobin Rev 8 1801; Critical Rev 2nd ser 34 1802.

Adelmorn the outlaw: a romantic drama. 1801, 1801, Dublin 1801, Philadelphia 1802, New York 1805, 1815; tr Ger 1829.
REVIEWS: Br Critic 18 1801; European Mag 39 1801; Monthly Mirror 11 1801; Critical Rev 2nd ser 34 1802.

Songs in Adelmorn the outlaw. 1801.

Alfonso, King of Castile: a tragedy. 1801, 1802, Philadelphia 1802, Philadelphia, Baltimore and Washington 1802, Philadelphia 1810, New York 1811.
REVIEWS: Br Critic 20 1802; Critical Rev 2nd ser 34 1802; European Mag 41 1802; Monthly Mirror 13 1802.

The wild wreath. Ed M. E. Robinson 1804. Contains 4 poems by Lewis.

The bravo of Venice: a romance translated from the German [of J. H. Zschokke]. '1805' [1804], 1805 (2nd edn), 1807 (5th edn), 1809, Baltimore 1809 (as Abaellino, the bravo of Venice), London 1818 (7th edn), 1826 (8th edn), Boston 1829, London 1830, 1834, 1839, [1844], 1856 etc; New York 1972 (facs of 1st edn, with introd by D. P. Varma); abridged as Rugantino: the bravo of Venice [1810?], 1823, Durham 1837; tr Fr (as Le brigand de Venise) 1806.
REVIEWS: Br Critic 25 1805; Critical Rev 3rd ser 5 1805; European Mag 48 1805.

Rugantino, or the bravo of Venice: a grand romantic melodrama. 1805, 1806, Dublin 1809, New York 1810, London 1820, Boston and New York 1822.
REVIEW: Critical Rev 3rd ser 7 1806.

Adelgitha, or the fruits of a single error: a tragedy. 1806 (4 edns), New York 1808, 1812, London 1817, Philadelphia 1823, London 1829 (in Cumberland's British Theatre vol 39), Boston [1858], New York [1858?] (as French's Modern Standard Drama no 323).
REVIEWS: Monthly Rev n.s. 50 1806; Critical Rev 3rd ser 11 1807.

Feudal tyrants, or the Counts of Carlsheim and Sargans: a romance, taken from the German [of C. B. E. Naubert]. 4 vols 1806, 1807, 1807; tr Fr 1810.
REVIEWS: Critical Rev 3rd ser 11 1807; Monthly Rev n.s. 53 1807.

The wood daemon, or the clock has struck: a grand romantic melodrama. [1807], Boston 1808.
REVIEW: European Mag 51 1807.

Romantic tales. 4 vols 1808, 2 vols New York 1809, 1 vol London 1838 (selection), 1848 (selection). Separate tales often rptd.
REVIEWS: Critical Rev 3rd ser 1808; Br Critic 33 1809; GM n.s. 2 1809.

Venoni, or the novice of St Mark's: a drama. 1809, New York 1809, Philadelphia 1810, London 1829.
REVIEW: Br Critic 36 1810.

Monody on the death of Sir John Moore. 1809.
REVIEW: Monthly Rev n.s. 61 1810.

Timour the tartar: a grand romantic melodrama. [1811], Dublin 1811, New York 1812, Boston 1813, London 1829, New York 1830, Baltimore 1842, London [1850?], 1868.

One o'clock or the knight and the wood demon: a grand musical romance. [1811], Dublin 1812, New York 1813, London 1824 etc.
REVIEW: Br Critic 40 1812.

Poems. 1812.

Rich and poor: a comic opera. 1812, 1818, 1823.

The harper's daughter, or love and ambition: a tragedy. By Schiller (Kabale und Liebe). Philadelphia 1813. Originally performed 1803; for ms copy, see headnote.

The isle of devils: a historical tale [in verse] founded on an anecdote in the annals of Portugal. Kingston Jamaica 1827, London 1912, Philadelphia 1978.

Journal of a West India proprietor kept during a residence in the island of Jamaica. 1834, 1845 (as Journal of a residence among the negroes in the West Indies), 1861; ed M. Wilson 1929; New York [1969].

Tales of mystery. Ed G. Saintsbury 1891. Selections from Ann Radcliffe, Lewis and Maturin.

Lewis also translated, with others, Anthony Hamilton, Fairy tales and romances, *1849. In 1899 appeared an edn of his trn of Hamilton,* Les quatres Facardins, *with continuations by Lewis and the Duc de Lévis.* Les mystères de la Tour Saint-Jean, *4 vols Paris 1819, is described on title page as 'par Lewis, auteur du Moine', but cannot be identified as a trn of any known work of his.* Tales of terror [in verse], with an introductory dialogue, *1801, 1808 (2nd edn), is wrongly attributed to Lewis.* Tales of terror and wonder, *ed H. Morley 1887 and* Tales in verse of terror and wonder, *ed L. E. Smith, Girard KS [1925], combine poems from this collection with Lewis's* Tales of wonder. *Summers lists various other spurious attributions, imitations, parodies and plagiarisms.*

§2

Mathias, T. J. The pursuits of literature. 1797. 4th dialogue contains a denunciation of The monk.

Impartial strictures on the poem called The pursuits of literature and particularly a vindication of the romance of The monk. 1798.

[Baron-Wilson, M.] The life and correspondence of Lewis, with many pieces never before published. 2 vols 1839.

Johnston, G. P. The first book printed by James Ballantyne. Edinburgh Bibl Soc Pbns 1 pt 4 1894. On Apology for tales of terror.

Bortone, G. Fra il voto e l'amore: note critiche sul Monaco del Lewis. Naples 1908.

Church, E. A bibliographical myth. MP 19 1922. On Tales of terror, 1801.

Emerson, O. F. Monk Lewis and the Tales of terror. MLN 38 1923.

Coykendall, F. A note on The monk. Colophon n.s. no 1 1935. Detailed bibliographical analysis.

Peck, L. F. Lewis and the Larpent catalogue. HLQ 5 1942.

Todd, W. B. The early editions and issues of The monk, with a bibliography. SB 2 1949.

Guthke, K. S. Some bibliographical errors concerning the romantic age. PBSA 51 1957. On Lewis's sources and authorship.

Guthke, K. S. Some unpublished letters of Lewis. N & Q 202, May, Sep 1957.

Parreaux, A. The publication of The monk. Paris 1960.

Peck, L. F. A life of Lewis. Cambridge MA 1961.

Guthke, K. S. Lewis' The twins: text and commentary. HLQ 25 1962. Includes the hitherto unpbd The twins: or is it he or his brother? from the Larpent ms.

Peck, L. F. An early copy of The monk. PBSA 57 1963.

Peck, L. F. On the date of the Tales of wonder. ELN 2 1964.

Lévy, M. Le manuscrit du Moine. Caliban 3 1965.

Peck, L. F. New poems by Lewis. Archiv 153 1966.

Bishop, M. A terrible tangle. TLS 19 Oct 1967. On the authorship of Tales of terror 1801.

Anderson, H. The ms of Lewis's The monk: some preliminary notes. PBSA 62 1968.

Irwin, J. J. Monk Lewis. Boston 1976.

Carnochan, W. B. and D. W. Donaldson. The presentation copy of Monk Lewis's Oberon's henchman. BC 30 1981.

Lévy, M. The monk: bibliographie selective et critique. Bulletin de la Societé d'Études Anglo-Americaines des XVIIe et XVIIIe Siècles 21 1985. [PG]

John Gibson Lockhart 1794–1854

See col 2189.

Samuel Lover 1797–1868

Collections

Characteristic sketches of Ireland and the Irish, by Carleton, Lover and Mrs Hall. Dublin 1845, Halifax 1846, 1849, 1852 (as Tales and stories of Ireland). Lover's contributions are Paddy Mullonney's travels in France; A legend of Clanmacnoise; Ballads and ballad singers.

Poetical works. 1868, New York 1869, London and New York [1870?], Boston and New York 1872, New York 1875, London and New York [1880], New York 1884, 1897, Boston 1902, 1903.

Legends and tales of Ireland. [c. 1900], 1995. Prose and verse. With T. Croker.

Tales from the works of Samuel Lover and other authors. [c. 1900.]

Collected writings. Ed J. J. Roche 10 vols Boston 1901–3 (Treasure Trove edn).

Dramatic works . . . . New York [1901?].

Works. Ed J. J. Roche 6 vols Boston 1902 (New Lib edn).

§1

The parson's horn-book. 2 pts Dublin 1831 (2 edns). Anon. Prose and verse.

Legends and stories of Ireland. Illustr W. Harvey and Lover. Ser 1 1831, Dublin 1832; ser 2 1834, 1844; 2 vols 1860, 1861, Liverpool [1890?], London 1893; ed D. J. O'Donoghue 1899; Nottingham [c. 1900] etc. Prose.

Popular tales and legends of the Irish peasantry. Ed and illustr Lover, Dublin 1834, 1837. Prose.

Rory O'More: a national romance. 3 vols 1837 (illustr Lover), Durham 1839 (rev), Philadelphia 1846, London 1859, [1879] (2 edns), [1884], New York 1886, London [c. 1890], [1891], 1893, Nottingham 1893; ed D. J. O'Donoghue, London 1898; Boston 1901. A dramatisation was pbd 1837 (in Webster's Acting National Drama vol 2), [1840], 1883 (in Dicks's Standard Plays no 356).

The white horse of the peppers: a comic drama in two acts. 1838 (in Webster's Acting National Drama vol 5) (2 issues), [1883?] (in Dicks's Standard Plays no 441). Prose.

The hall porter: a comic drama in two acts. 1839 (in Webster's Acting National Drama vol 7), 1884 (in Dicks's Standard Plays no 520). Prose.

The happy man: an extravaganza in one act. 1839 (in Webster's Acting National Drama vol 79), Boston [1858], London 1883 (in Dicks's Standard Plays no 328), New York [1883]. Prose.

Songs and ballads. 1839, New York 1847, Philadelphia 1847, London 1858.

Handy Andy: a tale of Irish life. 1842, New York 1843, London 1845, 1846, 1849, Philadelphia 1850, London 1851, New York 1851, 1854, London 1854, 1855, 1862, [1863] (illustr J. Proctor), 1867, 1869, New York 1877, London [1884] (2 edns), [1885], New York [1885], London [1886], New York 1888, London [c. 1890], [1891], 1892, New York 1892, Nottingham [c. 1893], London [1893], [c. 1895], Liverpool [1895?]; ed C. Whibley, London 1896; ed D. J. O'Donoghue 1898, Boston 1901, 1902, London 1904 (with 24 illustr by Lover), New York 1904, 1906; ed E. Rhys, London 1907 (EL), 1908, 1909, [1912]; Boston 1927, New York [1931], ed S. O'Faolain, Dublin [1945] (abridged); London 1954 (EL). Prose.

Treasure trove: the first of a series of accounts of Irish heirs: a romantic tale of the last century. 1844 (illustr Lover), New York 1844, London [1856] (as He would be a gentleman: or treasure trove), rptd New York 1866, 1872, London 1873, 1887, New York and Montreal 1873, New York 1862 (as Irish heirs), London 1890, 1893; ed D. J. O'Donoghue 1899 (as Treasure trove). Prose.

The lyrics of Ireland, edited and annotated by Lover. 1858, 1884 (as Poems of Ireland, to which is added Lover's Metrical tales).

Rival rhymes in honour of Burns, with curious illustrative matter, collected and edited by 'Ben Trovato' [Lover]. 1859.

Metrical tales and other poems. 1860 (illustr W. Harvey and others), 1884 (with Poems of Ireland).

Original songs for the Rifle Volunteers. 1861. With C. Mackay and T. Miller.

MacCarthy More, or possession nine points of the law: a comic drama in two acts. [1861] (in T. H. Lacy's Acting edition of plays vol 51).

Tom Crosbie and his friends. New York 1878.

Barney the baron: a farce in one act; [and] The happy man: an extravaganza in one act. [1883] (J. Dicks's Standard Plays no 328), New York [1910?].

Further stories of Ireland. Ed D. J. O'Donoghue 1899.

§2

Samuel Lover. Dublin Univ Mag Feb 1851.

The life, genius and writings of Lover. Temple Bar Aug 1868.

Bernard, W. B. The life of Lover, artistic, literary and musical, with selections from his unpublished papers and correspondence. 2 vols 1874.

Symington, A. J. Lover: a biographical sketch, with selections from his writings and correspondence. 1880.

Symington, A. J. In Poets and the poetry of the century, ed A. H. Miles, vol 9 1894. With a selection from Lover's poems.

Layard, G. S. Lover as a graphic humourist. Mag of Art 19 1896.

Schmid, F. Samuel Lover. Cent Mag 3 1897.

Lover contributed to The English Bijou Almanack *for 1840 and worked as an illustrator and composer; he also edited collections of Irish tales.* [JRdeJJ]

Felix Macdonogh 1768?–1836

§1

The hermit in London: or sketches of English manners. 5 vols 1819–20 (anon), 1 vol New York 1820, 2 vols Philadelphia 1820, 3 vols 1821, 1822, 2 vols [1850?]; tr Fr 1820–1.

The hermit in the country: or sketches of English manners. 4 vols 1820–2, 2 vols New York 1820, 3 vols 1823.

The hermit abroad. 4 vols 1823; tr Fr (as L'Hermite rodeur, 1824).

The hermit in Edinburgh: or sketches of manners and real characters and scenes in the drama of life. 3 vols 1824; tr Fr 1826.

The Highlanders: a tale. 3 vols 1824, 2 vols New York 1824.

Gratitude, a poetical essay: with other poems and translations. 1825.

The heroine of the peninsula: or Clara Matilda of Seville. 2 vols 1826.

Attributed works

Poetical essays and translations from the Latin, French, & Italian languages, by F. B. Macdonogh Esq. Edinburgh 1803. [PG]

Mary Jane Mackenzie

Geraldine, or modes of faith and practice: a tale by a lady. 3 vols London and Edinburgh 1820, 1821, 2 vols Boston 1821.

Lectures on parables selected from the New Testament. 1822, 1822, 1824 (4th edn), 1825 (5th edn), 1835 (7th edn); ser 2 1833.

Lectures on miracles selected from the New Testament. 1823, 1825, 1827 (4th edn).

Private life: or varieties of character and opinion. 2 vols London and Edinburgh 1829, New York 1829, London 1830, 1835. [PG]

William Maginn 1793–1842

See col 2191.

Frederick Marryat 1792–1848

Incomplete mss of Mr Midshipman Easy, Percival Keene *and* Masterman Ready *are in the Pierpont Morgan Library New York. The ms, virtually complete, of* The settlers in Canada *is in the library of King's School, Canterbury. Mss of letters and private papers are in Beinecke Library Yale University, British Library, Edinburgh University Library, Greenwich Maritime Museum, New York Public Library, Pierpont Morgan Library etc.*

Bibliographies

Anderson, J. P. In David Hannay's Life of Frederick Marryat, 1889.
Sadleir, M. In his Excursions in Victorian bibliography, 1922.
— In his XIX century fiction: a bibliographical record, 2 vols 1951.
Gautier, M.-P. In his Captain Frederick Marryat, Paris 1973.

Collections

Works. 2 vols Philadelphia 1836, 14 vols Leipzig 1839–42, 17 vols London 1873–8.
Novels: the King's own edition. Ed W. L. Courtney 24 vols 1896–9.
Novels. Ed R. B. Johnson 24 vols 1896–8, 26 vols 1929–30.
Sämmtliche Werke. 42 vols Braunschweig 1835–9, 26 vols Stuttgart 1843–6.
Oeuvres complètes. 26 vols Paris 1836–8, 60 vols 1838–41.

Selections

Readings from Marryat, arr. Herbert Hayens. [1924].
Dale, H. (ed). The Marryat book: scenes from the works of Captain Marryat. 1930.

§1

A code of signals for the use of vessels employed in the merchant service. 1817, 1837 (rev), 1841 (last edn rev Marryat).

A suggestion for the abolition of the present system of impressment in the naval service. 1822.

The naval officer: or scenes and adventures in the life of Frank Mildmay. 3 vols 1829, 1 vol 1836, 1839 etc, Paris 1840, London [1873] (with memoir by Florence Marryat); illustr H. R. Millar, introd D. Hannay 1897. Tr Ger 1835, Fr 1838.
REVIEWS: Athenaeum, 8 Apr 1829; NMM, May 1829; United Service Jnl Mar 1829; Edinburgh Rev 52, 1830.

The King's own. 3 vols 1830, 1 vol Paris 1834, 3 vols London 1836, 1 vol 1838 etc; 1874 (with memoir by Florence Marryat); illustr F. H. Townsend, introd D. Hannay 1896; introd W. C. Russell 1906; introd R. B. Johnson 1912. Tr Ger 1835, Fr 1837.
REVIEWS: United Service Jnl June 1830; NMM, Aug 1830; [Lister, T. H.] Edinburgh Rev 52, 1830; Metropolitan Mag, July 1836.

Newton Forster: or the merchant service. 3 vols 1832, 1 vol Paris 1834, London 1838 etc; illustr E. J. Sullivan, introd D. Hannay 1897. Adapted for the stage by John F. Savile 1888?. Tr Ger 1836; Fr 2 vols 1837.
REVIEWS: Metropolitan Mag, Jan 1832; Westminster Rev 16, 1832.

Peter Simple. Serialised to end of ch 42 Metropolitan Mag, June 1832–Sep 1833; 3 vols Philadelphia and Baltimore 1833–4, London 1834, 1 vol Paris 1834; illustr R. W. Buss 3 vols London 1837, 1 vol 1838 etc; illustr J. A. Symington, introd D. Hannay 1895; introd W. C. Russell 1904; introd R. B. Johnson 1907; ed M. Sadleir 2 vols 1929 (with Buss's illustrations); introd H. Bacon 1984. Tr Fr 1834, Ger 1835, Polish 1973.
REVIEWS: Metropolitan Mag Dec 1833; United Service Jnl, Dec 1833; NMM, Jan 1834.

Jacob Faithful. Serialised Metropolitan Mag, Sep 1833–Oct 1834. 3 vols Philadelphia 1834, London 1834, 1834, 1 vol Paris 1834, 3 vols London 1835; illustr R. W. Buss 3 vols, 1837, 1 vol 1838, Leipzig 1842 etc; illustr H. M. Brock, introd D. Hannay 1895; introd R. B. Johnson 1912; ed G. Saintsbury 2 vols 1928 (with 12 plates by Buss); introd D. Veale 1936. Tr Fr, Ger 1836, Danish 1933. Adapted for the stage by John T. Haines 1884.
REVIEW: NMM, Nov 1834.

The Pacha of many tales. 2 vols Philadelphia and Baltimore 1834, 3 vols London 1835, 1 vol Paris 1835, London 1838. The stories appeared intermittently Metropolitan Mag, June 1831–May 1835. Tr Ger 1835, Fr 1837.
REVIEW: Metropolitan Mag, June 1835.

The diary of a blasé. Serialised Metropolitan Mag, June 1835–July 1836; Philadelphia 1836. Subsequently pbd as Diary on the Continent, in Olla podrida, *below*.

Stories of the sea (The pirate and the three cutters, Moonshine). New York 1836.

The pirate and the three cutters, with illustrations by C. Stanfield 1836, 2 vols Philadelphia 1836, 1 vol Paris 1836, 15 pts London 1845, 1861 (with a memoir) etc; illustr E. J. Sullivan, introd D. Hannay 1897. Tr Ger 1836, Fr 1837.
REVIEWS: United Service Jnl, Jan 1836.

Japhet in search of a father. Serialised Metropolitan Mag, Nov 1834–Jan 1836; 4 pts New York 1835–6, 3 vols London 1836, 1836, 1 vol Paris 1836, London 1838 etc; illustr H. M. Brock, introd D. Hannay 1895. Tr Fr, Ger, 1836.
REVIEWS: The Times, 31 Dec 1835; Athenaeum, 2 Jan 1836; Spectator, 2 Jan 1836; NMM, Feb 1836; GM Apr 1836.

Mr Midshipman Easy. 1st 4 chs appeared Metropolitan Mag, Aug 1836; 3 vols 1836, 1 vol Paris 1837, London 1838 etc; illustr F. Pegram, introd D. Hannay 1896; introd W. C. Russell 1904; introd R. B. Johnson 1906; ed O. Warner 1954; introd C. Lloyd 1969; 1982 (Pen). Tr Ger, 1836, Fr 1837, Ital 1933.
REVIEWS: Athenaeum, 10 Sep 1836; Monthly Rev, Oct 1836; Metropolitan Mag, Sep 1836.

Snarleyyow: or the dog fiend. Serialised Metropolitan Mag, Jan 1836–July 1837; 3 vols 1837, 1 vol Philadelphia 1837, Paris 1837, London 1847 (as The dog fiend) etc; illustr H. R. Millar, introd D. Hannay 1897. Tr Fr 1837.
REVIEWS: Athenaeum, 24 Jun 1837; NMM, Jul 1837; Dublin Univ Mag 10, 1837.

The ocean wolf: or the channel outlaw. Play performed Bowery theatre New York, Oct 1837. Apparently unpbd.

The phantom ship. Serialised NMM, Mar 1837–Aug 1839; 3 vols 1839, 1 vol Paris 1839, London 1847 etc; illustr H. R. Millar, introd D. Hannay 1896; introd W. C. Russell 1906; ed M. W. Disher 1948. Tr Fr, Ger, 1839, Danish 1874.
REVIEW: Athenaeum, 20 Apr 1839.

A diary in America, with remarks on its institutions. 2 pts 6 vols 1839, Philadelphia 1839–40; ed J. Zanger 1960 (with bibliography); ed S. W. Jackman, New York 1963 (abridged).
REVIEWS: Athenaeum 6 July 1839, 13 July 1839, 4 Jan 1840; [Johnstone, C.] Tait's Edinburgh Mag 6, 1839; 7, 1840; [Lockhart, J. G.] Quart Rev 64, 1839; [Empson, W.] Edinburgh Rev 70, 1839; Southern Literary Messenger, Apr 1841.

Poor Jack. 12 monthly pts illustr C. Stanfield 1840, 1 vol 1840, Paris 1841 etc; introd D. Hannay 1897. Tr Ger 1840, Fr 1841.
REVIEWS: United Service Jnl, July 1840, Jan 1841.

Olla podrida. 3 vols 1840, 1 vol Paris 1840, 3 vols London 1842, 1 vol 1849 etc. Diary on the Continent 1st pbd Metropolitan Mag, 1836 as Diary of a blasé; the shorter pieces partly in same jnl, partly in NMM; Moonshine in Keepsake and in Stories of the sea, New York 1836.
REVIEWS: Metropolitan Mag, Dec 1840; United Service Jnl Jan 1841.

Masterman Ready: or the wreck of the Pacific, written for young people. 3 vols 1841–2, 1 vol Paris 1842, London 1845 etc; introd D. Hannay, illustr F. Pegram 1897, introd R. B. Johnson 1906, introd R. Armstrong 1970, introd J. Seelye 3 vols New York 1976. Tr Ger 1843, Fr 1845, Du 1880.
REVIEWS: Lit Gazette, 10 July 1841; United Service Jnl, July 1841; [Eastlake, E.] Quart Rev 74, 1844.

Joseph Rushbrook: or the poacher. Serialised weekly as The poacher,

Era, Dec 1840–May 1841; 3 vols 1841, 1 vol Paris 1841 (with A recontre), London 1846 (as The poacher) etc.
REVIEWS: Lit Gazette, 10 July 1841; Athenaeum, 7 Aug 1841; [Poe, E. A.] Graham's Mag, Sep 1841.

Percival Keene. 3 vols 1842, 1 vol Paris 1842, London 1848, 1857 (with memoir); introd R. B. Johnson 1906. Tr Fr 1843, Ger 1843.
REVIEWS: Athenaeum, 10 Sep 1842; Monthly Rev, Oct 1842; [Johnstone, C.] Tait's Edinburgh Mag 9, 1842.

Narrative of the travels and adventures of Monsieur Violet in California, Sonora and western Texas. 3 vols 1843, 1 vol 1843, 1849 (as Travels and romantic adventures of Monsieur Violet among the Snake Indians and wild tribes of the great western prairies).
REVIEW: Athenaeum, 2 Dec 1843.

The settlers in Canada, written for young people. 2 vols 1844 etc; illustr Gilbert and Dalziel 1860; introd R. B. Johnson 1906; ed O. Warner 1956. Tr Fr 1852; Norwegian 1906; Danish 1932.
REVIEWS: [Johnstone, C.] Tait's Edinburgh Mag 11, 1844; Athenaeum, 21 Sep 1844; Ainsworth's Mag 6, 1844.

The mission: or scenes in Africa, written for young people. 2 vols 1845; illustr J. Gilbert 1860. Tr Ger 1851, Fr 1853.
REVIEWS: NMM, Aug 1845; Athenaeum, 9 Aug 1845.

The privateer's-man, one hundred years ago. Serialised NMM, Aug 1845–June 1846. 2 vols 1846, 1 vol Paris 1846, Leipzig 1846; introd Tony Harrison 1970. Tr Polish 1937, Swedish 1938.
REVIEWS: Athenaeum, 18 Jul 1846; NMM, Aug 1846.

The children of the New forest. Planned for pt issue; only pt 1 (chs 1–4) issued Apr 1847; 2 vols 1847, Leipzig 1848; illustr Frank Marryat 1847, 1849 etc; illustr J. Gilbert 1853; introd R. B. Johnson 1907; 1948 (Puffin); introd O. Warner 1955; ed D. Butts 1991. Tr Fr 1854, Danish 1932, Polish 1934.
REVIEWS: Athenaeum, 24 Apr 1847; Examiner, 1 May 1847.

The little savage. 2 vols 1848–9 (pbd posthumously by Frank S. Marryat, who completed the work from ch 3 of vol 2 and illustr it); illustr J. Gilbert 1852, 1853, illustr A. W. Cooper and J. Gilbert 1893, 1889, 1907. Tr Fr 1859.
REVIEWS: NMM, Jan 1849; Lit Gazette, 3 Mar 1849.

Valerie: an autobiography. Serialised to end of vol 2 ch 3 NMM, July 1846–Feb 1847; 2 vols 1849 etc. Finished by another hand and pbd posthumously.
REVIEW: Lit Gazette, 23 Jun 1849. Tr Ger, 1850.

Many pirated edns of Marryat's books were pbd in America; see Sadleir, XIX century fiction, Bibliographies, *above.*

Contributions to periodicals

Marryat contributed mainly to Metropolitan Mag *(which he owned and ed 1832–6) and* NMM. *Some pieces, sometimes with variations of title, were pbd in more than 1 periodical. List below excludes material that later appeared in book form.*

Novels and novel writing. Metropolitan Mag, Nov 1832, Oct 1834.

The cavalier of Seville: a tragedy. Metropolitan Mag, Mar, Apr, May 1833, rev as The monk of Seville in 3-vol edns of Olla podrida and subsequently omitted.

The gipsy: or 'Whose son am I?' Metropolitan Mag, Sep 1834. Comedy in 3 acts.

Mr Willis's 'Pencillings by the way'. Metropolitan Mag, Jan 1836.

Confessions and opinions of Ralph Restless. NMM, July, Aug, Sep, Oct 1837, Mar 1838.

The history of a genius. Mirror 29, 1837.

Authors of the present day. New-York Mirror, 4 Nov 1837.

Lines. NMM, Apr 1838. Poem.

The fairy's wand: a tale of Windsor park in the days of the Merry Monarch. NMM, Mar 1840.

First discovery of Van *Demons'* land. George Cruikshank's Omnibus, 1842.

How to raise the wind. Ibid.

Collaborative works

Marryat collaborated with George Cruikshank in providing sketches for engravings, including The progress of a midshipman: exemplified in the career of Master Blockhead. *In seven plates and a frontispiece. 1820.*

Published letters

In Florence Marryat's life and letters of Captain Marryat (*see below*). Separate letters to GM, May 1820; Metropolitan Mag, Sep 1834; London Gazette, 26 Mar, 20 Aug 1825; Albion, 20 Oct 1838 (*see bibliography in Gautier's Captain Frederick Marryat,* Bibliographies, *above*).

Attributed works

The floral telegraph: a new mode of communication by floral signals. 1836 (anon; ascribed by the 'editor' to 'Horace Honeycomb', who wrote the dedication); 1850 (re-issued under Marryat's name). Doubtful authorship; see Sadleir's XIX century fiction.

Rattlin the reefer. 1836. Anonymous novel by Edward Howard sponsored by Marryat and hence attributed to him. Howard's other books also sometimes attributed to Marryat: The old commodore, 1837; Outward bound, 1838; Jack ashore, 1840; Sir Henry Morgan the buccaneer, 1842.

Imitations

Aytoun, W. E. The flying dutchman: a tale of the sea. 1842; rptd in W. Hamilton, Parodies of the works of English and American authors, 1889.

Harte, Bret. Mr Midshipman Breezy: a naval officer. By Captain M—rry—t, RN. In his Condensed novels, 1871.

§2

[Wilson, J. and J. Hogg]. Noctes ambrosianae lxvi. Blackwood's Mag, July 1834.

Naval novelists. Fraser's Mag, May 1838.

Horne, R. H. In his A new spirit of the age. 1844.

Obits: Athenaeum 12 Aug 1848; Illus London News, 19 Aug 1848; GM, Dec 1848.

Whitehead, C. Memoir of Captain Marryat, RN CB. Bentley's Misc, Nov 1848.

H[urton], W. Marryat's sea stories. Dublin Univ Mag, Mar 1856.

Redding, C. In Yesterday and to-day, 1863.

[Doran, J]. Marryat. Temple Bar, Dec 1872.

Marryat, Florence. Life and letters of Captain Marryat. 2 vols 1872.

Escott, T. H. S. Land and sea. London Soc Jan 1873.

[Hannay, J]. Sea-novels: Captain Marryat. Cornhill Mag, Feb 1873.

Hannay, D. Life of Frederick Marryat. 1889.

Iddesleigh, Lord. Marryat as novelist. Monthly Rev Sep 1904.

Saintsbury, G. In his The English novel, 1913.

Conrad, J. Tales of the sea. Outlook, 1898, rptd in Notes on life and letters, 1921.

Warner, O. Captain Marryat: a rediscovery. 1953.

Gautier, M.-P. Captain Frederick Marryat: l'homme et l'oeuvre. Paris, 1973. [DH]

Charles Robert Maturin 1780–1824

The original ms version of Bertram *is at Abbotsford, Sir Walter Scott's home, Melrose, Scotland; licensing versions of* Bertram *and other plays by Maturin are in the Larpent Collection in the Huntington. Letters to Archibald Constable, the Edinburgh publisher, and copies of letters from Constable to Maturin, are in the NLS, Edinburgh; correspondence with Messrs Hurst and Robinson, the publishers of* The Albigenses, *and other letters relating to Maturin's literary production, are in the BL, while letters to John Murray, the London publisher, are in the offices of John Murray Ltd, London; the Bodleian holds letters to Henry Colburn, publisher of* The Milesian chief.

Bibliographies

Summers, M. In his A Gothic bibliography, [1941].

Sadleir, M. In his XIX century fiction: a bibliographical record, 2 vols 1951.

Fierobe, C. In his C. R. Maturin (1780–1824): l'homme et l'œuvre, Lille and Paris 1974.

Durkan, M. J. A checklist of works by C. R. Maturin. Eire (Univ of Florida) 1 1977.

Frank, F. S. In his Gothic fiction: a master list of twentieth century criticism and research, Westport CT 1988. Secondary material.

Selections

Tales of mystery. Ed G. Saintsbury 1891. Selections from Mrs Radcliffe, Lewis and Maturin.

§1

Fatal revenge: or the family of Montorio, by Dennis Jasper Murphy. 3 vols 1807, 2 vols New York [1808], 4 vols London 1824, 1 vol 1840 ('4th edn'), 1841; 3 vols New York 1974 (facs of 1st edn, with introd by M. Lévy); Stroud 1994 (with introd by J. Cowley); tr Fr 1822.
REVIEW: [Scott, W.] Quart Rev 3 1810.

The wild Irish boy, by the author of Montorio. 3 vols 1808, 2 vols New York 1808, 3 vols London 1814, 4 vols 1824, 1839; 3 vols New York 1977 (facs of 1st edn, with introd by E. F. Bleiler); 3 vols New York and London 1979 (facs of 1st edn, with introd by R. L. Wolff); tr Fr 1828.
REVIEWS: Annual Rev 7 1808; Satirist 2 1808.

The Milesian chief: a romance by the author of Montorio and The wild Irish boy. 4 vols 1812, 2 vols Philadelphia and New York 1812; 4 vols New York and London 1979 (facs of 1st edn, with introd by R. L. Wolff); tr Fr 1828.
REVIEWS: Critical Rev 4th ser 1 1812; Monthly Rev n.s. 67 1812.

Bertram, or the Castle of St Aldobrand: a tragedy. 1816 (7 edns), Boston 1816, New York 1816, Philadelphia 1816, London 1817, 1817, New York 1817, Philadelphia 1822, Baltimore 1824, London 1827, 1829, New York 1847, 1848, London 1864, 1865, 1884, 1956; Oxford 1992 (facs of 1st edn, with introd by J. Wordsworth); ed J. N. Cox, in his Seven Gothic dramas 1789–1826, Athens OH 1992; tr Fr 1821.
REVIEWS: Antijacobin Rev 50 1816; Augustan Rev 3 1816; Br Critic n.s. 5 1816; Br Lady's Mag 3 1816; Br Rev 8 1816; [Coleridge, S. T.] Courier 29 Aug–11 Sep 1816; Eclectic Rev n.s. 6 1816; Monthly Rev n.s. 80 1816.

Manuel: a tragedy in five acts by the author of Bertram. 1817, 1817, 1817, Baltimore 1817, New York 1817, Philadelphia 1817.
REVIEWS: Br Lady's Mag 5 1817; European Mag 71 1817; Monthly Rev n.s. 83 1817.

Women, or pour et contre: a tale by the author of Bertram etc. 3 vols Edinburgh 1818, 2 vols New York 1818, Philadelphia 1818; 3 vols New York and London 1979 (facs of 1st edn, with introd by R. L. Wolff); tr Fr 1818.
REVIEWS: Br Critic n.s. 9 1818; [Scott, W.] Edinburgh Rev 30 1818; Monthly Rev n.s. 86 1818; Quart Rev 19 1818; Br Lady's Mag 3rd ser 2 1819.

Fredolfo: a tragedy in five acts. 1819, Philadelphia 1819.
REVIEWS: Monthly Mag 48 1819; Theatrical Inquisitor 15 1819.

Sermons. 1819, 1821.

Melmoth the wanderer: a tale by the author of Bertram. 4 vols Edinburgh 1820, 1821, 2 vols Boston 1821, New York 1835, 3 vols London 1892 (with memoir and bibliography); ed W. F. Axton, Lincoln NE 1961, London 1966; ed D. Grant 1968, rptd with introd by C. Baldick, 1989 (WCp); ed A. Hayter, Harmondsworth 1977; ed D. P. Varma 1993; tr Fr 1821, 1954, 1965, Ger 1821, Rus 1976, 1983, Romanian 1983. Dramatised by B. West [1823], [1830?].
REVIEWS: Blackwood's Mag Nov 1820; Eclectic Rev n.s. 14 1820; NMM 14 1820; Edinburgh Mag n.s. 8 1821; Edinburgh Rev 35 1821; Monthly Rev n.s. 94 1821; [Croker, J. W.] Quart Rev 24 1821.

The Albigenses: a romance by the author of Bertram etc. 4 vols 1824, 1824, 3 vols Philadelphia 1824; 4 vols New York 1974 (facs of 1st edn, with introd by D. Kramer); tr Fr 1825.
REVIEWS: Br Critic n.s. 21 1824; Edinburgh Literary Gazette no 55 Feb 1824; Edinburgh Mag n.s. 14 1824; Westminster Rev 1 1824; Monthly Rev n.s. 106 1825.

Five sermons on the errors of the Roman Catholic Church. Dublin 1824, 1826.

Leixlip Castle: an Irish family legend. Literary Souvenir 1825; in The Grimoire and other supernatural stories, ed M. Summers, 1936.

The sybil's prophecy: a dramatic fragment. Literary Souvenir 1826.

Attributed works

Lines on the battle of Waterloo: prize poem. Dublin 1816. Attributed to Maturin by his anon biographer in NMM, May 1827, but pbd under the authorship of John Shee, an undergraduate at Trinity College, Dublin.

The universe: a poem. 1821. The title page bears Maturin's name, but most or all was probably written by James Wills.

§2

The writings of Maturin. London Mag 3 May 1821.

Conversations of Maturin. NMM May–June 1827.

Recollections of Maturin. NMM Aug, Oct 1827.

Memoranda of Maturin. Douglas Jerrold's Shilling Mag 3 1846.

James Wills, D. D. Dublin Univ Mag 86 1875. On the poem The universe.

Maturin and the novel of terror. TLS 26 Aug 1920.

Cook, D. Maturin MSS at Abbotsford. TLS 16 Sep 1920.

Correspondence of Sir W. Scott and Maturin. Ed E. Ratchford and W. H. McCarthy, Austin TX 1937; rptd New York 1980.

Buchan, A. M. Maturin's birth date. N & Q 8 July 1950.

Kramer, D. Maturin. New York 1973. [PG]

Caroline Maxwell

Alfred of Normandy, or the ruby cross: an historical romance. 2 vols 1808.

Lionel, or the impenetrable command: an historical romance. 2 vols 1809.

The Earl of Desmond, or O'Brien's cottage: an Irish story. 3 vols 1810.

Feudal tales: being a collection of romantic narratives and other poems. [1810?]

Laura, or the invisible lover: a novel. 3 vols 1811.

Malcolm Douglas, or the sibylline prophecy: a novel. 2 vols [1812?].

The actress, or countess and no countess: a novel. 4 vols 1823.

Beauties of English and Scottish history. 1825.

The history of the Holy Bible: being an abridgement of the Old and New Testament. 1827.

The juvenile edition of Shakespeare: adapted to the capacities of youth. 1828. [PG]

William Hamilton Maxwell 1792–1850

Bibliographies

Sadleir, M. In his XIX century fiction: a bibliographical record, 2 vols 1951.

§1

O'Hara: or 1798. 2 vols 1825. Anon.

Stories of Waterloo and other tales. 3 vols 1829, 1 vol 1833, 1834, 1850 etc.

Wild sports of the West, with legendary tales and local sketches. 2 vols 1832, 1833, New York 1833, 1 vol London 1847, 1849; illustr F. Gillett [1915]; ed Earl of Dunraven 1915; tr Irish 1933.

The Hamilton wedding: a humorous poem. 1833.

The field-book: or sports and pastimes of the United Kingdom, compiled from the best authorities, ancient and modern. 1833.

The dark lady of Doona. 1834, 1846, [1854?], 1862, 1913; tr Fr 1834.
My life, by the author of Stories of Waterloo. 3 vols 1835, 2 vols New York 1835, 1 vol 1838 (as The adventures of Captain Blake: or my life), 3 vols 1846, 1 vol 1849 etc.
The bivouac: or stories of the Peninsular War. 3 vols 1837, 1 vol 1839, 1880.
The victories of the British armies; with anecdotes illustrative of modern warfare. 2 vols 1839, 1 vol 1868 (as The victories of Wellington and the British armies), 1885, 1891.
Life of Field-Marshal His Grace the Duke of Wellington. 3 vols 1839–41, 1845–6, 1 vol 1852 (abridged); tr Ger 1840.
Rambling recollections of a soldier of fortune. Dublin 1842, 1848; illustr Phiz 1850, 1857 (as Flood and field: or the recollections of a soldier of fortune).
Memoirs of Sir Robert Peel. 2 vols 1842.
The fortunes of Hector O'Halloran and his man Mark Antony O'Toole. 13 pts illustr [R. Doyle] and J. Leech 1842–3, 1851, 1853, [1882] etc.
Wanderings in the Highlands and Islands, with sketches taken on the Scottish border: being a sequel to Wild sports of the West. 2 vols 1844, 1 vol 1853 (as Sports and adventures in the Highlands etc).
Hints to a soldier on service. 2 vols 1845.
History of the Irish rebellion in 1798, with memoirs of the Union and Emmett's insurrection in 1803. 1845; illustr G. Cruikshank 1864, 1887.
Peninsular sketches, by actors on the scene. 2 vols 1845, [1860?] (as Stories of the Peninsular war: or Peninsular sketches).
Captain O'Sullivan: or adventures, civil, military, and matrimonial, of a gentleman on half pay. 3 vols 1846, 1 vol New York 1846, London 1858 (as Adventures of Captain O'Sullivan).
Hill-side and Border sketches, with legends of the Cheviots and the Lammermuir. 2 vols 1847, 1 vol New York and Philadelphia 1847, 2 vols London 1849 (as Legends of the Cheviots and the Lammermuir: a companion to Wild sports of the West), 1 vol 1852 (as Border tales and legends etc).
The Irish movements: their rise, progress and certain termination, with a few broad hints to patriots and pikemen. 1848.
Brian O'Linn: or luck is everything. 3 vols 1848, 1 vol 1856 (as Luck is everything: or the adventures of Brian O'Linn).
Erin-Go-Bragh: or Irish life pictures. 2 vols 1859 (with a memoir of Maxwell by W. Maginn), 1 vol 1860.
Terence O'Shaughnessy's first attempt to get married. In Tales from Bentley vol 1, 1859.
Maxwell contributed to Nimrod's Sporting, *1838, and to* Pic-Nic Papers *pt 1 1870.*

§2

Maginn, W. W. H. Maxwell. Bentley's Misc Apr 1840. Prefixed to Erin-Go-Bragh 2 vols 1859.
Dublin Univ Mag Aug 1841.
The Times 16 Jan 1851. Obituary.

Mary Meeke d. 1816?

Bibliographies

Blakey, D. In her Minerva Press, 1939.
Summers, M. In his Gothic bibliography, [1941].

§1

Count St Blancard, or the prejudiced judge: a novel. 3 vols 1795; ed D. P. Varma and introd by J. Garrett 1977.
The Abbey of Clugny: a novel. 3 vols 1796.
The mysterious wife: a novel, by Gabrielli. 4 vols 1797.
Palmira and Ermance: a novel. 3 vols 1797.
The Sicilian. 4 vols 1798.
Ellesmere: a novel. 4 vols 1799.
Harcourt: a novel, by Gabrielli. 4 vols 1799.
Anecdotes of the Altamont family: a novel, by the author of the Sicilian etc. 4 vols 1800.
Which is the man? a novel. 4 vols 1801.
Mysterious husband: a novel, by Gabrielli. 4 vols 1801.
Independence: a novel, by Gabrielli. 4 vols 1802; tr Fr 1804.
Midnight weddings: a novel. 3 vols 1802, 1814; tr Fr 1820.
Amazement!: a novel. 3 vols 1804.
The old wife and young husband. 3 vols 1804.
The nine days' wonder: a novel. 3 vols 1804.
Something odd!: a novel, by Gabrielli. 3 vols 1804.
The wonder of the village: a novel. 3 vols 1805.
Something strange: a novel, by Gabrielli. 4 vols 1806.
Julian: or my father's house. 4 vols 1807.
'There's a secret: find it out': a novel. 4 vols 1808.
Laughton Priory: a novel, by Gabrielli. 4 vols 1809.
Stratagems defeated: a novel, by Gabrielli. 4 vols 1811.
Matrimony the height of bliss or extreme of misery: a novel. 4 vols 1812.
Conscience: a novel. 4 vols 1814.
The Spanish campaign, or the Jew: a novel. 3 vols 1815.
The veiled protectress: or the mysterious mother: a novel. 5 vols 1819.
What shall be, shall be: a novel. 4 vols 1823.
The parent's offering to a good child: a collection of interesting tales. [1825.]
The birthday present, or pleasing tales of amusement and instruction. New York 1830.

Translations

A tale of mystery, or Celina. 4 vols 1813. Ducray-Duminil, F. G., Coelina, ou l'Enfant du mystère.
Lobenstein village. 4 vols 1804. LaFontaine, A. J. H., Theodor, oder Kultur und Humanitat.
Elizabeth, or the exiles of Siberia. 1807. Cottin, S. R., Elisabeth, ou les éxiles de Sibèrie.
Mrs Meeke also translated Mme du Deffan's Unpublished correspondence, *1810, and completed Mrs Collyer's translation of Klopstock's* Messiahs.
For a listing of reviews and notices of Meeke's work, see Ward (1972).

Attributed or spurious works

Murray House. 3 vols 1804. Sometimes attributed to Meeke but actually by Eliza Parsons. [CC]

Mary Russell Mitford 1787–1855

Mss, mostly correspondence, are in Berkshire County Local Studies Lib, the Bodleian, the BL (including a sonnet and a diary for 1819–23), Harvard (including several stories and a prompt ms for Rienzi*), the Huntington, and the John Rylands Univ Lib of Manchester.*

Bibliographies

Kunitz, S. J. In his British authors of the nineteenth century, New York 1936.
Sadleir, M. In his XIX century fiction: a bibliographical record, 2 vols 1951.
Hart, R. J. Mary Russell Mitford . . .: a bibliography. Thesis submitted for Fellowship of the Lib Assoc, July 1981. Berkshire County Local Studies Lib.

Collections

Works, prose and verse. Philadelphia 1841.
Dramatic works. 2 vols 1854.

§1

Poems. 1810, 1811 (with addns).
Christina, the maid of the South Seas: a poem. 1811.

Ode to genius. [1812.]
Watlington Hill: a poem. 1812.
Narrative poems on the female character. Vol 1 1813. No more pbd.
Julian: a tragedy in five acts. 1823, 1823, 1823, New York 1823, London 1829, 1829 (in Cumberland's British theatre), Philadelphia 1831.
Our village: sketches of rural character and scenery. 5 vols 1824–32 (vol 1 rptd 1824, 1825), 3 vols 1835, 2 vols Paris 1839, 2 vols London 1848, 1852, 1 vol 1862 (as Children of the village), 1881 (as Village tales and sketches); illustr F. Barnard et al 1889 (selection); ed E. Rhys 1891 (selection); ed A. T. Ritchie, illustr H. Thomson 1893 (selection); ed E. Gollancz 1900 (selection); ed A. T. Ritchie, illustr H. Thomson 1902, 1910 (with additional illustrations by A. Rawlings); illustr C. E. Brock 1904 (as Sketches of English life and character) (selection); illustr S. A. Forbes 1909, Chicago 1910, London 1928; 1936 (EL); illustr J. Hassall 1947, 1949, 1982 (WCp). First pbd in Lady's Mag 1819.
Foscari: a tragedy. 1826, 1827 etc, 1829 (in Cumberland's British theatre).
Foscari and Julian: tragedies. 1827.
Dramatic scenes, sonnets and other poems. 1827.
Dramatic scenes. 1832.
Rienzi: a tragedy. 1828, 1828, 1828 etc, New York 1829, London 1829 (in Cumberland's British theatre).
Mary, Queen of Scots: a scene in English verse. 1831.
Charles the First: an historical tragedy in five acts. 1834, Philadelphia 1835, London [1885] (in Dicks' Standard Plays).
Belford Regis: or sketches of a country town. 3 vols 1835, Philadelphia 1835, 1 vol London 1846, [1849]; ed L. S. Jast 1942.
Sadak and Kalasrade, or the waters of oblivion: a romantic opera. [1836.]
Country stories. 1837, 1850; illustr G. Morrow 1895.
Recollections of a literary life: or books, places and people. 3 vols 1852, 1859, 1 vol 1883 (as Recollections and selections from my favourite poets and prose writers).
Atherton and other tales. 3 vols 1854, 1 vol Boston 1854.
Stories of village and town life: or word pictures of old England. Ed J. P. Briscoe and E. M. P. Knight 1915. A collection of stories first pbd in various annuals.

Letters

The life of Mary Russell Mitford in a selection from her letters. Ed A. G. L'Estrange 3 vols 1870, 1870, 2 vols New York 1870, 5 vols London 1870–2.
Letters to C. Boner. In R. M. Kettle, Memoirs and letters of Charles Boner… with letters of Mary Russell Mitford to him during ten years. 2 vols 1871, 1876.
The letters of Mary Russell Mitford: second series. Ed H. F. Chorley 2 vols 1872.
The friendships of Mary Russell Mitford in letters from her literary correspondents. Ed A. G. L'Estrange 2 vols 1882, 1 vol New York 1882.
Correspondence with C. Boner and J. Ruskin. Ed E. Lee [1914], Chicago [1915].
The letters of Mary Russell Mitford. Selected with an introd by R. B. Johnson. 1925.

Miss Mitford contributed 4 tales to Mrs C. Johnstone, Edinburgh tales, *3 vols 1845–6, and edited Finden's* Tableaux of the affections: paintings by W. Perring, *1837, 1838, 1840. She also edited* Stories of American life by American writers, *3 vols 1830, and selections of American children's stories as* Tales for young people, *3 vols 1835, and* Tales and stories, *1866, and* Fragments des Oeuvres d'Alexandre Dumas, *1846.*

§2

[Unsigned.] GM Aug 1828.
Maginn, W. A. A gallery of literary characters no XII. Fraser's Mag May 1831, rptd in The Maclise portrait gallery of illustrious literary characters, ed W. Bates [1873].
Croker, T. C. My village versus Our village. 1833.
Collas, A. In his Authors of England with illustrative notices, 1838.
[Smith, W. H.] Miss Mitford's Recollections. Blackwood's Mag Mar 1852.
[Unsigned] Miss Mitford, credited to Monthly Rev in Eclectic Mag New York Apr 1853.
Oliphant, M. O. Mary Russell Mitford. Blackwood's Mag June 1854.
Hall, S. and A. Mary Russell Mitford. Eclectic Mag Aug 1866.
Manning, A. M. R. Mitford. Macmillan's Mag Feb 1870.
Oliphant, M. O. Miss Austen and Miss Mitford. Blackwood's Mag Mar 1870.
Martineau, H. In her Biographical sketches 1852–75, 1877.
Roberts, W. J. Mary Russell Mitford: the tragedy of a blue-stocking. 1913.
Hill, C. Mary Russell Mitford and her surroundings. 1920.
Watson, V. G. M. R. Mitford. 1949.
Duncan-Jones, C. M. Miss Mitford and Mr Harness: records of friendship. 1954.
Miller, B. (ed). Elizabeth Barrett to Miss Mitford; unpublished letters. 1954.
Coles, W. A. M. R. Mitford: the inauguration of a literary career. BJRL 40 1957.
Coles, W. A. Magazine and other contributions by M. R. Mitford and Thomas Noon Talfourd. SB 12 1958.
Lauterbach, C. E. Let the printer do it. N & Q Jan 1963. On Miss Mitford's typographical devices.
Lewis, J. M. R. Mitford letters. BM Quart 29 1965.
Kelley, P. and R. Hudson. The Browning correspondence. 14 vols 1984–98. [SH]

David Macbeth Moir 1798–1851

Collections

Poetical works. Ed T. Aird 2 vols 1852 (with memoir).

§1

The bombardment of Algiers and other poems. Edinburgh 1816. Anon.
The legend of Genevieve with other tales and poems by Delta. Edinburgh 1825.
The life of Mansie Wauch, tailor in Dalkeith, written by himself. Edinburgh 1828 (anon); illustr G. Cruikshank 1839 (rev and enlarged), 1853, 1880; ed T. F. Henderson [1902]; illustr C. M. Hardie 1911. First pbd in Blackwood's Mag Oct 1824–Dec 1828.
The bridal of Borthwick. In The Club book, ed A. Picken, 3 vols 1831; ed W. Hazlitt 1841.
Outlines of the ancient history of medicine. 1831, [1931].
Memoir of Galt. 1841. Prefixed to Annals of the parish in Blackwood's Standard Novels series.
Domestic verses by Delta. Edinburgh 1843 (priv ptd), 1843, 1871.
Sketches of the poetical literature of the past half-century. Edinburgh 1851, 1852, 1856.
The Roman antiquities of Inveresk. Edinburgh 1860. First pbd in Statistical account of Scotland, 1845.

Moir also wrote several medical works, the final chs of John Galt, The last of the lairds, *nearly 400 contributions to* Blackwood's Mag, *and various memoirs and periodical articles. The Blackwood Collection in the NLS includes over 500 letters from Moir to the Blackwood family.*

§2

[Maginn, W.] Gallery of literary characters no 11: Dr Moir. Fraser's Mag Sep 1833; rptd in his A gallery of illustrious literary characters, ed W. Bates [1873].
Blackwood's Mag Aug 1851. Obituary.
[Rev of Poetical works.] Eclectic Rev 96 1852.
Gilfillan, G. In his Galleries of literary portraits vol 2, Edinburgh 1856.

Douglas, C. The Blackwood group. [1897.]
MacCurdy, E. A literary enigma: the Canadian boat song. Stirling 1936. Attributed to Moir and Lockhart.
Robson, E. H. A. Preparation for a study of metropolitan Scots of the first half of the nineteenth century as exemplified in Mansie Wauch. 1937.
Needler, G. H. The lone shieling: origins and authorship of the Blackwood Canadian boat song. Toronto 1941. Attributed to Moir.
Nolte, E. Moir as Morgan Odoherty. PMLA 72 1957.
Nolte, E. A letter from Morgan Odoherty. Stud in Scottish Lit 2 1965.
Little, G. L. Christabess, by S. T. Colebritche esq [a parody by Moir in Blackwood's Mag June 1819]. MLR 56 1961.

Sydney, Lady Morgan 1776–1859

See Sydney Owenson, below.

James Justinian Morier 1780–1849

Bibliographies

Sadleir, M. In his XIX century fiction: a bibliographical record, 2 vols 1951.

Collections

Sämmtliche werke. 15 vols Braunschweig 1837.

§1

Memoir of a campaign with the Ottoman army, 1800. 1801.
A journey through Persia, Armenia and Asia Minor to Constantinople in the years 1808 and 1809, including an account of the mission under Sir Harford Jones to the Shah of Persia. 1812, 1816; tr Fr 1813, Ger 1815.
A second journey through Persia, Armenia and Asia Minor to Constantinople between the years 1810 and 1816, with a journal of the voyage to the Brazils and Bombay to the Persian Gulf and an account of the Embassy under Sir G. Ouseley. 1818; tr Fr 1818, Ger 1820, Ital 1820.
The adventures of Hajji Baba of Ispahan. 3 vols 1824, 1824 (with preface), 3 vols Paris 1824, 2 vols Philadelphia 1824, 1 vol London 1835 (rev), Philadelphia 1835, London 1849 (rev), 1856, 1863, Philadelphia [1880?], Manchester 1892; introd by E. G. Browne 2 vols Chicago and London 1895, 1 vol New York 1926; introd by G. Curzon, illustr H. R. Millar 2 vols London and New York 1895, New York 1896, 1 vol London 1902, 1912; ed C. J. Wills London 1897 (with introd by Sir F. Goldsmid), 1989 (rev); introd by C. E. Beckett, illustr H. R. Millar [1899?], 1900, 1924; illustr H. R. Millar 1904; London and Toronto 1914; ed C. W. Stewart London 1923, [1924]; preface by W. Scott, illustr H. Guilbeau 2 vols New York 1947, 1 vol [1947]; [1948]; introd by R. Jennings 1949; introd by R. D. Altick 1954; tr Ger 1824, 1913, Fr 1824, 1933, Cz 1877; Persian, 1905, Ital, 1985.
REVIEWS: Quart Rev 30 1824; Blackwood's Mag Jan 1824; Quart Rev 39 1829.
The adventures of Hajji Baba, of Ispahan, in England. 2 vols 1828, Philadelphia 1828, New York 1828, 1 vol London 1835 (rev), Paris 1835, London 1850, 1856, 1863; ed L. S. Jast, London and New York 1925, London [1925], 1942; tr Ger 1829.
Zohrab the hostage. 3 vols 1832, 1832 (rev), 1833 (rev with notes), 2 vols New York 1833, 1 vol Paris 1833, London 1836, 1837, 1856, 1864; tr Swed, 1834.
REVIEW: Quart Rev 48 1832.
Ayesha: the maid of Kars. 3 vols 1834, 1834, 2 vols Philadelphia 1834, 1 vol Paris 1834, 1843 (with Zohrab the hostage), London 1846; tr Ger 1836, Swed 1836.
The man of honour, and The reclaimed. 2 vols 1834.
Abel Allnutt: a novel. 3 vols 1837, 2 vols Philadelphia 1837, 1 vol Paris 1837.
An oriental tale. [1839], Brighton 1839. Printed for sale in aid of Sussex County Hospital.
The adventures of Tom Spicer, who advertised for a wife: a poem. 1840 (priv ptd).
The Mirza. 3 vols 1841, 1 vol Paris 1842; tr Ger 1842.
Literary contributions by various authors in aid of the funds of the hospital for consumption and diseases of the chest, edited by Mrs Leicester Stanhope. 1846. Contains contributions by Morier.
Misselmah: a Persian tale. Brighton 1847.
Martin Toutrond: a Frenchman in London in 1831. 1849 (anon), 1849 (signed), 1952. Written in French by Morier and translated by himself.
The adventures of Hajji Baba in Turkey, Persia and Russia. Philadelphia 1855; (as The life and adventures of the celebrated oriental traveller Hajji Baba in Persia, Turkey and Russia) 1860, [1880]. Compilation.
The life and adventures of the celebrated oriental traveller Hajji Baba. 5 vols Philadelphia [1859?]. Compilation.
Morier also 'edited' with a preface W. Hauff, The banished: a Swabian historical tale, *3 vols 1839, and* St Roche: a romance from the German, *3 vols 1847.* DNB *challenges the veracity of this ascription, however, arguing that Morier's name was attached merely to gain prestige, while he had no involvement whatsoever in these works. He also translated the travel writings of J. Scott-Waring into Fr as* Voyage de l'Inde à Chryas, *1813. Morier was also a regular contributor to* Bentley's Misc *1837–42.*

§2

James Morier. Fraser's Mag Feb 1833.
Maginn, W. In his A gallery of illustrious literary characters, ed W. Bates [1873].
Zeidler, K. J. Beckford, Hope and Morier als Vertreter des orientalischen Romans. Leipzig 1909.
The sun and the pen. TLS 22 July 1949.
Moussa-Mahmoud, F. Orientals in picaresque (Hope, Morier, Meadows Taylor). Cairo Stud in Eng 1962.
Weinberger, A. I. The Middle-Eastern writings of James Morier, traveller, novelist and creator of Hajji Baba. Dissertation Abstracts International no 1290A, 1985.
Krotkoff, G. Hammer-Purgstall, Hajji Baba and the Moriers. International Jnl of Middle East Stud 19 1987.
Pandit, P. Orientalist discourse and its literary representations in the works of four British travel writers: James Morier, Alexander Kinglake, Richard Burton and Gertrude Bell. Dissertation Abstracts International no DA9109496, 1991. [AM]

Henrietta Rouviere (afterwards Mosse), Henrietta Rouviere Mosse d. 1835

Bibliographies

Summers, M. In his A Gothic bibliography, [1941].

§1

Lussington Abbey: a novel. 2 vols 1804; tr Fr 1807.
The heirs of Villeroy: a romance. 3 vols 1806.
A peep at our ancestors: an historical romance. 4 vols 1807.
The old Irish baronet, or manners of my country: a novel. 3 vols 1808.
Arrivals from India, or time's a great master: a novel. 4 vols 1812.
Craigh-Melrose Priory, or memoirs of the Mount Linton family: a novel. 4 vols 1816; tr Fr 1817.
A bride and no wife: a novel. 4 vols 1817.
A father's love and a woman's friendship: or the widow and her daughters. 5 vols 1825.
Gratitude and other tales. 3 vols 1826.
Woman's wit & man's wisdom, or intrigue: a novel. 4 vols 1827.
The Blandfords, or fate and fortune: a novel. 4 vols 1829.
For a listing of reviews and notices of Rouviere's works, see Ward (1972, 1977).
[PG]

William Mudford 1782–1848

§1

A critical enquiry into the moral writings of Dr Samuel Johnson. 1802 (anon), 1803.

Augustus and Mary, or the maid of Buttermere: a domestic tale. 1803.

Nubilia in search of a husband, including sketches of modern society, and interspersed with moral and literary disquisitions. 1809 (anon), 1809 (2nd edn, containing 2 additional chs), 1809 (4th edn), Philadelphia 1809.

The contemplatist: a series of essays upon morals and literature. 1810.

The life and adventures of Paul Plaintive esq, an author, compiled from original documents, and interspersed with specimens of his genius, in prose and poetry, by Martin Gribaldus Swammerdam (his nephew and executor). 2 vols 1811.

A critical examination of the writings of Richard Cumberland esq. 2 vols 1812, 1812, 1 vol 1812 (as The life of Richard Cumberland esq, embracing a critical examination of his various writings), 2 vols 1814.

The historical account of the battle of Waterloo: comprehending a circumstantial narrative of the whole events of the war of 1815. Pt 1 1816, 1817 (as An historical account of the campaign in the Netherlands in 1815).

The five nights of St Albans. 3 vols Edinburgh 1829 (anon), 2 vols Philadelphia 1833, 3 vols London 1835, 1 vol [1878], [c. 1890].
REVIEW: [Lockhart, J. G.] Blackwood's Mag 26, Oct 1829.

The Premier. 3 vols 1831. Anon.

The iron shroud: or Italian revenge. Glasgow 1839 (anon), Paisley 1839, rptd in Tales and trifles from Blackwood's, *below*, vol 1; rptd in Romantic Gothic tales 1790–1840, ed G. R. Thompson, New York 1979; rptd in Tales of terror from Blackwood's Mag, ed R. Morrison and C. Baldick, Oxford 1995 (WCp).

Stephen Dugard: a novel, by the author of Five knights [*sic*] of St Albans. 3 vols 1840, 1 vol [1860].

Tales and trifles from Blackwood's and other popular mags. 2 vols 1849.

Attributed works

Arthur Wilson: a study. 3 vols 1872. Anon.

Mudford also prefixed a life of James Beattie to Beauties from the writings of Beattie, *1809, and a critique of Goldsmith to his edn of the* Essays, *1804. He translated several works from the Fr, including Helvétius,* De l'esprit *and Mme de Grafigny,* Lettres d'une Péruvienne, *edited several papers at different times and was a frequent contributor to* Blackwood's Mag. *For details of his edn of the* British novelists, *1810–17, see also M. Sadleir,* XIX century fiction: a bibliographical record *vol 2, pp. 141–2. For a fuller listing of reviews and notices of Mudford's works, see Ward (1972).*

§2

Guthke, K. S. Georg Büchner und Mudford. Archiv 198 1961. [PG]

Amelia Opie, née Alderson 1769–1853

Bibliographies

Block, A. In his The English novel 1740–1850, 1961.

Collections

Works. 12 vols in 11 Boston 1827.

Works. 2 vols New York 1835.

Works. 3 vols Philadelphia [1841] (with biographical sketch), 1848, New York 1974 (facs).

Miscellaneous tales. 12 vols 1845–7.

§1

The dangers of coquetry: a novel. 2 vols [1790]. Anon.

The father and daughter: a tale in prose, with an epistle from the maid of Corinth to her lover, and other poetical pieces. 1801, 1801 (2nd edn), 1804 (4th edn), 1809 (6th edn), Georgetown 1812, Washington 1812, New York 1814, London 1819 (8th edn), Boston 1827, London 1844 (10th edn), 1994 (facs); tr Fr 1802, Ital 1817 (as L'Agnese. Dramma semi-serio, per musica, music by Luigi Buonavoglia).
REVIEW: Monthly Rev June 1801.

Poems. 1802, 1803, 1804, 1806, 1808, 1811, New York 1978 (facs).
REVIEWS: Edinburgh Rev Oct 1802; Br Critic Nov 1802; Critical Rev Dec 1802; Monthly Rev Dec 1802.

An elegy to the memory of the late Duke of Bedford, written on the evening of his interment. 1802, New York 1978 (facs, with Psyche and other poems).
REVIEWS: Monthly Rev May 1802; Critical Rev Dec 1802.

Adeline Mowbray, or the mother and daughter: a tale. 3 vols 1804, 1805, 1 vol Edinburgh 1805, Georgetown 1808, London 1810, Boston 1827, London 1844, 1844 (with The welcome home and The Quaker and The young man of the world), New York 1974 (facs), introd by J. Winterson, London 1986, Oxford 1995 (facs); tr Fr 1806.
REVIEWS: Critical Rev Feb 1805; Br Critic June 1805; Monthly Rev Nov 1806.

Simple tales. 4 vols 1806, 1806, 1809 (3rd edn), 1815 (4th edn), 2 vols Georgetown 1807, 1810, Boston 1827; tr Fr 1815 (as Étrennes à mon fils, ou simples contes à l'usage de la jeunesse).
REVIEWS: Edinburgh Rev July 1806; Critical Rev Aug 1806; Monthly Rev Aug 1807; Br Critic May 1808.

The warrior's return and other poems. 1808, Philadelphia 1808, New York 1808, 1978 (facs, with The black man's lament).
REVIEWS: GM July 1808; Monthly Rev Dec 1808; Br Critic Aug 1809.

The black velvet pelisse and The mother and son. New York 1810; The black velvet pelisse (pbd alone) New York 1815, 1815.

The robber; and The revenge. New York 1810.

The brother and sister. Philadelphia 1811.

Murder will out. New Haven 1812, New York 1818, 1844 (in The omnibus of modern romance).

Temper, or domestic scenes: a tale. 3 vols 1812, 2 vols New York 1812, Boston 1812, 4 vols London 1813 (3rd edn), 1827; tr Fr 1813 (as Emma et Saint-Aubin, ou caractères et scènes de la vie privée).
REVIEWS: Br Critic May 1812; Monthly Rev June 1812; Critical Rev Aug 1812; GM Nov 1812.

Tales of real life. 3 vols 1813, 1816 (3rd edn), Boston 1827.
REVIEW: Monthly Rev Nov 1813.

Edgar et Alfred (with Maria Edgeworth's Conseils à mon fils, ou les deux familles). Paris 1814. Not separately pbd in Eng.

La dissipatrice ou lady Ellen et lady Anna. Paris, 1815. Not separately pbd in Eng; tr Rus 1819 (as Ladi Elena).

Valentine's Eve. 3 vols 1816, 1816, 2 vols Boston 1816, 1 vol 1827; tr Fr 1816 (as Catherine Shirley, ou la veille de la Saint-Valentin).
REVIEW: Monthly Rev Apr 1816.

The cabinet, containing an elegant collection of entertaining stories designed for the amusement of boys and girls by Mrs Opie, Madame de Montfolieu and others. Poughkeepsie NY 1818.

New tales. 4 vols 1818, 1819 (3rd edn), 2 vols New York 1818, Philadelphia 1818, Boston 1827, Paris 1831; tr Fr 5 vols 1818 (as Étrennes aux jeunes gens, ou nouveaux contes moraux).
REVIEWS: Br Critic July 1818; Edinburgh Mag Sep 1818.

Tales of the heart. 4 vols 1820, 2 vols New York 1820; tr Fr 1831.
REVIEW: Edinburgh Mag Aug 1820.

Madeline: a tale. 2 vols 1822, Boston 1827; tr Fr 3 vols 1822, 1822 (as Madeline ou memoires d'une jeune écossaise).

The negro boy's tale, a poem addressed to children. Norwich 1824.

Illustrations of lying, in all its branches. 2 vols 1825, 1825, Boston 1826, 1827, New York 1827, Exeter NH 1829, 1832, Hartford CT 1837; ed T. O. Summers, Nashville 1882, Hartford CT 1883.

Tales of the Pemberton family, for the use of children. 1825, 1826.
The black man's lament: or how to make sugar. 1826. Verse.
Detraction displayed. 1828, New York 1828. A manual showing how to defeat calumny.
A wife's duty: a tale. 1828, 1847.
Happy faces: or benevolence and selfishness; and The revenge. [1830?], 1847.
White lies; The welcome home, or the ball. Paris 1833, 1862.
Lays for the dead. 1834, 1840.
The stage coach and other tales on lying. 1845, Boston 1845.
Tales of trials: told to my children. Boston 1845.
Mrs Arlington. Henry Woodville. The ruffian boy. Three novels by Mrs Opie. Paris 1846.
The ruffian boy; and After the ball: or the two Sir Williams. 1858.
Mrs Arlington; or, all is not gold that glitters. [1864?]
Mrs Opie also contributed a memoir to Lectures on painting, *1809, by her husband, John Opie. She pbd a number of tales, poems etc in* GM, The Annual Anthology, Friendship's Offering, European Mag, Finden's Tableaux, *and other periodicals between 1795 and 1841; her poetry also appears in anthologies such as Bethune's* British female poets, *F. J. Stainforth's* Poetical scrapbook *and Rowton's* Female poets of Great Britain. *Several of her poems, including 'Fatherless Fanny', 'Poor Owen', 'The orphan boy's tale', and 'The suicide', were pbd as lyrics set to music by Edward Smith Biggs, William Horsley, Thomas Wright, and others. The* London Mag *pbd a letter from Opie about William Hayley in a long review article on his* Memoirs *in Nov 1824. To Mrs Margaret Roberts,* Duty: a novel, *1814, New York 1815; tr Fr 1816, she contributed a character of the author; this article was rptd in* GM *in Jan 1815. Marie Thérèse Kemble, W. T. Moncrieff, James Pocock and Thomas Welsh wrote melodramas based on tales by Mrs Opie, including* The Lear of common life, Love and duty, *and* Twenty years ago!

§2

Lines occasioned by reading Mrs Opie's affecting tale of The father and the daughter. GM Aug 1806.
Review of Women as they are (by C. Gore). Edinburgh Rev July 1830.
GM Jan 1854. Obituary.
Brightwell, C. L. Memorials of the life of Amelia Opie, from her letters, diaries and other mss. Norwich 1854, 1854, New York 1975 (facs).
Mrs Opie. Leisure Hour 3 1854.
Hall, Mrs A. M. Memoirs of Mrs Opie. Art Jnl 6 1854.
Brightwell, C. L. Memoir of Amelia Opie. 1855.
Kavanagh, J. In her English women of letters vol 2, 1863.
Martineau, H. In her Biographical sketches 1852–75, 1877.
Hall, Mrs A. M. Retrospect of a long life. 2 vols 1883.
Hall, S. C. Retrospect of a long life. 2 vols 1883.
[Ritchie, Lady.] Mrs Opie. Cornhill Mag Oct 1883; rptd in her A book of sibyls, 1883.
Robertson, E. S. In her English poetesses, 1883.
Ross, J. A. In her Three generations of Englishwomen: memoirs and correspondence of Mrs John Taylor, Mrs Sarah Austin and Lady Duff Gordon, 2 vols 1888.
Amelia Opie. Temple Bar Aug 1893.
Earland, A. John Opie and his circle. 1911.
Menzies-Wilson, J. and H. Lloyd. Amelia: the tale of a plain friend. Oxford 1937.
Todd, Janet (ed). Dictionary of British women writers 1660–1800. 1985. [PP]

Sydney Owenson, afterwards Lady Morgan

1776–1859

Bibliographies

Sadleir, M. In his XIX century fiction: a bibliographical record, 2 vols 1951.

§1

Poems. Dublin 1801.
St Clair: or the heiress of Desmond, by S. O. Dublin 1803, London 1803, Philadelphia 1807, 2 vols London 1812 (corrected and greatly enlarged); ed P. Garside 1995; tr Fr 1813, Du 1816.
REVIEWS: Monthly Mag 17 1804; Monthly Rev 43 1804; Antijacobin Rev 40 1811; Br Critic 38 1811.
A few reflections occasioned by the perusal of a work entitled 'Familiar epistles to F. J—s esq on the present state of the Irish stage'. Dublin 1804. Dedication subscribed S.O.
Twelve original Hibernian melodies. [1805.]
The novice of Saint Dominick. 4 vols '1805' [1806], 1806, New York 1807, Philadelphia 1807, 1808, 1823; tr Fr 1817.
REVIEWS: Monthly Mag 20 1806; Monthly Rev 52 1807; Antijacobin Rev 30 1808.
The wild Irish girl: a national tale. 3 vols 1806, 1 vol 1807, New York 1807, Philadelphia 1807, Boston 1808, London 1808, 3 vols 1813, 1 vol Philadelphia 1822, London 1846 (rev), Hartford CT 1850, London 1850, 1856, New York 1855, 1857, 1867, Hartford CT 1855, London 1879, New York 1883; ed R. L. Wolff, New York and London 1978; introd by B. Brophy 1986; ed J. Wordsworth, Oxford 1995; tr Ger 1809, Fr 1813.
REVIEWS: Critical Rev ser 3 no 9 1806; Flowers of Lit 5 1806; Literary Jnl 2 1806; Monthly Mag 2 1807; Monthly Mirror 1 1807; Monthly Rev 57 1808.
Comic opera. The first attempt: or the whim of a moment. Dublin 1807.
The lay of an Irish harp: or metrical fragments. 1807, Philadelphia 1807, New York 1808, Philadelphia [181–?].
REVIEWS: Annual Rev 6 1807; Oxford Rev 2 1807; Monthly Rev 57 1808; Br Critic 33 1809.
Patriotic sketches of Ireland written in Connaught. 2 vols 1807, 1 vol Baltimore 1809.
Woman: or Ida of Athens. 4 vols 1809, 2 vols Philadelphia, New York and Baltimore 1809.
The missionary: an Indian tale. 3 vols 1811 (4 edns), New York 1811, London 1859 (extensively rev as Luxima, the prophetess: a tale of India).
O'Donnel: a national tale. 3 vols 1814, 1814, 1815, New York 1816, London 1835, 1 vol 1835 (rev), 1836, 1850, 1895.
France. 2 vols 1817, 1817, Philadelphia 1817, 1817, London 1818 (with additional notes); tr Fr 1817.
Florence Macarthy: an Irish tale. 4 vols 1818, 1818, 1819, 1 vol 1839, 1856; tr Fr 1819.
Italy. 2 vols 1821, 3 vols 1821 (text differs in part from that of the 2-vol edn), 2 vols New York 1821; tr Fr 1821, Ital 1821. Notes on law, statistics and literary disputes, with appendix on the state of medicine by Sir Thomas Charles Morgan.
Letters to the reviewers of Italy. 1821.
The life and times of the Salvator Rosa. 2 vols 1824, Paris 1824, 1 vol 1846, 1855; tr Fr 1824.
Absenteeism. 1825.
The O'Briens and the O'Flahertys: a national tale. 4 vols 1827, 1827, 1827, 1828, Philadelphia 1828, 1 vol 1838, 1856; ed R. S. Mackenzie 2 vols New York 1856, 1869; tr Fr 1828.
The book of the boudoir. 2 vols 1829, 1829, New York 1829, London 1836. Autobiographical sketches.
France in 1829–30. 2 vols 1830.
Dramatic scenes from real life. 2 vols 1833, New York 1833.
The Princess: or the Beguine. 3 vols 1835, Paris 1835; tr Fr 1835, Ger 1835.
Woman and her master. 2 vols 1840, Philadelphia 1840.
The book without a name. 2 vols 1841. With Sir T. C. Morgan.
Letter to Cardinal Wiseman. 1851.
Passages in my autobiography. 1859, New York 1859.
Memoirs: autobiography, diaries and correspondence. Ed W. H. Dixon 2 vols 1862, 1863, 1 vol 1863.

Both France *and* Italy *aroused considerable controversy, to which Lady Morgan replied.*

§2

Fitzpatrick, W. J. The friends, foes and adventures of Lady Morgan. Dublin 1859, 1860 (enlarged as Lady Morgan: her career literary and personal etc). First pbd in the Irish Quart Rev July 1859.
Gleig, G. R. Blackwood's Mag Feb 1863. Review of the Memoirs.
Kavanagh, J. In her English women of letters vol 2, 1863.
Maginn, W. In his A gallery of illustrious literary characters, ed W. Bates [1873].
Temple Bar Feb 1893.
Stevenson, L. The wild Irish girl: the life of Sydney Owenson, Lady Morgan. 1936.
Moraud, M. I. Une irlandaise libérale en France sous la Restauration: Lady Morgan. Paris 1954.
Flanagan, T. In his Irish novelists, New York 1959.
Bolster, R. French romanticism and the Irish myth. Hermathena 99 1964. [CC]

Emma Parker, 'Emma de Lisle'

Bibliographies

Summers, M. In his A Gothic bibliography, [1941].

§1

A soldier's offspring, or the sisters: a tale. 2 vols 1810.
Elfrida, heiress of Belgrove: a novel. 4 vols 1811.
Fitz-Edward, or the Cambrians: a novel interspersed with pieces of poetry. 3 vols 1811.
Virginia, or the peace of Amiens: a novel. 4 vols 1811.
Aretas: a novel. 4 vols 1813.
The guerrilla chief: a novel. 3 vols 1815, 1817; tr Ger 1817.
Self-deception: in a series of letters. 2 vols 1816.
Important trifles: chiefly appropriate to females on their entrance into society. 1817.

Attributed or spurious works

Eva of Cambria, or the fugitive daughter: a novel by Emma de Lisle. 3 vols 1811.
Ora and Juliet, or influence of first principles: a novel. 4 vols 1811.
Alinda, or the child of mystery: a novel. 4 vols 1812.
These titles have been attributed to 'Emma de Lisle' as a result of a mistake when printing Eva of Cambria: *for the true author, see Amelia Beauclerc, above.*

For a listing of reviews and notices of Parker's works, see Ward (1972). [PG]

Eliza Parsons née Phelps c. 1748–1811

Bibliographies

Summers, M. In his A Gothic bibliography, [1941].

§1

The history of Miss Meredith: a novel. 2 vols 1790, 1790, 1 vol Dublin 1791.
The errors of education: a novel. 3 vols 1791, 2 vols Dublin 1792.
Woman as she should be: or memoirs of Mrs Menville. 4 vols 1793, 2 vols Dublin 1793.
Ellen and Julia: a novel. 2 vols 1793.
Castle of Wolfenbach: a German story. 2 vols 1793, 1794, 1 vol 1835; ed D. P. Varma 1968.
Lucy: a novel. 3 vols 1794.
The voluntary exile. 5 vols 1795, 2 vols Dublin 1795.
The mysterious warning: a German tale. 4 vols 1796; ed D. P. Varma 1968.
Women as they are: a novel. 4 vols 1796.
The girl of the mountains: a novel. 4 vols 1797, 2 vols Dublin 1798.
An old friend with a new face: a novel. 3 vols 1797.
Anecdotes of two well-known families, written by a descendant and dedicated to the first female pen in England: prepared for the press by Mrs Parsons. 3 vols 1798.
The valley of St Gothard: a novel. 3 vols Brentford 1799.
The miser and his family: a novel. 4 vols Brentford 1800, Dublin 1801.
The peasant of Ardenne Forest: a novel. 4 vols Brentford 1801; tr Fr 1803.
The mysterious visit: a novel founded on facts. 4 vols Brentford 1802.
Murray House: a plain unvarnished tale. 3 vols Brentford 1804.
Summers notes this novel sometimes attributed to Mrs Meeke.
The convict or navy lieutenant: a novel. Brentford 1807.

Translations

The intrigues of a morning: or an hour in Paris. A farce adapted from Molière's Monsieur de Pourceaugnac and produced at Covent Garden, 18 Apr 1792.
Love and gratitude: or traits of the human heart. Six novels translated from Augustus La Fontaine. 3 vols Brentford 1804.

Attributed or spurious works

Summers notes an attribution of the following to Parsons:
Rosetta: a novel. 4 vols 1805.
For a listing of reviews and notices of E. Parsons' works, see Ward (1979, 1972). [CF]

Thomas Love Peacock 1785–1866

The principal repositories of literary mss, private correspondence and family papers are the British Library and the Carl H. Pforzheimer Collection of Shelley and His Circle New York Public Library; smaller collections are in the Bodleian, Harvard, Princeton, Yale, and the Berg Collection New York Public Library. Peacock's official correspondence and steam navigation papers in the India Office Records have not been catalogued. Details of individual mss and letters will appear in IELM *vol 4 pt 4 and in the forthcoming* Letters, *ed N. A. Joukovsky.*

The present listing of Peacock's works is the most extensive to date, comprising all known edns, trns and adaptations as well as all known contributions to periodicals. All separate reprints and all reviews and other critical articles on Peacock are listed through 1875. Most reprintings of individual poems and prose selections in periodicals or anthologies are excluded, as are most musical settings. Edns containing three or more novels are listed under Collections and selections. Contributions to periodicals *does not repeat items that appear in* §1. *Posthumously ptd mss are included with Peacock's correspondence in* Letters and papers.

Bibliographies and reference works

Catalogue of the library of the late Thos Love Peacock, esq. . . . which will be sold at auction by Messrs Sotheby, Wilkinson & Hodge. 11–12 June 1866, rptd in Sale catalogues of libraries of eminent persons, vol 1: Poets and men of letters, ed A. N. L. Munby 1971.
Van Doren, C. Bibliography of Peacock's published writings. In his Life, 1911, §2, *below*.
Brett-Smith, H. F. B. and C. E. Jones. Bibliographical notes in Halliford edn of Works, *below*. Index bibliography in vol 1, 1934, with Peacockiana to 1933.
Sadleir, M. In his XIX century fiction: a bibliographical record, 2 vols 1951.
Read, B. The critical reputation of Thomas Love Peacock, with an annotated enumerative bibliography of works by and about Peacock from February 1800 to June 1958. Unpbd PhD thesis, Boston Univ 1959.
Read, B. Thomas Love Peacock: an enumerative bibliography. BB 24, 1963–4.
Ward, W. S. Contemporary reviews of Thomas Love Peacock: a supplementary list for the years 1805–1820. BB 25, 1967.

Madden, L. A short guide to Peacock studies. Critical Survey 4, 1970.
Ward, W. S. In his Literary reviews in British periodicals 1798–1820: a bibliography, 2 vols New York 1972. Also in his Literary reviews ... 1821–1826, New York 1977.
Gooch, B. N. S. and D. S. Thatcher. In their Musical settings of early and mid-Victorian literature: a catalogue, New York 1979.
Prance, C. A. The characters in the novels of Thomas Love Peacock, 1785–1866, with bibliographical lists. Lewiston NY 1992.
Donovan, J. P. Thomas Love Peacock. In Literature of the Romantic period: a bibliographical guide, ed M. O'Neill, Oxford 1998.

Collections and selections

Headlong Hall, Nightmare Abbey, Maid Marian, Crotchet Castle, 'with corrections, and a preface, by the author'. No 57 of Bentley's Standard Novels 1837. Preface signed The author of Headlong Hall, dated 4 Mar 1837. Various authorities mention an 1849 reprint, but this appears to be a ghost. Bentley's plates were purchased by Ward & Lock in Feb 1856 and used for separate edns of Headlong Hall and Nightmare Abbey, 1856 (*below*), and Maid Marian and Crotchet Castle, 1856 (*below*), as well as an edn of all 4 novels, listed in Athenaeum, 7 Aug 1858 (no known copies).
REVIEWS: Guide, 22 Apr 1837; Examiner, 28 May 1837.
[Selected poetry]. In Inheritors of unfulfilled renown, [ed T. L'Estrange], Belfast [1866?] (preface dated Christmas Eve 1865) (priv ptd). Anon. Texts of Peacock's poetry often altered by L'Estrange to include Belfast place names. Only known copy in a private collection.
The works of Thomas Love Peacock, including his novels, poems, fugitive pieces, criticisms etc, with a preface by the Right Hon. Lord Houghton, a biographical notice by his granddaughter, Edith Nicolls, and portrait. Ed H. Cole 3 vols 1875. Vols 1–2 Novels; vol 3 Poetry and miscellanea. A 4th vol was projected in 1879 but not pbd. Epitaph on Margaret Love Peacock (pbd in Nicolls's notice), independently ptd in Dickens's Dictionary of the Thames, from Oxford to the Nore, 1880 (from tombstone in Shepperton churchyard) (anon); tr Latin by E. D. A. Morshead, Westminster versions, ed H. F. Fox, Oxford 1906.
REVIEWS: [N. McColl] Athenaeum, 26 Dec 1874, 9 Jan 1875; (R. G[arnett]), Examiner, 23, 30 Jan 1875; Standard, 2 Feb 1875; Spectator, 6 Feb 1875; Saturday Rev, 20 Feb 1875; (J. Davies), Contemporary Rev, Apr 1875; [A. I. Shand] Edinburgh Rev 142, July 1875.
[Novels, with Calidore and miscellanea]. Ed R. Garnett 10 vols '1891' [1891–2]. Introd to Headlong Hall rptd in Garnett's Essays of an ex-librarian, 1901; also in EL edn of Headlong Hall and Nightmare Abbey, [1908].
[Novels and Rhododaphne]. Introds by G. Saintsbury, illustr F. H. Townsend, except Headlong Hall and Nightmare Abbey, illustr H. R. Millar, 5 vols 1895–7 (Macmillan's Illus Standard Novels), rptd 1927 (Macmillan's Illus Pocket Classics). Maid Marian and Crotchet Castle, rptd 1955 (Macmillan's Pocket Lib). Introds rptd in Saintsbury's Prefaces and essays, 1933.
Songs from the novels. Ed R. B. Johnson [1902].
Novels. 1903.
Works [novels]. 2 vols [1905–6] (New Universal Lib).
Poems. Ed R. B. Johnson [1906] (ML and New Universal Lib).
The plays of Thomas Love Peacock, published for the first time. Ed A. B. Young 1910.
[Selections]. Ed W. H. Helm [1911] (Regent Lib).
The Halliford edn of The works of Thomas Love Peacock. Ed H. F. B. Brett-Smith and C. E. Jones 10 vols 1924–34. Vol 1 Biographical introd and Headlong Hall, 1934; vol 2 Melincourt, 1924; vol 3 Nightmare Abbey and Maid Marian, 1924; vol 4 The misfortunes of Elphin and Crotchet Castle, 1924; vol 5 Gryll Grange, 1924; vol 6 Poems, 1927; vol 7 Poems and plays, 1931; vol 8 Essays, memoirs, letters and unfinished novels, 1934; vol 9 Critical and other essays, 1926; vol 10 Dramatic criticisms and trns and other essays, 1926. Detailed bibl and textual notes at the end of each novel or vol. General indexes, addenda and corrigenda in vol 1. Indexes to verse in vol 7. Details of excluded, lost, doubtful and alien works in vol 8 appendix 6.
Selections. Ed H. F. B. Brett-Smith 1928.
Three novels: Headlong Hall, Nightmare Abbey, Crotchet Castle. Introd by J. Mair 1940 (Nelson Classics).
The pleasures of Peacock. Ed B. R. Redman, New York 1947.
Novels. Ed D. Garnett 1948, 2 vols 1963 (corrected).
A Peacock selection. Ed H. L. B. Moody 1966 (Macmillan's Eng Classics).
Novels: Headlong Hall, Nightmare Abbey, The misfortunes of Elphin, Crotchet Castle. Introd by J. B. Priestley, notes by B. Lloyd Evans 1967 (Pan Bestsellers of Lit).
Memoirs of Shelley and other essays and reviews. Ed H. Mills 1970.
Nightmare Abbey, The misfortunes of Elphin, Crotchet Castle. Ed C. B. Dodson, New York 1971 (Rinehart Edns).

§1

Answer to the question, Is history or biography the more improving study? by Master T. L. Peacock, aged 14. The monthly preceptor: or juvenile library, pt 1, Feb 1800; monthly pts re-issued as The juvenile library (later The juvenile encyclopaedia), 6 vols 1800–3. Poem, awarded an 'extra prize' in an essay contest.
The monks of St Mark. '1804' [1805?] (priv ptd). 8° halfsheet ptd in same style and presumably at same time as the Palmyra volume, *below*. 2 known copies, both NYPL. Poem followed by initials T. L. P. and date Sep 1804, but this was date of composition, not of printing. *See* Joukovsky, 1994, Letters and papers, *below*.
Palmyra and other poems, by T. L. Peacock. '1806' [1805], 1812 (with The genius of the Thames, *below*) (extensively rev); The old man's complaint adapted (as Words of an old man) [by T. L'Estrange], Verses and metrical translations, Belfast 1866 (priv ptd) (only known copy in a private collection).
REVIEWS: Literary Jnl, Dec 1805; Monthly Mag suppl, 31 Jan 1806; Br Critic, Feb 1806; Critical Rev, Feb 1806; [Moody, C. L.] Monthly Rev, Mar 1806; Lady's Monthly Museum, June 1806; Br Critic, Jan 1808; Literary Annual Register, Mar 1808; Poetical Register for 1806–7 (pbd 1811).
The genius of the Thames: a lyrical poem in two parts, by Thomas Love Peacock. 1810, 1812 (with Palmyra and other poems, *below*) (rev); Stanzas written at sea, set to music by W. A. Nield [1816] (as The harbour of peace).
REVIEWS: Br Critic, Aug 1810; Satirist, Aug 1810; Antijacobin Rev, Sep 1810; GM, Oct 1810; Critical Rev, Dec 1810; Monthly Mag suppl, 31 Jan 1811; Eclectic Rev, Feb 1811; [Hodgson, F.] Monthly Rev, June 1811; Satirist, Dec 1811 (excerpts from other revs); Poetical Register for 1810–11 (pbd 1814).
The genius of the Thames, Palmyra and other poems, by T. L. Peacock, 'second edition'. 1812, 1817 (re-issued with only title and contents pp. reset).
REVIEW: [Hodgson, F.] Monthly Rev, Mar 1813.
The philosophy of melancholy: a poem in four parts, with a mythological ode, by T. L. Peacock. 1812.
REVIEWS: Critical Rev, Mar 1812; Antijacobin Rev, Apr 1812; Eclectic Rev, Oct 1812; New Rev, Feb 1813; New Annual Register for 1812 (pbd 1813).
Αναπαιστοι. [c. 1812–13?] (priv ptd) (anon) (no known copies), rptd in T. Forster prolegomena to his Philosophia musarum, Bruges '1845' [prolegomena dated 27 Feb 1846] (anon). Greek anapestic ode. *See* Joukovsky, 1992, §2 *below*.
Sir Hornbook, or Childe Launcelot's expedition: a grammatico-allegorical ballad, [illustr H. Corbould]. '1814' [1813] (anon), 1815 ('second edition'), 1815 ('third edition'), 1817 ('fourth edition'), 1818 ('fifth edition'); ed 'Felix Summerly' [H. Cole] with illustra-

tions redrawn for the Home Treasury ser 1843 (anon), 1846, 1855, [c. 1855?] (with the ballad of Chevy Chase, as 'The favorite ballads of Chevy Chase & Sir Hornbook'); Tokyo 1984 (facs of '1814' edn). Children's book. Some authorities mention an 1845 edn, but this appears to be an error for 1846. Tr Rus 1988 (with Nightmare Abbey, Gryll Grange etc).

REVIEWS: European Mag, Jan 1814; Br Critic, May 1814; Literary Panorama, May 1814; [Barbauld, A. L.] Monthly Rev, June 1814; The juvenile rev: or moral and critical observations on children's books pt 1, 1817.

Sir Proteus: a satirical ballad, by P. M. O'Donovan esq. 1814. Poem with extensive notes.

Headlong Hall. '1816' [1815] (anon), Philadelphia 1816, London 1816 ('second edition') (rev), 1822 ('third edition') (rev), 1837 (Bentley's Standard Novels, *above*) (slightly rev), New York 1845 ('first American edition') (with Nightmare Abbey) (Wiley and Putnam's Lib of Choice Reading), rptd 1848 (Putnam's Choice Lib), rptd 1850, London 1856 (ptd from Bentley's plates with unauthorised use of Peacock's name on title page) (with Nightmare Abbey), New York [1887] (with Nightmare Abbey) (Putnam's Knickerbocker Nuggets); ed R. Garnett [1908] (rptd from his 1891 edn, with Nightmare Abbey) (EL); 1929 (with Nightmare Abbey) (WC); ed J. Tamagnan, Paris 1958 (abridged); introd by P. M. Yarker 1961 (with Nightmare Abbey) (EL); ed M. Baron and M. Slater, Oxford 1987 (with Gryll Grange) (WCp); Ware 1995 (with Nightmare Abbey) (Wordsworth Classics); introd by R. Bradbury, Columbia SC 1997 (rptd from Works 1875); Love and opportunity, rptd in Morning Chron, 27 Dec 1815; Chorus, rptd 'with its last new reading' (as Song of the Headlong Ap-Headlong) in Leigh Hunt, On poems of joyful impulse, Musical Times, 15 Mar 1854.

REVIEWS: Critical Rev, Jan 1816; La Belle Assemblée, Feb 1816; NMM, 1 Feb 1816; Eclectic Rev, Apr 1816, rptd Analectic Mag (Philadelphia), July 1816; Literary Panorama, Apr 1816; Br Lady's Mag, Sep 1816; Monthly Rev, Mar 1817; Broadway Jnl (New York), 17 May 1845.

Prologue to J. Tobin's The faro table: or the guardians (Drury Lane, 5 Nov 1816). 1816 (prologue ascribed to 'E. Peacock, esq.'), New York 1817; prologue also ptd Morning Chron, 6 Nov 1816 ('by Mr. Peacock'). Peacock's epilogue not ptd.

Melincourt, by the author of Headlong Hall. 3 vols 1817, 2 vols Philadelphia 1817, 1 vol London 1856 (with new preface dated Mar 1856) (as Melincourt: or Sir Oran Haut-ton), rptd [1884] (Select Lib of Fiction, with cover title Miss Melincourt: or ten thousand a year) (only known copy in a priv collection); The flower of love, rptd Literary Gazette, 15 Mar 1817; The city of Novote and The borough of Onevote, ed W. H. D. Rouse, Election scenes in fiction, London and Glasgow 1929 (Blackie's Eng Texts); ed H. G. Nicholas, To the hustings: election scenes from English fiction, 1956; Cimmerian Lodge, illustr F. Butler, Berkeley CA 1976 (Poltroon Press, c. 100 copies). Tr Fr 2 vols 1818.

REVIEWS: Literary Gazette, 22 Mar 1817; Critical Rev, May 1817; NMM, 1 May 1817; Monthly Mag, 1 June 1817; Monthly Rev, July 1817; Amer Monthly Mag, July 1817; North Amer Rev, Sep 1817; Br Critic, Oct 1817 (tentatively ascribes authorship to Sir William Drummond); Portfolio (Philadelphia), Apr 1818; [Chorley, H. F.] Athenaeum, 19 Apr 1856.

The Round Table: or King Arthur's feast, embellished with eighteen engravings. [1817]. Anon but announced as by the author of Sir Hornbook in Edinburgh Rev, Nov 1817. Children's book.

Rhododaphne, or the Thessalian spell: a poem. 1818 (anon), Philadelphia 1818; rptd in Southern Literary Messenger (Richmond VA), June–July 1843 (attribution to Richard Dabney questioned and eventually withdrawn, July, Sep, Oct 1843). P. B. Shelley's review, written in 1818 and intended for Examiner, 1st ptd with his Notes on sculptures in Rome and Florence, ed H. B. Forman 1879 (priv ptd).

REVIEWS: Literary Gazette, 21 Feb 1818; La Belle Assemblée, Mar 1818; rptd in Athenaeum: or Spirit of the Eng magazines (Boston), July 1818; Monthly Mag, 1 Apr 1818; Literary Panorama, May 1818; Amer Monthly Mag, Nov 1818; Monthly Rev, Feb 1819, quoted in Fireside Mag (Stamford), Apr 1819; Virginia Evangelical and Literary Mag, May 1819 (ascribes authorship to Dabney for first time); Analectic Mag (Philadelphia), Jan 1820.

Nightmare Abbey, by the author of Headlong Hall. 1818, Philadelphia 1819, London 1837 (Bentley's Standard Novels, *above*) (rev), New York 1845 ('first American edition') (with Headlong Hall) (Wiley and Putnam's Lib of Choice Reading), rptd 1848 (Putnam's Choice Lib), rptd 1850, London 1856 (ptd from Bentley's plates with unauthorised use of Peacock's name on title page) (with Headlong Hall), New York [1887] (with Headlong Hall) (Putnam's Knickerbocker Nuggets); ed R. Garnett [1908] (rptd from his 1891 edn, with Headlong Hall) (EL); ed C. E. Jones 1923 (corrected type facs of 1818 edn) (Oxford Misc); 1929 (with Headlong Hall) (WC); ed J.-J. Mayoux, Paris 1936 (with Fr trn) (with The misfortunes of Elphin); introd by J. B. Priestley 1947 (with Crotchet Castle) (Novel Lib), rptd New York 1964; ed C. Connolly, Great English short novels, 1953 (without Peacock's notes); introd by P. M. Yarker, London 1961 (with Headlong Hall) (EL); New York 1964 (Norton Lib); ed A. R. Tompkins, London 1966 (Blackie's Medallion Eng Texts); ed W. E. Buckler, Minor classics of nineteenth-century fiction, Boston 1967 (Riverside Edns); ed R. Wright, Harmondsworth 1969 (with Crotchet Castle) (Penguin Eng Lib); introd by J. Wordsworth, Oxford 1992 (facs of 1818 edn); ed K. H. Brown, Masterpieces of the English short novel, New York 1992 (text rptd from Connolly edn); introd by M. Butler, illustr P. Forster 1994 (Folio Soc); Ware 1995 (with Headlong Hall) (Wordsworth Classics); Seamen three: a song, illustr M. Lock, Kingston (Ont.) 1991 (Locks' Press, 160 copies); radio adaptation by D. Cleverdon (BBC 3rd Programme Dec 1949) (unpbd); dramatisation by A. Sharp (Westminster theatre 27 Feb 1952), in Plays of the year, vol 7 1953, separately rptd 1971 (Ginn Drama Texts); by H. Nicholson in The second book of one-act plays, 1954 (as Port and a pistol); by E. Zeal (Edinburgh Festival Aug 1987) (unpbd). Ms Fr trn mentioned by R. Garnett in introd to his 1891 edn is at Harvard. Tr Ger 1913, 1989, Fr 1936 (*above*), 1993, Ital [1952], 1958 (with Crotchet Castle), Portuguese 1958, Sp 1975, Rus 1988 (with Gryll Grange etc).

REVIEWS: Tickler, 1 Dec 1818; Literary Jnl, 5 Dec 1818; Literary Gazette, 12 Dec 1818; European Mag, Mar 1819; Western Rev and Miscellaneous Mag (Lexington KY), Sep 1819; Monthly Rev, Nov 1819; Broadway Jnl (New York), 17 May 1845.

The four ages of poetry. Ollier's Literary Misc no 1 (only issue) 1820 (anon); [Belfast 1863] (priv ptd [for T. L'Estrange]) (anon); ed H. Cole, Works, London 1875; ed H. B. Forman, The prose works of Percy Bysshe Shelley, vol 3 1880; ed A. S. Cook, Boston 1891 (with Shelley's Defence); ed R. Garnett, Calidore and miscellanea, London '1891' [1892]; ed H. F. B. Brett-Smith, Oxford 1921 (Percy Reprints) (with Shelley's Defence and Browning's Essay on Shelley), 1923 (corrected); ed J. E. Jordan, Indianapolis IN 1965 (with Shelley's Defence) (Lib of Liberal Arts); ed D. Bromwich, Romantic critical essays, Cambridge 1987 (with abridged text of An essay on fashionable literature) (Cambridge Eng Prose Texts). Tr Portuguese 1985 (with Wordsworth's Preface and Shelley's Defence), Rus 1988 (with Nightmare Abbey, Gryll Grange etc). Often anthologised.

Maid Marian, by the author of Headlong Hall. 1822 (prefatory note dated 15 Mar 1822), 1837 (Bentley's Standard Novels, *above*) (slightly rev), 1856 (ptd from Bentley's plates) (with Crotchet Castle); ed F. A. Cavanagh 1912 (abridged) (Macmillan's Eng Lit for Secondary Schools); ed H. Newbolt, The greenwood: a collection of literary readings relating to Robin Hood, 1925 (Teaching of Eng); ed A. S. Cairncross, Edinburgh [1935] (Self Study Eng);

illustr A. Kashian, Felinfach (Dyfed) 1992 (illus facs of R. Garnett '1891' edn); The friar of Rubygill, rptd [Solihull] 1987 (Cherub Press, 65 copies); operatic adaptation by J. R. Planché (Covent Garden 3 Dec 1822) [1822], New York 1823; songs, duets, glees, choruses etc from opera London [1822]; music of opera by H. R. Bishop [1822]; dramatic adaptation of opera [c. 1825] (Hodgson's Juvenile Drama); concert adaptation by C. LeFleming 1939 (as The singing friar). Tr Ger 1823, Fr 1826, 1855, Serbo-Croat 1957.
REVIEWS: Monthly Rev, Apr 1822; Monthly Mag, May 1822; NMM, 1 May 1822; General Weekly Register, 5 May 1822, rptd in Monthly Literary Register, 1 June 1822; La Belle Assemblée, June 1822; London Museum, 10 Aug 1822; Literary Gazette, 23 Nov 1822; Literary Speculum, [Dec 1822]; Literary Chron, 7 Dec 1822; Kaleidoscope (Liverpool), 10 Dec 1822.

The misfortunes of Elphin, by the author of Headlong Hall. 1829; introd by R. W. Chapman 1924 (with Crotchet Castle) (WC); illustr H. W. Bray, Newtown (Montgomeryshire) 1928 (Gregynog Press, 250 copies) (with Peacock's spelling of Welsh names 'corrected'); ed J.-J. Mayoux, Paris 1936 (with Fr trn) (with Nightmare Abbey); illustr B. Eve, Felinfach (Dyfed) 1991 (without Peacock's notes); Seithenyn passages from chs 2 and 11 rptd in J. B. Priestley, Fools and philosophers: a gallery of comic figures from English literature, London 1925; The war-song of Dinas Vawr, set to music by C. Harper, Wrexham 1933 (with Welsh trn by E. Roberts); adapted as Amer Indian war song in [Charles Mackay], Periodical literature of the North American Indians, Bentley's Misc, June 1837. Tr Fr 1936 (*above*).
REVIEWS: Literary Gazette, 7 Mar 1829; Cambrian Quart Mag, Apr 1829; Westminster Rev 10, Apr 1829; NMM, 1 Apr 1829; Athenaeum, 6 May 1829; Monthly Rev, June 1829.

Crotchet Castle, by the author of Headlong Hall. 1831, 1837 (Bentley's Standard Novels, *above*) (slightly rev), 1856 (ptd from Bentley's plates) (with Maid Marian); introd by H. Morley 1887 (Cassell's Nat Lib); introd by R. W. Chapman 1924 (with The misfortunes of Elphin) (WC); introd by J. B. Priestley 1947 (with Nightmare Abbey) (Novel Lib), rptd New York 1964; introd by K. Hopkins, illustr P. Reddick 1964 (Folio Soc); ed R. Wright, Harmondsworth 1969 (with Nightmare Abbey) (Penguin Eng Lib); The pool of the diving friar rptd in Br Ladies' Newspaper, 13 Jan 1838; tr Ital 1958 (with Nightmare Abbey).
REVIEWS: Literary Gazette, 19 Feb 1831; [White, J.] Athenaeum, 5 Mar 1831; Cambrian Quart Mag, 1 Apr 1831; Mirror of Lit, Amusement and Instruction, 2 Apr 1831; Examiner, 3 Apr 1831; Metropolitan, May 1831; Monthly Rev, May 1831; Literary Beacon, 18 June 1831; [Fonblanque, A.] Westminster Rev 15, July 1831; [W. Maginn?] Fraser's Mag, Aug 1831; NMM, Oct 1831.

Appendix to Report from the select committee on steam navigation to India. House of Commons, 14 July 1834. Contains Peacock's Memorandum respecting the application of steam navigation to the internal and external communications of India, Sep 1829; Steam navigation in India, and between Europe and India, 2 Dec 1833; Estimate of the probable expense of placing two iron steam vessels on the river Euphrates at Bussora, and navigating the same from Bussora to Bir and back, 16 Apr 1834; other papers delivered to the committee by Peacock.

Paper money lyrics, and other poems. 1837 (priv ptd [for H. Cole], 100 copies) (preface dated 20 July 1837) (anon); 7 lyrics previously ptd [by H. Cole] in Guide, Apr–June 1837 (The three little men, 22 Apr; Prœmium of an epic, 21 May; Pan in town, 28 May; A mood of my own mind, 4 June; Chorus of Scotch economists, 11 June; The wise men of Gotham, and Love and the flimsies, 18 June) (all anon); Love and the flimsies, and Chorus of bubble buyers, rptd in Bentley's Misc, Aug, Sep 1838 (both anon); preface rptd [Solihull] 1979 (Cherub Press, 100 copies).

A whitebait dinner at Lovegrove's at Blackwall, July 1851. [1851] (priv ptd) (anon); literal Latin trn [1851] (lithographed from ms) (anon but by Peacock); ed H. Cole, Works, 1875 (Greek and Latin with Eng verse trn by Lord Broughton). Leaflet containing Greek poem. Only known copies BL and NYPL.

Horæ dramaticæ. Fraser's Mag, Mar 1852 (Querolus: or the buried treasure), Apr 1852 (The Phaëthon of Euripides), Oct 1857 (The Flask of Cratinus) (first 2 nos signed M. S. O.; no 3, By the author of Headlong Hall); ed H. Cole, Works, 1875; ed R. Garnett, Calidore and miscellanea '1891' [1892].

In statuam Roberti Peel, baronetti, quam in vico fori, prope terminum occidentalem, cives Londinienses erigendam decreverunt: epigrammata anathematica ad singula baseos latera. 1854 (priv ptd, 25 copies). Anon. Four Latin epigrams with notes. Only known copy at Lehigh Univ Bethlehem PA. *See* Joukovsky, 1988, §2 *below*.

Memoirs of Percy Bysshe Shelley. Fraser's Mag, June 1858 (pt 1), Jan 1860 (pt 2), Mar 1862 (suppl notice) (all signed T. L. Peacock); ed H. Cole, Works, 1875; ed H. F. B. Brett-Smith 1909 (with Shelley's letters to Peacock); ed B. H. Clark, Great short biographies of the world, New York 1928 (without Peacock's notes or suppl notice); ed H. Wolfe, The life of Percy Bysshe Shelley, as comprised in the Life . . . by Thomas Jefferson Hogg, the Recollections . . . by Edward John Trelawny, and the Memoirs . . . by Thomas Love Peacock, 2 vols London 1933 (text and notes rptd from Brett-Smith's edn) (with Shelley's letters to Peacock); ed H. Mills 1970 (with other essays and reviews); brief extract ptd [H. Wallis], Thomas Love Peacock on the portraits of Shelley, 1911. Tr Rus 1988 (with Nightmare Abbey, Gryll Grange etc).
REVIEWS: Shelley and Lord Eldon, Sat Rev, 28 Jan 1860; (R. Garnett) Shelley in Pall Mall, Macmillan's Mag, June 1860; [A. S. Kinnear] Quart Rev 110, Oct 1861, rptd Living Age (Boston), 7 Dec 1861; (R. Garnett) Shelley, Harriet Shelley and Mr T. L. Peacock, in his Relics of Shelley, 1862.

Unpublished letters of Percy Bysshe Shelley, from Italy – 1818 to 1822. Fraser's Mag, Mar 1860, postscript May 1860 (both signed T. L. Peacock); ed H. Cole, Works, 1875; Peacock's introd and notes rptd, with a more complete collection of Shelley's letters to Peacock, in edns of Memoirs by Brett-Smith, 1909, and Wolfe, 1933, *above*.

Gryll Grange, by the author of Headlong Hall. Fraser's Mag, Apr–Dec 1860; 1861 (rev), Harmondsworth 1947, Gloucester 1984 (Pocket Classics); ed M. Baron and M. Slater, Oxford 1987 (with Headlong Hall) (WCp). Tr Rus 1988 (with Nightmare Abbey etc).
REVIEWS: Critic, 2 Mar 1861; Spectator, 2 Mar 1861; London Rev, 9 Mar 1861; Sat Rev, 16 Mar 1861; Westminster Rev 19, Apr 1861.

Gl'inganNati, the deceived: a comedy performed at Siena in 1531, and Aelia Laelia Crispis, by T. L. Peacock. 1862; expurgated text of Peacock's trn of Gl'ingannati New Var edn of Shakespeare, Twelfe Night, ed H. H. Furness Philadelphia 1901; ed E. Bentley, The genius of the Italian theatre, New York 1964.
REVIEWS: Parthenon, 23 Aug 1862; Sat Rev, 30 Aug 1862; [Collier, J. P.] Athenaeum, 6 Sep 1862.

Contributions to periodicals

[Letter signed 'P.']. Morning Chron, 8 Apr 1814.

Rich and poor: or saint and sinner. Traveller, 9 July 1821 (signed 'Dives'), rptd Examiner, 22 July 1821; Globe and Traveller, 27 Aug 1825 (unsigned); Guide, 6 May 1837 (with new headnote); rptd with Paper money lyrics, 1837; ed H. Cole, Works, 1875 (with 2 additional stanzas). Poem, often ptd in other newspapers, sometimes with considerable additions and variations – see discussion of authorship and publishing history, prompted by attribution to R. H. Barham, in N & Q 27 July, 24, 31 Aug, 5, 19 Oct 1867. Version in Drakard's Stamford News, 20 July 1821, attributed to John Clare by E. Robinson, introd to Clare's The parish: a satire, Harmondsworth 1986.

Llyn-y-dreiddiad-vrawd: or the pool of the diving friar. NMM, June

1826 (anon); incorporated in Crotchet Castle, 1831 (slightly rev). Poem.

Moore's Epicurean. Westminster Rev 8, Oct 1827. Anon.

Touchandgo. Globe and Traveller, 24 Jan 1829. Anon. Poem.

Moore's Letters and journals of Byron. Westminster Rev 12, Apr 1830. Anon.

Randolph's Memoirs &c of Thomas Jefferson. Westminster Rev 13, Oct 1830. Anon.

London Bridge. Westminster Rev 13, Oct 1830. Anon.

The fate of a broom: an anticipation. Examiner, 14 Aug 1831 (anon); added as a note to Crotchet Castle, 1837 (Bentley's Standard Novels); rptd with Paper money lyrics, 1837. Poem.

On steam navigation to India. Edinburgh Rev 60, Jan 1835. Anon.

Lord Mount Edgcumbe's Musical reminiscences. London Rev 1, Apr 1835. Signed M.S.O.

French comic romances. London Rev 2, Oct 1835. Signed M.S.O.

The épicier. London Rev 2, Jan 1836. Signed M.S.O.

Bellini. London Rev 2, Jan 1836. Signed M.S.O.

The legend of Manor Hall, by the author of Headlong Hall. Bentley's Misc, Jan 1837, rptd in The Bentley ballads, ed J. Doran 1858, 1861, 1866; ed J. Sheehan, 1869. Poem.

Recollections of childhood, by the author of Headlong Hall: The Abbey House. Bentley's Misc, Feb 1837, rptd in Tales from Bentley, vol 1 1859; ed R. Garnett, Calidore and miscellanea '1891' [1892].

Promotion BY Purchase and by NO Purchase: or a dialogue between Captain A— of — and Colonel Q— of the —. Guide, 29 Apr 1837 (anon), rptd with Paper money lyrics, 1837 (as Byp and Nop: promotion . . . between Captain A. and Colonel Q.). Poem.

The new year: lines on George Cruikshank's illustration of January in the Comic Almanack for 1838, by the author of Headlong Hall. Bentley's Misc, Jan 1838. Poem.

[Letters signed 'Philatmos']. The Times, 3, 7 Nov 1838, 14 May 1842.

Gastronomy and civilization. Fraser's Mag, Dec 1851. Essay, written in collaboration with his daughter Mary Meredith and signed M.M.

Chapelle and Bachaumont, by the author of Headlong Hall. Fraser's Mag, Apr 1858.

Demetrius Galanus: Greek translations from Sanskrit, by the author of Headlong Hall. Fraser's Mag, Nov 1858.

Müller and Donaldson's History of Greek literature. Fraser's Mag, Mar 1859. Signed T. L. Peacock.

Newark Abbey, August 1842, with a reminiscence of August 1807. Fraser's Mag, Nov 1860. (signed T. L. Peacock); rptd Sidcot Somerset 1995, Gruffyground Press, 200 copies). Poem.

Peacock also contributed opera criticism to the Globe and Traveller (1830) and the Examiner (1831–4). See lists in Halliford edn of Works, *vol 9 appendix 1.*

Letters and papers

[Shelley, P. B. and M. W.] History of a six weeks' tour through a part of France, Switzerland, Germany and Holland. 1817 (anon). Includes revised versions of 2 letters from P. B. Shelley to 'T. P. Esq.'

Shelley, P. B. Essays, letters from abroad, translations and fragments. Ed M. W. Shelley 2 vols '1840' [1839]. Includes 13 letters to 'T. L. P., Esq.'

[Forster, T.]. Epistolarium: or the correspondence of the Forster family, letters and essays, vol 2 Bruges 1850 (priv ptd). Includes a Latin letter signed T. L. P.

Middleton, C. S. Shelley and his writings. 2 vols 1858. Contains revised versions of 2 letters from P. B. Shelley to 'a friend' [Peacock].

Hogg, T. J. The life of Percy Bysshe Shelley. 2 vols 1858. Preface contains a letter from Peacock to M. W. Shelley with the false signature L. T.

Unpublished letters of Percy Bysshe Shelley, 1860, *above*. 17 letters from P. B. Shelley and pt of 1 from M. W. Shelley, ed Peacock with notes.

[Cole, H.] Biographical notes, [1874] (§2, *below*). Prints ms poems, letters and portions of 1818 diary.

Works, ed H. Cole 1875 (Collections, *above*). Some ms material in Cole's Biographical notes pubd in Edith Nicolls's Biographical notice in vol 1; ms poems in vol 3.

The prose works of Percy Bysshe Shelley. Ed H. B. Forman 4 vols 1880. Text of Shelley's letters includes passages not printed by Peacock.

Shelley and Mary. [Ed J. Shelley] 3 (sometimes 4) vols [1882] (priv ptd, c. 12 copies distributed). Includes 13 letters to P. B. Shelley and 10 to M. W. Shelley.

The last day of Windsor Forest. National Rev, Sep 1887 (with prefatory note by R. G[arnett]); ed R. Garnett, Calidore and miscellanea, '1891' [1892], rptd Nat Rev, June 1933 (new prefatory note). Reminiscence, probably written c. 1862.

Garnett, R. Introd to Headlong Hall, 1891. Contains new letter to E. T. Hookham.

Calidore: a fragment of a romance. In Calidore and miscellanea, ed R. Garnett '1891' [1892]. Incomplete text of ms.

A letter from Percy B. Shelley to T. Peacock, July, MDCCCXVI. [Campden Gloucestershire] 1901 (Essex House Press, 50 copies).

Young, A. B. Unpublished songs by T. L. Peacock. N & Q 5 Dec 1908, 16 Jan 1909. Songs from ms plays.

Young, A. B. Ahrimanes by Thomas Love Peacock. MLR 4, 1909. Corrections by H. F. B. Brett-Smith in ibid.

Young, A. B. T. L. Peacock's Essay on fashionable literature. N & Q 2, 23 July 1910. Incomplete text of ms.

Plays, ed A. B. Young 1910 (Collections, *above*). 1st complete pbn of The dilettanti, The circle of Loda, The three doctors.

Letters to Edward Hookham and Percy B. Shelley, with fragments of unpublished manuscripts. Ed R. Garnett, Boston 1910 (priv ptd for Bibliophile Soc, 483 copies). Includes Ahrimanes, Calidore, 4 other fragmentary tales.

Van Doren, C. Life, 1911 (§2, *below*). Contains extract from new letter and other ms material priv ptd by H. Cole and R. Garnett.

Ingpen, R. Shelley in England: new facts and letters from the Shelley-Whitton papers. 1917. Contains details of Peacock's correspondence as Shelley's executor, including 2 letters by him and 3 letters to him.

A bill for the better promotion of oppression on the Sabbath day. Illustr L. Fraser, Plaistow 1926 (Curwen Press, 50 copies). Poem.

Halliford edn of Works, 1924–34 (Collections, *above*). Includes ms poetry and plays in vol 7; ms essays, unfinished novels, letters, diary etc in vol 8; extracts from cookery mss in vol 9 appendix 2. Contains 79 letters by Peacock and 10 letters to him.

Brett-Smith, H. F. B. The L'Estrange-Peacock correspondence. E & S 18, 1933.

The Athenians: being correspondence between Thomas Jefferson Hogg and his friends Thomas Love Peacock, Leigh Hunt, Percy Bysshe Shelley and others. Ed W. S. Scott 1943 (Golden Cockerel Press, 500 copies).

Shelley at Oxford: the early correspondence of P. B. Shelley with his friend T. J. Hogg, together with letters of Mary Shelley and T. L. Peacock, and a hitherto unpublished prose fragment by Shelley. Ed W. S. Scott 1944 (Golden Cockerel Press, 500 copies).

New Shelley letters. Ed W. S. Scott 1948. Includes correspondence with T. J. Hogg pbd in Scott's 2 previous vols, *above*.

Green, D. B. Two letters of Thomas Love Peacock. PQ 40, 1961.

Shelley and his circle 1773–1822. 8 vols to date Cambridge MA 1961–86. Vols 1–4 ed K. N. Cameron; vols 5–8 ed D. H. Reiman. Catalogue edn of mss in Carl H. Pforzheimer Lib (now NYPL), including Ahrimanes, shorter poems, verse translations, correspondence and East India Company examination paper on Ryotwar and zemindarry settlements.

The letters of Percy Bysshe Shelley. Ed F. L. Jones 2 vols Oxford 1964. Lists earlier printings of Shelley's letters to Peacock and prints most of Peacock's letters to Shelley in the notes.
Gallon, D. N. T. L. Peacock's later years: the evidence of unpublished letters. RES 20, 1969. Contains extracts from Peacock's letters to Lord Broughton. Corrections by P. Hawkins in ibid 21, 1970.
Johnson, D. The true history of the first Mrs Meredith and other lesser lives. New York 1972, London 1973 (adds index). Contains memorandum on Voltaire and 3 new letters to Peacock.
A dialogue on idealities. In H. Kjellin, Talkative banquets: a study of the Peacockian novels of talk. Stockholm 1974.
Joukovsky, N. A. Thomas Love Peacock on Sir Robert Peel: an unpublished satire. MP 73, 1975.
Joukovsky, N. A. A dialogue on idealities: an unpublished manuscript by Thomas Love Peacock. YES 7, 1977.
The letters of Mary Wollstonecraft Shelley. Ed B. T. Bennett 3 vols Baltimore 1980–8. Includes new letters to Peacock as well as new letter from Peacock to Lady Shelley in vol 3, appendix 1.
Joukovsky, N. A. Peacock before Headlong Hall, 1985 (§2, *below*). Contains extracts from Peacock's letters to Thomas Forster.
Mendelson, A. The Peacock-Meredith cookbook project: long-sundered manuscripts and unanswered questions. Biblion 2, 1993.
Joukovsky, N. A. Thomas Love Peacock's manuscript Poems of 1804. SB 47, 1994. Includes 4 new poems and new information about 24 others.
Madden, M. and L. Thomas Love Peacock, George and Mary Meredith, and John William Parker, Jr. Victorian Periodicals Rev 27, 1994. Contains new letter to Parker.
Joukovsky, N. A. Peacock and his 'pet politician': an unpublished Latin squib on the coalition against Palmerston. MLR 91, 1996.

§2

[Spedding, J.]. Tales by the author of Headlong Hall. Edinburgh Rev 68, Jan 1839; rptd in his Reviews and discussions, literary, political and historical, not relating to Bacon, 1879 (rev).
[Langley, H.]. Headlong Hall and Night-mare Abbey. US Mag and Democratic Rev, June 1845.
[Obituaries]. Examiner, 3 Feb 1866; Sunday Times, 4 Feb 1866; Daily Telegraph, 7 Feb 1866; Athenaeum, 10 Feb 1866; GM, Mar 1866.
[Hannay, J.]. Recent humourists: Aytoun, Peacock, Prout. North Br Rev 45, Sep 1866, rptd Living Age (Boston), Oct 1866, rptd Eclectic Mag (New York), Dec 1866.
Hutson, C. W. Peacock's Headlong Hall. Southern Mag (Baltimore), Feb 1873.
Smith, G. B. Thomas Love Peacock. Fortnightly Rev, Aug 1873, rptd in his Poets and novelists, 1875; tr Fr in Revue Britannique 1, 1874.
[Cole, H.]. Thomas Love Peacock: biographical notes from 1785 to 1862. [1874] (priv ptd, 10 copies). Copies BL, Bodleian.
Nicolls, E. Biographical notice in Works, ed H. Cole 1875 (Collections, *above*). Family memoir based largely on Cole's Biographical notes, [1874], *above*.
F. R. D. Two forgotten satires. Yale Literary Mag, Mar 1875.
Buchanan, R. Thomas Love Peacock: a personal reminiscence. New Quart Mag 4, Apr 1875, rptd Living Age (Boston), 17 July 1875, rptd in his A poet's sketchbook, 1883, rptd in his A look round literature, 1887.
[Pollock, W. H.]. Thomas Love Peacock. Temple Bar, May 1875, rptd Eclectic Mag (New York), July 1875.
G[osse], E. W. Thomas Love Peacock. London Soc, June 1875.
Collins, M. Thomas Love Peacock: versifier and humourist. St James's Mag, Sep 1875.
Saintsbury, G. Thomas Love Peacock. Macmillan's Mag, Apr 1886, rptd Living Age (Boston), 22 May 1886, rptd in his Essays in English literature 1780–1860, 1890, rptd in his Collected essays and papers, vol 2 1923.
[Abbott, E.]. Peacock. Temple Bar, May 1887, rptd Living Age (Boston), 11 June 1887.
Strachey, E. Recollections of Thomas Love Peacock. In Calidore and miscellanea, ed R. Garnett '1891' [1892].
Johnson, R. B. Thomas Love Peacock, satirist. Novel Rev, Aug 1892.
Stoddard, R. H. Thomas Love Peacock. In his Under the evening lamp, New York 1892.
Reichel, H. R. Thomas Love Peacock. Trans of Liverpool Welsh Nat Soc 15, 1899–1900.
Axon, W. E. A. The juvenile library. Library ns 2, 1901. Identifies and reprints Peacock's first pbd work.
Paul, H. The novels of Peacock. Nineteenth Cent, Apr 1903, rptd Living Age (Boston), 18 July 1903, rptd Eclectic Mag (New York), Sep 1903, rptd in his Stray leaves, 1906.
Young, A. B. The life and novels of Thomas Love Peacock. Norwich 1904. Univ of Freiburg inaugural dissertation, priv ptd.
Williams, C. Thomas Love Peacock. Library ns 7, 1906.
Boynton, H. W. Thomas Love Peacock. Atlantic Monthly, Dec 1906.
Young, A. B. T. L. Peacock: contributions to periodicals. N & Q 6 July 1907. Includes some mistaken attributions.
Young, A. B. T. L. Peacock and the overland route. N & Q 17 Aug 1907. Bibl data on Peacock's evidence before parliamentary committees.
Young, A. B. T. L. Peacock's literary remains. N & Q 20 Mar 1909.
Young, A. B. Thomas Love Peacock's plays. N & Q 10 July 1909.
Freeman, A. M. Thomas Love Peacock: a critical study. 1911. Suggests Peacock as probable author of Le mois Bubblose: or the A. S. S. Company, London Mag, Feb 1825.
Van Doren, C. The life of Thomas Love Peacock. 1911. 1st scholarly biography.
Vincent, L. H. Thomas Love Peacock. In his Dandies and men of letters, Boston 1913.
Butterworth, S. News for bibliophiles. Nation, 18 Dec 1913. Identifies Charles Abraham Elton as author of an essay On the poetry of Nonnus, London Mag, Oct, Nov 1822, attributed to Peacock by H. Cole and A. B. Young.
Hartley, L. C. Thomas Love Peacock. Manchester Quart 34, 1915.
Draper, J. W. The social satires of Thomas Love Peacock. MLN 33–4, 1918–19.
Gilson, J. P. [Letter to the editor]. The Times, 19 Mar 1923. Suggests Peacock as author of 2 pamphlets in defence of Sir Home Popham in 1804–5.
Brett-Smith, H. F. B. Biographical introd to Halliford edn of Works, vol 1 1934. Still the most reliable full-length biography.
White, N. I. In his The unextinguished hearth: Shelley and his contemporary critics, Durham NC 1938. Suggests Peacock as possible author of Dinner by the amateurs of vegetable diet (extracted from an old paper), London Mag, July 1821.
Robinson, E. Thomas Love Peacock: critic of scientific progress. Annals of Science 10, 1954. Attributes to Peacock a letter on iron steamers signed 'Cerberus' in Spectator, 9 Sep 1854. DNB authoritatively attributes this letter to Peacock's friend Macgregor Laird.
Fain, J. T. Peacock's essay on steam navigation. South Atlantic Bull 35, 1970. Confirms Peacock's authorship of article in Edinburgh Rev.
Joukovsky, N. A. The first printing of Peacock's The pool of the diving friar. N & Q 219, 1974.
Joukovsky, N. A. A mistaken Peacock attribution: A can of cream from Devon. Ibid 220, 1975.
Joukovsky, N. A. The composition of Peacock's Melincourt and the date of the Calidore fragment. ELN 13, 1975.
Joukovsky, N. A. The French translation of Peacock's Melincourt. N & Q 221, 1976.
Joukovsky, N. A. Peacock before Headlong Hall: a new look at his early years. Keats-Shelley Memorial Bull 36, 1985. Much new information about his family background and early life.

Joukovsky, N. A. A new 'little book' by Thomas Love Peacock. MP 85, 1988. Text and trn of his scatological Latin epigrams on Sir Robert Peel.

Joukovsky, N. A. The lost Greek anapests of Thomas Love Peacock. MP 89, 1992. Text and trn of his Greek anapestic ode on Christ. [NAJ]

Constantine Henry Phipps, Marquis of Normanby 1797–1863

The English in Italy. 3 vols 1825. Anon.

Matilda: a tale of the day. 1825 (anon), 2 vols 1825, 1825, 1 vol Philadelphia 1825, 2 vols London 1826 (4th edn); tr Fr 1826, Ger 1827.

REVIEWS: Monthly Rev n.s. 107 1825; [T. Hamilton] Blackwood's Mag Jan 1826; [W. S. Rose] Quart Rev 33 1826.

Historiettes: or tales of continental life, by the author of The English in Italy. 3 vols 1827.

The English in France, by the author of The English in Italy. 3 vols 1828, 1828, 2 vols Philadelphia 1829.

Yes and no: a tale of the day, by the author of Matilda. 2 vols 1828, 2 vols Philadelphia 1828; tr Fr 1830.

Clorinda, or the necklace of pearls: the tale of a bystander. In the Keepsake for 1829; tr Sp 1830.

The English at home, by the author of The English in Italy. 3 vols 1830, 2 vols New York 1830.

The contrast, by the author of Matilda, Yes and no etc. 3 vols 1832, 2 vols Philadelphia 1833.

Lord Normanby's farewell to Ireland. Dublin 1839.

A year of revolution, from a journal kept in Paris in 1848. 2 vols 1857; tr Fr 1858.

The Congress and the Cabinet. 1859, 1859 (5th edn); tr Fr 1860, Ital 1860.

An historical sketch of Louise de Bourbon, Duchess-Regent of Parma. 1861.

A vindication of the Duke of Modena from the charges of Mr Gladstone, from official documents. 1861, 1861; tr Fr 1862, Ital 1862.

The following of the above titles are attributed to Eyre Evans Crowe by DNB *and, more recently, by Wolff in his* Nineteenth-century fiction: a bibliographical guide, *5 vols New York 1981–6:* The English in Italy, Historiettes, The English in France *and* The English at home. *Several of the Marquis of Normanby's speeches were also pbd.* [PG]

Andrew Picken 1788–1833

§1

Tales and sketches of the West of Scotland, by Christopher Keelivine. Glasgow 1824, Edinburgh 1824. Mary Ogilvie rptd from above [1840?] (6th edn), illustr R. Cruikshank; tr Ger 1824.

The sectarian: or the Church and the Meeting-house. 3 vols 1829 (anon), 1834 (as Oldwood village: or the sectarian).

The dominie's legacy. 3 vols 1830, 1831, 2 vols Philadelphia 1833.

Travels and researches of eminent English missionaries, including an historical sketch of the progress and present state of some of the principal Protestant missions of late years. 1830.

The Club book: being original tales etc by various authors, edited by the author of the Dominie's legacy. 3 vols 1831, 1831, 2 vols New York 1831, 1836. Picken contributed The deer-stalkers of Glenskiach, Eisenbach, The three Kearneys, all of which were rptd in the Romancist and Novelist's Lib 1840–1. The other contributors included Galt, Hogg, Cunningham, James, Jerdan and Moir.

The Canadas as they at present commend themselves to the enterprize of emigrants, colonists and capitalists, compiled and condensed from original documents furnished by John Galt. 1832, 1836.

Traditionary stories of old families, and legendary illustrations of family history, with notes historical and biographical. 2 vols 1833, 1 vol Philadelphia 1833.

Waltham: a novel. 1833, 1835.

The Black Watch. 3 vols 1834, 2 vols Philadelphia 1835.

Picken also wrote A life of John Wesley, *tales for* Fraser's Mag *and a narrative entitled* Experience of life, *which remains unpbd.*

§2

Brown, R. Memoirs of Ebenezer Picken, poet, and of Andrew Picken, novelist. In Paisley Burns Club publications, Paisley 1879. [PG]

Mary Pilkington, née Hopkins 1766–1839

Bibliographies

Summers, M. In his A Gothic bibliography, [1941].

§1

Miscellaneous poems. 2 vols London and Cambridge 1796, London 1799.

Edward Barnard, or merit exalted: containing the history of the Edgerton family. 1797; tr Fr 1812.

Obedience rewarded and prejudice conquered: or the history of Mortimer Lascells. 1797.

A mirror for the female sex: historical beauties for young ladies. 1798, 1799, Hartford CT 1799, Dublin 1800 (as Historical beauties for young ladies), London 1804, 1811.

Tales of the cottage: or stories, moral and amusing. Written on the plan of that celebrated work, Les Veillées du château by Madame Genlis. 1798, 1799, 1800, Philadelphia 1800, London 1803, 1807, 1816; tr Fr 1804.

Tales of the Hermitage: written for the instruction and amusement of the rising generation. 1798, 1799, 1800, Philadelphia 1800, New York 1802, London 1805, 1809, 1811, 1815, New Haven CT 1820; tr Ital 1805.

Biography for boys: or characteristic histories. 1799, 1800, Dublin 1800, London 1805, 1808, Philadelphia 1809, London 1815.

Biography for girls: or moral and instructive examples. 1799, 1800 (3rd edn), 1806, 1809, Philadelphia 1809.

Henry or the foundling, to which are added the prejudiced parent, or the virtuous daughter: tales calculated to improve the mind and morals of youth. 1799.

The spoiled child: or indulgence counteracted. 1799.

The Asiatic princess. 2 vols 1800.

Edward: a tale for young persons. 1800. Adapted from Dr J. Moore's Edward: various views of human nature, 1796.

New tales of the castle: or the noble emigrants. 1800, Dublin 1801, London 1803, 1809, 1814; tr Fr 1804.

Marvellous adventures: or the vicissitudes of a cat. 1802, Baltimore 1814.

Mentorial tales for the instruction of young ladies just leaving school. 1802, Philadelphia 1803, 1811.

Memoirs of celebrated female characters. 1804, 1811.

Crimes and characters: or the new foundling. 3 vols 1805.

Violet vale: or Saturday night. Dublin 1806.

The calendar, or monthly recreations: chiefly consisting of dialogues between an aunt and her nieces. 1807.

The disgraceful effects of falsehood, and the fruits of early indulgence: exemplified in the histories of Percival Pembroke and Augustus Fitzhue. 1807.

Ellen: heiress of the castle. 3 vols 1807.

The history of Edward Mandewill. 1808.

The ill-fated mariner: or Richard the runaway. 1809.

Sinclair: or the mysterious orphan. 4 vols 1809.

Parental care producing practical virtue: or youthful errors conquered by judicious advice. Characteristic incidents, drawn from real life: or the history of the Rockinghams. 1810.

A reward for attentive studies: or moral and entertaining stories. London and Stroud [1810?].
Original poems. London and Cambridge 1811.
The history of the Rockinghams: interspersed with a description of the inhabitants of Russia and a variety of interesting anecdotes of Peter the Great. 1812.
Memoirs of Mrs Pilkington. [1812.]
Margate!!! or sketches amply descriptive of that celebrated place of resort, with its environs. 1813.
The sorrows of Caesar: or the adventures of a foundling dog. 1813.
The novice, or the heir of Montgomery Castle: a novel by Matthew Moral Esq. 3 vols 1814.
Celebrity, or the unfortunate choice: a novel. 3 vols 1815.
The shipwreck: or misfortune the inspirer of virtuous sentiments. 1819.

Attributed works

Delia: a pathetic and interesting tale. 4 vols 1790, 2 vols Dublin 1790.
Rosina: a novel. 5 vols 1793, 3 vols Dublin 1793.
The subterranean cavern, or memoirs of Antoinette de Montflorance. 4 vols 1798, 2 vols Dublin 1805.
The accusing spirit, or De Courcy and Eglantine: a romance. 4 vols 1802.

The above 4 titles, attributed to Miss Pilkington in a Minerva Lib catalogue of 1814, are probably the work of another author.

The force of example: or the history of Henry and Caroline. 1797. Listed in ESTC as attributed to Mrs Pilkington by Algar.
The budget, or moral and entertaining fragment: representing the punishment of vice and the reward of virtue. 1799. Attributed to Mrs Mary Pilkington by National Union catalogue.
Fitzherbert: a novel. 1808. Only listed in Summers.

Mary Pilkington also compiled a number of other school books and didactic works, including an abridgement of Goldsmith's History of the earth, *several devotional works, and a translation (selection) of J. F. Marmontel's* Moral tales.

For a listing of reviews and notices of M. Pilkington's works, see Ward (1979, 1972). [PG]

Elizabeth Plunkett, née Gunning 1769–1823

Bibliographies

Block, A. In his The English novel 1740–1850, 1961.
Summers, M. In his A Gothic Bibliography, [1941].

§1

The packet. 4 vols 1794, 2 vols Dublin 1794.
REVIEW: Br Critic Nov 1794.
Lord Fitzhenry. 3 vols 1794, 2 vols Dublin 1794.
REVIEWS: Br Critic Dec 1794; Critical Rev Dec 1794.
The foresters [altered from the Fr]. 4 vols 1796, 2 vols Dublin 1796.
REVIEW: Br Critic Oct 1796.
The orphans of Snowdon. 3 vols 1797.
REVIEW: Critical Rev Dec 1797.
The gypsy countess. 4 vols 1799, 2 vols Dublin 1799. Tr Fr 1802 (as La Bohémienne par infortune, ou la comtesse d'Ossington).
REVIEWS: Br Critic Nov 1799; Critical Rev Dec 1799; Monthly Rev May 1800.
The village Library; for the use of young persons. 1802.
REVIEWS: Critical Rev Oct 1802, May 1803; Monthly Rev Feb 1803.
Family stories; or evenings at my grandmother's, intended for young persons of eight years old. 2 vols 1802; tr Fr 2 vols 1803 (as Contes de famille, ou les soirées de ma grand'mère).
REVIEW: Critical Rev Aug 1802.
A sequel to family stories. 1802.
The exile of Erin. 3 vols 1808, Alexandria VA 1809.
Dangers through life; or, the victim of seduction. 3 vols 1810.
REVIEW: Critical Rev Apr 1810.
The man of fashion: a tale of modern times. 2 vols 1815.
Memoirs of Madame de Barneveldt. 2 vols 1795. Translated from the Fr.
REVIEWS: Analytical Rev Nov 1795; Br Critic Nov 1795; Monthly Rev Nov 1795.
The farmer's boy. 4 vols 1802. Translated from the Fr of Deuray Dumesuil.
The heir apparent. 3 vols 1802. Rev version of a novel by Susannah Minifie Gunning.
REVIEWS: Critical Rev Aug 1802; Monthly Rev Feb 1803.
Malvina. 1803. Translated from the Fr of Mme Cottin.
Conversations on the plurality of worlds. 1808. Translated from the Fr of Fontenelle.
The wife with two husbands. 1803. Translated from the Fr of R. G. Guilbert. Play.
Sentimental anecdotes. 1811. Translated from the Fr of Baroness de Montolieu.

§2

Literary memoirs of living authors of Great Britain. 2 vols 1798, New York 1970 (facs).
A biographical dictionary of the living authors of Great Britain and Ireland. 1816, Detroit 1966 (facs).
GM Aug 1823. Obituary.
Todd, Janet (ed). Dictionary of British women writers 1660–1800. 1985.

In 1791 Elizabeth Gunning (Plunkett) was at the centre of a society scandal, which was discussed at times throughout the year in columns in GM, London Chron, *and* Morning Post, *as well as in a number of Horace Walpole's letters to the Barry sisters. Susannah Gunning's pam on the subject,* A letter from Mrs Gunning, addressed to his Grace The Duke of Argyll, *was reviewed in periodicals such as* Analytical Rev, Monthly Rev *and* Critical Rev, *as was Essex Bowen's* A Statement of facts, in answer to Mrs Gunning's Letter, Addressed to His Grace the Duke of Argyll. *At least two anonymous writers also pbd pams on the subject, and it is discussed at length in General John Gunning's* Memoirs. *Susannah Gunning's novel* The memoirs of Mary *is loosely based on the incident, and Elizabeth Gunning repeatedly makes oblique references to the scandal in* The packet. [PP]

John William Polidori 1795–1821

Bibliographies

Summers, M. In his A Gothic bibliography, [1941].

§1

On the punishment of death. The Pamphleteer vol 8 1813.
An essay upon the source of positive pleasure. 1818.
Ximenes: a 'dramatic action' in five acts, the wreath and other poems. 1819.
The vampyre by the Right Honourable Lord Byron [or rather J. W. Polidori]. 1819, re-issued as The vampyre: a tale 1819 (anon), Paris 1821, rptd as The vampyre: a tale related by Lord Byron to Dr Polidori 1830, rptd as by Lord Byron [or rather by J. W. Polidori], illustr F. Gilbert 1884, preface by D. K. Adams and illustr H. E. Spencer, Pasadena CA 1968, introd by R. Ash Tring, Herts 1973; tr Fr 1819, Ger 1819, 1820, Ital (and ascribed to Byron), 1829. Also pbd in NMM Apr 1819, and attributed by the publisher to Byron; subsequently repudiated by him and claimed by Polidori. Preface of 1st edn contains an 'extract of a letter, containing an account of Lord Byron's residence in the island of Mitylene', which has been ascribed to John Mitford, R. N. (1782–1831). See N & Q 3rd ser vol 7, 201. Marschner's opera based on The vampire.
Ernestus Berchtold: or the modern Oedipus. A tale. 1819. Anon.
The diary of Dr John William Polidori, 1816, relating to Byron, Shelley, etc. Ed W. M. Rossetti 1911.
Sketches of his travels by J. W. P. pbd with text by R. Bridgens in 1821.

Attributed works

DNB has:

The fall of the angels: a sacred poem. 1821 (anon) and re-issued with author's name the same year.

For a listing of reviews and notices of Polidori's works, see Ward (1972).

§2

Rieger, J. Polidori and the genesis of Frankenstein. Stud in Eng Lit 1500–1900 3 1963.

MacDonald, D. L. Poor Polidori: a critical biography of the author of The vampyre. 1991. [CF]

Robert Pollok 1798–1838

See col 419.

John Poole 1786?–1872

See col 1982.

Anna Maria Porter 1780–1832

Bibliographies

Summers, M. In his A Gothic bibliography, [1941].

§1

Artless tales. 2 vols 1793–5. Anon.

Walsh Colville, or a young man's first entrance into life: a novel. 1797, 1833, New York 1974.

Octavia. 3 vols 1798; tr Fr [1799?].

The lake of Killarney: a novel. 3 vols 1804, 2 vols Philadelphia 1810, 1 vol London 1838, 1853, 1857 (as Rose de Blaquière: or the lake of Killarney).

A sailor's friendship; and A soldier's love. 2 vols 1805, Baltimore 1810.

The Hungarian brothers. 3 vols 1807, 1808, 1814, 1819, 2 vols Exeter NH 1825, 1 vol Exeter NH 1827, 1 vol London 1831 [new preface], 1832, Exeter NH 1836, London 1839, 1847, 1856, 3 vols 1870, 1872; tr Fr 1818.

Don Sebastian, or the house of Braganza: an historical romance. 4 vols 1809, 2 vols Exeter NH 1835, 4 vols London 1838, 1 vol [1850?]; tr Fr 1820, Ger 1821.

Ballad, romances and other poems. 1811, Philadelphia 1816.

The recluse of Norway. 4 vols 1814, 4 vols New York 1814, 2 vols Philadelphia 1815, 4 vols 1816, 1 vol Washington 1834, 1852; tr Fr 1815.

Tales of pity on fishing, shooting and hunting, intended to inculcate in the mind of youth sentiments of humanity toward the brute creation. 1814.

The Knight of Saint John: a romance. 3 vols 1817, 1817, 2 vols New York 1817, 3 vols London 1818, 1 vol 1851, 1852, 3 vols 1853; tr Fr 1818.

The fast of St Magdalen: a romance. 3 vols 1818, 1819, 2 vols Boston 1819, New York 1819; tr Fr 1819.

The village of Mariendorpt: a tale. 4 vols 1821, 2 vols Boston 1821; tr Fr 1821.

Roche-Blanche, or the hunters of the Pyrenees: a romance. 3 vols 1822, 2 vols Boston 1822; tr Fr 1822.

Honor O'Hara: a novel. 3 vols 1826, 2 vols New York 1827; tr Fr 1827.

Tales round a winter's hearth, by Jane and Anna Maria Porter. 2 vols 1826. Anna Maria contributed Glenrowan, Lord Howth, Jeannie Halliday. Jane Porter wrote the remainder.

Coming out: and the field of the forty footsteps. By Jane and Anna Maria Porter. 3 vols 1828. Vols 1 and 2 comprise Coming out by A. M. Porter, vol 3 consists of J. Porter's The field of the forty footsteps.

The barony. 3 vols 1830, New York 1830.

Attributed or spurious works

Gilmour: ou le dernier Lockinge, roman historique des deux roses d'Angleterre, par A. M. Porter [or rather an anonymous writer]. Traduit de l'anglais par J. Cohen. 3 vols 1829.

The tuileries: an historical romance. 1831. (Summers).

For a listing of reviews and notices of A. M. Porter's works, see Ward (1979, 1972, 1977).

§2

Jerdan, W. National portrait gallery. 1834.

Elwood, A. K. In her Memoirs of the literary ladies of England vol 2, 1843.

Vaughan, H. From Anne to Victoria. 1931.

De La Mare, W. In his Material of fiction, 1933.

Jones, A. H. In her Ideas and innovations: best sellers of Jane Austen's age, 1986, ch 5. [CF]

Jane Porter 1776–1850

Bibliographies

Summers, M. In his A Gothic bibliography, [1941].

§1

Thaddeus of Warsaw. 4 vols 1803, 1804, 1805, 1806, 1809, 2 vols Boston 1809, 4 vols New York 1809, 1 vol New York 1810, 4 vols London 1812, 1816, 1817, 2 vols New York 1817, Philadelphia 1817, 1818, 1819, New York 1820, Battleborough VT 1824, 3 vols London 1826, 2 vols Exeter NH 1829, 1 vol London 1831 (illustr, rev and new introd by the author), Paris 1831, New York [1831?], 1832, Exeter NH 1832, London 1835, Exeter NH 1839, 1845 (illustr and rev), 2 vols Hartford CT 1845, Chicago [1845?], 2 vols Hartford CT 1848, 1 vol London 1853, 1854, New York 1857, 1860, Philadelphia 1868, 1880, New York 1881, 1882, 1884, 1886, 1898, 191–?; tr Fr 1809, Ger 1825.

A sketch of the campaigns of Count Alexander Suwarrow Rymnikski [*sic*]. 1804.

Aphorisms of Sir Philip Sidney. 2 vols 1807.

The Scottish chiefs: a romance. 5 vols London and New York 1810, 3 vols Philadelphia 1810, 1811, 2 vols Battleborough VT 1814, London 1816, Philadelphia 1819, 2 vols Hartford CT 1823, 4 vols London 1825, Exeter NH 1827, 2 vols London 1831, 3 vols Exeter NH 1834, 3 vols Hartford CT 1834, 2 vols London 1835 (rev, illustr, new introd, notes), [1840] (rev, with plates), 1840, Dublin 1841, 3 vols Hartford CT 1846, 2 vols London 1850 (rev), 1 vol 1853, 1854, [1855], 1857, Halifax 1859, London 1860, [1860], Halifax 1860, London 1862, Halifax 1862, New York 1866, Philadelphia 1869, London 1870, Philadelphia 1870, London 1879, 1880, 1882, 1886, New York 1891 (rev), Chicago 1899, London 1900 (illus), New York [1903?], London 1904, New York 191–?; ed K. D. Wiggin and N. A. Smith London 1921, New York 1921, 1927, London 1956; tr Fr 1814.

The pastor's fireside: a novel. 4 vols 1817, 1817, 2 vols New York 1818, London 1821, 1822, 2 vols 1832, 1846, 1849, 1 vol 1856, 1880; tr Fr 1817, Ger 1822.

Duke Christian of Luneburg [*sic*]: or tradition [*sic*] from the Hartz. 3 vols 1824, 1824, 2 vols Boston 1824; tr Fr 1824, Ger 1825.

Tales round a winter hearth. By Jane and Anna Maria Porter. 2 vols 1826. 3 tales by Anna Maria Porter: the rest by Jane Porter.

Coming out; and The field of forty footsteps, by Jane and Anna Maria Porter. 3 vols 1828, New York 1828, 2 vols London 1831. Anna Maria wrote Coming out (vols 1 and 2); Jane wrote The field of the forty footsteps which makes up vol 3.

The following works by J. Porter were produced but not pbd:

Switzerland: a play (Feb 1819) and Owen, Prince of Powys: a play (Jan 1822).

Young hearts: a novel by a recluse; with a preface by Miss Jane Porter. 3 vols 1834.

Of doubtful attribution

The two princes of Persia: addressed to youth by I. [*sic*] Porter. 1801. Ward and NSTC attribute to J. Porter.

Bannockburn, a novel. London and Edinburgh 3 vols 1821 (anon), 2 vols Philadelphia 1822. A sequel to The Scottish chiefs. NSTC attributes to J. Porter.

Sir Edward Seaward's narrative of his shipwreck and consequent discovery of certain islands in the Caribbean Sea; with a detail of many extraordinary and highly interesting events of his life from 1733 to 1749. By W. O. Porter. Ed Jane Porter 1831, 3 vols New York 1831, 1 vol London 1832, 2 vols 1841, 1 vol abridged 1852, 1856, London and Edinburgh 1878, London and New York 1879 (introd by W. H. G. Kingston), 1883, 1884. Usually attributed to Jane Porter, or to William Ogilvie Porter.

For a listing of reviews and notices of J. Porter's works, see Ward (1972, 1977).

§2

Jerdan, W. National portrait gallery. 1834.

Miss Jane Porter. Fraser's Mag Apr 1835.

Elwood, A. K. Memoirs of the literary ladies of England. 1843.

Hall, A. M. Memoirs of Jane Porter. Art Jnl 2 1850.

Maginn, W. In his A gallery of illustrious characters, ed W. Bates [1873].

Wilson, M. A romantic novelist. In her These were Muses, 1924.

Vaughan, H. From Anne to Victoria. 1931.

Domhnall Ó Grianna. Jane Porter: historical novelist. 1937.

Jones, A. H. Ideas and innovations: best sellers of Jane Austen's age. New York 1986, ch 4.

Joukovsky, N. A. Jane Porter's first novel: the evidence of an unpublished letter. N & Q 235 Mar 1990. [CF]

Ann Radcliffe, née Ward 1764–1823

Common-place book and journal for May–Nov 1822 in Boston Public Lib; one letter held at Princeton.

Bibliographies

Summers, M. In his A Gothic bibliography, [1941].

Spector, R. D. In The English Gothic, Westport CT 1984.

Frank, F. S. In Guide to the Gothic: an annotated bibliography of criticism, Metuchen NJ 1984.

Frank, F. S. In The first Gothics: a critical guide to the English Gothic novel, New York 1987.

Collections

Works. 13 vols 1797–1811.

Poems. 1815, 1816, 1845. A collection of the poetical pieces in the novels.

Novels, with a memoir by Scott. 1824.

Poetical works. 2 vols 1834.

Novels. [1877.]

Tales of mystery. Ed G. Saintsbury 1891. Selections from Mrs Radcliffe, Lewis and Maturin.

In Anglistica and Americana. Hildesheim 1971 (facs). Novels, Gaston de Blondeville and A journey made in the summer of 1794.

In Gothic novels. New York 1972–4 (facs). Novels and Gaston de Blondeville.

Novels. 1987. (Folio Soc.)

§1

The Castles of Athlin and Dunbayne: a Highland story. 1789 (anon), 1793, Philadelphia 1796, Boston 1797, London 1799, 1811, 1821, 1824, 1826, 1827, 1836 etc; New York 1970 (facs); ed D. Varma, New York 1972 (Gothic Novels ser, facs); 1987 (Folio Soc); ed A. Milbank, Oxford 1995 (WCp); tr Fr 1797.

REVIEWS: Scots Mag 51, Apr 1789; Critical Rev 68, Sep 1789; Monthly Rev 81, Dec 1789.

A Sicilian romance. 2 vols 1790 (anon), 1792, Philadelphia 1795, London 1796, 1809, 1818, 1821, 1 vol 1826, 1830 etc; ed R. D. Spector and M. Tucker 2 vols New York 1971 (facs); ed D. Varma, New York 1972 (Gothic Novels ser, facs); 1987 (Folio Soc); ed A. Milbank, Oxford 1993 (Wcp); tr Ger 1792, Fr 1797 etc, Sp 1819, Rus 1819, Ital 1883, 1889.

REVIEWS: Monthly Rev n.s. 3, Sep 1790; Scots Mag 52, Sep 1790; Critical Rev n.s. 1, Mar 1791.

The romance of the forest, interspersed with some pieces of poetry. 3 vols 1791 (anon), 1792, 2 vols Dublin 1792, 3 vols London 1794, 1795, Boston 1795, London 1796, 1799, 2 vols Dublin 1801, London 1806, 1 vol 1810, 1816, 3 vols 1820, 1824, 1825, 2 vols Boston 1835, 1 vol 1846, Philadelphia 1872; ed D. M. Rose 1904; 3 vols New York 1970 (facs); ed D. Varma, New York 1974 (Gothic Novels ser, facs); 1987 (Folio Soc); ed C. Chard, Oxford 1986 (WCp); tr Ger 1793, Fr 1796 etc, 1869, Ital 1871.

REVIEWS: Critical Rev 4, Apr 1792; Monthly Rev 8, May 1792; Scots Mag 54, June 1792.

The mysteries of Udolpho: a romance, interspersed with some pieces of poetry. 4 vols 1794, 1794, 3 vols Dublin 1794, 4 vols 1795, Boston 1795, Worcester MA 1795, London 1799, 3 vols Dublin 1800, 4 vols London 1803, 1806 etc, 1824 (with a memoir), 3 vols Philadelphia 1828, London 1844; ed D. M. Rose 2 vols 1903; ed R. A. Freeman 2 vols [1931] (EL); ed B. Dobrée, Oxford 1966 (WCp 1980); tr Ger 1795, Fr 1797, 1808 etc, 1864, 1869, 1984, Rus 1818.

REVIEWS: Critical Rev 11, Aug 1794; GM 62, Sep 1794; Monthly Rev 15, Nov 1794.

A journey made in the summer of 1794 through Holland and the western frontier of Germany. 1795, Dublin 1795; tr Fr 1795.

REVIEWS: Critical Rev 14, July 1795; Monthly Rev 18, Nov 1795.

The Italian, or the confessional of the black penitents: a romance. 3 vols 1797, 1797, 2 vols New York 1797, Dublin 1797, 3 vols London 1811, 1824 etc; illustr P. Ross 1956 (as The confessional of the black penitents); ed D. Varma, New York 1974 (Gothic Novels ser, facs); 1987 (Folio Soc); ed F. Garber, Oxford 1968 (WCp 1981); tr Fr 1794 etc, Ger 1797, 1801, Sp 1836, Ital [1944].

REVIEWS: Monthly Rev 22, Mar 1797; Critical Rev 23, June 1798.

Gaston de Blondeville, or the Court of Henry III keeping festival in Ardenne: a romance; St Alban's Abbey: a metrical tale; with some poetical pieces, [and] a memoir of the author [by T. N. Talfourd] with extracts from her journals. 4 vols 1826, Philadelphia 1826, 2 vols 1834, 1839. Vols 3–4 of the first edn have the half-title Posthumous works of Mrs Radcliffe, and were rptd (in part) as Poetical works 2 vols 1834; tr Fr 1826.

REVIEW: Scots Mag n.s. 18 1826.

On the supernatural in poetry. NMM and Literary Jnl 16 1826.

Summers lists many spurious attributions, adaptations etc. Mary Ann Radcliffe's Manfroné *and the novels of Eliza Radcliffe were sometimes confused with the work of Ann Radcliffe to their authors' financial advantage. On Fr and Ger false attributions, see A. A. S. Wieten,* Mrs Radcliffe: her relation towards romanticism; with an appendix on the novels falsely ascribed to her. *Amsterdam 1926.*

§2

Barbauld, L. In The British Novelists vol 43. 1810.

Mrs Radcliffe. NMM 9 1823. Obit.

Scott, Sir W. Mrs Ann Radcliffe. In The lives of the novelists, Edinburgh 1825.

Lefèvre-Deumier, J. Célébrités anglaises: Ann Radcliffe. Paris 1895.

Godey's Lady's Book and Amer Mag 45 1852.

Lang, A. Mrs Radcliffe's novels. In his Adventures among books, 1905. First pbd in Cornhill Mag July 1900.

Summers, M. A great mistress of romance: Ann Radcliffe. Trans Royal Soc of Lit [1917]; rptd in his Essays in petto, 1928.

MacIntyre, C. F. Ann Radcliffe in relation to her time. New Haven CT 1920.

Arnaud, P. Un document inédit: le contrat des Mysteries of Udolpho. Études Anglaises 20 1967.

Arnaud, P. Ann Radcliffe et le fantastique: essai de psychobiographie. Paris 1976. [AMbk]

Regina Maria Roche, née Dalton 1764?–1845

Bibliographies

Summers, M. In his A Gothic bibliography, [1941].
Schroeder, N. Regina Maria Roche, popular novelist 1789–1834: the Rochean canon. Bibl Soc of America 73 1979.

§1

The Vicar of Lansdowne: or country quarters. 2 vols 1789, 1800, Baltimore 1802; tr Fr 1789, Ger 1790.
The maid of the hamlet: a tale. 2 vols 1793, 1800 (2nd edn), 1 vol Boston 1801, 1 vol Dublin 1802, 2 vols London 1821, 1833; tr Fr 1801.
The children of the Abbey: a tale. 4 vols 1796, 1797 (2nd edn), 1798 (3rd edn), 2 vols Cork 1798, New York 1798, 4 vols London 1800 (4th edn), Philadelphia 1800, London 1805 (5th edn), 2 vols New York 1805, Dublin 1809, 4 vols London 1810 (6th edn), Philadelphia 1812, 3 vols New York 1816, 4 vols Philadelphia 1818, 2 vols Hartford CT 1822, 4 vols London 1825 (10th edn), Glasgow 1826, 3 vols Exeter 1827, Exeter NH 1834, 1 vol London 1843, 1862, Philadelphia 1881, London 1882, New York 1895; tr Fr 1797, 1801, Sp 1845, 1868.
Clermont: a tale. 4 vols 1798, Dublin 1799, Philadelphia 1802, London 1836; ed D. P. Varma 1968; tr Fr 1798.
Nocturnal visit: a tale. 4 vols 1800, Philadelphia 1801, introd F. G. Atkinson 1977; tr Fr 1801, Ger 1801.
Alvondown Vicarage: a novel. 2 vols 1807. Anon.
The discarded son, or the haunt of the banditti: a tale. 5 vols 1807, 2 vols New York 1807, 5 vols London 1825; tr Fr 1820.
The houses of Osma and Almeria, or the Convent of St Ildefonso: a tale. 3 vols 1810, 1 vol Philadelphia 1810.
The Monastery of St Columb, or the atonement: a novel. 5 vols 1812, 1813, 2 vols New York and Philadelphia 1813.
Trecothick Bower: or the lady of the West Country; a tale. 3 vols Philadelphia and Boston '1814' [1813].
The Munster cottage boy: a tale. 4 vols [1819].
Bridal of Dunamore, and Lost and won: two tales. 3 vols 1823; tr Fr 1824.
The tradition of the castle: or scenes in the Emerald Isle. 4 vols '1824' [1823]; tr Fr 1824.
The castle chapel: a romantic tale. 3 vols 1825; tr Fr 1825.
Contrast. 3 vols 1828, 2 vols New York 1828.
The nun's picture. 3 vols 1836, 1843.

Attributed or spurious works

London tales: or reflective portraits. 2 vols 1814. Anon.
Plain tales, by Mrs Roche. 2 vols 1814.
Anna, or Edinburgh: a novel. 2 vols 1815.
The above 3 titles were almost certainly written by another author, styling herself as Mrs Roche. See also Schroeder, above.
For a listing of reviews and notices of Roche's work, see Ward (1972, 1979).
[CC]

Mrs Ross

§1

The cousins, or a woman's promise and a lover's vow: a novel. 3 vols 1811. Anon.
The marchioness!!! or the matured enchantress, by lady–. 3 vols 1813.
The strangers of Lindenfeldt, or who is my father? a novel. 3 vols 1813.
The modern calypso, or widow's captivation: a novel. 4 vols 1814.
The family estate, or lost and won: a novel. 3 vols 1815.
Paired – not matched, or matrimony in the nineteenth century: a novel. 4 vols 1815, 2 vols Philadelphia 1816.
The balance of comfort, or the old maid and married woman: a novel. 3 vols '1817' [1816], 1817 (2nd edn), 1817 (3rd edn), 2 vols New York 1817, 3 vols London 1818 (4th edn); tr Fr 1818.

Attributed works

The bachelor and the married man: or the equilibrium of 'the balance of comfort'. 3 vols 1817 (anon), 2 vols New York 1818.
The physiognomist: a novel. 3 vols 1818, 2 vols New York 1820.
Hesitation: or to marry or not to marry? 3 vols 1819, 2 vols New York 1819.
Tales of the imagination. 3 vols 1820.
The woman of genius. 3 vols 1821–2.
Fire-side scenes. 3 vols 1825.
These 6 titles, though attributed in most catalogues to Mrs Ross, form a separate sequence, and are perhaps the work of Elizabeth B. Lester. [PG]

Charles Rowcroft 1798–1856

§1

Tales of the colonies: or, the adventures of an emigrant. (Serialised in the British Queen and Statesman Mag 8 Oct 1842–24 June 1843.) 3 vols 1843, 1845 (4th edn), 1847 (5th edn), 1858 (7th edn), 1875, 1884; abridged as The Australian Crusoes, Philadelphia 1853, London 1856, 1860, New York 1877, London 1886 (abridged). Later edns employ a variety of titles i.e. Tales of Australia 1886, The perils and adventures of Mr William Thornley nd, 1916.
The man without a profession. 3 vols 1844.
The bushranger of Van Diemen's land. (Originally pbd Hood's Mag May 1845–Sep 1846.) 3 vols 1846, New York 1846, rptd as The bush ranger: or, Mark Brandon the convict, London 1869; rptd as Brandon the bushranger, 1914, 1929.
Currency and railways: being suggestions for the remedy of the present railway embarrassments. 1846.
Fanny, the little milliner: or, the rich and the poor. (Originally pbd in 12 monthly numbers Dec 1844–Nov 1845.) 1846, New York 1849, London 1853.
Tales of the colonies: or, the adventures of an emigrant. Second ser. 3 vols 1846.
Chronicles of 'the Fleet prison'. From the papers of the late Alfred Seedy Esq. (Serialised in Hood's Mag May 1845–Feb 1846.) 3 vols 1847, rptd as Recollections of the Fleet prison 1 vol 1860, 1861.
The triumph of woman: a Christmas story. 1848.
Evadne, or an empire in its fall. 3 vols 1850, rptd 1 vol 1861 as A Roman maiden.
An emigrant in search of a colony. 1851, 1861.
Confessions of an Etonian. (Originally pbd in shorter form as Tick; or memoirs of an Old Eton Boy, NMM Jan–Dec 1848.) 3 vols 1852, 1860, 1 vol 1861, 1 vol 1868.
Footprints in foreign lands. 1864.

Contributions to periodicals

Rowcroft assumed the editorship of Hood's Mag and Comic Misc *following the death of Thomas Hood on 3 May 1845 until Dec 1845, and perhaps later. The indexes of* Hood's Mag *for this period list Rowcroft as the author of 20 items of verse, 12 items of prose, numerous reviews and verses, and 2 serialised novels. He also wrote for the* Courier *and the* British Queen and Statesman, *both of which he may have edited for a short time.*

§2

Zinkhan, E. J. Charles Rowcroft: information, corrections, additions. Australian Literary Stud 11 (2) Oct 1983. [LA]

William Pitt Scargill (Unitarian Minister) 1787–1836

An essay on war. nd.
Essays on various subjects. 1815.
Moral discourses principally intended for young people. 1816.

Blue-stocking Hall: a work of fiction designed to inculcate the various duties of domestic life. 3 vols 1827, 2 vols New York 1828, 3 vols London 1829.
Truckleborough Hall: a novel. 3 vols 1827.
Penelope, or love's labour lost: a novel. 3 vols 1828, 1829.
Rank and talent: a novel. 3 vols 1829, 1835, 1 vol 1856.
Recollections of a Blue-coat boy: or a view of Christ's hospital. 1829.
Tales of a briefless barrister. 3 vols 1829, 1831.
Tales of my time. 3 vols 1829.
The peace of the country: a letter to the Freeholders of Suffolk on ... the election of two independent representatives. 1830, 1830.
Atherton: a tale of the last century. 3 vols 1831.
The usurer's daughter, by a contributor to Blackwood's Mag. 3 vols 1832, 1 vol 1853.
A reformer's reasons for voting for Earl Jermyn. [1832].
The Puritan's grave. 3 vols 1833, 1 vol 1846.
The autobiography of a Dissenting Minister. 1834 (anon), 1835, 1835, 1835 (4th edn), 1843 (6th edn).
Provincial sketches. 1835.
The widow's offering: a selection of tales and essays. Ed M. A. Scargill 2 vols 1837, 1856 (unauthorised, as The English sketch book), 1857 (authorised 2nd edn, as Essays and sketches).

Attributed works

Truth: a novel, by the author of Nothing. 3 vols 1826. No book entitled 'Nothing' can be located.
Elizabeth Evanshaw, the sequel of 'Truth': a novel. 3 vols 1827.
Scargill contributed to NMM *and the* Atlas *newspaper regularly.* [AM]

Honoria Scott

Amatory tales of Spain, France, Switzerland and the Mediterranean: containing the fair Andalusian, Rosolia of Palermo, and the Maltese portrait: interspersed with pieces of original poetry. 4 vols 1810.
Sketch of the life and character of Her Royal Highness the Princess Amelia. 1810.
The vale of Clyde: a tale. 2 vols 1810.
A winter in Edinburgh, or the Russian brothers: a novel. 3 vols 1810, 1822.
Strathmay, or scenes in the North illustrative of Scottish manners etc: a tale. 2 vols Edinburgh 1813, 1814 (as The Castle of Strathmay, or scenes in the North illustrative of Scottish manners and society: a tale).
Honoria Scott may or may not have been the pseudonym of Mrs Susan Fraser, author of Camilla de Florian, and other poems, *1809, and* Poems, *1811.* [PG]

Lady Caroline Lucy Scott, née Douglas 1784–1857

BL holds an agreement of Scott's with publishers R. Bentley; the Nat Lib of Scotland holds a letter from her to Sir Walter Scott.
A marriage in high life. Edited by the authoress of Flirtation [Lady Charlotte Bury]. 2 vols 1828 (anon), 1 vol Philadelphia 1833 (Novelist's Mag), 1 vol Paris 1836, 1857 (new edn), Philadelphia [187–?] (new edn); tr Fr nd (attributed to Joanna Baillie), Ger 1837.
Trevelyan. 3 vols 1833 (anon), 2 vols Philadelphia 1834, 3 vols London 1834 (2nd edn), 1 vol Paris 1835, 1 vol London 1837 (Bentley's Standard Novels), 1855, 1861 (Routledge's Railway Lib).
REVIEW: Athenaeum 2 Nov 1833.
Exposition of the types and antitypes of the Old and New Testament. 1856.
The old grey church: a novel. 3 vols 1856 (anon).
REVIEW: (George Eliot) in Silly novels by lady novelists, Westminster Rev 66, Oct 1856.
Incentives to Bible study: Scripture acrostics: a Sabbath pastime for young persons. [1860.]
Acrostics: historical, geographical, and biographical. [1863.] [JW]

Michael Scott 1789–1835

§1

Tom Cringle's log. 2 vols Edinburgh 1833, 1834, 1 vol Paris 1836, Edinburgh 1842 etc, New York [1883]; ed M. Morris, illustr J. A. Symington 1895; illustr H. Edwards, New York 1899; ed E. Rhys [1915?] (EL); ed W. McFee, illustr M. Schaeffer, New York 1927; ed J. Webber 1956 (abridged). First pbd in Blackwood's Mag 1829–33 (anon).
The cruise of the Midge, by the author of Tom Cringle's log. 2 vols Edinburgh 1836, 1 vol Paris 1836, Edinburgh 1842, London 1878; illustr F. Brangwyn 1894. First pbd in Blackwood's Mag 1834–5 (anon).

§2

Douglas, G. In his Blackwood group, 1897.

Sir Walter Scott 1771–1832

Quotation marks in '2nd' edn etc indicate a re-issue of an earlier edn with a new title page, or an issue made up of sheets from more than one genuine edition.

Translations are selectively listed. For the numerous Russian translations see Walter Scott, comp I. M. Levidova, Moscow 1958 (in Rus).

Almost all mss by or relating to Scott are now in public libraries. The Pierpont Morgan Lib, New York, has the largest single collection of Scott's own works, including the Journal, The lady of the lake, Rokeby, The bridal of Triermain, *part of* Waverley, Guy Mannering, The antiquary, The tale of Old Mortality, The black dwarf, Ivanhoe, The monastery, Peveril of the Peak, Saint Ronan's Well, Woodstock, Anne of Geierstein, *the first ser of* Tales of a grandfather, *the* Life of Napoleon *and* The Doom of Devorgoil. *The NLS, Edinburgh, owns* Marmion, The lord of the Isles, *most of* Waverley, The heart of Mid-Lothian, Quentin Durward, Redgauntlet, *the two ser of* Chronicles of the Canongate (The two drovers *is missing),* The betrothed, *and minor works.* Harold the Dauntless *and a small part of* The lay of the last minstrel *are in the Huntington.* The pirate *is in Princeton. The BL has* Kenilworth *and* The tapestried chamber. The Fortunes of Nigel, Count Robert of Paris, *the fifth ser of* Tales of a grandfather, *and a vol of misc minor prose works are in King's School, Canterbury.* The bride of Lammermoor, *and memoirs of* Goldsmith, Johnson *and part of* Sterne *are in the Signet Lib, Edinburgh.* Castle dangerous *is in the NY Soc Lib. The unpbd* The Siege of Malta *is in NYPL.* The talisman *is in the State Historical Museum, Moscow. Harvard has the* Life of Swift. *The largest collection of mss relating to Scott is in the NLS. It contains the Abbotsford Collection acquired in 1931–2 and the Walpole Collection of about 6,000 letters to Scott purchased from Abbotsford by Sir Hugh Walpole in 1921 and bequeathed by him to the library, together with Scott's interleaved set of the novels, with his ms corrections (used for the Magnum opus edn and by Messrs A. & C. Black for their rev texts).* The abbot *is in the possession of John Murray, London, and* Rob Roy *is in private hands in Britain, as is the first vol of* Minstrelsy of the Scottish Border *from the interleaved set of the* Poetical works. *For locations of proofs and of portions of mss, see the article by G. Dyson cited below. The principal Scott material in the NLS, including the entire Walpole Collection, was pbd on microfilm by Harvester Press in 1986–7. The interleaved set was pbd on microfiche by Aberdeen Univ Press and Pergamon Press in 1987.*

Bibliographies etc

[Chambers, R.?] Manuscripts of Sir Walter Scott. Chambers's Edinburgh Jnl 14 Feb 1835.
Quérard, J. M. Scott. In his La France littéraire, ou dictionnaire bibliographique des savants, 12 vols Paris 1827–64 (vol 8 1836).

Cadell, R. [firm]. Descriptive catalogue of the various edns of the novels, poetry, prose writings and life of Sir Walter Scott Bart. Edinburgh 1850.
The Scott exhibition 1871: catalogue of the exhibition held at Edinburgh in July and August 1871 on occasion of the commemoration of the centenary of the birth of Sir Walter Scott. [Ed W. S. Maxwell, J. Drummond and D. Laing,] Edinburgh 1872.
Anderson, J. P. Bibliography. In C. D. Yonge, Life of Sir Walter Scott, 1888.
The fate of Sir Walter Scott's manuscripts. Chambers's Jnl 6 ser 1 1898.
Fitzgerald, P. Early issues of the Waverley novels. N & Q 10 Mar 1900.
Ball, M. Bibliography. In her Sir Walter Scott as a critic of literature, New York 1907.
Crockett, W. S. The manuscript of Redgauntlet. Scotsman, 1 Dec 1923. Identifies owners of many Scott mss.
R., R. S. Scott manuscripts. TLS 8 Nov 1923.
Sir Walter Scott's 'Magnum opus'. New York 1930.
Ruff, W. Yale's collection of Walter Scott. Yale Univ Lib Gazette 6 1931.
Worthington, G. A bibliography of the Waverley novels. 1931. First edns only.
Catalogue of an exhibition of portraits, manuscripts and relics held by the Sir Walter Scott Centenary Committee, Glasgow, at the McLellan Galleries, Glasgow, June 8th–June 16th 1932. [Glasgow 1932.]
Catalogue of the Sir Walter Scott exhibition in the National Gallery of Scotland, Edinburgh, July 1 to September 30 1932. Edinburgh 1932.
Cook, D. Scott first editions. TLS 18 Aug 1932.
Heron, F. W. Scott in San Francisco. TLS 1 Sep 1932.
M[eikle], H. W. and M. R. D[obie]. Scott and his contemporaries: National Library papers. Scotsman 16 Dec 1932.
Scott centenary exhibition, 1932 [organised by D. Cook]. Barnsley 1932.
A Scott exhibition [Messrs J. and E. Bumpus]. TLS 27 Oct 1932.
Sir Walter Scott, author of the Waverley novels: list of the autograph manuscripts and the editions of his works in a commemorative exhibition, 1832–1932 [Columbia Univ Lib]. New York 1932.
Symington, J. A. Sir Walter Scott centenary exhibition, October 1932 [Brotherton Lib, Leeds Univ]. Oxford 1932.
Van Antwerp, W. C. A collector's comment on his first editions of the works of Sir Walter Scott. San Francisco 1932.
Van Antwerp, W. C. On collecting Scott. Colophon 14 1933.
Stevenson, E. E. D. Sir Walter Scott: a bibliography of the contemporary editions of the chief poems. Upbd Diss, London Univ School of Librarianship and Archives 1936.
Ruff, W. A bibliography of the poetical works of Sir Walter Scott 1796–1832. Trans Edinburgh Bibl Soc 1 1937, 1938 (additions and corrections).
National Library of Scotland. Catalogue of manuscripts vol 1. Edinburgh 1938.
Cook, D. and W. M. Parker. Additions to Scott's poems. TLS 15–22 Nov 1941; reply 13 Dec.
Corson, J. C. A bibliography of Sir Walter Scott: a classified and annotated list of books and articles relating to his life and works 1797–1940. Edinburgh and London 1943.
Poston, M. L. Addenda to Worthington. TLS 29 May 1943.
Leclaire, L. Scott, Sir Walter (1771–1832). In A general analytical bibliography of the regional novelists of the British Isles 1800–1950, Paris 1954.
Hillhouse, J. T. Sir Walter Scott. In The English romantic poets and essayists: a review of research and criticism, ed L. H. Houtchens and C. W. Houtchens, New York 1957; with ch rev A. Welsh 1966.
Strout, A. L. A bibliography of articles in Blackwood's Magazine volumes 1 through 18 1817–1825. Lib Bull 5, Texas Technological College, Lubbock TX 1959.
The Tinker Library: a bibliographical catalogue of the books and manuscripts collected by Chauncey Brewster Tinker. Ed R. F. Metzdorf, New Haven CT 1959.
Dyson, G. The manuscripts and proof sheets of Scott's Waverley novels. Trans Edinburgh Bibl Soc 4 1960.
Ruff, W. and W. Hellstrom. Some uncollected poems of Sir Walter Scott: a census. N & Q 212 Aug 1967.
The Earl Larrison collection of Sir Walter Scott. Univ of Idaho Lib Pbns 1, Moscow ID 1968.
Johnson, E. Sir Walter Scott in the Fales Library. New York Univ Lib Bibl Ser 4, New York 1968.
Bell, A. S. The Walter Scott manuscripts in the National Library of Scotland. TLS 9 July 1971.
Duval, K. D. [firm]. Scott and his Scotland: a catalogue to mark the bicentenary of the birth of Sir Walter Scott. Pitlochry 1971.
Exposîcão comemorativa do il centenário de Walter Scott, Lisboa, 16–26 de Fevereiro de 1971 [Instituto Britânico em Portugal]. [Lisbon 1971.]
Sale catalogues of libraries of eminent persons, vol 1: poets and men of letters. Ed A. N. L. Munby 1971.
Scott and his Scotland: the catalogue of an exhibition in Lockwood Memorial Library, together with a catalogue of Scott's works in the rare book room [State University of New York at Buffalo]. [Buffalo NY 1971.]
Sir Walter Scott 1771–1971: a bicentenary exhibition [NLS]. Edinburgh 1971.
Sir Walter Scott 1771–1971: a bicentenary exhibition. Wahlert Memorial Library, Cultural Ser no 3, Dubuque IA 1971.
Walter Scott, 1771–1832: a book exhibit arranged by the British Council [London]. 1971.
Bell, A. Scott's manuscripts and the collector. Manuscripts 24 1972.
Ward, W. S. Scott, Sir Walter. In his Literary reviews in British periodicals 1798–1820: a bibliography with a supplementary list of general articles on literary subjects, 2 vols New York and London 1972.
Bell, A. Scott manuscripts in Edinburgh libraries. In Scott Bicentenary essays, ed Bell, 1973.
Anderson, W. E. K. Scott. In The English novel: select bibliographical guides, ed A. E. Dyson, 1974.
Rubenstein, J. Sir Walter Scott: a reference guide. Boston and London 1978.
Webbert, C. A. Scottiana Idahoensis: a descriptive catalogue of the Sir Walter Scott collection in the University of Idaho Library. Moscow ID 1978.
Mack, D. S. Scottish literary manuscripts at Stirling University library. Scottish Literary Jnl suppl 20 1984.
Alexander, J. H. Some items in the Walpole Collection at King's School, Canterbury. Scott Newsletter 6 1985.
B[ell], A. S. Scott for Scotland. BC 35 1986. On the interleaved set of the novels.
[Brown, I. G. (ed).] Sir Walter Scott's Magnum Opus and the Pforzheimer manuscripts: essays to commemorate the acquisition of two great collections by the National Library of Scotland. Edinburgh 1986.
Hewitt, D. The Magnum Opus and the Pforzheimer manuscripts. Scott Newsletter 8 1986.
Hurst, C. The Dunston Collection. Bodleian Lib Record 12 1986.
Mitchell, J. Scott holdings in the library at Schloss Corvey. Scott Newsletter 8 1986.
Scott's interleaved Waverley novels (the Magnum Opus: National Library of Scotland MSS 23001–41): an introduction and commentary. Ed I. G. Brown, [Oxford and Aberdeen] 1987.
Kohler, C. C. Scott abroad: catalogue of a collection of editions of

Walter Scott's writings published outside Britain in English and in translation. Dorking 1989.
Rubenstein, J. Sir Walter Scott: an annotated bibliography of scholarship and criticism, 1975–1990. [Aberdeen 1994].
Todd, W. B. and A. Bowden. Sir Walter Scott: a bibliographical history 1796–1832. New Castle DE 1998.

Handbooks etc

Notices and anecdotes illustrative of the incidents, characters, and scenery described in the novels and romances of Sir Walter Scott Bart, with a complete glossary for all his works. Paris 1833. Glossary rptd New York 1974.
Cornish, S. W. The Waverley manual, or hand-book of the chief characters, incidents, and descriptions in the Waverley novels, with critical breviates from various sources. Edinburgh 1871.
Rogers, M. The Waverley dictionary: an alphabetical arrangement of all the characters in Sir Walter Scott's Waverley novels, with a descriptive analysis of each character and illustrative selections from the text. Chicago 1879.
Grey, Henry. A key to all the Waverley novels in chronological sequence. 1881.
Husband, M. F. A. A dictionary of the characters in the Waverley novels of Sir Walter Scott. 1910.
Burr, A. Sir Walter Scott: an index placing the short poems in his novels and in his long poems and dramas. Cambridge MA 1936.
Bradley, P. An index to the Waverley novels. Metuchen NJ 1975.

The Abbotsford Library

C[ochrane], J. G. Catalogue of the library at Abbotsford. Edinburgh 1838.
Gordon, G. H. Sir Walter Scott and the catalogue of the Abbotsford Library. GM n.s. 38 1852.
Muir, J. Burns at Abbotsford. Bookman [London] 55 1919.
Falconer, J. A. Two manuscripts at Abbotsford. Archiv 160 1931. Trns of Ger plays.
Williams, H. Dean Swift's library, with a facsimile of the original sale catalogue and some account of two manuscript lists of his books. Cambridge 1932.
S., P. P. Scott's library: exhibits at Abbotsford. Scotsman 18 June 1934.
S., P. P. Sir Walter Scott: unpublished manuscripts at Abbotsford. Scotsman 30 Apr 1937.
Mennie, D. M. Sir Walter Scott's unpublished translations of German plays. MLR 33 1938.
Parker, W. M. Scott's book marginalia. TLS 21 Sep–5 Oct 1940.
Parker, W. M. More Scott marginalia. TLS 3–17 May 1941.
Corson, J. C. Scott's boyhood collection of chapbooks. Bibliotheck 3 1962.
Corson, J. C. Some American books at Abbotsford. Bibliotheck 4 1963.
Montgomerie, W. William Macmath and the Scott ballad manuscripts. Stud in Scottish Lit 1 1963.
Buchan, D. D. Nicol, Scott and the ballad collectors. Ariel 2 1971.
Real, H. J. and H. J. Vienken. 'A pretty mixture': books from Swift's library at Abbotsford House. BJRL 67 1984.
Pinkerton, J. M. Demonology in the library of Abbotsford. Bull du Bibliophile 1 1985.
Key, N. Sir Walter Scotts Bibliotheck zu Abbotsford. Imprimatur 12 1987.

Collections

The works of Walter Scott Esq. 156 vols Zwickau 1821–31.
Works. Tr Fr 84 vols Paris 1828–33 (A. J. B. Defauconpret), 14 vols Paris 1840–1 (A. Montémont), 22 vols Paris [1851–2] (Montémont and L. Barré), 25 vols Paris 1840–2 (L. Vivien); Ger 27 vols Danzig 1825–7; Danish 44 vols Copenhagen 1832–[58] (F. Schaldemose).
The prose works of Sir Walter Scott. 8 vols Paris 1834. Novels, plays, miscellaneous prose works.

Poems

Works. 5 vols Edinburgh 1806. Minstrelsy, Sir Tristrem, Lay, Ballads and lyrical pieces. Composite edn.
Works. 6 vols Edinburgh 1808. Adds Marmion. Composite edn.
Works. 8 vols Edinburgh 1812. Adds Lady of the lake, Don Roderick. Composite edn.
Works. 9–[10] vols Edinburgh 1813–[17]. Various composite edns adding Rokeby and (in later issues) Lord of the isles.
Poetical works. 5 vols Baltimore 1812–13, 6 vols Philadelphia 1813, 6 vols New York 1818–19, 12 vols Edinburgh 1820, 10 vols Edinburgh 1821 (for 1820), 7 vols Paris 1821, 1826, 8 vols Edinburgh 1822 (for 1821), 10 vols Edinburgh 1823, 7 vols Fredericksburg VA 1824, 7 vols Philadelphia 1824, 10 vols Edinburgh 1825, 1 vol Frankfurt-am-Main 1826, 1 vol Brunswick 1827, 1 vol Paris 1827 (with memoir by J. W. Lake), 5 vols Philadelphia 1827, 7 vols Boston 1827–8, 11 vols Edinburgh 1830 (contains the dramas, new essays on ballad poetry and new introds to The lay, Marmion, etc, and was issued in 8vo and 18mo, vol 11 being sold separately to complete the edns of 1821, 1823 and 1825), 1 vol Philadelphia 1830 (with rpt of memoir by J. W. Lake), 1 vol Paris 1831; tr Fr 1832 (A. Montémont).
Poetical works. [Ed J. G. Lockhart] 12 vols Edinburgh 1833–4, often rptd in 12 and 1 vol edns; ed G. Gilfillan 3 vols Edinburgh 1857; ed F. T. Palgrave 1866 etc (Globe); ed W. M. Rossetti 1870 etc; ed W. B. Scott 1883 etc; ed W. Minto 2 vols Edinburgh '1888' [1887]; ed J. Dennis 5 vols 1892 (Aldine); ed J. Logie Robertson, Oxford 1894 etc; ed A. Lang 2 vols 1895 (Dryburgh); ed H. E. Scudder, Cambridge MA 1900.
 Ruff, W. Interleaved copies of Scott's poems. N & Q 181 1941.
 Millgate, J. Scott the cunning tailor: refurbishing the Poetical works. Library 11 1989.
 McMullin, B. J. Volume XI of Scott's Poetical works in octavo, 1830. Library 13 1991.

Novels

The first collected edns of the novels were issued in Edinburgh in 3 formats between 1819 and 1833, in 41, 53 and 41 vols, as follows.
Novels and tales (Waverley–Montrose). 8vo 12 vols 1819, 1822 (sometimes dated 1821–2), 12mo 16 vols 1821, [new edn] 1825 (for 1824), 18mo 12 vols 1823.
Historical romances (Ivanhoe–Kenilworth). 8vo 6 vols 1822; 12mo 8 vols 1822; 18mo 6 vols 1824.
Novels and romances (Pirate–Quentin Durward). 8vo 7 vols 1824 (for 1823), 12mo 9 vols 1824, 18mo 7 vols 1825 (for 1824).
Tales and romances (St Ronan's Well–Woodstock). 8vo 7 vols 1827, [new edn] 7 vols 1834, 12mo 9 vols 1827, 18mo 7 vols 1828 (for 1827, sometimes dated 1827–8).
Tales and romances (Chronicles of the Canongate–Castle Dangerous). 8vo 7 vols 1833, 12mo 8 vols 1833, 18mo 6 vols 1833.
Introductions, and notes and illustrations. 8vo 2 vols 1833, 12mo 3 vols 1833, 18mo 3 vols 1833.
Waverley novels. 31 vols Boston 1820–[34] [Parker's 1st edn], 45 vols Boston 1826–9 (Parker's 2nd edn).
The novels of Sir Walter Scott. 30 vols Paris 1831–3 (Baudry's Foreign Library: Collection of ancient and modern British novels and romances).
Waverley novels. 48 vols Edinburgh 1829–33 (author's last revision with notes, known as the 'Magnum opus' edn), 48 vols Edinburgh 1830–4. Edns followed at average rate of one every 2 years, the best known being: Fisher's edn, 48 vols 1836–9; Cabinet edn, 25 vols Edinburgh 1841–3; Abbotsford edn, 12 vols Edinburgh 1842–7; Library edn, 25 vols Edinburgh 1852–3; Centenary edn (text rev with notes by D. Laing), 25 vols Edinburgh 1870–1; Dryburgh edn (text again rev), 25 vols 1892–4; Border edn (unrev text but with notes by A. Lang), 48 vols Edinburgh 1892–4; Standard edn, 25 vols 1895–7; Victoria edn 25

vols 1897; Edinburgh Waverley, 48 vols Edinburgh 1901–3; Soho edn, 25 vols 1904; Fine Art Scott, 25 vols (illus) [1910]; New Annotated edns of the Waverley novels, ed C. B. Wheeler, Oxford 1914–24 (only 7 vols pbd); New Crown edn, 25 vols 1932; Edinburgh edn, 30 vols 1993– . Tr Ger 50 vols 1822–31 (W. Gerhard, E. Berthold etc), 25 vols 1851–2 (C. Hermann, F. Richter etc), 12 vols 1876–7 (B. Tschischwitz); Swed 26 vols 1853–8; Danish 21 vols 1855–71.

Selections

The dance of death, and other poems. Philadelphia 1816.
Miscellaneous poems. Edinburgh 1819, 1820.
The search after happiness; or, The quest of Sultaun Solimaun, with other poems. Philadelphia 1820.
The poetry contained in the novels, tales and romances of the author of Waverley. 1822.
The beauties of Sir Walter Scott and Thomas Moore Esq., selected from their works, with historical and explanatory notes. Philadelphia 1826, 1828 ('10th' edn).
Beauties of the Waverley novels. Boston 1828.
Tales and essays. Paris 1829.
The genius and wisdom of Sir Walter Scott, comprising moral, religious, political, literary, and social aphorisms selected carefully from his various writings, with a memoir. 1839.
The Waverley sketch book, or a collection of the most striking pictures and interesting events in the Waverley novels. Ed C. Olliffe, Paris 1840.
Diamonds from the Waverley mines, or maxims, observations and reflections selected from the novels of Sir Walter Scott. Ed J. Cauvin 1872.
Lyrics, dramas and miscellaneous pieces. Edinburgh 1875.
Historical scenes from Scott's novels, ed E. J. Irving 1882.
Pictures of Scottish life from the Waverley novels. Ed E. J. Irving 1882.
The lyrics and ballads of Sir Walter Scott. Ed A. Lang 1894.
Tales from Scott. Ed E. Sullivan 1894.
Scottish selections from the Waverley novels with explanatory lists of Scottish words for use in schools. Ed J. K. Craigie, Oxford 1916.
Selections from the poems of Sir Walter Scott. Ed A. H. Thompson, Cambridge 1922.
The Scott book: scenes from the novels. Ed W. P. Borland 1924.
The week-end Scott, being selected passages from the Waverley novels. Ed J. T. Christie 1931.
The Waverley pageant: the best passages from the novels of Sir Walter Scott, selected, with critical introductions. Ed H. Walpole 1932.
Short stories by Sir Walter Scott. Ed D. Cecil, Oxford 1934 (WC).
Songs and lyrics of Sir Walter Scott. Ed H. J. C. Grierson, Edinburgh 1942.
Selections from the prose of Sir Walter Scott. Ed J. C. Trewin 1952.
One crowded hour. Ed James Sutherland 1963.
Sir Walter Scott on novelists and fiction. Ed I. M. Williams 1968.
Selected poems of Sir Walter Scott. Ed T. Crawford, Oxford 1972.
Supernatural tales. Ed C. Grant 1974.
The supernatural short stories of Sir Walter Scott. Ed M. Hayes 1977.
The prefaces to the Waverley novels. Ed M. A. Weinstein, Lincoln NE 1978.
Scott on himself: a selection of the autobiographical writings of Sir Walter Scott. Ed D. Hewitt, Edinburgh 1981.
The two drovers and other stories. Ed G. Tulloch, Oxford 1987 (WC).

§1

Short poems

For single sheet poems (priv ptd) and contributions to miscellanies, song-books etc, see W. Ruff, Bibliography, *above, and the following items.*

Juvenile lines, from Virgil. 1782. Ptd in Lockhart, 1837 (title from 1847 edn).
On a thunderstorm. 1783. Ptd in Lockhart, 1837.
  Rait, R. S. Scott and The bee. TLS 16 Sep 1920; reply 23 Sep. Parallels with On a thunderstorm and The lay.
  Fairbrother, E. H. Lines written by Walter Scott when a child. N & Q 2 Apr 1927.
On the setting sun. 1783. Ptd in Lockhart, 1837.
The triumph of constancy. c. 1796.
  Emerson, O. F. Scott's early translations from Bürger. JEGP 14 1915.
  Parsons, C. O. Scott's translation of Bürger's Das Lied von Treue. JEGP 33 1934.
The lamentation of the faithful wife of Asan Aga. c. 1797.
  Low, D. H. The first link between English and Serbo-Croat literature. Slavonic Rev 3 1924.
The erl-king. 1798. Ptd in Kelso Mail 1 Mar 1798.
  Ruff, W. Walter Scott and the Erl-King. EStudien 69 1934.
The shepherd's tale (1799).
  Parsons, C. O. Two notes on Scott. N & Q 4 Feb 1933.
The battle of Killiekrankie (1803).
  Reliques of Walter Scott. Chambers's Edinburgh Jnl 29 Dec 1832. Translation.
  Strout, A. L. An unpublished ballad-translation by Scott: The battle of Killiecrankie; reply by J. C. Corson. MLN 54 1939.
Gilpin Horner to Demonia: Christmas 1805.
  Parsons, C. O. Walter Scott in pandemonium. MLR 38 1943.
Justice Law (1806).
  Justice Law, by Sir Walter Scott Baronet, sung at the meeting of Lord Melville's friends after his acquittal. In The Court of Session garland, [ed J. Maidment,] Edinburgh 1839; rptd 1871, 1888.
  Walter Scott's song on Lord Melville's trial. N & Q 12 Feb 1870; replies 26 Mar, 7 May.
  Crowley, J. Sir Walter Scott's The lawyer and the bishop. Juridical Rev 62 1950.
Address written for Miss Smith (1807). In Forget Me Not 1833.
Prologue to Helga (1812).
  Parker, W. M. Scott's prologue to [G. S. Mackenzie's] Helga. TLS 4 Jan 1941.
  Dean, D. R. Scott and Mackenzie: new poems. PQ 52 1973.
The Ettricke garland (1815).
  Campbell, C. The Ettricke garland. Trans of the Hawick Archaeological Soc, Session 1922.
  Mack, D. S. The Ettricke garland by Scott and Hogg: a note. Bibliotheck 7 1975.
Hymn for the Czar (1816).
  Reliques of Walter Scott. Chambers's Edinburgh Jnl, 29 Dec 1832.
Jock o' Hazeldean (1816).
  [Graham, A.] Jock o' Hazeldean [signed A. G. S.]. Border Mag 12 1907.
  Watson, G. Jock o' Hazeldean. Border Mag 12 1907.
  Kelley, M. W. Jock of Hazeldean and Child 293 E. MLN 46 1931.
  Zug, C. G. III. Scott's Jock of Hazeldean: the recreation of a traditional ballad. Jnl of American Folklore 86 1973.
The battle of Sempach. In Blackwood's Edinburgh Mag 2 1818.
  Mennie, D. M. A MS variant of Sir Walter Scott's Battle of Sempach. Anglia Beiblatt 49 1938.
Epilogue. In [John Galt's] The appeal, Edinburgh 1818.
A Bannatyne garland, qhuairin the president speaketh (Finis, quoth the Knight of Abbotsford). Edinburgh [1823].
Epilogue to the drama based on St Ronan's Well. Edinburgh Weekly Jnl 9 June 1824.
The bonnets of Bonnie Dundee. In The Christmas Box 1828 (for 1827) and Literary Gazette 8 Dec 1827.
  Leaves from a note-book: a traveller's tale. Macmillan's Mag 61 1889.
  M., J. Sir Walter Scott. Scotsman 28 Aug 1920; reply 2 Oct.
  Robertson, S. A. Bonnie Dundee. TLS 28 Feb 1929; replies 7 Mar–4 Apr.

Hewitt, D. The development of The bonnets of bonny Dundee. Scott Newsletter 1 1982; reply 2 1983.

The death of Keeldar. In The Gem 1829 (for 1828).

REVIEWS: Athenaeum 15 Oct 1828; Monthly Rev 3rd ser 9 1828.

Farewell address written for Mrs Henry Siddons (1830).

REVIEW: Edinburgh Literary Jnl 3 Apr 1830.

Lines addressed to Miss Jarman. In Cornucopia Britannia 26 Nov 1831.

Groves, D. Lines addressed to Miss Jarman, of the Theatre-Royal: a poem by Walter Scott. Scott Newsletter 9 1986.

'Tis well the gifted eye which saw (1831).

C., W. S. Scott's last verses. Glasgow Herald 4 Apr 1925; reply 7 Apr.

King Gathol's chair. In Fraser's Mag 4 1831.

Verses written by the Countess of Wollenluss request (1832).

Kerr, J. B. On supposed unpublished verses by Sir Walter Scott. History of the Berwickshire Naturalists' Club 9 1879; rptd 1880.

Sir Walter Scott [signed Hermes]. N & Q 9 Aug 1879.

The last verses of Walter Scott: Lockhart's search for a manuscript. The Times 19 Aug 1932; reply 25 Aug.

Additional lines to Burns's Scots wha hae (nd).

Frere, H. B. E. Walter Scott and Burns. Macmillan's Mag 26 1872.

Hilson, Oliver. Sir Walter Scott and Bannockburn. Scotsman 12 Jan 1927; replies 15 Jan.

New love-poems by Sir Walter Scott, discovered in the narrative of an unknown love episode with Jessie — of Kelso. Ed D. Cook, Oxford 1932.

Ruff, W. and W. Hellstrom. Scott's authorship of the songs in Daniel Terry's plays. Stud in Scottish Lit 5 1968.

Longer poems and fiction

The chase, and William and Helen: two ballads from the German of Gottfried Augustus Bürger. Edinburgh 1796. A few of the original sheets re-issued with new title page, London 1807.

REVIEWS: Critical Rev 2nd ser 20 1797; [J. Aikin.] Monthly Rev n.s. [2nd] 23 1797.

Studies

Emerson, O. F. The earliest English translations of Bürger's Lenore: a study in English and German romanticism. Western Reserve Univ Bulletins n.s. 18 1915.

Moldenhauer, G. Estudio filológico de una tradducción española de The wild huntsman de Sir Walter Scott. Instituto de Filología Moderna 2 1963.

Goetz of Berlichingen, with the iron hand: a tragedy, translated from the German of Goethe. 1799 (a few copies having 'By William Scott'), New York 1814, Paris 1826.

REVIEW: Critical Rev 2nd ser 26 1799.

[Lockhart, J. G.] Horae Germanicae, no 19: Goetz of Berlichingen, a tragedy by Goethe. Blackwood's Edinburgh Mag 16 1824.

The eve of Saint John: a Border ballad. Kelso 1800; tr Ger 1816 (with The bridal of Triermain); Rus 1824 (V. A. Zhukovsky); Fr 1826 [A. J. B. Defauconpret]; Du 1834; Polish 1835.

Studies

Crockett, W. S. The Eve of St John. Scotsman, 20 Jan 1920.

Reizov, B. G. V. A. Zukovskij perevodčik Val'tera Skotta [V. A. Zhukovsky translator of Walter Scott]. In Russko-evropeĭskie literaturnye sujazi: sbornik statej k 70-letiju so dnja rǒzdenija akademika Alekseev [Russian–European literary connections: a volume of articles dedicated to the 70th birthday of Academician M. P. Alekseev], Moscow 1966.

The lay of the last minstrel. 1804 (priv ptd), 1805 [1st edn], 1805 (2nd edn), 1806 (3rd–5th edns), 1807 (6th edn), 1808 (8th edn, with Ballads and lyrical pieces (a few copies having an appendix of additional short poems), re-issued 1810), 1808 (9th edn), 1809 (10th edn), 1810 (11th edn), 1811 (12th edn), 1812 (13th edn), 1816 (15th edn), 1821 [Murray's edn], 1823 (16th edn), 1825 (new edn, re-issued 1830), Philadelphia 1805, 1806, 1807, 1810, Charleston 1806, New York 1806, 1811, 1811, Boston 1807, 1810, 1828, Baltimore 1811, 1812, Savannah GA 1811; ed with notes, Edinburgh 1868; ed J. Morison, Glasgow 1873; ed J. S. Phillpotts 1874; ed W. Henkel, Berlin 1877; ed S. C. Dev 1880; ed W. Minto, Oxford 1886 (rev 1920); ed G. H. Stuart and E. H. Elliot 1889; abridged and ed T. Lattimer 2 vols 1890; ed M. G. Glazebrook 1894; ed W. J. Addis [1895]; ed J. H. Flather 1896; ed G. T. Warner [1896]; ed A. H. Reynar and C. Clarkson 1901; ed W. J. Alexander, Toronto 1901; ed J. Cusack 1904; ed J. W. Young [1904]; ed A. E. Jenkins [1904]; ed F. W. Ticknor 1905; ed J. W. B. Adams 1905; introd by A. D. Innes 1905; ed F. Marshall [1905]; introd by A. B. Coverton [1910]; ed S. G. Dunn, Bombay 1912; ed T. T. Jeffery [1914]; ed M. A. Allen, Boston [1915]; ed H. J. Findlay, London and Toronto [1920]; ed G. A. Sheldon 1932.

TRANSLATIONS: Ger 1820 (P. A. Storck), 1823 (C. H. W[eise]: free), 1824 (W. Alexis), 1828 (F. Lenning), 1857 (A. Neidhardt), [1895] (C. Cornelius); Fr 1821 [A. Pichot], 1824 (M. A. P.), 1826 [A. J. B. Defauconpret], 1865 (L. Barré); Polish 1822, 1838 (A. E. Odyniec), 1874; Rus 1822 [M. T. Kachenovsky: prose), 1823; Ital 1828 (C. F.), 1829 (A. G. G.), 1829 (F. Cusani), 1834 (E. Liberatore: prose), 1841 (G. G.), 1858 (C. Rusconi); Du 1840, 1845; Sp 1843 (D. P. Piferrer: prose); Swed 1872 (J. Sand); Jap 1983 (S. Takerou); Chinese [1988].

REVIEWS: [Barbauld, A. L.] Annual Rev 3 1804 (1805); Br Critic 26 1805; Critical Rev 3rd ser 5 1805; Eclectic Rev 2 1806; Edinburgh Rev 6 1805 [Jeffrey, F.; rptd in his Contributions to the Edinburgh Rev vol 2, 1844]; Imperial Rev 4 1805; Lady's Monthly Museum 15 1805, 16 1806; Literary Jnl 5 1805; Monthly Mag 19 suppl 1805; Monthly Mirror 22 1806; [Muirhead, L.] Monthly Rev n.s. [2nd] 49 1806; New Annual Register 25 1804 (1805); Poetical Register 5 1805; Scots Mag 67 1805.

Studies

Schetky, J. C. Illustrations of Walter Scott's Lay of the last minstrel. 1808, 1810.

Sir Walter Scott's MSS. Literary Gazette 26 Oct 1833.

On The lay of the last minstrel [signed A Borderer]. N & Q 10 May 1851; replies 7 June–23 Aug.

Brown, W. Records of Eskdalemuir. Hawick Archaeological Soc [1869–74] 1872. On Gilpin Horner.

Terry, F. C. B. Parallel lines. N & Q 2 June 1883.

Natorp, O. Zu Walter Scotts Lay of the last minstrel. Archiv 72 1884.

Staake, P. A critical introduction to Sir Walter Scott's Lay of the last minstrel. In Programm der Realschule zu Meerane i./S. 1888, Meerane 1888.

Wilson, W. E. The original of Lord Cranstoun's goblin page in The Lay of the last minstrel. N & Q 2 Apr 1892.

Franke, E. Quellen des Lay of the last minstrel von W. Scott. Archiv 101 1898.

Crockett, W. S. A Scott centenary. Border Mag 10 1905.

W., M. B. Sir Walter Scott and one of his reviewers. Chambers's Jnl 6 ser 8 1905. Robert Sym.

Pearce, J. W. Miscellaneous notes. MLN 22 1907. On Schiller and The lay.

Rait, R. S. Scott and The bee. TLS 16 Sep 1920; reply 23 Sep. Parallels with On a thunderstorm and The lay.

E., J. C. The lay of the last minstrel: a bibliographical find. Glasgow Herald 24 June 1922.

Johnston, R. F. The lay of the last minstrel. TLS 11 Aug 1932.

Swanzy, T. E. The lay of the last minstrel. TLS 4 Aug 1932.

Beck, R. Walter Scott: Aldarminning. Lögrjetta 28 1933.

Dyer, F. E. A line in Scott. TLS 17 Dec 1938.

Ballads and lyrical pieces. Edinburgh 1806 [1st edn], 1806 (2nd edn), 1810 (4th [3rd] edn), 1812 (4th edn), 1819 (5th edn), 1820 ('5th' edn), Boston 1807, Baltimore 1811, New York 1811, 1818 (with The vision of Don Roderick); tr Ger 1817 (H. Schubart).

REVIEWS: Annual Rev 5 1806 (1807); Le Beau Monde 1 1807; La Belle Assemblée 2 suppl 1807; Br Critic 32 1808; [Montgomery, J.]

Eclectic Rev 3 1807; Flowers of Lit 5 1806; Literary Annual Register 1 1807; Monthly Mag 22 suppl 1807; Monthly Mirror 22 1806; [Finlay, J.] Monthly Rev n.s. [2nd] 53 1807; Oxford Rev 1 1807; Poetical Register 6 1806–7 (1811); Scots Mag 68 1806.

Marmion: a tale of Flodden Field. Edinburgh 1808 ([1st], 2nd, 3rd, 4th edns), 1810 (5th, 6th edns), 1811 (7th, 8th edns), 1815 (9th edn), 1821 (10th edn), 1825 (new [11th] edn, re-issued 1830), 1825 (12th edn, re-issued [1830]), 1830, Boston 1808, 1810, 1827, Philadelphia 1808, 1809, 1810, Baltimore 1811, 1812, 1815, New York 1811, 1811, 1816, 1818, 1829, Zwickau 1825, Milwaukee 1831; ed E. E. Morris 1869; ed with notes, Edinburgh 1873; ed F. S. Arnold 1886; ed M. Macmillan 1887; ed T. Bayne, Oxford 1889; ed with notes 1895 (canto 1); ed J. H. B. Masterman 1895; ed G. T. Warner [1895]; ed T. W. Berry, Newport Shropshire and London [1899]; ed J. Lees [1900]; ed A. Mackie 1900; ed R. P. Davidson 1902; ed F. Marshall [1904]; introd by H. Morley 1904; ed G. Kendall 1905; ed E. Lee 1908; ed G. B. Aiton 1909; introd by R. F. Cholmeley [1910]; ed F. Allen 1912; ed H. J. Findlay, London and Toronto [1921]; ed E. C. Black, Boston [1927].

TRANSLATIONS: Fr 1820 (I. J. B.), 1820 [A. Pichot], 1823 (M. A. P.), 1826 [A. J. B. Defauconpret]; Ger 1822 (F. P. E. Richter), 1827 (S. May), 1857 (A. Neidhardt); Danish 1824 (L. A. Welker [F. Schaldemose]: free); Rus 1828 (from Fr: prose), 1834 (extract); Ital 1828 (F. Cusani: prose), 1832 (M. Amari), 1834 (E. Liberatore: prose), 1858 (C. Rusconi).

REVIEWS: Annual Rev 7 1808 (1809); Antijacobin Rev 38 1811; [Twiss, H.] Le Beau Monde 3 1808; Belfast Monthly Mag 1 1808; La Belle Assemblée 4 1808; Br Critic 31 1808, 36 1810; Cabinet 4 1808, 5 1808, n.s. 2 1809; Critical Rev 3rd ser 13 1808; Cyclopaedian Mag 2 1808 (copied from La Belle Assemblée); (Montgomery, J.) Eclectic Rev 4 1808; [Jeffrey, F.] Edinburgh Rev 12 1808; Eng Censor 1 1809; Literary Panorama 4 1808; [Twiss, H.] London Rev 1 1809; Monthly Mag 25 suppl 1808; Monthly Mirror n.s. 4 1808; [Merivale, J. H.] Monthly Rev n.s. [2nd] 56 1808; New Annual Register 29 1808 (1809); Poetical Register 7 1808–9 (1812); Satirist 2 1808, 4 1809; Scots Mag 70 1808; Universal Mag n.s. 9 1808.

Studies

Query to Mr Scott respecting a passage in Marmion. Monthly Mirror n.s. 4 1808.

French translation of Marmion. Port Folio 3rd ser 2 1823.

On a passage in Marmion [signed A. Borderer]. N & Q 15 Mar 1851.

Van Lennep's Heer van Culemberg [signed Senex]. N & Q 19 Jan 1861; reply 2 Feb.

Rolfe, W. J. The text of Scott's Marmion. Literary World 16 1885.

Krummacher, M. Zu Scotts Marmion. Archiv 77 1887.

Rolfe, W. J. Editions of Marmion. Athenaeum 4 Jan 1890 (also letters from M. Macmillan 26 Oct, 16 Nov 1889, and T. Bayne 2 Nov 1889).

Bayne, T. Young Lochinvar. N & Q 27 Apr 1895; replies 6 and 20 July.

Evans' notes on Scott's Marmion. Redditch 1899.

C., B. L. R. Scott's Lochinvar. N & Q 2 Oct 1909; replies 23 Oct, 6 and 27 Nov.

Hofmann, G. Entstehungsgeschichte von Sir Walter Scotts Marmion. Königsberg 1913.

Cowley, J. Lockhart and the publication of Marmion. PQ 32 1953.

Alexander, J. H. Marmion: studies in interpretation and composition. Salzburg 1981.

The lady of the lake: a poem. Edinburgh 1810 ([1st], 2nd–5th, '6th', 6th, '7th', '8th' edns), 1811 (9th edn), 1814 (10th edn), 1816 (11th edn), 1819 (12th edn), 1825 (new [13th] edn, 14th edn re-issued 1830), 1830 (new [15th] edn, re-issued 1832), Boston 1810, 1810, 1823, New York 1810, 1811, 1813, 1813, 1818, 1827, 1829, 1831, 1831, Philadelphia 1810, 1824, 1828, Baltimore 1811, 1812, Montpelier VT 1813, Paris 1822, Albany NY 1823; ed F. Schlesius, Königsberg 1850; ed L. J. Woodroffe c. 1870; ed with notes 1871–2; ed R. W. Taylor 1875; ed with notes 1880; ed W. J. Rolfe, Boston 1885; ed with notes [1887]; ed with notes [1890]; ed B. Foster and J. Gilbert 1891; ed W. Minto, Oxford 1891, rev 1923; ed W. J. Morice 3 vols 1891; ed G. H. Stuart 1891; ed W. K. Leask 1895; ed J. Marshall [1895]; ed J. H. B. Masterman 1896; ed A. E. Woodward 1896; ed C. E. Brock 1898 [for 1897]; ed W. E. W. Collins 1900; ed J. Lees [c. 1900]; ed R. G. McKinlay 1900; ed L. D. Syle [1903]; ed R. M. Alden [1904]; ed G. B. Airy and A. Lang 1904; ed F. Masson [1904]; introd by H. Morley 1904; ed W. H. Spragge 1905; ed E. A. Packard 1908; ed C. L. Thomson [1908]; introd by J. V. Saunders 1910; ed K. N. Colville with an essay by R. Scott, Bombay 1813; ed O. J. Stevenson [1915]; ed A. R. Weekes [1916]; ed W. A. Cowperthwaite [1919]; ed E. C. Black, Boston [1921]; ed W. H. Hamilton 1932; abridged and ed G. A. Sheldon 1932; ed H. G. Bennett 1935; ed I. F. Anderson 1959.

TRANSLATIONS: Fr 1813 (E. de [Bon]), 1821 [A. Pichot], 1826 [A. J. B. Defauconpret]; Ger 1819 (J. A. Storck), 1819 (A. H. Schubart: free), 1822 (W. Alexis), 1828 (F. Haas), 1830 (C. W. Asher), 1853 (F. Friedmann), 1857 (A. Neidhardt), 1863 (F. F. von Pechlin), 1865 (H. Viehoff), 1867 (L. Altenbernd), 1869 (L. Freytag), 1871 (K. E. Overbeck), [1877] (E. Ernst); Ital 1821 (P[allavicini, P.], rev 1826), 1821 (G. Indelicato), 1829 (C. C.: prose), 1831 (A. T.), 1834 (E. Liberatore: prose); Polish 1822 (K. Kalinówski [Sienkiewicz]), 1838 (A. E. Odyniec); Cz 1828 (F. L. Čelakovsky); Rus 1828 (from Fr: prose); Swed 1828 (L. Arnell); Sp 1830 [M. de Rementería y Fica: prose], 1981 (J. M. Gonzalez Cremona); Danish 1836 (P. D. Ibsen), 1871 (A. Munch); Portuguese 1842; Jap 1881 (S. Takada: unpbd), 1884 (T. Shoyo), 1894 (U. Sjioi), 1915 (M. Baba).

REVIEWS: Antijacobin Rev 38 1811; La Belle Assemblée 2nd ser 1 1810, 2 suppl 1811; Br Critic 36 1810; Christian Observer 9 1810; Critical Rev 3rd ser 20 1810; Eclectic Rev 6 1810; [Jeffrey, F.] Edinburgh Rev 16 1810; European Mag 58 1810 (signed M); Hibernia Mag 2 1810; Literary Panorama 8 1810; Monthly Mag 29 suppl 1810; Monthly Mirror n.s. 8 1810; [Hodgson, F.] Monthly Rev n.s. [2nd] 62 1810; New Annual Register 31 1810 (1811); Poetical Register 8 1810–11 (1814); Port Folio n.s. 4 1810; [Ellis, G.] Quart Rev 3 1810; Satirist 10 1812; Scots Mag 72 1810; Universal Mag n.s. 15 1811; Walker's Hibernian Mag 26 1811 (copies Edinburgh Rev); Weekly Register 30 June 1810.

Studies

[Letter to the editor on The lady of the lake] [signed Xn]. Edinburgh Christian Instructor 1 1810.

Mr Walter Scott's poetry. Monthly Mirror n.s. 8 1810. Letters from P. A. T. and Britannicus.

Brackenridge, H. A. An epistle to Walter Scott, written at Pittsburg during the sitting of the term. Philadelphia 1811.

Parallel passages from Walter Scott's Lady of the lake and Tasso's Gerusalemme liberata. Dublin Examiner 1 1816.

[Two translations of The lady of the lake.] Annual Register 63 1821.

N., P. E. Idaean vine. N & Q 26 Oct 1867; replies 21 Mar–18 Apr 1868, 7 Nov 1874, 19 Dec 1874.

Titius, A. Über Scotts Lady of the lake. In Programm der Realschule I. O. zu Iserlohn, 1870.

Airy, G. B. On the topography of The lady of the lake. 1873; rptd in The lady of the lake, ed A. Lang, 1904.

Prosch, W. Critical essay on W. Scott's Lady of the lake. In Programm der Grossherzoglichen Realschule zu Offenbach a. M. 1876, Offenbach 1876.

Löwe, H. An exact account on Sir Walter Scott's poem The lady of the lake. Rostock 1878.

Rehdans, W. J. An exact account and critical examination of Sir Walter Scott's poem The lady of the lake. In Beilage zum Programm des Königl. kathol. Gymnasiums zu Culm, August 1878, Culm 1878.

Rehdans, W. J. An exact account and critical examination of Sir Walter Scott's poem The lady of the lake: continuation. In Wissenschaftliche Beilage zum Programm des Königlichen Gymnasiums zu Strasburg W.-Pr., Easter 1880, Strasburg [1880].

Rolfe, W. J. The text of Scott's Lady of the lake. Critic 3 1883.
Wiencke, O. Über Walter Scotts The lady of the lake: ein kritischer Versuch. Ploen 1886.
Krummacher, M. Zu Scotts Lady of the lake. Archiv 76–7 1886–7.
Bouchier, J. Scott, Lady of the lake. N & Q 10 Oct 1896; replies 24 Oct.
Benner, F. Poetik W. Scott's in seiner Lady of the lake mit Hinweisen auf Byron's Siege of Corinth und Burns' poems. Ludwigslust 1899.
Müller, A. Lady of the lake: allusions. N & Q 4 Jan 1908; replies 15 Feb.
Shearer, J. E. The story of The lady of the lake, from Sir Walter Scott's poem [with] The lady of the lake, by J. A. Madden. Stirling 1909.
Neilson, G. Roderick Dhu: his poetical pedigree. Scottish Historical Rev 8 1910.
Parker, W. M. La donna del lago. TLS 16 Jan 1937; reply 23 Jan.
Corson, J. C. Goblin's cave, Mount Benvenue. N & Q 10 Apr 1943.
Ambrose, M. E. La donna del lago: the first Italian translations of Scott. MLR 67 1972.

The vision of Don Roderick: a poem. Edinburgh 1811 (priv ptd), 1811 [1st edn], 1811 (2nd edn, with other poems), 1815 [3rd edn] (with The field of Waterloo etc), 1821 (4th edn, with The field of Waterloo etc), Boston 1811, 1811, New York 1811, 1818 (with Ballads and lyrical pieces), Philadelphia 1811, 1811, Calcutta 1812, Baltimore 1813; tr Fr 1821 [A. Pichot], 1827 [A. J. B. Defauconpret]; Rus 1828 (A. Lazarev: prose); Sp 1829 (A. Tracia (A. Aicart)); Ital 1841 (F. Ferrari: free).

REVIEWS: Br Critic 38 1811; Christian Observer 11 1812; Critical Rev 3rd ser 23 1811; Eclectic Rev 7 1811; Edinburgh Monthly Mag and Rev 1 1811; [Jeffrey, F.] Edinburgh Rev 18 1811; General Chron 2 suppl 1811; Glasgow Mag 2 1811; Military Panorama 1 1813; [Hodgson, F.] Monthly Rev n.s. [2nd] 65 1811; New Annual Register 32 1811 (1812); Poetical Register 8 1810–11 (1814); Port Folio n.s. 6 1811; [Erskine?, W.] Quart Rev 6 1811; Scourge 2 1811; (J. H.) Universal Mag n.s. 16 1811.

Studies

Van Patten, N. A newly discovered issue of Scott's The vision of Don Roderick. Library 4th ser 18 1937.
Todd, W. B. Scott's Vision of Don Roderick 1811. BC 14 1965.
Hafter, M. Z. The Spanish version of Scott's Don Roderick. SiR 13 1974.

Rokeby: a poem. Edinburgh 1813 ([1st], 2nd, '3rd', 4th, 5th edns), 1815 (6th edn), 1821 (7th edn), Baltimore 1813, Boston 1813 (3 edns), Charlestown 1813, Philadelphia 1813, 1813, 1827, New York 1818; ed R. W. Taylor 1888; ed M. Macmillan 1889; tr Ger 1816 (G. C. Richard), 1822 (F. W. Moser: free), 1822 (F. P. E. Richter), 1822 (J. A. Storck); Fr 1820 [A. Pichot], 1823 (M. A. P.), 1827 [A. J. B. Defauconpret]; Rus 1823 (Nn. Vv.: prose); Polish 1826 (W. Malecka); Danish 1828 (C. F. Holm: free); Ital 1829 (F. Cusani), 1832 (G. Gabussi), 1834 (E. Liberatore: prose), 1858 (C. Rusconi); Sp 1829 (M. de Rementería y Fica).

REVIEWS: Antijacobin Rev 44 1813; La Belle Assemblée n.s. 7 1813; Br Critic 42 1813; Br Rev 4 1813; Country Mag 1 1813; Critical Rev 4th ser 3 1813; Drakard's Paper 31 Jan 1813; Dublin Mag 1 1813 (mostly from Monthly Rev); (Montgomery, J.) Eclectic Rev 9 1813; (signed S. W. X. Z.) European Mag 63 1813; [Everett, E.] General Repository 4 1813; Literary Panorama 13 1813; [Hodgson, F.] Monthly Rev n.s. [2nd] 70 1813; New Annual Register 34 1813 (1814); New Rev 2 1813; Port Folio 3rd ser 1–2 1813; [Ellis, G.] Quart Rev 8 1812; Satirist n.s. 2 1813; Scots Mag 75 1813; Scourge 5 1813; (W. G. T.) Theatrical Inquisitor 2 1813.

Studies

S., G. Pedigree of the Rokeby family. GM 95, Sep 1825.
A few hours with Scott, being sketches in the way of supplement to the two poems of The lord of the isles and of Rokeby, by one of his old readers. Edinburgh 1856.
Littledale, H. Notes on Sir Walter Scott's Rokeby, with critical introduction, paraphrase of Canto I, and map of Rokeby district. Bombay [1890].

The bridal of Triermain: or the vale of St John, in three cantos. (Anon.) Edinburgh 1813 ([1st]–3rd edns), 1814 (4th edn), 1817 (5th edn), 1819 (4th [6th] edn, with Harold the dauntless), Philadelphia 1813, 1813, Zwickau 1827; tr Fr 1821, 1827 [A. J. B. Defauconpret]; Rus 1825 (P. K.: prose, from Fr), 1825–6 (N. Zaborovsky: prose); Sp 1830 [M. de Rementería y Fica: prose]; Ital 1833 (G. Barbieri).

REVIEWS: Critical Rev 4th ser 3 1813; Drakard's Paper 18 Dec 1813; Eclectic Rev 10 1813; Ladies' Monthly Museum 2nd ser 17 1814; Monthly Mag 48 1819; [Hodgson, F.] Monthly Rev n.s. [2nd] 73 1814; Port Folio 3rd ser 2 1813; [Ellis, G.] Quart Rev 9 1813; Scots Mag 75 1813; Town Talk 4 1813.

C., S. K. [R. P. Gillies?]. Extempore to Walter Scott Esq on the publication of the new edition of the Bridal of Triermain. [1819.]

Waverley: or 'tis sixty years since. (The first of the novels, all anon.) 3 vols Edinburgh 1814 ([1st], 2nd, '3rd', 3rd, '4th' edns), 1814 (for 1815, 5th edn), 1816 (6th edn), 1817 (7th edn), 1821 (8th edn), 2 vols Boston 1815, 1822, 1829, 3 vols New York 1815, 2 vols New York 1819, 1821, 1822, 1828, 1829, 1 vol Boston 1820, 1 vol Hartford CT 1821, 3 vols Paris 1821, 3 vols Philadelphia 1821, 4 vols Zwickau 1822, 2 vols Exeter NH 1824, 2 vols Philadelphia 1825, 1 vol Chicago [1829]; ed A. R. Allinson 1892; ed E. E. Smith 1902; ed A. D. Innes, Oxford 1909; ed E. Penner, Bielefeld 1914; ed with notes [1939]; ed A. Hook, Harmondsworth 1972 (Pen); ed C. Lamont, Oxford 1981, 1986 (WC).

TRANSLATIONS: Fr, 1818 (J. Martin), 1826 (A. J. B. Defauconpret), 1867 (A. Pey and L. Bailleul), 1880 (A. Chaillot), 1883 (E. Scheffter); Ger 1821 (W. A. Lindau: free), 1822 (W. L.), 1822 (B. J. F. von Halem, rev 1825), 1826 (M. Richter), 1828 (L. Tafel), 1829, 1840 (C. Herrmann), 1840 (K. Immer and H. Clifford), 1844–6 (K. Richter), 1877 (B. Tschischwitz), [1883–4] (L. Proescholdt), [1886] (M. von Borch), 1905 (E. Walter), 1979 (G. Reichel); Ital 1822 (V. Soncini), 1830 (G. B. Bazzoni), 1837 (C. Rusconi), 1844 (C. Rusconi: retranslation), 1934 (C. Alvaro), 1951 (S. Palazzi); Hungarian 1823; Du 1824, 1858 (S. J. van den Bergh), 1872 (M. P. Lindo), 1893 (G. Keller); Swed 1824–6, 1963 (A. Ljungberg); Danish 1826 (A. P. Liunge), 1832 (F. Schaldemose); Rus 1827; Polish 1830 (T. Świderska, rev Z. Glinka 1955), 1875, 1959 (T. Tatarkiewicz), 1989; Sp, 1835 (P. de Xérica), 1836, 1907 (F. G. Brito and I. C. Lapuya), 1959 (J. P. Rivas); Portuguese 1844 (C. Lopes de Moura), 1845 (A. J. Ramalho e Sousa); Cz 1875, 1925 (Z. M. Kuděj), 1962 (H. Skoumalová); Romanian 1944 (A. Iacobescu); Hungarian 1949 (J. Bókai), 1976 (I. Bart); Slovak 1956 (V. Szathmáry-Vlčková); Slovenian 1987 (M. Mihelic).

REVIEWS: Antijacobin Rev 47 1814; Br Critic n.s. 2 1814; [Scott, John] Champion 24 July 1814; Critical Rev 5th ser 1 1815; [Jeffrey, F.] Edinburgh Rev 24 1814, 33 1820; Monthly Museum 2 1814; [Merivale, J. H.] Monthly Rev n.s. [2nd] 75 1814; NMM 2 1814; New Annual Register 35 1814; Port Folio 3rd ser 5 1815; [Croker, J. W.] Quart Rev 11 1814; Scots Mag 76 1814; Scourge 8 1814.

Studies

On the character of Edward Waverly [*sic*]. In Essays, poems and letters on various subjects, 1815.
Murthly Castle, the supposed original of Tully-Veolan [signed *D*]. Edinburgh Mag 1 1817.
Eve, H. W. Notes to Scott's Waverley. 1875, rev 1901.
Hole, W. Pictures from Waverley. Edinburgh 1886.
Hart, A. Sir Walter Scott and Waverley Abbey. Saturday Rev of Politics 25 Aug 1900.
Cross, W. L. An earlier Waverley. MLN 17 1902.
Siebert, A. Untersuchungen zu Walter Scotts Waverley. Berlin [1902], 1903.
Carruth, W. H. The relation of Hauff's Lichtenstein to Scott's Waverley. PMLA 18 1903.

Willcock, J. Capt Wogan. N & Q 9 Apr 1904.
Drummond, J. Tully-Veolan. Scotsman 4 July 1908; replies 8–16 July.
Tullyveolan [signed R]. Scotsman 4 Aug 1910; replies 6–9 Aug.
Saintsbury, G. E. B. July 7 1814: the centenary of Waverley. Everyman 3 July 1914.
Williams, A. M. Waverley, July 7 1814. Glasgow Herald 4 July 1914.
Crockett, W. S. The centenary of Waverley. Records of the Glasgow Bibl Soc 4 1914–15.
Grant, A. Memories of Waverley. Scotsman 26 June 1915; replies 29 June–3 July; rptd in his On the wings of the morning, 1917.
Peterson, C. T. The writing of Waverley. Amer BC 18 1967.
Poynton, O. Observations on the first edition of Waverley. Private Lib 4 1971.
Garside, P. D. Dating Waverley's early chapters. Bibliotheck 13 1986.
Garside, P. D. Popular fiction and national tale: hidden origins of Scott's Waverley. Nineteenth Cent Lit 46 1991.

Guy Mannering: or the astrologer, by the author of Waverley. 3 vols Edinburgh 1815 ([1st], '2nd', 2nd, 3rd edns), 1817 (4th edn), 1820 ('6th' [5th], 6th edns), 2 vols Boston 1815 (1st Amer edn), 1815, 1816 (2nd Amer edn), 2 vols New York 1818, 1820, 2 vols Philadelphia 1820, 1822, 1823, 1826, 1 vol Boston 1821, 1829, 1 vol Hartford CT 1821, 1822, 3 vols Paris 1821, 1826, 4 vols Zwickau 1822, 3 vols Berlin 1823, 4 vols Paris 1823, 1826, 2 vols Exeter NH 1824, 1 vol Paris 1830, 1831, 3 vols Leipzig 1831, 2 vols Paris 1831, 3 vols Pest 1831; ed A. D. Innes, Oxford 1910; ed J. H. Boardman 1913; ed R. F. Winch 1913; ed E. W. Case, New York 1919 (abridged); ed Y. W. Cann 1930 (abridged); ed with notes [1938].

TRANSLATIONS: Fr 1816 (J. Martin), 1822 [A. J. B. Defauconpret], 1823 (A. and P. Chaillot), 1882 (E. Scheffter); Ger 1816 (W. A. Lindau), 1828 (L. Tafel), 1840–1 (Oelckers), 1841 (K. Immer and H. Clifford), 1844–6 (W. Gerhard), 1876 (B. Tschischwitz), 1908 (E. Walter); Swed 1822 (S. N. Wahrman); Danish 1823 (C. W. Hviding), 1826 (F. Schaldemose), 1987 (L. Pihl); Du 1824–5, 1872 (M. P. Lindo), 1893 (G. Keller); Ital 1824 (G. Barbieri), 1829 (A. D. C.), 1836 (C. Rusconi), 1844 (C. Rusconi: retranslation); Rus 1824 (from Fr), 1993 (A. M. Shadrin); Sp 1835 (P. de Xérica), 1838 [E. de Ochoa], 1843 (P. A. O'Crowley), 1906 (E. López y Fernández); Portuguese 1842–3, 1908–9 (K. d'Avellar); Polish 1828 (F. S. Dmochowski), 1974 (A. Przedpełska-Trzeciakowska), 1975 (W. Lewik); Slovak 1964 (E. Chmelová); Romanian 1976 (P. G. Anastasis).

REVIEWS: Antijacobin Rev 48 1815; Augustan Rev 1 1815; La Belle Assemblée n.s. 11 1815; Br Critic n.s. 3 1815; Br Lady's Mag 1 1815; Br Rev 6 1815; Champion 9 Apr 1815; Critical Rev 5th ser 1 1815; Eclectic Rev 2nd ser 3 1815; European Mag 67 1815; GM 85 1815; Literary Panorama n.s. 2 1815; Mentor 11 Oct–1 Nov 1817; Monthly Mag 30 Jan 1815; [Merivale, J. H.] Monthly Rev n.s. [2nd] 77 1815; NMM 3 1815; New Annual Register 36 1815; [Tudor, W.] North Amer Rev 1 1815; Port Folio 4th ser 2 1816; [Croker, J. W.] Quart Rev 12 1815; Scots Mag 77 1815; Theatrical Inquisitor 6 1815; Tradesman n.s. 15 1815.

Studies

Illustrations of Guy Mannering: Carlaverock Castle. Edinburgh Literary Gazette 22 Aug–5 Sep 1829.
[French, G. J.] The foundation of Scott's Guy Mannering: adventures of James Annesley [signed G. I. F.]. GM n.s. 14 1840.
Parallel passages from two tales elucidating the origin of the plot of Guy Mannering. Ed G. J. French, Manchester 1855.
Bouchier, J. Guy Mannering. N & Q 11 Mar 1899; replies 3 June–15 July. On 'timber-tones'.
Murray, R. Jean Gordon, the Meg Merrilies of Sir Walter Scott. Border Mag 7 1902.
Reith, J. Was John Leyden the prototype of Dominie Sampson? Gallovidian 4 1902.
Goodfellow, J. C. John Caspar Leyden: an historical retrospect, explanatory and critical. Trans of the Hawick Archaeological Soc for 1903.
Leyden and Dominie Sampson [signed Septuagenarian]. Scotsman 27 Feb 1903; replies 28 Feb–18 Mar.
B[oulter], W. C. Scott's Guy Mannering and Antiquary. N & Q 28 July 1906; reply 11 Aug.
F., J. E. The original of Dominie Sampson, a Melrose eccentric. Scotsman 20 June 1906; reply 23 June.
McMillan, D. In Guy Mannering land. Glasgow Herald 13 Jan 1910.
Dick, C. H. Dirk Hatteraick's cave. Glasgow Herald 8 June 1912.
Lang, J. Madge and Jean Gordon. In her North and south of Tweed: stories and legends of the Borders, 1913.
[Seccombe, T.] A review of January 1815. TLS 21 Jan 1915.
Miller, F. Andrew Crosbie, advocate, a reputed original of Paulus Pleydell in Guy Mannering. [1919.]
Norval. Old Mortality [for Guy Mannering]: a date in Scottish history. N & Q 12 June 1937.
Millgate, J. Guy Mannering in Edinburgh: the evidence of the manuscript. Library 32 1977.

The Lord of the Isles: a poem. Edinburgh 1815 ([1st], 2nd, '3rd', 4th edns, '5th' edn (re-issued 1830)), Boston 1815, New York 1815, 1818, 1818 (for 1819), Philadelphia 1815, Paris 1821, Zwickau 1821–2; ed T. Bayne, Oxford 1866; ed J. H. Flather 1902; ed W. K. Leask 1903 (for 1902); ed H. B. Cotterill 1903; ed G. Eyre-Todd, Glasgow [1913]; ed F. Marshall [1915]; ed W. K. Leask 1918 (re-edited); tr Fr 1821 [A. Pichot], 1827 [A. J. B. Defauconpret]; Ger 1821 (F. P. E. Richter), 1830 (C. W. Asher), 1857 (A. Neidhardt), 1864 (W. Hertzberg), [1867] (R. Jachmann), 1876; Polish 1826 (W. Malecka); Ital 1827 (L. Bassi), 1828 (F. Cusani: prose), 1834, 1852 (F. Ferrari), 1858 (C. Rusconi); Rus 1827 (prose); Danish 1829 (C. N. Block); Sp 1830 (prose); Portuguese 1839 (prose).

REVIEWS: American Monthly Mag 3 1818 (signed G, largely copied from Critical Rev); Antijacobin Rev 50 1816; Augustan Rev 1 1815; La Belle Assemblée n.s. 11 1815; Br Critic n.s. 3 1815; Br Lady's Mag 1 1815; Br Rev 6 1815; Champion 15 Jan 1815; Critical Rev 5th ser 2 1815 (signed M); Eclectic Rev n.s. 3 1815 (C. N., perhaps Cornelius Neale); [Jeffrey, F.] Edinburgh Rev 24 1815; European Mag 67 1815; GM 85 1815; Literary Panorama n.s. 2 1815; Mentor 11 Oct–1 Nov 1817 (signed Erasmus); Monthly Mag 30 Jan 1815; [Hodgson, F.] Monthly Rev n.s. [2nd] 76 1815; NMM 3 1815; New Annual Register 36 1815 (1816); North Amer Rev 1 1815; Port Folio 3rd ser 6 1815 (signed C); [Ellis, G.] Quart Rev 13 1815; Scots Mag 77 1815; Theatrical Inquisitor 6 1815; Tradesman n.s. 5 1815.

Studies

Davos sum, non Oedipus: on the interpretation of old Scottish words [signed Davos]. Scots Mag 77 1815.
A few hours with Scott, being sketches in the way of supplement to the two poems of The Lord of the Isles and of Rokeby, by one of his old readers. Edinburgh 1856.
Winged Skye [signed A Scot]. N & Q 1 Jan 1898; replies 22 Jan–12 Mar 1898, 30 May 1908.

The field of Waterloo: a poem. Edinburgh 1815 ([1st], '2nd', 3rd edns), Boston 1815, New York 1815, Paris 1821, Philadelphia 1815, Burlington VT 1816, Hudson NY 1816, Lexington KY 1816; ed T. J. Allman [1874]; tr Fr 1821; Ger 1825 (J. V. Cirkel); Rus 1827; Swed 1830; Ital 1831 (A. D.).

REVIEWS: Antijacobin Rev 49 1815; Augustan Rev 1 1815; La Belle Assemblée n.s. 12 suppl 1815; Br Critic n.s. 4 1815; Br Lady's Mag 2 1815; Champion 5 Nov 1815; Christian Observer 14 1815; Critical Rev 5th ser 2 1815; [Conder, J.] Eclectic Rev n.s. 4 1815; European Mag 69 1816; Ladies' Monthly Museum n.s. 3 1815; Literary Panorama n.s. 3 1815; Liverpool Mag 1 1816; Monthly Rev n.s. [2nd] 78 1815; New Annual Register 36 1815 (1816); Portico 1 1816; Scourge 10 1815; Theatrical Inquisitor 7 1815 (signed J).

Studies

Walter Scott. Port Folio 4th ser 1 1816.
Dean, D. R. Four notes on Scott. Stud in Scottish Lit 10 1972. Includes variant reading for The field of Waterloo.

The antiquary, by the author of Waverley and Guy Mannering. 3 vols Edinburgh 1816 ([1st] and 2nd edns), 1818 ('5th', 5th edns), 1821 (6th edn), 2 vols New York 1816, 1818, 1820, 3 vols New York 1820, 1 vol Boston 1821, 1821, 1 vol Hartford CT 1821, 3 vols Paris 1821, 2 vols Philadelphia 1821, 1826, 3 vols Berlin 1822, 4 vols Zwickau 1822, 2 vols Exeter NH 1824, 1 vol Paris 1830, 2 vols Paris 1831, 3 vols Pest 1831; ed F. A. Cavenagh, Oxford 1914; ed with notes [1939]; ed D. Hewitt, Edinburgh and New York 1995 (Edinburgh edn of the Waverley novels 3).

TRANSLATIONS: Fr 1817 (M. Nevill (S. de Maraize)), 1821 [A. J. B. Defauconpret], 1823, 1827 (A. and P. Chaillot), 1882 (E. Scheffter); Ger 1823 (H. Döring), 1824–5, 1826, 1828 (L. Tafel), 1840 (K. Immer and H. Clifford), 1840–1 (Oelckers), 1851 ([C.] Herrmann), 1876 (B. Tschischwitz), 1905 (E. Walter), 1914 (O. von Schaching); Ital 1823–4 (P. Borsieri), 1830 (C. Vandoni), 1830, 1844 (C. Rusconi), 1961 (F. Ferrara); Danish 1824 (C. W. Hviding), 1856–8, 1864 (L Moltke); Sp 1824, 1828, 1831, 1834, 1892, 1930 (J. Zamacois), 1950 (M. O. Ramos), 1975, 1976, 1977 (M. Conill and J. Beltran), 1980 (S. Ruiz); Du 1825, 1873 (M. P. Lindo), 1893 (G. Keller); Rus 1825–6 (P. K. and N. K.: from Fr), 1845; Swed 1827 (T. Sundler); Polish 1828 (E. Glücksberg); Cz 1929 (A. Tvrdek); Slovenian, 1955.

REVIEWS: Antijacobin Rev 50 1816; Augustan Rev 3 1816; Br Critic n.s. 5 1816; Br Lady's Mag 4 1816; Critical Rev 5th ser 3 1816; Dublin Examiner 1 1816; [Jeffrey, F.] Edinburgh Rev 33 1820; European Mag 70 1816; GM 86 1816; Monthly Rev n.s. [2nd] 82 1817; NMM 5 1816; New Annual Register 37 1816; [Croker, J. W.] Quart Rev 15 1816; Scots Mag 78 1816.

Studies

E., S. Some account of Andrew Gemmels, a Scottish beggar, supposed to be the original of Edie Ochiltree. Edinburgh Mag 1 1817.

French criticism on The antiquary. Scots Mag 79 1817.

Illustration of the novel of The antiquary. Lady's Mag 2nd ser 10 1820.

Hall, A. C. Sir Walter Scott's works. Literary Gazette 10 Oct 1829. Andrew Gemmells.

Edie Ochiltree. Chambers's Edinburgh Jnl 26 May 1838.

A day amongst the scenery of The antiquary. Chambers's Edinburgh Jnl, 25 Nov 1843.

O., J. H. I. Walter Scott's Antiquary. J. Sabin & Sons' Amer Bibliopolist 4 1872.

Pickford, J. The Antiquary. N & Q 28 Oct 1876; replies 9 Dec. Original of Fairport.

Edie Ochiltree. Scotsman 28 Jan 1890; replies 30 Jan.

Clouston, W. A. Jonathan Oldbuck and the 'praetorium' in Scott's Antiquary. N & Q 16 May 1891; replies 4 July.

Lang, A. Allusions in Scott's Antiquary. N & Q 19 Dec 1891; reply 13 Feb 1892.

B., J. T. Scott's Antiquary. N & Q 5 Nov 1892; reply (on Dr Orkborne) 3 Dec.

Bouchier, J. Scott's Antiquary. N & Q 29 Oct 1898; reply 11 Mar. History of Sister Margaret.

C., H. F. Walter Scott's Antiquary. N & Q 2 Apr 1898; replies 4 June–16 July. Setting sun.

Anderson, D. B. The Kaim of Kinprunes. In his The vale of Anwoth and other essays, 1899.

E., K. P. D. Scott: epitaph in The antiquary. N & Q 24 July 1909.

P., A. S. Mistake of Scott's. N & Q 9 Mar 1912; replies 13 Apr. Setting sun.

Schultz, J. R. Sir Walter Scott and Chaucer. MLN 28 1913.

Stookes, S. A decaying hamlet and Sir Walter Scott. Scotsman 13 Jan 1913.

Cavenagh, F. A. Scott: The antiquary. N & Q 1 Aug 1914; replies 22 Aug–12 Sep 1914, 30 Aug 1924. Sources of quotations.

Chevalier, W. A. C. The antiquary and Pickwick. Dickensian 10 1914.

[Seccombe, T.] Scott and the invader. TLS 28 Oct 1915.

Holthausen, F. Die Geschichte von Martin Waldeck in W. Scotts The antiquary. Anglia Beiblatt 29 1918.

Holthausen, F. Zur vergleichenden Märchen- und Sagenkunde, 2: Weiteres zur Geschichte von Martin Waldeck. Anglia Beiblatt 31 1920.

Chapman, R. W. Scott's Antiquary. RES 19 1943. Possible textual errors.

Tales of my landlord, collected and arranged by Jedediah Cleishbotham [The black dwarf; Old Mortality]. 4 vols Edinburgh 1816 ([1st] edn), 1817 (2nd, 3rd edns), '1817' [1818] (4th edn), 1819 ('4th' [5th] edn), 1819 ('6th' edn), 4 vols Philadelphia 1817, 1818, 1818, 4 vols New York 1817 (2nd Amer edn), 1818, 1820, 1820, 3 vols Philadelphia 1820, 1823, 1826, 1832, 1 vol Boston 1821, 1 vol Hartford CT 1821, 4 vols Paris 1821, 4 vols Berlin 1822–3, 2 vols Exeter NH 1829, 1 vol Paris 1831, 3 vols Pest 1831; tr Fr 1817 [A. J. B. Defauconpret], 1835 (A. Montémont); Ital 1822 (G. Barbieri), 1844 (C. Rusconi); Sp 1826 (F. A[ltés] y G[urena]), 1838 (A. B[ergnes]); Danish 1825 (F. Schaldemose); Portuguese 1838.

REVIEWS: Br Critic n.s. 7 1817; Br Lady's Mag 5 1817; Br Rev 9 1817; Critical Rev 5th ser 4 1816; Eclectic Rev n.s. 7 1817; Edinburgh Christian Instructor 14 1817 [T. McCrie, rptd Glasgow 1824, Philadelphia and New York 1843, Edinburgh 1845, and in his Miscellaneous writings, Edinburgh 1841]; Edinburgh Rev 28 1817, 33 1820 [F. Jeffrey, rptd in his Contributions to the Edinburgh Rev, 1844]; Independent no 3 1816; Monthly Mag 42 1817; Monthly Rev n.s. [2nd] 82 1817; NMM 6 1817; New Annual Register 37 1816; [Palfrey, J. F.] North Amer Rev 5 1817; Portfolio Political and Literary, 14–21 Dec 1816; Quart Rev 16 1817; Scots Mag 78 1816.

The black dwarf. 2 vols Zwickau 1822; ed P. D. Garside, Edinburgh and New York 1993 (Edinburgh edn of the Waverley novels 4a); tr Ger 1819 (W. A. Lindau), 1829, 1844–6 (E. Berthold), 1851 (F. Rottenkamp), 1904 (E. Walter), 1989 (F. Dietschreit); Du 1824 (H. Riedel), 1824; Rus 1824, 1992; Danish 1862 (L. Moltke); Swed 1825, 1913 (E. Grafström); Polish 1826, 1875; Fr 1851 (L. Barré), 1863 [A. and P. Caillot], 1888 (D. de La Monnoye); Ital 1829 (F. Meneghezzi), 1934 (A. Pardini: from Fr); Sp 1829 (P. H. B.), 1832 [F. Altés y Gurena], 1897 (P. Moura), 1907 (C. S. Gonzalez), 1982 (J. P. Mauras); Portuguese 1838 (C. Lopes de Moura), 1844, 1915 (C. Lima); Slovak 1976 (R. Krajčková); Hungarian 1981 (I. Bart), 1994 (G. Donga); Serbo-Croatian 1987 (L. Drzic).

Studies

A., J. Some account of Bowed Davie, the supposed original of the Black Dwarf. Edinburgh Monthly [Blackwood's] Mag 1 1817.

Account of David Ritchie, the original of the Black Dwarf. Edinburgh Mag 1 1817 (perhaps by T. Pringle, based on Scott); rev by W. Chambers as The life and anecdotes of the Black Dwarf or David Ritchie, Edinburgh 1820, and as The life and anecdotes of David Ritchie, the original of Sir Walter Scott's Black Dwarf, Edinburgh 1885.

[Chambers, W.] The hermit of Manor. Chambers's Edinburgh Jnl 27 Apr 1833.

Brown, J. The Black Dwarf's bones. In his Horae subsecivae, Locke and Sydenham, with other occasional papers, Edinburgh 1858.

Murray, A. D. Tweedside in the eighteenth century. Trans of the Hawick Archaeological Soc 1863.

Veitch, J. The Vale of the Manor and the Black Dwarf. Blackwood's Mag Sep 1890; rptd in his Border essays, Edinburgh and London 1896.

Old Mortality. 4 vols Zwickau 1822; ed J. A. Nicklin 1875; ed A. T. Flux 1900; ed W. K. Leask 1905; ed with notes 1905; ed H. B. George, Oxford 1906; ed A. J. Grieve [1907]; ed W. M. Parker 1958 (EL); ed A. Calder, Harmondsworth 1975 (Pen); ed D. S. Mack as The tale of Old Mortality, Edinburgh and New York 1993 (Edinburgh edn of the Waverley novels 4b); ed P. Davidson and J. Stevenson, 1993 (WC); tr Ger 1820–1 (W. A. Lindau), 1823 (E. Berthold), 1824, 1828, 1841 (K. Andrae), 1841 (K. Immer and H.

Clifford), 1876 (B. Tschischwitz), 1953 (R. Schaller); Danish 1824–5 (C. J. Boye), 1834, 1864 (L. Moltke); Du 1824, 1874 (M. P. Lindo), 1894 (G. Keller); Rus 1824 (V. Sots), 1986 (A. Bobovich); Swed 1824; Ital 1825 (G. Barbieri), 1830, 1835 (C. R.); Fr 1827 [A. and P. Chaillot], 1855 (La Bédollière), 1882 (P. Louisy); Portuguese 1831 (C. Lopes de Moura), 1906, 1978 (L. Pereira Gil); Polish 1828 (F. S. Dmochowsky); Sp 1839, [1870?], 1907 (C. S. González); Cz 1844 [W. Spinky]; Slovak 1954 (V. Szathmáry-Vičková); Hungarian 1964 (T. Szinnai); Lithuanian 1984 (V. Petrauskas); Latvian 1994 (O. Sarma).

Studies

[Grahame, J.] Vindication of the Scottish Presbyterians and Covenanters against the aspersions of the author of Tales of my landlord, by a member of the Scottish bar. Glasgow 1817.

On the political and religious tendency of the work entitled Tales of my landlord [signed D]. Scots Mag 79 1817.

Localities of Tillitudlem and other scenes mentioned in the tale of Old Mortality [signed T]. Edinburgh Mag 4 1819.

Aiton, W. A history of the rencounter at Drumclog and battle at Bothwell Bridge in the month of June 1679, with an account of what is correct and what is fictitious in the Tales of my landlord respecting these engagements, and reflections on political subjects. Hamilton 1821.

Old Mortality's counterpart. Weekly Entertainer n.s. 4 1821.

Young, G. J. Morton and Evandale. In Great characters of fiction, ed M. E. Townsend, 1893.

Winch, R. F. Glossary and notes on Sir Walter Scott's Old Mortality. [1894.]

Barrett, J. A. S. Old Mortality and Sir Walter Scott. Leisure Hour Oct 1902.

Clarke, T. Notes on Scott's Old Mortality. (Normal Tutorial Ser) [1905.]

Bell, A. M. Old Mortality: is Habakkuk Mucklewrath drawn from Alexander Peden? Scotsman 18 Feb 1910; replies 1–22 Mar.

Williams, A. M. Geography of Old Mortality. Glasgow Herald 21 Dec 1912.

[Seccombe, T.] The centenary of Old Mortality. TLS 11 Jan 1917.

Craig-Brown, T. Scott: a surprise and a correction. TLS 29 July 1920; replies 5 Aug–14 Oct; rptd Scotsman 30 July 1920; replies 2 Aug–9 Dec. 'Sound, sound the clarion'.

Harold the dauntless: a poem. Anon. Edinburgh 1817, New York 1817, Zwickau 1827; tr Fr 1820, 1826 [A. J. B. Defauconpret], 1863 (L. Barré); Ger 1822 (W. von Morgenstern); Danish 1825 (F. Schaldemose); Ital 1833 (G. Barbieri), 1858 (C. Rusconi).
REVIEWS: Blackwood's Edinburgh Mag 1 1817; Critical Rev 5th ser 5 1817; Dublin Examiner 2 1817; Eclectic Rev n.s. 7 1817 (by C. N., perhaps Cornelius Neale); Literary Gazette, 15 Mar 1817; Monthly Mag 48 1819; Monthly Rev n.s. [2nd] 84 1817; NMM 7 1817; Scots Mag 79 1817.

Studies

'Oaken' [signed N. M. & A.]. N & Q 10 Aug 1895; replies 24 Aug, 12 Oct.

Hillhouse, J. T. Sir Walter's last long poem. HLQ 16 1952.

Rob Roy, by the author of Waverley. 3 vols Edinburgh 1818 (for 1817; [1st edn]), 1818 ('2nd', '3rd', 4th edns), 2 vols New York 1818 (3 edns), 1821, 2 vols Philadelphia 1818, 1818, 1818 (2nd Philadelphia edn), 1821, 1824, 1 vol Boston 1821, 1 vol Hartford CT 1821, 3 vols Paris 1821, 3 vols Berlin 1822, 4 vols Zwickau 1822, 1 vol Paris 1831, 3 vols Pest 1831; ed A. T. Flux 1903; ed R. S. Rait, Oxford 1908; ed C. B. Wheeler, Oxford 1914; ed E. R. Musgrove, New York 1919 (abridged); ed with notes 1933; ed J. Sutherland 1995 (EL); ed I. Duncan 1998 (WC); tr Fr 1817 (A. J. B. D[efauconpret]), 1818 [A. F. Villemain], 1822, 1835, 1855 (La Bédollière], 1881 (P. Louisy); Ger 1819, 1820–1 (W. A. Lindau), 1826 (H. Schubart), 1828 (E. W.), 1840 (C. Herrmann), 1904 (E. Walter), 1957 (C. Hoeppener); Danish 1821 (C. J. Boye), 1842 (F. Schaldemose), 1870 (L. Moltke); Swed 1824–5; Ital 1825 (G. Barbieri), 1830 (G. Crippa), 1844 (C. Rusconi), 1956 (S. Palazzi), 1974 (G. Baldi); Du 1826, 1874 (M. P. Lindo), 1894 (G. Keller), 1930 (E. B. Koster); Sp 1826 (F. A[ltés] y G[urena]), 1828 (V. F. D. M.), 1828, 1837 (E. de C. V.), 1882 (J. Riera y Bertrán), 1896 (Amador de Castro), 1924 (M. Ortega y Gasset), [c. 1930] (T. Orts-Ramos), 1986 (H. Garcia); Rus 1829; Polish 1830, 1875 (M. Grubecki), 1947 (A. Tretiaka), 1968 (T. Świderska, rev S. Garczyński), 1989 (N. D. Volpin); Cz 1844 (W. Špinky), 1927 (P. Moudrá), 1959 (E. and E. Tilschovi); Hungarian 1959 (T. Szinnai), 1987 (A. Katona); Norwegian 1972 (O. Nilsen); Romanian 1976 (P. Comarnescu); Georgian 1978 (A. Cheishvili); Indonesian 1978; Albanian 1980 (V. Gjymshana); Bulgarian 1982 (T. Atanasova); Lithuanian 1991 (J. Subatavicius and M. Kazlauskait).
REVIEWS: Analectic Mag 11 1818; Antijacobin Rev 53 1818; Anti-Unionist 31 Jan–7 Feb 1818; Br Critic n.s. 9 1818; Br Lady's Mag n.s. 2 1818; Br Rev 11 1818; Edinburgh Observer 7 Mar 1818 [copied from Literary Gazette]; Edinburgh Rev 29 1818, 33 1820 [F. Jeffrey, rptd in his Contributions to the Edinburgh Rev, 1844]; European Mag 73 1818; GM 88 1818; Literary and Political Examiner 1 1818; Literary and Statistical Mag 2 1818; Literary Gazette 17 Jan 1818; Monthly Mag 45 1818; Monthly Rev n.s. [2nd] 85 1818; [Channing, E. T.] North Amer Rev 7 1818; Northern Star 2 1818; Quart Rev 26 1821 [N. Senior, rptd in his Essays on fiction, 1864]; [Morehead, R.] Scots Mag n.s. 2 1818; Scotsman 3 Jan 1818; Theatrical Inquisitor 12 1818; Visitor 1 1817.

Studies

Memoirs of Rob Roy Macgregor and some branches of his family. Blackwood's Edinburgh Mag 2 1817.

Letter to the author of Rob Roy [signed Nicol Jarvie tertius]. Blackwood's Edinburgh Mag 2 1818.

Rob Roy. La Belle Assemblée n.s. 26 1822, 28 1823.

Rob Roy. Mirror of Lit 1 1823.

Rob Roy. Gleaner 2 1824.

Airy, O. Source of quotation in Rob Roy. N & Q 25 Oct 1884; replies 15 Nov.

Schüler, M. Quellenforschung zu Scotts Roman Rob Roy. Leipzig 1901.

MacCunn, F. A. The original of Die Vernon. Good Words Aug 1905.

Handley, G. M. Notes on Scott's Rob Roy. [1910] (Normal Tutorial Ser).

Wheeler, C. B. Scott's Rob Roy. N & Q 13 June 1914; replies 27 June–18 July. References.

Craik, H. Rob Roy and Swift. TLS 28 Mar 1918.

[Seccombe, T.] The centenary of Rob Roy. TLS 3 Jan 1918.

Lupton, E. B. A Dickens scene with a Scott prototype. Dickensian 16 1920.

Scott's Rob Roy [signed Lecteur]. Scotsman 22 Sep 1920; replies 25 Sep. Source in Beaumarchais.

Millgate, J. Scott as annotator: the example of Rob Roy. Bibliotheck 12 1985.

Tales of my landlord: second series [The heart of Mid-Lothian]. 4 vols Edinburgh 1818 ([1st]–3rd edns), 4 vols New York 1818, 4 vols Philadelphia 1818, 1818 (2nd Philadelphia edn), 1821 (3rd Philadelphia edn), 2 vols New York 1820, 1 vol Boston 1821, 1 vol Hartford CT 1821, 4 vols Paris 1821, 3 vols Berlin 1822 (2nd edn), 5 vols Zwickau 1822, 3 vols Philadelphia 1826, 2 vols Philadelphia 1829, 1 vol Paris 1831; ed J. H. Boardman 1907; ed W. M. Parker 1956 (EL); introd by D. Daiches, New York [1969]; ed C. Lamont 1982 (WC); ed T. Inglis 1994 (Pen); tr Fr 1818 [A. J. B. Defauconpret], 1829 [A. and P. Chaillot], 1830, 1866 (A. Pey and L. Bailleul), 1855 (La Bédollière), 1884 (L. D. de La Monnoye); Ger 1821 (M. W. Schmidt), 1822 (free: ed W. V. Schmidt), 1822–4 (W. A. Lindau), 1826 (S. May), 1828 (E. W.), 1836 (A. Wagner), 1841 (E. Susemihl), 1842 (K. Immer and H. Clifford), 1876, 1877 (B. Tschischwitz), 1907 (E. Walter), 1955 (W. Wilhelm); Danish 1822, 1834 (C. J. Boye); Ital 1823 [T. Grossi?], 1832 (B. Finoli), 1847 (C. Rusconi); Swed 1824, 1926 (M. A.

Goldschmidt); Du 1825, 1872 (M. P. Lindo), 1894 (G. Keller); Rus 1825 (A. and Z.); Polish 1827 (F. S. Dmochowski); Sp 1831, 1833 (P. de Xérica), 1907 (F. Mora), c. 1988 (F. Toda); Portuguese 1844 (C. Lopes de Moura), 1906 (K. d'Avellar); Norwegian 1949 (J. Øen); Cz 1958 (J. Fastrová); Slovak 1977 (D. Slobodnik); Hungarian 1980 (G. Horváth Laszlo); Jap 1988.

REVIEWS: Antijacobin Rev 55 1818; [Mackenzie, H.] Blackwood's Edinburgh Mag 3 1818; Br Critic n.s. 10 1818; Br Lady's Mag 3rd ser 1 1818; Br Rev 12 1818; Clydesdale Mag 1 1818; Eclectic Rev n.s. 12 1819; Edinburgh Advertiser 14 Aug 1818 (abridged from The New Times); Edinburgh Reflector 5–19 Aug 1818; Edinburgh Rev 33 1820 [F. Jeffrey, rptd in his Contributions to the Edinburgh Rev, 1844]; Fireside Mag 1 1819; GM 88 1818 (rptd from The New Times); Green Man 12 Dec 1818; Literary and Statistical Mag 1 1818; Literary Gazette 8 Aug 1818; Literary Jnl and General Misc 8–15 Aug 1818; Monthly Mag 46 1818; Monthly Rev n.s. [2nd] 87 1818; NMM 10 1818; Quart Rev 26 1821 [N. W. Senior, rptd in his Essays on fiction, 1864]; Scots Mag 3 1818; Scotsman 1 Aug 1818.

Studies

Criminal trials illustrative of the tale entitled The heart of Mid-Lothian, published from the original record: with a prefatory notice including some particulars of the life of Captain John Porteous. Edinburgh 1818.

[Goldie, T.] Jeany and Effie Deans. Dumfries and Galloway Courier c. Dec 1818.

On the history of fictitious writing in Scotland, with remarks on the tale entitled The heart of Mid-Lothian [signed O]. Edinburgh Mag n.s. 3 1818.

The heart of Midlothian. Literary Chron 22 May 1819.

The heart of Midlothian. Ayrshire Mirror 1 1821.

Heart of Mid Lothian: true story of Jeanie and Effie Deans. Daily Visiter 1 1822.

McDiarmid, J. The real history of Jeanie Deans. In his Sketches from nature, Edinburgh and London 1830.

Biographical sketch of Helen Walker, a gentlewoman of heaven's making. Schoolmaster 29 Sep 1832.

Helen Walker. Sharpe's London Mag 12 Dec 1846.

Oakley, J. H. I. Sir Walter Scott's geography. N & Q 30 Nov 1872.

Fowler, D. Shakespeare and Scott: Measure for measure and The heart of Mid-Lothian, Isabella and Jeanie Deans. Rose-Belford's Canadian Monthly and National Rev 1 1878.

P., S. Sir Walter Scott: The heart of Midlothian; Mat Prior, The thief and cordelier, a ballad. N & Q 22 Feb 1879.

The heart of Midlothian, rescued from a batch. Saturday Rev of Politics 13 June 1891.

Bouchier, J. Jeanie Deans and la soeur Simplice. N & Q 16 Dec 1893.

Young, G. J. Jeanie Deans. In Great characters of fiction, ed M. E. Townsend, 1893.

Gärdes, J. Walter Scott als Charakterzeichner in The heart of Midlothian. Vegesack 1904.

B[ell], A. M. A Scottish heroine. Scotsman 1 Feb 1905.

Hewison, J. K. The prototype of Effie Deans: a graceful act by Scott. Scotsman 5 May 1906.

Handley, G. M. Notes on Scott's Heart of Midlothian. [1907] (Normal Tutorial Ser).

Trent, W. P. The Heart of Midlothian. Sewanee Rev 17 1909.

Bell, A. M. Jeanie Deans. TLS 10 Oct 1918.

[Seccombe, T.] The heart of Midlothian, 4th June 1818. TLS 6 June 1918; replies 13 June.

Esdaile, A. The National Library of Scotland: The heart of Midlothian. Lib Assoc Record 38 1936.

The heart of Midlothian: slips in quotation [signed Philoscotus]. N & Q 22 Apr 1939.

Tales of my landlord: third series [The bride of Lammermoor; A legend of Montrose]. 4 vols Edinburgh 1819 ([1st], '2nd', '3rd' edns), 4 vols New York 1819, 4 vols Philadelphia 1819, 1 vol Boston 1821, 1822, 1 vol Hartford CT 1821, 3 vols Hartford CT 1821, 2 vols New York 1821, 4 vols Paris 1821, 3 vols Philadelphia 1822, 1826, 4 vols Berlin 1823, 1 vol Philadelphia 1826, 1 vol Paris 1831.

REVIEWS: Antijacobin Rev 56 1819; Blackwood's Edinburgh Mag 5 1819; Br Lady's Mag 3rd ser 3 1819; Br Rev 14 1819; Eclectic Rev 2nd ser 12 1819; Edinburgh Monthly Rev 2 1819; Edinburgh Rev 33 1820 [F. Jeffrey, rptd in his Contributions to the Edinburgh Rev, 1844]; Fireside Mag 1 1819; Kaleidoscope 6 July 1819 (rptd from Literary Gazette); Literary Chron 26 June–3 July 1819; Literary Gazette 26 June–3 July 1819; Man of Kent 10 July 1819; Miniature Mag 3 1819; Monthly Mag 47 1819; Monthly Rev n.s. 89 1819; NMM 12 1819; Quart Rev 26 1821 [N. W. Senior, rptd in his Essays on fiction, 1864]; Scots Mag n.s. 4 1819 [R. Morehead] (Montrose only), 5 1819; Scotsman 26 June 1819; Western Rev 1 1819.

The bride of Lammermoor. 3 vols Zwickau 1823; ed J. H. Boardman 1908; ed F. Robertson 1991 (WC); ed J. H. Alexander, Edinburgh and New York 1995 (Edinburgh edn of the Waverley novels 7a); tr Fr 1819 [A. J. B. Defauconpret], 1821, 1855 (La Bédollière), 1886 (D. de La Monnoye), [c. 1948] (L. Labat); Ger 1820 (W. A. Lindau, rev 1822), 1826, 1828 (A. Ludwig), 1844 (W. Sauerwein), 1844–6 (H. von Montenglaut), 1876, [1892] (A. Tuhten), 1895 (H. Lobedan), 1905 (E. Walter); Danish 1823 (C. J. Boye), 1871 (L. Moltke); Ital 1824 (G. Barbieri), 1829 (G. Sormani), 1835 (C. Rusconi), 1847 (C. Rusconi: retranslation), 1951 (O. Previtali), 1956 (B. Onofri); Du 1826, 1873 (M. P. Lindo), [1955] (T. A. Moro), [1964] (E. Giphart); Rus 1827; Polish 1828 (F. S. Dmochowski), 1875 (M. Grubecki), 1965 (K. Tarnowska); Sp 1828 (L. C. B.), 1831 (P. de Xérica), 1909 (M. de la Torre), 1914 (J. Lleonart and C. R. Bracons), 1943 (C. de Castro), 1986 (R. Vazquez Zamora); Portuguese 1836; Greek 1865; Hungarian 1874 (K. L. Palóczy), 1967 (I. Kulin); Jap 1880 (T. Shoyo: adapted); Finnish 1883 [J. L. F. Kron]; Swed 1918 (E. Thall), 1947 (R. Hallén), 1962 (H. Åkerhielm), 1963 (N. Holmberg); Cz 1925 (K. Vít), 1985 (L. Vokrová); Slovak 1980 (E. Castiglione); Lithuanian 1995 (E. Kuosaite-Jasinskiene).

Studies

Lines descriptive of the catastrophe of the Bride of Lammermuir. Literary Gazette 28 Aug 1819.

S., G. Tales of my landlord. Literary Gazette 7 Oct 1820. Source for Caleb's ruse.

Théâtre de la Porte-Saint-Martin: La fiancée de Lammermoor. Le Globe 29 Mar 1828.

Markland, J. H. The bride of Lammermoor. N & Q 5 Jan 1856.

The Bride of Lammermoor [signed Sp]. N & Q 4 June 1870. Edgar of Wedderlie or Woderlie.

Mayer, S. R. T. The bride of Baldoon. N & Q 14 Aug 1875.

Wilson, H. S. The bride of Lammermoor. GM 263, Dec 1887.

The scenery of The bride of Lammermoor. Chambers's Jnl 25 May 1889.

C., W. L. The Lyceum Ravenswood. Murray's Mag 8 1890.

Pickford, J. A note on The bride of Lammermoor. N & Q 13 Dec 1890; replies 3 Jan–18 Apr 1891.

Saintsbury, [G. E. B.] The two tragedies: a note. Blackwood's Edinburgh Mag Sep 1897; reply and rejoinder Dec.

Rutherford, M. [W. H. White]. Sir Walter Scott's use of the supernatural in The bride of Lammermoor. In his Pages from a journal, with other papers, 1900.

Pickford, J. The bride of Lammermoor. N & Q 16 Jan 1909; replies 23 Jan–13 Feb.

Crichton-Browne, J. Hamlet and Lammermoor. Contemporary Rev 98 1910.

[Seccombe, T.] The bride of Lammermoor. TLS 5 June 1919; replies 19 June–14 Aug.

McCombie, F. The completion of The bride of Lammermoor. N & Q 221 Oct 1976.

A legend of Montrose. 2 vols Zwickau 1823, 2 vols Paris 1826; ed H. F. M. Simpson 1896; ed A. T. Flux 1903; ed W. K. Leask 1903; ed G. S.

Gordon, Oxford 1908; ed R. Prowde [1908]; ed M. Sen, Calcutta 1916; ed F. A. Cavenagh, Oxford 1924; ed J. H. Alexander as A Legend of the wars of Montrose, Edinburgh and New York 1995 (Edinburgh edn of the Waverley novels 7b); tr Fr 1819 [A. J. B. Defauconpret], 1821, 1823, 1851 (L. Barré), 1855 (La Bédollière), 1895 (D. de La Monnoye); Ger 1821 (S. May), 1821 (G. Lotz: free), 1829, 1844–6 (H. von Montenglaut), 1851 (F. Rottenkamp); Ital 1822 (V. Lancetti), 1833 (D. E. G.), 1847 (C. Rusconi), 1949 (S. Palazzi); Rus 1824 (from Fr), 1829, 1983 (N. D. Volpin and N. N. Arbeneva), 1994 (G. Zlatogova); Danish 1825 (C. J. Boye), 1825 (P. Thorsen: free); Du 1825, 1841 (W. Moll); Swed 1826; Sp 1827 (B. C.), 1827 ([P. de] Xérica), 1831 (G. Morales), 1833, 1908 (C. S. Gonzalez), 1941; Polish 1828 (K. Korwell); Portuguese 1837 (M. P. C. C. d'A.), 1842 (M. A. da Silva), 1908; Finnish 1871 (J. Krohn); Cz 1954 (Z. Graždanskaja: from Rus); Slovak, 1974 (M. Majerčíková); Romanian 1977 (P. G. C. Anastasis); Jap 1979 (S. Akira); Serbo-Croatian 1983 (L. Z. Simic).

Studies

The real Dugald Dalgetty. GM 301 1906.

Allemandy, V. H. Notes on Scott's Legend of Montrose. [1911] (Normal Tutorial Ser).

Shepard, J. S. Where Scott found Dugald Dalgetty. The Month July 1911.

Mackie, J. D. Dugald Dalgetty and the Scottish soldiers of fortune. Scottish Historical Rev 12 1915.

Symon, J. D. Marischal's most martial alumnus. Aberdeen Univ Rev 3 1915.

Lowe, C. A new Dugald Dalgetty: did Scott know of Sir Andrew Melvill when he created his soldier of fortune? Book Monthly 14 1918.

Owen, W. Scott in Italian. TLS 25 Sep 1937.

Ivanhoe: a romance, by the author of Waverley. 3 vols Edinburgh 1820 (for 1819, [1st edn]: 2 impressions), 1820 ('2nd', 2nd edns), 1821 (3rd edn), 1 vol Boston 1820, 1823, 2 vols Philadelphia 1820, 1820 (2nd American edn), 1820 (3rd Amer edn), 1823 (4th Amer edn), 1823, 1827, 1828, 1 vol Hartford CT 1821, 3 vols Paris 1821, 1825, 3 vols Berlin 1822, 1822, 1 vol Philadelphia 1823, 2 vols New York 1823, 4 vols Zwickau 1823, 1 vol Paris 1831, 4 vols Paris 1832; ed A. Mackay [1883]; ed C. E. Theodosius, Oxford 1900; ed J. Higham 1899; ed A. M. Hitchcock 1901; ed C. E. T. Dracass 1904 (for 1903); ed F. H. Stoddard [1904]; ed G. L. Turnbull [1904]; ed P. L. MacClintock 1904; ed with notes 1904; ed R. J. Cunliffe [1915]; ed F. A. Cavenagh, Oxford 1921; ed H. G. Bennett 1935; introd by H. J. C. Grierson 1952 (for 1953); ed A. J. Brayley 1964; ed A. N. Wilson, Harmondsworth 1982 (Pen). ed G. Tulloch, Edinburgh 1988 (Edinburgh Edition of the Waverley Novels 8); ed I. Duncan, Oxford 1996 (WC).

TRANSLATIONS: Du 1820 (W. L. H. K. Henke), 1824, 1872 (M. P. Lindo), 1894 (G. Keller), 1948 (P. J. Schepers), [1951] (E. Schrijver), 1975 (P. de Zeeuw and J. Gzn), 1979 (M. Hilverda), 1980 (M. Bakker), [1981] (P. Schultink); Fr 1820 [A. J. B. Defauconpret], 1822, 1826 [A. and P. Chaillot], 1829 (A. Montémont), 1855 (La Bédollière), 1861 (L. Barré), 1863 (A. Dumas), 1863 (V. Perceval), 1880 (P. Louisy), [1910], 1911 (H. Mansvic), 1928 (C. Hamon), 1994 (L. Vivien); Ger 1820, 1824 (S. May), 1826 (K. Immermann), 1826 (Meyer), 1826 (E. von Hohenhausen), 1827 (L. Tafel), 1840 (K. Immer and H. Clifford), 1841 (E. Susemihl), 1876 (B. Tschischwitz), [1877] (O. Randolf), 1879 (H. Loewe), 1880 (R. Koenig), 1904 (E. Walter), c. 1925 (R. Zoozmann), [1930] (K. Merländer), c. 1952 (C. Hoeppener), 1976 (C. Mandelartz), 1977 (R. Hermann); Rus 1820 (Velichko: extract), 1826 (Kovtyrev), 1978 (E. Beketova), 1993 (B. Vlasov); Swed 1821–2, 1912 (H. Hultenberg), 1917 (O. H. Dumrath), 1977 (H. Gyllander), 1979 (H. Akerhielm), c. 1984 (N. Holmberg); Danish 1822 (C. J. Boye), 1827 (N. F. Berg), 1899 (P. V. Grove), 1977 (P. Steenstrup), [c. 1980] (L. Kellberg: abbreviated G. J. Jorgensen); Ital 1822 (G. Barbieri), 1829 (F. Cusani), 1829 (A. Clerichetti), 1849 (C. Rusconi), 1869, 1920 (A. Fidi), 1934 (L. Torretta), 1939 (A. Farinelli), 1949 (S. Palazzi), 1951 (L. O. Foglino), 1952 (U. Dettore), 1952 (A. Severino), 1953 (D. Pilla), 1956 (M. S. Ferrari), 1956 (R. Paccarié), [1982] (V. Brinzi), 1984 (M. Neri), 1987 (G. Spina), 1991 (D. Piraino); Sp 1825 [J. de Mora], 1826 (J. M. X.), 1831, 1833, 1841, 1843, 1857, 1883 (J. Tomás y Salvany), 1891, 1911, 1924, 1935, 1945, 1946 (A. Giménez Ortiz), 1947, 1950 (J. A. Sarriols), 1950 (V. Scholz), 1951, [1959], 1975 (J. M. Fernandez), 1975 (M. Gimenez), 1976 (J. Alarcon Benito), 1976 (R. Conde Obregon: adapted), 1976 (C. Vergara), 1977 (M. Conill and J. Beltran), 1978 (J. M. Carbonell Barbera), 1978 (P. Penalver), 1978 (E. Sanchez Pascual), 1979 (M. T. Diaz Valcarcel), 1980 (S. Alba Rico), 1980 (I. Gardenas Rebollo), 1981 (N. Sanz y Ruiz de la Pena), 1982 (J. M. Balil Siro), 1983 (G. D'Efak), 1983 (A. Echeverria), 1984 (M. Jimenez Sales), 1984 (R. J. Rodriguez de Vera), 1985 (I. Bonet), 1986 (G. Costabal); Hungarian 1829 (A. Thaisz), 1906 (G. G. Ilona), 1955 (T. Szinnai), 1993 (I. Bart and S. Weores); Polish 1829 (F. S. Dmochowski), 1865, 1948 (S. Draczko); Portuguese 1837 (E. P. da Camera), 1838 (A. J. Ramalho e Sousa), 1905, 1948 (A. Vilalva), 1979 (S. Leonardos), 1980 (B. Silveira), 1980 (P. Tavares), 1986 (R. C. Iglesias); Greek 1847 (L. D. Lampise), 1976 (E. Bartzinopoulos), 1985; Cz 1865, 1926 (A. Starý), 1956 (J. Kraus), 1956 (L. Vokrová); Finnish 1870 [J. Krohn]; Jap, 1886 (K. Ushiyama), 1910 (M. Ohara), 1915 (K. Omachi), 1981 (K. Takezaku); Icelandic 1910 (Th. Gíslason); Lithuanian 1922, 1979 (B. Mejeryte, from Rus); Norwegian 1929 (C. T. Ebbell), 1972 (U. Gleditsch), 1972 (F. Iversen), 1979 (N. Kobro), 1986 (D. Haug); Catalan [c. 1930] (C. A. Jordana); Irish 1937 (S. MacGrianna); Turkish 1946–9 (A. Givda), 1975 (V. Dilacar), 1975 (B. Pirhasan), 1986 (M. Onol); Slovak 1958 (E. Felberová and S. Felber); Latvian 1971 (A. Bauga); Armenian 1975 (A. Gukasjan, from Rus); Macedonian 1975 (S. Serafinov); Kazakh 1976 (A. Atygaev); Burmese 1977 (Aung Khant); Thai 1977 (Saitharn); Chinese 1978, 1990 (S. Lin and I. Wei); Basque 1980; Bulgarian 1980 (M. Rankova and T. Atanasova), 1992 (R. Slaveikov); Georgian 1980, 1991 (V. Celidze); Serbo-Croatian 1980 (L. Tucakovic), 1987 (M. Maras); Malayalam 1982 (M. Sadasivan); Bengali 1986 (N. Morshed); Slovenian 1992 (V. Levstik); Estonian 1994 (A. Hansen).

REVIEWS: Blackwood's Edinburgh Mag 6 1819; Br Rev 15 1820; Champion 9–15 Jan 1820; Comet 1 1820; Dublin Mag 1 1820; Eclectic Rev n.s. 13 1820; Edinburgh Monthly Rev 3 1820; Edinburgh Rev 33 1820 [F. Jeffrey, rptd in his Contributions to the Edinburgh Rev, 1844]; Ladies' Monthly Museum 3rd ser 11 1820; Literary Chron 1–8 Jan 1820; Literary Gazette 25 Dec 1819; [Scott, John] [Baldwin's] London Mag 1 Jan 1820; [Gold's] London Mag 1 1820; Lonsdale Mag 1 1820; Monthly Mag 49 1820; Monthly Rev n.s. [2nd] 91 1820; NMM 13 1820; Port Folio 4th ser 9 1820 (rptd from Blackwood's Edinburgh Mag), 13 1822 (rptd from Monthly Rev); Quart Rev 26 1821 [N. W. Senior, rptd in his Essays on fiction, 1864]; [Morehead, R.] Scots Mag n.s. 6 1820; Scotsman 25 Dec 1819; Western Rev 2 1820.

Studies

Critique of Ivanhoe. Salt-Bearer 1 1820–1.

H., J. Strictures on Ivanhoe. Edinburgh Mag 6 1820.

Romances and the drama: on public taste and manners, and the history of the Knights Templars in reference to the romance of Ivanhoe. Spirit of the Magazines 1 1820.

[Eagles, J.] Letter to Eusebius. Blackwood's Mag 59 1846.

J., F. W. Two slips in Ivanhoe. N & Q 18 Nov 1882; reply 10 Feb 1883.

van Rensselaer, G. The original of Rebecca in Ivanhoe. Cent Illust Monthly Mag 24 1882.

B., A. W. 'Fusty bandias' and 'Strike pantnere'. N & Q 7 Mar 1891; replies 25 Apr–18 July.

Miss Gratz, the original of Rebecca of York. Border Mag 4 1899.

McGovern, J. B. The trysting oak in Ivanhoe. N & Q 13 July 1901; reply 17 Aug.

Abramczyk, R. Über die Quellen zu Walter Scotts Roman Ivanhoe. Halle 1903.

Rebecca of Ivanhoe [signed Dominie Sampson]. N & Q 9 July 1904; replies 3 Sep.

Turnbull, C. F. Notes on Scott's Ivanhoe. [1906] (Normal Tutorial Ser).

Kerlin, R. T. Scott's Ivanhoe and Sydney's Arcadia. MLN 22 1907.

Pearce, J. W. Miscellaneous notes. MLN 22 1907. Debt to Shenstone.

Bortone, G. Fra il voto e l'amore: note critiche sul Monaco del Lewis, sul Templaro dello Scott, sull' Arcidiacono dell' Hugo, sull' Abate dello Zola, sullo Scorpione dell Prévost etc. Naples 1908.

Farrie, H. Ivanhoe. In his Highways and byways in literature, 1910.

Forsythe, R. S. Two debts of Scott to Le morte d'Arthur. MLN 27 1912.

Porterfield, A. W. Ivanhoe translated by Immermann. MLN 28 1913.

Jacobs, J. The original of Scott's Rebecca. Pbns of the American Jewish Historical Soc 22 1914.

[Seccombe, T.] Ivanhoe, Dec 1819–Dec 1919. TLS 18 Dec 1919.

Abrahams, I. The original of Scott's Rebecca. TLS 1 Jan 1920.

Pedersen, V. H. Walter Scott in Denmark: the transfer of literary form as exemplified by a comparison of Ivanhoe and Valdemar Sejr. In The romantic heritage: a collection of critical essays, ed Karsten Engelberg, Copenhagen 1983.

Millgate, J. Making it new: Scott, Constable, Ballantyne, and the publication of Ivanhoe. Stud in Eng Lit 1500–1900 34 1994.

The monastery: a romance, by the author of Waverley. 3 vols Edinburgh 1820 [1st edn], 1820 ('2nd' edn), 1 vol Boston 1820, 2 vols New York 1820, 1820, 1822, 2 vols Philadelphia 1820, 1820, 1821, 1825, 1827, 1 vol Hartford CT 1821, 3 vols Paris 1821, 1821, 2 vols Berlin 1822, 4 vols Zwickau 1824, 1 vol Paris 1832; tr Fr 1820 [A. J. B. Defauconpret], 1823, 1830 (A. Montémont), [1850] (L. Barré), 1884 (P. Louisy); Ger 1821 (K. L. M. Müller), 1826 (D. Diez), 1828 (C. Mogg), 1840–1 (F. Funck), 1901 (T. Bergfeldt), 1906 (E. Walter); Danish 1823–4 (A. Rasmussen), 1843 (F. Schaldemose), 1867 (L. Moltke); Ital 1823 (G. Barbieri), 1832–3 (V. Soncini), 1835 (A. S.), 1847 (C. Rusconi); Swed 1826, 1879 (M. A. Goldschmidt); Rus 1829 (B. T.), 1993 (V. D. Metalnikov and M. A. Kopachki); Polish 1830, 1875; Sp 1840 (E. de Ochoa), 1841 (L. de C.), 1907 (F. Mora), 1941 (F. Cabañas Ventura), 1978, 1983; Portuguese 1842 (J. M. de Sales Ribeiro), 1911 (K. d'Avellar).

REVIEWS: Antijacobin Rev 58 1820; La Belle Assemblée n.s. 21 1820; Blackwood's Edinburgh Mag 6 1820; Br Rev 15 1820; Dublin Mag 1 1820; Eclectic Rev n.s. 14 1820; Edinburgh Monthly Rev 4 1820; European Mag 77 1820; GM 90 1820; Ladies' Monthly Museum 3rd ser 11 1820; Literary Chron 1 Apr 1820; Literary Gazette 25 Mar 1820; [Baldwin's] London Mag 1 1820 [John Scott]; [Gold's] London Mag 1 1820; Lonsdale Mag 1 1820; Monthly Mag 49 1820; Monthly Rev n.s. [2nd] 91 1820; NMM 13 1820; Port Folio 4th ser 9 1820; Quart Rev 26 1821 [N. W. Senior, rptd in his Essays on fiction, 1864]; Scots Mag n.s. 6 1820; Scotsman 25 Mar 1820; Western Rev 2 1820.

Studies

S., R. [Letter to editor on White Lady.] GM 90 1820; replies Oct and suppl.

W., E. S. Morse. N & Q 28 June 1884; replies 12 July–2 Aug 1884, 6 Mar 1886, 18 Feb–3 Mar 1888.

Freer, J. Elwyndale and its three towers. Hist of the Berwickshire Naturalists' Club 13 1890.

Moulton, R. G. Scott's Monastery: a romance of the early Reformation. Chautauquan 20 1895.

[Seccombe, T.] Scott's Monastery (March 1820) and Abbot (Sep 1820). TLS 9 Sep 1920.

The abbot, by the author of Waverley. 3 vols Edinburgh 1820 [1st edn], 3 vols Paris 1820, 1821, 1 vol Boston 1820, 2 vols New York 1820, 2 vols Philadelphia 1820, 1821 (3 edns), 1825, 1 vol Hartford CT 1821, 3 vols Berlin 1822, 4 vols Zwickau 1824, 1 vol Paris 1832; ed H. Corstorphine 1905; ed with notes [1938]; tr Fr 1820, 1821 (A. J. B. Defauconpret), 1830 (A. Montémont), 1850 (L. Barré), 1886 (P. Louisy), 1991 (K. De Bondt); Ger 1821 (W. A. Lindau), 1823 (H. Müller), 1826, 1828 (L. Tafel), 1828, 1840–1 (F. Funck), 1876, 1877 (R. Springer), [1903] (T. Bergfeldt), 1906 (E. Walter); Ital 1821 (G. Barbieri), 1833 (A. B.), 1835 (S. P.), 1847 (C. Rusconi), 1890, 1951 (A. Salvatore), 1975 (V. Comacci); Danish 1823 (A. Rasmussen), 1845 (F. Schaldemose), 1890 (F. W. Horn); Swed 1824–5, 1826–7; Rus 1825 [Politovsky], 1993 (V. P. Korkiia and O. G. Sosina); Polish 1830 (F. S. Dmochowski); Sp 1832 (F. M.), 1845 (F. A. Fernel), 1908 (N. Eztévanez); Du 1834 (J. F. Thieme), 1868 (L. Moltke), 1908, 1978 (from Ital); Portuguese 1844 (J. M. de Sales Ribeiro); Hungarian 1971 (B. László); Korean 1991 (S. Sin).

REVIEWS: Antijacobin Rev 59 1820; La Belle Assemblée n.s. 22 1820; [Lockhart, J. G.] Blackwood's Edinburgh Mag 7 1820; Dublin Mag 2 1820; Eclectic Rev n.s. 14 1820; Edinburgh Monthly Rev 4 1820; European Mag 78 1820; GM 90 1820; Glasgow Mag 1 1820; Kaleidoscope 19 Sep 1820; Ladies' Monthly Museum 3rd ser 12 1820; Literary Chron 9 Sep 1820; Literary Gazette, 2 Sep 1820; [Scott, John] [Baldwin's] London Mag 2 1820; [Gold's] London Mag 2 1820; Lonsdale Mag 1 1820; Monthly Mag 50 1820; Monthly Rev n.s. [2nd] 93 1820; NMM 14 1820; Newcastle Mag 1 1820; New Hibernian Mag 1 1820; Port Folio [4th ser] 10 1820; Quart Rev 26 1821 [N. W. Senior, rptd in his Essays on fiction, 1864]; Scots Mag n.s. 7 1820; Scotsman 9 Sep 1820; Scottish Episcopal Rev (Literary and Statistical Mag) 1 1820 (B. C. C., Oxford); Western Rev 3 1820.

Studies

[Lockhart, J. G.] Extracts from Mr Wastle's diary, no 3. Blackwood's Edinburgh Mag 7 1820.

Rāmānatha Bhārgava. A companion to Mary Queen of Scots, including papers with answers on the text and general grammar. 3rd edn Allahabad 1901.

Wilson, S. Notes on Mary Queen of Scots, with summary, analysis, grammatical notes, model questions with answers etc. Calcutta 1901.

Reinert, M. Untersuchungen zu Scotts Roman Der Abt. Erlangen 1914.

Kenilworth: a romance, by the author of Waverley. 3 vols Edinburgh 1821 [1st edn], 1821 (2nd edn), 2 vols Paris 1821, 3 vols Paris 1821, 1 vol Boston 1821, 1 vol Hartford CT 1821, 2 vols New York 1821, 1821, 2 vols Philadelphia 1821 [1st Amer edn], 1821 (2nd Amer edn), 1821 (3rd Amer edn), 1824 (4th Amer edn), 1824, 1827, 4 vols Zwickau 1824, 3 vols Paris 1828, 1 vol Philadelphia 1831, 1 vol Paris 1832; ed E. Gilliat [1900]; ed E. S. Davies 1901; ed with notes 1902; ed O. Smeaton 1903; ed W. K. Leask 1904; ed J. H. Flather 1904; ed A. D. Innes 1911; ed J. H. Castleman, New York 1918; introd H. J. C. Grierson 1952 (for 1953); ed J. H. Alexander, Edinburgh and New York 1993 (Edinburgh edn of the Waverley novels 11); tr Fr 1821 (Collet), 1821 [A. J. B. Defauconpret], 1821 (J. T. Parisot), 1828, 1881 (L. D. de La Monnoye); Ger 1821 (G. Lotz: free), 1822 (E. von Hohenhausen), 1827 (L. Tafel), 1828, 1840 (K. Immer and H. Clifford), 1840–1, 1876, [1877] (O. Randolf), 1877 (B. Tschischwitz), 1879 (E. Susemihl), 1891 (R. Koenig), 1905 (E. Walter); Ital 1821 (G. Barbieri), 1831 (V. Calnetti [V. Lancetti]), 1832 (L. R.), 1849 (C. Rusconi); Rus 1823 ([Irakly Karpov]: from Fr); Danish 1824–5 (J. C. Lange and H. F. Hellesen), 1836 (F. Schaldemose), 1863 (L. Moltke); Swed 1824–5, 1879, 1917 (W. T. Steads, rev E. Lundquist); Du 1825, 1896 (G. Keller); Polish 1828 (E. Rykaczewski); Sp 1831 (P. H. B.), 1831 ([P. de] Xérica), 1832 (V. Pagasartundua: from Fr), 1854, 1906 (F. G. Brito), 1940 (P. Pedraza y Pérez), [1959] (B. V. Raluy), 1975 (I. R. Romo); Portuguese 1841–2 (A. J. Ramalho e Sousa); Cz [1870?] (D. Hanušova), 1965 (V. Henzl); Polish 1870, 1958 (E. Rykczewski); Norwegian 1910 (C. T. Ebbell), 1946 (J. Solheim); Slovak 1965 (J. Šimo); Hungarian 1971 (B. László); Jap 1975 (S. Natsuo); Bulgarian 1985 (K. Todorova); Korean 1990 (C. Hwang).

REVIEWS: Academic 1 Feb 1821; Blackwood's Edinburgh Mag 8 1821; Br Rev 17 1821; Dublin Inquisitor 1 1821; Edinburgh Monthly Rev 5 1821; European Mag 79 1821 (signed D); Examiner, 11 Mar 1821 (signed G); GM 91 1821; Independent 20 Jan–3 Feb 1821; Kaleidoscope 30 Jan 1821; Ladies' Monthly Museum n.s. 13 1821; Lady's Mag n.s. 2 1821; Literary Chron 20–7 Jan 1821; Literary Gazette 20 Jan 1821; [probably Scott, John] [Baldwin's] London Mag 3 1821; [Gold's] London Mag 3 1821; Lonsdale Mag 2 1821; Mirror of Lit 8 1826; Monthly Rev n.s. [2nd] 94 1821; NMM 1 1821; Newcastle Mag 1 1821; New Edinburgh Rev 5 1821; New Hibernian Mag 2 1821; Port Folio [4th ser] 11 1821; Quart Rev 26 1821 [N. W. Senior, rptd in his Essays on fiction, 1864]; [Morehead, R.] Scots Mag n.s. 8 1821; Scotsman 13–20 Jan 1821; Weekly Entertainer n.s. 2 1821; Western Rev 4 1821.

Studies

Additional remarks on Kenilworth, in a letter from the country [signed Caledonia]. Edinburgh Mag n.s. 8 1821.

The book worm, no 8. European Mag 80 1821. Secret memoirs of Robert Dudley.

[Errors in Kenilworth.] GM 91 1821.

The history of Kenilworth castle. [Arliss's] Pocket Mag 7 1821.

Illustrations. Examiner 5 Aug 1821.

Kenilworth festivities. Weekly Entertainer n.s. 3 1821.

Laneham, R. Laneham's letter describing the magnificent pageants presented before Queen Elizabeth at Kenilworth Castle in 1575, repeatedly referred to in the romance of Kenilworth. 1821, 1824, 1825 (rev).

Origin of the story of Kenilworth. European Mag 79 1821.

Original story on which the romance of Kenilworth is founded. Literary Chron 27 Jan 1821.

Tighe, H. U. An historical account of Cumner, with some particulars of the traditions respecting the death of the Countess of Leicester, also an extract from Ashmole's Antiquities of Berkshire relative to that transaction and illustrative of the romance of Kenilworth. Oxford 1821, 1821.

Kenilworth illustrated; or the history of the castle. GM 92 1822.

Laneham's letter describing the magnificent pageant before Queen Elizabeth at Kenilworth Castle. GM 92 1822.

Bartlett, A. D. An historical and descriptive account of Cumnor Place Berks, with biographical notices of the Lady Amy Dudley and of Anthony Forster, followed by some remarks on the statements in Sir Walter Scott's Kenilworth. Oxford and London 1850.

Pettigrew, T. J. An inquiry into the particulars connected with the death of Amy Robsart (Lady Dudley) at Cumnor Place, Berks, Sep 8 1560; being a refutation of the calumnies charged against Sir Robert Dudley K. G., Anthony Forster, and others. 1859.

S., W. Amy Robsart and Cumnor Hall. London Soc 10 1866.

Adlard, G. Amye Robsart and the Earl of Leycester: a critical inquiry into the authenticity of the various statements in relation to the death of Amye Robsart, and of the libels on the Earl of Leycester. 1870.

Jackson, J. E. Amye Robsart. Nineteenth Cent 11 Mar 1882.

The death of Amy Robsart. Macmillan's Mag 53 1885.

Rye, W. The murder of Amy Robsart: a brief for the prosecution. 1885.

Gairdner, J. The death of Amy Robsart. Eng Historical Rev 1 1886.

Sidney, P. Who killed Amy Robsart? being some account of her life and death; with remarks on Sir Walter Scott's Kenilworth. 1901.

Boardman, J. H. Notes on Scott's Kenilworth. [1903] (Normal Tutorial Ser).

Wolf, M. Walter Scott's Kenilworth: eine Untersuchung über sein Verhältnis zur Geschichte und zu seinen Quellen. Leipzig 1903.

Alexander, J. H. The first American editions of Scott's Kenilworth. Bibliotheck 18 1992–3.

The pirate, by the author of Waverley. 3 vols Edinburgh 1822 [for 1821: 1st edn], 1822 ('2nd', '3rd' edns), 2 vols Albany NY 1822, 3 vols Berlin 1822, 1 vol Boston 1822, 2 vols Boston 1822, 1 vol Hartford CT 1822, 2 vols New York 1822 (3 edns), 3 vols Paris 1822, 2 vols Philadelphia 1822, 1822, 1826, 4 vols Zwickau 1824, 3 vols Paris 1826, 1 vol Paris 1832; tr Fr 1822 [A. J. B. Defauconpret], 1822, 1855 (La Bédollière), 1889 (R. de Cérisy); Ger 1822 (G. Lotz), 1822 (A. H. M. Montenglaut), 1822 (S. H. Spiker), 1825 (G. W. Becker), 1825 (H. Döring), 1828 (C. Mogg), 1829, 1842 (K. Immer and H. Clifford), 1861 (F. Richter), 1907 (E. Walter); Du 1825 (S. van Goor), 1896 (G. Keller); Danish 1827–8 (F. Schaldemose and H. G. Brill), 1828–9 (H. Goss); Swed 1827–8; Ital 1828 (V. Ferrario), 1828 (A. G. G.), 1849 (C. Rusconi), 1904 (L. Matteucci: abridged); Rus 1829 (M. Voskresensky: from Fr), 1865, 1991 (A. Onoskovich-Jatsyna), 1992 (V. Davidenkova), 1993 (L. Shelgunov); Sp 1830 [from Fr], 1887, 1905, 1922 (E. Xammar), 1929 (J. M. Huertas y Ventosa), 1941 (F. Cabañas Ventura), 1975 (A. Rodriguez); Bulgarian 1979 (B. Mindov).

REVIEWS: Babbler 1 Jan 1822; Blackwood's Edinburgh Mag 10 1821; Brighton Mag 1 1822; Br Critic n.s. 17 1822; Christian Observer 22 1822; European Mag 81 1822; Examiner 30 Dec 1821 (signed Q); GM 91 1821–2; Kaleidoscope 8 Jan 1822 (rptd from Examiner); Ladies' Monthly Museum 3rd ser 15 1822; Lady's Mag n.s. 3 1822; Literary Chron 5–12 Jan 1822; Literary Gazette 22 Dec 1821; [Baldwin's] London Mag 5 1822 [W. Hazlitt, rptd in his Collected works vol 11, 1904]; Lonsdale Mag 3 1822; Mirror 30 Dec 1821–13 Jan 1822; Monthly Rev n.s. [2nd] 97 1822; NMM 4 1822; New Edinburgh Mag 4, 6 1822; New Edinburgh Rev 2 1822; Quart Rev 26 1822 [N. W. Senior, rptd in his Essays on fiction, 1864]; Scots Mag n.s. 9 1821; Scotsman, 29 Dec 1821; Scottish Episcopal Rev 3 1822; Weekly Entertainer n.s. 5 1822.

Studies

A few brief notes on the novel of The pirate. Newcastle Mag n.s. 1 1822.

[Sale of The pirate in New York.] Family Gazette 1 1822.

W., T. On a song in Scott's Pirate: Fire on the main-top. N & Q 9 Aug 1851.

Scott's Minna and Brenda. Border Mag 8 1903.

Sir Walter Scott in Shetland. Scotsman 2 Sep 1903; reply 7 Sep.

Bayne, T. Scott's Pirate: two readings. N & Q 23 Mar 1912.

Fea, A. The real Captain Cleveland. 1912.

Hanford, J. H. The manuscript of Scott's The pirate. Princeton Univ Lib Chron 18 1957.

McMullin, B. J. The publication of Scott's The pirate. Bibliotheck 16 1989.

The fortunes of Nigel, by the author of Waverley. 3 vols Edinburgh 1822 ([1st], '2nd', '3rd' edns), 2 vols Albany NY 1822, 3 vols Berlin 1822, 1822, 1 vol Boston 1822, 2 vols New York 1822, 3 vols Paris 1822, 2 vols Philadelphia 1822, 1822, 1825, 4 vols Zwickau 1824, 1 vol Paris 1832; ed E. S. Davies 1902; ed with notes 1904; ed S. V. Makower, Oxford 1911; ed J. C. Corson 1969 (EL); tr Fr 1822 [A. J. B. Defauconpret], 1822 [Collet], 1828, 1836 (M. A. Montémont), 1890 (M. E. Toudouze), 1890 (R. de Cérisy); Danish 1823 (F. Schneider), 1855 (V. Herrmann); Ger 1824 (F. Meyer), 1827 (S. May), 1828, 1829 (A. Ludwig), 1841 (F. Funck), 1851 (C. Herrmann); Swed 1827, 1827; Ital 1829 (G. Barbieri), 1834 (C. B.), 1849 (C. Rusconi); Rus 1829, 1993 (I. V. Bursianin and N. L. Rakhmanova); Polish 1830 (F. S. Dmochowski); Du 1834 (G. L. van Oosten van Staveren); Sp 1836 (P. de Xérica); Hungarian 1975 (A Kászonyi).

REVIEWS: La Belle Assemblée n.s. 26 1822; [Howison, W.?] Blackwood's Edinburgh Mag 11 1822; East Lothian Mag 1 1822; Eclectic Rev n.s. 18 1822; Edinburgh Rev 37 1822 [F. Jeffrey, rptd in his Contributions to the Edinburgh Rev, 1844]; European Mag 81 1822; Examiner 3 June 1822 (signed Q); Gazette of Fashion 2 1822; General Weekly Register 2–9 June 1822; GM 92 1822; Kaleidoscope 11–18 June 1822 (mostly rptd from Examiner); Ladies' Monthly Museum n.s. 16 1822; Lady's Mag n.s. 3 1822;

Literary Chron 1 June 1822; Literary Gazette 1–8 June, 19 Oct 1822; Literary Museum 1–15 June 1822; Literary Speculum 2 [1822]; Lonsdale Mag 3 1822; Monthly Censor 1 1822; Monthly Literary Register 1 1822; Monthly Mag 53 1822; Monthly Rev n.s. [2nd] 98 1822; NMM 5 1822; Quart Rev 27 1822; Scots Mag n.s. 10 1822; Scotsman 1 June 1822; Weekly Entertainer (abridged from Literary Gazette) n.s. 6 1822.

Studies

Remarks on The fortunes of Nigel. Newcastle Mag n.s. 1 1822.

Singular anachronism in The fortunes of Nigel. Newcastle Mag n.s. 1 1822.

MacRitchie, D. Pronunciation of Nigel. N & Q 13 Oct 1894; reply 29 Dec.

Parry, A. W. and W. E. Griffith. Notes on Scott's Fortunes of Nigel. [1904] (Normal Tutorial Ser).

Müller, P. Die Quellen zu Walter Scotts Roman The fortunes of Nigel. Leisnig 1913.

Halidon Hill: a dramatic sketch from Scottish history. Edinburgh 1822 ([1st], '2nd' edns), New York 1822, Paris 1822, Philadelphia 1822; tr Danish 1822 (K. L. Rahbek); Fr 1822, 1826 (A. J. B. Defauconpret), 1828; Ger 1823 (W. A. Lindau), 1825 (Dr Adrian), 1826 (H. Döring); Swed 1825; Rus 1828 (D. E.: from Fr, prose).

REVIEWS: Brighton Mag 2 1822; Br Critic n.s. 18 1822; Dundee Mag 1 1822; East Lothian Mag 1 1822; Eclectic Rev n.s. 18 1822; European Mag 82 1822; Gazette of Fashion 2 1822; GM 92 1822; Kaleidoscope 2–9 July 1822; Ladies' Monthly Museum n.s. 16 1822; Lady's Mag n.s. 3 1822; Literary Chron 29 June 1822; Literary Gazette 29 June 1822; Literary Melange 10 July 1822; Literary Museum 4, 10 1822; Literary Register 1 1822; Literary Speculum 2 1822; [Smith, James] [Baldwin's] London Mag 6 1822; Monthly Censor 1 1822; Monthly Literary Register 2 1822; Monthly Mag 54 1822; Monthly Rev n.s. [2nd] 98 1822; NMM 6 1822; Newcastle Mag n.s. 1 1822; New Edinburgh Rev 3 1822; New European Mag 1 1822; Port Folio [4th ser] 14 1822; Scots Mag n.s. 11 1822; Scottish Episcopal Rev 3 1822; Weekly Entertainer, n.s. 6 1822.

Peveril of the Peak, by the author of Waverley. 4 vols Edinburgh 1822 [for 1823: 1st edn], 1823 ('2nd' edn), 4 vols Berlin 1823, 1 vol Boston 1823, 4 vols Leipzig 1823, 2 vols New York 1823, 1823, 4 vols Paris 1823, 2 vols Philadelphia 1823, 3 vols Philadelphia 1823, 1826, 5 vols Zwickau 1824, 1 vol Paris 1832; tr Fr 1823 [A. J. B. Defauconpret], 1824, 1836 (A. Montémont), 1891 (P. Louisy); Danish 1825 (L. Flamand and P. S. Pedersen [P. S. Martin]), 1864 (L. Moltke); Du 1825–7; Swed 1825–6; Ital 1828 (P. Costa), 1833 (G. Crippa), 1852 (C. Rusconi); Ger 1829, 1844–6 (J. Körner), 1852 ([C.] Herrmann); Rus 1830 (Pt 1 [A. I. Pisarev], Pts 2–5 S. Aksakov: from Fr), 1988 (M. I. Bekker and N. L. Emeliannikova); Sp 1836 (W. Montes), 1908 (T. Meabe), 1933 (F. Cabañas Ventura); Hungarian 1874 (J. Frecksay).

REVIEWS: La Belle Assemblée n.s. 27 1823; Br Critic n.s. 19 1823; Br Mag 1 1823; Citizen 17 Jan 1823; Eclectic Rev n.s. 20 1823; Edinburgh Univ Jnl 8 Jan 1823; European Mag 83 1823; Examiner 2 Feb 1823; GM 93 1823; Hermes 25 Jan 1823; Kaleidoscope n.s. 3 1822–3; Ladies' Monthly Museum n.s. 17 1823; Lady's Mag n.s. 4 1823; Literary Chron 25 Jan–1 Feb 1823; Literary Gazette 18 Jan 1823; Literary Museum 25 Jan–8 Feb 1823; Literary Register 25 Jan–1 Feb 1823; [Baldwin's] London Mag 7 1823 [W. Hazlitt, rptd in his Collected works vol 1, 1904]; London Rev 1 1829; Manchester Iris 2 1823; Mirror of Lit 1 1823; Monthly Literary Register 3 1823 (rptd from Literary Register); Monthly Mag 55 1823; Monthly Rev n.s. [2nd] 100 1823; NMM 7 1823; New European Mag 2 1823; Nic-Nac 1 1823; Repository of Modern Lit 1 1823; Scots Mag n.s. 12 1823 (signed Beta); Theatre n.s. 2 1823; Weekly Entertainer n.s. 7 1823.

Studies

Earl and Countess of Derby: Peveril of the Peak. Scots Mag n.s. 12 1823.

[Extract with comment.] Apollo Mag 1 1823.

Remarks on Peveril of the Peak. Newcastle Mag n.s. 2 1823.

Remarks on Peveril of the Peak from a correspondent. Ephemera 17 Feb 1823.

[Wilks, M.?] Historical notices of two characters in Peveril of the Peak. Literary Gazette 26 Apr–3 May 1823; rptd as Historical notices of Edward and William Christian: two characters in Peveril of the Peak, 1823.

The spectre dog of Peel Castle, the Manthe Dhoo of Peveril of the Peak. Borderland 1 1894.

Lorenzen, H. L. Peveril of the Peak: ein Beitrag zur literarischen Würdigung Sir Walter Scotts. Berlin 1912.

Millgate, J. Adding more buckram: Scott and the amplification of Peveril of the Peak. Eng Stud in Canada 13 1987.

Millgate, J. Proofing Peveril. Bibliotheck 17 1990.

MacDuff's cross: a drama. In A collection of poems, chiefly manuscript, ed Joanna Baillie, 1823; tr Ger 1824 (W. A. Lindau).

Quentin Durward, by the author of Waverley. 3 vols Edinburgh 1823 [1st edn], 1823 ('2nd' edn), 3 vols Berlin 1823, 1 vol Boston 1823, 2 vols New York 1823, 3 vols Paris 1823, 1827, 2 vols Philadelphia 1823, 1823, 1826–7, 4 vols Zwickau 1824, 1 vol Paris 1832, 4 vols Paris 1832; ed H. W. Ord 1898; ed with notes 1902; ed W. K. Leask 1906; ed R. W. Bruère [1907]; ed W. Murison, Cambridge [1907]; ed P. F. Willert, Oxford 1907; ed J. Wilson [1908]; ed A. Ll. Eno 1909; ed C. B. Wheeler, Oxford 1920; ed M. W. and G. Thomas [1966]; ed S. Manning 1992 (WC); tr Fr 1823 [A. J. B. Defauconpret], 1824, 1825 (A. and P. Chaillot), 1830 (A. Montémont), [1838] (L. Vivien), [1849] (L. Barré), [1855] (La Bédollière), 1866 (A. Pey), 1878, 1885 (H. Van Looy), [c. 1973] (J. Lefevre: adaptation); Ger 1823 (K. L. M. Müller), 1823 (S. H. Spieter), 1826 (L. Tafel), 1827 (H. Döring), 1840 (K. Immer and H. Clifford), 1840–1 (Oelckers), 1865 (A. Stein), 1876 (B. Tschischwitz), [1879] (O. Randolf), 1881 (R. Koenig), 1907 (E. Walter); Du 1824, 1896 (G. Keller), 1981 (H. Kost), 1987 (C. van Eijsden); Ital 1824–7, 1827 (L. Ferreri), 1831 (D. F. C. and G. Crippa), 1834 (L. Salvadori), 1844 (G. Barbieri), 1849 (C. Rusconi), 1890, 1909 (E. di Monale: abridged), 1920 (A. Fidi), 1951 (S. Palazzi); Swed 1824; Danish 1825 [A. Rasmussen], 1837 (F. Schaldemose), 1861 (L. Moltke), 1884 (W. Horn), 1978 (S. Jensen); Rus 1826–7 (A. I. Pisarev), 1835, 1865, 1973, 1978 (M. A. Shishmareva); Polish 1827 (F. Kopczewski), 1875 (M. Grubecki); Sp 1827 (F. A[ltés] y G[urena]), 1834, 1841, 1883, 1884 (C. Navarro), [c. 1902] (J. Pérez Mauras), 1916, 1934 (M. T. de Llanos), 1950 (V. Scholz), 1979 (C. Sempall), 1980 (J. J. Llopis), 1985 (A. Vallve); Portuguese 1838 (C. Lopez de Moura), 1838–9 (A. J. Ramalho e Sousa), [1885?] (J. de Magalhães), 1906 (K. d'Avellar), 1949 (J. Rosado), 1976 (H. Donato), 1978 (L. Pereira Gil); Cz 1925 (Z. M. Kuděj), 1960 (M. Rejl); Hungarian 1928, 1957 (N. Szávai and E. Máthé), 1966 (A. Katona, E. Máthé, and N. Szávai); Norwegian 1940 (H. Lavik), 1972 (J. Brinchmann), 1975 (L. Toklum); Greek [1946]; Slovak 1958 (V. Szathmáry-Vičková); Azerbaijanian, 1976 (M. Rzaguluzada); Serbo-Croatian, 1983 (I. Devcic-Torbica); Armenian 1985; Kazakh 1987 (M. Mamasanov); Lithuanian 1987 (J. Subatavicius); Bulgarian 1992 (N. Rozeva); Romanian 1992 (S. Dimulescu); Latvian [1993] (P. Kalva).

REVIEWS: Apollo Mag 1 1823; La Belle Assemblée n.s. 28 1823; Br Critic n.s. 19 1823; Br Mag 1 1823; Citizen 9 May 1823; Eclectic Rev n.s. 20 1823; Edinburgh Literary Gazette 17 May–11 June 1823; European Mag 83 1823; Examiner 1 June 1823; GM 93 1823; Hive nos 35–6 [1822]; Kaleidoscope 13–27 May 1823; (Tell, J.) Knight's Quart Mag 1 1823; Ladies' Monthly Museum n.s. 18 1823; Lady's Mag n.s. 4 1823; Literary Chron 24 May–7 June 1823; Literary Gazette 10–17 May 1823; Literary Museum 2–10 May 1823; Literary Register 10–17 May 1823; London Rev 1 1829; Manchester Iris 24 May 1823; Mirror of Lit 2 1823; Monthly Mag 55–6 1823; Monthly Rev n.s. [2nd] 101 1823; [Hugo, V.] La Muse Française 1 1823; NMM 8–9 1823; Newcastle Mag n.s. 2 1823; New European Mag 2 1823 (signed J); Repository of Mod Lit 1 1823; Scots Mag n.s. 12 1823; Scotsman 21 May 1823; Weekly Entertainer n.s. 7 1823.

Studies

Chit chat. Citizen n.s. 1 1823.

Historical illustrations of Quentin Durward selected from the Memoirs of Philip de Comines and other writers. 1823.

Louis XI and Charles the Bold as delineated in Quentin Durward. Phrenological Jnl and Misc 1 1824.

Oliver the Dain, or Devil. Literary Gazette 10 Sep 1831.

Mann, M. F. Quentin Durward. Anglia 12 1889.

Armstrong, T. P. Anachronisms in Quentin Durward. N & Q 19 Sep 1891.

Armstrong, T. P. Quentin Durward. N & Q 30 Apr 1892; replies 4 June.

Scott's Quentin Durward. GM 272 Mar 1892.

Handley, G. M. Notes on Scott's Quentin Durward. [1908] (Normal Tutorial Ser).

Williams, A. M. Sources of Quentin Durward. Glasgow Herald 4 Oct 1913.

Wheeler, C. B. Quentin Durward. N & Q Oct 1919; reply Nov.

Rendall, V. A Scott error. TLS 30 Apr 1938.

St Ronan's Well, by the author of Waverley. 3 vols Edinburgh 1824 [for 1823: 1st edn], 1824 ('2nd' edn), 3 vols Berlin 1824, 1 vol Boston 1824, 2 vols New York 1824, 1824, 3 vols Paris 1824, 2 vols Philadelphia 1824, 1824, 1827, 4 vols Zwickau 1824, 1 vol Paris 1832; ed M. Weinstein as Saint Ronan's Well, Edinburgh and New York 1995 (Edinburgh edn of the Waverley novels 16); tr Fr 1824 [A. J. B. Defauconpret], 1824 (Collet), 1826 (A. J. B. Defauconpret: [retranslation]); Ger 1824 (S. May), 1826, 1827 (E. von Hohenhausen), 1829, 1844–6 (E. von Hohenhausen); Du 1825; Ital 1825 (G. Barbieri), 1833 (B. Finoli), 1833 (S. A.), 1852 (C. Rusconi); Danish 1826 (H. G. N. Nyegaard and P. S. Petersen [P. S. Martin]); Swed 1826; Rus 1828 (M. Voskresensky, from Fr); Sp 1841 (E. de Ochoa).

REVIEWS: Bazar 1–22 Jan 1824; La Belle Assemblée n.s. 29 1824; Br Critic n.s. 21 1824; Cambridge Quart Rev 1 1824; Edinburgh Literary Gazette 31 Dec 1823; Examiner 4 Jan 1824; GM 93 1823; Gleaner 2 1824; Kaleidoscope 6 Jan 1824; Ladies' Monthly Museum n.s. 19 1824; Lady's Mag n.s. 5 1824; Literary Chron 27 Dec 1823 [from the Leeds Intelligencer], 3–10 Jan 1824; Literary Gazette 27 Dec 1823 [from the Leeds Intelligencer], 2 Jan 1824; Literary Museum 27 Dec 1823–2 Jan 1824; Literary Olio 1 1824; Literary Sketch-Book 10 Jan 1824 (rptd from Literary Gazette); London Rev 1 1829; Monthly Mag 57 1824; Monthly Rev n.s. [2nd] 103 1824; Newcastle Mag n.s. 3 1824; New European Mag 4 1824; Northern Observer 31 Dec 1823–7 Jan 1824; Phrenological Jnl 1 1823–4; Port Folio [4th ser] 17 1824; Scots Mag n.s. 13 1823; Scotsman 31 Dec 1823; Universal Rev 1 1824; Weekly Entertainer n.s. 9 1824; Weekly Mag or Literary Observer 3–10 Jan 1824; Western Luminary 3 Jan 1824.

Studies

Scottish watering places: Innerleithen. Chambers's Edinburgh Jnl 1 June 1833.

Collyer, J. M. 'The catastrophe' in St Ronan's Well. Athenaeum 4 Feb 1893.

Redgauntlet: a tale of the eighteenth century, by the author of Waverley. 3 vols Edinburgh 1824 ([1st], '2nd' edns), 3 vols Berlin 1824, 1 vol Boston 1824, 2 vols Exeter NH 1824, 2 vols New York 1824, 3 vols Paris 1824, 2 vols Philadelphia 1824, 1824, 1827, 4 vols Zwickau 1825, 1 vol Paris 1832; ed with notes [1938]; ed K. Sutherland, Oxford 1985 (WC); ed G. A. M. Wood with D. Hewitt, Edinburgh and New York 1997 (Edinburgh edn of the Waverley novels 17); tr Fr, 1822, 1824 [A. J. B. Defauconpret], 1827, 1831 (A. Montémont), 1836 (H. Alber), 1885 (E. Scheffter); Ger 1822 (W. A. Lindau), 1824 (H. Döring), 1824 (S. May), 1826 (C. Weil), 1827 (M. Richter), 1828 (E. W.), 1844–6 (K. Richter), 1851 ([C.] Herrmann]; Swed 1824, 1826; Danish 1824–5 (F. Schneider), 1856 (C. J. Boye); Du 1825; Ital 1825 (G. Barbieri), 1825, 1830 (B. Finoli), 1852 (C. Rusconi); Rus 1825 (extract), 1828 (from Fr); Sp 1828 (V. F. D. M.), 1833 (F. de O.), 1858 (E. de C. V.); Cz 1925 (Z. M. Kudej); Hungarian 1972 (I. Bart).

REVIEWS: La Belle Assemblée n.s. 30 1824; Birmingham Spectator 26 June–17 July 1824; Br Critic n.s. 22 1824; European Rev 1 1824; Examiner 11 July 1824; GM 94 1824; Hive 4 [1824]; Kaleidoscope 20 July 1824 (rptd from Literary Museum); Ladies' Monthly Museum n.s. 20 1824; Lady's Mag n.s. 5 1824; Literary Chron 19 June 1824; Literary Gazette 19 June 1824; Literary Magnet 1 1824; Literary Museum n.s. 5 1824; [Baldwin's] London Mag 10 1824; London Rev 1 1829; Metropolitan Literary Jnl 1 1824; Monthly Critical Gazette 1 1824; Monthly Rev n.s. [2nd] 104 1824; NMM 11 1824; Newcastle Mag n.s. 3 1824; New European Mag 4 1824; News of Lit and Fashion 19–26 June 1824; Oxford Quart Mag 1 1825; Parlour Fire-Side 26 June–3 July 1824 [copied from Literary Chron]; Philomathic Jnl 1 1824; Phrenological Jnl 1 1823–4; Port Folio [4th ser] 18 1824; Scots Mag n.s. 14 1824; Scotsman 16 June 1824; Somerset House Gazette 19 June 1824; United States Literary Gazette 15 Aug 1824; Universal Rev 1 1824; Weekly Entertainer n.s. 10 1824 [rptd from Literary Gazette]; [Fonblanque, A.?] Westminster Rev 2 1824.

Studies

MacRitchie, D. The proof-sheets of Redgauntlet. Longman's Mag 35 1900.

Knothe, F. Untersuchungen zu Redgauntlet von Walter Scott. Görlitz 1913.

MacRitchie, D. The proof sheets of Redgauntlet. TLS 11 Sep 1924.

Lascelles, M. Scott and the art of revision. In Imagined worlds: essays on some English novels and novelists in honour of John Butt, ed M. Mack and I. Gregor, 1968; rev in her Notions and facts: collected criticism and research, Oxford 1972.

Wood, G. A. M. The great reviser: or the unknown Scott. Ariel 2 1971.

Wood, G. A. M. The manuscripts and proofsheets of Redgauntlet. In Scott bicentenary essays, ed A. Bell, 1973.

Wood, G. A. M. Scott's continuing revision: the printed texts of Redgauntlet. Bibliotheck 6 1973.

Tales of the Crusaders, by the author of Waverley [The betrothed; The talisman]. 4 vols Edinburgh 1825 [1st edn], 4 vols Berlin 1825, 1 vol Boston 1825, 2 vols Boston 1825, 4 vols New York 1825, 1825, 4 vols Paris 1825, 4 vols Philadelphia 1825, 3 vols Philadelphia 1825, 6 vols Zwickau 1826, 2 vols Paris 1832; tr Fr 1825 (A. J. B. Defauconpret: 2nd edn 1830); Ger 1825 (S. May), 1826 (A. Schäfer), 1828 (H. Döring); Du 1826, 1894 (G. Keller); Ital 1826, 1836 (G. Paganucci).

REVIEWS: La Belle Assemblée 3rd ser 1 1825; Br Critic 3rd ser 1 1825; Captain Rock in London 9–23 July 1825; Dublin and London Mag 1 1825; Dumfries Monthly Mag 1 1825; European Rev 2 1826; Examiner 27 June [from the Scotsman], 3 July 1825 (signed Q); GM 95 1825; Imperial Mag 7 1825; Isis 25 June–2 July 1825; Ladies' Monthly Museum n.s. 22 1825; Lady's Mag n.s. 6 1825; Literary Chron 25 June–2 July 1825; Literary Gazette 25 June–2 July 1825; Literary Magnet 4 1826; [Baldwin's] London Mag n.s. 2 1825; London Rev 1 1829; Monthly Mag 59 1823; Monthly Rev n.s. [2nd] 107 1825; NMM 14 1825; Newcastle Mag n.s. 4 1825; News of Lit and Fashion 25 June 1825; Parthenon 25 June–23 July 1825; Repository of Arts 3rd ser 6 1825; Scots Mag n.s. 16 1825; Scotsman 22 June 1825; United States Literary Gazette 1 Sep 1825; Weekly Entertainer n.s. 12 1825.

Study

The Crusaders. News of Lit and Fashion 9 July 1825.

The betrothed. Tr Du 1825–6 (W. L. H. K. Henke); Ger 1825 (S. May [F. Mayer]), 1851 (A. Schäfer), 1909 (E. Walter); Ital 1826 (G. Barbieri), 1826–7 (G. Pagnucci), 1856 (C. Rusconi); Swed 1826; Danish 1827 (A. Rasmussen), 1847–8 (F. Schaldemose), 1856; Rus 1828 (N. Sh[igaev]); Sp 1840 (P. Mata), 1907 (F. Mora); Portuguese 1911 (K. d'Avellar); Chinese 1990 (Lin Shu).

The talisman. Ed W. Melven 1897, ed H. B. George, Oxford 1897; ed E. Gilliat 1897; ed with notes 1904; ed G. L. Turnbull [1905]; ed H. Williams [1905]; ed W. K. Leask 1906; ed A. S. Gaye, Cambridge 1906; ed F. Treudley 1909; ed C. B. Wheeler, Oxford 1919; ed F. K. Ball, Boston [1928]; ed with notes [1938]; ed W. M. Parker 1956 [for 1957] (EL); tr Sp 1825 [J. de Mora], 1826, 1826 [J. N. Gallego and E. de Tapia], 1908 (M. A. Corral), 1942 (L. Jordá), 1977 (M. Conill and J. Beltran); Du 1826, 1826–7, 1955 (L. Ruys); Danish 1826–7 (A. E. Boye), 1826–7 (A. Rasmussen), 1830, 1849; Ger 1826, 1840 (K. Immer and H. Clifford), 1841, 1877 (B. Tschischwitz), 1881 (R. Koenig), 1898 (W. Sauerwein), 1907 (E. Walter), [1924] (O. Ebermann), [1960] (J. Hubalek), c. 1993 (T. Leitner); Ital 1826 (G. Barbieri), 1826 (G. Paganucci), 1856 (C. Rusconi), 1924 (abridged), 1949 (S. Palazzi), 1953 (M. Giussani: abridged), [1957] (L. Theodoli), 1983 (V. Brinzi), [c. 1985] (G. Benvenuto and S. Pierdonati); Polish 1826 (F. D[mochowski]), 1875 (M. Grubecki); Rus 1826 (extract), 1827, 1988 (B. T. Gribanov), 1994 (G. Zlatogova), 1991 (P. A. Obolenskii); Fr 1830 (A. Montémont), 1851 (L. Barré), 1861 (A. and P. Chaillot), 1892 (P. Louisy), 1991 (C. Franken); Portuguese 1835–6, 1837 (C. L. de Moura), 1945 (A. Vilalva), 1978 (L. Pereira Gil); Finnish 1880; Catalan 1922 (C. Capdevila); Cz 1926 (P. Holý), 1926 (F. Krupička), 1959 (V. Kovalová); Hungarian 1929, 1963 (I. Szász and M. Vajda), 1993 (Z. Majatinyi); Hebrew, 1929–30 (S. Mohilewer); Irish 1936 (N. Ó Domhnaill); Thai [c. 1950]; Bengali, 1985 (S. Raha), 1986 (N. Morshed); Chinese [1990] (S. Lin); Estonian 1995 (H. Kivisepp), c. 1995 (V. Kuusik).

Study

Barter, A. Notes on Scott's Talisman. [1904] (Normal Tutorial Ser).

Woodstock: or the cavalier, by the author of Waverley. 3 vols Edinburgh 1826 [1st edn], 3 vols Berlin 1826, 1 vol Boston 1826, 2 vols New York 1826, 1826, 3 vols Paris 1826, 2 vols Philadelphia 1826, 1826, 4 vols Zwickau 1826, 1 vol Paris 1832; ed B. Perry 1897; ed H. Costorphine 1900; ed with notes 1904; ed J. S. C. Bridge, Oxford 1908; ed A. S. Gaye 1911; introd by J. C. Corson 1969 (EL); tr Fr 1826 (A. J. B. Defauconpret), 1827, 1837 (A. Montémont), 1851 (L. Barré), 1885 (H. Van Looy), 1887 (E. Scheffter); Ger 1826 (C. F. Michaelis), 1826 (C. Weil), 1827, 1829 (G. N. Bärmann), 1874 (R. Koenig); Rus 1826 (extract), 1829 (S. de Shaplet: from Fr), 1829 (A. Gerasimova: from Fr), 1993 (E. N. Petrova and A. N. Teterevnikova); Swed 1826–7 (C. R.), 1882; Danish 1827 (A. Rasmussen), 1856 (A. E. Boye), 1862 (L. Moltke); Ital 1828 (V. Lancetti), 1829, 1834 (G. Crippa), 1852 (C. Rusconi), 1924 (abridged), 1950 (S. Palazzi), 1968 (M. R. Schisano); Du 1831, [1875] (P. J. Andriessen); Sp 1831, 1906–7 (C. S. Gonzalez), 1922 (F. Cabañas Ventura); Polish 1837; Portuguese 1837 (C. Lopes de Moura), 1843–4, 1909 (K. d'Avellar); Cz 1929 (P. Moudrá); Hungarian 1978 (G. Szegö).

REVIEWS: Br Critic 3rd ser 3 1826; Dublin and London Mag 2 1826; Dumfries Monthly Mag 2 1826; Eclectic Rev n.s. 25 1826; GM 96 1826; Inspector 1 1826; Kaleidoscope 2–30 May 1826; Ladies' Monthly Museum n.s. 23 1826; Lady's Mag n.s. 7 1826; Literary Chron 29 Apr–6 May 1826; Literary Gazette 29 Apr–13 May 1826; [Baldwin's] London Mag n.s. 5 1826; London Rev 1 1829; Mirror of Lit 7 1826; Monthly Mag n.s. 1 1826; Monthly Rev 3rd ser 2 1826; NMM 18 1826; Newcastle Mag n.s. 5 1826; Panoramic Misc 1 1826; Repository of Arts 3rd ser 7 1826; Scots Mag n.s. 18 1826; Spectrum 1 June 1826; [Barker, C.?] Westminster Rev 5 1826.

Studies

The ancient palace of Woodstock. Mirror of Lit 7 1826.

Blunders in the new novel of Woodstock [signed Oculus]. Mirror of Lit 7 1826.

Illustrations of Woodstock. Mirror of Lit 7 1826.

Memoir of Sir Walter Scott. Mirror of Lit 7 1826.

Some observations on the character of Cromwell as delineated in the novel of Woodstock. Phrenological Jnl and Misc 3 1826.

Moulton, R. G. Scott's Woodstock: a romance of the English Revolution. Chautauquan 20 1895.

Sir Walter Scott's Woodstock [signed Devoniensis]. N & Q 26 July 1902; replies 30 Aug–27 Dec.

Evans, H. A. The good devil of Woodstock. N & Q 9 May 1903.

Handley, G. M. Notes on Scott's Woodstock. [1904] (Normal Tutorial Ser).

Todd, W. B. Twin titles in Scott's Woodstock (1826). PBSA 45 1951.

Chronicles of the Canongate [1st ser: Croftangry's introd; The Highland widow; The two drovers; The surgeon's daughter]. 2 vols Edinburgh 1827 [1st edn], 1828 (2nd edn), 2 vols New York 1827, 1827, 2 vols Paris 1827, 2 vols Philadelphia 1827 (3 edns), 1828, 2 vols Berlin 1828, 1 vol Boston 1828, 1 vol Paris 1832; tr Fr 1827 (A. J. B. Defauconpret), 1828, 1831 (A. Montémont); Swed 1827, 1828 (L. Arnell); Danish 1828 (A. P. Liunge and E. C. Broager), 1869 (L. Moltke); Du 1828; Ger 1828 (K. L. Kannegiesser); Ital 1828 (N. Tommaseo), 1828–9 (G. Giglioli), 1829 (V. Soncini), 1831 (G. Barbieri), 1856 (C. Rusconi); Rus 1829 (extract), 1830 (from Fr); Sp 1907 (R. M. Lopez).

REVIEWS: Atlas 4 Nov 1827; [Wilson, J.] Blackwood's Edinburgh Mag 22 Nov 1827; Examiner 4 Nov 1827 (signed Qi); GM 97 1827; Kaleidoscope 30 Oct 1827; Ladies' Monthly Museum n.s. 26 1827; Lady's Mag n.s. 8 1827; Literary Chron 3 Nov 1827; Literary Gazette 27 Oct–3 Nov 1827; [Southern, S.] [Baldwin's] London Mag n.s. 9 1827; London Rev 1 1829; London Weekly Rev 20 Oct–3 Nov 1827; Mirror of Lit 27 Oct–17 Nov 1827; Monthly Mag n.s. 4 1827; NMM 21 1827; Scotsman 3 Nov 1827.

Study

Chronicles of the Canongate [signed Oculus]. Mirror of Literature, 1 Dec 1827.

Introductory. Tr Rus 1827, 1827, 1828, 1829, 1830.

The Highland widow. Tr Rus 1828 (extract), 1828; Ital 1829 (G. Crippa); Fr 1853 (A. Colincamp), 1879 (A. Chaillot), 1894; Finnish [1913] (V. Hameen-Antilla); Sp 1983, 1991 (F. Toda).

Studies

Dickins, L. Scott's masterpiece. Englishwoman 19 1913.

Hippoclydes. The Song of Hybrias the Cretan. N & Q 180 1941; reply 181 1941.

The two drovers. Tr Rus 1833 (M. Ivanenko); Ger 1981 (W. Franke), 1984 (H. Raykowski); Hungarian 1981 (I. Bart); Sp 1991 (F. Toda).

The surgeon's daughter. Tr Rus 1830; Polish 1836 (E. Cezary [Glückberg]); Fr 1853 (Michelant); Ger 1902 (K. L. Kannegiesser), 1904 (E. Walter).

Study

Krishnaswami, P. R. Sir Walter Scott's Indian novel The surgeon's daughter. Calcutta Rev Oct 1919.

Chronicles of the Canongate, second series, by the author of Waverley [Croftangry's introd; The fair maid of Perth]. 3 vols Edinburgh 1828 [1st edn], 1828 ('2nd' edn), 3 vols Berlin 1828, 2 vols Boston 1828, 2 vols New York 1828, 3 vols Paris 1828, 2 vols Philadelphia 1828, 1828, 3 vols Zwickau 1828, 1 vol Paris 1832, ed E. W. Jackson 1902; tr Danish 1828–9 (S. Meisling), 1860 (L. Moltke); Du 1828, 1896 (G. Keller), 1987 (C. van Eijsden and A. Crone); Fr 1828 (A. J. B. Defauconpret), 1829, 1831 (A. Montémont), 1837 (A. and P. Chaillot), 1852 (L. Barré), 1855 (La Bédollière), 1883 (D. de La Monnoye), 1911 (H. Mansvic); Ger 1828, 1829 (J. Körner), 1830 (G. von Krämer), 1844 (T. Oelckers), 1876, 1877 (R. Springer); Ital 1829 (G. Barbieri), 1834–5 (L. L.), 1836, 1856 (C. Rusconi), 1885; Rus 1829 (M. Voskrensky: from Fr), 1986 (N. D. Volpin); Swed 1829, 1829–30 (G. Eriksson), 1830 (L. Arnell), 1880, 1916 (M. A. Goldschmidt); Sp 1835, 1836 (J. M. Moralejo), 1836 [from Fr], 1907 (N. Estévanez); Finnish 1878 (J. L. F. Krohn); Portuguese 1907; Cz 1929 (Z. Franta); Polish 1965 (K. Tarnowska); Romanian 1975 (S. Dimulescu); Slovak 1976 (D. Slobodník: adapted); Ukrainian 1983 (N. Matuzova); Bengali 1985 (S. Raha).

REVIEWS: Athenaeum 21 May 1828; Atlas 18 May 1828; Examiner 1

June 1828 (signed Q.); GM 98 1828; Le Globe 10 May, 25 June 1828; L'Indicatore Genovese 12 July 1828 [G. Mazzini, rptd in his Scritti editi ed inediti vol 1, Imola 1906]; Ladies' Monthly Museum 27 1828; Lady's Mag n.s. 9 1828; Literary Chron 17 May 1828; Literary Gazette 17 May 1828; London Rev 1 1829; London Weekly Rev 17 May 1828; Mirror of Lit June 1828 suppl; Newcastle Mag 7 1828; Olio 17 May–21 June 1827; Repository of Arts 3rd ser 12 1828 (signed Reginald Hildebrand); Southern Rev 2 1828.

Studies

Drummond, P. R. Sir Walter Scott: supplementary. In his Perthshire in bygone days: one hundred biographical essays, 1879.

Maclagan, N. ['Behold the Tiber'.] N & Q 19 Sep 1891; replies 3 Oct 1891–13 June 1908.

Porter, A. The town of The fair maid of Perth. Great Thoughts from Master Minds 21 1894.

Wespy, P. The historical foundation of Walter Scott's tale of The fair maid of Perth. Abhandlung zum Jahresbericht des städtischen Realgymnasiums zu Chemnitz für Ostern 1894. Chemnitz 1894.

Macdonald, J. The origin and growth of the tradition 'Ecce Tiber! Ecce Campus Martius!' as applied to the Tay and the Inches of Perth. Proc of the Soc of Antiquaries of Scotland 33 1899.

Jack, J. W. Scott's view from the 'Wicks of Baiglie'. Scotsman 27 July 1901; replies 29–31 July.

Handley, G. M. Notes on Scott's Fair maid of Perth. [1908] (Normal Tutorial Ser).

Baxter, P. Perth and Sir Walter Scott. Perth 1932.

My aunt Margaret's mirror, The tapestried chamber, Death of the laird's Jock, A scene at Abbotsford [approved by Scott]. Keepsake 1829 (for 1828).

REVIEWS: Athenaeum 12 Nov 1828; Edinburgh Literary Jnl 15 Nov 1828; Literary Gazette 1 Nov 1828; [Knight, C., and St Leger, F. B. B.] [Baldwin's] London Mag 3rd ser 2 1828.

My aunt Margaret's mirror, The tapestried chamber. Paris 1829; tr Fr 1829; Ital 1830 (A. Fumagalli), 1834, 1858 (C. Rusconi), 1982 (I. Loffredo), 1985 (D. Ruotolo); Sp 1830 (from Fr), 1838 (J. Muñoz y Castro), 1996 (F. Toda); Ger 1851 (F. Rottenkamp), 1904 (E. Walter). My aunt Margaret's mirror, tr Rus 1829, 1831; Portuguese 1941 (J. Marinho). The tapestried chamber, tr Rus 1829 (V. Prakhov); Hungarian 1981 (I. Bart).

Study

Parsons, C. O. Scott's prior version of The tapestried chamber. N & Q 207, Nov 1962.

Anne of Geierstein: or the maiden of the mist, by the author of Waverley. 3 vols Edinburgh 1829 [1st edn], 2 vols New York 1829, 1829, 3 vols Paris 1829, 2 vols Philadelphia 1829, 5 vols Zwickau 1829, 3 vols Berlin 1829–30, 1 vol Boston 1831, 2 vols Boston 1833; ed C. B. Wheeler, Oxford 1920; introd by D. Frew [1926]; tr Fr 1829 (A. J. B. Defauconpret), 1829 (J. Cohen), 1836 (A. Montémont), 1883, 1887 (D. de La Monnoye), 1890; Ger 1829 (G. N. Bärmann), 1829–30, 1830 (G. von Krämer), 1846 (E. Elsenhans), 1908 (E. Walter); Rus 1829 (extract), 1830 (S. de Shaplet), 1994; Du 1830–[1834], 1895 (G. Keller); Ital 1830 (V. Lancetti), 1830–1 (F. Cusani), 1835 (C. Rusconi), 1858 (C. Rusconi: retranslation); Danish 1831–2, 1840 (F. Schaldemose); Sp 1831–2, 1832?, 1909 (I. L. Lapuya); Swed 1832; Portuguese 1843 (A. J. Ramalho e Sousa), 1911 (K. d'Avellar).

REVIEWS: Athenaeum 3 June 1829; Edinburgh Literary Gazette 16–30 May 1829; Edinburgh Literary Jnl 16 May 1829; Examiner 14 June 1829; GM 99 1829; Ladies' Museum 5th ser 1 1829; Literary Gazette 9–16 May 1829; Mirror of Lit 16–30 May 1829; Monthly Rev n.s. [2nd] 11 1829; Newcastle Mag 8 1829; New Scots Mag 1 1829; Olio 3 1829; Revue de Paris 2 1829; Southern Rev 4 1829; Spectator 6 June 1829; Westminister Rev 11 1829.

Studies

S[tanley], E. 'The mauvais pas': a scene in the Alps, illustrating a passage in the novel of Anne of Geierstein. Blackwood's Edinburgh Mag 26 1829.

S., W. G. Sir Walter Scott and Erasmus. N & Q 8 June 1850.

Bayne, T. Anne of Geierstein: two readings. N & Q 5 Mar 1910; replies 26 Mar–30 Apr.

Wheeler, C. B. Anne of Geierstein. N & Q 3 Apr 1920; replies 17 Apr–1 May.

The house of Aspen; a tragedy. Keepsake 1830 (for 1829). Pbd separately Hamburg 1829, Paris 1830, Philadelphia 1830; tr in Le Keepsake français, Paris 1830; tr Ital 1830, 1928 (V. Folco); Swed 1835 [J. A. Fahlroth].

REVIEWS: Athenaeum 11 Nov 1829; Edinburgh Literary Gazette 26 Dec 1829; Edinburgh Literary Jnl 24 Oct 1829; GM 99 1829; Monthly Rev 3rd ser 12 1829.

The doom of Devorgoil: a melo-drama; Auchindrane: or the Ayrshire tragedy. Edinburgh 1830, New York 1830, Paris 1830.

REVIEWS: Athenaeum 24 Apr 1830; Br Mag 1 1830; Edinburgh Literary Jnl 24 Apr 1830; GM 100 1830; Ladies' Museum 1 1830; Literary Gazette 17 Apr 1830; Mirror of Lit 15 1830; Monthly Repository and Rev n.s. 4 1830; Monthly Rev 3rd ser 14 1830.

Auchindrane, tr Ital 1830, 1928 (V. Folco).

Tales of my landlord, fourth and last series [Count Robert of Paris; Castle Dangerous]. 4 vols Edinburgh 1832 [for 1831: 1st edn], 1 vol Paris 1831, 3 vols Philadelphia 1831, 1832, 3 vols New York 1832, 3 vols Paris 1832, 3 vols Boston 1834; tr Ger 1832 (G. N. Bärmann); Portuguese 1842.

REVIEWS: Athenaeum 3–10 Dec 1831; Atlas 25 Dec 1831; La Belle Assemblée 15 1832; Border Mag 1 1831; Edinburgh Literary Jnl 3 Dec 1831; Fraser's Mag 5 1832; GM 101 1831; Ladies' Museum n.s. 2 1831; Literary Gazette 3 Dec 1831; Mirror of Lit 12–17 Dec 1831; Monthly Mag n.s. 13 1832; Monthly Rev 4th ser 1 1832; Spectator 3 Dec 1831.

Count Robert of Paris. Tr Fr 1831 (A. J. B. Defauconpret), 1832 (A. Montémont); Danish 1832 (S. Schaldemose), 1832–3 (A. Rasmussen); Du 1832 (H. Riedel); Ger 1832, 1844 (W. Sauerwein), 1907 (E. Walter); Ital 1832 (G. Barbieri), 1832 (V. Lancetti), 1852, 1858 (C. Rusconi); Rus 1833 (S. de Shaplet), 1988 (B. T. Gribanov); Swed 1833; Sp 1834; Cz 1925 (O. Potměšil).

Studies

S[anderson], H. K. St J. Scott's Count Robert of Paris. N & Q 12 Oct 1907; reply 7 Dec. Latin quotation.

R[endall], V. Notes on Scott's Count Robert of Paris. N & Q 17 Nov 1934; reply 15 Dec. Errors in Latin quotations.

Gamerschlag, K. The making and un-making of Sir Walter Scott's Count Robert of Paris. Stud in Scottish Lit 15 1980.

Castle Dangerous. Ed G. N. Bärmann, Zwickau 1833; tr Fr 1831, 1832 (A. J. B. Defauconpret); Danish 1833 (F. Schaldemose); Ger 1833, 1851 (F. Rottenkamp), 1904 (E. Walter); Rus 1833 (S. de Shaplet); Swed 1835; Sp 1840 (A. Mata), 1844 (F. A. Fernell), 1907 (F. Bellido); Portuguese (G. M. Martins), 1842; Ital 1843 (L. M.), 1858 (C. Rusconi).

The siege of Malta. Unpbd.

Studies

Frendo, C. S. Sir W. Scott's Siege of Malta. Malta Chron 2–7 Nov 1932.

K[ing], H. G. L. The siege of Malta. N & Q 17 Jan 1942; reply 21 Feb.

Wright, S. F. The siege of Malta: founded on an unfinished romance by Sir Walter Scott. 1942.

Sultana, D. E. The siege of Malta rediscovered: an account of Sir Walter Scott's last novel and his last journey. Edinburgh 1977.

Millgate, J. The limits of editing: the problem of Scott's The siege of Malta. BRH 82 1979.

Miscellaneous prose works

Miscellaneous prose works. 6 vols Edinburgh 1827, 6 vols Boston 1829.

The prose works of Sir Walter Scott: supplementary volume, containing notes, historical and illustrative, by the author, glossary etc. 9 vols Paris 1827–34. Essays (Chivalry, Romance, Drama) 2 vols Paris 1828.

Autobiography of Sir Walter Scott Bart. Philadelphia 1831, 1846. Compilation from introds to poetical works and novels.

Prose works. Ed J. G. Lockhart 28 vols Edinburgh 1834–6. Cited below as PW. A later issue adds (with new vol 29–30 half-titles) a re-issue of the 1830 History of Scotland. In a further edn of 30 vols, Edinburgh 1870–1, the 2 additional vols contain Letters on demonology and witchcraft, Religious discourses, and Memoir of George Bannatyne.

Sir Walter Scott on novelists and fiction. Ed I. Williams 1968.

Sir Walter Scott's Edinburgh Annual Register. Ed K. Curry, Knoxville TN 1977.

Disputatio juridica, de cadaveribus damnatorum. Edinburgh 1792. Thesis, priv ptd. Not rptd.

R. Southey and W. S. Rose's translations of Amadis de Gaul. Edinburgh Rev 3 1803. PW 18.

J. Sibbald's Chronicle of Scotish poetry. Edinburgh Rev 3 1803. Not rptd.

Godwin's Life of Geoffrey Chaucer. Edinburgh Rev 3 1804. PW 17.

G. Ellis's Specimens of the early English poets. Edinburgh Rev 4 1804. PW 17.

The works of Thomas Chatterton [ed Southey and Cottle]. Edinburgh Rev 4 1804. PW 17.

Sir John Froissart's Chronicles tr T. Johnes. Edinburgh Rev 5 1805. PW 19.

Colonel T. Thornton's Sporting tour. Edinburgh Rev 5 1805. PW 19.

W. Godwin's Fleetwood: or the new man of feeling. Edinburgh Rev 6 1805. PW 18.

Mrs Hudson and Mrs Donat's The new practice of cookery, and Culina famulatrix medicinae rev A Hunter. Edinburgh Rev 6 1805. PW 19.

Report of the committee of the Highland Society ... [upon] Ossian, and The poems of Ossian &c. containing the poetical works of James Macpherson ed M. Laing. Edinburgh Rev 6 1805. Not rptd.

The works of Edmund Spenser ed H. J. Todd. Edinburgh Rev 7 1805. PW 17.

G. Ellis's Specimens of early English metrical romances; J. Ritson's Ancient Engleish metrical romanceës. Edinburgh Rev 7 1806. PW 17.

[Beresford's] The miseries of human life. Edinburgh Rev 9 1806. PW 19.

W. Herbert's Miscellaneous poetry. Edinburgh Rev 9 1806. PW 17.

R. H. Cromek's Reliques of Robert Burns. Quart Rev 1 1809. PW 17.
  Low, D. A. Scott's criticism of The jolly beggars. Bibliotheck 5 1969.

R. Southey's translation of Chronicle of the Cid. Quart Rev 1 1809. PW 18.

J. Barrett's An essay on the earlier part of the life of Swift. Quart Rev 1 1809. Not rptd.

Sir J. Carr's Caledonian sketches. Quart Rev 1 1809. PW 19.

T. Campbell's Gertrude of Wyoming. Quart Rev 1 1809. PW 17.

R. Cumberland's John de Lancaster: a novel. Quart Rev 1 1809. PW 18.

[Croker's] The battles of Talavera. Quart Rev 2 1809. PW 17.

Of the living poets of Great Britain. Edinburgh Annual Register for 1808 1 1810. Rptd in Curry.

View of the proposed and adopted changes in the administration of justice in Scotland. Edinburgh Annual Register for 1808 1 1810. Rptd in Curry.

D. J. Murphy [C. Maturin]'s Fatal revenge; or, The family of Montorio. Quart Rev 3 1810. PW 18.

J. Graham's British Georgics. Quart Rev 3 1810. Not rptd.

T. Evans's Old ballads and J. Aikin's Essays on song writing and Vocal poetry. Quart Rev 3 1810. PW 17.

Cursory remarks upon the French order of battle, particularly in the campaigns of Buonaparte. Edinburgh Annual Register for 1809 2 1811. Rptd in Curry.

The inferno of Altisidora. Edinburgh Annual Register for 1809 2 1811. Rptd in Curry.

On the present state of periodical criticism. Edinburgh Annual Register for 1809 2 1811. Rptd in Curry.

R. Southey's The curse of Kehama. Quart Rev 5 1811. PW 17.

Introduction. In Border antiquities of England and Scotland [ed J. Greig] 2 vols [1812–17]. PW 7.
  REVIEWS: Antijacobin Rev 42 1812; [Foster, J.] Eclectic Rev n.s. 10 1818; Edinburgh Mag 1 1817.
  Studies
  Mudford, W. Curious literary case. Literary Gazette 7 Nov 1818; rptd in [W. J. Fitzpatrick,] Who wrote the Waverley novels? 1856.
  Corson, J. C. The border antiquities. Bibliotheck 1 1956.
  Todd, W. B. The early editions and issues of Scott's Border antiquities. SB 9 1957.
  Corson, J. C. A supplementary note on The border antiquities. Bibliotheck 3 1960.

Account of the poems of Patrick Carey, a poet of the 17th century. Edinburgh Annual Register for 1810 3 1812. Not rptd.

Biographical memoir of John Leyden M. D. Edinburgh Annual Register for 1811 4 1813. PW 4.

Extracts from a journal kept during a coasting voyage through the Scottish islands. Edinburgh Annual Register for 1812 5 1814. Complete diary rptd in Lockhart's Life of Scott.

Abstract of the Eyrbiggia-saga. In Illustrations of northern antiquities, Edinburgh 1814. PW 5.

[J. Austen's] Emma: a novel. Quart Rev 14 1815. Partly rptd in Williams.
  Studies
  Miss Austen and Sir Walter Scott. Tait's Edinburgh Mag 3 1833.
  Squire, W. B. Walter Scott and Jane Austen. TLS 14 Nov 1918; replies 21 Nov–5 Dec.

Paul's letters to his kinsfolk. Edinburgh 1816 ([1st], 2nd, 3rd edns), 1817 (4th edn), Philadelphia 1816, 2 vols Zwickau 1826; tr Du 1817 (N. Messchaert); Fr 1822 (A. Pichot); Ger 1822 (K. L. M. Müller), 1828 (S. May); Rus 1826 (G. P.: from Fr), 1827 (M. P[ano]v: from Fr); Swed 1826; Ital 1828.
  REVIEWS: Antijacobin Rev 50 1816; Augustan Rev 2 1816; Br Critic n.s. 5 1816; Br Lady's Mag 3 1816; Eclectic Rev n.s. 5 1816; GM 86 1816; Monthly Rev n.s. [2nd] 80–1 1816; Scots Mag 78 1816; Theatrical Inquisitor 8 1816.
  Studies
  Harrison, R. Haydon's notes on Waterloo etc. N & Q 30 Aug 1856.
  Sir Walter Scott on the Prussians. Spectator 4 Sep 1915.

History of Europe, 1814. Edinburgh Annual Register for 1814 7 1816. Not rptd.

Culloden papers. Quart Rev 14 1816. PW 20. Rptd with the introd to Rob Roy as The highland clans, Edinburgh 1856.

Byron's Childe Harold's pilgrimage, canto III and The prisoner of Chillon, a dream; and other poems. Quart Rev 16 1816. PW 4: rptd as a continuation of the 1824 memoir.

Alarming increase of depravity among animals. Blackwood's Edinburgh Mag 2 1817. Not rptd.

History of Europe, 1815. Edinburgh Annual Register for 1815 8 1817. Not rptd.

Notices concerning the Scottish gypsies. Edinburgh Monthly Mag 1817. PW 19 (in part).

[Scott's] Tales of my landlord. Quart Rev 16 1817. PW 19.
  Studies
  Sir Walter Scott reviewed by himself! NMM 46 1836.
  Lang, A. Scott his own reviewer. Sketch 5 Dec 1894.
  Lightfoot, M. Scott's self-reviewal: manuscript and other evidence. Nineteenth-Cent Fiction 23 1968.
  Garside, P. Scott's self-reviewal reviewed. Scott Newsletter 17 1990.

The search after happiness, or the quest of Sultaun Soolimaun. Sale-Room 1817.

Remarks on General Gourgaud's account of the campaign of 1815. Blackwood's Edinburgh Mag 4 1818. Not rptd.

Chivalry. In Encyclopaedia Britannica, suppl to 4th–6th edns, vol 3, pt 1, 1818. PW 6. Ed C. D. Yonge, Belfast 1889. Tr Ital [1834?] (G. Vegezzi), 1991 (E. Villari).

Remarks on [Mary Shelley's] Frankenstein, or the modern Prometheus: a novel. Blackwood's Edinburgh Mag 2 1818. PW 18.

To the veiled conductor of Blackwood's Edinburgh Magazine. Blackwood's Edinburgh Mag 3 1818. Not rptd.

Maturin's Women; or pour et contre: a tale. Edinburgh Rev 30 1818. PW 18.

Sir Howard Douglas on the passage of rivers: an essay on the principles and construction of military bridges, and on the passage of rivers in military operations. Quart Rev 18 1818. Not rptd.

James Kirkton's The secret and true history of the Church of Scotland. Quart Rev 18 1818. PW 19.

Letters from the Hon Horace Walpole to George Montagu Esq. Quart Rev 19 1818. Not rptd.

Byron's Childe Harold's pilgrimage, canto IV. Quart Rev 19 1818. PW 17.

Recollections of Sir Walter Scott [by S]. Edinburgh Evening Courant 11 Aug 1871.

Description of the regalia of Scotland. Edinburgh 1819, 1824, 1827 (unauthorised reprint), 1830, etc.

Garside, P. D. Two descriptions of the regalia. Scott Newsletter 2 1983.

Drama. In Encyclopaedia Britannica, suppl to 4th–6th edns, vol 3, pt 2, 1819. PW 6. Tr Fr 1828; Portuguese 1838.

REVIEW: Scotsman 27 Feb 1819.

The late Duke of Buccleuch and Queensberry. Edinburgh Weekly Jnl 12 May 1819. PW 4.

To the Editor of the Edinburgh Weekly Journal [signed L. T.]. Edinburgh Weekly Jnl 8 Sep 1819. On Peterloo. Rptd in G. McMaster's Scott and society, 1981.

The late Lord Somerville. Edinburgh Weekly Jnl 27 Oct 1819. PW 4.

The visionary [signed 'Somnambulus']. Edinburgh Weekly Jnl 1–15 Dec 1819. Rptd as The visionary, nos 1–3, Edinburgh 1819 (for 1820). Ed Peter Garside, Cardiff 1984.

[King George III.] Edinburgh Weekly Jnl 9 Feb 1820. PW 4.

To those inhabitants of the regality of Melrose. [Melrose] 1820. Broadside. Not rptd.

[Account of the coronation of George IV.] Edinburgh Weekly Jnl 25 July 1821. Rptd in Examiner 5 Aug 1821 and in Lockhart's Life of Scott.

Sir Walter Scott's account of the coronation. Examiner 5 Aug 1821.

Hints addressed to the inhabitants of Edinburgh, and others, in prospect of his majesty's visit, by an old citizen. Edinburgh 1822.

Sketch of the life and character of the late Lord Kinedder. Edinburgh 1822 (priv ptd). Not rptd.

Romance. In Encyclopaedia Britannica, suppl to 4th–6th edns, vol 6, pt 1, 1824 (signed N. N.). PW 6.

Lord Byron. Edinburgh Weekly Jnl 19 May 1824. PW 4. Tr Rus 1825.

Alexander Campbell. Edinburgh Weekly Jnl 19 May 1824. Not rptd.

Letters to and from Henrietta, Countess of Suffolk, and her second husband, the Hon George Berkeley. Quart Rev 30 1824. PW 19.

Lives of the novelists. 2 vols Berlin 1825, 2 vols Paris 1825, 2 vols Philadelphia 1825, 3 vols Zwickau 1826, 2 vols Boston 1826, 1 vol Paris 1832. Pirated from Ballantyne's novelist's library; *see* Edited works, *below*. Tr Du 1826 (H. Riedel); Fr 1826; Ger 1826 (L. Rellstab); Rus 1826, 1826; Swed [1834] (J. Krohn). Introd by A. Dobson 1906 (WC), introd by G. Saintsbury [1910] (EL).

REVIEWS: [Lockhart, J. G.] (Paris edn) Quart Rev 34 1826; (Philadelphia edn) United States Literary Gazette 1 Sep 1825.

[Galt's] The omen. Blackwood's Mag 20 1826. PW 18.

The currency [signed 'Malachi Malagrowther']. Edinburgh Weekly Jnl 22 Feb–8 Mar 1826. Rptd as A letter to the editor of the Edinburgh Weekly Jnl from Malachi Malagrowther Esq on the proposed change of currency and other late alterations as they affect, or are intended to affect, the kingdom of Scotland, Edinburgh 1826 ([1st], '2nd', '3rd', '4th' edns); A second letter etc, Edinburgh 1826 ([1st], '2nd', '3rd' edns); A third letter etc, Edinburgh 1826 ([1st], '2nd', '3rd' edns). The first edn of the first letter entitled Thoughts on the proposed change of currency. PW 21. Introd by D. Simpson and A. Wood (with Croker's 2 letters; *see below*), Shannon 1972; introd by P. H. Scott, Edinburgh 1981.

REVIEWS: Literary Chron 4–25 Mar 1826; Monthly Rev 3rd ser 1 1826; [Bisset, A.?] Westminster Rev 10 1829.

Studies

[Croker, J. W.] To Malachi Malagrowther, Esq (signed E. Bradwardine Waverley). Courier 6–9 Mar 1826; rptd as Two letters on Scottish affairs from Edward Bradwardine Waverley Esq to Malachi Malagrowther Esq, 1826, 1826.

Eunomia, with brief hints to country gentlemen and others of tender capacity on the principles of the new sect of political economical philosophers termed Eunomians, with some strictures upon banks and the banking system, in answer to the Right Hon Sir John Sinclair Bart, Malachi Malagrowther [etc.] 1826.

To Sir Malachi Malagrowther [signed T. MacRosty]. Scotsman 8–15 Mar 1826.

Wood, G. A. M. The great reviser: or the unknown Scott. Ariel 2 1971.

Provincial antiquities and picturesque scenery of Scotland, with descriptive illustrations by Sir Walter Scott Bart. 2 vols 1826. Issued in 10 pts 1819–26. Rptd (no illus) in PW 7.

REVIEWS: [Greenwood, F. W. P.] Christian Examiner and General Rev May 1829; Literary Chron 27 Nov 1819; Literary Gazette 6 Dec 1823; [Wainewright, T. G.] [Baldwin's] London Mag 1 1820 (signed Janus Weathercock).

Memoirs of Samuel Pepys Esq, ed Richard, Lord Braybrooke. Quart Rev 33 1826. PW 20.

Memoirs of the Life of John Philip Kemble by James Boaden; Reminiscences of Michael Kelly. Quart Rev 34 1826. PW 20.

The life of Napoleon Buonaparte. 9 vols Edinburgh 1827 [1st, '2nd', 2nd edns], 2 vols Exeter NH 1827, 1828, 1832, 1834, 3 vols New York 1827, 1827, 1828, 9 vols Paris 1827 (3 edns), 6 vols Stuttgart 1827, 35 vols Stuttgart 1827–9, 3 vols Philadelphia 1827, 1827, 18 vols Zwickau 1827–8; 1 vol Paris 1828; ed W. Sorge, Berlin [1916]; tr Danish 1827–30 (H. G. N. Nyegaard and A. P. Liunge), 1828 (F. Schaldemose: abridged); Du 1827 (C. H. Immerzeel: part), 1827 (J. G. Swaving), 1865; Fr 1827 [partly F. T. Licquet]; Ger 1827–8 (G. N. Bärmann), 1827–8 (J. von Theobald), 1827–30 (Meyer and Müller), 1834 (F. Beck); Ital 1827, 1827–8 (V. Pecchioli), 1828–9 (L. Toccagni and A. Clerichetti); Norwegian 1827 (H. A. Bjerregaard and C. N. Schwach); Rus 1827 (P. S. Maltsev), 1827, 1831–2 (S. de Shaplet), 1833; Sp, 1827, 1830 (M. L.); Swed 1827–30.

REVIEWS: American Quart Rev 1 1827; La Belle Assemblée 6 1827; [Channing, W. E.] Christian Examiner and Theological Rev 4 1827, rptd as Remarks on the character of Napoleon Bonaparte occasioned by the publication of Scott's Life of Napoleon, Boston 1827; Christian Spectator n.s. 2 1828; Eclectic Rev n.s. 28 1827; GM 97 1827; Le Globe 28 July–25 Aug (C. A. Sainte-Beuve), rptd in vol 1 (1874) of his Premiers Lundis, 3 vols Paris 1874–5; Literary Chron 1 Apr 1826; Literary Gazette 30 June 1827; London Weekly Rev 30 June–14 July 1827; Monthly Rev 3rd ser 6 1827; NMM 20 1827; Politische Annalen 26 1828 (Heinrich Heine), rptd in his Sämmtliche Werke vol 3, Hamburg 1876; Southern Rev 1 1828, 2 1828; [Mill, J. S.] Westminster Rev 9 1828.

Studies

[Caze, J. F.] Réfutation de la vie de Napoléon de Sir Walter Scott. 2 vols Paris 1827.

General La Fayette and Sir Walter Scott (signed Dikaios). Scotsman 12 Sep 1827.

G[ourgaud, G.] Réfutation de la vie de Napoléon par Sir Walter Scott. 2 pts Paris 1827.
Lettre de Sir Walter Scott et réponse du général Gourgaud, avec notes et pièces justificatives. Paris 1827.
Réfutation de la vie de Napoléon par Sir Walter-Scott, par le cte de ***, ex-général de la garde. Brussels 1827.
Remarks on the character of Napoleon Bonaparte, occasioned by the publication of Scott's Life of Napoleon. 1827.
Bonaparte, L. Réponse à Scott sur son Histoire de Napoléon. Stuttgart 1828, Paris 1829; tr Eng 1829 (W. H. Ireland), 1829; Ger 1829; Ital 1829, 1831; Sp 1831 (M. Gomez); tr from Ital and ed A. Kinloch 1861.
Channing, W. E. Analysis of the character of Napoleon Bonaparte, suggested by the publication of Scott's Life of Napoleon. 1828.
Sorell, T. S. Notes on the campaign of 1808–1809 in the north of Spain, in reference to some passages in Lieut.-Col. Napier's History of the war in the Peninsula, and in Sir Walter Scott's Life of Napoleon Bonaparte. 1828.
Lee, H. The life of the Emperor Napoleon, with an appendix containing an examination of Sir Walter Scott's Life of Napoleon Bonaparte. 1834 (vol 1 only).
Ruff, W. Cancels in Sir Walter Scott's Life of Napoleon. Trans Edinburgh Bibl Soc 3 1957.
Gettman, R. A. Colburn-Bentley and the march of intellect. SB 9 1958.
B. J. McMullin. Notes on cancellation in Scott's Life of Napoleon. SB 45 1992.
[The Duke of York.] Edinburgh Weekly Jnl 10 Jan 1827. PW 4. 1827, Newcastle 1827. Tr Du 1827 (E. C. Brygmann); Ger 1827.
[Remarks.] First Edinburgh theatrical fund dinner. Edinburgh Weekly Jnl 28 Feb 1827. Rptd in Waverley novels 41 1832.
Life of Napoleon. Edinburgh Weekly Jnl 19 Sep 1827. In reply to Gourgaud. Rptd in Lockhart, Life of Scott; translated in Lettre de Sir Walter Scott et réponse du général Gourgaud, avec notes et pièces justificatives, Paris 1827.
On the supernatural in fictitious composition and particularly on the works of Ernest Theodore William Hoffmann. Foreign Quart Rev 1 1827. PW 18. Tr Rus 1829.
Hennig, J. Goethe's translation of Scott's criticism of Hoffmann. MLR 51 1956.
The works of John Home Esq by Henry Mackenzie. Quart Rev 36 1827. PW 19.
On planting waste lands. Quart Rev 36 1827. Review of Robert Monteath's The forester's guide and profitable planter. PW 21. Tr Swed (B. G. Bredburg) in J. C. A. Blauel, Om lärkträdets användbarhet ut i skogshushallingen, Stockholm 1832.
Studies
Withers, W. A letter to Sir Walter Scott Bart, exposing certain fundamental errors in his late Essay on planting, and containing observations on the pruning and thinning of woods and maxims for profitable planting. 1828.
Billington, W. Facts, observations, etc., being an exposure of the misrepresentations of the author's Treatise on planting contained in Mr Withers's Letters to Sir Walter Scott Baronet, and to Sir Henry Steuart Baronet, with remarks on Sir Walter Scott's Essay on planting and on certain parts of Sir Henry Steuart's Planter's guide. Shrewsbury 1830.
Religious discourses by a layman. 1828 ([1st edn], '2nd' edn), Kingston Canada 1828, New York 1828, Paris 1828, Philadelphia 1828, Bethany VA 1831; tr Du 1828; Fr 1828; Ger 1828.
REVIEWS: Athenaeum 7 May 1828; Literary Gazette 3 May 1828; Monthly Repository n.s. 2 1828; Monthly Rev 3rd ser 8 1828; NMM 24 1828; Repository of Arts 1 July 1828 (signed Reginald Hildebrand).
Study
G., A. Sir Walter Scott as a sermon-writer. Border Mag 15 1910.

Oeuvres de Molière ed M. Auger and Histoire de la vie et des ouvrages de Molière by J. Taschereau. Foreign Quart Rev 2 1828. PW 17.
On ornamental plantations and landscape gardening. Quart Rev 37 1828. Review of The planter's guide by Sir Henry Steuart. PW 21.
Salmonia: or days of fly-fishing [by Sir Humphry Davy]. Quart Rev 38 1828. PW 20.
Tales of a grandfather: being stories taken from Scottish history [1st ser]. 3 vols Edinburgh 1828 ([1st edn: for 1827], 2nd, '3rd', '4th', 5th edns), 1829 (6th edn), 2 vols Berlin 1828, 2 vols Boston 1828, 1828, 2 vols New York 1828, 2 vols Paris 1828, 2 vols Philadelphia 1828; tr Fr 1828; Ger 1828 (K. L. Kannegiesser); Rus 1828 (extract: from Fr), 1831 (M. M[ikhailovich]); Du 1832–4 (G. E. Gerrits).
REVIEWS: Athenaeum 22 Feb 1828; La Belle Assemblée 7 1828; Le Globe 26 Mar 1828; Literary Gazette 22–9 Dec 1827; Monthly Rev n.s. 10 1829; NMM 24 1828; New Scots Mag 1 1829.
Study
Bisset, A. Sir Walter Scott. In his Essays on historical truth, 1871.
Tales of a grandfather, being stories taken from Scottish history: second series. 3 vols Edinburgh 1829 (for 1828), (new edn) 1829, Paris 1829, 3 vols Zwickau 1829, 2 vols Boston 1829, 2 vols New York 1829, 1831, 1 vol Paris 1829, 2 vols Philadelphia 1829; tr Fr 1828; Ger 1829 (G. Bärmann).
REVIEWS: Athenaeum 3 Dec 1828; Edinburgh Literary Jnl 29 Nov 1828; Le Globe 4 Feb 1829; Literary Gazette 22–9 Nov 1828; London Weekly Rev 29 Nov 1828; Monthly Rev 3rd ser 10 1829; Pocket Mag 2 1829; Westminster Rev 10 1829 [probably A. Bisset].
Alexander Lord Pitsligo's Thoughts concerning man's condition. Blackwood's Mag 25 1829. Not rptd.
Revolutions of Naples in 1647 and 1648; Masaniello and the Duke of Guise. Foreign Quart Rev 4 1829. Not rptd.
The adventures of Hajji Baba of Ispahan in England [by Morier]; The Kuzzilbash: a tale of Khorasan. Quart Rev 39 1829. PW 18.
Joseph Ritson's Annals of the Caledonians, Picts and Scots, and of Strathclyde, Cumberland, Galloway and Murray. Quart Rev 41 1829. PW 20.
Patrick Fraser Tytler's History of Scotland. Quart Rev 41 1829. PW 21.
Tales of a grandfather, being stories taken from Scottish history: third series. 3 vols Edinburgh 1830 (for 1829), 2 vols Boston 1830, 1834, 2 vols New York 1830, 1 vol Paris 1830, 2 vols Paris 1830, 2 vols Philadelphia 1830; tr Fr 1830; Ger 1830 (G. N. Bärmann).
REVIEWS: Edinburgh Literary Gazette 26 Dec 1829; Edinburgh Literary Jnl 19 Dec 1829; Literary Gazette 19 Dec 1829; New Scots Mag 2 1829.
Tales of a grandfather [ser 1–3]. Ed with notes, Edinburgh 1846; introd by F. W. Farrar 3 vols Edinburgh 1888 (for 1887); abridged and ed J. Hutchison 1908; ed P. Giles 1909; selected and ed R. K. Gordon 1925; abridged and ed E. Ginn, Boston [1925]; tr Fr 1828 (A. J. B. Defauconpret); Swed 1828–33; Danish 1833–9 (L. H. Wiimh); Du 1836.
The history of Scotland. 2 vols 1830, 2 vols Cambridge MA 1830, 2 vols Darmstadt 1830–1, 2 vols New York 1830, 2 vols Paris 1830, 2 vols Philadelphia 1830, 1 vol Paris 1838; tr Fr 1830–2 ([A. J. B.] Defauconpret), 1837 (A. Montémont); Ger 1830 (G. N. Bärmann), 1830–1 (F. Vogel); Rus 1831, 1832 (extracts); Ital 1836 (C. Rusconi).
REVIEWS: [Robertson, J.] Aberdeen Mag 2 1832, rptd in Selections from The Aberdeen Mag contributed during the years 1831 and 1832, Aberdeen 1878; Athenaeum 9 Dec 1829; Edinburgh Literary Gazette 5 Dec 1829; Edinburgh Literary Jnl 12 Dec 1829–13 Mar 1830; GM 100 1830; Imperial Mag 12 1830; Literary Gazette 28 Nov 1829–13 Mar 1830; Monthly Repository and Rev n.s. 4 1830; Monthly Rev 3rd ser 13 1830; New Scots Mag 2 1829.
Letters on demonology and witchcraft. 1830 [1st edn], 1831 (2nd edn), New York 1830, 1831, 1832, 1833, 1835, 1836, 1845; introd by H. Morley 1884; ed R. Lamont Brown, Wakefield 1968; tr Rus 1830

(extracts); Fr 1832 ([A. J. B.] Defauconpret), 1838 (A. Montémont); Ger 1833 (G. N. Bärmann); Ital 1839 (G. Barbieri); Sp 1876, 1976 (A. Bergnes de Las Casas), 1994 (A. Merlino); Portuguese 1977 (L. Costa).

REVIEWS: [Robertson, J.] Aberdeen Mag 1 1831, rptd in Selections from The Aberdeen Mag contributed during the years 1831 and 1832, Aberdeen 1878; Athenaeum 18 Sep 1830; Edinburgh Literary Jnl 2 Oct 1830; Fraser's Mag 2 1830; GM 100 1830; Imperial Mag 12 1830; Ladies' Museum 2 1830; Literary Gazette 18–25 Sep 1830; Monthly Repository n.s. 4 1830; Monthly Rev 3rd ser 15 1830; Phrenological Jnl 7 1831.

Studies

Collin de Plancy, J. A. S. Walter Scott. In his Dictionnaire infernal, ou répertoire universel des êtres, des personnages, des livres, des faits et des choses qui tiennent aux apparitions, 3rd (rev) edn, Paris and Lyons 1844.

Parsons, C. O. Manuscript of Scott's Letters on demonology and witchcraft. N & Q 22 Apr 1933.

Robert Southey's The pilgrim's progress, with a life of John Bunyan. Quart Rev 43, Oct 1830. PW 18.

Tales of a grandfather, being stories taken from the history of France [4th ser]. 3 vols 1831 (for 1830), 2 vols New York 1831, 2 vols Paris 1831, 2 vols Philadelphia 1831, 2 vols Boston 1834; tr Fr 1831; Ger 1831 (G. N. Bärmann); Swed 1832–3.

REVIEWS: Athenaeum 25 Dec 1830, 8 Jan 1831; Literary Gazette 25 Dec 1830; Monthly Rev 4th ser 1 1831; NMM 33 1831.

Robert Pitcairn's Trials, and other proceedings, in matters criminal, before the high court of justiciary in Scotland. Quart Rev 44 1831. PW 21.

[Annotations.] In [Boswell's] Life of Samuel Johnson, ed J. W. Croker. 1831, 1835, 1848.

Bowden, A. and W. B. Todd. Scott's commentary on The journal of a tour to the Hebrides. SB 78 1995.

Posthumously published works

Reliquiae Trottcosienses. Harper's NMM 78 1889 (in part); Nineteenth Cent Oct 1905 (in part).

Maxwell-Scott, M. M. Sir Walter Scott on his 'gabions'. Nineteenth Cent 58 1905.

Private letters of the seventeenth century. Scribner's Mag 14 1893 (in part); ed D. Grant, Oxford 1947 (complete).

Studies

Parker, W. M. The origin of Scott's Nigel. MLR 34 1939.

Maxwell, J. C. A deletion in Scott's Private letters of the seventeenth century. N & Q 214, Feb 1969.

Tour on the Continent, August 1815.

Study

Parker, W. M. Scott's continental tour in 1815. Blackwood's Mag May 1969.

On the present state of historical composition. [1808?].

Study

Baker, W. and J. H. Alexander. The Walpole collection at Canterbury: On the present state of historical composition. Scott Newsletter 5 1984.

Letters on reform.

Studies

Garside, P. D. Scott's Essay on reform, 1830: new information. Scott Newsletter 6 1985.

Garside, P. D. Scott's second Letter on reform: a transcript of the Canterbury manuscript. Scott Newsletter 7 1985.

Garside, P. D. Scott's first Letter on reform: an edited version. Scott Newsletter 8 1986.

Review of [Thomas Robson's] The British Herald.

Alexander, J. H. Scott's review of The British Herald. Wordsworth Circle 18 1987. Summary with extracts.

Tales of a grandfather—France: second series [5th ser]. Ed W. Baker and J. H. Alexander as Tales of a grandfather: the history of France (second series), DeKalb IL 1996. From an unfinished ms.

Study

Baker, W. Sir Walter Scott's Tales of a grandfather—France: second series. In Scott and his influence, ed J. H. Alexander and D. Hewitt, Aberdeen 1983.

Letters and journal

Original letter of Sir Walter Scott. London Weekly Rev 8 Sep 1827. To Archibald Park.

Letters of Sir Walter Scott addressed to the Rev R. Polwhele, D. Gilbert Esq, F. Douce Esq &c. 1832 [1st edn], 1832 ('2nd' edn).

Letters between James Ellis Esq and Walter Scott Esq. Newcastle-upon-Tyne 1850.

Markland, J. H. The bride of Lammermoor. N & Q 5 Jan 1856. To Markland.

Patterson, J. Memoir of Joseph Train, F. S. A. Scot., the antiquarian correspondent of Sir Walter Scott. Glasgow and Edinburgh 1857.

Original portrait and unpublished letters of Sir Walter Scott. Leisure Hour 1 July, 5 Aug 1871.

Tribute to Walter Scott on the one hundredth anniversary of his birthday, by the Massachusetts Historical Society, August 15 1871. Boston 1872. To an unknown correspondent, 2 Feb 1826.

Young, T. Sir Walter Scott on the Scottish metrical psalms: a letter believed to be unpublished. Life & Work 6 1884. To Charles McCombie.

Letters from and to Charles Kirkpatrick Sharpe Esq. Ed A. Allardyce 2 vols Edinburgh and London 1888.

Journal 1825–32. Ed D. Douglas 2 vols Edinburgh 1890, 1891, 1910, 1927, 2 vols New York 1890; rev J. G. Tait and W. M. Parker 3 vols Edinburgh 1939–46, 1 vol Edinburgh 1950; ed W. E. K. Anderson, Oxford 1972.

Studies

Leaves from a notebook: Sir Walter Scott's Journal. Macmillan's Mag 63 1890.

Swinburne, A. C. The Journal of Sir Walter Scott, 1825–1832. Fortnightly Rev May 1891; rptd in his Studies in prose and poetry, 1894.

Masson, D. The last years of Sir Walter Scott. In his Edinburgh sketches and memories, 1892.

Grierson, H. J. C. Scott's Journal. TLS 8 Aug 1936.

Tait, J. G. The missing tenth of Sir Walter Scott's Journal. Edinburgh 1936.

Tait, J. G. Sir Walter Scott's Journal and its editor. Edinburgh 1938.

Chapman, R. W. A problem in editorial method. E & S 27 1941.

Anderson, W. E. K. The Journal. In Scott bicentenary essays, ed A. Bell, 1973.

Douglas, G. B. S. Scott and the Shortreeds (unpublished letters of Sir Walter Scott). Scots Mag n.s. 5 1890.

[Report of a visit to Ashiestiel.] History of the Berwickshire Naturalists' Club 14 1893. To A. Pringle, Nov 1810.

Familiar letters of Sir Walter Scott. [Ed D. Douglas] 2 vols Edinburgh 1894, Boston 1894.

W., J. Letters of Sir Walter Scott: find of 103 at Galashiels. Scotsman 7 Nov 1894. To G. Craig.

Robertson, A. I. An interesting letter and verses of Sir Walter Scott. Life & Work 17 1895. To D. Stewart of Garth.

Four letters of Sir Walter Scott, James Hogg, Alfred Tennyson, and John Gibson Lockhart, facsimiled from the originals in the possession of James Falconer, Dundee. Dundee 1897. To Lockhart.

Hadden, J. C. George Thomson, the friend of Burns: his life & correspondence. 1898.

Hartwig, O. Zur ersten englischen Übersetzung der Kinder- und Hausmärchen der Brüder Grimm, mit ungedruckten Briefen von Edgar Taylor ... Walter Scott. Centralblatt für Bibliothekswesen 15 1898.

Lady Louisa Stuart: selections from her manuscripts. Ed J. A. Home, Edinburgh 1899.

Hughes, [M. A.] Letters and recollections of Sir Walter Scott. Ed H. G. Hutchinson [1904].

The letters of Sir Walter Scott and Charles Kirkpatrick Sharpe to Robert Chambers 1821–45 with original memoranda of Sir Walter Scott, printed from manuscripts in the possession of C. E. S. Chambers, Edinburgh. Edinburgh 1904 [for 1903].

Letters hitherto unpublished, written by members of Sir Walter Scott's family to their old governess [Miss Millar]. [Ed. P. A. Wright-Henderson] 1905.

Sim, J. D. S. [Report of his speech at the 11th annual dinner of the Edinburgh Sir Walter Scott Club, 21 Oct 1904.] Edinburgh Sir Walter Scott Club Annual Report 11 1905.

Craig-Brown, T. Sir Walter Scott on the yeomanry: an unpublished letter. Scotsman 23 Dec 1907.

[Russell, C.] Some letters of Sir Walter Scott. Blackwood's Mag Nov 1908. To Mrs and Miss Clephane.

Interesting find at H. M. Exchequer Office Edinburgh: Sir Walter Scott and Linlithgow Palace. Scotsman 11 Nov 1910. To W. Adam.

Unpublished Scott letters. Border Mag 15 1910. To W. Ross and Sir A. Keith.

Fletcher, W. G. D. Some unpublished letters of Sir Walter Scott. The Antiquary 49 1913.

C.-B., T. Sir Walter Scott's family affairs: his brother-in-law's fortune. Scotsman 28 Oct 1920.

Leishman, J. F. Scott and the Ballantynes. History of the Berwickshire Naturalists' Club 25 1923.

Books and other things: a review of current Scots letters, by the editor. Scots Mag 7 1927. Letter to Atchison (?) and Paterson.

Cook, D. Lockhart's treatment of Scott's letters. Nineteenth Cent Sep 1927.

Cook, D. Murray's mysterious contributor: unpublished letters of Sir Walter Scott. Nineteenth Cent Apr 1927.

Scrymgeour, N. The worst of Sir Walter. Scots Mag 7 1927. To Sir William Knighton.

Butler, H. J. and H. E. Sir Walter Scott and Maria Edgeworth: some unpublished letters. MLR 23 1928.

Cook, D. Scott letters . . . literary treasures. Glasgow Herald 23 Nov 1928.

A Scott letter: the authorship of Waverley. The Times 3 Aug 1928. To S. Warren.

Partington, W. The private letter-books of Sir Walter Scott: selections from the Abbotsford manuscripts, with a letter to the reader from Hugh Walpole. 1930, New York 1930.

Simon, J. A. Sir Walter Scott. In his Comments and criticisms, ed D. R. Evans, [1930]. To Southey.

Williams, A. M. Scott and his contemporaries: some letters. Scottish Country Life 17 1930.

Gray, W. F. Sir Walter's postbag: unpublished letters. Scotsman 2–7 Oct 1931.

Another Scott MS. Scotsman 11 Oct 1932. To J. E. Shortreed.

Bullough, G. A letter of Crabbe to Scott. TLS 22 Sep 1932.

Ellis, S. M. Followers of Sir Walter. Bookman 82 1932. To A. Trail.

Gordon, S. The wizard and the misty isle. S. M. T. Mag 8 1932. To Highland Soc of London.

Gray, W. F. Friends of Sir Walter: unpublished letters. Cornhill Mag n.s. 73 1932.

Gray, W. F. Letters to Sir Walter Scott. Glasgow Herald 3–6 Sep 1932. From M. Edgeworth and J. Baillie.

Gray, W. F. Some unpublished letters to Sir Walter Scott. National Rev 99 1932.

Grierson, H. J. C. Scott, Shelley and Crabbe. TLS 15 Sep 1932.

Grierson, H. J. C. Scott's letters: a correction. TLS 29 Sep 1932.

H., O. E. Sir Walter Scott and Douce. Bodleian Quart Record 7 1932.

Heron, F. W. Scott in San Francisco. TLS 1 Sep 1932. To J. Train.

The letters of Scott. Ed H. J. C. Grierson etc 12 vols 1932–7. Notes and index to Sir Herbert Grierson's edition of the letters of Sir Walter Scott, by J. C. Corson, Oxford 1979.

Parker, W. M. Scott and the antiquaries: the Surtees correspondence. Scots Mag n.s. 17 1932.

Parker, W. M. Scott as a letter-writer, a study of the many mss: some peculiarities of handwriting, spelling and punctuation. John o' London's Weekly 27 1932.

Partington, W. Sir Walter's post-bag: more stories and sidelights from his unpublished letter-books. 1932.

R[endall], V. Walter Scott: Latin misprints. N & Q 1 Oct 1932. To John Rutherfurd.

Scott letter for Jedburgh. Jedburgh Gazette 16 Sep 1932.

Some unpublished letters of Sir Walter Scott from the collection in the Brotherton Library. Ed J. A. Symington, Oxford 1932.

Strout, A. L. Scott and Swift. TLS 21 Apr 1932.

Reddie, L. N. Sir Walter Scott in the Court of Session. N & Q 24 June 1933. To the Lord Advocate.

Swaen, A. E. H. A letter from Sir Walter Scott to James Ballantyne. Neophilologicus 18 1933.

Grierson, H. J. C. Sir Walter as correspondent: experiences in editing Scott's letters. Glasgow Herald 22 Nov 1934.

Parker, W. M. William Motherwell: his correspondence with Sir Walter Scott. Scots Mag n.s. 24 1935.

Parker, W. M. Chambers and Scott: unpublished letters of the literary stars. Weekly Scotsman 4 Apr 1936. From R. Chambers.

Cook, D. Lockhart's treatment of Scott's letters. Nineteenth Cent Sep 1937.

The correspondence of Sir Walter Scott and Charles Robert Maturin with a few other allied letters. Ed F. E. Ratchford and W. H. McCarthy Jr, Austin 1937.

K[ing], H. G. L. A Scott letter: meaning of 'assessed'. N & Q 28 Aug 1937; reply 11 Sep. Letter to A. Lang.

Parker, W. M. Some of Scott's Aberdeen correspondents. N & Q 20 Feb 1937.

Dunn, M. T. A bookcase and its contents: mementoes of Scott, Burns and the Black Douglas. Scots Mag n.s. 29 1938.

Lambert, M. and J. T. Hillhouse. The Scott letters in the Huntington Library. HLQ 2 1939.

Harman, R. N. An unpublished letter of Sir Walter Scott. Yale Univ Lib Gazette 14 1940.

Jones, W. P. Three unpublished letters of Scott to Dibdin. HLQ 3 1940.

Tenbury discoveries. TLS 20 Sep 1941.

Parker, W. M. Scott as amicus curiae. Juridical Rev 55 1943.

Parker, W. M. Sir Walter Scott's quotations. N & Q 6 May 1944; replies 3 June–12 Aug.

Struve, G. Scott letters discovered in Russia. BJRL 28 1944; rptd Manchester 1945.

Aspinall, A. Walter Scott's baronetcy: some new letters. TLS 25 Oct 1947.

Aspinall, A. Some new Scott letters. TLS 27 Mar, 10 and 24 Apr 1948.

Häusermann, H. W. A new Scott letter. RES 25 1949.

Scott, D. F. S. Sir Walter Scott. In his Some English correspondents of Goethe, 1949. One letter from Scott.

Struve, G. Russian friends and correspondents of Sir Walter Scott. Comparative Lit 2 1950.

Miller, C. W. Letters from Thomas White of Virginia to Scott and Dickens. In English studies in honor of James Southall Wilson, ed F. Bowers, Charlottesville VA 1951.

R., A. M. L. Thomas Pringle and Sir Walter Scott. Quart Bull South African Public Lib 6 1951. 5 letters to Scott.

Downs, N. Two unpublished letters of Sir Walter Scott. MLN 69 1954.

Adams, R. M. A letter by Sir Walter Scott. MP 54 1956.

Green, F. C. Scott's French correspondence. MLR 52 1957.

Guthke, K. S. Die erste Nachwirkung von Herders Volksliedern in England. Archiv 193 1957. 10 letters from M. G. Lewis to Scott.
Guthke, K. S. Some unpublished letters of M. G. Lewis. N & Q May 1957. One letter to Scott.
Maxwell, J. C. An uncollected Scott letter. RES n.s. 9 1958.
The Tinker Library: a bibliographical catalogue of the books and manuscripts collected by Chauncey Brewster Tinker. Ed R. F. Metzdorf, New Haven CT 1959. Lists letters to S. E. Brydges and Miss Wagner of Liverpool, and from Alexander Murray.
Enkvist, N. E. Sir Walter Scott, Lord Bloomfield and Bernadotte. Studia Neophilologica 32 1960.
Green, D. B. New letters of Sir Walter Scott 1813–1831. N & Q Jan–Mar 1961.
McDonald, W. U. Jr. A letter of Sir Walter Scott to William Scott on the Jeffrey–Swift controversy. RES n.s. 12 1961.
Kies, P. P. An unpublished letter of Scott. Research Stud Washington State Univ 30 1962.
Massey, I. Mary Shelley, Walter Scott, and Maga. N & Q 207 Nov 1962.
Parker, W. M. Lady Davy in her letters. Quart Rev Jan 1962.
Russell, N. H. New letters of Sir Walter Scott. RES n.s. 14 1963.
Wood, G. A. M. Letters between Sir Walter Scott and the Marquis of Lothian. N & Q 209, Oct–Dec 1964.
McClary, B. H. Washington Irving to Walter Scott: two unpublished letters. Stud in Scottish Lit 3 1965.
Wood, G. A. M. The date of a Scott letter. N & Q 212, Jan 1967. To A. Seward.
Wood, G. A. M. Sir Walter Scott and Sir Ralph Sadler: a chapter in literary history. Stud in Scottish Lit 7–8 1969–71.
Hewitt, D. S. What should we do about Scott's letters? Scottish Literary News 2 1971.
Low, D. A. Walter Scott and Williamina Belsches. TLS 23 July 1971.
Robinson, K. E. and P. Roberts. Sir Walter Scott and John Bell of Newcastle-on-Tyne: some unpublished correspondence. YES 2 1972.
Albrecht, W. P. An unpublished letter by Sir Walter Scott. N & Q 218, Feb 1973. To J. Pringle.
Carnie, R. H. and M. F. Moran. Sir Walter Scott and the Maitland Club. Stud in Scottish Lit 12 1974.
Prévost, W. A. J. Joseph Train's letter to Sir Walter Scott concerning Wandering Willie. Scottish Stud 20 1976.
Bell, A. The letters of Sir Walter Scott in the Norton Downs collection: an address given on the occasion of the dedication of the Medieval Studies Room, Trinity College, Hartford, CT. Hartford CT 1979.
Bell, A. The letters of Sir Walter Scott: problems and opportunities. In Editing correspondence: papers given at the 14th annual conference on editorial problems, ed J. A. Dinard, New York 1979.
Horn, P. L. An unpublished letter of Sir Walter Scott. ELN 16 1979.
Downs, N. An unpublished note of Sir Walter Scott. N & Q 225 Feb 1980. To Rev E. B. Ramsay; corrects dates of 2 letters of 1825.
Hewitt, D. S. The survey of the letters of Sir Walter Scott. Scottish Literary Jnl 7 1980.
Sutherland, K. Walter Scott's highland minstrelsy and his correspondence with the Maclean Clephane family. Scottish Literary Jnl 9 1982.
Alexander, J. H. George Ellis on Rokeby: a background note. Scott Newsletter 3 1983.
Garside, P. Scott and the regalia. In Scott and his influence, ed J. H. Alexander and D. Hewitt, Aberdeen 1983.
Mellown, E. W. An unpublished letter from Walter Scott to George Canning, and Canning's reply. Scotia 7 1983.
Groves, D. 'Your humble servant': a new letter from Sir Walter Scott. Scott Newsletter 6 1985. To Edinburgh Evening Post.
Groves, D. Sir Walter Scott to Thomas Pringle: a letter. Scott Newsletter 7 1985.
Groves, D. Walter Scott to Alexander Balfour. Scott Newsletter 13 1988.
Richardson, T. C. Sir Walter Scott, John Lockhart, and Sir William Knighton: an unpublished Scott letter. Stud in Scottish Lit 24 1989.
Groves, D. Scott, Alexander Murray, and oriental languages: a new letter. Scott Newsletter 16 1990. To Principal Baird.
Groves, D. Alexander Peterkin. Scott Newsletter 19 1991.
Two Scott letters. Scott Newsletter 18 1991. To C. Erskine and Miss Pringle of Clifton and Haining.
Groves, D. 'Oh these terrible books': Scott and Mackintosh Mackay. Scott Newsletter 20 1992.
Groves, D. 'The usual faults of youthful production': Scott's advice to a young poet. Scott Newsletter 21–2 1992–3.
Ashe, A. H. Two letters of Sir Walter Scott, 1812. N & Q 238 1993. To and from M. Edgeworth.

Edited works

An apology for Tales of terror. Kelso 1799. Priv ptd in 12 copies, of which one has variant title: Tales of terror.

Studies

Cook, W. B. The first work of the Ballantyne Press. N & Q 8 Aug 1874.
Johnston, G. P. The first book printed by James Ballantyne, being An apology for Tales of terror; with notes on Tales of wonder and Tales of terror. Pbns Edinburgh Bibl Soc 1 1896.
Johnston, G. P. Note to a paper entitled The first book printed by James Ballantyne. Pbns Edinburgh Bibl Soc 9 1913.
Sadleir, M. Tales of terror. TLS 7 Jan 1939.

Minstrelsy of the Scottish Border. 2 vols Kelso 1802 [1st edn], 3 vols Edinburgh 1803 (2nd edn), 1806 (3rd edn), 1810 (4th edn), 1812 (5th edn), 1821 (5th [6th] edn), 3 vols Boston 1810, 1 vol Philadelphia 1813; tr Ger 1818 (H. Schubart: selection); Fr 1826 (Artaud); ed T. F. Henderson 4 vols Edinburgh, London and New York 1902, 1 vol 1931, 1932; ed and arranged A. Noyes 1908.

REVIEWS: Annual Rev 1 for 1802 (1803), 2 for 1803 (1804); [Ellis, G.] Br Critic 19 1802, [probably Ellis, G.] 23 1804; Critical Rev 2nd ser 39 1803; [Stoddart, J.] Edinburgh Rev 1 1803; Literary Jnl 16 Aug 1803; Monthly Mag 25 Jan 1803, 28 July 1804; Monthly Mirror 13 1802; Monthly Register 3 1803; Monthly Rev n.s. [2nd] 42 1803, [Muirhead, L.] 45 1804; Poetical Register 2 1802, 3 1803; Scots Mag 64 1802.

Studies

[Review of Minstrelsy in Poetical works vols 1–2.] Dublin Univ Rev 1 1833.
Veitch, J. The original ballad of the Dowie Dens. Blackwood's Edinburgh Mag June 1890.
Russell, H. J. M. The antiquity of the ballad of Auld Maitland. History of the Berwickshire Naturalists' Club 18 1901.
Scott's Minstrelsy of the Scottish Border. Athenaeum 27 Dec 1902.
[Whibley, C.] The Border minstrelsy. Blackwood's Edinburgh Mag Nov 1902.
Crockett, W. S. The making of the Minstrelsy (1802–1902). Bookman [London] 23 1903.
Border ballads. Edinburgh Rev Oct 1906.
Elliot, F. The trustworthiness of Border ballads as exemplified by Jamie Telfer i' the fair Dodhead and other ballads. Edinburgh and London 1906.
REVIEW: A. Lang, Scottish Historical Rev 4 1906.
Elliot, F. Further essays on Border ballads. Edinburgh 1910.
REVIEW: G. Douglas in Scottish Historical Rev 7 1910; replies 8 1910–11.
Lang, A. The mystery of Auld Maitland. Blackwood's Mag June 1910; discussed in Glasgow Herald 3 June.
Lang, A. Sir Walter Scott and the Border minstrelsy. 1910.
Miller, F. The ballad of Kinmont Willie. Archiv 127 1911.

Wilson, W. E. The making of the Minstrelsy: Scott and Shortreed in Liddesdale. Cornhill Mag n.s. 73 1932.
Weir, J. L. Thoughts on the Minstrelsy of the Scottish border. N & Q 11 Sep 1938.
Dobie, M. R. The development of Scott's Minstrelsy: an attempt at a reconstruction. Trans Edinburgh Bibl Soc 2 1940.
Chapman, R. W. Cancels in Scott's Minstrelsy. Library 4th ser 23 1943.
Montgomerie, W. Sir Walter Scott as ballad editor. RES n.s. 7 1956.
Zug, C. G. III. Sir Walter Scott and the ballad forgery. Stud in Scottish Lit 8 1970.
Harry, K. W. The sources and treatment of traditional ballad-texts. Unpbd PhD diss, Aberdeen Univ 1975.
Zug, C. G. III. The ballad editor as antiquary: Scott and the Minstrelsy. Jnl of the Folklore Institute 13 1976.
Zug, C. G. III. Sir Walter Scott, Robert Jamieson, and the new Minstrelsy. Music and Letters 57 1976.

Sir Tristrem: a metrical romance by Thomas of Ercildoune. Edinburgh 1804 [1st edn], 1806 (2nd edn), 1811 (3rd edn), 1819 (4th edn), Paris 1837.
REVIEWS: [Southey, R.] Annual Rev 3 for 1804 (1805); Br Critic 25 1805; [Taylor, W. of Norwich] Critical Rev 3rd ser 3 1804; [Ellis, G.] Edinburgh Rev 4 1804; Monthly Mag, 28 Jan 1805; Monthly Rev n.s. [2nd] 48 1805; Poetical Register 6 1806–7.
Study
M., F. Remarks on Sir W. Scott's Sir Tristrem. GM 103 1833.

Rasselas, by Samuel Johnson LLD. 1805.
Studies
Kolb, G. J. Sir Walter Scott, 'editor' of Rasselas. MP 89 1992.
Lloyd, B. C. The discovery of Scott as 'editor' and 'author of the advertisement' in the illustrated edition of Rasselas. Scott Newsletter 23–4 1993–4.

Original memoirs written during the first great civil war; being the life of Sir Henry Slingsby and memoirs of Capt Hodgson. Edinburgh 1806.
REVIEW: Scots Mag 69 1807.

The life of John Dryden, by Walter Scott Esq. 1808.

The works of John Dryden now first collected in eighteen volumes, illustrated with notes historical, critical and explanatory, and a life of the author, by Walter Scott Esq. 18 vols 1808, 1821; rev G. Saintsbury 18 vols Edinburgh 1882–93; Memoirs of John Dryden 2 vols Paris 1826; tr Fr 1826; The life of John Dryden, ed B. Kreissman, Lincoln NE 1963.
REVIEWS: Analectic Mag 2 1813 (signed P); Annual Rev 7 for 1808 (1809); Br Critic 35 1810; [Hallam, Henry] Edinburgh Rev 13 1808; (Pye) London Rev 1 1809; Monthly Mag, 30 Jan 1809; [Symmons, C.] Monthly Rev n.s. [2nd] 58 1809; Satirist 2 1808; Scots Mag 70 1808.
Studies
Warton's Dryden. Br Rev 4 1812.
Dryden: illustrations by T. Holt White [signed Aegrotus]. N & Q 18 Oct 1851.
Saintsbury's Dryden. Saturday Rev of Politics 14 July 1883.
Falle, G. Sir Walter Scott as editor of Dryden and Swift. UTQ 36 1967.

Memoirs of Capt George Carleton an English officer. Edinburgh 1808, 1809 (4th edn); ed A. W. Lawrence 1929.
REVIEWS: Annual Rev 7 for 1808 (1809); Antijacobin Rev 30 1808; Br Critic 32 1808; Eclectic Rev 4 1808; Literary Panorama 4 1808; Scots Mag 70 1808.
Studies
Carleton's Memoirs of an English officer [signed Beta]. N & Q 13 Nov 1858; replies 1 Jan–12 Mar 1859.
Parnell, A. Dean Swift and the Memoirs of Captain Carleton. Eng Historical Rev 6 1891.

Queenhoo-Hall: a romance. In Queenhoo-Hall, a romance, and Ancient times, a drama, by the late Joseph Strutt, 4 vols Edinburgh 1808.
REVIEWS: Br Critic 32 1808; Literary Panorama 4 1808; Scots Mag 70 1808.

Memoirs of Robert Cary, Earl of Monmouth written by himself, and Fragmenta regalia being a history of Queen Elizabeth's favourites by Sir Robert Naunton. Edinburgh 1808, Lee Priory [London] 1823, 1824.
REVIEWS: Br Critic 34 1809; Scots Mag 70 1808.
Study
Solly, E. Cary's Memoirs. N & Q 5 July 1873.

The life of Edward Lord Herbert of Cherbury, written by himself. Edinburgh 1809.

The State papers and letters of Sir Ralph Sadler knight-banneret. 2 and 3 vols (with A. Clifford) Edinburgh 1809. Biographical memoir rptd PW 4.
REVIEWS: Critical Rev 3rd ser 21 1810; [Napier, M.] Edinburgh Rev 16 1810; Quarterly Rev 4 1810.
Study
Wood, G. A. M. Sir Walter Scott and Sir Ralph Sadler: a chapter in literary history. Stud in Scottish Lit 7–8 1969–71.

A collection of scarce and valuable tracts, on the most interesting and entertaining subjects, but chiefly such as relate to the history and constitution of these kingdoms, selected from an infinite number in print and manuscript in the royal, Cotton, Sion and other public, as well as private, libraries, particularly that of the late Lord Somers: the second edition, revised, augmented and arranged by Walter Scott Esq. 13 vols 1809–15. 'Somers tracts'.
REVIEW: Literary Panorama 6 1809.
Study
Kinney, A. F. Two unique copies of Stephen Gosson's Schoole of abuse (1579): criteria for judging nineteenth century editing. PBSA 59 1965.

English minstrelsy: being a selection of fugitive poetry from the best English authors, with some original pieces hitherto unpublished. 2 vols Edinburgh 1810.
REVIEW: Br Critic 35 1810.
W., L. A. English minstrelsy. N & Q 29 Feb 1908; replies 28 Mar.

The poetical works of Anna Seward with extracts from her literary correspondence. 3 vols Edinburgh 1810.
REVIEWS: Antijacobin Rev 41 1812; Br Rev 2 1811; Critical Rev 3rd ser 1811; Eclectic Rev 7 1811; European Mag 58 1810; Literary Panorama 9 1911; Scots Mag 73 1811.

The ancient British drama. 3 vols 1810.
Study
Ruddick, B. Scott on the drama: a series of ascriptions. Scott Newsletter 14 1989.

The memoirs of the Duke of Sully, prime minister to Henry the Great. 5 vols 1810.

Memoirs of Count Grammont, by Anthony Hamilton. 2 vols 1811; tr Fr 1811.

The Castle of Otranto, by Horace Walpole. Edinburgh 1811.

Secret history of the court of James the First. 2 vols Edinburgh 1811.

The modern British drama. 5 vols 1811.

Memoirs of the reign of King Charles the First, by Sir Philip Warwick, Knight. Edinburgh 1813.

The works of Jonathan Swift DD, Dean of St Patrick's, Dublin: containing additional letters, tracts and poems, not hitherto published, with notes and a life of the author, by Walter Scott Esq. 19 vols Edinburgh 1814 [1st edn], 1824 (2nd edn). Memoirs of Jonathan Swift DD, Dean of St Patrick's Dublin, 2 vols Paris 1826; tr Fr 1826.
REVIEWS: [Jeffrey, F.] Edinburgh Rev 27 1816; Scots Mag 76 1814.
Studies
Easton, W. Twelve volumes of Sir Walter Scott's corrected proofs of the works of Jonathan Swift DD. nd.

Falle, G. Sir Walter Scott as editor of Dryden and Swift. UTQ 36 1967.
Potter, L. H. The text of Scott's edition of Swift. SB 22 1969.
Thompson, P. V. Suppressed names in Swift's letters 1735. N & Q 216, Feb 1971.

The letting of humours blood in the head vaine &c., by S. Rowlands. Edinburgh 1814, 1815.

An essay of the nature and actions of the subterranean (and for the most part) invisible people. Edinburgh 1815 (priv ptd).

Memorie of the Somervilles. 2 vols Edinburgh 1815.
REVIEW: Monthly Rev n.s. [2nd] 86 1818.

The history of Donald the Hammerer. In [E. Burt,] Letters from a gentleman in the north of Scotland, 5th edn 2 vols 1818 (re-issued 1822) (vol 1), Glasgow 1876.

Some particulars regarding the family of Invernahyle, copied from a manuscript in the possession of Dr Thomson, late of Appin, by Joseph Train. Scottish Jnl 29 Jan 1848.

Trivial poems and triolets, written in obedience to Mrs Tomkin's commands by Patrick Carey. 1819 (re-issued 1820).
REVIEWS: Ladies' Monthly Museum 3rd ser 12 1820; Literary Chron 3 June 1820; Literary Gazette 27 May 1820; Monthly Rev n.s. [2nd] 95 1821.

Memorials of the Haliburtons. Edinburgh 1820, 1824.
Cook, D. Scott first editions. TLS 18 Aug 1932; replies 1–29 Sep.

Northern memoirs calculated for the meridian of Scotland, to which is added the contemplative and practical angler, writ in the year 1658 by Richard Franck. Edinburgh 1821.

Ballantyne's novelist's library. 10 vols 1821–4.
REVIEWS: [Lockhart, J. G.] Blackwood's Edinburgh Mag 15 1824; Ladies' Monthly Museum n.s. 14 1821; Literary Chron 8 Sep 1821; Literary Gazette 27 Jan 1821–22 Jan 1825; Monthly Rev n.s. [2nd] 108 1825.
Study
Faulkner, P. Scott as editor of Bage. N & Q Oct 1970.

Chronological notes of Scottish affairs, from 1680 till 1701, being chiefly taken from the diary of Lord Fountainhall. Edinburgh 1822.
REVIEW: Edinburgh Mag 10 1822 (letter from T. D. Lauder, Dec 1822).

Military memoirs of the great civil war, being the military memoirs of John Gwynne, etc. Edinburgh 1822.
REVIEWS: Literary Chron 16 Nov 1822; Literary Gazette 2–9 Nov 1822.

Lays of the Lindsays. Edinburgh 1824. Suppressed.
Studies
Stronach, G. The evolution of a popular song. Dunedin Mag 1 1913.
Stronach, G. Lays of the Lindsays. Dunedin Mag 1 1913.

Auld Robin Gray: a ballad, by Lady Anne Barnard. Edinburgh 1825 (Bannatyne Club).

The Bannatyne miscellany; containing original papers and tracts chiefly relating to the history and literature of Scotland, vol 1. Edinburgh 1827 (Bannatyne Club). [Ed with D. Laing.]

Memoirs of the Marchioness de la Rochejaquelein. Edinburgh 1827.

Proceedings in the court-martial held upon John, Master of Sinclair, Captain-lieutenant in Preston's regiment, for the murder of Ensign Schaw of the same regiment, and Captain Schaw of the Royals, 17th October 1708 with correspondence respecting that transaction. Edinburgh 1828 (Roxburghe Club).

Memoir of George Bannatyne. In Memorials of George Bannatyne, 1545–1608, Edinburgh 1829 (Bannatyne Club).
Study
The Bannatyne Club. Edinburgh Literary Jnl 20 Mar 1830.

Trial of Duncan Terig alias Clerk and Alexander Bane Macdonald, for the murder of Arthur Davis, Sergeant in General Guise's Regiment of Foot, June MDCCLIV. Edinburgh 1831 (Bannatyne Club).

Memoirs of the insurrection in Scotland in 1715, by John, Master of Sinclair, with notes and introductory notice by Scott. Edinburgh 1858 (Abbotsford Club).

[Projected edn of Shakespeare]
Studies
Crockett, W. S. Sir Walter Scott's Shakespeare. Bookman 61 1921.
Crockett, W. S. Scott and Shakespeare: new light on a publishing project. Glasgow Herald 5 July 1930.
Parker, W. M. Scott's knowledge of Shakespeare. Quart Rev July 1952.
Rao, B. Scott's proposed edition of Shakespeare. Indian Jnl of Eng Stud 6 1965.

Dramatisations etc

Calcraft, J. W. [Cole, J. W.?]. Leaves from the portfolio of a manager, 5: On the dramas from the Waverley novels. Dublin Univ Mag 37 1851.
The Waverley dramas: a series of the original plays founded on the novels. Glasgow 1872.
Hamilton, W. Sir Walter Scott. In his Parodies of the works of English and American authors, 6 vols 1884–9 (vol 3 1886).
White, H. A. Sir Walter Scott's novels on the stage. (Yale Stud in Eng 76) New Haven CT and London 1927.
Pope-Hennessy, U. Scott and the theatre: stage versions of the Waverleys. Scots Mag n.s. 17 1932.
W., S. Scott's songs set to music. N & Q 9 Mar 1940; reply by H. G. L. K[ing] 23 Mar.
L., R. E. Dramatized versions of Scott's novels. N & Q 25 Jan 1941.
Dunlop, J. G. Scott's novels: dramatized versions. N & Q 2 June 1945; reply by J. C. Corson 14 July.
Chancellor, P. British bards and continental composers. Musical Quart 46 1960.
Carlton, W. J. George Hogarth: a link with Scott and Dickens. Dickensian 59 1963.
Parsons, C. O. Chapbook versions of the Waverley novels. Stud in Scottish Lit 3 1966.
Parsons, C. O. Scott's sixpenny public. Columbia Lib Columns 16 1967.
Ruff, W. and W. Hellstrom. Scott's authorship of the songs in Daniel Terry's plays. Stud in Scottish Lit 5 1968.
Ford, R. M. The Waverley burlesques. Nineteenth Cent Theatre Research 6 1978.
Mitchell, J. The Walter Scott operas: an analysis of operas based on the works of Sir Walter Scott. University AL 1978.
Ford, R. Dramatisations of Scott's novels: a catalogue. Oxford 1979.
Diller, H.-J. Ivanhoe auf der englischen Bühne des 19 Jahrhunderts. In Anglistentag 1980 Giessen: Tagungsbeiträge und Berichte im Auftrage des Vorstandes, ed H. Grabes, Grossen Linden 1981.
Fiske, R. Scotland in music: a European enthusiasm. Cambridge 1983.
Mitchell, J. A list of Walter Scott operas. In Scott and his influence, ed J. H. Alexander and D. Hewitt, Aberdeen 1983.
Parsons, C. O. Magic lantern lectures on Sir Walter Scott. Columbia Lib Columns 34 1985.
Bolton, H. P. Sir Walter Scott on BBC. Scott Newsletter 12 1988.
Mitchell, J. The Scott operas of Lionel Lackey. Scott Newsletter 13 1988.
Williams, G. J. Guy Mannering and Charlotte Cushman's Meg Merrilies: gothic novel, play, and performance. In When they weren't doing Shakespeare: essays on nineteenth century British and American theatre, ed J. L. Fisher and S. Watt, Athens GA and London 1989.
Bolton, H. P. Scott dramatized. 1992. An exhaustive list.
Kent, D. A. and D. R. Ewen (ed). Romantic parodies, 1797–1831. 1992.
Mitchell, J. More Scott operas: further analyses of operas based on the works of Sir Walter Scott. Lanham, New York, and London 1996.

§2

A fuller listing of secondary material up to 1940 may be found in J. C. Corson's bibliography, above; for more recent material, see the two bibliographies (above) by J. Rubenstein, whose help with this entry is gratefully acknowledged.

Textual, bibliographical, source and influence studies

W. B. Todd and A. Bowden have given substantial and invaluable help with this entry. Their analytical bibliography (see above) includes 68 Sessions (legal) papers, mostly in the Signet Lib, Edinburgh.

Anachronisms of the author of Waverley. GM 91 1821.

[Chambers, R.] Illustrations of the author of Waverley, being notices and anecdotes of real characters, scenes, incidents etc presumed to be described in his works. Edinburgh 1822, 1825, 1884.

Warner, R. Illustrations, historical, biographical and miscellaneous, of the novels by the author of Waverley, with criticisms, general and particular. 3 vols 1823–4.

[De Quincey, T.] Walladmor: Sir Walter Scott's German novel. [Baldwin's] London Mag 10 1824.

Plagiarisms of the author of Waverley. Emmet 10–17 Jan 1824.

The originals of some of the characters in the Waverley novels. News of Lit and Fashion 25 June 1825.

[Gebhardt, C. N.] Sir Walter Scott und seine deutschen Uebersetzer. In Ueberlieferungen zur Geschichte, Literatur und Kunst der Vor- und Mitwelt, ed F. A. Ebert, [Dresden 1827].

[Maurice, F. D.?] Sir Walter Scott and Goethe. Athenaeum 27 May 1829.

Skene, James. A series of sketches of the existing localities alluded to in the Waverley novels, etched from original drawings by James Skene Esq. Edinburgh 1829.

Parallel passages. Aberdeen Mag 1 Sep 1831. On the poems.

Landscape illustrations of the prose and poetical works of Sir Walter Scott Bart with portraits of the principal female characters. 24 pts 1832–3.

F[orsyth]. The Waverley anecdotes, illustrative of the incidents, characters, and scenery described in the novels and romances of Sir Walter Scott Bart. 2 vols 1833, 2 vols Boston MA 1833; rev edn 1 vol 1849.

[De Quincey, T.] Autobiography of an English opium-eater: recollections of Charles Lamb. Tait's Edinburgh Mag n.s. 5 1838; rptd in his Works, 17 vols Edinburgh 1862–71 (vol 17 1871) and in his Collected writings, ed D. Masson, 14 vols Edinburgh 1889–90 (vol 14 1890). On Walladmor.

Hagberg, C. A. Cervantes et Walter Scott: parallèle littéraire soumis à la discussion publique l'avant-midi du 21 nov. 1838. Lund 1838.

de Saint-Maurice Cabany, E. Découverte inattendue d'un roman posthume et inédit de Sir Walter Scott. Paris 1854. On Moredun.

Moredun, narration de l'année 1210: roman posthume et inédit de Sir Walter Scott, transcrit sur le manuscrit original signé W. S. et précédé d'une introduction par E. de Saint-Maurice Cabany. 3 vols Paris 1855; rev as Moredun, a tale of the twelve hundred and ten, by W. S., 3 vols 1855; correspondence in Athenaeum 6 Jan–9 June 1855.

Brandl, A. Die Aufnahme von Goethes Jugendwerken in England. Goethe-Jahrbuch 3 1882.

Dickson, N. The Bible in Waverley: or Sir Walter Scott's use of the sacred Scriptures. Edinburgh 1884.

Sime, W. Scott's influence in French literature. In his To and fro, or views from sea and land, 1884.

d'Ovidio, F. Appunti per un parallelo fra Manzoni e Walter Scott. In Atti R. Accad. Scienze, Naples 1886.

[Smith, G. C.] New editions of Walter Scott. Nation [New York] 18 May 1893.

Hallays, A. W. Scott et le romantisme français. Journal des Débats 26 July 1898.

Maigron, L. Le roman historique à l'époque romantique: essai sur l'influence de Walter Scott. Paris 1898, 1912.

Maigron, L. Walter Scott et la littérature française. Revue Française d'Édimbourg 3e année 4 1899.

Blumenhagen, K. Sir Walter Scott als Übersetzer. Rostock 1900; reviewed by A. R. Hohlfeld in Studien zur vergleichenden Literaturgeschichte 3 1903.

Dotti, M. Delle derivazioni nei Promessi sposi di Alessandro Manzoni dai romanzi di Walter Scott. Pisa 1900.

Hertel, H. Die Naturschilderungen in Walter Scotts Versdichtungen. Leipzig 1900.

Roesel, L. K. Die litterarischen und persönlichen Beziehungen Sir Walter Scotts zu Goethe: ein Beitrag zu Studien über das Verhältnis der deutschen Litteratur zur englischen am Ende des 18. und Beginn des 19. Jhrs. Leipzig 1901.

Freye, W. The influence of Gothic literature on Sir Walter Scott. Rostock 1902.

Bouchier, J. Local and personal proverbs in the Waverley novels. N & Q 14–21 May 1904.

Henderson, J. S. Heine and Sir Walter Scott. Temple Bar 129 1904.

Wenger, K. Historische Romane deutscher Romantiker: Untersuchungen über den Einfluss Walter Scotts. Berne 1905.

Agnoli, G. Gli albori del romanzo storico in Italia e i primi imitatori di Walter Scott. Piacenza 1906.

Fassò, L. Saggio di ricerche intorno alla fortuna di Walter Scott in Italia. Reale Accademia delle Scienze di Torino, Atti 41 1906.

François, V. E. Sir Walter Scott and Alfred de Vigny. MLN 21 1906.

Bayne, T. Sir Walter Scott's quotations. Glasgow Herald 25 Apr, 2 May 1907.

Korff, H. A. Scott und Alexis: eine Studie zur Technik des historischen Romans. Heidelberg 1907.

Colville, J. Scott and German romantics. Glasgow Herald 21 Aug 1909.

Crockett, W. S. The Scott originals: an account of notables and worthies, the originals of characters in the Waverley novels. Edinburgh 1912 (for 1911), 1932 (rev).

Forsythe, R. S. Two debts of Scott to Le morte d'Arthur. MLN 27 1912.

Hertel, Hugo. Waverley in France. Dunedin Mag 2 1914.

Kent, W. H. Walter Scott and the Catholic revival. Catholic World Nov 1914.

Kohler, H. F. Walladmor von Willibald Alexis: Untersuchung des Romans in seinem Verhältnis zu Walter Scott. Marburg 1915.

Sigmann, L. Die englische Literatur von 1800–1850 im Urteil der zeitgenossischen deutschen Kritik. (Anglistische Forschungen 55) Heidelberg 1918.

Devonshire, J. M. The 'decline' of Sir Walter Scott in France. Fr Quart 1 1919.

Price, L. M. English–German literary influences: bibliography and survey. (Univ of California Pbns in Mod Philology 9) Berkeley CA 1919.

Wojciechowski, K. Pan Tadeusz Mickiewicza a romans Waltera Scotta. Crakow 1919.

Cargill, A. Sir Walter Scott and his 'anonymous' quotations. Scotsman 20 Nov 1920; replies 22–7 Nov.

Lieder, P. R. Scott and Scandinavian literature: the influence of Bartholin and others. Smith College Stud in Mod Langs 2 1920.

Churchman, P. H. and E. A. Peers. A survey of the influence of Sir Walter Scott in Spain. Rev Hispanique 55 1922.

Crockett, W. S. Some Scott discoveries. Scotsman 9–16 Feb 1924.

Peers, E. A. Studies in the influence of Sir Walter Scott in Spain. Rev Hispanique 68 1926.

Cochrane, R. A forgotten skit of Sir Walter's. Sir Walter Scott Quart 1 1927. 'The aspirations of Christopher Corduroy'.

Gray, W. F. Some forgotten writings of Walter Scott. Quart Rev July 1930. Contributions to John Ballantyne's periodical The Sale-Room.

Perés, R. D. A Spanish tribute. Tr R. M. Macandrew. Scotsman Sir Walter Scott centenary suppl 21 Sep 1932.
Dunbabin, R. L. A quotation in Scott. TLS 18 May 1933. Incorrect Latin in the novels.
Parker, W. M. How the Waverley novels were produced. Scots Mag n.s. 18 1933.
Ruff, W. Scott's printers. TLS 7 Sep 1933.
Dargan, E. P. Scott and the French romantics: a list of the first French translations of the Waverley novels. PMLA 49 1934.
Randall, D. A. Waverley in America. Colophon n.s. 1 1935.
Cook, D. Scott's 1814 diary. TLS 22 Aug 1936.
Hillhouse, J. T. The Waverley novels and their critics. [1936.]
Cook, D. The Waverleys in French: Scott's authorship revealed in 1822. TLS 17 July 1937.
Bogner, H. F. Sir Walter Scott in New Orleans 1818–32. Louisiana Historical Quart 21 1938.
Gaelic spelling in Scott's writings [signed Quare]. N & Q 15 Jan 1938; reply 2 Apr.
Mennie, D. M. Sir Walter Scott's unpublished translations of German plays. MLR 33 1938.
Corson, J. C. Verses on the death of Scott. N & Q 2 Dec 1939.
The secret of Scott's authorship of the Waverley novels [signed Rhedecynian]. N & Q 4 Jan 1941; replies 8, 22 Feb, 29 Mar.
Bisson, L. A. Amédée Pichot: a romantic Prometheus. Oxford 1943.
Brightfield, M. F. Lockhart's Quarterly contributors. PMLA 59 1944.
Kern, J. D. An unidentified review, possibly by Scott. MLQ 6 1945.
Stevenson, P. R. Sir Walter Scott's diary. TLS 15 Nov 1947.
Klančar, A. J. Scott in Yugoslavia. Slavonic and East European Rev 27 1948.
Mayo, R. D. The chronology of the Waverley novels: the evidence of the manuscripts. PMLA 63 1948.
McDonald, T. P. Sir Walter Scott's fee book. Juridical Rev 62 1950.
Rodrigues, A. G. A novelística estrangeira em versão portuguesa no período pré-romântico. Boletim da Biblioteca da Universadade de Coimbra 20 1951.
Thomas, L. H. C. Walladmor: a pseudo-translation of Sir Walter Scott. MLR 46 1951.
Brown, T. J. The detection of faked literary MSS. BC 2 1953.
Ruff, W. An uncollected preface by Sir Walter Scott. N & Q 199, Nov 1954.
Parker, W. M. Correcting Scott's text. TLS 9 Dec 1955.
Altick, R. The English common reader: a social history of the mass reading public 1800–1900. Chicago 1957.
Gordan, J. D. Sir Walter Scott: autograph manuscript of Bizarro a Calabrian tale of recent date. BNYPL 61 1957.
Kaser, D. Waverley in America. PBSA 51 1957. Early American edns.
Levidova, I. M. (comp). Walter Scott. Moscow 1958. List of Russian translations.
Gettman, R. A. A Victorian publisher: a study of the Bentley papers. Cambridge 1960.
Nuñez de Arenas, Manuel. Simples notas acerca de Walter Scott in España. In L'Espagne: des luminères au romantisme, ed R. Marrast, Paris 1963.
Ewing, D. C. The three volume novel. PBSA 61 1967.
Ruff, W. and W. Hellstrom. Some uncollected poems of Sir Walter Scott: a census. N & Q 212 1967.
Hayden, J. O. The Satanic school: Sir Walter Scott. In his The romantic reviewers 1802–1824, Chicago 1968.
Romagnoli, S. Narratori e prosatori del romanticismo. In Storia della letteratura italiana vol 8, ed E. Cecchi and N. Sapegno, Milan 1968.
Hood, F. C. Scott and his printers. TLS 3 Apr 1969; replies 17–24 Apr.
Scott: the critical heritage. Ed J. O. Hayden 1970.
Béreaud, J. G. A. La traduction en France à l'époque romantique. Comparative Lit Stud 8 1971.
Petrov, R. Pred 200-godisninata ot rozdenieto ne Voltar Skot [Walter Scott's 200th anniversary]. Bibliotekar: Durzhavna Biblioteka Vasil Kolarov 18 1971.
Tippkötter, H. Walter Scott, Geschichte als Unterhaltung: eine Rezeptionsanalyze der Waverley novels. Frankfurt 1971.
Ash, M. Scott and historical publishing: the Bannatyne and Maitland Clubs. Abertay Hist Soc Pbns 16 1972.
Collingwood, F. Printer to Sir Walter Scott. Lib Rev 23 1972.
Massmann, K. Die Rezeption der historischen Romane Sir Walter Scotts in Frankreich (1816–1832). Heidelberg 1972.
Nielsen, J. E. Sir Walter Scott. N & Q 217 1972. Danish trns.
Cooney, S. Scott's anonymity: its motives and consequences. Stud in Scottish Lit 10 1973.
Katona, A. The impact of Sir Walter Scott in Hungary. In Scott bicentenary essays, ed A. Bell, Edinburgh 1973.
Lazu, E. Opera lui Walter Scott în România. Analele Universităţii Bucureşti: limbi germanice 22 1973.
Ochojski, P. M. Waverley ueber alles: Sir Walter Scott's German reputation. In Scott bicentenary essays, ed A. Bell, Edinburgh 1973.
Ruff, W. Deceptions in the works of Scott, or lying title-pages. In Scott bicentenary essays, ed A. Bell, Edinburgh 1973.
Benedetti, A. Le traduzioni italiane da Walter Scott e i loro anglicismi. Accademia Toscana di Scienze e Lettere La Colombaria Studi 33, Florence 1974.
Zug, C. G. III. Sir Walter Scott and George Thomson the friend of Burns. Stud in Scottish Lit 12 1974.
Hardman, Phillippa. A note on some 'lost' manuscripts. Library 30 1975.
Punzo, F. R. Walter Scott in Italia 1821–1971. (Biblioteca di Studi Inglesi 31) Bari 1975.
Alexander, J. H. The reviewing of Walter Scott's poetry 1805–1817. In his Two studies in romantic reviewing vol 2, Salzburg 1976.
Gamerschlag, K. Sir Walter Scott und die Waverley novels: eine Übersicht den Gang der Scottforschung von den Anfangen bis heute. Erträge der Forschung 9 1978.
Alexander, J. H. The reception of Scott's poetry by his correspondents 1796–1817. 2 vols Salzburg 1979.
Gamerschlag, K. Die Korrektur der Waverley novels: text-kritische Untersuchungen zu einer Autor-Korrektor-Beziehung. Bonn 1979.
Hargreaves, G. D. British printers on galley proofs. Library 6 ser 1 1979.
Brückner, U. Walter Scott, Dichter und Bibliophile. Marginalien 79 1980.
Rubenstein, J. 'This applause is worth having': Lady Louisa Stuart as critic of Sir Walter Scott. Scottish Literary Jnl 7 1980.
Alexander, J. H. The treatment of Scott in reviews of the English romantics. YES 11 1981.
Pujals Fontrodona, E. Las lineas generales del romanticismo inglés y su repercusión limitida a Byron y Scott en España. Filologia Moderna 71–3 1981.
Kelly, G. Toward a critical edition of the Waverley novels. Scott Newsletter 1 1982.
Ambrose, M. Scott, Sicily and Michele Amari. In Scott and his influence, ed J. H. Alexander and D. Hewitt, Aberdeen 1983.
Kelly, G. A proposal to carry out a critical edition of Sir Walter Scott's Waverley novels at the University of Alberta. In Scott and his influence, ed J. H. Alexander and D. Hewitt, Aberdeen 1983.
Nielsen, J. E. Sir Walter Scott's reception in nineteenth century Denmark. In Scott and his influence, ed J. H. Alexander and D. Hewitt, Aberdeen 1983.
A[lexander], J. H. The Waverley novels project. Scott Newsletter 4 1984.
Gamerschlag, K. Some thoughts on editing the Waverley novels. Archiv 22 1984.
Lyons, M. The audience for romanticism: Walter Scott in France, 1815–1851. European History Quart 14 1984.

Garside, P. Rob's last raid: Scott and the publication of the Waverley novels. In Author/publisher relations during the eighteenth and nineteenth centuries, ed R. Myers and M. Harris, Oxford 1985.
Kelly, G. Toward an edition of Scott's Waverley novels: computer technology and the idea of the text. In Studies in Scottish fiction: nineteenth century, ed H. W. Drescher and J. Schwend, Frankfurt 1985.
Garside, P. Scott as a political journalist. RES n.s. 37 1986.
Hewitt, D. The new Edinburgh Edition of the Waverley novels. Scott Newsletter 8 1986.
Kaiser, G. R. '... impossible to subject titles of this nature to criticism': Walter Scotts Kritik als Schlüssel zur Wirkungsgeschichte E. T. A. Hoffmans im 19 Jahrhundert. In Kontroversen, alte und neue, 9: Deutsche Literatur in der Weltliteratur: Kulturnation statt politischer Nation?, ed A. Schöne, F. N. Mennemeier and C. Wiedemann, Tübingen 1986.
Hewitt, D. The Edinburgh Edition of the Waverley novels: the transmission of the texts. Scott Newsletter 10 1987.
Millgate, J. Scott's last edition: a study in publishing history. Edinburgh 1987.
Garside, P. D. Henry Mackenzie, the Scottish novel and Blackwood's Mag. Scottish Literary Jnl 15 1988.
Lamont-Brown, R. Walter Scott in Japan: a listing of translations and translators 1880–1986. Scott Newsletter 12 1988.
Marrast, R. Ediciones perpinanesas de Walter Scott en castellano (1824–1826). Romanticismo (Atti del IV Congresso sul romanticismo Spagnolo e Ispanomericano, Universita di Genova) 3–4 1988.
Ruddick, B. Scott and the drama: a series of ascriptions. Scott Newsletter 14 1989.
Hewitt, D. The Edinburgh Edition of the Waverley novels: a progress report. Scott Newsletter 18 1991.
Alexander, J. H. and P. Garside. Editing the Waverley novels. Reviewing Romanticism, ed P. W. Martin and R. Jarvis, 1992.
Alexander, J. H. The Edinburgh Edition of the Waverley novels: an informal history. Scott Newsletter 21–2 1992–3.

General critical and biographical studies

Walter Scott's poems. Monthly Mirror n.s. 5 1809.
C., S. T. Walter Scott. The Courier 15 Sep 1810.
Mr Walter Scott's poetry. Monthly Mirror n.s. 8 1810.
[Review of Byron's English bards and Scotch reviewers.] Antijacobin Rev 37 1810. On Scott's poetry.
Walter Scott Esq. Hibernian Mag 3 1811.
[Letters to editor on Scott's poetry.] Monthly Mag 33 1812.
Remarks on the poems of Walter Scott. Cosmopolite 11 June 1812.
Critical sketches of living poetical characters in Edinburgh. Scots Mag 75 1813.
[Barnes, T.] Portraits of authors, no 3: Mr Walter Scott. Champion 12 Feb 1814.
H., G. C. Parallel between Scott and Campbell. Port Folio 3rd ser 4 1814.
Observations in reply to strictures on Walter Scott's poetry. Monthly Museum 1 1814.
Which is the best poet, Lord Byron or Walter Scott Esq? Reasoner 1 1814.
Berguer, L. T. Stanzas inscribed to Walter Scott Esq. Edinburgh 1815.
P., W. Letters from Edinburgh. North Amer Rev 1 1815.
Notice of Walter Scott. Analectic Mag and Naval Chron 8 1816.
[Watkins, J. and F. Shoberl.] Scott, Walter, Esq. In A biographical dictionary of the living authors of Great Britain and Ireland, 1816.
Of the modern poets: Walter Scott [signed B]. Literary Gazette 12 Apr 1817.
W., J. Memoir of Walter Scott, Esq. NMM 10 1818.
Walter Scott. Port Folio 4th ser 5 1818.
[Wilson, J.] Essays on the Lake School of poetry, No. 1: Wordsworth's White doe of Rylstone. Blackwood's Edinburgh Mag 3 1818.
The works under the name of Walter Scott. Kaleidoscope 24 Nov 1818.
Biographical memoir of Walter Scott. Miniature Mag 3 1819.
[Lockhart, J. G.] Peter's letters to his kinsfolk. 3 vols Edinburgh 1819 ('2nd' [for 1st] edn), 1819 ('3rd' [for 2nd] edn).
On the poetry of Walter Scott. NMM 11 1819.
Remarks on Walter Scott's poetry. Leeds Literary Observer 1 1819.
Remarks philosophical and literary on the poetry of Byron and Scott. GM 89 1819.
Visit to Walter Scott. Fireside Mag 1 1819.
The author of Waverley. Kaleidoscope n.s. 1 1820–1.
Burns, Scott, Byron and Campbell. Kaleidoscope n.s. 1 1820–1.
D., W. F. On the living novelists. [Gold's] London Mag 2 1820.
In The adversaria. Port Folio [4th ser] 10 1820. On the prose and verse.
A letter to the author of Waverley, Ivanhoe etc on the moral tendency of those popular works. Monthly Rev n.s. [2nd] 93 1820.
Memoir of Sir Walter Scott Bart. European Mag 78 1820.
Memoir of Sir Walter Scott Bart. [Gold's] London Mag 2 1820.
The novels of the author of the Tales of my landlord. Kaleidoscope 22 Feb 1820.
On the living novelists, 2: The author of Waverley. NMM 13 1820.
Pichot, A. Essai sur la vie et les ouvrages de W. Scott. In Romans poétiques, traduits de l'anglais (en prose) par le traducteur des oeuvres de lord Byron, 8 vols Paris 1820–1 (vol 1).
The real author of Waverley, Rob Roy, etc. Champion 12 Aug 1820.
The Scotch novels. Newcastle Mag 1 1820.
Scott, Byron, Herbert and Moore. Kaleidoscope 29 Feb 1820.
[Scott, John.] Living authors no 1: The author of the Scotch novels. [Baldwin's] London Mag 1 1820.
Sir Walter Scott and the Scotch novels. Déjeuné, 21 Oct 1820.
Sir Walter Scott pronounced not to be the author of Tales of my landlord. Kaleidoscope 8 Aug 1820; debate continued 5 Sep–31 Oct.
[Talfourd, T. N.] On the living novelists no 2: the author of Waverley [signed T. D.]. NMM 13 1820; rptd in his Critical and miscellaneous writings, Philadelphia 1842 etc.
Touchstone, Timothy. A letter to the author of Waverley, Ivanhoe, &c. on the moral tendency of those popular works. 1820.
Walter Scott and the greater and minor theatres. Champion 24 June 1820.
[Adolphus, J. L.] Letters to Richard Heber Esq, containing critical remarks on the series of novels beginning with Waverley and an attempt to ascertain their author. 1821, 1822; reviewed in Monthly Rev n.s. [2nd] 97 1822, and New Edinburgh Rev 1 1821 (rptd in Port Folio 4th ser 13 1822).
The author of Waverley. Lady's Mag n.s. 2 1821.
The author of Waverley. Weekly Entertainer n.s. 4 1821.
Chit chat. Citizen 1 1821.
Critique on Sir Walter Scott's remarks on novelists and dramatists. Literary Chron 29 Sep–6 Oct 1821.
Decease of Jedediah Cleishbotham. European Mag 80 1821.
Memoir of Sir Walter Scott. Gleaner 1 1821.
Memoir of Sir Walter Scott. New Hibernian Mag 2 1821.
Nasmyth, A. Sixteen engravings from real scenes supposed to be described in the novels and tales of the author of Waverley. 1821.
Observations on the author of Waverley. Imperial Mag 3 1821.
On the genius and writings of Sir Walter Scott. Literary Speculum 1 1821.
Pichot, A. Notice sur Sir Walter Scott et ses écrits. Paris 1821.
[R. F. St Barbe.] Semihorae biographicae no 3. Blackwood's Edinburgh Mag 8 1821.
[Senior, N. W.] Novels by the author of Waverley. Quart Rev 26 1821; rptd in his Essays on fiction, 1864.

Sir Walter Scott's account of the coronation. Examiner 5 Aug 1821.
Warton and Scott. Kaleidoscope n.s. 2 1821–3.
Additional reasons for believing that Sir Walter Scott is not the author of the Scotch novels. Newcastle Mag n.s. 1–2 1822–3.
American critique on an English author. Kaleidoscope n.s. 3 1822–3.
The author of Waverley. Citizen 1 1822.
Historical characters in Sir Walter Scott's novels. Kaleidoscope n.s. 3 1822–3.
Life of Sir Walter Scott. Port Folio 4th ser 13 1822.
Lord Byron and Sir Walter Scott. [Baldwin's] London Mag 5 1822.
Memoir of Sir Walter Scott. Gazette of Fashion 1 1822.
The poetry contained in the novels, tales and romances of the author of Waverley. Monthly Censor 1 1822.
Portraitures of modern poets, no 4. Ladies' Monthly Museum n.s. 15 1822.
The Scotch novels. Kaleidoscope n.s. 3 1822–3.
The Scotch novels; or an exposé of the prose-spinning school. Gazette of Fashion 1 1822.
Sir Walter Scott. Examiner 8 Sep 1822.
Sir Walter Scott. Ladies' Monthly Museum n.s. 15 1822.
A sketch of old England, by a New England man. New Voyages and Travels 8 1822.
Strictures on the poets of the present day, no 3. La Belle Assemblée n.s. 26 1822.
[The author of Waverley]. Edinburgh Literary Gazette 21 1823.
The author of Waverley. Literary Chron 21 June 1823.
The author of Waverley. Manchester Iris 2 1823.
Biography: Sir Walter Scott. Magnet 2 1823.
Bob Tickler on the authorship of the Scotch novels. Newcastle Mag n.s. 2 1823.
Clarendon, F. Modern novelists. New European Mag 3 1823.
The court of claims. New European Mag 3 1823.
An elucidation of some of the characters in the Scotch novels. Weekly Entertainer n.s. 8 1823.
Memoir of Sir Walter Scott. Manchester Iris 2 1823.
On anonymous publications [signed Z]. Literary Chron 26 July 1823.
On the Scotch novels. Manchester Iris 2 1823.
On the writings of Sir Walter Scott. Literary Register 19 July 1823.
[Patmore, P. G.] Letter 47: Sir Walter Scott. In Letters on England by Victoire count de Soligny, translated from the original MSS, 2 vols 1823 (vol 2).
Poetry and poets, no 2. Nic-Nac, 14 June 1823.
[The Scotch novels.] Monthly Mag 56 1823.
[Scott, Robert.] Memoir of Sir Walter Scott. Repository of Mod Lit 1 1823.
The Scottish novels. Northern Observer 1 1823.
Scottish novels of the second class. Scots Mag n.s. 13 1823.
Shakespeare v. the author of Waverley. Ephemera 14 Apr 1823.
Sir Walter Scott. Citizen n.s. 1 1823.
Sir Walter Scott. Kaleidoscope n.s. 4 1823–4.
Sir Walter Scott. Mirror of Lit 1 1823.
[Taylor, H.] Recent poetical plagiarisms and imitations. [Baldwin's] London Mag 8–9 1823–4.
W., S. The praise of W. S. by S. W. 1823.
A discourse on the comparative merits of Scott and Byron as writers of poetry. Western Luminary 1 1824.
Hazlitt, W. The spirits of the age, no 4: Sir Walter Scott. NMM and Literary Jnl 10 1824; rev in his The spirit of the age, or contemporary portraits, 1825, 1825; in his Collected works vol 4, 1902.
Historical delinquency of the Scotch novels. London Christian Instructor 7 1824.
Letters to literati no 4. Edinburgh Literary Gazette 28 Jan 1824.
[Lord Byron on the authorship of the Scotch novels.] NMM 10 1824.
[Mistakes in the Scotch Novels.] Mirror of Lit 3 1824.
[Opinion of Sir Walter Scott.] GM 94 1824.
P., G. A discourse on the comparative merits of Scott and Byron as writers of poetry, delivered before a literary institution in 1820. No place 1824; rptd in The living poets of England, ed A. Pichot, 2 vols Paris 1827 (vol 2).
The poet, no 5. Newcastle Mag n.s. 3 1824.
Portraits of Sir Walter Scott. Literary Chron 20 Nov 1824.
Report of an adjudged law-case, not to be found in the books: Shakespeare v. The author of Waverley [signed C]. Scots Mag n.s. 15 1824.
Sir Walter Scott and the Scotch novels. Kaleidoscope n.s. 5 1824–5.
Sketches of living characters, no 3. Literary Sketch Book 6–13 Mar 1824.
The Waverley novels. Citizen n.s. 2 1824.
[Anecdotes of Scott.] Weekly Entertainer n.s. 11 1825.
Author of the Scotch novels. Kaleidoscope n.s. 6 1825–6.
Bad English in the Scotch novels. Examiner 9–16 Oct 1825.
Bad English in the Scotch novels. Signed 'Indignator'. Kaleidoscope n.s. 6 1825–6.
Edinburgh chit-chat. News of Lit and Fashion 2 July 1825.
Letter from Senex on Sir Walter Scott. Blackwood's Edinburgh Mag 18 1825.
Letters from Posterity to the author of Waverley, 1 [signed Posterity]. Metropolitan Quart Mag 1 1825.
London chit-chat. News of Lit and Fashion 25 June 1825.
[Mudie, R.] The Scottish novelist. In his Attic fragments of characters, customs, opinions and scenes, by the author of Modern Athens and Babylon the Great, 1825.
Pichot, A. Voyage historique et littéraire en Angleterre et en Écosse. 3 vols Paris 1825; tr 1825.
Rory O'Rourke Esq to the editor. Dublin and London Mag [1] 1825. Scott in Dublin.
Rose's translation of Orlando furioso. Universal Rev 2 1825.
Scott (Walter). In A. V. Arnault et al, Biographie nouvelle des contemporains, 20 vols Paris 1820–5 (vol 19 1825).
Sir Walter Scott. Drama, or Theatrical Pocket Mag n.s. 1 1825.
[Sir Walter Scott.] Dumfries Monthly Mag 1 1825.
Sir Walter Scott. Kaleidoscope n.s. 6 1825–6.
Sir Walter Scott and the Scottish novels [signed Omega]. GM 95 1825.
Sir Walter Scott at Killarney. News of Lit and Fashion 17 Sep 1825.
Sir Walter Scott: blarney. Kaleidoscope n.s. 6 1825–6.
Sir Walter Scott in Ireland. Examiner 24 July 1825.
Ariosto and Scott. Bolster's Quart Mag 1 1826.
[Danton, P.] On the dramatic powers of the author of Waverley [signed Pi]. Blackwood's Edinburgh Mag 19 1826.
Graves, H. M. An essay on the genius of Shakespeare, with critical remarks on the characters of Romeo, Hamlet, Juliet and Ophelia, together with some observations on the writings of Sir Walter Scott. 1826.
[Hazlitt, W.] Sir Walter Scott, Racine and Shakespear. In his The plain speaker: opinions on books, men and things, 2 vols 1826 (vol 2); rptd in his Collected works vol 7, 1903.
Pichot, A. Vues pittoresques de l'Écosse, dessinées d'après nature par F. A. Pernot avec un texte explicatif extrait en grande partie des ouvrages de Sir Walter Scott par Am. Pichot. Paris 1826.
The Scotch novels. Kaleidoscope n.s. 7 1826–7.
Sir Walter Scott. Kaleidoscope n.s. 7 1826–7.
Sir Walter Scott. Lady's Mag n.s. 7 1826.
Sir Walter Scott in France. Kaleidoscope n.s. 7 1826–7.
Sir Walter Scott in Ireland. Bolster's Quart Mag 1 1826.
Sir Walter Scott not the author of Waverley, Scotch novels. Kaleidoscope n.s. 7 1826–7.
Sketches of living poets, no 1. Spirit and Manners of the Age 2 1826.
An account of the first Edinburgh Theatrical Fund dinner held at Edinburgh on Friday 23rd February 1827; containing a correct and authentic report of the speeches, which include, among other interesting matter, the first public avowal, by Sir Walter

Scott, of being the author of the Waverley novels. Edinburgh 1827.

B., M. L. Sir Walter Scott. Mirror of Lit 17 Feb 1827.

[Hazlitt, W.] Why the heroes of romances are insipid. NMM 20 1827; rptd in his Collected works vol 12, 1904.

[Historical romance. By J. G. Lockhart or J. A. Heraud.] Quarterly Rev 35 1827.

Jacob, K. G. Walter Scott: ein biographisch-literarischer Versuch für die Leser seiner Werke. Cologne 1827.

Memoir of Sir Walter Scott [signed L]. In The living poets of England: specimens of the living British poets, with biographical and critical notices and an essay on English poetry, ed A. Pichot, 2 vols Paris 1827.

Poetry of the Waverley novels. Retrospective Rev 2nd ser 1 1827.

Sir Walter Scott, the avowed author of the Waverley novels. Mirror of Lit 3 Mar 1827.

Sketches of Parisian society, politics and literature. NMM 19 1827.

[Southern, H.?] Sir Walter Scott and the Waverly novels. [Baldwin's] London Mag n.s. 7 1827.

[Maurice, F. D.] Sketches of contemporary authors, no 9: Sir Walter Scott. Athenaeum 11 Mar 1828.

Mazzini, G. Essays by Walter Scott (Saggi di Gualtiero Scott). L'Indicatore Genovese 1828; rptd In Scritti editi ed inediti di Giuseppe Mazzini vol 1, Imola 1906.

Sir Walter Scott Bart. In Public characters: biographical and characteristic sketches, with portraits, of the most distinguished personages of the present age, 2 vols 1828 (vol 2).

[Lake, J. W.?] Abbotsford. The Anniversary, or poetry and prose for 1829. 1829 (for 1828).

On Sir Walter Scott as a novelist. Edinburgh Literary Gazette 30 May 1829.

On Sir Walter Scott as a poet. Edinburgh Literary Gazette 15 Aug 1829.

Pichot, A. Souvenirs d'enfance de Walter-Scott. Revue de Paris 2 1829.

Gordon, P. L. Personal memoirs, or reminiscences of men and manners at home and abroad during the last half century, with occasional sketches of the author's life: being fragments from the portfolio of Pryse Lockhart Gordon, Esq. 2 vols 1830.

[Maginn, W,] The gallery of illustrious literary characters, no 6: Sir Walter Scott. Fraser's Mag 2 1830; rptd in The Maclise portrait-gallery of illustrious literary characters with memoirs by William Bates, 1883.

[Senior, N. W.] Peveril of the Peak, Quentin Durward, St Ronan's Well, Redgauntlet, Tales of the Crusaders, Woodstock, Chronicles of the Canongate. London Rev 1 1830; rptd in his Essays on fiction, 1864.

[Cunningham, A.] Abbotsford. Athenaeum 13–20 Aug 1831.

[Cunningham, A.] Living literary characters, no 1: Sir Walter Scott [signed C]. NMM 31 1831.

Jerdan, W. Sir Walter Scott Bart. In his National portrait gallery of illustrious and eminent personages of the nineteenth century, with memoirs, pt 27, 1831.

Letters to certain persons, Epistle 1: To Miss Jane Porter [signed Peter Puff]. Aberdeen Mag 1 1831.

[Peabody, W. B. O.] Waverley novels. North Amer Rev 32 1831.

Sir Walter Scott: Portsmouth. Annual Register 1831. Chron.

Biographical sketch of Sir Walter Scott. Penny Mag 31 Oct 1832.

Brydges, S. E. Caractère littéraire de Sir Walter Scott, par Sir Edgerton Brydges, communiqué par l'auteur (traduction). Bibliographie Universelle des Sciences, Belles-Lettres et Arts, rédigée à Genève, 51 1832; further translated as Der literarische Charakter Scotts, Magazin für die Literatur des Auslandes 3 1833.

C., J. An inquiry into the merits of the Scottish novels. Border Mag 1 1832.

C., J. S. Memoirs of Sir Walter Scott. Lady's Mag 1 1832.

[Chambers, R.] Life of Sir Walter Scott. Chambers's Edinburgh Jnl 1 suppl [6 Oct 1832]; rptd New York 1832.

Cunningham, A. Some account of the life and works of Sir Walter Scott Bart. Athenaeum 6 Oct 1832; rptd Boston 1832; tr Fr (free) Bibliothèque Universelle des Sciences, Belles-Lettres et Arts 51 1832.

Cursory observations on the death of Sir Walter Scott, addressed chiefly to the inhabitants of Edinburgh. Edinburgh 1832.

Death of Sir Walter Scott. Edinburgh Evening Courant 24 Sep 1832.

[Fox, W. J.] On the intellectual character of Sir Walter Scott. Monthly Repository 6 1832.

Funeral of Sir Walter Scott. Edinburgh Evening Courant 27 Sep 1832.

Funeral of Sir Walter Scott. Scotsman 29 Sep 1832.

[Lauder, T. D.] Funeral of Sir Walter Scott, by an eyewitness. Tait's Edinburgh Mag 2 1832.

[Lister, T. H.] The Waverley novels. Edinburgh Rev 55 Apr 1832.

[Lytton, E. G. E. L. Bulwer.] Death of Sir Walter Scott [signed The author of Eugene Aram]. NMM 35 1832.

[Maginn, W.] The death of Sir Walter Scott. Fraser's Mag 6 1832; rptd in The Fraserian papers of the late William Maginn LL. D. annotated, with a life of the author by R. Shelton Mackenzie DCL, New York 1857.

Martineau, H. Characteristics of the genius of Scott. Tait's Edinburgh Mag 2 1832; rptd in her Miscellanies, 2 vols Boston 1836 (vol 1).

Memoir of Sir Walter Scott Baronet. Imperial Mag 2 ser 2 1832.

Memoir of Sir Walter Scott Bart. Court Jnl 6 Oct 1832.

Notices of the life and writings of the late Sir Walter Scott Bart. Mirror of Lit 20 suppl 1832.

On the political tendency of Sir Walter Scott's writings. Schoolmaster 29 Sep 1832.

[Pichot, A.] Walter Scott. Revue de Paris 42 1832.

Public meeting in honour of Sir Walter Scott. Edinburgh Evening Courant 6 Oct 1832.

Saint-Beuve, C. A. Mort de Sir Walter Scott. Le Globe 27 Sep 1832; rptd in his Premiers Lundis, 3 vols Paris 1874–5 (vol 2 1874).

Sir Walter Scott as a lawyer. Legal Observer 6 Oct 1832.

Sir Walter Scott as a novelist. Greenock Advertiser 1 Oct 1832.

Sir Walter Scott Bart. GM 102 Oct 1832.

Sir Walter Scott's visit to Ireland [signed O'G]. Dublin Penny Jnl 15 Dec 1832.

A summary account of Sir Walter Scott Bart, the Scottish novelist. Edinburgh [1832].

Vedder, D. Memoir of Sir Walter Scott Bart with critical notices of his writings, compiled from various authentic sources. Dundee 1832.

Cunningham, A. Biographical and critical history of the literature of the last fifty years. Athenaeum 26 Oct–28 Dec 1833; rptd Paris 1834.

G., A. A day with Sir Walter Scott. Metropolitan 6 1833.

Galt, J. In his The autobiography of John Galt, 2 vols 1833 (vol 2).

Hall, B. Sir Walter Scott's embarkation at Portsmouth in the autumn of 1831. In his Fragments of voyages and travels, 3rd ser, 3 vols Edinburgh 1833 (vol 3).

d'Haussez, C. le M. de L., baron. A visit to Abbotsford. In his Great Britain in 1833, 2 vols 1833 (vol 2).

The land of Scott. Chambers's Edinburgh Jnl 20 Apr–27 July 1833.

McVickar, J. Tribute to the memory of Sir Walter Scott Baronet. New York 1833.

Madden, R. R. Sir Walter Scott. In his The infirmities of genius illustrated by referring the anomalies in the literary character to the habits and constitutional peculiarities of men of genius, 2 vols 1833 (vol 2).

Martineau, H. The achievements of the genius of Scott. Tait's

Edinburgh Mag 2 1833; rptd in her Miscellanies, 2 vols Boston 1836 (vol 1).

Nayler, B. S. A memoir of the life and writings of Walter Scott, the wizzard of the north, the great unknown, the author of Waverley. Amsterdam 1833.

[Peabody, W. B. O.] Sir Walter Scott. North Amer Rev 36 1833.

Scott's novels. American Monthly Rev 4 1833.

Sir Walter Scott and Constable and Company. Tait's Edinburgh Mag 2 1833

Allan, George. Life of Sir Walter Scott Baronet with critical notices of his writings [begun by W. Weir]. Edinburgh 1834 [issued in pts 1832–4], Philadelphia 1835.

H., J. Recollections of the author of Waverley. NMM 42 1834.

Hogg, James. Familiar anecdotes of Sir Walter Scott. New York 1834; rptd as The domestic manners and private life of Sir Walter Scott, Glasgow, Edinburgh and London 1834, 1838, New York 1834, Edinburgh 1846, 1882, Stirling 1909; Memoirs of the author's life and Familiar anecdotes of Sir Walter Scott, ed D. S. Mack, Edinburgh and London 1972; Anecdotes of Sir Walter Scott, ed D. S. Mack, Edinburgh 1983.

Mézières, L. Walter Scott. In his Histoire critique de la littérature anglaise depuis Bacon jusqu'au commencement du dix-neuvième siècle, 3 vols Paris 1834 (vol 3).

Pichot, A. Le perroquet de Walter Scott: esquisses de voyages; légendes, romans; contes biographiques et littéraires. 2 vols Paris 1834; rptd with Les chiens de Walter Scott in his L'écolier de Walter Scott: contes biographiques (Collection Michel Lévy), Paris 1860.

[Pichot, A.] Soirées d'Abbotsford, chroniques et nouvelles, recueillies dans les salons de Walter Scott. Paris 1834.

Chambers, R. Scott, (Sir) Walter. In his Lives of illustrious and distinguished Scotsmen, 4 vols Glasgow 1832–5 (vol 4, 1835).

[Develey, E.] Guide pour les lecteurs des romans de W. Scott et de Cooper, par un amateur. Paris and Lausanne 1835.

[Gillies, R. P.] Recollections of Sir Walter Scott. Fraser's Mag 12–13 1835–6; rptd as Recollections of Sir Walter Scott Bart 1837 (for 1836).

Howitt, W. The great modern poets great reformers. Tait's Edinburgh Mag n.s. 2 1835.

Irving, W. Abbotsford and Newstead Abbey. Philadelphia 1835.

Lodge, E. Sir Walter Scott. In his Portraits of illustrious personages of Great Britain . . . with biographical and historical memoirs of their lives and actions. 12 vols 1823–35 [for 1836] (vol 12 1835).

A parallel of Shakspeare and Scott: being the substance of three lectures on the kindred nature of their genius, read before the Literary and Philosophical Society of Chichester 1833 and 1834. 1835.

Ritchie, L. Scott and Scotland, with twenty-one highly finished engravings from original drawings by George Cattermole Esq. Heath's Picturesque annual for 1835.

Chateaubriand, F. R. A., Viscount. Walter Scott. In his Essai sur la littérature anglaise, et considérations sur le génie des hommes, des temps et des révolutions, 2 vols Brussels 1836 (vol 2).

Hall, B. The Countess [Purgstall] and Walter Scott. In his Schloss Hainfeld, or a winter in Lower Styria, Edinburgh and London 1836.

Wright, G. N. Landscape-historical illustrations of Scotland and the Waverley novels from drawings by J. M. W. Turner, Balmer, Bentley, Chisholm . . . comic illustrations by G. Cruickshank, descriptions by the Rev G. N. Wright. 2 vols [1836–8].

Cooper, J. F. Recollections of Europe. 2 vols 1837 (vol 2: Letter 2).

Lockhart, J. G. Memoirs of the life of Sir Walter Scott. 7 vols Edinburgh and London 1837–8, 10 vols Edinburgh and London 1839 etc; ed A. W. Pollard 5 vols 1900 (adds material from the Narrative, *below*); ed S. M. Francis 5 vols Boston and New York 1902. Abridged as Narrative of the life of Sir Walter Scott Bart begun by himself and continued by J. G. Lockhart, Esq, 2 vols Edinburgh and London 1848; 2nd edn Life of Sir Walter Scott Bart begun by himself and continued by J. G. Lockhart, Esq, 1 vol Edinburgh 1853 etc.

Sir Walter Scott as a lawyer. Legal Observer or Jnl of Jurisprudence 1 Apr 1837.

Bucke, C. A letter intended (one day) as a supplement to Lockhart's Life of Sir Walter Scott. 1838.

[Carlyle, T.] Memoirs of the life of Scott. Westminster Rev 28 1838; rptd as Sir Walter Scott in his Critical and miscellaneous essays, 5 vols 1840 (vol 5); reviewed in Hesperian 1 1838.

C[larke], J. F. Scott and Shakespeare. Western Messenger 5 1838.

Cooper, J. F. Sir Walter Scott and Mr Cooper. Knickerbocker 11 1838; reply by Wamba 12 1838.

Guide pittoresque du voyageur en Écosse, orné de 120 vues, représentant les principaux édifices, les curiosités naturelles, les châteaux remarquables, et tous les lieux cités par Walter Scott, par les auteurs du Guide pittoresque du voyageur en France. Paris 1838.

[Keble, J.] Life and writings of Sir Walter Scott. Br Critic 24 1838; rptd as Life of Sir Walter Scott in his Occasional papers and reviews, Oxford and London 1877.

L[andon], L. E. Female portrait gallery from Sir Walter Scott, by the author of The improvisatrice. NMM and Humorist 52 1838; rev in L. Blanchard, Life and literary remains of L. E. L., 2 vols 1841 (vol 2).

M'Donald, G. Life of Sir Walter Scott Bart. 1838.

[Prescott, W. H.] Memoirs of Sir Walter Scott. North Amer Rev 46 1838; rptd as Sir Walter Scott in his Biographical and critical miscellanies, 1845.

The trustees and son of the late Mr James Ballantyne. Refutation of the misstatements and calumnies contained in Mr Lockhart's Life of Sir Walter Scott, Bart respecting the Messrs Ballantyne. 1838 (3 edns), 1839, Boston 1838.

Brühl, M. Denkwürdigkeiten aus Walter Scott's Leben, mit besonderer Beziehung auf seine Schriften, nach Lockhart's Memoirs of the life of Sir W. Scott und den besten Original-Quellen bearbeitet. 5 vols Leipzig 1839–41.

Dickens, C. The Ballantyne humbug handled. Examiner 31 Mar, 29 Sep 1839; rptd in his To be read at dusk, 1898, and Miscellaneous papers, 2 vols 1911 (vol 1).

Lockhart, J. G. The Ballantyne-humbug handled, in a letter to Sir Adam Fergusson by the author of Memoirs of the life of Sir Walter Scott. Edinburgh and London 1839.

The Lockhart and Ballantyne controversy. Tait's Edinburgh Mag 6 1839.

[Maginn, W.] Epaminondas Grubb, or Fenimore Cooper, versus the memory of Sir Walter Scott. Fraser's Mag 19 1839; rptd in his Miscellaneous writings, 5 vols New York 1857 (vol 5).

Moir, G. Sir Walter Scott. In his Treatises on poetry, modern romance and rhetoric, being the articles under these heads contributed to the Encyclopaedia Britannica seventh edition, Edinburgh 1839.

Reply to Mr Lockhart's pamphlet entitled The Ballantyne-humbug handled by the authors of a Refutation. 1839.

[Chambers, R.] A conversation with Sir Walter Scott. Chambers's Edinburgh Jnl 7 Mar 1840.

[Miller, H.] The Scott monument. Witness 19 Aug 1840; rptd in his Leading articles on various subjects, ed J. Davidson, Edinburgh 1870, 1890.

Opie, A. A. Recollections of an authoress. Chambers's Edinburgh Jnl 25 Jan 1840; rev in C. L. Brightwell, Memorials of the life of Amelia Opie selected and arranged from her letters, diaries and other manuscripts, Norwich 1854.

Taylor, G. Memoir of Robert Surtees Esq. In R. Surtees, The history and antiquities of the County Palatine of Durham, 4 vols 1816–40 (vol 4 1840); rev as A memoir of Robert Surtees Esq (Publications of the Surtees Society), Durham [1852].

Chapters on English poetry: Scott, Byron and their imitators. Tait's Edinburgh Mag n.s. 8 1841.
Minor heroines of Scott. Chambers's Edinburgh Jnl 10 1841.
Plates to illustrate all editions of Sir Walter Scott's novels, engraved on steel from the original drawings by J. M. Turner, Allom, George Cruickshank etc. People's Edition 67 nos [1842–6].
Scott, John [of Gala]. Journal of a tour to Waterloo and Paris in company with Sir Walter Scott in 1815. 1842.
[Spalding, W.] Scott, Sir Walter. In Encyclopaedia Britannica 7th edn, 21 vols Edinburgh 1842 (vol 19).
Ballantyne, Mrs J. Rambling reminiscences of Sir Walter Scott and some of his friends. Chambers's Edinburgh Jnl 28 Oct–4 Nov 1843, 7 Sep 1844.
Morrison, J. Random reminiscences of Sir Walter Scott, of the Ettrick Shepherd, Sir Henry Raeburn, &c. &c. Tait's Edinburgh Mag 10–11 1843–4.
Sir Walter Scott in Cyclopaedia of English literature, ed R. Chambers, 2 vols Edinburgh 1843–4 (vol 2).
Jeffrey, F. In his Contributions to the Edinburgh Rev, 4 vols 1844.
Browne, J. A free examination of Sir Walter Scott's opinions respecting 'popery' and the penal laws as collected from Mr Lockhart's 'Life' and from various passages in Sir Walter Scott's works, with some remarks on the true genius and character of Catholicism. Edinburgh 1845.
Howitt, W. Sir Walter Scott. In his Homes and haunts of the most eminent British poets, the illustrations by W. and G. Measom, 2 vols 1847 (vol 2).
Walter Scott: has history gained by his writings? Fraser's Mag 36 1847.
Richardson, D. L. Sir Walter Scott and Lord Byron. In his Literary chit-chat, with miscellaneous poems and an appendix of prose papers, Calcutta 1848.
Whipple, E. P. English poets of the nineteenth century. In his Essays and reviews, 2 vols New York 1848–9 (vol 1 1848).
Moir, D. M. Sketches of the poetical literature of the past half-century, in six lectures delivered at the Edinburgh Philosophical Association. Edinburgh and London 1851.
Particulars and conditions of sale of copyrights, the property of the trustees of the late Robert Cadell, publisher, Edinburgh, consisting of the entire copyrights, steel plates, woodcuts, stereotype plates, etc, of the works of Sir Walter Scott Bart to be sold by auction . . . at the London Coffee House, Ludgate Hill, London. Edinburgh [1851].
Belfast, F. R. Chichester, Earl of. Scott. In his Poets and poetry of the 19th century, 1852.
Macleod, D. Life of Sir Walter Scott. New York 1852.
Buckley, T. A. W. Sir Walter Scott. In his The dawnings of genius exemplified and exhibited in the early lives of distinguished men. 1853.
[Matthews, G. K.] Abbotsford and Sir Walter Scott. 1853, 1854 (rev).
Stendhal [H. Beyle]. Walter Scott et la Princesse de Clèves. In his Racine et Shakespeare: Études sur le romantisme. Paris 1854.
Stowe, H. E. B. Melrose, Dryburgh, Abbotsford. In her Sunny memories of foreign lands, 2 vols 1854 (vol 1).
F[itzpatrick], W. J. Who wrote the Waverley novels? being an investigation into certain mysterious circumstances attending their production, and an inquiry into the literary aid which Sir Walter Scott may have received from other persons. 1856; rev edn as Who wrote the earlier Waverley novels? an essay, showing, on evidence amounting to moral demonstration, that Sir Walter Scott's relation to Waverley, Guy Mannering, Rob Roy, and the Tales of my landlord, was, at the most, that of an editor. Second edition. Completely re-written, and strengthened by a mass of new and well-authenticated facts. 1856.
French, G. J. An enquiry into the origin of the authorship of some of the earlier Waverley novels. Bolton 1856.
Gordon, G. H. Note on the Waverley novels. N & Q 13 Dec 1856.
Llewyvein. The subtleties of Scott's names. Knickerbocker 48 1856.
Ruskin, J. Of modern landscape. In his Modern painters, 5 vols 1843–60 (vol 3 1856); rptd in his Works vol 5, 1904.
Borrow, G. In his The Romany Rye, a sequel to Lavengro, 2 vols 1857 (vol 2).
Gordon, G. H. The Waverley novels. N & Q 20 June 1857.
Patterson, J. Memoir of Joseph Train F. S. A. (Scot.), the antiquarian correspondent of Sir Walter Scott. Glasgow and Edinburgh 1857.
[Bagehot, W.] The Waverley novels. Nat Rev 6 1858; rptd in his Literary studies, 2 vols 1879 (vol 2).
Jeaffreson, J. C. Walter Scott. In his Novels and novelists from Elizabeth to Victoria, 2 vols 1858 (vol 2).
White, James. Robert Burns and Sir Walter Scott: two lives. 1858.
Masson, D. Scott and his influence. In his British novelists and their style, being a critical sketch of the history of British prose fiction, Cambridge 1859.
M[oi]r, G. and W. E. A[ytoun?]. Sir Walter Scott. In Encyclopaedia Britannica 8th edn, 22 vols Edinburgh 1853–60 (vol 19 1859).
Eberty, F. Walter Scott: ein Lebensbild, aus englischen Quellen zusammengestellt. 2 vols Breslau 1860; tr Du, Amsterdam 1869.
Leslie, C. R. Autobiographical recollections by the late Charles Robert Leslie R. A. Ed T. Taylor 2 vols 1860.
P., W. F. British novelists: Richardson, Miss Austen, Scott. Fraser's Mag 61 1860.
Abbotsford papers, no. 1: The early days of Sir Walter Scott Bart. Border Mag 1 1863.
Anderson, W. Scott, Sir Walter. In his The Scottish nation, or the surnames, families, literature, honours and biographical history of the people of Scotland, 3 vols Edinburgh 1860–3 (vol 3 1863).
Leland, C. G. The skeptics of the Waverley novels. Continental Monthly 3 1863.
Lytton, E. G. E. L. Bulwer. On some authors in whose writings knowledge of the world is eminently displayed. Blackwood's Edinburgh Mag 94 1863; rptd in his Caxtonia: a series of essays on life, literature and manners, 2 vols Edinburgh and London 1863 (vol 2).
Pierson, W. The epic poems of Walter Scott compared with the like poetry of Thomas Moore. Jahresbericht über die Dorotheenstädtische Realschule 1863, Berlin 1863.
Taine, H. A. In his Histoire de la littérature anglaise, 4 vols Paris 1863–4 (vol 3).
Elze, K. Sir Walter Scott. 2 vols Dresden 1864; tr Danish, Copenhagen 1878.
Senior, N. W. Sir Walter Scott. In his Essays on fiction, 1864.
Palgrave, F. T. Sir Walter Scott. In The poetical works of Sir Walter Scott, 1866.
[Harkom, J. M.] Sir Walter Scott: the character of his genius and the moral influence his works are fitted to exercise. 1867.
Gladstone, W. E. History of the Scott Monument, Edinburgh. Chester Courant 1868; rptd in J. Colston, The Scott Monument, Edinburgh, and Sir Walter Scott Bart, Edinburgh 1881, 1890.
Jellett, J. H. The poetry of Sir Walter Scott. In his The afternoon lectures on literature and art [5th ser], Dublin and London 1869.
Schmidt, H. J. Walter Scott und seine Bedeuting für unsere Zeit. Westermann's Jahrbuch der Illustrirten deutschen Monatshefte, Apr–June 1869; rptd in his Bilder aus dem geistigen Leben unserer Zeit, Leipzig 1870.
Sir Walter Scott at college [signed C]. N & Q 6 Mar 1869.
Walter Scott at work. Chambers's Jnl 4 ser [6] 1869.
Allibone, S. A. Scott, Sir Walter. In A critical dictionary of English literature and British and American authors, 3 vols Philadelphia and London 1859–71 (vol 2 1870).
Gilfillan, G. Life of Sir Walter Scott Baronet. Edinburgh 1870, 1871, 1884.
Rossetti, W. M. [Memoir.] In The poetical works of Sir Walter Scott, ed Rossetti, 1870.

Scott's heroines. 4 pts Macmillan's Mag 22 1870, 62–4 1890–1.
Ballantyne & Co. The history of the Ballantyne Press and its connection with Sir Walter Scott Bart. Edinburgh and London 1871.
Ballantyne, J. The last days of Sir Walter Scott. Edinburgh Evening Courant 16 Aug 1871.
Chambers, R. Life of Scott, with Abbotsford notanda by R. Carruthers. 1871, 1894 [for 1893] (rev).
Gibson, J. Reminiscences of Sir Walter Scott. Edinburgh 1871.
Gleig, G. R. The life of Sir Walter Scott, reprinted with corrections and additions from the Quarterly Rev [1868]. Edinburgh 1871.
Hogg, A. A. Incidents in the life of Sir Walter Scott, including a full account of Carterhaugh hand ba'. Hawick Archaeological Soc 1871.
Hunnewell, J. F. The lands of Scott. Edinburgh and Boston 1871.
Leary, T. H. L. Sir Walter Scott as a poet: a centenary study. GM 231 1871.
Lockhart, C. S. M. The centenary memorial of Sir Walter Scott Bart. 1871.
Mackenzie, R. S. Sir Walter Scott: the story of his life. Boston 1871.
[Oliphant, M. O. W.] A century of great poets from 1750 downwards, no 2: Walter Scott. Blackwood's Edinburgh Mag Aug 1871.
Scott considered as a poet. Temple Bar 33 1871.
Sir Walter Scott as a lawyer [signed M]. Jnl of Jurisprudence 15 1871.
Sproat, G. M. Sir Walter Scott as a poet. Edinburgh 1871.
[Stephen, L.] Some words about Sir Walter Scott. Cornhill Mag 24 1871; rptd in his Hours in a library [1st ser], 1874.
What has Scott done for Scotland? Leisure Hour 5 Aug 1871.
Young, J. C. A memoir of Charles Mayne Young, tragedian, with extracts from his son's journal. 2 vols 1871.
Andree, R. In Walter Scott's Heimat. Die Illustrirte Welt 20 1872.
[Forman, H. B.] Walter Scott: a centenary tribute. London Quart Rev 38 1872.
The Scott Exhibition 1871: catalogue of the exhibition held at Edinburgh in July and August 1871 on occasion of the commemoration of the centenary of the birth of Sir Walter Scott. [Ed W. S. Maxwell, J. Drummond and D. Laing,] Edinburgh 1872; re-issued 1874 as A descriptive account of the portraits, busts, published writings and manuscripts of Sir Walter Scott Bart collected and exhibited at Edinburgh on occasion of the Scott centenary in 1871.
Smith, G. The lamps of fiction: an address delivered by Prof Goldwin Smith at the Toronto celebration of the Scott centenary 1871. Canadian Jnl of Science, Lit and History n.s. 13 1872; rptd in his Lectures and essays, Toronto 1881.
Yonge, C. D. Walter Scott. In his Three centuries of English literature, 1872.
Constable, T. Archibald Constable and his literary correspondents. 3 vols Edinburgh 1873.
Ruskin, J. Letters 31 (Wat of Harden), 32 (Sandy Knowe), and 33 (Aunt Jessie). In his Fors clavigera: letters to the workmen and labourers of Great Britain, 9 vols Orpington 1871–87 (vol 3 1873); rptd in his Works vol 27, 1907.
Ferrier, S. E. Recollections of visits to Ashistiel and Abbotsford. Temple Bar 40 1874.
Bouchier, J. Characteristic names in the Waverley novels. N & Q 16 Oct 1875.
Shairp, J. C. The Homeric element in the poetry of Scott. Good Words 1875; rptd in his Aspects of poetry, being lectures delivered at Oxford, Oxford 1881, Boston 1882.
Sinclair, J. Sir Walter Scott. In Sketches of old times and distant places, 1875.
Ticknor, G. Life, letters, and journals of George Ticknor. 2 vols Boston 1876, London 1876.
Doyle, F. H. Walter Scott. In his Lectures on poetry delivered at Oxford, 1877.
Rogers, C. Genealogical memoirs of the family of Sir Walter Scott Bart of Abbotsford with a reprint of his Memorials of the Haliburtons. 1877.
Hardy, J. Report of the meetings of the Club for the year 1878. History of the Berwickshire Naturalists' Club 8 1878. On Ashiestiel.
Hutton, R. H. Sir Walter Scott. 1878 (EML).
Veitch, J. The history and poetry of the Scottish Border: their main features and relations. Glasgow 1878, (rev) 2 vols Edinburgh and London 1893.
Wedgwood, J. Scott and the romantic reaction. Contemporary Rev 33 1878.
Canning, A. S. G. Philosophy of the Waverley novels. 1879.
Kerr, J. B. On supposed unpublished verses by Sir Walter Scott. History of the Berwickshire Naturalists' Club 9 1879.
Sir Walter Scott. Church Quart Rev 8 1879.
[Colston, J.] History of the Scott Monument, Edinburgh, to which is added a biographical sketch of Sir Walter Scott Bart. Edinburgh 1881, 1890.
Oliphant, M. O. W. Walter Scott. In her The literary history of England in the end of the eighteenth and beginning of the nineteenth century, 3 vols 1882 (vol 2).
Stevenson, R. L. A gossip on romance. Longman's Mag 1 1882; rptd in his Memories and portraits, 1887.
Tuckerman, B. In his A history of English prose fiction from Sir Thomas Malory to George Eliot, New York 1882, London 1882.
Welsh, A. H. Scott. In his Development of English literature and language, 2 vols Chicago and London 1882 (vol 2).
Dennis, J. Sir Walter Scott. In his Heroes of literature: English poets, a book for young readers, 1883.
Emerson, R. W. Walter Scott: remarks at the celebration by the Massachusetts Historical Soc of the centennial anniversary of his birth, Boston, August 15 1871. In his Miscellanies, 1884.
Courthope, W. J. The liberal movement in English literature, 4: The revival of romance: Scott, Byron, Shelley. National Rev 5 1885; rptd in his The liberal movement in English literature, 1885.
Lang, A. To Sir Walter Scott Bart. In his Letters to dead authors, 1886.
[Minto, W.] Scott, Sir Walter. In Encyclopaedia Britannica 9th edn, 33 vols Edinburgh 1875–1903 (vol 21 1886).
Wood, James. The life of Sir Walter Scott Bart: a sketch. Edinburgh 1886.
Bleibtreu, K. Walter Scott. In his Geschichte der englischen Litteratur in der Renaissance und Klassicität, 2 vols Leipzig [1887–8] (vol 2).
Jebb, R. C. Homer and Walter Scott. In his Homer: an introduction to the Iliad and the Odyssey, Glasgow 1887, 1887, 1888.
Körting, G. Walter Scott. In his Grundriss der Geschichte der englischen Litteratur von ihren Anfängen bis zur Gegenwart, Münster 1887.
Veitch, J. Modern period: Sir Walter Scott. In his The feeling for nature in Scottish poetry, 2 vols Edinburgh and London 1887 (vol 2).
Maxwell-Scott, M. M. Catalogue of the armour and antiquities at Abbotsford. Edinburgh 1888.
Yonge, C. D. Life of Sir Walter Scott (with a bibliography by J. P. Anderson). 1888.
Woodruff, E. H. Scott at work. Scribner's Mag 5 1889.
Evans, J. A. Dryden and Scott. Temple Bar 90 1890.
Oliphant, M. O. W. The Shakspeare of Scotland. In her Royal Edinburgh: her saints, kings, prophets and poets, 1890.
Stoddard, E. Characters of Scott. Lippincott's Monthly Mag 45 1890.
Canning, T. Catholicism in the Waverley novels. Dublin Rev Oct 1891.
Lang, A. The poems of Sir Walter Scott. In his Essays in little, 1891.
Smiles, S. A publisher and his friends: memoir and correspondence of the late John Murray with an account of the origin and progress of the house 1768–1843. 2 vols 1891.

Somerville, T. Sir Walter Scott. In his George Square, Glasgow, and the lives of those whom its statues commemorate, Glasgow [1891].

Swinburne, A. C. The journal of Sir Walter Scott 1825–32. Fortnightly Rev May 1891; rptd in his Studies in prose and poetry, 1894.

Cresswell, H. Observations on 'the tale-telling art' in Sir Walter Scott's introductions to the Waverley novels. The Author 2 1892.

Foster, J. The chronology of the Waverley novels. Library 4 1892.

Mallock, W. H. Are Scott, Dickens and Thackeray obsolete? Forum 14 1892.

Newmark, N. Scott's legal lore. Green Bag 4 1892.

R., E. Constable and Sir Walter Scott. Temple Bar 96 1892.

Smith, William. Ruskin and Carlyle on 'Sir Walter Scott'. Igdrasil 3 1892.

Maxwell-Scott, M. M. Abbotsford: the personal relics and antiquarian treasures of Sir Walter Scott. 1893.

Opitz, G. Die stabreimenden Wortbindungen in den Dichtungen Walter Scott's, I. Trebnitz 1893.

Stevenson, R. Scott's voyage in the Lighthouse yacht. Scribner's Mag 14 1893.

Table talk (signed Sylvanus Urban). GM 275 1893.

Walker, Hugh. Sir Walter Scott. In his Three centuries of Scottish literature, 2 vols Glasgow 1893 (vol 2).

Wilkie, J. Homer and Walter Scott. Scots Mag n.s. 11 1893.

Arnold, E. L. The historical novel as illustrated by Sir Walter Scott. Atalanta 7 1894.

The ethics of Sir Walter Scott. London Quart Rev 82 1894.

Hutton, R. H. Sir Walter Scott. In Criticisms on contemporary thought and thinkers selected from the Spectator, 2 vols 1894 (vol 2).

Minto, W. Scott. In his The literature of the Georgian era, ed W. Knight, Edinburgh and London 1894.

Munger, T. T. The head of Sir Walter Scott. Century Mag 47 1894.

S., J. B. An unexplored chapter in the life of Sir Walter Scott. Scotsman 26 Dec 1894; replies 27–9 Dec. Scott's churchmanship.

Saintsbury, G. E. B. The historical novel. Macmillan's Mag 70 1894; rptd in his Essays in English literature 1780–1860: 2nd ser, 1895, and in The collected essays and papers of George Saintsbury 1875–1920, 4 vols 1923–4 (vol 3 1923).

S[kene], F. M. F. Personal recollections of Sir Walter Scott. Argosy 57 1894.

Hannigan, D. F. The Waverley novels after sixty years. Westminster Rev 144 1895.

Burgess, S. The law in Scott. In The lawyer in history, literature, and humour, ed W. Andrews, 1896.

Quiller-Couch, A. T. Scott and Burns. In his Adventures in criticism, 1896.

Saintsbury, G. In his A history of nineteenth century literature (1780–1895), 1896.

Scott, Adam. The story of Sir Walter Scott's first love with illustrative passages from his life and works. Edinburgh 1896.

Canning, A. S. G. Walter Scott's historical novels. In his History in fact and fiction: a literary sketch, 1897.

Duncan, M. Sir Walter Scott as a novelist. Scots Mag n.s. 21 1897.

Gilfillan, G. Why Burns is more popular than Scott with the masses. In Burnsiana, comp J. D. Ross, 6 vols Paisley 1892–7 (vol 6 1897).

Herford, C. H. In his The age of Wordsworth, 1897.

Jack, A. A. Essays on the novel as illustrated by Scott and Miss Austen. 1897.

Napier, G. G. The homes and haunts of Sir Walter Scott, Bart. Glasgow 1897.

Oliphant, M. O. Annals of a publishing house: William Blackwood and his sons, their magazine and friends. 2 vols Edinburgh and London 1897.

Palgrave, F. T. Landscape in recent poetry: Scott and Byron. In his Landscape in poetry from Homer to Tennyson, with many illustrative examples, 1897.

Saintsbury, G. Sir Walter Scott. Edinburgh and London 1897.

Scott's methods and originals. Quart Rev Oct 1897.

Stearns, F. P. Walter Scott. In his Modern English prose writers, New York and London 1897.

Stephen, L. Scott, Sir Walter. In Dictionary of national biography, ed Stephen, 63 vols 1885–1900 (vol 51 1897; rev vol 17 1909).

[Stephen, L.] The story of Scott's ruin. Cornhill Mag n.s. [3rd] 2 1897; rptd in his Studies of a biographer, 4 vols 1898 (vol 2).

Walton, H. E. A Catholic tribute to Sir Walter Scott. The Month 92 1898.

The Waverley novels. In Novels and novelists: chapters on the Waverley novels including the recent editions, with other novel articles, 1898.

Bouchier, J. Sir Walter Scott's Scottish dialect. N & Q 23 Sep 1899; replies 21 Oct 1899–3 Feb 1900.

Hay, James. Sir Walter Scott. 1899.

Oliphant, J. Scott and Jane Austen. In his Victorian novelists, 1899.

Omond, T. S. In his The romantic triumph, Edinburgh and London 1900.

Beers, H. A. Walter Scott. In his A history of English romanticism in the nineteenth century, New York 1901.

Gaebel, K. Beiträge zur Technik der Erzählung in den Romanen Walter Scotts. Marburger Studien zur englischen Philologie 2 1901.

Howells, W. D. Scott's Rebecca and Rowena, and Lucy Ashton; Scott's Jeanie Deans and Cooper's lack of heroines. In his Heroines of fiction, 2 vols New York and London 1901 (vol 1).

Hudson, W. H. Sir Walter Scott. 1901.

Chesterton, G. K. The position of Sir Walter Scott. In his Twelve types, 1902.

Crockett, W. S. The Scott country. 1902, 1930 (rev).

Crockett, W. S. Sir Walter Scott: some of his homes and haunts. Bookman [London] 21 1902; rptd in W. S. Crockett and J. L. Caw, Sir Walter Scott, 1903.

Ker, W. P. Sir Walter Scott. In Chambers's Cyclopaedia of English literature, ed David Patrick et al, 3 vols 1901–3 (vol 3 1903).

Millar, J. H. Sir Walter Scott. In his A literary history of Scotland, 1903.

Ranken, T. E. Sir Walter Scott and mediaeval Catholicism. Month Feb 1903.

Sir Walter Scott as a churchman. Chambers's Jnl 6th ser 6 1903.

Gwynn, S. Scott. In his The masters of English literature, 1904.

Hughes, [M. A.] Letters and recollections of Sir Walter Scott. Ed H. G. Hutchinson [1904].

The letters of Sir Walter Scott and Charles Kirkpatrick Sharpe to Robert Chambers 1821–45, with original memoranda of Sir Walter Scott: printed from manuscripts in the possession of C. E. S. Chambers, Edinburgh. [Edinburgh] 1904.

S., D. Scott and Glasgow. Border Mag 9 1904.

Symons, A. Was Sir Walter Scott a poet? Atlantic Monthly 94 1904. Reply by G. Smith, 95 1905.

Ainger, A. Scott, 1771–1832. In his Lectures and essays, 2 vols 1905 (vol 1).

Brandes, G. Historical naturalism. In his Main currents in nineteenth century literature, 6 vols 1901–5 (vol 4 1905).

Canning, A. S. G. History in Scott's novels: a literary sketch. 1905.

Crockett, W. S. Abbotsford. 1905; abridged edn 1912.

Dawson, W. J. The Waverley novels; Scott's greatness. In his The makers of English fiction, 1905.

Laidlaw, W. Recollections of Sir Walter Scott 1802–4. Ed J. Sinton, Trans Hawick Archaeological Soc 1905.

Letters hitherto unpublished, written by members of Sir Walter Scott's family to their old governess. Ed P. A. Wright-Henderson 1905.

Macartney, M. H. H. Scott's use of the preface. Longman's Mag 46 1905.
O'Donoghue, D. J. Sir Walter Scott's tour in Ireland in 1825, now first fully described. Glasgow and Dublin 1905; rptd 1976.
Steuart, A. F. A journey with Sir Walter Scott in 1815. Chambers's Jnl 6th ser 8 1905. Robert Bruce's 1815 diary.
Woodberry, G. E. Great masters of literature, 2: Scott. McClure's Mag 25 1905; rptd in his Great writers, New York 1907.
Fyfe, W. T. Edinburgh under Sir Walter Scott. 1906.
Gest, J. M. The law and lawyers of Sir Walter Scott. Amer Law Register 54 1906; rptd in his Lawyer in literature, 1913.
Goudielock, D. M. The lodge of Sir Walter Scott: a historical sketch of Lodge St David No 36, Edinburgh, reprinted from The Scottish Masonic Historical Dictionary 1906. Glasgow 1906.
Lang, Andrew. Sir Walter Scott. 1906.
Norgate, G. Le G. The life of Sir Walter Scott. 1906.
[Bailey, J. C.] The Waverley novels. TLS 5 Apr 1907; rptd in his Poets and poetry, being articles reprinted from the Literary Supplement of The Times, Oxford 1911.
Ball, M. Sir Walter Scott as a critic of literature. New York 1907.
Brooke, S. A. Sir Walter Scott. In his Studies in poetry, 1907.
Redfern, O. The wisdom of Sir Walter: criticisms and opinions collected from the Waverley novels and Lockhart's Life of Sir Walter Scott. 1907.
Young, C. A. The Waverley novels: an appreciation. Glasgow 1907.
B., J. O. Sir Walter Scott's tutor. Scotsman 26 Aug 1908; replies 28 Aug. Rev James Mitchell.
Crockett, W. S. Footsteps of Scott. Edinburgh 1908.
Eyre-Todd, G. To the homes and haunts of Scott and Burns by the Caledonian Railway. [Glasgow c. 1908]; tr Fr L. Martin-Wabnitz, nd.
Fraser, G. M. Sir Walter Scott and the Aberdonians. In his The lone shieling with other literary and historical sketches, Aberdeen 1908.
Jackson, H. Sir Walter Scott. In his Great English novelists, [1908].
[Bailey, J. C.] Scott's poetry. TLS 19 Aug 1909; rptd in his Poets and poetry, being articles reprinted from the Literary Supplement of The Times, Oxford 1911.
Ballantyne, Hanson & Co. The Ballantyne Press and its founders 1796–1908. Edinburgh 1909.
Burton, R. Modern romanticism: Scott. In his Masters of the English novel: a study of principles and personalities, New York 1909.
Franke, P. W. Der Stil in den epischen Dichtungen Walter Scotts. Berlin 1909.
MacCunn, F. Sir Walter Scott's friends. Edinburgh and London 1909.
Skene, James. Memories of Sir Walter Scott. Ed Basil Thomson 1909; correction by A. M. Williams, Glasgow Herald, 5 Jan 1910.
Symons, A. Sir Walter Scott (1771–1832). In his The romantic movement in English poetry, 1909.
Canning, A. S. G. Sir Walter Scott studied in eight novels. 1910.
Petri, A. Über Walter Scotts Dramen (2 pts). Jahres-Bericht über die Herzogliche Realschule zu Schmölln S.-A., Schmölln 1910–11.
Sime, W. L. Scott's style. Scotsman 6 Aug 1910; replies 8–16 Aug.
Verrall, A. W. The prose of Walter Scott. Quart Rev 213 1910; rptd in his Collected literary essays classical and modern, ed M. A. Bayfield and J. D. Duff, Cambridge 1913.
Watson, G. Scott's Liddesdale raids. Border Mag 15 1910.
Chubb, E. W. The heroism of Sir Walter Scott. In his Stories of authors British and American, 1911.
Streissle, A. Personifikation und poetische Beseelung bei Scott und Burns. Heidelberg 1911.
Synge, M. B. Sir Walter Scott (1771–1832). In Great Scotsmen: an historical reading book for schools, 1911.
Thompson, G. W. Wilhelm Hauff's specific relation to Walter Scott. PMLA 26 1911.
Watson, J. Waverley novels [signed Ian MacLaren]. In From a northern window: papers critical, historical and imaginative, ed F. Watson, 1911.
Elton, O. In his Survey of English literature 1780–1830, 2 vols 1912 (vol 1). Chs on Scott rev and pbd separately as Sir Walter Scott, 1924.
Morgan, A. E. Scott and his poetry. 1912.
Ripari, R. Romantic and non-romantic elements in the works of Walter Scott. Castello 1912.
Watt, L. M. Scott. In his Scottish life and poetry, 1912.
Mackay, A. M. Sir Walter Scott as a freemason: an account of his connection with the fraternity. [Edinburgh 1913.]
MacRitchie, D. Waverley in France. Dunedin Mag 2 1913.
Olcott, C. S. The country of Sir Walter Scott. Boston and New York 1913, London 1913.
Saintsbury, G. E. B. Scott and Miss Austen. In his The English novel, 1913.
Steiger, O. Die Verwendung des schottischen Dialekts in Walter Scotts Romanen. Darmstadt 1913.
A century of Waverley. Nation [New York] 30 July 1914.
Erskine, John. Walter Scott. Columbia Univ Quart 17 1914–15; abridged as The Waverley novels in his The delight of great books, 1928.
Graham, J. E. Scott's Catholic tendencies. Catholic Univ Bull 20 1914.
Leask, W. K. The centenary of Waverley. Thistle 6 1914.
Macleod, K. Sir Walter Scott's madfolk. Thistle 6 1914.
Watson, G. Literary blunders of the author of Waverley. Trans Hawick Archaeological Soc 1914; rptd as Literary blunders of Sir Walter Scott, Hawick 1914.
Windakiewicz, S. Walter Scott i Lord Byron w odniesieuniu do Polskiej poezyi romantycznej. Crakow 1914.
Cecchi, E. Miss Austen e Walter Scott; Byron, Scott e Taine. In his Storia della letteratura inglese nel secolo XIX. Milan 1915 (vol 1 only).
Cochrane, R. The Ballantynes of Kelso and a forgotten skit by Sir Walter Scott. Border Standard 6 Feb 1915.
Cruse, A. Sir Walter Scott. 1915.
Graham, W. Notes on Sir Walter Scott. MLN 30 1915. Mottoes.
Henderson, T. F. Sir Walter Scott. In The Cambridge history of English literature, ed A. W. Ward and A. R. Waller, 15 vols Cambridge 1907–27 (vol 12 1915).
Rendall, V. Sir Walter Scott and golf. Scottish Historical Rev 12 1915.
Walthew, R. Music in the Waverley novels. Musical Opinion Apr–May 1915.
Leask, W. K. Scott's poetry. Thistle 8 1916.
Anstice, R. H. The poetical heroes of Sir Walter Scott. Aberdeen 1917.
Eckenrode, H. J. Sir Walter Scott and the South. North American Rev Oct 1917.
Harendrakumar Mukhopadhaya. The supernatural in Scott. Calcutta 1917.
Rogers, J. F. The healthiest of men. Scientific Monthly 5 1917.
Chisholm, J. Sir Walter Scott as a judge: his decisions in the Sheriff Court of Selkirk. Edinburgh 1918.
The decline of Sir Walter Scott! In Peace of mind: essays and reflections, August 1914–September 1917, 1918.
Cook, D. Scott and the booksellers: a vital link in the story of the poet-novelist's financial disaster. Bookman [London] 56 1919.
Ker, W. P. Sir Walter Scott. Anglo-French Rev 2 1919; rptd in his Collected essays, 2 vols 1925 (vol 1).
Dobie, W. G. M. Law and lawyers in the Waverley novels. Juridical Rev 32 1920.
Rait, R. S. Scott and The bee. TLS 16 Sep 1920; reply 23 Sep.
Withington, R. Scott's contribution to pageantic development: a note on the visit of George IV to Edinburgh in 1822. SP 17 1920.
Buchan, J. Sir Walter Scott. 1932.
Grierson, H. J. C. Sir Walter Scott Bart: a new life supplementary to, and corrective of, Lockhart's biography. 1938.

Gell, W. Reminiscences of Sir Walter Scott's residence in Italy 1832. Ed J. C. Corson, Toronto 1953; rptd London 1957.
Quayle, E. The ruin of Sir Walter Scott. 1968.
Johnson, E. Sir Walter Scott: the great unknown. 2 vols New York and London 1970.
Sultana, D. The journey of Sir Walter Scott to Malta. Gloucester and New York 1986.
Sultana, D. From Abbotsford to Paris and back: Sir Walter Scott's journey of 1815. Stroud 1993.
Sutherland, John. The life of Walter Scott: a critical biography. Oxford 1995. [JHA]

Sir Martin Archer Shee 1769–1850

See col 1983.

Mary Wollstonecraft Shelley, née Godwin 1797–1851

The major surviving mss are located in the Abinger Collection held on deposit at the Bodleian. These include the mss of Mary Shelley's journals, Frankenstein, Mathilda, The fields of fancy, *a memoir of William Godwin (unfinished), a short story entitled* Cecil *(unfinished), and miscellaneous drafts, letters and papers. Other mss are located in the Bodleian Shelley Papers. These include* Proserpine, Midas, Relation of the death of the family of the Cenci *(trn), research notes for* Valperga, *a memoir of P. B. Shelley (unfinished), and several notebooks containing Mary Shelley's transcriptions of Shelley's poetry and prose. Most of these items are available in annotated photo facs in* Mss of the younger romantics: Shelley, gen ed D. H. Reiman, 9 vols New York and London 1985– , *or in* Bodleian Shelley mss, gen ed D. H. Reiman, 23 vols New York and London 1986– *(see below for details). See also* Indexes to the Bodleian Shelley mss, Bodleian Shelley mss, vol 23, ed T. Tokoo and B. C. Barker-Benfield, New York and London 1986– . *Mary Shelley's prose trn of* Apuleius' story of Cupid and Psyche *is located in the Mary Shelley notebook in the Lib of Congress; and her short story for children,* Maurice, or the fisher's cot, *is in the private archive of the Dazzi family in San Marcello, Italy. One of her mss works has never been found:* Hate, *a story begun in 1814.*

Bibliographies

Wise, T. J. In his A Shelley library, 1924 (priv ptd), rptd New York 1971 (facs), 1982.
Keats–Shelley Journal. 1952– . Contains annual bibliography.
Lyles, W. H. Mary Shelley: an annotated bibliography. New York and London 1975.
Frank, F. S. Mary Shelley's Frankenstein: a register of research. Bull of Bibliography 40 1983.
Spector, R. D. In his The English Gothic: a bibliographic guide to writers from Horace Walpole to Mary Shelley, Westport CT 1984.
Clemit, P. In Literature of the Romantic period: a bibliographical guide, ed M. O'Neill, Oxford 1998.

Collections and selections

Tales and stories. Ed R. Garnett 1891, rptd with introd by J. Russ, Boston 1975.
Collected tales and stories. Ed C. E. Robinson, Baltimore and London 1976, rptd 1990 (with original engravings).
The Mary Shelley reader. Ed B. T. Bennett and C. E. Robinson, New York 1990.
The novels and selected works. Gen ed N. Crook with P. Clemit 8 vols 1996.

§1

For contemporary reviews, see Lyles, Bibliographies, above.

Prose fiction

Frankenstein: or the modern Prometheus. 3 vols 1818 (anon); 2 vols 1823 (rev); 1 vol 1831 (rev with introd signed 'M. W. S.', Bentley's Standard Novels, several reprints); 1855 (Parlour Lib); Boston 1869; [c. 1870] (Cottage Lib); introd by H. R. Haweis 1882 (several reprints); 1883 (English lib of standard works, vol 3); 1893 (Masterpiece Lib), 1897 (illus); ed E. Rhys 1912 (EL, several reprints); illustr N. Carbe, New York 1932 (1818 text); engraved L. Ward, New York and Toronto 1934; ed E. L. Pearson, illustr E. Henry, New York 1934; New York 1939 (in Horror omnibus); New York 1957, 1960, 1961; introd by M. M. Threapleton, New York 1963; introd by R. E. Dowse and D. J. Palmer 1963 (EL); ed H. Bloom 1965 (Signet); introd by R. D. Spector, New York, Toronto and London 1967; ed P. Fairclough, introd by M. Praz 1968 (in Three Gothic novels) (Pen); ed M. K. Joseph 1969 (Oxford English Texts), rptd 1980 (WCp); ed J. Rieger, Indianapolis 1974, Chicago and London 1982 (1818 text with variants); ed L. Wolf, New York 1977, rev 1993; introd by D. Johnson, New York 1981; illustr B. Moser, introd by J. C. Oates, New York 1984; ed M. Hindle 1985, rev 1992 (Pen) (1831 text with variants); engraved L. Ward, illustr A. Ruiz, New York 1988; ed B. T. Bennett and C. E. Robinson, New York 1990 (in Mary Shelley reader) (1818 text); ed P. Lyons 1992 (EL) (1818 text); ed J. H. Smith, Boston 1992; ed M. Butler 1993 (Pickering Women's Classics), rptd 1994 (WCp) (1818 text with variants); introd by J. Wordsworth, Spelsbury 1993 (facs of 1823 edn); ed D. L. Macdonald and K. Scherf, Peterborough Ontario 1994 (1818 text with variants); ed N. Crook 1996 (Novels and selected works vol 1) (1818 text with variants); ed P. Hunter 1996 (Norton) (1818 text); ed C. E. Robinson, 2 vols New York and London 1996 (in Frankenstein mss, Mss of the younger romantics: Shelley, vol 9) (annotated photo facs of Bodleian Abinger mss dep. c. 534 and dep. c. 477/1); tr Fr 1821, 1922, 1932, 1945, 1947, 1964, 1965, 1967, 1968, Ger 1912, 1948, 1964, 1969, 1970, 1971, 1972, 1975, Ital 1914, 1944, 1952, 1966, 1973, 1975, Sp 1945, 1947, 1959, 1966, 1969, 1971, 1972, 1973, Jap 1953, 1959, 1969, 1972, 1973, Bengali 1955, Portuguese 1957, 1974, Polish 1958, Arabic 1959, Malayalam 1959, Swed 1959, 1974, Serbo-Croat 1960, Urdu [1960?], Rus 1965, Cz 1966, 1969, 1969, Danish 1966 (1818 text), 1977, Du 1968, Greek 1971, Slovenian 1971, Turkish 1971, Finnish 1973, Romanian 1973, Norwegian 1976.
Valperga: or the life and adventures of Castruccio Prince of Lucca. 3 vols 1823, rptd Norwood PA 1978 (facs); introd by J. Wordsworth, Spelsbury 1995 (facs); ed N. Crook 1996 (Novels and selected works, vol 3) ed S. Curran New York 1997; ed T. Rajan, Peterborough Ontario 1998; tr Ger 1824.
The last man. 3 vols 1826, 1826, Paris 1826; 2 vols Philadelphia 1833; Hadleigh Essex 1951 (in M. Spark, Child of light: a reassessment of Mary Shelley) (abridged); ed H. J. Luke Jr, Lincoln NE 1965, rptd with introd by B. Aldiss 1985, rptd with introd by A. K. Mellor, Lincoln NE 1993; ed M. D. Paley, Oxford 1994 (WCp); ed J. Blumberg with N. Crook 1996 (Novels and selected works, vol 4); ed A. McWhir, Peterborough Ontario 1996.
The fortunes of Perkin Warbeck: a romance. 3 vols 1830, rptd Norwood PA 1976 (facs); 1830 ('revised, corrected and illustrated with a new introduction by the author'); 2 vols Philadelphia 1834; 1 vol 1857 (Railway Lib); ed D. D. Fischer 1996 (Novels and selected works, vol 5).
Lodore. 3 vols 1835; 1 vol New York 1835; Paris 1835 (corrected); 1844; 1846; Philadelphia [1865] (retitled The beautiful widow); New York 1893 (retitled The beautiful widow); ed F. Stafford 1996 (Novels and selected works, vol 6); ed L. Vargo, Peterborough Ontario 1997.
Falkner: a novel. 3 vols 1837, rptd Folcroft PA 1975 (facs); 1 vol New York 1837; 2 vols New York 1837; ed P. Clemit 1996 (Novels and selected works, vol 7).
Mathilda. (Written 1819–20.) Ed E. Nitchie, Chapel Hill NC 1959, rptd Folcroft PA 1972; ed E. B. Murray, New York and London 1988 (in Facsimile of Bodleian ms Shelley d. 1, pt 1, Bodleian Shelley mss, vol 4) (portion, annotated photo facs); ed B. T.

Bennett and C. E. Robinson, New York 1990 (in Mary Shelley reader); ed J. Todd 1991 (Pickering Women's Classics), rptd 1992 (Pen) (retitled Matilda) with Mary Wollstonecraft, Mary and Maria; ed P. Clemit 1996 (in Novels and selected works, vol 2) (retitled Matilda); ed A. Weinberg, New York and London 1997 (in Additional materials in the hand of Mary W. Shelley: mss Shelley adds. c. 5 and Shelley adds. d. 8, Bodleian Shelley mss, vol 22) (portion, annotated facs); tr Ital 1980.

The fields of fancy. (Written 1819.) Ed E. Nitchie, Chapel Hill NC 1959 (ch 1 only); ed E. B. Murray, New York and London 1988 (in Facsimile of Bodleian ms Shelley d. 1, pt 1, Bodleian Shelley mss, vol 4) (portion, annotated photo facs); ed P. Clemit 1996 (in Novels and selected works, vol 2).

Verse plays

Proserpine, a mythological drama in two acts. (Written 1820.) Includes two lyrics by P. B. Shelley. In Winter's Wreath for 1832 [1831] (rev); ed A. H. Koszul 1922 (in Proserpine & Midas: two unpublished mythological dramas), rptd Folcroft PA 1974 (facs); ed B. T. Bennett and C. E. Robinson, New York and London 1992 (in Mary Shelley's plays and her translation of the Cenci story: Bodleian mss Shelley adds. d. 2 and adds. e. 13, Bodleian Shelley mss, vol 10) (annotated photo facs); ed P. Clemit 1996 (in Novels and selected works, vol 2).

Midas. (Written 1820.) Includes two lyrics by P. B. Shelley. Ed A. H. Koszul 1922 (in Proserpine & Midas: two unpublished mythological dramas), rptd Folcroft PA 1974 (facs); ed B. T. Bennett and C. E. Robinson, New York and London 1992 (in Mary Shelley's plays and her translation of the Cenci story: Bodleian mss Shelley adds. d. 2 and adds. e. 13, Bodleian Shelley mss vol 10) (annotated photo-facs); ed P. Clemit 1996 (in Novels and selected works, vol 2).

Poetry

Absence: Ah! he is gone – and I alone! In Keepsake for 1831 [1830]; ed T. J. Wise 1924 (priv ptd) (in A Shelley library), rptd New York 1971 (facs), New York 1982.

A dirge: This morn, thy gallant bark, love. (Written 1827.) In Keepsake for 1831 [1830], rptd in P. B. Shelley, Poetical works, 4 vols 1839 (variant), *see* Other works, *below*; ed B. T. Bennett, Baltimore and London 1980–8 (in Letters of Mary Wollstonecraft Shelley, vol 2) (variant); ed D. Wu, Oxford and Cambridge MA 1994, rptd 1995 (in Romanticism: an anthology) (edited from ms and subtitled 'To the air of Phillida, adieu, love!'); ed P. Clemit 1996 (in Novels and selected works, vol 2) (1839 text).

Stanzas: I must forget thy dark eyes' love-fraught gaze. In Keepsake for 1833 [1832].

Stanzas: How like a star you rose upon my life. In Keepsake for 1839 [1838].

Stanzas: O come to me in dreams, my love! In Keepsake for 1839 [1838]; ed R. G. Grylls 1952 (in Keats–Shelley Memorial Bull 4) (variant entitled 'To the dead'); ed D. Wu, Oxford and Cambridge MA 1994, rptd 1995 (in Romanticism: an anthology) (edited from ms).

O listen while I sing to thee. nd (written 1838) ('Canzonet, with accompaniment for the harp or piano forte'); ed D. Wu, Oxford and Cambridge MA 1994, rptd 1995 (in Romanticism: an anthology).

Orpheus. (Written 1821.) With P. B. Shelley. Ed R. Garnett 1862 (in Relics of Shelley); ed N. Crook, New York and London 1991 (in Shelley's Charles the First notebook: Bodleian ms Shelley adds. e. 17, Bodleian Shelley mss, vol 12) (annotated photo facs); ed N. Crook 1996 (in Novels and selected works, vol 2).

The choice: a poem on Shelley's death. Ed H. B. Forman 1876 (priv ptd), rptd Folger PA 1973; ed P. R. Feldman and D. Scott-Kilvert, Oxford 1987, rptd Baltimore and London 1995 (in Journals of Mary Shelley 1814–1844) (variant dated July 1823).

On reading Wordsworth's lines on Peel [*sic*] castle. (Dated 8 Dec 1825.) In R. G. Grylls, Mary Shelley: a biography, 1938, rptd Norwood PA 1977, Philadelphia 1978, New York 1982; ed P. R. Feldman and D. Scott-Kilvert, Oxford 1987, rptd Baltimore and London 1995 (in Journals of Mary Shelley 1814–1844); ed D. Wu, Oxford and Cambridge MA 1994, rptd 1995 (in Romanticism: an anthology).

Fragment: Tribute for thee, dear solace of my life. In R. G. Grylls, Mary Shelley: a biography, 1938, rptd Norwood PA 1977, Philadelphia 1978, New York 1982 (annotated 'To Jane with The last [man]'); ed P. R. Feldman and D. Scott-Kilvert, Oxford 1987, rptd Baltimore and London 1995 (in Journals of Mary Shelley 1814–1844).

Tempo è ben di morire. (Dated 1833.) In E. Nitchie, Mary Shelley: author of Frankenstein, New Brunswick NJ 1953.

La vida es sueño. In E. Nitchie, Mary Shelley: author of Frankenstein, New Brunswick NJ 1953 (dated 1834); in J. de Palacio, Mary Shelley dans son oeuvre, Paris 1969 (variant dated 1833).

Other works

History of a six weeks' tour through a part of France, Switzerland, Germany, and Holland: with letters descriptive of a sail round the lake of Geneva, and of the glaciers of Chamouni. 1817. (With P. B. Shelley; contains Mary Shelley's History of a six weeks' tour and two of her letters from Geneva.) 1829; ed Mary Shelley 2 vols 1840 [1839] (in P. B. Shelley, Essays, letters from abroad, translations and fragments (retitled journal of a six weeks' tour), *see below*); ed C. Elton 1894 introd by J. Wordsworth, Spelsbury 1989, rptd 1991 (facs); ed E. B. Murray, Oxford 1993 (in P. B. Shelley, Prose works, vol 1); ed J. Moskal 1996 (in Novels and selected works, vol 8).

P. B. Shelley, Posthumous poems. Ed Mary Shelley 1824 (with preface); London, New York and Melbourne 1889 (in 1 vol with P. B. Shelley, Poetical works, and Essays, letters from abroad, translations and fragments); introd by J. Wordsworth, Spelsbury 1991 (facs).

Memoirs of William Godwin. In W. Godwin, Caleb Williams, 1831 (Bentley's Standard Novels), rptd 1849; ed P. Clemit 1996 (in Novels and selected works, vol 2).

Lives of the most eminent literary and scientific men of Italy, Spain and Portugal. In vols 86–8 of Cabinet cyclopaedia, ed D. Lardner, 3 vols 1835–7. With D. Brewster, J. Montgomery and others. (Mary Shelley's contributions include the lives of the Italian writers Petrarch, Boccaccio, Machiavelli, Metastasio, Goldoni, Alfieri, Monti and Foscolo, and all the Spanish and Portuguese lives with the possible exception of Ercilla.) 2 vols Philadelphia 1841 (retitled Lives of eminent literary and scientific men of Italy).

Lives of the most eminent literary and scientific men of France. In vols 102–3 of Cabinet cyclopaedia, ed D. Lardner, 2 vols 1838–9; 2 vols Philadelphia 1840 (retitled Lives of the most eminent French writers).

P. B. Shelley, Poetical works. Ed Mary Shelley 4 vols 1839 (with preface and notes, prints Queen Mab with omissions); 1 vol '1840' [1839] (rev) (with added postscript, includes Swellfoot the tyrant, Peter Bell III and Queen Mab complete); 1 vol 1841 (omits Queen Mab); 4 vols 1846; 1 vol Philadelphia 1846; 3 vols London 1847 (rev, prints Queen Mab, cantos 1–2); 1 vol Philadelphia 1847; London 1847 (in 1 vol with P. B. Shelley, Essays, letters from abroad, translations and fragments); 1 vol 1850; 1 vol Philadelphia 1851; 3 vols London 1853; 1 vol 1853; 1854 (in 1 vol with P. B. Shelley, Essays, letters from abroad, translations and fragments); 3 vols Boston 1855; 1 vol London 1856; 3 vols 1857; 2 vols Boston 1857 (with memoir by J. Lowell); 1 vol London 1862; 3 vols 1866; 3 vols 1869; 1 vol 1869; ed H. B. Forman 4 vols 1876–7, 1882 (with notes by Mary Shelley); 1 vol Philadelphia [1884]; 3 vols Boston 1889; London, New York and Melbourne 1889 (in 1 vol with P. B. Shelley,

Posthumous poems, and Essays, letters from abroad, translations and fragments); ed E. Dowden 1 vol 1890; ed T. Hutchinson 1 vol Oxford 1904 (several reprints), new edn corrected G. Matthews, Oxford 1970, rptd 1995.

P. B. Shelley, Essays, letters from abroad, translations and fragments. Ed Mary Shelley 2 vols '1840' [1839] (with preface); 2 vols New York 1840; 2 vols Philadelphia 1840; 1 vol 1845; 1847 (in 1 vol with P. B. Shelley, Poetical works); 1852 (new edn); 1854 (in 1 vol with P. B. Shelley, Poetical works); 2 vols 1856; London, New York and Melbourne 1889 (in 1 vol with P. B. Shelley, Posthumous poems, and Poetical works).

Relation of the death of the family of the Cenci. (Trn from Ital.) Ed Mary Shelley '1840' [1839] (in P. B. Shelley, Poetical works); ed B. T. Bennett and C. E. Robinson, New York and London 1992 (in Mary Shelley's plays and her translation of the Cenci story: Bodleian mss Shelley adds. d. 2 and adds. e. 13, Bodleian Shelley mss, vol 10) (annotated facs).

Rambles in Germany and Italy, in 1840, 1842 and 1843. 2 vols 1844, rptd Folcroft PA 1975 (facs); ed J. Moskal 1996 (in Novels and selected works, vol 8).

Memoir of Percy Bysshe Shelley. (Unfinished.) In T. J. Hogg, The life of Percy Bysshe Shelley, 1858 (portions); ed A. Weinberg 1997 (in Additional materials in the hand of Mary W. Shelley: mss Shelley adds. c. 5 and Shelley adds. d. 6, Bodleian Shelley mss, vol 22) (annotated facs).

Memoirs and correspondence of the late William Godwin. (Unfinished.) In C. Kegan Paul, William Godwin: his friends and contemporaries, 2 vols 1876 (portions); ed P. Clemit 1999, (in Lives of the great romantics by their contemporaries, ser 3, vol 1, portions).

The necessity of a belief in the heathen mythology: to a Christian. (Unfinished essay.) Ed. A. H. Koszul 1922 (in Proserpine & Midas: two unpublished mythological dramas), rptd Folcroft PA 1974; ed E. W. Sunstein 1981 (in Keats–Shelley Memorial Bull 32); ed J. Blumberg 1993 (in Mary Shelley's early novels).

A history of the Jews. (Unfinished.) Ed J. Blumberg 1993 (in Mary Shelley's early novels).

Tales and stories

A tale of the passions. In Liberal no 2, Jan 1823 (anon), Weekly Entertainer n.s. 7 1823 (anon), Romancist and Novelist's Library 1 1839 (retitled A tale of the passions: or the death of Despina); ed R. Garnett 1891, rptd with introd by J. Russ, Boston 1975 (in Tales and stories) (retitled A tale of the passions: or the death of Despina); ed C. E. Robinson, Baltimore and London 1976, rptd 1990 (in Collected tales and stories).

Recollections of Italy. In London Mag 9, Jan 1824 (anon); ed C. E. Robinson, Baltimore and London 1976, rptd 1990 (in Collected tales and stories); ed B. T. Bennett and C. E. Robinson, New York 1990 (in Mary Shelley reader).

The bride of modern Italy. In London Mag 9, Apr 1824 (anon); ed C. E. Robinson, Baltimore and London 1976, rptd 1990 (in Collected tales and stories); ed B. T. Bennett and C. E. Robinson, New York 1990 (in Mary Shelley reader).

The sisters of Albano. In Keepsake for 1829 [1828], Friendship's Offering, Boston 1847; ed R. Garnett 1891, rptd with introd by J. Russ, Boston 1975 (in Tales and stories); ed J. A. Hammerton, nd (in Masterpiece Lib of Short Stories); ed C. E. Robinson, Baltimore and London 1976, rptd 1990 (in Collected tales and stories).

Ferdinand Eboli: a tale. In Keepsake for 1829 [1828], Friendship's Offering, Boston 1845, Keepsake: a gift for the holidays, New York 1854; ed R. Garnett 1891, rptd with introd by J. Russ, Boston 1975 (in Tales and stories); ed C. E. Robinson, Baltimore and London 1976, rptd 1990 (in Collected tales and stories).

The mourner. In Keepsake for 1830 [1829]; ed R. Garnett 1891, rptd with introd by J. Russ, Boston 1975 (in Tales and stories); ed C. E. Robinson, Baltimore and London 1976, rptd 1990 (in Collected tales and stories).

The evil eye. In Keepsake for 1830 [1829]; ed R. Garnett 1891, rptd with introd by J. Russ, Boston 1975 (in Tales and stories); ed C. E. Robinson, Baltimore and London 1976, rptd 1990 (in Collected tales and stories).

The false rhyme. In Keepsake for 1830 [1829], Athenaeum, 11 Nov 1829, Polar Star 2 1830, Casket no 5, May 1830, American Keepsake, New York [1835]; ed J. A. Hammerton nd (in Masterpiece library of short stories); ed R. Garnett 1891, rptd with introd by J. Russ, Boston 1975 (in Tales and stories); ed C. E. Robinson, Baltimore and London 1976, rptd 1990 (in Collected tales and stories); ed B. T. Bennett and C. E. Robinson, New York 1990 (in Mary Shelley reader).

Transformation. In Keepsake for 1831 [1830], Spirit of the Annuals, Philadelphia 1831, Tale Book 2nd ser, Paris 1835 (Baudry's European Lib), International Monthly Mag 3, Apr 1851; ed R. Garnett 1891, rptd with introd by J Russ, Boston 1975 (in Tales and stories); introd by P. Haining, New York 1967 (in Gentlewomen of evil); ed A. H. Norton, New York 1968 (in Masters of horror); ed C. E. Robinson, Baltimore and London 1976, rptd 1990 (in Collected tales and stories); ed B. T. Bennett and C. E. Robinson, New York 1990 (in Mary Shelley reader).

The Swiss peasant. In Keepsake for 1831 [1830], Tale Book 1st ser, Paris 1834 (Baudry's European Lib), Friendship's Offering, Boston 1845, Tale Book, Königsberg 1859; ed R. Garnett 1891, rptd with introd by J. Russ, Boston 1975 (in Tales and stories); ed C. E. Robinson, Baltimore and London 1976, rptd 1990 (in Collected tales and stories).

The dream. In Keepsake for 1832 [1831], Leaflets of Memory (Philadelphia) 1846, Friendship's Offering (Philadelphia) 1855; ed R. Garnett 1891, rptd with introd by J. Russ, Boston 1975 (in Tales and stories); ed P. Haining, New York 1972, rptd Baltimore 1973 (in Gothic tales of terror); ed C. E. Robinson, Baltimore and London 1976, rptd 1990 (in Collected tales and stories); ed B. T. Bennett and C. E. Robinson, New York 1990 (in Mary Shelley reader).

The brother and sister: an Italian story. In Keepsake for 1833 [1832], Match-making and other tales (Philadelphia) 1832; ed R. Garnett 1891, rptd with introd by J. Russ, Boston 1975 (in Tales and stories); ed C. E. Robinson, Baltimore and London 1976, rptd 1990 (in Collected tales and stories); tr Fr 1832 (in Le Salmagondis).

The invisible girl. In Keepsake for 1833 [1832], Match-making and other tales (Philadelphia) 1832, Keepsake: a gift for the holidays (New York) 1854; ed R. Garnett 1891, rptd with introd by J. Russ, Boston 1975 (in Tales and stories); ed C. E. Robinson, Baltimore and London 1976, rptd 1990 (in Collected tales and stories).

The smuggler and his family. In Original compositions in prose and verse 1833; ed C. E. Robinson, Baltimore and London, 1976, rptd 1990 (in Collected tales and stories).

The mortal immortal: a tale. In Keepsake for 1834 [1833], Casquet of Lit nd, Casquet of Lit 1873, Lib of Choice Lit, Philadelphia 1890; ed R. Garnett 1891, rptd with introd by J. Russ, Boston 1975 (in Tales and stories); ed D. L. Sayers 1931 (in Great short stories of detection, mystery and horror 2nd ser); introd by J. Agate 1934 (in A century of thrillers: from Poe to Arlen); ed S. Moskowitz, Cleveland OH 1966, rptd Westport CT 1974 (in Masterpieces of science fiction); ed C. E. Robinson, Baltimore and London 1976, rptd 1990 (in Collected tales and stories); ed B. T. Bennett and C. E. Robinson, New York 1990 (in Mary Shelley reader).

The elder son. In Heath's Book of Beauty, 1835 [1834]; ed R. Garnett 1891, rptd with introd by J. Russ, Boston 1975 (in Tales and stories); ed C. E. Robinson, Baltimore and London 1976, rptd 1990 (in Collected tales and stories).

The trial of love. In Keepsake for 1835 [1834], Coronet (Philadelphia) nd (retitled Angeline and Faustina: or the trial of love); ed B. A. Booth, Berkeley 1938 (in A cabinet of gems); ed C. E. Robinson, Baltimore and London 1976, rptd 1990 (in Collected tales and stories); ed J. Sutherland, Oxford 1996 (in Oxford book of English love stories).

The parvenue. In Keepsake for 1837 [1836], Amaranth: or token of remembrance (Boston) 1848, Remember me: a token of love for 1855 (Philadelphia) [1854]; ed R. Garnett 1891, rptd with introd by J. Russ, Boston 1975; ed L. Melville and R. Hargreaves, New York 1930 (in Great English short stories); ed C. E. Robinson, Baltimore and London 1976, rptd 1990 (in Collected tales and stories).

Euphrasia: a tale of Greece. In Keepsake for 1839 [1838], Leaflets of Memory, Philadelphia 1847, Keepsake: a gift for the holidays, New York 1851 (retitled The brother: a tale of Greece); ed R. Garnett 1891, rptd with introd by J. Russ, Boston 1975 (in Tales and stories) (omits the six introductory paragraphs to the story); ed C. E. Robinson, Baltimore and London 1976, rptd 1990 (in Collected tales and stories).

Roger Dodsworth: the reanimated Englishman. In C. Redding, Yesterday and to-day, 1863; ed C. E. Robinson, Baltimore and London 1976, rptd 1990 (in Collected tales and stories); ed B. T. Bennett and C. E. Robinson, New York 1990 (in Mary Shelley reader).

The heir of Mondolfo. In Appleton's Jnl n.s. 2, Jan 1877; ed R. D. Spector, New York 1963 (in Seven masterpieces of Gothic horror); ed C. E. Robinson, Baltimore and London 1976, rptd 1990 (in Collected tales and stories).

Valerius: the reanimated Roman. (Unfinished.) Ed C. E. Robinson, Baltimore and London 1976, rptd 1990 (in Collected tales and stories).

An eighteenth-century tale: a fragment. Ed C. E. Robinson, Baltimore and London 1976, rptd 1990 (in Collected tales and stories).

Maurice, or the fisher's cot. Ed. C. Tomalin 1998.

Contributions to periodicals

Madame d'Houtetot. (Essay.) In Liberal no 3 1823 (anon); ed P. Clemit 1996 (in Novels and selected works, vol 2).

Giovanni Villani. (Essay.) In Liberal no 4 1824 (anon); ed B. T. Bennett and C. E. Robinson, New York 1990 (in Mary Shelley reader) (extract); ed P. Clemit 1996 (in Novels and selected works, vol 2).

On ghosts. (Essay.) In London Mag 9 Mar 1824 (signed $\Sigma\varsigma$); ed B. T. Bennett and C. E. Robinson, New York 1990 (in Mary Shelley reader); ed P. Clemit 1996 (in Novels and selected works, vol 2).

Defence of Velluti. In Examiner 11 June 1826 (letter signed 'ANGLO-ITALICUS'); ed B. T. Bennett, Baltimore and London 1980–8 (in Letters of Mary Wollstonecraft Shelley, vol 1).

The English in Italy. (Review.) In Westminster Rev 6, Oct 1826 (anon); ed B. T. Bennett and C. E. Robinson, New York 1990 (in Mary Shelley reader); ed P. Clemit 1996 (in Novels and selected works, vol 2).

A visit to Brighton. (Essay.) In London Mag 16, Dec 1826 (anon); ed P. Clemit 1996 (in Novels and selected works, vol 2).

Illyrian poems – feudal scenes. (Review.) In Westminster Rev 10, Jan 1829 (anon), rptd in A. W. Raitt, Prosper Mérimée, New York and London 1970; ed P. Clemit 1996 (in Novels and selected works, vol 2).

Modern Italy. (Review.) In Westminster Rev 11, July 1829 (anon); ed B. T. Bennett and C. E. Robinson, New York 1990 (in Mary Shelley reader) (extract); ed P. Clemit 1996 (in Novels and selected works, vol 2).

Loves of the poets. (Review.) In Westminster Rev 11, Oct 1829 (anon); ed B. T. Bennett and C. E. Robinson, New York 1990 (in Mary Shelley reader); ed P. Clemit 1996 (in Novels and selected works, vol 2).

Cloudesley: a tale. (Review.) In Blackwood's Edinburgh Mag 27, May 1830 (anon); ed B. T. Bennett and C. E. Robinson, New York 1990 (in Mary Shelley reader) (extract); ed P. Clemit 1996 (in Novels and selected works, vol 2).

The bravo: a Venetian story. (Review.) In Westminster Rev 16, Jan 1832 (anon); ed P. Clemit 1996 (in Novels and selected works, vol 2).

Mary Shelley's second defence of Velluti. (Letter to Examiner dated 23 June 1826, signed 'Anglo: Italicus'.) Ed F. L. Jones, Norman OK 1944 (in Letters of Mary W. Shelley, vol 2); ed B. T. Bennett, Baltimore and London 1980–8 (in Letters of Mary Wollstonecraft Shelley, vol 1).

Letters, journals, etc

Shelley and Mary: a collection of letters and documents of a biographical character in the possession of Sir Percy and Lady Shelley. Ed Lady Jane and Sir Percy F. Shelley 4 vols 1882 (priv ptd).

The romance of Mary W. Shelley, John Howard Payne and Washington Irving. Boston 1907, rptd Norwood PA 1978. (The Payne–Shelley letters, with remarks by F. B. Sanborn.)

Letters, mostly unpublished. Ed H. H. Harper, Boston 1918, rptd Folcroft PA 1972.

Harriet and Mary: being the relations between Percy Bysshe Shelley, Harriet Shelley, Mary Shelley and Thomas Jefferson Hogg as shown in letters between them. Ed W. S. Scott 1944, rptd Norwood PA 1978.

Letters of Mary W. Shelley. Ed F. L. Jones 2 vols Norman OK 1944.

Mary Shelley's journal. Ed F. L. Jones, Norman OK 1947.

Two Mary Shelley letters. Ed C. L. Cline, N & Q 195 1950.

Eight letters by Mary Wollstonecraft Shelley. Ed E. Nitchie, Keats–Shelley Memorial Bull 3 1950.

My best Mary: selected letters. Ed M. Spark and D. Stanford 1953, rptd Folcroft PA 1972 (facs).

Mary Shelley to Maria Gisborne: new letters 1818–22. Ed F. L. Jones, SP 52 1955.

Mary Shelley, Walter Scott and Maga. Ed I. Massey, N & Q 207 1962.

Letters of Mary Wollstonecraft Shelley. Ed B. T. Bennett 3 vols Baltimore and London 1980–8.

Journals of Mary Shelley 1814–1844. Ed P. R. Feldman and D. Scott-Kilvert 2 vols Oxford 1987, rptd 1 vol Baltimore and London 1995.

Selected letters of Mary Wollstonecraft Shelley. Ed B. T. Bennett, Baltimore and London 1995.

Attributed or spurious works

Mounseer Nongtongpaw. 1808 (anon). (Verses.) Ed I. and P. Opie, Oxford 1980 (in A nursery companion); ed J. Moskal 1996 (in Novels and selected works, vol 8). Attributed by I. and P. Opie, Oxford 1980 (in A nursery companion), rejected by E. W. Sunstein 1996 (A William Godwin letter and young Mary Godwin's part in Mounseer Nongtongpaw, KSJ 45), and by N. Crook 1996 (Novels and selected works, vol 1).

The pole. (Tale.) In Court Mag 1, Aug and Sep 1822, Eng Annual 1836; ed R. Garnett 1891, rptd with introd by J. Russ, Boston 1975 (in Tales and stories); ed B. A. Booth, Berkeley 1938 (in A cabinet of gems); ed C. E. Robinson, Baltimore and London 1976, rptd 1990 (in Collected tales and stories). Pbd under the name of the author of Frankenstein but largely written by C. Clairmont (B. A. Booth, The pole: a story by Claire Clairmont?, ELH 5 1938).

1572 Chronique du temps de Charles IX. (Review.) In Westminster Rev 13, Oct 1830 (anon); ed P. Clemit 1996 (in Novels and selected works, vol 2). External evidence lacking. Noticed by J. de Palacio, Paris 1969 (in Mary Shelley dans son oeuvre); accepted by W. H. Lyles, New York and London 1975 (in Mary Shelley: an annotated bibliography), by E. W. Sunstein, Baltimore and London 1989, rev 1991 (in Mary Shelley: romance and reality), and by N. Crook 1996 (in Novels and selected works, vol 1).

Night scene: I see thee not, my gentlest Isabel. (Verses.) In Keepsake for 1831 [1830] (signed 'by Mary S.'). Attributed by E. Nitchie, New Brunswick NJ 1953 (in Mary Shelley: author of Frankenstein), by J. de Palacio, Paris 1969 (in Mary Shelley dans son oeuvre), and by W. H. Lyles, New York and London 1975 (in Mary Shelley: an annotated bibliography).

E. J. Trelawny, Memoirs of a younger son. 3 vols 1831 (anon), New York 1832, 1 vol 1835 (anon), [1856] (Parlour Lib); ed R. Garnett 1890; ed H. N. Brailsford 1914; ed E. C. Mayne, Oxford 1925 (WC); ed W. St Clair, Oxford 1974; tr Fr 1860, Gaelic 1936. Editorial help attributed by E. Nitchie, New Brunswick NJ 1953 (in Mary Shelley: author of Frankenstein).

The pilgrims. In Keepsake for 1838 [1837] (anon), Snow-flake: a Christmas, new-year and birthday gift, Philadelphia (anon) (retitled The pilgrims: a tale of chivalry). External evidence lacking. Accepted by R. Garnett 1891, rptd with introd by J. Russ, Boston 1975 (in Tales and stories), by C. E. Robinson, Baltimore and London 1976, rptd 1990 (in Collected tales and stories), and by E. W. Sunstein, Baltimore and London 1989, rev 1991 (in Mary Shelley: romance and reality).

Alas I weep my life away. (Verses in journal entry for 14 Sep 1831.) Proposed by E. Nitchie, New Brunswick NJ 1953 (in Mary Shelley: author of Frankenstein), accepted by E. W. Sunstein, Baltimore and London 1989, rev 1991 (in Mary Shelley: romance and reality).

Struggle no more my soul with the sad chains. (Verses in journal entry for 16 Sep 1841.) Proposed by E. Nitchie, New Brunswick NJ 1953 (in Mary Shelley: author of Frankenstein), accepted by E. W. Sunstein, Baltimore and London 1989, rev 1991 (in Mary Shelley: romance and reality).

Elysian fields: an addition? (Written 1815 or 1816.) Addition to P. B. Shelley, Elysian fields, in Mary Shelley's hand. Ed E. B. Murray, Oxford 1993 (in P. B. Shelley, Prose works, vol 1). Attributed by E. B. Murray.

Items tentatively attributed, but with little consent, are Rome in the first and nineteenth century, in NMM *10 Mar 1824 (anon); The Italian novelists, in* Westminster Rev *7 Jan 1827 (anon); Lacy de Vere, in* Forget-Me-Not *for 1827 [1826] (anon); The Ritter von Reichenstein, in* Bijou *for 1828 [1827] (anon); The division of the earth in imitation of Spenser, from the German of Schiller, in* Bijou *for 1829 [1828] (signed 'M. S.'); The song of the sword, from the German of C. T. Korner, in* Bijou *for 1829 [1828] (signed 'M. S.'); The magician of Vicenza, in* Forget-Me-Not *for 1829 [1828] (anon); Ode, from the German of Klopstock, to Meta, in* Bijou *for 1830 [1829] (signed 'M. S.'); Rittrato di Ugo Foscolo, in* Bijou *for 1830 [1829] (signed 'M. S.'); To glory: from the Italian of Ciapetti, in* Bijou *for 1830 [1829] (signed 'M. S.'); review of W. Godwin,* Cloudesley, *in* NMM *28, Apr 1830 (anon); Byron and Shelley on the character of Hamlet, in* NMM *29, Nov 1830 (anon); Living literary characters no 2: the honourable Mrs Norton, in* NMM *33, Feb 1831 (anon); Living literary characters no 4: James Fenimore Cooper, in* NMM *33, Apr 1831 (anon); review of T. Moore,* The life and death of Edward Fitzgerald, *in* Westminster Rev *16, Jan–Apr 1832 (anon); Ode to ignorance, in* Metropolitan Mag *9, Jan 1834 (signed 'M. W. S.'); W. Godwin, Jr, Transfusion: or the orphans of Unwalden 3 vols 1835, 1 vol New York 1837 (editorial help); The silver lady, in* Keepsake *for 1838 [1837] (anon); Modern Italian romances, in* Monthly Chron *2, Nov 1838 (anon); Portuguese literature, in* Monthly Chron *3, Jan 1839 (anon); Spanish romantic drama, in* Monthly Chron *3, June 1839 (anon); The convent of Chaillot; or, Vallière and Louis XVI, in* Keepsake *for 1844 [1843] (anon); The ghost of private theatricals, in* Keepsake *for 1844 [1843] (signed 'M. S.'); review of C. A. Halstead,* Richard the Third, *in* Athenaeum *3, 10 Aug 1844 (anon).*

§2

Textual/bibliographical studies

Dilke, Charles W. The Liberal. N & Q ser 8, 4 1893.

Koszul, A. H. Notes and corrections to Shelley's History of a six weeks' tour. MLR 2 1906.

Booth, B. A. The pole: a story by Claire Clairmont? ELH 5 1938.

Jones, F. L. Unpublished fragments by Shelley and Mary. SP 45 1948.

Taylor, C. H. Jr. In his The early collected editions of Shelley's poems: a study in the history and transmission of the printed text. New Haven CT 1958.

Marshall, W. H. In his Byron, Shelley, Hunt, and the Liberal. Philadelphia 1960.

Nitchie, E. Shelley at Eton: Mary Shelley vs Jefferson Hogg. Keats–Shelley Memorial Bull 11 1960.

Massey, I. The first editions of Shelley's poetical works: some manuscript sources. KSJ 16 1967.

de Palacio, J. *See* Biographical studies, *below*.

Murray, E. B. Shelley's contribution to Mary's Frankenstein. Keats–Shelley Memorial Bull 29 1978.

Murray, E. B. Changes in the 1823 edition of Frankenstein. Library 6th ser 3 1981.

Mellor, A. K. *See* Biographical studies, *below*.

Barker-Benfield, B. C. Shelley's Guitar. Oxford 1992.

Bennett, B. T. Finding Mary Shelley in her letters. In Romantic revisions, ed R. Brinkley and K. Hanley, Cambridge 1992.

Bennett, B. T. Feminism and editing Mary Shelley: the editor and/or? the text. In Palimpsest: editorial theory in the humanities, ed G. Bornstein and R. G. Williams, Ann Arbor MI 1993.

Ketterer, D. The corrected Frankenstein: twelve preferred readings in the last draft. ELN 33 1995.

Ketterer, D. (De)Composing Frankenstein: the import of altered character names in the last draft. Stud in Bibliography 49 1996.

Leader, Z. In his Revision and romantic authorship, Oxford 1996.

Sunstein, E. W. A William Godwin letter and young Mary Godwin's part in Mounseer Nongtongpaw. KSJ 45 1996.

Clemit, P. From The fields of fancy to Matilda: Mary Shelley's changing conception of her novella. Romanticism 3 1997.

O'Neill, M. Trying to make it as good as I can: Mary Shelley's editing of Shelley's poetry and prose. Romanticism 3 1997.

Robinson, C. E. Editing and conceptualizing the Frankenstein notebooks. KSJ 46 1997.

Biographical studies

Gilfillan, G. In his Second gallery of literary portraits, Edinburgh 1850.

Moore, H. Mary Wollstonecraft Shelley. Philadelphia 1886.

Marshall, Mrs Julian (F. A.). The life and letters of Mary Wollstonecraft Shelley. 2 vols 1889, rptd New York 1982.

Rossetti, L. M. Mrs Shelley. 1890 (Eminent Women ser).

Church, R. Mary Shelley. 1928.

Grylls, R. G. Mary Shelley: a biography. Oxford 1938, rptd Norwood PA 1977, Philadelphia 1978, New York 1982.

Spark, M. Child of light: a reassessment of Mary Shelley. Hadleigh Essex 1951, 1987 (rev) (retitled Mary Shelley).

Nitchie, E. Mary Shelley: author of Frankenstein. New Brunswick NJ 1953.

de Palacio, Jean. Mary Shelley dans son oeuvre. Paris 1969.

Norman, S. Mary Wollstonecraft Shelley. In Shelley and his circle vol 3, ed K. N. Cameron, Cambridge MA 1970.

Dunn, J. Moon in eclipse: a life of Mary Shelley. 1978.

Mellor, A. K. Mary Shelley: her life, her fiction, her monsters. New York 1988.

Sunstein, E. W. Mary Shelley: romance and reality. Baltimore and London 1989, rev 1991. [PC]

Mrs Sherwood, Mary Martha Butt, née Sherwood 1771–1851

Bibliography

Cutt, N. M. Mrs Sherwood and her books for children. 1974.

Collections

Works. 7 vols New York 1834, 16 vols 1855.

The garland. Berwick 1835.

Home stories for the young. [1852].
Mrs Sherwood's popular tales. 1860.
Mrs Sherwood's juvenile tales. 1861.
'The Lily series'. 6 vols New York 1869.
The works of Mrs Sherwood. Being the only uniform edition ever published in the United States. New York 1871.
The juvenile library. By Mrs Sherwood. Containing a selection from her popular stories for young people. 1880 (illus).

§1

The traditions, a legendary tale. Written by a young lady. 2 vols 1795, 1796.
Margarita. (By the author of The traditions.) 4 vols 1799.
The history of Susan Gray, as related by a clergyman: designed for the benefit of young women when going into service. 1802, 1812 (8th edn), 1815, Andover MA 1817, London 1821, 1823, Wellington 1825, Philadelphia 1825, London [1830?], London and Wellington 1833, Lowell MA 1836, London 1869, Edinburgh 1870, London 1880, Edinburgh 1883, London 1887.
The history of Theophilus and Sophia. Wellington 1811, London 1818, Andover MA 1820, London 1822 (6th edn), Philadelphia 1830, London 1836.
The history of little Henry and his bearer. 1814 (anon), Wellington 1815, 2nd edn London 1818 (12th edn), 1819 (13th edn), 1820 (15th edn), 1823 (20th edn), 1825 (22nd edn), 1832, London and Edinburgh 1841 (as Little Henry and his bearer), London 1850 (37th edn), 1854 (illus), 1859, 1864, 1866 (includes The last days of Boosy), 1870 (with a preface by Mrs Kelly), Edinburgh 1870, 1871, London 1884, Worthing 1967 (contains The last days of Boosy by A. Macneil and T. Smith Wellington); tr Fr 1820, Ger New York 1850, Assamese 1853, Portuguese [nd].
The infant's progress, from the valley of destruction to everlasting glory. [1814?], 1847 (11th edn), 1851.
The Indian pilgrim: or the progress of the pilgrim Nazareenee (formerly called Goonah Purist, or the slave of sin) from the city of wrath of God to the city of Mount Zion. Delivered under the similitude of a dream. Wellington 1815, 1818, Boston 1828 (as The pilgrim of India).
The history of Lucy Clare. 1816, Wellington 1824 (14th edn), 1853, 1882, Edinburgh 1883. (Cutt indicates that this was begun in 1802 but not finished until 1810. Many reprints up to 1889.)
The ayah and her lady, an Indian story. Dublin 1816, 1822 (7th edn), Boston 1822, Madras 1828.
The history of Emily and her brothers. 1816, 1818 (3rd edn), Philadelphia 1819, London 1822 (9th edn), 1824 (12th edn).
The history of little George and his penny. Wellington 1816 (12th edn), Portland 1820.
Memoirs of Sergeant Dale, his daughter and the orphan Mary. Wellington 1815, London 1816 (3rd edn), 1821.
Stories explanatory of the Church catechism. Wellington 1817, 1820 7th edn, 1855 (introd by the Rev W. Meynell).
The busy bee. Wellington 1818, 1822 (6th edn), 1823 (7th edn).
A drive in the coach through the streets of London. Wellington, 1818, 1819 (3rd edn), 1824 (9th edn).
The history of the Fairchild family: or the child's manual: being a collection of stories calculated to shew the importance and effects of a religious education. 1818–47 (pt 3 with Mrs Streeten), 1818, 1819, 1822 etc, 1875 (with some account of the authoress by J. M.), [1902] (ed and introd by M. E. Palgrave), London and Edinburgh 1908 (retold by Jeanie Lang), 1913 (ed and abridged by Lady Strachey) (illus); tr Fr 1839, Ger 1839. (This was pbd in parts: Pt 1 first appeared in 1818, Pt 2 in 1842, Pt 3 in 1847.)
The little woodman and his dog Caesar. 1818, 1821 (5th edn), Philadelphia 1826, Wellington 1834 (16th edn), London [1850?] (21st edn), 1864, 1869, 1901; tr Fr 1841. (The work was frequently rptd throughout the nineteenth cent).
The rose: a fairy tale. Wellington 1818, 1820, 1823 (6th edn), 1828 (8th edn).
The errand boy. Wellington 1819, Boston 1821, Philadelphia 1830.
The hedge of thorns. 1819, 1821, 1825.
The orphan boy. Wellington 1819, Boston 1822 (8th edn).
Dudley Castle: a tale. 1820, [1834].
The Lambourne bell. [1820?], [1824?].
The golden clue. 1820.
The governess: or The little female academy. 1820, Wellington 1822 (3rd edn), New York 1827. (From the work of the same title by Sarah Fielding.)
The infirmary. 1821 (8th edn), 1846 (19th edn).
The iron cage. [1820?]
Little Arthur. Wellington 1820, 1824 (4th edn), 1826 (6th edn).
The little Sunday school child's reward. Wellington 1820, 1828 (15th edn).
The may-bee. Wellington 1820, 1821, New York [1820?], 1822, Wellington 1825.
The nursery maid's diary. [1820?]
Procrastination: or the evil of putting off till tomorrow which ought to be done today. [1820?]
The young mother. [1820?]
The blessed family. [1821], 1824 (4th edn), [1830?].
Charles Lorraine: or the young soldier drawn from scenes of real life. 5 pts. 1821, 1 vol 1822 (as The history of Charles Lorraine), [1866].
The history of George Desmond founded on facts which occurred in the East Indies and now published as a useful caution to young men going out to that country. 1821 (by M. M. Butt), Philadelphia 1828 (anon).
The history of Mary Saunders. 1821.
The infant's progress from the valley of destruction to everlasting glory. Wellington 1821, 1825, 1830, 1835.
Little Robert and the owl. 1821, 1824 (5th edn), Wellington 1825 (6th edn). (Rptd in The Children's Friend 1868.)
The recaptured negro. 1821 (2nd edn).
The two sisters. 1821.
The wishing cap. Wellington 1821, 1822 (5th edn), 1824 (7th edn), Philadelphia 1824 (as The wish: or little Charles), London [1871?].
The china manufactory. Wellington 1822.
Easy questions for a little child. Wellington 1822, 10th edn 1829.
The history of Henry Milner, a little boy, who was not brought up according to the fashions of this world. Pt 1 1822, 1823 (2nd edn), 1824 (3rd edn), 1835 (5th edn). (Pt 1 only pbd in 1822, 3 more pts were pbd later, the last in 1837.)
The potter's common. 4 pts. Wellington 1822–3.
The orphans of Normandy: or Florentin and Lucie. 1822, 1825 (2nd edn).
A general outline of profane history. 1823 (2nd edn).
The history of little Lucy and her Dhaye. Wellington 1823, Boston 1824, Wellington 1825 (2nd edn).
The infant's grave: a story of the northern part of France. 1823, Wellington 1825.
The lady of the manor: being a series of conversations on the subject of confirmation. Intended for the use of the middle and higher ranks of young females. 7 vols 1823–9, 1825–9 (2nd edn), 1831–4 (vol 1 is 1834 (4th edn), vols 2–5 are 1832–3 (3rd edn), vols 6–7 are 1831–2 (4th edn)), Philadelphia 1829.
Père la Chaise. Wellington 1823, 1827, 1834.
The history of Mrs Catherine Crawley. Wellington 1824.
A drive in the coach through the streets of London. A story founded on fact. 1824.
The history of Emily and her brothers. Wellington 1824 (12th edn).
The little beggars. 1824, 1830, Philadelphia [1830] (rev as The children of the Harz Mountains: or the little beggars).
The fountain of living waters. [1825?]

Juliana Oakley. 1825 (4th edn), New York 1825, 1833, London 1827, 1837.
My Uncle Timothy: an interesting tale for young persons. 1825.
The history of Emily and her mother. An extract from The governess. Wellington 1826, 1831 (4th edn); tr Fr 1825.
Julian Percival. Wellington 1826, Salem MA 1827.
The two dolls. Wellington 1826, 1830 (3rd edn).
Clara Stephens: or the white rose. Philadelphia 1827.
The dry ground. Wellington 1827, 1828, 1830, New Haven CT 1833.
Edward Mansfield. A narrative of facts. Wellington 1827, Salem MA 1827.
Ermina: or the second part of Juliana Oakley. Philadelphia 1827, 1831.
The gypsy babes: a story of the last century. Wellington 1827, Philadelphia 1827, 1850 (10th edn).
The lady in the arbour. Wellington 1827, New Haven CT 1833.
The pulpit and the desk. 1827.
Religious fashion: or the history of Anna. Philadelphia 1827.
The two sisters: or Ellen and Sophia. 1827, Philadelphia 1832 (as The broken Hyacinth).
The fawns. Wellington 1828, New Haven CT 1833 (as The two fawns).
The hills. Wellington 1828, 1831 (3rd edn).
The history of little George and his penny. Wellington 1828 (14th edn).
Home. Wellington 1828.
The idiot boy. Wellington 1828.
My Aunt Kate. Wellington 1828.
Poor Burruff. Wellington 1828, 1831 (4th edn).
The rainbow. Wellington 1828, 1831 (3rd edn).
The rosebuds. Wellington 1828.
Soffrona and her cat Muff. Wellington 1828.
Southstone's rock. Wellington 1828.
Susannah. 1828, Philadelphia 1829 (rev), London 1871 (rev S. Kelly).
The thunder storm. Wellington 1828.
Arzoomund. 1829.
Emancipation. Wellington 1829.
The little orphan. 1829.
Little Sally. 1829.
The mourning Queen. Wellington 1829.
The orange grove. Wellington 1829, New York 1842.
Common errors. [1830?]
The cottage in the woods. 2 pts [c. 1830].
Do what you can. 1830?
Do your own work. [1830?]
False colours. [1830?]
The flowers of the forest. 1830, 1832, 1834, 1835 (as Flores de Bosque), 1839; tr Portuguese 1835.
The golden chain. 1830 (illustr R. E. Bewick).
The governess: or the little female academy. 1830, 1832 (5th edn).
The hidden treasure. Wellington [1830?], [1837].
The history of Mary Saunders. Wellington [1830?].
The hop-picking. 1830.
The hidden treasure. [1830?], [1860?] (new edn).
Intimate friends. Wellington 1830, 1834.
It is not my business. [1830?]
Joan: or trustworthy. 2 pts [1830?].
The mail coach; and The old lady's complaint. [1830?]
A mother's duty. Wellington [1830?], [1860?].
Obedience. Berwick 1830, 1831.
The Oddingley murders. 1830, sequel 1830.
Old times. 2 pts [1830?].
The poor man of colour: or the sufferings, privations and death of Thomas Wilson in the suburbs of the British metropolis. [1830?]
Roxobel: or English manners and customs seventy years ago. 3 vols Wellington 1830–1.
The stolen fruit. Wellington [1830?], [1860?].
The turnpike-house. 2 pts [1830?].
The useful little girl and the little girl who was no use at all. Berwick 1830, 1832.
The young forester. 4 pts [1830?].
Everything out of its place. Wellington 1831, [184–?].
Hard times. 1831.
The father's eye. Berwick [1832].
The mountain ash. Berwick 1832.
The red morocco shoes. 1832.
The convent of St Clair. Berwick 1833.
The father's eye. Berwick 1833.
The latter days. 1833.
The little Momiere. 1833.
The nun. 1833, 1836, 1856 etc.
Victorian. 1833.
A visit to Grandpapa. Wellington [1833?].
Intimate friends. 1834 (2nd edn).
The lofty and the lowly. [1835.]
Sabbaths on the Continent. 1835.
Social tales for the young. [1835?], [1841], 1850 (as Family tales).
Dangerous sport. [between 1836 and 1847.]
Going to the fair. [between 1836 and 1847.]
The honey drop. [between 1836 and 1847.]
The Indian chief. [between 1836 and 1847.]
The lost trunk. [between 1836 and 1847.]
The red book. 1836.
Susan's first money. [between 1836 and 1847.]
The useful dog. [between 1836 and 1847.]
The monk of Cimiés. [1837], Ipswich [1855].
The parson's case of jewels. Berwick 1837.
The Bible. Wellington 1838.
The happy family. Wellington 1838.
The little negroes. Wellington 1838, 1846 (3rd edn).
The little woodman and his dog. 1838 (illus), [1860?], 1870.
Sea-side stories. [1838?]
Scenes from real life. [1838?] (contains The old lady's complaint, The mail coach, Economy, The Swiss cottage).
The little girl's keepsake. [184–?]
The druids of Britain. [1840?]
The happy family. [1840], 1870.
Duty is safety: or troublesome Tom. 1841 (in Holiday Keepsake), Philadelphia and New York 1847, London 1864 and 1877.
The Holiday Keepsake. 1841.
The Juvenile Forget-Me-Not. [1841.]
The history of John Marten, a sequel to the life of Henry Milner. 1844.
Joys and sorrows of childhood. [1844?]
Shanty the blacksmith: a tale of other times. [1844.]
Sunday entertainment. A collection of little pieces calculated to teach important truths to the reader. [1844–5.]
Caroline Mourdaunt: or the governess. 1845.
The De Cliffords: an historical tale. 1847 (by Mrs Sherwood, or rather by Sophia Streeten, afterwards Kelly, assisted by Mrs Sherwood).
The fairy knoll. 1848.
The golden garland of inestimable delights. 1849. With Sophia Kelly.
The story book of wonders. 1849.
Victorine Durocher. 1850. With Sophia Kelly. (Pbd with The young lord by C. Crosland.)
The mirror of maidens in the days of Queen Bess. 1851.
The two knights, or Delancy Castle: a tale of the Civil Wars. [1851.]
Boys will be boys: or the difficulties of a schoolboy's life. A schoolboy's mission. By Mrs Sherwood and her daughter Mrs Kelly. 1854, Halifax 1860.
Duty is safety: or troublesome Tom. [between 1859 and 1862.] (Extracted from the Holiday Keepsake. Also contains The white pigeon).

The cottage in the wood. 1860 (in Narrative tracts, moral and religious 2nd ser).
Grand Aunt's pictures and other tales. 1860 (tales are signed by Sophia Kelly).
John and James, and other tales. [186?]. With Sophia Kelly.
Duty is safety: or troublesome Tom. 1864 (5th edn), 1877.
The heron's plume. 1870.

Contributions to periodicals and collaborative works

In 1877 the Book Soc pbd the following from Holiday Keepsake, Juvenile Forget-me-not *and other annuals:* Duty is safety, The fall of pride, Frank Beauchamp: or the sailor's family, Grandmamma Parker, Jack the sailor boy, The lost trunk and the good nurse, Martin and the rose and nightingale, Think before you act, The traveller, Uncle Manners, The white pigeon. *Many of Mrs Sherwood's stories appeared in the* Youth's Mag *and a number were reissued in the* Children's Friend.

Mrs Sherwood wrote over a hundred tracts between 1818 and 1831, many of which are listed in Cutt (see Bibliography, above). She also wrote educational books.

Lamentations of old hospitality. In Marshall's Christmas Box 1831.
What is the world? In Fifty two stories of pluck, peril and romance for girls, ed H. A. Miles, 1896.
Little Robert and the owl. In Old fashioned tales, ed E. V. Lucas, 1905.

§2

The life of Mrs Sherwood, chiefly autobiographical, with extracts from Mr Sherwood's journal during his imprisonment in France and residence in India. Ed S. Kelly 1854, ed I. Gilchrist 1907 (abridged); ed F. H. J. Darton 1910 (enlarged). [DD]

Eleanor Sleath

Bibliographies

Summers, M. In his A Gothic bibliography, [1941].

§1

The orphan of the Rhine: a romance. 4 vols 1798, 2 vols Dublin 1802; ed D. P. Varma 1968.
Who's the murderer? or the mystery of the forest: a novel. 4 vols 1802; tr Fr 1819.
The Bristol heiress: or the errors of education. 5 vols 1809.
The nocturnal minstrel, or the spirit of the wood: a romance. 2 vols 1810; ed D. P. Varma, New York 1972 (facs).
Pyrenean banditti: a romance. 3 vols 1811.
Glenoven; or, The fairy palace. 1815. Only listed in Summers.
For a listing of reviews and notices of Sleath's works, see Ward (1972). [PG]

Horatio (Horace) Smith 1779–1849

Mss of letters to and from Leigh Hunt and to C. Redding are held in the Univ of Iowa Lib.

Bibliographies

Sadleir, M. In his XIX century fiction: a bibliographical record, 2 vols 1951.
Summers, M. In his A Gothic bibliography, [1941].
Wolff, R. L. In his Nineteenth-century fiction: a bibliographical catalogue, 5 vols 1981–6.

Collections

Poetical works. 2 vols 1846, 1 vol 1851, New York 1857.
Poetical works of Horace and James Smith. Ed E. Sargent, New York 1857, Boston 1858, 1859.
Poems. 1889.

§1

A family story. 3 vols 1800.
The runaway: or the seat of benevolence: a novel. 4 vols 1800.
Trevanion: or matrimonial errors: a novel. 4 vols 1801, Dublin 1801.
Horatio: or sketches of the Davenport family: a novel. 4 vols Richmond 1807.
Rejected addresses: or new theatrum poetarium. 1812, 1812 (2nd edn), 1812 (7th edn), 1812 (8th edn), 1817 (16th edn), 1833 (18th edn), New York 1871, London 1929, New York and London 1977 (introd by D. H. Reiman). By Horace and James Smith.
Horace in London: consisting of imitations of the first two books of the Odes of Horace. 1813, 1813, 1815 (4th edn). By Horace and James Smith.
First impressions, or trade in the West: a comedy in five acts. 1813, 1813, 1816.
Amarynthus the nympholept: a pastoral drama in three acts, with other poems. 1821, New York and London 1977 (1st edn rptd, introd by D. H. Reiman).
Gaieties and gravities: a series of essays, comic tales and fugitive vagaries. 3 vols 1825, 2 vols Philadelphia and New York 1825, 3 vols London 1826, 1826, New York 1852. Mainly rptd from the London Mag and NMM.
Brambletye House: or cavaliers and roundheads. 3 vols 1826, 1826, 1826, Boston 1826, Paris 1826, 1829, London 1833, 2 vols [1835], 1836, 1 vol New York 1837, 2 vols London 1837, 1839, etc; tr Fr 1826, Ger 1827.
The Tor Hill. 3 vols 1826, 2 vols Philadelphia 1826, 3 vols London 1827, Paris 1827, London 1835, 1 vol New York 1836, 1837, Hartford CT 1846; tr Fr 1827, Ger 1827.
Reuben Apsley: a novel. 3 vols 1827, 1827, 2 vols Philadelphia 1827, 3 vols London 1834, 1838; tr Fr 1827, Ger 1827.
Zillah: a tale of the Holy City. 4 vols 1828, 3 vols 1828, 2 vols New York 1829, 1 vol London 1839; tr Fr 1829.
The New Forest: a novel. 3 vols 1829, 2 vols New York 1829, 3 vols London 1830, 1 vol [18–?]; tr Ger 1830, Fr 1831.
The midsummer medley for 1830: a series of comic tales, sketches and fugitive vagaries, in prose and verse. 2 vols 1830, 1832.
Walter Colyton: a tale of 1688. 3 vols 1830, 1830, 2 vols New York 1830, 1 vol London [1857]; tr Fr 1836.
Festivals, games and amusements, ancient and modern. 1831, New York (with addns by S. Woodworth) 1831, 1832, 1833, 1836, 1839, 1841, 1842, 1844, 1862, 1868.
Tales of the early ages. 3 vols 1832, 2 vols New York 1832.
Gale Middleton: a story of the present day. 3 vols 1833, 2 vols Philadelphia 1834.
The involuntary prophet: a tale of the early ages. 1835. Part of an anthology also including W. Irving, Tales of the Alhambra, and F. R. de Chateaubriand, Last of the Abencerages.
The tin trumpet: or heads and tales, for the wise and waggish, to which are added poetical selections by the late Paul Chatfield MD [pseud], edited by Jefferson Saunders esq [pseud]. 2 vols 1836 (anon), Philadelphia 1836, 1 vol New York 1859, London 1869, New York 1869, London 1870, 1875, 1890 (signed).
A vision: on removal of Dr Mantell's collection from Brighton to the British Museum. 1838.
Jane Lomax: or a mother's crime. 3 vols 1838, 2 vols Philadelphia 1838, 3 vols London [1856], [1858], 1 vol [1877], [18–?].
The moneyed man: or the lesson of a life. 3 vols 1841, 2 vols Philadelphia 1841, 3 vols London 1843, 1 vol [1860].
Adam Brown: the merchant. 3 vols 1843, 1 vol New York 1843, 1857, 1865, London [18–?], nd. Issued serially in US in 1843.
Arthur Arundel: a tale of the English revolution. 3 vols 1844, 1 vol [1858], New York [186–?].
Love and mesmerism. 3 vols 1845, 1 vol New York 1846, 1863, 1867.
Esther: a tale of the sixth century. In Count Ludwig and other romances, ed Charles Dickens, New York 1845.
For Horace and James Smith's parodies, see col 455. Horace edited his brother's Memoirs, letters and comic miscellanies in prose and verse, *2 vols 1840, 1841; as well as H. W. Herbert,* Oliver Cromwell: an historical romance, *3 vols 1840, and D. MacCarthy,* Massaniello: an historical

romance, *3 vols 1842. It is not certain whether either one or both brothers wrote* Highgate tunnel, or the secret arch: an operatic tragedy in two acts, *1812. James and Horace contributed to the short-lived periodical,* The Pic Nic *(ed W. Combe),* Monthly Mirror, NMM *1821–49 and* London Mag. *Horace wrote prefaces for plays in* Bell's British Theatre *ser, as well as lyrics for comic musicals.*

§2

Sargent, E. Memoir of Horace Smith. Prefixed to Rejected addresses, New York 1871.
Beavan, A. H. James and Horace Smith. 1899.
Parker, W. M. The stockbroker author. Quart Rev 290 1952. [AM]

George Soane 1790–1860

See col 1985.

Elizabeth Isabella Spence 1768–1832

Bibliographies

Summers, M. In his A Gothic bibliography, [1941].

§1

Helen Sinclair: a novel, by a lady. 2 vols 1799.
The nobility of the heart: a novel. 3 vols 1805.
The wedding day: a novel. 3 vols 1807.
Summer excursions through parts of Oxfordshire, Gloucestershire, Warwickshire, Staffordshire, Herefordshire, Derbyshire, and South Wales. 2 vols 1809, 1809.
Sketches of the present manners, customs and scenery of Scotland. 2 vols 1811, 1811.
The curate and his daughter: a Cornish tale. 3 vols 1813.
The Spanish guitar: a tale for the use of young persons. 1815, Boston [18–?].
Letters from the North Highlands during the summer 1816. 1817.
A traveller's tale of the last century. 3 vols 1819.
Old stories. 2 vols 1822.
How to be rid of a wife, and the lily of Annandale: tales. 2 vols 1823.
Dame Rebecca Berry: or court scenes in the reign of Charles the Second. 3 vols 1827.

Attributed works

Memoirs of the Danby family: designed chiefly for the entertainment and improvement of young persons. 1799. Attributed to Spence by Block, though ESTC gives no author.
For a listing of reviews and notices of Spence's works, see Ward (1972, 1977). [PG]

Louisa Sidney Stanhope

Bibliographies

Blakey, D. In her Minerva Press, 1939.
Summers, M. In his A Gothic bibliography, [1941].

§1

Montbrasil Abbey, or maternal trials: a tale. 2 vols 1806. Anon.
The bandit's bride, or the maid of Saxony: a romance. 4 vols 1807, 1818, 3 vols Philadelphia 1820, Exeter NH 1825, 4 vol London 1827 (3rd edn), 3 vols Exeter NH 1829, 1832, 2 vols 1837, 3 vols Philadelphia 1859; tr Fr 1809.
Striking likenesses, or the votaries of fashion: a novel. 4 vols 1808.
The age we live in: a novel. 3 vols 1809.
Di Montranzo, or the novice of Corpus Domini: a romance. 4 vols 1810.
The confessional of Valombre: a romance. 4 vols 1812.
Madelina: a tale founded on facts. 4 vols 1814.
Treachery, or the grave of Antoinette: a romance interspersed with poetry. 4 vols 1815.
The nun of Santa Maria di Tindaro: a tale. 3 vols 1818.
The Crusaders: an historical romance of the twelfth century. 5 vols 1820.
The festival of Mora: an historical romance. 4 vols 1821, 1824.
The siege of Kenilworth: an historical romance. 4 vols 1824.
Runnemede: an ancient legend. 3 vols 1825.
The seer of Tiviotdale: a romance. 4 vols 1827.
The Corsair's bride: a legend of the sixteenth century. 3 vols 1830.
Sydney Beresford: a tale of the day. 3 vols 1835.
Rosaline, or the outlaw's bride: a romance. 1842 (in pts).
For a listing of reviews and notices of Stanhope's work, see Ward (1972, 1977). [CC]

'Rosalia St Clair'

Bibliography

Summers, M. In his A Gothic bibliography, [1941].

§1

The son of O'Donnel: a novel. 3 vols 1819.
The Highland Castle and the Lowland Cottage: a novel. 4 vols 1820.
Clavering Tower: a novel. 4 vols 1822.
The banker's daughters of Bristol, or compliance and decision: a novel. 3 vols 1824.
The first and last years of wedded life: a novel. 4 vols '1827' [1826].
Fashionables and unfashionables: a novel. 3 vols 1827.
Ulrica of Saxony: a romantic tale of the fifteenth century. 3 vols 1828.
Eleanor Ogilvie the maid of the Tweed: a romantic legend. 3 vols 1829.
The sailor boy, or the admiral and his protegée: a novel. 4 vols 1830.
The soldier boy, or the last of the Lyals: a novel. 3 vols 1831.
The doomed one, or they met at Glenylon: a tale of the Highlands. 3 vols 1832.
The pauper boy, or the ups and downs of life: a novel. 3 vols 1834.

Attributed works

Marston: a novel, by a lady. 3 vols 1835. The work of another author.
St Clair also translated anonymously The blind beggar, or the fountain of St Catherine: a novel, *4 vols 1817, from the Fr of F. G. Ducray-Duminil.* [PG]

Catherine, Lady Stepney, née Pollok, first married name Manners d. 1845

§1

Castle Nuovier: or Henry and Adelina. 2 vols 1806.
The Lords of Erith: a romance. 3 vols 1809.
The new road to ruin: a novel. 3 vols 1833.
The heir presumptive. 3 vols 1835.
The courtier's daughter. 3 vols 1838, 1841.
The three peers. 3 vols 1841.
Memoirs of Lady Russell and Lady Herbert, 1623–1723, compiled from original family documents by Lady Stepney. 1898.
For a brief biography of Lady Stepney and a portrait, see Colburn's NMM 51 *1837. For obituary, see* GM 24 *1845.* [EH]

Agnes Strickland 1796–1874

See col 2199.

Thomas Skinner Surr 1770–1847

Consequences, or adventures of Rraxall castle: a novel. 'By a gentleman'. 2 vols 1796, Dublin 1812 (as Modern adventures in fashionable life: or the Pryer family).
Christ's Hospital: a poem. 1797.
George Barnwell: a novel. 3 vols 1798, 2 vols Dublin 1798, Dublin

1799, Boston 1800, Philadelphia [1800], 3 vols London 1807 (as Barnwell: a novel), 1834 (6th edn), 1 vol [1857]; tr Fr [1799?].
Splendid misery: a novel. 3 vols 1801, 1802, 2 vols Dublin 1802, 3 vols London 1807, 1814; tr Ger 1802, Fr 1807.
A winter in London, or sketches of fashion: a novel. 3 vols 1806 (8 edns), 2 vols Baltimore 1808, 3 vols London 1824 (13th edn); tr Fr 1810.
The magic of wealth: a novel. 3 vols 1815, 2 vols Philadelphia 1815.
Richmond: or scenes in the life of a Bow Street Officer drawn up from his private memoranda. 3 vols 1827 (anon), 2 vols New York 1827; with introd by E. F. Bleiler, New York 1976. Also attributed to T. Gaspey.
Russell: or reign of fashion. 3 vols 1830.
Surr pbd several pams on banking.

Attributed and spurious works
The mask of fashion: a plain tale. 2 vols 1807. Attributed to Surr by Block and Bodleian, but other contemporary titles list this as the work of Charles Sedley.
For a listing of reviews and notices of Surr's works, see Ward (1979, 1972).

§2
Jones, A. H. Ideas and innovations: best sellers of Jane Austen's age. New York 1986, ch 6. [PG]

Elizabeth Thomas, née Dobson, 'Bridget Bluemantle', 'Martha Homely' b. 1771

Bibliography
Summers, M. In his A Gothic bibliography, [1941].

§1
Maids as they are not, and wives as they are: a novel by Mrs Martha Homely. 4 vols 1803. Not usually attributed to Thomas, but see next item.
The three old maids of the house of Penruddock: a novel by Mrs Bridget Bluemantle. 3 vols 1806. Introduction signed Martha Homely.
The husband and wife, or the matrimonial martyr: a novel. 3 vols 1808.
Monte video, or the officer's wife and her sister: a novel. 4 vols 1809, 2 vols Philadelphia 1816.
Mortimer Hall, or the labourer's hire: a novel. 4 vols 1811.
The vindictive spirit: a novel. 4 vols 1812.
The prison-house, or the world we lived in: a novel. 4 vols 1814.
The Baron of Falconberg: or Childe Harolde in prose. 3 vols 1815.
Purity of heart, or the ancient costume: a tale addressed to the author of Glenarvon by an old wife of twenty years. 1816, 1817.
Claudine, or pertinacity: a novel. 3 vols 1817.
The confession: or the novice of St Clare and other poems. 1818.
Serious poems: comprising The churchyard, Village sabbath, Deluge etc. 1831.
The convert: a tale of real life. 1840. Verse fiction.
The Georgian: or the Moor of Tripoli, and other poems. 1847.

Attributed or spurious works
Always happy: or anecdotes of Felix and his sister. 1813. Attributed by Summers to Thomas (under the pseudonym Mrs Bridget Bluemantle), but no copy discovered.
Woman, or minor maxims: a sketch. 1818, 1824 (as Helena Egerton: or traits of female character). Probably written by Maria Elizabeth Budden, though often attributed to Thomas as a result of both writers having pbd works titled Claudine.
For a listing of reviews and notices of Thomas's works, see Ward (1972). [PG]

Edward John Trelawny 1792–1881

See col 2203.

Frances Trollope, née Milton 1780–1863

Ms collections in Morris L. Parrish and Robert H. Taylor Collections, Princeton; Trollope Family Papers, UCLA; Anthony Trollope Collection, Univ of Illinois Lib, Urbana (includes early mss); John Murray archives, London.

Bibliographies
Sadleir, M. Trollope: a commentary. 1927. Appendix contains a calendar of events in the life of Frances Trollope and a bibliography.
Sadleir, M. In his XIX century fiction: a bibliographical record, 2 vols 1951.
Todd, J. (ed). Dictionary of British women writers. 1989.

§1
Domestic manners of the Americans. Illustr A. Hervieu 2 vols 1832 (4 edns), 1 vol New York 1832, Paris 1832 (in Eng) (Baudry's Foreign Lib), London 1839 (5th edn), New York 1894, 1894 (new edn), 1901, 1904, 1927 (ed M. Sadleir), 1949 (ed D. Smalley, illustr Hervieu), 1960, Barre MA 1969, Ann Arbor MI 1973 (micro), London 1974 (Folio Soc), Oxford 1984 (WCp); tr Du Te Haarlem 1833, Fr Paris 1833, 1841, 1848, Ger Kiel 1835, Sp Paris 1835.
REVIEWS: Athenaeum 230, 231 1832; [Hamilton. T.] Blackwood's Mag 31 1832; Edinburgh Rev 55 1832; GM 102 1832; Literary Gazette 24 Mar, 28 Apr 1832; Monthly Rev 127 1832; NMM 34, 35, 36 1832; Fraser's Mag 5 1832; North Amer Rev 36 1833; [Lockhart, J. G.] Quart Rev 47 1832; Tait's Edinburgh Mag 1 1832.
The refugee in America: a novel. 3 vols 1832, 2 vols New York 1833.
REVIEWS: Athenaeum 254, 257 1832; GM 102 1832; Literary Gazette 8 Sep, 20 Oct 1832; Monthly Rev 130 1833; Quart Rev 48 1833; Westminster Rev 18 1833.
The Abbess: a romance. 3 vols 1833, New York 1833, 2 vols 1833, London 1836, Philadelphia 1852 as The Abbess; or, the convent of St Catherine; a romance.
REVIEW: Spectator 6 1833.
The mother's manual, or illustrations of matrimonial economy: an essay in verse. 1833. Anon.
REVIEWS: Monthly Rev 131 1833; Spectator 6 1833.
Belgium and Western Germany in 1833. 2 vols 1834, Paris 1834 (Baudry's European Lib), Philadelphia 1834, London 1835 (2nd edn).
REVIEWS: Athenaeum 351, 356 1834; Metropolitan Mag 11 1834; Monthly Rev 134 1834; NMM 41 1834; Quart Rev 52 1834; Spectator 7 1834; Tait's Edinburgh Mag 1 1834; Westminster Rev 22 1835.
Tremordyn Cliff. 3 vols 1835.
REVIEWS: Athenaeum 411 1835; Spectator 8 1835.
Paris and the Parisians in 1835. 2 vols 1836, 1836 (2nd edn), 1 vol New York 1836, Paris 1836 (in Eng) (Baudry's European Lib); tr Ger Aachen 1836, Fr Paris 1911.
REVIEWS: Athenaeum 427, 428 1836; Fraser's Mag 13 1836; Literary Gazette 2, 9, 30 Jan 1836; Monthly Rev 139 1836; NMM 46 1836; Spectator 9 1836; Tait's Edinburgh Mag 3 1836; The Times 30 Jan 1836.
The life and adventures of Jonathan Jefferson Whitlaw: or scenes on the Mississippi. Illustr A. Hervieu 3 vols 1836, 1836 (2nd edn), Paris 1836 (in Eng) (Baudry's European Lib), 1836 (in Eng), London [1857] as Lynch law; or the life and adventures of Jonathan Jefferson Whitlaw.
REVIEWS: Athenaeum 453 1836; Literary Gazette 2 July 1836; Metropolitan Mag 16 1836; Spectator 9 1836; Mag of Domestic Economy 2 1837.
The vicar of Wrexhill. Illustr A. Hervieu 3 vols 1837, 1838 (2nd edn), 1 vol 1840 (Standard Novels), 1849, 1856, [1860] (Parlour Lib), New York 1975.
REVIEWS: Athenaeum 517 1837; Monthly Rev 144 1837; Spectator 10 1837; The Times 25 Oct 1837; [Thackeray, W. M.] Fraser's Mag 17 1838 (rptd in Famous reviews, ed R. B. Johnson, 1914);

Westminster Rev 28 1838; Dublin Rev 7 1839; Blackwood's Edinburgh Mag 64 1848.

Vienna and the Austrians, with some account of a journey through Swabia, Bavaria, the Tyrol, and the Salzbourg. Illustr A. Hervieu 2 vols 1838, 2 vols Paris 1838 (in Eng); tr Ger Leipzig 1838, Stuttgart 1966 as Briefe aus der Kaiserstadt, Fr Paris 1858.
REVIEWS: Athenaeum 538, 539 1838; Blackwood's Mag 43 1838; Monthly Rev 145 1838; Spectator 11 1838; The Times 14 Apr 1838; Quart Rev 65 1839–40.

A romance of Vienna. 3 vols 1838, 2 vols Philadelphia 1838.
REVIEWS: Athenaeum 566 1838; Monthly Rev 147 1838; Spectator 11 1838; The Times 4 Sep 1838.

The widow Barnaby. 3 vols 1839, 1 vol 1840 (Standard Novels), Paris 1840 (in Eng), London 1854, 1856, 1857, [1860] (Parlour Lib), 1881 (Notable Novels), New York 1885; tr Fr 1877.
REVIEWS: Athenaeum 584 1839; Monthly Rev 148 1839; Spectator 12 1839; Tait's Edinburgh Mag 6 1839; The Times 24 Jan 1839.

The life and adventures of Michael Armstrong, the factory boy. First pbd in 12 monthly nos 1839–40, 3 vols 1840, 2 vols New York 1840, Paris 1840 (in Eng) (Baudry's European Lib), 1876, 1888, 1968.
REVIEWS: Athenaeum 615 1839; NMM 55, 57 1839.

One fault: a novel. 3 vols 1840, Paris 1840 (in Eng), 1 vol London 1858, 1860.
REVIEWS: Athenaeum 631 1839; Literary Gazette no 1193 1839; Spectator 12 1839.

The widow married: a sequel to The widow Barnaby. Serialised in NMM May 1839–June 1840, illustr R. W. Buss 3 vols 1840, Paris 1840 (in Eng), [c. 1856], 1857.
REVIEW: Athenaeum 649 1840.

Charles Chesterfield: or the adventures of a youth of genius. Serialised in NMM July 1840–Nov 1841, illustr Phiz 3 vols 1841, 1846, [1858].
REVIEWS: Athenaeum 726 1841; Literary Gazette 25 Sep 1841; Tait's Edinburgh Mag 8 1841; The Times 8 Oct 1841.

The blue belles of England. Serialised in Metropolitan Mag Jan 1841–Jan 1842, 3 vols 1842, Paris 1842 (in Eng).
REVIEWS: Literary Gazette 18 Dec 1841; Athenaeum 738 1842; Monthly Rev 157 1842; Spectator 15 1842.

The ward of Thorpe-Combe. 3 vols 1842, 1 vol Paris 1842 (in Eng) (Baudry's European Lib), London 1857 as The ward; tr Fr Paris 1858.
REVIEWS: Athenaeum 754 1842; GM 18 1842; Literary Gazette 2 Apr 1842.

A visit to Italy. 2 vols 1842, 2 vols in 1 [185–?] as Italy and the Italians.
REVIEWS: Athenaeum 781, 782 1842; Literary Gazette 1 Oct 1842; Monthly Rev 159 1842; Spectator 15 1842; Tait's Edinburgh Mag 9 1842; Dublin Rev 14 1843; Mag of Domestic Economy n.s. 1 1843.

The Barnabys in America: or adventures of the widow wedded. Serialised in NMM Apr 1842–Sep 1843, illustr J. Leech 3 vols 1843, Paris 1843 (in Eng) (Baudry's European Lib), illustr J. Leech 3 vols London c. 1843 as The widow wedded; or, adventures of the Barnabys in America, c. 1857 as Adventures of the Barnabys in America, [1859] as Adventures of the Barnabys in America, a sequel to The widow Barnaby, illustr J. Leech 1859 as The widow wedded; or, adventures of the Barnabys in America.
REVIEW: Monthly Rev 162 1843.

Hargrave: or the adventures of a man of fashion. 3 vols 1843, 1843 (2nd edn).
REVIEWS: Athenaeum 806 1843; GM 20 1843; Literary Gazette 25 Mar 1843; NMM 67 1843.

Jessie Phillips: a tale of the present day. First pbd in 11 monthly pts 1842–3 as Jessie Phillips: a tale of the new poor law, illustr J. Leech 3 vols 1843, 1844.
REVIEWS: Ainsworth's Mag 4 1843; Athenaeum 835 1843; Mag of Domestic Economy n.s. 1 1843; NMM 67, 69 1843; Spectator 16 1843; Tait's Edinburgh Mag 10 1843.

The Laurringtons: or superior people. 3 vols 1844, 1846.
REVIEWS: Athenaeum 842 1843; Literary Gazette 9 Dec 1843; Spectator 16 1843; Tait's Edinburgh Mag 11 1844.

Young love; a novel. 3 vols 1844.
REVIEWS: Athenaeum 889 1844; Literary Gazette 26 Oct 1844; NMM 72 1844; Mirror n.s. 7 1845.

The Robertses on their travels. Serialised in NMM from May 1844–Jan 1846, 3 vols 1846.
REVIEW: GM 26 1846.

The attractive man: a novel. 3 vols 1846, 1864.
REVIEWS: Literary Gazette 25 Oct 1845; NMM 75 1845; Tait's Edinburgh Mag 12 1845.

Travels and travellers: a series of sketches. 2 vols 1846, 1 vol Paris 1846 (in Eng).
REVIEW: NMM 78 1846.

Father Eustace: a tale of the Jesuits. 3 vols 1847, nd (2nd edn), New York 1975.
REVIEWS: Literary Gazette 19 Dec 1846; NMM 79 1847.

The three cousins: a novel. 3 vols 1847, [1858].

Town and country: a novel. 3 vols 1848, 1 vol [1857] as The days of the Regency (George the Fourth); or town and country.
REVIEW: NMM 81 1847.

The young countess: or love and jealousy. 3 vols 1848, 1 vol [1859?] as Love and jealousy.
REVIEWS: Literary Gazette 11 Nov 1848; NMM 84 1848; Illus London News 14 1849.

The lottery of marriage: a novel. 3 vols 1849, 1 vol [c. 1860].
REVIEWS: Bentley's Misc 26 1849; Literary Gazette 12 May 1849; NMM 86 1849.

The old world and the new: a novel. 3 vols 1849.
REVIEWS: Bentley's Misc 26 1849; Literary Gazette 13 Nov 1849; NMM 87 1849.

Petticoat government: a novel. 3 vols 1850, 3 vols Paris 1850, 1 vol New York 1850, 1 vol London 1857, 3 vols 1858, New York 1873.

Mrs Mathews, or family mysteries: a novel. 3 vols 1851, 1 vol 1864.
REVIEWS: Literary Gazette 4 Oct 1851; NMM 93 1851.

Second love, or beauty and intellect: a novel. 3 vols 1851, c. 1861, 1875 (Blackwood's London Lib).

Uncle Walter: a novel. 3 vols 1852.
REVIEWS: Athenaeum 1305 1852; Bentley's Misc 32 1852; Illus London News 30 Oct 1852; Literary Gazette 11 Dec 1852; Spectator 25 1852.

The young heiress: a novel. 3 vols 1853, 1864, c. 1873 (4th edn).

The life and adventures of a clever woman, illustrated with occasional extracts from her diary. 3 vols 1854, 1864 (2nd edn).
REVIEWS: Literary Gazette 12 Aug 1854; Westminster Rev 62 1854.

Gertrude: or family pride. 3 vols 1855, 1864, 1 vol 1879 (Select Lib).
REVIEWS: Literary Gazette 8 Sep 1855; Saturday Rev 1 1855.

Fashionable life: or Paris and London. 3 vols 1856.
REVIEW: Literary Gazette 23 Aug 1856.

Contributions to periodicals

For Frances Trollope's periodical contributions, primarily to NMM *and* Bentley's Misc, *see Wellesley vol 5 1989.*

Editions

Trollope, T. A. A summer in Brittany. 2 vols 1840. Ed F. Trollope.
REVIEWS: Athenaeum 30 May, 6 June 1840; NMM 59 1840; The Times 30 Oct 1840; Quart Rev 68 1841.

Trollope, T. A. A summer in Western France. 2 vols 1841. Ed F. Trollope.
REVIEWS: Athenaeum 3, 17 July 1841; Monthly Rev 155 1841; Spectator 14 1841.

§2

Horne, R. H. A new spirit of the age. Vol 1 1844.

Trollope, T. A. What I remember. 3 vols 1887–9.

Trollope, F. E. Frances Trollope: her life and literary work from George III to Victoria. 2 vols 1895.
Pope-Hennessy, U. Three English women in America. 1929. On F. Trollope, F. Kemble, H. Martineau.
Bigland, E. The indomitable Mrs Trollope. 1953.
Johnston, J. The life, manners and travels of Fanny Trollope. 1978.
Heineman, H. Mrs Trollope: the triumphant feminine in the nineteenth century. 1979.
Ransom, T. Frances Trollope. 1995. [JJ]

George Walker 1772–1847

Bibliographies

Summers, M. In his A Gothic bibliography, [1941].

§1

The romance of the cavern: or the history of Fitz-Henry and James. 2 vols 1792. Anon.
The haunted castle: a Norman romance. 2 vols 1794. Anon.
The house of Tynian: a novel. 4 vols 1795, 2 vols Dublin 1796.
Theodore Cyphon, or the benevolent Jew: a novel. 3 vols 1796, 2 vols Dublin 1796, Philadelphia 1796, Alexandria VA 1803, 3 vols London 1823, 1 vol 1847; tr Ger 1797–9, Fr 1800.
Cinthelia: or a woman of ten thousand. 4 vols 1797; tr Fr [1798–9?].
The vagabond: a novel. 2 vols 1799, 1799, 1799, 1 vol Dublin 1800, Boston 1800 and Harrisonburg VA 1814 (as The vagabond: or practical infidelity); tr Fr 1807.
The three Spaniards: a romance. 3 vols 1800, 2 vols Dublin 1800, 1802, New York [1800?], 1801, 1817, 3 vols London 1821, New York 1829–30, 1831, Exeter NH 1832, Baltimore 1833, New York 1833, Baltimore 1834, Exeter NH 1836, 1839, 1842, Philadelphia 1851, 1 vol New York [1882]; tr Fr 1805, 1823.
Poems on various subjects. 1801, Philadelphia 1804.
Don Raphael: a romance. 3 vols 1803, 2 vols New York 1803.
Two girls of eighteen, by an old man. 2 vols 1806.
The adventures of Timothy Thoughtless: or the misfortunes of a little boy who ran away from boarding-school. 1813.
The travels of Sylvester Tramper through the interior of the south of Africa. 1813 (anon), 1813, 1816, 1817.
The battle of Waterloo: a poem. 1815.

Attributed or spurious works

Perseverance, or the third time best: a musical entertainment in two acts, by the author of the Busybody, a periodical work, Haunted castle. Dublin 1793. ESTC attributes to Walker, on the basis of other works cited on title page.
The midnight bell. 3 vols 1824. Attributed to Walker in NCBEL, but probably a confusion with the work of the same title by F. Lathom *(see col 944)*.

For a listing of reviews and notices of Walker's works, see Ward (1972, 1979). [PG]

Catherine George Ward, afterwards Mason b. 1787

Bibliographies

Summers, M. In his A Gothic bibliography, [1941].
Jackson, J. R. de J. In his Romantic poetry by women: a bibliography, 1770–1835, Oxford 1993.

§1

Poems. Edinburgh 1805, Coventry 1812.
The daughter of St Omar: a novel. 2 vols 1810.
My native land, or the test of heroism: a novel. 1813.
Tales of the glen. 1813. Poems.
The bachelor's heiress, or a tale without wonder! A novel. 3 vols 1814.
The son and the nephew, or more secrets than one: a novel. 3 vols 1814.
The Dandy family: or the pleasures of a ball night. [1815.] Verse.
Cottage stories: or tales of my grandmother. 1817, 1825.
A tributary poem on the death of the Princess Charlotte of Saxe-Coburg. [1817.]
Robertina, or the sacred deposit: a novel. 2 vols 1818.
Maid, wife and mother, or woman! A poem. 1819.
The thorn, or doubtful property. 1819, 1825, 1830.
Miscellaneous poems. 1820.
The mysterious marriage: or the will of my father. [1820], 1822, 1824, 4 vols 1824, 1 vol New York 1834, London [1857], [1860?], Wakefield [1873?] (as Rosa Clarendale and her unexpected marriage with the object of her devoted attention: or loveliness and virtue rewarded, pride and malignity defeated).
The rose of Claremont: or daughter, wife and mother. 2 vols [1820], [1821?], 1823.
The orphan boy: or test of innocence. 1821, 1822, New York 1835, London 1846.
Family portraits: or descendants of Trelawney. 1822, 1824, New York 1834.
The cottage on the cliff: a sea-side story. 1823, New York 1834, London [c. 1869], New York [1876].
The widow's choice: or one, two, three. 1823, 1824.
The first child: or the heiress of Monteith. 1824.
The mysteries of St Clair: or Mariette Mouline. 1824, Wakefield [1873?].
The fisher's daughter: or the wanderings of Wolf and the fortunes of Alfred, being the sequel to that so greatly admired and popular work entitled The cottage on the cliff. 1824, 1825, 1827, New York 1835, London 1836.
The forest girl, or the mountain hut: an original and interesting domestic tale. 1826, [1850?].
The knight of the white banner: or the secrets of the castle. 1827.
Adelaide and her children: a tale. [1828]; tr Fr 1834.
The eve of St Agnes: a novel. 4 vols 1831.
Alice Gray: a domestic novel. 3 vols 1833.

Many of Ward's works in her middle and later years were first pbd in pts, and then re-issued in collected form with a fresh title page. [PG]

Robert Ward, afterwards Plumer Ward (Member of Parliament) 1765–1846

§1

An enquiry into the foundation and history of the law of nations in Europe from the time of the Greeks and Romans to the age of Grotius. 2 vols 1795, Dublin 1795, London 1865.
A treatise of the relative rights and duties of belligerents and neutral powers in maritime affairs, in which the principles of the armed neutralities and the opinions of Hübner and Schlegel are fully discussed. 1801, 1875.
An essay on contraband: being a continuation of the treatise of the relative rights and duties of belligerent and neutral nations, in maritime affairs. 1801.
A view of the relative situations of Mr Pitt and Mr Addington previous to and on the night of Mr Patten's motion. 1804, 1804, 1804.
An enquiry into the manner in which the different wars of Europe have commenced during the last two centuries. 1804, 1805.
Tremaine: or the man of refinement. 3 vols 1825 (anon), 1825, 1825, Philadelphia 1825, London 1827, 1833, 1835 etc; tr Fr 1830.
REVIEW: Quart Rev 33 1826.
De Vere: or the man of independence. 4 vols 1827, 1827, 3 vols 1827, Philadelphia 1827, 2 vols New York 1831, 3 vols London 1831, 1833.
REVIEW: Quart Rev 36 1827.
Illustrations of human life. 3 vols 1837, Philadelphia 1837, 1 vol Paris 1837, 3 vols London 1838, Philadelphia 1838, London 1843.
Contains Atticus, St Lawrence, Fielding or society.
An historical essay on the real character and amount of the precedent of the Revolution of 1688, in which the opinions of

Mackintosh, Price, Hallam and Locke are initially considered. 2 vols 1838.

The reviewer reviewed. 1838 (anon), 1839. An answer to a review of An historical essay, *above*, in Edinburgh Rev, addressed to the editor of the Quart Rev.

Pictures of the world at home and abroad. 3 vols 1839, 1843. Contains Sterling, Penruddock, The enthusiasts. Sterling and Penruddock issued in 2 vols Philadelphia 1839.

De Clifford: or the constant man. 4 vols 1841, 3 vols Philadelphia 1841, 2 vols Paris 1841, 4 vols London 1846, 1858.

Ward also edited P. G. Patmore, Chatsworth: or the romance of a week, *3 vols 1844; and J. Hunter,* A true account of the alienation and recovery of the estates of the Offleys of Norton in 1754: with remarks on this version of the story *[by Ward], 1841.*

§2

Phipps, E. Memoirs of the political and literary life of Ward, with selections from his correspondence, diaries and unpublished literary remains. 2 vols 1850.

Robert Plumer Ward. Bentley's Misc Sep 1850.

Patmore, P. G. My friends and acquaintances. 3 vols 1855. Contains a number of Ward's letters.

Rosa, M. W. The silver fork school: novels of fashion preceding Vanity Fair. New York 1936. [AM]

Jane West 1758–1852

Bibliographies

Summers, M. In his A Gothic bibliography, [1941].

Block, A. In his The English novel 1740–1850, 1961.

§1

Miscellaneous poems, translations and imitations. 1780.

Miscellaneous poems, written at an early period of life. 1786.

The humours of Brighthelmstone. 1788. A poem.

Edmund: a tragedy. 1791.

Miscellaneous poems and a tragedy [Edmund surnamed Ironside]. York 1791, 1797, 1804.

The advantages of education, or the history of Maria Williams: a tale for very young ladies, by Mrs Prudentia Homespun. 2 vols 1793, Dublin 1799, London 1803, New York 1974 (facs).
REVIEW: Br Critic Feb 1804.

A gossip's story, and a legendary tale. 2 vols 1796, 1797, 1798 (3rd edn), 1799, 1 vol Dublin 1798, London 1799, Cork 1799, London 1804, 2 vols New York 1974 (facs).
REVIEWS: Analytical Rev Jan 1797; Monthly Rev Jan 1797; Br Critic Aug 1797; Critical Rev Oct 1797.

An elegy on the death of Edmund Burke. 1797.
REVIEWS: Br Critic Mar 1798; Critical Rev June 1798.

A tale of the times. 3 vols 1799, 1799, 2 vols Dublin 1799, Alexandria VA 1801, 3 vols London 1803, New York 1974 (facs).
REVIEWS: GM Feb 1799; Br Critic Apr 1799; Monthly Rev May 1799; Analytical Rev June 1799.

Poems and plays. 4 vols 1799–1805. Contains Adela, The minstrel, How will it end?
REVIEWS: Br Critic Sep 1799; July 1806; GM Oct 1799; Critical Rev Oct 1799; Monthly Rev Nov 1799.

Letters addressed to a young man on his first entrance into life. 3 vols 1801, 1802, 2 vols Charlestown MA 1803, London 1806, 1 vol New York 1806, London 1818 (6th edn).
REVIEWS: GM Aug 1801; Br Critic Sep, Oct, Nov 1801; Critical Rev Apr 1803.

The infidel father. 3 vols 1802.
REVIEW: Br Critic Apr 1803.

Letters to a young lady in which the duties and character of women are considered. 3 vols 1806, 1806, 1811, New York 1974 (facs).
REVIEWS: Critical Rev Apr 1806; Br Critic Dec 1806.

The mother: a poem in five books. 1809, 1810.
REVIEWS: Br Critic June 1809; Critical Rev July 1809; GM Nov 1810.

The refusal. 3 vols 1810, 2 vols Philadelphia 1810; tr Fr 4 vols 1813 (as Sidney, comte d'Avondel).
REVIEW: Br Critic July 1810.

Scriptural essays. 2 vols 1811, 1 vol 1816, 2 vols 1817.
REVIEW: GM Apr 1817.

The loyalists: an historical novel. 3 vols 1812, 2 vols Boston 1813.
REVIEWS: Critical Rev Sep 1812; Br Critic Oct 1812.

Alicia de Lacy: an historical romance. 4 vols 1814.
REVIEWS: Br Critic Nov 1814; Critical Rev July 1815.

Ringrove: or old fashioned notions. 2 vols 1827.

Translation

A select translation of The beauties of Massilon. 1812. Tr from the Fr.

§2

Literary memoirs of living authors of Great Britain. 2 vols 1798, New York 1970 (facs).

A biographical dictionary of the living authors of Great Britain and Ireland. 1816, Detroit 1966 (facs).

GM July 1852. Obituary.

Lonsdale, Roger (ed). Eighteenth-century women poets: an Oxford anthology. Oxford and New York 1989.

Blain, Clements and Grundy (ed). The feminist companion to literature in English. 1990.

In its suppl to the vols for 1799, and in Jan and Feb 1802, GM pbd letters discussing Jane West's social and literary standing; in Apr 1800 it printed a letter from West as well as two of her poems. [PP]

George Wilkins 1785–1865

§1

Body and soul. 2 vols 1822–3 (anon), 1823, 1823 (3rd edn, with additions and corrections), 1824, Philadelphia 1824.

The two rectors. 1824, 1825.

The village pastor. 1825.

The convert. 1826.

Other works

Wilkins also pbd around 30 sermons, apologies, histories and addresses on various issues concerning religious matters, and specifically the Church of England.

For a listing of reviews and notices of Wilkins's literary works, see Ward (1977). [PG]

John Wilson 1785–1854

See col 2205.

Mary Julia Young

Bibliographies

Summers, M. In his A Gothic bibliography, [1941].

Jackson, J. R. de J. In his Romantic poetry by women: a bibliography, 1770–1835, Oxford 1993.

§1

The family party. 3 vols 1791. Anon.

Genius and fancy: or dramatic sketches, by a lady. [1792?], 1795.

Adelaide and Antonine, or the emigrants: a tale. 1793. Poem.

Poems. 1798, [1801] (as The metrical museum: part I).

Rose-mount Castle, or false report: a novel. 3 vols 1798.

The East Indian, or Clifford Priory: a novel. 4 vols 1799.

Moss Cliff Abbey, or the sepulchral harmonist: a mysterious tale. 4 vols 1803.

Right and wrong, or the kinsmen of Naples: a romantic story. 4 vols 1803.
Donalda, or the witches of Glenshiel: a Caledonian legend. 2 vols 1805.
Memoirs of Mrs Crouch: including a retrospect of the stage during the years she performed. 2 vols 1806. Memoir.
A summer at Brighton: a modern novel. 3 vols 1807, 1807, 1807, 4 vols 1807 (with the 4th vol adding The story of the modern Laïs), 1807 (5th edn).
A summer at Weymouth, or the star of fashion: a novel. 3 vols 1808.
The heir of Drumcondra: or family pride. 3 vols 1810.

Translations
Lindorf and Caroline: or the danger of credulity, translated from the German of Professor Kramer [i.e. of C. B. E. Naubert]. 3 vols 1803.
Voltairiana: selected and translated from the French [of F. M. de Voltaire]. 4 vols 1805.
The mother and daughter: a pathetic tale. 3 vols 1804. From the Fr of J. B. C. Berthien.

Attributed works
Horatio and Amanda: a poem, by a young lady. 1777.
Innocence: an allegorical poem, by Miss Mary Young. 1790.
Poems, by Mrs G. Sewell. Egham and Chertsey 1803, 1803, 2 vols 1805 (with Essays, moral and religious).
Poems and essays. Chertsey 1809 (vol 3, sequel to Poems of 1805).
Trafalgar; a poem to the memory of Lord Nelson. Chertsey 1806.
The last 5 titles, all probably written by Mary (Young) Sewell, are sometimes erroneously identified with Mary Julia Young.

For a listing of reviews and notices of Mary Julia Young's works, see Ward (1979, 1972). [PG]

iii. The mid-nineteenth-century novel 1835–1870

This section has been restricted, with one or two exceptions, to novelists born after 1799 and before 1831.

Grace Aguilar 1816–47

A collection of Aguilar's papers (mss notebooks, including poems, short stories and a lecture) and printed books, some with inscriptions, is at Univ College London. An archive of her letters (also some of her mother's) is in the Southern History Collection, Univ of North Carolina.

Bibliography
Abrahams, B.-Z. In her Grace Aguilar: a centenary tribute. Transactions of the Jewish Historical Soc of England 16 1952.

Collections
Works. 8 vols 1861.
Works. 9 vols New York 1870 (new edn).

§1
The magic wreath of hidden flowers. 1835 (anon), Brighton 1839. Poems.
The spirit of Judaism. Ed I. Leeser, Philadelphia 1842, 1849 (2nd edn), Cincinnati [1863?], Philadelphia [1873] (3rd edn); tr Hebrew 1864.
The Perez family, a tale. 1843, Philadelphia 1847; rptd in Home scenes and heart studies, 1853, *below*.
Records of Israel. 1844, 1845; rptd in Home scenes and heart studies, 1853, *below*. Contains The edict: a tale of 1492 and The escape: a tale of 1755.
REVIEW: Athenaeum 869 1844.
The women of Israel: or characters and sketches from the Holy Scriptures and Jewish history. 2 vols 1844–5, 2 vols New York and Philadelphia 1851, 2 vols 1852 (2nd edn), 2 vols New York 1852 (illus), London 1853 (3rd edn), New York 1853, 1854, 1855, 1857, London 1860 (new edn), New York 1860, 1862, 1866, London 1870 (6th edn), New York 1870, 1871, 1872, London 1873 (8th edn), New York 1875, 1879–80, London 1880, New York 1881, 1883, 1884, London [1888], New York 1888, London 1889, New York 1889, 1891, 1895, 1900 (new edn), 1901, London [1904?], New York 1907, 1913.
The Jewish faith: its spiritual consolation, moral guidance, and immortal hope. [1846], Philadelphia 1864.
REVIEW: Athenaeum 1009 1847.
Home influence: a tale for mothers and daughters. 2 vols 1847, New York 1848, 1 vol London 1849 (2nd edn with a Memoir by Sarah Aguilar), New York 1850, London 1850, 1851, New York 1851, Boston 1854, New York 1854, London 1856 (7th edn), Boston 1857 (new edn), Leipzig 1859 (Tauchnitz), New York 1859 (new edn), London 1860, Boston 1860, New York 1862, 1863, 1866, London 1869 (24th edn illustr Sir J. Gilbert and M. E. Edwards), New York 1870, 1874, London 1875–7, 1881 (36th edn), New York 1881, 1882, 1883, 1884, 1885, 1887, 1888, London 1889, New York 1890, London 1892, Edinburgh 1892, London 1893, New York 1895, London 1896, New York 1897, London 1899, 1900, New York 1904, London [1905], New York 1907, 1910, 1918, London 1925, 1928 (new edn).
REVIEWS: Athenaeum 1017 1847; Spectator 20 1847; Dublin Rev 24 1848.
Josephine: or the edict and the escape. Philadelphia [184?]; rptd in Home scenes and heart studies, 1853, *below*.
Sabbath thoughts and sacred communings... together with a memoir of her life. Published for private circulation by a friend. Charleston 1850; ed Sarah Aguilar [1851?], 1853, 1854.
The vale of cedars: or the martyr. 1850, New York and Philadelphia 1850, London 1851 (2nd edn), New York and Philadelphia 1851, New York 1852, 1853, London 1856 (5th edn), 1860 (new edn), New York 1860, 1861, 1862, 1864, London 1869 (11th edn illustr Dalziel brothers and H. Anelay), New York 1870 (illus), 1875, 1880, 1883, 1888, 1889 (illus), London 1891 (illus), 1895, 1896, New York 1897, 1900 (new edn illus), London 1905, New York 1915, 1916; tr Ger 1860, 1862, Hebrew [1875], 1888.
REVIEW: Athenaeum 1194 1850.
The vale of cedars and other tales [from Home scenes and heart studies]. Introd by W. Jerrold and illustr T. H. Robinson 1902, Philadelphia 1902.
REVIEW: Dial 34 1903.
Woman's friendship: a story of domestic life. 1850, New York 1850, 1851, 1852, London 1856 (4th edn), New York 1857, 1859, London 1860 (new edn), New York 1864, 1867, London 1870 (11th edn illustr H. J. A. Miles, with a portrait of the author), New York 1871, London 1873, 1874 (14th edn), 1876, New York 1880, 1884, 1885, 1888, 1894, 1898, 1901 (new edn), London 1904 (new edn), 1905.
The mother's recompense: a sequel to Home influence. Ed S. Aguilar 1851, New York 1851, Philadelphia 1851, New York 1852, 1853, 1855, London 1856 (5th edn), New York 1857, 2 vols Leipzig 1859 (Tauchnitz), London 1860 (new edn), New York 1861, London 1862 (new edn illus), New York 1864, London 1869 (21st edn illustr H. J. A. Miles), New York 1870, 1871, 1873, 1877, 1879, 1880, 1882, 1884, 1887, 1889, [c. 1890] (Rainbow Lib), 1891, London 1896, 1899 (new edn), New York 1901, [1902], 1906, 1910, 1913, London 1928; tr Ger 1859, 1893.
The days of Bruce: a story from Scottish history. Ed S. Aguilar 2 vols 1852, 2 vols New York 1852, 1853, London 1854, New York 1854, London 1857, New York 1857, London 1860 (new edn), New York 1860, 1861, 1866, London 1868 (new edn), 1870 (14th edn illustr H. W. Briscoe), New York 1870, 1871, 1872, 1874, 1875, London 1876

(20th edn), New York 1878, 1879, 1883, 1886, 1887, 1891, 1893, 1894, London 1896, New York 1897, London 1900 (new edn), New York 1900, London 1903, New York 1903, 1904, London 1905 (illustr H. M. Brock), New York 1909, 1913.
REVIEW: Athenaeum 1292 1852.

The days of Bruce. Retold for boys and girls by A. F. Jackson. London and Edinburgh [1912] (illustr R. J. Williams), London 1929, Toronto 1930, Philadelphia nd.

Essays and miscellanies. Choice cullings from the manuscripts of Grace Aguilar, selected by her mother, Sarah Aguilar. Philadelphia 1853.

Home scenes and heart studies. 1853, New York 1853, 1854, London 1855 (3rd edn), 1860, New York 1868, London 1869 (8th edn illustr H. W. Briscoe), New York 1870, 1871, 1873, 1874, London 1876 (13th edn), New York 1876, 1878, London 1880 (15th edn), New York 1884, London 1886 (17th edn), New York 1888, 1890, London 1891, London and New York [1906?].

The triumph of love. Philadelphia 1872. Rptd from Home scenes and heart studies, 1853, *above*.

Lady Gresham's fete. In Every girl's stories, 1896. Rptd from Home scenes and heart studies, 1853, *above*.

History of the Jews in England. Chambers's Misc 1847.

de Orobio de Castro, B. Israel defended: or the Jewish exposition of the Hebrew prophecies, applied by the Christians to their Messiah. Tr from the Fr by Aguilar. (Original in Sp, never printed.) 1838 (priv ptd).

Tales from British history: Edmund the exiled prince and Wallace, the dauntless chief. 1908, New York [1908].

Tales from British history: Macintosh, the Highland chief. [1908] (with a facs of the author's ms).

§2

Memoirs of Grace Aguilar. New York 1847 (copy in Union Lib of PA, Philadelphia).

Hall, S. C. Pilgrimages to English shrines. Art Union Jnl 9 1852.

Grace Aguilar. Eclectic Rev n.s. 3, Feb 1858.

In DNB.

Isaacs, A. S. The young champion. One year in Grace Aguilar's childhood. Philadelphia 1913 (Jewish Publications Soc).

Schlueter, P. and J. (ed). An encyclopedia of British women writers. London and New York 1988.

William Harrison Ainsworth 1805–82

Bibliographies

Ellis, S. M. William Harrison Ainsworth and his friends. 2 vols 1911. See vol 2, pp. 345–83.

Locke, H. A. A bibliographical catalogue of the published novels and ballads of William Harrison Ainsworth. 1925.

Collections

Works. 14 vols 1850–1. With a memoir by S. L. Blanchard.

Collected works. 16 vols 1875, 31 vols 1878–80, 12 vols 1923.

There is no complete edn of Ainsworth's writings.

§1

Poems by Cheviot Ticheburn. 1822.

The maid's revenge, and A summer's evening tale with other poems by Cheviot Ticheburn. 1823.

Monody on the death of John Philip Kemble. Manchester 1823.

December tales. 1823.

The Boeotian. Manchester 1824.

The works of Cheviot Ticheburn, with the types of John Leigh. Manchester 1825.

Considerations on the best means of affording immediate relief to the operative classes in the manufacturing districts. 1826.

Letters from cockney lands. 1826, 1827.

Sir John Chiverton: a romance. 1826, 1827. Anon; in collaboration with J. P. Aston.

Mayfair, in four cantos. 1827.

Rookwood: a romance. 3 vols 1834 (anon), 1834, 2 vols Philadelphia 1834, 1835, 1836, 1837, Leipzig 1837, London 1850, 1851, 1853, 1857, 1875, 1878, 1884, 1891, 1892 etc; tr Fr 1836, Ger 1837.
REVIEWS: Athenaeum 3 May 1834; Examiner 18 May 1834; Fraser's Mag 9 1834.

Crichton. 3 vols 1837, Paris 1837, 2 vols New York 1837 etc, 3 vols London 1849 (rev), 1853, 1854, 1879, 1889, 1892 etc; tr Ger 1845, Fr 1858, Polish 1876. Also pbd in Ainsworth's Mag Jan 1848–Aug 1849.
REVIEWS: [Mahony, F.] Fraser's Mag 14 1836; Monthly Rev 1 1837; Examiner 27 Nov 1836 and 23 Apr 1837; Athenaeum 4 Mar 1837; Recent English romances, Edinburgh Rev 65 1837; Amer Quart Rev 13 1837.

Jack Sheppard: a romance. 3 vols 1839, 15 monthly pts 1840–1, Philadelphia 1840, 1 vol 1840, Paris 1841 etc, New York 1846 etc, Leipzig 1846, London 1854, 1856, 1862, 1865, 1879, 1884, 1891, 1893 etc; tr Fr 1873. First pbd in Bentley's Misc Jan 1839–Feb 1840.
REVIEWS: Literary Gazette 19 Oct 1839; Athenaeum 26 Oct 1839; [Forster, J.] Examiner 3 Nov 1839; William Ainsworth and 'Jack Sheppard' Fraser's Mag 21 1840.

The Tower of London: a historical romance. 13 monthly pts Jan–Dec 1840, 1 vol 1840, Paris 1841, Philadelphia 1841, London 1842, 1842, 1843, 1844, 1845, New York 1846 etc, London 1853, 1854, 1855, 1858, 1878, 1882, 1884, 1889, 1890, 1891, 1894 etc; tr Du 1843, Sp 1844, Fr 1858, Portuguese 1943.
REVIEW: Athenaeum 2 Jan 1841.

Guy Fawkes, or the gunpowder treason: an historical romance. 3 vols 1841, New York 1841, Paris 1841, Philadelphia 1841, London 1844, 1857, 1878, 1884, 1891 etc. First pbd in Bentley's Misc Jan 1840–Nov 1841; also pbd in Ainsworth's Mag July 1849–June 1850.
REVIEW: Athenaeum 14 Aug 1841.

Old Saint Paul's: a tale of the Plague and the Fire. 3 vols 1841, 12 monthly pts 1841–2, Paris 1842, London 1847, 1855, 1857, 1879, 1881, 1884, 1891 etc; tr Portuguese 1943. First pbd in Sunday Times 1841; also pbd in Ainsworth's Mag June–Dec 1846.
REVIEW: Athenaeum 18 Dec 1841.

The miser's daughter: a tale. 3 vols 1842, New York 1842, Paris 1842, London 1843, 1848, 1855, Leipzig 1862, London 1879, 1886, 1892 etc. First pbd in Ainsworth's Mag Feb–Nov 1842.
REVIEW: Athenaeum 5 Nov 1842.

Modern chivalry, or a new Orlando Furioso. 2 vols 1843. With Catherine Gore. First pbd in Ainsworth's Mag July–Dec 1843.

Windsor Castle: an historical romance. 3 vols 1843, 1 vol 1843, 11 monthly pts 1843–4, 1844, Leipzig 1844, London 1847, 1853, 1859, 1878, 1884, 1891, 1894 etc; tr Portuguese 1943. First pbd in Ainsworth's Mag July 1842–June 1843.
REVIEW: Athenaeum 1 July 1843.

Saint James's, or the Court of Queen Anne: an historical romance. 3 vols 1844, New York 1844, Leipzig 1844, London 1846, 1853, 1879, 1889; tr Fr 1858. First pbd in Ainsworth's Mag Jan–Dec 1844.

James the Second, or the revolution of 1688: an historical romance. 3 vols 1848, New York 1848 etc, Philadelphia 1848 etc, London 1854, 1890. First pbd in Ainsworth's Mag Jan–Dec 1847.

The Lancashire witches: a novel. 1849 (priv ptd), 3 vols 1849 (as The Lancashire witches: a romance of Pendle Forest), 2 vols Leipzig 1849, New York 1849 etc, London 1854, 1878, 1884 etc. First pbd in Sunday Times 1848; also pbd in Ainsworth's Mag July 1850–Sep 1853.
REVIEW: Athenaeum 6 Jan 1849.

Life and adventures of Mervyn Clitheroe. 12 monthly pts Dec 1851–Mar 1852, Dec 1857–June 1858, 1 vol 1858 (as Mervyn Clitheroe), 2 vols Leipzig 1858, London 1879, 1890; tr Ger 1859.

The Star Chamber: an historical romance. 2 vols 1854, 2 vols Leipzig

1854, London 1857, 1861, 1873, 1879, 1889, 1892 etc; tr Swed 1854. First pbd in Home Companion 1853.
The Flitch of Bacon, or the custom of Dunmow. 1854, Leipzig 1854, London 1855, 1874, 1879, 1889, 1892 etc; tr Du 1855. First pbd in NMM Jan 1853–May 1854.
Ballads: romantic, fantastical and humorous. 1855, 1872 (with memoir of Ainsworth by J. Crossley, and adding The combat of the thirty). Rptd from the novels.
The spendthrift: a tale. '1857' [1856], Leipzig 1856, London 1867, 1871, 1879, 1889, 1892 etc. First pbd in Bentley's Misc Jan 1855–Jan 1857.
The combat of the thirty, from a Breton lay of the fourteenth century. 1859. First pbd in Bentley's Misc Jan–May 1859.
Ovingdean Grange: a tale of the South Downs. 1860, Leipzig 1860, London 1865, 1870, 1876, 1879, 1882, 1891 etc. First pbd in Bentley's Misc Nov 1859–July 1860.
The constable of the tower: an historical romance. 3 vols 1861, Leipzig 1861, London 1862, 1880, 1881 etc. First pbd in Bentley's Misc Feb–Sep 1861.
The Lord Mayor of London, or city life in the last century. 3 vols 1862, 2 vols Leipzig 1862, London 1863, 1880 etc. First pbd in Bentley's Misc Jan–Nov 1862.
Cardinal Pole, or the days of Philip and Mary: an historical romance. 3 vols 1863, 2 vols Leipzig 1863, London 1864, 1880, 1881 etc. First pbd in Bentley's Misc Dec 1862–Nov 1863.
John Law the projector. 3 vols 1864, 2 vols Leipzig 1864, London 1866, 1881. First pbd in Bentley's Misc Nov 1863–Sep 1864.
The Spanish match, or Charles Stuart at Madrid. 3 vols 1865, Leipzig 1865, London 1865, 1880, 1894. First pbd in Bentley's Misc Nov 1864–Sep 1865 as The house of seven chimneys.
Auriol, or the elixir of life. [1865] (with The old London merchant, and A night's adventure in Rome [2 short stories]), 1868, [1875], 1875, 1881, 1890, 1892 etc. First pbd in Ainsworth's Mag Oct 1844–May 1845 and NMM July 1845–Jan 1846 as Revelations of London.
The Constable de Bourbon. 3 vols 1866, 2 vols Leipzig 1866, London 1878, 1880, New York 1882; tr Ger 1867. First pbd in Bentley's Misc Nov 1865–Aug 1866.
Old Court: a novel. 3 vols 1867, 2 vols Leipzig 1867, London 1878, 1880; tr Ger 1868. First pbd in Bentley's Misc Oct 1866–May 1867.
Myddleton Pomfret: a novel. 3 vols 1868, 2 vols Leipzig 1868, London 1878, 1881. First pbd in Bentley's Misc July 1867–Mar 1868.
The South Sea Bubble: a tale of the year 1720. 2 vols Leipzig 1868, [1871]. First pbd in Bow Bells 1868.
Hilary St Ives: a novel. 3 vols 1870, Leipzig 1869, London 1881. First pbd in NMM Feb–Dec 1869.
Talbot Harland. 1871, Leipzig 1870. First pbd in Bow Bells 1868.
Tower Hill. 1871, Leipzig 1871. First pbd in Bow Bells 1871.
Boscobel, or the Royal Oak: a tale of the year 1651. 3 vols 1872, 2 vols Leipzig 1872, London 1874, 1875, 1879, 1889. First pbd in NMM Jan–Dec 1872.
REVIEW: Spectator 1 Mar 1873.
The good old times: the story of the Manchester rebels of '45. 3 vols 1873, 2 vols Leipzig 1873, London 1874 (as The Manchester rebels of the fatal '45), 1880, 1884, 1890, 1892, 1893.
REVIEW: Athenaeum 18 Oct 1873.
Merry England, or nobles and serfs. 3 vols 1874, 2 vols Leipzig 1874, London [1875], New York 1879, 1881 (as The blacksmith outlaw, or Merry England). First pbd in Bow Bells 1874.
The goldsmith's wife: a tale. 3 vols 1875, 2 vols Leipzig 1875, London [1875]. First pbd in Bow Bells 1874.
Preston Fight, or the insurrection of 1715: a tale. 3 vols 1875, 2 vols Leipzig 1875, London [1877], 1879.
Chetwynd Calverley: a tale. 3 vols 1876, 2 vols Leipzig 1876, London [1877]. First pbd in Bow Bells 1876.
The leaguer of Lathom: a tale of the Civil War in Lancashire. 3 vols 1876, Leipzig 1877, London 1880.
The fall of Somerset. 3 vols 1877, 2 vols Leipzig 1877, London [1878]. First pbd in Bow Bells 1877–8.
Beatrice Tyldesley. 3 vols 1878, 2 vols Leipzig 1878, London [1879]. First pbd in Bow Bells 1878.
Beau Nash, or Bath in the eighteenth century. 3 vols [1879], 2 vols Leipzig 1879, London 1880, 1881, New York 1882, London 1889.
Stanley Brereton. 3 vols [1881], Leipzig 1881, London 1882, 1884, New York 1892. First pbd in Bolton Weekly Jnl 1881.

For Ainsworth's contributions to Ainsworth's Mag, Arliss's Pocket Mag, Bentley's Misc, Boeotian, Bolton Weekly Jnl, Book of Beauty, Bow Bells, Christmas Box, Edinburgh Mag, European Mag, Fraser's Mag, Home Companion, Keepsake, Literary Souvenir, London Mag, Manchester Courier, Manchester Iris, NMM *and* Sunday Times *see Bibliography in Ellis,* William Harrison Ainsworth and his friends *vol 2. For Ainsworth's prose contributions to* Fraser's Mag, Ainsworth's Mag, NMM, *and* Bentley's Misc, *see* Wellesley *vol 5, 1989. Ainsworth edited* Ainsworth's Mag *1842–June 1845 and Dec 1845–54,* NMM *1845–70 and* Bentley's Misc *1839–41 and 1854–68.*

§2

Horne, R. H. In his A new spirit of the age vol 2, 1844.
Friswell, J. H. In his Modern men of letters honestly criticised, 1870.
Maginn, W. In his A gallery of illustrious literary characters, 1830–8, ed W. Bates [1873]. Rptd from Fraser's Mag 10 1834.
Evans, J. The early life of William Harrison Ainsworth. Manchester Quart 1882.
Axon, W. E. A. William Harrison Ainsworth: a memoir. 1902.
Ellis, S. M. William Harrison Ainsworth and his friends. 2 vols 1911.
Hollingsworth, K. In his The Newgate novel 1830–47, Detroit 1963.
[GW]

'Mrs Alexander', Mrs Annie Hector, née French

1825–1902

§1

Kate Vernon. 3 vols 1854. Anon.
Agnes Waring: an autobiography edited [really written] by the author of Kate Vernon. 3 vols 1856. Anon.
The happy cottage. 1856. Anon.
Memorial of a beloved child. [1865.] Anon; ptd for private circulation.
Look before you leap. 2 vols 1865. Anon, 1882 (revised edn), New York 1882, [1886], London 1900 (new edn), 1909.
REVIEW: Athenaeum 18 Mar 1865.
Which shall it be? 3 vols 1866 (anon), 1867 (new edn), Boston [1874], New York 1874, London 1875 (4th edn), New York 1878, 1881, [1884], London 1886 (7th edn), New York [1887], Chicago [188?], London 1891 (8th edn), New York [1897?], London 1900.
The legend of the golden prayer etc. 1872. Poems.
The wooing o't. Serialised in Temple Bar June 1872–Nov 1873, 3 vols 1873, New York 1873, 1 vol London 1874 (new edn), New York 1874, London 1881 (6th edn), 1884 (7th edn), New York [188?], London 1890 (8th edn), 1893 (9th edn), London and New York 1899, New York [189?], London 1903.
REVIEW: Saturday Rev 8 Nov 1873.
Ralph Wilton's weird. Serialised in Temple Bar June 1875–Aug 1876, 2 vols 1875, New York 1875, 1 vol London 1878, New York 1878, [1886].
Her dearest foe. Serialised in Temple Bar June 1875–Aug 1876, 3 vols 1876, New York 1876, 1 vol London 1877 (new edn), 1878 (3rd edn), New York [1886], London 1887 (5th edn), 1895 (7th edn), New York [1896], London and New York 1899, London 1909, New York [19?]; tr Sp 1902, 1905.
REVIEW: Saturday Rev 3 June 1876.
The heritage of Langdale. 3 vols 1877, New York 1877, 1 vol London 1877 (new edn), 1894, 1901.

Maid, wife or widow? 1879, New York 1879, London 1880 (new edn), 1881, New York [1884], [1886], London 1895.
Moral songs. 1879 (illus), 1880.
The Freres. Serialised in Temple Bar Jan 1881–May 1882, 3 vols 1882, New York 1882, 1 vol London 1882, 1900.
The Australian aunt. New York [1882].
Valerie's fate. New York 1882, [1884]. Lonodn 1885 (with Mrs Vereker's courier maid), 1887, 1899 (new edn).
The admiral's ward. 3 vols 1883, 1 vol 1883, New York 1883, London 1884, Chicago [1886?], London 1900 (new edn).
The executor. 3 vols 1883, New York 1883, 1 vol London 1885, 1900 (new edn), New York [19?].
Holiday songs. 1884 (set to music by Lady Arthur Hill).
Mrs Vereker's courier maid. 1884, New York [1884]. First pbd in Gentleman's Annual, Christmas 1884. Rptd with Valerie's fate, 1885, *above*.
A second life. 3 vols 1885, Leipzig 1885 (Tauchnitz), New York 1885, 1 vol London [1895], 1904.
At bay. 1885, London and New York [1885], New York [1885], London [1887] (3rd edn). Rptd with Valerie's fate, New York 1885.
Beaton's bargain. 1886, New York 1886, London and New York [1887], New York 1893, Boston [18?], London and New York [19?].
By woman's wit. 2 vols 1886, Leipzig 1886 (Tauchnitz), New York 1886, 1887, London 1887, 1898 (new edn); tr Danish 1887.
Forging the fetters, and other stories. New York [1887], Chicago [189?], London [189?], New York [189?]. Contains Forging the fetters, The Irish refugee, Eveline Murray, The three sisters.
Forging the fetters, and other stories. New York 1887. Contains Forging the fetters, Mrs Vereker's courier maid, The Australian maid.
Forging the fetters. 1890.
Mona's choice. 3 vols 1887, 2 vols Leipzig 1887 (Tauchnitz), New York [1887], 1 vol London 1888, New York 1888, London 1889 (new edn), New York 1889, London 1898 (new edn); tr Polish, Warsaw 1888.
A life interest. Serialised in London Soc Apr 1887–Apr 1888, 3 vols 1888, 2 vols Leipzig 1888 (Tauchnitz), New York 1888, 1 vol London 1889, 1898 (new edn).
A crooked path. 3 vols 1889, 2 vols Leipzig 1889 (Tauchnitz), New York [1889], [1896], London 1909.
A false scent. 1889, New York [1889].
Blind fate. 3 vols 1890, New York 1890, Leipzig 1891 (Tauchnitz), 1 vol London 1892, 1897 (new edn).
Heart wins, and The Australian aunt. 1890.
A woman's heart. 3 vols 1891, 2 vols Leipzig 1891 (Tauchnitz), New York [1891], 1 vol London 1894.
Well won. 1891, New York 1891.
What gold cannot buy. Leipzig 1891 (Tauchnitz), London 1895, New York [189?], Chicago [18?], New York [1905?], London 1907, Cleveland OH [1916?].
For his sake. 3 vols 1892, 2 vols Leipzig 1892 (Tauchnitz), Philadelphia 1892, 1 vol London [1894?], 1907.
Mammon. 3 vols 1892, Leipzig 1892, New York [1892?], New York 1896, London 1897, New York 1901.
The snare of the fowler. 3 vols 1892, New York [1892], 2 vols Leipzig 1893 (Tauchnitz).
Found wanting. 3 vols 1893, 2 vols Leipzig 1893 (Tauchnitz), Philadelphia 1893, 1 vol London 1895.
Broken links. New York 1894.
A choice of evils. 3 vols 1894, 2 vols Leipzig 1894 (Tauchnitz), London 1898, 1907.
A ward in Chancery. 2 vols 1894, Leipzig 1894 (Tauchnitz), New York 1894, London 1895.
Mrs Chrichton's creditor. Philadelphia 1896, London 1897, Leipzig 1897 (Tauchnitz), Philadelphia 1897, London 1898 (new edn). First pbd in Lippincott's Monthly Mag Jan 1896.
A fight with fate. 1896, 2 vols Leipzig 1896 (Tauchnitz), Philadelphia 1897, London 1898, 1900 (new edn).
A golden autumn. 1896, 1897 (new edn), Philadelphia 1897, London 1898 (new edn), 1900, Philadelphia 1900, London 1908, [1922].
A winning hazard. 1896. Leipzig 1896 (Tauchnitz), New York 1896, London 1898, 1900.
Barbara, lady's maid and peeress. 1897, Leipzig 1897 (Tauchnitz), London 1898 (3rd edn), Philadelphia 1898, London 1899 (4th edn), 1900 (new edn).
The cost of her pride. 1898, 2 vols Leipzig 1899 (Tauchnitz), Philadelphia 1899, London 1900 (new edn).
Brown V. C. 1899, Leipzig 1899 (Tauchnitz), New York 1899, London [1900] (new edn), 1908.
The step-mother. 1899, 1900, Philadelphia 1900, 1901, London 1907.
Through fire to fortune. 1900, Leipzig 1900 (Tauchnitz), New York 1900, London 1903.
A missing hero. 1901, 1901 (2nd edn), Leipzig 1901 (Tauchnitz), New York 1901, London 1905.
The yellow fiend. 1901, New York 1901, Leipzig 1902 (Tauchnitz), London 1902, New York 1902.
Stronger than love. 1902, 2 vols Leipzig 1902 (Tauchnitz), New York 1902, London 1904, 1906.
Kitty Costello. 1904 (with a biographical note on the author by I. A. Hardy), Leipzig 1904 (Tauchnitz), London 1906.
The crumpled leaf. A Vatican mystery. 1911.

Contributions to periodicals and collaborative works

Billeted in Boulogne. Household Words 24 May 1856.
Two difficult cases. Household Words 8 Nov 1856.
Number five, Hanbury Terrace. Household Words 12 Dec 1857.
A peep at Presburg and Pesth. Temple Bar Mar 1879.
To be, or not to be. In Three notable stories by the Marquis of Lorne etc, 1890.
By special wire. In Miss Parson's adventure and other stories by W. C. Russell etc, 1894.
Mrs Norton. In Women novelists of Queen Victoria's reign, 1897.
Failure. In In memoriam by I. A. Hardy, [1904?]. Poem.

§2

Black, H. C. In her Notable women authors of the day, Glasgow 1893.
DNB 1901–1911.
Sutherland, J. The Longman companion to Victorian fiction, Harlow 1988.

William Edmondstoune Aytoun 1813–65

See col 530.

Robert Michael Ballantyne, pseud Comus 1825–94

Ballantyne used the pseudonym for stories for the nursery in order not to alienate his boy readers.

Bibliography

Quayle, E. R. M. Ballantyne: a bibliography of first editions. 1968.

Collected works

Ballantyne's miscellany. 18 pts 1863–86.
Tales of adventure by the sea. Selections from Ballantyne's miscellany. 1873.
Tales of adventure by flood, field and mountain. Selected from Ballantyne's miscellany. 1874.
Tales of adventure; or wild work in strange places. Selected from Ballantyne's miscellany. 1874.
Tales of adventure on the coast. Selected from Ballantyne's miscellany. 1875.
The coxwain's bride, or, the rising tide. A tale of the sea and other tales. 1891.

The Ballantyne series. Tales by R. M. Ballantyne. 1910–12.
The jolly kitten book. 1925.
Ballantyne omnibus for boys (The coral island, The gorilla hunters, Martin Rattler). [1932].

§1

Hudson's Bay; or, every-day life in the wilds of North America, etc. Edinburgh 1848 (priv circulated), 1857, New York 1857, Boston 1859 (illus by the author), 1897, 1902, 1904.
The northern coasts of America, and the Hudson's Bay Territories. A narrative of discovery and adventure (from P. F. Tytler's Historical view of the progress of discovery, with a continuation by R. M. Ballantyne). 1848, 1853.
Snowflakes and sunbeams; or, the young fur traders. 1848 (illus by the author), 1856; as The young fur traders, or snowflakes and sunbeams from the far north 1896, 1901, 1907, 1908, 1913, 1923, 1925, 1937, 1948, 1950.
Naughty boys; or, the sufferings of Mr Delteil by Champfleury. Illustr and ed R. M. and M. Ballantyne. 1855.
Three little kittens. A nursery tale. With verses and music. By Comus. 1856, 1857, 1860, 1863, 1874, 1925.
The butterfly's ball and the grasshopper's feast. Ed Comus. 1857.
Mister Fox. By Comus. 1857, 1860.
The life of a ship, from the launch to the wreck. By Comus. 1857.
My mother. By Comus. 1857.
The robber kitten. By Comus. 1857.
The coral island: a tale of the Pacific Ocean. 1858 (illus by the author), 1893, 1894, 1901, 1903, 1906, 1907, 1908, Edinburgh 1909, London 1910, 1912, 1914, 1916, 1927, 1931, 1932, 1933, 1934, 1935, 1937, 1947, 1948, 1949, 1952, 1953, 1955, 1957, 1960, 1965; tr Portuguese 1935, Afrikaans 1959. Abridgements 1931, 1932, 1935, 1937, 1946, 1947, 1948, 1950, 1955, 1958, 1959.
Handbook to the new gold fields: a full account of the richness and extent of the Fraser and Thompson River gold mines. Edinburgh 1858.
Martin Rattler: or a boy's adventures in the forests of Brazil. 1858, 1894, 1901, [1901], 1902, 1903, 1904, 1906, 1907, 1908, 1911, 1935, 1937, 1938, 1940, 1947, 1948, 1949, 1954, 1959, 1961. Abridgements 1906, 1920, 1939, 1940, 1963. Retold by Richard Musman 1966.
Ungava. A tale of Esquimaux-land. 1858 (illus by the author), 1899, 1901, 1903, 1904, 1908, 1915, 1916.
Environs and vicinity of Edinburgh. 1859 (Nelson's Handbooks for Tourists).
How not to do it. A manual for the awkward squad: or a handbook of directions written for the instruction of raw recruits in our Rifle Volunteer Regiments. By one of themselves i.e. R. M. Ballantyne. 1859 (illus).
The lakes of Killarney. 1859 (Nelson's Handbooks for Tourists).
Mee-a-ow! or good advice to cats and kittens. 1859.
Ships. The Great Eastern and lesser craft. 1859 (illus).
Discovery and adventure in the Polar seas and regions. With a narrative of the recent expeditions in search of Sir J. Franklin. 1860.
The dog Crusoe and his master. A tale of adventure in the Western prairies. [1860], 1861, Boston 1863, London 1900, 1901, 1903, 1905, 1907, 1908, 1910, 1911, 1913 (illustr D. Hardy), 1936, 1937, 1950, 1965, 1966; tr Esperanto 1951. Abridgement 1909. Retold and ed Constance Martin 1936.
The golden dream: or adventures in the Far West. [1860], 1861 (illus), 1914.
Mister Fox. Edinburgh [1860].
The volunteer levee: or the remarkable experiences of Ensign Sopht. Written and illus by himself. 1860.
The world of ice: or adventures in the Rocky Mountains. 1860 (illus); as Fast in the ice; or, adventures in the Polar regions 1863, New York and Philadelphia 1865, New York 1869.
The gorilla hunters. A tale of the wilds of Africa. 1861, 1901, 1903, 1905, 1908, 1910, 1911, 1921, 1930, 1934, 1935, 1937; adapted 1940; tr Fr 1937.
The red Eric: or, the Whaler's last cruise. A tale. 1861, 1862, 1904, 1910, 1911, 1914.
Away in the wilderness: or life among the Red Indians and fur-traders of North-America. 1863, New York 1863, Philadelphia 1869.
Fighting the whales. 1863, 1915.
Man on the ocean: a book for boys. 1863, [1873], 1874.
The wild man of the West: a tale of the Rocky Mountains. 1863, 1876, 1905, 1912, 1913, 1932.
Chasing the sun: or rambles in Norway. 1864.
Gasgoyne, the sandal-wood trader: a tale of the Pacific. 1864 (illus), 1915.
The lifeboat. A tale of our coast heroes. 1864 (illus), 1912, 1915.
Freaks on the Fells: or three months rustication. And why I did not become a sailor. 1865 (illus), 1913, 1923.
The lighthouse: being the story of a great fight between man and the sea. 1865 (illus), 1912, 1914, 1922, 1925, 1932.
Shifting winds. A tough yarn. 1866 (illus), Philadelphia 1868.
Funny animals: a picture book for the nursery. 1867.
A rescue in the Rocky Mountains. 1867.
Silver lake: or lost in the snow. 1867, 1949.
Fighting the flames. A tale of the London fire brigade. 1868 (illus), 1913, 1914.
Photographs of Edinburgh by A. Burns with descriptive letterpress by R. M. Ballantyne. Glasgow 1868.
Deep down. A tale of the Cornish mines. New York 1868, London 1869, 1886, 1912, 1913.
Erling the bold. A tale of the Norse sea-kings. 1869 (illus by the author), 1913, 1919.
Hunting the lions, or, the land of the negro. 1869 (illus).
Lost in the forest: or Wandering Will's adventure in South America. 1869.
Saved by the life-boat. A tale of wreck and rescue on the coast. 1869 (illus).
Sunk at sea: or the adventures of Wandering Will in the Pacific. 1869.
Up in the clouds: or balloon voyages. 1869 (illus).
The floating light of the Goodwin Sands. A tale. 1870 (illus by the author).
The kitten cousins by Doctor Smiles. [1870.]
The iron horse: or life on the line. A tale of the Grand National Trunk Railway. 1871 (illus).
The Norsemen in the West: or America before Columbus. 1872 (illus).
The pioneers. A tale of the Western wilderness: illustrative of the adventures and discoveries of Sir Alexander Mackenzie. 1872.
Life in the red brigade. A story for boys. 1873 (illus).
Black ivory. A tale of adventure among the slavers of East Africa. 1873 (illus).
The ocean and its wonders. 1874.
The pirate city: an algerine tale. 1875.
Rivers of ice. A tale illustrative of Alpine adventure and glacier action. 1876 (illus).
Under the waves: or diving in deep waters. A tale. 1876 (illus).
The settler and the savage. A tale of peace and war in South Africa. 1877 (illus).
In the track of the troops. A tale of modern war. 1878 (illus).
Jarwin and Cuffy. A tale. [1878] (illus), 1885.
Digging for gold: or adventures in California. 1879.
Six months at the Cape: or letters to Periwinkle from South Africa. 1879 (illus), 1879, 1888, 1897.
The lonely island: or, the refuge of the mutineers. 1880 (illus).
Philosopher Jack. A tale of the Southern seas. 1880 (illus).
Post haste. A tale of Her Majesty's mails. 1880 (illus).
The red man's revenge. A tale of the Red River flood. 1880 (illus).
The robber kitten. 1880.

The collected works of Ensign Sopht, late of the volunteers, illustrated by himself. Ed R. M. Ballantyne 1881.
My Doggie and I. 1881 (illus).
The giant of the North: or pokings round the Pole. 1882 (illus).
The kitten pilgrims: or, great battles and grand victories. [1882] (illus by the author).
The battery and the boiler: or adventures in the laying of submarine electric cables. 1883 (illus by the author).
Battles with the sea: or heroes of the lifeboat and rocket, being descriptive of our coast-saving apparatus with some account of the glorious war and of our grand victories. 1883.
The madman and the pirate. 1883 (illus).
Dusty diamonds cut and polished: a tale of city-Arab life and adventure. 1884 (illus), 1890.
The young trawler. A story of life and death and rescue on the North Sea. 1884 (illus).
The island queen: or dethroned by fire and water. A tale of the Southern hemisphere. 1885.
The rover of the Andes. A tale of adventure in South America. 1885.
Twice bought: a tale of the Oregon goldfields. 1885.
The prairie chief: a tale. 1886.
Red Rooney: or the last of the crew. 1886.
The fugitives: or the tyrant queen of Madagascar. 1887.
The big otter. A tale of the great nor' west. 1887.
Blue lights: or hot work in the Soudan. A tale of soldier life, in several of its phases. 1888 (illus).
The middy and the moors: an algerine story. 1888.
Blown to bits: or the lonely man of Rakata. A tale of the Malay archipelago. 1889 (illus by the author).
The crew of the Walter Wagtail. A story of Newfoundland. 1889 (illus).
The eagle cliff. A tale of the Western Isles. [1889.]
Charlie to the rescue. A tale of the sea and the Rockies. 1890 (illus by the author).
The garret and the garden: or low life high up, and Jeff Benson: or the young coastguardsman. 1890 (illus).
The buffalo runners. A tale of the Red River plains. 1891.
The hot swamp: a tale of old Albion. 1892.
Hunted and harried. A tale of the Scottish covenanters, etc. 1892.
Personal reminiscences in bookmaking. 1893.
The walrus hunters: a romance of the realms of ice. 1893 (illus).
Reuben's luck. A tale of the wild north. [1896.]

Short stories

Ballantyne issued a series of short stories as Ballantyne's miscellany 1863–86.

1. Fighting the whales. 1863.
2. Away in the wilderness. 1863.
3. Fast in the ice. 1863.
4. Chasing the sun, or rambles in Norway. 1864.
5. Sunk at sea. 1869.
6. Lost in the forest. 1869.
7. Over the Rocky Mountains. 1869.
8. Saved by the lifeboat. A tale of wreck and rescue. 1869.
9. The cannibal islands. 1869.
10. Hunting the lions; or, the land of the negro. 1869.
11. Digging for gold. 1879.
12. Up in the clouds; or, balloon voyages. 1869.
13. The battle and the breeze. 1869.
14. The pioneers. A tale of the Western wilderness. Illustrative of the adventures and discoveries of Sir Alexander Mackenzie. 1875.
15. The story of the Rock; or, building on the Eddystone. 1875.
16. Wrecked but not ruined. 1875.
17. The Thoroughgood family. 1883.
18. The lively poll. 1886.

Contributions to periodicals and collaborative works

A rescue in the Rocky Mountains. In Our Christmas party, by Old Merry 1867.
The fight on the green. In A. H. Miles, Fifty two stories for boys, 1889.
A gallant rescue. In Stories jolly, stories new, etc, 1889.
Ballantyne contributed extensively to periodicals, including the Scotsman, Sunday at Home, Good Words, Routledge's Mag for Boys, Quiver, Cassell's Illus Family Paper, Sabbath School Messenger, Old Merry's Annual, Life and Work, Union Jack, A1 Annual, Routledge's Every Boy's Annual, Young England, Young Men.

§2

Quayle, E. Ballantyne the brave: a Victorian writer and his family. 1967. [DD]

Mrs George Linnaeus Banks, Isabella Banks, née Varley 1821–97

The E. L. Burney Collection in the John Rylands Univ Lib of Manchester is the principal repository of papers, letters and notebooks of Banks. Manchester City Lib also has a small collection of mss and letters.

Collections

A uniform edn of her novels and stories commenced publication in Manchester and London in 1881 but was not completed.

§1

Ivy leaves: a collection of poems by I. Varley. 1844.
Peals from the belfry: lyrics. 1853.
The waif of the Wear. Serialised in Durham Chron 25 Dec 1863–8 Jan 1864, 1 vol Durham 1864, expanded into Stung to the quick, 1867, *below*.
Daisies in the grass: a collection of songs and poems. 1865. With G. L. Banks.
REVIEW: Athenaeum 1974 1865.
God's providence house: a story of 1791. 3 vols 1865, 1865 (2nd edn), 1 vol 1872, 1873, 1878 (new edn), 1880, 1885, 1887 (illus), 1907 (new edn), 1923.
REVIEW: Athenaeum 1970 1865.
Stung to the quick: a north country story. 3 vols 1867, 1 vol Manchester 1881, London 1892, 1893, 1897, 1903 (new edn).
The Manchester man. Serialised in Cassell's Family Mag Jan–Nov 1875, 3 vols 1876, 1 vol Altrincham 1876, London 1877, London and Manchester 1881 (4th edn), 1886 (6th edn), 1892, 1895, 1896 (illustr C. Green and H. Fitton), 1897 (10th edn), 1902 (11th edn), 1923, 1932, Altrincham 1954 (illustr E. Gee), London 1970 (introd by W. L. Webb), Altrincham and Manchester 1973.
REVIEWS: Athenaeum 2519 1876; Saturday Rev 41 1876; Spectator 78 1897.
Geoffrey Ollivant's folly. 1877, 1886.
Glory: a Wiltshire story. Serialised in Christian Globe 1876–7, 3 vols 1877, 1 vol Manchester 1881, London 1882 (illustr H. French and G. C. Banks), [1892], 1897, 1903 (new edn).
REVIEWS: Athenaeum 2603 1877; Graphic 27 Oct 1877; Saturday Rev 44 1877; Spectator 50 1877.
Caleb Booth's clerk: a Lancashire story. 3 vols 1878, London and Manchester 1882 (illustr R. B. Wallace and G. C. Banks).
Ripples and breakers: a volume of verse. 1878 (illustr J. Proctor and G. C. Banks), 1893 (new edn).
REVIEW: Spectator 53 1880.
Wooers and winners; or under the scars. A Yorkshire story. 3 vols 1880, 1 vol London and Manchester 1882 (illustr H. French and G. C. Banks), New York [1883].
Light work for leisure hours: designs in ornamental needlework. Derby 1881.
More than coronets. Serialised in Girl's Own Paper 1880, 3 vols 1881, 1 vol Manchester 1881 (illustr J. Copleston and G. C. Banks), London and Manchester 1882.
Through the night: tales of shades and shadows. London and

Manchester 1882 (illustr G. C. Banks), 1882 (new edn). Contains A world between, The pride of the Corbyns, Wraith haunted, The piper's ghost, St Cuthbert's cup, The fairies' cradle, My will, Judgment deferred, A dour weird, The white woman of Slaith, Larry's apprenticeship, The fate of the Fosbrookes, A new leaf, The Plainbury mystery.

The watchmaker's daughter and other tales. London and Manchester 1882 (illustr F. Dadd and G. C. Banks). Contains The watchmaker's daughter, The skeleton under the skirt, The puritan's will, The two valentines, Joe's first marriage, The old mill-wheel, Love me, love my dog, The house that James Sutton built for himself, The quilted petticoat, The Indian scarf, The runaway, Theresa Trevor's wedding dress, A wife's extravagance.

Forbidden to marry. 3 vols 1883, 1 vol London and Manchester 1885 (as Forbidden to wed).

REVIEWS: Athenaeum 2919 1883; Spectator 56 1883.

Sybilla and other stories. 3 vols 1884, 1 vol London and Manchester 1885, 1904. Contains Sybilla, By ways unknown, Old Elspa, Bessy and others, The first straw hat, The old schoolmaster, Church bells.

REVIEW: Athenaeum 2979 1884.

In his own hand. 3 vols [1885], 1 vol London and Manchester 1887 (illustr R. Pollitt and G. C. Banks), Manchester 1892.

REVIEW: Athenaeum 3033 1886.

The bridge of beauty: a fiction founded on fact. 1890 (illustr W. Dewar), 1893, [1894], [1901] (2nd edn, as The making of William Edwards: or the story of the bridge of beauty).

From the same nest: a homely tale. 1890, [1891].

Miss Pringle's pearls. 1890 (illustr F. Dadd), 1894.

A rough road: or how the boy made a man of himself. 1892, 1893 (illustr A. Pearse).

Bond-slaves. 1893.

REVIEWS: Athenaeum 3432 1893; Spectator 72 1894.

The slowly grinding mills. 3 vols 1893.

REVIEWS: Athenaeum 3426 1893, Spectator 71 1893.

Banks's stories and poems were pbd in a variety of periodicals, including Cassell's Family Mag, Family Herald, Girl's Own Paper and Manchester Guardian; *see the unpbd Catalogue to the E. L. Burney Collection in the John Rylands Univ Lib of Manchester. Banks contributed to various needlework jnls. Her many articles for* Manchester City News *are listed in Burney, below.*

§2

Mrs G. L. Banks. In Manchester faces and places vol 4, Manchester 1892.

Plarr, V. G. In Men and women of the time, Manchester and New York 1895 (14th edn).

The Times 6 May 1897.

Manchester Weekly Times 7 May 1897.

In DNB Suppl.

Burney, E. L. Mrs G. Linnaeus Banks. Manchester 1969.

'A. J. Barrowcliffe', Albert Julius Mott

Amberhill. 2 vols 1856, 1862.

Trust for trust. 3 vols 1859.

Normanton. 1862, 1865.

Barrowcliffe also pbd a number of pamphlets on various subjects under his real name, A. J. Mott.

'Cuthbert Bede', Edward Bradley 1827–89

Collections

Humour, wit and satire: containing i Book of beauty; ii Motley; iii Medley. [1885.]

§1

The adventures of Mr Verdant Green, an Oxford freshman; with numerous illustrations designed and drawn on the wood by the author. 1853.

The further adventures of Mr Verdant Green, an Oxford under-graduate: being a continuation of the Adventures of Mr Verdant Green, an Oxford freshman. With illustrations by the author. 1854.

Mr Verdant Green married and done for: being the third and concluding part of the Adventures of Mr Verdant Green, an Oxford freshman. 1857. The 3 pts have been frequently rptd together as Mr Verdant Green, with illustrations by the author.

The ratcatcher's daughter; illustrated, and dedicated (with permission) to the Honourable — by *Y*. [1854?]

Motley: prose and verse, grave and gay, with original illustrations by the author. 1855.

Love's provocations: being extracts taken in the most unmanly and unmannerly manner from the diary of Miss Polly C—. Illustrations by the author. 1855.

Photographic pleasure popularly portrayed with pen and pencil. 1855, 1859, [1864].

Medley. [1856.]

The shilling book of beauty, edited and illustrated by Cuthbert Bede. 1856. Written by Bede.

Tales of college life. 1856, 1862 (as College life). Contains 'Aeger', or mistaken identity; A long-vacation vigil; The only man left in college on Christmas day.

Nearer and dearer, a tale out of school: a novelette. Illustrated by the author. 1857.

Fairy fables, with illustrations by Alfred Crowquill. 1858.

Funny figures, by A. Funnyman (Cuthbert Bede). [1858.] 'One shilling plain: two shillings coloured', the latter with 24 coloured pictures.

Happy hours at Wynford Grange: a story for children. With coloured illustrations. 1859.

Glencreggan: or a highland home in Cantire, illustrated from the author's drawings. 2 vols 1861.

Our new rector: or the village of Norton, edited by Cuthbert Bede. 1861.

The curate of Cranston; with other prose and verse. 1862.

A tour in tartan-land. 1863.

The visitor's handbook to Rosslyn and Hawthornden. 1864.

The white wife; with other stories, supernatural, romantic and legendary, collected and illustrated by Cuthbert Bede. 1865.

The rook's garden: essays and sketches. 1865.

Mattins and Mutton's, or the Beauty of Brighton: a love story. 2 vols 1866.

Round the peat fire at Glenbrechy, with illustrations by the author. Xmas no of Once a Week 1869.

Little Mr Bouncer and his friend, Verdant Green, with illustrations by the author. [1873.]

Figaro at Hastings St Leonards. [1877.]

Fotheringhay and Mary, Queen of Scots: being an account, historical and descriptive, of Fotheringhay Castle, the last prison of Mary, Queen of Scots and the scene of her trial and execution, with illustrations by the author. 1886. First pbd in Leisure Hour 1865.

Betrothal ring of Mary Queen of Scots 1565: a description of the Darnley ring discovered in 1820 by a labourer, Robert Wyatt, when digging in the eastern mound on which stood the eastern keep of Fotheringhay Castle; printed for the Tercentenary of Mary Queen of Scots Exhibition held at Peterborough. 1887.

Argyll's highlands: or Mac Cailein Mor and the Lord of Lorne; with traditionary tales and legends of the County of Argyll and the Campbells and Macdonalds. Ed J. MacKay, Glasgow 1902.

'Cuthbert Bede' was a frequent contributor to Punch, All the Year Round, Field, GM, Once a Week, St James's Mag, London Rev, Quiver, Boy's Own Paper, Illus London News *and* N & Q. [EH]

Richard Doddridge Blackmore 1825–1900

Correspondence and literary papers are noted in LR. *Other unnoted archival material can be found in the Univ of Virginia Lib; Devon Record Office; Nat Lib of Wales; BL Manuscripts Collection; Huntington; Exeter Univ Lib; Bristol Univ Lib; Blackwood Papers, Nat Lib of Scotland; and the Walter H. Dunn Collection, Princeton.*

Bibliographies

Keogh, A. In W. L. Phelps, Essays on modern novelists, New York 1910, pp. 265–7.

Dunn, W. H. In his R. D. Blackmore: the author of Lorna Doone, 1956. *See also* Bernbaum and Carter *under* §2, *below.*

§1

Poems by Melanter. 1854.

Epullia [and other poems], by the author of Poems by Melanter. 1854.

The bugle of the Black Sea: or the British in the East, by Melanter. 1855.

The fate of Franklin. 1860.

The farm and fruit of old: an illustration in verse of the first and second Georgics of Virgil, by a market-gardener. 1862.

Clara Vaughan: a novel. 3 vols 1864, 1872 (rev); 12 edns 1874–92, 1894 (new edn), 1895, 1913.

Cradock Nowell: a tale of the New Forest. First pbd in Macmillan's Mag May 1865–Aug 1866. 3 vols 1866, 1873 (rev); 10 edns 1874–87, 1888 (new edn), 1893 (rev), 1902.

Lorna Doone: a romance of Exmoor. 3 vols 1869, 1873 (6th edn), New York 1875; pbd continuously between 1875–1908; ed H. S. Ward, 1908; 1910 (EL), 1911 (Macmillan's Pocket Classics), 1912, 2 vols 1913, Oxford 1913 (WC), ed H. Warren, Oxford 1914 (WC); ed R. O. Morris 1920. Pbd continuously between 1919–80, 1984 (Puffin Classics), 1991; tr Fr 1947.

The Georgics of Virgil, translated. 1871; ed R. S. Conway 1932.

The maid of Sker. First pbd in Blackwood's Mag Aug 1871–July 1872. 3 vols Edinburgh and London 1872, 1873, Hamburg 1878, Edinburgh and London 1879, 1888, 1890, 1893, 1895.

Alice Lorraine: a tale of the South Downs. First pbd in Blackwood's Mag Mar 1874–Apr 1875. 3 vols 1875, 1876 (6th edn rev), 1883, 1891, 1892, 1893, 1913, 1920; tr Polish 1885.

Cripps the carrier: a woodland tale. 3 vols 1876, 1877, 1881, 1883, 1887, 1890 (new edn), 1891.

Erema: or my father's sin. First pbd in Cornhill Mag Nov 1876–Nov 1877. 3 vols 1877, 1878, 1880, 1883, 1894, 1895.

Figaro at Hastings, St Leonards, with illustrations by the author. 1877.

Mary Anerley: a Yorkshire tale. First pbd in Fraser's Mag July 1879–Sep 1880. 3 vols 1880, 1881, 1894, 1913.

Christowell: a Dartmoor tale. First pbd in Good Words Jan–Dec 1881. 3 vols 1882, 1882, 1885, 1888, 1893, 1913.

The remarkable history of Sir Thomas Upmore Bart MP, formerly known as 'Tommy Upmore'. 2 vols 1884, 1884, 1885, 1894, 1902.

Humour, wit and satire: containing i Book of beauty; ii Motley; iii Medley, with numerous illustrations by the author. [1885].

Fotheringhay and Mary Queen of Scots: being an account, historical and descriptive, of Fotheringhay Castle, the last prison of Mary Queen of Scots and the scene of her trial and execution, with illustrations by the author. 1886. First pbd in Leisure Hour 1865.

Springhaven: a tale of the great war. First pbd in Harper's Mag Apr 1886–Apr 1887. 3 vols 1887, 1888, 1889 (new edn), 1894, 1909, 1925, 1928, 1969 (EL) with introd by R. L. Blackmore.

Betrothal ring of Mary Queen of Scots 1565: a description of the Darnley ring discovered in 1820 by a labourer, Robert Wyatt, when digging in the eastern mound on which stood the eastern keep of Fotheringhay Castle; printed for the Tercentenary of Mary Queen of Scots Exhibition held at Peterborough. 1887.

Kit and Kitty: a story of west Middlesex. 3 vols 1890, New York [1890], London 1894, 1913.

Perlycross: a tale of the western hills. 3 vols 1894, New York 1894, London 1894, 2 vols Leipzig 1895, London 1902, 1913.

Fringilla: a tale in verse. 1895.

Tales from the telling house. 1896, 1898, 1911.

Dariel: a romance of Surrey. First pbd in Blackwood's Mag Oct 1896–Oct 1897. 1897, New York 1897, 1900.

Argyll's highlands: or MacCailein Mor and the Lords of Lorne; with traditional tales. Ed J. Mackay, Glasgow 1902.

Contributions to periodicals

See Wellesley *vol 5, 1989.*

Buscombe: or, A Michaelmas goose. Harper's Mag Dec 1889. Poem.

§2

For a fuller list, see Q. G. Burris, Richard Doddridge Blackmore, *Urbana IL 1930, pp. 212–16.*

Smith, G. B. Mr Blackmore's novels. International Rev 7 1879.

The novels of Mr Blackmore. Blackwood's Mag Sep 1896.

Snell, F. J. The Blackmore country. 1906.

Phelps, W. L. Lorna Doone. In Essays on modern novelists, New York 1910.

Bernbaum, E. Blackmore and American cordiality. Southwest Rev 11 1925.

Bernbaum, E. On Blackmore and Lorna Doone: a selected bibliography, with brief comments. Lib Jnl 15 June 1925.

Burris, Q. G. Blackmore: his life and novels. Urbana IL 1930.

Elwin, M. In his Victorian wallflowers, 1934.

Etherington, J. R. M. Blackmore and his illustrators. N & Q 24 Mar 1945.

Etherington, J. R. M. Blackmore and a libel suit. N & Q 15 Dec 1945.

Etherington, J. R. M. Blackmore. New Eng Rev 13 1946.

Gill, W. W. and M. Words in Lorna Doone. N & Q 19 Oct, 30 Nov 1946.

Seybolt, P. S. Blackmore's Poems by Melanter. New Colophon 2 1950.

Dunn, W. H. R. D. Blackmore. N & Q 198, Nov 1953.

Hyde, W. J. Social propaganda in Blackmore. N & Q 199, Apr 1954.

Dunn, W. H. Blackmore: the author of Lorna Doone. 1956.

Buckler, W. E. Blackmore's novels before Lorna Doone. Nineteenth-Cent Fiction 10 1956.

Budd, K. The last Victorian: Blackmore and his novels. 1960.

Carter, J. A. Supplement to Blackmore bibliography. N & Q 207, Aug 1962. [DF]

Isa Blagden, Isabella Jane Blagden, 'Ivory Beryl' 1816/17–73

§1

Agnes Tremorne. 2 vols 1861.
  REVIEWS: Athenaeum 1744 1861; Saturday Rev 11 1861.

The cost of a secret. 3 vols 1863.
  REVIEW: Saturday Rev 15 1863.

The woman I loved, and the woman who loved me. 1865, Leipzig 1872 (Tauchnitz), New York [1886], Boston [18?].

Nora and Archibald Lee. 3 vols 1867, 1 vol New York 1867.

The crown of a life. 3 vols 1869.

Poems. Edinburgh and London 1873 (with a memoir [by Alfred Austin]).
  REVIEW: Athenaeum 2410 1874.

Blagden wrote stories and articles under the pseudonym 'Ivory Beryl'. Five of them are identified in Wellesley *vol 5, 1989.*

§2

Dearest Isa: Robert Browning's letters to Isabella Blagden. Ed with an introd by E. C. McAleer, Austin TX 1951; ed Sandra Donaldson with an introd by E. C. McAleer, 1990.

Blain, V., P. Clements and I. Grundy. The feminist companion to literature in English. 1990.

'Rolf Boldrewood', Thomas Alexander Browne

1826–1915

Bibliographies

Burke, K. Thomas Alexander Browne (Rolf Boldrewood): an annotated bibliography, checklist, and chronology. Cremorne NSW 1956.

Selections

Rolf Boldrewood. St Lucia, Queensland 1979 (Portable Australian Authors).

§1

The wild Australian. Serialised in the Australian Town and Country Jnl, 1877. Never pbd subsequently.
Ups and downs: a story of Australian life. 1878, 1890 (as The squatter's dream). The only complete version was pbd 1875 in the Australian Town and Country Jnl as The squatter's dream.
Old Melbourne memories. Melbourne 1884, London 1896 (rev), Melbourne and London 1969.
Robbery under arms: a story of life and adventure in the bush and in the goldfields of Australia. 3 vols 1888, 1 vol 1889, 1947, 1949, 1954, 1958, 1968 (abridged), 1972; tr Irish Gaelic Dublin 1936.
A colonial reformer. 3 vols 1890.
The miner's right: a tale of the Australian goldfields. 3 vols 1890.
A Sydney-side Saxon. 1891.
Nevermore. 3 vols 1892.
A modern buccaneer. 3 vols 1894.
The crooked stick: or Pollie's probation. 1895.
The sphinx of Eaglehawk: a tale of old Bendigo. 1895.
The sealskin cloak. 1896.
My run home. 1897.
Plain living: a bush idyll. 1898.
A romance of Canvas Town and other stories. 1898.
'War to the knife': or Tangata Maori. 1899.
Babes in the bush. 1900. First pbd 1876/77 in the Australian Town and Country Jnl as An Australian squire.
In bad company and other stories. 1901.
The ghost camp: or the avengers. 1902.
The Last Chance: a tale of the golden west. 1905.

§2

Clune, F. Captain Starlight: reckless rascal of 'Robbery under arms'. Melbourne 1945.
Brissenden, A. Rolf Boldrewood. Melbourne and London 1972.
[EH]

George Henry Borrow 1803–81

Borrow's mss and letters are widely dispersed. For details of locations, see M. Collie and A. Fraser, Bibliographies, *below. Major institutional holdings include (UK) BL, Cambridge Univ Lib, John Murray archive and Norfolk Record Office; (USA) Hispanic Soc of Amer New York, Huntington, HRHRC, Univ of Kentucky, NYPL (Berg), Rutgers Univ and Yale; (Canada) York Univ; (Russia) Nat Lib of Russia St Petersburg.*

Bibliographies

Knapp, W. I. In his Life, writings, and correspondence of Borrow, 2 vols 1899.
Thomas, E. In his George Borrow, 1912.
Wise, T. J. A bibliography of the writings in prose and verse of Borrow. 1914.
Stephen, G. A. In his Borrow House Museum: a brief account of the life of Borrow and his Norwich home, Norwich 1927.
Fréchet, R. In his George Borrow, Paris 1956.
Collie, M. and A. Fraser. George Borrow: a bibliographical study. Winchester 1984.
Vilarrubia, M. Borrow: a bibliographical addenda of secondary sources. BB, June 1990.

Collections

The works. 'Definitive' edn 6 vols 1899–1905. Contains Zincali, Bible in Spain, Lavengro, Romany rye, Wild Wales, Romano lavo-lil; completed 1928 with Celtic bards, chiefs and kings, ed H. G. Wright.
The works. Norwich edn ed C. K. Shorter 16 vols 1923–4. Includes unpbd ms material.
REVIEW: TLS, 28 Aug 1924.

Selections

An English Gypsy word-book: being Borrow's Romany vocabulary transposed. Ed Lord Lilford 1889.
Bohèmes et gypsies. Paris 1892. Trn of pt of Lavengro.
Isopel Berners. Ed T. Seccombe 1901. Extracted from Lavengro and The Romany rye.
Gipsy stories from Borrow's Bible in Spain. Ed W. H. D. Rouse [1905].
The stories of Antonio and Benedict Mol, from Borrow's Bible in Spain. Ed W. H. D. Rouse [1905].
The pocket Borrow. Ed E. Thomas 1912.
Selections from Borrow. Ed A. Burrell [1913].
Selections from Borrow. Ed J. G. Wilson [1914].
Wanderings in Spain: selections from The Bible in Spain. Ed F. A. Cavanagh 1914.
Readings from Borrow. Ed S. A. Richards [1921].
Borrow selections: with essays by Richard Ford, Leslie Stephen and George Saintsbury. Ed H. S. Milford, Oxford 1924.
The complete Newgate Calendar. Ed J. L. Rayner and G. T. Crook. 5 vols 1925–6.
Selections from Borrow. Ed W. E. Williams 1927.
Ballads of all nations, translated by Borrow: a selection. Ed R. B. Johnson 1927.
Celebrated trials. Ed E. M. Bierstadt. 2 vols New York and London 1928.
Isopel. Ed and tr M. J. Lavelle, Paris 1941.

§1

The Zincali: or an account of the Gypsies of Spain, with an original collection of their songs and poetry, and a copious dictionary of their language. 2 vols 1841, 1843, 1843, 1 vol 1846, 1861, 1869, 1872, 1882, 1888, 1893, 1901; introd E. Thomas 1914 (EL). Tr Ital (pts) 1878, Sp 1932.
REVIEWS: Athenaeum, 24 Apr, 1, 8 May 1841; [Bowring, J.] Westminster Rev, May 1841; [Chasles, P.] Revue des Deux Mondes, 1 Aug 1841; [Holme, F.] Blackwood's Mag, Sep 1841; [Merivale, H.] Edinburgh Rev 74, 1841; [Ford, R.] Br and Foreign Rev, June 1842.
The Bible in Spain: or the journeys, adventures, and imprisonments of an Englishman, in an attempt to circulate the scriptures in the peninsula. 3 vols 1843 (4 edns), 1 vol 1843 etc, ed U. R. Burke 2 vols 1896, ed U. R. Burke 1 vol 1899; introd E. Thomas 1906 (EL); 1906 (WC); ed P. Quennell 1959; introd W. Starkie 1961 (EL); introd T. Walker 1985. Tr Ger 1844, Fr 1845, 1967, Sp 1921, 1956, Ital [1943].
REVIEWS: [Dilke, C. W.] Athenaeum, 17, 24, 31 Dec 1842; [Lockhart, J. G.] Quart Rev 71, 1842; Examiner, 17 Dec 1842; Spectator, 17 Dec 1842; [Chasles, P.] Revue des Deux Mondes, 1 May 1843; [Ford, R.] Edinburgh Rev 64, 1843.
Lavengro: the scholar, the Gypsy, the priest. 3 vols 1851, 1 vol New York 1851, Paris 1851, Cincinatti 1852, London 1872, 1888, 1896; introd T. Watts[-Dunton] 1893; introd A. Birrell 1896; ed W. I. Knapp 1900; ed F. H. Groome 2 vols 1901; 1904 (WC); introd T. Seccombe 1906 (EL); ed E. Maxwell 1914; illustr B. Freedman, introd H. Walpole 1936; introd W. Starkie 1961 (EL). Tr Ger 1959, Rus 1967, Sp 1991.

REVIEWS: [Dilke, C. W.] Athenaeum, 8, 15 Feb 1851; [Aytoun, W. E.] Blackwood's Mag, Mar 1851; [Stirling, W.] Fraser's Mag, Mar 1851; [Forgues, E.-D.] Revue des Deux Mondes, 15 Mar 1851; [Ainsworth, W. H.] NMM, Mar 1851, [Hake, T. G.], Apr 1851; [Robberds, J. W.] Eclectic Rev, Apr 1851; [Donne, W. B.] Tait's Edinburgh Mag, May 1851; [Elwin, W.] Quart Rev 101, 1857.

The Romany rye: a sequel to Lavengro. 2 vols 1857, 1 vol New York 1857, 2 vols London 1858, 1 vol 1872, 1888, 1896, 1903; introd T. Watts-Dunton 1900; ed W. I. Knapp 1900; ed J. Sampson 1903; 1906 (EL); 1906 (WC); introd W. Starkie 1948.
REVIEWS: [Elwin, W.] Quart Rev 101, 1857; Athenaeum, 23 May 1857; [Montégut, E.] Revue des Deux Mondes, 1 Sep 1857.

Wild Wales: its people, language, and scenery. 3 vols 1862, 1 vol 1865, 1868, 1872, 1888, 1896, 1901 ('authoritative' edn); introd T. Watts-Dunton 1906 (EL); 1920 (WC); introd C. Price 1955; introd D. Jones 1958 (EL); illustr W. Rowlands, introd W. Condry, Llandysul 1995.
REVIEWS: Spectator, Dec 1862; [Lewes, G. H.] Cornhill Mag, Jan 1863.

Romano lavo-lil: word-book of the Romany, or English Gypsy language; with many pieces in Gypsy, illustrative of the way of speaking and thinking of the English Gypsies; with specimens of their poetry, and an account of certain Gypsyries or places inhabited by them, and of various things relating to Gypsy life in England. 1874, 1888, 1905.
REVIEWS: [Palmer, E. H.] Athenaeum, 25 Apr 1874; [Groome, F. H.] Acad 13 June 1874.

A supplementary chapter to The Bible in Spain, inspired by Ford's Hand-book for travellers in Spain. 1913 (priv ptd).

Celtic bards, chiefs and kings. Ed H. G. Wright 1928. Probably written 1857–60.
REVIEW: [Quennell, P.] New Statesman, 5 Jan 1929.

Contributions to periodicals

Borrow contributed trns, reviews etc to a number of periodicals, notably the following: NMM *7, 1823;* Monthly Mag *56–60, 1823–5;* Universal Rev, *1824–5;* London Mag *10, Dec 1824;* Panoramic Misc *1, 1826;* Athenaeum, *20 Aug 1836;* Illus London News, *8 Dec 1855;* Quart Rev *109, Jan 1861 (The Welsh and their literature);* Once a Week *6–9, 1862–3.*
For detailed listing see Collie and Fraser, Bibliographies, *above.*

Letters and diaries

A number of unpbd passages also appeared in works listed in §2 below.

Letters to the British and Foreign Bible Society. Ed T. H. Darlow 1911.
REVIEWS: TLS, 23 Nov 1911; New York Times, 25 Feb 1912.

Letters to his wife Mary Borrow. 1913 (priv ptd).

Letters to his mother Ann Borrow and other correspondents. 1913 (priv ptd).

George Borrow in Vienna: an unpublished letter. Ed C. K. Shorter [1914] (priv ptd).

An expedition to the Isle of Man in the year 1855: a hitherto unpublished diary by Borrow. Mannin 2–3 1914–15; Douglas 1915 (separately).

A journey to eastern Europe in 1844 (thirteen letters). Ed A. M. Fraser, Edinburgh 1981.

Letters to John Hasfeld 1835–1839. Ed A. M. Fraser, Edinburgh 1982.

Letters to John Hasfeld 1841–1846. Ed A. M. Fraser, Edinburgh 1984.

Editions

Celebrated trials and remarkable cases of criminal jurisprudence, from the earliest records to the year 1825. 6 vols 1825. Much, if not all, of preface by Sir R. Phillips, who directed the compilation.

Of the edns of scriptural trn with which Borrow was associated, his trn of St Luke into Spanish Romani is listed below. His role with the Manchu New Testament (St Petersburg 1835) and the Spanish New Testament (Madrid 1837) lay in the printing and manufacture; that was again his main function in regard to a trn of St Luke into Basque (Evangelioa San Lucasen Guissan: el Evangelio segun S Lucas, traducido al vascuence, Madrid 1838)*, but he also appears to have played a limited editorial role in its preparation.*

Translations in verse and prose

Faustus: his life, death, and descent into Hell, translated from the Ger [of F. M. von Klinger]. 1825, 1840, 1864. Anon.
REVIEWS: Literary Gazette, 16 July 1825; Monthly Mag, 1 Sep 1825; GM 95, 1825.

Romantic ballads, translated from the Danish, and miscellaneous pieces. Norwich 1826, London 1826, 1826, Norwich 1913.

Targum: or metrical translations from thirty languages and dialects. St Petersburg 1835; in Targum and the Talisman with other pieces, [1892] (facs).
REVIEW: [Hasfeld, J. P.] Athenaeum, 5 Mar 1836.

The talisman, from the Russian of Alexander Pushkin, with other pieces. St Petersburg 1835; in Targum and the Talisman, [1892] (facs).

Embéo e Majaró Lucas: brotoboro randado andré la chipe griega, acána chibado andré o Romanó, ó chipe es Zincales de Sesé; El evangelio segun S Lucas, traducido al Romani, ó dialecto de los Gitanos de España. [Madrid] 1837; Criscote e Majaró Lucas 1872.
REVIEW: [Usoz y Río, L. de] El Correo Nacional, 20 Apr 1838.

The sleeping bard: or visions of the world, death and hell, by Elis Wyn, translated from the Cambrian British. 1860.
REVIEWS: Borrow (anon), Quart Rev 109, 1861; [Montégut, E.] Revue des Deux Mondes, 15 Feb 1862.

The Turkish jester: or the pleasantries of Cogia Nasr Eddin Effendi, translated from the Turkish. Ipswich 1884.

The death of Balder, from the Danish of Johannes Ewald (1773). 1889.

Ode to Lewis Morris, from the Welsh of Goronwy Owen. Ed C. K. Shorter [1915] (priv ptd).

Welsh poems and ballads. Ed E. Rhys 1915.
REVIEW: [Seccombe, T.] Bookman (London) 48, Apr 1915.

The following are ballads, poems and tales priv ptd for T. J. Wise 1913, 1914 and rptd in Norwich edn 1923–4.

Alf the freebooter, Little Danneved and Swayne Trost, and other ballads. 1913.

Axel Thordson and fair Valborg: a ballad. 1913.

The brother avenged and other ballads. 1913.

Brown William, The power of the harp and other ballads. 1913.

Child Maidelvold and other ballads. 1913

The Dalby bear and other ballads. 1913.

Ellen of Villenskov and other ballads. 1913.

Emelian the fool: a tale translated from the Russian. 1913.

Ermeline: a ballad. 1913.

Finnish arts: or Sir Thor and Damsel Thure, a ballad. 1913.

The fountain of Maribo and other ballads. 1913.

The giant of Bern and Orm Ungerswayne: a ballad. 1913.

The gold horns, from the Danish of Adam Gottlob Oehlenschläger. Ed E. Gosse 1913.

Grimhild's vengeance: three ballads. Ed E. Gosse 1913.

Grimmer and Kamper, The end of Sivard Snarenswayne and other ballads. 1913.

Hafbur and Signe: a ballad. 1913.

King Diderik and the fight between the lion and dragon and other ballads. 1913.

King Hacon's death and Bran and the black dog: two ballads. 1913.

The king's wake and other ballads. 1913.

Little Engel: a ballad; with a series of epigrams from the Persian. 1913.

Marsk Stig: a ballad. 1913.

Marsk Stig's daughters and other songs and ballads. 1913.

The mermaid's prophecy and other songs relating to Queen Dagmar. 1913.

Mollie Charane and other ballads. 1913.

Niels Ebbesen and Germand Gladenswayne: two ballads. 1913.
The nightingale, The Valkyrie and raven, and other ballads. 1913.
Proud Signild and other ballads. 1913.
Queen Berngerd, The bard and the dreams and other ballads. 1913.
The return of the dead and other ballads. 1913.
The serpent knight and other ballads. 1913.
Signelil: a tale from the Cornish and other ballads. 1913.
The song of Deirdra, King Byrge and his brothers, and other ballads. 1913.
The songs of Ranild. 1913.
The story of Tim, translated from the Russian. 1913.
The story of Yvashka with the bear's ear, translated from the Russian. 1913.
The tale of Brynild and King Valdemar and his sister: two ballads. 1913.
Ulf van Yern and other ballads. 1913.
The Verner raven, The count of Vendel's daughter and other ballads. 1913.
Young Swaigder or the force of runes and other ballads. 1913.
The expedition to Birting's Land and other ballads. 1914.
Tord of Hafsborough and other ballads. 1914.

§2

For further titles see Stephen, Fréchet, Collie and Fraser, and Vilarrubia, Bibliographies, *above. The* George Borrow Bulletin, *issued by the George Borrow Soc since 1991, contains articles on Borrow's life and works. The Soc has published proceedings of conferences.*

Elwin, W. Roving life in England. Quart Rev 101, 1857. Reviews Lavengro, Romany rye.
Smiles, S. George Borrow. In his Brief biographies, Boston 1861.
Stephen, L. Country books. Cornhill Mag, Dec 1880, rptd in his Hours in a library, ser 3 1881.
Rommany rye. Standard, 1 Aug 1881. Obituary.
Elwin, W. Mr Borrow. Athenaeum, 6 Aug 1881. Obituary.
Hake, A. E. Recollections of Borrow. Athenaeum, 13 Aug 1881.
Watts[-Dunton], T. Reminiscences of Borrow. Athenaeum, 3–10 Sep 1881, rptd in his Old familiar faces, 1916.
Hake, A. E. George Borrow. Macmillan's Mag 45, Nov 1881. Obituary.
Webster, W. Borrow in Spain. Acad, 26 Nov 1881.
Tal-a-Hen. Borrow in Wales. Red Dragon 3, 1883.
Hake, A. E. George Borrow. DNB vol 5 1886.
Saintsbury, G. George Borrow. Macmillan's Mag, Jan 1886, rptd in his Essays in English literature 1780–1860, 1890.
Birrell, A. The office of literature. In his Obiter dicta, ser 2 1887.
Knapp, W. I. George Borrow. Chautauquan, Nov 1887.
Birrell, A. George Borrow. Reflector, 8 Jan 1888, rptd in his Res judicatae, 1892.
Montégut, E. Borrow, le gentilhomme bohémien. In his Écrivains modernes de l'Angleterre, Paris 1889.
Webster, W. Stray notes on Borrow's life in Spain. Jnl of Gypsy Lore Soc 1, 1889.
Whately, E. W. George Borrow. In his Personal and family glimpses of remarkable people, 1889.
Henley, W. E. Borrow: his vocation, ideals and achievements; himself. In his Views and reviews, 1890.
Smiles, S. In his A publisher and his friends, vol 2 1891.
Hake, T. G. In his Memoirs of eighty years, 1892.
Plane, J. Borrow: a sketch of his life and work. Eastern Daily Press, 17–19 Sep 1892.
Monkhouse, A. N. George Borrow. Manchester Quart 11, 1892, rptd in his Books and plays, 1894.
Harvey, E. Borrow: personal recollections. Eastern Daily Press, 1 Oct 1892.
Groome, F. H. George Borrow, etc. Bookman (London) Feb 1893.
Jessopp, A. Lavengro. Athenaeum, 8 Jul 1893.
Murray, J. Some authors I have known. Good Words, Feb 1895.
Lewis-Jones, W. George Borrow. Bangor 1895.
Dutt, W. A. Borrow in East Anglia. 1896.
Dutt, W. A. Borrow and East Anglia. Good Words, May 1897.
Knapp, W. I. The life, writings, and correspondence of Borrow, derived from official and other authentic sources. 2 vols 1899.
Johnson, L. O rare George Borrow! Outlook, 1 Apr 1899, rptd in his Post liminium, 1911.
Birrell, A. Borrow and his works. Quart Rev 189, Apr 1899.
Whibley, C. George Borrow. Blackwood's Mag, Apr 1899.
Stephen, L. Borrow and Gifford. Lit, 8 Apr 1899.
Findlater, J. H. George Borrow. Cornhill Mag, Nov 1899, rptd in her Stones from a glass house, 1904.
Jessopp, A. Lights on Borrow. Daily Chron, 30 Apr 1900.
Herzfeld, G. George Borrow. Archiv 107, 1901.
Seccombe, T. Borrow: his homes and haunts. Bookman (London), Feb 1902.
Watts-Dunton, T. George Henry Borrow. Chambers's Cyclopedia of Eng Lit vol 3 1903.
Euren, H. F. Norwich notables, 8: Borrow. Norwich Mercury, 4, 8 July 1903.
Seccombe, T. George Borrow. TLS, 10 July 1903.
McCormick, A. George Borrow, and the memorandum of his tour through Galloway. Gallovidian 7, 1905, rptd in his Words from the wild-wood, Glasgow 1912.
Shorthouse, J. H. The successor of Monsieur Le Sage. In his Life, letters and literary remains, vol 2 1905.
[Compton-]Rickett, A. George Borrow. In his The vagabond in literature, 1906.
Conan Doyle, A. In his Through the magic door, 1907.
Dutt, W. A. In his Some literary associations of East Anglia, 1907.
Shorter, C. K. To the immortal memory of Borrow. In his Immortal memories, 1907.
Walling, R. A. J. George Borrow: the man and his work. 1908.
Jenkins, H. Borrow in Russia. Nat Rev 54, 1909.
Blaesing, B. George Borrow. Marburg 1910.
Cantrill, T. C. and J. Pringle. Borrow's second tour in Wales. Y Cymmrodor 22, 1910; 1911 (separately).
Walker, H. In his Literature in the Victorian era, Cambridge 1910.
Thompson, T. W. Borrow's Gypsies. Jnl of Gypsy Lore Soc (n.s.) 3, 1910–11.
Hake, A. E. George Borrow. Acad, 10 June 1911.
Jenkins, H. Life of George Borrow, compiled from unpublished official documents, his works, correspondence etc. 1912.
Thomas, E. George Borrow: the man and his books. 1912.
More, P. E. George Borrow. Nation (New York), 27 June 1912, rptd in his Demon of the absolute, Princeton NJ 1928.
Shorter, C. K. Translation of Klinger's Faustus. N & Q, 15 Mar 1913.
Shorter, C. K. Borrow in Scotland. Fortnightly Rev, Apr 1913.
Hooper, J. Souvenir of the George Borrow celebration. Norwich 1913.
Beeching, H. C. George Borrow. Norwich 1913.
Beeching, H. C. The Borrow commemoration at Norwich. Cornhill Mag 35, 1913.
Shorter, C. K. George Borrow and his circle: wherein may be found many hitherto unpublished letters of Borrow and his friends. 1913.
Adams, M. In the footsteps of Borrow and FitzGerald. [1913].
Seccombe, T. George Borrow. Bookman (London), Oct 1913.
Leslie, S. Borrow in Spain. Dublin Rev 155, 1914.
Howells, W. D. The editor's easy chair. Harper's Monthly Mag, May 1914.
Ralli, A. George Borrow. Fortnightly Rev, 1 Oct 1915, rptd in his Critiques, 1927.
Rhys, E. Some unpublished prose miscellanies of Borrow. Y Cymmrodor 25, 1915.
Walker, H. In CHEL, vol 14 1916.

Schevill, R. Borrow: an English humourist in Spain. Univ of California Chron 18, May 1916; Berkeley CA 1916 (separately).
Hearn, L. George Borrow. In his Life and literature, New York 1917.
Thomas, E. In his A literary pilgrim in England, 1917.
Conan Doyle, A. Borrowed scenes. In his Danger! and other stories, 1918. Parody of Borrow.
Wright, H. G. The source of Matthew Arnold's Forsaken merman. MLR 13, 1918.
Elton, O. In his A survey of English literature 1830–80, vol 1 1920.
Shorter, C. K. The life of George Borrow. 1920.
Jerrold, W. Borrow's Joseph Sell. Cornhill Mag, Jan 1921.
Wright, H. G. Wild Wales: suppressed chapters. Welsh Outlook 9–10, 1922–3.
Wright, H. G. Borrow's Celtic bards, chiefs and kings. Quart Rev 479, 1924.
Blair, F. G. Fragments of three manuscripts in Borrow's autograph. Jnl of Gypsy Lore Soc 3rd ser 29, 1950.
Winstedt, E. O. Borrow's Hungarian-Romani vocabulary. Ibid 29–30 1950–1.
Boyle, A. The adventures of Joseph Sell and Tales of the wild and the wonderful. N & Q, 2 Feb 1952.
Yates, D. E. A leaf of Lavengro in Borrow's autograph. Jnl of Gypsy Lore Soc 3rd ser 31, 1952.
Hepworth, P. Original Borrow manuscripts acquired by Norwich Public Libraries. Ibid 32, 1953.
Fréchet, R. George Borrow: vagabond polyglotte, agent biblique, écrivain. Paris 1956.
Carter, J. and G. Pollard. The mystery of The death of Balder. Oxford 1969.
Fraser, A. M. The diaries of Borrow's walking tours. Jnl of Gypsy Lore Soc 3rd ser 49, 1970.
Fraser, A. M. Borrow's walking tours: the Welsh diary, 2–6 Sep 1854. Jnl of Gypsy Lore Soc (ser 3) 49, 1970.
Fraser, A. M. Borrow's walking tours: the Scottish diary, 4–7 Aug 1866. Jnl of Gypsy Lore Soc (ser 3) 50 1971.
Ridler, A. M. Sidelights on Borrow's Gypsy Luke. Bible Translator 33, July 1981.
Fraser, A. M. Borrow's wild Wales: fact and fabrication. Trans of Hon Soc of Cymmrodorion 1981.
Collie, M. Borrow's Joseph Sell. Nineteenth Cent Fiction 37, Sep 1982.
Collie, M. George Borrow eccentric. Cambridge 1982.
Fraser, A. M. The dismemberment of Borrow's remains. Antiquarian Bk Monthly Rev, May 1990.
Fraser, A. M. Los olvidados colaboradores de Borrow en España. Cuadernos Hispanoamericanos 524, Feb 1994.
Fraser, A. M. On the fringes of the Borrow canon. Borrow Bull, Autumn 1994.
Ridler, A. M. George Borrow as a linguist: images and contexts. Warborough 1996.
Fraser, A. M. Colonel Blood and Joseph Sell: reassessing the Borrow canon. Library 18, Mar 1996. [AMF]

Archibald Boyd

The Duchess, or woman's love and woman's hate: a romance. 3 vols 1850. Anon.
The Cardinal. 3 vols 1854.
The Crown ward. 3 vols 1856.

The Brontës

The Brontë Parsonage Museum is the principal repository of mss, correspondence, drawings and paintings, and memorabilia by or relating to the Brontës. Other major locations of Brontë mss include the BL; the Fitzwilliam Museum, Cambridge; the Harry Ransom Humanities Research Center, Univ of Texas at Austin; the Houghton Lib and Widener Collection, Harvard Univ; the Huntington Lib; Leeds Univ Lib (Brotherton Collection); the NYPL (Berg Collection); the Pierpont Morgan Lib (Bonnell Collection); and the Princeton Univ Libs (Robert H. Taylor Collection and Morris L. Parrish Collection). In addition to these, the John Rylands Univ Lib of Manchester, the King's School Canterbury, the NLS, the Rosenbach Lib, Rutgers Univ Lib, the State Univ of New York at Buffalo, the Univ of Missouri-Columbia, Wellesley College, Yale Univ and a substantial number of private collectors, chiefly in the United States, own one or more Brontë manuscripts. See also IELM vol 4 pt 1 1982.

Bibliographies and general works of reference

Turner, J. H. Haworth – past and present: a history of Haworth, Stanbury, & Oxenhope. Brighouse 1879, rptd 1971.
Anderson, J. P. Bibliography. In A. Birrell, Life of Charlotte Brontë, 1887.
Stuart, J. A. E. The Brontë country: its topography, antiquities, and history. 1888.
Wise, T. J. (ed). A reference catalogue of British and foreign autographs and manuscripts, part 1: the autograph of Charlotte Brontë. 1893 (priv ptd).
Transactions & publications of the Brontë Society. Bradford [later Haworth] 1895– .
Wood, B. A bibliography of the works of the Brontë family. Brontë Soc Trans 1 pt 1 1895; suppl 1 pt 6 1897.
Galloway, F. C. Descriptive catalogue of objects [including manuscripts] in the museum of the Brontë Society at Haworth. Bradford 1896.
Wroot, H. E. Relics of the Brontë family. Good Words 37, Feb 1896.
The London publishing houses: 4, Messrs Smith, Elder and Co. Bookman 21, Oct 1901.
Green, J. A. A catalogue of the Gleave Brontë Collection at the Moss Side Free Library, Manchester. Moss Side, Manchester 1905. List of additions 1907–16, Manchester 1916.
Field, W. T. Catalogue of the objects in the museum of the Brontë Society. Brontë Soc Trans 4 pt 18 1908.
Shorter, C. K. The early Brontë manuscripts. In The Brontës: life and letters, 2 vols 1908, vol 2 appendix 5.
Wood, B. Some bibliographical notes on the Brontë literature. Brontë Soc Trans 4 pt 21 1911.
Bibliography of recent Brontë literature. Brontë Soc Trans 5 pts 25–6 1915–16, 7 pt 40 1930.
Wise, T. J. A bibliography of the writings in prose and verse of the members of the Brontë family. 1917 (priv ptd); rptd 1965.
Wise, T. J. The Ashley Library: a catalogue of printed books, manuscripts, and autograph letters. 11 vols 1922–36; rptd 1971.
Cook, D. Brontë manuscripts in the Law Collection. Bookman 69, Nov 1925.
Symington, J. A. Roundhay Hall: the library of Col Sir Edward Allen Brotherton. Leeds 1926.
Symington, J. A. (comp). Catalogue of the Brontë Museum and Library. Haworth 1927; rptd 1967.
Wise, T. J. A Brontë library: a catalogue of printed books, manuscripts and autograph letters by the members of the Brontë family. 1929 (priv ptd).
Symington, J. A. The Bonnell Collection. Brontë Soc Trans 7 pt 40 1930.
Doubleday, W. E. (ed). Catalogue of the Brontë books and manuscripts. Hampstead [1931].
Hatfield, C. W. (comp). Catalogue of the Bonnell Collection in the Brontë Parsonage Museum. Brontë Soc Trans 8 pt 42 1932; rptd 1968.
Parrish, M. L. Victorian lady novelists: George Eliot, Mrs Gaskell, the Brontë sisters. First editions in the library at Dormy House, Pine Valley, New Jersey. 1933.
Ruff, W. First American editions of the Brontë novels: a complete bibliography. Brontë Soc Trans 8 pt 44 1934.
Christian, M. G. A census of Brontë manuscripts in the United

States. Trollopian 2–3 1947–8. Pt 1: mss of stories and poems by C. Brontë; pt 2: mags by C. and B. Brontë, book of poems by Charlotte and by Emily Brontë, mss of poems by Emily Brontë, mss of stories and poems by P. B. Brontë, mss of stories and poems by A. Brontë; pts 3–5: C. Brontë's letters.
Weir, E. M. Contemporary reviews of the first Brontë novels. Brontë Soc Trans 11 pt 57 1947.
Marchand, L. A. Description of the Symington Collection. Jnl of Rutgers Univ Lib 1948.
Marchand, L. A. An addition to the census of Brontë manuscripts. Nineteenth-Cent Fiction 4 1949. The Symington Collection.
Foxon, D. F. Binding variants in the Brontës' Poems. BC 2 1953.
Leclaire, L. A general analytical bibliography of the regional novelists of the British Isles 1800–1950. 1954. In Fr.
Huguenin, C. A. Brontëana at Princeton University: the Parrish Collection. Brontë Soc Trans 12 pt 65 1955.
Taylor, R. H. The singular anomalies. Princeton Univ Lib Chron 17 Winter 1956.
Christian, M. G. A guide to research materials on the major Victorians (part 2): the Brontës. Victorian Newsletter no 13 Spring 1958.
Randall, D. A. and S. Adelman. The first American edition of the Brontës' Poems. BC 9 1960. Response to query by J. Hayward in BC 8 1959.
Blackburn, R. H. (ed). The Brontë sisters: selected source materials for college research papers. Boston 1964.
Christian, M. G. The Brontës. In Victorian fiction: a guide to research, ed L. Stevenson, Cambridge MA 1964.
Nelson, J. G. First American reviews of the works of Charlotte, Emily and Anne Brontë. Brontë Soc Trans 14 pt 74 1964.
Foster, A. G. Analytical index of the contents of the Brontë Society Transactions vol 1 (1895)–vol 15 (1967) and index of authors. Keighley 1968 (Brontë Soc).
Hargreaves, G. D. The publishing of 'Poems by Currer, Ellis, and Acton Bell'. Brontë Soc Trans 15 pt 79 1969; Lib Rev 22 1970.
Cross, B. G. Annual checklists for the Brontë Society Transactions. 1970–81; continued by M. Klaus 1982–8, M. Klaus, G. Cross and R. Golen 1989.
Watt, I. The Brontës. In The British novel: Scott through Hardy. Northbrook IL 1973.
Winnifrith, T. The Brontës and their background: romance and reality. 1973.
Allott, M. The Brontës. In The English novel: select bibliographical guides, ed A. E. Dyson, 1974.
Allott, M. (ed). The Brontës: the critical heritage. London and Boston 1974.
Leeming, G. Who's who in Jane Austen and the Brontës. 1974.
Rauth, H. A survey of Brontë plays. Brontë Soc Trans 16 pt 84 1974. Summary of Univ of Innsbruck diss, Dramatisierungen von Leben und Werk der Brontë Schwestern, 1971.
Pinion, F. B. A Brontë companion: literary assessment, background, and reference. London and Basingstoke 1975.
Pollin, B. R. The Brontës in the American periodical press of their day: 193 reviews and comments annotated. Brontë Soc Trans 16 pt 85 1975.
Rosengarten, H. J. The Brontës. In Victorian fiction: a second guide to research, ed G. H. Ford, New York 1978.
Yablon, G. A. and J. R. Turner. A Brontë bibliography. London and Westport CT 1978.
Passel, A. Charlotte and Emily Brontë: an annotated bibliography. New York 1979.
Blake, K. Review of Brontë studies: 1975–1980, 1981–1987. In Dickens Stud Annual 10 1982, 18 1989.
Crump, R. W. (comp). Charlotte and Emily Brontë 1846–1915: a reference guide. Boston 1982. Additional vols for 1916–54, Boston 1985; 1955–83, Boston 1986.
Lloyd Evans, B. and G. Lloyd Evans. Everyman's companion to the Brontës. London, Melbourne and Toronto 1982.
Pollin, B. R. More contemporary American reviews of books by the Brontës. Brontë Soc Trans 18 pt 92 1982.
Rosenbaum, B. and P. White, comp. In IELM vol 4, pt 1 1982. The Brontës.
Walker, A. D. The correspondence of the Brontë family: a guide. Manchester 1982.
Chitham, E. and T. Winnifrith. Brontë facts and Brontë problems. London and Basingstoke 1983.
The Gordon bequest. Brontë Soc Trans 19 pts 1–2 1986.
Chaudhuri, B. Bibliography on demand: the Brontës: 1970–1985. Edmonton, Canada 1987.
Sixty treasures: the Brontë Parsonage museum. Haworth 1988.
Gordon, F. A preface to the Brontës. London and New York 1989.
Smith, W. E. The Brontë sisters: a bibliographical catalogue of first and early editions 1846–1860, with photographic reproductions of bindings and title pages. Los Angeles 1991.
Lemon, C. A centenary history of the Brontë Society 1893–1993. [Haworth] 1993.
Alexander, C. and J. Sellars. The art of the Brontës. Cambridge 1994. Includes catalogue of art work.
Lemon, C. (ed). Early visitors to Haworth: from Ellen Nussey to Virginia Woolf. Haworth 1996.
McNees, E. (ed). The Brontë sisters: critical assessments. 4 vols Robertsbridge and New York 1996.
Stoneman, P. Brontë transformations: the cultural dissemination of Jane Eyre and Wuthering Heights. London and New York 1996.
Orel, H. The Brontës: interviews and recollections. 1997.

Collections and selections: the Brontë family

For individual authors' works, see relevant sections below.

Poems by Currer, Ellis, and Acton Bell. 1846, '1846' [1848], Philadelphia 1848, '1905' [1904] (as Poems: by the Brontë sisters; with Selections from the literary remains of Ellis and Acton Bell, first pbd in Wuthering Heights and Agnes Grey, 1850).
REVIEWS: [Dobell, S.] Athenaeum 4 July 1846; Critic n.s. 4, 4 July 1846; B[utler, W. A.] Dublin Univ Mag 28, Oct 1846; Peterson's Mag (Philadelphia) 14, Sep 1848; Tribune (New York) 10 Aug 1848; Godey's Lady's Book (Philadelphia) 37, Oct 1848; Spectator 11 Nov 1848; Tait's Edinburgh Mag n.s. 15, Dec 1848; Critic n.s. 7, 15 Dec 1848; Literary Gazette 32, 30 Dec 1848; Rankin, J. E. The Bells and their chimes, Pictorial Nat Lib (Boston) Jan 1849.

Wuthering Heights and Agnes Grey, by Ellis and Acton Bell. A new edition revised, with a biographical notice of the authors, a selection from their literary remains, and a preface by Currer Bell. 1850.
REVIEWS: Examiner 21 Dec 1850; Athenaeum 28 Dec 1850; [Lewes, G. H.] Leader 1, 28 Dec 1850; Economist 9, 4 Jan 1851; Eclectic Rev, n.s. 1, Feb 1851.

Uniform edition of the life and works of the Brontë sisters, Currer, Ellis, and Acton Bell. 7 vols 1857–60. Vol 1 Life of Charlotte Brontë by Mrs Gaskell; vol 2 Jane Eyre; vol 3 Shirley; vol 4 Villette; vol 5 The professor by Currer Bell . . . to which are added the poems of Currer, Ellis, and Acton Bell: now first collected; vol 6 Wuthering Heights and Agnes Grey; vol 7 The tenant of Wildfell Hall.

The life and works of Charlotte Brontë and her sisters. 7 vols 1872–3, 1888–9. Vol 1 Jane Eyre; vol 2 Shirley; vol 3 Villette; vol 4 The professor, to which are added the poems of Currer, Ellis, and Acton Bell, and Cottage poems by the Rev Patrick Brontë; vol 5 Wuthering Heights and Agnes Grey; vol 6 The tenant of Wildfell Hall; vol 7 The life of Charlotte Brontë by Mrs Gaskell.

The works of Charlotte, Emily and Anne Brontë. Introd by F. J. S. 12 vols 1893, 1901 (Temple edn). Vols 1–2 Jane Eyre; vols 3–4 Shirley; vols 5–6 Villette; vol 7 The professor; vol 8 Poems of Charlotte, Emily, & Anne Brontë, with Cottage poems by Patrick Brontë;

vols 9–10 Wuthering Heights and Agnes Grey; vols 11–12 The tenant of Wildfell Hall.
The novels of the sisters Brontë: Thornton edn. Ed T. Scott, introd and notes to E. C. Gaskell's Life by Scott and B. W. Willett, 12 vols 1898–1901, Edinburgh 1905.
Life and works of Charlotte Brontë and her sisters: Haworth edn. With introds to the works by Mrs H. Ward, and an introd and notes to the Life [by E. C. Gaskell] by C. K. Shorter. 7 vols London and New York 1899–1900; rptd New York 1982. Vol 1 Jane Eyre (1899); vol 2 Shirley (1899); vol 3 Villette (1899); vol 4 The professor, with poems by Charlotte, Emily and Anne Brontë, and the Rev Patrick Brontë (1900); vol 5 Wuthering Heights and Agnes Grey (1900); vol 6 The tenant of Wildfell Hall (1900); vol 7 The life of Charlotte Brontë by E. C. Gaskell (1900).
The novels of Charlotte, Emily, and Anne Brontë. 7 vols 1901–7 (WC). Vol 1 Jane Eyre (1901); vol 2 Wuthering Heights (1901); vol 3 Shirley (1902); vol 4 Villette (1903); vol 5 The professor ... to which are added the poems of Charlotte, Emily, and Anne Brontë, introd by T. Watts-Dunton (1906); vol 6 The tenant of Wildfell Hall (1906); vol 7 Agnes Grey (1907).
Poems by Charlotte, Emily and Anne Brontë, now for the first time printed. New York 1902.
The complete works of Charlotte Brontë and her sisters. 7 vols 1905.
The novels of the sisters Brontë. Illustr E. Dulac, 10 vols London and New York 1905. Introd by F. J. S. as in 1893 12-vol edn of the works, *above*.
Agnes Grey, The professor, Poems, by the sisters Brontë. London and Glasgow [1908].
Brontë poems: selections from the poetry of Charlotte, Emily, Anne and Branwell Brontë. Ed A. C. Benson, New York and London 1915.
The orphans, and other poems: by Charlotte, Emily and Branwell Brontë. Ed T. J. Wise 1917 (priv ptd).
The Shakespeare Head Brontë. Ed T. J. Wise and J. A. Symington 19 vols Oxford 1931–8. Vols 1–2 Jane Eyre (1931); vol 3 The professor (1931); vols 4–5 Shirley (1931); vols 6–7 Villette (1931); vol 8 Wuthering Heights (1931); vol 9 Agnes Grey (1931); vols 10–11 The tenant of Wildfell Hall (1931); vols 12–15 The Brontës: their lives, friendships, and correspondence, in 4 vols (1932) (i, 1777–1843; ii, 1844–9; iii, 1849–52; iv, 1852–1928); vol 16 The poems of Emily Jane Brontë and Anne Brontë (1934); vol 17 The poems of Charlotte Brontë & Patrick Branwell Brontë (1934); vols 18–19 The miscellaneous and unpublished writings of Charlotte and Patrick Branwell Brontë, in 2 vols (i, 1936; ii, 1938). A twentieth vol, intended to provide bibl information, was proposed but never issued.
The Brontës: Heather edn. Arranged and introd by P. Bentley 6 vols 1949. Vol 1 Jane Eyre; vol 2 Shirley; vol 3 Villette; vol 4 Wuthering Heights and Agnes Grey; vol 5 The tenant of Wildfell Hall; vol 6 The lives and writings of the Brontës (includes Stories from Angria, The professor, Emma, Poems).
The Clarendon edition of the novels of the Brontës. General ed I. Jack 7 vols Oxford and New York 1969–92. Vol 1 Jane Eyre, ed J. Jack and M. Smith (1969); vol 2 Wuthering Heights, ed H. Marsden and I. Jack (1976); vol 3 Shirley, ed H. Rosengarten and M. Smith (1979); vol 4 Villette, ed H. Rosengarten and M. Smith (1984); vol 5 The professor, ed M. Smith and H. Rosengarten (1987); vol 6 Agnes Grey, ed H. Marsden and R. Inglesfield (1988); vol 7 The tenant of Wildfell Hall, ed H. Rosengarten (1992).
Charlotte Brontë, Patrick Branwell Brontë: choix établi et présenté par Raymond Bellour. Paris 1972.
The Brontë sisters: selected poems of Charlotte, Emily and Anne Brontë. Ed S. Davies, Cheadle 1976.
Poems by the Brontë sisters. Introd by M. R. D. Seaward, Wakefield 1978. Facs of 1846 Poems.
The Brontës: selected poems. Ed with introd and notes by J. R. V. Barker, London and Melbourne 1985 (EL).
Selected Brontë poems. Ed E. Chitham and T. Winnifrith, Oxford and New York 1985.
The juvenilia of Jane Austen and Charlotte Brontë. Ed F. Beer 1986 (Pen).
Angria & Gondal. Ed E. Maletzke, tr H. J. Schütz, Frankfurt 1987.

Letters

Shorter, C. The Brontës: life and letters. Being an attempt to present a full and final record of the lives of the three sisters, Charlotte, Emily, and Anne Brontë from the biographies of Mrs Gaskell and others, and from numerous hitherto unpublished manuscripts and letters. 2 vols London and New York 1908; rptd New York 1969.
The Brontës: their lives, friendships and correspondence. Ed T. J. Wise and J. A. Symington, 4 vols Oxford 1932 (Shakespeare Head Brontë); rptd in 2 vols 1980.
New acquisitions: letters from Emily, Anne, and Patrick. Mrs Gaskell's annotations. Brontë Soc Trans 12 pt 63 1953.
Spark, M. (ed). The Brontë letters. 1954; 1966 (new edn); rptd in The essence of the Brontës, London and Chester Springs PA 1993.
Three Brontë letters. Brontë Soc Trans 14 pt 74 1964.
Stephens, F. C. Hartley Coleridge and the Brontës. TLS 14 May 1970.
Gardiner, J. The world within: the Brontës at Haworth: a life in letters, diaries and writings. 1992.
Smith, M. Newly acquired Brontë letters, transcriptions and notes. Brontë Soc Trans 21 pt 7 1996.
Barker, J. The Brontës: a life in letters. 1997.

Biographical studies

For works on individual authors, see relevant sections below.
P., W. P. Jottings on Currer, Ellis, and Acton Bell. 1856.
Wright, W. The Brontës in Ireland, or, facts stranger than fiction. 1893, New York 1894, rptd 1981.
Richardson, F. (later F. Macdonald). The Brontës at Brussels. Woman at Home 2, July 1894.
Turner, J. H. A day at Haworth. [1894.]
Mackay, A. M. A crop of Brontë myths. Westminster Rev 144, Oct 1895; expanded in The Brontës: fact and fiction, 1897.
Scruton, W. Thornton and the Brontës. Bradford 1898; rptd 1968 (as The Brontës).
Duclaux, Mme (A. M. F. Robinson). Les soeurs Brontë. Revue de Paris 6, Dec 1899; 7, Jan 1900.
Henneman, J. B. The Brontë sisters. Sewanee Rev 9, Apr 1901. Review article on the Haworth edn.
Mackay, A. M. The Brontës: their fascination and genius. Bookman 27, Oct 1904 (special no on the Brontës).
[Smith, C. C. M.] The Brontës at Thornton. Bookman 27, Oct 1904; rptd in C. K. Shorter, The Brontës: life and letters vol 2.
Malham-Dembleby, J. The lifting of the Brontë veil: a new study of the Brontë family. Fortnightly Rev n.s. 87, Mar 1907.
Dimnet, E. Les soeurs Brontë. Paris 1910 (Les grands écrivains étrangers); tr L. M. Sill as The Brontë sisters, 1927.
Chadwick, Mrs E. H. (Esther Alice Chadwick). In the footsteps of the Brontës. 1914.
Clarke, I. C. Haworth parsonage: a picture of the Brontë family. [1927.]
Romieu, E. and G. Romieu. La vie des soeurs Brontë. Paris 1929. Tr R. Tapley as Three virgins of Haworth, being an account of the Brontë sisters, New York 1930, London 1931 (as The Brontë sisters).
Sugden, K. A. R. A short history of the Brontës. 1929.
Crevel, R. Les soeurs Brontë, filles du vent. Paris 1930.
O'Byrne, C. The Gaelic source of the Brontë genius. 1933; rptd Port Washington NY and London 1970.
Willis, I. C. The Brontës. 1933; rptd New York 1977.
Delafield, E. M. [E. E. M. de la Pasture] (comp and introd). The Brontës: their lives recorded by their contemporaries. 1935.

Edgerley, C. M. Elizabeth Branwell, the 'small, antiquated lady'. Brontë Soc Trans 9 pt 47 1937.
de Traz, R. La famille Brontë. Paris 1939.
White, W. B. The miracle of Haworth: a Brontë study. New York 1939.
Hinkley, L. L. The Brontës: Charlotte and Emily. New York 1945, London 1947.
Bentley, P. The Brontës. 1947.
The Brontës then and now: a symposium of articles reprinted from various issues of the Brontë Society Transactions. Shipley 1947.
Harrison, G. E. The clue to the Brontës. 1948.
Raymond, E. In the steps of the Brontës. 1948.
Hanson, L. and E. M. Hanson. The four Brontës: the lives and works of Charlotte, Branwell, Emily, and Anne Brontë. London, New York and Toronto 1949.
Braithwaite, W. S. The bewitched parsonage: the story of the Brontës. New York and Toronto 1950.
Lane, M. Mr Nicholls. Cornhill Mag 983 Summer 1950.
Whone, C. Where the Brontës borrowed books: the Keighley Mechanics' Institute. Brontë Soc Trans 11 pt 60 1950.
Holgate, I. The Brontës at Thornton: 1815–1820. Brontë Soc Trans 13 pt 69 1959.
Bluteau, J. La vie passionée des Brontës. Paris 1960.
Whitehead, P. The Brontës came here. [Halifax 1962.]
Maurat, C. Le secret des Brontë ou Charlotte Brontë d'après les juvénilia, ses lettres et ceux qui l'ont connue. Paris 1967. Tr M. Meldrum as The Brontës' secret, 1969.
Bentley, P. The Brontës and their world. 1969.
Morrison, N. B. Haworth harvest: the story of the Brontës. London and New York 1969.
Gérin, W. The Brontës: 1. The formative years; 2. The creative work. Writers and their work 232 and 236, 1973, 1974.
Cannon, J. The road to Haworth: the story of the Brontës' Irish ancestry. 1980, New York 1981.
Foister, S. The Brontë portraits. Brontë Soc Trans 18 pt 95 1985.
Chitham, E. The Brontës' Irish background. New York and London 1986.
Barker, J. The Brontës. 1995.
Lemon, C. (ed). Early visitors to Haworth. From Ellen Nussey to Virginia Woolf. Haworth 1996.

Selected criticism

C., T. C. Shirley, Jane Eyre and Wuthering Heights. Amer Rev n.s. 5, Mar 1850. Includes discussion of The tenant of Wildfell Hall.
Bayne, P. Currer Bell. Hogg's Instructor n.s. 4, May 1855; rptd as Ellis, Acton, and Currer Bell in Bayne's Essays in biography and criticism, 1st ser Boston and New York 1857; also in his Essays, biographical, critical, and miscellaneous, Edinburgh and London 1859.
[Rands, W. B.] Reading raids no VI – Currer, Ellis, and Acton Bell. Tait's Edinburgh Mag n.s. 22, July 1855.
Roscoe, W. C. The Miss Brontës. In Poems and essays by the late William Caldwell Roscoe, ed R. H. Hutton 2 vols 1860, vol 2.
[Smith, G. B.] The Brontës. Cornhill Mag 28, July 1873; rptd in his Poets and novelists: a series of literary studies, 1875.
Kinsley, W. W. The Brontë sisters. In his Views on vexed questions, Philadelphia 1881; rptd as The Brontë sisters, London, New York and Chicago 1899.
Oliphant, M. The sisters Brontë. In A. Sergeant et al, Women novelists of Queen Victoria's reign, 1897.
Saintsbury, G. Position of the Brontës as origins in the history of the English novel. Brontë Soc Trans 2 pt 9 1899.
Lord, W. F. The Brontë novels. Nineteenth Cent and After 53, Mar 1903.
Whitmore, C. H. The Brontës. In Woman's work in English fiction from the Restoration to the mid-Victorian period, London and New York 1910.
Meynell, A. Charlotte and Emily Brontë. Dublin Rev 148, Apr 1911; rptd in her Hearts of controversy, [1917]; revised in her Essays of to-day and yesterday, 1926.
Sinclair, M. The three Brontës. London, New York and Boston 1912; 1914 (2nd edn).
Chesterton, G. K. The Victorian age in literature. [1913.]
Drinkwater, J. The Brontës as poets. In Prose papers, 1917. First pbd as a rev of A. C. Benson's Brontë poems, 1915.
Masson, J. The Brontës as seen through French eyes. London Quart Rev 131, Jan 1919.
Dello Buono, C. J. (ed). Rare early essays on the Brontës. Darby PA 1980. 10 essays, pbd 1857–1943.

Patrick Brontë 1770–1861

See Collections and selections: the Brontë family, *above*.

§1

Winter-evening thoughts. A miscellaneous poem. London and Wakefield 1810; revised as Winter-night meditations, ptd in Cottage poems, 1811.
Cottage poems. Halifax 1811; rptd (with The rural minstrel) in facs, with introd by D. H. Reiman, New York and London 1977.
REVIEW: Eclectic Rev 8, Jan 1812.
The rural minstrel: a miscellany of descriptive poems. Halifax 1813; rptd (with Cottage poems) in facs, with introd by D. H. Reiman, New York and London 1977.
The cottage in the wood; or the art of becoming rich and happy. Bradford 1815; 1818 (2nd edn). Prose section rptd in Cottage Mag 6, June 1817, and separately in Bradford 1859, Bingley 1865.
On conversion. Pastoral Visitor July, Sep, Oct 1815; rptd by K. Lawson in Brontë Soc Trans 19 pt 6 1988.
The maid of Killarney; or, Albion and Flora, a modern tale; in which are interwoven some cursory remarks on religion and politics. 1818.
A sermon preached in the church of Haworth, on Sunday, the 12th day of September, 1824, in reference to an earthquake, and extraordinary eruption of mud and water, that had taken place ten days before, in the moors of that chapelry. Bradford 1824. Extract given under title Crow Hill earthquake, in J. Whalley, The wild moor: a tale founded on fact, Leeds 1869.
The phenomenon, or, an account in verse, of the extraordinary disruption of a bog, which took place in the moors of Haworth, on the 12th day [*sic*] of September, 1824: intended as a reward-book for the higher classes in Sunday-schools. Bradford 1824.
The signs of the times; or a familiar treatise on some political indications in the year 1835. Keighley 1835.
A brief treatise on the best time and mode of baptism, chiefly in answer to a tract of Peter Pontifex, alias the Rev M. S–, Baptist minister. Keighley 1836.
A funeral sermon for the late Rev William Weightman, M.A., preached in the church of Haworth, on Sunday, the 2nd of October, 1842, by the Rev Patrick Brontë, A.B., Incumbent. Halifax 1842.
On Halley's comet in 1835. The Bradfordian 1861. Poem dated 20 Oct 1835.
Poems of Currer, Ellis, and Acton Bell, with Cottage poems by the Rev Patrick Brontë. With The professor, in The life and works of Charlotte Brontë and her sisters vol 4, 1873 (*see* Collections, *above*).
Two sermons preached in the church of Haworth . . . Also A phenomenon, or an account in verse of the extraordinary disruption of a bog . . . Haworth [1885].
Poems of Charlotte, Emily & Anne Brontë, with Cottage poems by Patrick Brontë. In the works of Charlotte, Emily, and Anne Brontë, introd by F. J. S. 12 vols, vol 8. 1893.
Brontëana: The Rev Patrick Brontë A. B., his collected works and

life; the works, and The Brontës of Ireland. Ed J. H. Turner, Bingley 1898; rptd Darby PA 1978. Includes Cottage poems; The rural minstrel; The cottage in the wood; The maid of Killarney; The phenomenon; A sermon ... in reference to an earthquake; The signs of the times; A brief treatise on ... baptism; A funeral sermon for the late Rev William Weightman, M.A.; Fugitive pieces; On Halley's comet in 1835. Pt 2: The Brontës of Ireland.

The professor, with poems by Charlotte, Emily, and Anne Brontë, and the Rev Patrick Brontë. Introd by Mrs H. Ward in Haworth edn of Life and works of Charlotte Brontë and her sisters vol 4, London and New York 1900.

Letters

Letter to Leeds Mercury 15 Dec 1810 (signed 'Sydney').

A letter from a clergyman – in answer to a letter of sympathy on the loss of his wife. Cottage Mag 11, 1822; rptd in Letter from the Rev Patrick Brontë, on the death of his wife, Brontë Soc Trans 7 pt 41 1931; also in J. Lock and W. T. Dixon, A man of sorrow, 1965. Letter dated 27 Nov 1821.

Cremation. Letter ptd in Leeds Mercury 16 Mar 1844.

The Brontës at Thornton. Bookman 27, Oct 1904. Two letters to Mrs J. C. Franks; one to Rev J. C. Franks.

S[horter], C. K. A literary letter: more Brontë love letters. Sphere 23 Aug 1913. Letters between Mr Brontë and Mary Burder.

Goldring, M. Some unpublished Brontë manuscripts. Appendix to her Charlotte Brontë, the woman: a study, 1915, New York 1916. Two letters from Mr Brontë dated 4 Oct 1843 and 29 Feb 1844.

The Brontës: their lives, friendships and correspondence. Ed T. J. Wise and J. A. Symington 4 vols Oxford 1932 (Shakespeare Head Brontë); rptd in 2 vols 1980.

The Reverend Patrick Brontë and Mrs E. C. Gaskell: sources of biographer's information. Brontë Soc Trans 8 pt 43 1933. Letters from Mr Brontë used by Gaskell in her biography of Charlotte Brontë.

New acquisitions: letters from Emily, Anne and Patrick; Mrs Gaskell's annotations. Brontë Soc Trans 12 pt 63 1953. Letters dated 12 July 1850; two from [Jan 1853]; 8 July 1854; 31 Aug 1857.

Beckwith, F. Letters of the Rev Patrick Brontë to the Leeds Intelligencer. Brontë Soc Trans 13 pt 70 1960. Letters dated 16 Sep 1824; 15 Jan, 29 Jan, 5 Feb 1829; 6 May 1830.

Timings, E. K. 'A great fancy for arms': correspondence between the Reverend Patrick Brontë and the Ordnance office. Brontë Soc Trans 14 pt 71 1961. Letters dated 19 Nov 1841; 29 Nov 1841; 4 July 1848.

Three Brontë letters. Brontë Soc Trans 14 pt 74 1964. Letter from Mr Brontë to Eliza Brown, 10 June 1859.

Acquisition of Brontë drawings and a letter by Mr Brontë. Brontë Soc Trans 16 pt 85 1975. Letter dated 8 Aug 1831.

§2

Biographical and critical studies

The Rev Patrick Brontë. Illus London News 22 June 1861.

Mayor, J. E. B. Patrick Brontë. N & Q 2nd ser 12, 24 Aug 1861.

H. Mr Nicholls: Charlotte Brontë. N & Q 5th ser 12, 26 July 1879. Mainly on Mr Brontë.

H., L. L. Rev Patrick Brontë. N & Q 5th ser 12, 20 Sep 1879.

Yates, W. W. The Brontës at Dewsbury. Brontë Soc Trans 1 pt 3 1895.

Yates, W. W. The father of the Brontës: his life and work at Dewsbury and Hartshead, with a chapter on 'Currer Bell'. Leeds 1897.

Hatfield, C. W. and C. M. Edgerley (ed). The Reverend Patrick Brontë and Mrs E. C. Gaskell: sources of biographer's information. Brontë Soc Trans 8 pt 43 1933; pt 44 1934.

Holgate, I. The cottage in the wood. Brontë Soc Trans 13 pt 67 1957.

Hopkins, A. B. The father of the Brontës. Baltimore 1958; rptd New York 1968.

Prunty, M. Father of the Brontë sisters. Irish Digest 73, Dec 1961.

Lock, J. and W. T. Dixon. A man of sorrow: the life, letters, and times of the Rev Patrick Brontë 1777–1861. 1965.

Colloms, B. Victorian country parsons. 1977.

Pollard, A. The Brontës and their father's faith. E & S 37 1984.

Baumber, M. William Grimshaw, Patrick Brontë, and the evangelical revival. History Today 42, Nov 1992.

Textual/bibliographical studies

Defniel (pseud). A sermon by the Rev P. Brontë. N & Q 6th ser 1, 14 Feb 1880. Response by J. H. T[urner], N & Q 6th ser 1, 27 Mar 1880.

Whone, C. Where the Brontës borrowed books: the Keighley Mechanics' Institute. Brontë Soc Trans 11 pt 60 1950.

Stanley, B. E. Patrick Brontë's notebook. Brontë Soc Trans 14 pt 72 1962

Dewhirst, I. The Rev Patrick Brontë and the Keighley Mechanics' Institute. Brontë Soc Trans 14 pt 75 1965.

Myer, V. G. Patrick Brontë's The cottage in the wood and the plot of Jane Eyre. N & Q n.s. 233, Dec 1987.

Charlotte Brontë, later Nicholls, 'Currer Bell'

1816–55

See Collections and selections: the Brontë family, *above.*

§1

Jane Eyre: an autobiography, edited by Currer Bell. 3 vols 1847, New York [1847] etc, London 1848 (2nd edn with preface and dedication to W. M. Thackeray), 1848 (3rd edn), 1 vol New York 1848, London 1850 (4th edn), 2 vols Leipzig 1848 (Tauchnitz), 1850, 1 vol London 1857 (new edn), 1858 etc, 2 vols Philadelphia 1884; introd by C. K. Shorter, London, New York and Toronto [1889]; introd by H. P. Spofford, New York 1898; introd by W. R. Nicoll 1902 (with The Moores); introd by M. Sinclair, London and New York [1908] (EL); 1953; ed B. Dobree, London and Glasgow 1954; introd by M. Lane London and New York [1957] (EL); ed M. Shorer, Boston 1959; ed Q. D. Leavis 1966, 1985 (Pen); ed R. J. Dunn, New York and London 1971 (Norton Critical edn), New York 1987 (2nd edn); ed M. Smith 1973 (Oxford English Novels), 1980 (WC); introd by L. Hughes-Hallett, 2 vols New York 1991 (EL); ed B. Newman, Boston and New York 1996; ed M. Mason 1996 (Pen); ed R. A. Nemesvari, Peterborough, Ontario, 1999. *See also* Collections *above.*

TRANSLATIONS: Fr 1849 (abridged), 1854, 1855, 1859, 1883, [1932], [1944], 1946, 1946, [1947], [1947] (adapted), 1953, 1966; Ger [1864], 1867, 1888; Hungarian 1873; Danish 1884; Sp 1889, 1903 (2nd edn), 1941, [1944], 1958; Swed 1894, [1905]; Du [1942], 1946, 1947, [1948]; Portuguese 1944; Finnish [1945], [1954]; Ital [1946]; Hebrew 1947; Greek [1949]; Ukranian 1956, 1971; Georgian 1964; Polish 1971, 1974.

REVIEWS: Douglas Jerrold's Mag 6, July–Dec 1847; [Chorley, H. F.] Athenaeum 23 Oct 1847; Atlas 23 Oct 1847; Literary Gazette 23 Oct 1847; Tablet 23 Oct 1847; Weekly Chron 23 Oct 1847; Critic, (USA) 30 Oct 1847; NMM 81, Nov 1847; People's Jnl 13 Nov 1847; Observer 1 Nov 1847; Britannia 6 Nov 1847; Spectator 6 Nov 1847; Sun 6 Nov 1847; Era 14 Nov 1847; Bath Herald 20 Nov 1847; Howitt's Jnl 2, 20 Nov 1847; Economist 5, 27 Nov 1847; [Fonblanque, A. W.] Examiner 27 Nov 1847; [Lewes, G. H.] Fraser's Mag 36, Dec 1847; Mirror ser 4, 2 Dec 1847; Sunday Times 5 Dec 1847; [Lewes, G. H.] Westminster Rev 48, Jan 1848; Courier 1 Jan 1848; Christian Remembrancer 15, Apr 1848; Church of England Quart Rev 23, Apr 1848; Dublin Univ Mag 31, May 1848; Tait's Edinburgh Mag n.s. 15, May 1848; [Eagles, J.] Blackwood's Mag 64, Oct 1848; [Whipple, E. P.] North Amer Rev 141, Oct 1848; Forçade, E., Revue des Deux Mondes 5th ser 24, 1 Nov 1848; [Rigby, E. (later Lady Eastlake)] Quart Rev 84, Dec 1848 (rptd in Famous reviews, ed R. B. Johnson, 1914); Rankin, J. E., The Bells and their chimes, Pictorial Nat Lib (Boston) Jan 1849; Chasles, P., Revue des Deux Mondes 4, 1 Mar 1849; [Dauran-Forgues, E.]

Revue Britannique May 1849; [Lorimer, J.] North Br Rev 11, Aug 1849; [Bagshawe, H. R.] Dublin Rev 28, Mar 1850; NMM 95, July 1852; [Oliphant, M.] Blackwood's Mag 77, May 1855; A few words about Jane Eyre, Sharpe's London Mag 5, June 1855; [Sweat, M.] North Amer Rev 85, Oct 1857.

Shirley: a tale by Currer Bell. 3 vols 1849, 2 vols Leipzig 1849 (Tauchnitz), 1 vol New York 1850, London 1853 (new edn), 1857, etc; ed G. T. Bettany 1891; introd by M. Sinclair, London and New York [1908] (EL); ed P. Bentley, London and Glasgow 1953; introd by M. Lane, London and New York [1955] (EL); ed A. and J. Hook 1974 (Pen); ed M. Smith and H. Rosengarten, Oxford 1981 (WC). *See also* Collections, *above*.

TRANSLATIONS: Ger 1851; Swed 1854; Fr 1859, 1933; Cz 1906; Sp 1943.

REVIEWS: Daily News 31 Oct 1849; Athenaeum 3 Nov 1849; Atlas 3 Nov 1849; [Fonblanque, A.] Examiner 3 Nov 1849; Spectator 22, 3 Nov 1849; Observer 4 Nov 1849; Globe 9 Nov 1849; Britannia 10 Nov 1849; Economist 10 Nov 1849; [Howitt, W.] Standard of Freedom 10 Nov 1849; Weekly Chron 10 Nov 1849; Sun 14 Nov 1849; Critic (USA) 15 Nov 1849; Forçade, E. Revue des Deux Mondes 6th ser 4, 15 Nov 1849; Morning Herald 16 Nov 1849; Examiner (Richmond VA) 30 Nov 1849; [Clark, W. G.?] Fraser's Mag 40, Dec 1849; Dublin Univ Mag 34, Dec 1849; Eclectic Rev 26, Dec 1849; Albion (New York) n.s. 8, 1 Dec 1849; The Times 7 Dec 1849 (rptd Brontë Soc Trans 11 pt 60 1950); Portland Transcript 13, 8 Dec 1849; Morning Chron 25 Dec 1849; Amer Rev n.s. 1, Jan 1850; Church of England Quart Rev 27, Jan 1850; [Lewes, G. H.] Edinburgh Rev 91, Jan 1850; Westminster Rev 52, Jan 1850; Godey's Lady's Book 40, Feb 1850; Sartain's Union Mag 6, Feb 1850; [Bagshawe, H. R.] Dublin Rev 28, Mar 1850; Sharpe's London Mag 11, June 1850; NMM 81, Nov 1852; Globe 6 Dec 1852; Bells Weekly Messenger 11 Dec 1852; Nonconformist 15 Dec 1852; Sunday Times 2 Jan 1853.

Villette, by Currer Bell. 3 vols 1853, 1 vol Leipzig 1853 (Tauchnitz), New York 1853, London 1855, 1857, etc; introd by M. Sinclair, London and New York [1909] (EL); ed P. Bentley, London and Glasgow 1953; introd by M. Lane, London and New York [1957] (EL); ed G. Tillotson and D. Hawes, Boston 1971 (Houghton Mifflin edn); ed G. Phelps 1973 (Pan); ed M. Lilly, introd by T. Tanner 1979 (Pen), 1985; ed M. Smith and H. Rosengarten, Oxford and New York 1990 (WC); introd by S. Kemp 1993 (EL). *See also* Collections, *above*.

TRANSLATIONS: Finnish [1921]; Cz 1948; Flemish 1950.

REVIEWS: [Martineau, H.] Daily News 3 Feb 1853; Morning Advertiser 4 Feb 1853; Examiner 5 Feb 1853; Literary Gazette 5 Feb 1853; Globe 7 Feb 1853; Athenaeum 12 Feb 1853; Atlas 12 Feb 1853; Bells Weekly Messenger 12 Feb 1853; [Lewes, G. H.] Leader 12 Feb 1853; Spectator 12 Feb 1853; Weekly News and Chron 12 Feb 1853; Critic (USA) 15 Feb 1853; Guardian 23 Feb 1853; Magnet 28 Feb 1853; Eclectic Rev n.s. 5, Mar 1853; Sunday Times 13 Mar 1853; Forçade, E., Revue des Deux Mondes 7th ser 1, 15 Mar 1853; Nonconformist 16 Mar 1853; [Mozley, A.] Christian Remembrancer 25, Apr 1853; [Greg, W. R.] Edinburgh Rev 97, Apr 1853; [Lewes, G. H.] 'Ruth' and Villette, Westminster Rev n.s. 3, Apr 1853; Graham's Mag (Philadelphia) 42, May 1853; [Curtis, G. W.] Villette and Ruth, Putnam's Monthly Mag 1, May 1853; Dublin Univ Mag 42, Nov 1853; Edinburgh Guardian 3 Dec 1853.

The professor: a tale, by Currer Bell. 2 vols 1857 (with preface by A. B. Nicholls), Leipzig 1857 (Tauchnitz), 1 vol New York 1857, London 1860 (with Poems by Currer, Ellis, and Acton Bell), 1862, etc; 1891 (with Poems, and Cottage poems by P. Brontë); introd by M. Sinclair, London and New York [1910] (EL), 1922 (illustr E. Dulac); introd by M. Lane, London and New York [1954], 1969 (EL) (with Emma), London and Melbourne 1985 (re-set, new introd by A. Smith) (EL); 1948 (Pen); ed P. Bentley, London and Glasgow 1954 (with Tales from Angria, Emma: a fragment: together with a selection of poems by Charlotte, Emily and Anne Brontë; ed H. Glen 1989 (Pen)); ed M. Smith and H. Rosengarten, Oxford and New York 1991 (WC). *See also* Collections, *above*.

TRANSLATIONS: Fr 1858, 1878, 1882; Ger 1858; Ital 1890–1; Sp 1943.

REVIEWS: Economist 15, June 1857; Athenaeum 13 June 1857; Examiner 20 June 1857; Dublin Univ Mag 50, July 1857; Harper's NMM 15, Aug 1857; [Sweat, M.] North Amer Rev 85, Oct 1857.

Extracts from 6 early prose mss; The wounded stag (poem); Imitation: portrait de Pierre L'Hermite (devoir); and Sur la mort de Napoléon (devoir), all first pbd in Gaskell, The life of Charlotte Brontë vol 1, 1857.

Emma. Cornhill Mag Apr 1860 ('The last sketch', introd by W. M. Thackeray); Brontë Soc Trans 2 pt 10 1899; with The professor, 1949 (Heather edn); with The professor, 1954 (Collins), 1974; Cornhill Mag Autumn 1960 (introd by Margaret Lane); with The professor, 1969 (EL), 1985 (re-set); with The professor, 1987 (Clarendon edn).

The poems of Charlotte Brontë (Currer Bell). New York 1882, 1883, etc, 1900 (9th edn).

The story of Willie Ellin: fragments of an unpublished novel. Woman at Home 1 Dec 1898; rptd Brontë Soc Trans 9 pt 46 1936.

The Moores. First pbd in Jane Eyre, introd by W. R. Nicoll 1902, *above*; extracts rptd by J. R. Geer in An unpublished manuscript by Charlotte Brontë, Brontë Soc Trans 15 pt 76 1966; full text in appendix D of Shirley, 1979 (Clarendon edn).

Saul and other poems. Ed [T. J. Wise] 1913 (priv ptd).

The Red Cross Knight, and other poems. Ed T. J. Wise. Priv ptd 1917.

The Swiss emigrant's return, and other poems. Ed T. J. Wise 1917 (priv ptd).

Latest gleanings: being a series of unpublished poems selected from her early manuscripts. Ed C. K. Shorter 1918 (priv ptd).

The complete poems of Charlotte Brontë. Ed C. K. Shorter, now for the first time collected, with bibliography and notes by C. W. Hatfield 1923; rptd New York 1971.

The twelve adventurers, and other stories. Ed C. K. Shorter, assisted by C. W. Hatfield 1925.

Two unpublished manuscripts foreshadowing Villette. Brontë Soc Trans 7 pt 41 1931; also in Villette, appendix 1 1984 (Clarendon edn).

Legends of Angria: compiled from the early writings of Charlotte Brontë by F. E. Ratchford, with the collaboration of W. C. DeVane. New Haven CT 1933; rptd Port Washington NY, New York and London 1973.

The poems of Charlotte Brontë & Patrick Branwell Brontë. Oxford 1934 (Shakespeare Head Brontë).

Lettres et poésies d'amour de Charlotte Brontë. Tr P. Verdier, Paris–Bruxelles [1945].

Five novelettes: Passing events, Julia, Mina Laury, Captain Henry Hastings, Caroline Vernon. Transcribed from the original ms and ed W. Gérin 1971.

Two tales by Charlotte Brontë: The secret & Lily heart. Transcribed from the original ms and ed W. Holtz, Columbia MO 1978.

Ashworth: an unfinished novel by Charlotte Brontë. Ed M. Monahan, SP 80 1983. Portions of this ms and early draft fragments previously pbd by C. W. Hatfield in Charlotte Brontë and Hartley Coleridge, 1840, Brontë Soc Trans 10 pt 50 1940.

The poems of Charlotte Brontë. Ed T. Winnifrith, Oxford 1984.

Charlotte Brontë at Roe Head. Ed C. Alexander, in Jane Eyre 1987 (Norton Critical 2nd edn), *above*. The Roe Head jnl.

The poems of Charlotte Brontë: a new text and commentary. Ed V. A. Neufeldt, New York and London 1985 (Garland English Texts).

The Juvenilia of Jane Austen and Charlotte Brontë. Ed F. Beer 1986 (Pen).

An edition of the early writings of Charlotte Brontë. Ed C. Alexander 3 vols Oxford 1987–98. Vol 1 The Glass Town saga

1826–1832, (1987); vol 2 The rise of Angria 1833–1835: pt 1 1833–1834, pt 2 1834–1835 (1991); vol 3 The Angrian legend 1836–1839 (1998).

Unfinished novels. Introd by T. Winnifrith, Stroud 1993. The story of Willie Ellin, Ashworth, The Moores, Emma.

High life in Verdopolis, a story from the Glass Town saga. Ed C. Alexander 1995.

Individual early prose writings, published earlier than their appearance in collections or editions noted above

An adventure in Ireland. In C. K. Shorter, Charlotte Brontë and her circle, 1896.

The adventures of Ernest Alembert: a fairy tale. Ed T. J. Wise. 1896 (priv ptd). Also in Literary anecdotes of the nineteenth century, ed W. R. Nicoll and T. J. Wise, vol 2 1896; rptd 1967.

A leaf from an unopened volume: an unpublished romance by Charlotte Brontë [extracts]. Ed W. G. Kingsland, Poet-Lore 9, Spring 1897; complete text transcribed and ed C. Lemon, Haworth 1986. *See also* A. Edward Newton, Derby day and other adventures, Boston 1934 (limited edn); inserted facs of ms.

Tales of the Islanders: by Charlotte Brontë. Ed E. Markham, illustr B. Greer, Cosmopolitan Mag Oct 1911 (extract); rptd Nash's Mag Dec 1911. Complete text in Alexander, Early writings vol 1, 1987.

The four wishes: a fairy tale. Ed C. K. Shorter 1918 (priv ptd). Also in Strand Mag Dec 1918. This is ch 2 only of Visits in Verreopolis vol 2; complete text in Alexander, Early writings vol 1, 1987.

Napoleon and the spectre: a ghost story. Ed C. Shorter 1919 (priv ptd, extract from The green dwarf); extracts previously pbd in Early romances of Charlotte Brontë: 2, The green dwarf, ed W. G. Kingsland, Poet-Lore 9, Autumn 1897. First pbd complete in Alexander, Early writings vol 2 pt 1, 1991.

Unpublished juvenile manuscript by Charlotte Brontë [Blackwood's Young Men's Mag Dec (1) 1829]. Brontë Soc Trans 5 pt 29 1919.

Albion and Marina: a romantic love story by Charlotte Brontë, written at the age of fourteen years. Ed C. W. Hatfield, Brontë Soc Trans 6 pt 30 1920.

Conversations: a dialogue playlet in prose and verse [from Young Men's Mag Dec 1830]. Bookman 69, Dec 1925.

Conversations night [a playlet in the Young Men's Mag for Dec 1829]. In D. Cook, Miniature magazines of Charlotte Brontë: with unpublished poems from an original manuscript in Ashley Library, Bookman 71, Dec 1926.

The spell: an extravaganza: an unpublished novel. Ed G. E. MacLean 1931. Extracts previously pbd in Br Weekly 28 Mar 1895. Tr Y. Ryall as Le sortilège, Paris 1946.

'A visit to the Duke of Wellington's small palace situated on the banks of the Indince': unpublished short story by Charlotte Brontë. Brontë Soc Trans 8 pt 43 1933.

A Frenchman's journal: by Charlotte Brontë [from Young Men's Mag 2nd ser Nov 1830]. Transcribed by C. M. Edgerley, Brontë Soc Trans 10 pt 52 1942. Complete text in Alexander, Early writings vol 1, 1987.

'Four years ago'. In Charlotte Brontë, Patrick Branwell Brontë: choix établi et présenté par Raymond Bellour, Paris 1972 (as Quatre ans plus tôt).

An unpublished tale by Charlotte Brontë ['An interesting passage in the lives of some eminent men of the present time']. Ed. J. Chernaik, TLS 23 Nov 1973.

Charlotte Brontë juvenilia: first publication ['About 9 months after my arrival at the GT . . .']. Ed W. Baker, Literary Rev 5, 30 Nov–13 Dec 1979. Complete text in C. Alexander, Some new findings in Brontë bibliography, N & Q 228, June 1983.

Something about Arthur. Transcribed from the original ms and ed C. Alexander, Austin TX 1981.

The Poetaster: text and notes. Ed M. Monahan, SiR 20, Winter 1981.

Charlotte Brontë at Roe Head. Ed C. Alexander, in Jane Eyre, ed R. I. Dunn (Norton Critical 2nd edn), 1987. The Roe Head jnl.

Individual poems published earlier than their appearance in collected editions noted above

The orphans. Manchester Athenaeum Album, tr from Fr by Currer Bell, 1850; in The orphans and other poems, 1917 (*see* Collections, *above*).

Watching and wishing ['O! would I were the golden light']. Cornhill Mag 2, Dec 1860.

When thou sleepest. Cornhill Mag 4, Aug 1861.

Memory. In Reminiscences of Charlotte Brontë, by E. Nussey, Scribner's Monthly 2, May 1871 (extract); Cornhill Mag 20, Feb 1893; Critic (New York) 18 Feb 1893; Brontë Soc Trans 2 pt 10 1899; in Saul and other poems, 1913 (text from a later ms).

Poems by Charlotte Brontë, on the deaths of her sisters Emily ['My darling, thou wilt never know'] and Anne ['There's little joy in life for me']. Woman at Home 5, Dec 1896; in T. J. Wise, A bibliography of the writings in prose and verse of the members of the Brontë family, 1917.

'Long since as I remember well'. In A. H. Joline, Meditations of an autograph collector, New York and London 1902 (extract).

Lines on the celebrated Bewick ['The cloud of recent death is past away']. TLS 4 Jan 1907; in A. E. Hall, Illustrated guide to Haworth [1908] (2nd edn).

'A Roland for your Oliver'. In C. K. Shorter, The Brontës: life and letters vol 1, 1908. (According to Shorter this poem was first pbd in Whitehaven News (USA) 1876, but no pbn record can be found.)

Richard Coeur de Lion and Blondel: a poem by Charlotte Brontë. Ed C. K. Shorter 1912 (priv ptd).

Lament befitting these 'times of night' ['Lament for the Martyr who dies for his faith']. Ed G. E. MacLean, Cornhill Mag Aug 1916; ed MacLean 1916 (priv ptd, rptd from Cornhill Mag).

The violet: a poem written at the age of fourteen. Ed [C. K. Shorter]. [1916] (priv ptd).

Darius Codomannus. A poem by Charlotte Brontë written at the age of eighteen years. 1920 (priv ptd).

'The autumn day its course has run, the autumn evening falls'. In C. W. Hatfield, The early manuscripts of Charlotte Brontë: a bibliography, pt 3, Brontë Soc Trans 6 pt 34 1924.

'On seeing an ancient dirk in the armory of the Tower of All Nations. In D. Cook, Brontë manuscripts in the Law Collection, Bookman 69, Nov 1925.

An unfinished poem by Charlotte Brontë ['Morning was in its freshness still']. Brontë Soc Trans 7 pt 36 1926.

Miniature magazines of Charlotte Brontë: with unpublished poems from an original ms in Ashley Library ['Merry England, land of glory' and 'Harvest in Spain' (by 'UT')], by D. Cook, Bookman 71, Dec 1926.

Two unpublished poems by Charlotte Brontë ['Early wrapt in slumber deep', and 'Lines written beside a fountain in the grounds of York Villa'] transcribed by C. W. Hatfield. Brontë Soc Trans 7 pt 41 1931.

Review at Gazemba: lines, previously unpublished, by Charlotte Brontë. Brontë Soc Trans 8 pt 44 1934.

Huguenin, C. A. Charlotte Brontë's juvenile poem ['The trumpet hath sounded, its voice is gone forth']. Brontë Soc Trans 13 pt 66 1956.

Letters

Gaskell, E. C. The life of Charlotte Brontë. 2 vols 1857. First pbn of many letters by Charlotte Brontë. Haworth edn of Life and works, ed C. K. Shorter (1900), includes first pbn of additional letters to G. Smith, H. Martineau, the Rev P. Brontë.

Letter to the editor of the Christian Remembrancer. Christian Remembrancer n.s. 34, July 1857; rptd in W. R. Nicoll, Charlotte Brontë and one of her critics, Bookman 17, Nov 1899.

Two letters to John Stores Smith. Free Lance 7 Mar 1868; included in C. K. Shorter, The Brontës: life and letters, vol 2 appendix 6.

Unpublished letters of Charlotte Brontë. Hours at Home 11, June–Sep 1870. Letters to E. Nussey.

Reid, T. W. Charlotte Brontë: a monograph. Macmillan's Mag 34, Sep, Oct, Nov 1876; expanded into a book, London and New York 1877. Letters to E. Nussey and other correspondents.

The life and letters of Sydney Dobell, ed E. J. (Emily Jolly) 2 vols 1878, vol 1; *see also* C. W. H[atfield], Charlotte Brontë and Sydney Dobell: correspondence, 1851, Brontë Soc Trans 7 pt 36 1926. Four letters to Dobell.

The story of the Brontës, their home, haunts, friends and works: part second – Charlotte's letters. Ed E. Nussey, Bradford 1885–9. This book ptd but suppressed before pbn; title taken from the drop-head title. Letters chiefly to E. Nussey.

Williams, E. B. Extracts from some unpublished letters of Charlotte Brontë [to W. Smith Williams]. Macmillan's Mag 64, June (pt 1), July (pt 2), Aug (pt 3), 1891; included in C. K. Shorter, Charlotte Brontë and her circle, 1896.

Shorter, C. K. Charlotte Brontë and her circle. 1896. Previously unpbd letters to Ellen Nussey and other correspondents.

North, E. D. An interesting find: or, Thackeray and Charlotte Brontë. Bookman (New York) 6, Sep 1897. Supposed letter to Thackeray: *see* next entry.

Shorter, C. K. Some Brontë forgeries: a storm in a teacup. Bookman 13, Dec 1897. Refutation of claim in article by E. D. North, *above*.

Alfred Lord Tennyson: a memoir, by his son. 2 vols 1897, vol 1. Letter to Tennyson.

Yates, W. W. The father of the Brontës. 1897. Letter to L. Brooke.

The Brontës at Thornton. Bookman 27, Oct 1904. Two letters to Mrs J. C. Franks.

Shorter, C. The Brontës: life and letters. Being an attempt to present a full and final record of the lives of the three sisters, Charlotte, Emily and Anne Brontë from the biographies of Mrs Gaskell and others, and from numerous hitherto unpublished manuscripts and letters. 2 vols London and New York 1908; rptd New York 1969.

Charlotte Brontë. In Women as letter-writers: a collection of letters, ed A. M. Ingpen, 1909.

Spielmann, M. H. (ed). Charlotte Brontë's 'tragedy': the lost letters. The Times 29 July 1913; notes on the letters by M. H. Spielmann, The Times 30 July 1913. Rptd in Brontë Soc Trans 5 pt 24 1914; also in The love letters of Charlotte Brontë to Constantin Heger, ed T. J. W[ise]. 1914 (priv ptd). *See also* C. K. Shorter, The Brontës and their circle, 1914. C. Brontë's 4 letters to Constantin Heger, in Fr with trn.

Letters recounting the deaths of Emily, Anne and Branwell Brontë by Charlotte Brontë: to which are added letters signed Currer Bell and C. B. Nicholls. Ed T. J. Wise. 1913 (priv ptd).

Unpublished letter by Charlotte Brontë. Brontë Soc Trans 5 pt 29 1919. Letter to M. Brown.

Thackeray and Charlotte Brontë: being some hitherto unpublished letters by Charlotte Brontë. Ed C. K. Shorter 1919 (priv ptd).

Extracts from Charlotte Brontë's letters relating to Patrick Branwell Brontë and Mrs Lydia Robinson. In A complete transcript of the Leyland manuscripts showing the unpublished portions from the original manuscripts [in the Brotherton Collection], Brontë Soc Trans 6 pt 35 1925.

Charlotte Brontë and Sydney Dobell: correspondence, 1851. Brontë Soc Trans 7 pt 36 1926. First pbn of letter to Miss Martineau.

Charlotte Brontë. In The lost art: letters of seven famous women, ed D. Van Doren, New York 1929.

An account of her honeymoon . . . in a letter to Miss Catharine Winkworth. Ed T. J. Wise, Leeds 1930 (priv ptd).

The letters of 'K. T.'. Brontë Soc Trans 9 pt 47 1937. Pbn of two draft replies by C. Brontë.

Hatfield, C. W. Charlotte Brontë and Hartley Coleridge, 1840. Brontë Soc Trans 10 pt 50 1940.

Lettres et poésies d'amour de Charlotte Brontë. Tr P. Verdier, Paris–Bruxelles [1945].

Two letters from Charlotte Brontë to Mrs Gaskell. Brontë Soc Trans 12 pt 62 1952.

Two letters from Charlotte. Brontë Soc Trans 12 pt 64 1954. Letters to E. Kingston and W. S. Williams.

A letter from Charlotte to W. S. Williams. Brontë Soc Trans 12 pt 64 1954.

Martin, N. D. S. Two unpublished letters of Charlotte Brontë. Bodleian Lib Record 5, Oct 1955.

Brontëana at Princeton University: the Parrish Collection. Brontë Soc Trans 12 pt 65 1955. Letters to Henry Coburn, Smith, Elder and Co, and Ellen Nussey; letter to Smith, Elder and Co rptd in Brontë Soc Trans 16 pt 82 1972.

Two letters from Charlotte Brontë. Brontë Soc Trans 12 pt 65 1955. Letters to G. Smith and L. Wheelwright.

Bates, M. C. Charlotte Brontë and the Kay-Shuttleworths, with a new Brontë letter. Harvard Lib Bull 9 1955.

New acquisitions: letters from Charlotte to Francis Bennoch [and Lady Kay-Shuttleworth]. Brontë Soc Trans 13 pt 67 1957.

Letters and papers of Charlotte Brontë. In The Brontë sisters: selected source materials for college research papers, ed R. H. Blackburn, Boston 1964.

An unpublished letter by Charlotte Brontë. Brontë Soc Trans 15 pt 77 1967. Letter to Mlle Victoire Dubois.

Stephens, F. C. Hartley Coleridge and the Brontës. TLS 14 May 1970. Draft of letter to Coleridge.

Winnifrith, T. J. Charlotte Brontë's letters to Ellen Nussey. Durham Univ Jnl 63 1970. Study of Needham transcriptions; *see also* The Needham copies of Charlotte Brontë's letters to Ellen Nussey, in T. Winnifrith, The Brontës and their background: romance and reality, 1973, appendix B.

Charlotte Brontë manuscript and letters purchased. Brontë Soc Trans 16 pt 82 1972. Letters to Dr Wooler.

Choix d'écrits de jeunesse. Ed R. Bellour, Paris 1972.

A letter from Charlotte Brontë to Ellen Nussey returns to Haworth: an American gift. Brontë Soc Trans 16 pt 83 1973.

Lever, Sir T. Harriet Martineau and her novel Oliver Weld. Brontë Soc Trans 16 pt 84 1974. Letter to G. Smith.

Jackson, R. J. Charlotte Brontë to Lady Kay-Shuttleworth: an unpublished letter. Brontë Soc Trans 16 pt 84 1974.

Important Brontëana purchased. Brontë Soc Trans 16 pt 85 1975. Letter to W. S. Williams.

Two letters by Charlotte Brontë. Brontë Soc Trans 17 pt 87 1977. Letters to Mrs Holland and J. S. Smith (facs).

Lemon, C. An exciting chapter in the Society's history: purchase of forty-four autograph letters by Charlotte Brontë. Brontë Soc Trans 17 pt 90 1980. Letters to E. C. Gaskell, B. Brontë, E. Nussey and W. S. Williams.

Pollard, A. The Seton-Gordon Brontë letters. Brontë Soc Trans 18 pt 92 1982. Letters to Smith, Elder and Co.

Peters, M. An unpublished Brontë letter: the second edition of 'Jane Eyre'. Brontë Soc Trans 18 pt 92 1982. Letter to W. S. Williams.

The Gordon bequest. Brontë Soc Trans 19 pts 1–2 1986. Letter to Mrs Smith; tentatively dated by A. D. Walker in Charlotte letter dated, Brontë Soc Trans 19 pt 3 1987.

Whitehead, B. The Wooler letters. Brontë Soc Trans 19 pt 3 1987.

Über die liebe. Ed E. Maletzke, tr E. Groepler and H. J. Schütz, Germany 1988.

Smith, M. Charlotte Brontë's letters. Brontë Soc Trans 20 pt 1 1990.

Smith, M. A reconstructed letter. Brontë Soc Trans 20 pt 1 1990.

Alexander, C. Newby's chicanery: new Brontë letters. N & Q 240, June 1995.

Smith, M. (ed). The letters of Charlotte Brontë, with a selection of letters by family and friends. Vol 1: 1829–1847. Oxford 1995.

Devoirs (exercises in French)

Imitation: portrait de Pierre L'Hermite; Sur la nom de Napoléon. In E. C. Gaskell, The Life of Charlotte Brontë vol 1, 1857 (3rd edn 1857 corrects 'nom' to 'mort').

From an unpublished French essay of Charlotte Brontë. Bookman 7, Feb 1895. English extracts of La mort de Moïse.

An early essay by Charlotte Brontë [on Millevoye's La chute des feuilles]. Introd by M. H. Spielmann, Brontë Soc Trans 6 pt 34 1924. Previously pbd TLS 19 July 1923.

Four essays by Charlotte Brontë: the authentic fire in exercises in Brussels ['Human justice'; 'Athens saved by poetry'; 'The palace of death', tr D. Cornish; 'The sick girl', tr J. P. Inebnit]. Brontë Soc Trans 12 pt 62 1952. English trn only.

French essays by Charlotte and Emily ['La mort de Napoléon', tr M. Lane]. Brontë Soc Trans 12 pt 64 1954. Variant ms 'Sur la mort de Napoléon' pbd in E. C. Gaskell, The life of Charlotte Brontë vol 1, 1857 (incorrectly transcribed in 1st edn 'Sur la nom de Napoléon', corrected in 3rd edn).

More Brontë devoirs ['La chenille', 'La mort de Moïse', and 'La chute des feuilles', tr and ed P. Bentley]. Brontë Soc Trans 12 pt 65 1955.

Charlotte Brontë's 'Le nid': an unpublished manuscript. Tr and ed L. J. Dessner, Brontë Soc Trans 16 pt 83 1973. English trn only.

On the struggles of a poor and unknown artist: a devoir by Charlotte Brontë. Ed S. Lonoff, Brontë Soc Trans 18 pt 95 1985.

Lonoff, S. (ed). Charlotte and Emily Brontë: the Belgian essays. New Haven CT 1997.

Translations, editions and prefaces

Preface [to the 2nd edn of Jane Eyre, dedicating the work to W. M. Thackeray]. 1847 (2nd edn); *see* Jane Eyre, *above*.

Note to the third edition of Jane Eyre. 1848; *see* Jane Eyre, *above*.

Wuthering Heights and Agnes Grey: by Ellis and Acton Bell: a new edition, revised, with a biographical notice of the authors, a selection from their literary remains, and a preface by Currer Bell [pbd as Biographical notice of Ellis and Acton Bell, Editor's preface to the new edition of Wuthering Heights, and Selections from poems by Ellis and Acton Bell]. Ed C. Brontë 1850.

Preface [to The professor]. 1857, etc; *see* The professor, *above*.

Voltaire's Henriade, book 1. Tr C. Brontë. Ed C. K. Shorter 1917 (priv ptd). *See* E. L. Duthie, Charlotte Brontë's translation: The first canto of Voltaire's Henriade, Brontë Soc Trans 13 pt 69 1959.

A word to the Quarterly: Charlotte Brontë's rejected preface to Shirley. Brontë Soc Trans 16 pt 85 1975; in Shirley, 1979 (Clarendon edn), *above*.

§2

Textual/bibliographical studies

Wroot, H. E. The persons and places of the Brontë novels. Brontë Soc Trans vol 3 1906; rptd as Sources of Charlotte Brontë's novels: persons and places, suppl with Brontë Soc Trans 8 pt 45 1935. C. Brontë's novels only.

MacLean, G. E. Unpublished essays in novel writing by Charlotte Brontë. Brontë Soc Trans 5 pt 26 1916.

Suppressed passages: a collation of the earlier and later editions of Mrs Gaskell's Life of Charlotte Brontë. Brontë Soc Trans 6 pt 31 1921. Collation by C. W. Hatfield.

Hatfield, C. W. The early manuscripts of Charlotte Brontë: a bibliography. Brontë Soc Trans 6 pts 32–4 1922–4.

Clark, A. P. The manuscript collections of the Princeton University Library: an introductory survey. Princeton Univ Lib Chron 19, Spring/Summer 1958. On Charlotte Brontë mss.

Brooks, R. L. Unrecorded newspaper reviews of Charlotte Brontë's 'Shirley' and 'Villette'. PBSA 53 1959.

Brammer, M. M. The manuscript of The professor. RES n.s. 11, May 1960.

Passel, A. Charlotte Brontë: a bibliography of the criticism of her novels. BB 26 1969, 27 1970.

Harkness, B. The Clarendon 'Jane Eyre'. Nineteenth-Century Fiction 25, Dec 1970.

Jack, I. and M. Smith. The Clarendon 'Jane Eyre': a rejoinder. Nineteenth-Century Fiction 26, Dec 1971.

Langlois, E. Early critics and translators of 'Jane Eyre' in France. Brontë Soc Trans 16 pt 81 1971.

Stevens, J. A Brontë letter corrected. Brontë Soc Trans 16 pt 81 1971. Correction of transcription of letter from Charlotte Brontë to Miss Dixon in W. Gérin, Charlotte Brontë, 1967.

Stevens, J. Woozles in Brontëland: a cautionary tale. SB 24 1971. Study of errors in ptd version of Charlotte Brontë's letter to Mary Taylor, Sep 1848.

Rosengarten, H. J. Charlotte Brontë's Shirley and the Leeds Mercury. SEL 16 1976.

Peters, M. Charlotte Brontë: a critico-bibliographic survey 1945–1974. Br Stud Monitor 6 and 7 1976–7.

Parkison, J. Charlotte Brontë: a bibliography of 19th century criticism. BB 35 1978.

Alexander, C. Recent research on Charlotte Brontë's juvenilia. Brontë Soc Trans 18 pt 91 1981.

Sabol, R. C. and T. K. Bender. A concordance to Charlotte Brontë's Jane Eyre. New York 1981 (Garland Reference Lib of the Humanities).

Alexander, C. A bibliography of the manuscripts of Charlotte Brontë. Haworth and New York 1982.

Alexander, C. The early writings of Charlotte Brontë. Oxford and Buffalo NY 1983.

Alexander, C. Some new findings in Brontë bibliography. N & Q 228, June 1983.

Bemelmans, J. A Charlotte Brontë manuscript. N & Q 228, Aug 1983.

Smith, M. The manuscripts of Charlotte Brontë's novels. Brontë Soc Trans 18 pt 93 1983.

Dunn, R. I. (ed). Charlotte Brontë and her readers. In Jane Eyre, 1987 (Norton Critical 2nd edn).

Whitehead, B. The Wooler letters: discrepancies between the Wise and Symington Shakespeare Head transcripts of Charlotte Brontë's letters to Miss Wooler and Miss Catherine Wooler and the original letters .... Brontë Soc Trans 19 pt 4 1987.

Smith, M. Charlotte Brontë's letters. Brontë Soc Trans 20 pt 1 1990. List of unlocated mss.

Nudd, D. M. Bibliography of film, television and stage adaptations of Jane Eyre. Brontë Soc Trans 20 pt 3 1991.

Alexander, C. Editorial creations and editorial compromise: the art of the possible in the case of the Brontës. In The textual condition: rhetoric and editing, ed M. Blackburn, F. Muecke and M. Sankey, Sydney 1995.

Selected criticism

Letters/early comments on Jane Eyre

Lockhart, J. G. Letter to Mr and Mrs Hope 29 Dec 1847. In A. Lang, The life and letters of J. G. Lockhart vol 2, 1897.

Mitford, F. Letters to Miss Mitford 9 Jan, 18 Feb 1850, and to Mrs James 2 Apr 1850. In The letters of Elizabeth Barrett Browning, ed F. G. Kenyon, 1897.

Taylor, M. Letter to Charlotte Brontë 24 July 1848. In The Brontës: their lives, friendships and correspondence, ed Wise and Symington, vol 2.

Thackeray, W. S. Letter to W. S. Williams 23 Oct 1847. In The letters and private papers of W. M. Thackeray, ed G. N. Ray, vol 2 1947.

Eliot, G. Letter to Charles Bray 11 June 1848. In The George Eliot letters, ed G. S. Haight, vol 1 1954.

Letters/early comments on Shirley

Mitford, F. Letter to Mrs James 2 Apr 1850. In The letters of Elizabeth Barrett Browning, ed F. G. Kenyon, 1897.

Arnold, T. Unpublished letter to his sister Mary 15 Aug 1851. Alexander Turnbull Lib, Wellington NZ.

Winkworth, C. Letter to Eliza Paterson 5 Dec 1849. In Memorials of two sisters, Susanna and Catherine Winkworth, ed M. J. Shaen, 1908.

[Dobell, S.] Currer Bell. Palladium no 3, Sep 1850; rptd in his Life and letters, ed. E. J. (E. Jolly) vol 1, 1878; Brontë Soc Trans 5 pt 28 1918.

Letters/early comments on Villette

Arnold, M. Letter to Mrs Forster 14 Apr 1853. In Letters of Matthew Arnold, ed G. W. Russell, 1895.

Mitford, F. Letter to Mr Westwood Sep 1853. In The letters of Elizabeth Barrett Browning, ed F. G. Kenyon, 1897.

Thackeray, W. M. Letters to Lucy Baxter 11 Mar 1853, Mrs Carmichael-Smyth 25–8 Mar 1853 and Mrs Bryan Proctor 4 Apr 1853. In The letters and private papers of W. M. Thackeray, ed G. N. Ray, vol 3 1947.

Eliot, G. Letters to Mrs Bray 15 Feb and 12 Mar 1853. In The letters of George Eliot, ed G. S. Haight, vol 2 1954.

[Oliphant, M.] Modern novelists, great and small. Blackwood's Mag 77, May 1855.

[Cracroft, B.] Thackeray and Currer Bell. Oxford and Cambridge Mag 1, June 1856.

Montégut, É. Miss Brontë: sa vie et ses oeuvres. Revue des Deux Mondes 1 and 14 July 1857; rptd in Écrivains modernes de l'Angleterre, 1ère série, Paris 1885.

De Mouy, C. Romanciers anglais contemporains: Miss Brontë (Currer Bell). Revue Européene (Paris) 12 1860. Trn of extracts given by D. Newton-De Molina in A note on an early French view of Charlotte Brontë, Brontë Soc Trans 15 pt 80 1970.

'Selden, Camille'. Charlotte Brontë et la vie morale en Angleterre. In his L'esprit des femmes de notre temps, Paris 1865.

[Oliphant, M.] Novels. Blackwood's Mag 102, Sep 1867. Criticism mentioning Jane Eyre and Shirley.

Stephen, L. Hours in a library, no 17: Charlotte Brontë. Cornhill Mag 36, Dec 1877; rptd in his Hours in a library, 3rd ser 1879.

Swinburne, A. C. A note on Charlotte Brontë. 1877.

[Browne, J. H. B.] Charlotte Brontë. Westminster Rev 109, Jan 1878; rptd in his Essays critical and political vol 1, 1907.

Armitt, A. Jane Austen and Charlotte Brontë: a contrast. Modern Rev 3 1882.

Trollope, A. On English novelists of the present day. In An autobiography, 1883.

Holroyd, A. Keighley series of poems, tales, and sketches, no 4: Currer Bell and her sisters. Keighley [1887]. Rptd from Bradford Advertiser 1855.

Lang, A. Charlotte Brontë. Good Words 30, Apr 1889.

Oliphant, M. O. and F. R. Oliphant. The Victorian age of English literature vol 1, 1892.

Wood, B. The influence of the Moorlands on Charlotte and Emily Brontë. Bradford Argus 6 Jan 1894; Bradford Scientific Assoc 1894.

Harrison, F. Charlotte Brontë's place in literature. Forum 19, Mar 1895; rptd in his Studies in early Victorian literature, London and New York 1895.

Saintsbury, G. Three mid-century novelists. In his Corrected impressions, 1895.

Stead, J. J. Hathersage and Jane Eyre. Brontë Soc Trans 1 pt 4 1896.

Mathews, W. Charlotte Brontë: a tribute to her works and genius. 1897.

Munro, H. Charlotte Brontë. Univ Mag and Free Rev 9, Oct 1897.

Stead, J. J. The Shirley country, with map and illustrations. Brontë Soc Trans 1 pt 7 1897; revised in Brontë Soc Trans 4 pt 17 1907.

Howells, W. D. Thackeray's Ethel Newcome and Charlotte Brontë's Jane Eyre. In his Heroines of fiction vol 1, London and New York 1901. Rptd from Harper's Bazar 33, 15 Dec 1900.

Bonnell, H. H. Charlotte Brontë, George Eliot, Jane Austen: studies in their works. New York, London and Bombay 1902.

Chesterton, G. K. Charlotte Brontë. In Twelve types, 1902.

Gosse, E. The challenge of the Brontës. 1903 (priv ptd). Also in Brontë Soc Trans 2 pt 14 1904; rptd in his Some diversions of a man of letters, 1919; and in his Selected essays 2 1928.

Tiddeman, L. E. The novels of Charlotte Brontë. Westminster Rev 160, Dec 1903.

Garnett, R. The place of Charlotte Brontë in nineteenth-century fiction. Brontë Soc Trans 2 pt 14 1904; rptd in Charlotte Brontë 1816–1916: a centenary tribute, ed B. Wood, 1917.

Cazamian, L. Charlotte Brontë: Shirley. In Le roman social en Angleterre (1830–1850), Paris 1904, rev 1935, tr with a foreword by M. Fido 1973.

De Selincourt, E. The genius of the Brontës. Brontë Soc Trans 2 pt 15 1906.

Chesterton, G. K. Charlotte Brontë and the Realists. Brontë Soc Trans 4 pt 16 1907.

Magnus, L. Brontë criticism in English literature in the nineteenth century: an essay in criticism. 1909.

Ralli, A. Charlotte Brontë. Fortnightly Rev n.s. 94, Sep 1913.

Benson, A. C. The message of Charlotte Brontë to the nineteenth century. Brontë Soc Trans 5 pt 25 1915.

Biographical studies

Martineau, H. Obituary of Charlotte Brontë. Daily News 6 Apr 1855; rptd in her Biographical sketches, London and New York 1869.

Gaskell, E. C. The life of Charlotte Brontë. 2 vols 1857, 1857, 1857 (3rd edn 'revised and corrected'), 2 vols New York 1857; 2 vols Leipzig 1857, 1859 (Tauchnitz edns); 1858; 1860; in Life and works, 1872–3, vol 7, *see* Collections *above*; in Life and works, introd and notes by C. K. Shorter, New York and London 1900 (Haworth edn), vol 7, *see* Collections *above*; in Novels, introd and notes by T. Scott and B. W. Willett, 1898–1901 (Thornton edn), Edinburgh 1905, vol 12, *see* Collections *above*; ed W. Gérin 1973; ed A. Shelston 1975 (Pen). REVIEWS: [Lucas, S.] The Times 25 Apr 1857; [Skelton, J.] Fraser's Mag 55, May 1857; Tait's Edinburgh Mag n.s. 24, May 1857; [Dallas, E. S.] Blackwood's Mag 82, July 1857; Christian Remembrancer n.s. 34, July 1857; [Stephen, F.] Edinburgh Rev 106, July 1857; [Roscoe, W. C.] Nat Rev 5, July 1857; [Sweat, M.] North Amer Rev 85, Oct 1857.

Shepheard, H. A vindication of the clergy daughters' school, and of the Rev W. Carus Wilson, from the remarks in the Life of Charlotte Brontë. Kirkby Lonsdale 1857.

Carus Wilson, W. W. A refutation of the statements in 'The life of Charlotte Brontë' regarding the Casterton Clergy Daughters' School, when at Cowan Bridge. Weston-Super-Mare 1858.

Garland, F. A. Jane Eyre's school. Belgravia 5 1868.

Smith, J. S. A day with Charlotte Brontë in 1850. Free Lance (Manchester) 7 and 14 Mar 1868; ed K. Tillotson, Brontë Soc Trans 16 pt 81 1971.

Horne, R. H. Portraits and memoirs [Charlotte Brontë]. Macmillan's Mag 22, Sep 1870.

'E' [Ellen Nussey]. Reminiscences of Charlotte Brontë. Scribner's Monthly 2, May 1871; ed J. Waugh, Brontë Soc Trans 2 pt 10 1899.

Horne, R. H. Charlotte Brontë. In Letters of Elizabeth Barrett Browning addressed to Richard Hengist Horne, ed S. R. Townshend Meyer, 2 vols 1877, vol 2.

Reid, T. W. Charlotte Brontë: a monograph. 1877; rptd New York 1970. From articles in Macmillan's Mag 34, Sep–Nov 1876.

Bayne, P. Two great Englishwomen: Mrs Browning and Charlotte Brontë. 1881.

Adams, W. H. D. Charlotte Brontë. In his Celebrated Englishwomen of the Victorian era, 2 vols 1884, vol 1.

Scruton, W. The birthplace of Charlotte Brontë. 1884.

Birrell, A. Life of Charlotte Brontë. 1887.

Ritchie, A. My witches' cauldron. Macmillan's Mag 63, Feb 1891.

Shorter, C. K. Charlotte Brontë and her circle. London and New York

1896; rev as The Brontës and their circle, London and New York 1914.
Shorter, C. K. Mrs Gaskell and Charlotte Brontë. Woman at Home 5, May 1896.
Scruton, W. Reminiscences of the late Miss Ellen Nussey. Brontë Soc Trans 1 pt 8 1898.
Axon, W. E. A. Charlotte Brontë and Manchester. N & Q 9th ser 5, 9 June 1900.
Smith, G. M. Charlotte Brontë. Cornhill Mag n.s. 8, Dec 1900; rptd in George Smith: a memoir, with some pages of autobiography, ed Mrs G. M. Smith, 1902.
Shorter, C. K. Charlotte Brontë and her sisters. In Literary Lives ser, ed W. R. Nicoll, 1905.
Wroot, H. E. The late Rev A. B. Nicholls. Brontë Soc Trans 4 pt 16 1907.
Lee, S. Charlotte Brontë in London. Cornhill Mag n.s. 26, Mar 1909; rptd in Brontë Soc Trans 4 pt 19 1909.
Chadwick, Mrs E. H. Charlotte Brontë and Thackeray. Brontë Soc Trans 4 pt 21 1911.
Harper, J. Charlotte Brontë's Heger family and their school. Blackwood's Mag 191, Apr 1912.
Macdonald, F. The secret of Charlotte Brontë, followed by some reminiscences of the real Monsieur and Madame Heger. London and Edinburgh 1914.
Goldring, M. Charlotte Brontë the woman: a study. London 1915, New York 1916.
Brown, L. R. Charlotte Brontë and Belgium. Nineteenth Century and After 79, Apr 1916.
Green, J. J. The Brontë–Wheelwright friendship. Friends Quart Examiner 50 1916.
Shorter, C. K. Mrs Gaskell and Charlotte Brontë. Brontë Soc Trans 5 pt 26 1916.
Spielmann, M. H. Charlotte Brontë in Brussels. TLS 13 Apr 1916, rptd in Charlotte Brontë 1816–1916: a centenary tribute, ed B. Wood, 1917.
Wood, B. Charlotte Brontë 1816–1916: a centenary memorial prepared by the Brontë Society. Foreword by Mrs H. Ward. 1917, New York 1918.
Spielmann, M. H. The inner history of the Brontë–Heger letters. Fortnightly Rev 111, Apr 1919; rptd 1919.
Wroot, H. E. A Brontë relic [Charlotte Brontë's account book 1848–9]. Brontë Soc Trans 5 pt 29, 1919.
Dooley, L. Psychoanalysis of Charlotte Brontë, as a type of the woman of genius. Amer Jnl of Psychology 31, July 1920.
Langbridge, R. Charlotte Brontë: a psychological study. 1929; rptd 1972.
Benson, E. F. Charlotte Brontë. London, New York and Toronto 1932.
Rowse, A. L. The English past: evocations of persons and places. 1951.
Lane, M. The Brontë story: a reconsideration of Mrs Gaskell's Life of Charlotte Brontë. 1953, London and Glasgow 1969.
Bates, M. C. Charlotte Brontë and the Kay-Shuttleworths, with a new Brontë letter. Harvard Lib Bull 9 1955.
Crompton, M. Passionate search: a life of Charlotte Brontë. 1955; New York 1956.
Duthie, E. L. Charlotte Brontë and Constantin Heger. Contemporary Rev 187, Mar 1955.
Pearson, F. R. Charlotte Brontë on the East Yorkshire coast. [East Yorkshire] 1957.
The Cowan Bridge controversy [extracts from letters to The Leeds Mercury and The Halifax Guardian 1857]. In The Brontë sisters: selected source materials for college research papers, ed R. H. Blackburn, Boston 1964. *See also* Mr A. B. Nicholls and Mr Carus Wilson, in C. K. Shorter, The Brontës: life and letters, vol 2 appendix 8.
Gérin, W. Charlotte Brontë: the evolution of genius. Oxford 1967, 1968 (with corrections).
Winnifrith, T. Charlotte Brontë and Calvinism. N & Q 215, Jan 1970.
C. Brontë's relationship with E. Nussey.
Stevens, J. Mary Taylor, friend of Charlotte Brontë: letters from New Zealand and elsewhere. Auckland and Oxford 1972.
L[emon], C. H. 'Severe to the point of injustice': two letters by Harriet Martineau purchased. Brontë Soc Trans 16 pt 83 1973.
Pollin, B. R. Two letters concerning Charlotte Brontë in contemporary American journals. Brontë Soc Trans 16 pt 83 1973.
Peters, M. Unquiet soul: a biography of Charlotte Brontë. 1975, New York 1975.
Moglen, H. Charlotte Brontë: the self conceived. New York 1976.
Blom, M. H. Charlotte Brontë. Twayne's English Authors ser, London and Boston 1977.
Keefe, R. Charlotte Brontë's world of death. Austin TX 1979.
Lever, Sir T. Charlotte Brontë and George Smith. Brontë Soc Trans 17 pt 87 1977.
Pollard, A. Admiration and exasperation: Charlotte Brontë's relationship with William Makepeace Thackeray. Brontë Soc Trans 17 pt 88 1978.
Raymond, E. Charlotte Brontë and Elizabeth Gaskell – the fruitful friendship. Brontë Soc Trans 17 pt 89 1979.
Jones, M. George Smith's influence on the life of Charlotte Brontë. Brontë Soc Trans 18 pt 94 1984.
Barker, J. R. V. Subdued expectations: Charlotte Brontë's marriage settlement. Brontë Soc Trans 19 pts 1–2 1986.
Berg, M. Portrait of a life. Boston 1987.
Smith, M. New light on Mr Nicholls. Brontë Soc Trans 19 pt 3 1987.
Fraser, R. Charlotte Brontë. London and New York 1988.
Winnifrith, T. A new life of Charlotte Brontë. 1988.
A strange plant: Charlotte Brontë's friendship with Mrs Gaskell. Brontë Soc Trans 19 pt 8 1989.
Smith, M. The letters of Charlotte Brontë: some new insights into her life and writing. In The Brontë Soc and the Gaskell Soc joint conference, 1990: conference papers. [Haworth] 1992.
Lonoff, S. An unpublished memoir by Paul Heger. Brontë Soc Trans 20 pt 6 1992.
Whitehead, B. Charlotte Brontë and her 'dearest Nell': the story of a friendship. Otley 1993.
Gordon, L. Charlotte Brontë: a passionate life. 1994.
Bellamy, J. Mary Taylor, Ellen Nussey and Brontë biography. Brontë Soc Trans 21 pt 7 1996.
Smith, M. A window on the world: Charlotte Brontë's correspondence with her publishers. Brontë Soc Trans 21 pt 7 1996.

Patrick Branwell Brontë 1817–48

See Collections and selections: The Brontë family, *above.*

§1

Leyland, F. A. The Brontë family with special reference to Patrick Branwell Brontë. 2 vols 1886. 10 poems first pbd here.
The complete works of Emily Jane Brontë. Ed C. K. Shorter 2 vols 1910, *see* E. Brontë, *below*. 10 poems by P. B. Brontë incorrectly attributed to E. Brontë.
The odes of Quintus Horatius Flaccus, book 1, translated by Branwell Brontë. Ed J. Drinkwater 1923 (priv ptd); in The miscellaneous and unpublished writings of Charlotte and Patrick Branwell Brontë vol 2, 1938 (Shakespeare Head Brontë); in The poems of Patrick Branwell Brontë, ed V. A. Neufeldt 1990, *below*. Extract pbd previously in De Quincey memorials, ed A. H. Japp, vol 2 1891.
And the weary are at rest. Ed C. W. Hatfield 1924 (priv ptd).
Hatfield, C. W. Unpublished poems by Patrick Branwell Brontë. Brontë Soc Trans 7 pt 37 1927.

Branwell Brontë's flute book 1831–3. Introd by R. Rastall, Co. Kilkenny, Ireland 1980. Reproduction of ms in Bonnell collection.

The poems of Patrick Branwell Brontë. Ed T. Winnifrith, Oxford 1983 (Shakespeare Head Brontë).

The poems of Charlotte Brontë: a new text and commentary. Ed V. A. Neufeldt, New York and London 1985. 7 poems by 'UT' first pbd here.

Brother in the shadow: stories & sketches by Patrick Branwell Brontë. Transcribed by M. Butterfield, ed R. J. Duckett, Bradford 1988.

E. Flintoff. Some unpublished poems of Branwell Brontë. Durham Univ Jnl 81, June 1989.

The poems of Patrick Branwell Brontë: a new text and commentary. Ed V. A. Neufeldt, New York and London 1990.

The hand of the arch-sinner: two Angrian chronicles of Branwell Brontë. Reconstructed and ed with an introd, notes and commentary by R. G. Collins, initial transcription by J. Barnard, M. Collins, J. Bates and Collins, Oxford 1993. Texts: The life of Field Marshal the Right Honourable Alexander Percy, Earl of Northangerland...; and Real life in Verdopolis, a tale.

Branwell's Blackwood's Magazine. Introd by and ed C. Alexander, assisted by V. Benson and R. Alexander, Edmonton, Alberta 1995.

The works of Patrick Branwell Brontë. An edition, vol 1. Ed V. A. Neufeldt, New York and London 1997.

Individual poems published earlier than their appearance in collections noted above

Heaven and earth. Halifax Guardian 5 June 1841.

On the Melbourne ministry. Halifax Guardian 14 Aug 1841; Brontë Soc Trans 19 pt 8 1989.

Sonnet I. On Landseer's painting: 'The shepherd's chief mourner'. Bradford Herald 28 Apr 1842; in Unpublished poems by Patrick Branwell Brontë, Brontë Soc Trans 7 pt 37 1927.

Sonnet II. On the callousness produced by cares. Bradford Herald 5 May 1842; as Sonnet I in Halifax Guardian 7 May 1842; in F. A. Leyland, The Brontë family, 1886; also in W. Gérin, Branwell Brontë: a biography, 1961.

The Affghan War. Leeds Intelligencer 7 May 1842; in F. A. Leyland, The Brontë family, 1886.

Sonnet III. On peaceful death and painful life. Bradford Herald 12 May 1842; as Sonnet II in Halifax Guardian 14 May 1842; in F. A. Leyland, The Brontë family, 1886; also in W. Gérin, Branwell Brontë: a biography, 1961.

Caroline's prayer. On the change from childhood to womanhood. Bradford Herald 2 June 1842; Halifax Guardian 4 June 1842; in F. A. Leyland, The Brontë family, 1886. Extracts from Sir Henry Tunstall, *below*.

Song ['Should Life's first feelings be forgot', extract from 'How Eden like seem palace halls']. Bradford Herald 9 June 1842; Halifax Guardian 11 June 1842; in F. A. Leyland, The Brontë family, 1886; complete text pbd in The poems of Charlotte Brontë and Patrick Branwell Brontë, 1934 (Shakespeare Head Brontë). Extracts from 'How Eden like' also pbd in The complete works of Emily Jane Brontë vol 1, 1910; and in The orphans, and other poems, 1917, *see* Collections, *above*.

An epicurean's song. Bradford Herald 7 July 1842; Halifax Guardian 9 July 1842; in F. A. Leyland, The Brontë family, 1886.

On Caroline. Bradford Herald 12 July 1842; Halifax Guardian 14 July 1842; in F. A. Leyland, The Brontë family, 1886; extract pbd in I. Holgate, The key to 'Caroline', Brontë Soc Trans 13 pt 68 1958.

Noah's warning over Methuselah's grave [revised version of first 48 lines of Azrael]. Bradford Herald 25 Aug 1842; in F. A. Leyland, The Brontë family, 1886; earlier version and remaining text of Azrael pbd in Brontë Soc Trans 8 pt 43 1933 (as Azrael: or the eve of destruction: unpublished poem by Patrick Branwell Brontë).

Real rest. Halifax Guardian 8 Nov 1845; in F. A. Leyland, The Brontë family, 1886.

Penmaenmawr. Halifax Guardian 20 Dec 1845; in F. A. Leyland, The Brontë family, 1886.

Letter from a father on Earth to his child in her grave. Halifax Guardian 18 Apr 1846; in F. A. Leyland, The Brontë family, 1886; in The poems of Patrick Branwell Brontë, ed T. Winnifrith, 1983 (as 'From Earth – whose life-refreshing April showers'); in S. H. Goodacre, The published poems of Branwell Brontë, Brontë Soc Trans 19 pt 8 1989.

The end of all. Halifax Guardian 5 June 1847.

'Still and bright in twighlight shining'. In E. C. Gaskell, The life of Charlotte Brontë, 1857 (extract); in The complete works of Emily Jane Brontë, 1910 (extract, misattributed); complete text in The poems of Charlotte Brontë and Patrick Branwell Brontë, 1934 (Shakespeare Head Brontë).

'The man who will not know another'. In F. H. Grundy, Pictures of the past, 1879.

Sir Henry Tunstall. In F. A. Leyland, The Brontë family, 1886; in De Quincey memorials, ed A. H. Japp, vol 2 1891; in W. Gérin, Branwell Brontë: a biography, 1961 (extracts); complete text in The poems of Patrick Branwell Brontë, ed V. A. Neufeldt, 1990. Extracts pbd earlier in Bradford Herald 2 June 1842 and Halifax Guardian 4 June 1842 (both as 'Caroline's prayer: on the change from childhood to womanhood').

'Misery. Scene 1' ['How fast that courser fleeted by']. In Mrs Oliphant, Annals of a publishing house: William Blackwood and his sons, their magazine and friends vol 2, Edinburgh 1897 (extract).

'Augusta', 'Backward I look upon my life', 'Song: I saw her in the crowded hall', and 'The Rover'. In T. J. Wise, A bibliography of the writings in prose and verse of the members of the Brontë family, 1917.

Unpublished juvenile manuscript by Charlotte Brontë ['On the great bay of the Glass Town' (by 'UT'), 'Lines spoken by a lawyer on the occasion of the transfer of this magazine' (by 'WT'), and 'Lines spoken by one who was tired of dullness upon the same occasion' (by 'UT'), in 'Blackwood's Young Men's Magazine Dec (1) 1829']. Brontë Soc Trans 5 pt 29 1919. *See also* An edition of the early writings of Charlotte Brontë, ed C. Alexander, vol 1 1987.

'Addressed to "the tower of all nations"' (by 'UT'). In Albion and Marina: a romantic love story by Charlotte Brontë, Brontë Soc Trans 6 pt 30 1920.

'The Angrian welcome', 'Before our mighty Maker's throne', and 'Zamorna and Percy' (in appendix). In The complete poems of Charlotte Brontë, 1923 (misattributed).

'Harvest in Spain' (by 'UT'). In D. Cook, Miniature magazines of Charlotte Brontë: with unpublished poems from an original manuscript in Ashley Library. In Bookman 71, Dec 1926. *See also* The poems of Charlotte Brontë, ed V. A. Neufeldt, 1985; and An edition of the early writings of Charlotte Brontë, ed C. Alexander, vol 1 1987.

'Our hopes on earth seem wholly gone'. In Catalogue of the Bonnell Collection in the Brontë Parsonage Museum, 1932.

An unpublished poem written by Patrick Branwell Brontë in October, 1835 ['Song: written by Percy in 1813']. Brontë Soc Trans 8 pt 44 1934.

'Oh may America', 'Dirge of the Genii' (facs), and extracts from 'If you live by the sunny fountain', 'One day I went out awalking', 'The Ammon tree cutter', 'Ode to the cheif Genius Bany', 'Ode to Napoleon', 'Adress to the Genius &c', and 'W[h]ose that who ridest on the storm'. In F. E. Ratchford, The Brontës' web of childhood, New York 1941.

'Laussane: a dramatic poem by Young Soult' (extract), 'But now the night with dusky wings', and 'Caractacus' (extract). In J. Malham-Dembleby, The confessions of Charlotte Brontë, Bradford 1954 (priv ptd); complete texts ptd in The poems of Patrick Branwell Brontë, ed V. A. Neufeldt, 1990.

'While holy Wheelhouse far above'. In D. du Maurier, The infernal world of Branwell Brontë, 1961 (extract).

'High minded Frenchmen love not the ghost'. In The poems of Charlotte Brontë, ed T. Winnifrith, 1984. Poem possibly by Branwell.

Letters

Letter to Wordsworth. In E. C. Gaskell, The life of Charlotte Brontë, 1857; in The Brontës: their lives, friendships, and correspondence, ed Wise and Symington, vol 1 1932 (Shakespeare Head Brontë); rptd in The Letters of Charlotte Brontë, ed M. Smith, vol 1 Oxford 1995.

Letters to the editor of Blackwood's Magazine. In Mrs Oliphant, Annals of a publishing house: William Blackwood and his sons, their magazine and friends vol 1, Edinburgh 1897 (shortened version); letter of 4 Jan 1837 rptd in Brontë letters purchased, Brontë Soc Trans 16 pt 81 1971.

A complete transcript of the Leyland manuscripts showing the unpublished portions from the original documents [in the Brotherton Collection]. Collected and transcribed by J. A. Symington, arranged with notes by C. W. Hatfield, Brontë Soc Trans 6 pt 35 1925; Leeds 1925 (priv ptd). Letters to J. B. Leyland and J. Brown.

Two letters from Branwell [to J. Frobisher]. Brontë Soc Trans 12 pt 65 1955.

§2

Textual/bibliographical studies

Oakendale, W. (W. Dearden). Who wrote Wuthering Heights? Halifax Guardian 15 June 1867; rptd with commentary in Patrick Branwell Brontë and 'Wuthering Heights', Brontë Soc Trans 7 pt 37 1927.

Yates, W. W. Who wrote Wuthering Heights? More about Branwell Brontë. Dewsbury Reporter 24 Mar 1894.

Drinkwater, J. Patrick Branwell Brontë and his 'Horace'. In his A book for bookmen, 1926.

[Law, A.] Emily Jane Brontë and the authorship of Wuthering Heights. [1928.]

Gill, S. A manuscript of Branwell Brontë, with letters of Mrs Gaskell. Brontë Soc Trans 15 pt 80 1970.

Alexander, C. The early writings of Charlotte Brontë. Oxford and New York 1983. Substantial discussion of Branwell's mss and their chronology.

Goodacre, S. H. The published poems of Branwell Brontë. Brontë Soc Trans 19 pt 8 1989.

Neufeldt, V. A. A bibliography of the manuscripts of Patrick Branwell Brontë. New York and London 1993.

Biographical studies

Grundy, F. H. Patrick Branwell Brontë. In Pictures of the past: memories of men I have met, and places I have seen, 1879.

Leyland, F. A. The Brontë family with special reference to Patrick Branwell Brontë. 2 vols 1886; rptd 1973 (2 vols in 1).

Chadwick, E. A. Patrick Branwell Brontë, June 24, 1817–September 28, 1848: a vindication. Nineteenth Century and After 84, Aug 1918.

Law, A. Patrick Branwell Brontë. [1924.]

Gosse, E. W. The brother of the Brontës. In his Silhouettes, 1925.

Kinsley, E. E. Pattern for genius: a story of Branwell Brontë and his three sisters. 1939.

du Maurier, D. The infernal world of Branwell Brontë. 1960, 1972 (Pen).

Gérin, W. Branwell Brontë: a biography. 1961.

Rees, J. Profligate son: Branwell Brontë and his sisters. 1986.

Cheney, P. Another Branwell liaison? Brontë Soc Trans 21 pt 7 1996.

Emily Brontë, 'Ellis Bell' 1818–48

Collections

The complete works of Emily Jane Brontë, Ed C. K. Shorter 2 vols 1910, 1911.

See Collections and selections: the Brontë family, *above*.

Wuthering Heights, a novel, by Ellis Bell. 3 vols 1847 (vols 1 and 2 only; vol 3 is Agnes Grey by Acton Bell: *see* Anne Brontë, *below*); 1 vol New York 1848 ('By the Author of Jane Eyre'), also issued in 2 pts; 1 vol Boston 1848; 1 vol 1850 (with Agnes Grey; a new edition revised, with a biographical notice of the authors, a selection from their literary remains, and a preface by Currer Bell); 2 vols Leipzig 1851 (with Agnes Grey; 'copyright edition', Tauchnitz Collection of British Authors vols 201 and 202); 1 vol New York 1857; London 1858 (with Agnes Grey); New York 1878 (Seaside Lib); Boston 1891 etc; ed E. Rhys, London and New York 1907 (EL); introd by J. N. McIlwraith, New York 1907; in Emily Brontë: complete works, in 2 vols, introd by C. K. Shorter, vol 2 1911; introd by M. Sinclair 1921 (EL); ed H. W. Garrod 1930 (WC); Harmondsworth 1946 (Pen); introd by W. S. Maugham, Philadelphia 1949; introd by M. Schorer, New York 1950; introd by R. A. Gettmann, New York 1950; introd by B. McCullough, New York 1950; introd B. Dobrée, London and Glasgow 1953; introd by V. S. Pritchett, Boston 1956; with Selected poems, ed P. Henderson, introd by M. Lane 1957 (EL); ed G. Moore, New York 1959; ed T. C. Moser, New York 1962; ed W. M. Sale Jr, New York 1963, (Norton Critical edn) 1972 (2nd edn), 1990 (3rd edn (with R. Dunn)); ed D. Daiches 1965 (Pen); ed F. R. Flahiff, Toronto 1968; ed I. Jack 1981 (WC); ed H. Glen, London and New York 1988; introd by K. Frank, New York 1991; ed L. H. Peterson, Boston 1992; ed H. Osborne (with introd by M. Drabble, Selected poems ed P. Henderson) 1993 (EL); introd by P. Stoneman 1995 (WC).

TRANSLATIONS: Ger 1851, 1908, 1938 (rptd 1975), 1945 (rptd 1957, 1971), 1949 (rptd 1973), 1950, 1950, [1952]; Fr 1892, 1925 (rev 1947, 1989), 1927, 1934, 1937, 1943, 1944, 1948, 1963, 1971, 1972 (rptd 1990); Ital 1926, 1949, 1952, 1956, 1957, 1981; Swed 1927; Gaelic 1933; Romanian 1937, 1968; Sp 1940, 1959, 1963 (6th edn), 1969; Flemish 1945; Turkish 1946; Du 1947, 1985; Serbian 1952; Persian 1955, 1992; Rus 1956, 1960; Cz 1958, 1960; Hungarian 1962; Norwegian 1968; Sinhala 1970; Korean 1972; Hebrew 1990.

REVIEWS: Spectator 18 Dec 1847; [Chorley, H. F.] Athenaeum 25 Dec 1847; NMM 82, Jan 1848; John Bull 1 Jan 1848; Examiner 8 Jan 1848; Britannia 15 Jan 1848; Douglas Jerrold's Weekly Newspaper 15 Jan 1848; Atlas 22 Jan 1848; Morning Herald 22 Jan 1848; Economist 29 Jan 1848; Tait's Edinburgh Mag n.s. 15, Feb 1848; Harbinger (Boston and New York) 29 Apr 1848; Literary World (New York) 3, 29 Apr 1848; [Briggs, C. F.] Holden's Dollar Mag (New York) 1, May, June 1848; Albion (New York) n.s. 7, 6 May 1848; Examiner (Richmond VA) 9 May 1848; Nat Era (Washington) 11 May 1848; P[eck], G. W. Amer Rev (New York) 7, n.s. 1, June 1848; Peterson's Mag (Philadelphia) 13, June 1848; Sartain's Union Mag (New York) 2, June 1848; Union Mag of Lit and Art 2, June 1848; Godey's Lady's Book (Philadelphia) 37, July 1848; Graham's Mag (Philadelphia) 33, July 1848; [Whipple, E. P.] North Amer Rev 67, Oct 1848; Examiner 21 Dec 1850; Athenaeum 28 Dec 1850; [Lewes, G. H.] Leader 1, 28 Dec 1850; Economist 9, 4 Jan 1851; Eclectic Rev n.s. 1, Feb 1851.

Selections from poems by Ellis Bell. In Wuthering Heights and Agnes Grey: a new edition revised, with a biographical notice of the authors, a selection from their literary remains, and a preface, by Currer Bell, 1850. *See* Collections and selections, *above*.

Poems of Emily Brontë. Introd by A. Symons, London and New York 1906.

The complete poems of Emily Brontë. Ed C. Shorter, introd by W. R. Nicoll, in The complete works of Emily Brontë in 2 vols, vol 1 1910.

The complete poems of Emily Jane Brontë. Ed C. Shorter, arranged by C. W. Hatfield [1923], New York [1924].

Poèmes d'Emily Brontë. Tr M. Graham et G. Pelorson, introd par E. Jaloux, Paris 1933.

The poems of Emily Jane Brontë and Anne Brontë. Ed T. J. Wise and J. A. Symington, Oxford 1934 (Shakespeare Head Brontë).

Two poems: Love's rebuke, Remembrance, by Emily Brontë, with the Gondal background of her poems and novel. Ed F. E. Ratchford, Austin TX 1934 (priv ptd).

Gondal poems by Emily Jane Brontë, now first published from the ms in the British Museum. Ed H. Brown and J. Mott, Oxford 1938; rptd 1973.

The complete poems of Emily Jane Brontë. Ed from the manuscripts by C. W. Hatfield, New York and London 1941.

Les poésies d'Emily Brontë. Tr P. Pascal, introd by J. Boulenger, Paris 1943.

Poems, selected with an introduction by P. Henderson. 1947.

Les orages du coeur: un choix de poèmes. Tr M. Best, Paris 1950.

The complete poems of Emily Brontë. Ed P. Henderson 1951.

Selected poems of Emily Brontë. Ed M. Spark 1952; rptd in Spark's The essence of the Brontës: a compilation with essays, London and Chester Springs PA 1993.

Gondal's Queen: a novel in verse by Emily Jane Brontë, arranged with introduction and notes by F. E. Ratchford. Austin TX 1955.

Selected poems. Ed P. Henderson, in Wuthering Heights, introd by M. Lane 1957; introd by M. Drabble 1978 (EL).

Selected poems of Emily Brontë. In Wuthering Heights: text, sources, criticism, ed T. C. Moser, New York 1962.

Poèmes, 1836–1846; choisis et traduits d'après la leçon des manuscrits par Pierre Leyris; ed bilingue. Paris 1963.

Emily Brontë: présentation par Françoise d'Eaubonne; choix de textes, bibliographie, portraits, facsimiles. Paris 1964.

Quelques poèmes d'Emily Brontë traduits par J. Blondel. Études Brontëennes, Paris 1970.

Emily Brontë: a peculiar music; poems for young readers. Ed N. Lewis, London, Sydney and Toronto 1971.

Poems by Emily Brontë. Ed D. Thompson 1972.

Emily Brontë: poems. Ed R. Hartill 1973.

Le midi de la nuit: poèmes. Tr. J. Blondel, Pavillons-sous-Bois, France 1988.

Emily Jane Brontë: the complete poems. Ed J. Gezari 1992 (Pen).

The poems of Emily Brontë. Ed B. Lloyd-Evans 1992.

The poems of Emily Brontë. Ed D. Roper with E. Chitham, Oxford 1995.

Individual poems published earlier than their appearance in editions or collections noted above

A farewell to Alexandria ('I've seen this dell in July's shine'). Cornhill Mag 1 May 1860 (entitled The outcast mother).

Gleneden's dream ('Tell me, watcher, is it winter?'). In C. K. Shorter, Charlotte Brontë and her circle, 1896.

Written in the Gaaldine prison caves to A. G. A. ('Thy sun is near meridian height'). In C. K. Shorter, Relics of Emily Brontë, Woman at Home 5, Aug 1897; Bookman (New York) 6, Sep 1897.

An unpublished verse by Emily Jane Brontë. Brontë Soc Trans 8 pt 44 1934. ('A winter night on Haworth Moor': cancelled stanza from 'It was night and on the mountains'.)

'There shines the moon at noon of night', 'Thou standest in the greenwood now', 'Come, the wind may never again'. Facs in V. Moore, The life and eager death of Emily Brontë, 1936; first ptd in Gondal poems, 1938, *above*.

'Alcona, in its changing mood'. In H. Brown and J. Mott, The Gondal saga, Brontë Soc Trans 9 pt 48 1938. *See also* TLS 19 Mar 1938.

Letters, essays ('devoirs'), and diary papers

L'amour filial. Facs of essay with trn in Woman at Home, Sep 1894.

Diary papers:for 24 Nov 1834, in The Brontës: their lives, friendships and correspondence ed Wise and Symington, vol 1 1932; for 26 June 1837, in Brontë Soc Trans 12 pt 61 1951; for 30 July 1841 and 30 July 1845, in C. K. Shorter, Charlotte Brontë and her circle, London and New York 1896, rptd in The Brontës: their lives, friendships and correspondence vols 1 and 2, 1932. The diary papers are also reproduced in Gondal's queen, ed F. E. Ratchford, Austin TX 1955; The Brontë sisters: selected source materials for college research papers, ed R. H. Blackburn, Boston 1964; and Wuthering Heights, Norton Critical 3rd edn 1990.

Letters to Miss Ellen Nussey, 12 May 1843 and 9 February 1846, signed Emily J. Brontë. First ptd in C. K. Shorter, Charlotte Brontë and her circle, London and New York 1896.

Cornish, D. H. The Brontës' study of French. Includes translations of two essays, Portrait: Harold the night before Hastings, and Filial love. Brontë Soc Trans 11 pt 57 1947.

Five essays written in French by Emily Jane Brontë. Tr L. W. Nagel, introd and notes by F. E. Ratchford, Austin TX 1948; rptd Folcroft PA 1974. (The cat; Portrait: King Harold on the eve of the battle of Hastings; Filial love; A letter from one brother to another; The butterfly.)

Three essays by Emily Brontë [The cat; A letter from one brother to another; The butterfly]. Reprint of 3 of the essays in Five essays written in French . . ., tr L. W. Nagel (*see* previous entry), Brontë Soc Trans 11 pt 60 1950. English trn only.

Le palais de la mort. With trn by M. Lane. In French essays by Charlotte and Emily, Brontë Soc Trans 12 pt 64 1954. *See also* Listener 52, 11 Nov 1954.

Lettre (Ma chère Maman) [a 'devoir' dated 26 juillet]. Tr P. Bentley, in More Brontë devoirs, Brontë Soc Trans 12 pt 65 1955.

Gérin, W. Emily Brontë's French devoirs. In her Emily Brontë: a biography, Oxford 1971. French texts of Le chat; Portrait: le roi Harold avant la bataille de Hastings; Lettre ('Ma chère Maman'); L'amour filial; Lettre d'un frère à un frère; Le papillon; Le palais de la mort.

Lettre (Madame) [a 'devoir' dated 16 juillet]. In C. Lemon, An exciting chapter in the Society's history: purchase of forty-four autograph letters by Charlotte Brontë and a devoir by Emily Brontë, Brontë Soc Trans 17 pt 90 1980.

Lonoff, S. (ed). Charlotte and Emily Brontë: the Belgian essays. New Haven CT 1997.

Textual/bibliographical studies

Law, A. Emily Jane Brontë and the authorship of Wuthering Heights. Altham, Accrington [1925].

Cook, D. Emily Brontë's poems [some textual corrections and unpbd verses]. Nineteenth Cent and After 100, Aug 1926.

Willis, I. C. The authorship of Wuthering Heights. 1936. *See also* the same author's article, The authorship of Wuthering Heights, Trollopian 2, Dec 1947.

Brown, H. and J. Mott. The Gondal saga: unpublished verses by Emily Brontë. TLS 19 Feb 1938.

Ratchford, F. E. Correct text of Emily Brontë's poems. Brontë Soc Trans 10 pt 52 1942.

Watson, M. R. Wuthering Heights and the critics. Trollopian 3, Mar 1949.

Weir, E. M. Mr Henderson creates a controversy: his edition of Emily's poems. Brontë Soc Trans 12 pt 62 1952.

Isenberg, D. R. A Gondal fragment. Brontë Soc Trans 14 pt 72 1962.

A first edition of Wuthering Heights. Brontë Soc Trans 14 pt 74 1964.

Bracco, E. J. Emily Brontë's second novel. Brontë Soc Trans 15 pt 76 1966.

Maxwell, J. C. Emily Brontë's 'The palace of death'. Brontë Soc Trans 15 pt 77 1967.

Schmidt, E. T. From highland to lowland: Charlotte Brontë's editorial changes in Emily's poems. Brontë Soc Trans 15 pt 78 1968.

Larken, G. The shuffling scamp: some notes on Thomas Cautley Newby.... Brontë Soc Trans 15 pt 80 1970.
Merry, B. An unknown Italian dramatisation of Wuthering Heights [by B. Fenoglio]. Brontë Soc Trans 16 pt 81 1971.
Allott, M. (ed). Emily Brontë, Wuthering Heights: a casebook. 1973; 1992 (rev edn).
Petit, J.-P. (ed). Emily Brontë: a critical anthology. 1973 (Pen).
Barclay, J. M. (comp). Emily Brontë criticism 1900–1968: an annotated check list. New York 1974; expanded edn (1900–82) Westport CT and London 1984.
Rauth, H. Emily Brontës roman Wuthering Heights als Quelle für Bühnen und Film Versionen. Veröffentlichungen der Universität Innsbruck 84 1974.
Von Frank, A. J. An American defence of Wuthering Heights – 1848. Brontë Soc Trans 16 pt 84 1974. Reprint of rev in Holden's Dollar Mag (New York) June 1848.
Akiho, S. and T. Fujita (comp). A concordance to the complete poems of Emily Jane Brontë. Tokyo 1976.
Russian and French editions of Wuthering Heights. Brontë Soc Trans 17 pt 86 1976.
Ganner, H. Wuthering Heights in German translation. Brontë Soc Trans 17 pt 90 1980.
Winnifrith, T. Wuthering Heights: one volume or two? In E. Chitham and T. Winnifrith, Brontë facts and Brontë problems, 1983.
Roper, D. The revision of Emily Brontë's Poems of 1846. Library 6th ser 6 1984.
Sabol, C. R. and T. K. Bender. A concordance to Brontë's Wuthering Heights. New York and London 1984.
Hargreaves, G. D. The poems of Ellis Bell: the version printed in 1846 and the manuscript version. Brontë Soc Trans 21 pt 3 1994.

Selected criticism

Letters/early comments on Wuthering Heights

Charlotte Brontë, letter to W. S. Williams, 14 August 1848. In The Brontës: their lives, friendships and correspondence, ed Wise and Symington, vol 2 1932.
D. G. Rossetti, letter to W. Allingham, 19 September 1854. Letters of D. G. Rossetti ed. O. Doughty and J. R. Wahl vol 2 Oxford 1965.
[Dobell, S.] Currer Bell. Palladium no 3, Sep 1850; rptd in The life and letters of Sydney Dobell, ed E. J. [Emily Jolly], 2 vols 1878, vol 1; and in Brontë Soc Trans 5 pt 28 1918.
[Dallas, E. S.] Currer Bell. Blackwood's Edinburgh Mag 82, July 1857.
Oakendale, W. (W. Dearden) Who wrote Wuthering Heights? Halifax Guardian 15 June 1867; rptd as Patrick Branwell Brontë and Wuthering Heights, in Brontë Soc Trans 7 pt 37 1927.
Poetesses. Saturday Rev 23 May 1868.
Gosse, E. Emily Brontë. In The English poets: selections with critical introductions by various writers and a general introduction by Matthew Arnold, ed T. Humphry Ward, 4 vols London and New York 1880, vol 4.
Robertson, E. S. Emily Brontë. In English poetesses: a series of critical biographies, with illustrative extracts. London, Paris and New York 1883.
Swinburne, A. C. Emily Brontë. Athenaeum 16 June 1883; rptd in his Miscellanies, 1886.
F[othergill], J. Wuthering Heights. Temple Bar 81 1887.
Girl novelists of the time. Atlantic Monthly 60, Nov 1887.
De Wyzewa, T. Littérature anglaise: une soeur de Charlotte Brontë: Emily Brontë. Revue Bleue 29, 15 Aug 1891; rptd in Écrivains étrangers, 2nd ser, Paris 1897.
Garnett, R. Emily Brontë 1818–1848. In The poets and the poetry of the nineteenth century: Joanna Baillie to Jean Ingelow, ed A. H. Miles, 1891.
Keyworth, T. A new identification of Wuthering Heights. Bookman 3, Mar 1893.
Williams, A. M. Emily Brontë. Temple Bar 98, July 1893; rptd in Our early female novelists and other essays, Glasgow 1904.
Colton, A. W. Emily Brontë. Citizen (Philadelphia) 2, Mar 1896.
MacKay, Angus M. On the interpretation of Emily Brontë. Westminster Rev 150, Aug 1898.
Maeterlinck, M. In La sagesse et la destinée. Paris 1898; tr A. Sutro, Wisdom and destiny, London and New York 1898.
Saintsbury, G. The position of the Brontës as origins in the history of the English novel. Brontë Soc Trans 2 pt 9 1899.
Fotheringham, J. The work of Emily Brontë, and the Brontë problem. Brontë Soc Trans 2 pt 11 1900.
Gower, E. I. The sphinx of our modern literature. Friends Quart Examiner 44, Jan–Mar 1900.
Haldane, R. B. Emily Brontë's place in literature. Brontë Soc Trans 2 pt 12 1901.
Howells, W. D. The two Catharines of Emily Brontë. In his Heroines of fiction, 2 vols London and New York 1901, vol 1. Rptd from Harper's Bazar 33, 29 Dec 1900.
The genius of the moors. Academy 65, 3 Oct 1903.
Hopkins, M. M. Emily Brontë. Chicago 1903.
Sutcliffe, H. The spirit of the moors. Brontë Soc Trans 2 pt 13 1903; rptd in Charlotte Brontë 1816–1916: a centenary memorial, 1917.
Wilkins, M. E. Emily Brontë and Wuthering Heights. Booklover's Mag 1, May 1903.
Gleave, J. J. Emily Brontë: an appreciation. Manchester 1904.
Mew, C. The poems of Emily Brontë. Temple Bar 130, July 1904.
Longbottom, J. Wuthering Heights and Patrick Branwell Brontë. Yorkshire N & Q 1, Feb 1905.
Shorter, C. K. Wuthering Heights. In Charlotte Brontë and her sisters, 1905, 1906 (2nd edn).
Ward, Mrs H. Wuthering Heights. Brontë Soc Trans 2 pt 15 1906.
Malham-Dembleby, J. The lifting of the Brontë veil. Fortnightly Rev 81, Mar 1907.
Emily Brontë. TLS 5 Nov 1908.
Bridges, R. The poems of Emily Brontë. TLS 12 Jan 1911; rptd in Collected essays vol 9, 1932.
Malham-Dembleby, J. The key to the Brontë works: the key to Charlotte Brontë's Wuthering Heights, Jane Eyre, and her other works. 1911.
Meynell, A. Charlotte and Emily Brontë. Dublin Rev 148, Apr 1911; rptd in Hearts of controversy, London and New York 1917; rev in Essays of today and yesterday, 1926.
Moore, C. L. Another literary mare's-nest. Dial 53, 16 Oct 1912.
Vaughan, C. E. Charlotte and Emily Brontë: a comparison and a contrast. Brontë Soc Trans 4 pt 22 1912; rptd in Charlotte Brontë 1816–1916: a centenary tribute, 1917.
Spurgeon, C. F. E. Emily Brontë. In Mysticism in English literature, Cambridge 1913.
Smith, J. C. Emily Brontë: a reconsideration. In Essays and studies by members of the English association 5, ed O. Elton, Oxford 1914.
An unrecovered poetess. TLS 10 June 1915.
Powys, J. C. Emily Brontë. In Suspended judgments: essays on books and sensations, New York 1916.
Symons, A. Emily Brontë. Figures of several centuries, 1916; rev in Nation 23, 24 Aug 1918; rptd in Dramatis personae, Indianapolis 1923.
Allen, H. M. Emily Brontë – one hundred years after. Education 39, Dec 1918.
Roseveare, A. The poetry of Emily Brontë. Poetry Rev 9, Sep–Oct 1918.
Fenton, E. M. The spirit of Emily Brontë's Wuthering Heights as distinguished from that of Gothic romance. Washington Univ Stud (Humanistic ser) 8 1920.
Kavanagh, C. The symbolism of Wuthering Heights. 1920.

Biographical studies

Bell, C. (C. Brontë). Biographical notice of Ellis and Acton Bell, and editor's preface to the new edition of Wuthering Heights. In Wuthering Heights and Agnes Grey, new edn rev 1850.

E[bsworth], J. W. Emily Brontë ('Ellis Bell'). MacPhail's Edinburgh Ecclesiastical Jnl and Literary Rev no 164, Sep 1859.

[Kinsley, W. W.] The life and writings of Emily Brontë (Ellis Bell). Galaxy (New York) 15, Feb 1873.

Robinson, A. M. F. (Mme Duclaux). Emily Brontë. London and Boston 1883.

Salmon, A. L. A modern stoic: Emily Brontë. Poet-Lore 4 1892.

Shorter, C. K. Relics of Emily Brontë. Woman at Home 5, Aug 1897; rev Bookman (New York) 6, Sep 1897.

Sonnino, G. Il pensiero religioso di una poetassa inglese del secolo XIX: Emilia Giovanna Brontë. Nuova Antologia 5th ser 39 1904.

Chadwick, E. A. Emily Brontë. Nineteenth Century and After 86, Oct 1919.

Wilson, R. (Florence Romer Muir Wilson O'Brien). All alone: the life and private history of Emily Jane Brontë. London and New York 1928. US title: The life and private history of Emily Jane Brontë.

Simpson, C. Emily Brontë. London and New York 1929.

Dooley, L. Psychoanalysis of the character and genius of Emily Brontë. Psychoanalytic Rev 17, Apr 1930.

Edgerley, C. M. Emily Brontë: a national portrait vindicated. Brontë Soc Trans 8 pt 42 1932.

Moore, V. The life and eager death of Emily Brontë: a biography. 1936. *See* letter by C. W. Hatfield, Emily Brontë's 'lost love', TLS 29 Aug 1936.

Ocampo, V. Emily Brontë: terra incognita. Buenos Aires 1938.

Escombe, L. Emily Brontë et ses démons. Paris and Clermont 1941.

Hinkley, L. L. The Brontës: Charlotte and Emily. New York 1945, London 1947.

Evans, M. Byron and Emily Brontë. Life & Letters 57, June 1948.

Preston, A. H. John Greenwood and the Brontës: the Haworth stationer's notebook throws new light on Emily. Brontë Soc Trans 12 pt 61 1951.

Spark, M. and D. Stanford. Emily Brontë: her life and work. 1953, New York 1966. Pt 1, Biographical, rptd in M. Spark, The essence of the Brontës, London and Chester Springs PA 1993.

Crandall, N. Emily Brontë: a psychological portrait. Rindge NH 1957.

Stevenson, W. H. Emily and Anne Brontë. London and New York 1968.

Miller, M. J. Emily: the story of Emily Brontë. 1969.

Hewish, J. Emily Brontë: a critical and biographical study. 1969.

Gérin, W. Emily Brontë: a biography. Oxford 1971.

Benvenuto, R. Emily Brontë. Boston 1982.

Davies, S. Emily Brontë: the artist as a free woman. Manchester 1983.

Chitham, E. A life of Emily Brontë. London and New York 1987.

Winnifrith, T. and E. Chitham. Charlotte and Emily Brontë: literary lives. Basingstoke 1989.

Frank, K. A chainless soul: a life of Emily Brontë. Boston 1990.

Anne Brontë, 'Acton Bell' 1820–49

See Collections and selections: the Brontë family, *above*.

§1

Agnes Grey: a novel, by Acton Bell (Anne Brontë). 3 vols 1847 (vol 3 only; vols 1 and 2 are Wuthering Heights, by Ellis Bell [Emily Brontë]); 1 vol 1850 (with Wuthering Heights; a new edition revised, with a biographical notice of the authors, a selection from their literary remains, and a preface, by Currer Bell [Charlotte Brontë]); serialised weekly in Saturday Gazette (Philadelphia) 22 Dec 1849–19 Jan 1850; 1 vol Philadelphia [1850] (Agnes Grey: an autobiography, by the authors of Jane Eyre, Shirley, The tenant of Wildfell Hall, etc); 2 vols Leipzig 1851 (with Wuthering Heights; a new edition revised ... by Currer Bell, 'copyright edition', Tauchnitz Collection of British Authors vols 201 and 202); 1 vol 1858 (with Wuthering Heights); New York 1881; [1905] (with Poems by Charlotte, Emily, and Anne Brontë, introd by F. Masson); [1935]; 1908 (with The professor, Poems, by the sisters Brontë); New York 1910 (with Wuthering Heights in Complete works of Charlotte Brontë and her sisters); (with The tenant of Wildfell Hall) introd by M. Sinclair 1914 (EL), introd by P. Bentley 1954 (Collins), introd by M. Lane 1958 (EL); [1935]; ed H. van Thal, introd by F. Hughes 1966; 1969 (Folio Soc); introd by A. Smith 1985 (EL) (with Poems); ed A. Goreau 1988 (Pen). *See also* Collections, *above*.

TRANSLATIONS: Du 1853; Fr 1859, 1962 (rptd 1990); Ital 1956.

REVIEWS: Spectator 18 Dec 1847; [Chorley, H. F.] Athenaeum 25 Dec 1847; NMM Jan 1848; Britannia 15 Jan 1848; Douglas Jerrold's Weekly Newspaper 15 Jan 1848; Atlas 22 Jan 1848; [Peck, G. W.] Amer Rev June 1848; Albion (New York) n.s. 7, 5 Aug 1848; Nat Era (Washington) 4, 3 Jan 1850; Graham's Mag (Philadelphia) 36, Feb 1850; Peterson's Mag (Philadelphia) 17, Feb 1850; Godey's Lady's Book (Philadelphia) 40, Mar 1850; Sartain's Union Mag (New York) 6, Apr 1850; Examiner 21 Dec 1850; Athenaeum 28 Dec 1850; Economist 4 Jan 1851; Eclectic Rev n.s. 1, Feb 1851.

The tenant of Wildfell Hall, by Acton Bell. 3 vols 1848; reissued as 'Second edition', with preface, 1848; 1 vol, 'By Acton Bell, author of Wuthering Heights', New York 1848 (also 2 vols in paper wrappers); 1 vol 1854 (Parlour Lib edn); 'a new edition' 1858, 1867, etc; New York 1881 (Seaside Lib edn); 1904 (with The Professor); (with Agnes Grey) introd by M. Sinclair 1914 (EL), introd by P. Bentley 1954, introd by M. Lane 1958 (EL); New York 1962; 1966 (Folio Soc); with author's preface to second edn 1974 (WC); ed G. D. Hargreaves, introd by W. Gérin 1979 (Pen); introd by J. Weeks, Santa Barbara CA 1979; ed H. Rosengarten and M. Smith, Oxford and New York 1993 (WC). *See also* Collections, *above*.

TRANSLATIONS: Fr 1945, 1964, rptd 1991.

REVIEWS: [Chorley, H. F.] Athenaeum 8 July 1848; Spectator 8 July 1848; Morning Express (New York) 27 July 1848; Examiner 29 July 1848; Sunday News and Noah's Weekly Messenger 8, 30 July 1848; Sharpe's London Mag Aug 1848; Boston Post 3 Aug 1848; Albion (New York) n.s. 7, 5 Aug 1848; Literary World (New York) 3, 12 Aug 1848; Nat Era (Washington) 2, 24 Aug 1848; Holden's Dollar Mag (New York) 2, Sep 1848; Peterson's Mag (Philadelphia) 14, Sep 1848; Sartain's Union Mag (New York) 3, Sep 1848; Godey's Lady's Book (Philadelphia) 37, Oct 1848; Graham's Mag (Philadelphia) 33, Oct 1848; [Whipple, E. P.] North Amer Rev 67, Oct 1848 (rptd Brontë Soc Trans 13 pt 66 1956); J. E. Rankin, Pictorial Nat Lib (Boston) 2, Jan 1849; [Kingsley, C.] Fraser's Mag 39, Apr 1849.

Selections from poems by Acton Bell. In Wuthering Heights and Agnes Grey, a new edition revised, with a biographical notice of the authors, a selection from their literary remains, and a preface, by Currer Bell, 1850.

Dreams and other poems. 1917 (priv ptd).

The complete poems of Anne Brontë. Ed C. Shorter, introd by C. W. Hatfield, London and New York [1920].

The poems of Emily Jane and Anne Brontë. Ed T. J. Wise and J. A. Symington, Oxford 1934 (Shakespeare Head Brontë).

The poems of Anne Brontë: a new text and commentary. Ed E. Chitham, London and Totowa NJ 1979.

Anne Brontë's song book 1843–4. Introd by R. Rastall, Co. Kilkenny, Ireland, 1980. Reproduction of ms in Bonnell Collection.

Individual poems published earlier than their appearance in collections noted above

Oh, they have robbed me of the hope. In Agnes Grey (1847) ch 17.

Farewell to thee! but not farewell. In The tenant of Wildfell Hall (1848), vol 1 ch 19.

The three guides. Fraser's Mag 38, Aug 1848. Included in Selections from poems by Acton Bell, in 1850 edn of Wuthering Heights and Agnes Grey: *see* Collections, *above*.
Self-communion: a poem. Ed T. J. Wise 1900 (priv ptd).
Retirement ('O, let me be alone a while'). Attributed to E. Brontë in 1910 edn of her poems: *see* complete works of Emily Brontë vol 2, 1910, *above*.
Two poems by Anne Brontë ['A prisoner in a dungeon deep'; The shadow of Christ ('Take my friend this little token'); the latter is not by A. Brontë]. Brontë Soc Trans 7 pt 36 1926.
I will not mourn thee, lovely one. In A. Harrison and D. Stanford, Anne Brontë: her life and work, 1959.

Letters, diary papers, preface

Diary papers of 30 July 1841, 31 July 1845. In C. K. Shorter, Charlotte Brontë and her circle, London and New York 1896.
Letters of 4 January 1848 (to Ellen Nussey) and 18 January 1849 (to W. S. Williams). In C. K. Shorter, Charlotte Brontë and her circle, London and New York 1896.
Preface to the second edn. The tenant of Wildfell Hall, 2nd edn 1848; *see above*.
Letter to the Rev D. Thom, 30 Dec 1848. TLS 21 June 1923; given also in appendix 3 of The tenant of Wildfell Hall (Clarendon edn), Oxford 1992.
New acquisitions: letters from Emily, Anne and Patrick; Mrs Gaskell's annotations. Brontë Soc Trans 12 pt 63 1953. Letters to E. Nussey, 4 Oct 1847, 26 Jan 1848, 5 Apr 1849.

Textual/bibliographical studies

Anne Brontë's hymns. Baptist Messenger Mar 1891.
Hatfield, C. W. The last verses written by Anne Brontë. Brontë Soc Trans 8 pt 42 1932.
Christian, M. G. Manuscripts of stories and poems by Anne Brontë. In A census of Brontë manuscripts in the United States, part 2, Trollopian 2, Mar 1948.
Visick, M. Anne Brontë's last poem. Brontë Soc Trans 13 pt 69 1959.
Ekeblad, I.-S. The tenant of Wildfell Hall and Women beware women. N & Q n.s. 10, Dec 1963.
Hargreaves, G. D. Incomplete texts of The tenant of Wildfell Hall. Brontë Soc Trans 16 pt 82 1972.
Tiffany, L. K. Charlotte and Anne's literary reputation. Brontë Soc Trans 16 pt 84 1974.
Hargreaves, G. D. Further omissions in The tenant of Wildfell Hall. Brontë Soc Trans 17 pt 87 1977.
Easson, A. Anne Brontë and the glow-worms. N & Q n.s. 26, Aug 1979.
Rastall, J. R. Anne Brontë's song book. Clifden, Ireland 1980.
Peterson, N. J. The Marmion scene in The tenant of Wildfell Hall. American N & Q 23, Mar–Apr 1985.

Letters/early comments on The tenant of Wildfell Hall

Charlotte Brontë, letter to W. S. Williams, 14 August 1848. In The Brontës: their lives, friendships, and correspondence, ed Wise and Symington, vol 2.

Biographical studies

V. Brontë portraits. Bookman 1, Nov 1891.
Hale, W. T. Anne Brontë: her life and writings. Bloomington IN 1929.
Edgerley, C. M. Anne Brontë. Brontë Soc Trans 9 pt 48 1938.
Raymond, E. Exiled and harassed Anne. Brontë Soc Trans 11 pt 59 1949.
Brooke, S. Anne Brontë at Blake Hall: an episode of courage and insight. Brontë Soc Trans 13 pt 68 1958.
Gérin, W. Anne Brontë: a biography. London and New York 1959.
Harrison, A. and D. Stanford. Anne Brontë: her life and work. 1959.
Stevenson, W. H. Emily and Anne Brontë. London and New York 1968.
Le Guern, J. Anne Brontë 1820–1849: la vie et l'oeuvre. 2 vols Paris 1977.
Langland, E. Anne Brontë: the other one. Totowa NJ 1989.
Chitham, E. A life of Anne Brontë. Oxford and Cambridge MA 1991.
[CA and HJR]

Charles William Shirley Brooks 1816–74

See col 1996.

Robert Barnabas Brough 1828–60

See col 1997.

Frances Browne 1816–79

The star of Attéghéi; the vision of Schwartz; and other poems. 1844.
Lyrics and miscellaneous poems. Edinburgh 1848.
The Ericksons; [and] The clever boy: or consider another. Edinburgh 1852. At head of title: Two stories for my young friends.
Pictures and songs of home. [1856.]
Granny's wonderful chair and its tales of fairy times. 1857 (for 1856); ed R. L. Green 1963.
Our uncle the traveller's stories. 1859.
My share of the world, an autobiography [a novel]. 3 vols 1861.
The Castleford case. 3 vols 1862.
The orphans of Elfholm. [1862.]
The poor cousin. [1863.]
The young Foresters. [1864.]
The hidden sin: a novel. 3 vols 1866. Anon.
The exile's trust: a tale of the French Revolution, and other stories. [1869.]
The nearest neighbour and other stories. [1875.]
The dangerous guest: a story of 1745. [1886.]
The foundling of the Fens: a story of a flood. [1886.]
The first of the African diamonds. [1887].

Bulwer Lytton, Sir Edward George Earle Lytton, 1st Lord Lytton 1803–73

Bulwer Lytton published under a variety of names. For the first (and most prolific) two decades of his career he styled himself Edward Bulwer or Edward Lytton Bulwer. He was knighted in 1838: hence, generally, Sir Edward [Lytton] Bulwer. In 1843 he formally expanded his surname to Bulwer Lytton (generally without a hyphen): hence [Sir] Edward Bulwer Lytton. In 1866 he was raised to the peerage as Baron Lytton of Knebworth, and thereafter was usually styled simply Lord Lytton on title pages. His son, Edward Robert Bulwer Lytton (see col 765), with whom he is sometimes confused, was a poet (pseud Owen Meredith) and diplomat who became Viceroy of India and was created 1st Earl of Lytton in 1880.

The main repository of mss is the Hertfordshire County Record Office, Hertford. This includes the complete or partial autograph mss of all his novels (excepting Eugene Aram, The pilgrims of the Rhine, What will he do with it?, *and* The coming race*), the historical study* Athens: its rise and fall *(including an unpbd 3rd vol), the epic poem* King Arthur, *and the essay collection* Caxtoniana. *There are, in addition, fragments of two dozen unfinished novels, stories and plays, drafts of three dozen essays, 30 commonplace books filled with miscellaneous notes, several hundred letters, and countless thousands of lines of verse.*

Bibliographies

Wilstack, P. Dramatisations of Bulwer. Bookman (New York) July 1903.
Taft, W. H. III. Lytton as a literary critic. Unpbd diss, Princeton Univ 1942. For complete listing of prefaces, advertisements and dedicatory epistles to Bulwer's novels.

Zipser, R. A. Edward Bulwer-Lytton and Germany. Berne and Frankfurt 1974. For listings of German reviews of Bulwer.

Collections

Works

Philadelphia 1836, 10 vols London 1840, 24 vols New York 1854, 22 vols Philadelphia 1869, 25 vols London 1870–3 (Globe edn), 37 vols London and New York 1873–7 (Knebworth edn), 21 vols Philadelphia 1876–82 (Lord Lytton edn), 9 vols New York [1880s], 10 vols London [1880s], 13 vols [1880s], 6 vols Boston [1880s], 4 vols Charleston SC [1880s] (Dixie edn), 29 vols London 1895–8 (New Knebworth edn), 13 vols New York [1890s], 15 vols London [1890s], 20 vols Boston [1890s] (Univ edn); tr Ger (by F. Notter and G. Pfizer) 22 vols Stuttgart 1834–9, (by G. N. Bärmann and F. Notter) 19 vols Zwickau, Leipzig and Stuttgart 1834–43.

Novels

2 vols New York [1835], 2 vols Boston 1837, 1838, 2 vols Littlefield MA 1841, 2 vols Boston 1847, 2 vols New York 1854, 10 vols London 1856, 47 vols Edinburgh and London 1859–74 (Library edn), 47 vols Philadelphia 1860–74 (Library edn), 10 vols London 1862, 22 vols London and New York 1865–6, 11 vols [1868], 27 vols London 1877–8, 10 vols [1880–3], 25 vols Philadelphia 1883–5, 47 vols 1887 (Library edn), 28 vols London 1887–9 (Pocket Vol edn), 32 vols London, Glasgow and Manchester 1891 (Edn de luxe limited to 500 sets), 32 vols Boston 1891–2, 40 vols 1892–3, 30 vols New York 1892–8 (Athenaeum Soc), 16 vols Boston [1893], 31 vols [1893] (New Household edn), 35 vols 1893–1900 (Library edn), 10 vols New York 1896, 40 vols Boston 1896–8 (limited to 1,250 sets), 30 vols [1897–8], 15 vols [1890s]; tr Ger (by F. Notter and G. Pfizer) 13 vols Stuttgart 1838–43.

Poetry

Poetical works, Paris 1836 (Baudry); Poems, New York 1845; Poetical and dramatic works, 5 vols London 1848, 1852–4; Dramas and poems, Boston 1857, 1858; Poetical works, London and New York 1860; Dramas and poems, Boston 1863, 1864; Poems, London 1865.

Plays

Dramatic works, London 1841; Poetical and dramatic works, 5 vols London 1848, 1852–4; Dramas and poems, Boston 1857, 1858; Dramatic works, London and New York 1860, Leipzig 1860 (Tauchnitz), London and New York 1863; Dramas and poems, Boston 1863, 1864; Dramatic works, London and New York 1865, 1873.

Non-fictional prose

Critical and miscellaneous writings, 2 vols Philadelphia 1841; Miscellaneous prose works, 3 vols London 1868, 2 vols New York 1868, 4 vols Leipzig 1868 (Tauchnitz); Pamphlets and sketches, London and New York 1875; Quarterly essays, London and New York 1875.

Speeches

Speeches of Edward Lord Lytton now first collected with some of his political writings hitherto unpublished and a prefatory memoir by his son. 2 vols Edinburgh and London 1874.

Anthologies

The Bulwer Lytton birthday book. 1879.

The wit and wisdom of Edward Bulwer Lord Lytton (selected by C. Kent). London and New York 1883.

The wit and wisdom of E. Bulwer-Lytton (compiled by C. L. Bonney). New York 1885.

Beautiful thoughts (arranged by P. W. Wilson). New York 1900.

A Lytton treasury (selected by A. Broadbent). Manchester 1908.

§1

Novels

With the exception of a few significant twentieth-century reissues, the following lists are restricted to edns pbd during Bulwer's lifetime. For thirty or so years after his death his popularity and reputation remained immense, particularly in the USA, where there were numerous (generally undated) cheap reprints of his best-known novels by publishers such as Aldine, Belford Clarke, Cromwell, Estes and Lauriat, Lippincott, Little Brown, Lovell, Lupton, Merril and Baker, Mershon, Ogilvie, and Rand McNally, some of them appearing in such series as Famous Books by Famous Authors, World's Famous Books, World's Greatest Literature, the Handy Library, the Parchment Library, the Fireside College Library, the Escutcheon Library, the Illustrated Holiday Edition, and the American News Co. People's Edition.

Falkland. 1827 (anon), New York 1830, Philadelphia 1830, Paris 1833 (Baudry), London 1834, New York 1835, Philadelphia 1836, Leipzig 1842 (Tauchnitz), Exeter CT 1843, Philadelphia 1852, London 1967 (First Novel Lib); tr Fr Paris 1833, Danish (by J. R. Reiersen) Copenhagen 1856.
REVIEW: Montgomery, R. The age reviewed 1827.

Pelham: or the adventures of a gentleman. 3 vols London 1828 (2 edns) (anon), 2 vols New York 1828 (2 edns), 3 vols London 1829, 2 vols New York 1829, New York 1829, 1831, Paris 1832 (Baudry), 3 vols London 1833, 2 vols New York 1834, 2 vols London 1835 (includes Mortimer: or memoirs of a gentleman, the pilot story for Pelham), 2 vols New York 1835, Paris 1835 (Baudry), 2 vols New York 1836, Philadelphia 1836, 2 vols Boston 1837, Paris 1837 (Galignani), 2 vols London 1839, 2 vols Exeter CT 1839, London 1840, Littlefield MA 1841, New York 1842, Paris 1842 (Baudry), Leipzig 1842 (Tauchnitz), New York 1845, Boston 1847, London 1848, New York 1848, London 1853, New York 1853, London 1854, Boston 1854, London 1855, New York 1856, London 1857, 1858, 1860, New York 1860, 2 vols Edinburgh and London 1862, 2 vols New York 1862, 2 vols Philadelphia 1864, 1865, London 1866, New York 1867, Philadelphia 1867, Lincoln NE 1972; tr Ger (by G. N. Bärmann) 4 vols Zwickau 1833, (by F. Kottenkamp) 2 vols Stuttgart 1845, (by G. Pfizer) 5 vols Stuttgart 1858, Swed Stockholm 1843, Danish (by P. Saxild) 2 vols Copenhagen 1856; parodied as Pelham, second series, in Age 11 and 18 Oct 1829.
REVIEWS: Literary Gazette 7 June and 8 Nov 1828; Examiner 14 and 21 Sep 1828; Westminster Rev Jan 1829; North Amer Rev Apr 1829; Southern Rev May 1829; Fraser's Mag June 1830, Aug 1834 (by T. Carlyle, in Sartor Resartus); Br and Foreign Rev Dec 1836.

The disowned. 4 vols 1829, 3 vols 1829 (2 edns), 2 vols New York 1829, 3 vols 1833, Paris 1833 (Baudry), 2 vols London 1835 (includes prefatory essay On the different kinds of prose fiction), 2 vols New York 1835, London 1835, 1836, Philadelphia 1836, Exeter CT 1839, London, Edinburgh and Dublin 1840, Leipzig 1842 (Tauchnitz), New York 1845, London 1852, 1855, 1859, Edinburgh and London 1862, Philadelphia 1862, London and New York 1864 (2 edns), Philadelphia 1865; tr Ger (by C. Richard) 4 vols Aachen 1829, (by E. Susemihl) 2 vols Stuttgart 1845, (by F. Notter) 8 vols Stuttgart 1845, Danish (by J. R. Reiersen 2 vols Copenhagen 1857, Fr (by P. Lorain and M. Corréard) 2 vols Paris 1858.
REVIEWS: Literary Gazette 29 Nov 1828; Examiner 28 Dec 1828; Monthly Mag Jan 1829; Westminster Rev Jan 1829; Southern Rev May 1829; Fraser's Mag June 1830; NMM May 1831, Sep 1835.

Devereux. 3 vols 1829 (2 edns), 2 vols New York 1829, 2 vols London 1831, 2 vols New York 1831, Paris 1832 (Baudry), 3 vols London 1833, 2 vols New York 1835, London 1836, Paris 1836 (Baudry), 2 vols Boston 1837, London 1839, London and Dublin 1841, New York 1842, Leipzig 1842 (Tauchnitz), Exeter CT 1843, London 1852, London and New York 1852, London 1854, 1855, 2 vols Edinburgh and London 1860, 2 vols Philadelphia 1860, London 1861, 1862, London and New York 1864, 1865, 2 vols Philadelphia 1865; tr Danish (by F. Schaldemose) 3 vols Copenhagen 1856, Fr (by P. Lorain and W. L. Hughes) Paris 1859, 2 vols 1887.
REVIEWS: Literary Gazette 27 June and 4 July 1829; Athenaeum 15 and 22 July 1829; Spectator 25 July 1829; Examiner 9 Aug 1829; Westminster Rev Oct 1829; Fraser's Mag June 1830; NMM May 1831.

Paul Clifford. 3 vols 1830 (2 edns), 2 vols New York 1830 (2 edns), 2 vols New York 1832 (includes 'key' by Amer publishers), London 1833, Paris 1833 (Baudry), 2 vols London 1835, London, Edinburgh and Dublin 1835, 2 vols New York 1836, 2 vols Boston 1837, Paris 1837 (Galignani), London, Edinburgh and Dublin 1838, 1840, New York 1842, Exeter CT 1842, Leipzig 1842 (Tauchnitz), London 1848, 1850, 1854, 1860, 1861, 2 vols Edinburgh and London 1862, London and New York 1865, 1866; tr Fr (by J. Cohen) 4 vols Paris 1831, (by P. Lorain and V. Boileau) 2 vols Paris 1858, Swed Stockholm 1835, Ger (by E. Susemihl) 2 vols Stuttgart 1845, (by G. Pfizer) 7 vols Stuttgart 1845, Danish (by E. Levison) 2 vols Copenhagen 1856, shorthand (Pitman's Shorthand Lib) London nd.

REVIEWS: Literary Gazette 1 May 1830; Athenaeum 15 May 1830; Spectator 15 May and 25 Sep 1830; Age 23 May 1830; Fraser's Mag June 1830, Feb 1831; NMM May 1831.

Eugene Aram. 3 vols 1832, 2 vols New York 1832, Paris 1832 (Baudry), London 1833, London, Edinburgh, Dublin and Paris 1834, London 1836 (2 edns), 2 vols New York 1836, 1838, London, Edinburgh and Dublin 1840, New York 1840, Leipzig 1841, 1842 (Tauchnitz), Exeter CT 1843, London, Edinburgh and Dublin 1846, New York 1848, London 1849, London and New York 1851, London 1853, 1854, New York 1859, 2 vols Edinburgh and London 1861, 2 vols Philadelphia 1862, London and New York 1865, 1866, New York 1869, London 1903 (Cassell's Standard Lib), London [1949] (Mellifont Classics); tr Fr (by J. Cohen) 2 vols Paris 1832, (by A. J. B. Defauconpret) Paris 1842, (by M. Frater) 2 vols Paris 1873, Danish (by F. Schaldemose) 3 vols Copenhagen 1857, Ger, Stuttgart 1863, (by C. Richard) Leipzig nd, (by F. Notter) Halle nd; abridged (by W. G. Wills) as The strange case of Eugene Aram, Glasgow 1930 (Detective Story Club); dramatisations by W. T. Moncrieff as Eugene Aram: or Saint Robert's cave [1835], by E. W. H. Williams New Orleans 1874; parodied as Elizabeth Brownrigge (by W. Maginn) Fraser's Mag Aug and Sep 1832, as George de Barnwell by Sir E. L. B. L. B. B. L. L. B. B. B. L. L. L. Bart. (by W. M. Thackeray) Punch 3, 10 and 17 Apr 1847.

REVIEWS: Athenaeum 7 Jan 1832; Literary Gazette 7 Jan 1832; Fraser's Mag Feb 1832; Monthly Mag Feb 1832; Cab 3 Mar 1832; Literary Censor 17 Mar 1832; Edinburgh Rev Apr 1832; Thief 21 Apr 1832.

Godolphin. 3 vols 1833 (2 edns) (anon), 2 vols Philadelphia 1833, London, Edinburgh and Dublin 1840, 2 vols New York 1840, Paris 1840 (Baudry), Paris 1840 (Galignani), Leipzig 1841, New York 1842, Leipzig 1842 (Tauchnitz), London, Edinburgh and Dublin 1844, New York 1845, London 1850, Cincinnati 1851, London 1854, 1860, 1862, Edinburgh and London 1862, London and New York 1865, 1866, Philadelphia 1866, London 1867, New York 1873; tr Danish (by L. Moltke) 2 vols Copenhagen 1858, Ger (by G. N. Bärmann) Stuttgart 1863.

REVIEWS: Athenaeum 4 May and 10 Aug 1833; Spectator 4 May 1833; Literary Gazette 11 May 1833; Examiner 19 May 1833; NMM June 1833 (by Bulwer himself).

The last days of Pompeii. 3 vols 1834, 2 vols New York 1834, Paris 1834 (Baudry), 3 vols London 1835, 2 vols New York 1835, Leipzig 1835, 2 vols New York 1836, 2 vols Boston 1837, London 1839, Paris 1839 (Baudry), London, Edinburgh and Dublin 1840, New York 1842, Leipzig 1842 (Tauchnitz), Ithaca NY 1846, London 1849, 1850, Hartford CT 1851, London 1854, 1856, 2 vols Edinburgh and London 1860, 2 vols Philadelphia 1860, London 1861, 1865, 2 vols Philadelphia 1865, London 1866, 2 vols Philadelphia 1867, Philadelphia 1869, 2 vols Philadelphia 1870, Philadelphia 1871, London 1873, 1906 (EL), 1919 (Nelson's Classics), 1925 (Harrap's Standard Fiction Lib), New York 1926 (Macmillan Pocket Classics), Reading PA [1936?] (World's Greatest Lit ser), London 1957 (EL), 1968 (Heron Books); tr Ital (by F. Cusani) 3 vols Milan 1835–6, (by G. Barbieri) 5 vols Naples 1854, Naples 1902, Florence 1928, Ger (by J. Sporschil) 3 vols Leipzig 1835, (by F. Notter) 4 vols Stuttgart 1841, 6 vols 1845, Tubingen 1866, (by O. von Schaching) Regensburg nd, (by H. V. Schumacher) Berlin nd, (by B. Dedek) Berlin nd, (by O. von Czarnowski) Leipzig nd, (by K. Walther) Stuttgart nd, (by O. Hendel) Halle 188[?], St Louis [1900?], (by G. Bauer) Stuttgart [1921], (by G. Lehmann) Berlin 192[?], Fr 2 vols Brussels 1837, Tours 1842 (14 edns by 1864), Paris 1859, 1893, 1911, 1912, 1948, Du Ghent 1846, Danish (by J. R. Reiersen) 2 vols Copenhagen 1856, 1863, Sp Madrid 1897, (by C. Jimenez) Buenos Aires [1939?], Swed Stockholm 1909, Serbo-Croat (by R. Raikhard) Belgrade 1927, (by P. Moritz) Zagreb nd, Latvian (by O. Krolls) Riga [1935], Hungarian (by G. Mozes) Budapest nd, Cz (by P. Moudré) 5 vols Prague nd; abridged New York 1876, 1899, London 1906, 1913, 1914, 1916, 1920, as Fire and darkness (Books Within Books ser) 1927 (2 edns), 1929, by J. Field (Told to the Children ser) 1944, 1948, by E. Tydeman (Stories Told and Retold ser) 1961, by E. F. Dodd (Stories to Remember in Simple English ser) Madras 1961, by M. West (New Method Supplementary Readers stage 3) London 1966; dramatised by L. H. Medina 1858, by L. Griffa [1876], by J. Buckstone 1887, by E. Abbott (for use in schools) 1929, by C. Nuitter (in Fr) Paris 1869; parodied as The very last days of Pompeii (by R. Reece) [1878?]; adaptations as opera as Ione (by G. Peruzzini, music by E. Petrella) Milan [1858?], Naples [1860?], Rome 1863, New York 1863, Boston 1864, New York 1892 (all in Ital), Mexico City 1865 (in Sp), Malta [1865?] (in Eng), Lisbon 1869 (in Portuguese), as Nydia the blind girl of Pompeii (by G. Fox) 1892, as Pompeii, a dramatic vocal and symphonic poem for soloists, chorus, orchestra and organ (by B. Hollander, libretto by G. H. R. Dabbs) 1907.

REVIEWS: Athenaeum 27 Sep 1834; Literary Gazette 27 Sep 1834; Mirror 25 Oct 1834; Examiner 26 Oct 1834; NMM Nov 1834; New York Knickerbocker Nov 1834; New York Evening Post 20 Nov 1834; New York Morning Courier and Inquirer 21 Nov 1834; New York Albion 22 Nov 1834; GM Feb 1835; Dublin Univ Mag Mar 1835; North Amer Rev Apr 1835; Br and Foreign Rev Dec 1836.

The pilgrims of the Rhine. 1834, New York 1834, Paris 1834 (Baudry), New York 1836, Philadelphia 1836, Paris 1836, Frankfurt 1838, Exeter CT 1839, London 1840, London, Edinburgh and Dublin 1840, Leipzig 1842 (Tauchnitz), New York 1843 (2 edns), 1847, London 1850, 1854, 1860, Edinburgh and London 1861, Philadelphia 1861, London 1865, Philadelphia 1865, London 1866, New York 1867, Charleston SC 1872, London [1909] (EL); extracts: the story The maid of Malines rptd in The Lover's Lib New York 1871, and in Little Classics, Boston 1875; tr Fr (by J. Cohen) 2 vols Paris 1834, (by M. Defauconpret) 2 vols Brussels 1834, (by A. Dalamotte) of the stories The maid of Malines, The brothers and The tour of the virtues: a philosopher's tale (together with Arasmanes: or the seeker) St Petersburg 1866, Ger Quedlinburg 1834, Leipzig nd, Sp (by J. Muñoz y Castro) of The maid of Malines and The brothers, Havana 1838, Swed of The wooing of master fox, Stockholm 1851, Danish (by J. R. Reiersen) Copenhagen 1856, Rus of The brothers [1880], The wooing of master fox transcribed into 'phonotypic characters' by B. Pitman (as Renard the foks), Sinsinati [*sic*] [1863], 'engraved in phonic shorthand' by E. Boardman Burns (as Renard the fox), New York 1872, 188[?], 1897, 1901; The maid of Malines dramatised by W. B. Bernard as Lucille: or the story of a heart, 1836, [1857], [1883?].

REVIEWS: Literary Gazette 8 Feb 1834; Athenaeum 22 Feb 1834; Mirror 8 Mar 1834; Examiner 30 Mar 1834; Southern Literary Messenger 1834.

Rienzi: the last of the tribunes. 3 vols 1835, 2 vols New York 1836, Philadelphia 1836, Paris 1836 (Baudry), 1836 (Galignani), 3 vols London 1837, 2 vols Boston 1838, 2 vols Exeter CT 1839, London 1840 (title changed to Rienzi: the last of the Roman tribunes), New York 1842, Leipzig 1842 (Tauchnitz), London, Edinburgh and Dublin 1843, New York 1847, Paris 1847 (Baudry), London

1848 (with new appendix), 1851, 1854, 1858, New York 1860, 2 vols Philadelphia 1860, 2 vols Edinburgh and London 1861, London 1864, 2 vols Philadelphia 1865, London and New York 1866, London 1867, Philadelphia 1867, 2 vols Philadelphia 1869, New York 1871, London [1911] (EL), 1926 (Harrap's Standard Fiction Lib); tr Ital (by S. M. Maggioni) 2 vols Milan 1836, Florence 1892, Ger (by G. Pfizer) Stuttgart 1836, 1859, (by O. von Czarnowski) Leipzig 1836, (by G. N. Bärmann) Zwickau 1836, (by T. Roth) 1845, Sp, Bogotá 1849, (by J. P. Mauras) Barcelona [1917]; Greek 2 vols Athens 1850–2, Danish (by J. R. Reiersen) 2 vols Copenhagen 1855, Fr (by P. Lorain) 2 vols Paris 1859; adapted as opera by Richard Wagner, Dresden 1842.

REVIEWS: Athenaeum 12 Dec 1835; Examiner 13 Dec 1835; Literary Gazette 13 Dec 1835; Conservative 19 Dec 1835; Spectator 26 Dec 1835; Mirror 2 and 9 Jan 1836; London and Westminster Rev Apr 1836; Dublin Rev May 1836; GM June 1836; Parterre 4 June 1836; Br and Foreign Rev Dec 1836; Eclectic Rev June 1837; Dublin Rev Dec 1858.

Ernest Maltravers. 3 vols 1837, 2 vols New York 1837, London 1837, Paris 1837 (Baudry), 1837 (Galignani), 2 vols New York 1838, Leipzig 1838, London, Edinburgh and Dublin 1840, New York 1842, Leipzig 1842 (Tauchnitz), London 1851, 1854, 1857, 1861, London and New York 1862, 1865, 2 vols London 1867, London and New York 1873; tr Ger (by F. Kottenkamp) 2 vols Stuttgart 1845, Stuttgart 1859, Sp Havana 1845, Madrid 1857, Danish (by F. Schaldemose) 2 vols Copenhagen 1855, Fr (by Mlle Collinet and P. Lorain) Paris 1859, 1866, 1869, 1882, (by M. Frater) Paris 1873; dramatised by L. H. Medina [1860].

REVIEWS: Revue des Deux Mondes 1837; Literary Gazette 23 Sep and 11 Nov 1837; Mirror 14 Oct 1837; Monthly Mag Dec 1837; Fraser's Mag Jan 1838; Athenaeum 24 Mar 1838; Eclectic Rev July 1838.

Alice: or the mysteries. 3 vols 1838 (2 edns), 2 vols New York 1838, Paris 1838 (Baudry), 1838 (Galignani), Leipzig 1838, London, Edinburgh and Dublin 1840, Leipzig 1842 (Tauchnitz), London 1854, London and New York 1865, 1873; as Ernest Maltravers: or the Eleusinia, part the second, London 1851, London and New York 1862, 1866, 4 vols Philadelphia 1866, Philadelphia 1868; tr Danish (by A. Rung) 2 vols Copenhagen 1855, Fr Paris 1874.

REVIEWS: Literary Gazette 17 Mar 1838; Athenaeum 24 Mar 1838; Monthly Rev May 1838; Eclectic Rev July 1838.

Leila: or the siege of Granada. 1838, New York 1838, Philadelphia 1838, Cincinnati 1838, Berlin 1838, New York 1846 (as The enchanter: or the fall of Granada), London 1850, New York 1864, London 1867, New York 1873, Philadelphia 1873; tr Ger (by J. Zedner) Berlin 1837, Stuttgart 1863, Swed (by A. F. Dalin) Stockholm 1838, Danish (by F. Schaldemose) Copenhagen 1857; dramatised in Ital as L'Ebreo, Milan 1855; adapted as opera in Cz by E. Krasnohorska [pseud of Alzbeta Pechova], Prague 1868. As Leila: or the siege of Granada, with Calderon the courtier, London and Paris 1838, Paris 1838 (Baudry), 1838 (Galignani), Berlin 1838, Leipzig 1839, London 1850, 1851, 1853, 1855, 1856, Philadelphia 1860, Edinburgh and London 1861, London and New York 1865, Philadelphia 1865, London and New York 1866, 2 vols Philadelphia 1868.

REVIEWS: Mirror suppl no Apr 1838; Athenaeum 19 May 1838; Examiner 19 May 1838; Literary Gazette 19 May 1838; Spectator 19 May 1838; NMM June 1838.

Night and morning. 3 vols 1841 (2 edns), 2 vols New York 1841, Paris 1841 (Baudry), Leipzig 1843 (Tauchnitz), London, Edinburgh and Dublin 1845, 2 vols New York 1845, NewYork 1850, London 1851, 1854, New York 1854, London and New York 1859, 1862, 2 vols Edinburgh and London 1862, 2 vols Philadelphia 1862, 1865, London and New York 1865, 1873; tr Ger 2 vols Leipzig 1841, (by E. Susemihl) 2 vols Stuttgart 1845, (by G. Pfizer) 5 vols Stuttgart 1863, (by A. Tuhten) Leipzig nd, Hungarian (by P. Vajda) Budapest 1843, (by B. Mihály) 2 vols nd, Fr (by A. Tardieu) 2 vols Paris 1876, 1879, Sp (by A. de los Rios) Barcelona 1926; dramatised by J. Brougham, London nd.

REVIEWS: Literary Gazette 9 Jan 1841; Athenaeum 16 Jan 1841; Examiner 17 Jan 1841; Monthly Rev Feb 1841; Mirror 20 Feb and 10 Apr 1841; Monthly Mag May 1841.

Zanoni. 3 vols 1842, 2 vols New York 1842, New York (in extra edns of the mags New World 4 Apr and (as Zanoni: or the secret order) of Brother Jonathan 8 Apr) 1842, Paris 1842 (Baudry), 1842 (Galignani), Leipzig 1842 (Tauchnitz), 3 vols Amsterdam 1842, London, Edinburgh and Dublin 1845, New York 1850, London 1853, 1856, 1858, 2 vols Edinburgh and London 1861, 2 vols Philadelphia 1862, London and New York 1864, 1865, 2 vols Philadelphia 1865, Philadelphia 1867, New York 1871, 2 vols Philadelphia 1871; tr Ger (by G. Pfizer) 6 vols Stuttgart 1845, 1863, 3 vols Berlin 1858, Leipzig 1925, Danish (by L. Moltke) 2 vols Copenhagen 1857, Fr (by M. Sheldon and P. Lorain) Paris 1858, 2 vols Paris 1882, Paris 1924, Finnish, Helsinki 1908, 1909, Cz (by K. Weinfurter) 2 vols Prague 1919; dramatised by E. Perelli (in Ital) as Viola Pisani, 1873; parodied as Me (by B. Harte) in Californian 15 July 1865, later rptd as The dweller of the threshold.

REVIEWS: Athenaeum 26 Feb 1842; Examiner 26 Feb 1842; Literary Gazette 26 Feb 1842; Monthly Rev Apr 1842; City of London Mag Oct 1842; Theosophical Rev Sep 1902–Feb 1903.

The last of the barons. 3 vols 1843, New York 1843 (3 edns including extra nos of the mags Brother Jonathan and New World, both Feb 1843), 2 vols Leipzig 1843 (Tauchnitz), Paris 1843 (Baudry), London 1850, 1854, 2 vols Edinburgh and London 1861, 2 vols Philadelphia 1861, 1863, London and New York 1865, Philadelphia 1865, London and New York 1866, Philadelphia 1869; numerous posthumous Br reprints including London 1880 (Derry and Toms), 1888 (Cassell's Red Lib), Liverpool and Llandudno [1895?] (Home Instructor Lib), London 1906 (EL), 1908 (People's Lib), Oxford 1913 (Clarendon Press, ed F. C. Romilly), London 1944 (Lit of Yesterday and Today); tr Danish (by F. Schaldemose) 4 vols Copenhagen 1858, Fr (by P. Lorain and Mme Bressant) 2 vols Paris 1859; abridged (C. E. Smith) London and Edinburgh [1910] (Bulwer Lytton for Boys and Girls), London 1920, as Warwick the king-maker, (by F. J. Tickner), Edinburgh [1931] (Books within Books ser).

REVIEWS: Athenaeum 4 Mar 1843; Examiner 11 Mar 1843; Tait's Edinburgh Mag Apr 1843; Blackwood's Mag Sep 1845.

Lucretia: or the children of night. 3 vols 1846, New York 1846, 2 vols Leipzig 1846 (Tauchnitz), 3 vols London 1847 (includes prefatory essay A word to the public), New York 1847, Paris 1847 (Baudry), 1847 (Galignani), London 1853, 1855, 2 vols Philadelphia 1858, 2 vols Edinburgh and London 1863, London and New York 1865, 2 vols Philadelphia 1866, London 1867, Philadelphia 1868; tr Ger 3 vols Berlin 1846, Stuttgart 1863, Danish (by F. Schaldemose) 3 vols Copenhagen 1856.

REVIEWS: Literary Gazette 28 Nov, 5 and 12 Dec 1846; Athenaeum 5 Dec 1846; Examiner 5 and 12 Dec 1846; Spectator 12 Dec 1846; Dublin Univ Mag Mar 1847; Eclectic Rev Apr 1847; Edinburgh Rev Apr 1847; Westminster and Foreign Quart Rev Apr 1847.

Harold: the last of the Saxon kings. 3 vols 1848 (2 edns), New York 1848, Paris 1848 (Baudry), 2 vols Leipzig 1848 (Tauchnitz), 3 vols London 1849 (with new preface), 1851, London 1853, 1855, 2 vols Edinburgh and London 1861, 2 vols Philadelphia 1861, London and New York 1864, 2 vols Philadelphia 1865, London and New York 1866, ed G. E. Gomme 1897, London [1906] (EL), 1908 (Oxford Boys' Classics), London and New York 1908 (WC), London 1970 (EL); tr Ger (by E. Mauch) 8 vols Stuttgart 1848; Rus [1902] (abridged); dramatised by A. G. Butler, London 1892, 1906; abridged New York and New Orleans 1896 (for use in schools), as Harold at Hastings (by A. E. M. Bayliss) London and Edinburgh [1930] (Books within Books ser).

REVIEWS: Athenaeum 17 June 1848; Examiner 17 June 1848; Literary Gazette 17 June 1848; Spectator 17 June 1848, Illus London News 17 June and 1 July 1848; Hood's Mag July 1848; Mirror Monthly Mag July 1848; Sharpe's London Mag July 1848; Dublin Univ Mag Sep 1848; Fraser's Mag Oct 1848; Westminster and Foreign Quart Rev Oct 1848–Jan 1849.

The Caxtons: a family picture. Blackwood's Mag Apr 1848–Oct 1849, 3 vols Edinburgh and London 1849, 2 vols 1849, New York 1849, 2 vols Leipzig 1849 (Tauchnitz), Edinburgh and London 1853, 1854, London and New York 1854, 1855, London 1855, 1856, 2 vols Edinburgh and London 1859, 2 vols Philadelphia 1860, London 1862, New York 1863, 2 vols London and New York 1866 (2 edns), 2 vols Philadelphia 1867; tr Danish (by G. C. Jacobsen) 3 vols Copenhagen 1855, Fr (by E. Scheffter) Paris 1857.
REVIEWS: Spectator 13 Oct 1849; Athenaeum 27 Oct 1849; NMM Nov 1849; Westminster Rev Jan 1850; Fraser's Mag Jan 1850 (by C. Kingsley) and Mar 1856; Bentley's Quart Mar 1859.

'My novel' by Pisistratus Caxton: or varieties in English life. Blackwood's Mag Sep 1850–Jan 1853, 4 vols Leipzig 1851–2 (Tauchnitz), New York 1852, Paris 1852 (Galignani), 4 vols Edinburgh and London 1853, 2 vols 1853, 2 vols London and New York 1854, New York 1854, 2 vols London and New York 1855, 1856, 1857, 4 vols Edinburgh and London 1860, 4 vols Philadelphia 1860–5, 2 vols London and New York 1866 (2 edns), 4 vols Philadelphia 1867, 2 vols 1869; tr Danish (by M. Strom and G. C. Jacobsen) 8 vols Copenhagen 1855, Fr (by H. de l'Espine) 2 vols Paris [1861], 1877, Ger (by C. Kolb) 13 vols Stuttgart 1863; extracts in Momentous reflections by a lady to which is added by permission a pastoral sermon by Sir E. B. Lytton, London 1853.
REVIEWS: Literary Gazette 12 and 26 Feb 1853; John Bull 19 Feb 1853; Spectator 19 Feb 1853; Examiner 26 Feb 1853; Dublin Rev Mar 1853; Blackwood's Mag Feb 1855; Bentley's Quart Mar 1859.

What will he do with it? by Pisistratus Caxton. Blackwood's Mag June 1857–Jan 1859, 4 vols Leipzig 1857–8 (Tauchnitz), 4 vols Edinburgh and London 1859 (2 edns), New York 1859, 4 vols Edinburgh and London 1860, New York 1860, 3 vols Philadelphia 1860, New York 1863, 2 vols London and New York 1864, 1865, 3 vols Philadelphia 1867, London 1868, 2 vols Philadelphia 1868; tr Danish (by C. M. Gorm) 4 vols Copenhagen 1858–9, Fr (by A. Pichot and A. Courtois) 2 vols Paris 1860, 1882.
REVIEWS: Athenaeum 22 Jan 1859; Bentley's Quart Mar 1859; Nat Rev Apr 1859; North Amer Rev Apr 1859.

A strange story. All the Year Round 10 Aug 1861–8 Mar 1862, 2 vols Leipzig 1861–2 (Tauchnitz), 2 vols London 1862 (3 edns), New York 1862, Boston 1862, London 1863, Mobile AL 1863, London 1864, London and New York 1865 (2 edns), 2 vols Philadelphia 1865, 2 vols Edinburgh and London 1866, Philadelphia 1868, New York 1871, 1873, Berkeley CA 1973; tr Fr 6 vols Paris 1863, Ger Leipzig 1908; addendum Supplementary Chapter (typeset, and proof-corrected by Bulwer, but not included in the published text of the novel) in Victorian Literature and Culture 26 1997.
REVIEWS: Athenaeum 15 Feb 1862; Literary Gazette 8 Mar 1862; Examiner 22 Mar 1862; Eclectic Rev Apr 1862; Westminster Rev Apr 1862; Guardian 23 Apr 1862; Blackwood's Mag May 1862.

The coming race. Edinburgh and London 1871 (anon) (8 edns by 1873), New York 1871 (as The coming race: or the new Utopia), Toronto 1871, New York 1873 (2 edns), Leipzig 1873 (Tauchnitz), London 1928 (WC) (with The haunted and the haunters); tr Ger (by J. Piokowska) Leipzig 1874, Ital (by C. Casoretti) Milan 1874, Hungarian (by J. B. Fay) Budapest 1880, Fr (by R. Frary) Paris 1888, Sp Madrid [1893?].
REVIEWS: Athenaeum 27 May 1871; Saturday Rev 27 May 1871; Spectator 3 June 1871; Blackwood's Mag July 1871; Month July 1871; Fraser's Mag June 1874.

The Parisians. Blackwood's Mag Oct 1872–Jan 1874, 4 vols Edinburgh and London 1873, 4 vols Leipzig 1873 (Tauchnitz), 4 vols Edinburgh and London 1874, 2 vols New York 1874, New York 1874, Philadelphia 1874, Toronto 1874.
REVIEWS: Athenaeum 27 Dec 1873; Saturday Rev 27 Dec 1873; Fraser's Mag June 1874.

Kenelm Chillingly: his adventures and opinions. 3 vols Edinburgh and London 1873 (2 edns), 2 vols 1873, New York 1873 (2 edns), 4 vols Leipzig 1873 (Tauchnitz), 2 vols Philadelphia 1873 (2 edns), Toronto 1873; tr Du (by D. Beets) 2 vols Haarlem 1873; Finnish Helsinki 1883.
REVIEWS: Athenaeum 29 Mar 1873; Saturday Rev 5 Apr 1873; Spectator 12 Apr 1873; Academy 1 May 1873; Fraser's Mag June 1874.

Pausanias the Spartan (unfinished, ed Edward Robert Bulwer Lytton). 1876 (2 edns), New York 1876, Philadelphia 1876, Toronto 1876, Leipzig 1876 (Tauchnitz).
REVIEWS: Athenaeum 5 Feb 1876; Spectator 4 Mar 1876; Saturday Rev 25 Mar 1876.

Poetry

Ismael: an oriental tale, with other poems written between the age of thirteen and fifteen. 1820, 1821.

Delmour: or the tale of a sylphid, and other poems. 1823 (anon).

Sculpture: a poem which obtained the chancellor's medal at the Cambridge commencement July 1825. Cambridge 1825, 1828, New York 1831.

Weeds and wild flowers. Paris 1826 (priv ptd), Edinburgh 1826 (as Weeds and wild flowers: or stray rhymes from a journal in verse).

O'Neill: or the rebel. 1827 (anon), Paris 1829, New York 1835 (as The rebel and other tales in prose and verse); tr Fr (in prose, by H. Preble) Paris 1829.

The Siamese twins: a satirical tale of the times, with other poems. 1831 (2 edns), New York 1831.
REVIEWS: John Bull 23 Jan 1831; Athenaeum 29 Jan and 5 Feb 1831; Edinburgh Rev Mar 1831; Fraser's Mag Mar 1831; Monthly Rev Mar 1831; Amer Quart Rev June 1831.

Eva: a true story of light and darkness, The ill-omened marriage, and other tales and poems. 1842 (2 edns), Paris 1842 (Baudry), 1842 (Galignani), Leipzig 1842 (Tauchnitz).

The crisis: a satire of the day. 1845.

The new Timon: a romance of London. 4 pts 1846 (anon), London 1846 (4 edns), Philadelphia 1846, 1847, 1849, Leipzig 1849 (Tauchnitz), 1860; parodied in The new Timon and the poets (by A. Tennyson) Punch 28 Feb 1846.
REVIEWS: Athenaeum 3 Jan and 14 Mar 1846; Literary Gazette 10 Jan, 7 and 28 Feb 1846; Hood's Mag Feb and Mar 1846; Spectator 14 Mar 1846; Examiner 4 Apr 1846; North Amer Rev Apr 1847 (by J. R. Lowell); North Br Rev Aug 1847, Irish Quart Rev Sep 1852.

King Arthur. 3 pts 1848–9, 2 vols 1849, Leipzig 2 vols 1849 (Tauchnitz), 2 vols London 1851, 2 vols Philadelphia 1851, London 1870, New York 1871.
REVIEWS: Athenaeum 27 Jan 1849; Examiner 27 Jan 1849; Literary Gazette 3 Feb and 4 Aug 1849; Edinburgh Rev July 1849; Eclectic Rev Oct 1849; Illus Rev 15 Feb 1871; Fortnightly Rev Apr 1871.

St Stephens. Blackwood's Mag Jan–Mar 1860, Edinburgh and London 1860 (2 edns) (anon).

The boatman by Pisistratus Caxton. Edinburgh and London 1864.

The lost tales of Miletus. [1865] (priv ptd, limited to 12 copies), 1866, New York 1866, Leipzig 1866 (Tauchnitz), London 1867, New York 1872; tr Rus (by D. P. Oznobishin) 1871 (the poem 'Death and Sisyphus').

Plays

The Duchess de la Vallière. 1836 (3 edns), New York 1836, 1837, Paris 1837 (Baudry), 1837 (Galignani), 1838 (Baudry); tr Swed Stockholm 1837, Danish (by F. Schaldemose) Copenhagen 1839, Ger (by G. N. Bärmann) Stuttgart 1840.

The lady of Lyons: or love and pride. 1838 (11 edns by 1839), New York 1838, Berlin 1838, London 1841, 1843, New York 1844, Philadelphia and New York 1845, Clyde OH [1845], London 1846, New York and Baltimore 1846, New York 1848, London 1849, Leipzig 1849 (Tauchnitz), London 1851, 1852, 1855, 1858, 1859, 1860, New York [1860], London 1863, New York [1864], [1868, 'as produced by Edwin Booth'], London [1870?], New York [1870?, 'as produced, with many important excisions and alterations sanctioned by the author, under the management of Mr Fechter'], [1873?], (numerous, generally undated 'acting edns', Br and US, from 1850s onwards, plus several dozen later nineteenth-century reprints); tr Swed (by C. G. Jungberg) Stockholm 1839, Sp (by F. Megia) Havana 1841, Ital (by G. Guerini) Florence 1852, 'with a complete idiomatical and grammatical vocabulary for translation from English into French' New York [1872?], Eng text with notes in Ger for students Leipzig 1866, Berlin 1891; adapted as The latest edition of The lady of Lyons: or two-penny pride and penny-tence, a burlesque extravaganza (by H. J. Byron) [1858], [1859], as The lady of Lyons married and settled (by H. Merivale) 1878, as A metrical version of Lord Lytton's Lady of Lyons (by L. J. Chamberlen) 1914.

Richelieu: or the conspiracy. 1839 (9 edns), New York 1839, Philadelphia [1839?], Boston [1839?], Baltimore [1839?], Paris 1839 (Baudry), New York 1844, New York, Baltimore and Washington 1846, New York 1847, 1848, London 1850, 1856, New York 1860, London 1860, New York 1866 ('as performed by Edwin Booth', the first of c. 20 such edns), (numerous, generally undated 'acting edns', Br and US, from 1850s onwards); tr Du (by H. de Vries) Amsterdam 185[?], Ger [of Edwin Booth's version] New York 1882, Fr (by C. Samson) Paris 1897, Sp Madrid 1920; adapted as Cardinal Richelieu (prose adaptation by H. L. Williams) New York [1883], [1884], (by A. Goodrich) New York and London 1930 (this 'new version of Sir Edward Bulwer-Lytton's play' subsequently adapted for radio by C. Warburton New York [1939]); parodied as Richelieu re-dressed (by Robert Reece) [1873].

The sea-captain: or the birthright. 1839 (5 edns), New York 1839, Paris 1840 (Baudry), 1840 (Galignani), (several undated US edns, probably 1840s); tr Swed Stockholm 1845, Du (by J. van Lennep) Amsterdam 1859.

Money. 1840 (4 edns), 1841 (2 edns), Paris 1841 (Baudry), 1841 (Galignani), London 1842 (2 edns), New York 1845, London 1848, New York 1848, London 1851, 1853, 1856, 1863, (numerous, generally undated 'acting edns', mostly Br, from 1850s onwards); tr Fr Paris 1841, Swed, Stockholm 1843, 1848, Sp (by Don Victor Balaguer) nd; adaptated in prose (by H. L. Williams) New York [1883], [1884], in Fr (by M. P. de Guerville) Paris 1849; musical adaptation in Ger (by F. Kaiser) Vienna 1842.

Not so bad as we seem: or many sides to a character. 1851 (2 edns), New York 1851, Leipzig 1852, London 1853.

The rightful heir. 1868, New York 1868; tr Ger (by C. H. Simon) Leipzig 1869; parodied as The frightful heir: or who shot the dog? an original travestie on Lord Lytton's rightful heir (by F. C. Burnand) [1868?], as The right-fall heir: or the sea rover and the fall over (by H. T. Arden) nd.

Walpole: or every man has his price. Edinburgh and London 1869.

Darnley. (Unfinished drama in five acts, published in the Knebworth edn; *see* Collections, *above*).

Miscellaneous writings

Glenallan. Short story, 1826. In Life, letters and literary remains of Edward Bulwer by his son, 2 vols 1883.

Greville. Unfinished novel, 1828. In Life, letters and literary remains.

Lionel Hastings. Unfinished novel, nd. In Life, letters and literary remains.

Conversations with an ambitious student in ill health, with other pieces. New York 1832. Rptd from NMM.

Asmodeus at large. 1833 (anon), Philadelphia 1833. Rptd from NMM.

England and the English. 2 vols 1833 (2 edns), 2 vols New York 1833, Paris 1833 (Baudry), 1833 (Galignani), 2 vols London 1834, Paris 1834 (Baudry), 2 vols London 1836, Paris 1836 (Baudry), 2 vols New York 1838, London 1840, Leipzig 1841, Chicago 1970; tr Fr (by J. Cohen) 2 vols Paris 1833, 1835, 2 vols Brussels 1837, Danish (by F. Schaldemose) 2 vols Copenhagen 1835, Swed Norrkoping 1835; extracts (from Bk III) pbd as Survey of the state of education, aristocratic and popular, and of the general influences of morality and religion, 1833.
REVIEWS: Literary Gazette 22 and 29 June, 6 July, 17 Aug 1833; Athenaeum 27 July 1833 and 16 Aug 1834; Spectator 3 Aug 1833; Monthly Rev Aug 1833.

A letter to a late cabinet minister on the present crisis. 1834 (21 edns), Paris 1835 (Baudry), 1835 (Galignani), 1838 (Baudry).

The student: a series of papers. 2 vols 1835, 2 vols New York 1835, Philadelphia 1835, Paris 1835 (Baudry), 2 vols London 1836, 2 vols New York 1836, Boston 1838, Paris 1838 (Baudry), 2 vols London 1840, London, Edinburgh and Dublin 1840, Boston 1841, 2 vols Exeter CT 1843, 2 vols Philadelphia 1847, Boston 1854, 2 vols New York 1860; tr Fr (by M. Pichot) 2 vols Paris 1835, Danish (by I. C. Magnus) 2 vols Copenhagen 1837.

Athens: its rise and fall, with views of the literature, philosophy and social life of the Athenian people. 2 vols 1837, 2 vols New York 1837, Paris 1837 (Baudry), Leipzig 1837, 2 vols New York 1838, Leipzig 1843 (Tauchnitz); tr Danish (by I. Møller) 3 vols Copenhagen 1856, Ital (by F. Ambrosoli) 3 vols Milan 1857.
REVIEWS: Athenaeum 29 Apr and 6 May 1837; Blackwood's Mag July 1837; Mirror 15 July 1837; Fraser's Mag Sep 1837; Eclectic Rev Nov 1837.

Calderon the courtier. Short story. Philadelphia 1838, Cincinnati 1838, London 1850 (*see also* Leila: or the siege of Granada, *above*); tr Danish (by V. Hee) Copenhagen 1838.

Confessions and observations of a water-patient. NMM Sep 1845, London 1845, Baltimore [1845], Leipzig 1845 (Tauchnitz), London 1846, 1847, 1851, in Bulwer and Forbes on the water-treatment (ed with additional matter by R. S. Houghton) New York 1849; tr Du Amsterdam 1847; abridged South Orange NJ [1851?].

A word to the public. 1847, Leipzig 1847 (Tauchnitz). Originally pbd as prefatory essay to 2nd edn of Lucretia.

Letters to John Bull esq. on affairs connected with his landed property and the persons who live thereon. 1851 (11 edns).

Papers relative to the affairs of British Columbia: copies of despatches from the secretary of state for the colonies to the governor of British Columbia and from the governor to the secretary of state. 1859–62.

Caxtoniana: a series of essays on life, literature and manners. Blackwood's Mag Feb 1862–Oct 1863, 2 vols Edinburgh and London 1863, New York 1863, 1864, 2 vols Leipzig 1864 (Tauchnitz), New York 1868.

Lectures and speeches

Speech in the House of Commons on the second reading of the bill for reform of parliament. 1831.

Taxes on knowledge: debate in the House of Commons on the 15th June 1832 on Mr Edward Lytton Bulwer's motion for a select committee to consider the propriety of establishing a cheap postage on newspapers and other publications. 1832.

Speech delivered in the House of Commons upon the motion of Sir Eardley Wilmot for the immediate abolition of negro apprenticeship in the British colonies. 1838.

To the independent freemen and electors of the city of Lincoln. Lincoln 1848. 2 election addresses.

The question of unreciprocated copyright in Great Britain: a report

of the speeches and proceedings at a public meeting held at the Hanover Square rooms July 1 1851, Sir Edward Bulwer Lytton bart. in the chair. 1851.
Outlines of the early history of the east with explanatory descriptions of some of the more remarkable nations and cities mentioned in the Old Testament: a lecture delivered at the Royston Mechanics' Institute. Royston 1852.
Sir Edward Bulwer Lytton's speech delivered at the Leeds Mechanics' Institution. 1854.
Address of Sir Edward Bulwer Lytton to the associated societies of the University of Edinburgh on the occasion of his installation as their Honorary President. Edinburgh and London 1854, 1855.
Speech of Sir Edward Bulwer Lytton against the second reading of the foreign enlistment bill in the House of Commons. 1855.
Inaugural address delivered by Sir E. L. Bulwer Lytton bart. on his installation as Lord Rector of the University of Glasgow. Glasgow 1857.
The representation of the people bill: speech delivered in the House of Commons. Edinburgh and London 1859.
The new reform bill: speech delivered in the House of Commons. 1860.
The inaugural address of the Right Hon. Lord Lytton delivered at the congress of the British Archaeological Association. Hertford 1869.

Contributions to periodicals and annuals

Bulwer edited the NMM *from Nov 1831 to Aug 1833, and in this capacity contributed regularly to features such as the Monthly Commentary besides the more specific contributions listed below. He edited* Monthly Chronicle, *to which he similarly contributed in an editorial role, from Mar to Oct 1838.*

Short fiction

The first songstresses in town. Knight's Quart Mag Oct 1823.
Madame Catalani. Knight's Quart Mag Jan 1824.
Narenor: a tale. Knight's Quart Mag Apr–Aug 1824.
Too handsome for any thing (rptd in The student, *above*, as Ferdinand Fitzroy: or too handsome for any thing); A manuscript found in a madhouse. Literary Souvenir 1829.
Monos and Daimonos: a legend. NMM May 1830; rptd in The student, *above*.
De Lindsay: a tale. NMM June 1830.
The world as it is: a tale. NMM Nov 1831 (rptd in The student, *above*), New York 1898 (edn limited to 120 copies).
The law of arrest: a tale from facts. NMM Mar 1832; rptd in The student, *above*.
Hereditary honours: a tale of love and mystery. NMM May 1832.
The suicide of St Vallery. NMM June 1832.
The nymph of the Lurlei Berg: a tale. NMM Nov 1832.
The English abroad: or the prince of Seidlitz Powders. NMM Dec 1832.
Fi-Ho-Ti: or the pleasures of reputation. NMM Aug 1833; rptd in The student, *above*.
Arasmanes: or the seeker. Amulet 1834 (rptd in The student, *above*), Paris 1834 (Baudry), London 1905; tr Fr (by A. Dalamotte) with 3 stories from The pilgrims of the Rhine, St Petersburg 1866.
The choice of Phylias. Heath's Book of Beauty 1834; rptd in The student, *above*.
Puck's tale: or the love of a spirit. Angelo's Pic Nic: or table talk 1834.
Chairolas. Heath's Book of Beauty, 1836 (rptd in later edns of The student, *above*); as Chairolas prince of Paida in Chairolas prince of Paida with other tales (the other tales not by Bulwer), Philadelphia 1836.
The three sisters, translated from the Phoenician. Heath's Book of Beauty, 1838.
Zicci. Monthly Chron Mar–Aug 1838. Unfinished pilot story for Zanoni, often printed with Zanoni, and occasionally with Falkland, in collected edns of Bulwer's novels.
An episode in life. Heath's Book of Beauty, 1843.
The lawyer who cost his client nothing, from the Thresor d'histoires admirables et memorables de nostre temps, par Simon Goulart, Senslisien MDCXX. Keepsake 1848.
The confirmed valetudinarian. Keepsake 1851.
The haunted and the haunters: or the house and the brain. Blackwood's Mag Aug 1859; rptd in Tales from Blackwood (1st ser) Edinburgh and London 1858–61, vol 10, London and Glasgow 1905, London 1925 (introd by H. Armitage). From 1864 onwards often appended to edns of A strange story; frequently anthologised in twentieth-century collections of supernatural fiction.
A dream of the dead. Blackwood's Mag Sep 1859.

Poems

Poems to Zoë. Knight's Quart Mag June 1823.
Stanzas in the editorial; Sonnet written on the first leaf of Keats' poems; Despair; Song; To M—. Knight's Quart Mag Jan 1824.
Sonnet to A. T. on her birth-day. Knight's Quart Mag Apr 1824.
English manners or satiric sketches. NMM Apr 1830.
The poet's dream. Friendship's Offering 1832.
Elegy to the memory of H. W.; The consolations of sleep. NMM Aug 1833.
One of the crowd. In a letter to Lady Blessington, 1 Jan 1836, in The literary life and correspondence of the Countess of Blessington, ed R. R. Madden, 3 vols 1855.
Ode to a leafless tree in June. Heath's Book of Beauty 1839.
The wife to the wooer. Heath's Book of Beauty 1840.
First and last. Heath's Book of Beauty 1841.
Ode, the last separation. Keepsake 1841.
Jealousy. Keepsake 1842.
Content and desire. Heath's Book of Beauty 1844.
Youth's dirge. Heath's Book of Beauty 1845.
To the Hon Mrs Norton, 'the queenly spirit of a star'. The Drawing-Room Scrapbook 1847.
The first violets. Keepsake 1849.
The modern wooer. Keepsake 1855.

Drama

Eugene Aram: a tragedy. NMM Aug 1833; rptd in later edns of the novel Eugene Aram *above*.
The old dream. Once a Year, Christmas no 1868.

Essays and reviews

The lounger. 3 pts NMM Apr–June 1830.
The English poor. NMM Dec 1830.
Conversations with an ambitious student in ill health. 8 pts NMM Dec 1830–Mar 1832.
The spirit of society in England and France. Edinburgh Rev Jan 1831.
A letter to Doctor Southey poet laureate respecting a remarkable poem by a mechanic. NMM Apr 1831.
Literature considered as a profession. NMM Sep 1831.
Address to the public; How will the peers be gained?; Why may we blame the bishops?; Aristocracy in religion; Ourselves, our correspondents and the public [with S. C. Hall]; Living literary characters no 11: Samuel Rogers. NMM Nov 1831.
The times; A foreigner in England; Lord Brougham the man of the time; A knowledge of the world in men and books (rptd in The student, *above*); Romance and reality [review of novel by L. E. Landon]; Government and administration [headnote to Ebenezer Elliott's poem Byron and Napoleon: or they met in heaven]. NMM Dec 1831.
Asmodeus at large. 10 pts NMM Jan 1832–Feb 1833.
The new year; On English notions of morality; The universal education of the people essential to the public happiness (rptd, revised, as appendix A to England and the English, *above*). NMM Jan 1832.
The Quarterly Review: remarks in reply to the article therein enti-

tled 'The progress of misgovernment'; The state of the drama. NMM Feb 1832.
On the influence and education of women. NMM Mar 1832.
A few plain words on a great question; Upon the spirit of true criticism; The wilful misstatements of the Quarterly Review. NMM Apr 1832.
The recess; The contrast [review of novel by Lord Normanby]; Retrospective criticism [review of Laman Blanchard's poems]. NMM May 1832.
Our present state; Recent dramas; Fiesco: a tragedy, translated from the German of Schiller [review of trn by Colonel d'Aguilar]. NMM June 1832.
The politician, no I; Character of the last unreformed House of Commons; Another epic by the author of corn-law rhymes [review of Ebenezer Elliott's Spirits and men]. NMM July 1832.
The politician, no II; The true spirit of religious poetry: Montgomery's Messiah; Aristocracy. NMM Aug 1832.
The politician, no IV; Letter from Paris by Henry Pelham esq. to the editors of the New Monthly Magazine; Death of Sir Walter Scott. NMM Oct 1832.
To our friends, on preserving the anonymous in periodicals; The politician, nos V and VI; The 'True Sun': another argument against the taxes on knowledge; The difference between authors and the impression conveyed of them by their works (rptd in The student, *above*); Proposals for a literary union. NMM Nov 1832.
The politician, no VII. NMM Dec 1832.
The politician, nos VIII and IX; Count Pecchio's notions of England; The modern platonist; The faults of recent poets: poems by Alfred Tennyson; Letter to the editor of the Quarterly Review. NMM Jan 1833.
The politician, nos X and XI; On moral fictions: Miss Martineau's illustrations of political economy. NMM Feb 1833.
The politician, no XII; Position of independent labourers under the operation of the poor laws in England; Paul Louis Courier: his life and writings, a biographical criticism; Leigh Hunt's poetical works; The wondrous tale of Alroy [review of Disraeli's novel]. NMM Mar 1833.
The politician, no XIV. NMM May 1833.
The politician, no XV; Modern novelists and recent novels [including review of Bulwer's own novel Godolphin]. NMM June 1833.
View of the character of Goethe [review of Falk's Goethe tr by Mrs Austin]. NMM July 1833.
The editor's farewell; The politician, no XVIII; On the state of eloquence in England; An essay on breakfasts; Watering places. NMM Aug 1833.
Sir Egerton Brydges's autobiography. Edinburgh Rev July 1834.
Mrs Butler's American journal. Edinburgh Rev July 1835.
Prose fictions and their varieties. London Rev July 1835.
Sir Thomas Browne's works [review of Simon Wilkin's edn]. Edinburgh Rev Oct 1836.
Juliet's tomb in Verona. Heath's Book of Beauty, 1836; rptd in later edns of The student, *above*.
Paul de Kock; Chateaubriand on the literature of England. Edinburgh Rev Jan 1837.
The great metropolis. Edinburgh Rev July 1837.
Charles Lamb; Gray's works [review of John Mitford's edn]. London and Westminster Rev July 1837.
The position and prospects of the government; The history of the reign of Victoria I. Monthly Chron Mar 1838.
On art in fiction. 2 pts Monthly Chron Mar–Apr 1838.
Slavery and the new slave trade; The international law of copyright [with Sir David Brewster]. Monthly Chron Apr 1838.
The life and writings of Scott [review of J. G. Lockhart's biography]; Manners; Lord Brougham. Monthly Chron May 1838.
The present state of poetry. Monthly Chron June 1838.
Letters by an English member of parliament to M. De— of the chambre des députés (2 pts); Animal magnetism [with Dionysius Lardner] (2 pts). Monthly Chron June–July 1838.
Lady Blessington's novels. Edinburgh Rev July 1838.
Courts of British queens. London and Westminster Rev Aug 1838.
Lord Durham's mission. Monthly Chron Sep 1838.
The people's charter: Mr O'Connell and the English radicals. Monthly Chron Oct 1838.
Lord Lyndhurst's review of the last session – defence of the Whigs. Edinburgh Rev Oct 1839.
Present state and conduct of parties. Edinburgh Rev Apr 1840.
The reign of terror: its causes and results. Foreign Quart Rev July 1842.
Goldsmith [review of J. Forster's biography]. Edinburgh Rev July 1848.
Lord Lyndhurst and the war. Quart Rev June 1854.
Pitt and Fox. Quart Rev Sep 1855.
The disputes with America. Quart Rev June 1856.
Arrest of the five members by Charles the first. Quart Rev Oct 1860; rptd in Miscellaneous prose works *above* as Pym versus Falkland.
England and her institutions. Quart Rev Oct 1866.
Charles Lamb and some of his companions. Quart Rev Jan 1867.
Upon the employment of rhymed verse in English comedy. Blackwood's Mag Feb 1870.

Introductions and translations

Literary remains of the late William Hazlitt with a notice of his life by his son and thoughts on his genius and writings by E. L. Bulwer esq. MP and Mr Sergeant Talfourd MP. 2 vols 1836.
The poems and ballads of Schiller with a brief sketch of Schiller's life. 2 vols Edinburgh and London 1844, Leipzig 1844 (Tauchnitz), Edinburgh and London 1852, London 1870; tr Ger (of the introduction, by H. Kletke) Berlin 1848, [1890]. For subsequent pbs of individual poems in Bulwer's trn, *see* Bulwer entry in BL catalogue, 1956.
Sketches from life by the late Laman Blanchard with a memoir of the author by Sir Edward Bulwer Lytton bart. 3 vols 1846, 1849.
The odes and epodes of Horace: a metrical translation into English with introduction and commentaries. Blackwood's Mag Apr–Aug 1868, Edinburgh and London 1869, 2 vols Leipzig 1869 (Tauchnitz), New York 1870.

§2

Criticism

[Landon, L. E.] Living literary characters no 5, Edward Lytton Bulwer. NMM May 1831.
Review of the writings of Bulwer. Literary and Theological Rev (New York) Sep 1834.
Laube, H. Moderne Charackteristiken. 2 vols Mannheim 1835.
Willis, N. P. Pencillings by the way. 3 vols 1835.
Chorley, H. F. The authors of England. 1838.
[Bulwer Lytton, Rosina.] Bulwer's dramatic poetry. Dublin Univ Mag Mar and Apr 1840.
[Thackeray, W. M.] Epistles to the literati no 13. Fraser's Mag Jan 1840.
[Robertson, J.] Sir Lytton Bulwer. Westminster Rev May 1843.
Horne, R. H. A new spirit of the age. 2 vols 1844.
Gilfillian, G. Galleries of literary portraits. 2 vols Edinburgh 1845.
Powell, T. The living authors of England. 1849.
Jerdan, W. Autobiography. 4 vols 1852–3.
Alison, A. History of Europe from 1815 to 1852. Edinburgh 1853.
[Oliphant, M. O.] Bulwer. Blackwood's Mag Feb 1855.
Planché, G. Portraits littéraires. Paris 1855.
[Senior, N. W.] Sir E. Bulwer Lytton's novels. North Br Rev Aug 1855.
Jeaffreson, J. C. Novels and novelists from Elizabeth to Victoria. 2 vols 1858.
Mark Rochester (pseud of W. C. M. Kent). The Derby ministry, a series of cabinet pictures. 1858.

Masson, D. British novelists and their styles. 1859.
[Roscoe, W. C.] Sir E. B. Lytton: novelist, philosopher and poet. Nat Rev Apr 1859.
Senior, N. W. Essays on fiction. 1864.
Dallas, E. S. The gay science. 2 vols 1866.
Friswell, J. H. Modern men of letters honestly criticised. 1870.
Edward Bulwer Lord Lytton. Illus Rev 15 Feb 1871.
Böddeker, K. Über Bulwers Übersetzungen Schillerischer Gedichte. Archiv 49 1872.
Cooper, T. Men of the time. 1872 (8th edn).
Lord Lytton. Graphic 28 Dec 1872.
Reid, T. W. Cabinet portraits, sketches of statesmen. 1872.
[Blackwood, J.] The death of Lord Lytton. Blackwood's Mag Feb 1873.
Jowett, B. Lord Lytton the man and the author (funeral address in Westminster Abbey) to which is added a biography by M. Marsden. 1873.
Lord Lytton. Athenaeum 25 Jan 1873.
Lord Lytton as littérateur. Spectator 25 Jan 1873.
Maginn, W. A gallery of illustrious literary characters (1830–8) drawn by Daniel Maclise and accompanied by notices chiefly by William Maginn, republished from Fraser's Magazine. [1873.]
[Oliphant, M. O.] Lord Lytton, Blackwood's Mag Mar 1873.
[Stephen, L.] The late Lord Lytton as a novelist. Cornhill Mag Mar 1873.
[Storr, F.] Lord Lytton. Quart Rev Apr 1873.
Ten Brink, J. E. G. Bulwer-Lytton biografie en kritiek. Haarlem 1873.
Towle, G. M. Reminiscences of Lytton. Appleton's Jnl (New York) 15 and 22 Feb 1873.
The historical romance. Argosy May 1874.
Blavatsky, H. P. Isis unveiled. 2 vols New York 1877.
Heywood, J. C. How they strike me. Philadelphia 1877.
Mackay, C. Forty years' recollections of life, literature and public affairs from 1830 to 1870. 2 vols 1877.
Watt, J. C. Great novelists. Edinburgh 1880.
Walsh, W. S. Pen pictures of earlier Victorian authors. New York 1884.
Griswold, H. T. Home life of great authors. Chicago 1887.
Home, Mme Daniel Dunglas. D. D. Home: his life and mission. 1888.
Hamley, Sir E. Shakespeare's funeral and other papers. 1889.
Cooke, P. J. Bulwer Lytton's plays. [1894] (Battersea Polytechnic lectures on the English drama).
Goldhan, H. Über die Einwirkung des Goethischen Werthers und Wilhelm Meisters auf die Entwicklung Edward Bulwers. Anglia 16 1894.
Saintsbury, G. A history of nineteenth century literature. 1896.
Howells, W. D. A heroine of Bulwer's. Harper's Bazaar (New York) 25 Aug 1900.
Lord, W. F. Lord Lytton's novels. Nineteenth Cent and After Sep 1901.
A sketch from memory. Macmillan's Mag Mar 1901.
Nield, J. A guide to the best historical novels and tales. 1902.
Melville, L. The centenary of Bulwer-Lytton. Bookman 25 May 1903.
Musings without method: Bulwer's early novels. Blackwood's Mag May 1903.
Cazamian, L. Le roman social en Angleterre 1830–50. Paris 1904.
Recollections of a visit to Sir Edward Bulwer Lytton at Knebworth in 1857. Blackwood's Mag Jan 1905.
Melville, L. Victorian novelists. 1906.
Escott, T. H. S. Edward Bulwer first Lord Lytton, a social, personal and political monograph. 1910.
Letters of Bulwer-Lytton to Macready 1836–66. Hasark NJ 1911 (Carteret Book Club).
Buckley, J. A. and W. J. Williams. A guide to British historical fiction. 1912.
Chesterton, G. K. The Victorian age in literature, 1913.
Saintsbury, G. The English novel. 1913.
Baker, E. A. A guide to historical fiction. 1914.
Bell, E. G. Introductions to the prose romances, plays and comedies of Edward Bulwer Lord Lytton. Chicago 1914.
Sichel, W. Bulwer Lytton. Bookman Jan 1914.
Ward, L. Forty years of 'Spy', 1915.
Price, L. M. Karl Gutzow and Bulwer Lytton. JEGP July 1917.
Gosse, E. Some diversions of a man of letters. 1919.

Biographies and letters

Cooper, T. Lord Lytton, a biography. 1873.
[Bulwer Lytton, Edward Robert, 1st Earl (ed).] The life, letters and literary remains of Edward Bulwer Lord Lytton by his son. 2 vols 1883.
Devey, L. (ed). Letters of the late Edward Bulwer Lord Lytton to his wife, with extracts from her manuscript autobiography and other documents published in vindication of her memory. 1884.
[Lytton, Victor Alexander George Robert, 2nd Earl.] The life of Edward Bulwer first Lord Lytton by his grandson the Earl of Lytton. 2 vols 1913.
REVIEW: Gosse, E. Fortnightly Rev Dec 1913.
Frost, W. A. Bulwer Lytton, an exposure of the errors of his biographers. 1913.
Waddell, G. de R. Reminiscences and letters of Bulwer-Lytton. Century Mag July 1914.
Sadleir, M. Edward and Rosina 1803–1836. 1931 (the only vol pbd of a projected 3-vol biography entitled Bulwer a panorama).
The [2nd] Earl of Lytton K. G. Bulwer-Lytton. 1948.
Shattuck, C. Bulwer and Macready, a chronicle of the early Victorian theatre. Urbana IL 1958. Contains extensive correspondence.
Usrey, M. O. (ed). The letters of Sir Edward Bulwer-Lytton to the editors of Blackwood's Magazine 1840–73 in the National Library of Scotland. Unpbd diss, Texas Technical College 1963. [AB]

Rosina Anne Doyle Bulwer Lytton, née Wheeler, 1st Lady Lytton 1802–82

§1

Artaphernes the Platonist: or the supper at Sallust's, a roman fragment. Fraser's Mag Apr 1838. Short story.
Cheveley: or the man of honour. 3 vols 1839 (3 edns), 2 vols New York 1839, Paris 1839 (Baudry); parodied, in verse, as Lady Cheveley: or the woman of honour, 1839 (2 edns).
The budget of the Bubble family. 3 vols 1840, 2 vols New York 1840, Paris 1840 (Baudry), Paris 1840 (Galignani).
Bulwer's dramatic poetry. Dublin Univ Mag Mar and Apr 1840. An attack on her estranged husband in the guise of a review of his plays.
The Prince-Duke and the page: an historical novel. 3 vols 1841.
Bianca Cappello: an historical romance. 3 vols 1843, New York 1843.
Memoirs of a Muscovite. 3 vols 1844.
The man of the people. 3 vols 1845 (attrib – 'by the author of The Prince-Duke and the page').
The peer's daughter: a novel. 3 vols 1849, New York 1850.
Miriam Sedley, or the tares and the wheat: a tale of real life. 3 vols 1851.
The school for husbands: or Molière's life and times. 3 vols 1852, Philadelphia 1852.
Behind the scenes: a novel. 3 vols 1854, 2 vols New York 1854 (2 edns).
Very successful! 3 vols Taunton 1856, 1 vol [1857?].
Lady Bulwer Lytton's appeal to the justice and charity of the English public. 1857 (3 edns). Pam.
The world and his wife: or a person of consequence, a photographic novel. 3 vols 1858.
The household fairy. 1870. A manual 'for young housekeepers'.
Where there's a will there's a way. 3 vols 1871. Anon.
Shells from the sands of time. 1876. Essays and stories.

Attributed works

A blighted life, by the Right Hon Lady Lytton. 1880.
'Autobiography', apparently by RBL but *see* Sadleir *under* §2, *below*, p. 433, for refutation of authorship.

In her Life of Rosina Lady Lytton, *see* §2 *below, Louisa Devey attributes two further anonymously pbd novels to RBL. The first of these,* Mauleverer's divorce *(3 vols 1859), is in fact the work of Emma Robinson (see col 1392). The second,* Clumber Chase: or love's riddle solved by a royal sphinx, a tale of the Restoration *(3 vols 1871), is the only catalogued work of a certain George Gordon Scott. Devey claims that this was a pseud of RBL.*

§2

Refutation of an audacious forgery of the dowager Lady Lytton's name to a book [i.e. A blighted life] of the publication of which she was totally ignorant. 1880 (priv ptd).

Devey, L. (ed). Letters of the late Edward Bulwer Lord Lytton to his wife with extracts of her MS autobiography and other documents published in vindication of her memory. 1884, New York 1889.

Devy, L. (ed). Life of Rosina, Lady Lytton with numerous extracts from her MS autobiography and other original documents published in vindication of her memory. 1887 (2 edns).

Ellis, S. M. (ed). Unpublished letters from Lady Bulwer Lytton to A. E. Chalon R. A. 1914.

Sadleir, M. Edward and Rosina 1803–36. 1931. [AB]

Selina Bunbury 1802–82

§1

Early recollections: a tale. 1825 (anon); [1856] (2nd edn).
The pastor's tales. 1826 (anon).
A visit to my birthplace. Dublin 1826 (anon), Boston [1828] (Amer edn rev and improved), London 1855.
Annot and her pupil. Edinburgh 1827 (anon), Salem 1829, Edinburgh 1830, London 1830 (2nd edn).
Cabin conversations and castle scenes. An Irish story. 1827. Anon.
The Abbey of Innismoyle. Dublin 1828 (anon), 1829 (2nd edn), New York and Philadelphia 1845 (1st Amer edn).
Stories from church history. 1828. Anon.
Retrospectives: a soldier's story. 1829. Anon.
Eleanor. 1830. Anon.
Gertrude and her family. Dublin 1830. Anon.
My foster brother. 1833 (2nd edn). Anon.
Tales of my country. 1833. Anon.
My early adventures during the peninsular campaigns of Napoleon. Boston 1834. Anon.
Anecdotes of Peter the Great, Emperor of Russia. [1843.] Anon.
Coombe Abbey: an historical tale. Dublin 1843, 1844, London 1857 (new edn).
The castle and the hovel: or the two sceptics. 1844, 1864.
'I am so happy'. 1844.
Rides in the Pyrenees. 2 vols 1844, 1847, 1848.
REVIEWS: Athenaeum 886 1844; Spectator 17 1844.
The star of the court. 1844. 1845.
The blind girl of the moor, a shepherd's child. 1845.
The Indian babes in the wood. [1845?]
Recollections of Ireland. Dublin 1846. Anon.
The triumph of truth. [1846] (anon), [1847].
A happy new-year! [1847.]
Sketches in the life of Alfred the Great. 1847.
Evelyn: or a journey from Stockholm to Rome in 1847–8. 2 vols 1849.
A visit to the Catacombs. 1849.
The blind clergyman and his little guide. 1850.
The brother's sacrifice. A French story. [1851?]
Evelyn, or the maiden's secret. 1851.
The first offence, or the forged letter. 1851 (Stories for schools. SPCK).
Little Dora Playfair, or 'I won't go to school'. 1851.
Why are you afraid of the policeman? 1851 (Stories for schools. SPCK).
The happy land. 1852 (Stories for schools. SPCK).
Honesty and industry, or the violet seller. 1853 (Stories for schools. SPCK).
Life in Sweden, with excursions in Norway and Denmark. 2 vols 1853.
REVIEW: London Quart Rev 1 1853.
Glory, glory, glory. A story for little children. [1855?]
The lost one found. 1856.
Our own story. 3 vols 1856.
Silent John, or the picture of the good shepherd expounded. 1856, [1895] (SPCK).
A summer in northern Europe. 2 vols 1856.
REVIEW: Athenaeum 1491 1856.
Little Mary, or the captain's gold ring. 1857.
Russia after the war. 2 vols 1857.
REVIEW: Athenaeum 1541 1857.
Sir Guy d'Esterre. 2 vols 1858, 1 vol Dublin 1874.
REVIEW: Athenaeum 1593 1858.
My first travels. 2 vols 1859.
REVIEW: Athenaeum 1675 1859.
Edward, the infant-school boy. [1860].
Madame Constance: the autobiography of a Frenchwoman. Ed [actually written by] Bunbury. 2 vols 1861.
REVIEW: Athenaeum 1750 1861.
The recovered estate and other tales. 1862. Contains The recovered estate, The blind curate's child, Christmas Eve in the forests of Sweden.
Sampson the fisherman and his son. 1862.
The blind curate's child. 1863. First pbd in The recovered estate, 1862, *above*.
Florence Manvers. 3 vols 1865.
Lady Flora: or the events of a winter in Sweden, and a summer in Rome in the years 1846 and 1847. 2 vols 1870.
The smuggler's cave. [1897.]
Fanny the flower-girl, or honesty rewarded. New York [1911], Philadelphia nd.

Editions and translations

Evenings in the Pyrenees, comprising the stories of wanderers from many lands. Ed and arranged by Bunbury. 1845.
REVIEW: Athenaeum 931 1845.
Mullois, J. The Sunday of the people in France. Tr with an introd by Bunbury 1855.

Bunbury wrote for various journals, especially Fraser's Mag. *See* Wellesley *vol 5*.

§2

Crone, J. S. A concise dictionary of Irish biography. Dublin 1928.
Brady, A. M. and B. Cleeve. A biographical dictionary of Irish writers. Gigginstown, Ireland 1985.

Georgina, Lady Chatterton, Lady Henrietta Georgiana Marcia Lascelles Chatterton, née Iremonger 1806–76

§1

Aunt Dorothy's tale: or Geraldine Morton. 2 vols 1837. Anon.
REVIEWS: Athenaeum 503 1837; Spectator 10 1837.
A good match, The heiress of Drosberg and The cathedral chorister. 3 vols 1839, 1840, 1 vol 1868 (new edn).
REVIEWS: Athenaeum 633 1839; Spectator 12 1839.
Rambles in the south of Ireland during the year 1838. 2 vols 1839, 1839 (2nd edn).
REVIEWS: Athenaeum 601 1839; Spectator 12 1839.

Home sketches and foreign recollections. 3 vols 1841.
REVIEWS: in Athenaeum 708 1841; Dublin Univ Mag 18 1841; Spectator 14 1841.
Allanston, or the infidel. 3 vols 1843 (private edn?), 1844.
The Pyrenees, with excursions into Spain. 2 vols 1843.
REVIEWS: Athenaeum 810 1843; Spectator 16 1843.
Lost happiness, or the effects of a lie. A tale. 1845.
Reflections on the history of the kings of Judah. 1848.
Compensation. A story of real life thirty years ago. 2 vols 1856. Anon.
Life and its realities. 3 vols 1857.
The reigning beauty. 3 vols 1858.
The heiress and her lovers. 3 vols 1863.
REVIEWS: Athenaeum 1879 1863; Saturday Rev 16 1863.
Leonore, a tale: and other poems. Cambridge and London 1864, 1865 (new edn illus).
Quagmire ahead. 1864 (priv ptd).
Grey's court. 2 vols 1865, 1866. With E. H. Dering.
Oswald of Deira: a drama. 1867. Verse.
A plea for happiness and hope. 1867 (priv ptd).
Country coteries. 3 vols 1868.
Lady May: a pastoral. 1869. Verse.
The lost bride. 3 vols 1872, 1 vol 1875 (2nd edn).
REVIEW: Athenaeum 2330 1872.
Won at last. 3 vols 1874.
REVIEW: Athenaeum 2431 1874.
Convictions. 1875 (priv ptd).
Misgivings. 1875 (priv ptd).
The golden bird: a fairy legend of the south of Ireland. In The oak; original tales and sketches by Sir J. Bowring, Lady Chatterton and others, ed C. Rogers, 1869. Play.

Editions and translations

Extracts from the works of J. P. F. Richter. Selected by and tr Chatterton. 1859.
Memorials personal and historical of Admiral Lord Gambier. Ed Chatterton. 2 vols [1860], 1861, 1861 (2nd edn).
Selections from the works of Plato. Tr Chatterton. 1862.
Extracts from Aristotle's works. Selected by and tr Chatterton. 1875 (priv ptd).
Frassinetti, G. The consolation of the devout soul . . . . Tr Chatterton. 1876.

§2

Dering, E. H. Memoirs of Georgiana, Lady Chatterton. 1878, 1901 (2nd edn), [1911].
REVIEWS: Athenaeum 2640 1878; Dublin Rev 83 1878.
DNB

Henry Fothergill Chorley 1808–82

See col 2220.

Charles Clarke

Charlie Thornhill, or the dunce of the family: a novel. 3 vols 1863.
A box for the season: a sporting sketch. 2 vols 1864.
Which is the winner? or the first gentleman of his family. 3 vols 1864.
Crumbs from a sportsman's table. 2 vols 1865, [1869].
The flying scud: a sporting novel. 2 vols 1867 (anon), 1868 (3rd edn).
Tom Crackenthorpe: hunting and steeplechasing. 1867.
The Beauclercs, father and son: a novel. 3 vols 1867.
Lord Falconberg's heir: a novel. 2 vols 1868.
A forecastle frolic: being a round of stories for Christmas, conducted by Charles Clarke. [1868.]
Myra Gray, or sown in tears, reaped in joy: a novel. 3 vols 1870.
Calcraft's confessions: or coward-conscience. 1870.
Chips from an old block. [1871.]

Mary Cowden Clarke 1809–98

See col 2221.

Caroline Clive, née Meysey-Wigley 1801–73

Bibliography

Mitchell, C. (ed). Caroline Clive: a bibliography. Victorian Fiction Research Guide. St Lucia Qld. 1999.

§1

Essays on the human intellect, as controlled by God, and on our Saviour, considered in his character of man. By Paul Ferrol. 1827.
Anecdotes of the new poor laws. Nos 1 and 2. Birmingham nd. [1836].
IX poems by V. 1840, 1841, (enlarged to 18 poems) 1928 (with introd by E. Partridge). V was short for Vigolina, mock-Latin for Wigley.
REVIEWS: Quart Rev 66, Sep 1840, (attributed to H. N. Coleridge in Wellesley) but to J. G. Lockhart by J. Davies *see below*; [Coventry Patmore] Edinburgh Rev 104, Oct 1856.
I watched the heavens: a poem by V. 1842. Canto 1 of a projected longer poem.
Saint Oldooman: a myth of the nineteenth century; contained in a letter from the Bishop of Verulanum to the Lord Drayton. 1845. Anon. St Oldooman is the rector of 'Littlebitmore', i.e. Newman.
The Queen's ball: a poem by V. 1847. Based on a report that 150 dead people were invited to Queen Victoria's ball on 18 June 1847.
The glass-berg: a poem. 1851. About the Great Exhibition.
The valley of the Rea: by V. 1851.
The Morlas: a poem by V. 1853.
Paul Ferroll: a tale, by the author of IX poems by V. 1855, 1856 (4th edn, with a 'concluding notice' added), Leipzig 1856 (Tauchnitz), New York 1856, London 1858 (another '4th edn', but in fact the 5th), 1865, 1873, 1882, 1890, 1901, 1929 (with introd by E. Partridge), Oxford 1997 (introd by C. Mitchell); tr Fr (by Henriette Loreau) Paris 1858, (by Marie Souvestre) Paris 1859, Rus [St Petersburg?] 1859.
REVIEW: Athenaeum 1451, 18 Aug 1855.
Poems by the author of Paul Ferroll: including a new edition of IX poems by V with former and recent additions. 1856, 1872 (with 8 poems deleted and 8 others added), 1890 (as Poems by V [Mrs Archer Clive], with another 3 poems added and introd by A. Greathed, Clive's daughter).
Year after year: a tale by the author of Paul Ferroll and IX poems by V. 1858, Leipzig 1858.
Why Paul Ferroll killed his wife. 1860, Leipzig 1861, London 1861, 1861, 1862, 1864, 1882, 1901.
John Greswold. 2 vols 1864.

Translation

Guy of Warwick: a knight of Britain who in his day did many deeds of prowess and conquest in Germany, Italy and Denmark. Tr Clive. Ed William B. Todd, Austin TX 1968.

Contributions to periodicals

Clive contributed one article to Blackwood's Mag *and one to the* Fortnightly Rev *(see* Wellesley *vol 5). She also had a poem, 'The first morning of 1860', in the inaugural number of the* Cornhill Mag *(Jan 1860).*

§2

Mitford, M. R. Recollections of a literary life. 1852.
Anon [R. H. Hutton]. The author of Paul Ferroll. Nat Rev 12, Apr 1861.
Obits: The Times 16 July 1873; Athenaeum 2386, 19 July 1873.
Davies, J. Contemporary Rev 23, Jan 1874.
Saintsbury, G. A history of nineteenth century literature. 1896.
Sergeant, A. Mrs Archer Clive. In Women novelists of Queen Victoria's reign, 1897.
Clive, M. (ed). Caroline Clive: from the diary and family papers of Mrs Archer Clive (1801–73). 1949.

Browning, E. B. The letters of Elizabeth Barrett Browning to Mary Russell Mitford 1836–54. Ed M. B. Raymond and M. R. Sullivan 1983.

Lennox-Boyd, C. M. The literary career of Caroline Clive 1801–1873. Unpbd PhD thesis, Univ of London 1989. [PDE]

Henry Cockton 1807–53

The life and adventures of Valentine Vox, the ventriloquist. 1840, 1853 (rev).

Stanley Thorn. 3 vols 1841.

George St George Julian, the Prince of Swindlers. 1841, 1844.

Sylvester Sound the somnambulist. 1844.

The sisters, or England and France: a romance of real life. 1844, 1851 (with additions as The sisters: or the fatal marriages).

The love match. 1845.

The steward: a romance of real life. 1850.

Lady Felicia: a novel. 1852.

Percy Effingham: or the germ of the world's esteem. 2 vols 1853.

Charles Allston Collins 1828–73

A new sentimental journey. 1859. First pbd in All the Year Round June–July 1859.

The eyewitness: his evidence about many wonderful things. 1860. First pbd in All the Year Round 1859–60.

A cruise upon wheels: the chronicles of some autumn wanderings among the deserted post roads of France. 2 vols 1862, 1863, 1926.

The bar sinister: a tale. 2 vols 1864.

Strathcairn: a novel. 2 vols 1864.

At the Bar: a tale. 2 vols 1866.

Mortimer Collins 1827–76

§1

Idyls and rhymes. Dublin 1855.

Summer songs. 1860.

Who is the heir? a novel. 3 vols 1865.

Sweet Anne Page. 3 vols 1868.

The ivory gate. 2 vols 1869.

A letter to the Right Honourable Benjamin Disraeli MP. 1869.

The Vivian romance. 3 vols 1870.

Marquis and merchant. 3 vols 1871.

The inn of strange meetings and other poems. 1871.

The secret of long life. 1871. Essays.

The British birds: a communication from the ghost of Aristophanes. 1872.

The Princess Clarice: a story of 1871. 2 vols 1872.

Two plunges for a pearl. 3 vols 1872. First pbd in London Soc Jan–Nov 1871.

Squire Silchester's whim. 3 vols 1873.

Miranda: a midsummer madness. 3 vols 1873.

Mr Carington: a tale of love and conspiracy. 3 vols 1873. Pbd as by Robert Turner Cotton.

Transmigration. 3 vols 1874.

Frances. 3 vols 1874.

Sweet and twenty. 3 vols 1875.

Blacksmith and scholar and From midnight to midnight. 3 vols 1876. From midnight to midnight rptd separately, 1883.

A fight with fortune. 3 vols 1876.

You play me false: a novel, by Mortimer and Frances Collins. 3 vols 1878.

The village comedy, by Mortimer and Frances Collins. 3 vols 1878.

Pen sketches from a vanished hand, from the papers of the late Mortimer Collins, edited by Tom Taylor, with notes by the editor and Mrs Mortimer Collins. 2 vols 1879.

Thoughts in my garden, edited by Edmund Yates, with notes by the editor and Mrs Mortimer Collins. 2 vols 1880.

Selections from the poetical works. Ed F. P. Cotton 1886.

§2

Collins, Frances. Mortimer Collins: his letters and friendships, with some account of his life. 2 vols 1877.

(William) Wilkie Collins 1824–89

The majority of mss for novels, short stories and plays have survived in some form of draft and are now located in various libraries (see IELM *vol 4 pt 1 1982 for a comprehensive listing). In the UK,* Basil *is held in the* BL, No name *in the King's School, Canterbury, and the play* The lighthouse *in the Forster collection in the Victoria and Albert Museum. The remainder are mainly in the US with significant holdings in the Berg, Harvard, HRHRC, Huntington, Pierpont Morgan and Princeton collections. These libraries hold a large number of Collins's letters but many remain in private hands. The collected edn of Collins's letters is ed by W. Baker and W. M. Clarke, 1999.*

Bibliographies

For joint works, see also Dickens *entry, col 1181.*

Puttick & Simpson. Library of the late Wilkie Collins, Esq. 20 Jan 1890.

Sotheby, Wilkinson & Hodge. Catalogue of the original manuscripts by Charles Dickens and Wilkie Collins. 18 June 1890.

Sadleir, M. Excursions in Victorian bibliography. 1922, rptd 1974.

Brussel, I. R. Anglo-American first editions 1826–1900: East to West. 1935, rptd New York 1981.

Parrish, M. L. and E. V. Miller. Wilkie Collins and Charles Reade: first editions described with notes. 1940, rptd New York 1968.

Sadleir, M. XIX century fiction: a bibliographical record. 2 vols 1951, rptd New York 1969.

Andrew, R. V. A Wilkie Collins check-list. Eng Stud in Africa 3 1960; rptd in Wilkie Collins: a critical survey of his prose fiction with a bibliography, New York 1979.

Lohrli, A. Household Words: a weekly journal 1850–1859. Toronto 1973.

Beetz, K. H. Wilkie Collins: an annotated bibliography 1889–1976. Metuchen NJ 1978.

Gasson, A. Wilkie Collins: a collector's and bibliographer's challenge. Private Library 3rd ser vol 3:2, Summer 1980.

Wolff, R. L. Nineteenth-century fiction: a bibliographical catalogue vol 1, New York 1981.

Beetz, K. H. Wilkie Collins and The Leader. Victorian Periodicals Rev, vol 15 no 1, Spring 1982.

Oppenlander, E. A. Dickens' All the Year Round: descriptive index and contributor list. Troy NY 1984.

Todd, W. B. and A. Bowden. Tauchnitz international editions in English 1841–1955. New York 1988.

[Harlow, S.] Abbreviated bibliographic check list: Wilkie Collins. Canterbury 1990.

Peters, C. In The king of inventors: a life of Wilkie Collins, 1991.

Topp, C. W. Victorian yellowbacks & paperbacks 1849–1905 vol 1, Denver 1993– .

Jarndyce, catalogue 93. Wilkie Collins. Summer 1993.

Catalogue of St Petersburg public lib, 'Saltykov Shchedrin'.

Law, G. The serial publication in Britain of the novels of Wilkie Collins. Humanitas 33, 20 Feb 1995 (Waseda Univ Law Soc).

Law, S. Wilkie in the weeklies: the serialization and syndication of Collins's late novels. Victorian Periodicals Rev 30 1997.

Gasson, A. Wilkie Collins: an illustrated guide. Oxford 1998.

Collections

There is no complete edn of the works of Wilkie Collins although there have been several partial collections.

Sampson Low, 1861–5. Cheap and uniform edn of the novels and romances of Wilkie Collins with vignette illustrations (Antonina; Basil; Hide and seek; The dead secret; The Queen of hearts; The woman in white); also with No name in Low's Favourite Lib of Popular Books.

Smith Elder, popular edn, 1865–72. 10 titles, adding to Low's After dark, Armadale, and The moonstone.

Chatto & Windus, from 1875. Several cheap edns including the New Illus Lib, Piccadilly Novels and popular edns. By 1890, Chatto pbd 29 titles which continued to be issued in various formats well into the twentieth century.

Harpers, New York 1873–1902. 17 titles in a variety of forms including the Illus Lib Edn, Lib of Select Novels and Cheap Edn.

Collier, New York 1900. The works of Wilkie Collins in 30 vols, rptd New York 1970. Several titles were issued in unauthorised nineteenth-century edns: e.g. New York, Fireside, Lovell and Seaside Libs; Chicago, Lakeside Lib; Philadelphia, Peterson.

Tauchnitz, Leipzig 1856–90. 28 titles in 50 vols in the Collection of British Authors.

Modern publishers include Oxford (WCp), Alan Sutton (Stroud) and Dover (New York), all of whom have also issued various collections of short stories. The 1994 Complete shorter fiction (ed J. Thompson) includes several works not previously reissued or which had originally appeared in the US and not pbd in the UK. The Wilkie Collins Society (WCS) reprints short pieces not previously reprinted.

§1

Br and Amer edns of individual titles are listed in separate sequences.

Iolani; or, Tahiti as it was: a romance. Ed I. B. Nadel, Princeton 1999 [1844].

Memoirs of the life of William Collins, Esq, R.A.: with selections from his journals and correspondence. 2 vols 1848 (frontispiece portrait and illus titles), Wakefield 1978 (1 vol facs with new indexes).

Antonina; or, the fall of Rome: a romance of the fifth century. 3 vols [Feb] 1850, 3 vols [May] 1850 (2nd edn, rev with rev preface), 3 vols 1853 (1st edn sheets), 1861 (new preface and illus title by J. Gilbert), 1862, 1864, 1865 (Sampson Low), 1865 (Smith Elder), 1871, 1872, 1875 (8 illustrations by A. Concanen), [1877], 1889, 1895, 1896, 1897 (Chatto), 1897 (Routledge Railway Lib no 1245), 1905, 1908. New York 1850, 1868, 1873, 1874, 1877, 1893, 1898, 1900 (Collier vol 17), 1904, 1916. Leipzig 1863 (Tauchnitz vols 678–9); tr Ger Leipzig 1850.

Rambles beyond railways: or notes in Cornwall taken a-foot. 1851 (12 illustrations by H. C. Brandling), 1852 (2nd edn), 1861 (with The cruise of the Tomtit, first pbd Household Words 22 Dec 1855), 1865, Philadelphia [1871] (as Sights a-foot), London 1948, 1982.

Mr Wray's cash-box; or, the mask and the mystery: a Christmas sketch. (1852) [1851] (preface dated Dec 1851, frontispiece by J. E. Millais), 1852 (2nd edn, with shortened preface dated Jan 1852), 1991 (in Crime for Christmas, ed R. Dalby), Philadelphia [1862] (as The stolen mask; or the mysterious cash-box), Stroud 1996.

Basil: a story of modern life. 3 vols 1852, 1856 (Blackwood's London Lib), 1862 (with rev letter of dedication, rev text, frontispiece by J. Gilbert), 1865, 1871, 1872, 1875 (with 8 illustrations by M. F. Mahoney), 1877, 1885, 1887, 1889, 1890, 1894, 1897 (Downey 6d Lib), 1897 (Routledge Railway Lib), 1898 (Routledge Handy Novels no 19), 1901 (Butterworth), 1905, 1910, 1990 (WCp ed D. Goldman). New York 1853 (Appleton), Philadelphia [1860] (as The crossed path), New York [1873], 1874, 1880 (Seaside Lib vol 35 no 721), 1893, 1898, 1904, 1900 (in Collier vol 10), 1980. Leipzig 1862 (Tauchnitz vol 620).

Hide and seek. 3 vols 1854, 1861 (sub-titled The mystery of Mary Grice, rev text and new preface, frontispiece by J. Gilbert), 1863, 1865, 1866, 1871, 1872, 1875 (with 8 illustrations by M. F. Mahoney), 1876, 1877, [1881], 1889, 1891, 1897 (Routledge Railway Lib), 1898 (Routledge Handy Novels no 2), 1921. New York 1858 (Dick & Fitzgerald), Philadelphia 1862, New York [1873], 1874, 1877 (Seaside Lib vol 3 no 42), 1898, 1900 (Collier vol 11), 1904, 1981. Oxford 1993 (WCp ed C. Peters). Leipzig 1856 (Tauchnitz vols 370–1). Tr Rus St Petersburg 1858; Ger Sonderhausen 1864, Fr (by C. de Cendrey) Paris 1877.

After dark. 2 vols 1856 (6 stories with connecting narrative, 5 first pbd in Household Words and The angler's story of the lady of Glenwith Grange), 1859, 1862 (5 illustrations by [A. B. Houghton]), 1865, 1870, 1871, 1872, 1876, 1878 (4 illustrations), 1879, 1882, 1888, 1890 (Smith Elder), 1890 (Chatto & Windus, 4 illustrations), 1891 (illus title by W. Crane), 1894, 1907, 1908, 1925. New York [1856] (Dick & Fitzgerald), Philadelphia [1863], 1873, 1875 (3 illustrations by S. L. Fildes and E. A. Abbey, also includes Miss or Mrs?, The dead alive, The fatal cradle, 'Blow up with the brig!', The frozen deep, Fatal fortune), 1878 (Union Square Lib no 14), 1881 (Fireside Lib vol 8 no 104, Dime Novel Collection), 1893, 1899, 1900 (Collier vol 19). Leipzig 1856 (Tauchnitz vol 367). Tr Ger Lemgo 1859, Polish Lwow 1871, Du The Hague 1876.

Individual publication

The traveller's story of a terribly strange bed first pbd Household Words 24 Apr 1852 (as A terribly strange bed), 1924 (Holerth Lib no 52). The lawyer's story of a stolen letter first pbd Household Words Christmas 1854 (as The fourth poor traveller), New York 1854 (in The seven poor travellers), [1855]. The French governess's story of Sister Rose first pbd Household Words 7–28 Apr 1855 (as Sister Rose), Philadelphia 1855 (first separate edn, as Sister Rose, wrongly attributed to C. Dickens). The nun's story of Gabriel's marriage first pbd Household Words 16–23 Apr 1853 (as Gabriel's marriage); tr Ital Milan 1868. The professor's story of the yellow mask first pbd Household Words 7–28 July 1855 (as The yellow mask), Chicago 1876, 1879 (Seaside Lib no 551), 1879 (Appleton's New Handy-Vol ser), Philadelphia [187–?]. The lady of Glenwith Grange, 1947 (Atlantis Books no 2).

The dead secret. First pbd Household Words 3 Jan–13 June 1857 and Harper's Weekly 24 Jan–27 June 1857, Littell's Living Age, Boston 28 Feb–18 July 1857. 2 vols 1857, 1861 (new preface and frontispiece by J. Gilbert), 1865, 1871, 1872, 2 vols [1874?] (original sheets reissued), 1875, 1877, [1881], 1890, 1892, 1893, 1898, 1899, 1900 (Downey), 1901, 1906, 1929, Stroud 1986, Oxford 1997 (WCp ed I. Nadel). New York 1857 (Miller & Curtis), Philadelphia 1864, New York [1873], 1874, 1877 (Seaside Lib vol 1 no 14), 1881 (Fireside Lib vol 9 no 113), [1887] (Lovell's Lib vol 20 no 957), [188–?] (Lupton), 1893, 1899, 1900 (in Collier vol 16), 1902, 1979. Leipzig 1857 (Tauchnitz vols 386, 409 (includes A queen's revenge, first pbd Household Words 15 Aug 1857)). Tr Rus St Petersburg 1857, 1861; Fr (by E. D. Forgues) Paris 1858; Du Amsterdam 1858; Ger Leipzig 1862. *See also* Plays, *below*.

The Queen of hearts. 3 vols 1859 (11 stories with connecting narrative), 1862 (frontispiece by J. Gilbert), 1865, 1871, 1872, 1873, 1874, 1875 (8 illustrations by A. Concanen), 1877, 1885, [1886], 1893, [1911]. New York 1859, 1874, 1877 (Seaside Lib vol 2 no 32), 1882, 1885 (Seaside Lib Pocket Edn no 591), 1887 (Lovell's Lib vol 20 no 996), 1899, 1900 (Collier vol 14), 1902. Leipzig 1859 (Tauchnitz vol 493, as A plot in private life and other tales; includes Mad Monkton, The black cottage, The family secret, The biter bit). Tr Rus 1875.

Individual publication

The first story, The Queen of hearts, links Brother Owen's story of the black cottage, first pbd Harper's Monthly Mag Feb 1857 (as The siege of the black cottage). Brother Griffith's story of the family secret first pbd Nat Mag Nov 1856 (as Uncle George or the family mystery). Brother Morgan's story of the dream woman first pbd Household Words extra Christmas no Dec 1855 (as The ostler, 2nd pt of The Holly Tree Inn), 1874 (in The frozen deep and other stories, altered), Boston 1875 (as Alicia Warlock in Alicia Warlock and other stories), New York 1894 (in Love's random shot and other stories), Girard KS 1923 (abridged in Little Blue Book no 107); tr Rus 1875. Brother Griffith's story of Mad Monkton, first pbd Fraser's Mag Nov–Dec 1855 (as The Monktons of Wincot Abbey); tr Rus 1866. Brother Morgan's story of the dead hand first pbd Household Words 10 Oct 1857 (as [The double-bedded room], 2nd pt of The lazy tour of two idle apprentices). Brother Griffith's story of the biter bit, first pbd Atlantic Monthly Apr 1858 (as Who is the thief?), 1924 (Holerth Lib no 48). Brother Owen's story of The parson's scruple first pbd Household Words 1 Jan 1859 (as A new mind), Leipzig 1859 (in vol 11 of Novels and tales from Household Words, Tauchnitz vol 481). Brother Griffith's story of a plot in private life first pbd Harper's Monthly Mag Feb 1858 (as A marriage tragedy); tr Rus 1864, 1869. Brother Morgan's story of Fauntleroy first pbd Household Words 13 Nov 1858 (as A paradoxical experience), New York [1874] (in Remember, a keepsake), Chicago 1890 (in Readings and recitations from modern authors, as Fauntleroy the forger). Brother Owen's story of Anne Rodway first pbd Household Words 19–26 July 1856 (as The diary of Anne Rodway), Leipzig 1856 (in vol 2 of Novels and tales from Household Words, Tauchnitz vol 377).

The woman in white. First pbd All the Year Round 26 Nov 1859–25 Aug 1860 and Harper's Weekly 26 Nov 1859–Aug 1860. 3 vols [15 Aug] 1860. 1860 (2nd–7th edns, numbered on title pages, minor changes to text and chronology, all in 3 vols), 3 vols [Nov] 1860 (new edn), 1861 (new preface and illus title by J. Gilbert, further changes to chronology in response to criticism in The Times), 1863, 1865, 1871, 1872, 1875, 1877, [1879], [1880], 1889, 1890 (8 illustrations by F. A. Fraser), 1892, 1894, 1895 (with The moonstone), 1896 (with The moonstone), 1898, 1904 (Routledge Caxton Novels), 1906, 1908, 1910 (EL), 1910 (Nelson Classics), 1922 (WC), 1928, 1932, 1956 (Folio Soc, illustr L. Lamb), 1974 (Pen, ed J. Symons), Oxford 1980 (WCp, ed H. P. Sucksmith), London 1991 (EL, introd by N. Rance), 1992 (Folio Soc, illustr A. Pendle, introd by R. Rendell), Oxford 1996 (WCp ed by J. Sutherland). New York [15 Aug] 1860 (simultaneous with London edn), 1861, 1863, 1865, 1867, 1869, 1873, 1877 (Munro), [1877?] (Seaside Lib vol 1 no 10), 1878 (Union Square Lib no 4), 1880 (Seaside Lib), 1893, 1899, 1900, 1900 (Collier vols 1 and 2; vol 2 also includes The dead alive, The fatal cradle, Fatal fortune, Blow up the brig), 1902, 1964 (Limited Editions Club, illustr L. Rosoman, introd by V. Starrett), Boston 1969 (Riverside edn, introd by K. Tillotson), Leipzig 1860 (Tauchnitz vols 525–6). Tr Rus St Petersburg 1860; Fr 1861 (in Le Temps), (by E. D. Forgues), 2 vols Paris 1862 (Hetzel); Ger (by C. Buchele) Stuttgart 1862, 4 vols Vienna 1902; Du Amsterdam 1861, 1866. *See also* Plays, *below*.

For further pbn details, see A. Gasson, The woman in white: a chronological study, *in* WCSJ, *vol 2, 1982.*

No name. First pbd All the Year Round 15 Mar 1862–17 Jan 1863 and Harper's Weekly 15 Mar 1862–24 Jan 1863. 3 vols 1862, 3 vols 1863 (new edn), 1864 (frontispiece by J. E. Millais), 1865, 1866, 1869, 1870, 1872, 1873, 1875, 1876, 1877 (3 new illustrations by A. W. Cooper), 1885, 1886, 1890, 1895, 1896, 1904, 1921, 1928, 1932, 1967 (Doughty Lib no 2, introd by H. van Thal), Oxford 1986 (WCp, ed V. Blain), London 1992 (Folio Soc, illustr A. Pendle, introd by K. Robinson). Boston 2 vols 1863 (Fuller's Illus Lib, 8 illustrations), Richmond VA 1863 (West & Johnson), New York 1863, 1871, 1872, 1873, 1874, 1878 (Seaside Lib vol 13 no 250), 1878 (Union Square Lib no 24), [1883] (Seaside Lib Pocket Edn no 1119), 1899, 1900 (Collier vols 12 and 13; vol 13 also includes Mr Cosway and the landlady, Miss Mina and the groom), [1911], 1978. Leipzig 1863 (Tauchnitz vols 631–3). Tr Rus St Petersburg 1862; Fr (by E. D. Forgues) Paris, Hetzel, 2 vols 1863, 1863 (2nd edn); Ger Leipzig [1893], Du Amsterdam 1863. *See also* Plays, *below*.

My miscellanies. 2 vols 1863, [1874?] (original sheets reissued), 1875 (rearranged, 6-line addition to original preface, omitting Dramatic Grub Street; frontispiece portrait by Halpin and 8 illustrations by A. Concanen), [1877], [1879], 1885, 1893, 1898, 1899, Farnborough 1971. New York 1874, 1893, 1899, 1900 (Collier vol 20). Essays and stories previously pbd in Household Words (HW) or All the Year Round (ATYR).

Individual publication

Vol 1: Talk stoppers (HW 25 Oct 1856); A journey in search of nothing (HW 5 Sep 1857); A queen's revenge (HW 15 Aug 1857, Philadelphia 1866, Boston 1875 (in Alicia Warlock and other stories)); A petition to the novel-writers (HW 6 Dec 1856); Laid up in lodgings (HW 7–14 June 1856); A shockingly rude article (HW 28 Aug 1858); The great (forgotten) invasion (HW 12 Mar 1859); The unknown public (HW 21 Aug 1858); Give us room! (HW 13 Feb 1858); Portrait of an author, painted by his publisher (ATYR 18–25 June 1859); My black mirror (HW 6 Sep 1856, Boston 1875 (in Alicia Warlock)); Mrs Badgery (HW 26 Sep 1857, Leipzig 1857 (in vol 6 of Novels and tales from Household Words, Tauchnitz vol 416), Boston 1875 (in Alicia Warlock).

Vol 2: Memoirs of an adopted son (ATYR 20 Apr 1861, Boston 1875 (in Alicia Warlock); The bachelor bedroom (ATYR 6 Aug 1859); A remarkable revolution (HW 1 Aug 1857); Douglas Jerrold (HW 5 Feb 1859, Leipzig 1859 (in vol 11 of Novels and tales from Household Words, Tauchnitz vol 481)); Pray employ Major Namby! (ATYR 4 June 1859); The poisoned meal (HW 18 Sep–2 Oct 1858, Leipzig 1859 (in vol 10 of Novels and tales from Household Words, Tauchnitz vol 475)); My spinsters (HW 23 Aug 1856); Dramatic Grub Street (HW 6 Mar 1858); To think, or be thought for? (HW 13 Sep 1856); Save me from my friends (HW 16 Jan 1858); The cauldron of oil (ATYR 11 May 1861); Bold words by a bachelor (HW 13 Dec 1856); Mrs Bullwinkle (HW 17 Apr 1858).

Armadale. First pbd Cornhill Mag Nov 1864–June 1866 and Harper's New Monthly Mag Dec 1864–July 1866. 2 Vols 1866 (20 illustrations by G. H. Thomas), 2 vols 1866 (2nd edn), 2 vols 1866 (3rd edn), 1867 (with illus title and 4 other illustrations), 1869, 1871, 1872, 1874, 1876, 1877, 1879, 1884, 1885, 1886, 1890, 1891 (12 illustrations by G. H. Thomas), 1895, 1903, 1908, 1920, Oxford 1989 (WCp, ed C. Peters), London 1992 (Folio Soc, illustr A. Pendle, introd by T. Heald'1995 (Pen). New York 1866, 1871, [1873], 1874, 1893, 1899, 1900 (Collier vols 8, 9), 1902, 1977. Leipzig 1866 (Tauchnitz vols 838–40). Tr Ger Leipzig 1866, 1878; Fr Paris 1867, Du The Hague 1866, 1875, Rus St Petersburg 1871. *See also* Plays, *below*.

The moonstone: a romance. First pbd All the Year Round 4 Jan–8 Aug 1868 and Harper's Weekly 4 Jan–8 Aug 1868. 3 vols 1868, 3 vols 1868 (2nd edn), 1871 (rev text with new preface), 1875, 1876 (9 illustrations by G. du Maurier and F. A. Fraser), 1877, 1891, 1894, 1895, 1895 (with The woman in white), 1896 (with The woman in white), 1897, 1899, 1902, 1907, 1925 (Nelson Classics), 1928 (WC, introd by T. S. Eliot), 1944 (EL no 979, introd by D. L. Sayers), 1951 (Folio Soc, illustr E. La Dell), 1966 (Pen, ed J. I. M. Stewart), 1967 (Pan, introd by A. Burgess), 1982 (WCp, ed A. Trodd), London 1992 (EL, introd by C. Peters), 1992 (Folio Soc, illustr A. Pendle, introd by P. D. James). New York 1868, [1868] (Lovell), [1868] (Burt), 1869, [1873], 1874, 1874 (Garden City Publishing), 1875, 1882 (Lovell's Lib vol 1 nos 8–9), 1898, [189–?] (Burt's Home Lib), 1900, 1900 (Collier vols 6 and 7; vol 7 also includes The new Magdalen), 1905, 1908, [1908] (Burt's Home Lib), 1959 (Limited Editions Club, illustr A. Dignimont, introd by V. Starrett). Leipzig 1868 (Tauchnitz vols 972–3). Tr Rus Moscow 1868, 1873, 1895 and 31 edns 1911–92; Ger in Roman-Magazin des Auslandes 2, 2 vols Berlin 1868, (by E. Lehmann) 2 vols Berlin 1869; Ital Milan 1870; Fr (by Mme La comtesse Gedeon de Clermont-Tonnerre) Paris 1872; Dublin 1933. *See also* Plays, *below*.

Man and wife: a novel. First pbd Cassell's Mag 20 Nov 1869–30 July 1870 and Harper's Weekly 11 Dec 1869–6 Aug 1870. 3 vols 1870.

3 vols 1870 (2nd edn), 3 vols 1870 (3rd edn) 1871 (new preface), 1875 (12 illustrations by W. Small), 1877, 1887, 1889, 1890, 1893, 1897, 1902, 1903, 1907, 1932, Stroud 1990, Oxford 1995 (WCp ed N. Page). New York 1870 (2 states with textual changes), Toronto 1870, New York 1871, [1873], 1874, 1877 (Seaside Lib vol 2 no 22), 1879, 1893, 1899, 1900 (Collier vols 3 and 4; vol 4 also includes Miss or Mrs?, The frozen deep), 1902, 1911, 1916, 1983. Leipzig 1870 (Tauchnitz vols 1103–5). Tr Rus St Petersburg 1870; Du The Hague 1870; Fr (by C. Bernard-Derosne) 2 vols Paris 1872; Ital 2 vols Milan 1877; Ger Leipzig 1872. *See also* Plays, *below*.

Poor Miss Finch: a novel. First pbd in Harper's Weekly 2 Sep 1871–24 Feb 1872 and Cassell's Mag Oct 1871–Mar 1872. 3 vols 1872, 1873 (with 'note to present edition'), 1875 (12 illustrations by G. du Maurier and E. Hughes), 1889, [1890], [1895], 1897, 1906, 1913, Stroud 1994, Oxford 1995 (WCp ed C. Peters). New York 1872 (illus), Toronto 1872?, New York [1873], 1874, 1879 (Seaside Lib vol 32 no 634), 1893, 1899, 1900 (Collier vol 15), 1902. Leipzig 1872 (Tauchnitz vols 1200–1). Tr Rus St Petersburg 1873; Ger Leipzig 1874; Fr 2 vols Paris 1876, 1884.

Miss or Mrs? and other stories in outline. 1873 (with 'Blow up with the brig!': a sailor's story, and The fatal cradle), 1875 (includes A mad marriage, 6 illustrations), 1877, [1887], [1888], 1889, 1894, 1900, 1906, 1925, Stroud 1993. Toronto 1874?, Philadelphia [nd], New York 1891 (Mayfair ser no 3). Leipzig 1872 (Tauchnitz vol 1233, 1st issue without dedication, 2nd issue reset with dedication to Baron von Tauchnitz). Tr Fr Paris 1872; Ger Leipzig 1872; Du The Hague 1872; Rus 1873; Polish Lwow 1873. (Note 1st issue Tauchnitz and Fr edn precede 1st Eng edn).

Individual publication

Miss or Mrs? first pbd Graphic Christmas no 25 Dec 1871 (as Miss or Mrs? a Christmas story in twelve scenes), Harper's Weekly 30 Dec 1871–13 Jan 1872, New York 1900 (Collier vol 4). 'Blow up with the brig!': a sailor's story first pbd in The haunted house in All the Year Round extra Christmas number Dec 1859 (as The ghost in the cupboard room), New York 1900 (Collier vol 2). The fatal cradle: otherwise the heartrending story of Mr Heavysides first pbd in Tom Tiddler's ground in All the Year Round extra Christmas no Dec 1861 (as Picking up waifs at sea), New York 1900 (Collier vol 2). A mad marriage first pbd All the Year Round 17–24 Oct 1874 (as A fatal fortune), London and Boston 1875 (in Lotos leaves), Boston 1875 (as A sane madman, in Alicia Warlock and other stories), New York 1900 (in Collier vol 2).

The new Magdalen: a novel. First pbd Temple Bar Oct 1872–July 1873; Harper's Monthly Oct 1872–June 1873. 2 vols 1873, 1874, 1875 (7 illustrations by G. du Maurier and C. S. Reinhart), [1877], [1883], 1885, 1887, 1889, 1890, 1893, 1894, 1900, 1925, Stroud 1993. New York 1873, Toronto 1873, New York 1874, 1877 (Seaside Lib vol 4 no 76), 1881 (Fireside Lib vol 8 no 92), Chicago 1881, New York [1882] (Lovell's Lib vol 1 no 24), 1900 (Collier vol 7), 1902, 1903. Leipzig 1873 (Tauchnitz vols 1325–6). Tr Rus St Petersburg 1873; Du The Hague 1873; Fr (by C. B. Derosne) Paris 1873.

The frozen deep and other stories. 2 vols 1874 (with The dream woman and John Jago's ghost; or, the dead alive), 2 vols 1874 (original sheets reissued), 1875 (frontispiece by G. du Maurier and 8 illustrations by M. F. Mahoney), [1877], 1885, 1889, 1892, 1905, 1915. Leipzig 1874 (Tauchnitz vols 1455–6). Tr Fr (by C. de Cendrey) Paris 1879; Rus St Petersburg 1874; Du The Hague 1876.

Individual publication

The frozen deep, altered from the play, first pbd Temple Bar Aug–Oct 1874, Toronto 1874 (with The dream-woman, as Readings in America), Boston 1875 (with A terribly strange bed, illustr A. Fredericks), New York 1881 (Seaside Lib vol 48 no 971), 1900 (Collier vol 4); tr Rus July–Aug 1874, 1874, 1875, 1876. The dream woman, altered from the story in The Queen of hearts, first pbd Household Words extra Christmas no Dec 1855 (as The ostler, 2nd pt of The Holly Tree Inn), Toronto 1874, Boston 1875 (as Alicia Warlock in Alicia Warlock and other stories), 1923 (abridged in Little Blue Book no 107); tr Rus 1875. *See also* Plays, *below*. John Jago's ghost; or, the dead alive first pbd Home Jnl 27 Dec 1873–4 Feb 1874, New York Fireside Companion 29 Dec 1873–19 Jan 1874, and Canadian Monthly Jan–Feb 1874; Boston 1874 [1873] (as The dead alive), Toronto 1874 (as The dead alive), New York 7 Aug 1886 (Leisure Hour Lib, as The Morwick farm mystery), 1900 (Collier vol 2); tr Rus 1875, 1911.

The law and the lady: a novel. First pbd Graphic 26 Sep 1874–13 Mar 1875 and Harper's Weekly 10 Oct 1874–27 Mar 1875. 3 vols [Feb] 1876 [1875] 1875 (7 illustrations by S. L. Fildes, S. Hall and F. W. Lawson), [1877], [1884], 1885, 1889, 1898, 1903, 1908, 1913, Oxford 1992 (WCp, ed J. Bourne Taylor). New York 1875, Toronto 1875, Chicago [1876], New York 1877 (Seaside Lib vol 5 no 94), 1899, 1900 (Collier vol 5). Leipzig [Feb] 1875 (Tauchnitz vols 1475–6, precedes first Eng edn?). Tr Rus Moscow 1874–May 1875, 1875, 1877; Fr 2 vols Paris 1875; Du The Hague 1875; Ger Berlin 1875.

The two destinies: a romance. First pbd Harper's Bazar 25 Dec 1875–9 Sep 1876; Temple Bar Jan–Sep 1876. 2 Vols 1876, 1878, [1881], 1887, 1888, 1891, 1892, 1906. New York 1876, Toronto 1876, Chicago 1876 (Lakeside Lib vol 3 no 60), New York 1879 (Seaside Lib no 225), 1881 (Fireside Lib vol 9 no 117), 1883 (Waverley Lib vol 9 no 214), 1893, 1899, 1900 (Collier vol 18, with 5 of Little novels), 1905. Leipzig 1876 (Tauchnitz vol 1590). Tr Rus St Petersburg 1876, 1878; Du The Hague 1877; Ital Milan 1884; Fr Paris 1877, 1878, 1883.

The haunted hotel: a mystery of modern Venice, to which is added My lady's money. 2 vols '1879' [1878] (6 illustrations by A. Hopkins). The haunted hotel first pbd Belgravia Mag June–Nov 1878 and Canadian Monthly July–Dec 1878. [1879] (2nd edn), [1879], [1883], 1889, 1892, 1902, 1909, 1915, Stroud 1990. Toronto 1878 (1st edn in book form), New York 1887 (Seaside Lib Pocket Edn no 977), [1887] (Lovell's Lib no 1003), 1900 (Collier vol 22), 1975. Leipzig 1878 (Tauchnitz vol 1785). Tr Rus St Petersburg 1878; Du The Hague 1879; Fr Paris 1881, 1884, 1889; Ger 2 vols Berlin 1892. My lady's money first pbd Illus London News Christmas no 1877. Stroud 1990. New York 1878 (Harper's Half-Hour ser vol 45), 1885 (Harper's Handy ser, with The ghost's touch, and Percy and the prophet), 1885 (Seaside Lib Pocket Edn no 623), [1898] (Arrow Lib no 58), [nd] (Lovell's Lib no 686), 1978. Leipzig 1877 (Tauchnitz vol 1706, with Percy and the prophet), Tr Rus 1878.

A rogue's life: from his birth to his marriage. First pbd Household Words, 1–29 Mar 1856 as A rogue's life: written by himself (minor changes to text). 1879, 1889, 1890, 1903, Stroud 1984. New York 1879 (Appleton's New Handy-Vol ser), 1879 (Seaside Lib vol 25 no 487), [1890] (Seaside Lib Pocket Edn no 1347), 1893 (Armchair Lib), 1900 (Collier vol 30, with 2 of Little novels), 1985. Leipzig 1856 (in vol 1 of Novels and tales from Household Words conducted by Charles Dickens, Tauchnitz vol 376; 1st book pbn). Tr Sp New York 1892, 1897 (3rd edn).

The fallen leaves: first series. First pbd World 1 Jan–23 July 1879 and Canadian Monthly Feb 1879–Mar 1880. 3 vols 1879. 1880, 1881, 1886, 1889, 1893, 1899, Stroud 1994. Toronto 1879, New York 1900 (Collier vol 21). Leipzig 1879 (Tauchnitz vols 1833–4). Tr Rus Moscow 1880; Ger Berlin 1892.

Jezebel's daughter. First pbd Bolton Weekly Jnl and other syndicated Tillotson jnls Sep 1879–Jan 1880 (adapted from the 1858 play, The red vial). 3 vols 1880, 1880, 1882, 1887, 1889, 1897, 1901. New York 1880 [31 Jan] (Seaside Lib vol 34 no 696; 1st book pbn), 1900 (Collier vol 27). Leipzig 1880 (Tauchnitz vols 1895–6). Tr Rus Jan–July 1880, 1913; Du The Hague 1880.

Considerations on the copyright question addressed to an American friend. 1880. Also pbd Author June 1890 and International Rev (New York) June 1880, rptd Wilkie Collins Soc 1997.

The black robe. First pbd Sheffield & Rotherham Independent Suppl 2 Oct 1880–26 Mar 1881 (specially written for the Independent and other provincial newspapers) and Canadian

Monthly Nov 1880–June 1881. 3 Vols 1881, 3 vols 1881 (2nd edn), 1 vol 1881, [1884], 1885, 1889, 1892, 1897, 1901, Stroud 1994. New York 1881 (Seaside Lib), Chicago [1881], 1882, New York 1900 (Collier vol 23). Leipzig 1881 (Tauchnitz vols 1979–80). Tr Rus St Petersburg 1881, 1882; Ger Berlin 1882.

Heart and science: a story of the present time. First pbd Manchester Weekly Times Suppl and other provincial newspapers 22 July 1882–13 Jan 1883, and Belgravia Aug 1882–June 1883. 3 vols 1883, 1884, 1885, 1890, 1892, 1899, 1913, Stroud 1990. New York 1883 (Seaside Lib vol 76 no 1544; 1st book pbn), [1883] (Lovell's Lib vol 2 no 87), Chicago 1883, Toronto 1883, New York [1884] (Seaside Lib Pocket Edn no 167), Chicago 1888, New York 1900 (Collier vol 25), Toronto 1996 (ed S. Farmer). Melbourne 1883. Leipzig 1883 (Tauchnitz vols 2137–8). Tr Rus 1882?; Du The Hague 1883; Ital (by L. Cerracchini) Milan 1884; Ger Berlin 1886.

'I say no'. First pbd Glasgow Weekly Herald and other provincial newspapers Dec 1883–July 1884, and Harper's Weekly 22 Dec 1883–12 July 1884; London Society Jan–Dec 1884. 3 vols 1884, 1886, 1889, 1891, 1894, 1899, 1906. New York 1884 (1st edn, as 'I say no': or the love-letter answered), 1884 (Lovell's Lib vol 8 no 418), 1884 (Seaside Lib vol 92 no 1856), 1886, 1893, 1899, 1900 (Collier vol 29), 1916. Leipzig 1884 (Tauchnitz vols 2298–9). Tr Rus St Petersburg Mar–Aug 1884, Du The Hague 1884; 1884, 1887; Ger Berlin 1886; Fr (by C. Valdy) Paris 1888.

The evil genius: a domestic story. First pbd Leigh Jnl and Times and other provincial newspapers 11 Dec 1885–11 May 1886. (Prologue pbd separately with the same title, Bolton [1885]). 3 vols 1886. 1887, 1888, 1890, 1892, 1899. New York [1886] (Harper's Handy ser no 72; 1st book pbn), [1886] (Lovell's Lib vol 14 no 722), 1886 (Seaside Lib vol 102 no 2069), [1886] (Seaside Lib Pocket Edn no 764), Chicago 1886 (Donnelly's Lakeside Lib), [1895], New York 1900 (Collier vol 24), ed G. Law Peterborough Ontario 1994, Stroud 1995. Leipzig 1886 (Tauchnitz vols 2421–2). Tr Rus 1887; Ger Berlin 1887.

The guilty river. Bristol 1886 (Arrowsmith's Christmas Annual), 1887 (Bristol Lib no 19), 1899 (Bristol), 1909?, [1911] (Bristol), Stroud 1991. New York 1886 (Harper's Handy ser no 105), 1886 (Seaside Lib Pocket Edn no 896), [1886] (Fireside ser no 13), 1887, Boston 1887, New York [1887] (Lovell's Lib vol 17 no 839). Leipzig 1887 (Tauchnitz vol 2439, The guilty river and The ghost's touch).

Little novels. 3 vols 1887 (14 stories), 1887, London 1889, 1890, 1902. New York 1900 (Collier vols 10, 13, 14, 16, 18, 30), 1977, Melbourne 1887.

Individual publication

Mrs Zant and the ghost first pbd as The ghost's touch in Irish Fireside 30 Sep–14 Oct 1885, Harper's Weekly 23 Oct 1885; New York 1885 (Harper's Handy ser no 30, The ghost's touch and other stories, with My lady's money, and Percy and the prophet), Nottingham [1897] (Mason's Popular Stories no 1); tr Rus Jan 1888; Ital Milan 1895. Miss Morris and the stranger first pbd as How I married him in Spirit of the Times 24 Dec 1881, Belgravia Jan 1882. Mr Cosway and the landlady first pbd as Your money or your life in Belgravia Annual Christmas 1881, People's Lib 17 Dec 1881; New York 1881 (Seaside Lib vol 57 no 1164). Mr Medhurst and the princess first pbd as Royal love in Longman's Mag Christmas 1884. Mr Lismore and the widow first pbd as She loves and lies in Spirit of the Times 22 Dec 1883; New York 1885 (in Tales from many sources vol 4); tr Rus Feb 1884. Miss Jeromette and the clergyman first pbd as The clergyman's confession in World 4–18 Aug 1875, Canadian Monthly Aug–Sep 1875; Boston 1876 (in Golden treasures of poetry, romance, and art), 1880 (in Papyrus leaves). Miss Mina and the groom first pbd as A shocking story in Barnes' International Rev Nov 1878, Belgravia Annual Christmas 1878; New York [1878]. Mr Lepel and the housekeeper first pbd as The girl at the gate in Spirit of the Times 6 Dec 1884, Eng Illus Mag Jan 1885; New York 17 Aug 1885 (Seaside Lib vol 100 no 2030), 17 July 1886 (Leisure Hour Lib). Mr Captain and the nymph first pbd as The Captain's last love in Spirit of the Times 23 Dec 1876, Belgravia Jan 1877; New York 1880 (Seaside Lib vol 35 no 713). Mr Marmaduke and the minister first pbd as The mystery of Marmaduke in Spirit of the Times 28 Dec 1878, Temple Bar Jan 1879; tr Rus Feb 1879. Mr Percy and the prophet first pbd as Percy and the prophet in All the Year Round Extra Summer no 2 July 1877; New York 1877 (Harper's Half-Hour ser), 1885 (Harper's Handy ser no 30, in The ghost's touch and other stories); Leipzig 1877 (Tauchnitz vol 1706, with My lady's money). Miss Bertha and the Yankee first pbd as The duel in Herne Wood in Spirit of the Times 22 Dec 1877; New York 1880 (Seaside Lib vol 44 no 905); tr Rus 1878. Miss Dulane and my Lord first pbd as An old maid's husband in Spirit of the Times 25 Dec 1886, Belgravia Annual 1887. Mr Policeman and the cook first pbd as Who killed Zebedee? in Spirit of the Times 25 Dec 1880; New York 26 Jan 1881 (Seaside Lib vol 45 no 928).

The legacy of Cain. First pbd in Leigh Jnl and Times and other Tillotson syndicated newspapers Feb–July 1888. 3 vols '1889' [1888], Bolton [nd], 1889, 1891, 1915, 1932, Stroud 1993. New York 1888 (Lovell's Lib no 1176), [July] 1888 (both Harper and Lovell preceded Eng edn), 1888 (Seaside Lib Pocket Edn no 1095), 1900 (Collier vol 26). Leipzig 1888 (Tauchnitz vols 2554–5). Tr Du 1889, Ital (by L. Ceracchini) Milan 1890.

Blind love. Preface by Sir Walter Besant, 16 illustrations by A. Forestier. First pbd Illus London News 6 July–28 Dec 1889. Weekly parts 1–18 (to Ch 48) by Collins, completed by Besant (to Ch 64 and Epilogue), based on detailed synopsis prepared by Collins; also pbd in Penny Illus Paper from 12 Oct 1889. 3 Vols 1890, 3 vols 1890 (2nd edn), 1890, 1890 (special edn for sale only in India and Br colonies), 1891, 1907, 1910. New York 1890 (Appleton's Town & Country Lib), 1890 (Hurst) 1900 (Collier vol 28). Leipzig 1890 (Tauchnitz vols 2629–30). Tr Ger Stuttgart 1890.

The lazy tour of two idle apprentices; No thoroughfare; The perils of certain English prisoners. 1890 (with C. Dickens, 8 illustrations by A. Layard), 1895 (photolithographs redrawn).

Individual publication

The lazy tour of two idle apprentices first pbd Household Words 3–31 Oct 1857 Harper's Weekly 31 Oct–28 Nov 1857 and Leipzig 1857 (in vol 6 of Novels and tales from Household Words, Tauchnitz vol 416); Philadelphia [1857] (as The two apprentices with a history of their lazy tour, by Dickens), New York [1884] (by Dickens), Boston 1876 (in Christmas stories), New York 1896 (Reprinted pieces and The lazy tour of two idle apprentices, by Dickens). No thoroughfare first pbd in extra Christmas no of All the Year Round, 12 Dec 1867, and in extra Christmas no of Every Saturday (Boston), Dec 1867; Boston 1876 (in Christmas stories comprising No thoroughfare and The lazy tour of two idle apprentices); Leipzig 1868 (Tauchnitz vol 961); tr Rus Jan 1868, 1909; Swed Stockholm 1868; Sp Madrid [1890], Barcelona (by G. de Ayarza) [1923]. The perils of certain English prisoners first pbd in extra Christmas no of Household Words, Dec 1857, and Leipzig 1858 (in vol 7 of Novels and tales from Household Words, Tauchnitz vol 427); Philadelphia 1858 (by C. Dickens), 1871 (by Dickens and Collins).

Plays

A court duel!: a drama in three acts, adapted from the French by Collins (Soho Theatre 26 Feb 1850). Not pbd.

The lighthouse: a domestic melo-drama in two acts (Tavistock House 16 June 1855, priv performance; Royal Olym 10 Aug 1857). Not pbd. New York (New Theatre 21 Jan 1858).

The frozen deep: a drama in three acts (Tavistock House 6 Jan 1857). Not pbd. (Royal Olym 27 Oct 1866); rev 1866 (ptd but not pbd). *See* Under the management of Mr Charles Dickens: his production of The frozen deep, ed R. L. Brannan, Ithaca NY 1966.

The red vial: a drama in three acts (Royal Olym 11 Oct 1858). Not pbd. Plot used for Jezebel's daughter, 1880.

The woman in white (Surrey Theatre 3 Nov 1860); a drama in three acts (Leicester, Theatre Royal, 26 Aug 1870) (not pbd); in a prologue and four acts (Olym 9 Oct 1871). Rev and pbd by the author 1871. Reviews pbd in Specimens of criticism extracted from notices of 'The woman in white' in the press, 1871.

A message from the sea: a drama in three acts, with C. Dickens (Brit 7 Jan 1861). 1861; by J. Brougham, a drama in four acts, Dicks 459.

No name: a drama in five acts, by W. B. Bernard (not produced). 1863; 1870, a drama in four acts, pbd by the author. New York (Fifth Ave Theatre 7 June 1871, produced only in USA); De Witt 104.

Armadale: a drama in three acts altered from the novel (not produced). 1866 (25 copies pbd for the author); as Miss Gwilt: a drama in five acts (Liverpool, Alexandra 9 Dec 1875) (ptd but not pbd).

No thoroughfare: a drama in five acts, with C. Dickens (Theatre Royal Adel 26 Dec 1867). 1867; as L'abime (Vaudeville, Paris 2 June 1868) 1868; Dicks 1052. New York [1868], as Identity: or no thoroughfare by L. Lequel, French 348; De Witt 14.

Black and white: a love story in three acts, with C. Fechter (Theatre Royal Adel 29 Mar 1869). 1869 (ptd but not pbd). New York, De Witt 296.

Man and wife: a dramatic story in four acts (Prince of Wales 22 Feb 1873). 1870 (pbd by the author). (Opera House, Green Bay WI 8 Jan 1870) Ames 4, 1873; New York (Fifth Ave Theatre 13 Sep 1870).

The new Magdalen: a dramatic story in a prologue and three acts. (Olym 19 May 1873). 1873 (pbd by the author). New York (10 Nov 1873); Ames 112, 1882.

The dream woman: a mystery in four narratives and two parts (altered and enlarged for reading in public). 1873 (priv ptd for Collins's tour of the USA).

The dead secret, by E. J. Bramwell, adapted by the author's express permission (Royal Lyc 29 Aug 1877). 1877.

The moonstone: a dramatic story in three acts (Royal Olym 17 Sep 1877). 1877 (priv ptd for the convenience of the author, not pbd).

Rank and riches: a play in four acts and five tableaux (Adel 9 June 1883). Not pbd.

The evil genius (Vaudeville 30 Oct 1885, single performance to establish copyright). Not pbd.

For further bibliographical details of plays, see Sadleir 1922, and Parrish and Miller 1940, both under Bibliographies, *above, and* IELM. *For personal recollections of Collins and his plays, see §2, below.*

Miscellaneous works

Memorandum, relating to the life and writings of Wilkie Collins, 21 Mar 1862. In a letter to an unidentified Frenchman, quoted in Parrish and Miller (*see* Bibliographies, *above*).

Proceedings at the twentieth anniversary festival of the Royal General Theatrical Fund held April 12th, 1865. Report of Collins's speech, pbd Aug 1865.

A little fable [c. 1880]. Pbd by the Wilkie Collins Society July 1996.

Recollections of Charles Fechter, 18 Jan 1882. Ch in Charles Albert Fechter, by Kate Field.

Collins, Charles Allston (1828–1873) in Dictionary of National Biography 1882.

Love's random shot. New York 1884 (Seaside Lib vol 87 no 1770), 1884 (Seaside Lib Pocket Edn no 175), 1894 (with other stories, including The dream woman).

The use of gas in theatres or the air and the audience: considerations on the atmospheric influence of theatres. Written in 1881 and pbd New York 1885; rptd in The Mask 10 1924, Florence 1924, and WCSJ vol 6 1986.

Contribution to The art of authorship, literary reminiscences, methods of work, and advice to young beginners, ed G. Bainton, 1890.

Contributions to periodicals

Illuminated Magazine

The last stage coachman. Aug 1843; rptd Wilkie Collins Society Nov 1990.

Bentley's Miscellany

The twin sisters. Mar 1851.
A pictorial tour to St George Bosherville. May 1851 rptd WCS 1996.
The exhibition of the Royal Academy. 1 June 1851 rptd WCS 1999.
The picture galleries of England 1, The Earl of Ellesmere's collection. 1 July 1851.
The picture galleries of England 2, Northumberland House and Syon House. 1 Aug 1851.
The picture galleries of England 3, Dulwich Gallery. 1 Oct 1851.
A passage in the life of Mr Perugino Potts. Feb 1852
Nine o'clock. Aug 1852.

The Leader

A plea for Sunday reform. 27 Sep 1851.
Magnetic evenings at home: Letter I. To G. H. Lewes. 17 Jan 1852.
Magnetic evenings at home: Letter II. To G. H. Lewes. 14 Feb 1852.
Magnetic evenings at home: Letter III. To G. H. Lewes. 21 Feb 1852.
Magnetic evenings at home: Letter IV. To G. H. Lewes. 28 Feb 1852.
Magnetic evenings at home: Letter V. To G. H. Lewes. 6 Mar 1852.
Magnetic evenings at home: Letter VI. To G. H. Lewes. 13 Mar 1852.
The incredible not always impossible: To G. H. Lewes. 3 Apr 1852.
A word about a painted window. 11 Mar 1854.
La primise. 17 June 1854.
The courier of Lyons. 1 July 1854.
The arts. 8 July 1854.
A second batch of new books. 8 July 1854.
Les diamans de la Couronne. 15 July 1854.
Theatres. 29 July 1854.
Chaucer. 23 Dec 1854.
A batch of fictions. 6 Jan 1855.
William Etty, R.A. 27 Jan 1855.
The British Institution. 10 Feb 1855.
A new bookselling dodge. 10 Feb 1855.
Untitled paragraph in Literature section. 10 Feb 1855.
The warden. 17 Feb 1855.
Geoffrey Crayon's new sketch-book. 24 Feb 1855.
Four novels. 24 Mar 1855.
Mr Silk Buckingham. 31 Mar 1855.
The British artists. 21 Apr 1855.
A queer story. 16 June 1855 (in Suppl to The Leader).
The novels of M. Hendrick Conscience. 18 Aug 1855.
M. Forgues on the caricaturists of England. 25 Aug 1855.
For other works in The Leader *possibly by Collins, see Beetz,* Wilkie Collins and The Leader *(under* Bibliographies, *above).*

Household words

The National Gallery and the old masters. 25 Oct 1856.
The wreck of the Golden Mary. Extra Christmas no, Dec 1856 (with C. Dickens); New York Dec 1856 (*see* Dickens, *col 1238*).
A fair penitent. 18 July 1857.
The debtor's best friend. 19 Sep 1857.
Deep design on society. 2 Jan 1858.
The little Huguenot. 9 Jan 1858.
Thanks to Doctor Livingstone. 23 Jan 1858.
Strike! 6 Feb 1858.
A sermon for Sepoys. 27 Feb 1858.
A shy scheme. 20 Mar 1858.
Awful warning to bachelors. 27 Mar 1858.
Sea-breezes with the London smack. 4 Sep 1858.
Highly proper! 2 Oct 1858.
A clause for the new Reform Bill. 9 Oct 1858 (with C. Dickens).
Doctor Dulcamara, MP. 18 Dec 1858 (with C. Dickens).

Over the way, Trottle's report and (with C. Dickens) Let at last. In A house to let, extra Christmas no, Dec 1858.
Pity a poor Prince. 15 Jan 1859.
Burns. Viewed as a hat-peg. 12 Feb 1859.
A column to Burns. 26 Feb 1859.
A breach of British privilege. 19 Mar 1859.
A dramatic author. 28 May 1859.

All the Year Round
Sure to be healthy, wealthy and wise. 30 Apr 1859.
Occasional register. 30 Apr 1859 (with C. Dickens).
Occasional register. 7 May 1859 (with E. Yates).
The Royal Academy in Bed. 28 May 1859.
My advisers [?]. 18 June 1859.
The second sitting. 25 June 1859.
New view of society. 20 Aug 1859.
Small shot: cooks at college [?]. 29 Oct 1859.
My boys [?], 28 Jan 1860.
My girls [?], 11 Feb 1860.
Vidocq, French detective. 14–21 July 1860.
Boxing-Day. 22 Dec 1860.
A message from the sea. Extra Christmas no, Dec 1860 (with C. Dickens and others).
A night in the jungle. 3 Aug 1861.
A trial at Toulouse [?], 15 Feb 1862.
Notes of interrogation [?]. 10 May 1862.
Suggestions from a maniac. 13 Feb 1864.
To let. 18 June 1864.
The dead lock in Italy. 8 Dec 1866.

The World
The law and the lady (letter to the editor). 24 Mar 1875; rptd in appendix to WCp, 1992.

Spirit of the Times
The devil's spectacles. 20 Dec 1879. New York 25 June 1880 (Seaside Lib no 745 as The magic spectacles); 20–27 Dec 1884 in Bolton Weekly Jnl and other syndicated papers.
Fie! Fie! or the fair physician. 23 Dec 1882 (pbd simultaneously in special Christmas Suppl to Pictorial World). New York 5 Apr 1883 (Seaside Library no 1587).
The poetry did it: an event in the life of Major Evergreen. 26 Dec 1885 (and in Eng Illus Mag, Jan 1886).
The first officer's confession. 24 Dec 1887 (and in Bow Bells).

Pall Mall Gazette
Books necessary for a liberal education. 11 Feb 1886.
Wilkie Collins about Charles Dickens, from a marked copy of Forster's 'Dickens'. 20 Jan 1890; excerpts rptd in K. Robinson, Wilkie Collins, 1951.

Youth's Companion
Victims of circumstances discovered in records of old trials. 19 Aug 1886 (also pbd Boys' Own Paper, Oct 1886 and Sep 1887); rptd by Wilkie Collins Soc, Nov 1992.

The Globe
How I write my books. 26 Nov 1887; rptd as appendix C to Riverside edn of The woman in white, Boston 1969 and as appendix D to the World's Classics edn of The woman in white 1980.

Universal Review
Reminiscences of a story-teller. June 1888; rptd by Wilkie Collins Soc, Oct 1991.

Attributed and spurious works
John Jasper's secret: sequel to Edwin Drood, by Charles Dickens, the younger, and Wilkie Collins [H. Morford]. New York 1871, rptd 1898, 1901, 1905 (correctly attributed).

Parodies ('iana' and imitations)
Slow thoroughfare by Warles Chickens and Chilky Dollins. Banter 23 Dec 1867.
No thoroughfare; the book in eight acts. Mask vol 1, Feb 1868.
Parodies of Collins's titles in Punch 7–14 Mar 1868, rptd in Mokeanna! by F. C. Burnand, 1873.
The moonstone and moonshine. Mask vol 1, Aug 1868.
No thoroughfare by C—s D—s. Boston 1868, 1868 (2nd edn) (Bellamy Brownjohn & Domby).
No title by W—lk—e C—ll—ns. By Bret Harte, in Condensed novels, Boston 1871.
The Gwilty governess and the downy doctor; or, another good lady help gone wrong! A new sensation drama, in one prologue and two compartments by G. M. Layton (Brighton, Theatre Royal 31 July 1876).
Parody in The Bird o' Freedom, ed John Corlett, 13 Aug 1879.
The woman in tights by Wilkie Collins. By W. E. Rose, Weekly Dispatch 25 Feb 1883 (300-word parody competition).
See also Dickens, *col 1181*.

Adaptations
Films
The Moonstone. 1909, 1915 silent versions; USA 1934.
The new Magdalen. 1910, 1912, 1913, 1914 silent versions.
The dead secret. 1913. Directed by Stanner E. V. Taylor.
Armadale. 1916. Directed by Richard Garrick.
She loves and lies. 1920.
The woman in white. 1929. The last of several silent versions from 1912 with various titles such as The dream woman and Twin pawns; and as Crimes at the Dark House 1940; and The woman in white, USA 1948.
A terribly strange bed. Poland 1968. Directed by Witold Lesiewicz.
Basil. 1997. Direted by Radha Bharadwaj.

Television
The moonstone. 1959, 1972, 1996 (BBC); 1994 (Ger).
The woman in white. 1982, 1997 (BBC), 1994 (Ger).
Armadale. 1994 (Ger).

Radio
A terribly strange bed. Mar 1946.
Armadale. Apr 1948.
No name. 15 June–29 Aug 1952.
Poor Miss Finch, 1952.
The dream woman, July 1954.
Mr Lepel and the housekeeper. 19–23 July 1954.
Miss Bertha and the Yankee. 26–30 July 1954.
Blow up with the brig!. Sep 1957.
The dead secret. 1957, 1977.
The woman in white. 12 Oc t–28 Dec 1969.
A rogue's life. July 1979.
The moonstone. 14 Oct–18 Nov 1979; other adaptations from the mid 1940s.
Mrs Zant and the ghost. Aug 1982.
Basil. 1983.
Radio biography. Sep 1989.
No name. 22 Sep–27 Oct 1989, repeated 1995.
The dream woman. 3 Nov 1989.
The biter bit. 10 Nov 1989.
A terribly strange bed. 17 Nov 1989.
The stolen letter, 24 Nov 1989.
The dead hand. 1 Dec 1989.
Little novels. 31 Dec 1997–28 Jan 1998.
Mr Percy and the prophet. 21 Nov 1998.

§2
For additional material, see K. H. Beetz, Wilkie Collins: an annotated bibliography,1889–1976, *Metuchen NJ 1978; N. Page (ed),* Wilkie Collins:

the critical heritage, *1974; C. Peters,* The king of inventors: a life of Wilkie Collins *1991.*
Dickens, C. Letters of Charles Dickens. ed M. Dickens and G. Hogarth 1880–2; *see also* Pilgrim edn, ed M. House and G. Storey, Oxford 1965– .
Forgues, E.-D. William Wilkie Collins. Revue des Deux Mondes Nov 1855.
Yates, E. Men of mark: no 2 – W. Wilkie Collins. Train June 1857.
Wilkie Collins. Appleton's Jnl 3 Sep 1870.
Ainger, A. Mr Dickens's amateur theatricals: a reminiscence. Macmillan's Mag Jan 1871; rptd in Lectures and essays, 1905.
Forster, J. The life of Charles Dickens. 3 vols 1872–4; ed J. W. T. Ley 1928.
Jehu jun [T. G. Bowles], Men of the day, no 39, Mr Wilkie Collins. Vanity Fair 3 Feb 1872.
Mr Wilkie Collins. Once a Week 24 Feb 1872.
Olympic Theatre. The Times 21 May 1873 (review of The new Magdalen).
Wilkie Collins. Illus Rev 10 July 1873.
Mr Wilkie Collins's new novel. World 24 Feb 1875 (The law and the lady).
Mr Wilkie Collins and The Graphic. World 17 Mar 1875.
Celebrities at home no 81, Mr Wilkie Collins in Gloucester Place. World 26 Dec 1877.
Cooper, T. Wilkie Collins, Esq. Men of Mark fifth ser 1881.
Cook, D. The theatre: rank and riches. World 13 June 1883.
Kosmos [T. H. S. Escott]. Letters to eminent persons no 72, Mr Wilkie Collins. World 6 June 1883.
Trollope, A. An autobiography. 1883.
Von Wolzogen, E. Wilkie Collins: ein biographisch-kritischerver-such. Leipzig 1885.
Reade, C. L. and C. Charles Reade: a memoir. 1887.
Bancroft, S. and M. Mr and Mrs Bancroft: on and off the stage. 1888.
Quilter, H. A living story-teller. Contemporary Rev Apr 1888.
Death of Mr Wilkie Collins. Daily Telegraph 24 Feb 1889. Obituary.
Death of Mr Wilkie Collins. The Times 24 Feb 1889. Obituary.
The late Mr Wilkie Collins. Daily News 24 Feb 1889. Obituary.
Wilkie Collins dead. New York Times 24 Feb 1889. Obituary.
Yates, E. In memoriam – W. W. C. obit September 23rd 1889. World 25 Sep 1889.
The late Mr Wilkie Collins. Illus London News 28 Feb 1889.
Mr Wilkie Collins. Saturday Rev 28 Sep 1889. Obituary.
Wilkie Collins' last days. New York World 29 Sep 1889.
Caine, H. Wilkie Collins: personal recollections. Globe 4 Oct 1889.
Quilter, H. In memoriam amici. Universal Rev Oct 1889; rptd in Preferences in art, life and literature, 1892.
Lang, A. Mr Wilkie Collins's novels. Contemporary Rev Jan 1890.
Yates, E. The novels of Wilkie Collins. Temple Bar Aug 1890.
Swinburne, A. C. Wilkie Collins. Fortnightly Rev 52, Nov 1889; rptd in his Studies in prose and poetry, 1894. Obituary.
Dickens, C. Letters to Wilkie Collins. Selected by G. Hogarth, ed L. Hutton, 1892, New York 1892.
Beard, N. Some recollections of yesterday. Temple Bar July 1894.
Fitzgerald, P. Memoirs of an author. 1895.
Anderson, M. A few memories. 1896, New York 1896.
Waugh, A. Wilkie Collins: and his mantle. Academy and Lit 5 Apr 1902.
Cumming Walters, J. Books and their makers: a chat about Wilkie Collins. Ideas 22 July 1905.
Melville, L. Wilkie Collins. Temple Bar Sep 1903; rptd in Victorian novelists, 1906.
Reeve, W. Recollections of Wilkie Collins. Chambers's Jnl June 1906.
Caine, H. My story. 1908.
Lehmann, R. C. Memories of half a century. 1908.
Shore, W. T. Charles Dickens and his friends. 1909.
Winter, W. Old friends. New York 1909.
Fitz-Gerald, S. J. A. Dickens and the drama. 1910.
Archer, F. An actor's notebooks. 1912.
Compton-Rickett, A. Wilkie Collins. Bookman June 1912.
Lehmann, R. C. Charles Dickens as editor. 1912.
Winter, W. The wallet of time. New York 1913.
Crotch, W. W. The secret of Dickens. 1919.
Phillips, W. C. Dickens, Reade and Collins: sensation novelists. New York 1919.
Eliot, T. S. Wilkie Collins and Charles Dickens. TLS 4 Aug 1927; rptd in Selected essays: 1917–1932, 1932.
Ellis, S. M. Wilkie Collins, Le Fanu and others. 1931.
Sehlbach, H. Untersuchungen über die Romanskunst von Wilkie Collins. Jena 1931.

Biographies

Robinson, K. Wilkie Collins. 1951, 1974.
Davis, N. P. The life of Wilkie Collins. Urbana IL 1956.
Sayers, D. L. Wilkie Collins: a critical and biographical study. Ed R. L. Gregory Toledo OH 1977. Unfinished.
Clarke, W. M. The secret life of Wilkie Collins. 1988.
Peters, C. The King of inventors: a life of Wilkie Collins, 1991.
The Wilkie Collins Society Journal (WCSJ) 1981–1991; n.s. 1998– publishes biographical, critical, bibliographical and related material on Collins and his contemporaries. [AG]

Thomas Cooper 1805–92

See col 603.

Catherine Crowe, née Stevens 1800?–76

Bibliographies

Summers, M. In his A Gothic bibliography, [1941].

§1

Aristodemus: a tragedy. Edinburgh 1838.
Adventures of Susan Hopley: or circumstantial evidence. 3 vols 1841, 1 vol 1852 (sub-title differs).
Men and women: or manorial rights. 3 vols 1844.
The Seeress of Prevorst. 1845. From the Ger of A. J. C. Kerner.
The story of Martha Guinnis and her son. In The Edinburgh tales, ed C. I. Johnstone, vol 1, 1845.
The story of Lilly Dawson. 3 vols 1847, 1 vol 1852.
Pippie's warning: or mind your temper. 1848.
The night side of nature: or ghosts and ghost seers. 2 vols 1848, 1 vol 1882, [1892], [1904], Wellingborough 1986, 2 vols Stuttgart 1849 (Ger trn by C. Kolb).
Light and darkness: or mysteries of life. 3 vols 1850.
The adventures of a beauty. 3 vols 1852, 1 vol 1873.
The juvenile Uncle Tom's Cabin arranged for young readers. 1853, 1868 (as Uncle Tom's Cabin for children). From the novel by Harriet Beecher Stowe.
The cruel kindness: a romantic play in five acts. 1853.
Linny Lockwood: a novel. 2 vols 1854, 1 vol 1857.
Ghosts and family legends: a volume for Christmas. 1859.
Spiritualism and the age we live in. 1859.
The story of Arthur Hunter and his first shilling; with other tales. [1861.]
The adventures of a monkey: an interesting narrative. 1862. Also contains Blind Willie.
The lost portrait. In The midnight journey and other tales, 1871.

§2

Sergeant, A. In her Women novelists of Queen Victoria's reign, 1897.
Clapton, G. T. Baudelaire and Catherine Crowe. MLR 25 1930.
Hughes, R. Une étape de l'esthétique de Baudelaire: Catherine Crowe. Revue de Littérature Comparée 17 1937. [EH]

Charles Dickens 1812–70

Manuscripts

Most of the mss of Dickens's works are in the Forster Collection at the Victoria and Albert Museum, London; a small quantity, including a few leaves of Pickwick, *in BL; the ms of* Great expectations *in Wisbech Museum; and that of* Our mutual friend *in Pierpont Morgan Lib, New York; others in various libs or in private hands. The Forster Collection includes corrected proof-sheets and similar matter. A considerable number of letters, many still unpbd, are in private collections. See ms survey by A. Nisbet in* Victorian fiction: a guide to research, *below. For a convenient summary of the chief miscellaneous documents in private hands, see* B. Currie, Fishers of Books, Boston 1931. *Dickens's private life, which entered largely into his work, is illustrated in various museums connected with his name, notably Dickens House (48 Doughty St, London WC1 2 LF), the Birthplace Museum, Portsmouth, and Eastgate House, Rochester. The sale catalogues of his effects have been ptd and annotated. Dickens's mss, notes and corrected proofs from the Forster Collection, along with edns, imitations, etc from the Dexter Collection, are available elsewhere in microfilm copies.*

Charles Dickens's book of memoranda. Ed. F. Kaplan, New York 1981.

Smith, H. B. How Dickens wrote his books. Harper's Mag Dec 1924, rptd Strand Mag Feb 1925. Facs.

Ford, G. H. Dickens's notebook and Edwin Drood. Nineteenth Cent Fiction 6 1952.

Aylmer, F. John Forster and Dickens's memorandum book. Dickensian 51 1955. Reply by P. Pakenham, ibid.

Dickens' working notes for his novels. Ed with introd by H. Stone. Chicago 1987.

Bibliographies and reference works

Items dealing with single works or special subjects are included in the appropriate sections below. Many of the biographical and critical works listed below contain valuable bibliographies.

Catalogue of the beautiful collection of modern pictures, water-colour drawings and objects of art of Dickens, which will be sold by auction by Messrs Christie, Manson & Woods. [1870]; rptd in Dickens memento, 1884, and in Stonehouse's Catalogue, 1935, *below*.

Gad's Hill Place, Higham, by Rochester: catalogue of the household furniture, linen, about 200 dozen of superior wines and liquors, china, glass, horse, carriages, greenhouse plants, and other effects of the late Charles Dickens, which will be sold by auction by Messrs Thomas & Homan. Rochester [1870]. BM copy has buyers' names and prices in ms.

Charles Dickens's manuscripts. Chambers's Jnl 10 Nov 1877.

Pierce, G. A. The Dickens dictionary: a key to the characters and principal incidents in the tales of Dickens. Boston 1872; rptd with preface by C. Dickens jr 1878; 1880, 1894 (with addns by W. A. Wheeler), 1926, New York 1965 (rev), New York 1972.

De Fontaine, F. G. A cyclopaedia of the best thoughts of Dickens. 1873, 1883 (enlarged as The Fireside Dickens).

Forster, J. In his Life of Dickens vol 3, 1874.

Cook, J. Bibliography of the writings of Dickens. 1879.

[Shepherd, R. H.] The bibliography of Dickens. Manchester [1880]; rev and enlarged edns in Shepherd, Speeches of Dickens, 1884; and in his Plays and poems of Dickens vol 2, 1885.

Dickens memento: catalogue with purchasers' names and prices realised of the pictures, drawings and objects of art of the late Charles Dickens. Introd by F. Phillimore, Hints to collectors by J. F. Dexter [1884].

Johnson, C. P. Hints to collectors of original editions of the works of Dickens. 1885. *See* J. H. Slater's entries on Dickens in his Early editions, 1894.

Kitton, F. G. Dickensiana: a bibliography of the literature relating to Dickens and his writings. 1886, New York 1971. *See* C. F. Carty, Some addenda to Kitton's Dickensiana, Lib Collector 5 1903.

Victoria and Albert Museum, South Kensington. A catalogue of the printed books bequeathed by John Forster. 1888.

Victoria and Albert Museum. A catalogue of the paintings, manuscripts, autograph letters, pamphlets etc, bequeathed by Forster. 1893.

Kitton, F. G. The novels of Dickens: a bibliography and sketch. 1897, New York 1975.

Chapman & Hall Ltd. The works of Dickens and Thomas Carlyle, with full particulars of each edition and biographical introductions. [1900]. *See* B. W. Matz, Two great Victorian writers (Dickens and Carlyle). 1905. Describes the Chapman & Hall collected edns.

Eaton, S. (ed). Dickens rare print collection. Philadelphia [1900] (priv ptd).

Kitton, F. G. The minor writings of Dickens: a bibliography and sketch. 1900, New York 1970. *See* bibliography of Kitton's writings on Dickens, Dickensian 1 1905.

Dickens Fellowship, London. Dickens exhibition held at the Memorial Hall London, opened by P. Fitzgerald: catalogue of exhibits. Ed F. G. Kitton 1903.

Thomson, J. C. Bibliography of the writings of Dickens. Warwick 1904.

The Dickensian. 1905– . In progress. Index 1905–34, 1935; 1935–60, 1961. Cumulative analytical index 1905–74, compiled by F. T. Dunn, Hassocks 1976.

Williams, M. The Dickens concordance. 1907, Folcroft PA 1970, New York 1970.

Dickens Fellowship. The second Dickens exhibition at the New Dudley Gallery: catalogue with an introduction by J. W. T. Ley and P. Fitzgerald. 1908.

Dickens Fellowship. Catalogue of the third Dickens exhibition at the New Dudley Gallery, with an introduction by P. Fitzgerald. 1909.

Philip, A. J. A Dickens dictionary. 1909, Gravesend 1928 (rev and enlarged by W. L. Gadd), New York 1970.

Hammerton, J. A. The Dickens companion: a book of anecdote and reference. [1910]. Vol 18 of Charles Dickens Lib.

Brooklyn Public Library, New York. Dickens: a list of books and of references to periodicals in the Brooklyn Public Library. Brooklyn 1912.

Franklin Club of St Louis. An exhibition of books, prints, drawings, manuscripts and letters commemorative of the centenary of Dickens. [St Louis 1912].

Fyfe, T. A. Who's who in Dickens: a complete Dickens repertory in Dickens' own words. [1912], New York 1971, Folcroft PA 1971.

Pugh, E. W. The Dickens originals. 1912.

Victoria and Albert Museum. The Dickens exhibition, March to October 1912. 1912, 1912 (not illus).

Eckel, J. C. The first editions of the writings of Dickens: a bibliography. 1913, 1932 (rev and enlarged), New York 1972, Folcroft PA 1973, Havertown PA 1976. For criticism, *see* TLS 26 Jan 1933; Dickensian 9 1913 and 29 1933; Publisher's Weekly 31 Mar 1934; and A new Dickens bibliography, Dickensian 39–41 1943–5.

Grolier Club, New York. Catalogue of an exhibition of the works of Dickens. New York 1913 (introd by R. Cortissoz).

Anderson Galleries, New York. Dickens collection, Thackeray collection etc from the library of E. W. Coggeshall of New York. 2 vols New York 1916. A collection of autograph letters; Lib of Congress copy has prices in ms.

Dibelius, W. Dickens. Leipzig 1916, 1926 (rev). Extensive bibliography.

Miller, W. and T. W. Hill. Dickens's manuscripts. Dickensian 13 1917. Their locations listed.

Rosenbach, A. S. W. (ed). A catalogue of the writings of Dickens in the library of Harry Elkins Widener. Philadelphia 1918 (priv ptd). With texts of many letters and publishers' agreements; collection

now at Harvard. *See* E. Wolf and J. Fleming, Rosenbach: a biography, 1961.
American Art Assoc. The renowned collection of Dickens and Thackeray formed by George Barr McCutcheon. New York [1920].
Newton, A. E. The amenities of book collecting. 1920.
Cowan, R. E. and W. A. Clark jr (ed). The library of William Andrews Clark jr: vols 10–11, Cruikshank and Dickens. San Francisco 1921–3.
Dibelius, W. The Dickens collection formed by the late R. T. Jupp of London. New York 1922. *See* Sotheran's catalogue, Piccadilly ser 68 [1920]: the Dickens collection formed by R. T. Jupp, and relics of Mrs Winter.
Dibelius, W. The Dickens collection of the late W. G. Wilkins of Pittsburgh, Pennsylvania. New York 1922.
Sargent, G. H. Dickensiana in America. Bookman's Jnl Apr 1922.
Spencer, W. T. Dickensiana. In his Forty years in my bookshop, 1923.
Arnold, W. H. Ventures in book collecting. New York 1923.
Hopkins, A. A. and F. R. Newbury. A Dickens atlas. 1923.
Hayward, A. L. The Dickens encyclopaedia. 1924.
de Suzannet, A. Oeuvres de Dickens. Vol 1 of his Catalogue d'un choix de livres imprimés et manuscrits. 4 vols Biarritz 1925 (priv ptd).
British Library. Dickens: an excerpt from the general catalogue. 1926, 1960, 1975, 1996 (CD-Rom version).
American Art Assoc. The renowned collection of the works of Dickens formed by Thomas Hatton of Leicester, England. New York 1927. *See* Sotheby catalogue of the Hatton collection, [1931].
Delattre, F. Dickens et la France. Paris 1927.
American Art Assoc. The renowned collection of the works of Dickens formed by Mr and Mrs Edward C. Daoust. New York 1929.
Edgar, H. L. and R. W. G. Vail. Early American editions of the works of Dickens. BNYPL 33 1929; rptd with C. W. Cavanaugh, Charles Dickens, New York 1929.
Stevens, J. S. Quotations and references in Dickens. Boston 1929.
American Art Assoc. A Dickens collection of superlative merit: the library of Frederick W. Lehmann, St Louis. New York 1930.
Darwin, B. The Dickens advertiser. 1930, New York 1971.
Currie, B. John Forster and the Dickens manuscripts. In his Fishers of Books, Boston 1931.
Hatton, T. and A. H. Cleaver. A bibliography of the periodical works of Dickens, bibliographical, analytical and statistical. 1933, New York 1973. Illus, with facs. *See* E. B. Haynes, Dickensian 30 1934.
Rubens, C. The dummy library of Dickens at Gad's Hill Place; recollections of a pilgrimage as narrated to J. C. Bay. Chicago 1934 (priv ptd). *See* L. C. Staples, Dickensian 54 1958.
Unique items in famous Dickens collections. Dickensian 30–2 1934–6.
Stonehouse, J. H. (ed). Catalogue of the library of Dickens from Gadshill, sold by Sotheby's in 1878; rptd from Sotheran's Price current of literature, 1935. Valuable for listing of annotated public-reading copies; *see* Stonehouse's bibliography of reading edns in his Sikes and Nancy, 1921.
Pierce, D. Special bibliography: the stage versions of Dickens's novels. BB 16 1936.
Sawyer, C. J. A Dickens library: exhibition catalogue of the Sawyer collection. [Letchworth 1936] (priv ptd). *See* Sawyer's sales catalogues of 1931, 1936 and 1938; and collations in Sawyer and F. J. H. Darton, English books: a signpost for collectors, 1927.
de Suzannet, A. Catalogue of a further portion of the library of the Comte de Suzannet: the celebrated collection of materials concerning Dickens. [1938] (Sotheby & Co). For descriptions, *see* Dickensian 30 1934, TLS 23 July 1938.
Parrish, M. L. List of writings of Dickens compiled from the collection at Dormy House, Pine Valley, New Jersey. Philadelphia 1938. *See* G. H. Gerould, Princeton Univ Lib Chron 8 1946, and Additions to the Dickens collection at Princeton, 21 1959.
Gummer, E. N. Dickens's works in Germany 1837–1937. Oxford 1940.
Wilson, R. A. Translations of Dickens. BM Quart 14 1940.
Hill, T. W. A unique collection of music: a catalogue of the Miller collection of Dickens music at the Dickens House. Dickensian 37 1941.
Houtchens, L. H. and C. W. Three early works (wrongly) attributed to Dickens. PMLA 59 1944.
Free Library of Philadelphia. The life and works of Dickens: an exhibition from the collection of William M. Elkins of Philadelphia. Philadelphia 1946. *See* L. Stevenson, Victorian Newsletter no 3 1953.
Fridlender, I. V. Charles Dickens 1838–1945. Leningrad 1946. A bibliography of trns, reviews, books and articles in Russian.
Miller, W. The Dickens student and collector: a list of writings relating to Dickens and his works 1836–1945. Cambridge MA 1946; suppl Brighton 1947 (priv ptd); suppl Hove 1953 (priv ptd). *See* commentary and corrections in P. Calhoun and H. J. Heaney, Dickensiana in the rough, PBSA 41 1947; New York 1947 (ptd separately).
Fielding, K. J. Dickens: a survey. 1953, 1960 (rev), 1963 (rev) (Br Council pam).
Parke-Bernet Galleries. The distinguished collection of first editions, autographs etc by and relating to Dickens formed by Lewis A. Hird, Englewood, New Jersey. New York 1953.
Collins, P. A. W. Dickens's periodicals: articles on education – an annotated bibliography. [Leicester] 1957.
Dickson, S. A. The Arents collection of books in parts and associated literature. New York 1958.
Fielding, K. J. Dickens: a guide to research materials. Victorian Newsletter no 14 1958.
Finlay, I. F. Dickens in the cinema. Dickensian 54 1958. Lists films of Dickens's writings 1902–58. Note by E. Wagenknecht.
Gordan, J. D. Reading for profit: the other career of Dickens – an exhibition from the Berg Collection. New York 1958. Annotated chronological listing of reading edns, letters, prompt books etc dealing with the public readings.
Prades, J. Los libros de Dickens en España. Libro Español 1 1958.
Stange, G. R. Reprints of nineteenth-century British fiction. College Eng Dec 1959.
Carr, Sister M. C. (ed). Catalogue of the Dickens collection at the University of Texas. Austin 1961.
Dawson's Book Shop, Los Angeles. Books from the library of Dickens together with autograph letters etc from the Langstroth collections. Los Angeles [1961].
Ford, G. H. and L. Lane jr (ed). The Dickens critics. Ithaca NY 1961. Bibliography includes Checklist of Dickens criticism 1840–1960.
Dutu, A. and S. Alexandrescu. Dickens in Rumania; a bibliography for the 150th anniversary. Bucharest 1962 (UNESCO).
Fridlender, I. V. and I. M. Katarsky. Dickens: bibliografiya russkikh 1838–1960. Moscow 1962. Expanded edn of 1946 bibliography, *above*.
Gimbel, R. An exhibition of manuscripts and first editions selected and described. YULG 37 1962.
Nisbet, A. In Victorian fiction: a guide to research, ed L. Stevenson, Cambridge MA 1964.
Dickens Studies: a journal of modern research and criticism. Boston 1965–9.
Hardwick, M. and M. The Dickens companion. 1965.
McPherson, B. (ed). Dickens: catalogue, Alfred and Isabel Reed Dickens collection, Dunedin Public Library, New Zealand. Wellington [1965]. With J. S. Ryan, Dickens and New Zealand: a colonial image, selected from the periodical publications of Dickens with historical and biographical notes by A. W. Reed.
Carr, Sister L. A catalogue of the VanderPoel Dickens collection at the University of Texas. Austin 1968.

Charles Dickens 1812–1870: a centenary book exhibition. 1970.
Dickens 1812–1870. TLS 4 June 1970.
Dickens Studies Annual. 1970– (in progress).
Dickens Studies Newsletter (1970–83), continued as Dickens Quarterly (1983– in progress). In addition to reviews, articles and notes, includes an extensive quarterly bibliography of Dickens studies.
Dutch Dickensian [founded c. 1970]. Annual jnl with essays in Eng and Du, abstracts in Du and Eng.
Genet, M. Charles Dickens 1812–1870. Austin 1970. Exhibition catalogue of VanderPoel collection.
[Greaves, J. and G. Major.] The London of Charles Dickens, with foreword by M. Dickens. 1970, 1979. A guide to London locations associated with Dickens.
A guide to the Charles Dickens birthplace museum. Portsmouth 1970.
Victoria and Albert Museum. Charles Dickens: an exhibition to commemorate the centenary of his death. 1970.
Jarndyce Antiquarian Booksellers catalogues. 1970– (in progress). These have included Dickens materials from the outset; catalogues devoted exclusively to Dickens first appeared in 1984.
Catalogue of autograph manuscripts, original drawings and first editions of Charles Dickens from the collection of the late Comte Alain de Suzannet. Ed with foreword by M. Slater 1971.
Gold, J. The stature of Dickens: a centenary bibliography. Toronto 1971.
Charles Dickens: the J. F. Dexter collection: accessions to the general catalogue of printed books, manuscripts, prints and drawings. 1974.
Churchill, R. C. A bibliography of Dickensian criticism 1836–1975. 1975.
Burton, A. The Forster library as a Dickens collection. Dickens Stud Newsletter 9 1978.
Fenstermaker, J. J. Charles Dickens 1940–1975: an analytical subject index to periodical criticism of the novels and Christmas books. 1979.
DeVries, D. The Garland Dickens Bibliographies; later Dickens Bibliographies series. 1981– (in progress). *See under* §1, *below*. Vol eds: David Copperfield, R. J. Dunn 1981; Hard times, S. Manning 1984; Our mutual friend, J. J. Brattin and B. Hornback 1984; Christmas books, Christmas stories and other short fiction, R. F. Glancy 1985; Oliver Twist, D. Paroissien 1986; Great expectations, G. J. Worth 1986; Barnaby Rudge, T. J. Rice 1987; The old curiosity shop, P. Schlicke and P. Schlicke 1988; The Pickwick papers, E. Engel 1990; Martin Chuzzlewit, R. E. Lougy 1990; A tale of two cities, R. F. Glancy 1993; The Mystery of Edwin Drood, A. J. Cox, 1998; Dombey and Son L. Litvack 1999.
Cohn, A. M. and K. K. Collins. The cumulated Dickens checklist 1970–1979. Troy NY 1982.
Rosenbaum, B. and P. White. Charles Dickens 1812–70. In IELM, vol 4, 1800–1900, London and New York 1982.
Harris, K. and D. Parker. The Dickens House London. Dickens Stud Newsletter 14 1983.
Smith, W. E. Charles Dickens in the original cloth: a bibliographical catalogue. Los Angeles 1983.
The Dickens World. Annual from 1985.
The Dickens Companions. Ed M. Cotsell and S. Shatto 1986– (in progress). *See under* §1, *below*. Vol eds: Our mutual friend, M. Cotsell 1986; The mystery of Edwin Drood, W. Jacobson 1986; Bleak House, S. Shatto 1988; A tale of two cities, A. Sanders 1988; Oliver Twist, D. Paroissien 1992; Hard times, M. Simpson 1997.
Bentley, N., M. Slater and N. Burgis. The Dickens index. Oxford 1988.
Page, N. A Dickens chronology. 1988.
Chittick, K. The critical reception of Charles Dickens 1833–1841. New York 1989.
Levit, F. A Dickens glossary. New York 1990.
Pointer, M. Who's who in Dickens. 1995.
Newlin, G. Windows into Dickens: everyone in Dickens, every thing in Dickens. 4 vols Westport CT 1996.
Hawes, D. Who's who in Dickens. 1998.
Schlicke, P. Oxford reader's companion to Dickens. Oxford 1999.

Websites

Dickens House Museum web site: http://www.rmplc.co.uk/orgs/dickens/index.html
Dickens Project (Univ of California Santa Cruz) with bibliographies, conference information, etc. web site: http://humwww.ucsc.edu/Dickens/index.html
Charles Dickens Forum e-mail address: DICKNS-L@UCSBVM.ucsb.edu
Japanese web site, with e-texts, bibliographies, mailing lists, etc. web site: http://lang.nagoya-u.ac.jp/~matsuoka/Dickens.html#info

Collections

During Dickens's lifetime and the duration of the chief copyrights, the only authorised collected edns issued in England were pbd by Chapman & Hall. These edns were expanded from time to time, and in due course furnished with introductory or critical matter. After Dickens's death, similarly annotated edns were issued by other firms, and new artists were procured for the illustrations; only the more important of these edns are given here. The authorised edns are not all included because some varied merely in title, price and other technical details. Reprints not containing new material are omitted.

Editions published by Chapman & Hall

The works of Charles Dickens. 17 vols 1847–67; 1st ser 1847–52 also issued in weekly and monthly pts. The first systematic re-issue, known as the 'first cheap edition'. Frontispiece illustrations only. Contains some new prefaces; general Address to the reader about this edn in Pickwick papers 1847. *See* S. Nowell-Smith, The Cheap edition of Dickens's works (first ser) 1847–52, Library 5th ser 22 1967.
Library edition. 22 vols 1858–9. Frontispiece illustrations only. Includes Reprinted pieces 1858, from Household Words. Dedicated to John Forster. Re-issued in 30 vols (including later works) 1861–74, with new title pages and illustrations, including the original ones and addns by Marcus Stone, John Leech, Clarkson Stanfield et al.
The People's edition. 25 vols 1865–7. A re-issue of the Cheap edition, excluding prefaces etc.
Charles Dickens edition. 21 vols 1867–[75]. Mainly rptd from foregoing, with slight addns and revisions by Dickens, including the addn of running headlines and some new prefaces. This is the text most often rptd in later edns.
Household edition. 22 vols [1871–9]; issued in monthly pts. With new illustrations by F. Barnard, J. Mahoney et al. Includes Forster's Life of Dickens.
Illustrated Library edition. 30 vols 1873–6.
Gadshill edition. Introds, general essay and notes by A. Lang, 36 vols 1897–[1908]. Contains all the original illustrations, with many additional ones by Charles Green, Harry Furniss, Maurice Greiffenhagen et al. Vols 35–6 Miscellaneous papers (not previously collected), ed B. W. Matz 1908. Rptd in edn de luxe 38 vols 1903–[8], with Forster's Life of Dickens, 2 vols, added.
Authentic edition. 22 vols 1901–[6]. With the original illustrations and additional illustrations from the Gadshill edn.
Oxford India paper Dickens. 17 vols 1901–2. With Henry Frowde (afterwards Humphrey Milford). Copyright text, on thin paper, with the original illustrations. Forster's Life added 1907.
Biographical edition. Ed A. Waugh 19 vols 1902–3. With the original illustrations. Includes Collected papers (prefaces and minor works). Miscellaneous papers, ed B. W. Matz, as additional vol 1908.

Fireside Dickens. 23 vols 1903–7. Includes Forster's Life.
National edition. Ed B. W. Matz 40 vols 1906–8. Includes Miscellaneous papers, letters, speeches, plays and poems, and Forster's Life, together with the original illustrations, and portraits, facs and drawings.
Centenary edition. 36 vols 1910–11. With original illustrations. A reissue of the Gadshill edn, with Dickens's prefaces substituted for Lang's introds. Includes Miscellaneous papers.
Universal edition. 22 vols [1912].

Other editions

Only those collections which include important new material are listed. Larger series which include most Dickens titles are also listed.

Tauchnitz edition. Leipzig 1842–1918. At least from 1843 authorised by Dickens, who received payment for advance proofs of his works, for publication in Tauchnitz's 'Collection of British Authors', pbd for continental circulation only and prohibited from importation into Britain or any British colony. *See* J. Y. Southam, Dickensian 8 1912; P. H. Muir, BC 1955; W. B. Todd and A. Bowden, Tauchnitz international editions in English 1841–1955: a bibliographical history, New York 1988.
New Illus Lib edition. Introds by E. P. Whipple 29 vols New York 1876–7.
The works of Charles Dickens. 21 vols 1892–1925. Usually known as Macmillan edn. Rptd from 1st edns, with biographical and bibliographical introds by C. Dickens the younger. Includes Letters, ed G. Hogarth and M. Dickens 1893.
Rochester edition. 11 vols (all pbd) 1899–1901. Introds by George Gissing and notes by F. G. Kitton.
Temple edition. Ed W. Jerrold 35 vols 1899–1903. Incomplete. Illustr W. C. Cooke et al.
Imperial edition. 16 vols 1901–3. Incomplete; includes A critical study by George Gissing and topographical illustrations by F. G. Kitton.
London edition. 13 vols Edinburgh 1901–2. Topographical notes by F. G. Kitton. Includes Kitton's Dickens: his life, writings and personality, 2 vols [1902].
Autograph edition. Ed F. G. Kitton 15 vols 1903–8. Only 6 works pbd. Original and later illustrations, introds by Gissing, Saintsbury, Dowden et al; annotations, bibliography and topography by Kitton.
Everyman's Lib. 22 vols [1906–21]. Introds to Barnaby Rudge and A tale of two cities by W. Jerrold, to remainder by G. K. Chesterton.
Charles Dickens Lib. Ed J. A. Hammerton 18 vols [1910]. 1,200 illustrations in all, including the original ones and 500 specially drawn by Harry Furniss. Vol 17 The Dickens picture book (a compendium of information about illustrators of Dickens); vol 18 The Dickens companion (a biographical narrative with extracts, list of authorities, short-title bibliography etc).
Waverley edition. 30 vols 1913–18. With character-study illustrations by Charles Pears and coloured versions of F. Barnard's illustrations. Introds by G. B. Shaw, W. de Morgan, J. Galsworthy, A. C. Benson, H. Caine et al.
The Nonesuch Dickens. Ed A. Waugh, H. Walpole, W. Dexter and T. Hatton. 23 vols 1937–8. Text from Charles Dickens edn, 1867–75. Illustrations from original plates and blocks (over 800) bought from Chapman & Hall. Each work complete in one vol. Before Pilgrim edn 1965 (*see* Letters, *below*), fullest collection of letters, 3 vols, ed Dexter. Includes The life of our Lord and other minor items not in other edns; also Miscellaneous papers as Collected papers 2 vols. Each set has one of the printing blocks in a dummy book box uniform with the edn's binding. *See* Nonesuch Dickensiana: the Nonesuch Dickens: retrospectus and prospectus (by A. Waugh, T. Hatton et al), 1937.
The New Oxford Illustrated Dickens. 21 vols Oxford 1947–58. *See under* §1, *below*. With illustrations remade from the original drawings. Introds by the following: Sketches by Boz, T. Holme; The Pickwick papers, B. Darwin; Oliver Twist, H. House; Nicholas Nickleby, S. Thorndike; The old curiosity shop, Earl of Wicklow; Barnaby Rudge, K. Tillotson; Martin Chuzzlewit, G. Russell; Dombey and son, H. W. Garrod; David Copperfield, R. H. Malden; Bleak House, O. Sitwell; Hard times, D. Foot; Little Dorrit, L. Trilling; A tale of two cities, J. Shuckburgh; Great expectations, F. Page; Our mutual friend, E. S. Davies; The mystery of Edwin Drood, S. C. Roberts; Christmas books, E. Farjeon; Christmas stories, M. Lane; American notes and Pictures from Italy, S. Sitwell; Master Humphrey's clock and A child's history of England, D. Hudson; Uncommercial traveller and Reprinted pieces, L. C. Staples. Apart from the last-named items, the edn excludes Dickens's minor and non-fictional writings.
Signet Classics edition. 1960–82. Charles Dickens text except for Hard times and The mystery of Edwin Drood, both of which use first book edn. Vol eds: The Pickwick papers, S. Marcus; Oliver Twist, E. LeComte; Nicholas Nickleby, S. Marcus; Martin Chuzzlewit, M. Mudrick; Dombey and son, A. Pryce-Jones; David Copperfield, E. Johnson; Bleak House, G. Tillotson; Hard times, C. Shapiro; Little Dorrit, R. Altick; A tale of two cities, E. Johnson; Great expectations, A. Wilson; Our mutual friend, J. H. Miller; The mystery of Edwin Drood, J. Wright.
Penguin English Lib edition, later Penguin Classics. 1965– (in progress). Various texts used. Individual vol eds: Sketches by Boz, D. Walder; The Pickwick papers, R. L. Patten; Oliver Twist, P. Fairclough, introd by A. Wilson; Nicholas Nickleby, M. Slater; The old curiosity shop, A. Easson, introd by M. Andrews; Barnaby Rudge, G. Spence; Martin Chuzzlewit, P. N. Furbank; Dombey and son, P. Fairclough; David Copperfield, T. Blount; Bleak House, N. Page, introd by J. H. Miller; Hard times, D. Craig; Little Dorrit, J. Holloway; A tale of two cities, G. Woodcock; Great expectations, A. Calder; Our mutual friend, S. Gill; The mystery of Edwin Drood, A. J. Cox, introd by A. Wilson; American notes, J. S. Whitley and A. Goldman; Selected short fiction, D. A. Thomas.
The Clarendon Dickens. Ed J. Butt and K. Tillotson, Oxford 1966– . (in progress). The first edn based on a collation of texts, with textual variants and bibliographies. Vol eds: The Pickwick papers, J. Kinsley; Oliver Twist, K. Tillotson; The old curiosity shop, E. Brennan; Martin Chuzzlewit, M. Cardwell; Dombey and son, A. Horsman; David Copperfield, N. Burgis; Little Dorrit, H. P. Sucksmith; Great expectations, M. Cardwell; The mystery of Edwin Drood, M. Cardwell.
Norton edition. 1966– (in progress). Introd, notes, background sources and studies. Vol eds: Oliver Twist, F. Kaplan; David Copperfield, J. H. Buckley; Bleak House, G. H. Ford and S. Monod; Hard times, G. H. Ford and S. Monod; Great Expectations, E. Rosenberg.
World's Classics edition. 1982– (in progress). Texts based on the Clarendon edn where available, introd, notes, and chronology. Vol eds: The Pickwick papers, J. Kinsley; Oliver Twist, K. Tillotson; Nicholas Nickleby, P. Schlicke; The old curiosity shop, E. Brennan; Martin Chuzzlewit, M. Cardwell; Dombey and son, A. Horsman; David Copperfield, N. Burgis; Bleak House, S. Gill; Hard times, P. Schlicke; Little Dorrit, H. P. Sucksmith; A tale of two cities, A. Sanders; Great expectations, M. Cardwell, introd by K. Flint; Our mutual friend, M. Cotsell; The mystery of Edwin Drood, M. Cardwell.
Dickens on disk. Ed F. Levit, Wilmette IL 1991– (in progress). CD-Rom version.
Mandarin edition, introd by P. Ackroyd 1991.
The Everyman Dickens. Ed M. Slater 1994– (in progress). Texts based on the Charles Dickens edn (corrected), with original illustrations, plus introd, notes, chronology, text summary and survey of critical responses. Individual vol eds: The Pickwick papers, M. Andrews; Oliver Twist, S. Connor; Nicholas Nickleby,

D. Parker; Master Humphrey's clock and other stories, P. Mudford; The old curiosity shop, P. Schlicke; Barnaby Rudge, D. Hawes; Martin Chuzzlewit, M. Slater; Dombey and son, V. Purton; David Copperfield, M. Andrews; Bleak House, A. Sanders; Hard times, G. Smith; Little Dorrit, A. Easson; A tale of two cities, N. Page; Great expectations, R. Gilmour; The mystery of Edwin Drood, S. Connor; American notes and Pictures from Italy, L. Ormond and F. Schwarzbach; Plays, poems and prefaces, M. Slater; Holiday romance and other writings for children, G. Avery; The Christmas stories, R. Glancy; Journalism (4 vols), M. Slater and J. Drew.

Like the Dickens: the complete works. Parsipany NJ 1994. CD-Rom version.

E-texts (under construction) are available at web sites:
http://www-cgi.cs.emu.edu/cgi-bn/book/authorsearch?dickens
http://www.wonderland.org/works/Charles-Dickens

Studies of manuscripts and editions

The National edition of the works of Charles Dickens. Dickensian 2 1906.

Wilkins, W. G. First and early American editions of the works of Dickens. Dickensian 3 1907.

Completion of the National edition of Dickens's works. Dickensian 4 1908.

Wilkins, W. G. First and early American editions of the works of Charles Dickens. Cedar Rapids IA 1910; rptd New York 1968.

Wilkins, W. G. Early foreign translations of Dickens's works. Dickensian 7 1911.

Southton, J. Y. Authorised Leipzig edition of Dickens. Dickensian 8 1912.

Wilkins, W. G. Dickens and his first American publishers. Dickensian 9 1913.

H[ill], T. W. The Universal Dickens. Dickensian 9–10 1913–14.

Edgar, H. L. and R. W. G. Vail. Early American editions of the works of Charles Dickens. BNYPL 33 1929.

Dickens, M. Dickens and his French publishers. Dickensian 29 1933.

Brussel, I. R. Anglo-American first editions 1826–1900: east to west, 1935.

Straus, R. The forthcoming Nonesuch Dickens. Dickensian 33 1937.

Grubb, G. G. Dickens's pattern of weekly serialisation. ELH 9 1942.

Kennethe, L. A. [Dexter, W.] The Cheap edition. Dickensian 39 1943.

Dexter, W. The 'Library', 'People's' and 'Charles Dickens' editions. Dickensian 40 1944.

Butt, J. Dickens's notes for his serial parts. Dickensian 45 1949.

Muir, P. H. Note 55. Dickens and Tauchnitz. BC 4 1955.

Butt, J. and K. Tillotson. Dickens at work. 1957.

Fielding, K. J. The monthly serialisation of Dickens's novels. Dickensian 54 1958.

Fielding, K. J. The weekly serialisation of Dickens's novels. Dickensian 54 1958.

Butt, J. Dickens's manuscripts. YULG 36 1962.

Coolidge, A. C., jr. Charles Dickens as a serial novelist. Ames IA 1967.

Butt, J. Editing a nineteenth-century novelist: proposals for an edition of Dickens. English Stud Today: 2nd ser, Berne 1961. Rptd in Art and error: modern textual editing, ed R. Gottesman and S. Bennett, Bloomington IN 1970.

Editing Dickens. TLS 6 Apr 1967.

Nowell-Smith, S. The 'Cheap edition' of Dickens's works (first series). Library Sep 1967.

Collins, Philip. Dickens editions. TLS 16 Apr 1970. Replies by J. G. Philips, A. H. Chaplin, A. G. S. Enser, 30 Apr 1970, and J. M. Gladstone 14 May 1970.

Thomas, G. Publishing Dickens 60 years ago. Bookseller 18 Apr 1970.

Nowell-Smith, S. Editing Dickens. TLS 4 June 1970.

Patten, R. L. Proposal for an annotated edition of the works of Charles Dickens. Dickens Stud Newsletter 2 1971.

Bracher, P. Harper & Brothers: publishers of Dickens. BNYPL 79 1976.

Crum, M. English and American autographs in the Bodmeriana. Bibliotheca Bodmeriana, catalogues, 4. Cologny-Genève 1977. Describes ms.

Monod, S. The need for a Dickens concordance. Dickens Stud Newsletter 9 1978. *See* D. N. Dobrin, Dickens Stud Newsletter 11 1980.

Patten, R. L. Charles Dickens and his publishers. Oxford 1978.

Tyler, R. and J. F. Baker. Classic corner: the works of great writers available today: Charles Dickens. Bookviews 2 Dec 1978.

Low, A. The conservation of Charles Dickens's manuscripts. V & A Conservation Jnl Oct 1993. Web site: http://www.nal.vam.ac.uk/pubs/lowecons.html

§1

Sketches by Boz

Sketches by 'Boz' illustrative of every-day life and every-day people. Illustr George Cruikshank 2 vols 1836; second ser 1836. The ptd title page of ser 2 is dated 1837, the engraved 1836. It was actually pbd on 17 Dec 1836 (the preface being dated the same day). There are variants in both ser. The Sketches appeared originally at intervals in Monthly Mag, Bell's Weekly Mag, Morning Chron, Evening Chron, Bell's Life in London (signed 'Tibbs'), Lib of Fiction and Carlton Chron. For detailed list, *see* Appendix F, Letters of Dickens, ed M. House and G. Storey, vol 1, Oxford 1965. The earliest – Dickens's first appearance in print as an author – was A dinner at Poplar Walk (called Mr Minns and his cousin in ser 2) in Monthly Mag Dec 1833. Many items were substantially rev before republication: *see* J. Butt and K. Tillotson, Dickens at work, 1957, ch 2. After the first edn Dickens persuaded Chapman & Hall to purchase the copyright of both ser from John Macrone.

Bibliographies

Matz, B. W. A bibliographical note. Dickensian 1 1905.

Darton, F. J. H. Dickens: positively the first appearance – a centenary review with a bibliography of Sketches by 'Boz' by J. E. S. Sawyer and F. J. H. Darton. 1933. Includes original text of A dinner at Poplar Walk.

Dexter, W. Contemporary opinion on Dickens's earliest work. Dickensian 31 1935.

Dexter, W. The reception of Dickens's first book. Dickensian 32 1936.

Dexter, W. Macrone and the reissue of Sketches by Boz. Dickensian 33 1937.

Dexter, W. The library of fiction. Dickensian 32 1936. Reviews of The Tuggses at Ramsgate.

Editions

2 vols Philadelphia 1836 (ser 1 only, as Watkins Tottle and other sketches, illustrative of every-day life and every-day people; variants).

Calcutta 1837 (20 sketches from ser 2, as The new series of sketches by Boz).

Sketches by 'Boz' (both ser). 20 monthly pts Nov 1837–June 1839 (variants) with 40 illustrations by Cruikshank, 13 of them new.

1839, with new preface (the monthly pts in 1 vol; known as the first 8vo edn; variants).

Paris 1839 Baudry's European Lib edn.

Leipzig 1843 Tauchnitz Collection of British Authors no 50, as Sketches.

1850 Cheap edn (and in 20 weekly pts, and 5 monthly pts, July–Nov 1850; with new preface and frontispiece by Cruikshank).

1858 Library edn.

1867 Diamond edn, bound with Christmas books, illustr S. Eytinge, jr.

1868 Charles Dickens edn.

New York 1877 New Illus Lib edn, introd by E. P. Whipple.
Leipzig 1886 Tauchnitz Cabinet edn of English classics, as Sketches.
1892 Macmillan edn, introd by C. Dickens the younger.
1898 Gadshill edn, introd and notes by A. Lang. 2 vols.
1899 Temple edn, introd by W. Jerrold. 2 vols.
1902 Biographical edn, introd by A. Waugh.
1907 Everyman Lib edn, with introd by G. K. Chesterton.
1913–15 Waverley edn, illustr C. Pears and F. Barnard.
A dinner at Poplar Walk: being [Dickens's] first effusion 'in all the glory of print', reproduced in facsimile from the Monthly Magazine, Dec 1833. 1933 (priv ptd). With facs of page of 1847 Pickwick preface corrected by Dickens.
1938 Nonesuch edn, ed A. Waugh, H. Walpole, W. Dexter and T. Hatton.
1947 Scenes of London life, from Sketches by Boz. Ed J. B. Priestley. Selection.
1957 New Oxford Illus Dickens, introd by T. Holme.
1991 Mandarin edn, introd by P. Ackroyd.
1994, bound with Sunday under three heads and pieces from Bentley's Misc. In Dickens' journalism vol 1, ed M. Slater, *below*.
Harmondsworth 1995, Penguin Classics edn, introd and notes by D. Walder.

Commentary on the text

De Vries, D. Dickens's apprentice years: the making of a novelist. Hassocks 1976.

Imitations

[Grant, J.] Sketches in London. 1837–8. In shilling numbers, similar to Pickwick.
'Bos' (Thomas Peckett Prest). The sketch book, embellished with seventeen elegant engravings. [1838?]. Ostensibly, and partly in fact, a close imitation of Sketches by Boz, but from internal evidence written when Pickwick was advanced in monthly pbn and Oliver Twist begun.

Dramatisations

Buckstone, J. B. The Christening. 1834. The first dramatisation of a work by Dickens.
Dickens, C. The strange gentleman. 1836. Dickens's adaptation of his own story, The great Wingleberry duel, as a comic burletta. Revs of the production are collected in Dickensian 30 1934.
Stirling, E. Horatio Sparkins. 1840.

Reviews

See Chittick 1989 *under* Bibliographies and reference works, *above*.
[Hogarth, G.] Morning Chron 11 Feb 1836; Literary Gazette 13 Feb 1836, 24 Dec 1836; Satirist 14 Feb 1836; Sun 15 Feb 1836; Athenaeum 20 Feb 1836, 31 Dec 1836; Court Jnl 20 Feb 1836, 31 Dec 1836; Spectator 20 Feb 1836, 26 Dec 1836; Atlas 21 Feb 1836; Sunday Herald 21 Feb 1836; Sunday Times 21 Feb 1836; [Forster, J.] Examiner 28 Feb 1836; Weekly Despatch 28 Feb 1836; Metropolitan Mag Mar 1836; Monthly Rev Mar 1836, Feb 1837; Morning Post 12 Mar 1836; Chambers's Edinburgh Jnl 9 Apr 1836; [Buller, C.] Westminster Rev 27 1837; [Haywood, A.?] Quart Rev 59 1837; [Lewes, G. H.] Nat Mag Dec 1837; [Lister, T. H.] Edinburgh Rev 68 1838.

Pickwick papers

The posthumous papers of the Pickwick Club containing a faithful record of the perambulations, perils, travels, adventures and sporting transactions of the corresponding members, edited by 'Boz'. Only 46 pages of The Pickwick papers ms survive, in several locations; *see* Engel 1990 *under* Bibliographies, *below*. 20 (as 19) monthly pts Apr 1836–Nov 1837 except June 1837; illustr R. Seymour, d. Apr 1836 (pts 1–2), R. W. Buss (pt 3), H. K. Browne ('Phiz') (remainder).

Bibliographies

Fitzgerald, P. H. The history of Pickwick, an account of its characters, localities, allusions and illustrations; with a bibliography. 1891.
Dickens Fellowship, London. The Pickwick exhibition held at the New Dudley Gallery: catalogue of exhibits. Ed B. W. Matz and J. W. T. Ley 1907. Illus.
Davis, G. W. The posthumous papers of the Pickwick Club: some new bibliographical discoveries. 1928, Folcroft PA 1971, New York 1972.
Eckel, J. C. Prime Pickwicks in parts: census with complete collation, comparison and comment; foreword by A. Edward Newton, 11 plates. New York 1928.
The Lombard Street edition of Dickens: the Pickwick papers, with (biographical and bibliographical) introd by J. H. Stonehouse. 1931–2 (monthly pts). A reprint of the original text with plates and wrappers (except date and imprint) in facs, including the suppressed plates; modern advertisements inserted in the same style as in the original pts. Bound in 2 vols 1932.
Bay, J. C. The Pickwick papers: some bibliographical remarks. Chicago 1936, 1938 (rev); rptd in his Fortune of books, Chicago 1941.
Books about Pickwick. Dickensian 32 1936.
Dexter, W. How the press and public received the Pickwick papers. Nineteenth Cent 119, Mar 1936.
Dexter, W. and J. W. T. Ley. The origin of Pickwick: new facts now first published for the year of the centenary. 1936. Reprints from early reviews.
The English editions of Pickwick. Dickensian 32 1936.
Miller, W. and E. H. Strange. A centenary bibliography of the Pickwick papers. 1936. Reprints from early reviews.
Miller, W. Imitations of Pickwick. Dickensian 32 1936.
Shillingsburg, P. L. Paperback edns: The Pickwick papers. Dickens Stud Newsletter 3 1972.
Harries, J. M. Pickwick papers: a bibliographical curiosity. N & Q 218 Mar 1973. *See* reply by P. G. Scott, N & Q 218 Sep 1973.
Vann, J. D. Pickwick in the London newspapers. Dickensian 70 1974.
Engel, E. and M. King. Pickwick's progress: the critical reception of The Pickwick papers from 1836 to 1986. Dickens Quart 3 1986.
Engel, E. Pickwick papers: an annotated bibliography. New York 1990 (Garland Dickens Bibliographies).

Editions

There are innumerable variants in the earliest copies, and the exact bibliographical details are still undecided, owing to (i) inequality of demand for each pt in the early stages, and consequent use of material in various states of production; (ii) textual and pictorial changes made in the course of serial issue, though the main body was unaltered; (iii) insertion in bound-up copies of discarded or extra plates; (iv) the binding-up or improvisation of 'perfect' copies out of different-state but genuine monthly pts. See Eckel 1932 *under* Bibliographies and reference works, *above*.
1837 first single-vol edn, ptd from stereotype plates, with 2 new plates replacing Buss's illustrations.
Launceston, Tasmania 1838, with illustrations after Phiz.
Philadelphia 1838, 'with illustrations by Sam Weller jr [T. H. Onwhyn] and Alfred Crowquill [A. H. Forrester]'.
The posthumous papers of the Pickwick Club. Leipzig 1842 Tauchnitz Collection of British Authors no 2. 3 vols.
1847 Cheap edn (and in 31 weekly pts, 8 monthly pts, Apr–Sep 1847; frontispiece by C. R. Leslie and preface describing origin of Pickwick and Dickens's relations with R. Seymour).
1858 Library edn, with 2 illustrations by Browne. 2 vols.
1867 Charles Dickens edn, with 8 of the original illustrations.
New York 1876 New Illus Lib edn, introd by E. P. Whipple.
1886 Jubilee edn, introd by C. Dickens the younger. 2 vols.
1887 Victoria edn, introd by C. P. Johnson. 2 vols with facs of original

illustrations, including Buss's, and additional drawings by J. Leech.

1891, introd by J. Lubbock.

1892 Macmillan edn, introd by C. Dickens the younger.

1897 Gadshill edn, introd and notes by A. Lang. 2 vols.

1899 Rochester edn, introd by G. Gissing, notes by F. G. Kitton, frontispiece by S. Laurence, illustr E. H. 2 vols.

1899 Temple edn, introd by W. Jerrold. 3 vols.

1901–2 London edn, notes by F. G. Kitton and original illustrations.

1902 Autograph edn, introd by P. Fitzgerald, notes by F. G. Kitton, original and extra illustrations. 3 vols.

1902 Biographical edn, introd by A. Waugh, with original illustrations.

1903 Autograph edn, introd by P. Fitzgerald, notes by F. G. Kitton and original illustrations. 3 vols.

1906 National edn, with 60 illustrations.

1907 Everyman Lib edn, introd by G. K. Chesterton.

1909 Topical edn, introd by C. Van Noorden, notes by C. P. Johnson. 2 vols. (Original illustrations and prefaces, 223 additional pictures, etc.)

1910 Testimonial edn, introd by J. A. Hammerton, illustr H. Furniss.

1913–15 Waverley edn, introd by A. Lang, illustr C. Pears and F. Barnard.

1937 Nonesuch edn, ed. W. Dexter, H. Walpole, A. Waugh, and T. Hatton.

1947 New Oxford Illus Dickens, introd by B. Darwin.

New York 1949 Inner Sanctum edn, introd by C. Fadiman, illustr F. Banbery.

1953 Collins edn, introd by A. Waugh.

New York 1960 Washington Square edn. Rptd as a Collateral Classic 1967, introd by J. Mersand.

New York 1964 Laurel edn, introd by E. Johnson.

New York 1964 Signet Classics edn, afterword by S. Marcus.

New York 1969 Airmont edn, introd by B. Rowland.

Harmondsworth 1972, Penguin English Library edn, later Penguin Classics edn, ed with introd and notes by R. L. Patten, with original illustrations, maps and appendices.

1981 Folio Society edn, introd by C. Hibbert and illustr C. Keeping.

Oxford 1986 Clarendon edn, ed J. Kinsley.

Oxford 1988 World's Classics edn, ed with introd and notes by J. Kinsley and K. Tillotson.

1991 Mandarin edn, introd by P. Ackroyd.

1997 Everyman Dickens edn, ed with introd and notes by M. Andrews.

Harmondsworth 1998 Penguin Classics edn, ed M. Wormald.

Dickens's reading adaptations

Bardell and Pickwick; Mr Chops, the dwarf [from Going into society]; Mr Bob Sawyer's party: three readings, each in one chapter. nd (priv ptd). Both Pickwick items rptd Boston 1868 and in collections 1868, 1883, 1907, 1975, 1983. *See* Readings, *below*.

Commentary on the text

de Suzannet, A. The original manuscript of Pickwick papers. Dickensian 28 1932.

Miller, W. and E. H. Strange. The original Pickwick papers: the collation of a perfect first edition. Dickensian 29–31 1933–5.

Patten, R. L. The interpolated tales in Pickwick papers. Dickens Stud 1 1965.

Patten, R. L. The unpropitious muse: Pickwick's 'interpolated' tales. Dickens Stud Newsletter 1 1970.

Patten, R. L. Pickwick and the development of serial fiction. Rice Univ Stud 61 1975.

Imitations

'Bos' [T. P. Prest?]. The post-humourous notes of the Pickwickian club. 2 vols [1839?]. Issued weekly, May 1837–July 1839, 112 nos at 1d as The penny Pickwick, and 4d monthly; illus. *See* F. C. Rose, Dickensian 22 1926.

Pickwick in Boulogne. Boulogne Sep 1837.

The Pickwick Gazette, illustrated by Robert Cruikshank. 1837. 2 issues only, June–July.

Posthumous papers of the Cadgers' club. 1837–8.

Sam Weller's Pickwick jest book. Penny nos from 1 Nov 1837.

Sam Weller's sentiments on the Poor Law. Cleave's London Satirist 16 Dec 1837.

The beauties of Pickwick, by Sam Weller. 1838, 1883 (facs, introd on original of Sam Weller, note on piracies, and other comments, 'by a lover of Dickens's works'). Partly quotation, partly invention.

Mr Pickwick's collection of songs. [c. 1838].

'Poz'. The posthumous papers of the wonderful discovery club. [1838].

'Quiz'. Droll discussions and queer proceedings of the Magnum-Fundum club. [1838.]

Reynolds, G. W. M. Pickwick in America! 44 pts 1838–9. *See* F. C. Roe, Connoisseur 107 1941.

Winkle's journal (omitted in the Pickwick papers). Metropolitan Mag Oct 1838.

Pickwick in India. Madras 1839–40.

Pickwick's mirthful almanac for 1839.

Reynolds, G. W. M. Pickwick abroad: or the tour in France, illus. 1839, 1864, 1905. Appeared serially Dec 1837–June 1838 in Monthly Mag, of which Reynolds was then editor. Also issued in monthly pts from Jan 1839. The book issue contains a long preface defending the imitation, 41 steel engravings by 'Alfred Crowquill' (A. H. Forrester) and J. Phillips, and 33 woodcuts by G. W. Bonner (views of Paris). *See* W. Miller, G. W. M. Reynolds and Dickens, Dickensian 13 1917.

Dickens, C. Master Humphrey's clock nos 5–88 (2 May 1840–27 Nov 1841) passim. Pickwick and the Wellers revived.

Reynolds, G. W. M. Noctes Pickwickianae. Teetotaler 27 June–8 Aug 1840.

Ross, H. Mr Pickwick's hat-box. The New Monthly Belle Assemblée Jan–Nov 1840.

An omitted Pickwick paper: restored by Poz. The Token and Atlantic Souvenir. Boston 1841.

Reynolds, G. W. M. Pickwick married. Teetotaler 23 Jan–19 June 1841. Rptd and rev as The marriage of Mr Pickwick in his Master Timothy's book case, 1842. A tale occupying one-sixth of a long work.

The Pickwickian treasury of wit: or Joe Miller's jest book. 1846.

Viles, E. Marmaduke Midge, the Pickwickian legatee. [c. 1852].

[Besant, W. and J. Rice.] The death of Samuel Pickwick. In The case of Mr Lucraft and other tales, 2 vols 1876.

Mr Pickwick goes out pike fishing. The Shooting Times 1902.

Pickwick papers up to date. Gleam 19 June 1902.

Pickwick papers up to date. Punch 17 and 24 Dec 1902, 22 Apr 1903.

Reid, J. G. Pickwickians abroad. Shanghai 1913.

Harper, C. G. Mr Pickwick's second time. The Autocar 24 Dec 1921; rev and expanded as Mr Pickwick's second time on earth, 1927.

Young Pickwick's schooldays. nd.

Dramatisations

See Bolton 1987 *under* Studies and bibliographies of adaptations, *below*.

Stirling, E. The Pickwick club; or, the age we live in. 1837.

Rede, W. L. Peregrinations of Pickwick. 1837.

Moncrieff, W. T. Sam Weller; or, the Pickwickians. 1837.

Taylor, T. P. Boz; or, the Pickwick club. 1837.

Selby, C. Pickwickian adventures; or, the sayings and doings of the Pickwick club, 1837.

Murray, W. H. Scraps from Pickwick. Edinburgh 1837.

Nantz, F. C. Pickwick; or the sayings and doings of Sam Weller. Colchester 1837.
Moncrieff, W. T. Sam Weller's tour; or, the Pickwickians abroad. 1838.
Daly, A. Pickwick papers. New York 1868.
Albery, J. Pickwick. 1871.
Hollingshead, J. Bardell versus Pickwick. 1871.
Emson, F. E. The Weller family [Sam Weller's visit to his mother-in-law]; [The course of true love]. 1878.
Furtado, C. Gabriel Grub. 1879.
[Pemberton, J. E.?], T. H. Gem and F. Spinney. Bardell versus Pickwick. 1881.
Pollitt, R. The great Pickwick case. Manchester 1884.
Rowe, G. F. Jingle; or, the Pickwick club. New York 1887.
Burnand, F. C. and E. Solomon. Pickwick. 1889.
Parker, J. M. An evening with Pickwick. New York 1889.
Klein, C. Mr Pickwick. New York 1903.
Bengough, J. W. The breach of promise trial, Bardell v Pickwick. Toronto 1907.
Mr Pickwick's predicament. Film 1912. Produced by T. A. Edison.
Pickwick papers. Film, Vitagraph 1913.
Adventures of Mr Pickwick. Film 1921. Script by E. A. Baughan and E. Stannard. Directed by T. Bentley.
Hamilton, C. and F. C. Reilly. Pickwick. New York 1927.
Bardell against Pickwick. BBC Television 1938. Script by S. Harrison.
Pickwick papers. Film 1952. Written and directed by N. Langley.
Young, S. The Trial of Mr Pickwick. 1952.
Mankowitz, W. Pickwick. 1963.
The Pickwick papers. BBC Television serial 1985. Directed by B. Lighthill.

Reviews

See Chittick 1989 *under* Bibliographies and reference works, *above*.
Athenaeum 26 Mar 1836 (advertisement), 3 Dec 1836; Court Jnl Apr 1836; Atlas 3 Apr 1836; Bath Herald 9 Apr 1836, 11 June 1836, 9 July 1836, 6 Aug 1836; Fraser's Lit Chron 9 Apr 1836; Literary Gazette 9 Apr 1836, and many subsequent articles; (*see* particularly [W. Jerdan] 13 Aug 1836); Bell's Life in London 10 Apr 1836, 1 May 1836, 3 July 1836; News and Sunday Herald 10 Apr 1836; Spectator 16 Apr 1836; Lincoln Gazette 19 Apr 1836, 13 Sep 1836; Satirist 30 Apr 1836, 11 Dec 1836; Metropolitan Mag May 1836, and many subsequent articles; Sun 2 May 1836; Morning Post 11 May 1836; Bath Chron 12 May 1836; John Bull 12 June 1836, 11 Sep 1836; Sunday Times 12 June 1836; Brighton Guardian 15 June 1836, 10 Aug 1836; NMM Sep 1836; Examiner 4 Sep 1836, and many subsequent articles (*see* particularly [J. Forster] 2 July 1837, and 5 Nov 1837); [Poe, E. A.] Southern Lit Messenger Nov 1836, Sep 1837; [Buller, C.] Westminster Rev 27 1837; [Haywood, A.] Quart Rev 59 1837; Monthly Rev Feb 1837; Court Mag Apr 1837; Eclectic Rev Apr 1837; Chambers's Jnl 29 Apr 1837; Star 7 Oct 1837; Torch 14 Oct 1837; [Lewes, G. H.?] Nat Mag Dec 1837; [Lister, T. H.] Edinburgh Rev 68 1838; Fraser's Mag Oct 1838, Apr 1840; Chasles, P. Journal des Débats 13 Oct 1838; [Russell, C. W.] Dublin Rev 8 1840; [Patmore, C.?] North Br Rev 7 1847; [Whipple, E. P.] North Amer Rev 69 1849; [Hamley, E. B.] Blackwood's Mag Apr 1857; Saturday Rev 23 Feb 1861; Athenaeum 31 Mar 1866.

Studies and appreciations

Seymour, Mrs [Robert]. An account of the origin of the Pickwick papers. [1854] (priv ptd and apparently not circulated); ed F. G. Kitton, St Albans 1901 (priv ptd).
Calverley, C. S. An examination paper [on Pickwick papers]. [1857]; rptd in his Fly-leaves, Cambridge 1872 (2nd edn). *See* W. Besant, Dickensian 32 1936.
Dickens, C. The history of Pickwick. Athenaeum 31 Mar 1866; correction, 7 Apr 1866. On the Seymour claims.
Hassard, J. R. G. A Pickwickian pilgrimage. Boston 1881. Chiefly on London scenes.
Fitzgerald, P. H. The history of Pickwick. 1891.
Lockwood, F. The law and lawyers of Pickwick. [1894], [1896].
Fitzgerald, P. H. Pickwickian manners and customs. [1897], New York 1974, Folcroft PA 1974.
Neale, C. M. An index to Pickwick. 1897. Addenda, Dickensian 4 1908. Rptd Folcroft PA 1974.
Fitzgerald, P. H. Pickwickian studies. 1899, Folcroft PA 1977.
Grego, J. Pictorial Pickwickiana: Charles Dickens and his illustrators. 2 vols. 1899.
Hall, H. Mr Pickwick's Kent. 1899, Norwood PA 1975.
Fitzgerald, P. H. Bardell v. Pickwick, notes and commentaries. 1902.
Machen, A. In his Hieroglyphics, 1902.
Fitzgerald, P. H. The Pickwickian dictionary and cyclopaedia. [1903], New York 1974, 1975.
Bailey, W. H. Wellerisms and wit. Dickensian 1 1905.
Allbut, R. Sam Weller: a character sketch. Dickensian 2 1906.
Chesterton, G. K. The superiority of the Pickwick England. Dickensian 3 1907.
The Eatanswill gazette: official organ of the Eatanswill Club, Sudbury Suffolk – a journal devoted to Eatanswillian, Pickwickian and Dickensian humour and research. 4 nos Sudbury 1907–8. Founded chiefly to defend the theory that Eatanswill in the Pickwick papers represents Sudbury, but contains other minutiae.
Edgar, G. The Pickwickian Christmas. Dickensian 3 1907.
Ley, J. W. T. Is Sudbury Eatanswill? Dickensian 3 1907.
Barlow, G. The genius of Dickens. Contemporary Rev 94 1908.
Neale, C. M. A few more Pickwick references. Dickensian 4 1908.
Beisiegel, M. K. Notes on Dickens's Pickwick papers. 1910.
Neale, C. M. Pickwick and Charles Lamb. Dickensian 6 1910.
Dibelius, W. Zu den Pickwick papers. Anglia 35 1912.
Fitzgerald, P. H. Pickwick riddles and perplexities. 1912.
Matz, B. W. The inns and taverns of Pickwick. [1912].
Suddaby, J. The anonymous hot-pieman in Pickwick. Dickensian 10 1914.
Bowen, C. M. Dead souls and Pickwick papers. Athenaeum June 1916.

Oliver Twist

Oliver Twist; or, the parish boy's progress, by 'Boz'. In 24 monthly instalments, Bentley's Misc Feb 1837–Apr 1839 (except June and Oct 1837 and Sep 1838), illustr G. Cruikshank. The incomplete ms, consisting of 22 chs, is in the Forster Collection; scraps survive in the Berg Collection, the Dickens House and the Gimbel Collection. *See* Paroissien 1986 *under* Bibliographies, *below*.

Bibliographies

Dexter, W. Bentley's Miscellany. Dickensian 33 1937.
Patten, R. L. Paperback editions: Oliver Twist. Dickens Stud Newsletter 3 1972.
Paroissien, D. Oliver Twist: an annotated bibliography 1986 (Garland Dickens Bibliographies).

Editions

1838, 1838 (by Charles Dickens), illustr G. Cruikshank. 3 vols.
1839 (by Charles Dickens, 2nd edn), illustr G. Cruikshank. 3 vols.
Philadelphia 1839 [1838] not illus, 2 vols; 1839 illustr G. Cruikshank, 1 vol. These Philadelphia edns are unique texts, partly based on proofs of Bentley's Misc before Dickens's corrections.
Paris 1839. First European edn.
1840 (by 'Boz'), illustr G. Cruikshank.
1841 (by Charles Dickens, 3rd edn, with author's introd), illustr G. Cruikshank. 3 vols.
Leipzig 1843 Tauchnitz Collection of British Authors no 36, first as Oliver Twist, later as The adventures of Oliver Twist.

The adventures of Oliver Twist: or the parish boy's progress. New edn, rev and corrected. In 10 monthly pts and 1 vol 1846 (illustr and new cover by G. Cruikshank).
1850 Cheap edn (and in 19 weekly pts, 5 monthly pts, Dec 1849–Apr 1850; with new preface by Dickens and frontispiece by G. Cruikshank).
1858 Library edn.
1867 Charles Dickens edn (with rev preface).
Boston 1867 Diamond edn, illustr S. Eytinge jr.
New York 1876 New Illus Lib edn, introd by E. P. Whipple.
1892 Macmillan edn, introd by C. Dickens the younger.
1895 (with 26 water-colour drawings by G. Cruikshank); [ed J. Grego] [1903] (selections). Coloured drawings done specially by Cruikshank for a friend, F. W. Cosens, in 1866, though similar in design to the earlier line engravings. The 1903 edn contains Cruikshank's claim to have invented the substance of the novel. The 2 edns differ widely in colour reproduction.
1897 Gadshill edn, notes by A. Lang.
1899 Temple edn, introd by W. Jerrold. 2 vols.
1900 Autograph edn, introd by R. Garnett.
1900 Rochester edn, introd by G. Gissing, notes by F. G. Kitton.
1906 Biographical edn, introd by A. Waugh, with the original illustrations.
1907 Everyman Lib edn, introd by G. K. Chesterton.
1913–15 Waverley edn, introd by A. C. Benson, illustr C. Pears and F. Barnard.
New York 1918, introd by F. W. Pine.
1937 Nonesuch edn, ed W. Dexter, H. Walpole, A. Waugh and T. Hatton.
1949 New Oxford Illus Dickens, introd by H. House.
1950 Novel Lib edn, introd by G. Greene.
1954 Collins edn, introd by K. Hayens.
New York 1957 Washington Square edn, introd by E. Johnson.
1961 Signet Classics edn, afterword by E. LeComte.
1961 Heritage of Literature edn, introd and notes by S. H. Burton.
New York 1962 Rinehart edn, introd by J. H. Miller.
1962 Michael Joseph edn, ed D. Dickens, illustr R. Searle.
1963 Blackie edn, introd by A. R. Tompkins.
Harmondsworth 1966 Penguin English Lib edn, later Penguin Classics edn, ed with notes by P. Fairclough, introd by A. Wilson.
Oxford 1966 Clarendon edn, ed K. Tillotson.
1980 Pan edn, introd and notes by I. Ousby.
Toronto 1982 Bantam edn, introd by I. Howe.
Oxford 1982 World's Classics edn, ed with new introd by K. Tillotson.
1983 Macmillan Students' Novels edn, introd and notes by G. Williams.
1984 Longman Study Texts edn, ed R. Garland.
1984 Folio Soc edn, introd by C. Hibbert, illustr C. Keeping.
1991 Mandarin edn, introd by P. Ackroyd.
1992 Everyman's Lib edn, introd by M. Slater, with G. K. Chesterton's 1907 introd (*above*) as appendix.
New York 1993 Norton Critical edn, ed with notes, background sources and studies by F. Kaplan.
1993 New Windmill Classics edn, introd and notes by A. Worrall.
1994 Everyman Dickens edn, ed with introd and notes by S. Connor.
Harmondsworth 1998 Penguin Classics edn, ed P. Horne.

Dickens's reading adaptation

Sikes and Nancy: a reading from Oliver Twist. 1868 (priv ptd); rev as A reading by Charles Dickens 1870 (priv ptd). The 1870 text rptd, introd by J. H. Stonehouse, 1921 and in collections 1975, 1983. *See* Readings, *below, and* P. Collins, Sikes and Nancy: Dickens's last reading, TLS 11 June 1971.

Commentary on the text

Grubb, G. G. On the serial publication of Oliver Twist. MLN 56 1941.
Tillotson, K. Oliver Twist in three volumes. Library 18 1963.
Schweitzer, J. The chapter numbering in Oliver Twist. PBSA 60 1966.
Bowers, F. Review of Clarendon edn. Nineteenth-Cent Fiction 23 1968.
Wheeler, B. M. The text and plans of Oliver Twist. Dickens Stud Annual 12 1984.

Imitations

'Poz'. Oliver Twiss. [1838].
'Bos' [T. P. Prest?]. The life and adventures of Oliver Twiss, the workhouse boy. 79 pts 1838–9, 1 vol [1839].

Dramatisations

See Bolton 1987 *under* Studies and bibliographies of adaptations, *below.*
À Beckett, G. A. Oliver Twist. 1838.
Barnett, C. Z. Oliver Twist or the parish boy's progress. 1838.
Almar, G. Oliver Twist. 1838.
Greenwood, T. Boz's Oliver Twist. 1838.
Stirling, E. Oliver Twist. 1838.
Coyne, J. S. Oliver Twist. 1839.
Murray, W. H. W. Oliver Twist. Edinburgh, 1840.
Hazelwood, C. H. Oliver Twist. 1855.
Elphinstone, J. and F. Neale. Oliver Twist. 1855.
Mordaunt, J. Oliver Twist. 1856.
Jefferson, J. Oliver Twist. New York 1860.
Oxenford, J. Oliver Twist. 1868.
Johnstone, J. B. Oliver Twist. 1868.
Emson, F. E. Bumble's courtship. 1874.
Toole, J. L. The Artful Dodger. New York 1875.
Searle, C. Nancy Sikes. 1878.
Collingham, G. C. Oliver Twist. 1891.
Brand, O. Oliver Twist. 1903.
Carr, J. W. C. Oliver Twist. 1905.
Whyte, H. and R. Balmain. Oliver Twist. 1905.
Oliver Twist. Film, Vitagraph 1909. Produced by J. S. Blackton.
Oliver Twist. Film, Pathe 1910.
Oliver Twist. Film, Blom 1910.
Melville, W. and F. Melville. Oliver Twist. 1912.
Oliver Twist. Film 1912. Produced by C. Hepworth and T. Bentley.
Oliver Twist. Film, Paramount 1916. Produced by J. Young.
Oliver Twist, jr. Film 1921. Script by F. M. Willis. Directed by M. Webb.
Oliver Twist. Film 1922. Directed by F. Lloyd and H. Weil, with J. Coogan.
Oliver Twist. Film, Monogram 1933. Script by E. Meehan. Directed by W. Cowen.
Oliver Twist. Film 1948. Written and directed by D. Lean.
Oliver Twist. Film, United Artists 1951. Produced by R. Neame.
Bart, L. Oliver! 1960; film version 1968. Directed by C. Reed.
Oliver Twist. BBC television serial 7 Jan–1 Apr 1962. Script by C. Cox.
Oliver Twist. CBS television play 1982. Script by J. Goldman. Directed by C. Donner.
Oliver Twist. BBC television serial 1985. Script by A. Baron. Directed by G. Davies.

Reviews

See Chittick 1989 *under* Bibliographies and reference works, *above; for comprehensive list of reviews, see also* K. Tillotson's edn Oxford 1966 Clarendon, Appendix F.
[Forster, J.] [Buller, C.] Westminster Rev 29 1837; Examiner 12 Mar, 10 Sep, 19 Nov 1837, 18–25 Nov 1838, 25 Sep 1841; Carlton Chron 8 Apr, 16 May 1837; Southern Literary Messenger May 1837; Sun 1 July 1837, 1 May, 4 June, 1 Aug, 20 Nov 1838; Atlas 9 July, 5 Nov 1837, 6 Oct, 17 Nov 1838; Weekly Dispatch 13 Aug, 3 Sep, 12 and 25 Nov 1837; Morning Chron 2 Sep 1837; [Hayward, A.] Quart Rev 59,

Oct 1837; [Lewes, G. H.] Nat Mag and Monthly Critic Dec 1837; Torch 6 Jan 1838; Courier 5 Feb, 2 Mar, 3 Apr 1838; Bell's Weekly Messenger 6 May 1838; [Lister, T. H.] Edinburgh Rev 68, Oct 1838; Athenaeum 17 Nov 1838, 26 Oct 1839; Literary Gazette 24 Nov 1838; Spectator 24 Nov 1838; Dublin Univ Mag Dec 1838; Court Jnl 15 Dec 1838; Monthly Rev Jan 1839; [[Ford, R.] Quart Rev 64, June 1839; D[wight], J. S., Christian Examiner Nov 1839; [Thackeray, W. M.] Fraser's Mag Apr 1840; Parker's London Mag 2 Feb 1845; [Cleghorn T.?] North Br Rev 3 1845.

Studies and appreciations

Cruikshank, G. The origin of Oliver Twist. The Times 30 Dec 1871.

Cruikshank, G. The artist and the author. 1872. Cruikshank's claim to have originated Oliver Twist; *see* Forster, Life of Dickens vol 2, 1873.

Whipple, E. P. Atlantic Monthly Oct 1876.

Bayne, P. Studies in English Authors. Literary World 4 Apr 1879.

Manners-Smith, C. In the footsteps of Bill Sikes. Cassell's Mag Mar 1900.

Harper, C. G. In the track of Bill Sikes. London Mag Feb 1906.

Southton, J. Y. Bill Sikes's Hampton Tavern. Dickensian 7 1911.

'Sack, O.' [B. W. Matz]. Jacob's island and Bill Sikes's house. Dickensian 14 1918.

Nicholas Nickleby

The life and adventures of Nicholas Nickleby, containing a faithful account of the fortunes, misfortunes, uprisings, downfallings and complete career of the Nickleby family, edited by 'Boz', with illustrations by 'Phiz'. (Title on wrapper. On title page, The life and adventures of Nicholas Nickleby, by Charles Dickens). 20 (as 19) monthly pts (with variants) Apr 1838–Oct 1839. The ms is dispersed in various collections: nearly 100 pages are held in the Rosenbach Museum in Philadelphia; ch 9 is in the Dickens House Museum; there are several pages in the Dexter Collection in the BL, others in the Pierpont Morgan Lib, and half a page in the Free Lib of Philadelphia. Corrected proofs are in the Forster Collection.

Bibliographies

Strange, E. H. Notes on the bibliography of Nicholas Nickleby. Dickensian 33 1937.

A new Dickens bibliography: Nicholas Nickleby. Dickensian 40 1944.

Editions

Oct 1839 (with preface, and portrait of Dickens by Daniel Maclise, as The life and adventures of Nicholas Nickleby). 1 vol.

Philadelphia 1839. First American edn.

Paris 1839.

New York 1839.

Leipzig 1843 Tauchnitz Collection of British Authors no 47, as The life and adventures of Nicholas Nickleby.

1848 Cheap edn, with frontispiece from painting by T. Webster, engraved by T. Williams. (And in 30 weekly pts, 8 monthly pts, Oct 1847–May 1848).

1858 Library edn.

1867 Charles Dickens edn, with new preface.

Boston 1867 Diamond edn, illustr S. Eytinge jr.

New York 1873 Household edn, illustr C. S. Reinhart.

New York 1876 New Illus Lib edn, introd by E. P. Whipple.

1881, illustr F. Barnard.

1883, illustr J. Proctor.

1892 Macmillan edn, introd by C. Dickens the younger.

1897 Gadshill edn, introd by A. Lang. 2 vols.

1899 Temple edn, introd by W. Jerrold. 3 vols.

1900 Rochester edn, introd by G. Gissing, notes by F. G. Kitton. 2 vols.

1902 Biographical edn, introd by A. Waugh.

1906, illustr W. H. C. Groome.

1907 Everyman's Lib edn, introd by G. K. Chesterton.

1913–15, Waverley edn, introd by E. F. Benson, illustr C. Pears and F. Barnard.

New York 1931, illustr C. E. Brock.

1938 Nonesuch edn, ed W. Dexter, H. Walpole, A. Waugh and T. Hatton.

New York 1940 Heritage Club edn, illustr S. Spurrier.

Altrincham 1948 Cheshire Lib edn, illustr J. M. Currie.

1950 New Oxford Illus Dickens, introd by S. Thorndyke.

1953 Collins edn, introd by A. Waugh.

1968 Pan edn, introd and notes by A. Calder-Marshall.

Harmondsworth 1978 Penguin English Lib edn, later Penguin Classics edn, ed with introd and notes by M. Slater.

1982 Scholar facs edn, ed with introd by M. Slater (and in parts 18 Sep 1972–22 Jan 1973).

1982 Signet Classics edn, afterword by S. Marcus.

Toronto and London 1983 Bantam edn, introd by E. Johnson.

1986 Folio Soc edn, introd by C. Hibbert, illustr C. Keeping.

1990 World's Classics edn, ed with introd and notes by P. Schlicke.

1991 Mandarin edn, introd by P. Ackroyd.

1993 Everyman's Lib edn, introd by J. Carey, with G. K. Chesterton's 1907 introd (*above*) as appendix.

1994 Everyman Dickens edn, ed with introd and notes by D. Parker.

Harmondsworth 1999 Penguin Classics edn, ed M. Ford.

Dickens's reading adaptation

Nicholas Nickleby at the Yorkshire School: a reading in four chapters. [1861?] (priv ptd), nd (rev and 'in three chapters'), both rptd ('in four chapters') and in collections 1975, 1983. Facs rptd in parts, Ilkley 1973. *See* Readings, *below.*

Commentary on the text

de Suzannet, A. The original manuscript of Nicholas Nickleby. Dickensian 43 1947.

Slater, M. The composition and monthly publication of Nicholas Nickleby. 1972.

Imitations

'Bos' [T. P. Prest?]. Nickelas Nickelbery: containing the adventures of the family of Nickelbery, embellished with forty-two engravings. [1838?]. In weekly and monthly pts.

'Palette, Peter' [T. Onwhyn]. Thirty-two illustrations to Nicholas Nickleby. [1838–9], Ilkley 1973.

'La Creevy, Miss' [J. K. Meadows]. Heads from Nicholas Nickleby. From drawings by Miss La Creevy. [1839].

'Guess'. Scenes from the life of Nickleby married, with 22 plates by Quiz. 1840.

Dramatisations

See Bolton 1987 *under* Studies and bibliographies of adaptations, *below.*

Stirling, E. Nicholas Nickleby; or, Doings at Dotheboys Hall. 1838.

Pitt, G. D. Nicholas Nickleby; or, the schoolmaster at home and abroad. 1838.

Moncrieff, W. Nicholas Nickleby and Poor Smike; or, the victim of the Yorkshire school. 1839.

Horncastle, H. The savage and the maiden [alt title: Old Crummles and the phenomenon]. New York 1840.

Horncastle, H. The fortunes of Smike: or a sequel to Nicholas Nickleby. 1840.

The humbug or the savage and the maiden. New York 1842.

Boucicault, D. Smike; or, Nicholas Nickleby. New York 1859.

Halliday, A. Nicholas Nickleby. 1875.

Simms, H. Nicholas Nickleby. Brighton 1875.

Nicholas Nickleby. Film, Biograph 1903.

Nicholas Nickleby. Film, Thanhouser 1912.

Nicholas Nickleby. Film 1947. Script by J. Dighton. Directed by A. Cavalcanti.
Nicholas Nickleby. BBC television serial 18 Oct–20 Dec 1957. Script by V. Tilsley.
Nicholas Nickleby. BBC television serial 11 Feb–5 May 1968. Script by H. Leonard.
Edgar, D. The life and adventures of Nicholas Nickleby. 1980; teleplay 1982. Directed by T. Nunn and J. Caird.

Reviews

See Chittick 1989 *under* Bibliographies and reference works, *above*.
Athenaeum 31 Mar 1838; [Forster, J.] Examiner 1 Apr 1838, then irregularly until 27 Oct 1839; Weekly Chron 1 Apr 1838; Sun 2 Apr 1838; Literary Gazette 7 Apr 1838; Age 8 Apr 1838; Bells' New Weekly Messenger 8 Apr 1838; Penny Satirist 10 Nov 1838; [Cooke, J.?] Actors by Daylight 9 Feb 1839; Odd Fellow 9 Feb 1839; Town 7 Sep 1839; Court Jnl 5 Oct 1839; Fraser's Mag Apr 1840; Christian Remembrancer Dec 1842; [Croker, J. W.] Quart Rev 71 1843; [Cleghorn, T.?] North Br Rev 3 1845.

Studies

Thackeray, W. M. Dickens in France. Fraser's Mag Mar 1842. On a Parisian stage version of Nickleby. Illustr Thackeray.
Hayhurst, T. H. An appreciative estimate of the Grant brothers of Ramsbottom – the brothers Cheeryble. 1884.
Elliot, W. H. The country and church of the Cheeryble brothers. Selkirk 1893.
Humphreys, A. The Cheeryble brothers. Dickensian 1 1905.
Humphreys, A. The story of the 'Cheeryble' Grants. Manchester 1906.
Broughton, R. J. Squeers and Dotheboys Hall. Dickensian 7 1911.
Hardy, E. Yorkshire schools. Dickensian 7 1911.
Suddaby, J. The dramatic piracy of Nicholas Nickleby. Dickensian 7 1911.
Pascoe, C. E. Dickens in Yorkshire. [1912].
Thomson, W. R. Mrs Nickleby's tendermindedness. Dickensian 9 1913.
Mulgrew, F. A real Dotheboys Hall. Cornhill Mag Dec 1914.
Suddaby, J. The Shaw Academy trials. Dickensian 11 1915.
Clark, C. Charles Dickens and the Yorkshire schools. 1918, Folcroft PA 1975.

Master Humphrey's clock, The old curiosity shop, Barnaby Rudge

Master Humphrey's clock, by 'Boz' with illustrations by Hablot Browne, George Cattermole, Daniel Maclise, and Samuel Williams. 88 weekly pts and 20 monthly nos from 4 Apr 1840; 3 vols 1840–1 (by 'Charles Dickens') with preface to each vol, that to vol 3 being the preface to Barnaby Rudge. The old curiosity shop pbd 25 Apr 1840–6 Feb 1841; Barnaby Rudge 13 Feb–27 Nov 1841. Some variants in the periodical issues. The 'Clock' setting was not retained when the two long stories were pbd as separate works, and in most collected edns is usually included as a 'miscellany' vol.

Master Humphrey's clock

Bibliography

Gibson, F. Dickens's unique book: a bibliographical causerie. Dickensian 44 1948.

Editions

1841 'extra-illustrated' edn, 3 vols, illustr T. Sibson.
Philadelphia 1841, 1 vol, omits Barnaby Rudge, illustr Cattermole and Browne.
New York 1841, 2 vols, omits Barnaby Rudge.
Paris 1841, includes Master Humphrey's clock, The old curiosity shop, Thackeray's Yellowplush papers, but not Barnaby Rudge.
Leipzig 1846 Tauchnitz Collection of British Authors no 94. 3 vols. 1891, introd by F. Marzials.
1899 Gadshill edn, bound with Edwin Drood, introd and notes by A. Lang.
1903 Temple edn, bound with Great expectations, introd by W. Jerrold. 2 vols.
1908, illustr W. H. C. Groome, omits The old curiosity shop and Barnaby Rudge.
1913–15 Waverley edn, illustr C. Pears and F. Barnard.
1983–4, Nottingham Court Press facs of original issue in parts.
Master Humphrey's clock and other stories. Everyman Dickens edn, ed P. Mudford 1997.

Commentary on the text

de Saint Victor, Carol. Master Humphrey's clock: Dickens's 'lost' book. TSLL 10 1969.
Andrews, M. Introducing Master Humphrey. Dickensian 67 1971.
Chittick, K. A. The idea of a miscellany: Master Humphrey's clock. Dickensian 78 1972.

Reviews

See Chittick 1989 *under* Bibliographies and reference works, *above*.
Monthly Rev May 1840.

Imitations

'Bos' [T. P. Prest?]. Mister Humphrie's clock. 1840. Plagiarism of early sections of Master Humphrey's clock and The old curiosity shop.
'Parallel, J.' Jacob Parallel's hands to Master Humphrey's clock. [1840–1]. 12 illustrations, 4 depicting scenes from Master Humphrey's clock and 8 from The old curiosity shop.
[Nicholson, R.] Master Humphrey's clock: written by himself. Town 10 Nov 1841–26 Jan 1842. 'Continuation' of Master Humphrey's clock contains materials on prototypes from Nicholas Nickleby.
Reynolds, G. M. W. Master Timothy's bookcase. 1842.

Studies and appreciations

Rogers, C. Master Humphrey's clock. N & Q 30 July 1870.
Watson, H. B. North-country lore and legend: Master Humphrey's clock. Monthly Chron Nov 1887.
Kitton, F. G. Master Humphrey's clock: The old curiosity shop, Barnaby Rudge: a biographical and bibliographical sketch. Literary Rev 1 1892.
H., M. Dickens in Yorkshire. Athenaeum 20 Jan 1894.
Suddaby, J. Master Humphrey's clock. Dickensian 6 1910.

The old curiosity shop

The complete ms, number plans for chs 66–72 (the first extant number plans for a Dickens novel), and corrected proofs are in the Forster Collection; corrected galley proofs for chs 29, 30, 31 and 37 are in the Dexter Collection.

Bibliographies

A new Dickens bibliography: The old curiosity shop. Dickensian 40 1944.
Schlicke, P. and P. Schlicke. The old curiosity shop: an annotated bibliography. New York 1988 (Garland Dickens Bibliographies).

Editions

1841. The first edn of The old curiosity shop pbd independently of Master Humphrey's clock, ptd from the original plates with the original pagination. Where 'Clock' material has been excised Dickens added some new material. 4 extra illustrations by Browne added separately.
Philadelphia [1841?]. First American edn, bound in 1 vol with Samuel Warren's Ten thousand a year and Charles Lever's Charles O'Malley.
Philadelphia 1846. Bound in 1 vol with The Pickwick papers, with Master Humphrey's clock still in place, and illustrations by Cattermole, Browne and Gibson; omits Barnaby Rudge.
1848 Cheap edn (and in 20 weekly pts, 5 monthly pts June–Oct 1848),

without illustrations but with new frontispiece by Cattermole and new preface.
1858 Library edn. 2 vols. Bound with Reprinted pieces in vol 2.
1868 Charles Dickens edn, with 8 of the original illustrations, the 1848 preface and running descriptive headlines.
Boston 1869. A raised-letter edn which Dickens arranged during his second American tour to have printed for the blind.
Boston 1871 Illustrated Household edn, illustr S. Eytinge jr.
New York 1872, illustr T. Worth.
[1876] Household edn, illustr C. Green.
New York 1876 New Illus Lib edn, introd by E. P. Whipple. 2 vols.
1892 Macmillan edn, introd by C. Dickens the younger. Reprint of serial version without interpolations Dickens added for pbn as an independent vol.
1897 Gadshill edn, introd and notes by A. Lang. 2 vols.
1899 Temple edn, introd by W. Jerrold. 2 vols.
1901, illustr W. S. Brock.
1901 Rochester edn, introd by G. Gissing, notes by F. G. Kitton, illustr G. M. Brimlow, uses Master Humphrey's clock text of The old curiosity shop with Master Humphrey's clock material extracted and ptd separately. 2 vols.
1902 Biographical edn, introd by A. Waugh, with the original illustrations.
1904 Autograph edn, introd by G. Saintsbury, notes by F. G. Kitton, illustr various hands.
1905, illustr J. Jellicoe.
1906, illustr R. C. Pethrick.
1907 Everyman's Lib edn, introd by G. K. Chesterton.
1910 Charles Dickens Lib edn, illustr H. Furniss.
New York [1913], illustr F. Reynolds.
[1914] Waverley edn, illustr C. Pears and F. Barnard.
[c. 1925], illustr W. H. C. Groome.
1930, illustr R. Wheelwright.
1937–8 Nonesuch edn, ed W. Dexter, H. Walpole, A. Waugh and T. Hatton.
New York 1941 Heritage Club edn, introd by J. Winterich, illustr W. Sharp.
1951 New Oxford Illus Dickens, introd by Earl of Wicklow.
1953 Collins edn, introd by R. B. Johnson.
Harmondsworth 1972 Penguin Eng Lib edn, later Penguin Classics edn, ed with notes by A. Easson, introd by M. Andrews.
1987 Folio Soc edn, introd by C. Hibbert, illustr C. Keeping.
1991 Mandarin edn, introd by P. Ackroyd.
1995 Everyman's Lib edn, introd by P. Washington, with G. K. Chesterton's 1907 introd (*above*) as appendix.
1995 Everyman Dickens edn, ed with introd and notes by P. Schlicke.
Oxford 1997. Clarendon edn , ed E. M. Brennan.
Oxford 1998. Worlds Classics edn, ed E. M. Brennan.

Commentary on the text

Dickens books for the blind. Dickensian 12 1916.
Allen, E. At their fingers' ends. Dickensian 22 1926.
Staples, L. C. Shavings from Dickens's workshop unpublished fragments from the novels, IV: The old curiosity shop. Dickensian 50 1953.
Stevens, J. Woodcuts dropped into the text: the illustrations in The old curiosity shop and Barnaby Rudge. SB 20 1967.
Easson, A. The old curiosity shop: from manuscript to print. Dickens Stud Annual 1 1970.
Patten, R. The story-weaver at his loom: Dickens and the beginning of The old curiosity shop. In Dickens the Craftsman, ed R. B. Partlow, jr, Carbondale IL 1970.
Chittick, K. A. The idea of a miscellany: Master Humphrey's clock. Dickensian 78 1972.
Tick, S. The decline and fall of little Nell: some evidence from the manuscripts. Pacific Coast Philology 9 1974.
Brattin, J. J. Some old curiosities from The old curiosity shop manuscript. Dickens Quart 7 1990.

Imitations

'Bos' [T. P. Prest?]. Mister Humphrie's clock 1840. *See above*, Master Humphrey's clock, Imitations.
'Parley, P.' [S. G. Goodrich]. Parley's Penny Lib [1841]. Weekly periodical containing a pirated version of The old curiosity shop in 7 pts, collected in Dec 1841.
'Poz' [R. Nicholson]. Master Humphrey's turnip: a chimney-corner crotchet. Town, weekly 25 Apr–5 Dec 1840. Parody of The old curiosity shop.

Dramatisations

See Bolton 1987 *under* Studies and bibliographies of adaptations, *below*.
Cooper, F. F. Master Humphrey's clock. 1840.
Stirling, E. The old curiosity shop; or, one hour from Humphrey's clock. 1840.
Brougham, J. Little Nell and the Marchioness. 1867.
Bartlett, G. B. and W. G. Benham. Mrs Jarley's far-famed collection of waxworks. 1870.
Lander, G. The old curiosity shop. 1877.
The old curiosity shop. Film, Essanay 1909.
The old curiosity shop. Film, Thanhouser 1911.
The old curiosity shop. Film, Pathe 1912.
The old curiosity shop. Films 1914, 1921, 1935. Directed by T. Bentley.
Padmore, E. S. The old curiosity shop of Charles Dickens: dramatised as an ironical morality. 1917.
The old curiosity shop. BBC television serial Nov 1962–Feb 1963. Script by C. Cox.
Mister Quilp (retitled The old curiosity shop for video release). Musical feature film 1975. Script by L. and I. Kamp. Directed by M. Tuchner.
The old curiosity shop. BBC television serial 9 Dec 1979–1 Feb 1980. Script by W. Trevor.
The old curiosity shop. Animated feature film, Australia 1984. Script by A. Buzo. Directed by W. Gilbert.
The old curiosity shop. Disney Channel television Mar 1995. Directed by K. Connor.

Reviews

See Chittick 1989 *under* Bibliographies and reference works, *above*.
Metropolitan Mag 28, 29 1840, 30 1841; Fraser's Mag Apr 1840; [Forster, J.] Examiner 3 May, 31 May, 12 July, 16 Aug 1840, 4 Dec 1841; Reynolds, G. W. M. Teetotaller July 1840; [Hood, T.] Athenaeum 7 Nov 1840; [Linton, W. J.] Odd Fellow 3 1841; Bristol Mag and Western Literary Jnl 23 Jan 1841; Western Times (Exeter) 6 Mar 1841; Poe, E. A. Graham's Mag 18 May 1841; P[eabody], A. P. Christian Examiner 32 1842; Christian Remembrancer 14 Dec 1842; Illus Polytechnic Rev 22, 3 June 1843; [Cleghorn, T.] North Br Rev 3 May 1845.

Studies and appreciations

Landor, W. S. To Charles Dickens. Examiner 21 Sep 1844. Verse letter eulogising Nell.
Fitzgerald, E. Little Nell's wanderings. [1846]. In A Fitzgerald medley, ed C. Ganz, 1933.
Young, C. Little Nell. nd. Popular song.
Heavisides, E. M. Little Nell. In Poetical and prose remains of Edward Marsh Heavisides, 1850. Poem.
Butler, A. W. H. The death of little Nell. Quiver 2 1867. Poem.
Little Nell. Human Nature Aug 1871. Poem.
Pickford, J. The old curiosity shop. N & Q 21 Oct 1871.
Harte, B. Dickens in camp. In Poetical works, 1872.
Coleridge, S. Memoir and letters. 1873. Wilhelm Meister as influence.
Old curiosity shop. Pall Mall Gazette 1 Jan 1884. Portsmouth Street shop.

The old printer's curiosity shop: a reminiscence of the late Charles Dickens. Provincial and Colonial Press News 19 Feb 1884. Fetter Lane shop.
The characters of Charles Dickens drawn by Kyd. No 1 Quilp – The old curiosity shop. Fleet Street Mag 1, 10 Sep 1887.
The church of little Nell. Pump Court 3 Dec 1887.
Liston, W. L. The little Nell of Charles Dickens. Girl's Own Paper Dec 1889.
The old curiosity shop. Publisher's Circular 23 Apr 1890. Fetter Lane shop.
Kitton, F. G. Master Humphrey's clock: The old curiosity shop, Barnaby Rudge: a biographical and bibliographical sketch. Literary Rev 1 1892.
Ragan, H. In the footsteps of Dickens. Cosmopolitan 15 1893. Portsmouth Street shop.
Habben, F. H. The old curiosity shop. People 9 July 1899.
Stafford, D. In the steps of Dickens: the death-place of little Nell. Ludgate Sep 1900. Tong.
S., C. S. In the steps of little Nell. Illus London News 9 Sep 1905. Tong and Black Country.
'Sack, O.' [B. W. Matz]. Coventry and Dickens. Dickensian 2 1906.
Moore, E. H. Dickens and Birmingham. Dickensian 3 1907.
Where little Nell died. Dickensian 3 1907. Tong.
R., A. The old curiosity shop: traditional notes on the house immortalised by Charles Dickens as the home of little Nell and her grandfather. 1907. Portsmouth Street shop.
A[uden], J. E. Tong and the old curiosity shop. Dickensian 4 1908.
The old curiosity shop. Westminster Gazette 11 May 1908. Portsmouth Street shop.
Sawle, Rose, Lady Graves [Rose Caroline Paynter]. Sketches from the diaries of Rose Lady Graves Sawle. 1908. Prototype for Quilp.
Stafford, D. The resting place of little Nell. Great Thoughts 5 Dec 1908. Tong.
Davis, G. W. Dickens and Birmingham. Dickensian 5 1909.
The old curiosity shop: a picturesque survival. Daily Telegraph 4 Jan 1909. Portsmouth Street shop.
Day, J. B. The old curiosity shop. Daily Telegraph 5 Jan 1909.
Where little Nell died. English Illus Mag 41, July 1909. Tong.
Allbut, R. Old curiosity shop. I. Dickensian 6 1910.
The disappearance of Dickens's London. Bazaar 16 Sep 1910. Westminster Bridge shop.
F. The old curiosity shop. II. Dickensian 6 1910.
Hearn, A. J. The old curiosity shop. IV. Dickensian 6 1910.
'Jingle'. Literary legends and landmarks of London. Bystander 10 Aug 1910.
Little Bethel. Daily News 7 Mar 1910. Zoar Chapel.
Matz, B. W. When found. Dickensian 6 1910. Portsmouth Street shop.
Minster Abbey Church and Dickens. Dickensian 6 1910. Sheppey.
Polack, E. E. Humorous villains: a comparison between Daniel Quilp and Shakespeare's Richard the Third. Dickensian 6 1910.
Reade, C. T. The old curiosity shop. III. Dickensian 6 1910.
'Rutherford, Mark' [W. H. White]. Little Nell. In his Pages from a journal, with other papers, 1910.
Stafford, D. The birthplace of little Nell. Great Thoughts 21 May 1910. Bath.
Stafford, D. Dickens and the Midlands. Great Thoughts 11 June 1910.
Allbut, R. She lay at rest. Dickensian 7 1911. Poem.
Carlton, G. Was Daniel Quilp a real character or a caricature? Discovery of the flesh-and-blood original used by Dickens in The old curiosity shop. New York Times 16 July 1911.
Cross, A. E. B. Our ladies of sorrow and The old curiosity shop. Dickensian 7 1911. Link with De Quincey.
Van Noorden, C. Some Dickens discoveries. Strand Mag 42 1911. London topography.
Corfield, W. At the canal, Birmingham. Dickensian 8 1912.
Nabokoff, V. Charles Dickens: a Russian appreciation. Dickensian 8 1912.
Watson, L. Charles Dickens and the dissenters. N & Q 29 June 1912. Little Bethel.
Corfield, W. Demolition of Dickensian landmarks in Birmingham. N & Q 7, 11th ser 1913.
Corfield, W. Where was Little Bethel? Dickensian 9 1913.
Rogers, F. Little Bethel. Dickensian 9 1913.
Dexter, W. The old curiosity shop, Portugal Street, Lincoln's Inn Fields. In Charles Dickens: A Bookman extra number, 1914.
Dickens' little Nell? Death of lady born in the old curiosity shop. Daily News and Leader 13 May 1914. Miss Tice.
Hulme, H. Quilp's house. Dickensian 10 1914.
Matz, B. W. When found. Dickensian 10 1914. Miss Tice.
Carver, B. A ride to little Nell's haven. Cycling 49, 25 May 1915.
Matz, B. W. Memorials and tablets to Dickens. Dickensian 11 1915. Portsmouth Street shop.
Philip, A. J. Dickens' originals. IV. The old curiosity shop and little Nell. Millgate Monthly Aug 1915.
Seen by the tourist: little Nell's burial place. Cycling 50, 22 July 1915. Tong.
Fitzgerald, P. A Dickens perplexity. II. Little Nell's travels. Dickensian 12 1916.
Minck, J. M. Daniel Quilp. Dickensian 13 1917.
Thornton, C. Poetical tributes to Charles Dickens: Little Nell. Dickensian 13 1917.
The schoolmistress in literature: 14. Sophy Wackles and Miss Monflathers. Schoolmaster 28 Dec 1918.
Sharp, H. In defence of little Nell. Dickensian 14 1918.
McNaught, C. Dickens's Bevis Marks. Dickensian 15 1919.
W. London in little: the old curiosity shop. John o' London's Weekly 4 Oct 1919.
Smith, H. G. The art of Mr Slum: poets as advertisers. John o' London's Weekly 10 July 1920.

Barnaby Rudge: a tale of the riots of '80

The complete ms, including the original 3 chs composed 1839, and proofs for chs 17 and 18 are in the Forster Collection.

Bibliography

Rice, T. J. Barnaby Rudge: an annotated bibliography. New York, 1987. Garland Dickens Bibliographies.

Editions

1841, with the original illustrations; first separate edn; ptd from the stereotype plates of Master Humphrey's clock, vols 2–3, and retaining their pagination.
c. 1841 Parley's Penny Lib edn, with 20 engravings.
Philadelphia 1842. First American edn.
Paris 1842.
1849 Cheap edn (and in weekly parts Nov 1848–Apr 1849).
1858 Library edn. 2 vols, bound with Hard times in vol 2.
1865 People's edn. 2 vols.
1868 Charles Dickens edn, with 8 of the original illustrations and new running headlines.
1874 Household edn, illustr F. Barnard.
New York 1877 New Illus Lib edn, introd by E. P. Whipple. 2 vols, bound with Master Humphrey's clock and Edwin Drood.
1892 Macmillan edn, introd by C. Dickens the younger.
1897 Gadshill edn, introd and notes by A. S. Lang. 2 vols.
1899 Temple edn, introd by W. Jerrold. 2 vols.
1901 Rochester edn, introd by G. Gissing, notes by F. G. Kitton. 2 vols.
1902 Biographical edn, introd by A. Waugh, with original illustrations.
1905 Autograph edn, introd by A. Dobson, notes by F. G. Kitton, and the original illustrations. 3 vols.

1906, introd by A. A. Barter.
New York 1911 Anniversary edn, introd and notes by W. Jerrold.
1913–15 Waverley edn, illustr C. Pears and F. Barnard.
New York 1919, introd and notes by L. H. Vincent.
1937 Nonesuch edn, ed W. Dexter, H. Walpole, A. Waugh and T. Hatton.
New York 1944 Great Illus Classics edn, introd by M. L. Becker.
1950 Everyman's Lib edn, introd by G. K. Chesterton.
1953 Collins edn, introd by K. Hayens.
1954 New Oxford Illus edn, introd by K. Tillotson.
Harmondsworth 1973 Penguin English Lib edn, later Penguin Classics edn, introd and notes by G. Spence.
1987 Folio Soc edn, introd by C. Hibbert, illustr C. Keeping.
1991 Mandarin edn, introd by P. Ackroyd.
1997 Everyman Dickens edn, ed with introd and notes by D. Hawes.

Commentary on the text

Stevens, J. Woodcuts dropped into the text: the illustrations in The old curiosity shop and Barnaby Rudge. SB 20 1967.
Brattin, J. J. 'Secrets inside . . . to strike to your heart': new readings from Dickens's manuscript of Barnaby Rudge, ch 75. Dickens Quart 8 1991.

Imitation

'Bos' [T. P. Prest]. Barnaby Rudge. Illustr 'Phis' 1841.

Dramatisations

See Bolton 1987 *under* Studies and bibliographies of adaptations, *below.*
Selby, C. and C. Melville. Barnaby Rudge. 1841.
Barnett, C. Z. Barnaby Rudge. 1841.
Stirling, E. Barnaby Rudge; or, the riots in London in 1780. 1841.
Dillon, C. Barnaby Rudge. 1844.
Higgie, T. Barnaby Rudge; or, the murder at the Warren. 1841.
Almar, G. Barnaby Rudge. 1841.
Phillips, W. and H. Vining. Barnaby Rudge. 1866.
Wood, M. Dolly Varden. 1872.
Cave, J. Barnaby Rudge. 1876.
Simpson, E. Dolly Varden; or, the riots of 1780. Brighton 1889.
Stange, S. Dolly Varden. New York c. 1901.
Dexter, W. Dolly Varden. 1907.
Dolly Varden. Film 1913. Produced by T. A. Edison.
Barnaby Rudge. Films 1915, 1921. Directed by T. Bentley.
Barnaby Rudge. BBC television 1960. Script by M. Voysey.
Jones-Evans, E. The blue cockade. Southampton 1964.

Reviews

See Chittick 1989 *under* Bibliographies and reference works, *above.*
Poe, E. A., Saturday Post 1 May 1841; Cooke, J., Actor's Note Book 26 May 1841; Metropolitan Mag June, Sep, Dec 1841; [Forster, J.] Examiner 4 Dec 1841; [Hood, T.] Athenaeum 22 Jan 1842; Poe, E. A., Graham's Mag Feb 1842; Christian Remembrancer 4 1842; Southern Quart Rev 3 1843; [Cleghorn, T.?] North Br Rev 3 1845; [Murray, P. A.] Dublin Rev 21 1846.

Studies and appreciations

Salmon, R. S. Lord George Gordon's riots. N & Q 2nd ser 2, 13 Sep 1856.
Harte, B. Dolly Varden. In An episode of Fiddletown and other sketches, [1873].
Foulsham, F. In the footsteps of Barnaby Rudge. Royal Mag 5 1900.
Fraser, J. A. L. Gashford and his prototype. Dickensian 2 1906.
Philip, A. J. Blunders of Dickens and his illustrators. Dickensian 2 1906.
Macleod, J. A. The personality of Barnaby Rudge. Dickensian 5 1909.
Polack, E. E. Was Barnaby Rudge mad? Dickensian 7 1911.
The King's Head Chigwell. A short account of the historic 'Maypole' in Barnaby Rudge. [1912].
Rees, B. The polished villain and the uncouth villain. Dickensian 8 1912.
Wilkins, W. G. Barnaby Rudge and the Gordon riots. Dickensian 8 1912.
Roberts, H. Could Dickens describe a gentleman? Dickensian 9 1913.
'Sack, O.' [B. W. Matz]. Dickens's ravens. Dickensian 13 1917.
[Wilkins, W. G.] Poe and Dickens: a mystery cleared up. Pittsburg 1918.

Martin Chuzzlewit

The life and adventures of Martin Chuzzlewit, his relatives, friends and enemies: comprising all his wills and his ways, with an historical record of what he did, and what he didn't; showing, moreover, who inherited the family plate, who came in for the silver spoons, and who for the wooden ladles: the whole forming a complete key to the House of Chuzzlewit, edited by 'Boz', with illustrations by 'Phiz'. (Title on wrapper. On title page and for vol issue, The life and adventures of Martin Chuzzlewit, by Charles Dickens.) 20 (as 19) monthly pts, Jan 1843–July 1844 (with variants). The complete ms, preliminaries, number plans and corrected proofs are in the Forster Collection.

Bibliographies

A new Dickens bibliography: Martin Chuzzlewit. Dickensian 39 1943. Information superseded Dickensian 67 1971 and TLS 11 June 1971.
Nisbet, A. The mystery of Martin Chuzzlewit. In Essays critical and historical dedicated to L. B. Campbell. Berkeley and Los Angeles 1950.
Lougy, R. E. Martin Chuzzlewit: an annotated bibliography. New York 1990. (Garland Dickens Bibliographies).

Editions

The life and adventures of Martin Chuzzlewit. 1 vol collection of original monthly pts, with preface and the 38 original illustrations. 1844.
Leipzig 1844 Tauchnitz Collection of British Authors edn 57, as The life and adventures of Martin Chuzzlewit. 2 vols.
Paris 1844 Baudry's European Lib edn. 2 vols.
'1850' [1849] Cheap edn, with new preface, and frontispiece by F. Stone (and in 32 weekly pts, 8 monthly pts, May–Nov 1849).
1858 Library edn. 2 vols.
1867 Charles Dickens edn, with rev preface.
New York 1877 New Illus Lib edn. 2 vols, introd by E. P. Whipple.
1892 Macmillan edn, introd by C. Dickens the younger.
1899 Temple edn, introd by W. Jerrold. 3 vols.
New York 1899. 2 vols, introd and notes by A. Lang.
1902 Biographical edn, introd by A. Waugh, with original illustrations.
1907 Everyman Lib edn, introd by G. K. Chesterton.
1915 Waverley edn, introd by M. Pemberton, illustr F. Barnard. 2 vols.
1937 Nonesuch edn, bound with Christmas stories, ed W. Dexter, H. Walpole, A. Waugh and T. Hatton.
1951 New Oxford Illus Dickens, introd by G. Russell.
New York 1951 Heritage Club edn, introd by J. Winterich, illustr W. Manning.
1953 Collins edn, introd by K. Hayens.
New York 1965 Signet Classics edn, afterword by M. Mudrick.
New York 1965 Laurel edn, introd by E. Johnson.
Harmondsworth 1968 Penguin English Lib edn, later Penguin Classics edn, ed with introd and notes by P. N. Furbank.
Oxford 1982 Clarendon edn, ed M. Cardwell.
Oxford 1982 World's Classics edn, ed with new introd and notes by M. Cardwell.
1988 Folio Soc edn, introd by C. Hibbert, illustr C. Keeping.
1991 Mandarin edn, introd by P. Ackroyd.

1994 Everyman's Lib edn, introd by W. Boyd, with G. K. Chesterton's 1907 introd (*above*) as appendix.
1994 Everyman Dickens edn, ed with introd and notes by M. Slater.
Harmondsworth 1998 Penguin Classics edn, ed P. Ingham.

Dickens's adaptations

Mrs Gamp. 1858 (reading) (priv ptd, with The poor traveller); Boston 1868 (Mrs Gamp only); New York 1956 (facs of the author's prompt-copy, ed J. D. Gordan); and in collections 1975, 1983. *See* Readings, *below*.
An account of a late expedition into the North, for an amateur theatrical benefit, written by Mrs Gamp. Fragment composed for use on theatrical tour on behalf of Leigh Hunt 1847. Not pbd in Dickens's lifetime, but included in Forster's Life, bk 6 ch 1; priv ptd from ms as Mrs Gamp with the strolling players: an unfinished sketch by Charles Dickens, New York 1899; as A new Piljians Projiss, nd (facs of ms, illustr J. Leech, F. Barnard and F. W. Pailthorpe).

Commentary on the text

Butt, J. The serial publication of Dickens's novels: Martin Chuzzlewit and Little Dorrit. In his Pope, Dickens and others, Edinburgh 1969.
Brattin, J. J. A map of the labyrinth: editing Dickens's manuscripts. Dickens Quart 2 1985.
Metz, N. A. The companion to Martin Chuzzlewit. Dickens Companions ser. Forthcoming Mountfield East Sussex.

Imitations

'Bos'. Life and adventures of Martin Puzzlewhit. Lloyd's Penny Sunday Times from 15 Jan 1843.
'Syr' [S. A. Allen]. My own home and fireside: being illustrative of the speculations of Martin Chuzzlewit and Co, among the 'Wenom of the Walley of Eden'. Philadelphia 1846.

Dramatisations

See Bolton 1987 *under* Studies and bibliographies of adaptations, *below*.
Stirling, E. Martin Chuzzlewit; his friends, relations and enemies. 1844.
Webb, C. Martin Chuzzlewit; or, his wills and his ways, what he did and what he didn't. 1844.
Higgie, T. H. and T. H. Lacy. Martin Chuzzlewit; or, his wills and his ways, what he did and what he didn't. 1844. Differs considerably from Webb's version; *see* Bolton 1987 *under* Studies and bibliographies of adaptations, *below*.
Stirling, E. Mrs Harris: a farce. 1846.
Webster, B. Mrs Sarah Gamp's tea and turn out: a Bozzian sketch. 1846.
Cooper, F. F. Dealings with the firm of Gamp and Harris. 1846.
Fiske, S. Martin Chuzzlewit. New York 1864.
Wigan, H. Martin Chuzzlewit. 1868.
Dilley, J. J. and L. Clifton. Tom Pinch. 1881.
Martin Chuzzlewit. Film 1912. Produced by T. A. Edison.
Martin Chuzzlewit. Film, Biograph 1914.
Martin Chuzzlewit. BBC television 1964. Script by C. Cox.
Martin Chuzzlewit. BBC television serial Nov–Dec 1994. Script by D. Lodge.

Reviews

[Hickson, W. E.?] Westminster Rev 40 1843; Brother Jonathan 29 July 1843, rptd in Dickensian 10 1914; Christian Remembrancer Oct 1843; [Blanchard, S. L.] Ainsworth's Mag Jan 1844; Critic Jan 1844; Dublin Univ Mag Apr 1844; [Chorley, H. F.] Athenaeum 20 July 1844; Monthly Rev Sep 1844; Knickerbocker 24 Sep 1844; [Forster, J.] Examiner 26 Oct 1844; [Cleghorn, T.] North Br Rev 3 1845; [Howitt, W.] People's Jnl 1 June 1846; Eng Rev Dec 1848; Ecclesiastic and Theologian Oct 1855; Nat Rev 13 1861.

Studies and appreciations

Butler, Samuel. A translation, attempted in consequence of a challenge. Cambridge [1894]. Rptd from Eagle. A trn of an utterance of Mrs Gamp's (ch 19 of Martin Chuzzlewit) into Greek Homeric hexameters.
Harper, C. C. The Blue Dragon of Martin Chuzzlewit. Dickensian 1 1905.
Shore, W. T. On re-reading Martin Chuzzlewit. Dickensian 1 1905.
Matchett, W. Thomas Griffiths Wainwright: a notable Dickens model. Dickensian 2 1906.
Osborne, C. C. Mr Pecksniff and his prototype. Independent Rev Sep 1906.
Crandon, E. S. The last of Eden. Dickensian 5 1909.
Fitch, R. G. The last of Eden. Dickensian 5 1909.
How they hoaxed Dickens. Dickensian 6 1910.
Romayne, L. The Chuzzlewit family. Dickensian 6 1910.
Snyder, J. F. Charles Dickens in Illinois. Jnl of the Illinois State Historical Soc 3 1910.
Welsh, D. The Mississippi Eden. Harper's Mag 121 1910.
Cross, A. E. B. Martin Chuzzlewit: a few random remarks. Dickensian 12 1916.
Dutch drops. Dickensian 13 1917.
Keane, C. Mark Tapley: Charles Dickens's richest legacy to humanity. Dickensian 14 1918.
Chuzzlewit's Eden now a garden spot. Dickensian 16 1920.
Dickens's Martin Chuzzlewit and Theodore Roosevelt. Dickensian 16 1920.
Dickens and Sweeney Todd. Dickensian 16 1920.

Dombey and son

Dealings with the firm of Dombey and son wholesale, retail and for exportation, with illustrations by H. K. Browne. (Title on wrapper. On title page and for vol issue, Dombey and son.) 20 (as 19) monthly pts, Oct 1846–Apr 1848 (with variants). The complete ms, number plans and corrected proofs are in the Forster Collection.

Bibliographies

A new Dickens bibliography: Dombey and son. Dickensian 39 1943.
Levine, R. A. Paperback editions: Dombey and son. Dickens Stud Newsletter 3 1972.
Sadrin, A. Dombey and son: a selective bibliography. Cahiers Victoriens and Edouardiens 32 1990.
Litvack, L. Charles Dickens's Dombey and son: an annotated bibliography. New York 1999. Dickens Bibliographies ser.

Editions

New York 1847 [1847–8]; New York 1847–8 [monthly parts].
Boston 1847–8. Jones' Cheap edn.
1847 Tauchnitz Collection of British Authors no 119, first as Dealings with the firm of Dombey and son, later as Dombey and son. 3 vols.
1848 1 vol with preface and original illustrations.
Philadelphia 1848.
New York 1848. Library of Choice Reading.
1858 Cheap edn, with new frontispiece.
1859 Library edn. 2 vols.
1865 People's edn.
1867 Charles Dickens edn, with new preface.
New York 1877 New Illus Lib edn, introd by E. P. Whipple. 2 vols.
1892 Macmillan edn, with introd by C. Dickens the younger.
1897 Gadshill edn, introd and notes by A. Lang. 2 vols.
1899 Temple edn, introd by W. Jerrold. 3 vols.
1903 Biographical edn, introd by A. Waugh, with the original illustrations.
1907 Everyman's Lib edn, introd by G. K. Chesterton.
1908 Autograph edn, introd by E. Dowden, notes by F. G. Kitton and the original illustrations. 3 vols.

1910 London edn. 2 vols.
1913–15 Waverley edn, introd by L. Malet, illustr C. Pears and F. Barnard.
1937 Nonesuch edn, ed W. Dexter, H. Walpole, A. Waugh and T. Hatton.
New York 1950, introd by J. Cournos.
1950 New Oxford Illus edn, introd by H. W. Garrod.
1954, introd by M. Whyte.
New York 1957 Heritage Club edn, introd by J. T. Winterich.
New York 1963 Dell edn, introd by E. Johnson.
New York 1964 Signet Classics edn, afterword by A. Pryce-Jones.
Harmondsworth 1970 Penguin English Lib edn, later Penguin Classics edn, ed with notes by P. Fairclough and introd by R. Williams.
Oxford 1974 Clarendon edn, ed A. Horsman.
Oxford 1982 World's Classics edn, ed with notes and new introd by A. Horsman.
1984 Folio Society edn, introd by C. Hibbert.
1991 Mandarin edn, introd by P. Ackroyd.
1994 Everyman's Lib edn, introd by L. Hughes-Hallet, with G. K. Chesterton's 1907 introd (*above*) as appendix.
1997 Everyman Dickens edn, ed with introd and notes by V. Purton.
Harmondsworth 1998, Penguin Classics edn, ed D. Birch.

Dickens's reading adaptation

The story of little Dombey. [1858] (priv ptd), 1858, 1862, nd, Boston 1868; in collections 1975, 1983. *See* Readings, *below.*

Commentary on the text

Butt, J. and K. Tillotson. Dickens at work on Dombey and son. E & S n.s. 4 1951.
Tillotson, K. A lost sentence in Dombey and son. Dickensian 47 1951. *See* D. S. Bland, Dickensian 52 1956.
Staples, L. C. Shavings from Dickens's workshop: unpublished fragments from the novels, II. Dickensian 49 1953.
Herring, P. D. The number plans for Dombey and son: some further observations. MP 68 1970.

Imitations

Inquest on the late Master Paul Dombey. The Man in the Moon, ed A. Smith and A. B. Reach, Mar 1847.
Nicholson, R. Dombey and daughter: a moral fiction. [1847]. In penny nos.
Dombey and son finished: part the best and last. The Man in the Moon Feb 1848.
'Buz'. Dolby and father. New York 1868. Parody, in part, of Dombey and son, with characters from other works by Dickens and some serious attacks upon him.

Dramatisations

See Bolton 1987 *under* Studies and bibliographies of adaptations, *below.*
Taylor, T. P. Dombey and son; Good Mrs Brown the child stealer. 1847.
Brougham, J. Dombey and son. New York 1848.
Walcot, C. M. Edith; or, dealings with the firm of Dombey and son. New York 1848.
The Nipper; or one of the house(hold) of Dombey. New York 1848.
Sydney, W. Dombey and son; or good Mrs Brown the child stealer. 1849.
Brougham, J. Captain Cuttle: a few more scenes from the moral [*sic*] of Dombey and son. 1850.
Halliday, A. Heart's delight. Newcastle upon Tyne 1873.
What are the wild waves saying, sister? Film, Amer Mutoscope and Biograph 1903.
Dombey and son. Film 1918. Script by E. Stannard. Produced by M. Elvey.
Rich man's folly. Film 1931. Script by G. Jones and E. Paramore, jr. Directed by J. Cromwell.
Dombey and son. BBC television 1969. Script by H. Leonard. Directed by J. Craft.
Dombey and son. BBC television 1983. Script by J. A. Hall. Directed by R. Bennett.

Reviews

[Kent, W. C. M.] Sun 2 Oct 1846 and frequently thereafter; Economist 10 Oct, 7 Nov, 12 Dec 1846; Chambers's Jnl 24 Oct 1846; Athenaeum 31 Oct 1846; [Warren, S.] Blackwood's Mag Nov 1846; [Hickson, W. E.?] Westminster Rev 47 1847; [Patmore, C.?] North Br Rev 7 1847; Christian Remembrancer Oct 1847; Rambler Jan 1848; Dudley, A. Revue des Deux Mondes Mar 1848; People's Jnl 22 Apr 1848; Sharpe's London Mag May 1848; [Aytoun, W. E.] Blackwood's Mag Oct 1848; [Forster, J.] Examiner 28 Oct 1848; Eng Rev Dec 1848; [Whipple, E. P.] North Amer Rev 69 1849; Williams, S. F. Rose, Shamrock and Thistle June 1863; 'Nathaniel, Sir'. NMM June 1864.

Studies and appreciations

Sterry, S. The wooden midshipman. All the Year Round 29 Oct 1881.
Humpherys, A. The prototype of Polly Toodle. Dickensian 3 1907.
Allemandy, V. H. Notes of Dickens's Dombey and son. 1910.
B[rindley], H. B. Where was Mr Carker killed. Cambridge Review Apr 1911.
Matchett, W. A chat about Dombey. Dickensian 11 1915.

David Copperfield

The personal history, adventures, experiences and observations of David Copperfield the younger, of Blunderstone Rookery, (which he never meant to be published on any account), with illustrations by H. K. Browne. (Title on wrapper. On title page and for vol issue, The personal history of David Copperfield.) 20 (as 19) monthly pts, May 1849–Nov 1850 (with variants). The complete ms, number plans and corrected proofs are in the Forster Collection.

Bibliographies

A new Dickens bibliography: David Copperfield. Dickensian 39 1943.
Dunn, R. J. David Copperfield: an annotated bibliography. 1981. (Garland Dickens Bibliographies).

Editions

1850 The personal history of David Copperfield. 1 vol with preface.
Leipzig 1850 Tauchnitz Collection of British Authors no 175, as The personal history, adventures . . . of David Copperfield. 3 vols.
New York 1850. 2 vols.
1858 Cheap edn, with new preface.
1859 Library edn. 2 vols.
1867 Charles Dickens edn, with rev preface.
New York 1877 New Illus Lib edn, introd by E. P. Whipple. 2 vols.
1892 Macmillan edn, introd by C. Dickens the younger.
1897 Gadshill edn, introd and notes by A. Lang. 2 vols.
1899 Temple edn, introd by W. Jerrold. 3 vols.
1900, introd by W. K. Leask.
1903 Autograph edn, introd by G. Gissing, notes by F. G. Kitton, illustr H. M. Brock. 3 vols.
1903, introd and notes by A. A. Barter.
1903 Biographical edn, introd by A. Waugh, with the original illustrations.
1907 Everyman's Lib edn, introd by G. K. Chesterton.
Boston 1910, introd and notes by P. M. Buck, jr.
New York 1911, introd and notes by E. Fairley. 2 vols.
1912 Waverley edn, introd by H. Caine, illustr C. Pears and F. Barnard. 2 vols.
Oxford 1916, ed E. Kibblewhite.
Bath 1919 Readers' Classic edn, ed G. K. Chesterton, H. Jackson and R. B. Johnson with a large collection of critical appreciations.

New York 1928 Modern Readers edn, introd by A. Nevins. 2 vols.
Garden City NY 1936, ed H. S. Hughes. 2 vols.
1937 Nonesuch edn, ed W. Dexter, H. Walpole, A. Waugh and T. Hatton.
New York 1943 Great Illus Classics edn, introd by M. L. Becker.
New York 1950 Modern Lib edn, ed E. K. Brown.
1952 Collins Classics edn, introd by N. Collins.
New York 1952 Macmillan's Classics edn, afterword by C. Fadiman.
Boston 1958 Riverside edn, ed with introd and notes by G. H. Ford.
New York 1958 Pocket Books edn, introd by J. Mersand.
New York 1962 Signet Classics edn, afterword by E. Johnson.
New York 1965 Airmont edn, introd by M. M. Threapleton.
Harmondsworth 1966 Penguin English Lib edn, later Penguin Classics edn, ed with introd and notes by T. Blount.
1967 Pan edn, introd and notes by A. Calder-Marshall.
1971 Ultratype edn, introd by A. Wilson.
Oxford 1981 Clarendon edn, ed with introd by N. Burgis.
Oxford 1983 World's Classics edn, ed with new introd and notes by N. Burgis.
1983 Folio Soc edn, introd by C. Hibbert, illustr C. Keeping.
New York 1990 Norton Critical edn, ed with notes, background sources and studies by J. H. Buckley.
1991 Mandarin edn, introd by P. Ackroyd.
1991 Everyman's Lib edn, introd by M. Slater, with G. K. Chesterton's 1907 introd (*above*) as appendix.
New York 1991 Chelsea House edn, introd by H. Bloom.
1993 Everyman Dickens edn, ed with introd and notes by M. Andrews.
1995 Macmillan edn, bound with Hard times, introd by J. Peck.
Harmondsworth 1996, Penguin Classics edn, ed J. Tambling.
Oxford 1997 World's Classics edn, ed with introd and notes by A. Sanders.

Dickens's reading adaptation

David Copperfield: a reading in five chapters. nd (priv ptd), Boston 1868, London 1921 (reprint of 1st edn, with a note by J. H. Stonehouse summarising the Maria Beadnell correspondence and the relation between David Copperfield and Dickens's own life), New York 1995 (afterword by A. Bell); in collections 1975, 1983. *See* Readings, *below*.

Commentary on the text

Kidson, F. The King Charles's head allusion in David Copperfield. Dickensian 2 1906.
[Dexter, W.] The long and the short of it. Dickensian 35 1939.
Dexter, W. The favourite child. Dickensian 39 1943.
Dexter, W. and K. Bromhill [T. W. Hill]. The David Copperfield advertiser. Dickensian 41 1944.
Butt, J. Dickens's notes for his serial parts. Dickensian 45 1949.
King Charles in the china shop. Dickensian 45 1949.
Butt, J. The composition of David Copperfield. Dickensian 46–7, 1950–1.
Butt, J. David Copperfield: from manuscript to print. RES n.s. 1 1950.
Staples, L. C. Shavings from Dickens's workshop: unpublished fragments of his novels, I: David Copperfield. Dickensian 48 1952.
Muir, P. H. Note 53: the Tauchnitz David Copperfield, 1849. BC 4 1955.
Cowden, R. W. Dickens at work. Michigan Quart Rev 9 1970.
Gaskell, P. The textual history of David Copperfield. In his A new introduction to bibliography, Oxford 1972.
Millhauser, M. David Copperfield: some shifts of plan. Nineteenth-Cent Fiction 27 1972.
Hawes, D. David Copperfield's names. Dickensian 74 1978.
Brattin, J. J. Recent Norton Critical editions: David Copperfield . . . Hard times. Dickens Quart 8 1991.

Imitations

Coalfield, J. [pseud]. Micawber redivivus. [c. 1870].
McLean, R. Public examination of Wilkins Micawber, Esq. In Diversions of an articled clerk, 1892.
Fellow, C. Mr Chippendale of Fort Welcome. 1905.
Rust, S. J. David Copperfield and his friends: what they did in the great war. Dickensian 16 1920.
Graves, R. The real David Copperfield. 1933. Dickens's text rev at full length to 'sort what is true from what is false', with critical introd by way of justification.

Dramatisations

See Bolton 1987 *under* Studies and bibliographies of adaptations, *below*.
Almar, G. Born with a caul; or the personal adventures of David Copperfield. 1850.
Brougham, J. David Copperfield. Philadelphia 1850.
[Courtney, J.?] David Copperfield the younger, of Blunderstone Rookery. 1850.
Northall, D. K. David Copperfield. New York 1850.
Burnand, F. C. The Deal boatman. 1863.
Rowe, G. F. David Copperfield; or, Little Emily Micawber. 1866.
Halliday, A. Little Emily. 1869.
Murray, G. Lost Emily. 1870.
Hamilton, G. Em'ly. 1877.
Collette, C. Micawber. 1881.
Warren, T. G. and B. Landeck. Em'ly. 1903.
David Copperfield. Film, Thanhauser 1911.
David Copperfield. Film, Pathe 1912.
David Copperfield. Film 1912. Produced by F. Powell.
David Copperfield. Film 1913. Written and directed by T. Bentley.
Parker, L. N. The highway of life. 1914.
David Copperfield. Film 1922. Script by L. Skands. Directed by A. W. Sandberg.
The love stories of David Copperfield. Film, Phillips Film Co 1924.
David Copperfield. Film, MGM 1935. Script by H. Estabrook and H. Walpole. Directed by G. Cukor. With F. Bartholomew, E. M. Oliver and W. C. Fields, et al.
David Copperfield. BBC television 1956, 1966. Script by V. Tilsley.
David Copperfield. Film, CBS/Fox 1970. Script by J. Pulman. Directed by D. Mann. With E. Evans, L. Olivier, et al.
David Copperfield. BBC television 1974, 1976. Script by H. Whitemore.

Reviews

[Hervey, T. K.] Athenaeum 5 May 1849; Family Herald 28 July 1849; Rambler Sep 1849; [Chorley, H. F.] Athenaeum 23 Nov 1850; Spectator 23 Nov 1850; [Forster, J.] Examiner 14 Dec 1850; Fraser's Mag Dec 1850; [Masson, D.] North Br Rev 15 1851; [Phillips, S.] The Times 11 June 1851; Prospective Rev 7 July 1851; Southern Literary Messenger Aug 1851; [Oliphant, M.] Blackwood's Mag Apr 1855; Spectator 44 Dec 1861.

Studies and appreciations

'Munkshood' [W. J. Clarke]. Mr Micawber: typically considered. Bentley's Misc 56 1864.
Arnold, M. The incompatibles. Nineteenth Cent Apr 1881; rptd in his Irish essays, 1882.
Ansted, A. Reminiscences of David Copperfield's childhood. Good Words Apr and May 1894.
David Copperfield's birthplace. Black and White 7 Sep 1895.
Jerome, J. K. My favourite novelist and his best book. Munsey's Mag 19 1898.
Stockwell, N. Notes on Dickens's David Copperfield. 1904.
Romayne, L. The survival of Mrs Crupp. Dickensian 1 1905.
Matz, B. W. Blunderstone: a visit to David Copperfield's birthplace. Dickensian 2 1906.

Soray, W. Dickensian humbugs III: Uriah and some others. Dickensian 2 1906.
Bately, J. From Blunderstone to Yarmouth. Dickensian 5 1909.
Norris, E. A. Mr Peggotty, Gentleman. Dickensian 5 1909.
Nicoll, W. R. The true story of David Copperfield. Bookman extra no 1914.
Roe, F. G. Some remarks upon the Copperfield controversy. Dickensian 10 1914.
MacDuffie, M. Why I liked David Copperfield. Dickensian 11 1915.
Morten, W. V. James Sharman and Ham Peggotty. Dickensian 11 1915.
Watson, G. Wilkins Micawber: a sketch. Dickensian 14 1918.
Fraser, E. A. The psychology of Betsey Trotwood. Dickensian 16 1920.
Lupton, E. B. Oliver Goldsmith as the prototype of Mr Mell. Dickensian 16 1920.

Bleak House

Bleak House, with illustrations by H. K. Browne. 20 (as 19) monthly pts, Mar 1852–Sep 1853 (slight variants). Complete ms, memoranda and number plans and an incomplete set of corrected proofs are in the Forster Collection.

Bibliographies

A new Dickens bibliography: Bleak House. Dickensian 39 1943.
Blount, T. Bleak, bleaker, bleakest. Dickensian 67 1971. Review of recent edns of Bleak House.
Easson, A. Paperback editions of Bleak House. Dickens Quart 1984.

Editions

Leipzig 1852 Tauchnitz Collection of British Authors no 230. 4 vols. Originally issued in pts.
1853, with preface. 1 vol.
1858 Cheap edn.
1859 Library edn.
1868 Charles Dickens edn, with rev preface.
New York 1877 New Illus Lib edn, introd by E. P. Whipple. 2 vols.
1896 Macmillan edn, introd by C. Dickens the younger.
1897 Gadshill edn, introd and notes by A. Lang. 2 vols.
1899 Temple edn, introd by W. Jerrold. 3 vols.
1900 Rochester edn, introd by G. Gissing and notes by F. G. Kitton.
1903 Biographical edn, introd by A. Waugh.
1907 Everyman Lib edn, introd by G. K. Chesterton.
1908, illustr W. H. C. Groome.
1913–15 Waverley edn, introd by J. Galsworthy, illustr C. Pears and F. Barnard.
1938 Nonesuch edn, ed W. Dexter, H. Walpole, A. Waugh and T. Hatton.
1948 New Oxford Illus Dickens, introd by O. Sitwell.
New York 1951, introd by J. Cournos.
1953, introd by R. B. Johnson.
New York 1953, introd by D. Friede.
Boston 1956 Riverside edn, introd by M. D. Zabel.
New York 1964 Signet Classics edn, afterword by G. Tillotson.
New York 1965 Laurel edn, introd by E. Johnson.
1969, ed A. E. Dyson.
New York 1970 Rinehart edn, introd and notes by A. Guerard.
New York 1971 Crowell Critical Lib edn, ed D. DeVries with background material and selected criticism.
Harmondsworth 1971 Penguin English Lib edn, later Penguin Classics edn, ed with notes by N. Page and introd by J. H. Miller.
1976 Pan edn, introd and notes by A. Calder-Marshall.
New York 1977 Norton Critical edn, ed with notes, background sources and studies by G. H. Ford and S. Monod.
Toronto, New York, London and Sidney 1983 Bantam Classic edn, with excerpts from V. Nabakov's lectures on Bleak House.
New York 1985, ed with notes by G. H. Ford and S. Monod.
1985 Folio Soc edn, introd by C. Hibbert, illustr C. Keeping.
1991 Mandarin edn, introd by P. Ackroyd.
1991 Everyman's Lib edn, introd by B. Hardy, with G. K. Chesterton's 1907 introd (*above*) as appendix.
1994 Everyman Dickens edn, ed with introd and notes by A. Sanders.
Oxford 1996 World's Classics edn, ed with introd and notes by S. Gill.
Harmondsworth 1996 Penguin Classics edn, introd by N. Bradbury.
1996 Bedford Books edn, ed J. Carlisle.

Commentary on the text

Staples, L. C. Shavings from Dickens's workshop: unpublished fragments from the novels, V. Dickensian 50 1954.
Sucksmith, H. P. Dickens at work on Bleak House: a critical examination of his memoranda and number plans. RMS 9 1965.
Ford, G. H. The titles for Bleak House. Dickensian 65 1969.
DeVries, D. The Bleak House page-proofs: more shavings from Dickens's workshop. Dickensian 66 1970.
Monod, S. When the battle's lost and won: Dickens vs the compositors of Bleak House. Dickensian 69 1973.
Watson, J. L. Dickens at work on manuscript and proof: Bleak House and Little Dorrit. Jnl of the Australasian Univs Lang and Lit Assoc 45 1976.
Ford, G. and S. Monod. Textual notes in their edn of Bleak House, 1977.
Monod, S. 'Between two worlds': editing Dickens. In Editing nineteenth-century fiction, ed Jane Millgate, Toronto 1978.
Shatto, S. The companion to Bleak House. 1988.

Dramatisations

See Bolton, 1987, under Studies and bibliographies of adaptations, *below*.
Pitt, G. D. Bleak House, or the wandering spectre. 1853.
Lee, N. Bleak House. 1853.
Brougham, J. Bleak House. New York 1853.
Bleak House; or the ghost walk (alt, or the adventures of Jo the crossing sweeper). 1854.
Falconer, E. Bleak House; or, the ghost walk. 1854.
Randle, H. and F. Janauschek. Chesney Wold. Baltimore 1873.
Burnett, J. P. Jo; or, Bleak House. 1875.
Simpson, J. P. Lady Dedlock's secret. 1874.
Lander, G. Bleak House, or Poor Jo. 1876.
Woolf, B. E. Poor Jo. Boston 1876.
Weaver, H. A. Tom-All-Alone's. New York 1877.
Davenport, H. Poor Jo. 1878.
Jo, the crossing sweep. Film 1918.
Bleak House. Film, Ideal 1920. Script by W. J. Elliott. Directed by M. Elvey.
Kester, P. Lady Dedlock. New York 1923.
Bleak House. BBC television serial 1959. Script by C. Cox.
Mr Guppy's tale. BBC television 1969. Script by Whitemore, H.
Bleak House. BBC television serial 1985. 8 pts, 10 Apr–29 May. Script by A. Hopcraft. Directed by R. Devenish. With D. Rigg and D. Elliott.

Reviews

[Chorley, H. F.] Athenaeum 6 Mar 1852, 17 Sep 1853; Eng Rev July 1852; [Denman, T.] 6 articles in the Standard 13 Sep–5 Oct 1853 (rptd in Uncle Tom's cabin, Bleak House, slavery and slave trade; *see* H. Stone, Dickens and Harriet Beecher Stowe, Nineteenth-Cent Fiction 12 1958); Leader 5 Feb 1853; United States Mag and Democratic Rev Sep 1853; Illus London News 24 Sep 1853; Bentley's Misc 34 1853; [Brimley, G.] Spectator 24 Sep 1853. (rptd in his Essays, 1858); [Sargent, W.] North Amer Rev 77 1853; Bentley's Monthly Rev Oct 1853; Westminster Rev Oct 1853; [Forster, J.] Examiner 8 Oct 1853; [Riggs, C. F.] Putnam's Monthly Mag Nov 1853; Eclectic Rev Dec 1853; [Stothert, J. A.] Rambler Jan

1854; Blackwood's Mag Apr 1855; Ecclesiastic and Theologian Oct 1855; 'Nathaniel, Sir'. NMM June 1864.

Studies and appreciations

C., W. A Bleak House narrative in real life: a suit in the Irish Court of Chancery 1826–51. 1856.

Romayne, L. Turveydrop and Deportment. Dickensian 1 1905.

Ward, H. S. Topography of Bleak House. Dickensian 1 1905.

Handley, G. M. Notes of Dickens's Bleak House. 1910.

Suddaby, J. The crossing sweeper in Bleak House: Dickens and the original Jo. Dickensian 8 1912.

Weaver, F. My favourite Dickens novel. Dickensian 8 1912.

Fitzgerald, P. H. A Dickens perplexity. I: Lady Dedlock's flight. Dickensian 12 1916.

Hard times

Hard times, for these times. 1854. No illustrations. Not issued in pts, but pbd weekly in Household Words 1 Apr–12 Aug 1854. The complete ms, number plans and corrected proofs are in the Forster Collection. Eleven leaves of page proofs are in the Dexter Collection.

Bibliographies

Smith, A. Paperback editions of Hard times. Dickens Stud Newsletter 4 1973.

Manning, S. Hard times: an annotated bibliography. New York 1984 (Garland Dickens Bibliographies).

Editions

1854. First single-vol edn, with ch titles and division into 3 bks.

Leipzig 1854 Tauchnitz Collection of British Authors no 307, as Hard times. For these times.

New York 1854.

New York 1854.

1862 Library edn, illustr F. Walker.

1865 Cheap edn.

1868 Charles Dickens edn, bound with Pictures from Italy.

New York 1876 New Illus Lib edn, bound with Barnaby Rudge, introd by E. P. Whipple. 2 vols.

1898 Gadshill edn, bound with Hunted down, Holiday romance and George Silverman's explanation, introd and notes by A. Lang.

1899 Temple edn, introd by W. Jerrold.

1900 Autograph edn, bound with Bleak House, introd by R. Garnett.

Edinburgh 1901–2 London edn, bound with Sketches by Boz, notes by F. G. Kitton.

1903 Biographical edn, bound with Christmas books, introd by A. Waugh, with original illustrations.

1904 Macmillan edn, bound with Great expectations, introd by C. Dickens the younger.

1907 Everyman's Lib edn, introd by G. K. Chesterton. Rptd New York 1970, afterword by J. Richardson.

1912 Waverley edn, bound with No thoroughfare, introd by G. B. Shaw, illustr C. Pears and F. Barnard.

1954, afterword by J. M. Richardson.

1954 Collins edn, introd by F. Brereton.

1955 New Oxford Illus Dickens, introd by D. Foot.

New York 1958 Rinehart edn, introd by W. W. Watt.

New York 1960 Harper edn, introd by J. H. Middendorf.

New York 1961 Signet Classics edn, afterword by C. Shapiro.

New York 1964 Bantam edn, ed with introd by R. D. Spector.

New York 1965 Harper Classic edn, introd by W. Allen.

New York 1966 Norton Critical edn, ed with notes, background sources and studies by G. H. Ford and S. Monod. 2nd edn 1991.

Greenwich CT 1966 Fawcett Premier edn, introd by R. Williams.

New York 1966 Heritage Club edn, introd by J. Winterich.

Harmondsworth 1969 Penguin English Lib edn, later Penguin Classics edn, ed with introd and notes by D. Craig.

1970 Longman edn, commentary and notes by D. R. Elloway.

1971 Heinemann Educational edn, ed N. L. Clay.

Barre MA 1972 Imprint Soc edn, introd by M. Dickens.

1977 Pan edn, introd and notes by G. Levine.

St Albans 1977 Panther edn, foreword by A. Briggs.

London and New York 1978, introd by P. Collins.

1983 Macmillan Students' Novels edn, introd by J. Gibson.

1983 Folio Soc edn, introd by C. Hibbert, illustr C. Keeping.

1987 Methuen English Texts edn, introd, critical commentary and notes by T. Eagleton.

1988 Longman Study Texts edn, ed P. Cairns.

Oxford 1989 World's Classics edn, ed with introd and notes by P. Schlicke.

1991 Mandarin edn, introd by P. Ackroyd.

1994 Everyman Dickens edn, ed with introd and notes by G. Smith.

Harmondsworth 1995 Penguin Classics edn, introd by K. Flint.

1995 Macmillan edn, bound with David Copperfield, introd by J. Peck.

1995 Longman edn, ed E. Holden.

1995 New Windmill Classics edn, introd and notes by P. Thomas.

Peterborough Ontario 1996 Broadview edn, ed G. Law.

Cambridge 1996 Cambridge Univ Press edn, ed G. Jose.

Commentary on the text

Woodings, R. B. A cancelled passage in Hard times. Dickensian 60 1964.

Monod, S. Dickens at work on the text of Hard times. Dickensian 54 1968.

Bartrip, P. W. J. Household Words and the factory accident controversy. Dickensian 75 1979.

Brattin, J. J. Recent Norton Critical editions: David Copperfield ... Hard times. Dickens Quart 8 1991.

Simpson, M. The companion to Hard times. Dickens companions ser. Mountfield, East Sussex 1997.

Imitations

[Brough, R. B.] Hard times by Charles Dickens. Concluding as it ought to have been. Diogenes 4 1854.

[Brough, R. B.] Hard times by Charle Diggins. In Our miscellany, ed E. H. Yates and R. B. Brough, 1865.

Dramatisations

See Bolton 1987, under Studies and bibliographies of adaptations, *below*.

Cooper, F. F. Hard times. 1854.

Cowell, W. Hard times; or the self-made man. Boston 1854.

Pitt, G. D. Hard times but wait a little longer. 1854.

Robertson, T. W. Household Words. 1855.

Nation, W. H. C. Under the earth: or the sons of toil. 1867.

Hanworth, S. Mr Gradgrind's system. Llandudno 1906.

Hard times. Film 1915. Directed by T. Bentley.

Hard times. Granada television serial 1977. Script by A. Hopcraft. Directed by J. Irvin.

Hard times. BBC television serial Apr–May 1994. 4 pts. Directed by P. Barnes.

Reviews

[Dixon, W. H.] Athenaeum 12 Aug 1854; Economist Sep 1854; [Forster, J.] Examiner 9 Sep 1854; South London Athenaeum and Institution Mag Oct 1854; [Simpson, R.] Rambler n.s. 2 Oct 1854; Br Quart Rev 20 Oct 1854; [Sinnett, J.] Westminster Rev n.s. 6 1854; Graham's Mag 45, Nov 1854; [Oliphant, M.] Blackwood's Mag Apr 1855; W., A. Christian Examiner 59, Nov 1855.

Studies and appreciations

Hodgson, W. B. On the importance of the study of economic science. In Lectures on education delivered at the Royal Institution, 1855. *See* GM Sep 1854.

Ruskin, J. Footnote on Hard times. Cornhill Mag Aug 1860. In his Unto this last.

Whipple, E. P. Atlantic Monthly Mar 1877.
Rodd, W. B. Stephen Blackpool's prayer. Dickensian 6 1910.
Hearn, A. S. Dickens and schools. Dickensian 8 1912.
McCormick, I. C. A defence for Hard times. Dickensian 12 1916.
Doran, W. J. Hard times and these times. Dickensian 15 1919.

Little Dorrit

Little Dorrit, with illustrations by H. K. Browne. 20 (as 19) monthly pts, Dec 1855–June 1857 (variants). The complete ms, number plans and incomplete corrected proofs are in the Forster Collection. Corrected page proofs for bk 1, ch 4 and all No 2 are in the Dexter Collection.

Bibliography

A new Dickens bibliography: Little Dorrit. Dickensian 40 1944.

Editions

Leipzig 1856 Tauchnitz Collection of British Authors no 350. 4 vols. Originally issued in pts.
1857, with preface. 1 vol.
1859 Library edn.
1861 Cheap edn.
1868 Charles Dickens edn, with rev preface.
New York 1877 New Illus Lib edn, introd by E. P. Whipple. 2 vols.
1897 Gadshill edn, introd and notes by A. Lang. 2 vols.
1899 Macmillan edn, introd by C. Dickens the younger.
1899 Temple edn, introd by W. Jerrold. 3 vols.
1903 Biographical edn, introd by A. Waugh.
1908 Everyman's Lib edn, introd by G. K. Chesterton.
1913–15 Waverley edn, introd by E. Orczy, illustr C. Pears and F. Barnard.
1937 Nonesuch edn, ed W. Dexter, H. Walpole, A. Waugh and T. Hatton.
New York 1951, introd by J. Cournos.
1953 New Oxford Illus edn, introd by L. Trilling.
1959 Collins edn, introd by M. Whyte.
Harmondsworth 1967 Penguin Eng Lib edn, later Penguin Classics edn, ed with introd and notes by J. Holloway.
Toronto 1969 Macmillan College Classics edn, introd by R. D. McMaster.
Oxford 1979 Clarendon edn, ed with introd by H. P. Sucksmith.
Oxford 1979 World's Classics edn, ed with new introd and notes by H. P. Sucksmith.
New York 1980 Signet Classics edn, afterword by R. Altick.
1986 Folio Soc edn, introd by C. Hibbert, illustr C. Keeping.
1991 Mandarin edn, introd by P. Ackroyd.
Harmondsworth 1997. Penguin Classics edn, ed S. Wall, notes by H. Small.
1999 Everyman Dickens edn, ed with introd and notes by A. Easson.

Commentary on the text

Staples, L. C. Shavings from Dickens's workshop: unpublished fragments from the novels, III. Dickensian 49 1953.
Herring, P. D. Dickens's monthly number plans for Little Dorrit. MP 64 1966.
Butt, J. The serial publication of Dickens's novels: Martin Chuzzlewit and Little Dorrit. In Pope, Dickens and others, Edinburgh 1969.
Watson, J. L. Dickens at work on manuscript and proof: Bleak House and Little Dorrit. Jnl of the Australasian Univs Lang and Lit Assoc 45 1976.

Dramatisations

See Bolton 1987 *under* Studies and bibliographies of adaptations, *below*.
Cooper, F. F. Little Dorrit. 1856.
Albery, J. The two roses. 1870. The role of Digby Grant made famous by Henry Irving.
Brougham, J. Amy Dorrit. 1873.
The two roses. Film, Thanhauser 1910.
Little Dorrit. Film, Thanhauser 1913.
Little Dorrit. Film 1920. Directed by S. Morgan.
Little Dorrit. Film, Denmark 1930. Script by S. Ask. Directed by A. W. Sandberg.
Little Dorrit. Pt 1, Nobody's fault; pt 2, Little Dorrit's story. Film 1987. Written and directed by C. Edzard. With D. Jacobi and S. Pickering.

Reviews

[Dixon, W. H.] Athenaeum 1 Dec 1855, 6 June 1857; Illus Times 8 Dec 1855; Monthly Rev of Lit, Science and Art Jan 1856; Saturday Rev 22 Nov 1856; [Hanley, E. B.] Blackwood's Mag Apr 1857; [Forster, J.] Examiner 13 June 1857; Leader 27 June 1857; [Stephen, J. F.] Edinburgh Rev 106 1857 (reply by Dickens, Household Words 1 Aug 1857); [Stephen, J. F.?] Saturday Rev 4, 18 July 1857 (reply in Leader 11–18 July 1857); Knickerbocker Aug 1857; Hollingshead, J. Train Aug 1857; Trollope, A. Cornhill Mag 3 Feb 1861; Eclectic Rev Oct 1861.

Studies and appreciations

Fraser, W. A. Little Dorrit. Dickensian 3 1907.
Shaw, G. B. Dickens and Little Dorrit. Dickensian 4 1908.
Compagnon de la Marjolaine. Dickensian 5 1909.
Matchett, W. The neglected book. Dickensian 6 1910.
Kent, W. Little Dorrit and the Edinburgh Review. Dickensian 15 1919.

A tale of two cities

A tale of two cities, with illustrations by H. K. Browne. Appeared simultaneously in All the Year Round 30 Apr–26 Nov 1859, and in 8 (as 7) monthly pts, June–Dec 1859. The ms and number plans are in the Forster Collection. No proofs survive.

Bibliographies

Sawyer, C. J. and F. J. H. Darton. English books. Vol 2, 1927. Full collation of 1859 pts.
A new Dickens bibliography: A tale of two cities. Dickensian 41 1945.
Todd, W. B. Note 94: Dickens, A tale of two cities, 1859. BC 7 1958.
Glancy, R. F. A tale of two cities: an annotated bibliography. New York 1993 (Garland Dickens Bibliographies).

Editions

In Harper's Weekly 7 May–3 Dec 1859. First Amer appearance.
1859, with preface. 1 vol, with variants.
Philadelphia 1859, from advance proofs.
Leipzig 1859 Tauchnitz Collection of British Authors no 479. 2 vols. Originally issued in pts.
1864 Cheap edn, frontispiece by M. Stone.
Boston 1864.
1868 Charles Dickens edn.
New York 1877 New Illus Lib edn, introd by E. P. Whipple.
1893 Macmillan edn, introd by C. Dickens the younger.
1898 Gadshill edn, introd by A. Lang.
1899 Temple edn, introd by W. Jerrold.
Boston 1901, introd by H. B. Moore.
1902, introd and notes by H. M. Fitzgibbon.
1903 Biographical edn, introd by A. Waugh.
1905, introd by A. A. Barter.
New York 1906, introd by J. W. Linn.
1906 Everyman's Lib, introd by G. K. Chesterton.
1906 Biographical edn, introd by W. Jerrold.
1906, introd and notes by H. G. Buehler and L. Mason.
New York 1908, introd by J. W. Abernathy.
New York 1910 Longmans English Classics edn, introd by F. W. Roe.
1911, introd by W. Magennis.
1911 World's Classics edn, introd and notes by Mrs F. S. Boas.

1913–15 Waverley edn, illustr C. Pears and F. Barnard.
1915, introd by A. R. Weekes.
Boston nd, introd by G. A. Sherwell.
1920, introd and notes by G. Todhunter.
Boston 1922, ed A. B. DeMille.
Lincoln NE 1925, introd by E. J. Erwin.
New York 1926 Modern Readers' edn, introd by W. C. Phillips.
Philadelphia 1930, introd by P. Warner.
Boston 1930, ed E. O. Wiggins.
1934 Scholar's Lib edn, introd by G. K. Chesterton and notes by G. Boas.
Chicago 1934, introd by I. Kincheloe.
1937 Nonesuch edn, ed W. Dexter, H. Walpole, A. Waugh and T. Hatton.
New York 1942 Great Illus Classics edn, with foreword by M. L. Becker, illustr H. K. Browne and F. Barnard.
1949 New Oxford Illus edn, introd by J. Shuckburgh.
New York 1950 Modern Lib edn, introd by E. Wagenknecht.
1952 Collins edn, introd by S. Dark.
New York 1957 Signet Classics edn, afterword by E. Johnson.
1957 London Eng Lit edn, introd by B. Osbourn.
New York 1958 Longman edn, introd by S. H. Burton.
New York 1958 Harper edn, introd by M. D. Zabel.
New York 1960 Signet Classics edn, afterword by J. Mersand.
New York 1962 Macmillan edn, afterword by C. Fadiman.
New York 1962 Collier edn, introd by S. Marcus.
Boston 1962 Riverside edn, introd by P. Pickrel.
Evanston IL 1963 Harper's Modern Classics edn, introd by J. C. Mellon.
New York 1963 Airmont edn, introd by D. G. Pitt.
New York 1964 Longman edn, with appendices and notes by D. K. Swan.
1966 Medallion edn, introd by A. R. Tompkins.
New York 1968 Cambridge Book edn, introd by F. B. Tromley.
New York 1969, introd by A. A. Adrian.
New York nd Harper edn, introd by W. Allen.
Harmondsworth 1970 Penguin English Classics edn, later Penguin Classics edn, ed with introd and notes by G. Woodcock.
New York 1971 Amsco School edn, ed H. I. Christ.
New York 1973 Pocket Books edn, with 48-page reader's guide.
New York 1978 Avenel edn, introd by H. Weitzner.
1980 Pan edn, introd by I. Ousby.
Cape Town 1980, ed with notes by M. M. Green.
1984 Macmillan Students' Novels edn, introd by J. Gibson.
1985 Folio Soc edn, introd by C. Hibbert, illustr C. Keeping.
1986, bound with David Copperfield and Great expectations as vol 2 of The annotated Dickens, ed with introd by E. Guiliano and P. Collins.
Oxford 1988 World's Classics edn, ed with introd and notes by A. Sanders.
New York 1990 and London 1993 Everyman's Lib edn, introd by S. Schama, with G. K. Chesterton's 1906 introd (*above*) as appendix.
1991 Mandarin edn, introd by P. Ackroyd.
1993 Reader's Digest edn, afterword by M. H. Dobkin.
1994 Everyman Dickens edn, ed N. Page.
New York 1995 Chelsea House edn, introd by H. Bloom.

Dickens's reading version

The Bastille prisoner: a reading. [1861?] (priv ptd). Arranged by Dickens, but never used. Rptd in collections 1975, 1983. *See* Readings, *below*.

Commentary on the text

Tucker, D. The text of the Oxford Illustrated Dickens A tale of two cities: some shortcomings noted. N & Q 223 1978.
Tucker, D. Dickens at work on the manuscript of A tale of two cities. Études Anglaises 32 1979.
Sanders, A. The companion to A tale of two cities. 1988. Includes unpbd variants from Dickens's ms.

Dramatisations

See Bolton 1987 *under* Studies and bibliographies of adaptations, *below*.
Taylor, T. A tale of two cities. 1860.
Cooper, F. F. The tale of two cities: or the incarcerated victim of the Bastille. 1860. This is essentially the same play as that attributed to H. J. Rivers, A tale of two cities; or, the horrors of the Bastille, 1860.
Simpson, J. P. and H. C. Merivale. All for her. 1875.
Wills, F. and F. Langbridge. The only way. 1899. With Sir John Martin-Harvey as Carton.
A tale of two cities. Film, Selig 1908.
A tale of two cities. Film, Vitagraph 1911. Directed by W. Humpreys.
A tale of two cities. Film, Fox 1917. Written and directed by F. Lloyd.
The only way. Film 1926. Directed by H. Cox.
A tale of two cities. Film, MGM 1935. Script by W. P. Lipscomb and S. N. Berman. Directed by J. Conway. With R. Colman as Carton.
The only way. BBC television 1948.
A tale of two cities. BBC television opera 1953. Script by A. Benjamin.
A tale of two cities. BBC television serial 1957. Script by J. K. Cross.
A tale of two cities. Film, Rank 1958. Script by T. E. B. Clarke. Directed by R. Thomas. With Dirk Bogarde as Carton.
A tale of two cities. BBC television serial 1965. Script by C. Cox.
A tale of two cities. BBC television serial 1980. Script by P. Harding. Directed by M. E. Briant.
A tale of two cities. CBS television 1980. Script by J. Gay. Directed by J. Goddard.
Francis, M. A tale of two cities. Greenwich, London 1994.

Reviews

[Kent, W. M. C.] Sun 11 Aug 1859; Literary Gazette 29 Oct 1859; Weekly Herald and Mercury 12 Nov 1859; Sanders, Otley Budget 3 Dec 1859, 19 Jan 1860; Athenaeum 10 Dec 1859; [Forster, J.] Examiner 10 Dec 1859; Observer 11 Dec 1859; Weekly Dispatch 11 Dec 1859; Daily News 14 Dec 1859; Daily Telegraph 16 Dec 1859; Critic n.s. 19, 17 Dec 1859; [Stephen, J. F.] Saturday Rev 17 Dec 1859; Morning Post 21 Dec 1859; Morning Star 24 Dec 1859; Morning Herald 26 Dec 1859; Atlas 31 Dec 1859; Press 31 Dec 1859; Morning Chron 2 Jan 1860; Sunday Times 22 Jan 1860; Dublin Univ Mag 55, Feb 1860; Eclectic Rev Oct 1861.

Studies and Appreciations

Coleman, J. The truth about The dead heart and A tale of two cities. New Rev 1 1889. *See* E. W. Philips, Watts Phillips: artist and playwright, 1891, *and* C. R. Dolmetsch, Dickens and The dead heart, Dickensian 55 1959.
Dr Manette's house. Dickensian 1 1905.
Handley, G. M. Notes of Dickens's Tale of two cities. 1907.
Polock, E. E. A tale of two cities: an appreciation. Dickensian 4 1908.
Hunter, R. W. G. A tale of two cities and the French revolution. Dickensian 8 1912.
Polack, E. E. Mr Jarvis Lorry. Dickensian 9 1913.
Sharp, C. The Crunchers. Dickensian 10 1914.
Wilson, C. The originals of Sidney Carton and Stryver, Q. C. Dickensian 10 1914.
Bennet, A. Sidney Carton. Dickensian 11 1915.

Great expectations

Great expectations. Pbd weekly in All the Year Round 1 Dec 1860–3 Aug 1861. The complete ms and notes are in the Wisbech and Fenland Museum. Corrected proofs for chs 1–4, 51–7, and most of 58, are in the Forster Collection; a further 177 pages of corrected proofs are in the Pierpont Morgan Lib. Colour microfilm of ms and related papers in Wisbech and Fenland Museum produced 1978.

Bibliographies

Edgar, H. le R. and R. W. G. Vail. Early American editions of Great expectations. BNYPL 22 1929.

Rosenberg, E. A preface to Great expectations: the pale usher dusts his lexicons. Dickens Stud Annual 2 1972.

DeVries, D. Paperback editions of Great expectations. Dickens Stud Newsletter 5 1974.

Worth, G. J. Great expectations: an annotated bibliography. New York 1986 (Garland Dickens Bibliographies).

Dundeck, J. M. Note 551: A new first American edition of Great expectations. BC 43 1994.

Editions

In Harper's Weekly 24 Nov 1860–3 Aug 1861. First Amer appearance.

New York 1860.

1861, with variants. 3 vols, each consisting of one of the 3 stages of Pip's expectations. No issue in pts, no illustrations.

Philadelphia 1861, from advance proofs, illustr John McLenan.

Leipzig 1861 Tauchnitz Collection of British Authors no 547. 2 vols.

1862, with frontispiece and illus title page by M. Stone.

1863 Cheap edn.

1864 Library edn, illustr M. Stone.

1868 Charles Dickens edn.

New York 1877 New Illus Lib edn, introd by E. P. Whipple.

1898 Gadshill edn, introd and notes by A. Lang.

1903 Biographical edn, bound with Uncommercial traveller, introd by A. Waugh.

1903 Temple edn, bound with Master Humphrey's clock, introd by W. Jerrold. 2 vols.

1904 Macmillan edn, bound with Hard times, introd by C. Dickens the younger.

1907 Everyman's Lib edn, introd by G. K. Chesterton.

1914 Waverley edn, introd by W. A. Dunkerley, illustr C. Pears and F. Barnard.

New York 1931, introd by E. M. Clark.

Edinburgh 1937, with preface by G. B. Shaw.

1937–8 Nonesuch edn, ed W. Dexter, H. Walpole, A. Waugh and T. Hatton.

New York 1939 Heritage Club edn, introd by J. Winterich.

New York 1942 Great Illus Classics edn, introd by M. L. Becker.

1947, with new introd by G. B. Shaw.

New York 1948 Rinehart edn, introd by E. Davis. 1972 (2nd edn).

Cleveland 1952, introd by C. C. Livensparger.

1953 Collins edn, introd by K. Hayens.

1953 New Oxford Illus edn, introd by F. Page.

New York 1956 Pocket Books edn, introd by E. Wagenknecht.

1958 Heritage of Literature edn, introd by H. M. Burton.

New York 1961 Harper's Modern Classics edn, introd by L. Lane.

New York and London 1962 Collier edn, introd by F. Chapman.

Boston 1962 Riverside edn, introd by M. Engel and notes by L. G. Dickens.

Evanston IL 1963 Harper's Modern Classics edn, introd by C. McKee.

New York 1963 Signet Classics edn, afterword by A. Wilson.

Indianapolis and New York 1964 Lib of Literature edn, introd by L. Crompton.

1964 Great Writing in English edn, notes by J. M. Stutt.

1964 Panther edn, introd by M. Lane.

1964 London edn, introd by G. C. Rosner.

New York 1964 Classics Ser edn, introd by M. M. Threapleton.

New York 1965 Harper Classics edn, introd by W. Allen.

Harmondsworth 1965 Penguin Eng Lib edn, later Penguin Classics edn, ed with introd and notes by A. Calder.

Toronto and New York 1965 Odyssey edn, introd by R. D. McMaster.

London and New York 1966 Macmillan edn, introd by L. Stevens.

1971 Heinemann Education edn, ed N. L. Clay.

New York 1973 Pocket Books edn, introd by W. W. Winters.

London and New York 1973 Collins edn, introd K. Hayens.

1974 Pan edn, introd by J. Symons.

1977, bound with Oliver Twist and A tale of two cities, introd by M. Fido.

New York 1977 Spring Books edn, introd by J. Steinbach.

1981 Folio Soc edn, introd by C. Hibbert, illustr C. Keeping.

Cape Town 1981, ed with notes by A. M. Potter.

1982 Macmillan Education edn, introd by J. Gibson.

1983 Longman Study Texts edn, introd by T. Pearce.

1991 Mandarin edn, introd by P. Ackroyd.

1992 Everyman's Lib edn, introd by M. Slater, with G. K. Chesterton's 1907 introd (*above*) as appendix.

1992 Puffin edn, ed A. Calder.

1992 Longman edn, ed E. Holden.

1993 New Windmill Classics edn, introd and notes by P. Thomas.

Oxford 1993 Clarendon edn, ed M. Cardwell.

Oxford 1994 World's Classics edn, ed M. Cardwell, introd by K. Flint.

1994 Macmillan edn, introd by R. D. Sell.

1994 Everyman Dickens edn, ed with introd and notes by R. Gilmour.

Cambridge 1995, ed T. Seward.

New York 1996 Chelsea House edn, introd by H. Bloom.

Boston 1996 Case Stud in Contemporary Criticism edn, ed with notes by J. Carlisle.

1996 Henderson edn, ed J. Heppell.

Harmondsworth 1997 Penguin Classics edn, ed C. Mitchell, introd by D. Trotter.

New York 1999. Norton Critical edn, ed E. Rosenberg.

Dickens's reading adaptation

Great expectations: a reading in three stages. 1861 (priv ptd, never publicly delivered). Rptd in collection 1975. *See* Readings, *below.*

Commentary on the text

Hargrave, W. A trifle light as air, being a strange story of a Dickens misprint. Connoisseur 4 1902. On a misprint in ch 26.

Dexter, W. The end of Great expectations. Dickensian 34 1938.

Staples, L. The manuscript of Great expectations. Dickensian 43 1947.

Calhoun, P. M. The court of appeals. Appeal 24: rarity of Great expectations. New Colophon 1 1948.

Randall, D. A. The court of appeals. Answer to appeal 24: Great expectations. New Colophon 2 1949.

Carter, J. Further answers to appeal 24: Great expectations. New Colophon 2 1949.

Butt, J. Dickens's plan for the conclusion of Great expectations. Dickensian 45 1949.

Rosenberg, E. Small talk in Hammersmith: ch 23 of Great expectations. Dickensian 69 1973.

Rosenberg, E. Last words on Great expectations: a textual brief on the six endings. Dickens Stud Annual 9 1981.

Paroissien, D. The companion to Great expectations. Dickens Companions ser. Forthcoming Mountfield East Sussex.

Imitations

Carey, P. Jack Maggs. 1997.

Noonan, M. Magwitch. 1982.

Roe, S. Estella: her expectations. 1982.

Dramatisations

See Bolton 1987 *under* Studies and bibliographies of adaptations, *below.*

Great expectations: a drama, in three stages. Founded on, and compiled from, the story of that name, by Charles Dickens. 1861 (priv ptd). A copyrighting device. Bolton and Worth claim Dickens was probably not the playwright.

de Marguerittes, J. Great expectations. Philadelphia 1861.

Aiken, G. L. Great expectations. New York 1861.
Woolf, B. E. Great expectations. Boston 1861.
Menken, A. I. Great expectations. 1862.
Gilbert, W. S. Great expectations. 1871.
Scott, S. My unknown friend. New York 1872.
Tees, L. C. Botany Bay. 1881.
Rix, W. J. Pip's patron. 1892.
Great expectations. Film, Paramount 1917. Written and directed by P. West.
Great expectations. Film, Nordisk 1921. Script by L. Skands. Directed by A. W. Sandberg.
Great expectations. Film, Universal 1934. Script by G. Unger. Directed by S. Walker.
Guinness, A. Great expectations. 1939.
Great expectations. Film 1946. Written and directed by D. Lean.
Great expectations. BBC television serial 1959. Script by C. Cox.
Great expectations. BBC television serial 1967. Script by H. Leonard.
Great expectations. Film 1971. Directed by L. H. Ginner.
Great expectations. NBC television play 1974. Script by S. Yellen. Directed by J. Hardy.
Great expectations. Film 1974. Script by S. Yellen. Produced by R. Fryer.
Great expectations. BBC television serial 1980. Script by J. A. Hall. Directed by J. Amyes.
Great expectations. Film, Disney 1989. Script by J. Goldsmith. Directed by K. Connor.
Great expectations. Film, 20th-Century Fox 1996. Directed by A. Cuarón. With A. Bancroft and R. de Niro.
Great expectations. BBC television serial 1999. Script by T. Marchant. Directed by J. Jarrold.

Reviews

[Chorley, H. F.] Athenaeum 13 July 1861; Literary Gazette n.s. 7, 13 July 1861; [Forster, J.] Examiner 20 July 1861; Saturday Rev 20 July 1861; [Townsend, M?] Spectator 20 July 1861; Critic 10 Aug 1861; [Whipple, E. P.] Atlantic Monthly Sep 1861; Eclectic Rev Oct 1861; [Dallas, E. S.] The Times 17 Oct 1861; [Trotter, L. J.] Dublin Univ Mag Dec 1861; A., J. Ladies Companion and Monthly Mag 20 1861; Westminster Rev Jan 1862; Br Quart Rev 35, Jan 1862; [Capes, J. M. and J. E. E. D. Acton] Rambler Jan 1862; [Oliphant, M.] Blackwood's Mag May 1862, June 1871.

Studies and appreciations

Cassidy, J. Children in Dickens's novels. Pip and his adventures. Chatterbox 1895.
Plummer, J. The original Miss Havisham. Dickensian 2 1906.
Fitch, F. Great expectations. Dickensian 3 1907.
Fitch, F. Dickens and Walworth. Dickensian 4 1908.
Joe Gargery's forge. Dickensian 4 1908.
Gadd, W. L. The lonely church on the marshes. Dickensian 5 1909.
Philip, A. J. With Pip in Kent. United Methodist Mag Mar 1909.
Romayne, L. The genius of Wemmick. Dickensian 5 1909.
Matchett, W. The strange case of Great expectations. Dickensian 9 1913.
Richards, T. A. Joe Gargery and his recollections of Dickens. Strand Mag 45, Apr 1913.
Copeland, C. T. Dickens's best book. Dickensian 8 1914.
Sharp, H. Herbert Pocket, Gentleman. Dickensian 11 1915.

Our mutual friend

Our mutual friend. With illustrations by Marcus Stone. 20 (as 19) monthly pts, May 1864–Nov 1865. The complete ms and number plans are in the Pierpont Morgan Lib; corrected proofs are in the Berg Collection of New York Public Lib.

Bibliographies

Miller, W. and T. W. Hill. Charles Dickens's manuscripts. Dickensian 13 1917.
Hopkins, A. A. An important sale of Dickens manuscripts. Dickensian 22 1926.
Fymore, A. H. W. A Dickens manuscript. N & Q 187 1944.
A new Dickens bibliography: Our mutual friend. Dickensian 40 1944.
Fisher, B. F. IV. Paperback editions: Our mutual friend. Dickens Stud Newsletter 5 1974.
Brattin, J. J. and B. G. Hornback. Our mutual friend: an annotated bibliography. New York 1984 (Garland Dickens Bibliographies).

Editions

Leipzig 1864–5 Tauchnitz Collection of British Authors no 730. 4 vols. Originally issued in pts.
In Harper's New Monthly Mag June 1864–Dec 1865.
1865, with 'Postscript in lieu of a preface'. 2 vols, sometimes bound as a single vol.
New York 1865.
Philadelphia 1865.
New York 1866. 4 vols.
1867 Cheap edn.
Boston 1867 Diamond edn, illustr S. Eytinge, jr.
1867 Library edn. 2 vols.
1868 Charles Dickens edn.
New York 1875 Household edn, illustr J. Mahoney.
New York 1877 New Illus Lib edn, introd by E. P. Whipple. 2 vols.
1895 Macmillan edn, introd by C. Dickens the younger.
1898 Gadshill edn, introd and notes by A. Lang. 2 vols.
1903 Biographical edn, introd by A. Waugh.
1908 Everyman's Lib edn, introd by G. K. Chesterton.
1913–15 Waverley edn, introd by W. De Morgan, illustr C. Pears and F. Barnard.
1938 Nonesuch edn, ed W. Dexter, H. Walpole, A. Waugh and T. Hatton.
New York 1951 Great Illus Classics edn, introd by A. Klots, jr.
1952 New Oxford Illus edn, introd by E. S. Davies.
1955 Collins edn, introd by J. K. Jerome.
1957 Macdonald Illus Classics edn, introd by J. B. Priestley.
New York 1957 Heritage Club edn, introd by J. Winterich.
New York 1960 Random House edn, introd by M. Engel.
New York 1964 Signet Classics edn, afterword by J. H. Miller.
Harmondsworth 1971 Penguin Eng Lib edn, later Penguin Classics edn, ed with introd and notes by S. Gill.
New York 1978 Bounty edn, introd by H. Weitzner, illustr E. G. Dalzeil.
Oxford 1989 World's Classics edn, ed with introd and notes by M. Cotsell.
1991 Mandarin edn, introd by P. Ackroyd.
1994 Everyman's Lib edn, introd by A. Sanders, with G. K. Chesterton's 1908 introd (*above*) as appendix.
Harmondsworth 1997 Penguin Classics edn, ed A. Poole.

Commentary on the text

Field, K. Our mutual friend in manuscript. Scribner's Monthly Aug 1874.
Stone, M. Mr Marcus Stone, R. A., and Charles Dickens. Dickensian 8 1912.
Boll, E. The plotting of Our mutual friend. MP 42 1944. Prints Dickens's number plans. *See* J. D. Winslow, The number plans for Our mutual friend, Dickens Stud Newsletter 9 1978 for corrections.
Shea, F. X. No change of intention in Our mutual friend. Dickensian 63 1967.
Shea, F. X. Mr Venus observed: the plot change in Our mutual friend. Papers on Lang and Lit 4 1968.
Winslow, J. D. The number plans for Our mutual friend: a note. Dickens Stud Newsletter 9 1978.

Imitations

Busch, F. The mutual friend. New York 1975. Primarily about Dickens and Dolby.

Dramatisations

See Bolton 1987 *under* Studies and bibliographies of adaptations, *below.*

Rowe, G. F. Our mutual friend. New York 1866. Rev as Found drowned; or, Our mutual friend 1870.

Farnie, H. B. The golden dustman. 1866.

Hazlewood, C. H. The dustman's treasure; or, Wegg and Boffin. 1866.

Rogers, F. The dustman's golden mound; or, the will of John Harmon in the old Dutch bottle. 1866.

Fulton, C. Jenny Wren; or, the doll's dressmaker and her friends. New York 1867.

Brougham, J. Gold dust. New York 1871.

Eugene Wrayburn. Film 1911. Directed by T. A. Edison.

Our mutual friend. Film, Nordisk 1919. Directed by A. W. Sandberg.

Our mutual friend. BBC television serial 1958–9. Script by F. Lindstrom.

Our mutual friend. BBC television serial 1976. Script by J. Jones and D. Churchill.

Reviews

London Rev 30 Apr 1864–28 Oct 1865 (reviews of each no and of the whole novel); [Guernsey, A. H.] Harper's New Monthly Mag June and Aug 1864, Nov 1865; [Chorley, H. F.] Athenaeum 28 Oct 1865; [Forster, J.] Examiner 28 Oct 1865; Eclectic Rev Nov 1865; Saturday Rev 11 Nov 1865; New York Times 22 Nov and 14 Dec 1865; [Dallas, E. S.] The Times 29 Nov 1865; Christian Spectator Dec 1865; Reader 9 Dec 1865; Young Englishwoman 9 Dec 1865; [James, H.] Nation (New York) 21 Dec 1865; Annual Register for 1865; Westminster Rev n.s. 29 1866.

Studies and appreciations

Stockton, F. R. My favourite novelist and his best book. Munsey's Mag 1897.

Miniken, E. M. Betty Higden. Dickensian 4 1908.

The mystery of Edwin Drood

The mystery of Edwin Drood. With twelve illustrations by S. L. Fildes, and a portrait. In 6 monthly pts, Apr–Sep 1870 (Dickens's death in June 1870 having cut short the announced 12 pts). The ms, complete except for 5 paragraphs from ch 1, a list of projected titles, the 'Sapsea fragment', number plans, and the corrected proof for no 5 only are in the Forster Collection. A complete proof, originally sent to Sir Luke Fildes, is in the Beinecke Lib of Yale Univ. Forster prints a cancelled ch, How Mr Sapsea ceased to be a member of the Eight Club (Life, bk 11 ch 2). The ch order in the pts seen through the press by Forster has been criticised by some commentators, as departing from Dickens's intentions.

Bibliographies

Gadd, G. F. The history of a mystery: a review of solutions to Edwin Drood. Dickensian 1 1905.

Matz, B. W. The mystery of Edwin Drood: a bibliography. Dickensian 7 1911.

Matz, B. W. A bibliography of Edwin Drood: part II. Dickensian 24–5, 1928–9.

Lehman-Haupt, C. F. Studies on Edwin Drood. Dickensian 31 1935.

A new Dickens bibliography: The mystery of Edwin Drood. Dickensian 41 1945.

Fisher, B. F. IV. Paperback editions: The mystery of Edwin Drood. Dickens Stud Newsletter 8 1977.

Essential Edwin Drood: a bibliographic catalogue. 1995.

Cox, A. S. Charles Dickens's The mystery of Edwin Drood: an annotated bibliography. New York 1998. Dickens Bibliographies ser.

Editions

1870, with 12 illustrations by S. L. Fildes and a portrait. 1 vol.

In Every Saturday (Boston) 9 Apr–17 Sep 1870.

Leipzig 1870 Tauchnitz Collection of British Authors no 1100. 2 vols.

Boston 1870 (from advance proofs).

1873 Library edn, bound with Master Humphrey's clock, Hunted down, Holiday romance, and George Silverman's explanation.

1875 Charles Dickens edn, ptd from 1873 edn and bound with Master Humphrey's clock, Hunted down, Holiday romance, and George Silverman's explanation.

New York 1877 New Illus Lib edn, introd by E. P. Whipple.

1899 Gadshill edn, bound with Master Humphrey's clock, introd and notes by A. Lang. 2 vols.

1903 Biographical edn, bound with Reprinted pieces, introd by A. Waugh.

1913–15 Waverley edn, introd by H. A. Vachell, illustr C. Pears and F. Barnard.

1915 Everyman Lib edn, introd by G. K. Chesterton.

1923 Macmillan edn, introd by C. Dickens the younger.

1937–8 Nonesuch edn, ed W. Dexter, H. Walpole, A. Waugh and T. Hatton.

New York 1941 Heritage edn, introd by V. Starrett.

1952, introd by 'Michael Innes' [J. I. M. Stewart].

1956 Collins edn, introd by C. D. Lewis.

1956 New Oxford Illus edn, introd by S. C. Roberts.

New York 1961 Signet Classics edn, afterword by J. Wright.

1964 World's Classics edn, introd by C. Williams.

New York 1966 Airmont Classics edn, introd by N. F. Budgey.

Oxford 1972 Clarendon edn, ed with introd and notes by M. Cardwell.

Oxford 1972 World's Classics edn, ed with new introd by M. Cardwell.

Harmondsworth 1974 Penguin Eng Lib edn, later Penguin Classics edn, ed with notes by A. J. Cox, introd by A. Wilson.

Canterbury 1980. Facs of original serial pts.

1982 Folio Soc edn, ed A. J. Cox, introd by C. Hibbert, illustr C. Keeping.

1991 Mandarin edn, introd by P. Ackroyd.

1996 Everyman Dickens edn, ed with introd and notes by S. Connor.

Harmondsworth 1998 Penguin Classics edn, ed J. Maule.

Commentary on the text

Carden, P. Dickens's number plans for The mystery of Edwin Drood. Dickensian 27 1931.

Ford, G. H. Dickens's notebook and Edwin Drood. Nineteenth-Cent Fiction 6 1952. *See* F. Aylmer and P. Pakenham, Dickensian 51 1955.

Jacobson, W. The companion to The mystery of Edwin Drood. 1986.

Cox, D. R. The Every Saturday page proofs of The mystery of Edwin Drood. Dickensian 90 1994.

Dramatisations

See Bolton 1987 *under* Studies and bibliographies of adaptations, *below.*

Deleon, T. C. The mystery of Edwin Drood. Chicago 1870. Rev as Jasper, New York 1871.

Stephens, W. The mystery of Edwin Drood (of Cloisterham) (The mystery of Cloisterham) (Lost). 1871.

Carr, J. C. The mystery of Edwin Drood. 1907.

Trial of John Jasper for the murder of Edwin Drood: verbatim report of the proceedings by J. W. T. Ley. 1914. Report of a mock trial, G. K. Chesterton as judge, G. B. Shaw as juryman.

Mystery of Edwin Drood. Film, Ideal 1914. Directed by H. Blaché.

Mystery of Edwin Drood. Film, Universal 1935. Script by J. L. Balderston, G. Unger, L. Atlas and B. King. Directed by S. Walker.

The mystery of Edwin Drood. Film 1993. Written and directed by T. Forder.

Reviews

Annual Register for 1870; Athenaeum 2 Apr, 17 Sep 1870; [Broome, F. N.] The Times 2 Apr 1870; Graphic 9 Apr 1870; Every Saturday 7 May 1870; Academy 14 May, 22 Oct 1870; Saturday Rev 17 Sep 1870; Guardian 28 Sep 1870; Spectator 1 Oct 1870; Lawrenny, H. Academy 22 Oct 1870; NMM 22 Oct 1870; [Woods, G. B.] Old and New Nov 1870; Dublin Rev n.s. 16 1871; [Oliphant, M.] Blackwood's Mag June 1871.

Studies and appreciations

[Edwards, H. S.] The mystery of Edwin Drood: suggestions for a conclusion. Cornhill Mag Mar 1884.
Meynell, A. How Edwin Drood was illustrated. Century Mag Feb 1884.
Proctor, R. A. Watched by the dead: a loving study of Dickens' half-told tale. 1887.
Fildes, L. The mysteries of Edwin Drood. The Times 3 Nov 1905. Replies by A. Lang and J. W. T. Ley, The Times 10, 21 Nov 1905.
Lang, A. The puzzle of Dickens' last plot. 1905.
Matz, B. W. Solving The mystery of Edwin Drood. Dickensian 1 1905.
Walters, J. C. Clues to Dickens' Mystery of Edwin Drood. 1905.
Gadd, G. F. Datchery, the enigma. The case for Tartar. Dickensian 2 1906.
Perugini, K. (née Dickens). Edwin Drood and Dickens's last days. Pall Mall Mag June 1906.
Charles, E. Keys to the Drood mystery. 1908.
Matchett, W. Mr Datchery. Dickensian 4 1908.
Matz, B. W. The mystery of Edwin Drood: Dickens's half-told tale. Bookman Mar 1908.
Walters, J. C. Desultory thoughts on Drood. Dickensian 4 1908.
J[ackson], H. About Edwin Drood. Cambridge 1911.
Walters, J. C. Drood and Datchery. Dickensian 7 1911.
Nicoll, W. R. The problem of Edwin Drood. 1912. With bibliography by B. W. Matz, rev from Dickensian 1911.
Walters, J. C. Andrew Lang and Dickens's puzzles. Dickensian 8 1912.
Walters, J. C. The complete mystery of Edwin Drood . . . the history, continuations and solutions 1870–1912. 1912.
Fennell, C. A. M. 'The opium-woman' and 'Datchery' in The mystery of Edwin Drood. Cambridge 1913.
King, P. The secret of the Drood mystery. Dickensian 9 1913.
Matchett, W. A talk around Drood. Dickensian 10 1914.
Saunders, M. The mystery in the Drood family. Cambridge 1914.
Walters, J. C. Edwin Drood continued. Dickensian 10 1914.
Saunders, M. The mystery in the Drood family. Dickensian 11 1915.
Walters, J. C. The devotion of John Jasper. Dickensian 11 1915.
Suddaby, J. A night amongst the Drood opium dens. Dickensian 12 1916.
Edwin Drood number (Mar). Dickensian 15 1919: Carden, P. T., Datchery: the case for Tartar restated; Saunders, M., Dickens, Drood and Datchery; Squire, J. C., The Drood mystery insoluble; Walters, J. C., Drood and Datchery.

Sequels and continuations

'Kerr, O. C.' [R. H. Newell]. The cloven foot: being an adaptation [of Edwin Drood] to American scenes, characters, customs and nomenclature. New York 1870; rev Piccadilly Annual 1870. Complete adaptation with conclusion and critical introd.
[Morford, H. et al]. John Jasper's secret: a sequel to Dickens' unfinished novel. Philadelphia 1871–2 (in pts), 1871, London 1872; rptd as by W. Collins and C. Dickens the younger, New York 1901.
'The spirit pen of Charles Dickens, through a medium' [T. P. James]. The mystery of Edwin Drood. Battleboro VT 1873.
'Vase, Gillan' [Elizabeth Newton]. A great mystery solved: being a sequel to The mystery of Edwin Drood. 3 vols 1878, 1 vol [1914].
C[risp], W. E. The mystery of Edwin Drood completed. Ed M. L. C. Grant [1914]. 21 addnl chs.
Kavanagh, M. A new solution of The mystery of Edwin Drood. 1919, 1922 (with Dickens's text).
Carden, P. T. The murder of Edwin Drood: an attempted solution. 1920.

Christmas books

Dickens wrote five short books for Christmas, A Christmas carol 1843, The chimes 1844, The cricket on the hearth 1845, The battle of life 1846 *and* The haunted man 1848, *each pbd individually (see below). They were collected, with a preface and frontispiece by J. Leech, as* Christmas books *in 1852 Cheap edn of Works (17 weekly pts, 4 monthly pts, June–Sep 1852).*

Bibliographies

'Secutor' [pseud]. Early issues of first edns: Dickens's Christmas books. Bookman's Jnl and Print Collector 14 May 1920.
Glancy, R. F. Dickens's Christmas books, Christmas stories and other short fiction: an annotated bibliography. New York 1985 (Garland Dickens Bibliographies).

Collected editions

A Christmas carol in prose; The chimes; The cricket on the hearth. Leipzig 1846 Tauchnitz Collection of British Authors no 91.
New York 1849. First collection (without Haunted man).
1852 Cheap edn.
The battle of life; The haunted man. Leipzig 1856 Tauchnitz Collection of British Authors no 358.
1859 Library edn.
1861 New York, illustr F. O. C. Darley and J. Gilbert.
Boston 1867 Diamond edn, bound with Sketches by Boz, illustr S. Eytinge, jr.
1868 Charles Dickens edn, with rev preface.
New York 1876 New Illus Lib edn, introd by E. P. Whipple.
1886 A Christmas carol and The chimes, introd by H. Morley.
1886 A Christmas carol and The chimes, introd by R. Haweis.
1892 Macmillan edn, introd by C. Dickens the younger.
1897 Gadshill edn, introd by A. Lang.
1899 Temple edn, introd by W. Jerrold. 2 vols.
1903 Biographical edn, bound with Hard times, introd by A. Waugh, with original illustrations.
1905, introd by S. Laurence. 2 vols.
1905 A Christmas carol and The cricket on the hearth, ed with introd by J. M. Sawin and I. M. Thomas.
New York 1905 A Christmas carol and The cricket on the hearth, introd and illustr G. A. Williams.
1907 Everyman's Lib edn, introd by G. K. Chesterton.
[1912] Centenary edn, introd by C. Shorter, illustr C. Green and L. Rossi, 5 pts.
1913–15 Waverley edn, introd by G. K. Chesterton, illustr C. Pears and F. Barnard.
1923, introd by H. Strang.
New York and Boston 1928 A Christmas carol and The cricket on the hearth, ed with notes by E. Tourison.
1938 Nonesuch edn, ed A. Waugh, H. Walpole, W. Dexter and T. Hatton.
New York 1946 Christmas stories: A Christmas carol, The chimes, The cricket on the hearth, introd by M. L. Becker.
1954 Collins edn, introd by D. N. Brereton.
1954 New Oxford Illus Dickens, introd by E. Farjeon.
New York 1965 A Christmas carol and The chimes, Harper edn, introd by W. Allen.
Harmondsworth 1971 Penguin Eng Lib edn, later Penguin Classics edn, ed with introd and notes by M. Slater. 2 vols.
New York 1986 A Christmas Carol and other Christmas stories, introd by F. Busch.
1988 Folio Soc edn, introd by C. Hibbert, illustr C. Keeping.
Oxford 1988 World's Classics edn, ed with introd and notes by R. Glancy.

1991 Mandarin edn, introd by P. Ackroyd.
Cheltenham 1995 A Christmas carol and The cricket on the hearth, ed F. Green.

Reviews

Union Mag Feb 1846; Douglas Jerrold's Weekly 12 Dec 1846; [Thackeray, W. M.] A grumble about the Christmas books, Fraser's Mag Jan 1847; The Times 25 Dec 1847; Fraser's Mag 43 1851; Literary World 24 Dec 1869.

Studies and appreciations

[Fitzgerald, P.] Charles Dickens in relation to Christmas. Graphic Christmas No 25 Dec 1870.
Dorr, J. C. R. Christmas and its literature. Book Buyer 2 1885.
Kitton, F. G. Some famous Christmas stories. Lib Rev Jan 1893.
Dickens, C., the younger. The Christmas books of Charles Dickens. Good Cheer 1895.
Hadden, J. C. Christmas with Dickens. Family Friend 35 1904.
Van Noorden, C. Charles Dickens and the spirit of Christmas. Eng Illus Mag Dec 1904.
Ley, J. W. T. The apostle of Christmas. Dickensian 2 1906.
The Christmas books of Charles Dickens. Young Man Dec 1907.
Stewart, R. L. The Christmas spirit of Dickens. Dickensian 3 1907.
Watts-Dunton, T. Dickens and Father Christmas. A Yule-tide appeal for the babes of Famine Street. Nineteenth Cent and After 62 1907.
Frith, J. C. Dickens's Christmas tales. Book Monthly Dec 1919.

A Christmas carol

A Christmas carol, in prose: being a ghost story of Christmas, with illustrations by John Leech. 1843. The variants of the title page and endpapers of the 'first issue' are a matter of controversy. *See* J. C. Eckel 1932 *under* Bibliographies and reference works, *above*; C. J. Sawyer and F. J. H. Darton, English books vol 2, 1927, ch 7; Bookman (London) Dec 1931; TLS 14, 28 Jan 1932. The ms is in the Pierpont Morgan Lib.

Bibliographies

Newton, A. E. The greatest book in the world. Atlantic Monthly 132 1923. Rptd in The greatest little book in the world and other papers, Boston 1925.
Osborne, E. A. The facts about A Christmas carol. 1937.
Rust, S. J. At the Dickens House. Legal documents relating to the piracy of A Christmas carol. Dickensian 34 1938.
Newton, A. E. Rare books, manuscripts etc collected by the late A. Edward Newton. Parke-Bernet Galleries, 3 vols New York 1941. Proof-sheets of A Christmas carol in vol 1.
Calhoun, P. and H. J. Heaney. Dickens's Christmas carol after a hundred years: a study in bibliographical evidence. PBSA 39 1945.
Butt, J. A Christmas carol: its origin and design. Dickensian 51 1955.
Gimbel, R. The earliest state of the first edition of Dickens' A Christmas carol. Princeton Univ Lib Chron 19 1958.
Todd, W. B. A Christmas carol. BC 10 1961.
Davis, P. The lives and times of Ebeneezer Scrooge. New Haven CT 1990.
Mortimer, J. Poorhouse, pamphlets and Marley's Ghost. New York Times 24 Dec 1993. Discovery of original ms of Christmas carol.

Separate editions

A Christmas carol in prose. Leipzig 1843, 1847 Tauchnitz Collection of British Authors edn (unnumbered).
New York 1844.
Philadelphia 1844.
Paris 1844.
1858 Cheap edn.
Boston 1871, notes by A. J. Demarest.
1877 Household edn, illustr F. Barnard.
New York 1882, ed A. F. Blaisdell.
Leipzig 1888 Tauchnitz Cabinet edn of Eng classics.
1890, 1897. A Christmas carol. Facs of original ms, introd by F. G. Kitton.
Groningen 1901 (in English), with notes by K. ten Bruggencate.
1907, introd by W. P. Treloar, illustr J. Leech and F. Barnard.
1912, introd by C. Shorter, illustr C. Green.
Leipzig 1916 Tauchnitz Pocket Lib edn.
1922 facs of second edn (*not* first, as claimed), introd by G. K. Chesterton, preface by B. W. Matz.
New York 1924, introd by J. W. McSpadden, illustr E. F. Everett.
Boston 1934, introd by S. Leacock, illustr G. Ross.
Philadelphia 1938, introd by L. Barrymore, illustr E. Shinn.
New York 1956, 1967, facs of first edn, introd by E. Johnson.
New York 1963, afterword by C. Fadiman, illustr J. Groth.
New York 1966 Bantam Pathfinder edn, notes, background material and ed H. E. Vittum.
New York 1967. Facs of ms, text of first edn, with preface by F. B. Adams, jr, introd by M. Dickens.
New York 1976. The annotated Christmas carol, ed with introd, notes and bibliography by M. P. Hearn.
Louisville KY 1977 Braille edn.
New Haven CT 1993, facs of autograph ms, introd by J. Mortimer.
1994 Longman edn, ed G. Barton.
1995 Reader's Digest edn, illustr A. Rackham, R. Buchanan and B. Buchanan, afterword by A. Newton.
Kansas City 1995 Hallmark Cards edn, ed C. Marsh, illustr G. Head.
New York 1996, afterword by P. Glassman.

Dickens's reading version

A Christmas carol reading edition. 1857, rev Boston 1868, Paderborn 1980. Rptd in collections 1907, 1975, 1983. *See* Readings, *below.*
A Christmas carol: the public reading version. New York 1971. Facs of Dickens's prompt-copy, introd and notes by P. Collins.

Imitations

[Hewitt, H.] A Christmas ghost story. 1844 (Peter Parley's Lib). Plagiarisation.
[Swepstone, W. M.] Christmas shadows. A tale of the times. 1850.
Alger, H., jr. Job Warner's Christmas. Harper's New Monthly Mag 28 1863.
Harte, F. B. The haunted man: a Christmas story, by Ch-r--s D-c-k-n-s. [1865]. In his Condensed novels, New York 1867. Parody of A Christmas carol.
A., F. The final stave of A Christmas carol. Punch 129 1905.
Waterhouse, K. The Cratchit factor. Punch 275 1978.

Dramatisations

See Bolton 1987 *under* Studies and bibliographies of adaptations, *below.*
Stirling, E. A. Christmas carol; or, past, present and future. 1844.
Webb, C. A Christmas carol; or Scrooge the miser's dream. 1844.
Barnett, C. Z. A Christmas carol; or, the miser's warning. 1844.
Cooper, F. F. A Christmas carol. 1854.
Taylor, T. A Christmas carol. 1860.
Buckstone, J. C. Scrooge. 1901.
Scrooge. Film 1901. Produceed by R. W. Paul. Directed by W. R. Booth.
A Christmas carol. Film, Essanay 1908.
A Christmas carol. Film 1910. Directed by T. A. Edison.
Scrooge. Film, Hepworth 1913.
A Christmas carol. Film 1914. Written and directed by H. Shaw.
The right to be happy. Film 1916. Script by E. J. Clawson. Directed by R. Julian.
Scrooge. Film, Paramount 1935. Script by H. F. Mear. Directed by H. Edwards. With S. Hicks as Scrooge.
A Christmas carol. Film, MGM 1938. Script by H. Butler. Directed by E. L. Marin.

A Christmas carol. BBC television play 1950. Script by E. Fawcett.
A Christmas carol. Film, Renown 1951. Script by N. Langley. Directed by B. D. Hurst. With A. Sim as Scrooge.
A Christmas carol. Television film 1954. Script by M. Anderson. Directed by R. Levy.
Carol for another Christmas. ABC television film 1964. Script by R. Serling. Directed by J. L. Makiewicz.
Scrooge. Film 1970. Script by L. Bricusse. Directed by R. Neame. With A. Finney as Scrooge.
A Christmas carol. Animated cartoon. ABC television 1971. Drawn by R. Williams. Directed by C. Jones. Narrated by M. Redgrave, A. Sim, M. Hordern.
The stingiest man in town. Animated cartoon, NBC television 1978. Script by R. Muller. Directed by A. Rankin, jr.
A Christmas carol. BBC television 1979. Script by E. Morgan. With M. Hordern as Scrooge.
An American Christmas carol. Television film 1979. Directed by E. Till.
Mickey's Christmas carol. Animated cartoon, Disney 1983. Written and directed by B. Mattinson.
A Christmas carol. Film 1984. Script by R. O. Hirson. Directed by C. Donner. With G. C. Scott as Scrooge.
Scrooged. Film 1988. Script by M. Glazer and M. O'Donoghue. Directed by R. Donner. With B. Murray.
Blackadder's Christmas carol. Television film 1988. Script by R. Curtis and B. Elton. Directed by R. Boden. With R. Atkinson.
The Muppets' Christmas carol. Puppet film 1992. Script by J. Juhl. Directed by B. Henson.
Stewart, P. A Christmas carol. 1993.
Mortimer, J. A Christmas carol. 1994.
Ebbie. Television film 1995. Script by P. Redford and E. Redlich. Directed by G. Kaczender.

Reviews

[Mackay, C.] Morning Chron 9 Dec 1843; Evening Sun 22 Dec 1843; [Chorley, H. F.] Athenaeum 23 Dec 1843; Britannia 23 Dec 1843; [Forster, J.? or L. Hunt?] Examiner 23 Dec 1843 (on authorship, *see* P. Collins, in Dickens the craftsman, ed R. B. Partlow, jr, 1970, and A. Brice, Dickens Stud Newsletter 3 1972); John Bull 23 Dec 1843; Illus London News 23 Dec 1843; Literary Gazette 23 Dec 1843; Spectator 23 Dec 1843; Weekly Dispatch 24 Dec 1843; Morning Post 26 Dec 1843; Bell's Weekly Messenger 30 Dec 1843; [Russell, C. W.] Dublin Rev 15 1843; [Blanchard, L.] Ainsworth's Mag Jan 1844 (on authorship, *see* A. de Suzannet, Dickensian 34 1938); Mag of Domestic Economy Jan 1844; [Hood, T.] Hood's Mag Jan 1844; Sunday Times 7 Jan 1844; [Thackeray, W. M.] Fraser's Mag Feb 1844; 'Bon Gaultier' [T. Martin] Tait's Edinburgh Mag Feb 1844; GM Feb 1844; Illus Mag Feb 1844; [Clark, S. G.] Knickerbocker Mar 1844; [Starkey, D. P.] Dublin Univ Mag Apr 1844; Westminster Rev 41 1844 (review of R. H. Horne); Sammons, W. L., Sam Sly's African Jnl 15 Aug 1844; Northern Star 21 Dec 1844.

Studies and appreciations

Rann, E. H. The story of Dickens's Christmas carol. Cassell's Mag Dec 1907.
Jaques, E. T. [pseud]. Charles Dickens in Chancery: being an account of his proceeding in respect of the Christmas carol with some gossip in relation to the old law courts at Westminster. 1914; rptd New York 1972.
McNulty, J. H. Dickens's Christmas carol and ours also. Dickensian 16 1920.

The chimes

The chimes: a goblin story of some bells that rang an old year out and a new year in. 1845 (for 1844). Illustr Daniel Maclise, John Leech, Richard Doyle and Clarkson Stanfield. Slight variants. The ms and corrected proofs are in the Forster Collection; proofs in the Dexter Collection.

Separate editions

Leipzig 1845 Tauchnitz Collection of British Authors edn (unnumbered).
Philadelphia 1845.
New York 1845.
Paris 1845.
1858 Cheap edn.
Leipzig 1873 Tauchnitz edn, notes by F. H. Ahn.
Groningen 1883 (in English), notes by K. ten Bruggencate.
1912, introd by C. Shorter, illustr C. Green.
Leipzig 1916 Tauchnitz Pocket Lib edn.
1931, introd by E. Wagenknecht, illustr Arthur Rackham.
New York [1937], introd by E. Dickens Hawksley.
1983, facs of 1845 edn.

Dickens's reading version

The chimes: reading edition. 1858, [1868?] (rev and priv ptd with Sikes and Nancy, from Oliver Twist); in collections 1975, 1983. *See* Readings, *below*.

Study of the text

Slater, M. Dickens (and Forster) at work on The chimes. Dickens Stud 2 1966.

Imitations

[Planché, M. A., later Mrs H. S. Mackarness]. Old Jolliffe: not a goblin story, by the spirit of a little bell awakened by The chimes. 1845.
The wedding bells: an echo of The chimes. 1846 (for 1845).
Chamerovzov, L. A. The yule log, for everybody's Christmas hearth. 1847.
[Planché, M. A., later Mrs H. S. Mackarness]. The sequel to Old Jolliffe, written in the same spirit, by the same spirit. 1849.

Dramatisations

See Bolton 1987 *under* Studies and bibliographies of adaptations, *below*.
Lemon, M. and G. A. À Beckett. The chimes: a goblin story. 1844. Authorised by Dickens.
Stirling, E. The chimes; a goblin story of some bells that rang an old year out and a new year in. In three peals. 1844.
Atkyns, S. The chimes; a goblin story of some bells that rang an old year out and a new year in. 1844.
Edwards, E. The chimes; a goblin story of the old church bells. 1844.
Hazlewood, C. Some bells that rang an old year out and a new year in [The chimes] 1862.
The chimes. Film 1914. Directed by T. Bentley.
The chimes. Film 1914. Directed by H. Blaché.

Reviews

[Russell, C. W.] Dublin Rev Dec 1844; Morning Chron 17 Dec 1844; Evening Sun 18 Dec 1844; Morning Herald 19 Dec 1844; Liverpool Mercury 20 Dec 1844; Morning Advertiser 20 Dec 1844; Apprentice and Trades Weekly Register 21 Dec 1844; [Chorley, H. F.] Athenaeum 21 Dec 1844; Atlas 21 Dec 1844; Britannia and Conservative Jnl 21 Dec 1844; [Hunt, L.] Examiner 21 Dec 1844; Illus London News 21 Dec 1844; Literary Gazette 21 Dec 1844; Mirror of Lit 21 Dec 1844; Northern Star 21, 28 Dec 1844; Spectator 21 Dec 1844; Tablet 21 Dec 1844; Weekly Chron 21 Dec 1844; Bell's Life in London 22 Dec 1844; Observer 22 Dec 1844; Weekly Dispatch 22 Dec 1844; Morning Post 23 Dec 1844; Liverpool Courier 25 Dec 1844; The Times 25 Dec 1844; John Bull 28 Dec 1844; Sentinel 28 Dec 1844; World 28 Dec 1844; Globe 31 Dec 1844; Christian Remembrancer Jan 1845; Douglas Jerrold's Shilling Mag Jan 1845; Eclectic Rev Jan 1845; Economist 18 Jan 1845; [Forster, J.] Edinburgh Rev 81 1845; [Hood, T.] Hood's Mag Jan

1845; Tait's Edinburgh Mag Jan 1845; Critic 1 Jan 1845; Economist 18 Jan 1845; Parker's London Mag Feb 1845; New Monthly Belle Assemblée Feb 1845; Illuminated Mag Feb 1845; 'Bon Gaultier' [T. Martin] Tait's Edinburgh Mag Apr 1845; [Cleghorn, T.] North Br Rev 3 1845.

The cricket on the hearth

The cricket on the hearth: a fairy tale of home. 1846 (for 1845). Illustr Daniel Maclise, John Leech, Richard Doyle, Clarkson Stanfield and Edwin Landseer. The ms is in the Pierpont Morgan Lib.

Separate editions

Leipzig 1846 Tauchnitz Collection of British Authors edn (unnumbered).
New York 1846.
New York 1846.
Boston 1846.
Paris 1846.
1858 Cheap edn.
Hamburg 1872 (in English).
Berlin 1873 (in English).
1887, 1904, bound with selections from Sketches by Boz, introd by H. Morley.
New York 1898, introd by J. Jefferson.
1906, introd by H. Caine.
1912, introd by C. Shorter, illustr L. Rossi.
Leipzig 1916 Tauchnitz Pocket Lib edn.
1933, introd by W. de la Mare, illustr Hugh Thomson.
Guildford 1981, facs of ms, introd by A. Sanders.

Dickens's reading version

The cricket on the hearth: reading edition. 1858; in collection 1975. *See* Readings, *below*. Prompt-copies are in the Berg Collection, NYPL, and the William M. Elkins Collection, Free Lib of Philadelphia.

Commentary on the text

Fielding, K. J. The manuscript of The cricket on the hearth. N & Q 197 July 1952.

Imitation

The beetle under the fender. Mephystopheles 10, 17, 31 Jan, 7 Feb 1846.

Dramatisations

See Bolton 1987 *under* Studies and bibliographies of adaptations, *below*.
Smith, A. R. The cricket on the hearth, a fairy tale of home. 1845.
Stirling, E. The cricket on the hearth, a fairy tale of home. 1845.
Webster, B. N. The cricket on the hearth, a fairy tale of home. 1846.
Archer, T. The cricket on the hearth. Three chirps. 1846.
Lucas, W. J. The cricket on the hearth. 1846.
Barnett, C. Z. The cricket on the hearth; or, the carrier and his wife. 1846.
Townsend, W. T. The cricket on the hearth: a fairy tale of home. In three chirps 1846.
Blanchard, E. L. The cricket on our hearth. 1846. Burlesque.
Rayner, B. F. The cricket on the hearth. 1846.
Halford, J. The cricket on the hearth. 1855.
Boucicault, D. Dot. A fairy tale of home. New York 1859.
Williams, F. The cricket on the hearth. 1877.
Cricket on the hearth. Film, Biograph 1909. Directed by D. W. Griffith.
Cricket on the hearth. Film, Biograph 1914. Produced by A. Hale.
The cricket on the hearth. Film, Biograph 1923. Script by C. F. Cooke. Directed by L. Johnston.
Cricket on the hearth. Film, Realm Television Productions 1949. Directed by S. Martin.
Cricket on the hearth. Animated cartoon 1968. With voices by D. Thomas and M. Thomas.

Reviews

Literary Annual Register 1845; [Heraud, J. A.] Athenaeum 20 Dec 1845; Bell's Weekly Messenger 21, 27 Dec 1845; Era 21 Dec 1845; Observer 21 Dec 1845; Morning Post 22 Dec 1845; [Thackeray, W. M.] Morning Chron 24 Dec 1845; Morning Herald 25 Dec 1845; Atlas 27 Dec 1845; Britannia 27 Dec 1845; Critic 27 Dec 1845; [Forster, J.? or L. Hunt?] Examiner 27 Dec 1845 (on authorship, *see* P. Collins, in Dickens the Craftsman, ed R. B. Partlow, jr, 1970, and A. Brice, Dickens Stud Newsletter 3 1972); Illus London News 27 Dec 1845; John Bull 27 Dec 1845; Literary Gazette 27 Dec 1845; The critic on the art (of humbug) v The cricket on the hearth, Mephystopheles 27 Dec 1845, 10, 17, 24, 31 Jan 1846; Mirror of Lit 27 Dec 1845; Northern Star 27 Dec 1845; Pictorial Times 27 Dec 1845; Spectator 27 Dec 1845; The Times 27 Dec 1845; Weekly Chron 27 Dec 1845; Sentinel 28 Dec 1845; Weekly Dispatch 28 Dec 1845; London Jnl 2 Jan 1846; Economist 3 Jan 1846; Chambers's Jnl 17 Jan 1846; Oxford and Cambridge Rev Jan 1846; People's Jnl Jan 1846; Macphail's Edinburgh Ecclesiastical Jnl Feb 1846; Union Mag Feb 1846.

Studies and appreciations

Baker, H. L. An essay on Dickens and The cricket on the hearth. Detroit 1868.
Goodburn, G. The cricket on the hearth. An early criticism. Dickensian 13 1917.

The battle of life

The battle of life: a love story. 1846. Dickens's name on ptd title page, not on engraved. Illustr Daniel Maclise, John Leech, Richard Doyle and Clarkson Stanfield. Variants. The ms is in the Pierpont Morgan Lib.

Bibliographies

Schaw Miller, A. G. Dickens's Battle of life. TLS 31 July 1937.
Carter, J. W. The battle of life: round three. Antiquarian Bookman 33 1964.
Todd, W. B. The battle of life: round six. BC 15 1966.

Separate editions

Paris 1847, bound with The cricket on the hearth.
New York 1847.
Philadelphia 1847.
Leipzig 1856 Tauchnitz edn, bound with The haunted man. Dated 1847 but not apparently issued as a separate vol.
1888, 1904, introd by H. Morley.
1912, introd by C. Shorter, illustr C. Green.
Leipzig 1918 Tauchnitz Pocket Lib edn.

Dramatisations

See Bolton 1987 *under* Studies and bibliographies of adaptations, *below*.
Harris. The battle of life. Dublin 1846.
Robertson, T. W. The battle of life. [1846?].
Smith, A. [R.] The battle of life, dramatised from early proofs of the work, by the express permission of the author. 1846.
Atkyns, S. The battle of life. 1847.
Archer, T. The battle of life. 1847.
Lyon, T. E. Battle of life; a love story. 1847.
Somerset, C. A. The battle of life. 1847.
Pitt, G. D. The battle of life. 1847.
Stirling, E. The battle of life. 1847.
Davenport, J. M. [J. B. Marriage?]. The battle of life. Norwich 1847.
Nation, W. H. C. The battle of life. 1867.
Dickens, C., the younger. The battle of life. 1873.
Ellis, W. and P. Greenwood. Marion. 1891.

Reviews

Morning Advertiser 21 Dec 1846; Morning Post 21 Dec 1846; Globe 23 Dec 1846; Morning Chron 24 Dec 1846; [Marston, J. W.]

Athenaeum 26 Dec 1846; Atlas 26 Dec 1846; Britannia 26 Dec 1846; Critic 26 Dec 1846; Daily News 26 Dec 1846; [Forster, J.] Examiner 26 Dec 1846; Literary Gazette 26 Dec 1846; Northern Star 26 Dec 1846; Spectator 26 Dec 1846; Weekly Chron 26 Dec 1846; Weekly Dispatch 27 Dec 1846; Tait's Edinburgh Mag Jan 1847; [Philips, S.] The Times 2 Jan 1847; London Jnl 9 Jan 1847; Dublin Univ Mag 29 Jan 1847; [Patmore, C.?] North Br Rev 7 1847; Howitt's Jnl 1 1847; North Br Rev Feb 1848.

The haunted man

The haunted man and the ghost's bargain: a fancy for Christmas time. 1848. Illustr John Leech, Clarkson Stanfield, John Tenniel and F. Stone. Variant ms formerly in Carl H. Pforzheimer Lib, New York; presently in private collection.

Bibliography

Matz, B. W. When found. Dickensian 18 1922. Reports sale of Haunted man ms.

Separate editions

Leipzig 1848 Tauchnitz Collection of British Authors edn (unnumbered).
New York 1849.
1891, introd by H. Morley.
1912, introd by C. Shorter, illustr C. Green.
New York 1914, facs of 1st edn.
Leipzig 1918 Tauchnitz Pocket Lib edn.

Dickens's reading version

W. C. M. Kent, Dickens as a reader, 1872, and Sotheran (Jan 1879) record a copy of the 1848 edn prepared by Dickens as a reading; but this reading was never used. In collection 1975. *See* Readings, *below.*

Imitations

'Buz'. The haunted druggist, or Bogey's speculation. 1849.
The haunted shopman; or, the ghost's bad bargain. The Man in the Moon 4, Jan 1849.

Dramatisations

See Bolton 1987 *under* Studies and bibliographies of adaptations, *below.*
Lemon, M. The haunted man and the ghost's bargain. A fancy for Christmas. 1848, 1863.
[Atkyns, S.?] The haunted man and the ghost's bargain. 1848.
Somerset, C. A. The haunted man. 1848.
Robertson, T. W. The haunted man. Boston, Lincs 1849.
Brougham, J. The haunted man New York. 1849.
The haunted shopkeeper; or a queer ghost story about a goblin. 1849. Farce.
[Walcott, C.?] The haunted man. New York 1849.

Reviews

Morning Herald 18 Dec 1848; Morning Post 21 Dec 1848; Spectator 21 Dec 1848; The Times 21 Dec 1848; [Marston, J. W.] Athenaeum 23 Dec 1848; Altas 23 Dec 1848; [Forster, J.] Examiner 23 Dec 1848; Literary Gazette 23 Dec 1848; Spectator 23 Dec 1848; Bell's Life 24 Dec 1848; Bell's New Weekly Messenger 24 Dec 1848; Weekly Chron 24 Dec 1848; Sunday Times 24 Dec 1848; Daily News 25 Dec 1848; Morning Chron 25 Dec 1848; Bell's Weekly Messenger 30 Dec 1848; Macphail's Edinburgh Ecclesiastical Jnl Jan 1849; Man in the Moon 4, Jan 1849; Mirror Monthly Mag Jan 1849; Sharpe's London Mag Jan 1849; Tait's Edinburgh Mag Jan 1849; Family Friend 1 1849.

Christmas stories

The items collected under the title Christmas stories *in most edns of the* Collected works *appeared in* Household Words 21 Dec 1850, *the* Extra Christmas numbers *of* Household Words 1851–8 *('containing the amount of one regular number and a half'), and the* Extra Christmas numbers *of* All the Year Round 1859–67 *('containing the amount of two ordinary numbers'). All these nos contained contributions by other authors also. Dickens's contributions to the 1850, 1852 and 1853 nos were rptd in* Reprinted pieces 1858, *and many edns of the* Christmas stories *exclude these (and his 1851 contribution) or exclude his 1850 contribution (as an essay, not a story). His contributions have frequently been rptd singly or in groups of two or three.*

Household Words

21 Dec 1850. A Christmas tree. The whole issue is called simply Christmas number.
21 Dec 1850. Christmas in the frozen regions (with R. McCormick).
Christmas 1851. What Christmas is as we grow older. Whole issue called Extra number for Christmas.
Christmas 1852. The poor relation's story; The child's story. In A round of stories by the Christmas fire.
Christmas 1853. The schoolboy's story; Nobody's story. In Another round of stories by the Christmas fire.
Christmas 1854. The first poor traveller; The road. In The seven poor travellers.

Dickens's reading adaptation

The poor traveller, bound with Boots at the Holly-Tree Inn and Mrs Gamp. 1858; in collections 1975, 1983. *See* Readings, *below.*

Dramatisations

See Bolton 1987 *under* Studies and bibliographies of adaptations, *below.*
Johnstone, J. B. The seven poor travellers; of the fireside stories of a Christmas eve. 1855.
Hicks, N. T. The seven poor travellers: a Christmas eve's romance at Mr Richard Watts' charity, Rochester. 1855.
Pitt, G. D. The seven poor travellers; life's faults and follies. 1855.
The seven poor travellers. 1855.
Cooper, F. F. The seven poor travellers, or Heart-strings and purse-strings. 1855.
Digges, W. Doubledick; or, friendship and love. Halifax 1875.

Christmas 1855. The guest; The boots; The bill. In The Holly-Tree Inn. Draft of proposed story outline in Huntington Museum.

Dickens's reading version

Boots at the Holly-Tree Inn, bound with The poor traveller and Mrs Gamp 1858; in collections 1868, 1975, 1983. *See* Readings, *below.*

Dramatisations

See Bolton 1987 *under* Studies and bibliographies of adaptations, *below.*
Johnstone, J. B. The Holly Tree Inn. 1856.
Hazlewood, C. H. Tales of the Holly Tree Inn. 1856.
Seaman, W. The Holly Tree Inn; or, the adventures of a snowed up traveller. 1856.
Webster, B. Holly tree inn; or, the juvenile elopement to Gretna Green. 1856.
Berenger, Mrs. O. Holly Tree Inn. 1891.
Boots at the Holly Tree Inn. BBC television 1957.
The runaways. Film, Coronet [1976].

Christmas 1856. The wreck of the Golden Mary. The Wreck, excluding John Steadiman's account. Draft of proposed story outline in Huntington Museum. *See* Poems, doubtful and supposititious, *below.*

Editions

1935, introd by W. H. D. Rouse.
1955, introd by J. van Thal, illustr J. Dugan.

Dramatisations

See Bolton 1987 *under* Studies and bibliographies of adaptations, *below.*
Seaman, W. The wreck of the Golden Mary. 1857.
Townsend, W. T. The wreck of the Golden Mary. 1857.
Young, H. The child's prayer. 1860.

Studies and appreciations

Matz, B. W. A child's hymn in The wreck of the Golden Mary. Dickensian 12 1916.

Suddaby, J. The wrecked dying-child near Natal, its lifelong effect on Dickens. Dickensian 6 1910.

Christmas 1857. The perils of certain English prisoners, and their treasure in women, children, silver and jewels. Chs 1 and 3 by Dickens, ch 2 by Wilkie Collins.

Editions

1923, illustr M. Urquhart.

1924, introd by J. Drinkwater.

Dramatisations

[Hazlewood, C. H.?] The perils of certain English prisoners, and their treasure in women, children, silver and jewels. 1858.

Young, H. Silver Store Island [The black flag]; or, Pedro Mendez the South American Pirate. 1858.

Baynham, W. The Island of Silver Store; or, the prisoners' perils. Brighton 1858.

Travers, W. The Island of Silver Store; or, the pirate of the Carabees. 1858.

Cooper, F. F. Silver Store Island; or, the British flag of the South American pirate. 1858.

The pirate chief; or, the black flag and the treacherous Sambo. 1858.

Reviews

[Lucas, S.] The Times 4 Dec 1857; Saturday Rev 26 Dec 1857.

Christmas 1858. Going into society; Let at last (in collaboration with Wilkie Collins). In A house to let.

Dickens's reading version

Mr Chops the dwarf, bound with Bardell and Pickwick and Mr Bob Sawyer's party. [1861?]; in collection 1975. *See* Readings, *below.*

Review

[Stephen, J. F.?] Saturday Rev 25 Dec 1858.

All the Year Round

Christmas 1859. The mortals in the house; The guest in Master B.'s room; The ghost in the corner room; connecting links. In The haunted house.

Review

Critic 17 Dec 1859.

Studies and appreciations

Mr Dickens and his haunted house. Spiritual Mag 1 1860.

Mr Howitt and Mr Dickens. Spiritual Mag 1 1860.

Christmas 1860. A message from the sea. Ch 1 and opening of ch 3 by Dickens, chs 2 and 5 by Dickens and Wilkie Collins.

Dramatisations

See Bolton 1987 *under* Studies and bibliographies of adaptations, *below.*

Brougham, J. A message from the sea. [America, 1860?]

Dickens, C. and W. Collins. A message from the sea. 1861. Persons of the drama and outline of the plot only. Pbd for copyright purposes. *See* M. Morley, Dickensian 52 1956.

Hazlewood, C. H. A message from the sea. 1861.

Cline, T. S. A message from the sea. Boston 1861.

Russell, E. R. Stolen money; or, a message from the sea. 1863.

Study

Carlton, W. J. Captain Morgan – alias Jorgan. Dickensian 53–4 1957–8.

Christmas 1861. Tom Tiddler's ground. Chs 1, 6, 7. One ms page is in Dickens House; another in Gimbel Collection.

Study

C., E. Mr Mopes the Hermit. London Society 1 1862. *See* F. G. Kitton, The Dickens Country 1911, and A. E. B. Cross, Dickensian 26 1930.

Christmas 1862. Somebody's luggage. 1 His leaving it till called for; 2 His boots; 7 His brown-paper parcel; 10 His wonderful end. Draft of Dickens's instructions for prospective contributors is in the Huntington Museum. The ms of His brown-paper parcel (with one page missing) is in Harvard.

Reviews

[Dallas, E. S.] The Times 4 Dec 1862; Saturday Rev 20 Dec 1862.

Christmas 1863. Mrs Lirriper's lodgings. Chs 1, 7. Draft of Dickens's instructions for prospective contributors is in the Huntington Museum. One page of ms is in the Alfred and Isabel Reed Dickens Collection, Dunedin Public Lib, New Zealand.

Dickens's reading version

Mrs Lirriper's lodgings. 1866; in collection 1975. Never performed. *See* Readings, *below.*

Reviews

[Dallas, E. S.] The Times 3 Dec 1863; Saturday Rev 12 Dec 1863.

Christmas 1864. Mrs Lirriper's legacy. Chs 1, 7.

Reviews

[Dallas, E. S.] The Times 2 Dec 1864; Saturday Rev 10 Dec 1864.

Christmas 1865. Doctor Marigold's prescriptions. Chs 1, 7.

Dickens's reading version

Doctor Marigold [1866]; in collections Boston 1868, London 1907, 1975, 1983. *See* Readings, *below.* Dickens's prompt-copy is in the Berg Collection, NYPL.

Dramatisation

Byron, H. J. Uncle Dick's Sophy. 1869, with Henry Irving.

Reviews

[Dallas, E. S.] The Times 6 Dec 1864; Saturday Rev 16 Dec 1864.

Christmas 1866. Mugby Junction. Barbox Brothers; Barbox Brothers & Co; Main line, The boy at Mugby; No 1 branch line; The signal man. Draft instructions for prospective contributors in Huntington Museum. Two pages of corrected proofs are in the Gimbel Collection in Yale.

Dickens's reading version

Barbox brothers. The boy at Mugby. The signalman. [1867]; in collection 1975. *See* Readings, *below.* Dickens's prompt-copy is in the Berg Collection, NYPL.

Imitations

Astle, J. The gal at Mugby. Cheltenham 1867.

'Lyulph' [H. R. Lumley]. A girl at a railway junction's reply. [1867].

First class. Routledge's Christmas Annual. 1868.

Dramatisations

The signalman. Film for television 1955. Directed by N. Zucker.

The signalman. Film, Dynamic 1955. With M. Woolley.

The signalman. BBC television film 1976. Directed by L. G. Clark. With D. Elliott.

Reviews

[Dallas, E. S.] The Times 5 Dec 1866; [Kent, C.] Sun 7 Dec 1866; Saturday Rev 15 Dec 1866.

Study

'Sack, O.' [i.e. B. W. Matz]. Mugby Junction and the Grand Magazine. Dickensian 8 1912.

Christmas 1867. No thoroughfare. By Charles Dickens and Wilkie Collins. Overture and Act III entirely by Dickens, Act II entirely by Collins. Other 'acts' in collaboration.

Editions

No thoroughfare. Every Saturday. Extra Christmas number 1867.

Leipzig 1868 Tauchnitz Collection of British Authors no 961.

No thoroughfare. 1997. Website http://www.why.net/home/jrusk/collins/thor/thor_ttl.htm

Imitations

Slow thoroughfare. By Warles Chickens and Chilky Dollins. Banter 23 Dec 1867.

No thoroughfare: the book in eight acts. Mask Feb 1868. Parody.

No throughfare [*sic*]. By C—s D—s, Bellamy Brownjohn and Domby. Boston 1868. A parody with reference also to Dickens's readings and Amer notes.

Dramatisations

See Bolton 1987 *under* Studies and bibliographies of adaptations, *below.*

Dickens, C. and W. Collins. No thoroughfare. 1867. Collins's ms and ms prompt-book for the part of Obenreizer are in the Gimble Collection, Yale.

Sherwell, L. R. and F. Williams. No thoroughfare. Boston 1867.

Lequel, L. Identity, or no thoroughfare: a drama. New York 1868.

Hazlewood, H. C., jr. No thoroughfare beyond Highbury; or, the maid, the mother and the malicious mountaineer. 1868. Burlesque.

Grossmith, G. No thoroughfare. 1869. Burlesque.

Brand, O. No thoroughfare; or, the story of a foundling. 1903.

Review

[Dallas, E. S.] The Times 27 Dec 1867.

Bibliographies

Pierpont, R. Letter to the editor. Dickensian 4 1908. Describes 1868 edn.

Notes on sales: Dickens's Christmas numbers. TLS 25 Dec 1924.

Pierpont, R. Dickens's Christmas numbers. TLS 8 Jan 1925.

Thomas, D. A. Contributors to the Christmas numbers of Household Words and All the Year Round. Dickensian 69–70 1973–4.

Davies, H. N. The Tauchnitz extra Christmas numbers of All the Year Round. Library 5th ser 33 1978. Attributions.

Collected editions

[1859]. Christmas stories from Household Words (1850–8).

Leipzig 1862 Tauchnitz Collection of British Authors no 609. Christmas stories: The haunted house, A message from the sea, and Tom Tiddler's ground.

Boston 1867 Diamond edn, illustr S. Eytinge, jr. Dickens's portions of Christmas numbers first removed by Dickens for this edn and pbd together as Christmas stories; only 9 stories included, not in chronological order. *See* Glancy, Dickens's Christmas books, 1985, Bibliographies, *below*.

Leipzig 1867 Tauchnitz Collection of British Authors no 888. Somebody's luggage, Mrs Lirriper's luggage, and Mrs Lirriper's legacy.

Leipzig 1867 Tauchnitz Collection of British Authors no 894. Doctor Marigold's Prescription and Mugby Junction.

1868 Household Words Christmas stories 1851–8; 9 vols 1906.

[1868] Christmas stories from All the Year Round. 9 pts; 1 vol 1868, 9 vols [1907].

1871 Christmas stories from Household Words and All the Year Round. Charles Dickens edn, with stories in chronological order.

1874 Christmas stories from Household Words and All the Year Round, Illus Lib edn.

1898 Christmas stories from Household Words and All the Year Round. Gadshill edn, introd by A. Lang and illustr A. J. Goodman. 2 vols.

1900 The Holly Tree Inn and The seven poor travellers, introd by W. Jerrold.

New York 1906 Stories from the Christmas numbers of Household Words and All the Year Round 1852–1867, introd and notes by C. Dickens the younger.

1908 The Holly Tree Inn and A Christmas tree, introd and illustr G. A. Williams.

1910 Christmas stories, Everyman's Lib, introd by G. K. Chesterton.

New York 1911 Christmas stories, introd and notes by A. Lang, J. Forster, P. Fitzgerald et al.

New York 1927 A Christmas tree and What Christmas is as we grow older. Introd by W. L. Phelps.

1956 Christmas stories, New Oxford Illus edn, introd by M. Lane.

1996 Christmas stories, Everyman Dickens, ed with introd and notes by R. Glancy.

Studies and appreciations

Ellis, F. M. Dickens's Christmas stories. Christian Realm Dec 1903.

Fitzgerald, P. Boz and Christmas. Pears' Christmas Annual 1904.

Readings

For reading-texts of individual items, see under Novels, Christmas books, Christmas stories, *above.*

Bibliography

Stonehouse, J. H. A first bibliography of the reading editions of Dickens's works. In his edn of Sikes and Nancy, 1921.

Collected editions

The poor traveller; Boots at the Holly-Tree Inn; and Mrs Gamp. 1858 (priv ptd), 1858, nd.

Barbox brothers; The boy at Mugby; and The signalman: three readings, each in one chapter. [1866] (priv ptd).

Bardell and Pickwick; Mr Chops the dwarf; Mr Bob Sawyer's party: three readings, each in one chapter. nd (priv ptd).

The readings of Dickens, as condensed by himself. Boston 1868, London 1883, 1907. 10 readings. Items also issued separately Boston 1867–8.

Readings from the works of Dickens as arranged and read by himself. Ed J. Hollingshead 1907. 10 readings.

Charles Dickens: the public readings. Ed P. Collins, Oxford 1975.

Charles Dickens: Sikes and Nancy and other public readings. Ed P. Collins, Oxford 1983 (World's Classics edn).

Contemporary accounts

See notes in Pilgrim Letters *from 1854 onwards for many further accounts.*

The Times 2 Jan 1854, 8 Jan 1869.

Leader 4 July 1857.

Saturday Rev 19 June 1858, 9 May 1868.

[Hollingshead, J.] Critic 4 Sep 1858; rptd in his Today vol 2, 1865 and his Miscellanies vol 3, 1874; also as Introd to his 1907 edn of Readings, *above*.

Manchester Guardian 1861–7; Dickensian 34 1938.

Harper's Weekly 28 Dec 1867.

Yates, E. Tinsley's Mag Feb 1869.

Illus London News 19 Mar 1870.

Field, K. Pen photographs of Dickens's readings. Boston [1868], 1871 (rev and enlarged). *See* her diary in L. Whiting, Kate Field: a record, 1899.

Kent, W. C. M. Dickens as a reader. 1872, Farnborough 1971, New York 1973.

Dolby, G. Dickens as I knew him: the story of the reading tours 1866–70. 1885, 1912, New York 1970. *See* J. G. Ollé, Dickens and Dolby, Dickensian 54 1958.

Murray, D. C. Recollections. 1908. Ch 4.

Studies and appreciations

Dexter, W. For one night only: an account of the famous readings. Dickensian 37–8 1941–2.

Dexter, W. The readings in America. Dickensian 38 1942.

Dexter, W. ('L. A. Kennethe'). The unique reading books. Dickensian 39 1943.

Murphy, T. and R. Dickens as a professional reader. Quart Jnl of Speech 33 1947.

Fielding, K. J. Dickens and Thomas C. Evans. N & Q 186 Mar 1951. *See* G. G. Grubb, Dickensian 48 1952.

Williams, E. Readings from Dickens. Introd by B. Darwin 1953 (limited edn), 1954. Williams's Notes on the adaptations compare his versions with Dickens's.

Murphy, T. Interpretation in the Dickens period. Quart Jnl of Speech 41 1955.

Gordon, J. D. (ed). Mrs Gamp: a facsimile of the author's prompt copy. New York 1956. Discusses Dickens's methods.

Gordon, J. D. Reading for profit: the other career of Dickens. BNYPL Sep 1958. Also pbd separately.

Collins, P. Dickens's public readings: the performer and the novelist. Stud in the Novel 1 1969.

Fitzsimons, R. The Charles Dickens show: an account of his public readings 1858–1870. 1970.
Collins, P. The Dickens reading copies in Dickens House. Dickensian 68 1972.
Collins, P. Dickens's public readings: texts and performances. Dickens Stud Annual 3 1974.
Collins, P. Dickens's public readings: the kit and the team. Dickensian 74 1978.

Plays, poems and other minor works and papers
Bibliographies
Most of the shorter items have been listed in the bibliographies by Shepherd, Kitton, Hammerton and Eckel (see Bibliographies and reference works, *above), and have been collected in the vols listed below. Only separate reprints issued in Dickens's lifetime, or subsequently pbd with comment or other supplementary matter, or items identified since the most generally available collection of his papers* (ed Matz 1908) *are included here.*
Dexter, W. Dickens's early dramatic productions (from The strange gentleman to The lamplighter). Dickensian 33–4 1937–8.
The Lord Chamberlain's copies of Dickens's plays. Appendix G. Letters of Dickens, ed M. House and G. Storey, [Pilgrim edn] vol 1 Oxford 1965.
Glancy, R. Dickens's Christmas books, Christmas stories, and other short fiction. New York 1985.

Collections
The plays and poems of Dickens, with a few miscellanies in prose now first collected. Ed R. H. Shepherd 2 vols 1885. An earlier edn, 2 vols 1882, containing No thoroughfare, was withdrawn through copyright difficulties.
Poems and verses. Ed F. G. Kitton 1903.
Plays and poems. In Collected papers vol 2, 1937 (Nonesuch). The fullest collection.
Complete plays and selected poems. 1970.
The strange gentleman and other plays. Ed J. Tillett 1972.

Plays
O'Thello: an operatic burlesque (unpbd). Performed privately by Dickens's family and friends, 1833. Facs of fragments, Dickensian 13 1917, 26 1930. Included in Nonesuch, Collected papers, *above*.
Hayward, C. Charles Dickens and Shakespeare: or the Irish Moor of Venice, O'Thello, with music. Dickensian 73 1977.
The village coquettes: a comic opera in two acts, the music by John Hullah. 1836, Leipzig 1845 (in L. Hilsenberg, Modern English comic theatre), Amsterdam [1868?] (in Modern English comedies and farces no 1); rptd [1878] (facs), 1883 (in Dicks, Standard plays). First production 6 Dec 1836, St James's Theatre.
Songs, choruses and concerted pieces in the operatic burletta of The village coquettes. 1837.
The following songs were pbd separately (Hullah's music, Dickens's words): The child and the old man 1836, Some folks who have grown old 1836, How beautiful at eventide 1836, No light bound of stag 1836, My fair home 1851, The cares of the day 1858, Autumn leaves 1871. Reviews in Dickensian 30 1934.
The strange gentleman: a comic burletta, in two acts, by 'Boz', first performed at the St James's Theatre on Thursday September 29 1836. 1837 (with frontispiece by 'Phiz'), 1871 (without frontispiece). Variants; in some copies extra frontispiece by F. W. Pailthorpe. J. C. Eckel 1932 (*see* Bibliographies and reference works, *above*) mentions another reprint but gives no data.
The strange gentleman. [1883] (in Dicks, Standard plays), 2 pts 1904, 1928 (priv ptd, illus with reproductions from original drawings by John Leech, John Orlando Parry et al). Dickens's first publicly produced play; a version as a short story, The great Winglebury duel, appeared in Sketches by Boz 1st ser 1836.
Adrian, A. A. The demise of The strange gentleman. Dickensian 51 1955. On the 1873 revival.
Hill, T. W. Dickens and his ugly duckling. Dickensian 37 1941.
Is she his wife? or something singular: a comic burletta in one act. [1872?]. The earliest known surviving edn. A unique copy of the real 1st edn – nd, presumably about 1837 – was destroyed by fire in 1879. A reprint of the text had been made from it and was issued at Boston in 1877. Play produced at St James's Theatre London 6 Mar 1837. *See* R. H. Shepherd, A lost work of Dickens, Pen Oct 1880, and J. C. Eckel 1932 *under* Bibliographies and reference works, *above*.
The lamplighter: a farce by Charles Dickens (1838) now first printed from a manuscript in the Forster Collection at the South Kensington Museum. 1879; ed W. L. Phelps, New York 1926 (with The lamplighter's story). Discovered and ptd by R. H. Shepherd. Never produced or ptd in Dickens's lifetime. Written as a farce for Macready (*see* his Diaries) but withdrawn. The substance was turned into a tale and included in The Pic Nic Papers as The lamplighter's story.
Mr Nightingale's diary: a farce in one act, by — [Dickens and Mark Lemon]. 1851 (priv ptd), Boston 1877 (some copies with frontispiece by F. W. Pailthorpe). Produced at Devonshire House 16 May 1851, both authors in the cast. *See* L. W. Fisher, Lemon, Dickens and Mr Nightingale's diary: a Victorian farce, Univ of Victoria Eng Literary Stud, Monograph Ser no 41, 1988 (text of Lemon's autograph draft with version rev by Lemon and Dickens for performance).
Horne, R. H. Bygone celebrities, II: Mr Nightingale's diary. GM May 1871.
Collins, W. Wilkie. The lighthouse. Acted at Dickens's Tavistock House Theatre, 19 June 1856. Prologue and Song of the wreck by Dickens; text of play rev by him during rehearsal. Ms (incomplete) in Berg Collection, NYPL.
The frozen deep: a drama, in three acts, by Wilkie Collins; not published. 1866. 'not published' is part of title page. The play was produced at Dickens's house, 6 Jan 1857; in supervising rehearsals he rewrote much of the play himself. *See* introd to Collins's version as a story-reading, Readings and writings in America, 2 vols 1874.
Berger, F. Letter about The frozen deep. Dickensian 10 1914.
Brannan, R. L. (ed). Under the management of Mr Charles Dickens: his production of The frozen deep. Ithaca NY 1966. Prints the 1857 ms prompt-copy, shows the extent of Dickens's contributions, and gives details of the production, reviews etc.
No thoroughfare: a drama in five acts (altered from the Christmas story for performance on the stage), by Charles Dickens and Wilkie Collins [with the collaboration of C. S. Fechter]. 1867. Produced 26 Dec 1867. Possibly variants. *See* Christmas numbers 1867, *above*.

Study of plays
Fitz-Gerald, S. J. A. Dickens and the St James's Theatre. Dickensian 16 1920.

Poems
Dexter, W. The love romance of Dickens, told in his letters to Maria Beadnell. 1936. Includes 4 poems written in Maria Beadnell's album 1829–31, and The bill of fare (1831).
See A. de Suzannet Maria Beadnell's album. Dickensian 31 1935.
A fable (not a Gay one). Lines written in Ellen Beard's album 1834. Dickensian 28 1932.
The ivy green, a Christmas carol and Gabriel Grub's song. In Pickwick papers 1836–7.
Song of the month no 8 (Of all the months in the twelve that fly). Bentley's Misc Aug 1837. Unsigned. *See* W. Dexter, The song of August, Dickensian 35 1939, and W. J. Carlton, The death of Mary Hogarth, Dickensian 63 1967.

To Ariel. 1838. Written in Priscilla Horton's album 26 Oct 1838. Ariel was one of her stage-roles. *See* Dickensian 30 1934.

The loving ballad of Lord Bateman. Illustr George Cruikshank. 1839, 1841, 1870 (rev, by Dickens?). On authorship, *see* A. L. Haight, Colophon, New York 1939 and Pilgrim Letters vol 1, p. 536n. Dickens wrote the preface and notes and adapted at least part of the text, based on a traditional ballad. Rptd 'by Charles Dickens and W. M. Thackeray' 1969, with note by L. C. Staples.

Examiner 1841. The fine old English gentleman (7 Aug), The quack doctor's prescription (14 Aug), Subjects for painters: after Peter Pindar (21 Aug). Signed W. *See* Forster, Life bk 2 ch 12.

Prologue to The patrician's daughter: a tragedy in five acts by J. Westland Marston. Produced 10 Dec 1842, Drury Lane; pbd 1841 without the Prologue. Prologue in Sunday Times 11 Dec 1842 (and other jnls); another version in Letters vol 1, 1880.

A word in season. In Keepsake, ed Countess of Blessington 1844. Signed Charles Dickens.

Prologue to The elder brother, by Fletcher and Massinger, spoken to Miss Kelly at a benefit performance at her theatre by Dickens's company, 3 Jan 1846.

Daily News 1846. The British lion: a new song but an old story (24 Jan, signed Catnach), The hymn of the Wiltshire labourers (14 Feb, signed Charles Dickens). The Hymn rptd in Gems from the spirit mine, pbd by the League of Universal Brotherhood, 1850.

Charade sent to Henry Riley Bradbury 3 June 1847; rptd Pilgrim Letters vol 5 appendix A.

Elegy written in a country churchyard. Parody sent to Mary Boyle 3 Dec 1849. *See* Dickensian 16 1920 (facs); rptd Pilgrim Letters vol 5 appendix H.

Starr, H. W. Dickens's parody of Gray's Elegy. Dickensian 51 1955.

New song. Signed T. Sparkler. In letter to Mark Lemon, 25 June 1849.

Prologue ('Prologues and epilogues, in good old days'), hitherto unpublished. Dickensian 37 1941. To Jerrold's The housekeeper?

Prologue and The song of the wreck for Wilkie Collins's The lighthouse. 1855.

Prologue to Wilkie Collins's The frozen deep. 1856.

Doubtful or supposititious play and poems

The strategems of Rozanza: a Venetian comedietta by C. J. H. Dickens. 1828. The existence of this ms, not in Dickens's handwriting, has been reported; apparently unpbd, its authenticity is not established. Probably a trn of a Goldoni play. *See* Dickensian 22 1926 and J. W. T. Ley, note to his edn (1928) of Forster's Life, bk 1 ch 4.

Household Words 1850–1. Hiram Power's Greek slave (26 Oct 1850); Aspire! (25 Jan 1851). These poems, often attributed to Dickens through a misunderstanding of the Household Words contributors' book, are by E. B. Browning and another. *See* A. Lohrli, Greek slave mystery, N & Q 211, Feb 1966.

Child's hymn. In The wreck of The Golden Mary, Household Words Christmas no 1856. Attributed to Dickens on evidence of a letter to Rev R. H. Davies (Forster's Life bk 11 ch 3), probably misunderstood. *See* B. W. Matz, Dickensian 12 1916.

The blacksmith. All the Year Round 30 Apr 1859. Attributed to Dickens on the evidence of Rev T. B. Lawes (Forster's Life bk 8 ch 5), but challenged by F. G. Kitton, Literature 15 Sep 1900, referring to the 'office' set of All the Year Round (now lost). *See* W. Miller and J. Suddaby, Dickensian 11 1915.

Other minor works and papers

Sunday under three heads: as it is; as Sabbath Bills would make it; as it might be made. By Timothy Sparks. 1836 (illustr H. K. Browne); 1884 (facs, introd); Manchester [1884] (facs, introd); London 1994, bound with Sketches by Boz and pieces from Bentley's Misc, in Dickens' journalism vol 1, ed M. Slater, *below*.

Contemporary reviews. Dickensian 32 1936.

Johnson, E. Dickens and the bluenose legislator. Amer Scholar 17 1948.

A newly discovered Dickens fragment. Ed G. Seawim, Dickensian 54 1958. Theatrical Advertisement, Extraordinary, in Bentley's Misc Feb 1837. *See* note by M. Morley, Dickensian 57 1961.

Sketches of young gentlemen, dedicated to the young ladies, with six illustrations by Phiz. 1838. Anon. *See below*, Sketches of young couples.

Memoirs of Joseph Grimaldi, edited by 'Boz' with illustrations by George Cruikshank. 2 vols 1838 (variants); rev C. Whitehead 1846; 1853, 1866, 1884; ed P. Fitzgerald 1903; ed R. Findlater 1968. Dickens wrote a preface and rewrote Grimaldi's ms; 'he has not swelled the quantity of matter, but materially abridged it' (preface).

The suppressed letter respecting Grimaldi. Dickensian 34 1938. A suppressed prefatory note, ptd in part in Forster, Life bk 2 ch 2.

Stott, R. T. Boz's Memoirs of Grimaldi. BC 15 1966. Bibliographical.

Sketches of young couples, with an urgent remonstrance to the gentlemen of England (being bachelors or widowers) on the present alarming crisis, by the author of Sketches of young gentlemen, with six illustrations by Phiz. 1840. Anon. Rptd with Sketches of young gentlemen as Sketches of young couples and young gentlemen, by Boz 1846, and with Sketches of young ladies as Sketches of young couples, young ladies, young gentlemen, by Quiz, illustr Phiz, [1869]. Quiz (Edward Caswall) was the author of Sketches of young ladies, 1837, to which Dickens's Sketches of young gentlemen, 1838, was a riposte.

The Pic Nic papers, by various hands. Edited by Charles Dickens, with illustrations by George Cruikshank, Phiz etc. 3 vols 1841. Variants. Introduction (in vol 2) and The lamplighter's story (in vol 1) by Dickens; the latter adapted from the farce, The lamplighter (*see above*, Plays). The farce and the story rptd, ed W. L. Phelps, New York 1926.

Grubb, G. G. and L. Mason. Dickens and J. C. Neal's Charcoal sketches. Dickensian 46 1950.

American notes

American notes for general circulation. 2 vols 1842 (variants); Tauchnitz Collection of British Authors no 32, Leipzig 1842; Cheap edn 1850 (and in 12 weekly pts, 3 monthly pts, May-July 1850; with preface, and frontispiece by C. Stanfield); Charles Dickens edn 1868 (with rev preface and postscript). A suppressed chapter, Introductory and necessary to be read, is given in Forster, Life bk 3 ch 8. The 1868 postscript, 'to be added to all future editions', was pbd in All the Year Round 6 June 1868 as A debt of honour. Harmondsworth 1975, Penguin Eng Lib edn, later Penguin Classics edn, ed A. Goldman and J. S. Whitley; 1997 Everyman Dickens edn, bound with Pictures from Italy, ed L. Ormond and F. Schwarzbach; Harmondsworth 1998, Penguin classics edn, ed P. Ingham.

Bibliographies

Wilkins, W. G. American parodies on American notes. Dickensian 4 1908. *See* his Dickens and America, 1911.

Fielding, K. J. American notes and some English reviewers. MLR 59 1964.

Bracher, P. The Lea and Blanchard edition of Dickens's American notes, 1842. PBSA 63 1969.

Bracher, P. The New York Herald and American notes. Dickens Stud 5 1969.

Bracher, P. The early American editions of American notes: their priority and circulation. PBSA 69 1975.

Reviews

Athenaeum 22, 29 Oct 1842; Examiner 22–9 Oct 1842; Literary Gazette 22 Oct 1842; Mirror 28 Oct 1842; [Payne, G. P.] Ainsworth's Mag Nov 1842; Dublin Monthly Mag Nov 1842; Fraser's Mag Nov 1842; Monthly Rev Nov 1842; [Hood, T.] NMM Nov 1842; Tait's Edinburgh Mag Nov 1842; [Chapman, M.]

Liberator 18 Nov 1842; Chambers's Jnl 19–26 Nov 1842; [Warren, S.] Blackwood's Mag Dec 1842; Bradshaw's Jnl Dec 1842; Christian Remembrancer Dec 1842; Knickerbocker Dec 1842; S., J. London Univ Mag 1 1842; [Spedding, J.] Edinburgh Rev 76 1843 (enlarged in his Reviews and discussions, 1979. Reply by Dickens, The Times 16 Jan 1843); [Thompson, J. T.] New Englander Jan 1843; [Felton, C.] North Amer Rev 56 1843; Southern Literary Messenger Jan 1843; [Wiseman, N.] Dublin Rev 15 1843; [Hickson, W. E.?] Westminster Rev 40 1843; [Croker, J. W.] Quart Rev 71 1843; National Quart Rev Sep 1860; Whipple, E. P. Atlantic Monthly Apr 1877.

Parodies

'Quickens, Quarles'. English notes, intended for very extensive circulation! Boston 1842; ed J. Jackson and G. H. Sargent, New York 1920. A parody and retort to American notes. Not by E. A. Poe, as often conjectured.

'Buz'. Current American notes. nd. A close parody; includes material transcribed from American notes.

Studies and appreciations

[Cary, T. G.] Letter to a lady in France with answers to enquiries concerning the books of Capt Marryat and Mr Dickens. Boston 1843, 1844.

[Wood, Henry.] Change for American notes: in letters from London to New York, by an American lady. 1843.

Overs, John. Evenings of a working man, with a preface relative to the author by Charles Dickens. 1844. *See* G. G. Grubb, Dickensian 49 1953.

Adshead, J. The fictions of Dickens on solitary confinement. In his Prisons and prisoners, 1845. On American notes, ch 7.

Tellkampf, J. L. Remarks on American notes. In his Essays on law reform, 1859.

Some notes on America to be rewritten: suggested, with respect, to Charles Dickens esq. Philadelphia 1868.

[Tallack, W.] Dickens's prison fiction. 1894. Issued by the Howard Assoc.

Dickensian special numbers on Dickens and America: Aug 1909, Aug 1910, Sep 1916, Apr 1926, Dec 1941.

Jackson, J. Dickens in Philadelphia. Philadelphia 1912 (priv ptd).

Pictures from Italy

Pictures from Italy, the vignette illustrations on wood by Samuel Palmer. 1846; Tauchnitz Collection of British Authors no 103, Leipzig 1846; 1865 Cheap edn; 1868 Charles Dickens edn; ed D. Paroissien 1973; 1997, Everyman Dickens, bound with American notes, ed L. Ormond and F. Schwarzbach. Appeared in part in Daily News 21 Jan–11 Mar 1846, as Travelling letters written on the road, by Charles Dickens.

Reviews

Athenaeum 23 May 1846; The Times 1 June 1846; Chambers's Jnl 20 June 1846; London Jnl 20 June 1846; GM July 1846; Tait's Mag July 1846; Literary Gazette 18 July 1846; [Murray, P. A.] Dublin Rev 21 1846; Macphail's Edinburgh Ecclesiastical Jnl Sep 1846.

Study

'Savonarolo, Don Jeremy' [F. S. Mahony]. Facts and figures from Italy, addressed to Charles Dickens. 1847. Prefatory note by Dickens.

Autobiographical fragment. Written c. 1845–6; not pbd by Dickens. In Forster, Life bk 1 ch 2.

Circular sent to the friends of Leigh Hunt about performances for his benefit, June 1847; rptd Pilgrim Letters vol 5 appendix B. *See* Dickensian 36 1940.

Broadsheet for the friends of Leigh Hunt about performances for his benefit, at Liverpool, July 1847; rptd Pilgrim Letters vol 5 appendix C.

An appeal to fallen women. Pamphlet [1847], written in connection with Miss Coutts's Home for fallen women. Rptd in Collected papers (Nonesuch edn), in Johnson 1952 (Biographies, *below*), and in Pilgrim Letters vol 5 appendix D.

Proposed prospectus for the Provident union of literature, science and art, [November] 1847; rptd in Pilgrim Letters vol 5 appendix E.

Explanation of the mark table used in Urania cottage, 29 Aug 1848; rptd in Pilgrim Letters vol 5 appendix F.

Bill of one of Dickens's conjuring performances at Bonchurch 1849; rptd in Pilgrim Letters vol 5 appendix G.

[Charles Dickens]. (Proof.) [Private and Confidential]. Brackets thus on title page. A pamphlet denouncing the forgeries of Thomas Powell, prepared by Dickens 1849 (priv ptd) and sent to various English and Amer newspapers. *See* W. Partington, Should a biographer tell? Atlantic Monthly Aug 1947; rptd with addns, Dickensian 43 1947 (reply by W. J. Carlton, Atlantic Monthly Aug 1947).

The life of our Lord, written expressly for his own children, 1849. 1934, 1970, Philadelphia 1981; rptd 1995 in Everyman Dickens, Holiday romance and other writings for children, ed G. Avery. Not intended for pbn; written 1846. *See* Dickensian 30 1934.

Prayer at night. Written for his children, c. 1849. Pbd by J. Suddaby, Dickensian 5 1909, and in Mr and Mrs Charles Dickens, ed W. Dexter 1935.

Emigration. [February 1850?]. Unpbd in Dickens's lifetime; ptd in Pilgrim Letters vol 6 appendix E.

A child's history of England, with a frontispiece by F. W. Topham (in each vol). Vol 1 1852, vol 2 1853, vol 3 1854; Tauchnitz Collection of British Authors (unnumbered), Leipzig 1853; 1 vol 1863. Slight variants. Originally appeared intermittently in Household Words 25 Jan 1851–10 Dec 1853. Illustr Marcus Stone 1873. Rptd 1995 in Everyman Dickens, Holiday romance and other writings for children, ed G. Avery.

Topham's illustration to A child's history of England. Dickensian 3 1907.

To be read at dusk. In Keepsake for 1852, ed M. Power; pirated in Harper's New Monthly Mag Jan 1852. Rptd 1852 (priv ptd); ed F. G. Kitton 1898 (with other stories, etc, *below*). The 1852 edn is probably a forgery; *see* J. Carter and H. G. Pollard, An enquiry into the nature of certain nineteenth-century pamphlets, 1934, and J. Carter, TLS 26 July 1934.

The late Mr Justice Talfourd. [1854]. Private pre-print of the article in Household Words 25 Mar 1854.

Address of the English author to the French public, 17 January 1857. Prefixed to P. Lorain's authorised trn of Nicholas Nickleby, 2 vols Paris 1857. Rptd in Collected papers (Nonesuch).

The lazy tour of two idle apprentices. In collaboration with Wilkie Collins. Originally appeared in Household Words 3–31 Oct 1857. Rptd [1875] (in part in Joseph Sly, King's Arms and Royal Hotel, Lancaster), 1890 (illus), with No thoroughfare and The perils of certain English prisoners (*see* Christmas numbers, *above*). Rptd in part as The bride's chamber, ed with introd by H. Stone, illustr K. Jacobi, Santa Monica CA 1996.

The case of the reformers in the [Royal] Literary Fund; stated by Charles W. Dilke, Charles Dickens and John Forster. [1858] (priv ptd). Followed by A summary of facts in answer to allegations… [1858] (priv ptd by the Committee), and The Answer to the Committee's summary of 'facts' [1858] (priv ptd). For Dickens's substantial authorship of the reformers' pamphlets, *see* Speeches, ed K. J. Fielding, Oxford 1960.

Hunted down: a story, with an account of Thomas Griffiths Wainewright the poisoner. [1870]. Originally in New York Ledger 7–20 Aug, 3 Sep 1859; also in All the Year Round 4–11 Aug 1860; Leipzig 1860 Tauchnitz Collection of British Authors no 536, with Uncommercial traveller; Philadelphia [1861] (with

Lamplighter and other novelettes). The account of Wainewright is by John Camden Hotten.

Matchett, W. Thomas Griffiths Wainewright: a notable Dickens model. Dickensian 2 1906.

Matchett, W. The lesson of Hunted down. Dickensian 6 1910.

Curling, J. Janus Weathercock: the life of Thomas Griffiths Wainewright. 1938. Ch 7, As Dickens saw him.

Procter, A. A. Legends and lyrics, with an introduction by Charles Dickens. New edn, with addns, illus 1866. Introd included in later edns and in the Complete works, 1905.

Holiday romance. Our Young Folks (Boston) Jan, Mar, Apr, May 1868; rptd in All the Year Round 25 Jan, 8 Feb, 14 Mar, 4 Apr 1868; [1875] (Charles Dickens edn). Rptd 1920 with decorations by D. M. Palmer; pt 1 (The trial of William Tinkling) [1912] with illustrations by S. B. Pearce; pt 2 (The magic fishbone) [1911] with illustrations by S. B. Pearce; [1921] by F. D. Bedford; Oxford 1939 by P. Bray; by H. Knight 1964. New York 1976 facs of Our Young Folks as The king of the golden river, A Holiday romance, Petsetilla's posy, by J. Ruskin, C. Dickens and T. Hood. Rptd 1995 Everyman Dickens, Holiday romance and other stories for children, ed G. Avery, with illustrations by G. C. White and J. Gilbert.

George Silverman's explanation. Atlantic Monthly Jan–Mar 1867; rptd in All the Year Round 1, 15, 29 Feb 1868; [1875] (Charles Dickens edn, with Drood); Northridge CA 1984, introd and notes by H. Stone.

Batterson, R. F. The manuscript and text of Dickens's George Silverman's explanation. PBSA 73 1979.

The great international walking match of February 29th, 1868 (broadside, priv pbd, Boston).

East London Hospital for Children, reprinted by permission of Charles Dickens esq from All the Year Round Dec 19th 1868. nd. Original mag title, New uncommercial samples: A small star in the east.

Religious opinions of the late Reverend Chauncey Hare Townshend, published as directed in his will, by his literary executor [Charles Dickens]. 1869. Explanatory introd by Dickens.

An unpublished satirical sketch by Dickens. Ed and introd by G. Storey. Dickensian 74 1978.

Supposititious article

Women in the home. Preface to A summary account of prizes for common things offered and awarded by Miss Burdett Coutts at the Whitelands Training Institute. 1856 [by A. B. Coutts, copied by Dickens]. *See* K. J. Fielding, Women in the home: an article Dickens did *not* write, Dickensian 47 1951.

Periodicals edited by Dickens

Dickens contributed many items to his periodicals and, particularly for his weeklies (in which almost all contributions were unsigned), accepted responsibility for the tenor as well as the quality of whatever he pbd; so he often silently rewrote or otherwise amended his colleagues' work. Many stories and essays by other contributors were rptd, especially in America, as his work.

Bibliographies

B. W. Matz. Writings wrongly attributed to Dickens. Chambers's Jnl 16 Aug 1924, rptd in Dickensian 21 1925. Incomplete.

'T. Kent Brumleigh' (T. W. Hill). Journalistics. Dickensian 48 1952. A list of Dickens's journalistic works.

The letters of Charles Dickens. Ed M. House and G. Storey, Oxford 1965 (Pilgrim edn). Vol 1 Appendix F.

Lohrli, A. Household Words: a weekly journal 1850–1859 conducted by Charles Dickens. Toronto 1973. Table of contents, list of contributors and their contributions based on the Household Words office book.

DeVries, D. Dickens's apprentice years: the making of a novelist. Appendix A. Hassocks 1976.

Oppenlander, E. A. Dickens's All the Year Round: descriptive index and contributor list. Troy NY 1984.

Atkinson, D. Appendix: Dickens's journalism. In The Dickens index, ed N. Bentley, M. Slater and N. Burgis, Oxford 1988.

M. Slater (ed). Dickens' journalism. 1995 (Everyman Dickens edn). Vol 2 Appendix B, vol 3 Appendix C.

Periodicals

Bentley's Miscellany. Monthly from Jan 1837. Dickens was its first editor and resigned 31 Jan 1839. Contents included Oliver Twist and sundry shorter items, mostly signed; *see below*.

Prospectus for Bentley's Miscellany. Ptd from Dickens's ms. In The letters of Charles Dickens, ed M. House and G. Storey, Oxford 1965 (Pilgrim edn). Vol 1 Appendix D.

Extraordinary Gazette. Speech of his Mightiness on opening the second number of Bentley's Miscellany. 1837. Pam, illustr H. K. Browne. Rptd with illustration, Dickensian 26 1930, 34 1938.

Daily News. From 21 Jan 1846. Dickens was its first editor and resigned 9 Feb 1846. Contents included his Travelling letters, rptd as Pictures from Italy (*see above*), also other contributions, mostly signed. Facs of opening no pbd with Jubilee no, 21 Jan 1896. Dummy issue 19 Jan 1846 (rare) with contributions by Dickens.

Household Words. Weekly 30 Mar 1850–28 May 1859, when it was incorporated into All the Year Round. Also in monthly pts and 19 half-yearly vols. Cheap edn, 19 vols 1868–73. Charles Dickens the younger revived the mag and its title 1881. Contents included A child's history of England, Hard times, Christmas stories and numerous unsigned essays; *see below*. Extensive reprinting Leipzig 1851–6 Tauchnitz Collection of British Authors no 199 as Household Words. Conducted by Charles Dickens, 36 vols, Leipzig 1856–9 Tauchnitz Collection of British Authors no 376 as Novels and tales reprinted from Household Words, 11 vols; rptd 1868–73, with variants, 19 vols, also monthly parts; *see* A. Lohrli 1973 *under* Bibliographies, *above*.

The Household Narrative of Current Events. Monthly Apr 1850–Dec 1855; nos for Jan–Mar 1850 pbd retrospectively. Bound, 6 vols. A news suppl to Household Words.

The Household Words Almanac. Annually 1856, 1857.

All the Year Round. Weekly from 30 Apr 1859. Also in monthly pts and half-yearly vols. Edited by Dickens until his death, and by C. Dickens the younger thereafter; incorporated 1895 in the revived Household Words. Bound, 20 vols 1859–68 (with General index, 1868); new ser 1868–88. Contents included A tale of two cities, The uncommercial traveller, Great expectations, Christmas stories and some unsigned essays; *see below*.

New weekly illustrated periodical, Once a Week. 1859. Prospectus by Bradbury & Evans, with a statement, Mr Charles Dickens and his late publishers, about their differences with him.

Collections from Dickens's periodicals

Novels and tales reprinted from Household Words, conducted by Charles Dickens. 11 vols Leipzig 1856–9 (Tauchnitz Collection of British Authors no 376).

Reprinted pieces. 1858. Vol 8 of the Library edn of the Works. 31 anon contributions to Household Words 1850–6.

Wills, W. H. Old leaves gleaned from Household Words. 1860. Dedication acknowledges Dickens's helpful revisions. One essay, A plated article, appears both here and in Dickens's Reprinted pieces, 1858.

The Gad's Hill Gazette. [1860–6]. A family mag mainly ed H. F. Dickens, to which Dickens contributed. Produced partly in ms and partly on a small private press, for domestic use only. *See* Dickensian 6, July 1910 (facs) and P. Fitzgerald, Recreations of a literary man, vol 1, 1882 (facs). Not rptd; incomplete runs in some libraries, notably NYPL and Yale.

Dickens, H. F. The history of the Gad's Hill Gazette. Dickensian 25 1929.

The uncommercial traveller. 1861 [1860]. 16 articles in All the Year Round 1860, collected in 17 chs. Leipzig 1860 (Tauchnitz Collection of British Authors no 536, with Hunted down), 2nd ser 1866 [1865], in Cheap edn (3rd ser) of the Works (11 further contributions), rptd in Charles Dickens edn 1868. 8 further contributions, first pbd 1863–9, added in Uncommercial traveller, [1873] (Illus Lib edn of the Works). One more, first pbd 1869, added in Gadshill edn of the Works, 1898.
REVIEWS: Morning Chron 10 Jan 1861; [Stephen, J. F.?] Saturday Rev 23 Feb 1861.

The Mudfog papers etc by Charles Dickens, now first collected. 1880, introd by George Bentley; Leipzig 1880 (Tauchnitz Collection of British Authors no 1935); Gloucester 1984, introd by S. Michell. From Bentley's Misc 1837–8. Now usually included in Works in vol containing Sketches by Boz.

To be read at dusk, and other stories, sketches and essays by Charles Dickens, now first collected. 1898. Introd by F. G. Kitton, claiming that 24 of the 46 items had not been included in any previous bibliography. Items from Bentley's Misc, Examiner and Household Words. Includes one item (By rail to Parnassus) not by Dickens but by Henry Morley. New York 1897.

Collected papers. Ed A. Waugh 1903. In the Biographical edn of the Works. Contains Sketches of young gentlemen, Sketches of young couples, items from Bentley's Misc etc, and the Prefaces, Addresses to the reader, Editorial announcements etc from successive edns of the novels and from the periodicals.

Miscellaneous papers. Ed B. W. Matz 2 vols 1908. In Gadshill edn of the Works 1908, National edn 1908, Biographical edn (1 vol) 1908, Centenary edn 1911, Universal edn (1 vol) 1914. Also rptd separately. 140 items, mostly newly rptd, from Morning Chron, Examiner, Household Words, All the Year Round etc. One item (The restoration of Shakspeare's Lear to the stage) not by Dickens: *see* Supposititious contributions, *below*. Miscellaneous papers is not included in most subsequent edns of the Works, but some use this title to describe items usually collected as 'Reprinted pieces', sometimes with other miscellaneous works.

Collected papers. 2 vols 1937. In the Nonesuch edn of the Works. Editorial note signed by all 4 editors. Adds 16 items not in Matz's Miscellaneous papers. One item (The restoration of Shakspeare's Lear to the stage) not by Dickens: *see* Supposititious contributions, *below*.

The uncollected writings of Charles Dickens. Ed H. Stone, Harmondsworth 1969. 2 vols.

Dickens' journalism. Ed M. Slater and J. Drew 1994– (in progress). Dent Uniform edn, later Everyman Dickens edn. 4 vols. Vol 1 Sketches by Boz and other early papers, 1833–39 (1994); vol 2 The amusements of the people and other papers: reports, essays, reviews, 1834–51 (1995); vol 3 Gone astray and other papers, 1851–59; vol 4 The uncommercial traveller and other papers, 1859–69.

Studies

Grant, J. The newspaper press. 2 vols 1871. Vol 2 ch 3, The Daily News.

Dickens, C., the younger. Dickens as an editor. Eng Illus Mag Aug 1889.

Fitzgerald, P. H. Memoirs of an author. 2 vols 1894. Vol 1 ch 1, Dickens and Household Words. *See* Fitzgerald *under* Biographies, *below*.

Crow, J. Reminiscences of thirty-five years. 1895. On the Daily News.

McCarthy, J. and J. R. Robinson. The Daily News jubilee. 1896. Chs 1–2.

Hollingshead, J. Fifty years of Household Words. Household Words Jubilee no 26 May 1900. *See* Hollingshead *under* Personal recollections, *below*.

Fitzgerald, P. H. Household Words memories. Household Words 28 Mar 1903.

Thomas, W. M. An old Household Words man. Household Words 28 Mar 1903.

Robinson, J. R. Fifty years of Fleet Street. 1904.

Escott, T. H. S. Literature and journalism. Fortnightly Rev Jan 1912.

Fitzgerald, P. H. Some memories of Dickens and Household Words. In The Dickens souvenir, ed D. C. Calthrop and M. Pemberton, 1912.

Lehmann, R. C. (ed). Dickens as editor: letters written by him to W. H. Wills, his sub-editor. 1912.

Quail, J. Dickens and the Daily News. Nineteenth Cent Oct 1920.

Van Dyke, C. A talk with Dickens's office-boy. Bookman (New York) Mar 1921.

Dexter, W. Bentley's Miscellany. Dickensian 33 1937.

Rust, S. J. The first number of the Daily News. Dickensian 34 1938.

Dexter, W. Dickens's contributions to Household Words. Dickensian 35 1939. Articles of which Dickens was part-author.

Grubb, G. G. Dickens's editorial methods. SP 40 1943.

Grubb, G. G. The editorial policies of Dickens. PMLA 58 1943.

Grubb, G. G. Dickens's influence as an editor. SP 42 1945.

Buckler, W. E. Dickens's success with Household Words. Dickensian 46 1950.

Grubb, G. G. Dickens and the Daily News: the origin of the idea. In Booker memorial studies, ed H. Shine, Chapel Hill NC 1950.

Buckler, W. E. Dickens the paymaster. PMLA 66 1951. *See* G. G. Grubb, Dickensian 51 1955.

Buckler, W. E. Household Words in America. PBSA 45 1951.

Grubb, G. G. Dickens and the Daily News. Nineteenth-Cent Fiction 6–7 1952–3.

Grubb, G. G. The American edition of All the Year Round. PBSA 47 1953.

Collins, P. 'Keep Household Words imaginative!' Dickensian 52 1956.

Grubb, G. G. Dickens rejects. Dickensian 52 1956.

Collins, P. Dickens's periodicals: articles on education. [Leicester] 1957.

Adrian, A. A. Dickens as verse editor. MP 58 1960.

Collins, P. Dickens as editor: some uncollected fragments. Dickensian 56 1960.

Collins, P. The significance of Dickens's periodicals. REL 2 1961.

Lohrli, A. Household Words on American English. Amer Speech 37 1962.

Easson, A. Dickens, Household Words, and a double standard. Dickensian 60 1964.

Collins, P. 'Inky fishing-nets': Dickens as editor. Dickensian 61 1965. His revision of contributors' work.

Lohrli, A. Household Words and its office book. Princeton Univ Lib Chron 26 1965.

Ryan, J. S. (ed). Dickens and New Zealand. Wellington 1965. Articles from Household Words and All the Year Round.

Stone, H. Dickens and composite writing (in Household Words). Dickens Stud 3 1967.

Stone, H. Dickens and the idea of a periodical. Western Humanities Rev 21 1967.

Stone, H. New writings by Dickens. Dalhousie Rev 47 1967.

Contributions to periodicals

Stories and sketches collected in Sketches by Boz, *the novels and Christmas stories are not listed here.*

Contributions to Bentley's Miscellany

The public life of Mr Tulrumble, once mayor of Mudfog. Jan 1837.

The pantomime of life. Mar 1837.

Some particulars concerning a lion. May 1837.

Full report of the first meeting of the Mudfog Association for the Advancement of Everything. Oct 1837.

Full report of the second meeting of the Mudfog Association for the Advancement of Everything. Sep 1838.

Familiar epistle from a parent to a child aged two years and two months. Feb 1839.

Contributions to the Morning Chronicle 1834–42

Report from Edinburgh on preparations for the Grey festival. 17 Sep 1834.
Report of the Edinburgh dinner to Lord Grey. 18 Sep 1834.
The christening. 14 Oct 1834. Review.
Report on meeting of Birmingham liberals. 1 Dec 1834.
Report of Southwark parish meeting. 5 Dec 1834.
The story without a beginning. 18 Dec 1834.
Election report from Colchester. 10 Jan 1835.
Election report from Braintree. 12 Jan 1835.
Election report from Chelmsford. 13 Jan 1835.
Election report from Sudbury. 14 Jan 1835.
Election report from Bury St Edmunds. 17 Jan 1835.
The maid of Castile. 22 Jan 1835. Review.
Election report from Exeter. 2 May 1835.
The Colosseum. 8 July 1835.
Grand Colosseum fete. 10 July 1835.
Zarah. 8 Sep 1835. Review.
The christening. 29 Sep 1835. Review.
Rival pages. 9 Oct 1835. Review.
The reopening of the Colosseum. 13 Oct 1835.
Truth, or a glass too much. 20 Oct 1835. Review.
The king's command. 27 Oct 1835. Review.
The Castilian noble and the contrabandista 4 Nov 1835. Review.
Report of speech by Lord John Russell in Bristol. 11 and 12 Nov 1835.
Report of political dinner at Bath. 13 Nov 1835.
Reopening of the Adelphi under Mrs Nisbett's management. 17 Nov 1835.
The dream at sea. 24 Nov 1835. Review.
Report on the fire at Hatfield House. 2 and 4 Dec 1835.
Report on the Northamptonshire election. 16 and 19 Dec 1835.
One hour, or a carnival ball. 12 Jan 1836. Review.
The waterman. 15 Jan 1836. Review.
Brown's horse. 19 Jan 1836. Review.
Report of foundation stone laying by Lord Melbourne. 22 Jan 1836.
Rienzi. 4 Feb 1836. Review.
Report of reform dinner at Ipswich. 28 May 1836.
Report of Norton/Melbourne trial. 23 June 1836.
A letter to Lord Ashley. 20 Oct 1842. Review.
The agricultural interest. 9 Mar 1844. Review.

Contributions to the Examiner 1837–49

Joan of Arc. 3 Dec 1837. Review.
Pierre Bertrand. 17 Dec 1837. Review.
The ages of female beauty. 28 Jan 1838. Review.
Sporting. Edited by Nimrod. 28 Jan 1838. Review.
Report of coronation fair in Hyde Park. 1 July 1838.
Refutations of the misstatements... in Mr Lockhart's Life of Sir Walter Scott. 2 Sep 1838. Review.
Hood's Comic annual for 1839. 3 Feb 1839. Review.
Scott and his publishers II. 31 Mar 1839.
The boy's country book. 7 Apr 1839. Review.
Scott and his publishers III. 29 Sep 1839. Review.
Lady of Lyons. 26 July 1840. Review.
Snoring for the millions. 27 Dec 1842.
Harlequin and William Tell. 31 Dec 1842. Review.
Macready as Benedick. 4 Mar 1843. Review.
Report of the commissioners appointed to inquire into the condition of the persons variously engaged in the University of Oxford. 3 June 1843.
La Favorita. 21 Oct 1843. Review.
Juvenile imprisonment in the metropolis. 18 Dec 1843.
The night side of nature. 26 Feb 1848. Review.
Ignorance and crime. 22 Apr 1848.
Ignorance and its victims. 29 Apr 1848.
The Chinese junk. 24 June 1848.
The drunkard's children. 8 July 1848. Review.
Narrative of the expedition... the River Niger. 19 Aug 1848. Review.
A truly British judge. 19 Aug 1848.
The poetry of science. 9 Dec 1848. Review.
The American panorama. 16 Dec 1848.
Judicial special pleading. 23 Dec 1848.
Edinburgh Apprentice School Association. 30 Dec 1848.
The rising generation. 30 Dec 1848. Review.
The paradise at Tooting. 20 Jan 1849.
The Tooting farm. 27 Jan 1848.
A recorder's charge. 3 Mar 1849.
Prison and convict discipline. 10 Mar 1849.
Rush's conviction. 7 Apr 1849.
The verdict for Drouet. 21 Apr 1849.
Capital punishment. 5 May 1849.
Virginia and Black-eyed Susan. 12 May 1849. Review.
False reliance (re. the Rush murder). 2 June 1849.
Drainage and health in the metropolis. 14 July 1849.
An American in Europe. 21 July 1849. Review.
The sewers' commission. 4 Aug 1849.
Demoralisation and total abstinence. 27 Oct 1849.
Macready as King Lear. 27 Oct 1849. Review.
Central criminal court. 8 Dec 1849.
Court ceremonies. 15 Dec 1849.

Contributions to The Times

International copyright (letter). 16 Jan 1843; rptd in Collected papers (Nonesuch) and Pilgrim Letters vol 3, pp. 422–4.
On behalf of the Miss Lowes (letter, with T. Carlyle and J. Forster). 1 Nov 1855; rptd Examiner 3 Nov 1855; Pilgrim Letters vol 7 Appendix F.
Public executions (letters). 14, 17 Nov 1849; rptd as pam, 1849; Pilgrim Letters vol 5 pp. 644–5, 651–4.
Personal. 7 June 1858. *See below,* Household Words 12 June 1858.
Dramatic rights in fiction (letter). 12 Jan 1861. Rptd in Collected papers (Nonesuch).
The earthquake shock in England (letter). 8 Oct 1863. Rptd in Collected papers (Nonesuch).
Denying rumours about his state of health (letter). 2 Sep 1867; Nonesuch Letters vol 3 p. 543.

Contributions to the Daily News

Address to the reader. 21 Jan 1846. Rptd in G. G. Grubb, Dickens and the Daily News: the early issues, Nineteenth-Cent Fiction 6 1952.
Letter to the Editor. Signed A. Constant Reader, 22 Jan 1846. With reply by Dickens as editor. About misprints in opening number.
Crime and education (letter). 4 Feb 1846.
Letters on social questions. Capital punishment (letters). 23, 28 Feb, 9, 13 and 16 Mar 1846. 3 letters in this ser (9, 13 and 16 Mar 1846) have been rptd in Collected papers (Nonesuch); also as a pam 1849. 2 further letters have been rptd later: 23 Feb 1846, in TLS 12 Aug 1965, ed K. Tillotson 28 Feb 1846, in The law as literature, ed L. Blom-Cooper 1961.
The election for Finsbury (letter denying that he was a candidate). 23 Nov 1861. Rptd in Letters (Nonesuch edn).

Contributions to Household Words

During his lifetime Dickens rptd 2 collections of his writings from Household Words, *as* Reprinted pieces *and* The uncommercial traveller. *In 1908 B. W. Matz gathered all of Dickens's identifiable journalism, along with Dickens's plays and poems, as* Miscellaneous papers *(2 vols in the National edn). In 1937 Walter Dexter rptd this material, plus other items of Dickens's journalism, as* Collected papers *(2 vols in the Nonesuch edn). In 1968 Harry Stone gathered Dickens's collaborative pieces of journalism as* The uncollected writings of Charles Dickens, Household Words

1850–59. *In 1995 Michael Slater included a generous selection of Dickens's contributions to* Household Words *in* The Dent Uniform Edn of Dickens' journalism (later Everyman Dickens), vol2 and 3.
A preliminary word. 30 Mar 1850.
The amusements of the people. 30 Mar and 13 Apr 1850.
Valentine's day at the post office (with W. H. Wills). 30 Mar 1850.
A bundle of emigrants' letters (with C. Chisholm). 30 Mar 1850.
A child's dream of a star. 6 Apr 1850. Rptd with illustrations by H. Billings, Boston MA 1871.
Perfect felicity in a bird's-eye view. 6 Apr 1850.
The household narrative. 13 Apr 1850.
Some account of an extraordinary traveller. 20 Apr 1850.
Supposing! 20 Apr, 10 Aug 1850, 7 June, 6 Sep 1851, 10 Feb 1855.
Pet prisoners. 27 Apr 1850.
The heart of mid-London (with W. H. Wills). 4 May 1850.
From the Raven in the happy family. 11 May, 8 June, 24 Aug 1850.
The begging-letter writer. 18 May 1850.
A card from Mr Booley. 18 May 1850.
A walk in the workhouse. 27 May 1850.
A popular delusion (with W. H. Wills). 1 June 1850.
Old lamps for new ones. 15 June 1850.
The Sunday screw. 22 June 1850.
Chips. 6 July 1850.
The old lady of Threadneedle Street. 6 July 1850.
A detective police party. 27 July, 10 Aug 1850.
A paper-mill (with M. Lemon). 31 Aug 1850.
Three 'Detective' anecdotes. 14 Sep 1850.
Chips: the individuality of locomotives. 21 Sep 1850.
Foreigners' portraits of Englishmen (with W. H. Wills and E. Murray). 21 Sep 1850.
Two chapters on bank note forgeries, chapter 2 (with W. H. Wills). 21 Sep 1850).
The doom of English wills (with W. H. Wills). 28 Sep, 5 Oct 1850. Rptd from ms as Ecclesiastical registries, Collected papers (Nonesuch edn).
The 'good' hippopotamus. 12 Oct 1850.
A poor man's tale of a patent. 19 Oct 1850.
Lively turtle. 26 Oct 1850.
A crisis in the affairs of Mr John Bull. 23 Nov 1850.
Mr Booley's view of the last Lord Mayor's show. 30 Nov 1850.
A December vision. 14 Dec 1850.
Mr Bendigo Buster on our national defences against education (with H. Morley). 28 Dec 1850.
The last words of the old year. 4 Jan 1851.
Railway strikes. 11 Jan 1851.
Plate glass (with W. H. Wills). 1 Feb 1851.
Red tape. 15 Feb 1851.
Births: Mrs Meek, of a son. 22 Feb 1851.
A monument of French folly. 8 Mar 1851.
My mahogany friend (with M. L. Boyle). 8 Mar 1851.
Bill-sticking. 22 Mar 1851.
Chips: small beginnings (with W. H. Wills). 5 Apr 1851.
Spitalfields (with W. H. Wills). 5 Apr 1851.
Common-sense on wheels (with W. H. Wills and E. Murray). 12 Apr 1851.
The metropolitan protectives (with W. H. Wills). 26 Apr 1851.
Cain in the fields (with R. H. Horne). 10 May 1851.
The Guild of Literature and Art. 10 May 1851.
The finishing schoolmaster. 17 May 1851.
The wind and the rain (with H. Morley). 31 May 1851.
Epsom (with W. H. Wills). 7 June 1851.
On duty with Inspector Field. 14 June 1851.
The tresses of the day star (with C. Knight). 21 June 1851.
A few conventionalities. 28 June 1851.
The Great Exhibition and the little one (with R. H. Horne). 5 July 1851.
A narrative of extraordinary suffering. 12 July 1851.
Our watering place. 2 Aug 1851.
Whole hogs. 23 Aug 1851.
A flight. 30 Aug 1851.
One man in a dockyard (with R. H. Horne). 6 Sep 1851. Rptd, ed P. Collins, Dickensian 59 1963.
Shakspeare and Newgate (with R. H. Horne). 4 Oct 1851.
Our school. 11 Oct 1851.
Sucking pigs. 8 Nov 1851.
Chip: homeopathy. 15 Nov 1851.
A free (and easy) school (with H. Morley). 15 Nov, 6 Dec 1851.
A black eagle in a bad way (with E. Murray and H. Morley). 22 Nov 1851.
My uncle (with W. H. Wills). 6 Dec 1851.
A curious dance round a curious tree (with W. H. Wills). 17 Jan 1852. Rptd [1860?] with title of main text preceded by '1852'; the article is followed by an extract from The Times headed 1860 and an appeal for St Luke's Hospital headed Contrast between 1852 and 1860. Rptd in Wills, Old leaves, 1860.
Chip: the fine arts in Australia. 13 Mar 1852.
A sleep to startle us. 13 Mar 1852.
Post-office money-orders (with W. H. Wills). 20 Mar 1852. Rptd 1852 (in part, anon) in Methods of employment, as Remarks by Charles Dickens esq; 1860 in W. H. Wills, Old leaves.
Drooping buds (with H. Morley). 3 Apr 1852.
A plated article (with W. H. Wills). 24 Apr 1852.
First fruits (with G. A. H. Sala). 15 May 1852.
Betting-shops. 26 June 1852.
Our honourable friend. 31 July 1852.
Our vestry. 28 Aug 1852.
Boys to mend (with H. Morley). 11 Sep 1852.
North American slavery (with H. Morley). 18 Sep 1852.
Our bore. 9 Oct 1852.
Lying awake. 30 Oct 1852.
Discovery of a treasure near Cheapside (with H. Morley). 13 Nov 1852.
Trading in death. 27 Nov 1852.
Where we stopped growing. 1 Jan 1853.
Chip: the ghost of the Cock Lane ghost wrong again. 15 Jan 1853.
Down with the tide. 5 Feb 1853.
Proposals for amusing posterity. 12 Feb 1853.
Received, a blank child (with W. H. Wills). 19 Mar 1853.
H. W. (with H. Morley). 16 Apr 1853.
Home for homeless women. 23 Apr 1853.
The spirit business. 7 May 1853.
In and out of jail (with W. H. Wills and H. Morley). 14 May 1853.
Idiots (with W. H. Wills). 4 June 1853.
The noble savage. 11 June 1853.
A haunted house. 23 July 1853.
Gone astray. 13 Aug 1853. Rptd with illustrations by Ruth Cobb, from old prints and from photographs by T. W. Tyrell, and introd and notes by B. W. Matz, 1912.
Frauds on the fairies. 1 Oct 1853.
Things that cannot be done. 8 Oct 1853.
The long voyage. 31 Dec 1853.
On Her Majesty's service (with E. Murray). 7 Jan 1854.
Fire and snow. 21 Jan 1854.
Chip: ready wit. 4 Feb 1854.
On strike. 11 Feb 1854.
The late Mr Justice Talfourd. 25 Mar 1854. Priv pre-ptd 1854; *see* Minor works, *above.*
Hidden light (verse, with 'M. Berwick', i.e. A. Procter). 26 Aug 1854.
It is not generally known. 2 Sep 1854.
Legal and equitable jokes. 23 Sep 1854.
To working men. 7 Oct 1854.
Our French watering place. 4 Nov 1854.

An unsettled neighbourhood. 11 Nov 1854.
Reflections of a Lord Mayor. 18 Nov 1854.
Mr Bull's somnambulist. 25 Nov 1854.
The lost Arctic voyagers (with J. Rae). 2, 9 and 23 Dec 1854.
That other public. 3 Feb 1855.
Gaslight fairies. 10 Feb 1855.
Prince Bull. A fairy tale. 17 Feb 1855.
Gone to the dogs. 10 Mar 1855.
Fast and loose. 24 Mar 1855.
The thousand and one humbugs. 21, 28 Apr and 5 May 1855.
The toady tree. 26 May 1855.
Cheap patriotism. 9 June 1855.
Smuggled relations. 23 June 1855.
The great baby. 4 Aug 1855.
Our commission. 11 Aug 1855.
The worthy magistrate. 25 Aug 1855.
A slight depreciation of the currency. 3 Nov 1855.
Out of town. 29 Sep 1855. Rptd as Pavilionstone, with biographical preface describing Folkestone and the writing of Little Dorrit by P. Fitzgerald, [1902].
Our almanac. 24 Nov 1855.
Insularities. 19 Jan 1856.
A nightly scene in London. 26 Jan 1856.
The friend of the lions. 2 Feb 1856.
Why? 1 Mar 1856.
Proposals for a national jest-book. 3 May 1856.
Railway dreaming. 10 May 1856.
The demeanour of murderers. 14 June 1856.
Out of season. 28 June 1856.
Nobody, somebody and everybody. 30 Aug 1856.
The murdered person. 11 Oct 1856.
Murderous extremes. 3 Jan 1857.
Stores for the first of Apr. 7 Mar 1857.
The Samaritan Institution. 16 May 1857.
The best authority. 20 June 1857.
Duelling in France (with E. Lynn). 27 June 1857.
Curious misprint in the Edinburgh Review. 1 Aug 1857.
Well-authenticated rappings. 20 Feb 1858.
An idea of mine. 13 Mar 1858.
Please to leave your umbrella. 1 May 1858.
Personal. 12 June 1858; first ptd in The Times 7 June 1858; rptd in many contemporary newspapers and jnls. Dickens's statement about his marital difficulties. Rptd in Mr and Mrs Charles Dickens, ed W. Dexter, 1935. Not in Collected papers (Nonesuch edn).
A clause for the new reform bill (with W. Collins). 9 Oct 1858.
Doctor Dulcamara, M. P. (with W. Collins). 18 Dec 1858.
New Year's Day. 1 Jan 1859.
All the Year Round (announcement). 28 May 1859.
A last household word. 28 May 1868.

Contributions to All the Year Round

Occasional register (with W. Collins). 30 Apr 1859.
The poor man and his beer. 30 Apr 1859.
Five new points of criminal law. 24 Sep 1859.
Leigh Hunt: a remonstrance. 24 Dec 1859.
The Tattlesnivel bleater. 31 Dec 1859.
Without a name. 21 Jan 1860.
Note. 25 Feb 1860.
The young man from the country. 1 Mar 1862.
An enlightened clergyman. 8 Mar 1862.
Rather a strong dose. 21 Mar 1863.
The martyr medium. 4 Apr 1863.
Working men's clubs (with E. Ollier). 26 Mar 1864.
Our suburban residence: private character. 19 May 1866.
The late Mr Stanfield. 1 June 1867.
Debt of honour. 6 June 1868
New series of All the Year Round (address announcing a new series). 19 and 26 Sep 1868.
A slight question of fact. 13 Feb 1869.
Robert Keeley (with H. Merivale). 10 Apr 1869. Rptd, ed P. Collins, Dickensian, 60 1964.
Landor's Life (rev). 24 July 1869.

Miscellaneous contributions

The Early Closing Movement. Letter to the Committee of the Metropolitan Drapers' Association 28 March 1844. Pbd in The Student and Young Man's Advocate, Jan 1845. Rptd in Collected papers (Nonesuch edn); in Pilgrim Letters vol 4 p. 88.
Threatening letter to Thomas Hood, from an Ancient Gentleman. Contribution to Hood's Mag and Comic Misc, May 1844.
The spirit of chivalry in Westminster Hall. Douglas Jerrold's Shilling Mag Aug 1845.
Dreadful hardships endured by the shipwrecked crew of The London, chiefly for want of water. Contribution sent to Punch [1849?] but not pbd. Facs in M. H. Spielmann, The history of Punch, 1895.
To be read at dusk. In Keepsake for 1852, ed M. Power. Rptd 1852 (priv ptd); ed F. G. Kitton 1898 (with other stories, etc, *above*). The 1852 edn is probably a forgery; *see* J. Carter and H. G. Pollard, An enquiry into the nature of certain nineteenth-century pamphlets, 1934, and J. Carter, TLS 26 July 1934.
In memoriam W. M. Thackeray. Cornhill Mag Feb 1864.
On Mr Fechter's acting. Atlantic Monthly Aug 1869. Rptd Leeds [1872].

Doubtful or supposititious contributions to periodicals

The restoration of Shakspeare's Lear to the stage. Examiner 4 Feb 1838. Misattributed to Dickens by B. W. Matz when collecting Dickens's journalism for Miscellaneous papers. *See* W. J. Carlton, Dickens or Forster? Some King Lear criticisms re-examined. Dickensian 61 1965.
Trade songs: the blacksmith (? by Dickens or B. W. Procter). All the Year Round 30 Apr 1859.
Dress in Paris (? by Dickens). All the Year Round 28 Feb 1863.
A neat sample of translation (? by Dickens). All the Year Round 27 Jan 1866.

Letters and speeches

Letters pbd separately or in small collections are not listed here if they have been rptd in the collected edns, unless they appeared in vol form or with useful ancillary material. Those dealing with particular works or themes are entered under the appropriate works above. All previous collections are being superseded by the Pilgrim *edn, 1965– , below. K. J. Fielding's edn of the* Speeches, *below, contains particulars of earlier pbn of individual speeches and these are not given here.*

Speeches literary and social by Dickens, now first collected, with chapters on Dickens as a clear writer, poet and public reader. [Ed R. H. Shepherd] 1870; rev and with a bibliography as The speeches of Dickens 1841–70, 1884; with introd by B. Darwin [1937]. On the origins and method of Shepherd's collection, *see* K. J. Fielding, textual introd to his edn of Speeches. 2 further speeches added to National edn, 1908; 7 further to Nonesuch edn of Collected papers, 1937.
Speeches, letters and sayings of Dickens, to which is added a sketch of the author by George Augustus Sala, and Dean Stanley's sermon. New York 1870. Text of speeches from Shepherd's 1870 edn. Contains also some of the poems, a note on the readings and a biographical introd.
The letters of Dickens, edited by his sister-in-law [Georgina Hogarth] and his eldest daughter [Mamie (Mary) Dickens]. 3 vols 1880–2, 2 vols 1882, 1 vol 1893; with Letters to Wilkie Collins, 2 vols 1908 (National edn of Works). Much revision and re-

arrangement between edns; *see* A. A. Adrian, Georgina Hogarth and the Dickens circle, Oxford 1957, ch 13, and preface to Pilgrim edn of the letters, vol 1 Oxford 1965. Contains Dickens's diary 1837–41 (incompletely and inaccurately): so does Nonesuch edn of the letters, vol 1. Complete transcript for 1838–9 in Pilgrim edn, vol 1. Only one other Dickens diary has survived, for 1867 (unpbd). *See* W. J. Carlton, The Dickens diaries, Dickensian 55 1959.

REVIEWS: Athenaeum 29 Nov 1879; Spectator 29 Nov, 6 Dec 1879; Minto, W. Fortnightly Rev Dec 1879; Brownell, W. C. Nation 4 Dec 1879; Saturday Rev 6 Dec 1879; Literary World 12 Dec 1879, 18 Nov 1881; The Times 27 Dec 1879; 'Browne, Matthew' (W. B. Rands) Contemporary Rev Jan 1880; Scribner's Monthly Mag Jan 1880; Atlantic Monthly Feb 1880; Didier, E. L. North Amer Rev Mar 1880; [Cullen, P.?] Dublin Rev 3rd ser 3 1880; Temple Bar Apr 1880; Westminster Rev n.s. 58 1880.

Hans Christian Andersen's correspondence. Ed F. Crawford [1891]. Letters to and from Dickens. *See* E. Munksgaard, H. C. Andersen's visits to Dickens, Copenhagen 1937 (6 letters in facs), and E. Bredsdorff, Hans Anderson and Charles Dickens, Cambridge and Copenhagen 1956.

Letters of Dickens to Wilkie Collins 1851–70. Selected by Miss G. Hogarth. Ed L. Hutton 1892.

Furniss, H. A. Shakespeare's birthday and a reminiscence of Dickens. Pall Mall Mag Apr 1906. His speech about Shakespeare at the Garrick Club 1854; not collected.

Dickens and Maria Beadnell. Ed G. P. Baker 1908 (Boston Bibliophile Soc) (with notes by J. H. Stonehouse); St Louis 1908 (priv ptd for W. K. Bixby, owner of the ms letters). *See* Piccadilly notes (Henry Sotheran) no iv 1933 for history of the letters and their discovery by J. H. Stonehouse. *See* also Dickensian 29 1933.

The Dickens–Kolle letters, supplemental to the letters from Dickens to Maria Beadnell. Ed H. B. Smith and H. H. Harper 1910 (Boston Bibliophile Soc).

Payne, E. F. and H. H. Harper. The romance of Dickens and Maria Beadnell Winter. 1929 (Boston Bibliophile Soc). A commentary on the foregoing and other newly discovered material.

Otto, K. Der Verlag Bernhard Tauchnitz 1837–1912. Leipzig 1912. Letters to his German publisher.

Dickens as editor: letters written by him to William Henry Wills, his sub-editor. Ed R. C. Lehmann 1912.

Letters to Mark Lemon. Ed T. J. Wise 1917 (priv ptd).

Clark, C. Dickens and his Jewish characters. 1918. Letters, with commentary.

Clark, C. The story of a great friendship: Dickens and Clarkson Stanfield, with seven unpublished letters. 1918.

Clark, C. Dickens and Talfourd, with three unpublished letters [on copyright]. 1919.

Notes and comments on certain writings in prose and verse by Richard Henry Horne. 1920 (priv ptd). 6 letters.

Clark, C. Dickens and the begging-letter writer; with a letter. 1923.

The unpublished letters of Dickens to Mark Lemon. Ed W. Dexter 1927.

Payne, E. F. and H. H. Harper. The charity of Charles Dickens. 1929 (Boston Bibliophile Soc). Narrative embodying some correspondence and the pam by Dickens about the foundation, with the aid of Miss Burdett Coutts, of a home for fallen women. *See* An appeal to fallen women [1847] *under* Minor works, *above*.

The letters of Dickens to the Baroness Burdett-Coutts. Ed C. C. Osborne 1931. Selection with narrative.

Dickens to his oldest friend: some unpublished letters to Thomas Beard, with a foreword by Sir Henry Fielding Dickens. 1931 (priv pbd). 5 pbd letters, one unpbd facs and A fable (facs), with brief comment.

Dickens to his oldest friend: the letters of a lifetime. Ed W. Dexter 1932. The whole available correspondence with notes, introd and facs. *See* B. Darwin (ed), Dickens and his oldest friend, Bookman (New York) Oct 1931–Jan 1932.

Dickens's letters to Charles Lever. Ed F. V. Livingston, introd by H. E. Rollins, Cambridge MA 1933.

Mabbott, T. O. Correspondence of John Tomlin. N & Q 6 Jan 1934.

Mr and Mrs Charles Dickens: his letters to her. Ed W. Dexter 1934.

The love romance of Dickens, told in his letters to Maria Beadnell (Mrs Winter). Ed W. Dexter 1936.

The letters of Dickens. Ed. W. Dexter 3 vols 1938 (Nonesuch). The fullest collection, until superseded by the Pilgrim edn.

Rolfe, F. P. The Dickens letters in the Huntington Library. HLQ 1 1938.

Rolfe, F. P. Additions to the Nonesuch edition of Dickens's letters. HLQ 5 1942.

Rolfe, F. P. More letters to the Watsons. Dickensian 38 1942.

[Dexter, W.] Adventures among Dickens's letters. Dickensian 39 1943.

Altick, R. D. Dickens and America: some unpublished letters. Pennsylvania Mag of History 73 1949.

House, H. A new edition of Dickens's letters. Listener 18 Oct 1951; rptd in his All in due time, 1955.

The heart of Dickens. Ed E. Johnson, New York 1952, London 1953 as Letters from Dickens to Angela Burdett Coutts 1841–1865.

Grubb, G. G. Some unpublished correspondence of Dickens and Chapman & Hall. Boston Univ Stud in Eng 1 1955.

Rust, J. D. Dickens and the Americans: an unnoticed letter. Nineteenth-Cent Fiction 11 1957.

Griffith, B. W. Dickens the philanthropist: an unpublished letter. Nineteenth-Cent Fiction 12 1958.

Monod, S. Une amitié française de Dickens: lettres inédites à Philoclès Régnier. Études Anglaises 11 1958.

Letters of English authors from the collection of Robert H. Taylor: a catalogue. Princeton 1960.

Selected letters. Ed F. W. Dupee, New York 1960. Introd pbd as The other Dickens, Partisan Rev 27 1960.

The speeches of Charles Dickens. Ed K. J. Fielding, Oxford 1960, Hassocks 1988. *See* M. H. Miller, Dickens at the English charity dinner, Quart Jnl of Speech 47 1961. The convention of oratory on such occasions.

Carr, Sr M. C. Catalogue of the Dickens collection at the University of Texas. Austin 1961. Particulars of 146 letters, many unpbd, with quotations.

Monod, S. Misères et splendeurs d'une carrière littéraire. Les Lettres Françaises 27 Sep 1962. 19 unpbd letters.

Grylls, R. G. Dickens and Holman Hunt. Texas Stud in Lit and Lang 6 1964. 3 unpbd letters.

Mistler, J. Un grand éditeur [Louis Hachette] et ses auteurs. Revue des Mondes 15 July 1964.

Smith, S. M. An unpublished letter from Dickens to Disraeli. N & Q 204 June 1964.

The Pilgrim edition of the letters of Charles Dickens. Ed M. House, G. Storey et al, Oxford 1965– (in progress). First complete edn.

Collins, P. Some uncollected speeches by Dickens. Dickensian 73 1977.

Roos, D. A. Dickens at the Royal Academy of Arts: a new speech and two eulogies. Dickensian 73 1977.

Selected letters of Charles Dickens. Ed D. Paroissien 1985. Based on the Nonesuch edn and arranged thematically.

Long, W. F. Dickens and the coming of rail to Deal: an uncollected speech and its context. Dickensian 85 1989.

Long, W. F. Rejecting the golden dustman: an uncollected letter. Dickensian 94 1998.

§2

Personal recollections and memoirs

References to Dickens occur in numerous contemporary biographies and vols of reminiscence. They can be traced through his more intimate friendships, for which see J. W. T. Ley, The Dickens circle, 1918, *and* W. T. Shore, Dickens and his friends, 1909. *A number of extracts are given in* J. A. Hammerton, The Dickens companion, 1910, *and in* Peeps at Dickens: pen pictures from contemporary sources, Dickensian passim. *The following select list includes only writers not previously mentioned whose personal contacts with Dickens have more than casual interest.*

Willis, N. P. Dashes at life. New York 1845.

Jeffrey, F. Life of Lord Jeffrey, with a selection from his correspondence, by Lord Cockburn. 2 vols Edinburgh 1852.

Jerdan, W. Autobiography. 4 vols 1852–3.

Knight, C. Passages of a working life. 3 vols 1864–5.

Fields, J. T. Some memories of Dickens. Atlantic Monthly Aug 1870; rev and enlarged in his Yesterdays with authors, 1872; rptd as In and out of doors with Dickens, Boston 1876. *See* J. T. Fields: biographical notes and personal sketches, Boston 1881.

Hall, S. C. A book of memories of great men and women of the age, from personal acquaintance. 1870.

Hodder, G. Memories of my time. 1870.

Ainger, A. Mr Dickens's amateur theatricals. Macmillan's Mag Jan 1871; rptd in his Lectures and essays vol 2, 1905.

Andersen, H. C. In his Pictures of travel, New York 1871. Pp. 267–93, A visit at Dickens's house. *See* R. N. Bain's Life of Andersen, 1895, and H. C. Andersen's correspondence (*above*, Letters).

C[hristian], E. E. Reminiscences of Dickens, from a young lady's diary. Englishwoman's Domestic Mag June 1871; rev and enlarged as Recollections of Dickens, his family and friends, Temple Bar Apr 1888. *See* J. C. Maxwell, Mrs Christian's reminiscences of Dickens, RES n.s. 2 1951, and W. J. Carlton, Who was the lady? Dickensian 60 1964.

Collier, J. P. An old man's diary, forty years ago. 4 pts 1871–2 (priv ptd).

Horne, R. H. Byegone celebrities; I, The guild of literature and art of Chatsworth; II, Mr Nightingale's diary. GM Feb, May 1871; rptd with addns in Letters of E. B. Browning to R. H. Horne vol 2, 1887. *See* K. J. Fielding, Dickens and R. H. Horne, English 9 1952.

Young, J. C., A memoir of C. M. Young. 2 vols 1871.

Marryat, F. Life and letters, by Florence Marryat. 2 vols 1872.

Chorley, H. F. Autobiography; with memoir and letters. Ed H. G. Hewlett 2 vols 1873. *See his* Charles Dickens, Athenaeum 18 June 1870.

Jerdan, W. Personal reminiscences. Ed R. H. Stoddard 1874.

Macready, W. C. Reminiscences and selections from his diaries and letters. Ed F. Pollock 2 vols 1875.

Horne, R. H. John Forster: his early life and friendships. Temple Bar Apr 1876.

Mackay, C. Forty years' recollections 1830–70. 2 vols 1877.

Martineau, H. Autobiography. 3 vols 1877.

Clarke, C. and M. C. Clarke. Recollections of writers. 1878. *See* Mary Cowden Clarke, My long life, 1896.

Compton, H. Memoir by C. and E. Compton. 1879.

Lever, C. J. Life, by W. J. Fitzpatrick. 2 vols 1879.

Hall, S. C. Retrospect of a long life, from 1815 to 1883. 2 vols 1883.

Carlyle, T. Thomas Carlyle: a history of his life in London 1838–81, by J. A. Froude. 2 vols 1884. *See* Carlyle's letters, ed C. R. Sanders, BJRL 38 1956.

Cole, H. Fifty years of the public life of Sir Henry Cole. 2 vols 1884.

Yates, E. Recollections and experiences. 2 vols 1884. Vol 1 ch 9, vol 2 ch 11.

Dickens, M. Dickens at home. Cornhill Mag Jan 1885. *See* Biographies, *below.*

Mason, E. T. Personal traits of British authors, vol 3. New York 1885.

Hullah, J. Life, by his wife. 1886.

Frith, W. P. My autobiography and reminiscences. 3 vols 1887–8. *See* his daughter Mrs E. M. Ward's Memories of ninety years, [1924].

Mackay, C. Through the long day: memorials of a literary life. 2 vols 1887.

Pollock, F. Personal reminiscences. 2 vols 1887.

Trollope, T. A. What I remember. 2 vols 1887. Vol 2 ch 7.

Toole, J. L. Reminiscences. Ed J. Hatton 1888. *See* 'Cuthbert Bede', Dickens and Toole, London Figaro 15 Apr 1874, rptd in Dickensian 28 1932.

Rogers, S. Samuel Rogers and his contemporaries, by P. W. Clayden. 2 vols 1889.

Collins, W. W. About Dickens, from a marked copy of Forster's Life. Pall Mall Gazette 20 Jan 1890. *See* N. P. Davis, Life of Wilkie Collins, Urbana IL 1956.

Houghton, Lord (R. M. Milnes). Life, letters and friendships, by T. W. Reid. 2 vols 1890.

Dickens, C., the younger. Introds to Works, Macmillan edn, 21 vols 1892–1925.

Latimer, E. W. A girl's recollection of Dickens. Lippincott's Mag Sep 1893.

[Beard, N.] Some recollections of yesterday. Temple Bar July 1894. By the son of Dickens's lifelong friend, Thomas Beard.

Jeaffreson, J. C. A book of recollections. 2 vols 1894.

Ritchie, Lady [A. T., née Thackeray]. Chapters from some memories. 1894.

Sala, G. A. H. Things I have seen and people I have known. 2 vols 1894. Vol 1 chs 2–3.

Dickens, C., the younger. Glimpses of Dickens. North Amer Rev May–June 1895.

Hollingshead, J. My lifetime. 2 vols 1895. *See* F. A. Gibson, Dickensian 62 1966.

Sala, G. A. H. Life and adventures. 2 vols 1895. Vol 1 chs 6–8, 25–8.

Locker-Lampson, F. My confidences. 1896.

Dickens, M. A. A child's memories of Gad's Hill. Strand Mag Jan 1897.

Morley, H. Life, by H. S. Solly. 1898. Chs 10–11.

Linton, E. [Mrs Lynn Linton]. My literary life. 1899.

Hollingshead, J. In his According to my lights, 1900.

Boyle, Mary: her book. Ed C. Boyle 1901.

Cross, C. Dickens, a memory. New Liberal Rev 2 1901.

Anderson, J. R. An actor's life. 1902.

Perugini, K. [née Dickens]. Dickens as a lover of art and artists. Mag of Art Jan–Feb 1903.

Priestley, Lady [Eliza]. The story of a lifetime. 1904. Includes letters etc from her uncle, W. H. Wills.

Perugini, K. [née Dickens]. Edwin Drood and the last days of Dickens. Pall Mall Mag June 1906.

Hood, T. Thomas Hood: his life and times, by Walter Jerrold. 1907. *See* J. C. Reid, Thomas Hood, 1963.

Martin, T. Memories of Dickens. Great Thoughts 28 Sep 1907.

Browning, R. Life and letters. Ed Mrs S. Orr 1908 (rev).

Lehmann, R. C. Memories of half a century. 1908. Ch 7. *See* J. Lehmann, Ancestors and friends, 1962.

Hogarth, G. How Dickens wrote. Evening News 10 Nov 1909.

Dickens, A. T. Reminiscences of Dickens. Great Thoughts 12 Nov 1910.

Dickens, H. F. Dickens at work. Lloyd's Weekly News 6 Feb 1910.

Stone, M. Some recollections of Dickens. Dickensian 6 1910, 8 1912.

Ainsworth, W. H. William Harrison Ainsworth and his friends, by S. M. Ellis. 2 vols 1911.

Dickens, A. T. My father and his friends. Nash's Mag Sep 1911.

Dickens, M. A. My grandfather as I knew him. Nash's Mag Oct 1911.

Perugini, K. [née Dickens]. My father's love for children. Dickensian 7 1911.

Perugini, K. [née Dickens]. Thackeray and my father. Pall Mall Mag Aug 1911.

Russell, W. H. Life, by J. B. Atkins. 2 vols 1911.

'Schoolfellow and friend.' Recollections of Dickens. Dickensian 7 1911.

Dickens, A. T. New chapters from the life of Dickens. Cosmopolitan Mag 52 1912.

Dickens, M. A. My father in his home life. Ladies' Home Jnl 29 1912.
Drew, E. Dickens as I knew him. Tit-Bits 10 Feb 1912.
Macready, W. C. Diaries. Ed W. Toynbee 2 vols 1912. *See* P. Collins, Macready and Dickens: some family recollections, Dickens Stud 2 1966.
Ritchie, Lady [A. T., née Thackeray]. Charles Dickens as I remember him. Pall Mall Mag Mar 1912; rev in her From the porch, 1913, Freeport NY 1971.
Wiggin, K. D. A child's journey with Dickens. Boston 1912.
Berger, F. Reminiscences, impressions and anecdotes. [1913]. Ch 3.
Norton, C. E. English friends, from his letters and journals. Ed S. Norton and M. A. de W. Howe, Scribner's Mag 53 1913.
Dickens, H. F. Chat about Dickens. Harper's Mag July 1914.
Jerrold, D. Douglas Jerrold, dramatist and wit, by Walter Jerrold. [1918].
Fields, Mrs A. A. Diaries. In Memories of a hostess, ed M. A. de W. Howe, Boston 1922. Ch 5, With Dickens in America. *See* unpbd diaries, ed L. C. Staples, Dickensian 47 1951.
E. M. Ward's Memories of ninety years, [1924].
Hughes, J. L. Personal reminiscences relating to Dickens. Jnl of Education 101 1925.
Berger, F. Memories of Dickens. Living Age 332 1927.
Dickens, H. F. Memories of my father. 1928, New York 1972.
Berger, F. 97. 1932. Ch 1. (Selected articles pbd to celebrate the author's 97th birthday.)
Dickens, C., the younger. Reminiscences of my father. Windsor Mag Christmas suppl 1934. Rptd with foreword by M. A. Dickens, New York 1972.
Dickens, H. F. Recollections. 1934.
Perugini, K. [née Dickens]. Foreword to Mr and Mrs Charles Dickens: his letters to her. Ed W. Dexter 1935. *See* Gladys Storey, Dickens and daughter, 1939.
Thackeray, W. M. Letters and private papers. Ed G. N. Ray 4 vols Oxford 1945–6. Also many allusions and criticisms in essays; *see especially* Jerome Paturot 1843, Charity and humour (English humourists, 1853), *and above* under Novels. *See also* K. Perugini 1911, *above*; C. R. Williams, The personal relations of Dickens and Thackeray, Dickensian 35 1939; C. Mauskopf, Thackeray's attitude to Dickens's writing, Nineteenth-Cent Fiction 21 1967.
Smith, S. Letters. Ed N. C. Smith 2 vols Oxford 1953.
'Eliot, George'. Letters. Ed G. S. Haight 7 vols Oxford 1954–6.

Obituaries

The Times, 10 June 1870 (leading article); rptd with obituary of Dickens (11 June 1870) in Eminent persons: biographies reprinted from The Times 1870–9, 1880.
[Fraser, G.] Saturday Rev 11 June 1870.
Spectator 11 June 1870.
Dickens in Poets' corner. Illus London News 15 June 1870.
[Dennet, J. R.] Nation 16 June 1870.
The late Charles Dickens. Illus London News 18 June 1870.
Graphic 18 June 1870.
[Hutton, R. H.] The genius of Dickens. Spectator 18 June 1870; rptd in his Brief literary criticisms, 1906.
Jowett, B. Sermon in Westminster Abbey 19 June 1870. 1870. Rptd in his Sermons biographical and miscellaneous, 1899.
Stanley, A. P. Sermon preached in Westminster Abbey June 19, 1870. 1870; rptd in his Sermons on special occasions, 1882.
Austin, A. Temple Bar July 1870, Jan 1875.
Englishwoman's Domestic Mag 1 July 1870.
Fraser's Mag July 1870.
Gentleman's Jnl 1 July 1870.
[Helps, A.] Macmillan's Mag July 1870.
Jerrold, B. Charles Dickens: in memoriam. GM July 1870. Rptd in The best of all good company, 1871.
Eclectic Mag Aug 1870.
Mitchell, D. G. Hours at Home Aug 1870.
St James's Mag Aug 1870.
Victoria Mag Aug 1870.
Conway, M. D. Footprints of Charles Dickens Harper's New Monthly Mag Sep 1870.
Hill, B. A pilgrimage. Lippincott's Mag Sep 1870.
'Meteor'. Illus Mag Sep 1870.
Ham, J. P. Parables of fiction: a memorial discourse on Dickens. 1870.

Critical studies up to 1920

Special chs in general histories of English literature are not included. The Dickensian *has recorded these as they have appeared from 1905 onwards, and has also rptd earlier pieces from time to time.*

Some thoughts on arch-waggery and, in especial, on the genius of Boz. Court Mag Apr 1837. Rptd in Dickensian 4 1908.
[Lister, T.] Dickens's tales. Edinburgh Rev 68 1838.
Charles Dickens and his works. Fraser's Mag Apr 1840.
Wilson, J. ['Christopher North']. Speech at Edinburgh banquet for Dickens, 25 June 1841. Rptd in Dickensian 12 1916 from Edinburgh Advertiser 29 June 1841.
Rymer, J. M. Popular writing. Queen's Mag 1 1842.
Whitman, W. Boz and democracy. Brother Jonathan 26 Feb 1842. Rptd in his Rivulets of prose, New York 1928.
Horne, R. H. In the first chapter of his A new spirit of the age vol 1, 1844. *See* E. B. Browning's 2 letters to Horne, 1844, priv ptd 1919 as Dickens and other spirits of the age.
Boz versus Dickens. Parker's London Mag Feb 1845.
[Cleghorn, T.?]. Writings of Dickens. North Br Rev 3 1845.
Dickens and Thackeray. English Rev Dec 1848.
[Eagles, J.] A few words about novels. Blackwood's Mag 64 1848.
[Whipple, E. P.] North Amer Rev 69 1849; rptd in his Literature and life, 1851.
Heavisides, E. M. Charles Dickens. The poetical and prose remains of E. M. Heavisides. 1850.
The genius and characters of Dickens. Working Man's Friend and Family Instructor 21 Aug 1852.
Shelton, F. W. On the genius of Dickens. Knickerbocker May 1852.
Cruikshank, G. A letter from Hop-o'-my-thumb to Charles Dickens esq. [1854]. Rptd from George Cruikshank's Mag Feb 1854.
Dickens. Ecclesiastic and Theologian 17 1855.
[Oliphant, M.] Blackwood's Mag Apr 1855, June 1871.
Talbot, G. F. The genius of Dickens. Putnam's Monthly Mag Mar 1855.
Trollope, A. The warden. 1855. Dickens as Mr Popular Sentiment, ch 15. *See* L. Stevenson, Dickens and the origin of The warden, Trollopian 2 1947.
Taine, H. Dickens: son talent et ses oeuvres. Revue des Deux Mondes 1 Feb 1856; rptd in his Histoire de la littérature anglaise vol 5, Paris 1863–4; tr Edinburgh 1871.
[Hamley, E. B.] Remonstrance with Dickens. Blackwood's Mag Apr 1857.
[Stephen, J. F.] Mr Dickens as a politician; light literature and the Saturday Review. Saturday Rev 3 Jan, 11 July 1857. Replies in Leader 18 July 1857, and by J. Hollingshead, Dickens and his critics, Train Aug 1857; rptd in his Essays vol 2, 1865, and in his Miscellanies vol 3, 1874. *See above,* Novels (Little Dorrit).
Bagehot, W. Nat Rev 7 1858; rptd in his Literary studies vol 2, 1879.
Jeaffreson, J. C. In his Novels and novelists vol 2, 1858.
Masson, D. British novelists and their styles. 1859. Ch 4. Enlarged from North Br Rev 15 1851.
[Turner, G.] Dickens and his reviewers. Welcome Guest 1 1860.
Galloway, A. H. A critical dissertation on some of the writings of Dickens. Liverpool [1862?].
Williams, S. F. Dickens: a series of criticisms. Rose, Shamrock and Thistle 3–4 1863–4.
Fitzgerald, P. H. Two English essayists: Lamb and Dickens. In Afternoon lectures on literature and art, 1864.

[McCarthy, J.] Westminster Rev n.s. 26 1864; rptd in his Con amore, 1868.
Gourdault, J. Les privilégiés et les pauvres gens dans les romans de Dickens. Revue des Cours Littéraires 2 1865.
Whipple, E. P. The genius of Dickens. Atlantic Monthly May 1867.
[Norton, C. E.] North Amer Rev Apr 1868.
Sala, G. A. H. Sensationalism in literature. Belgravia Feb 1868.
Dickens's moral services to literature. Spectator 17 Apr 1869.
Dickens's use of the Bible. Temple Bar Sep 1869.
Stott, G. Contemporary Rev Jan 1869.
Trollope, A. St Paul's Mag July 1870.
Harte, F. B. Dickens in camp. In his Poetical works, Boston 1871.
London Quart Rev 35 1871.
Two English novelists: Dickens and Thackeray. Dublin Rev Apr 1871.
Buchanan, R. W. The good genie of fiction. St Paul's Mag Feb 1872.
Lewes, G. H. Dickens in relation to criticism. Fortnightly Rev Feb 1872. *See* G. S. Haight, Dickens and Lewes, PMLA 71 1956.
Peacock, W. F. Dickens's nomenclature. Belgravia Apr–May 1873.
Hutton, R. H. The dispute about Dickens. Spectator 7 Feb 1874. Rptd in his Criticisms of contemporary thought and thinkers vol 1, 1894.
Irving, W. Charles Dickens: an essay. 1874.
Bulwer and Dickens: a contrast. Temple Bar Jan 1875.
Davey, S. Darwin, Carlyle and Dickens. 1875.
'Browne, Matthew' (W. B. Rands). The letters of Dickens. Contemporary Rev Jan 1880.
Canning, A. S. G. Philosophy of Dickens. 1880.
[Cullen, P.] The letters of Dickens. Dublin Rev Apr 1880.
Ruskin, J. Fiction, fair and foul. Nineteenth Cent June 1880–Oct 1881; rptd in On the old road vol 2, 1885. Numerous brief references to Dickens throughout Ruskin's career; *see* Index to Works, ed E. T. Cook and A. D. O. Wedderburn, 1902–12.
Watt, J. C. Great novelists: Scott, Thackeray, Dickens, Lytton. Edinburgh 1880.
Morris, M. Fortnightly Rev Dec 1882.
Cook, D. Dickens as a dramatic critic. Longman's Mag May 1883.
Trollope, A. Autobiography. 1883. Ch 13.
Howells, W. D. Dickens's Christmas books. In his Criticism and fiction, New York 1891.
Lang, A. Dickens. In his Essays in little, 1891. *See* list of Lang's writings on Dickens, Dickensian 41 1945; and R. L. Green, Andrew Lang: real reader of Dickens, Dickensian 57 1961.
Harrison, F. Dickens's place in literature. [1894]; rptd in his Studies in early Victorian literature, 1895.
Howells, W. D. In his My literary passions, New York 1895.
Lilly, W. S. Four English humorists of the nineteenth century. 1895. Dickens, Thackeray, George Eliot and Carlyle.
Saintsbury, G. In his Corrected impression, 1895. 2 papers on Dickens rev in his Collected essays vol 2, 1923, Folcroft PA 1974.
Rideal, C. F. Dickens' heroines and women-folk. [1896] (rev).
Murray, D. C. First the critics, and then a word on Dickens. In his My contemporaries in fiction, 1897.
Gissing, G. Dickens: a critical study. 1898, 1903 (rev, in Imperial edn of the Works), New York 1974, Folcroft PA 1974.
Henley, W. E. Some notes on Dickens. Pall Mall Mag Aug 1899.
Meynell, A. Dickens as a writer. Pall Mall Gazette 11–18 Jan 1899.
Hughes, J. L. Dickens as an educator. New York 1900.
Jerome, J. K. My favourite novelist and his best book. Munsey's Mag Apr 1900.
Howells, W. D. In his Heroines of fiction vol 1, New York 1901.
Swinburne, A. C. Charles Dickens Quart Rev 1902. Rptd with addns, especially on Oliver Twist, ed T. Watts-Dunton 1913; rptd (part) in Swinburne as critic, ed C. K. Hyder, 1972.
[Thompson, F.] Mrs Boythorn and her canary. Academy 19 July 1902.
Chesterton, G. K. and F. G. Kitton. Charles Dickens. 1903.
Lord, W. F. Dickens. Nineteenth Cent Nov 1903.
Meynell, A. Dickens as a man of letters. Atlantic Monthly Jan 1903.
Baillie-Saunders, M. The philosophy of Dickens: a study of his life and teaching as a social reformer. 1905.
Chesterton, G. K. Charles Dickens. 1906; rptd as Dickens: a critical study, New York 1911, as Dickens: the last of the great men, introd by A. Woollcott, New York 1942, and as Charles Dickens, introd by S. Marcus, New York 1965, London 1975.
Gissing, G. Dickens. In Homes and haunts of English authors, 1906.
Johnson, R. B. Dickens as artist. Book Monthly Jan 1906.
Sibbald, W. A. Dickens revisited. Westminster Rev Jan 1907.
Leffmann, H. About Dickens: being a few essays on themes suggested by the novels. Philadelphia 1908 (priv ptd).
More, P. E. The praise of Dickens. In his Shelbourne essays 5th ser, New York 1908.
Pugh, E. W. Dickens: the apostle of the people. 1908.
Barlow, G. The genius of Dickens. [1909], Folcroft PA 1977.
Christian, E. B. V. Leaves of the lower branch: the attorney in life and letters. 1909.
Gissing, G. In his Views and reviews, 1909.
Fyfe, T. A. Dickens and the law. Edinburgh 1910.
Smith, M. S. C. (ed). Studies in Dickens. New York 1910. Revs, appreciations etc.
Spielmann, M. H. How Dickens improved his style. Graphic 12 Mar 1910. Facs of ms.
Canning, A. S. G. Dickens and Thackeray studied in three novels [Pickwick, Nickleby, Vanity Fair]. 1911.
Chesterton, G. K. Appreciations and criticisms of the works of Dickens. 1911; rptd as Criticisms and appreciations of the works of Dickens, 1933, and as Chesterton on Dickens, introd by M. Slater, 1992. Collects introds to Everyman Lib.
Moses, B. Dickens and his girl heroines. 1911.
Walters, J. C. Phases of Dickens: the man, his message and his mission. 1911.
Beerbohm, M. Dickens, by G—rge M—re. In A Christmas garland, 1912. A parody of George Moore which is also an oblique criticism of Dickens.
Canning, A. S. G. Dickens studied in six novels. 1912.
Charles Dickens: a Bookman (London) extra number. 1912. By various writers; chiefly reprints of prefaces, essays etc. Numerous illustrations previously pbd in other forms. Rptd 1914.
Escott, T. H. S. Dickens: his work, age and influence. London Quart Rev 117 1912.
Jerome, J. K. Dickens. Pall Mall Gazette 7 Feb 1912.
Lightwood, W. R. In Dickens street. 1912. Stud in Dickens characters.
Meynell, A. Notes of a reader of Dickens. Dublin Rev Apr 1912. Rptd as Dickens as a man of letters in her Hearts of controversy, 1917.
Nabokoff, V. Dickens: a Russian appreciation. Dickensian 8 1912. Tr from Retch 25 Jan 1912.
Pugh, E. W. The Dickens originals. 1912, New York 1975.
Whipple, E. P. Dickens: the man and his work. 2 vols Boston 1912.
Crotch, W. W. Dickens, social reformer. 1913.
Shaw, G. B. On Dickens. Dickensian 10 1914. Numerous references to Dickens in Prefaces, etc; introds to Hard times, 1912, Great expectations, 1937 and 1947. *See* A. Henderson, Bernard Shaw, New York 1956, ch 55; H. F. and J. R. Brooks, Dickens in Shaw, Dickensian 59 1963; and Shaw on Dickens, ed D. H. Lawrence and M. Quinn, New York 1985.
Bennet, A. R. Charles Dickens and the railway. Locomotive 15 Apr 1915.
Crotch, W. W. The pageant of Dickens. 1915, 1916 (rev).
Powys, J. C. In his Visions and revisions, 1915, New York 1978.
Crotch, W. W. The soul of Dickens. 1916.
Leacock, S. Fiction and reality: a study of the art of Dickens. In his Essays and literary studies, 1916.

Gordon, E. H. The naming of characters in the works of Dickens. Lincoln NE 1917.

de Laski, E. The psychological attitude of Dickens towards surnames. Amer Jnl of Psychology 29 1918.

Burton, R. E. Dickens: how to know him. Indianapolis 1919.

Crotch, W. W. The decline [in Dickens's reputation] – and after! Dickensian 15 1919.

Crotch, W. W. The secret of Dickens. 1919.

Phillips, W. C. Dickens, Reade and Collins, sensation novelists. New York 1919.

[Woolf, V.] Dickens by a disciple. TLS 27 Mar 1919.

Crotch, W. W. The touchstone of Dickens. 1920.

Darwin, F. In his Springtime and other essays, 1920.

Zweig, S. Drei Meister: Balzac, Dickens, Dostojewski. Leipzig 1920; tr 1930. Incorporated into his Die Baumeister der Welt vol 1, 1920, tr 1939. Essay on Dickens tr in Dial Jan 1923.

Gissing, G. Critical studies of the works of Dickens. Ed T. Scott, New York 1924. 9 introds from works ed Gissing. The same introds ed B. W. Matz as The immortal Dickens, 1925. *See* P. Coustillas, Gissing's writings on Dickens, Dickensian 61 1965.

Special periods and aspects

Lester, C. E. Dickens. In his Glory and shame of England vol 2, New York 1841, 1866 (rev).

The reception of Dickens. United States Mag Apr 1842.

Report of the dinner given to Dickens in Boston, 1 February 1842. Boston 1842.

Literary lions: Dickens. Pictorial Times 20 Apr 1844.

Howitt, W. The people's portrait gallery: Dickens. People's Jnl 3 June 1846.

'Morna' [T. M. O'Keefe]. The battle of London life: or Boz and his secretary, with six [five] designs on stone by George Sala. 1849.

Powell, T. The living authors of England, New York 1849, London 1851 (rev as Pictures of the living authors of Britain). *See above,* Minor works, Proof: private and confidential 1849.

Yates, E. Mr Thackeray, Mr Yates and the Garrick Club: the correspondence and facts. 1859 (priv ptd). *See* Garrick Club: correspondence, 1858 (priv ptd), and Garrick Club: report of the committee, 1858 (priv ptd).

Clark, L. G. Letters from Dickens. Harper's Mag Aug 1862.

The Charles Dickens Dinner: an authentic record of the public banquet on Nov 2nd 1867 prior to his departure for the United States, with a report of the speeches; with a preface by W[illiam] C[harles] [Mark] K[ent]. 1867. Speeches by Dickens, Lytton, Trollope et al.

Reeve, L. A. Portraits of men of eminence, with biographical memoirs, vol 4. 1867.

Sherwood, J. D. Visits to the homes of authors: Dickens. Hours at Home July 1867.

Clark, L. G. Appleton's Jnl 6 Aug 1870.

[Putnam, G. W.] Four months with Dickens, during his first visit to America. Atlantic Monthly Oct–Nov 1870.

Grant, J. The newspaper press. 2 vols 1871. Vol 1 ch 12, The Morning Chronicle; vol 2 ch 3, The Daily News.

The parents of Dickens. Lippincott's Mag June 1874.

Kent, W. C. M. Dickens as a journalist. Time Dec 1881.

Fitzgerald, P. H. Recreations of a literary man. 2 vols 1882. Vol 1 Dickens as an editor; Dickens at home.

Payn, J. The youth and middle age of Dickens. 1883. Rptd from Chambers's Jnl.

Payn, J. Some literary recollections. 1884.

Powell, T. Leaves from my life. Frank Leslie's Sunday Mag Feb 1887.

Pemberton, C. T. E. Charles Dickens and the stage. 1888.

Hone, P. Diary. Ed B. Tuckerman 2 vols New York 1889. Vol 2 Dickens's reception in USA 1842.

Axon, W. E. A. Dickens and shorthand. Manchester [1892]. Dickens as a reporter.

Aronstein, P. Dickens und Carlyle. Anglia 18 1896.

Williamson, E. S. Glimpses of Dickens. Toronto 1898.

Fitzgerald, P. H. John Forster, by one of his friends. 1903.

McCarthy, J. Portraits of the sixties. 1903. Ch 2.

Robinson, J. R. Dickens and the Guild of Literature and Art. Cornhill Mag Jan 1904.

Bowes, C. C. The associations of Dickens with Liverpool. Liverpool 1905. Introd by E. A. Browne.

Furniss, H. A Shakespeare birthday: a reminiscence of Dickens. Pall Mall Mag Apr 1906.

Welch, D. Dickens in Genoa. Harper's Monthly Mag Aug 1906.

Welch, D. Dickens in Switzerland. Harper's Monthly Mag Apr 1906.

Wells, G. The tale of Dickens, told by a local man to local people. Rochester 1906.

Benham, W. Dickens in Kent. In his Memorials of old Kent, 1907.

Matz, B. W. Dickens as a journalist. Fortnightly Rev May 1908.

Beazell, W. P. (ed). Account of the Boz Ball in New York 14 February 1842, reprinted from the New York Aurora-Extra. Cedar Rapids IA 1909 (priv ptd). *See* A. Nisbet, The Boz Ball, Amer Heritage 9 1957.

Tull, E. M. Dickens and Reading. Reading [1909].

Winter, W. Old friends: literary recollections. New York 1909.

Fitz-Gerald, S. J. A. Dickens and the drama. 1910, New York 1971.

Snyder, J. F. Dickens in Illinois. Jnl of Illinois State Historical Soc 3 1910.

Wilkins, W. G. Dickens and America. 1911.

Calthrop, D. C. and M. Pemberton (ed). The Dickens souvenir of 1912. 1912.

Renton, R. John Forster and his friendships. 1912. Chs 4–5.

Fiedler, F. Dickens' Belesenheit. Archiv n.s. 40 1920.

Studies and bibliographies of adaptations

Dramatisations

Wistach, P. Dramatisations of Dickens. Bookman 14 1891.

Woolcott A., Mr Dickens goes to the play. The Dickensian plays, players, and the theatre. New York 1922.

Pierce, D. Special bibliography: the stage versions of Dickens' novels. Bull of Bibliography and Dramatic Index 22 Jan, 8 May and 13 Sep 1937.

Morley, M. A series of articles in Dickensian 1946–56 identifying dramatisations of Dickens's works.

Fawcett, F. D. Dickens the dramatist on stage, screen and radio. 1952. Includes incomplete listing of dramatisations.

Zambrano, A. L. Feature motion pictures adapted from Dickens. Dickens Stud Newsletter 5 1974 and 6 1975.

Zambrano, A. L. Dickens and film. New York 1977. Lists film versions of Dickens's works.

Bolton, H. P. Dickens dramatised. 1987. Annotated calendar of dramatisations of Dickens's works.

Pointer, M. Dickens on the screen: the film, television and video adaptations. Metuchen NJ 1995.

Music

Lightwood, J. T. Dickens and music. 1912, New York 1970.

Ley, J. W. T. Some comic songs that Dickens knew. Dickensian 26–7 1930–1.

Ley, J. W. T. The songs of Silas Wegg. Dickensian 26 1930.

Ley, J. W. T. The sea songs of Dickens. Dickensian 27 1931.

Ley, J. W. T. Some hymns and songs of childhood. Dickensian 27 1931.

Ley, J. W. T. The songs Dick Swiveller knew. Dickensian 27 1931.

Ley, J. W. T. More songs of Dickens's day. Dickensian 28 1932.

Ley, J. W. T. Sentimental songs in Dickens. Dickensian 28–9 1932–3.

Ley, J. W. T. The sporting songs of Dickens. Dickensian 28 1932.

O'Sullivan, D. Charles Dickens and Thomas Moore. Stud (Dublin) 37 1948.

Dickens's illustrators and illustrations

For extra illustrations to particular works, see under individual entries above. The following entries include only (1) general collections of illustrations or commentaries on them; (2) works dealing with an illustrator's relations with Dickens; not general biographies of the artists.

Barnard, F. A series of character sketches from Dickens. [1879]. Lithographed. 6 plates. Re-issued in photogravure in 1887 uniformly with 2 further sers (6 plates each) pbd in 1884 and 1885 respectively. All the 18 plates in photogravure were re-issued later in 6 sections for subscribers, with letterpress by T. Archer.

Kitton, F. G. 'Phiz' [Hablot Knight Browne]: a memoir. 1882.

Thomson, D. C. Life and labours of Hablot Knight Browne, 'Phiz'. 1884.

'Kyd' (J. C. Clarke). The characters of Dickens portrayed in original water colour sketches. [c. 1887].

Archer, T. Dickens: a gossip about his life, works and characters, with eighteen full-page character sketches (reproduced in photogravure) by Frederick Barnard, and other illustrations by well-known artists, in six sections for subscribers only. [1895?], [1902].

Gibson, C. D. People of Dickens. New York 1897. 6 plates.

Grego, J. Pictorial Pickwickiana: Dickens and his illustrators, with 350 drawings and engravings [by various artists who illustrated original or early edns of Dickens]. 2 vols 1899. Commentary and bibliographical notes are not confined to The Pickwick papers.

Kitton, F. G. Dickens and his illustrators. 1899, Amsterdam 1972, New York 1973. All the recognised illustrators, with 22 portraits and 70 unpbd illustrations, and bibliography.

Eaton, S. Dickens rare print collection. Philadelphia [1900] (priv ptd).

Kitton, F. G. (ed). Dickens illustrations: facsimilies of the original drawings, sketches and studies for illustrations by Cruikshank, Browne, Leech, Stone and Fildes. 1900.

Van Noorden, C. Quaint errors by Dickens's illustrators. English Illus Mag 29 May 1903.

Fraser, W. A. The illustrators of Dickens. Dickensian 2 1906.

Cecil, L. One of Dickens's exponents: George Cattermole. Crown 20 Apr 1907.

Layard, G. S. Suppressed plates, wood engravings etc. 1907.

Scenes and characters from the works of Dickens: being 866 drawings by various artists printed from the original woodblocks engraved for 'The Household edition' 1908. With an introductory note.

Hammerton, J. A. The Dickens picture-book: a record of the Dickens illustrators. [1910]. Vol 17 of The Charles Dickens Lib. *See above,* Collected works.

Ley, J. W. T. Robert William Buss. Dickensian 6 1910.

Crowdy, W. L. Famous Dickens pictures. 1912. Reproduction of 12 illustrations by Charles Green, with brief introd.

Lewin, F. G. Characters from Dickens: a portfolio of 20 Vandyck gravures from the drawings of F. G. L., introduced by B. W. Matz. 1912.

Browne, E. A. Phiz and Dickens. 1913. By the artist's son.

Cohn, A. M. A bibliographical catalogue of the printed works illustrated by George Cruikshank. 1914.

Cohn, A. M. George Cruikshank: a catalogue raisonné. 1924.

Fraser, C. L. Characters from Dickens. [1924]. 18 coloured plates and decorations. Foreword by H. Macfall.

Reynolds, F. The Buchanan portfolio of characters from Dickens. Glasgow [1925]. 14 coloured plates.

Nonesuch Dickensiana. 1937. 1 A. Waugh, Dickens and his illustrators; 2 T. Hatton, A bibliographical list of the original illustrations to the works of Dickens.

Dickens illustrations. TLS 19 May 1945. *See* TLS 7 Apr–19 May 1945.

Millican, J. N. B. Phiz without sparkle. Dickensian 41 1945.

Yarre, D'A. P. Dickens without Phiz? Dickensian 42 1946.

Weitenkampf, F. American illustrators of Dickens. Boston Public Lib Quart 5 1953.

Johannsen, A. (ed). Phiz illustrations from the novels of Dickens. Chicago 1956. 516 etchings from 7 novels.

Bentley, N. Dickens and his illustrators. In Charles Dickens 1812–1870, ed E. W. F. Tomlin, 1969.

Cohen, J. R. Strained relations: Charles Dickens and George Cattermole. Dickens Stud Annual 1 1970.

Harvey, J. Victorian novelists and their illustrators. London and New York 1971.

Miller, G. E. Postcard Dickensiana 1900–1920. Dickensian 71 1975.

Johnston, W. R. Alfred Jacob Miller: would-be illustrator. Walters Art Gallery Bull Dec 1977.

Buchanan-Brown, J. Phiz! The book illustrations of Hablot Knight Browne. Newton Abbot 1978.

Steig, M. Dickens and Phiz. Bloomington IN 1978.

Cohen, J. R. Charles Dickens and his original illustrators. Columbus OH 1980.

Turpin, J. Maclise as a Dickens illustrator. Dickensian 76 1980.

Patten, R. L. George Cruikshank's life, times and art. 2 vols New Brunswick NJ 1992, 1996.

Topographical studies up to 1920

Pemberton, T. E. Dickens's London. Guildford 1876, New York 1973.

Frost, T. In Kent with Dickens. 1880.

Langton, R. Dickens and Rochester. 1880.

Rimmer, A. About England with Dickens. 1883, 1899.

Allbut, R. London rambles 'en zigzag' with Dickens. [1886].

Hughes, W. R. A week's tramp in Dickens-land, together with personal reminiscences of the Inimitable Boz. 1891.

Dickens, C., the younger. Disappearing Dickensland. North Amer Rev June 1893.

Fitzgerald, P. H. Bozland: Dickens' places and people. 1895, Detroit 1970.

Dickens, C., the younger. Notes on some Dickens places and people. Pall Mall Mag July 1896.

Trumble, A. In jail with Dickens. 1896. A study of the prisons described by Dickens.

Allbut, R. Rambles in Dickens's land. 1899, 1903 (rev), New York 1977.

'Miltoun, Francis' (F. M. Milburg). Dickens' London, with many illustrations and plans. 1904.

Ward, H. S. and C. W. B. Ward The real Dickens land, with an outline of Dickens's life. 1904.

Fitzgerald, P. H. Boz and Bath. Bath 1905.

Kitton, F. G. The Dickens country. 1905, 1911, 1925.

Harris, E. Gad's Hill Place and Dickens. Rochester 1910.

Harris, E. Dickensian Chatham. Rochester 1911.

Nicklin, J. A. Dickens-land, pictured by E. W. Haslehurst. 1911.

Thomson, W. R. In Dickens Street. 1912, New York 1977, Folcroft PA 1978.

Smith, F. H. In Dickens' London: twenty-two photogravure proofs reproducing charcoal drawings. New York 1914, 1916.

For further topographical studies, see Bibliography of B. W. Matz, Dickensian 21 1925.

Biographies

[Friswell, J.] Dickens: a critical biography. 1858 (Our contemporaries no 1).

Mackenzie, R. S. Life of Dickens, with personal recollections and anecdotes. Philadelphia [1870].

Perkins, F. B. Dickens: a sketch of his life and work. New York 1870, Folcroft PA 1973.

Sala, G. A. H. Charles Dickens. [1870]; with Speeches, letters and sayings of Dickens, New York [1870], Farnborough 1970. Enlarged from Daily Telegraph 10 June 1870.

[Taverner, H. T. and J. C. Hotten]. Dickens: the story of his life, by the author of the Life of Thackeray. [1870]; with Speeches by Dickens [1873], Folcroft PA 1978.

Watkins, W. Dickens, with anecdotes and recollections of his life. [1870].

Hammond, R. A. The life and writings of Charles Dickens: a memorial volume. 1871, New York 1972.

Hanaford, P. A. Life and writings of Dickens: a woman's memorial volume. Boston 1871.

Jerrold, W. B. The best of all good company: a [monthly] series. 1871–2. Pt 1 A day with Dickens, June 1871. Includes short life, personal appreciation, account of friendships and facs of handwriting. *See* GM July 1870.

Forster, J. The life of Dickens. 3 vols 1872–4 (revisions in successive edns of each vol), 2 vols 1876 (Library edn), 1879 (illus); rev and abridged G. Gissing 1903; Memorial edn, ed B. W. Matz 2 vols 1911 (500 portraits, facs etc); ed G. K. Chesterton 2 vols 1927 (EL); ed J. W. T. Ley 1928 (notes embody much new matter); ed A. J. Hoppé 2 vols 1966 (EL).

REVIEWS: Wilson, H. Examiner 9 Dec 1871; Saturday Rev 9 Dec 1871; Literary World 15–22 Dec 1871, 22 Nov 1872; The Times 26 Dec 1871; Payn, J. Chambers's Jnl 13–20 Jan 1872, 1 Feb 1873, 21 Mar 1874; Stack, J. H. Fortnightly Rev Jan 1872; Fraser's Mag Jan 1872; [Elwin, W.] Quart Rev 132 1872; Atlantic Monthly Feb 1872; Buchanan, R. St Paul's Mag Feb 1872; Guardian 6 Mar 1872, 22 Jan 1873; Sheldon, F. North Amer Rev Apr 1872; Athenaeum 16 Nov 1872; Examiner 16 Nov 1872, 14 Feb 1874; Br Quart Rev 57 1873, 59 1874; Atlantic Monthly Feb 1873; Temple Bar May 1873; [Hutton, R. H.] Spectator 7 Feb 1874; Lang, A. Academy 21 Feb 1874.

Carlton, W. J. Postscripts to Forster. Dickensian 58 1962. Letters to Forster from readers of Life.

Stoddard, R. H. Anecdote biographies of Thackeray and Dickens. New York 1874.

Langton, R. Dickens and Rochester. 1880. Rptd with addns from Papers of Manchester Literary Club. Partly incorporated in following.

Jones, C. H. A short life of Dickens, with selections from his letters. New York 1880.

Ward, A. W. Charles Dickens. 1882 (EML). *See* his Dickens (a lecture), in Science lectures 2nd ser, Manchester 1870.

Langton, R. The childhood and youth of Dickens, with retrospective notes and elucidations, from his books and letters. Manchester 1883 (priv ptd), 1891 (enlarged and rev), 1912, New York 1974. Supplements and controverts Forster.

Dickens, M. Charles Dickens, by his eldest daughter. 1885, 1911, New York 1977.

Marzials, F. T. Life of Dickens. 1887. Contains bibliography by J. P. Anderson.

Kitton, F. G. Dickens by pen and pencil, including anecdotes and reminiscences collected by his friends and companions. 1890. Suppl 1890; additional illustrations 1891.

Dickens, M. My father as I recall him. [1897], New York 1974.

Matz, B. W. Dickens: the story of his life and writings. [1902]. Rptd from Household Words 14 June 1902. *See* Bibliography of B. W. Matz, Dickensian 21 1925.

Kitton, F. G. Dickens: his life, writings and personality. 2 vols Edinburgh [1902], 1 vol nd. *See* Bibliography of F. G. Kitton, Dickensian 1 1905.

Shore, W. T. Dickens. 1904, Folcroft PA 1977.

Fitzgerald, P. H. The life of Dickens as revealed in his writings. 2 vols 1905.

Ellison, O. Charles Dickens, novelist. [1908].

Shore, W. T. Dickens and his friends. 1909.

Shore, W. T. Charles Dickens. 1910.

Moses, B. Charles Dickens. 1912.

Fitzgerald, P. H. Memories of Dickens, with an account of Household Words and All the Year Round and of the contributors thereto. Bristol 1913, New York 1971.

Bookman extra number–Charles Dickens. 1914.

Dibelius, W. Dickens. Leipzig 1916, 1926 (rev). Extensive bibliography. *See* his Englische Romanskunst, Berlin 1910, 1922 (rev).

Ley, J. W. T. The Dickens circle: a narrative of the novelist's friendships. 1918, New York 1972.

Dark, S. Charles Dickens. 1919.

Nicoll, W. R. Dickens's own story: sidelights on his life and personality. 1923, Folcroft PA 1976.

Dexter, W. Dickens: the story of the life of the world's favourite author. 1927.

Dickens, H. F. Memories of my father. 1928. *See* Personal recollections, *above*.

'Ephesian' [C. E. B. Roberts]. This side idolatry. 1928. A biography in the form of a novel.

Straus, R. Dickens: a portrait in pencil. 1928, 1938 (as A portrait of Dickens).

Payne, E. F. and H. H. Garper. The romance of Charles Dickens and Maria Beadnell Winter. Boston 1929.

Wagenknecht, E. The man Dickens: a Victorian portrait. Cambridge MA 1929, Norman OK 1965 (rev).

Stonehouse, J. H. Green leaves: new chapters in the life of Dickens. 1930–1 (priv ptd), 1931 (rev and enlarged), New York 1973.

Darwin, B. Charles Dickens. 1933.

Dent, H. C. The life and characters of Dickens. 1933.

Leacock, S. Dickens: his life and work. 1933.

'Kingsmill, Hugh' [H. K. Lunn]. The sentimental journey: a life of Dickens. 1934.

Boarman, J. C. and J. L. Harte. Boz: an intimate biography of Charles Dickens. Boston 1935.

Wright, T. The life of Dickens. 1935. *See* his Autobiography, 1936: ch 14 on Dickens and Ellen Ternan.

Dybowski, R. Dickens. Warsaw 1936. With bibliography of Polish trns.

Pope-Hennessy, U. Dickens. 1945.

Lemonnier, L. Dickens. Paris 1946; tr Paris 1947.

Pearson, H. Dickens: his character, comedy and career. 1949.

Aylmer, F. Dickens incognito. 1950.

Lindsay, J. Dickens: a biographical and critical study. 1950.

Symons, J. Dickens. 1951.

Graham, E. The story of Charles Dickens. 1952.

Johnson, E. Dickens: his tragedy and triumph. 2 vols New York 1952; rev and abridged 1977.

Nisbet, A. Dickens and Ellen Ternan. 1952.

Fielding, K. J. Dickens: a survey. 1953, 1960 (rev), 1963 (rev) (Br Council pam).

Harrison, M. Dickens: a sentimental journey in search of an unvarnished portrait. 1953.

Bowen, W. H. Dickens and his family. Cambridge 1956.

Fielding, K. J. Dickens: a critical introduction. 1958, 1965 (rev and enlarged).

Katarsky, I. M. Dickens. Moscow 1960.

Priestley, J. B. Dickens: a pictorial biography. 1961.

Clair, C. Charles Dickens: life and character. 1963.

Wagenknecht, E. Dickens and the scandal-mongers. Norman OK 1965.

Hibbert, C. The making of Dickens. 1967.

Cooper, L. A hand upon the time: a life of Charles Dickens. New York 1968, London 1971. [Children's book]

Fido, M. Charles Dickens: an authentic account of his life and times. 1970.

Lazarus, M. A tale of two brothers. 1973.

Greaves, J. Dickens at Doughty Street. 1975.

Mankowitz, W. Dickens of London. 1976.

MacKenzie, N. and J. Dickens: a life. Oxford 1979.

Allen, M. Charles Dickens's childhood. 1988.

Kaplan, F. Dickens: a biography. 1988.

Ackroyd, P. Dickens. 1990.

Tomalin, C. The invisible woman: the story of Nelly Ternan and Charles Dickens. 1990.
Smith, G. Charles Dickens: a literary life. 1996. [PS]

Benjamin Disraeli, 1st Earl of Beaconsfield

1804–81

The Hughenden Papers, the most important collection of Disraeli mss, formerly housed at Hughenden Manor, is now for the most part in the Bodleian. Microfilm copies (University Microfilms 1970) are in the Cambridge and Syracuse univ libs. Other mss can be located by reference to IELM and the pbd vols of Benjamin Disraeli letters, *below. Large cols of letters are in the Royal Archives, Windsor Castle; the Liverpool Lib and Records Office; the BL; Belvoir Castle Archives; and at Christ Church, Oxford, and Queens University, Kingston, Ontario. Private owners include the Earl of Bradford, Lord Rothschild, and D. Mopsik of Dallas, Texas.*

Bibliographies

Angus, G. Contributions to a bibliography of Disraeli. N & Q 29 Apr–8 June 1893.
Aronstein, P. In Disraelis Leben und dichterische Werke, Anglia 17 1895.
Sadleir, M. In Excursions in Victorian bibliography, 1922.
Sadleir, M. In XIX century fiction, vol 2 1951.
Dahl, C. In Victorian fiction: a guide to research, ed L. Stevenson, Cambridge MA 1964. Secondary.
Stewart, R. W. Writings of Benjamin Disraeli. In R. Blake, Disraeli, '1966' [1967].
Levine, R. In Benjamin Disraeli, New York 1968 (Twayne's English Authors).
Stewart, R. W. Benjamin Disraeli: a list of writings by him, and writings about him. Metuchen NJ 1972 (Scarecrow Author Bibliographies). Contains full listings of Disraeli's works, works attributed to him, trns, contemporary reviews, later edns, reviews of edns, secondary materials and reviews of secondary materials; invaluable.
Dahl, C. In Victorian fiction: a second guide to research, ed. G. H. Ford, New York 1978. Continues 1964 guide, *above*.
Disraeli Newsletter. Pbd by the Disraeli Project, Queens University, Kingston, Ontario 1976–7, continued as Disraeli Project Newsletter 1978–81. Brief notes on Disraeli and his work; individual items therein not separately listed here.

Collections

Works of Disraeli the younger. 2 vols Philadelphia 1839, 1 vol 1845, 1850.
Works. Uniform edn (Bryce). 4 vols London and New York 1853 (revised texts).
Works. Uniform edn (Routledge). 1858. Rptd as Uniform Shilling edn, 10 vols 1862–3.
Novels and tales. New edn (Warne). 5 vols 1866.
Novels and tales. Collected edn (Longmans), with preface by Disraeli, 10 vols 1870–1 (revised texts). Endymion added 1881.
Novels and tales. Hughenden edn. 11 vols 1881. Includes portrait, engravings and biographical sketch.
REVIEW: Edinburgh Rev 155 1882.
Seaside Lib edn (Munro). 12 vols New York 1881.
Novels. Primrose edn (Routledge). 8 vols 1888. Vivian Grey to Sybil.
Works. Empire edn (Dunne). Ed E. Gosse, with biographical preface by R. Arnot, 20 vols London and New York 1904–5.
Works. Centenary edn. Ed L. Wolf 1904. Only Vivian Grey and The young duke pbd.
Novels. Uniform edn (Lane). Ed Earl of Iddesleigh [W. S. Northcote], 9 vols 1905–6.
Novels and tales. Bradenham edn (Davies). Ed P. Guedella, 12 vols 1926–7, New York 1934. Introds rptd in Guedella, Idylls of the Queen, 1937.
Novels and tales. Uniform edn (Lane: Bodley Head). 11 vols 1927–8.
Novels and tales. Tr Ger 1846 (Sämtliche Schriften).

Selections

Wit and wisdom of Benjamin Disraeli. Ed H. G. Calcraft, London and New York 1881, 1883 (new edn).
Tales and sketches. Ed J. L. Robertson 1891. Collects from periodicals True story, Carrier pigeon, Consul's daughter, Walstein, Speaking Harlequin, Midland ocean, Ibrahim pacha, Court of Egypt, Valley of Thebes, Egyptian Thebes, Shoubra, Bosphorus, Interview with a great Turk, Munich.
Young England. Ed B. N. Langdon-Davies, illustr Byam Shaw 4 vols 1904. (Vivian Grey, Coningsby, Sybil, Tancred).
Alroy, Popanilla, Count Alarcos, Ixion in heaven. Ed Iddesleigh '1906' [1905] (New Pocket Lib).
The young duke 'a moral tale, though gay,' The rise of Iskander & The infernal marriage. Introd by Iddesleigh '1906' [1905] (New Pocket Lib).
Selections from the novels. Ed and introd by Eric Forbes-Boyd 1964 (Falcon Prose Classics).
Jerusalem by moonlight, and The Hebrew race. Berkeley Heights NJ 1965.
Sayings of Disraeli. Ed R. Blake 1992.

§1

Rumpel Stilts Kin: a dramatic spectacle, by 'B. D.' and 'W. G. M.' [Disraeli, W. G. Meredith]. Glasgow [1823?]; ed and introd by M. Sadleir 1952 (priv ptd).
Vivian Grey. Vols 1–2 1826, vols 3–5 1827 (2 edns); 4 vols 1827 (3rd edn); 2 vols Philadelphia 1827; 5 vols in 4 1833 (authorship first acknowledged); rev edn with preface, 1 vol 1853 (Uniform edn, Bryce); rev edn 1870 (Longmans); original text ed and introd by L. Wolf, 2 vols 1904; rev text ed B. N. Langdon-Davies, illustr Byam Shaw (see Young England, *above*) 1904; ed Iddesleigh 1906; ed H. Van Thal, introd by S. Nettell 1968 (First Novel Lib); tr Ger 1827, Danish 1840–1. Keys to characters rptd from Star Chamber in 10th edn 1827.
The voyage of Captain Popanilla. 1828; Philadelphia 1828; illustr Maclise, London 1829; rev edn in Works, Uniform edn (Bryce) 1853 (with Ixion); in Novels and tales, Collected edn (Longmans) 1870 (with Alroy); ed Iddesleigh 1906 (with Alroy and Ixion); ed P. Guedella 1934; tr Fr 1866.
The young duke. 3 vols 1831, 2 vols New York 1831; in Works, Uniform edn (Bryce) 1853; in Novels and Tales, Collected edn (Longmans) 1871 (with Count Alarcos); 1 vol [1888], [1894]; ed Wolf 1905 (with Vivian Grey); ed Iddesleigh 1906 (with The rise of Iskander and The infernal marriage).
Contarini Fleming: a psychological autobiography. 4 vols 1832; 2nd edn as Contarini Fleming or the psychological romance, 4 vols 1834; as The Young Venetian: or the victim of imagination, by 'Granville Jones', 4 vols Glasgow 1834; with new preface, 3 vols '1846' [1845] (with Alroy); in Works, Uniform edn (Bryce) 1853; in Novels and tales, Collected edn (Longmans) 1871 (with The rise of Iskander); ed Iddesleigh 1905; tr Ger 1846, Fr 1863.
The wondrous tale of Alroy. 3 vols 1832 (with The rise of Iskander); 1834 (new edn); 3 vols 1846 (with Contarini Fleming); in Novels and tales, Collected edn (Longmans) 1871 (with Ixion in heaven, The infernal marriage, and Popanilla); as Miriam Alroy: a romance of the twelfth century, New York 1881 (Seaside Lib); as Alroy: a romance [1888]; ed Iddesleigh 1906 (with Popanilla, Count Alarcos, and Ixion in heaven) (New Pocket Lib); tr Ger 1833, Hebrew 1883. Dramatised by P. P. Grunfeld 1896 and 1906 (2 versions).
Ixion in heaven. NMM Dec 1832–Feb 1833. Rpt in Works, Uniform edn (Bryce) 1853 (with The infernal marriage, Popanilla, Count Alarcos); in Novels and tales, Collected edn (Longmans) 1871 (with Alroy); illustr J. Austen 1925; in Novels and tales,

Bradenham edn 1926 (with Popanilla); introd by E. Partridge 1927 (with W. E. Aytoun's burlesque Endymion).

Velvet lawn: a sketch. Wycombe 1833.

The infernal marriage. NMM July–Oct 1834. Rptd in Works, Uniform edn (Bryce) 1853 (with Ixion in heaven); in Novels and tales, Collected edn (Longmans) 1871 (with Alroy); ed Iddesleigh 1906 (with The young duke); in Novels and tales, Bradenham edn 1926 (with Popanilla); introd by E. Partridge, illustr W. Jackson 1929; tr Fr 1853.

The revolutionary epick. 2 vols 1834; rev edn 1864; in The revolutionary epick and other poems, ed W. D. Adams 1904 (with Count Alarcos and The Dunciad of today).

Henrietta Temple: a love story. 3 vols 1837; rev edn in Works, Uniform edn (Bryce) 1853; in Novels and tales, Collected edn (Longmans) 1871; ed Iddesleigh 1906; in Novels of high society from the Victorian age, ed A. Powell 1947; introd by A. Herd 1969; tr Ger 1837, Fr 1850, Swed 1859, Rus 1859 etc, Hungarian 1861, Greek 1862, Polish 1882.

Venetia. 3 vols 1837, Philadelphia 1837, rev text in Works, Uniform edn (Bryce) 1853 (1 vol), 2 vols 1858, in Novels and tales, Collected edn (Longmans) 1870, 1 vol [1888]; ed Iddesleigh 1906, [German student edn] 1915; tr Greek 1889.

The tragedy of Count Alarcos. 1839, 1847 (priv ptd); in Works, Uniform edn (Bryce) 1853 (with Ixion in heaven); in Novels and tales, Collected edn (Longmans) 1870 (with The young duke); ed Adams 1904 (with The revolutionary epick); ed Iddesleigh 1906 (with Alroy).

Coningsby: or the new generation. 3 vols 1844 (3 edns); Philadelphia 1844; New York 1844; London 1847 (4th edn); 1 vol New York 1849 (with new preface) (5th edn); in Works, Uniform edn (Bryce) 1853; in Works, Uniform edn (Routledge) 1859; in Novels and tales, Collected edn (Longmans) 1870; ed F. Hitchman 1889; introd by W. K. Leask, illustr C. A. Shepperson 1900; ed B. N. Langdon-Davies, illustr B. Shaw 1904; ed Iddesleigh 1905; ed B. N. Langdon-Davies 1911 (EL); ed P. Guedella 1926 (Bradenham edn); preface by A. Maurois 1931 (WC); introd by W. Allen 1948 (Chiltern Lib); ed B. Langdon-Davies *(see above)* 1961 (Capricorn); ed A. Briggs 1962 (Signet); ed M. Elwin 1968 (Heron); ed S. M. Smith, New York 1982 (WCp); ed T. Braun, Harmondsworth 1983 (Pen); tr Ger 1844–5, Fr 1846 (introd by P. Chasles), 1975 (preface by A. Maurois), Hungarian 1862, 1891.

Sybil: or the two nations. 3 vols 1845, 1 vol Philadelphia 1845, Leipzig 1845 (Tauchnitz), in Works, Uniform edn (Bryce) 1853; in Novels and tales, Collected edn (Longmans) 1871; 1882; introd by H. D. Traill, illustr F. Pegram 1895; ed Iddesleigh 1905; introd by Walter Sichel 1925 (WC); ed V. Cohen, illustr F. Pegram 1934 (Scholar's Lib); introd by J. G. Watson, Harmondsworth 1954 (Pen); introd by A. N. Jeffares 1957 (Nelson Classics); ed T. Braun, introd by R. A. Butler, Harmondsworth 1980 (Pen); ed S. Smith 1981 (WCp); tr Ger 1846 etc, Fr 1847 etc, Du 1889.

Tancred: or the new crusade. 3 vols 1847; 1 vol Leipzig 1847 (Tauchnitz), Philadelphia [1847?]; in Novels and tales, Collected edn (Longmans) 1871; ed Iddesleigh 1905. Several reprints in 1970s; tr Ger 1847, 1914 (postscript by O. Levy), 1936, Fr 1851, Rus 1878, Polish 1879, Hebrew 1883. Dramatisation by E. Millbank produced London 1923.

Lothair. 3 vols 1870 (7 edns); New York 1870; Leipzig 1870 (Tauchnitz); 1 vol 1870 (with General Preface to Novels and tales, Longmans Collected edn); introd by A. N. Jeffares 1957 (Nelson Classics); ed V. Bogdanor 1975 (Oxford English Novels); tr Fr 1870 etc, Rus 1870 etc, Hungarian 1871 etc, Ital 2 vols 1871–2 (introd by R. M. Stuart), Ger 1872, 1874.

Endymion. 3 vols 1880; 1 vol New York 1880 (2 edns); in Novels and tales, Collected edn (Longmans, with Memoir) 1881; introd by E. Gosse, New York 1905; tr Rus 1880 etc, Fr 1881, Ger 1881, Polish 1881–3.

Unfinished novel (untitled; generally known as Falconet). 3 pts in The Times Jan 1905; rptd in New York Times Jan–Feb 1905; in W. F. Monypenny and G. E. Buckle, The Life of Benjamin Disraeli, 1910–20, *below*, and in Novels, and tales, Bradenham edn, 1926–7 (with Endymion).

Selected political writings and speeches

An inquiry into the plans, progress and policy of American mining companies. 1825 (3 edns).

Lawyers and legislators: or notes on the American mining companies. 1825.

The present state of Mexico, as detailed in a report presented to the General Congress by the Secretary of State for the Home Department and Foreign Affairs, at the opening of the Session in 1825. 1825.

England and France: or a cure for the ministerial Gallomania. 1832.

What is he? 1833, 1833 (rev edn); rptd in Lord Beaconsfield on the constitution, ed F. Hitchman [1884] (with Vindication of the English Constitution).

The crisis examined. 1834 (2 edns).

Vindication of the English Constitution in a letter to a noble and learned lord. 1835; ed F. Hitchman [1884] (with What is he?); ed F. A. Hyndman [1895]; in Whigs and Whiggism 1913, *below*; 1969 (facs).

The letters of Runnymede. First pbd in The Times Jan–May 1836; Exeter 1836 (unauthorised?); first complete edn 1836; 1836 (with The spirit of Whiggism); ed W. Hutcheon 1913 (in Whigs and Whiggism); ed F. Hitchman 1885 (with The spirit); ed F. Bickley, illustr M. Travers 1923 (Abbey Classics).

The spirit of Whiggism. First pbd in The Times June–July 1836; 1836 (with The letters of Runnymede); ed W. Hutcheon 1913 (in Whigs and Whiggism).

Speech in the House of Commons, Friday 15 May 1846. 1846.

England and Denmark: ... speech in the House of Commons 19 April 1848. 1848.

The new Parliamentary reform: speech in the House of Commons, Tuesday June 20 1848. 1848.

The Parliament and the Government: speech on the labours of the Session, August 30 1848. 1848.

Financial policy: speech in the House of Commons, June 30 1851. 1851.

Address delivered to the members of the Manchester Athenaeum on the 3 October 1844. In the importance of literature to men of business, 1852.

Lord George Bentinck: a political biography. 1852 (5 edns, 4th and 5th rev), 1858, 1872 (8th edn, rev with preface), 1874, 1881; ed C. Whibley 1905; tr Ger 1853.

Parliamentary reform, House of Commons 25 March 1852. 1852.

Mr Disraeli to Colonel Rathbone. 1857 [1858]. Letters on the annexation of Oude.

Parliamentary reform, House of Commons Feb 28 1859. 1859.

Public expenditure: speech in the House of Commons June 3 1862. 1862.

Mr Gladstone's finance 1853–62. 1862. Speeches in the House of Commons 24 Feb 1860, 8 Apr 1862.

Speech to the Oxford Diocesan Society, October 30 1862. 1862.

Church policy: speech at a public meeting of the Oxford Diocesan Society for the augmentation of small livings in the Sheldonian Theatre November 25 1864. 1864.

'Church and Queen': five speeches 1860–4, edited with a preface by a member of the University of Oxford [Frederick Lygon]. 1865.

Speech in defence of Church establishment. Br Quart Rev 41 1865.

Two speeches in the City of Edinburgh on 29 and 30 October 1867. 1867.

Speeches on Parliamentary reform 1848–66. Ed M. Corry 1867.

The Prime Minister on Church and State: speech at the Hall of the Merchant Taylors Company, June 17 1868. [1868].

Speeches on the Conservative policy of the last thirty years. Ed J. F. Bulley [1870], 4th edn enlarged 1874.

Speech at the banquet of the National Union of Conservative and Constitutional Associations at the Crystal Palace, Monday June 24 1872. 1872; Wiesbaden 1968 (with commentaries by D. Daiches, J. Holloway et al: Eng and Ger).

Speech at Free Trade Hall Manchester, April 3 1872. [1872]; rptd in Representative British orations, ed C. Adams, vol 3, 1884; rptd 1885 as A voice from the grave.

Mr Osborne Morgan's Burials Bill: speech [by Disraeli] moving the rejection, House of Commons, March 26 1873. 1873.

Inaugural address delivered to the University of Glasgow, November 19 1873. 1873 (on his installation as rector).

Speech at Aylesbury, 20 September 1876. 1876. On the Eastern question.

Selected speeches. Ed T. E. Kebbel 2 vols 1882.

Whigs and Whiggism: political writings. Ed W. Hutcheon 1913; New York 1914. Contains What is he?, Crisis examined, Vindication of the English constitution, Letters of Runnymede, Spirit of Whiggism, and various unrptd articles from The Times 1837–41, Morning Post 1835, Press 1853 and Fraser's Mag 1835–6.

The radical Tory: Disraeli's political development illustrated from his original writings and speeches. Ed H. W. J. Edwards [1937].

Contributions to periodicals

See Tales and sketches; Selected political writings and speeches; *and Stewart's bibliography, above.*

Letters and journals

The unfinished diary of Disraeli's journey to Flanders and the Rhineland. [1824]. Ed C. L. Cline, Univ of Texas Stud in Eng 1943.

Home letters . . . 1830–1. Ed R. Disraeli, London and New York 1885, 1886(?) (2nd edn), 1887 (*see below*).

Correspondence with his sister. Ed R. Disraeli 1886; rptd with Home letters, *above*, and additional letters as Lord Beaconsfield's letters 1830–52 1928; ed A. Birrell 1928 as Home Letters . . . 1830–52; tr Fr 1889.

A new sheaf of Disraeli letters: hitherto unpublished correspondence with his sister Sarah. Ed C. I. Freed, Amer Hebrew 15 Apr 1927.

Letters of Disraeli to Lady Bradford and Lady Chesterfield. Ed Marquis of Zetland, 2 vols London and New York 1929; tr Fr 1930, Cz.

Some early letters of Lord Beaconsfield. Ed E. T. Cook, Sat Rev 21 and 28 May 1932.

Letters from Benjamin Disraeli to Frances Anne, Marchioness of Londonderry 1837–61. Ed with introd by [Edith Helen,] Marchioness of Londonderry 1938.

Benjamin Disraeli's letters to Robert Carter. Ed H. J. Hoeltje, PQ 31 1952.

Disraeli's fan mail. Ed B. R. Jerman, Nineteenth-Century Fiction 9 1954.

Five letters from Benjamin Disraeli to his sister Sarah. Ed C. L. Cline, Univ of Texas Lib Chron 8 1967.

Benjamin Disraeli and R. Shelton Mackenzie: unpublished letters. Ed D. W. Tutein, Victorian Newsletter 31 1967.

Disraeli's Reminiscences. Ed H. M. and M. Swartz, London and New York 1975.

Benjamin Disraeli letters. Ed J. A. W. Gunn, J. Matthews, D. M. Shurman, M. G. Weibe, J. B. Conacher et al, 5 vols [thus far] Toronto 1982– . Vol 1 1815–34; vol 2 1835–7; vol 3 1838–41; vol 4 1824–7; vol 5 1848–51. The Disraeli Project at Queens Univ, Kingston, Ontario, plans to publish as near complete an edition as possible of the letters. It will include those published in earlier collections. The total will be over 10,000.

Works edited by Disraeli

The life of Paul Jones, from original documents in the possession of John Henry Sherburne, Register of the Navy of the United States. 1825. Preface by Disraeli.

Curiosities of literature by Isaac D'Israeli. With a view of the life and writings of the author, edited by his son. 3 vols 1849. This was the first of several of the elder Disraeli's works edited by his son, probably with help from Sarah Disraeli. Others followed at uneven intervals for a number of years. Formal collections are Works 7 vols 1858–9; 6 vols 1867–8; 6 vols New York 1880–1 (standard edn), rptd Hillesheim 1969.

Works attributed to Disraeli

A modern Aesop and The Dunciad of today. Star Chamber May 1826; Dunciad pbd with The revolutionary epick 1904; both Aesop and Dunciad ed M. Sadlier 1928. Since there is a ms of Aesop among the Disraeli papers, its authorship is clear; Sadlier supports the attribution of Dunciad, but Stewart in his bibliography, *above*, rejects it.

Key to Vivian Grey. 1827. Pamphlet (probably by Disraeli).

A year at Hartlebury: or the election, by Cherry and Fair Star. 1834. Ed E. Henderson and J. Matthews, London and Toronto, 1983. Generally accepted as by Disraeli and his sister Sarah.

The present crisis: or the Russo-Turkish war. By Coningsby. 1853; tr Ger 1854. Probably not by Disraeli.

For other works attributed to Disraeli, see Stewart's bibliography, above.

§2

Thackeray, W. M. Coningsby. Morning Chron 13 May 1844; rptd in Contributions to the Morning Chron, ed G. N. Ray 1955.

Thackeray, W. M. Coningsby. Pictorial Times 25 May 1844.

[North, W.] Anti-Coningsby: or the new generation grown old, by an embryo MP. 2 vols 1844.

Strictures on Coningsby . . . With remarks on the present state of parties and the character of the age. 1844.

Key to the characters in Coningsby. 1844.

Forcade, E. De la jeune Angleterre. Revue des Deux Mondes 1 Aug 1844.

A new key to the characters in Coningsby. [1845].

Thackeray, W. M. Sybil. Morning Chron 13 May 1845; rptd Ray, *above*.

Lowell, J. R. North Amer Rev 65 1847 (rev of Tancred); rptd in Round table, 1913.

[Thackeray, W. M.] Codlingsby, by B. de Shrewsberry esq. Punch Jan–June 1847; rptd in Novels by eminent hands, in Miscellanies: prose and verse vol 2, 1856. Parody of Coningsby.

Milnes, R. M. Mr Disraeli's Tancred: the emancipation of the Jews. Edinburgh Rev 86 1847.

[Lewes, G. H.] Coningsby. Br Quart Rev 10 1849.

Francis, G. H. Disraeli: a critical biography. 1852.

Hayward, A. Mr Disraeli: his character and career. Edinburgh Rev 97 1853.

Aytoun, W. E. Disraeli: a biography. Blackwood's Mag 75 1854. Rev of Francis, *above*.

Gilfillan, G. In A third gallery of portraits vol 1, Edinburgh 1854; rptd in his Galleries of literary portraits, Edinburgh 1856.

[MacKnight, T.?] Disraeli: a literary and political biography. 1854.

Gleig, G. R. The Right Honourable Benjamin Disraeli. Blackwood's Mag 104, Aug 1868.

M'Gilchrist, J. Life of Disraeli. London and New York [1868] (Cassell's Biographies).

Hamley, E. B. Lothair. Blackwood's Mag 108, June 1870.

Hayward, A. Lothair. Macmillan's Mag 22, June 1870.

Challemel-Lacour, P. Le roman politique en Angleterre. Revue des Deux Mondes 15 July 1870. Review of Lothair.

Collins, M. The literary character of Mr Disraeli. Br Quart Rev 52, July 1870; rptd in his Pen sketches vol 2, 1879.

Ingle, J. Lothair and its author. 1870. Lecture.

Milnes, R. M. Disraeli's Lothair. Edinburgh Rev 132 1870.

Simpson, R. Lothair. North Br Rev 52 1870.

[Bret Harte, F.] Lothaw: or the adventures of a gentleman in search of religion, by Mr Benjamins. [1871]; rptd in his Condensed novels, Boston and London 1871; separately 1871. Parody of Lothair.

[W., E.] Lothair, the critics, and the Rt Hon Benjamin Disraeli's General Preface to all his works. [1872?]. Verse.

Stephen, L. Mr. Disraeli's novels. In Hours in a Library ser 2, 1876.

Brandes, G. Benjamin Disraeli jarl af Beaconsfield: en litteraer charakteristik. Copenhagen 1878; tr Ger 1879, Eng 1880 as Lord Beaconsfield: a study.

Cucheval-Clarigny, A. Lord Beaconsfield et son temps. Revue des Deux Mondes n.s. 35–6 1879; rptd separately 1880.

Hitchman, F. The public life of Beaconsfield. 2 vols 1879.

[Lester, H. F.] Ben D'Ymion, by the author of Loafair. Punch Dec 1880; rptd in H. F. Lester, Ben D'Ymion and other parodies 1887. Parody of Endymion.

Ewald, A. C. Disraeli and his times. 2 vols 1881.

Greg, W. R. The great twin brethren [Disraeli and Napoleon III]. In Miscellaneous essays vol 1, 1881.

MacColl, M. Lord Beaconsfield. Contemporary Rev 39 1881.

Manners, J. [later Duchess of Rutland]. Some personal recollections of the later years of the Earl of Beaconsfield. 1881 (3 edns).

O'Connor, T. P. and A. Foggo. Disraeli: a biography. 2 vols [1881].

Sichel, W. S. The wit and humour of Lord Beaconsfield. Macmillan's Mag 44, June 1881.

Skelton, J. A last word on Disraeli. Contemporary Rev 39 1881.

Bauer, B. Disraelis romantischer und Bismarcks socialistischer Imperialismus. Chemnitz 1882.

Walpole, S. Lord Beaconsfield's speeches. Edinburgh Rev 155 1882. Review of Kebbel's Selected speeches, *above*, and of the Hughenden edn.

Sichel, W. S. Disraeli as a landscape painter. Time 18 1885.

Harrison, F. The romance of the peerage: Lothair. In Choice of books, 1886; rptd in Modern English essays, ed Ernest Rhys 1922.

Saintsbury, G. Benjamin Disraeli, Earl of Beaconsfield. Mag of Art 9 1886.

Kebbel, T. E. The life of Lord Beaconsfield. London and Philadelphia 1888.

Philipson, D. Disraeli's Coningsby and Tancred. In The Jew in English fiction, Cincinnati 1889.

Brewster, F. C. Disraeli in outline. London and Philadelphia 1890. Biography with abridgements of the novels.

Froude, J. A. Lord Beaconsfield. 1890 (Prime Ministers of Victoria ser); New York 1890; 1915 (EL).

Fraser, W. A. Disraeli and his day. 1891 (2 edns). Anecdotes.

Lake, H. Personal reminiscences of . . . Disraeli. [1891].

Aronstein, P. Disraelis Leben und dichterische Werke. Anglia 17 1895.

Harrison, F. Benjamin Disraeli. In Studies in early Victorian literature, 1895.

Skelton, J. The table talk of Shirley. 1895. Includes reminiscences of Disraeli.

Greenwood, F. Characteristics of Lord Beaconsfield. Cornhill Mag n.s. 1 1896.

Traill, H. D. The political novel. In New fiction, 1897.

Sichel, W. S. Disraeli and the colonies. Blackwood's Mag 167, Apr 1900.

Whibley, C. Disraeli the younger. In Pageantry of life, 1900.

de Vogüé, E.-M. La littérature impérialiste: les romans de Benjamin Disraeli. Revue des Deux Mondes n.s. 3 1901.

Garnett, R. Shelley and Lord Beaconsfield. In Essays of an ex-librarian, 1901.

Muret, M. Lord Beaconsfield, un homme d'état Israélite. In L'esprit juif, Paris 1901.

Bryce, J. Beaconsfield. In Studies in contemporary biography, 1903.

Cazamian, L. Disraeli: le toryisme social. In his Le roman social en Angleterre 1830 to 1850, Paris 1903; tr Eng London and Boston 1973.

Meynell, W. Benjamin Disraeli: an unconventional biography. 2 vols London and New York 1903; rev edn London and Toronto 1927 as The man Disraeli.

'Melville, Lewis' [L. S. Benjamin]. The novels of Disraeli. Fortnightly Rev Nov 1904; rptd in Victorian novelists, 1906.

Samuel, H. B. Two dandy novels. Acad & Lit 67 1904. On Vivian Grey and Bulwer-Lytton's Pelham.

Sichel, W. S. Disraeli: a study in personality and ideas. London and New York 1904.

Kebbel, T. E. Lord Beaconsfield and other Tory memories. 1907.

Ward, A. D. The political and social novel. CHEL vol 13 1907.

Monypenny, W. F. and G. E. Buckle. The life of Benjamin Disraeli. 6 vols London and New York 1910–20; rev edn 2 vols 1929 (the standard life).

Schmitz, O. A. H. Die Kunst der Politik: Lord Beaconsfield. Berlin 1911; Munich 1914 (2nd edn).

Baring, E. (Earl of Cromer). Disraeli. 1912; rptd in Political and literary essays, 1st ser 1913. Review of first 2 vols of Monypenny and Buckle, *above*.

Cecil, A. Disraeli: the first two phases. Quart Rev 218 1913. Review of first 2 vols of Monypenny and Buckle, *above*.

More, P. E. Disraeli and Conservatism. Atlantic Monthly 116 1915; rptd London and Boston 1915 in Aristocracy and justice (Shelburne essays 9th ser).

Heur, E. Entstehungsgeschichte von Disraelis Erstlingsroman Vivian Grey. Berlin 1925 (diss).

Raymond, E. T. Disraeli: the alien patriot. London and New York 1925.

Cline, C. L. Disraeli on the grotesque in literature. RES 16 1940. Argues from a paper in the Hughenden coll that a portion of the review of Vivian Grey is by Disraeli himself.

Cline, C. L. The failure of Disraeli's Contarini Fleming. N & Q 1 Aug 1942. Effect of financial failure of the novel on Disraeli's career.

Jerman, B. R. The young Disraeli. Princeton and London 1960.

Moers, E. The dandy: Brummell to Beerbohm. New York 1960.

Stewart, R. W. The publication and reception of Disraeli's Vivian Grey. Quart Rev 298 1960.

Jerman, B. R. The production of Disraeli's trilogy. PBSA 1964.

Blake, R. The dating of Endymion. RES n.s. 17 1966.

Smith, S. (ed). Mr. Disraeli's readers: letters written to Disraeli and his wife by nineteenth-century readers of Sybil. Nottingham 1966 (Nottingham Univ Misc no 2).

Blake, R. Disraeli. London and New York '1966' [1967]. Second in importance only to Monypenny and Buckle.

Blake, R. Disraeli the novelist. Trans Royal Soc Lit 1967. Includes comments on changes in texts of novels.

Levine, R. A. Benjamin Disraeli. New York 1968 (Twayne's English Authors).

Jones, Annabel. Disraeli's Endymion: a case study. In Essays in the history of publishing, ed A. Briggs 1974.

Stewart, R. W. Disraeli's novels reviewed 1826–1968. Metuchen NJ 1975.

Davis, R. W. Disraeli. Boston and Toronto 1976 (Lib of World Biography).

Hibbert, C. Disraeli and his world. London and New York 1978 (well illustrated).

Korniki, P. F. Notes on the reception of Disraeli in Japan. Disraeli Newsletter 6 1981. Reception of Coningsby.

Bradford, S. Disraeli. 1983.

Vincent, J. R. Disraeli. Oxford and New York 1990.

Millar, M. S. and M. G. Weibe. 'This power so vast . . . and so generally misunderstood': Disraeli and the press in the 1840s. Victorian Periodicals Rev 25, Summer 1992.

Shannon, R. The age of Disraeli, 1868–1881. 1992.
Weintraub, S. Disraeli: a biography. Harmondsworth and New York 1993. [CD]

Annie Edwardes, Annie Edwards (until 1871), née Jones c. 1830–96

§1

The morals of May Fair. 3 vols 1858 (anon), 1 vol 1862, [1863], New York 1865, London 1874 (new edn), 1878, New York 1873 (pbd as Philip Earnscliffe: or the morals of May Fair), [1886], [1889].
Creeds. 3 vols 1859. Anon.
REVIEW: Athenaeum 1640 1859.
The world's verdict. 3 vols 1860, 1861. Anon.
REVIEW: Athenaeum 1735 1861.
A point of honour. 2 vols 1863 (anon), 1 vol 1875 (new edn), New York [1875], [1876], London 1885 (new edn), New York [1886], 1887 (pbd as 'He' and 'she': or a point of honour), [1889], [1899].
REVIEW: Nation (New York) 24 1877.
The ordeal for wives. 3 vols 1864 (anon), 1865, New York 1872, [1873], 1883 (pbd as Delicate ground), 1898.
Miss Forrester: a novel. 3 vols 1865, New York 1866, 1873, London 1880, London and New York 1889.
REVIEW: Athenaeum 1980 1865.
Archie Lovell: a novel. Serialised in Temple Bar Jan–Dec 1866. 3 vols 1866, 2 vols 1867, Leipzig 1867 (Tauchnitz), New York 1867, 1 vol London 1867 (new edn), New York 1868, 1869, London 1871 (new edn), New York [1879], London 1881, (new edn), New York 1883, London [1899], 1902.
Steven Lawrence: yeoman. Serialised in Temple Bar Apr 1867–May 1868. 3 vols 1868, 1 vol New York 1868, 2 vols Leipzig 1869 (Tauchnitz), 1 vol London 1873 (new edn), 1875, New York 1883, [1886].
Susan Fielding. Serialised in Temple Bar Dec 1868–Dec 1869. 3 vols 1869 (anon), New York [1869] (illustr S. Eytinge and W. Homer), 1 vol New York [1870], 1 vol London 1873, New York 1883, [1886], London 1893 (new edn), 1900, London and New York 1900.
Ought we to visit her? Serialised in Temple Bar Dec 1870–Dec 1871. 3 vols 1871, New York [1871], 2 vols Leipzig 1872 (Tauchnitz), 1 vol London 1872, 1885, London and New York 1900, London 1901.
REVIEWS: Athenaeum 2297 1871; Spectator 44 1871; Nation (New York) 14 1872.
A vagabond heroine. Serialised in Temple Bar Jan–July 1873. 1 vol 1873, Leipzig 1873 (Tauchnitz), New York 1873, [1878], London 1879, New York 1884 (pbd as A Spanish story. With Rival charms, in 1 vol).
REVIEWS: Athenaeum 2373 1873; Nation (New York) 17 1873.
Estelle: a novel. New York 1874.
Leah a woman of fashion. Serialised in Temple Bar Nov 1874–Oct 1875. 3 vols 1875, 2 vols Leipzig 1875 (Tauchnitz), 1 vol London 1876, New York [1879], 1884 (pbd as A woman of fashion), [1886], London 1899.
REVIEWS: Acad 8 1875; Athenaeum 2498 1875; Saturday Rev 40 1875; Nation (New York) 22 1876.
A blue-stocking. Serialised in Temple Bar Aug–Nov 1877. 1 vol 1877, Leipzig 1877 (Tauchnitz), New York 1877, London 1878, New York 1884 (pbd as Rival charms. With A Spanish story, in 1 vol).
REVIEWS: Athenaeum 2608 1877; Nation (New York) 26 1878.
Jet: her face or her fortune? Serialised in Temple Bar Feb–June 1878. 1 vol 1878, Leipzig 1878 (Tauchnitz), New York 1878, [1886], [1889].
REVIEWS: Athenaeum 2640 1878; Nation (New York) 27 1878.
Vivian the beauty. Serialised in Temple Bar Aug–Dec 1879. 1 vol 1879, Leipzig 1879 (Tauchnitz), New York 1880, [1886].
REVIEW: Athenaeum 2719 1879.
A ballroom repentance. Serialised in Temple Bar Jan–Aug 1882. 2 vols 1882, Leipzig 1882 (Tauchnitz), New York [1882]; 1 vol London 1883, New York [1886], London 1900.
REVIEW: Athenaeum 2857 1882.
At the eleventh hour. New York 1882.
A Girton girl. Serialised in Temple Bar Jan–Dec 1885. 3 vols 1885, 2 vols Leipzig 1885 (Tauchnitz), New York 1885, 1 vol London 1886.
REVIEWS: Athenaeum 3027 1885; Nation (New York) 42 1886; Spectator 59 1886.
A playwright's daughter. [1886], Leipzig 1886 (Tauchnitz, pbd with Bertie Griffiths), New York 1886, [1889].
REVIEW: Nation (New York) 43 1886.
Pearl-powder. Serialised in Temple Bar Jan–Aug 1890. 2 vols 1890, Leipzig 1890 (Tauchnitz), Philadelphia [1890].
REVIEW: Athenaeum 3272 1890.
The adventuress. Serialised in Temple Bar July–Oct 1894. 1 vol 1894.
REVIEW: Athenaeum 3490 1894.
A plaster saint. 1899.
REVIEW: Athenaeum 3754 1899.

Contributions to periodicals

Bertie Griffiths. Temple Bar Jan 1867.
Forgotten goddess: Mme de Girardin. Temple Bar Nov 1885.

§2

Boase, F. Modern English biography. Suppl 1912.
Sutherland, J. The Longman companion to Victorian fiction. Harlow 1988.

'George Eliot', Mary Ann Evans, later Cross 1819–80

The ms Scenes of clerical life *is in the Pierpont Morgan Lib, New York; the mss of all other major works are in the BL. The largest collection of letters is at Yale: other collections are to be found in the BM, the NLS, Princeton, the Berg Collection in the NYPL, the Huntington and Coventry Public Lib. George Eliot's diary for 1879 is in the Berg Collection; other journals and diaries are at Yale. Yale also has several notebooks, including the 'Quarry' for* Felix Holt; *The Quarry for* Romola *is at Princeton; Harvard has the main* Middlemarch *Quarry, though 2 other* Middlemarch *notebooks are in the Folger.*

Bibliographies etc

Sutton, C. W. George Eliot: a bibliography. Papers of Manchester Literary Club 1881.
Anderson, J. P. In O. Browning, Life of George Eliot, 1890.
Waldo, F. and G. A. Turkington. In M. Blind, George Eliot, Boston 1904.
Mudge, I. G. and M. E. Sears. A George Eliot dictionary. 1924.
Muir, P. H. A bibliography of the first editions of books by George Eliot. Bookman's Jnl suppl 1927–8.
Parrish, M. L. In her Victorian lady novelists: first editions in the library at Dormy House, Pine Valley New Jersey. 1933.
Barry, J. D. The literary reputation of George Eliot's fiction. BB 22 1959.
Harvey, W. J. In Victorian fiction, ed L. Stevenson, Cambridge MA 1964.
Fulmer, C. M. George Eliot: a reference guide. Boston 1977.
Knoepflmacher, U. C. In Victorian fiction: a second guide to research, ed G. Ford, New York 1978.
Levine, G. An annotated critical bibliography of George Eliot. Brighton 1988.

Collections

Novels: illustrated edition. 6 vols 1867–[78].
Wise, witty and tender sayings. Ed A. Main, Edinburgh 1872.
The George Eliot birthday book. Ed A. Main, Edinburgh 1878.
Works: cabinet edition. 24 vols 1878–[85].
Works: fireside edition. 12 vols New York 1885.

Works: 8 vols Chicago 1886.
Works: edition de luxe. 12 vols Boston 1886–7.
Complete poetical works. New York 1888.
Complete poems. Ed M. Browne, Boston 1889.
Works: Rosehill edition. 24 vols Boston 1893–5.
Works: standard edition. 21 vols Edinburgh 1895.
Works. 24 vols New York 1895.
Works: Foleshill edition. 12 vols Boston 1900, Toronto 1902.
Works: Nuneaton edition. 20 vols Boston 1900.
Works: library edition. 10 vols 1901.
Works: Riverside edition. 22 vols Boston and New York 1907.
Works: large paper edition. 25 vols Boston and New York 1908.
Works: illustrated copyright edition. 21 vols 1908–11.
Works: Clarendon edition, in progress, Oxford 1980– .
Collected poems. Ed L. Jenkins 1989.

§1

Scenes of clerical life. 2 vols Edinburgh 1858, London 1859, 1860, 1863 (with Silas Marner), 1868 etc, New York 1858, Leipzig 1859; ed A. Mattheson, Oxford 1909 (WC); ed W. W. Fowler and E. Limouzin 1916; ed M. Macmillan 1924; ed D. Lodge 1973 (Pen); ed T. A. Noble, Oxford 1985 (in Clarendon edn); tr Fr 1884, Ger 1885. First pbd in Blackwood's Mag: The sad fortunes of the Rev Amos Barton, Jan–Feb 1857; Mr Gilfil's love story, Mar–June 1857; Janet's repentance, July–Nov 1857.

REVIEWS: [Lucas, S.] The Times 2 Jan 1858; Literary Gazette 23 Jan 1858; Atlantic Monthly May 1858; Saturday Rev 29 May 1858; Nat Rev Oct 1858; Edinburgh Rev 110, July 1859.

Adam Bede. 3 vols Edinburgh 1859 (7 edns), Edinburgh and London 1862 (10th edn), New York 1859, 2 vols Leipzig 1859; ed L. J. Wylie, New York 1915; ed S. W. Patterson, New York 1923; ed G. S. Haight, New York 1949; ed G. Bullett 1953; ed M. H. Goldberg, New York 1956; ed S. Gill 1980 (Pen); tr Ger 1860, Fr 1861, Du 1870, Hungarian 1888.

REVIEWS: [Jewsbury, G.] Athenaeum 26 Feb 1859; Literary Gazette 26 Feb 1859; Saturday Rev 26 Feb 1859; [Collins, W. L.] Blackwood's Mag Apr 1859; [Dallas, E. S.] The Times 12 Apr 1859; [Chapman, J.] Westminster Rev Apr 1859; North Br Rev May 1859; [Mozley, A.] Bentley's Quart Rev July 1859; Edinburgh Rev 110, July 1859; Atlantic Monthly Oct 1859; Dublin Rev Nov 1859.

The lifted veil. Blackwood's Mag July 1859; rptd with Silas Marner in Works 1878, *above*; ed B. Gray 1985.

The mill on the Floss. 3 vols Edinburgh 1860, 2 vols 1860, 1 vol 1861 (corrected), 1862 (5th edn), New York 1860, Boston 1860; ed I. Ausherman, New York 1913; ed R. O. Morris London 1913; ed J. M. Dorey, Boston 1914; ed H. T. Eaton, Boston 1928; ed M. E. Clark, Chicago 1929; ed M. Herzberg, Boston 1929; ed G. Bullett 1953; ed M. H. Goldberg, New York 1956; ed G. S. Haight, Boston 1961; ed G. S. Haight, Oxford 1980 (in Clarendon edn); tr Ger 1861, Fr 1863, Du 1870.

REVIEWS: [Jewsbury, G.] Athenaeum 7 Apr 1860; Saturday Rev 14 Apr 1860; [Collins, W. L.] Blackwood's Mag May 1860; Tait's Edinburgh Mag May 1860; [Dallas, E. S.] The Times 19 May 1860; Atlantic Monthly June 1860; [Hutton, R. H.] Nat Rev 11, July 1860 (with review of Scenes of clerical life and Adam Bede); Westminster Rev July 1860; North Br Rev 33, Aug 1860; [Robertson, J. C.] Quart Rev 108, Oct 1860 (with review of Scenes of clerical life and Adam Bede); Dublin Univ Mag 57, Feb 1861.

Silas Marner: the weaver of Raveloe. Edinburgh 1861 (7 edns), London 1864 (with Scenes of clerical life), 1868 etc; ed B. Carmen, Boston 1895; ed R. Herrick, New York 1895; ed E. L. Gulick 1899; ed R. Garnett 1905; ed J. R. Colby, New York 1906; ed F. T. Baker, New York 1911; ed E. Harrington, New York 1930; ed K. M. Lobb 1958; ed Q. D. Leavis 1967 (Pen); tr Ger 1861, Fr 1862, Hungarian 1885.

REVIEWS: [Jewsbury, G.] Athenaeum 6 Apr 1861; Literary Gazette 6 Apr 1861; London Rev 6 Apr 1861; Saturday Rev 13 Apr 1861; [Dallas, E. S.] The Times 29 Apr 1861; Englishwoman's Domestic Mag May 1861; Ludlow, J. M. Elsie Venner and Silas Marner, Macmillan's Mag Aug 1861; Dublin Univ Mag 59, Apr 1862; [Smith, A.] North Br Rev 38, Feb 1863.

Romola. 3 vols 1863, 1865 (illus), 2 vols 1880 etc, 1 vol New York 1863, 2 vols Leipzig 1863; ed G. Biagi 2 vols 1907; ed C. B. Wheeler 1916; ed V. Meynell, Oxford 1929 (WC); ed A. Brown, Oxford 1993 (in Clarendon edn); tr Ger 1864, Du 1864, Fr 1887. First pbd, illustr Leighton, Cornhill Mag July 1862–Aug 1863.

REVIEWS: Athenaeum 11 July 1863; [Hutton, R. H.] Spectator 18 July 1863; Saturday Rev 25 July 1863; London Rev 1 Aug 1863; Br Quart Rev 38, Oct 1863; Westminster Rev 80, Oct 1863.

Brother Jacob. Cornhill Mag July 1864; rptd with Silas Marner in Works, 1878, *above*; ed B. Gray 1989; tr Ital 1880.

Felix Holt the radical. 3 vols Edinburgh 1866, 2 vols Edinburgh 1866, Leipzig 1867; ed V. Meynell, Oxford 1913 (WC); ed F. C. Thomson, Oxford 1980 (in Clarendon edn); tr Ger 1867, Du 1867, Hungarian 1874.

REVIEWS: [Morley, J.] Saturday Rev 16 June 1866; Athenaeum 23 June 1866; [Hutton, R. H.] Spectator 23 June 1866; [Dallas, E. S.] The Times 26 June 1866; London Rev 30 June 1866; [Collins, W.] Blackwood's Mag July 1866; Chambers's Jnl 11 Aug 1866; [James, H.] Nation (New York) 16 Aug 1866; Contemporary Rev Sep 1866; [Venables, G. S.] Edinburgh Rev Oct 1866; London Quart Rev Oct 1866; [Sedgwick, A. G.?] North Amer Rev Oct 1866.

Address to working men, by Felix Holt. Blackwood's Mag Jan 1868.

The Spanish gypsy: a poem. Edinburgh and London 1868 (3 edns), 1875 (5th edn), Boston 1868.

REVIEWS: [Hamly, E. B.] Blackwood's Mag June 1868; London Rev 6 June 1868; [Morley, J.] Macmillan's Mag July 1868; St James's Mag July 1868; Nation (New York) 2 July 1868; Saturday Rev 4 July 1868; [Pollock, J.] St Paul's Mag Aug 1868; [Bayne, P.] Br Quart Rev Oct 1868; [Milnes, R. M.] Edinburgh Rev Oct 1868; [Skelton, J.] Fraser's Mag Oct 1868; [Forman, H. B.] London Quart Rev Oct 1868; [James, H.] North Amer Rev Oct 1868.

Agatha. 1869 (priv ptd). First pbd in Atlantic Monthly 1869. 2nd edn a forgery. *See* J. Carter and H. G. Pollard, An enquiry into the nature of certain nineteenth-century pamphlets, 1934.

Brother and sister: sonnets by Marian Lewes. 1869 (priv ptd). A forgery. *See* Agatha, *above*.

How Lisa loved the King. Boston 1869, 1883. First pbd in Blackwood's Mag May 1869.

Armgart. Macmillan's Mag, Atlantic Monthly, July 1871.

Middlemarch: a study of provincial life. 4 vols Edinburgh 1872, London 1873, 1 vol 1874 (corrected), 2 vols Berlin 1872, New York 1872; ed W. F. Neff, New York 1926; ed G. Bullett 1930; ed R. M. Hewit, Oxford 1947 (WC); ed G. S. Haight, Boston 1956; ed Q. Anderson, 1963; ed F. Kermode 1964; ed W. J. Harvey 1965 (Pen); ed D. Carroll, Oxford 1986 (in Clarendon edn); tr Ger 1872–3, Du 1873, Hungarian 1874–5, Fr 1890. First pbd in 8 bks, Dec 1871–Dec 1872.

REVIEWS: Athenaeum 2 Dec 1871, 3 Feb, 30 Mar, 1 June, 27 July, 7 Dec 1872; Examiner 2 Dec 1871, 3 Feb, 30 Mar, 8 June, 27 July, 5 Oct, 7 Dec 1872; [Hutton, R. H.] Spectator 16 Dec 1871, 3 Feb, 30 Mar, 1 June, 5 Oct, 7 Dec 1872; [Collins, W. L.] Blackwood's Mag Dec 1872; Saturday Rev 7, 21 Dec 1872; [Houghton, Lord]. Edinburgh Rev 137, Jan 1873; [Simcox, E.] Acad 1 Jan 1873; [Colvin, S.] Fortnightly Rev 19 Jan 1873; [James, H.] Galaxy Mar 1873, rptd in his House of fiction, ed L. Edel 1957; Atlantic Monthly Apr 1873; [Hutton, R. H.] Br Quart Rev Apr 1873; [Forman, H. B.] London Quart Rev Apr 1873; [Parry, T. S.?] North Amer Rev 116, Apr 1873; [Laing, R.] Quart Rev 134, Apr 1873; [Smith, G. B.] St Paul's Mag May 1873; [McCarthy, J.] The story of two worlds, Catholic World Sep 1873.

The legend of Jubal, and other poems. Edinburgh 1874, Boston

1874, Toronto 1874; tr Du 1888. The legend of Jubal first pbd Macmillan's Mag May 1870.

REVIEWS: Simcox, G. A. Academy 16 May 1874; [Minto, W.] Examiner 16 May 1874; Saturday Rev 13 June 1874; [James, H.] North Amer Rev Oct 1874.

Daniel Deronda. 4 vols Edinburgh and London 1876, 1877, 1 vol 1877, New York 1876; ed F. R. Leavis, New York 1961; ed E. L. Jones 2 vols 1964 (EL); ed G. Handley, Oxford 1984 (in Clarendon edn); tr Ger 1876, Swed 1878, Ital 1882–3, Hebrew 1893. First pbd in 8 bks Jan–Sep 1876.

REVIEWS: Athenaeum 29 Jan, 4 Mar, 1, 29 Apr, 3 June, 1, 29 July, 2 Sep 1876; Examiner 29 Jan, 4 Mar, 1 Apr, 3 June, 5 Aug, 2 Sep 1876; [James, H.] Nation (New York) 24 Feb 1876; [Hutton, R. H.] Spectator 8 Apr, 10 June, 29 July 1876; Saturday Rev 16, 23 Sep 1876; Br Quart Rev Oct 1876; Edinburgh Rev 144, Oct 1876; [Dicey, A. V.?] Nation (New York) 12, 19 Oct 1876; Colvin, S. Fortnightly Rev Nov 1876; [James, H.] Daniel Deronda: a conversation, Atlantic Monthly Dec 1876, rptd in F. R. Leavis, The great tradition 1948; [Whipple, E. P.] North Amer Rev Jan 1877; Romance of modern scepticism: Daniel Deronda, Church Quart Rev Oct 1877; Kaufmann, D. George Eliot and Judaism: an attempt to appreciate Daniel Deronda, tr from the Ger by J. W. Ferrier, 1877.

A college breakfast party. Macmillan's Mag July 1878.

Impressions of Theophrastus Such. Edinburgh 1879, New York 1879, Leipzig 1879; ed N. Henry 1994; tr Ger 1880 (in part).

REVIEWS: Examiner 7 June 1879; Nation (New York) 19 June 1879; Saintsbury, G. Acad 28 June 1879; Br Quart Rev July 1879; [Allen, G.] Fortnightly Rev July 1879; Fraser's Mag July 1879; [Mallock, W. H.] Edinburgh Rev Oct 1879; [Eggleston, E.] North Amer Rev Nov 1879.

Essays and leaves from a note-book. Ed C. L. Lewes, Edinburgh 1884, New York 1884, Leipzig 1884.

REVIEWS: [Jacobs, J.] Athenaeum 23 Feb 1884; Saturday Rev 8 Mar 1884; [Beeching, H. C.] Acad 15 Mar 1884.

Early essays. 1919 (priv ptd). Not rptd from mss, as the preface claims, but from cuttings of George Eliot's contributions to the Coventry Herald exhibited in 1919.

Essays. Ed T. Pinney 1963.

Selected essays, poems and other writings. Ed A. S. Byatt and N. Warren 1990 (Pen).

Selected critical writings. Ed R. Ashton, Oxford 1992 (WC).

Letters, journals and notebooks

George Eliot's life as related in her letters and journals, arranged and edited by her husband J. W. Cross. 3 vols Edinburgh 1885.

Letters from George Eliot to Elma Stuart 1872–80. Ed R. Stuart 1909.

The letters of George Eliot, selected by R. B. Johnson. 1926.

George Eliot's family life and letters. Ed A. Paterson 1928.

Quarry for Middlemarch. Ed A. Kitchel, Berkeley CA 1950.

The George Eliot letters. Ed G. S. Haight 9 vols New Haven CT 1954–78. First complete edn.

Some George Eliot notebooks: an edition of the Carl H. Pforzheimer Library's George Eliot holograph notebooks. Ed W. Baker, Salzburg 1976.

Middlemarch notebooks: a transcription. Ed J. C. Pratt and V. A. Neufeldt, Berkeley CA 1979.

George Eliot's blotter: a commonplace book. Ed D. Waley 1980.

A writer's notebook 1854–1879 and uncollected writings. Ed J. Wiesenfarth, Charlottesville VA 1981.

New George Eliot letters at the Huntington. Ed R. Ashton. HLQ 54 1991.

The journals of George Eliot. Ed M. Harris and J. Johnston, Cambridge 1999.

Translations

The life of Jesus critically examined, by David Friedrich Strauss, translated from the fourth German edition. 3 vols 1846, 1 vol 1892; ed P. C. Hodgson 1973. Begun by Rufa Brabant and completed anon by Eliot.

The essence of Christianity, by Ludwig Feuerbach, translated from the second German edition by Marian Evans. 1854, New York 1857, London 1957.

Ethics, by Benedict de Spinoza, translated by George Eliot. Ed T. Deegan, Salzburg 1981.

§2

Morley, J. George Eliot's novels. Macmillan's Mag Aug 1866.

[Lancaster, H. H.] George Eliot's novels. North Br Rev Sep 1866.

James, H. The novels of George Eliot. Atlantic Monthly Oct 1866.

[Bayne, P.] George Eliot. Br Quart Rev 45, Jan 1867.

[Rands, W. B.] George Eliot as a poet. Contemporary Rev July 1868.

McCarthy, J. George Eliot and George Lewes. Galaxy 7, June 1869.

Hutton, R. H. In his Essays theological and literary, 2 vols 1871.

Smith, G. B. George Eliot. St Paul's Mag May 1873.

Carpenter, J. E. Religious influences in current literature: George Eliot. Unitarian Rev 3, Apr 1875.

[Marzials, F. T.] George Eliot and Comtism. London Quart Rev Jan 1877.

Dowden, E. In his Studies in literature 1789–1877, 1878.

Brown, J. C. The ethics of George Eliot's works. Edinburgh 1879.

[Shand, A. I.] Contemporary literature: novelists. Blackwood's Mag Mar 1879.

Axon, W. E. A. George Eliot's use of dialect. Eng Dialect Soc Misc 1880.

[Stephen, L.] George Eliot. Cornhill Mag Feb 1881.

Paul, C. K. George Eliot. Harper's New Monthly Mag May 1881.

Simcox, E. George Eliot. Nineteenth Cent May 1881.

Call, W. M. W. George Eliot: her life and writings. Westminster Rev July 1881.

Sully, J. George Eliot's art. Mind 6, July 1881.

[Bayne, P.] Shakespeare and George Eliot. Blackwood's Mag Apr 1883.

Blind, M. George Eliot. 1883, Boston 1904 (rev and enlarged).

Cooke, G. W. George Eliot: a critical study of her life, writings and philosophy. 1883.

Myers, F. W. H. George Eliot. In his Essays modern, 1883.

Cleveland, R. E. George Eliot's poetry, and other studies. 1885.

Druskowitz, H. In her Drei englische Dichterinnen, Berlin 1885.

George Eliot. Br Quart Rev Apr 1885.

George Eliot's life. London Quart Rev 64, July 1885.

James, H. The life of George Eliot. Atlantic Monthly May 1885.

Montégut, É. In his Écrivains modernes de l'Angleterre ser 1, Paris 1885.

Morley, J. The life of George Eliot. Macmillan's Mag Apr 1885.

[Oliphant, M.] The life and letters of George Eliot. Edinburgh Rev 161, Apr 1885.

Wolzogen, E. von. George Eliot: eine biographisch-kritische Studie. Leipzig 1885.

Yonge, C. M. George Eliot and her critics. Monthly Packet May 1885.

Harrison, F. The life of George Eliot. In his Choice of books and other literary pieces, 1886. Rptd from Fortnightly Rev.

Conrad, H. George Eliot: ihr Leben und Schaffen dargestellt nach ihren Briefen und Tagebüchern. Berlin 1887.

Browning, O. Life of George Eliot. 1890.

Jacobs, J. In his George Eliot, Matthew Arnold, Browning, Newman: essays and reviews from the Athenaeum, 1891.

Negri, G. George Eliot: la sua vita e i suoi romanzi. 2 vols Milan 1891.

Whiting, M. B. George Eliot as a character artist. Westminster Rev Oct 1892.

Bender, H. George Eliot: ein Lebensbild. Hamburg 1893.

Westermarck, H. George Eliot och den engelska naturalistika romanen. Helsingfors 1894.

Harrison, F. In his Studies in early Victorian literature, 1895.

Lilly, W. S. In his Four English humourists of the nineteenth century, 1895.
Saintsbury, G. In his Corrected impressions, 1895.
Linton, E. L. George Eliot. 1897.
Newdigate-Newdegate, A. E. The Cheverels of Cheverel Manor. 1898.
Linton, E. L. In her My literary life, 1899.
Oliphant, J. In his Victorian novelists, 1899.
Brownell, W. C. In his Victorian prose masters, New York 1901.
Thomson, C. L. George Eliot. 1901.
Stephen, L. George Eliot. 1902 (EML).
Gould, G. M. Biographic clinics: the origin of the ill-health of De Quincey, Carlyle [et al]. 6 vols 1903–9. Vol 2 1904 is on George Eliot.
Johnson, M. L. George Eliot and George Combe. Westminster Rev 156, Nov 1906.
Olcott, C. S. George Eliot: scenes and people in her novels. New York 1910.
Deakin, M. H. The early life of George Eliot. Manchester 1913.
Block, L. J. The poetry of George Eliot. Sewanee Rev 26, Jan 1918.
Clifford, Mrs W. K. George Eliot: some personal recollections. Bookman (London) Oct 1927.
Beaty, J. Middlemarch from notebook to novel: a study of George Eliot's creative method. Urbana IL 1960.
Haight, G. S. George Eliot: a biography. Oxford 1968, rev 1969.
Sutherland, J. A. Lytton, John Blackwood and the serialisation of Middlemarch. Bibliotheck 7 1974–5.
Anderson, R. F. Negotiating for The mill on the Floss. Publishing History 2 1977.
Anderson, R. F. 'Things wisely ordered': John Blackwood, George Eliot and the publication of Romola. Publishing History 11 1982.
Ashton, R. George Eliot: a life. 1996.
There are two jnls devoted to George Eliot scholarship: The George Eliot Review, *pbd annually by the George Eliot Fellowship, and* George Eliot–George Henry Lewes Studies, *published annually at De Kalb IL.*
[RA]

Sarah Ellis, née Stickney Mrs William Ellis

1799–1872

Bibliographies

Allibone, S. A. A critical dictionary of English literature, and British and American authors, living and deceased. London and Philadelphia 1859. Contains a detailed account of Ellis's major publications before 1859, together with quotations from some review notices.
Smith, J. Descriptive catalogue of friends' books. 1867, suppl 1893.

Collections and selections

The select works of Mrs Ellis. New York 1843–4. (The women of England, The daughters of England, The wives of England and The mothers of England, also The poetry of life.)
The prose works of Mrs Ellis. New York 1844. (The poetry of life, Pictures of private life, A voice from the vintage, The women of England, The daughters of England, The wives of England and The mothers of England.)
The brother and sister and other tales. New York 1844. Rptd from Fisher's Juvenile Scrap-book. Contains The brother and sister, True greatness, The youthful instructor, The citizen king, Love me, love my dog, The value of a name, Winter's evening, The inquisitive boy, The dame's school, Affection, Ancient castles, Little Arthur, or, the unwilling philosopher, Harvest night.
The select works of Mrs Ellis. New York 1845. (The poetry of life, Pictures of private life, 1st and 2nd ser., A voice from the vintage.)
The family monitor and domestic guide. New York 1844, 1848, 1849, 1850. (The women of England, The daughters of England, The wives of England, and The mothers of England.)
Guide to social happiness. New York 1847, 1850. (The poetry of life, Pictures of private life and A voice from the vintage).
The English woman's family library, containing The women of England (vol 1); The daughters of England (vol 2); Family secrets, or hints to those who would make home happy (vols 3–5); The wives of England (vol 6). nd.

§1

The lament of the peasant's daughter. In Kaleidoscope Dec 1824.
The negro slave. 1832.
Contrasts, a series of twenty drawings designed by S. Stickney. 1832.
Pictures of private life. 3 sers 1833–7, 1844 (6th edn), New York 1844, 1845, London 1850 (7th edn). Rptd in The prose works of Mrs Ellis, New York 1844; ser 1 and 2 rptd in Select works of Mrs Ellis, New York 1845; rptd in Guide to social happiness, New York 1847, 1850. Pretension, from ser 3 of Pictures of private life, ptd separately Philadelphia 1837. Ser 1 prefaced by an Apology for fiction.
The poetry of life. 2 vols 1835, Philadelphia 1843, New York 1845; rptd in The prose works of Mrs Ellis, New York 1844; rptd in Guide to social happiness, New York 1847.
REVIEW: Athenaeum 29 Feb 1840.
Home, or the iron rule: a domestic story. 3 vols 1836, New York 1836, London 1843.
The women of England, their social duties and domestic habits. 1839, New York [1839], London [1839] (2nd edn), Philadelphia 1839 (in 2 vols), London [1843], New York 1843, London [1844], New York 1845, London [1846], 5th edn nd, 6th edn nd, 9th and 10th edns 1850, 12th–21st edns nd. Also illus edn nd. Rptd in The family monitor, New York 1844, 1848, 1849, 1850; rptd in The prose works of Mrs Ellis, New York 1844; in The English woman's family library nd.
The sons of the soil: a poem. [1840], 1860.
Summer and winter in the Pyrenees. 1841 (2nd edn), New York 1842.
Family secrets, or hints to those who would make home happy. 3 vols 1841–2, New York 1841, London 1842, Philadelphia 1842, London [1846], [1853]; rptd in The English woman's family library nd.
Dangers of dining out, or hints to those who would make home happy. New York 1842, London 1843, 1845, 1857, 1873. (Extracts from vol 1 of Family secrets.) Somerville Hall, or hints to those who would make home happy. New York 1842, 1845, 1846. (Extract from vol 1 of Family secrets.) First impressions, or hints to those who would make home happy. New York 1842, London 1849, 1855, 1873. (Extracts from vol 2 of Family secrets.)
The daughters of England, their position in society, character and responsibilities. [1842], New York 1842, 1843, 1844, London [1845, 1846], New York 1848, London [1853]; rptd in The family monitor, New York 1844, 1848, 1849, 1850; rptd in The prose works of Mrs Ellis, New York 1844; in The English woman's family library nd.
A voice from the vintage, on the force of example. 1843, New York 1843, 1844, (with additional ch) London 1857 (3rd edn), 1860.
REVIEW Athenaeum 24 Apr 1858.
Mrs Ellis's housekeeping made easy. New York 1843.
The wives of England, their relative duties, domestic influence, and social obligations. 1843, New York 1843, 1844, London [1846], New York 1848, London [1853]; rptd in The family monitor, New York 1844, 1848, 1849, 1850; rptd in The prose works of Mrs Ellis, New York 1844; in The English woman's family library nd.
The mothers of England, their influence and responsibility. 1843, New York 1844, 1845, London [1853]; rptd in The family monitor, New York 1844, 1848, 1849, 1850; rptd in The prose works of Mrs Ellis, New York 1844.
The Irish girl and other poems. New York 1844. Rptd from Fisher's Juvenile Scrap-book, and from The Aurora Borealis[?].

The brother and sister and other tales. New York 1844, 1848. Rptd from Fisher's Juvenile Scrap-book; *see* Collections and selections, *above*.
The minister's family, or hints to those who would make home happy. New York 1844. (Extract from vol 2 of Family secrets.)
Progressive education for young ladies. (School prospectus) [1845?].
Rawdon house, or hints on the formation of character at school. [1845?]
Look to the end, or the Bennets abroad. 2 vols 1845, New York 1845, 1857.
REVIEW: Athenaeum 15 Feb 1845.
The young ladies' reader, or extracts from modern authors. 1845.
REVIEW: Athenaeum 10 May 1845.
Temper and temperament, or varieties of character. 2 vols 1846, New York 1846.
The island queen: a poem. 1846.
REVIEW: Athenaeum 17 Jan 1846.
Prevention better than cure, or the moral wants of the world we live in. 1847, New York 1847.
Fireside tales, for the young. 4 vols [1848–9]. Rptd from Fisher's Juvenile Scrap-book.
Social distinction, or Hearts and homes. 3 vols [1848–9] (sometimes titled Hearts and homes), 4 vols 1850, New York 1857.
Self-deception, or the history of a human heart. Serialised in the Morning Call 1850–2, New York 1851, 2 vols London 1860.
Fireside stories. New York 1850. (Selection from vols 1 and 2 of Family secrets.)
The value of health. 1854.
My brother, or the man of many friends. 1855.
The education of character, with hints on moral training. 1856.
REVIEW: Athenaeum 31 Jan 1857.
The mother's mistake, a tale. [1856.] (Prefaced by unattributed but probably authorial Sketch of the literary career of Mrs Ellis.)
Friends at their own fireside, or pictures of the private life of the people called Quakers. 2 vols 1858.
REVIEW: Athenaeum 19 June 1858.
The mothers of great men. 1859, 1861, 1874, 1883.
REVIEW: Athenaeum 4 June 1859.
The widow Green and her three nieces. 1859, [1862], [1865].
REVIEW: Athenaeum 21 Jan 1859.
Chapters on wives. 1860, New York 1860.
REVIEW: Athenaeum 14 July 1860.
Janet, one of many: a story in verse. 1862.
REVIEW: Athenaeum 4 Oct 1862.
The brewer's family. 1863, New York 1867; rptd as The brewer's son, London 1881.
Madagascar: its social and religious progress. London and Edinburgh 1863.
William and Mary, or the fatal blow. 1865.
Share and share alike, or the grand principle. 1865.
The beautiful in nature and in art. 1866.
REVIEW: Athenaeum 7 July 1866.
Northern roses, a Yorkshire story. 3 vols 1868.
The education of the heart; woman's best work. London and Aylesbury 1869.
REVIEW: Athenaeum 11 June 1870.

Contributions to periodicals

Mrs Ellis edited Fisher's Juvenile Scrap-book *1840–8*, Fisher's Drawing-room Scrap-book *1843–5, and the* Morning Call, *a table-book of literature and art, vols 1–4, 1850–2. To these periodicals she also contributed the major part of the contents, both prose and verse, during the period of her editorship.*

From The home life and letters, *below, it is clear that Mrs Ellis also contributed a considerable amount to various (unnamed) journals, writing particularly on educational, missionary and temperance subjects.*

The two nights; The widow's child; The brook and the bird; The Irish girl. In The Aurora Borealis, a literary annual, 1833.
All is vanity; City missions. In The Christian Keepsake and Missionary Annual, 1835.

§2

Ellis, J. E. Life of William Ellis, missionary to the South Seas and to Madagascar. 1873. By Mrs Ellis's step-son.
Bayley, Mrs. The life and letters of Mrs Sewell. 1889. (Mrs Sewell and Mrs Ellis were sisters-in-law.)
The home life and letters of Mrs Ellis, compiled by her nieces. 1893. The main source for information about Mrs Ellis.
Hay, A. G. Afterglow memories. 1905. Memoir of Rawdon House School.

For a series of jokes at Mrs Ellis's expense, see Punch, *vol 5 1843, p. 258; vol 6 1844, p. 128; vol 7 1844, p. 199; vol 8 1845, p. 78; vol 10 1846, pp. 115, 137. Douglas Jerrold's series* Mrs Caudle's curtain lectures, *in* Punch *vols 8–9, 1845–6, mentions Mrs Ellis, and his following series* Capsicum House, *in* Punch *vols 12–13, 1847, was clearly modelled on her school, Rawdon House, at Hoddesdon in Hertfordshire.* [HT-M]

Lady Georgiana Charlotte Fullerton 1812–85

§1

Ellen Middleton: a tale. 3 vols 1844.
Grantley Manor: a tale. 3 vols 1847.
The old Highlander and other verses. 1849 (priv ptd).
Lady-Bird: a tale. 3 vols 1852.
The life of St Frances of Rome. 1855.
The Countess de Bonneval: her life and letters. 2 vols 1858. Originally pbd in Fr.
Apostleship in humble life: a sketch of the life of Elisabeth Twiddy. [1860] (Our Lady's Little Books).
Our Lady's Little Books. 4 nos 1860–1. Ed Lady Georgiana Fullerton.
Laurentia: a tale of Japan. 1861.
Rose Leblanc. 1862.
Too strange not to be true: a tale. 3 vols 1864.
Constance Sherwood: an autobiography of the sixteenth century. 3 vols 1865.
A stormy life: a novel. 3 vols 1867.
The helpers of the Holy Souls. 1868.
Mrs Gerald's niece. 3 vols 1869.
The gold-digger and other verses. Edinburgh 1872.
Dramas from the lives of the saints: Germaine Cousin, the shepherdess of Pibrac. [1872.]
Life of Luisa de Carvajal. 1873.
Seven stories. 1873.
A sketch of the life of the late Father H. Young. 1874.
The life of Mère Marie de la Providence. 1875.
The notary's daughter; [and] The house of Penarvan. 2 vols 1878. Adapted from the Fr of L. d'Aulney and J. Sandeau.
The miraculous medal: life and visions of Catherine Labouré. 1880.
A will and a way. 3 vols 1881.
The fire of London: a play. [1882.]
The life of Elisabeth Lady Falkland 1585–1639. 1883.

§2

Craven, A. The life of Lady Georgiana Fullerton, translated from the French by H. J. Coleridge. 1888.
Yonge, C. M. In A. Sergeant et al, Women novelists of Queen Victoria's reign, 1897.
Taylor, F. M. The inner life of Lady Georgiana Fullerton, with notes of retreat and diary. [1899.]
Lockhead, M. Two minor Victorian novelists: Lady Georgiana Fullerton and Mrs Norton. Quart Rev 293 1955.
Barker, J. Lady Georgiana Fullerton: a Bournemouth benefactor. Bournemouth 1991.

Elizabeth Cleghorn Gaskell, née Stevenson

1810–65

Gaskell's surviving mss are mainly located in the United Kingdom. The chief holdings are in Leeds in the Brotherton Lib of the Univ; in Manchester in the John Rylands Univ Lib of Manchester (combining the holdings of the Univ and the former John Rylands Lib) and in the Central Public Lib. Holders in the USA include the Houghton Lib, Harvard Univ, and the Berg Collection, NYPL. For listings of holdings, see J. A. V. Chapple and A. Pollard, Letters of Mrs Gaskell, Manchester 1966 (appendix B); J. G. Sharps, Mrs Gaskell's observation and invention, Fontwell Sussex 1970 (bibliography (b)); IELM 4 1800–1900 (A–G), 1982; and D. Sutton (ed), Location register of English literary manuscripts and letters: 18th and 19th centuries, 1995.

Bibliographies of primary material

Green, J. A. A bibliographical guide to the Gaskell collection in Moss Side Library. Manchester 1911. Includes vol contents of collections; the material is now in the Manchester Central Lib.

Sadleir, M. In his Excursions in Victorian bibliography, 1922. 'Editiones principes' only.

Northup, C. S. In G. D. Sanders, Elizabeth Gaskell, New Haven CT 1929. Includes vol contents of collections and reprints after 1865.

Quinn, M. Elizabeth Gaskell and nineteenth-century literature: manuscripts from the John Rylands University Library, Manchester: a history and a guide to the research publications microfilm collection. Manchester 1989.

Collections

The works. 17 vols Leipzig 1849–67. Eng lang edns pbd by Tauchnitz for circulation on the Continent only. Includes Gaskell's edn of Cummins's Mabel Vaughan (*see* §1 *below*); The life of Charlotte Brontë 2 vols 1857 (replaced by rev and corrected edn 2 vols 1859); Ruth 2 vols; Sylvia's lovers 2 vols; and Wives and daughters 3 vols. For dates and contents of 3 vols of collected pieces, *see* §1, *below*, and Northup, *above*.

Novels and tales. 7 vols 1872–3 (illustr G. du Maurier); variously reissued. Details of vols and contents in Green, *above*.

Novels and tales. 8 vols 1892–4 pocket edn. Details of vols and contents in Green, *above*.

The works: Knutsford edn. Ed A. W. Ward 8 vols 1906. Biographical and critical introds; omits The life of Charlotte Brontë and a few shorter items. For details of vols and contents, *see* §1, *below*, and Green and Northup, *above*.

The novels and tales: WC edn. Ed C. K. Shorter 11 vols 1906–19. Biographical and critical introds; includes The life of Charlotte Brontë; vol 10 includes a few misattributed items (*see* Attributed or spurious works *below*). For details of vols and contents *see* §1, *below*, and Northup, *above*.

Selections

For lifetime gatherings of stories and other items, see §1, below. Only selections edited or with a significant introd are given below.

Cousin Phillis and other tales. Introd by T. Seccombe 1912 (EL); introd by M. Lane 1970 (EL). Contains Cousin Phillis, My lady Ludlow, Half a life-time ago, Right at last, The sexton's hero.

The sexton's hero and other tales. Introd by A. S. Whitfield, Tokyo 1932. Contains The sexton's hero, The squire's story, The Manchester marriage, The half-brothers.

The cage at Cranford and other tales. Introd by P. Beard 1937. Contains The cage at Cranford, The grey woman, The Manchester marriage, Half a life-time ago, Cousin Phillis.

Cousin Phillis and other tales. Ed A. Easson 1981 (WCp). Contains Lizzie Leigh, The old nurse's story, Half a life-time ago, Lois the witch, The crooked branch, Curious, if true, Cousin Phillis.

Elizabeth Gaskell: four short stories. Introd by A. Walters 1983. Contains The well of Pen Morfa, The Manchester marriage, Libbie Marsh's three eras, Lizzie Leigh.

My lady Ludlow and other stories. Introd by E. Wright 1989 (WCp). Contains My lady Ludlow, An accursed race, The doom of the Griffiths, The poor Clare, The half-brothers, Mr Harrison's confessions, Round the sofa (preface and links).

A dark night's work and other stories. Ed S. Lewis 1992 (WCp). Contains A dark night's work, Libbie Marsh's three eras, Six weeks at Heppenheim, Cumberland sheep-shearers, The grey woman.

Curious, if true: strange tales by Mrs Gaskell. Introd by J. Uglow 1995. Contains The old nurse's story, The poor Clare, Lois the witch, The grey woman, Curious, if true.

The moorland cottage and other stories. Ed S. Lewis 1995 (WCp). Contains The moorland cottage, The sexton's hero, Christmas storms and sunshine, The well of Pen Morfa, The heart of John Middleton, Morton Hall, My French master, The Manchester marriage, Crowley Castle.

§1

See also collected edns and selections. Edns pbd during Gaskell's lifetime and subsequent edns with significant critical or textual material are given below. In addition, her work in Dickens's Household Words *and* All the Year Round *appeared in reprints of those jnls in America and Germany.*

Libbie Marsh's three eras. 3 weekly pts Howitt's Jnl 1, 5–19 June 1847 (as Life in Manchester: Libbie Marsh's three eras. By Cotton Mather Mills, Esq [pseudonym]); rptd Liverpool [1850], [1850]; in Lizzie Leigh and other tales 1855, Leipzig 1855; in The grey woman and other tales 1865, Philadelphia 1865; Knutsford edn vol 1 1906; WC edn vol 8 1913; introd by J. A. V. Chapple, Lancashire and Cheshire Antiquarian Soc reprints 3 1968; tr Fr 1854.

The sexton's hero. Howitt's Jnl 2, 4 Sep 1847; rptd Manchester 1850 (with Christmas storms and sunshine); 1851 (in Christian Socialist 1, Mar); 1855 (with Christmas storms and sunshine); in Lizzie Leigh and other tales 1855, Leipzig 1855; 1859 (in The Parish Mag 1); in Cousin Phillis and other tales 1865; Knutsford edn vol 1 1906; WC edn vol 7 1911; tr Fr 1867.

Christmas storms and sunshine. Howitt's Jnl 3, 1 Jan 1848; rptd Manchester 1850 (with The sexton's hero); 1851 (in Christian Socialist 1, Mar–Apr); 1855 (with Sexton's hero); in Lizzie Leigh and other tales 1855, Leipzig 1855; in The grey woman and other tales 1865, Philadelphia 1865; Knutsford edn vol 2 1906; WC edn vol 8 1913; tr Fr 1864.

Mary Barton: a tale of Manchester life. 2 vols 1848 (anon), 1849, 1849, 1 vol New York 1849, Leipzig 1849, 2 vols London 1850, 1 vol 1854 (includes 2 lectures by W. Gaskell on the Lancashire dialect), New York 1855, London 1861, New York 1864, London 1865, Knutsford edn vol 1 1906; WC edn vol 1 1906; introd by T. Seccombe 1911 (EL); introd by L. Cooper 1947; introd by M. Brightfield, New York 1958; introd by K. Dick, London 1966; introd by M. Lane 1967 (EL); ed S. Gill 1970 (Pen); ed E. Wright 1987 (WCp); ed A. Easson Halifax 1993; ed A. Easson, introd J. Uglow 1994 (EL); ed M. Daly 1996 (Pen); ed A. Shelston 1996 (EL pbk); tr Du 1849, Fr 1849 (abridged), 1856, 1956, Ger 1849–50?, Rus 1861 (in part), 1936, 1963, Hungarian 1875, Sp 1879, 1922, Serbo-Croat 1955, Polish 1956, Cz 1960, Romanian 1960, Ital 1981.

REVIEWS: [Chorley, H. F.] Athenaeum 21 Oct 1848; Britannia 21 Oct 1848; Literary Gazette 28 Oct 1848; Standard of Freedom 28 Oct 1848; NMM Nov 1848; Atlas 4 Nov 1848; [Forster, J.] Examiner 4 Nov 1848; John Bull 4 Nov 1848; Inquirer 11 Nov 1848; Critic 15 Nov 1848; Morning Post 24 Nov 1848; Economist 25 Nov 1848; Sun 30 Nov 1848; Eclectic Rev 25 Jan 1849; British Quart Rev 1 Feb 1849; [Tayler, J. J.] Prospective Rev 1 Feb 1849; Manchester Guardian 28 Feb 1849; Bradford, J. Christian Examiner (Boston) Mar 1849; [Greg, W. R.] Edinburgh Rev Apr 1849 (rptd in his Mistaken aims and attainable ideals of the artisan class, 1876); [Kingsley, C.] Fraser's Mag Apr 1849; W. E. [Ellis, W. and M.] Westminster and Foreign Quart Apr 1849.

The last generation in England [expanded as Cranford]. Sartain's Union Mag 5, July 1849; rptd Cranford (ed E. P. Watson) 1972 and 1980; Cranford (ed P. Keating) 1976; Cranford (ed Watson, introd Mitchell) 1998.

Hand and heart. 5 pts Sunday School Penny Mag 2, July–Aug, Oct–Dec 1849; rptd 1855 (with Bessy's troubles at home); in Lizzie Leigh and other tales 1855, Leipzig 1855; in The grey woman and other tales 1865, Philadelphia 1865; Knutsford edn vol 3 1906; WC edn vol 8 1913.

Martha Preston [rev as Half a life-time ago]. Sartain's Union Mag 6, Feb 1850.

Lizzie Leigh. 3 weekly pts Household Words 1, 30 Mar–13 Apr 1850; rptd New York 1850 (in Harper's New Monthly Mag, as by Dickens), 1850, 1851 (in Irving Offering, as by Dickens), 1854 (in Pearl Fishing), Philadelphia nd (1855?); in Lizzie Leigh and other tales 1855, Leipzig 1855, London 1865; Knutsford edn vol 2 1906; WC edn vol 8 1913; tr Ital 1868, Fr 1882.

The well of Pen Morfa. 2 weekly pts Household Words 2, 16–23 Nov 1850; rptd in Lizzie Leigh and other tales 1855, Leipzig 1855, London 1865; Knutsford edn vol 2 1906; WC edn vol 8 1913.

The moorland cottage. 1850 (illustr Birket Foster), Boston 1851, New York 1851, 1859; introd by W. Nicoll London 1898 (with Cranford); Knutsford edn vol 2 1906; WC edn vol 3 1907; tr Portugese 1962 (2nd edn).

REVIEWS: Athenaeum 21 Dec 1850; Britannia 21 Dec 1850; Examiner 21 Dec 1850; Leader 21 Dec 1850; Standard of Freedom 21 Dec 1850; Morning Post 23 Dec 1850; Guardian 24 Dec 1850; [?Whewell, W.] Fraser's Mag 43, Jan 1851; Ladies' Companion 1 Feb 1851; Harper's New Monthly Mag (New York) Mar 1851; Godey's Lady's Book (Philadelphia) June 1851.

The heart of John Middleton. Household Words 2, 28 Dec 1850; rptd in Lizzie Leigh and other tales 1855, Leipzig 1855, London 1865; Knutsford edn vol 2 1906; WC edn vol 8 1913.

The sexton's hero and Christmas storms and sunshine. Manchester 1850, 1855.

Mr Harrison's confessions. Ladies' Companion 3, Feb–Apr 1851; rptd in Lizzie Leigh and other tales 1855, Leipzig 1855; in Cousin Phillis and other tales 1865; Knutsford edn vol 5 1906; WC edn vol 7 1911; ed G. Handley 1995 (EL pbk) with Cranford; tr Fr 1866.

Cranford. 9 irregular weekly pts Household Words 4–7, 13 Dec 1851–21 May 1853; rptd 1853, 1853, New York 1853, London 1855 (Cheap edn), New York 1855, London 1864 (illus), nd (1864?), New York 1864, Leipzig 1867; introd by A. T. Ritchie London 1891 (illustr H. Thomson); introd by B. Herford 1898; introd by W. Nicoll 1898 (with The moorland cottage); 1898 (illustr H. M. Brock); introd by E. V. Lucas 1899; 1902 (illustr T. H. Robinson); 1905 (illustr C. E. Brock); introd by J. M. Dent 1904 and 1906 (EL); Knutsford edn vol 2 1906; introd by R. B. Johnson 1907 (rptd in his Women novelists, 1918); WC edn vol 3 1907; ed G. A. Payne 1914 (with introd by Lucas 1899); ed N. Hepple 1921; introd by A. Thérive 1940; introd by E. Jenkins 1947 (with Cousin Phillis); introd by A. Thirkell 1951; introd by D. Ascoli 1952; introd by F. Swinnerton 1954 (EL); introd W. Buckler, Boston 1967; ed P. Keating 1976 (Pen) with Cousin Phillis, The last generation in England and The cage at Cranford; ed E. P. Watson 1972 and 1980 (WCp) with The last generation in England and The cage at Cranford; ed G. Handley 1995 (EL pbk) with Mr Harrison's confessions; ed E. P. Watson, introd by C. Mitchell 1998 (WCp) with The last generation in England and The cage at Cranford; tr Du 1854, 1947, Fr 1856, 1940, 1945, 1981, Ger [1857], 1950, 1959, 1982, 1983, Hungarian 1884, 1959, Sp 1931, 1943, 1958, Portuguese 1943, Ital 1950, 1951, Jap 1953, 1986, Chinese 1957, Swed 1960, Finnish 1963, Serbo-Croat 1965, Norwegian 1967, Polish 1970, Romanian 1970, Rus 1973, Bulgarian 1986.

REVIEWS: [Chorley, H. F.] Athenaeum 25 June 1853; John Bull 25 June 1853; Westminster Rev July 1853; [Lewes, G. H.] Leader 2 July 1853; Examiner 23 July 1853; Inquirer 30 July 1853; Tait's Edinburgh Mag Aug 1853; Nonconformist 3 Aug 1853; New York Daily Times 15 Aug 1853; Harper's New Monthly Mag (New York) Sep 1853; Graham's Mag (Philadelphia) Oct 1853; Peterson's Mag (Philadelphia) Oct 1853; GM Nov 1853; NMM Dec 1855.

Bessy's troubles at home. Sunday School Penny Mag n.s. 2, Jan–Apr 1852; rptd 1855 (with Hand and heart); in Lizzie Leigh and other tales 1855, Leipzig 1855; in The grey woman and other tales 1865, Philadelphia 1865; Knutsford edn vol 3 1906; WC edn vol 8 1913.

The old nurse's story. In A round of stories by the Christmas fire, Household Words Extra Christmas Number 6, 18 Dec 1852; rptd in Lizzie Leigh and other tales 1855, Leipzig 1855, London 1865; Knutsford edn vol 2 1906; WC edn vol 8 1913.

Ruth. 3 vols 1853, 2 vols Leipzig 1853, 1 vol Boston 1853, London 1855 (Cheap edn), 2 vols 1857, 1 vol 1861; Knutsford edn vol 3 1906, WC edn vol 2 1906; introd by M. Lane 1967 (EL); ed A. Shelston 1985 (WCp); ed A. Easson 1997 (Pen); tr Fr 1854, 1856, 1866.

REVIEWS: Morning Advertiser 12 Jan 1853; [Chorley, H. F.] Athenaeum 15 Jan 1853; Sharpe's London Mag 15 Jan 1853; Spectator 15 Jan 1853; [Forster, J.] Examiner 22 Jan 1853; John Bull 22 Jan 1853; [Lewes, G. H.] Leader 22 Jan 1853; Literary Gazette 22 Jan 1853; Observer 23 Jan 1853; Nonconformist 26 Jan 1853; Britannia 29 Jan 1853; Inquirer 29 Jan 1853; Morning Post 29 Jan 1853; GM Feb 1853; NMM Feb 1853; Putnam's Monthly (New York) Feb 1853; Critic 1 Feb 1853; Guardian 2 Feb 1853; Manchester Examiner and Times 2 Feb 1853; Bentley's Misc 3 Feb 1853; Atlas 5 Feb 1853; Sun 12 Feb 1853; Sunday Times 20 Feb 1853; Eliza Cook's Jnl 26 Feb 1853; New York Daily Times 26 Feb 1853; Ladies' Companion Mar 1853; Literary World (New York) 26 Mar 1853; English Rev Apr 1853; Peterson's Mag (Philadelphia) Apr 1853; [Beard, J.] Tait's Edinburgh Mag Apr 1853; [Lewes, G. H.] Westminster Rev Apr 1853; Graham's Mag (Philadelphia) May 1853; [Ludlow, J. M. F.] North Br Rev (Edinburgh) May 1853; Prospective Rev May 1853; [Curtis, G. W.] Putnam's Monthly (New York) May 1853; Montégut, É. Revue des Deux Mondes (Paris) 1 June 1853 (rptd in his Écrivains modernes de l'Angleterre vol 2 1889); Christian Observer July 1853; GM July 1853; New Quart Rev 2 1853; Hedouin, A. Athenaeum Français (Paris) 31 May 1856.

Morton Hall. 2 weekly pts Household Words 8, 19–26 Nov 1853; rptd in Lizzie Leigh and other tales 1855, Leipzig 1855, London 1865; Knutsford edn vol 2 1906; WC edn vol 8 1913.

My French master. 2 weekly pts Household Words 8, 17–24 Dec 1853; rptd in Lizzie Leigh and other tales 1855, Leipzig 1855, London 1865; Knutsford edn vol 2 1906; WC edn vol 8 1913; tr Fr 1866.

The squire's story. In Another round of stories by the Christmas fire, Household Words Extra Christmas Number 8, 19 Dec 1853; rptd in Lizzie Leigh and other tales 1855, Leipzig 1855, London 1865; Knutsford edn vol 2 1906; WC edn vol 8 1913.

North and south. 22 weekly pts Household Words 10, 2 Sep 1854–27 Jan 1855; rptd 2 vols 1855 (rev), 2 vols 1855 (rev), 1 vol Leipzig 1855, New York 1855, London 1859, New York 1860, 1864, London 1865; Knutsford edn vol 4 1906; WC edn vol 4 1908; introd by E. A. Chadwick 1914 (EL); introd by E. Bowen 1951; ed D. Collin, introd by M. Dodsworth 1970 (Pen); ed A. Easson 1973 and 1982 (WCp); ed J. Uglow 1993 (EL pbk); ed P. Ingham 1995 (Pen); ed A. Easson, introd by S. Shuttleworth 1998 (WCp); tr Du 1856, Fr 1859, 1865, Sp 1930, Romanian 1979.

REVIEWS: Spectator 31 Mar 1855; [Chorley, H. F.] Athenaeum 7 Apr 1855; [Lewes, G. H.] Leader 14 Apr 1855; Manchester Weekly Advertiser 14 Apr 1855; Examiner 21 Apr 1855; [Oliphant, M.] Blackwood's Edinburgh Mag May 1855; Graham's Mag (Philadelphia) June 1855; Guardian 22 Aug 1855; Nat Rev Oct 1855; Montégut, É. Revue des Deux Mondes (Paris) 1 Oct 1855 (rptd in his Écrivains modernes de l'Angleterre vol 2 1889).

Hand and heart and Bessy's troubles at home. 1855.

Lizzie Leigh and other tales. 1855 (Cheap edn), Leipzig 1855.

Contains Lizzie Leigh, The well of Pen Morfa, The heart of John Middleton, Disappearances, The old nurse's story, Traits and stories of the Huguenots, Morton Hall, My French master, The squire's story, Company manners, Mr Harrison's confessions, Libbie Marsh's three eras, The sexton's hero, Christmas storms and sunshine, Hand and heart, Bessy's troubles at home. (For 1865 collection with title but not contents identical, *see* separate entry, *below*.)

REVIEWS: Critic 1 Oct 1855; Athenaeum 20 Oct 1855.

Half a life-time ago [rev from Martha Preston]. 3 weekly pts Household Words 12, 6–20 Oct 1855; rptd in Round the sofa 1859, 1859, 1861; Knutsford edn vol 5 1906; WC edn vol 9 1913.

The poor Clare. 3 weekly pts Household Words 14, 13–27 Dec 1856; rptd in Round the sofa 1859, 1859, 1861; Knutsford edn vol 5 1906; WC edn vol 9 1913.

The life of Charlotte Brontë, by E. C. Gaskell [1st work with Gaskell named on title page]. 2 vols 1857, Leipzig 1857, London 1857 (rev), 1857 (rev and corrected), New York 1857, 1 vol London 1858, 2 vols New York 1858, Leipzig 1859 (rev and corrected), 1 vol London 1859, 1860 (Cheap edn), 2 vols New York 1861, 1862, 1 vol London 1862; ed C. K. Shorter 1900 (Haworth edn); introd by B. Willett 1905; introd by M. Sinclair 1908 (EL); WC edn vol 11 1919; introd by M. Lane 1947; introd by A. Huxley Geneva 1970; introd by W. Gérin 1971 (EL); ed W. Gérin 1971 (Folio Soc); ed A. Shelston 1975 (Pen); introd by J. Uglow 1992 (EL pbk); ed A. Easson 1996 (WCp); ed G. Handley, introd by J. Uglow 1997 (EL pbk); ed E. Jay 1997 (Pen); tr Ger 1859, Fr 1877, 1945, 1972, Sp 1945, Jap 1980, 1982.

REVIEWS: [Chorley, H. F.] Athenaeum 4 Apr 1857; Daily News 4 Apr 1857; Saturday Rev 4 Apr 1857; Spectator 4 Apr 1857; Examiner 11 Apr 1857; [Hunt, T.] Leader 11 and 18 Apr 1857; Observer 12 Apr 1857; Critic 15 Apr 1857; Economist 18 Apr 1857; Englishwoman's Rev 18 Apr 1857; Weekly Dispatch 19 Apr 1857; The Times 23 Apr 1857; Inquirer 25 Apr 1857; Manchester Weekly Examiner and Times 25 Apr and 2 May 1857; [Skelton, J.] Fraser's Mag May 1857; Ladies' Companion May 1857; Tait's Edinburgh Mag May 1857; Boston Evening Transcript 1 May 1857; Sun 1 May 1857; Guardian 6 May 1857; Manchester Guardian 7 May 1857; Evening Post (New York) 15 May 1857; New York Daily Times 15 May 1857; New York Herald 20 May 1857; English Churchman 28 May, 4 and 11 June 1857; Eclectic Rev June 1857; GM June 1857; Nat Mag June 1857; New Quart Rev 6 1857; Putnam's Monthly (New York) June and Sep 1857; [Dallas, E. S.] Blackwood's Edinburgh Mag July 1857; Christian Observer July 1857; Christian Remembrancer July 1857; [Stephen, J. F.] Edinburgh Rev July 1857; Graham's Illus Mag (Philadelphia) July 1857; [Roscoe, W. C.] Nat Rev July 1857; Russell's Mag (Charleston) July 1857; [Martineau, H.] Westminster Rev July 1857; [Lawrance, H.] British Quart Rev 1 July 1857; Independent (New York) 12 July 1857; Amer Church Monthly (New York) Aug 1857; Emerson's United States Mag (New York) Sep 1857; Godey's Lady's Book (Philadelphia) Sep 1857; [Sweat, M. J.] North Amer Rev (Boston) Oct 1857; Shepheard, H. A vindication of the clergy daughters' school, and of the Rev W. Carus Wilson, from the remarks of The life of Charlotte Brontë, 1857.

The doom of the Griffiths. Harper's New Monthly Mag 16, Jan 1858; rptd in Round the sofa 1859, 1859, 1861; in Lois the witch and other tales, Leipzig 1861; Knutsford edn vol 5 1906; WC edn vol 9 1913; tr Danish 1871.

An incident at Niagara Falls [from Mabel Vaughan: *see* Edition etc, *below*]. Harper's New Monthly Mag 17, June 1858.

My lady Ludlow. 14 weekly pts Household Words 18, 19 June–14 Aug, 28 Aug–25 Sep 1858; rptd New York 1858; in Round the sofa 1859, 1859, 1861; Knutsford edn vol 5 1906; WC edn vol 9 1913; tr Fr 1947.

The sin of a father [rptd as Right at last]. Household Words 18, 27 Nov 1858; rptd in Right at last and other tales 1860, New York 1860; in Cousin Phillis and other tales, Leipzig 1867; Knutsford edn vol 7 1906; WC edn vol 10 1915.

The Manchester marriage. In A house to let, Household Words Extra Christmas Number 19, 7 Dec 1858; rptd in Right at last and other tales 1860, New York 1860; in Cousin Phillis and other tales, Leipzig 1867; Knutsford edn vol 5 1906; WC edn vol 10 1915; tr Fr 1867.

Round the sofa. 2 vols 1859, 1859, 1 vol 1861 (as My lady Ludlow and other tales included in Round the sofa); Knutsford edn vol 5 1906; WC edn vol 9 1913. Contains Round the sofa (frame and links), My lady Ludlow, An accursed race, The doom of the Griffiths, Half a life-time ago, The poor Clare, The half-brothers; tr Fr 1860.

REVIEWS: Spectator 19 Mar 1859; Saturday Rev 25 June 1859.

The half-brothers. In Round the sofa 1859; first pbn. Rptd in Round the sofa 1859, 1861; in Lois the witch and other tales, Leipzig 1861; Knutsford edn vol 5 1906; WC edn vol 9 1913; tr Ger 1979.

Lois the witch. 3 weekly pts All the Year Round 1, 8–22 Oct 1859; rptd in Right at last and other tales 1860, New York 1860; New York 1861 (as The maiden martyr: a tale of New England witchcraft); in Lois the witch and other tales, Leipzig 1861; Knutsford edn vol 7 1906; WC edn vol 10 1915; tr Ger 1915.

The ghost in the garden room [rptd as The crooked branch]. In The haunted house, All the Year Round Extra Christmas Number 2, 13 Dec 1859; rptd in Right at last and other tales 1860, New York 1860; in Lois the witch and other tales, Leipzig 1861; Knutsford edn vol 7 1906; WC edn vol 10 1915; tr Danish 1871, Ger 1974.

Right at last and other tales. 1860, New York 1860. Contains Right at last (originally The sin of a father), The Manchester marriage, Lois the witch, The crooked branch (originally The ghost in the garden room).

Curious, if true. Cornhill Mag 1, Feb 1860; rptd in The grey woman and other tales 1865, Philadelphia 1865; in Cousin Phillis and other tales, Leipzig 1867; Knutsford edn vol 7 1906; WC edn vol 8 1913.

The grey woman. 3 weekly pts All the Year Round 4, 5–19 Jan 1861; rptd in Lois the witch and other tales, Leipzig 1861; in The grey woman and other tales 1865, Philadelphia 1865; Knutsford edn vol 7 1906; WC edn vol 8 1913.

Lois the witch and other tales. Leipzig 1861. Contains Lois the witch, The grey woman, The doom of the Griffiths, The half-brothers, The crooked branch.

Six weeks at Heppenheim. Cornhill Mag 5, May 1862; rptd in The grey woman and other tales 1865, Philadelphia 1865; in Cousin Phillis and other tales, Leipzig 1867; Knutsford edn vol 7 1906; WC edn vol 8 1913; tr Fr 1868.

A dark night's work. 5 weekly pts All the Year Round 8–9, 24 Jan–21 Feb 1863; rptd 1863 (illustr G. du Maurier), New York 1863, Leipzig 1863, London 1864; Knutsford edn vol 7 1906; WC edn vol 10 1915; tr Du 1864, Ger 1865, 1894, Fr 1867, Hungarian 1875, Portuguese 1883.

REVIEWS: Reader 9 May 1863; Observer 10 May 1863; New York Times 26 May 1863; Athenaeum 30 May 1863; John Bull 30 May 1863; Westminster Rev July 1863; Guardian 29 July 1863.

Sylvia's lovers. 3 vols 1863, 1863, 1863 (rev), 1 vol 1863 (illustr G. du Maurier), 2 vols Leipzig 1863, 1 vol New York 1863; Knutsford edn vol 6 1906; WC edn vol 5 1909; introd by T. Seccombe 1910; introd by E. A. Chadwick 1911 (EL); introd by A. Pollard 1964 (EL); ed A. Sanders 1982 (WCp); ed S. Foster 1996 (Pen); ed N. Henry 1997 (ELpbk); tr Ger 1863, Du 1864, Fr 1865, Finnish 1958; Japanese 1997.

REVIEWS: Morning Advertiser 26 Feb 1863; Sun 27 Feb 1863; [Jewsbury, G.] Athenaeum 28 Feb 1863; Reader 28 Feb 1863; Observer 1 Mar 1863; John Bull 7 Mar 1863; Weekly Dispatch 15 Mar 1863; New York Times 23 Mar 1863; Morning Post 26 Mar 1863; Examiner 28 Mar and 11 Apr 1863; Englishwoman's Domestic Mag Apr 1863; Westminster Rev Apr 1863; Daily News 3 Apr 1863; Saturday Rev 4 Apr 1863; Morning Herald 6 Apr 1863; Manchester Daily Examiner and Times 14 Apr 1863; Nat Mag May

1863; Peterson's Mag (Philadelphia) May 1863; Nonconformist 6 May 1863; Godey's Lady's Book and Mag (Philadelphia) June 1863; Harper's New Monthly Mag (New York) June 1863; Guardian 29 July 1863.

Cousin Phillis. 4 monthly pts Cornhill Mag 8–9, Nov 1863–Feb 1864; rptd New York 1864; in Cousin Phillis and other tales 1865, Leipzig 1867 (title but not contents identical with previous; *see* separate entries, *below*); Knutsford edn vol 7 1906; WC edn vol 7 1911; introd by E. Jenkins 1947 (with Cranford); ed P. Keating 1976 (Pen) with Cranford; tr Fr 1866, 1867, 1981, Hungarian 1867, Ger 1912, Sp 1920, 1946, Ital 1929, Swed 1960.

REVIEW: Godey's Lady's Book and Mag (Philadelphia) Aug 1864.

The cage at Cranford. All the Year Round 10, 28 Nov 1863; rptd WC edn vol 3 1907; rptd Cranford (ed Watson) 1972 and 1980; Cranford (ed Keating) 1976; Cranford (ed Watson, introd Mitchell) 1998.

How the first floor went to Crowley Castle [rptd as Crowley Castle]. In Mrs Lirriper's lodgings, All the Year Round Extra Christmas Number 10, 3 Dec 1863; rptd Knutsford edn vol 7 1906; WC edn vol 10 1915.

Wives and daughters: an every-day story. 18 monthly pts (illustr G. du Maurier) Cornhill Mag 10–13, Aug 1864–Jan 1866 and Littell's Living Age (New York) 27 May 1865–3 Feb 1866 (from advance sheets); rptd 2 vols 1866 (illustr G. du Maurier), 1 vol New York 1866, 3 vols Leipzig 1866; Knutsford edn vol 8 1906; WC edn vol 6 1910; introd by T. Seccombe 1912; introd by R. Lehmann 1948; introd by M. Lane 1966 (EL); ed F. Smith, introd by L. Lerner 1969 (Pen); ed A. Easson 1987 (WCp); ed P. Morris 1996 (Pen); tr Ger 1867, Du 1868, Fr 1868, 1930.

REVIEWS: Nation (New York) 14 Dec 1865; [James, H.] Nation (New York) 24 Feb 1866 (rptd in H. James, Notes and reviews, 1921); Round Table (New York) 24 Feb 1866; New York Times 26 Feb 1866; Manchester Examiner and Times 27 Feb 1866; Harper's New Monthly Mag (New York) Mar 1866; [Chorley, H. F.] Athenaeum 3 Mar 1866; Spectator 17 Mar 1866; Saturday Rev 24 Mar 1866; Manchester Guardian 1 May 1866.

Cousin Phillis and other tales. 1865 (illustr G. du Maurier). Contains Cousin Phillis, Company manners, Mr Harrison's confessions, The sexton's hero.

The grey woman and other tales. 1865 (illustr G. du Maurier), Philadelphia 1865. Contains The grey woman, Curious, if true, Six weeks at Heppenheim, Libbie Marsh's three eras, Christmas storms and sunshine, Hand and heart, Bessy's troubles at home, Disappearances.

Lizzie Leigh and other tales. 1865 (illustr G. du Maurier). Contains Lizzie Leigh, The well of Pen Morfa, The heart of John Middleton, The old nurse's story, Traits and stories of the Huguenots, Morton Hall, My French master, The squire's story.

Cousin Phillis and other tales. Leipzig 1867. Contains Cousin Phillis, Six weeks at Heppenheim, Curious, if true, Right at last, The Manchester marriage.

On visiting the grave of my stillborn little girl [sonnet 1836]. Knutsford edn vol 1 1906; rptd in Private voices: the diaries of Elizabeth Gaskell and Sophia Holland, ed J. A. V Chapple and A. Wilson, Keele 1996.

Two fragments of ghost stories. Knutsford edn vol 7 1906; WC edn vol 10 1915.

Contributions to periodicals and collaborative works

Sketches among the poor – No 1 [poem with W. Gaskell; no other issued]. Blackwood's Edinburgh Mag 41, Jan 1837; rptd 1897 (in Temperance Star); Knutsford edn vol 1 1906; WC edn vol 10 1915; Mary Barton (ed S. Gill) 1970; Mary Barton (ed E. Wright) 1987; Mary Barton (ed A. Easson) Halifax 1993.

Clopton Hall. In W. Howitt, Visits to remarkable places, 1840; rptd Knutsford edn vol 1 1906; WC edn vol 7 1911.

Cheshire customs. In W. Howitt, The rural life of England, 1840 (2nd edn) pp. 589–90. From Gaskell's letter to M. Howitt, pbd in Chapple and Pollard, Letters, *below*, pp. 28–33; identified by C. A. Martin, Elizabeth Gaskell's contributions to the works of William Howitt, Nineteenth-Cent Fiction 40 1985–6. *See also* W. Howitt p. 461 for Manchester Christmas trees, identified by J. A. V. Chapple and J. G. Sharps.

Disappearances. Household Words 3, 7 June 1851; rptd in Lizzie Leigh and other tales 1855, Leipzig 1855; in The grey woman and other tales 1865, Philadelphia 1865; Knutsford edn vol 2 1906; WC edn vol 8 1913. *See also* [W. H. Wills], A disappearance, Household Words 3, 21 June 1851 (rptd in Leipzig 1855 edn); [J. and W. Gaunt], A disappearance cleared up, Household Words 4, 21 Feb 1852; [H. Morley], Character-murder, Household Words 19, 8 Jan 1859, which follow up and challenge Gaskell's piece. *See also* S. Butler, Life of Samuel Butler vol 1, 1896.

Review of Anon, Spiritual alchemy. Athenaeum 13 Dec 1851.

Review of Longfellow, The golden legend. Athenaeum 13 Dec 1851.

The schah's English gardener. Household Words 5, 19 June 1852; rptd Knutsford edn vol 7 1906; WC edn vol 10 1915.

Cumberland sheep-shearers. Household Words 6, 22 Jan 1853; rptd Knutsford edn vol 3 1906; WC edn vol 10 1915.

Traits and stories of the Huguenots. Household Words 8, 10 Dec 1853; rptd in Lizzie Leigh and other tales 1855, Leipzig 1855, London 1865; Knutsford edn vol 2 1906; WC edn vol 8 1913.

Modern Greek songs. Household Words 9, 25 Feb 1854; rptd Knutsford edn vol 3 1906; WC edn vol 7 1911.

Company manners. Household Words 9, 20 May 1854; rptd in Lizzie Leigh and other tales 1855, Leipzig 1855; in Cousin Phillis and other tales 1865; Knutsford edn vol 3 1906; WC edn vol 7 1911.

An accursed race. Household Words 12, 25 Aug 1855; rptd in Round the sofa 1859, 1859, 1861; Knutsford edn vol 5 1906; WC edn vol 9 1913.

Shams. Fraser's Mag 67, Feb 1863.

An Italian institution. All the Year Round 9, 21 Mar 1863; rptd Knutsford edn vol 6 1906; WC edn vol 7 1911.

Robert Gould Shaw. Macmillan's Mag 9, Dec 1863; tr Ger 1864?

French life. 3 monthly pts Fraser's Mag 69, Apr–June 1864; rptd Knutsford edn vol 7 1906; WC edn vol 7 1911.

Review of Torrens, Lancashire lessons. The Reader 5, 25 Mar 1865. The Reader 6, 18 Nov 1866, states that Gaskell was an early contributor; other contributions not yet identified.

Published letters and diary

Letters and printed sources before Chapple and Pollard 1966 *(below) are not cited unless they contain letters not included there or other relevant material. For pbn details of letters before 1966, see* J. G. Sharps, Mrs Gaskell's observation and invention, 1970 (bibliography (b) iv) *and* Chapple and Pollard, appendix B.

[Winkworth, S.] Letters and memorials of Catherine Winkworth. Ed her sister 2 vols Clifton 1883–6 (priv ptd). Abridged as Memorials of two sisters, Susanna and Catherine Winkworth, ed M. J. Shaen, 1908.

[Otto, C.] Der verlag Bernhard Tauchnitz. Leipzig 1912.

[Huxley, L.] The house of Smith Elder. 1923 (priv ptd).

Diary 1835–8. Ed C. Shorter 1923 (priv ptd) as My diary: the early years of my daughter Marianne; ed J. A. V. Chapple and A. Wilson in Private voices: the diaries of Elizabeth Gaskell and Sophia Holland, Keele 1996.

Letters of Mrs Gaskell and C. E. Norton, 1855–1865. Ed J. Whitehill 1932.

The letters of Mrs Gaskell. Ed J. A. V. Chapple and A. Pollard, Manchester 1966.

Gill, S. A manuscript of Branwell Brontë, with letters of Mrs Gaskell. Brontë Soc Trans 12 1970.

McCready, H. W. Elizabeth Gaskell and the cotton famine in

Manchester: some unpublished letters. Trans of the Historic Soc of Lancashire and Cheshire 123 1971.
Chapple, J. A. V. and J. G. Sharps. Elizabeth Gaskell: a portrait in letters. Manchester 1980.
Benn, J. M. Some unpublished Gaskell letters. N & Q 225, Dec 1980.
Chapple, J. A. V. Elizabeth Gaskell: two unpublished letters to George Smith. Études Anglaises 33 1980.
Unsworth, A. Two versions of a Gaskell letter. N & Q 227, Aug 1982.
Collin, D. W. The composition and publication of Elizabeth Gaskell's Cranford. BJRL 69 1986–7 (appendix II).
Dingley, R. J. Mrs Gaskell: an unpublished letter. N & Q 233, Sep 1988.
Chapple, J. A. V. Before 'crutches and changed feelings': five early letters by Elizabeth Gaskell (née Stevenson). Gaskell Soc Jnl 4 1990.
Chapple, J. A. V. Unofficial lives: Elizabeth Gaskell and the Turner family in Charles Parish, The history of the Literary and Philosophical Society of Newcastle upon Tyne vol 2, 1896–1989. Newcastle upon Tyne 1990.
Unsworth, A. A new Gaskell letter. N & Q 235, Mar 1990.
Stonehouse, S. A letter from Mrs Gaskell. Brontë Soc Trans 20 1991.

Edition, introductions, prefaces

[Cummins, M.] Mabel Vaughan, by the author of the Lamplighter. Ed Mrs Gaskell 1857; rptd Leipzig 1857; WC edn vol 10 1915 (preface only); tr Fr 1858, Ger 1861. Gaskell provided preface plus some annotation and interpolated material.
Preface to C. Vecchi, Garibaldi at Caprera, 1862; rptd WC edn vol 10 1915.

Attributed or spurious works

Our Manchester correspondent: Emerson's lectures. Howitt's Jnl 2, 11 Dec 1847. Attribution in J. G. Sharps, Mrs Gaskell's observation and invention.
Letter of enquiry. Howitt's Jnl 2, 18 Dec 1847. Initialled C. M. M., perhaps for Gaskell's pseudonym of Cotton Mather Mills; attribution in Sharps, *above*.
The deserted mansion. Fraser's Mag 44, July 1851. This and the following 5 items attributed by A. Unsworth and A. Q. Morton, Mrs Gaskell anonymous: some unidentified items in Fraser's Magazine, Victorian Periodicals Rev 14 1981.
Uncle Peter. 2 monthly pts in Fraser's Mag 48, Oct–Nov 1853.
Sermons and sermonizers. Fraser's Mag 55, Jan 1857.
A visit to Eton. Fraser's Mag 56, Sep 1857.
A fear for the future that women will cease to be womanly. Fraser's Mag 59, Feb 1859.
Some passages from the history of the Chomley family. Fraser's Mag 72, Sep 1865.
Bran [poem]. Household Words 8, 22 Oct 1853; rptd WC edn vol 10 1915, trn by W. Gaskell; *see* A. Lohrli, Household Words: conducted by Charles Dickens, Toronto 1973.
Prose introduction to The scholar's story [poem]. In Another round of stories by the Christmas fire, Household Words Extra Christmas Number 8, 19 Dec 1853; rptd WC edn 10 1915. Attributed in J. A. Green, Bibliographical guide to the Gaskell collection in the Moss Side library, 1911; the poem is a trn by W. Gaskell; *see* Lohrli, *above*.
Two lectures on Lancashire dialect. By the author of Mary Barton. 1854. By W. Gaskell; rptd from Mary Barton 1854.
A few words about 'Jane Eyre'. Sharpe's London Mag n.s. 6, June 1855. Possibly by F. Smedley; includes extract from letter accepted by Chapple and Pollard, Letters, *above*; the Gaskell attribution discussed by Sharps, *above*.
A Christmas carol. Household Words 14, 27 Dec 1856; rptd WC edn vol 10 1915. Author unknown; misattributed by C. K. Shorter; *see* Lohrli, *above*.
The siege of the black cottage. Harper's New Monthly Mag 14, Feb 1857. By Wilkie Collins; misattributed in G. Durfee, Index to Harper's New Monthly Mag, 1885.
The half-brothers. Dublin Univ Mag 52, Nov 1858. Identical in title only with story in Round the sofa, 1859.
A column of gossip from Paris. 3 pts (the third as A letter of gossip from Paris) Pall Mall Gazette, 25 and 28 Mar, 25 Apr 1865. Attribution by Sharps, *above*.
A parson's holiday. 5 pts Pall Mall Gazette 11, 15, 17, 21 Aug, 5 Sep 1865. Attribution by Sharps, *above*.

§2

Secondary criticism: guides

Barry, J. D. In Victorian fiction: a guide to research, ed L. Stevenson, Cambridge MA 1964.
Selig, R. L. Elizabeth Gaskell: a reference guide. Boston 1977.
Welch, J. E. Elizabeth Gaskell: an annotated bibliography 1929–1975. New York 1977.
Barry, J. D. In Victorian fiction: a second guide to research, ed G. H. Ford, New York 1978.
Schor, H. M. Elizabeth Gaskell: a critical history and a critical revision. Dickens Stud Annual 19 1990.
Weyant, N. S. Elizabeth Gaskell: an annotated bibliography of English language sources 1976–1991. Metuchen NJ and London 1994.

Criticism to 1920

Jeaffreson, J. C. In his Novels and novelists from Elizabeth to Victoria vol 2, 1858.
Green, H. In his Knutsford: its traditions and history, 1859 (2nd edn).
[Greg, W. R.] False morality of lady novelists. Nat Rev 8, Jan 1859; rptd in his Literary and social judgments, 1868.
de Moüy, C. Romanciers anglais contemporains: mistress Gaskell. Revue Européenne 17, 1 Sep 1861.
[Anon.] Mrs Gaskell. Saturday Rev 18 Nov 1865.
[Anon.] Obituary: Mrs Gaskell. Inquirer 24, 18 Nov 1865.
[Chorley, H. F.] Obituary. Athenaeum 18 Nov 1865.
[Dicey, E.] Mrs Gaskell. Nation (New York) 1, 7 Dec 1865.
D. [Masson, D.] Mrs Gaskell. Macmillan's Mag 13, Dec 1865.
[Milnes, R. M. (Lord Houghton)] Occasional notes. Pall Mall Gazette 2, 14 Nov 1865.
[Greenwood, F.] (Editorial conclusion to) Wives and daughters. Cornhill Mag 13, Jan 1866.
[Anon.] Obituary memoirs: Mrs Gaskell. GM 4th ser 1, Feb 1866.
[Anon.] Mrs Gaskell. Englishwoman's Domestic Mag 3rd ser 2, Mar 1866.
Belloc, L. S. Elizabeth Gaskell et ses ouvrages. In Cousine Phillis . . ., tr E. D. Forgues, Paris 1867.
[Parr, H.] Mrs Gaskell. British Quart Rev 45, 1 Apr 1867.
G. B. S. [Smith, G. B.] Mrs Gaskell and her novels. Cornhill Mag 29, Feb 1874.
Minto, W. Mrs Gaskell. Fortnightly Rev n.s. 24, 1 Sep 1878.
Keegan, P. Q. Mrs Crowe's and Mrs Gaskell's novels. Victoria Mag 33, May 1879.
Morley, H. In his Of English literature in the reign of Victoria, Leipzig 1881; rptd as A first sketch of English literature, 1912.
[Oliphant, M.] The old saloon (no VI): the literature of the last fifty years. Blackwood's Edinburgh Mag 141, June 1887.
Oliphant, M. and F. R. In their Victorian age of English literature, 1892.
Lyall, E. In A. Sergeant et al, Women novelists of Queen Victoria's reign, 1897.
Cazamian, L. In his Le roman social en Angleterre (1830–1850), Paris 1903; tr M. Fido (The social novel in England 1830–1850) 1973.
Cross, W. L. In his The development of the English novel, 1905.
[Coleridge, M. E.] Mrs Gaskell. TLS 14 Sep 1906; rptd in her Gathered leaves, 1910.

Lewis, M. In his Victorian novelists, 1906.
Ritchie, A. T. Mrs Gaskell. Cornhill Mag n.s. 21, Dec 1906; rptd in her Blackstick papers, 1908.
Lewis, M. The centenary of Mrs Gaskell. Nineteenth Century and After 67, Sep 1910.
Ward, A. W. In memoriam: Elizabeth Cleghorn Gaskell. Cornhill Mag n.s. 29, Oct 1910; rptd in his Collected papers: historical, literary, travel and miscellaneous vol 4, 1920.
Ritchie, A. T. A discourse on modern sibyls. English Assoc pam no 24, Oxford 1913.
Ward, A. W. The political and social novel ... Mrs Gaskell. In The nineteenth century, CHEL 1917.

Biographies
A. W. W. [Ward, A. W.] In DNB. 1890.
Chadwick, E. H. Mrs Gaskell: haunts, homes and stories. 1910, 1913 (rev).
Haldane, E. S. Mrs Gaskell and her friends. 1930.
Hopkins, A. B. Elizabeth Gaskell: her life and work. 1952.
Gérin, W. Elizabeth Gaskell: a biography. Oxford 1976.
Uglow, J. Elizabeth Gaskell: a habit of stories. 1993.
In addition, see the following.
The George Eliot letters. Ed G. S. Haight 9 vols Oxford 1954–78.
The letters of Charles Dickens. Ed M. House, G. Storey and K. Tillotson 10 vols Oxford 1965– (in progress).
Elizabeth Gaskell: the critical heritage. Ed A. Easson 1991. [AE]

Margaret Gatty née Scott 1809–73

§1
The fairy godmothers and other tales. 1851.
Parables from nature. 5 ser 1855–71. Frequently rptd, especially the earlier ser, and tr Ger, Swed, Fr, Danish, Rus and Ital, 1856–80. Ser 1–2 rptd 1885 with memoir by J. H. Ewing.
'Worlds not realised'. 1856, 1869 (with Proverbs illustrated, *below*).
Proverbs illustrated. 1857, 1869 (with 'Worlds not realised', *above*).
The poor incumbent: a tale. 1858.
Legendary tales. 1858. Illustr Phiz.
Aunt Judy's tales. 1859.
The human face divine and other tales. 1860.
Aunt Judy's letters. 1862. Illus.
Red snow and other parables from nature. 1862.
British seaweeds, drawn from Professor Harvey's Phycologia Britannica. 1863, 2 vols 1872.
Aunt Sally's life. 1865.
Domestic pictures and tales. 1866.
Waifs and strays of natural history. 1871.
A book of emblems, with interpretations thereof. 1872.
The book of sundials. 1872.
Mrs Gatty also founded and contributed constantly to Aunt Judy's Mag for Children, *from May 1866.*

§2
Maxwell, C. Mrs Gatty and Mrs Ewing. 1949.

William Gilbert 1804–90

§1
On the present system of rating for the relief of the poor in the metropolis. [1857.]
Dives and Lazarus: the adventures of an obscure medical man in a low neighbourhood. 1858.
Margaret Meadows. 1859.
The weaver's family. [1860.]
Shirley Hall asylum: the memoirs of a monomaniac. 2 vols 1863.
De profundis: a tale of the social deposits. 2 vols 1864, 1 vol 1866.
Dr Austin's guests. 2 vols 1866.
The magic mirror: a round of tales for young and old. 1866.
The washerwoman's foundling. 1867.
The wizard of the mountain. 2 vols 1867.
The doctor of Beauweir: an autobiography. 2 vols 1868.
King George's middy. 1869.
Sir Thomas Branston. 3 vols 1869.
Lucrezia Borgia. 2 vols 1869.
The seven-leagued boots. [1869.]
The landlord of the Sun. 3 vols 1871.
Martha. 3 vols 1871.
Clara Levesque. 3 vols 1872.
Contrasts: dedicated to the ratepayers of London. 1873.
Facta non verba. 1874.
Disestablishment considered from a church point of view. 1875.
The city: an inquiry into the corporation, its liberty companies, and the administration of their charities and endowments. 1877.
Nothing but the truth. 1877.
James Duke, costermonger: another tale of the social deposits. 1879.
Mrs Dubosq's bible. [1879.]
Memoirs of a cynic. 3 vols 1880.
Modern wonders of the world, or the new Sinbad. 1881.
Legion, or the modern demoniac. 1882.

Contributions to periodicals
Gilbert contributed to Good Words; Good Words for the Young; St Paul's Mag; Temple Bar; Cornhill Mag; Contemporary Rev; Fortnightly Rev; Sunday Mag; Britannia; Belgravia; People's Mag.

§2
In DNB. [BM]

James Grant 1822–87

§1
The romance of war: or the Highlanders in Spain [France and Belgium]. 4 vols 1846–7.
Adventures of an aide-de-camp: or a campaign in Calabria. 3 vols 1848.
Memoirs and adventures of Sir William Kirkaldy of Grange. Edinburgh 1849.
The Scottish Cavalier: an historical romance. 3 vols 1850.
Memorials of the Castle of Edinburgh. 1850, Edinburgh 1862.
Bothwell: or the days of Mary Queen of Scots. 3 vols 1851.
Memoirs and adventures of Sir John Hepburn. 1851.
Jane Seton, or the King's Advocate: a Scottish historical romance. 2 vols 1853.
Philip Rollo: or the Scottish musketeers. 2 vols 1854.
Frank Hilton: or 'the Queen's Own'. 1855.
The Yellow Frigate: or the three sisters. 1855.
Harry Ogilvie, or the Black Dragoons: new edition. 1856.
The phantom regiment: or stories of 'ours'. [1856], [1964].
The Highlanders of Glen Ora. 1857, 1862 (as Laura Everingham: or the Highlanders of Glen Ora).
Memoirs of James Marquis of Montrose. 1858.
Arthur Blane: or the hundred cuirassiers. [1858.]
Hollywood Hall: a tale of 1715. 1859, 1861 (as Lucy Arden: or Hollywood Hall).
Legends of the Black Watch or Forty-Second Highlanders. 1859.
The Cavaliers of fortune: or British heroes in foreign wars. 1859, 1873 (as British heroes in foreign wars).
Mary of Lorraine: an historical romance. 1860.
Oliver Ellis: or the Fusiliers. 1861.
Jack Manly: his adventures by sea and land. 1861.
Dick Rodney: or the adventures of an Eton boy. '1863' [1862.]
The Captain of the Guard. 1862.
Letty Hyde's lovers: or the Household Brigade. 1863.
Second to none: a military romance. 3 vols 1864.

The adventures of Rob Roy. 1864.
The King's Own Borderers: a military romance. 3 vols 1865.
The Constable of France and other military historiettes. 1866.
The white cockade: or faith and fortitude. 3 vols 1867.
First love and last love: a tale of the Indian Mutiny. 3 vols 1868.
The girl he married: a novel. 3 vols 1869.
The secret dispatch: or the adventures of Captain Balgonie. 1869.
Lady Wedderburn's wish: a tale of the Crimean War. 3 vols 1870.
Only an ensign: a tale of the retreat from Cabul. 3 vols 1871.
Under the Red Dragon: a novel. 3 vols 1872.
British battles on land and sea. 3 vols [1873–5], 4 vols [1884–8], [1896–7].
Fairer than a fairy: a novel. 3 vols 1874.
Shall I win her? the story of a wanderer. 3 vols 1874.
The Queen's cadet and other tales. 1874.
One of the six hundred: a novel. 3 vols 1875.
Did she love him? a novel. 3 vols 1876.
Morley Ashton: a story of the sea. 3 vols 1876.
Cassell's illustrated history of India. 2 vols [1876–7].
Six years ago: a novel. 2 vols 1877.
Vere of Ours, the Eighth or King's: a novel. 3 vols 1878.
The Ross-shire Buffs. [1878.]
The Lord Hermitage: a novel. 3 vols 1878.
The Royal Regiment and other novelettes. [1879.]
The Duke of Albany's Own Highlanders: a novel. 3 vols 1880.
Cassell's old and new Edinburgh. 3 vols [1880–3].
Lady Glendonwyn: a novel. 3 vols 1881.
Derval Hampton: a story of the sea. 2 vols 1881.
The Cameronians: a novel. 3 vols 1881.
Violet Jermyn: or tender and true. 1882.
The 'Scots Brigade' and other tales. 1882.
Jack Chaloner: or the Fighting Forty-Third. [1883.]
The dead tryst, and A haunted life. [1883.]
Miss Cheyne of Essilmont. 3 vols 1883.
The Master of Aberfeldie. 3 vols 1884.
Colville of the Guards. 3 vols 1885.
The Royal Highlanders, or the Black Watch in Egypt. [1885.]
Cassell's history of the war in the Soudan. 6 vols [1885–6].
Dulcie Carlyon: a novel. 3 vols 1886.
The tartans of the clans of Scotland. 1886, Ware 1992 (as The clans and tartans of Scotland).
Playing with fire: a story of the Soudan war. 1887.
Love's labour won: a novel. 3 vols 1888, 1889.
The Scottish soldiers of fortune: their adventures and achievements in the armies of Europe. 1889, 1890.

§2

Ellis, S. M. In his Mainly Victorian, [1925].

Gerald Griffin 1803–40

Collections

Works. 8 vols 1842–3. Vol 1 Life; vol 2 The collegians; vol 3 Tales of the Munster festivals; vol 4 The rivals, and Tracy's ambition; vol 5 Holland-tide; vol 6 The Duke of Monmouth; vol 7 Talis qualis: or tales of the jury room; vol 8 Poetical works.
The poetical and dramatic works. Dublin 1857, 1867, 1926.

Selections

Irish poetic gems from Mangan, Moore and Griffin. Dublin 1887.

§1

'Holland-tide': or Munster popular tales. 1827, 1827, Dublin and London 1857, Dublin 1891. Anon.
Tales of the Munster festivals, containing Card drawing; The half sir; and Suil Dhubh the coiner. 3 vols 1827, 1829, 1848, Dublin 1857 (as Card-drawing, The half sir and Suil Dhuv the coiner), 1 vol Dublin 1859, New York 1868, New York 1896; ed R. L. Wolff, New York and London 1979; tr Ger 1829.
The collegians. 3 vols 1829, 1829, 2 vols New York 1829, 1847, 1848, Dublin 1857, London 1857, 1861 (as The colleen bawn: or the collegian's wife), 1867, 1887, 1896, New York 1898, 1906; ed P. Colum 1918 etc; ed R. L. Wolff, New York and London 1979; ed J. Cronin, Belfast 1992; tr Ger 1843. For the dramatisation by Dion Boucicault, *see col 1994, below.*
The rivals: Tracy's ambition. 3 vols 1829, 1830, 2 vols New York 1830, London 1842, 1851, Dublin 1857; ed J. Cronin, Lille 1978; ed R. L. Wolff, New York and London 1979.
The Christian physiologist: tales illustrative of the five senses . . . with moral and explanatory introductions. 1830, New York and Boston 1853 (as Tales of the five senses), Dublin 1854, New York 1854 (as The offering of friendship), [c. 1886] (as The offering of friendship). Stories also rptd separately, Dublin 1854, *see below.*
The invasion: a tale. 4 vols 1832, 1 vol Dublin and London [1861], New York 1896.
Tales of my neighbourhood. 3 vols 1835, 2 vols Philadelphia 1836; ed R. L. Wolff, New York and London 1979.
The Duke of Monmouth: a historical novel. 3 vols 1836, 2 vols Philadelphia 1837, 3 vols London 1841, 1 vol Dublin 1857, New York 1880, 1896.
The fate of Cathleen: a Wicklow story. 1841. First pbd in The rivals, *above.*
Gisippus: a play in five acts. 1842, 1842, New York 1848.
Talis qualis: or tales of the jury room. 3 vols 1842, Dublin 1846, 1 vol London 1857, Dublin 1857, 1867, New York [c. 1885]; ed R. L. Wolff, New York and London 1979.
The poetical works. 1843 (Works vol 8), 1851.
The young Milesian and the selfish Crotarie. '1854' [1853], 1903 (as Eagna the bard or the selfish Crotarie). First pbd in The Christian physiologist.
The kelp-gatherer: an Irish tale. Dublin 1854. First pbd in The Christian physiologist, *above.*
The day of trial: an Irish tale. Dublin 1854.
The voluptuary cured: an Irish tale. Dublin 1854. First pbd in The Christian physiologist, *above.*
The beautiful Queen of Leix, or the self-consumed: an Irish tale. Dublin 1854. First pbd in The Christian physiologist, *above.*
A story of Psyche. Dublin 1854. First pbd in The Christian physiologist, *above.*
The day of trial: an Irish tale. Dublin '1854' [1853].
Card-drawing, the half sir, and Suil Dhuv the coiner. Dublin 1857.
Poems. Dublin 1886.
Poetical works. Dublin 1926. Includes Gisippus, *above.*

§2

Griffin, D. The life of Gerald Griffin. 1843 (Works vol 1), Dublin [1857] (rev); ed R. L. Wolff, New York and London 1979; tr Ger 1847.
Gill, W. S. Gerald Griffin: poet, novelist, Christian Brother. Dublin [1940].
Mannin, E. Two studies in integrity: Griffin and the Reverend Francis Mahony. 1954.
Cronin, J. Gerald Griffin (1803–1840): a critical biography. Cambridge 1978.
Davis, R. B. Gerald Griffin. Boston 1980. [CC]

Anna Maria Hall, née Fielding 1800–81

Selections

Tales of Irish life and character. Edinburgh and London 1909.

§1

Sketches of Irish character. 2 vols 1829; ser 2, 1 vol 1831; combined in 1 vol 1842 (illus edn, rev with additions and 1 omission).

Chronicles of a school room. 1830.
The buccaneer: a tale. 3 vols 1832. Anon.
The outlaw. 3 vols 1835.
Tales of woman's trials. 1835.
Uncle Horace: a novel. 3 vols 1837. Anon.
Lights and shadows of Irish life. 3 vols 1838. First pbd in NMM.
The Hartopp jubilee, or profit from play: a volume for the young. [1839.]
Marian: or a young maid's fortunes. 3 vols 1840.
Characteristic sketches of Ireland and the Irish, by Carleton, Lover, and Mrs S. C. Hall. Dublin 1842, 1845.
Number one: a tale. 1844.
Little Chatterbox: a tale. 1844.
The Whiteboy: a story of Ireland in 1822. 2 vols 1845, 1 vol 1855, [1884], 1887.
The forlorn hope: a story of Old Chelsea. [1846.]
Stories and studies from the chronicles and history of England. 2 vols 1847. With Mrs J. Foster.
Uncle Sam's money-box. 1848.
Midsummer Eve: a fairy tale of love. 1848, 1870. First pbd in Art Jnl.
The old governess: a story. [1848]; rptd in Stories of the governess, *below*, 1852.
Grandmamma's pockets. Edinburgh 1849, London [1880].
Seven tales, by seven authors. Ed F. E. Smedley 1849, 1860. Contains The last in the lease by Mrs Hall.
Pilgrimages to English shrines. 2 ser 1850–3.
Stories of the Irish peasantry. Edinburgh 1850. First pbd in Chambers's Jnl.
The whisperer. Edinburgh 1850.
The swan's egg. Edinburgh 1851.
Stories of the governess. 1852. The old governess first pbd 1848, *above*; The governess rptd separately, *below*, 1858.
The worn thimble: a story of woman's duty and woman's influence. 1853.
The drunkard's Bible. 1854.
Popular tales and sketches. 1856.
The two friends: a sketch. [1856.]
A woman's story. 3 vols 1857.
The lucky penny and other tales. 1857.
Turns of fortune. 1858. Also contains The figured satin.
There is no hurry and Deeds – not words: tales. 1858.
The unjust judge. 1858. With A. M. Sergeant's Be just before you are generous. Rptd from The Art-Union 1840.
All is not gold that glitters: a tale. 1858.
Cleverness: a tale. 1858.
The governess: a tale. 1858. First pbd in Stories of the governess, *above*, 1852.
The private purse and Tattle: tales. 1858.
Wives and husbands: a tale. 1858.
Daddy Dacre's school: a story for the young. 1859.
Mamma Milly. [1860.]
The golden casket, edited by M. Howitt. [1861.] Contains William and his teacher by Mrs Hall.
Union Jack. [1861.]
Can wrong be right? A tale. 2 vols 1862.
Building a house with a teacup. [1863.]
Fanny's fancies. [1863.]
The village garland: tales and sketches. 1863.
Nelly Nowlan and other stories. 1865.
Ronald's reason: or the little cripple. [1865], [1890] (with other stories).
The cabman's cat. [1865.]
'God save the Green!': a few words to the Irish people. [1866.]
The playfellow and other stories. 1866.
The way of the world and other stories. 1866.
The prince of the Fair family: a fairy tale. [1867.]
Alice Stanley and other stories. 1868.
The fight of faith: a story. 2 vols 1869.
The rift in the rock: a tale in two parts. [1871.]
Digging a grave with a wine glass. [1871.]
Chronicles of Cosy Nook: a book for the young. 1875.
Boons and blessings: stories and sketches to illustrate the advantages of temperance. 1875.
John Harding's locket. [1875.]
Annie Leslie and other stories. [1877.]
Mrs Hall also conducted St James's Mag, *1861, and* Sharpe's London Mag *from 1845. In addn to her novels and tales she pbd plays and miscellaneous hack-work as well as several books of travel with her husband S. C. Hall.*

§2

Maginn, W. In his A gallery of illustrious literary characters, ed W. Bates [1873].
Hall, S. C. Retrospect of a long life. 1883.
Keane, M. Mrs. S. C. Hall: a literary biography. Gerrards Cross 1997.
[EH]

James Hannay 1827–73

See col 2234.

John Berwick Harwood 1828–?

Poems. 1849.
The bridal and the bridle: or our honeymoon-trip in the East, in 1850. 1851. Travel.
Stamboul, and the sea of gems. 1852. Travel.
Falconbeck Hall: a novel. 3 vols 1854.
The serf-sisters: or the Russia of to-day. 1855.
Lord Lynn's wife. 2 vols 1864. Anon.
Lady Flavia. 3 vols 1865.
Odd neighbours. 3 vols 1865.
Major Peter. 3 vols 1866.
Plain John Orpington. 3 vols 1866.
Lord Ulswater: a novel. 3 vols 1867.
Miss Jane, the bishop's daughter. 3 vols 1867.
Lady Livingston's legacy: a novel. 3 vols 1874.
Sir Peregrine's heir. 3 vols 1875.
Helena Lady Harrogate: a tale. 3 vols 1878.
Paul Knox, pitman. 3 vols 1878.
The tenth earl. 3 vols 1880.
Young Lord Penrith. 3 vols 1880.
The merchant prince: being the fortunes of Bertram Oakley. 3 vols 1882.
One false, both fair: or a hard knot. 3 vols 1884.
Within the clasp: a story of the Yorkshire jet-hunters. Serialised in Cassell's Family Mag 1884. New York [1884], 1885.
Ralph Raeburn and other tales. 3 vols 1885. Ralph Raeburn 1st pbd in Cassell's Family Mag 1882 as Ralph Raeburn's trusteeship.
Sir Robert Shirley, bart. 3 vols 1886.
The Lady Egeria, or brought to light: a novel. New York 1890.
John Berwick Harwood also contributed short stories to Once a Week *and* Cassell's Family Mag. [EH]

Sir Arthur Helps 1813–75

See col 2235.

Thomas Hughes 1822–96

Bibliographies

Parrish, M. L. and B. K. Maun. Charles Kingsley and Thomas Hughes: first editions in the library at Dormy House. 1936.

Mack, E. C. and W. H. G. Armytage. Thomas Hughes: the life of the author of Tom Brown's school days. 1952. *See* pp. 292–6.

§1

History of the Working Tailors' Association. [1850.] Tracts on Christian Socialism ii.

A lecture on the slop-system, especially as it bears upon the females engaged in it, delivered at Reading. Exeter 1852.

King's College and Mr Maurice. 1854.

Tom Brown's school days, by an old boy. Cambridge 1857 (5 edns), Boston 1857 and later (as School days at Rugby), London 1858, Leipzig 1858, London 1859, 1860, 1861, 1865, 1868, 1869, 1870, New York 1870 and later, London 1871, 1874, Chicago [1876] and later, London 1877, 1878, 1879, 1880, Philadelphia [1881] and later, London 1882, 1884, 1885, 1886, 1888, as Tom Brown at Rugby Boston [1888] and later (as Tom Brown at Rugby), London 1890, 1896, 1897, 1898; numerous 20th-cent edns incl Everyman (1906) and WC (1989); tr Ger 1867, Fr 1876, Swed 1878.
REVIEWS: Spectator 2 May 1857; Saturday Rev 3 Oct 1857; The Times 9 Oct 1857; [Stephen, J. F.] Edinburgh Rev 107 1858.

The scouring of the white horse: or the long vacation ramble of a London clerk, illustrated by Richard Doyle. Cambridge '1859' [1858] (2 edns), Boston 1859, London 1859, 1889 (with The ashen faggot; a tale for Christmas), 1892.
REVIEW: Examiner 4 Dec 1858.

Account of the lock-out of engineers 1851–2, prepared for the National Association for the Promotion of Social Science. Cambridge 1860.

Tom Brown at Oxford, by the author of Tom Brown's school days. 3 vols Cambridge 1861 (2 edns), Boston 1861 and later, Philadelphia [1861] and later, New York 1861 and later, London 1864, 1865, 1869, 1870, 1871, 1872, 1874, 1875, 1877 (2 edns), 1878, 1879, 1880, 1883, 1885, 1886, 1888, 1889, 1903, 1905, 1906, 1910, 1914, 1921, 1924, 1929.
REVIEWS: Atlantic Monthly 8 1861; Critic 23 Nov 1861; Spectator 23 Nov 1861; Athenaeum 30 Nov 1861; Examiner 14 Dec 1861; Saturday Rev 14 Dec 1861.

Tracts for priests and people, no 1: Religio laici. Cambridge 1861 (4 edns). Afterwards included in Tracts for priests and people, ser i.

The struggle for Kansas. Appended to J. M. Ludlow, A sketch of the history of the United States, Cambridge 1862.

The cause of freedom: which is its champion in America, the North or the South? [1863.]

A layman's faith. 1868.

Alfred the Great. 3 pts 1869, 1871, Boston 1871 and later, London 1873, 1874, 1877, 1878, 1881, 1887, 1898, 1907.

Memoir of a brother. 1873 (5 edns), Boston 1873, London 1874, Boston 1875.

Lecture on the history and objects of co-operation, delivered at Manchester, 22nd April 1878. Manchester 1878.

The old church: what shall we do with it? 1878.

The manliness of Christ. 1879, 1880, Boston 1880 and later, New York 1880 and later, London 1894, Philadelphia 1895, London 1907.

Rugby, Tennessee: being some account of the settlement founded on the Cumberland plateau by the Board of Aid to Land Ownership. 1881, New York 1881.

Memoir of Daniel Macmillan. 1882, 1882 (corrected), 1883.

G. T. T. – Gone to Texas; letters from our boys. 1884 (2 edns).

Address by his honour Thos Hughes, Q.C., on the occasion of the presentation of a testimonial in recognition of his services to the cause of co-operation, 6th December 1884. Manchester 1885.

Life and times of Peter Cooper. 1886.

James Fraser, second Bishop of Manchester: a memoir 1818–1885. 1887 (2 edns), 1888, 1889.

Co-operative production: an address delivered at the Annual Co-operative Congress, Carlisle. Manchester [1887].

Church reform and defence: an address delivered in Wadham College Hall, Oxford, Advent Sunday, 1886. 1887.

David Livingstone. 1889 (2 edns), 1890, 1891, 1893, New York 1897 and later, London 1901, 1906, 1908, 1912.

Co-operative faith and practice: an address. Manchester [1890].

Fifty years ago: a layman's address to Rugby School, Quinquagesima Sunday, 1891. [1891.]

Vacation rambles. 1895.

Early memories for the children. 1899 (priv ptd).

Some letters of Thomas Hughes. Economic Rev 24 1914.

Fragments of autobiography. Ed H. C. Shelley, Cornhill Mag Mar–May 1925.

Hughes also wrote introds to J. R. Lowell, Biglow Papers, *1859; J. F. D. Maurice,* Christian Socialism, *1898 etc. For Hughes's contributions to* Contemporary Rev, Macmillan's Mag *and* Quart Rev, *see* Wellesley *vol 1, Toronto 1966; for his contributions to* Fraser's Mag *see* Wellesley *vol 2, Toronto 1972; for his contributions to* Dark Blue, *see* Wellesley *vol 4, Toronto 1987.*

§2

Ritchie, J. E. In his British Senators, 1869.

Cooper, T. In his Men of mark, 7 vols 1876–83.

Hinton, R. J. In his English radical leaders, New York 1878.

Ludlow, J. M. Thomas Hughes and Septimus Hansard. Economic Rev 6 1896.

Cornish, J. F. Thomas Hughes. Macmillan's Mag 74 1896. Obituary.

Tollemache, L. A. In his Essays, mock essays and character sketches. 1898.

Selfe, S. Chapters from the history of Rugby School, together with notes on the characters and incidents depicted in Tom Brown's school days. Rugby 1910.

Mack, E. C. and W. H. G. Armytage. Thomas Hughes: the life of the author of Tom Brown's school days. 1952. [GW]

Jean Ingelow 1820–97

See col 622.

Douglas William Jerrold 1803–57

See col 2002.

Geraldine Endsor Jewsbury 1812–80

The BL holds 609 reports which Geraldine Jewsbury prepared as publisher's reader for Richard Bentley from 8 Feb 1860 until 8 Jan 1875. It also holds letters from Jewsbury to Richard Bentley, George Bentley, and Mrs A. Bentley, 1860–74. The Nat Lib of Scotland holds her ms Reminiscences of Jane Carlyle *(1866). For other British holdings of her letters see LR 1, pp. 515–6. Jewsbury's letters to William Hepworth Dixon, editor of the* Athenaeum, *are held in the Special Collections of the Lib at UCLA. The Alexander Turnbull Lib in Wellington, New Zealand, holds 8 letters from Jewsbury to Thomas Carlyle, 1840–1, and an extensive collection of her letters to Walter Mantell, 1857–80.*

Collection

The collected writings of Geraldine Jewsbury, micro. Marlborough, Wilts, 1994.

§1

Zoe: the history of two lives. 3 vols 1845, 1 vol New York 1845, new 3-vol edn London 1852, 1 vol New York 1873 (Lib of Select Novels no 52), first edn rptd London and New York 1975 (Garland's ser of Victorian Fiction: Novels of Faith and Doubt), 1 vol edn rptd London 1989 (Virago Modern Classics, introd S. Foster).
REVIEWS: [Chorley, H. F.] Athenaeum 1 Feb 1845; Fraser's Mag 32, Nov 1845; Manchester Examiner and Times 29 Apr 1848.

The half sisters: a tale. 2 vols 1848 (Chapman and Hall's monthly ser vols 16–17), 1 vol New York 1848, 1 vol Cheap edn London 1854 (Select Lib of Fiction) rptd [1861?] (Parlour Lib vol 230), 8th edn 1 vol 1866; ed J. Wilkes, Oxford 1994 (WCp).
REVIEWS: [Chorley, H. F.] Athenaeum 18 Mar 1848; Literary Gazette 1848.
Marian Withers. 3 vols 1851. First pbd in Manchester Examiner and Times 5 Jan–18 May 1850.
REVIEWS: [Hepworth Dixon, W.] Athenaeum 30 Aug 1851; [Lewes, G. H.] Leader 30 Aug 1851.
The history of an adopted child. '1853' [1852], New York 1853.
Constance Herbert. 3 vols 1855, 1 vol New York 1855 as Constance Herbert: a novel, new edn 1 vol London 1864, rptd [1882] (Select Lib).
REVIEWS: Athenaeum 24 Mar 1855; [Oliphant, Margaret] Blackwood's Mag 77, May 1855; [Eliot, George] Westminster Rev n.s. 8, July 1855.
Angelo: or the pine forest in the Alps. [1855] (illus), 1864 (2nd edn).
REVIEW: Athenaeum 1 Dec 1855.
The sorrows of gentility. 2 vols 1856, 2nd edn 1 vol nd, partly pbd in The Ladies' Companion 1850. Dedicated to John Forster.
REVIEW: Athenaeum 31 May 1856.
Right or wrong. 2 vols 1859.

Contributions to periodicals

For Jewsbury's contributions to Fraser's Mag, Westminster Rev *and* Temple Bar, *see* Wellesley *vol 5, 1989.*
Douglas Jerrold's Shilling Mag: To-day, 3 1846; Things of importance, 3 1846; Social barbarisms: hiring a servant, 4 1846; The lower orders, 5 1847; The civilisation of 'the lower orders', 6 1847; How Agnes Worral was taught to be respectable, 5 1847 (fiction). *See also* M. C. Fryckstedt, Geraldine Jewsbury and Douglas Jerrold's Shilling Magazine, ES 66 1985.
Seventeen tales for Household Words, 1850–9.
Jewsbury reviewed about 2,000 books for the Athenaeum *between 1849 and 1880. They are listed in* M. C. Fryckstedt, Geraldine Jewsbury's Athenaeum reviews: a mirror of mid-Victorian attitudes to fiction, *Uppsala 1986; see also her* New sources on Geraldine Jewsbury and the woman question, Research Studies *51, June 1983.*

Letters

Selections from the letters of Geraldine Endsor Jewsbury to Jane Welsh Carlyle. Ed Mrs A. Ireland 1892.
Wilkes, J. Walter Mantell, Geraldine Jewsbury, and race relations in New Zealand. New Zealand Jnl of History 22, Oct 1988. Includes extracts from Jewsbury's letters to Mantell.

Translations, edition and preface

Mazzini, G. The works of Thomas Carlyle. Br and Foreign Rev 16, Oct 1843. Tr from Ital.
Mazzini, G. Dante Allighieri. Foreign Quart Rev 33, Apr 1844. Tr from Ital.
Lady Morgan's memoirs: autobiography, diaries and correspondence. 2 vols 1862 (preface by William Hepworth Dixon), 3 vols Leipzig 1863, 2nd edn 1 vol London 1863, 1st edn rptd New York 1975. Jewsbury provided the connecting narrative for vol 1, 191ff, and all of vol 2.
Herschel, Mrs J. Caroline Herschel. 1878, 1879 (2nd edn). Jewsbury wrote the preface, but signed it with the author's initials.

§2

Sutton, C. W. In DNB.
Mercer, E. Geraldine Endsor Jewsbury. Manchester Quart 17, Oct 1898.
Howe, S. Geraldine Jewsbury: her life and errors. 1935.
Clarke, N. Ambitious heights: writing, friendship, love – the Jewsbury sisters, Felicia Hemans, and Jane Welsh Carlyle. 1990. [JW]

Julia Kavanagh 1824–77

§1

The Montyon prizes. [1846.]
The three paths: a story for young people. 1848, rptd as Saint Gildas; or the three paths [Boston] 1856.
Madeleine: a tale of Auvergne. 1848, 1851, 1852, New York 1852, 1 vol London 1857, New York 1875, 1 vol London [1884].
Nathalie: a tale. 3 vols 1850, 2 vols 1851, 1 vol 1859, New York 1864.
Woman in France during the eighteenth century. 2 vols 1850, Philadelphia 1850, London 1864.
Women of Christianity, exemplary for acts of piety and charity. 1852.
Daisy Burns: a tale. 3 vols 1853, New York 1853, 2 vols London 1853, 1865, New York 1866.
Grace Lee: a tale. 3 vols 1855, New York [1875].
Rachel Gray: a tale, founded on fact. 1856, New York 1856.
Adèle: a tale. 3 vols 1858, New York 1858, 2 vols London 1858, 3 vols 1862.
A summer and winter in the two Sicilies. 2 vols 1858.
Seven years and other tales. 1859, Boston 1859, 3 vols London '1860' [1859], New York 1860, 1870.
French women of letters: biographical sketches. 2 vols '1862' [1861].
English women of letters: biographical sketches. 2 vols 1862, 2 vols '1863' [1862].
Queen Mab: a novel. 3 vols 1863, 2 vols 1863, 3 vols in 1 New York 1864, 1 vol London nd [after 1892].
Beatrice: a novel. 2 vols 1864, New York 1865, 3 vols London 1865.
Sybil's second love: a novel. 3 vols 1867, 2 vols 1867.
Dora: a novel. 3 vols 1868, New York 1868.
Silvia. 3 vols 1870.
Bessie: a novel. 3 vols 1872.
John Dorrien: a novel. 3 vols 1875, 1 vol 1893.
The pearl fountain and other fairy tales. 1876.
Two lilies: a novel. 3 vols 1877.
Forget-me-nots. 3 vols 1878. Short stories.

§2

Macquoid, K. S. In A. Sergeant et al, Women novelists of Queen Victoria's reign, 1897. [LA]

Annie Keary 1825–79

§1

Mia and Charlie: or a week's holiday at Ryedale rectory. 1855 (anon), 1856, 1860.
Sidney Grey. A tale of school life. 1856 (anon), 1857, 1860 (2nd edn), New York [186?], London [1883] (new edn pbd as Sidney Grey: or a year from home).
The heroes of Asgard and the giants of Jotunheim: or the week and its story. With E. Keary. 1857 (anon), [1860] (pbd as Christmas week and its stories), 1871 (pbd as The heroes of Asgard; illustr Huard), 1872, 1880 (new edn), London and New York 1883, New York 1893, London 1897, New York 1898, 1900, [1904?], 1906, 1909, Philadelphia [191?], London 1924, 1930 (illustr C. E. Brock), 1932 (illustr Huard); London and New York 1904 (rev and abridged by C. H. Morss), London 1909, 1914, 1918; 1905 (adapted for use in schools with an introd by M. R. Earle), 1907; London and Glasgow [1924] (adapted and arranged by H. Hayens).
The rival kings: or overbearing. 1857 (anon), 1860, 1861 (new edn).
Blind man's holiday: or short tales for the nursery. 1857 (anon), 1860 (illustr J. Absolon), 1883 (new edn).
Through the shadows. 3 vols 1859 (anon).
REVIEW: Athenaeum 1654 1859.
An early Egyptian history for the young. Cambridge and London 1861 (anon), 1863 (new edn). With E. Keary.
Janet's home. 2 vols Cambridge and London 1863 (anon), 1 vol

London 1864, 1872, 1875, 1882 (new edn), New York [1883], London 1885, London and New York 1890.
REVIEW: Saturday Rev 17 1864.
Little Wanderlin and other fairy tales. Cambridge and London 1865, London 1873 (new edn), 1896. With E. Keary.
Clemency Franklyn. 2 vols 1866 (anon), 1867, London and New York 1871 (new edn), London 1882, London and New York 1888.
REVIEW: Saturday Rev 21 1866.
Oldbury. 3 vols 1869, Leipzig 1874 (Tauchnitz), London 1875 (2nd edn), Philadelphia [1876?], New York [1880?], London 1886 (new edn) 1888, 1891, Philadelphia [189?].
REVIEW: Spectator 42 1869.
The nations around Palestine. 1870, 1875, London and New York 1893 (pbd as The nations around Israel), London 1894.
REVIEWS: Athenaeum 2228 1870; Nation (New York) 11 1870.
Castle Daly. Serialised in Macmillan's Mag Feb 1874–July 1875. 3 vols London 1875, Leipzig 1875 (Tauchnitz), 2 vols London 1876 (new edn), 1889, Philadelphia [189?], London 1892, 1894, 1902, Philadelphia [1911?].
REVIEWS: Athenaeum 2490 1875; Nation (New York) 21 1875; Spectator 50 1877.
A York and a Lancaster rose. 1876, 1877, New York [1882?], London 1888 (new edn), 1890, London and New York 1894, London 1896, 1904, 1909.
A doubting heart. Serialised in Macmillan's Mag June 1878–Dec 1879. 3 vols 1879, New York [1879?], 1 vol London 1880, New York [1880?], London 1882 (new edn), 1884, 1891, London and New York 1895. With K. Macquoid.
REVIEW: Athenaeum 2717 1879; Spectator 53 1880.
Father Phim. 1879, 1962 (ed with an introd by G. Avery).

Articles, editions and letters

Runic legend. Good Words 18 1877.
Letters of Annie Keary. Selected, with a preface by E. Keary. [1883.]
Enchanted tulips, and other verses for children. By A., E. and M. Keary. 1914. Ed M. Keary.

§2

[Keary, E.] Memoir of Annie Keary by her sister. 1882, 1883 (2nd edn).
In DNB.

Charles Kingsley 'Parson Lot' 1819–75

Major collections include the Kingsley papers in the British Library and the Morris L. Parrish collection Princeton University.

Bibliographies

Northup, C. S. A register of bibliographies of the English language and literature. New Haven CT 1925.
Parrish, M. L. and B. K. Mann. Charles Kingsley and Thomas Hughes. First editions in the library at Dormy House. 1936.
Barrett, H. M. A bibliography of Charles Kingsley. 1936.
Thorp, M. F. The Kingsley collection. Princeton Univ Lib Chron 8, 1946.
Sadleir, M. XIX century fiction: a bibliographical record based on his own collection. 2 vols Cambridge 1951.
Wainwright, A. D. The Morris L. Parrish collection of Victorian novelists. Princeton Univ Lib Chron 18, 1956.
Clark, A. P. The ms collections of the Princeton University Library. Princeton Univ Lib Chron 19, 1958.
Barry, J. D. In Victorian fiction: a guide to research, ed L. Stevenson, Cambridge MA 1964.
Campbell, R. A. Charles Kingsley: a bibliography of secondary studies. Pt I, Bull of Bibliography 33, Feb–Mar 1976; pt II, Apr–June 1976.
Barry, J. D. In Victorian fiction: a second guide to research, ed G. H. Ford, Cambridge MA 1978.
Harris, S. Charles Kingsley: a reference guide. Boston 1981.
Wolff, R. L. Nineteenth century fiction: a bibliographical catalogue. Vol 2 1985.

Collections

Works. 28 vols 1880–5, 1888–9.
The Sixpenny edition of the novels. 7 vols 1889.
The Pocket edition of Charles Kingsley's works. 1895.
Works. Ed M. Kingsley 7 vols 1898–9.
Novels, poems and memories. 14 vols 1899.
The life and works. 19 vols 1901–3.

§1

Separately ptd sermons and short tracts are omitted here. These are listed in full in Thorp's biography, below. For Kingsley's articles in periodicals see Wellesley *vol 5 1989.*

The saint's tragedy, with a preface by Professor Maurice. 1848, 1851, 1855, 1859, 1861, 1908.
On English composition; On English literature. In Introductory lectures delivered at Queen's College London, 1849.
Twenty-five village sermons. 1849, 1852 (rev), 1857, 1861 (with other sermons, as Town and country sermons), 1867, 1868, 1872, 1877, 1880, 1894 etc.
Alton Locke, tailor and poet: an autobiography. 2 vols 1850 (anon), New York 1850, London 1851, 1852, 1856 (with preface addressed to the working men of Great Britain), Leipzig 1857 (Cheap edn), 1862 (with a new preface To the undergraduates of Cambridge), 1865, 1875, 1876 (with a prefatory memoir by Thomas Hughes), 1877, 1879, 2 vols 1881 (with Hughes's memoir, Eversley edn), 1889, 1892, [1893] etc; ed H. van Thal 1967 (EL), 1969; ed E. A. Cripps Oxford 1983 (WCp), 1987.
Cheap clothes and nasty, by Parson Lot. 1850, 1851, 1876.
The application of associative principles and methods to agriculture: a lecture. 1851.
Yeast: a problem. 1851 (anon), New York 1851, London 1855, 1856 New York, London 1859 (4th edn, with new preface), 1867, 1870, 2 vols Leipzig 1875, London 1877, 1879, 1881, 1888, 1893, 1895, 1994, ed A. Sutton. 1st pbd Fraser's Mag, July–Dec 1848.
Who are the friends of order? 1852.
Phaethon: or loose thoughts for loose thinkers. Cambridge 1852, 1854, 1859.
Sermons on national subjects. 1852, 1872 (as The King of the Earth, and other sermons preached in a village church), 1873.
Hypatia: or new foes with an old face. 2 vols 1853, Boston 1854, 1855, 1856, 1 vol London 1856, 2 vols Leipzig 1857, Boston 1858, 1862, London 1863, 1874, 1876, 1879, 2 vols 1881, 1889, 1891, 1895, 1897, 1899, 1902, 1903, 1905, 1925 etc. 1st pbd Fraser's Mag, Jan 1852–Apr 1853.
Alexandria and her schools. Cambridge 1854.
Sermons on national subjects: second series. 1854, 2 vols 1872, 1880.
Who causes pestilence? 1854.
Brave words for brave soldiers and sailors. 1855.
Glaucus: or the wonders of the shore. Cambridge 1855, Boston 1855, London 1856 (3rd edn, corrected and enlarged), 1859 (enlarged and illus), 1862, 1873, 1879, 1886, 1890, 1904. 1st pbd North Br Rev, Nov 1854.
Sermons for the times. 1855, 1858, 1872, 1878.
Sermons for sailors. [1855], 1885 (as Sea sermons).
The country parish: a lecture. In Lectures to ladies on practical subjects, Cambridge 1855, 1857.
Westward Ho! or the voyages and adventures of Sir Amyas Leigh, Knight, of Burrough in the County of Devon, in the reign of her most Glorious Majesty Queen Elizabeth, rendered into modern English by Charles Kingsley. 3 vols Cambridge 1855, 1855 (2nd edn), Leipzig 1855, Boston 1855, Cambridge 1861, 1865, 1867, 1869, London 1873, 1876, 1879, 2 vols 1881, 1894, 1896, 1898; ed W. K. Leask 1899, [1900], [1901]; 2 vols 1901, 1902, [1903], 1904, 1905, 1910;

ed J. T. Winterich, New York 1947; ed L. A. G. Strong London 1953; ed J. A. Williamston 1955; ed. M. W. and G. Thomas 1957; 1989.
The heroes: or Greek fairy tales for my children, with 8 illustrations by the author. Cambridge '1856' [1855], Boston 1856, Cambridge and London 1859 (2nd edn), 1862, 1864, London 1868, 1873, 1875, 1879, 1885, 1887, 1889, 1899, 1900, 1902; ed. T. H. Robinson 1902; ed. E. Gardner 1902; ed A. E. Roberts 1903; ed. C. A. McMurry 1907; ed. C. Mayne 1913; ed. F. K. Ball 1917; ed. E. M. Wilmot-Buxton 1920; ed. E. Gardner, Cambridge 1940; 1980.
Two years ago: a novel. 3 vols Cambridge 1857, 1859, 1877, 1879, 2 vols London 1881, 1889, 1902, 1903, [1904] etc.
Andromeda and other poems. 1858, Boston 1858, 1862.
Miscellanies reprinted chiefly from Fraser's Magazine and the North British Review. 2 vols 1859.
The good news of God: sermons. 1859, 1866, 1872, 1878, 1881 etc.
The massacre of the innocents: an address. [1859].
Sir Walter Raleigh and his time, with other papers. Boston 1859.
The limits of exact science as applied to history: an inaugural lecture. Cambridge 1860.
New miscellanies. Boston 1860.
Ode performed in the Senate-House Cambridge, composed for the installation of his Grace the Duke of Devonshire, Chancellor of the University. Cambridge 1862.
Speech of Lord Dundreary on the great Hippocampus question. Cambridge 1862.
The Gospel of the Pentateuch: a set of parish sermons. 1863, 1864, 1872, 1878, 1881.
The water-babies: a fairy tale for a land-baby with two illustrations by J. Noel Paton. 1863, 1869, Boston and New York 1870, London 1871, 1872, 1878, 1879, 1885 (100 illustrations by Linley Sambourne), 1889, 1903, 1904, 1905, [1905], 1906, [1907], [1908], 1908, 1909 (3 edns), 1912, 1913 etc, ed E. Thorndike 1935; ed C. M. Martin 1945, 1948, 1955; ed M. Robson 1978, 1979, 1980, 1983, 1984; 1984 (facs 1885 edn); adapted W. Hall 1987, 1989, 1990, 1992, 1993; ed B. Alderson 1995.
Hints to stammerers, by a minute philosopher. 1864. Also issued as The irrationale of speech.
The Roman and the Teuton: a series of lectures delivered before the University of Cambridge. Cambridge 1864; ed F. M. Müller 1875, 1879.
Mr Kingsley and Dr Newman: a correspondence on the question whether Dr Newman teaches that truth is no virtue. 1864.
'What, then, does Dr Newman mean?': a reply to a pamphlet lately published by Dr Newman. 1864; ed W. Ward, Oxford 1913 (with Newman's Apologia).
David: four sermons preached before the University of Cambridge. 1865, 1874 (5 sermons).
Hereward the Wake: 'last of the English'. 2 vols Cambridge 1866, Boston 1866, London 1867, 1877, 1879, 1881, 1890, 1908, [1909], 1911 (with introd and notes), 1912, 1914; ed L. A. G. Strong 1954. 1st pbd Good Words, Jan–Dec 1865.
A game-law ballad ... a rough rhyme on a rough matter. 1866?.
Three lectures delivered at the Royal Institution on the ancien régime before the French Revolution. 1867.
The fens. 1867.
The water of life and other sermons. 1867, 1868, 1872, 1881, 1890, 1891.
Discipline and other sermons. 1868, 1872, 1881.
The two breaths: an address. 1869.
Women and politics. 1869.
The hermits. 3 pts [1868], 1 vol 1878, 1880, 1891.
Madam How and Lady Why: or first lessons in earth-lore for children. 1870 (illus), 1872, 1880, 1889, 1897 etc. 1st pbd Good Words for the Young, Nov 1868–Oct 1869.
At last: a Christmas in the West Indies, with illustrations. 2 vols 1871, 1872, 1874, 1880, 1889, 1910.
Poems: collected edition. 1872, 1878 (enlarged), 1879, 1880 (enlarged as vol 1 of Works), 2 vols 1884 (enlarged), 1889, 1913, 1927.
Town geology. 1872, 1879.
Plays and Puritans, and other historical essays. 1873, 1880, 1889.
Prose idylls, new and old. 1873, 1880, 1889.
Westminster sermons. 1874, 1877, 1890.
Health and education. 1874.
Lectures delivered in America in 1874. 1875.
American notes: letters from a lecture tour 1874. Ed R. B. Martin, Princeton 1958.
Letters to young men on betting and gambling. 1877.
True words for brave men. 1878, 1879, 1914.
All Saints Day and other sermons. Ed W. Harrison 1878.
Historical lectures and essays. 1880 (Works vol 17), 1889.
Sanitary and social lectures and essays. 1880 (Works vol 18), 1889.
Literary and general lectures and essays. 1880 (Works vol 20).
Scientific lectures and essays. 1885 (Works vol 19).
From death to life: fragments of teaching to a village congregation, with letters on the life after death, edited by his wife. 1887.
Words of advice to schoolboys, collected from hitherto unpublished notes and letters. Ed E. F. Johns 1912.
The tutor's story, by the late Charles Kingsley, revised and completed by his daughter 'Lucas Malet' [M. St L. Harrison]. 1916, 1920. This story, of which c. 150 foolscap pp. were left in ms by Kingsley, seems to have been written about 1863.
Kingsley also contributed prefaces etc to the following: Things to come: being lectures on the third chapter of the second Epistle of St Peter, 1851; *C. B. Mansfield,* Paraguay, Brazil and the Plate, *edited with a sketch of the author's life, 1856;* The history and life of J. Tauler with 25 of his sermons, *1857; H. Brooke,* The fool of quality, *1859;* The pilgrim's progress, *1860.*

§2

Criticism Pre-1920

Parson, F. Charles Kingsley. People's Journal 11, 1851.
Revolutionary literature. Quart Rev 89, Sep 1851.
Bayne, P. Charles Kingsley. Hoggs' Instructor, 11 Feb 1854.
Kingsley as a lyric poet. Chambers's Jnl 23, June 1855.
Modern novelists – great and small. Blackwood's Mag 77, May 1855.
Aytoun, W. E. The Rev Charles Kingsley. Blackwood's Mag 77, June 1855.
The novels and poems of the Rev Charles Kingsley. Nat Rev 1, July 1855.
Modern light literature – science. Blackwood's Mag 78, Aug 1855.
Charles Kingsley. Tait's Edinburgh Mag 22, Oct 1855.
Modern light literature – travellers' tales. Blackwood's Mag 78, Nov 1855.
Phillips, S. Essays from The Times (2nd ser). 1855.
Rigg, J. H. The writings of Charles Kingsley. London Quart Rev 8, Apr 1857, repr in his Modern Anglican theology 1857.
The genius of the Rev Charles Kingsley. Dublin Univ Mag 49, June 1857.
Mr Kingsley's novels. Christian Remembrancer 34, Oct 1857.
Brimley, G. In his Essays, 1858.
Sowerby, Y. B. Companion to Mr Kingsley's Glaucus. Cambridge 1858.
Masson, D. In his British novelists and their styles, Cambridge 1859.
Greg, W. R. Mr Kingsley's literary excesses. Nat Rev 10, Jan 1860.
A clerical Chricton. Chambers's Jnl 3rd ser 13, Jan 1860.
Coltharp, S. R. Cambridge and Kingsley on American affairs. Christian Examiner 75, Nov 1863.
Dr Newman and Mr Kingsley. Sat Rev, 17 Feb 1864.
Our contemporaries. Dublin Rev 54, Apr 1864.
Mr Kingsley and Dr Newman. London Quart Rev, 23 Oct 1864.
Greg, W. R. In his Literary and social judgments, 1868, Boston 1873.
Friswell, J. H. In his Modern men of letters honestly criticised, 1870.
Phillips, S. In his Essays from The Times, 2 vols 1871.

Towle, G. M. Charles Kingsley. Appleton's Jnl 6, Dec 1871.
Allibone, S. A. A critical dictionary of English literature. Vol 2 Philadelphia 1872.
McCarthy, J. The Reverend Charles Kingsley. Galaxy 14, Aug 1872.
Helps, A. Charles Kingsley. Macmillan's Mag, Feb 1874. Obituary.
Death of Canon Kingsley. The Times, 25 Jan 1875.
Charles Kingsley: his standing as an author and poet. New York Times, 14 Feb 1875.
Burlingame, E. L. Charles Kingsley. Appleton's Jnl 13, Feb 1875.
Dyer, J. Charles Kingsley, parson, poet and politician. Penn Monthly 6, Mar 1875.
Escott, T. H. S. Charles Kingsley. Belgravia 26, Mar 1875.
King, R. J. Charles Kingsley. Fraser's Mag 11, Mar 1875.
Recollections of Kingsley. Good Words 16, 1875.
James, H. Life and letters of Charles Kingsley. Nation (New York) 24, 1876.
Page, H. A. The Chartism of Kingsley. Good Words 17, 1876.
Boyd, A. K. H. Charles Kingsley. Fraser's Mag 15, Feb 1877.
Mayer, S. R. T. The poetry of Charles Kingsley and Clough. St James's Mag 31, Mar 1877.
Hosmer, G. W. Memoirs of Charles Kingsley. Unitarian Rev 9, Apr 1878.
Schmidt, J. Portraits aus den Neunzehnten Jahrhundert. Berlin 1878.
Bayne, T. Charles Kingsley. St James's Mag 36, Sep 1879.
Stephen, L. In his Hours in a library, ser 3 1879, rptd New York 1894.
Henley, W. E. In The English poets, ed T. H. Ward vol 4 1880.
Chambers cyclopedia of English literature (3rd edn). Ed R. Chambers vol 7 New York 1880.
Rigg, J. H. Modern Anglican theology. 1880 (3rd edn). Includes memoir of Kingsley.
Mr Kingsley as a novelist. Spectator 55, 28 Jan 1882.
Stanley, A. P. Sermons at Westminster. 1882.
Tuckerman, B. In his A history of English prose fiction, New York 1882.
Besly, E. F. S. Charles Kingsley: his life and works. Doncaster 1883.
Davies, G. J. In his Successful preachers, 1884.
Müller, M. In his Biographical essays, 1884.
Thomson, J. In his Satires and profanities, 1884.
Maurice, F. D. In The life of Frederick Denison Maurice. 2 vols 1885.
Tulloch, J. In his Movements of religious thought in the nineteenth century, 1885.
Whipple, E. P. In his Some noted princes, authors and statesmen of our time, New York 1885.
Dowden, E. In his Transcripts and studies, 1887 (2nd edn).
Japp, A. H. In his Leaders upward and onward: brief biographies of noble workers, 1887.
Cochrane, R. In Great thinkers and workers, 1888.
DeVries, D. M. Charles Kingsley: schets van karakter en deukbielden met bloemlezing mit zijne geschiften. Amsterdam 1888.
Nielsen, F. Charles Kingsley og den kristelige socialisme i England. Copenhagen 1888.
Stedman, E. C. In Victorian poets, Boston 1888 (rev edn).
Cross, W. In his The development of the English novel, New York 1889.
Mallock, M. M. Charles Kingsley. Dublin Rev 24, 1890.
Ellis, J. J. Charles Kingsley. New York 1890.
Gosse, E. W. In The life of Philip Henry Gosse, 1890.
Japp, A. H. In his Good men and true, 1890 (7th edn).
Martineau, J. In his Essays, 4 vols 1890–1.
Lang, A. In his Essays in little, New York 1891.
Parsons, J. C. In his English versification, Boston 1891.
Suffield, R. R. Charles Kingsley. Library 3. Reading Jan 1891.
Gibbins, H. De B. In his English social reformers, 1892.
Groser, H. G. Charles Kingsley. In his The poets and the poetry of the century, vol 5 1892.
Kaufmann, M. Charles Kingsley: Christian socialist and social reformer. 1892.
Kirk, J. F. In A supplement to Allibone's critical dictionary of English literature, vol 2 Philadelphia 1892.
Marriott, J. A. R. Charles Kingsley, novelist. 1892.
Montégut, E. Ecrivains moderne de l'Angleterre. 3rd ser Paris 1892.
Groser, H. G. Charles Kingsley. Prefixed to a selection from the poems in The poets and the poetry of the century, ed A. H. Miles vol 5 1893 etc.
Groth, E. Charles Kingsley als Dichter und Sozial-reformer. Leipzig 1893.
Ludlow, J. M. Some of the Christian socialists of 1848 and the following years. Economic Rev 3, Oct 1893.
Ludlow, J. M. Some of the Christian socialists of 1848 and the following years. Economic Rev 4, Jan 1894.
Ogilvie, G. S. Hypatia: a play in four acts founded on Charles Kingsley's novel. 1894.
Pancoast, H. S. In his An introduction to English literature, New York 1894.
Russell, P. In his A guide to British and American novels, 1894.
Harrison, F. In his Studies in early Victorian literature, 1895.
Raleigh, W. In his The English novel, 1895 (2nd edn).
Saintsbury, G. In his A history of nineteenth century literature, New York 1896.
Tupper, F. Charles Kingsley as novelist. Citizen 2, 1896.
Hunt, T. W. In his Representative English and prose writers, New York 1897.
Müller, F. M. Literary recollections. Cosmopolis 5, Jan 1897.
Rose, J. H. In his The rise of democracy. 1897.
Shorter, C. In his Victorian literature: sixty years of books and bookmen, New York 1897.
Rogers, A. In his Men and movements in the English church, New York 1898.
Saintsbury, G. In his A short history of English literature, New York 1898.
Scudder, V. D. In her Social ideals in English letters, Boston 1898.
Cross, W. In his The English novel, New York 1899.
[L., F.,] Charles Kingsley as a novelist, Acad 57, 26 Aug 1899.
McCarthy, J. In his Reminiscences, vol 2 1899.
Paul, C. K. In his Memories, 1899.
Stubbs, C. W. Charles Kingsley and the Christian social movement. 1899.
Stoddard, F. H. in his The evolution of the English novel, New York 1900.
Beers, H. A. In his A history of English romanticism in the nineteenth century, New York 1901.
Mayor, J. B. In his Chapters on English metre, Cambridge 1901.
Paul, H. In his Men and letters, 1901.
Müller, G. A. G. (ed). In her The life and letters of Friedrich Max Müller, 2 vols 1902.
Saintsbury, G. In his A history of criticism, vol 2 Edinburgh 1902; 1911 (rev edn).
Cazamian, L. Kingsley et Thomas Cooper: étude sur une source d'Alton Locke. 1903
Cazamian, L. Le roman social en Angleterre 1830–50. Paris 1903.
McCabe, J. Hypatia. Critic 43, Sep 1903.
Woodworth, A. V. Christian socialism in England. 1903.
Lord, W. F. Kingsley's novels. Nineteenth Cent 55, June 1904.
Moulton, C. W. (ed). In his Library of literary criticism, vol 7 Buffalo NY 1904.
Review of Le roman social en Angleterre. Nation 78, 16 June 1904.
Dawson, W. J. In his The makers of English fiction, New York 1905.
Whitcomb, S. L. In his The study of a novel, Boston 1905.
Benjamin, L. S. In his Victorian novelists, 1906.
Lord, W. F. The Kingsleys. In his The mirror of the century, 1906.
Saintsbury, G. In his A history of criticism, vol 3 Edinburgh 1906.

Saintsbury, G. In his A history of English prosody, vol 1 1906, vol 3 1910.
Goldberg. F. S. Kingsley and the social problems of his day. Westminster Rev 167, Jan 1907.
Sweet, F. H. Charles Kingsley. Book News Monthly 25, June 1907.
Alden, R. M. In his An introduction to poetry, New York 1909.
Dierlamm, G. Die flugschriften Literatur der chartisten Bewegung und ihr Widerhall in der öffentlichen Meinung. Leipzig 1909.
Magnus, L. In his English literature in the nineteenth century, New York 1909.
Merker, B. Die historischen Quellen zu Kingsleys Roman Hypatia. Wurzburg 1909.
Wedgwood, J. In her Nineteenth century teachers and other essays, 1909.
Chapman, E. M. In his English literature and religion 1800–1900, 1910.
Dyboski, R. Charles Kingsley i socyalizin chrzescijanski w Anglii. Krakow 1910.
Saintsbury, G. In his Historical manual of English prosody, 1910.
Walker, H. In The literature of the Victorian era, Cambridge 1910.
Benson, A. C. The leaves of the tree. In his Studies in biography, 1911. Also pbd North Amer Rev 194, 1911.
Keller, L. Charles Kingsley und die religiö-sozialen Kämpfe in England in 19. Jahrhundert. Berlin [1911].
Noel, C. In his Socialism in church history, Milwaukee WI 1911.
Chope, R. P. The historical basis of Kingsley's Westward Ho! [1912].
Boynton, P. H. In London in English literature, Chicago 1913.
Chesterton, G. K. In his The Victorian age in literature, New York 1913.
Saintsbury, G. In his The English novel, 1913.
Storr, V. F. In his The development of English theology in the nineteenth century, vol 1 New York 1913.
Walker, H. In his Outlines of Victorian literature, Cambridge 1913.
Vulliamy, C. E. Charles Kingsley and Christian socialism. 1914.
Burton, R. In his Masters of the English novel: a study of principles and personalities, New York 1915.
Hearn, L. In his Interpretations of literature, vol 1 New York 1915.
Nairne, A. Poems by Charles Kingsley. Chester 1915.
Waugh, A. In his Reticence in literature and other papers, 1915.
Hearn, L. In his Appreciations of poetry, 1916.
Phelps, W. L. In his The advance of the English novel, New York 1916.
Hearn, L. In his Life and literature, New York 1917.
Jacobson, A. Charles Kingsleys Beziehungen zu Deutschland. Heidelberg 1917.
Savage, O. M. In her Rhythm in prose illustrated from authors of the nineteenth century, 1917.
Whiteford, R. N. In his Motives in English fiction, New York 1918.
Benjamin, L. S. ('Lewis Melville'). The centenary of Charles Kingsley. Contemporary Rev, 115, June 1919.
Courtney, J. E. Charles Kingsley. Fortnightly Rev, June 1919.
Patton, J. In her The English village: a literary study, 1750–1850, New York 1919.
Roberts, R. E. Charles Kingsley 1819–1875. Bookman 56, June 1919.
Williams, S. T. Yeast: a Victorian heresy. North Amer Rev 212, 1920.
Blore, G. H. In Victorian worthies, 1920.
Perry, B. In his A study of prose fiction, Boston 1920 (rev edn).
Rauschenbusch, W. In his Christianity and the social crisis, New York 1920.
Raven, C. E. Christian socialism 1848–1854. 1920.
Russell, F. T. In her Satire in the Victorian novel, New York 1920.
Ward, Sir A. The political and social novels of Charles Kingsley. In Cambridge history of English literature, vol 13 1922.
For individual reviews of Kingsley's novels in periodicals see Harris, 1981, Bibliographies, *above.*

Biographies

Charles Kingsley: his letters and memories of his life, edited by his wife. 2 vols 1877 etc; abridged 1 vol New York 1877; rptd as vols 1–4 of The life and works, London 1901–2. 2 vols 1879 (for 1878), 1881.
Baldwin, S. E. Charles Kingsley. Ithaca NY 1934.
Thorp, M. F. Charles Kingsley 1819–1875. Princeton NJ 1937.
Kendall, G. Charles Kingsley and his ideas. 1947.
Pope-Hennessy, U. Canon Charles Kingsley: a biography. 1948.
Martin, R. B. The dust of combat: a life of Charles Kingsley. New York 1960.
Reboul, M. Charles Kingsley: le formation d'une personalité et son affirmation littéraire. Paris 1973.
Chitty, S. The beast and the monk: a life of Charles Kingsley. New York 1975.
Colloms, B. Charles Kingsley: the lion of Eversley. 1975. [EC]

Henry Kingsley, 'Granby Dixon' 1830–76

Bibliographies

Ellis, S. M. Henry Kingsley. 1931. With Kingsley's contributions to magazines.
Thirkell, A. Henry Kingsley. Nineteenth-Cent Fiction 5, 1951.
Wolff, R. L. Henry Kingsley. Harvard Lib Bull 13, 1959.

Collections

Novels. 7 vols 1872, 1885.
Novels. Ed C. K. Shorter 8 vols 1894–5.

Selections

Selections. Ed J. S. D. Mellick 1982.

§1

The recollections of Geoffrey Hamlyn. 3 vols 1859, Boston 1859, London 1860, Leipzig 1864 (2 vols in 1), London 1872, 1885, [1891] (with memoir by C. K. Shorter), '1909' [1910] etc, Oxford 1924 (WC).
Ravenshoe. 3 vols 1861, 1862, Boston 1862, 1864, London 1864, 1872, 1875, 1885, 1900, 1903, 1906, 1907, 1908, 1909, 1910 etc, Oxford 1925 (WC), London 1956, 1970.
Austin Elliot. 2 vols 1863 (3 edns), Boston 1863, 1865, 1866, 1872, 1885, Oxford 1932 (WC).
The Hillyars and the Burtons: a story of two families. 3 vols 1865, 1866, Boston 1866, London 1870, 1895 (with note on Old Chelsea Church by C. K. Shorter).
Leighton court: a country house story. 2 vols 1866, Boston 1866, London 1867, 1875.
Silcote of Silcotes. 3 vols 1867, New York 1869.
Mademoiselle Mathilde. 3 vols 1868, 1 vol 1870, 1885. 1st pbd GM.
Stretton. 3 vols 1869, New York 1869, London 1870, 1879, 1885.
Tales of old travels re-narrated. 1869, 1871.
The boy in grey and other stories and sketches. 1871.
Hetty and other stories. New York 1869, London 1871, 1885.
The lost child. 1871.
Old Margaret and other stories. 2 vols 1871, 1872, 1885, 1895.
The Harveys. 2 vols 1872, 1872 (rev), 1885 [1910].
Valentin: a French boy's story of Sedan. 2 vols 1872, [1874] (rev), 1885.
Hornby Mills and other stories. 2 vols 1872, 1873, 1885.
Oakshott castle, by Mr Granby Dixon, edited by Henry Kingsley. 3 vols 1873, 1878.
Reginald Hetherege. 3 vols 1874, 1875.
Number seventeen. 2 vols 1875, 1876, 1879.
Fireside studies. 2 vols 1876.
The Grange garden: a romance. 3 vols 1876.
The mystery of the island. 1877.

§2

Geoffrey Hamlyn. North Br Rev 31, 1859.
The Hillyars and the Burtons. North Amer Rev 101, 1865.

Quiller-Couch, A. T. In his Adventures in criticism, 1896.
Lord, W. F. In his The mirror of the century, 1906.
'Melville, Lewis' (L. S. Benjamin). In his Victorian novelists, 1906.
Russell, G. W. E. In his Selected essays, 1914. [EC]

William Henry Giles Kingston, 'Barrington Beaver' 1814–80

Collections

Tales for old and young of all classes by many writers. Ed W. H. G. Kingston. 1862, 1863.
Tales for all ages by W. H. G. Kingston and S. E. De Morgan, M. Doyle and others. 1863.
Popular sea tales. [189?] (illus).

§1

The frontier fort: or stirring times in the North-west territory of British America. nd.
How Britannia came to rule the waves. nd.
Michael Penguyne: or fisher life on the Cornish coast. nd.
The Circassian chief. A romance of Russia. 3 vols 1843, [1860].
Lusitanian sketches of the pen and pencil. 1844.
The prime minister. An historical romance. 1845.
The albatross: a tale of the sea. 1849.
The Ocean Queen and the spirit of the storm. A new fairy tale of the southern seas. 1851 (illus).
Peter the whaler: his early life, and adventures in Arctic regions. [1851], 1852, New York 1853, London 1882 (as Peter Trawl; or the adventures of a whaler), 1890, [1901], [1904].
The pirate of the Mediterranean. A tale of the sea. 1851.
Manco, the Peruvian chief: or an Englishman's adventures in the country of the Incas. [1852], 1853, [187?], London and Glasgow [1917?].
Mark Seaworth: a tale of the Indian Ocean. 1852 (illus).
Blue Jackets: or chips off the old block: a narrative of the gallant British seamen, and of the principal events in the naval service during the reign of Queen Victoria. 1854.
Western wanderings: or a pleasure tour in the Canadas. [1855], 1856.
Salt water: or the sea life and adventures of Neil D'Arcy, the midshipman. 1857.
The early life of old Jack: a sea tale. [1858], [1859].
Fred Markham in Russia: or the boy travellers in the land of the Czar. 1858 (illustr R. T. Landells).
Old Jack: a man-of-war's man and south-sea whaler. 1859, 1869 (with The early life of old Jack).
Round the world: a tale for boys. 1859, 1861, Boston 1862.
Will Weatherhelm: or the yarn of an old sailor, about his early life and adventures. [1859], 1860, 1879 (illus).
The boatswain's song: a tale of the sea. [1860], 1896.
The cruise of the 'Frolic': or yachting experiments of Barnaby Brine. 1860, 1866, 1884, 1885.
Digby Heathcote: or the early days of a country gentleman's son and heir. 1860.
Ernest Bracebridge: or school days. 1860 (illus).
The grateful Indian: a tale of Rupert's land. [1860.]
My first voyage to southern seas. 1860 (illus), 1869.
The boy's own book of boats, including vessels of every rig and size to be found floating on the waters in all parts of the world. 1861 (illus), [1867] (as The boy's own book of boats with complete instructions on how to make sailing models), 1868.
Jack Buntline: or life on the ocean. 1861.
My first cruise: or notes from Pringle Rushforth's sea log. [1861.]
My travels in many lands narrated for my young friends. [1861], 1862.
Salt water: or the life and adventures of Neil D'Arcy, the midshipman. 1861.
The seven champions of Christendom. 1861.
True blue: or the life and adventures of a British seaman of the old school. 1862.
The fire-ships. A tale of the last naval war. 1862, [1872] (as Ronald Morton: or the fire ships: a story of the last naval war).
Hearty words for British sailors afloat and ashore. 1862.
Marmaduke Merry the midshipman: or my early days at sea. 1862, 1864, 1870.
Adventures of Dick Onslow among the red skins. By Barrington Beaver. 1863, Boston 1864, London 1870, 1876.
Our sailors: or anecdotes of the engagements and other gallant deeds of the British navy during the reign of Her Majesty Queen Victoria. 1863.
Our soldiers or anecdotes of the campaigns and gallant deeds of the British army during the reign of Her Majesty Queen Victoria. 1863.
The three midshipmen. 1863 (illus), 1896. Originally pbd in Kingston's Mag.
The log house by the lake. A tale of Canada. [1864.]
Anthony Waymouth: or the gentlemen adventurers. 1865, Boston 1865.
The Gilpins and their fortunes. An Australian tale. [1865.]
Paul Luggershull: or the lightship. A tale of the coast. [1865?]
Philip Mavor: or life amongst the Kaffirs. [1865.]
Rob Nixon, the old white trapper. A tale of central British North America. [1865].
The young foresters and other tales. New York 1865, Philadelphia 1883.
Mountain Moggy: or the stoning of the witch. A tale for the young. [1866.]
My first cruise. Followed by The travelling tinman, The beautiful gate and The Chimaera. [1866] (Cassell's Story Books for the Young).
Washed ashore: or the tower of Stormont Bay. 1866, 1868, [1936].
Foxholme Hall: a legend of Christmas and other tales for boys. 1867 (illus), New York 1869.
Frozen up: or my polar experiences. 1867.
Infant amusements: or how to make a nursery happy. With practical hints to parents and nurses on the moral and physical training of children. 1867.
Paul Gerard, the cabin boy. 1867.
Ralph Clavering: or we must try before we can do. 1867.
Taking tales for cottage homes. Ed W. H. G. Kingston [1867].
Count Ulrich von Lindberg: a tale of the Reformation in Germany. [1868.]
The perils and adventures of Harry Skipwith by sea and by land. 1868.
The pirates' treasure: a legend of Panama and other tales for boys. 1868.
Three hundred years ago: or the martyr of Brentwood. [1868], Dublin 1868, Philadelphia 1868.
The last lock: a tale of the Spanish Inquisition. 1869.
Our fresh and salt water tutors. A story of that good old time our schooldays at the Cape. Ed W. H. G. Kingston. 1869.
At the South Pole: or the adventures of R. Pengelly. [1870] (illus).
John Deane of Nottingham: his adventures and exploits: a tale of the times of William of Orange and Queen Anne. 1870.
Little Ben Hadden: or do right whatever comes of it. [1870.]
Off to sea: or the adventures of jovial Jack Junker on his road to fame. [1870.]
The royal merchant: or events in the days of Sir Thomas Gresham, as narrated in the diary of E. Verner, whilom his page and secretary during the reigns of Queens Mary and Elizabeth. 1870.
The pirate's treasure. A tale of Panama. 1870.
Sunshine bill. [1870.]
In the eastern seas: or the regions of the bird of paradise. 1871.
In the wilds of Africa. A tale for boys. 1871.
The fortunes of the 'Ranger' and 'Crusader'. A tale of two ships and the adventures of their passengers and crews. [1872.]

On the banks of the Amazon: or a boy's journal of his adventures in the tropical wilds of South America. 1872, 1906.
The adventures of Harry Skipwith by sea and land. 1873 (illus).
The history of little Peter the ship-boy. 1873.
The trapper's son. A story of the Canadian west. [1873.]
Waihoura: or the New Zealand girl. [1873.]
The young whaler: or the adventures of Archibald Hughson. London and Boston 1873.
The history of little Peter the ship-boy. 1874, Philadelphia nd.
Stories of the sagacity of animals. 1874 (illustr H. Weir).
The African trader: or the adventures of Harry Bayford. 1875, 1888, Boston nd (as The African trader and Waihoura: or the New Zealand girl).
The south sea whaler: a story of the loss of the 'Champion' and the adventures of her crew. 1875.
The three lieutenants: or naval life in the nineteenth century. 1875.
Archibald Hughes, the young Shetlander. 1876.
The child of the wreck: or the loss of the Royal George. 1876.
The cruise of the 'Dainty': or rovings in the Pacific. 1876.
My first voyage to southern seas. A book for boys. 1876.
Snow shoes and canoes: or the early days of a fur trader in the Hudson's Bay territory. 1876 (illus), London and Edinburgh 1913.
The three commanders: or active service afloat in modern days. 1876.
Virginia: a centennial story. Boston [1876].
The wanderers: or adventures in the wilds of Trinidad and up the Orinoco. 1876 (illus), 1883.
At the South Pole: or the adventures of Richard Pengelly, mariner. 1877 (4th edn).
The voyage of the 'Steadfast': or the young missionaries in the Pacific. 1877, 1878.
Yachting tales. 1877.
The young llanero. 1877 (illustr W. S. Stacey and S. Paget).
In the Rocky Mountains. 1878, 1906.
The three admirals, and the adventures of their young followers. 1878 (illustr J. R. Wells and C. J. Staniland), 1883, 1886.
With axe and rifle: or the western pioneers. 1878, 1887 (4th edn).
The frontier fort: or stirring times in the North-west territory of British America. [1879.]
The grateful Indian and other stories. 1879.
In New Granada: or heroes and patriots. A tale for boys. 1879.
Mary Liddiard: or the missionary's daughter. 1879.
Voyages and travels of Count Funnibos and Baron Stilkin. [1880.]
Hendricks the hunter: or the border farm: a tale of Zululand. 1880.
Adventures in the far west. 1881.
Dick Cheveley: his adventures and misadventures. 1881, 1908 (EL).
The heir of Kilfinnan. A tale of the shore and ocean. 1881.
Arctic adventures. 1882 (illus), 1888.
Ned Garth: or made prisoner in Africa. 1882.
The two voyages: or midnight and daylight. 1882.
Adventures in Africa. 1883.
Charley Laurel: a story of adventure by sea and land. 1883.
Adventures among the Indians: or scouting with General Custer. Chicago 1884.
Afar in the forest. A tale of adventure in North America. 1884.
From powder boy to admiral. A story of naval adventure. 1884, 1886.
Mate of the 'Lily': or notes from Harry Musgrave's log book. [1885], 1890.
Among the redskins: or over the Smoky Mountains. 1887.
The settlers: a tale of Virginia. 1887.
The heroic wife: or the wanderers on the Amazon. 1888.
Norman Vallery: or how to overcome evil with good. 1888.
The boy who sailed with Blake. 1889.
The lily of Leyden. 1889.
Twice lost. Edinburgh and New York 1889.
The golden grasshopper. A story of the days of Sir Thomas Gresham, Kt. 1890.
The trapper's son. [1890?]
Captain Mugford or our salt and fresh water tutors. 1891.
The ferryman of Brill and other stories. 1891.
The two whalers: or adventures in the Pacific. 1891.
The boatswain's son and other stories. 1896 (illus).
Ben Haddon: or do right, whatever comes of it. 1897.
The mines and its wonders. 1898.
The last look. A tale of the Spanish Inquisition. 1899.
The cruise of the 'Mary Rose': or here and there in the Pacific. 1901.

Pamphlets on emigration

Emigrant manuals (The British colonies described; Preparations for the voyage; Employment on the voyage; Arrival in the colony). 1850. (Emigrant tracts nos 14, 15, 16, 17 and 50.)
The emigrant voyager's manual. 1850.
How to emigrate; or, the British colonists: a tale. 1850.
The emigrant's home; or, how to settle. A story of Australian life. [1855], 1856.
The silver skates: a story. With a preface by W. H. G. Kingston. 1867.
Kingston edited the Colonial Mag and East India Rev *1849–51;* Kingston's Mag for Boys *1859–63;* Union Jack *1880.*

§2

Kingsford, M. R. The life, work and influence of Kingston. Toronto 1947. [DD]

Letitia Elizabeth Landon 1802–38

See col 629.

George Alfred Lawrence 1827–76

§1

The marriage of Marie Antoinette with the Dauphin: a prize poem recited in Rugby School, June 20 1845. Rugby 1845.
Songs of feast, field and fray, by Δ. 1853.
Guy Livingstone: or thorough. 1857 (anon), 1863 (6th edn); ed S. Kaye-Smith 1928.
Sword and gown. 1859. First pbd in Fraser's Mag.
Barren honour: a tale. 2 vols 1862. First pbd in Fraser's Mag.
Border and Bastille. 1863, New York 1866. Includes Songs of feast, field and fray, *above.*
A bundle of ballads. 1864.
Maurice Dering, or the quadrilateral: a novel. 2 vols 1864, Leipzig 1864.
Sans merci: or kestrels and falcons. 3 vols 1866, 1866.
Brakespeare: or the fortunes of a free lance. 3 vols 1868.
Breaking a butterfly: or Blanche Ellerslie's ending. 3 vols 1869.
Anteros: a novel. 3 vols 1873.
Silverland. 1873.
Hagarene. 3 vols 1874.

§2

Edinburgh Rev 108 1858. Review of Guy Livingstone.
Montégut, E. In his Écrivains modernes de l'Angleterre ser i, Paris 1885.
Roberts, W. G. A. Lawrence's Songs of feast, field and fray. TLS 4, 18 July 1935.
Fleming, G. H. Lawrence and the Victorian sensation novel. Tucson AZ 1952.

'Holme Lee', Harriet Parr 1828–1900

Maude Talbot. 3 vols 1854.
Thorney Hall: a story of an old family. 1855.
Gilbert Massenger. 1855.
Kathie Brande: a fireside history of a quiet life. 2 vols 1856.

Sylvan Holt's daughter. 3 vols 1858.
Against wind and tide. 3 vols 1859.
Hawksview: a family history of our own times. 1859.
Legends from Fairy Land: narrating the history of Prince Glee and Princess Trill, the cruel persecutions and condign punishment of Aunt Spite, the adventures of the great Tuflongbo, and the story of the blackcap in the giant's well. 1860, 1908, 1988.
The Wortlebank diary and some old stories from Kathie Brande's portfolio. 3 vols 1860.
The wonderful adventures of Tuflongbo and his elfin company, in their journey of little content through the enchanted forest. 1861 Cambridge Univ Lib.
Warp and woof: or the reminiscences of Doris Fletcher. 3 vols 1861.
Tuflongbo's journey in search of ogres, with some account of his early life, and how his shoes got worn out. 1862.
Annis Warleigh's fortunes. 3 vols 1863.
The true pathetic history of Poor Match. 1863, [1863] (as Poor Match: his life, adventures and death).
In the silver age: essays – that is, dispersed meditations. 2 vols 1864.
The life and death of Jeanne d'Arc, called 'The Maid'. 2 vols 1866.
Mr Wynyard's ward. 2 vols 1867.
Basil Godfrey's caprice. 3 vols 1868.
Contrast: or the schoolfellows. 1868.
For richer, for poorer. 3 vols 1870.
Maurice and Eugénie de Guérin: a monograph. 1870.
Her title of honour. 1871.
The beautiful Miss Barrington. 3 vols 1871.
Echoes of a famous year. 1872.
Country stories, old and new, in prose and verse. 2 vols 1872.
Katherine's trial. 1873.
The vicissitudes of Bessie Fairfax. 3 vols 1874.
This work-a-day world. 3 vols 1875.
Ben Milner's wooing. 1876.
Straightforward. 3 vols 1878.
Mrs Denys of Cote. 3 vols 1880.
A poor squire. 2 vols 1882.
Loving and serving. 3 vols 1883.

Joseph Thomas Sheridan le Fanu 1814–73

Ms material in Cambridge Univ Lib (Le Fanu family archive); Brotherton Lib, Univ of Leeds (Bennett Papers); Trinity College Dublin (diaries of W. R. Le Fanu); Public Record Office of Northern Ireland (Dufferin and Ava Papers); Nat Lib of Ireland (Butt Papers, Joly mss, and microfilm of other material); Victoria and Albert Museum (Forster Papers); Univ of Illinois (Bentley correspondence). See W. R. Le Fanu, Notebooks of Sheridan Le Fanu *in* Long Room *14/15 1977.*

Le Fanu purchased the Dublin Univ Mag *in July 1861 and disposed of it in 1870; he acted as editor for all but the first and final months of this period; see W. J. Mc Cormack,* 'Never put your name to an anonymous letter': serial reading in The Dublin University Magazine 1861–69 *YES 26 1996.*

Collections and Selections

The Purcell Papers, with a memoir by A. P. Graves. 3 vols 1880.
The watcher and other weird stories. 1894.
A chronicle of Golden Friars and other stories. 1896.
Poems. Ed A. P. Graves 1896.
Madam Crowl's ghost and other tales of mystery. Ed M. R. James 1923.
Green tea and other ghost stories. Sauk City WI 1945.
Best ghost stories. Ed E. F. Bleiler, New York 1964.
Ghost stories and mysteries. Ed E. F. Bleiler, New York 1975.
Collected works. 20 titles in facs of 1st edns, ed D. Varma, New York 1977.
Der besessene Baronet und andere Geistergeschichten. Frankfurt 1981.
Der ehrenwerte richter Harbottle: vier unheimliche Geschichten. Zurich 1982.
Ein Bild des malers Schalken und andere Geistergeschichten. Frankfurt 1983.
The illustrated J. S. Le Fanu. Wellingborough 1988.

§1

The cock and anchor: being a chronicle of old Dublin city. Anon. 3 vols Dublin, London and Edinburgh 1845, Dublin 1847, 1848, 1851 (as Sir Henry Ashwoode, the forger), London 1873 (amended as Morley Court), 1895, Dublin [1913], London 1962. Never serialised.
The fortunes of Colonel Torlogh O'Brien: a tale of the wars of King James. Anon Dublin and London 1847, 1851, 1855, [1891], 1896, 1897, 1899. Anon. Issued in parts prior to book pbn.
Ghost stories and tales of mystery. Dublin and London 1851. Anon.
The house by the church-yard. 3 vols 1863, 1866, [1870], New York 1886, London 1899, Dublin 1904, London 1968, Belfast 1992; tr Cz 1972, Ger 1977, Polish 1977. Serialised in the Dublin Univ Mag.
Wylder's hand; a novel. 3 vols 1864, 1865, [1870], [1903], 1963, New York 1978; tr Jap 1981. Serialised in the Dublin Univ Mag.
Uncle Silas; a tale of Bartram-Haugh. 3 vols 1864, 1865, 1 vol 1865, 2 vols Leipzig 1865, [1871], New York 1878, London 1893, 1899, Dublin 1904, London [1913], 1926, 1940; ed E. Bowen 1947; New York 1966; ed Mc Cormack, Oxford 1981; tr Swed 1866, Fr 1877, Ger 1972, Jap 1980 (2 vols), Polish 1987. Serialised in the Dublin Univ Mag commencing as Maud Ruthyn.
Guy Deverell. 3 vols 1865, 2 vols Leipzig 1865, 1 vol 1866, [1869], New York 1984. Serialised in the Dublin Univ Mag.
All in the dark. 2 vols 1866, [1869], [1898]. Serialised in the Dublin Univ Mag.
The tenants of Malory: a novel. 3 vols 1867, [1872]. Serialised in the Dublin Univ Mag.
A lost name. 3 vols 1868. Serialised in Temple Bar.
Haunted lives: a novel. 3 vols 1868. Serialised in the Dublin Univ Mag.
My own story: or, loved and lost. 9 pts. Serialised in the Dublin Univ Mag, Sep 1868–May 1869, never issued in book form.
The Wyvern mystery: a novel. 3 vols 1869, 1889, [1904], Stroud 1994. Serialised in the Dublin Univ Mag.
Checkmate. 3 vols 1871, New York 1873, London [1876], [1898]. Serialised in Cassell's Mag.
The rose and the key. 3 vols 1871, [1893], 1900, New York 1982, Stroud 1994. Serialised in All the Year Round.
Chronicles of Golden Friars [tales]. 3 vols 1871.
In a glass darkly [tales]. 3 vols 1872, 1884, 1886, 1897, 1923, 1929, 1947; ed R. Tracy, Oxford 1993; tr Ital 1981, Ger 1982, Sp 1987.
Willing to die. 3 vols 1873. Serialised in All the Year Round.

Individual stories posthumously published in single-volume form

De vliegende draak (The room in the Dragon Volant, tr Du). Haarlem [187?].
The bird of passage. New York 1878.
The evil guest. 1895.
No escape. Waterford 1942.
A strange adventure in the life of Miss Laura Mildmay. [1947.]
Borrhomeo the astrologer. Edinburgh 1985.
No attempt has been made to list separate pbn of certain stories (e.g. 'Carmilla' from In a glass darkly*) which have been reproduced on many occasions with varying degrees of textual integrity.*

§2

Le Fanu, W. R. Seventy years of Irish life. 1893.
Brown, Nelson. Sheridan Le Fanu. 1951.
Ellis, S. M. Wilkie Collins, Le Fanu, and others. 1951.

Achilles, Jochen. Sheridan Le Fanu und die schauerromantische Tradition. Tubingen 1991.

McCormack, W. J. Sheridan Le Fanu. Stroud 1997. 3rd edn of Sheridan Le Fanu and Victorian Ireland (1980), with additional material. [WJ MCC]

Charles James Lever 1806–72

Mss and correspondence relating to Lever can be found in the Huntington; Royal Irish Acad; Parrish Collection, Princeton; Houghton Lib, Harvard; Bulwer-Lytton Collection, Hertfordshire Record Office; and Blackwood Papers, NLS.

Collections

The military novels, illustrated by George Cruikshank and 'Phiz'. 9 vols nd.

Works. 34 vols 1876–8. Harry Lorrequer edn.

Novels, edited by his daughter [Julia Kate Neville]. 37 vols 1897–9.

§1

The confessions of Harry Lorrequer. Dublin 1839, London 1845, 2 vols 1847, 1857, 1872, 1882, 1884; pbd continuously between 1893 and 1905. Ed 'Lewis Melville' (L. S. Benjamin), London [1907] (EL), 1928 (abridged), [1937] (Nelson Classics), Dublin 1945 (abridged); tr Fr 1859.

Diary and notes of Horace Templeton, late Secretary of Legation. Philadelphia [1840?], 2 vols London 1848, [1878].

Charles O'Malley, the Irish dragoon, edited by Harry Lorrequer. 2 vols Dublin 1841, London 1842, 1845, 3 vols Leipzig 1848, 2 vols London 1857, 1876, 1879, 1884, 1888, 1892, 1893, 1897, 1903, 1905, 1906, 1909, 1912, 1947 (abridged).

Our mess. 3 vols Dublin 1843–4, London 1857, 1876, 1885. Vol 1 Jack Hinton; vols 2–3 Tom Burke of 'Ours'.

Jack Hinton. First pbd as part of Our mess. Dublin 1845, 2 vols Leipzig 1849, Dublin 1857, London 1876, 1885, 1886, 1890, 1892, 1893, 1899, 1905.

Tom Burke. First pbd as vols 2–3 of Our mess. 3 vols Leipzig 1849, Dublin 1857, 2 vols London 1876, 1886, 1892, 1893, 1899, 1902, 1904, 1906.

Arthur O'Leary: his wanderings and ponderings in many lands. 3 vols 1844, 1845, 1 vol 1856 (as Adventures of Arthur O'Leary), 1877, 1886, 1892, 1906.

St Patrick's Eve. 1845, 1871 (with A rent in the cloud etc).

Nuts and nutcrackers. 1845, 1857.

Tales of the trains. 1845.

The O'Donoghue: a tale of Ireland fifty years ago. Dublin 1845, Leipzig 1845, Dublin 1858, London 1868, 1876, 1887, 1893, 1898 (new edn).

The Knight of Gwynne: a tale of the time of the Union. 1847, 1858, 1867, 1877, 1889.

The Martins of Gro' Martin. 1847, 1856, 3 vols Leipzig 1856, 2 vols London 1878.

Confessions of Con Cregan, the Irish Gil Blas. 2 vols [1849], 1854, 1860, 1876, 1 vol 1891, 1892.

Roland Cashel. 1850, 3 vols Leipzig 1858, 2 vols London 1858, 1864, 2 vols 1877.

The Daltons: or three roads in life. 2 vols 1850–2, 1859, 1876.

Maurice Tiernay: the soldier of fortune. 1852, [1855], 2 vols 1861, 1878.

The Dodd family abroad. 2 vols 1852–4, 1859, 1877, 1890.

Sir Jasper Carew: his life and experiences. [1855], 2 vols Leipzig 1861, London 1878.

The fortunes of Glencore. 3 vols 1857, 2 vols Leipzig 1857, London 1875, 1878.

Davenport Dunn: or the man of the day. 1857–9, 3 vols Leipzig 1859, 2 vols London 1877; tr Fr 1861.

One of them. 1860, 2 vols Leipzig 1860, London 1861, 1877.

A day's ride. 2 vols 1863, 1878; tr Du 1913.

Barrington. 1863, 2 vols Leipzig 1863, 1 vol London 1878.

Cornelius O'Dowd upon men, women and other things in general. 3 ser 1864–5, 1 vol 1874. First pbd in Blackwood's Mag.

Luttrell of Arran. 1865, 2 vols Leipzig 1865, 1 vol London 1877.

A rent in a cloud. [1865], 1871, 1878 (with St Patrick's Eve etc).

Tony Butler. First pbd in Blackwood's Mag Oct 1863–Jan 1865. 3 vols Edinburgh 1865, 2 vols Leipzig 1866, Edinburgh 1878.

Sir Brook Fossbrooke. First pbd in Blackwood's Mag May 1865–Nov 1866. 3 vols Edinburgh 1866, 2 vols Leipzig 1867, Edinburgh 1878.

The Bramleighs of Bishop's Folly. 3 vols 1868, 1877.

Paul Gosslett's confessions in law and the Civil Service. 1868, 1924. First pbd in St Paul's Mag.

That boy of Norcott's. 1869, 1878 (with A rent in a cloud, *above*, etc).

Lord Kilgobbin: a tale of Ireland in our own time. 3 vols 1872, 1877, 1906.

Gerald Fitzgerald the Chevalier. 1899. First pbd in Dublin Univ Mag; rptd 27 years after Lever's death.

Lever edited Dublin Univ Mag *1835–72 and from 1835 was also a regular contributor to* Blackwood's Mag. *See* Wellesley *vol 5 1989.*

§2

The works of Lever. Blackwood's Mag Apr 1862.

Friswell, J. H. In his Modern men of letters, 1870.

Fitzpatrick, W. J. Life of Lever. 2 vols 1879.

Notes on Charles Lever. Rev of Revs Jan 1896.

Downey, E. Lever: life in his letters. 2 vols 1906.

Rolfe, F. P. Letters of Lever to his wife and daughter. Huntington Lib Bull no 10 1936.

McHugh, R. Charles Lever. Stud 27 1938.

Stevenson, L. Dr Quicksilver. 1939.

Genn, F. Books in general. New Statesman 5 Sep 1942.

Hennig, J. Lever and Rodolphe Toepffer. MLR 43 1948. [DF]

George Henry Lewes 1817–78

See col 2550.

Eliza Lynn Linton, née Lynn 1822–98

Linton's letters are in the ms collections at the Beinecke Lib, Yale; Univ of Illinois Lib; Nat Lib of Australia; NLS; Pierpont Morgan Lib, New York; Princeton; UCLA Research Lib; and Duke Univ Lib, Durham NC, with lesser holdings in other libs.

Selections

The mad Willoughbys and other tales. 1875. Rptd from New Quart Mag.

With a silken thread, and other stories. 3 vols 1880. Rptd from Household Words, All the Year Round, Queen, et al.
REVIEWS: Saturday Rev 5 June 1880; Acad 21 Aug 1880.

The girl of the period, and other social essays. 2 vols 1883. Rptd from Saturday Rev.
REVIEWS: The Times 22 Nov 1883; Acad 12 Jan 1884; Spectator 9 Feb 1884. (For the controversy surrounding the original pbns of these essays, *see below under* Contributions to periodicals.)

An octave of friends, with other silhouettes and stories. 1891. Rptd from London Soc and other periodicals.

Freeshooting: extracts from the works of Mrs Lynn Linton. Selected and with an introd by G. F. S. 1892.
REVIEW: Acad 4 June 1892.

'Twixt cup and lip, etc. [1896.] Stories. Rptd from All the Year Round and other periodicals.

§1

Azeth, the Egyptian, by E. L. 3 vols 1847.
REVIEWS: Literary Gazette 16 Jan 1847; Athenaeum 23 Jan 1847; Ainsworth's Mag Feb 1847; NMM Feb 1847; Westminster Rev July

1847; Examiner 23 Oct 1847. *See also* F. E. Trollope, Frances Trollope: her life and literary work, 1895.
Amymone: a romance in the days of Pericles. 3 vols 1848.
REVIEWS: Literary Gazette 12 Aug 1848; Athenaeum 26 Aug 1848; Bentley's Misc Sep 1848; NMM Sep 1848; Examiner 2 Sep 1848; The Times 15 Sep 1848; Edinburgh Rev Oct 1850. *See also* Walter Savage Landor to Eliza Lynn on her Amymone, Examiner 22 July 1848; The Brontës: their lives, friendships, and correspondence, ed T. Wise, vol 2, 1932.
Realities: a tale. 3 vols 1851.
REVIEWS: Spectator 24 May 1851; Leader 31 May 1851; Bentley's Misc June 1851; NMM June 1851; Athenaeum 14 June 1851. *See also* G. H. Lewes, The lady novelists, Westminster Rev July 1852; G. Haight, George Eliot and John Chapman, with Chapman's diaries, 1940.
Witch stories. 1861, 1881, New York 1972.
REVIEWS: Athenaeum 28 Dec 1861; All the Year Round 15 Mar 1862.
The Lake country, illustrated by W. J. Linton. 1864.
REVIEWS: Examiner 3 Dec 1864; Reader 3 Dec 1864; London Rev 10 Dec 1864.
Grasp your nettle: a novel. 3 vols 1865.
REVIEWS: Illus London News 24 June 1865; Reader 1 July 1865; Athenaeum 15 July 1865; London Rev 9 Sep 1865.
Lizzie Lorton of Greyrigg: a novel. 2 vols 1866, New York 1866, 1871 (5th edn).
REVIEWS: Athenaeum 5 May 1866; Examiner 12 May 1866; Saturday Rev 14 July 1866; Spectator 21 July 1866.
Sowing the wind. 3 vols 1867, 1890, New York 1890.
REVIEWS: Athenaeum 9 Mar 1867; London Rev 16 Mar 1867; Examiner 23 Mar 1867; Saturday Rev 23 Mar 1867. *See also* T. Tinsley, Random recollections of an old publisher vol 2, 1900.
Ourselves: essays on women. 1869, New York 1869, London 1870, New York 1870, London 1884, 1893. First pbd in Routledge's Mag 1868.
REVIEWS: Pall Mall Gazette 10 1869; Athenaeum 21 Aug 1869; Illus London News 4 Sep 1869; Blackwood's Mag 108 1870.
The true history of Joshua Davidson, Christian and communist, by anon. 1872, 1873, Philadelphia 1873 with 2nd edn under title The life of Joshua Davidson, London 1901 (11th edn), 1916, New York 1975; tr Du 1915.
REVIEWS: Graphic 30 Nov 1872; Examiner 11 Jan 1873; Contemporary Rev Apr 1873. *See also* New England Mag Apr 1892; Walter de la Mare, Some women novelists of the seventies, in The eighteen-seventies, ed H. Granville-Barker, 1929.
Patricia Kemball. 3 vols 1875, Philadelphia 1875, 1893. Serialised in Temple Bar Feb 1874–Feb 1875.
REVIEWS: Graphic 5 Dec 1874; Examiner 26 Dec 1874; Westminster Rev Jan 1875; Acad 6 Mar 1875.
The atonement of Leam Dundas. 3 vols 1877. Serialised in Cornhill Mag Aug 1875–June 1876.
REVIEWS: Athenaeum 27 May 1876; Saturday Rev 19 June 1876; Graphic 24 June 1876; Br Quart Rev July 1876; Westminster Rev July 1876; Examiner 1 July 1876; Spectator 12 Aug 1876.
The world well lost. 2 vols 1877, New York 1877, 1890. Serialised in Belgravia Jan–Dec 1877.
REVIEWS: Athenaeum 22 Dec 1877; Contemporary Rev Jan 1878; Saturday Rev 26 Jan 1878; Acad 2 Feb 1878; Examiner 2 Feb 1878; Br Quart Rev Apr 1878.
Misericordia, a story. New York 1878.
A night in a hospital. 1879. Essay. Rptd from Belgravia.
Under which lord? 1879, New York 1976. Serialised in GM Jan–Dec 1879.
REVIEWS: Athenaeum 15 Nov 1879; Saturday Rev 29 Nov 1879; Illus London News 13 Dec 1879; Br Quart Rev Jan 1880; Westminster Rev Jan 1880. *See also* B. Tuckerman, A history of English prose fiction, 1882.
The rebel of the family. 3 vols 1880, New York 1880, 1886. Serialised in Temple Bar Jan–Dec 1880.
REVIEWS: Examiner 3 Jan, 2 Oct 1880; Saturday Rev 20 Nov 1880; Athenaeum 4 Dec 1880; Br Quart Rev Jan 1881; Acad 19 Feb 1881.
'My Love!' 3 vols 1881, New York 1881. Serialised in the Bolton Evening News.
REVIEWS: Br Quart Rev July 1881; Athenaeum 9 July 1881; Acad 30 July 1881; Saturday Rev 13 Aug 1881.
Ione. 3 vols 1883, New York 1883 with title Ione Stewart, 1884. Serialised in Temple Bar Jan–Dec 1880.
REVIEWS: Athenaeum 8 Dec 1883; Saturday Rev 26 Jan 1884; Westminster Rev Apr 1884. *See also* G. Gissing, London and the life of literature in late Victorian England: the diary of George Gissing, novelist, ed P. Coustillas, 1978.
The autobiography of Christopher Kirkland. 3 vols 1885, New York 1976. Fictionalised autobiography.
REVIEWS: Contemporary Rev Apr 1886; Acad 25 July 1885; Athenaeum 25 July 1885; Saturday Rev 1 Aug 1885; Spectator 3 Oct 1885.
Stabbed in the dark. [1885], New York [1886]. Novella.
Rift in the lute: a tale. Glasgow [1885].
Paston Carew, millionaire and miser. 1886, New York [1886]. Serialised in Temple Bar Jan–Dec 1886.
REVIEW: St James's Gazette 23 Nov 1886.
Through the long night. 3 vols 1888, New York 1888. Serialised in The People.
REVIEWS: Saturday Rev 24 Nov 1888; Athenaeum 1 Dec 1888; Acad 15 Dec 1888; Spectator 29 Dec 1888.
About Ireland. 1890. Rptd in expanded form from the New Rev 1 1889.
About Ulster, 1892.
The one too many. 3 vols 1894, New York 1894. Serialised in the Lady's Pictorial 1893.
REVIEWS: Athenaeum 17 Mar 1894; Spectator 31 Mar 1894; Acad 14 Apr 1894.
In haste and at leisure. 3 vols 1895, New York [1895] with the title The new woman; in haste and at leisure.
REVIEWS: Queen 23 Mar 1895; Acad 30 Mar 1895; Athenaeum 30 Mar 1895; Graphic 27 Apr 1895; Spectator 27 Apr 1895; Bookman Feb 1896.
Dulcie Everton. 2 vols 1896.
My literary life, with a prefatory note by Beatrice Harraden. 1899. Rptd from Woman at Home.
The second youth of Theodora Desanges, with an introduction by G. S. Layard. 1900.

Contributions to periodicals

Listed chronologically based on first pbn in each jnl. This list includes the major periodicals to which Linton contributed, but does not include all her periodical pbns in her prolific career. See also Wellesley.
Ainsworth's Mag 1844–6. For listing, *see* Wellesley vol 3, plus The national convention of the gods (poem) May 1844, A wreath (poem) June 1844.
Metropolitan Mag. Song of the fairies (poem) July 1845, Lorenzo's moonlight adventure (story) Nov 1845, To Lucy, on receiving a lock of her hair (poem) Dec 1845, Psycholene, the ice-queen; a seasonable tale Dec 1845, Fanny Lawson's new bonnet (story) Apr 1846, To Lucy, on hearing that her flower of fate had died (poem) Apr 1846, The vision (poem) Apr 1846, Courtship and matrimony (story) Aug 1846.
NMM 1847–9. *See* Wellesley vol 3.
Morning Chron (newspaper) 1848–51. 6 articles monthly, on social subjects.
Chambers' Edinburgh Jnl. The picnic to Watendlath (story) 6 Dec 1851, That stitch in time 29 June 1889, The treatment of servants 20 July 1889, Our young folks 14 Sep 1889, Our margins 15 Mar

1890, Invalids 7 June 1890, Admirable, but – 2 Aug 1890, Possessing one's soul 4 Oct 1890, Huffy people 28 Mar 1891, Bolts from the blue 3 May 1891, The art of happiness 4 July 1891, That supple backbone 19 Sep 1891, The science of society 7 Nov 1891, Old maids 26 Mar 1892, Old songs and new saws 7 Oct 1893, The ethics of hotel life 18 Nov 1893, A practical philosopher 12 May 1894, From turmoil to repose 17 Nov 1894, Irrepressibles 21 Sep 1895, Social crimes 25 Jan 1896.

Chambers' Repository of Instructive and Amusing Tracts. Grace Ayton (story) 2 vols 1853.

Household Words 1853–9. For listing of her contributions and Dickens's evaluations of them, *see* A. Lohrli (comp), Household Words; a weekly journal 1850–1859, 1973.

English Republic. Mary Wollstonecraft 3 1854, A homily (poem) 4 1854.

Nat Mag. 22 stories and articles from 1857–9.

Fraser's Mag 1857–70. *See* Wellesley vol 2.

North Br Rev 1857, 1869. *See* Wellesley vol 1.

Literary Gazette. 1858–60. Regular book reviews.

All the Year Round. Commons and kings 26 May 1860, The family at Fenhouse (story) 22 Dec 1860 (rptd in With a silken thread 1880), John Wilson 29 Nov 1862, Canker in the bud 14 Nov 1868, The white witch of Combe Andrew (story) 23 Dec 1871 (rptd in With a silken thread 1880), Dear Davie (story) 18 Mar 1870 (rptd in With a silken thread 1880), Galloping Dick (story) 17 Feb 1873 (rptd in With a silken thread 1880), Misericordia (story) 1, 8, 15 Jan 1881, 'Twixt cup and lip (story) 18 Aug 1883 (rptd in 'Twixt cup and lip, etc 1896).

London Rev 1860–2. Regular essays satirising English women.

Temple Bar 1861–88. *See* Wellesley vol 3.

London Soc. My first soirée July 1864, Rose Blackett and her lovers Nov 1864, Faithful and true July–Sep 1865, Snowed up with a burglar Christmas No 1865, An octave of friends (story) Jan, Mar, July, Sep 1872, Madame Dufour Feb 1873. (All of these stories were rptd in An octave of friends 1891.)

Saturday Rev 1866–75. For listings, *see* M. Bevington, The Saturday Review 1855–1867, 1941. For reactions to these satiric essays and especially to The girl of the period (25 1868), *see* Tomahawk 2 1868; Punch 55 1868; Fun 7 1868; Eclectic Rev 15 1868; Judy 2 1868, 3 1868; Temple Bar 24 1868; Victoria 11 1868, 12 1869, 15 1870; A. Trollope, The Vicar of Bullhampton, 1870; Macmillan's Mag 19 1869; Contemporary Rev 11 1869; St Paul's Mag 2 1869; Belgravia 9 1869; Pall Mall Gazette 10 1869; Girl of the Period Misc 1869; Tinsley's Mag 5 1870. *See also* Examiner 18 Apr 1874; G. S. Layard, Mrs Lynn Linton: her life, letters, and opinions, 1901; H. Corkran, Celebrities and I, 1902; J. E. Panton, Leaves from a life, 1908. *See also* reviews of Modern women and what is said of them, Ourselves, and The girl of the period, and other social essays.

Tinsley's Mag. Our lake-land 1 1867, A story of the hills (story) 1 1867, Guernsey in midwinter 2 1868, Secrets 2 1868, Fussy folk 4 1869.

St Paul's Mag 1867. *See* Wellesley vol 3.

Galaxy. Clementina Kinniside (story) 5, May 1868.

Broadway. Walter Savage Landor 2 1869.

Atlantic Monthly. The Channel Islands 25 1870, Let us be cheerful 25 1870, Old friends with a new face 30 1872, An old English home 32 1873.

Macmillan's Mag. 1870. *See* Wellesley vol 1.

Queen. Regular contributions from 1870s to the late 1890s.

Punch. On being taken up and put down again 7 Jan 1871.

Dark Blue 1872. *See* Wellesley vol 4.

Good Words. Lost lambs Jan 1873.

Cornhill Mag 1873–6. *See* Wellesley vol 1. For reaction to On the side of the maids (29 1874), *see* Cornhill Mag 29 1874.

World. Jezebel à la mode 8 July 1874.

New Quart Mag 1874–8. *See* Wellesley vol 2.

Belgravia. Woman's place in nature and society May 1876 (for reactions, *see* Victoria Mag 28 1876; Examiner 27 May 1876 and 1 July 1876), Old maids June 1876, From dreams to waking (story) 30 and 31 1876, The world well lost (novel) Jan–Dec 1877 (pbd separately in 1877), Our scholastica Sep 1878, Pictures from Venice Dec 1878, A Florentine orphanage Jan 1879, A night in a hospital July 1879 (rptd separately in 1879), The young lions (story) Nov 1879, Under the snow 40 1880, My compatriot (story) Nov 1883, Medea Fortune (story) Apr 1885.

GM. Masks 240 1877, A Summer in the south 242 1878, Under which lord? (novel) Jan–Dec 1879 (pbd separately in 1879), Netley Hospital 247 1879, History in little 256 1884, On the way home 257 1884.

Nat Rev 1885–95. *See* Wellesley vol 2.

Fortnightly Rev 1885–96. *See* Wellesley vol 2. For reaction to Pasteur's life and labours (Aug 1885), *see* W. E. Gladstone, Dawn of creation and of worship, Nineteenth Cent Nov 1885. Linton's response was pbd in The origin of creation: the conflict between Genesis and geology [1884]. For reaction to the 1887–9 essays on the history of women, *see* Millicent Fawcett, The enfranchisement of women, Fortnightly Rev Apr 1889.

Forum. The tyranny of fashion Mar 1887, On things social June 1887, The pains of fear May 1888, Are good women characterless? Feb 1889, Democracy in the household Oct 1889, Mrs Grundy's kingdom Feb 1890 (criticised in Rev of Revs Mar 1890), The revolt against matrimony Jan 1891.

Universal Rev. M. Zola's idée mère May 1888, The philosophy of marriage Sep 1888, An unfinished history (story) Feb–Mar 1889, The new and the old Feb 1890.

New Rev 1889–95. *See* Wellesley vol 3.

For criticism of Linton's views expressed in the symposium Candour in English *fiction* 2 *(Jan 1890), see* Rev of Revs *Jan 1890; of* Nearing the rapids *(Mar 1894), see* Rev of Revs *Mar 1894; of her views expressed in the symposium* The tree of knowledge *(June 1894), see* Rev of Revs *June 1894.*

Nineteenth Cent 1891–2. *See* Wellesley vol 2. For response to The wild women as politicians (July 1891), *see* Mona Caird, A defence of the so-called 'wild women', Nineteenth Cent May 1892; to Partisans of the wild women (Mar 1892), *see* Isabel Burton, Sir Richard Burton: an explanation and a defence, New Rev Nov 1892; to A picture of the past (Nov 1892), *see* Herbert Maxwell, Walling the cuckoo, Nineteenth Cent Dec 1892.

Albemarle Rev. On echoes Jan 1892.

Pall Mall Mag. Society – the remnant 1 1893. For criticism, *see* Rev of Revs Sep 1893.

Idler 1893–7. Regular participant in Idler forums.

English Illus Mag. A counterblast Oct 1893. A reply to Lady Colin Campbell, A plea for tobacco, in English Illus Mag Oct 1893.

Young Woman. The ideal husband 3 1894, A study in wives 5 1896.

North Amer Rev. Cranks and crazes Dec 1895.

Collaborative works

Modern women and what is said of them: a reprint of the series of articles in the Saturday Review. [Anon, with many of the essays later identified as Linton's.] With an introd by Mrs Lucia Gilbert Calhoun, New York 1868.

REVIEWS: [Henry James] Nation 7 1868; Atlantic Monthly 22 1868.

The order of creation: the conflict between Genesis and geology. A controversy between W. E. Gladstone, Max Müller, T. H. Huxley, M. Réville, E. Lynn Linton. New York [1886].

Women novelists of Queen Victoria's reign: a book of appreciations. Ed A. Sergeant et al 1897. Linton's essay was on George Eliot.

REVIEW: Queen 28 Aug 1897.

§2

See above for reviews and responses to specific writings.

Landor, W. S. To Eliza Lynn in his Last fruit 1853, and in Letters of Walter Savage Landor, ed S. Wheeler, 1899.

Eliot, George. Letters vols 1–4. Ed G. Haight, 1954–5.
Swinburne, A. C. Note on Charlotte Brontë [1877]. In Complete Works 14, ed E. Gosse and T. J. Wise, 1926; On the death of Mrs Lynn Linton 1898 in Works 6 1927; *see also* Swinburne letters vols 4–6, ed C. Lang 1959–62.
Bowker, R. R. London as a literary centre. Harper's New Monthly Mag 77 1888.
Frith, W. P. My autobiography and reminiscences vol 2, 1888.
Pall Mall Gazette 11 Apr 1890.
Black, Helen C. Notable women authors of the day. 1893, rptd Freeport NY 1974.
Tweedie, Mrs A. A chat with Mrs Lynn Linton. Temple Bar July 1894.
Tooley, Sarah A. Mrs Lynn Linton. Woman at Home 5 1897.
The Times 16 July 1898.
Acad 30 July 1898.
Athenaeum 23 July 1898.
Besant, Walter. E. Lynn Linton. Queen 23 July 1898.
Gould, Frederick. Chats with pioneers of modern thought. 1898.
Harraden, Beatrice. Mrs Lynn Linton. Bookman Sep 1898.
Pollock, Walter Herries. Mrs Lynn Linton. Saturday Rev 1 June 1901. This and the following 1901 pbns were reviews of G. S. Layard's biography of Linton (*see below*).
Paston, George [Emily Morse Symonds]. A censor of modern womanhood. Fortnightly Rev 1 Sep 1901.
Athenaeum 18 May 1901.
Acad 25 May 1901.
The Times 29 May 1901.
Tinsley, W. In Random recollections of an old publisher vol 2, 1905.
Carr, J. C. Some eminent Victorians: personal recollections in the world of art and letters. 1908.
Crozier, J. B. In My inner life, being a chapter in personal evolution and autobiography vol 2, 1908.
McCarthy, J. Our book of memories: letters of Justin McCarthy to Mrs Campbell Praed. Ed Mrs C. Praed 1912.
Francillion, R. E. Mid-Victorian memories. [1914.]
Clodd, E. Memories 1916.

Textual/bibliographical criticism

Belflower, James. The life and career of Elizabeth Lynn Linton: Victorian woman of letters. Unpbd PhD diss, Duke Univ 1968.

Biographies

Layard, G. S. Mrs Lynn Linton: her life, letters, and opinions. 1901.
Anderson, N. F. Woman against women: a life of Eliza Lynn Linton. Bloomington IN 1987. [NFA]

Thomas Henry Lister 1800–42

§1

Granby: a novel. 3 vols 1826 (3 edns), 1838.
Herbert Lacy. 3 vols 1828.
Epicharis: an historical tragedy. 1829.
Arlington: a novel. 3 vols [1832].
Anne Grey: a novel, by Harriet Lister, edited by the author of Granby. 3 vols 1834.
The life and administration of Edward first Earl of Clarendon: with original correspondence and authentic papers never before published. 3 vols 1837–8.
An answer to the misrepresentations contained in an article [by J. W. Croker] on the life of Clarendon in no 124 of the Quarterly Review. 1839.
Hulse House. 1860.

§2

Moers, E. In her Dandy, 1961.

George MacDonald 1824–1905

The major collection of mss and letters is in the Beinecke Lib, Yale. Others are in the NLS, BL, Harvard, Wheaton College IL and Dr Williams Lib, London. For a full list, see Sadler, under Letters, below.

Bibliographies

Bulloch, J. M. A centennial bibliography of George MacDonald. Aberdeen 1925.
[Hutchinson, B.] George MacDonald, 1824–1905. Book Collector and Lib Monthly Apr 1969.
Jordan, M. N. George MacDonald: a bibliographical catalogue and record. Fairfax VA 1984.
Shaberman, R. B. George MacDonald: a bibliographical study. Detroit and Winchester 1990.

Collections and selections

Dealings with the fairies. 1867. Includes The light princess, first pbd in Adela Cathcart 1864; The giant's heart, first pbd in Illus London News Dec 1863; The shadows, first pbd in Adela Cathcart 1864; Cross purposes, first pbd in Beeton's Christmas Annual 1862; The golden key.
Works of fancy and imagination. 10 vols 1871. Includes Within and without; A hidden life; Shorter poems; Phantastes; The portent, first pbd in Cornhill Mag May–July 1860; The light princess; The giant's heart; The shadows; Cross purposes; The golden key; The carasoyn; Little Daylight, first pbd in At the back of the north wind in Good Words for the Young; The broken swords, first pbd in Monthly Christian Spectator Oct 1854; The wow o' Rivven, first pbd in Good Words Feb 1864; The cruel painter, first pbd in Adela Cathcart 1864; The castle: a parable, first pbd in Adela Cathcart 1864; The gray wolf, first pbd in Robert Falconer 1868; Uncle Cornelius his story.
The light princess and other stories. 1874. (Reissue of Works 1871 edn, vol 8.)
Cross purposes and other stories. 1874. (Reissue of Works 1871 edn, vol 9.)
The gifts of the child Christ and other tales. 2 vols London and Leipzig 1882 (Tauchnitz). Includes The gifts of the child Christ; The history of Photogen and Nycteris, first pbd in The Graphic Christmas 1879; The butcher's bills; Stephen Archer; Port in a storm, first pbd in Argosy Nov 1866; If I had a father (drama). REVIEW: Athenaeum 29 Apr 1882.
Stephen Archer and other tales. 1883, Whitethorn CA 1994. Contents are the same as The gifts of the child Christ, 1882, *above*.
Parables and ballads and Scotch songs by George MacDonald. 1884. (Reissue of Works 1871 edn, vol 4.)
Poems by George MacDonald. Selected by V. D. S. and C. F. New York 1887.
The light princess and other fairy stories. [1890.] Includes The light princess; The giant's heart; The golden key.
The poetical works of George MacDonald. 2 vols 1893.
The light princess and other fairy tales. New York 1893. Introd rptd as 'The fantastic imagination' in A dish of orts. Includes The light princess; The giant's heart; The shadows; Cross purposes; The golden key; The carasoyn; Little Daylight.
Fairy tales by George MacDonald. Ed and introd by Greville MacDonald. 1904. Reissued in 5 pts as The fairy tales of George MacDonald '1904' [1905–6]. Includes contents of The light princess and other fairy tales, 1893, *above*, plus The day boy and the night girl.
Short stories. London and Glasgow 1928. Includes The light princess; The giant's heart; The golden key; Cross purposes.
The light princess and other tales: being the complete fairy stories of George MacDonald. Introd by R. L. Green. London and New York 1961. Includes contents of Fairy tales by George MacDonald, 1904, *above*.

Evenor. Introd by L. Carter. New York and London 1972. Includes The wise woman; The carasoyn; The golden key.

The gifts of the child Christ: fairytales and stories for the childlike. Ed G. E. Sadler 2 vols Grand Rapids MI and Oxford 1973. Includes The gifts of the child Christ; The history of Photogen and Nycteris; The shadows; Little Daylight; The golden key; Cross purposes; The wise woman; The castle; Port in a storm; Papa's story, first pbd in Illus London News Dec 1865; The light princess; The giant's heart; The carasoyn; The gray wolf; The cruel painter; The broken swords; The wow o' Rivven; Uncle Cornelius; The butcher's bills; Birth, dreaming, death, first pbd in Adela Cathcart 1864.

The golden key and other stories. Elgin IL and London 1978. Includes The light princess; Little Daylight; The day boy and the night girl.

The Christmas stories of George MacDonald. Elgin IL and Tring 1982. Includes abridged versions of My uncle Peter; Papa's story; The gifts of the child Christ.

§1

Within and without: a dramatic poem. 1855, 1857, 1871 (in Works of fancy and imagination), New York 1872, London 1884 (in reissue of vol 1 of Works of fancy and imagination), 1893 (in Poetical works, *below*).

Poems. 1857, 1864 (as A hidden life and other poems), 1871 (in Works of fancy and imagination), New York 1872 (as A hidden life and other poems), London 1893 (in Poetical works, *below*).

Phantastes: a faerie romance for men and women. 1858, Boston 1870, London 1871 (in Works of fancy and imagination), New York 1885, London 1894 as Phantastes: a faerie romance illustr J. Bell (an edn suppressed by Greville MacDonald), 1905 (ed and introd by Greville MacDonald, illustr A. Hughes), Philadelphia [1911] (with The portent), 1915 (EL, introd by Greville MacDonald), New York 1954 (ed A. Freemantle, introd by W. H. Auden, with Lilith), 1962 (introd by C. S. Lewis, with Lilith), New York 1970 (introd by L. Carter, London 1971), Tring 1982 (introd by C. S. Lewis), Woodbridge 1982 (introd by D. Brewer), 1983 (EL, introd by D. Holbrook), Whitethorn CA 1994; tr Du 1975, Ital 1977, Ger 1982, 1984.

David Elginbrod. 3 vols 1863, 1 vol 1871, 2 vols Leipzig 1871 (Tauchnitz), 1 vol Boston 1872, New York 1879, 189?, 1897, London 1900, 1906, New York 1917, London 1921, Boston and Philadelphia nd, London, Toronto, Melbourne and Sydney 1927, Minneapolis 1984? (rev by M. Phillips as The tutor's first love), Whitethorn CA 1996; tr Ger 1873.
REVIEW: Athenaeum 17 Jan 1863.

Adela Cathcart. 3 vols 1864, 1 vol Boston 1875, New York 1882, London 1882 (heavily rev with 7 original stories omitted and 3 new ones inserted), 1890, 1905, Philadelphia [1911], Whitethorn CA 1994. 1864 edn contains The light princess; The bell: a sketch in pen and ink; Birth, dreaming and death; The curate and his wife; The shadows; The broken swords; My Uncle Peter; The giant's heart; The two Gordons (poem); A child's holiday; The cruel painter; The castle: a parable. 1882 edn contains Birth, dreaming and death; The curate and his wife; My Uncle Peter; The two Gordons; A child's holiday; The lost lamb; The snow fight; An invalid's winter.

The portent: a story of the inner vision of the highlanders, commonly called the second sight. First pbd in Cornhill Mag May–July 1860. 1864 (much rev), 1871 (in Works of fancy and imagination), New York 1885, 1902, London [1909] as The portent and other stories, Philadelphia 1911 (with Phantastes), London 1924 Centenary edn (rptd from 1909 edn, 100 copies only), San Francisco, London, etc 1979 introd by G. E. Sadler, Whitethorn CA 1994.

Alec Forbes of Howglen. 3 vols 1865, 2 vols Leipzig 1865 (Tauchnitz), 1 vol London 1867, New York 1872, 1880, 1891?, London 1900, 1901, 1906, Philadelphia 1911, London 1921, London, Toronto, Melbourne and Sydney 1927, Whitethorn CA 1995.
REVIEW: Athenaeum 17 June 1865.

Annals of a quiet neighbourhood. Serialised in Sunday Mag Oct 1865–Sep 1866. 3 vols '1867' [1866], 1 vol 1867, 2 vols Leipzig 1867 (Tauchnitz), 1 vol New York 1867, New York and Boston 1873, London 1874, New York 1879 (Seaside Lib), London 1884, New York 1895 (Franklin Square Lib), Philadelphia [1911], Whitethorn CA 1995.
REVIEW: Br Quart Rev Jan 1867.

Unspoken sermons (Ἔπεα Ἄπτερα): series one. '1867' [1866], '5th edn' 1874, New York 1890?, London 1890?, Whitethorn CA 1997.
REVIEW: Br Quart Rev Apr 1867.

The disciple and other poems. 1867.

Guild court: a London story. Serialised in Good Words Jan–June 1867. 3 vols '1868' [1867], 1 vol New York 1868, London 1881, New York 1881, London 1905, Philadelphia [1911], abridged by D. Hamilton, Wheaton IL 1986 (as The prodigal apprentice), Whitethorn CA 1992; tr Fr 1869 (as Lucy Barton).

Robert Falconer. Serialised in Argosy Dec 1866–Nov 1867. 3 vols 1868 (enlarged from Argosy version), 1 vol 1868 (pirated binding of Argosy version), 1870, Boston 1876, New York 1881 (Seaside Lib), London 1895? ('new and enlarged edn'), [1896] (abridged in The Masterpiece Lib), New York 189?, London 1900, 1907 ('new edn'), Philadelphia [1911], London, Toronto, Melbourne and Sydney 1927, Minneapolis 1984? (as The musician's quest), Whitethorn CA 1996.
REVIEWS: Athenaeum 4 July 1868; Fortnightly Rev July 1868.

The seaboard parish. Serialised in Sunday Mag Oct 1867–Aug 1868. 3 vols 1868, 1 vol New York 1868, London 1869, New York and London 1871, London 1872, New York 1879 (Seaside Lib), London 1886 ('4th edn', illus), Philadelphia [1911], abridged by D. Hamilton, Wheaton IL 1985, Whitethorn CA 1995.

England's antiphon. 1868 (in 3 sections, also as 1 vol), Philadelphia nd (before 1880), Whitethorn CA 1996. Anthology and literary criticism.

The miracles of Our Lord. 1870, New York 1870, Philadelphia and New York nd, London 1886, Whitethorn CA 1996. Sermons.

At the back of the north wind. Serialised in Good Words for the Young Nov 1868–Oct 1870. '1871' [1870], New York 1871, London and Glasgow 1886, 1900 ('new edn'), Philadelphia and London 1909 (illustr M. L. Kirk), London 1910?, London and Glasgow 1911, Philadelphia 1914 (simplified by E. Lewis), 1919 (illustr J. Willcox Smith), London and Glasgow 1926, Philadelphia 1926, New York and Akron OH 1927 (illustr F. Brundage), New York 1930 (illustr D. Bedford), 1950 (illustr G. and D. Hauman), Garden City NY 1956 (illustr C. Brown), London and New York 1956 (illustr E. H. Shephard), London and Glasgow 1958, 1960 (illustr A. Hughes, in To the land of fair delight: three Victorian tales of the imagination), New York 1963 (illustr C. Mozley), 1964 (illustr H. Dinnerstein, afterword by C. Fadiman), 1976 (preface by G. Sadler), London 1978 (reprint of Blackie edn of 1900 but introd by C. Duriez), 1979 (with The princess and the goblin and The princess and Curdie), Harmondsworth 1984, Whitethorn CA 1992, Harmondsworth 1994 (new Puffin edn); tr Polish [1958], Jap 1977, Ger 1981, Norwegian 1982.

Ranald Bannerman's boyhood. Serialised in Good Words for the Young Nov 1869–Oct 1870. 1871, New York 1871, London 1877, Philadelphia 1879, London 1884, Boston 1889, London and Glasgow nd, Boston nd, London and Glasgow 1911, Whitethorn CA 1993.

The princess and the goblin. Serialised in Good Words for the Young Nov 1870–June 1871. '1872' [1871], New York 1871, London 1884, London and Glasgow '1888' [1887], Boston 1889, London and Glasgow '1900' [1899] (illustr A. Hughes), Boston 1907,

Philadelphia 1907, London and Glasgow 1911 (illustr H. Stratton), Boston 1913 (simplified by E. Lewis), Philadelphia 1920 (illustr J. W. Smith), New York 1926 (illustr F. D. Bedford), New York 1927 (illustr F. Brundage), 1928 (illustr E. Mackinstry), Philadelphia [1934?] (illustr M. L. Kirk), London 1948 (illustr A. Hughes), London and New York 1949, New York 1951 (illustr N. S. Unwin), [1955] (simplified by M. Tommasini), London and Glasgow [1956?] (illustr W. Nickless), Glasgow 1957 (abridged), New York [1959], London and Glasgow 1960 (illustr J. Paton), Harmondsworth 1964 (illustr A Hughes), Ann Arbor MI 1967 (microfilm), New York 1967, Middletown CT 1970 (abridged by O. Jones, with The princess and Curdie), 2 vols London 1971 (Braille edn), London and Glasgow 1973, Elgin IL and London 1978, London 1979 (with At the back of the north wind and The princess and Curdie), 1979 (abridged), Basingstoke 1987 (abridged), Oxford 1987 (illustr A. Hughes), Edinburgh 1989, London 1993 (illustr A. Hughes), 1990 (illustr L. Thomas), 1990 (ed R. McGillis, with The princess and Curdie), Whitethorn CA 1993, London 1996 (illustr A. Hughes); tr Hebrew 1965.

The vicar's daughter: an autobiographical story. Serialised in Sunday Mag 1871–2. 3 vols 1872, 2 vols Leipzig 1872 (Tauchnitz), 1 vol London 1881, 1893 ('new edn'), 1905, Whitethorn CA 1992.

Wilfrid Cumbermede. Serialised in St Paul's Mag Nov 1870–Dec 1871 and in Scribner's Monthly Mag Nov 1870–Mar 1872. 3 vols '1872' [1871], 1 vol New York 1872, 2 vols Berlin 1872, 1 vol London 1872 ('2nd edn'), Chicago and St Louis 1881, London 1884 ('4th edn'), 1893, 1901, Philadelphia [1911], Whitethorn CA 1997.

Gutta Percha Willie, the working genius. Serialised as The history of Gutta Percha Willie in Good Words for the Young 1872. 1873, Boston 1873, London 1874, London and Glasgow 1887 (as The history of Gutta Percha Willie), New York 1900, London '1901' [1900] (as The history of Gutta Percha Willie), Philadelphia 1903, London 1917, Philadelphia nd, Whitethorn CA 1993.

Malcolm. Serialised in Glasgow Weekly Herald. 3 vols 1875, 1 vol Philadelphia 1875, 3 vols London 1876 ('2nd edn'), 2 vols Leipzig 1876 (Tauchnitz), 1 vol London 1877 ('3rd edn'), Philadelphia 1877, 1879 ('4th edn'), New York 1880, 189?, London 1900, 1901, Philadelphia [1911], London 1913, 1927, Minneapolis 1982 (rev by M. Phillips as The fisherman's lady), Whitethorn CA 1995; The fisherman's lady tr Du 1992?.

REVIEW: Canadian Monthly Apr 1875.

The wise woman. Serialised in Good Things Dec 1874–July 1875 (as A double story). 1875 (as The wise woman: a parable), New York 1876 (as A double story), Boston 1876 (as A double story), [1879] (as Princess Rosamond, a double story), London [1883] (as The wise woman), Boston [1884] (as A double story), London 1895 (as The lost princess: or the wise woman), Elgin IL [1905] (as A double story by George MacDonald), Elgin IL and Chicago 1905 (as A double story, with a short story by E. L. Vincent and 5 essays), London and New York 1965 (as The lost princess: a double story), 1972 (in Evenor, ed Lin Carter, with The carasoyn and The golden key), Grand Rapids MI and Oxford 1973 (in The gifts of the child Christ, as The wise woman or the lost princess: a double story), Elgin IL 1978 (as The lost princess: a double story), Leominster and Grand Rapids MI 1992 (ed G. E. Sadler illustr B. Oberdieck), Whitethorn CA 1993; tr Swed 1980, Danish 1985.

REVIEW: Athenaeum 29 Jan 1876.

Thomas Wingfold, curate. Serialised in Day of Rest Jan–Dec 1876. 3 vols 1876, 1 vol New York 1876, 1879, [1880], London 1883, 1886, 1893, 1901, Philadelphia [1911], Minneapolis 1985 (rev by M. Phillips as The curate's awakening), Whitethorn CA 1997.

REVIEWS: Athenaeum 11 Nov 1876; Fortnightly Rev Jan 1877.

St George and St Michael. Serialised in Graphic Apr–Oct 1875. 3 vols '1876' [1875], 2 vols Leipzig 1876 (Tauchnitz), 1 vol New York [1876?], London 1878 ('2nd edn'), Edinburgh 1878, New York 1880, London [1892] ('new edn'), 1900, 1910 ('another edn'), Philadelphia [1911], Wheaton IL 1986 (rev by D. Hamilton as The last castle), Whitethorn CA 1997.

The marquis of Lossie. Serialised in Glasgow Weekly Mail and in Lippincott's Mag Nov 1876–Sep 1877. 3 vols 1877, 1 vol Philadelphia 1877, Chicago 1877, 2 vols Leipzig 1877 (Tauchnitz), 1 vol London 1878 ('2nd edn'), New York 1881, Boston [1886], London [1900 or 1901] (in The Sixpenny Series of Copyright Books), 1900, Philadelphia [1911], London 1913 (in Everett's Lib), 1927, Minneapolis 1982 (rev by M. Phillips as The marquis' secret), Whitethorn CA 1995.

Sir Gibbie. Serialised in Glasgow Weekly Mail Jan–Mar 1879. 3 vols 1879, 1 vol Philadelphia 1879, New York 1879, 2 vols Leipzig 1880 (Tauchnitz), 1 vol London 1880 ('another edn'), 1900, 1906, Philadelphia 1911, London 1914 (EL introd by Greville MacDonald), 1927, New York 1963 (abridged by E. Yates), London and Glasgow 1967 (abridged by E. Yates), Minneapolis [1983] (abridged by M. Phillips as The baronet's song), Whitethorn CA 1991; tr Norwegian 1984 (tr of M. Phillips's abridgement).

REVIEWS: Athenaeum 14 July 1879; Br Quart Rev Oct 1879.

Paul Faber, surgeon. 3 vols '1879' [1878], 1 vol Philadelphia 1879, New York 1879, London 1881, 1883, 1886, Philadelphia [1911], Whitethorn CA 1992.

A book of strife, in the form of the diary of an old soul. 1880 (priv ptd 'for the author', ptd on one side of the leaf only), 1885, London and New York 1889, London 1897 (in Rampolli, *below*), 1905 (in The diary of an old soul and translations of other spiritual verse, i.e. Rampolli rptd), 1905 (as previous item but without the other poetic works, by Fifield then by Dent), 1924. Poem.

Mary Marston. 3 vols 1881, 1881 ('5th edn'), 2 vols Leipzig 1881 (Tauchnitz), 1 vol New York 1881, Philadelphia 1881, London 1894, 1905, 1908, Whitethorn CA 1996.

Castle Warlock: a homely romance. Serialised as 'Warlock o' Glen Warlock' in Wide Awake (Boston) and as 'Castle Warlock, a homely romance' in Glasgow Weekly Mail Jan–May 1897. Boston 1881 (as 'Warlock o' Glen Warlock: a homely romance'), 1881 (i.e. another Boston edn of 1881), New York 1881, 1882, 3 vols London 1882, 1 vol 1883 ('2nd edn'), 3 vols Berlin nd (between 1883 and 1885?) (in Ascher's Collection of English Authors), 1 vol Boston 1885, London 1900, Whitethorn CA 1991.

REVIEWS: Athenaeum 21 May 1882; Spectator 24 June 1882.

Orts. 1882, Boston 1883 (as The imagination and other essays), London 1893 (enlarged edn, as A dish of orts: chiefly papers on the imagination, and on Shakspere [*sic*]), 1895, 1905, 1908 (illustr C. Cuneo and G. H. Evison), Whitethorn CA 1996.

Weighed and wanting. Serialised in Sunday Mag Jan–Dec 1882. 3 vols 1882, 1 vol Boston 1882, New York 1882, 1883, London 1883, 1900, 1905, Whitethorn CA 1996.

REVIEWS: Athenaeum 4 Nov 1882; Saturday Rev 25 Nov 1882; Spectator 24 Mar 1883.

Donal Grant. 3 vols 1883, 1 vol New York 1883, Boston 1883, London 1884 ('2nd edn'), New York [1884], London 1892 ('new edn'), New York [189?], London 1901, Minneapolis 1983 (rev by M. Phillips as The shepherd's castle), Whitethorn CA 1991.

The princess and Curdie. Serialised in Good Things Jan–June 1877. '1883' [1882] (illustr Allan), Leipzig 1883 (Tauchnitz), Philadelphia 1883, New York [1883] (subtitled A girl's story), London and Glasgow 1888, '1900' [1899] (illustr H. Stratton), New York 1900, Philadelphia 1908 (illustr M. L. Kirk), London and Glasgow 1912, Philadelphia 1914 (simplified by M. L. Kirk), Philadelphia 1926 (illustr G. A Kay), New York 1927 (illustr F. Brundage), 1927 (illustr D. P. Lathrop), London and New York 1949 (illustr C. Folkard), New York 1954 (illustr N. S. Unwin), London and Glasgow 1956, New York 1960 (illustr H. Stratton), London and Glasgow 1961 (illustr J. Paton), Harmondsworth 1966 (illustr H. Stratton), Middletown CT 1970 (abridged by O. Jones, with The princess and the goblin), London 1970, London and Glasgow 1973, Elgin IL and London

1978, London 1979 (with At the back of the north wind and The princess and the goblin), 1979 (abridged by J. Watson), 1990 (ed R. McGillis, with The princess and the goblin), Whitethorn CA 1993.

Unspoken sermons (Ἔπεα Ἄπτερα): series two. 1885, 1886 ('another edn'), Whitethorn CA 1997.

What's mine's mine. 3 vols 1886, 1 vol 1886, Boston 1886, New York 1886 (3 separate New York edns in 1886), London 1892, 1900, Whitethorn CA 1991.

REVIEW: Athenaeum 5 June 1886.

Home again. 1887, New York 1888, London 1893, 1902, New York [1911], Whitethorn CA 1992.

The elect lady. 1888, New York 1888, Whitethorn CA 1992.

Unspoken sermons (Ἔπεα Ἄπτερα): series three. 1889, Whitethorn CA 1997.

A rough shaking. Serialised in Atalanta Oct 1889–Sep 1890. '1891' [1890], New York 1890, Boston 1891, London 1900, New York 1904, Whitethorn CA 1991.

There and back. Serialised in The Sun Sep 1889–Aug 1890. 3 vols 1891, 1891 ('2nd edn'), Boston [1891], Minneapolis 1986 (rev by M. Phillips as The baron's apprenticeship), Whitethorn CA 1991.

REVIEW: Athenaeum 25 Apr 1891.

The flight of the shadow. 1891, New York 1891, London 1894, 1902, New York [1911], Whitethorn CA 1994.

The hope of the gospel. 1892, New York 1892, Whitethorn CA 1996. Sermons.

Heather and snow. 2 vols 1893, 1 vol 1893, New York 1893, Whitethorn CA 1996.

Poetical works. 2 vols 1893, 2 vols 1911 (fine-paper edn), 1915, Whitethorn CA 1997.

Scotch songs and ballads. Aberdeen 1893 (from vol 2 of Poetical works, *above*).

Lilith: a romance. 1895, New York 1895, London 1924 (ed Greville MacDonald), New York 1954 (ed A. Fremantle, introd by W. H. Auden), London 1962 (introd by C. S. Lewis, with Phantastes), New York 1969 (introd by L. Carter), Tring 1982 (introd by C. S. Lewis), Whitethorn CA 1994; tr Du 1975, Ger 1977, 1983.

The hope of the universe. Ptd in Sunday Mag 1892. Abridged as an anti-vivisectionist pam [1896]. Final sermon in The hope of the gospel.

Salted with fire. Serialised in Glasgow Weekly Mail Jan–May 1897. 1897, New York 1897, London 1900, Whitethorn CA 1996.

Far above rubies. Ptd in The Sketch Christmas 1898. New York 1899?, New Jersey 1913, Whitethorn CA 1996.

Letters

An expression of character: the letters of George MacDonald. Ed G. E. Sadler, Grand Rapids MI 1994.

Translations, editions, etc

Twelve of the spiritual songs of Novalis; done into English by George MacDonald. Arundel 1851 (priv ptd). Another trn 1873 (priv ptd). 1873 trn rptd in Exotics 1876 and Rampolli 1897, *below*.

Exotics: a translation [in verse] of the spiritual songs of Novalis, the hymn-book of Luther, and other poems from the German and Italian. 1876.

REVIEW: Athenaeum 10 May 1876.

A threefold cord: poems by three friends. Ed George MacDonald. 1883 (priv ptd), 1884 (as A threefold chord), 1893 (in Poetical works). By George MacDonald, John Hill MacDonald and Greville Matheson.

Preface to Letters from Hell by L. W. J. S. 1884.

The tragedie of Hamlet, prince of Denmarke: a study, with the text of the folio of 1623. 1885, 1905, 1924, Whitethorn CA 1996.

Preface to For the right by K. E. Franzos tr J. Sutter. 1887, 1889.

A cabinet of gems, cut and polished by Sir Philip Sidney; now for the more radiance presented without their setting by George MacDonald. 1892.

Rampolli: growths from a long-planted root. Being translations, new and old, chiefly from the German, along with A year's diary of an old soul. 1897, 1905 (as The diary of an old soul and translations of other spiritual verse), Whitethorn CA 1995.

Anthologies

Cheerful words from the writings of George MacDonald. Ed E. E. Brown, introd by J. T. Fields, Boston 1880.

Selections from the writings of George MacDonald: or help for weary souls. Ed J. Dewey, New York 1885.

Beautiful thoughts from George MacDonald. Ed E. W. Dougall, New York 1894.

Daily readings from George MacDonald. Ed J. Dobson 1905.

The pocket George MacDonald. Ed A. H. Hyatt 1906, Boston 1907?.

Light to live by. Ed F. M. Nicholson, London and Edinburgh 1909.

A book of life from the works of George MacDonald. Ed W. L. T. and S. M. T. 1913.

Gathered grace. Ed E. Yates, introd by L. C. Coulson, Cambridge nd (c. 1930).

George MacDonald: a selection. Ed and introd by C. S. Lewis 1946.

The world of George MacDonald: selections from his works of fiction. Ed R. Hein, Wheaton IL 1978.

Getting to know Jesus. Ed W. A. Hutchinson, introd by C. S. Kilby, New Canaan CT 1980.

The heart of George MacDonald. Ed R. Hein, Wheaton IL 1994.

George MacDonald: a devotional guide to his writings. Ed G. W. Deddo and C. A. Deddo, Edinburgh 1996.

§2

Kinnear, A. S. Mr George MacDonald's novels. North Br Rev Sep 1866.

Bayne, P. Works by George MacDonald. Br Quart Rev Jan 1868.

George MacDonald as a teacher of religion. London Quart Rev Jan 1869.

Rands, W. B. ('Henry Holbeach'). George MacDonald. Contemporary Rev Dec 1872, rptd Eclectic Mag (New York) 248.

M'Crie, G. A word to George Eliot and George MacDonald. In The religion of our literature, 1875.

Shand, A. I. Recent Scotch novels. Edinburgh Rev Apr 1876.

Geddes, W. D. George MacDonald as a poet. Blackwood's Mag Mar 1891.

Selby, T. G. George MacDonald and the Scottish school. In The theology of modern fiction, 1896.

Wilson, S. L. The theology of George MacDonald. In The theology of modern literature, Edinburgh 1899.

Johnson, J. George MacDonald: a biographical and critical appreciation. '1906' [1905].

Obits: 19 Sep 1905 (The Times), 21 Sep 1905 (Br Weekly), 23 Sep 1905 (Athenaeum, Daily News, Spectator), Nov 1905 (Bookman).

MacDonald, R. George MacDonald: a personal note. In From a northern window, 1911.

MacDonald, Greville. George MacDonald and his wife. 1924.

McGillis, R. F. George MacDonald – the Lilith manuscripts. Scottish Literary Jnl Dec 1977.

Raeper, W. George MacDonald. 1987.

Webster, A. George MacDonald's influence on Scottish religion: Robert Falconer's plan for emptying hell. nd.

North Wind: *journal of the George MacDonald Soc is published annually.*

[DSR]

Anne Manning 1807–79

§1

A sister's gift: conversations on sacred subjects. 1826.

Stories from the history of Italy, from the invasion of Alaric to the present time. 1831.

Village belles. 3 vols 1833, 1859.
The maiden and married life of Mary Powell, afterwards Mistress Milton. 1849, 1855, 1859 (with Deborah's diary), 1860, 1866, 1874. First pbd in Sharpe's Mag 1849. *See* Deborah's diary, *below.*
The household of Sir Thomas More. 1851, 1860, 1870, 1887, 1896 etc. First pbd in Sharpe's Mag.
Queen Philippa's golden booke. [1851.]
The colloquies of Edward Osborne, citizen and cloth worker of London. 1852.
The drawing room table book. 1852.
Cherry & Violet: a tale of the Plague. 1853.
The provocations of Madame Palissy. 1853.
Chronicles of Merry England. 1854.
Claude the colporteur. 1854.
Jack and the tanner of Wymondham. 1854.
The hill side: illustrations of some of the simplest terms used in logic. 1854.
Some account of Mrs Clarinda Singlehart. 1855.
The adventures of the Caliph Haroun al Raschid. 1855.
A Sabbath at home. 1855.
The Old Chelsea Bun House: a tale. 1855.
Tasso and Leonora: the commentaries of Ser Pantaleone degli Gambacorti. 1856.
The week of darkness: a short manual for the use and comfort of mourners. 1856.
Helen and Olga: a Russian tale. 1857.
Lives of good servants. 1857.
The good old times: a tale of Auvergne. 1857.
An English girl's account of a Moravian settlement. 1858. Ed Anne Manning.
Deborah's diary. 1858. Sequel to Mary Powell, *above.*
The year nine: a tale of the Tyrol. 1858.
The ladies of Bever Hollow. 2 vols 1858.
Poplar House Academy. 2 vols 1859.
Valentine Duval: an autobiography of the last century. 1860.
Town and forest. 1860.
The day of small things. 1860.
Chronicle of Ethelfled. 1861.
Family pictures. 1861.
The cottage history of England. 1861.
A noble purpose nobly won. 2 vols 1862. On Joan of Arc.
Bessy's money: a tale. 1863.
Meadowleigh. 2 vols 1863.
The Duchess of Trajetto. 1863.
The interrupted wedding. 1864.
Belforest: a tale. 2 vols 1865.
Selvaggio: a tale of Italian country life. Edinburgh 1865.
Miss Biddy Frobisher: a saltwater story. 1866.
The Lincolnshire tragedy: passages in the life of the Faire Gospeller, Mistress Anne Askewe, recounted by Nicholas Moldwarp. 1866.
The masque at Ludlow and other romanesques. 1866.
Diana's crescent. 2 vols 1868.
Jacques Bonneval. 1868.
The Spanish barber: a tale. 1869.
Margaret More's Tagebuch. 1870.
One trip more, and other stories. 1870.
Compton Friars. 1872.
The lady of limited income. 2 vols 1872.
Lord Harry Bellair. 2 vols 1874.
Monks Norton. 2 vols 1874.
Heroes of the desert: the story of the lives of Moffat and Livingstone. 1875.
An idyll of the Alps. 1876.
Anne Manning contributed articles and stories to Golden Hours *1868–76, a mag ed Dr Whittemore. The following serials, not rptd, were pbd there:* Madame Prosni and Madame Bleay, *1868;* Rosita, *1869;* On the Grand Tour, *1870;* Octavia Solaro, *1871;* Illusions dispelled, *1871. The only book pbd under her own name was* Stories from the history of Italy, *1831.*

§2

Yonge, C. M. In A. Sergeant et al, Women novelists of Queen Victoria's reign, 1897.

Katharine Macquoid, Katharine Sarah Gadsden Macquoid, née Thomas 1824–1917

§1

A bad beginning: a story of a French marriage. 2 vols 1862 (anon), 1866, 1872 (new edn) [1884] (new edn).
REVIEW: Athenaeum 1830 1862.
Piccalilli: a mixture. 1862 (anon).
Chesterford and some of its people. 3 vols 1863.
By the sea. 2 vols 1864, 1876.
Hester Kirton. 3 vols 1864, 1870 (new edn), Philadelphia 1871 (new edn), London 1880 (new edn), New York [1880].
REVIEW: Athenaeum 1911 1864.
Charlotte Burney. 3 vols 1867. Later re-written and pbd as Mrs Rumbold's secret 1888, *below.*
REVIEW: Athenaeum 2095 1867.
Elinor Dryden's probation. 3 vols 1867. Revised edn pbd as Elinor Dryden 1878.
REVIEW: Athenaeum 2063 1867.
Wild as a hawk. 3 vols 1868, 1874 (new and rev edn), New York 1874 (pbd as A charming widow: or wild as a hawk).
REVIEW: Athenaeum 2130 1868.
Forgotten by the world. 3 vols 1869 (anon), 1873, 1876 (new edn), New York [1876], London and New York [1884] (new edn).
REVIEW: Athenaeum 2200 1869.
Patty. Serialised in Macmillan's Mag Jan–Nov 1871, 2 vols 1871, London and New York 1871, 2 vols Leipzig 1872 (Tauchnitz), 2 vols London 1872, New York 1872, London 1873 (new edn), [New York] [1879], London 1883 (new edn).
REVIEWS: Athenaeum 2301 1871; Saturday Rev 33 1871; Spectator 45 1872.
Rookstone. 3 vols 1871, Philadelphia 1871.
REVIEW: Athenaeum 2279 1871.
Miriam's marriage. 3 vols 1872, 1874.
REVIEW: Athenaeum 2348 1872.
Pictures across the channel. 2 vols 1873, 2 vols Leipzig 1873 (Tauchnitz). Stories.
REVIEW: Athenaeum 2359 1873.
Too soon: a study of a girl's heart. 3 vols 1873, New York 1873, Leipzig 1874 (Tauchnitz), New York 1881, London 1892 (new and rev edn), 1893.
REVIEW: Athenaeum 2383 1873.
A charming widow: or wild as a hawk. New York 1874. First pbd as Wild as a hawk, 1868, *above.*
Through Normandy. 1874 (illustr T. R. Macquoid), 1875 (2nd edn), New York [1875], London 1877 (new edn), [1880?], [1890?], 1895.
REVIEWS: Saturday Rev 38 1874; London Quart and Holborn Rev 43 1875.
Diane. 2 vols 1875, Leipzig 1876 (Tauchnitz), London 1879 (new and rev edn).
My story: a novel. 3 vols 1875, Leipzig 1875 (Tauchnitz), New York 1875.
REVIEW: Athenaeum 2459 1874.
The evil eye and other stories. 1876 (illustr T. R. and P. Macquoid), 1879 (new edn), 1881 (new edn).
REVIEW: Spectator 50 1877.
Lost rose and other stories. 3 vols 1876, 1 vol 1880 (new edn).
REVIEW: Athenaeum 2557 1876.

Doris Barugh: a Yorkshire story. Serialised in Good Words Jan–Dec 1877, 3 vols 1878.
REVIEW: Athenaeum 2615 1877.
The mill of St Herbot: a Breton story. New York 1877.
Through Brittany. Vol 1 (no more pbd) 1877 (illustr T. R. Macquoid), [1880], 1895, [1898?].
REVIEWS: London Quart and Holborn Rev 49 1877; Saturday Rev 44 1877.
The fisherman of Auge: a story. New York 1878.
REVIEW: Nation 27 1878.
The awakening: a tale of English life. New York 1879.
The Berkshire lady: a romance. 1879, 1880.
REVIEW: Athenaeum 2706 1879.
Pictures and legends from Normandy and Brittany. With T. R. Macquoid. 1879, New York 1881, London 1888, 1895.
REVIEWS: Athenaeum 2670 1878; Nation 33 1881.
In the sweet spring-time: a love story. 3 vols 1880.
REVIEW: Athenaeum 2727 1880.
Beside the river: a story of the Ardennes. 3 vols 1881, 2 vols Leipzig 1881 (Tauchnitz), New York [1881], London 1892 (new and rev edn), 1893.
REVIEW: Spectator 54 1881.
In the Ardennes. 1881 (illustr T. R. Macquoid), 1888, 1895.
REVIEW: Spectator 54 1881.
Little Fifine and other tales. 3 vols 1881.
REVIEW: Athenaeum 2814 1881.
Esau Ruswick. New York 1882.
A faithful lover. 3 vols 1882, Leipzig 1882 (Tauchnitz), London 1892 (new and rev edn), 1893.
REVIEWS: Athenaeum 2851 1882; Spectator 55 1882.
Poor Roger and other tales. New York [1882].
About Yorkshire. With T. R. Macquoid. 1883 (illustr T. R. Macquoid), 1888.
Her sailor love. 3 vols 1883, New York [1883].
REVIEWS: Athenaeum 2897 1883; Spectator 56 1883.
At the red glove. 3 vols 1885, New York 1885, 3 vols London 1886 (2nd edn), 1 vol 1887 (illustr C. S. Reinhart), Leipzig 1892.
REVIEWS: Athenaeum 3034 1885; Dublin Rev 98 1886; Spectator 59 1886.
Louisa. 3 vols 1885, 2 vols New York 1885, 1 vol London 1885, 1886 (new edn), 1888.
REVIEW: Athenaeum 3000 1885.
Under the snow. [1885] (SPCK).
Joan Wentworth. 1886 (illustr G. Browne), New York 1886.
REVIEW: Athenaeum 3082 1886.
The little vagabond: a story of Checco: a tale of Perugia. [1886]. (SPCK).
REVIEW: Athenaeum 3082 1886.
Sir James Appleby, Bart: a novel. 3 vols 1886, New York [1886].
REVIEWS: Athenaeum 3084 1886; Spectator 60 1887.
A strange company. [1886] (SPCK).
At 'The Peacock'. [1887] (SPCK).
The back windows of the Hotel Ste. Barbe. [1887] (SPCK).
Gone: a story of some years ago. [1887] (SPCK), New York [188?].
Jeanne Dupont. [1887] (SPCK).
Mère Suzanne and other stories. [1887] (SPCK), New York [1887].
The story of Yves: a Breton legend. [1887] (SPCK).
Mrs Rumbold's secret: or the story of Charlotte Burney. 1888. First pbd as Charlotte Burney, 1867, *above*.
Puff: an autobiography. Ed [i.e. written by] K. Macquoid. [1888] (SPCK).
Elizabeth Morley: a novel. Bristol 1889, New York [1889].
REVIEW: Athenaeum 3210 1889.
Pepin: the dancing bear. 1889 (illustr P. Macquoid).
Roger Ferron and other stories. 2 vols 1889.
At an old chateau. New York 1890, London 1891.
REVIEWS: Athenaeum 3320 1891; Dublin Rev 109 1891.
Cosette. 2 vols 1890, 1 vol 1891 (new edn).
REVIEWS: Athenaeum 3251 1890; Dublin Rev 107 1890.
The haunted fountain. 1890, New York [1890], Toronto [1890?].
The old courtyard. New York [1890].
Drifting apart: a story. 1891.
REVIEW: Athenaeum 3313 1891.
The Prince's whim and other stories. 1891.
Maisie Derrick. 2 vols 1892, Leipzig 1892, Montreal [1892].
REVIEW: Athenaeum 3363 1892.
Miss Eyon of Eyon Court. 1892, 1895.
Berris. 2 vols 1893, Leipzig 1893, New York [1900].
REVIEW: Athenaeum 3412 1893.
Appledore Farm. 3 vols 1894.
In an orchard. 2 vols 1894.
REVIEW: Athenaeum 3463 1894.
His last card. 1895.
REVIEWS: Academy 49 1896; Spectator 76 1896.
In the volcanic Eifel: a holiday ramble. With G. Macquoid. 1896 (illustr T. Macquoid), New York 1896.
REVIEW: Dial 22 1897.
The story of Lois. 1898, [1898] (3rd edn).
REVIEWS: Academy 53 1898; Athenaeum 3683 1898.
A ward of the King: a romance. 1898, New York 1899.
REVIEWS: Athenaeum 3714 1898; Bookman 15 1899; Dial 28 1900.
In Paris: a handbook for visitors to Paris in the year 1900. With G. Macquoid. 1900 (illustr T. R. Macquoid), Boston 1900.
REVIEW: Athenaeum 3780 1900.
His heart's desire: a romance. 1903, 1903 (2nd edn).
REVIEWS: Athenaeum 3946 1903; Bookman 24 1903.
Pictures in Umbria. London and New York 1905 (illustr T. R. Macquoid).
REVIEWS: Bookman 28 1905; Nation 81 1905.
A village chronicle. 1905 (illustr Forestier).
REVIEW: Athenaeum 4059 1905.
Captain Dallington. Bristol 1907.
REVIEW: Athenaeum 4179 1907.
Molly Montague's love story. [1911.]
REVIEW: Bookman 41 1911.

Contributions to periodicals and collaborative works

A desperate race. Routledge's Xmas Annual 1872.
The fires of St John. Illus London News Christmas 1879.
The little town by the Seine. Illus London News Christmas 1880.
A night of terror. Illus London News Christmas 1883.
Amelia Blandford Edwards. In Women novelists of Queen Victoria's reign, 1897.
Julia Kavanagh. In Women novelists of Queen Victoria's reign, 1897.
Macquoid's stories and travel articles were pbd in a variety of periodicals, including Belgravia, Chambers's Jnl, Eclectic Mag, English Illus Mag, Harper's Mag, Leisure Hour, Lippincott's Mag, Macmillan's Mag, Sunday Mag, Temple Bar. *See also* Wellesley *vol 5*.

§2

In Who was who 1916–28.
Sutherland, J. The Longman companion to Victorian fiction. Harlow 1988.
Blain, V., P. Clements and I. Grundy. The feminist companion to literature in English. 1990.

Blanche Marryat, Charlotte Blanche Marryat, later Mrs Lynal Thomas b. 1827

Bibliography

Kirk, J. F. Suppl to Allibone's Critical dictionary of English literature. Philadelphia 1891.

§1
Briars and thorns: a novel. Bentley's Misc Jan 1866–Feb 1867, 3 vols 1867. [DH]

Frank Marryat, Francis Samuel Marryat 1826–55

Bibliographies
Allibone, S. A. Critical dictionary of English literature. Philadelphia 1870.

§1
Borneo and the Indian archipelago, with drawings of costume and scenery. 1848.
REVIEW: Spectator 15 Jan 1848; Athenaeum 22 Jan and 12 Feb 1848.
Gold quartz mining in California: practical observations during a residence of two years, 1850–51, and 1852 in the mining districts of that country. 1852.
Mountains and molehills, or recollections of a burnt journal. With illustrations by the author. 1855, New York 1855; ed M. E. Wilbur, Stanford CA 1952.
REVIEW: Spectator 10 Feb 1855; Athenaeum 3 Mar 1855.

Collaborative works
Ed and illustr Frederick Marryat. The little savage. 2 vols 1848–9.

§2
Boase, F. Modern English biography. 1897. [DH]

Anne Marsh, later Marsh-Caldwell, née Caldwell 1791–1874

Two old men's tales: The deformed and The Admiral's daughter. 2 vols 1834, 1834.
Tales of the woods and fields: a second series of 'the two old men's tales'. 3 vols 1836, 1 vol 1850 (as A country vicarage; and, Love and duty). A country vicarage pbd separately New York 1845 (as Louisa Mildmay).
The triumphs of time. 3 vols 1844. Contains Sealed orders; The previsions of Lady Evelyn; A soldier's fortune.
Mount Sorel: or the heiress of the de Veres. 2 vols 1845, 1 vol [1856].
Emilia Wyndham. 3 vols 1846, 1 vol 1848, 2 vols Leipzig 1852.
Father Darcy. 2 vols 1846, 1 vol [1857].
Norman's Bridge: or the modern Midas. 3 vols 1847, 1 vol 1850, [1855].
The Protestant Reformation in France: or the history of the Hugonots. 2 vols 1847.
Angela: a novel. 3 vols 1848, 1 vol [1855], [1875].
Mordaunt Hall, or a September night: a novel. 3 vols 1849, 1 vol 1853.
The previsions of Lady Evelyn; with the conclusion. 1849. An earlier version pbd in The triumphs of time, *above*, 1844.
Tales of the first French Revolution, collected by the author of 'Emilia Wyndham'. 1849. 4 stories adapted from the Fr, 2 of which were first pbd in The triumphs of time, *above*, 1844.
Bellah: a tale of La Vendée. From the Fr (of O. Feuillet). 1850. Trn.
Lettice Arnold: a tale. 1850, [1856], [1876].
The Wilmingtons: a novel. 3 vols 1850, 1 vol 1852.
Adelaide Lindsay: a novel, edited by the author of 'Emilia Wyndham'. 3 vols 1850, 1 vol 1852, 1877.
Ravenscliffe. 3 vols 1851, 2 vols Leipzig 1852, 1 vol London [1855].
Time, the avenger. 3 vols 1851, 1 vol 1853.
Castle Avon. 3 vols 1852, 2 vols Leipzig 1852, 1 vol London [1855].
Helen's fault: a tale for the young. 1853.
The Longwoods of the Grange. 3 vols 1853, 1 vol 1862, New York [186?] (as Edith's legacy).
Aubrey. 3 vols 1854, 2 vols Leipzig 1854, 1 vol London [1857], [1875].
The song of Roland, as chanted before the Battle of Hastings, by the minstrel Taillefer. 1854. Trn.
The heiress of Haughton: or the mother's secret. 3 vols 1855, 2 vols Leipzig 1855, 1 vol London [1858].
Evelyn Marston. 3 vols 1856, 2 vols Leipzig 1856, 1 vol London [1860].
The rose of Ashurst. 3 vols 1857, 2 vols Leipzig 1857, 1 vol London 1859.
Charley and Georgy: or the children at Gibraltar. 1861.
Heathside Farm: a tale of country life, edited by the author of 'Two old men's tales'. 2 vols 1863. [EH]

John Westland Marston 1819–90

See col 2007.

Harriet Martineau 1802–76

The chief repositories of Martineau correspondence are the Bancroft Library Berkeley CA and Birmingham University Library (which also holds the mss of the autobiography). Other significant collections of mss material (mainly correspondence) are held at the Armitt Trust, Ambleside, BL, Bodleian, Harvard, Hertford County Record Office, Manchester College Oxford, Trinity College Cambridge, University College London, Wellesley College MA, Dr Williams's Library and Yale. Some mss are in family archives.

Bibliographies
Rivlin, J. B. Harriet Martineau: a bibliography of her separately printed books. BNYPL, May–July, Oct 1946–Jan 1947.

§1
Devotional exercises ... for the use of young persons. 1823, 1832 (enlarged as Devotional exercises, to which is added A guide to the study of the scriptures).
Christmas-Day: or the friends: a tale. [1825], 1834 (5th edn).
Addresses; with prayers and original hymns for the use of families and schools. By a lady. 1826, 1838 (2nd edn).
Principle and practice: or the orphan family. Wellington (Salop) 1827.
The rioters: or a tale of bad times. Wellington 1827.
The turn-out: or patience the best policy. Wellington 1829.
Traditions of Palestine. 1830.
The essential faith of the universal church: deduced from the sacred records. 1831.
The friends: a continuation of Christmas-Day. 1831 (3rd edn).
Sequel to Principle and practice: or the orphan family: a tale. Wellington 1831.
Five years of youth: or sense and sentiment. 1831.
Illustrations of political economy. 9 vols 1832–4. Includes Life in the wilds, 1832; The hill and the valley, 1832; Brooke and Brooke farm, 1832; Demerara, 1832; Ella of Garveloch, 1832; Weal and woe in Garveloch, 1832; A Manchester strike, 1832; Cousin Marshall, 1832; Ireland, 1832; Homes abroad, 1832; For each and for all, 1832; French wines and politics, 1833; The charmed sea, 1833; Berkeley the banker, 1833; Messrs Vanderput and Snoek, 1833; The loom and the lugger and Sowers not reapers, 1833; Cinnamon and pearls, 1833; A tale of the Tyne, 1833; Briery creek, 1833; The three ages, 1833; The Farrers of Budge row, 1834; The moral of many fables, 1834. Collected edns, 1843–5, 1859, 1862, 1884, 1887.
REVIEWS: Spectator, 4 Feb, 3 Mar, 7 July, 4 Aug, 8 Sep 1832, 2 Mar, 28 Sep, 9 Nov 1833; Athenaeum 11 Feb, 19 May, 8 Sep, 27 Oct 1832, 28 Dec 1833; Monthly Repository 6, Feb, Mar, June 1832, 8, May 1834; Examiner, 8 July, 16 Sep 1832, Apr 1834; Tait's Edinburgh Mag, Aug 1832, Apr, June 1833; Poor Man's Advocate, 29 Sep 1832; NMM 37, Apr 1833; Fraser's Mag 8, Nov 1833; Dublin Univ Mag 6, Nov 1835.
The faith as unfolded by many prophets: an essay ... addressed to the disciples of Mohammed. 1832.
Providence as manifested through Israel. 1832.
Poor laws and paupers illustrated. 4 pts 1833–4. 1, The parish: a tale;

2, The hamlets: a tale; 3, The town: a tale; 4, The land's end: a tale.
REVIEWS: Monthly Repository 7, 1833; Spectator, 1 June 1833.
Illustrations of taxation. 5 pts 1834. Includes 1, The park and the paddock; 2, The tenth haycock; 3, The Jerseymen meeting; 4, The Jerseymen parting; 5, The scholars of Arneside.
REVIEWS: NMM 41, June 1834; Athenaeum, 26 July 1834.
The tendency of strikes and sticks . . . [1834].
Miscellanies. 2 vols [Boston] 1836.
Society in America. 3 vols 1837.
REVIEWS: Athenaeum, 13 May 1837; The Times, 30 May 1837; Tait's Edinburgh Mag, July 1837.
How to observe: morals and manners. 1838.
REVIEWS: Quart rev 63, Jan 1839.
Retrospect of western travel. 3 vols 1838.
REVIEWS: Athenaeum, 3 Feb 1838; Spectator, 3 Feb 1838; Athenaeum, 10 Feb 1838; Eclectic Rev, Mar 1838; Tait's Edinburgh Mag, Apr 1838; Edinburgh Rev 67, Apr 1838.
Deerbrook: a novel. 3 vols 1839. New edns 1858, 1859, 1870, 1878, 1892.
REVIEWS: Athenaeum, 6 Apr 1839; Spectator, 13 Apr 1839; Edinburgh Rev 69, July 1839; Blackwood's Edinburgh Mag 47, Feb 1840; Westminster Rev 34, Sep 1840.
Guides to service. 1838–9. The lady's maid; The maid of all-work; The housemaid.
The martyr age of the United States of America. 1840.
The hour and the man: an historical romance. 3 vols 1841.
REVIEWS: Tait's Edinburgh Mag, Jan 1841; Eclectic Rev, Apr 1841.
The playfellow: a series of tales. 4 vols 1841. The settlers at home (rptd separately 1853, 1856); The peasant and the prince (rptd separately 1856); Feats on the fiord (rptd separately 1844, 1846, 1856, 1883 etc); The Crofton boys (rptd separately 1856).
REVIEWS: Athenaeum, 20 Mar, 11 Sept 1841, 5 Feb 1842.
Life in the sick-room: essays by an invalid. 1844.
REVIEW: Hood's Mag, 1844.
Dawn island: a tale. Manchester 1845. Pbd on behalf of the Anti-Corn Law League.
Forest and game-law tales. 3 vols 1845–6. 1, Merdhin (rptd separately 1852); The manor and the eyrie; The staunch and their work; Old landmarks and old laws; 2, The bishop's flock and the bishop's herd; Heathendom in Christendom; Four years at Maude-Chapel farm; 3, Gentle and simple.
Letters on mesmerism. 1845.
The billow and the rock: a tale. 1846.
REVIEW: Quart Rev 85, Apr 1847.
The land we live in. 4 vols 1847. With Charles Knight.
Eastern life, present and past. 3 vols 1848.
REVIEWS: NMM 83, June 1848; Westminster Rev 49, July 1848; Blackwood's Edinburgh Mag 64, Aug 1848; Br Quart Rev 8, Nov 1848; Prospective Rev, Nov 1848.
Household education. 1849.
The history of England during the thirty years' peace 1816–46. 2 vols 1849–50, 1855 (rev as History of the peace 1816–46), 4 vols [1877–8].
REVIEWS: Br Quart Rev, May 1850; Quart Rev 91, June 1852.
Two letters on cow-keeping. [1850?].
Letters on the laws of man's nature and development. 1851. With H. G. Atkinson.
REVIEW: Prospective Rev, May 1851.
Introduction to the history of the peace from 1800 to 1815. 1851, 1878.
Half a century of the British empire: a history of the kingdom and the people from 1800 to 1850. Pt 1 [1851]. Only pt 1 pbd.
Letters from Ireland. 1852. Rptd from Daily News.
A complete guide to the English Lakes. Windermere [1855].
Guide to Windermere, with tours to the neighbouring lakes and other interesting places. Windermere [1854], [1854], [1856].
The factory controversy: a warning against meddling legislation. Manchester 1855.
A history of the American compromises. 1856. Rptd with addns from Daily News.
Sketches from life . . . illustrated. [1856].
British rule in India: a historical sketch. 1857.
Corporate tradition and national rights: local dues on shipping. [1857].
Guide to Keswick and its environs. Windermere [1857].
Suggestions towards the future government of India. 1858.
Endowed schools of Ireland. 1859. Rptd from Daily News.
England and her soldiers. 1859.
Survey of the Lake District. 1860.
Health, husbandry and handicraft. 1861.
Biographical sketches. 1869, 1877 (enlarged and with autobiographical sketch). Rptd from Daily News.
Harriet Martineau's autobiography, with memorials by Maria Weston Chapman. 3 vols 1877, 1878, 1879, 1881, ed G. Weiner 2 vols 1983.
REVIEWS: Blackwood's Mag 121, Apr 1877; Fortnightly Rev 21, Apr 1877; Quart Rev 143, Apr 1877; Contemporary Rev 29, May 1877; Macmillan's Mag 36, May 1877; Westminster Rev, July 1877; Nineteenth Cent, Aug 1877; Temple Bar 53, Aug 1878.
The Hampdens: an historiette. 1880. Illustr J. E. Millais.

Contributions to periodicals

Harriet Martineau was a prolific contributor to periodicals. Listings are to be found in the following:
Lohrli, A. Household Words: A weekly journal 1850–1859. Toronto and Buffalo 1973.
Mineka, F. E. The dissidence of dissent: the Monthly Repository, 1806–1838. Chapel Hill NC 1944.
Webb, R. K. A handlist of contributions to the Daily News by Harriet Martineau 1852–1866. 1959.
Contributions to Cornhill Mag, Edinburgh Rev, Macmillan's Mag, NMM, Quart Rev, Westminster Rev *are listed in* Wellesley *vol 5. See also* G. G. Yates (ed), Harriet Martineau on women, 1985, and E. S. Arbuckle, Harriet Martineau in the London Daily News: selected contributions, 1852–1866, New York 1994.
Characteristics of the genius of Scott. Tait's Edinburgh Mag 2, Dec 1832.
The achievements of the genius of Scott. Tait's Edinburgh Mag 2, Jan 1833.
A month at sea. Penny Mag 6, Oct–Nov 1837.
Letters on mesmerism. Athenaeum, Nov 1844. Earlier version of a work of same title; *see* §1, *above*.
Surveys from the mountain. People's Jnl, 1846–7.
A thought about old and new times. Ibid.
Lake and mountain holidays. Ibid 2, 1847.
Homes for the people: household education 2–5, 1847–8. Rptd as Household education, 1849.
Ara force: a sketch. People's Jnl 3, 1847.
Survey from the pyramid. Ibid 3, 1847.
The holy land. I–IX. Ibid 3–5, 1847–8.
Shakspere's house. Ibid 4, 1848.
The old governess. Leader, 9 Nov 1850. 13 further articles 1850–1 rptd in Sketches from life, 1856.
Flood and its lessons. Chambers's Jnl, July 1859.
Drought and its lessons. Ibid 1859. Rptd in Health, husbandry and handicraft, 1861.
Our farm of two acres. Once a Week 1, 1859. 1st of a regular ser of contributions 1859–65.
The student: his health. Once a Week 2, 1860. Rptd with rest of health ser in Health, husbandry and handicraft, 1861.
Representative men: series. Once a Week 4–6, 1861–2.
Historiettes: series. Once a Week 6–9, 12, 13, 1862–5.

Letters

Harriet Martineau's letters to Fanny Wedgwood. Ed E. S. Arbuckle. Stanford CA 1983.

Harriet Martineau: selected letters. Ed. V. Sanders. Oxford 1990.

Editions and introductions

Mind amongst the spindles: a miscellany. Introd by Martineau, Boston 1845.

The positive philosophy of Auguste Comte freely translated and condensed. 2 vols 1853.

Pauli, R. Simon de Montfort, Earl of Leicester, the creator of the House of Commons. Tr U. M. Goodwin, introd by Martineau 1876.

Attributed works

Mary Campbell: or the affectionate granddaughter. Wellington 1828. Included in Rivlin bibliography.

My servant Rachel. 1838.

§2

Horne, R. H. In his A new spirit of the age, vol 2 1844.

Miller, Mrs F. Fenwick. Harriet Martineau. 1884.

Martineau, James. The early days of Harriet Martineau. Daily News, 30 Dec 1884.

Payn, J. In his Literary recollections, 1884.

Fawcett, Mrs Henry. Some eminent women of our times. 1889.

Hamilton, C. J. Women writers: their works and ways. 1893. 2nd ser.

Webb, R. K. Harriet Martineau: a radical Victorian. 1960.

Pichanick, V. K. Harriet Martineau: the woman and her work, 1802–76. Ann Arbor MI 1980.

Sanders, V. Reason over passion: Harriet Martineau and the Victorian novel. 1986.

Hoecker-Drysdale, S. Harriet Martineau: first woman sociologist. 1993.

Hunter, S. Harriet Martineau: the poetics of moralism. Aldershot 1995. [VS]

Augustus Septimus Mayhew 1826–76

The greatest plague of life: adventures of a lady in search of a good servant, illustrated by George Cruikshank. [1847.] With his brother Henry Mayhew.

The good genius that turned everything into gold, or the Queen Bee and the magic dress: a Christmas fairytale. 1847. With Henry Mayhew.

Whom to marry and how to get married, illustrated by George Cruikshank. [1848.] With Henry Mayhew.

The image of his father: or one boy is more trouble than a dozen girls, illustrated by 'Phiz'. 1848. With Henry Mayhew.

The magic of kindness: or the wondrous story of the good Huan, illustrated by George Cruikshank and Kenny Meadows. [1849], [1869] (illustr Walter Crane). With Henry Mayhew.

Living for appearances: a tale. 1855. With Henry Mayhew.

Kitty Lamere or a dark page in London life: a tale. 1855.

Paved with gold, or the romance and reality of London streets: an unfashionable novel, illustrated by H. K. Browne. 1858.

The finest girl in Bloomsbury: a serio-comic tale of ambitious love. 1861.

Blow-hot – blow cold: a love story. 1862.

Faces for fortunes. 3 vols 1865.

The comic almanack. 1870 etc. With Henry Mayhew.

Fanny N. Mayne

§1

Jane Rutherford: or, the miners' strike. By a friend of the people. The True Briton n.s. 1–2, 9 June–20 Oct 1853.

Jane Rutherford; or, the miners' strike. By a friend of the people. 1854.

Contributions to periodicals

Editor, The True Briton, vols 1–2, 1851–2; n.s. vols 1–2 1853. (Afterwards incorporated into The Illustrated People's Paper, Apr–June 1854.)

Attributed Works

The perilous nature of the penny periodical press. 1851.

The life of Nicholas I. Emperor of Russia: with a short account of Russia and the Russians. 1855.

Voyages and discoveries in the Arctic regions. Vol 7 of The Traveller's Lib. 1855, 1856.

§2

Kestner, Joseph A. Fanny Mayne's Jane Rutherford and the tradition of the social-protest novel in England. Stud in the Novel 19 1987. [JAK]

George Meredith 1828–1909

Manuscripts

The principal repository of Meredith mss is the Beinecke Rare Book and Manuscript Lib at Yale, particularly the Altschul col. It includes mss of much of Meredith's fiction (Celt and Saxon, The egoist, Harry Richmond, *mss A and B of* One of our conquerors, The tragic comedians, *partial versions of* Diana of the Crossways, The amazing marriage, *and* Lord Ormont and his Aminta) *together with notebooks and miscellaneous papers, including some reader's reports for Chapman and Hall, and much poetry and correspondence. Other significant holdings are in the Pierpont Morgan Lib (mss of* Diana of the Crossways, Lord Ormont and his Aminta, and The amazing marriage) *and Huntington (a partial version of* Diana of the Crossways, *poetry, and many of Meredith's reader's reports for Chapman and Hall). A full account is given in* IELM.

Bibliographies

Forman, M. B. A bibliography of the writings in prose and verse of George Meredith. 1922.

Forman, M. B. Meredithiana: being a supplement to the bibliography of Meredith. 1924.

Coolidge, B. A catalogue of the Altschul collection of Meredith in the Yale University Library. New Haven CT 1931 (priv ptd).

Hudson, R. B. The Altschul collection of Meredith seventeen years later. YULG 22 1948.

Sawin, H. L. Meredith: a bibliography of Meredithiana 1920–53. BB 21 1955.

Stevenson, L. In Victorian poets: a guide to research, ed F. E. Faverty, Cambridge MA 1956, 1968 (rev).

Cline, C. L. In Victorian fiction: a guide to research, ed L. Stevenson, Cambridge MA 1964.

Collie, M. George Meredith: a bibliography. Toronto and Buffalo 1974.

Beer, G. In Victorian fiction: a second guide to research, Ed G. H. Ford, New York 1978.

Olmsted, J. C. George Meredith: an annotated bibliography of criticism 1925–1975. New York and London 1978.

Hogan, R. S., L. Sawin and L. L. Merrill (ed). A concordance to the poetry of George Meredith. 2 vols New York and London 1982.

Stone, J. S. Errata in Michael Collie's bibliography of George Meredith. BB 43 1986.

Collections

The fullest description of the collected edns of Meredith's work is to be found in Collie, above; see also Forman.

Collected ('new') edition. 14 vols 1885–95. Omits The amazing marriage. Meredith corrected his novels for this edn. Colonial edns ptd from its plates.

Edition de luxe. 36 vols 1896–8, 1910–11. Includes fiction and poetry, miscellaneous prose, bibliography by A. Esdaile, and variant readings. Texts revised by Meredith. American counterpart is Boxhill edn New York 1896–8.

Library edition (also known as New Popular edition and Revised edition). 18 vols 1897–8. Text of Edition de luxe.

Pocket edition. 18 vols 1902 [1901]–6. Most titles rptd from plates of Library edn.

Memorial edition. 27 vols 1909–11, New York 1909–12. Most complete edn, substantially the same text as Edition de luxe. Vol 27 includes various readings (alterations in the text of the prose between first edn and Memorial edn).

Standard edition. 15 vols 1914–20. Rpts plates of Memorial edn.

Mickleham edition. 18 vols 1922–4. Rpts plates of Memorial edn.

Collected Poems

Poetical works. Ed G. M. Trevelyan 1912.

Selected poems. Ed G. Hough, Oxford 1962.

The poems of George Meredith. Ed P. Bartlett 2 vols New Haven CT and London 1978. Complete edn, including much previously unpbd material.

George Meredith: selected poems. Ed K. Hanley, Manchester 1983.

§1

There is a substantial listing of reviews of individual works in Forman, Meredithiana, *in* Bibliographies, *above. See also* George Meredith: the critical heritage, *ed I. Williams 1971, which reprints a selection of significant reviews. The following pbns by L. T. Hergenhan list some reviews not in* Meredithiana: A critical consideration of the reviews of the novels of George Meredith (down to The egoist), unpbd PhD thesis, Univ of London 1960; The reception of George Meredith's early novels, Nineteenth-Century Fiction 19 1964; Meredith's attempts to win popularity: contemporary reactions, SEL 4 1964; *and* Meredith achieves recognition: the reception of Beauchamp's career and The egoist, TSLL 11 1969.

Poems. 1851, New York 1898, London 1909, New York 1909 (adds poems from Modern love, Scattered poems).

The shaving of Shagpat: an Arabian entertainment. '1856' [1855], 1865, 1872, 1900 (selection), 1912; ed F. M. Meynell, illustr H. Guilbeau, New York 1955; London 1988; tr Fr 1921.

Farina: a legend of Cologne. 1857, 1865, 1868, 1898 (in Short stories); tr Ger 1931.

The ordeal of Richard Feverel: a history of father and son. 3 vols 1859, 2 vols Leipzig 1875 (rev, Tauchnitz), London 1 vol 1878 (rpts 1875 text), London 1885, Boston 1888, London 1890, 1899, 1901, New York 1906, London 1910; ed F. W. Chandler, New York 1917; ed R. Sencourt, London 1935; ed L. Stevenson, New York 1950 (Mod Lib); ed N. Kelvin, New York 1961; ed C. J. Hill, New York 1964; ed C. L. Cline, Boston 1971; ed J Halperin, Oxford 1984 (WCp); tr Fr 1865 in Revue des Deux Mondes (abridged), 1938, Ital 1873, Cz 1902, Ger 1904, 1912, 1961, Hungarian 193(?), Rus 1932, 1984, Finnish 1953, Serbo-Croat 1957, 1965, 1967.

Evan Harrington: or he would be a gentleman. First pbd Once a Week 11 Feb–13 Oct 1860. New York 1860, 3 vols London 1861, 1 vol 1866, 1885, Melbourne and Sydney 1888, London 1889, [1911]; ed G. F. Reynolds, New York 1922; London 1983; tr Fr 1910, 1934.

Modern love, and poems of the English roadside, with poems and ballads. 1862; foreword E. Cavazza, Portland ME 1891, London 1892 (adds The sage enamoured, The honest lady), Boston 1892, 1894, 1895, Portland ME 1898 (rpt 1910); ed R. Le Gallienne, New York 1909, London 1922; ed C. Day Lewis 1948; ed S. Regan, Peterborough 1988; introd by G. Beer, 1995 (Pen); tr Fr 1910, 1930, Jap 1958.

Emilia in England. 3 vols 1864, 1 vol 1886 (as Sandra Belloni); tr Fr 1864 in Revue des Deux Mondes (abridged), 1865.

Rhoda Fleming: a story. 3 vols 1865, 2 vols New York 1888, 1 vol Melbourne and Sydney 1889, London 1890, 1901; tr Ger 1905, 1964, Cz 1927.

Vittoria. First pbd in Fortnightly Rev 15 Jan–1 Dec 1866. 3 vols '1867' [1866], Boston 1888, 1 vol London 1890.

The adventures of Harry Richmond. First pbd in Cornhill Mag Sep 1870–Nov 1871, 3 vols 1871, 1871, 1 vol '1886' [1885] (rev), Boston 1886, Melbourne and Sydney 1887, London 1889, 1901, 1912; ed L. T. Hergenhan, Lincoln NE 1970; tr Ger [1904], Fr 1948.

Beauchamp's career. First pbd in Fortnightly Rev Aug 1874–Dec 1875. 3 vols '1876' [1875], 2 vols Leipzig 1876 (Tauchnitz), London 1889, Melbourne and Sydney 1889, London 1913; ed G. M. Young 1950 (WC); ed M. Harris, Oxford 1988 (WCp); tr Fr 1928.

The house on the beach: a realistic tale. First pbd in New Quart Mag Jan 1877. New York 1877, 1878, London '1894' [1895] (adds The tale of Chloe and The case of General Ople and Lady Camper), New York 1898 (rev in Short stories); tr Fr 1929.

The egoist: a comedy in narrative. First pbd as Sir Willoughby Patterne The Egoist in Glasgow Weekly Herald 21 June 1879–10 Jan 1880. 3 vols 1879, New York 1879, 1 vol 1880, New York 1880, 3 vols London 1880, 2 vols New York [1888], 1 vol London 1890; ed W. C. Brownell, New York 1901, Leipzig 1910, London 1912; ed Lord Dunsany 1947 (WC); ed L. Stevenson, Boston 1958; ed A. Wilson, New York 1963; ed G. Woodcock 1968 (Pen); ed R. M. Adams, New York 1979; ed M. Harris, Oxford 1992 (WCp); The egoist arranged for the stage, ed A. Sutro 1920 (priv ptd), and ed L. Sawin, Athens OH 1981; tr Rus 1894, Fr 1904, 1924, 1949, 1962, Ger 1905, 1925, 1932, 1955, Ital 1922, 1929, Serbo-Croat 1953, 1962, Portuguese 1959, Hungarian 1964, Romanian 1966, Lithuanian 1976.

The tragic comedians: a study in a well-known story, enlarged from the Fortnightly Review. First pbd in abbreviated form in Fortnightly Rev Oct 1880–Feb 1881 as The tragic comedians: a study in an old story. 2 vols 1880, 1881, 1 vol 1881, 1881, New York 1881, Leipzig 1881 (Tauchnitz); ed C. K. Shorter London 1891 (rev), 1892, Boston 1892, London [1914], 1946; tr Ger 1908, 1909, Fr 1909, 1927, Ital 1951.

Poems and lyrics of the joy of earth. 1883, 1883, 1894, 1895.

Diana of the Crossways: a novel, considerably enlarged from the Fortnightly Review. First pbd (26 chs only) in Fortnightly Rev June–July and Sep–Dec 1884. 3 vols 1885 (3 edns), 1 vol New York 1885 (incomplete mag version), New York 1885, Melbourne and Sydney 1887, London 1890, New York 1891, London 1901, 1909; ed A. Symons, New York [1930?], London 1980 (Virago); tr Ger 1886, 1905, 1962, Ital 1906, 1909, 1953, Cz 1928, Fr 2 vols 1931, Portuguese 1967.

Ballads and poems of tragic life. 1887, Boston 1887, London 1894, 1897.

A reading of earth. 1888, Boston 1888, London 1895, New York and London 1901.

Jump-to-glory Jane: a poem. 1889 (priv ptd); illustr L. Housman 1892.

The case of General Ople and Lady Camper. First pbd in New Quart Mag July 1877. New York 1890, 1891, '1894' [1895] (with The tale of Chloe and The house on the beach), New York 1898 (in Short stories), 1900; tr Fr 1931, Ital 1944, Polish 1977.

The tale of Chloe: an episode in the history of Beau Beamish. First pbd in New Quart Mag July 1879. New York 1890, 1891, London '1894' [1895] (with The house on the beach and The case of General Ople and Lady Camper), New York 1898 (in Short stories), Portland ME 1899, London 1900; tr Fr 1908 in Mercure de France, 1931, Ger 1923, 1925, 1949, Ital 1944.

One of our conquerors. First pbd in abbreviated form in Fortnightly Rev Oct 1890–May 1891, and in the Australasian 29 Nov 1890–2 May 1891. 3 vols 1891 (2 edns), 2 vols Leipzig 1891, 1 vol Melbourne and Sydney 1891, Boston 1891, London 1892; ed M. Harris, St Lucia, Queensland 1975; tr Fr 1935.

Poems: The empty purse, with Odes to the comic spirit, to youth in memory and verses. 1892, 1895.

Lord Ormont and his Aminta: a novel. First pbd in abbreviated form in Pall Mall Mag Dec 1893–July 1894. 3 vols 1894, 1 vol New York 1894, London 1895, 2 vols Leipzig 1895 (Tauchnitz); tr Ger 1907, Serbo-Croat 1968.
The tale of Chloe and other stories. '1894' [1895], 1895.
The amazing marriage. First pbd in abbreviated form in Scribner's Mag Jan–Dec 1895. 2 vols 1895, New York 1895, London 1896, 1896, 1 vol 1896 (rev), 2 vols Leipzig 1897; tr Du 1896 in De Gids (selection), Fr 1939.
On the idea of comedy and the uses of the comic spirit: a lecture delivered at the London Institute, February 1st 1877. First pbd in New Quart Mag Apr 1877. 1897, New York 1897; ed L. Cooper, Ithaca NY 1956; tr Fr 1897, Ger 1910, Jap 1953.
Selected poems. 1897, New York 1897. Meredith's selection.
Odes in contribution to the song of French history. 1898, New York 1898; tr Fr 1916.
Short stories: The tale of Chloe, The house on the beach, Farina and The case of General Ople and Lady Camper. New York 1898.
A reading of life, with other poems. 1901.
Twenty poems. 1909.
Last poems. 1909.
Poems written in early youth (published in 1851), Poems from Modern love (first edition) and Scattered poems. 1909, New York 1909.
Celt and Saxon. First pbd in Fortnightly Rev Jan–Aug 1910 and Forum New York Jan–Nov 1910. 1910, New York 1910. Uniform with 'Library' or 'New Popular' edn.
The friend of an engaged couple. Ed M. Harris. Sydney Stud in English 6 1980.

Contributions to periodicals

Many of the occasional works are collected in Miscellaneous prose, *vol 23 of the* Memorial edition, *above. Items in that vol are marked* 'Mem' *below. For serial pbn of prose works, see §1 above; for poetry, see Bartlett's edn in* Collections, *above. Most of Meredith's contributions to* Fortnightly Rev, Fraser's Mag, National Rev *and* Westminster Rev *are in* Wellesley.

Songs from the dramatists. Fraser's Mag Nov 1854. Review and trn.
A story-telling party. Once a Week 24 Dec 1859.
Leading articles and weekly news notes. Ipswich Jnl 1860–8 (some identified and quoted in R. L. Newby, Three faces of Meredith in the Ipswich Journal, McNeese Rev 28 1981–2; George Meredith and the Ipswich Journal, Ball State Univ Forum 28 1982; George Meredith and the Ipswich Journal, N & Q 30 1983; George Meredith and the Governor Eyre case again, N & Q 35 1988).
Correspondence from the seat of war in Italy. Morning Post 22 June–24 July 1866 (Mem).
The anecdotalist. Pall Mall Gazette 2 Mar 1868; The cynic of society, 28 Mar 1868; The consummate epicure, 25 Apr 1868; A working Frenchwoman, 30 Apr 1868; The third-class carriage, 23 May 1868; English country inns, 27 June 1868. Essays.
Mistral's Mireio, tr H. Crichton. Pall Mall Gazette 27 Mar 1869. Review and trn.
Up to midnight. Graphic 21 Dec 1872–18 Jan 1873; rptd Graphic 1–8 Feb 1913; in book form Boston 1913 (incomplete). Essays.
A pause in the strife. Pall Mall Gazette 9 July 1886. Article (Mem).
Leslie Stephen. Author Apr 1904 (Mem).
The contributions of Meredith to the Monthly Observer, January–July 1849. Ed M. B. Forman 1928 (priv ptd).

Letters, journals etc

Letters, collected and edited by his son [W. M. Meredith]. 2 vols 1912. Selections pbd Scribner's Mag Aug–Oct 1912.
The letters of George Meredith. Ed C. L. Cline, 3 vols Oxford 1970. *For letters not in Cline's edn, see* IELM.
The notebooks of George Meredith. Ed G. Beer and M. Harris, Salzburg 1983.

Introductions

Most of Meredith's introductions are collected in Miscellaneous prose, *vol 23 of the* Memorial edition, *above. Items in that vol are marked* 'Mem' *below.*

The cruise of the Alabama and the Sumter: from the private journals and other papers of Commander R. Semmes. 1864. Introductory and concluding chs by Meredith.
Introduction. In Thackeray, The four Georges, 1903 (Mem).
Introduction. In Lady Duff Gordon, Letters from Egypt, 1904 (Mem).
Introduction. In The Japanese spirit by Yoshimaburo Okakura, 1905 (Mem).
Introduction. In Collected poems of Dora Sigerson Shorter, 1907 (Mem).

§2

See Forman, Meredithiana, *in* Bibliographies, *above, for a comprehensive list of obituaries.*

McCarthy, J. Novels with a purpose. Westminster Rev July 1864, rptd in his Con amore: or critical studies, 1868.
Shore, A. The novels of Meredith. Br Quart Rev 69, 1879.
Courtney, W. L. Meredith's novels. Fortnightly Rev June 1886.
Shaw, F. L. George Meredith. New Princeton Rev Apr 1887.
Stevenson, R. L. Books which have influenced me. Br Weekly 13 May 1887, rptd in his Essays in the art of writing, 1905.
Wilde, O. The decay of lying: a dialogue. Nineteenth Century Jan 1888, rptd in his Intentions, 1891.
Watson, W. Fiction – plethoric and anaemic. Nat Rev Oct 1889.
Bainton, G. In his Art of authorship, 1890. Quotes Meredith's advice on novel writing.
Henley, W. E. In his Views and reviews, 1890.
Le Gallienne, R. George Meredith. Some characteristics. 1890.
More, P. E. The novels of Meredith. Atlantic Monthly Oct 1890, rptd in his Shelburne essays ser 2, New York 1905.
Gosse, E. In his Gossip in a library, 1891.
Lynch, H. George Meredith: a study. 1891.
Ross, J. In her Early days recalled, 1891.
Wilde, O. The critic as artist. In his Intentions, 1891.
Wilde, O. The soul of man under Socialism. Fortnightly Rev Feb 1891.
Dolman, F. Meredith as a journalist. New Rev 8 1893.
Bridges, R. In his Overheard in Arcady, 1894.
Dowden, E. Meredith's poetry. In his New studies in literature, 1895.
Mr Meredith's novels. Edinburgh Rev 181 Jan 1895.
Schwob, M. In his Spicilege, Paris 1896.
Smith, G. The women of Meredith. Fortnightly Rev May 1896.
Robertson, J. M. Concerning preciosity. Yellow Book 13 1897.
Shaw, G. B. Meredith on comedy. Sat Rev 27 Mar 1897.
Wilson, S. L. In his Theology of modern literature, 1899.
Brownell, W. C. In his Victorian prose masters, New York 1901.
Legras, C. In his Chez nos contemporains d'Angleterre, Paris 1901.
Leonard, R. M. Politics in Meredith's novels. New Liberal Rev 2 1901.
Jerrold, W. C. George Meredith: an essay towards appreciation. 1902.
Samuel Richardson and Meredith. Macmillan's Mag Mar 1902.
O., H. [Harold Owen]. Mr Meredith on the future of Liberalism, Home Rule and Imperialism, education and the use of votes. Manchester Guardian 2 Feb 1903. Interview.
Burnand, F. C. In his Records and reminiscences, 2 vols 1904.
Sharp, W. In his Literary geography, 1904.
Stead, W. T. Character sketch: Meredith. Rev of Reviews 29 1904.
Legouis, E. L'égoiste de Meredith. Revue Germanique 1 1905.
Moffatt, J. Mr Meredith on religion. Hibbert Jnl 3 1905.
Pigou, A. C. The optimism of Browning and Meredith. Independent Rev 6 1905.
Trevelyan, G. M. Optimism and Mr Meredith: a reply. Independent Rev 6 1905.

Cordelet, H. La femme dans l'oeuvre de Meredith. Revue Germanique 2 1906.
de Selincourt, B. Meredith's hymn to colour. Independent Rev 11 1906.
Henderson, M. S. (later Gretton). Some thoughts underlying Meredith's poems. International Jnl of Ethics 16 1906.
Quiller-Couch, A. T. Meredith's poetry. In his From a Cornish window, Bristol and London 1906.
S[idgwick], A. S. and E. M. In their Henry Sidgwick: a memoir, 1906.
Trevelyan, G. M. The poetry and philosophy of George Meredith. 1906.
Bailey, E. J. The novels of George Meredith: a study. New York 1907.
Greene, H. C. George Meredith. Atlantic Monthly June 1907.
Henderson, M. S. (later Gretton). George Meredith: novelist, poet, reformer. 1907. Chs 14–17, on the poems, are by B. de Selincourt.
Magnus, L. The succession of Mr Meredith. Fortnightly Rev Dec 1907.
Short, T. S. On some of the characteristics of Meredith's prose-writing. 1907.
Curle, R. H. P. Aspects of George Meredith. 1908.
Meredith and the Jews. Jewish Chron 14 Feb 1908.
Barrie, J. M. George Meredith. 1909.
Chesterton, G. K. The moral philosophy of Meredith. Contemporary Rev July 1909.
Clodd, E. Meredith: some recollections. Fortnightly Rev July 1909.
Davray, H. D. Meredith: souvenirs et réflexions. Revue Hebdomadaire 5 June 1909.
Forman, M. B. Meredith: some early appreciations. 1909.
Hammerton, J. A. George Meredith in anecdote and criticism. 1909, Edinburgh 1911 (rev). Quotes many contemporary reviews not rptd elsewhere.
Matz, B. W. Meredith as publisher's reader. Fortnightly Rev Aug 1909.
Moffatt, J. Meredith: a primer to the novels. 1909.
Thomson, J. James Thomson 'B.V.' on Meredith. 1909.
Dick, E. Meredith: drei Versuche. Berlin 1910.
Frey, E. Die Dichtungen Merediths. Zurich 1910.
Lubbock, P. The collected works of Meredith. Quart Rev 212 1910.
McKechnie, J. Meredith's allegory The shaving of Shagpat re-interpreted. 1910.
Watson, F. Meredith and education. Nineteenth Century Feb 1910.
Beach, J. W. The comic spirit in George Meredith. 1911.
Forman, M. B. Meredith and the Monthly Observer. 1911.
Henderson, A. In his Interpreters of life and the modern spirit, 1911.
Hyndman, H. M. In his Record of an adventurous life, New York 1911.
Jack, A. A. Meredith – intellectual poetry. In his Poetry and prose: being essays on modern English poetry, 1911.
Brendel, A. Die Technik des Romans bei Meredith. Munich 1912.
Collins, J. P. Conversations with Meredith. Pall Mall Mag 50 1912.
Figgis, D. Meredith: the philosopher in the artist. In his Studies and appreciations, 1912.
Jones, D. M. English writers and the making of Italy. London Quart Rev 118 1912.
Ross, J. In her Fourth generation, 1912.
Seccombe, T. In DNB, 2nd suppl, vol 2, 1912.
Benedetti, A. Meredith: poeta. Palermo 1913.
Chesterton, G. K. In his Victorian age in literature, 1913.
Foote, G. W. Meredith: freethinker. Eng Rev 13 1913.
Frey, E. Die Romane Merediths: ein Versuch. Winterthur 1913.
Torretta, L. Meredith: romanziere, poeta, pensatore. Naples 1913.
Bedford, H. The heroines of Meredith. 1914.
Hartog, W. G. Meredith, France and the French. Fortnightly Rev Oct 1914.
Harris, F. In his Contemporary portraits, New York 1915.
Photiadès, C. Meredith: sa vie – son imagination – son art – sa doctrine. Paris 1910; tr 1916.
Symons, A. Meredith as a poet. In his Figures of several centuries, 1916.
Lee, J. Meredith's literary relations with Germany. MLR 12 1917.
Morley, J. In his Recollections, 2 vols 1917. Vol 1 ch 4 on Meredith.
Thomas, E. In his Literary pilgrim in England, 1917.
Campbell, O. J. Some influences of Meredith's philosophy upon his fiction. Wisconsin Stud in Lang & Lit 2 1918.
Crees, J. H. E. George Meredith: a study of his works and personality. Oxford 1918.
MacCarthy, D. Meredith's method. In his Remnants, 1918.
Quiller-Couch, A. T. The poetry of Meredith. In his Studies in literature, Cambridge 1918.
Sully, J. In his My life and friends, 1918.
Butcher, A. M. Memories of George Meredith, O. M. 1919.
Ellis, S. M. George Meredith: his life and friends in relation to his work. 1919.
Trevelyan, G. M. Englishmen and Italians. PBA 9 1919.
Watson, A. F. Meredith and Italy. Fortnightly Rev Feb 1919.
Dimond, C. Music in the novels of Meredith. Nineteenth Century May 1920.
Galland, R. George Meredith and British criticism. 1923.
Galland, R. George Meredith les cinquante premières années (1828–1878). Paris 1923.
Stevenson, L. The ordeal of George Meredith. New York 1953.
Hudson, R. B. The publishing of Meredith's Rhoda Fleming. SB 6 1954.
Beer, G. Meredith's revisions of The tragic comedians. RES n.s. 14 1963.
Hergenhan, L. T. Meredith's revisions of Harry Richmond. RES n.s. 14 1963.
Beer, G. Some compositors' misreadings of The tragic comedians. N & Q 209 1964.
Hergenhan, L. T. Meredith's use of revision: a consideration of the revisions of Richard Feverel and Evan Harrington. MLR 59 1964.
Measures, J. E. Meredith's Diana of the Crossways: revisions and reconsiderations. Unpbd PhD thesis, Univ of Wisconsin 1966.
Nowell-Smith, S. The printing of George Meredith's The amazing marriage. Library 21 1966.
Sage, J. A. S. The making of Meredith's The amazing marriage. Unpbd PhD thesis, Ohio State Univ 1967.
Cotton, J. R. Evan Harrington: an analysis of George Meredith's revisions. Unpbd PhD thesis, Univ of Southern California 1968.
Harris, M. Serial versions of Meredith's One of our conquerors. N & Q 219 1974.
Shaheen, M. Y. On the manuscripts of The amazing marriage. N & Q 220 1975.
Roth, L. Meredith's revisions of The egoist. Unpbd PhD thesis, Kent State Univ 1983.
Simpson, D. A. A critical edition of The tragic comedians by George Meredith. Unpbd DPhil thesis, Oxford Univ 1989.
Spånberg, S-J. The adventures of Harry Richmond: the unpublished parts. Studia Anglistica Upsaliensia 72 1990.
Ives, M. A. George Meredith's publications in the New Quarterly Magazine: a critical edition of The house on the beach, On the idea of comedy, The case of General Ople and Lady Camper and The tale of Chloe. Unpbd PhD thesis, Univ of Virginia 1991.
[MH]

Eliza Meteyard, 'Silverpen' 1816–79

Collections

Wedgwood trio. Merion PA 1967 (3 books rptd in 1 vol).

§1

Struggles for fame: a novel. 3 vols 1845, 1847.
The doctor's little daughter. 1850, 1872.

Lilian's Golden hours. Illus. '1857' [1856], 1858.
Dr Oliver's maid: a story in four chapters. 1857.
Dora and her papa: a story for children. Illus. 1860, 1869.
Mainstone's housekeeper. 3 vols 1860, 1864, 1865.
The Delft jug. 1861.
Give bread, gain love: a tale. 1861, 1869.
The little museum keepers. 1861.
The hallowed spots of ancient London: historical, biographical and antiquarian sketches. 1862, rptd 1870.
Lady Herbert's gentlewomen. 3 vols 1862.
The life of Josiah Wedgwood from his private correspondence and family papers. Illus. 2 vols 1865, 2 vols 1970 (facs with introd by R. W. Lightbown), 2 vols New York 1971, Stoke-on-Trent 1980 (facs).
A group of Englishmen: being records of the younger Wedgwoods and their friends. 1871.
The Nine Hours' Movement: industrial and household tales. 1872.
Wedgwood and his works. 1873.
Memorials of Wedgwood. 1874.
The Wedgwood handbook: a manual for collectors. 1875.
The children's isle: a story for the young. Illus. 1878.
Choice examples of Wedgwood art. 1879.
Joe Fulwood's trust. 1883.

Contributions to periodicals

Life of an authoress. Tait's Edinburgh Mag Dec 1843–Apr 1844.
Art in Spitalfields. People's Jnl 1845.
Life's contrasts. Howitt's Jnl 2 Jan 1847.
The angel of the unfortunate. Howitt's Jnl 1847.
The worm towards the sun. Douglas Jerrold's Shilling Mag 1847.
The great question of Ragged Schools. Eliza Cook's Jnl 11 Aug 1849.
Lucy Dean: the noble needlewoman. Eliza Cook's Jnl 16 Mar 1850. Rptd in The slaughter-house of mammon, ed S. A. Winn and L. M. Alexander, West Cornwall CT 1992.
My work as a decorator. Sharpe's London Mag 1855.
Dr Oliver's maid. Sharpe's London Mag 1856.
Holy homes. Sharpe's London Mag 1857, 1858.
Mistress of St John's. Sharpe's London Mag 1859 and Littell's Living Age 1873.
Primroses on the bar. Sharpe's London Mag 1859.
Bridget of the moor. Reliquary 1860.
Love steps of Dorothy Vernon. Reliquary 1860.
St Benedicts in the Holme. Reliquary 1860.
A sketch from Wroxeter. Sharpe's London Mag 1860.
Through the snow: a tale. Sharpe's London Mag 1861.
Great Yarmouth; semi-Dutch town. Good Words 1866.
Plates and dishes. Good Words 1866.
Meteyard was a regular contributor to Howitt's Jnl, Eliza Cook's Jnl, Household Words *and* Douglas Jerrold's Shilling Mag. *She also pbd in periodicals ranging from the* Reliquary *to the* Working Man's Friend and Family Instructor. *After mid-1846 she was a frequent writer for* Douglas Jerrold's Weekly Newspaper, *and for the* Forest of Dean Examiner. [LA]

John Mills d. c. 1885

The old English gentleman: or the fields and the woods. 3 vols 1841, 1841, 1854.
The stage coach: or the road of life. 3 vols 1843.
D'Horsay: or the follies of the day, by a man of fashion. 1844; ed J. Grego 1902 (with introd, sketch of D'Orsay's career, key to the characters mentioned in the satire and bibliography of works written by Mills).
The English fireside: a tale of the past. 3 vols 1844.
The days of old. In The Edinburgh tales vol 2, 1845.
The old hall: or our hearth and homestead. 3 vols 1845.
The sportsman's library. Edinburgh 1845.
Christmas in the olden time: or the wassail bowl. [1846.]
The life of a foxhound. 1848, 1849, 1861, 1892, [1910], 1921.
A capful of moonshine: or 'tis not all gold that glitters. 1849.
Our county. 3 vols 1850.
The belle of the village. 3 vols 1852.
The life of a racehorse. 1854, 1861.
The wheel of life. 1855.
The flyers of the hunt. Illustr J. Leech. 1859, 1865.
Stable secrets: or Puffy Doddles, his sayings and sympathies. 1863.
Too fast to last. 3 vols 1881, [1882].
On the spur of the moment. 3 vols 1884.
Jack Cherton of Sydney. [1906.]

Dinah Maria Mulock, later Craik 1826–87

§1

Michael the miner. 1846. Children's book.
How to win love: or Rhoda's lesson. 1848, [1866] (new edn), [1883]. Children's book.
REVIEWS: Athenaeum 20 May 1848; (Smedley, Frank) Sharpe's London Mag 7 1848.
Cola Monti: or the story of a genius. 1849, [1864] (illus), [1883], [1899]. Children's book.
REVIEWS: Chambers's Edinburgh Jnl 24 Nov 1849; [Smedley, Frank] Sharpe's London Mag 9 1849.
The Ogilvies. 3 vols 1849, 1850, 1855, Leipzig 1863, London [1895] (Oxford Lib), [1902].
REVIEWS: Chambers's Edinburgh Jnl 19 Jan 1850; Colburn's New Monthly Mag 87 1849; Dublin Univ Mag 36 1850; [Smedley, Frank] Sharpe's London Mag 10 1849.
Olive. 3 vols 1850, 1851, 1854, 2 vols Leipzig 1866, London 1875, [1877] (new edn), [1893] (Oxford Lib).
REVIEWS: Colburn's New Monthly Mag 90 1850; Chambers's Edinburgh Jnl 4 Jan 1851; Colburn's New Monthly Mag 95 1851; Dublin Univ Mag 37 1851.
The half-caste: an old governess's tale. First pbd in Chambers's Papers for the People 12 1851. 1880, 1897.
Alice Learmont: a fairy tale. 1852, 1859, 1878; tr Fr [187?]. Children's book.
Bread upon the waters: a governess's life. 1852, Leipzig 1865.
The head of the family. 3 vols 1852, 1854, 2 vols Leipzig 1858, London 1874 (new edn), 1890 (illustr Walter Crane), [1895] (Oxford Lib), [1916].
REVIEWS: Colburn's New Monthly Mag 94 1852; [Hall, Anna Maria] Sharpe's London Mag 15 1852; in 'Recent novels', Edinburgh Rev 97 1853.
Agatha's husband. 3 vols 1853, 1858, Leipzig 1860, London 1861 (Parlour Lib), 1865 (6th edn), 1875 (illustr Walter Crane), 1906; tr Ger 1861.
REVIEWS: Athenaeum 1 Jan 1853; Colburn's New Monthly Mag 97 1853; in 'Recent novels', Dublin Univ Mag 42 1853; in 'Recent novels', Edinburgh Rev 97 1853 [by Greg, W. R.]; in 'Books and their authors', Sharpe's London Mag n.s. 2 1853 [by Hall, Anna Maria].
Avillion and other tales. 3 vols 1853, 1854. Includes Avillion; or, the happy isles; The last of the Ruthvens (Chambers's Papers for the People 5, 1850); The self-seer (Fraser's Mag, Jan–Mar 1849); The sculptor of Bruges (Chambers's Edinburgh Jnl, 20 Feb 1847); The Italian's daughter (Chambers's Edinburgh Jnl, 27 Nov 1847); The daughter of Heremon (Sharpe's London Mag, Dec 1848); King Tolv (as The wife of King Tolv, Sharpe's London Mag, June 1850); Erotion (Dublin Univ Mag, Oct 1847); Cleomenes the Greek (Bentley's Misc, July 1849); The story of Hyas (as Hyas the Athenian, Fraser's Mag, July 1848); The cross on the snow mountains (Dublin Univ Mag, Feb 1849); The Rosecrucian (Dublin Univ Mag, Feb 1847); Antonio Melidori (Chambers's Papers for

the People 5, 1850); The two homes: a story for wives (Chambers's Edinburgh Jnl, 17 Apr 1847); Minor trials (Chambers's Edinburgh Jnl, 10 Oct 1846); Adelaide, being fragments from a young wife's diary (Sharpe's London Jnl, Aug 1852); The old mathematician (Douglas Jerrold's Shilling Mag, May 1848); The half-caste (Chambers's Papers for the People 12, 1851); Miss Letty's experiences; A bride's tragedy (Sharpe's London Jnl, Aug–Sep 1848); 'Tis useless trying (Chambers's Edinburgh Jnl, 4 Sep 1847); The only son (Chambers's Edinburgh Jnl, 1 May 1847); The doctor's family (Chambers's Edinburgh Jnl, 2 Jan 1847); All for the best (Chambers's Edinburgh Jnl, 29 May 1847); The story of Elizabeth Sirani (Chambers's Edinburgh Jnl, 31 July 1847); A life episode.

REVIEW: Athenaeum 19 Nov 1853.

A hero: Philip's book. 1853, 1857, 1860 (new edn), 1875 (new edn), 1889. Children's book.

REVIEW: Dublin Univ Mag 43 1854.

The little Lychetts. 1855. Children's book.

John Halifax, gentleman. 3 vols 1856, 2 vols Leipzig 1857, London 1857 (rev edn), 1859 (4th edn), [1864] (12th edn), [1870] (17th edn), [1895] (39th edn), [1906] (EL), 1907, 1914 (Oxford edn), 1925, 1961 (EL); tr Du [186?], Sp 1890, Ger 1891.

REVIEW: In 'New novels', Athenaeum 26 Apr 1856.

Nothing new: tales. 1857, 1861, 1869. Short stories. Lord Erlistoun (Nat Mag, May 1857); Alwyn's first wife (Fraser's Mag, Jan–Feb 1855); M. Anastasius (as A ghost story, Household Words, 24 Mar 1855); The water cure (Dublin Univ Mag, Apr 1855); The double house (Fraser's Mag, Aug 1856); The last house in C— Street, (Fraser's Mag, Oct 1856); A family in love; A low marriage (National Mag, Nov 1856).

A woman's thoughts about women. Essays. 1858, 1859, Leipzig 1860, London 1869; tr Swed 1861, Danish 1869. First pbd in Chambers's Edinburgh Jnl 2 May–19 Dec 1857.

Domestic stories. 1859, Leipzig 1862. Philip Armytage; or the blind girl's love (Dublin Univ Mag, June 1847) and the following stories from Avillon and other tales: The last of the Ruthvens, The Italian's daughter, The two homes, Minor trials, Adelaide, The old mathematician, The half-caste, Miss Letty's experiences, A bride's tragedy, 'Tis useless trying, The only son, The doctor's family, All for the best.

A life for a life. 3 vols 1859, 2 vols Leipzig 1859, London 1860 (new edn, rev), 1865, 1871, 1903; tr Ger 1877.

REVIEWS: Athenaeum 6 Aug 1859; Christian Remembrancer 38 1859.

Poems. [1859], 1860, Leipzig 1868, London 1872.

Romantic tales. 1859, Leipzig 1861. From Avillon and other tales: Avillon, The self-seer, The sculptor of Bruges, The daughter of Heremon, King Tolv, Erotion, Cleomenes the Greek, The story of Hyas, The cross on the snow mountains, The Rosecrucian, Antonio Melidori, The story of Elisabetta Sirani, A life episode.

Our year: a child's book in prose and verse. Cambridge 1860, Leipzig 1860.

Studies from life. 1861, Leipzig 1867. Essays first pbd in Chambers's Edinburgh Jnl: Old stones (22 Aug 1857); Silence for a generation (12 June 1858); Going out to play (6 Mar 1858); Want something to read (8 May 1858); War sparkles (24 Mar 1855); An old soldier's coming home (as A soldier's coming home, 1 Sep 1855); Poor people's children (21 Apr 1855); Travelling companions (25 July 1857); Through the powder-mills (3 Nov 1855); Brother Jonathan's pet (16 Jan 1858); Literary ghouls (21 Aug 1858); About mothers-in-law (10 July 1858); Our lost cat (as Our lost pet, 29 May 1858); My babes in the wood (11 Sep 1858); The man of men (25 Sep 1858); Lost (13 Feb 1858).

Mistress and maid. First pbd in Good Words, Jan–Dec 1862. Leipzig 1862, 2 vols London 1863, 1864, [1897], [1916].

The fairy book. 1863, 1865, 1868 (Golden Treasury), 1913 (illustr Warwick Goble), [1922] (illustr Louis Rhead), 1923, 1979 etc. Children's book.

Christian's mistake. 1865, Leipzig 1865, London [1866], 1901.

REVIEW: Athenaeum 18 Feb 1865.

A New Year's gift for sick children. Edinburgh 1865. Poems and essays.

A noble life. 2 vols 1866, Leipzig 1866, London [1869], 1902 (new edn); tr Rus [1890].

REVIEWS: Nation 1 Mar 1866 [James, Henry]; Athenaeum 3 Mar 1866; London Rev 17 Mar 1866.

Two marriages. 2 vols 1867, Leipzig 1867, London 1880 (new edn), 1904. Two novellas: John Browerbank's wife, Parson Garland's daughter.

The woman's kingdom. First pbd in Good Words Jan–Dec 1868. 2 vols Leipzig 1868, 3 vols London 1869, 1870; tr Ger 1869.

REVIEWS: Athenaeum 31 Oct 1868; Saturday Rev 6 Feb 1869.

A brave lady. First pbd in Macmillan's Mag May 1869–Apr 1870. 3 vols 1870, 2 vols Leipzig 1870, London [1871], 1899, 1903.

REVIEWS: Athenaeum 19 Mar 1870; Saturday Rev 2 Apr 1870.

The unkind word and other stories. 2 vols 1869, 2 vols 1870, [1874]. Essays, reviews, short stories. The unkind word (Good Words, May–June 1864); A child's life: sixty years ago; His young lordship (Argosy, Oct 1866); Elizabeth and Victoria: from a woman's point of view (Victoria Mag, 1864); A woman's book [Queen Victoria's highland journal]; The age of gold (Macmillan's Mag, Feb 1860); On living in perspective (as Living in perspective, Fraser's Mag, Oct 1866); Sermons (Cornhill Mag, Jan 1864); The House of Commons: from the ladies' gallery (Cornhill Mag, Oct 1863); A few words about sorrow (Macmillan's Mag, Jan 1861); A hedge-side poet [James Reynolds Withers] (Macmillan's Mag, Apr 1860); The last great exhibition: its beginning (as Five shillings worth of the great world's fair, Good Words, May 1862); The last great exhibition: its end (Macmillan's Mag, Dec 1862); To novelists – and a novelist [George Eliot] (Macmillan's Mag, Apr 1861); Bodies and souls (Macmillan's Mag, Oct 1864); Blind! (Macmillan's Mag, Nov 1860); Children of Israel (Macmillan's Mag, Apr 1863); Give us air (Good Words, Jan 1861); In the ring (All the Year Round, 18 Jan 1865); A dreadful ghost (Once a Week, 15 Feb 1862); Meadowside House (Good Words, Jan 1864); In her teens (Macmillan's Mag, July 1864); Clothes (as On the subject of clothes, Macmillan's Mag, Jan 1860); The history of a hospital (Macmillan's Mag, July 1862); Death on the seas (Macmillan's Mag, Feb 1866); To parents (All the Year Round, 9 July 1864); Misery-mongers (All the Year Round, 7 Apr 1866); An old Scotch love-story; A garden party; The tale of two walks, told to sick children (as Strolls with invalid children, Once a Week, 6 Apr and 4 May 1867).

Fair France: impressions of a traveller. 1871, Leipzig 1872. Incorporates La belle France: a glimpse (Good Words, Sep–Oct 1867) and We four in Normandy (St Paul's, Oct 1870–Jan 1871).

Hannah. First pbd in St Paul's, Feb–Dec 1871; 2 vols Leipzig 1871, 2 vols London 1872, 1875, 1904, [1916].

REVIEWS: In 'Recent novels', Acad 2 (1871) by H. Lawrenny [i.e. Edith Simcox]; Athenaeum 18 Nov 1871.

Little Sunshine's holiday: a picture from life. 1871, 1881 (new edn). Children's book.

The adventures of a Brownie, as told to my child. 1872, 1893, 1900 etc. Children's book.

My mother and I: a girl's love-story. First pbd in Good Words Jan–July 1874. 1874, Leipzig 1874, London 1904; tr Fr 1887.

The little lame prince and his travelling cloak. 1875 (illustr J. M. Ralston), 1877, 1886, 1918 (illustr Maria L. Kirk), etc. Children's book.

Sermons out of church. 1875, Leipzig 1875, London 1881. Essays.

Songs of our youth. 1875. Poems.

The laurel bush: an old-fashioned love story. First pbd in Good Words June–Nov 1876. Montreal 1876, London 1877, 1890.

A legacy: being the life and remains of John Martin, schoolmaster and poet. 2 vols 1878. Biography and edited journal.
REVIEW: Athenaeum 13 Apr 1878.
Young Mrs Jardine. First pbd in Good Words Jan–Dec 1879. 3 vols 1879, 2 vols Leipzig 1879, [1880], [1916].
REVIEW: Athenaeum 25 Oct 1879.
Thirty years: poems new and old. 1880, 1881.
Children's poetry. 1881.
His little mother and other tales and sketches. 1881. [1882] (new edn), Leipzig 1882. Contains His little mother; Poor Prin; Two little tinkers (Sunday Mag, Feb–Mar 1877); The postman's daughter (Sunday Mag, Sep 1877); About travelling and travellers (Good Words, Dec 1878); Save the children (Sunday Mag, Mar 1879); Sinless sabbath-breaking (Catholic Presbyterian, 1879); De mortuis [Sydney Dobell] (Good Words, May 1879).
Plain speaking. 1882, Leipzig 1882. Essays. Contains Decayed gentlewomen; An island of the blest; How she told a lie; A ruined palace; and the following rptd from Good Words: The tide at the flood (as The tide at the turn, Apr 1880); Victims and victimisers (July 1880); 'Odd' people (Oct 1880); A little music (Nov 1880); Conies (Feb 1881); On novels and novel makers (May 1881); Light in darkness (Jan–Feb 1882).
Miss Tommy: a medieval romance. 1884, Leipzig 1884.
An unsentimental journey through Cornwall. First pbd in English Illus Mag Feb–July 1884. 1884.
About money and other things. 1886. Essays and children's stories. About money (Contemporary Rev, Sep 1886); Six happy days in a houseboat (as A holiday afloat, Good Words, Sep 1884); Life and its worth (Sunday Mag 1884); Story of a little pig (Macmillan's Mag, Jan 1883); Genius: its aberrations and its responsibilities (Good Words, Apr 1855); My sister's grapes; Sisterhoods (as About sisterhoods, Longman's Mag, Jan 1883); Facing the world: a story for boys (in Plucky Boys, Boston [1884]; A Paris atelier (Good Words, May 1886); Kiss and be friends: a Whitsuntide wander (English Illus Mag, Dec 1885).
King Arthur – not a love story. 1886, Leipzig 1886; tr Norwegian 1886.
Fifty golden years. [1887]. Jubilee souvenir.
An unknown country. 1887. Travel. First pbd in English Illus Mag from Jan 1887.
REVIEW: London Quarterly Rev 69 1887.
Concerning men and other papers. 1888. Essays. Concerning men (Cornhill Mag, Oct 1887); For better for worse (Contemporary Rev, Apr 1887); A house of rest (Murray's Mag, June 1886); Work for idle hands (Cornhill Mag, July 1887); Our island sports (Good Words, Oct 1887); Merely players (Nineteenth Cent, Sep 1886); Miss Anderson in the 'Winter's Tale' (Woman's World, Dec 1887).
Poems. 1888.

Contributions to periodicals and collaborative works

Stories and translations from Tasso. Chambers's Edinburgh Jnl, 18 Apr, 13 June, 19 Sep, 24 Oct 1846.
The strawberry girl. Chambers's Edinburgh Jnl, 15 Aug 1846.
Quintin Matsys, blacksmith of Antwerp. Chambers's Miscellany of Instructing and Entertaining Tracts 19 [1847].
Too handsome: a tale. Sharpe's London Mag, 27 Nov 1847.
Forgiveness: a tale. Keepsake, 1848.
Matilda of Scotland. The Book of Beauty, 1848.
History of a household. Sharpe's London Jnl, May–July 1849.
The King's shilling. Sharpe's London Jnl, July 1851.
Arndt's night underground. In Six pleasant companions for spare hours, Boston [1852].
Little Lizzie and the fairies. In Six pleasant companions for spare hours, Boston [1852].
Sunny hair's dream. In Six pleasant companions for idle hours, Boston [1852].
The young ship-carver. In Tony the sleepless, Boston [1852].
Our flitting: a household sketch. Nat Mag, Feb 1857.
The Papal excommunication. Macmillan's Mag, May 1860.
In King Arthur's land: a week's study of Cornish life. Good Words, Jan 1867.
A city at play. Macmillan's Mag, May 1868.
Johnny's opinion of himself. Good Words for the Young, Nov 1868.
The first Sunday of Lent. Macmillan's Mag, June 1868.
The dog with a conscience and the dog without. Good Words for the Young, Mar–Apr 1869.
The last news of the fairies. Good Words for the Young, Mar 1870.
Twenty-six hours. Cornhill Mag, May 1871.
Fighting in the dark. Good Words, Sep 1873.

Translations, editions and prefaces

A French country family, by Henriette de Witt. Tr Fr 1867.
M de Barante: a memoir, by F. P. G. Guizot. Tr Fr 1869.
Motherless: or a Parisian family, by Henriette de Witt. Tr Fr 1871.
Twenty years ago: from the journal of a girl in her teens. 1871. Ed Mulock.
Is it true? Tales curious and wonderful. 1872. Ed Mulock.
An only sister, by Henriette de Witt. Tr Fr 1873.
A Christian woman, by Henriette de Witt. Preface 1882.

Attributed or spurious works

Will Denbigh, nobleman. 1877. Probably written by Emily Fox.

§2

Hutton, R. H. Novels by the authoress of John Halifax. North Br Rev 29 1858.
[Parr, H.] The author of John Halifax. Br Quart Rev 44 1866.
Oliphant, M. Mrs Craik. Macmillan's Mag 57 1887.
Parr, L. In A. Sergeant et al, Women novelists of Queen Victoria's reign, 1897; rptd as The author of John Halifax, gentleman: a memoir, 1898.
Reade, A. L. The Mellards and their descendants; with memoirs of Dinah Maria Mulock. 1915.
Mitchell, S. Dinah Mulock Craik. 1983. [SM]

Sir Charles Augustus Murray 1806–95

§1

Travels in North America during the years 1834, 1835 and 1836, including a summer residence with the Pannee tribe of Indians and a visit to Cuba and the Azore Islands. 2 vols 1839, 1854 (rev).
The prairie-bird. 3 vols 1844, 1 vol 1845, 1857, [1874].
Hassan, or the child of the Pyramid: an Egyptian tale. 2 vols 1857, 1901.
Nour-ed-dyn, or the light of the faith: an Eastern fairy tale. [1883.]
A short memoir of Mohammed Ali, founder of the Vice-Royalty of Egypt. Ed H. Maxwell 1898.

§2

Maxwell, H. The Hon Sir Charles Murray KCB: a memoir. 1898.

John Mason Neale 1818–66

See col 643.

William Johnson Neale 1812–93

Bibliographies

Summers, M. In his Gothic bibliography, [1941].

§1

Cavendish: or the patrician at sea. 1831, 1832.
The lauread: a satire. 1833.
The Port Admiral: a tale of the war. 3 vols 1833.

Will Watch, from the auto-biography of a British officer. 3 vols 1834.
The Priors of Prague. 3 vols 1836.
Gentleman Jack: a naval story. 3 vols 1837.
The flying Dutchman: a legend of the High Seas. 3 vols 1839.
The law of parliamentary elections. 1839.
Paul Periwinkle: or the pressgang. 1841 (illustr 'Phiz').
The naval surgeon. 3 vols 1841.
History of the mutiny at Spithead and the Nore: with an enquiry into its origin and treatment, and suggestions for the prevention of future discontent in the Royal Navy. 1842.
The Captain's wife. 3 vols 1842.
The lost ship: or the Atlantic steamer. 3 vols 1843.
A letter to the Attorney General Sir W. W. Follett, suggesting some amendments in the proposed new County Courts Bill. 1844.
Scapegrace at sea: or soldiers afloat and sailors ashore. 3 vols 1863 (2nd edn).

John Henry Newman 1801–90

See col 2246.

Caroline Norton 1808–77

See col 646.

Laurence Oliphant 1829–88

Mss and letters to and from Oliphant are located in Amphill, Hammond and Foreign Office Papers in the Public Record Office, London; Blackwood Papers in the NLS; Broadland Papers in the Hampshire County Record Office and the Historical Manuscripts Commission, London; Harris/Oliphant Papers in the rare book and manuscript library at Columbia Univ, New York; the India Office Lib, London; the Royal Geographical Soc, London; and Times Newspapers Ltd.

§1

A journey to Katmandu with the camp of Jung Bahadoor, including a sketch of the Nepaulese Ambassador at home. 1852.
The Russian shores of the Black Sea in the autumn of 1852, with a voyage down the Volga, and a tour through the country of the Don Cossacks. Edinburgh 1853, 1853 (enlarged), 1854, 1970 (rptd).
The coming campaign. Edinburgh 1855, 1856 (as The Trans-Caucasian campaign of the Turkish army under Omar Pascha: a personal narrative).
Minnesota and the Far West. Edinburgh 1855.
The Trans-Caucasian provinces the proper field of operation for a Christian army. Edinburgh 1855.
Narrative of the Earl of Elgin's mission to China and Japan in the years 1857, 58, 59. 2 vols Edinburgh 1859, 2 vols Oxford 1970; tr Fr 1860, Ital 1869.
Patriots and filibusters: incidents of political and exploratory travel, reprinted from Blackwood's Magazine with corrections and additions. Edinburgh 1860.
Universal suffrage and Napoleon the Third. 1860.
On the present state of political parties in America. Edinburgh 1866.
Piccadilly: a fragment of contemporary biography. First pbd in Blackwood's Mag Mar–Sep 1865. 1866, Edinburgh 1870, 1874; ed M. Sadleir 1928.
The land of Gilead, with excursions in the Lebanon. Edinburgh 1880.
The land of Khemi: up and down the Middle Nile. Edinburgh 1882.
Traits and travesties, social and political. Edinburgh 1882. Largely rptd from Blackwood's Mag. Includes The autobiography of a joint-stock company, The adventures of a war correspondent, etc.
Altiora Peto. 2 vols Edinburgh 1883, 1884.
A trip to the north-east of Lake Tiberias in Jaulan. 1885.
Haifa: or life in modern Palestine. 1885, Edinburgh 1887.
Sympneumata: or evolutionary forces now active in man. Edinburgh 1885.
Masollam. A problem of the period. 3 vols Edinburgh 1886.
Episodes in a life of adventure: or moss from a rolling stone. Edinburgh 1887. Rptd from Blackwood's Mag.
Fashionable philosophy and other sketches. Edinburgh 1887. Rptd from Nineteenth Cent and Blackwood's Mag. Dramatic sketches and stories, mainly satirical.
The star in the East. 1887. A pamphlet written for Mohammedans.
Scientific religion: or higher possibilities of life and practice through the operation of natural forces, with an appendix by a clergyman of the Church of England [Haskett Smith]. 1888.

Contributions to periodicals

See Wellesley *vol 5 1989.*

§2

Liesching, L. F. Personal reminiscences of Oliphant. [1891.]
Barry, W. F. Laurence Oliphant. Quart Rev Oct 1891.
Oliphant, M. O. Memoir of Oliphant and of Alice Oliphant his wife. 2 vols Edinburgh 1891.
Fairbairn, E. Laurence Oliphant. Westminster Rev May 1892.
Scott, C. N. Oliphant: supplementary contributions to his biography. 1895.
Owen, R. D. My perilous life in Palestine. 1928. By Oliphant's second wife.
Kent, M. An errant genius. Cornhill Mag Nov 1936.
Schneider, H. and G. Lawton. A prophet and a pilgrim, being the incredible history of Thomas Lake Harris and Laurence Oliphant. New York 1942.
Henderson, P. The life of Oliphant. 1956.
Dearden, S. Laurence Oliphant. Cornhill Mag 169 1956.
Ryan, A. P. Laurence Oliphant. Listener 31 May 1956.
Taylor, Anne. Laurence Oliphant 1829–1888. Oxford 1982. [DF]

Margaret Oliphant, née Wilson, Mrs Oliphant, Mrs Margaret Oliphant, Mrs M. O. W. Oliphant, Margaret Oliphant Wilson Oliphant, Margaret Oliphant W. Oliphant, M. O. W. O. 1828–97

The main collections of mss are in the NLS, BL, Berg Collection (NPYL), Houghton Lib (Harvard), Columbia Univ Lib and Huntington Lib.

Bibliographies

Clarke, J. S. Margaret Oliphant: 1828–1897. A bibliography. St Lucia, Queensland 1986; Non-fictional writings: a bibliography. St Lucia, Queensland 1997. Victorian Fiction Research Guides 11 and 26.
Trela, D. J. and J. S. Clarke. Margaret Oliphant: a secondary bibliography. West Cornwall CN 1998.

Collection

Oliphant: the collected writings of Margaret Oliphant (1828–1897). Marlborough: Adam Matthew Publications 1995. 80 reels of positive microfilm.
Chronicles of Carlingford. 5 vols 1986–9. The rector and the doctor's family; The perpetual curate; Salem Chapel; Miss Marjoribanks; Phoebe; Junior.

§1

Passages in the life of Mrs Margaret Maitland, of Sunnyside written by herself. 3 vols 1849, 1849, 1850, 1851, New York 1851, London 1855 (Parlour Lib 125, 1 episode omitted), New York 1856, London 1860, 1876 (Parlour Lib), New York, nd (Stratford edn), Leipzig 1862 (Tauchnitz).
REVIEW: Fraser's Mag 42, Nov 1850.
Merkland. A story of Scottish life. 3 vols '1851' [1850], 1851, New York

1854 (retitled Merkland, or self sacrifice), London 1855 (Parlour Lib 159, abridged), Philadelphia nd [1864] (retitled Self-sacrifice), New York nd (retitled Self-sacrifice).

Caleb Field. A tale of the Puritans. 1851, New York 1851, London 1852, nd [c. 1860s] (with Orphans, Select Lib of Fiction 36), 1876 (in Heart and cross and other stories, Select Lib of Fiction 323), nd [c. 1880s].

John Drayton, being a history of the early life and development of a Liverpool engineer. 2 vols 1851 [Aug and Nov], 1853.
REVIEW: [Jewsbury, Geraldine] Athenaeum 6 Sep 1851.

Memoirs and resolutions of Adam Graeme, of Mossgray. Including some chronicles of the Borough of Fendie. 3 vols 1852 [reprint], 3 vols 1854?, 1859 (Hurst and Blackett's Standard Lib 6), Berlin 1872 (Asher's Collection of English Authors, British and American), London 1897.
REVIEWS: The Leader 17 Apr 1852; Scotsman 19 May 1852; [Syme, E.] Westminster Rev 58, July 1852.

The Melvilles. 3 vols 1852 [Apr].

Katie Stewart. First pbd Blackwood's Mag July–Nov 1852 and Littell's Living Age 8 Jan–5 Feb 1853. New York 1852, Edinburgh and London '1853' [Dec 1852], (retitled Katie Stewart: a true story), 1855 (2nd edn), 1875, [c. 1890] (illus), 1892 (retitled Katie Stewart and other tales; includes John Rintoul and A railway junction, 1st pbd Blackwood's Mag Oct 1873 and Littell's Living Age 29 Nov 1873).

Aílieford. A family history. 3 vols 1853, New York 1855, Philadelphia [c. 1865] (retitled The lost love).

Harry Muir. A story of Scottish life. 3 vols 1853, 1853, New York 1853, London 1876 (Select Lib of Fiction 317), nd [c. 1880s].

The quiet heart. First pbd Blackwood's Mag Dec 1853–May 1854 and Littell's Living Age 22 Apr–10 June 1854. Edinburgh and London 1854 (reprint), New York 1854, [c. 1858].

Magdalen Hepburn. A story of the Scottish Reformation. 3 vols 1854, New York 1854, 1856, nd [c. 1869], London 1876 (Select Lib of Fiction 333), Glasgow nd [c. 1890s].

Zaidee: a romance. First pbd Blackwood's Mag Dec 1854–Dec 1855 and Littell's Living Age 10 Feb 1855–5 Jan 1856. 3 vols Edinburgh and London '1856' [1855], Boston 1856.

Lilliesleaf: being a concluding series of passages in the life of Mrs Margaret Maitland, of Sunnyside, written by herself. 3 vols 1855, 3 vols 1856, Boston nd [c. 1857], London 1858?, nd [1876] (Select Lib of Fiction 336, retitled Lilliesleaf: or passages in the life of Mrs Margaret Maitland, of Sunnyside), nd [c. 1880s].

Christian Melville. '1856' [1855] ('by the author of Matthew Paxton' on title page, but Mathew Paxton was by Oliphant's brother, William Wilson), 1873.

The Athelings or the three gifts. First pbd Blackwood's Mag June 1856–June 1857 and Littell's Living Age 19 July 1856–11 July 1857. 3 vols Edinburgh and London 1857, New York 1857.
REVIEW: [Meredith, George] Westminster Rev 68 n.s. 12, Oct 1857.

The days of my life. An autobiography. 3 vols 1857, New York 1857, London 1876 (Select Lib of Fiction 316), nd [c. 1890s].
REVIEWS: Spectator 21 Feb 1857; Saturday Rev 28 Mar 1857.

Orphans. A chapter in a life. '1858' [1857], 1860, 1863, Philadelphia 1866 (with Caleb Field), London 1876 (collected in Heart and cross and other stories, Select Lib of Fiction 323; includes Heart and cross, Caleb Field and Orphans), nd [c. 1880s] (contents as preceding).

The laird of Norlaw. A Scottish story. 3 vols 1858, New York 1859, 1860, London nd [1861] (Standard Lib 15), 2 vols Berlin 1872 (Asher), London 1897, 1913.
REVIEW: [Jewsbury, Geraldine] Athenaeum 27 Nov 1858.

Sundays. '1858' [1857], 1861. Non-fiction.

Agnes Hopetoun's schools and holidays. The experiences of a little girl. '1859' [1858], Boston 1859, London 1862, 1872, 1874 (illus), 1880, 1884, 1897 (illus). Children's book.

Lucy Crofton. '1860' [1859], New York 1860, London 1878 (Select Lib of Fiction 377), nd [c. 1885], nd [c. 1890s], New York 1887, Glasgow nd [c. 1890s].
REVIEWS: [Jewsbury, Geraldine] Athenaeum 21 Jan 1860; Examiner 21 Jan 1860.

The house on the moor. 3 vols '1861' [1860], 1861, 1876 (Select Lib of Fiction 334), 1912.
REVIEWS: [Jewsbury, Geraldine] Athenaeum 1 Dec 1860; Spectator 1 Dec 1860.

The last of the Mortimers. A story in two voices. 3 vols '1862' [1861], New York 1862, Leipzig 1862 (Tauchnitz), London 1875 (Select Lib of Fiction 277), 1878, nd [c. 1880s].

The executor (first pbd Blackwood's Mag May 1861 and Littell's Living Age 22 June 1861); The rector (Blackwood's Mag Oct 1861 and Littell's Living Age 12 Oct 1861); The doctor's family (Blackwood's Mag Oct 1861–Jan 1862 and Littell's Living Age 16 Nov 1861–1 Mar 1862), pbd as The chronicles of Carlingford. Boston nd [1862], New York 1863, Edinburgh and London 1863 (retitled The rector and the doctor's family; Br edns omitted The executor), 1863, 1865, 1869 (Blackwood's Standard Novels), Leipzig 1870 (Tauchnitz), Edinburgh and London 1870, [c. 1890], 3 vols 1894 (includes The doctor's family, Salem Chapel, The rector, The perpetual curate), 1897 (as preceding), New York 1975 (in Novels of Faith and Doubt, ed R. L. Wolff), Oxford 1986 (WCp) (introd by M. Williams, retitled The Doctor's family and other stories, includes The rector and The executor), London 1986 (introd by P. Fitzgerald, titled The rector and the doctor's family); tr Fr The doctor's family, Paris 1866 (in S. Bellonia, etc).
REVIEW: Reader 6 June 1863.

The life of Edward Irving, Minister of the National Scotch Church, London. Illustrated by his journals and correspondence. 2 vols 1862, New York 1862, London 1862 (2nd edn rev), 1864 (3rd edn rev), nd [1865] (Hurst and Blackett's Standard Lib 30), nd [1873], nd [c. 1880s], 1897.
REVIEWS: [Chorley, H. F.] Athenaeum 19 Apr 1862; [Story, R. H.] Macmillan's Mag 7, May 1862; [Maurice, F. D.] Spectator 21 June 1862; [Smith, W.] North Br Rev 37, Aug 1862.

Salem Chapel. First pbd Blackwood's Mag Feb 1862–Jan 1863 and Littell's Living Age 15 Mar–13 Dec 1862. 2 vols Edinburgh and London 1863, 1863, New York 1863 (titled Chronicles of Carlingford), Edinburgh and London 1865, 1869, 2 vols Leipzig 1870 (Tauchnitz), Edinburgh and London 1873, 1881 (Blackwood's Standard Novels), [c. 1890], 1894 and 1897 (titled Chronicles of Carlingford), London 1907 (EL, introd by W. Robertson Nicoll), Dundee 1908, London 1914 (Nelson Sixpenny Classics 144), New York 1975 (in Novels of Faith and Doubt, ed R. L. Wolff), London 1986 (introd by P. Fitzgerald).
REVIEWS: Reader 14 Feb 1863; [Hutton, R. H.] Spectator 14 Feb 1863; Athenaeum 6 Mar 1863; The Times 10 Mar 1863.

Heart and cross. 1863 (sequel to Orphans and Lucy Crofton), New York 1863, London 1876, nd [c. 1880s] (rptd in Heart and cross and other stories, including Caleb Field and Orphans).

The perpetual curate. First pbd Blackwood's Mag June 1863–Sep 1864 and Littell's Living Age 27 June 1863–8 Oct 1864. 3 vols Edinburgh and London 1864, New York 1865, Edinburgh and London 1865, 1869, [c. 1878] (Blackwood's Standard Novels), c. 1890, 2 vols Leipzig 1870 (Tauchnitz), New York 1976 (ed R. L. Wolff, Novels of Faith and Doubt 90), London 1987 (introd by P. Fitzgerald).
REVIEWS: [Hutton, R. H.] Spectator 5 Nov 1864; Reader 19 Nov 1864; Eclectic and Congregational Rev 120, Dec 1864.

A son of the soil. First pbd Macmillan's Mag Nov 1863–Apr 1865 and Littell's Living Age 9 Jan 1864–6 May 1865, New York 1865, 2 vols London 1866, New York 1871, 1872, 1877, 1883, 1886, 1894.
REVIEWS: [Hutton, R. H.] Spectator 21 Apr 1866; [Jewsbury, Geraldine] Athenaeum 9 June 1866.

Agnes. 3 vols '1866' [1865], New York 1866, London nd [1867] (Hurst and Blackett's Standard Lib 35; this and subsequent Hurst and Blackett edns abridged), 1897, nd [1912] (Hurst and Blackett's Sevenpenny Copyright Novels), 2 vols Leipzig 1866 (Tauchnitz).
REVIEWS: Morning Post 3 Nov 1865; Reader 11 Nov 1865.

Miss Marjoribanks. First pbd Blackwood's Mag Feb 1865–May 1866 and Littell's Living Age 11 Mar 1865–12 May 1866. 3 vols Edinburgh and London 1866, Boston nd [1866], Edinburgh and London 1866, New York 1867 (Lib of Select Novels 268), Edinburgh and London 1869, 2 vols Leipzig 1869 (Tauchnitz), New York 1881 (Seaside Lib 959), Edinburgh and London nd [c. 1890], 1894 (in collected Chronicles of Carlingford), 1897, London 1908 (Collins' Pocket Classics, illus), Leicester 1969 (introd by Q. D. Leavis), New York and London 1976 (ed R. L. Wolff, Novels of Faith and Doubt 91), London 1988 (introd by P. Fitzgerald).
REVIEWS: [Hutton, R. H.] Spectator 26 May 1866; Daily Rev (Edinburgh) 28 May 1866; Christian Remembrancer 52, June 1866; Glasgow Herald 13 June 1866.

Madonna Mary. First pbd Good Words Jan–Dec 1866 and Littell's Living Age 27 Jan–22 Dec 1866. 3 vols '1867' [1866], Boston '1867' [1866], New York 1866 (Lib of Select Novels 282), London 1875 (Select Lib of Fiction 296), 1880.
REVIEW: Morning Post 9 Nov 1866.

Brownlows. First pbd Blackwood's Mag Jan 1867–Feb 1868 and Littell's Living Age 16 Feb 1867–29 Feb 1868. 3 vols Edinburgh and London 1868, Boston 1868, New York 1868 (Lib of Select Novels 310), London nd [1912] (Everett's Sevenpenny Lib).
REVIEW: Daily News 14 Apr 1867.

The minister's wife. 3 vols 1869, New York 1869 (Lib of Select Novels 330), 2 vols Leipzig 1869 (Tauchnitz), London 1913 (Everett's Sevenpenny Lib, abridged), 1915.
REVIEWS: Nonconformist 16 June 1869; [Jeaffreson, J. Cordy] Athenaeum 26 June 1869; Vanity Fair 24, July 1869.

Historical sketches of the reign of George II [biography]. Serialised in Blackwood's Mag beginning with The Queen (Feb 1868) and concluding with The painter (Aug 1869), rptd in Littell's Living Age 9 May 1868–18 Sep 1869. 2 vols Edinburgh and London 1869, Boston nd [1869], Edinburgh and London 1870, 1875 [rev edn].

The three brothers. First pbd St Paul's Mag June 1869–Sep 1870 and Appleton's Jnl 12 June 1869–24 Sep 1870, 3 vols 1870. New York 1870.
REVIEWS: Spectator 16 July 1870; Saturday Rev 23 July 1870; Br Quart Rev 52, Oct 1870.

John. A love story. First pbd Blackwood's Mag Nov 1869–July 1870 and Littell's Living Age 11 Dec 1869–30 July 1870. 2 vols Edinburgh and London 1870, New York 1870, Edinburgh nd [1875], nd [c. 1890s].

Francis of Assisi. 1870 (Sunday Lib for Household Reading), 9 additional printings by Macmillan up to 1907, 1 Philadelphia and 5 different New York publishers ptd edns beginning in the 1890s.

Squire Arden. First pbd Glasgow Evening Post 13 June–26 Sep 1870. 3 vols 1871, New York 1874, London 1875 (Select Lib of Fiction 280), 1880 nd.
REVIEW: Nonconformist 27 Sep 1871.

Memoir of Count de Montalembert, peer of France, Deputy for the Department of Doubs. A chapter of recent French history. 2 vols Edinburgh and London 1872, 2 vols Leipzig 1872 (Tauchnitz); tr Fr Paris 1875.
REVIEW: [Tulloch, John] Blackwood's Mag 112, Nov 1872.

Ombra. 3 vols 1872, New York 1872, London 1875 (Select Lib of Fiction 285), nd [c. 1880s], 2 vols Leipzig 1872 (Tauchnitz).
REVIEW: Br Quart Rev 56, July 1872.

At his gates. First pbd Good Words Jan–Dec 1872 and Scribner's Monthly Jan–Dec 1872. 3 vols 1872, New York 1873, London 1873, 1873 (Select Lib of Fiction 159), 1875 (Routledge's Railway Lib 665), 1885?, 1888.
REVIEWS: Manchester Guardian 1 Nov 1872; Saturday Rev 23 Nov 1872; Guardian 15 Jan 1873.

May. 3 vols 1873, New York 1873, 2 vols Leipzig 1873 (Tauchnitz), London 1875 (Select Lib of Fiction 271), nd [c. 1880s].
REVIEW: [Collins, W. Lucas] Blackwood's Mag 113, June 1873.

Innocent. A tale of modern life. First pbd Graphic 4 Jan–28 June 1873 and Littell's Living Age 19 Apr–27 Sep 1873, 3 vols 1873 [reprint], New York 1873, 2 vols Leipzig 1873 (Tauchnitz), London 1874, 1874 (4th edn, illus), 1892, nd [c. 1900s], Chiswick nd.
REVIEWS: Saturday Rev 28 June 1873; [Hutton, R. H.] Spectator 19 July 1873.

For love and life. 3 vols 1874 (sequel to Squire Arden), 2 vols Leipzig 1874 (Tauchnitz), London 1875 (Select Lib of Fiction 276), New York 1879 (Seaside Lib vol 25 no 497), London 1880 (4th edn), 1886.
REVIEW: Graphic 23 May 1874.

A rose in June. First pbd Cornhill Mag Mar–Aug 1874 and Littell's Living Age 18 Apr–5 Sep 1874. Boston 1874 (illustr George du Maurier), 2 vols London 1874, Leipzig 1874 (Tauchnitz), London 1875 (Hurst and Blackett's Standard Lib 46), nd [c. 1880s], 1897, Paris 1889 (tr Fr by Marie Cartier).
REVIEWS: The Times 1 Sep 1874; Saturday Rev 10 Oct 1874; Br Quart Rev 61, Jan 1875.

The story of Valentine and his brother. First pbd Blackwood's Mag Jan 1874–Feb 1875 and Littell's Living Age 28 Feb 1874–27 Mar 1875. 3 vols Edinburgh and London 1875, New York 1875, Edinburgh and London 1875, 2 vols Leipzig 1875 (Tauchnitz), Edinburgh and London 1892, 1897.
REVIEWS: Nonconformist 24 Feb 1875; Br Quart Rev 61, Apr 1875.

Whiteladies. First pbd Good Words Jan–Dec 1875. 3 vols 1875 [reprint], New York 1875 (Leisure Hour ser), 2 vols Leipzig 1875 (Tauchnitz), London 1876 (illustr A. Hopkins and H. Woods), 1879, nd [1881?] (Piccadilly Novel ser), nd [1898], 1904 (illus).

The curate in charge. First pbd Macmillan's Mag Aug 1875–Jan 1876 and Littell's Living Age 13 Nov 1875–19 Feb 1876. 2 vols 1876 [4 reprints], 1876 [6th edn], New York 1876, Leipzig 1876 (Tauchnitz), London 1877 (7th edn), 1883, 1884, 1885, 1894, 1905, Gloucester 1987 (introd by M. Williams).
REVIEWS: Nonconformist 19 Jan 1876; Manchester Guardian 3 Apr 1876.

An odd couple. First pbd Graphic Christmas no 1875. Philadelphia 1876 (International ser), New York 1879 (Seaside Lib vol 23 no 452).

Phoebe, Junior: a last chronicle of Carlingford. 3 vols 1876, New York 1876 (Lib of Select Novels 468), 2 vols Leipzig 1876 (Tauchnitz), London 1877 (Hurst and Blackett's Standard Lib 48), nd [c. 1880s], New York 1977 (ed R. L. Wolff, Novels of Faith and Doubt 92), London 1989 (introd by P. Fitzgerald).
REVIEWS: [Townsend, M.] Spectator 17 June 1876; Br Quart Rev 64, July 1876.

Trials and triumphs. New York 1876 (not separately pbd).

The makers of Florence: Dante, Giotto, Savonarola and their city. History and biography. Partially serialised in Macmillan's Mag July 1874–Oct 1876. London and New York 1876 (illustr C. H. Jeens and Prof Delamotte), 1877 (preface by author), 1881 (cheap edn, at least 5 reprints up to 1889), 1891 (extra illus edn, at least 7 further reprints up to 1914), New York nd [c. 1880], beginning 1896 1 Philadelphia and 7 New York imprints by various publishers.
REVIEW: [Symonds, J. A.] Academy 16 Dec 1876.

Dante. Edinburgh and London 1877 (Foreign Classics for English Readers, ser ed Oliphant), Philadelphia 1877, Edinburgh and London 1879, 1881, 1887, 1898, 1906.

Mrs Arthur. 3 vols 1877, New York 1877 (Lib of Select Novels 488), 2 vols Leipzig 1877 (Tauchnitz), London 1891.
REVIEW: [Saintsbury, George] Academy 9 June 1877; Daily News 4 Sep 1877.

Carita. First pbd Cornhill Mag June 1876–Aug 1877, Littell's Living Age 1 July 1876–1 Sep 1877 and Harper's Weekly 1 July 1876–1 Sep 1877. 3 vols 1877 [rptd, illus], New York 1877 (illus, Lib of Select Novels 492), 2 vols Leipzig 1877 (Tauchnitz), London 1878 (illus), 1883 (4 illustrations), 1885 (Popular Lib of Standard Works), 1885.
REVIEW: Daily News 4 Oct 1877.

Young Musgrave. First pbd Macmillan's Mag Jan–Dec 1877. 3 vols 1877, New York 1878 (Seaside Lib vol 11 no 210), London 1878, 1883, 1886, 1894.
REVIEWS: [Blind, Mathilde] Athenaeum 15 Dec 1877; Examiner 15 Dec 1877.

Dress. 1878 (Art at Home ser, 7 illustrations), Philadelphia 1879 (Art at Home ser).

The primrose path. A chapter in the annals of the kingdom of Fife. 3 vols 1878, New York 1878, 1878 (Seaside Lib vol 20 no 391), 2 vols Leipzig 1878 (Tauchnitz), London 1886, 1888, 1892, 1909, Dundee and London nd [c. 1909], 1921, 1922.

The fugitives. First pbd Good Words Christmas no 1879. New York 1879, 1879 (Franklin Square Lib 86), London 1880?, 2 vols Leipzig 1890 (Tauchnitz; rptd with The duke's daughter (new title of Lady Jane) as The duke's daughter, and the fugitives), 3 vols Edinburgh and London 1890 (as preceding).

Molière. With Francis Tarver. Edinburgh and London 1879 (Foreign Classics for English Readers 6), 1887?, 1898, 1902.

Within the precincts. First pbd Littell's Living Age 12 Jan 1878–8 Mar 1879 and Cornhill Mag Feb 1878–Apr 1879. 3 vols 1879 (illus), New York 1879 (Franklin Square Lib 44), 3 vols Leipzig 1879 (Tauchnitz), London 1879 (illus), 1883 (illus), 1885 (illus, Popular Lib of Standard Works).
REVIEWS: Nonconformist 2 Apr 1879; London 5 Apr 1879.

The greatest heiress in England. 3 vols '1880' [1879], 3 vols 1880 (2nd edn), 2 vols Leipzig 1880 (Tauchnitz), New York 1880, London 1886, 1888, 1891.
REVIEWS: Examiner 20 Dec 1879; Daily News 1 Jan 1880.

A beleaguered city. Being a narrative of certain recent events in the city of Semur, in the Department of the Haute Bourgogne. A story of the seen and the unseen. First pbd New Quart Mag Jan 1879. London and New York '1880' [1879] (ch 9 added), New York 1879 (pbd with The awakening by Katherine S. Macquoid), London and New York 1881, nd (Macmillan's Colonial Lib 43), 1889, 1892, 1897, 1900, London 1910 (Macmillan's Sevenpenny ser), 1913, 1930 (The Caravan Lib, title shortened to A beleaguered city), New York 1944 (introd by E. Wagenknecht), Westport CT 1970 (in Six novels of the supernatural), Oxford 1988 (WCp) ed M. Williams in A beleaguered city and other stories, including Earthbound, Old lady Mary, The land of darkness, The library window); tr Fr Paris 1911 (by Henri Bremond), Paris 1925.
REVIEWS: Glasgow Herald 3 Feb 1879; Daily News 20 Jan 1880; Pall Mall Gazette 15 Mar 1880.

He that will not when he may. First pbd Littell's Living Age 1 Nov 1879–7 Aug 1880 and Macmillan's Mag Nov 1879–Nov 1880. 3 vols London and New York 1880 [reprint], New York 1880 (Franklin Square Lib 149), London and New York 1881 (2nd edn), 2 vols Leipzig 1881 (Tauchnitz), London and New York 1883, 1886, 1892.
REVIEWS: Scotsman 28 Sep 1880; Spectator 16 Oct 1880.

Cervantes. Edinburgh and London 1880 (Foreign Classics for English Readers 11), Philadelphia nd [1881], Edinburgh and London 1887?, 1898.

Queen Victoria. First pbd as Queen Victoria in Harper's New Monthly Mag June 1880; expanded as The life of the Queen in Graphic 28 June 1880. 1880 (unauthorised pbn), New York 1880 (retitled The Queen, unauthorised pbn, 44 illustrations), rev as The Queen's record reign in Graphic, Diamond Jubilee no, 1 June 1897 (illus), London, Paris, New York and Melbourne 1900 (retitled Queen Victoria. A personal sketch, illus, text headed The domestic life of the Queen, 4pp by anonymous author to bring narrative to Victoria's death), London, Paris, New York and Melbourne 1901.

No 3, Grove road, Hampstead. First pbd Good Cheer, Christmas no of Good Words, Dec 1880. New York 1880 (Seaside Lib vol 43 no 875), rptd with The two Marys (*see below*).

Harry Joscelyn. 3 vols 1881, New York 1881 (Franklin Square Lib 183), 1881 (Seaside Lib vol 48 no 1004), 2 vols Leipzig 1881 (Tauchnitz), London 1887 (Standard Lib), nd [1893] (Standard Lib of Fiction), 1898, nd [c. 1900s] (Sun-dial Lib).
REVIEWS: Pall Mall Gazette 26 Apr 1881, St James's Gazette 9 May 1881.

In trust: a story of a lady and her lover. First pbd Littell's Living Age 6 Aug–29 Oct 1881 and Fraser's Mag Feb 1881–Jan 1882. New York 1881 (Seaside Lib vol 51 no 1049), 3 vols London 1882, 2 vols Leipzig 1882 (Tauchnitz), London 1882, 1883, 1885 [reprint] (Modern Novel Lib), 1887 [reprint], 1892, 1893, 1894.
REVIEW: [Townsend, Meredith] Spectator 28 Jan 1882.

The literary history of England in the end of the eighteenth and beginning of the nineteenth century. 3 vols 1882 [reprint with preface], 3 vols New York 1882, 2 vols 1883, 2 vols New York and London 1886, 3 vols 1889, 3 vols 1895, 3 vols 1897, 3 vols nd (Macmillan's Colonial Lib 17–19).

Lady Jane. First pbd Good Words Jan–June 1882, Littell's Living Age 18 Mar–30 June 1882 and Potter's Amer Monthly Mar–Aug 1882. New York 1882 (Seaside Lib vol 65 no 1319), 1882 (Franklin Square Lib 259), 3 vols Edinburgh and London 1890 (retitled The duke's daughter, pbd with The fugitives, *see above*), 2 vols Leipzig 1890 (Tauchnitz), Stuttgart 1894 (tr Ger by F. Mangold, retitled Die Herzogstochter).

A little pilgrim in the unseen.
The textual history of Oliphant's supernatural stories is particularly complex. These were her most popular works and were frequently rptd individually and in various collections. First pbd in Macmillan's Mag *May 1882 and* Littell's Living Age *27 May 1882; additional story* The little pilgrim goes up higher, Macmillan's Mag *Sep 1882 and* Littell's Living Age *30 Sep 1882. 1882 [2 reprints], Boston 1882 (retitled* A little pilgrim*), New York 1882* (Seaside Lib *vol 71 no 1449, pbd with F. Anstey's* The black poodle*), London 1883 [4 reprints], 17 further reprints between 1884 and 1910, 1912 (Shilling edn) [rptd 1915], 1920* (Macmillan's Two Shilling Theological Lib*)*.

Boston nd [1889?] (titled Further experiences of a little pilgrim, includes The land of darkness), 1889 (titled The little pilgrim. Further experiences, includes The little pilgrim in the seen and the unseen, On the dark mountains, The land of darkness), Leipzig 1891 (Tauchnitz), Boston 1889 (titled Stories of the seen and the unseen, includes A little pilgrim in the unseen (single story), The little pilgrim goes up higher, The open door, Old lady Mary, The portrait, The little pilgrim in the seen and unseen, The land of darkness, and On the dark mountains), 1900 (as preceding), 1907 (as preceding), Chicago 1913 (retitled A little pilgrim in the seen and the unseen, includes A little pilgrim in the unseen (retitled In the unseen), The little pilgrim goes up higher, The little pilgrim in the seen and the unseen, On the dark mountains, The land of darkness).

It was a lover and his lass. 3 vols 1883, New York 1883 (Franklin Square Lib 294), 3 vols Leipzig (Tauchnitz), London nd [1894] (Standard Lib 53), 1897, 1904, nd [1911] (Hurst and Blackett's Sevenpenny Copyright Novels, abridged), 1951 (unabridged).
REVIEWS: Scotsman 28 Feb 1883; Saturday Rev 10 Mar 1883.

The ladies Lindores. First pbd Blackwood's Mag Apr 1882–May 1883 and Littell's Living Age 3 June 1882–2 June 1883. 3 vols Edinburgh and London 1883, New York 1883, 1883 (Lovell's Lib vol 3 no 124), 1883 (Seaside Lib vol 81 no 1647), 3 vols Leipzig 1884 (Tauchnitz).
REVIEWS: St James's Gazette 9 May 1883; Pall Mall Gazette 30 May 1883; Br Quart Rev 78, July 1883.

Hester. A story of contemporary life. 3 vols 1883, 1883, New York

1883, London 1884, New York 1884, 1884 (Franklin Square Lib 359), 3 vols Leipzig 1884 (Tauchnitz), London 1888, 1891, 1984 (introd by J. Uglow).

REVIEWS: [Townsend, Meredith] Spectator 22 Dec 1883; [Henley, W. E.] Academy 5 Jan 1884; Daily News 11 Jan 1884; [Julia Wedgwood] Contemporary Rev 45, Mar 1884.

The lady's walk. First pbd Longman's Mag Dec 1882–Jan 1883 and Littell's Living Age 20 Jan 1883. New York 1883 (Seaside Lib vol 84 no 1697), London 1897 (rev and expanded, also includes The ship's doctor, first pbd Good Words Apr 1868), 1898, 1900, 1905.

Sheridan. 1883 (EML), New York 1883, 1887, London 1889, 1889 (bound with J. A. Symonds's Sidney and David Masson's De Quincey), New York 1894?, London 1896, New York nd [c. 1900s] (Makers of Lit), New York 1901, London 1902 (Lib edn), New York and London 1902, London and New York 1906, London 1909 (Pocket edn).

The wizard's son. A novel. First pbd Littell's Living Age 21 Apr–29 Dec 1883 and Macmillan's Mag Nov 1882–Mar 1884. 3 vols 1884, New York 1884, nd [1884] (Lovell's Lib vol 6 no 326), 1884 (Franklin Square Lib), 3 vols Leipzig (Tauchnitz), London 1884, 1888, 1894.

REVIEW: Daily News 16 Aug 1884.

Sir Tom [sequel to The greatest heiress in England]. First pbd Bolton Weekly Jnl and District News, and Farnsworth Weekly Jnl and Observer 20 Jan–14 July 1883; Nottinghamshire Guardian 26 Jan–20 July 1883; Weekly Mail (Cardiff) 27 Jan–11 Aug 1883. New York 1883 (Franklin Square Lib 327), nd [1883] (Lovell's Lib vol 4 no 175), 1883 (Seaside Lib vol 84 no 1703), 3 vols London 1884, 1884, 1885, 1889, 1893.

Madam. First pbd Longman's Mag Jan 1884–Jan 1885. New York 1884 (Franklin Square Lib 435), 3 vols London 1884 [30 Dec 1884], 3 vols 1885, 1885, New York 1885 (Seaside Lib Pocket Edn no 345), London 1887 [reprint], 1891, 1892, 1894, 1901 (dramatised version adapted by Mrs G. W. Steevens (Christina Rogerson) in A motley crew).

REVIEWS: Guardian 28 Jan 1885; The Times 28 May 1885.

Old lady Mary. First pbd Blackwood's Mag Jan 1884 and Littell's Living Age 26 Jan–2 Feb 1884. Boston 1884, New York nd [1884], Edinburgh and London 1885 (includes The open door (first pbd Blackwood's Mag Jan 1882 and Littell's Living Age 4 Feb 1882), collection titled Two stories of the seen and unseen. The open door. Old lady Mary), 1890 (as preceding), 1902 (collection titled Stories of the seen and the unseen, includes The open door, The portrait (first pbd Blackwood's Mag Jan 1885 and Littell's Living Age 31 Jan 1885), The library window (first pbd Blackwood's Mag Jan 1896 and Littell's Living Age 1 Feb 1896), Old lady Mary), Mokelumne Hill CA 1971 (as preceding); Boston 1889 (collection titled Stories of the seen and unseen, includes Old lady Mary, The open door, The portrait, A little pilgrim in the unseen, The little pilgrim goes up higher, The little pilgrim in the seen and unseen, The land of darkness, On the dark mountains), Boston 1900 (as preceding); Boston 1907 (as preceding); Edinburgh 1985 (ed M. K. Gray, Selected short stories of the supernatural, Assoc for Scottish Literary Stud 15, includes The secret chamber, Earthbound, Old lady Mary, The portrait, The land of darkness, The library window).

The prodigals and their inheritance. First pbd Good Words Christmas no 1884. New York nd [1885] (Seaside Lib 1919 and Pocket Edn no 321), 2 vols London 1894 [reprint], 1905, 1906.

REVIEWS: [Bennett, Arnold] Woman 30 Apr 1894; [Courtney, W. L.] Daily Telegraph 4 May 1894; Daily Chron 16 May 1894.

Oliver's bride: a true story. First pbd Bolton Weekly Jnl and District News, and Newcastle Weekly Chron 18 Apr–9 May 1885; Nottinghamshire Guardian 24 Apr–15 May 1885; Glasgow Weekly Mail 6–27 June 1885; Carlisle Express and Examiner 9–28 Nov 1885. New York 1885 (pbd with Rhoda Broughton's Mrs Smith of Longmains and Thomas Hardy's A mere interlude), New York 1885 (Lovell's Lib vol 12 no 602), London 1886 (added ch), reserialisation in Darlington and Stockton Times 10–31 Oct 1891, 1895 [reprint], nd [c. 1900].

REVIEW: [Noble, James Ashcroft] Academy 13 Mar 1886.

A country gentleman and his family. First pbd Atlantic Monthly Jan 1885–Feb 1886. 3 vols London 1886, New York 1886, 1886 (Franklin Square Lib 507, retitled A country gentleman), 1886 (Lovell's Lib vol 14 no 717, retitled A country gentleman), 1886 (Seaside Lib Pocket Edn 902), 2 vols Leipzig 1886 (Tauchnitz), London and New York 1887, 1888, 1894, London nd [c. 1900] (Success Club Lib), nd (Macmillan's Colonial Lib 16).

REVIEWS: [Noble, James Ashcroft] Academy 24 Apr 1886; Pictorial World 20 May 1886; Guardian 2 June 1886.

Effie Olgilvie. The story of a young girl. First pbd Scottish Church June 1885–May 1886. 2 vols Glasgow 1886, New York 1886, 1886 (Harper's Handy ser 82), 1886 (Seaside Lib Pocket Edn 827), Glasgow 1888, London nd (Macmillan's Colonial Lib 27).

REVIEW: Glasgow Herald 17 Sep 1886.

A house divided against itself [sequel to A country gentleman and his family]. First pbd Chambers's Jnl 3 Jan–5 Dec 1885 and Littell's Living Age 31 Jan 1885–3 Jan 1886. 3 vols Edinburgh and London 1886, New York 1886 (Franklin Square Lib 511), 1886 (Seaside Lib Pocket Edn 703), London nd (Macmillan's Colonial Lib 37).

REVIEWS: Scotsman 11 Oct 1886; Spectator 20 Nov 1886.

A poor gentleman. First pbd Leisure Hour Jan–Dec 1886. New York 1886 (Seaside Lib Pocket Edn 902), 1887 (Lovell's Lib vol 19 no 295), 1887, 3 vols London 1889.

REVIEW: [Noble, James Ashcroft] Spectator 27 July 1889.

The son of his father. First pbd Bolton Weekly Jnl and District News 17 Apr–23 Oct 1886; Farnworth Weekly Jnl and Observer 17 Apr–30 Oct 1886; Leigh Jnl and Times, Tyldesley Weekly Jnl and Atherton Times, Pendlebury and Swinton Jnl, Eccles and Patricroft Jnl 16 Apr–29 Oct 1886; Weekly Irish Times 24 Apr–23 Oct 1886. New York 1886 (Franklin Square Lib 554), 1886 (Lovell's Lib vol 17 no 381), 1886 (Seaside Lib Pocket Edn 880), 3 vols London 1887, 1888, nd [1889], nd [c. 1893] (Popular Two Shilling Novels), 1897.

REVIEW: [Townsend, Meredith] Spectator 16 July 1887.

The makers of Venice. Doges, conquerors, painters and men of letters. 3 chs previously pbd as articles, including A soldier of fortune (Blackwood's Mag Apr 1885), A Venetian dynasty (Contemporary Rev Aug 1886), Marco Polo (Blackwood's Mag Sep 1887). London and New York 1887 (illustr R. R. Holmes), 1888 (2nd edn) [2 reprints], 1889, 1891, 1892 (extra illustration), 1893, 1898, 1898, 1905, at least 9 further cheap edns pbd in New York (4), New York and Boston, Chicago (2), Philadelphia and Springfield OH.

REVIEW: [Wilde, Oscar] Woman's World 2, Mar 1888.

The second son. First pbd Atlantic Monthly Feb 1887–Feb 1888. T. B. Aldrich, poet and editor of Atlantic Monthly, is listed as co-author; his minimal alterations were intended to limit Amer piracy of Oliphant's works. 3 vols 1888, 1888, New York 1888, London 1894, nd (Macmillan's Colonial Lib 63).

REVIEWS: Pall Mall Gazette 20 Feb 1888; [Noble, James Ashcroft] Spectator 25 Feb 1888.

Joyce. First pbd Blackwood's Mag May 1887–Apr 1888. 3 vols 1888, New York 1888, London 1889 (2nd edn), 1891, nd (Macmillan's Colonial Lib 71).

REVIEWS: Br Weekly 11 May 1888; Saturday Rev 12 May 1888; Guardian 30 May 1888.

A memoir of the life of John Tulloch. Edinburgh and London 1888, 1888 (2nd edn), 1889 (3rd edn).

Cousin Mary. First pbd Welcome Jan–Aug 1887. nd [1888] (illus), 1890, 1892, nd [1896].

The land of darkness. Along with some further chapters in the

experiences of the little pilgrim. 3 stories originally pbd as The little pilgrim in the seen and unseen (Scottish Church July 1885), The land of darkness (Blackwood's Mag Jan 188)7 and On the dark mountains (Blackwood's Mag Nov 1888). London and New York 1888 (reprint), Boston 1889, 1889 (retitled Further experiences of a little pilgrim, includes A little pilgrim in the unseen and The little pilgrim goes up higher).
REVIEWS: Scotsman 31 Dec 1888; [Hutton, R. H.] Spectator 5 Jan 1889; [de Mattos, Katherine] Athenaeum 19 Jan 1889.

Neighbours on the green. First pbd as My neighbour Nelly (Cornhill Mag Feb 1868 and Littell's Living Age 7 Mar 1868), Lady Denzil (Cornhill Mag Apr 1868), The stockbroker at Dinglewood (Cornhill Mag Sep 1868), Mrs Merridew's fortune (Cornhill Mag Sep 1869 and Littell's Living Age 9 Oct 1969), Lady Isabella (Cornhill Mag Mar–Apr 1871 and Littell's Living Age 15 Apr–20 May 1871), The scientific gentleman (Cornhill Mag Nov–Dec 1872 and Littell's Living Age 11–25 Jan 1873), The barley mow (Graphic Christmas 1877), An elderly romance (Cornhill Mag Nov 1879 and Littell's Living Age 13 Dec 1879), My faithful Johnny (Cornhill Mag Nov–Dec 1880 and Littell's Living Age 11 Dec 1880–15 Jan 1881). 3 vols London and New York 1889, 1889 (2nd edn), Leipzig 1889 (Tauchnitz) (abridged, includes 1st 4 stories only), London and New York 1891, 1901, 1904.
REVIEWS: [Noble, James Ashcroft] Spectator 30 Mar 1889; Illus London News 6 Apr 1889.

Lady Car. The sequel of a life [sequel to The ladies Lindores]. First pbd Longman's Mag Mar–July 1889. 1889 [2 reprints], New York 1889 (Franklin Square Lib no 657), London 1890 (Royal Lib), 1891.
REVIEWS: Saturday Rev 6 July 1889; [James's Ashcroft Noble] Spectator 6 July 1889; St James's Gazette 17 July 1889.

A house of peace. 1890 (sketch on Royal Hospital for Incurables, copy at NLS).

The mystery of Mrs Blencarrow. First pbd Manchester Weekly Times, Birmingham Weekly Post, Yorkshire Weekly Post, Carlisle Express and Examiner 30 Nov–28 Dec 1889; Weekly Mail (Cardiff) 7 Dec 1889–4 Jan 1890. nd [1889], 1890, Chicago 1894, nd [1900s] (titled The mystery of Blengarrow [*sic*]), London nd [1900s] (Br Empire Lib and Sun Dial Lib), New York nd [1900s] (includes unidentified story not by Oliphant titled Winny).
REVIEWS: [Saintsbury, George] Academy 23 Aug 1890; Scots Observer 23 Aug 1890.

Sons and daughters. A novel. First pbd Blackwood's Mag Mar–Apr 1890 and Littell's Living Age 5 Apr–24 May 1890. Edinburgh and London 1890, 1891.
REVIEWS: Life 13 Sep 1890; [Saintsbury, George] Academy 4 Oct 1890.

Kirsteen. The story of a Scotch family seventy years ago. First pbd Macmillan's Mag Aug 1889–Aug 1890. 3 vols 1890 (reprint), New York 1890 (Franklin Square Lib 683), London 1891 [reprint], 2 vols Leipzig 1891 (Tauchnitz), London 1895, 1898, 1900 (Two Shilling Lib), nd (Macmillan's Colonial Lib 115), 1984 (EL, introd by M. Williams).
REVIEWS: Scotsman 13 Oct 1890; [Wallace, William] Academy 8 Nov 1890; Guardian 19 Nov 1890; [Noble, James Ashcroft] Spectator 13 Dec 1890; [James, Henry] Notes on novelists with some other notes 1915.

Royal Edinburgh. Her saints, kings, prophets and poets. One ch pbd as Margaret of Scotland, Eng Illus Mag Nov 1889. London and New York 1890 (also a large paper edn, illustr George Reid), 1891 (2nd edn), 1893, 5 further imprints c. 1890s by New York publishers.

Janet. First pbd Lady's Pictorial 4 Jan–28 June 1890 (titled Janet, the story of a governess). 3 vols 1891, 1893, New York 1895 (retitled The story of a governess), London nd [c. 1911] (Hurst and Blackett's Sevenpenny Copyright Novels).

Memoir of the life of Laurence Oliphant and of Alice Oliphant, his wife. 2 vols Edinburgh and London 1891 (6 reprints in 1891, labelled 2nd to 7th edns), 2 vols New York 1891, 2 vols Leipzig 1891 (Tauchnitz), Edinburgh and London 1892 (includes preface to the new edn answering critics).
REVIEWS: [Townsend, Meredith] Spectator 30 May 1891; [Allardyce, Alexander] Blackwood's Mag 150, July 1891.

The heir presumptive and the heir apparent. First pbd Birmingham Weekly Post, Newcastle Weekly Chron, Yorkshire Weekly Post, Hereford Times 18 Oct 1890–11 Apr 1891; Newport and Market Drayton Advertiser 25 Oct 1890–2 May 1891; likely pbn in unidentified New York newspaper. New York 1891 (Lovell's International ser 156), 3 vols London 1892, 2 vols Leipzig 1892 (Tauchnitz), London 1893, nd (Macmillan's Colonial Lib 146).
REVIEWS: Manchester Guardian 22 Nov 1892.

The railwayman and his children. First pbd Sun Mag (Paisley and London) Oct 1890–Sep 1891. 3 vols 1891, New York 1891, nd [1891] (Lovell's International ser 177), London 1892, 2 vols Leipzig 1892 [Heinemann and Balestier] (The English Lib 77–8), nd London (Macmillan's Colonial Lib 133).
REVIEWS: Anti-Jacobin 12 Dec 1891; [Collyer, J. M.] Athenaeum 19 Dec 1891; Speaker 2 Jan 1892.

Jerusalem. The holy city. Its history and hope. New York and London 1891 (illustr Hamilton Aide and F. M. Good), 1893 (2nd edn), 1985.

The marriage of Elinor. First pbd Good Words Jan–Dec 1891. New York 1891, 3 vols London 1892 (2 reprints in 1 vol), 2 vols Leipzig 1892 [Heinemann and Balestier] (The English Lib 95–6), London nd (Macmillan's Colonial Lib 138), nd [c. 1911] (Hurst and Blackett's Sevenpenny Copyright Lib).
REVIEW: Nat Rev 19, Apr 1892.

Diana. The history of a great mistake. First pbd Blackwood's Mag Feb–July 1892. 2 vols Edinburgh and London 1892 (retitled Diana Trelawny. The history of a great mistake), New York and Chicago 1892 (title as serialised), Leipzig 1893 [Heinemann and Balestier] (The English Lib 168).
REVIEW: Queen 20 Aug 1892.

Katie Stewart and other tales. 1892. Includes John Rintoul (first pbd Blackwood's Mag Mar–Apr 1853 and Littell's Living Age 9 Apr–14 May 1853), A railway junction (Blackwood's Mag Oct 1873 and Littell's Living Age 29 Nov 1873).

The cuckoo in the nest. First pbd Victorian Mag (Dec 1891–Nov 1892), 3 vols 1892 (3 reprints in 1892), New York 1892, 2 vols Leipzig 1892 [Heinemann and Balestier] (The English Lib 156–7), London 1893 (5th edn) (illustr G. H. Edwards), 1894 (6th and Popular edn), 1901, nd [c. 1900s] (abridged and with altered paragraphing), nd [1910 and 1912] (Hurst and Blackett's New Lib of Sevenpenny Copyright Novels), 1934.
REVIEWS: Manchester Guardian 20 Sep 1892; [Collyer, J. M.] Athenaeum 24 Sep 1892.

The Victorian age of English literature. 2 vols 1892, 2 vols New York 1892 (Francis Romano Oliphant listed as joint author), 2 vols New York 1892, nd [1892?], 2 vols Leipzig 1893 [Heinemann and Balestier] (The English Lib 171–2), 2 vols London 1897.

Lady William. First pbd Lady's Pictorial, 3 Jan–27 June 1891. 3 vols London and New York 1893, London 1894, 1894 (Macmillan's Colonial Lib 162).
REVIEWS: Manchester Guardian 23 Jan 1894; [Collyer, J. M.] Athenaeum 10 Feb 1894; [Bennett, Arnold] Woman 18 Apr 1894.

The sorceress. First pbd Gentlewoman 2 July 1892–7 Jan 1893; Newcastle Weekly Courant 2 July–23 Dec 1892; Bolton Weekly Jnl and District News, Farnworth Weekly Jnl and Observer 10 Sep 1892–4 Mar 1893; Leigh Jnl and Times, Tyldesley Weekly Jnl and Atherton Times, Eccles and Patricroft Jnl, Pendlebury and Swinton Jnl 9 Sep 1892–3 Mar 1893. 3 vols 1893, New York 1893 (Broadway ser 22), 2 vols Leipzig 1893 (Tauchnitz), London 1894, 1895, nd [1897] (Piccadilly Novel ser).

REVIEWS: [Collyer, J. M.] Athenaeum 11 Mar 1893; The Times 5 Apr 1893; [Noble, James Ashcroft] Spectator 29 Apr 1893.

Thomas Chalmers. Preacher, philosopher and statesman. 1893 (English Leaders of Religion ser), Boston and New York 1893, London 1896, 1905, 1912.

Historical characters of the reign of Queen Anne. First serialised in Century as The princess Anne (Apr 1893), The queen and the duchess (May 1893), The author of Gulliver (July 1893), The author of Robinson Crusoe (Sep 1893), Addison, the humorist (Sep 1894). New York 1894 (abridged), London and New York 1894 (2 additional chs on William Penn).

REVIEW: [Tattersall, Hiram] Academy 2 Mar 1895.

Sir Robert's fortune. The story of a Scotch moor. First pbd Atalanta Oct 1893–Sep 1894. New York 1894, London 1895, 2 vols Leipzig 1896 (Tauchnitz), London 1902 (2 reprints) (Methuen's Sixpenny Lib, abridged), 1905.

REVIEWS: Daily News 25 May 1895; Pall Mall Gazette 27 May 1895.

Who was lost and is found. First pbd Blackwood's Mag June–Nov 1894. Edinburgh and London 1894, New York '1895' [1894], Edinburgh and London 1898.

REVIEWS: Observer 7 Nov 1894, [Shand, A. Innes] Blackwood's Mag 156, Dec 1894.

A house in Bloomsbury. First pbd Young Woman Oct 1893–Sep 1894. 2 vols 1894 (2 reprints), New York 1894, London 1895, 1901, nd [c. 1900s].

REVIEWS: [Bennett, Arnold] Westminster Gazette 24 Aug 1894; [Noble, James Ashcroft] Spectator 29 Sep 1894.

Two strangers. 1894 (Autonym Lib), 1895, New York 1895.

REVIEWS: [Bennett, Arnold] Woman 29 May 1895; Cambridge Rev 30 May 1895.

'Dies Irae'. The story of a spirit in prison. Edinburgh and London '1894' [1895].

REVIEW: Manchester Guardian 15 Jan 1895.

Old Mr Tredgold. A story of two sisters. First pbd Longman's Mag June 1895–May 1896. New York 1895, London 1896 (Colonial Lib edn), 1896 (reprint) (retitled Old Mr Tredgold), 2 vols Leipzig 1897 (Tauchnitz) (retitled Old Mr Tredgold), London 1898.

REVIEWS: Glasgow Herald 21 Mar 1896; Daily News 9 Apr 1896; Morning Post 9 Apr 1896; The Times 30 May 1896.

The makers of modern Rome. London and New York 1895 (illustr Henry P. Rivière and Joseph Pennell, also a large paper edn), 1896, 1897.

A child's history of Scotland. '1895' [1896] (The children's study), 1896 (retitled A history of Scotland for the young, expanded), New York nd [1898], London 1899 (2nd impression, retitled A child's history of Scotland), 1901, 1909.

Jeanne D'Arc. Her life and death. New York and London 1896 (Heroes of the Nations ser), 1899, 1905, New York 1908, Garden City NY 1926.

The two Marys. First pbd Macmillan's Mag Sep 1872–Jan 1873. 1896 (also contains Grove Road, Hampstead (first pbd Good Cheer, Christmas no of Good Words, 1880), originally titled No. 3, Grove Road, Hampstead), 1897, 1905, 1906, 1907, 1918 (last 3 items may contain only The two Marys).

REVIEWS: Daily News 6 July 1896; Manchester Guardian 22 July 1896; Pall Mall Gazette 30 July 1896.

The unjust steward, or, the minister's debt. London and Edinburgh 1896, Philadelphia 1896, London and Edinburgh 1899.

REVIEW: Englishwoman 5, Mar 1896.

The ways of life. Two stories. First pbd as Mr Sandford, Cornhill Mag Apr–May 1888 and Littell's Living Age 9–16 June 1888, and The strange story of Mr Robert Dalyell, Cornhill Mag Jan–Mar 1892. 1897 (preface On the ebb tide, story retitled The wonderful history of Mr Robert Dalyell), New York 1897, Leipzig 1897 (Tauchnitz), London 1898, 1919 (Murray's Two-Shilling Lib).

REVIEWS: Manchester Guardian 18 May 1896; [Graves, C. L.] Spectator 29 May 1896; Daily Chron 2 June 1896; [Courtney, W. L.] Daily Telegraph 7 July 1897.

Annals of a publishing house. William Blackwood and his sons, their magazine and friends. 2 vols Edinburgh and London 1897 (reprint), 1898. (Vol 3 written by Mrs Gerald Porter after Oliphant's death.) 3 vols New York 1897–8.

A widow's tale and other stories. Includes The lily and the thorn (Good Words Christmas no 1877), Queen Eleanor and fair Rosamond (Cornhill Mag Jan–Feb 1886), Mademoiselle (Cornhill Mag Nov–Dec 1889), The story of a wedding tour (St James's Gazette 30 June–3 July 1894 and St James's Budget 29 June–6 July 1894), A widow's tale (Cornhill Mag July–Sep 1893), The whirl of youth (Nat Observer 7–28 Oct 1893), John (Pall Mall Mag Mar 1894 as sequel to The story of a wedding tour), The heirs of Kellie, an episode of family history (Blackwood's Mag Mar 1896 and Littell's Living Age 11–18 Apr 1896), The strange adventures of John Percival (Chambers's Jnl 2–30 May 1896). Edinburgh and London 1898 (reprint) (introd by J. M. Barrie), New York 1899.

REVIEWS: Daily Chron 7 June 1898; St James's Gazette 21 Sep 1898.

That little cutty; Dr Barrere; Isabel Dysart. That little cutty first pbd Home Christmas 1880; Dr Barrere first pbd Eng Illus Mag Dec 1884 and Littell's Living Age 16 Jan 1886, Isabel Dysart first pbd Chambers's Jnl 7–28 Jan 1893. London and New York 1898.

REVIEW: [Nicoll, W. Robertson] Sketch 12 Oct 1896.

The autobiography and letters of Mrs M. O. W. Oliphant. Edinburgh and London 1899 (reprint) (ed Annie [Mrs Harry] Coghill), 1899 (abridged), New York 1899, Leicester 1974 (introd by Q. D. Leavis), Chicago and London 1988 (introd by L. Langbauer, letters omitted, retitled The autobiography of Mrs Oliphant), Oxford 1990 (ed with notes and introd by Elisabeth Jay, based on original mss, retitled The autobiography of Margaret Oliphant: the complete text).

REVIEWS: [O'Connor, T. P.] Sunday Telegraph 30 Apr 1899; [Millar, J. H.] Blackwood's Mag 165, May 1899; Manchester Guardian 2 May 1899; [Street, G. S.] Pall Mall Gazette 4 May 1899; Saturday Rev 20 May 1899; Guardian 24 May 1899; [Nicoll, W. Robertson] Br Weekly 1 June 1899.

Contributions to books and collaborative works

John Rintoul, or, the fragment of the wreck. First pbd Blackwood's Mag Mar–Apr 1853 and Littell's Living Age 9 Apr–14 May 1853. In Tales from Blackwood, Edinburgh and London 1860, nd (retitled John Rintoul).

A boy of Fife. In Victoria Regia, a miscellany of prose and verse, ed Adelaide A. Proctor, 1861.

Introduction to Robert Herbert Story, Life and remains of Robert Lee, D.D., 2 vols '1870' [1869].

Preface to Sergeant Leahy, The art of swimming in the Eton style, 1875 (illustr F. Tarver).

Postscript to preface of Geraldine Macpherson, Memoirs of the life of Anna Jameson, 1878.

A railway junction, or, the romance of Ladybank. First pbd Blackwood's Mag Oct 1873 and Littell's Living Age 29 Nov 1873. In Tales from Blackwood, Edinburgh and London 1878 (retitled A railway junction).

The secret chamber. First pbd Blackwood's Mag Dec 1876 and Littell's Living Age 6 Jan 1877. In Tales from Blackwood, Edinburgh and London 1878, rptd Blackwood's Mag Oct 1967 (abridged), London and Edinburgh 1978 (in Scottish tales of magic and mystery, ed Marion Lochead), Edinburgh 1985 (in Margaret Oliphant. Selected short stories of the supernatural, ed Margaret K. Gray).

The two Mrs Scudamores. First pbd Scribner's Monthly Dec 1871–Jan 1872 and Blackwood's Mag Dec 1871–Jan 1872. In Tales from Blackwood, Edinburgh and London 1879.

A Christmas tale. First pbd Blackwood's Mag Jan 1857 and Littell's

Living Age 21 Feb 1857. In Tales from Blackwood, Edinburgh and London 1879 (retitled Witcherley ways: a Christmas tale, abridged).

Preface to Selections from Cowper's poems, London and New York 1883 [rptd 1892 and 1905] (Golden Treasury ser).

An anxious moment [story]. In The new amphion: being the book of the Edinburgh University Union fancy fair, Edinburgh 1886 (book intended as fund-raiser for the student union).

The sisters Brontë. In Women novelists of Queen Victoria's reign: a book of appreciations, 1897.

Prologue to Robert Wilson, The life and times of Queen Victoria, London, Paris, New York and Melbourne 1900. Earlier edns in 1887, 1888, 1891–3. Oliphant's prologue appears only in 1900.

The golden rule. First pbd in Black and White 22 Aug 1891, Newcastle Weekly Courant and Hampshire Telegraph and Sussex Chron 26 Dec 1891. In Stories from Black and White, 1893.

Contributions to periodicals

Material rptd in book form generally not listed here. Most of Oliphant's novels and many short stories are listed above though originally serialised.

For Oliphant's contributions to the following periodicals, see Wellesley: Blackwood's Mag, *254 reviews and articles and 34 short stories or novels from 1852–97;* Contemporary Rev, *4 articles;* Cornhill Mag, *4 reviews and 16 stories or novels;* Edinburgh Rev, *6 reviews;* Fraser's Mag, *1 article, 2 works of fiction;* Longman's Mag, *4 works of fiction;* Macmillan's Mag, *9 reviews, 9 works of fiction;* New Quart Mag, *1 work of fiction;* New Rev, *1 article,* St Pauls, *1 novel.*

Atalanta: Mary's brother, Oct 1892; story. Things in general, Oct 1893–Sep 1894; monthly editorial on literature, travel and social issues. A maiden's mind, Dec 1895.

Athenaeum: The complaints of authors, 7 Feb 1891; unsigned, against Tillotson's unauthorised republication of The heir presumptive and the heir apparent.

Black and White: A chance encounter, 12 Dec 1891.

Court and Society Rev: The story of an anonymous letter, 16 Nov–14 Dec 1887. Oliphant's son Cyril a part owner of this periodical.

English Illus Mag: Heidelberg, Oct 1884. Margaret of Scotland, Nov 1889; included in Royal Edinburgh. Edinburgh, Oct 1890.

Forum (New York): Success in fiction, May 1889.

Good Words: Madam Saint-Ange, Christmas no 1867. The count's daughters, Christmas no 1874 and Littell's Living Age 30 Jan–6 Feb 1875. A party of travellers, Mar–June 1879. Anthony Trollope, Feb 1883. San Remo, Feb 1893. The Queen, June 1897.

Harper's New Monthly Mag: Queen Victoria, June 1880.

Illus London News: A divided pair, 6 Feb 1892 suppl, illustr E. F. Brewthall.

Lady's Pictorial: Elisabeth, Christmas no 1890.

McClure's Mag: A visitor and his opinions, Dec 1893 also Littell's Living Age 20 May 1893 and Blackwood's Mag Apr 1893.

Nat Mag: Eben, a true story, Nov–Dec 1857 and Littell's Living Age 26 Dec 1857.

Nat Observer: The member's wife, 4–11 Mar 1893.

Pall Mall Mag: The mysterious bridegroom, Mar 1895; sequel to John.

Scribner's Monthly: Norah, the story of a wild Irish girl, May–June 1871.

Sharpe's London Mag: Annie Orme: how Annie Orme was settled in life, and what we did to help it on. By her aunt, Miss Rachel Sinclair, mantua-maker, Lasswade, Sep–Oct 1852 and Littell's Living Age 20 Nov 1852.

St James's Gazette: A series of 21 articles on social, political and literary issues headed A fireside commentary, running from 11 Jan–8 June 1888, continued under various titles until 24 Aug 1888, all but the last article rptd in St James's Budget 5–8 days after Gazette's pbn.

St James's Mag: Isabell Carr, Oct–Nov 1861 and Littell's Living Age 23 Nov, 21 Dec 1861.

St Nicholas (New York, children's mag, 6 articles with general title Windsor Castle): The Order of the Garter, Mar 1876; The captive prince, May 1876; The baby king, July 1876; The Tudors, Aug 1876; The Stuarts, Sep 1876; Queen Victoria, Oct 1876.

Spectator: The rights of women, 7 Mar 1874. The study of history at Eton, 29 Jan 1876. Memorials of a quiet life, 8 July 1876. The Christian doctrine of sin, 12 Aug 1876. Post mortem, 13 Aug 1881. Mrs Oliphant and Bishop Wilberforce, 6 Jan 1883. Life on the lagoons, 21 June 1884. Are women a 'represented class', 1 Nov 1884. Hurrish, 30 Jan 1886. Principal Tulloch, 20 Feb 1886. The story of the nations: Ireland, 14 Jan 1888. A commentary from my chair, 7, 14, 21 and 28 Dec 1889, followed by A commentary in an easy chair, 4 Jan–8 Nov 1890 (possibly terminated by the death of Oliphant's son on 8 Nov 1890). Aunt Anne, 6 Aug 1892. The apology of age to youth, 24 Dec 1892. Venice, 24 June 1893. Prayers for the dead, 15 Dec 1894. The seen and the unseen, 1 Feb 1896. The land of the dollar, 13 Feb 1897.

Victoria Mag: A story of a voice, Aug–Sep 1863.

The Weekly Irish Times: A chance encounter, 6 Aug 1892.

Windsor Comet and Bazaar News: The dirty little angel, 6 Nov 1888.

Wit and Wisdom: Advice to our young women readers, 9 Apr 1892.

Poetry

The Christian knight's vigil. A chant, addressed to a young minister on the even of his ordination. The English Presbyterian Messenger Dec 1850.

The shadow on the way. Blackwood's Mag June 1853.

From India. Blackwood's Mag Jan 1857.

The nation's prayer. Blackwood's Mag Jan 1862.

In the garden. Blackwood's Mag Aug 1863; rptd in Garden memories, ed Mary W. G. Wilson, Edinburgh, London and Boston nd.

Amen. – In the cathedral of St Andrews. Blackwood's Mag Oct 1863.

Day and night. Blackwood's Mag Jan 1865.

The innermost room. Blackwood's Mag Mar 1867.

Alfred Tennyson. Spectator 15 Oct 1892.

A farewell. Spectator 2 Mar 1895.

22nd June 1897. Blackwood's Mag June 1897.

Miscellaneous writings

On the edge of the world I lie, I lie. In Autobiography and letters, p. 438.

An elderly lover. 1885 (priv ptd 52 pp., copies at NLS). Drama.

§2

Obituaries and posthumous appreciations: Daily News 18 June 1897, [W. Robertson Nicoll] Br Weekly 1 July 1897; [Norman NacColl] Athenaeum 3 July 1897; Speaker 3 July 1897; [Meredith Townsend] Spectator 3 July 1897; Speaker 3 July 1897; [Christabel Coleridge] Monthly Packet 93 n.s. 14, Aug 1897; [Gertrude Slater] Westminster Rev 148, Dec 1897; [Stephen Gwynn] Edinburgh Rev 190, July 1899; [Anne Thackeray Ritchie] From the Porch 1913: 21–8; Henry James, Notes on Novelists 1914.

Porter, Mrs Gerald. Annals of a publishing house, vol 3 1898.

Colby, R. and V. The equivocal virtue: Mrs Oliphant and the Victorian literary marketplace. 1966.

M. Williams, Margaret Oliphant: a critical biography, London and New York, 1986.

Jay, E. Mrs Oliphant: a fiction to herself: a literary life, Oxford 1995. [DT]

Francis Paget, Francis Edward Paget, W. Churne, F. E. P. 1806–82

§1

Caleb Kniveton, the incendiary: a tale. 1833.

A sermon on Acts 20:25–27. 1834.

Lectures upon the seven sentences uttered by our blessed Lord on the cross. 1839.
A discourse concerning prayer. 1840.
A selection of psalms and hymns. 1840.
A tale of the village. 3 vols 1840 (abridged).
Tales of the village. The Englishman's Lib vol 9 1840.
Tales of the village children. The Juvenile Englishman's Lib vol 1 1840, 1843 (4th edn).
A treatise of repentance and of fasting. 1840.
The Church of England: man's companion in the closet. 1841.
St Antholin's; or, old churches and new: a tale for the times. 1841.
Tales of the village. Second ser. The Englishman's Lib vol 16 1841.
Tales of the village. Third ser. The Englishman's Lib vol 18 1841, 1843.
The idolatry of covetousness: a sermon. 1842.
Milford Malvoisin; or, pews and pewholders. 1842.
The pageant; or, pleasure and its price: a tale for the upper ranks of society. 1843.
A tract upon tomb-stones. 1843, 1847, rptd 1853.
The warden of Berkingholt; or, rich and poor. 1843.
The churchman's calendar for 1844. 1843.
The hymns of the Church. 1843.
The hope of the Katzekopfs; or, the sorrows of selfishness: a fairy tale. The Juvenile Englishman's Lib vol 2 1844, 2nd edn '1846' [1845], rptd 1916 as The self-willed prince; or, the hope of the Katzekopfs; retold in short words (illus).
Room for all. Tracts for Englishmen no 11 1844.
Sermons on duties of daily life. 1844, Philadelphia 1844, New York 1844.
The Christian's day. 1845, 1846, 1857 (4th edn).
The living and the dead: a course of practical sermons on the burial service. 1845.
Luke Sharp; or, knowledge with religion: a tale of modern education. 1845, New York 1846.
Tales of the village children. Second ser. The Juvenile Englishman's Lib vol 5 1845.
Sursum Corda: aids to private devotion. 1847, 1859 (2nd edn).
Sermons for the saints' days. 1848.
The destinies of God's temples: a sermon. 1849.
The Church the sojourner's resting-place. Sermons preached at St Barnabas. 1850.
Prayers in behalf of the Church and her children in times of trouble. 1850 (2nd edn).
Daily prayers for labouring lads. 1851.
The preacher in the wilderness: a sermon. 1852.
Psalms, hymns, anthems and introits. 1853.
The owlet of Owlstone Edge. '1856' [1855], 1858 (4th edn), 1869 (5th edn).
The parish and the priest: colloquies. 1858.
Sermons for special occasions. 1858.
The curate of Cumberworth; and the vicar of Roost: tales. 1859, 1860 (2nd edn).
Daily prayers for young women, who have been taught in church schools. 1859.
The heart-stone. 1860. Rptd from the Penny Post.
The pancake bell. 1860. From Tales of the village children.
Prayers for the Queen, and for these kingdoms. 1861.
Lucretia; or, the heroine of the nineteenth century. 1868.
Eigenwillig; or, the self-willed: a fairy extravaganza. 1870. Poem.
Some account of Elford Church. 1870.
The effect and influence of the Passion upon our hearts. Plain preaching for a year vol 1 1873.
The journey and the journey's end. Plain preaching for a year vol 3 1873.
Suffering. Plain preaching for a year vol 2 1873.
Helps and hindrances to the Christian life: plain village sermons for a year. 2 vols 1874.
As men live so they die. Plain preaching ser 7 1875.
Better late than never, and For a small moment forsaken. Plain preaching ser 9 1875.
Reasons of the hope that is in us: eight papers of questions for candidates under instruction for confirmation. 1875.
A student penitent of 1695. 1875.
Homeward bound: the voyage and the voyagers, the pilot and the port. 1876.
Of sowing beside all waters. Plain preaching for poor people ser 6 1878.
Paget edited, with J. F. Russell, The Juvenile Englishman's Lib, *21 vols illus '1845' [1844–9].* [LA]

Julia Pardoe 1804–62

The BL holds mss of Pardoe's agreements with publisher R. Bentley, plus mss of her plays Louise de Lignarolles (1838) *and* Breach of Promise (1841). *For holdings of her letters including those relating to her applications to the Royal Literary Fund see LR 2, p. 728. Mss of 34 letters plus a ballad, poem and memoranda are held by Brown Univ Lib.*

Collections

Miss Pardoe's complete works. Philadelphia 1846, rptd [1859]. Contains only: The confessions of a pretty woman, The jealous wife, The rival beauties, The wife's trials (by Emma Jane Worboise) and The romance of the harem.
[Historical works.] New York 1887.

§1

Lord Morcar of Hereward: a romance of the times of William the Conqueror. 4 vols in 2 1829 (anon), 1837 (new edn).
Traits and traditions of Portugal: collected during a residence in that country. 2 vols [1833] (micro Cambridge MA [198-?]), Philadelphia 1834, 1834 (2nd edn).
REVIEWS: Athenaeum 2 Nov 1833; (Christian Johnstone) Tait's Edinburgh Mag o.s. 4, Jan 1834.
Speculation: a novel. 3 vols 1834, 2 vols New York 1834, 3rd edn 2 vols in 1 New York [and London?] 1847.
REVIEW: Athenaeum 10 May 1834.
The Mardens; and the Daventrys: tales. 3 vols 1835, 2 vols Philadelphia 1835.
REVIEW: Athenaeum 28 Feb 1835.
The city of the sultan, and domestic manners of the Turks, in 1836. 2 vols 1837 (micro Cambridge MA [1988]), Philadelphia 1837 (in 2-vol edn and also in Select Circulating Lib, ed Adam Waldie, vol 10), 2nd [London] edn 3 vols 1838, 3rd edn 3 vols 1845, 4th edn 1 vol 1854, 5th edn 1 vol 1855 (with title, The city of the sultan, and domestic manners of the Turks, with steam voyage up the Danube, and bound with Pardoe's Confessions of a pretty woman).
REVIEWS: Athenaeum 3 June 1837; [Cameron, Hugh] British and Foreign Rev 7, July 1838.
The beauties of the Bosphorus. Illustr W. H. Bartlett. 1838, rptd 1839, [1840], [1850?], new edn 1855 (bound with William Beattie's The Danube, with new Appendix and 10 new plates, micro Ann Arbor MI 1991), new edn [1874] (with title, Picturesque Europe).
The river and the desert: or recollections of the Rhone and the Chartreuse. 2 vols in 1 1838, Philadelphia 1838 (in 2-vol edn and also in Select Circulating Lib, ed Adam Waldie, vol 11).
REVIEW: Athenaeum 24 Mar 1838.
The romance of the harem. 3 vols 1839, 2 vols Philadelphia 1839; new edns 1842, 1857, Philadelphia [188?]. Novel.
REVIEW: Athenaeum 9 Feb 1839.
The city of the Magyar, or Hungary and her institutions in 1839–40. 3 vols 1840 (micro New York 1974), 3 vols in 1 Leipzig 1842; tr Ger 1842.
REVIEWS: Athenaeum 28 Nov and 5 Dec 1840; Fraser's Mag 23, Mar 1841.

The Hungarian castle. 3 vols 1842 (micro Washington 1986, Lib of Congress), New York [1842] (with title, Hungarian tales and legends), 1855 (3rd edn).

The confessions of a pretty woman. 3 vols 1846, 1 vol New York [1846], London [184-?] (bound with Charles Augustus Murray's The prairie-bird), London 1855 (bound with Pardoe's The city of the sultan), new edn [1860] (Parlour Lib).

Louis the Fourteenth, and the court of France in the seventeenth century. 3 vols 1847 (micro Washington 1983 Lib of Congress), 2 vols New York 1847, 3 vols London 1847 (2nd edn), 2 vols New York 1848, 3 vols London 1849 (with index) (3rd edn), 2 vols New York 1851, rptd 1855, 1865, 1868, 1874, 3 vols London 1886 (illus) (new edn), 3 vols New York 1887, 1901, new 3-vol edn London and New York 1902, new 6-vol edn New York 1905.
REVIEWS: Athenaeum 6 and 13 Mar 1847; [Kirwan, A. V.] Fraser's Mag 35, June 1847.

The rival beauties: a novel. 3 vols 1848 (2 edns), 1 vol New York 1850 (Select Novels no 3), new 1-vol edn London 1867 (Parlour Lib), 1 vol Philadelphia nd (with subtitle, a love story).

The court and reign of Francis the First, King of France. 2 vols 1849, 2 vols Philadelphia 1849, 2 vols London 1850 (2nd edn), new 3-vol edn London and New York 1887 (including memoir of Pardoe), new 3-vol edn London and New York 1901 (preface by Adolphe Cohn) (micro Washington 1986 (LC)), new 3-vol edn New York 1905.
REVIEW: Br Quart Rev 11, May 1850.

Flies in amber. 3 vols 1850. Short stories.

The life of Marie de Medicis. 3 vols 1852 (2 edns), new 3-vol edns 1890 and New York 1890, new 3-vol edn London and New York 1902, 2 new 6-vol edns New York 1905 (including one of 100 copies).
REVIEWS: Athenaeum 12 June 1852; Edinburgh Rev 96, Oct 1852; Blackwood's Edinburgh Mag 78, Oct 1855.

Louise de Lignerolles: a tragic drama in five parts. 1854 (Lacy's Acting Edn no 204), micro New York 1968.

Reginald Lyle. 3 vols 1854, 1 vol New York 1854.

The jealous wife: a novel. 3 vols 1855, 1 vol New York 1855, new 1-vol edn London [1860] (Parlour Lib), Philadelphia 1876 (with subtitle, a love story).

Lady Arabella: or the adventures of a doll. 1856 (illustr George Cruikshank).

Pilgrimages in Paris. 1857. Partly pbd in Fraser's Mag 27–8, Mar–Oct 1843.

Abroad and at home: tales here and there. [1857.]

The poor relation: a novel. 3 vols 1858.

Episodes of French history, during the Consulate and the First Empire. 2 vols 1859, 1 vol New York 1859, 1 vol London 1859 (new edn).

A life-struggle. 2 vols 1859, 1 vol New York 1860.

The rich relation. [1862] (Bentley's Standard Novels).

Contributions to periodicals

For Pardoe's numerous contributions to annuals, see A. Boyle, An index to the annuals *vol 1, 1967.*

Collaborative work, translation, editions, etc

Sorelli, G. La peste, poema. Tr from Ital 1834.

Seven tales by seven authors. Ed F. E. Smedley 1849 (includes Pardoe's story, The will), new edns 1860 and 1867 (with title, The Colville family).

George, A. Memoirs of the Queens of Spain ... Ed with an introduction and notes by ... Julia Pardoe. 2 vols 1850, 2 vols New York 1850 (with title, Annals of the Queens of Spain).

A thousand and one days: a companion to the Arabian Nights. 1857, Baltimore 1858 (Pardoe wrote the introd). Reissued Baltimore 1860, with title, Hassan Abdallah; or the enchanted keys, and other tales: a companion to the Arabian Nights. Reissued New York and Baltimore 1869, with title, The enchanted keys, and other tales: a companion to the Arabian Nights.

Attributed/spurious works

The nun, a poetical romance, and two others. [1822] (attributed by Halkett and Laing).

The adopted heir. Philadelphia [186-?] (Nat Union Catalogue; not in BL).

The earl's secret. Philadelphia 1865 (Nat Union Catalogue; not in BL, and would have to be posthumous pbn).

The wife's trials: a novel. Probably by Emma Jane Worboise; attributed in BL Catalogue and Halkett and Laing.

§2

Memoir of Pardoe in 1887 edn of The court and reign of Francis the First.

Lee, Elizabeth. In DNB.

Cross, N. The common writer: life in nineteenth-century Grub Street. Cambridge 1985. [JW]

James Payn 1830–98

Mss located in Nat Lib of Scotland; Pierpont Morgan Lib; Berg Collection, NYPL. See also LR.

Bibliographies

Wolff, R. L. In his Nineteenth-century fiction: a bibliographical catalogue, 5 vols 1981–6.

See Wellesley *vol 5 1989.*

Collections and selections

In E. H. Yates's Wrecked in port: a novel. New York. 1873.

Rebecca's remorse. In The general's will and other stories. 1892.

Aunt Sue's Panic. In Twenty-four novelettes. Augusta ME 1896.

A faithful retainer. In Short story classics. 1907, Toronto. 1907.

§1

Stories from Boccaccio and other poems. 1852

Poems. Cambridge 1853.
REVIEW: Athenaeum 21 Jan 1854.

Stories and sketches. 1857, Edinburgh 1857.
REVIEW: Literary Gazette 25 Apr 1857.

Furness Abbey and its neighbourhood. Windermere [1858], [1862], London [1863], [1864] (as A description of Furness Abbey and its neighbourhood), [1869], 187-? (4th edn).

Leaves from lakeland. [1858], 1880, 1889.

The Foster brothers. 1859, New York 1859, London [1870], [1881], [1884], 1886, 1899.

A handbook to the English lakes. 1859, [1860?] (2nd edn), 1890 (10th edn).

The Bateman household. 1860. Rptd from Chambers's Jnl.

Richard Arbour, or the family scapegrace. Edinburgh 1861, then as The family scapegrace: or Richard Arbour, London [1869], 1887, 1901.

Meliboeus in London. Cambridge 1862.

Lost Sir Massingberd. A romance of real life. 2 vols 1864, 1865 (3rd edn), 1869, Philadelphia [1870], London 1878 (4th edn), New York 1879, London 1881, '1891' [1892], 1896, 1905, Salem NH 1976, New York 1976, London 1980.
REVIEW: Athenaeum 11 June 1864.

Married beneath him. 3 vols Cambridge '1865' [1864], 1866, 1867, [1869] (4th edn), New York 1879, Philadelphia [18—?], London 1886, 1892, New York 1899.
REVIEW: Athenaeum 14 Jan 1865.

People, places and things. 1865, 1876 (new edn as Humorous stories about people, places and things), 1881, 1893 (both with revised title).

The Clyffards of Clyffe. 3 vols '1866' [1865], 1867, Philadelphia 1871, New York 1880, [1881], London 1887, New York 1890, 1899.
Mirk Abbey. 3 vols 1866, 1869, 1882, 1889. Rptd from Chambers's Jnl.
Carlyon's year. 2 vols New York 1867, London 1868, 1874, 1882, New York 1882, 1883, London 1888.
REVIEW: Athenaeum 25 Apr 1868.
The Lakes in sunshine: being photographic and other pictures of the Lake District of Westmoreland and north Lancashire. With descriptive letterpress by James Payn. 2 vols Windermere 1867–70, 1 vol London 1867, 1868, 1870, 1871, 1872.
Lights and shadows of London life. 1867.
Bentinck's tutor, one of the family. A novel. 1868, 1881, 1883.
REVIEW: Athenaeum 7 Mar 1868.
Blondel Parva. 2 vols 1868.
A beggar on horseback; or a county family (American edn of A county family). New York 1869, 1878, 1881.
A county family. A novel. 3 vols 1869, [1871], 1881, 1897.
REVIEW: Athenaeum 9 Oct 1869.
Found dead. 1869 (2nd edn), Leipzig 1869 (Tauchnitz), New York 1869, 1879, Leipzig 1880 (Tauchnitz), New York 1882, [1883 new edn], Leipzig 1883 (Tauchnitz), 1884, 1902, 1928.
Maxims by a man of the world. 1869.
A perfect treasure. An incident in the early life of Marmaduke Drake, esq. 1869, 1870 (2nd edn), 1890, 1918.
Gwendoline's harvest. A novel. 2 vols 1870, New York 1870, Leipzig 1870 (Tauchnitz as Gwendolin's harvest), London 1872, New York 1878, London 1880, 1881.
Like father, like son. A novel. 3 vols 1871, 2 vols Leipzig 1871 (Tauchnitz), New York 1871 (as Bred in the bone; or like father like son), London 1872, New York 1872 (as Bred in the bone; or like father like son), London 1880, 1881, Leipzig 1885 (Tauchnitz), London 1888, Leipzig 1892 (Tauchnitz), 1893, 1903, 1928, 1929; tr Ger 4 vols 1872–3.
Not wooed, but won. A novel. 2 vols 1871, Leipzig 1871 (Tauchnitz), New York 1871 (as Won – not wooed), London 1873, 1881, Leipzig 1890 (Tauchnitz), 1892, London 1895, Leipzig 1895 (Tauchnitz), 1902, 1905, 1908, 1930 (Tauchnitz).
REVIEW: Athenaeum 1 July 1871.
Cecil's tryst. A novel. 3 vols 1872, New York 1872, 1 vol Leipzig 1872 (Tauchnitz), 1 vol London 1874, 1881, New York 1881, 1 vol Leipzig 1883 (Tauchnitz), 1887, London 1890, 1 vol Leipzig 1896 (Tauchnitz, 2 edns).
At her mercy. 3 vols 1872, 1874, 2 vols Leipzig 1874 (Tauchnitz), New York 1874, 1879, London 1881, 1885, Leipzig 1891 (Tauchnitz), 1900.
REVIEW: Athenaeum 25 Apr 1874.
A woman's vengeance. 3 vols 1872, 2 vols Leipzig 1872 (Tauchnitz), London 1874 (2nd edn), New York 1883, Leipzig (Tauchnitz), 1884, 1886, London 1888, Leipzig (Tauchnitz) 1893, 1897, 1911, 1925, 1929.
REVIEW: Athenaeum 12 Oct 1872.
In the heart of a hill, and other stories. 1873, Leipzig (Tauchnitz) 1883, 1894, 1903, 1927.
Murphy's master, and other stories. 2 vols 1873, Leipzig 1873 (Tauchnitz), New York 1873, London 1881, New York 1881, Leipzig (Tauchnitz) 1887, 1894, 1909.
REVIEW: Athenaeum 15 Mar 1873.
The best of husbands. 3 vols 1874, 2 vols Leipzig 1874 (Tauchnitz), New York 1874, London 1876, [1897], New York 1878, New York 1882, 2 vols Leipzig (Tauchnitz) 1892, 1895, 1900.
Walter's word. A novel. 3 vols 1875, 2 vols Leipzig 1875 (Tauchnitz), London 1876 (2nd edn), 1879, 1887, 1889.
Fallen fortunes. 3 vols 1876, 2 vols Leipzig 1876 (Tauchnitz), New York 1876, London [1880], [New York 1880], London 1891, Leipzig 1905 (Tauchnitz).
REVIEW: Acad 4 Nov 1876.
Halves, a novel, and other tales. 3 vols 1876, 2 vols Leipzig 1876 (Tauchnitz as Halves; a novel), New York 1876, London 1877, New York [1878], Leipzig 1919 (Tauchnitz).
What he cost her. 3 vols 1877, 2 vols Leipzig 1877 (Tauchnitz), New York 1877, London 1879, 2 vols Leipzig (Tauchnitz) 1893, 1903.
REVIEW: Acad 7 July 1877.
By proxy. 2 vols 1878, 2 vols Leipzig 1878 (Tauchnitz), 1 vol London 1878, Leipzig (Tauchnitz) 1891, 1893 (Tauchnitz), London 1898, Leipzig (Tauchnitz) 1919, 1920.
REVIEW: Acad 29 June 1878.
Less black than we're painted. 3 vols 1878 (2 edns), 2 vols Leipzig 1878 (Tauchnitz), New York 1878, 2 vols Leipzig 1883 (Tauchnitz), London 1885, 1888, 1893, Leipzig 1894 (Tauchnitz), London 1898, Leipzig 1906 (Tauchnitz).
Under one roof: an episode in a family history. 3 vols 1879, New York 1879, Toronto 1879, London 1881, 1882, 2 vols Leipzig (Tauchnitz), 1886, 1890, 1894, 1906, 1920.
REVIEW: Acad 1 Nov 1879.
High spirits, being certain stories written in them. 3 vols 1879, 1 vol Leipzig 1879 (Tauchnitz), New York 1879, London 1880, Leipzig 1881 (Tauchnitz), New York 1882, London 1884, 1885, 1890, 1 vol Leipzig 1892 (Tauchnitz), London 1894, Leipzig (Tauchnitz) 1895, 1905, 1920, 1930.
REVIEW: Acad 1 Nov 1879.
A confidential agent. 3 vols 1880, 1881 (2nd edn), 2 vols Leipzig 1881 (Tauchnitz), London 1886, 2 vols Leipzig 1889 (Tauchnitz), London 1890, 1892, 2 vols Leipzig (Tauchnitz) 1894, 1900, Leipzig 1902.
REVIEW: Acad 11 Dec 1880.
From exile. 3 vols 1881, 2 vols Leipzig 1881 (Tauchnitz), New York 1881, 1 vol London 1889, 2 vols Leipzig (Tauchnitz) 1889, 1894, 1920.
A marine residence and other stories. 1881, 1894.
A grape from a thorn. 3 vols 1881, New York 1881, 1882 (2nd edn), 2 vols Leipzig 1882 (Tauchnitz), London 1883, 1884, 1885, Leipzig 1888 (Tauchnitz), 1890, London 1892, 2 vols Leipzig 1899 (Tauchnitz), London 1902.
REVIEW: Athenaeum 24 Dec 1881.
Some private views, being essays from the Nineteenth Century Review, with some occasional articles from The Times. 1881, Leipzig (Tauchnitz) 1882, 1883, 1889, 1902.
REVIEW: Athenaeum 11 Feb 1882.
Two hundred pounds reward, and other tales. 1881, 1887.
For cash only. A novel. 3 vols [1882], 2 vols Leipzig 1882 (Tauchnitz), New York 1882, London 1883, 2 vols Leipzig 1883 (Tauchnitz), London 1885, 1890, 1893, 2 vols Leipzig 1921 (Tauchnitz).
REVIEW: Athenaeum 6 May 1882.
Kit: a memory. 3 vols New York 1882, London 1883, New York 1883, 2 vols Leipzig (Tauchnitz) 1883, 1887, 1892, 1893, London 1896, Leipzig (Tauchnitz) 1912, 1924.
REVIEW: Athenaeum 27 Jan 1883.
Thicker than water. 3 vols 1883, New York 1883, London 1884, 1885, New York 1889, London 1891.
REVIEW: Athenaeum 22 Sep 1883.
The youth and middle age of Charles Dickens. 1883. Rptd from Chambers's Jnl.
The canon's ward. 3 vols 1884, 2 vols Leipzig 1884 (Tauchnitz), New York 1884, 1885, 1886, 2 vols London 1891, 2 vols Leipzig (Tauchnitz) 1897, 1919, 1924.
REVIEW: Athenaeum 26 Jan 1884.
Some literary recollections. 1884 (3 edns), Leipzig 1884 (Tauchnitz), New York 1884, London 1885 (4th edn), New York 1889, Leipzig 1894 (Tauchnitz), 1907 (Tauchnitz).
REVIEW: Athenaeum 4 Oct 1884.
A bitter reckoning. New York 1885.
In peril and privation. Stories of marine disaster retold. 1885 (illus), New York 1885, London 1888 (2nd edn).

The luck of the Darrells. A novel. 3 vols 1885, 2 vols Leipzig 1885 (Tauchnitz), New York 1885, London 1886, London and New York 1893, New York 1889, Leipzig 1917 (Tauchnitz), 1931 (Tauchnitz).
REVIEWS: Athenaeum 10 Oct 1885; Acad 16 Oct 1885.

The talk of the town. 2 vols 1885 (2 edns, illustr H. Furniss), New York 1884, 1 vol Leipzig 1885 (Tauchnitz), New York [1885], London 1887, 1889, 1 vol Leipzig (Tauchnitz) 1892, 1898, 1910.
REVIEWS: Acad 24 Jan 1885: Athenaeum 31 Jan 1885.

The heir of the ages. 3 vols 1886, 2 vols Leipzig 1886 (Tauchnitz), New York 1886, London 1887, Leipzig 1887 (Tauchnitz), London 1888, Leipzig 1897 (Tauchnitz), 1900 (Tauchnitz).
REVIEWS: Athenaeum 12 June 1886; Acad 3 July 1886.

Glow-worm tales. 1st ser. 3 vols 1887, 1 vol Leipzig 1887 (Tauchnitz), New York [1887], London 1888, 1 vol Leipzig 1888 (Tauchnitz), London 1889, 1 vol Leipzig 1930 (Tauchnitz).
REVIEWS: Athenaeum 7 May 1887; Acad 14 May 1887.

Glow-worm tales. 2nd ser. Leipzig (Tauchnitz) 1887, 1888, 1902.

Holiday tasks: being essays written in vacation time. 3 vols 1887, 1 vol Leipzig 1887 (Tauchnitz), London 1888, 1889, 1 vol Leipzig (Tauchnitz) 1889, 1902, 1907.
REVIEW: Athenaeum 19 Feb 1887.

The eavesdropper: an unparalleled experience. 1888, New York 1888.

The mystery of Mirbridge. 3 vols 1888, 2 vols Leipzig 1888 (Tauchnitz), New York 1888, London 1889, 1890, 1 vol Leipzig 1892 (Tauchnitz), London 1894, Leipzig (Tauchnitz) 1894, 1914, 1916, 1924.
REVIEWS: Athenaeum 30 June 1888; Acad 7 July 1888.

A prince of the blood. A novel. 3 vols 1888 (2 edns), 2 vols Leipzig 1888 (Tauchnitz), New York 1888, London 1890 (4th edn), 1893, Leipzig (Tauchnitz) 1897, 1900, 1908.
REVIEWS: Acad 10 Dec 1887; Athenaeum 10 Dec 1887.

The burnt million. 3 vols New York [1889], London 1890, 2 vols Leipzig 1890 (Tauchnitz), New York 1890, London 1891, Leipzig (Tauchnitz) 1896, 1897, 1909, 1919.
REVIEWS: Athenaeum 3 May 1890; Scots Observer 17 May 1890; Acad 2 June 1890; Spectator 28 June 1890; Harper's Monthly suppl 4 Aug 1890.

Notes from the [Illustrated London] News. 1890, New York 1890.
REVIEW: Athenaeum 21 June 1890.

The word and the will: a novel. 3 vols 1890, 2 vols Leipzig 1890 (Tauchnitz), New York [1890], London 1891, 1892, 2 vols Leipzig (Tauchnitz) 1892, 1919, 1924.
REVIEWS: Athenaeum 27 Sep 1890; Scots Observer 25 Oct 1890; Acad 1 Nov 1890.

Sunny stories and some shady ones. 1891, Leipzig 1891 (Tauchnitz), New York 1891, Leipzig 1905 (Tauchnitz), 1911.
REVIEWS: Athenaeum 30 May 1891; Scots Observer 30 May 1891.

A stumble on the threshold. A novel. 2 vols 1892, New York 1892, London 1893 (2nd edn), 2 vols Leipzig 1893 (Tauchnitz), 1913.
REVIEWS: Spectator 10 Dec 1892; Athenaeum 24 Dec 1892; Catholic World Feb 1893.

A modern Dick Whittington: or a patron of letters. 2 vols 1892, Leipzig 1892 (Tauchnitz), New York 1892, London 1893, 2 vols Leipzig 1895 (Tauchnitz), London 1898, 2 vols Leipzig 1903 (Tauchnitz).
REVIEWS: Athenaeum 16 July 1892; Acad 20 Aug 1892; Spectator 5 Nov 1892.

A trying patient. 1893, Leipzig 1893 (Tauchnitz), London 1895, Leipzig 1896 (Tauchnitz), 1922 (Tauchnitz). Short stories.

Gleams of memory: with some reflections. 1894, Leipzig 1894 (with The eavesdropper) (Tauchnitz), 1909 (with The eavesdropper) (Tauchnitz).
REVIEW: Athenaeum 17 Nov 1894.

In market overt. 1895 (illustr W. Paget), Leipzig 1895 (Tauchnitz), Philadelphia 1895, Leipzig 1902 (Tauchnitz).
REVIEWS: Athenaeum 18 May 1895; Spectator 17 Aug 1895.

The disappearance of George Driffell. 1896 Leipzig 1896, (Tauchnitz), London 1917.
REVIEWS: Acad 25 June 1896; Athenaeum 4 July 1896.

Another's burden. 1897, Leipzig 1898 (as Another's burden and two essays) (Tauchnitz), 1907 (as Another's burden and two essays) (Tauchnitz).
REVIEW: Athenaeum 11 Dec 1897.

The backwater of life: or essays of a literary veteran, with a biographical introduction by Sir Leslie Stephen. 1899, Leipzig (Tauchnitz) 1900, 1918, 1925.
REVIEWS: Bookman Jan 1900; Athenaeum 13 Jan 1900; New York Times 14 Apr 1900.

Payn was a prolific novelist and a long-time contributor to Household Words *and* Chambers's Jnl, *being co-editor of the latter from 1857 to 1861. He was editor of the* Cornhill Mag *from June 1883 to June 1896.*

Contributions to periodicals, collaborative works and anthologies

Once a Week. 6 July–26 Oct 1867.
Belgravia. Oct 1876–Oct 1881.
Belgravia Annual. 1877–83.
Belgravia Holiday Nos. 1877–83.
For Cornhill Mag, Nineteenth Cent, Longman's Mag *and* Westminster Rev, *see* Wellesley *vol 5 1989.*
Halves. In S. Morley, Aileen Ferrers: a novel, New York 1875 (vol 1), 1876 (vol 2).
Jebb's mantelpiece. In Humbling of the memblings, New York 1883.
Patient Kitty. In Romantic tales, New York [1885].
Forum. Closing of the doors, 7 1888.
Idler. Feb 1892–Dec 1893.
Rebecca's remorse. In Stories from Black and White, 1893, New York 1893.
Chapman's Mag. A noiseless burglar, May 1895.
Living Age. Backwater of life, 1 June 1895.
In Stories by English authors, New York 1896.

§2

Payn, J., Some literary recollections. 1884, 1885.
Reading, W. H. and H. H. In their The boyhood of living authors. New York 1887.
Payn, J. Gleams of memory: with some reflections. 1894.
Spectator 4 May 1895.
Harris, I. Great Thoughts Oct 1896.
Obits: The Times 26 Mar 1898, New York Times 26 Mar and 9 Apr 1898, Athenaeum 2 Apr 1898; Critic 2 Apr 1898; Spectator 2 Apr 1898, Bookman May 1898.
Acad suppl 30 Apr 1898.
Stephen, L. Cornhill Mag May 1898; rptd Living Age 4 June 1898.
Payn, J. The backwater of life: or essays of a literary veteran, with a biographical introduction by Sir Leslie Stephen. 1899.
Stephen, L. In DNB.
'Melville, L.' (L. S. Benjamin). In his Victorian novelists, 1906.
Reiding, W. H. In his Friends and acquaintances, Cornhill Mag Mar 1910.
Weyman, S. T. James Payn, editor. Cornhill Mag Jan 1910.
Russell, G. W. E. In his Afterthoughts, 1912.
Nicoll, W. R. In his A bookman's letters, 1913.
Russell, G. W. E. In his Selected essays, 1914.
Huxley, L. James Payn, 1830–98. Cornhill Mag Mar 1930.
In The letters of George Meredith, ed C. L. Cline, 3 vols Oxford 1970.
DLB vol 18 Detroit 1983.
Sutherland, J. In The Longman companion to Victorian fiction, 1988.
Van Arsdel, R. T. In The 1890s: an encyclopedia of British literature, art, and culture, ed G. A. Cevasco, 1993.
In The letters of Robert Louis Stevenson, ed B. A. Booth and E. Mehew, 8 vols New Haven CT 1994–5.

Wegener, F. Henry James on James Payn: a forgotten critical text. New England Quart Mar 1994. [DA]

Samuel Phillips 1814–54

Caleb Stukely. 3 vols Edinburgh 1844, 1854, 1862.
Letters from the Orient, by Countess Hahn-Hahn, translated by the author of Caleb Stukely. 1845.
The literature of the rail. 1851.
Essays from the Times: being a selection from the literary papers which have appeared in that journal. 1851; ser 2, 1854. Both ser, 2 vols 1871.
Memoir of the Duke of Wellington. 1852 (anon), 1856. Usually attributed to Phillips.
Guide to the Crystal Palace and park. 1854.
The Portrait Gallery of the Crystal Palace. 1854.
We're all low people there, and other tales. 1854.
Phillips was also editor of the Literary Gazette; *for his career, see obituary in The Times 17 Oct 1854.*

Watts Phillips 1825–74

See col 2014.

Charles Reade 1814–84

The principal repositories of Reade's notebooks and notecards are the London Lib and the Morris L. Parrish Col at Princeton (details of the latter are given in Smith, Bibliographies, *below). Mss and correspondence relating to Reade can also be found in Huntington; Wellcome Institute for the History of Medicine; Yale; and the Harper Col, Pierpont Morgan Lib. Twenty-four playscripts written or co-written by Reade are held in the Lord Chamberlain's Plays Col at the BL.*

Bibliographies

Sadleir, M. In his Excursions in Victorian bibliography, 1922.
Elwin, M. In his Reade: a biography, 1930.
Parrish, M. L. Wilkie Collins and Reade. 1940.
Rives, L. In her Reade: sa vie, ses romans, Toulouse 1940.
Burns, W. In Victorian fiction: a guide to research, ed L. Stevenson, Cambridge MA 1964.
Smith, E. E. In his Charles Reade, 1976.

Collections and selections

Works. 20 vols 1884–94 (new edn, illustr), 17 vols 1895–6 (Uniform lib edn), 17 vols New York 1895 (lib edn), 9 vols New York [1895?] (new edn), 18 vols Boston [1899] (Cabinet edn, illustr), 13 vols London and New York [nd] (Colonial Press), 13 vols Chicago [nd], 12 vols New York [19?] (deluxe edn) etc, 17 vols New York 1970– (rpt of 1895 edn).
Selections from the works of Charles Reade, with introduction by Mrs A. Ireland. 1891.
Plays by Charles Reade. Ed with introd and notes by M. Hammet, Cambridge 1986. Contains Masks and faces, The courier of Lyons and It is never too late to mend.

§1

For plays, see below.

Peg Woffington: a novel. 1853, Boston 1855, London 1857, Boston 1864, London 1868, Boston 1869, Leipzig 1872 (Tauchnitz), London [1872], New York 1887, London 1899 (introd by A. Dobson, illustr H. Thomson), [1901], 1905 (introd by R. Garnett), 1911 (Nelson's Classics), 1914, 1917, 1929. With Christie Johnstone, *below.*
Christie Johnstone: a novel. 1853, 1854, Boston 1855, London 1857, Boston 1859, Boston 1864, Boston 1868, London 1868, 1872, Leipzig 1873 (Tauchnitz), New York 1878, London 1888, 1890, 1893, 1894, New York 1895, London 1907, 1929.
Peg Woffington and Christie Johnstone. 1893, 1895, [1905?] (illustr D. Chamberlain), 1906, 1908, 1929, New York 1992 (rpt of 1929 edn).
Clouds and sunshine. Bentley's Misc June–Sep 1854; Art: a dramatic tale, Bentley's Misc Dec 1853–Jan 1854, Boston 1855.
It is never too late to mend: a matter of fact romance. 3 vols 1856, 1856, 2 vols Boston 1856, 2 vols Leipzig 1856 (Tauchnitz), 1 vol London 1857 (illustr), Boston 1858, London 1868, Boston 1869, London [1872], 1890, 1893, 1896, 1899, 1900, 1907 (illustr P. Hardy), 1908, 1927, 1948. The gold diggers. Extract from It is never too late to mend, London and Edinburgh [1927].
The course of true love never did run smooth. 1857, 1868, [1873], 1888, Boston [1890], London 1890, 1891, 1896, 1906, 1910. Contains The bloomer; Art: a dramatic tale; Clouds and sunshine, *above.* With Singleheart and doubleface, 1896.
Propria quae maribus: a jeu d'esprit, and The box tunnel: a fact. Bentley's Misc Nov 1853, Boston 1857. Propria quae maribus is the same story as The bloomer, *above.*
White lies: a story. LJ 11 July–5 Dec 1857, 3 vols 1857, 1 vol Boston 1858, Boston 1860, London 1868, Boston 1869, New York 1870, London 1872 (as Double marriage: or white lies), New York 1877, 1891.
Cream. 1858, 1859, [1873]. Contains Jack of all trades: a matter-of-fact romance (Illustrated London News 1856, Harper's Mag Dec 1857–May 1858), The autobiography of a thief. The autobiography of a thief and other stories, New York 1870. The autobiography of a thief and other histories. 1882 (new edn), 1890, 1896, 1903 etc.
A good fight and other tales. New York 1859. Contains The autobiography of a thief; Jack of all trades; A good fight (first pbd in Once a week 2 July–1 Oct 1859). A good fight. London 1910 (ed A. Lang). 1937 (ed H. A. Trebble). A good fight was expanded into The cloister and the hearth, 1861, *below.*
It is never too late to mend: proofs of its prison revelations. 1859. Pamphlet.
Love me little, love me long. 2 vols 1859, New York 1859, Leipzig 1859, London 1868, Boston 1869, London 1873, 1896.
The eighth commandment. 1860.
Monopoly versus property. 1860. Pamphlet.
The cloister and the hearth: a tale of the Middle Ages. 4 vols 1861, 1861 (rev), 1 vol New York 1861, London 1862, 1863, 2 vols Leipzig 1864 (Tauchnitz), London 1868, Philadelphia [1868?], Boston 1869, London 1870, Boston 1871, Boston 1872, London 1873, Boston 1875, Boston 1876, New York [1877], New York 1878, 4 vols London 1894 (ed W. Besant), 1895, 1896, 1898, 1 vol 1900, 1901, 1902 (illustr M. B. Hewerdine), 1903 (illustr M. Lalau), 1905 (Nelson's Classics), 1905 (ed A. C. Swinburne, EL), 1907, 1909 (illustr B. Shaw), 1912 (illustr G. Browne), London and New York 1915 (ed with introd and notes by C. B. Wheeler), London 1915 (illustr C. Keene and M. Sankey), New York 1920 (ed with introd and notes by O. E. Hart), London 1922 (illustr E. Paul), New York 1924, 1928, London 1929 (ed with introd and notes by Y. W. Cann), 1930, Philadelphia 1930, London 1931, London and New York 1932 (introd by H. W. Van Loon, illustr L. Ward), London and Glasgow 1933, London 1938 (introd and notes by H. Osborne), New York 1942, 1944, 1946, London [1946], 1948 (EL), 1952 (EL), [1953] (introd by R. Liddell), New York [1961] (with critical and biographical material by B. A. Booth), London 1967 (EL), 1968 (Heron Bks). Gerard and Margaret, extract from The cloister and the hearth, London and Edinburgh 1927, 1931. Gerard and Denys, extract from The cloister and the hearth, London and Edinburgh 1928. Come over and stay till domesday, extract from The cloister and the hearth, New York 1937.
Hard cash: a matter-of-fact romance. All the Year Round 28 Mar–26 Dec 1863 (as Very hard cash), 3 vols 1863, 1864, 1 vol New York 1864, 3 vols Leipzig 1864 (Tauchnitz), 1 vol London 1868, Boston 1869, London [1872], New York 1876, London 1890, Glasgow [1890?], London 1895, 1898, [1906], 1907, 1909, 1913, 1914, 1932. The

loss of the Agra, extract from Hard cash, 1920, London and Glasgow 1929.

Griffith Gaunt: or jealousy. Argosy Dec 1865–Nov 1866, 3 vols 1866, 1 vol Boston 1866, 3 vols 1867, 1868 (5th edn), 1869, New York 1869, Boston 1869, London [1872], 1896.

Foul play, by Dion Boucicault and Reade. Once a Week 4 Jan–20 June 1868, 3 vols 1868, 1 vol Boston 1868, Montreal 1868, London 1869, Philadelphia 1869, Boston 1869, Boston 1871, London [1873], 1896, 1927.

Put yourself in his place. Cornhill Mag Mar 1869–July 1870, 3 vols 1870, Leipzig 1870, 1 vol New York 1870, London 1871, 1876, Leipzig 1900 (Tauchnitz), London 1932.

A terrible temptation: a story of the day. Cassell's Mag Apr–Sep 1871, 3 vols 1871, 1 vol Boston 1871, Leipzig 1872, London [1882], Leipzig 1885 (Tauchnitz).

To the editor of the Daily Globe, Toronto: a reply to criticism. 1871. Pamphlet.

The legal vocabulary. 1872. Pamphlet.

The wandering heir. Graphic Dec 1872, Toronto 1872, Boston 1873, New York 1873, London 1875, Leipzig 1880 (Tauchnitz), London 1882, 1905, 1924, 1932.

Cremona violins: four letters reprinted from the Pall Mall Gazette [19–31 Aug 1872]. Gloucester 1873. Rptd in G. A. Dissmore's The violin gallery, Des Moines 1890. Facs rpt of The violin gallery, New York [1967?].

A simpleton: a story of the day. London Soc Aug 1872–Sep 1873, 2 vols Leipzig 1874 (Tauchnitz), 3 vols 1873, 1 vol New York 1873, London 1907.

A hero and a martyr: a true and accurate account of the heroic feats and sad calamity of James Lambert. 1874, New York 1875.

Trade malice: a personal narrative, and The wandering heir: a matter of fact romance. 1875.

The jilt: a novel. Belgravia Mar–June 1877, New York 1877. The jilt later pbd as the title story in some edns of selected stories. Also pbd in Good stories of men and other animals, 1884 *below*.

A woman-hater. Blackwood's Mag June 1876–June 1877, 3 vols 1877, 1 vol New York 1877, 3 vols Edinburgh 1877, London 1896.

Golden crowns: Sunday stories. Manchester [1877].

The coming man: letters contributed to Harper's Weekly. New York 1878.

Dora: or the history of a play. 1878. Pamphlet.

Singleheart and doubleface: a matter-of-fact romance. Life 8 June–7 Sep 1882 and Harper's Mag 1882. New York 1882, London 1884, Leipzig 1884 (Tauchnitz). Also pbd in Good stories of man and other animals, 1884 *below*.

Readiana: comments on current events. 1883, New York 1884, London 1896.

Good stories of man and other animals. 1884, New York 1884, London and New York 1898, London 1924.

The jilt and other stories. 1884, 1891 (new edn).

A perilous secret. Temple Bar Sep 1884–May 1885, 2 vols 1884, 1 vol New York 1884, London 1885, 1891, 1915.

The picture. Harper's Mag Mar–Apr 1884, New York 1884. Also pbd in Good stories of man and other animals, 1884, *above*.

Bible characters. 1888, New York 1889.

Androgynism: or woman playing at man. English Rev Aug–Sep 1911. From an unpbd ms.

Plays

For performance dates see Hammet, above.

Peregrine Pickle, a biographical play, in five acts. Oxford [1851] (priv ptd).

The ladies' battle, or un duel en amour: a comedy in three acts. [1851] (translator's preface signed C. R.), Boston [1855], London 1877 (rev).

Angelo: a tragedy, in four acts. 1851.

The lost husband: a drama in four acts. 1852, 1872.

Gold! a drama in five acts. [1853], 1899.

The courier of Lyons, or the attack upon the mail: a drama in four acts. Translated from the French of Mssrs Moreau, Siraudin and Delacour. [1854], 1856, Cambridge 1895 (rev as The Lyons mail, a play in three acts), London 1909.

The King's rival: a drama in five acts by Tom Taylor and Reade. 1854, New York 1860.

Masks and faces, or before and behind the curtain: a comedy in two acts by Tom Taylor and Reade. 1854, Boston 1855, London 1867, [1895?], [1898].

Two loves and a life: a drama in four acts by Tom Taylor and Reade. 1854, [1899].

Poverty and pride, a drama in five acts, being the authorised English version of 'Les pauvres de Paris'. 1856.

The hypochondriac, adapted to the English stage from the Malade imaginaire of Molière. 1857.

Le faubourg Saint-Germain: pièce en deux actes. Paris 1859.

It's never too late to mend: a drama in four acts. [1865] (BL edn contains notes by the author), [1873] (rev in five acts), Toulouse 1940 (rpt of 1890 edn with preface and notes by L. Rives. Priv ptd).

Dora; a pastoral drama, in three acts. Founded on Tennyson's poem. 1867, Boston [1869].

The double marriage: a drama in five acts by August Maquet and Reade. [1867].

Foul play: a drama in four acts by Dion Boucicault and Reade. [1868], [1871?], 1883 (rev as Foul play: a drama in a prologue and five acts by Reade).

Rachel the reaper: a rustic drama in three acts. 1871.

Kate Peyton, or jealousy: a drama in a prologue and four acts. 1872, 1883 (rev).

The well-born workman: or a man of the day. 1878 (adapted from Put yourself in his place, *above*).

The countess and the dancer, or high life in Vienna: a comedy drama in four acts. 1883.

Love and money: an original drama in prologue and four acts by Reade and Henry Pettitt. 1883. Serialised in Adelaide Observer July–Sep 1884.

Nance Oldfield: a comedy in one act. [1884?] (priv ptd).

Drink. Ed David Baguley, London Ontario 1991.

For Reade's periodical contributions, see Wellesley *vol 5, 647. Also 'Born to good luck',* Adelaide Observer Oct 1883. *Short story.*

§2

Reade's novels. Blackwood's Mag Oct 1869.

Archer, W. In his English dramatists, 1882.

Besant, W. The novels of Reade. GM Apr 1882.

'Ouida' (M. L. de la Ramée). Reade. GM Apr 1882.

Buchanan, R. Personal recollections of Reade. Pall Mall Gazette 16 Apr 1884; rptd in his Look round literature, 1887.

Littledale, R. F. Reade. Academy 19 Apr 1884.

Courtney, W. L. Reade's novels. Fortnightly Rev Oct 1884; rptd in his Studies new and old, 1889.

Swinburne, A. C. Reade. Nineteenth Century Oct 1884; rptd in his Miscellanies, [1886].

Fields, A. An acquaintance with Reade. Century Mag Nov 1884.

Reade, Compton. Charles Reade. Contemporary Rev 45 1884.

Reade, C. L. and C. Reade, dramatist, novelist, journalist: a memoir compiled chiefly from his literary remains. 2 vols 1887.

Howells, W. D. My literary passions. New York 1895.

Quiller-Couch, A. T. In his Adventures in criticism, 1896.

Coleman, J. Reade as I knew him. 1903.

Lord, W. F. Reade's novels. Nineteenth Century Aug 1903; rptd in his Mirror of the century, 1906.

Ahlers, E. Reades Romane und ihr Verhältnis zu ihren literarischen Vorbildern. Münster 1914.

Phillips, W. C. Dickens, Reade and Collins: sensation novelists. New York 1919.
Allen, P. Mrs Stirling, Reade and Mlle Rachel. Anglo-French Rev July 1920.
Sutcliffe, E. G. Charles Reade's notebooks. SP 1930.
Elwin, M. Charles Reade: a biography. 1931.
Burns, W. More Reade notebooks. SP 1945.
Booth, B. A. Trollope, Reade and 'Shilly-Shally'. Trollopian Mar and June 1947.
Martin, R. B. Manuscripts and correspondence of Charles Reade. Princeton University Library Chron Winter 1959.
Clareson, T. D. Charles Reade's letter book. From shadow to substance. Princeton University Library Chronicle, Winter 1986.
[JE and DF]

Thomas Mayne Reid 1818–83

§1

The Rifle Rangers: or adventures of an officer in southern Mexico. 2 vols 1850, 1853, [1857], [1871], 1891 etc.
The scalp hunters: or romantic adventures in northern Mexico. 3 vols 1851, 1852, [1886], 1892 etc.
The desert home: or the adventures of a lost family in the wilderness. 1852, [1884]. At head of title: The English family Robinson.
The boy hunters: or adventures in search of a white buffalo. 1852, [1884], [1892].
The young voyageurs: or the boy hunters in the north. [1853], Paris [1877], London [1884].
The forest exiles: or the perils of a Peruvian family amid the wilds of the Amazon. [1854] (for 1855).
The white chief: a legend of northern Mexico. 3 vols 1855, [1871].
The hunters' feast: or conversations around the camp fire. [1855], [1860], [1871].
The quadroon: or a lover's adventures in Louisiana. 3 vols 1856, Paris 1858.
The bush-boys: or the history and adventures of a Cape farmer and his family in the wild karoos of southern Africa. 1856, [1884].
The young yägers: or a narrative of hunting adventures in southern Africa. 1857, 1884, Paris 1859.
The war-trail: or the hunt of the wild horse. 1857, Paris 1861.
The plant hunters: or adventures among the Himalaya mountains. 1858, Paris 1859, London [1884], [1892].
Ran away to sea: an autobiography for boys. [1858], 1884.
Oçeola. New York 1858, 3 vols London 1859, [1861] (as The half blood), Paris 1873, London [1890].
The boy tar: or a voyage in the dark. [1859 for] 1860, Paris 1861, London [1884].
A hero in spite of himself. 3 vols 1860, 1 vol 1863 (as The tiger-hunter). Adapted from the Fr of L. de Bellemare.
Odd people: being a popular description of singular races of men. 1860, Paris 1862, London [1884].
Quadrupeds, what they are, and where found: a book of zoology for boys. [1860], 1867.
The wood-rangers. 3 vols 1860. Adapted from the Fr of L. de Bellemare.
Bruin: or the grand bear hunt. 1861, Paris 1863, [1884].
The wild huntress. 3 vols 1861, 1865, 1871, Paris [1875], [1890].
The maroon. 3 vols 1862, [1864], Paris [1874], London [1891].
Croquet. 1863, 1865, 1866, New York 1869.
Garibaldi rebuked by one of his best friends: being a letter addressed to him by Captain Mayne Reid. 1864.
The cliff climbers: or the lone home in the Himalayas. [1864], Paris 1865, London [1872], [1888].
The ocean waifs. 1864, [1871]; tr Fr [1869?].
The white gauntlet: a romance. 3 vols [1865], Paris 1865, London [1872].
The boy slaves. [1865], Paris [1869], London [1872].
The headless horseman: a strange tale of Texas. 2 vols 1866, [1868], [1874], [1888].
Afloat in the forest. 1866, [1868].
The bandolero: or a marriage among the mountains. 1866, [1867] (as The mountain marriage: or the Bandolero), [1873].
The guerilla chief and other tales. 1867, [1871], [1891].
The giraffe hunters. 3 vols 1867, [1868], Paris [1869].
The child wife: a tale of the two worlds. 3 vols 1868, 1888.
The fatal cord: a tale of backwood retribution. [1869], [1872] (with The falcon rover).
The white squaw. [1870], [1871] (with The yellow chief).
The yellow chief: a romance of the Rocky Mountains. [1870], [1871] (with The white squaw).
The castaways: a story of adventure in the wilds of Borneo. 1870, Paris [1872].
The lone ranche: a tale of the Staked Plain. 2 vols 1871.
A zigzag journey through Mexico. In Wonderful adventures: a series of narratives of personal experiences among the native tribes of America, [1872].
The finger of fate: a romance. 2 vols 1872, Paris 1873.
The death shot: a romance of forest and prairie. 3 vols 1873, 1884.
Gaspar, the gaucho: a tale of the Gran Chaco. Paris [1874], [1879 for] 1880, [1884].
The flag of distress: a story of the South Sea. 3 vols 1876, 1879.
Gwen Wynn: a romance of the Wye. 3 vols 1877, 1889.
The Queen of the Lakes: a romance of the Mexican valley. 1879.
The free lances: a romance of the Mexican valley. 3 vols 1881, [1888].
The chase of Leviathan: or adventures on the ocean. Paris 1882, [1884 for] 1885.
The lost mountain: a tale of Sonora. Paris [1883], [1884 for] 1885.
Love's martyr: a tragedy in five acts. Perth [1884].
The land of fire: a tale of adventure. [1884], Paris 1885.
The Vee Boers: a tale of adventure in Southern Africa. Paris [1884], London [1885], [1907].
The pierced heart and other stories. [1885.]
The Star of Empire: a romance. 1886, [1888].
No quarter! 3 vols 1888.
The naturalist in Siluria. 1889.
Stories of strange adventures, by Captain Mayne Reid and others. 1890.
Stories of bold deeds and brave men. By Mayne Reid and others. Beeton's Annual [1893]. Contains An adventure in the Vermilion Sea.
A dashing dragoon: the Murat of the American army (Philip Kearny). New York 1913 (Mag of History extra no 22).
Mayne Reid also edited Frederick Whittaker, The cadet button *and Charles Beach,* Lost Lenore.

§2

Reid, E. Mayne Reid: a memoir of his life. 1890.
Reid, E. Captain Mayne Reid: his life and adventures. 1900.
Steele, J. Captain Mayne Reid. Boston 1978.

George William McArthur Reynolds 1814–79

§1

The pbn dates of Reynolds's fiction are difficult to determine definitively. Most were first serialised in one or another popular jnl, usually one edited by Reynolds, and then issued and reissued in vol form by various publishers for decades. The dates listed here are those of the first serialised pbn. Reynolds also wrote a number of short stories for various jnls he edited, none of which is noted here. The most complete bibliography is that contained in E. F. Bleiler's reprint edn of Wagner the wehr-wolf, *New York 1975.*
The youthful imposter. 3 vols Paris 1835; rptd as The parracide, 1847.
Songs of twilight, by Victor Hugo. 1836. Tr from the Fr.

The Baroness. Monthly Mag 1837–8.
Pickwick abroad: or the tour in France. 1837–8.
Alfred de Rosann. 1838. (Also known as Alfred and Life in Paris.)
The appointment: a tale. Isis 1839.
Grace Darling, or the heroine of the Fern Islands. 1839.
Modern writers of France. 2 vols 1839.
The drunkard's tale. Teetotaler 1840. (Also known as The drunkard's progress.)
The last day of a condemned, by Victor Hugo. 1840. Tr from the Fr.
Noctes Pickwickiane. Teetotaler 1840. Tract.
Robert Macaire in England. Illustr 'Phiz'. 3 vols 1840.
Sister Anne: a novel by Paul de Kock. 1840. Tr from the Fr.
The steam-packet: a tale of the river and the ocean. 1840.
Master Timothy's bookcase, or The magic lanthorn [*sic*] of the world. 1841.
Pickwick married. 1841.
Sequel to Don Juan. 1843.
Mysteries of London. 2 vols 1844–6; ser 2, 2 vols 1846–8; ed Trefor Thomas 1 vol Keele 1996.
Faust: a romance of the Second Empire. 1845–6.
The French self instructor. 1846.
Wagner the wehr-wolf. 1846–7; rptd New York 1975, ed E. F. Bleiler.
The days of Hogarth, or the mysteries of old London. 1847–8.
The coral island, or the hereditary curse. 1848–9.
The mysteries of the Court of London. 1st ser 1848–50; 2nd ser 1850–2; 3rd ser 1852–3; 4th ser 1853–5.
The pixy, or the unbaptized child. 1848.
The bronze statue, or the virgin's kiss. 1849.
The seamstress, or the white slaves of England. 1850.
Kenneth, a romance of the highlands. 1851.
Mary Price: or, the memoirs of a servant-maid. 2 vols 1851–2.
Pope Joan, or the female pontiff. 1851.
The massacre of Glencoe, a historical tale. 1852–3.
Soldier's wife. 1852–3.
Joseph Wilmot: or the memoirs of a man servant. 2 vols 1853–4.
Rosa Lambert. 1853–4.
The Rye house plot, or Ruth, the conspirator's daughter. 1853–4. (In US The royal favorite or The mysteries of the court of Charles II or The mysteries of the merry monarch's court.)
May Middleton, the history of a fortune. 1854–5.
Agnes: or beauty and pleasure. 2 vols 1855–7.
Ellen Percy: or the memoirs of an actress. 2 vols 1855–7. (Also known as Mary Glentworth.)
Loves of the harem, or a romance of Constantinople. 1855.
Omar, a tale of the Crimean war. 1855–6.
Leila, or the star of Mingrella. 1856.
Margaret, or the discarded queen. 1856–7.
The Empress Eugenie's boudoir. 1857.
Canonbury House: or the Queen's prophecy. 1857–8.
The young Duchess, or the memoirs of a woman of quality. A sequel to Ellen Percy. 1857–8.
Mary Stuart. 1859.
The self instructor. 1861 (lessons from Reynolds' Misc).
The young fisherman, or the spirits of the lake. 1861.
Reynolds edited the Monthly Mag *1837–8;* Teetotaler *1840–1;* London Jnl *1845–6;* Reynolds's Misc, *1846–69;* Reynolds's Political Instructor, *1849–50;* Reynolds's Weekly Newspaper *1850–9, and* Bow Bells *1864–8.*

§2

Mischievous literature. Bookseller July 1868. A long article dealing with Reynolds and including an incomplete list of his works, without dates.
Obits: Reynolds Weekly Newspaper 22 June 1879; Bookseller 3 July 1879.
G. W. M. Reynolds. Saturday Rev 6 Feb 1886.
Jay, Frank. Peeps into the past. London Jnl 16 Oct 1918.
Reynolds and penny fiction. TLS 24 Jan 1924.
Centenary edn, Reynolds Weekly News, 7 May 1950.
Bleiler, E. F. Introduction and bibliography in reprint of Wagner the wehr-wolf, New York 1975.
James, L. and J. Saville. G. W. M. Reynolds. In Dictionary of labour biography, 1976. [AH]

Leitch Ritchie 1800?–65

Friendship's Offering. 1824–44. Ed Ritchie 1842–4.
Head-pieces and tail-pieces by a travelling artist. 1826. Short stories.
Tales and confessions. 1829, 1833 (with 2 additional stories as London nights' entertainments).
The game of life. 2 vols 1830.
The romance of history: France. 3 vols 1831, [1872] (illustr T. Landseer).
Schinderhannes, the robber of the Rhine. 1833, 1878 (as The robber of the Rhine).
The library of romance. 15 vols 1833–5. Ed Ritchie.
Wanderings by the Loire. 1833 (illustr J. M. W. Turner).
Wanderings by the Seine. [1834–5] (illustr J. M. W. Turner).
The magician. 3 vols 1836.
Beauty's costume: a series of female figures in the dresses of all times and nations with descriptions by Leitch Ritchie. 2 vols 1838–9.
The poetical works of Thomas Pringle with a sketch of his life by Leitch Ritchie. 1838.
Windsor Castle and its environs.... 1840, 1848.
The Wye and its associations: a picturesque ramble. 1841.
A view of the opium trade, historical, moral and commercial. 1843.
The British world in the East.... 2 vols 1847.
Wearyfoot Common. 1855.
The new shilling. 1857.
Winter evening. 2 vols 1859.
The midnight journey [by Ritchie] and other tales [by Mrs Crowe and others] reprinted from Chambers's Journal. 1871. Also contains The night at home, by Ritchie.
Ritchie also contributed The Cheatrice Packman *to* The Club-Book, *ed A. Picken 3 vols 1831, and* The storm lights of Anzasia *to* The tale book, *Königsberg 1859, as well as the letterpress to 9 of Heath's* Picturesque Annuals *1832–40.*

Emma Robinson 1814–90

The BL holds the ms of the version licensed for performance of Richelieu in love, *plus correspondence with the publisher R. Bentley (1863–4). Ms biographical materials are held in Kremers Reference Files, Univ of Wisconsin-Madison. For British holdings of other letters, see LR 2, p 801.*

Bibliographies

Summers, M. In his A Gothic bibliography, [1941].

§1

Whitefriars: or the days of Charles the Second: an historical romance. 3 vols '1844' [1843] (anon), 2nd and 3rd edns 1844 (3rd edn micro Cambridge MA [19—?]), 1 vol New York [1847] (illus), 1 vol London 1851 (Routledge's Railway Lib), reissued 1853 (Routledge's Standard Novels), rptd many times until the end of the cent and finally in 1903 (Half-forgotten Books ser, introd by E. A. Baker, sub-titled, or the court of Charles II), 1-vol edn Philadelphia [1877] (sub-titled, or the times of Charles II), new 1-vol edn 1884, rptd several times until 1892, other edns London and New York [1898?], London 1909 (The People's Lib no 88); tr Ger 1845, Fr 1858. Adapted into play by William Thompson Townsend, 1844.
REVIEW: Athenaeum 30 Dec 1843.
Richelieu in love; or, the youth of Charles I: an historical comedy in

Margaret Forster: a dream within a dream. Preface by Mrs Sala. 1897, 1899.

McKenzie, J. (ed). Letters of George Augustus Sala to Edmund Yates: in the Edmund Yates Papers, University of Queensland Library. St Lucia, Australia 1993.

Dingley, R. (ed). The land of the golden fleece: George Augustus Sala in Australia and New Zealand in 1885. Canberra 1995.

Contributions to periodicals

Periodicals Sala edited and contributed to include:

Chat c. 1848–9.

Conservative Mag Aug 1850.

Temple Bar. Sala was editor Nov 1860–Jan 1863, contributor 1860–8. For a list of his contributions, *see* Wellesley vol 5.

Banter 2 Sep 1867–20 Jan 1868.

Sala's Jnl 30 Apr 1892–11 Apr 1894.

Newspapers and mags for which Sala wrote regularly include:

Household Words 1851–6. Sala's contributions are listed in Anne Lohrli, Household Words . . . table of contents, list of contributors and their contributions, Toronto 1973.

Illus Times 1855–early 1860s.

The Welcome Guest 1858–60.

Daily Telegraph 1857–95. Sala wrote leaders, often two on a single day, special correspondent's reports, reviews, including art reviews, and other articles.

All the Year Round 1859–69. Sala's contributions are listed in Ella Ann Oppenlander, Dickens's All the Year Round: descriptive index and contributor list, New York 1984.

Cornhill Mag 1860. Sala's contributions are listed in Wellesley vol 5.

Illus London News 1860–87 (intermittently). Sala's columns were 'Echoes of the week' and 'Playhouses'. From 18 June to 1 Oct 1887 'Echoes of the week' was continued in Entertainment Gazette and from 2 Mar 1890 to 27? Jan 1895 in Sunday Times.

Notes and Queries. Sala contributed dozens of notes between the early 1860s and the late 1880s.

Belgravia Nov 1866–June 1878.

Bow Bells Annual 1868–88. Sala contributed to or 'edited' the issues entitled The poor prisoners [1868], Stories with a vengeance [1882], Mrs General Mucklestrap's four tall daughters, a culinary romance, by George Augustus Sala, and other stories [1886], Right round the world, with some stories I found on it [1887] (all but 2 stories by Sala), Not a friend in the world, a story of a Christmas dinner, by George Augustus Sala, and other stories [1888?]. The issues entitled Terrible tales [1873] and Dead men tell no tales; but live men do [1884], solely by Sala, are listed above among his individual works.

Contributions to collaborative works

Harlequin Billy Taylor, or the Flying Dutchman and the King of Raritongo. Invented and written by Mr George Ellis and the Brothers [G. A. and C. K.] Sala. 1851. Play.

Funeral procession of Arthur, Duke of Wellington. (panorama). [By Henry Alken and Sala.] [1852.]

The boy's birth-day book: a collection of tales, essays, and narratives of adventure. [1859.]

Marston Lynch: a personal biography. By Robert Brough. 1860. Novel. Sala wrote last para and prefatory Memoir of the author.

Belle Boyd, in camp and prison: written by herself. 2 vols 1865. Introd by 'George Augusta [*sic*] Sala'.

The Biglow papers, by James R. Lowell. 1865. Introd by Sala.

The autocrat of the breakfast-table, by Oliver Wendell Holmes. 1865, 1866. Introd by Sala.

Artemus Ward, his book. 1865. Introd by Sala.

Major Jack Downing. 1865. Introd by Sala.

The Nasby papers by Petroleum V. Nasby. 1865, 1866. Introd by Sala.

Artemus Ward, his travels. 1865. Introd by Sala.

The Orpheus C. Kerr papers. 1865. Introd by Sala.

Yankee drolleries: the most celebrated works of the best American humorists. 1866, 1869, 1870, 1872 etc. Introds by Sala.

The complete correspondence and works of Charles Lamb, vol 1. 1868. Essay by Sala.

James Spence & Co: St Paul's cathedral and its churchyard. 1868. Advertising brochure. Essay by Sala.

Love's cross-currents: a year's letters. By A. C. Swinburne. [1871?]. Novel. May have been partly written by Sala.

Crystal Palace first mule and donkey show. 1874. Advertising brochure. Essay by Sala.

Mornings at Bow Street, by J. Wight. 1875. Essay by Sala.

Fanmakers Company: catalogue of competitive exhibition of fans held at Drapers Hall, 2–11 July 1878. 1878. Essay by Sala.

The showman's panorama, by Codlin and Short [John Latey, jun]. 1880. Introd by Sala.

The dogaressa, by W. G. Melmontí. Tr Clare Brun. '1887' [1886]. Preface by Sala.

Books and mags illustrated or partly illustrated by Sala include:

A word with Punch, by Alfred Bunn. [1847.]

A bowl of punch, by Albert Smith. [1848.]

The man in the moon. 1847[?]–9.

The battle of London life, or Boz and his secretary, by Morna [Thomas O'Keefe]. [1849.]

The April fool book: for the wise men of the west, by Morna [Thomas O'Keefe]. [1849.]

§2

Arnold, Matthew. Friendship's garland. 1871.

Forster, John. The life of Charles Dickens. 1872.

Yates, Edmund. Recollections and experiences. 1884.

Vizetelly, Henry. Glances back through seventy years. 1893.

Obits: The Times 9 Dec 1895, Daily Telegraph 9 Dec 1895, Illus London News 14 Dec 1895, Athenaeum 14 Dec 1895.

Tinsley, William. Random recollections of an old publisher. 1900.

Straus, Ralph. Sala: the portrait of an eminent Victorian. 1942.

Edwards, P. D. Dickens's 'Young men': George Augustus Sala, Edmund Yates, and the world of Victorian journalism. Aldershot 1997. [PDE]

Adelaide Sartoris, née Kemble 1816–79

§1

A week in a French country house. 1867, Boston 1867 (3 edns), rptd Boston 1868 with her Medusa, and other tales (Loring's Railway Novels), rptd London 1902 with preface by Anne Thackeray Ritchie, illustr Lord Leighton, New York 1902, 3rd London impression 1903. Another edn 1909. Serialised in Cornhill Mag 15, Feb–Apr 1867.

REVIEW: Athenaeum 27 July 1867.

Medusa, and other tales. 1868, Boston [186-?], 1868 with her A week in a French country house. 3 stories first pbd Cornhill Mag 9, Apr 1864, 10, Oct 1864, and 12, Dec 1865. Rptd with 4 new stories and title Past hours, 2 vols 1880.

REVIEW: Athenaeum 27 June 1868.

§2

Jameson, Anna. Memoirs and essays illustrative of art, literature, and social morals. 1846.

Middleton, Miss. In DNB.

See also biographies of Sartoris's sister Fanny Kemble by L. S. Driver, Chapel Hill 1933, C. Wright, 1972, D. Marshall, 1977, and J. C. Furnas, New York 1982. [JW]

Marmion W. Savage 1803–72

The Falcon family: or young Ireland. 1845, 1854.

The bachelor of the Albany. 1848; ed B. Dobrée 1927.

My uncle the curate: a novel. 3 vols 1849.
Reuben Medlicott: or the coming man. 3 vols 1852.
Sketches, legal and political, by the Rt Hon R. L. Sheil. 1855. Ed Savage.
Clover Cottage. 1856. Tom Taylor's Comedietta, Nine points of the law, was founded on this.
The woman of business, or the lady and the lawyer: a novel. 3 vols 1870.

Elizabeth Missing Sewell 1815–1906

Collections

Tales by the author of Amy Herbert. 10 vols 1858–62.

§1

Stories on the Lord's Prayer. Rptd from The cottager's monthly visitor for 1840. 1841?, New York 1843 (as The rector's visits), London 1851 (as Stories illustrative of the Lord's Prayer).
Amy Herbert, by a lady. 2 vols 1844. Ed W. Sewell.
Gertrude. 2 vols 1845. Ed W. Sewell.
Laneton Parsonage: a tale for children on the practical use of a portion of the Church Catechism. 3 pts 1846–8. Ed W. Sewell.
A friend in disguise and The fate of a favourite. 1847?; also pbd in The Churchman's Companion 1847.
Margaret Percival. 2 vols 1847. Ed W. Sewell. A sequel by E. E. Hale, entitled Margaret Percival in America, Boston 1850.
The sketches: three tales. 1848. With W. Adams and W. Sewell.
The child's first history of Rome. 1849.
Was it a dream? and The new churchyard. 1849.
The Earl's daughter. 1850. Ed W. Sewell.
A journal kept during a summer tour for the children of a village school. 3 pts 1852. Travel.
A first history of Greece. 1852.
The experience of life. 1853.
Katharine Ashton. 2 vols 1854.
Cleve Hall. 2 vols 1855.
Ivors. 2 vols 1856.
Ursula: a tale of country life. 2 vols 1858.
History of the early Church from the first preaching of the Gospel to the Council of Nicea for the use of young persons. 1859.
Impressions of Rome, Florence, and Turin. 1862.
Ancient history of Egypt, Assyria, and Babylonia. 1862, 1870.
A glimpse of the world. 1863.
Principles of education, drawn from nature and revelation, and applied to female education in the upper classes. 2 vols 1865; rev Mrs G. J. Chitty and L. H. M. Soulsby 1914.
The journal of a home life. 1867, New York 1867 (as Home life).
After life. 1868. A sequel to the preceding. The 2 vols were pbd together in an abridged form in 1891 as Home and after life.
What can be done for our young servants? [1873.]
Some questions of the day. 1875.
Popular history of France from the earliest period to the death of Louis XIV. 1876.
Note-book of an elderly lady. 1881. Rptd from Monthly Packet.
Letters on daily life. 1885. Rptd from Monthly Packet. Essays.
Outline history of Italy from the fall of the Western Empire. 1895 (preface by L. H. M. Soulsby).
Conversations between youth and age. 1896.
The autobiography of Elizabeth M. Sewell, edited by her niece Eleanor L. Sewell. 1907.

Elizabeth Sewell also pbd devotional works and textbooks, and edited several works by her brother William, below.

§2

Owen, M. C. The Sewells of the Isle of Wight. Manchester [1906] (priv ptd). [EH]

William Sewell 1804–74

Bibliographies

Crichton, W. J. In Sewell's Microscope of the New Testamen t, 1878.

§1

An essay on the cultivation of the intellect by the study of dead languages. 1830.
Hora philologica: or conjectures on the structure of the Greek language. Oxford 1830.
A clergyman's recreation: or sacred thoughts in verse. 1831, 1835 (as Sacred thoughts in verse). Anon.
An introduction to the Dialogues of Plato. 1841.
The first voyage of Rodolph the voyager, by G. D. L. 1844.
The second voyage of Rodolph the voyager. Ed W. Sewell 1844. Written by Sewell.
Uncle Peter's fairy tales: the first story, containing the history and adventures of little Mary, Queen of the great island of Brakarakakaka, by Uncle Peter. 1844.
Hawkstone: a tale of and for England in 184—. 2 vols 1845. Anon.
The Agamemnon of Aeschylus, translated literally and rhythmically. 1846.
The Georgics of Virgil, with the text of Heyne; literally and rhythmically translated by W. Sewell. 1846, Oxford 1854 (Eng text only).
The sketches: three tales. 1848. With E. M. Sewell and W. Adams.
The Odes and Epodes of Horace, translated literally and rhythmically. 1850.
The University Commission: or Lord John Russell's postbag of April 27, 1850. 4 pts Oxford 1850 (pt 4 sub-title differs). Anon. Sketch.
Uncle Peter's fairy tale for the nineteenth century. 1869. Anon. Ed E. M. Sewell. Novel.
The giant. 1871. Ed E. M. Sewell. Cover sub-titled: a witch's story for English boys.
Mrs Britton's letter touching the Europa troubles. 1871.
Poems of bygone years. 1871. Ed E. M. Sewell. Anon. Attributed to William Sewell.
Diaries, reminiscences and poems, Mar 7 1866–May 1874. Microfilm copy produced by Library of Congress from mss vols in family ownership.

Sewell also pbd many sermons and theological works, the more important of which are listed at col 2668, and edited several works by his sister Elizabeth, above. A few ephemeral works are unrecorded here.

§2

Owen, M. C. The Sewells of the Isle of Wight. Manchester [1906] (priv ptd).
James, L. A forgotten genius: Sewell of St Columba's and Radley. 1945. [EH]

Elizabeth Sara Sheppard 1830–62

Charles Auchester: a memorial. 3 vols 1853.
Counterparts: or the cross of love. 3 vols 1854.
My first season, by Beatrice Reynolds. Edited by the author of 'Counterparts' and 'Charles Auchester'. 1855. Written by Sheppard.
The double coronet: a novel. 2 vols 1856.
Round the fire: six stories. 1856.
Rumour. 3 vols 1858.
Almost a heroine. 3 vols 1859.

John Palgrave Simpson 1807–87

See col 2021.

Catherine Sinclair 1800–64

Modern accomplishments: or the march of intellect. 1836.
Modern society, or the march of intellect: the conclusion of Modern accomplishments. 1837.
Hill and valley: or hours in England and Wales. Edinburgh 1838.
Holiday house: a series of tales. Edinburgh 1839, [1856] (as Holiday house: a book for the young) etc.
Shetland and the Shetlanders: or the northern circuit. 1840.
Scotland and the Scotch: or the western circuit. 2 pts 1840, 1859 (rev).
Modern flirtations: or a month at Harrowgate. 3 vols Edinburgh 1841.
Scotch courtiers and the Court. Edinburgh 1842. A poem of Victoria's visit to Scotland.
Jane Bouverie: or prosperity and adversity. Edinburgh 1846, 1855 (as Jane Bouverie and how she became an old maid).
The journey of life. 1847.
The lives of Caesars: or the juvenile Plutarch. [1847], [1862] (abbreviated as Anecdotes of the Caesars).
The business of life. 2 vols 1848.
Sir Edward Graham: or railway speculators. 3 vols 1849, 1854 (as The mysterious marriage: or Sir Edward Graham).
Lord and Lady Harcourt: or country hospitalities. 1850, [1856] (as Country hospitalities: or Lord and Lady Harcourt).
The kaleidoscope of anecdotes and aphorisms. 1851.
Beatrice: or the unknown relatives. 3 vols 1852. Preface also rptd separately as a tract, Modern superstition, 1857.
A letter on the principles of the Christian faith, by Hannah Sinclair. 1852. Ed Catherine Sinclair.
Popish legends: or Bible truths. 1852.
Frank Vansittart: or the model schoolboys. 1853.
Lady Mary Pierrepoint. 1853.
London homes: including The murder hole, The drowning dragoon, The priest and the curate, Lady Mary Pierrepoint, & Frank Vansittart. 6 pts 1853.
The priest and the curate: or the two diaries. 1853.
Cross purposes: a novel. 3 vols 1855, [1857] (as Torchester Abbey, or cross purposes: a tale).
The cabman's holiday: a tale. 1855.
Charlie Seymour: or the good and bad choice. 1856 (4th edn).
Memoirs of the English Bible. [1858.]
Sketches and stories of Wales and the Welsh. [1860] (3 edns).
Letters for children with pictures. 6 nos Edinburgh 1863–4. 'Hieroglyphic' stories in letter-form.
The first of April picture letter. Edinburgh 1864.

Francis Edward Smedley 1818–64

§1

Seven tales by seven authors. 1849, 1850. Ed Smedley; includes his Mysteries of Redgrave Court.
Frank Fairleigh: or scenes from the life of a private pupil. 1850 (illustr G. Cruikshank), 1854, 1866, 1878, 1892, 1904.
Lewis Arundel: or the railroad of life, with illustrations by 'Phiz'. 1852, [1855], 2 vols 1892, 1898.
The fortunes of the Colville family, or a cloud and its silver lining: a Christmas story. 1853.
Harry Coverdale's courtship and all that came of it, illustrated by 'Phiz'. 1855.
Mirth and metre. 1855. With E. H. Yates.
Gathered leaves: being a collection of the poetical writings of the late F. E. Smedley, with a memorial preface by Edmund Yates. 1865.
Last leaves from Beechwood. Ed W. Brailsford, Enfield 1867. Poems.
The 'wicked Lady Ferrers': a legend of Markyate Cell in Flamstead, being the poem of F. E. Smedley entitled Maude Allinghame, extracted from Mirth and metre, with an introductory note, forming an attempt to solve the mystery of 'The lady highwayman' by W. B. Gerish. Bishop's Stortford 1911.
Smedley also edited George Cruikshank's Mag *1854*.

§2

Ellis, S. M. In his Mainly Victorian, 1925.

Menella Bute Smedley 1820–77

See col 670.

Albert Richard Smith 1816–60

§1

Beauty and the beast, illustrated by Alfred Crowquill. [1843?].
The wassail-bowl. 2 vols 1843, 1848 (as Comic sketches from The wassail-bowl).
The adventures of Mr Ledbury and his friend Jack Johnson. 3 vols 1844, 1847.
The adventures of Jack Holyday; with something about his sister. 1844.
The fortunes of the Scattergood family. 3 vols 1845, 1853.
The Marchioness of Brinvilliers, the poisoner of the seventeenth century: a romance of old Paris; etchings by John Leech. 1846, 1856, 1860, 1886.
The physiology of evening parties. [1846?], 1849 (as The natural history of evening parties), 1872.
The man in the moon. Ed Albert Smith and Angus B. Reach 5 vols 1847–9.
The natural history of 'stuck-up' people. 1847, 1872.
The natural history of the ballet girl. 1847, 1872.
The natural history of the gent. 1847, 1872.
The natural history of the flirt. 1848, 1872.
The natural history of the idler upon town. 1848, 1872.
The struggles and adventures of Christopher Tadpole at home and abroad, illustrated by John Leech. 1848, 1853, 1864, 1897.
A bowl of punch. 1848.
A pottle of strawberries to beguile a short journey or a long half-hour. 1848.
The Pottleton legacy: a story of town and country life. 1849 (illustr H. K. Browne).
Gavarni in London: sketches of life and character; with illustrative essays by popular writers, edited by Albert Smith. 1849, 1859 (as Sketches of London life and character).
A month at Constantinople. 1850.
Comic tales and sketches. 1852.
Pictures of life at home and abroad. 1852.
The momentous question: a lay in three fyttes. 1852 (priv ptd).
The story of Mont Blanc. 1853, 1854 (enlarged), 1860 (with a life by E. H. Yates).
The English hotel nuisance. 1855.
To China and back: being a diary kept out and home. [1859.]
Wild oats and dead leaves. 1860.
The London medical student. Edited by Arthur Smith. 1861.

§2

Thorington, J. M. Mont Blanc sideshow: the life and times of Albert Smith. Philadelphia 1933.
Fitzsimons, R. The baron of Piccadilly: the travels and entertainments of Albert Smith, 1816–60. 1967.

Alexander Smith 1829–67

See col 671.

John Sterling 1806–44

See col 2199.

Elizabeth Wheeler Stone 1803–61?

§1

The art of needlework from the earliest ages ... edited by the Countess of Wilton. 1840, 1841 (3rd edn).
William Langshawe, the cotton lord. 2 vols 1842.
REVIEWS: Athenaeum 1 Oct 1842; Examiner 5 Nov 1842.
The young milliner. 1843.
REVIEW: Athenaeum 6 May 1843.
Miss Pen and her niece; or the old maid, and the young one. 3 vols 1843.
Sir Eustace de Lucie, a romance. In vol 3 of Miss Pen and her niece, 1843.
The widow's son. Chambers's Misc 1 1844.
Chronicles of fashion, from the time of Elizabeth to the early part of the nineteenth century, in manners, amusements, banquets, costumes, etc. 1845, 1846.
Mr Dalton's legatee, a very nice woman. 3 vols 1850.
Ellen Merton; or the pic-nic. 1856.
God's acre; or, historical notices relating to churchyards. 1858.
Angels. 1859.
A handbook to the Christian year, for young people. 1860.

Contributions to periodicals

The royal sneeze. Ainsworth's Mag 1, Feb 1842.
Matrimony. Ainsworth's Mag 1, Mar 1842.
The Duke of Wellington and Richard Coeur de Lion. Ainsworth's Mag 2, Nov 1842.

Attributed works

Three incidents, strictly true [in verse]. Worthing 1873.

§2

Kestner, J. A. Elizabeth Stone's William Langshawe, the cotton lord and The young milliner as condition-of-England novels. BJRL 67 1985.
Kestner, J. A. Protest and reform: the British social narrative by women, 1827–1867. Madison WI 1985. [JAK]

Robert Smith Surtees 1803–64

Collections

Sporting novels: with all the coloured plates from the original editions. 6 vols nd (priv ptd), [1926].
Novels. 10 vols 1930.

§1

The horseman's manual: being a treatise on soundness, the law of warranty and generally on the laws relating to horses. 1 vol 1831.
Jorrocks' jaunts and jollities: or the hunting, shooting, racing, driving, sailing, eating, eccentric and extravagant exploits of that renowned sporting citizen, Mr John Jorrocks of St Botolph Lane and Great Coram Street; with illustrations by Phiz (H. K. Browne). First pbd in New Sporting Mag July 1831–Sep 1834; 1 vol 1838, 1839, 1843 (illustr Henry Alken), 1869 (rev and enlarged), 1874 etc.
Handley Cross, or the spa hunt: a sporting tale. First pbd in New Sporting Mag Mar 1838–Dec 1839 as The Handley-Cross Hounds (The Gin-and-Water Hunt for first 2 instalments Mar, Apr 1838; 1 illustration Nov 1839 by H. K. Browne); 3 vols 1843 (rev and enlarged, no illustrations); 17 monthly pts Mar 1853–Oct 1854 (rev and enlarged); 1 vol 1854 as Handley Cross: or Mr Jorrocks's hunt, illustr John Leech; 1888 (new illustrations); 1891, 1892 etc.
REVIEWS: [Lockhart, J. G.] Quart Rev 71, Mar 1843; Sunday Times 26 Mar 1843; Ainsworth's Mag 3, June 1843.
Hillingdon Hall, or the cockney squire: a tale of country life. First pbd in New Sporting Mag Feb 1843–June 1844 (up to ch 24) illustr G. Tattersall and H. Heath; completed and rev 3 vols 1845; 1 vol 1888 (with coloured illustrations).
REVIEW: Brighton Gazette 16 Jan 1845.
The analysis of the hunting field: being a series of sketches of the principal characters that compose one; the whole forming a slight souvenir of the season. First pbd in Bell's Life in London and Sporting Chron 12 Oct 1845–26 Apr 1846; 1 vol 1846 rev (illustr Henry Alken).
Hawbuck Grange: or the sporting adventures of Thomas Scott esq. First pbd in Bell's Life in London 25 Oct 1846–27 June 1847; 1 vol rev 1847 (illustr 'Phiz'); [1888], 1891, 1892 etc.
Mr Sponge's sporting tour. First pbd in New Monthly Mag and Humorist Jan 1849–Apr 1851 as Soapey Sponge's sporting tour; 13 monthly pts 1852–3 (illustr John Leech); 1853, [1888], 1892, 1893 etc.
REVIEW: New Sporting Mag n.s. 25, Jan 1853.
Young Tom Hall's heart-aches and horses. First pbd in New Monthy Mag and Humorist Oct 1851–Jan 1853. Incomplete. Ed E. D. Cuming 1926 as Young Tom Hall, his heart-aches and horses, illustr G. D. Armour.
Ask Mamma: or the richest commoner in England. 13 monthly pts 1857–8 (illustr John Leech), 1 vol 1858, [1888], 1892, 1903, 1904 etc.
An encyclopaedia of rural sports or complete account (historical, practical, and descriptive) of hunting, shooting, fishing, racing, etc by Delabere P. Blaine, esq. A new edn rev and corrected (ed R. S. Surtees) 1858.
Plain or ringlets? 13 monthly pts 1859–60 (illustr John Leech); 1860, [1888], 1892, 1900 etc.
Mr Romford's hounds. 12 monthly pts May 1864–Apr 1865 (illustr John Leech and 'Phiz' (H. K. Browne)); 1865 (as Mr Facey Romford's hounds); 1892, 1911.

Collections of articles

Thoughts on hunting and other matters. Ed E. D. Cuming 1925.
The hunting tours of Surtees. Ed E. D. Cuming 1927.
Town and country papers. Ed E. D. Cuming 1929.
Surtees also helped to found New Sporting Mag *which he edited 1831–6.*

§2

The novels of Surtees. TLS 28 Dec 1916.
Frith, W. P. In his John Leech, 1891.
'O'Neill, M.' (Nesta Skrine) Novels by Surtees. Blackwood's Mag Apr 1913.
Fairfax-Blakeborough, J. Handley Cross. The Field 29 Apr 1916.
Cuming, E. D. R. S. Surtees: creator of Jorrocks. 1924.
O'Neill, M. (Nesta Skrine). The author of Jorrocks. Blackwood's Mag June 1924.
Guthrie, D. Some new Surtees letters. The Field 3 Apr 1948.
Cooper, L. R. S. Surtees: a biography. 1952.
Collison, R. L. A Jorrocks handbook. 1964.
Blain, V. H. A study of R. S. Surtees as novelist with special reference to his textual revisions. Unpbd B.Lit thesis, Oxford 1970.
Gash, N. Robert Surtees and early Victorian society. Oxford 1993. [VHB]

Jemima, Baroness Tautphoeus née Montgomery 1807–93

§1

The initials: a novel. 3 vols 1850, 1853, 2 vols Leipzig 1854, London 1858, 1863 (6th edn).
Cyrilla: a tale. 3 vols 1853, 2 vols Leipzig 1853, 1872; tr Ger 1854.
Quits: a novel. 3 vols 1857, 2 vols Leipzig 1858, London 1860, 1864; tr Ger [1863].
At odds: a novel. 2 vols 1863, Leipzig 1863, 1 vol London 1873.

§2

Thorpe, L. Baroness Tautphoeus, an early Victorian novelist. Eng Misc (Rome) 13 1962.

Philip Meadows Taylor 1808–76

Letters and book contracts can be found in the BL and the Nat Lib of Scotland. The Nat Lib of Ireland also holds copies of Meadows Taylor's family tree and coat of arms.

Bibliographies.

Simmons, J. C. Philip Meadows Taylor and the Anglo-Indian novel with a checklist of his writings. BNYPL 75 1971.

Gupta, B. K. India in English fiction 1800–1970. Metuchen NJ 1973.

Finkelstein, D. Philip Meadows Taylor 1808–1876: a bibliography. Victorian Fiction Research Guides. St Lucia, Queensland, 1990.

§1

Sketches in the Deccan. 1837.

Confessions of a thug. 3 vols 1839, 1858, 1873 etc; Oxford 1916 (WC), 1938 (ed F. Yeats-Brown), New York 1967, London 1974, New Delhi 1985, Oxford 1986.

Tippoo Sultaun: a tale of the Mysore War. 3 vols 1840, 1880, 1883, 1887, 1888, 1890, 1896, 1898, 1912, New Delhi 1986.

Tara: a Mahratta tale. 3 vols 1863, 1874, 1881, 1884, 1888, 1898, New Delhi '1986' [1985].

Ralph Darnell. 3 vols 1865, 1879, 1883, 1889, 1896, 1898.

The people of India. 6 vols 1868–75.

A student's manual of the history of India from the earliest period to the present. 1870, 1871, 1877, 1879, 1883, 1896, 1904.

Seeta. 3 vols 1873, 1880, 1881, 1887, 1888, 1890, 1894, 1898, 1912.

The story of my life. Edited by his daughter, Edinburgh 1877, 1878, 1882, 1899, 1903, 1920 (with introd and notes), 1989.

A noble Queen: a romance of Indian history. Serialised in The Overland Mail Feb–Dec 1875. 3 vols 1878, 1880, 1882, 1888, 1890, 1892, 1896, 1898.

Contributions to periodicals

See Wellesley *vol* 5.

Legends of the Dekhan: the fatal armlet. The Keepsake 1841.

The great cat and dog question. Household Words 1, 18 May 1850.

Ancient remains at the village of Jiwarji near Firozabad on the Bheema. Jnl of the Bombay Branch of the Royal Asiatic Soc 3, Jan 1851.

Sketch of the topography of East and West Berar, in reference to the production of cotton. Jnl of the Royal Asiatic Soc 20 1863.

Descriptions of cairns, cromlechs, kistvaens and other Celtic Druidical or Scythian monuments in the Dekhan. Trans of the Royal Irish Acad 24 1865.

Letters from Egypt, 1863–1865. Fraser's Mag 72, Nov 1865.

The midnight search. The Belgravian Annual, Christmas 1869.

On prehistoric archaeology of India. Jnl of the Ethnological Soc 1 1869.

Description of the contents of a cairn at Hyat Nagger in the Dekhan. Proc of the Royal Irish Acad 19 1870.

Collaborative works

The Oriental Annual or Scenes in India. 2 vols 1839–40, 1842, 1843.

The afternoon lectures on English literature and art. 2nd ser. 1864.

Letters

Letters from Meadows Taylor esq. Written during the Indian Rebellion 1857. 1857 (priv ptd).

The letters of Philip Meadows Taylor to Henry Reeve. Ed P Cadell. 1947.

§2

Our portrait gallery. No. xviii Captain Philip Meadows Taylor. Dublin Univ Mag 17, Apr 1841.

[Hilda Gregg.] The Indian Mutiny in fiction. Blackwood's Mag 161, Feb 1897.

Dunn, T. O. Meadows Taylor: his autobiography and novels. Calcutta Rev 291, Jan 1918.

Singh, B. Meadows Taylor and other predecessors of Kipling. In his A survey of Anglo-Indian fiction, Oxford 1934.

Pritchett, V. S. Books in general. New Statesman 8 Nov 1941.

Mansukhani, G. S. Philip Meadows Taylor: a critical survey. Bombay 1951.

Edwardes, M. The articulate hero: Philip Meadows Taylor. Twentieth Cent Sep 1953.

Finkelstein, D. Corrigendum to the Wellesley Index concerning articles attributed to Philip Meadows Taylor. Victorian Periodicals Rev Summer 1990. [DF]

William Makepeace Thackeray, Pseudonyms:

(ὁ Ψευδαγωγος), A Gentleman of the Footguards (Blue), A Literary Snob, Bashi-Bozouk, Brown the Elder, Folkstone Canterbury, Fitzroy Clarence, John Corks, E. L. B. L. B. B. L. L. B. B. B. L. L. L., Henry Esmond, G. S. F. B., George Savage Fitz-Boodle, Major Gahagan, Gamma, Gobemouche, Hibernis Hibernoir, Leonitus Androcles Hugglestone, J. P. R. Jeames, T. M., T. B. McPuvel, Thaddeus Molony, Frederick Haltamount de Montmorency, Goliah Muff, Robert Muff, Lady Nimrod, Ninethousundndninundredannintynine, Our Fat Contributor (F. C.), Dr Solomon Pacifico, Arthur Pendennis, Under Petty, Philodicky, Pleaceman X, C. Jeames de la Pluche, Je—mes Plush, Dorothea Julia Ramsbottom, Harry Rollicker, B de Shrewsbury, Wilhelmina Amelia Skeggs, John Small, Ikey Solomons, Spec, T., T. T., M. A. T., Michael Angelo Titmarsh, F. Tudge, Brian Tuggles Tuggles, L. E. U., W., Launcelot Wagstaff, Théophile Wagstaff, Charles Yellowplush. 1811–63

Major repositories of manuscripts include Beinecke Lib, Yale, BL, Charterhouse School, Harvard Lib, HRHRC Austin TX, Huntington, Pierpont Morgan Lib, New York, Princeton Lib, Nat Lib of Scotland, Trinity College Cambridge. See also: Schulz, H. C. English Literary Manuscripts in the Huntington Library. HLQ 31 1968.

Colby, R. A. and J. Sutherland. Thackeray's Manuscripts: A preliminary census of library locations. Costerus n.s. 2 1974. For additions to Colby and Sutherland see Thackeray Newsletter nos 1, 3, 6, 7, 8, 11, 12, 14–16, 18, 19, 21, 22, 28, 30, 32, 38 1975–93.

Lange, T. V. Appendix: the Robert H. Taylor collection. Costerus n.s. 2 1974.

Sutherland, J. Manuscript sources. In his Thackeray at work. 1974.

Harden, E. F. Manuscript sources. In his Emergence of Thackeray's serial fiction. Athens GA 1979.

Bell, A. Some recent acquisitions of publishing archives by the Nat Lib of Scotland. Publishing History 3 1978.

Bibliographies (Primary)

Shepherd, R. H. The bibliography of Thackeray: the published writings in prose and verse and the sketches and drawings from 1829 to 1880. 1881, 1887 (rev and enlarged in his edn of Sultan Stork and other stories).

Johnson, C. P. Hints to collectors of original editions of the works of Thackeray, 1885.

Johnson, C. P. The earlier writings of Thackeray. 1888.

Anderson, J. P. In H. C. Merivale and F. T. Marzials, Life of Thackeray, 1891.

Spielmann, M. H. Thackeray's hitherto unidentified contributions to Punch: with a complete bibliography from 1845 to 1848. 1899.

Williams, W. J. In Works of Thackeray: biographical edition, vol 13 1899.

Dickson, F. S. Bibliography of Thackeray in the United States. In J. G. Wilson, Thackeray in the United States, vol 2 1904.

'Melville, Lewis' (L. S. Benjamin). In his William Makepeace Thackeray, vol 2 1910. Supersedes the bibliography in his Life of Thackeray, 1899.

The Thackeray centenary exhibition at the old Charterhouse. 1911.

Catalogue of an exhibition commemorating the hundredth anniversary of the birth of William Makepeace Thackeray (1811–1863). New York 1912.

The library of William D. Lambert: part II. New York 1914.

Van Duzer, H. S. A Thackeray library: first editions and first publications, portraits, water colours, etchings, drawings and manuscripts. New York 1919.

The renowned collection of first editions of Charles Dickens and William Makepeace Thackeray. Formed by G. B. M[cCutheon]. New York 1926.

Parrish, M. L. Catalogue of an exhibition of the works of Thackeray. Philadelphia 1940.

Ray, G. N. Articles newly identified as Thackeray's. In his edn of Letters and private papers of Thackeray, vol 2 Cambridge MA 1945.

Gordan, J. D. Thackeray. BNYPL May 1947. Catalogue of Berg collection.

Ray, G. N. Thackeray and Punch: 44 newly identified contributions. TLS 1 Jan 1949.

White, E. M. Thackeray's contributions to Fraser's Magazine. SB 19 1966.

Shillingsburg, P. L. A census of imprints to 1965. In his Pegasus in harness. 1992.

Harden, Edgar F. A Check-list of Contributions by William Makepeace Thackeray to newspapers, periodicals, books, and serial part issues: 1828–1864. 1996.

See also section 2 for bibliographical and textual studies of primary materials as well as for bibliographies of secondary materials.

Collections

Works. Library edn 22 vols 1867–9 (2 more vols 1885–6); Cheaper illus edn 24 vols 1877–9; De luxe edn 26 vols 1878–86 (with memoir by L. Stephen); Standard edn 26 vols 1883–6; Pocket edn 27 vols 1887–93; ed H. E. Scudder 22 vols Boston 1889 (fuller than preceding English edns); Biographical edn 13 vols 1898–9 (with introds by A. T. Ritchie and biographical sketch by L. Stephen rptd from DNB); New Century Lib 14 vols 1899–1900.

Prose works. Ed W. Jerrold 30 vols 1901–3.

Works. Ed 'Lewis Melville' (from vol 8) 20 vols 1901–7, 1911 (rptd from 1st edns and including much new matter); London edn 13 vols 1903 (topographical introds by J. McVicar in vols 1–12; vol 13 is Melville's Life of Thackeray, first pbd 2 vols 1899); Oxford edn 17 vols 1908 (introds by G. Saintsbury; much new matter); Centenary biographical edn 26 vols 1910–11 (enlarged from Biographical edn, above).

§1

Contributions to periodicals are not listed here. The most comprehensive list is Harden's 1996 Checklist. *For contemporary reviews of individual works, see* D. Flamm *and* Tillotson *and* Hawes, *in §2 below*

Flore et Zéphyr: ballet mythologique par Théophile Wagstaff. 1836; ed S. A. Muresianu, New York 1991. 9 lithographed plates; no text.

The Yellowplush correspondence. Fraser's Mag Nov 1837–July 1838; Philadelphia 1838, Paris 1841, New York 1852, 1853 (as The Yellowplush papers); ed P. Shillingsburg, New York 1991; see also Miscellanies *below*.

Some passages in the life of Major Gahagan. NMM, Feb 1838–Feb 1839; Philadelphia 1839 (no known copy); New York 1866; ed P. Shillingsburg, New York 1991; see also Miscellanies and Confessions of Fitz-Boodle, 1852, *below*.

An essay on the genius of George Cruikshank. Westminster Rev, June 1840; 1840; ed W. E. Church 1884.

The Paris sketch book, by Mr Titmarsh. 2 vols 1840, 1866 (rptd), New York 1852, 1853, 1865 (rptd). Several of the sketches rptd from Fraser's Mag, NMM, National Standard, Corsair (New York).

Comic tales and sketches, edited and illustrated by Mr Michael Angelo Titmarsh. 2 vols 1841, 1848. Vol 1, The Yellowplush papers; vol 2, Some passages in the life of Major Gahagan, The professor (from Bentley's Misc Sep 1837), The Bedford Row conspiracy (from NMM Jan–Apr 1840), Stubbs's calendar (from Comic Almanac 1839).

The second funeral of Napoleon, in three letters to Miss Smith of London; and The chronicle of the drum, by Mr M. A. Titmarsh. 1841; See also Miscellanies.

The Irish sketch-book, by Mr M. A. Titmarsh. 2 vols 1843, 1845 (reissue), 1 vol New York [1843], 1847, London 1857, New York 1864, Philadelphia 1864.

The luck of Barry Lyndon: a romance of the last century. Fraser's Mag Jan–Dec 1844; 2 vols New York 1852–3, 1 vol 1856 (rev, as The memoirs of Barry Lyndon Esq); ed M. Anisman, New York 1970; ed A. Sanders, Oxford (WCp) 1984; See also Miscellanies.

Jeames's diary. Punch, 2 Aug 1845–7 Feb 1846; New York 1846, 1853.

Notes of a journey from Cornhill to Grand Cairo, by way of Lisbon, Athens, Constantinople and Jerusalem, performed in the steamers of the Peninsular and Oriental Company, by Mr M. A. Titmarsh. 1846, 1846 (with postscript signed W. M. T.), 1850, 1864, 1865 (rptd), New York 1846, 1848, 1850, 1852 (rptd).

The snobs of England, by one of themselves. Punch, 28 Feb 1846–27 Feb 1847; 1848 (as The book of snobs), omitting chs 17–23), New York 1852 (complete), 1853 (rptd), London 1855, 1856, 1865 (rptd), New York 1864; ed G. K. Chesterton, London 1911; ed John Sutherland, Brisbane 1978.

Vanity Fair: pen and pencil sketches of English society. 20 monthly pts Jan 1847–July 1848; Vanity Fair: a novel without a hero, 1848, 2 pts New York 1848, 1 vol 1848, 3 vols Leipzig 1849, 1 vol London 1853 (rev), 1863 (rptd), 3 vols Cambridge MA 1865; 2 vols New York 1865; ed J. E. Wells 2 vols New York 1928; ed P. E. More 2 vols Garden City NY 1935; ed J. W. Beach, New York 1950; ed G. H. Ford, New York 1958; ed G. and K. Tillotson 1963; ed Gilbert Phelps, London 1967; ed J. I. M. Stewart, 1968 (Pen); ed F. E. L. Priestley, New York 1969; ed J. Sutherland, Oxford 1983 (WCp); ed P. Shillingsburg, New York 1989; ed P. Shillingsburg, New York 1994 (Norton Critical Edn).

Mrs Perkins's ball, by Mr M. A. Titmarsh. 1847 (3 edns), 1866 (rptd), 1898 (facs).

The history of Samuel Titmarsh and the great Hoggarty diamond. Fraser's Mag Sep–Dec 1841; New York 1848 (as The great Hoggarty diamond), London 1849 (with original title), 1849 (new edn), 1852, 1857, 1865 (reissued with new title pages), Leipzig 1849; see also Miscellanies below.

'Our street', by Mr M. A. Titmarsh. 1848, 1848, 1864 (rptd).

The history of Pendennis: his fortunes and misfortunes, his friends and his greatest enemy. 24 monthly pts Nov 1848–Dec 1850; 2 vols 1849–50, 8 pts New York, 1849–50, 3 vols Leipzig 1849–50, 2 vols New York 1850, 1854, 1855, 1858, 1860 (rptd), 1 vol London 1856 (rev), 1863 (rptd); ed D. Hawes (Pen) 1972; ed P. Shillingsburg, New York 1991; ed J. Sutherland, Oxford 1994 (WCp).

Doctor Birch and his young friends, by Mr M. A. Titmarsh. 1849, 1864 (rptd), Paris 1849, New York 1853, London 1856, 1857 (rptd), New York 1867.

Miscellanies: prose and verse. 8 vols Leipzig 1849–57. Vol 1 (1849) contains The great Hoggarty diamond, The book of snobs; vol 2 (1851) The Kickleburys abroad, A legend of the Rhine, Rebecca and Rowena, The second funeral of Napoleon, The chronicle of the drum; Vol 3 (1856) The tremendous adventures of Major Gahagan, The fatal boots, Ballads; Vol 4 (1856) Memoirs of Mr Charles J. Yellowplush, The diary of C. Jeames de la Pluche, esq, Cox's diary; Vol 5 (1856) Sketches and travels in London; Vol 6

(1856) Memoirs of Barry Lyndon; Vol 7 (1857) A little dinner at Timmins's, The Bedford Row conspiracy, Fitz-Boodle papers, A shabby genteel story; Vol 8 (1857) Men's wives.

The Kickleburys on the Rhine, by Mr M. A. Titmarsh. 1850, 1850, 1851 (with Preface being an essay on thunder and small beer), Frankfurt 1851, New York 1851, Leipzig 1851, London 1866, New York 1867.

Stubbs's calendar: or the fatal boots. New York 1850; see also Miscellanies.

Rebecca and Rowena: a romance upon romance, by Mr M. A. Titmarsh. 1850, Paris 1850, Leipzig 1852. Revision of Proposals for a continuation of Ivanhoe, Fraser's Mag Aug–Sep 1846.

The history of Henry Esmond esq, a colonel in the service of Her Majesty Q. Anne, written by himself. 3 vols 1852, 2 vols Leipzig 1852, 1 vol New York 1852, 3 vols London 1853, 1 vol 1858 (rev), 1866 (rptd); ed T. C. Snow and W. Snow 1909 (annotated); ed G. N. Ray, New York 1950; ed J. Sutherland, London 1970 (Pen); ed E. Harden, New York 1989; ed D. Hawes, Oxford 1991 (WCp).

The confessions of Fitz-Boodle; and some passages in the life of Major Gahagan. New York 1852; see also Miscellanies.

A shabby genteel story and other tales. New York 1852, London 1853, 1853 (enlarged), 1864; ed D. J. Taylor, as A shabby genteel story and other writings. London 1993 (EL). See also Miscellanies. Contains The professor, The Bedford Row conspiracy, A little dinner at Timmins's (from Punch 27 May–29 July 1848).

Men's wives. Fraser's Mag March–Nov 1843; New York 1852, London 1853, 1859 (rptd); see also Miscellanies.

Jeames's diary, A legend of the Rhine and Rebecca and Rowena. New York 1853, 1859 (rptd); see also Miscellanies.

Mr Brown's letters to a young man about town; with the Proser and other papers. Punch 1845, 1848–51; New York 1853, London 1859, 1866 (rptd); see also Miscellanies.

Punch's prize novelists, The fat contributor and Travels in London. Punch 1844–5, 1847–8, 1850; New York 1853, 1859, 1865, 1868 (rptd); London 1856 (as Novels by eminent hands); Leipzig 1867 (with Sketches and travels); see also Miscellanies. Contains also Going to see a man hanged, from Fraser's Mag Aug 1840.

The English humourists of the eighteenth century: a series of lectures delivered in England, Scotland and the United States of America. 1853, 1853 (rev), Leipzig 1853, New York 1853, 1854, 1858, 1860, 1864 (rptd), 1867 (new ed), London 1858, 1863 (rptd); ed E. Regel 6 vols Halle 1885–91; ed W. L. Phelps, New York 1900. Notes by G. Hodder.

The Newcomes: memoirs of a most respectable family, edited by Arthur Pendennis esqre. 24 monthly pts Oct 1853–Aug 1855; Harper's Mag Nov 1853–Oct 1855; 2 vols 1854–5, 4 vols Leipzig 1854–5, 2 vols New York 1855, 1856, 1859, 1865, 1867, 1868 (rptd), 1 vol London 1860 (rev), 1863 (rptd).

The rose and the ring, or the history of Prince Giglio and Prince Bulbo: a fireside pantomime for great and small children, by Mr M. A. Titmarsh. 1855 (for 1854), 1855, 1855, New York 1855, London 1866, 1867; ed G. N. Ray, New York 1947 (ms facs).

Miscellanies: prose and verse. 4 vols 1855–7, 1861, 1865. Vol 1 (4 pts) 1855 contains Ballads, The book of snobs, The fatal boots (i.e. Stubbs's calendar) and Cox's diary (i.e. Barber Cox from Comic almanac 1840), The tremendous adventures of Major Gahagan (i.e. Some passages in the life of Major Gahagan); vol 2 (3 pts) 1856 contains: The memoirs of Mr Charles J. Yellowplush and the diary of C. Jeames de la Pluche esq, Sketches and travels in London (including Mr Brown's letters to a young man), Novels by eminent hands (i.e. Punch's prize novelists), Character sketches (from Heads of the people 1840–1); vol 3 (3 pts) 1856 contains The Memoirs of Barry Lyndon esq, Burlesques (A legend of the Rhine, Rebecca and Rowena), A little dinner at Timmins's, The Bedford Row conspiracy; vol 4 (3 pts) 1857 contains The Fitz-Boodle papers, Men's wives (omitting The —'s wife), A shabby genteel story, The history of Samuel Titmarsh and the great Hoggarty diamond.

Ballads. Boston 1856. See also Miscellanies.

A little dinner at Timmins's and The Bedford Row conspiracy. Leipzig 1857, New York 1867; see also A shabby genteel story and Miscellanies.

Christmas books. 1857. Contains Mrs Perkins's ball, 'Our street', Doctor Birch and his young friends.

The Virginians: a tale of the last century. 24 monthly pts Nov 1857–Oct 1859; Harper's Mag Dec 1857–Oct 1859; New York Semi-weekly Tribune Nov 1857–Oct 1859, New York Weekly Tribune Nov 1857–Oct 1859; 2 vols 1858–9, 4 vols Leipzig 1858–9, 1 vol New York 1859, London 1863 (rev); ed G. Saintsbury and J. L. Robertson 1911; ed G. Sorensen, unpbd diss Univ of Minnesota 1966.

The four Georges: sketches of manners, morals, court and town life. Cornhill Mag July–Oct 1860; Harper's Mag Aug–Nov 1860; New York 1860, 1862, 1864 (rptd), 1860 (new ed), London 1861, 1861, 1862, 1866 (rptd), Leipzig 1861; ed G. Meredith and T. Bayne 1903.

Lovel the widower. Cornhill Mag Jan–June 1860; Harper's Mag Feb–July 1860; New York 1860, London 1861 (rev).

A leaf out of a sketch book 1861 (a T. J. Wise forgery).

The adventures of Philip on his way through the world, shewing who robbed him, who helped him, and who passed him by. Cornhill Mag Jan 1861–Aug 1862; Harper's Mag Feb 1861–Sep 1862; 3 vols 1862, 2 vols Leipzig 1862, 1 vol New York 1862; Columbia SC 1864.

Roundabout papers. Cornhill Mag Jan 1860–Feb 1863; 1863, 1864 (rptd), New York 1863, 1864 (rptd); ed J. E. Wells, New York 1925 (from ms).

Miscellanies. 6 vols New York 1864. Rptd from New York edns of 1852–3.

Denis Duval. Cornhill Mag March–June 1864; Harper's Mag Apr–Aug 1864; New York 1864, London 1867, Leipzig 1867; ed J. Schacht, unpbd diss Univ of Illinois 1949.

Early and late papers hitherto uncollected. Ed J. T. Fields, Boston 1867. From Fraser's Mag, Quart Rev, Cornhill Mag etc 1841–63.

Miscellanies vol 5. Boston 1870. Contains Catherine (from Harper's Mag May 1839–Feb 1840), Christmas books, Ballads etc.

The students' quarter: or Paris five and thirty years since. [1874?]. From Corsair (New York), 24 Aug 1839–18 Jan 1840. All except More aspects of Paris life rev and rptd in The Paris sketch book, 1840.

The orphan of Pimlico: and other sketches, fragments and drawings. 1876. Notes by A. I. Thackeray.

Sultan Stork and other stories and sketches (1829–44), now first collected [by R. H. Shepherd]. 1887. From Snob 1829, Fraser's Mag 1829, 1842, Nat Standard 1833–4, The Times 1837, Ainsworth's Mag 1842 etc.

Reading a poem. 1891 (priv ptd). From Britannia 1, 8 May 1841.

The Heroic Adventures of M. Boudin. Harpers' New Monthly 1891; Syracuse 1980 (first book edn).

Loose sketches, an eastern adventure etc. 1894. Loose sketches by M. A. Titmarsh from Britannia 1 May–5 July 1841; An eastern adventure of the fat contributor from Punch's pocket-book 1847; Preface to Sketches after English landscape painters by L. Marvy 1850.

The hitherto unidentified contributions of W. M. Thackeray to Punch, with a complete authoritative bibliography from 1845 to 1848. Ed M. H. Spielmann 1899.

Mr Thackeray's writings in the National Standard and the Constitutional. Ed W. T. Spencer 1899.

Stray papers: being stories, reviews, verses, and sketches 1821–47. Ed 'Lewis Melville' 1901. Subtitle should read 1829–51.

The new sketch book: being essays now first collected from the Foreign Quarterly Review. Ed R. S. Garnett 1906.

The knights of Borsellen: a hitherto unpublished romance. Harper's Mag July 1911. Notes by Lady Ritchie.

Thackeray's contributions to the Morning Chronicle. Ed G. N. Ray, Urbana IL 1955. *See* E. M. White, SB 19 1966.
Letters from a club arm-chair. Ed H. Summerfield, Nineteenth-Century Fiction 18 1964.
'Bluebeard at Breakfast': An Unpublished Thackeray Manuscript. Ed J. McMaster. Dickens Studies Annual 8 1980.
Early Verse by 'Unfortunate W. Thackeray'. Ed J. McMaster. Victorian Newsletter 62 1982.
William Makepeace Thackeray: An Uncollected Paris Letter from 'The Constitutional'. Ed R. Pearson. N&Q 238 1993.

Letters

A collection of letters of Thackeray 1847–55. Ed J. O. Brookfield, Scribner's Mag Apr–Oct 1887; 1887.
Thackeray's letters to an American family. Ed L. W. Baxter, Century Mag Nov 1903–Mar 1904; 1904.
Some family letters of Thackeray, together with recollections by his kinswoman B. W. Cornish. 1911.
Unpublished letters. Ed C. K. Shorter 1916 (priv ptd).
Thackeray and Edward FitzGerald, a literary friendship: unpublished letters and verses by Thackeray. Ed C. K. Shorter 1916 (priv ptd). Introd by Lady Ritchie.
Letters of Anne Thackeray Ritchie, with forty-two additional letters from her father. Ed H. Ritchie 1924.
The letters and private papers of Thackeray. Ed G. N. Ray 4 vols Cambridge MA 1945–6; Ed G. N. Ray 4 vols Cambridge MA 1945–46; The letters and private papers of Thackeray. A supplement. Ed E. F. Harden 2 vols New York 1994.
Hardy, C. E. ed. John Bowes and the Bowes Museum. Newcastle upon Tyne 1970.
Landow, G. P. Some new Thackeray letters. ELN 10 1973.
Meyer, H. E. Thackeray's letters to Baron Tauchnitz. N&Q 219 1974.
Harden, E. F. Thackeray and his publishers: two uncollected letters concerning Vanity Fair and Esmond. Papers on Language and Literature 12 1976.
Harden, E. F. Thackeray's 'Rebecca and Rowena': a further document. N&Q 222 1977.
Weinstein, M. A. A Thackeray letter dated and his verses explained. N&Q 222 1977.
Harden, E. F. Thackeray and the Carlyles: seven further letters. Studies in Scottish literature 14 1979.
McCrimmon, B. Thackeray to Panizzi, 1848. Manuscripts 33 1981.
Scharnhorst, G. An uncollected letter from Thackeray to James T. Fields. Amer N&Q 24 1985.
Harden, E. F. Selected letters. 1997.

§2

Biographies

'Taylor, Theodore'. Thackeray: the humourist and the man of letters. 1864, New York 1864 (enlarged).
Trollope, A. Thackeray. 1879 (EML).
Ritchie, A. Biographical Introductions. In Centenary Biographical Edition of Thackeray's Works. 1910. Rptd in The two Thackeray's, New York 1988.
Melville, L. William Makepeace Thackeray. 1910.
Dodds, J. Thackeray: a critical portrait. New York 1941.
Stevenson, L. The showman of Vanity Fair. New York 1947.
Tillotson, G. Thackeray the novelist. Cambridge 1954.
Ray, G. N. Thackeray: the uses of adversity. 1955; Thackeray: the age of wisdom. 1958.
Forster, M. Memoirs of a Victorian gentlemen. 1978.
Monsarrat, A. An uneasy Victorian: Thackeray the man, 1811–1863. 1980.
Ferris, I. William Makepeace Thackeray. Boston 1983.
Peters, C. Thackeray's universe: shifting worlds of imagination and reality. 1987.

Textual and Bibliographical Criticism

Gulliver, H. S. Thackeray's literary apprenticeship. Valdosta GA 1934.
Randall, D. A. Notes towards a correct collation of the first edition of Vanity Fair. PBSA 42 1948.
Winegarner, L. Thackeray's contributions to the British and Foreign Review. JEGP 47 1948.
Stokes, G. C. Thackeray as historian: two newly identified contributions to Fraser's Magazine. Nineteenth-Century Fiction 22 1967.
Hawes, D. Thackeray and the National Standard. RES 23 1972.
Sutherland, J. Thackeray's patchwork: a note on the composition of the eleventh chapter of Henry Esmond. YES 1 1971.
Sutherland, J. A date for the early composition of Vanity Fair. ES 53 1972.
Shillingsburg, P. L. Thackeray texts: a guide to inexpensive editions. Costerus n.s. 2 1974.
Sorensen, G. C. Thackeray texts and bibliographical scholarship. Costerus n.s. 2 1974.
Sutherland, J. The composition of Thackeray's Philip. YULG 48 1974.
Sutherland, J. Thackeray at work. 1974.
Sutherland, J. Thackeray's notebook for Henry Esmond. Costerus n.s. 2 1974.
Sutherland, J. A Vanity Fair mystery: the delay in publication. Costerus n.s. 2 1974.
Shillingsburg, P. L. Thackeray's Pendennis: a rejected page of manuscript. HLQ 38 1975.
The Thackeray Newsletter. 1975– . Frequent bibliographical and textual notes, not cited separately.
Goodwin, K. L. Towards an ideal edition of Vanity Fair. N&Q 221 1976; *see* Shillingsburg, P. L. N&Q 222 1977.
Harden, E. F. Thackeray's Miscellanies. PBSA 71 1977.
James, E. William Makepeace Thackeray's The Newcomes in America. Proof 5 1977.
Roos, D. A. A new speech by Thackeray. N&Q 222 1977.
Gaskell, P. Thackeray, Henry Esmond, 1952. In his From writer to reader: studies in editorial method. Oxford 1978.
Oram, R. W. Thackeray translations of German poetry and his Weimar commonplace book. N&Q 223 1978.
Shillingsburg, P. L. Textual problems in editing Thackeray. In Editing nineteenth-century fiction. J. Millgate ed. New York 1978.
Harden, E. F. The emergence of Thackeray's serial fiction. Athens GA 1979.
Shillingsburg, P. L. Editorial problems are readers' problems. Browning Institute Stud 9 1981.
Shillingsburg, P. L. Final touches and patches in Vanity Fair: the first edition. Stud in the Novel 13 1981.
Shillingsburg, P. L. Pendennis revised. Etudes Anglaises 34 1981.
Shillingsburg, P. L. The printing, proof-reading, and publishing of Thackeray's Vanity Fair: the first edition. SB 34 1981; rev in Pegasus in harness 1992.
Oram, R. W. The confederate Thackeray: Evans and Cogswell's The adventures of Philip. Amer Bk Collector n.s. 4 1983.
Harden, E. F. Thackeray's English Humourists and Four Georges. Newark DE 1985.
Sutherland, J. The genesis of Thackeray's Denis Duval. RES 37 1986.
Sutherland, J. Thackeray and France, 1842. N&Q 228 1986.
Goldfarb, S. Repeated discomposure: a Vanity Fair textual problem. ELN 24 1987.
Oram, R. W. 'Catalogues of war': Thackeray's 'Essay on Pumpernickel'. Victorians Inst Jnl 15 1987.
Shillingsburg, P. L. Thackeray and Punch; Bradbury and Evans and Smith, Elder. Thackeray Newsletter 26 1987.
Clarke, M. A mystery solved: Ainsworth's criminal romances censured in Frasers's by J. Hamilton Reynolds, not Thackeray. Victorian Periodicals Rev 23 1990.

Shillingsburg, P. L. Pegasus in harness: Victorian publishing and W. M. Thackeray. Charlottsville VA 1992.

Secondary Criticism: Bibliographies

Flamm provides a comprehensive listing of reviews; Tillotson and Hawes's Critical heritage *and Collins's* Interviews and recollections *reprint the most important ones.*

Stevenson, L. William Makepeace Thackeray. In Victorian fiction: a guide to research, ed Stevenson, Cambridge MA 1964.

Flamm, Dudley. Thackeray's critics: an annotated bibliography of British and American criticism 1836–1901. Chapel Hill NC 1967.

Thackeray studies. Thackeray Newsletter (semi-annual) 1975– .

Olmsted, J. C. Thackeray and his twentieth century critics: an annotated bibliography 1900–1975. New York 1977.

Vann, J. D. Unrecorded reviews of Thackeray's Paris sketch-book. PBSA 71 1977.

Colby, R. A. In Victorian fiction: a second guide to research. Ed G. H. Ford 1978.

Colby, R. A. Thackeray studies, 1975–79. Studies in the novel 13 1981.

Colby, R. A. Thackeray studies, 1979–1982. Dickens Studies Annual 1983.

Goldfarb, S. William Makepeace Thackeray: an annotated bibliography 1976–1987. New York 1989.

Shillingsburg, P. L. Thackeray studies, 1983–1993. Dickens Studies Annual 1994.

Collections of Criticism

Tillotson, G. and Hawes, D. (ed). Thackeray: the critical heritage. 1968.

Welsh, A. (ed) Thackeray: a collection of critical essays. Teaneck NJ 1968.

Sundell, M. G. (ed) Twentieth century interpretations of 'Vanity Fair': a collection of critical essays. Teaneck NJ 1969.

Collins, P. (ed). Thackeray: interviews and recollections, 2 vols 1983.

Bloom, H. (ed). William Makepeace Thackeray: modern critical views. New York 1987.

Bloom, H. (ed). William Makepeace Thackeray's Vanity Fair: modern critical interpretations. New York 1987.

Landmark Works of Criticism, pre–1920:

Note that the bibliographies of secondary materials by Flamm, Olmsted, and Goldfarb above combine to list nearly all Thackeray criticism to 1987.

Dickens, C. In memoriam W. M. T. Cornhill Mag Feb 1864.

Bagehot, W. Sterne and Thackeray. Nat Rev Apr 1864; rptd in his Literary studies, 1879.

Senior, N. W. In his Essays on fiction, 1864.

Taylor, B. Thackeray. Atlantic Monthly Mar 1864.

[Grego, J.] Thackerayana: notes and anecdotes illustrated by nearly 600 sketches by Thackeray. 1875, 1901.

Irvine, J. W. A study for Colonel Newcome. Nineteenth Cent Oct 1893.

Howells, W. D. In his My literary passions. New York 1895.

Saintsbury, G. A consideration of Thackeray. Oxford 1931. Introds rptd from Oxford edn of Thackeray's works.

Spielmann, M. H. In his History of Punch, 1895.

'Melville Lewis' (L. S. Benjamin). Some aspects of Thackeray. 1911.

Brownell, W. C. In his Victorian prose masters, New York 1901.

Whibley, C. William Makepeace Thackeray. 1903.

Mudge, I. G. and M. E. Sears. A Thackeray dictionary. 1910. [PLS]

Charlotte Elizabeth Browne, later Phelan, later Tonna, 'Charlotte Elizabeth' 1790–1846

The following institutions have correspondence by Charlotte Elizabeth Tonna: The Dreer Collection, The Historical Soc of Pennsylvania, Philadelphia; BL; Nat Lib of Ireland, Dublin; John Rylands Univ Lib of Manchester; NLS. The Nat Lib of Ireland holds ms and other poems. Mss of three poems are in the possession of Joseph A. Kestner; see his Three unpublished manuscripts of poems by Charlotte Elizabeth Tonna, Papers on Lang and Lit *23, Spring 1987, which includes transcriptions.*

Collections

Tales and illustrations: chiefly intended for young persons. Dublin 1829, 1854.

The works of Charlotte Elizabeth. With an introduction by Mrs H. B. Stowe. 3 vols New York 1844–5.

The works of Charlotte Elizabeth. With an introduction by Mrs H. B. Stowe. 2 vols New York 1844, 1845 (2nd edn), 1846 (4th edn), 1847 (5th edn), 1848 (6th edn), 1849 (7th edn), 1850 (8th edn), 1852.

Posthumous and other poems. 1846.

The minor poems of Charlotte Elizabeth, written especially for juvenile readers. Dublin 1848.

Short stories for children. [1st ser]. Dublin 1854 (6th edn), New York 1857, Edinburgh 1861.

Short stories for children. 2nd ser. Dublin 1854.

Juvenile stories for juvenile readers. By Charlotte Elizabeth and other writers. Dublin 1858.

Juvenile tales for juvenile readers. 1861.

Little tales for little readers. Edinburgh 1861.

Charlotte Elizabeth's stories. 8 vols New York 1868.

Selections

Novelle scelte ed instruttive: tradotte dall'inglese de Carlotta Elizabetta, ed altri. Dublin 1828.

In The British female poets, ed G. W. Bethune, Philadelphia 1854.

§1

The Glow-worm. Dublin 1820, 1831 (3rd edn).

The Shepherd boy and the deluge. 1823.

Zadoc, the outcast of Israel: a tale. 1825.

Osric: a missionary tale; with The garden, and other poems. Dublin 1826, New York 1845, 1847 [reissue].

Osric [and Izram] and other poems. New York 1848.

Philip and his garden. Dublin 1826, another edn 1826 (as Philip, and his garden: and other tales suitable for Sabbath schools), New York 1843.

Anne Bell: or, the faults. Dublin 1826.

Perseverance; or, Walter and his little school. 1826.

The Grandfather's tales. 4 pts (with individual title pages dated 1823, 1824, 1825, 1826). 1826.

Rachel: a tale. 1826, 1862.

The simple flower. Dublin 1826 (2nd edn).

Consistency. 1826.

Izram, a Mexican tale; and other poems. 1826, New York 1845, 1847 [reissue].

The net of lemons. 1826.

The hen and her chickens. Dublin 1827 (3rd edn).

A visit to St George's chapel, Windsor, on the evening succeeding the funeral of his late Royal Highness the Duke of York. 1827. Poem.

Edward, the orphan boy, a tale founded on facts. Clapham 1827.

The bird's nest. Dublin 1827 (5th edn), 1828 (6th edn).

The system; a tale of the West Indies. 1827, 1832.

The moth. Dublin [1828?].

The willow tree. Dublin 1828.

A friendly address to converts from the Roman Catholic Church. 1828.

The fortune teller. Dublin 1829, 1832 (2nd edn).

The swan. Dublin 1829.

The Rockite, an Irish story. 1829, 1846 [4th edn enlarged].
REVIEW: Athenaeum 91 1829.

Maternal martyrdom: a fact, ilustrative [*sic*] of the improved spirit of popery, in the nineteenth century. [1830?]

Little oaths. Dublin 1830.

A respectful appeal to the primates and prelates of the church, on the present crisis. [1830?]

The burying ground. Dublin 1830.
A letter to a friend, containing a few heads for consideration, on subjects that trouble the Church. 1831.
The baby. Dublin 1831 (2nd edn).
The wasp. Dublin 1831 (2nd edn).
'Try again'. Dublin 1831 (2nd edn).
Answering again. Dublin 1831.
The fragments. Dublin 1831 (2nd edn).
An address to the Christian friends and supporters of the British and Foreign Bible Society. 1831.
The dying sheep. Dublin 1832 (2nd edn).
The girl's best ornament. Boston 1832.
The museum. Dublin 1832, 1837 (3rd edn).
The happy mute; or, the dumb child's appeal. c. 1832, 1833 (2nd edn rev), 1835 (4th edn enlarged).
The Bible the best book. Dublin 1832 (3rd edn).
The bow in the cloud. Dublin 1832 (3rd edn).
Combination: a tale founded on facts. 1832, New York 1844.
REVIEW: American Biblical Repository, 2nd ser 11 (1844).
Ireland's crisis. 1832.
White lies. Dublin 1833 (3rd edn).
The oak-grove. Dublin 1833 (2nd edn).
Derry, a tale of the revolution. 1833 (also called The Siege of Derry; or, suffering of the Protestants), 1847 (10th edn), 1873.
Good and bad luck. Dublin 1834 (3rd edn).
Grumbling. Dublin 1834, [1850?].
A few words on the Eightieth Psalm. 1835.
The mole. Dublin 1835.
The Newfoundland fisherman. A true story. [1835?]
The deserter. Dublin 1836; tr Fr (by P. F. J. Braure) 1853.
Letter writing. Dublin 1836 (2nd edn).
Chapters on flowers. 1836, 1844 (6th edn).
Floral biography; or chapters on flowers. New York 1840, 1853 (8th edn), 1886.
The industrious artist. Dublin 1836 (2nd edn).
Alice Benden, or, the bowed shilling. 1838.
Passing thoughts. 1838.
Letters from Ireland. 1837, 1838.
Glimpses of the past. 1839.
The Lady Flora Hastings. A brief sketch. Thames Ditton 1839.
The flower garden; or, chapters on flowers, a sequel to floral biography. New York 1840.
Helen Fleetwood. First serialised in The Christian Lady's Mag, Sep 1839–Mar 1841. 1841, New York 1844, London 1846, 1848, 1852.
Conformity: a tale. 1841.
Falsehood and truth. Liverpool 1841.
A peep into number ninety [of Tracts for the Times by J. H. Newman]. 1841.
The bee. New York 1842, 1864.
Backbiting. New York 1842, 1854. Another edn (with The visit) 1854, Philadelphia 186?.
Dangers and duties. A tale. 1841.
'Principalities and powers in heavenly places'. 1842.
The flower of innocence: or, Rachel: a true narrative: with other tales. New York 1842.
The simple flower and other tales. New York 1842.
Israel's ordinances. A few thoughts on their perpetuity respectfully suggested in a letter to the Right Rev the Bishop of Jerusalem. 1843.
Second causes; or, up and be doing. Dublin 1843.
Promising and performing. New York 1843.
The glory of Israel; or, letters to Jewish children on the early history of their nation. Philadelphia 1843.
The two carpenters. New York [18?].
Jack, the dumb boy. New York [18?].
James Orwell, the mountain cottager. New York [184?].
Judah's lion. 1843; tr Fr Toulouse 1855.
The wrongs of woman. 4 pts (Milliners and dress-makers, The forsaken home, The little pin-headers, The lace-runners) 1843–4; New York 1843–4 (The wrongs of woman: milliners and dress-makers), 1843 (as The wrongs of women [*sic*]), 1843 (The wrongs of woman), 1844, London 1845 (4th edn), 1852; [another edn of pt 1] Milliners and dressmakers [*sic*], New York 1843 (3rd edn); 1844 (3rd edn), [another edn of part 3] The little pin-headers, in I. Kovacevic, Fact into fiction, Leicester 1975.
Ridley, Latimer, Cranmer, and other English martyrs. New York 1844.
The simple flower. New York [184?].
Female martyrs of the English reformation. New York 1844.
The Church visible in all ages. 1844.
The yew-tree. New York 1844.
Kindness to animals. 1844, 1876 (rev edn).
Mesmerism. A letter to Miss Martineau. 1844.
Judaea capta. An historical sketch of the siege and destruction of Jerusalem by the Romans. 1845. Tr Ger Stuttgart 1858.
The convent bell; and other poems. New York 1845. (Contains Convent bell only.)
A simple flower and other tales. New York 1845.
The angel child: ballad. Boston 1845.
Posthumous and other poems. 1846.
Wants and wishes. New York 1846.
The Snow-ball. New York 1846.
Richard and Rover. New York 1846.
Days of old. Philadelphia 1847.
The faithful dogs. New York [18?].
The rose-bud. New York 1848.
The red berries. New York 1848.
War with the saints. (Stories of the crusade against the Albigenses.) 1848 (2nd edn). War with the saints: Count Raymond of Toulouse, and the Crusade against the Albigenses under Pope Innocent III, New York 1848 (2nd edn). Count Raymound [*sic*] of Toulouse, and the crusade against the Albigenses under Pope Innocent III, New York 1860.
Humility before honor. Albany NY 1849.
Memoir of John Britt: the happy mute. Compiled from the writings, letters, and conversation of Charlotte Elizabeth. 1850.
Grumbling. Dublin [1850?].
Bible characteristics. 1851.
The peep of day. 1852, tr Mpongwe, Gabon, West Africa 1852.
Wants and wishes. New York 1854.
Protection: or, the candle and the dog. New York 1854.
Stories from the Bible. To which is added, Paul the martyr of Palestine. 1861.
Philip and his garden. With other stories. 1861.
The star. New York nd.
Little George Bell. 1861.
The boat. New York [18?].
The two servants. New York 1908.

Prefaces

S., L. Meditations: or, remains of L. S. 1834.
Renoult, J. B. Answer of Mr Renoult . . . to his father. 1834.
Seymour, C. Twenty-six sermons. 1835.
Myers, A. M. Both One in Christ. 1840.

Editions

Fox, J. The English martyrology, abridged from Foxe [*sic*], by Charlotte Elizabeth. 1840.

Works published

The perils of the nation. An appeal to the legislature, the clergy, and the higher and middle classes. 1843.
REVIEW: The Times 2 May 1843.

Contributions to periodicals

Editor, The Christian Lady's Mag, 1834–46; The Protestant Annual 1840; 1841 (2nd edn, as Protestant Christian Keepsake, 1841); The Protestant Mag 1841–4.

Works attributed to Tonna

Robert and Frederick. 1842.

Remedies suggested for some of the evils which constitute 'the perils of the nation'. 1844.

§2

Tonna, C. E. Personal recollections. 1841, New York 1844 (2 edns), 3rd edn continued to the close of her life. London 1847, New York 1850; London 1854 (4th edn), New York 1858.

REVIEW: [Hall, E. B.] Christian Examiner (Boston) 39 July 1845.

Mrs Tonna. GM 180, Oct 1846. Obituary.

Tonna, L. H. J. A Memoir of Charlotte Elizabeth: embracing the period from the close of her personal recollections to her death. New York 1847, Bristol 1852.

Balfour, C. L. A sketch of Charlotte Elizabeth. 1854.

Alexander, J. H. [pseud] [Jean Hester Buggs]. From darkness to light. Sheffield 1974.

Fryckstedt, M. C. Charlotte Elizabeth Tonna: a forgotten Evangelical writer. Studia Neophilologica 52 1980.

Kestner, J. A. Protest and reform: the British social narrative by women, 1827–1867. Madison WI 1985. [JAK]

Camilla Toulmin, later Crosland, Mrs Newton Crosland; 'Emma Grey', 'Mrs MaCarthy', 'Helena Herbert' 1812–95

§1

The little Berlin wool worker; or, cousin Caroline's visit. 1844.

Lays and legends illustrative of English life. 1845, 1852. Illus.

Poems. 1846.

Partners for life; a Christmas story. 1847.

Is it meekness or vanity? a tale. Miniature Lib of Fiction vol 6 1848.

Stratagems; a story. 1849.

Toil and trial; a story of London life. 1849.

The young lord, and other tales. (With Victorine Durocher by Mrs Sherwood) 1849, 1850.

Lydia; a woman's book. 1852.

English tales and sketches. 1853.

The gentleman of the family; a tale. Miniature Lib of Fiction vol 8 1853.

Stray leaves from shady places. 1853.

Memorable women; the story of their lives. 1854, [1870] (4th edn).

Hildred, the daughter. 1855.

Light in the valley; my experiences of spiritualism. 1857.

The neglected child; a tale. Miniature Lib of Fiction vol 12 1858.

Mrs Blake. 1862.

The island of the rainbow: a fairy tale. '1866' [1865]. Illus.

The diamond wedding: a Doric story; and other poems. 1871.

Hubert Freeth's prosperity. 1873.

Stories of the city of London. 1880. Illus.

Landmarks of a literary life, 1820–1892. 1893.

Contributions to periodicals

Poems

Dirge for a suicide. Reynolds's Misc 20 May 1848.

He loves but me. Reynolds's Misc 11 Sep 1852.

The mother's dream. Reynolds's Misc 6 Jan 1855.

Stories

The orphan milliners: a story of the West End. Illuminated Mag Apr 1844.

A railroad adventure. Ainsworth's Mag Mar 1845.

A story of the factories. Lloyd's Entertaining Jnl 11 July 1846.

The secret. New Monthly Belle Assemblée Dec 1848; rptd Reynolds's Misc 20 Jan 1849.

Mrs Jenkins's evening party. Sharpe's London Mag 1870.

Toulman first appeared in print in the Booleg Beauty *1838, and she contributed to* Chambers's Edinburgh Mag *for 54 years. She served as editor of the* Ladies Companion, *the* New Monthly Belle Assemblée *1848–9, and as sub-editor of* Friendship's Offering. *The majority of her work is in the form of poems, stories, and periodical articles.* [LA]

Anthony Trollope 1815–82

The most important collections of letters and private papers are held in the Taylor and Parrish Collections at Princeton, in the NLS and Bodleian. Locations of mss of individual texts, where known, are listed under titles.

Bibliographies and reference works

Lavington, M. In T. H. S. Escott, Anthony Trollope, 1913.

Sadleir, M. In his Excursions in Victorian Bibliography, 1922.

Irwin, M. L. Anthony Trollope: a bibliography. New York 1926.

Sadleir, M. Trollope: a bibliography. 1928, 1934 (rev), 1964, 1977.

Sadleir, M. In his XIX century fiction: a bibliographical record. 1951.

Tingay, L. O. The Trollope collector. 1985, 1992 (rev as Anthony Trollope: a collector's catalogue 1847–1990).

Collections

The following excludes collections solely of short fiction or of non-fictional contributions to periodicals. Photo-reproductions of early edns are included only when of scholarly interest.

Tauchnitz's British Authors. 90 vols Leipzig 1858–84 (includes 45 titles).

Library of Select Novels. New York 1862–77 (includes 12 titles).

Select Library of Fiction. 1866–80 (includes 27 titles).

Chronicles of Barsetshire. 8 vols 1878–9 (includes 6 titles).

Franklin Square Library. New York 1879–84 (includes 16 titles).

Railway Library. 1880–4 (includes 30 titles).

Seaside Library. New York 1881–4 (includes 46 titles).

Popular works. 1883–5 (includes 9 titles).

Collector's edn. Philadelphia 30 vols 1900–2 (the 6 Barsetshire and 6 Palliser novels).

New Pocket Library. 16 vols 1902–6 (includes 13 titles).

Everyman's Library. 10 vols 1907–29 (8 titles, including the Barsetshire novels).

World's Classics. 1907–48 (38 titles).

New Cent Library. 1913–14 (the 6 Barsetshire novels).

Nelson's Classics. 1917–52 (the 6 Barsetshire novels).

Shakespeare Head edn. Ed M. Sadleir 14 vols Oxford 1929 (the 6 Barsetshire novels and An autobiography).

Oxford Trollope. Ed F. Page and M. Sadleir 16 vols 1948–54 (includes 9 titles).

Penguin (originally Penguin English Lib; later Penguin Classics) 1967– (includes 17 titles).

The Pallisers 1973.

The Pallisers 14 vols New York 1979 (5 titles).

World's Classics. Oxford 1980–96 (49 vols, including 50 titles).

Selected works of Anthony Trollope. 62 vols New York 1981 (includes 36 titles).

Folio Soc edn. 1989– (includes 32 titles, newly illus).

Trollope Soc edn. 1989– (includes 32 titles, from the same setting as above, and with the original illustrations).

Everyman Paperback Library 1993– (includes 5 titles to 1997) (ELp).

Selections

The following excludes selections solely of short fiction or of non-fictional contributions to periodicals.

The Warden and Barchester Towers. New York 1870 (Lib of Select Novels), London 1914, New York 1936, 1948 (abridged), Boston 1966.

The Warden and Doctor Thorne. 1914.
Novels and stories. London 1946 (Barchester Towers, Malachi's cove, The Turkish bath, Mary Gresley, Father Giles of Ballymoy, Dr Wortle's school).
Nina Balatka and Linda Tressel. London 1946 (WC), 1991 (WC).
The Pallisers (abridged). 1974, New York 1975.
The Barchester chronicles (abridged). 1982.
Malachi's cove and other stories and essays. Padstow 1985.
An illus Autobiography and How the 'Mastiff's' went to Iceland. Gloucester 1987.
Barchester Towers, Miss Mackenzie and Cousin Henry. 1995.

§1

Novels

Photo-reproductions of early edns and details of illustrations are included below only when of scholarly interest.

The Macdermots of Ballycloran. 3 vols 1847, 1 vol [1859], 1861, 1865, 1866 (Select Lib of Fiction), Philadelphia [1870], London 1871, 1880 (Railway Lib), New York 1882 (Seaside Lib), New York 1894, London 1906 (New Pocket Lib), 3 vols New York 1979, 1981 (Selected works of Anthony Trollope), 1 vol New York 1988, Oxford 1989 (WC), London 1991 (Trollope Soc and Folio Soc edn).
REVIEWS: Critic 5 1847; Spectator 20 1847; [Chorley, H. F.] Athenaeum 1020 1847; John Bull 27 1847; Douglas Jerrold's Weekly Newspaper 29 May 1847; Howitt's Jnl of Lit and Popular Progress 1 1847; NMM n.s. 80 1847.

The Kellys and the O'Kellys, or landlords and tenants: a tale of Irish life. 3 vols 1848, 1 vol 1859, New York 1859, London 1866 (Select Lib of Fiction), 1871, 1880 (Railway Lib), New York 1882 (Seaside Lib), London 1906 (New Pocket Lib), 1929 (WC), New York 1937, 3 vols New York 1979, Oxford 1982 (WC), London 1992 (Trollope Soc and Folio Soc edn).
REVIEWS: [Chorley, H. F.] Athenaeum 1081 1848; Douglas Jerrold's Weekly Newspaper 22 July 1848; NMM n.s. 83 1848; Sharpe's London Mag 7 1848; The Times 7 Sep 1848.

La Vendée: an historical romance. 3 vols 1850, 1874 (Select Lib of Fiction), 1880 (Railway Lib), New York 1981 (Selected works of Anthony Trollope), 1994 (WC).
REVIEWS: Examiner 15 June 1850; [Chorley, H. F.] Athenaeum 1184 1850.

The Warden. 1855, Leipzig 1859 (Tauchnitz's British Authors), New York 1862, 1870 (Lib of Select Novels, with Barchester Towers), Philadelphia 1870, London 1878 (Chronicles of Barsetshire), New York 1885 (Seaside Lib), New York 1892, Philadelphia 1900 (Collector's edn), London 1902 (New Pocket Lib), 1904, 1906, 1907 (EL), New York 1907, London 1914 (New Cent Lib), 1914 (with Doctor Thorne), [1917?], 1918 (WC), 1925, 1925, New York 1925, 1925, London 1926, New York 1926, Boston 1926, London [1927?], 1928, 1929 (Nelson's Classics), Oxford 1929 (Shakespeare Head), New York 1931, 1932, 1935, 1936 (with Barchester Towers), London 1944, Bognor 1946 (abridged for children), London 1946, 1947 (abridged), New York 1948 (abridged, with Barchester Towers), London 1949, 1950, 1950 (abridged), New York 1950, London 1952 (Oxford Trollope), 1955, 1955, 1955, New York 1955, 1960, London 1961, 1961, New York 1962, 1964, Boston 1966 (with Barchester Towers), London 1967, New York 1968, London 1976, Oxford 1980 (WC), London 1984 (Pen), 1994 (ELp), 1995 (Trollope Soc and Folio Soc edn).
REVIEWS: Examiner 6 Jan 1855; Spectator 28 1855; [Jewsbury, G.] Athenaeum 1422 1855.
TRANSLATIONS: Fr (C. Berthoud) (serialised), L'union libérale, Neuchâtel 1879, 1879, (J. Staquet) Brussels 1946, Paris 1947; Ital (A. Lombardo), Milan 1951, (L. Berti) Milan 1952; Finnish, Helsinki 1953; Chinese, Beijing [1959]; Norwegian, Oslo 1966.

Barchester Towers. 3 vols 1857, 1 vol 1858, 2 vols Leipzig 1859 (Tauchnitz's British Authors), New York 1860, 1 vol London 1862, New York 1870 (Lib of Select Novels, with The Warden), Philadelphia 1870, 2 vols London 1878 (Chronicles of Barsetshire), 1 vol New York 1881 (Seaside Lib), 2 vols 1892, Philadelphia 1900 (Collector's edn), 1 vol London 1902 (New Pocket Lib), New York 1902, London 1903, 1904, 1906 (EL), 1906, 1908, New York 1908, Philadelphia 1908, London 1909, 1913, New York 1923, London 1924, 1925, 1925 (WC), New York 1925, Boston 1926, New York 1926, London [1927?], 1928, 2 vols Oxford 1929 (Shakespeare Head), London 1931, New York 1936 (with The Warden), London 1941, 2 vols 1941, 1 vol New York 1945, London 1946, 1946, 1946 (abridged), 1946 (in Novels and stories), 1947, 1948, Canada 1948 (abridged), New York 1948 (abridged, with The Warden), London 1949, New York 1949, London 1952, 1952 (abridged), Cleveland OH 1952, London 1953 (Oxford Trollope), 1956 (abridged), 1957, New York 1958, 1959, 1962, London 1963 (abridged), New York 1963, 1963, London 1966 (abridged), Boston 1966 (with The Warden), London [1966?], 2 vols 1974, 1 vol 1977, 1980, Oxford 1980 (WC), London 1983 (Pen), 1987, 1994 (ELp), 1995 (Trollope Soc and Folio Soc edn), Oxford 1996 (WC).
REVIEWS: Examiner 16 May 1857; Spectator 30 1857; Leader 8 1857; [St John, H.] Athenaeum 1544 1857; Saturday Rev 3 1857; Eclectic Rev n.s. 2 1857; [Dallas, E. S.] The Times 13 Aug 1857; [Meredith, G.] Westminster Rev n.s. 12 1857; Montégut, E. Le roman des moeurs en Angleterre, Revue des Deux Mondes 2nd ser 17 1858.
TRANSLATIONS: Fr (L. Bartel), Paris 1886; Swed (H. Jernström), Stockholm 1947; Norwegian, Oslo 1951; Slovene (I. Cankar), Lublijana 1951; Ital (A. Lombardo), Milan 1952, (V. Sanna) Turin 1956; Rus, Moscow 1970.

The three clerks: a novel. 3 vols '1858' [1857], 1 vol 1859, 1860, New York 1860, 1865, 2 vols Berlin 1874, 1 vol New York 1886 (Seaside Lib), London 1900, 1903, 1904 (New Pocket Lib), 1907 (WC), 1932 (simplified), New York 1981, 3 vols 1981 (Selected Works of Anthony Trollope), Gloucester 1986, Oxford 1989 (WC), London 1992 (Trollope Soc and Folio Soc edn).
REVIEWS: Saturday Rev 4 1857; Spectator 30 1857; Examiner 19 Dec 1857; Leader 8 1857; [Jewsbury, G.] Athenaeum 1574 1857.
TRANSLATION: Hebrew 1958.

Doctor Thorne: a novel. 3 vols 1858, 1 vol New York 1858 (Lib of Select Novels), 2 vols Leipzig 1858 (Tauchnitz's British Authors), 1 vol London 1859, 1865 (Select Lib of Fiction), New York 1866, London 1871, 1879 (Chronicles of Barsetshire), 1880 (Railway Lib), 2 pts New York 1882 (Seaside Lib), 2 vols 1892, Philadelphia 1900 (Collector's edn), 1 vol London 1902 (New Pocket Lib), 1906, 1909, 1909 (EL), 1914, 1914 (with The Warden), 1924, 1925, 1926 (WC), Boston 1926, London [1927?], 1928, 2 vols Oxford 1929 (Shakespeare Head), 1 vol London 1947, 1949, 1957 (simplified), Cambridge MA 1959, New York 1961, London 1968, 1978, Oxford 1980 (WC), London 1991 (Pen), 1996 (Trollope Soc and Folio Soc edn), 1997 (ELp).
REVIEWS: Examiner 29 May 1858; Leader 9 1858; Spectator 31 1858; [Jewsbury, G.] Athenaeum 1597 1858; Saturday Rev 5 1858; Harper's Mag 17 1858.
TRANSLATIONS: Du (van Weterheene), Amsterdam 1860; Danish, Copenhagen 1861, (L. Pihl) Copenhagen 1988; Fr (serialised), Revue Britannique Jan–Nov 1863, Naumburg 1863, Paris 1863, Paris 1864; Ger (A. Kretzschmar), Wurzen 1863, Zurich 1954; Norwegian (O. Berthung), Oslo 1951–2.

The Bertrams: a novel. 3 vols 1859, 1 vol New York 1859, 2 vols Leipzig 1859 (Tauchnitz's British Authors), 1 vol London 1860, 1866 (Select Lib of Fiction), 1871, Manchester Weekly Times suppl 30 Jan 1876–9 June 1877, New York 1879 (Franklin Square Lib), London 1880 (Railway Lib), 1905 (New Pocket Lib), 3 vols New York 1981 (Selected Works of Anthony Trollope), 1 vol Gloucester 1986, New York 1987, Oxford 1991 (WC), London 1993 (Trollope Soc and Folio Soc edn).

REVIEWS: Spectator 32 1859; [Jewsbury, G.] Athenaeum 1639 1859; Illus London News 34 1859; Saturday Rev 7 1859; Examiner 2 Apr 1859; Leader 10 1859; [Dallas, E. S.] The Times 23 May 1859; Bentley's Quart Rev 1 1859; Nat Rev 9 1859; NMM 115 1859; Forgues, E. D. Romans de la vie anglaise, Revue des Deux Mondes 2nd ser 29 1860.
TRANSLATIONS: Ger (A. Kretzschmar), Wurzen 1859–60; Du, Sneed 1860; Danish 1863; Fr (serialised), Revue Nationale Apr–Oct 1864, Paris 1866.

Castle Richmond: a novel. 3 vols 1860, 1 vol New York 1860, 2 vols Leipzig 1860 (Tauchnitz's British Authors), 1 vol London 1861, 1866 (Select Lib of Fiction), 1871, 1880 (Railway Lib), New York 1882 (Seaside Lib), London 1906 (New Pocket Lib), 3 vols New York 1979, 1981 (Selected Works of Anthony Trollope), 1 vol London 1984, London 1989, 1994 (Trollope Soc and Folio Soc edn).
REVIEWS: [Jewsbury, G.] Athenaeum 1699 1860; Saturday Rev 9 1860; Spectator 33 1860; Br Quart Rev 32 1860; Harper's Mag 21 1860; Forgues, E. D. Romans de la vie anglaise, Revue des Deux Mondes 2nd ser 29 1860.
TRANSLATIONS: Danish 1860; Ger (A. Kretzschmar), Wurzen 1860; Fr (serialised), Revue Britannique Jan–Nov 1861, Naumburg 1863; Du, Amsterdam 1862.

Framley Parsonage (ms Vaughan Lib, Harrow School). Cornhill Mag 1–3, Jan 1860 [Dec 1859]–Apr 1861 illustr J. E. Millais, 3 vols 1861, 1 vol 1861, New York 1861, 2 vols Leipzig 1861 (Tauchnitz's British Authors), 1 vol London 1879 (Chronicles of Barsetshire), New York 1879 (Franklin Square Lib), 1884 (Seaside Lib), 2 vols 1892, Philadelphia 1900, 1 vol London 1903 (New Pocket Lib), 1904, 1906, 1906 (EL), 1908, 1909 (illustr J. E. Millais), Philadelphia 1909, London 1914 (New Cent Lib), 1924, 1925 (Nelson's Classics), 1925 (illustr J. E. Millais), 1926 (WC), Boston 1926, London [1927?] (illustr J. E. Millais), 1928, 2 vols Oxford 1929 (Shakespeare Head), 1 vol London 1941, 1947, 1947, 1978, Oxford 1980 (WC), London 1984 (Pen), New York 1989, London 1996 (Trollope Soc and Folio Soc edn), 1997 (ELp).
REVIEWS: [Dixon, W. H.] Athenaeum 1747 1861; Examiner 20 Apr 1861; Saturday Rev 11 1861; London Rev 2 1861; Br Quart Rev 34 1861; Eclectic Rev 8th ser 1 1861; 'J. A.' Sharpe's London Mag n.s. 19 1861; Westminster Rev n.s. 20 1861; Amer Theological Rev 3 1861; Dublin Univ Mag 59 1862.
TRANSLATIONS: Rus, St Petersburg 1861; Ger (A. Kretzschmar), Wurzen 1864; Norwegian, Oslo 1952.

Orley Farm (ms Taylor Collection, Princeton). 20 monthly pts Mar 1861–Oct 1862 (illustr J. E. Millais); Harper's Mag 22–6; May 1861–Dec 1862, London 2 vols 1861–2 (illustr J. E. Millais); 1 vol New York 1862 (illustr J. E. Millais); 3 vols Leipzig 1862 (Tauchnitz's British Authors), 1 vol London 1868 (Select Lib of Fiction), 1871, 1880 (Railway Lib), 1880, 2 pts New York 1882 (Seaside Lib), 3 vols 1905, 2 vols London 1906 (New Pocket Lib), 1 vol 1910, 1935 (WC), 2 vols 1935 (WC), 1 vol New York 1950, London 1951 (abridged), New York 1981 (illustr J. E. Millais), Oxford 1985 (WC), London 1993 (Trollope Soc and Folio Soc edn).
REVIEWS: [Dixon, W. H.] Athenaeum 1741 1861; Spectator 35 1862; [Dixon, W. H.] Athenaeum 1823 1862; Saturday Rev 14 1862; [Hutton, R. H.?] Spectator 33 1862; London Rev 5 1862; Examiner 25 Oct 1862; Mr Trollope and the lawyers, London Rev 5 1862; [Lewes, G. H., J. F. W. Herschel or J. W. Kaye] Cornhill Mag 6 1862; [Dallas, E. S.] The Times 26 Dec 1862; Home and Foreign Rev 2 1863; Nat Mag 13 1863; Nat Rev 16 1863; [Smith, A.] Novels and novelists of the present day, North Br Rev 38 1863; Amer Presbyterian Theological Rev n.s. 1 1863; Dublin Univ Rev 61 1863; Harper's Mag 26 1863; North Br Rev 40 1864.
TRANSLATIONS: Du, Amsterdam 1864; Rus, St Petersburg 1864; Ger (C. Markgraff), Wurzen 1864; Fr (serialised), Revue Nationale Mar 1865–Aug 1866.

The struggles of Brown, Jones and Robinson, by one of the firm. Cornhill Mag 4–5, Aug 1861–Mar 1862, New York 1862 (Lib of Select Novels), London 1870, New York 1882 (Seaside Lib), 1981 (Selected Works of Anthony Trollope), Oxford 1992 (WC).
REVIEWS: Amer Theological Rev 1862; Harper's Mag 25 1862; Br Quart Rev 53 1871; Westminster Rev n.s. 39 1871.

Rachel Ray: a novel (ms Arents Collection, NYPL). 2 vols 1863, 1 vol New York 1863 (Lib of Select Novels), 2 vols Leipzig (Tauchnitz's British Authors), 1 vol London 1864 (illustr J. E. Millais), 1866 (Select Lib of Fiction), 1871, 1880 (Railway Lib), New York 1884 (Seaside Lib), London 1906 (New Pocket Lib), 1924 (WC), New York 1952, 1980, 2 vols 1981 (Selected Works of Anthony Trollope), 1 vol Oxford 1988 (WC), London 1990 (Trollope Soc and Folio Soc edn), 1995 (Pen).
REVIEWS: [Jeaffreson, J. C.] Athenaeum 1877 1863; [E. Dicey?] Reader 2 1863; Saturday Rev 16 1863; Mr Trollope's caricature: Rachel Ray, Spectator 36 1863; London Rev 31 1863; [Dallas, E. S.] The Times 25 Dec 1863; Amer Presbyterian Theological Rev n.s. 2 1864; Harper's Mag 28 1864; Westminster Rev n.s. 25 1864.
TRANSLATIONS: Rus, St Petersburg 1864; Fr, Paris 1869.

The small house at Allington (ms Huntington). Cornhill Mag 6–9, Sep 1862–Apr 1864 (illustr J. E. Millais), Harper's Mag 25–9, Dec 1862–June 1864, 2 vols London 1864 (illustr J. E. Millais), 1 vol New York 1864, 3 vols Leipzig 1864 (Tauchnitz's British Authors), 1 vol London 1864, 2 vols 1879 (Chronicles of Barsetshire), 2 pts New York 1883 (Seaside Lib), 3 vols 1892, Philadelphia 1900 (Collector's edn), 2 vols London 1906 (New Pocket Lib), 1906, 1 vol 1909 (EL), 1909 (illustr J. E. Millais), 1914 (New Cent Lib), 1925 (illustr J. E. Millais), Boston 1926, London [1927?] (illustr J. E. Millais), 2 vols 1928, Oxford 1929 (Shakespeare Head), London 1939 (WC), 1 vol 1948 (Nelson's Classics), 1948, 1950 (WC), 1950, 1979, Oxford 1980 (WC), London 1991 (Pen), 1997 (Trollope Soc and Folio Soc edn).
REVIEWS: [Jeaffreson, J. C.] Athenaeum 1900 1864; Reader 3 1864; Spectator 37 1864; Illus London News 44 1864; London Rev 8 1864; Saturday Rev 17 1864; North Br Rev 40 1864; Amer Presbyterian Theological Rev n.s. 2 1864; Washburn, W. T. North Amer Rev 99 1864; Westminster Rev n.s. 26 1864.
TRANSLATIONS: Rus, St Petersburg 1864; Fr, Paris 1866; Norwegian, Oslo 1952.

Can you forgive her? (ms Beinecke Lib, Yale). 20 monthly pts Jan 1864–Aug 1865 (illustr H. K. Browne and E. Taylor); 2 vols 1864–5 (illustr H. K. Browne and E. Taylor); 1 vol New York 1865, 3 vols Leipzig 1865 (Tauchnitz's British Authors), 1 vol London 1866, 1868 (Select Lib of Fiction), 1871, 1880 (Railway Lib), 3 vols New York 1893, Philadelphia 1900 (Collector's edn), 2 vols London 1906 (New Pocket Lib), 1938 (WC), 1948 (Oxford Trollope), 1 vol 1972 (Pen), 1973 (The Pallisers), Oxford 1982 (WC), London 1989 (Trollope Soc and Folio Soc edn), 1994, 1994 (ELp).
REVIEWS: Westminster Rev n.s. 28 1865; Saturday Rev 20 1865; [Jewsbury, G.] Athenaeum 1975 1865; Spectator 38 1865; James, H. Nation 1 1865; Month 3 1865.
TRANSLATIONS: Danish 1866; Du, Amsterdam 1867.

Miss Mackenzie (ms Berg Collection, NYPL). 2 vols 1865, 1 vol New York 1865 (Lib of Select Novels), London 1868 (Select Lib of Fiction), 1871, 2 vols Berlin 1876, 1 vol London 1880 (Railway Lib), New York 1881 (Seaside Lib), London 1924 (WC), 2 vols New York 1981 (Selected works of Anthony Trollope), 1 vol 1987, Oxford 1988 (WC).
REVIEWS: Saturday Rev 19 1865; Spectator 38 1865; [Jewsbury, G.] Athenaeum 1953 1865; London Rev 10 1865; Reader 5 1865; Dublin Univ Mag 65 1865; James, H. Nation 1 1865; Westminster Rev n.s. 28 1865; [Dallas, E. S.] The Times 23 Aug 1865.
TRANSLATION: Du, Arnhem 1876.

The Belton estate (ms Huntington). Fortnightly Rev 1–3, 15 May 1865–1 Jan 1866, Littell's Living Age 88, July 1865–Jan 1866, 3 vols London '1866' [1865], 1 vol New York 1866 (Lib of Select Novels),

Philadelphia 1866, 2 vols Leipzig 1866 (Tauchnitz's British Authors), 1 vol London 1866, 1868 (Select Lib of Fiction), 1880 (Railway Lib), New York 1882 (Seaside Lib), 2 vols 1912, 1 vol London 1923 (WC), Oxford 1985 (WC), New York 1985, London 1991 (Trollope Soc and Folio Soc edn).

REVIEWS: James, H. Nation 2 1866; Spectator 3 1866; [Wilberforce] Athenaeum 1997 1866; Saturday Rev 21 1866; London Rev 12 1866; Harper's Mag 32 1866; Contemporary Rev 3 1866; Forgues, E. D. Le roman anglais contemporain, Revue des Deux Mondes 2nd ser 69 1867.

TRANSLATIONS: Fr (serialised), Revue Nationale Jan–July 1867, (E. Daillac) Paris 1875; Du (Lindo), Dordrecht 1867; Rus, St Petersburg 1871.

The Claverings (ms Taylor Collection, Princeton). Cornhill Mag 13–15, Feb 1866–May 1867 (illustr M. E. Edwards), Galaxy 1–3, May 1866–Mar 1867, Littell's Living Age 88–92 1866–7, in pts New York 1866–7, 1 vol New York 1866 (illustr M. E. Edwards, Lib of Select Novels), 2 vols London 1867 (illustr M. E. Edwards), New York 1867, 2 vols Leipzig 1867 (Tauchnitz's British Authors), 1 vol London 1871 (illustr M. E. Edwards), Boston 1871, London 1910, 1924 (WC), New York 1977 (illustr M. E. Edwards), Oxford 1986 (WC), London 1994 (Trollope Soc and Folio Soc edn).

REVIEWS: [Oliphant, M.] Blackwood's Mag 102 1867; Amer Presbyterian Theological Rev n.s. 5 1867; Spectator 40 1867; Living Age 93 1867; London Rev 14 1867; Saturday Rev 23 1867; Knight, J. Fortnightly Rev n.s. 1 1867; [Jewsbury, G.] Athenaeum 2068 1867; Harper's Mag 36 1867; Gorter, S. De Gids 3 1868.

TRANSLATIONS: Du (J. C. van Deventer), Dordrecht 1867; Rus, St Petersburg 1867; Norwegian, Stavanger 1875.

Nina Balatka: the story of a maiden of Prague (ms Arents Collection, NYPL). Blackwood's Mag 100–1, July 1866–Jan 1867, Littell's Living Age 91–2, 13 Oct 1866–9 Feb 1867, 2 vols Edinburgh 1867 (anon), 1 vol Leipzig 1867 (Tauchnitz's British Authors), Boston 1867, Edinburgh 1879 (with attribution to Trollope), London 1946 (WC, with Linda Tressel), 2 vols New York 1981 (Selected Works of Anthony Trollope), 1 vol Oxford 1991 (WC, with Linda Tressel), London 1996 (Trollope Soc and Folio Soc edn).

REVIEWS: [Chorley, H.] Athenaeum 2053 1867; London Rev 14 1867; [Hutton, R. H.?] Spectator 40 1867; Examiner 11 May 1867.

TRANSLATION: Chinese [1959?].

The last chronicle of Barset (ms Beinecke Lib, Yale). 32 weekly nos 1 Dec 1866–8 July 1867 (illustr G. H. Thomas), 2 vols 1867 (illustr G. H. Thomas), 1 vol New York 1867, 3 vols Leipzig 1867 (Tauchnitz's British Authors), 2 vols London 1869 (illustr G. H. Thomas), 1 vol 1872 (illustr G. H. Thomas), 2 vols 1876 (illustr G. H. Thomas), 1879 (Chronicles of Barsetshire), 2 pts New York 1883 (Seaside Lib), 3 vols 1892, Philadelphia 1900 (Collector's edn), 2 vols London 1906, 1909 (EL), 1 vol 1909 (illustr G. H. Thomas), 1910, 1914 (New Cent Lib), 2 vols 1924, 1 vol 1925 (illustr G. H. Thomas), 2 vols 1926 (Nelson's Classics), 1 vol Boston 1926, London [1927?] (illustr G. H. Thomas), 2 vols 1928, 4 vols Oxford 1929 (Shakespeare Head), 2 vols London 1932 (WC), 1 vol 1949, 1957 (abridged), Toronto 1961, New York 1964, Cambridge MA 1964, London 1967 (Pen), 1967, 2 vols 1969, 1 vol Oxford 1980 (WC), London 1980, 1993 (ELp), 1997 (Trollope Soc and Folio Soc edn).

REVIEWS: [Oliphant, M.] Blackwood's Mag 102 1867; Saturday Rev 24 1867; Spectator 40 1867; Examiner 20 July 1867; London Rev 15 1867; [Jewsbury, G.] Athenaeum 2075 1867; Br Quart Rev 46 1867; Harper's Mag 36 1867.

TRANSLATIONS: Du, Arnhem 1869; Swed (M. Angström), Stockholm 1945; Norwegian, Oslo 1952.

Linda Tressel. Blackwood's Mag 102–3, Oct 1867–May 1868, Littell's Living Age 95–7 1867–8, 2 vols Edinburgh 1868 (anon), 1 vol Boston 1868, Edinburgh 1879 (with attribution to Trollope), London 1946 (WC, with Nina Balatka), 2 vols New York 1981 (Selected Works of Anthony Trollope), 1 vol Oxford 1991 (WC, with Nina Balatka).

REVIEWS: [Jeaffreson, J. C.] Athenaeum 2117 1868; Br Quart Rev 48 1868; Nation 6 1868; Spectator 41 1868.

Phineas Finn: the Irish Member (ms Beinecke Lib, Yale). Saint Paul's Mag 1–4, Oct 1867–May 1869 (illustr J. E. Millais), Littell's Living Age 95–101 1867–9, New Eclectic 1–4 1867–9, New York 1868, 2 vols London 1869 (illustr J. E. Millais), 1 vol 1869 (Select Lib of Fiction), 3 vols Leipzig 1869 (Tauchnitz's British Authors), 1 vol London 1870, 1871, 1880 (Railway Lib), 2 pts New York 1882 (Seaside Lib), 3 vols 1893, Philadelphia 1901 (Collector's edn), 2 vols London 1911, 1929 (EL), 1937 (WC), 1949 (Oxford Trollope), 1 vol 1968, 1972 (Pen), 1973 (The Pallisers), Oxford 1982 (WC), London 1989 (Trollope Soc and Folio Soc edn), 1997 (ELp).

REVIEWS: Spectator 42 1869; Saturday Rev 27 1869; Harper's Mag 38 1869; 'M. B.', Contemporary Rev 12 1869; Dublin Rev n.s. 13 1869; [Rands, W. B.] Contemporary Rev 12 1870; De Gids 7 1870.

TRANSLATIONS: Du (J. H. Aronier), Arnhem 1870; Rus, St Petersburg 1873.

He knew he was right (ms Pierpont Morgan Lib, New York). 32 weekly nos 17 Oct 1868–22 May 1869 (illustr Marcus Stone), 8 monthly pts Nov 1868–June 1869 (illustr Marcus Stone), Every Saturday 6–7, Oct 1868–May 1869, Eclectic Mag 71–3 1868–9, 2 vols 1869 (illustr Marcus Stone), 2 pts New York 1869, 3 vols Leipzig 1869 (Tauchnitz's British Authors), 1 vol New York 1870, London 1871 (Select Lib of Fiction), 1871, 1880 (Railway Lib), 1948 (WC), Brisbane 1974, New York 1983, Oxford 1985 (WC), London 1993 (ELp), 1994 (Trollope Soc and Folio Soc edn).

REVIEWS: Harper's Mag 38 1869; Saturday Rev 27 1869; Public Opinion 13 1869; Spectator 42 1869; [Broome, F. N.] The Times 26 Aug 1869; Br Quart Rev 50 1869; [Oliphant, M.] Blackwood's Mag 107 1870.

TRANSLATIONS: Du (J. C. van Deventer), Schiedam 1870; Rus, St Petersburg 1870.

The vicar of Bullhampton (ms Houghton Lib, Harvard). 11 monthly pts July 1869–May 1870 (illustr H. Woods), Lippincott's Mag 4–5 1869–70, 2 vols Philadelphia 1869–70, 1 vol London 1870 (illustr H. Woods), 1 vol Philadelphia 1870, New York 1870, 2 vols Leipzig 1870 (Tauchnitz's British Authors), 1 vol London 1871 (illustr H. Woods), 1875 (Select Lib of Fiction), 1880 (Railway Lib), New York 1883 (Seaside Lib), 2 vols 1906, 1 vol London 1924 (WC), New York 1979, Gloucester 1983, Oxford 1988 (WC), London 1997 (Trollope Soc and Folio Soc edn).

REVIEWS: [Collyer] Athenaeum 2218 1870; [Oliphant, M.] Blackwood's Mag 107 1870; Saturday Rev 29 1870; [Dasent, G.] The Times 3 June 1870; Harper's Mag 41 1870.

TRANSLATIONS: Rus, Moscow 1870, St Petersburg 1873; Du (J. C. van Deventer), Schiedam 1872.

Sir Harry Hotspur of Humblethwaite (ms Beinecke Lib, Yale). Macmillan's Mag 22–3, May–Dec 1870, Lippincott's Mag 5–6 1870, '1871' [1870], 1871, New York 1871, 1871 (Lib of Select Novels), Leipzig 1871 (Tauchnitz's British Authors), London 1879 (Select Lib of Fiction), New York 1879 (Seaside Lib), London 1880 (Railway Lib), 1928 (WC), 1948, New York 1981, 1986, Stroud 1990, Oxford 1991 (WC), London 1992 (Trollope Soc and Folio Soc edn).

REVIEWS: [Dasent, G.] The Times 16 Nov 1870; [MacColl, N.] Athenaeum 2247 1870; Spectator 43 1870; Saturday Rev 30 1870; Harper's Mag 42 1871; Heijse, J. H. C., De Gids 1873.

TRANSLATIONS: Du (S. J. Andriessen), Amsterdam 1871; Rus, St Petersburg 1871.

Ralph the heir (ms Houghton Lib, Harvard). 19 monthly pts Jan 1870–July 1871 (illustr F. A. Fraser), suppl to Saint Paul's Mag 5–8, Jan 1870–July 1871 (illustr F. A. Fraser), suppl to Appleton's Jnl 3–5, Feb 1870–May 1871, 3 vols 1871, 1 vol 1871, New York 1871, 2 vols Leipzig 1871 (Tauchnitz's British Authors), 1 vol London 1872

(illustr F. A. Fraser), 1872 (Select Lib of Fiction), 1880 (Railway Lib), New York 1886 (Seaside Lib), 2 vols London 1939 (WC), 1 vol New York 1978, Oxford 1990 (WC), London 1996 (Trollope Soc and Folio Soc edn).
REVIEWS: [Collyer] Athenaeum 2268 1871; Spectator 44 1871; [Dasent, G.] The Times 17 Apr 1871; Examiner 22 Apr 1871; Saturday Rev 31 1871; Bristed, C. A. North Amer Rev 112 1871; Graphic 3 1871; Br Quart Rev 54 1871; Harper's Mag 43 1871.
TRANSLATIONS: Rus, St Petersburg 1871; Danish 1872; Swed, Stockholm 1874.

The Golden Lion of Granpere. Good Words 13, Jan–Aug 1872 (illustr F. A. Fraser); Feb–Sep 1872 Harper's Mag 44–5 (illustr F. A. Fraser); London 1872, New York 1872 (illustr F. A. Fraser), Leipzig 1872 (Tauchnitz's British Authors), London 1873 (illustr F. A. Fraser), 1875, 1885, New York 1885 (Seaside Lib), London 1924 (EL), 1946 (WC), New York 1981 (Selected Works of Anthony Trollope), Oxford 1993 (WC).
REVIEWS: Spectator 45 1872; [Collyer] Athenaeum 2326 1872; Saturday Rev 33 1872; Nation 15 1872; Harper's Mag 45 1872; Old and New 6 1872.
TRANSLATIONS: Du (van Westerheene), Amsterdam 1872; Ger (L. Kayser), Leipzig 1873; Rus, St Petersburg 1873.

The Eustace diamonds (ms Taylor Collection, Princeton). Fortnightly Rev 16–19, July 1871–Feb 1873, Galaxy 12–15, Sep 1871–Jan 1873, New York 1872, 3 vols London '1873' [1872], 1 vol 1873, 2 vols Berlin 1873, 1 vol London 1874 (Select Lib of Fiction), 1881 (Railway Lib), 2 vols Philadelphia 1902 (Collector's edn), New York 1903, 1 vol London 1930 (WC), New York 1947, 2 vols London 1950 (Oxford Trollope), 1 vol New York 1951 (abridged), London 1968, 1969 (Pen), 1973 (The Pallisers), Oxford 1983 (WC), London 1990 (Trollope Soc and Folio Soc edn).
REVIEWS: [Collyer] Athenaeum 2348 1872; Spectator 45 1872; [Broome, F. N.] The Times 30 Oct 1872; Nation 15 1872; Saturday Rev 34 1872; Harper's Mag 46 1872.
TRANSLATIONS: Du (J. W. Straatman), Groningen 1873, Amsterdam 1873; Rus, St Petersburg 1873.

Lady Anna (ms Taylor Collection, Princeton). Fortnightly Rev 19–21, Apr 1873–Apr 1874, Australasian 1873–4, 2 vols Leipzig 1873 (Tauchnitz's British Authors), London 1874, 1 vol New York 1874 (Lib of Select Novels), Toronto 1874, London 1875 (Select Lib of Fiction), Detroit 1878, London 1880 (Railway Lib), New York 1882 (Seaside Lib), London 1936 (WC), 1942, 2 vols New York 1981 (Selected Works of Anthony Trollope), 1 vol 1984, Gloucester 1986, Oxford 1990 (WC), London 1990 (Trollope Soc and Folio Soc edn).
REVIEWS: [MacColl, N.] Athenaeum 2424 1874; Saintsbury, G. Academy 5 1874; Saturday Rev 37 1874; Nation 19 1874; [Dasent, G.] The Times 24 July 1874; Harper's Mag 49 1874.
TRANSLATION: Rus, Vestnik Evropy 1873–4, Moscow 1874.

Phineas redux (ms Beinecke Lib, Yale). Graphic 8–9, 19 July 1873–10 Jan 1874 (illustr F. Holl), 2 vols '1874' [1873] (illustr F. Holl), 1 vol New York 1874, 3 vols Berlin 1874, 1 vol London 1875 (Select Lib of Fiction), 1881 (Railway Lib), 2 pts New York 1883 (Seaside Lib), 3 vols 1893, Philadelphia 1902 (Collector's edn), 2 vols London 1911, 1937 (WC), 1951 (Oxford Trollope), 1 vol 1973 (The Pallisers), Oxford 1983 (WC), London 1990 (Trollope Soc and Folio Soc edn), 1997 (ELp).
REVIEWS: Spectator 47 1874; [Collyer] Athenaeum 2411 1874; Simcox, E. Academy 5 1874; Saturday Rev 37 1874; Dicey, A. V. Nation 18 1874; Harper's Mag 49 1874.
TRANSLATION: Rus, St Petersburg 1874.

Harry Heathcote of Gangoil: a tale of Australian bush life (ms Beinecke Lib, Yale). Graphic 8 Christmas no 1873 (illus), Littell's Living Age 120, 24 Jan–7 Mar 1874, New York 1874, Leipzig 1874 (Tauchnitz's British Authors), London 1874, 1874 (illus), 1883 (Railway Lib), New York 1885 (Seaside Lib), Glasgow 1885, London 1963, New York 1981 (Selected Works of Anthony Trollope), Gloucester 1986, New York 1987, Oxford 1992 (WC).
REVIEWS: Harper's Mag 48 1874; [Collyer] Athenaeum 2454 1874; Saturday Rev 38 1874; Saintsbury, G. Academy 6 1874; Br Quart Rev 61 and 62 1875; [Hutton, R. H.] Spectator 48 1875; Owen, F. M. Academy 7 1875; Westminster Rev n.s. 47 1875.
TRANSLATION: Rus, St Petersburg 1875.

The way we live now (ms Pierpont Morgan Lib, New York). Old and New 9–11, Jan 1874–May 1875 (omits chs 77–100), 20 monthly pts Feb 1874–Sep 1875 (illustr L. Faulkes), 2 vols 1875 (illustr L. Faulkes), 1 vol New York 1875, 4 vols Leipzig 1875 (Tauchnitz's British Authors), 2 vols London 1876, 2 pts New York 1883 (Seaside Lib), 1 vol London 1892, 2 vols 1941 (WC), 1 vol New York 1950, London 1969, Indianapolis 1974, Oxford 1982 (WC), New York 1982, London 1992 (Trollope Soc and Folio Soc edn), 1994 (Pen).
REVIEWS: [MacColl, N.] Athenaeum 2418 1874 and 2487 1875; [Townsend, M.] Spectator 48 1875; Saturday Rev 40 1875; [Barker, Lady] The Times 24 Aug 1875; Examiner 28 Aug 1875; Nation 21 1875; Harper's Mag 51 1875; Westminster Rev n.s. 48 1875.
TRANSLATION: Rus, St Petersburg 1877.

The Prime Minister (ms Arents Collection, NYPL). 8 monthly pts Jan 1875–June 1876, 4 vols 1876, 1 vol New York 1876, 4 vols Leipzig 1876 (Tauchnitz's British Authors), 1 vol Toronto 1876, London 1877, New York 1877, 1877, Philadelphia 1877, London 1878[?] (Select Lib of Fiction), 1881 (Railway Lib), 2 pts New York 1886 (Seaside Lib), 3 vols 1893, Philadelphia 1902 (Collector's edn), 2 vols London 1938 (WC), 1952 (Oxford Trollope), 1 vol 1973 (The Pallisers), Oxford 1984 (WC), London 1991 (Trollope Soc and Folio Soc edn), 1994 (Pen).
REVIEWS: [MacColl, N.] Athenaeum 2512 1875 and 2540 1876; Nation 23 1876; [Townsend, M.] Spectator 49 1876; Littledale, R. F. Academy 10 1876; [Shand, A. I.] The Times 18 Aug 1876; Harper's Mag 53 1876; Saturday Rev 42 1876.
TRANSLATION: Rus, St Petersburg 1877.

The American Senator (ms Taylor Collection, Princeton). Temple Bar 47–50, May 1876–July 1877, 3 vols 1877, 1 vol New York 1877 (Lib of Select Novels), 1877 (Seaside Lib), Toronto 1877, Detroit 1877, 3 vols Leipzig 1877 (Tauchnitz's British Authors), 1 vol London 1878, 1931 (WC), New York 1940, 1979, 3 vols 1981 (Selected Works of Anthony Trollope), Oxford 1986 (WC), London 1994 (Trollope Soc and Folio Soc edn).
REVIEWS: [Cook] Athenaeum 2590 1877; Saturday Rev 43 1877; Examiner 21 July 1877; [Shand, A. I.] The Times 10 Aug 1877; Nation 25 1877; Spectator 51 1877; Canadian Monthly 12 1877; Harper's Mag 55 1877; Crawley, T. W. Academy 12 1877.
TRANSLATION: Danish, Copenhagen 1877.

Is he Popenjoy? a novel. All the Year Round 39–41, 13 Oct 1877–13 July 1878, 3 vols 1878, 1 vol New York (Franklin Square Lib), 3 vols Leipzig 1878 (Tauchnitz's British Authors), 1 vol London 1879 (Select Lib of Fiction), 1880 (Railway Lib), New York 1883 (Seaside Lib), 2 vols 1907, London 1944 (WC), 1 vol Oxford 1986 (WC).
REVIEWS: [Collyer] Athenaeum 2636 1878; Saturday Rev 45 1878; Littledale, R. F. Academy 13 1878; Harper's Mag 57 1878; [Shand, A. I.] The Times 14 Sep 1878; Spectator 51 1878.
TRANSLATIONS: Ger, Strasburg 1878; Rus, St Petersburg 1878.

An eye for an eye (ms Parrish Collection, Princeton). Whitehall Rev 24 Aug 1878–1 Feb 1879, 2 vols 1879, 1 vol 1879, 1 vol 1879 (Select Lib of Fiction), New York 1879 (Franklin Square Lib), Leipzig 1879 (Tauchnitz's British Authors), New York 1880 (Seaside Lib), London 1881 (Railway Lib), 1966, 2 vols New York 1979, 1981 (Selected Works of Anthony Trollope), 1 vol Oxford 1992 (WC), London 1993 (Trollope Soc and Folio Soc edn).
REVIEWS: [Collyer] Athenaeum 2672 1879; Littledale, R. F. Academy 15 1879; Spectator 52 1879; Saturday Rev 47 1879; Nation 28 1879.

TRANSLATIONS: Fr (A. Davy), Neuchâtel 1879, Brussels 1946; Polish, St Petersburg 1881; Hungarian, Budapest 1887; Flemish, Antwerp 1955.

John Caldigate (ms Arents Collection, NYPL). Blackwood's Mag 123–5, Apr 1878–June 1879, 3 vols 1879, 1 vol New York 1879 (Franklin Square Lib), 1879 (Seaside Lib), 3 vols Leipzig 1879 (Tauchnitz's British Authors), 1 vol London 1880 (Railway Lib), 1885, 2 vols New York 1907, 1 vol London 1946 (WC), 1972, Oxford 1993 (WC), London 1995 (Trollope Soc and Folio Soc edn).
REVIEWS: [Sergeant] Athenaeum 2694 1879; Purcell, E. Academy 16 1879; Spectator 52 1879; Examiner 2 Aug 1879; [Shand, A. I.] The Times 8 Aug 1879; Saturday Rev 48 1879; Harper's Mag 59 1879; Nineteenth Cent 8 1880.

Cousin Henry: a novel (ms Beinecke Lib, Yale). Manchester Weekly Times (suppl) and North Br Weekly Mail 8 Mar–24 May 1879, New York 1879 (Seaside Lib), 2 vols London 1879, 1 vol Leipzig 1879 (Tauchnitz's British Authors), New York 1879 (Franklin Square Lib), London 1881 (Railway Lib), New York 1882, London 1929 (WC), 2 vols New York 1981 (Selected Works of Anthony Trollope), 1 vol Oxford 1987 (WC), London 1993 (Trollope Soc and Folio Soc edn).
REVIEWS: [Collyer] Athenaeum 2712 1879; [Hawthorne, J.] Spectator 53 1879; Examiner 25 Oct 1879; Saturday Rev 48 1879; Wallace, W. Academy 16 1879; [Shand, A. I.] The Times 6 Nov 1879; Harper's Mag 60 1880; Bidwell, W. H. Eclectic Mag 94 1880.
TRANSLATION: Fr (H. Martel), Paris 1881.

The Duke's children: a novel (ms Beinecke Lib, Yale). All the Year Round 43–5, 4 Oct 1879–24 July 1880, 3 vols 1880, 1 vol New York 1880 (Seaside Lib), 1880 (Franklin Square Lib), 3 vols Leipzig 1880 (Tauchnitz's British Authors), 1 vol London 1880 (Select Lib of Fiction), 1881 (Railway Lib), 3 vols New York 1893, Philadelphia 1902 (Collector's edn), 2 vols London 1938 (WC), 1 vol 1954 (Oxford Trollope), 1973 (The Pallisers), Oxford 1984 (WC), London 1991 (Trollope Soc and Folio Soc edn).
REVIEWS: [Cook] Athenaeum 2744 1880; Saturday Rev 49 1880; Spectator 53 1880; Illus London News 76 1880; Sedgwick, A. G. Nation 31 1880; Nineteenth Cent 8 1880; Harper's Mag 61 1880; Westminster Rev n.s. 58 1880.
TRANSLATIONS: Rus, St Petersburg 1880; Hungarian, Budapest 1881.

Dr Wortle's school: a novel (ms Beinecke Lib, Yale). Blackwood's Mag 127–8, May–Dec 1880, New York 1880 (Franklin Square Lib), 2 vols London 1881, 1 vol New York 1881 (Seaside Lib), Leipzig 1881 (Tauchnitz's British Authors), London 1881 (Railway Lib), 1928 (WC), 1946 (in Novels and stories), Oxford 1984 (WC), London 1989 (Trollope Soc and Folio Soc edn).
REVIEWS: [Collyer] Athenaeum 2777 1881; Saturday Rev 51 1881; Critic 1 1881; Nation 32 1881; [Shand, A. I.] The Times 16 Apr 1881; Harper's Mag 62 1881; Westminster Rev n.s. 60 1881.
TRANSLATIONS: Du, Arnhem 1881; Rus, St Petersburg 1881.

Ayala's angel (ms Beinecke Lib, Yale). Cincinnati Commercial 6 Nov 1880–23 July 1881; 3 vols London 1881, 1 vol New York 1881 (Franklin Square Lib), 1881 (Seaside Lib), 3 vols Leipzig 1881 (Tauchnitz's British Authors), 1 vol London 1884 (Railway Lib), 1929 (WC), 1964 (abridged), Oxford 1986 (WC), London 1989 (Trollope Soc and Folio Soc edn).
REVIEWS: [Cook] Athenaeum 2795 1881; Illus London News 78 1881; Saturday Rev 49 1881; [Dillwyn, E. A.] Spectator 54 1881; [Shand, A. I.] The Times 16 July 1881; Critic 1, 16 July and 13 Aug 1881; Nation 33 1881; Harper's Mag 63 1881; Westminster Rev n.s. 60 1881.
TRANSLATIONS: Rus, Moscow 1882, St Petersburg 1898; Hungarian, Budapest 1890.

The fixed period: a novel (ms Hatcher Lib, Univ of Michigan). Blackwood's Mag 130–1, Oct 1881–Mar 1882, 2 vols Edinburgh 1882, 1 vol New York 1882 (Franklin Square Lib), 1882 (Seaside Lib), 3 vols Leipzig 1882 (Tauchnitz's British Authors), 2 vols New York 1981 (Selected Works of Anthony Trollope), 1 vol Ann Arbor MI 1990, Oxford 1993 (WC), London 1997 (Trollope Soc and Folio Soc edn).
REVIEWS: [Collyer] Athenaeum 2837 1882; [Hutton, R. H.] Spectator 55 1882; Saturday Rev 53 1882; [Shand, A. I.] The Times 12 Apr 1882; Nation 34 1882; Harper's Mag 65 1882; Westminster Rev n.s. 62 1882.

Marion Fay: a novel (ms Taylor Collection, Princeton). Graphic 24–5, 3 Dec 1881–3 June 1882 (illustr W. Small), Illus Sydney News 1881–2 (illustr W. Small), 3 vols 1882, 1 vol New York 1882 (Franklin Square Lib), 1882 (Seaside Lib), 2 vols Leipzig 1882 (Tauchnitz's British Authors), 1 vol London 1883, 2 vols New York 1981 (Selected Works of Anthony Trollope), 1 vol Ann Arbor MI 1982 (illustr W. Small), Oxford 1992 (WC), London 1997 (Trollope Soc and Folio Soc edn).
REVIEWS: [Collyer] Athenaeum 2852 1882; Saturday Rev 54 1882; Nation 35 1882; Critic 2 1882; [Lock] Spectator 55 1882; Harper's Mag 65 1882.
TRANSLATIONS: Norwegian (W. S. Juell), Christiana 1883; Rus, Vestnik Evropy nos 3–9 1883, 1883.

Kept in the dark: a novel (ms Hatcher Lib, Univ of Michigan). Good Words 23 May–Dec 1882 (illustr J. E. Millais), 2 vols 1882 (illustr J. E. Millais), 1 vol New York 1882 (Franklin Square Lib), 1882 (Seaside Lib), Leipzig 1882 (Tauchnitz's British Authors), New York 1978 (illustr J. E. Millais), Gloucester 1987, Oxford 1992 (WC), London 1997 (Trollope Soc and Folio Soc edn).
REVIEWS: [Collyer] Athenaeum 2873 1882; Henley, W. E. Academy 22 1882; Nation 35 1882; Graphic 26 1882; [Lock] Spectator 56 1883; Br Quart Rev 77 1883; Harper's Mag 66 1883; Westminster Rev n.s. 63 1883.
TRANSLATION: Du, Haarlem 1883.

Mr Scarborough's family (ms Taylor Collection, Princeton). All the Year Round 49–52, 27 May 1882–16 June 1883, 3 vols 1883, 1 vol New York 1883 (Franklin Square Lib), 1883 (Seaside Lib), 1883, 3 vols Hamburg 1883, 1 vol London 1885, New York 1886, London 1946 (WC), Gloucester 1984, Oxford 1989 (WC).
REVIEWS: [Collyer] Athenaeum 2898 1883; [Townsend, M.] Spectator 56 1883; Wallace, W. Academy 23 1883; Saturday Rev 55 1883; Nation 36 1883; Br Quart Rev 78 1883; Westminster Rev n.s. 64 1883; Harper's Mag 67 1883.

The Landleaguers (ms Taylor Collection, Princeton). Life 16 Nov 1882–4 Oct 1883, 3 vols 1883, 1 vol 1883, New York 1883 (Seaside Lib), 3 vols 1979, 3 vols 1981 (Selected Works of Anthony Trollope), 1 vol Gloucester 1991, Oxford 1993 (WC), London 1995 (Trollope Soc and Folio Soc edn).
REVIEWS: Continent 2 1882; Purcell, E. Academy 34 1883; [Collyer] Athenaeum 2926 1883; Continent 4 1883; [Church, A. J.] Spectator 56 1883; Saturday Rev 57 1884; Westminster Rev n.s. 65 1884.
TRANSLATION: Du (A. A. Deenik), Haarlem 1885.

An old man's love (ms Taylor Collection, Princeton). 2 vols Edinburgh 1884, 1 vol New York 1884 (Franklin Square Lib), 1884 (Seaside Lib), 1884, 1884, Leipzig 1884 (Tauchnitz's British Authors), New York 1885, London 1936 (WC), 2 vols New York 1981 (Selected Works of Anthony Trollope), 1 vol Gloucester 1984, Oxford 1991 (WC).
REVIEWS: Dawkins, C. E. Academy 25 1884; Saturday Rev 57 1884; [Collyer] Athenaeum 2945 1884; [Shand, A. I.] The Times 14 Apr 1884; Br Quart Rev 80 1884; Wedgwood, J. Contemporary Rev 46 1884; Harper's Mag 69 1884; Westminster Rev n.s. 66 1884.
TRANSLATIONS: Rus (serialised), Izyashchnaya Literature 1884; Hungarian, Budapest 1884, 1886; Du, Arnhem 1885.

Short fiction

In the following list, collections and selections of Trollope's short fiction are numbered. Individual stories are listed separately and each entry includes the numbers of the collections and selections in which it appears.

Collections and selections

Tales of all countries (1st ser). 1861, 1931 (WC), New York 1981 (Selected Works of Anthony Trollope). **(1)**
REVIEWS: Saturday Rev 12 1861; Spectator 35 1861.

Tales of all countries (2nd ser). 1863, New York 1981 (Selected Works of Anthony Trollope). **(2)**
REVIEWS: Reader 1 1863; Saturday Rev 15 1863; Spectator 36 1863; Nat Rev 16 1863.

Lotta Schmidt and other stories. 1867, 1870 (Select Lib of Fiction), 1871, Berlin 1874, London 1880 (Railway Lib), New York 1981 (Selected Works of Anthony Trollope). **(3)**
REVIEWS: Saturday Rev 24 1867; Spectator 40 1867; [Jewsbury, G.] Athenaeum 2091 1867; Br Quart Rev 46 1867.

An editor's tales. 1870, 1871 (as Mary Gresley and an editor's tales in Select Lib of Fiction), 1871 (as Mary Gresley and an editor's tales), 1873, 1880 (Railway Lib), New York 1981 (Selected Works of Anthony Trollope). **(4)**
REVIEWS: [Doran, J.] Athenaeum 2230 1870; Public Opinion 18 1870; Saturday Rev 30 1870; Graphic 2 1830; [Rands, W. B.] Contemporary Rev 15 1870; Spectator 43 1870; Br Quart Rev 52 1870.

Why Frau Frohmann raised her prices, and other stories. '1882' [1881], 1882 (as Frau Frohmann and other stories), New York 1882 (Franklin Square Lib), 1882 (Seaside Lib), Leipzig 1883 (Tauchnitz's British Authors omitting Alice Dugdale), New York 1981 (Selected Works of Anthony Trollope). **(5)**
REVIEWS: Baker, A. Academy 21 1882; [Collyer] Athenaeum 2829 1882; Saturday Rev 52 1882; [Hutton, R. H.] Spectator 55 1882; Nation 34 1882; Critic 2 1882; Harper's Mag 65 1882.

Alice Dugdale and other stories. Leipzig 1883 (Tauchnitz's British Authors), New York 1883 (Seaside Lib). **(6)**
TRANSLATIONS: Danish (L. Kornelius) 1885; Hungarian, Budapest 1897.

La Mère Bauche and other stories. Leipzig 1883 (Tauchnitz's British Authors), New York 1884 (Seaside Lib). **(7)**

The mistletoe bough and other stories. Leipzig 1883 (Tauchnitz's British Authors). **(8)**

The O'Conors of Castle Conor with Aaron Trow. 1924. **(9)**

Short stories. 1928. **(10)**

Three tales. Paris 1946. **(11)**

The parson's daughter and other stories. 1949. **(12)**

The Spotted Dog and other stories. 1950. **(13)**

Mary Gresley and other stories (contains Katchen's Caprices [by F. E. Trollope?] erroneously attributed to AT). 1951, Philadelphia 1974. **(14)**

The journey to Panama and Malachi's cove. Berlin 1951.

Complete short stories. 5 vols Fort Worth 1979–83, London 1990–1. **(15)**

The two heroines of Plumplington and other stories. 1981. **(16)**

Collected short stories (contains Katchen's Caprices [by F. E. Trollope?] erroneously attributed to AT). New York 1981 (Selected Works of Anthony Trollope). **(17)**

The Spotted Dog and other stories. Gloucester 1983. **(18)**

An unprotected female at the Pyramids and other stories. Gloucester 1984. **(19)**

Early short stories. Ed J. Sutherland Oxford 1994 (WC). **(20)**

Later short stories. Ed J. Sutherland Oxford 1995 (WC). **(21)**

The collected shorter fiction. Ed J. Thompson 1992. **(22)**

Individual stories

Relics of General Chassé. Harper's Mag 20 1860; in 1, 3, 7, 11, 17, 20, 22, *above*.

The O'Conors of Castle Conor. Harper's New Monthly Mag 21 1860; in W. S. Walsh (ed), Treasure trove vol 2, 1875; in Half hours with great novelists, Chicago [1875?]; in L. Melville and R. Hargreaves (ed), Great English short stories, New York 1930; in 1, 3, 7, 9, 10, 11, 12, 14, 17, 20, 22, *above*.

The courtship of Susan Bell. Harper's New Monthly Mag 21 1860; in Outstanding short stories (abridged) 1958; in 1, 3, 9, 14, 17, 20, 22, *above*.
TRANSLATION: Swed (O. P. Behm and F. Hjertberg), Stockholm 1912.

An unprotected female at the Pyramids. Cassell's Illus Family Paper 6 and 13 Oct 1860; in 1, 3, 8, 14, 17, 20, 22, *above*.

The Chateau of Prince Polignac. Cassell's Illus Family Paper 20 and 27 Oct 1860; in 1, 3, 7, 12, 17, 20, 22, *above*.

Miss Sarah Jack of Spanish Town Jamaica. Cassell's Illus Family Paper 3 and 10 Nov 1860; in 1, 3, 8, 17, 20, 22, *above*.

John Bull on the Guadalquivir. Cassell's Illus Family Paper 17 and 24 Nov 1860; in Great stories of the nineteenth century, Paris 1944; in 1, 3, 8, 17, 18, 20, 22, *above*.
TRANSLATIONS: Rus, 1884; Ger, Vienna 1928

The banks of the Jordan (also pbd as A ride across Palestine). London Rev 5 1861; in 2, 9, 17, 20, 22, *above*.

Mrs General Talboys. London Rev 5 1861; in Tales by English authors, New York 1896; in 2, 8, 17, 20, 22, *above*.

The parson's daughter of Oxney Colne. London Rev 5 1861; in 2, 9, 17, 20, 22, *above*.
TRANSLATION: Danish (H. M. Berg), Copenhagen 1964.

The man who kept his money in a box. Public Opinion 2 and 9 Nov 1861 (literary suppl); in 2, 11, 17, 18, 20, 22, *above*.
TRANSLATION: Rus, 1888.

The house of the Heine brothers in Munich. Public Opinion 16 and 23 Nov 1861 (literary suppl); in 2, 9, 17, 20, 22, *above*.

Returning home. Public Opinion 30 Nov (literary suppl) and 7 Dec 1861; in 2, 17, 20, 22, *above*.

Aaron Trow. Public Opinion 14 and 21 Dec 1861; in 2, 7, 10, 17, 18, 20, 22, *above*.

The mistletoe bough. Illus London Rev 21 Dec 1861 (Christmas suppl); in 2, 9, 17, 21, 20, 22, *above*.

George Walker at Suez. Public Opinion 28 Dec 1861; in 2, 7, 17, 20, 22, *above*.

The journey to Panama. In A. A. Proctor (ed), Victoria Regia, 1861; in English short stories (3rd ser) 1927 (WC); in H. D. Thomson and G. C. Ramsay (ed), The big book of great short stories, [1927?]; in C. H. Lockitt (ed), Short stories of the past, 1949; in R. Mullen (ed), Malachi's cove and other stories and essays, Padstow 1985; in 4, 15, 17, 18, 20, 22, *above*.

La Mère Bauche. In English short stories (3rd ser), 1927 (WC); in J. Hampden (ed), Great English short stories vol 2, 1940, 1944; in P. Bayley (ed), Loves and deaths, 1972; in R. Mullen (ed), Malachi's cove and other stories and essays, Padstow 1985; in 1, 8, 11, 13, 14, 17, 20, 22, *above*.

The widow's mite. Good Words 4 [Jan] 1863; in 4, 18, 20, 22, *above*.

The two generals. Good Words 4 [Dec] 1863; in 4, 11, 17, 20, 22, *above*.

Miss Ophelia Gledd. In A welcome, 1863; in R. Mullen (ed), Malachi's cove and other stories and essays, Padstow 1985; in 4, 17, 20, 22, *above*.

Malachi's cove. Good Words 5 [Dec] 1864; Littell's Living Age 84 1865; in Tales, travels, plays selected from Asher's collection vol 4, Berlin 1875; in H. Walker (ed), English short stories – nineteenth century, 1914; in O. J. Campbell and R. A. Rice (ed), Book of narratives, New York 1917; in J. A. Hammerton (ed), Masterpiece lib of short stories vol 8, 1923; in F. H. Pritchard (ed), Short stories of yesterday, 1929; in J. Hampden (ed), Selected English stories vol 2, 1932; in A century of thrillers, 1934, Edinburgh 1937 (simplified); in B. A. Cerf and H. C. Moriarty (ed), Bedside book of famous British stories, New York 1940; in Novels and stories, 1946; in J. G. Fyfe (ed), Short stories of the nineteenth century, 1958; in J. Bayley (ed), Loves and deaths, 1972; in R. Mullen (ed), Malachi's cove and other stories and essays, Padstow 1985; in 4, 11, 14, 16, 17, 18, 20, 22, *above*.
TRANSLATIONS: Fr, Bibliothèque Universelle et Revue Suisse 29

1867; Latvian, Riga [1875?]; Ger, Ulm 1946; Ital, Turin 1948, Rome 1953.

Father Giles of Ballymoy. Argosy 1 1866; in Novels and stories, 1946; in R. Mullen (ed), Malachi's cove and other stories and essays, Padstow 1985; in 4, 13, 14, 17, 21, 22, *above*.

The gentle Euphemia. Fortnightly Rev 4 1866; in 17, 19, 22, *above*.

Lotta Schmidt. Argosy 2 1866; in World's great stories of love and romance, [1867?]; in 4, 17, 18, 21, 22, *above*.

The adventures of Fred Pickering. Argosy 2 1866 (as The misfortunes of Fred Pickering); in 4, 17, 21, 22, *above*.

The last Austrian who left Venice. Good Words 8 1867; in 4, 17, 21, 22, *above*.

The Turkish bath. Saint Paul's Mag 5 1869; Galaxy 8 1869; Littell's Living Age 103 1869; in Novels and stories, 1946; in 5, 15, 17, 21, 22, *above*.

Mary Gresley. Saint Paul's Mag 5 1869; in 5, 15, 17, 21, 22, *above*.

Josephine de Montmorenci. Saint Paul's Mag 5 1869; Galaxy 8 1869; in 5, 17, 21, 22, *above*.

The Panjandrum. Saint Paul's Mag 5, Jan–Feb 1870; Galaxy 9, Feb–Mar 1870; in 5, 17, 21, 22, *above*.

The Spotted Dog. Saint Paul's Mag 5, Mar–Apr 1870; Galaxy 9, Apr–May 1870; Littell's Living Age 105, Apr–May 1870; in 5, 13, 14, 17, 21, 22, *above*.

Mrs Brumby. Saint Paul's Mag 6 1870; in 5, 17, 21, 22, *above*.

Christmas Day at Kirkby Cottage. Routledge's Christmas Annual 1870; in B. A. Booth (ed), A cabinet of gems, Berkeley CA 1938, 1947; in E. Wagenknecht (ed), A fireside book of yuletide tales, Indianapolis 1948; in 17, 19, 21, 22, *above*.

Never, never – never, never. Sheets for the Cradle 6, 8 and 10 Dec 1875, 1971; in 19, *above*.

Christmas at Thompson Hall. Graphic 15 Christmas no 1876 (illustr 'W. R.'), New York 1877 (illustr 'W. R.'), London 1885 (illustr 'W. R.', under title Thompson Hall), Boston 1894, 1901, Racine WI 1979; in 6, 17, 21, 22, *above*.

REVIEW: Harper's Mag 55 1877.

TRANSLATIONS: Ger, Familienbibliothek 5th ser no 19, Einsideln 1891, Berlin 1912.

Why Frau Frohmann raised her prices. Good Words 18, Feb–May 1877, Racine WI 1978; in 6, 17, 18, 21, 22, *above*.

The telegraph girl. Good Words 18 Christmas no 1877, New York 1882; in 6, 17, 21, 22, *above*.

TRANSLATION: Ger, Berlin 1912.

The lady of Launay (ms Huntington). 6 weekly nos 6 Apr–11 May and in 2 monthly nos May–June in Light 1 (ed R. Buchanan) 1878, New York 1878, 1878 (Seaside Lib), Racine WI 1978; in 6, 17, 21, 22, *above*.

Alice Dugdale. Good Words 19 Christmas no 1878, Racine WI 1980; in 6, 7, 13, 17, 21, 22, *above*.

Catherine Carmichael. Masonic Mag 6 Christmas no 1878; in 17, 19, 21, 22, *above*.

Not if I know it. Life (New York) Christmas no 1882, New York 1883 (Seaside Lib); in 17, 19, 21, 22, *above*.

The two heroines of Plumplington. Good Words 23 Christmas no 1882, Harper's Bazaar [Dec] 1882, New York 1883 (Seaside Lib), 1883, London 1953, Racine WI 1980; in 17, 18, 21, 22, *above*.

Plays

Did he steal it? 1869, Princeton 1952.

The noble jilt (ms Wrenn Lib, Univ of Texas). 1923.

Did he steal it? and The noble jilt. New York 1981 (Selected Works of Anthony Trollope).

Non-fictional works

Travel literature

The West Indies and the Spanish Main. 1859, New York 1860, Leipzig 1860 (Tauchnitz's British Authors), London 1968, 1968, Gloucester 1985.

REVIEWS: [St John, H.] Athenaeum 1671 1859; Spectator 32 1859; Saturday Rev 8 26 Nov and 3 Dec 1859; [Dallas, E. S.] The Times 6 Jan and 18 Jan 1860; Br Quart Rev 31 1860; North Amer Rev 90 1860; Harper's Mag 21 1860; Quart Rev 108 1860.

TRANSLATIONS: Fr (excerpts) (L. Étienne), Bibliothèque Universelle et Revue Suisse 16 1863; Sp (chs 17–20 only) (R. Fernandez), San José (Costa Rica) 1925.

North America (ms private collection). 2 vols 1862, 1 vol New York 1862, 2 vols Philadelphia 1862, 3 vols Leipzig 1862 (Tauchnitz's British Authors), 1 vol London 1866, New York 1951, 2 vols London 1968, 1 vol 1968 (Pen, abridged), 2 vols 1986, 1 vol New York 1986, 2 vols Gloucester 1987.

REVIEWS: [Dixon, W. H.] Athenaeum 1804 1862; Saturday Rev 13 1862; Spectator 35 1862; [Lucas, S.] The Times 11 June 1862; Chambers's Jnl 3rd ser 17 1862; [Lewes, G. H. or Greenwood, F.] Cornhill Mag 6 1862; Dublin Univ Mag 60 1862; Harper's Mag 25 1862; [Lathbury, D. C.] Home and Foreign Rev 1 1862; Presbyterian Quart Rev 11 1862; Fraser's Mag 66 1862; [Hamley, E. B.] Blackwood's Mag 92 1862; Br Quart Rev 36 1862; Cooke, J. R. North Amer Rev 95 1862; [Cecil, R.] The Confederate struggle and recognition, Quart Rev 112 1862.

TRANSLATION: Ger (A. Diezmann), Leipzig 1862.

Australia and New Zealand (ms Nat Lib of Australia). Australasian 22 Feb 1873–20 June 1874, 2 vols 1873, 6 vols Melbourne 1873, 1 vol 1873, 3 vols Leipzig 1873 (Tauchnitz's British Authors), London 1874 (as 4 separate books), 1884 (as 4 separate books), chs 3–4 of New Zealand in A. H. and A. W. Reed, The story of Otago, Wellington NZ 1947, 1 vol Melbourne 1966 (abridged as Trollope's Australia), St Lucia Queensland 1967 (omitting chs on New Zealand), 2 vols London 1968, Gloucester 1987 (omitting chs on New Zealand).

REVIEWS: [Dilke, C. W.] Athenaeum 2366 1873; [Broome, F. N.] The Times 12 Apr 1873; Saturday Rev 35 1873; Br Quart Rev 57 1873; Spectator 46 1873; Simcox, E. Fortnightly Rev n.s. 13 1873; Horne, R. H. Contemporary Rev 22 1873.

TRANSLATION: Du, Leiden 1875.

South Africa (ms Huntington). 2 vols 1878, Leipzig 1878 (Tauchnitz's British Authors), 1 vol London 1879 (abridged and with new matter), 1939 (abridged), 2 vols 1968, 1 vol Cape Town 1973, 2 vols Gloucester 1987.

REVIEWS: [Chesson, F. W.?] Athenaeum 2625 1878; Saturday Rev 45 1878; Trotter, C. Academy 13 1878; Spectator 51 1878; The Times 18 Apr 1878; [Brackenbury, H.] Blackwood's Mag 124 1878; Br Quart Rev 57 1878; Church Quart Rev 7 1878.

Iceland. Fortnightly Rev 30 1878, 1878.

How the 'Mastiffs' went to Iceland. 1878, New York 1981 (Selected Works of Anthony Trollope).

TRANSLATION: Icelandic (B. Guethmundsson), Reykjavik 1960.

Other non-fictional works

The Civil Service as a profession. [1861–3?] (priv ptd), in Four lectures, ed M. L. Parrish, 1938, Philadelphia 1976.

The present condition of the northern states of the American Union. [1861–3?] (priv ptd), in Four lectures, ed M. L. Parrish, 1938, Philadelphia 1976.

Hunting sketches. Pall Mall Gazette 9 Feb–15 Mar 1865, 1865, Hartford CT 1929, New York 1933, London 1952, New York 1967, 1981 (Selected Works of Anthony Trollope).

Travelling sketches. Pall Mall Gazette 3 Aug–6 Sep 1865, 1866, New York 1981 (Selected Works of Anthony Trollope).

Clergymen of the Church of England. Pall Mall Gazette 20 Nov 1865–25 Jan 1866, 1866, Leicester 1974.

Prospectus for Saint Paul's Mag. 1867.

On English prose fiction as a rational amusement. [1869?] (priv ptd), in Four lectures, ed M. L. Parrish, 1938, Philadelphia 1976.

The commentaries of Caesar. Edinburgh 1870 (Ancient Classics for English Readers), Philadelphia 1872, New York 1981 (Selected Works of Anthony Trollope).

REVIEWS: [Rumsey] Athenaeum 2224 1870; Spectator 43 1870; Br Quart Rev 52 1870; Dublin Rev n.s. 28 1877.

Higher education for women. [1869/70?] (priv ptd), in Four lectures, ed M. L. Parrish, 1938, Philadelphia 1976.

Thackeray. 1879 (English Men of Letters), New York 1879, Toronto 1879, New York 1880 (Franklin Square Lib), 1887, 1894, 1894, 1906, Detroit 1968.

REVIEWS: Ward, T. H. Academy 15 1879; Br Quart Rev 70 1879; Westminster Rev n.s. 56 1879; [Rands, W. B.] Contemporary Rev 35 1879; Appleton's Jnl n.s. 7 1879; Fraser's Mag n.s. 20 1879; Harper's Mag 59 1879; Nation 29 1879; Scribner's Monthly 18 1879; Spectator 52 1879; [Thomson, J. 'B.V.'] Cope's Tobacco Plant 2 1880.

TRANSLATION: Ger (L. Katscher), Leipzig 1880.

London tradesmen. Pall Mall Gazette 10 July–7 Sep 1880, ed M. Sadleir 1927, New York 1970.

The life of Cicero (ms Parrish Collection, Princeton). 2 vols 1880, New York 1881, 1981 (Selected Works of Anthony Trollope).

REVIEWS: Critic 1 1881; Fowler, W. W. Academy 19 1881; Saturday Rev 51 1881; [Collins, W. L.] Blackwood's Mag 129 1881; [Clayton, J.] Spectator 54 1881; Springfield Republican 22 Mar 1881; Harper's Mag 62 1881; Westminster Rev n.s. 59 1881; Nation 33 1881; [Piele] Athenaeum 2806 1881.

Lord Palmerston (ms Taylor Collection, Princeton). 1882, New York 1981 (Selected Works of Anthony Trollope).

REVIEWS: Academy 22 1882; Saturday Rev 54 1882; [Bourne, H. R. F.] Athenaeum 2852 1882; Br Quart Rev 76 1882; Westminster Rev n.s. 62 1882; Nation 36 1883.

An autobiography (ms BL). 2 vols Edinburgh 1883, 1 vol New York 1883, 1883 (Franklin Square Lib), 1883 (Seaside Lib), Leipzig 1884 (Tauchnitz's British Authors), New York 1905, London 1923 (WC), Oxford 1929 (Shakespeare Head), London 1946, Berkeley CA 1947, London 1950, New York 1960, London 1962, Oxford 1980 (WC), Gloucester 1987 (in An illus Autobiography and How the 'Mastiffs' went to Iceland), London 1996.

REVIEWS: The Times 28 Sep, 12 and 13 Oct 1883; Graphic 28 1883; Saturday Rev 56 1883; [Townsend, M.] The boyhood of Anthony Trollope, Spectator 56 1883; Tribune 20 and 23 Oct 1883; Littledale, R. F. Academy 24 1883; [Hutton, R. H.] Mr Trollope as critic, Spectator 56 1883; [Hutton, R. H.], Spectator 56 1883; [Collins, W. L.] Blackwood's Mag 134 1883; [Morley, J. and M. A. Ward] Macmillan's Mag 49 1883; Contemporary Rev 44 1883; Tanzer, A. Nation 37 1883; Continent 4 (two articles) 1883; Norman, H. Theories and practice in modern fiction, Fortnightly Rev n.s. 34 1883; Literary World 14 1883; Hawthorne, J. The maker of many books, Manhattan 2 1883; Month 40 1883; Br Quart Rev 79 1884; Critic n.s. 1 1884; [Shand, A. I.] The literary life of Anthony Trollope, Edinburgh Rev 1884; 'Sylvanus Urban' Trollope upon novel-writing, GM 256 1884; Harper's Mag 68 1884; [E. C. Whitehurst] Westminster Rev n.s. 65 1884; Atlantic Monthly 53 1884; Dronsart, M. Une autobiographie du romancier Anthony Trollope, Correspondant n.s. 101 1884.

Four lectures. Ed M. L. Parrish 1938.

The New Zealander (ms Taylor Collection, Princeton). Ed N. J. Hall, Oxford 1972.

Editions

British sports and pastimes. 1868.

Saint Paul's Mag. Oct 1867–Oct 1869.

Trollope, F. Salmagundi. In Salmagundi: Byron, Allegra and the Trollope family, ed N. J. Hall, 1975.

Contributions to periodicals

Collections

The following collections reprint some of Trollope's periodical contributions.

The tireless traveller. 1941, 1978.

Miscellaneous essays and reviews. Ed N. J. Hall, New York 1981.

Writings for Saint Paul's Magazine. Ed J. Sutherland, New York 1981. Omits editorial postscript to essay In Babyland, Nov 1869.

The Irish famine: six letters to the Examiner 1849/50. 1987.

Other individual contributions

For Trollope's non-fictional contributions to Blackwood's Mag, Cornhill Mag, Dublin Univ Mag, Fortnightly Rev, Nineteenth Cent and St Paul's Mag, *see* Wellesley *vol 5 1989*.

Irish distress. Examiner 25 Aug 1849.

The real state of Ireland. Examiner 30 Mar, 6 Apr, 11 May, 1 June, 15 June 1850.

History of the Post Office in Ireland. In Third report of the Postmaster General, Appendix J, Parliamentary Papers 1857.

Two letters on 'American literary piracy'. Athenaeum 1819 2 Sep and 1826 22 Oct 1862.

Four letters defending T. A. Trollope's Lenten journey in Umbria. Athenaeum 1832 6 Dec 1862, 1835 27 Dec 1862, 1863 3 Jan 1863, 1864 10 Jan 1863.

The American question. Pall Mall Gazette 7 Feb 1865.

England and America. Pall Mall Gazette 25 Feb 1865.

Ladies in the hunting field. Pall Mall Gazette 28 Feb 1865. Letter.

The Public school calendar 1865. Pall Mall Gazette 2 Mar 1865. Review.

The American conflict. Pall Mall Gazette 16 Mar 1865.

Accusations against Lord Brougham. Pall Mall Gazette 20 Mar 1865.

Usurers and clerks in public offices. Pall Mall Gazette 23 Mar 1865.

What is a job? Pall Mall Gazette 28 Mar, 8 May and 28 June 1865.

The American war. Pall Mall Gazette 6 Apr 1865.

The election of M. Paradol to the French Academy. Pall Mall Gazette 12 Apr 1865.

Letter-article on American Civil War. Pall Mall Gazette 17 Apr 1865.

Letter-article on the assassination of Lincoln. Pall Mall Gazette 5 May 1865.

REVIEW: Mistaken estimates of self, Saturday Rev 19 1865.

A Zulu in search of a religion. Pall Mall Gazette 10 May 1865.

Letter on the American Secession. Pall Mall Gazette 2 June 1865.

The Civil Service. Pall Mall Gazette 27 July 1865.

Anglican sisterhoods. Pall Mall Gazette 11 Sep 1865.

Letter-article on England and the USA. Pall Mall Gazette 8 Jan 1866.

The Sabbath Question. Pall Mall Gazette 5 Feb 1866.

Letter-article on Lord John Russell and the Saturday Rev. Pall Mall Gazette 18 July 1866.

Curates' incomes. Pall Mall Gazette 24 July 1866.

Robert Bell. Pall Mall Gazette 13 Apr 1867.

Irish prison fare. Pall Mall Gazette 16 May 1867.

Copyright in England and America. Pall Mall Gazette 13 Mar 1868.

Letter-article on impeachment of the US president. Pall Mall Gazette 15 June 1868.

The United States. Pall Mall Gazette 11 July 1868.

Letter on his political characters. Daily Telegraph 1 Apr 1869.

Letter on rumour of lawsuit with Tauchnitz. Pall Mall Gazette 21 May 1869.

Letter-article on Australia. Daily Telegraph 23 Dec 1871.

Letter-articles on Australia. Signed Antipodean. Daily Telegraph 13 Feb, 13 Mar, 2, 9, 10, 17, 23, 29 Oct, 24, 28 Dec 1872.

Letter on C. Reade's play Shilly Shally. Pall Mall Gazette 16 July 1872.

Letter on C. Reade's play Shilly Shally. Daily Telegraph 6 Aug 1872.

Letter on rumour of law suit with Tauchnitz. New York Herald 25 Nov 1872.

4 letters complaining of the train-service to Basle. The Times 24, 28 Sep, 27 Nov and 10 Dec 1874.

Letter-articles on South Africa. North Br Weekly Mail Oct–Dec 1877; also ptd in Aberdeen Weekly Press, Cardiff Times, Glasgow Weekly Mail, Manchester Weekly Times, Northern Echo, Northern Whig, Preston Guardian; rptd in Cape Times Nov

1877–Feb 1878, and in Eastern Star, Grocott's Penny Mail, Observer [Port Elizabeth], Queenstown Representative.

Letters

Letter from Anthony Trollope describing a visit to California 1875. HLQ Oct 1939, San Francisco 1946.
The letters of Anthony Trollope. Ed B. A. Booth, 1951.
Hamer, M. Forty letters of Anthony Trollope. YES 3 1973.
Corbett, J. P. Two more Trollope letters. N & Q 225 1980.
Hall, N. J. Trollope's letters to Harriet and Mary Knower. Princeton Univ Lib Chron 43 1981.
The letters of Anthony Trollope. Ed N. J. Hall, Stanford CA 1983.
Dustin, J. E. A new Trollope letter. Amer N & Q 23 1985.

§2

Bibliographical and textual criticism

Adams, R. A. The text of Phineas Redux. Colophon n.s. 3 1938.
Chapman, R. W. The text of Phineas Redux. RES 17 1941. Replies by G. Bone, RES 17 1941, C. B. Tinker, RES 18 1942.
Chapman, R. W. The text of Trollope's Autobiography. RES 17 1941.
Chapman, R. W. The text of Trollope's novels. RES 17 1941.
Chapman, R. W. The text of Trollope. TLS 25 Jan, 1 Mar and 22 Mar 1941.
Chapman, R. W. Trollope's American senator. TLS 21 June and 12 July 1941.
Chapman, R. W. The text of Trollope's Autobiography. N & Q 181 1941.
Wade, A. The text of Trollope. TLS 10 Jan 1942.
Chapman, R. W. A correction in Trollope. TLS 7 Mar 1942.
Chapman, R. W. The text of Trollope's Ayala's angel. MP 39 1942.
Tinker, C. B. and R. W. Chapman. The text of Trollope's Phineas Redux. RES 18 1942.
Chapman, R. W. The text of Trollope's Sir Harry Hotspur. N & Q 186 1944.
Chapman, R. W. The text of Phineas Finn. TLS 15 Apr 1944. Replies by S. Nowell-Smith, TLS 15 Apr 1944, R. L. Purdy, TLS 29 July 1944.
Chapman, R. W. Textual criticism: a provisional bibliography. Trollopian 1 1945.
Chapman, R. W. The text of Barchester Towers. TLS 30 Aug 1947. Reply by B. H. P. Fisher, TLS 4 Oct 1947.
Taylor, R. H. The manuscript of Trollope's The American Senator. PBSA 41 1947.
Gerould, W. G. and J. T. A guide to Trollope. Princeton 1948.
Taylor, R. H. The Trollopes write to Bentley. Nineteenth-Cent Fiction 3 1948.
Chapman, R. W. The text of Miss Mackenzie. Nineteenth-Cent Fiction 3 1949.
Tingay, L. O. Trollope's first novel. N & Q 195 1950.
Tingay, L. O. The reception of Trollope's first novel. Nineteenth-Cent Fiction 6 1951.
Helling, R. A century of Trollope criticism. Helsinki 1956.
Tingay, L. O. Trollope's popularity: a statistical approach. Nineteenth-Cent Fiction 11 1956.
Bicanic, S. A missing page of The Claverings. Studia Romantica et Anglica Zagrabiensia 8 1959.
Booth, B. A. Author to publisher: Anthony Trollope and William Isbister. Princeton Univ Lib Chron 24 1961.
Edwards, P. D. Trollope changes his mind: the death of Melmotte in The way we live now. Nineteenth-Cent Fiction 18 1963.
Hornback, B. G. Anthony Trollope and the calendar of 1872; the chronology of The way we live now. N & Q 208 1963.
Edwards, P. D. Trollope and the reviewers: three notes. N & Q 213 1968.
Ray, G. N. Trollope at full length. HLQ 31 1968.
Hamer, M. Working diary for The last chronicle of Barset. TLS 24 Dec 1971.
Terry, R. C. Three lost chapters of Trollope's first novel. Nineteenth-Cent Fiction 27 1972.
Hamer, M. Chapter divisions in early novels by Anthony Trollope. N & Q 218 1973.
Wittig, E. W. Significant revisions in Trollope's The Macdermots of Ballycloran. N & Q 218 1973.
Hall, N. J. An unpublished manuscript on a proposed history of world literature. Nineteenth-Cent Fiction 29 1974.
Clark, J. W. The language and style of Anthony Trollope 1975.
Edwards, P. D. Trollope and All the Year Round. N & Q 221 1976.
Sutherland, J. A. In his Victorian novelists and publishers, 1976.
Edwards, P. D. Trollope's working papers as evidence of his contributions to Saint Paul's. Victorian Periodicals Newsletter 10 1977.
Hall, N. J. Millais's illustrations for Trollope. Univ of Pennsylvania Lib Chron 42 1977.
Crawford, M. Barchester Towers: an allusion and a note on composition. N & Q 224 1979.
Hall, N. J. Trollope and his illustrators. 1980.
Bailey, J. W. The Duke's children: rediscovering a Trollope manuscript. Yale Lib Gazette 57 1982.
Overton, W. In his The unofficial Trollope, 1982.
Srebrnik, P. T. Trollope, James Virtue and Saint Paul's Magazine. Nineteenth-Cent Fiction 37 1982.
Sutherland, J. A. Trollope at work on The way we live now. Nineteenth-Cent Fiction 37 1982; rptd in his Victorian fiction: writers, publishers, readers, 1995.
Hall, N. J. Seeing Trollope's Autobiography through the press: the correspondence of William Blackwood and Henry Merivale Trollope. Princeton Univ Lib Chron 47 1986.
Sutherland, J. A. The commercial success of The way we live now: some new evidence. Nineteenth-Cent Fiction 40 1986.
Sutherland, J. A. Trollope, publishers and the truth. Prose Studies 10 1987.

Pre-1920 criticism

The following are useful reference works.

Smalley, D. In Victorian fiction: a guide to research, ed L. Stevenson, Cambridge 1964.
Smalley, D. (ed). Trollope: the critical heritage. 1969.
Skilton, D. In his Anthony Trollope and his contemporaries, 1972.
Olmsted, J. C. and J. E. Welch. The reputation of Anthony Trollope: an annotated bibliography 1925–1975. 1978.
ap Roberts, R. Anthony Trollope. In Victorian fiction: a second guide to research, ed G. H. Ford, New York 1978.
Lyons, A. K. Anthony Trollope: an annotated bibliography of periodical works by and about him in the United States and Great Britain to 1900. Greenwood SC 1985.

Mr Trollope's novels. Nat Rev 7 1858.
[Kinnear, A. S.] Mr Trollope's novels. North Br Rev n.s. 1 1864.
'Cuthbert Bede' [Bradley, E.]. Some recollections of Mr Anthony Trollope. Graphic 26 1882.
[Hutton, R. H.] From Miss Austen to Mr Trollope. Spectator 55 1882.
Morris, M. Anthony Trollope: a poem. Graphic 26 1882.
Bryce, J. The death of Anthony Trollope. Nation 36 1883.
Freeman, E. A. Anthony Trollope. Macmillan's Mag 47 1883.
James, H. Anthony Trollope. Cent Mag n.s. 4 1883.
[Meetkerke, C. E.] Anthony Trollope. Blackwood's Mag 133 1883.
The novels of Anthony Trollope. Dublin Rev 3rd ser 9 1883.
Pollock, W. H. Anthony Trollope. Harper's Mag 66 1883.
English character and manners as portrayed by Anthony Trollope. Westminster Rev n.s. 67 1885.
Harrison, F. Anthony Trollope's place in literature. Forum 19 1895; in his Studies in early Victorian literature, 1895.
Saintsbury, G. In his Corrected impressions, 1895.
Saintsbury, G. In his History of nineteenth century literature, 1896.
Ker, W. P. In his Romance, 1909.

Obituaries

[Bourne, H. R. F.] Athenaeum. 2876 1882.
Graphic 26 1882.
[Hutton, R. H.] Spectator 45 1882.
Illus London News 81 1882.
Literary World (Boston) 13 1882.
Littledale, R. F. Academy 22 1882.
[Ward M. A.] The Times 7 Dec 1882.
Oliphant, M. Obituary. Good Words 24 1883.

Biographies

Escott, T. H. S. Anthony Trollope: his work, associates and literary originals. 1913.
Sadleir, M. Trollope: a commentary. 1927.
Snow, C. P. Trollope. 1975.
Super, R. H. Trollope in the Post Office. Ann Arbor MI 1981.
Pope-Hennessy, J. Anthony Trollope. 1986.
Terry R. C. (ed). Trollope: interviews and recollections. 1987.
Super, R. H. The chronicler of Barsetshire. Ann Arbor MI 1988.
Terry, R. C. Trollope chronology. 1989.
Mullen, R. Anthony Trollope: a Victorian in his world. 1990.
Hall, N. J. Trollope: a biography. 1991.
Glendinning, V. Trollope. 1992. [DS]

Thomas Adolphus Trollope 1810–92

§1

A summer in Brittany. Ed F. Trollope 2 vols 1840.
A summer in Western France. Ed F. Trollope 2 vols 1841.
Impressions of a wanderer in Italy, Switzerland, France, and Spain. 1850.
The girlhood of Catherine de'Medici. 1856.
A decade of Italian women. 2 vols 1859. Life of Vittoria Colonna pbd separately New York 1859.
Tuscany in 1849 and in 1859. 1859.
Filippo Strozzi: a history of the last days of the old Italian liberty. 1860.
La Beata. 2 vols 1861, 1861, 1 vol 1862 (also contains A Tuscan Romeo and Juliet).
Paul the Pope [Paul V] and Paul the Friar [Pietro Sarpi]: a story of an interdict. 1861.
A Lenten journey in Umbria and the Marches. 1862, [1865?] (as Travels in Central Italy).
Marietta: a novel. 2 vols 1862.
Giulio Malatesta: a novel. 3 vols 1863, 1 vol New York [nd] (as The sealed packet).
Beppo the conscript: a novel. 2 vols 1864, 1 vol 1865.
Lindisfarn Chase: a novel. 3 vols 1864, 1 vol [1884].
A history of the Commonwealth of Florence from the earliest independence of the commune to the fall of the Republic in 1531. 4 vols 1865.
Gemma: a novel. 3 vols 1866.
Artingale Castle. 3 vols 1867.
Leonora Casaloni: a novel. 2 vols 1868.
The dream numbers: a novel. 3 vols 1868.
The Garstangs of Garstang Grange. 3 vols 1869, 1 vol Philadelphia [1870?] (as Garstang Grange).
A siren. 3 vols 1870.
Durnton Abbey: a novel. 3 vols 1871.
The Stilwinches of Combe Mavis: a novel. 3 vols 1872.
Diamond cut diamond: a story of Tuscan life and other stories. 2 vols 1875.
The Papal Conclaves as they were and as they are. 1876.
A family party in the Piazza of St Peter and other stories. 3 vols 1877.
A peep behind the scenes at Rome. 1877. First pbd in pt in Standard.
The story of the life of Pius the Ninth. 2 vols 1877.
Sketches from French history. 1878.
The homes and haunts of the Italian poets. 2 vols 1881. With F. E. Trollope.
What I remember. 3 vols 1887–9, 1 vol 1973 (abridged).
The General Election: a working man's advice. Budleigh Salterton 1892. Single sheet.
Trollope edited F. E. Trollope's trns from Stieler, Paulus and Kaden pbd as Italy from the Alps to Mount Etna.

§2

Mahoney, J. L. T. A. Trollope: a Victorian man of letters. Univ of Rochester Lib Bull 15 1960. [EH]

Eliot Warburton 1810–52

See col 2305.

Samuel Warren 1807–77

Mss and correspondence are in the NLS; Inner Temple, London; and Trinity College Lib, Cambridge.

Collections

Works. 4 vols 1847–71, 5 vols 1854–5, 4 vols 1871–4.

§1

Passages from the diary of a late physician, with notes and illustrations by the editor. 2 vols New York 1831 (pirated), 2 vols London 1832 (anon; vol 3, signed, 1838), 1841, 1842, 2 vols 1844, 2 vols 1848, 1 vol 1848, 1853, 1864, 1868, 1871 [1884]; tr Fr 4 vols 1834; Ger 2 vols 1843, 2 vols Leipzig 1844. First pbd in Blackwood's Mag 1830–7.
A popular and practical introduction to law studies. 1835, 1845 (rewritten and enlarged), 2 vols 1863 (rewritten and enlarged).
Select extracts from Blackstone's commentaries. 1837.
Adventures of an attorney in search of practice. 1839.
The opium question. 1840, 1860.
Ten thousand a-year. 3 vols 1841, 2 vols Paris 1842, London 1845, 1854, 1855, 1859, 1871, [1884], [1887], 1899, 1900, 1903 (ed by C. T. Brady); tr Ger 1843, 3 vols Leipzig 1845. First pbd in Blackwood's Mag; dramatised by R. B. Peake [1886].
Now and then. 1847, Leipzig and Paris 1848, London 1848, 1854.
The moral, social and professional duties of attorneys and solicitors. 1848, 1851.
Letter to the Queen on a late court martial (Captain G. Douglas). 1850.
The lily and the bee: an apologue of the Crystal Palace. 1851, 1854 (rev).
The Queen or the Pope? Edinburgh 1850–1 (6 edns).
A manual of the Parliamentary Election Law. 1852, 1857.
The intellectual and moral development of the present age. Edinburgh 1853, 1854 (2nd edn).
The law and practice of election committees. 1853.
Miscellanies, critical, imaginative and juridical, contributed to Blackwood's Magazine. 2 vols 1855.
An abridgement of Blackstone's Commentaries. 1855, 1856.
The experiences of a barrister. Originally pbd in Blackwood's Mag as The lawyer detective. 1856, New York 1859, London 1878, New York 1976.
Labour: its rights, difficulties, dignity and consolations. 1856.

Contributions to periodicals

See Wellesley *vol 5.*

Letters

Correspondence between Warren and C. Phillips relative to the trial of corvoisier with a preface and appendix. 1849.

§2

Atlay, J. B. Author of Ten thousand a-year. Cornhill Mag Oct 1907. [DF]

Edwin Waugh 1817–90

See col 690.

Charles Whitehead 1804–62

See col 692.

George John Whyte-Melville 1821–78

Bibliographies

Freeman, J. C. Whyte-Melville: a bibliography. BB 19 1949.

Collections

Works. Ed H. Maxwell 24 vols 1898–1902.
Works. 25 vols nd (Library edn).

§1

Horace translated into English verse. 1850.
Digby Grand: an autobiography. 2 vols 1853.
Tilbury Nogo: or passages in the life of an unsuccessful man. 2 vols 1854.
General Bounce: or the lady and the locusts. 2 vols 1855.
Kate Coventry: an autobiography. 1856.
The Arab's ride to Cairo: a legend of the desert. Edinburgh [1857?]. Verse.
The interpreter: a tale of the war. 1858.
Holmby House: a tale of old Northamptonshire. 2 vols 1860.
Market Harborough: or how Mr Sawyer went to the shires. 1861, 1862 (with Inside the bar), Feltham 1984.
Good for nothing: or all down hill. 2 vols 1861.
Inside the bar: or sketches at Soakington. 1862 (with Market Harborough).
The Queen's Maries: a romance of Holyrood. 2 vols 1862.
The gladiators: a tale of Rome and Judaea. 3 vols 1863.
The Brookes of Bridlemere. 3 vols 1864.
Cerise: a tale of the last century. 3 vols 1866.
'Bones and I': or the skeleton at home. 1868.
The white rose. 3 vols 1868.
M. or N.: 'similia similibus curantur'. 2 vols 1869.
Songs and verses. 1869, 1924.
Contraband: or a losing hazard. 2 vols 1871.
Sarchedon: a legend of the great Queen. 3 vols 1871.
Satanella: a story of Punchestown. 2 vols 1872.
The true cross: a legend of the Church. 1873. Verse.
Uncle John: a novel. 3 vols 1874.
Katerfelto: a story of Exmoor. 1875.
Sister Louise: or the story of a woman's repentance. 1876.
Rosine. 1877.
Riding recollections. 1878 (7 edns), 1880 (edns 8–9), [1885], 1898, 1933, 1985.
Roy's wife: a novel. 2 vols 1878.
Black but comely: or the adventures of Jane Lee. 3 vols 1879.
The bones at Rothwell: a lecture. [Rothwell 1903.]
Hunting poems. 1911.

§2

'Melville, Lewis' (L. S. Benjamin). In his Victorian novelists, 1906.
Ellis, S. M. In his Mainly Victorian, [1925].
Fortescue, J. In The eighteen-sixties, 1932 (Royal Soc of Lit).
Freeman, J. C. Whyte-Melville and Galsworthy's Bright beings. Nineteenth-Cent Fiction 5 1951.

William Gorman Wills 1828–91

See col 2027.

Mrs Henry Wood, née Ellen Price 1814–87

§1

Danesbury House. Glasgow, Scottish Temperance League 1860.
For better, for worse. 1861. Pbd anon in Temple Bar 1–3 1861. Pbd in USA as For better, for worse, Philadelphia 1862. Included in a list of Mrs H. Wood's novels pbd by T. B. Peterson & Brothers, Philadelphia, 1862 as Better for worse. Wrongly attributed in Nat Union Cat to Marion Harland.
East Lynne. 3 vols 1861. First pbd in NMM 118–22 1860–1.
The Elchester College boys. In The golden casket. A treasury of tales for young people, ed Mary Howitt [1861]. Also pbd in J. Cassell, Cassell's story books for the young, 1866.
The Channings. 3 vols 1862. First pbd in The Quiver 1 1861.
Mrs Halliburton's troubles. 3 vols 1862. First pbd in The Quiver 2 1862.
The shadow of Ashlydyat. 3 vols 1863. First pbd in NMM 123–9 1861–3.
The foggy night at Offord: a Christmas gift for the Lancashire Fund. 1863; rptd in The unholy wish, 1890.
Verner's pride. 3 vols 1863. First pbd in Once a Week 7–8 1862.
A race for life. In Shilling books for leisure hours, [1863]. First pbd in The Leisure Hour 1861.
The lost bank note. In The Leisure Hour 1863.
William Allair: or running away to sea. 1864. First pbd in The Quiver 2–3 1862–3; rptd 1905. Children's book.
Lord Oakburn's daughters. 3 vols 1864. First pbd in Once a Week 10–11 1864.
Oswald Cray. 3 vols Edinburgh 1864. First pbd in Good Words 1864.
Trevlyn Hold: or Squire Trevlyn's heir. 3 vols 1864. Pbd in USA as Squire Trevlyn's heir, Philadelphia 1862; pbd as Squire Trevlyn's heir in The Quiver 3–4 1863–4.
Mildred Arkell: a novel. 3 vols 1865. Pt pbd in NMM 101–2 1854 and 114–15 1858–9.
St Martin's Eve: a novel. 3 vols 1866. Pt pbd in NMM 99 1853 and 103–4 1855; pt pbd in USA as Castle Wafer: or the plain gold ring, New York [1868].
Elster's folly: a novel. 3 vols 1866. Part pbd in NMM 112 1858.
Lady Adelaide's oath. 3 vols 1867, 1889 (as Lady Adelaide). Pbd in Temple Bar 17–19 1866–7; first pbd in USA as The castle's heir. A novel in real life, Philadelphia 1862; pbd also as Out of the deep, Boston 1876.
A life's secret. 2 vols 1867. First pbd in The Leisure Hour 1862.
Orville College: a story. 2 vols 1867.
The Red Court Farm: a novel. 3 vols 1868. Pt pbd in NMM 117 1859; pbd abridged in USA as The Red Court Farm: and the nobleman's wife, Philadelphia [c. 1868] ('issued here in advance of the publication of the work in Europe').
Anne Hereford: a novel. 3 vols 1868. Pbd in The Argosy 5–6 1867–8. First pbd in USA as The mystery. A story of domestic life, Philadelphia 1862 ('printed from the author's manuscript, purchased from Mrs Henry Wood, in advance of the publication of the work in Europe').
Roland Yorke: a novel. 3 vols 1869. A sequel to The Channings, *above*. First pbd in The Argosy 7–8 1868–9.
Bessy Rane: a novel. 3 vols 1870. First pbd in The Argosy 9 1870.
George Canterbury's will: a novel. 3 vols 1870. Pt pbd in Bentley's Misc 44–5 1858–9; pbd in Tinsley's Mag 4–5 1869–70 and The Argosy 10 1870.
Dene Hollow: a novel. 3 vols 1871. First pbd in The Argosy 11–12 1871; ch 4 first pbd as The ghost of the Hollow Field, in Routledge's Christmas Annual 1867; pt pbd as A light and a dark Christmas, Philadelphia [1866].
Within the maze: a novel. 3 vols 1872. First pbd in The Argosy 13–14 1872.

The master of Greylands: a novel. 3 vols 1873. First pbd in The Argosy 15–16 1873.
Johnny Ludlow. 6 ser 1874–89. First pbd in The Argosy.
Told in the twilight. 3 vols 1875. Contains Parkwater and 10 shorter stories. Parkwater pbd in The Argosy 19–20 1875; pbd in USA as Parkwater: or a race with time, New York [c. 1862].
Bessy Wells. 1875. First pbd in The Sunday Mag 1875.
Adam Grainger and other stories. 1876.
Edina: a novel. 3 vols 1876. First pbd in The Argosy 21–2 1876.
Parkwater; with four other tales. 1876. First pbd in Told in the twilight, 1875.
Our children. 1876. Non-fiction.
Pomeroy Abbey: a romance. 3 vols 1878. Pt pbd in NMM 115–17 1859; pbd in The Argosy 25–6 1878; pbd in USA as Pomeroy Abbey: or the old keep, New York [c. 1862].
Court Netherleigh: a novel. 3 vols 1881. Pt pbd in NMM 106 1856 and Bentley's Misc 42–4 1857–8; pbd in The Argosy 31–2 1881.
About ourselves. 1883. Non-fiction.
Lady Grace and other stories. 3 vols 1887. 1 vol as Lady Grace. A novel, 1890. Lady Grace first pbd in The Argosy 43–4 1887.
The story of Charles Strange: a novel. 3 vols 1888. Pt pbd in Bentley's Misc 45–6 1859; pbd in The Argosy 45 1888; pbd in USA as The recollections of Charles Strange, New York [c. 1862]; pbd abridged as The Red Court Farm: and the nobleman's wife, Philadelphia 1865.
Featherston's story. A tale. By Johnny Ludlow (Mrs Henry Wood) 1889.
The unholy wish and other stories. 1890. The unholy wish first pbd in NMM 97–8 1853.
Summer stories from the Argosy, by Mrs Henry Wood and other authors. 2 pts 1890. 3 short stories, all pbd in The unholy wish, 1890, *above*.
The house of Halliwell: a novel. 3 vols 1890. Pt pbd in Bentley's Misc 38–40 1855–6.
Ashley and other stories. 1897. Ashley first pbd in NMM 107 1856; pbd in USA as The heir to Ashley, New York [1862].

Contributions to periodicals

The Argosy, a periodical acquired by Mrs H. Wood in 1867 and edited by her 1867–87 and after her death by her son C. W. Wood, contains novels and many short stories by Mrs H. Wood. 1867–99.

§2

Wood, C. W. Memorials of Mrs Henry Wood. 1894. First pbd in The Argosy 1887.
Sergeant, Adeline. In Women novelists of Queen Victoria's reign, 1897.
Tinsley, William. Random recollections of an old publisher. 1900.
Burgauer, Rolf. Mrs Henry Wood. Persönlichkeit und Werk. Zurich 1950. [PM]

Emma Jane Worboise, later Guyton 1825–87

Collections

Works. 26 vols [1882–99].
Works. 41 vols 1882–91.

§1

Alice Cunningham. 1846.
The autobiography of Maude Bolingbroke. 1849, 1864 (2nd edn), 1882, 1890 (new edn).
Helen Bury: or the errors of my early life. Bath [1850], [1852], London [1860] (illustr B. Foster), 1868, 1885, 1890 (new edn).
Amy Wilton: or lights and shades of Christian life. Bath [1851], [1852], London 1853 (new edn), 1883, 1890.
The wife's trials and triumphs. 1855, 1858, 1859, New York 1860, London 1865 (3rd edn), 1876 (6th edn), 1877, 1887 (new edn), 1894 (13th edn), 1906.
REVIEW: Athenaeum 1435 1855.
Grace Hamilton's school-days. Bath [1856], London 1868 (new edn), 1895, 1903 (new edn), 1908.
Veiled hearts. 3 vols 1856.
Kingsdown Lodge. Bath [1858], [186?], London 1869 (new edn), 1895, 1903 (new edn).
The life of Thomas Arnold D. D. 1859, 1865 (2nd edn), 1870 (3rd edn), 1885 (pbd as The life of Dr Arnold), 1897.
REVIEW: Athenaeum 1641 1859.
Millicent Kendrick: or the search after happiness. 1862, 1864, 1865 (3rd edn), 1888, 1903 (19th edn), [c. 1905] (new edn).
Married life: or the story of Philip and Edith. 1863, 1865 (2nd edn), 1870 (4th edn), 1872 (5th edn), 1890 (new edn).
Lottie Lonsdale: or the chain and its links. 1863, 1865, 1871 (new edn), 1877, 1887 (new edn), 1893, 1894, 1908.
REVIEW: Athenaeum 1885, 1863.
Labour and wait: or Evelyn's story. 2 vols 1864 and 1867, 1 vol 1867 (pbd as Evelyn's story: or labour and wait), 1871, 1877 (new edn), 1894 (12th edn), 1907.
Lillingstones of Lillingstone. 1864, 1865, 1871, New York 1872 (illus), New York 1873, London 1877, 1887 (new edn), 1894 (11th edn).
REVIEW: Athenaeum 1907 1864.
Campion Court: a tale of the days of the ejectment two hundred years ago. 1864, 1867 (3rd edn), 1871 (4th edn), 1872, 1877, 1887 (11th edn), 1894 (12th edn), 1909.
Thornycroft Hall: its owners and its heirs. 1864 (2nd thousand), 1866 (5th thousand), 1903 (new edn), 1906.
St Beetha's: or the heiress of Arne. London and Ipswich 1865, London 1866, [188?] (4th edn), 1898, 1903 (new edn), 1907.
St Julian's wife. 1866, 1877 (new edn), 1887, 1894 (14th edn), 1896, 1899.
Violet Vaughan: or the shadow of Warneford Grange. 1866, 1883, 1899, 1903 (new edn), 1908.
Hymns and songs for the Christian church; and poems. 1867, 1871.
REVIEW: Athenaeum 2072 1867.
Margaret Torrington, or the voyage of life. 1867, 1868, 1907, 1909, 1927.
The fortunes of Cyril Denham. London and Aylesbury 1868, London 1869, 1875 (new edn), 1903 (10th edn), 1908, 1927.
Singlehurst Manor: or a story of a country life. London and Ipswich 1868, 1869, London 1875 (2nd edn), 1908.
Overdale: or the story of a pervert. London and Ipswich 1869, London 1898 (new edn), 1903, 1927.
Grey and gold. London and Ipswich 1870, London 1871 (2nd edn), 1888 (12th edn), 1898, 1903, 1927.
REVIEW: Athenaeum 2219 1870.
Mr Montmorency's money. 1870, 1903 (new edn), 1927.
REVIEW: Athenaeum 2256 1871.
Nobly born. 1871, 1904 (new edn), 1927.
REVIEW: Athenaeum 2300 1871.
Canonbury Holt: a life's problem stated. 1872, 1904 (new edn).
Chrystabel: or clouds with silver linings. 1872, 1873, 1886 (8th edn), 1898, 1899, 1903 (new edn).
REVIEW: Athenaeum 2325 1872.
Our new house: or keeping up appearances. 1873, '1890' [1891] (7th edn).
The house of bondage. 1873, 1904 (12th edn).
REVIEW: Athenaeum 2403 1873.
Husbands and wives. 1873, 1876, 1906.
REVIEW: Athenaeum 2370 1873.
Hearts-ease in the family. 1874, 1890 (new edn).
REVIEW: Athenaeum 2447 1874.
Emilia's inheritance. 1874, [1900?] (13th edn), 1906 (new edn).
Oliver Westwood: or overwhelming the world. 1875, 1878, 1906.
Father Fabian, the monk of Malham Tower. 1875, 1876, 1904 (20th edn), [c. 1905] (21st edn).
REVIEW: Acad 7 1875.

Lady Clarissa. 1876, 1885, 1904 (16th edn).
REVIEW: Acad 10 1876.
Robert Wreford's daughter. 1877, [c. 1905], 1914.
REVIEW: Acad 13 1878.
The grey house at Endlestone. 1877, 1905 (new edn).
REVIEW: Acad 13 1878.
The Brudenells of Brude. 1878, 1885 (4th edn), 1905 (new edn).
A woman's patience. 1879, 1905 (new edn).
REVIEW: Athenaeum 2721 1879.
Joan Carisbroke. 1880, 1903 (new edn).
REVIEW: Athenaeum 2744 1880.
The heirs of Errington. 1881, 1904 (13th edn).
REVIEW: Athenaeum 2797 1881.
The story of Penelope. 1881, [1884?], 1905 (new edn).
REVIEWS: Acad 20 1881; Athenaeum 2825 1881.
Sissie. 1882, 1883 (2nd edn), 1890 (5th edn), 1903.
REVIEW: Athenaeum 2854 1882.
Warleigh's trust. 1883, 1887, 1890 (new edn), 1906.
REVIEW: Acad 25 1884.
The Abbey Mill. 1883, 1890, 1905.
Fortune's favourite. 1885, 1890 (new edn), 1905.
Esther Wynne. 1885, 1890 (new edn), 1907.
REVIEW: Athenaeum 2993 1885.
His next of kin. 1887, 1890 (2nd edn), 1903 (13th edn).
Charles Eversley's choice. A true story. 1895.
Uncle Austin. Burton Holme. The legend of Warleigh Place. A round of stories for Christmas circles. By E. Worboise, M. Farmingham et al. [1872.]
Blott, J. S. In Christo: a memoir of the late Samuel Blott of Bassingbourne. 1865. Preface by Worboise.
Worboise was a regular contributor to Christian World Mag, *and was its editor from 1866 to 1886. Many of her novels first appeared in serial form in* Christian World Mag.

§2

In DNB.
Sutherland, J. The Longman companion to Victorian fiction. 1987.
Blain, V., P. Clements and I. Grundy. The feminist companion to literature in English. 1990.

Charlotte Mary Yonge 1823–1901

Bibliographies

Laski, M. and K. Tillotson. In A chaplet for Charlotte Yonge, ed G. Battiscombe and M. Laski, 1965.

Collections

Novels and tales: new edition. 40 vols 1879–99.

§1

Le Château de Melville: ou recréations du cabinet d'étude. 1839.
Abbey Church, or self control and self conceit. 1844, 1872 (with Mystery of the cavern).
REVIEW: Christian Remembrancer 26 1853.
Scenes and characters: or eighteen months at Beechcroft. 1847.
REVIEW: Christian Remembrancer 26 1853.
Kings of England: a history for young children. 1848, 1852 (4th edn).
REVIEW: Christian Remembrancer 26 1853.
Henrietta's wish, or domineering: a tale. 1850.
REVIEW: Christian Remembrancer 26 1853.
Kenneth: or the Rear Guard of the Grand Army. 1850.
REVIEW: Christian Remembrancer 26 1853.
Langley School. 1850.
REVIEW: Christian Remembrancer 26 1853.
Landmarks of history. 3 vols 1852–7. Ancient history: from the earliest times of the Mahometan conquest, 1852; Middle ages: from the reign of Charlemagne to that of Charles V, 1853; Modern history: from the Reformation to the fall of Napoleon, 1857, 1882 (6th edn, Modern history: from the Reformation to the French Revolution).
REVIEW: Christian Remembrancer 26 1853.
The two guardians: or home in this world. 1852, 1861.
REVIEW: Christian Remembrancer 26 1853.
The heir of Redclyffe. 2 vols 1853, 1854, 1868 (17th edn); ed A. Meynell 1909 (EL); ed C. Haldane 1965; ed B. Dennis 1997 (WCp).
REVIEW: Nat Rev 12 1860.
The herb of the field. 1853, 1887.
The castle builders: or the deferred confirmation. 1854, 1859.
Heartsease: or the brother's wife. 2 vols 1854, 1862, 1868 (10th edn).
REVIEWS: Fraser's Mag 50, Nov 1854; Nat Rev 12 1860.
The little Duke: or Richard the fearless. 1854, 1857, 1891; ed E. Mason 1910 (EL).
The history of the life and death of the good Knight Sir Thomas Thumb. 1855, 1859.
The Lances of Lynwood. 1855, 1857, 1894 (abridged); ed L. M. Crump 1911 (EL).
The railroad children. 1855.
Ben Sylvester's word. 1856.
The daisy chain: or aspirations; a family chronicle. 2 vols 1856, 1868 (9th edn) etc, 1988 (Virago, with introd by B. Dennis).
REVIEW: Nat Rev 12 1860.
Harriet and her sister. [1848?], 1856 (3rd edn).
Leonard the Lion-heart. 1856.
Dynevor Terrace: or the clue of life. 2 vols 1857, 1858, 1860.
REVIEW: Nat Rev 12 1860.
The instructive picture book: lessons from the vegetable world. 1857.
The Christmas mummers. 1858, 1876 (with 6 other stories as The Christmas mummers and other stories).
The chosen people: a compendium of sacred and Church history for school-children. 1859.
Conversations on the catechism. 3 vols 1859–63: The commandments, 1859; To the end of the creed, 1859; Means of grace, 1863.
Friarswood Post Office. 1860.
Hopes and fears: or scenes from the life of a spinster. 2 vols 1860, 1861.
REVIEW: Nat Rev 12 1860.
The mice at play. 1860.
The strayed falcon. 1860.
The pigeon pie. 1860, 1861.
The Stokesley secret. 1861, 1862, 1892 (with Countess Kate).
The young step-mother: or a chronicle of mistakes. 1861.
Biographies of good women. 2 ser 1862–5.
Countess Kate. 1862.
The sea spleenwort. 1862.
A history of Christian names. 2 vols 1863, 1884.
The apple of discord. 1864.
A book of golden deeds of all times and all lands. 1864, 1871 etc.
Historical dramas. 1864.
The trial: more links of the daisy chain. 2 vols 1864, 1868 (4th edn), 1870, 1996.
The Wars of Wapsburgh. 1864.
The clever woman of the family. 2 vols 1865, 1867, introd by G. Battiscombe 1985 (Virago).
The dove in the eagle's nest. 2 vols 1866, 1 vol 1870; ed E. Hull 1908 (EL).
The Prince and the page: a story of the last Crusade. 1865.
The Danvers papers: an invention. 1867.
The six cushions. 1867.
Cameos from English history. 9 vols 1868–99. From Rollo to Edward II, 1868; The wars in France, 1871; The Wars of the Roses, 1877; Reformation times, 1879; England and Spain, 1883; Forty years of Stewart rule (1603–43), 1887; The rebellion and restoration

(1642–78), 1890; The end of the Stewarts (1662–1748), 1896; The eighteenth century, 1899.
The chaplet of pearls: or the white and black Ribaumont. 2 vols 1868.
New ground. 1868.
The pupils of St John the Divine. 1868.
A book of worthies, gathered from the old histories and now written anew. 1869.
Key-notes of the first lessons for every day in the year. 1869.
The seal: or the inward spiritual grace of confirmation. 1869.
The caged lion. 1870.
Little Lucy's wonderful globe. 1871.
Musings over the Christian year and Lyra innocentium, together with a few gleanings of recollections of the Rev J. Keble, gathered by several friends. 1871.
A parallel history of France and England, consisting of outlines and dates. 1871.
Pioneers and founders: or recent workers in the mission field. 1871.
A history of France. In An historical course for schools, ed E. A. Freeman, 1872.
In memoriam Bishop Patteson. 1872.
P's and Q's: or, the question of putting upon. 1872.
Questions on the Prayer-book. 1872.
Mystery of the cavern. nd. Serialised in Monthly Packet Jan–Dec 1867, issued with 2nd edn of Abbey Church, 1872.
Aunt Charlotte's stories of English history for the little ones. 1873.
The pillars of the house: or, under wode, under rode. 4 vols 1873, 2 vols 1875.
Life of John Coleridge Patteson, missionary Bishop to the Melanesian Islands. 2 vols 1874, 1874 (3rd edn abridged), 1878 (6th edn).
Aunt Charlotte's stories of French history for the little ones. 1874.
Lady Hester: or Ursula's narrative. 1874.
Questions on the collects. 1874.
Questions on the epistles. 1874.
Questions on the gospels. 1874.
Aunt Charlotte's stories of Bible history for the little ones. 1875.
My young Alcides: a faded photograph. 2 vols 1875.
Aunt Charlotte's stories of Greek history for the little ones. 1876.
Eighteen centuries of beginnings of Church history. 1876.
The three brides. 2 vols 1876.
Womankind. 1876.
Aunt Charlotte's stories of German history for the little ones. 1877.
Aunt Charlotte's stories of Roman history for the little ones. 1877.
The disturbing element: or chronicles of the Blue-bell Society. 1878.
A history of France. In History primers, ed J. R. Green, 1878.
The story of the Christians and Moors of Spain. 1878.
Burnt out: a story or mothers' meetings. 1879, 1880.
Magnum bonum: or Mother Carey's brood. 3 vols 1879.
Bye-words: a collection of tales new and old. 1880.
Love and life: an old story in eighteenth-century costume. 2 vols 1880.
Verses on the gospels for Sundays and holydays. 1880.
English history reading books, adapted to the requirements of the New Code of 1880. Standards II–VI. 5 vols [1881]–3; revised edn 5 vols with The young student's English history reading book, 1885.
Frank's debt. 1881, 1882.
How to teach the New Testament. 1881.
Lads and lasses of Langley. 1881. 5 stories.
Practical work in Sunday schools. 1881.
Questions on the Psalms. 1881.
Wolf. 1881.
Given to hospitality. 1882.
Langley little ones: six stories. 1882.
Pickle and his page-boy, or unlooked for. 1882.
A pictorial history of the world's great nations. 1882.
Sowing and sewing: a Sexagesima story. 1882.
Talks about the laws we live under: or at Langley nightschool. 1882.
Unknown to history: a story of the captivity of Mary of Scotland. 2 vols 1882, 1884.
English Church history, adapted for use in day and Sunday schools and for general reading. 1883.
Landmarks of recent history 1770–1883. 1883.
Stray pearls: memoirs of Margaret de Ribaumont, Viscountess of Bellaise. 2 vols 1883.
New national poetry cards. Nos 1–6. Ed and annotated 1883.
The armourer's prentices. 1884.
Langley adventures. 1884.
Nuttie's father. 2 vols 1885.
Pixie lawn. In Please tell me a tale: a collection of short original stories for children, 1885.
The two sides of the shield. 2 vols 1885.
Astray: a tale of a country town. 1886. With M. Bramston, C. Coleridge and E. Stuart.
Black looks. In Just one more tale, 1886.
Chantry House. 2 vols 1886, 1887.
The little rick-burners. 1886.
A modern Telemachus. 2 vols 1886.
Teachings on the catechism: for the little ones. 1886.
The Victorian halfcentury: a jubilee book. 1886.
Nurse's pocket. In Jack Frost's little prisoners, 1887.
Under the storm: or Steadfast's charge. 1887.
What books to lend and what to give. 1887.
Beechcroft at Rockstone. 2 vols 1888.
Deacon's book of dates: a manual of the world's chief historical landmarks, and an outline of universal history. 1888.
Hannah More. 1888.
Nurse's memories. 1888.
Our new mistress: or changes at Brookfield Earl. 1888.
Preparation of prayer-book lessons. 1888.
The cunning woman's grandson: a tale of Cheddar a hundred years ago. 1889.
Neigh-bour's fare. In Stories jolly, stories new, 1889.
The parent's power: address to the conference of the Mother's Union. 1889.
A reputed changeling: or three seventh years two centuries ago. 2 vols 1889.
Life of HRH the Prince Consort. 1890.
More bywords. 1890.
The slaves of Sabinus: Jew and Gentile. 1890.
The constable's tower: or the times of Magna Charta. 1891.
Old times at Otterbourne. 1891.
Two penniless princesses. 2 vols 1891.
Westminster historical reading books. 6 vols 1891–2. Simple stories relating to English history; Twelve stories from early English history; Twenty stories and biographies from 1066 to 1485; The Tudor period, with biographies of leading persons; The Stewart period, with biographies of leading persons; The Hanoverian period, with biographies of leading persons.
An old woman's outlook in a Hampshire village. 1892.
The cross roads: or a choice in life: a story for young women and older girls. 1892.
That stick. 2 vols 1892.
Chimes for the mothers: a reading for each week in the year. 1893.
The girl's little book. 1893.
Grisly Grisell, or the laidly lady of Whitburn: a tale of the Wars of the Roses. 2 vols 1893.
Strolling players: a harmony of contrasts. 1893. With C. Coleridge.
The treasures in the marshes. 1893.
The cook and the captive: or Attalus the hostage. 1894.
The rubies of St Lo. 1894.

The story of Easter. 1894.
The Carbonels. 1895.
The long vacation. 1895.
The release: or Caroline's French kindred. 1896.
The wardship of Steepcoombe. 1896.
The pilgrimage of the Ben Beriah. 1897.
Founded on paper: or uphill and downhill between the two jubilees. 1898.
John Keble's parishes: a history of Hursley and Otterbourne. 1898.
The patriots of Palestine: a story of the Maccabees. 1898.
The herd boy and his hermit. 1900.
The making of a missionary: or daydreams in earnest. 1900.
Modern broods: or developments unlooked for. 1900.
Reasons why I am a Catholic, and not a Roman Catholic. Ed G. Ireland, Blackburn 1901.

C. M. Yonge edited and contributed to three journals: Monthly Packet *1851–94;* Monthly Paper of Sunday Teaching *1860–75; and* Mothers in Council *1890–1900. Much of her work was first serialised in* Monthly Packet, Churchman's Companion *and* Mag for the Young.

Her uncollected contributions to periodicals include:
Children's literature of the last century. Macmillan's Mag 20 1869.

Editions and translations

Marie Thérèse de Lamourous, foundress of La Misericorde, at Bordeaux. A biography abridged from the French [of F. Pouget]. 1858.
Two years of school-life, by E. F. L. de Pressense. Ed and tr Yonge 1865.
The population of an old pear-tree; or Stories of insect life by E. J. van Bruyssel. Ed and tr Yonge 1870.
A storehouse of stories. 2 ser 1870–2.
Life and adventures of Count Beugnot, Minister of State under Napoleon I. Ed from the Fr 2 vols 1871.
Scripture readings for schools and families. 1871.
Dames of high estate, by H. de Witt. Ed 1872.
Recollections of a page at the court of Louis XVI, by C. A. F. Felix, conte d'Hezecques. Ed from the Fr 2 vols 1873.
Recollections, Le Harivel de Gonnerville (Amyar Olivier), pbd by contess de Mirabeau. Ed from the Fr 2 vols 1875.
A man of other days, recollections of the marquis Henry Joseph Costa de Beauregard, selected from his papers by his great-grandson. 2 vols 1877.
Youth of Queen Elizabeth, by L. Wiesener. 1879.
Aunt Charlotte's evenings at home with the poets: a collection of poems for the young, with conversations, arranged for twenty-five evenings. 1881.
Beneath the Cross. Readings for children on our Lord's seven sayings, by F. Wilford. Ed 1881.
Catherine of Arragon and sources of the English Reformation, by A. Du Boys. 1881.
Behind the hedges, by H. de Witt. Tr 1882. (Later rptd [nd] as The loyalists; or The war in the Vendée.)
Historical ballads. 3 vols 1882. (Vol 3 as Historical poetry.)
Sparks of light, by H. de Witt. Ed 1882.
Shakespeare's plays for schools, abridged and annotated. 5 pts 1883.
Charity. 1884.
Faith. 1884.
Hope. 1884.
Memoirs of Marshal Bugeaud from his private correspondence and original documents, 1784–1849, by count H. d'Ideville. Ed from the Fr 2 vols 1884.
Mercy and peace. 1884.
Higher reading book for schools, colleges and general use. [1885.]
Chips from the royal image, fragments of the Eikon basilike, by J. Gauden. Ed 1887.
A child's guide to the Book of Common Prayer, by E. Esdaile. Ed 1900.

Prefaces and introductions

Journal of the Lady Beatrix Graham, sister of the Marquis of Montrose. 1871.
Sermons by G. C. Harris. 1875.
Sintram and his companions and Undine. 1896.

Collaborations

Historical selections: a series of readings in English and European history. 2 vols 1868–70. With E. Sewell.
Aunt Charlotte's stories of American history. 1883. With J. H. Hastings Weld.
The miz-maze, or the Winkworth puzzle: a story in letters by nine authors. 1883. With F. Awdry, M. Bramston, C. R. Coleridge, F. M. Peard et al.
Strolling players. A harmony of contrasts. 1893. With C. Coleridge.

§2

Coleridge, C. R. Charlotte Mary Yonge: her life and letters. 1903. With bibliography.
Charlotte Mary Yonge. Church Quart Rev 57 1904.
Romanes, E. Charlotte Mary Yonge: an appreciation. 1908.
Bailey, S. Charlotte Mary Yonge. Cornhill Mag Aug 1934.
Battiscombe, G. Charlotte Mary Yonge: the story of an uneventful life. 1943.
Mare, M. and A. C. Percival. Victorian best-seller: the world of Charlotte Yonge. 1947.
Dodds, M. H. Jane Austen and Charlotte Yonge. N & Q 30 Oct 1948.
Avery, G. In her Nineteenth-century children, 1965.
Battiscombe, G. and M. Laski (ed). A chaplet for Charlotte Yonge. 1965. Contains essays by G. Battiscombe, K. Briggs, L. Cooper, A. Fairfax-Lucy, A. Gillie, R. Harris, E. Jenkins, M. Kennedy, M. Laski, V. Powell, C. Storr, K. Tillotson.
Tillotson, K. The heir of Redclyffe. In her Mid-Victorian studies, 1965.
Chapman, R. In his Faith and revolt: studies in the literary influence of the Oxford Movement, 1970.
Jay, E. In her Faith and doubt in Victorian Britain, 1986. [BD]

iv. The late-nineteenth-century novel 1870–1900

This section has been restricted to writers born between 1830 and 1865 whose more important works were written before 1900.

Francis Adams, Francis William Lauderdale Adams, Agnes Farrell, Frank Hawkesbury 1862–93

Ms collections in Nat Lib of Australia, Canberra (Palmer Papers, poetry by Adams, plus letters); Univ of British Columbia Lib (Angeli-Dennis Collection, letters between Adams, his widow Edith Dean, and W. M. Rossetti).

Bibliography

Tasker, M. Francis Adams: a research guide. Victorian Fiction Research Guide 24. St Lucia, Queensland 1996.

§1

Henry and other tales. 1884. Poetry.
Leicester: an autobiography. 1885; rptd London and Boston 1894 with minor revisions as A child of the age. Novel.
Madeline Brown's murderer. Melbourne 1886. Novel.
Australian essays. London and Melbourne 1886, 1892. Essays.
Poetical works. London and Brisbane 1887. Poetry.
Songs of the army of the night. Sydney 1888, 1890, 1892, 1894, London and New York 1910 (revision titled Songs of the army of the night and the mass of Christ, ed H. S. Salt). Poetry.

John Webb's end: Australian bush life. 1891, Canberra 1995. Novel.
The Melbournians. London and Sydney 1892. Novel.
Australian life. 1892. Short stories.
The Australians: a social sketch. 1893. Social commentary.
REVIEW: Rev of Revs 7, May 1893; Bookman 4, 20 May 1893.
The New Egypt: a social sketch. Ed J. W. Longsdon 1893. Social criticism.
A child of the age. London and Boston 1894, New York 1977. Novel. Revised version of Leicester, an autobiography 1885.
Tiberius: a drama. Ed and introd by W. M. Rossetti 1894. Play.
REVIEW: Bookman 6, Aug 1894.
[Farrell, Agnes.] Lady Lovan. 1895. Novel. Pbd posthumously; the use of a pseud may not have been Adams's own decision.
Essays in modernity: criticisms and dialogues. London and New York 1899. Essays.
REVIEW: Bookman 16, Sep 1899.

Contributions to periodicals (short stories and essays not collected elsewhere)

Tennyson. Victorian Rev (Melbourne) 11, Jan–Feb 1885.
Arnold. Victorian Rev (Melbourne) 11, Mar–Apr 1885.
Leonard. Australasian 9 May 1885.
Dante Rossetti. Victorian Rev (Melbourne) 12, June–July 1885.
My Rose (a memory of the commune). Once a Month (Melbourne) 15 Oct 1885.
Introduction to Othello. Victorian Rev (Melbourne) 13, Jan 1886.
Nellie: a tale of the mutiny. Australasian 27 Mar, 3 Apr, 10 Apr 1886. (Previously pbd as Jack's heroine in Family Herald 4 June 1881.)
The church and the stage. Queensland Rev 1, 3 June 1886.
The prose works of Marcus Clarke. Sydney Quart Mag 4, 2 June 1887.
Australian civilisation. A gaol flogging. Sydney Bull 26 Nov 1887.
Realism. Centennial 1, 1 Aug 1888.
The contemporary stage. Centennial 1, 4 Nov 1888.
Matthew Arnold. Centennial 1, 6 Jan 1889.
Shakspere [*sic*]: an address for the Brisbane Literary Circle. Centennial 1, 8 Mar 1889.
Australian criticism and the reaction against Gordon. Centennial 2, 7 Feb 1890.
Apropos of Mr R. L. Stevenson: a protest. Centennial 2, 10 May 1890.
A note on Mr Herbert Spencer. Centennial 3, 2 Sep 1890.
The labour movement in Australia. Fortnightly Rev n.s. 50, Aug 1891.
Tennyson. New Rev 10, Mar 1894.

The above list of Adams's contributions to periodicals, contemporary reviews and other secondary materials is very selective. A comprehensive listing of all known pbns by and about Adams is available in Tasker, Francis Adams: a research guide, *under Bibliography, above. Much of Adams's work as a journalist, particularly in Australia, was unsigned.*

§2

Obits: Daily Chron 5 Sep 1893 (letter from Frank Harris), 6 Sep 1893 (letter from H. S. Salt and report of inquest), 7 Sep 1893 (letter from H. W. M[assingham]; Gill, F. Table Talk (Melbourne) 22 Sep 1893.
Turnbull, C. Australian lives. Melbourne 1965. Ch on Adams first pbd separately as These tears of fire: the story of Francis Adams, Melbourne [1949].
Seccombe, T. Francis Adams. In DNB 1901, 1968.
Murray-Smith, S. Francis Adams. In Australian dictionary of biography, vol 3 1851–1890, Melbourne 1969.
Britain, I. M. Francis Adams: the Arnoldian as socialist. Historical Stud 15, Oct 1972.
Britain, I. M. Francis Adams. In Dictionary of labour biography vol 5, ed J. M. Bellamy and J. Saville, 1979.
Tasker, M. Francis Adams. In The 1890s: an encyclopedia of British literature, art and culture, New York 1993. [MT]

Grant Allen, i.e. Charles Grant Blairfindie Allen

1848–99

§1

Physiological aesthetics. 1877.
The colour-sense, its origin and development: an essay in comparative psychology. 1879.
Anglo-Saxon Britain. [1881.] At head of title: Early Britain.
The evolutionist at large. 1881, 1884 (rev).
Vignettes from nature. 1881.
The colours of flowers as illustrated in the British flora. 1882.
Colin Clout's calendar: the record of a summer, April–October. 1883, 1901.
Flowers and their pedigrees. 1883.
Nature studies. [1883.] With Andrew Wilson, Thomas Foster, Edward Clodd and R. A. Proctor.
Biographies of working men. 1884.
Philistia. 3 vols 1884. Pbd under the pseud 'Cecil Power'.
Strange stories. 1884. Contains 16 stories first pbd in Cornhill Mag, Longman's Mag and Belgravia, under the pseud 'J. Arbuthnot Wilson'.
Babylon. 3 vols 1885.
Charles Darwin. 1885.
The miscellaneous and posthumous works of Henry Thomas Buckle. 2 vols 1885. Ed Allen.
Kalee's shrine. Bristol 1886. With May Cotes.
In all shades: a novel. 3 vols 1886.
For Maimie's sake: a tale of love and dynamite. 1886.
Common sense science. Boston [1886].
The beckoning hand and other stories. 1887.
A terrible inheritance. [1887.]
Force and energy: a theory of dynamics. 1888.
This mortal coil: a novel. 3 vols 1888.
The white man's foot. 1888.
The devil's die: a novel. 3 vols 1888.
Falling in love, with other essays on more exact branches of science. 1889.
The tents of Shem: a novel. 3 vols 1889.
Dr Palliser's patient. 1889, 1893.
The jaws of death. [1889], 1896.
A living apparition. [1889.]
The great taboo. 1890.
Wednesday the tenth: a tale of the South Pacific. Boston [1890], [1898] (as The cruise of the Albatross).
The sole trustee. [1890.]
Recalled to life. Bristol [1891].
What's bred in the bone: £1000 prize novel. 1891.
Dumaresq's daughter: a novel. 3 vols 1891.
The Duchess of Powysland: a novel. 3 vols 1892.
Science in Arcady. 1892.
The tidal Thames with twenty full-page photogravure plates printed on India paper, and other illustrations, after original drawings by W. L. Wyllie and descriptive letterpress by Grant Allen. [1892] (subscriber's edn in 5 pts), [1892].
The Attis of Caius Valerius Catullus, translated into English verse with dissertations on the myth of Attis, on the origin of tree-worship, and on the Galliambic metre. 1892 (550 copies).
The scallywag. 3 vols 1893.
Michael's Crag. 1893. At head of title: Mr Grant Allen's new story.
Ivan Greet's masterpiece, etc. 1893.
Blood Royal: a novel. 1893.
An army doctor's romance. [1893.]
At market value: a novel. 2 vols 1894.
The lower slopes: reminiscences of excursions round the base of Helicon, under-taken in early manhood. 1894. Poems.
Post-prandial philosophy. 1894. First pbd in Westminster Gazette.

In memoriam George Paul Macdonell. 1895.
The British barbarians: a hill-top novel. 1895. A parody by H. D. Traill, entitled The barbarous Britishers: a tip-top novel, pbd 1896.
The story of the plants. 1895, [1908] (as Plant life).
The woman who did. 1895.
Under sealed orders: a novel. 3 vols 1895.
Moorland idylls. 1896. Natural science.
A splendid sin. 1896.
An African millionaire: episodes in the life of the illustrious Colonel Clay. 1897, 1980.
The evolution of the idea of God: an inquiry into the origins of religions. 1897, 1903 (rev and abridged), 1931.
Cities of Belgium. 1897.
Florence. 1897.
Paris. 1897, 1903 (4th edn, rev and enlarged).
Tom, unlimited: a story for children. 1897. Pbd under the pseud 'Martin Leach Warborough'.
The type-writer girl. 1897. Pbd under the pseud 'Olive Pratt Rayner'.
Flashlights on nature. New York 1898, London 1899.
Linnet: a romance. 1898.
The incidental Bishop. 1898.
Venice. 1898.
The European tour: a handbook for Americans and colonists. 1899.
Rosalba: the story of her development; with other episodes of the European Movement, more especially as they affected the Monti Berici, near Vicenza. 1899. Pbd under the pseud 'Olive Pratt Rayner'.
Miss Cayley's adventures. 1899.
Twelve tales with a headpiece, a tailpiece, and an intermezzo: being select stories chosen and arranged by the author. 1899.
Hilda Wade. 1900. First pbd in Strand Mag.
The natural history of Selborne, by Gilbert White. 1900. Ed Allen.
County and town in England, together with some annals of Churnside. 1901. First pbd in Pall Mall Gazette 1881–2.
In nature's workshop. 1901.
Selwyn Utterton's nemesis. In Strange happenings, 1901.
Sir Theodore's guest and other stories. Bristol 1902.
Evolution in Italian art. 1903, 1907, 1908.
The hand of God and other posthumous essays together with some reprinted papers. 1909.
A few ephemeral works are unrecorded here.

§2

Harrison, F. Grant Allen: an address. 1899.
Clodd, E. Grant Allen: a memoir, with a bibliography. 1900.
Le Gallienne, R. In his Attitudes and avowals, 1910. [EH]

'F. Anstey', Thomas Anstey Guthrie 1856–1934

Bibliographies

Turner, M. J. A bibliography of the works of F. Anstey (Thomas Anstey Guthrie). 1931 (priv ptd).

Collections

Humour and fantasy. 1931. Includes Vice versa; The tinted Venus; A fallen idol; The brass bottle; The talking horse; Salted almonds.

§1

Vice versâ: or a lesson for fathers. 1882, 1883 (rev), 1894 (with addns). Dramatised by E. Rose C (Gai 9 Apr 1883); French 1802.
The giant's robe. 1884.
The black poodle and other tales. 1884.
The tinted Venus: a farcical romance. Bristol 1885, London 1898. Dramatised as A vision of Venus, by H. Pleon. F. (Brit 20 Mar 1893). Dick 1025.
A fallen idol. 1886.
Burglar Bill and other pieces for the use of the young reciter. [1888], [1892] (enlarged as Mr Punch's young reciter); ed C. L. Graves 1931 (with Mr Punch's model music-hall songs and dramas, *below*, as The young reciter and model music-hall).
The pariah. 3 vols 1889.
Voces populi. 2 ser 1890–2. From Punch.
Tourmalin's time cheques. Bristol [1891], 1905 (as The time bargain: or Tourmalin's cheque book), 1986 (as Tourmalin's time cheques).
The travelling companions: a story in scenes. 1892, 1908. From Punch.
Mr Punch's model music-hall songs and dramas collected, improved, and re-arranged from 'Punch'. 1892; ed C. L. Graves 1931 (with Mr Punch's young reciter, *above*, as The young reciter and model music-hall).
The talking horse and other tales. 1892.
Mr Punch's pocket Ibsen: a collection of some of the master's best-known dramas condensed, revised and slightly re-arranged for the benefit of the earnest student. 1893, 1895 (enlarged). Parodies.
The man from Blankley's and other sketches. 1893. From Punch.
Under the rose: a story in scenes. [1894.] From Punch.
Lyre and lancet: a story in scenes. 1895.
The statement of Stella Maberly, written by herself. 1896. Anon.
Puppets at large: scenes and subjects from Mr Punch's show. 1897.
Baboo Jabberjee BA. 1897. From Punch.
Love among the lions: a matrimonial experiment. [1898.] From Idler Mag.
Paleface and Redskin, and other stories for boys and girls. [1898.]
The brass bottle. 1900. From Strand Mag. Dramatised 1911.
A Bayard from Bengal: being some account of the magnificent and spanking career of Chunder Bindabun Bhosh .... 1902. From Punch.
Only toys! 1903. From Strand Mag.
Salted almonds. 1906.
Winnie: an everyday story. In In a good cause, 1909.
Vice versâ, a farcical fantastic play in 3 acts. 1910.
The brass bottle, a farcical fantastic play in 4 acts. 1911 (H 13 Mar 1907).
In brief authority. 1915.
Percy and others: sketches mainly reprinted from Punch. 1915.
The last load: stories and essays. 1925.
The man from Blankley's, a comedy of the early nineties. 1927. (P. O. W. 25 Apr 1901; rev H. 24 Mar 1906).
Four Molière comedies, freely adapted. 1931.
Three Molière plays, freely adapted. 1933.
A long retrospect. 1936. [LS]

Sabine Baring-Gould 1834–1924

§1

The chorister: a tale of King's College Chapel in the Civil Wars. Cambridge [1854]. Anon.
The path of the just: tales of holy men and children. 1857.
Iceland: its scenes and sagas. 1863.
The book of were-wolves: being an account of a terrible superstition. 1865.
Post-mediaeval preachers: some account of the most celebrated preachers of the 15th, 16th and 17th centuries; with outlines of their sermons and specimens of their style. 1865.
Curious myths of the Middle Ages. 2 ser 1866–8.
The silver store, collected from mediaeval, Christian and Jewish mines. 1868, 1887 (with addns), 1898 (with addns). Poems.
Through flood and flame: a novel. 3 vols 1868.
Curiosities of olden times. [1869.]
The origin and development of religious belief. 2 pts 1869–70.
In exitu Israel: an historical novel. 2 vols 1870, 1 vol New York 1871 (as Gabrielle André).

Only a ghost!, by Irenaeus the Deacon. 1870. Sometimes attributed to Baring-Gould.
Legends of Old Testament characters, from the Talmud and other sources. 2 vols 1871.
The lives of the saints. 17 vols 1872–89, 16 vols 1897–8 (rev). 2 vols of selected reprints pbd Lampeter 1990 as Lives of the British saints and Lives of the Northumbrian saints.
How to save fuel. 1874.
Yorkshire oddities, incidents and strange events. 2 vols 1874.
Some modern difficulties: nine lectures. 1875.
The Vicar of Morwenstow: a life of Robert Stephen Hawker MA. 1876, 1876 (rev), 1899 (rev).
Ernestine: a novel. [By Wilhelmine von Hillern.] 2 vols 1879. Tr from the Ger by Baring-Gould.
Germany present and past. 2 vols 1879.
Mehalah: a story of the salt marshes. 2 vols 1880.
Germany. 1883.
John Herring: a West of England romance. 3 vols 1883, 1884.
Please tell me a tale: a collection of short original stories for children. 1885. Baring-Gould contributed Gottlob's picture.
Just one more tale: a second collection of stories for children, being a companion volume to Please tell me a tale. 1886. Baring-Gould contributed Wow Wow.
Court Royal: a story of cross currents. 3 vols 1886.
Germany. 1886, [1905] (rev), 1921 (rev and enlarged by J. MacCabe). With A. Gilman. A different work from Germany, *above*, 1883.
Golden Feather. [1886.]
Little Tu'penny. 1887.
Jack Frost's little prisoners: a collection of stories for children from four to twelve years of age. 1887. Baring-Gould contributed The Schnabelweid plot and The cats' tree.
Red spider. 2 vols 1887.
The Gaverocks: a tale of the Cornish coast. 3 vols 1887.
Richard Cable the lightshipman. 3 vols 1888.
Eve: a novel. 2 vols 1888.
The Pennycomequicks: a novel. 3 vols 1889.
Grettir the outlaw: a story of Iceland. [1889], '1890'.
Historic oddities and strange events. 2 ser 1889–91. Ser 2 also pbd as Freaks of fanaticism and other strange events.
Arminell: a social romance. 3 vols 1890.
Jacquetta and other stories. 1890.
My Prague pig and other stories for children. 1890.
Old country life. 1890.
Songs and ballads of the West: a collection made from the mouths of the people by S. Baring-Gould and H. Fleetwood Sheppard. 4 pts [1890], 1 vol [1905] (rev C. J. Sharp as Songs of the West).
Fifteen pounds. [1891.]
In troubadour-land: a ramble in Provence and Languedoc. 1891.
Urith: a tale of Dartmoor. 3 vols 1891.
Margery of Quether and other stories. 1891.
In the roar of the sea: a tale of the Cornish coast. 3 vols 1892.
Strange survivals: some chapters in the history of man. 1892.
Through all the changing scenes of life. [1892.]
The tragedy of the Caesars. 2 vols 1892.
Mrs Curgenven of Curgenven. 1893, 3 vols 1893.
Cheap Jack Zita. 3 vols 1893.
The two John Brents. [1893.]
A book of fairy tales retold. 1894.
Colour in composition. In On the art of writing fiction, [1894].
The deserts of southern France: an introduction to the limestone and chalk plateaux of ancient Aquitaine. 2 vols 1894.
The Icelander's sword, or the story of Oraefa-dal. 1894.
Kitty alone: a story of three fires. 3 vols 1894.
The Queen of Love: a novel. 3 vols 1894.
English minstrelsie: a national monument of English song. 8 vols Edinburgh 1895–[7]. Collated and ed Baring-Gould.
A book of nursery songs and rhymes. 1895. Ed Baring-Gould.
A garland of country song: English folk songs with their traditional melodies. Collected and arranged by S. Baring-Gould and H. Fleetwood Sheppard. 1895.
Fairy tales from Grimm. 1895. Introd by Baring-Gould.
Noémi. 1895.
Old English fairy tales. 1895.
Dartmoor idylls. 1896.
The broom-squire. 1896.
Perpetua: a story of Nimes in AD 213. 1897.
Guavas the tinner. 1897.
Bladys of the Stewponey. 1897.
The life of Napoleon Bonaparte. 1897.
A study of St Paul: his character and opinions. 1897.
An armory of the western counties (Devon and Cornwall): from unpublished manuscripts of the XVI century. Exeter 1898. With R. Twigge.
Domitia. 1898.
An old English home and its dependencies. 1898.
A book of the West: introduction to Devon and Cornwall. 2 vols 1899.
Pabo the priest. 1899.
The crock of gold. [1899.] Fairy tales.
Furze bloom: tales of the western moors. 1899.
A book of Dartmoor. 1900.
Winefred: a story of the chalk cliffs. 1900.
In a quiet village. 1900.
A book of Brittany. 1901.
Bath waters, by Preston King, with an historical sketch by S. Baring-Gould. [1901.]
The Frobishers: a story of the Staffordshire potteries. 1901.
Royal Georgie. 1901.
Brittany. 1902.
Nebo the nailer. 1902.
Miss Quillet. 1902.
Chris of all-sorts. 1903.
Amazing adventures, drawn by H. B. Neilson and written by S. Baring-Gould. [1903.]
A book of North Wales. 1903.
A book of ghosts. 1904.
Siegfried: a romance. 1904. Founded on Wagner's operas.
In Dewisland. 1904.
A book of South Wales. 1905.
A book of the Riviera. 1905.
A memorial of Horatio Lord Nelson. 1905.
Monsieur Pichelmère and other stories. 1905.
A book of the Rhine from Cleve to Mainz. 1906.
The lives of the British saints: the saints of Wales and Cornwall and such Irish saints as have dedications in Britain. 4 vols 1907–13, 1 vol Lampeter 1990 (abridged). With J. Fisher.
A book of the Cevennes. 1907.
Devon. 1907.
James Lawless innkeeper. 1907 (50 copies priv ptd).
Nero. 1907.
A book of the Pyrenees. 1907.
Devonshire characters and strange events. 1908.
Cornish characters and strange events. 1909.
A history of Sarawak under its two white Rajahs 1839–1908. 1909. With C. A. Bampfylde.
Cornwall. Cambridge 1910.
Family names and their story. 1910.
The land of Teck and its neighbourhood. 1911.
Cliff castles and cave dwellings of Europe. 1911.
Sheepstor. Plymouth 1912.
A book of folk-lore. [1913.]
Early reminiscences 1834–1864. 1923.

Further reminiscences 1864–1894. 1925.

Folk songs of the West Country, collected by Sabine Baring-Gould; annotated from the manuscripts at Plymouth Library and with additional material by Gordon Hitchcock. Newton Abbot 1974.

Baring-Gould also wrote a number of devotional and theological works, and contributed introds to several books on folk-lore and theology. A few ephemeral works are unrecorded here.

§2

Ellis, S. M. In his Mainly Victorian, [1925].

Powys, L. A Devonshire gentleman. North Amer Rev 121 1925.

Purcell, W. Onward Christian soldier: a life of Sabine Baring-Gould, parson, squire, novelist, antiquary, 1834–1924. 1957.

Reeves, J. The everlasting circle. 1960.

Hyde, W. J. The stature of Baring-Gould as a novelist. Nineteenth-Cent Fiction 15 1961.

Dickinson, B. H. C. Sabine Baring-Gould: squarson, writer and folk-lorist, 1834–1924. Newton Abbot 1970.

Kirk-Smith, H. 'Now the day is over': the life and times of Sabine Baring-Gould 1834–1924, squire and rector of Lew Trenchard. Boston, Lincs 1997. [EH]

Sir James Matthew Barrie 1860–1937

See col 2029.

Arthur Christopher Benson 1862–1925

See col 2313.

Sir Walter Besant 1836–1901

Collections of letters in the archives of Chatto & Windus, Royal Literary Fund, A. P. Watt; also in Dr William's Lib, London. See also Chatto & Windus production records.

§1

Studies in early French poetry. 1868, (2 impressions to 1877), Boston 1877, New York 1975 (reprint of 1868 edn).

The French humourists. 1873, Boston 1874, New York [1972].

Our work in Palestine. New York 1873.

Book of French: grammatical exercises, history of the language, etc. 1877.

Gaspard De Coligny. 1879 (New Plutarch ser; 2 impressions), New York 1879 (Harper's Half-Hour ser), 1879 (New Plutarch ser), [1879?] (Harper's School Classics), London 1894, 1905 (St Martin's Lib).

Rabelais. 1879 (Blackwood's Foreign Classics for English Readers; 2 impressions to 1885), Philadelphia [1879], London 1898.
REVIEW: Athenaeum 2 Aug 1879.

On the buying of books. 1881. First pbd in Temple Bar.

The revolt of man. 1882, (9 impressions to 1890), Leipzig 1882, New York 1882 (Seaside Lib), 1882, London 1896, 1898 (2 impressions to 1901), 1912.
REVIEWS: Westminster Rev July 1882; Spectator 28 Oct 1882.

All sorts and conditions of men. First pbd in Belgravia Jan–Dec 1882. 3 vols 1882, New York 1882 (Harper's Franklin Square Lib), [1882] (Caldwell's Berkeley Lib), [1882], [1882], [1882], [1882], London 1883 (Piccadilly Lib, 23 impressions to 1923 including 1883 'GR' (George Robertson) edn), 1884 (14 impressions to 1897), New York [188?], [188?], Philadelphia [188?], London 1897 (4 impressions to 1908), 1902 (St Martin's Lib), Toronto 1910, Chicago [19??], Boston [nd], St Clair Shores MI 1971.
REVIEWS: Acad 7 Oct 1882; Athenaeum 7 Oct 1882; Saturday Rev 14 Oct 1883; Spectator 21 Oct 1882; British Quart Rev Jan 1883; Westminster Rev Jan 1883.

The captain's room. 3 vols 1883, 1883 (Piccadilly Lib, 9 impressions to 1901 including 1883 'GR' (George Robertson) edn), 1884 (6 impressions to 1901), New York 1884 (The Leisure Hour Lib), [188?] (Franklin Square Lib), [188?] (The Seaside Lib).
REVIEWS: Athenaeum 17 Mar 1883; Academy 24 Mar 1883; British Quart Rev Apr 1883; Westminster Rev July 1883.

All in a garden fair. First pbd in Good Words Jan–Dec 1883. 3 vols 1883, New York 1883 (Franklin Square Lib), [1883] (Seaside Lib), [1883] (Lovell's Lib), London 1884 (Piccadilly Lib, 11 impressions to 1908 including 1883 'GR' (George Robertson) edn), 1885 (9 impressions to 1908), Chicago [189?] (Household edn), London 1912, [1919] (World's Best Lib).
REVIEWS: Athenaeum 24 Nov 1883; Saturday Rev 22 Dec 1883; Westminster Rev Apr 1884.

The life and achievements of E. H. Palmer. 1883, New York 1883; tr Ger Gotha 1884.
REVIEWS: Athenaeum 9 June 1883; Acad 16 June 1883.

Life in a hospital: an East End chapter. [1883.]

Readings in Rabelais. 1883. First pbd in GM.
REVIEWS: Saturday Rev 22 Dec 1883; Athenaeum 5 Jan 1884.

The art of fiction: a lecture. 1884, Boston 1884, [1884], London 1902, New York 1902.
REVIEW: Saturday Rev 31 May 1884.

Dorothy Forster. First pbd in The Graphic Jan–Dec 1884. 3 vols 1884, 1884 (Piccadilly Lib, 18 impressions to 1928 including 1884 'GR' (George Robertson) edn), Leipzig 1884, New York [1884] (Seaside Lib), London 1886 (10 impressions to 1898), New York 1886, [1887] (Franklin Square Lib), [188?] (Munro's Lib), Portway 1967.
REVIEW: Athenaeum 14 June 1884.

Uncle Jack [etc]. 5 tales. 1885, 1885 (2 impressions to 1894), 1886 (7 impressions to 1892), New York 1883 (Seaside Lib, 2 tales), 1885 (Harper's Handy ser, 3 tales), [1885] (Lovell's Lib, 2 tales), [1885?] (2 tales).
REVIEWS: Athenaeum 6 June 1885; Westminster Rev July 1885.

Children of Gibeon. First pbd in Longman's Mag Jan–Dec 1886. 3 vols 1886 (2 impressions), Leipzig 1886, New York [1886] (Franklin Square Lib), [1886] (Seaside Lib), London 1887 (Piccadilly Lib, 8 impressions to 1909 including 1887 'GR' (George Robertson) edn), 1888 (3 impressions to 1894), 1902, New York [19??].
REVIEWS: Athenaeum 20 Nov 1886; Acad 27 Nov 1886; Blackwood's Mag Dec 1886; Murray's Mag Jan 1887.

The Holy Rose. First pbd in All the Year Round Christmas 1886. 1886, New York 1886 (Franklin Square Lib), [1886] (Seaside Lib), [1886] (Lovell's Lib).

Twenty-one years' work 1865–86 (Palestine Exploration Fund). 1886 (with addns).
REVIEW: Athenaeum 2 Oct 1886.

The world went very well then. First pbd in Illus London News July–Dec 1886. New York [1886] (Franklin Square Lib), [1886] (Seaside Lib), 3 vols London 1887, Leipzig 1887, London 1887 (Piccadilly Lib, 5 impressions to 1912 including 2 1887 'GR' (George Robertson) edns), New York [1887] (Lovell's Lib), [188?], London 1889 (6 impressions to 1912), Liverpool 1919 (World's Best Lib).
REVIEWS: Athenaeum 30 Apr 1887; Saturday Rev 7 May 1887.

To call her mine. New York 1887 (Franklin Square Lib), [1887] (Lovell's Lib), [1887?].

Katherine Regina. Bristol [1887], New York 1887 (Franklin Square Lib), 1887 (Seaside Lib), [1887], Leipzig 1888; tr Polish Warsaw 1888.
REVIEW: Athenaeum 12 Nov 1887.

Herr Paulus. 3 vols 1888, 1888 (Piccadilly Lib, 2 impressions in 1888 including 'GR' (George Robertson) edn), New York 1888 (Franklin Square Lib), Leipzig 1888, New York [1888] (Seaside Lib), San Francisco [1888], London 1890, New York [193?].
REVIEWS: Athenaeum 28 Apr 1888; Westminster Rev July 1888.

The inner house. Bristol 1888, New York 1888 (Franklin Square Lib), 1888 (Lovell's Lib), Leipzig 1888, New York [1888] (Seaside Lib).

The eulogy of Richard Jefferies. 1888 (3 impressions to 1905), New York 1888.
REVIEW: Athenaeum 8 Dec 1888.

Fifty years ago. First pbd in The Graphic, Jubilee no, June 1887. 1888, New York [1888], London 1892.
REVIEW: Athenaeum 31 Mar 1888.

The doubts of Dives. Bristol [1889] (Arrowsmith's Bristol Lib), New York [1889?] (Aldine edn pbd as The lament of Dives).

The bell of St Paul's. First pbd in Longman's Mag Jan–Dec 1889. 3 vols 1889, New York 1889 (Franklin Square Lib), [1889] (Seaside Lib), London 1890 (Piccadilly Lib, 3 impressions to 1908 including 1889 'GR' (George Robertson) edn), Leipzig 1890, London 1891.

For faith and freedom. First pbd in Illus London News July–Dec 1888. 3 vols 1889, 1889 (Piccadilly Lib, 7 impressions to 1915 including 1889 'GR' (George Robertson) edn), New York 1889 (Franklin Square Lib), [1889] (Seaside Lib), [1889] (Lovell's Household Lib), Leipzig 1890, London 1891 (2 impressions to 1892), 1902 (2 impressions to 1911).
REVIEWS: Athenaeum Mar 1889; Pall Mall Gazette Mar 1889; Spectator Mar 1889.

To call her mine, etc. 1889, 1891 (Piccadilly Lib, 4 impressions to 1903 including 1889 'GR' (George Robertson) edn), 1891.

Armorel of Lyonesse. First pbd in Illus London News Jan–June 1890. 3 vols 1890, New York 1890, [1890?], [1890?], London 1891 (Piccadilly Novels, 17 impressions to 1949), Leipzig 1891, London 1893 (3 impressions to 1907), New York [189?], London 1909, Liverpool [1919] (World's Best Lib).
REVIEW: Athenaeum 22 Nov 1890.

Captain Cook. 1890 (English Men of Action, 5 impressions to 1925).
REVIEW: Athenaeum 22 Mar 1890.

The demoniac. Bristol [1890] (Arrowsmith's Bristol Lib), New York [1890], [1890], [1890], [1890] (Seaside Lib), [189?].

The holy rose, etc. (The holy rose; The last mass; The inner house; Even with this; Camilla's last string) 1890 (4 impressions to 1896), 1892.
REVIEW: Athenaeum 22 Mar 1890.

The 'Literary handmaid of the Church'. 1890.

Correspondence on the distribution of pensions to literature. 1890.

St Katherine's by the Tower. First pbd in The Graphic Jan–June 1891. 3 vols 1891, New York 1891 (Franklin Square Lib), [1891], [1891] (Fireside ser), London 1892 (Piccadilly Novels, 2 impressions to 1892 including an 1891 Colonial edn), 1893, New York [189?].

Verbena camellia stephanotis etc (The doubt of Dives; The demoniac; The doll's house — and after). 1892, New York 1892 (Franklin Square Lib), Leipzig 1892, London 1894; The doll's house — and after tr Ger Hamburg 1891.
REVIEW: Athenaeum 13 Aug 1892.

The ivory gate. First pbd in Chambers's Jnl Jan–Sep 1892. 3 vols 1892, New York 1892, Leipzig 1892 (English Lib), London 1893 (3 impressions to 1912 including 1892 Colonial edn and 1912 Lever Brothers edn), 1894, 1910, Liverpool 1919 (World's Best Lib).
REVIEW: Athenaeum 15 Oct 1892.

London. 1892, New York 1892, London 1894 (6 impressions to 1924), 1904 (St Martin's Lib, 2 impressions to 1910).
REVIEW: Athenaeum 8 Oct 1892.

General work of the society. 1892 (Palestine Exploration Fund).

The history of London. 1893 (8 impressions to 1913).

The society of authors. 1893.

The rebel queen. First pbd in Illus London News Jan–June 1893. 3 vols 1893, New York 1893, London 1894 (2 impressions including 1893 Colonial edn), 1895; New York 1975; tr Du 1895.

Beyond the dreams of avarice. First pbd in Tit-Bits July–Dec 1894. 1895, New York 1895, Leipzig 1895, London 1896 (3 impressions to 1921), 1897 (3 impressions to 1900).

In deacon's orders, etc (In deacon's orders; Peer and heiress; The equal women; The shrinking shoe; Quarantine island; In three weeks; One and two; A night with Tantalus; The solid gold reef company ltd; To the third and fourth generation; King David's friend). 1895, New York 1895, London 1897 (2 impressions to 1902), 1898 (2 impressions to 1900), New York [1970], 1976 (In deacon's orders).

Palestine Exploration Fund, Thirty years' work in the Holy Land. 1895.

Westminster. 1895. First pbd in Pall Mall Mag Sep–Dec 1894. New York [1894], London 1897 (3 impressions to 1925), 1907.

The city of refuge. First pbd in Pall Mall Mag Mar–Oct 1896, 3 vols 1896, New York [1896], London 1897 (3 impressions including 2 1896 Colonial edns), 1899.

The master craftsman. First pbd in Chambers's Jnl Jan–June 1896, 2 vols 1896 (2 impressions), New York [1896], [1896] (The Fortnightly Lib), Leipzig 1896, London 1897 (3 impressions to 1897 including 2 1896 Colonial edns), 1899.

A fountain sealed. First pbd in Illus London News Jan–Mar 1897. 1897, New York [1897], Leipzig 1896, London 1898.

The rise of empire. [1897] (2 impressions to 1898), New York 1897.

Alfred: a lecture. 1898 (3 impressions to 1899).

The changeling. 1898, New York [1898], London 1899.

The orange girl. (1st pbd in Lady's Pictorial Jan–June 1899. 1899 (8 impressions to 1900 including a Colonial edn), New York 1899, Leipzig 1899, London 1901 (3 impressions to 1906), 1904 (2 impressions to 1921), 1922.

The pen and the book. 1899.

South London. First pbd in Pall Mall Mag Jan–Apr 1898. '1899' [1898], New York [1898], London 1912.

The alabaster box. First pbd Leisure Hour Oct 1899–Mar 1900. 1900 (3 impressions), New York 1900, London 1904.

The fourth generation. 1900 (3 impressions), New York [1900], Leipzig 1900, London 1901; tr Rus St Petersburg 1901.

East London. 1901, New York 1901, London 1902.

The lady of Lynn. First pbd in Queen Jan–June 1901. 1901, New York 1901, Leipzig 1901, London 1904, 1912.

The story of King Alfred. 1901.

Autobiography. 1902, New York 1902, St Clair Shores MI 1971.

A five year's tryst and other stories. 1902, 1905.

London in the eighteenth century. 1902 (Survey of London, 3 impressions to 1925), New York 1903.

No other way. First pbd in the Lady's Realm Nov 1901–Oct 1902. 1902, New York 1902, London 1906 (2 impressions to 1911), 1908.

London in the time of the Stuarts. 1903 (Survey of London).

As we are and as we may be (The endowment of the daughter; From thirteen to seventeen; The people's palace; Sunday morning in the city; A riverside parish; St Katherine's by the Tower; The upward pressure; The land of romance (the United States); The land of reality (the United States); Art and the people; The amusements of the people; The associated life). 1903.

Essays and historiettes (King René of Anjou; The failure of the French reformation; Théophile de Viau; Alfred de Musset; Henry Murger; Froissart's love story; The story of a fair Circassian; Over Johnson's grave; The first society of British authors; Literature as a career). 1903, New York [1970].

The Thames. 1903 (Fascination of London).

London in the time of the Tudors. 1904 (Survey of London), 1989.

Medieval London. 2 vols (vol 1 historical and social; vol 2 Ecclesiastical) 1906 (Survey of London).

Early London: Prehistoric, Roman, Saxon and Norman. 1908 (Survey of London).

London in the nineteenth century. 1909 (Survey of London).

London city. 1910 (Survey of London).

London north of the Thames. 1911 (Survey of London).

London south of the Thames. 1912 (Survey of London).

Collaborative works

Jerusalem: the city of Herod and Saladin. 1871 (3 impressions to 1891), New York 1889, London 1899 ('fourth edn enlarged'), 1908 (St Martin's Lib). With E. H. Palmer.

Stewart's local examination series. 1877–82. With R. J. Griffiths.

Constantinople. 1879. With W. J. Brodribb.

Sir Jocelyn's cap. Longman's Mag Dec 1884–Jan 1885. With W. H. Pollock.

How can a love and appreciation of art be best developed among the masses of the people? In W. Tuckwell, Art and handwork for the people, 1885.

British copyright. In G. H. Putnam, The question of copyright, New York 1891.

The charm and other drawing room plays (The charm; The voice of love; Peer and heiress; Loved I not honour more; The shrinking shoe; The glove; The spy; The wife's confession). 1896, New York [1897], London 1898. With W. Pollock.

A riverside parish. In R. A. Woods et al, The poor in great cities, 1896.

The memory cell. In Charles Hyne, For Britain's soldiers, 1900.

The Strand district. 1902. With G. E. Mitton (Fascination of London).

Westminster. 1902. With G. E. Mitton (Fascination of London).

Holborn and Bloomsbury. 1903. With G. E. Mitton (Fascination of London).

Shoreditch and the East End. 1908. With others (Fascination of London).

Works written in collaboration with James Rice

Ready-money Mortiboy. First pbd in Once a Week Jan–June 1872. 3 vols 1872, 1873, 1877 (16 impressions to 1912 including 1912 Lever Brothers edn), 1877 (13 impressions to 1897), New York 1879 (Lib of Famous Fiction), 1880 (Seaside Lib), Leipzig 1884, London 1887 (Lib edn), New York 1888, London 1901 (3 impressions to 1912), 1908, Liverpool 1919 (World's Best Lib), London 1926 (Pocket Classics), Bath 1974. Dramatic version, as Ready money, by Rice and W. Maurice, was produced at the Court Theatre, 12 Mar 1874.

My little girl. First pbd in Once a Week Dec 1872–May 1873. 3 vols 1873, New York 1872, Boston 1873, London 1877 (11 impressions to 1893), 1877 (14 impressions to 1894), 1887 (Lib edn), New York [1888], London 1909.

The golden butterfly. First pbd in World Jan–Oct 1876. 3 vols 1876, Toronto 1876, London 1877 (22 impressions to 1912 including Longman's Colonial edn), 1877 (23 impressions to 1895 including 1899 Daily Telegraph edn), New York 1877, 1877, [1877], [1877], [1878] (Seaside Lib), Leipzig 1883, London 1887 (Lib edn), New York 1888 (Lib edn), London 1895 (7 impressions to 1909), Philadelphia [18??], London 1907 (5 impressions to 1928).
REVIEW: Saturday Rev 2 Dec 1876.

The case of Mr Lucraft and other tales (From the supernatural; The case of Mr Lucraft; The mystery of Joe Morgan; An old, old story; Lady Kitty; The old four-poster; My own experience – from fairy-land; Titania's farewell – from fact; On the Goodwin; Edelweis; Love finds the way; The death of Samuel Pickwick; When the ship comes home). 2 vols 1876, 1877 (6 impressions to 1891), 1877 (9 impressions to 1891), 1888 (Lib edn), New York [1888] (Lib edn), [188?] (Seaside Lib).

This son of Vulcan. First pbd in London Society July 1875–Oct 1876. 3 vols 1876, 1877 (10 impressions to 1894), 1877 (13 impressions to 1902), New York [187?], London 1887 (Lib edn), New York 1888 (Lib edn).

With harp and crown. 3 vols 1875, Boston 1876, London 1877 (9 impressions to 1892), 1877 (12 impressions to 1915 including 1915 The Khaki Lib), 1887 (Lib edn), New York 1888 (Lib edn).

Such a good man. 1877.

Le chien d'or. The Graphic, Summer no, 1878.

The monks of Thelema. First pbd in World Jan–Oct 1878. 3 vols 1878, 1878 (11 impressions to 1894), Toronto 1878, London 1880 (13 impressions to 1892), New York [1883] (Seaside Lib), London 1887 (Lib edn, 3 impressions to 1910), New York 1888 (Lib edn), London 1906.
REVIEW: Westminster Rev Jan 1879.

By Celia's arbour. First pbd in The Graphic Sep 1877–Mar 1878. 3 vols 1878, 1878 (13 impressions to 1912), New York 1878, [1878] (Seaside Lib), London 1880 (14 impressions to 1900), 1888 (Lib edn, 3 impressions to 1904), New York 1888 (Lib edn), Leipzig 1893, London 1908.

'Twas in Trafalgar's Bay. New York 1879 (Harper's Half-Hour ser), 1879 (Union Square Lib), [1879?] (Seaside Lib), London 1880 (10 impressions to 1898), 1881 (10 impressions to 1893), New York [1882] (Waverley Lib).

Shepherds all and maidens fair. New York 1878 (Harper's Half-Hour ser), [1878] (Seaside Lib), 1882 (Fireside Lib).

Sweet Nelly, my heart's delight. New York 1879 (Franklin Square Lib), 1880 (Seaside Lib, with Henry James, A bundle of letters).

'Twas in Trafalgar's Bay and other stories ('Twas in Trafalgar's Bay; Shepherds all and maidens fair; Such a good man; Le chien d'or). 1879 (2 impressions), 1888 (Lib edn), New York [1888] (Lib edn).

The seamy side. First pbd in Time July 1879–June 1880. 3 vols 1880, 1 vol 1880 (14 impressions to 1907), New York 1880 (Seaside Lib), 1880, London 1881 (13 impressions to 1898), 1888 (Lib edn), New York 1888 (Lib edn).
REVIEW: Athenaeum Jan–June 1880.

The chaplain of the Fleet. First pbd in The Graphic Dec 1880–June 1881. 3 vols 1881, 1881 (11 impressions to 1894 including 2 1881 'GR' (George Robertson) edns), New York 1881 (Franklin Square Lib), 1881 (Seaside Lib), London 1883 (12 impressions to 1910), 1888 (Lib edn, 2 impressions to 1900), New York 1888 (Lib edn), London 1902 (2 impressions to 1909), 1914 (Wayfarer's Lib).
REVIEW: Athenaeum Jan–June 1881.

Sir Richard Whittington. 1881 (New Plutarch ser), New York 1881, [1881?] (Makers of History), [1881?], London 1894 (2 impressions to 1902), 1905 (St Martin's Lib).
REVIEW: Athenaeum 22 Oct 1881.

The ten years' tenant and other stories (Ten years' tenant; Sweet Nelly, my heart's delight; Over the sea with a sailor). 3 vols 1881, 1881 (8 impressions to 1895 including 'GR' (George Robertson) edn 1881), 1882 (7 impressions to 1893), New York [1883] (Seaside Lib), [1885] (Romantic Tales), London 1888 (Lib edn, 2 impressions to 1906), New York [1888] (Lib edn).
REVIEWS: Athenaeum Jan–June 1881; Westminster Rev Apr 1881.

So they were married. New York 1882 (Franklin Square Lib), [1882] (Lovell's Lib).

Contributions to periodicals

For Besant's contributions to the British Quart Rev, Contemporary Rev, Cornhill Mag, Longman's Mag, Macmillan's Mag, Nat Rev, New Rev, Nineteenth Cent, *and* Temple Bar, *see* Wellesley *vol 5 1989.*

Charles Reade's novels. GM Aug 1882.

An East End chapter. GM Apr 1883.

Besant edited the Author *1890–1901.*

Letters and journals

Sir Walter Besant's 'Bourbon' journal, Aug 1863. 1933.

Editions

The literary remains of C. F. T. Drake. 1877. Ed Besant, with a memoir.

The new Plutarch, lives of men and women of action. 1879 etc. Ed partly by Besant.

The survey of Western Palestine. By C. R. Conder. 1881. Ed E. H. Palmer and Besant.

The Fascination of London series. 12 vols 1902–8. Ed Besant (The Strand district; Westminster; Hampstead and Marylebone;

Chelsea; Holborn and Bloomsbury; The Thames; Hammersmith, Fulham and Putney; Kensington; Mayfair, Belgravia and Bayswater; Clerkenwell and St Lukes; Hackney and Stoke Newington; Shoreditch and the East End).
The survey of London. 10 vols 1902–12. Ed Besant. *See also* individual vols listed *above*.

Introductions and prefaces
Collins, Wilkie. Blind love. 1890. Completed and with a preface by Besant.
Hake, A. E. Suffering London. 1892. With an introd by Besant.
Wallis, D. Dorothy Wallis. 1892. With an introd by Besant.
Athenian Society. The Athenian Oracle. [1892.] With a prefatory letter by Besant.
Reade, Charles. The cloister and the hearth. 1893. With an introd by Besant.
Haynes, A. E. Man-hunting in the desert. 1894. With an introd by Besant.
Round, J. H. The commune of London. 1899. With a prefatory letter by Besant.
Bowker, A. Alfred the Great. 1899. With an introd by Besant.
Defoe, Daniel. A journal of the plague year. 1900. With an introd by Besant.
Gates, W. G. Illustrated history of Portsmouth. 1900. With an introd by Besant.
Locks, W. A. East London antiquities. 1902. With an introd by Besant.

Attributed or spurious works
When George the Third was king. 2 vols 1872. (Wrongly attributed to Besant by BL Catalogue.)

§2
Eliot, S. His generation read his stories: Walter Besant, Chatto and Windus and All sorts and conditions of men. Publishing History 21 1987.
Eliot, S. Unequal partnership: Besant, Rice and Chatto 1876–1882. Publishing History 26 1989.
Feltes, W. Literary capital and the late Victorian novel. 1993. [SE]

Matilda Barbara Betham-Edwards 1836–1919

§1
The white house by the sea. 2 vols 1852, 1857, 1 vol 1864 (new edn), 1875 (new edn), [1882], Leipzig 1911 (Tauchnitz), London 1913, 1930.
Charlie and Ernest: or play and work. Edinburgh 1859, 1878 (new edn).
Now or never. Edinburgh 1859, London [1877] (new edn).
REVIEW: Saturday Rev 8 1859.
Holiday among the mountains: or scenes and stories of Wales. 1860, 1861 (illustr F. J. Skill), 1880 (new edn), New York [1880?].
Ally and her school-fellow. [1861], 1872 (new edn).
Little bird red and little bird blue [in 4 acts and in verse]. 1861, New York [1862?], London [1883].
John and I. 3 vols 1862 (anon), 1 vol 1876 (new edn).
Scenes and stories of the Rhine. 1862, 1863 (illustr F. W. Key).
Snow-flakes and the stories they told the children. 1862, [1862] (illustr H. K. Browne), 1881, 1883 (new edn), London and New York [1884]. Verse.
Doctor Jacob. 3 vols 1864, 1 vol 1868, Boston 1869, Leipzig 1884 (Tauchnitz), New York 1884, [1885], 1888, London 1890 (new edn).
REVIEW: Saturday Rev 17 1864.
The primrose pilgrimage: a woodland story. 1864 (illustr T. Macquoid), 1865. Verse.
Lisabee's love-story. 3 vols 1865 (anon); 1876 (new edn).
The wild flower of Ravensworth. 3 vols 1866 (anon); 1876 (new edn).
A winter with the swallows, 1866, 1867.
Through Spain to the Sahara. 1867, 1868.
REVIEW: Saturday Rev 25 1868.
Dr Campany's courtship and other tales. 1868. Contains Dr Campany's courtship, The burg-keeper's secret, Out of the world, Schloss Schaubek, A letter, The boarding-house in the Rue Buffon, A madman's story, The Canstatt conspirators, An eastern love-story, Lucia.
Kitty. Serialised in Temple Bar May 1868–Apr 1869, 3 vols 1869, New York 1870, 1 vol London 1872, 1877 (new edn), New York 1882, London 1882, 1883, 1884, 1891 (new edn), 1907.
REVIEWS: Nation (New York) 12 1871; Saturday Rev 32 1871.
The Sylvestres. Serialised in Good Words Jan–Dec 1871, 3 vols 1871, 1 vol Leipzig 1872 (Tauchnitz), Philadelphia 1872, London 1877 (new edn), New York 1882.
REVIEWS: Athenaeum 2296, Oct 1871; Nation (New York) 14 1872.
Holiday letters from Athens, Cairo and Weimar. 1873.
Mademoiselle Josephine's Fridays and other stories. 1874, 1875. Contains Mademoiselle Josephine's Fridays, Episodes in the life of a musician, Two letters that crossed, Christmas in the desert, Leaves from a lost diary, At the world's end, Ruth in the garden, Philomena, My cousin Rénée, Two winter days.
Felicia. 3 vols 1875, 2 vols Leipzig 1875 (Tauchnitz), London 1877 (new edn), [1879] (new edn).
Minna's holiday: or country cousins, and other stories. 1875, 1876. Contains Minna's holiday, The dream-mamma, Bob's belongings, The runaway girls in green.
Walking with the world. Philadelphia 1875.
Bridget. 3 vols 1877, 1884 (new edn), [1886].
REVIEW: Spectator 50 1877.
A year in western France. 1877.
REVIEW: Saturday Rev 43 1877.
Brother Gabriel: or on the banks of the Loire. 3 vols 1878, 2 vols Leipzig (Tauchnitz), London 1895 (new edn), 1901 (rev edn).
REVIEW: Spectator 51 1878.
Friends over the water: a series of sketches of French life. London and Edinburgh 1879 (illus).
Holidays in eastern France. 1879, New York 1879.
REVIEW: Saturday Rev 47 1879; Spectator 52 1879.
Forestalled; or the life quest. 2 vols 1880, Leipzig 1880 (Tauchnitz), New York [1880], London 1890, New York [1891?] (authorised edn).
REVIEW: Spectator 53 1880.
Six life studies of famous women. London and New York 1880 (illus). Also pbd in separate parts [1880], 184 (Famous Women Lib): 1 Fernan Caballero; 2 Alexandrine Tinne; 3 Caroline Herschel; 4 Marie Pape-Carpentier; 5 Elizabeth Carter; 6 Matilda Betham.
REVIEW: Saturday Rev 50 1880.
The starry blossom, and other stories for the young. 1881.
Exchange no robbery. Serialised in Fraser's Mag Feb–May 1882. Exchange no robbery, and other novelettes. 2 vols '1883' [1882], Leipzig 1882 (Tauchnitz), New York [1882]. Contains Exchange no robbery, A Japanese bride, Fernande, Priest and maiden, Désillusioné, The three B. A.'s, Two winter days by the sea, A Christmas cabful.
Disarmed! 2 vols 1883, 1 vol Leipzig 1883 (Tauchnitz), New York [1883], London 1891 (new and rev edn), 1894.
Pearla: or the world after an island. Serialised in Good Words Jan–Dec 1883, 3 vols 1883, 1 vol New York [1883], Leipzig 1884 (Tauchnitz), London [1892] (illustr D. Knowles), Bristol and London 1913 (new edn).
Love and mirage: or the waiting on an island, and other tales. 21 vols 1884, New York 1884, London 1885, New York [1889], London 1890. Contains Love and mirage, Stories from windows, A dream of millions, Dropped from the clouds.
REVIEW: Spectator 58 1885.
Poems. 1884, 1907 (rev and enlarged new edn).

The flower of doom: or the conspirator, and other stories. 1885, New York 1885, London 1887, 1890 (3rd edn). Contains The flower of doom, Love and manuscript, A group of immortals, The rebuke amid roses.
REVIEW: Spectator 58 1885.
Half-way: an Anglo-French romance. New York 1885, 2 vols London 1886, New York 1886, London 1889 (new and rev edn), 1892, 1893.
Next of kin wanted. 2 vols 1887, Leipzig 1887 (Tauchnitz), New York [1887], London 1911.
The parting of the ways. 3 vols 1888, 1 vol Leipzig 1888 (Tauchnitz), London 1890, New York [1890], London 1891.
REVIEW: Murray's Mag 3 May 1888.
For one and the world. 2 vols 1889, Leipzig 1889 (Tauchnitz), New York [1890], London 1895.
The roof of France, or the Causses of the Lozère. 1889.
A romance of the wire. New York [c. 1890], London [1891].
A dream of millions, and other tales. 1891, 1892, Leipzig 1892 (Tauchnitz). Contains A dream of millions, A romance of the cloister, Isabelle's waiting, Father Chrystal's elixir, The halt on the way, The romance of a French parsonage, The message.
A north-country comedy. 1891, 1892, Philadelphia 1892, London 1897.
The romance of a French parsonage: or the double sacrifice. 2 vols 1891, Leipzig 1891 (Tauchnitz), New York [c. 1891], London 1892, 1916. First pbd in A dream of millions, 1891, *above*.
France of to-day: a survey, comparative and retrospective. New York [1892], 2 vols Leipzig 1892–4 (Tauchnitz), London 1892–4.
Two aunts and a nephew. 1892, Leipzig 1892 (Tauchnitz), London 1897 (new edn), Bristol 1902.
The curb of honour. 1893, New York [1893], London 1894.
A romance of Dijon. 1894, New York 1894, Leipzig 1895 (Tauchnitz), London 1896.
REVIEW: Dial 18 1895.
The dream-Charlotte: a story of echoes. 1896, Leipzig 1896 (Tauchnitz), New York 1896, London 1898.
The golden bee, and other recitations. [1896].
A blue book for sale: comedietta. 1898.
Reminiscences. 1898, 1898 (new edn), 1903 (new and rev edn).
A storm-rent sky: scenes of love and revolution. 1898, Leipzig 1898 (Tauchnitz), London 1898 (2nd edn), 1911, 1917.
Anglo-French reminiscences 1875–1899. '1900' [1899], Leipzig 1900 (Tauchnitz).
The lord of the harvest. 1899, Leipzig 1899 (Tauchnitz), Edinburgh and London 1913 (introd by F. Harrison, WC), Woodbridge 1983 (introd by C. N. Smith).
REVIEW: Bookman 17 1899.
A Suffolk courtship. 1900, Leipzig 1900 (Tauchnitz).
East of Paris: sketches in the Gâtinais, Bourbonnais and Champagne. 1902 (illustr H. E. Detmold), Leipzig 1902 (Tauchnitz), New York 1902.
REVIEW: Bookman 23 1902.
Mock beggar's hall: a story. 1902, Leipzig 1902 (Tauchnitz).
Barham Brocklebank M. D. 1903, Leipzig 1903 (Tauchnitz).
A humble lover. 1903, Leipzig 1903 (Tauchnitz).
REVIEW: Bookman 23 1903.
Home life in France. 1905, [1905] (3rd edn), Chicago 1905, London 1907, '1907' [1908] (5th edn), [1913] (6th edn). Some of these papers first pbd in Cornhill and other mags.
REVIEWS: Dial 39 1905; Nation (New York) 81 1905.
Martha Rose, teacher. 1906, Leipzig 1906 (Tauchnitz).
A close ring: or episodes in the life of a French family. Bristol 1907.
Literary rambles in France. 1907, Chicago 1907.
REVIEWS: Dial 43 1907; London Quart Rev of Books 108 1907; Nation (New York) 86 1908.
French vignettes: a series of dramatic episodes 1787–1871. 1909, 1909 (2nd edn), New York 1909.
REVIEW: Bookman 37 1909.
French men, women and books: a series of nineteenth century studies. 1910, Chicago 1911.
REVIEWS: Bookman 38 1910; Dial 50 1911; Nation (New York) 92 1911.
Unfrequented France: by river and mead and town. 1910 (illus), 1910 (2nd edn), New York [1910].
REVIEW: Bookman 39 Suppl 1910.
Friendly faces of three nationalities. 1911 (illus).
REVIEW: Bookman 40 1911.
In the heart of the Vosges and other sketches by a 'devious traveller'. 1911, Chicago 1912.
REVIEWS: Bookman 41 Suppl 1911; Dial 53 1912.
In French-Africa: scenes and memories. 1912 (illus), [1913], Chicago [1913].
From an Islington window: pages of reminiscent romance. 1914, Leipzig 1914 (Tauchnitz).
Under the German ban in Alsace and Lorraine. [1914.]
Hearts of Alsace: a story of our time. 1916.
Twentieth-century France, social, intellectual, territorial. 1917 (illus).
REVIEWS: Bookman 53 1917; Punch 152 1917; Nation (New York) 106 1918.
War poems. Bristol [1917].
Mid-Victorian memories, with a personal sketch by Mrs Sarah Grand. 1919, New York 1919.
REVIEW: Nation (New York) 111 1920.

Contributions to periodicals

Blanche. Once a Week 17 and 24 Mar 1866.
Kabyles. Once a Week 6 July 1867.
Hattie's dream. Once a Week 7 and 14 Dec 1867.
Christmas in the desert. Warne's Christmas Annual 1867. Rptd in Mademoiselle Josephine's Fridays, 1874, *above*.
My cousin Renée. Once a Week Christmas 1867. Rptd in Mademoiselle Josephine's Fridays, 1874, *above*.
Cottage homes for working children. Good Words 11 1870.
English orphans in Paris. Good Words 19 1878.
French vineyards. Sunday Mag no 24 1895.
The Lycée Fénélon for girls. Chambers's Jnl 81 1904.
Old and young conscripts. Chambers's Jnl 81 1904.
General William Booth: a character sketch. Independent Rev 4 1905.
The vanished salon, or the lost art of conversation. Chambers's Jnl 83 1906.
Betham-Edwards contributed to the Daily News *for many years. See also* Wellesley *vol 5*.

Translations, editions

[d'Houdetot, C. F. A.] Bombonnel the panther-slayer. Tr Betham-Edwards 1887.
Young, A. Travels in France during the years 1787, 1788 and 1789. Ed with an introd, biographical sketch and notes by Betham-Edwards. 1889, 1890 (3rd edn), 1905, 1906.
Poems of Owen Meredith (the Earl of Lytton). Selected and introduced by Betham-Edwards. London and New York [1890].
Marteilhe, J. Passages in the life of a galley-slave. Tr Betham-Edwards 1895.
Young, A. Autobiography. With selections from his correspondence. Ed Betham-Edwards 1898.
French fireside poetry, with metrical translations and an introduction by the late Matilda Betham-Edwards, edited by B. Miall. 1919, Boston 1921.
REVIEW: Bookman 57 Suppl 1919.

§2

Black, H. C. In her Notable women authors of the day, Glasgow 1893.
The Times 7 Jan 1919.
In DNB 1912–21.

Blain, V., P. Clements and I. Grundy. The feminist companion to literature in English. 1990.
See also col 1750.

Clementina Black 1853–1922

A collection of Black's corespondence and other documents in the R. L. Wolff Collection is described in Wolff's Nineteenth century fiction: a bibliographical catalogue, *vol 1, New York and London 1981.*

Bibliography

Glage, A. In her Clementina Black: a study in social history and literature, Heidelberg 1981.

§1

A Sussex idyl. 1877, New York 1877, 1878. Novel.
Orlando. 3 vols 1879, 1880. Novel.
REVIEW: The Times 5 Feb 1880.
Mericas. Serialised in Dublin Univ Mag Apr–June 1879. Mericas, and other stories. 1880, 1881. Contains Mericas, An artist, Topsy, The troubles of an automaton.
Miss Falkland, and other stories. 1892. Contains Miss Falkland, The professor's piano, Captain Lackland, Moonlight and floods, In a London street, A long day.
REVIEWS: Athenaeum 3370 1892; Bookman 2 1892.
An agitator. 1894, New York 1895. Novel.
REVIEWS: Athenaeum 3501 1894; Rev of Revs 10 1894.
The truck acts: what they do and what they ought to do. 1894. With S. N. Fox. (Issued by the Women's Trade Union Assoc.)
The Princess Désirée. Serialised in Longman's Monthly Mag Sep–Dec 1896, 1 vol 1896 (illustr J. Williamson), New York 1896. Novel.
The pursuit of Camilla. 1899, Philadelphia 1900. Novel.
REVIEW: Bookman 17 1899.
The rhyme of the factory act. 1900.
Some current objections to factory legislation for women. In B. Webb, The case for the factory acts, 1901.
Frederick Walker. London and New York [1902] (illus), London [1913].
REVIEWS: Nation (New York) 75 1902; London Quart Rev 99 1903.
High treason: a romance of the days of George II. 1902. Novel.
Kindergarten plays [in verse]. 2 vols 1903.
London tailoresses. [1905.]
Sweated industry and the minimum wage. 1907 (with an introd by A. G. Gardiner), [1910].
REVIEW: Ethics 18 1907–8.
Caroline. 1908. Novel.
REVIEWS: Bookman 33 1908; Punch 134 1908.
Makers of our clothes. 1909. With A. Meyer.
The Linleys of Bath. 1911, 1926 (rev new edn with an introd by G. Saintsbury), 1971 (with a new introd by the Countess of Rosse and a pedigree of the Linley family compiled by Sir A. Wagner).
REVIEWS: Bookman 41 1911; Punch 172 1927.
A new way of housekeeping. [1918.]
REVIEWS: Bookman 54 1918; TLS 1 Aug 1918.
Woman in industry from seven points of view. 1908. With G. M. Tuckwell and others.

Translations, editions, etc

Bréal, A. Rembrandt. Tr Black, London and New York [1902].
REVIEW: Bookman 22 1902.
Rolland, R. Millet. Tr Black, London and New York [1902].
Partsch, J. Central Europe. Tr Black 1903, London and New York 1915.
Mauclair, C. Auguste Rodin. Tr Black 1905, New York 1905.
Gray, B. K. A modern humanist. Miscellaneous papers. With an appreciation by Black. 1910.
The Cumberland letters: being the correspondence of Richard Dennison Cumberland and George Cumberland, between the years 1771 and 1784. Ed Black 1912.
REVIEW: Bookman 43 1912.
Married women's work. Ed Black 1915, London and New York 1980 (facs reprint), London 1983, 1990.
REVIEW: Dublin Rev 158 1916.
Black's numerous articles and pbd letters are listed in Glage, below. See also Wellesley *vol 5 1989.*

§2

Cameron, M. Clementina Black: a character sketch. The Young Woman 1 1892–3.
The Times 20 Dec 1922.
Glage, L. Clementina Black: a study in social history and literature. Heidelberg 1981.
Banks, O. In The biographical dictionary of British feminists vol 2, Hemel Hempstead 1990.

William Black 1841–98

Collections

New and revised edition of the novels. 28 vols 1892–8.

§1

James Merle: an autobiography, edited by William Black. Glasgow 1864. Written by Black.
Love or marriage?: a novel. 3 vols 1868.
In silk attire: a novel. 3 vols 1869.
Kilmeny. 3 vols 1870.
The monarch of Mincing-Lane: a novel. 3 vols 1871.
A daughter of Heth. 3 vols 1871.
Mr Pisistratus Brown, MP, in the Highlands. 1871. Rptd from Daily News with addns.
The strange adventures of a phaeton. 2 vols 1872.
A Princess of Thule. 3 vols 1874.
The maid of Killeena and other stories. 1874.
Three feathers: a novel. 3 vols 1875.
Madcap Violet. 3 vols 1876.
Lady Silverdale's sweetheart and other stories. 1876.
Green pastures and Piccadilly. 3 vols 1877.
Macleod of Dare: a novel. 3 vols '1879' [1878].
Goldsmith. 1878 (EML).
White wings: a yachting romance. 3 vols 1880.
Sunrise: a story of these times. 3 vols 1881.
The beautiful wretch; The four MacNicols; The pupil of Aurelius: three stories, in three volumes. 3 vols 1881.
Yolande: the story of a daughter. 3 vols 1883.
Adventures in Thule: three stories for boys. 1883.
Shandon Bells: a novel. 3 vols 1883.
Judith Shakespeare: a romance. 3 vols 1884.
White heather: a novel. 3 vols 1885.
The wise women of Inverness: a tale, and other miscellanies. 1885.
Sabina Zembra: a novel. 3 vols 1887.
In far Lochaber. 3 vols 1888.
The strange adventures of a house-boat. 3 vols 1888.
The penance of John Logan, and two other tales. 1889.
Nanciebel: a tale of Stratford-on-Avon. New York 1889.
The new Prince Fortunatus. 3 vols 1890.
Stand fast, Craig-Royston!: a novel. 3 vols 1890.
Donald Ross of Heimra. 3 vols 1891.
Wolfenberg. 3 vols 1892.
The magic ink and other tales. 1892.
The handsome Humes. 3 vols 1893.
Highland cousins. 3 vols 1894.
Briseis. 1896.
Wild Eelin: her escapades, adventures, and bitter sorrows. 1898.
With the eyes of youth, and other sketches. 1903.

§2

Reid, T. W. William Black, novelist: a biography. 1902.
'Melville, Lewis' (L. S. Benjamin). In his Victorian novelists, 1906.
Scene and sentiment: Black reaches his centenary. TLS 8 Nov 1941.

Mary Elizabeth Braddon, later Maxwell 1835–1915

Ms collections in Houghton Lib, Harvard, and the Robert Lee Woolf Collection, HRHRC, Austin TX.

Bibliographies

Sadleir, M. Nineteenth-century fiction. 2 vols 1951.
Summers, M. A Gothic bibliography. [1941.]
Woolf, R. L. Nineteenth century fiction. 5 vols 1981–6.

§1

Three times dead: or the secret of the heath. [1860] (in penny pts, undated), 1861 (as The trail of the serpent: or three times dead), 1864 (serialised in Halfpenny Jnl as Three times dead: or the trail of the serpent), 1866 (as The trail of the serpent); tr Fr Charles Bernard-Derosne 2 vols Paris 1864.
Garibaldi and other poems. 1861.
The Lady Lisle. 1862, 1867 (rev). Tr Fr C. Bernard-Derosne, Paris 1863.
Lady Audley's secret. First ptd in Robin Goodfellow and Sixpenny Mag; after book pbd, serialised in London Jnl. 3 vols 1862, 2 vols Leipzig 1862, 1 vol London 1863; tr Fr J. Bernard-Derosne 2 vols Paris 1863, 1873 (rev and corrected).
REVIEWS: [Mansel, Henry] Sensation Novels Quart Rev 113 1863; Miss Braddon, New Rev 2 1863; The morality of modern novels, New Rev 1 1863; The popular novels of the year, Fraser's Mag 68 1863; [Smith, Alexander] Novels and novelists of the day, North Br Rev 38 1863.
Ralph the bailiff and other tales. 1862, [1866] (with 4 more stories, including Lost and found, the subplot cut out of Henry Dunbar, 1864), [1870] (yellowback, with an extra story later in Weavers and weft, 1877); tr C. Bernard-Derosne, Paris 1864.
Captain of the Vulture. 1863, 1867 (rev); tr C. Bernard-Derosne, Paris 1863.
The lawyer's secret. Philadelphia 1863. (A story in Ralph the bailiff, 1862.)
Aurora Floyd. 3 vols 1863, 2 vols Leipzig 1863, 1 vol London 1864, 1890, New York [c. 1890]; tr Fr C. Bernard-Derosne 2 vols Paris 1863, Polish Przeckland T. Marenicza 1 vol Warsaw 1883.
REVIEWS: Athenaeum 31 Jan 1863; Saturday Rev 31 Jan 1863; Henry James, Notes and reviews, Cambridge MA 1921, rptd from The Nation 9 Nov 1865. *See also* reviews of Lady Audley's Secret, *above*.
Eleanor's victory. 3 vols 1863 (illustr George du Maurier), 2 vols Leipzig 1863, 1 vol Richmond VA 1864, London [1873?]; tr Fr C. Bernard-Derosne 2 vols Paris 1864.
John Marchmont's legacy. 3 vols 1863, 1 vol 1864, 2 vols Leipzig 1864; tr Fr C. Bernard-Derosne 2 vols Paris 1864.
Henry Dunbar: the story of an outcast. Serialised as The outcasts in the London Jnl 1863–4. 3 vols 1864, 2 vols Leipzig 1864, 1 vol London 1865; tr Fr C. Bernard-Derosne 2 vols Paris 1865. (Excised subplot pbd as Lost and found in Ralph the bailiff, [1866].)
The doctor's wife. 3 vols 1864, 2 vols Leipzig 1864, 1 vol London 1865; tr Fr C. Bernard-Derosne 2 vols Paris 1867.
Only a clod. 3 vols 1865, 1 vol (nd), 2 vols Leipzig 1865; tr Fr C. Bernard-Derosne 2 vols Paris 1869.
Sir Jasper's tenant. 3 vols 1865, 2 vols Leipzig 1866, 1 vol London [1867?]; tr Fr C. Bernard-Derosne 2 vols Paris 1868.
The lady's mile. 3 vols 1866, 2 vols Leipzig 1866, 1 vol London 1867; tr Fr C. Bernard-Derosne 2 vols Paris 1870.
REVIEWS: Saturday Rev 12 May 1866; [Jewsbury, G.] Athenaeum 2 June 1866; Youth as depicted in modern fiction, Christian Remembrancer 52 1866.
The black band: or the mysteries of midnight. (Under pseud Lady Caroline Lascelles) 1867, New York 1867 (as What is this mystery?).
Circe: three acts in the life of an artist, by Babington White. 2 vols 1867. Anon.
Rupert Godwin. First pbd in the Halfpenny Jnl as The banker's secret, 1864–5. 3 vols 1867, 2 vols Leipzig 1867, 1 vol London [1870?] (serialised in Paris, Jnl Pour Tous and in America, New York Mercury); tr Fr C. Bernard-Derosne 2 vols Paris 1868, Sp Alfredo Elias y Pujol, 1 vol New York 1902.
Birds of prey: a novel. 3 vols 1867, 1 vol 1868; tr Fr C. Bernard-Derosne 2 vols Paris 1874.
Charlotte's inheritance. 3 vols 1868, 1 vol 1868, [c. 1890]; tr Fr C. Bernard-Derosne 2 vols Paris 1874.
Run to earth. 3 vols 1868 (Anon). (Originally pbd in the London Jnl as Diavola: or, The woman's battle, 1866–7. 1 vol (nd), New York 1867 (as Daughter: or, The ballad singer of Wapping, by M. E. Braddon); tr Fr C. Bernard-Derosne 2 vols Paris 1874.
Dead Sea fruit. 3 vols 1868, 1 vol (nd), 1891; tr Fr C. Bernard-Derosne 2 vols Paris 1874.
Fenton's quest: a novel. 3 vols 1871, 1 vol (nd), 1902.
The Lovels of Arden. 3 vols 1871, 1 vol [1872?], New York 1872.
Robert Ainsleigh. 3 vols 1872, 1 vol [1872]. (Amer edn as Bound to John Company.)
To the bitter end: a novel. 3 vols 1872, 1 vol 1873, New York 1873.
Milly Darrell and other tales. 3 vols 1873, 1 vol [1873], Chicago 1880 (as My sister's confession and other stories).
Strangers and pilgrims: a novel. 3 vols 1873, 1 vol [1873], 2 vols Leipzig 1873.
Lucius Davoren, or publicans and sinners: a novel. 3 vols 1873, 1 vol [1874].
Taken at the flood: a novel. 3 vols 1874, 1 vol [1874]; tr Du 2 vols The Hague 1875.
Lost for love: a novel. 3 vols 1874, 1 vol [1875], New York 1875, London 1887.
A strange world: a novel. 3 vols 1875, 1 vol [1875].
Hostages to fortune. 3 vols 1875, 1 vol New York 1875, London [1876].
Dead men's shoes. 3 vols 1876, 1 vol 1876.
Joshua Haggard's daughter. 3 vols 1876, 1 vol 1877, [1885?] (as Joshua Haggard); tr Fr Marie Létant 2 vols Paris 1879.
REVIEW: Rev C. Kent, Weekly Registrar and Catholic Standard 2 Dec 1876.
Weavers and weft, and other tales. 3 vols 1877, 1 vol 1877, Amer edn 1877 (only title story, sub-titled Love that hath us in his net).
An open verdict: a novel. 3 vols 1878, 1 vol 1878, [c. 1890].
Vixen: a novel, by the author of Lady Audley's secret. 3 vols 1879, 1 vol 1879.
The cloven foot: a novel. 3 vols 1879.
The missing witness: an original drama in four acts. [1880.]
The story of Barbara: her splendid misery and her gilded cage. Originally pbd in The world as splendid misery. 3 vols [1880], 1 vol (nd); tr Fr Marie Létang [Létant] 1 vol Paris 1881.
Just as I am: a novel. 3 vols [1880], 1 vol [1880].
Asphodel: a novel. 3 vols 1881, 1 vol [1881], 3 vols Leipzig 1881.
Boscastle, Cornwall, an English engadine. 1881 (rptd from The World, 1880).
Dross, or the root of evil: a comedy in four acts. [1881 or 1882], (rev in three acts in Under the red flag and other tales [1886]).
Married beneath him: a comedy in four acts. [1881 or 1882].
Marjorie Daw: a household idyl in two acts. [1881], [1886] (in Under the red flag and other tales), New York [1886].
Mount Royal: a novel. 3 vols 1882, 1 vol (nd).
Flower and weed: a novel. 1882 (Mistletoe Bough Annual), Leipzig 1883, London [1883] (and other tales).
The golden calf: a novel. 3 vols 1883, 1 vol [1883], Leipzig 1883.

Phantom fortune: a novel. 3 vols 1883, 1 vol 1884; tr Polish H. J. Boguska 3 vols [1883, 1884].
Under the red flag. 1883 (Mistletoe Bough Annual), [1886] (and other tales; includes several Babington White stories from Belgravia); tr Polish H. J. Boguska, Warsaw 1884.
Ishmael. 3 vols [1884], 1 vol (nd).
Dudley Carleon. Philadelphia 1884. (A story in Ralph the bailiff, 1862.)
Wyllard's weird: a novel. 3 vols [1885], 1 vol [18??]; tr Polish Maryl Falenskiéj 1 vol Warsaw 1889.
One thing needful: a novel. 3 vols 1886. (Cut by the county, *below*, comprises end of vol 2 and whole of vol 3); tr Polish (One thing needful only) 1 vol Warsaw 1886.
Cut by the county. [1886] (on its own; see One thing needful, *above*).
Mohawks. 3 vols [1886], 1 vol (nd), New York [c. 1890].
The good Hermione, a story for the Jubilee year, by Aunt Belinda. 1887.
In great waters and other tales. Leipzig 1887.
Like and unlike. 3 vols [1887], 1 vol (nd).
The fatal three. 3 vols [1888], 1 vol (nd), [c. 1890].
George Caulfield's journey. Philadelphia 1888. (Originally pbd in Mistletoe Bough 1879, rptd in Flower and weed and other tales [1883]).
The day will come: a novel. 3 vols [1889], 1 vol 1893.
One life, one love: a novel. 3 vols 1890, 1 vol (nd).
Gerard, or the world, the flesh and the devil: a novel. 3 vols 1891, 1 vol 1892.
The Venetians: a novel. 3 vols 1892, 1 vol 1893.
All along the river: a novel. 3 vols 1893, (vol 3 contains several short stories originally pbd in Mistletoe Bough), 1 vol (nd; without stories), 3 vols Leipzig 1893.
The Christmas hirelings. 1894 (illustr F. W. Townshend).
Thou art the man. 3 vols [1894].
Sons of fire: a novel. 3 vols [1896], 1 vol (nd).
London pride: or when the world was younger. 1896.
Under love's rule. 1897.
REVIEW: The Era 1895 (of the serialisation as The little auntie).
In high places. 1898.
Rough justice. 1898.
His darling sin. [1899.]
REVIEW: Athenaeum 15 Nov 1899.
The infidel: a story of the great revival. [1900.]
REVIEW: Barker, W. The Primitive Methodist Quart 1901.
The conflict. 1903.
A lost Eden. 1904.
The rose of life. 1905.
The white house. 1906.
Dead love has chains. 1907.
Her convict. 1907.
During Her Majesty's pleasure. 1908.
Our adversary. 1909.
The woman I remember. The Press Album. Ed T. Catling 1909.
Beyond these voices. 1910.
The green curtain. 1911.
Miranda. 1913.
Mary. 1916.
Several Halfpenny Jnl *novels pbd in bk form only in America:* Oscar Bertrand: or the black band unmasked, *New York nd;* The Octoroon: or the lily of Louisiana, *New York nd;* The white phantom: or the nameless child, *New York nd;* The factory girl: or all is not gold that glitters. A romance of real life, *New York nd; also one* Temple Bar *novel,* For better, for worse, *Philadelphia nd.*

Letters

Woolf, R. L. Devoted disciple: the letters of Mary Elizabeth Braddon to Sir Edward Bulwer-Lytton, 1862–73. HLB 22.1, 1974.

Contributions to periodicals and collaborative works

Mary Braddon contributed to the Halfpenny Jnl, Reynold's Misc, London Jnl, Sixpenny Mag, Welcome Guest, Temple Bar, St James Mag, All the Year Round. *She edited* Belgravia *1866–76, the* Belgravia Annual *1867–76, and* Mistletoe Bough *1878–92. She also contributed to the* Sporting Mag *under the pseuds of Gilbert Forrester and 'a Member of the Burton Hunt'. She also contributed* Jonnie, *by Alphonse Daudet (anon), and* Le Pétrolium: ou les Saloperies Parisiennes, *by Zorgon-Gola (anon) to Mr Punch's prize novelists,* Punch *99, 29 Nov 1890 and 100, 28 Feb 1891. She edited* My sister Caroline: a novellette *(anon) 1870, which reappeared as the title story in* My sister's confession and other stories: a novel, *ed M. E. Braddon, Chicago 1880 (the rest of the stories are by Braddon, originally in* Milly Darrel *and* Ralph the bailiff*);* The summer tourist: a book for long and short journeys by rail, road, or river, *1871 (and wrote one of the stories);* Put to the test *(by Ada Buisson, originally pbd 1865), 1876;* Only a woman *1878;* Madeline's mystery: a novel *(by Major E. Rogers; originally* A modern sphinx, *1881), [1882];* Married in haste: a novel *[1882 or 1883], New York 1885; and* On her Majesty's service. *She revised* Aladdin: or the wonderful lamp; Sinbad the sailor: or the old man of the sea; Ali Baba: or the forty thieves *[1880] (illustr Gustave Doré and others). Braddon abridged Sir Walter Scott's novels in the Penny edn [1881–2], 16 vols and 1 vol. She also wrote several plays which were produced and never pbd, including her first literary endeavour,* The loves of Arcadia, *1860, a comedietta, written under her stage name, Mary Seyton, as well as several which were neither produced nor pbd.*

§2

Textual and bibliographical criticism

Austin, R. N & Q ser 11, 11 1915.
Bolt, F. N & Q ser 11, 11 1915.
Ratcliffe, T. N & Q ser 11, 11 1915.
Sparke, A. N & Q ser 11, 11 1915.
Sadleir, M. Notes on Lady Audley's secret. TLS 11 May 1940.
MacAlister, I. TLS 26 Sep 1942.
Sadleir, M. Miss Braddon. TLS 10 Oct 1942.
Summers, M. Miss Braddon. TLS 29 Aug 1942.
Summers, M. Miss Braddon's Black band. TLS 24 Apr 1943.
Evans, F. B. TLS 21 Oct 1944.
Evans, F. B. TLS 23 Dec 1944.
Summers, M. Mr Babington White. TLS 20 Sep 1944.
Summers, M. The black band scandal. TLS 17 Feb 1945.
Heywood, C. Flaubert, Miss Braddon and George Moore. Comparative Lit 12 1960.
Heywood, C. The return of the native and Miss Braddon's The doctor's wife: a probable source. Nineteenth-Cent Fiction 18 1964.
Heywood, C. Miss Braddon's The doctor's wife: an intermediary between Madame Bovary and The return of the native. Revue de Littérature Comparée 38 1964.
Hutchison, B. Miss M. E. Braddon, 1837–1915. Book Collector and Lib Monthly 20 1969.
See also notes by A. N. Q., J. R., Mac and B. B. in N & Q *ser 11, 11 1915.*

Other criticism

Oliphant, M. Sensation novels. Blackwood's Edinburgh Mag 91 1862.
Baits for suicide: Lady Audley's secret and Aurora Floyd. The Medical Critic and Psychological Jnl 3 1863.
Oliphant, M. Novels. Blackwood's Edinburgh Mag 94 1863.
Sensation novels. The Medical Critic and Psychological Jnl 13 1863.
[MacCarthy, J.] Novels with a purpose. Westminster Rev 82 1864.
Novels and life. Saturday Rev 13 Feb 1864.
Our female sensation novelists. Christian Remembrancer 46 1864.
Rae, W. F. Sensation novelists: Miss Braddon. North Br Rev 4 1865.
Novels, past and present. Saturday Rev 21, 14 Apr 1866.
Novel-reading. Saturday Rev 16 Feb 1867.
Oliphant, M. Novels. Blackwood's Edinburgh Mag 102 1867.

Sala, G. A. The cant of modern criticism. Belgravia 4 1867.
Sala, G. A. On the sensational in literature and art. Belgravia 4 1868.
Bastard literature by Miss Braddon. Spectator 57 1884.
Hatton, J. Miss Braddon at home: a sketch and an interview. London Soc 58 1888.
Dickens, M. A. Miss Braddon at home. Windsor Mag 6 1897.
Oliphant, M. Annals of a publishing house: William Blackwood and his sons. 2 vols Edinburgh 1897.
Holland, C. Fifty years of novel writing: Miss Braddon at home. Pall Mall Mag 48 1911.
Miss Braddon at home. Daily Telegraph 4 Oct 1913.
Maxwell, W. B. Time gathered. 1937.
Sadleir, M. TLS 2 Oct 1937.
Yates, E. Celebrities at home. First ser. London 1877.

Biographies

Braddon, M. E. Autobiographical article. Idler Feb 1893.
Braddon, M. E. Autobiographical article. Theatre Sep 1894.
Memoir. The Times 5 Feb 1915.
Sadleir, M. Things past. 1944.
Woolf, R. L. Sensational Victorian: the life and fiction of Mary Elizabeth Braddon. New York 1979. [HK]

Rhoda Broughton 1840–1920

Archives of Richard Bentley and son (on microfilm); Macmillan Papers pre-1939 in BL and Univ of Reading; Broughton's papers and correspondence, Chester Record Office (available only through Dr Tamie Watters Cole, embargoed); letters to J. B. Pinker, Berg Collection, NYPL.

§1

Not wisely, but too well: a novel. Serialised in Dublin Univ Mag 67–8, Aug 1865–July 1866; revised and enlarged 3 vols 1867 (Tinsley); 2 vols Leipzig 1867 (Tauchnitz); 1 vol London 1868; New York 1868 (rptd 1870); London 1869; 1870 (Tinsley's Popular Half-crown Novels, rptd 1871); New York 1873 (rptd 1901; 1873 imprint microfilm [197?]); 1 vol London 1875 (Bentley, rptd 1878, 1883, 1887, 1892); New York 1878; New York 1886; New York [1887]; 1875 edn rptd 1899 (Macmillan); introd by F. King, ed H. van Thal 1967 (Cassell First Novel Lib); Stroud, Glos and Dover NH 1993.

Cometh up as a flower: an autobiography. mss held by Ethel Arnold in 1920. Serialised in Dublin Univ Mag 68–9, July 1866–Jan 1867; greatly enlarged 2 vols 1867 (Bentley, rptd twice 1867); further rev after newspaper criticism 1 vol 1867 (rptd 1868, 1868, 1870, 1871, 1872, 1873, 1874, 1876, 1877, 1878, 1883, 1889, 1890, 1895); Leipzig 1867 (Tauchnitz); New York 1867 (rptd 1868, 1870, 1872; 1867 imprint microfilm Cambridge MA [1967?]); New York 1872 (with Good-bye, sweetheart! in double columns); New York 1878; New York [1886]; New York [1887]; New York 1901; London 1899 (Macmillan reprint of 1 vol 1867 Bentley edn); 1900 (Macmillan Six Penny Ser, rptd 1907); 1910 (Macmillan Seven Penny Ser); Stroud, Glos and Dover NH 1993; tr Fr 1869 (by August de Viguerie, preface Gustave Droz, rptd 1901).

Red as a rose is she: a novel. Serialised in Temple Bar May 1869–Mar 1870; 3 vols 1870 (Bentley); 1 vol 1870 (Bentley, rptd 1872, 1876, 1887, 1895); 2 vols Leipzig 1870 (Tauchnitz); New York 1870 (rptd 1872, 1897, 1901; 1872 imprint microfilm Cambridge MA 1967); New York 1878; New York [1886]; New York [1887]; London 1899 (Macmillan reprint of 1 vol 1870 Bentley edn).

'Good-bye, sweetheart!': a tale. Serialised in Temple Bar July 1871–July 1872; 3 vols 1872 (Bentley); 2 vols Berlin 1872; 1 vol London 1873 (Bentley, rptd 1882, 1890); New York 1872 (rptd 1891, 1901); New York 1873 (with Cometh up as a flower in double columns); New York 1877; New York 1880; New York 1886; New York [1886]; New York [1887]; London 1899 (Macmillan reprint of 1873 Bentley edn, microfilm [197?]).

Nancy: a novel. 3 vols 1873 (Bentley); 2 vols Leipzig 1873 (Tauchnitz); 1 vol 1874 (Bentley, rptd 1878, 1887, 1893); New York 1874 (rptd 1890, 1891, 1895); New York [1879?]; New York [1884]; New York [1887]; 1900 (Macmillan reprint of 1874 Bentley edn; microfilm Cambridge MA [1967?]); [191?] (Macmillan Seven Penny Ser); dramatised as Sweet Nancy by Robert Buchanan, 1890, ptd 1914; tr Danish 1876.

Tales for Christmas Eve. Five collected short ghost stories. 1873 (Bentley); Leipzig '1872' [1873] (Tauchnitz); as Twilight stories 1879 (Bentley); as Twilight stories, introd by H. van Thal 1947; New York 1948; with 7 previously uncollected stories as Rhoda Broughton's ghost stories: and other tales of mystery and suspense, introd by M. Wood, Stamford 1995; Under the cloak in Reign of terror: the third Corgi book of great Victorian horror stories, ed M. Parry, 1977; Behold, it was a dream in The lifted veil: the book of fantastic literature by women 1800–World War II, introd by A. S. Williams, New York 1992; in The Penguin book of classic fantasy by women, introd by A. S. Williams, 1992 (Xanadu), Harmondsworth 1995; The truth, the whole truth and nothing but the truth in Victorian ghost stories by eminent women writers, ed R. Dalby, New York 1988; Poor pretty Bobby tr Ger by Auguste Scheibe in Novellenschatz des Auslandes vol 14, [1875?].

Joan: a tale. 3 vols 1876 (Bentley, rptd 1876); 2 vols Leipzig 1876 (Tauchnitz); 1 vol 1877 (Bentley, rptd 1880, 1883, 1887, 1890?, 1893); New York 1877 (rptd 1882, 1891); New York 1879; New York [1886]; New York [1887]; 1899 (Macmillan reprint of 1877 Bentley edn); 1911 (Macmillan Seven Penny Ser).

Second thoughts. 2 vols 1880 (Bentley); 2 vols Leipzig 1880 (Tauchnitz); 1 vol 1880 (Bentley, rptd 1885, 1893); New York 1880 (microfilm Cambridge MA [1967?]); New York 1880 (with Miss Litton's lovers); Chicago 1881; New York [1882]; New York [1883]; 1898 (Macmillan reprint of 1880 1 vol Bentley edn); New York [190?]; tr Ital [1883] (by A. Brigola).

Belinda: a novel. Serialised in Temple Bar Jan 1883–Jan 1884; 3 vols 1883 (Bentley); 2 vols Leipzig 1883 (Tauchnitz); 1 vol 1884 (Bentley, rptd 1887, 1898); New York 1883 (rptd 1884); New York [1883?]; New York [1883?]; New York [188?]; New York and Chicago [188?]; 1899 (Macmillan reprint of 1884 1 vol Bentley edn); St Clair Shores MI 1970 (reprint of 1883 New York edn); introd by T. Watters, 1984.

Betty's visions and Mrs Smith of Longmains. Collected short work. [1886]; New York [1886]; Betty's visions, New York [1886?] (with Ugly Barrington by Mrs Hungerford, 'the Duchess'); Mrs Smith of Longmains, New York [1885/6?] (with Oliver's bride by Mrs Oliphant, A mere interlude by Thomas Hardy).

Doctor Cupid: a novel. 3 vols 1886 (Bentley); 1 vol Leipzig 1886 (Tauchnitz); 1 vol 1887 (Bentley, rptd 1891); New York [1886]; New York and Montreal [1887] (microfilm [197?]); Philadelphia 1887; New York [189?] (microfilm Cambridge MA 1968); 1899 (Macmillan reprint of 1887 1 vol Bentley edn; microfilm [197?]); dramatised as That Doctor Cupid! by Robert Buchanan, 189?.

Alas!: a novel. Serialised in Temple Bar Jan–Dec 1890; 3 vols 1890 (Bentley); 2 vols Leipzig 1890 (Tauchnitz); New York [1890] (microfilm Ottawa 1981); 1 vol 1891 (Bentley, rptd 1895; microfilm Ottawa 1985); New York [1890/1?]; 1899 (Macmillan reprint of 1891 1 vol Bentley edn; microfilm Ottawa 1983).

A widower indeed. 1891 (rptd 1892); Leipzig 1891 (Tauchnitz); New York 1891 (microfilm, [196?]). With Elizabeth Bisland (Wetmore).

Mrs Bligh: a novel. Serialised in Temple Bar Sep–Dec 1892; 1892 (Bentley, rptd twice 1892); Leipzig 1892 (Tauchnitz); New York 1892; 1898 (Macmillan reprint of 1892 Bentley edn).

A beginner. Serialised in Temple Bar Jan–June 1894; 1894 (Bentley, rptd twice 1894); Leipzig 1894 (Tauchnitz); New York 1894; 1898 (Macmillan reprint of 1894 Bentley edn).

Scylla or Charybdis? Serialised in Temple Bar June–Dec 1895; 1895 (Bentley, rptd 1897); Leipzig 1895 (Tauchnitz); New York 1895

(rptd 1912; 1895 imprint microfilm [197?]); 1899 (Macmillan reprint of 1895 Bentley edn).
Dear Faustina. Serialised in Temple Bar Jan–June 1897; 1897 (Bentley); Leipzig 1897 (Tauchnitz); New York 1897 (microfilm Cambridge MA 1968); 1898 (Macmillan reprint of 1897 Bentley edn, rptd 1900).
The game and the candle. Serialised in Temple Bar Jan–May 1899; 1899 (Macmillan, rptd 1902); New York 1899 (rptd 1912; 1912 imprint microfilm Cambridge MA 1968); Leipzig 1899 (Tauchnitz).
Foes in law. Serialised in Temple Bar Sep–Dec 1900; 1900 (Macmillan, rptd 1901, 1906; 1900 imprint microfilm Cambridge MA 1968); 1900 (Macmillan, rptd 1905); Leipzig 1901 (Tauchnitz); New York 1906 (Grosset and Dunlap reprint of Macmillan 1905 imprint).
Lavinia. Serialised in Temple Bar Jan–Nov 1902; 1902 (Macmillan, rptd 1902, 1906); Leipzig 1903 (Tauchnitz).
A waif's progress. 1905 (Macmillan, rptd 1906); 1909 (Macmillan, microfilm Cambridge MA [1967?]).
Mamma. 1908 (Macmillan); Leipzig 1909 (Tauchnitz); 1910 (Macmillan Seven Penny Ser).
The devil and the deep sea. 1910 (Macmillan); Leipzig 1910 (Tauchnitz).
Between two stools. 1912 (rptd twice 1912, [1913], pbk); Leipzig 1912 (Tauchnitz).
Concerning a vow. 1914; Leipzig 1914 (Tauchnitz).
A thorn in the flesh. 1917 (rptd three times 1917).
A fool in her folly. With an appreciation by Mrs Belloc Lowndes. 1920.

Contributions to periodicals and collaborative works

Entry on herself in The art of authorship: personally contributed by leading authors of the day, ed George Bainton, 1890.
Girls past and present. Ladies Home Jnl Sep 1920. Essay.
Broughton pbd some short stories in Temple Bar *and other jnls, some of which were later collected in* Tales for Christmas Eve *and* Ghost stories.

Attributed or spurious work

'Jerry' and other stories. Philadelphia 1889.
Valerie: or half a truth. Chicago [188?].
Both are held in the Cleveland Public Lib Dime Novel Collection; neither appears in bibliographies or is mentioned in reviews.

'-iana'

Lang, Andrew. From Professor Forth to the Rev Mr Casaubon. In Old friends: essays in epistolatory parody, 1890.
[Delafield, E. M.] The Bazalgettes. 1935. Pastiche of Broughton's motifs in a vol designed in imitation of the Bentley 1 vol edns.
There were many parodies of Broughton's novels in periodicals in the 1870s and 1880s, and many imitative novels in a 'Broughton-and-water' school by such authors as Annie Edwardes, Mrs G. W. Godfrey, Mrs Hungerford ('the Duchess'), Helen Mathers and Florence Marryat.

§2

[Austin, A.] The novels of Miss Broughton. Temple Bar May 1874.
Brunetière, F. Romans de Miss Rhoda Broughton. In Le roman naturaliste: ouvrage couronné par l'académie française, Paris 1883 (essay omitted from later edns).
[Lynn Linton, E.] Miss Broughton's novels. Temple Bar June 1887.
Shaw, G. B. Fiction and truth (1887). In Bernard Shaw's nondramatic literary criticism, ed Stanley Weintraub, Lincoln NE 1972.
Rhoda Broughton. Men and Women of the Day Feb 1889.
[White, G.] To Miss Rhoda Broughton. In Letters to eminent hands, Derby 1892.
Oliphant, Mrs M. O. W. Rhoda Broughton. In The Victorian age of English literature vol 2, 1892.
Miss Rhoda Broughton. Ludgate Monthly Apr 1893.
Blaize de Bury, Y. In Les romanciers anglais contemporains. Paris 1900.
Black, H. C. Rhoda Broughton. In Notable women authors of the day, 1906.
Two veteran novelists. The Times (women's suppl) 19 Nov 1910.
Sichel, W. Rhoda Broughton. Bookman Aug 1917.
Miss Rhoda Broughton. The Times 7, 10, 11 June 1920 (5 items).
Rhoda Broughton dead. New York Times 7 June 1920.
Arnold, E. Rhoda Broughton as I knew her. Fortnightly Rev 2 Aug 1920.
Ellis, S. M. Rhoda Broughton. Bookman July 1920.
Curtis, M. In DNB 1912–1921, 1927.
Addleshaw, S. A Victorian novelist – Rhoda Broughton. Church Quart Rev July–Sep 1939.
Sadleir, M. Rhoda Broughton. In Things past, 1944.
Walbank, A. Miss Broughton. In Queens of the circulating library: selections from Victorian lady novelists, 1950.
Ketcham, C. H. A woman's arm: George Eliot and Rhoda Broughton. N & Q 199, Mar 1954.
Sadleir, M. Broughton, Rhoda (1840–1920), Broughtoniana. In XIX century fiction: a bibliographical record based on his own collection, 1951. [SJS]

Oliver Madox Brown 1855–74

§1

Gabriel Denver. 1873.
The dwale bluth, Hebditch's legacy and other literary remains, with a memoir and two portraits. Ed W. M. Rossetti and F. Hueffer 2 vols 1876. Prefixed is a Lament by P. B. Marston. Contains the original version of Gabriel Denver, as The black swan.

§2

Marston, P. B. Oliver Madox Brown. Scribner's Mag July 1876.
Ingram, J. H. Oliver Madox Brown: a biographical sketch. 1883.
Ingram, J. H. In the poets and poetry of the century, ed A. H. Miles, vol 8, 1893 etc.

Robert Buchanan 1841–1901

See col 722.

Frances Hodgson Burnett 1849–1924

The Scribner Archive at Princeton holds much of Mrs Hodgson Burnett's professional correspondence, and ms materials relating to her life and work are held by many libs in Britain and the US, notably Manchester Central Lib and NYPL.

§1

That lass o' Lowries. New York and London 1877. First pbd in Scribner's Mag 1876. Adapted for the stage with Julius Magnus, New York 1878.
Dolly: a love story. Philadelphia and London 1877; as Vagabodia, New York 1883.
Surly Tim and other stories. New York and London 1877.
'Theo': a love story. Philadelphia and London 1877.
Pretty Polly Pemberton: a love story. Philadelphia 1877, London 1878. First pbd in Peterson's Mag.
Our neighbour opposite. 1878.
Kathleen: a love story. Philadelphia and London 1878.
A quiet life: and the tide on the moaning bar. Philadelphia 1878; as The tide on the moaning bar. – A quiet life, London 1879. First pbd in Peterson's Mag.
Miss Crespigny: a love story. Philadelphia 1878, London 1879. First pbd in Peterson's Mag.
Earlier stories: first ser. New York 1878, London 1879.
Earlier stories: second ser. New York 1878, London 1879.
Howarth's. London and New York 1879.

Jarl's daughter and other stories and other novelettes. Philadelphia 1879. First pbd in Peterson's Mag.

Lindsay's luck: a fascinating love story. New York and London 1879. First pbd in Peterson's Mag.

Natalie and other stories. 1879.

Louisiana. New York 1880 with That lass o' lowries, London 1880.

Esmeralda: a comedy drama in four acts (with William Gillette). Produced New York 1881; pbd New York 1881; as Young folk's ways, London 1883.

A fair barbarian. Boston and London 1881.

Through one administration. Boston and London 1883; New York 1969 (reprint of 1883 edn with introd by Robert Lee White).

Little Lord Fauntleroy. Illustr Reginald B. Birch. New York and London 1886; first pbd in St Nicholas Mag Nov 1885–Oct 1886; The real Lord Fauntleroy, adapted from the novel for the stage and produced London and New York 1888; Little Lord Fauntleroy; a drama in three acts founded on the story of the same name, New York and London 1889. Since 1886 Little Lord Fauntleroy has been frequently rptd on both sides of the Atlantic, including: London 1888 ('Eighth edn'), 1908, 1925 (illustr C. E. Brock), 1937, 1962 (Dent's Children's Illus Classics), 1974, 1981, 1984 (Puffin Storybooks), Oxford 1993 (WCp, with an introd by Dennis Butts); New York 1889, 1890, 1891, 1895, 1902, 1911, 1914, 1930, 1936, 1954, 1977, 1981, 1986, 1987.

TRANSLATIONS INCLUDE: Fr 1888; Ger 1888; Swed 1919; Cz 1920; Ital 1920; Jap 1921; Polish 1922; Slovene 1925; Icelandic 1928; Hebrew 1955; Sp 1957; Chinese 1974; Korean 1980; Portuguese 1982; Rus 1992.

A woman's will: or Miss Defarge. 1887; as Miss Defarge, with John Habberton's Brueton's bayou, Philadelphia 1888. First pbd in Lippincott's Mag (Philadelphia), Dec 1886.

The fortunes of Philippa Fairfax. 1888. First pbd in Semi-Weekly Inter Ocean Mag, Chicago (Oct–Nov 1886); produced as a play, Phyllis, London 1888.

Sara Crewe: or what happened at Miss Minchin's. 1887; New York 1888. A little unfairy princess, Burnett's stage-adaptation of Sara Crewe, produced London 1902; A little princess produced London 1902, New York 1903; A little princess: being the whole story of Sara Crewe now told for the first time, New York and London 1905; The little princess: a play for children and grown-up children in three acts, New York and London 1911. Since 1887 Sara Crewe and A little princess have often been rptd on both sides of the Atlantic, including: London 1888, 'Twentieth thousand' 1891, 1905, 1961 (Puffin Storybooks), facs of first edn 1969, 1975; New York 1888, 1889, 1891, 1894, 1903, 1905, 1915, 1922, 1928, 1935, 1940, 1967, 1974, 1975, 1981, 1987.

TRANSLATIONS OF SARA CREWE OR A LITTLE PRINCESS INCLUDE: Ger 1909; Swed 1920; Fr 1950; Jap 1957; Polish 1959; Hebrew 1970; Taiwan 1983; Korean 1984; Rus 1992.

Editha's burglar: a story for children. Boston 1888; Editha's burglar and Sara Crewe, London 1888. First pbd in St Nicholas Mag 7, May 1880. Adapted as a play with Stephen Townesend and produced as Nixie, London 1890.

The pretty sister of José. New York, London 1889. Adapted as a play and produced New York, London 1903.

Little Saint Elizabeth and other stories. New York, London 1890. First pbd in St Nicholas Mag 1888–9.

Children I have known. 1892; as Giovanni and the other children who have made stories, New York 1892.

The showman's daughter (a play) with Stephen Townesend. Produced Worcester 1891; London 1892.

The Drury Lane Boys' Club. Washington 1892. Essay.

The one I knew the best of all: a memory of the mind of a child. New York and London 1893. First pbd in Scribner's Mag 1893; facs of London edn 1974; reprint of New York edn, New York 1980. Autobiography.

The captain's youngest: Piccino and other child stories. 1894; as Piccino and other child stories, New York 1894.

The two little pilgrims' progress: a story of the city beautiful. New York and London 1895; tr Turkish 1930.

A lady of quality: being a most curious, hitherto unknown history as related by Mr Isaac Bickerstaff but not presented to the world of fashion through the pages of the Tatler and now for the first time written down. New York and London 1896; with Stephen Townesend, a play adapted from the novel, produced New York 1897, London 1899.

His Grace of Osmond: being the portion of that nobleman's life omitted in the relation of his lady's story presented to the world of fashion under the title of A lady of quality. New York and London 1897.

The first gentleman of Europe (a play). With Constance Fletcher, produced New York and London 1897.

In connection with the De Willoughby claim. New York and London 1899. That man and I, a play derived from the novel by Frances Hodgson Burnett, produced New York and London in 1904.

The making of a marchioness. New York and London 1901. (The first part of the book serialised in Cornhill Mag Jun–Aug 1901.)

The methods of Lady Walderhurst. New York 1901; London 1902.

In the closed room. New York and London 1904; New York [1905?].

The dawn of a tomorrow. New York 1906; London 1907. The play adapted from the novel by Frances Hodgson Burnett produced in New York 1909, Liverpool and London 1910.

Racketty Packetty house. New York 1906; London 1907. First pbd in St Nicholas Mag Dec 1906–Jan 1907. Produced as play New York 1912.

The troubles of Queen Silver Bell. New York 1906; London 1907. First pbd in St Nicholas Mag Oct 1906.

The cozy lion as told by Queen Crosspatch. New York 1907; London 1972. First pbd in St Nicholas Mag Feb–Mar 1907.

The shuttle. New York and London 1907.

The good wolf. New York 1908. First pbd in Children's Mag.

The spring cleaning as told by Queen Crosspatch. New York 1908; London 1973. First pbd in St Nicholas Mag Dec 1908–Jan 1909.

Barty Crusoe and his man Saturday. New York 1909. First pbd in Children's Mag.

The land of the blue flower. 1909, New York 1912; tr Ger 1922. First pbd in Children's Mag London 1912.

The secret garden. New York 1911. First pbd in The American Mag Nov 1910–Aug 1911. London, illustr Charles Robinson, 1911. Since 1911 The secret garden has been frequently rptd on both sides of the Atlantic, including: London 1927, 1950 ('New Windmill'), 1951 (Puffin Storybooks), 1957, 1966, 1975 (Dent's Children's 'Illus Classics'), 1983, Oxford 1987 (WCp, with an introd by Dennis Butts); New York 1911 ('2nd edn'), 1915, 1938, 1962, 1971, 1977, 1987, 1988.

TRANSLATIONS: Cz 1920; Lettish 1929; Hebrew 1960; Swed 1960; Finnish 1965; Korean 1977; Jap 1978; Fr 1980; Arabic 1982; Sp 1986; Ger 1987; Thai 1990; Chinese 1991.

My robin. New York 1912, London 1913. Autobiographical essay.

The lost prince. New York and London 1915; tr Finnish 1918; Hebrew 1979; Korean 1988. First pbd in St Nicholas Mag 1915.

The way to the house of Santa Claus: a Christmas story for very small boys in which every little reader is the hero of a big adventure. New York, London 1916. A picture book.

T. Tembaron. New York and London 1913; tr Swed 1918.

The little hunchback Zia. New York and London 1916.

The white people. New York 1917; London 1920.

The head of the house of Coombe. New York and London 1922; tr Swed 1923. First pbd in Good Housekeeping Mag.

Robin. New York and London 1922. First pbd in Good Housekeeping Mag.

Kate Douglas Wiggin: a sketch of her life with an appreciation. Boston 1924.
In the garden. Boston 1925. Essays.

Fiction and drama for children
For details of pbn, see above.
Little Lord Fauntleroy. 1886.
Sara Crewe: or what happened at Miss Minchin's (A little princess). 1887.
Editha's burglar: a story for children. 1888.
Little Saint Elizabeth and other stories. 1890.
Children I have known (Giovanni and the other children who have made stories). 1892.
The captain's youngest: Piccino and other child stories (Piccino and other child stories). 1894.
The two little pilgrims' progress: a story of the city beautiful. 1895.
Racketty packetty house. 1906.
The troubles of Queen Silver Bell. 1906.
The cosy lion as told by Queen Crosspatch. 1907.
The good wolf. 1908.
The spring cleaning as told by Queen Crosspatch. 1908.
Barty Crusoe and his man Saturday. 1909.
The land of the blue flower. 1909.
The secret garden. 1911.
The lost prince. 1915.
The way to the house of Santa Claus: a Christmas story for very small boys in which every little reader is the hero of a big adventure. 1916.

Contributions to periodicals and collaborative works
A city of groves and flowers. St Nicholas Mag 20, June 1893.
When he decides. In Before he is twenty: five perplexing phases of the boy question considered, with Mrs Lyman Abbot et al, New York 1894.
How Winnie hatched the little rooks. St Nicholas Mag 34, Nov 1906.
The Christmas in the fog. Good Housekeeping Mag 59, Dec 1914.
The woman in the other stateroom. Good Housekeeping Mag 60, Mar 1915.
The attic in the house on Long Island. Good Housekeeping Mag 62, May 1916.
The passing of the kings. Good Housekeeping Mag 68, Mar 1919.
The house in the dismal swamp. Good Housekeeping Mag 70, Apr 1920.

Contributions to periodicals for children
How Winnie hatched the little rooks. St Nicholas Mag 34, Nov 1906.

'iana' or imitations
That lass o' lowries. Punch 13 Oct–17 Nov 1877. Parodies.

§2
Stoddard, R. H. Frances Hodgson Burnett. In Essays from 'The critic', Boston 1882.
Alcott, L. M. Little Lord Fauntleroy. The Book Buyer Mag, New York, Dec 1886.
Burnett, Vivian. The romantick lady (Frances Hodgson Burnett): the life story of an imagination. New York 1927.
Thwaite, Ann. Waiting for the party: the life of Frances Hodgson Burnett (1849–1924). 1974.
The secret garden. Ed with an introd by Dennis Butts, Oxford 1987 (WCp).
Little Lord Fauntleroy. Ed with an introd by Dennis Butts, Oxford 1993 (WCp). [DB]

Samuel Butler 1835–1902

See col 2327.

Kathleen Mannington Caffyn, née Hunt, 'Iota'
1853–1926

§1
Kooroona: a tale of South Australia. Oxford 1871.
A yellow aster. 3 vols 1894, 1 vol 1894 (12th edn), 2 vols Leipzig 1894 (Tauchnitz), New York 1894, [1895], London 1899, 1912.
REVIEWS: Athenaeum 3460 1894; Bookman 6 1894; Saturday Rev 77 1894; Spectator 72 1894.
Children of circumstance. 3 vols 1894, 1894 (2nd edn).
REVIEWS: Acad 46 1894; Bookman 7 1894; Saturday Rev 78 1894; Spectator 73 1894.
A comedy in spasms. 1895 (Zetgeist Lib), New York and London [1895].
REVIEWS: Athenaeum 3539 1895; Critic 24 1895.
Miss Milne and I. New York [1895].
A quaker grandmother. 1896.
REVIEW: Athenaeum 3597 1896.
Poor Max. 1898, Philadelphia 1898.
REVIEWS: Acad 53 1898; Athenaeum 3673 1898.
Anne Maulever. 1899, 2 vols Leipzig 1899 (Tauchnitz), Philadelphia 1899, London 1902, 1903, 1906.
REVIEWS: Athenaeum 3734 1899; Bookman 16 1899; Saturday Rev 87 1899; Spectator 82 1899.
The minx. New York [1899], London 1900.
REVIEWS: Athenaeum 3784 1900; Dial 29 1900; Spectator 84 1900.
The happenings of Jill. 1901.
He for God only. 1903, 1905.
REVIEWS: Acad 64 1903; Athenaeum 3939 1903.
At a rest house of the foothills. 1904 (Daily Mail. Registration copy).
Patricia: a mother. 1905, New York 1905, London 1906.
Smoke in the flame. 1906, 1907.
The magic of May. 1908.
REVIEW: TLS 21 May 1908.
'Whoso breaketh an hedge'. 1909.
REVIEW: Athenaeum 4283 1909.
Dorinda and her daughter. 1910.
REVIEW: TLS 17 Nov 1910.
The fire-seeker. 1911.
REVIEW: TLS 16 Nov 1911.
Two ways of love. 1913.
Mary Mirrilies. 1916.

Collaborative works
Victims of Circe. In Coo-ee, tales of Australian life by Australian ladies, ed H. P. Martin, [1891].
Lenchen. In By creek and gully, ed L. Fisher, 1899.

§2
In Who was who 1916–28.
Sutherland, J. The Longman companion to Victorian fiction. Harlow 1988.
Blain, V., P. Clements and I. Grundy. (ed) The feminist companion to literature in English. 1990.

Sir Thomas Henry Hall Caine 1853–1931

Bibliographies
Gibbon, W. C. In his Bibliographical account of works relating to the Isle of Man vol 2, 1939.

§1
Richard III and Macbeth; the spirit of romantic play in relationship to the principles of Greek and of Gothic art, and to the picturesque interpretations of Mr Henry Irving: a dramatic study. 1877.
Recollections of Dante Gabriel Rossetti. 1882, 1929 (rev).

Sonnets of three centuries: a selection. 1882. Ed Hall Caine.
Cobwebs of criticism: a review of the first reviewers of the 'Lake', 'Satanic', and 'Cockney' schools. 1883.
The shadow of a crime. 3 vols 1885.
The Deemster: a romance. 3 vols 1887. Dramatised as The Bishop's son, 1910.
Life of Samuel Taylor Coleridge. 1887.
A son of Hagar: a romance of our time. 3 vols 1887.
The bondman: a new saga. 3 vols 1890. Dramatised as The bondman play, 1906.
The little Manx nation. 1891.
The scapegoat: a romance. 2 vols 1891.
Capt'n Davy's honeymoon; The last confession; The blind mother. 1893.
The little Man island: scenes and specimen days in the Isle of Man. Douglas 1894.
The Manxman. 1894. Dramatised as Pete, 1908 [with L. N. Parker].
Yan, the Icelander: home sweet home, a lecture story. Greeba Castle [1896].
The Christian: a story. 1897. Dramatised 1907.
The Eternal City. 1901. Dramatised as The eternal question, 1910.
The prodigal son. 1904.
Drink: a love story on a great question. [1908.]
My story. 1908.
The white prophet. 2 vols 1909.
King Edward: a prince and a great man: a pen portrait. 1910. Rptd from Daily Telegraph.
The woman thou gavest me: being the story of Mary O'Neill. 1913.
King Albert's book. 1914. Ed Hall Caine.
The drama of three hundred and sixty-five days: scenes in the Great War. 1915. Rptd from Daily Telegraph.
Our girls: their work for the war. 1916.
The master of Man: the story of a sin. 1921.
The woman of Knockaloe: a parable. 1923.
Life of Christ. 1938.

§2

Kenyon, C. F. Hall Caine: the man and the novelist. 1901.
MacCarthy, D. In his Portraits, 1931.
Norris, S. Two men of Manxland. 1947.

Mona Caird, Mona Alice Henryson-Caird, née Alison 1858–1932

§1

Lady Hetty: a story of Scottish and Australian life. 3 vols 1875 (anon); tr Ger 1876.
REVIEW: Athenaeum 2469 1875.
Whom nature leadeth [by G. Noel Hatton]. 3 vols 1883.
REVIEW: Athenaeum 2924 1883.
One that wins: the story of a holiday in Italy. 2 vols 1887 (anon), New York [1887].
For money or for love. New York [1889]; rptd in A romance of the moors, 1891, *below*.
The wing of Azrael: a novel. 3 vols 1889, New York 1889, London 1890.
REVIEW: Athenaeum 3213 1889.
A romance of the moors. Bristol [1891], New York 1891, Leipzig 1892. Contains A romance of the moors, For money or for love, The yellow drawing-room.
The daughters of Danaus. 1894.
A sentimental view of vivisection. [1894], [1895]. Pam.
Some truths about vivisection. 1894. Pam.
The savagery of vivisection. [1894/5?] Pam.
Beyond the pale: an appeal on behalf of the victims of vivisection. [1896.]
The morality of marriage and other essays. 1897, 1898. Originally pbd in North Amer Rev, Westminster Rev, Fortnightly Rev and Nineteenth Cent.
REVIEW: Ethics 9 1898.
The pathway of the gods. 1898. Novel.
REVIEW: Bookman 15 1898.
The proposed Pasteur Institute at Chelsea Bridge. [189?] Pam.
The sanctuary of mercy. [189?]
Legalized torture. Ilfracombe [18??]
The inquisition of science. 1903.
The logicians. An episode in dialogue. [1905.]
Romantic cities of Provence. 1906 (illus).
REVIEWS: Bookman 31 Suppl 1906; Dial 41 1906; Nat Geographic 18 1907.
Personal rights: an address. [1913.] Pam.
The stones of sacrifice. 1915.
The great wave. 1931.
REVIEW: Bookman 80 1931.

Contributions to periodicals

Is marriage a failure? Daily Telegraph 1888.
The emancipation of the family. North Amer Rev 150 1890.
Is vivisection logically justifiable? Humane Rev 1 1900.
The duel of the sexes. Fortnightly Rev 84 (n.s. 78) 1905.
Positivism. A ridiculous god. Monthly Rev 25 1906.
See also Wellesley *vol 5*.

§2

Mrs Mona Caird in a new character. Rev of Revs 7 1893.
The Times 5 Feb 1932.
In Who was who 1929–40.

Ada Cambridge, 'A. C.' Later Mrs George Frederick Cross 1844–1926

Principal collections of unpbd mss, typescripts and correspondence by or relating to Ada Cambridge, are at the Mitchell Lib, State Lib of New South Wales; Fryer Lib, Univ of Queensland; La Trobe Lib, State Lib of Victoria; and at the Huntington. Publishing contracts and correspondence are located in the papers of R. Bentley & Son (BL, Univ of Illinois, and UCLA; microfilmed by Chadwyck-Healey), Kegan Paul, Trench, Trübner (London; and microfilmed by Chadwyck-Healey), W. Heinemann (Reed Book Services, Rushden, Northants), and A. P. Watt (in particular at the Wilson Lib, Univ of North Carolina, Chapel Hill). For location of additional ms collections, see Bibliography in A. Tate under §2, below. See also Letters §1, below.

Bibliographies

Miller, E. M. In his Australian literature from its beginnings to 1935, 2 vols Melbourne 1940.
Miller, E. M. and F. T. Macartney. In their Australian literature, a bibliography to 1938, extended to 1950. Sydney 1956.
Andrews, B. and W. H. Wilde. In their Australian literature to 1900: a guide to information sources. Detroit 1980.
Barton, P. In her Ada Cambridge: writing for her life, in A bright and fiery troop: Australian women writers of the nineteenth century, ed D. Adelaide, Ringwood Victoria 1988.
Morrison, E. Bibliographical note. In Cambridge, a woman's friendship, ed Morrison, 1988; *see §1, below*. (Specific focus on serial fiction.)
Adelaide, D. In her Bibliography of Australian women's literature: 1795–1990, Pt Melbourne, Australia 1991.
Bradstock, M. and L. Wakeling. Appendix: the works of Ada Cambridge, and Bibliography. In their Rattling the orthodoxies, 1991; *see §2, below*.
Tate, A. Bibliography. In her Ada Cambridge, 1991; *see §2, below*.
Duwell, M. and L. Hergenhan (ed, with M. Ehrhardt and C. Hetherington). Ada Cambridge. In The Australian literary

studies guide to Australian writers: a bibliography 1963–1995. St Lucia, Queensland 2nd edn 1997. (Secondary bibliography.)
See also the Australian literature electronic database (AUSLIT), Univ College Lib, Australian Defence Force Acad, Canberra ACT. (Continually updated.)

Collections

Hymns on the Litany. Oxford and London 1865. (By 'A. C.')

Hymns on the Holy Communion. '1866' [1865] (with Preface by Rev R. H. Baynes), New York 1866 (with addn to Prefatory note).
REVIEW: Contemporary Rev 1, Jan–Apr 1866.

The manor house and other poems. 1875. Includes poems first pbd in Sunday Mag 1869–73, and in Good Words 1875.

Unspoken thoughts. 1887 (anon); ed P. Barton, Campbell ACT 1988 (with background notes). Includes poems first pbd in Australasian (Melbourne) 1880–6. *See also* Barton (1987) and S. Thomas, under §2, *below.*
REVIEWS: Age (Melbourne) 3 Sep 1887; Pall Mall Gazette 10 Sep 1887; Argus (Melbourne) 1 Oct 1887; Australasian 8 Oct 1887; Brisbane Courier 24 Oct 1887; Saturday Rev 29 Oct 1887.

At midnight and other stories. 1897 (illustr P. Frenzeny), Toronto [1897?]. Includes At midnight, first pbd as A honeymoon adventure in Sydney Mail 20 Dec 1884–3 Jan 1885; A breath of the sea, first pbd in Leisure Hour 1893; The wind of destiny, first pbd in Windsor Mag 1896; A sweet day, first pbd as A peer's romance, Windsor Mag 1897; 'One of these little ones', first pbd as A chaperon, Windsor Mag 1895. Stories rptd in Australian Town and Country Jnl (Sydney) 9 Oct 1897–27 Aug 1898 (pbd at irregular intervals, with At midnight appearing as In the dead of the night).
REVIEWS: Australasian 11 Dec 1897; Australian Town and Country Jnl (Sydney) 11 Dec 1897; Sydney Mail 18 Dec 1897; Athenaeum 22 Jan 1898; Bookman (London) Feb 1898.

The hand in the dark and other poems. 1913. Includes poems (rev) from Unspoken thoughts, and poems first pbd in Centennial Mag and in Australasian.
REVIEWS: Bookman (London) Aug 1913 (E. Thomas); Lone Hand (Sydney) 1 Aug 1913; Acad 11 Oct 1913.

§1

Works pbd separately after first pbn in serial form often incorporate significant textual modification.

The two surplices: a tale. 1865 ('Reprinted from the Churchman's Companion'). Moral tale.

Little Jenny. 1867 (illus). Moral tale.

The vicar's guest: a tale. London and New York 1869. Moral tale.

My guardian: a story of the fen country. London, Paris and New York [1878] (illustr F. Dicksee), New York 1879 (Appletons' Lib of Choice Novels), 1879 (G. Munro's Seaside Lib 25 no 486; and G. Munro's Seaside Lib Pocket Edn no 1967), 1892 (Appletons' Town and Country Lib no 89), Toronto [1892?] (Nat Publishing Co, Red Letter Ser), New York [1905] (A. L. Burt's Cornell Lib). First pbd in Cassell's Family Mag Dec 1876–June 1877.
REVIEWS: British Quart Rev Jan 1879; Literary World (Boston) 15 Feb 1879 and 23 Apr 1892; Publishers' Weekly (New York) 12 Mar 1892; New York Times 28 Mar 1892.

In two years' time. 2 vols 1879. First pbd in Australasian 4 Jan–5 Apr 1879.
REVIEW: Spectator 8 May 1880.

A mere chance. 3 vols 1882, 1 vol New York 1882 (G. Munro's Seaside Lib 64 no 1294). First pbd in Australasian 10 July–20 Nov 1880.
REVIEWS: Acad 18 Feb 1882; Athenaeum 18 Feb 1882 (W. Wallace); Melbourne Rev Apr 1882; Saturday Rev 8 Apr 1882; Sydney Mail 15 Apr 1882.

A marked man: some episodes in his life. 3 vols 1890 (rev), 1 vol New York 1890 (Lovell's International Series no 113), New York 1890 (G. Munro's Seaside Lib Pocket Edn no 1583), London 1891 ('Popular Edn'), Melbourne, Sydney and London 1891 (Colonial Edn) (Petherick's Collection of Favourite & Approved Authors no 59), New York [1896?] (Lenox and Summer Ser); ed D. Adelaide, London, North Ryde NSW and New York 1987 (Australian Women Writers Ser). First pbd in Age July 1888–5 Jan 1889 (as A black sheep: some episodes in his life), and in Manchester Weekly Times Suppl 28 June–10 Oct 1890. *See also* Zinkhan (1993), under §2, *below.*
REVIEWS: Athenaeum 20 Sep 1890; Manchester Examiner and Times 20 Sep 1890; Speaker 20 Sep 1890; Manchester Guardian 23 Sep 1890; Acad 11 Oct 1890 (G. B. Smith); Scots Observer 11 Oct 1890; Illus London News 1 Nov 1890; Queen 1 Nov 1890; Graphic 8 Nov 1890; Lady's Pictorial 15 Nov 1890; Spectator 27 Dec 1890; Argus 24 Jan 1891; Westminster Rev Feb 1891; Argus 7 Mar 1891; Australasian Critic 1 Apr 1891; Sydney Quart Mag June 1891.

The three Miss Kings: a novel. 1891, Melbourne and London 1891 (as The three Miss Kings, by 'Mrs Cross') (Lib of Australian Authors), New York 1891 (as The three Miss Kings: an Australian story, Appletons' Town and Country Lib no 75) ('Authorized Edn'), 1891 (G. Munro's Seaside Lib Pocket Edn no 2139), London 1892 (2nd edn; 'Seventh Thousand'), New York 1892 (M. J. Ivers Amer Ser), London 1897 ('Eighth Thousand'), 1899 ('Popular Edn'), New York [1905?] (A. L. Burt's Cornell Lib), [1907?] (A. L. Burt's Ivy Series of Fiction); ed A. Tate, London 1987 (Virago Modern Classics no 244). First pbd in Australasian 23 June–15 Dec 1883.
REVIEWS: Manchester Guardian 23 June 1891; Athenaeum 4 July 1891; Publishers' Weekly 4 July 1891; Queen 25 July 1891; Saturday Rev 25 July 1891; Literary World 1 Aug 1891; Acad 22 Aug 1891; Tinsley's Mag Sep 1891; Australasian Critic 1 Sep 1891 (M. Gaunt); Argus 12 Sep 1891; Age 10 Oct 1891; Leader (Melbourne) 17 Oct 1891; Sydney Mail 17 June 1899.

Not all in vain. 3 vols 1892, 1 vol New York 1892 (Appletons' Town and Country Lib no 87) (includes Publishers' Note), London 1892 (2nd edn; 'Sixth Thousand') (plates from Appleton), Melbourne and London 1892 (by 'Mrs Cross', Lib of Australian Authors). First pbd in Australasian 6 Dec 1890–18 Apr 1891.
REVIEWS: Publishers' Weekly 13 Feb 1892; Athenaeum 12 Mar 1892; Critic (New York) 19 Mar 1892; Queen 19 Mar 1892; Acad 26 Mar 1892 (G. B. Smith); Argus 2 Apr 1892; Spectator 9 Apr 1892; World 13 Apr 1892; Age 16 Apr and 28 May 1892; Saturday Rev 16 Apr 1892; Sydney Mail 30 Apr 1892.

A little minx: a sketch. 1893 (incorporates and modifies Sydney Mail serial, *below*, and short story The unseen foe, pbd in Centennial Mag Aug 1889), New York 1893 (Appletons' Town and Country Lib no 114). First pbd Sydney Mail 17 Oct–5 Dec 1885.
REVIEWS: New York Times 3 Apr 1893; Literary World 8 Apr 1893; Athenaeum 29 Apr 1893; Queen 29 Apr 1893; Bookman (London) May 1893; Acad 10 June 1893 (J. S. Little); Nation 29 June 1893; Critic 29 July 1893. *See also* Champion (Melbourne) 19 Dec 1896.

A marriage ceremony. 2 vols 1894 (rev), 1 vol 1894 ('Third Edn') ('For India and the Colonies Only'), New York 1894 (Appletons' Town and Country Lib no 133), Toronto [1894?] (UK sheets), London [1895?] ('Fourth Edn'). First pbd in Australasian 15 Nov 1884–21 Feb 1885 (as Mrs Carnegie's husband). Rptd in Toronto Daily Star 12 Dec 1901–7 Feb 1902.
REVIEWS: Publishers' Weekly 17 Feb 1894; Speaker 24 Feb 1894; Books and Notions (Toronto) Mar 1894; Athenaeum 3 Mar 1894; Spectator 17 Mar 1894; Acad 24 Mar 1894 (G. B. Smith); Literary World 24 Mar 1894; Lady's Pictorial 21 Apr 1894; Saturday Rev 8 Sep 1894; Critic 21 July 1894; Queen 24 Feb 1904.

Fidelis: a novel. 3 vols 1895 (also 2nd edn), 1 vol 1895 (3rd edn) (Colonial Edn), 1895 ('Fourth Edn') ('Hutchinson's Select Novels'), New York 1895 (Appletons' Town and Country Lib no 167).
REVIEWS: Athenaeum 13 Apr 1895; Lady's Pictorial 4 May 1895; Acad 11 May 1895; Publishers' Weekly 18 May 1895; Queen 18 May 1895; New York Times 25 May 1895; Spectator 25 May 1895;

Literary World 1 June 1895; Saturday Rev 8 June 1895; Bookman (London) Sep 1895; Nation 3 Oct 1895.

A humble enterprise. London, New York and Melbourne 1896 (illustr St Clair Simmons), 1896 (2nd edn) (Colonial Edn), New York 1896 (Appletons' Town and Country Lib no 196), London, New York and Melbourne nd (Lily Ser no 24), New York [1905?] (A. L. Burt's Cornell Lib), London, Melbourne and Toronto nd (Girls' Favourite Lib). First pbd in Australasian 19 Dec 1891 (Xmas story, as 'The charm that works').
REVIEWS: Athenaeum 8 Aug 1896; Australasian 8 Aug 1896; Literary World 8 Aug 1896; Critic 22 Aug 1896; Acad 29 Aug 1896; Queen 29 Aug 1896; Tatler (Melbourne) 14 Aug 1897; Publishers' Weekly 18 July 1898.

Materfamilias. London, New York and Melbourne [1898] (illustr R. Potter), New York 1898 (Appletons' Town and Country Lib no 242). Includes 6 stories (rev) first pbd in Woman at Home Oct 1895–Sep 1897 (illustr R. Potter et al): Deposed, My voyage to Australia, My baby, An unexpected legacy, An experiment in matchmaking, and The silver wedding-day.
REVIEWS: Publishers' Weekly 11 June 1898; Athenaeum 25 June 1898; New York Times 25 June 1898; Literary World 9 July 1898; Literature 30 July 1898; Sydney Mail 30 July 1898; Illus London News 6 Aug 1898; Australasian 13 Aug 1898; Bookman (New York) Oct 1898.

Path and goal. 1900 (also 2nd edn; and Colonial Edn), New York 1900 (as Path and goal: a novel, Appletons' Town and Country Lib no 293).
REVIEWS: Acad 8 Sep 1900; Athenaeum 8 Sep 1900; Spectator 15 Sep 1900; Bookman (London) Oct 1900; Saturday Rev 6 Oct 1900; Br Australasian 18 Oct 1900; Acad 3 Nov 1900; Queen 3 Nov 1900 (D. Sladen); Literature 24 Nov 1900; Age 29 Dec 1900, Australian Town and Country Jnl 23 Feb 1901 (F. C. Rhodes).

The devastators. 1901 (also Colonial Edn), New York 1901 (Appletons' Town and Country Lib no 304). Incorporates The end of the story (rev) first pbd in Lady's Realm Nov 1898.
REVIEWS: Acad 17 Aug and 24 Aug 1901; Punch 28 Aug 1901; Athenaeum 14 Sep 1901; Publishers' Weekly 12 Oct 1901; Queen 19 Oct 1901.

Thirty years in Australia. 1903 (also Colonial Edn); ed M. Bradstock and L. Wakeling, Kensington NSW 1989. Incorporates (rev) Thirty years in Australia: some memories, Empire Rev July 1901–Dec 1902; and Toby: a memory, Quiver 1902. Rptd in Woman's World (Melbourne) 1 Mar 1923–1 July 1925 (truncated). *See also* Bradstock and Wakeling (1990), under §2, *below*. Autobiography.
REVIEWS: Saturday Rev 14 Mar 1903; Athenaeum 28 Mar 1903; Acad and Lit 4 Apr 1903; Country Life 4 Apr 1903; Punch 22 Apr 1903; Bulletin 25 Apr 1903; Bookman (London) May 1903; Book Lover (Melbourne) 1 May 1903; Illus London News 2 May 1903; Queen 16 May 1903. *See also* Woman's World 1 Feb 1923.

Sisters: a novel. 1904 (also Colonial Edn); ed N. Cato, Ringwood Victoria 1989 (Penguin Australian Women's Lib). Individual chs incorporate the following stories (rev): A painful interview, Chapman's Mag 1897; Solving the difficulty, Longman's Mag 1897; The ambushed enemy, Windsor Mag 1898.
REVIEWS: Punch 5 Oct 1904; Athenaeum 15 Oct 1904; Queen 5 Nov 1904; Book Lover 1 Dec 1904.

A platonic friendship. 1905; London and Bombay [1906?] (Bell's Indian and Colonial Lib no 642).
REVIEWS: Queen 30 Dec 1905, Lady's Pictorial 23 June 1906.

A happy marriage. 1906, London and Bombay [1906?] (Bell's Indian and Colonial Lib no 686).
REVIEWS: TLS 28 Sep 1906; Acad 20 Oct 1906; Queen 17 Nov 1906.

The eternal feminine. 1907, London and Bombay [1907?] (Bell's Indian and Colonial Lib no 754).
REVIEWS: TLS 17 Oct 1907; Athenaeum 16 Nov 1907.

The retrospect. [1912] (also a Colonial edn). Autobiography.
REVIEW: Acad 31 Aug 1912.

The making of Rachel Rowe. London, New York, Toronto and Melbourne 1914 (illustr S. Adamson).
REVIEW: TLS 15 Oct 1914.

A woman's friendship. Ed E. Morrison, Kensington NSW 1988 (Colonial Texts Ser). Includes The Reform Club (previously unpbd). First pbd in Age 31 Aug–26 Oct 1889. *See also* Morrison (1990), under §2, *below*.

Contributions to periodicals and newspapers

For contributions to periodicals and newspapers later pbd in collections, or pbd separately, see Collections and §1, above. For additional contributions pbd by or attributed to Cambridge, or rptd in anthologies, see AUSLIT (above) and the bibliographies in Bradstock and Wakeling, and in Tate, under §2, below.

The false love. Once a Week 17, 19 Oct 1867. Poem.
From the battlefield: good night. Sydney Mail 18 Feb 1871. Poem.
Gifts of grace. Sunday Mag n.s. 1 1872. Poem.
Counsel. Sydney Mail 16 Mar 1872. Poem.
A great secret. Sydney Mail 20 Jan 1872. Poem.
Bachelor troubles. Australasian 31 Aug 1872. Short story.
The history of six hours. Australasian 15 Feb 1873. Short story.
At sea. Australasian 28 June 1873. Short story.
Up the Murray. Australasian 27 Mar–17 July 1875. Novel.
Rachel Lindsay: a South Australian story. Chambers's Jnl 55 1878. Anon.
The captain's charge. Sydney Mail 26 July–6 Sep 1879. Novel.
Dinah. Australasian 6 Dec 1879–24 Feb 1880. Novel.
Missed in the crowd. Australasian 8 Oct 1881–4 Mar 1882. Novel.
A girl's ideal. Age 10 Dec 1881–14 Jan 1882; and Australian Town and Country Jnl 24 Dec 1881–18 Mar 1882. Novel.
Across the grain. Australasian 7 Oct–23 Dec 1882. Novel.
Mrs Carlisle's enemy. Australasian 8–15 Mar 1884. Novella.
A successful experiment. Australasian 3–17 May 1884. Novella.
Under favourable circumstances. Australasian 27 Dec 1884. Short story.
Against the rules: an episode. Australasian 28 Nov 1885–23 Jan 1886. Novel.
The story of a summer. Australian Jnl (Melbourne) 21, Mar 1886.
Notes of an Australian snowstorm. Age 11 June 1887. Sketch.
The perversity of human nature. Illus Australian News (Christmas story) Dec 1887. Novel.
By the night express: an episode (illus). Centennial Mag (Melbourne and Sydney) 1, Aug 1888. Short story.
A face at the window. Australian Jnl 24, Dec 1888. Short story.
America in Samoa. Centennial Mag 1, July 1889. Poem.
The unseen foe. Centennial Mag 2, Aug 1889. Short story.
A memory. Centennial Mag 2, Sep 1889. Poem.
Evening. Centennial Mag 2, Nov 1889. Poem.
My father-in-law. Bulletin 20 Sep 1890. Short story.
Not sufficient funds. Bulletin 20 Dec 1890. Short story.
The second Mrs Jowker: a bush sketch. Bulletin 10 Oct 1891. Short story.
Tasma [Jessie Couvreur]. Queen 95, 13 Jan 1894. Essay.
Studies in Australian child-life: a new Australian writer (illus). Rev of Revs for Australasia (Melbourne) 7, 20 Oct 1895. Essay on Ethel Turner.
A third officer and a girl (illustr W. Paget). Queen 108, 24 Nov 1900. Also pbd New York Press 25 Nov 1900. Short story.
The human document: a suggestion. Lyceum Annual 1901. Essay.
Toby: a memory (illus). Quiver Annual 1902. Sketch.
For the third time of asking (illus). Quiver Annual 1907. Short story.
The return. Australasian 5 Jan 1907. Short story.
The retrospect. Atlantic Monthly 103, Jan 1909. Essay.

Weather permitting: the story of an outdoor Christmas (illus). Quiver Annual 1909. Short story.
The worms that turned (illus). Quiver Annual 1909. Short story.
A patent of nobility. Atlantic Monthly 106, Oct 1910. Essay.
The lonely seas. Atlantic Monthly 108, July 1911. Essay.
The privy slanderer: an unusual story with an unusual moral (illus). Quiver Annual 1911. (See also editorial and reader response to this story.)
Hobbled. North Amer Rev 197, Mar 1913. Essay.
The Statue of Liberty (New York). Lone Hand 1 May 1916. Poem.
The haunted house. North Amer Rev 207, Feb 1918. Essay.
Nightfall. Atlantic Monthly 130, Aug 1922. Essay.
25th April, 1923. Woman's World, Apr 1923. Poem.
Cambridge may have collaborated in two articles pbd under her husband's name: G. F. Cross, The modern pulpit, *and* The modern pulpit: a last word, *Melbourne Rev 4 1879.*

Other publications

[Verse addn to Auld lang syne.] Blake's Musical Misc no 42, Baltimore nd (copy in Univ of Virginia Lib).
The towns of Victoria: Western District (as 'Ada Cross') (illus). In Picturesque atlas of Australasia, ed A. Garran, 3 vols Sydney 1886 (vol 2) (in collaboration with J. Smith and A. Semple); facs edn Sydney 1974. Essay.
[Untitled contribution.] In Illustrated guide to Beechworth and vicinity, Beechworth, Victoria 1892. Essay.
A sedative. In Childhood in bud and blossom: a souvenir book of the children's hospital bazaar, ed J. Lake (illustr E. Fahey and N. Carter), Melbourne 1900. Short story.

Letters

[Letters.] In Dear Robertson: letters to an Australian publisher, ed A. W. Barker, Sydney 1982. Prints 7 letters from Cambridge to G. Robertson.
[Inscriptions.] In E. Zinkhan, Ada Cambridge: a poetry manuscript and holograph inscriptions in America, formerly part of the James Carleton Young Collection. In Bibliographical Soc of Australia and New Zealand Bull 14 1990 (issued 1991). Discusses unpbd mss and prints 4 Cambridge inscriptions.
See also Cambridge, Unspoken thoughts, *ed Barton, under Collections, above. Prints one letter from Cambridge to A. G. Stephens.*

§2

This is a selective list. For additional secondary material, see works cited under Bibliographies, above.

Greene, C. M. Australian writers. Universal Rev 3 1889.
Falk, D. To A. C. Centennial Mag 2 Jan 1890. Poem.
Byrne, D. Ada Cambridge. In his Australian writers, 1896.
Turner, H. G. and A. Sutherland. In their The development of Australian literature, 1898.
Dolman, F. Australian authors of to-day. Cassell's Mag 29 Dec 1899–May 1900 (with photo).
Stephens, A. G. Notes on books: a clergyman's wife. Bulletin 25 Apr 1903; rptd in A. G. Stephens: his life and work, ed V. Palmer, Melbourne 1941.
Women in literature: popular novelist: Ada Cambridge. Melbourne Herald 20 Feb 1912 (with photo); rptd in Weekly Times (Melbourne) 24 Feb 1912. Anon.
Spencer, G. Ada Cambridge: the doyen of Australian novelists (with photo). Woman's World 1 Jan 1922. Interview.
Taylor, F. How I became a writer: by Ada Cambridge (with photo). Woman's World 1 May 1924. Interview.
Obits: Argus (Melbourne) 21 July 1926 (anon); The Times 21 July 1926, 22 July 1926 (photo), 24 July 1926 (by Rev Heard); Argus 23 July 1926 (with photo) (anon); Australasian 24 July 1926 (anon); Stephens, A. G. Sydney Morning Herald 31 July 1926; [Bruce, M. G.] Woman's World 1 Aug 1926.
Baker, K. A. Williamstown novelist: Ada Cambridge. Williamstown Chron 1 June 1945. (The erection of a memorial plaque.)
Morrison, E. Bibliographical revisionism: the novels of Ada Cambridge. In Books, libraries and readers in colonial Australia, ed E. Morrison and M. Talbot, Melbourne 1985.
Barton, P. Re-opening the case of Ada Cambridge. Australian Literary Stud 13 Oct 1987. (Publication history of Unspoken thoughts.)
Thomas, S. Ada Cambridge's Unspoken thoughts. Notes & Furphies (Australia) 18 1987. (Publication history.)
Bradstock, M. and L. Wakeling. Ada Cambridge and the first thirty years. Australian Lit Stud 14 May 1990. (Discusses textual variance.)
Morrison, E. Editing a newspaper novel for the Colonial Texts Series: A woman's friendship. In Editing in Australia, ed P. Eggert, Melbourne 1990.
Bradstock, M. and L. Wakeling. Rattling the orthodoxies: a life of Ada Cambridge. Ringwood, Victoria 1991.
Tate, A. Ada Cambridge: her life and work 1844–1926. Carlton, Victoria 1991.
Zinkhan, E. Ada Cambridge: A marked man, the Manchester Weekly Times Suppl, and late-nineteenth-century fiction publication. Bibliographical Soc of Australia and New Zealand Bull 17 1993. (On serial and book pbn, and textual variance.)
See also Zinkhan (1990/1991), under Letters, above. [EJZ]

Bernard Edward Joseph Capes 1854–1918

Mss located in NLS.

Bibliographies

In An index to Blackwood's Mag 1901–1980, ed D. Finkelstein, Aldershot 1995.
See also Wellesley *vol 5 1989.*

Selections

In The black reaper: tales of terror, ed H. Lamb, Wellingborough 1989.
An eddy on the floor. In Victorian ghost stories, ed M. Cox and R. A. Gilbert, Oxford 1991.
A ghost-child in The mammoth book of Victorian and Edwardian ghost stories, ed R. Dalby, 1995, rptd as The giant book of classic ghost stories, 1997.
Dark dignum. In Twelve Victorian ghost stories, ed M. Cox, Oxford 1997.

§1

The mill of silence. Chicago and New York 1897, London 1902.
REVIEWS: The Chap-Book 15 May 1897; Acad 26 July 1902.
The lake of wine. 1898, New York 1898, London 1906, [1919].
REVIEWS: Literary World 27 May 1898; Spectator 28 May 1898; Bookman June 1898; Athenaeum 4 June 1898; Dial 1 Aug 1898; Bookman (USA) Oct 1898.
Adventures of the Comte de la Muette during the reign of terror. Edinburgh 1898, New York 1898.
REVIEWS: Spectator 25 June 1898; Acad Suppl 2 July 1898; Literature 2 July 1898; Speaker 30 July 1898; Literary World 19 Aug 1898; Athenaeum 3 Sep 1898; Dial 16 Feb 1899.
The mysterious singer. Bristol 1898.
REVIEWS: Acad Suppl 3 Sep 1898; Literary World 23 Sep 1898.
At a winter's fire. 1899, New York 1899, 1906, Freeport NY 1969.
REVIEWS: Spectator 17 June 1899; Literature 1 July 1899; Literary World 14 July 1899; Dial Aug 1899; Athenaeum 12 Aug 1899; New York Times 12 Aug 1899; Bookman (USA) Oct 1899.
Our lady of darkness. Edinburgh and London 1899, New York 1899.
REVIEWS: Literature 30 Sep 1899; Spectator 30 Sep 1899; Speaker

7 Oct 1899; Literary World 13 Oct 1899; Blackwood's Mag Nov 1899; Athenaeum 23 Dec 1899; Outlook 6 Jan 1900; Dial 1 Feb 1900.

From door to door. A book of romances, fantasies, whimsies and levities. Edinburgh 1900, New York 1900, London 1904.
REVIEWS: Acad 19 May 1900; Literature 9 June 1900; Athenaeum 16 June 1900; New York Times 18 Aug 1900.

Joan Brotherhood. 1900.
REVIEWS: Literature 9 June 1900; Literary World 26 Oct 1900; Acad 3 Nov 1900; Literature 10 Nov 1900; Spectator 17 Nov 1900; Outlook 24 Nov 1900.

Love like a gipsy. A romance. 1901.
REVIEWS: Acad 19 Oct 1901; Spectator 2 Nov 1901; Athenaeum 23 Nov 1901; Literature 23 Nov 1901; Literary World 20 Dec 1901; Acad 11 Jan 1902; Outlook 11 Jan 1902.

Plots. 1902.
REVIEWS: Acad 15 Mar 1902; Literary World 4 Apr 1902; TLS 11 Apr 1902; Athenaeum 19 Apr 1902; Outlook 17 May 1902.

A castle in Spain: certain memories of Robin Louis, ex-major of His Majesty's 109th Regiment of Foot. 1903.
REVIEWS: Acad 14 Feb 1903; TLS 20 Feb 1903; Acad 21 Feb 1903; Outlook 7 Mar 1903; Spectator 21 Mar 1903; Athenaeum 11 Apr 1903.

The secret in the hill. 1903.
REVIEWS: Athenaeum 14 Nov 1903; Outlook 14 Nov 1903; TLS 20 Nov 1903; Acad 21 Nov 1903; Spectator 21 Nov 1903; Athenaeum 28 Nov 1903.

The extraordinary confessions of Diana Please. 1904.
REVIEWS: TLS 2 Sep 1904; Acad 10 Sep 1904; Literary World 7 Oct 1904; Outlook 5 Nov 1904.

The vanishing cheques. [1904.]

A jay of Italy. 1905, [1915].
REVIEWS: TLS 21 July 1905; Acad 29 July 1905; Spectator 12 Aug 1905; Athenaeum 19 Aug 1905.

The romance of Lothengrin, founded on Wagner's opera. 1905, Boston 1905.
REVIEWS: TLS 21 July 1905; Acad 12 Aug 1905; Athenaeum 26 Aug 1905; New York Times 21 Oct 1905.

Bembo: a tale of Italy. New York 1906.
REVIEWS: New York Times 9 June 1906; Dial 1 Sep 1906.

Loaves and fishes. 1906, 1909.
REVIEWS: Acad 7 Apr 1906; Athenaeum 28 Apr 1906.

The rogue's tragedy. 1906 (2 edns).
REVIEWS: TLS 24 Aug 1906; Acad 25 Aug 1906; Outlook 25 Aug 1906; Athenaeum 27 Oct 1906.

The great skene mystery. 1907, 1910.
REVIEWS: TLS 26 July 1907; Outlook 27 July 1907; Spectator 10 Aug 1907; Acad 5 Oct 1907.

Amaranthus. A book of little songs. 1908.
REVIEWS: Spectator 12 Sep 1908; Bookman Oct 1908; Athenaeum 7 Nov 1908.

The green parrot. 1908, 1922.
REVIEWS: TLS 8 Oct 1908; Acad 17 Oct 1908; Outlook 24 Oct 1908; Athenaeum 31 Oct 1908; Spectator 26 Dec 1908.

The love of St Bel. 1909.
REVIEWS: TLS 18 Mar 1909; Outlook 17 Apr 1909; Athenaeum 24 Apr 1909.

Historical vignettes. 1910, New York 1910 (enlarged edn), London 1912, Boston 1962, Salem NH 1962, Boston 1963.
REVIEWS: TLS 13 Oct 1910; Outlook 29 Oct 1910; Athenaeum 3 Dec 1910; Bookman Apr 1911.

Why did he do it? 1910, New York 1910.
REVIEWS: Outlook 19 Feb 1910; Athenaeum 5 Mar 1910; TLS 10 Mar 1910; New York Times 30 Apr 1910.

The will and the way. 1910.

Jemmy Abercraw. 1910, New York 1911, London [1913], [1928].
REVIEWS: Outlook 10 Sep 1910; Athenaeum 17 Sep 1910; Spectator 15 Oct 1910.

Gilead Balm, knight errant. His adventures in search of the truth. 1911, New York 1911, Toronto 1911.
REVIEWS: Athenaeum 28 Jan 1911; Outlook 28 Jan 1911; Bookman Feb 1911; Acad 11 Feb 1911.

The house of many voices. 1911.
REVIEWS: TLS 10 Aug 1911; Athenaeum 26 Aug 1911; Outlook 16 Sep 1911; Bookman Dec 1911.

Jessie Bazley. 1912.

Bag and baggage. 1913.
REVIEW: Athenaeum 25 Jan 1913.

The pot of basil. 1913.
REVIEWS: TLS 7 Aug 1913; Athenaeum 9 Aug 1913; Bookman Sep 1913.

The story of Fifine. 1914, 1919, 1920.
REVIEWS: TLS 2 July 1914; Athenaeum 4 July 1914; Spectator 19 Sep 1914.

The fabulists. 1915.
REVIEWS: Athenaeum 13 Mar 1915; TLS 18 Mar 1915; Outlook 20 Mar 1915.

Moll Davis. A comedy. [1916.]
REVIEWS: TLS 10 Feb 1916; Outlook 26 Feb 1916.

If age could. 1916.
REVIEWS: TLS 26 Oct 1916; Bookman Nov 1916.

Where England sets her feet. A romance. [1918], 1920, 1925.
REVIEWS: TLS 21 Mar 1918; Outlook 23 Mar 1918; Athenaeum Apr 1918.

The skeleton key. New York 1918, London 1919 (introd by G. K. Chesterton), New York 1920, London 1921, New York 1921, London 1923, 1925, 1929 (as The mystery of the skeleton key).
REVIEWS: TLS 17 Apr 1919; Athenaeum 18 Apr 1919; New York Times 27 June 1920; Spectator 19 July 1919.

Contributions to periodicals

Capes was editor of Theatre *from Jan 1890 to Oct 1890 and co-editor from Nov 1890 to May 1892. He also contributed to the* Illus London News.

Pearson's Mag. Dark dignum, June 1897.
The Idler. A true princess, July 1898.
Dome. The passing ghost (poem), June 1899; The accursed cordonnier, May–July 1900.
Strand. Wanted – a bicycle, June 1899.
Outlook. Ignorance for its own sake, 10 June 1899.
Literature. 'The air hath bubbles', 9 Sep 1899.
Pall Mall Mag. Oct 1899–June 1907.
T. P.'s Weekly. 10 Apr 1903–24 July 1903.
Cassell's Mag. A double pretender, July 1906.
Harmsworth's London Mag. Nov 1906–Dec 1911.
Lady's Realm. May 1907–Oct 1910.
The story-teller. Sep 1907–Jan 1912.
Current literature. Christmas feast, Jan 1909. Poem.
Athenaeum. The voice, 2 Jan 1909. Poem.
English Review. Fouquier-Tinville, Sep 1909.
Living Age. Clipping the currency, 9 Oct 1909; Pleasures of eating, 19 Sep 1914.
Blackwood's Mag. Pleasures of eating, July 1914.
Cornhill Mag. La morgue littéraire, Nov 1917.

§2

Books of my childhood. T. P.'s Weekly 6 Feb 1903.
The making of a novelist. T. P.'s Weekly 10 Apr 1903.
News notes (photo and note). Bookman Aug 1908.
The Times 4 Nov 1918. Obituary.
The Times 8 Nov 1918. Biographical.
Sutherland, J. In his The Longman companion to Victorian fiction, 1988.
DLB vol 156 Detriot 1995. [DA]

Rosa Nouchette Carey 1840–1909

Mss of 27 letters in Bentley Archives, Univ of Illinois Lib (micro); 3 letters in Huntington.

Bibliographies

Crisp, J. Rosa Nouchette Carey. Victorian Fiction Research Guides 16. St Lucia, Queensland 1989.

Selections

The Rosa Nouchette Carey birthday book, with portrait of author. Comp H. M. Burnside [1901].

§1

Nellie's memories: a domestic story. 3 vols 1868, 1874 (2nd edn), 1880, New York [1880], London 1892 ('new edn'), 1898 (reissue of previous item), London and New York 1900 (abridged edn for schools), New York [190?], London [1920], [nd].
REVIEWS: Pall Mall Gazette 3 Dec 1868; Athenaeum 5 Dec 1868.

Wee Wifie. 2 vols 1869, 1887 (rev with 'several, fresh chapters'), New York [1887], London 1901 (reissue of 1887 edn), [1920].
REVIEW: Athenaeum 11 Dec 1869.

Barbara Heathcote's trial. 3 vols 1871, 1883, New York [1885], London 1898 (reissue of 1883 edn), Philadelphia 1909, [1922].
REVIEWS: Athenaeum 4 Nov 1871; Graphic 11 Nov 1871.

Robert Ord's atonement. 3 vols 1873, 1884, New York [1885], [1887], London 1898 (reissue of 1884 edn).
REVIEW: Athenaeum 17 May 1873.

Wooed and married. 3 vols 1875, 1875, Philadelphia 1876, London 1882 (reissue of 1875 edn), New York [1887], London 1898 (reissue), New York [nd], [1922].

Heriot's choice. First pbd Monthly Packet 24 July 1877–Oct 1879. 3 vols 1879, 1890, 1898 (reissue), [1921].
REVIEWS: Athenaeum 10 Jan 1880; Davies, J. Acad 7 Feb 1880; Graphic 14 Feb 1880.

Queenie's whim. 3 vols 1881, New York [1887], London 1889, 1898 (reissue), [1923].
REVIEWS: Lang, L. B. Acad 12 Mar 1881; Graphic 19 Mar 1881; Athenaeum 2 Apr 1881.

Mary St John. 3 vols 1882, 1891, 1898 (reissue), [1924].
REVIEWS: Acad 9 Dec 1882; Athenaeum 23 Dec 1882.

Esther (subsequently Esther Cameron's story). First pbd Girl's Own Paper 6 Oct 1883–15 Mar 1884. [1887], Philadelphia [1887], London [1907] (Leisure Hour Monthly Lib), [1914], [nd]; tr Sp [1927].

Not like other girls. 3 vols 1884, New York [1884], 1885, 1898 (reissue), Philadelphia 1907, 2 vols Leipzig (nd in Tauchnitz Edn Complete List 1 Dec 1911), London [1921].
REVIEWS: Saintsbury, G. Acad 22 Mar 1884; Athenaeum 22 Mar 1884; Nation 22 May 1884; Graphic 7 June 1884.

Aunt Diana. First pbd Girl's Own Paper 21 Mar–26 Sep 1885. [1888], New York [1888], [nd], London [1906] (Leisure Hour Monthly Lib), Philadelphia 1909, London [1914].

For Lilias. 3 vols 1885, New York [1885], London 1892, 1898 (reissue), Philadelphia 1904, New York [1915].
REVIEWS: Wallace, W. Acad 26 Sep 1885; Athenaeum 26 Sep 1885; Graphic 7 Nov 1885.

Merle's crusade. First pbd Girl's Own Paper 2 Oct 1886–9 Apr 1887. [1889], New York [1889], [nd], Philadelphia 1903, London [1906] (Leisure Hour Monthly Lib), [1914], [nd] (with L. Keith, A lass and her lover, and E. Everett-Green, Joint guardians).

Uncle Max. 3 vols 1887, 1887, New York [1887], London 1898, New York [190?], [nd].
REVIEWS: Littledale, R. Acad 5 Feb 1887; Athenaeum 5 Feb 1887; Graphic 26 Mar 1887.

Only the governess. 3 vols 1888, '1889' [1888], New York [1888], London 1898 (reissue of '1889' edn), Philadelphia [1915], [1922].
REVIEWS: Sharp, W. Acad 17 Mar 1888 (with M. Ward, Robert Elsmere, and G. Moore, Confessions of a young man); Athenaeum 17 Mar 1888; Graphic 24 Mar 1888.

Our Bessie. First pbd Girl's Own Paper 6 Oct 1888–23 Mar 1889. [1891], [nd] (Carey Lib for Girls), [1906] (Leisure Hour Monthly Lib), [1914], [nd] (with L. Becke, Tom Wallis, and F. C. Houston, The woman of the well); tr Fr 1897.

The search for Basil Lyndhurst. (Basil Lyndhurst in subsequent British edns.) 3 vols 1889, New York [1889] (Munro), [1889] (Lovell), 1894, London 1899 (reissue), Philadelphia 1908, London [1924].
REVIEWS: Athenaeum 15 June 1889; Graphic 13 July 1889; Saintsbury, G. Acad 20 July 1889.

Lover or friend? 3 vols 1890, New York [1890], London 1893, 1899 (reissue), [1923].
REVIEWS: Athenaeum 27 Sep 1890; Barnett Smith, G. Acad 11 Oct 1890; Spectator 25 Oct 1890; Graphic 8 Nov 1890.

Averil. First pbd Girl's Own Paper 4 Oct 1890–14 Mar 1891. [1891], [nd] (2 different edns pbd Religious Tract Soc), [1907] (Leisure Hour Monthly Lib), [nd] (Girl's Own Paper); tr Fr 1902.

'But men must work'. 1892, with Mrs Romney in Lippincott's Monthly Mag 51 1893, with Mrs Romney 1899, Leipzig [nd in Tauchnitz Edn Complete List 1 Dec 1911].
REVIEWS: Cotterell, G. Acad 3 Sep 1892; Athenaeum 3 Sep 1892; Graphic 15 Oct 1892.

Little Miss Muffet. First pbd Girl's Own Paper 1 Oct 1892–18 Mar 1893. Philadelphia 1893, London [1894], [nd], [nd] (Girl's Own Paper), [1908] (Leisure Hour Monthly Lib).

Sir Godfrey's grand-daughters. 3 vols 1892, Leipzig 1892, Philadelphia 1892, London 1895, 1899 (reissue).
REVIEWS: Athenaeum 5 Nov 1892; Ashcroft Noble, J. Acad 24 Dec 1892; Spectator 28 Jan 1893; Graphic 25 Mar 1893.

Mrs Romney. First pbd with 'But men must work' in Lippincott's Monthly Mag 51 1893. 1894, with 'But men must work' 1899.
REVIEWS: Graphic 13 Oct 1894; Literary World (Boston) 27 1896.

Tiney's birthday gift. In Eighteen stories for girls, ed C. Peters, [1894].

The old, old story. 3 vols 1894, Philadelphia 1894, London 1897, 1898 (reissue), 2 vols Leipzig (nd in Tauchnitz Edn Complete List 1 Dec 1911), London [1920].
REVIEWS: Athenaeum 29 Sep 1894; Spectator 20 Oct 1894; Acad 3 Nov 1894.

Cousin Mona. First pbd Girl's Own Paper 30 Mar–21 Sep 1895. Philadelphia 1896, London [1897], [1908] (Leisure Hour Monthly Lib), [1914] (Girl's Own Paper).

My little Boy Blue. New York and Chicago 1895. Children's book.

The mistress of Brae Farm. 1896, Philadelphia 1897, London 1899 (reissue of 1896 edn), [1920].
REVIEWS: Literary World (Boston) 27 1896; Graphic 6 Mar 1897; Spectator 26 June 1897.

Dr Luttrell's first patient. 1897, Philadelphia 1897.
REVIEWS: Athenaeum 6 Nov 1897; Literary World (Boston) 28 1897.

Other people's lives. 1897, Philadelphia 1898, London 1902.
REVIEWS: Athenaeum 8 Jan 1898 (title given as 'Other people's sins'); Literature 16 Apr 1898.

Mollie's prince. 1898, Philadelphia '1899' [1898], 1912.
REVIEWS: Acad 1 Oct 1898; Athenaeum 29 Oct 1898; Literature 4 Mar 1899.

My Lady Frivol. Illustr B. Newcombe 1899, Philadelphia 1900, London [nd], [nd].
REVIEW: Literature 6 Jan 1900.

Twelve notable good women of the nineteenth century. 1899 (illus). Biography.
REVIEWS: Literature 6 Jan 1900; New York Times 31 Mar 1900.

Life's trivial round. Illustr S. Aldridge 1900, Philadelphia 1900.
REVIEWS: Athenaeum 16 June 1900; New York Times 23 June 1900.

Rue with a difference. 1900 (listed in Macmillan's Colonial Lib), Philadelphia 1901.
REVIEWS: Acad 13 Oct 1900; Acad 3 Nov 1900; Literature 3 Nov 1900; [Bennett, A.] Hearth and Home 22 Nov 1900; Athenaeum 24 Nov 1900; Bookman Jan 1901.
Herb of grace. 1901 (listed in Macmillan's Colonial Lib), Philadelphia 1901, 2 vols Leipzig (nd in Tauchnitz Edn Complete List 1 Dec 1911).
REVIEWS: Acad 21 Sep 1901; Bookman Oct 1901; Athenaeum 11 Jan 1902.
The highway of fate. 1902 (listed in Macmillan's Colonial Lib), Philadelphia 1902, 2 vols Leipzig (nd in Tauchnitz Edn Complete List 1 Dec 1911).
REVIEWS: Acad 20 Sep 1902; Athenaeum 11 Oct 1902.
Effie's little mother. [1903] (with Cat's cradle by E. Marshall). Children's story.
A passage perilous. 1903 (listed in Macmillan's Colonial Lib), Philadelphia 1903, 2 vols Leipzig (nd in Tauchnitz Edn Complete List 1 Dec 1911).
REVIEWS: Acad 26 Sep 1903; New York Times 24 Oct 1903; Athenaeum July–Dec 1903.
At The Moorings. 1904 (listed in Macmillan's Colonial Lib), Philadelphia 1904, 2 vols Leipzig (nd in Tauchnitz Edn Complete List 1 Dec 1911).
REVIEWS: Acad 5 Nov 1904; New York Times 12 Nov 1904; Athenaeum 24 Dec 1904; Bookman Apr 1905.
The household of Peter. 1905 (listed in Macmillan's Colonial Lib), Philadelphia 1905.
REVIEW: Athenaeum 21 Oct 1905.
'No friend like a sister'. 1906, 1906 (Macmillan's Colonial Lib), Philadelphia 1906.
REVIEW: Athenaeum 13 Oct 1906.
The angel of forgiveness. 1907, 1907 (Macmillan's Colonial Lib), Philadelphia 1907.
The sunny side of the hill. 1908, 1908 (Macmillan's Colonial Lib), Philadelphia 1908.
REVIEWS: Acad 17 Oct 1908; Athenaeum 17 Oct 1908; Bookman Nov 1908; New York Times 20 Feb 1909.
The key of the unknown. With photograph of author 1909, Philadelphia 1909.
REVIEWS: Athenaeum 2 Oct 1909; New York Times 30 Oct 1909.

Contributions to periodicals

An Oxford idyll. Argosy 1886. Short story.
Marquise. Lady's Realm 1896/7; rptd in Twenty-six ideal stories for girls [1899]. Short story.
Joan and her public. Lady's Realm 1896/7. Short story.
Hercules. Girl's Own Paper 9 Oct 1897. Short story.
Mademoiselle. Lady's Realm 1897/8. Short story.

Attributed works

Novels by 'Le Voleur' attributed to Carey by BL Cat.
By order of the brotherhood: a story of Russian intrigue. 1895, 1895 (Macmillan's Colonial Lib), [1913].
REVIEW: Barnett Smith, G. Acad 1 June 1895.
For love of a Bedouin maid. 1897.
REVIEWS: Acad 6 Nov 1897; Spectator 22 Jan 1898.
In the Tsar's dominions. Illustr E. Dyer 1899.
REVIEW: Spectator 14 Jan 1899.
The Champington mystery. 1900.

§2

Tooley, S. Some women novelists. Woman at Home 1897.
Black, H. Notable women authors of the day. 1906.
Obits: The Times 20 July 1909; New York Times 20 July 1909; Athenaeum 24 July 1909; Graphic 31 July 1909; Bookman Aug 1909.

For works of criticism, see J. Crisp, Rosa Nouchette Carey, Victorian Fiction Research Guide 16, St Lucia, Queensland 1989. [JC]

'Lewis Carroll', Charles Lutwidge Dodgson

1832–98

The manuscript booklet of Alice's adventures under ground *(the precursor of* Alice's adventures in Wonderland*) is in the BL. No complete manuscripts of* Alice's adventures in Wonderland, Through the looking-glass *or* The hunting of the Snark *have come to light. Four family manuscript magazines, almost entirely by Dodgson, survive:* Useful and instructive poetry *at the Fales Lib, New York Univ;* The rectory umbrella *and* Mischmasch *at the Houghton Lib Harvard; and* The rectory magazine *at HRHRC. Nine volumes of the surviving diaries are at the BL, one at Princeton. Important collections of manuscripts and first edns are, in addition to the locations mentioned above, at the Berg Collection NYPL, Bodleian, Univ of Br Columbia Lib Vancouver, Bryn Mawr College Lib Bryn Mawr PA; Christ Church Lib Oxford, Columbia Univ Lib, Huntington, Pierpont Morgan Lib, Muniments Room Castle Arch Museum Guildford, Surrey, Osborne Collection Toronto, and Rosenbach. Some of the most valuable material still resides in private collections. Collections of Carroll's original photographs are in most of the above and at the National Portrait Gallery and the National Museum of Photography, Film and Television (Bradford).*

Bibliographies and reference works

Catalogue of the furniture, personal effects and library of . . . Carroll. Oxford 1898.
Collingwood, S. D. The life and letters of Carroll. 1898.
Williams, S. H. A bibliography of the writings of Carroll. 1924.
Parrish, M. L. A list of the writings of Carroll . . . collected by Morris L. Parrish. Pine Valley NJ 1928. A supplementary list . . . 1933.
Williams, S. H. and F. Madan. A handbook of the literature of the Rev. C. L. Dodgson. Oxford 1931. Suppl: F. Madan, Oxford 1935.
Green, R. L. Revision of Williams and Madan as The Lewis Carroll handbook. Oxford 1962.
Crutch, D. Revision of Green. Folkstone 1979.
Catalogue of an exhibition at Columbia University to commemorate the one hundredth anniversary of the birth of Carroll. New York 1932.
De Sausmarez, F. B. Theatricals at Oxford; with prologues by Carroll. Nineteenth Cent, Feb 1932.
Livingston, F. V. The Harcourt Amory collection of Carroll in the Harvard College Library, Cambridge MA 1932.
Madan, F. The Carroll centenary in London. 1932. Exhibition catalogue.
Weaver, W. Carroll correspondence numbers. New York 1940 (priv ptd).
Green R. L. Carroll and the St James's Gazette. N & Q Apr 1945.
Black, D. Discovery of Carroll documents. N & Q, Feb 1953.
Green, R. L. Lewis Carroll's fugitive pieces. TLS, 31 July 1953.
Green, R. L. Lewis Carroll's periodical publications. N & Q, Mar 1954.
Weaver, W. The mathematical manuscripts of Carroll. Princeton Univ Lib Chron, Autumn 1954; also The Parrish collection of Carrolliana, ibid 1955/6, updated Autumn 1970.
Bond, W. H. The publication of Alice's adventures in Wonderland. HLB, Autumn 1956.
Weaver, W. Alice in many tongues. Madison WI 1964.
Smith, R. D. H. Alice one hundred. Victoria 1966. Carroll collection at Univ of Br Columbia Lib.
Goodacre, S. H. Lewis Carroll's Easter greeting. N & Q July 1972.
Goodacre, S. H. Carroll's 1887 corrections to Alice. Library, June 1973.
Goodacre, S. H. The listing of the Snark. Burton-on-Trent 1974.
Lewis Carroll and Hatfield House. 1975. Exhibition catalogue.
Cohen, M. N. (ed). Lewis Carroll's photographs of nude children.

Philadelphia PA 1978, rptd as Lewis Carroll, photographer of children: four nude studies, New York 1979.
Thoiron, P. Index et concordance pour Alice's adventures in Wonderland. Paris 1979.
Guiliano, E. Lewis Carroll: an annotated international bibliography 1960–77. Charlottesville VA 1980.
Stern, J. (ed). Lewis Carroll's library. New York 1981.
Tanis, J. and J. Dooley (ed). Lewis Carroll's The hunting of the Snark. Los Altos CA 1981.
Cohen, M. N. Lewis Carroll and Alice 1832–1982. New York 1982. Morgan Lib exhibition catalogue.
Preston, M. J. A concordance of the verse of Carroll. New York 1985.
Taylor, R. N. Lewis Carroll at Texas. Austin TX 1985.
Colquhoun, D. The Alice concordance. Adelaide 1986.
Preston, M. J. A KWIC concordance to Carroll's 'Alice's adventures in Wonderland' and 'Through the looking-glass'. New York 1986.
Fordyce, R. Lewis Carroll: a reference guide. Boston 1988.
Lovett, C. C. and S. B. Lewis Carroll's Alice: an annotated checklist of the Lovett collection. Westport CT 1990.
Sewell, B. W. Much of a muchness. South Charleston WV 1992 (priv ptd). List of US edns of Alice.

Collections and selections

In spite of some of the titles below, no complete edition of Carroll's literary works exists.

Further nonsense verse and prose. Ed L. Reed 1926.
Collected verse. New York 1929.
Collected verse. London 1932, New York 1933. More inclusive than above.
Logical nonsense: the works of Carroll. Ed P. C. Blackburn and L. White, New York 1934.
The Russian journal and other selections. Ed J. F. McDermott, New York 1935.
Complete works. New York 1936, London 1949.
Mathematical recreations of Carroll. New York 1958.
Gardner, M. The games and puzzles of Carroll. Scientific Amer, Mar 1960.
Works. Ed R. L. Green 1965.
The magic of Carroll. Ed J. Fisher, London and New York 1973.
Complete illustrated works. Ed E. Guiliano, New York 1982.

§1

The following works by Dodgson appeared under his real name or his famous pseudonym Lewis Carroll or other pseudonyms, or as anon. The Crutch Carroll handbook, 1979 *(col 1492) contains detailed information about most of the following items and others omitted here.*

The fifth book of Euclid treated algebraically. Oxford 1858, 1868 (rev).
Rules for court circular. Oxford 1860, 1862.
A syllabus of plane algebraical geometry, part I. Oxford 1860.
Notes on the first two books of Euclid. Oxford 1860.
Photographs. [Oxford 1860].
The formulae of plane trigonometry. Oxford 1861.
Endowment of the Greek professorship. [Oxford 1861].
General list of [mathematical] subjects. Oxford 1863.
The enunciations of the propositions of Euclid, books I and II. Oxford 1863, 1873 (rev).
Croquet castles for five players. [Oxford 1863].
Examination statute. [Oxford 1864].
The new examination statute. Oxford 1864.
A guide to the mathematical student, part I. Oxford 1864.
American telegrams. [Oxford] 1865.
The new method of evaluation as applied to π. [Oxford] 1865.
The dynamics of a parti-cle. Oxford 1865.
Alice's adventures in Wonderland. 1865 (edn suppressed), London and New York 1866; London 1886 (rev); numerous later edns; 9th edn, 86th thousand, 1897 is Dodgson's last rev edn. Reliable modern edns of the two Alice books: EL Children's Classics 1992 and Gardner (ed), The annotated Alice, 1960 (*col 1499*). Hundreds of trns exist into some 70 languages; some firsts are Ger 1869, Fr 1869, Ital 1872, Du (abridged) 1875, Danish 1875, Rus 1923 (by Vladimir Nabokov). The book has been rptd hundreds of times, with John Tenniel's illustrations and with illustrations by other artists, including Peter Newell 1901, Arthur Rackham 1907, Marie Laurencin 1930, Mervyn Peake 1946, Ralph Steadman 1967, Salvador Dali 1969, Barry Moser 1982. *See* The illustrators of Alice in Wonderland and Through the looking-glass, ed G. Ovenden 1972.
REVIEWS: 1865: Reader, 18 Nov; Press, 25 Nov; Publishers' Circular, 8 Dec; Bookseller, 12 Dec; Guardian, 13 Dec; Athenaeum, 16 Dec; Illus London News, 16 Dec; Illus Times, 16 Dec; London Rev, 23 Dec; Pall Mall Gazette, 23 Dec; Spectator, 23 Dec; The Times, 26 Dec. 1866: Art-Jnl; Monthly Packet, 1 Jan; John Bull, 20 Jan; Westminster Rev, Apr; Literary Churchman, 5 May; Sunderland Herald, 25 May; Aunt Judy's Mag, 1 Jun; Contemporary Rev, 1 Oct; Examiner, 15 Dec; Daily News, 19 Dec; Scotsman, 22 Dec; Spectator, 22 Dec; Weekly Dispatch, 23 Dec. 1867: Kind Words, Jan; Pall Mall Gazette, 19 Jan. Later reviews: The Times, 13 Aug 1868; Contemporary Rev, May 1869.
Castle-Croquet for four players. [Oxford] 1866.
The elections to the Hebdomadal Council. Oxford 1866.
Condensation of determinants. 1866.
The deserted parks. Oxford 1867.
An elementary treatise on determinants. 1867.
The offer of the Clarendon trustees. Oxford 1868.
The telegraph-cipher. [Oxford 1868].
Alphabet-cipher. [Oxford 1868].
Fifth book of Euclid. Oxford 1868.
Algebraical formulae. Oxford 1868.
Phantasmagoria and other poems. 1869.
The Guildford gazette extraordinary. [Guildford] 1869.
Songs from Alice's adventures in Wonderland. 1870. With additions by Dodgson.
Algebraical formulae and rules. Oxford 1870.
Arithmetical formulae and rules. Oxford 1870.
Suggestions for committee to consider the expediency of reconstituting senior studentships at Christ Church. [Oxford 1871].
To all child readers of Alice's adventures in Wonderland [Oxford] 1871.
Through the looking-glass, and what Alice found there. London 1872 [1871], Boston and New York 1872. 4th edn, 61st thousand, 1897, is Dodgson's last rev edn. For modern edns, *see* Alice's adventures, *above*. Early trns: Ital c. 1900, Jap 1920, Ger 1923, Rus 1923, Cz 1923, Braille 1925. *See* W. Weaver, Alice in many tongues, 1964 for more trns (*col 1492*); The illustrators of Alice, ed Ovenden *above* for more illus edns.
REVIEWS: 1871: Globe, 15 Dec; Athenaeum, 16 Dec; Examiner, 16 Dec; Illus London News, 16 Dec; Aunt Judy's Mag, Christmas vol; Saturday Rev, 30 Dec; Spectator, 30 Dec.
The new belfry of Christ Church, Oxford. Oxford 1872.
The enunciations of Euclid I–VI. Oxford 1873.
The vision of the three T's: a threnody. Oxford 1873.
Objections . . . against certain proposed alterations in the Great Quadrangle. Oxford 1873.
A discussion of the various methods of procedure in conducting elections. Oxford 1873.
The blank cheque, a fable. Oxford 1874.
Notes by an Oxford chiel. Oxford 1874.
Suggestions as to the best method of taking votes, where more than two issues are to be voted on. Oxford 1874.
Examples in arithmetic. Oxford 1874.
Euclid, book V, proved algebraically. Oxford 1874.
Euclid, bks I and II. Ed Dodgson. Oxford 1875, 1882 (rev).

Professorship of comparative philology. Oxford 1876.
A method of taking votes on more than two issues. [Oxford] 1876.
The hunting of the Snark: an agony in eight fits. 1876. Rptd 18 times between 1876 and 1910. The original illustrations were by Henry Holiday; among the artists who have reillustrated the poem are Peter Newell 1903, Mervyn Peake 1941, Ralph Steadman 1975, Quentin Blake 1976. For a comprehensive list of edns, trns and illustrators *see* Tanis and Dooley (eds) 1981 (*col 1493*), which contains a reliable modern edn.
REVIEWS: 1876: (Andrew Lang) Academy, 8 Apr; Athenaeum, 8 Apr; Graphic, 15 Apr; Saturday Rev, 15 Apr; Spectator, 22 Apr; Standard, 24 Apr; Vanity Fair, 29 Apr.
An Easter greeting to every child who loves 'Alice'. [Oxford] 1876, 1880.
Fame's penny-trumpet. [Oxford] 1876.
Word-links: a game for two players. [Oxford 1878].
Euclid and his modern rivals. 1879, 1885 (rev); suppl 1885.
REVIEWS: Vanity Fair, 12 Apr 1879; Eng Mechanic, 2 May 1879; Saturday Rev, 10 May 1879.
Doublets: a word-puzzle. 1879, 1880.
Lanrick: a game for two players. Oxford 1881.
Analysis of the responsions-lists. [Oxford] 1882.
Mischmasch: a word-game. [Oxford] 1882.
Lawn tennis tournaments: the true method of assigning prizes. 1883.
Rhyme? and reason? 1883.
Christmas greetings from a fairy to a child. [1884].
Twelve months in a curatorship. Oxford 1884; suppl, post script Oxford 1884.
The principles of parliamentary representation. 1884; suppl 1885.
The proposed procuratorial cycle. [Oxford] 1885, 1886.
The proctorial cycle to be voted on in Congregation. [Oxford] 1885.
Suggestions as to election of proctors. [Oxford] 1885, 1886.
A tangled tale. 1885.
Three years in a curatorship. Oxford 1886.
Remarks on report of finance committee. Oxford 1886.
Remarks on Mr Sampson's proposal ... that common room shall pay rent. [Oxford] 1886.
Observations on Mr Sampson's new proposal. Oxford 1886.
The game of logic. 1886, 1887.
Alice's adventures under ground. 1886; ed M. Gardner, New York 1965. Followed by other edns.
Curiosa mathematica, part I: a new theory of parallels. 1888.
The nursery Alice. 1889, 1890; ed M. Gardner, New York 1966.
Sylvie and Bruno. 1889.
Circular billiards, for two players. [Oxford 1890].
Eight or nine wise words about letter-writing. Oxford 1890.
A postal problem. [Oxford?] 1891; suppl 1891.
Syzygies: a word puzzle. [Oxford?] 1891.
Curiosissima curatoria. Oxford 1892.
Challenge to logicians. [Oxford?] 1892.
Syzygies and Lanrick: a word-puzzle and a game. 1893.
Curiosa mathematica, part II: pillow-problems thought out during sleepless nights. 1893, 1893 (2nd edn).
Sylvie and Bruno concluded. 1893.
A disputed point in logic. Oxford 1894.
A theorem in logic. [Oxford] 1894.
A logical puzzle. [Oxford] 1894.
Logical nomenclature. [Oxford] 1895.
Symbolic logic, part I: elementary. 1896.
Resident women-students. Oxford 1896.
Three sunsets and other poems. 1898.
The Carroll picture book. 1899, New York 1961 (as Diversions and digressions). Both contain items pbd for the first time.
The story of Sylvie and Bruno. Ed E. H. Dodgson 1904.
Feeding the mind. 1907; ed S. H. Goodacre, New York 1984.
Some rare Carrolliana. 1924 (priv ptd).
The rectory umbrella and mischmasch. 1932.
Useful and instructive poetry. Ed D. Hudson 1956.
The Carroll circular. Ed T. Winkfield, Leeds no 1 1972, no 2 1974.
The rectory magazine. Austin TX 1975.
Lewis Carroll's symbolic logic part I and part II. Ed W. W. Bartley III, New York 1977.
The wasp in a wig. New York 1977
The Oxford pamphlets, leaflets, and circulars of C. L. Dodgson. Ed E. Wakeling, Charlottesville VA 1993.
The mathematical pamphlets of C. L. Dodgson and related pieces. Ed F. F. Abeles, Charlottesville VA 1994.

Contributions to periodicals and collaborative works

Dodgson contributed fiction, prose articles, verse, games and puzzles to various publications. Some of these appear also in the Dodgson family magazines, in the volumes of poetry Dodgson published or in later collections of his works.

The lady of the ladle. Whitby Gazette, 31 Aug 1854.
Wilhelm Von Schmitz. Whitby Gazette, 7 Sep 1854.
Poetry for the millions, and The dear gazelle. Comic Times, 18 Aug 1855.
She's all my fancy painted him. Comic Times, 8 Sep 1855.
Hints for etiquette. Comic Times, 13 Oct 1855.
Photography extraordinary. Comic Times, 3 Nov 1855.
Solitude. Train, Ye carpette knyghte. Train, Mar 1856.
The path of roses. Train, May 1856.
Novelty and romancement. A broken spell. Train, Upon the lonely moor. Train, Oct 1856.
The three voices. Train, Nov 1856.
The sailor's wife. Train, Apr 1857
The palace of humbug. Oxford Critic, May 1857.
Hiawatha's photographing. Train, Dec 1857.
A photographer's day out. South Shields Amateur Mag, 1860.
Photographic exhibition. Illus Times, Jan 1860.
Faces in the fire. All the Year Round, Feb 1860.
After three days. Temple Bar, July 1861.
A sea dirge. College Rhymes, Oct term 1861.
The dream of fame. College Rhymes, Oct term 1861.
An index to 'In memoriam'. Co-edited with his sisters 1862.
Ode to Damon from Chloë. College Rhymes no 2, [1862?].
Those horrid hurdy-gurdies! College Rhymes no 2 [1862?]
Only a woman's hair. College Rhymes, Lent term 1862.
Melancholetta. College Rhymes, Lent term 1862.
Stolen waters. College Rhymes, Summer term 1862.
Poeta fit non nascitur. College Rhymes no 7, [1862].
Disillusionised. College Rhymes no 7, [1862].
The lang coortin'. College Rhymes, Oct term 1862.
Beatrice. College Rhymes, Oct term 1862.
The majesty of justice. College Rhymes, Lent term 1863.
Size and tears. College Rhymes, Summer term 1863.
Atalanta in Camden Town. Punch, 27 July 1867.
Castle-croquet: a game for four players. Aunt Judy's Mag, Aug 1867.
Bruno's revenge. Aunt Judy's Mag, Dec 1867.
Puzzles from Wonderland. Aunt Judy's Mag, Dec 1870.
Some popular fallacies about vivisection. Fortnightly Rev, 1 June 1875.
Doublets. Vanity Fair, 1879–81. A series of word puzzles, their rules, answers and methods of scoring that appeared between 29 Mar 1879 and 9 Apr 1881.
Practical hints on teaching long multiplication worked with a single line of figures. Educational Times, 1 Nov 1879.
A tangled tale. Monthly Packet, Feb 1880–Nov 1882. The individual 'knots' or problems of what became the book of this title.
What hand may wreathe thy natal crown. The garland of Rachel. Oxford 1881 (priv ptd).

Dreamland. Aunt Judy's Mag, July 1882.
A complete postal guide. The Times, 1 Sep 1883.
Parliamentary elections. St James's Gazette, 5 July 1884.
Redistribution. St James's Gazette, 11 Oct 1884.
Notes on Question 7695. Educational Times, 1 May 1885.
Who so shall offend one of those little ones. St James's Gazette, 22 July 1885.
Mischmasch. Court Circular, 2 Dec 1886.
To find the day of the week for any given date. Nature, 31 Mar 1887.
'Alice' on the stage. Theatre, Apr 1887.
The stage and the spirit of reverence. Theatre, June 1888.
Question 9588. Educational Times, 1 June 1888.
Something or nothing. Educational Times, 1 June 1888.
Question 9636. Educational Times, 1 July 1888.
Question 9995. Educational Times, 1 Feb 1889.
Syzygies. Lady, 23 July 1891–2 June 1892. Another series of word games comprising 48 sets of puzzles with rules and notes.
Question 11530. Educational Times, 1 May 1892.
Advertisement [about Through the looking-glass]. The Times, 2 Dec 1893. Followed by [announcement about] Through the looking-glass, ibid, 6 Mar 1894.
A logical paradox. Mind, July 1894. Seven replies followed.
What the tortoise said to Achilles. Mind, Dec 1894. Two replies followed.
Question 12650. Educational Times, 1 Feb 1895.
Address. St Mary Magdalen Church Mag (St Leonards-on-Sea), 1897; rptd in The Carroll picture book, 1899, *above*. Delivered at the children's service on Harvest Thanksgiving Day.
Question 13614. Educational Times, 1 Sep 1897.
Brief method of dividing a given number by 9 or 11. Nature, 14 Oct 1897.
Abridged long division. Nature, 20 Jan 1898.
Question 14122. Educational Times, 1 Feb 1899.
La guida di Bragia. Queen, 18 Nov 1931. Written c. 1850.

Letters to the press

Carroll frequently wrote letters to the editors of papers and journals.

The science of betting. Pall Mall Gazette, 19/20 Nov 1866; rptd The Times, 20 Nov 1866. Letter of correction, 21 Nov 1866.
The organisation of charity. Pall Mall Gazette, 24 Jan 1867.
Woodstock elections. Oxford Univ Herald, 28 Nov 1868.
Original research. Pall Mall Gazette, 29 Oct 1874.
Architecture in Oxford. Pall Mall Gazette, 3 Nov 1874. Another with same title, ibid, 5 Nov 1874.
Vivisection as a sign of the times. Pall Mall Gazette, 12 Feb 1875.
Vivisection. Pall Mall Gazette, 16 Feb 1875.
Natural science at Oxford. Pall Mall Gazette, 19 May 1877.
Clerical fellowships. Pall Mall Gazette 4 June 1877.
Is it well to have our children vaccinated? Eastbourne Chron, 18 Aug 1877. Two more on the same subject, ibid, 8, 22 Sep 1877.
Purity of election. St James's Gazette, 4 May 1881.
Christ Church, Oxford. Observer, 5 June 1881.
Traitors in the camp. St James's Gazette, 30 Dec 1881.
Oxford responsions. Guardian, 2 Feb 1882.
Education for the stage. St James's Gazette, 27 Feb 1882. A second letter with same title, ibid, 6 Mar 1882.
[On Gladstone and the cloture]. St James's Gazette, 23 Mar 1882.
A letter about Shakespeare for young people. Aunt Judy's Mag, Apr 1882.
Lawn tennis tournaments. St James's Gazette, 12 Aug 1882.
The fallacies of lawn tennis tournaments. St James's Gazette, 1 Aug 1883. Two more on same subject, 4, 21 Aug 1883.
Proportionate representation. St James's Gazette, 15 May 1884. Three more on same subject, 19, 27 May, 5 June 1884.
[On 'The showerbath']. St James's Gazette, 7 Aug 1884.
Vivisection vivisected. St James's Gazette, 19 Mar 1885.
Hydrophobia curable. St James's Gazette, 21 Oct 1885.
Election gains and losses. St James's Gazette, 4 Dec 1885.
Children in theatres. St James's Gazette, 19 July 1887.
Tristan d'Acunha. St James's Gazette, 10 Apr 1888.
What to call a 'telephone-message'. St James's Gazette, 17 Jan 1889.
Mrs Fawcett and the stage children. St James's Gazette, 20 July 1889.
Stage children. Sunday Times, 4 Aug 1889; rptd in Theatre, Sep 1889.
Sylvie and Bruno. St James's Gazette, 10 Jan 1890. Explaining purpose of book.
The fasting man. St James's Gazette, 10 Apr 1890.
Eight hours movement. Standard, 19 Aug 1890.
An Oxford scandal. St James's Gazette, 6 Dec 1890.

Letters, diaries etc.

Three more volumes of Dodgson's letters are projected: to his illustrators; to Henry Savile Clarke, who produced the first Alice on the professional stage; and his public letters. Dodgson both produced with his electric pen and had printed numerous circulars, letters he sent to multiple recipients; most are recorded in the Crutch Handbook *1979 and will be included in the projected volumes of public letters.*

Six letters by Carroll. 1924 (priv ptd).
Tour in 1867. Philadelphia 1928; ed J. F. McDermott, New York 1935 (as The Russian journal). Diary.
Two letters to Marion. Bristol 1932 (priv ptd).
A selection from the letters of Carroll to his child-friends. Ed E. M. Hatch 1933.
Diaries. Ed R. L. Green 2 vols 1953.
Some Oxford scandals: seven 'letters to the editor'. 1978.
Letters. Ed M. N. Cohen with assistance of R. L. Green 2 vols 1979. Followed by The Selected letters, 1982, 1989 (2nd edn).
Lewis Carroll and the Kitchins. Ed M. N. Cohen, New York 1980.
Lewis Carroll and the house of Macmillan. Ed M. N. Cohen and A. Gandolfo 1987.
Diaries. Ed E. Wakeling 10 vols 1994– .

Introductions and prefaces

Dodgson wrote numerous introductions, prologues and prefaces to his own works, frequently adding or altering them in later edns. The most famous is the advertisement in the 2nd edn of Symbolic logic, part I, *where he contradicts the 'silly story' about his having presented certain books to Queen Victoria. He wrote only a few prefatory pieces for works other than his own. See F. B. de Sausmarez,* Theatricals at Oxford; *with prologues by Carroll,* Nineteenth Cent *Feb 1932.*

Prologue. College Rhymes, Michaelmas term 1862.
Introduction. In E. G. Wilcox, The lost plum-cake, 1897.
Prologue to a play. Strand Mag, Apr 1898. Written 1873.

§2

Excerpts from more than a hundred reminiscences of Dodgson by family, colleagues, friends and others are collected in Lewis Carroll, *ed Cohen, 1989, below. Obituaries not listed below appeared on 15 Jan 1898 in* The Times, St James's Gazette, Daily Telegraph, Daily Chron, Daily Mail *and* Daily Graphic. *Others appeared in* Independent, *20 Jan;* Sat Rev, *22 Jan;* Acad, *22 Jan;* Critic *(New York), 22 Jan;* Punch, *29 Jan;* Dial *(Chicago), 1 Feb.*

Anon. Lewis Carroll. London, 4 May 1878.
Salmon, E. Literature for the little ones. Nineteenth Cent, Oct 1887.
[Leader on Carroll]. Standard, 26 Oct 1888.
Arnold, E. Social life in Oxford. Harper's Mag, July 1890.
Hatch, B. In memoriam: Charles Lutwidge Dodgson. Guardian, 19 Jan 1898. Another as Lewis Carroll. Strand Mag, Apr 1898.
H[ewett], W. H. The late Carroll. Eastbourne Gazette, 19 Jan 1898.
Thompson, H. L. Lewis Carroll. Oxford Mag, 26 Jan 1898. Obituary.
[Cowley-Brown, G. J.]. Personal recollections of the author of 'Alice in Wonderland'. Scottish Guardian, 28 Jan 1898.
Holiday, H. The Snark's significance. Academy, 29 Jan 1898.
Thomson, E. G. Lewis Carroll. Gentlewoman, 29 Jan, 5 Feb 1898.
Strong, T. B. Lewis Carroll. Cornhill Mag, Mar 1898. Obituary.

Lang, A. The death of Lewis Carroll. In At the sign of the ship, Longman's Mag, Mar 1898.
[Fowler, T.]. Our Carroll memorial. St James's Gazette, 11 Mar 1898.
Collingwood, S. D. The life and letters of Carroll. 1898.
Maitland, E. A. Childish memories of Carroll. Quiver, 1899.
Bowman, I. The story of Carroll. 1899.
Powell, F. Y. In O. Elton, Frederick York Powell, 1906.
Furniss, H. Recollections of Carroll. Strand Mag, Jan 1908.
Ffooks, M. Alice in Dorsetland. Dorset Yearbook, 1928.
Arnold, E. M. Reminiscences of Carroll. Atlantic Monthly, June 1929. Also Windsor Mag, Dec 1929.
Lewis Carroll interrupts a story. Children's Newspaper, 7 Feb 1931.
De la Mare, W. Lewis Carroll. 1932.
Reed, L. The life of Carroll. 1932.
Mileham, H. R. Lewis Carroll. The Times, 2 Jan 1932.
Strong, T. B. Mr Dodgson: Carroll at Oxford. The Times, 27 Jan 1932.
H[ayes], G. B. Recollections of Carroll. Christian Science Monitor, 23 Feb 1932.
Hargreaves, A. and C. The Carroll that Alice recalls. New York Times, 1 May 1932. Another version (as Alice's recollections of Carrollian days), Cornhill Mag, July 1932.
Standen, I. Lewis Carroll as I remember him. Queen, 20 July 1932.
Shute, E. L. Lewis Carroll as artist. Cornhill Mag, Nov 1932.
Rowell, E. M. 'To me he was Mr Dodgson'. Harper's Mag, Feb 1943.
Lennon, F. B. Victoria through the looking-glass: the life of Carroll. New York 1945; London 1947 (as Lewis Carroll: a biography); New York 1962 (rev).
Atkinson, G. Memories of Carroll. Hampshire Chron, 13 Mar 1948.
Gernsheim, H. Lewis Carroll, photographer. 1949, 1951 (rev).
Green, R. L. The story of Carroll. 1949.
Dodgson, V. Lewis Carroll. London Calling, 28 June 1951.
Taylor, A. L. The white knight: a study of C. L. Dodgson. Edinburgh 1952.
Hudson, D. Lewis Carroll. 1954, 1976 (rev). Biography.
Shawyer, E. Lewis Carroll. Observer, 14 Feb 1954.
Green, R. L. Carroll's first publication. TLS, 13 Sep 1957.
Hatch, E. Recollections of Carroll. Listener, 30 Jan 1958. Followed by recollections by E. H. B. Skimming, H. T. Stretton and E. G. Shawyer, 6 Feb 1958.
Black, D. The theory of committees and elections. Cambridge 1958.
Godman, S. Carroll's final corrections to Alice. TLS, 2 May 1958.
Gardner, M. The annotated Alice. New York 1960, 1995 (rev). Followed by More annotated Alice. New York 1990.
Gardner, M. The annotated Snark. New York 1962, London 1967.
Black, D. The central argument in Carroll's The principles of parliamentary representation. Papers on Non-Market Decision Making, Fall 1967.
Cohen, M. N. and R. L. Green, Carroll's loss of consciousness. BNYPL, Jan 1969.
Black, D. Lewis Carroll and the theory of games. Amer Economic Rev, May 1969.
Black, D. Lewis Carroll and the Cambridge mathematical school of p.r.; Arthur Cohen and Edith Denman. Public Choice, Spring 1970.
Ovenden, G. (ed). The illustrators of Alice. 1972.
Goodacre, S. H. The illnesses of Lewis Carroll. Practitioner, Aug 1972.
Hankey, M. Tea with Carroll. Daily Telegraph, 15 Dec 1972.
Gattégno, J. Lewis Carroll: une vie d'Alice à Zénon d'Elée. Paris 1974; tr. R. Sheed as Lewis Carroll: fragments of a looking-glass, New York 1976.
Heath, P. The philosopher's Alice. 1974.
Goodacre, S. H. Carroll's rejection of the 60th thousand of Through the looking-glass. BC, Summer 1975.
Cohen, M. N. Carroll comes to school. Ad Lucem (mag of the Oxford High School for Girls), 1975; rptd in Jabberwocky, Winter 1976.
Rivers, K. Memories of Carroll. [McMaster Univ] Lib Research News, Jan 1976.
Cohen, M. N. 'Alice under ground'. New York Times Bk Rev, 9 Oct 1977. Concealed portrait at the end of the ms of Alice's adventures under ground.
Cohen, M. N. The electric pen. Illus London News, Christmas 1976.
Kelly, R. Lewis Carroll. New York 1977, 1990.
Tenniel's Alice. Cambridge MA 1978.
Goodacre, S. H. An enquiry into a certain Carroll pamphlet (Some popular fallacies about vivisection). BC, Autumn 1978.
Clark, A. Lewis Carroll: a biography. London and New York 1979.
Cohen, M. N. (ed). The Russian journal II. New York 1979. A record kept by Henry Parry Liddon of a tour with Dodgson in 1867.
Hancher, M. The Tenniel illustrations to the 'Alice' books. Columbus OH 1985.
Cohen, M. N. (ed). Lewis Carroll: interviews and recollections. 1989.
Schiller, J. (comp). Alice's adventures in Wonderland: an 1865 printing re-described. Kingston NY 1990.
Cohen, M. N. Lewis Carroll: a biography. New York and London 1995.
McLean, I., A. McMillan and B. L. Monroe. Duncan Black and Lewis Carroll. Jnl of Theoretical Politics, Apr 1995.
McLean, I. and A. B. Urken. Classics of social choice. Ann Arbor MI 1995.
Cohen, M. N. Reflections in a looking glass: a centennial celebration of Lewis Carroll, photographer. New York 1998. [MNC]

Mary Cholmondeley 1859–1925

Mss: 83 letters held in Bentley Archives, Univ of Illinois (micro); series of letters to H. Newbolt held in R. L. Wolff Collections, HRHRC.

Bibliographies

Wolff, R. L. Nineteenth century fiction: a bibliographical catalogue. New York and London 1981.
Crisp, J. Mary Cholmondeley. Victorian Fiction Research Guide 6, St Lucia, Queensland 1981.

§1

The Danvers jewels. First pbd Temple Bar Jan–Mar 1887, anon. [1887], with Sir Charles Danvers New York 1890, anon, London 1898 ('new edn'), anon, with Sir Charles Danvers New York 1900 (reissue), London 1902.
REVIEW: Punch 22 Oct 1887.

Sir Charles Danvers. First pbd Temple Bar May–Dec 1889, anon. 2 vols 1889, anon, 1890, anon, with The Danvers jewels New York 1890, anon, London 1895 ('new edn'), anon, with The Danvers jewels New York 1900 (reissue), London 1902.
REVIEWS: Graphic Nov 1889; Athenaeum 9 Nov 1889; Saturday Rev 7 Dec 1889; Spectator 8 Feb 1890; Guardian 24 Dec 1890.

Diana Tempest. First pbd Temple Bar Jan–Dec 1893. 3 vols 1893, 2 vols Leipzig 1893, London 1894 ('new edn'), 1900, 1900, with portrait and biographical sketch New York 1900, London 1909, [1913].
REVIEWS: Sketch Nov 1893; Athenaeum 18 Nov 1893; Bookman Dec 1893; [Cotterell, G.] Acad July–Dec 1893; Lang, A. Longmans Jan 1894; Lyttelton, E. Nat Rev Jan 1894; Dial (Chicago) 1 Jan 1894; The Times 12 Jan 1894; Punch 27 Jan 1894; Spectator 3 Feb 1894, 28 Apr 1894; Bookman May 1894; Saturday Rev 9 Dec 1894; Acad 9 Dec 1899.

A devotee: an episode in the life of a butterfly. First pbd Temple Bar Aug–Oct 1896. London and New York 1897.
REVIEW: Bookman (New York) Sep 1897.

Red pottage. 1899, (New York) 1899, London 1900 ('fifth edn'), 2 vols Leipzig 1900, London [1904], 1905 ('new and cheaper edn'), [1914]; introd by D. Tindall 1968; New York 1976 (with W. Besant, In deacon's orders).

REVIEWS: Literature July–Dec 1899; Spectator 28 Oct 1899; Saturday Rev 11 Nov 1899; Acad 18 Nov 1899; Athenaeum 18 Nov 1899; Dial (Chicago) 16 Dec 1899; The Times 25 Dec 1899; [Payne, H. G.] Bookbuyer Feb 1900; Lyttleton, E. Nat Rev Mar 1900; Nation 29 Mar 1900; Canadian Mag Apr 1900; Ball, T. I. Guardian 11 Apr 1900 (letter); Critic July 1900; [Gwynn, S. L.] Edinburgh Rev July 1900; Harper's Weekly July 1900; Acad 21 July 1900.

Dick's ordeal. In L. B. Walford et al, Life's possibilities, 1899. Short story.

REVIEW: Literature Dec 1899.

We twain. In The book of beauty – Era King Edward VII 1902, Pearson's Mag Jan–June 1903. Poem.

Moth and rust: together with Geoffrey's wife and The pitfall. 1902; 'and other stories', New York 1902 (with addn of Let loose), Leipzig 1903, London [1907], [1912]; tr Fr 1906. Geoffrey's wife first pbd Graphic Summer 1885, Let loose Temple Bar Apr 1890, The pitfall Monthly Rev Dec 1901.

REVIEWS: Athenaeum 6 Dec 1902; Monthly Rev Jan 1903.

Prisoners (fast bound in misery and iron). First pbd Lady's Realm Nov 1905–Oct 1906, American Mag Nov 1905–May 1906. 1906, New York 1906, Toronto 1906, London [1908], 2 vols Leipzig [listed in Tauchnitz Edn Complete List Sep 1910].

REVIEWS: Acad Sep 1906; Stoddart, J. T. Bookman Oct 1906.

The lowest rung, with the Hand on the latch, St Luke's summer and The understudy. 1908, Leipzig (listed in Tauchnitz Edn Complete List Sep 1910), as The hand on the latch, New York 1909. The understudy first pbd Windsor Mag Dec 1907–May 1908, The lowest rung Aug 1908, St Luke's summer Cassell's Mag 1908; preface also pbd Pall Mall Mag July–Dec 1908 as The skeleton in a novelist's cupboard.

Notwithstanding. 1913, Leipzig 1913, as After all, New York 1913, 1915.

REVIEW: Bookman Nov 1913.

Polydore in England. In King Albert's book: a tribute to the Belgian king and people..., ed H. Caine, 1914. Essay.

Under one roof: a family record. 1918. Autobiography.

REVIEW: Bookman May 1918.

The romance of his life, and other romances. 1921. First pbd as The romance of his life, Scribner's Mag Aug 1909; Votes for men, Cornhill Mag July 1909.

Contributions to periodicals

Geoffrey's wife. Graphic Summer 1885; rptd in Moth and rust, 1902. Short story.

The cottager at home. Murray's Mag July–Dec 1889. Essay.

Let loose. Temple Bar Apr 1890, Living Age 17 May 1890; rptd in New York edn of Moth and rust, 1902. Short story.

Run to earth. Monthly Packet Feb–Mar 1893. Short story.

A latter-day prophet. Temple Bar Dec 1894. Biography.

A day in Teneriffe. Monthly Packet Nov 1896, Chautauquan Sep 1901. Travel.

A second day in Teneriffe. Monthly Packet Dec 1896. Travel.

An art in its infancy. Monthly Rev June 1901, Living Age 27 July 1901, Bookman (New York) Aug 1901. Essay on advertising.

The pitfall. Monthly Rev Dec 1901; rptd in Moth and rust, 1902. Short story.

In the small hours. Lady's Realm Dec 1907. Short story.

The skeleton in a novelist's cupboard. Pall Mall Mag July–Dec 1908; also pbd as Preface to The lowest rung, 1908. Essay.

Votes for men. Cornhill Mag July 1909, Harpers Bazaar Jan 1910; rptd in The romance of his life, 1921. Short story.

Vicarious charities: a dialogue. Cornhill Mag July 1909. Essay.

The romance of his life. Scribner's Mag Aug 1909; rptd in The romance of his life and other romances, 1921. Short story.

§2

Obits: The Times 17 July 1925, 18 Aug 1925 (will); New York Times 16 July 1925.

[Gwynn, S. L.] Some recent novels of manners. Edinburgh Rev July 1900.

Lubbock, P. Mary Cholmondeley: a sketch from memory. 1928.

Kent, M. A novelist of yesterday. Cornhill Mag Feb 1935.

Colby, V. Devoted amateur: Mary Cholmondeley and Red pottage. EIC Apr 1970.

Crisp, J. Mary Cholmondeley. Victorian Fiction Research Guide 6, St Lucia, Queensland 1981. [JC]

Mrs William Kingdon Clifford, Sophia Lucy Clifford, née Lane 1846–1929

For letters to and from Lucy Clifford, see LR. *Notable collection in* BL.

§1

Children busy, children glad, children naughty, children sad. London 1881, New York 1881; tr Ger.

The dingy house at Kensington. New York 1882 (first pbd in Quiver 1872).

Anyhow stories: moral and otherwise. 1882 (contains The new mother, rptd in Oxford book of modern fairy tales, ed A. Laurie, 1994), 1885 (as Anyhow stories for children and containing an additional story Wooden Tony, rptd in Beyond the looking glass, ed J. Cott, 1974).

Mrs Keith's crime: a record. 1885, New York 1885, Leipzig 1893.

Under mother's wing. 1885.

Very short stories and verses for children. 1886.

Love-letters of a worldly woman. 1891, Leipzig 1892, New York 1892, Chicago 1894.

Aunt Anne. 2 vols Leipzig 1892, New York 1892, London 1893; tr Ger 1895.

The last touches and other stories. 1892, New York 1892, Leipzig 1893.

An interlude. 1893. With W. H. Pollock. Play.

Marie May or, changed aims. 1893.

A wild proxy. 1893, New York 1893, Leipzig 1893; tr Ger nd.

A flash of summer. New York 1894, London 1895, Leipzig 1896.

A grey romance. 1894.

A honeymoon tragedy. 1896. Play.

Mere stories. 1896, Leipzig 1909.

The dominant note, and other stories. New York 1897.

A woman alone. 1898, Leipzig 1901, New York 1901. Play.

A supreme moment. 1899; tr Ger 1889. Play.

The likeness of the night. 1900, New York 1900. Play.

A long duel. 1901, New York 1901. Play.

Woodside Farm. 1902, New York 1902 (as Margaret Vincent), Leipzig 1902.

The search-light. 1903, New York 1925. Play.

A honeymoon tragedy. 1904.

The getting well of Dorothy. 1904, Leipzig 1907, New York 1917; tr Du nd.

The modern way. 1906, Leipzig 1907.

The shepherd's purse. 1906. Play.

Proposals to Kathleen. New York 1908.

Plays: Hamilton's second marriage; Thomas and the princess; The modern way. 1909, New York 1910.

Sir George's objection. 1910, New York 1910, Leipzig 1925.

George Wendern gives a party, by John Inglis (pseud). New York 1912.

The house in Marylebone; a chronicle. 1917.

Mr Webster, and others. 1918.

Miss Fingal. 1919, New York 1919, Leipzig 1928.

Eve's lover, and other stories. New York 1924, Leipzig 1924.

Letters

M. Demoor and M. Chisholm, Bravest of women and finest of friends: Henry James's letters to Lucy Clifford. Eng Literary Stud 80, Summer 1999.

Contributions to periodicals and collaborative works

Lucy Clifford contributed stories to numerous periodicals, among them the Daily Mail, London Illus News *and* Strand Mag. *For a selection of contributions to periodicals, see* Wellesley *vol 5 1989.*

The troubles of Chattie and Mollie. Quiver [187?].

About Nellie. Quiver 1872.

The last scene of the play. In Voluntaries for an East London Hospital, 1887.

A ridiculous tragedy. Tauchnitz Mag Jan 1892.

Luck for him. Cassell's Family Mag 1895–6.

The likeness of the night. Anglo-Saxon Rev 4 1899–1901.

A remembrance of George Eliot. Nineteenth Century Rev July 1913.

§2

Delille, E. Mrs W. K. Clifford. The Novel Rev July 1892.

Mrs W. K. Clifford. Whitehall Rev 9 Dec 1893. Anon.

Dickens, M. A. A chat with Mrs W. K. Clifford. Windsor Mag 1899.

Kellner, L. Die Cliffords. Die Nation. Wochenschrift für Politik, Wolfswirtßchaft und Literatur 14 Apr 1906, 440–3.

Randell, W. L. Mrs W. K. Clifford. Bookman Jan 1920.

The Times 22 Apr 1929. Obituary.

Shell, H. Clifford's The new mother and the menace of the lower classes. TCW May 1990.

Chisholm, M. Mrs W. K. Clifford. A brief appreciation. In Advances in applied Clifford algebra, Mexico 1993.

Demoor, M. Self-fashioning at the turn of the century: the discursive life of Lucy Clifford (1846–1929). Jnl of Victorian Culture 4 1999. [MD]

James Maclaren Cobban 1849–1903

Mss located in Nat Lib of Scotland; Pierpont Morgan Lib; Royal Literary Fund.

Bibliographies

In Nineteenth century readers' guide to periodical literature 1890–1899, ed H. G. Cushing and A. V. Morris, 2 vols New York 1944.

See also Wellesley *vol 5 1989.*

In Nineteenth-century fiction: a bibliographical catalogue based on the collection formed by Robert Lee Wolff, 5 vols New York 1981–6.

§1

The cure of souls. A novel. [1879], 1899 (new edn).

By telegraph. New York [187?], London 1880, 1889.

Tinted vapours: a nemesis. New York 1885, 1890 (2 impressions, as A nemesis, or tinted vapors).

Master of his fate. Edinburgh and London 1890, New York 1890 (as Julius Courtney, or master of his fate), 1891, Elstree 1987 (facs of 1890 edn).

REVIEWS: Scots Observer 21 Dec 1889; Edinburgh Medical Jnl Feb 1890.

The horned cat. New York [1891].

Sir Ralph's secret. 1891.

REVIEW: Acad 28 Nov 1891.

A reverend gentleman. 1891, 1903, New York 1950, 1983.

REVIEWS: Nat Observer 14 Nov 1891; Acad 21 Nov 1891.

A soldier and a gentleman. New York 1891, London 1904.

REVIEW: Acad 24 Sep 1904.

The red sultan. The remarkable adventures in western Barbary of Sir Cosmo Mac Laurin, Bart. of Monzie in the county of Perth. 3 vols 1893, Chicago 1894, London and Edinburgh [1917], London [1924].

REVIEWS: Nat Observer 10 June 1893; Bookman July 1893.

The burden of Isabel. 3 vols 1893, New York 1893, London 1894 (new edn).

REVIEWS: Pall Mall Gazette 9 Jan 1894; Nat Observer 6 Jan 1894; Acad 17 Feb 1894.

White Kaid of the Atlas. 1894.

The avenger of blood. 1895 (illustr J. Gülich).

REVIEW: Acad 22 June 1895.

The king of Andaman. A saviour of society. 1895, New York 1895.

The tyrants of Kool-Sim. 1896 (illustr J. B. Fisher), 1896 (2 edns, frontispiece A. Wright).

Wilt thou have this woman? 1897, Philadelphia 1897.

REVIEW: Acad 10 Apr 1897.

Her Royal Highness's love affair. 1897.

The angel of the covenant. 1898, New York 1899.

REVIEWS: Acad 29 Oct 1898; New York Times 24 June 1899.

An African treasure. A tale of the great Sahara. 1899 (2 edns), New York 1900.

Pursued by the law. 1899, New York 1899.

REVIEW: Outlook 8 Apr 1899.

Cease fire! A story of the Transvaal war of '81. 1900, 1919.

REVIEW: Bookman Apr 1900.

I'd crowns resign. 1900.

REVIEW: Bookman Dec 1900.

The golden tooth. 1901, New York 1901.

REVIEW: New York Times 10 Aug 1901.

A royal exchange. New York 1901.

The life and deeds of Earl Roberts, V. C. etc. 4 vols Edinburgh 1901–[1902] (illus) (vol 4 London), London nd.

REVIEW: Acad 9 Mar 1901.

The green turbans. [1902], New York [1902].

REVIEWS: Athenaeum 15 Mar 1902; Acad 22 Mar 1902.

The last alive. 1902, 1912.

REVIEW: Bookman Dec 1902.

The iron hand. 1904.

REVIEW: Acad 6 Feb 1904.

The terror by night. 1905.

REVIEW: Athenaeum 2 Sep 1905.

The missing partner. 1913.

Contributions to periodicals

Belgravia. Feb 1881–Apr 1883.

Scots Observer. 6 Apr 1889–27 July 1889.

Strand Mag. Feb–Aug 1891.

Chambers's Jnl. 1891–4.

Yuletide (Cassell's Christmas Annual). The avenger of blood, 1894.

Cassell's Mag. Awr Tom, Mar 1895.

Ludgate Mag. One of the nameless, Dec 1896.

Pall Mall Mag. El mansor and Haïda, Mar 1904.

For Blackwood's Mag, Longman's Mag *and* Temple Bar, *see* Wellesley *vol 5 1989.*

§2

Stuart, A. Montrose and Argyll in fiction. Blackwood's Mag Jan 1899. Discusses Cobban's Angel of the covenant.

Sutherland, J. In his The Longman companion to Victorian fiction, 1988. [DA]

Mary Coleridge 1861–1907

See col 725.

'Hugh Conway', Frederick John Fargus 1847–85

A life's idylls and other poems. 1879, Bristol 1887.

Called back. Bristol 1884, 1885 (with life of the author).

Bound together: tales. 2 vols 1884.

Chewton-Abbot and other tales. 1884. Only Chewton-Abbot is by Conway.

Dark days. Bristol 1885.

Slings and arrows. Bristol 1885.
At what cost and other stories. [1885.]
A family affair: a novel. 3 vols 1885.
A cardinal sin: a novel. 3 vols 1886.
Carriston's gift; A fresh start; Julian Vanneck; and A dead man's face. Bristol 1886.
'Somebody's' story. [1886.] An exact reproduction of Conway's original ms.
Living or dead: a novel. 3 vols [1886].

Marie Corelli 1855–1924

Selection

The beauties of Marie Corelli; selected and arranged, with the author's permission, by Annie Mackay. 1897.

§1

A romance of two worlds: a novel. 2 vols 1886, 1 vol 1887.
Vendetta! or the story of one forgotten: a novel. 3 vols 1886, 1 vol 1887.
Thelma: a society novel. 3 vols 1887, 1 vol 1888. Dramatised by V. Mitchell 1941.
Ardath: the story of a dead self. 3 vols 1889, 1 vol 1890.
My wonderful wife!: a study in smoke. 1889.
Wormwood: a drama of Paris. 3 vols 1890, 1 vol 1895 (7th edn).
The hired baby with other stories and social sketches. Leipzig 1891.
The silver domino: or side whispers, social and literary. 1892. Anon.
The soul of Lilith. 3 vols 1892, 1 vol 1893.
Barabbas: a dream of the world's tragedy. 3 vols 1893, 1 vol 1894, 1909 (44th edn), 1961 (59th edn, rptd).
The sorrows of Satan, or the strange experience of one Geoffrey Tempest, millionaire: a romance. 1895, 1952 (68th edn).
The murder of Delicia. 1896; rptd in Delicia and other stories, *below*, 1907.
The mighty atom. 1896.
Cameos: short stories. [1896.]
Ziska: the problem of a wicked soul. Bristol 1897, [1911], London 1960, 1989.
Jane: a social incident. 1897.
The modern marriage market. 1898. With Lady Jeune, F. A. Steele, Susan Countess of Malmesbury.
Boy: a sketch. 1900.
The greatest queen in the world: a tribute to the Majesty of England, 1837–1900. 1900.
The master-Christian. 1900.
Patriotism or self-advertisement?: a social note on the war. 1900 (6th edn).
A Christmas greeting of various thoughts, verses and fancies. 1901.
The passing of the great queen: a tribute to the noble life of Victoria Regina. 1901.
'Temporal Power': a study in supremacy. 1902.
The vanishing gift: an address on the decay of the imagination, delivered before the Philosophical Institution, Edinburgh, on the evening of 19th November 1901. Edinburgh [1902].
The Avon star: a literary manual for the Stratford-on-Avon season of 1903. Stratford-on-Avon [1903]. Ed Corelli.
The plain truth of the Stratford-on-Avon controversy, concerning the fully-intended demolition of old houses in Henley Street and the changes proposed to be effected on the national ground of Shakespeare's birthplace. 1903.
God's good man: a simple love story. 1904.
The strange visitation of Josiah McNason: a Christmas ghost story. 1904.
Free opinions freely expressed on certain phases of modern social life and conduct. 1905.
Faith versus flunkeyism: a word on the Spanish royal marriage. 1906.
The treasure of heaven: a romance of riches. 1906.
Delicia and other stories. 1907. Delicia first pbd as The murder of Delicia, *above*, 1896.
Woman, or suffragette? A question of national choice. 1907.
Holy orders: the tragedy of a quiet life. 1908.
The devil's motor: a fantasy. [1910]. First pbd in A Christmas greeting, *above*, 1901.
The life everlasting: a reality of romance. 1911.
Innocent, her fancy and his fact: a novel. 1914, 1921.
Eyes of the sea: [a tribute to the Grand Fleet and the Grand Fleet's commander]. [1917.]
Is all well with England?: a question. [1917.]
The young Diana: an experiment of the future: a romance. 1918.
My 'little bit'. 1919.
The love of long ago, and other stories. 1920.
The secret power: a romance of the time. 1921.
Love – and the philosopher: a study in sentiment. 1923.
Open confession to a man from a woman. [1925.]
Poems. Ed B. Vyver 1925.
A few ephemeral works are unrecorded here.

§2

Carr, K. Miss Marie Corelli. 1901.
Murray, H. In his Robert Buchanan and other essays, 1901.
Coates, T. F. G. and R. S. W. Bell. Marie Corelli: the writer and the woman. 1903.
Vyver, B. Memoirs of Marie Corelli, with an epilogue by J. Cuming Walters. [1930.]
Elwin, M. Nine best sellers. In his Old gods falling, 1939.
Bullock, G. Marie Corelli: the life and death of a best-seller. 1940.
Jaggard, W. Marie Corelli. N & Q 13 Mar, 24 Apr 1943.
Bullock, G. The Corelli wonder. Life & Letters 41 1944.
Sadleir, M. The camel's back: or the last tribulation of a Victorian publisher. In Essays presented to Sir Humphrey Milford, Oxford 1948.
Bigland, E. Marie Corelli; the woman and the legend: a biography. 1953.
Scott, W. S. Marie Corelli: the story of a friendship. 1955.
Masters, B. Now Barabbas was a rotter: the extraordinary life of Marie Corelli. 1978. [EH]

Leslie Cope Cornford 1867–1927

Mss located in Lib of Congress. See also LR.

Bibliographies

In Nineteenth century readers' guide to periodical literature 1890–1899, ed H. G. Cushing and A. V. Moris, New York 1944.
See also Wellesley *vol 5 1989.*

§1

Captain Jacobus. Certain passages from the memoirs of Anthony Langford. 1896, New York 1896, 1906.
REVIEW: Literary World 27 Nov 1896.
The master-beggars. 1897, Philadelphia 1897, London 1914, 1914 (as The master beggars of Belgium), New York 1915 (as The master beggars of Belgium).
REVIEWS: Acad 10 Apr 1897; Speaker 10 Apr 1897; Literary World 13 Apr 1897; Nat Observer 17 Apr 1897; Bookman May 1897; Dial 16 May 1897; New York Times 5 June 1897.
Sons of adversity. A romance of Queen Elizabeth's time. 1898, Boston 1898, London 1902, 1905.
REVIEWS: Literary World 17 June 1898; Acad Suppl 18 June 1898; Spectator 2 July 1898; Dial 1 Aug 1898.
Robert Louis Stevenson. Edinburgh and London 1899, 1900 (2nd edn), New York 1900.

REVIEWS: Bookman Dec 1899; Literature 23 Dec 1899; New York Times 13 Jan 1900; Dial 16 July 1900.
Travellers for ever. Sketches and fantasies. 1899.
REVIEWS: Literature 13 Jan 1900; Literary World 7 Feb 1900.
Travellers by the way: roadside sketches, impressions. 1899.
English composition. A manual of theory and practice. 1900.
REVIEWS: Outlook 20 Oct 1900; Spectator Suppl 3 Nov 1900; Acad 24 Nov 1900; Literary World 15 Feb 1901.
Northborough Cross. 1901.
REVIEWS: Spectator 20 Apr 1901; Literature 4 May 1901; Athenaeum 18 May 1901; Literary World 24 May 1901; Acad 1 June 1901.
The last buccaneer: or the trustees of Mrs A. 1902, Philadelphia 1902.
REVIEWS: Spectator 27 Dec 1902; Athenaeum 3 Jan 1903; Outlook 10 Jan 1903; Literary World 16 Jan 1903; T. P.'s Weekly 13 Feb 1903.
Essay-writing for schools. 1903, New York 1903, London 1904, 1914.
REVIEWS: Literary World 18 Sep 1903; Dial 16 Dec 1903.
The canker at the heart. Being studies from the life of the poor in the year of grace 1905. 1905.
REVIEW: Bookman Feb 1906.
Parson Brand, and other voyagers' tales. 1906.
REVIEWS: Bookman June 1906; Athenaeum 2 June 1906.
The defenceless islands. A study of the social and industrial conditions of Great Britain and Ireland. 1906.
REVIEW: Athenaeum 28 July 1906.
London pride and London shame. 1910, 1912.
The price of home rule. 1910.
'No surrender!' Being the story of the siege of Derry, 1688–9. Westminster 1911.
Troubled waters. Edinburgh and London 1911.
William Ernest Henley. 1913, Boston and New York 1913, New York 1972.
REVIEWS: Athenaeum 26 Apr 1913; Outlook 17 May 1913; Bookman June 1913; Dial 16 Sep 1913.
Echoes from the fleet. 1914 (2 impressions).
REVIEW: Spectator 19 Dec 1914.
The Lord High Admiral, and others. 1915.
REVIEW: Athenaeum 4 Dec 1915.
With the grand fleet. 1915.
The secret of consolation. 1916.
The merchant seaman in war. 1918, New York 1918.
REVIEWS: TLS 10 Jan 1918; Spectator 30 Mar 1918.
The British navy, the navy vigilant. 1918, 1920.
The fairy man. London and Toronto 1919, New York 1919.
The Paravane adventure. 1919, New York 1919.
REVIEW: TLS 15 Jan 1920.
The designers of our buildings. 1921.
A century of sea trading, 1824–1924. The General Steam Navigation Company, Limited. 1924.
REVIEW: TLS 11 Sep 1924.
The sea carriers, 1825–1925. 1925.
REVIEW: TLS 12 Nov 1925.
Interpretations. 1926, Port Washington NY 1970.
REVIEW: TLS 8 July 1926.

Contributions to periodicals

Cornford trained as an architect but later turned to journalism and writing. He contributed to the Standard, St James's Gazette *and the* Sketch, *among others, and was naval correspondent of the* Morning Post *1914–18. He was the first editor of the* Roedean School Mag.

Nat Observer. The invitation to the road, 27 Jan 1894; A certain arbour, 10 Mar 1894.
Black and White. 24 Aug 1895–25 Sep 1897.
Outlook. 19 Mar 1898–21 Oct 1905.
Pall Mall Mag. The golden messias, Dec 1899.
Monthly Rev. Feb–Oct 1905.
Living Age. Apostle of Port Royal, 3 Nov 1894; 26 Oct 1907–10 Jan 1920.
Lippincott's Mag. Northborough Cross, July 1914.
Edinburgh Rev. Siege by water, Oct 1916.
Nat Rev. Feb 1917–Sep 1919.
Nineteenth Cent. The future of the navy, June 1920.
English Rev. Politicians at war, June 1923; New knowledge, Oct 1923.

Collaborative works and translations

Additional notes. In Lyra heroica (school edn), ed W. E. Henley, 1900, 1903, 1906, 1908, 1912. With W. W. Greg.
Notes and elucidations to Henley's Lyra heroica, 1900. With W. W. Greg.
Mouse-land. A new story. Text by A. Snellen, tr A. Thieme and L. C. Cornford, 1910.
The great deeds of the Black Watch. 1915. With F. W. Walker.
Roedean School. 1927. With F. R. Yerbury.

Introductions

Introd and notes to The memoirs of Admiral Lord Charles Beresford, written by himself, 2 vols 1914, 1916 (4th edn).

§2

The Times 5 Aug 1927. Obituary.
Cornford, C. The first editor of the Magazine. In memoriam Leslie Cope Cornford. Roedean School Mag Nov 1927. [DA]

Vivian Cory, 'Victoria Cross/Crosse' d. 1930

§1

The woman who didn't. 1895, 1895 (2nd edn), London and Boston 1895, Boston 1895, London [1896], 1909, New York [1922?] (4th edn).
REVIEW: Athenaeum 3542 1895.
Paula: a sketch from life. 1896, [1897], New York [19??], London [1905] (9th edn), London and New York [1907?] (12th edn), New York [1908?], London [1917], 1923 (23rd edn), 1935.
REVIEWS: Academy 50 1896; Athenaeum 3599 1896.
A girl of the Klondike. [1899], New York [19??], London 1921, [1936].
REVIEW: Athenaeum 3723 1899.
Anna Lombard. 1901, [1901] (19th edn), [1902], New York [1907], London 1908, 1930 (39th edn), [1934?]; tr Ital [1947].
REVIEW: Athenaeum 3835 1901.
Six chapters of a man's life. London, Newcastle-on-Tyne and New York 1903, New York [1904?], London 1908, 1917, London and Felling-on-Tyne [1918], New York [192?], London 1923, 1936.
Tomorrow? London, Newcastle-on-Tyne and New York 1904, London 1904 (7th edn), New York [1904], London and Felling-on-Tyne 1910, New York 1914, London 1917, 1923 (25th edn), [1936].
REVIEW: Athenaeum 4005 1904.
Life on my heart. 1905, 1905 (19th edn), 1914, New York 1915.
REVIEW: Punch 128 1905.
The religion of Evelyn Hastings. London and Newcastle-on-Tyne 1905, New York [19??], [1908], London [1917], 1921, 1923.
REVIEW: Athenaeum 4035 1905.
Six women. [1906], New York [1906], [19??], London 1912, New York [1915].
Life's shop window. 1907, New York [1907?], 1908 (8th edn), [1909], London [1912], 1923, 1935.
Five nights. 1908, New York [1908?], London 1911, 1918, [1919], 1921, [1935].
Bal Krishna. The love of Kusama. Introd [really written] by Cory [1910], [1911].
The eternal fires. [1910], New York [1910?], London [1917], 1918, 1921.
Self and the other. [1910], [1911], New York 1911, London 1918.
REVIEW: TLS 12 Jan 1911.

The life sentence, 1912, New York 1914, London 1921.
The night of temptation. [1912], [1913], New York 1914, London 1916, 1932.
REVIEW: TLS 12 Dec 1912.
The greater law. 1914, New York 1914 (pbd as Hilda against the world).
REVIEW: Saturday Rev 118 1914.
Daughters of heaven. 1920, New York [1920?], London 1921, New York [1921?], London 1922. Contains The bachelor, The price of an hour, The butterflies' dance, Their honeymoon, Triumph, More cruel than the beast of prey, Playing the game, The vision of love, The ride into life.
Over life's edge. [1921], New York 1921, London 1922, New York [1922], London 1926, 1929.
The beating heart. 1924, New York [1924?], London 1928. Contains The kiss in the wilderness, Colour, A novel elopement, Village passion, The vengeance of Pasht, The jewel casket, Supping with the devil.
Electric love. 1929, New York [1929?], London 1931, 1933; tr Fr 1947.
The unconscious sinner. 1930, New York [1930?], London 1931, 1932.
The husband's holiday. 1932, 1933.
The girl in the studio. 1934, New York [1934], London 1935; tr Ital 1947.
Martha Brown M. P.: a girl of tomorrow. 1935, 1936.
REVIEW: London Mercury 32 1935.
Jim. 1937, 1938.

§2

Stokes, S. Pilloried. 1929, New York 1929.
Blain, V., P. Clements, and I. Grundy. The feminist companion to literature in English. 1990.

Hubert Montague Crackanthorpe 1870–96

Bibliographies

Danielson, H. In his Bibliographies of modern authors, 1921.
Harris, W. A bibliography of writings about Crackanthorpe. Eng Fiction in Transition 6 1963.

Collections

Collected stories, 1893–7, together with an appreciation by Henry James. Gainesville FL 1969.

§1

Wreckage: seven studies. 1893.
Sentimental studies; and, A set of village tales. 1895.
Vignettes: a miniature journal of whim and sentiment. 1896.
Last studies. 1897.

§2

Crackanthorpe, D. Hubert Crackanthorpe and English realism in the 1890s. 1977.
Johnson, L. Poetry and fiction: reflections on three nineteenth century authors: Herbert P. Horne, Hubert Crackanthorpe, William Johnson Cory. Edinburgh 1982.

Francis Marion Crawford 1854–1909

Bibliographies

Moran, J. C. An F. Marion Crawford companion. Westport CT 1981.

Collections

Uncanny tales. 1911, New York 1911 (as Wandering ghosts).

§1

Our silver: a letter addressed to George S. Coe, esq., chairman of the executive council of the American Bankers' Association. New York 1881.
Mr Isaacs: a tale of modern India. 1882.
Doctor Claudius: a true story. 1883.
To leeward. 2 vols '1884' [1883].
A Roman singer. 2 vols 1884 (May).
An American politician: a novel. 2 vols 1884 (Nov).
Zoroaster. 2 vols 1885.
A tale of a lonely parish. 2 vols 1886.
Saracinesca. 3 vols Edinburgh 1887 (Apr).
Marzio's crucifix. 2 vols 1887 (Oct).
Paul Patoff. 3 vols 1887 (Nov).
With the immortals. 2 vols 1888.
Greifenstein. 3 vols 1889 (Apr).
Sant' Ilario. 3 vols 1889 (Aug).
A cigarette-maker's romance. 2 vols 1890.
Khaled: a tale of Arabia. 2 vols 1891 (May).
The witch of Prague. 3 vols 1891 (July).
The three fates. 3 vols 1892 (Apr).
Don Orsino. 3 vols 1892 (Nov).
The children of the King: a tale of southern Italy. 2 vols 1893 (Feb).
The novel: what it is. New York 1893 (Mar), London 1893 (May). Literary criticism.
Pietro Ghisleri. 3 vols 1893 (June).
Marion Darche: a story without comment. 2 vols 1893 (Oct).
Katharine Lauderdale. 3 vols 1894 (Mar).
The upper berth. 1894 (May). Also contains By the waters of Paradise.
Love in idleness: a Bar Harbour tale. 1894 (Oct).
The Ralstons. 2 vols 1895 (Jan).
Constantinople. 1895 (Oct). Travel.
Casa Braccio. 2 vols 1895 (Nov).
Adam Johnstone's son. 1896 (Apr).
Bar Harbor. New York 1896 (July). First pbd in Scribner's Mag 1894. Travel.
Taquisara. 2 vols New York and London 1896 (Oct).
A rose of yesterday. 1897 (June).
Corleone: a tale of Sicily. 2 vols 1897 (Oct).
Ave Roma Immortalis: studies from the chronicles of Rome. 2 vols 1898, 1 vol 1903. History.
Via Crucis: a romance of the Second Crusade. 1899.
In the palace of the king: a love story of old Madrid. 1900 (Oct).
The rulers of the south: Sicily, Calabria, Malta. 2 vols 1900 (Nov), 1 vol 1905 (as Southern Italy and Sicily and the rulers of the south). History.
Marietta: a maid of Venice. 1901.
Francesca da Rimini: a play in four acts. New York 1902 (Apr) (12 copies only), Nashville 1980 (200 copies); tr Fr by Marcel Schwob, Paris 1902, London [1914] (abridged).
Cecilia: a story of modern Rome. 1902 (Oct).
Man overboard! 1903 (July).
The heart of Rome: a tale of the 'lost water'. 1903 (Oct).
Whosoever shall offend.... 1904.
Soprano: a portrait. 1905 (Sep), New York 1905 (as Fair Margaret).
Gleanings from Venetian history. 2 vols 1905 (Dec), 1 vol 1907, 2 vols New York 1905 (as Salve Venetia), 1909 (as Venice: the place and the people). History.
A lady of Rome. 1906.
Arethusa. 1907 (Oct).
The little City of Hope: a Christmas story. 1907 (Nov), [1908].
The primadonna: a sequel to 'Soprano'. 1908 (Mar).
The diva's ruby: a sequel to 'Soprano' and 'Primadonna'. 1908 (Oct).
The White Sister. 1909 (May).
Stradella: an old Italian love tale. 1909 (Sep).
The undesirable governess. 1910.
The White Sister: romantic drama in three acts. New York 1937. With W. Hackett. A dramatised version of the 1909 novel written in that year.

§2

Elliott, M. H. My cousin F. Marion Crawford. 1934.
Contenti, A. Esercizi di nostalgia: La Roma spirita di F. Marion Crawford. Rome 1992. [EH]

Samuel Rutherford Crockett 1860–1914

§1

Dulce cor: being the poems of Ford Berêton. 1886. 'Ford Berêton' was Crockett's pseud.
The Stickit minister and some common men. 1893. Stories.
The playactress. 1894.
The lilac sunbonnet. 1894.
Mad Sir Uchtred of the hills. 1894.
The raiders: being some passages in the life of John Faa, Lord and Earl of Little Egypt. 1894.
Bog-myrtle and peat: tales chiefly of Galloway gathered from the years 1889 to 1895. 1895.
The men of the moss hags: being a history of adventure taken from the papers of William Gordon of Earlstoun in Galloway and told over again. 1895.
Sweetheart travellers: a child's book for children, for women, and for men. 1895.
The grey man. 1896.
The smugglers of the Clone. In Tales of our coast, 1896.
Cleg Kelly, Arab of the city. 1896.
The surprising adventures of Sir Toady Lion with those of General Napoleon Smith: an improving history of old boys, young boys, good boys, bad boys, big boys, little boys, cow boys, and tom-boys. 1897.
Lads' love. 1897.
Lochinvar. 1897.
The standard bearer. 1898.
The red axe. 1898.
The Black Douglas. 1899.
Kit Kennedy, country boy. 1899.
Ione March. 1899.
Joan of the sword hand. 1900.
The Stickit minister's wooing, and other Galloway stories. 1900.
Little Anna Mark. 1900.
Love idylls. 1901.
The silver skull. 1901.
Cinderella: a novel. 1901.
The firebrand. 1901.
The dark o' the moon; being certain further histories of the folk called 'raiders'. 1902.
Flower-o'-the-corn. 1902.
The adventurer in Spain. 1903.
The banner of blue. 1903.
The loves of Miss Anne. 1904.
Raiderland: all about grey Galloway, its stories, traditions, characters, humours. 1904.
Red Cap tales. 2 ser 1904–8. Abbreviated versions of some of Scott's novels. 2nd ser called Red Cap adventures.
Strong Mac. 1904.
The cherry ribband. 1905.
Sir Toady Crusoe. 1905.
Maid Margaret of Galloway: the life story of her whom four centuries have called 'The fair maid of Galloway'. 1905.
Kid McGhie: a nugget of dim gold. 1906, New York 1906 (as Fishers of men).
The white plumes of Navarre: a romance of the wars of religion. 1906.
Me and Myn. 1907.
Little Esson. 1907.
Vida: or the Iron Lord of Kirktown. 1907.
Deep Moat Grange. 1908.
Princess Penniless. 1908.
The bloom o' the heather. 1908.
The men of the mountain. 1909, 1910.
Rose of the wilderness. 1909.
The seven wise men. 1909. First pbd in The bloom o' the heather, *above*, 1908.
The dew of their youth. 1910.
Young Nick and old Nick: yarns for the year's end. [1910.]
The lady of the hundred dresses. 1911.
Love in Pernicketty Town. [1911.]
The smugglers: the odyssey of Zipporah Katti, being some chronicles of the last raiders of Solway. [1911.]
Anne of the barricades. [1912.]
The Moss Troopers. 1912.
Sweethearts at home. [1912.]
Sandy's love affair. 1913.
A tatter of scarlet: adventurous episodes of the commune in the Midi 1871. 1913.
Silver sand. 1914.
Hal o' the Ironsides. 1915.
The azure hand: a novel. [1917.]
The white Pope, called 'The Light out of the East'. Liverpool [1920].
Rogues' Island. 1926.
Crockett also wrote forewords to Carlyle's Montaigne *and other essays, 1897 etc.*

§2

Dudgeon, P. Glossaries to Crockett's The Stickit minister, The raiders, The lilac sunbonnet. 1895.
Harper, M. M. Crockett and grey Galloway: the novelist and his works. [1907.]
Donaldson, I. M. The life and work of Samuel Rutherford Crockett. Aberdeen 1989.

John Davidson 1857–1909

See col 727.

'George Douglas', George Douglas Brown 1869–1902

§1

Love and a sword: a tale of the Afridi war. 1899. Pbd under the pseud 'Kennedy King'.
The house with the green shutters. 1901.

§2

Lennox, C. George Douglas Brown: a biographical memoir, and reminiscences by Andrew Melrose. 1903.
Muir, E. In his Latitudes, 1924.
Veitch, J. George Douglas Brown. 1952.

Ernest Dowson 1867–1900

See col 731.

Sir Arthur Conan Doyle 1859–1930

Bibliographies

De Waal, R. B. The world bibliography of Sherlock Holmes and Dr Watson. A classified and annotated list of materials relating to their lives and adventures. 1974.
De Waal, R. B. The international Sherlock Holmes. A companion volume to The world bibliography of Sherlock Holmes and Dr Watson. 1980.
Green, R. L. and J. M. Gibson. A bibliography of A. Conan Doyle. The Soho Bibliographies vol 23, 1983. Foreword by G. Greene.

Collections and selections

Works of Arthur Conan Doyle. Author's edn. Preface and notes by the author. 12 vols 1903. Incomplete.

The poems of Arthur Donan Doyle – Collected edn. Author's foreword. 1922.

The Conan Doyle [short] stories. Author's preface. 1929. Incomplete.

The Crowborough edition of the works of Sir Arthur Conan Doyle. 24 vols 1930. Incomplete, new introd only.

The Conan Doyle historical romances. 2 vols 1931, 1932. Preface by the author's widow, 1932. Incomplete.

The Professor Challenger stories. 1952.

The complete Napoleonic stories. 1956. Incomplete.

Conan Doyle centennial series. Afterword by J. Tracy. The non-historical non-Holmes novels. 1980.

The unknown Conan Doyle. Ed J. M. Gibson and R. L. Green 3 vols 1982 (2 edns), 1986. Uncollected stories, essays in photography, letters to the press.

The uncollected Sherlock Holmes. Comp with introd by R. L. Green 1983. Self-parodies, plays, poems, speeches and other writings on Sherlock Holmes.

The Oxford Sherlock Holmes. General ed O. Dudley Edwards; editors R. L. Green, W. W. Robson and C. Roden. 9 vols Oxford 1993.

The World's Classics Sherlock Holmes. 9 vols Oxford 1994. The Oxford Sherlock Holmes revised.

The complete Sherlock Holmes and other detective stories. Introd by O. Dudley Edwards 1994.

The complete Brigadier Gerard. Introd by O. Dudley Edwards, Edinburgh 1995 (Canongate Classics 57).

§1

A study in scarlet. 1888. First pbd Beeton's Christmas Annual 1887.

The mystery of Cloomber. 1888. First pbd Pall Mall Budget 30 Aug–8 Nov 1888, Pall Mall Gazette 10–29 Sep 1888.

Micah Clarke his statement as made to his three grand-children Joseph, Gervas, and Reuben during the hard winter of 1734. 1889.

Mysteries and adventures. [1889.] As The gully of Bluemandsdyke and other stories, [1892]. Stories first pbd in London Soc 1881–5, rptd by its editor against author's wish. Amer edn as My friend the murderer and other mysteries and adventures.

The captain of the Polestar and other tales. 1890. Stories first pbd 1881–90.

The firm of Girdlestone: a romance of the unromantic. 1890. First pbd People 27 Oct 1889–13 Apr 1890.

The sign of four. 1890. First pbd Lippincott's Mag Feb 1890 as The sign of the four, or the problem of the Sholtos.

The white company. 3 vols 1891. First pbd Cornhill Mag Jan–Dec 1890.

The doings of Raffles Haw. 1892. First pbd Answers 12 Dec 1891–27 Feb 1892.

The adventures of Sherlock Holmes. 1892. First pbd Strand Mag July 1891–June 1892.

The great shadow. 1892.

The refugees: a tale of two continents. 3 vols 1893. First pbd Harper's Mag Jan–June 1893.

Jane Annie; or, the good conduct prize. 1893. A comic opera written with J. M. Barrie, music by E. Ford.

The great shadow and Beyond the city. [1893.] Beyond the city first pbd Good Cheer, special Christmas no of Good Words 1891; pbd as separate book 1912.

The memoirs of Sherlock Holmes. 1893. First pbd Strand Mag Dec 1892–Dec 1893.

An actor's duel and The winning shot. [1894.] The winning shot first pbd in Bow Bells 11 July 1883; An actor's duel misattributed.

Round the red lamp: being facts and fancies of medical life. 1894. Stories, some first pbd 1890–4, others new.

The parasite. 1894. First pbd Lloyd's Weekly Newspaper 11 Nov–2 Dec 1894.

The Stark Munro letters, being a series of sixteen letters written by J. Stark Munro, M. B., to his friend and former fellow-student, Herbert Swanborough, of Lowell, Massachusetts, during the years 1881–1884. 1895. First pbd Idler Oct 1894–Nov 1895.

The exploits of Brigadier Gerard. 1896. First pbd in Strand Mag Dec 1894–Dec 1895.

Rodney Stone. 1896. First pbd Strand Mag Jan–Dec 1896 as Rodney Stone, a reminiscence of the ring.

Uncle Bernac: a memory of the Empire. 1897. First pbd Manchester Weekly Times 8 Jan–5 Mar 1897.

The tragedy of the Korosko. 1898. First pbd Strand Mag May–Dec 1897.

A duet with an occasional chorus. 1899, rev edn with 2 additional chs 1910.

The green flag and other stories of war and sport. 1900. Stories 1st pbd 1893–1900.

The hound of the Baskervilles: another adventure of Sherlock Holmes. 1902. First pbd Strand Mag Aug 1901–Apr 1902.

Adventures of Gerard. [1903.] First pbd Strand Mag Aug 1902–May 1903.

The return of Sherlock Holmes. 1905. First pbd Strand Mag Oct 1903–Dec 1904.

Sir Nigel. 1906. First pbd Strand Mag Dec 1905–Dec 1906.

Round the fire stories. 1908. First pbd 1892, 1897–1900, 1903, 1908.

The last galley: impressions and tales. 1911. Stories 1st pbd 1892, 1908–11.

The lost world. [1912.] Being on account of the recent amazing adventures of Professor George E. Challenger, Lord John Roxton, Professor Summerlee, and Mr E. D. Malone of the 'Daily Gazette'. First pbd Strand Mag Apr–Nov 1912.

The poison belt. [1913.] First pbd Strand Mag Mar–July 1913.

The valley of fear. 1915. First pbd Strand Mag Sep 1914–May 1915.

His last bow: some reminiscences of Sherlock Holmes. 1917. First pbd in Strand Mag 1892, 1908, 1910, 1911, 1913, 1917.

Danger! and other stories. 1918. First pbd 1890, 1911–14, 1916, 1918.

Three of them. A reminiscence. 1923. First pbd Strand Mag 1918, 1922–3.

The land of mist. [1925.] First pbd Strand Mag July 1925–Mar 1926 as The land of mist or the quest of Edward Malone.

The case-book of Sherlock Holmes. 1927. First pbd Strand Mag 1921–7.

The Maracot Deep and other stories. [1929.] First pbd Strand Mag 1927–9.

The field bazaar. A Sherlock Holmes pastiche. 1934. First pbd Edinburgh Univ Student 20 Nov 1896 in support of university's student appeal for a new cricket pavilion.

The blood-stone tragedy. A Druidical story. 1995. Ed C. and B. Roden with an afterword by O. Dudley Edwards. First pbd Cassell's Saturday Jnl 16 Feb 1884.

Plays

Jane Annie, or The good conduct prize. 1893 (with J. M. Barrie). *See above.*

Foreign policy. A one-act play adapted from the short story A question of diplomacy (in Round the red lamp 1894). Performed 3, 6–9 June 1893, revived 1910. Unpbd.

Waterloo. (Also known as A story of Waterloo.) Adapted from the short story A straggler of '15 (in Round the red lamp 1894). Performed by Sir Henry Irving and subsequently by H. B. Irving, 1894, 1895, 1905 etc. Pbd 1907.

Halves. A prologue and three acts based on the novel by James Payn (1876). Performed 1899.

Sherlock Holmes. A drama in four acts. Co-author W. Gillette. Performed 1899–1902 by Gillette with many revivals. Pbd 1922.

A duet. A one-act comedy adapted from A duet. Performed 1902. Pbd 1903.
Brigadier Gerard. A four-act comedy. Performed 1906.
The fires of fate. A four-act modern morality play adapted from The tragedy of the Korosko. Performed 1909–10.
The house of Temperley. A melodrama of the Ring, adapted from Rodney Stone. Performed 1910.
A pot of caviare. A one-act play adapted from the eponymous short story (in Round the fire stories 1908). Performed 1910.
The speckled band: an adventure of Sherlock Holmes. A three-act play adapted from the eponymous short story, originally The Stonor case. Performed 1910, 1911, 1921. Pbd 1912.
The crown diamond. An evening with Sherlock Holmes.... A one-act play rewritten as The Mazarin stone (Case-book). Performed 1921, pbd 1958.

Poems

Songs of action. 1898. 28 poems, most previously pbd.
Songs of the road. 1911. 33 poems, most previously unpbd.
The guards came through and other poems. 1919. 17 poems, most unpbd.

Prose

(1) Contemporary history

The great Boer war. 1900, rev 1901, 1902.
The British campaign in France and Flanders 1914. 1916.
The British campaign in France and Flanders 1915. 1917.
The British campaign in France and Flanders 1916. 1918.
The British campaign in France and Flanders 1917. 1918.
The British campaign in France and Flanders 1918. 1919.
The British campaigns in Europe 1914–18. 1928. (The 6 vols reduced to slightly more than half with new material.)

(2) Literary criticism

The immortal memory. 1901. Address to the Edinburgh Burns Club 23 Mar 1901.
Through the magic door. 1907. Remotely based on Before my book-shelf, 6 pt ser in Great Thoughts 5 May–30 June 1894.
The future of Canadian literature. With an introd by C. and B. Roden. 1994. Address to Canadian Club of Montreal 4 June 1914. First pbd in Addresses delivered before the Canadian Club of Montreal 1914–15 season.

(3) Polemic

The war in South Africa – its cause and conduct. 1902.
The fiscal question treated in a series of three speeches. 1905.
An incursion into diplomacy. 1906.
The story of Mr George Edalji. 1907. First pbd Daily Telegraph 11, 12 Jan 1907.
The crime of the Congo. 1909.
Divorce law reform: an essay. [1909.]
Why he is now in favour of home rule. 1911. First pbd Belfast Evening Telegraph 22 Sep 1911.
The case of Oscar Slater. [1912.]
Civilian national reserve. [1914.]
Great Britain and the next war. 1914. First pbd Fortnightly Rev Feb 1913.
To arms! With preface by F. E. Smith. [1914.]
The world war conspiracy: Germany's long drawn plot against England. [1914.] First pbd Daily Chron 27 Aug 1914.
The German war. 1914. First pbd with previous 3 items Daily Chron 18, 26 Sep, 10, 26 Oct, 23 Nov 1914.
Western wanderings. [1915.] First pbd Cornhill Mag Jan–Apr 1915.
The outlook on the war. [1915] First pbd Daily Chron 25 Oct 1915.
An appreciation of Sir John French. [1916.] First pbd Daily Chron 20 Dec 1915.
A visit to three fronts June 1916. 1916. First pbd Daily Chron 13, 15, 20, 22, 27, 29 June 1916.
Supremacy of the British soldier. [1917.] First pbd Daily Chron 18 Apr 1917.

(4) Autobiography

Memories and adventures. 1924, rev 1930. First pbd Strand Mag 1897, 1900, 1906, 1916–18, 1923–4.

(5) Religion

The new revelation. 1918.
Life after death. 1918.
The vital message. 1919. First pbd Nash's Pall Mall Mag May–Oct 1919.
Our reply to the cleric. 1920.
Spiritualism and rationalism with a drastic examination of Mr Joseph M'Cabe. 1920. A reply to Joseph McCabe, Is spiritualism based on fraud? The evidence given by Sir A. C. Doyle and others drastically examined.
The wanderings of a spiritualist. 1921. First pbd Weekly Dispatch 29 May–10 July 1921.
The coming of the fairies. 1921. First pbd in pt Strand Mag Dec 1920, Mar 1921.
Spiritualism: some straight questions and direct answers. [1922.]
The case for spirit photography. [1922.]
Our American adventure. [1923.] First pbd as The adventures of a spiritualist in America, Lloyd's Sunday News 3 Sep–17 Dec 1922.
Our second American adventure. [1924.]
The early Christian church and modern spiritualism. [1925.]
Psychic experiences. [1925.] First pbd Pearson's Mag Apr 1924.
The history of spiritualism. 2 vols 1926. First pbd Light 7, 14, 21, 28 Feb, 7, 14, 21 Mar, 4, 11, 18 Apr 1925; Strand Mag Sep 1920, May 1921; Quart Trans of the Br College of Psychic Science Oct 1922, Oct 1924.
Pheneas speaks: direct spirit communications in the family circle. 1927.
What does spiritualism actually teach and stand for? [1928.]
A word of warning. [1928.]
An open letter to those of my generation. 1929.
Our African winter. 1929.
The Roman Catholic church. A rejoinder. 1929. A reply to Rev Herbert Thurston, S.J., Modern spiritualism.
The edge of the unknown. 1930. First pbd Strand Mag 1919–21, 1927–8, etc.

(6) Criminology

Strange studies from life containing three hitherto uncollected tales. Based on the Annals of true crime. A profile of the author by P. Trevor, ed P. Ruber 1963. First pbd Strand Mag Mar–June 1901.

§2

Criticism

Prothero, R. E. Noticeable books: Micah Clarke. Nineteenth Cent 26, Aug 1889.
Bell, J. The adventures of Sherlock Holmes. Bookman (London) Dec 1892.
Some notable beginners in Chambers's Journal. Chambers's Jnl 19 Jan 1895. (ACD's first story, The mystery of Sassasa Valley, in Chambers's 6 Sep 1879.)
Cromwell, A. and H. S. Maclauchlan. Dr Conan Doyle and his stories. Windsor Mag 4, Oct 1896.
Cromie, R. Dr C. Doyle's place in modern literature. Twentieth Cent 2, May 1901.
S[idgwick], F. The hound of the Baskervilles at fault (An open letter to Dr Watson). Cambridge Rev 23, Jan 1902. (Inaugurated the endless pursuit of alleged Watsonian literary solecisms on the facetious assumption of Holmes–Watson actual existence.)

Wodehouse, P. G. The pugilist in fiction. Sandow's Mag 8, Mar 1902. (By ACD's most eminent literary heir.)
[Lang, A.] The novels of Sir Arthur Conan Doyle. Quart Rev 200, July 1904.
Maurice, A. B. Sherlock Holmes and his creator. Collier's Mag 41, 15 Aug 1908.
Hawthorne, J. Riddle stories, introducing American stories in The Lock and Key Library vol 10, 1909. (See also vol 8 in the ser anthologising the first 3 Holmes short stories.)
Knox, R. A. Studies in the literature of Sherlock Holmes, [Oxford] Blue Book vol 1, July 1912. (Notwithstanding its schoolboy humour, the classic anatomy of the Holmes story.)
Wells, C. The technique of the mystery story. Introd by J. B. Eisenwein [for his Home Correspondence School, its representative plagiarisms noted in R. F. Stewart, ... And also a detective: chapters on the history of detective fiction, 1980]. 1913.
Depken, F. Sherlock Holmes, Raffles, und Ihre Vorbilder. 1914.
Chesterton, G. K. A handful of authors. 1953. (Includes Sherlock Holmes, combining Daily News essays of 2 Sep 1901, 23 Mar 1907).
Baring-Gould, W. S. (ed). The annotated Sherlock Holmes. 2 vols 1968.
Dakin, D. M. A Sherlock Holmes commentary. 1972.
Pointer, M. The public life of Sherlock Holmes. 1975. (Stage, screen, radio dramatisations.)
Tracy, J. W. The encyclopaedia Sherlockiana. 1977.
Redmond, D. A. Sherlock Holmes: a study in sources. 1982.
Shreffler, P. A. (ed). The Baker Street reader: cornerstone writings about Sherlock Holmes. 1984.
Orel, H. (ed). Critical essays on Sir Arthur Conan Doyle. 1992.

Biographies

Lamond, J. Arthur Conan Doyle: a memoir. Epilogue by Jean, Lady Conan Doyle. 1931.
Pearson, H. Conan Doyle: his life and art. 1943.
Carr, J. D. The life of Sir Arthur Conan Doyle. 1949.
Nordon, P. [Weil]. Sir Arthur Conan Doyle: L'homme et l'oeuvre. 1964. Tr by F. Partridge, abridged, as Conan Doyle 1966.
Higham, C. The adventures of Conan Doyle: the life of the creator of Sherlock Holmes. 1976.
Baker, M. The Doyle diary. The last great Conan Doyle mystery, with a Holmesian investigation into the strange and curious case of Charles Altamont Doyle. 1978. (Includes diary and art work by ACD's father in Montrose Royal Lunatic Asylum, 1889).
Symons, J. Portrait of an artist: Conan Doyle. 1979.
Edwards, O. Dudley. The quest for Sherlock Holmes: a biographical study of Arthur Conan Doyle. 1983, rev 1984.
Lellenberg, J. L. (ed). The quest for Sir Arthur Conan Doyle: thirteen biographers in search of a life. 1987. (Critiques of Conan Doyle biographies to date.)
Stavert, G. A study in Southsea; the unrevealed life of Dr Arthur Conan Doyle. 1987.
Redmond, C. Welcome to America, Mr Sherlock Holmes. 1987. (Conan Doyle's tour of North America 1894.)
Orel, H. (ed). Sir Arthur Conan Doyle: interviews and recollections. 1991.
ACD: The Jnl of the Arthur Conan Doyle Soc, ed C. Roden et al, 1989– publishes textual matter, criticism, discoveries in ACD data. [ODE]

George Louis Palmella Busson Du Maurier
1834–96

Collections

Novels of George Du Maurier. 1947.

§1

English society at home from the collection of 'Mr Punch'. 1880.
Society pictures drawn by George du Maurier; selected from 'Punch'. 2 vols 1891.
Peter Ibbetson; with an introduction by his cousin, Lady ***** (Madge Plunket). 2 vols 1892, 1 vol 1892, [1936], 1969. First pbd in Harper's Mag.
Trilby. 3 vols 1894, 1 vol 1895, 1931, 1947, 1956, 1982 (first complete and unexpurgated edn entitled Svengali). First pbd in Harper's Mag.
English society sketched by George Du Maurier. 1897.
The Martian: a novel. 1897.
Social pictorial satire. 1898.
A legend of Camelot: pictures and poems, etc. 1898.
Pictures by George Du Maurier. 1911. Illustrations from Punch 1865–8.

Letters

The young George Du Maurier: a selection of his letters, 1860–67. Ed D. Du Maurier 1951.

§2

Gilder, J. L. and J. B. Trilbyana: the rise and progress of a popular novel. 1895.
Moscheles, F. In Bohemia with Du Maurier. 1896.
Armstrong, T. Reminiscences of Du Maurier. 1912.
Wood, T. M. George Du Maurier, the satirist of the Victorians: a review of his art and personality. 1913.
Lucas, E. V. George du Maurier at thirty-three. Cornhill Mag Oct 1934; rptd in his All of a piece, 1937.
Du Maurier, D. The Du Mauriers. 1937.
Feipel, L. N. The American issues of Trilby. Colophon 2 1937.
Millar, C. C. H. George Du Maurier and others. 1937.
Lanoire, M. Un anglo-français, Du Maurier. Revue de Paris 15 Mar 1940.
Trilby reappears. TLS 3 Apr 1948.
Whiteley, D. P. George du Maurier: his life and work. 1948.
Stevenson, L. Du Maurier and the romantic novel. Essays by Divers Hands 30 1960.
Ormond, L. George Du Maurier. 1969.
Kelly, R. The art of George du Maurier. Aldershot 1996. [EH]

Amelia B. Edwards, Amelia Ann Blandford Edwards 1831–92

The Amelia B. Edwards Archive in the Lib of Somerville College Oxford is the principal repository of mss, letters, notebooks and proofs. Her correspondence with Petrie is held by the Petrie Museum of Egyptian Archaeology, Univ College London; other papers and correspondence are in the Lib, Univ College London; documents relating to Edwards and the founding of the Chair of Egyptology are in the Records Office, Univ College London.

§1

My brother's wife; a life history. 1855, 1862, 1864, New York 1865, London 1874 (new edn), New York 1875, London 1892, 1894.
REVIEW: Athenaeum 1451 1855.
The ladder of life: a heart history. 1856, 1857, 1862, 1864, New York 1864, [1866?], 1872, London 1874, New York 1875, 1882, 1883, London 1892, 1894.
A summary of English history: from the Roman conquest to the present time. 1856, New York [1856?], London 1859 (new edn), 1860, 1864, 1871 (new edn rev), 1878 (new edn illus); Boston 1857 (pbd as Outlines of English history), 1858, [186?] (Amer edn corrected and continued to 1866), 1878, 1886.
The young marquis: or a story from a reign. 1857, 1859.
Hand and glove: a tale. 1858, 1859, [1860?], Leipzig 1865 (Tauchnitz), London 1865 (new edn), New York 1866, London 1874 (new edn).
REVIEW: Athenaeum 1599 1858.
The history of France from the conquest of Gaul to the Peace of 1856. London and New York 1858, 1880 (new edn continued to the death of the Prince Imperial, by Thomas Archer).
The photographic historical portrait gallery. 1860, 1864.

Sights and stories: being some account of a holiday tour through the north of Belgium. 1862 (illus).
REVIEW: Athenaeum 1788 1862.
The story of Cervantes. 1862, 1863, [1875], 1878.
Barbara's history. 3 vols 1863, 3 vols 1864, 2 vols 1864, 2 vols Leipzig 1864 (Tauchnitz), 1 vol London 1864, 2 vols New York 1864, London 1865 (new edn), New York 1877, [1883], London 1897, 1903; tr Fr, Ger, Ital.
REVIEWS: Athenaeum 1888 1864; Saturday Rev 17 1864.
No hero: an autobiography. Calcutta 1863. Rptd from Englishman's Weekly Literary Jnl.
Rachel Noble's experience. 1863.
Ballads. 1865.
Half a million of money: a novel. 2 vols Leipzig 1865 (Tauchnitz), 3 vols London 1865, 3 vols 1866 (2nd edn), 3 vols 1866 (3rd edn), 1 vol 1866 (new edn rev), New York 1866, 1867, London 1868, New York 1868, 1870, [New York 1877], New York [1889], London 1892 (4th edn).
REVIEWS: Athenaeum 1989 1865; Fortnightly Rev 3 1866.
Miss Carew. 2 vols Leipzig 1865 (Tauchnitz), 3 vols London 1865, 2 vols London 1865 (2nd edn), 3 vols New York 1865, London 1875 (new edn), New York [1880]. Stories.
REVIEW: Athenaeum 1969 1865.
Debenham's vow. 3 vols 1869, 2 vols Leipzig 1870 (Tauchnitz), 3 vols London 1870, 1 vol New York 1870, London 1876 (new edn); tr Ger 1873.
REVIEWS: Athenaeum 2198 1869; Saturday Rev 28 1869.
In the days of my youth. 3 vols 1872, 2 vols Leipzig 1873 (Tauchnitz), 3 vols London 1873, 1 vol Philadelphia 1874, 1 vol London 1875; tr Ger 1876.
REVIEW: Athenaeum 2358 1873; Saturday Rev 35 1873.
Monsieur Maurice, a new novelette, and other tales. 3 vols 1873, Leipzig 1873 (Tauchnitz), 1 vol London 1876. Contains Monsieur Maurice, Vendetta, An engineer's story, The cabaret of the break of day, The story of Ernest Christian Schoeffer, The new pass, The service of danger. Monsieur Maurice rptd in Five Victorian ghost stories, ed with an introd by E. F. Bleiler, New York 1971.
REVIEW: Athenaeum 2392 1873.
Untrodden peaks and unfrequented valleys: a midsummer ramble in the Dolomites. 1873 (illus), Leipzig 1873 (Tauchnitz), London 1889 (2nd edn), London and New York '1890' [1889], London 1898, [19??] (3rd edn), Boston 1987 (introd by P. Levine).
REVIEWS: Athenaeum 2385 1873; Dial 10 1890.
A thousand miles up the Nile. '1877' [1876] (illus), New York 1877, 2 vols Leipzig 1878 (Tauchnitz), Boston [1888] (2nd edn), New York [1888?], Philadelphia [1888?], London 1888 (2nd edn rev), London and New York 1889, 1890, New York 1890, London and New York 1891, Boston 1897, London 1899 (new edn), New York [1902], London 1993 (reprint of rev 2nd edn); tr Polish 1880.
REVIEWS: Athenaeum 2573 1877; London Quart and Holborn Rev 52 1877; Spectator 50 1877.
Lord Brackenbury: a novel. Serialised in Graphic. 3 vols 1880, 2 vols Leipzig 1880 (Tauchnitz), [New York 1880], 1 vol London 1881 (new edn), 1897, 1903.
REVIEW: Athenaeum 2761 1880.
The story of Tanis. [New York 1885?] (illus), np 1886. Pam.
The provincial and private collections of Egyptian antiquities in Great Britain. [Westbury on Trym 1888.]
Bubastis, an historical study. np 1890.
Recent discoveries in Egypt. [New York] 1890. Pam.
Pharoahs, fellas and explorers. 1891, New York 1891, 1892, 1902.
REVIEW: Dial 13 1892.
The eleventh of March. A welcome: original contributions in poetry and prose. 1863. Rptd in Miss Carew, 1865, *above.*
Home thoughts and home scenes. Original poems by J. Ingelow and others. 1865.
The four-fifteen express. Mixed sweets from Routledge's Annual. [1867.]

Translations, editions

Loviot, F. A lady's captivity among the Chinese pirates. Tr Edwards [1858], 1930.
A poetry book of elder poets. Selected and arranged with notes by Edwards. 1879.
REVIEW: Athenaeum 2675 1879.
A poetry book of modern poets. Selected and arranged with notes by Edwards. 1879.
Maspero, G. C. Egyptian archaeology. Tr Edwards 1887 (illus), 1889, 1895, 1902 (5th edn rev and enlarged).
Edwards wrote numerous stories and articles for many different newspapers and jnls.

§2

Macquoid, K. S. Amelia Blandford Edwards. In Women novelists of Queen Victoria's reign, 1897.
Betham-Edwards, M. Reminiscences. 1898.
Winslow, W. C. The queen of Egyptology, Amelia B. Edwards. [Cleveland 1892?] Rptd from Amer Antiquarian 1892. Pam.
In DNB Suppl.

'George Egerton', Mary Chavelita Dunne, later Clairmonte, afterwards Bright 1859–1945

Boston Univ Lib holds the major collection of Egerton's papers, including letters. Ms copies of some plays performed but unpbd are in NYPL.

Bibliography

The works of George Egerton. In Ten contemporaries. Notes toward their definitive bibliography, [first series] ed J. Gawsworth 1932. Includes George Egerton. A keynote to Keynotes.

§1

Keynotes. 1893, 1894, Boston and London 1977, 1983 (with Discords, introd by M. Vicinus).
REVIEWS: Athenaeum 3 Feb 1894; Acad 17 Feb 1894; Saturday Rev 3 Mar 1894.
Discords. 1894, 1983 (with Keynotes, introd by M. Vicinus).
REVIEWS: Acad 2 Mar 1895; Athenaeum 23 Mar 1895; Saturday Rev 30 Mar 1895.
Symphonies. 1897.
REVIEWS: Acad Fiction Suppl 12 June 1897; Athenaeum 10 July 1897; Saturday Rev 25 Sep 1897.
Fantasias. London and New York 1898.
REVIEWS: Acad Fiction Suppl 8 Jan 1898; Athenaeum 9 Apr 1898.
The wheel of God. A tale. 1898.
REVIEWS: Spectator 25 June 1898; Athenaeum 6 Aug 1898.
Rosa Amorosa. The love-letters of a woman. 1901. Novel.
REVIEWS: Acad 25 May 1901; Athenaeum 29 June 1901.
Flies in amber. 1905.

Periodical contributions

A lost masterpiece: a city mood, Aug '93. Yellow Book 4 Jan 1895.
The captain's book. Yellow Book 6 July 1895.

Letters

A leaf from the Yellow Book. The correspondence of George Egerton. Ed Terence de Vere 1958.

Translations

Ola Hansson. Young Ofeg's ditties. Tr from Swed by George Egerton, 1895.
REVIEWS: Saturday Rev 30 Mar 1895; Acad 6 Apr 1895.
Knut Hamsun. Hunger. Tr from Norwegian by George Egerton, 1899, 1921.
REVIEW: Acad 24 June 1899.

§2

Burgin, G. B. How women writers work. Idler 10 Sep 1896.

Foerster, E. Die Frauenfrage in den Romanen Englischer Schriftstellerinnen der Gegenwart. Marburg 1907. [MH]

Juliana Horatia Ewing, née Gatty 1841–85

Collections

Uniform edition. 18 vols 1894–6. Complete; vol 17, Miscellanea (later called Tales of the Khoja), consists of uncollected articles, tales and trns from Aunt Judy's Mag, London Soc etc. Vol 18 is H. K. F. Eden's life, *below*.

Jackanapes, Daddy Darwin's dovecot, and The story of a short life. 1916 (EL).

Mrs Overtheway's remembrances and other stories. 1916 (EL).

The Ewing omnibus, containing Jackanapes, Mrs Overtheway's remembrances, Daddy Darwin's dovecot, and other stories. 1935.

§1

Melchior's dream and other tales. 1862, 1869, 1888 (5th edn with 3 additional stories), 1891. First pbd in Monthly Packet 1861.

Mrs Overtheway's remembrances. 1869 (illus), 1984. Originally appeared in Aunt Judy's Mag 1866–8.

The brownies and other tales. 1870, 1871, 1954 (Dent Children's Illus Classics).

A flat iron for a farthing: or some passages in the life of an only son. 1872, 1883 (illustr Mrs Allingham), [189?].

Lob Lie-by-the fire: or, the luck of Lingborough. 1874 (illustr G. Cruickshank), 1885 (illustr R. Caldecott), New York 1917, London 1964 (Dent Children's Illus Classics). 4 of the 5 stories were first pbd in Aunt Judy's Mag; Lob had not appeared before.

Six to sixteen: a story for girls. 1876 (illustr Mrs H. Allingham). First pbd in Aunt Judy's Mag 1872.

Jan of the windmill: a story of the plains. 1876, 1885 (illustr H. Paterson), 1905, 1914 (Queens Treasure ser). First appeared in Aunt Judy's Mag as The miller's thumb 1872–3.

A great emergency and other tales. 1877, 1887. First pbd in Aunt Judy's Mag 1873–5.

We and the world: a book for boys. 1880, 1886, 1893. First appeared in Aunt Judy's Mag 1877–9.

Old fashioned fairy tales. [1882] (illus). First pbd in Aunt Judy's Mag 1870–6.

Brothers of pity and other tales of beasts and men. [1882.] First pbd in Aunt Judy's Mag 1876–9.

Blue and Red: or the discontented lobster: his history related in verse. [1883.] First appeared in Aunt Judy's Mag 1881.

Verse books for children. 6 vols [1883], 1 vol [1888] (as A soldier's children and five other tales in verse). Illustr R. André. Vols entitled: The dolls' wash; Master Fritz; Our garden; A soldier's children; A sweet little dear; Three little nest birds. First pbd in Aunt Judy's Mag.

A week spent in a glass pond by the great water beetle. [1883.]

Jackanapes. 1884 (illustr R. Caldecott), [1910?]. First pbd in Aunt Judy's Mag Oct 1879.

Daddy Darwin's dovecot. A country tale. 1884 (illustr R. Caldecott). First pbd in Aunt Judy's Mag 1881.

Verse books for children. Second ser. 6 vols [1884], 1 vol [1888] (as The blue bells on the lea and ten other tales in verse). Illustr R. André. Vols entitled The blue bells on the lea; Dolls' housekeeping; Little boys and wooden horses; Papa Poodle, and other pets; Tongues in trees; 'Touch him if you dare'. First pbd in Aunt Judy's Mag 1866–80.

Poems of child life and country life. 6 vols [1885], 1 vol [1888] (as Mother's birthday review and seven other tales in verse. Illustr R. André. Vols entitled Baby, puppy, kitty; Convalescence; Grandmother's spring; The mill stream; Mother's birthday review; The poet and the brook. First pbd in Aunt Judy's Mag 1874–83.

The story of a short life. [1885?] (illustr G. Browne). Originally appeared in Laetus sorte mea in Aunt Judy's Mag 1882.

Mary's meadow, and Letters from a little garden. 1886 (illustr G. Browne). First pbd in Aunt Judy's Mag 1883–4.

Dandelion clocks and other tales. [1887] (illustr G Browne). First pbd in Aunt Judy's Mag 1875–7.

The peace egg and a Christmas mumming play. [1887] (illustr G. Browne). First pbd in Aunt Judy's Mag 1884.

Snapdragons. A tale of Christmas Eve and old Father Christmas; an old fashioned tale of the young days of a grumpy old godfather. 1888 (illustr G. Browne). (Snapdragons was first pbd in Lob Lie-by-the-fire).

Leaves from Juliana Horatia Ewing's 'Canada home' gathered and illustrated by Elizabeth S. Tucker, together with eight water colour drawings by Mrs Ewing's own hand. Boston and London 1896.

Also vols of verse and prose. See H. K. F. Gatty (later Eden), Juliana Horatia Ewing and her books, *1885.*

§2

Gatty (later Eden), H. K. F. Juliana Horatia Ewing and her books. 1885 (in Uniform edn, *above*).

Marshall, E. In A. Sargeant et al, Women novelists of Queen Victoria's reign, 1897.

Juliana Ewing's world: morality with fun. TLS 9 Aug 1941.

Maxwell, C. Mrs Gatty and Mrs Ewing. 1949.

Laski, M. Mrs Ewing, Mrs Molesworth and Mrs Hodgson Burnett. 1951.

Avery, G. Mrs Ewing. 1961. [DD]

'Michael Fairless', Margaret Fairless Barber 1869–1901

Collections

The complete works of Michael Fairless. 1931.

§1

The gathering of Brother Hilarius. 1901.

The roadmender. 1902; ed M. E. Dowson 1926 (with addns). First pbd in The Pilot.

The child king: four Christmas writings. 1902.

The grey brethren and other fragments in prose and verse. 1905.

Stories told to children. Ed 'M. E. Dowson' (W. S. Palmer) 1914, 1923. Contents first pbd in The grey brethren, 1905, *above*.

§2

'Dowson, M. E.' (W. S. Palmer) and A. M. Haggard. Michael Fairless: her life and writings. 1913.

'Lanoe Falconer', Mary Elizabeth Hawker 1848–1908

§1

Mademoiselle Ixe. 1891 (for 1890).

Cecilia de Noël. 1891.

The Hôtel d'Angleterre and other stories. 1891.

Shoulder to shoulder: a tale of love and friendship. [1891.]

The wrong prescription. In Tavistock tales by Gilbert Parker etc, 1893.

Old Hampshire vignettes. 1907.

'Lanoe Falconer' also contributed The short story to On the art of writing fiction, *1894.*

§2

Phillipps, E. M. Lanoe Falconer. Cornhill Mag Feb 1912.

Phillipps, E. M. Lanoe Falconer (author of Mademoiselle Ixe). 1915.

John Meade Falkner 1858–1932

Bibliographies

Pollard, H. G. Some uncollected authors: J. M. Falkner. Book Collector 9 1960.

§1

Handbook for travellers in Oxfordshire. 1894.
The lost Stradivarius. Edinburgh 1895, Oxford 1954 (WC).
Moonfleet. 1898.
A history of Oxfordshire. 1899.
Handbook for Berkshire. 1902.
The nebuly coat. 1903, Oxford 1954 (WC).
Bath in history and social tradition. 1918.
Poems. [1933.]
A midsummer night's marriage. Edinburgh 1977. Edn limited to 100 copies. First pbd in Nat Rev, 1896.

§2

Pritchett, V. S. In his Living novel, 1946.
Warren, K. John Meade Falkner, 1858–1932: a paradoxical life. Lewiston NY and Lampeter 1995.

'Violet Fane' 1843–1905

See col 733.

Benjamin Leopold Farjeon 1843–1903

§1

Grif: a story of Australian life. Dunedin NZ 1866, 2 vols 1870.
Shadows on the snow: a Christmas story. Dunedin NZ 1866, London [1904].
Joshua Marvel. 3 vols 1871.
London's heart. 3 vols 1873.
Christmas stories: Blade o'grass; Golden grain; and Bread and cheese and kisses. 3 pts in 1 1874.
Jessie Trim: a novel. 3 vols 1874.
Love's victory: a novel. 2 vols 1875.
At the sign of the silver flagon. 3 vols 1876.
The Duchess of Rosemary Lane: a novel. 3 vols 1876.
The house of white shadows: a novel. 3 vols 1884.
Christmas angel. [1885.]
Great Porter Square: a mystery. 3 vols 1885.
The sacred nugget: a novel. 3 vols 1885.
Self-doomed. [1885.]
The golden land: or links from shore to shore. 1886.
In a silver sea. 3 vols 1886.
The nine of hearts. [1886.]
Three times tried. [1886.]
A secret inheritance. 3 vols 1887.
The tragedy of Featherstone: a novel. 3 vols 1887.
Devlin the barber. 1888.
Miser Farebrother: a novel. 3 vols 1888.
Toilers of Babylon. 3 vols 1888.
The blood white rose. [1889.]
Doctor Glennie's daughter: a story of real life. 1889.
A strange enchantment. 1889.
A young girl's life: a novel. 3 vols 1889.
Basil and Annette: a novel. 3 vols 1890.
The mystery of M. Felix: a novel. 3 vols 1890.
The peril of Richard Pardon: a novel. 1890.
A very young couple: a novel. 1890.
For the defence: a realistic and sensational story of human nature. 1890.
The shield of love. 1891 (Arrowsmith's Christmas Annual).
The death trance. [1893.]
The march of fate: a novel. 3 vols 1893.
The last tenant. [1893.]
Something occurred. 1893.
Aaron the Jew: a novel. 3 vols 1894.
The betrayal of John Fordham. 1896.
Miriam Rozella. 1898.
Samuel Boyd of Catchpole Square: a mystery. 1899.
The mesmerists: a novel. 1900. Also contains The mesmerist: an original play in four acts.
The pride of race, in five panels. 1901.
The mystery of the Royal Mail. 1902.
The Amblers. 1904. Completed by Eleanor Farjeon.
The clairvoyante. 1905.
Mrs Dimmock's worries. 1906.
Stories by Farjeon also appeared in the following collections: In Australian wilds, *ed P. Mennell 1889;* Seven Xmas eves, *1894, and* Fifty-two stories of the British Empire, *ed A. H. Miles 1900.*

§2

B. L. Farjeon. Victoria Mag 32 1879.
Bok, E. W. B. L. Farjeon. Author (Boston) 3 1891.
Reed, A. H. Ben and Eleanor Farjeon and Dunedin. Wellington NZ 1973.

Frederic William Farrar 1831–1903

§1

Eric, or little by little: a tale of Roslyn School. Edinburgh 1858.
Julian Home: a tale of college life. Edinburgh 1859.
St Winifred's: or the world of school. Edinburgh 1862.
The three homes: a tale for fathers and sons. [1873] (under the pseud 'F. T. L. Hope'), 1896 (signed), 1903.
Darkness and dawn, or scenes in the days of Nero: an historic tale. 2 vols 1891.
Gathering clouds: a tale of the days of St Chrysostom. 2 vols 1895.
Allegories. 1898.
Verses. [1905] (for private circulation).
Farrar also pbd many sermons and theological works, the more important of which are listed col 2652.

§2

Farrar, R. The life of Frederick William Farrar. 1904.
Russell, G. W. E. Sketches and snapshots. 1910.
'Kingsmill, Hugh' (H. K. Lunn). After Puritanism 1850–1900. 1929.

George Manville Fenn 1831–1909

Collections

The bag of diamonds and three bits of paste. 1900. Contains The bag of diamonds; The dark house; Eve at the wheel; The chaplain's craze.

§1

'Cabby'. 1864.
Featherland: or how the birds lived at Greenlawn. 1866, 1896.
Hollowdell Grange: or holiday hours in a country home. 1866.
Original penny readings: a series of short sketches. 3 vols 1866–7, 1 vol 1889 (abridged as In jeopardy and other stories of peril).
Bent, not broken: a tale. 3 vols 1867.
Christmas penny readings: original sketches for the season. 1867.
Webs in the way. 3 vols 1867.
Mad: a story of dust and ashes. 3 vols 1868.
Begumbagh: an episode of the Indian Mutiny. 1869 (Christmas no of Chambers's Jnl).
By birth a lady: a tale. 3 vols 1871.
The sapphire cross: a novel. 3 vols 1871.
Midnight webs. 1872. Stories. Contains Smith's ditty (variant edn of

Begumbagh); Aboard the Sea-mew; Under the tree-ferns; Violets in the snow (later pbd with Dutch the diver); Nil des (later pbd with Dutch the diver).
A book of fair women, edited by George Manville Fenn. [1873.] Poems.
'Ship ahoy!': a yarn in thirty-six cable lengths. 1873 (Once a Week Christmas Annual). Anon.
Sixty per cent: a domestic ditty. 1874 (Once a Week Christmas Annual).
Jack in the box. 1875 (Once a Week Christmas Annual).
'Land ahead!': or leaves of shamrock. 1876 (Once a Week Christmas Annual).
Thereby hangs a tale: a novel. 3 vols 1876.
A little world. 3 vols 1877, 1 vol [1882] (as Poverty Corner), [1907].
Pretty Polly: a farce in fyttes. 3 vols 1878.
Begumbagh: a tale of the Indian Mutiny, and other stories. 1879, [1893] (with different stories). A variant edn of Begumbagh pbd in Midnight webs as Smith's ditty.
Goblin Rock: the tale of a light at sea. 1879 (Once a Week Christmas Annual).
The parson o' Dumford: a tale. 3 vols 1879, 1 vol [1883], 1906.
The clerk of Portwick: a tale. 3 vols 1880.
Adventures of working men. [1881], [1883] (as My patients).
Friends I have made. [1881], [1883] (as Cobweb's father and other tales).
Off to the wilds: being the adventures of two brothers. 1881.
The vicar's people: a story of a stain. 3 vols 1881, 1 vol [1885], [1888].
Eli's children: the chronicles of an unhappy family. 3 vols 1882.
Dutch the diver: or a man's mistake. [1883]. Also contains 2 short stories previously pbd in Midnight webs.
In the king's name: or the cruise of the 'Kestrel'. 1883.
Middy and ensign, or the jungle station: a tale of the Malay Peninsula. 1883, 1910.
Nat the naturalist: or a boy's adventures in the eastern seas. 1883, 1899, 1905, [1911], [1926].
The new mistress: a tale. 3 vols 1883, 1 vol 1891.
The golden magnet: a tale of the land of the Incas. 1884, 1901, [1934].
The Rosery folk: a country tale. 2 vols 1884.
The silver cañon: a tale of the western plains. 1884.
Sweet Mace: a Sussex legend of the iron times. 3 vols 1884, 1 vol [1885].
Bunyip land: the story of a wild journey in New Guinea. 1885, [1894], [1929].
The dark house: a knot unravelled. 1885.
Eve at the wheel: a tale of three hundred virgins. 1885.
Menhardoc: a story of Cornish nets and mines. 1885, [1894], 1911 (as The boys of Menhardoc).
Morgan's horror: a romance of the 'West Countree'. 1885.
Some stained pages: a story of life. 3 vols 1885, 1 vol [1888] (as The story of Antony Grace).
A terrible coward; and, Son Philip. [1885.]
Brownsmith's boy. 1886, 1892.
The chaplain's craze: being the mystery of Findon Friars. 1886.
Double cunning: the tale of a transparent mystery. 3 vols 1886, 1 vol 1886.
The Master of the Ceremonies: a novel. 3 vols 1886.
Patience wins: or war in the works. 1886, 1893.
The bag of diamonds. [1887.]
Devon boys: a tale of the north shore. 1887, 1905, [1930].
Lord John: or a search for gold. [1887.]
One maid's mischief: a novel. 3 vols 1887.
This man's wife: a novel. 3 vols 1887.
Yussuf the guide: being the strange story of the travels in Asia Minor of Burne the lawyer, Preston the professor, and Lawrence the sick. 1887, [1894].
Commodore Junk. 1888.
Dick o' the Fens: a tale of the great east swamp. 1888, 1906, [1936].
In marine armour: being the adventures of Abel Dane. [1888], [1927].
The man with a shadow. 3 vols 1888.
Mother Carey's chicken: her voyage to the unknown isle. 1888, 1893.
The traveller. Illustr J. Finnemore, ed G. C. Haité 1888. Poem.
Crown and sceptre: a West Country story. [1889], [1907].
A cure of souls. 1889 (Christmas no of Good Words).
The lass that loved a soldier. 3 vols 1889.
Of high descent: a novel. 3 vols 1889. Serialised in Good Words as The haute noblesse.
Quicksilver: or the boy with no skid to his wheel. 1889, 1897.
Staunch: a story of steel. [1889], [1927] (as Staunch as steel).
Three boys: or the chiefs of the Clan Mackhai. 1889.
Three people's secret: a tale of the faculty. [1889.]
Cutlass and cudgel. [1890], 1911, [1914].
A double knot: a novel. 3 vols 1890.
A fluttered dovecote. [1890], 1899.
Lady Maude's mania: a tragedy in high life. 1890.
Mass' George: or a boy's adventures in the old savannahs. [1890.]
The mutiny of the 'Helen Gray'. [1890.]
The Mynns' mystery. 1890.
Burr junior: his struggles and studies at Old Browne's school. [1891], 1916.
Mahme Nousie. 2 vols 1891.
'Nolens volens': or the adventures of Don Lavington. [1891], [1896] (as The adventures of Don Lavington).
Princess Fédor's pledge, and other stories. [1891.]
The Rajah of Dah. 1891.
Sawn off. 1891. Also contains The gilded pill.
Syd Belton: the boy who would not go to sea. 1891.
To the West. 1891.
The crystal hunters: a boy's adventures in the higher Alps. [1892], [1936].
The Dingo boys: or the squatters of Wallaby Range. 1892.
Gil the gunner: or the youngest officer in the East. [1892].
The Grand Chaco: a boy's adventures in an unknown land. [1892], [1907] (as Rob Harlow's adventures), [1935].
King of the castle: a novel. 3 vols 1892.
The weathercock: being the adventures of a boy with a bias. [1892.]
The black bar. 1893.
Blue jackets: or the log of the Teaser. [1893], [1912].
In mid-air. [1893], [1924].
Nurse Elisia. 2 vols 1893.
Sail-ho!: or a boy at sea. [1893], [1907].
Steve Young: or the voyage of the 'Hvalross' to the icy seas. [1893], [1910].
A sylvan courtship. [1893.]
Witness to the deed. 3 vols 1893.
First in the field: a story of New South Wales. [1894], [1936].
Fire Island: being the adventures of uncertain naturalists in an unknown track. 1894.
In an alpine valley. 3 vols 1894.
A life's eclipse. [1894.]
Real gold: a story of adventure. 1894.
The star-gazers. 3 vols 1894.
The tiger lily: a story of two passions. 2 vols 1894.
The vast abyss: being the story of Tom Blount, his uncles, and his cousin Sam. [1894.]
The White Virgin. 2 vols 1894.
Cormorant Crag: a tale of the smuggling days. [1895], [1912], [1935].
Diamond Dyke, or the lone farm on the veldt: a story of South African adventure. 1895.
An electric spark. 1895.
Planter Jack: or the cinnamon garden. [1895.]
The queen's scarlet: being the adventures and misadventures of Sir Richard Frayne. 1895.

The Black Tor: a tale of the reign of James I. 1896.
The case of Ailsa Gray. 1896.
Cursed by a fortune. 1896.
In honour's cause: a tale of the days of George the First. [1896], [1936].
Jack at sea: or all work and no play made him a dull boy. [1896.]
Roy Royland, or the young castellan: a tale of the Civil War. 1896.
Sappers and miners: or the flood beneath the sea. 1896, [1899].
Smith's weakness: the simple tale of an uphill fight. [1896.]
Frank and Saxon: a tale of the days of Good Queen Bess. [1897.]
High play: a comedy off the stage. 1897.
The little skipper: a son of a sailor. [1897.]
Vince the rebel: or the sanctuary in the bog. 1897.
Draw swords!: in the horse artillery. 1898.
Jungle and stream: or the adventures of two boys in Siam. 1898, [1935].
Nic Revel: a white slave's adventures in alligator land. 1898.
Our soldier boy. [1898.]
The silver salvors: a tale of a treasure found and lost. [1898.]
A woman worth winning. 1898.
A crimson crime. 1899.
Fix bay'nets!: or the regiment in the hills. 1899.
In the mahdi's grasp. [1899], [1935].
King o' the beach: a tropic tale. [1899.]
Ned Leger: the adventures of a middy on the Spanish Main. [1899.]
The Vibart affair. 1899.
Young Robin Hood. [1899.]
Charge!: a story of Briton and Boer. [1900.]
King Robert's page. [1900.]
Old gold: or the cruise of the 'Jason' brig. [1900.]
Uncle Bart: the tale of a tyrant. [1900.]
The cankerworm: being episodes of a woman's life. 1901.
Ching, the Chinaman and his middy friends. [1901.]
A dash from Diamond City. [1901.]
The king's sons. [1901.]
The kopje garrison: a tale of the Boer War. 1901.
Pulabad: or the bravery of a boy. 1901.
Running amok: a story of adventure. 1901.
Black shadows. 1902.
Coastguard Jack. [1902.]
The lost middy: being the secret of the smugglers' gap. [1902.]
A meeting of Greeks and the tug of war. 1902.
The peril finders. [1902.]
Stan Lynn: a boy's adventures in China. 1902.
Two rough stones; and, A bad day's fishing. [1902.]
Fitz the filibuster. [1903.]
It came to pass. 1903.
The kings' esquires: or the jewel of France. 1903.
Memoir of Benjamin Franklin Stevens. 1903. Biography.
Walsh the wonder-worker. 1903.
Will of the mill. [1903.]
A young hero. [1903.]
Blind policy. 1904.
Coming home to roost: a tale of a Welsh haven. 1904.
Glyn Severn's school-days. 1904.
The khedive's country: the Nile Valley and its products; edited by G. Manville Fenn. 1904.
Marcus: the young centurion. [1904.]
The ocean cat's-paw: the story of a strange cruise. [1904.]
The powder monkey. [1904.]
To win or to die: a tale of the Klondike gold craze. [1904.]
Nephew Jack: his cruise for his uncle's craze. [1905.]
Shoulder arms!: a tale of two soldiers' sons. 1905.
So like a woman. 1905.
Trapper Dan: a story of the backwoods. [1905.]
Aynsley's case. 1906.
Dead man's land: being the voyage to Zimbambangwe of certain and uncertain blacks and whites. [1906.]
Hunting the skipper: or the cruise of the 'Seafowl' sloop. [1906.]
'Tention!: a story of boy-life during the Peninsular War. 1906.
The traitor's gait and other stories. 1906.
A country squire: being an impossible story. 1907.
George Alfred Henty: the story of an active life. 1907. Biography.
Trapped by Malays: a tale of bayonet and kris. 1907.
Sir Hilton's sin: a novel. 1908, [1920], [1924].
Jack, the rascal: a country story. [1909.]
George Manville Fenn also contributed stories to Once a Week *and to various annuals and collections. He edited the* World of wit and humour, *and collaborated on several plays.* [EH]

Jane Helen Findlater 1866–1946

§1

The green graves of Balgowrie. 1896, 1896 (3rd edn), New York 1896, London 1898, New York [19??], London [1904] (5th edn), 1914, New York [1914].
REVIEWS: Athenaeum 3579 1896; Nation 98 1914; New York Times 8 Mar 1914; Outlook Apr 1914.
A daughter of strife. 1897, New York 1897.
Rachel. 1899. New York 1899, London 1902, 1920.
REVIEWS: Athenaeum 3727 1899; Nation 69 1899.
Tales that are told. With M. Findlater. 1901.
REVIEW: Athenaeum 3841 1901.
The story of a mother. 1902, 1903.
The affair at the inn. 1904, Boston and New York 1904. With M. Findlater, K. D. Wiggin and A. McAulay.
Stones from a glass house. 1904.
All that happened in a week: a story for little children. 1905, [1919].
The ladder to the stars. 1906, New York 1906.
REVIEWS: Acad 71 1906; Athenaeum 4122 1906; The Times 5 Oct 1906; New York Times 20 Oct 1906; Spectator 97 1906; Dial 42 1907.
Crossriggs. 1908, 1908 (2nd edn), 1910, New York 1913, London [1914], [1919], 1924, 1926, 1986 (introd by P. Binding). With M. Findlater.
REVIEWS: Athenaeum 4203 1908; Spectator 100 1908; TLS 7 May 1908; Nation 96 1913.
Penny Monypenny. 1911, 1912, New York 1913, London [1918]. With M. Findlater.
REVIEWS: Athenaeum 4385 1911; Punch 141 1911; Saturday Rev 112 1911; Spectator 107 1911; Bookman 41 1912; Nation 96 1913; New York Times 2 Mar 1913.
Robinetta. 1911, Boston and New York [1911]. With M. Findlater, K. D. Wiggin and A. McAulay.
REVIEW: Athenaeum 4361 1911.
Seven Scots stories. 1912 (illustr H. W. Kerr), New York 1913.
REVIEWS: Bookman 43 1912; New York Times 2 Mar 1913; Outlook 103 1913; Saturday Rev 115 1913; Spectator 110 1913.
Content with flies. 1916, New York 1916. With M. Findlater.
REVIEWS: Bookman 50 1916; Dial 61 1916; Nation 103 1916; New York Times 3 Dec 1916; Spectator 116 1916; TLS 6 Apr 1916.
Seen and heard before and after 1914. 1916, New York 1916, London 1917. Stories. With M. Findlater.
REVIEWS: TLS 30 Nov 1916; Dial 62 1917; Nation 104 1917; New York Times 13 May 1917; Spectator 118 1917.
A green grass widow and other stories. 1921.
REVIEW: Bookman 60 1921; Punch 160 1921.
Beneath the visiting moon. 1923. With M. Findlater.
REVIEWS: Bookman 64 1923; TLS 3 May 1923; New Statesman 12 May 1923.

Contributions to periodicals

The other grace. Nat Rev 29 1897.
The sisters of Balgowrie. Living Age 212 1897.

Between two. Living Age 216 1898.
George Borrow. Cornhill Mag 80, Nov 1899.
Point of view. Nat Rev 32 1899.
The Scot of fiction. Atlantic Monthly 84 1899.
The art of narration. Nat Rev 34 1900.
The slum movement in fiction. Nat Rev 35 1900.
Great war novels. Nat Rev 37 1901.
Religious novels. Nat Rev 39 1902.
The islander. New England Mag 28 1903.
Observations on modern tragedy. Nat Rev 42 1904.
Fiction: is it deteriorating? Nat Rev 43 1904.
United States: the land of effort. Nat Rev 45 1905.
Ibsen the reformer. Nat Rev 48 1907.
Bairn-keeper. Living Age 260 1909.
Novels of Fogazzaro. Living Age 260 1909.
Ower young to marry yet. Living Age 264 1910.
Three sides to a question. Living Age 264 1910.
Charlie over the water. Living Age 268 1911.
Compulsory rations. Living Age 296 1918.

§2

Mackenzie, E. The Findlater sisters. Literature and friendship. 1964.
Blain, V., P. Clements and I. Grundy. The feminist companion to literature in English. 1990.
Nichols, J. M. Rediscovering the novels of Mary and Jane Findlater. ELT 37 1994.

Mary Williamina Findlater 1865–1963

§1

Sonnets and songs. 1895
Over the hills. 1897, New York 1897.
REVIEWS: Athenaeum 3655 1897; Nation 98 1914; New York Times 8 Mar 1914; Outlook Apr 1914.
Betty Musgrave. 1899, 1899 (2nd edn), New York 1913.
REVIEWS: Athenaeum 3742 1899; Punch 116 1899; Nation 97 1913; New York Times 7 Dec 1913.
A narrow way. 1901, New York [nd].
REVIEWS: Athenaeum 3828 1901; Punch 120 1901; Nation 97 1913; New York Times 7 Dec 1913.
Tales that are told. 1901. With J. Findlater.
REVIEW: Athenaeum 3841 1901.
The rose of joy. 1903, New York 1903.
REVIEWS: Athenaeum 3961 1903; Bookman 25 1903.
The affair at the inn. 1904, Boston and New York 1904. With J. Findlater, K. D. Wiggin and A. McAulay.
A blind bird's nest. 1907, 1909 (illus).
REVIEWS: Bookman 31 1907; Punch 132 1907.
Crossriggs. 1908, 1908 (2nd edn), 1910, New York 1913, London [1914], [1919], 1924, 1926, 1986 (introd by P. Binding). With J. Findlater.
REVIEWS: Athenaeum 4203 1908; Spectator 100 1908; TLS 7 May 1908; Nation 96 1913.
Penny Monypenny. 1911, 1912, New York 1913, London [1918]. With J. Findlater.
REVIEWS: Athenaeum 4385 1911; Punch 141 1911; Saturday Rev 112 1911; Spectator 107 1911; Bookman 41 1912; Nation 96 1913; New York Times 2 Mar 1913.
Robinetta. 1911, Boston and New York [1911]. With J. Findlater, K. D. Wiggin and A. McAulay.
REVIEW: Athenaeum 4361 1911.
Tents of a night. 1914, New York [1914].
REVIEWS: Athenaeum 4522 1914; Bookman 47 1914; New York Times 6 Sep 1914; Saturday Rev 118 1914; Spectator 112 1914.
Content with flies. 1916, New York 1916. With J. Findlater.
REVIEWS: Bookman 50 1916; Dial 61 1916; Nation 103 1916; New York Times 3 Dec 1916; Spectator 116 1916; TLS 6 Apr 1916.
Seen and heard before and after 1914. 1916, New York 1916, London 1917. Stories. With J. Findlater.
REVIEW: TLS 30 Nov 1916; Dial 62 1917; New York Times 13 May 1917; Spectator 118 1917.
Beneath the visiting moon. 1923. With J. Findlater.
REVIEWS: Bookman 64 1923; TLS 3 May 1923; New Statesman 12 May 1923.

Contributions to periodicals

Void of understanding. Cornhill Mag 80, Sep 1899.
Amid the orchids. Scribner's Mag 37, May 1905.
To an old lady: poem. Outlook 105 1913.

§2

The Times 26 Nov 1963.
Mackenzie, E. The Findlater sisters. Literature and friendship. 1964.
Nichols, J. M. Rediscovering the novels of Mary and Jane Findlater. ELT 37 1994.

Percy Hetherington Fitzgerald 1834–1925

Roman candles. 1861.
The night mail: its passengers, and how they fared at Christmas. 1862.
The story of the Incumbered Estates Court. 1862. From All the Year Round.
Mildrington the barrister: a romance. 2 vols 1863. Anon.
Two English essayists: Charles Lamb and Charles Dickens. 1863.
The Rev Alfred Hoblush and his curacies: a memoir. 1863.
Bella donna, or the cross before the name: a romance. 2 vols 1864. Pbd under the pseud 'Gilbert Dyce'.
The life of Laurence Sterne. 2 vols 1864.
'Le sport' at Baden: a picture of watering-place life and manners. 1864.
Fairy Alice. 2 vols 1865.
A famous forgery: being the story of the unfortunate Dr Dodd. 1865.
Never forgotten. 3 vols 1865.
Charles Lamb: his friends, his haunts and his books. 1866.
Charles Townshend: wit and statesman. 1866.
Jenny Bell: a story. 3 vols 1866.
The second Mrs Tillotson: a story, reprinted from All the Year Round. 3 vols 1866.
Polly: a village portrait. 2 vols 1867. Anon.
School days at Saxonhurst, illustrated by 'Phiz'. 1867.
Seventy-five Brooke Street: a story. 3 vols 1867.
The dear girl. 3 vols 1868.
Diana Gay: or the history of a young lady. 3 vols 1868. First pbd in Belgravia.
The life of David Garrick from original family papers. 2 vols 1868, 1899 (rev).
Autobiography of a small boy. 1869. Anon.
Fatal zero: a Homburg diary. 2 vols 1869, 1 vol 1886.
Proverbs and comediettas written for private representation. 1869.
Beauty Talbot. 3 vols 1870.
Principles of comedy and dramatic effect. 1870.
The Kembles: an account of the Kemble family. 2 vols [1871].
Two fair daughters. 3 vols 1871.
Life and adventures of Alexander Dumas. 2 vols 1873.
The middle-aged lover: a story. 2 vols 1873.
The romance of the English stage. 2 vols 1874.
The life of Samuel Johnson [by Boswell], edited with new notes. 3 vols 1874, 1888.
The life, letters and writings of Charles Lamb, edited with notes. 6 vols 1876, 4 vols 1882.
The parvenu family: or Phoebe, girl and wife. 3 vols 1876.
Little Dorinda: who won and who lost her! [1878.]

Croker's Boswell and Boswell: studies in the life of Johnson. 1880.
The life of George the Fourth. 2 vols 1881.
The world behind the scenes. 1881.
Young Coelebs. 3 vols 1881.
A new history of the English stage. 2 vols 1882.
The Royal Dukes and Princesses of the family of George III: a view of court life and manners for seventy years 1760–1830. 2 vols 1882.
Recreations of a literary man: or does writing pay? 2 vols 1882.
Kings and Queens of an hour: records of love, romance, oddity and adventure. 2 vols 1883.
The lady of Brantome. 1884.
The life and times of William IV. 2 vols 1884.
Puppets: a romance. 3 vols 1884.
The art of the stage as set out in Lamb's dramatic essays, with a commentary. 1885.
Lives of the Sheridans. 2 vols 1886.
The book fancier: or the romance of book collecting. 1886.
A day's tour: a journey through France and Belgium .... 1887.
Chronicles of Bow Street police office .... 2 vols 1888.
The life and times of John Wilkes, MP .... 2 vols 1888.
Life of Mrs Catherine Clive. 1888.
Music-hall land. [1890.]
King Theodore of Corsica. 1890.
The story of 'Bradshaw's Guide'. 1890.
Words for the worldly. [1890.]
Life of James Boswell. 2 vols 1891.
Editing à la mode: an examination [of G. Birkbeck Hill's Boswell]. [1891.]
The history of Pickwick .... 1891.
Three weeks at Mopetown: or humours of a hydro. 1891.
The art of acting. 1892.
The bachelor's dilemma and other stories, gay and grave. [1892.]
Henry Irving: a record of twenty years at the Lyceum. 1893, 1895 (rev).
Memoirs of an author. 2 vols 1894.
The Savoy Opera and the Savoyards. 1894.
Bozland: Dickens' places and people. 1895.
Stonyhurst memories: or six years at school. 1895.
Pickwickian manners and customs. [1897.]
A critical examination of Dr G. Birkbeck Hill's 'Johnsonian' editions. 1898.
The good Queen Charlotte. 1899.
The Pickwickian dictionary and cyclopaedia. [1902.]
John Forster. 1903.
Lightning tours. 1903.
Pickwickian wit and humour. 1903.
The Garrick Club. 1904.
Lady Jean: the romance of the great Douglas cause. 1904.
Robert Adam. 1904.
The life of Charles Dickens, as revealed in his writings. 2 vols 1905.
Sir Henry Irving: a biography. 1906.
Josephine's troubles: a story of the great Franco-German war of 1870–1. [1907.]
Shakespearian representation: its law and limits. 1908.
Samuel Foote: a biography. 1910.
Boswell's autobiography. 1912.
Jane Austen: a criticism and appreciation. 1912.
An output: a list of writings on many divine subjects, of sculptures, dramas, music, lectures, tours, collections, clubs, and public donations, being a record of work done during a long and busy life, 1850–1912. [1912] (for private circulation).
Pickwick riddles and perplexities. 1912.
Memories of Charles Dickens. 1913.
Worldlyman: a modern morality of our day .... [1913.]
Fitzgerald also wrote a number of books on Roman Catholicism, London etc.

Jessie Fothergill 1851–91

Mss: Letters in archives of Kegan Paul, Trench, Trübner & Henry S. King 1858–1912 (micro), archives of Richard Bentley & Son 1829–98 (micro).

Bibliographies

Crisp, J. Jessie Fothergill. Victorian Fiction Research Guide 2. St Lucia, Queensland 1980.

§1

Healey: a romance. 3 vols 1875, '1884' [1883], New York [1885], London 1900.
REVIEWS: Athenaeum 14 Aug 1875; Saintsbury, G. Acad 4 Sep 1875; Spectator 2 Oct 1875.
Aldyth: or 'Let the end try the man'. 2 vols '1877' [1876], 1891, 1899.
REVIEWS: Athenaeum 3 Feb 1877; Graphic 10 Feb 1877; Saturday Rev 24 Feb 1877; Alleyne, F. M. Acad 10 Mar 1877; Spectator 5 May 1877.
The first violin. 3 vols 1877 (unpbd, *see* M. Sadleir, XIX Century Fiction 1951), first pbd anon Temple Bar Jan–Dec 1878, 'by J. F.' 3 vols 1878, New York 1878, 2 vols Leipzig 1878, 'by J. F.' London 1879, New York [1894], London 1899, New York 1900, [190?], 1904, London 1909, New York [1915]; tr Fr 1887. Dramatised versions: New York 1896 (*see* Dramatic compositions copyrighted in the US 1870 to 1916, Washington 1918); New York 1897 (ibid); London [1898] (*see* Nineteenth century readers guide to periodical lit) 1899; (*see* DNB 1908–9).
REVIEWS: Athenaeum 2 Nov 1878; Saturday Rev 8 Mar 1979.
Probation. First pbd anon Temple Bar Jan–Dec 1879, 3 vols 1879, New York 1879, London 1880, 2 vols Leipzig 1881, New York [189?], London 1899.
REVIEW: Graphic 21 1880.
The Wellfields. 3 vols 1880, New York 1880, London 1881, 1900; tr Polish 2 vols 1887.
REVIEWS: Athenaeum 18 Sep 1880; Spectator 2 Oct 1880; Owen, F. W. Acad 16 Oct 1880.
Made or marred. 1881, New York 1881, with 'One of three' 1881.
REVIEWS: Barnett Smith, G. Acad 20 Aug 1881; Athenaeum 27 Aug 1881; Graphic 17 Sep 1881; Spectator 21 Oct 1881.
'One of three'. 1881, with Made or marred New York 1881.
REVIEWS: Henley, W. E. Acad 27 Aug 1881; Athenaeum 27 Aug 1881; Graphic 17 Sep 1881.
Kith and kin. First pbd Temple Bar Jan–Dec 1881, 3 vols 1881, 1882, 1899, 1903; tr Polish 1883.
REVIEWS: Athenaeum 22 Oct 1881; Saturday Rev 22 Oct 1881; Monkhouse, C. Acad 29 Oct 1881; Graphic 5 Nov 1881; Spectator 27 May 1882.
Peril. First pbd Temple Bar Jan–Dec 1884, 3 vols 1884, 2 vols Leipzig 1885, New York [1885].
REVIEWS: Ashcroft Noble, J. Acad 26, July–Dec 1884; Athenaeum 8 Nov 1884; Graphic 29 Nov 1884; Saturday Rev 6 Dec 1884.
Borderland: a country-town chronicle. 3 vols 1886, 1887, New York [1887], London 1899.
REVIEWS: Barnett Smith, G. Acad 18 Dec 1886; Athenaeum 1 Jan 1887; Graphic 8 Jan 1887; Spectator 5 Mar 1887.
The lasses of Leverhouse. First pbd Bolton Weekly Jnl 1878–9 (according to author's note in next item), 1888 ('revised and corrected'), New York 1888, London [1913].
REVIEWS: Athenaeum 2 June 1888; Acad 23 June 1888; Graphic 11 Aug 1888.
From Moor Isles; a love story. First pbd Temple Bar Jan–Nov 1888, 3 vols 1888, 1894, 1900.
REVIEWS: Athenaeum 13 Oct 1888; Sharp, W. Acad 27 Oct 1888; Spectator 24 Nov 1888; Murray's Mag July–Dec 1888.
A march in the ranks. 3 vols 1890, nd, New York nd, London [1910].
REVIEWS: Ashcroft Noble, J. Acad 22 Feb 1890; Spectator 22 Feb 1890; Nation 4 Sep 1890.

Oriole's daughter. 3 vols 1893, 1893, New York [1893?].
REVIEWS: Athenaeum 15 Apr 1893; Spectator 22 Apr 1893; Barrow Allen, J. Acad 20 May 1893.

Contributions to periodicals

Temple Bar: 'Some American recollections' Feb 1886; 'Wuthering Heights' Dec 1887; 'Flowers and fire' Aug 1889.

§2

Obits: The Times 31 July 1891; Athenaeum 1 Aug 1891; Illus London News 8 Aug 1891; Walford, L. B. Critic New York 29 Aug 1891.
Gardiner, L. 'Jessie Fothergill's novels'. Novel Rev n.s. 1 1892.
Black, H. Notable women authors of the day. 1906.
Crisp, J. Jessie Fothergill. Victorian Fiction Research Guide 2. St Lucia, Queensland 1980. [JC]

Christina Catherine Fraser-Tytler, afterwards Liddell 1848–19??

§1

Sweet Violet, and other stories. 1869.
A Rose and a Pearl. 1870.
Jasmine Leigh. 1871, 1885.
Margaret. 2 vols 1872.
Mistress Judith: a Cambridgeshire story. 2 vols 1873.
Jonathan: a novel. 2 vols 1876, 1 vol 1887.
Making or marring. 1879.
The other half of the world. [1881.]
Songs in minor keys. 1881.
Songs of the twilight hours. [1909.]
Is sickness the will of God? 1906.
Debt. 1913.
A shepherd of the sheep: the life-story of an English parish-priest told by his wife. 1916. Biography. [EH]

Richard Garnett 1835–1906

See col 2343.

Charles Gibbon 1843–90

§1

Dangerous connexions: a novel. 3 vols 1864, 1 vol 1875.
The dead heart: a tale of the Bastille. 1865.
Robin Gray: a novel. 3 vols 1869, 1 vol 1872, 1877.
For lack of gold: a novel. 3 vols 1871, 1 vol 1873, 1877.
For the king. 2 vols 1872, 1 vol [1880].
In honour bound. 3 vols 1874, 1 vol [1880].
What will the world say?: a novel. 3 vols 1875, 1 vol 1880.
In love and war: a romance. 3 vols 1877, 1 vol [1880].
The life of George Combe, author of The constitution of man. 2 vols 1878. Biography.
In pastures green and other stories. 1880.
Queen of the Meadow: a novel. 3 vols 1880, 1 vol 1880.
The braes of Yarrow: a romance. 3 vols 1881.
A heart's problem. 2 vols 1881.
The flower of the forest: a romance. 1882.
The golden shaft. 3 vols 1882.
Of high degree: a story. 3 vols 1883.
By mead and stream: a novel. 3 vols 1884.
Fancy free and other stories. 3 vols 1884. Contains Fancy free, One of his inventions, and Loving a dream. Also pbd 1884 in 2 separate vols as Fancy free, and Loving a dream and One of his inventions.
In Cupid's wars: a novel. 3 vols 1884.
Garvock: a romance. 3 vols [1885].
A hard knot: a novel. 3 vols 1885, 1 vol 1886.
Heart's delight: a novel. 3 vols 1885.
Amoret: a romance. [1886.]
Clare of Claresmede: a romance. 3 vols 1886.
A maiden fair and other stories. [1886.]
A princess of Jutedom: a novel. 3 vols 1886, 1 vol 1887.
The shadow of wrong: a romance. [1886.]
Paying the penalty. [1887.]
Beyond compare: a story. 3 vols 1888.
Blood-money and other stories. 2 vols 1889.
A strange wooing: a story of the period. 1890.
Charles Gibbon also edited the Casquet of Lit. [EH]

R. Murray Gilchrist, Robert Murray Gilchrist

1868–1917

Main holding of mss in NYPL. See also LR.

Bibliographies

In A dictionary of English authors: biographical and bibliographical, ed R. F. Sharp, 1904, rptd Detroit 1978.
In Nineteenth century readers' guide to periodical literature 1890–1899, ed H. G. Cushing and A. V. Morris, New York 1944.
In Nineteenth-century fiction: a bibliographical catalogue based on the collection formed by Robert Lee Wolff, 5 vols New York 1981–6.

Selections

In Selected English short stories, ed H. Walker, 1930.
The basilisk. In The Daedalus book of decadence (Moral ruins), ed B. Stableford, Sawtry 1990, 1993.
Witch in-grain. In The Second Daedalus book of decadence: the black feast, ed B. Stableford, Sawtry 1992.

§1

Passion the plaything. A novel. 1890.
REVIEWS: Scots Observer 19 July 1890; Acad 16 Aug 1890.
Frangipanni. 1893 (Regent Lib).
REVIEW: Bookman Jan 1894.
Hercules and the marionettes. 1894 (illustr C. P. Sainton).
The stone dragon and other tragic romances. 1894, New York and London 1984 (facs of 1894 edn).
REVIEWS: Nat Observer 24 Feb 1894; Acad 7 Apr 1894.
A peakland faggot. Collected short stories. 1897, 1926.
REVIEW: Acad Suppl 10 July 1897.
Willowbrake. 1898.
REVIEWS: Athenaeum 6 Aug 1898; Bookman Oct 1898; Nation 6 Oct 1898.
The rue bargin: a story. 1898 (Sylvian series).
REVIEWS: Athenaeum 5 Nov 1898; Acad 19 Nov 1898.
Nicholas and Mary and other Milton folk. 1899.
The courtesy dame. 1900.
REVIEW: Athenaeum 8 Sep 1900.
The labyrinth. A romance. 1902.
REVIEWS: Acad 22 Mar 1902; Athenaeum 22 Mar 1902; Bookman Apr 1902; TLS 4 Apr 1902.
Natives of Milton. 1902.
REVIEWS: TLS 17 Oct 1902; Athenaeum 18 Oct 1902.
Beggar's manor. 1903.
REVIEWS: TLS 3 July 1903; Athenaeum 4 July 1903; Acad 11 July 1903; Bookman Aug 1903.
Lords and ladies. Stories. 1903.
REVIEW: Athenaeum 17 Oct 1903.
The gentle thespians. 1908.
REVIEW: Athenaeum 21 Mar 1908.
Good-bye to market: a collection of stories. Leek 1908.
REVIEW: Athenaeum 29 July 1908.
The abbey mystery: a novel. 1908.
The two Goodwins. 1908.
REVIEWS: Athenaeum 13 Feb 1909; Bookman Apr 1909.

Pretty Fanny's way. 1909.
Willowford Woods. 1911, 1921 (abridged).
REVIEWS: Athenaeum 26 Aug 1911; Bookman Sep 1911.
The first born. [1911.]
REVIEWS: Athenaeum 9 Sep 1911; Bookman Oct 1911.
The secret tontine. 1912.
Damosel Croft. A novel. [1912.]
The Dukeries. 1913 (Beautiful England ser, illustr E. W. Haslehust).
Roadknight. A novel. [1913.]
REVIEW: Bookman June 1913.
Weird wedlock. 1913.
The chase. A story. 1914, 1921.
REVIEW: Athenaeum 6 Dec 1914.
Ripon & Harrogate. 1914 (Beautiful England ser, painted by E. Haslehust).
Scarborough and neighbourhood. 1914 (Beautiful England ser, painted by E. Haslehust).
Under cover of night. 1914.
REVIEW: Athenaeum 12 Sep 1914.
Honeysuckle rogue: a novel. 1917.
The climax. A comedy in one act. London and Glasgow 1928 (Repertory Plays no 67).

Contributions to periodicals

Ludgate Mag. In the land of romance, Apr 1892.
Nat Observer. 2 July 1892–3 Feb 1894.
Yellow Book. Crimson weaver, July 1895.
Pall Mall Mag. Nov 1900–June 1904.
Windsor Mag. For owd time's sake, Feb 1902.
Temple Bar. The charity of widow Ogden, June 1906.
The Idler. Apr 1906–June 1910.
Cornhill. My dowager, Sep 1912.

§2

Sharp, E. A. In her William Sharp (Fiona Macleod): a memoir, 1910, New York 1910, 2 vols 1912.
The Times 7 Apr 1917. Obituary.
Phillpotts, E. Letter. TLS 12 Apr 1917.
Phillpots, E. Bookman June 1917.
Moult, T. Bookman Oct 1926. [DA]

George Gissing 1857–1903

The three main sources of material are the Beinecke Library at Yale, which contains much family correspondence, the letters to Bertz and miscellaneous correspondents and mss of poems and short stories, and of The town traveller; *the Berg Collection NYPL, which also holds much family correspondence and letters to many minor correspondents and mss of short stories and of* Demos, The emancipated, New Grub Street *and* Will Warburton; *the Lilly Library, Indiana University, which has acquired the material formerly held by the Carl H. Pforzheimer Library, that is numerous letters, including the most significant ones to literary agents, and mss of early work in verse and prose and of* Isabel Clarendon, Charles Dickens: a critical study, By the Ionian sea, The private papers of Henry Ryecroft *(first version) and* Veranilda. *Other important collections are in the Huntington, which possesses the mss of* Thyrza, The nether world, Denzil Quarrier, Born in exile, In the year of jubilee, Eve's ransom, The whirlpool *and* The crown of life; *Colgate University Library (letters and mss of short stories); the Boston Public Library (letters to Ellen Gissing); the Pierpont Morgan Library (letters and early mss); HRHRC (letters and the ms of* Workers in the dawn); *the Turnbull Library, Wellington NZ (ms of* Our friend the charlatan); *the University of Illinois at Urbana-Champaign (letters to H. G. Wells) and the Royal Society for the Protection of Birds (letters to W. H. Hudson and one chapter of* A life's morning). *Further details will be found in the* Location register, vol 1 1988 *and* IELM, vol 4 pt 1. *Many items of current and permanent interest will be found in the* Gissing Newsletter 1965–1990 *and in the* Gissing Jnl *1991–* .

Bibliographies

Danielson, H. In his Bibliographies of modern authors, 1921.
Wise, T. J. The Ashley Library, vols 2 1922, 9 1927, 10 1930.
Quinn, J. Complete catalogue of the library of John Quinn, Anderson Galleries, 10 Dec 1923.
Scott, T. In his edn of Gissing, Critical studies of the works of Charles Dickens, New York 1924.
Notes on sales. TLS, 3 Mar 1927.
Kern, J. The library of Jerome Kern, Anderson Galleries, 7–10 July 1929.
Sotheby catalogue, 19 June 1930.
Cutler, B. D. and V. Stiles. Modern British authors: their first editions. 1930.
Schwartz, J. In his 1100 obscure points, 1931.
Books for sale. Publishers' Weekly, 23 Apr 1932.
Adams, G. M. How and why I collect George Gissing. Colophon pt 18, 1934. Facs of Account of books 1880–98.
The first editions of Gissing's works. More Books, Boston, Feb 1936.
Niebling, R. F. The Adams-Gissing collection. YULG, Jan 1942.
Wing, D. The Adams-Gissing collection. YULG, Jan 1944.
Notes on recent acquisitions. YULG, Jan 1946 and Apr 1947.
Ransom, W. Selective check lists of press books. New York 1947.
Sadleir, M. Nineteenth-century fiction. 2 vols 1951.
Recent acquisitions. YULG, July 1952.
Bibliographical notes on Gissing. Eng Fiction in Transition 1 no 1, Fall–Winter 1957, Spring–Summer 1958, Autumn 1958, Spring 1959; 3 no 2, 1960; 4 no 1, 1961; Eng Lit in Transition 6 no 4, 1963; 7 nos 1 and 2, 1964; 8 no 5, 1965; 9 no 4, 1966; 11 no 1, 1968; 14 no 1, 1971.
Daniels, E. From a Gissing collection. Philobiblon (Colgate Univ Lib), June 1961.
Gordan, J. D. New in the Berg Collection 1959–61. Exhibition NYPL 1964.
Coustillas, P. Gissing's short stories: a bibliography. Eng Lit in Transition 7 no 2, 1964. For addns see Gissing Newsletter, then Gissing Jnl passim.
Korg, J. George Gissing. In Victorian fiction: a guide to research, ed L. Stevenson, Cambridge MA 1964.
A creative century: selections from the twentieth century collections at the University of Texas 1964.
Gordan, J. D. Novels in manuscript. An exhibition from the Berg collection NYPL 1965. On ms of New Grub Street.
Coustillas, P. Gissing's writings on Dickens. A biobibliographical survey. Dickensian, Autumn 1965.
Gordan, J. D. An anniversary exhibition. The Henry W. and Albert A. Berg collection 1940–1965 NYPL 1965. The holograph diaries.
Schulz, H. C. English literary manuscripts in the Huntington. HLQ, May 1968. Mss of 8 Gissing novels, his memorandum book and 8 letters.
Coustillas, P. Collecting George Gissing. Book Collecting and Lib Monthly, May 1968.
Coustillas, P. In search of Gissing memories in Switzerland. Book Collecting and Lib Monthly, Dec 1968.
Spiers, J. and P. Coustillas. A George Gissing bibliography. Book Collecting and Lib Monthly, Sep–Nov 1969.
Howard-Hill, T. H. Bibliography of British literary bibliographies. 1969.
Coustillas, P. Gissing's writings on Dickens: a bibliographical survey 1969, rptd 1971. With 2 uncollected articles on Dickens.
Koike, S., G. Kamo, C. C. Kohler and P. Coustillas. Gissing East and West. 1970.
Coustillas, P. Gissing's library. Gissing Newsletter, Apr 1971.
Spiers, J. and P. Coustillas. The rediscovery of George Gissing. Nat Book League, 1971.
Szladits, L. L. New in the Berg collection 1965–69. NYPL 1971.

Korg, J. George Gissing: a survey of research and criticism. Br Stud Monitor, Summer 1973.
Krishnamurti, G. The eighteen-nineties. A literary exhibition. Nat Book League, 4–21 Sep 1973.
Wolff, J. J. George Gissing: an annotated bibliography of writings about him. De Kalb IL 1974.
Victorian social fiction: an exhibition catalogue. Ed M. Jefferson 1975.
Collie, M. George Gissing: a bibliography. 1975, 1985 (rev).
Halperin, J. The Gissing revival 1961–1974. Stud in the Novel, Spring 1976.
The English novel: twentieth-century criticism. Vol 1, Defoe through Hardy. Ed R. J. Dunn, Chicago 1976.
Victorian fiction: a second guide to research. Ed G. Ford, New York 1978.
Foley, A. M. George Gissing 1857–1903. In Research guide to biography and criticism, vol 1 ed W. Beacham, Washington DC 1985.
Cagle, W. R. and D. Gossy. Two hundred and fifty years of the British novel 1740–1989, Lilly Lib, Indiana Univ, Bloomington 1990.
George Gissing. Jarndyce illus catalogue 85, Spring 1992, introd by P. Coustillas.
F[reeman], A. George Gissing 1857–1903. Books, manuscripts and letters. A chronological catalogue of the Pforzheimer Library. Bernard Quaritch 1992.
[Loomis, R.]. George Gissing. Yarmouth ME 1994. Catalogue 50 of Sumner & Stillman.
Freeman, A. George Gissing (1857–1903): an exhibition of books, manuscripts and letters from the Pforzheimer collection in the Lilly Library. Bloomington IN 1994.

Selections

Selections autobiographical and imaginative from the works of George Gissing, with biographical and critical notes by his son [A. C. Gissing]. Introd by V. Woolf 1929; New York 1929.
Short stories of to-day and yesterday. Introd by F. H. P[ritchard] 1929. Contains The prize lodger, Miss Rodney's leisure, The firebrand, A victim of circumstances, An inspiration, The justice and the vagabond, One way of happiness, An old maid's triumph, The poet's portmanteau, A charming family, Our Mr Jupp, Comrades in arms.
Six short stories. Ed F. Badolato, Treviso 1973. Contains Spellbound, The schoolmaster's vision, The fate of Humphrey Snell, The light on the tower, An inspiration, A victim of circumstances.
The salt of the earth and other stories. Ed F. Badolato, Brescia 1978. Contains title story, A charming family, A lodger in Maze Pond, The scrupulous father, A daughter of the lodge, One way of happiness, The justice and the vagabond.
Three short stories by George Gissing. Introd by John Michell, Christmas 1984 (priv ptd). Contains A poor gentleman, Under an umbrella, The prize lodger.
Aphorisms and reflections. Ed with introd by P. F. Kropholler, Edinburgh 1989.
The day of silence and other stories. Ed P. Coustillas 1993 (EL). Contains Lou and Liz, title story, Fleet-footed Hester, In honour bound, Their pretty ways, The fate of Humphrey Snell, An inspiration, The foolish virgin, One way of happiness, A freak of nature, A poor gentleman, Humplebee, The scrupulous father, A daughter of the lodge, Christopherson, Miss Rodney's leisure.

§1

For contemporary reviews see Gissing: the critical heritage, *ed P. Coustillas and C. Partridge, 1972. Only the major reviews not rptd or listed in the book are given here. For reviews in* London Figaro, *see P. Coustillas,* Gissing and the London Figaro, Gissing Jnl *Oct 1991; for those in the Australian and NZ press see C. M. Wyatt and P. Coustillas,* Gissing Down under, Gissing Newsletter *Oct 1988–July 1989; for those in the Chicago press see R. L. Selig and P. Coustillas,* Gissing Jnl, *Apr 1993, Jan–Apr 1994, Jan 1995, Oct 1995; for those in the* Boston Evening Transcript, *see Bonnie Zare and P. Coustillas,* Gissing Jnl *July 1997. For Jap pbns see headnote to* Short stories *below.*

Workers in the dawn: a novel. 3 vols 1880; 2-vol stillborn edn New York (Bowling Green Press), introd by R. West 1930 (proofs at Yale and Lilly Lib); ed R. Shafer 2 vols New York 1935, 3 vols in 1 1968, 3 vols in 1 1976; ed P. Coustillas, Brighton and New York 1985.
REVIEW: (A. Besant) Nat Reformer, 22 Aug 1880.
The unclassed: a novel. 3 vols 1884, 1895 (rev, preface by Gissing), 1895 (Colonial edn); New York 1896 (rev, preface by Gissing), c. 1898; London 1901, 1905, 1911, 1915, 1930 (Essex Lib); New York 1968; ed J. Korg, Hassocks 1976, Cranbury NJ 1976; ed J. Korg, Brighton and New York 1983. Tr Jap 1998.
REVIEWS: Manchester Guardian, 24 Dec 1895; Detroit Free Press, 18 May 1896; Boston Sunday Post, 24 May 1896; Buffalo Commercial, 30 May 1896; Illus Buffalo Express, 31 May 1896; San Francisco Call, 31 May 1896; Buffalo Courier, 7 June 1896; (G. H. Payne) Commercial Advertiser (New York), 13 June 1896.
Demos: a story of English socialism. 3 vols 1886 (anon), 1 vol 1886 (anon); New York 1886 (anon); 2 vols Leipzig (Tauchnitz) 1886 (anon); London 1888; serialised in Manchester Weekly Times, 20 July 1889–1 Feb 1890; London 1890, 1892, 1897, 1908 (Smith & Elder, John Murray), [1915] (Wayfarer's Lib), introd by M. Roberts, 1927, 1928; introd by M. Roberts, New York, c. 1929, introd by J. Korg 1971; ed P. Coustillas, Brighton 1972, rptd Hassocks 1974, rptd Brighton and New York 1982. Tr Fr 1890, Rus in Vestnik Evropy, Jan–May 1891, Ger 3 vols 1892, 3 vols in 1 1893, Polish in Niwa, 15 July 1891–15 May 1892.
REVIEWS: Whitehall Rev, 8 Apr 1886; Manchester Examiner and Times, 26 May 1886; Dublin Rev, July 1886.
Isabel Clarendon. 2 vols 1886; ed P. Coustillas 2 vols Brighton 1969; ed P. Coustillas 2 vols in 1 Brighton 1982.
Thyrza: a tale. 3 vols 1887, 1891; Melbourne 1891 (Colonial edn); London 1892, 1895, 1907 (Smith & Elder, John Murray), introd by M. Roberts 1927, rptd 1928; introd by M. Roberts, New York [1929]; introd by M. Roberts, London (Nash's Great Novel Lib) [1930]; 3 vols in 1 New York 1969; ed J. Korg, Hassocks 1974, Cranbury NJ 1974; ed J. Korg, Brighton and New York 1984. Tr Rus in Vsemirnaia biblioteka Dec 1891–July 1892, Fr 1928 (abridged), Ital 1939, Romanian 1985.
REVIEWS: Globe, 23 May 1887; Dublin Rev, July 1887.
A life's morning. Serialised Cornhill Mag, Jan–Dec 1888; 3 vols 1888; Philadelphia 1888; London 1889, 1890, 1892, 1914 (Smith & Elder, John Murray), 1919, introd by M. Roberts 1927, rptd 1928; introd by M. Roberts, New York [1929]; Kyoto 1961 (abridged); 3 vols in 1 New York 1969; ed P. Coustillas, Brighton and New York 1984.
REVIEWS: Murray's Mag, Jan 1889; Dublin Rev, Jan 1889; Scottish Rev, Apr 1889.
The nether world: a novel. 3 vols 1889; New York 1889; London 1890 [1889], 1890; Melbourne 1890 and 1891 (Colonial edns); London 1903 (Smith & Elder, John Murray), 1907, introd by M. Roberts 1927, rptd 1928; introd by M. Roberts, New York [1929]; introd by W. Allen, London 1973 (EL, rptd 1975, 1982, 1986); introd by J. Goode, Brighton 1974; introd by J. Goode, Brighton and New York 1982; ed. S. Gill, Oxford 1992 (WCp, 3 printings by 1998). Tr Rus in Vestnik Evropy, July–Oct 1898, Jap 1992.
REVIEWS: Manchester Examiner and Times, 27 Apr 1889; Scots Observer, 4 May 1889; San Francisco Chron, 9 June 1889; Dublin Rev, July 1889, Oct 1890; New York Times, 16 Sep 1889; (A. Lang) Longman's Mag, Sep 1889, Daily Chron, 23 Aug 1890.
Selections: A Gissing–Hardy reader, with notes by T. Hilding Svartengren. Stockholm 1916. 4 chs from the novel.
The emancipated: a novel. 3 vols 1890, 1893, 1894 (Colonial edn), 1895, 1895 (Colonial edn); Chicago 1895, 1897; London 1901, 1911; 3 vols in 1 New York 1969; ed P. Coustillas, Hassocks 1977, Cranbury NJ 1977; introd by J. Halperin, London 1985.

REVIEWS: Deutsche Presse, 4 May 1890; Scotsman, 16 Dec 1893; Daily Telegraph, 29 Dec 1893; World, 21 Feb 1894.

New Grub Street: a novel. 3 vols 1891 (twice); 2 vols Leipzig (Tauchnitz) 1891; London 1891; Melbourne 1891 (Colonial edn); London 1892, 1893, 1904; Troy NY 1904; New York 1905; London 1908 (Smith & Elder, John Murray), [1910]; introd by H. Hansen, New York 1926 (Mod Lib, many reprints until 1942); introd by M. Roberts, London 1927, rptd 1928; introd by M. Roberts, New York c. 1928; introd by G. W. Stonier, London 1958 (WC); New York [1961] (Dolphin Bks); introd by I. Howe, Boston 1962 (Riverside edn), 1965; ed B. Bergonzi, Harmondsworth 1968 (Pen, 16 printings by 1998); New York 1985 (Mod Lib); ed J. Halperin, Halifax 1992; ed J. Goode, Oxford 1993 (WCp, 3 printings by 1998); Ware 1996 (Wordsworth Classics); ed D. J. Taylor, London 1997 (EL); dramatisation as 'Decline and rise' by R. Morris, Geneva 1973. Tr Rus in Knizhki Nedeli, Nov 1891–May 1892, Ger in Pester Lloyd suppl, Budapest, 29 Dec 1891–30 Apr 1892, 1986 (Andere Bibliothek), rptd 1993, Fr in Journal des Débats, (daily edn) 23 Feb–3 June 1901, (weekly edn) 1 Mar–14 June 1901, in vol 1902, 1978, Jap 1969, 1988 (rev), Romanian 1978, Swed 1982, Chinese 1986 (2 different trns), Greek 1995, Korean 1995.

REVIEWS: Manchester Examiner and Times, 16 Apr 1891; Leeds Mercury, 11 May 1891; Dublin Rev, July 1891; Tauchnitz Mag, Aug 1891.

Denzil Quarrier: a novel. 1892; New York 1892; London 1892 (Colonial edn); Leipzig 1892 (Continental edn); London 1894 (Colonial edn), 1911; Leipzig 1911 (Eng Lib); New York 1969; ed J. Halperin, Hassocks 1979, rptd [1987].

REVIEWS: Beacon (Boston), 20 Feb 1892; Manchester Guardian, 1 Mar 1892; The Times, (weekly edn) 18 Mar 1892; St James's Gazette, 25 Mar 1892; Literary News, Mar 1892.

Born in exile: a novel. 3 vols 1892; Melbourne 1892 (Colonial edn); London 1893, 1894, 1895 (Colonial edn), 1896, [1910] (Nelson's Lib); 3 vols in 1 New York 1968; introd by W. Allen, London 1970 (Gollancz Classics); ed P. Coustillas, Hassocks 1978; introd by G. Tindall, London 1985; ed. D. Grylls 1993 (EL). Tr Fr 1932 (abridged), Ital 1955, 1969, Jap 1988.

REVIEWS: Bookman, June 1892; Leeds Mercury, 8 June 1892; The Times (weekly edn) 8 July 1892.

The odd women. 3 vols 1893; New York 1893; London 1893 (Colonial edn), 1894, 1901, 1905, [1907] (Nelson's Lib), 1911, 1915, introd by F. Swinnerton 1968; New York, introd by F. Swinnerton 1968, 3 vols in 1 New York 1969, 1971 (13 printings by 1998, with introd by M. R. Fox from 6th [1978]); introd by M. Walters, London 1980 (Virago Classics, 8 printings by 1995); New York 1983 (New Amer Lib, 6 printings by 1993); Harmondsworth 1993 [1994] (Pen, 3 printings by 1998; ed Arlene Young, Peterborough, Ontario 1998 (Broadview Literary Texts); dramatisation by M. Meyer 1993. Tr Swed 1980, Fr 1982, Jap 1988 (2 trns), Ger 1997, rptd 1999.

REVIEWS: Beacon (Boston), 15 Apr 1893; New York Times, 24 Apr 1893; Westminster Gazette, 28 Apr 1893; News and Courier (Charleston SC), 30 Apr 1893; San Francisco Chron, 7 May 1893; Birmingham Daily Post, 19 June 1893.

In the year of jubilee. 3 vols 1894, 1894 (Colonial edn), 1894 [1895], 1895; New York 1895 (bowdlerised); London 1901; New York [1905]; London 1911, introd by W. Plomer 1947; New York 1969; introd by G. Tindall, notes by P. F. Kropholler Hassocks 1976, Cranbury NJ 1976; New York 1982 (bowdlerised); introd by J. Halperin, London 1987; ed P. Delany 1994 (EL).

REVIEWS: Birmingham Daily Post, 24 Dec 1894; Westminster Gazette, 18 Jan 1895; The Times, (weekly edn) 15 Mar 1895; Commercial Advertiser (New York), 24 July 1895; (J. N. Hilliard) Union and Advertiser (Rochester NY), 24 Aug 1895; (D[ouglas] S[laden]) Queen, 7 Sep 1895.

Eve's ransom. Serialised Illus London News, 5 Jan–30 Mar 1895; 1895 (twice), 1895 (Colonial edn); New York 1895; London 1901, 1911; New York 1912; London 1929 (Essex Lib); New York 1969, 1980. Tr Fr in Revue de Paris, 1 Apr–15 May 1898, in vol 1898, [1907], Rus in Zhivopisnoe Obozrenie nos 29–36, 1898, Danish in Samfundet 2 Jan–18 Feb 1900, in vol 1900, Du 1904.

REVIEWS: (J. N. Hilliard) Union and Advertiser (Rochester NY), 13 Apr 1895; (G. Strong) Star, 18 Apr 1895; San Francisco Chron, 19 May 1895.

Sleeping fires. 1895, 1896; New York 1896; London 1927; introd by Masanobu Oda, Tokyo 1930 (4 printings by 1943); introd by P. Coustillas, Hassocks 1974; Lincoln NE 1983. Tr Jap 1988.

REVIEWS: (St Barbe) Queen, 28 Dec 1895; Lloyd's Weekly Newspaper, 12 Jan 1896; Newcastle Daily Leader, 6 Feb 1896; The Times, (weekly edn) 28 Feb 1896; San Francisco Chron, 26 Apr 1896.

The paying guest. 1895 [1896]; New York 1895 [1896]; Tokyo 1936, 1953 (at least 15 printings by 1977); New York 1968; ed F. Badolato, Treviso 1973; ed I. Fletcher, Brighton 1982.

REVIEWS: New Age, 30 Jan 1896; Philadelphia Record, 31 Jan 1896; Black and White, 1 Feb 1896; San Francisco Chron, 2 Feb 1896; Birmingham Daily Post, 24 Feb 1896; (Paperknife) Hearth and Home, 2 Apr 1896; The Times, (weekly edn) 5 June 1896.

The whirlpool. 1897 (3 printings), 1897 (Colonial edn); New York [1898] (5 printings); London 1901, 1911, 1915, introd by M. Evans 1948; New York 1969; ed P. Parrinder, Hassocks 1977, Cranbury NJ 1977; ed P. Parrinder, Brighton and New York 1984; introd by G. Tindall, London 1984; ed W. Greenslade 1997 (EL). Tr Jap 1989.

REVIEWS: Leeds and Yorkshire Mercury, 19 Apr 1897; Daily Mail, 20 Apr 1897; (Barbara) Woman, 21 Apr 1897; (E. Gosse) St James's Gazette, 23 Apr 1897; Athenaeum, 24 Apr 1897; Westminster Gazette, 7 May 1897; The Times, (weekly edn) 20 Apr 1897; Cleveland Leader, 3 Apr 1898.

Human odds and ends: stories and sketches. 1898 [1897], 1897 (Colonial edn), 1901, 1911, 1915; New York 1977. Contains Comrades in arms, The justice and the vagabond, The firebrand, An inspiration, The poet's portmanteau, The day of silence, In honour bound, The prize lodger, Our Mr Jupp, The medicine man, Raw material, Two collectors, An old maid's triumph, The invincible curate, The tout of Yarmouth bridge, A well-meaning man, A song of sixpence, A profitable weakness, The beggar's nurse, Transplanted, A parent's feeling, Lord Dunfield, The little woman from Lancashire, In no-man's land, At high pressure, A conversion, A free woman, A son of the soil, Out of the fashion.

REVIEWS: Daily Mail, 2 Nov 1897; Birmingham Daily Post, 27 Dec 1897; The Times, (weekly edn) 25 Feb 1898.

Charles Dickens, a critical study. 1898 (Victorian Era); New York 1898; London (Imperial edn) 1902 (rptd 1903, 1904, 1912, [1913], [1914], [1922], [1923], [1925]), 1903 (Victorian Era); New York 1904, 1912, 1924; London 1926, 1928; India 1928 (Colonial edn); London 1929; Port Washington NY 1966; St Clair Shores MI 1972; New York 1974; St Clair Shores MI 1976. Tr Jap 1988.

REVIEWS: Glasgow Evening News, 17 Feb 1898; The Times, (weekly edn) 18 Feb 1898; Daily Mail, 22 Feb 1898; New Age, 3 March 1898; Birmingham Daily Post, 26 Mar 1898; The Times, (weekly edn) 8 Apr 1898; Idler, Apr 1898; Detroit Free Press, 28 May 1898; Bibliothèque Universelle (Lausanne), July 1898. *For other revs of this title see* P. Coustillas, Gissing's writings on Dickens: a bio-bibliographical survey, 1969.

The town traveller. 1898 (twice), 1898 (Colonial edn); New York 1898; Toronto 1898; London [1902], [1919], 1927, 1956; New York 1968; ed P. Coustillas, Brighton 1981, rptd [1983].

REVIEWS: New Age, 15 Sep 1898; (Sarah Volatile) Hearth and Home, 29 Sep 1898; Black and White, 10 Oct 1898; Sun (Baltimore), 26 Nov 1898; The Times, (weekly edn) 2 Dec 1898.

The crown of life. 1899, 1899 (Colonial edn); New York 1899, nd; Toronto 1899; London [1905], 1927; New York 1969; ed M. Ballard, Hassocks 1978, rptd [1987].

REVIEWS: Providence Sunday Jnl, 29 Oct 1899; (Socius) New Age, 2 Nov 1899; Public Opinion (New York), 30 Nov 1899; San Francisco Chron, 28 Jan 1900; The Times, 13 Apr 1900; The Times, (weekly edn) 20 Apr 1900.

The works of Charles Dickens. 11 vols (6 titles) 1899–1901 (Rochester edn). Introds by Gissing, notes by F. G. Kitton.

Our friend the charlatan. 1901, 1901 (Colonial edn); New York 1901; London [1903], [1906]; New York 1969; ed P. Coustillas, Hassocks 1976, Cranbury NJ 1976.
REVIEWS: Birmingham Daily Post, 21 June 1901; Daily Mail, 25 June 1901; (E. A. Bennett) Hearth and Home, 4 July 1901; The Times, (weekly edn suppl) 5 July 1901; Daily Graphic, 6 July 1901; Standard, 19 July 1901; Vanity Fair, 8 Aug 1901; Commercial Advertiser (New York), 10 Aug 1901; Book Buyer (New York), Aug 1901.

By the Ionian sea: notes of a ramble in southern Italy. Serialised in Fortnightly Rev, May–Oct 1900; 1901, 1905 (twice), 1905 (Colonial edn); New York 1905; London 1917; New York [1917]; Portland ME 1920; London 1921, introd by V. Woolf (Travellers' Lib), London and New York 1933; foreword by F. Swinnerton, London 1956, rptd 1961, rptd 1963; Tokyo 1958 (abridged); Chester Springs PA 1963; Tokyo 1970 (abridged); Reggio Calabria 1980 (abridged); London 1986; Marlboro VT 1991; Loanhead 1992 (priv ptd); Evanston IL 1996. Tr Jap 1947, 1988, 1994 (rev), Ital 1957, 1962, 1971, 1993, Fr 1997. Selections: Bartlesville OK, Christmas 1943 (priv ptd).
REVIEWS: Globe, 29 June 1901; Queen, 29 June 1901; (E. A. Bennett) Hearth and Home, 4 July 1901; The Times, (weekly edn suppl) 19 July 1901; (W. S. Maugham) Sunday Sun, 11 Aug 1901, rptd in W. S. Maugham, A traveller in romance: uncollected writings 1901–1964, 1984; Bookman, Aug 1901; New York Times Book Rev, 20 May 1905.

Forster's life of Charles Dickens. Abridged and rev New York 1902; London 1903 [1902], 1907, nd (vol 20 of Special authorised edition of the works of Charles Dickens).
REVIEWS: Daily Telegraph, 17 Oct 1902; Morning Post, 4 Dec 1902; Book Lover (Melbourne), Dec 1902.

The private papers of Henry Ryecroft. 1903 (4 times); New York 1903; London 1903 (Colonial edn, twice), 1904 (twice), 1905; New York 1905; London 1906 (twice); New York 1906; London 1907; New York 1907; London 1908 (twice), 1909, 1910; New York 1910; London 1912 (twice); New York [1912]; Toronto [1912]; London 1913, 1914, 1915; New York 1915, [1915] (Wayfarer's Lib); London 1918; introd by P. E. More, New York [1918] (Mod Lib, many reprints until 1942); London 1921; New York 1921; introd by T. Seccombe, Portland ME 1921; London 1923, 1926; New York 1927 (EL); London 1928 (twice); introd by T. Seccombe, Portland ME 1928; London 1930, 1939 (64th thousand), introd by C. Chisholm 1953, 1954, introd by C. Chisholm 1961; New York, introd by V. S. Pritchett 1961 (Signet Classics), [1961] (Dolphin Books); introd by C. Chisholm, London 1964 (EL); introd by J. S. Collis and bibl notes by P. Coustillas, Brighton 1982, rptd 1983; ed M. Storey, Oxford 1987 (WCp). Tr Jap in Shumi, July 1909 (selection), 1912, 1924, 1927–8 (selection), 1960 (many reprints), 1995, Du 1920, 1989, Swed 1929, 1963 (selection), Ital 1957 (7 printings by 1964), 1990, Korean 1960, 1979, Fr 1966, Chinese 1969, 1987.
REVIEWS: Leeds and Yorkshire Mercury, 3 Feb 1903; Yorkshire Post, 4 Feb 1903; Irish Times, 6 Feb 1903; Birmingham Daily Post, 27 Feb 1903; New York Times Book Rev, 28 Feb 1903; Standard, 12 March 1903; Weekly Critical Rev (Paris), 12 Mar, (Theodore Davidson) 30 Apr 1903; (H. Murray) Sunday Sun, 15 Mar 1903; (V. Woolf) Guardian, 13 Feb 1907.
Selections: Books and the quiet life, being some pages from The private papers of Henry Ryecroft, chosen by W[aldo] R. B[rowne], Portland ME 1914, rptd 1922; Ragged veterans: selections from The private papers of Henry Ryecroft, np Christmas 1930; George Gissing on the ownership of books, being some excerpts from that wise and delightful volume The private papers of Henry Ryecroft, Muscatine IA 1937; George Gissing contemplates his ancient penholder, [Muscatine IA] 1938; Stray leaves from The private papers of Henry Ryecroft, Westport CT 1942; The day I granted to my better genius: selections from The private papers of Henry Ryecroft, 1944; The private papers of Henry Ryecroft, ed F. Badolato, Rome 1991.

Veranilda: a romance. 1904 (twice), 1904 (Colonial edn, twice), 1905; New York 1905 (twice); London 1929 (WC); New York 1968; ed P. Coustillas, Brighton 1987.
REVIEWS: St James's Gazette, 28 Sep 1904; Daily Graphic, 28 Sep 1904; Morning Leader, 5 Oct 1904; Black and White, 8 Oct 1904; Sketch, 12 Oct 1904; To-Day, 12 Oct 1904; Birmingham Daily Post, 14 Oct 1904; Glasgow Herald, 15 Oct 1904; Yorkshire Post, 19 Oct 1904; Standard, 26 Oct 1904; (T. Lloyd) Sunday Sun, 20 Nov 1904; Rapid Rev, Nov 1904; (Charbon) Hearth and Home, 1 Dec 1904; Liverpool Daily Post, 7 Dec 1904; New York Sat Rev of Books, 31 Dec 1904.

Will Warburton: a romance of real life. Serialised New Age, 5 Jan–8 June 1905, Yorkshire Weekly Post, 7 Jan–20 May 1905, Adelaide Observer, 7 Jan–20 May 1905; 1905; New York 1905; London [1908], 1915; New York [1916] (Wayfarer's Lib); London 1929 (WC); New York 1969; ed Colin Partridge, Brighton 1981; introd by J. Halperin, London 1985.
REVIEWS: World, 27 June 1905; (A. N. M[onkhouse]) Manchester Guardian, 28 June 1905; (F. G. Bettany) Sunday Times, 9 July 1905; Daily Graphic, 12 July 1905; (L.) Sunday Sun, 16 July 1905; Truth, 20 July 1905; Vanity Fair, 20 July 1905; Yorkshire Post, 26 July 1905; (Charbon) Hearth and Home, 27 July 1905; Rapid Rev, Aug 1905; (Max Meyerfeld) Die Nation (Berlin), 12 Aug 1905; Observer, 13 Aug 1905; Leeds and Yorkshire Mercury, 15 Aug 1905.

The House of Cobwebs and other stories. [All Eng and Amer edns up to 1971 carry the introductory survey by T. Seccombe.] 1906 (twice); New York 1906 (1st edn bears 'second impression' on title page); London 1907; New York 1907; London 1914; New York [1915] (Wayfarer's Lib); London 1919, 1923, 1926; Tokyo c. 1927; London 1931; Osaka 1949 (selection); 2 vols Tokyo 1953 (selection, many printings); Kyoto c. 1958 (selection); Freeport NY 1971. Contains title story, A capitalist, Christopherson, Humplebee, The scrupulous father, A poor gentleman, Miss Rodney's leisure, A charming family, A daughter of the lodge, The riding-whip, Fate and the apothecary, Topham's chance, A lodger in Maze Pond, The salt of the earth, The pig and whistle. Tr Jap, 2 vols 1946, 2 vols 1951, 2 vols 1953. Many reprints.
REVIEWS: Rapid Rev, May 1906; Tribune, 30 May 1906; Standard, 8 June 1906; Daily Mail, 11 June 1906; Daily Graphic, 14 June 1906; (Charbon) Hearth and Home, 14 June 1906; Public Opinion, 15 June 1906; (F. G. Bettany) Sunday Times, 17 June 1906; Yorkshire Post, 20 June 1906.

An heiress on condition. Philadelphia 1923 (priv ptd).

Sins of the fathers and other tales. Introd by V. Starrett, Chicago 1924. Contains title story, Gretchen, R. I. P., Too dearly bought.

Critical studies of the works of Charles Dickens. New York 1924, 1965. Contains 9 introds to Rochester edn, including 3 unpubd, and Dickens in memory. Introd and bibliography of Gissing by T. Scott.

The immortal Dickens. 1925; New York 1969. Same contents as Critical studies but with introd by B. W. M[atz]. No bibliography.

A victim of circumstances and other stories. Preface by A. C. Gissing 1927; Boston and New York 1927; New York 1971. Contains title story, One way of happiness, The fate of Humphrey Snell, A despot on tour, The elixir, The light on the tower, The schoolmaster's vision, The honeymoon, The pessimist of Plato road, The foolish virgin, Lou and Liz, The tyrant's apology, Spellbound, Our learned fellow-townsman, Fleet-footed Hester.

A Yorkshire lass. New York 1928 (priv ptd).

Hope in vain. [Winchester] 1930 (priv ptd). Poem.

Brownie, rptd from the Chicago Tribune, with six other stories attributed to him [Gissing]. Ed G. E. Hastings, V. Starrett and T. O. Mabbott, New York 1931. Contains title story, The warden's daughter, Twenty pounds, Joseph Yates' temptation, The death-clock, The serpent-charm, Dead and alive.

Stories and sketches. Ed A. C. Gissing 1938. Contains Phoebe, Letty Coe, Snapshall's youngest, His brother's keeper, Under an umbrella, A calamity at Tooting, A Yorkshire lass, The hapless boaster, The ring finger, The peace bringer, The friend in need, A drug in the market, Of good address, Humble felicity, A man of leisure.

George Gissing's commonplace book. Ed J. Korg, New York 1962.

Notes on social democracy. Introd by J. Korg 1968. Articles 1st pbd in Pall Mall Gazette, 9, 11, 14 Sep 1880.

George Gissing: essays and fiction. Ed P. Coustillas, Baltimore and London 1970. Contains The hope of pessimism, Along shore, All for love, The last half-crown, Cain and Abel, The quarry on the heath, The lady of the dedication, Mutimer's choice, Their pretty way.

My first rehearsal and My clerical rival. Ed P. Coustillas 1970.

Six sonnets on Shakespearean heroines. Introd by P. Coustillas 1982.

A freak of nature: or Mr Brogden, City clerk. Ed P. Coustillas, Edinburgh 1990.

George Gissing: lost stories from America. Ed R. L. Selig, Lewiston NY 1992. Contains A terrible mistake, A mother's hope, A test of honor, The artist's child (the 2 versions), An English coast-picture, Too wretched to live, A game of hearts, How they cooked me, The portrait, The mysterious portrait, The picture, One farthing damages.

George Gissing's essay on Robert Burns. Ed J. Korg, Lewiston NY 1992.

The poetry of George Gissing. Ed B. Postmus, Lewiston NY 1995.

Short stories

Besides the original pbn data, only reprints and trns in periodicals, foreign collections and general anthologies are noted here. The Eng collections of Gissing's short stories are listed under Individual works *and under* Selections. *A still useful though partly superseded bibliography is to be found in* P. Coustillas, Gissing short stories: a bibliography, ELT 7 no 2, 1964. *For Jap pbns in Eng, bilingual edns and trns, a complex subject outside the scope of the present bibliography, see* S. Koike, Gissing in Japan, BNYPL Nov 1963 *and* P. Coustillas, The romance of Japanese editions, Gissing Newsletter July 1988 *and* Gissing Jnl *passim.*

The sins of the fathers. Chicago Tribune, (Sat suppl) 10 Mar 1877, rptd in Troy Times, 14 July 1877.

R. I. P. Ibid, 31 Mar 1877.

Too dearly bought. Ibid, 14 Apr 1877.

The death-clock. Chicago Daily Tribune, 21 Apr 1877.

Too wretched to live. Chicago Daily News, 24 Apr 1877, rptd in Stud in Bibliography, 1983.

The serpent-charm. Chicago Daily Tribune, 28 Apr 1877.

The warden's daughter. Chicago Evening Jnl, 28 Apr 1877, rptd as The warder's daughter, Chicago Daily News, 18 May 1877.

A terrible mistake. Nat Weekly, 5 May 1877.

Gretchen. Chicago Tribune, (illus suppl) 12 May 1877.

A mother's hope. Alliance, 12 May 1877.

Twenty pounds. Chicago Evening Jnl, 19 May 1877.

A game of hearts. Chicago Daily News, 28 May 1877.

Joseph Yates' temptation. Chicago Post, 2 June 1877.

A test of honor. Alliance, 2 June 1877, rptd TLS, 12 Dec 1980.

How they cooked me. Chicago Daily News, 4 June 1877, rptd Gissing Jnl, Apr 1991.

The portrait. Chicago Daily News, 18 June 1877, rptd ELT 33 no 3, 1990.

The artist's child. Alliance, 30 June 1877, rptd Tinsleys' Mag, Jan 1878 (rev).

An English coast-picture. Appletons' Jnl, July 1877.

The mysterious portrait. Chicago Daily News, 6 July 1877, rptd Chicago Daily News, 16 July 1877 and ELT 33 no 3, 1990.

Dead and alive. Chicago Daily Tribune, 14 July 1877.

One farthing damages. Chicago Post, 28 July 1877, rptd Chicago Post, 2 Aug 1877 and Gissing Newsletter, Oct 1986.

Brownie. Chicago Daily Tribune, 29 July 1877.

The picture. Chicago Daily News, 14 Aug 1877, rptd ELT 33 no 3, 1990.

Phoebe. Temple Bar, Mar 1884. Tr Ger in Aus fremden Zungen, 1891 and vol 3 of Bibliothek der fremden Zungen, Das Kind und andere Novellen, 1892.

Letty Coe. Temple Bar, Aug 1891, rptd Living Age, 3 Oct 1891.

A victim of circumstances. Blackwood's Mag, Jan 1893; rptd with introd by John Michell, Christmas 1986 (priv ptd). Tr Ital in Un'ispirazione ed altre novelle, ed F. Badolato, Como 1970 and Novara 1975 (rev).

Lou and Liz. Eng Illus Mag, Aug 1893, rptd in Working-class stories of the 1890s, ed P. J. Keating 1971. Tr Fr in Nouvelles choisies, ed P. Coustillas, Lille 1980.

The day of silence. Nat Rev, Dec 1893, rptd Living Age, 30 Dec 1893. Tr Fr in Revue Bleue, 5 Oct 1895 and Nouvelles choisies, 1980.

Fleet-footed Hester. Illus London News, Christmas 1893.

The muse of the halls. Eng Illus Mag, Christmas 1893.

Under an umbrella. To-Day, 6 Jan 1894.

Our Mr Jupp. Eng Illus Mag, Mar 1894. Tr Fr in Le Monde Moderne, May 1901 and Nouvelles anglaises de la Belle Epoque, ed P. Coustillas, Lille 1984.

A capitalist. Nat Rev, Apr 1894. Tr Ital in Un'ispirazione ed altre novelle 1975.

The honeymoon. Eng Illus Mag, June 1894.

Comrades in arms. Eng Illus Mag, Sep 1894, rptd in Short stories of the nineties, ed D. Stanford 1968, and in Love stories with introd by Rosamunde Pilcher 1990. Tr Fr in Revue Bleue, 4 Mar 1899 and Nouvelles anglaises de la Belle Epoque 1984.

The pessimist of Plato Road. Eng Illus Mag, Nov 1894.

A midsummer madness. Eng Illus Mag, Dec 1894.

The salt of the earth. Minster, Jan 1895. Tr Fr in Revue Bleue, 17 Mar 1928, Ital in Un'ispirazione ed altre novelle 1975.

A lodger in Maze pond. Nat Rev, Feb 1895, rptd Ainslee's, June 1926. Tr Fr in Revue Bleue, 16 Mar 1895, Ital in Un'ispirazione ed altre novelle 1975.

The poet's portmanteau. Eng Illus Mag, Feb 1895, rptd Union and Advertiser (Rochester NY), 21 Mar 1896.

In honour bound. Eng Illus Mag, Apr 1895, rptd Living Age, 25 May 1895.

The friend in need. To-Day, 4 May 1895.

A drug in the market. Ibid, 11 May 1895.

Of good address. Ibid, 18 May 1895.

By the kerb. Ibid, 25 May 1895.

His brother's keeper. Chapman's Mag, June 1895.

A calamity at Tooting. Minster, June 1895.

Humble felicity. To-Day, 1 June 1895.

A man of leisure. Ibid, 8 June 1895.

The tyrant's apology. Eng Illus Mag, July 1895.

Their pretty ways. Lloyd's Weekly Newspaper, 15 Sep 1895.

The fate of Humphrey Snell. Eng Illus Mag, Oct 1895.

The medicine man. Sketch, 9 Oct 1895.

Raw material. Ibid, 16 Oct 1895.

Two collectors. Ibid, 23 Oct 1895. Tr Fr in Gaulois du Dimanche, 29–30 Oct 1898.

An old maid's triumph. Ibid, 30 Oct 1895.

The invincible curate. Ibid, 6 Nov 1895.

The tout of Yarmouth bridge. Ibid, 13 Nov 1895, rptd and tr Fr in Nouvelles victoriennes, ed C. Larrière, Paris 1991.

A well-meaning man. Sketch, 20 Nov 1895.
A song of sixpence. Ibid, 27 Nov 1895.
An inspiration. Eng Illus Mag, Dec 1895, rptd Canterbury Times (NZ), 23 Jan 1896. Tr Fr in Revue Hebdomadaire, 11 Mar 1899 and Nouvelles choisies 1980, Ital in Un'ispirazione ed altre novelle 1970, 1975 (rev).
A profitable weakness. Sketch, 4 Dec 1895.
The beggar's nurse. Ibid, 11 Dec 1895.
Transplanted. Ibid, 25 Dec 1895. Tr Fr in Gaulois du Dimanche, 28–29 Oct 1899.
The foolish virgin. Yellow Book, Jan 1896, rptd in selections from Yellow Book 1928, 1949, 1950, 1964, 1967, 1974, 1982; British prose and poetry, ed I. Fletcher 1987. Tr in Ital Un'ispirazione ed altre novelle 1970, 1975 (rev).
A parent's feelings. Sketch, 1 Jan 1896.
Lord Dunfield. Ibid, 15 Jan 1896.
The little woman from Lancashire. Ibid, 29 Jan 1896.
In no-man's land. Ibid, 12 Feb 1896.
At high pressure. Ibid, 19 Feb 1896.
A conversion. Ibid, 26 Feb 1896, rptd Commercial Advertiser (New York), 17 Mar 1896.
A free woman. Sketch, 4 Mar 1896.
A son of the soil. Ibid, 11 Mar 1896, rptd Commercial Advertiser (New York), 26 Mar 1896.
Out of fashion. Sketch, 18 Mar 1896.
Our learned fellow-townsman. New York Times, 20 Mar 1896, rptd Eng Illus Mag, May 1896.
Simple Simon. Idler, May 1896, rptd Harmsworth Mag, Dec 1900 (bowdlerised); Gissing Jnl, Jan 1995.
Joseph. Lloyd's Weekly Newspaper, 17 May 1896; rptd Gissing Newsletter, Jan 1988.
The justice and the vagabond. Eng Illus Mag, June 1896. Tr Ital in Un'ispirazione ed altre novelle 1970, 1975 (rev).
The firebrand. Eng Illus Mag, July 1896; tr Ger in Victorian Stories, ed R. Fenzl, Munich 1990.
A Yorkshire lass. Cosmopolis, Aug 1896, rptd Canterbury Times (NZ), 4 Feb 1897; as vol New York 1928 (priv ptd).
The prize lodger. Eng Illus Mag, Aug 1896, rptd in Victorian short stories 2: the trials of love, ed H. Orel 1990; tr Ger in Love and marriage, ed R. Fenzl, Munich 1996.
The schoolmaster's vision. Eng Illus Mag, Sep 1896, tr Fr in Nouvelles choisies 1980.
The light on the tower. Eng Illus Mag, Jan 1897.
The hapless boaster. Illus London News, 11 Sep 1897.
Spellbound. Eng Illus Mag, Oct 1897, rptd in England in literature, ed H. McDonnell et al, Glenview IL 1979.
A despot on tour. Strand Mag, Jan 1898.
The ring finger. Cosmopolis, May 1898.
One way of happiness. Eng Illus Mag, June 1898. Tr Ital in Un'ispirazione ed altre novelle 1970, 1975 (rev). Tr Fr Nouvelles choisies 1980.
The peace bringer. Lady's Realm, Oct 1898.
A freak of nature. Harmsworth Mag, Feb 1899 (bowdlerised as Mr Brogden, City clerk), rptd as vol from ms with introd by P. Coustillas, Edinburgh 1990.
The elixir. Idler, May 1899.
Fate and the apothecary. Lit, 6 May 1899; rptd with introd by John Michell, Christmas 1987 (priv ptd). Tr Ital Un'ispirazione ed altre novelle 1975.
A poor gentleman. Pall Mall Mag, Oct 1899, rptd in Selected short stories, 2nd ser 1921 (WC), and in Rekenschap, Amsterdam, Sep 1997. Tr Fr in Revue Bleue, 17 Mar 1900 and Nouvelles choisies 1980, Polish in Czas (Krakow), 19–23 Apr 1902, Ger in Englische Erzähler, ed R. Kraushaar, Zurich 1964, Ital in Un'ispirazione ed altre novelle 1975.
Snapshall's youngest. Sphere, 17 Feb 1900.
Humplebee. AS Rev, Mar 1900, rptd in Short stories by great authors, ed W. van Maanen, Zwolle 1924, 1931, 1937; Great English short stories, ed L. Melville and R. Hargreaves 1931. Tr Ital in Un'ispirazione ed altre novelle 1975, Fr in Nouvelles choisies 1980.
At nightfall. Lippincott's Monthly Mag, May 1900.
The house of cobwebs. Argosy, Aug 1900, rptd in English short story in transition, ed H. E. Gerber, New York 1967; Fiction 100, ed J. H. Pickering, New York 1974.
The scrupulous father. Truth (New York), Dec 1900, rptd Cornhill Mag, Feb 1901; Great love stories of all nations, ed R. Lynd 1932, 1970; Victorian short stories, ed H. Orel 1987. Tr Ital in Un'ispirazione ed altre novelle 1970, 1975 (rev), Fr in Nouvelles choisies 1980.
A charming family. Illus London News, 4 May 1901, rptd in A seven seas sampler, ed M. Stewart, Berlin 1961. Tr Ital in Un'ispirazione ed altre novelle 1970, 1975 (rev), Fr in Nouvelles choisies 1980.
A daughter of the lodge. Illus London News, 17 Aug 1901, rptd in Selected English short stories, 3rd ser 1927 (WC). Tr Ital in Un'ispirazione ed altre novelle 1970, 1975 (rev), Fr in Nouvelles choisies 1980.
The riding whip. Illus London News, 22, 29 Mar 1902.
Christopherson. Illus London News, 20 Sep 1902, rptd in Selected English short stories, 1st ser 1914 (WC). Tr Ital in Un'ispirazione ed altre novelle 1975, Fr in Nouvelles choisies 1980.
Topham's chance. Daily Mail, 9 Dec 1903, rptd Tasmanian Mail, 28 May 1904.
Miss Rodney's leisure. T. P.'s Weekly, Christmas 1903. Tr Fr in Nouvelles choisies 1980.
The pig and whistle. Graphic, Christmas 1904, rptd in Short stories by great authors, 1924, 1931, 1937; The story survey, ed H. Blodgett, Chicago 1939. Tr Swed in Allt för alla, 12 Dec 1924.
An heiress on condition. Philadelphia 1923 (priv ptd).
My first rehearsal. ELT 9 no 1, 1966, rptd in My first rehearsal and My clerical rival, ed P. Coustillas 1970.
The last half-crown. In George Gissing: essays and fiction, Baltimore and London 1970.
Cain and Abel. In Ibid.
The quarry on the heath. In ibid.
The lady of the dedication. In ibid.
Mutimer's choice. In ibid.
My clerical rival. In My first rehearsal and My clerical rival, ed P. Coustillas 1970.

Contributions to periodicals and to collaborative works

For the serialisation of short stories see under Bibliographies *and titles of collections of short stories.*

Ravenna. Prize Poem 1873. Owens College Mag, Feb 1874, rptd in Manchester University verses, ed Sir A. Hopkinson 1913; Selections autobiographical and imaginative 1929.
To truth. Owens College Mag, May 1875, rptd in Manchester University verses, ed Sir A. Hopkinson 1913.
Our Shaksperean studies. Owens College Mag, Jan 1876. Unsigned.
Art notes. Commonwealth (Boston), 28 Oct 1876. Unsigned.
Notes on social democracy. Pall Mall Gazette, 9, 11, 14 Sep 1880, rptd in Notes on social democracy, 1968.
Correspondence from England. Vestnik Evropy, Feb, May, Aug, Nov 1881, Feb, May, Aug, Nov 1882.
Letter. Daily News, 6 Feb 1883, rptd in Collected letters vol 2.
On Battersea bridge. Pall Mall Gazette, 30 Nov 1883, rptd in Selections autobiographical and imaginative, 1929.
Song. Temple Bar, Nov 1883, rptd N & Q, Dec 1960.
The new censorship of literature. Pall Mall Gazette, 15 Dec 1884, rptd in George Moore, Literature at nurse, ed P. Coustillas, Hassocks 1976; Realismustheorien in England (1692–1912), ed W. F. Greiner and F. Kemmler 1979.

Christmas on the Capitol. Bolton Evening News, 28 Dec 1889, rptd in Selections autobiographical and imaginative, 1929.

Bainton, G. The art of authorship. 1890. Includes letter from Gissing, rptd in Collected letters vol 3.

The pronunciation of Greek. The Times, 25 Feb 1891, rptd in Collected letters vol 4.

Why I don't write plays. Pall Mall Gazette, 10 Sep 1892; rptd in Collected letters vol 5.

Gosse, E. Questions at issue. 1893. Includes letter from Gissing in Appendix 1, Tennyson – and after?, rptd in Collected letters vol 5.

The speech of characters in fiction. Nat Observer, 27 Jan 1894, rptd in Collected letters vol 5.

Mr George Gissing. Pearson's Weekly, 30 June 1894, rptd in Collected letters vol 5.

Who should be laureate? Idler, Apr 1895, rptd in Collected letters vol 5.

The place of realism in fiction. Humanitarian, July 1895, rptd in Selections autobiographical and imaginative, 1929; G. L. Barnett, Nineteenth-century British novelists on the novel, 1971; Gissing on fiction, ed J. and C. Korg 1978; Realismustheorien in England (1692–1912), ed W. F. Greiner and F. Kemmler 1979; W. Greiner and G. Stilz, Naturalismus in England 1880–1920, 1983; Victorian novelists after 1885, ed I. D. Nadel and W. E. Fredeman, Dictionary of Literary Biography vol 18 1983; Collected letters vol 5.

Novelists and their works. Ludgate, Nov 1895, rptd in Collected letters vol 6.

The immediate future of the British empire. Minster, Jan 1896.

The reviewer reviewed. Westminster Gazette, 22 Jan 1897, rptd in Collected letters vol 6.

The old school. Dinglewood Mag (Colwyn Bay), 1897, rptd in P. Coustillas, George Gissing at Alderley Edge, 1969.

Mr George Gissing at home. Acad, 19 Mar 1898, rptd Bookman, May 1898; Collected letters vol 7.

At the grave of Alaric. Daily Chron, 31 May 1898, rptd in Selections autobiographical and imaginative, 1929.

Tyrtaeus. Rev of the Week, 4 Nov 1899, rptd Gissing Newsletter, July 1974. Tr Fr in Gaulois du Dimanche, 25–26 Nov 1899 (abridged).

The coming of the preacher. Lit, 6 Jan 1900, rptd Gissing Newsletter, July 1974.

Mr George Gissing on vegetarianism. Life and Beauty, Aug–Sep 1900, rptd in Collected letters vol 8.

The bed of Odysseus. Student (Edinburgh), Jan 1901, rptd in rev version of The private papers of Henry Ryecroft.

Dickens in memory. Lit, 21 Dec 1901, rptd Critic (New York), Jan 1902; Critical studies of the works of Charles Dickens, 1924; The immortal Dickens, 1925.

Nel centenario di Vittor Hugo. Piccolo Giornale di Trieste (Piccolo della Sera), 26 Feb 1902, rptd in Collected letters vol 8.

Mr Swinburne on Dickens. TLS, 25 July 1902, rptd in P. Coustillas, Gissing's writings on Dickens, 1969.

Mr Kitton's Life of Dickens. TLS, 15 Aug 1902, rptd in P. Coustillas, Gissing's writings on Dickens, 1969.

The homes and haunts of Dickens. Nottinghamshire Guardian, 16 Aug 1902, rptd in Home and haunts of famous authors, 1906.

An English academy. Daily Chron, 27 Jan 1903, rptd in Collected letters vol 9.

The death of the children. Eng Rev, Apr 1914, rptd ibid, Jan 1920 (rev); Literary Digest (New York), 13 Mar 1920. Poem.

Published letters, diaries, notebooks

Articles containing only a few letters have been omitted, as they are mentioned in Collected letters of George Gissing.

Stevenson, M. C. Letters from Gissing. T. P.'s Weekly, 27 Dec 1912.

Letters to Edward Clodd from George Gissing. 1914 (priv ptd).

Letters to an editor [C. K. Shorter]. 1915 (priv ptd).

Goodspeed, E. J. A letter of Gissing's [to Martha McC. Barnes, 1897]. Nation, 17 Aug 1916, rptd in Collected letters vol 6.

Letters of George Gissing 1899–1903 [to Clara E. Collet]. 1916 (priv ptd, 6 copies).

Clodd, E. In his Memories, 1916.

Two letters from George Gissing to Joseph Conrad. Ed G. Jean-Aubry 1926.

Letters of George Gissing to members of his family. Ed A. and E. Gissing 1926, 1927; Boston 1927; London 1931; New York 1970 (Kraus, Haskell House).

Autobiographical notes with comments upon Tennyson and Huxley in three letters to Edward Clodd. 1930 (priv ptd).

George Gissing and H. G. Wells: their friendship and correspondence. Ed R. A. Gettmann 1961, Urbana IL 1961.

The letters of George Gissing to Eduard Bertz 1887–1903. Ed Arthur C. Young 1961, New Brunswick NJ 1961, Westport CT 1980.

George Gissing's commonplace book. Ed J. Korg, serialised BNYPL, Sep–Nov 1961; in vol New York 1962.

The letters of George Gissing to Gabrielle Fleury. Ed P. Coustillas, serialised in part BNYPL, Sep–Nov 1964; in vol New York 1964 [1965].

Henry Hick's recollections of George Gissing, together with Gissing's letters to Henry Hick. Ed P. Coustillas 1973.

The letters of George Gissing to Edward Clodd. Ed P. Coustillas 1973.

Garland, B. Bibliographical notes: two Gissing letters. Wake Forest Univ Lib Newsletter, May 1975.

London and the life of literature in late Victorian England: the diary of George Gissing, novelist. Ed P. Coustillas, Hassocks 1978, Lewisburg PA 1978. Tr Ital in F. Badolato, Da Venezia allo stretto di Messina, Rome 1989 (selections).

Coustillas, P. George Gissing and Ivan Turgenev, including two letters from Turgenev. 1981.

Landscapes and literati. Ed D. Shrubsall and P. Coustillas, Wilton 1985. Gissing/W. H. Hudson correspondence.

Brief interlude. Ed P. Coustillas, Edinburgh 1987. Letters to Edith Sichel.

George Gissing at work: a study of his notebook 'Extracts from my reading'. Ed P. Coustillas and P. Bridgwater, Greensboro NC 1988.

The collected letters of George Gissing. Ed P. F. Mattheisen, A. C. Young and P. Coustillas, 9 vols Athens OH 1990–7.

George Gissing's American notebook: notes – G. R. G. – 1877. Ed B. Postmus, Lewiston NY 1993.

George Gissing's memorandum book: a novelist's note book 1895–1902. Ed B. Postmus, Lewiston NY 1996; Salzburg 1997.

Editions and introductions

The works of Charles Dickens. 11 vols (6 titles) 1899–1901 (Rochester edition). Introds by Gissing, notes by F. G. Kitton.

Introd to David Copperfield. New York 1903 (Autograph edn); rptd in Gissing Jnl Jan 1997.

Introd to David Copperfield (Rochester edn). Dickensian, Spring 1981.

§2

Textual and bibliographical criticism

Spencer, W. T. Forty years in my bookshop. 1923. Ch 16.

Bibliographica. Constable's Monthly List, Feb 1925.

Ransom, W. Private presses and their books. New York 1929.

Books and mss in the London sale-rooms. Bookman, Oct 1931.

Wolff, J. J. Gissing's revision of The unclassed. Nineteenth-Cent Fiction, June 1953.

Harper, K. E. and B. A. Booth. Russian translations of nineteenth-century English fiction. Ibid, Dec 1953.

Gordan, J. D. George Gissing (1857–1903): an exhibition from the Berg collection. NYPL 1954.

Collie, M. The revision of Gissing's New Grub street. YES 4, 1974.

Korg, J. Cancelled passages in Gissing's The unclassed. BNYPL, Summer 1977.

Coustillas, P. Sidelights on Gissing's publishing career. Gissing Newsletter, July 1986.

Coustillas, P. Recent work and close prospects in Gissing studies. ELT 32 no 4, 1989.

Selected obituaries

29 Dec 1903: Birmingham Daily Gazette, Birmingham Daily Mail, Boston Evening Transcript, Daily Chron (leader and obituary), Daily Express, Daily Mail, Daily Mirror, Daily News, Daily Telegraph, Echo, Glasgow Herald, Globe, Leeds and Yorkshire Mercury, Leeds Daily News, Manchester Courier, Manchester Evening Chron (leader and paragraphs), Manchester Evening News, Morning Post, New York Herald, New York Times, Pall Mall Gazette, St James's Gazette, San Francisco Chron, Scotsman, Standard, [H. H. Child] The Times, Westminster Gazette, Yorkshire Daily Express.

30 Dec 1903: Age (Melbourne), Birmingham Daily Gazette, Bristol Daily Mercury, Bristol Times and Mirror (leader and obituary), Daily Express, Daily Graphic, (C. F. G. Masterman) Daily News, Glasgow Herald (leader), Leeds and Yorkshire Mercury, Leeds Daily News, Liverpool Daily Post, Liverpool Mercury (leader), Manchester Courier (leader and obituary), Manchester Guardian (leader), Morning Leader, New York Daily Tribune (leader), Scotsman, (J. D[erry]) Sheffield Daily Independent, Sheffield Daily Telegraph, Vossische Zeitung (Berlin) (evening edn), Western Daily News (leader), Wolverhampton Chron, Yorkshire Daily Observer, Yorkshire Herald, Yorkshire Post.

31 Dec 1903: (A man of Kent) Br Weekly, Daily Graphic (leader).

1 Jan 1904: Literary World, Public Opinion, The Times (weekly edn), Vossische Zeitung (Berlin) (morning edn).

2 Jan 1904: Athenaeum, Graphic, (L. F. Austin) Illus London News, Labour Leader, Manchester City News, New York Times Sat Rev, Nottinghamshire Guardian, Outlook, Pilot, Publishers' Weekly, St Jean-de-Luz Gazette, Sat Rev, Speaker, Spectator, Sphere (also 9 Jan), Wakefield and West Riding Herald (also 9 Jan), Wakefield Express.

3 Jan 1904: (Hubert [Bland]) Sunday Chron, Manchester.

6 Jan 1904: To-Day, (C. K. S[horter]) Tatler.

8 Jan 1904: Church Times, (Harry Beswick) Clarion, (John o' London) T. P.'s Weekly.

9 Jan 1904: (G. C. Williamson and W. M. Colles) Acad and Lit, (W. F. Black) Labour Leader, (Max Meyerfeld) Die Nation, Westminster Gazette.

11 Jan 1904: (Morley Roberts) Westminster Gazette.

13 Jan 1904: (J. C. H[adden]) Wolverhampton Chron.

15 Jan 1904: (Morley Roberts) Church Times (also 29 Jan), (Alys Hallard [Alice Ward]) Weekly Critical Rev (Paris).

16 Jan 1904: (C. F. K[eary]) Athenaeum.

17 Jan 1904: (G. W. Foote) Freethinker.

19 Jan 1904: Bookseller.

30 Jan 1904: Outlook.

1 Feb 1904: (E. W. Hornung; Alys Hallard [Alice Ward]) Author.

1 Mar 1904: (Mimnermus) Literary Guide.

Mar 1904: Critic (New York).

Pre-1920 criticism

Items rptd in Gissing: the critical heritage, *ed P. Coustillas and C. Partridge 1972, are omitted.*

Collet, C. George Gissing's novels: a first impression. Charity Organization Rev, Oct 1891.

Dolman, F. The social reformer in fiction. Westminster Rev, May 1892.

T[repka], N. Jerzy Moore i Jerzy R. Gissing. Ateneum (Warsaw), Nov 1893.

Fitch, G. H. The best work of George Gissing. San Francisco Chron, 13 Oct 1895.

George Gissing. Owens College Union Mag, Dec 1895.

Hilliard, J. N. An eminent English writer: Mr George Gissing and his work. Union and Advertiser (Rochester NY), 21 Mar 1896.

Meyer, A. N. Neglected books II: Mr Gissing's The odd women. Bookman (New York), Mar 1896.

Krout, M. H. Woman's kingdom: The odd women. Daily Inter Ocean (Chicago), 7 Nov 1896.

A. R. O[rage]. George Gissing. Labour Leader, 14, 21 Nov 1896, rptd Gissing Newsletter, Apr 1983.

Cummings, A. M. George Gissing's Gloom. Boston Evening Transcript, 9 Oct 97, rptd Current Lit, Jan 1898.

Is pessimism necessary? Critic, 5 Mar 1898.

Jerzy Gissing. Prawda (Warsaw), 30 May 1898.

White, G. A novelist of the hour. Sewanee Rev, July 1898, rptd in Collected articles on George Gissing, ed P. Coustillas 1968.

Michaelis, K. W. George Gissing. Boston Evening Transcript, 9 Nov 1898.

Bertz, E. Gissing. In Goldenes Buch der Weltlitteratur, ed W. Spemann, Berlin 1901.

Courtney, W. L. George Gissing. Eng Illus Mag, Nov 1903.

Bateson, M. [Mrs W. E. Heitland]. Mr George Gissing. Guardian, 6 Jan 1904.

Sturmer, H. and A. Ransom. George Gissing: two appreciations. Week's Survey, 9 Jan 1904.

Shan F. Bullock estimates art of late George Gissing. Chicago Evening Post, 16 Jan 1904.

Ley, J. W. T. Friday notes. T. P.'s Weekly, 22 Jan 1904.

Waugh, Arthur. George Gissing. Fortnightly Rev, 1 Feb 1904, rptd Living Age, 19 Mar 1904; Eclectic Mag, May 1904; in his Reticence in literature, 1915.

M. George Gissing. An appreciation. Book Lover (Melbourne), 1 Feb 1904.

Zangwill, I. George Gissing. To-Day, 3 Feb 1904, rptd Reader Mag, May 1904; Gissing Newsletter, Oct 1971.

MacCarthy, J. Politics and literature in England. Independent (New York), 18 Feb 1904.

Björkman, E. George Gissing. Bookman, Feb 1904.

(K[lara] J[ohanson]). George Gissing. Stockholms Dagblad, 17 Apr 1904.

Dinglewood Mag (Colwyn Bay), Apr 1904. Gissing no.

W. C. Jerzy Gissing. Prawda (Warsaw), 9 July 1904.

Richardson, J. J. George Gissing. Manchester Quart, July 1904.

Bullock, Shan F. George Gissing in Chicago. Chicago Evening Post, 27 Aug 1904.

Wells, H. G. George Gissing: an impression. Monthly Rev, Aug 1904, rptd Living Age, 1 Oct 1904; Eclectic Mag, Nov 1904; George Gissing and H. G. Wells, ed R. A. Gettmann 1961.

The 'broken and abnormal career' of George Gissing. Literary Digest, 24 Sep 1904.

[Roberts, Morley]. The exile of George Gissing. Albany Mag, Christmas 1904.

MacCarthy, J. George Gissing. King, 21 Jan 1905.

Davray, H. D. Causerie littéraire: George Gissing. Semaine littéraire (Geneva), 4 Aug 1906.

Harrison, A. George Gissing. Nineteenth Cent, Sep 1906, rptd Living Age, 27 Oct 1906; George Gissing: critical essays, ed J.-P. Michaux 1981.

Rzewuski, S. Georges Gissing. Figaro (suppl littéraire), 13 Oct 1906.

The thought of George Gissing. Manchester Univ Mag, May 1908.

Lang, Andrew. The bookman's character. Morning Post, 9 Oct 1908.

Schaefer, A. George Gissing: Sein Leben und seine Romane. Marburg 1908.

Hirata, K. George Gissing. Shinshosetsu, June 1909. 1st article on Gissing in Japan.

C[harles] B[onnier]. George Gissing: le milieu réfractaire. In his Milieux d'art, [1910].

Svartengren T. H. Studies in the language of George Gissing as represented by The crown of life. Umeå 1910.
Chapman E. M. In his English literature in account with religion, Boston and New York 1910.
J. C. M. George Gissing. Glasgow Herald, 20 May 1911.
Johnson, L. About Dickens. Acad (suppl), 24 Feb 1912, rptd from Acad, 22 Apr 1899.
Choisy, H. Un romancier social: George Gissing. Wissen und Leben (Zurich), 15 Nov 1912.
Pugh, E. An inverted idealist, and Swinnerton, F. The real Gissing. Bookman, Dec 1912.
Wells, H. G. The truth about Gissing. Rhythm (literary suppl), Dec 1912, rptd New York Times Rev of Books, 12 Jan 1913.
Seccombe, T. Gissing, George. In DNB suppl 1912. *See* P. Coustillas, Thomas Seccombe writes the Gissing entry in the DNB, Gissing Newsletter, Oct 1977–Jan 1978.
Swinnerton, F. George Gissing: a critical study. 1912; New York 1912; London 1923; New York 1923; Port Washington NY 1966.
Roberts, Morley. The private life of Henry Maitland. 1912; New York 1912; London 1923 (rev); New York 1923 (rev); ed M. Bishop, London 1958. Biography disguised as a novel. *See* P. Coustillas, The publication of The private life of Henry Maitland, in Twilight of dawn: studies in English literature in transition, ed O. M. Brack jr, Tucson AZ 1987.
Kennedy, J. M. In his English literature 1880–1905, 1912.
Fehr, B. In his Streifzüge durch die neueste englische Literatur, Strassburg 1912.
Benson, A. C. George Gissing. Manchester Guardian, 5 Mar 1913. With leader, A Manchester memorial to Gissing, and letter to the ed proposing to found a scholarship, also ptd in The Times and Yorkshire Post of 5 Mar and Spectator of 8 Mar.
Project of dishonour. Manchester City News, 8 Mar 1913. Protest against the Gissing memorial. Correspondence in next 3 nos.
Fuller, E. George Gissing: his life and art. Brown Alumni Monthly (Providence RI), Mar 1913.
Grüenbaum, D. George Gissing. Nordisk Tidskrift, 1913.
Björkman, E. George Gissing. In his Voices of to-morrow, 1913.
Nicoll, W. R. George Gissing. In his A bookman's letters, 1913.
Adcock, A. St John. In his Booklover's London, 1913 (passim).
The trail of Gissing. Bookman (New York), Feb 1914.
Gissing the extraordinary. Bookman (New York), Mar 1914.
Bookman, Jan 1915. Gissing no.
Pond, L. H. George Gissing. East and West (Bombay), Feb 1915.
Walker, Hugh. Some essayists of yesterday. In his English essay and essayists, 1915.
Douglas, Norman. Old Calabria. 1915. Ch 36.
Young, W. T. in A. W. Ward and A. R. Waller, The Cambridge history of English literature vol 13 1916.
Adcock, A. St John. A novelist who is slowly coming into his own. Boston Evening Transcript, 1 June 1918.
Kranendonk, A. G. van. George Gissing's Ry[e]croft en 'Frank Rozelaar'. Groot Nederland, July 1918.
Horn, W. George Gissing über das dichterische Schaffen. Archiv für das Studium der neueren Sprachen und Literaturen, July 1918.
Follett, W. In his The modern novel, New York 1918.
Roberts, Morley. George Gissing: what is a classic? Bookman's Jnl, 19 Dec 1919.
Follett, H. T. and W. George Gissing. In their Some modern novelists, 1919.
Cunliffe, J. W. George Gissing. In his English literature during the last half-century, 1919.

Biographies

Anderson, J. George Gissing as he is. Boston Evening Transcript, 13 June 1896 rptd Current Lit, Aug 1896 (abridged).
Hilliard, J. N. The author of The Whirlpool. Book Buyer, Feb 1898, rptd in part in Mr George Gissing at home, Acad suppl 5 Mar 1898.
See P. Coustillas, A confession unwisely revealed: the uneasy relationship between Gissing and John Northern Hilliard, Gissing Jnl, Jan 1993.
Sykes, T. T. George Gissing, and Bowes A. Gissing's Cheshire schooldays. Alderley Edge and Wilmslow Advertiser, 22 Jan 1904, rptd in P. Coustillas, George Gissing at Alderley Edge, 1969, 1971.
Gissing et al. Dinglewood Mag (Colwyn Bay), Apr 1904. Gissing no.
Wilkins, A. S. George Robert Gissing. Owens College Union Mag, Jan 1904.
[Lister, E.] Some recollections of George Gissing. GM, Feb 1906.
Harrison, A. George Gissing. Nineteenth Cent and After, Sep 1906.
Roberts, M. The private life of Henry Maitland. 1912; New York 1912; London 1923 (rev); ed Morchard Bishop 1958. Biography disguised as fiction.
Clodd, E. Memories. 1916. Recollections with letters.
Stearns, G. A. George Gissing in America. Bookman, Aug 1926.
Harrison, A. Frederic Harrison: thoughts and memories. 1926.
Gissing, E. George Gissing: a character sketch. Nineteenth Cent and After, Sep 1927.
Gissing, A. C. George Gissing – some aspects of his life and work. Nat Rev, Aug 1929.
Donnelly, M. C. George Gissing: grave comedian. Cambridge MA 1954; Millwood NY 1973.
Adams, R. M. George Gissing and Clara Collet. Nineteenth-Cent Fiction, June 1956.
Gettmann, R. A. Bentley and Gissing. Nineteenth-Cent Fiction, Mar 1957.
Young, A. C. George Gissing's friendship with Eduard Bertz. Nineteenth-Cent Fiction, Dec 1958.
Coustillas, P. George Gissing à Manchester. EA, July–Sep 1963.
Korg, J. George Gissing: a critical biography. Seattle 1963; London 1965 (rev); Seattle 1979 (rev); Brighton 1980.
Coustillas, P. Henry Hick's recollections of Gissing. HLQ 29, 1966; London 1973 (with Gissing's letters to Henry Hick).
Tindall, G. The born exile: George Gissing. 1974; New York 1974.
Collie, M. George Gissing: a biography. Folkestone 1977; Hamden CT 1977.
Brook, C. George Gissing and Wakefield. Introd by P. Coustillas, Wakefield 1980, 1992 (rev).
Coustillas, P. Gissing and Crackanthorpe: a note on their relationship. N & Q, Oct 1981.
Halperin, J. Gissing: a life in books. 1982, 1987.
Selig, R. L. Gissing's benefactor at the Chicago Tribune. EA, Oct–Dec 1985.
Coustillas, P. Gissing's reminiscences of his father: an unpublished manuscript. ELT 32 no 4, 1989.
Coustillas, P. 'Found him a genial fellow, well disposed': the relationship between Gissing and Herbert Heaton Sturmer. Gissing Jnl, July 1994. [PC]

Sir Edmund Gosse 1845–1928

See col 2345.

Nat[haniel] Gould, 'Verax' 1857–1919

Selections

A stable mystery, and other stories. [1921.] Contains A stable mystery; His last chance; Chased by fire.

§1

The double event: a tale of the Melbourne Cup. [1891], [1898]. First pbd in Australia in serial form as With the tide.
Jockey Jack. 1892.

Running it off: or hard hit. 1892.
Banker and broker. [1893.]
Harry Dale's jockey 'Wild Rose': her life and adventures. [1893.]
Stuck up. 1894.
Thrown away: or Basil Ray's mistake. 1894.
On and off the turf in Australia. [1895.]
Only a commoner. [1895.]
The doctor's double: an Anglo-Australian sensation. [1896.]
The magpie jacket: a tale of the turf. 1896.
The Miners' Cup: a Coolgardie romance. [1896.]
Town and bush: stray notes on Australia. 1896.
Who did it? 1896.
Horse or blacksmith? 1897, [1899] (as Hills and dales).
A lad of mettle. [1897.]
Not so bad after all. 1897.
Seeing him through: a racing story. 1897.
The famous match: being the story of a great race. [1898.]
A gentleman rider: a tale of the Grand National. [1898.]
Golden ruin. [1898.]
Landed at last. [1898.]
Racecourse and battlefield. [1898.]
The dark horse. [1899.]
The old mare's foal. [1899.]
The pace that kills. [1899.]
A dead certainty. [1900.]
His last plunge. [1900.]
A rank outsider. [1900.]
The roar of the ring. [1900.]
The sporting annual: for sportsmen and sportswomen at home and abroad. 1900. Ed Gould. Contains Gould's Chased by fire.
Sporting sketches: being recollections and reflections on a variety of subjects connected with sport, horses and horsemen, never before published. [1900], [1921] (as Sporting stories), [1925] (as Sporting sketches).
A racecourse tragedy. [1901.]
Settling day. [1901.]
A stable mystery. [1901.]
Warned off. [1901.]
Broken down. [1902.]
His last chance, by Nat Gould, and other stories. [1902.] Also contains Gould's Chased by fire, 1st pbd in The sporting annual, *above*, 1900.
In royal colours. [1902.]
King of the Ranges: a blend of fact and fiction. [1902.]
Life's web. [1902], [1904] (as A near thing).
A racing sinner. [1902.]
Blue cap. [1903.]
Bred in the bush. [1903.]
Raymond's ride. [1903.]
The runaways: a new and original story. [1903.]
The silken rein. [1903.]
The three wagers. [1903.]
The gold whip. [1904.]
In low water. [1904.]
The outcast: a new and original story. [1904.]
The rajah's racer. [1904.]
The second string. [1904.]
A bit of a rogue: a new and original story. [1905.]
The boy in green. [1905.]
One of a mob. 1905.
The selling plater. 1905.
The story of Black Bess, as told by her owner, and written by Nat Gould. [1905.]
A hundred to one chance. [1906.]
The lady trainer. [1906.]
The pet of the public: a new and original story. [1906.]
A sporting squatter. [1906.]
A straight goer. [1906.]
The chance of a lifetime. [1907], [1909], [1910] (as The lottery colt). Original title re-used 1910 for a new work, *below*.
Charger and chaser. [1907.]
The Little Wonder. [1907.]
A stroke of luck: a new and original story. [1907.]
A bird in hand: a new and original story. [1908.]
The dapple grey. [1908.]
The top weight. [1908.]
Whirlwind's year. 1908.
The buckjumper. 1909.
The jockey's revenge. 1909.
The magic of sport, mainly autobiographical. 1909. Autobiography.
The pick of the stable: a new and original story. [1909.]
A reckless owner. [1909.]
The stolen racer. [1909.]
The chance of a lifetime: a novel founded on Nat Gould's drama of the same name. [1910], [1915]. A different work from same title 1907, *above*.
A great coup. [1910.]
The lucky shoe. [1910.]
Queen of the Turf: a new and original story. [1910.]
The roarer. [1910.]
A cast off. [1911.]
The king's favourite. [1911.]
The phantom horse: a new and original story. 1911.
Good at the game. [1912.]
Left in the lurch: a new and original story. 1912.
A member of Tatt's. [1912.]
The trainer's treasure. [1912.]
The best of the season: a new and original story. 1913.
A fortune at stake. 1913.
The head lad. [1913.]
The flyer: a new and original story. 1914.
A gamble for love. 1914.
Never in doubt. 1915.
The white arab: a new and original story. 1915.
The Wizard of the Turf. 1915.
Breaking the record. 1916.
Lost and won: a tale of sport and war. 1916.
A turf conspiracy. [1916.]
A northern crack. 1917.
The smasher. [1917.]
Fast as the wind. [1918.]
A race for a wife. [1918.]
The rider in khaki. [1918.]
The steeplechaser. [1918.]
Won on the post. 1918.
At starting price. [1920.]
A chestnut champion. [1920.]
Odds on. [1920.]
Racing rivals. [1920.]
The silver star. [1920.]
The sweep winner. [1920.]
The blue ribbon. [1921.]
The Demon wins. [1921.]
A Derby winner. [1921.]
In the paddock. [1921.]
A long shot. [1921.]
The man from Newmarket. [1921.]
The Rake. [1921.]
A bad start. [1922.]
A dangerous stable. [1922.]
A great surprise. 1922.
Sold for a song. 1922.

Beating the favourite. 1923.
A brilliant season. 1923.
The challenge. 1924.
First in the field. 1924.
Riding to orders. 1925.
The major's mascot. 1926. Short stories.
The racing adventures of Barry Bromley. 1926.
The exploits of a race-course detective. 1927.
Trainers' tales. 1927.
Most titles reissued more than once and a number of abridgements produced for the Mellifont Racing Series. [EH]

Sarah Grand 1854–1943

Major collection of letters in Bath Reference Lib; 70 letters in Sadleir Collection UCLA.

Bibliography
Huddleston, J. Sarah Grand: a bibliography. Victorian Fiction Research Guide 1. St Lucia, Queensland 1979.

Selections
The breath of life. Ed G. Singers-Bigger, Bath 1933 (priv ptd).

§1

Two dear little feet. 1873.
Constance of Calais. Libretto by Mrs D. Chambers McFall, music by Francis Edward Gladstone. 1884.
Ideala: a study from life. Warrington, Lancs 1888 (priv ptd, anon), London 1888 (anon), 1889 (anon), 1893, New York 1893, 1894, Chicago [1899?].
REVIEWS: Saturday Rev 66, Sep 1888; Spectator 62, Jan 1889; Nation 57, Nov 1893.
A domestic experiment. Edinburgh 1891.
The heavenly twins. Warrington, Lancs 1892 (priv ptd, anon), London 1893, New York 1893, London 1893 (Colonial Lib), 1894, 1895 (Popular Six-Shilling Novels), 1901, New York 1901, London 1912 (Sixpenny Novels), 1923 (with foreword by Sarah Grand); tr Du 1895, Ger 1898.
REVIEWS: Critic 23, Oct 1893; Lippincott's Mag 52 1893; [W. T. Stead] Rev of Revs 10 1894.
Singularly deluded. First pbd Blackwood's Mag 1892. Edinburgh 1893, New York 1893 (Seaside Lib), 1895, [189?], 1899.
Our manifold nature. 1894, New York 1894, Leipzig 1894 (Tauchnitz), New York 1971 (Books for Libs). Short stories; tr Ger 1907.
REVIEWS: Spectator 72, Apr 1894; Saturday Rev 78, Sep 1894.
The Beth book. New York 1897, Toronto 1897, London 1898, 1979; tr Ger 1898.
REVIEWS: Rev of Revs 16 1897 (including portrait); Spectator 79, Nov 1897.
Modern man and maid. 1898, New York 1898.
The tenor and the boy. (Central section from The heavenly twins.) 1899.
Babs the impossible. First pbd Harper's Bazaar 33 1900, Lady's Realm 8–9 1900–1, New York 1900, London 1901.
REVIEWS: Macmillan's Mag Sep 1900; Athenaeum 3834 1901; Dial 30 1901.
The human quest: being some thoughts in contribution to the subject of the art of happiness. 1900.
Emotional moments. 1908, Leipzig 1908 (Tauchnitz). Short stories.
Adnam's orchard. 1912, New York 1913.
REVIEW: TLS 24 Oct 1912.
The winged victory. 1916, New York 1916.
REVIEW: Athenaeum 4609 1916.
Variety. 1922. Short stories.

Contributions to periodicals
Essays
Morals and manners of appearance. Humanitarian 3 1893.
The new aspect of the woman question. North Amer Rev 158 1894.
Man of the moment. North Amer Rev 158 1894.
The modern girl. North Amer Rev 158 1894, Temple Mag 2 1898.
A page of confessions. Woman at Home 3 1894.
Marriage questions in fiction: the standpoint of the typical modern woman. Fortnightly Rev 375 1898.
The modern young man. Temple Mag 2 1898.
The new woman and the old. Lady's Realm 4 1898.
Does marriage hinder a woman's self-development? Lady's Realm 5 1898–9.
Some recollections of my schooldays. Lady's Mag 1 1901.
The modern English girl. Canadian Mag 10 1901.
Preface to 'Bartholomew's' As they are, 1908.
Case of the modern spinster. Pall Mall Mag 51 1913.
Case of the modern married woman. Pall Mall Mag 51 1913.
Introd. In M. M. Betham-Edwards, Mid-Victorian memories, 1919.

Stories
Mamma's music lessons. Aunt Judy's Mag 1878.
School revisited. Aunt Judy's Mag 1880.
The great typhoon. Aunt Judy's Mag 1881.
Kane a soldier servant. Temple Bar 92 1891, Littell's Living Age 190 1891, rptd in Our manifold nature.
Janey, a humble administrator. Temple Bar 93 1891, Littell's Living Age 191 1891, rptd in Our manifold nature.
Boomellen. Temple Bar 94 1892, Littell's Living Age 193 1892, rptd in Our manifold nature.
Eugenia. Temple Bar 99 1893, rptd in Our manifold nature.
Ah man. Woman at Home 1 1894, rptd in Our manifold nature.
The undefinable. New Rev 11 1894, Cosmopolitan 17 1894, rptd in Emotional moments.
A momentary indiscretion. Cosmopolitan 20 1895.
The wrong road. English Illus Mag 1895, rptd in Emotional moments.
She was silent. Lady's Realm 1 1897, rptd in Emotional moments.
The baby's tragedy. Lady's Realm 3 1897–8, rptd in Emotional moments.
When the door opened. Idler 12 1897, rptd in Emotional moments.
A new sensation. Windsor Mag 1899, rptd in Emotional moments.
The man in the scented coat. Lady's World 1904, rptd in Emotional moments.
One of the olden time. Pall Mall Mag 98 n.s. 14 1911, rptd in Variety.

§2

Cotton, J. J. Madame Grand. Macmillan's Mag Sep 1900.
McFall, H. Sarah Grand. Biograph & Rev 11 1902.
Black, H. Notable women authors of the day. 1906.
Foerster, E. Die Frauenfragen in den Romanen englischer Schriftstellerinnen der Gegenwart (George Egerton, Mona Caird, Sarah Grand). Marburg 1907.
Huddleston, J. Sarah Grand. St Lucia, Queensland 1979.
Kersley, G. Darling Madame. 1983. [JM]

'Sydney C. Grier', Hilda Caroline Gregg 1868–1933

Letters regarding the pbn of her works are located in the Blackwood Papers, Nat Lib of Scotland.

§1

In furthest Ind. 1894.
An uncrowned king. 1896 (first serialised in Blackwood's Mag 1895–6), 1903, 1907.
His excellency's English governess. 1896 (serialised in Girl's Own Guide 1896).

Peace with honour. 1897 (serialised in Argosy 1897).
A crowned queen: the romance of a minister of state. 1898, 1907.
Like another Helen. 1899.
The kings of the East. 1900, 1907.
The warden of the marshes. 1901 (serialised in Argosy 1901), 1905, 1912.
Prince of the captivity. 1902.
The advanced guard. 1903, 1912.
The great proconsul. The memoirs of Mrs Hester Ward. 1904. Novel.
On the winning side. 1904.
For triumph or truth? A tale of thrilling adventure. 1904.
The letters of Warren Hastings to his wife. (Letters introduced and annotated by S. C. Grier.) 1905.
The heir. 1906.
The power of the keys. 1907.
The heritage. 1908.
A young man married. 1909, 1912.
The path to honour. 1909, 1913.
The prize. 1910.
The keepers of the gate. 1911.
One crowded hour. 1912.
Writ in water. 1913.
A royal marriage. 1914.
The rearguard. 1915.
England hath need of thee. 1916.
The kingdom of waste lands. 1917.
The princess's tragedy. 1918.
Berringer of Bandeir. 1919.
The strong hand. 1920.
The flag of the adventurer. 1921.
Out of prison. 1922.
Two strong men. 1923.
A brother of girls. Some experiences of Major William Barnes. 1925.

Contributions to periodicals

What came of a clergyman's fortnight. (Short story.) Cassell's Family Mag 17 1890–1.
A six weeks' wooing. (Short story.) Cassell's Family Mag 20 1893–4.
Stratford's love story. (Short story.) Argosy 65 [1897?].
An Indian mutiny in fiction. Blackwood's Mag 7388, Feb 1897.
Early Victorian fiction. Blackwood's Mag 7419, May 1897.
John Nicholson of Delhi. Blackwood's Mag 7517, Feb 1898.
The medical woman in fiction. Blackwood's Mag 7579, July 1898.
A good turn. (Short story.) Blackwood's Mag 7600, Sep 1898.
Deaconess Chriemhild's romance. (Short story.) Argosy 69 [1900?].
[DF]

Sir Henry Rider Haggard 1856–1925

Norfolk Records Office at Norwich has much material, including holographs of early mss; other important collections include the Cassell Collection (Cassell Ltd, 35 Red Lion Square, London), and Columbia Univ Lib, New York.

Bibliography

McKay, G. L. A bibliography of the writings of Sir Rider Haggard. 1930.
Scott, J. E. A bibliography of the works of Sir Henry Rider Haggard 1856–1925. 1947.

§1

Cetywayo and his white neighbours. 1882, 1888 (with addns), 1893 (5th edn); reissued as A history of the Transvaal, New York 1899, London 1900.
Dawn. 3 vols 1884, New York 1887, Leipzig 1892 (Tauchnitz).
Thc witch's head. 3 vols 1885, New York 1885, London 1887, 1888, Leipzig 1887 (Tauchnitz).
King Solomon's mines. 1885. 'Fifty-third thousand' illustr W. Paget 1887; 1891, 1898; 'revised edition with thirty-two illustrations by Russell Flint' 1905; 1907, 1915; illustr Charles Keeping 1961; illustr A. R. Whitear 1963; ed Dennis Butts 1989 (Oxford WCp). New York 1885, 1887, 1888, 1904, 1920, etc. Leipzig 1886 (Tauchnitz). Tr Fr 1890, Afrikaans 1938, Sp 1973, Korean 1983, etc.
She. First pbd in Graphic 1886–7. 1887, 1888, 1891, 'new and revised edition' 1896, 1899, 1913, 1915, 1920; 1925 (special film edn); illustr Hookway Cowles 1952; illustr Will Nickless 1959; ed Daniel Karlin 1991 (Oxford WCp). New York 1887, 1888, 1911, etc. 'An operatic spectacular drama' by R. C. White, New York 1887. Tr Du 1934, Ger 1970, etc.
Jess. First pbd in Cornhill Mag 1886–7. 1887; 'new and revised edition' illustr Maurice Greiffenhagen 1896. Chicago 1887; Leipzig 1887 (Tauchnitz).
Allan Quatermain. First pbd in Longman's Mag 1887. 1887, 1891, 1904, 1918; illustr Hookway Cowles 1949; illustr Will Nickless 1955; ed Dennis Butts 1995 (Oxford WCp). New York 1887, 1888, 1894, 1899, etc. Leipzig 1887 (Tauchnitz). Tr Icelandic 1906, Swahili 1935, Sp 1965, etc.
A tale of three lions. New York 1887. First pbd in Atalanta 1887. Rptd in Allan's wife, London 1889, 1951.
Mr Meeson's will. First pbd in Illus London News Summer 1888. 1888, 'Fifteenth thousand' 1894. New York 1888. Leipzig 1888 (Tauchnitz). Tr Polish 1889.
Maiwa's revenge: or the war of the little hand. 1888, 1891, 1916; 'new edition' 1923; illustr Hookway Cowles 1965. New York, Chicago 1888. Leipzig (Tauchnitz) 1888.
My fellow laborer and the wreck of the 'Copeland'. First pbd in Collier's Once a Week 1888. New York 1888, 1897.
Colonel Quaritch VC. 3 vols 1888, 1 vol 1915, New York 1888, Leipzig 1889 (Tauchnitz); tr Ger 1891.
Cleopatra. First pbd in Illus London News 1889. 1889, 1913, 1924; illustr Hookway Cowles 1958; New York 1889; Leipzig 1889 (Tauchnitz). Fr opera by G. Sandré 1905. Tr Ger 1925, Rus 1991.
Allan's wife and other tales. 1889, 1891, 1914. Chicago and New York 1889 etc.
Beatrice. 1890, 'fourth edition' 1892, 1903, 1915. Chicago 1890. Leipzig 1890 (Tauchnitz). Tr Ger 1891; Swed 1913.
The world's desire. 1890. With Andrew Lang; first pbd in New Rev 1890. 'New edition' illustr Maurice Greiffenhagen 1894; illustr Geoffrey Whittam 1953. New York 1890. Leipzig 1891 (Tauchnitz).
Eric Brighteyes. 1891, 'fourth edition' 1895, 1949. New York 1891. Leipzig 1891 (Tauchnitz).
Nada the lily. 1892; illustr Cyrus Cuneo 1896; illustr Will Nickless 1951. New York 1892. Tr Polish 1894.
An heroic effort. (A plea for contributions to the Universities' Mission to Central Africa.) 1893.
Montezuma's daughter. 1893, 1896; illustr Hookway Cowles 1948; 'thirteenth impression' 1958. New York 1893, 1909, etc. Tr Czech 1923, Hebrew 1975, etc.
The people of the mist. 1894; illustr Cyrus Cuneo 1906; illustr Jack Matthews 1951. New York 1894. Leipzig 1894 (Tauchnitz).
Church and State. 1895.
Joan Haste. First pbd in Pall Mall Mag 1894–5. 1895. New York 1895. Tr Polish 1896.
Heart of the world. New York 1895, London 1896, 1907, 1926, etc; illustr Hookway Cowles 1954. Tr Lettish 1934; Irish 1937.
The wizard. Bristol 1896; illustr Newton Whittaker, London 1940. New York 1896. Leipzig 1897 (Tauchnitz).
Dr Therne. 1898. Leipzig 1899 (Tauchnitz).
A farmer's year. First pbd in Longman's Mag 1898–9. 1899; 'new impression' 1906.
The last Boer War. 1899; '30th thousand' 1900.
Swallow. 1899, New York [1898]. Leipzig 1899 (Tauchnitz).
Black heart and white heart, and other stories. 1900. Leipzig 1900 (Tauchnitz). New York 1911.

House of mercy . . . An appeal. 1900.
Lysbeth. 1901. Leipzig 1901 (Tauchnitz). New York 1907.
A winter pilgrimage. First pbd in Queen 1901. 1901. Leipzig 1902 (Tauchnitz).
Rural England. 2 vols 1902, 1906.
Pearl Maiden. 1903, 1906. New York [1902]. Leipzig 1903 (Tauchnitz).
Stella Fregelius. First pbd in TP's Weekly 1902–3. 1904, Leipzig 1904 (Tauchnitz).
The brethren. 1904, 1910, 1929; illustr Hookway Cowles 1952. New York 1904, Leipzig 1904 (Tauchnitz). Tr Icelandic 1916.
Ayesha: the return of She. First pbd in Windsor Mag 1904–5. 1905; illustr Hookway Cowles 1956; illustr Will Nickless 1957. Toronto 1905. Leipzig 1905 (Tauchnitz).
A gardener's year. 1905. First pbd in Queen 1904.
Report on Salvation Army colonies. 1905, 1905 (rev as The poor and the land).
Back to the land: a plea for state-directed colonisation. 1905.
The way of the spirit. 1906. Leipzig 1906 (Tauchnitz).
Benita. 1906; illustr Hookway Cowles. As The spirit of Bambatse. New York 1906. Leipzig 1907 (Tauchnitz).
Fair Margaret. 1907. As Margaret New York 1907. Leipzig 1907 (Tauchnitz).
The real wealth of England. An address delivered on behalf of Dr Barnardo's homes. 1907.
The ghost kings. 1908, 1912.
The yellow god. New York 1908, London 1909.
The lady of Blossholme. First pbd in The British Weekly 1909 as The lady of heavens. 1909, New York 1908. Leipzig 1909 (Tauchnitz). Tr Swed 1911.
Morning star. 1910, New York 1910, Leipzig 1910 (Tauchnitz).
Queen Sheba's ring. 1910; illustr Geoffrey Whittam 1953. New York 1910. Leipzig 1910 (Tauchnitz). Tr Rus 1962.
Regeneration: an account of the social work of the Salvation Army. 1910.
The Mahatma and the hare. 1911, New York 1911.
Red eve. New York 1911. Leipzig 1911 (Tauchnitz).
Rural Denmark. 1911; 'New edition' 1917.
Marie. 1912; illustr Hookway Cowles 1959. New York 1913. Leipzig 1913 (Tauchnitz). Tr Sp 1951.
Child of storm. 1913.
A call to arms. 1914 (priv ptd).
Letter to the Right Hon Lewis Harcourt from Sir Rider Haggard relating to his visit to Rhodesia and Zululand. 1914.
The wanderer's necklace. 1914, New York 1914. Leipzig 1914 (Tauchnitz).
The holy flower. First pbd in The Windsor Mag 1913–14. 1915; illustr Hookway Cowles 1954. As Allan and the holy flower. New York 1915.
The after-war settlement and employment of ex-service men. 1916.
The ivory child. 1916; illustr Hookway Cowles 1958. New York 1916.
Finished. 1917; illustr Hookway Cowles 1962. New York 1921, etc.
Love eternal. 1918, New York 1918.
Moon of Israel. 1918, Toronto 1918. Tr Esperanto 1928.
When the world shook. 1919, New York 1919.
The ancient Allan. 1920, New York 1920.
Smith and the Pharaohs, and other tales. Bristol 1920. New York 1921.
She and Allan. First pbd in Story Mag 1919–20. 1921, New York 1921.
The virgin of the sun. 1922, New York 1922.
Wisdom's daughter. 1923, New York 1923. Leipzig 1923 (Tauchnitz).
Heu-Heu. 1924, New York 1924. Leipzig 1924 (Tauchnitz).
Queen of the dawn. 1925, New York 1925.
The days of my life. 2 vols 1926. First pbd in Strand Mag 1926, but expanded in book form.
The treasure of the lake. 1926, New York 1926.
Allan and the ice gods. 1927, New York 1927. Leipzig 1927 (Tauchnitz).
Mary of Marion Isle. 1929. As Marion Isle. New York 1929.
Balshazzar. 1930, New York 1930.

Contributions to periodicals and collaborative works

The tale of Isandhlwana and Rorke's Drift. In The true story book, ed Andrew Lang, 1893.
A wedding gift by H. Rider Haggard. In Harry Furniss's Christmas annual for 1905, 1905.

Letters or journals

Rudyard Kipling to Rider Haggard. Ed Morton Cohen 1965.
The private diaries of Sir Henry Rider Haggard. Ed D. S. Higgins 1980.

Translations or introductions or commendatory verses

Haggard, Ella. Life and its author with a memoir by H. Rider Haggard. 1890.
Jebb, B. (Mrs). A strange career. Life and adventures of John Gladwyn Jebb with an introduction by H. Rider Haggard. 1894.
Wilmot, Alexander. Monomotopa (Rhodesia), its monuments and its history with preface by H. Rider Haggard. 1896.
Dutt, William A. The king's homeland with an introduction by H. Rider Haggard. 1904.
Adams, Thomas. Garden city and agriculture with an introductory address by H. Rider Haggard. [1905.]
Home Counties (pseud, i.e. J. W. Robertson Scott). The case for the government with introductions by the Duchess of Hamilton and Brandon . . . and Mr H. Rider Haggard. 1908.

'iana' or imitations

Bess. A companion to Jess. (By John De Morgan.) New York 1887.
He. By the authors of It, King Solomon's wives, and Bess. (By Andrew Lang and W. H. Pollock.) 1887.
He. (By John De Morgan.) New York 1887.
It. (By John De Morgan.) New York 1887.
King Solomon's treasures. (By John De Morgan.) New York 1887.
King Solomon's wives: or the phantom mines by Hyder Ragged. (By Sir Henry Chartres Biron.) 1887.
'Me', or the story of the window curtains: a companion to She. Chicago 1887.

§2

Haggard, L. R. The cloak that I left: a biography. 1951.
Ellis, H. F. The niceties of plagiarism. Atlantic Monthly Jan 1959.
Cohen, M. Rider Haggard: his life and works. 1960.
Higgins, D. S. Rider Haggard: the great storyteller. 1981.
Butts, D. King Solomon's mines. Edited with a critical introd, Oxford 1989 (WCp).
Karlin, D. She. Edited with a critical introd, Oxford 1991 (WCp).
Butts, D. Allan Quatermain. Edited with a critical introd, Oxford 1995 (WCp). [DB]

Philip Gilbert Hamerton 1834–94

See col 2353.

Thomas Hardy 1840–1928

Manuscripts

Ms materials are described in individual entries.

The original manuscripts and papers of Thomas Hardy: a collection on microfilm. E. P. Microform, Wakefield, Yorkshire 1976. Includes most, but not all, of the mss material in the British Isles.
Thomas Hardy's The return of the native. Ed S. Gatrell, New York 1986. Photo facs of all ms materials relating to the novel.
Thomas Hardy's Tess of the d'Urbervilles. Ed S. Gatrell, 2 vols New York 1986. Photofacs of all ms materials relating to the novel).

Bibliographies and reference works

Hodgson & Co. A catalogue of the library of Hardy. 1938.

Purdy, R. L. Hardy: a bibliographical study. Oxford 1954, 1968 (rev). The standard work of reference for primary texts.

Bunnosuke, Y. Bibliography of Hardy in Japan. Tokyo 1957.

Bowden, A. The Hardy collection. LCUT 7 1962.

Gerber, H. E. and W. E. Davis. Thomas Hardy: an annotated bibliography of writings about him (to 1978). 2 vols De Kalb IL 1973, 1983.

Carter, K. Thomas Hardy in the Dorset County Library. Thomas Hardy Soc Rev 6 1980 and 7 1981.

Foote, I. Thomas Hardy in Russian translation and criticism (to 1978). The Thomas Hardy Year Book 11 1984.

Draper, R. and M. Ray. An annotated critical bibliography of Thomas Hardy. 1989.

Jedrzejewski, J. The Polish translations of Thomas Hardy. Thomas Hardy Jnl 7 1991.

Collections and selections

The first English one-vol edns of 8 of the novels listed below were issued or reissued by Sampson, Low at various dates between 1881 and 1894; they were issued from 1887 onwards in matching bindings and might thus be held to constitute a first col of much of Hardy's fiction. The history of the development of the texts of Hardy's poems between individual and collected vols is complex; for description and analysis, see introd to vol 1 of S. Hynes ed, Complete poetical works, *below.*

Wessex novels (rev). 16 vols 1895–6 (illustr H. Macbeth-Raeburn).
REVIEW: Bookman May 1895.

Uniform edition (some vols rev). 19 vols 1902–3.

[Works]: Wessex edition (rev). 24 vols 1912–31 (illustr with photographs H. Lea); rptd in part as Autograph edition (some vols reset and rev), 20 vols New York 1915; Anniversary edition, 21 vols New York 1920; rptd with additional material as New Wessex edition, London 1974–7.
REVIEWS: Spectator, Sphere 18 May 1912; Daily News 20 May 1912; T. P.'s Weekly 24 May 1912; Observer 2 June 1912; Guardian 6 June 1912; Saturday Rev 22 June 1912; Bookman (New York) July 1912; Observer 7 Sep 1912; Athenaeum 12 Oct 1912; Athenaeum 9 Nov 1912; Daily News 13 Nov 1912; Athenaeum 7 Dec 1912; Saturday Rev 22 Mar 1913.

Selected poems. 1916, 1917 (copy of 1916 with ms rev Dorset County Museum), 1921, 1929 (rev and enlarged as Chosen poems; copy of 1917 with ms rev Dorset County Museum).
REVIEWS: Saturday Rev 21 Oct 1912; Morning Post 27 Oct 1916; New Statesman 4 Nov 1916; Nation 11 Nov 1916; TLS 23 Nov 1916; Boston Evening Transcript 23 Dec 1916; Bookman Dec 1916; Living Age 13 Jan 1917; Daily News 26 Jan 1917.

[Works]: Mellstock edition [de luxe] (some vols rev; copies of Wessex edn with ms rev Dorset County Museum). 37 vols 1919–20.

Collected poems. 1919 (copy of Selected poems 1916 with ms rev Dorset County Museum), 1923, 1928 (copy of 1923 with ms rev Dorset County Museum), 1930.
REVIEWS: Morning Post 17 Oct 1919; Athenaeum 7 Nov 1919; Nation 8 Nov 1919; Outlook 8 Nov 1919; Saturday Rev 15 Nov 1919; TLS 27 Nov 1919; Saurday Rev 29 Nov 1919; Observer 30 Nov 1919; Westminster Gazette 6 Dec 1919; Bookman's Jnl 12 Dec 1919; TLS 18 Dec 1919; Liverpool Post 28 Jan 1920; Bookman, London Mercury Jan 1920.

The short stories of Thomas Hardy. 1928.

Variorum edition of the complete poems of Thomas Hardy. Ed J. Gibson 1978.

The complete poetical works of Thomas Hardy. Ed S. Hynes, 5 vols Oxford 1982–95.

Thomas Hardy: the excluded and collaborative stories. Ed P. Dalziel, Oxford 1992, as An indiscretion in the life of an heiress and other stories, Oxford 1994 (WCp).

§1

Fiction

For priv ptd or uncollected contributions to books, periodicals and newspapers, see R. L. Purdy, A Bibliographical study, *above. The first English edns of novels that appeared in serial form were universally revised by Hardy; the same is true of all vols in the Wessex novels edn of 1895–6 and the Wessex edn of 1912–31; the notation '(rev)' has not been appended to entries for these vols. It is also the case that prefaces were added or altered in all fiction vols in both Wessex novels and Wessex edns. The textual relationship between American and English serialisations and early editions is in many cases complex, and cannot fully be indicated in this abbreviated listing; for further details see the WCp editions of individual works where available, and S. Gatrell,* Hardy the creator, *below. Hardy's novels have been very widely issued in hbk and pbk in Britain and the United States, particularly since 1978; the texts have almost universally followed those of the Wessex edn, above. Only versions that have been critically edited are listed here. Hardy's novels have been translated into almost every known language, but it has proved impossible to provide accurate inclusive information concerning such translations.*

Desperate remedies: a novel. 3 vols 1871 (anon), 1 vol New York 1874 (rev), London 1889 (rev), 1892, 1896, 1912, 1920.
REVIEWS: Athenaeum 1 Apr 1871; Morning Post 13 Apr 1871; Echo 21 Apr 1871; Spectator 22 Apr 1871; Saturday Rev 30 Sep 1871; Harper's New Monthly Mag June 1874.

Under the greenwood tree: a rural painting of the Dutch school. 2 vols 1872 (anon; printer's ms Dorset County Museum), 1 vol 1873, New York 1873, London 1876 (illustr R. Knight), 1896, as Under the greenwood tree or the Mellstock quire: a rural painting of the Dutch school 1902, 1912, 1920 (copy of 1912 with ms rev Dorset County Museum), 1928; ed S. Gatrell, Oxford 1985 (WCp).
REVIEWS: Athenaeum 15 June 1872; Graphic 29 June 1872; Evening Standard 2 July 1872; Pall Mall Gazette 5 July 1872; Saturday Rev 28 Sep 1872; Guardian 2 Oct 1872; Echo 11 Oct 1872; Spectator 2 Nov 1872.

A pair of blue eyes: a novel. 3 vols 1873, 1 vol New York 1873, London 1877, 2 vols Leipzig 1884, 1895, 1912, 1920 (rev; copy of 1912 with ms rev Dorset County Museum) ed A. Manford, Oxford 1985 (WCp). First pbd Tinsley's Mag Sep 1872–July 1873 (illustr J. Pasquier, printer's ms (fragmentary) Berg Col, NYPL), Semi-weekly New York Tribune 26 Sep–16 Dec 1873.
REVIEWS: Athenaeum, Spectator 28 June 1873; Nation (New York) 10 July 1873; Graphic 12 July 1873; Saturday Rev 2 Aug 1873; Times 9 Sep 1873; Southern Mag (Baltimore MD) Sep 1873; Pall Mall Gazette 25 Oct 1873; John Bull 20 May 1876; Liverpool Weekly Albion 15 Sep 1877; Examiner 13 Oct 1877.

Far from the madding crowd. 2 vols 1874 (illustr H. Paterson (Allingham)), 1 vol New York 1874, 2 vols London 1875 (rev), 1 vol 1877 (rev), 2 vols Leipzig 1878 (rev), 1895 (reviewed Dial (Chicago) 1 July 1895), 1901 (pbk rev; printer's copy, page proofs Signet lib Edinburgh), 1902 (rev), 1912, 1919 (rev; copy of 1912 with ms rev Dorset County Museum); ed R. Schweik, New York 1986; ed S. Falck-Yi; Oxford 1993 (WCp). First pbd anon in Cornhill Mag Jan–Dec 1874 (printer's ms Yale, ms fragments Dorset County Museum), Every Saturday 31 Jan–24 Oct 1874, Littell's Living Age 31 Jan 1874–9 Jan 1875, Eclectic Mag Mar 1874–Feb 1875, Semi-weekly New York Tribune 26 Jun–15 Dec 1874.
REVIEWS: Spectator 3 Jan 1874; Spectator 7 Feb 1874; Academy 14 Feb 1874; Spectator 14 Mar 1874; Echo 28 Nov 1874; World 2 Dec 1874; Athenaeum, Examiner 5 Dec 1874; Graphic, John Bull 12 Dec 1874; Spectator 19 Dec 1874; Nation (New York) 24 Dec 1874; Morning Post 28 Dec 1874; Athenaeum2 Jan 1875; Observer 3 Jan 1875; Saturday Rev 9 Jan 1875; Times 25 Jan 1875; British Quart Rev, Westminster Rev Jan 1875; Pictorial World 6 Feb 1875; Manchester Guardian 24 Feb 1875; Harper's New Monthly Mag, Scribner's Monthly Mar 1875; Revue des Deux Mondes 18 Dec 1875.
Dramatisation (by Hardy and J. Comyns Carr) as The mistress of the farm (for details *see* Purdy, A bibliographical study, *above*).

REVIEWS: (as Far from the madding crowd): Whitehall Rev 2 Mar 1882; Athenaeum, Era 4 Mar 1882; Punch 11 Mar 1882; Liverpool Daily Post 13 Mar 1882; Theatre 1 Apr 1882; Academy 13 May 1882.

The hand of Ethelberta: a comedy in chapters. 2 vols 1876 (illustr G. Du Maurier), 1 vol New York 1876, Leipzig 1876, London 1877, 1895, 1912, 1920 (copy of 1912 with ms rev Dorset County Museum). First pbd Cornhill Mag July 1875–May 1876 (rev proofs Yale), New York Times 20 June 1875–9 Apr 1876.

REVIEWS: Athenaeum 15 Apr 1876; World 19 Apr 1876; Spectator 22 Apr 1876; Saturday Rev 6 May 1876; Academy, Examiner 13 May 1876; Times 5 June 1876; Literary World (Boston) June 1876; Guardian 19 July 1876; Westminster Rev July 1876; Morning Post 5 Aug 1876; Atlantic Monthly, Harper's New Monthly Mag Aug 1876; Century (New York) Nov 1876; Scribner's Monthly Nov 1876.

The return of the native. 3 vols 1878 (map of scene drawn by Hardy, Dorset County Museum; for photo facs of all ms material, *see* S. Gatrell ed under Manuscripts, *above*), 1 vol New York 1878, Leipzig 1879, London 1880, 1895, 1912, 1920 (copy of 1912 with ms rev Dorset County Museum); ed S. Gatrell, Oxford 1990 (WCp). First pbd Belgravia Jan–Dec 1878 (illustr A. Hopkins, printer's ms University College Dublin, National University of Ireland), Harper's New Monthly Mag Feb 1878–Jan 1879.

REVIEWS: Evening Standard 2 May 1878; Academy, Athenaeum, Examiner, John Bull, London Quart Rev, Vanity Fair 30 Nov 1878; Daily Telegraph 3 Dec 1878; Times 5 Dec 1878; Graphic 7 Dec 1878; Illus London News 14 Dec 1878; Morning Post 27 Dec 1878; Contemporary Rev Dec 1878; Saturday Rev 4 Jan 1879; Observer 5 Jan 1879; British Quart Rev, Westminster Rev Jan 1879; Literary World (Boston) 1 Feb 1879; Guardian 5 Feb 1879; Spectator 8 Feb 1879; Nation (New York) 27 Feb 1879; International Rev Feb 1879; Blackwood's Mag, Harper's New Monthly Mag Mar 1879; Atlantic Monthly, Scribner's Mag Apr 1879; New Quart Mag July 1879; Atlantic Monthly Nov 1879; Liverpool Weekly Albion 10 Jan 1880.

Fellow-townsmen. New York 1880. First pbd New Quart Mag n.s. 2 1880, Harper's Weekly 17 Apr–15 May 1880. Collected in Wessex tales, *below*.

The trumpet-major: a tale. 3 vols 1880, 1 vol New York 1880, London 1881 (rev), 1895, 1902 (rev), 1912, 1920; ed R. Nemesvari, Oxford 1991 (WCp). First pbd Good Words Jan–Dec 1880 (illustr J. Collier; printer's ms Royal Library Windsor Castle), Demorest's Monthly Mag Jan 1880–Jan 1881 (variant version).

REVIEWS: Saturday Rev 6 Nov 1880; John Bull, Queen 13 Nov 1880; Daily News 18 Nov 1880; Scotsman 19 Nov 1880; Athenaeum, Court Jnl 20 Nov 1880; Pall Mall Gazette, St James' Gazette 23 Nov 1880; Examiner, Graphic, Public Opinion, Vanity Fair 27 Nov 1880; Vanity Fair 1 Dec 1880; Academy 11 Dec 1880; Spectator 18 Dec 1880; Morning Post 21 Dec 1880: Nation (New York) 6 Jan 1881; Literary World (Boston) 15 Jan 1881; British Quart Rev, Westminster Rev Jan 1881; Times 1 Feb 1881; Whitehall Rev 3 Feb 1881.

A Laodicean: a novel. 3 vols 1881, 1 vol New York 1881, Leipzig 1882 (rev), London 1882 (rev), 1896, 1912, 1920 (copy of 1912 with ms rev Dorset County Museum); ed J. Gatewood, Oxford 1991 (WCp). First pbd Harper's New Monthly Mag (European edn) Dec 1880–Dec 1881 (illustr G. Du Maurier; rev galleys and page proofs Library of Congress) and in Amer edn Jan 1881–Jan 1882.

REVIEWS: Athenaeum 31 Dec 1881; Nation (New York) 3 Jan 1882; St James' Gazette 4 Jan 1882; Academy 7 Jan 1882; World 11 Jan 1882; Saturday Rev, Vanity Fair 14 Jan 1882; Morning Post 19 Jan 1882; Court Circular, Daily News 28 Jan 1882; Literary World (Boston) Jan 1882; Globe 17 Feb 1882; Critic (New York) 25 Feb 1882; Spectator 4 Mar 1882; Observer 2 Apr 1882.

Two on a tower: a romance. 3 vols 1882 (2nd impression rev 1883), 1 vol New York 1882, Leipzig 1883 (rev), London 1883 (rev), 1895, 1912, 1920 (copy of 1912 with ms rev Dorset County Museum); ed S. Ahmad, Oxford 1993 (WCp). First pbd Atlantic Monthly May–Dec 1882 (ms, part printer's copy, Harvard).

REVIEWS: Athenaeum, Saturday Rev 18 Nov 1882; Daily News 12 Dec 1882; Literary World (Boston), Pall Mall Gazette 16 Dec 1882; Morning Post 28 Dec 1882; St James' Gazette 16 Jan 1883; World 31 Jan 1883; Spectator 3 Feb 1883.

The romantic adventures of a milkmaid: a novel. New York [1883] (illustr C. S. Reinhart), London 1913 (rev for A changed man). First pbd Graphic 25 June 1883 (printer's ms Pierpont Morgan Library, New York), Harper's Weekly 23 Jun–4 Aug 1883.

REVIEWS: Literary World (Boston) 28 July 1883; Nation (New York) 20 Sep 1883.

The Mayor of Casterbridge: the life and death of a man of character. 2 vols 1886, 1 vol New York 1886 (rev), as The mayor of Casterbridge: a story of a man of character, London 1887 (rev), 1895 (copy of impression of 1887 with ms rev Yale; reviewed Bookman July 1895, Literary World Rev (Boston) 10 Aug 1895), as The life and death of the mayor of Casterbridge: a story of a man of character 1902, 1912, 1920 (copy of 1912 with ms rev Dorset County Museum); ed D. Kramer, Oxford 1987 (WCp). First pbd Graphic (printer's ms, incomplete, Dorset County Museum) and Harper's Weekly 2 Jan–15 May 1886 (variant text) (both illustr R. Barnes).

REVIEWS: Globe 14 May 1886; Whitehall Rev 20 May 1886; Daily Telegraph, Stage 27 May 1886; Athenaeum, Saturday Rev 29 May 1886; Spectator, St James' Gazette 5 June 1886; Literary World (Boston) 12 June 1886; John Bull 19 June 1886; World 23 June 1886; Scotsman 24 June 1886; Critic (New York) 3 July 1886; Pall Mall Gazette 9 July 1886; Morning Post 16 July 1886; Critic (New York) 17 July 1886; Guardian 28 July 1886; Dial (Chicago), Westminster Rev July 1886; Nation (New York) Aug 1886; Vanity Fair 4 Sep 1886; Times 9 Sep 1886; Daily News 30 Sep 1886; Harper's New Monthly Mag Nov 1886.

The woodlanders. 3 vols 1887, 1 vol New York 1887, London 1887 (rev), 1895, 1912 (impression of 1895 rev, fragmentary proofs Dorset County Museum), 1920 (copy of 1912 rev Dorset County Museum); ed D. Kramer, Oxford 1981, 1985 (WCp). First pbd Macmillan's Mag May 1886–Apr 1887 (printer's ms Dorset County Museum), Harper's Bazar 15 May 1886–9 Apr 1887 (variant text).

REVIEWS: Dublin Evening Mail 20 Mar 1887; Athenaeum, Spectator 26 Mar 1887; Land and Water, Saturday Rev, St James' Gazette 2 Apr 1887; Globe 5 Apr 1887; Morning Post 6 Apr 1887; Academy 9 Apr 1887; Daily Telegraph 12 Apr 1887; Literary World 15 Apr 1887; Critic (New York) 16 Apr 1887; World 20 Apr 1887; Times 27 Apr 1887; Cambridge Rev 4 May 1887; Graphic, John Bull, Sphinx 7 May 1887; Literary World (Boston) 14 May 1887; Nation (New York), Pall Mall Gazette 19 May 1887; Leeds Mercury 25 May 1887; Daily News 28 May 1887; Literary World (Boston) 11 June 1887; Guardian 29 June 1887; Westminster Rev June 1887; Dial (Chicago), Harper's New Monthly Mag, Holborn Rev, London Quart July 1887; Revue des Deux Mondes 1 July 1888; Deutsche Rundschau 1889.

Wessex tales: strange, lively, and commonplace. 2 vols 1888 (contents a, d, e, f, g *below*), 1 vol New York 1888 (with portrait), London 1889, 1896 (adds An imaginative woman), 1912 (with addn to preface; adds b and c *below*; omits An imaginative woman), 1920 (with addn to preface) (copy of 1912 rev Dorset County Museum); ed K. King, Oxford 1991 (WCp). Includes (in Hardy's final arrangement): (a) The three strangers (first pbd Longman's Mag Mar 1883 (printer's ms Berg Col, NYPL), Harper's Weekly 3–10 Mar 1883); dramatised as The three wayfarers New York 1893 (typescript and ms Univ of California, Berkeley), Boston 1930, Dorchester 1935, produced London 1893, 1900, Dorchester 1911, London 1913, Oxford 1926 (reviewed The Times 5

June 1893; Stage 8 June 1893; Athenaeum, Saturday Rev 10 June 1893; Era 22 July 1893; W. Archer, The theatrical 'world' for 1893, New York and London 1894); (b) A tradition of eighteen hundred and four (first pbd Harper's Christmas Dec 1882 as A legend of the year eighteen hundred and four); (c) The melancholy hussar of the German legion (first pbd Bristol Times and Mirror 4 and 11 Jan 1890 etc as The melancholy hussar (printer's ms Huntington) reviewed Literary World 25 July 1890; Academy 2 Aug 1890); (d) The withered arm (first pbd Blackwood's Mag Jan 1888); (e) Fellow-townsmen (*see above*, 1880); (f) Interlopers at the Knap (first pbd Eng Illustr Mag May 1884); (g) The distracted preacher (first pubd New Quart Mag n.s. 1 1879 (printer's ms private col) and Harper's Weekly 19 Apr–17 May 1879 (variant text); reviewed Literary World (Boston) 25 Oct 1879.

REVIEWS OF COL: Morning Post 21 May 1888; Glasgow Herald 25 May 1888; The Times 2 June 1888; Graphic 9 June 1888; Nation (New York) 28 June 1888; Athenaeum 30 June 1888; Harper's New Monthly Mag, Public Opinion (New York) June 1888; Literary World 27 July 1888; Spectator 28 July 1888; Westminster Rev July 1888; Critic (New York) 8 Aug 1888.

A group of noble dames. 1891, New York 1891, Leipzig 1891, London 1896, 1912, 1920. Includes The first Countess of Wessex (first pbd Harper's New Monthly Mag Dec 1889; illustr A. Parsons and S. C. Reinhart); Barbara of the house of Grebe; The Marchioness of Stonehenge; Lady Mottisfont; The Lady Icenway; Squire Petrick's lady; Anna, Lady Baxby (these 6 bowdlerised in Graphic 1 Dec 1890 (printer's ms Library of Congress), more or less unbowdlerised in Harper's Weekly 29 Nov–20 Dec 1890); The Lady Penelope (Longman's Mag Jan 1890 (printer's ms, including material used to integrate the story into the volume, Library of Congress)); The Duchess of Hamptonshire as The impulsive lady of Croome Castle (Light 6–13 Apr 1878; Harper's Weekly 11–18 May 1878), as Emmeline; or passion versus principle (Independent (New York) 7 Feb 1884); The Honourable Laura as Benighted travellers (Bolton Weekly Jnl 17 Dec 1881, Harper's Weekly 10–17 Dec 1881).

REVIEWS: Anti-Jacobin, Speaker 6 June 1891; Morning Post 8 June 1891; Literary World 12 June 1891; Saturday Rev 20 June 1891; National Observer 27 Jun 1891; St James' Gazette 1 July 1891; Athenaeum 4 July 1891; Pall Mall Gazette, World 8 July 1891; Nation (New York) 23 July 1891; Illustr London News 25 July 1891; Book Buyer, Review of Reviews July 1891; Literary World (Boston), Spectator 1 Aug 1891; Academy 22 Aug 1891; Nat Rev Aug 1891; Critic (New York) 12 Sep 1891; Harper's New Monthly Mag Sep 1891; Archiv 1891.

Tess of the d'Urbervilles: a pure woman faithfully presented by Thomas Hardy. (For photo facs of ms material, *see* S. Gatrell edn under Manuscripts, *above*.) 3 vols 1891 (ms of prefatory note, ms of revised title page Dorset County Museum), 1892 (rev), 1 vol New York 1892 (Harper's Bazar text and illustr), Leipzig 1892, London 1892 (rev with preface), New York 1892 (new and rev edn includes chs omitted from serial, but not revisions made for English edns), New York 1893 (includes c. half of the revisions made for English edns), 1895 (copy of London 1892 rev, Berg Coll, NYPL), 1900 (pbk rev), 1902 (rev), 1912 (includes 'General preface to the novels and poems'; ms of part of ch 10 omitted from earlier edns Dorset County Museum; rev proof of preliminary matter Univ of California, Berkeley), New York 1915 (rev), 1919 (copy of 1912 rev for this and subsequent edns), 1920, 1926 (illustr V Gribble); ed J. Grindle and S. Gatrell, Oxford 1983 (rev 1986), 1988 (WCp), this text also in ed S. Elledge, New York (3rd edn) 1990. First pbd, omitting some chs, in Graphic 4 July–26 Dec 1891 (illustr H. von Herkomer et al; incomplete printer's ms BL); chs 10–11 ptd as Saturday night in Arcady in Nat Observer (Edinburgh) 14 Nov 1891 (printer's ms ff. 1–8 HRHRC; f. 9 Bathurst–Glenesk papers, Leeds; f. 10 Berg Col NYPL; ff. 11–13 Taylor Col, Princeton); ch 14 as The midnight baptism in Fortnightly Rev May 1891; in Nottinghamshire Guardian (unrev), in Harper's Bazar 18 July–26 Dec 1891 (11 of 25 Graphic illustr) (ch 4 in Eclectic Mag June 1891); rptd complete in John O'London's Weekly 24 Oct 1925–10 July 1926 (introductory note).

REVIEWS: Star 23 Dec 1891; Nat Observer, Speaker 26 Dec 1891; Daily Chron 28, 30 Dec 1891; Pall Mall Gazette 31 Dec 1891; St James' Gazette 7 Jan 1892; Athenaeum, Illustr London News 9 Jan 1892; Times, World 13 Jan 1892; Saturday Rev 16 Jan 1892; Spectator 23 Jan 1892; Morning Post 30 Jan 1892; Independent (New York) 5 Feb 1892; Academy 6 Feb 1892; Literary World (Boston) 13 Feb 1892; Chicago Evening Jnl 20 Feb 1892; Punch 27 Feb 1892; Bookman, New Rev, Rev of Reviews Feb 1892; Blackwood's Mag, Book Buyer, Novel Rev, Westminster Rev Mar 1892; Critic (New York), National Observer 16 Apr 1892; Nation (New York) 28 Apr 1892; Dial (Chicago), Nat Rev, Quart Rev Apr 1892; Atlantic Monthly May 1892; Literary World (Boston) 4 June 1892; Harper's New Monthly Mag June 1892; Fortnightly Rev 1 July 1892; Novel Rev July 1892; Gentleman's Mag Sep 1892; Illustr London News 5 Nov 1892; Bookman, Longman's Mag Nov 1892; Book Buyer Dec 1892; Archiv London 1892. Dramatised 1894–5, produced New York 2 Mar 1897 (rev L. Stoddard; reviewed Critic (New York) 6 Mar 1897; Critic (New York) 13 Mar 1897; New Century Rev Aug 1898), produced Dorchester 1924, London 1925 (reviewed New Statesman 26 Sep 1925; London Mercury Oct 1925), 1929 (rev Hardy); ed M. Roberts in Tess in the theatre, Toronto 1950.

Life's little ironies: a set of tales with some colloquial sketches entitled A few crusted characters. 1894 (1 leaf of copy, proofs rev Dorset County Museum), New York 1894, Leipzig 1894, London 1896 (impression of 1894, with preface), 1912 (rev, omits preface and stories (b) and (c) in Wessex tales, *above*; adds Prefatory note, and An imaginative woman from Wessex tales), 1920 (copy of 1912 rev Dorset County Museum). Includes (in Hardy's final arrangement) An imaginative woman (first pbd Pall Mall Mag Apr 1894, illustr A. Goodman, printer's ms Aberdeen Univ Lib); The son's veto (Illustr London News 1 Dec 1891, illustr A. Forestier, printer's ms Bibliotheca Bodmeriana, Geneva); For conscience' sake (Fortnightly Rev Mar 1891, printer's ms John Rylands Univ Lib of Manchester); A tragedy of two ambitions (Universal Rev Dec 1888, illustr G. Lambert, printer's ms John Rylands Univ Lib of Manchester); On the western circuit (Eng Illustr Mag Dec 1891, illustr W. Paget, ms Central Lib Manchester, and Harper's Weekly, illustr W. Smedley); To please his wife (Black and White 27 June 1891, illustr W. Hennessy); The fiddler of the reels (Scribner's Mag May 1893, illustr W. Hatherell); A few crusted characters ([as Wessex folk in Harper's New Monthly Mag Mar–June 1891, illustr A. Parsons and C. Green, draft ms Berg Col, NYPL]).

REVIEWS: Russkoe Bogatstvo Jan 1894; St. James' Gazette 9 Mar 1894; National Observer, To-day 10 Mar 1894; Speaker 17 Mar 1894; Woman 21 Mar 1894; Literary World 23 Mar 1894; Athenaeum 24 Mar 1894; Times 30 Mar 1894; Saturday Rev 31 Mar 1894; Westminster Gazette Mar 1894; Guardian 4 Apr 1894; Spectator 21 Apr 1894; Bookman, Book Buyer Apr 1894; Critic (New York) 5 May 1894; Literary World 11 May 1894; Academy 2 June 1894; Dial (Chicago) 16 Jun 1894; Goodey's Mag Jul 1894; Author 1 Sep 1894; Archiv 1894.

The spectre of the real. To-day 17 Nov 1894 (illustr H. Millar) (printer's copy typescript, proofs F. B. Adams) with Florence Henniker; rptd in In scarlet and grey: stories of soldiers and others by Florence Henniker (Hardy's share acknowledged), London and Boston 1896; Thomas Hardy: the excluded and collaborative stories, ed P. Dalziel, Oxford 1992.

REVIEWS: Speaker 1 Aug 1896; New Saturday 26 Sep 1896; Academy 24 Oct 1896; Spectator 31 Oct 1896; Critic (New York) 23 Jan 1897.

Jude the obscure. 1896 (for 1895, as vol 8 of Wessex novels edn, *above*; incomplete ms Fitzwilliam Museum, Cambridge; rev proofs Signet Library, Edinburgh), New York 1896 (for 1895), Leipzig 1896 (rev), 1903 (rev), 1912 (ms of postscript to preface Yale), New York 1915 (rev), 1920 (copies of 1912 with ms rev Dorset County Museum, Adams); ed P. Ingham, Oxford 1985 (WCp). First pbd abridged and modified as The simpletons, then as Hearts insurgent in Harper's New Monthly Mag Dec 1894–Nov 1895 (illustr W. Hatherell). Extract from part 1 ch 10 rptd in Animal's Friend as A merciful man, Dec 1895.

REVIEWS (serial): Harper's Weekly (New York) 8 Dec 1894; Critic (New York) 4 Jan 1895; Critic (New York) 11 Jan 1895; Spectator 9 Feb 1895; Critic (New York) 14 Sep 1895; Literary World 27 Sep 1895; Critic (New York) 12 Oct 1895.

REVIEWS (book): Daily Telegraph 1 Nov 1895; Morning Post 7 Nov 1895; St James' Gazette 8 Nov 1895; Pall Mall Gazette 12 Nov 1895; Guardian, Woman, World (New York) 13 Nov 1895; Graphic 16 Nov 1895; Sun (New York) 20 Nov 1895; Athenaeum, Lady's Pictorial 23 Nov 1895; Weekly Sun 1 Dec 1895; Harper's Weekly (New York), Speaker 7 Dec 1895, Weekly Sun, World (New York) 8 Dec 1895; National Observer 14 Dec 1895; Critic (New York) 28 Dec 1895; Yorkshire Daily Post 30 Dec 1895; Bookselling Dec 1895; Daily Chronicle 1 Jan 1896; Illustr London News, Literary World (Boston) 11 Jan 1896; Chapbook 15 Jan 1896; Blackwood's Mag, Bookman, Bookman (New York), Cosmopolis, Free Rev Jan 1896; Dial (Chicago) 1 Feb 1896; Nation (New York) 6 Feb 1896; Saturday Rev 8 Feb 1896; Academy, Idler, Our Day, Westminster Rev Feb 1896; Liverpool Daily Post 20 Mar 1896; Internazionale Litteraturberichte (Leipzig, in German) 30 Apr 1896; New Ireland Rev Apr 1896; National Rev May 1896; Fortnightly Rev 1 June 1896; Yorkshire Post 8 Jun 1896; Nuova Antologia (in Italian) 16 June 1896; Savoy (review-essay by H. Ellis) Oct 1896.

The well-beloved: a sketch of a temperament. 1897 (as vol 17 in Wessex novels edn, *above*, radically altered from serial), New York 1897, London 1903 (rev), 1912, 1920 (copy of 1912 rev Dorset County Museum); ed T. Hetherington, Oxford 1986 (WCp). First pbd as The pursuit of the well-beloved in Illustr London News (illustr W. Paget) and Harper's Bazar 1 Oct–17 Dec 1892.

REVIEWS: Daily Chron 18 Mar 1897; Graphic, Saturday Rev 20 Mar 1897; Daily Mail 23 Mar 1897; Westminster Gazette, Woman, World 24 Mar 1897; Literary World 26 Mar 1897; Academy, Speaker 27 Mar 1897; Star 29 Mar 1897; Pall Mall Gazette, St James' Gazette 31 Mar 1897; Morning Post 1 Apr 1897; Academy, Globe 3 Apr 1897; Globe 5 Apr 1897; Guardian 7 Apr 1897; Athenaeum 10 Apr 1897; Literary Digest, Literary World (Boston), 15 May 1897; Dial (Chicago) 16 May 1897; Bookman (New York), Book Buyer, Critic (New York) May 1897; Times 8 June 1897; Academy 4 Dec 1897.

A changed man, The waiting supper and other tales. 1913, 1920. Includes A changed man (first pbd Sphere 21–28 Apr 1900, printer's ms Berg Coll NYPL); The waiting supper (Murray's Mag Jan–Feb 1888 and Harper's Weekly 31 Dec 1887–7 Jan 1888); Alicia's diary (Manchester Weekly Times 15–22 Oct 1887); The grave by the handpost (St James's Budget 30 Nov 1897, printer's ms priv coll); Enter a dragoon (Harper's New Monthly Mag Dec 1900); A tryst at an ancient earthwork (Detroit Post 15 Mar 1885 printer's ms HRHRC); What the shepherd saw (Illustr London News 5 Dec 1881); A committee-man of the Terror (Illustr London News 22 Nov 1896, printer's ms and galleys Berg Coll NYPL, reviewed Academy 12 Dec 1896); Master John Horseleigh, Knight (Illustr London News 12 June 1893, printer's ms HRHRC; The Duke's reappearance (Saturday Rev 14 Dec 1896, printer's ms HRHRC); A mere interlude (Bolton Weekly Jnl 17–24 Oct 1885); The romantic adventures of a milkmaid (1883, *above*).

REVIEWS OF COL: Daily Chron, Daily Mail, Daily News 24 Oct 1913; World 28 Oct 1913; TLS 30 Oct 1913; Athenaeum, Saturday Rev, Westminster Gazette 1 Nov 1913; Nation 8 Nov 1913; Sphere 15 Nov 1913; Punch 19 Nov 1913; Bookman, Das Literarische Echo Dec 1913.

An indiscretion in the life of an heiress. 1934 (priv ptd); in Thomas Hardy: the excluded and collaborative stories, ed P Dalziel, Oxford 1992. First pbd Harper's Weekly 29 June–27 July 1878, New Quart Mag 1878 (rev); a reworking of part of The poor man and the lady, Hardy's first novel, now lost.

Our exploits at West Poley. Ed R. L. Purdy, Oxford 1952; in Thomas Hardy: the excluded and collaborative stories, ed P Dalziel, Oxford 1992. First pbd Household (Boston) Nov 1892–Apr 1893.

Hardy, E. Hardy: plots for five unpublished stories. London Mag Nov 1958 (mss in Dorset County Museum); *see also* S. Gatrell, The early stages of Hardy's fiction, under Textual matters, *below*.

Poetry

For first appearance and mss of single poems, and priv ptd or uncollected contributions to books, periodicals and newspapers, see R. L. Purdy, A bibliographical study, *and S. Hynes,* Complete poetical works, *above.*

Wessex poems and other verses, with thirty illustrations by the author. 1898 (printer's ms and illustrations Birmingham City Museum), New York 1899, London 1903 (rev), 1907 (rev), 1912 (with Poems of the past and the present), 1920 (rev, with Poems of the past and the present); in Complete poetical works, ed S. Hynes, vol 1 Oxford 1982.

REVIEWS: British Weekly 22 Dec 1898; Outlook, Speaker 24 Dec 1898; Globe, St James' Gazette 28 Dec 1898; Literature 31 Dec 1898; Daily Telegraph, Glasgow Herald 4 Jan 1899; Times 5 Jan 1899; Pall Mall Gazette 6 Jan 1899; Saturday Rev 7 Jan 1899; Westminster Gazette 11 Jan 1899; Academy, Athenaeum 14 Jan 1899; Outlook 28 Jan 1899; Bookman, Critic (New York) Feb 1899; Literature 4 Mar 1899; Literary World (Boston) 18 Mar 1899; Bookman Mar 1899; Dial (Chicago) 16 Apr 1899; London Quart Rev Apr 1899; Nation (New York) 22 June 1899; Westminster Rev Aug 1899; Academy 18 Nov 1899; Academy 9 Dec 1899.

Poems of the past and the present. 1902 (for 1901) (printer's ms Bodleian), 1902 (rev), 1903 (rev), 1912 (with Wessex poems), 1920 (rev, with Wessex poems), in Complete poetical works, ed S. Hynes, vol 1 Oxford 1982.

REVIEWS: Academy 23 Nov 1901; Glasgow Herald 28 Nov 1901; Manchester Guardian 4 Dec 1901; Public Opinion (New York) 19 Dec 1901; Speaker 21 Dec 1901; Times 26 Dec 1901; Literature 28 Dec 1901; Das Literarische Echo Dec 1901; Athenaeum 4 Jan 1902; Saturday Rev 11 Jan 1902; Nation (New York) 23 Jan 1902; Bookman, North Amer Rev Jan 1902; Literary World (Boston) 1 Feb 1902; Atlantic Monthly Feb 1902; Spectator 5 Apr 1902; Dial (Chicago) 1 May 1902.

Time's laughingstocks and other verses. 1909 (printer's ms Fitzwilliam Museum, Cambridge), 1910 (rev), 1913 (with The dynasts pt 3, rev), 1915, 1920 (rev).

REVIEWS: Daily Telegraph 8 Dec 1909; Scotsman, TLS 9 Dec 1909; Country Life 11 Dec 1909; Daily News 13 Dec 1909; Guardian 14 Dec 1909; Glasgow Herald 15 Dec 1909; Westminster Gazette 18 Dec 1909; Nation 19 Dec 1909; Das Literarische Echo Dec 1909; Athenaeum 8 Jan 1910; Pall Mall Gazette 13 Jan 1910; Saturday Rev 15 Jan 1910; Cambridge Rev 20 Jan 1910; Living Age, Spectator 29 Jan 1910; Queen 5 Feb 1910; Bookman Feb 1910; Academy 12 Mar 1910; English Rev Mar 1910.

Satires of circumstance: lyrics and reveries with miscellaneous pieces. 1914 (printer's ms Dorset County Museum), 1915 (rev), 1919 (Wessex edn with Moments of vision, rev), 1920 (rev).

REVIEWS: TLS 19 Nov 1914; Daily News, Saturday Rev 21 Nov 1914; Sunday Times 22 Nov 1914; Academy, Daily Express, Globe 26 Nov 1914; Academy, Athenaeum, Country Life 28 Nov 1914; Daily Telegraph 2 Dec 1914; New Statesman, Westminster Gazette 19 Dec 1914; Morning Post 24 Dec 1914; Pall Mall Gazette 29 Dec 1914;

Boston Evening Transcript 30 Dec 1914; Living Age, Outlook, Spectator 2 Jan 1915; New York Times Book Rev 24 Jan 1915; British Weekly Jan 1915; Guardian 2 Feb 1915; Nation (New York) 4 Feb 1915; Dial (Chicago) 24 June 1915.

Moments of vision and miscellaneous verses. 1917 (printer's ms Magdalene College, Cambridge), 1919 (pocket edn, rev), 1919 (Uniform edn, rev; copy of 1917 with ms rev F. B. Adams), 1919 (Wessex edn with Satires of circumstance, rev), 1920 (rev).
REVIEWS: Glasgow Herald 6 Dec 1917; Morning Post, Westminster Gazette 8 Dec 1917; Land and Water, TLS 13 Dec 1917; Daily News 14 Dec 1917; Cambridge Mag, New Statesman 15 Dec 1917; Nation, Outlook, Saturday Rev 22 Dec 1917; Literary World 3 Jan 1918; Sphere 12 Jan 1918; Living Age, Manchester Weekly Times 26 Jan 1918; Dial (Chicago) 31 Jan 1918; Athenaeum Jan 1918; Poetry Rev Jan–Feb 1918; Guardian 1 Mar 1918; Queen 2 Mar 1918; Mercure de France (Paris), Spectator 16 Mar 1918; Church Quart Oct 1918; English Rev 1918.

Late lyrics and earlier with many other verses. 1922 (printer's ms Dorset County Museum), 1922 (rev), 1922 (Uniform edn, rev), 1926 (Wessex edn with The famous tragedy of the queen of Cornwall, rev).
REVIEWS: Times 8 May 1922; Daily News, Guardian, Morning Post, Pall Mall Gazette 23 May 1922; Times 29 May 1922; Nation and Athenaeum 27 May 1922; TLS 1 June 1922; Nation and Athenaeum, New Statesman 3 June 1922; Saturday Rev 24 June 1922; Rev of Reviews Jun 1922; Spectator 8 July 1922; Bookman, New Republic 19 Jul 1922; London Mercury 22 July 1922; London Quart Rev July 1922; New York Times Book Rev 24 Sep 1922; Contemporary Rev Sep 1922; Fortnightly Rev 2 Oct 1922; Literary Rev (New York) 7 Oct 1922; Scribner's Mag Nov 1922; Nation (New York) 31 Dec 1922; Outlook 3 Jan 1923; Church Quart Rev Jan 1923.

Human shows, far phantasies, songs, and trifles. 1925 (printer's ms Yale), 1925 (rev; proof of 1925 with ms rev Dorset County Museum), New York 1925, 1931 (Wessex edn with Winter words).
REVIEWS: TLS 3 Dec 1925; Nation and Athenaeum 5 Dec 1925; Observer 6 Dec 1925; Sunday Times 13 Dec 1925; Saturday Rev, Spectator 19 Dec 1925; Boston Evening Transcript 2 Jan 1926; Nation (New York) 20 Jan 1926; Literary Rev (New York), New Statesman 23 Jan 1926; Bookman, Fortnightly Rev Jan 1926; Living Age 6 Feb 1926; London Mercury Feb 1926; New Republic 3 Mar 1926; Atlantic Monthly Mar 1926; New Criterion Apr 1926; Dial (Chicago) May 1926; Dublin Mag July–Sep 1926.

Winter words in various moods and metres. 1928 (ms Queen's College, Oxford), New York 1928, 1931 (Wessex edn with Human shows). Partially serialised Daily Telegraph 19 Mar–26 Sep 1928.
REVIEWS: TLS 4 Oct 1928; Spectator 6 Oct 1928; Nation and Athenaeum 13 Oct 1928; Truth 17 Oct 1928; Observer 21 Oct 1928; John O'London's Weekly, T. P.'s Weekly 27 Oct 1928; Saturday Rev 10 Nov 1928; Life and Letters Nov 1928; Poetry Rev Nov–Dec 1928; New York Evening Post 8 Dec 1928; New York Times Book Rev 9 Dec 1928; New York Herald Tribune 23 Dec 1928; Landmark, London Mercury Dec 1928.

Plays

For dramatisations by the Hardy players, see R. L. Purdy, A bibliographical study, *above.*

The dynasts: a drama of the Napoleonic wars. Pt 1 1903 (for 1904), 1904 (rev); pt 2 1905 (for 1906); pt 3 1908, 1910 (printer's mss of all three parts BL, ms draft of pt 3 Dorset County Museum); The dynasts: an epic-drama of the war with Napoleon, 1 vol 1910, 1913 (Wessex edn), 1919 (vol 2 of Poetical works; copy of 1910 with ms rev and typescript list of corrections Princeton), 1920 (ms list of corrections Dorset County Museum), 1920 (Wessex edn rev; typecript/ms lists of revisions Dorset County Museum), 1926 (1919 rev), 3 vols 1927 (ms list of corrections Dorset County Museum); in vols 4 and 5 of Complete poetical works, ed S Hynes, Oxford 1995. Abridged version produced by H. Granville-Barker 25 Nov 1914–30 Jan 1915, including specially written prologue and epilogue; reviewed Daily Express, Daily News, Pall Mall Gazette 26 Nov 1914, New Statesman, T. P.'s Weekly 5 Dec 1914, TLS 10 Dec 1914, Spectator 12 Dec 1914, New Republic 26 Dec 1914.
REVIEWS (pt 1): Daily Chron, Daily Express, Daily Telegraph, Morning Post 13 Jan 1904; Daily News, Pall Mall Gazette 14 Jan 1904; TLS 15 Jan 1904; Country Life 16 Jan 1904; To-day 20 Jan 1904; Westminster Gazette 21 Jan 1904; Academy, Athenaeum, Black and White, New York Daily Tribune 23 Jan 1904; TLS, T. P.'s Weekly 29 Jan 1904; New York Times, Saturday Rev 30 Jan 1904; Daily Paper 3 Feb 1904; New York Times Sat Rev 6 Feb 1904; Literary World, TLS 12 Feb 1904; Speaker 13 Feb 1904; Spectator 20 Feb 1904; Nation (New York) 25 Feb 1904; Chicago Daily Tribune 27 Feb 1904; Bookman Feb 1904; Literary Digest 26 Mar 1904; Monthly Rev Mar 1904; Mercure de France Apr 1904; Dial (Chicago) 16 May 1904; Atlantic Monthly, Critic (New York) May 1904; Independent Rev Oct 1904.
REVIEWS (pt 2): Daily Express, Daily Graphic, Daily News, Tribune 9 Feb 1906; Daily Chron, Evening Standard 12 Feb 1906; TLS 16 Feb 1906; Westminster Gazette 17 Feb 1906; Tatler 21 Feb 1906; Star 22 Feb 1906; Guardian, T. P.'s Weekly 23 Feb 1906; Rev of Reviews 1 Mar 1906; Academy 3 Mar 1906; Literary World 15 Mar 1906; Globe 16 Mar 1906; New York Times, Speaker 17 Mar 1906; Independent 5 Apr 1906; Outlook, Spectator 7 Apr 1906; Mercure de France 15 Apr 1906; Nation (New York) 19 Apr 1906; Dial (Chicago) 16 May 1906; Current Lit May 1906; Book News Monthly, Forum July 1906; Putnam's Monthly (New York) Nov 1906.
REVIEWS (pt 3): Daily Chron 12 Feb 1908; Morning Leader 14 Feb 1908; Daily News 17 Feb 1908; Daily Telegraph 19 Feb 1908; Country Life 20 Feb 1908; Outlook, Westminster Gazette 22 Feb 1908; Guardian 24 Feb 1908; Tatler 26 Feb 1908; TLS 27 Feb 1908; Star 29 Feb 1908; Pall Mall Gazette, T. P.'s Weekly 6 Mar 1908; Guardian 11 Mar 1908; Academy 14 Mar 1908; Literary World 15 Mar 1908; Spectator 21 Mar 1908; Nation (New York) 16 Apr 1908; Evening Post (New York) 18 Apr 1908; Edinburgh Rev Apr 1908; Mercure de France 1 May 1908; New York Times Sat Rev of Books 2 May 1908; Athenaeum, Dial (Chicago) 16 May 1908; Westminster Rev May 1908; Current Lit June 1908; Bookman, Bookman (New York) July 1908; La Phalange (Paris) 15 Oct 1908; Das Literarische Echo 1908; Quart Rev Jan 1909; Journal des Débats (Paris) 15 Sep 1909
REVIEWS (1 vol edn):Academy 24 Dec 1910; Westminster Gazette 21 Jan 1911.

The play of Saint George. Cambridge 1921 (priv ptd), New York 1928 (with modernised version by R. S. Loomis).

The famous tragedy of the Queen of Cornwall. 1923 (illustr Hardy), 1924 (rev), 1926.
REVIEWS: Daily News, Evening News, Guardian, TLS 15 Nov 1923; Country Life 17 Nov 1923; Sunday Times 18 Nov 1923; Westminster Gazette 28 Nov 1923; Spectator 8 Dec 1923; Nation and Athenaeum, Saturday Rev 29 Dec 1923; New York Times Book Rev 30 Dec 1923; London Mercury, Yale Literary Mag Dec 1923; Nation (New York) 9 Jan 1924; New Republic 27 Feb 1924; Forum June 1924; Neophilologus July 1924. Produced Dorchester 28 Nov 1923 (production reviewed Daily Express, Morning Post, The Times 29 Nov 1923; Saturday Rev, Weekly Westminster 8 Dec 1923)

Autobiography

The life and work of Thomas Hardy. Ed M. Millgate 1984 (typescripts with ms rev Dorset County Museum). First pbd with posthumous revisions as The early life of Hardy 1840–91 by F. E. Hardy, 1928, New York 1928; and The later years of Hardy 1892–1928 by F. E. Hardy, 1930, New York 1930. Collected as The life of Thomas Hardy 1962, New York 1962.

Editions, essays and introductions

Select poems of William Barnes, chosen and edited with a preface and glossorial notes. 1908, 1922 (for 1921), 1933.
REVIEWS: Athenaeum 26 Dec 1908, Contemporary Rev Apr 1909.

Hardy's personal writings: prefaces, literary opinions, reminiscences. Ed H. Orel, Lawrence KS 1966. Includes prefaces to Wessex edn of novels and poetry and to works by others; also How I built myself a house (first pbd Chambers's Jnl 18 Mar 1865); The Dorsetshire labourer (Longman's Mag July 1883), rptd as The Dorset farm labourer, Dorchester 1884; The Rev William Barnes BD (Athenaeum 16 Oct 1886), rptd in L. Johnson, The art of Thomas Hardy, *below*; The profitable reading of fiction (Forum Mar 1888); Candour in English fiction (New Rev Jan 1890); The science of fiction (New Rev Apr 1891); The tree of knowledge (New Rev Apr 1894); Memories of church restoration (Soc for the protection of ancient buildings, general meeting, London 1906), rptd Cornhill Mag Aug 1906 (rev); Dorset in London (The society of Dorset men in London, 1908); Maumbury ring (The Times 9 Oct 1908); The ancient cottages of England (The preservation of ancient cottages, 1927).

Letters and notebooks

The architectural notebook of Thomas Hardy. Ed C. Beatty, Dorchester 1966 (ms Dorset County Museum). Foreword by J. Summerson.

The collected letters of Thomas Hardy. Ed R. L. Purdy and M. Millgate, 7 vols Oxford 1978–88.

The personal notebooks of Thomas Hardy. Ed R. Taylor 1978. Includes Memoranda I, Memoranda II, Schools of painting, Trumpet-Major notebook and extracts from typescripts of The life and work, *above* (all documents Dorset County Museum).

The literary notebooks of Thomas Hardy. Ed L. Björk, 2 vols 1985. Includes Literary notes I, Literary notes II, '1867' notebook (all documents Dorset County Museum). First pbd in part as The literary notes of Thomas Hardy, 2 vols Gothenburg 1974.

Thomas Hardy's 'Studies, specimens &c.' notebook. Ed P. Dalziel and M. Millgate, Oxford 1994 (ms Yale).

§2

For detailed and annotated listing of all writing about Hardy to 1978, see Gerber and Davis, under Bibliographies, *above. The texts of some of the contemporary reviews listed above may be found in* Thomas Hardy and his readers, *ed L. Lerner and J Holmstrom 1968;* Thomas Hardy: the critical heritage, *ed R. Cox 1970; and* Thomas Hardy: critical assessments, *ed G. Clarke, 4 vols Mountfield, East Sussex 1993 (not always reliable).*

Textual matters

Much significant textual information is given in the introds to the modern critical edns listed above under individual titles and cols.

Beach, J. News for bibliophiles. Nation (New York) 1 Feb 1912.
Chase, M. Hardy from serial to novel. Minneapolis 1927.
Weber, C. Hardy in America. Waterville ME 1946 (rev).
Weber, C. The manuscript of Hardy's Two on a tower. PBSA 40 1946.
Paterson, J. The genesis of Jude the obscure. SP 57 1960.
Paterson, J. The making of The return of the native. Berkeley CA 1960.
Wheeler, O. Four versions of The return of the native. Nineteenth-Century Fiction 14 1960.
Kramer, D. A query concerning the handwriting in Hardy's manuscripts. PBSA 57 1963.
Riesner, D. ber die Genesis von Thomas Hardys The return of the native. Archiv 200 1963. Corrective of Paterson, The making, *above*.
Riesner, D. Kunstprosa in der Werkstatt: Hardys The mayor of Casterbridge 1884–1912. In Festschrift für Walter Hübner, Berlin 1964.
Schweik, R. The 'duplicate' manuscript of Hardy's Two on a tower: a correction and a comment. PBSA 60 1966.
Kramer, D. Two 'new' texts of Hardy's The woodlanders. SB 20 1967.
Schweik, R. The early development of Hardy's Far from the madding crowd. TSLL 9 1967.
Macleod, A. A textual study of Thomas Hardy's A group of noble dames. Unpbd diss, Univ of Notre Dame 1968.
Pinion, F. The composition of The return of the native. TLS 21 Aug 1970.
Kramer, D. Revisions and vision: Thomas Hardy's The woodlanders. BNYPL 75 1971.
Schweik, R. A first draft chapter of Hardy's Far from the madding crowd. English Studies 53 1972.
Gatrell, S. A critical edition of Thomas Hardy's Under the greenwood tree. Unpbd diss, Oxford Univ 1973.
Winfield, C. The manuscript of Hardy's Mayor of Casterbridge. PBSA 67 1973.
Grindle, J. A critical edition of Thomas Hardy's Tess of the d'Urbervilles. Unpbd diss, Oxford Univ 1974 (pbd Oxford 1983 ed J. Grindle and S. Gatrell, *above*).
Laird, J. The shaping of Tess of the d'Urbervilles. Oxford 1975.
Ingham, P. The evolution of Jude the obscure. RES 27 1976.
Sutherland. J. Victorian novelists and publishers. 1976.
Ahmad, S. Thomas Hardy's last revision of A pair of blue eyes. PBSA 72 1978.
Gaskell, P. From writer to reader: studies in editorial method. Oxford 1978. On The woodlanders.
Millgate, M. The making and unmaking of Hardy's Wessex edition. In Editing nineteenth-century fiction, ed J. Millgate, New York 1978.
Weiner, S. Thomas Hardy and his first American publisher: a chapter from the Henry Holt archives. Princeton Chron 39 1978.
Ahmad, S. Emma Hardy and the ms of A pair of blue eyes. N & Q 224 26 1979.
Dobrinsky, J. Un inédit de Thomas Hardy: quatre schémas pour un adaptation dramatique de Jude. Etudes Anglaises 32 1979.
Gatrell, S. An examination of some revisions to printed versions of The dynasts. Library 6th ser 1 1979.
Gatrell, S. Hardy the creator: Far from the madding crowd. In Critical approaches to the fiction of Thomas Hardy, ed D. Kramer 1979.
Gatrell, S. Hardy, house-style, and the aesthetics of punctuation. In The novels of Thomas Hardy, ed A. Smith 1979.
Ahmad, S. The genesis of the Wessex edition of Hardy's works. PBSA 77 1981.
Schweik, R. and M. Piret. Editing Hardy. Browning Institute Studies 9 1981.
Manford, A. The 'texts' of Thomas Hardy's map of Wessex. Library 6th ser 4 1982.
Gatrell, S. The early stages of Hardy's fiction. Thomas Hardy Annual 2 1984.
[Greenland, R.] Notes and queries. Thomas Hardy Jnl 3 1987. On edns of Desperate remedies.
Gatrell, S. Hardy the creator: a textual biography. Oxford 1988.
Greenland, R. Hardy in the Osgood, McIlvaine and Harper (London) editions. Thomas Hardy Jnl 4 1988.
Greenland, R. A preliminary note on the Tauchnitz editions of Thomas Hardy's works. Thomas Hardy Jnl 4 1988.
Manford, A. Who wrote Thomas Hardy's novels?: a survey of Emma Hardy's contribution to the manuscripts of her husband's novels. Thomas Hardy Jnl 6 1990.
Ray, M. 'The fiddler of the reels': a textual study. Thomas Hardy Jnl 9 1993.

Criticism to 1920

Boucher, L. Le roman pastoral en Angleterre. Revue des Deux Mondes 18 Dec 1875.
The Wessex labourer. Examiner 15 July 1876.

Living novelists: Thomas Hardy. London 22 Sep 1877.
Paul, K. Mr Hardy's novels. New Quart Mag Oct 1879.
Mr Hardy's novels. Br Quart Rev Apr 1881.
Ellis, H. Hardy's novels. Westminster Rev 120 1883; rptd and expanded 1896, 1928; in his From Marlowe to Shaw, ed J. Gawsworth 1950.
Kegan Paul, C. The rustic of George Eliot and Thomas Hardy. Merry England May 1883.
Purves, J. Mr Thomas Hardy's rustics. Time n.s.1 1885.
Barrie, J. Thomas Hardy: the historian of Wessex. Contemporary Rev Aug 1889.
Steuart, J. (Roderick Random pseud). Letters to living authors: to Mr Thomas Hardy. Wit and Wisdom 28 Sep 1889; rptd in Letters to living authors 1890.
Minto, W. The work of Thomas Hardy. Bookman Dec 1891.
Modern men: Thomas Hardy. National Observer Feb 1891.
[Lehman, R.] Mr Punch's agricultural novel. Bo and the blacksheep, a story of *the* sex. Punch 7 May 1892. Parody of Tess of the d'Urbervilles.
Newton-Robinson, J. A study of Mr Thomas Hardy. Westminster Rev Feb 1892.
Sharp, W. Thomas Hardy and his novels. Forum July 1892.
Trent, W. The novels of Hardy. Sewanee Rev Nov 1892.
Preston, H. Thomas Hardy. Century July 1893.
Alden, H. Thomas Hardy. Harper's Weekly 8 Dec 1894.
Johnson, L. The art of Thomas Hardy. 1894, 1923 (rev with ch on the poetry by J. Barton).
Macdonell, A. Thomas Hardy. 1894, New York 1895.
Trent, W. Hardy as a novelist. Citizen (Philadelphia) 1896.
Johnson, L. Mr Thomas Hardy. Academy 12 Nov 1898.
Pène-Huette, L. Thomas Hardy. Nouvelle Revue Internationale 15 Nov 1900.
Gosse, E. The historical place of Mr Meredith and Mr Hardy. International Quart Sep 1901.
Howells, W. D. In his Heroines of fiction, New York 1901.
[Mallock, W]. The popular novel. Quart Rev July 1901.
Frye, P. Nature and Thomas Hardy. Independent (New York) 10 July 1902.
Turnbull, M. Two delineators of Wessex. GM Nov 1903.
Brunnemann, A. Thomas Hardy. Aus Fremden Zungen 15 Apr 1904.
Ortensi, U. Litterati contemporanei: Thomas Hardy. Emporium July 1904.
Wright, E. The novels of Thomas Hardy. Quart Rev Apr 1904.
Bates, E. The optimism of Thomas Hardy. International Journal of Ethics July 1905.
Dawson, W. In The makers of English fiction, 1905.
Moss, M. The novels of Thomas Hardy. Atlantic Monthly Sep 1906.
Roz, F. Thomas Hardy. Revue des Deux Mondes 1 July 1906.
Garrett, L. The essence of Hardyism. Monthly Rev June 1907.
Hirn, Y. Thomas Hardy. Finsk Tidskrift for Vitterhet, Konst och Politik 1907.
Montfort, E. Reflexions à propos de Thomas Hardy. Les Marges Paris 1908.
Durrant, W. The disciple of destiny. Fortnightly Rev June 1909.
Phelps, W. The novels of Thomas Hardy. North Amer Rev Oct 1909.
Garwood, H. Hardy: an illustration of the philosophy of Schopenhauer. Philadelphia 1911.
Hedgcock, F. A. Essai de critique: Hardy, penseur et artiste. Paris 1911.
Lee, V. (pseud of Violet Paget). The handling of words: Thomas Hardy. Eng Rev Sep 1911.
Noyes, A. The poetry of Thomas Hardy. North Amer Rev July 1911.
Abercrombie, L. Hardy: a critical study. 1912, New York 1927 (abridged).
Dickinson, T. Thomas Hardy's The dynasts. North Amer Rev Apr 1912.
Forsyth, P. The pessimism of Thomas Hardy. Living Age 23 Nov 1912.
Powell, G. The weird of Wessex. Oxford and Cambridge Rev Aug 1912.
Roz, F. In Le roman anglais contemporain, Paris 1912.
Ushihara, Tōji. Hardy no Josei. Teikoku Bungaku (Tokyo) Jan 1912.
Beerbohm, M. A sequelula to The dynasts: a Christmas garland. 1913. Parody.
Chesterton, G. In The Victorian age in literature. 1913.
Lea, H. Hardy's Wessex. 1913.
Thomas, E. Thomas Hardy of Dorchester. Poetry and Drama 1 1913.
Aronstein, P. Thomas Hardy. Germanisch-Romanische Monatsschrift 6 1914.
Williams, H. The Wessex novels of Thomas Hardy. North Amer Rev Jan 1914.
Little, J. Thomas Hardy: our greatest prose poet. East and West (Bombay) Mar, Apr 1915.
Arch, R. The freethought of Thomas Hardy. Freethinker 7 May 1916.
Child, H. Thomas Hardy. 1916.
Duffin, H. C. Hardy: a study of the Wessex novels. 1916, 1921 (with appendix on the poems and The dynasts), 1937 (rev).
Freeman, J. Thomas Hardy. In The moderns: essays in literary criticism. 1916, New York 1917.
Shaw, C. Thomas Hardy and the ancient anguish of the earth. Methodist Rev Mar 1916.
Berle, L. W. George Eliot and Hardy: a contrast. 1917.
Follett, H. and W. The historian of Wessex. Atlantic Monthly Sep 1917.
Utter, R. The work of Thomas Hardy. Sewanee Rev Apr 1917.
Gosse, E. Mr Hardy's lyrical poems. Edinburgh Rev Apr 1918, rptd as The lyrical poetry of Thomas Hardy in Some diversions of a man of letters 1919.
Hogben, L. Thomas Hardy and democracy. Socialist Rev Apr–June 1918.
Quiller-Couch, A. T. The poetry of Hardy. In Studies in literature, vol 1 1918.
Stewart, H. Thomas Hardy as a teacher of his age. North Amer Rev Oct 1918.
Fairley, B. Notes on the form of The dynasts. PMLA 34 1919.
Murry, J. M. The poetry of Thomas Hardy. Athenaeum 7 Nov 1919, rptd in Aspects of literature, 1920.
Okada, Tetsuzo. Thomas Hardy no The dynasts. Teiyu Rinri Kai: Rinri Koen Shu (Tokyo) Aug, Sep 1919.
Fairley, B. Thomas Hardy's lyrical poems. Canadian Bookman July 1920.
Gilbert-Cooper, E. The debt of Mr Thomas Hardy to Indian philosophy. Hindustan Rev Mar 1920.
Symons, A. Thomas Hardy. Dial (Chicago) Jan 1920.

Biographies

Gittings, R. Young Thomas Hardy. 1975.
Gittings, R. The older Hardy. 1978.
Millgate, M. Thomas Hardy: a biography. Oxford 1982.

Special journals

The Thomas Hardy Journal. Pbd 3 times a year by the Thomas Hardy Society, P. O. Box 1438, Dorchester, Dorset DT1 1YH, England. Free to members. Includes correspondence, essays, reviews, notes, images, and an annual survey of criticism in jnls; ed S. Curtis. Vols 1 (1985)– . Preceded by The Thomas Hardy Society Newsletter (quarterly) 1–60, 1970–84, and The Thomas Hardy Review (annually) 1974–83.
Thomas Hardy Annual 1–5. Includes essays, reviews and an annual bibliography of criticism (vol 1 1978–81); ed N. Page 1982–6.
The Thomas Hardy Year Book (annual, but irregular). Includes notes and essays; occasional issues devoted to monographs. 1 (1970)– . St Peter Port, Guernsey. [SG]

Beatrice Harraden 1864–1936

Things will take a turn. 1889, 1895, 1910 (adapted from the story by), 1915 (rev).
Master Roley. 1889.
A new book of the fairies. 1891, 1897, 1915 (new edn).
Ships that pass in the night. 1893, 1894, 1899, 1901, 1912, 1920, 1931.
In varying moods: short stories. 1894, 1906, 1910.
Untold tales of the past. 1897, 1927.
Hilda Strafford and the remittance man. 1897, 1906, 1915.
The fowler. 1899.
Katharine Frensham: a novel. 1903, 1909, 1927.
The scholar's daughter. 1906, 1908, 1912.
Interplay. 1908, 1911, 1919, 1925.
Out of the wreck I rise. 1912, 1914, 1920.
The guiding thread. 1916.
Where your treasure is. 1918.
Spring shall plant. 1920.
Thirteen all told: tales. 1921.
Patuffa. 1923, 1926.
Youth calling. 1924.
Rachel. 1926.
Search will find it out. 1928. [DF]

Joseph Hatton 1841–1907

Provincial papers: being a collection of tales and sketches. 1861.
Bitter sweets: a love story. 3 vols 1865. Dramatised as Two May days, 1871.
Against the stream. 3 vols 1866.
The Tallants of Barton: a tale of fortune and finance. 3 vols 1867, 1 vol 1868.
Not in society: a posthumous story edited by Joseph Hatton. 1868, [1877] (rptd with other tales by Hatton). Adaptation of an unpbd work by Vaughan Morgan entitled Brompton and Islington.
Pippins and cheese. 1868.
Christopher Kenrick: his life and adventures. 2 vols 1869.
Reminiscences of Mark Lemon, together with Mark Lemon's revised text of Falstaff. At head of title: With a show in the north. 1871, 1872 (as With a show in the north).
Kites and pigeons: a novelette. [1872.] Dramatised as Birds of a feather: a serio-comic play, [1872].
The valley of poppies. 2 vols 1872.
In the lap of fortune: a story 'stranger than fiction'. 3 vols 1873.
Clytie: a novel of modern life. 3 vols 1874. Dramatised [1874].
Romantic Caroline: a farcical comedy in one act founded upon the three-act comedy of Barrière and Thiboust. [1874.]
The Queen of Bohemia: a novel. 2 vols 1877.
Cruel London: a novel. 3 vols 1878.
Liz: a drama. [1879.] With A. Matthison.
Much too clever: a comedy. [1879.] With J. Oxenford.
Three recruits and the girls they left behind them: a novel. 3 vols 1880.
Today in America: studies for the old world and the new. 2 vols 1881.
'The new Ceylon': being a sketch of British North Borneo or Sabah. 1881.
Journalistic London: being a series of sketches of famous pens and papers of the day. 1882.
The dove's nest. 1883. In Society Novelettes, vol 2.
A modern Ulysses: being the life, loves, adventures, and strange experiences of Horace Durand. 3 vols 1883, 1 vol 1888 (as Captured by cannibals).
Newfoundland, the oldest British colony: its history, its present condition, and its prospects in the future. 1883. With M. Harvey.
Henry Irving's impressions of America. 2 vols 1884.
John Needham's double: a story founded on fact. [1885.]
Behind a mask: a romance of real life. [1886.] Bow Bells Annual, 1885–6.
The old house at Sandwich: the story of a ruined home, as developed in the strange revelations of Hickory Maynard. 2 vols 1887.
The Park Lane mystery. Bristol [1887].
The gay world: a novel. 3 vols 1887.
By order of the Czar: the tragic story of Anna Klosstock queen of the ghetto. 3 vols 1890 (2nd edn).
Club-land, London and provincial. 1890.
Old lamps and new: an after-dinner chat. [1890.]
The Princess Mazaroff: a romance of the day. 2 vols 1891.
Cigarette papers for after-dinner smoking. 1892. Essays and sketches.
The fate of Fenella, by Helen Mathers [et al]. 1892. Hatton wrote ch 8.
In jest and earnest: a book of gossip. 1893.
Under the Great Seal. 3 vols 1893.
Tom Chester's sweetheart: tale of the press. [1895.]
When Greek meets Greek: a novel. 1895.
The banishment of Jessop Blythe: a novel. 1895.
'A world afloat'. [1897.]
The dagger and the cross. 1897.
The Vicar: a novel. 1898.
The white King of Manoa: an Anglo-Spanish romance, being the life, loves, and adventures of David Yarcombe, protégé and fellow-voyager of Sir Walter Raleigh, Knight. 1899.
When rogues fall out: a romance of old London. 1899.
In male attire: a romance of the day. 1900.
A vision of beauty. 1902.
The life and work of Alfred Gilbert. 1903.
Hatton also wrote works on cocoa, tobacco, etc, and edited E. W. Streeter, Great diamonds, *1882, and J. L. Toole,* Reminiscences, *1889.*

George Alfred Henty 1832–1902

Bibliographies

Dartt, R. L. G. A. Henty: a bibliography. 1971.
Newbolt, P. G. A. Henty 1832–1902: a bibliographical study of his publishers, illustrators, designers and notes on the production methods used in his books. 1996.

Collections and selections

Redskin and cowboy. A tale of the western plains. 1892 (illustr A. Pearse), New York c. 1905, London 1920, 1925, 1939, 1953, 1954, 1958. (Contains Redskin and cowboy, Burton and son, and The ranch in the valley.)
Tales from the works of G. A. Henty. 1893.
Yule logs. 1898.
Yule tide yarns. 1899.
Tales from the works of G. A. Henty. 1915.

§1

Out on the Pampas: or the young settlers. 1871 (for 1870), New York nd, Chicago nd, London 1910.
The young franc-tireurs and their adventures in the Franco-Prussian war. 1872, 1898, 1902, 1909, 1910, 1921.
The march to Coomassie. 1874 (2nd edn).
The young buglers. A tale of the Peninsular War. 1879, New York nd, London 1880, 1898, 1902, 1909, 1910, 1954.
The cornet of horse. A tale of Marlborough's wars. 1881 (illus).
In times of peril. 1881.
Facing death or the hero of the Vaughan pit. A tale of the coal miner. Chicago nd, London 1882, 1887? (illustr G. Browne).
Under Drake's flag: a tale of the Spanish Main. 1882, 1910.
Friends though divided: a tale of the Civil War. 1883.
Jack Archer: a tale of the Crimea. 1883.

By sheer pluck: a tale of the Ashanti war. 1884, 1885 (illustr G. Browne), New York nd.
With Clive in India: or the beginnings of an empire. 1884 (illustr G. Browne), New York 1897, London 1920, 1953.
St George for England: a tale of Cressy and Poitiers. 1884, 1885 (illustr G. Browne), New York 1895, Chicago nd, London 1916, 1954, 1965.
In freedom's cause: a story of Wallace and Bruce. 1885 (illustr G. Browne), 1886, 1996.
The lion of the north: a tale of the times of Gustavus Adolphus and the Wars of Religion. 1885 (illus), 1886, New York 1897, London 1905, 1906.
True to the old flag. A tale of the American War of Independence. 1885 (illustr G. Browne), 1890, Glasgow and Toronto 1896.
Yarns on the beach: a bundle of tales. 1885, 1886, 1892 (illus).
The young colonists: a story of life in South Africa. 1885, as The young colonists: a story of the Zulu and Boer Wars 1897 (illus), 1898.
The dragon and the raven: or the days of King Alfred. 1886, 1995.
For name and fame: or through Afghan passes. 1886 (illustr G. Browne), New York [189?].
Through the fray: a tale of the Luddite riots. 1886 (illus).
With Wolfe in Canada: or the winning of a continent. 1886 (illus), Chicago nd, London 1887, 1920, 1953, 1958.
The young Carthaginians: or a struggle for empire. A story of the times of Hannibal. 1886 (illustr C. J. Staniland), 1887, New York nd, London 1905, 1906.
The bravest of the brave: or with Peterborough in Spain. 1887 (illus), 1914.
A final reckoning: a tale of bush life in Australia. 1887, Rahway NJ [c. 1904?].
Sturdy and strong: or how George Andrews made his way. 1887 (illus), New York nd, London 1888, 1899.
Bonnie Prince Charlie: a tale of Fontenoy and Culloden. 1887 (illustr G. Browne), 1888, New York 1898, London 1917, 1955.
The sovereign reader: scenes from the life and reign of Queen Victoria. 1887, 1900.
In the reign of terror: adventures of a Westminster boy. 1888.
For the temple: a tale of the fall of Jerusalem. 1888, 1995.
The lion of St Mark: a story of Venice in the fourteenth century. 1889.
By pike and dyke: a tale of the rise of the Dutch republic. 1889, Toronto nd, New York nd, Chicago nd, London 1890, 1905, 1996.
The cat of Bubastes: a tale of ancient Egypt. 1888, 1889, 1907, 1908, 1936.
Orange and green: a tale of the Boyne and Limerick. 1888 (illustr G. Browne), New York nd, Chicago nd, London 1910.
Captain Bailey's hair: a tale of the goldfields in California. 1889, 1896, 1905.
One of the 28th: a tale of Waterloo. 1889, New York 1897, London 1907, 1908, 1955.
With Lee in Virginia: a story of the American Civil War. 1889, 1890, 1997.
By England's aid: or the freeing of the Netherlands (1585–1604). 1890, 1891 (illustr A. Pearse), Chicago nd.
By right of conquest: or with Cortez in Mexico. 1890 (illustr W. S. Stacey), Philadelphia nd, London 1891, 1910, 1957, 1997.
A chapter of adventures: or through the bombardments of Alexandria. 1890 (illus), 1891, 1899, 1911.
Maori and settler: a story of the New Zealand war. 1891 (illustr A. Pearse), 1899, 1911, 1960.
Beric the Briton: a story of the Roman invasion. London and New York 1892, London 1893, 1922, 1959, 1996.
Condemned as a nihilist. A story of escape from Siberia. New York 1892 (illus), 1893, 1926.
The dash for Khartoum: a tale of the Nile expedition. 1892.
Held fast for England: a tale of the siege of Gibraltar. 1892 (illustr G. Browne).
The ranch in the valley. A novel. New York 1892, 1923. (Pbd in Redskin and cowboy.)
In Greek waters: a story of the Grecian War of Independence (1821–1827). New York 1892 (illustr W. S. Stacey), London 1893.
Winning his spurs: a tale of the Crusades. 1892, 1965.
Rujub the juggler. A novel. 1893, New York [1901?], London 1903.
St Bartholomew's eve: a tale of the Huguenot wars. London and New York 1893 (illus), London 1894, 1911, 1997.
A Jacobite exile: being adventures of a young Englishman in the service of Charles XII of Sweden. 1894.
Through the Sikh wars: a tale of the conquest of the Punjaub. 1894.
Wulf the Saxon: a story of the Norman conquest. 1894, 1895 (illus), New York 1902.
In the heart of the Rockies: a story of adventure in Colorado. 1895.
The tiger of Mysore: a story of the war with Tippoo Saib. 1895, 1913, 1995.
When London burned: a story of Restoration times and the Great Fire. 1895.
A woman of the Commune. A tale of two sieges of Paris. 1895.
At Agincourt: a tale of the white hoods of Paris. 1896, 1897, 1912.
Bears and dacoits. A tale of the Ghanuts. 1896, 1901.
A knight of the White Cross: a tale of the siege of Rhodes. 1896.
On the Irrawaddy: a story of the first Burmese war. 1896 (illus), 1897.
Surly Joe. The story of a true hero. 1896.
With Cochrane the dauntless. A tale of the exploits of Lord Cochrane in South American waters. London and New York 1896 (illus), 1897, 1908, 1909, 1959.
A march on London: being a story of Wat Tyler's insurrection. 1897 (illus), 1898.
The Queen's cup. A novel. 1897.
With Frederick the Great: a story of the Seven Years War. 1897 (illus), 1898, 1908, 1909.
With Moore at Corunna. 1897 (illus), 1898, 1908, 1909, 1959.
Both sides of the border: a tale of Hotspur and Glendower. 1898 (illus), 1899.
Colonel Thorndyke's secret. 1898.
At Aboukir and Acre: a story of Napoleon's invasion of Egypt. 1899 (illus), New York 1903.
Cuthbert Hartington. A tale of two sieges of Paris. 1899 (illus), 1916 (as Two sieges; or, Cuthbert Hartington's adventures).
The lost heir. 1899 (illus), Chicago nd.
No surrender. A tale of the rising in La Vendée. 1899, 1900, 1939.
On the Spanish Main. A tale of Cuba and the buccaneers. 1899.
A roving commission: or through the black insurrection of Hayti. New York 1899 (illus), London 1900.
Won by the sword. A tale of the Thirty Years War. New York 1899, London 1900, 1956.
With Buller in Natal: or a born leader. A tale. 1900, 1901.
At the point of the bayonet: a tale of the Mahratta War. New York 1901 (illus), London 1902.
In the Irish brigade: a tale of war in Flanders and Spain. 1901.
John Hawke's fortune: a story of Monmouth's rebellion. 1901.
Out with Garibaldi. A story of the liberation of Italy. 1901 (illus).
Queen Victoria. Scenes from her life and reign. 1901.
The sole survivors. 1901.
With Roberts to Pretoria. A tale of the South African war. 1901 (illus), 1902.
At duty's call. 1902.
In the hands of the cave dwellers. 1903.
To Herat and Cabul: a story of the first Afghan War. 1902.
With the British legion. A story of the Carlist wars. 1902, 1903.
The treasure of the Incas: a tale of adventure in Peru. 1903.
With Kitchener in the Sudan: a story of Athara and Omduran. 1903 (illus), New York 1905, London 1916.

By conduct and courage: a story of the days of Nelson. 1904, 1905.
Through three campaigns: a story of Chitral, Tirah and Ashantee. 1904.
With the allies to Pekin: a tale of the relief of the legations. 1904.
In the hands of the Malays and other stories. 1905 (illus).
A soldier's daughter, and other stories. 1906, [1905].
A search for a secret. 1911.
Charlie Marryat. From With Clive in India, 1920.
The plague ship. 1923.
Henty contributed extensively to boys' periodicals including Boys, Longman's Christmas Annual, *and the* Union Jack *which he edited after the death of W. H. G. Kingston.*
See G. Arnold, Held fast for England: G. A. Henty imperialist boys' writer *1980.* [DD]

'John Oliver Hobbes', Pearl Mary Teresa Craigie
1867–1906

Collections
The tales of John Oliver Hobbes. 1894.

§1
Some emotions and a moral. 1891.
The sinner's comedy. 1892.
A bundle of life. 1893.
A study in temptations. 1893.
The gods, some mortals and Lord Wickenham. 1895.
The herb-moon: a fantasia. 1896.
The school for saints: part of the history of the Right Honourable Robert Orange, M. P. 1897.
The ambassador: a comedy in four acts. 1898.
A repentance: an original drama in one act. 1899.
Osbern and Ursyne: a drama in three acts. 1900.
Robert Orange: being a continuation of the history of Robert Orange, M. P., and a sequel to The school for saints. 1900.
The serious wooing: a heart's history. 1901.
The wisdom of the wise: a comedy in three acts. 1901.
Love and the soul hunters. 1902.
Tales about temperaments. 1902.
Imperial India: letters from the East. 1903.
The artist's life. 1904. Critical essays.
Letters from a silent study. 1904.
The science of life. 1904.
The vineyard. 1904.
The flute of Pan: a romance. 1905. Originally written as a play and on its failure converted into a novel.
The dream and the business. 1906.

§2
Archer, W. In his Real conversations, 1904.
Courtney, W. L. In his Feminine note in fiction, 1904.
Richards, J. M. The life of John Oliver Hobbes told in her correspondence with numerous friends, with a biographical sketch by her father John Morgan Richards. 1911.
Clarke, I. C. In her Six portraits, 1935.
Maison, M. John Oliver Hobbes: her life and work. 1976.

'Frances Cashel Hoey', Frances Sarah Hoey, née Johnston 1830–1908

Nat Lib of Ireland holds 114 ms letters from Hoey to the publisher Edmund Downey, and 4 to other people. Univ of Illinois Lib holds 43 of her letters to the publisher Bentley and 8 to Grant Richards.

Bibliography
Edwards, P. Frances Cashel Hoey: a bibliography. St Lucia, Queensland 1982.

§1
A house of cards: a novel. 3 vols 1868, 1 vol [1871]. First pbd in Tinsley's Mag Mar 1868–Feb 1869.
REVIEWS: [? Romer] Athenaeum 21 Nov 1868; Spectator 8 Feb 1873.
Falsely true: a novel. 3 vols 1870, revised edn 1 vol 1890, [1901].
REVIEWS: [? Romer] Athenaeum 3 Sep 1870; [R. H. Hutton?] Spectator 24 Sep 1870.
Buried in the deep, and other tales. 1871[?], 1873. Title story first pbd in Chambers's Jnl 4–25 Feb 1865.
REVIEW: Spectator 8 Feb 1873.
A golden sorrow. 3 vols 1872, 2 vols Leipzig 1872, 1 vol New York [1872?], new edn London 1880, New York [1881?]. First pbd in Chambers's Jnl 6 Jan 1872–25 May 1872.
REVIEWS: [? Romer] Athenaeum 1 June 1872; Saturday Rev 22 May 1880; [R. H. Hutton?] Spectator 8 June 1872.
Out of court. 3 vols 1874, 1 vol [1881?]. First pbd in The Australasian 4 Oct 1873–30 May 1874.
REVIEWS: [Hepworth Dixon] Athenaeum 21 Mar 1874; [R. H. Hutton?] Spectator 14 Mar 1874; (A. Lang) Acad Apr 1874; The Times 21 Aug 1874.
The blossoming of an aloe and The queen's token. 3 vols 1875, 1 vol New York [1875?], The blossoming of an aloe (on its own) London 1876, New York 1881, The queen's token (on its own) London 1889, New York 1889, Boston 1889. The blossoming of an aloe first pbd in Chambers's Jnl 29 Aug–26 Dec 1874, The queen's token in London Soc May–Sep 1874.
REVIEWS: [R. H. Hutton?] Spectator 2 Jan 1875; The Times 25 Jan 1875; London Soc Feb 1875; (G. Saintsbury) Acad 13 Feb 1875.
No sign, and other tales. [1876.] First pbd in New Quart Mag Apr–Oct 1875.
Griffith's double. 3 vols 1876. First pbd in All the Year Round 4 Dec 1875–5 Aug 1876.
REVIEWS: [? Collyer] Athenaeum 5 Aug 1876; (G. Saintsbury) Acad 16 Sep 1876; [O. J. F. Crawfurd] New Quart Mag Oct 1876; [R. H. Hutton?] Spectator 7 Oct 1876.
Kate Cronin's dowry. New York [1877]. First pbd in New Quart Mag Jan 1877.
All, or nothing. 3 vols 1879, 1 vol New York 1879, London 1888, [1901?]. First pbd in All the Year Round 13 July 1878–8 Mar 1879.
REVIEWS: [R. H. Hutton?] Spectator 29 Mar 1879; [D.? Cook] Athenaeum 5 Apr 1879; (R. Littledale) Acad 17 May 1879.
The question of Cain. 3 vols 1882, 1 vol New York [1882?], New York [1882?], rev edn London 1890, [1900?]. First pbd in All the Year Round 26 Mar 1881–10 Dec 1882.
REVIEWS: (L. Lang) Acad 28 Jan 1882; [? Collyer] Athenaeum 11 Feb 1882; Graphic 18 Feb 1882; [R. H. Hutton?] Spectator 18 Feb 1882.
The lover's creed. 3 vols 1884, 1 vol New York 1884, New York 1884. First pbd in Belgravia Jan–Dec 1884.
REVIEWS: (C. Dawkins) Acad 13 Dec 1884; [A.? Sergeant] Athenaeum 29 Nov 1884; [Captain Clarke] Spectator 13 Dec 1884; Graphic 27 Dec 1884; Saturday Rev 27 June 1885.
A stern chase, a novel. 3 vols 1886, New York 1886, London 1886, 1886, 1 vol London 1888, New York 1889. First pbd in All the Year Round 29 Aug 1885–1 May 1886.
REVIEWS: [A.? Sergeant] Athenaeum 5 June 1886; (R. Littledale) Acad 19 June 1886; [William Wallace] Spectator 26 June 1886; Graphic 31 July 1886; Saturday Rev 28 Aug 1886.
His match, and more. 1890. Summer no of Household Words 26 June 1890.

Contributions to periodicals
Among the journals to which Hoey contributed regularly were Chambers's Jnl *(1865–75),* Temple Bar *(1867–78),* Dublin Rev *(1865–81),* The Spectator *(1871?–95),* The Australasian *(1873–1908?),* New Quart Mag *(1875–8). For her contributions to* Temple Bar, Dublin Rev, *and* New

Quart Mag, *see* Wellesley *vol 5, for those to other journals, see the bibliography by Edwards listed above.*

Translations

Hoey translated 35 books from Fr into Eng, including two of Jules Verne's novels, and contributed to two other books. These are listed in the bibliography by Edwards.

Attributed works

William Tinsley, in his Random recollections of an old publisher *(1900), asserted that Hoey was the author of 1 novel pbd as the work of Edmund Yates,* A righted wrong *(3 vols 1870), and pt-author of 4 others,* Land at last *(3 vols 1865),* A forlorn hope *(3 vols 1867),* Black sheep *(3 vols 1867), and* The rock ahead *(3 vols 1868). Yates's family and friends disputed the assertion and Hoey herself did not corroborate it. There is insufficient evidence to justify the attribution of the novels in question to Hoey, even conjecturally. The arguments for and against her possible authorship, or pt-authorship, are considered by Edwards in the introd to his bibliography of Hoey's works.*

§2

Tinsley, W. Random recollections of an old publisher. 1900.

Escott, T. Anthony Trollope: his work, associates and literary originals. 1913. According to Escott, Trollope helped spread the story about Hoey's authorship of parts or the whole of some of Edmund Yates's novels.

Shaw, C. M. Bernard's brethren. 1939. Bernard Shaw was Hoey's cousin.

Edwards, P. D. Dickens's 'young men': George Augustus Sala, Edmund Yates, and the world of Victorian journalism. Aldershot 1997. [PDE]

'Anthony Hope', Sir Anthony Hope Hawkins

1863–1933

§1

A man of mark. 1890, 1895.
Father Stafford. 1891.
Mr Witt's widow: a frivolous tale. 1892.
A change of air. 1893.
Half a hero. 2 vols 1893.
Sport Royal and other stories. 1893.
The Dolly dialogues. 1894, 1896, [1901].
The god in the car. 2 vols 1894.
The indiscretion of the Duchess: being a story concerning two ladies, a nobleman, and a necklace. Bristol 1894, (as Arrowsmith's Christmas Annual, [1897]).
The prisoner of Zenda: being the history of three months in the life of an English gentleman. Bristol [1894]; ed R. L. Green 1966 (EL) (with Rupert of Hentzau, *below*).
The chronicles of Count Antonio. 1895.
Comedies of courtship. 1896.
The heart of Princess Osra. 1896.
Phroso: a romance. 1897.
Rupert of Hentzau: being the sequel to a story by the same writer entitled the Prisoner of Zenda. Bristol [1898].
Simon Dale. 1898.
The King's mirror. 1899.
Quisanté. 1900.
Tristram of Blent: an episode in the story of an ancient house. 1901.
The intrusions of Peggy. 1902.
Double harness. 1904.
A servant of the public. 1905.
Sophy of Kravonia. Bristol 1906.
Tales of two people. 1907.
The great Miss Driver. 1908.
Dialogue. 1909. Eng Assoc lecture.
Second string. 1910.
Mrs Maxon protests. 1911.
The New (German) Testament: some texts and a commentary. 1914.
Militarism, German and British. 1915.
A young man's year. 1915.
Why Italy is with the Allies. 1917.
Captain Dieppe. [1918.]
Beaumaroy home from the wars. 1919.
Lucinda. [1920.]
Little Tiger: a novel. [1925.]
Memories and notes. [1927.]

§2

Mallet, C. Anthony Hope and his books: being the authorized life of Sir Anthony Hope Hawkins. 1935.

Putt, S. G. The prisoner of the prisoner of Zenda: Hope and the novel of society. EIC 6 1956.

Margaret Raine Hunt, Mrs Alfred W. Hunt

1831–1912

§1

Magdalen Wynyard. By Averil Beaumont (pseud). 1872.
Thornicroft's Model. By Averil Beaumont (pseud). 1873.
Under seal of confession. By Averil Beaumont (pseud). 1874.
This indenture witnesseth. 3 vols 1875.
The hazard of the die. 3 vols 1878.
Basildon. 2 vols 1879, New York 1879.
The leaden casket. New York 1880. Novel.
The posy ring. New York 1881 (rptd from Gentleman's Annual 1880).
Barrington's fate. 1883, Boston 1883.
Self-condemned. 3 vols 1883.
Our grandmothers' gowns. 1884.
That other person. 3 vols 1885, New York 1887, Philadelphia 1887.
Richmondshire. Illustr J. M. W. Turner, with descriptions by M. Hunt and an introd by M. B. Huish. 1891.
Mrs Juliet. 1892.
A black squire. 1894.
The governess. Preface by Ford Madox Ford. 1912. With Violet Hunt.

Editions

Grimm's household tales. Tr and ed Margaret Hunt, etc. Introd by A. Lang 1884. [MD]

William Henry Hudson 1841–1922

Bibliographies

Wilson, G. F. A bibliography of the writings of Hudson. 1922.

Collections

Collected works. 24 vols 1922–3.
A Hudson anthology, arranged by Edward Garnett. 1924.
Hudson's South American romances: The purple land; Green mansions; El Ombú [etc]. 1930.
Birds of wing and other wild things: selections from the works of Hudson by H. F. B. Fox. 1930.
The best of Hudson. Ed O. Shepard, New York 1949.
Works: uniform edition. 1951– .

§1

The purple land that England lost: travels and adventures in the Banda Oriental, South America. 2 vols 1885.
A crystal age. 1887 (anon), 1906 (with signed preface).
Ralph Herne. In Youth 12 1888, New York 1923 (limited edn). Hudson's first story; not separately rptd in England, but included in Collected works, 1922–3, *above*.
Fan: the story of a young girl's life. 3 vols 1892. Pbd under the pseud 'Henry Harford'.

The naturalist in La Plata. 1892.
Birds in a village. 1893, [1920] (with Poems of birds by various writers).
Idle days in Patagonia. 1893.
British birds, with a chapter on structure and classification by Frank E. Beddard. 1895.
Birds in London. 1898.
Nature in Downland. 1900.
Birds and man. 1901.
El Ombú [and other tales]. 1902, 1909 (as South American sketches).
Hampshire days. 1903.
Green mansions: a romance of the tropical forest. 1904.
A little boy lost. 1905.
The land's end: a naturalist's impressions in West Cornwall. 1908.
Afoot in England. 1909.
A shepherd's life: impressions of the South Wiltshire downs. 1910, 1987 (as The illustrated shepherd's life).
Adventures among birds. 1913.
Far away and long ago: a history of my early life. 1918, 1931 (rev).
Birds in town and village. 1919.
The book of a naturalist. [1919.]
Birds of La Plata. 2 vols 1920.
Dead man's plack, and An old thorn. 1920, 1924 (also contains poems).
A traveller in little things. 1921.
A hind in Richmond Park. Ed M. Roberts 1922.
Rare, vanishing & lost British birds. 1923. Compiled from Hudson's notes by L. Gardiner.
153 letters. Ed E. Garnett 1923. 1925 (as Letters from W. H. Hudson to Edward Garnett).
Men, books and birds, with notes, some letters, and an introduction by Morley Roberts. 1925.
Mary's little lamb. 1929. Rptd from The book of a naturalist.
Birds of a feather: unpublished letters. Ed D. Shrubsall, Bradford-on-Avon 1981.
Landscapes and literati: unpbd letters of W. H. Hudson and George Gissing. Ed D. Shrubsall and P. Coustillas, Salisbury 1985.

Hudson also contributed notes to P. L. Sclater, Argentine ornithology, *2 vols 1888–9, and a preface to P. Fountain,* The great deserts and forests of North America, *1901; he pbd a few periodical articles, and a number of pams, the latter mostly for the Soc for the Protection of Birds.*

§2

R., E. The work of Hudson. Eng Rev Apr 1909.
Rhys, E. Hudson, rare traveller. Nineteenth Cent July 1920.
Curle, R. W. H. Hudson. Fortnightly Rev Oct 1922.
Roberts, M. Hudson: a portrait. 1924.
Salt, H. S. Hudson as I saw him. Fortnightly Rev Feb 1926.
Ford, F. M. W. H. Hudson. Amer Mercury 37 1936.
Hamilton, E. W. H. Hudson. 1946.
Liandrat, F. Hudson, naturalist: sa vie et son oeuvre. Lyons 1946.
Tomalin, R. W. H. Hudson. 1954.
Frederick, J. T. William Henry Hudson. New York 1972.
Shrubsall, D. W. H. Hudson: writer and naturalist. 1978.
Wilson, J. W. H. Hudson: the colonial's revenge. [1981.]
Tomalin, R. W. H. Hudson: a biography. 1982.
Thomas, H. A memory of W. H. Hudson. Wakefield 1984.
Ronner, A. D. W. H. Hudson: the man, the novelist, the naturalist. New York 1986.
Miller, D. W. H. Hudson and the elusive paradise. 1990.

Henry James 1843–1916

The largest surviving collection of James papers is in the Houghton Library Harvard University, which holds the manuscript of the revised American; *most of the revised* Portrait of a lady; *journals and diaries; notebooks; typescripts of* The other house, The outcry, Guy Domville *(with extensive annotations by James); a fragment of* The turning point of my life; *preliminary statements and copy for* The sense of the past; *a preliminary statement for* Mrs Max *and* A note for the K. B. case; *preliminary statement and copy of* The ivory tower; The middle years; *a fragment of* Hugh Merrow; *and some shorter articles. The Henry E. Huntington Library holds a manuscript of* Four meetings. *Other North American libraries holding Henry James collections are Alderman Library University of Virginia, Berg Collection New York Public Library, Beinecke Library Yale University, Library of Congress, HRHRC University of Texas at Austin, Columbia University Library and Duke University Library. Appendix VI in* Letters vol 4 ed L. Edel *gives locations for James letters.*

Bibliographies

Henry James Rev *annually includes an analytic bibliographical essay on a selected James text.*
Foley, R. M. Criticism in American periodicals of the work of Henry James from 1866 to 1916. Washington DC 1944, rptd 1970.
Gard, R. Henry James: the critical heritage. London and New York 1968.
Ricks, B. Henry James: a bibliography of secondary works. Metuchen NJ 1975 (Scarecrow Author Bibliographies).
McColgan, K. Henry James 1917–1959: a reference guide. Boston 1979.
Scura, D. Henry James 1960–1974: a reference guide. Boston 1979.
Taylor, L. Henry James 1866–1916: a reference guide. Boston 1982.
Edel, L. and D. H. Laurence. A bibliography of James. 1957, 1961 (rev); rev with J. Rambeau 1982 (Soho Bibliographies).
Budd, J. Henry James: a bibliography of criticism 1975–1981. Westport CT and London 1983.
The library of Henry James: from inventory, catalogues, and library lists. Ed L. Edel and A. Tintner, Henry James Rev 4, 1983.
Bradbury, N. An annotated critical bibliography of Henry James. 1987.

Collections

[Novels and tales]. 14 vols 1883, 1886–7.
Novels and tales: New York edition. 26 vols New York 1907–18, 1961–5; 24 vols 1908–9, 1913.
Uniform tales. 14 vols 1915–20, 7 vols Boston 1917–18.
Novels and stories. Ed P. Lubbock 35 vols 1921–3.
The art of the novel: critical prefaces [to New York edn, *above*]. Ed R. P. Blackmur, New York 1934.
American novels and stories. Ed F. O. Matthiessen, New York 1947.
Complete plays. Ed L. Edel, Philadelphia 1949, London 1949.
Ghostly tales. Ed L. Edel, New Brunswick NJ 1948 [1949].
Complete tales. Ed L. Edel 12 vols 1962–5, Philadelphia 1962–5.
Tales of Henry James. Ed M. Aziz 3 vols of projected 12, 1973–84.
Novels 1871–80. Ed W. T. Stafford, New York (Viking Lib of America) 1983.
Novels 1881–86. Ed W. T. Stafford, New York (Viking Lib of America) 1985.
Novels 1886–90. Ed D. M. Fogel, New York (Viking Lib of America) 1989.

§1

James was an inveterate reviser, freely revising not only from serial to book but from 1 edn to the next, and even from 1 impression to the next within a single edn. For serial pbn of separate tales, see Edel and Laurence with Rambeau, Bibliographies, *above. Selected modern reprints are included below (for references to 'New York edn' see* Collections, *above). See also Section E Translations, in Edel and Laurence with Rambeau,* Bibliographies, *above.*

A passionate pilgrim, and other tales. Boston 1875. A passionate pilgrim, The last of the Valerii, Eugene Pickering, The madonna of the future, The romance of certain old clothes, Madame de Mauves. Tr (A passionate pilgrim) Fr 1876 (Revue des Deux Mondes), Ger 1876, Hungarian 1877.

Transatlantic sketches. Boston 1875, Leipzig 1883 (rev as Foreign parts).

Roderick Hudson. Boston 1876 [1875], 3 vols London 1879 (rev), 1 vol 1880, Boston 1882 (rev), London 1888; ed L. Edel, New York 1960; ed T. Tanner, Oxford 1980 (New York edn) (WC); ed G. Moore and P. Crick 1986 (1879 edn) (Pen). 1st pbd Atlantic Monthly, Jan–Dec 1875. Tr Swed 1877, Fr 1884, Ger 2 vols 1876, Ital 1960.

The American. Boston 1877, London [1877] (unauthorised), 1879; ms facs 1976, the version of 1877 revised in autograph and typescript for New York edn of 1907, reproduced in facs from the original in Houghton Lib, Harvard Univ, with introduction by R. G. Dennis 1976; ed W. Spengemann 1986 (1879 edn) (Pen). 1st pbd Atlantic Monthly, June 1876–May 1877. Dramatic version 1891 (2 impressions, priv ptd); acted at Opera Comique London 26 Sep 1891. Tr Ger 1877 (2 versions), 1878 (3rd version), Polish 2 vols 1879, Rus 1880 (weekly Novoye Vremya), Fr 1880 (République Française), 2 vols 1884; Swed 1884, 1944, 1960 (3 versions), Ital 1934, Slovene 1956, Korean 1957, Jap 1958, 1959 (2 versions).

French poets and novelists. 1878, Leipzig 1883 (rev), London 1884 (rev); ed L. Edel, New York 1964.

Watch and ward. Boston 1878; ed L. Edel London 1960. 1st pbd Atlantic Monthly, Aug–Dec 1871.

The Europeans. 2 vols 1878, Boston 1879 [1878], London 1879; ed E. Sackville-West 1952; ed L. Edel 1967 (with Washington Square, *below*); ms facs New York 1979; ed T. Tanner with P. Crick, London 1984 (1st edn) (Pen); I. Campbell Ross, Oxford 1985 (1st edn) (WC). 1st pbd Atlantic Monthly, July–Oct 1878. Tr Fr 1955, Ger 1894 (Die Romanwelt).

Daisy Miller. New York 1879 [1878], 2 vols London 1879 (with An international episode and Four meetings), 1 vol 1880, New York 1883 (with An international episode, The diary of a man of fifty, A bundle of letters), London 1888, New York 1892 (with An international episode), 1900; ed J. Gooder, Oxford 1985 (New York edn) (WC); ed G. Moore with P. Crick, London 1986 (1878 edn with Pandora, The Patagonia, Four meetings) (Pen); 1st pbd Cornhill Mag, June–July 1878. Dramatic version 1882 (priv ptd), Boston 1883. 1st pbd Atlantic Monthly, April–June 1883. Tr Fr 1883 (Revue Britannique), 1886, Rus 1898 (Zhivopisnoye Obozreniye), 1946, Danish 1920; Ital 1930, Jap 1941, Bengali 1956, Korean 1957, Serbo-Croat 1958, Ger 1958, Sp 1958, Polish 1961, Turkish 1963.

An international episode. New York 1879, 2 vols London 1879 (with Daisy Miller and Four meetings), 1 vol 1880, New York 1883 (with Daisy Miller, The diary of a man of fifty, A bundle of letters), 1892 (with Daisy Miller), 1902; ed S. Gorley Putt, London 1985 (Pen). 1st pbd Cornhill Mag, Dec 1878–Jan 1879. Tr Rus 1880 (weekly Novoye Vremya), Fr 1886, Jap 1915, 1956 (2 versions), Danish 1920.

The madonna of the future and other tales. 2 vols 1879, 1 vol 1880, 1888. Vol 1 The madonna of the future, Longstaff's marriage, Madame de Mauves; vol 2 Eugene Pickering, The diary of a man of fifty, Benvolio. Tr (the madonna of the future) Fr 1876 (Revue des Deux Mondes), Ger 1876, 1958, Rus 1876 (Pcheia), 1877, Swed 1893.

Confidence. 2 vols 1880 [1879], Boston 1880 [1879], 1880, London 1 vol 1880, 1881, 1882, Boston 1891; ed H. Ruhm, New York 1962 (from ms). 1st pbd Scribner's Monthly, Aug 1879–Jan 1880. Tr Ital, 1946.

Hawthorne. 1879, New York 1880, London 1883, 1887, 1902 (EML); ed W. M. Sale jr, Ithaca NY 1956; ed T. Tanner, London 1967.

A bundle of letters. Boston [1880], New York [1880], (both unauthorised), New York 1880 (with The diary of a man of fifty), London 1883 (with Daisy Miller, An international episode, The diary of a man of fifty). 1st pbd Parisian, 18 Dec 1879. Tr (A bundle of letters) Rus 1882 (Vestnik Yevropy).

Washington Square. New York 1881 [1880], 2 vols London 1881 (with The pension Beaurepas, A bundle of letters), 1 vol 1881, 1889; ed L. Edel 1967 (with The Europeans, *above*); ed M. LeFanu, London 1982 (WC) (1st Eng edn); ed B. Lee 1984 (1881 edn) (Pen). 1st pbd Cornhill Mag, June–Nov 1880; Harper's New Monthly Mag, July–Dec 1880. Tr Rus 1881 (Zagranichnyi Vestnik), Ital 1950 (2 versions), Jap 1950, Sp 1951, 1952, 1958 (3 versions), Hebrew 1952, Serbo-Croat 1953, Fr 1953, Greek c. 1953, Ger 1956, Portuguese c. 1956, Korean 1960.

The portrait of a lady. 3 vols 1881, 1 vol Boston 1882 [1881], 1 vol London 1882; ed G. Greene, Oxford 1947 (WC); ed L. Edel, Boston 1956; ed R. D. Bamberg New York 1975 (1st edn) (Norton); ed G. Greene with N. Bradbury, Oxford 1981 (New York edn) (WC); ed G. Moore with P. Crick London 1986 (New York edn) (Pen). 1st pbd Macmillan's Mag Oct 1880–Nov 1881; Atlantic Monthly, Nov 1880–Dec 1881. Tr Fr 1933, Ital 1943, 1963 (2 versions), Port 1944, Sp 1944, 1958 (2 versions), Swed 1947, Ger 1950, Finnish 1955, Urdu 1958.

The point of view. 1882 (priv ptd).

The siege of London, The pension Beaurepas, and The point of view. Boston 1883, Leipzig 1884 (rev with A passionate pilgrim replacing The pension Beaurepas).

Portraits of places. 1883, Boston 1884, Leipzig 1884 (truncated).

Notes on a collection of drawings by Mr George du Maurier. 1884. Catalogue of Fine Art Society exhibition.

A little tour in France. Boston 1885 [1884], 1900, London 1900, Boston 1907, 1914. 1st pbd as En provence in Atlantic Monthly, July–Nov 1883, Feb, Apr–May 1884.

Tales of three cities. Boston 1884, London 1884. The impressions of a cousin; Lady Barberina; A New England winter.

The art of fiction. Boston 1885 [1884], London 1887 [1888?], 1889. Pbd with Walter Besant's essay of same title; rptd in The house of fiction, ed L. Edel 1957.

The author of Beltraffio. Boston 1885. The author of Beltraffio, Pandora, Georgina's reasons, The path of duty, Four meetings. The author of Beltraffio, ed F. Kermode, London 1986 (New York edn with The figure in the carpet, The lesson of the master, The private life, The middle years, The death of the lion, The next time, John Delavoy) (Pen); Pandora, ed J. Gooder Oxford 1985 (New York edn with Daisy Miller, The Patagonia, Four meetings) (WC).

Stories revived. 3 vols 1885, 2 vols 1885. Vol 1 The author of 'Beltraffio', Pandora, The path of duty, A day of days, A light man; vol 2 Georgina's reasons, A passionate pilgrim, A landscape-painter, Rose-Agathe; vol 3 Poor Richard, The last of the Valerii, Master Eustace, The romance of certain old clothes, A most extraordinary case.

The Bostonians. 3 vols 1886, New York 1886, 1 vol London 1886; ed P. Rahv, New York 1945; ed L. Trilling, London 1952; ed I. Howe, New York 1956 (Mod Lib); ed L. Edel, London 1967; ed C. R. Anderson 1984 (1st English edn) (Pen); ed R. W. Gooder Oxford 1984 (1st edn) (WC). 1st pbd Century Mag, Feb 1885–Feb 1886. Tr Fr 1955, Ger 1964.

The Princess Casamassima. 3 vols 1886, 1 vol New York 1886, London 1887, 1888; ed L. Trilling 2 vols New York 1948; ed D. Brewer with P. Crick, London 1987 (1st edn) (Pen). 1st pbd Atlantic Monthly, Sep 1885–Oct 1886. Tr Danish 1887, Ger 1954, Serbo-Croat 1958.

Partial portraits. 1888, New York 1888, London 1894.

The reverberator. 2 vols 1888, 1 vol New York 1888, London 1888; ed S. Nowell-Smith, 1949; ed P. Horne, Oxford 1989 (New York edn with A London life) (WC). 1st pbd Macmillan's Mag, Feb–July 1888.

The Aspern papers; Louisa Pallant; The modern warning. 2 vols 1888, New York 1888, 1 vol London 1890; The Aspern papers, ed S. Gorley Putt 1976 (New York edn with The real thing and The papers) (Pen); ed A. Poole, Oxford 1983 (New York edn with The private life, The middle years, The death of the lion) (WC); ed A. Curtis, London 1984 (New York edn with The turn of the screw) (Pen); The Aspern papers 1st pbd Atlantic Monthly, Mar–May 1888. Tr (The Aspern papers) Fr 1920 (Journal des Débats), 1929,

Ital 1944, 1946 (2 versions), Sp 1944 [1946], 1949, 1950 (3 versions), Swed 1951, Ger 1953, Cz 1959, Flemish 1959.

A London life; The Patagonia; The liar; Mrs Temperly. 2 vols 1889, New York 1889, 1 vol London 1889, Leipzig 1891 (omitting Patagonia); A London life, ed P. Horne, Oxford 1989 (New York edn with The reverberator) (WC).

The tragic muse. 2 vols Boston 1890, 3 vols London 1890, 1 vol 1891; ed L. Edel, New York 1960; ed R. P. Blackmur, New York 1961. 1st pbd Atlantic Monthly, Jan 1889–May 1890.

Daudet, A. Port Tarascon. New York 1891 [1890], London 1891 [1890]. Tr James. 1st pbd Harper's New Monthly Mag, June–Nov 1890.

The lesson of the master: The marriages; The pupil; Brooksmith; The solution; Sir Edmund Orme. New York 1892, London 1892; The lesson of the master, ed F. Kermode, London 1986 (New York edn with The figure in the carpet, The author of Beltraffio, The private life, The middle years, The death of the lion, The next time, John Delavoy) (Pen). Tr Fr 1922 (Revue Hebdomadaire), Sp 1949.

The real thing, and other tales. New York 1893, London 1893. The real thing, Sir Dominick Ferrand, Nona Vincent, The chaperon, Greville Fane. The real thing, ed S. Gorley Putt, London 1976 (New York edn with The Aspern papers and The papers) (Pen). Tr (The real thing) Rus 1893 (Vestnik Yevropy), Danish 1948, Ger 1958.

Picture and text. New York 1893.

The private life; The wheel of time; Lord Beaupré; The visits; Collaboration; Owen Wingrave. 1893, 2 vols New York 1893. Vol 1 The private life (including Lord Beaupré and The visits); vol 2 The wheel of time (including Collaboration and Owen Wingrave). The private life, ed F. Kermode, London 1986 (New York edn with The lesson of the master, The figure in the carpet, The author of Beltraffio, The middle years, The death of the lion, The next time, John Delavoy) (Pen); ed A. Poole, Oxford 1983 (New York edn with The Aspern papers, The middle years, The death of the lion) (WC). Tr Ital 1946.

Essays in London and elsewhere. 1893, New York 1893.

Theatricals. New York 1894, London 1895. Tenants, Disengaged (acted Hudson Theatre New York 11 Mar 1909).

Guy Domville. 1894 (priv ptd). Acted St James's Theatre 5 Jan 1895.

Theatricals: second series. 1895 [1894], New York 1894. The album, The reprobate (acted Royal Court Theatre 14 Dec 1919).

Terminations. 1895, New York 1895. The death of the lion, The Coxon fund, The middle years, The altar of the dead. The death of the lion and The middle years, ed F. Kermode, London 1986 (New York edn with The figure in the carpet, The lesson of the master, The author of Beltraffio, The next time, The private life, John Delavoy) (Pen); The death of the lion and The middle years, ed A. Poole, Oxford 1983 (New York edn with The Aspern papers and The private life) (WC). Tr (The altar of the dead) Fr 1925 (Revue de Paris), Ger 1932 (Corona), Ital 1934, 1943, Sp 1949.

Embarrassments. 1896, New York 1896, London 1897. The figure in the carpet, Glasses, The next time, The way it came. The figure in the carpet, ed F. Kermode, London 1986 (New York edn with The lesson of the master, The author of Beltraffio, The next time, The private life, John Delavoy, The death of the lion, The middle years) (Pen). Tr Fr 1922, 1957, Ger 1958.

The other house. 2 vols 1896, New York 1896, 1 vol London 1897; ed L. Edel 1948. 1st pbd Illus London News, 4 July–26 Sep 1896.

The spoils of Poynton. 1897, New York 1897; ed L. Edel, London 1967; ed B. Richards, Oxford 1982 (New York edn) (WC); ed D. Lodge with P. Crick, London 1987 (New York edn) (Pen). 1st pbd as The old things in Atlantic Monthly, Apr–Oct 1896. Tr Fr 1928 (Revue de Paris), 1929, Serbo-Croat 1959.

What Maisie knew. 1898 [1897], Chicago 1897; ed D. Jefferson with D. Grant, London 1980 (New York edn) (WC); ed P. Theroux with P. Crick 1985 (New York edn) (Pen). 1st pbd Chapbook, 15 Jan–1 Aug 1897; New Rev, Feb–Sep 1897 (rev and abridged). Tr Danish 1919, Fr 1947, Ger 1955.

John Delavoy. New York 1897 (priv ptd); ed F. Kermode, London 1986 (with The figure in the carpet, The author of Beltraffio, The lesson of the master, The private life, The middle years, The death of the lion, The next time) (Pen).

In the cage. 1898, Chicago 1898, New York 1906; ed M. D. Zabel 1958. Tr Fr 1959, Ital 1933.

The two magics: The turn of the screw; Covering end. 1898, New York 1898; The turn of the screw ed D. Kimbrough, New York 1966 (Norton); ed A. Curtis, London 1984 (New York edn with The Aspern papers) (Pen); New York 1991 (1st edn rptd) (Dover Thrift); ed T. J. Lustig, London 1992 (New York edn with Sir Edmund Orme, Owen Wingrave, The friends of the friends) (WC); ed K. Murdock with A. Lloyd Smith 1993 (EL). Turn of the screw 1st pbd Collier's Weekly, 27 Jan–16 Apr 1898. Tr (Turn of the screw) Fr 1929, Ital 1932, 1934, 1960 (3 versions), Portuguese 1943, Sp 1945, 1946 (2 versions), Danish 1950, Du 1951, Swed 1951, Ger 1953, 1954, 1962 (3 versions), Korean 1957, Arabic 1958, Jap 1958, 1962 (2 versions), Polish 1959, Serbo-Croat 1960.

The awkward age. 1899, New York 1899; ed L. Edel 1967; ed V. Jones, Oxford 1984 (1st bk edn) (WC); ed R. Blythe, London 1987 (1899 edn) (Pen); ed C. Ozick 1993 (EL). 1st pbd Harper's Weekly, 1 Oct 1898–7 Jan 1899. Tr Fr 1956.

The soft side. 1900, New York 1900. The great good place, 'Europe', Paste, The real right thing, The great condition, The tree of knowledge, The abasement of the Northmores, The given case, John Delavoy, The third person, Maud-Evelyn, Miss Gunton of Poughkeepsie.

The sacred fount. New York 1901, London 1901; ed L. Edel, New York 1953, London 1959 (rev).

The wings of the dove. 2 vols New York 1902, London 1902; ed H. Read 1948; ed R. P. Blackmur, New York 1958; ed J. Bayley with P. Crick, London 1965 (New York edn) (Pen); ed J. D. Crowley with R. A. Hocks, New York 1978 (New York edn) (Norton); ed P. Brooks, Oxford 1984 (New York edn) (WC). Tr Fr 1953, Ger 1962.

The better sort. 1903, New York 1903. Broken wings, The Beldonald Holbein, The two faces, The tone of time, The special type, Mrs Medwin, Flickerbridge, The story in it, The beast in the jungle, The birthplace, The papers. The beast in the jungle and The birthplace, ed R. Gard, London 1990 (1st book edn, with The third person, Broken wings, The jolly corner, The velvet glove, Crapy Cornelia, The bench of desolation) (Pen). Tr (The beast in the jungle) Fr 1928 (Revue Hebdomadaire), Ital 1943, 1946, Swed 1948, Ger 1958.

The ambassadors. 1903, New York 1903; ed L. Edel, Boston 1960; ed S. P. Rosenbaum, New York 1966; ed C. Butler, Oxford 1985 (New York edn) (WC); ed H. Levin, London 1986 (New York edn) (Pen); ed S. P. Rosenbaum, New York 1994 (New York edn) (Norton). 1st pbd North Amer Rev, Jan–Dec 1903. Tr Fr 1950, Serbo-Croat 1955, Ger 1956, Polish 1960.

William Wetmore Story and his friends. 2 vols Edinburgh 1903, Boston 1903.

The golden bowl. 2 vols New York 1904, London [1905]; ed R. P. Blackmur, New York 1952; ed V. Llewellyn-Smith, Oxford 1983 (1st Eng edn) (WC); ed G. Vidal with P. Crick, London 1985 (New York edn) (Pen). Tr Fr 1954, Serbo-Croat 1960, Ger 1964.

The question of our speech; The lesson of Balzac. Boston 1905. 2 lectures.

English hours. 1905, Boston 1905, 1914; London 1989.

The American scene. 1907, New York 1907; ed W. H. Auden, New York 1946; ed L. Edel, London 1968.

Views and reviews. Ed L. Phillips, Boston 1908.

Julia Bride. New York 1909.

Italian hours. 1909, Boston 1909, ed T. Follini, London 1986, ed J. Auchard, University Park, PA 1992.

The finer grain. New York 1910, London 1910. The velvet glove, Mora Montravers, A round of visits, Crapy Cornelia, The bench of desolation. The velvet glove, Crapy Cornelia, The bench of desolation, ed R. Gard 1990 (1st bk edn, with The jolly corner, The third person, Broken wings, The beast in the jungle, The birthplace) (Pen).

The Henry James year book. Ed E. G. Smalley, Boston [1911], London [1912]. Introds by James and W. D. Howells.

The outcry. [1911], New York 1911.

A small boy and others. New York 1913, London 1913. An autobiography continued in Notes of a son and brother and Middle years, *below*; collected as Autobiography, ed F. W. Dupee, New York 1956.

Notes of a son and brother. New York 1914, London 1914.

Notes on novelists. 1914, New York 1914.

The question of the mind. [1915].

Pictures and other passages from Henry James. Ed R. Head 1916, New York [1917].

The ivory tower. [1917], New York 1917; Notes for The ivory tower, New York [1947].

The sense of the past. [1917], New York 1917.

The middle years. [Ed P. Lubbock] [1917], New York 1917.

Gabrielle de Bergerac. New York 1918.

Within the rim. [1919].

Travelling companions. New York 1919. Travelling companions, The sweetheart of M. Briseux, Professor Fargo, At Isella, Guest's confession, Adina, De Grey: a romance.

A landscape painter. New York 1919 [1920]. A landscape painter, Poor Richard, A day of days, A most extraordinary case. A landscape painter, ed R. Gard, London 1990 (Pen).

Refugees in Chelsea. [1920] (priv ptd).

Master Eustace. New York 1920. Master Eustace, Longstaff's marriage, Théodolinde, A light man, Benvolio.

Notes and reviews. Ed P. de Chaignon La Rose, Cambridge MA 1921.

The scenic art. Ed A. Wade, New Brunswick NJ 1948.

Eight uncollected tales. Ed E. Kenton, New Brunswick NJ 1950. The story of a year, My friend Bingham, The story of a masterpiece, A problem, Osborne's revenge, Gabrielle de Bergerac, Crawford's consistency, The ghostly rental.

Daumier, caricaturist. [1954].

The American essays. Ed L. Edel, New York 1956.

The future of the novel: essays on the art of fiction. Ed L. Edel, New York 1956, London 1957 (with variations, as The house of fiction).

The painter's eye: notes and essays on the pictorial arts. Ed J. L. Sweeney 1956.

Parisian sketches. Ed L. Edel and I. D. Lind, New York 1957.

Literary reviews and essays on American, English and French literature. Ed A. Mordell, New York [1957].

French writers and American women. Ed P. Buitenhuis, Branford CT 1960.

Letters and papers

See also Section B Contributions to books, Section C Published letters, and Section D Contributions to periodicals in Edel and Laurence with Rambeau, Bibliographies, *above. For location of letter mss see* Letters, ed L. Edel vol 4 Appendix, *below. For early responses to James see Foley, Criticism in American periodicals and Gard, Critical heritage,* Bibliographies, *above.*

The American volunteer motor-ambulance corps in France. 1914.

Letters to an editor [Clement Shorter]. 1916 (priv ptd).

Letters. Ed P. Lubbock 2 vols 1920, New York 1920.

'A most unholy trade': being letters on the drama. Cambridge MA 1923 (priv ptd).

Three letters to Joseph Conrad. 1926 (priv ptd).

Letters to Walter Berry. Paris 1928 (priv ptd).

Letters to A. C. Benson and Auguste Monod. 1930.

Theatre and friendship: commentary by Elizabeth Robins. 1932.

Notebooks. Ed F. O. Matthiessen and K. B. Murdock, New York 1947. Tr Fr 1954.

Henry James and Robert Louis Stevenson: a record of friendship and criticism. Ed J. A. Smith 1948.

Harlow, V. Thomas Sergeant Perry. Durham NC 1950.

Selected letters. Ed L. Edel, New York 1955.

James and the Bazar letters. Ed L. Edel and L. H. Powers, BNYPL, Feb 1958, rptd in E. G. Jordan and W. M. Gibson, eds, Howells and James: a double billing, New York 1958.

Henry James and H. G. Wells: a record of friendship. Ed L. Edel and G. N. Ray 1958.

Parisian sketches: letters to the New York Tribune 1875–1876. Ed L. Edel and I. D. Lind 1958.

Selected literary criticism. Ed M. Shapira with introd F. R. Leavis 1963.

Letters to Macmillan. Ed S. Nowell-Smith 1967.

Henry James letters. Ed L. Edel 4 vols Cambridge MA 1974–84.

Henry James literary criticism. Ed L. Edel and M. Wilson 2 vols New York and Cambridge 1984 (Lib of America).

The art of criticism: Henry James on the theory and practice of fiction. Ed W. Veeder and S. M. Griffin, Chicago and London 1986.

The complete notebooks of Henry James: the authoritative and definitive edition. Ed L. Edel and L. H. Powers, New York and Oxford 1987.

The critical muse: selected literary criticism. Ed R. Gard 1987 (Pen).

Henry James and Edith Wharton: letters 1900–1915. Ed L. H. Powers, New York and London 1990.

The correspondence of Henry James and the house of Macmillan 1877–1914. Ed R. S. Moore 1993.

§2

Howells, W. D. James's Passionate pilgrim and other tales. Atlantic Monthly, Apr 1875. Henry James jr, Century, Nov 1882. Editor's study, Harper's New Monthly Mag, Oct 1888. Mr Henry James's later work, North Amer Rev, Jan 1903. All rptd in Discovery of a genius, ed A. Mordell, New York 1961.

Newburgh, M. L. H. Mr Henry James jr and his critics. Literary World, 14 Jan 1882.

Brownell, W. C. James's Portrait of a lady. Nation, 2 Feb 1882.

Tilley, A. The new school of fiction. Nat Rev, Apr 1883.

Fawcett, E. Henry James's novels. Princeton Rev new ser 14, 1884.

Scudder, H. E. James, Crawford and Howells. Atlantic Monthly, June 1886.

Conrad, J. James: an appreciation. North Amer Rev, Jan 1905, rptd in his Notes on life and letters, 1921.

Cary, E. L. The novels of James. New York 1905.

Brownell, W. C. In his American prose master, New York 1909.

Fullerton, M. The art of James. Quart Rev 212 1910.

Paget, V. The handling of words. Eng Rev, June 1910.

Hueffer, F. M. James: a critical study. 1913.

'West, Rebecca' (C. I. Andrews). Henry James. 1916.

Freeman, J. In his Moderns, 1916.

Lubbock, P. Henry James. Quart Rev 226, 1916.

Powys, J. C. In his Suspended judgements, New York 1916.

Scott, D. In his Men of letters, 1916.

Sherman, S. P. The aesthetic idealism of James. Nation, 5 Apr 1917, rptd in his On contemporary literature, New York 1917.

Beach, J. W. The method of James. New Haven CT 1918, Philadelphia 1954 (enlarged).

Cairns, W. B. Character-portrayal in the work of James. Univ of Wisconsin Stud in Lang and Lit no 2, 1918.

[James no]. Little Rev, Aug 1918.

Eliot, T. S. In memory of Henry James. Egoist 5, 1918; rptd in The question of Henry James: a collection of critical essays, ed F. W. Dupee, London and New York 1945.

Pound, E. The middle years. Egoist 5, 1918.

Pound, E. Brief note. Little Rev 5, 1918.
Liljegren, S. B. American and European in the works of James. Lund 1919.
Pound, E. In his Instigations, New York 1920, rptd in his Make it new, New Haven CT 1935.
Lubbock, P. In his Craft of fiction, 1921.
Harvitt, H. How Henry James revised Roderick Hudson: a study in style. PMLA 39, 1924.
Havens, R. The revision of Roderick Hudson. PMLA 40, 1925.
Gegenheimer, A. F. Early and late revisions in Henry James's A passionate pilgrim. Amer Lit 16, 1945.
Gettman, R. A. Henry James's revision of The American. Amer Lit 16, 1945.
Dunbar, V. A source for Roderick Hudson. MLN 63, 1948.
Dunbar, V. The revision of Daisy Miller. MLN 65, 1950.
Humphries, S. M. Henry James's revisions for The ambassadors. N & Q 1, 1954.
Schulz, M. F. The Bellegardes' feud with Christopher Newman: a study of Henry James's revision of The American. Amer Lit 27, 1955.
Traschen, I. Henry James and the art of revision. Philological Quart 35, 1956.
Traschen, I. James's revisions of the love affair in The American. New England Quart 29, 1956.
Krause, S. J. James's revisions of the style of The portrait of a lady. Amer Lit 30, 1958.
Tartella, V. James's Four meetings: two texts compared. Nineteenth Cent Fiction 15, 1960.
Durkin, M. B. Henry James's revisions of the style of The reverberator. Amer Lit 33, 1961.
Shumsky, A. James again: the New York edition. Sewanee Rev 70, 1962.
Stafford, W. T. The ending of James's The American: a defense of the early version. Nineteenth Cent Fiction 18, 1963.
Ohmann, C. Daisy Miller: a study of changing intentions. Amer Lit 36, 1964.
Aziz, M. Four meetings: a caveat for James critics. EIC 18, 1968.
Bazzanella, D. J. The conclusion to The portrait of a lady re-examined. Amer Lit 41, 1969.
Bercovitch, S. The revision of Rowland Mallet. Nineteenth Cent Fiction 24, 1969.
Aziz, M. Revisiting The pension Beaurepas: the tale and its texts. EIC 23, 1973.
Reynolds, L. J. Henry James's new Christopher Newman. Stud in the Novel 5, 1973.
Taylor, L. J. The portrait of a lady and the Anglo-American press: an annotated checklist 1880–1886. Resources for Amer Literary Study 5, 1975.
Baym, N. Revisions and thematic change in The portrait of a lady. Mod Fiction Stud 22, 1976.
Girling, H. K. On editing a paragraph of The princess Casamassima. Lang and Style 8, 1976.
Timms, D. The governess's feelings and the argument from textual revision of The turn of the screw. YES 6, 1976.
Taylor, L. J. Contemporary critical response to Henry James's The Bostonians: an annotated checklist. Resources for Amer Literary Study 7, 1977.
Tuttleton, J. W. Re-reading The American: a century since. Henry James Rev 1, 1980.
Leitch, T. M. The editor as hero: Henry James and the New York edition. Henry James Rev 1981.
Parker, H. Henry James 'In the wood': sequence and significances of his literary labours 1905–1907. Nineteenth Cent Fiction 38, 1984.
Anesko, M. 'Friction with the market': Henry James and the profession of authorship. Oxford 1986.
Habegger, A. Henry James's rewriting of Minny Temple's letters. Amer Lit 4, 1986.
Horne, P. Henry James and revision. Oxford 1990.

Biographies

James, H. Autobiography, A small boy and others, Notes of a son and brother, The middle years. Ed F. W. Dupee, New York 1956, rptd Princeton NJ 1983.
Edel, L. The life of Henry James. 5 vols London 1953, 1962, 1963, 1969, 1972; 2 vols Harmondsworth 1977 (rev); rev as Henry James: a life, London 1987.
Kaplan, F. Henry James: the imagination of genius. 1992. [NB]

Richard Jefferies, John Richard Jefferies 1848–87

The largest coll of mss which includes mss of pbd and unpbd works, drafts, notebooks, letters and agreements with publishers, is in the BL. Two pbd mss and 5 letters are at the Richard Jefferies Museum, Coate, Swindon. For smaller holdings in the UK and USA, see Miller and Matthews, *below.*

Bibliographies

Dartnell, G. E. Richard Jefferies. Wiltshire Archaeological and Natural History Mag 26 June 1893, bibliographical addenda 28 June 1895.
Miller, G. and H. Matthews. Richard Jefferies: a bibliographical study. Aldershot 1993.

Collections

The collector's edition of Richard Jefferies. 5 vols (begun as The collected edition but not completed) 1947–8. Ed with introds and notes by S. J. Looker. Titles listed separately under §1, *below.*
The uniform edition of works by Richard Jefferies. 6 vols 1948–9 (discontinued). Ed with introds and notes by C. H. Warren. Titles listed separately under §1, *below.*

Selections

Thoughts from the writings of Richard Jefferies, selected by H. S. H. Waylen. 1895.
Richard Jefferies: A little book of nature thoughts, selected by T. C. Watkins. Portland ME 1903.
The pocket Richard Jefferies: being passages chosen from the nature writings of Jefferies by A. H. Hyatt. 1905.
Selections from Richard Jefferies, with an introduction and notes by F. W. Tickner. 1909. Extracts from books, essays with unmarked omissions.
A calendar of nature for the year 1911 from the works of Richard Jefferies: selections by F. G. H[eath]. 1910. Short extracts.
Out of doors with Richard Jefferies. Ed E. F. Daglish 1935. Complete book and 7 essays.
Richard Jefferies: selections of his work, with details of his life and circumstance, his death and immortality by Henry Williamson. 1937. Wide selection of book extracts and essays.
Jefferies' England: nature essays by Richard Jefferies, edited with an introduction, notes and check lists by S. J. Looker. 1937. Selected essays with many omissions.
Readings from Richard Jefferies: an anthology of the countryside chosen and edited by R. Hook. 1940. Extracts from books and essays with unstated retitling, omission and revision.
The sun and the earth: passages from the works of Richard Jefferies, decorations by G. Gardiner. Northwood, Middlesex [c. 1943]. Pamphlet.
Jefferies' countryside: nature essays by Richard Jefferies edited with an introduction and notes by S. J. Looker. 1944. Book extracts, essays with unmarked omissions.
Richard Jefferies' London, edited with an introduction and notes by S. J. Looker. 1944. Book extracts, essays with unmarked omissions.
A Richard Jefferies anthology, gathered by G. P. Insh. Glasgow 1945. Book extracts, essays with unmarked omissions.

The spring of the year and other nature essays by Richard Jefferies, edited with an introduction and notes by S. J. Looker. 1946. Book extracts, essays with unstated omission and revision.

Summer in the woods: a selection from the works of Richard Jefferies with four drawings by S. H. de Roos. Amsterdam 1947. Four essays, one incomplete.

The Jefferies companion, selected and arranged with an introduction and notes by S. J. Looker. 1948. Wide selection of passages from books and essays with Looker's usual concealed cuts.

The essential Richard Jefferies, selected with an introduction by M. Elwin. 1948. One complete work, large extracts and complete essays.

The pageant of summer and other essays by Richard Jefferies, selected and arranged by A. Rossabi. 1979. Essays and a passage from one novel.

Rural England by Richard Jefferies, edited with notes by F. Nodzu. Tokyo [c. 1980]. One book extract, one complete and five abridged essays.

Richard Jefferies. Under the acorns: a selection of nature essays illustrated and introduced by P. and C. Cholerton. Stratford-upon-Avon 1982. Ten essays.

Richard Jefferies. Landscape with figures: an anthology of prose chosen and introduced by R. Mabey. Harmondsworth 1983. Extracts and essays, one possibly not by Jefferies.

An illustrated anthology. The eye of the beholder: Richard Jefferies. Introd by C. McKelvie. Southampton 1987. Extracts, and essays of which some not proven by Jefferies.

A rook book: an anthology of writings by Richard Jefferies illustrated [and selected] by N. Parry. Market Drayton 1988. Untitled and unreferenced extracts.

The Wessex landscape of Richard Jefferies by Anthony Clare Lees. Swindon 1990. Photographs illustrated with short extracts.

Country vignettes: descriptive passages selected from the writings of Richard Jefferies, with seven engravings by A. Christmas. Buxton 1991. Extracts from 4 books and an essay.

Beloved land: a Richard Jefferies anthology edited by C. McKelvie. Shrewsbury 1994. Eleven essays and one retitled extract.

§1

Reporting, editing & authorship: practical hints for beginners in literature. [1873]. Pamphlet.
REVIEW: Athenaeum 21 June 1873.

A memoir of the Goddards of North Wilts: compiled from ancient records, registers and family papers. Coate, Swindon [1873], with addenda and omissions priv rptd by D. Goddard, Cleveland OH 1912, introd by R. G. H. Goddard, Newbury 1987 for the Goddard assoc.
REVIEWS: Reliquary Aug 1873, Athenaeum 30 Aug 1873, New England Historical and Genealogical Register Apr 1874.

Jack Brass, emperor of England. 1873. Pamphlet.

The scarlet shawl: a novel. 1874, [1877] ('new edition', issued in cloth and as 'yellowback'), with A female nihilist by E. Lavigne tr G. S. Edwards [1880], 1996.
REVIEWS: Athenaeum 1 Aug 1874, Examiner 22 Aug 1874, Graphic 29 Aug 1874, Westminster Rev 1 Oct 1874.

Restless human hearts: a novel. 3 vols 1875 (later reissued 3 vols in 1).
REVIEWS: Athenaeum 20 Mar 1875, Graphic 3 Apr 1875, Academy 10 Apr 1875, Spectator 28 Aug 1875.

Suez-cide!! or how Miss Britannia bought a dirty puddle and lost her sugar-plums. 1876, 1876 ('second edition'), '1876' [1893] (forgery of 1st edn probably by J. H. Ashworth, detectable by spelling 'Anthony' rather than 'Antony' on p. 8, line 11). Pamphlet.

World's end, a story in three books: I Facts, II Persons, III Results. 3 vols 1877, 1996.
REVIEWS: Queen 4 Aug 1877, Sat Rev 11 Aug 1877, World 22 Aug 1877, Athenaeum 25 Aug 1877, Graphic 25 Aug 1877, Spectator 20 Oct 1877, Academy 24 Nov 1877.

The gamekeeper at home: sketches of natural history and rural life (anon). First pbd Pall Mall Gazette Dec 1877 and Jan–Apr 1878, 1878, 1878 ('second edition'), 1878 ('third edition'), 1879 ('third edition'), Boston 1879 ('third edition'), illustr C. Whymper, London '1880' [1879], illustr Whymper Boston 1880, London 1881 ('new edition', rptd 1887, 1889), illustr Whymper 1890 ('new edition', rptd 1892, 1896, 1905, 1906 Waterloo lib, 1910 [1s. net ser], 1914 Waterloo lib, 1914, 1924 'reprinted', 1937 'cheap edition'), illustr Whymper Boston 1890 ('new edition'), London [1927] (Collins' Kings' way classics), illustr D. Constable [1929] ([Collins' illustrated pocket classics], rptd [c. 1938] and issued in [Collins' illustrated school classics], New univ soc, and Lib of classics), introd by G. N. P[ocock] 1932 (Dent's Kings treasuries of lit), introd by Henry Williamson 1935 (Travellers' lib), in Out of doors with Richard Jefferies ed E. F. Daglish 1935 (Open air lib), illustr photographs [1938] ([Collins' enterprise ser]), introd by Williamson 1940 (Saint Giles lib), introd by C. H. Warren 1948 (Uniform edn), with The amateur poacher, introd by D. Ascoli 1948 (WC, rptd 1951, 1960), illustr Whymper Rhyl 1973 ('facsimile edition'), with The amateur poacher, introd by R. Fitter Oxford 1978 (WCp, rptd 1979, 1981, 1983), illustr Whymper Rhyl 1985, illustr Whymper Alton 1988 (Classic reprint).
REVIEWS: Edinburgh Rev July 1878, Live Stock Jnl Literary Suppl 5 July 1878, Spectator 13 July 1878, Examiner 20 July 1878, World 24 July 1878, Acad 27 July 1878, John Bull 27 July 1878, Saturday Rev 10 Aug 1878, Liverpool Weekly Albion 17 Aug 1878, Morning Post 20 Aug 1878, Non-Conformist 21 Aug 1878, Daily News 22 Aug 1878, Broad Arrow 24 Aug 1878, Whitehall Rev 24 Aug 1878, Land and Water 31 Aug 1878, Zoologist Mag Sep 1878, Scotsman 3 Sep 1878, Standard 3 Sep 1878, Br Quart Rev Oct 1878, Sporting Gazette 12 Oct 1878, Westminster Rev Jan 1879, Guardian 5 Mar 1879, Gentleman's Mag Apr 1879, Blackwood's Mag Apr 1879.

Wild life in a southern county, by the author of The gamekeeper at home. First pbd Pall Mall Gazette May–Dec 1878, 1879, Boston 1879, London 1879 ('second edition'), 1880 ('third edition'), 1881 ('new edition', rptd 1889, 1892, 1893, 1897, 1902, 1903), Boston 1889, retitled An English village Boston 1903 (rptd 1904), London [1908] ([Nelson's shilling lib]), [1917] (Nelson's lib of general lit, rptd [c. 1919]), 1925, 1927 (Edinburgh lib of non-fiction bks), introd by Henry Williamson 1934 (Travellers' lib), 1937 ('cheap edition'), introd by W. Beach-Thomas illustr G. E. Collins 1937, introd by F. Brereton illustr M. Anderson [1939] (Lib of classics, also in [Canterbury classics] and [Collins' illustrated school classics]), introd by Williamson 1940 (Saint Giles lib), introd and notes by S. J. Looker illustr C. F. Tunnicliffe 1949 (Collector's edn), introd by D. Hawkins illustr Tunnicliffe, Bradford-on-Avon 1978.
REVIEWS: Standard 26 Feb 1879, Scotsman 27 Feb 1879, Athenaeum 1 Mar 1879, Sat Rev 1 Mar 1879, John Bull 1 Mar 1879, Bailey's Mag Mar 1879, Acad 15 Mar 1879, North Br Daily Mail 19 Mar 1879, Globe 27 Mar 1879, Week 27 Mar 1879, Eng Independent 27 Mar 1879, Blackwoods Mag Apr 1879, Br Quart Rev Apr 1879, Westminster Rev Apr 1879, Edinburgh Rev July 1879, Spectator 19 July 1879, Chambers's Jnl 23 Aug 1879, Church Quart Rev Oct 1879.

The amateur poacher, by the author of The gamekeeper at home and Wild life in a southern county. First pbd Pall Mall Gazette Nov 1877 and March–July 1879, 1879, Boston 1879, London 1881 ('second edition'), 1881 ('new edition', rptd 1889, 1893, 1896, 1901, 1903, 1905, 1909 Waterloo lib, 1914 Waterloo lib, 1914, 1925), [1911] (Nelson's lib of notable bks), introd by Henry Williamson 1934 (Travellers' lib), with The gamekeeper at home, 1948 (WC), rptd 1951, 1960, Rhyl 1973 ('facsimile edition', rptd 1977), with The gamekeeper at home 1978 (WCp), rptd 1979, 1981, 1983, illustr D. Bown Rhyl 1985.

REVIEWS: Sat Rev 1 Nov 1879, Acad 15 Nov 1879, Examiner 22 Nov 1879, Br Quart Rev Jan 1880, Westminster Rev Jan 1880, Albion 15 Mar 1880, Daily News 15 Mar 1880, Graphic 15 Mar 1880, John Bull 15 Mar 1880, Scotsman 15 Mar 1880, Chambers's Jnl 18 Sep 1880.

Greene ferne farm. First pbd Time Apr 1879–Feb 1880, 1880, Hounslow [1947], introd and notes by A. Rossabi, London 1986 (Grafton classic). Novel.

REVIEWS: Live Stock Jnl Literary Suppl 13 Feb 1880, Athenaeum 21 Feb 1880, Court Jnl 28 Feb 1880, Public Opinion 28 Feb 1880, Examiner 6 Mar 1880, Spectator 6 Mar 1880, Scotsman 23 Mar 1880, Acad 27 Mar 1880, Graphic 27 Mar 1880, The Times 27 Mar 1880, Br Quart Rev Apr 1880, Westminster Rev Apr 1880, Vanity Fair 8 May 1880.

Hodge and his masters. First pbd Standard Sep 1879–Jan 1880, 2 vols 1880, 1890 ('new edition'), rev abridged and introd by Henry Williamson and illustr photographs 1937, rev abridged introd and retitled A classic of English farming: Hodge and his masters by Williamson 1946 (rptd 1948), introd by C. H. Warren 1949 (Uniform edn), introd by R. Williams 2 vols 1966 (Fitzroy edn), introd and notes by A. Rossabi 1979, introd by A. Richardson illustr photographs Stroud 1992.

REVIEWS: Examiner 3 Apr 1880, Athenaeum 10 Apr 1880, Acad 17 Apr 1880, Field 1 May 1880, Live Stock Jnl Literary Suppl 14 May 1880, Public Opinion 29 May 1880, Spectator 29 May 1880, Sat Rev 19 June 1880, Br Quart Rev July 1880, Edinburgh Rev July 1880, Westminster Rev July 1880, Chambers's Jnl 2 Oct 1880.

Round about a great estate. First pbd Pall Mall Gazette Jan–Apr 1880, 1880, Boston 1880, London 1881 ('new edition', rptd 1891, 1894, 1903), 1925, 1937 ('cheap edition'), with Red deer with introd by C. H. Warren 1948 (Uniform edn), introd by John Fowles illustr G. Arnold Bradford-on-Avon 1987 (Centenary edn).

REVIEWS: Athenaeum 14 Aug 1880, Acad 21 Aug 1880, Globe 27 Aug 1880, Sat Rev 28 Aug 1880, Live Stock Jnl Literary Suppl 3 Sep 1880, Br Quart Rev Oct 1880.

Wood magic: a fable. 2 vols 1881, New York 1881, London [1882] ('new edition', reissued [1887]), New York [1883?], introd by C. J. L[ongman] illustr E. V. B[oyle] 1893 ('new edition', Silver lib, rptd 1894), 1899 ('new impression', Silver lib, rptd 1903, 1907, 1912, 1916, 1924), abridged introd and retitled Sir Bevis: a tale of the fields by E. J. Kelley Boston 1899 (rptd 1900), introd by D. C. Fraser illustr L. Steele London [1928] (Collins' illustrated pocket classics, reissued [1940?], rptd [c. 1945 and 1955], also in [Collins' copyright reward ser] and Collins' illustrated school classics), introd by Fraser illustr Steele [1930] (Collins' Canterbury classics), 1934 (Swan lib), introd by Fraser illustr A. E. Kennedy [1939] ([Collins' enterprise ser]), 1969, introd by Richard Adams New York 1974, London 1976.

REVIEWS: Athenaeum 4 June 1881, Pall Mall Gazette Literary Suppl 11 June 1881, Acad 18 June 1881, Spectator 18 June 1881, John Bull 25 June 1881, Sat Rev 16 July 1881, Truth 21 July 1881, Land 23 July 1881, The Times 19 Aug 1881, Br Quart Rev Oct 1881, Westminster Rev Oct 1881, Harper's New Monthly Mag European Edn Dec 1881.

Bevis: the story of a boy. 3 vols 1882, abridged [by G. A. Henty] illustr A. V. Poncy 1891 (reissued [1892] 'new and cheaper edition', rptd 1893, rptd [1894?] 'new and cheaper edition'), introd by E. V. Lucas 1904 (rptd 1905, reissued 1908 'popular edition', rptd 1908), introd by Lucas New York 1905, introd by Lucas London 1910 (Reader's lib, rptd 1913, 1920, 1928), introd by Lucas illustr H. Rountree 1913, introd by G. N. Pocock 1930 (EL, rptd 1936, 1945, 1950, 1956, new introd by Henry Williamson 1966, 1981), introd by Lucas illustr E. H. Shepard 1932 (rptd 1943, 1948, 1951, 1955, 1958, 1967, 1972), abridged introd and retitled Bevis and Mark by G. N. Pocock 1937 (Dent's Kings treasuries of lit, rptd 1938, 1946, 1950, 1952, 1956, 1959, 1964), abridged and introd by H. Strang 1939, abridged retitled Bevis at home and illustr D. G. Knowland 1940, in Stories of adventure selected with an introd by M. Laski 1946, introd by C. H. Warren 1948 (Uniform edn), abridged and introd by R. Harding illustr F. Jennens [1949], abridged and introd by B. Jackson 1974 (Puffin, rptd 1976, 1984), introd and notes by P. Hunt: Oxford 1989 (WCp); Tr Fr(selections) by G. d'Hangest, 1939, and (selections retitled Adventures in New Formosa) by H. Kerst, 1945.

REVIEWS: Forestry June 1882, Literary World 16 June 1882, Acad 5 Aug 1882, Athenaeum 12 Aug 1882, World 23 Aug 1882, Pall Mall Gazette 24 Aug 1882, Harper's New Monthly Mag European Edn Jan 1883.

Kiss and try: a tale of St. Valentine. Illustr [J. Nash], first pbd London Soc Feb 1877, in vol 1 of Society novelettes by C. F. Burnard et al 2 vols 1883, vol 1 rptd as No rose without a thorn 1886. Short story.

Out of the season. Illustr [A. Claxton], first pbd London Soc Sep 1876, in vol 2 of Society novelettes by C. F. Burnard et al 2 vols 1883, vol 2 rptd as The dove's nest and other tales by J. Hatton et al 1886. Short story.

Nature near London. First pbd Standard Aug 1880–Dec 1882, 1883, 1887, 1889 ('new edition', rptd 1892, 1897, 1900, 1901, 1904, 1909 'new impression'), 1893 (hand-made-paper edn), 1905 (fine-paper edn, rptd 1913), introd by T. C. Watkins New York 1907, illustr R. Dollman London 1908 (St Martin's illustrated lib of standard authors), illustr Dollman Philadelphia 1908, London 1937 (Phoenix lib), 1941 (Pelham lib), introd by H. Clarke 1980 ('facsimile edition'). Essays.

REVIEWS: Pall Mall Gazette 25 Apr 1883, St James Gazette 27 Apr 1883, Athenaeum 5 May 1883, Sat Rev 19 May 1883, Br Quart Rev July 1883, Acad 28 July 1883, Harper's New Monthly Mag Jan 1884, Spectator 5 Jan 1884, Chambers's Jnl 12 Apr 1884.

The story of my heart: my autobiography. 1883, Boston 1883, introd by C. J. Longman portrait by W. Strang London 1891 ('second edition', Silver lib, rptd 'third edition' to 'tenth impression' 1891, 1894, 1896, 1898, 1901, 1904, 1906, 1910), Boston 1893, San Francisco [1897?] (Lark classics), Portland ME 1898 (Old world ser, rptd 1900, 1905, 1909), Boston [1903] ([Handy vol Cambridge classics]), introd by Longman London 1907 (Pocket edn, rptd 1908, 1911, 1913, 1917, 1920, 1922, 1926, 1930), New York 1908, introd by Longman illustr E. W. Waite London 1912 (also in limited edn 100 copies and issued New York 1913), Tokyo 1921, New York [1923] ([Wayside ser]), illustr E. White London 1923 (also in limited edn 225 copies and issued New York 1924), [1927] (Collins' kings' way classics), introd by Longman 1933 (Swan lib edn, rptd 1936), Girard KS [1935] ([Big blue bks]), introd by G. B. Harrison illustr G. Hermes Harmondsworth 1938 (Pen), London 1946, with first draft of ms introd and notes by S. J. Looker illustr photographs 1947, in The essential Richard Jefferies ed M. Elwin 1948, introd by C. H. Warren and Longman 1949 (Uniform edn), introd and notes by E. E. Speight Tokyo 1949 (Kenyusha pocket English ser, rptd 1954, 1955, 1956, 1959, 1961, 1964, 1966, 1968), introd by E. Jennings London 1968, introd by A. Rossabi 1979; tr Ger by H. Jahn 1906, Jap 1939 by S. Jugaku (rptd 1993).

REVIEWS: Acad 3 Nov 1883, Athenaeum 8 Dec 1883, Westminster Rev Jan 1884.

Red deer. 1884 (a few dated 1883), illustr H. Tunaley and J. Charlton 1892 ('second edition' Silver lib, rptd 'third edition' to 'seventh impression' 1894, 1900, 1903, 1908, 1911), with Round about a great estate with introd by C. H. Warren 1948 (Uniform edn), illustr N. McReddie Salisbury 1989.

REVIEWS: Acad 12 Jan 1884, Knowledge 25 Jan 1884, Athenaeum 9 Feb 1884, Forestry Feb 1884, Westminster Rev July 1884.

The life of the fields. 1884, 1888 ('new edition', rptd 1889, 1891, 1892, 1898, 1900, 1903, 1904), 1893 (hand-made-paper edn, rptd 1899), 1902 (fine-paper edn, rptd 1904, 1906, 1908, 1912, 1921, 1927), introd by T. C. Watkins New York 1907, illustr M. U. Clarke London '1908' [1907] (St Martin's illustrated lib of standard authors, rptd 1908), illustr Clarke Philadelphia 1908, London 1937 (Phoenix lib), introd and notes by S. J. Looker illustr A. M. Parker 1947 (Collector's edn), Oxford 1983 (rptd 1989). Essays collected from periodicals.

REVIEWS: St James Gazette 9 June 1884, Derby Mercury 18 June 1884, Pall Mall Gazette 30 June 1884, Sat Rev 12 July 1884, Athenaeum 13 Sep 1884, Hardwicke's Science Gossip Nov 1884, Spectator Literary Suppl 6 Dec 1884.

The dewy morn: a novel. 2 vols 1884, 1891 ([Bentley's favourite novels]), 1900, introd by L. Lerner 1982 (A Wildwood rediscovery).

REVIEWS: Acad 6 Sep 1884, Athenaeum 6 Sep 1884, Pall Mall Gazette 12 Sep 1884, St James Gazette 17 Sep 1884, Graphic 20 Sep 1884, World 24 Sep 1884, Spectator 4 Oct 1884, Sat Rev 18 Oct 1884.

After London: or wild England, pt I: The relapse into barbarism, pt II: Wild England. 1885, New York 1885, London 1886, 1905 ('new edition', reissued 1906 'colonial edition' and 1908 'popular edition'), New York 1906, London 1911 (Readers' lib), 1929 (New readers' lib), with Amaryllis at the fair with introd by D. Garnett 1939 (EL, rptd 1948), New York 1975 (Arno press collection: science fiction), with The great snow with introd by John Fowles Oxford 1980 (WCp, rptd 1980); tr Fr 1992. Novel.

REVIEWS: Athenaeum 11 Apr 1885, Pall Mall Gazette 11 Apr 1885, Acad 18 Apr 1885, World 20 May 1885, Spectator 4 July 1885, Sat Rev 11 July 1885, Westminster Rev July 1885, Harper's New Monthly Mag European Edn Oct 1885.

The open air. 1885, New York 1886 (Harper's handy ser), London 1889 ('new edition', rpt 1890, 1893, 1900, 1901, 1905 'new impression', 1909 'new impression'), 1893 (hand-made-paper edn), 1904 (fine-paper edn, rptd 1907, 1909, 1912, 1920, 1926), introd by T. C. Watkins New York 1907, illustr R. Dollman London 1908 (St Martin's illustrated lib of standard authors, rptd 1913), illustr Dollman Philadelphia 1908, London [1914] (Wayfarer's lib, also New York [1914], rptd 1920), 1937 (Phoenix lib), introd by C. H. Warren 1948 (Uniform edn), introd and notes by S. J. Looker illustr A. M. Parker 1948 (Collector's edn), introd by R. Mabey 1981 (Wildwood House rediscoveries). Essays collected from periodicals.

REVIEWS: Sat Rev 6 Dec 1885, Br Quart Rev Jan 1886.

Amaryllis at the fair: a novel. 1887, New York 1887 (Harper's Franklin Square lib), London 1891 (reissued [1896] and [c. 1898]), introd by E. Garnett 1904 (reissued 1906, 1906 'colonial edition', 1908 'popular edition'), introd by Garnett New York 1906, introd by Garnett London 1911 (Readers' lib), introd by Garnett 1927 (New readers lib), with After London with introd by D. Garnett 1939 (EL, rptd 1948), introd by E. Garnett 1940 (Nelson's classic, rptd [c. 1944]), introd by W. Girvan 1948, 1950 (Classics bk club), introd by A. Rossabi 1980, introd by D. Buxton Stroud 1992 (Pocket classics).

REVIEWS: Sat Rev 9 Apr 1887, Pall Mall Gazette 21 Apr 1887, Acad 23 Apr 1887, World 27 Apr 1887, Athenaeum 30 Apr 1887, Murray's Mag May 1887, Graphic 28 May 1887, Westminster Rev Aug 1887.

Preface to The natural history of Selborne by Gilbert White. 1887 (Camelot ser), '1887' [1892?] (Scott lib, rptd [1894?], [1899?], [1911]), [c. 1893–1905] (issued in [Union lib], [Oxford lib], [Brocade ser?], Brotherhood lib and [Emerald lib]), illustr G. E. Lodge, M. U. Clarke, C. W[hymper] et al [1896], [1905] (reissued in Evergreen lib and Peacock's univ ser).

Field and hedgerow: being the last essays of Richard Jefferies collected by his widow. 1889, 1889 (large-paper edn limited to 200 copies), 1889 ('second edition'), 1890 ('new edition' Silver lib, rptd 1891, 1892, 1895, 1897), 1900 ('new impression' Silver lib, rptd 1904, 1907, 1910, 1916, 1926), introd and notes by S. J. Looker illustr A. M. Parker 1948 (Collector's edn), Oxford 1982 (poem My chaffinch omitted).

REVIEWS: Scotsman Jan 1889, Morning Post Feb 1889, Sat Rev 9 Feb 1889, Acad 2 Mar 1889, Selborne Mag May 1889.

The toilers of the field. Short story from ms, essays and journalism from Fraser's Mag, Longman's Mag and The Times, ed and preface by C. J. Longman. 1892, 1892 (large-paper edn limited to 105 copies), 1893 ('new edition'), 1894 ('new edition' Silver lib), 1898 ('new impression' Silver lib, rptd 1901, 1904, 1907), introd V. Neuberg omitting Longman's preface 1981.

REVIEWS: Bookman Dec 1892, Devizes Gazette 1 and 8 Dec 1892, Spectator 17 Dec 1892, Acad 31 Dec 1892, Athenaeum 7 Jan 1893, Critic 7 Jan 1893, Dial 16 Feb 1893.

The early fiction of Richard Jefferies, edited by G. Toplis, with a rare portrait. 1896, 1896 (large-paper edn limited to 50 copies). Two poems, an essay and 4 short stories from North Wilts Herald, June–Oct 1866.

Jefferies' land: a history of Swindon and its environs, edited with notes by G. Toplis. With map and illustrations. First pbd North Wilts Herald Oct 1867–Feb 1868, 1896, 1896 (large-paper edn limited to 50 copies).

T. T. T. First pbd North Wilts Herald 2 Feb 1867. Wells 1896. Short story.

Nature and eternity: with other uncollected papers. With preface [by T. B. Mosher?] Portland ME 1902, rptd 1907 ('second edition'). Three essays from Longman's Mag June 1894, May and July 1895.

The hills and the vale. With an introduction by Edward Thomas. 1909, 1911 (Readers lib), Oxford 1980. Essays, 3 from ms, 15 from periodicals, collected by Thomas.)

The nature diaries and note-books of Richard Jefferies with an essay A tangle of autumn, now printed for the first time. Edited with an introduction and notes by S. J. Looker. Billericay 1941, 1941 (limited edn 105 copies). Extracts from 4 of Jefferies' notebooks.

REVIEWS: N &Q 29 Nov 1941, Poetry Quart Winter 1941.

Beauty is immortal: Felise of The dewy morn, with some hitherto uncollected essays and manuscripts. Edited by S. J. Looker. Illustr L. Cattermole painting and facs. Worthing 1948 (Worthing cavalcade). Extracts from The dewy morn, 5 pieces from ms, 4 from Cassell's Mag Aug 1876–June 1877 and one from Mag of Art June 1877. Includes material possibly not by Jefferies).

REVIEW: TLS 26 Feb 1949.

Chronicles of the hedges and other essays, edited with an introduction and notes by S. J. Looker, illustrated with pencil drawings by Richard Jefferies & by his uncle J. L. Jefferies. 1948, 1950 (Country bk club). Essays and journalism, 47 from periodicals, chiefly Land, St James Gazette, Pall Mall Gazette and Live Stock Jnl, and 31 from ms. Includes material possibly not by Jefferies.

REVIEWS: TLS 29 May 1948, Out of Doors July–Aug 1948.

Nature diaries and note-books of Richard Jefferies, edited with an introduction and notes by S. J. Looker. 1948. Transcriptions of 16 of Jefferies' notebooks, illustr facs.

REVIEW: Spectator 3 Sep 1948.

The old house at Coate, and other hitherto unpublished essays. Edited with an introduction and notes by S. J. Looker. Wood engravings by A. M. Parker 1948, Cambridge MA 1948, London 1970 (Essay index reprint ser), Bradford-on-Avon 1985 (omitting some of Looker's notes). Autobiographical fragment and other material from ms.

REVIEW: Saturday Rev 21 May 1949.

Field and farm: essays now first collected, with some from mss. Edited with an introduction and notes by S. J. Looker. With illustrations by Richard and J. L. Jefferies. 1957, 1958 (Country bk club). Periodical sources: Live Stock Gazette, Pall Mall Gazette, St James Gazette and The Times, 1877–87. Includes material possibly not by Jefferies.

REVIEWS: The Times 25 July 1957, Country Life 15 Aug 1957, TLS 30 Aug 1957.

Landscape and labour: essays and letters now first collected with an introduction, notes and bibliography by J. Pearson. Drawings by U. Sieger. Bradford-on-Avon 1979. From 10 periodicals, 1871–83.

REVIEWS: Annual report and bulletin of the Richard Jefferies soc 1978–9, Swindon Evening Advertiser 4 Sep 1979.

By the brook, edited with an introduction by G. Miller. Wisbech 1981 (also special issue limited to 20 copies). Essay from ms, with original etching by A. Neal.

The birth of a naturalist: an unpublished chapter from Round about a great estate, edited and introduced by G. Miller, with engravings by N. Parry. Market Drayton 1985 (also special issue, with watercolour paintings by Parry replacing the engravings, limited to 20 copies).

Return to Jefferies' land. Illustr photographs Salisbury 1985. Last 10 pts of Jefferies' History of Malmesbury, first pbd North Wilts Herald July–Oct 1867.

Contributions to periodicals

Jefferies wrote nearly 300 pieces – essays, articles, stories and serialised works – for 35 periodicals. He revised and selected many of these for book publication and many more have been collected by a series of editors since his death (see §1, above). There are also a considerable number of unsigned periodical pieces for which claims of Jefferies' authorship have been made, with or without adequate documentary support. Some of these, including a group of 59 on farming topics in Live Stock Jnl 1877–87, have not been reprinted. For a detailed guide to all known contributions, their book publication, textual variation, and problems of attribution, see Miller and Matthews, *Bibliographies, above, and Keith, §2 below. The following list is of works signed or otherwise claimed by Jefferies but not yet published in book form.*

The grave of the last abbot. Wilts and Glo'stershire Standard 12 June 1869. Poem

History of Cirencester. Pts I–XI. Wilts and Glo'stershire Standard 12 Mar–29 Oct 1870.

The man of the future. Swindon Advertiser 19 June 1871.

A natural system of national defence. Pts I–III. Swindon Advertiser 26 June, 3 July, 10 July 1871.

The future of farming. The Times 15 Oct 1873. Letter.

The future of farming. Fraser's Mag Dec 1873.

Swindon: its history and antiquities. Wiltshire Archaeological and Natural History Mag Mar 1874.

A railway-accidents bill. Fraser's Mag May 1874.

The power of the farmers. Fortnightly Rev 1 June 1874.

The Shipton accident. Fraser's Mag Feb 1875.

On allotment gardens. New Quart Mag Apr 1875.

Local taxation. Wilts and Glo'stershire Standard 1 Jan 1876. Letter.

The Monkbourne mystery. NMM Jan 1876. Short story.

The spirit of modern agriculture. New Quart Mag July 1876.

The rise of Maximin, emperor of the occident, compiled by Lucius, keeper of the imperial archives at Iscapolis. NMM Oct 1876–July 1877. Novel.

A midnight skate. London Soc Dec 1876. Short story.

Which is the way? Cassell's Family Mag Dec 1876.

A great agricultural problem. Fraser's Mag Mar 1878.

The future of the dairy. Live Stock Jnl Almanack 1879.

Mound restorers. Land 24 Dec 1881.

Humanity and natural history. Knowledge 5 Jan 1883.

Machiavelli: a study. Nineteenth Century and After Sep 1948 (from ms).

§2

Obituaries

Pall Mall Gazette 15 and 16 Aug 1887, Daily News 16 Aug 1887, Morning Post 16 Aug 1887, Standard 16 Aug 1887, The Times 16 Aug 1887, North Wilts Herald 19 Aug 1887, Acad 20 Aug 1887, Athenaeum 20 Aug 1887, Swindon Advertiser 20 Aug 1887, World 24 Aug 1887, Sat Rev 27 Aug 1887.

Criticism to 1920

Salt, H. S. The story of a heart. Today June 1888.

Garnett, E. Richard Jefferies. Universal Rev Nov 1888.

Salt, H. S. The gospel according to Richard Jefferies. Pall Mall Gazette 15 Nov 1888.

Henley, W. E. Jefferies. In Views and reviews: essays in appreciation, 1890.

Greenwood, F. Richard Jefferies. Scot's Observer 2 Aug 1890.

Graham, P. A. The magic of the fields (Richard Jefferies). In Nature in books: some studies in biography, 1891.

Foley, C. A. Woman in the works of Richard Jefferies. Scots Mag Feb 1891.

Salt, H. S. Richard Jefferies. Temple Bar June 1891.

Fotheringham, W. B., et al. The pernicious works of Richard Jefferies. Pall Mall Gazette 8 Sep 1891, and subsequent controversy 11, 12, 16–18, 21, 22 Sep and 3 Oct 1891. Also relevant comment in Nottingham Daily Express 17 Sep 1891 and National Reformer 18 Oct 1891.

Garnett, R. Richard Jefferies. In DNB, 1892.

Q[uiller]-C[ouch], A. T. A literary causerie: the country as 'copy'. Speaker 30 Sep 1893, rptd with revision in Adventures in criticism, 1896.

Salt, H. S. Richard Jefferies: a study. 1894, rptd as Richard Jefferies: his life and ideals, 1905.

Ellwanger, G. H. Afield with Jefferies. In Idyllists of the countryside, 1896.

Saintsbury, G. Jefferies. In A history of nineteenth-century literature, 1896.

Symons, A. Richard Jefferies. In Studies in two literatures, 1897.

Crawfurd, O. Richard Jefferies: field-naturalist and litterateur. Idler Oct 1898.

Hudson, W. H. Nature in downland, 1900. In ch 1.

Bucke, R. M. Richard Jefferies. In Cosmic consciousness: a study of the evolution of the human mind, Philadelphia 1901.

Avebury, Rt Hon Lord. Richard Jefferies. In Essays and addresses 1900–1903, 1903.

Salt, H. S. The faith of Richard Jefferies. Westminster Rev Aug 1905 (rptd as pam 1906).

Rickett, Arthur. Richard Jefferies. In The vagabond in literature, 1906.

Salmon, A. L. Richard Jefferies: an attempt at an appreciation. In Literary rambles in the west of England, 1906.

Thomas, Edward. Richard Jefferies. In British country life in autumn and winter, [1907].

Thomas, Edward. The fiction of Richard Jefferies. Readers' Rev July 1908.

Jackson, H. Richard Jefferies. In All manner of folk: interpretations and studies, 1912.

Masseck, C. J. Richard Jefferies: étude d'une personalité. Paris 1913.

Foerster, N. The vogue of Richard Jefferies. PMLA Dec 1913.

Thorn, A. F. Richard Jefferies and civilization. [1914]. Revised and rptd as The life-worship of Richard Jefferies, [1920]. Pamphlet.

Masseck, C. J. Richard Jefferies: an attempt at an estimate. Washington Univ Stud Apr 1914.

Thomas, Edward. Richard Jefferies. In A literary pilgrim in England, 1917.

Coleridge, G. Richard Jefferies and the unknown god. Nineteenth Century and After Mar 1920.

Textual/bibliographical criticism

Letters and commentary on the forged edn of Suez-cide!! in The Clique 3, 10, 17, 24 June and 1, 22, 29 July 1893.

Hunt, P. A note on the text, in Bevis, Oxford 1989 (WCp).

Miller, G. and H. Matthews. Richard Jefferies: a bibliographical study. Aldershot 1993.

Keith, W. J. The Jefferies canon. Oxford 1995. Pamphlet.

Essential post-1920 criticism

Leavis, Q. D. Lives and works of Richard Jefferies. Scrutiny Mar 1938.

Keith, W. J. Richard Jefferies: a critical study. Toronto 1965.

Biographies

Besant, Walter. The eulogy of Richard Jefferies. 1888.

Thomas, Edward. Richard Jefferies: his life and work. 1909.

Looker, S. J. and C. Porteous. Richard Jefferies, man of the fields: a biography and letters. 1964.

Matthews, H. and P. Treitel. The forward life of Richard Jefferies: a chronological study. Oxford 1994. [GM]

Edward Jenkins, John Edward Jenkins 1838–1910

Much material relevant to the publishing history of Jenkins's work can be found in the publishers' archives for Strahan & Co and Swan Sonnenschein. These archives have been republished in microfilm versions by Chadwyck-Healey Ltd, Cambridge 1972–4.

§1

Jenkins, E. and A. P. Stewart. The medical and legal aspects of sanitary reform. Ed M. W. Flinn 1867, rptd Leicester 1969. Jenkins's contribution, The legal aspects of sanitary reform, had first been given as a paper to the 1866 Manchester Social Science Congress and printed in the Trans of the Nat Assoc for the Promotion of Social Science 1866.

Ginx's baby. 1870, 2nd edn with author's note 1870, 1871 (6th edn), 1872 (People's edn), 1874 ('32nd edn' Dublin), Dublin 1877 (36th edn illus).

The coolie: a journey to British Guiana to inquire into his rights and wrongs. 1871. First serialised in Good Words.

Lord Bantam. 2 vols 1872, 1-vol edn 1872, Cheap edn Dublin 1877.

Little Hodge. 1872, 14th thousand 1874, Cheap edn illus Dublin 1877. The novel is linked to an article on agricultural discontent in Good Words 1872.

Glances at inner England. 1874.

Edwards, E. and J. Raymond. A legal handbook for architects. 1874.

The devil's chain. 1876, 10th thousand with new Preface 1876, Cheap edn '26th thousand' Dublin 1877.

Lutchmee and Dilloo: a story of West Indian life. 3 vols Dublin 1876–7. First serialised in Evening Hours.

The captain's cabin. Dublin 1876, 10th thousand Dublin 1877.

The Christian citizen. 1877.

Jobson's enemies. 1879–82 (first pbd in 6 pt issues), 3-vol edn 1882, 1-vol edn 1886, Stereotype edn 1888.

Lisa Lena. 2 vols 1880.

A paladin of finance. 1882.

A week of passion. 1884.

A secret of two lives. 1886.

Pantalas. 1897.

Political pamphlets

Barney Geoghegan, M. P. and Home Rule at St Stephens. 1872. First pbd in St Paul's Mag.

A blot on the Queen's head. 1876, 90th thousand illus 1876. This, and the following entry, were contributions to the pam wars surrounding Disraeli's Royal Titles Bill.

Ben changes the motto. nd [1876].

The shadow on the Cross: the present crisis of the Turkish question. 1877.

Janus, or, the double faced Ministry. 1877.

Haverholme, or, the apotheosis of Jingo. 1878.

Contributions to periodicals

Jenkins contributed to Contemporary Rev, Fraser's Mag, St Paul's Mag, Good Words, Fortnightly Rev, *and other jnls. See* Wellesley *vol* 5.

§2

In DNB.

Maidment, B. What shall we do with the starving baby – Edward Jenkins and Ginx's baby. Literature and History 6, Autumn 1980.

Maidment, B. Victorian publishing and social criticism – the case of Edward Jenkins. Publishing History 11, Winter 1982. [BM]

Jerome Klapka Jerome 1859–1927

Selections

A miscellany of sense and nonsense from the writings of Jerome K. Jerome, selected by the author with many apologies. 1923.

The other J. K. Jerome. Ed M. Green 1984.

Three men in an omnibus: his funniest writings. Ed M. Green 1984. Contains Three men in a boat with selections from six other books.

§1

On the stage – and off: the brief career of a would-be actor. 1885.

The idle thoughts of an idle fellow: a book for an idle holiday. [1886.]

Stage-land: curious habits and customs of its inhabitants. 1889.

Three men in a boat (to say nothing of the dog). Bristol 1889.

Diary of a pilgrimage (and six essays). Bristol 1891. Essays rptd 1982 as Evergreens and other short stories.

Told after supper. 1891, 1985 (as After supper ghost stories).

Novel notes. 1893. Rptd from Idler.

John Ingerfield and other stories. 1894.

Sketches in lavender, blue and green. 1897.

The second thoughts of an idle fellow. 1898.

Three men on the bummel. Bristol [1900].

The observations of Henry. Bristol 1901.

Paul Kelver: a novel. 1902.

Tea-table talk. 1903.

Tommy and Co. 1904.

Idle ideas in 1905. [1905.] Contents previously pbd New York 1904 in American wives and others.

The passing of the third floor back, and other stories. 1907. Dramatised 1910.

The angel and the author – and others. 1908.

They and I. 1909.

Malvina of Brittany. 1916.

All roads lead to Calvary. [1919].

Anthony John: a biography. 1923.

My life and times. [1926].

Jerome also wrote a number of plays.

§2

Walkley, A. B. In his Playhouse impressions, 1892.

Connolly, J. Jerome K. Jerome: a critical biography. 1982.

'H. Ogram Matuce', Charles Francis Keary 1848–1917

Mss located in NLS; Berg Collection, NYPL.

Bibliographies

In Nineteenth century readers' guide to periodical literature 1890–1899, ed H. G. Cushing and A. V. Morris, 2 vols New York 1944.

See also Wellesley *vol 5 1989.*

Collections

The posthumous poems of C. F. Keary. Oxford 1923 (introd by J. Bailey).
REVIEW: TLS 7 June 1923.

§1

The mythology of the Eddas: how far of true Teutonic origin. 1882. Rptd from the Trans Royal Soc of Lit.
REVIEW: Antiquary Sep 1883.

Outlines of primitive belief among the Indo-European races. 1882.

The morphology of coins. 1886, Chicago 1970.

A marriage de convenance. 2 vols 1890 (2 edns), [1893] (in Unwin's novel series, as 1 vol).
REVIEWS: Scots Observer 31 May 1890; Athenaeum 14 June 1890; Spectator 5 July 1890.
The Vikings in Western Christendom A. D. 789 to A. D. 888. With a map and tables. '1891' [1890].
REVIEWS: Athenaeum 7 Mar 1891; Mag of Amer History Apr 1891; Dial July 1891; Nation 3 Sep 1891; Spectator 19 Sep 1891; English Historical Rev Jan 1892.
Norway and the Norwegians. 1892, New York 1892, 1896 (with additional chapter by E. Tindall).
REVIEWS: Nat Observer 16 July 1892; Nation 2 Mar 1893.
The two Lancrofts. 3 vols 1893, 1 vol 1894.
REVIEWS: Athenaeum 26 Aug 1893; Spectator 26 Aug 1893; Acad 23 Sep 1893; Bookman Oct 1893; Nat Observer 11 Nov 1893.
Herbert Vanlennart. '1896' [1895].
REVIEWS: Athenaeum 21 Dec 1895; Bookman Jan 1896; Bookman (USA) Feb 1896; Acad 22 Feb 1896; Dial 1 June 1896.
The journalist. 1898.
REVIEWS: Athenaeum 24 Sep 1898; Acad 1 Oct 1898; Bookman Oct 1898; New York Times 21 Jan 1899.
A wanderer. From the papers of the late H. Ogram Matuce. 1901.
REVIEWS: Bookman Oct 1895; Bookman (USA) Nov 1895.
'Twixt dog and wolf. 1901.
REVIEWS: Pall Mall Gazette 10 Dec 1901; Athenaeum 25 Jan 1902.
The brothers: a fairy masque. 1902.
REVIEWS: TLS 20 June 1902; Acad 21 June 1902.
High policy. 1902.
REVIEWS: Acad 23 June 1902; TLS 29 Aug 1902; Athenaeum 6 Sep 1902.
India: impressions. 1903.
Rigel: An autumn mystery. 1903. Verse drama.
REVIEW: Athenaeum 27 Feb 1904.
Bloomsbury. A novel. 1905.
REVIEWS: Acad Suppl 18 Mar 1905; Athenaeum 29 Apr 1905.
The mount. 1909, Leipzig 1911 (Tauchnitz).
REVIEWS: Athenaeum 18 Sep 1909; TLS 28 Oct 1909; Bookman Dec 1909.
The pursuit of reason. Cambridge 1910.
REVIEWS: TLS 26 Jan 1911; Athenaeum 20 May 1911; New York Times 2 July 1911.
Religious hours. 1916. Poems.
REVIEW: TLS 25 Jan 1917.

Contributions to periodicals and collaborative works

Numismatic Chronicle. The coinages of Western Europe, 1878, 1879.
Trans Royal Soc of Lit. 1879, 1880.
Mind. The Homeric words for 'soul', Oct 1881.
Acad. Review of Henning's Das deutsche Haus in seiner historischen Entwickelung, 29 July 1882.
Antiquary. Apr–July 1883.
Wessex and England to the Norman Conquest. In A catalogue of English coins in the British Museum, Anglo-Saxon ser, vol 2, 1887, rptd 1970. With H. A. Grueber.
Eng Historical Rev. 1890, 1892.
Nat Observer. 30 Sep 1893–3 Mar 1894.
Athenaeum. The Junian controversy, 26 Mar 1898.
Living Age. Philosophy of impressionism, 18 June 1898.
Boyesen, H. H. A history of Norway from the earliest times. With a new chapter on the recent history of Norway by C. F. Keary. 1900.
Edinburgh Rev. Oct 1901–July 1903. *See also* Wellesley vol 5.
Fortnightly Rev. Apr 1902–Nov 1902. *See also* Wellesley vol 5.
Pall Mall Mag. Apr 1902–Mar 1906.
Independent Rev. Oct–Dec 1904.
Philosophical Rev. Matter in ancient and modern philosophy, Jan 1908.
English Rev. Sep 1909–July 1911.
Koanga. Opera in three acts by F. Delius. Original text by Keary. 1935, [1980] (revised text). 1st performance 30 May 1899, St James's Hall, London.
For contributions to Bentley's Quart Rev, Blackwood's Mag, Contemporary Rev, Fraser's Mag, Macmillan's Mag, Nat Rev-II, Nineteenth Cent *and the* New Rev, *see* Wellesley *vol 5*.

Editions and introductions

The dawn of history: an introduction to pre-historic study. Ed C. F. K[eary] 1878, New York 1879, 1883, 1885, London 1888 (new edn), New York 1889 (new edn), 1892 (new edn), 1900, 1904, 1906 (new edn), 1911, 1912, 1921.
Synopsis of the contents of the British Museum. Department of coins and medals. A guide to the Italian medals exhibited in the King's Library. 1881 (plates), 1893 (plates, 2nd edn).
Henfrey, H. W. A guide to the study of English coins from the conquest to the present time. Rev edn and introd by Keary 1885.
The Francis letters. By Sir Philip Francis and other members of the family. Ed B. Francis and E. Keary, with a note on the Junius controversy by C. F. Keary, 2 vols [1901].

§2

Bookman Oct 1893.
Obits: The Times 27 Oct 1917; New York Times 28 Oct 1917; Blackwood's Mag Dec 1917.
Sutherland, J. In The Longman companion to Victorian fiction, 1988. [DA]

Rudyard Kipling 1865–1936

As a result of gifts and bequests, Kipling's mss are now widely located; major collections are to be found as follows: BL: mss, limited and rare edns of Kipling's books, autograph notes, poems, photographs, vols from Kipling's mother's and father's libs, pirated edns and trns into foreign languages – 1,200 vols in all (see BM Quart 14 1940; Index of mss in the BL, Cambridge 1984–6*). The Kipling papers, Univ of Sussex Lib: business and legal papers, correspondence (family and other correspondents), literary mss, press-cuttings, papers of Kipling's children, papers of Kipling's father (letters, drawings, press-cuttings) (see* Kipling Jnl Mar 1983*). Dalhousie Univ Lib: 1,200 first edns and associated copies, 300 vols of Kiplingiana, bibliographies and biographies, 200 Kipling items in trn, copyright printings, periodical collection (including files of* Pioneer, Week's News, United Services College Chron*); a total of 2,757 vols mainly drawn from J. McGregor Stewart's collection judged the most comprehensive of all collections (see* The Stewart Kipling Collection, Dalhousie Rev Summer 1956*. Univ of Texas Lib: rare and first edns including runs of the Indian Lib series, revised galley proofs, holographs, a total of 3,093 vols (see* The Kipling collection at the Univ of Texas, LCUT, Summer 1952*. Lib of Congress: letters from collections of W. R. Carpenter and H. Dunscombe Colt. The following libs also hold letters and literary mss:* NYPL, *Bodleian, Pierpont Morgan Lib (New York). For a full list of locations and their contents, see:* IELM vol 4 pt 2; A guide to archives and manuscripts in the United States, ed P. M. Hamer, New Haven CT 1961.

Bibliographies

Prideaux, W. F. Mr Kipling's Allahabad books; a bibliographical essay. N & Q ser 9 1 Feb 1898.
Knowles, F. L. Bibliography of first editions in A Kipling primer. 1900.
Lane, J. Rudyard Kipling: a bibliography 1881–9. In R. Le Gallienne, Rudyard Kipling: a criticism, 1900.
Livingston, L. S. The works of Rudyard Kipling; the description of a set of the first editions of his books in the library of a New York collector. New York 1901.
Powell, F. Y. Rudyard Kipling. Eng Illus Mag n.s. 30 Dec 1903, 30 Jan 1904.
Young, W. A. Uncollected Kipling items. N & Q 8 1913.
Martindell, E. W. A bibliography of the works of Kipling 1881–1921.

Bookman's Jnl, J. F. Drake London and New York 1922, London 1923 (enlarged).

Livingston, F. V. Bibliography of the works of Kipling. New York 1927; suppl 1938.

REVIEW: TLS 5 May 1927.

Chandler, L. H. A summary of the works of Kipling, including items ascribed to him. New York 1930.

Catalogue of the works of Kipling exhibited at the Grolier Club 1929. New York 1930.

Ballard, E. A. Catalogues intimate and descriptive of my Kipling collection: books, manuscripts and letters. Philadelphia 1935 (priv ptd).

Ehrsam, T. G. and R. H. Deily. In their Bibliographies of twelve Victorian authors, New York 1936; suppl MP 37 1939.

Ballard, E. A. The renowned collection of first editions, autograph letters and manuscripts of Rudyard Kipling. New York Parke-Bernet Galleries 1942.

BM [Dept of ptd books] catalogue of ptd books: accessions: Rudyard Kipling. 1949.

Stewart, J. McG. Kipling: a bibliographical catalogue. Ed A. W. Yeats, Toronto 1959.

REVIEWS: [Dobree, B.] Crit Quart 2 1960; Dalhousie Rev 39 1960; UTQ 29 1960; TLS 2 Sep 1960; RES n.s. 13 1962.

Gerber, H. E. and E. Lauterbach. Rudyard Kipling; an annotated bibliography of writings about him. Eng Fiction in Transition 3 1960; suppl 8 1965.

Harbord, R. E. The reader's guide to Rudyard Kipling's work. 8 vols 1961–72.

Yeats, A. W. Kipling collections in the James McGregor Stewart and the University of Texas libraries. *See* An appraisal of resources for literary investigations. Dissertation Abstracts 1961.

Princeton Univ Lib. Something of Kipling 1865–1965, an exhibition in the Princeton University Library. Princeton 1965.

Cornell, L. L. Kipling's uncollected newspaper writings. In Kipling in India, 1966.

Monteiro, G. Rudyard Kipling: early printings in American periodicals. PBSA 61 1967.

Collections

Collected works

Indian Railway Library. 6 vols Lahore 1888.

Lovell's authorized edition. 11 vols New York 1890–1.

Tauchnitz edition. 19 vols Leipzig 1890–1926.

English Library. 9 vols London 1891–7.

Edition de luxe. 38 vols 1897–1938.

Outward Bound edition. 36 vols New York 1897–1937.

American pocket edition (manuscript edition). 33 vols New York 1898–1932.

American trade edition. 31 vols New York 1898–1932.

Brushwood edition. 15 vols New York 1898–9.

Swastika edition. 15 vols New York 1899.

Uniform edition. 29 vols 1899–1938.

English pocket edition. 37 vols 1907–38.

Bombay edition. 31 vols 1913–38.

Seven Seas edition. 27 vols New York 1914–26.

Service Kipling. 34 vols 1914–15.

Miniature edition. 10 vols New York 1921.

New World edition. 13 vols New York 1923.

Mandalay edition. 26 vols New York 1925–6.

English school edition. 8 vols 1926–51.

American school edition. 3 vols New York 1932.

Compact edition. 16 in 6 vols New York 1936–7.

Sussex edition. 35 vols 1937–9. A posthumous edn incorporating revisions made by Kipling during his last years. Contains vols of prose and verse hitherto uncollected (*see* vols 25, 29, 30).

Everybody's Kipling. 6 vols 1938.

Burwash edition. 28 vols 1941. Text as Sussex but contents arranged differently.

Sussex and Burwash are the only edns containing all acknowledged and authorised works, and are identical in content. Cited as SBE, below.

Library edition. 24 vols 1949–51.

Young People's edition. 7 vols 1954.

Centenary edition. 23 vols 1965.

Selections

Soldier tales. 1896, New York 1896 (as Soldier stories).

The Kipling reader. 1900 (contains 10 stories and 9 poems previously collected), 1901 (rev); 1908 (illus; 13 stories, 5 of which were in 1st edn, and 8 poems, 7 of which were in 1st edn).

Kipling stories and poems every child should know. New York 1909. 14 stories and 26 poems.

The Appleton readers. 2 vols New York 1912. Vol 1 10 stories and 10 poems; vol 2 9 poems and 9 stories.

Selected stories. Ed W. L. Phelps, New York 1921. 13 stories.

A Kipling anthology: prose. 1922. Selections from Life's handicap.

The one volume Kipling. New York 1928. Contains The light that failed, The city of dreadful night, The story of the Gadsbys, 77 poems and 91 stories already collected, and 4 stories collected (with Kipling's authority) for the first time: The last relief, For one night only, The legs of Sister Ursula, The lamentable comedy of willow wood.

Humorous tales. New York 1928. 15 stories and 9 poems.

Selected stories. 1929. Contents as The Kipling reader.

Humorous tales. 1931. 20 stories and 9 poems.

Animal stories from Rudyard Kipling. 1932. 11 stories and 8 poems.

All the Mowgli stories. 1933. 3 stories and 3 poems from The jungle book, 5 stories and 5 poems from The second jungle book, and 1 story and 1 poem from Many inventions.

Collected dog stories. 1934. 8 stories, 5 poems and first pbn of A sea dog.

A Kipling pageant. New York 1935. 37 stories, 52 poems and new foreword.

More selected stories. 1940. 9 poems and 9 stories.

A Kipling treasury. 1940. 8 stories and 10 poems.

Twenty-one tales. 1946.

Ten stories. 1947.

A choice of Kipling's prose. Ed W. S. Maugham 1952. 16 stories.

Kipling: a selection of his stories and poems. Ed J. Beacroft 2 vols New York 1956.

Kipling: short stories selected. Ed E. Parone, New York 1960.

The fifty best short stories. Ed R. Jarrell, New York 1961.

The Kipling sampler: selections from a great story-teller's best. Ed A. Greendale, Greenwich CT 1962.

In the vernacular – the English in India: short stories by Kipling. Ed R. Jarrell, New York 1963.

The English in England: short stories by Kipling. Ed R. Jarrell, New York 1963.

Short stories. Ed A. Rutherford 2 vols 1971.

Selected stories. Ed S. Kemp 1987.

A choice of Kipling's prose. Selected and introd by C. Raine 1987.

The man who would be king and other stories. Ed L. Cornell 1987.

Selected stories. Ed A. Rutherford 1990.

War stories and poems. Ed A. Rutherford 1990.

Mrs Bathurst. Ed L. Lewis, introd by J. Bayley 1991.

Verse

The Cornhill booklet: occasional poems. Boston 1900 (unauthorised).

Collected verse. New York 1907 (3 edns), illus edn 1910. Contains all the poems in Departmental ditties and other verses, Ballads and barrack-room ballads, The seven seas and The five nations. The fires is pbd for the first time as the introd. London 1912 (omits The sacrifice of Er-Heb otherwise the text is that of the Amer edn).

REVIEWS: Nation (New York) 86 1908; Independent (New York) 70, 5 Jan 1911; Athenaeum 30 Nov 1912; [Newbolt, Henry] Book Monthly 10, Jan 1913.

Songs from books. Verses that had previously appeared in prose volumes, many expanded into poems of several stanzas. New York 1912, Toronto 1912, London 1913 (containing additional material).

REVIEWS: Independent (New York) 74, 16 Jan 1913; Spectator 25 Oct 1913; Bookman 45, Dec 1913.

Twenty poems. 1918, Toronto 1918 (2 edns), London 1937 (limited edn in aid of The Rudyard Kipling Memorial Fund). The sons of Martha, For all we have and are, The holy war collected for the first time although all previously pbd in mags and separate edns.

Kipling's verse: inclusive edition 1885–1918. 1919, New York 1919, London 1921 (2nd edn). Contains all the poems in Departmental ditties and other verses 1899, Barrack-room ballads and other verses 1892 (except When 'Omer smote 'is bloomin' lyre), The seven seas 1896, The five nations 1903, Songs from books 1913, The years between 1919, and 13 additional poems previously pbd.

Uncollected verse: inclusive edition 1881–1922. Priv ptd and without permission, for E. W. Martindell and E. A. Ballard, in 1922 in edn of 12 copies, containing many poems uncollected elsewhere, some not by Kipling.

A Kipling anthology: verse. 1922, New York 1922.

Songs of youth. 1924, New York 1925.

A choice of songs. 1925 (with one unpbd poem).

Sea and Sussex. 1925 (with one ubpbd poem), New York 1926.

Songs of the sea. 1927 (with one poem rptd from periodical), New York 1927.

Verse: inclusive edition, 1885–1926. 1927, New York 1927. Contains, in addition to the poems in the edn of 1921, 8 poems from Land and sea tales 1923, 19 poems and 2 scenes from Gow's witch in Debits and credits 1926, 1 poem from Songs of the sea, 6 poems previously uncollected and 1 poem not previously pbd, also 2 chapter headings not previously included.

Selected poems. 1931.

East of Suez. 1931. A selection of stanzas from Departmental ditties and other verses, Barrack-room ballads and The seven seas.

Verse: inclusive edition 1885–1932. 1933, Toronto 1933, New York 1934. Contains, in addition to the poems in the edn of 1927, verses from Limits and renewals 1932, the verses from Brazilian sketches 1927, and 12 miscellaneous poems.

REVIEWS: Mercure de France 149, 15 July 1921; Bookman 61, Dec 1921; [le Gallienne, R.] Munsey's Mag 68, Nov 1919, rptd in Around the world with Kipling, 1926; [de Selincourt, B.] Observer 22 Oct 1933; TLS 14 Dec 1933; Bookman 85, Dec 1933.

Kipling: sixty poems. 1939. Contains 59 poems from all vols through to Verse: inclusive edition 1933.

The definitive edition of Rudyard Kipling's verse. 1940, New York 1940. Omits early and miscellaneous uncollected verse rptd only in Sussex edn (vol 25) and Burwash edn (vol 28). Many of the verses omitted from Schoolboy lyrics, Echoes etc are now collected in Early verse, ed A. Rutherford, 1986. Other verses by Kipling remain uncollected.

So shall ye reap: poems for these days. 1941.

A choice of Kipling's verse. Ed T. S. Eliot 1941.

A Kipling anthology. Ed W. G. Bebbington 1964.

Selected verse. Ed J. Cochrane 1977.

Early verse by Rudyard Kipling. Ed A. Rutherford 1986.

Rudyard Kipling: the complete verse. Ed M. M. Kaye 1990.

Selected poetry. Ed C. Raine 1992.

Rudyard Kipling: selected poems. Ed P. Keating 1993.

§1

Schoolboy lyrics. Lahore 1881 (c. 50 copies priv ptd). Rptd in SBE except The night before.

REVIEWS: Book Buyer (New York) June 1899; Bookman (New York) 10 Dec 1899.

Echoes, by two writers. Lahore 1884. 32 poems by Kipling, 7 by his sister.

REVIEW: Colophon n.s. 111 no 3 1938.

Quartette, by four Anglo-Indian writers. Lahore 1885. Prose and verse by Kipling, his sister and parents. 2 stories by Kipling subsequently rptd; for 2 stories and 5 poems, no authorised reprint.

Departmental ditties and other verses. Lahore 1886 (1st edn, 26 poems); Calcutta 1886 (2nd edn, 5 additional poems); Calcutta 1888 (3rd edn, 10 additional poems); London 1890 (4th edn, 1st Eng, 10 additional poems, excluding Diana of Ephesus never included in later edns); London 1891 (6th edn, including a Glossary); London 1897 (9th edn, illus); Calcutta 1898 (Thacker's deluxe edn); London 1899 (Newnes's cheap edn); New York 1899; London 1904 (Methuen's 1st edn); tr Swed 1891, Du 1892, Ger 1895, 1915, Danish 1906, Fr 1907, 1908.

REVIEWS: [Lang, A.] Longman's Mag Oct 1886; [Hunter, Sir W.] Acad 1 Sep 1888; Daily News (London) 15 Mar 1890; Athenaeum 26 Apr 1890; Critic 20 Dec 1890; Dial Feb 1891; Nation 16 Apr 1891; Critic (New York) 12 Dec 1891; Acad 1 May 1897.

Plain tales from the hills. Calcutta 1888 (40 stories, 32 rptd from Civil & Military Gazette); New York 1890 (with letter from Kipling); London 1890; New York 1897 (1st Amer collected edn, Outward Bound vol 1); 1897 (1st Eng collected edn); 1897 (Edition de luxe vol 1); 1899 (Macmillan Uniform edn); Ed A. Rutherford, Oxford 1987 (WCp); Ed H. R. Woudhuysen, London 1987 (Pen); 1994 (Pen).

REVIEWS: Saturday Rev, 9 June 1888; [Lang, A.] Daily News 2 Nov 1889; [Ward, Mrs H.] The Times 25 Mar 1890; [Henley, W. E.] Scots Observer 3 May 1890; Literary World (Boston) 10 May 1890; Lippincott's Monthly Mag (Philadelphia) Oct 1890; Nation (New York) Dec 1890.

Soldiers three. Allahabad 1888, 1889 (2nd and 3rd Indian edns), London 1890. 7 stories, 6 rptd from Week's News, 1993 (Pen); tr Fr 1908, 1926.

REVIEWS: Athenaeum 26 Apr 1890; Book Buyer n.s. 7, 9 Oct 1890; Westminster Rev Dec 1890; Fortnightly Rev Nov 1891; Dial 1 Dec 1896; Spectator 23 Mar 1899.

The story of the Gadsbys. Allahabad 1888, 1889 (2nd Indian edn), London 1890 (1st and 2nd Eng edns), New York 1890; tr Swed 1897, Fr 1905, Sp 1923. 8 scenes, 6 rptd from Week's News.

In black and white. Allahabad 1888, 1889 (2nd Indian edn), London 1890, New York 1897 (collected edn), London 1897 (collected edn); tr Rus 1897, Fr 1909. 8 stories, 7 rptd from Week's News.

REVIEWS: Athenaeum 13 Sep 1890; [Whibley, C.] Scots Observer 20 Sep 1890.

Under the deodars. Allahabad 1888, 1889 (2nd edn), London 1890, New York 1890; tr Fr 1910, 1925 (limited edn). 6 stories, 5 rptd from Week's News.

REVIEW: Saturday Rev 10 Aug 1889.

The phantom rickshaw and other stories. Allahabad 1888, 1889 (2nd edn), London 1890. 4 stories rptd from Quartette and Week's News.

Wee Willie Winkie and other child stories. Allahabad 1888, 1889 (2nd edn), London 1890, New York 1890, London 1989 (Pen); tr Swed 1908. 4 stories, 3 rptd from Week's News.

REVIEW: Athenaeum 27 Dec 1890.

The courting of Dinah Shadd and other stories. 1890, New York 1890. With essay by A. Lang. 6 stories rptd from mags; 2nd edn substitutes The record of Badalia Herodsfoot for The incarnation of Krishna Mulvaney.

REVIEW: New York Herald 14 Sep 1890.

Departmental ditties, barrack-room ballads and other verses. New York 1890. Rptd from Scots Observer and Eng Illus Mag.

The light that failed. London, New York, Sydney and Melbourne Jan

1891 (Lippincott's Mag edn, 12 chs, with happy ending); New York 1890 (Lovell's Westminster ser no 25, 12 chs, authorised); New York 1890 (Lovell's authorised edn, 14 chs, with sad ending); London and New York 1891 (1st Macmillan edn, 15 ch version, with sad ending and poem Mother o'mine and Preface); New York 1899 (Doubleday and McClure's first edn, 15 chs); London 1899 (Macmillan Uniform edn); New York 1903 (Doubleday's illus edn); New York 1925 (Renard's illus edn); London 1989 (Pen); tr Du 1892, 1911, Ger 1899, Swed 1899, 1900, Fr 1900, 1911, 1936, Danish 1905, 1922.

REVIEWS: Speaker 24 Jan 1891; Spectator 31 Jan 1891; Literary World (Boston) 28 Feb 1891; [Barrie, J. M.] Contemporary Rev 59, Mar 1891; [Johnson, L.] Acad 4 Apr 1891; Critic (New York) 4 Apr 1891; Athenaeum 18 Apr 1891; Literary World (London) n.s. Apr 1891; National Observer n.s. 25 Apr 1891; [Gosse, E.] Century Mag Oct 1891, rptd in Questions at issue 1893; GM Aug 1892; [Beerbohm, M.] Saturday Rev, 14 Feb 1903 (review of stage production).

The city of dreadful night and other sketches. Allahabad 1890 (suppressed). 7 articles on Calcutta from The Pioneer, 10 sketches that had appeared in Civil & Military Gazette, 1 from The Pioneer; 4 not in SBE.

The city of dreadful night and other places. Allahabad 1891, London 1891; tr Ger 1900, Norwegian 1901. 8 articles and 3 travel sketches.

The Smith administration. Allahabad 1891 (suppressed). 20 stories from Civil & Military Gazette, all but 3 later included in From sea to sea.

Letters of marque. Allahabad 1891, London 1891. Both edns suppressed. 19 letters from The Pioneer.

American notes. New York 1891. Pirated extracts from letters sent to The Pioneer.

Mine own people. New York 1891. Introd by Henry James. 12 stories, 6 from The courting of Dinah Shadd.

REVIEWS: Literary World (Boston) 9 May 1891; Nation (New York) 11 June 1891; [James, H.] Introduction 1891, rptd in Views and reviews, 1908, and in Gilbert, E. L. (ed), Kipling and the critics 1965.

Life's handicap: being stories of mine own people. 1891, New York 1891; ed A. O. J. Cockshut, Oxford 1987 (WCp); tr Swed 1891, Danish 1906 (16 tales), 1918, Fr 1928. All stories from Mine own people except A conference of the powers, plus 17 stories, all but 3 rptd from periodicals.

REVIEWS: Edinburgh Rev July 1891; Nat Observer n.s. 29 Aug 1891; Literary World (Boston) 12 Sep 1891; Spectator 26 Sep 1891; [Lynd, R.] Bookman 1 Oct 1891; [Johnson, L.] Acad 17 Oct 1891; Westminster Rev n.s. Oct 1891; Blackwood's Mag Nov 1891; Fortnightly Rev Nov 1891; [Oliphant, M.] Blackwood's Mag Nov 1891; Quart Rev July 1892.

Soldiers three; The story of the Gadsbys; In black and white. 1892, 1895 (rev), New York 1895. With 2 stories from Civil & Military Gazette not previously collected.

Wee Willie Winkie; Under the deodars; The phantom rickshaw and other stories. 1892, 1895, New York 1895 (rev and including 2 stories not in the Eng edn from St James's Gazette and Civil & Military Gazette).

The Naulahka. 1892, New York 1892; tr Danish 1894, 1911, Swed 1898, Fr 1900, 1908, Polish 1901, Ital 1932, Cz 1937. Rptd from Century Mag with ch headings added. In collaboration with Wolcott Balestier.

REVIEWS: Nat Observer n.s. 16 July 1892; Literary World (London) n.s. 22 July 1892; Speaker 23 July 1892; Athenaeum 30 July 1892; [Gosse, E.] Literary World (Boston) 30 July 1892; Book Buyer (New York) n.s. Aug 1892; Bookman (London) Aug 1892; Dial Aug 1892; [Cope, G.] GM Aug 1892; Spectator 6 Aug 1892; Saturday Rev 20 Aug 1892; Atlantic Monthly Oct 1892; Nation (New York) 6 Oct 1892; Westminster Rev n.s. Nov 1892; Edinburgh Rev Oct 1899.

Barrack-room ballads and other verses. 1892. As Ballads and barrack-room ballads, New York 1892 (although the titles differ the contents are the same; all but 8 poems were rptd from books and mags); New York 1893 (2nd edn with 4 additional poems); London 1989 (Methuen Centenary edn); tr Ger 1911, 1936, Fr 1920; Soldier songs from Barrack-room ballads tr Ger 1910; Soldier songs tr Norwegian 1902.

REVIEWS: Nat Observer (Edinburgh) 7 May 1892; [Archer, W.] Pall Mall Gazette 7 May 1892; Spectator 7 May 1892; Athenaeum 14 May 1892; Saturday Rev 14 May 1892; Literary World (London) n.s. 20 May 1892; [Johnson, L.] Acad 28 May 1892; Literary World (Boston) 18 June 1892; Nation (New York) 7 July 1892; Critic (New York) 9 July 1892; [Quiller-Couch, A.] English Illus Mag Sep 1893; Fortnightly Rev Nov 1893; Independent (New York) 28 Dec 1893; Forum (New York) Dec 1896.

Many inventions. 1893, New York 1893; tr Du 1893, Ger 1893 (rptd 1900, 1903, 1921), Swed 1898, Sp 1926. 14 stories, 9 rptd from periodicals and 2 poems.

REVIEWS: Literary World 30 Jan 1893; Saturday Rev 17 June 1893; [Lynd, R.] Bookman July 1893; Acad 1 July 1893; Athenaeum 8 July 1893; Spectator 15 July 1893; Book Buyer (New York) n.s. Aug 1893; Dial 16 Aug 1893; Critic (New York) 19 Aug 1893; Nation (New York) 14 Sep 1893; Independent (New York) 26 Oct 1893; [Saintsbury, G.] in unidentified periodical rptd in A last vintage: essays and papers, 1950.

The jungle book. 1894, New York 1894 (with variants); London 1908 (English edn with Detmold illustrations); New York 1913 (Amer edn with Detmold illustrations); New York 1932 (Amer edn with Wiese illustrations); New York 1932 (Amer school edn, 7 stories rptd from periodicals and 7 new poems), London 1989 (Penguin Jungle book and Second jungle book); ed W. W. Robson, Oxford 1992 (WCp); tr Fr 1899, Ger 1901, Danish 1918, Polish 1923, 1931, Ital 1928, Du 1934; Romanian 1935.

REVIEWS: Bookman June 1894; Spectator 2 June 1894; Athenaeum 16 June 1894; Saturday Rev 16 June 1894; Academy 30 June 1894; Book Buyer (New York) n.s. July 1894; Nation (New York) 5 July 1894; Critic (New York) 21 July 1894; London Quart Rev Jan 1896.

The second jungle book. 1895, New York 1895 (textual variation), London 1895 (2nd edn, rev), New York 1932 (Amer school edn, 8 stories rptd from periodicals and 8 (3 previously pbd) poems and 2 verse headings); ed W. W. Robson Oxford 1987 (WCp); London 1994 (Puffin); tr Fr 1899, 1919, 1925, 1930, 1936, Ger 1899, Polish 1903, 1923, 1934, Lithuanian 1926, 1936, Ital 1929, Cz 1933, Du 1935, Romanian 1935, Hungarian 1943.

REVIEWS: [Crockett, S. R.] Bookman (New York) Feb 1895; Forum June 1895; Book Buyer (New York) n.s. Nov 1895; Critic (New York 23 Nov 1895; Dial 1 Dec 1895; Athenaeum 29 Feb 1896; Atlantic Monthly Mar 1896.

The two jungle books. 1924, New York 1925, London 1941, 2 vols 1948; tr Rus 1924, 1926.

Out of India. New York 1895. City of the dreadful night and other places, Letters of marque rptd without authority.

The seven seas. 1896, New York 1896, illus edn London 1905; tr Swed 1918. Fr 1924. The Eng edn contained 47 poems, 13 first pbd here; the Amer edn 44. 3 of the poems in the Eng edn had already appeared in the Amer edn of Barrack-room ballads.

REVIEWS: Book Buyer Nov 1896; Book Buyer (New York) ser 3 Nov 1896, rptd in Genius and other essays, 1910; Critic Nov 1896; Acad 14 Nov 1896; Saturday Rev 21 Nov 1896, rptd in Living Age (Boston) 18 Dec 1896; Spectator 21 Nov 1896; Bookman Dec 1896; Rev of Reviews Dec 1896; Nation 10 Dec 1896; Nation (New York) 10 Dec 1896; Literary World (Boston) 26 Dec 1896; [Norton, C. E.] Atlantic Monthly Jan 1897; Bookman (New York) Jan 1897; Dial 1 Feb 1897; Independent (New York) 4 Feb 1897, [Howells, W. D.] McClure's Mag Mar 1897; Poet Lore n.s. 1 no 2 Apr 1897; London

Quart Rev Jan 1898; Atlantic Monthly Dec 1899; [Ferguson, J. de Lancy] Forum (New York) Sep 1913.

The Kipling birthday book. 1896, New York 1896. Quotations from verses in Civil & Military Gazette not otherwise rptd.

'Captains courageous': a story of the Grand Banks. 1897 (serialised in McClure's Mag and Pearson's Mag), New York 1897 (slight textual variants); ed J. de L. Ferguson, New York 1959; ed L. Ormond, Oxford 1995 (WCp), London 1995 (Pen); tr Swed 1897, 1898, Ger 1902, Fr 1903, 1906, 1932, Cz 1904, Danish 1905, Icelandic 1907, Du 1911, Sp 1918, Polish 1930.
REVIEWS: McClure's Mag May 1897; Acad 30 Oct 1897; Athenaeum 30 Oct 1897; Bookman Nov 1897; Harper's Monthly Mag (New York) Nov 1897; Critic (New York) 6 Nov 1897; Literature (London and New York) 6 Nov 1897; Atlantic Monthly Dec 1897; Independent (New York) 9 Dec 1897; London Quart Rev Jan 1898; Nation (New York) 6 Jan 1898.

An almanac of twelve sports. 1898, New York 1898, London 1899. Verses to drawings by W. Nicholson.
REVIEW: Acad 4 Dec 1897.

The day's work. 1898, New York 1898. Ed A. Rutherford, Oxford 1987 (WCp); ed C. Phipps, London 1990 (Pen); tr Swed 1898, Ger 1900, 1927, Norwegian 1900, Cz 1930. 12 stories rptd from periodicals.
REVIEWS: Acad 15 Oct 1898; Athenaeum 15 Oct 1898; Literature (New York) 15 Oct 1898; Spectator 15 Oct 1898; Bookman Nov 1898; Cosmopolis (London) Nov 1898; Critic (New York) Nov 1898; Literary World (Boston) 26 Nov 1898; Bookman (New York) Dec 1898; [Gwynn, S.] Macmillan's Mag Dec 1898; Atlantic Monthly (Boston) Jan 1899.

A fleet in being. 1898, New York 1913; tr Ger 1899, 1900, Swed 1899, Danish 1909, 1915, 1916. 6 articles from The Times and The Morning Post.
REVIEW: Spectator 24 Dec 1898.

Stalky & Co. 1899, New York 1899. 9 stories from mags and 1 poem; The complete Stalky & Co. 1929, New York 1930 (adds 5 stories and 4 poems, 4 previously collected in other vols, 1 hitherto uncollected); The complete Stalky & Co., ed I. Quigley, Oxford 1987 (WCp); tr Swed 1899, Danish 1903, 1918, Fr 1903, Ger 1909, 1928, Romanian 1932, Sp 1944.
REVIEWS: Arena 21 1899; Calcutta Rev 1899; Athenaeum 14 Oct 1899; Literature (London) 14 Oct 1899; Spectator 21 Oct 1899; Literature (New York) 27 Oct 1899; Spectator 28 Oct 1899; Bookman Nov 1899; Literary World (Boston) 25 Nov 1899; Dial 1 Dec 1899; Scottish Rev Jan 1900; Nation (New York) 4 Jan 1900; Acad 17 Mar 1900; Mercure de France (Paris) May 1903.

From sea to sea. New York 1899, London 1900; tr Ger 1900 (2 vols), Swed 1901, Danish 1913, Fr 1904 as Lettres du Japon, pt 1 of From sea to sea, 1912 as Chez les Américaines, pt 2 of From sea to sea, Polish 1904 (11 letters from From sea to sea). Rev versions of Letters of marque, The Smith administration, City of the dreadful night and other places.
REVIEWS: Bookman Jan 1899; New York Times 10 June 1899; Bookman (New York) July 1899; Dial (Chicago) 1 July 1899; Literary World 8 July 1899; Nation (New York) 7 Sep 1899; Athenaeum 3 Mar 1900; Literary World n.s. 9 Mar 1900; Literature 10 Mar 1900; Spectator 24 Mar 1900; [Lynd, R.] Bookman Apr 1900.

With number three, Surgical and medical, and new poems by Rudyard Kipling; also letters from Julian Ralph, Charles E. Hands and Douglas Story. Santiago 1900. 3 poems and 2 stories written by Kipling during the Boer War and 4 poems written previously.

Kim. 1901 (serialised in McClure's Mag and Cassell's Mag); New York 1901; London 1901 (2nd edn); New York 1912 (American Quarto edn); 1936 (Canadian school edn); 1939, (Sun dial press edn) New York 1950; New York 1962 (preface by J. I. M. Stewart); New York 1962 (preface by C. E. Carrington); New York 1962 (preface by A. L. Rowse); ed A. Sandison, Oxford 1987 (WCp); ed E. Said, 1987 (Pen); London 1994 (Penguin Popular Classics); tr Fr 1902, 1921, 1931, 2 vols 1932, 1936, Swed 1902, Cz 1903, 1936, Danish 1906, 1918, Ger 1908, 1909, Ital 1920, 1922, Sp 1921, Polish 1926, Romanian 1937.
REVIEWS: Literary World n.s. 4 Jan 1901; Book Buyer (New York) n.s. Oct 1901; [Lynd, R.] Bookman Oct 1901; Bookman (New York) Oct 1901; World's Work Oct 1901; Speaker n.s. 5 Oct 1901; Spectator 5 Oct 1901; Independent (New York) 10 Oct 1901; Athenaeum 26 Oct 1901; Critic (New York) Nov 1901; Nation (New York) 14 Nov 1901; Atlantic Monthly Dec 1901; Blackwood's Mag Dec 1901; Bookman (New York) Dec 1901; Literary World (Boston) 1 Dec 1901; Atlantic Monthly Apr 1902.

Just so stories for little children. 1902 (12 stories, 11 rptd from periodicals, and 9 poems); New York 1902, collected edn New York 1903 (including The tabu tale not collected elsewhere and not rptd until SBE vol 16); Just so song book 1903, music by E. German; Amer extra-illus edn New York 1912; Eng extra-illus edn 1913; Just so stories painting books for children 1922–3; New York 1923; school edn London 1930; New York 1932; 4 vols New York 1942 (with Rojanovsky illustrations); New York 1952 (with illustrations by Nicolas); 1987 (Pen): ed L. Lewis, Oxford 1995 (WCp); tr Swed 1902, Fr 1903, Ger 1903, 1929, Cz 1904, Danish 1904, 1914, Ital 1910, 1924, 1948, Eng and Polish 1921, 1922, Rus 1929, Romanian 1939, Sp 1943.
REVIEWS: Spectator 4 Oct 1902; Nation (New York) 23 Oct 1902; [Chesterton, G. K.] Bookman Nov 1902, rptd Bookman (New York) Dec 1902; Anglo-American Mag (Toronto) Dec 1902; Book Buyer (New York) n.s. Dec 1902; Dial 1 Dec 1902; Outlook (New York) 6 Dec 1902; Atlantic Monthly 91, May 1903; English Illus Mag Jan 1904.

The five nations. 1903, New York 1903; tr Fr 1920. 54 poems, 28 not previously pbd.
REVIEWS: Academy 3 Oct 1903; Athenaeum 10 Oct 1903; [Gwynn, S.] Pilot 10 Oct 1903, rptd Eclectic Mag of Foreign Lit (New York) 10 Oct 1903; Independent (New York) 15 Oct 1903; Saturday Rev 31 Oct 1903; Bookman (New York) Nov 1903; [Archer, W.] Critic (New York) Nov 1903; [Cooper, F. T.] World's Work Nov 1903; [Waugh, A.] Book Monthly 1 Nov 1903; Dial 16 Nov 1903; Atlantic Monthly Dec 1903; Out West (Los Angeles) Mar 1904; Atlantic Monthly Jan 1918.

The muse among the motors. 1904 (pbd by The Daily Mail). A series of 14 poems that had appeared in The Daily Mail.

Traffics and discoveries. 1904, New York 1904; ed H. Lee, London 1992 (Pen); stories from tr Swed 1903, 1905. 11 stories and 11 poems rptd from mags.
REVIEWS: Bookman (New York) Oct 1904; Athenaeum 8 Oct 1904; Saturday Rev 15 Oct 1904; Independent (New York) 20 Oct 1904; [Lynd, R.] Bookman Nov 1904; Critic (New York) Nov 1904; Literary World (Boston) Nov 1904; Catholic World (New York) Dec 1904; Current Literature (New York) Dec 1904; Reader Mag Dec 1904; Outlook (New York) 3 Dec 1904; North Amer Rev 11 May 1911.

Puck of Pook's Hill. 1906, New York 1906; London 1987 (Pen); ed D. Mackenzie, Oxford 1993 (WCp); London 1995 (Penguin Popular Classics); tr Swed 1906, Danish 1907, Ger 1912, Polish 1924, Fr 1930, 1931. 10 stories rptd from periodicals in Britain and America, and 16 poems.
REVIEWS: Independent (New York) 4 Oct 1906; Nation (New York) 4 Oct 1906; Acad 6 Oct 1906; Athenaeum 6 Oct 1906; Saturday Rev 6 Oct 1906; Spectator 13 Oct 1906; [Noyes, A.] Bookman Nov 1906; Bookman (New York) Dec 1906; Book News Monthly Dec 1906; Book News Monthly (Philadelphia) Dec 1906; Current Literature (New York) Dec 1906; Living Age (Boston) 1 Dec 1906; Contemporary Rev May 1907.

Letters to the family: notes on a recent trip to Canada. Toronto 1908, 1910, New York 1913. 8 articles rptd from newspapers, later

included in Letters of travel; 7 poems later included in Songs from books and verse.
REVIEWS: Independent (New York) 16 Jan 1913; Spectator 25 Oct 1913; Bookman Dec 1913.

Actions and reactions. 1909 (8 stories rptd from periodicals, and 8 poems), New York 1909 (contents the same but slight textual variants); tr Fr 1911, Ger 1913, Danish 1914.
REVIEWS: Spectator 9 Oct 1909; Athenaeum 16 Oct 1909; T. P.'s Weekly 22 Oct 1909; Bookman Nov 1909; [Bennett, A.] New Age 4 Nov 1909, rptd in Books and Persons 1917; Nation (New York) 11 Nov 1909; Current Literature (New York) Feb 1910.

Abaft the funnel. New York 1909 (unauthorised), 1909 (authorised), 1st Eng printing vol 30 SBE 1938. 8 stories written by Kipling for Civil & Military Gazette while en route for England 1889–90.
REVIEW: Bookman (New York) Dec 1909.

Kipling stories and poems every child should know. New York 1909, illus edn 1938. 26 poems, 11 stories and extracts from 3 other stories.

Rewards and fairies. 1910, New York 1910 (textual variants), London 1926 (school edn, rev), 1987 (Pen); ed D. Mackenzie, Oxford 1993 (WCp, with Puck of Pook's Hill); tr Danish 1915, Fr 1935. 11 stories, 9 from periodicals, 23 poems.
REVIEWS: Spectator 8 Oct 1910; Nation (New York) 20 Oct 1910; Athenaeum 22 Oct 1910; Bookman (London) Nov 1910; Current Literature Jan 1911; North Amer Rev 11 May 1911.

A history of England. 1911, New York 1911; school edn Oxford 1911, rev 1930; tr Fr 1930. Prose text by C. R. L. Fletcher, 23 poems by Kipling, rptd in various verse collections and in SBE.
REVIEWS: Spectator 5 Aug 1911; Athenaeum 19 Aug 1911.

Songs from books. New York 1912, Toronto 1912, London 1913 (with many addns). Poems from prose vols, many expanded.

The new army in training. New York 1914, London 1915; tr Danish 1915. A rev ser of 6 articles from the Daily Telegraph Dec 1914.
REVIEW: Spectator 13 Feb 1915.

France at war. 1915, New York 1915; tr Danish 1915, Fr 1915. 6 articles which had appeared simultaneously in Great Britain and Amer.
REVIEW: Athenaeum 4 Dec 1915.

Fringes of the fleet. 1915, New York 1915 (Hearst edn), Toronto 1915; tr Danish 1916. 6 articles written for the Ministry of Information.
REVIEWS: Spectator 20 Jan 1916; Nation (New York) 10 Feb 1916.

Tales of 'the trade'. 1916. 3 articles rptd from The Times made available to Amer newspapers; Eng edn 25 copies only; Tales of the trade, Fringes of the fleet. tr Sp 1916.

Sea warfare. 1916, New York 1917; tr Danish 1917, Swed 1917, Fr 1919. Fringes of the fleet with 6 poems, Tales of 'the trade' with 1 poem, Destroyers at Jutland rptd from newspapers with 1 poem.
REVIEW: Dial 19 Apr 1917.

The war in the mountains. 1917, New York 1917. 5 pams stitched together which had appeared in the Daily Telegraph and the New York Tribune in June 1917; tr Ital 1917 and pbd in Ital mags and as a pam.

A diversity of creatures. 1917, New York 1917, London 1994 (Pen); tr Danish 1918, Fr 1919. 14 stories and 14 poems, 12 of the stories and part of 1 of the poems previously pbd in periodicals.
REVIEWS: Athenaeum 18 May 1917; Nation (New York) 24 May 1917.

The eyes of Asia. New York 1918; tr Fr 1921. 4 letters rptd from newspapers. Not collected in Eng edn until SBE vols 26 and 20.
REVIEW: Dial 30 Nov 1918.

The graves of the fallen. 1919 (HMSO). Rev 1928 as War graves of the empire and issued by Times publishing company. Much is by Kipling but only 1 epitaph included in SBE.

The years between. 1919, New York 1919. 45 poems and a collection of epitaphs, all but 11 poems and the epitaphs previously pbd in periodicals.
REVIEWS: TLS 10 Apr 1919; New Republic 19 Apr 1919; Bookman May 1919; Spectator 3 May 1919; [Eliot, T. S.] Athenaeum 9 May 1919; Dial 31 May 1919; Literary Digest 31 May 1919; Bookman (New York) July 1919; Nation (New York) 26 July 1919.

Letters of travel (1892–1913). 1920, New York 1920, Eng college edn London 1938, Amer college edn New York 1941. 3 sers of letters: From tideway to tideway, Letters to the family, Egypt of the magicians; in collected edns (SBE) a further ser is added, Brazilian sketches.
REVIEWS: TLS 10 June 1920; Spectator 19 June 1920; Bookman's Jnl (London) 2 July 1920; [Woolf, V.] Athenaeum 16 July 1920.

The Irish Guards in the Great War edited and compiled from their diaries and papers. Vol 1 The first battalion; vol 2 The second battalion and appendices. 1923, New York 1923.
REVIEWS: TLS 19 Apr 1923; [Blunden, E.] Nation and Athenaeum 28 Apr 1923; Bookman May 1923; New Statesman 2 June 1923; New York World 22 July 1923; [Patterson, I.] New York Tribune Book News and Rev 5 Aug 1923; [Hay, A.] New York Times Book Rev 2 Sep 1923.

Land and sea tales. 1923, New York 1923, London 1925; tr Danish 1924. 11 stories and 8 poems, 1 story and 7 poems pbd for the first time.
REVIEWS: TLS 29 Nov 1923; New Statesman 8 Dec 1923; Saturday Rev 8 Dec 1923; [Massingham, H. J.] Nation and Athenaeum 5 Jan 1924.

Debits and credits. 1926, New York 1926, London 1993 (Pen). 14 stories and 21 poems, all of the stories and 2 of the poems pbd previously.
REVIEWS: TLS 16 Sep 1926; Saturday Rev 18 Sep 1926; New York Evening Post Literary Rev Oct 1926; Saturday Rev of Lit 2 Oct 1926; [Wilson, E.] New Republic 6 Oct 1926; Outlook 6 Oct 1926; Literary Digest International Book Rev (USA) Nov 1926; Nation (New York) 17 Nov 1926.

A book of words. 1928, New York 1928. Collection of 31 addresses delivered by Kipling 1906–27, 11 pbd previously in pam form. Eng college edn 1938 Sussex vol 25 with 6 additional addresses, 4 of which had appeared previously as pams; Amer college edn, New York 1941 Burwash vol 24 follows the text of the Sussex edn. 31 speeches; 6 added in SBE.
REVIEWS: [Petrie, Sir C. A.] Outlook 31 Mar 1928; [Shanks, E.] Saturday Rev 31 Mar 1928; TLS 26 Apr 1928; Bookman May 1928; Contemporary Rev June 1928; Revue Anglo-Américaine (Paris) Feb 1929.

Thy servant a dog. 1930, New York 1930; tr Cz 1931, Du 1931, Fr 1931, Swed 1931. 3 dog stories, 2 previously pbd. As Thy servant a dog and other dog stories, London 1938 (adds 2 stories and 2 poems not previously collected).

Limits and renewals. 1932, New York 1932, London 1944 (Pen); tr Cz 1934. 14 stories and 19 poems; 4 of the stories pbd previously in periodicals, 7 of the stories and 1 poem pbd separately for copyright.
REVIEWS: TLS 7 Apr 1932; Saturday Rev of Lit 23 Apr 1932; Spectator 23 Apr 1932; Bookman May 1932; New Republic 25 May 1932.

Souvenirs of France. 1933; tr Fr 1933. Sketches rptd from newspapers.

Collected dog stories. 1934, New York 1934. 9 stories and 5 poems, all but one of which pbd previously.

All the Puck stories. 1935. Comprising Puck of Pook's Hill 1906 and Rewards and fairies 1910.

Something of myself. 1937, New York 1937, London 1977 (Pen); ed T. Pinney, Cambridge 1990; tr Fr 1938 with bibliography of the Fr edns of Kipling.
REVIEWS: TLS 20 Feb 1937; Observer 21 Feb 1937; Nation 27 Feb 1937; Saturday Rev of Lit 27 Feb 1937; New York Herald Tribune Books 28 Feb 1937; [Wilson, E.] New Republic 24 Mar 1937; American Mercury June 1937; [Williams, O.] Criterion July 1937;

[Phelps, W. L.] Yale Rev Summer 1937; Queen's Quart Autumn 1937.
Brazilian sketches. New York 1940.

Stories, poems and speeches published separately

This list does not include over 120 items ptd separately for copyright purposes, or the hundreds of pirated edns.

The seven nights of creation. Calcutta 1886. Poem of 145 lines, 80 only in SBE.
Further information. Calcutta 1886.
The song of the women. Calcutta 1888.
One word more. [Calcutta 1888.] As One viceroy resigns in Departmental ditties.
The ballad of east and west. New York 1889.
My great and only. Allahabad 1890.
'Cleared'. Edinburgh 1890.
The record of Badalia Herodsfoot. [1890.]
My lord the elephant. Boston 1892.
When earth's last picture is painted. New York 1892, 1896, 1905.
My first book. 1894, New York 1919.
In sight of Mount Monadnock. Northampton MA 1894, Boston 1904.
His Excellency. Rutlam Canada 1895, Bombay 1899. Not in SBE.
Rudyard Kipling's regrets. New Haven CT 1896. Poem Mulvaney's regrets from Yale Lit Mag. Not in SBE.
Recessional. New York 1897, 1898, London 1914, 1917.
The vampire. 1897, New York 1898 (priv ptd), Boston 1898 etc.
Mandalay. New York 1898.
The destroyers. 1898, HMS Kipling edn 1939.
The man who would be king. New York 1899.
The drums of the Fore and Aft. New York 1899.
The brushwood boy. New York 1899, 1907, London 1907.
The betrothed. New York 1899.
Black Jack. New York 1899. Unrevised story from Soldiers three.
The absent-minded beggar. 1899.
Kipling masterpieces. New York 1899. 5 stories ptd as separate booklets.
The incarnation of Krishna Mulvaney. New York 1899.
The courting of Dinah Shadd. New York 1899.
Without benefit of clergy. New York 1899.
Bobs. Montreal 1899.
Ten gems. New York 1899. Separate booklets of Belts, The betrothed, Danny Deever, Fuzzy Wuzzy, Gunga Din, Mandalay, Recessional, Tommy, The vampire, The undertaker's horse.
Our Bobs. Boston 1900.
A new auld lang syne. Bloemfontein 1900.
The sin of witchcraft. 1901. Letter rptd from The Times; not in SBE.
The science of rebellion: a tract for the times. 1901.
The houses. 1902.
The islanders. 1902. 25 copies limited edn.
The settler. 1903.
The rowers. 1903.
The gipsy trail. Boston 1904, 1905. Rptd from Century Mag Dec 1892.
The foreloper. 1904. Pbd later as The Voortrekker.
The captive. 1904.
They. 1905, New York 1906.
The army of a dream. 1905.
Letter on a possible source of The tempest. Providence RI 1906 (priv ptd), New York 1916. Rptd from Spectator 1898.
South Africa. New York 1906. Copyright issue, rptd from Standard 1906. Not in SBE.
The sons of Martha. New York 1907 (1st and 2nd edns), Chicago 1907 (3rd edn).
The claims of art. 1907.
Doctors: an address. 1908; tr Ger 1937.
With the night mail: a story of 2000 A. D. New York 1909.
A song of the English. 1909, 1915, National Bands edn 1919.
A patrol song. 1909.
A doctor's work. St Louis 1910.
If—. New York 1910, London 1914 (1st and 2nd edns), 1915 (Waterloo Free Buffet edn), 1935 (Silver Jubilee edn), 1937.
The dead king. 1910.
The spies' march. 1911.
Why snow falls at Vernet. Mansfield UK 1911 (in Pages from the Merrythought), 1923 (priv ptd), 1963 (priv ptd). Not in SBE.
The female of the species. New York 1912.
Ulster: a poem. Belfast 1912, Ely 1914 (priv ptd).
France. New York 1913, London 1915.
Some aspects of travel. New York 1914, 1914.
For all we have and are. 1914.
The Tunbridge Wells speech. 1914. Issued as The secret bargain and the Ulster plot by The League of British Covenanters and as Rudyard Kipling's indictment of a government by the Daily Express.
The children's song. 1914, 1918.
Hymn before action. 1914, 1915.
A call to the nation. 1915. Speech; not in SBE.
The new army in training. 1915.
National bands. 1915. In SBE as The soul of a battalion.
Tales of the trade: 1. Some work in the Baltic; 2. Business in the Sea of Marmora; 3. Ravages and repairs. 1916 (priv ptd), New York 1916 (priv ptd).
The holy war. 1917, 1918.
Hymn of the free peoples. New York 1917.
The war in the mountains. New York 1917; Sussex edn vol 26; tr Danish 1917, Sp 1917.
Mesopotamia. 1917.
Kipling's message. 1918. Speech; not in SBE.
To fighting Americans. 1918. Not in SBE.
The Irish Guards. 1918. Poem.
Values in life. Indianapolis 1918, San Francisco 1920, Pittsburgh 1924, Illinois 1939 as Kipling speaks to the young man.
In the interests of the brethren. New York 1918.
Justice. 1919.
The feet of the young men. New York 1920.
England and the English. 1920, 1920 (2nd edn), New York and Toronto 1921 as The mind of the English.
Some notes on a bill. Little Rock AR 1920 (priv ptd). Poem rptd from Author (Boston) 1891; not in SBE.
The first assault upon the Sorbonne [in English and French]. New York 1922 (limited edn; rptd in SBE).
The King's pilgrimage. 1922.
Independence. 1923, New York 1924.
Michigan twins. 1923.
The glory of the garden. Manchester 1923.
The Janeites. New York 1924.
The potted princess. New York 1925 (priv ptd).
Collah-wallah and the poison stick. New York 1925 (priv ptd).
They and The brushwood boy. 1925, New York 1926.
The shipping industry. 1925, 1925 (2nd edn).
Address at Stationers' Hall. 1925 (1st and 2nd edns).
On dry-cow fishing as a fine art. Cleveland OH 1926 (priv ptd).
The art of fiction. 1926.
A rector's memory: St Andrews: two poems. 1926.
The legs of Sister Ursula. San Francisco 1927.
A tour of inspection. New York 1928 (priv ptd).
Supplication of the black Aberdeen. 1928, New York 1929.
Two lives. 1928. For the Kipling Soc.
The lamentable comedy of willow wood. San Francisco 1929.
Address at Milner Court. 1929.
The English way. 1929, New York 1929.

The benefactors. New York 1930.
His apologies. 1932, New York 1932.
Selections from the freer verse Horace. New York 1932 (copyright edn, rptd from Magdalene College Mag 1932), Liverpool 1965 (priv ptd). Not in SBE.
Neighbours. 1932.
The day of the dead. 1932.
The fox meditates. 1933.
Two forewords. New York 1935.
Hymn of breaking strain. 1935.
Ham and the porcupine: a just so story. 1935 (in The Princess Elizabeth gift book), New York 1935 (copyright pam), Kipling Jnl 25 1958. Not in SBE.
The Maltese cat. 1936, New York 1936.
Toomai of the elephants. 1937.
Teem: a treasure-hunter. New York 1938.
The appeal. San Francisco 1940.
Tommy. 1943.
For uncollected items, unauthorised edns, poems set to music, copyright and miscellaneous reprints, see J. McG. Stewart, Bibliographical catalogue, Toronto 1959.

Contributions to periodicals and collaborative works

Some of Kipling's early contributions to newspapers in India have now been pbd; see Kipling's India: uncollected sketches 1884–88, ed T. Pinney, 1986. *See also* L. Cornell, Kipling in India, 1966 *for a chronological list of Kipling's writing Oct 1882–Mar 1889, pp 167–84.*

Before being collected in books, many stories and poems by Kipling were pbd simultaneously in periodicals and newspapers in Britain and America. For initial location, see IELM vol 4 pt 2; Wellesley vol 5 1989.

Lister, R. J. A catalogue of a portion of the library of Edmund Gosse. 1893, 1924 (in E. H. Cox, Library of Edmund Gosse). Poem.
Barry, J. A. Steve Brown's bunyip and other stories with introductory verses by R. Kipling. 1893.
Ralph, J. War's brighter side. 1901. Prose and verse.
Landon, P. (ed). Helio-tropes: or new posies for sundials. 1904. Poem.
Young, A. B. F. The complete motorist with a letter from R. Kipling. 1904.
Humières, A. E. R. Through isle and empire of Great Britain with a prefatory letter by R. Kipling. 1905.
Baden-Powell, R. S. S. Sketches in Mafeking. 1907. Verses.
Rice, W. and F. The little book of limericks. 1910. Rptd from periodicals.
Lowther, H. C. From pillar to post. 1911. Poem.
The King's book of Quebec. Ottawa 1911. Article.
The Kipling reader. New York 1912 (How to bring up a lion, rptd from Ladies' Home Jnl 1902), New York 1962 (in Everyman's arm, ed S. P. Johnson).
Newton, W. D. War. 1914. Introd by Kipling.
Chevrillon, A. Britain and the War. 1917. Preface.
Greek national anthem rendered into English by R. Kipling. 1918.
Q. Horati Flacci carmen liber quintus. Oxford 1920, 1920 (rev), 1922 (rev). 3 poems, collected; 2nd and subsequent edns also contain uncollected prose version.
Bland-Sutton, J. The story of a surgeon. 1929. Introd by Kipling.
Tusser, T. Five hundred points of good husbandry. Ed E. V. Lucas 1931. Benediction.
Cave, E. et al. Ant antics. 1933. Limerick.
Atholl, Duchess of, and J. C. French. India and the report of the joint select committee. [1934.] Prose message affixed.
Also uncollected prose and verse in bibliographical, biographical and critical studies, catalogues and Kipling Jnl 1927– (in progress). *See also the unauthorised pams ptd privately (a few copies only) for E. W. Martindell and A. E. Ballard, of which bound vols are in Bodleian with the titles* Flies in amber, More flies in amber, Still more flies in amber – *128 prose items, many not by Kipling. Most are drawn from the Indian newspapers and from* United Services Coll Chron *and* St James's Gazette.

Letters

More than 6,000 letters by Kipling are preserved in over 138 libs all over the world, and items are still appearing in sales rooms. In Britain the Univ of Sussex, the BL and the Bodleian have significant holdings. A collected edn of Kipling's letters is in progress, ed T. Pinney, 1990– .

Other sources of published letters include:

Letters from Kipling to Guy Paget 1919–36. 1936 (12 copies, priv ptd).
Carrington, C. E. Rudyard Kipling. 1955. Authorised biography.
Cohen, M. N. Kipling to Rider Haggard: the record of a friendship. 1965.

About 20 uncollected letters may be found in Kipling Jnl, *and usually not more than one in each of the following:*

Year boke of the sette of odd volumes. 1892.
Letters to A. P. Watt. 1892 (letter), 1893 (2), 1902 (3), 1924 (4).
Wilson, B. The tenth island. 1897.
The school budget: no 13. Horsmonden 1898 (rptd in Academy, Critic etc).
Bullen, F. T. The cruise of the 'Cachalot'. 1898.
Clemens, A. M. A ken of Kipling. New York 1899.
Knowles, F. W. A Kipling primer. Boston 1899.
Lawrence, A. Sir Arthur Sullivan. 1899.
Joline, A. H. Meditations of an autograph collector. New York 1902.
The Times and the publishers. 1906 (priv ptd).
The surplus. 1909 (Salvation Army pbn), 1913 (in Census surplus and Empire), 1924 (in The Salvation Army: British Empire exhibition handbook).
Bordeaux, H. Guynemer, knight of the air. 1918.
Proc Amer Acad of Arts & Letters 11 1921.
Maitland, E. M. The log of HMA R 34. 1921.
Leslie, S. Mark Sykes: his life and letters. 1923.
Cushing, H. The life of William Osler. 1925.
Cook, T. A. The sunlit hours. New York 1925.
A letter from Kipling to Joseph Conrad. 1926.
Haggard, H. R. The days of my life. 1926.
Hall, A. V. South Africa and other poems. 1926.
Lawrence, W. R. The India we served. 1928.
Lemperley, P. Among my books. Cleveland OH 1929.
Jones, D. A. The life and letters of Henry Arthur Jones. 1930.
Trowbridge, U. and A. Marshall. John Lord Montagu of Beaulieu. 1930.
Lucas, E. V. Postbag diversions. 1934.
Rice, H. C. Kipling in New England. Brattleboro VT 1936, 1951 (rev).
Letter to R. D. Bloomfield. Daily Express 18 Jan 1936.
Hillman, A. and W. W. Skeat. Salem the mouse-deer: wonder stories of the Malayan forest. 1938.
Catalogue of the William Inglis Morse collection. Dalhousie Univ Lib 1938.
Letter to G. B. Burgin. Daily Telegraph 4 Jan 1940; Kipling Jnl 53 1940.
Green, R. L. A. E. W. Mason. 1952.
Hovelaque, B. Lettres de guerre à André Chevrillon. Revue des Deux Mondes 15 Sep 1959.
Cohen, M. N. Rider Haggard: his life and works. 1960.

§2

Current scholarship about Kipling is listed in MLA, YWES and BRH; a significant amount of it appears in The Kipling Jnl (1927–), *ed G. H. Webb, pbd 4 times a year. For an annotated bibliography covering the years up to 1965, see* H. E. Gerber and E. S. Lauterbach, English Fiction in Transition 3 1960; suppl 8 1965. *Textual and bibliographical matters are dealt with in* R. E. Harbord. The reader's guide to Rudyard Kipling's work, 8 vols 1961–72. *An early report on Kipling's work as it appears on film can be found in* The Kipling Jnl Sep 1935, *and a more current essay on the subject in* Rudyard Kipling: the man, his work and his world, ed J. Gross, 1975.

Textual matters

Ames, C. L. The suppressed works of Rudyard Kipling. Bookman (London) Jan 1893.
Henley, W. E. Concerning Atkins. Pall Mall Mag 21 1900.
Mr Kipling's accuracy [on Mandalay]. Literature 6 Jan 1900.
Pierpoint, R. Kipling's City of the day and night. N & Q 3 Jan 1903.
Turnbull, T. E. Mr Kipling's titles. Academy 25 Mar 1905.
Pierpoint, R. Dust builds on dust: Kipling's Recessional. N & Q 16 Nov 1907.
Pierpoint, R. Kipling on Shakespeare. N & Q 31 Oct 1908.
Adam, F. A. S. Parodies of Kipling. N & Q 14 Aug 1909.
Corfield, W. Parodies of Kipling. N & Q 11 Dec 1909.
Meany, E. A lost Kipling poem. Century Mag Jan 1909.
Pierpoint, R. Parodies of Kipling. N & Q 9 Oct 1909.
Swithin, St. Kipling and the swastika. N & Q 3 Sep 1910; 17 Sep 1910; 8 Oct 1910; 22 Oct 1910.
Thompson, J. W. The origin of Kipling's rhyme of the three captains. N & Q 8 Feb 1912.
Ferguson, J. De Lancey. A note on the Foreloper. Bookman (New York) Mar 1914.
Wainewright, J. B. Got haven. N & Q 16 May 1914.
Thacker, J. G. The seven seas. N & Q 26 June 1915.
Pierpoint, R. Stalky & co. N & Q 26 June 1920; 17 July 1920; 7 Aug 1920; 9 Oct 1920.
Waterhouse, F. A. The literary fortunes of Kipling. Yale Rev July 1921.
Ames, C. L. Kipling and the critics. Kipling Jnl Jan 1928.
Beresford, G. C. Schoolboy lyrics and juvenilia. Kipling Jnl Oct 1928.
Ferguson, J. De Lancey. The germ of the Joyous adventure. Kipling Jnl Apr 1928.
Bazley, B. Kipling among the critics. Kipling Jnl Apr 1930; July 1930; Oct 1930.
Chandler, L. H. Kipling's verse headings. Kipling Jnl 1930.
News and notes: sales of Kipling's poems. Kipling Jnl Dec 1933.
Maurois, A. Kipling and his works from a French point of view. Kipling Jnl June 1934.
News and notes: referring to Kipling's letter of 6 January 1934 'explaining' The sons of Martha. Kipling Jnl Mar 1934.
Williamson, H. S. Masonic references in the works of Rudyard Kipling. Kipling Jnl Sep 1934.
Williamson, H. S. A Masonic note: on the origin of the names Learoyd and Mulvaney. Kipling Jnl Oct 1938.
Martindell, E. W. Some uncollected Kipling writings. Kipling Jnl Oct 1939; Dec 1939; Apr 1940; July 1940.
Weygandt, A. M. Kipling's reading and its influence on his poetry. Philadelphia 1939.
Martindell, E. W. Some early critics of Kipling. Kipling Jnl Dec 1940; Apr 1941.
Milburn, C. H. The song of an outsider. Kipling Jnl July 1940.
The origins of Proofs of Holy Writ. Kipling Jnl Oct 1940.
Martindell, E. W. Kiplingiana: origins of the Rhyme of the three sealers and Hymn before action. Kipling Jnl July 1941.
Kipling's barrack-room language. Amer Speech Dec 1943.
McMunn, G. The original Gunga Din. Kipling Jnl July 1943.
Yeats, A. W. The autograph adjunct to a literary career. Kipling Jnl Dec 1952.
Concerning Danny Deever and a murder at Ranikhet, India in 1886. Kipling Jnl July 1954.
Green, R. L. The chronology of Stalky & co. Kipling Jnl Dec 1954.
Ames, C. L. Lalun, the Baragun. Kipling Jnl July 1955.
Carrington, C. E. Some conjectures about The light that failed. Kipling Jnl Mar 1958.
Green, R. L. Two notes on The jungle book. Kipling Jnl Dec 1958.
Harbord, R. E. The reader's guide to Rudyard Kipling's work. 8 vols 1961–72.
Cornell, L. L. The authenticity of Rudyard Kipling's Uncollected Newspaper Writings: 1882–88. ELT 8 1965.
Corrit, J. Just so and jungle stories: a note on origins. Kipling Jnl Mar 1969.
Shippey, T. Borrowing and independence in Kipling's story of Muhammed Din. MLR 67 1972.
Lyman, P. Notes on American notes. Kipling Jnl 1982.
Orel, H. Rudyard Kipling and the establishment: a humanistic dilemma. South Atlantic Quart 81 1982.
Burt, J. The Kipling papers at Sussex. Kipling Jnl Mar 1983.
Danny Deever's death – and Dinapore. Kipling Jnl Dec 1983.
Stewart, D. H. Aspects of language in Kim. Kipling Jnl June 1983.
Karim, E. Kipling's uncollected poem New year's resolutions. VP 23 Summer 1985.
Parry, A. Reading formations in the Victorian periodical press: the reception of Kipling 1888–1891. Lit and History Autumn 1985.
Hunter, A. Kipling to Clifford: a rediscovered correspondence. N & Q 231 June 1986.
Pinney, T. Kipling in the libraries. ELT 29 1986.
Pinney, T. Unrecorded Kipling. Kipling Jnl Dec 1986.
Fedorowich, K. That look: an unpublished story by Rudyard Kipling. Kipling Jnl June 1988.
Unfinished verses. Kipling Jnl Sep 1988.
Leenerts, C. Kipling's fumes of the heart: an introduction to The eyes of Asia. Literary Criterion (Mysore) 6 1990.

Criticism up to 1920

Lang, A. [Three reviews 1886–9]; rptd Kipling Jnl 32 1965.
Barrie, J. M. The man from nowhere. The British Weekly (London) 2 May 1890.
Henley, W. E. The new writer. Scots Observer 3 May 1890.
Wilde, O. The function and value of criticism. The Nineteenth Cent July, Sep 1890; rptd and expanded in Intentions, 1891.
Adams, F. W. L. Rudyard Kipling. Fortnightly Rev Nov 1891; rptd in Essays in modernity, 1899.
Barrie, J. M. Mr Kipling's stories. Contemporary Rev Mar 1891.
Gosse, E. W. Rudyard Kipling. Century Mag Oct 1891; rptd in his Questions at issue, 1893.
James, H. [Introduction.] In Mine own people, New York 1891; rptd in his Views and reviews, 1908, and in E. L. Gilbert (ed), Kipling and the Critics, 1965.
Lang, A. Mr Kipling's stories. In his Essays in little, 1891; rptd in Gilbert, *below*, 1965.
Lynd, R. The works of Kipling. Bookman (London) Oct 1891.
Cope, G. The books of Kipling. GM Aug 1892.
Gosse, E. W. Wolcott Balestier. Century Mag Apr 1892; rptd in his Portraits and sketches, 1912.
Meynell, A. The soldier's poet. Merry England Apr 1893.
Crockett, S. R. On some tales of Mr Kipling's. Bookman (London) Feb 1895.
Robinson, E. K. Kipling in India. McClure's Mag 7 1896.
Howells, W. D. The laureate of the larger England. McClure's Mag 8 1897.
Murray, D. C. In his My contemporaries in fiction, 1897.
Norton, C. E. The poetry of Rudyard Kipling. Atlantic Monthly Jan 1897.
Forster's notebook of Kipling. Birmingham 1898.
Graz, F. Beiträge zu einer Kritik Kiplings. Leipzig 1898.
Gwynn, S. The madness of Mr Kipling. Macmillan's Mag Dec 1898.
Millar, J. H. The works of Mr Kipling. Blackwood's Mag Oct 1898.
Adams, F. W. L. In his Essays in modernity, 1899.
Buchanan, R. The voice of the hooligan. Contemporary Rev Dec 1899.
Clemens, W. M. A ken of Kipling. New York 1899.
Kinnosuké, A. A Japanese view of Kipling. Arena 21 1899.
Laneir, H. W. Mr Kipling's cynical jingoism. Dial June 1899.
Lawton, W. C. Kipling the artist. New York 1899.
Livingston, L. S. Kipling's first book. New York 1899.

Mansfield, M. F. and A. Wessels. Kiplingiana. New York 1899.
'Monkshood, G. F.' (W. J. Clarke). Kipling: an attempt at appreciation. 1899, 1913 (rev as Kipling: his life and work).
Norton, C. E. Kipling: a biographical sketch. New York 1899.
Parker, W. B. The religion of Mr Kipling. New York 1899.
Roberton, W. The Kipling guide book. Birmingham 1899.
Robinson, E. K. Rudyard Kipling as journalist. Literature 4 1899.
Teneung, G. F. An apocalypse of Kipling. Independent 30 Mar 1899.
Walker, A. H. Mr Kipling's schoolmasters and schoolboys. Bookman (London) June 1899.
Knowles, F. L. A Kipling primer. Boston 1899.
Johnston, C. Rudyard Kipling. Calcutta Rev 109 1899.
Besant, W. Is it the voice of the hooligan? Contemporary Rev Jan 1900.
Dawborn, R. H. M. Opium in India: a medical interview with Kipling. Therapeutic Gazette (Detroit) 15 Nov 1900.
Le Gallienne, R. Kipling: a criticism. 1900.
Le Gallienne, R. et al. Around the world with Kipling. 1926.
de Vogüé, E. M. La littérature impérialiste: Disraeli et Kipling. Revue des Deux Mondes 1 May 1901.
Dowden, E. The poetry of Mr Kipling. New Liberal Rev Feb 1901.
Russell, C. E. Are there two Kiplings? Cosmopolitan (New York) 31 1901.
Archer, W. In his Poets of the younger generation, 1902.
Beerbohm, M. Kipling's entire. Saturday Rev 14 Feb 1903; rptd in his Around theatres, 1953.
Gwynn, S. Mr Kipling as poet and prophet. Pilot 8 1903.
Powell, F. Y. Rudyard Kipling [with bibliography]. Eng Illus Mag 30 1903.
Freeman, L. R. The inimitable cruelty of Kipling. Overland Monthly (San Francisco) Apr 1904.
Lynd, R. Traffics and mafficks: the strange case of Mr Kipling. Bookman Nov 1904.
Chesterton, G. K. In his Heretics, 1905.
Dalrymple, C. M. Kiplings Prosa. Marburg 1905.
Stoddard, C. W. Kipling at Naulahka. Nat Mag 22 1905.
Marcosson, I. F. Rudyard Kipling. Book News Monthly Dec 1906.
Millard, F. B. How Kipling discovered America. Bookman (New York) Jan 1908.
Bennett, A. Rudyard Kipling. The New Age 4 Nov 1909; rptd in Books and persons, 1917.
Leeb-Lundberg, W. Word-formation in Kipling. Lund 1909, Cambridge 1909.
London, J. 'These bones shall rise again'. In his Revolution and other essays, New York 1910.
Charles, C. Kipling: his life and works. 1911.
Hooker, W. B. The later works of Mr Kipling. North Amer Rev May 1911.
Young, W. A. A dictionary of the characters and scenes in the stories and poems of Kipling 1886–1911. 1911, 1921 (rev); rev J. H. McGrivring 1967 (as A Kipling dictionary).
Forbes, E. A. Across India with Kim. World's Work (Chicago) 24 1912.
Jackson, K. The eighteen-nineties. 1913, 1922 (rev).
Durand, R. A handbook to the poetry of Kipling. 1914.
Sarath-Roy, A. R. Kipling seen through Hindu eyes. North Amer Rev Feb 1914.
Falls, C. Kipling: a critical study. 1915.
Hopkins, R. T. Kipling: a character study: life, writings and literary landmarks. 1915, 1921 (rev).
Hopkins, R. T. Kipling: a literary appreciation. 1915.
Munson, A. Kipling's India. New York 1915.
Palmer, J. L. Rudyard Kipling. 1915.
Harris, F. Rudyard Kipling. Pearson's Mag 37 1917; rptd in his Contemporary portraits, New York 1919 (priv ptd).
Matthews, B. These many years. New York 1917.
'Monkshood, G. F.' The less familiar Kipling and Kiplingiana. 1917, 1922 (rev), 1936 (rev).
Gerould, K. F. The remarkable rightness of Kipling. Atlantic Monthly Jan 1918.
Hart, W. M. Kipling the story teller. Berkeley 1918.
Hutton, M. Kipling. McGill Univ Mag 17 1918; rptd in his Many minds, New York 1928.
Eliot, T. S. Kipling redivivus. Athenaeum 9 May 1919.
Hackett, F. The light that failed. New Republic 19 Apr 1919.
Sherwood, J. B. Kipling's women. Fine Arts Jnl (Chicago) 37 1919.
Chevrillon, A. La poésie de Kipling. Revue des Deux Mondes 15 Apr 1920; rptd in his Three studies in English literature, 1923.
Worster, W. J. A. Merlin's isle: a study of Kipling's England. [1921.]

Obituaries

Chicago Tribune 10 July 1926 (premature), rptd Kipling Jnl Sep 1933; Daily Telegraph 18 Jan 1936; The Manchester Guardian 18 Jan 1936; [Gwynne, H. A.] Morning Post 18 Jan 1936; The Times 18, 20, 21 Jan 1936; Sunday Times 19 Jan 1936; Daily Mail 20 Jan 1936; News Chron 20 Jan 1936; New Statesman and Nation 25 Jan 1936; TLS 25 Jan 1936; Unity (Chicago) 3 Feb 1936; New York Times Book Rev 9 Feb 1936; Kipling Jnl Mar 1936; Round Table Mar 1936; Mercure de France 15 Mar 1936; Commonwealth 23, 10 Apr 1936; Spectator 24 June 1936; Catholic World (New York) 109, Aug 1936.

Biographies

Norton, C. E. Kipling: a biographical sketch. New York 1899.
Palmer, J. L. Rudyard Kipling. 1915.
Hopkins, R. T. Kipling: a character study: life, writings and literary landmarks. 1915.
Carrington, C. Rudyard Kipling, his life and work. 1955, 3rd edn with revisions 1978.
Wilson, A. The strange ride of Rudyard Kipling. 1977.
Birkenhead, Lord. Rudyard Kipling. New York 1978.
Ricketts, H. The unforgiving minute: a life of Rudyard Kipling. 1999. [AP]

Andrew Lang 1844–1912

See col 2362.

Emily Lawless 1845–1913

See col 761.

'Vernon Lee' 1856–1935

See col 2369.

Richard Le Gallienne 1866–1947

§1

My lady's sonnets. [Liverpool] 1887 (priv ptd).
Volumes in folio. 1889. Poems.
George Meredith: some characteristics. 1890.
The student and the body-snatcher. [1890.] With R. K. Leather.
The book-bills of Narcissus: an account rendered. [Derby] 1891, 1895 (3rd edn, rev).
English poems. 1892.
A fellowship in song. [Rugby 1893.] With Alfred Hayes and Norman Gale.
The religion of a literary man. 1893.
Young lives. 1893.
Limited editions: a prose fancy; together with Confessio Amantis: a sonnet. 1893 (priv ptd).

Bits of old Chelsea. 1894. With Lionel Johnson.
Prose fancies. 2 ser 1894–6.
Robert Louis Stevenson and other poems. 1895.
The quest of the golden girl. 1896.
Retrospective reviews. 2 vols 1896.
If I were God. 1897.
Rubáiyát of Omar Khayyám: a paraphrase. 1897.
The romance of Zion Chapel. 1898.
The worshipper of the image. 1899.
Sleeping Beauty and other prose fancies. 1900.
The beautiful lie of Rome. 1900.
Rudyard Kipling. A criticism. 1900.
Travels in England. 1900.
The life romantic. 1901.
Perseus and Andromeda: the story retold. New York 1903.
Odes from the Divan of Hafiz freely rendered. 1903.
An old country house. 1903.
The burial of Romeo and Juliet. 1904.
How to get the best out of books. 1904.
Romances of old France. New York 1905.
Omar repentant. 1908. Poems.
Painted shadows. 1908.
Little dinners with the Sphinx and other prose fancies. 1909.
Attitudes and avowals, with some retrospective reviews. 1910.
New poems. 1910.
Orestes: a tragedy. New York 1910.
The loves of the poets. New York 1911.
October vagabonds. 1911.
The maker of rainbows, and other fairy-tales and fables. 1912.
The lonely dancer and other poems. 1914.
The highway to happiness. 1914.
Vanishing roads and other essays. 1915.
The silk-hat soldier and other poems. 1915.
Pieces of eight. 1918.
The junk man and other poems. New York 1920.
A jongleur strayed. New York 1922.
Old love stories retold. 1924.
The romantic nineties. 1926; ed H. M. Hyde 1952.
There was a ship. [New York] 1930.
Le Gallienne also edited Hazlitt's Liber Amoris, *1893, A. H. Hallam's* Poems, *1893, and Walton's* Compleat angler, *1896, and translated Wagner's* Tristan *into verse, 1909.*

§2

Archer, W. In his Poets of the younger generation, 1902.

Bertha Leith-Adams, Laffan, Bertha Jane de Courcy 1837–1912

Ms collections in NLS (Blackwood Papers).

§1

Nancy's work, a church story. 1876. Novel.
Winstowe. 1877. Novel.
Georgie's wooer. New York 1878.
Madelon Lemoin. 1879, 1885, Philadelphia 1879, 1887. Novel.
My land of Beulah. 1880, 1890, 1891, Philadelphia 1891, 1894. Short stories.
Aunt Hepsy's foundling. New York 1880, London 1881, [1884], Philadelphia 1887. Novel.
Cosmo Gordon. 1882. Novel.
Expiated and other stories. 1882.
Geoffrey Stirling. 1883, 1885, 1893, 1905, Philadelphia 1887, 1894. Novel.
Lady Deane. 1882. Short stories.
My brother Sol. 1883. Short stories.
A song of jubilee, and other poems. 1887, 1890. Poetry.
The great bank robbery. 1889.
Louis Draycott. 1889, 1890, 1893. Novel.
REVIEW: Athenaeum 11 Jan 1890.
Bonnie Kate: a story from a woman's point of view. 1891, 1894. Novel.
REVIEW: Athenaeum 25 July 1891.
A garrison romance. 1892, 1895. Novel.
REVIEW: Athenaeum 27 Feb 1892.
The Peyton romance. 1892, 1895. Novel.
The cruise of the Tomahawk; the story of a summer's holiday in prose and rhyme, by Mrs R. S. de Courcy Laffan, assisted by 'Stroke' and 'Bow'. 1892.
Colour-Sergeant No 1 Company. 2 vols 1894, 1897, 1903. Novel.
The old pastures: a story of the woods and fields. 1895. Novel.
The prince's feathers. 1899. Novel.
Accessory after the fact. 1899. Short stories.
Cruel calumny. 1901. Short stories.
The dream of her life. 1902. Short stories.
What Hector had to say. 1902. Short stories.
The Vicar of Dale End. 1902. Novel.
Their experiment. 1904. Plays and songs.
Poems. 1907.
Dreams made verity. 1910. Essays and stories.
The story of the brotherhood of hero dogs. 1910.
Short plays and a memory. 1912.

Contributions to periodicals

La Tarentule. A memory. Centennial June 1890.
A simple hero. Serialised in The Oakleaf (newsletter of the 22nd Cheshire Regiment), vol 1, Oct–Dec 1896.
Leith-Adams contributed to All the Year Round, *edited the* Kensington Mag, *and in 1900 pbd the famous song, 'Good-bye, Daddy'. She lectured, e.g. on fictional literature as a calling for women, at the Sesame Club (rptd in* Dreams made verity, *1910).*

§2

In Helen C. Black, Notable Women authors of the day. Glasgow 1893.
Blain, V., P. Clements and I. Grundy (ed). The feminist companion to literature in English. New Haven CT and London 1990.
Sutherland, J. The Longman companion to Victorian fiction. 1988.
[MT]

Mary Linskill, 'Stephen Yorke' 1840–91

Ms correspondence, publishers' agreements, registration certificate held at BL and NLS. Small section of diary (c. 1 year) held by Whitby Literary and Philosophical Soc.

§1

Tales of the North Riding by Stephen Yorke (Cornborough Vicarage, Theo's escape, Squire Hesildene's sorrow, Taught by adversity, Thorpe-Houe Farm). 2 vols 1871, 1893 (new edn 1 vol), 1902, 1904.
REVIEW: Athenaeum 3 June 1871.
Cleveden by Stephen Yorke. 2 vols 1875, 1892 (new edn 1 vol), 1900, 1909, 1980.
REVIEWS: Athenaeum 1 Jan 1876; Graphic 1 Jan 1876; Spectator 2 Dec 1876.
Carl Forrest's faith. 1883.
REVIEWS: Athenaeum 27 Oct 1883; Spectator 24 Nov 1883.
Between the heather and the northern sea. Serialised in Good Words 25 1884. 3 vols 1884, 1890 (new edn 1 vol), 1891, 1893, 1899, 1903.
REVIEWS: Acad 29 Nov 1884; Athenaeum 29 Nov 1884; Saturday Rev 3 Jan 1885; Graphic 17 Jan 1885.
The magic flute. 1884.
REVIEWS: Acad 18 Oct 1884; Athenaeum 8 Nov 1884; Spectator 8 Nov 1884.
A lost son, and The glover's daughter. 1885. A lost son serialised in

Leisure Hour 34 1885. The glover's daughter first pbd in Good Words Christmas suppl [Good Cheer] 1872.
REVIEWS: Acad 12 Sep 1885; Graphic 19 Sep 1885; Athenaeum 3 Oct 1885; Saturday Rev 10 Oct 1885.
Pictures from Whitby (essay). Good Words 26 1885.
A garland of seven lilies (novel). 1886, 1895 (new edn).
The haven under the hill. Serialised in Good Words 27 1886. 3 vols 1886, 1891 (new edn 1 vol), 1892, 1894, 1900.
REVIEWS: Acad 9 Oct 1886; Athenaeum 30 Oct 1886; Saturday Rev 20 Nov 1886; Spectator 29 Jan 1887; Graphic 26 Feb 1887.
In exchange for a soul. Serialised in Sunday Mag 16 1887. 3 vols 1887, 1888 (new edn 1 vol), New York 1889, new edn with memoir of author by John Hutton rptd from Good Words London 1892; 1894 (new edn with memoir), 1900, 1902 (new edn with memoir), 1909.
REVIEWS: Athenaeum 29 Oct 1887; Saturday Rev 5 Nov 1887; Acad 19 Nov 1887; Spectator 3 Dec 1887.
Hagar: a North Yorkshire pastoral. 1887; in Good Words Christmas suppl [Good Cheer] 1882.
REVIEWS: Athenaeum 10 Dec 1887; Spectator 24 Mar 1888.
Robert Holt's illusion, and other stories (Godwyn; Raith Wyke). 1888, 1898 (new edn). Robert Holt's Illusion first pbd Good Words Christmas suppl [Good Cheer] 1873, Littell's Living Age 120 1873. Godwyn first pbd Good Words Christmas suppl [Good Cheer] 1875. Raith Wyke first pbd Good Words Christmas suppl [Good Cheer] 1874.
REVIEWS: Saturday Rev 2 June 1888; Athenaeum 9 June 1888; Graphic 18 Aug 1888; Spectator 13 Oct 1888.
Vignettes of a northern village (George Gatonby's return to Hild's Haven; Antholin Vereker; Ladies of Leventhorpe). Series in Good Words 29 1888. George Gatonby first pbd Littell's Living Age 177 1887.
For pity's sake, and The lost leader (tales). 1 vol 1892. For pity's sake first pbd in Littell's Living Age 129/130 1875. The lost leader pbd in Good Words Christmas suppl [Good Cheer] 1878.

§2

Quinlan, David, and Arthur Frederick Humble. Mary Linskill: the Whitby novelist. Whitby 1969.
Stamp, C. S. Mary Linskill. Whitby 1980. [BG]

H. D. Lowry, Henry Dawson Lowry 1869–1906

Mss located in Berg Collection, NYPL. See also LR.

Bibliographies

Symons, A. J. H. D. Lowry, 1869–1906. (Memoir and bibliography.) 1925 (priv ptd).
In Nineteenth-century fiction: a bibliographical catalogue based on the collection formed by Robert Lee Wolff, 5 vols New York 1981–6.

Collections and selections

A dream of daffodils. Last poems arranged for the press by G. E. Matheson and C. A. Dawson Scott 1912 (memoir by E. A. Preston).
REVIEWS: TLS 24 Oct 1912; Athenaeum 16 Nov 1912.
Beauty's lover. In Short stories of the 'nineties, ed D. Stanford. 1968.

§1

Prisoners of the earth, and other stories. New York 1893.
Wreckers and methodists, and other stories. 1893.
REVIEWS: Nat Observer 14 Oct 1893; Acad 18 Nov 1893.
Women's tragedies. 1895 (Keynote series), Boston 1895.
Make believe. 1896 (illustr C. Robinson).
REVIEW: Acad 26 Dec 1896.
A man of moods. 1896.
The happy exile. 1898 (etchings by E. P. Pimlett). Sketches.
REVIEW: Acad 6 Nov 1898.
The valley of the shadow. Extract from 'The Morning Post', Wednesday, 7th March, 1900. [1900.]
The first to die. In Strange happenings: being stories by W. C. Russell, W. E. Norris, Grant Allen, et al, 1901.
The hundred windows. 1904. Poems.

Contributions to periodicals and collaborative works

Lowry became editor of the Ludgate Mag *in 1897 and also joined the* Morning Post. *He contributed to the* English Illus Mag *and* Sylvia's Jnl *among others. In 1895 he joined the* Pall Mall Gazette *and later* Black and White.
Pall Mall Gazette. The great Ko-Ko, 12 Jan 1884.
Cornish Mag. Aug 1898–Apr 1899.
Chambers's Jnl. 28 Jan 1893–1901.
Nat Observer. 15 Aug 1893–3 Mar 1894.
Strand Mag. Feb 1895–Oct 1895.
Ludgate Mag. The pen that remembered, Dec 1897.
Sunday Mag. Nov 1897–Dec 1901.
The Idler. The collector's tragedy, June 1899.
Pall Mall Mag. Alone, Nov 1900; Song of the road, Sep 1901. Poems.
Acad. Luck in artistic work, 12 Jan 1901.
New Liberal. June–Dec 1902.
Good Words. Making a story, May 1903.
Bookman. Rev of C. Marriott's Genevra. Oct 1904.
Wheal darkness. [1927.] With C. A. D. Scott.
REVIEW: TLS 10 Nov 1927.
For contributions to London Quart Rev, National Rev, New Rev *and* Temple Bar, *see* Wellesley *vol 5* 1989.

§2

Henderson, T. F. In DNB 1901–11.
Morning Post 23 Oct 1906. Obituary.
A dream of daffodils. Last poems arranged for the press by G. E. Matheson and C. A. Dawson Scott 1912 (memoir by E. A. Preston).
Symons, A. J. H. D. Lowry, 1869–1906. (Memoir and bibliography.) 1925 (priv ptd).
From four who are dead. Messages to C. A. D. Scott (Lowry's cousin). 1926 (introd by M. Sinclair).
Sutherland, J. In The Longman companion to Victorian fiction, 1988. [DA]

'Lucas Malet', Mary St Leger Kingsley, later Harrison 1852–1931

§1

Mrs Lorimer: a sketch in black and white. 2 vols 1882.
Colonel Enderby's wife: a novel. 3 vols 1885, 1 vol 1885.
A counsel of perfection. 1888.
Little Peter: a Christmas morality for children of any age. 1888.
The wages of sin: a novel. 3 vols 1891.
The Carissima: a modern grotesque. 1896.
The gateless barrier. 1900.
The history of Sir Richard Calmady: a romance. 2 vols 1901, 1 vol 1901.
The far horizon. 1906.
The score. 1909.
The wreck of the golden galleon. 1910.
Adrian Savage: a novel. 1911.
The tutor's story: an unpublished novel by the late Charles Kingsley, revised and completed by his daughter Lucas Malet. 1916, 1920.
Damaris: a novel. 1916.
Deadham Hard: a romance. 1919.
The tall villa: a novel. 1920.
Da Silva's widow and other stories. [1922.]
The survivors: a novel. 1923.
The dogs of want: a modern comedy of errors. [1924.]
The private life of Mr Justice Syme: a novel. [1932.] Left unfinished at her death and completed by Gabrielle Vallings.

§2

Archer, W. In his Real conversations, 1904.

Courtney, W. L. In his Feminine note in fiction, 1904.

'Edna Lyall', Ada Ellen Bayly 1857–1903

§1

Won by waiting: a story of home life in France and England. 1879, 1886 (rev).

Donovan: a novel. 3 vols 1882.

We two: a novel. 3 vols 1884.

In the golden days: a novel. 3 vols 1885.

Autobiography of a slander. 1887.

Knight-errant: a novel. 3 vols 1887.

Their happiest Christmas. 1889.

Derrick Vaughan, novelist. 1889.

A hardy Norseman: a novel. 3 vols 1890.

Max Hereford's dream: a tale. 1891.

To right the wrong. 3 vols 1894.

Doreen: the story of a singer. 1894.

How the children raised the wind: a tale. 1896.

The autobiography of a truth. 1896.

Mrs Gaskell. In A. Sergeant et al, Women novelists of Queen Victoria's reign, 1897.

Wayfaring men: a novel. 1897.

Hope the hermit: a novel. 1898.

In spite of all: a novel. 1901.

The Burges letters: a record of child life in the Sixties. 1902. Autobiography.

The hinderers: a story of the present time. 1902.

§2

Payne, G. A. Edna Lyall: an appreciation, with biographical and critical notes. [1903.]

William Sharp, 'Fiona Macleod' 1855–1905

Collections

Works of 'Fiona Macleod': Uniform edition. Arranged by Mrs William Sharp, 7 vols London and New York 1910.

Selected writings of William Sharp. Arranged by Mrs William Sharp, 5 vols London and New York 1912.

§1

Writings published under the name William Sharp

The human inheritance, the new hope, motherhood. 1882.

Dante Gabriel Rossetti: a record and a study. 1882.

Earth's voices, transcripts from nature, sospitra, and other poems. 1884.

Jack Noel's legacy: a story for boys. Young Folks' Paper 1886. A serial.

The sonnets of this century. Ed and arranged, with a critical introd on the sonnet, by William Sharp 1886. Rptd several times. After 1900, title changed to Sonnets of the nineteenth century.

Life of Percy Bysshe Shelley. 1887.

Under the banner of St James: a romance of the discovery of the Pacific. Young Folks' Paper 1887. A serial.

Life of Heinrich Heine. London and New York 1888.

Romantic ballads and poems of phantasy. 1888 (Second printing in 1889 contains 1 new poem and rev preface).

The secret of the seven fountains: a story for boys. Young Folks' Paper 1888. A serial.

The sport of chance: a novel. 3 vols 1888. First pbd in People's Friend (Dundee) 1887 as A deathless hate.

Children of tomorrow: a romance. 1889, New York 1890.

Life of Robert Browning. 1890.

Sospiri di Roma. Rome 1891.

A fellowe and his wife. London and New York 1892. With B. W. Howard.

Flower o' the vine: romantic ballads and sospiri di Roma. New York 1892.

The life and letters of Joseph Severn. London and New York 1892.

The Pagan Review. Ed W. H. Brooks. No 1 (all pbd) Aug 1892. Ed and written entirely by Sharp under various pseuds.

The red rider: a romance of the Garibaldian campaign in the two Sicilies. Weekly Budget 1892. A serial.

The last of the Vikings, being the adventures in the East and West of Sigurd, the Boy King of Norway. Old and Young 1893. A serial.

Fair women in painting and poetry. 1894.

Vistas. Derby and Chicago 1894.

The gipsy Christ and other tales. Chicago 1895. Pbd as Madge o' the Pool, the gipsy Christ and other tales, 1897.

Ecce puella and other prose imaginings. 1896.

Wives in exile: a comedy in romance. Boston 1896. Pbd London 1898.

Silence farm: a novel. 1899.

Progress of art in the XIX century. London and Edinburgh, Philadelphia and Toronto 1902.

Literary geography. 1904.

Writings published under the pseud 'Fiona Macleod'

Pharais: a romance of the isles. Derby 1894, Chicago 1895.

The mountain lovers. London and Boston 1895.

The sin-eater and other tales. Edinburgh and Chicago 1895.

The washer of the ford and other legendary moralities. Edinburgh [May] and Chicago [June] 1896.

Green fire: a romance. London [Nov] and New York 1896.

From the hills of dream: mountain songs and island runes. Edinburgh [Dec] 1896. Rev and pbd as From the hills of dream: threnodies, songs and other poems, Portland ME 1901, 1904. Rev and pbd as From the hills of dream: threnodies and songs and later poems, 1907.

The shorter stories of Fiona Macleod, rearranged with additional tales. 3 vols Edinburgh [Mar 1897].

The laughter of Peterkin: a retelling of old tales of the Celtic wonderland. [Oct] 1897.

The dominion of dreams. London and New York 1899.

The divine adventure: Iona: by sundown shores: studies in spiritual history. 1900.

Celtic: an essay. Contemporary Rev May 1900. Rev and pbd separately as Celtic: a study in spiritual history, Portland ME 1901.

The house of Usna: a drama. Nat Rev July 1900. Pbd separately Portland ME 1903.

The immortal hour. Fortnightly Rev 68, Nov 1900. Pbd separately as The immortal hour: a drama in two acts, Portland ME 1907, Edinburgh and London 1908.

The winged destiny: studies in the spiritual history of the Gael. 1904.

Where the forest murmurs: nature essays. London and New York 1906.

A little book of nature thoughts, selected from the writings of 'Fiona Macleod' by Mrs William Sharp with a foreword by Roselle Lathrop Shields. Portland ME 1908. Pbd as A little book of nature, Edinburgh and London 1909.

Songs and poems, old and new. 1909.

At the turn of the year: essays and nature thoughts. Illustr H. C. Preston Macgown, London and Edinburgh 1913.

The hills of ruel, and other stories. Illustr Margery H. Lawrence, New York 1921.

From May 1879 to Dec 1905 Sharp contributed articles, sketches and poems to Fortnightly Rev, Nineteenth Cent, Examiner, Chambers's Jnl, Good Words, Athenaeum, Acad, Portfolio, Art Jnl, Nat Rev, Atlantic Monthly, Literature, Harper's Mag, Quart Rev, Pall Mall Mag, Evergreen, Savoy, Dome, Eng Illus Mag, Contemporary Rev,

Country Life *and* North Amer Rev, *both under his own name and (1895–1905) as 'Fiona Macleod'. He also edited several volumes in the Canterbury Poets ser and several anthologies.*

§2

Rhys, E. The new mysticism. Fortnightly Rev June 1900.
Noble, J. A. William Sharp. In Poets and poetry of the century, ed A. H. Miles, 1903, vol 8.
Tynan, K. William Sharp and 'Fiona Macleod'. Fortnightly Rev Mar 1906.
Gilman, L. The art of Fiona Macleod. North Amer Rev 5 Oct 1906.
Janvier, C. A. Fiona Macleod and her creator William Sharp. North Amer Rev 5 Apr 1907.
Rhys, E. William Sharp and 'Fiona Macleod'. Century Mag May 1907.
Sharp, E. A. William Sharp (Fiona Macleod); a memoir compiled by his wife. 1910; 2 vols 1912 (with a bibliography of Sharp's writings).
Le Gallienne, R. The mystery of Fiona Macleod. Forum Feb 1911.
Kelman, J. Celtic revivals of paganism. In his Among famous books, 1912.
More, P. E. Fiona Macleod. In his The drift of romanticism, Boston 1913.
Parker, W. M. Dreamer and critic: William Sharp (Fiona Macleod). In his Modern Scottish writers, Edinburgh 1917.
Evans, B. I. William Sharp. In English poetry in the later nineteenth century. 1933.
Waugh, A. Fiona Macleod: a forgotten mystery. Spectator 14 Aug 1936.
Iorio, J. J. A Victorian controversy: William Sharp's letters on motherhood. Colby Literary Quart 4 1957.
Garbaty, T. J. Fiona Macleod: defence of views and her identity. N & Q 205, Dec 1960.
Halloran, W. F. W. B. Yeats and William Sharp: the archer vision. ELN 6 1969.
Alaya, F. William Sharp – 'Fiona Macleod': 1855–1905. Cambridge MA 1970.
Halloran, W. F. William Sharp as bard and craftsman. VP 10 1972.
Murray, I. Children of tomorrow: a Sharp inspiration for Dorian Gray. Durham Univ Jnl 80 1987.
Meyers, T. L. The sexual tensions of William Sharp: a study of the birth of Fiona Macleod, incorporating two lost works, Ariadne in Naxos and 'Beatrice'. New York 1996.
Halloran, W. F. W. B. Yeats, William Sharp, and Fiona Macleod: a Celtic drama: 1887 to 1897. Yeats Annual No 13 1998. [WFH]

William Hurrell Mallock 1849–1923

Bibliographies

Nickerson, C. C. A bibliography of the novels of Mallock. Eng Fiction in Transition 6 1963.

§1

Poems. 1867 (priv ptd).
The parting of the ways: a poetic epistle. 1867.
Newdigate Prize poem: The Isthmus of Suez. Oxford 1871.
Every man his own poet: or the inspired singer's recipe book. Oxford 1872. Anon.
The new republic: or culture, faith, and philosophy in an English country house. 2 vols 1877; ed J. M. Patrick, Gainesville FL 1950. Novel.
Lucretius. Edinburgh 1878.
The new Paul and Virginia: or Positivism on an island. 1878.
Is life worth living? 1879.
Poems. 1880.
A romance of the nineteenth century. 2 vols 1881.
Social equality: a short study in a missing science. 1882.
Atheism and the value of life: five studies in contemporary literature. 1884.
Property and progress: or a brief enquiry into contemporary social agitation in England. 1884. A reply to H. George, Progress and poverty.
The landlords and the national income: a chart showing the proportion borne by the rental of the landlords to the gross income of the people. 1884.
The old order changes: a novel. 3 vols 1886.
In an enchanted island: or a winter's retreat in Cyprus. 1889.
A human document: a novel. 3 vols 1892.
Labour and the popular welfare. 1893, 1894 (with Appendix).
Verses. 1893. Partly rptd from the 1880 collection, *above*.
The heart of life. 3 vols 1895.
Studies of contemporary superstition. 1895.
Classes and masses, or wealth, wages and welfare in the United Kingdom: a handbook of social facts for political thinkers and speakers. 1896.
Aristocracy and evolution: a study of the rights, the origin and the social functions of the wealthier classes. 1898.
The individualist. 1899. Novel.
Doctrine and doctrinal disruption: being an examination of the intellectual position of the Church of England. 1900.
Lucretius on life and death. 1900. A very free adaptation of Lucretius in the metre of FitzGerald, Omar Khayyám.
The fiscal dispute made easy: or a key to the principles involved in the opposite policies. 1903.
Religion as a credible doctrine: a study of the fundamental difficulty. 1903.
The veil of the temple: or from night to twilight. 1904.
The reconstruction of belief. 1905.
A critical examination of Socialism. New York and London 1907, London 1908.
An immortal soul. 1908. Novel.
The nation as a business firm: an attempt to cut a path through jungle. 1910.
Social reform as related to realities and delusions: an examination of the increase and distribution of wealth from 1801 to 1910. 1914.
The limits of pure democracy. 1918, 1924 (abridged as Democracy, with an introd by the Duke of Northumberland).
Capital, war and wages: three questions in outline. 1918.
Memoirs of life and literature. 1920.

§2

Shaw, G. B. Socialism and superior brains: a reply to Mr Mallock. 1909.
Nickerson, C. C. Mallock's contributions to the Miscellany. VS 6 1962.

Augusta Marryat 1834–98

Bibliographies

Kirk, J. F. Suppl to Allibone's Critical dictionary of English literature. Philadelphia 1891.
Wolff, R. L. Nineteenth-century fiction. New York and London 1984.

§1

Lost in the jungle: a story of the Indian Mutiny. With illustrations by D. H. Friston. '1877' [1876].
Left to themselves: a boy's adventures in Australia. With original illustrations. [1878.] Reissued as Young Lamberts: a boy's adventures in Australia, 1891.
The reverse of the shield, or the adventures of Grenville Le Merchant during the Franco-Prussian war. With illustrations and map. [1879.]
The snow maiden. With tales by others in The penny library of Catholic tales, no XI, [1890.]

Contributions to periodicals

The major's diplomacy (short story). Belgravia vol 91, Dec 1896.

Collaborative works

Illustr E. M. Norris The children's pic-nic. '1868' [1867].

Introd by E. M. Norris. Paul Howard's captivity, and why he escaped. 1876, New York 1876. [DH]

Emilia Marryat, later Norris 1835–75

Bibliographies

Allibone, S. A. Critical dictionary of English literature. Philadelphia 1870.

Kirk, R. F. Suppl to Allibone's Critical dictionary of English Literature. Philadelphia 1891.

Wolff, R. L. Nineteenth-century fiction. New York and London 1984.

§1

Temper: a tale. 3 vols 1854, 1 vol New York 1859.

Henry Lyle, or life and existence. 2 vols 1856, 1 vol New York [nd].

Long evenings, or stories for my little friends. Illustr J. Absolon '1861' [1860], [1878].

Every-day. 5 essays on human behaviour. 1862.

Harry at school: a story for boys. Illustr J. Absolon 1862 [1861], New York 1884.

A week by themselves. Illustr C. A. Edwards '1865' [1864].

What became of Tommy. Illustr J. Absolon '1866' [1865], New York 1865.

The early start in life. Illustr J. Lawson 1867.

The children's pic-nic, and what came of it. Illustr A. Marryat '1868' [1867], New York [nd].

Gerald and Harry, or the boys in the north. Illustr J. B. Zwecker '1868' [1867].

The stolen cherries, or tell the truth at once. Illustr F. A. Fraser '1869' [1868], [1881].

Theodora: a tale for girls. Illustr G. Hay 1870, New York [1883].

Adrift on the sea, or the children's escape. With illustrations. '1871' [1870].

Alda Graham, and her brother Philip. Illustr G. Hay '1872' [1871], New York 1883.

Geoffry's great fault. Illustr D. H. Friston. 1873, New York [nd].

Snowed up, or the hut in the forest. Illustr D. H. Friston 1874.

Amongst the Maoris: a book of adventure. With illustrations. [1874], New York c. 1877.

The sea-side home and the smugglers' cave. Illustr E. N. Downard 1875.

Paul Howard's captivity and why he escaped: founded on fact. Illustr E. N. Downard, introd by A. Marryat 1876, New York 1876.

Contributions to periodicals

Captain Marryat at Langham. Cornhill Mag 16, Aug 1867.

§2

Boase, F. Modern English biography, suppl. 1921. [DH]

Florence Marryat, later Mrs Ross Church, later Mrs Francis Lean 1838–99

Bibliographies

Kirk, J. F. Suppl to Allibone's Critical dictionary of English literature. Philadelphia 1891.

Sadleir, M. XIX century fiction. 1951.

Wolff, R. L. Nineteenth-century fiction. New York and London 1984.

§1

Love's conflict. 3 vols 1865, 2 vols Leipzig 1865, 1 vol London 1869, New York 1880.

Too good for him. 3 vols 1865, 1 vol 1868, Boston 1869.

Woman against woman. 3 vols 1865, 1 vol Boston 1866, London 1869 etc.

For ever and ever: a drama of life. 3 vols 1866, 2 vols Leipzig 1866, 1 vol Boston 1867, 1 vol London 1869 etc.

The girls of Feversham. 1 vol New York 1866 etc, 2 vols London 1869, 1 vol Boston 1869, New York 1877 etc.

The confessions of Gerald Estcourt. 3 vols 1867, 2 vols Leipzig 1867, 1 vol Boston 1867, 1 vol London 1869 etc. Retitled Gerald Estcourt: his confessions, 1908.

'Gup': sketches of Anglo-Indian life and character. 1868. Rptd from Temple Bar.

Nelly Brooke: a homely story. 3 vols 1868, 1 vol Boston 1868, 2 vols Leipzig 1869, 1 vol London 1869 etc.

Véronique: a romance. 3 vols 1869, 2 vols Leipzig 1869, 1 vol Boston 186?.

A star and a heart. Boston 186? etc, Leipzig 1876 (with An utter impossibility), New York 1880 etc.

Petronel: a novel. 3 vols 1870, 1 vol Boston 1870, 2 vols in 1 Leipzig 1870, 1 vol New York 1877 etc.

Captain Norton's diary, and other stories. Philadelphia 1870, New York 1887.

The poison of asps: a novelette. New York 1871 etc, Leipzig 1876 (with other stories).

Her lord and master: a tale. 3 vols 1871, 2 vols Leipzig 1872, 1 vol New York 1871 etc, 1 vol London 189?.

The prey of the gods: a novel. 3 vols 1871, 1 vol Boston 1871, New York 1871 etc, 1 vol London 1872, Leipzig 1872.

Life and letters of Captain Marryat. 2 vols 1872, 1 vol Leipzig 1872, 2 vols New York 1872.
REVIEW: Athenaeum 12 Oct 1872; Saturday Rev 19 Oct 1872; Spectator 2 Nov 1872.

Mad Dumaresque: a novel. 3 vols 1873, 2 vols Leipzig 1873, 1 vol New York 1887, 1 vol London 1904.

Sybil's friend, and how she found him. New York 1873, 1874.

'No intentions': a novel. 3 vols 1874, 2 vols Leipzig 1874, 1 vol New York 1878 etc.

Fighting the air: a novel. 3 vols 1875, 2 vols Leipzig 1875, 1 vol New York 1887.

Open! sesame! 3 vols 1875, 1 vol Chicago 1875, London 1876, Boston 1878, Hamburg 1880, New York 1887.

Hidden chains. 3 vols 1876. Tales rptd from Temple Bar etc.

'My own child': a novel. 3 vols 1876, 2 vols Leipzig 1876, 1 vol New York 1876 etc.

A lucky disappointment, and other stories. Boston 1876 etc, Leipzig 1876, New York 1878 etc.

Four irrepressibles, or the tribe of Benjamin; their summer with Aunt Agnes, what they did, and what they undid. Boston c. 1877.

Her father's name: a novel. 3 vols 1876, 2 vols Leipzig 1877, 1 vol 1878, New York 1886 etc.

A harvest of wild oats: a novel. 3 vols 1877, 2 vols Leipzig 1877, 1 vol New York 1877 etc, London 188?.

A little stepson: a tale. 2 vols 1878, 1 vol Leipzig 1878, New York 1881 etc. Retitled Scrappie, or a little stepson, 1888.

Written in fire: a novel. 3 vols 1878, 2 vols Leipzig 1878, 1 vol New York 1878 etc; tr Polish 1886.

Ange. A novel. New York 1879 etc.

A broken blossom: a novel. 3 vols 1879, 2 vols in 1 Leipzig 1879, 1 vol New York 1879 etc.

Her world against a lie: a romance. 3 vols '1879' [1878], 2 vols Leipzig 1879, 1 vol New York 1887 etc.

The root of all evil. 3 vols '1880' [1879], 1 vol New York 1880 etc, 2 vols Leipzig 1880, 1 vol London 1894 etc.

The fair-haired Alda: a novel. 3 vols 1880, 3 vols Leipzig 1880, 1 vol New York 1880 etc.

With Cupid's eyes: a novel. 3 vols 1881, 2 vols Leipzig 1881, 1 vol New York 1881 etc.

My sister the actress: a novel. 3 vols 1881, 1 vol 1881 etc, New York 1881 etc.
How they loved him: a novel. 3 vols 1882, 1 vol New York 1889; tr Swed 1881?.
Phyllida, a life drama. 3 vols 1882, 2 vols Leipzig 1882, 1 vol New York 1882 etc, 1 vol 1883.
A moment of madness, and other stories. 3 vols 1883, 1 vol Leipzig 1883, New York 1884. Rptd from Temple Bar.
Peeress and player: a novel. 3 vols 1883, 1 vol New York 1884 etc, 1 vol London 1900? etc.
Facing the footlights: a novel. 3 vols 1883, 1 vol New York 1883 etc, 2 vols in 1 Leipzig 1884, 1 vol 1914.
The ghost of Charlotte Cray, and other stories. Leipzig 1883, New York 1884.
Old contrairy, and other stories. New York 1884.
Under the lilies and roses: a novel. 3 vols 1884, 2 vols Leipzig 1884, 1 vol New York 1884 etc, 1886 etc.
The heart of Jane Warner: a novel. 3 vols '1885' [1884], 2 vols Leipzig 1885, 1 vol New York 1885 etc; tr Ger 1886.
The heir presumptive: a love story. 3 vols 1885, 2 vols Leipzig 1886, 1 vol New York 1886 etc.
Spiders of society: a novel. 3 vols 1886, 2 vols Leipzig 1887.
The master passion: a novel. 3 vols 1886, 2 vols Leipzig 1886, 1 vol New York 1886 etc.
Tom Tiddler's ground. Account of a visit to North America. 1886.
REVIEW: [R. Brown] Acad 16 Oct 1886.
Miss Harrington's husband: a novel. New York 1886, 1891; tr Polish 1887.
A daughter of the tropics: a novel. 3 vols 1887, 2 vols Leipzig 1888.
Driven to bay: a novel. 3 vols 1887, 2 vols Leipzig 1887, 1 vol New York 1887 etc.
Why not? New York 1887.
Gentleman and courtier: a romance. 3 vols 1888, 1 vol New York 1888; tr Polish 1888.
On circumstantial evidence. 3 vols 1889, 1 vol New York 1889.
Mount Eden: a romance. 3 vols 1889, 1 vol New York 1889 etc.
The nobler sex. 1 vol New York 188? etc, 3 vols London 1892.
Blindfold: a novel. 3 vols 1890, 2 vols Leipzig 1890, 1 vol New York 1890.
Brave heart and true: a novel. 3 vols 1890, 1 vol New York 1890, 2 vols Leipzig 1891.
A scarlet sin. 2 vols 1890, 1 vol New York 1890, Leipzig 1891; tr Polish 1909.
A fatal silence. 3 vols 1891, 1 vol New York 1891, 2 vols Leipzig 1892, 1 vol London 1892 etc.
The risen dead: a novel. 2 vols 1891, 1 vol New York 1891, Leipzig 1891, 1 vol London 1893.
There is no death. On spiritualism. 1891 etc, New York 1891 etc, Leipzig 1892, Philadelphia 1917 etc; tr Greek 1929.
REVIEW: Athenaeum 12 Sep 1891.
Women of the future (1891), or what shall we do with our men? (Lecture c. 1891, apparently unpbd.)
The little marine and the Japanese lily, or the land of the rising sun. A book for boys. 1891 etc, New York 1892.
How like a woman! A novel. 3 vols 1892, 1 vol New York 1892 etc, 1 vol London 1893 etc.
Parson Jones: a novel. 3 vols 1893, 1 vol New York 1893, 1 vol London 1895 etc.
A bankrupt heart. 3 vols 1894, 1 vol New York 1894.
The beautiful soul. 1894 etc, New York 1895.
The Hampstead mystery: a novel. 3 vols '1894' [1893].
The dead man's message: an occult romance. New York 1894.
The spirit world. 1894 etc, New York 1894, Leipzig 1894.
At heart a rake. 1895, New York 1895, 2 vols Leipzig 1895.
The dream that stayed. 1896, 2 vols Leipzig 1897.
The strange transfiguration of Hannah Stubbs. 1896, Leipzig 1896.
In the name of liberty. 1897, Chicago and New York 1898.
The blood of the vampire. 1897, 2 vols Leipzig 1897.
A passing madness. 1897, Leipzig 1897.
An angel of pity. 1898.
A soul on fire. 1898, Leipzig 1898.
Why did she love him? 1898.
A rational marriage. 1899, New York 1899.
The folly of Alison. 1899.
Iris the avenger. 1899, Leipzig 1899.
A blighted name. 1901.
The luckiest girl in Yorkshire and other stories. 1907.
Saint and sinner. [1914.]
Besides novels, Florence Marryat wrote 'an enormous quantity of journalistic work, about one hundred short stories, and numerous essays, poems, and recitations' (Black, Notable women authors of the day).

Collaborative works
Miss Chester (play). With Sir C. L. Young. 1875.
Her world against a lie (dramatised novel). With G. F. Neville. 1880.
Where the chain galls. In Twenty novelettes, by twenty prominent novelists, New York 1889.
The lost diamonds: a tale of plot and passion. With C. Ogilvie. 1891.
Stray recollections of P. C. Challice, 999X. In C. I. M. Graves, Seven Xmas eves, being the romance of a social evolution, 1894?
The summer holiday. With D. St Aubin etc. 1898.
The gamekeeper. With H. Macpherson. Unpbd? Produced Aquarium Theatre, Brighton 16 May 1898.

Prefaces and introductions
Marryat, Frederick. Frank Mildmay. 1873.
Marryat, Frederick. The king's own. 1874.
Church, E. R. An actress's love story. 1888.
Williams, later Fitzgerald, later Davies, B. The clairvoyance of Bessie Williams. Ed Florence Marryat 1893.

Attributed works
Marryat, E. Temper: a tale. 3 vols 1854, 1 vol New York 1859.
Church, E. R. The hospital boy. Philadelphia 1870.

§2

Black, H. C. Notable women authors of the day. Glasgow 1893.
Obits: The Times 28 Oct 1899; Athenaeum 4 Nov 1899.
Lee, E. In DNB suppl 1901.
Boase, F. In Modern English biography, suppl to vol 3, 1921.
Sutherland, J. A. In Longman companion to Victorian fiction, 1988.
[DH]

Helen Buckingham Mathers, later Reeves

1853–1920

Comin' thro' the rye: a novel. 3 vols 1875. Anon.
The token of the silver lily. 1877. A poem.
As he comes up the stair. 1878.
'Cherry ripe!' a romance. 3 vols 1878.
'Land o' the leal'. 1878. Anon. Also contains Stephen Hatton.
My Lady Green Sleeves. 3 vols 1879.
Story of a sin: a sketch. 1882.
Sam's sweetheart. 3 vols 1883.
Eyre's acquittal: a sequel to Story of a sin. 3 vols 1884.
Jock o' Hazelgreen. 1884. Also contains As he comes up the stair, 'Land o' the leal' and 2 short stories.
Found out: a story. [1885.]
Murder or manslaughter? a novel. [1885.]
The fashion of this world. [1886.]
Blind justice: a story. 1890.
The mystery of no 13: a novel. 1891. Later pbd in Venus Victrix and other stories, *below*, 1902.

My Jo, John: a novel. 1891. Later pbd in Venus Victrix and other stories, *below*, 1902.
The fate of Fenella, by Helen Mathers [et al]. 1892. Mathers wrote ch 1.
T'other dear charmer: a novel. 1892.
A study of a woman, or Venus Victrix: a novel. 1893. Later pbd in Venus Victrix and other stories, *below*, 1902.
What the glass told: a novel. 1893. Later pbd in Venus Victrix and other stories, *below*, 1902.
A man of to-day: a novel. 3 vols 1894.
The lovely Malincourt: a novel. 1895.
The juggler and the soul. 1896.
The rebel. 1896.
The sin of Hagar. 1896.
Bam Wildfire: a character sketch. 1898.
Becky. 1900.
Cinders: a novel. 1901.
'Honey'. 1902.
Venus Victrix and other stories. 1902. Contains Venus Victrix; The mystery of no 13; What the glass told; My Jo, John.
Dahlia and other stories. 1903.
'Dimples'. 1903.
The face in the mirror and other stories. 1903.
Griff of Griffthscourt. 1903.
The new Lady Teazle and other stories. 1903.
'Side-shows'. 1904.
The ferryman. 1905.
Tally ho! 1906.
Pigskin and petticoat. 1907.
The pirouette and other stories. 1907 (2nd edn).
Gay Lawless. 1908.
Love, the thief. 1909.
Man is fire: woman is tow, and other stories. [1912.]

Gertrude Townshend Mayer, née Dalby

1840/1–1932

§1

Sir Hubert's marriage. 3 vols 1876.
The fatal inheritance, and other stories. 1878.
Belmore. 1880. Moxon's Select Novelettes no 2.
English women of letters. 2 vols 1894, rptd Freeport NY 1973. Covers women writers from Margaret, Duchess of Newcastle, to Lucie Duff Gordon, and includes unpbd letters from Mary Shelley to the Leigh Hunts. Adapted from articles in Temple Bar, 1882–94.

Contributions to periodicals

For Gertrude Townshend Mayer's articles in Temple Bar, *1882–1900, see* Wellesley *vol 5. As well as those collected into* English women of letters, *these include articles on several literary figures of the early nineteenth century.*

§2

DNB on her husband Samuel Ralph Townshend Mayer, by G. C. Boase. [JW]

L. T. Meade, i.e. Elizabeth (Lillie) Thomasina Meade, Mrs Toulmin Smith 1844–1914

Ashton-Morton. 1866. anon.
Lettie's last home. 1875.
Great St. Benedict's. 1876 (illus), 1876 (pbd by 'Elizabeth Thomas'). Reissued as Dorothy's story, 1931.
Those boys. 1876. By 'Aunt Penn'.
Scamp and I. 1876, rptd 1877, 1883, 1891, 1923.
David's little lad. 1877, rptd 1878, 1888.
A knight of today. 1877. Illus.
Little trouble-the-house. 1877. By 'Aunt Penn'.
Bel-Marjory. 1878, rptd 1894, 1927.
White lilies and other tales. 1878.
Your brother and mine: a cry from the great city. 1878. Reissued 1884, 1923 (as Outcast Robin).
The children's kingdom. 1879, rptd 1889.
Dot and her treasures. 1879, rptd 1886, 1923, 1930.
The floating light of Ringfinnan and Guardian angels. 1879, rptd 1904.
Water gipsies. 1879, rptd 1884.
Andrew Harvey's wife. 1880, rptd 1908.
A dweller in tents. 1880.
Mou-setse, a negro hero. 1880.
Mother Herring's chicken. 1881 (illus), rptd 1908.
The children's pilgrimage. 1883, rptd 1893, 1902.
Hermie's rose-buds. 1883, rptd 1890.
How it all came round. 1883 (illus), rptd 1885, 1892, 1909.
A London baby. 1883, rptd 1891, 1899.
The autocrat of the nursery. 1884 (illus), rptd 1893, 1920.
A band of three. 1884 (illus), rptd 1886.
Scarlet anemones. 1884.
The two sisters. 1884.
The angel of love. 1885 (illus), rptd 1892, 1896, 1914.
Faithful friends: stories of struggle and victory. 1885.
A little silver trumpet. 1885 (illus), rptd 1890, 1909, 1916, 1918, 1921. Adapted for BBC TV and the modernised version by T. Bennett pbd 1980.
A world of girls. 1886 (illus), rptd many times up to 1902.
Beforehand. 1887, rptd 1889.
Daddy's boy. 1887 (illus), rptd 1892.
The O'Donnells of Inchfawn. 1887.
The palace beautiful. 1887 (illus), rptd 1889, 1890, 1902, 1909.
'Sweet Nancy'. 1887 (illus), rptd 1894, 1899, 1903, 1908, 1914, 1916, 1922, 1925, 1928, 1930, 1933.
Deb and the duchess. 1888 (illus), rptd 1892.
The lady of the forest. 1888 (illustr J. B. Yeats), rptd 1894.
The little princess of Tower Hill. 1888.
Nobody's neighbours. 1888 (illus), rptd 1920, 1928.
Engaged to be married. 1889 (illus), rptd 1895. Later issued as Daughters of today, 1916, rptd 1921, 1923.
A farthingful. 1889.
The golden lady. 1889.
The house of surprises. 1889. Illus.
Marigold. 1889. Illus.
Polly: a new-fashioned girl. 1889. Illus.
Poor Miss Carolina. 1889.
The Beresford prize. 1890 (illus), rptd 1895.
Dickory Dock. 1890.
Frances Kane's fortune. 1890.
A girl of the people. 1890 (illus), rptd 1912.
Heart of gold. 1890.
Just a love story. 1890 (illus). Pbd as The Beauforts 1900; *see below*.
The children of Wilton Chase. 1891. Illus.
Hepsy Gipsy. 1891 (illus), rptd 1912.
The Honourable Miss. 1891.
Little Mary, and other stories. 1891 (illus), rptd 1929.
A sweet girl graduate. 1891 (illus), rptd 1902.
What really happened. 1891.
Bashful fifteen. 1892 (illus), rptd 1902.
Four on an island. 1892. Illus.
The medicine lady. 1892, rptd 1893, 1901.
Out of the fashion. 1892 (illus), rptd 1894.
A ring of rubies. 1892, rptd 1893, 1903, 1921, 1937.
Beyond the blue mountains. 1893 (illus), rptd 1903, 1931.
Jill, a flower girl. 1893 (illus), rptd 1910, 1936.
A young mutineer. 1893. Illus.

Betty, a school girl. 1894. Illus.
In an iron grip. 1894, rptd 1895.
A life for a love. 1894, rptd 1895.
Red Rose and Tiger Lily. 1894 (illus), rptd 1902.
A soldier of fortune. 1894, rptd 1895, 1896.
Girls new and old. 1895. Illus.
Minister. 1895. Illus.
A princess of the gutter. 1895, rptd 1910, 1922.
The voice of the charmer. 1895, rptd 1896, 1910.
Andrew Sargeant's wedding. 1896. Illus.
Catalina: art student. 1896. Illus.
A girl in ten thousand. 1896.
Good luck. 1896, rptd 1904, 1905.
A little mother to the others. 1896 (illus), rptd 1898, 1900, 1902.
Merry girls of England. 1896 (illus), rptd 1902.
Playmates. 1896. Illus.
A son of Ishmael. 1896, rptd 1900.
The white Tzar. 1896.
Bad little Hannah. 1897 (illus), rptd 1898, 1900, 1922.
A handful of silver. 1897. Illus.
The way of a woman. 1897, rptd 1898, 1899, 1900.
Wild Kitty. 1897. Illus.
A bunch of cherries. 1898. Illus.
Cave perilous. 1898 (illus), rptd 1905, 1935.
The cleverest woman in England. 1898, rptd 1908.
The girls of St Wode's. 1898 (illus), rptd 1904.
On the brink of a chasm. 1898, rptd 1899.
The rebellion of Lil Carrington. 1898 (illus), rptd 1902.
The siren. 1898, rptd 1902.
An adventuress. 1899, rptd 1900, 1921.
All sorts. 1899.
The desire of men. 1899, rptd 1901, 1905.
The kingfisher's egg. 1899.
Light o' the morning. 1899 (illus), rptd 1924.
The odds and the evens. 1899. Illus.
A public school boy. 1899. Memoir.
The Beauforts. 1900 (illus), rptd 1910, 1914, 1935. Previously pbd as Just a love story, 1890.
A big temptation. 1900.
A brave poor thing. 1900.
Daddy's girl. 1900 (illus), rptd 1912.
Seven maids. 1900. Illus.
A sister of the Red Cross. 1900 (illus), rptd 1931.
The temptation of Olive Latimer. 1900. Illus.
The time of roses. 1900.
Wages. 1900, rptd 1901.
The blue diamond. 1901, rptd 1902.
Cosey Corner, or, How they kept a farm. 1901. Illus.
Girls of the true blue. 1901. Illus.
The new Mrs Lascelles. 1901 (illus), rptd 1903. Later edn pbd as Mother Mary.
The secret of the dead. 1901.
A stumble by the way. 1901, rptd 1902.
Through peril for a wife. 1901, rptd 1907.
A very naughty girl. 1901. Illus.
Wheels of iron. 1901, rptd 1902.
The wooing of Monica. 1901, rptd 1914, 1921, 1933.
Confessions of a court milliner. 1902.
A double revenge. 1902, rptd 1905.
Drift. 1902, rptd 1903.
Girls of the forest. 1902. Illus.
Margaret. 1902.
The Princess who gave away all, and The naughty one of the family. 1902.
Queen Rose. 1902. Illus.
The rebel of the school. 1902 (illus), rptd 1921.
The squire's little girl. 1902, rptd 1929.
The burden of her youth. 1903, rptd 1905, 1915.
By mutual consent. 1903.
A gay charmer. 1903. Illus.
The Manor School. 1903. Illus.
Peter the pilgrim. 1903. Illus.
Resurgam. 1903.
Rosebury. 1903, rptd 1905.
Stories from the old, old Bible. 1903 (illus), rptd 1911.
That brilliant Peggy. 1903, rptd 1905.
Tic-Tac-Too. 1903. Illus.
The witch maid. 1903, rptd 1921.
The adventures of Miranda. 1904.
At the back of the world. 1904.
Bride of to-morrow. 1904.
Castle poverty. 1904.
The girls of Mrs Pritchard's School. 1904. Illus.
The lady cake-maker. 1904, rptd 1906.
Love triumphant. 1904, rptd 1911.
A madcap. 1904 (illus), rptd 1908.
A maid of mystery. 1904, rptd 1906.
A modern tomboy. 1904. Illus.
Nurse Charlotte. 1904, rptd 1915.
Petronella, and The coming of Polly. 1904. Illus.
Silenced. 1904.
Bess of Delaney's. 1905, rptd 1913.
A bevy of girls. 1905 (illus), rptd 1921.
Dumps: a plain girl. 1905. Illus.
The face of Juliet. 1905.
His mascot. 1905.
Little wife Hester. 1905, rptd 1908, 1916, 1920.
Loveday. 1905 (illus), rptd 1908, 1914.
Old Readymoney's daughter. 1905 (illus), rptd 1910.
The other woman. 1905, rptd 1912, 1929.
Virginia. 1905, rptd 1908.
Wilful cousin Kate. 1905. Illus.
The colonel and the boy. 1906. Illus.
From the hand of the hunter. 1906.
The girl and her fortune. 1906, rptd 1909.
A golden shadow. 1906, rptd 1924, 1938.
The heart of Helen. 1906.
The hill-top girl. 1906. Illus.
The home of sweet content. 1906, rptd 1907.
In the flower of her youth. 1906.
The maid with the goggles. 1906, rptd 1914, 1922.
Sue: the story of a little heroine and her friend. 1906. Illus.
Turquoise and ruby. 1906. Illus.
Victory. 1906.
The chateau of mystery. 1907.
The curse of the Feverals. 1907.
A girl from America. 1907. Illus.
The home of silence. 1907, rptd 1908.
Kindred spirits. 1907.
The lady of delight. 1907.
The little school-mothers. 1907. Illus.
The love of Susan Cardigan. 1907.
The red cap of liberty. 1907.
The red ruth. 1907, rptd 1911, 1917, 1929.
The scamp family. 1907. Illus.
Three girls from school. 1907. Illus.
The aim of her life. 1908.
Betty of the rectory. 1908 (illus), rptd 1911.
The Court-Harman girls. 1908. Illus.
The courtship of Sybil. 1908.
Hetty Beresford. 1908.
Little Josephine. 1908, rptd 1912.

A lovely fiend, and other stories. 1908.
Sarah's mother. 1908. A later edn pbd as Colonel Tracy's wife, 1910, rptd 1914.
The school favourite. 1908. Illus.
The school queens. 1908. Illus.
Aylwyn's friends. 1909. Illus.
Betty Vivian. 1909 (illus), rptd 1921.
Blue of the sea. 1909, rptd 1911.
Brother or husband. 1909, rptd 1910.
The fountain of beauty. 1909.
I will sing a new song. 1909.
The necklace of Parmona. 1909, rptd 1912.
The princess of the revels. 1909. Illus.
The pursuit of Penelope. 1909.
The stormy petrel. 1909.
Wild Heather. 1909, rptd 1911.
The ABC girl. 1910, rptd 1911.
Belinda Traherne. 1910.
Colonel Tracy's wife. 1910, rptd 1914. Previously pbd as Sarah's mother, 1908.
A girl of to-day. 1910.
Lady Anne. 1910, rptd 1911.
Micah Faraday, adventurer. 1910.
Miss Gwendoline. 1910.
Nance Kennedy. 1910.
Pretty-girl and the others. 1910. Illus.
Rosa Regina. 1910. Illus.
A wild Irish girl. 1910. Illus.
A bunch of cousins, and The barn 'boys'. 1911. Illus.
Desborough's wife. 1911.
The doctor's children. 1911 (illus), rptd 1927.
For dear Dad. 1911. Illus.
The girls of Merton College. 1911. Illus.
Mother and son. 1911.
'Ruffles'. 1911, rptd 1914, 1920, 1935, 1939 (abridged).
The soul of Margaret Rand. 1911.
Twenty-four hours: a novel of to-day. 1911, rptd 1912.
Corporal Violet. 1912, rptd 1934.
The girl from Spain. 1912.
The great Lord Masareene. 1912, rptd 1914.
The house of black magic. 1912, rptd 1917.
Kitty O'Donovan. 1912 (illus), rptd 1927.
Lord and Lady Kitty. 1912, rptd 1913.
Love's cross roads. 1912, rptd 1935, 1939 (abridged).
Peggy from Kerry. 1912. Illus.
The Chesterton girl graduates. 1913. Illus.
The girls of Abinger Close. 1913. Illus.
The girls of King's Royal. 1913. Illus.
Once of the angels. 1913. Pbd under the pseud of 'Evelyn Beacon'.
The passion of Kathleen Duveen. 1913 rptd 1921, 1935.
A band of mirth. 1914.
Elizabeth's prisoner. 1914, rptd 1920, 1925.
A girl of high adventure. 1914.
Her happy face. 1914.
The queen of joy. 1914. Illus.
The darling of the school. 1915. Illus.
The daughter of a soldier. 1915. Illus.
Greater than gold. 1915, rptd 1917.
Jill the irresistible. 1915 (illus), rptd 1927.
Daughters of today. 1916, rptd 1921, 1923. Previously pbd as Engaged to be married, 1889.
Hollyhock: a spirit of mischief. 1916. Illus.
Madge Mostyn's nieces. 1916. Illus.
The maid indomitable. 1916.
Mother Mary. 1916. Illus. Previously pbd as The new Mrs Lascelles, 1901.
Better than riches. 1917. Illus.
The fairy godmother. 1917. Illus.

Collaborative works

Under the dragon throne. (With Robert K. Douglas) 1897.
A master of mysteries: the adventures of John Bell – ghost explorer. (With Robert Eustace, i.e. Robert Eustace Barton) 1898 (illus), rptd 1901. First pbd in Cassell's Mag 1897.
The brotherhood of the seven kings. (With Robert Eustace) 1899 (illus), rptd 1900, 1903. First pbd in Strand Mag 1898.
The Gold Star Line. (With Robert Eustace) 1899. Illus.
The Sanctuary Club. (With Robert Eustace) 1900 (illus), rptd 1906. First pbd in Strand Mag 1899 as 'Stories of the Sanctuary Club'.
The lost square. (With Robert Eustace) 1902, rptd 1904.
The sorceress of the Strand. (With Robert Eustace) 1903 (illus). First pbd in Strand Mag 1902–3. One of these stories, 'Madame Sara', rptd in 'The rivals of Sherlock Holmes: early detective stories', ed Hugh Greene, 1970.
The oracle of Maddox Street. (With Robert Eustace) 1904. First pbd in Pearson's Mag 1902.
This troublesome world. (With Clifford Halifax, i.e. Edgar Beaumont) 1893, rptd 1901, 1905.
Stories from the diary of a doctor. (With Clifford Halifax) 1894 (illus), rptd 1910. First pbd in Strand Mag 1893.
Dr Rumsey's patient. (With Clifford Halifax) 1896, rptd 1897.
Stories from the diary of a doctor: 2nd ser. (With Clifford Halifax) 1896, rptd 1901. First pbd in Strand Mag 1895.
Where the shoe pinches. (With Clifford Halifax) 1900.
A race with the sun. (With Clifford Halifax) 1901. Illus. Rptd in The crooked counties: further rivals of Sherlock Holmes, ed Hugh Greene, 1973, rptd 1976.
Stories from the diary of a doctor: 3rd ser. (With Clifford Halifax) 1901. First pbd in Strand Mag 1895.

Short stories

Jack Daring's conqueror. Little snow-flakes, being the Sunday Mag Christmas stories for the young. 1881.
The least of these my brethren. Sunday Mag 1881.
Little black sheep. Sunday Mag 1881.
Paths of peace. Sunday Mag Christmas no for 1881.
Behind the tapestry. Cassell's Family Mag 10 1883–4.
Bluebell's hero. Quiver Christmas Suppl 1884.
Bessie: a sketch. Quiver 1885.
The gems she wore. Sunday Mag 15 1886.
In the second place. Quiver 1890.
A bonnie creature. Sunday Mag 19 1890.
From two points of view. Parents' Review 1 1890–1.
The yellow dragon vases. Atalanta 5 1891–2.
A young blue-stocking. Ludgate Monthly 2 1891–2.
The under dog. Sunday Mag 1892.
Aunt Cassandra. Young Woman 1 1892–3.
A golden fleece. Sunday Mag 22 1893.
A horrible fright. Strand Mag 8 1894, rptd in Strange tales from The Strand, 1991.
The little old lady. Woman at Home 3 1894–5.
Stories from the diary of a court dressmaker. Woman at Home 3 1894–5. 7 stories.
Sally. Chambers's Jnl 72 1895.
A very up-to-date girl. Woman at Home 4 1895–6.
A case of cross-purposes. Woman at Home 5 1895–6.
Rachel Merrick's engagement. Young Woman 4 1895–6.
For fame and fortune: a series of short stories. Young Woman 5 1896–7. 12 stories.
A swift temptation. Temple Mag 2 1897–8.
The love adventures of Primrose Ward. Windsor Mag 7 1898.
The sloping desk. Young Woman 7 1899.
The cherub of Chancery Lane. Young Woman 8 1899–1900.

A strange insanity. Cassell's Mag 29 1899–1900.
The mysteries of Greystones. Girl's Realm Annual 2 1899–1900.
Over the cliff. Lady's Word 1 1900.
The purple bag. Girl's Realm Annual 3 1900–1.
The revolt of Dinah Rashleigh. Sunday Strand 1 1900.
Robbery with compensation. Sunday Strand 1 1900.
The best brother-in-law in the world. Lady's World 3 1901.
The bride's secret. Lady's World 3 1900–1.
The ruby bracelet. Lady's World 3 1900–1.
Yours Philip Mortimer. Lady's World 3 1900–1.
The great pink pearl. Harmsworth Mag 6 1901.
A race for a wife. Lady's World 3 1901.
Great Aunt Alicia: a Christmas ghost story. Girl's Realm 4 1901–2.
The visiting card: a series of short stories. Lady's World 4 1902.
Eyes of terror. Strand Mag 26 1903.
Roland Trevor's secret. Sunday Strand 8 1903.
The rays of magic. Woman at Home 18 1904–5.
The magic earrings. Woman at Home 20 1905–6.
The man from Johannesburg. London Mag 16 1906.
The ordeal of Sybil West. Girl's Realm 10 1907–8.
Accepted: a story of the Royal Academy. Girl's Realm 10 1907–8.
Jessica's dilemma. Girl's Realm 11 1908–9.
The ordeal of Cicely Blunt. Quiver 1909.
Love stories of real life. Strand Mag 39 1910.
Colour blindness. In The storyteller: a magazine of clever fiction, ed Arthur Spurgeon, 1907.

Short stories as joint author

Richard Maitland – consul. (With R. K. Douglas) Chambers's Jnl 71 1894, 72 1895, rptd in Brains and bravery, 1903 (illus).
Stories of the Red Cross. (With Clifford Halifax) Pearson's Mag 4 1897.
Adventures of a man of science. (With Clifford Halifax, i.e. Edgar Beaumont) Strand Mag 12 1896; 13 1897.
The blue laboratory. (With Robert Eustace, i.e. Robert Eustace Barton) Cassell's Family Mag 23 1896–7.
Where the air quivered. (With Robert Eustace) Strand Mag 16 1898.
The secret of Emu Plain. (With Robert Eustace) Cassell's Mag 27 1898–9.
The arrest of Captain Vandeleur. (With Robert Eustace) Harmsworth Mag 2 1899.
Mr Bovey's unexpected will. (With Robert Eustace) Harmsworth Mag 2 1899.
The D Line. (With Robert Eustace) Windsor Mag 11 1899–1900.
The outside ledge: a cablegram mystery. (With Robert Eustace) Harmsworth Mag 5 1900, rptd in A treasury of Victorian detective stories, ed E. F. Bleiler, 1980.
A terrible railway ride. (With Robert Eustace) Harmsworth Mag 4 1900.
Followed. (With Robert Eustace) Strand Mag 20 1900.
Mrs Reid's terror. (With Robert Eustace) Harmsworth Mag 6 1901.
The heart of a mystery. (With Robert Eustace). Windsor Mag 14 1901.
Spangle-winged. (With Clifford Halifax) Strand Mag 22 1901.
The mystery of Susanna Tankerville. (With Clifford Halifax) Woman at Home 12 1901–2.
The black ball. (With Robert Eustace) Cassell's Mag 35 1902–3.
Uninsured. (With Robert Eustace). Woman at Home 14 1902–3.
The face in the dark. (With Robert Eustace) Harmsworth Mag 10 1903, rptd in Great short stories of detection, mystery and horror, ed D. L. Sayers, 1928, vol 1.

Short stories in collections

What really happened by Mrs Meade and others. 1891.
Fifty-two stories of heroism in life and action for girls, by L. T. Meade, S. Doudney, G. Stebbing and other writers. Ed A. H. Miles 1895. Illus.
Fifty-two stories of pluck, peril and romance for girls, by L. T. Meade etc. Ed A. H. Miles 1896. Illus.
Fifty-two stories of duty and daring for girls by Countess Norraikow, L. T. Meade and other writers. 1897.
Fifty-two holiday stories for girls, by L. T. Meade, Mary E. Wilkins and Sarah Doudney. 1898.
The kingfisher's egg, by L. T. Meade and E. Walton, G. R. Glasgow and O. Molesworth. 1899.
Sweet bright-eyes: a volume of original pictures, stories and verses. By. L. T. Meade and others. 1899. Illus.
Fifty-two stirring stories for girls, by L. T. Meade, S. Doudney, R. Overton and other writers. 1900.
In storyland: a volume of original pictures, stories and verses. Written by G. S. Henty, L. T. Meade and others. 1900.
Sunny days: a volume of original pictures, stories and verses. Written by L. T. Meade and others. 1900. Illus.
A golden apple, by L. T. Meade and other stories by M. B. Manwell, Eliza F. Pollard etc. 1901.
Queen of the day by L. T. Meade and other stories by M. B. Manwell and Frances E. Crompton, etc. 1902.
That little French baby etc and other stories by L. T. Meade and L. L. Weedon. 1905.
Seaside story book, with tales by G. Manville Fenn, L. T. Meade et al. 1907.
Seaside holiday frolics, with stories by L. T. Meade, G. Manville Fenn, A. J. Daniels etc. 1910.
Golden hours story book, by L. T. Meade, G. Manville Fenn, M. A. Hoyer, L. Molesworth etc. 1912.
Happy playmates: a volume of original pictures, stories and verses written by G. Manville Fenn, L. T. Meade and E. Everett-Green, etc. Ed A. J. Fuller 1913.

Contributions to periodicals

One in the thousand. Sunday Mag 14 1885.
Authors: an English editor's view. Literary World (Boston) 24 May 1890.
Carmen Sylva: Queen of Roumania. Sunday Mag 19 1890.
The children of the highways. Sunday Mag 19 1890.
English girls and their colleges. 8 articles in Lady's Pictorial, Dec 1891 and Jan 1892.
The Atalanta scholarship and school of fiction: from the Editor's standpoint. Atalanta 6 1892–3.
The children's country holidays. Atalanta 6 1892–3.
Winter resorts. Atalanta 6 1892–3.
How I write my books. Young Woman 1 1893.
Girton College. Atalanta 7 1893–4.
Newnham College. Atalanta 7 1893–4.
Antwerp: an old Flemish city. Sunday Mag 23 1894.
Sir Edward Burne-Jones: the painter of eternal youth. Sunday Mag 23 1894.
G. F. Watts: painter of the eternal truths. Sunday Mag 23 1894.
Cheltenham Ladies College. (Girls' schools of to-day.) Strand Mag 9 1895.
St Leonard's and Great Harrowden Hall. (Girls' schools of to-day.) Strand Mag 9 1895.
Sir Edward Burne-Jones. Strand Mag 10 1895.
Children past and present. The Parents' Rev 6 1896, 7 1896.
A school of fiction. New Cent Rev 1 1897.
At what age should girls marry? Young Woman 7 1898–9.
Red letter days. Sunday Mag 1899.
How I began. Girl's Realm 3 1900–1.
The friends I loved when I was young. Sunday Mag 1901.
Story writing for girls. Academy and Literature Fiction Suppl 1903.
L. T. Meade edited Atalanta, *vols 1–6 1887–93. The first vol (1887–8) was edited jointly with Alicia A. Leith, the 2nd and 3rd vols (1888–90) with John C. Staples, and vol 6 with A. Balfour Symington.* [JG]

Leonard Merrick, originally Miller 1864–1938

Bibliographies

Danielson, H. In his Bibliographies of modern authors, 1921.

Collections

The call from the past, and other stories. [1910], 1924.
Works. 12 vols 1918–19. Introd to each vol by M. Hewlett, W. D. Howells, N. Munro, H. G. Wells et al.
A chair on the boulevard. [1919.]
The Leonard Merrick omnibus. 1950.

§1

Mr Bazalgette's agent. 1888.
Violet Moses. 3 vols 1891.
The man who was good: a novel. 2 vols 1892.
This stage of fools. 1896.
Cynthia: a daughter of the Philistines. 2 vols 1896, 1897.
One man's view. 1897.
The actor manager. 1898.
The worldlings. 1900.
When love flies out o' the window. 1902.
Conrad in quest of his youth: an extravagance of temperament. 1903.
The quaint companions. 1903.
Whispers about women. 1906.
The House of Lynch. 1907.
The man who understood women, and other stories. 1908.
All the world wondered, and other stories. 1911.
The position of Peggy Harper. 1911.
While Paris laughed; being pranks and passions of the poet Tricotrin. [1918.]
To tell you the truth. [1922.]
Four stories. 1925.
The little dog laughed. [1930.]

'Henry Seton Merriman', Hugh Stowell Scott 1862–1903

Collections

Works. 14 vols 1909–10.

§1

Young Mistley. 2 vols 1888. Anon.
The phantom future. 2 vols 1888.
Suspense. 3 vols 1890.
Prisoners and captives. 3 vols 1891.
The slave of the lamp. 2 vols 1892.
From one generation to another. 2 vols 1892.
From Wisdom Court. 1893. With S. G. Tallentyre.
With edged tools. 3 vols 1894.
The grey lady. 1895.
Flotsam: the study of a life. 1896.
The money-spinner and other character notes. 1896. With S. G. Tallentyre.
The sowers. 1896.
In Kedar's tents. 1897.
Roden's corner. 1898.
Dross. Chicago and New York 1899.
The isle of unrest. 1900.
The velvet glove. 1901.
The vultures. 1902.
Barlasch of the Guard. 1903.
The last hope. 1904.
Tomaso's fortune and other stories. 1904.

§2

Cox, H. T. Henry Seton Merriman. New York 1967.

William Minto 1845–93

See col 2371.

Mary Louisa Molesworth née Stewart, 'Ennis Graham' 1839–1921

The collection of Molesworth mss and papers assembled by the late Ruth Robertson is held privately.

Bibliography

Green, R. L. In his Mrs Molesworth, 1961 (Bodley Head monograph).
In The cuckoo clock and The tapestry room, New York 1976 (Garland Classics of Children's Lit ser). Contains bibliography of Molesworth's books for children, pp. vii–xv.

Collections

Happy story land. A volume of stories and verses. By M. Molesworth, A. Hoyer, E. Nesbit, F. E. Weatherley, etc. 1911.
Stories by Mrs Molesworth. Compiled by S. Baldwin, illustr E. Cooke, New York 1922, rptd 1935. Includes The cuckoo clock; The six poor little princesses; Too bad; Carrots; Mary Ann Jolly; Basil's violin; The reel fairies; The blue dwarfs; Good night Winny.
Fairy stories by Mrs Molesworth. Ed R. L. Green 1957.

§1

Lover and husband. 3 vols 1870.
She was young and he was old. 3 vols 1872.
Not without thorns. 3 vols 1873.
Cicely: a story of three years. 3 vols 1874.
Tell me a story. 1875 (illustr W. Crane), 1879 (3rd edn), 1894.
'Carrots': just a little boy. By Ennis Graham. 1876 (illustr W. Crane), 1880, 1891, Boston [1895?], London 1920 (illustr M. V. Wheelhouse), 1957.
REVIEW: [R. H. Hutton] Spectator 9 Dec 1876.
The cuckoo clock. 1877 (illustr W. Crane), New York 1877, Chicago 1877, London 1882, 1886, London and New York 1889, 1893 (with The tapestry room), New York [1895], London and New York 1896, London 1903, London and New York 1904 (with The tapestry room), 1907, London 1913, New York 1913, London and Philadelphia 1914 (illustr M. L. Kirk), Philadelphia 1916, 1917 (in Fairies and goblins from storyland), London 1919 (with Crane illustrations), New York 1921, 1922 (*see* Collections, *above*), 1925 (with The tapestry room), Akron OH 1927 (illustr F. W. Williams), Philadelphia, New York and London 1930 (illustr F. S. Cooke), London 1931 (illustr C. E. Brock), New York 1931 (with The tapestry room), London 1933, 1939 (illustr Crane), 1941 (illustr Brock, Pen), New York 1947 (with The tapestry room), London 1948 (illustr S. Green), 1952, London and New York 1954 (illustr E. H. Shepard, Dent Children's Illus Classics ser), Glasgow 1959 (illustr C. Ruffinelli), New York 1976 (with The tapestry room, in Garland Classics of Children's Lit ser introd by A. Bull), London 1980 (illustr Brock), New York 1980 (photofacs of 1931 edn illustr Brock), New York 1987 (Dell Yearling Classic), 1988 (Puffin, based on lst edn).
REVIEWS: [R. H. Hutton] Spectator 1 Dec 1877; Independent 29, 6 Dec 1877; Nation 25, 6 Dec 1877; Literary World 8 Jan 1878; St Nicholas 5, Feb 1878.
Hathercourt rectory. 1878.
Grandmother dear. A book for boys and girl. 1878 (illustr W. Crane), 1900.
REVIEWS: Nation 27, 19 Dec 1878; Literary World 10, 15 Feb 1879; Independent 31, 20 Mar 1879.
The tapestry room. A child's romance. 1879 (illustr W. Crane), New York 1887, London 1949 (illustr Crane), 1957, New York 1976 (with The cuckoo clock). *See also* The cuckoo clock, *above*.
REVIEWS: [R. H. Hutton] Spectator 13 Dec 1879; Independent 32, 11 Mar 1880.

A Christmas child. A sketch of a boy-life. 1880 (illustr W. Crane).
REVIEWS: Literary World 4 Dec 1880; Independent 32, 9 Dec 1880; Nation 31, 9 Dec 1880.
Miss Bouverie. A novel. 1880, 1901.
A Christmas posy. 1881 (illustr W. Crane), 1888.
The adventures of Herr Baby. 1881 (illustr W. Crane), London and New York 1886.
REVIEW: [R. H. Hutton] Spectator 10 Dec 1881.
Hermy, the story of a little girl. 1881 (illustr M. E. Edwards), 1890, 1898, 1911.
REVIEW: Literary World 11, 4 Dec 1881.
Hoodie. 1882 (illustr M. E. Edwards), 1897.
Rosy. 1882 (illustr W. Crane), 1886.
Summer stories for boys and girls. 1882.
Two little waifs. 1883 (illustr W. Crane), New York 1977 (introd by R. L. Green, with The children of the castle).
The boys and I: a child's story for children. 1883. (illustr M. E. Edwards), [1899].
The little old portrait. 1884, 1916 (as Edmée: a tale of the French revolution).
Christmas tree land. 1884 (illustr W. Crane), rptd 1981.
Lettice: a tale. 1884.
REVIEW: [R. H. Hutton] Spectator 5 July 1884.
'Us'. An old fashioned story. 1885 (illustr W. Crane), 1900.
A charge fulfilled. 1886.
The abbey by the sea, and another story, Felix, an outcast, from the French. 1887.
Four winds farm. 1887 (illustr W. Crane), New York 1977 (introd by R. L. Green, with The children of the castle).
Little Miss Peggy. Only a nursery story. 1887 (illustr W. Crane).
Lost, stolen or strayed. 1887.
Marrying and giving in marriage. A novel. 1887.
The palace in the garden. A story for children. 1887 (illustr H. M. Bennett), [1923].
Silverthorns. 1887.
Five minutes' stories. London and New York 1888.
Four ghost stories. 1888.
A Christmas posy. 1888.
French life in letters. 1889. (Macmillan's Primary Ser in Fr).
The third Miss St Quentin. 1889.
The rectory children. 1889 (illustr W. Crane).
That girl in black and bronze. 2 tales. 1889 (2nd edn).
Cheri's second escapade. 1889.
A house to let. 1889.
Neighbours. A novel. 1889 (illustr M. E. Edwards).
The old pincushion: or Aunt Clothilda's guests. 1889 (illustr M. L. Attwell), 1910.
Nesta, or fragments of a little life. 1889.
Great Uncle Hoot-Toot. 1889 [illustr G. Browne].
A house to let. 1889.
The story of a spring morning, and other tales. 1890, 1923.
The children of the castle. 1890 (illustr W. Crane), New York 1977, (Introd by R. L. Green, with Four Winds Farm).
Twelve tiny tales. 1890.
Family troubles (Mr Nobody). 1890 [illustr W. J. Morgan].
The green casket and other stories. 1890. Two stories from this collection were rptd as Leo's post office.
Little Mother Bunch. 1890 (illus), [c. 1912].
Nurse Heatherdale's story. 1891 (illustr L. L. Brooke).
Sweet content. A tale. 1891 (illus), 1908.
The red grange: a tale. 1891 (illustr G. Browne), 1913.
Lucky ducks and other stories. 1891 (illustr W. J. Morgan).
The bewitched lamp. 1891.
The black letter saints. London and New York 1892.
An enchanted garden: fairy stories. 1892 (illustr W. H. Hennessy).
Farthings: the story of a stray and a waif. 1892.
The girls and I: a veracious history. 1892 (illus).
Imogen: or only eighteen. 1892 (illustr H. A. Bone).
Leona: a tale. 1892.
The man with the pan-pipes and other stories. London and New York 1892 (illustr W. J. Morgan), rptd 1892.
The next-door house. A tale. 1893, 1914.
Robin redbreast: a story for girls. 1892 (illus).
Stories of the saints for children. 1892 (illus).
Blanche: a story for girls. '1894' [1893].
Mary: a nursery story for very little children. 1893 (illus).
The next-door house. 1893.
Studies and stories. 1893.
The thirteen black pigs and other stories. 1893 (illustr W. J. Morgan).
Hollow Tree House, and other stories. 1894. By Mrs Molesworth 'and others'.
My new home. 1894 (illustr L. L. Brooke), rptd 1968 (ed G. Avery).
Olivia: a story for girls. 1894, Philadelphia 1895 (illus).
The smugglers' cave and other stories. 1894. By Mrs Molesworth and others.
The story of a spring morning and other tales. 1894 (illustr M. E. Edwards).
Buttercups and daisies. A volume of stories, by J. S. Winter, Mrs Molesworth, etc. [1894.]
The carved lions. 1895 (illus), 1947 (ed M. Laski in Victorian tales for girls), 1960 (ed G. Avery), 1964 (ed R. L. Green, illustr L. Hart).
Cosy corner stories. 1895 (illus), 1941, 1948, 1954. Stories by Molesworth, E. Bennett etc.
Opposite neighbours and other stories. 1895.
Sheila's mystery. 1895 (illus).
The story shop. 1895. By Mrs Molesworth and others.
White turrets. A tale. [1895], 1896.
Friendly Joey and other stories. 1896.
The oriel window. 1896 (illus).
Philippa. A novel. Philadelphia 1896 (illustr L. L. Brooke), London and Edinburgh 1897.
Uncanny tales. 1896, rptd New York 1976.
Meg Langholme, or the day after tomorrow. 1897.
Miss Mouse and her boys. 1897.
Stories for children in illustration of the Lord's prayer. 1897.
Not quite true. 1898 (Nister's Holiday Annual).
Greyling Towers: a story for the young. 1898, 1918.
The laurel walk. 1898.
The magic nuts. 1898.
The third Miss St Quentin. 1898.
The children's hour. 1899.
The grim house. 1899.
This and That, a tale of two tinies. 1899 (illustr H. Thomson).
The house that grew. 1900 (illus).
The three witches, etc. A tale. 1900.
'My Pretty' and her little brother 'Too' and other stories. 1901 (illus).
The blue baby and other stories. 1901.
The wood-pigeons and Mary. 1901.
The blue baby and other stories. 1901, 1904 (illus).
Peterkin. 1902 (illus).
The mystery of the pinewood and Hollow tree house. 1903.
The ruby ring. London and New York 1904 (illustr R. M. M. Pitman), 1957.
The bolted door, and other stories. 1906 (illustr L. Baumer).
Jasper: a story for children. 1906 (illustr G. D. Hammond).
The wrong envelope, and other stories. 1906. (Contains A ghost of the Pampas by B. R. Molesworth.)
The little guest: a story for children. 1907 (illus).
Fairies – of sorts. 1908 (illustr G. D. Hammond).
The February boys: a story for children. 1909 (illustr M. L. Attwell).
The story of a year. 1910 (illustr G. D. Hammond).
Tales told in the twilight. An illustrated story book for children.

1911. Stories by Mrs Molesworth, Helen J. Wood, L. T. Meade, J. S. Winter, M. A. Hover, Edric Vredenburg and others.
Fairies afield. 1911 (illustr G. D. Hammond).

Contributions to periodicals and collaborative works

Juliana Horatia Ewing. 1886. Rptd in A peculiar gift, ed L. Salway, 1976.
The best books for children. II. Pall Mall Gazette 29 Oct 1887.
Bainton, G. (ed). The art of authorship. 1890. Contains contribution by Mrs Molesworth.
For the little ones. In Women's mission, ed A. Burdett Coutts 1893.
Hans Christian Andersen. 1893. Rptd in A peculiar gift, ed L. Salway, 1976.
On the art of writing fiction for children. Atalanta May 1893; rptd in A peculiar gift, ed L. Salway, 1976.
How I write my children's stories. Little Folks July 1894.
Story-writing. Monthly Packet Aug 1894.
A cry from the far west. Macmillan's Mag Dec 1897.
Story-reading and story-writing. Chambers's Jnl 75, Nov 1898.
A ramble about childhood. Girl's Own Annual 20, Oct 1898–Sep 1899, Feb 1899.
Mrs Molesworth was a regular contributor to girls' mags, especially Atalanta, *the* Girl's Own Paper *and* Every Girl's Annual. *Many of her stories were serialised in these mags.*

§2

Swinburne, A. C. Charles Reade. Nineteenth Cent 16, Oct 1884.
Salmon, E. Juvenile literature as it is. 1888.
L[ow?], F. H. A popular writer for children. Mrs Molesworth. Westminster Budget 20 Oct 1893.
Swinburne, A. C. The golden age. Daily Chron 31 Mar 1896.
Tooley, S. A. Some women novelists. Mrs Molesworth. Woman at Home Dec 1897.
Swan, H. Girls' Christian names: their history, meaning and association. 1900. (Quotes article by Mrs Molesworth.)
Robson, I. S. Story weavers: or, writers for the young. 1900.
Woolf, B. S. Children's classics. Mrs Molesworth and Carrots. Quiver 41, June 1906.
The Times 22 July 1921. Obituary (anon). *See also* New York Times c. 22 July 1921.
Day, C. Noble boys. Saturday Rev of Lit 15, 14 Nov 1936.
Baker, M. J. Mary Louisa Molesworth. Junior Bookshelf 12, Mar 1948.
Laski, M. Mrs Ewing, Mrs Molesworth and Mrs Hodgson Burnett. 1950.
Green, R. L. Notes on Mrs Molesworth. TLS 17 Nov 1950.
Green, R. L. Mrs. Molesworth and her books. Library World Nov 1951.
Green, R. L. Mrs. Molesworth. Junior Bookshelf July 1957.
In The letters of A. C. Swinburne, ed C. Y. Lang, New Haven CT 1959–62, vols 4, 5, 6.
Green, R. L. Mrs Molesworth. 1961 (Bodley Head Monograph ser).
Alison, D. The Scottish contribution to children's literature part 2. Lib Rev 20, no 5 1965–6.
Cooper, J. In Children's Book History Soc Newsletter, 1996. [DD and SJS]

George Moore 1852–1933

Letters and other mss are to be found in the Nat Lib of Ireland, Bibliothèque Nationale Paris, Brotherton Lib Univ of Leeds, Berg Collection NYPL, HRHRC, Univ of Washington and Beinecke Lib Yale Univ; smaller collections are in Special Collections Arizona State Univ, Boston Public Lib, BL, Univ of California Berkeley, Fitzwilliam Museum Cambridge, Cornell, Duke, Elgar Foundation, Univ of Florida, Houghton Lib Harvard, Huntington, Lilly Library Univ of Indiana, Univ of Illinois, Special Collections Univ of Kansas, Letterkundig Museum The Hague, Univ of London, Fales Collection NY Univ, State Univ of NY Buffalo, Pforzheimer Lib, Princeton, Univ of Virginia.

Bibliographies

Korg, J. In Victorian fiction: a guide to research, ed L. Stevenson, Cambridge MA 1964.
Jernigan, E. J. George Moore's 're-tying of bows': a critical study of the eight early novels and their revisions. Unpd PhD thesis, KS State Univ 1966.
Noël, J. C. In his George Moore: l'homme et l'oeuvre, Paris 1966. Includes extensive, although incomplete, primary and secondary bibliographies in Fr.
Gilcher, E. (1). A bibliography of George Moore. DeKalb IL 1970.
Gerber, H. E. In Anglo-Irish literature: a review of research, ed R. J. Finneran, New York 1976.
Gerber, H. E. In Dictionary of Irish literature, ed R. Hogan, Westport CT and London 1979.
Gerber, H. E. In Recent research on Anglo-Irish writers, ed R. J. Finneran, New York 1983.
Gilcher, E. Supplement to a bibliography of George Moore, Westport CT and Gerrards Cross 1988.
Langenfeld, R. George Moore: an annotated secondary bibliography of writings about him. New York 1987. Incorporates material previously published in ELT.

Collections

Works: Tauchnitz collection of British authors, 13 titles in 19 vols Leipzig 1895–1927; Brentano uniform edn, 10 vols New York 1912–21 (3 titles later replaced by rev texts); Carra edn, 21 vols Liveright New York 1922–4 with 2 suppl vols 1924 and 1926; Uniform edn, 17 titles in 20 vols Heinemann 1924–33, reissued as Ebury edn, 20 vols 1936–8 (since 1942 again Uniform edn).
In minor keys: the uncollected short stories of George Moore. Ed D. B. Eakin and H. E. Gerber, London and Syracuse NY 1985, 1987.
Selected plays of George Moore and Edward Martyn. Ed D. B. Eakin and B. Case. Gerrards Cross and Washington DC 1995.

§1

For uncollected articles published in periodicals as well as prefaces and diverse writings contributed to works by others see Gilcher (1), above.

Worldliness: a comedy in three acts. c. 1874. Frequently cited as Moore's earliest ptd work, but existence doubtful; see Gilcher (1) *above*.
Flowers of passion. '1878' [1877]; with Pagan poems, 1881 (*below*), New York and London 1978 (facs). Poems.
REVIEWS: (as A bestial bard) World, 28 Nov 1877; Truth, 6 Dec 1877; Examiner, 26 Jan 1878; Figaro, 6 Feb 1878.
Martin Luther: a tragedy in five acts, with Bernard Lopez. 1879. Verse play.
Pagan poems. 1881; with Flowers of passion (*above*), New York and London 1978 (facs).
Les cloches de Corneville. c. 1883. Trans with Augustus Moore of lyrics from Clairville and Planquette operetta. Produced 1883. Pamphlet; only known copy at Arizona State Univ.
A modern lover. 3 vols 1883, New York 1984 (facs), 1 vol London 1885 (rev), New York 1890; rewritten as Lewis Seymour and some women, 1917 (*below*).
REVIEWS: Athenaeum, 7 July 1883; St James's Gazette, 11 July 1883; Acad, 14 July 1883; Spectator, 18 Aug 1883; Pall Mall Gazette, 28 Sep 1883; Henry Norman Fortnightly, Dec 1883.
A mummer's wife. '1885' [1884], '1886' [1885] (rev), 1894 (rev), 1918 (rev), 1933 (Uniform), Chicago 1889 (as An actor's wife), New York 1903, 1917 (Brentano), 1917 (rev) (Brentano), 1922 (Carra), 1966 with foreword by W. Miller (Blue & Gold Lib), 1967 (Washington Square Press). Tr Fr 1888, Du 1886.
REVIEWS: Acad, 29 Nov 1884; Graphic, 29 Nov 1884; Pall Mall

Gazette, 5 Dec 1884; Athenaeum, 13 Dec 1884; Spectator, 17 Jan 1895; Sat Rev, 14 Feb 1885; Time, Nov 1884.

Literature at nurse: or circulating morals. 1885; with introd by P. Coustillas, Hassocks and Atlantic Highlands NJ 1976 (facs); with A mere accident, 1887 (*below*), New York 1978 (facs), and in Victorian novelists after 1885, ed I. Nadel and W. E. Fredeman, Detroit MI 1983. Pamphlet on selection of books at Mudie's lib.
REVIEW: Westminster Rev, Oct 1886.

La ballade de l'amant de coeur. Signed 'Pagan'. c. mid 1880s; rev in Confessions of a young man, New York 1917 (*below*) and all subsequent edns. Pamphlet; only known copy in Fayant collection Cornell Univ.

A drama in muslin: a realistic novel. Serialised Court and Soc Rev, 14 Jan–1 July 1886; 1886 (rev); with introd by A. N. Jeffares, Gerrards Cross 1981 (facs); rewritten as Muslin, 1915 (*below*). Tr Rus 1887, Du 1888, Ger 1978.
REVIEWS: Bat, 6 July 1886; Pall Mall Gazette, 14 July 1886; Acad, 17 July 1886; Athenaeum, 24 July 1886; Sat Rev, 24 July 1886.

A mere accident. London and New York 1887; with Literature at nurse, 1885 (*above*), New York 1978 (facs); rewritten as John Norton in Celibates, 1895 (*below*). Tr Fr in Revue International (Rome), 25 May–5 July 1887.
REVIEWS: (G. B. Shaw) Pall Mall Gazette, 19 July 1887; Acad, 23 July 1887; Athenaeum, 30 July 1887; Sat Rev, 13 Aug 1887.

Parnell and his island. 1887 (rev), 1891. Sketches. Previously tr Fr as Lettres sur l'Irlande, Figaro, 31 July–4 Sep 1886, and as Terre d'Irlande, Paris 1886.
REVIEWS: Daily Telegraph, 14 Feb 1887; Athenaeum, 26 Mar 1887; Acad, 2 Apr 1887; Lady's Pictorial, 4 Apr 1887; Evening News, 13 May 1887; Literary World (Boston), 11 June 1887; Westminster Rev, June 1887.

Confessions of a young man. Pt serialised Time July–Nov 1887; 1888 (rev), 1889 (rev), 1904 (rev), Leipzig 1905 (Tauchnitz), London 1918 (rev), Eng text (facs) with notes and introd in Jap by Minoru Toyoda, Tokyo 1927; expanded with articles from Impressions and opinions, 1891 (*below*); London 1926, 1928 (Travellers Lib), 1933 (Uniform), 1933 (Windmill Lib), London and Toronto 1935, 1939 (Pen), 1961 (Digit Books); New York 1888, 1915 (Brentano), with introd by F. Dell 1917 (Mod Lib), 1943 (facs), St Clair Shores MI 1971 (facs), 1904 (rev), 1917 (rev) (Brentano), with introd by R. M. Coates 1959 (Capricorn Books) (facs), with Avowals, 1919 (*below*), New York 1923 (Carra); semi-var ed S. Dick, Montreal and London 1972. Tr Fr in Revue Indépendent, Mar–Aug 1888, 1889 (rev), Cz 1910, Ital 1929, Jap 1939, Ger (1904 text) 1988.
REVIEWS: Acad, 17 Mar 1888; Athenaeum, 31 Mar 1888; Hawk, 10 Apr 1888; New York Times, 30 Sep 1888, 20 Sep 1891; Revue Indépendent (Paris), Oct 1888.

Spring days: a realistic novel – prelude to 'Don Juan'. Serialised Evening News, 3 Apr–31 May 1888; 1888 (rev), 1912 (rev with preface), New York (as Shifting love) 1891, 1912 (rev) (Brentano), 1922 (Carra), Leipzig 1912 (rev) (Tauchnitz).
REVIEWS: Athenaeum, 8 Sep 1888; Acad, 22 Sep 1888.

Mike Fletcher: a novel. 1889, 1899, New York 1889, New York and London 1977 (facs).
REVIEWS: Athenaeum, 21 Dec 1889; Acad, 28 Dec 1889; Spectator, 8 Feb 1890.

Impressions and opinions. 1891, 1913 (rev), New York 1891, 1972 (facs); 1913 (rev) (Brentano). Previously pbd articles on lit and art.
REVIEWS: (A. Symons) Acad, 21 Mar 1891; Speaker, 21 Mar 1891; St James's Gazette, 2 Apr 1891; Lady's Pictorial, 4 Apr 1891; Sat Rev, 18 Apr 1891; New Rev, 23 Apr 1891; Book Buyer, June 1891; New York Times, 21 June 1891; Athenaeum, 25 July 1891; Critic (New York), 19 Sep 1891; Dial (Chicago), Oct 1891; Bookman (London), Apr 1913; Literary World (Boston), 4 July 1891; New York Times, 11 May 1913; Mercure de France, May 1913.

Vain fortune. Serialised as by 'Lady Rhone' Lady's Pictorial, 4 July–17 Oct 1891; [1891] (rev), 1895 (rev), New York 1892, 1892 (rev). Tr Du 1895.
REVIEWS: Athenaeum, 7 Nov 1891; Lady's Pictorial, 7 Nov 1891; Sat Rev, 7 Nov 1891; Speaker, 7 Nov 1891; Acad, 12 Dec 1891; New York Times, 13 Mar 1892; Book Buyer, Mar 1892; Dial Apr, 1892; Literary World (Boston), 9 Apr 1892; [A. Bennett] Woman, 8 May 1895.

Modern painting. 1893, 1897 (enlarged), New York 1893, 1898 (enlarged), 1906, 1923 (with Degas from Impressions and opinions, 1891, *above*) (Carra). Art criticism previously pbd in Speaker. Tr Cz 1909.
REVIEWS: (W. Pater) Daily Chron, 10 June 1893; (R. Fry) Cambridge Rev, 22 June 1893; New York Times, 26 June 1893; Bookman, Aug 1893; Sketch, 30 Aug 1893; Westminster Rev, Sep 1893; Sat Rev, 7 Oct 1893; Critic, 14 Oct 1893; Spectator, 18 Nov 1893; Modern Art (Boston), 1 July 1894.

The strike at Arlingford: play in three acts. 1893, New York 1893; in Selected plays, 1995 (Collections, *above*). Produced London and Manchester Feb 1893.
REVIEWS: Athenaeum, 26 Aug 1893; New York Times, 29 Oct 1893; Literary World (Boston), 30 Dec 1893.

Esther Waters: a novel. Pt serialised as Pages from the life of a work-girl, Pall Mall Gazette, 2–4, 6–7, 9–14 Oct 1893; 1894 (rev), Chicago 1894 (facs), with introd and notes by M. Brown, New York 1958 (Norton Lib) (facs), with introd and bibliographical notes by H. Gerber, Chicago (Pandora) 1977 (facs), London 1899 (rev), 1920 (rev), 1926 (rev), 1932 (Uniform), with introd by C. D. Medley 1936 (EL), London and Toronto 1936, with George Moore colloquy London 1936 (Pen), with introd by W. Allen 1962 (EL), London and New York 1965 (EL), with introd by G. Hough London 1964 (WC), with introd and notes by D. Skilton London 1983 (WC), with introd by H. Laurie London 1990 (ELp), with introd and additional notes and material 1994 (ELp), Leipzig 1894 (English Lib), Chicago and New York 1899 (rev), New York 1917 (Brentano), with introd and text analysis by L. Stevenson, Boston MA 1963 (semi-var), New York 1921 (rev) (Brentano), 1922 (Carra), with Moore colloquy 1932 (Blue & Gold), with introd by B. Evans 1936 (Premier World Classics); dramatised for stage 1911, Wessex films 1948, BBC Radio 4 c. 1964–5, BBC2 TV 1977, BBC Radio 4 1978. Tr Danish 1895, Rus 1895, 1973, Swed 1900, Ger 1904, 1977, Fr 1907, 1933 (rev), Ital 1934, 1959, Jap 1989.
REVIEWS: Daily Chron, 28 Mar 1894; (A. Quiller-Couch) Speaker, 31 Mar 1894; Athenaeum, 28 Apr 1894; Bookman, May 1894; Sat Rev, 5 May 1894; Sketch, 9 May 1894; The Times, 15 May 1894; Critic (New York), 19 May 1894; Acad, 26 May 1894; Spectator, 2 June 1894; New York Times, 10 June 1894; Literary World, 30 June 1894; Düsseldorfer Zeitung (Berlin), 12 Sep 1904; Jnl des Débates (Paris), 8 May 1907; L'Éclair (Paris), 31 Mar 1907.

The Royal Academy. 1895. New Budget extra no 1. Report of Royal Acad exhibition, New Budget, 9 May 1895.

Celibates. 1895, New York 1895, with introd by Temple Scott 1915 (Brentano), Leipzig 1895 (Tauchnitz). Includes Mildred Lawson, rev from An art student in Today, Spring 1895, and John Norton, rev from A mere accident, 1887 (*above*), and Agnes Lahens. Tr (Agnes Lahens) Norwegian 1895–6, Rus 1897, Cz 1905 (Mildred Lawson, with other stories from The untilled field, 1903, *below*).
REVIEWS: New York Times, 2 June 1895; [A. Bennett] Woman, 19 June 1895; Critic (New York), 22 June 1895; Bookman, July 1895; Athenaeum, 13 July 1895; Sat Rev, 27 July 1895; (W. D. Howells) Harper's Weekly, 27 July 1895; Literary World, 10 Aug 1895; Dial (Chicago), 16 Aug 1895; The Times, 6 Sep 1895; Yellow Dwarf [H. Harland] Yellow Book, Oct 1895; Overland (San Francisco), Feb 1896.

Evelyn Innes. 1898, (with Sister Teresa, 1901, *below*) New York and London 1975 (facs), London 1898 (rev), 1901 (rev), 1908 (rev), 1929, New York 1898, 1923 (Carra), 2 vols Leipzig 1898 (Tauchnitz). Tr Ger 1904 (rev).

REVIEWS: Daily Chron, 8 June 1898; Pall Mall Gazette, 10 June 1898; Sat Rev, 11 June 1898; (G. Atherton) Vanity Fair, 16 June 1898; (A. T. Quiller-Couch) Speaker, 18 June 1898; (R. Cortissoz) New York Tribune, 19 June 1898; Westminster Gazette, 22 June 1898; (J. G. Huneker) Musical Courier (New York), 22 June 1898; St James's Gazette, 22 June 1898; Acad, 25 June 1898; Outlook, 25 June 1898; Athenaeum, 2 July 1898; Bookman, July 1898; Book Buyer (New York), Aug 1898; Dial, Aug 1898; Literary World, 6 Aug 1898; Die Nation (Berlin), 13 Aug 1898; The Times, 6 Sep 1898.

The bending of the bough: a comedy in five acts. 1900, 1900 (rev), Chicago and New York 1900, Chicago 1969; in Selected plays, 1995 (Collections, *above*). Preface pbd separately New York 1900 (pamphlet). Produced Dublin 1900.

REVIEWS: Illus London News, 17 Mar 1900; Bookman, Apr 1900; (William Archer) Critic, May 1900; Athenaeum, 9 June 1900.

Sister Teresa. 1901, (with Evelyn Innes, 1898, *above*) New York and London 1975 (facs), London 1901 (rev), 1909 (rev), 1929, New York 1901, 1918 (Brentano), 1923 (Carra), 2 vols Leipzig 1901 (rev) (Tauchnitz). Tr Ger 1905 (rev).

REVIEWS: (A. Bennett) Acad, 20 July 1901; Freeman's Jnl (Dublin), 26 July 1901; Contemporary Rev, Aug 1901; Athenaeum, 3 Aug 1901; New York Times, 24 Aug 1901; The Times, 30 Aug 1901; Independent, 19 Sep 1901; (H. T. Peck) Bookman (New York), Nov 1901.

The untilled field. [Six stories previously published in Irish as An t-ur-gort (Dublin) 1902], 1903, New York (facs) 1970, London 1914 (rev), 1926 (rev), 1931 (rev), 1932 (Uniform), Philadelphia 1903, New York 1923 (with The lake, 1905, *below*) (Carra), Leipzig 1903 (rev) (Tauchnitz); with introd by T. R. Henn, Gerrards Cross and Toronto 1976 (facs); with introd by T. Brown, Gloucester and Dublin 1990. Short stories. Tr Cz (3 stories) 1905, Ger (3 stories) 1902–3.

REVIEWS: Acad 2 Aug 1902; Daily Chron 27 Apr 1903; Acad and Lit 16 May 1903; Independent 11 June 1903; Critic July 1903; Macmillan's July 1903; New York Times 29 Aug 1903; Munsey's (New York) Nov 1903.

The lake. 1905, 1905 (rev), 1921 (rev), 1932 (Uniform); with afterword by R. A. Cave, Gerrards Cross 1980; New York 1906, 1986 (facs); with Confessions of a young man, 1887 (*above*) 1923 (rev) (Carra); Leipzig 1906 (rev) (Tauchnitz). Tr Fr 1923, Ital 1933.

REVIEWS: TLS, 10 Nov 1905; Acad, 18 Nov 1905; Athenaeum, 2 Dec 1905; Sat Rev, 2 Dec 1905; (J. G. Huneker) New York Times, 17 Feb 1906; Outlook, Mar 1906; Edinburgh Rev, Apr 1906; Dial, 16 Apr 1906; North American, June 1906; Lit Digest (New York), 4 Aug 1906.

Reminiscences of the impressionist painters. Scribner's (New York), Feb 1906; Dublin 1906 (rev); rev and included in Hail and farewell: vale, 1911 (*below*) 1914. Tr Ger '1907' [1908], 1973.

Memoirs of my dead life. 1906, 1915 (expanded), 1921 (rev), 1928 (rev) (Uniform), New York '1907' [1906] (expurgated), 1920 (rev and expanded), 1960 (facs), 1923 (Carra), Leipzig 1906 (Tauchnitz) (rev). Tr Cz (End of Marie Pellegrin) c. 1905, Fr (End of Marie Pellegrin) 1918, (Resurgam) 1920, (Bring in the lamp) 1922, (2 stories omitted) 1922, (1 story restored) 1828, Ger 1907, (Lovers of Orelay) 1925, (reprint of 1907 with 4 stories omitted) 1926, Swedish (4 stories) 1927, Chinese (only Euphorion in Texas) 1929, Ital (3 stories omitted) 1945.

REVIEWS: Sat Rev, 7 July 1906; Athenaeum, 28 July 1906; (J. G. Huneker) New York Times, 5 Oct 1906; Nation (New York), 17 Jan 1907; Current Lit, Apr 1907.

The apostle. Dublin and Boston 1911; London 1923 (rev), New York 1911. Play, rev as The passing of the Essenes, 1930 (*below*); tr Ger 1911.

REVIEWS: Athenaeum, 22 July 1911; Literary Guide and Rationalist Rev, 1 Aug 1911; Current Lit (New York) Oct 1911; (M. C. Maguire) Irish Rev (Dublin), Oct 1911.

Hail and farewell: a trilogy. Vol 1 Ave; vol 2 Salve; vol 3 Vale. 1911, 1912, 1914, Vale (rev) 1915, 2 vols 1925 (rev), 3 vols (Uniform) 1933, 1 vol with introd and notes by R. Cave, Gerrards Cross and Montreal 1976, Gerrards Cross and Washington 1985 (facs), New York 3 vols 1911, 1912, 1914, 1923 (Carra), Leipzig 1912, 1912, 1914 (Vale rev) (Tauchnitz).

REVIEWS: TLS, 19 Oct 1911; [R Ross] TLS, 14 Nov 1912; Manchester Guardian, 24 Oct 1911; New York Times, 3 Dec 1911, 1 Dec 1912, 19 Apr 1914; Athenaeum, 25 Nov 1911, 26 Oct 1912; Sat Rev, 25 Nov 1911; Independent, 21 Dec 1911; Current Lit, Jan 1912; Irish Rev, Jan 1912; Bookman, Feb 1912; Sat Rev, 7 Mar 1914; Acad, 16 May 1914; Spectator, 27 June 1914; Yale Rev, Oct 1912.

Esther Waters: a play. London and Boston 1913, Lanahan, New York and London (rev) (2 versions) 1985. Produced London 1911.

REVIEW: Athenaeum, 1 Feb 1913.

Elizabeth Cooper: a comedy in three acts. Dublin, London and Boston 1913; rewritten as The coming of Gabrielle, 1920 (*below*) 1920. Produced London 1913, Paris (in Fr) 1914. Tr Fr as Clara Florise 1920.

Muslin (revision of A drama in muslin, 1886, *above*). 1915, 1932 (Uniform), New York 1915 (Brentano), 2 vols 1922, Leipzig 1920 (Tauchnitz).

REVIEWS: TLS, 16 Sep 1915; New York Times, 9 Jan 1916.

The brook Kerith: a Syrian story. 1916, 1916 (rev), 1921 (rev), 1927 (Uniform), illus 1929, 1952 (Pen), London and Toronto 1937, New York 1916, with preface 1916 (rev), 1917 (Brentano), 1923 (rev) (Carra), illus 1929, 1936, illus 1956, with introd by W. J. Miller 1969 (Black & Gold Lib), 2 vols Leipzig 1920 (Tauchnitz); partially dramatised as The apostle, 1911 (*above*) 1923 and again as The passing of the Essenes, 1930 (*below*) 1930. Tr Fr 1927.

REVIEWS: Boston Evening Transcript, 12 Aug 1916; Daily Express, 29 Aug 1916; (J. G. Huneker) New York Sun, 31 Aug 1916; Sat Rev, 2 Sep 1916; Observer, 3 Sep 1916; Outlook, 9 Sep 1916; Westminster, Gazette, 9 Sep 1916; Zion's Herald (Boston), 13 Sep 1916; TLS, 14 Sep 1916; (E. Garnett) Dial (New York), 21 Sep 1916; (L. Gilman) North Amer Rev (New York), Dec 1916; Bookman (New York), Mar 1917.

Lewis Seymour and some women (rev of A modern lover, 1883, *above*). New York 1917 (Brentano), 1923 (Carra), London 1917, Paris 1918 (Standard col).

REVIEWS: New York Times, 25 Feb 1917; TLS, 22 Mar 1917; Sat Rev, 7 Apr 1917.

A story-teller's holiday. 1918, 2 vols 1928 (rev with introd by E. Longworth and with Ulick and Soracha, 1926, *below*, replacing Albert Nobbs) (Uniform), New York 1918, 1923 (Carra), 2 vols 1928 (rev), 1 vol 1929, with introd by W. J. Miller, New York 1929 (Black & Gold Lib) (facs). Tr Ger (Albert Nobbs) 1928.

REVIEWS: (J. G. Huneker) Bookman (New York), Dec 1918; Smart Set, Dec 1918; Dial (New York), 14 Dec 1918; (B. De Casseres) New York, Sun 5 Jan 1919.

Avowals. 1919, 1924 (rev) (Uniform), New York 1919, (with Confessions of a young man, 1887, *above*) 1923 (Carra), 1926.

REVIEWS: (V. Woolf) TLS, 30 Oct 1919; Eng Rev, Dec 1919; Nation, 6 Dec 1919, 21 Jan 1920; Town Topics, 6 Dec 1919; Observer, 21 Dec 1919; Current Opinion, Jan 1920; Nation (New York), 21 Feb 1920; (D. MacCarthy) New Statesman, 30 July 1921.

The coming of Gabrielle (rev of Elizabeth Cooper, 1913, *above*). 1920, New York 1921, Leipzig 1923 (rev) (Tauchnitz); in Selected plays, 1995 (Collections, *above*). Produced London July 1923.

Héloïse and Abélard. 2 vols 1921, 1 vol 1925 (rev) (Uniform), 2 vols New York 1921, 1923 (rev) (Carra), 1 vol 1931, 1932 (Black & Gold Lib). Fragments (additions and corrections) 1921 (pamphlet), added to subsequent edns New York 1921 et seq.

In single strictness. 1922, New York 1922, 1923 (rev) (Carra); rptd (with Albert Nobbs replacing Wilfrid Holmes) as Celibate lives, 1927 (*below*). Tr Sp (Henrietta Marr and Wilfrid Holmes) 1942.

Conversations in Ebury street. 1924, 1930 (rev) (Uniform), 1969 (facs), New York 1924 (Carra).
Pure poetry: an anthology. 1924, New York 1924, 1925, 1973.
The pastoral loves of Daphnis and Chloe, done into English (from Longus). 1924, 1927, with Peronnik the fool (*below*) 1933 (Uniform), illus 1954, with Perronik [sic] the fool, New York 1924 (Carra), illus 1934, illus 1977.
Pure poetry: an anthology. Ed Moore 1924; as An anthology of pure poetry, ed with an introd by Moore, New York 1924, 1973.
Peronnik the fool. New York with Daphnis and Chloe (*above*) 1924 (Carra), 1926, Chapelle-Réanville (rev) 1928, London with The pastoral loves of Daphnis and Chloe; 1924 (*above*) 1933 (Uniform), illus 1933.
Ulick and Soracha. 1926, New York 1926, rev and included in A story-teller's holiday, 1918 (*above*) 1928.
Celibate lives (reprint of In single strictness, 1922, *above*, with Hugh Monfert replaced by Alfred Nobbs from A story-teller's holiday) 1927 (Uniform), 1968, New York 1927, Leipzig 1927 (Tauchnitz). Tr Fr (Albert Nobbs) 1971, Ger (Albert Nobbs) 1928.
The making of an immortal. New York and London 1927. Play, produced London Apr 1928. Tr Fr, Revue des Deux Mondes, 15 Jan 1930.
The passing of the Essenes: a drama in three acts (rev of The apostle 1923 *above*). 1930; in Selected plays, 1995 (Collections, *above*); 1931 (rev), 1938; New York 1930. Produced London Oct 1931.
Aphrodite in Aulis. London and New York 1930, New York (rev) 1931, London (rev) 1931 (Uniform).
A flood. New York 1930, Folcroft PA 1973 (facs), Norwood PA 1976 (facs), Philadelphia 1978 (facs), rptd in In minor keys, 1985 (Collections, *above*).
The talking pine. Paris 1931 (pamphlet), Folcroft PA 1976 (facs), Norwood PA 1977 (facs), Philadelphia 1978 (facs), Tempe AZ, 1948 (priv ptd pamphlet).
A communication to my friends. 1933, New York 1974 (facs), Folcroft PA 1974 (facs), Norwood PA 1976 (facs). Used as preface to Uniform 1933 and Ebury 1937 edns of A mummer's wife, '1885', *above*.
Diarmuid and Grania: a play in three acts (with William Butler Yeats). Introd by W. Becker, Dublin 1951 (pamphlet); Chicago 1974 (pamphlet), included in var edn of Yeats's plays, London and New York 1966. Produced Dublin Oct 1901.
La vie singular d'Albert Nobbs. Paris 1977. Produced Paris 1977; in Eng trn by A. McClelland, London 1978, New York 1982; in another Eng trn at Niagara-on-the-Lake (Ont., Canada) 1982. Dramatisation of Albert Nobbs by S. Benmussa.

Letters

See Gilcher's primary and Langenfeld's secondary bibliographies above for numerous letters included in several dozen biographies and memoirs of Moore's contemporaries, some of which are rptd in collections listed below.
Moore versus Harris. Ed G. Bruno, Detroit 1921, Chicago 1925, Folcroft PA 197? (facs), Norwood PA 1977 (facs).
A letter to the editor of The Times. 1925 (priv ptd pamphlet).
Letters to Ed Dujardin 1886–1922. Ed and tr from Fr 'John Eglinton' [W. K. Magee], New York 1929, Folcroft PA 197? (facs), Norwood PA 1977 (facs).
George Moore in quest of locale: two letters to W. T. Stead. Introd by J. McClelland, Berkeley CA 1931 (priv ptd, pamphlet).
Letters from George Moore: the Greek background of Aphrodite in Aulis, P. J. Dixon, London Mercury, Nov 1934.
George Moore: letters of his last years. Notes by V. M. Crawford, London Mercury and Bookman, Dec 1936.
Letters of George Moore (with an introduction by John Eglinton to whom they were written,) Bournemouth 1942 (priv ptd), Folcroft PA 1970 (facs), Norwood PA 1975 (facs).
George Moore on authorship. Cherry Plain NY 1949 (priv ptd).
Letters to Lady Cunard 1895–1933. Ed and introd by R. Hart-Davis, London and New York 1957, Westport CT 1979 (facs).
George Moore's letters to Edmund Gosse, W. B. Yeats, R. I. Best, Nancy Cunard, and Mary Hutchinson. Ed C. J. Burkhart, unpbd Phd thesis, Univ of MD 1958.
George Moore in transition: letters to T. Fisher Unwin and Lena Milman 1894–1910. Ed and commentary H. E. Gerber, Detroit 1968.
Letters of George Moore to his brother, Colonel Maurice Moore. Ed S. MacDonncha, unpbd diss Nat Univ of Ireland Galway 1972–3.
From naturalism to lyrical realism: fourteen unpublished letters from George Moore to Frans Netscher. Ed J. R. Riewald, Eng Stud, Apr 1977.
George Moore to Edward Elgar: eighteen letters on Diarmuid and Grania and operatic dreams. Ed E. Kennedy, ELT 21:3 1978.
Letters of George Moore 1863–1901. Ed R. S. Becker, unpbd PhD diss Univ of Reading 1980.
George Moore's correspondence with the mysterious countess. Ed and introd D. B. Eakin and R. Langenfeld, Victoria (BC, Canada) 1984.
George Moore on Parnassus: letters 1900–1933. Ed, notes and commentary H. E. Gerber, Newark DE, London and Toronto 1988.

§2

[Noble, J. A.]. An English disciple of Zola. Spectator, 17 Jan 1885.
Boycotting on the bookstalls: a note on George Moore. Court and Soc Rev, 15 July 1886.
Buchanan, R. The modern young man as critic. Universal Rev, Jan–Apr 1889, rptd in his The coming terror 1891.
Lanza, C. A rising novelist: George Moore. New York World, 29 Apr 1889.
Carpenter, G. R. Three critics: Mr Howells, Mr Moore, and Mr Wilde. Andover Rev, Dec 1891.
[White, G.]. To George Moore Esq. In Letters to eminent hands, "i", Derby 1892.
Pater, W. Mr George Moore as an art critic. Daily Chron, 10 June 1893, rptd in his Uncollected essays, Portland ME 1903, and Sketches and reviews, New York 1919.
Johnson, L. Mr George Moore's success. Daily Chron, 28 Mar 1894.
Peck, H. T. The rise of George Moore. Bookman (New York), June 1895, expanded as George Moore in his The personal equation, New York 1898.
Murray, D. C. Under French encouragement – George Moore. In his My contemporaries in fiction, 1897.
Morton, E. English novelists as dramatists. Bookman (New York), Aug 1898.
Montague, G. H. Mr George Moore. Harvard Monthly, Jan 1901.
[Huneker, J. G.]. Interview. Musical Courier (New York), 24 July 1901.
Cowley-Brown, J. S. The English Zola. Reedy's Mirror (St Louis MO), 1 Aug 1901.
Bennett, A. George Moore. In his Fame and fiction: an enquiry into certain popularities, 1901.
Archer, W. Real conversations: George Moore. 1904, New York 1904.
Chesterton, G. K. The moods of George Moore. In his Heretics, 1904, New York 1904.
Herts, R. D. George Moore the mundane. In Depreciations, New York 1914.
Huneker, J. G. Literary men who loved music. In Overtones: a book of temperaments, New York 1904.
Quinn, John. George Moore in Irish literatiure. Ed J. McCarthy, New York 1904.
Reid, F. The novels of George Moore. Westminster Rev, Aug 1909.
Murdoch, W. G. Blaikie. George Moore: an appreciation. In his Memories of Swinburne, with other essays, Edinburgh 1910.
Beerbohm, M. Dickens by G**rge M**re. In his A Christmas garland, London and New York 1912. Parody.

Weygandt, C. Edward Martyn and George Moore. In his Irish plays and playwrights, Boston and New York 1913.
Mitchell, S. L. George Moore. Dublin and London 1916, New York 1916.
Greg, F. J. George Moore – novelist of the hour. Vanity Fair (New York), Nov 1916.
Lucas, E. V. His fatal beauty: or the Moore of Chelsea, 1917 (priv ptd, pamphlet). Satiric skit included in Chelsea matinee, 20 Mar 1917.
Sherman, S. P. The aesthetic naturalism of George Moore. In his On contemporary literature, New York 1917.
Lanza, C. My friendship with George Moore, three thousand miles away. Bookman (New York), July 1918.
Clark, B. H. George Moore dogmatizes on the drama. New York Sun, 4 Aug 1918.
Williams, H. George Moore. In his Modern English writers: being a study of imaginative literature, 1918.
Eagle, Solomon [J. C. Squire]. Shakespeare's women and Mr George, Moore, and The bible as raw material. In Books in general, 1919.
[Woolf, V.]. A born writer. TLS, 29 July 1920.
Freeman, J. A portrait of George Moore in a study of his work. 1922, New York 1922.
Hone, J. The life of George Moore. 1936, New York 1936.
Hone, J. M. The Moore of Moore Hall. 1939. [EG]

Arthur Morrison 1863–1945

Mss located in Bancroft Lib, Univ of California; Berg Collection, NYPL; Colgate Univ Lib, Hamilton NY; Pierpont Morgan Lib, New York; Princeton; Rochester Univ. See also LR.

Bibliographies

In Index to short stories, ed I. T. E. Firkins, New York 1923 (2nd edn).
In Nineteenth century readers' guide to periodical literature 1890–1899, ed H. G. Cushing and A. V. Morris, 2 vols New York, 1944.
In Index to the Strand Magazine, 1891–1950, ed G. Beare, Westport CT 1982.
Calder, R. Arthur Morrison: a commentary with an annotated bibliography of writings about him. ELT 28 1985.
See also Wellesley *vol* 5 1989.

Selections

Arthur Morrison. 1929. Selected stories.
In Great tales of mystery, ed R. C. Bull, 1960, 1964, 1966, 1968.
In Short stories of the 'nineties, ed D. Stanford 1968.
In The rivals of Sherlock Holmes, ed H. Greene, 1970, 1971.
In Working-class stories of the 1890s, ed P. J. Keating, 1971.
In The crooked counties, ed H. Greene, 1973, 1976 (as The further rivals of Sherlock Holmes).
Best Martin Hewitt detective stories. New York 1976.
In Rivals of Sherlock Holmes, ed A. K. Russell, Secaucus NJ 1979.
In A treasury of Victorian detective stories, ed E. F. Bleiler, 1979.
In British poetry and prose 1870–1905, ed I. Fletcher, Oxford 1987.
In Victorian short stories vol 2, ed H. Orgel, 1990.
In Victorian tales of mystery and detection, ed M. Cox, Oxford 1992, 1993 (as Victorian detective stories).

§1

The shadows around us: authentic tales of the supernatural. 1891.
REVIEW: Literary World 9 Jan 1891.
Tales of mean streets. 1894, 1895 (2nd edn), 1895 (3rd edn), Boston 1895, Leipzig 1895 (Tauchnitz), New York 1895, London 1896 (4th edn), 1898 (5th edn), 1903 (6th edn), 1906 (7th edn), 1911, 1912, 1913 [9th edn], New York 1921, London 1927, Bath 1967, New York 1970, Woodbridge CT 1983, Chicago 1997.
REVIEWS: Pall Mall Gazette 19 Nov 1894; Athenaeum 24 Nov 1894; Nat Observer 22 Dec 1894; Bookman Jan 1895, rptd Bookman (USA) Mar 1895; Pall Mall Gazette 4 Jan 1895; Literary World 18 Jan 1895; Methodist Times 21 Feb 1895; Spectator 9 Mar 1895; New York Times 27 Apr 1895; Critic 15 June 1895; Nation 11 July 1895; Harper's Mag Suppl 4 Oct 1895; New York Times 26 Mar 1922.
Martin Hewitt, investigator. 1894, New York and London 1894, New York 1907, 1971, Philadelphia 1971, Westport CT 1975, London 1976, Salem NH 1976, New York 1976, 1977, Leicester 1978.
REVIEWS: Literary World 1 Feb 1895; Acad 2 Feb 1895; New York Times 13 Apr 1907.
Chronicles of Martin Hewitt. Being the second series of the Martin Hewitt, investigator. 1894, 1895 (2nd edn), New York 1896, London 1901, 1905?, Boston 1907, Freeport NY 1971, Leicester 1978; tr Swed 1896.
REVIEWS: Athenaeum 21 Dec 1895; Literary World 27 Dec 1895; Acad 1 Feb 1896; Spectator 18 Apr 1896; Dial 16 Nov 1896.
Zig-zags at the zoo. 1895.
Adventures of Martin Hewitt (3rd ser). 1896.
REVIEW: Literary World 20 Nov 1896.
A child of the Jago. 1896, Chicago 1896, Leipzig 1897 (Tauchnitz), New York 1906, London 1907, New York 1911, London 1913, New York 1911, London 1946 (Pen), 1969 (ed P. J. Keating), St Albans 1969, Woodbridge, Suffolk 1969, Glasgow 1971, Chicago 1995 (introd by A. Miller), London 1996 (introd by P. Miles); tr Swed 1898.
REVIEWS: Saturday Rev 28 Nov 1896; Blackwood's Mag Dec 1896; Bookman Dec 1896, rptd Bookman (USA) Jan 1897; St James's Gazette 2 Dec 1896; St James's Gazette 8 Dec 1896; Acad 12 Dec 1896; Athenaeum 12 Dec 1896; Fortnightly Rev Jan 1897; Br Rev 9 Jan 1897; Literary World 22 Jan 1897; Critic 24 Apr 1897; Quart Rev Oct 1902.
The Dorrington deed-box. 1897, 1901, 1902, Paris 1912.
REVIEWS: Literature 23 Oct 1897; Athenaeum 13 Nov 1897; Literary World 19 Nov 1897.
To London town. 1899, Chicago 1899, Leipzig 1899 (Tauchnitz).
REVIEWS: Acad 16 Sep 1899; Spectator 16 Sep 1899; Athenaeum 23 Sep 1899; Bookman Nov 1899; Outlook 23 Dec 1899.
Cunning Murrell. 1900, New York 1900, Woodbridge, Suffolk 1977.
REVIEWS: Acad 22 Sep 1900; Athenaeum 29 Sep 1900; Bookman Oct 1900; Literary World 5 Oct 1900; Spectator 6 Oct 1900; Acad 3 Nov 1900; Outlook 15 Dec 1900; Bookman (USA) Feb 1901.
The hole in the wall. 1902, Leipzig 1902 (Tauchnitz), New York 1902, London 1903, New York 1903, London 1905, 1947 (introd by V. S. Pritchett), 1956, 1972, 1978, Woodbridge, Suffolk 1982.
REVIEWS: Acad 13 Sep 1902; Acad 20 Sep 1902; Spectator 20 Sep 1902; Athenaeum 27 Sep 1902; New York Times 27 Sep 1902; Harper's Weekly 4 Oct 1902; Outlook 11 Oct 1902; Literary World 24 Oct 1902.
The red triangle: being some further chronicles of Martin Hewitt, investigator. 1903, 1904, Boston 1903, New York 1905, 1907, Freeport NY 1970.
REVIEW: Acad 6 June 1903.
The green eye of Goona. Stories of a case of tokay. 1904, Boston 1904 (as The green diamond), Leipzig 1905 (Tauchnitz), Boston 1907 (as The green diamond), New York 1908 (as The green diamond).
REVIEWS: New York Times 17 Sep 1904; Bookman (USA) Oct 1904; Athenaeum 1 Oct 1904; Spectator 15 Oct 1904; Arena Mar 1905; Reader Mar 1905.
Divers vanities. 1905, Leipzig 1905 (Tauchnitz).
REVIEWS: TLS 29 Sep 1905; Spectator 30 Sep 1905; Acad 7 Oct 1905; Athenaeum 4 Nov 1905.
Chronicles of Martin Hewitt, detective. Boston 1907, London 1908, 1919.
The seller of hate. 1907.
Green ginger. 1909, Leipzig 1909 (Tauchnitz), New York 1909, 1910,
REVIEWS: TLS 11 Feb 1909; Spectator 20 Feb 1909; Bookman Mar

1909; Outlook 16 Mar 1909; Athenaeum 10 Apr 1909; New York Times 18 Sep 1909.
The painters of Japan. 2 vols 1911, New York 1911. First pbd Macmillan's Mag Aug–Dec 1902.
Fiddle o' dreams and more. 1933.
REVIEW: TLS 30 Nov 1933.

Contributions to periodicals and collaborative works
Morrison joined W. E. Henley's Nat Observer, *later working for* Macmillan's Mag.
Palace Journal. 24 Apr 1889–25 Dec 1889.
Nat Observer. 17 Dec 1892–17 Mar 1892.
Windsor Mag. Adventures of Martin Hewitt, Jan–June 1896; The Dorrington deed-box, Jan–June 1897.
Chap-Book. Ingrates at Bagshaw's, 15 Nov 1895; A vision of Toyokuni, 1 Aug 1895.
That brute Simmons. In Stories by English authors, 1896, 1904 (play with H. C. Sargent).
Bookman. How to write a short story, Mar 1897.
Saturday Rev. A county council improvement, 8 May 1897.
Pall Mall Mag. Feb 1901–Sep 1905.
One more unfortunate. In The May book, 1901.
Cornhill Mag. Family budgets, Apr 1901.
T. P.'s Weekly. William Ernest Henley, 24 July 1903.
The Story-Teller. The thing in the upper room, May 1910.
Harmsworth's London Mag. Dec 1902–Jan 1913.
The dumb-cake. New York 1907, 1919. With R. Pryce. Play.
Lippincott's Mag. Oct 1912–Oct 1913.
For contributions to the New Rev, *see* Wellesley *vol* 5.

Introductions
Exhibition of Japanese prints (Fine Art Soc). 1909.
Exhibition of Japanese screens painted by the old masters (Royal Soc of Br Artists). 1910.
Catalogue of an exhibition of Chinese painting. 1911.
Exhibition of Japanese screens decorated by the old masters (Royal Soc of Br Artists). 1914.

§2
Bookman Jan 1895.
Lang, A. At the sign of the ship. Longman's Mag June 1895.
Daily News 12 Dec 1896. Interview.
[C. R.] Acad 12 Dec 1896.
Bookman (USA) Jan 1897. Portrait.
Traill, H. D. The new realism. Fortnightly Rev Jan 1897.
Traill, H. D. In his The new fiction and other essays on literary subjects, 1897.
Jay, Rev A. O. Fortnightly Rev Feb 1897. Letter.
Great Thoughts 24 Apr 1897.
Rook, C. Chap-Book 15 Aug 1897.
Acad 4 Dec 1897.
Blatchford, R. In his My favourite books, 1900, 1911.
Findlater, J. H. The slum movement in fiction. Nat Rev May 1900.
Dark, S. Crampton's Mag July 1902.
T. P.'s Weekly 28 Nov 1902.
Bookman July 1905.
Authors at work. Bookman Nov 1908.
Williamson, K. In his W. E. Henley: a memoir, 1930, rptd Brooklyn NY 1974, 1982.
The Times 5 Dec 1945. Obituary.
Bell, J. A study of Arthur Morrison. Essays & Studies 1952.
Keating, P. J. Biographical study. In A child of the Jago, 1969.
Keating, P. J. In his The working classes in Victorian fiction, 1971.
Krzack, M. In Victorian writers and the city, ed J. P. Hulin and P. Coustillas, Lille 1979.
Severn, D. The damned and innocent: two novels by Arthur Morrison. London Mag Feb 1980.
Krzack, M. Preface. In Tales of mean streets, Woodbridge, Suffolk 1983.
DLB vols 70, 135, 197.
Sutherland, J. In The Longman companion to Victorian fiction, 1988.
Calder, R. L. In The 1890s: an encyclopedia of British literature, art, and culture, ed G. A. Cevasco, New York 1993. [DA]

Neil Munro, 'Hugh Foulis' 1863–1930

Mss located in Berg Collection, NYPL; Princeton. See also LR.

Bibliographies
In An index to Blackwood's Magazine 1901–1980, ed D. Finkelstein, Aldershot 1995.
See also Wellesley *vol* 5 1989.

Collections and selections
In Shorter lyrics of the twentieth century, 1900–1922, ed W. H. Davies, 1922.
Works. Uniform edition. 9 vols Edinburgh and London 1923.
The poetry of Neil Munro. Edinburgh and London 1931 (ed and introd by J. Buchan), Stevenage 1987.
In The pirate ship (various authors). London and Glasgow 1933.
The works of Neil Munro. Inveraray edn. 9 vols Edinburgh and London 1935.
Para Handy tales. Edinburgh and London 1955 (1st 3 pts of Para Handy and other tales), 1965, 1969, 1981.
Para Handy, the collected stories (including 15 previously uncollected). Edinburgh 1992 (introduced and annotated by B. D. Osborne and R. Armstrong).
REVIEW: TLS 7 Jan 1932.

§1
The lost pibroch, and other sheiling stories. Edinburgh and London 1896, 1898, 1902, 1903 (5th edn), 1910 (6th edn), 1925, 1935 (Inveraray edn with Jaunty Jock and Ayrshire idylls), 1948 (Inveraray edn reprint with Jaunty Jack and Ayrshire idylls); tr Gaelic 1913.
REVIEWS: Blackwood's Mag May 1896; Bookman May 1896; Acad 13 June 1896.
John Splendid: the tale of a poor gentleman, and the little wars of Lorn. Edinburgh and London 1898 (5 impressions), Toronto 1898, Edinburgh and London 1899, 1903, 1905 (7th edn), 1910 (8th edn), 1915, 1920, 1923, 1923 (Uniform edn), 1924, 1929, 1931 (twice), 1935 (Inveraray edn), 1936, 1943 (Inveraray edn), 1945 (Inveraray edn), 1948 (Inveraray edn), Edinburgh 1994 (introd by B. D. Osborne); tr Gaelic 1931.
REVIEWS: Spectator 24 Sep 1898; Bookman Oct 1898 (symposium on John Splendid); Athenaeum 1 Oct 1898; Acad 10 Oct, 12 Nov 1898; Bookman (USA) Dec 1898; Blackwood's Mag Jan 1899; Critic Feb 1899; New York Times 11 Feb 1899; Dublin Mag Oct/Dec 1931.
Gilian the dreamer. His fancy, his love and his adventure. 1899, New York 1899, Toronto 1899, Edinburgh and London 1923 (Uniform edn), 1935 (Inveraray edn), 1948 (Inveraray edn), Edinburgh 1935 (Inveraray edn); tr Gaelic 1940.
REVIEWS: Spectator 14 Oct 1899; Athenaeum 21 Oct 1899; Acad 28 Oct 1899; Blackwood's Mag Nov 1899; Bookman Nov 1899; Bookman (USA) Dec 1899.
Doom castle. A romance. Edinburgh and London 1901, New York 1901, Edinburgh and London 1923 (Uniform edn), Edinburgh 1925, Edinburgh and London 1948 (Inveraray edn reprint), Edinburgh 1978, 1996 (introd by B. D. Osborne).
REVIEWS: Athenaeum 15 June 1901; Bookman Aug 1901.
The shoes of fortune. 1901 (illus), New York 1901, 1902, Edinburgh and London 1923 (Uniform edn), 1925, 1930, 1932, 1935 (Inveraray edn), 1948 (Inveraray edn).
REVIEW: Bookman Dec 1901.

Children of the tempest. A tale of the outer isles. Edinburgh and London 1903, 1905, 1923 (Uniform edn), 1935 (Inveraray edn), 1948 (Inveraray edn); tr Gaelic 1933.
REVIEWS: TLS 24 July 1903; Athenaeum 8 Aug 1903.
Erchie, my droll friend. Edinburgh and London 1904, 1905.
The Vital Spark and her queer crew. Edinburgh and London 1906, 1920.
REVIEW: Bookman June 1906.
The daft days. Edinburgh and London 1907, New York and London 1907 (as Bud: a novel), Edinburgh and London 1909, 1911 (4th impression), 1912, 1915, 1916, 1918, 1920, 1923 (Uniform edn), 1924, 1925, 1928, 1931, 1933, 1935 (Inveraray edn), 1939 (Inveraray edn), 1948 (Inveraray edn), 1953 (Inveraray edn).
REVIEWS: Athenaeum 25 May 1907; Bookman June 1907; Acad 8 June 1907.
Fancy farm. Edinburgh and London 1910, 1917, 1923 (Uniform edn), 1935 (Inveraray edn), 1948 (Inveraray edn reprint).
REVIEWS: TLS 1 Dec 1910; Bookman Feb 1911.
In Highland harbours with Para Handy, S. S. Vital Spark. Edinburgh and London 1911.
Ayrshire idylls. 1912 (illustr G. Houston), New York 1912 (illustr G. Houston), 1923 (illustr G. Houston), Edinburgh and London 1923 (new edn), 1926, 1935 (Inveraray edn with The lost pibroch, and other sheiling stories, and Jaunty Jock), 1948 (Inveraray edn with The lost pibroch, and other sheiling stories, and Jaunty Jock).
REVIEWS: Athenaeum 14 Dec 1912; TLS 26 Dec 1912.
The new road. 1914, Edinburgh and London 1919, Toronto 1919, Edinburgh and London 1923 (Uniform edn), 1930, 1935 (Inveraray edn), 1948 (Inveraray edn), 1969, Edinburgh 1994 (introd by B. D. Osborne).
REVIEWS: TLS 2 July 1914; Athenaeum 4 July 1914; Bookman Aug 1914.
Jaunty Jock, and other stories. Edinburgh and London 1918, 1919 (3rd impression), (Uniform edn), 1931.
REVIEWS: TLS 1 Nov 1918; Bookman Jan 1919.
Hurricane Jack of the Vital Spark. Edinburgh and London 1923.
The history of the Royal Bank of Scotland, 1727–1927. Edinburgh 1928 (priv ptd).
REVIEW: TLS 2 Aug 1928.
The brave days. A chronicle from the north. Edinburgh 1931 (introd by G. Blake), 1934 (introd by G. Blake).
REVIEWS: Bookman Jan 1932; TLS 7 Jan 1932.
Para Handy and other tales. Edinburgh and London 1931, 1933, 1937, 1941, 1942, 1943 (twice), 1945, 1947, 1948, 1951, Edinburgh 1980.
REVIEW: TLS 7 Jan 1932.
The looker-on. (Essays rptd from the Glasgow Evening News, ed and introd by G. Blake.) Edinburgh 1933, 1935.
Erchie & Jimmy Swan. 1969, Edinburgh 1972, Greenock 1987, 1989, Edinburgh 1993 (with 59 previously uncollected stories, introd and annotated by B. D. Osborne and R. Armstrong), Edinburgh 1996 (with 59 previously uncollected stories, introd and annotated B. D. Osborne and R. Armstrong).
Neil Munro's Para Handy. Port Glasgow 1986.
Neil Munro's Jimmy Swan. Greenock 1988.
Neil Munro's Erchie. Greenock 1987, 1989.

Contributions to periodicals, collaborative works and anthologies

Munro edited the Glasgow Evening News *1918–24. Much of his poetry was pbd in jnls, particularly* Blackwood's Mag.
Blackwood's Mag. Oct 1893–Aug 1917. *See also* Wellesley *vol 5 1989*.
Bookman. Dec 1896–Jan 1913 (sporadic).
Living Age. Heather, 16 Jan 1897; Two exiles, 4 Mar 1899. Poems.
Good Words. Jan 1899–Dec 1901.
Bookman (USA). Rudyard Kipling, May 1899.
The imaginative boy. In A volunteer haversack containing contributions of certain writers to the Queen's Rifle Volunteer Brigade: The Royal Scots, ed A. S. Walker, Edinburgh 1902.
Cassell's Mag. The silver drum, Jan 1903.
Stevenson: the man and his work. In Robert Louis Stevenson: a Bookman extra number 1913, 1913.
In Songs & sonnets for England in time of war, 1915.
In A treasury of war poetry: British and American poems of the world war 1914–1919, ed G. H. Clarke, [1919].
In Valour and vision: poems of the war, ed J. T. Trotter, 1920.
In Ballads and poems. By members of the Glasgow Ballad Club (4th ser). Edinburgh 1924.
For the New Rev, *see* Wellesley *vol 5*.

Editions, introductions, etc

Introd to Poems by Robert Burns. [1904], 1906 (Red Letter Lib), New York 1928.
The Clyde river and Firth. Painted by M. Y. and J. Young Hunter. Described by N. Munro. 1907.
Introd to The old Highlands: being papers read before the Gaelic Society of Glasgow 1895–1906. 1908.
Scottish university verses, 1918–1923. Ed Munro, Aberdeen 1923.
Introd to A. Robertson, The Ogha Mor or the tale-man on his elbow, tr Rev A. MacKinnon, Glasgow and London 1924.
Of the western isle; forty woodcuts by Stephen Bone. 1925. Description by N. Munro.
Introd to Dr W. H. Drummond's complete poems. [1926.]

§2

New writers (with portrait). Bookman Apr 1896.
Bookman (USA) Jan 1898.
Stuart, A. Montrose and Argyll in fiction. Blackwood's Mag Jan 1899 Discusses Munro's John Splendid.
Stewart, A. W. The author of Gilian the dreamer. Sunday Mag Jan 1900.
MacArthur, J. Bookman (USA) Apr 1900.
A novelist of the north. Young Man Mar 1902.
Acad 1 Aug 1903.
Portrait. Bookman July 1903.
Meldrum, D. S. July 1915.
Obits: [Glasgow] Evening News 22 Dec 1930; Graham, R. B. C. [Glasgow] Evening News 23 Dec 1930; The Times 23 and 24 Dec 1930; New York Times 23 Dec 1930.
Blake, G. Introd to The brave days. Edinburgh 1931. Contains biographical material.
Hendry, B. Neil Munro: the Gael in literature. Bookman 1931.
Wernitz, H. Neil Munro und die nationale Kulturbewegung in modernen Schottland. Berlin 1937.
Sutherland, J. In The Longman companion to Victorian fiction, 1988.
Donald, S. In the wake of the Vital spark: Para Handy's Scotland. Glasgow 1994, 1996.
DLB vol 156. Detroit 1995.
Osborne, B. D. Introds to John Splendid, Edinburgh 1994, The new road, Edinburgh 1994, and Doom castle, 1996.
Völkel, H. Das literarische Werk Neil Munros. Frankfurt-am-Main 1996. [DAPA]

Edith Nesbit 1858–1924

Fabian papers at Nuffield College include letters about Nesbit's involvement with the Fabian Soc. Letters to her agents are in the Berg Collection, NYPL. Letters to the Soc of Authors are in the BL, and to H. G. Wells in the Wells papers at the Univ Lib of Illinois at Urbana-Champaign. Parts of her correspondence with her publishers are in the Macmillan papers at the BL and in the John Lane papers in the HRHRC, Austin TX. Jocelyn Nixon's private archive contains several ms notebooks of poems (some extracted from periodi-

cals), and some correspondence. The Doris Langley Moore archive contains transcripts of many letters from Nesbit.

Bibliographies

Moore, D. L. E. Nesbit, a biography. 1933. A list of her writings is included at the end.

Streatfeild, N. Magic and the magician. 1958. Contains a brief list of writings. This list was expanded for the Bodley Head monograph 1960.

Goodacre, S. His bibliography included at the end of J. Briggs, A woman of passion: the life of E. Nesbit, 1987.

§1

Lays and legends. 1886.
The lily and the cross. 1887, New York 1887.
The star of Bethlehem. 1887, New York 1887.
The better part, and other poems. 1888.
The message of the dove. 1888, New York 1888.
Landscape and song. 1888, New York 1888.
Leaves of life. London and New York 1888.
Carols and sea songs. 1889, New York 1889.
Songs of two seasons. Illustr J. McIntyre, 1890.
The voyage of Columbus, a narrative in verse. 1892.
Sweet lavender (verses). 1892, New York 1892.
Lays and legends. Second ser (verses) 1892.
Grim tales. 1893.
Something wrong. 1893.
The Marden mystery. Chicago 1894.
Pussy tales. 1895.
Doggy tales. 1895.
Rose leaves. 1895.
A pomander of verse. 1895, Chicago 1895.
As happy as a king. 1896.
In homespun. 1896, Boston 1896. Vol 22 in the Keynote Ser.
The children's Shakespeare. Ed E. Vredenburg, no 1532, 1897, Philadelphia 1900. Reissued in 1910 as Children's stories from Shakespeare, and in 6 vols as The Gem Shakespeare Library [1914?]. For details, *see* 1910 *below.*
Royal children of English history. 1897.
Songs of love and empire. 1898.
Pussy and doggy tales. 1899, New York 1900. A combined edn of the two 1895 vols, with new material.
The story of the treasure seekers, being the adventures of the Bastable family in search of a fortune. Illustr G. Browne (15) and L. Baumer (2) 1899, New York 1899. Rptd often, then reissued both separately and as 1st pt of The complete story of the Bastable family 1929, with later reprintings; reset with original illustrations 1958; new edn with illustrations by C. Leslie 1958 (Pen); pbd together with The would-be-goods, illustr S. Einzig, with introd by N. Streatfield, 1966 (Nonesuch Cygnet).
The secret of Kyriels. 1899, Philadelphia 1899.
The book of dragons. Illustr H. R. Millar, with decorations by H. Granville Fell, London and New York 1900, rptd 1901.
Nine unlikely tales for children. Illustr H. R. Millar (8), C. Shepperson (20), frontispiece by M. Bowley, 1901, New York 1901. Rptd often up to 1928, then taken over by Ernest Benn, and further rptd.
The would-be-goods, being the further adventures of the treasure seekers. Illustr A. H. Buckland (17) and J. Hassell (2) 1901, New York 1901. Often rptd; reset with the original illustrations 1958; new edn, illustr C. Leslie, 1958 (Pen); pbd with The treasure seekers, illustr S. Einzig, with introd by N. Streatfield, 1966 (Nonesuch Cygnet).
To wish you every joy. 1901.
Thirteen ways home. 1901.
The revolt of the toys, and what comes of quarrelling. 1902, New York 1902.
Five children and it. Illustr H. R. Millar 1902, New York 1905. Often rptd. Reset with the original illustrations 1957; new edn with the original illustrations 1959 (Pen).
The red house. Illustr A. L. Kellar 1902, New York 1902. Several reprints.
The rainbow queen, and other stories. 1903.
Playtime stories. 1903.
The literary sense. 1903, New York 1903.
The phoenix and the carpet. Illustr H. R. Millar 1904, New York 1904. Often rptd. Facs of 1st edn 1956; new edn with the original illustrations 1959 (Pen).
The new treasure seekers. Illustr G. Browne (31) and L. Baumer (2) 1904, New York 1904. Often rptd. Reset with illustrations by C. W. Hodges 1949; new edn with original illustrations 1958 (Pen).
The story of the five rebellious dolls. 1904, New York 1904.
Pug Peter and other stories for boys and girls. Leeds and London 1905. Anon.
Oswald Bastable and others. Illustr C. E. Brock (7) and H. R. Millar (13) 1905.
The rainbow and the rose. London, New York and Bombay 1905.
The story of the amulet. Illustr H. R. Millar 1906, New York 1906. Often rptd; reset with the original illustrations 1957; new edn with original illustrations 1959 (Pen).
The railway children. Illustr C. E. Brock 1906, New York 1906. Often rptd; new edn 1948; new edn with original illustrations 1960 (Pen); new edn illustr P. Kay 1989.
The incomplete amorist. Illustr C. F. Underwood 1906, New York 1906.
Man and maid. 1906.
The enchanted castle. Illustr H. R. Millar 1907, New York 1907. Often rptd; facs of lst edn 1957; reset edn illustr L. Lamb 1957.
Twenty beautiful stories from Shakespeare ... retold by E. N. Ed E. T. Roe, Chicago 1907, rptd 1926.
The old nursery stories. 1908. No 1 of The Children's Bookcase Ser (later books in the series were by other authors).
The house of Arden, a story for children. Illustr H. R. Millar 1908, New York 1909. Often rptd; reset edn illustr D. E. Walduck 1949.
Jesus in London, a poem. 1908.
Ballads and lyrics of socialism 1883 to 1908. 1908. Pbd for the Fabian Soc.
Harding's luck. Illustr H. R. Millar 1909, New York 1910. Several reprints; reset edn illustr D. E. Walduck 1949.
These little ones. Illustr S. Pryse 1909.
Cinderella, a play with twelve songs to popular airs. 1909.
Daphne in Fitzroy Street. 1909, New York 1909 (as The house with no address), rptd London 1914 with the revised title.
Garden poems. London and Glasgow 1909.
The magic city. Illustr H. R. Millar 1910. Further reprints.
Children's stories from Shakespeare, with When Shakespeare was a boy by Dr F. J. Furnivall. 1910, Philadelphia 1912. A reissue of the 1897 vol with new title and illustrations; rptd in The Gem Shakespeare Lib 6 vols [1914?].
Fear. 1911.
The wonderful garden, or the three C's. Illustr H. R. Millar 1911. Further rptd.
Ballads and verses of the spiritual life. 1911.
Dormant. 1911, New York 1912 (as Rose Royal).
The magic world. Illustr H. R. Millar (21) and S. Pryse (3) London and New York 1912, 2nd impression London 1924. Further rptd.
Our new story book. 1913, New York 1913.
Wet magic. Illustr H. R. Millar 1913. Further rptd.
Wings and the child, or the building of magic cities. 1913, New York 1913.
The incredible honeymoon. New York 1916, London 1921.
The New World Literary Series, book two. Ed H. C. Wylde, London and Glasgow 1921.

The lark. 1922.
Many voices. 1922.
To the adventurous. 1923.
Five of us, and Madeleine. 1925, New York 1926; 2nd impression London 1926; further rptd.
The Bastable children. Preface by C. Morley, New York 1925. A reprint of the 3 Bastable books. Often rptd. English edn pbd under the title Complete history of the Bastable family, with illustrations by G. Browne, L. Baumer, A. H. Buckland and J. Hassall, 1928.

Undated works

Fading light. Illustr A. Warne Browne, W. Hagelberg, London and New York.
May-time and play-time. London and New York.
Miss Mischief. London and New York c. 1891.
Off to fairyland. London and New York.
Fairies (a shaped book). London.
Sunnylands. London and New York.
Bright eyes. London and New York. A book in the shape of a butterfly.
Songs of the cornfield. London. A book in the shape of a straw hat and sickle.

Books edited or arranged by E. Nesbit

Spring songs and sketches; Summer songs and sketches; Autumn songs and sketches; Winter songs and sketches. A series of illustrated books of verses, selected and arranged by E. N. and R. Ellice Mack. London and New York 1886. A similar series of books – for Morning, Noon, Eventide and Night – was pbd in 1887.
River sketches. Words selected and written by E. N. London and New York 1887.
Winter snow; In the spring time; The time of roses; Autumn leaves. A series of books, with contents selected and arranged by E. N. London and New York 1888.
Lilies and heartsease; Daisy days; Falling leaves. A similar series of books, ed E. N. and R. E. Mack. London and New York 1888.
By land and sea. Poems selected by E. N. London and New York 1888.
The life of happy children, by C. Brooke, A. Hoatson and E. Bland. Selected and arranged by E. N. London and New York 1889.
Songs of Scotland. Selected by E. N., illustr H. Bellingham Smith, G. E. Corner, and G. Gorsky. 1890.
The girl's own birthday book. Selected and arranged by E. N. 1894.
Poets' whispers, a birthday book. Quotations selected and arranged by E. N. 1895.

Collaborative works

The prophet's mantle (in collaboration with Hubert Bland, under the pseud 'Fabian Bland'). 1885, Chicago 1889.
Easter-tide, by E. N. and C. Brooke. 1888, New York 1888.
All round the year, by E. N. and C. Brooke. 1888.
The lilies round the cross (with Helen J. Wood). 1889, New York 1889.
Life's sunny side (poems by E. N. and others). 1890, New York 1890.
Told by the fireside (short stories by E. N. and others). 1890.
Twice four (short stories by E. N. and others). 1891.
Story upon story, and every word true (by E. N. and others). 1892.
Contributions to the following books of verse and prose, pbd 1893: Flowers I bring and songs I sing; Our friends and all about them; Listen long and listen well; Sunny tales for snowy days; Told by the sunbeams and me; What really happened; We've tales to tell.
Contributions to 15 of the Nister's Holiday Annuals between 1893 and 1915.
Contributions to the following books of verse and prose, pbd in 1894: Hours in many lands; Tales that are true for brown eyes and blue; Tales to delight from morning till night; Fur and feathers, tales for all weathers; All but one, told by the flowers; Lads and lasses.
A graven image (short stories by E. N. and O. Barron). 1894.
The Butler in Bohemia (short stories, written in collaboration with O. Barron). 1894.
Contributions to the following books of verses and prose pbd 1895: Tick tock, tales of the clock; Stories in a shell; Treasures from storyland; Friends in fable, a book of animal stories; Rosy cheeks and golden ringlets.
Dulcie's lantern, and other stories (by E. N. and others). 1895.
Holly and mistletoe, a book of Christmas verse (with Norman Gale and Richard le Gallienne). 1895.
Once upon a time, the favourite nursery tales (retold by E. N. and others). London and New York 1897. Much of this material was included in later Nister edns – e.g. Little Red Riding Hood and other nursery tales (undated) and Favourite fairy tales (1912), where E. N. is named as one of several authors.
Dinna Forget (poems by E. N. and others). London 1897, New York 1898.
Tales told in the twilight (very short stories by E. N. and others). London and New York 1897.
Dog tales, and other tales, by E. N. and others. Ed E. Vredenburg 1898.
A book of dogs, being a discourse on them, with many tales and wonders, gathered by E. N. London and New York 1898.
Contributions to Father Tuck's Annual. 1900.
Cat tales (with Rosamund Bland). London and New York 1904.
Days of delight. Ed E. Vredenburg 1910. In Father Tuck's Golden Gift Ser. There are possibly 19 vols in the ser. Only a few have Nesbit contributions. Father Tuck's Welcome Gift Ser may also date from this time – *see* undated section, *below*.
Children's stories from English history, told by E. N. and Doris Ashley. 1910. Rptd material from Royal children of English history 1897; reissued 1914.
My sea-side-story book, by E. N. with G. Manville Fenn. London and New York 1911.
Favourite fairy tales, retold by E. N. and others. 1911.
Battle songs, chosen by E. N. 1914.
Essays, by Hubert Bland. Ed 'E. Nesbit Bland' 1914.

Undated collaborative works

Sunny hours. In Father Tuck's Welcome Gift Series, No 401. There were 6 vols in this series, some of which may have had E. N. contributions. The numbering suggests a date before 1910 (*see* Golden Gift Ser under that year, *above*).
My farmyard story book, by E. N. and others. London and New York.
Stories for all times, by E. N. and others. London and New York.
Hallowe'en house, by Mrs Molesworth, E. N. and others. London and New York.
Round the hearth, by E. N. and others, ed and arranged by Robert Ellice Mack.
Merry playtimes, a picture book for boys and girls (by E. N. and others). London and New York.
Our own story book (by E. N. and others). London and New York.
Merry companions (by E. N. and others). London and New York.
In picture land, a book of pictures and stories for little ones (by E. N. and others). London and New York.
Blue eyes and cherry pies (by E. N. and others). London and New York.
The beautiful world, and other poems (by E. N. and others). London and New York.

Contributions to periodicals

E. Nesbit was a prolific contributor to periodicals of all descriptions. Her first contribution was a 'set of verses with a moral tag' in The Sunday Mag *in 1874 (not yet precisely identified). The 1st positively identified contribution was a set of verses 'A year ago' in Good Words Dec 1876. The following lists the more important of the rest of her huge output:*

Argosy. Over 30 contributions 1877–97.
Atalanta. At least 8 contributions 1891–8.
Black and White. 4 chs from children's books 1899–1907.
Daily Chron. Weekly articles for children Apr–July 1910.
Girls Own Paper. My school days Oct 1896–Sep 1897.
Home Chimes. Short stories 1887–9.
Illus London News. Chs from children's books 1896–1901.
London Mag. Chs from children's books 1903–6.
Longman's Mag. 4 adult short stories and poems 1890–1.
The Neolith, an experimental mag, pbd quarterly under the direction of E. N., Graily Hewitt, F. Ernest Jackson, and Spencer Pryse. 4 issues only pbd (3 with Nesbit stories).
Pall Mall Mag. Chs from children's books 1893–5.
Sketch. Adult short stories and poems 1893–5.
Strand Mag. July 1899–Aug 1913. Large sections of many of her most important children's books, from The book of dragons to Wet magic (111 contributions in all).
Weekly Dispatch. Numerous contributions Jan 1882–Mar 1892. In the middle years a poem and/or a short story appeared virtually every week.

§2

Kentish Express 10 May 1924. Obituary.
Moore, D. Langley. E. Nesbit, a biography. 1933, 1936, 1951, rev edn Philadelphia and New York 1966, London 1967.
Streatfield, N. Magic and the magician: E. Nesbit and her children's books. London and New York 1958.
Bell, A. E. Nesbit. 1960, New York 1964, rev London 1968.
Briggs, J. A woman of passion, the life of E. Nesbit 1858–1924. London and New York 1987, rev edn Harmondsworth 1989 (Pen).
E. N. was the subject of a BBC TV play by Ken Taylor in 1973 in the series The Edwardians. *A version of the series was pbd in book form:* The Edwardians, *by P. Brent, 1972 (E. N. pp. 147–67).* [SHG]

Lady Augusta Noel 1838–1902

Effie's friends: or chronicles of the woods and shore. 1865. Anon.
The story of Wandering Willie. 1870.
The life and times of Conrad the squirrel: a story for children. 1872.
Owen Gwynne's great work. 2 vols 1875.
From generation to generation. 2 vols 1879; ed J. Gore 1929.
Faith and unfaith. In In a good cause: a collection of stories, poems, and illustrations, 1885.
Hithersea Mere. 3 vols 1887.
The wise man of Sterncross. 1901.

'Ouida', Marie Louise de la Ramée 1839–1908

Selections

The silver Christ, [and] A lemon tree, Le Selve, An Altruist, Toxin. 1898.

§1

'Held in bondage', or Granville de Vigne: a tale of the day. 3 vols 1863. First pbd in NMM as Granville de Vigne: a tale of the day, Jan 1861–June 1863.
Strathmore: a romance. 3 vols 1865. First pbd in NMM.
Chandos: a novel. 3 vols 1866.
Under two flags: a story of the household and the desert. 3 vols 1867.
Cecil Castlemaine's gage, and other novelettes. Collected and rev by the author. 1867. First pbd in Bentley's Misc.
Idalia: a romance. 3 vols 1867. First pbd in NMM Mar 1865–Feb 1867.
Tricotrin: the story of a waif and stray. 3 vols 1869.
Puck: his vicissitudes, adventures, observations, conclusions, friendships, and philosophies, related by himself. 3 vols 1870.
Folle-Farine. 3 vols 1871.
A dog of Flanders, and other stories. 1872. First pbd in Lippincott's Mag.
Pascarèl: only a story. 3 vols 1873.
Two little wooden shoes: a sketch. 1874.
Signa: a story. 3 vols 1875.
In a winter city: a sketch. 1876.
Ariadnê: the story of a dream. 3 vols 1877.
Friendship: a story. 3 vols 1878.
Moths: a novel. 3 vols 1880.
Pipistrello and other stories. 1880.
A village commune. 2 vols 1881.
In Maremma: a story. 3 vols 1882.
Bimbi: stories for children. 1882.
Frescoes, etc: dramatic sketches. 1883.
Wanda. 3 vols 1883.
Princess Napraxine. 3 vols 1884.
A rainy June: a novelette. [1885.]
Othmar. 3 vols 1885.
Don Gesualdo. 1886.
A house party: a novel. 1887.
Guilderoy. 3 vols 1889.
Ruffino etc. 1890. Contains Ruffino; An orchard; Trottolino; The bullfinch.
Syrlin. 3 vols 1890.
Santa Barbara, etc. 1891. Tales.
The tower of Taddeo. 3 vols 1892.
The new priesthood. 1893. A protest against vivisection.
Two offenders. 1894.
The silver Christ, and A lemon tree. 1894.
Toxin: a sketch. 1895.
Views and opinions. 1895. Essays.
Le Selve. 1896.
An altruist. 1897.
Dogs. 1897.
The Massarenes: a novel. 1897.
Le Strega and other stories. 1899.
Critical studies. 1900.
The waters of Edera. 1900.
Street dust and other stories. 1901.
Helianthus: a novel. 1908. Unfinished.
Ouida contributed various articles from 1897 onwards to Fortnightly Rev, Nineteenth Cent, North Amer Rev *and other jnls. She also wrote several articles in Italian for* Nuova Antologia.

§2

Burnand, F. C. Strapmore! a romance by Weeder. 1878. First pbd in Punch 1878.
Street, G. S. An appreciation of Ouida. In his Quales ego, 1896.
Beerbohm, M. In his More, 1899.

Gilbert Parker, Sir Horatio Gilbert George Parker 1860–1932

Mss located in: Berg Collection, NYPL; Boston Public Lib; Columbia Univ Lib; Dartmouth College Lib, Hanover NH; Harvard Univ Lib; Hove Public Lib; Lib of Congress; Lilly Lib, Indiana Univ; McGill Univ, Montreal; Mitchell Lib, Sydney; Newberry Lib; NYPL; Ohio State Univ; Pierpont Morgan Lib; Princeton; Public Archives of Canada, Ottawa; Douglas Lib, Queen's Univ, Kingston, Ontario; Saint Lawrence Univ, Canton, New York; Simon Fraser Univ, Burnaby, BC; Smith College, Northampton MA; Univ of British Columbia; Univ of California, Berkeley; United Church Archives, Toronto; Univ of North Carolina at Chapel Hill; Univ of Toronto; Yavapai Club, Prescott AZ. See also LR.

Bibliographies

In A dictionary of English authors: biographical and bibliographical, ed R. F. A. Sharp, 1904, rptd Detroit 1978.

Adams, E. M. Bibliography of Sir Gilbert Parker. [Toronto 1933.]
Barry, N. H. Bibliography of Rt Hon Sir Gilbert Parker, bart. [Toronto] 1933.
In Nineteenth century readers' guide to periodical literature 1890–1899, ed H. G. Cushing and A. V. Morris, New York 1944.
In G. Fridén, The Canadian novels of Sir Gilbert Parker: historical elements and literary technique, Copenhagen 1953.
In J. C. Adams, Seated with the mighty: a biography of Sir Gilbert Parker, Ottawa 1979.
Wolff, R. L. In his Nineteenth-century fiction: a bibliographical catalogue, 5 vols 1981–6.
In E. Waterson, Gilbert Parker and his works, Toronto 1989.
See also Wellesley *vol 5 1989*.

Collections and selections

In Camdem town. In a good cause: stories and verses on behalf of the hospital for sick children. 1909.
The works of Gilbert Parker. Imperial edn. 1913 (18 vols), New York 1912–23 (Imperial edn 23 vols).
Pocket edition of selected works of Sir Gilbert Parker. 10 vols 1926.
The going of the white swan: an extract. Sioux City IA 1928.
A hazard of the north. In The Oxford book of adventure stories, ed J. Bristow, Oxford 1995.

§1

Sir William C. F. Robinson, G.C.M.G. [Melbourne 1890?] Rptd from Centennial Mag July 1889.
Round the compass in Australia. 1892 (illus), Sydney and Adelaide 1892, 1897 (illus).
REVIEWS: Nat Observer 23 July 1892.
Pierre and his people. Tales of the far north. 1892, Chicago 1894 (2nd edn), 1895 (3rd edn), Toronto 1897, New York 1903, London 1905, 1906 (illus), 1908, 1911, New York 1912 (Imperial edn), London 1913 (2 edns), 1913 (Imperial edn), New York 1916, London 1925, 1926 (Pocket edn), Freeport NY 1969.
REVIEW: Nat Observer 3 Dec 1892.
Patrol of the Cypress hills. New York [c. 1893].
The chief factor: a tale of the Hudson's Bay Company. New York 1893.
Mrs Falchion. A novel. 1893, 1894 (new edn), Chicago 1895 (3rd edn), New York 1896 (4th edn), London 1896, New York 1898 (new edn), Toronto 1898, New York 1903, London [1909] (illus), New York 1912 (Imperial edn), London 1913 (Imperial edn), 1914, New York 1916, [1920].
REVIEWS: Nat Observer 3 June 1893; New York Times 11 June 1898; Acad 22 July 1893.
The march of the white guard. [1893] (in Tavestock tales), New York 1902, London 1913 (Imperial edn with The trespasser), New York 1913 (Imperial edn with The trespasser).
The translation of a savage. New York 1893, London 1894, New York 1897, 1898 (new edn), Toronto 1898, New York 1903, London 1908, New York 1909, London 1913 (Imperial edn with The pomp of the Lavilettes and At the sign of the eagle), New York 1913 (Imperial edn with The pomp of the Lavilettes and At the sign of the eagle), London 1926 (Pocket edn).
REVIEWS: Nat Observer 30 June 1894; Acad 21 July 1894; New York Times 11 June 1898.
The trespasser. Arrowsmith's Christmas annual 1893, 1893, Akron OH 1893, New York 1894, Toronto 1898, Akron OH 1906, New York 1906, London 1910, 1913 (Imperial edn with The march of the white guard), New York 1913 (Imperial edn with The march of the white guard), Laurel NY 1976.
REVIEWS: Nat Observer 18 Nov 1893; New York Times 11 June 1898.
A lover's diary: songs in sequence. 1894, Cambridge [MA] and Chicago 1894, London and New York 1898, New York 1898, Toronto 1898, New York 1900, 1904, 1910, London 1913 (Imperial edn as A lover's diary with Embers), New York 1913 (Imperial edn as A lover's diary with Embers). Poems.
REVIEWS: Chap-Book 1 June 1894; Nat Observer 16 June 1894.
The trail of the sword. Akron OH 1894, New York 1894, London 1895, 1896 (4th edn), Akron OH 1897, London 1898 (6th edn), Toronto 1898, London 1899, 1900 (new edn), New York 1901, London 1903, 1905, New York 1906 (de luxe edn), London 1908, 1909, New York 1911, London 1913 (Imperial edn with When Valmond came to Pontiac), New York 1913 (Imperial edn with When Valmond came to Pontiac), London 1914, 1926 (Pocket edn), London 1927; tr Fr Quebec 1898, Swed 1911.
REVIEW: New York Times 11 June 1898.
When Valmond came to Pontiac. The story of a lost Napoleon. 1895, Chicago 1895, New York 1896 (3rd edn), Toronto 1897, London 1901, New York 1904, London 1911, 1913 (Imperial edn with The trail of the sword), New York 1913 (Imperial edn with The trail of the sword), London 1926 (Pocket edn), 1927, 1985.
An adventurer of the north. 1895, Chicago 1895, New York 1895, 1896, 1897 (2nd edn), 2 vols Chicago 1897 (An adventurer of the north and A Romany of the snows), London and New York 1898 (as A Romany of the snows), 2 vols New York 1898, Toronto [1898] (as A Romany of the snows), New York 1900, 1904 (as A Romany of the snows), London 1908 (4th edn), New York 1906 (as A Romany of the snows), 1910, London 1911 (5th edn), New York 1912 (Imperial edn as A Romany of the snows), London 1913 (Imperial edn as A Romany of the snows), [1918], [1920], [1923] (6th edn), 1926 (Pocket edn), 1930, Freeport NY 1969.
REVIEWS: Bookman Jan 1896; New York Times 12 Dec 1896.
The seats of the mighty. Being the memoirs of Captain Robert Moray, etc. 1896 (6 edns), Toronto 1896 (2 edns), London 1897 (7th, 8th, 9th edns), New York 1897, 1898, London 1899 (10th edn), 1900 (11th edn), New York 1901, 1902 (12th edn), Toronto 1902, London 1904 (13th edn), New York 1905 (2 edns), Toronto 1905, London 1906 (14th edn), 1907 (15th edn), 1908 (16th edn), 1909, London and Glasgow [1910], London 1910 (17th edn), 1912 (18th, 19th edns), 1913 (Imperial edn), New York 1913 (Imperial edn), London [1914], 1918 (20th edn), 1919, New York 1919, London [1920], 1924, Leipzig 1924 (Tauchnitz), London 1926 (Pocket edn), 1927, New York 1927, London 1929, New York 1931, Toronto 1971 (introd by E. Waterston), Laurel NY 1976, Ottawa 1981, Lancaster PA 1982 (ed J. C. Adams), London 1985, Toronto 1987 (play, ed J. Ripley). Dramatised by Parker (unpbd) and performed at Her Majesty's Theatre, London, 28 Apr 1897.
REVIEWS: Atlantic Monthly Aug 1896; Harper's Mag Aug 1896; New York Times 11 June 1898; New York Times 4 May 1913.
There is a sorrow on the sea. 1896 (in Tales of our coast), New York 1896, London 1913 (Imperial edn with Michel and Angèle and John Enderby), New York 1913 (Imperial edn with Michel and Angèle and John Enderby).
The pomp of the Lavilettes. Boston and New York [1896], London 1897 (2 edns), 1900, 1908 (3rd edn), 1913, 1913 (Imperial edn with The translation of a savage and At the sign of the eagle), New York 1913 (Imperial edn with The translation of a savage and At the sign of the eagle), London 1926 (Pocket edn).
REVIEWS: Chap-Book 15 May 1897; Acad 23 Oct 1897; Acad Suppl 30 Oct 1897.
The battle of the strong. A romance of two kingdoms. 1898 (3 edns), Boston and New York 1898, New York 1898, Toronto 1898, New York 1898, London and New York 1899, Boston and New York 1899, Cambridge MA 1899, Leipzig 1899 (Tauchnitz), London 1903 (5th edn), 1907 (6th edn), 1911 (7th edn), 1913 (Imperial edn), New York 1913 (Imperial edn), London [1919], [1920], 1923 (8th edn), [1924], 1926 (Pocket edn), Leipzig 1926 (Tauchnitz), London 1927, Leipzig 1930 (Tauchnitz), Laurel NY 1976.
REVIEWS: Acad 5 Nov 1898; New York Times 5 Nov, 10 Dec 1898; Outlook 4 Feb 1899.

The hill of pains. Boston [1899], Laurel NY 1976.

The liar. Boston 1899 (unauthorised edn).

The lane that had no turning: and other associated tales concerning the people of Pontiac; together with certain 'parables of provinces'. London and New York 1899 (as Born with a golden spoon), London 1900, New York 1900 (2 edns), Toronto 1900, London 1902 (illustr F. E. Schoonover), New York 1902, London 1909, [1913], 1913 (Imperial edn), New York 1913 (Imperial edn), London [1920], Laurel NY 1976 (as Born with a golden spoon).
REVIEWS: Literary World 2 Nov 1900; Athenaeum 3 Nov 1900; New York Times 3 Nov 1900.

The right of way. Being the story of Charley Steele and another. New York 1900, London 1901, New York 1901 (2 edns), New York and London 1901, Toronto 1901 (with different title page plus illus), New York 1904, London 1905, [1911], 1913 (Imperial edn), New York 1913 (Imperial edn), London [1919], 1920, 1924, 1926 (Pocket edn), New York 1928, Laurel NY 1976; tr Irish 1937. Dramatised by E. W. Presbry and performed at Hollis Street Theatre, Boston, 30 March 1980.
REVIEWS: Bookman Oct 1901; Bookman (USA) Oct 1901; Athenaeum 12 Oct 1901; Literary World 1 Nov 1901; Empire Rev Nov 1901; Acad 9 Nov 1901; Atlantic Dec 1910.

An unpardonable liar. Chicago 1900 (an unauthorised edn of The liar).
REVIEW: New York Times 7 July 1900.

Donovan Pasha and some people of Egypt. 1902, Toronto [1902], New York 1902, Leipzig 1903 (Tauchnitz), London [1912], 1913 (Imperial edn), New York 1913 (Imperial edn), London [1920], 1930, London and New York 1950.
REVIEWS: TLS 10 Oct 1902; Acad 18 Oct 1902; New York Times 18 Oct 1902; Bookman Dec 1902.

Old Quebec, the fortress of New France. Illus London and New York 1903, Toronto 1903, New York 1904, Bowie MD 1992 (facs of 1904 edn). With C. G. Bryan.

A ladder of swords: a tale of love, laughter and tears. 1904, New York and London 1904, Toronto 1904, New York 1905, London 1908, 1912, New York 1912, London [1914] (Wayfarer's Lib), 1926 (Pocket edn).
REVIEWS: New York Times 4 Sep 1904; TLS 9 Sep 1904; Acad 24 Sep 1904; Bookman Oct 1904; Athenaeum 24 Oct 1904.

A national policy: our fiscal system and imperial reciprocity. A speech. Gravesend 1904. Rptd from Gravesend Standard.

Report of an address entitled 'Our imperial responsibilities in the Transvaal'. 1904.

Canada as a nation. To the editor of the Standard (Montreal). Westminster [1905?].

The weavers: a tale of England and Egypt of fifty years ago. Illus 1907, New York and London 1907, Toronto 1907, Leipzig 1908 (Tauchnitz), London 1911, Leipzig 1911 (Tauchnitz), London 1913 (Imperial edn 2 vols), New York 1913 (Imperial edn 2 vols).
REVIEWS: New York Times 28 Sep 1907; Athenaeum 5 Oct 1907; TLS 10 Oct 1907; Bookman Nov 1907; Acad (Fiction Suppl) 9 Nov 1907.

The land for the people: small ownerships and land banks. 1908 (preface A. J. Balfour), 1909.

Embers. Being a book of verses. Plymouth 1908 (ptd for priv circulation), New York 1913 (Imperial edn with additional poems with A lover's diary).

Northern lights. 1909, New York, London and Toronto 1909 (with illus and different title page), New York 1912, 1912 (Imperial edn), 1913 (Imperial edn).
REVIEWS: TLS 16 Sep 1909; Athenaeum 9 Oct 1909; New York Times 16 Oct 1909.

Cumner's son, and other South Sea folk. [1910], New York and London 1910, Toronto 1910, London and New York 1913 (Imperial edn).
REVIEW: New York Times 14 Jan 1911.

Small ownership and a national land bank. 1910.

The going of the white swan. New York 1912. Rptd from An adventurer of the north.
REVIEW: New York Times 8 Dec 1912.

Home rule and the colonial analogy. 1912.

John Enderby. New York 1913 (Imperial edn with Michel and Angèle and 'There is a sorrow on the sea').

At the sign of the eagle. New York 1913 (Imperial edn with The translation of a savage and The pomp of the Lavilettes).

The judgment house. 1913, 1913 (Imperial edn), New York 1913 (Imperial edn), New York and London 1913, Toronto [1913] (illustr W. Hatherall), Leipzig 1914 (Tauchnitz), London 1915 (4th edn), New York and London 1922, London 1924, 1932, Laurel NY 1976.

You never know your luck: being the story of a matrimonial deserter. Illus [1914], New York 1914, Toronto 1914, London 1915, New York 1915, London [1916], 1916, 1917, [1919], New York 1919 (Imperial edn with Wild youth), London [1920].
REVIEWS: New York Times 23 Mar 1913; Athenaeum 23 Aug 1913; TLS 28 Aug 1913; New York Times 7 June 1914; TLS 25 Mar 1915; Athenaeum 17 Apr 1915.

The United States and this war: a word in season. 1915 (Speech to the Pilgrims' Soc, 15 Apr 1915).

Is England apathetic? A reply by Sir Gilbert Parker, Bart. 1915. Originally pbd in the New York Times 14 Aug 1915.

What is the matter with England? Criticism and a reply. 1915.

Defence of British policy towards the United States. New York 1915. Rptd from the New York American.

The world in the crucible: an account of the origins of the Great War and conduct of the Great War. 1915, New York 1915.
REVIEWS: New York Times 20 June 1915; TLS 1 July 1915; Athenaeum 17 July 1915.

The money master. 1915, New York and London 1915, Toronto [1915], New York 1916 (Imperial edn), 1927.
REVIEWS: TLS 16 Sep 1915; New York Times 19 Sep 1915; Athenaeum 16 Oct 1915.

Two years of war. 1916. Interview with Assoc Press of the United States of America.

The world for sale. 1916, New York and London 1916, Toronto 1916, New York 1917 (Imperial edn), Toronto 1919, [1926].
REVIEWS: New York Times 17 Sep 1916; TLS 21 Sep 1916; New York Times 29 Apr 1917.

Wild youth and another with Jordan is a hard road. [1918], New York 1919 (Imperial edn as Wild youth with You never know your luck), Philadelphia and London 1919, Toronto 1919, London 1920, 1927.
REVIEWS: TLS 6 Feb 1919; New York Times 16 Feb 1919.

No defence. [1920], New York 1920, Philadelphia and London 1920, Toronto [1920], New York 1923 (Imperial edn).
REVIEWS: New York Times 12 Sep 1920; TLS 23 Sep 1920.

Carnac. [1922], New York 1922, 1922, Toronto 1922, 1922 (as Carnac and as Carnac's folly), Philadelphia and London 1922 (as Carnac's folly, 2 edns), 1923 (Imperial edn as Carnac's folly), 1924.
REVIEWS: New York Times 24 Sep 1922; TLS 28 Sep 1922.

The power and the glory. A romance of the great La Salle. New York and London 1925 (2 edns), Toronto 1925, London 1927.
REVIEWS: New York Times 4 Oct 1925.

Tarboe: the story of a life. 1927, New York 1927, Toronto 1927, London 1930.
REVIEWS: New York Times 25 Sep 1927; TLS 13 Oct 1927.

The promised land. A story of David in Israel. 1928, Toronto 1928, New York 1929, London 1931, 1938.
REVIEWS: TLS 6 Sep 1928; New York Times 13 Jan 1929.

Gilbert Parker and Beerbohm Tree stage The seats of the mighty: in Washington (1896) and London (1897): the promptbooks for the productions at Her Majesty's Theatre, London, 28 Apr 1897. Ed J. Ripley, Toronto 1986.

Contributions to periodicals, collaborative works and anthologies

Parker was a journalist on the Sydney Herald. *He came to England in 1889 and worked as a journalist writing for a number of newspapers and jnls.*

Dominion Churchman. In memoriam: Rev Francis W. Kirkpatrick, Jan 1885. Poem.
Church Guardian. The hidden things, 17 Jan 1885.
The Week. 26 Mar–22 Oct 1885. Poems.
Daily Br Whig. 14 Apr 1885–15 Apr 1885. Poems.
Sydney Mail. 5 Mar 1887–30 Apr 1887.
Sydney Bulletin. 24 July 1886, 28 Aug 1886. Poems.
Illus Sydney News. 16 Oct 1886–Dec 1886.
Centennial Mag. Aug 1888–Dec 1889.
Leslie's Weekly (New York). Contributions from 1890.
Independent. 29 Jan 1891–31 Mar 1892; 1 Nov 1915.
Good Words. May 1891–1898.
Anti-Jacobin. 28 Mar–18 Apr 1891.
Living Age. 8 Aug 1891–8 May 1897; 7 Sep 1912; 18 Oct 1913.
Nat Observer. 10 Oct 1891–18 Aug 1894.
The Speaker. 27 June–12 Dec 1891.
Eng Illus Mag. Nov 1891–June 1895.
Literary Opinion. Sep 1891–Jan 1892.
Good Cheer (Christmas edn of Good Words). The chief factor, 1892.
The Week. Close up, 16 Dec 1892. Poem.
Illus London News. 24 Dec 1892–7 Oct 1893.
March of the white guard. In Tavestock tales [1893].
McClure's Mag. June 1893–Sep 1894.
Lippincott's Mag. June 1893–Jan 1895.
The Critic. To the Emporer, dead, aged five: poem to Henley's daughter, 24 Mar 1894.
Pall Mall Mag. Mar 1894–Dec 1900.
Dial. It is enough that in this burdened time, 1 Aug 1894. Poem.
Outlook. 4 Aug 1894.
The Idler. Sep 1894–Apr 1895.
Chap-Book. 1 Nov 1894–1 Oct 1895.
Scribner's Mag. Jan 1895; Dec 1913; May 1922.
Spectator. Nay, Lady, though I love thee I make pause, 27 Apr 1895. Poem.
Atlantic Monthly. May 1894–June 1899.
Saturday Rev. Porfirio Diaz, President of Mexico, 10 Aug 1895; Small ownerships and land banks, 20 Nov 1909.
Chambers's Jnl. The bombadier. 3 Aug 1895.
New York Times. Nor king nor country, 1–6 Apr 1896.
The Globe (Toronto). Nor king nor country, 2 Apr–9 May 1896.
There is a sorrow on the sea. In Tales of our coast, 1896, New York 1896, 1901, Freeport NY 1970.
The Century (New York). The little bell of honor, Apr 1896.
Routledge (children's mag). The stolen bonds, Feb 1897.
Canadian Mag. Dec 1897–Aug 1928.
Strand Mag. Jan 1898–Sep 1923.
Fortnightly Rev. July 1899; Mar 1911; July 1912; Sep 1913; July 1919.
Saturday Evening Post. 29 Sep 1900–29 Feb 1908.
Harper's Monthly Mag. Oct 1900–May 1913.
In Treasury of Canadian verse, ed T. H. Rand, 1900.
Youth's Companion (Boston). Contributions from 1900.
Nineteenth Cent. May 1901; Oct 1910–Aug 1913.
By Farcalladen Moor. In The May book, 1901. Poem.
Bookman. Dec 1901; June 1913; Dec 1921.
Windsor Mag. Dec 1901–Aug 1908.
Empire Rev. Life in Canada under the old régime, June 1902; First years of British rule in Canada, Aug 1902.
North Amer Rev. July 1902; Dec 1907.
Current Lit. Nov 1904.
Delineator. When swallows homeward fly, Dec 1905.
Booklover's Mag. Watching the rise of Orion, Mar 1906.
Cosmopolitan. Mar 1906; Dec 1910–Jan 1913.
Harmsworth's Mag. Apr/May 1906–Oct 1912.
Everybody's. Feb–July 1906.
The Story-Teller. Nov 1907–May 1922.
Cornhill Mag. The lodge beyond, July 1908.
Colliers. Norah, 25 Dec 1909.
The land, the people and the state: a case for small ownership and a handbook. 1910. With R. Dawson.
English Rev. Land purchase and land banks, June 1911.
Hearst's Mag. The money master, 1913–14.
Munsey's Mag (New York). Feb–Sep 1914.
Sunset. War maker, Nov 1914.
In Horrors and atrocities of the Great War, ed L. Marshall, Philadelphia 1915.
New York Times Current History Mag. Sep 1915–Dec 1918; Jan 1923.
To the memory of a friend. In Herbert Beerbohm Tree, ed M Beerbohm, New York [c. 1918].
The Mentor. The author and motion pictures, Dec 1921.
Art and Decoration. Impressions of the motion picture as industry and art, Jan 1922.
Views on the general situation in Great Britain. In Empire Club addresses, Toronto 1923.
Primary Education, Popular Educator. Little Garaine, 18 Sep 1826. Poem.

For contributions to Macmillan's Mag, National Rev (London), *and* New Rev, *see* Wellesley *vol 5 1989.*

Introductions, forewords and prefaces

Introd to E. P. Johnson, The moccasin maker, Toronto 1913.
Preface to P. C. Creswick et al, Kent's care for the wounded, 1915.
Foreword to A. L. Lewis, The life of John Travers Lewis, [1930?].

§2

Bliss, C. Chap-Book 1 Nov 1894.
The novelist of the far north. Young Man, Dec 1895. Interview.
Thorold, W. J. Massey's Mag Feb 1897.
Comer, C. A. P. Critic Oct 1898.
Rutledge, J. L. Acta Victoriana Apr 1904.
Cooper, J. A. Canadian Mag Oct 1905.
Douglas, J. Sir Gilbert Parker as plagiarist. The Star Dec 1909 and Dec 1910.
Need, B. M. Some hidden sources of fiction: a paper read before the Historical Society of Dauphin County, Pennsylvania. Philadelphia 1909 (priv ptd). Compares Parker's Seats of the mighty with N. B. Craig's Memoirs of Major Robert Stobo.
Northwest and Gilbert Parker. Nation Feb 1913.
Canadian Mag Aug 1926. Interview.
Obits: The Times 7 Sep 1932; The Mail and Empire [Toronto] 7 Sep 1932; Adock, A. St J. Bookman Oct 1932; Verte, I. Canadian Bookman Oct 1932; Pomeroy, E. Educational Courier Feb 1933; Elson, J. M. Onward Dec 1933.
Stanley, C. In DNB 1931–1940.
Adams, J. C. Seated with the mighty: a biography of Sir Gilbert Parker. Ottawa 1979.
Sutherland, J. In the Longman companion to Victorian fiction, 1988.
Waterson, E. Gilbert Parker and his works. Toronto 1989.
DLB vol 99 Detroit 1990. [DA]

Walter Pater 1839–94

See col 2376.

Frances Mary Peard 1835–1923

§1

The wood-cart, and other tales of the south of France. 1867, rptd [1892] as Tales of the south of France.

One year: or a story of three homes. London and New York 1869, Leipzig 1869, Boston 1871.
Unawares: a story of an old French town. 1870, Boston 1872, Leipzig 1872, other edns [1877], New York [1882], 1888 (subtitled, or the notary's plot).
REVIEW: (J. R. Wise) Westminster Rev n.s. 38, July 1870.
The history of the Prayer Book. [1870.]
The rose-garden. 1872 (2 edns), Boston 1872, Leipzig 1872, other edns 1874, 1882, 1903.
REVIEWS: Athenaeum 24 Feb 1872; Saturday Rev 33 1872; (J. R. Wise) Westminster Rev n.s. 42, July 1872.
Thorpe Regis. 1874, Boston 1874 (micro New York 1984), Leipzig 1874.
REVIEWS: Athenaeum 14 Feb 1874; (J. R. Wise) Westminster Rev n.s. 45, Apr 1874.
A winter story. 1875, Leipzig 1876, Boston 1877 (Town and Country ser).
A madrigal and other stories. 1876, Leipzig 1877.
Cartouche. 2 vols 1878, 1 vol New York 1879, Leipzig 1879.
Mother Molly. 1880, New York 1880, Leipzig 1881 (for children), other edns London and New York 1881, 1896, new edn illustr M. V. Wheelhouse 1914 (The Queen's Treasures ser).
REVIEW: Athenaeum, 13 Nov 1880.
The white month. 1880.
Schloss and town. 3 vols 1882, 2 vols Leipzig 1882; pbd in US in 1 vol as Castle and town, New York 1882 (Seaside Lib no 1253), Philadelphia 1882.
Jeannette: a story of the Huguenots. London and New York '1883' [1882] (for children).
Princess Alethea. '1883' [1882], New York 1882 For children.
Contradictions. 2 vols 1883, 2 vols Leipzig 1883.
The Ashelden schoolroom. London and New York '1884' [1883] For children.
Near neighbours. 2 vols 1885, 1 vol 1885, 1 vol Leipzig 1885.
REVIEW: Athenaeum 31 Jan 1885.
Alicia Tennant. 2 vols 1886, 1 vol Leipzig 1886.
REVIEW: Athenaeum 3 Apr 1886.
Scapegrace Dick. [1886] (for children).
Prentice Hugh. 1887, London and New York [189?] For children.
Madame's grand-daughter. [1887], New York [1887], Leipzig 1887.
Two studios. [1887] (for children).
The belfry at Bruges. 1888.
His cousin Betty. 3 vols 1888.
To horse and away. [1888], London and New York [189?].
The country cousin. 3 vols 1889, 1 vol New York 1889.
Paul's sister. 3 vols 1889. Serialised in Temple Bar 85–7, Jan–Dec 1889.
The blue dragon. London and New York [1890] (for children).
The locked desk. [1890] (for children).
Mademoiselle: a story of the siege of Paris. 1890, New York 1891 (two edns); tr Ger 1894.
The abbot's bridge. [1891], New York [1891] For children.
The secret of the organ loft. [1891] (Penny Popular Lib).
The baroness: a Dutch story. 2 vols 1892, 1 vol New York 1892; tr Du 1892.
The swing of the pendulum. 2 vols 1893, 1 vol New York 1894 (Harper's Franklin Square Lib no 742), micro Washington 1986 (Lib of Congress).
Catherine. '1894' [1893], New York 1893.
An interloper: a novel. 2 vols 1894, 1 vol New York 1894; serialised in Temple Bar 101–2, Jan–Aug 1894.
Jacob and the raven: with other stories for children. '1896' [1895] (illus), New York 1895.
The career of Claudia. 1897; serialised in Temple Bar 109–10, Nov 1896–Apr 1897.
Donna Teresa. 1899, Leipzig 1900; serialised in Temple Bar 117–18, June–Oct 1899.
Number one and number two. London and New York 1900, Leipzig 1901.
The ring from Jaipur. 1904, Leipzig 1905.
REVIEW: Athenaeum 3 Dec 1904.
The flying months. 1909, Leipzig 1909.
REVIEW: Athenaeum 15 May 1909.

Contributions to periodicals

For Peard's nineteenth-century contributions to Temple Bar, St Paul's Mag *and* Cornhill Mag, *see* Wellesley *vol 5 1989. In 1903 she contributed to the* Cornhill Mag *an article on her uncle John Whitehead Peard; she also contributed regularly to Charlotte Yonge's* Monthly Packet.

Collaboration

Howitt, Mary. The angel unawares and other stories. nd. (Includes Peard's Margie's remembrances.)

§2

Weyman, S. J. Frances Mary Peard. Cornhill Mag Apr 1924.
Harris, M. J. Y. Memoirs of Frances Mary Peard. Torquay 1930.
[JW]

Francis Charles Philips 1849–1921

§1

As in a looking glass. 2 vols 1885, 1 vol 1889, 1908.
Jack and three Jills: a novel. 2 vols 1886, 1 vol 1891, 1911.
A lucky young woman: a novel. 3 vols 1886, 1 vol 1890, 1910.
Social vicissitudes. 1886.
The dean and his daughter. 3 vols 1887, 1 vol 1897 (5th edn), [1909]. Dramatised 1891 with S. Grundy as The dean's daughter.
The strange adventures of Lucy Smith. 2 vols 1887, 1 vol [1912].
Little Mrs Murray. 2 vols 1888, 1 vol 1889.
The fatal Phryne. 2 vols 1889, 1 vol [1890]. With C. J. Wills.
Young Mr Ainslie's courtship. 2 vols 1889, 1 vol 1890.
A daughter's sacrifice: a novel. 2 vols 1890, 1 vol New York [1890]. With P. Fendall.
A French marriage: a novel. 1890.
Margaret Byng: a novel. 2 vols 1890. With P. Fendall.
The Scudamores: a novel. 2 vols 1890. With C. J. Wills.
Sybil Ross's marriage: the romance of an inexperienced girl. 1890. With C. J. Wills.
Extenuating circumstances: a novel. 1891.
A maiden fair to see. 1891. With C. J. Wills.
'My face is my fortune': a novel. 2 vols 1891. With P. Fendall.
Madame Valerie: a novel. 1892.
Constance: a novel. 3 vols 1893.
One never knows. 3 vols 1893, 1 vol 1909, [1920].
A doctor in difficulties. 1894.
Mrs Bouverie. 2 vols 1894.
The test of ridicule. 1894 (in Miss Parson's adventure by W. C. Russell, and other stories by other writers).
A devil in nun's veiling: a novel. 1895.
A question of colour. 1895, 1898.
The worst woman in London and other stories. 1895.
The luckiest of three: a novel. 1896.
An undeserving woman and other stories. 1896.
Poor little Bella. 1897.
Men, women and things. 1898.
A woman of the world's advice. 1901. Short stories.
Disciples of Plato. 1908. With P. Fendall.
A honeymoon – and after. 1910. With P. Fendall.
The matrimonial country and other stories. 1910.
That wicked Miss Keane. 1911.
The dancer in blue. [1913.] With L. Brooke.
Judas, the woman. 1914. With A. R. T. Philips.
My varied life. 1914. Autobiography.

The man and the woman. 1916. With A. R. T. Philips.
A white sin. 1916. With R. Strong. [EH]

Mrs Campbell Praed, Rosa Caroline Praed, née Murray-Prior 1851–1935

The John Oxley Lib, Brisbane, and the Australian Nat Lib, Canberra, hold files of Praed correspondence, notebooks and personal papers. The Mitchell Lib, Sydney, holds papers of Praed's father.

Bibliographies

Tiffin, C. Rosa Praed (Mrs Campbell Praed) 1851–1935: a bibliography. Victorian Fiction Research Guide 15. St Lucia, Queensland 1989.
Tiffin, C. and L. Baer. The Praed papers: a listing and index. Brisbane 1994.

§1

An Australian heroine. By R. Murray Prior. 3 vols 1880, 1 vol 1883.
Policy and passion: a novel of Australian life. 3 vols 1881, 1 vol 1881, 1887 (as Longleat of Kooralbyn: or Policy and passion: a novel of Australian life).
Nadine: the study of a woman. 2 vols 1882, 1 vol 1883, New York 1883.
Moloch: a story of sacrifice. 3 vols 1883, 1884, Philadelphia 1887.
Zéro: a story of Monte Carlo. Temple Bar 70–1 1884, 2 vols 1884, 1 vol 1884, Leipzig 1884, New York 1884; tr Ger 1884.
Australian life: black and white. 1885. Part fiction, part memoir.
Affinities: a romance of today. 2 vols 1885, 1 vol Leipzig 1885, New York [1885].
The head station: a novel of Australian life. 3 vols 1885, 2 vols Leipzig 1886, 1 vol New York [1886], 1890.
'The right honourable': a romance of society and politics. 3 vols 1886, 1 vol 1887, New York 1887. With Justin McCarthy.
The brother of the shadow: a mystery of today. 1886, New York 1976.
Miss Jacobsen's chance: a story of Australian life. Leader (Melbourne) Aug–Dec 1886, 2 vols '1886' [1887], 1 vol 1890.
The bond of wedlock: a tale of London life. 2 vols 1887, 1 vol 1887 (omitting epigraphs), 1987 (introd by L. Spender), Canberra 1993 (introd by E. Webby).
The rebel rose: a novel. 3 vols 1888 (anon), New York 1888; as The rival princess: a London romance of today by Justin McCarthy MP and Mrs Campbell Praed 1890.
The ladies' gallery: a novel. Queenslander July 1888–Apr 1889, 3 vols 1888, 1 vol Toronto 1888, New York 1888, London 1890, Melbourne 1890. With Justin McCarthy.
The grey river. 1889. By Justin McCarthy, Mrs Campbell Praed and Mortimer Menpes. Travel.
The romance of a station. 2 vols [1889], 1 vol [1889], Sydney [1889].
The soul of Countess Adrian: a romance. (First episode only) Gentleman 26 Oct 1888, 1891, New York [1891].
The romance of a châlet: a story. 2 vols '1892' [1891], 1 vol Philadelphia '1892' [1891], London 1892.
December roses: a novel. Sala's Jnl Apr–July 1892, New York 1892, Bristol '1892' [1893].
Why I don't write plays. Pall Mall Gazette 8 Sep 1892. Essay.
Outlaw and lawmaker. 3 vols 1893, 1 vol 1894, New York 1894, 1988 (introd by D. Spender).
Christina Chard: a novel. Queen July–Nov 1893, 1 vol New York 1893, 3 vols 1894, 1 vol 1894.
Mrs Tregaskiss: a novel of Australian life. Queen July–Dec 1895, Age (Melbourne) July 1895–Jan 1896, 1 vol New York 1895, 3 vols London 1896, 1 vol 1896.
Nùlma: an Anglo-Australian romance. 1897, New York 1897.
The scourge-stick. 1898.
Madam Izàn: a tourist story. 1899, New York 1899.
As a watch in the night: a dream of waking and dream, in five acts. '1901' [1900].
'Company': a love episode. Queenslander 22 Aug 1901. Short story.
The insane root: a romance of a strange country. 1902, New York [1902], 1908.
Dwellers by the river. [1902]. Short stories.
My Australian girlhood: sketches and impressions of bush life. 1902. Memoir.
Fugitive Anne: a romance of the unexplored bush. '1902' [1903], New York 1903, 1908.
The Ghost. 1903, [1906].
The other Mrs Jacobs: a matrimonial story. 1903, [1906].
Nyria. 1904; tr Du [190?].
Some loves and a life: a study of a neurotic woman. 1904, 1906.
The maid of the river: an Australian girl's love story. 1905.
The lost Earl of Ellan: a story of Australian life. Serialised in Age (Melbourne) Dec 1905–May 1906; Canadian Mag 26–7, Jan–Dec 1906. 1906, 1908.
The luck of the Leura. 1907. Short stories.
Stubble before the wind. 1908. Short stories.
By their fruits: a novel. 1908.
A summer wreath. 1909. Short stories.
The romance of Mademoiselle Aïssé. 1910.
Opal fire. 1910, 1912.
The body of his desire: a romance of the soul. 1912.
Our book of memories: letters from Justin McCarthy to Mrs Campbell Praed. 1912, Boston 1912, Toronto 1912 (memoir).
The mystery woman. 1913.
Lady Bridget in the never-never land: a story of Australian life. 1915, New York 1915, London 1916, 1987 (introd by P. Gilbert).
Sister sorrow: a story of Australian life. 1916.
Soul of Nyria: the memory of a past life in ancient Rome. [1931]. Occult memoir.

Praed contributed some 20 stories to anthologies and periodicals, half of which were not collected. She also pbd about 20 biographical, travel or social sketches. These are listed in Tiffin, Bibliographies, above.

§2

'La Quenouille' [M. H. Foott]. Our Queensland novelist. Queenslander 25 Jan 1895.
Byrne, D. Australian writers. 1896.
McCarthy, J. Mrs Campbell Praed. Eng Illus Mag Mar 1904.
Roderick, C. In mortal bondage: the strange life of Rosa Praed. Sydney 1948. [CT]

Richard Pryce 1864–1942

§1

Dieudonnée: a study, by Richard Ap Rhys. 1884.
An evil spirit. 2 vols 1887, 1 vol (rev) 1892.
The ugly story of Miss Wetherby. 1889.
Just impediment. 2 vols 1890, 1 vol [1892].
Deck-chair stories. 1891.
Miss Maxwell's affections: a novel. 2 vols 1891, 1 vol 1892.
The quiet Mrs Fleming. 1891.
Time and the woman: a novel. 2 vols 1892, 1 vol 1893.
Winifred Mount: a novel. 2 vols 1894, 1 vol 1895.
The burden of a woman. 1895.
Elementary Jane. 1897.
Jezebel. 1900.
The successor: a novel. 1904.
Towing-Path Bess and other stories. 1907.
Christopher. 1911.
David Penstephen. 1916.
The statue in the wood. 1918.
Romance and Jane Weston. 1924.
Morgan's Yard. 1932.

Pryce also wrote several plays. [EH]

'Q', Sir Arthur Thomas Quiller-Couch 1863–1944

Collections

My best book. Fowey 1912 (edn limited to 300 copies).
Selected stories by Q chosen by the author. [1921.]
The Duchy edition of tales and romances by Q. 30 vols 1928.
Poems. 1929.
Q's mystery stories. 1937.
Cambridge lectures. 1943.
Shorter stories. 1944.
Q anthology: a selection of the prose and verse. Ed F. Brittain 1948.
Selected short stories. Harmondsworth 1957.

§1

Athens: a poem. [Bodmin] 1881.
Dead Man's Rock: a romance. 1887, 1898, 1900.
The astonishing history of Troy Town. 1888.
The splendid spur: being memoirs of the adventures of Mr John Marvel, a servant of His late Majesty King Charles I, in the years 1642–3; written by himself; edited in modern English by Q. 1889. Written by Quiller-Couch.
The blue pavilions. 1891, 1892.
Noughts and crosses: stories, studies and sketches. 1891.
A blot of ink, by René Bazin. 1892. Tr from the Fr by Quiller-Couch and P. M. Francke.
I saw three ships, and other winter's tales. 1892.
The Warwickshire Avon. 1892.
The delectable Duchy: stories, studies and sketches. 1893.
Green bays: verses and parodies. 1893, 1930 (new and enlarged edn).
Fairy tales, far and near. 1895.
Wandering heath: stories, studies and sketches. 1895.
Adventures in criticism. 1896, Cambridge 1924.
Ia. 1896.
Poems and ballads. 1896.
St Ives, by Robert Louis Stevenson. 1898. Completed from ch 31 by Quiller-Couch.
The ship of stars. 1899.
Historical tales from Shakespeare. 1899, 1905.
Old fires and profitable ghosts: a book of stories. 1900.
The laird's luck and other fireside tales. 1901.
The Westcotes. Bristol 1902.
The white wolf and other fireside tales. 1902.
The adventures of Harry Revel. 1903.
Two sides of the face: midwinter tales. Bristol 1903.
The collaborators: or the comedy that wrote itself. 1903.
Hetty Wesley. 1903.
Fort Amity. 1904.
Shakespeare's Christmas and other stories. 1905.
Shining ferry. 1905.
From a Cornish window. Bristol 1906.
Sir John Constantine: memoirs of his adventures at home and abroad and particularly in the island of Corsica beginning with the year 1756, written by his son Prosper Paleologus otherwise Constantine and edited by 'Q' (A. T. Quiller-Couch). 1906. Written by Quiller-Couch.
The Mayor of Troy. 1906.
Major Vigoureux. 1907.
Poison Island. 1907.
Merry-Garden and other stories. 1907.
True Tilda. Bristol 1909.
Corporal Sam and other stories. 1910.
Lady Good-for-Nothing: a man's portrait of a woman. 1910.
The sleeping beauty and other fairy tales from the Old French, retold. Illustrated by Edmund Dulac. [1911.]
Brother Copas. Bristol 1911.
Hocken and Hunken: a tale of Troy. Edinburgh 1912.
The roll call of honour: a new book of golden deeds. [1912.]
The vigil of Venus and other poems. 1912.
In powder & crinoline: old fairy tales retold. Illustr Kay Nielsen. [1913.]
News from the Duchy. Bristol 1913.
Poetry. 1914.
Nicky-Nan, reservist. Edinburgh 1915.
On the art of writing: lectures delivered in the University of Cambridge 1913–1914. Cambridge 1916.
Memoir of Arthur John Butler. 1917.
Mortallone and Aunt Trinidad: tales of the Spanish Main. Bristol 1917. Contains The keys of Mortallone (pbd separately 1932), Aunt Trinidad, and Captain Knot.
Foe-Farrell. 1918.
Shakespeare's workmanship. 1918.
Studies in literature. 3 ser Cambridge 1918–29.
On the art of reading: lectures delivered in the University of Cambridge 1916–1917. Cambridge 1920.
Charles Dickens and other Victorians. Cambridge 1925.
Honourable men – Livingstone; Lincoln; Gordon. [1925.] Rptd from Roll call of honour, *above*.
Victors of peace – Florence Nightingale; Pasteur; Father Damien. [1926]. Rptd from Roll call of honour, *above*.
The age of Chaucer. [1926.]
A lecture on lectures. 1927.
The poet as citizen and other papers. Cambridge 1934.
Memories & opinions: an unfinished autobiography. Ed S. C. Roberts, Cambridge 1944.
The whimsical history of Bluebeard, by Charles Perrault. New York 1952. Tr from the Fr.
Castle Dor. 1962. Completed by D. du Maurier.
Exploring Shakespeare's country 100 years ago. Ed S. D. Ludlum 1985. Articles first pbd in Harper's New Monthly Mag, 1891.

Editions

The golden pomp: a procession of English lyrics from Surrey to Shirley. 1895.
The story of the sea. 2 vols 1895–6.
The Oxford book of English verse 1250–1900. Oxford 1900.
The world of adventure: a collection of stirring scenes and moving accidents. 36 pts 1904–5. Selections from The world of adventure were pbd in 6 vols as The black, blue, brown, green, grey and red adventure books, 1904–5.
The pilgrim's way: a little scrip of good counsel for travellers. 1906.
Select English classics. 1908– .
The Oxford book of ballads. Oxford 1910.
The Oxford book of Victorian verse. Oxford 1912.
The King's treasuries of literature. 1920– .
The works of Shakespeare. 39 vols Cambridge 1921–66 (New Cambridge edn). The comedies were edited by Quiller-Couch and J. D. Wilson, the tragedies and histories by Wilson alone.
The Oxford book of English prose. Oxford 1925.
The Cambridge shorter Bible. Cambridge 1928. With A. Nairne and T. R. Glover.
Pages of English prose 1390–1930. Oxford 1930.

§2

Archer, W. In his Poets of the younger generation, 1902.
Brittain, F. Arthur Quiller-Couch: a biographical study of Q. Cambridge 1947.
Rowse, A. L. Quiller-Couch: a portrait of 'Q'. 1988. [EH]

James Rice 1843–82

See under Sir Walter Besant, col 1459.

Mrs J. H. Riddell, i.e. Charlotte Elizabeth Lawson Cowan 1832–1906

Selections

The collected ghost stories. Ed E. F. Bleiler, New York and London 1977.

§1

Zuriel's grandchild. [1855?], 1873 (as Joy after sorrow).
The ruling passion. 3 vols 1857, 1896. Pbd under the pseud 'Rainey Hawthorne'.
The moors and the fens. 3 vols 1858. Pbd under the pseud 'F. G. Trafford'.
The rich husband: a novel of real life. 3 vols 1858. Anon.
Too much alone, by F. G. Trafford. 3 vols 1860.
City and suburb, by F. G. Trafford. 3 vols 1861.
The world in the Church, by F. G. Trafford. 3 vols 1863 (2nd edn).
George Geith of Fen Court: a novel by F. G. Trafford. 3 vols 1864.
Maxwell Drewitt: a novel by F. G. Trafford. 3 vols 1865.
Phemie Keller: a novel by F. G. Trafford. 3 vols 1866.
The race for wealth: a novel. 3 vols 1866. First pbd in Once a Week.
Far above rubies: a novel. 3 vols 1867 (2nd edn).
The miseries of Christmas. In Routledge's Christmas Annual, 1867.
Austin Friars: a novel. 3 vols 1870. Rptd from Tinsleys' Mag.
A life's assize: a novel. 3 vols 1871. First pbd in St James's Mag Apr 1868–Feb 1870.
The Earl's promise: a novel. 3 vols 1873.
Home, sweet home: a novel. 3 vols 1873.
Fairy water: a Christmas story. [1873] (as Routledge's Christmas Annual), 1878.
Mortomley's estate: a novel. 3 vols 1874.
Frank Sinclair's wife and other stories. 3 vols 1874.
The uninhabited house. [1875] (as Routledge's Christmas Annual), [1883] (with The haunted river).
Above suspicion: a novel. 3 vols 1876.
Her mother's darling: a novel. 3 vols 1877.
The haunted river: a Christmas story. In Routledge's Christmas Annual 1877, [1883] (with The uninhabited house).
The disappearance of Mr Jeremiah Redworth. In Routledge's Christmas Annual, [1878].
The mystery in Palace Gardens: a novel. 3 vols 1880. First pbd in London Soc.
Alaric Spenceley: or a high ideal. 3 vols 1881.
The senior partner: a novel. 3 vols 1881.
The curate of Lowood: or every man has his golden chance. [1882.] With 3 stories by other authors.
Daisies and buttercups: a novel. 3 vols 1882.
The Prince of Wales's garden party and other stories. 1882.
A struggle for fame: a novel. 3 vols 1883.
Susan Drummond: a novel. 3 vols 1884. First pbd in London Soc 1883 as Three wizards and a witch.
Weird stories. 1884, 1946.
Berna Boyle: a love story of the County Down. 3 vols 1884.
Mitre Court: a tale of the great city. 3 vols 1885. First pbd in Temple Bar.
For Dick's sake. [1886.]
The government official: a novel. 3 vols 1887. Anon. With A. H. Norway.
Miss Gascoigne: a novel. 1887.
Idle tales. 1888.
The nun's curse: a novel. 3 vols 1888.
Princess Sunshine and other stories. 2 vols 1889.
A mad tour: or a journey undertaken in an insane moment through Central Europe on foot. 1891.
The head of the firm: a novel. 3 vols 1892.
The rusty sword: or thereby hangs a tale. [1894.] First pbd in Dawn of day, 1893.
A silent tragedy: a novel. 1893.
The banshee's warning and other tales. 1894.
Did he deserve it? 1897.
A rich man's daughter. 1897.
Handsome Phil and other stories. 1899.
The football of fate. 1900.
Poor fellow! 1902.
Mrs Riddell also revised Sir C. P. Roney's How to spend a month in Ireland, *1874.*

§2

Black, H. C. In her Notable women authors of the day, 1893.

Elizabeth Robins, 'C. E. Raimond' 1862–1952

The Fales Lib, New York Univ, is the principal repository of mss, typescripts, diaries, correspondence, family papers, scrapbooks and records by or relating to Robins. For locations of other mss materials, see Thomas, Bibliography, below.

Bibliography

Thomas, S. Elizabeth Robins (1862–1952): a bibliography. Victorian Fiction Research Guide 22. St Lucia, Queensland 1994. Addendum: Robins, E. The herstory of a button. Introd by J. E. Gates. American Voice 19 1990.

§1

Alan's wife: a dramatic study in three scenes. Introd by W. Archer 1893 (anon). Rptd without Archer's introd in New woman plays, ed L. Fitzsimmons and V. Gardner, 1991, and in Female playwrights of the nineteenth century, ed A. Scullion, 1996; tr Swed 1895. Based on Befriad, by E. Ameen. With F. Bell.
George Mandeville's husband. By C. E. Raimond. 1894, New York 1894, micro Louisville KY [1966?] (Wright Amer Fiction).
The new moon. By C. E. Raimond. 1895, New York 1895, micro Louisville KY [1966?] (Wright Amer Fiction).
Below the salt. By C. E. Raimond. 1896, Chicago 1896 (as The fatal gift of beauty and other stories), London 1900 (2 edns), micro Louisville KY [1966?] (Wright Amer Fiction). Contains A lucky sixpence, Confessions of a cruel mistress, The Portman memoirs, The fatal gift of beauty, 'Gustus Frederick, Vroni, Below the salt. The stories A lucky sixpence and 'Gustus Frederick were dropped for the Amer edn. Robins's name appeared on the title page of the 1900 British edn.
The open question: a tale of two temperaments. By C. E. Raimond. 1898 (2 impressions), 1899, 2 vols Leipzig 1899 (Tauchnitz), New York 1899, London 1907, 1913, 1915, micro Louisville KY [1966?] (Wright Amer Fiction). Robins's name appeared on the title pages of the 2nd impression of the British edn in Dec 1898 and in the 3rd issue of the Amer edn in 1899.
The magnetic north. 1904, 2 vols Leipzig 1904 (Tauchnitz), New York 1904, Toronto 1904, Melbourne 1904, London 1906, 1909, 1910, 1915 (Nelson's Lib), 1919, micro Louisville KY 1963, Upper Saddle River NJ 1969, micro Woodbridge CT [1971?] (Amer Fiction).
A dark lantern: a story with a prologue. 1905, Leipzig 1905 (Tauchnitz), New York 1905, 1913 (Macmillan's Fiction Lib), micro Woodbridge CT [1971?] (Amer Fiction).
The convert. 1907 (2 edns), New York 1907, Leipzig 1908 (Tauchnitz), New York 1910, 1912 (Macmillan's Standard Lib), 1913 (Macmillan's Fiction Lib), London 1919, micro Woodbridge CT [1971?] (Amer Fiction), London 1980 (introd by J. Marcus), Old Westbury NY 1980 (introd by J. Marcus).
Under the southern cross. New York 1907, rptd in Cassell's Mag 46 1908, Woodbridge CT [1971?]. Novella.
Votes for women: a play in three acts. Chicago 1907, London [1909?], [192?], rptd in How the vote was won and other suffragette plays,

ed D. Spender and C. Hayman, 1985. 1907 script, ed J. E. Gates, in Modern drama by women 1880s–1930s: an international anthology, ed K. E. Kelly, London and New York 1996.
Woman's secret. Letchworth [1907], rptd in Way stations, 1913, *below*, micro New Haven CT 1976 (History of Women 6098). Pam.
'Come and find me!' Serialised in Century Mag n.s. 51–3 1907–8. 1908, New York 1908 (as Come and find me), London 1914, New York 1917, micro Woodbridge CT [1971?] (Amer Fiction).
The mills of the gods. Serialised in Fortnightly Rev 83–4 June–July 1908. New York 1908, rptd in The mills of the gods and other stories 1920, *below*, micro Woodbridge CT [1971?] (Amer Fiction). Novella.
The Florentine frame. 1909, New York 1909, Leipzig 1909 (Tauchnitz), London 1915, 1929 (2 edns), micro Woodbridge CT [1971?] (Amer Fiction).
Why? 1910, rptd in Way stations 1913, *below*, micro New Haven CT 1976 (History of Women 6097). First pbd in Everybody's Mag Dec 1909 and Votes for Women 3 Dec 1909–4 Feb 1910. Pam.
Under his roof. [1912], serialised in Good Housekeeping May 1913, rptd in The mills of the gods and other stories 1920, *below*, and Anthology of British women writers, ed D. Spender and J. Todd, 1989. Short story.
'Where are you going to . . .?' Serialised in shorter form as My little sister, McClure's Mag 40, Dec 1912–Jan 1913. [Jan] 1913, Leipzig 1913 (Tauchnitz), New York 1913 (as My little sister), [Toronto?] 1913, New York 1915 (Crown Novels), London 1916.
Way stations. [Feb] 1913, Leipzig 1913 (Tauchnitz), New York 1913, micro Glen Rock NJ [1976?] (Gerritsen Collection of Women's History 2407), micro New Haven CT 1977 (History of Women 6936). Political commentary.
What can I do? [c. 1914.] Pam.
Camilla. Serialised in Cosmopolitan 63–5 Oct–Sep 1917. New York 1918, London 1918.
The messenger. Serialised in Century Mag n.s. 75–6 Nov 1918–July 1919. New York 1919, London [1919] (as The messenger: a novel).
The mills of the gods and other stories. 1920. Miss Cal, The Derrington ghost, Under his roof, Monica's village, The Threlkeld ear, The mills of the gods, The tortoise-shell cat.
Time is whispering. 1923, New York 1923, London 1925.
Ancilla's share: an indictment of sex antagonism. 1924 (anon), Westport CT 1976 (Pioneers of the Women's Movement), micro Glen Rock NJ nd (Gerritsen Collection of Women's History 2406). Social criticism.
The secret that was kept: a study in fear. A novel. [1926], New York 1926, Leipzig 1926 (Tauchnitz), London 1928, 1930.
Prudence and Peter: a story for children about cooking out-of-doors and indoors. Serialised in Time and Tide 1 1920. 1928, New York 1928. With O. Wilberforce.
Ibsen and the actress. 1928, New York 1973 (Studies in Drama 39). Essay.
Theatre and friendship: some Henry James letters. 1932, New York 1932, London 1934 (Life and Letters), Freeport NY 1969. Memoir.
Both sides of the curtain. 1940, New York [1940?], Toronto [1940?]. Autobiography.
Portrait of a lady, or the English spirit old and new. Letchworth 1941. Memoir of E. Yates Thompson. Pam.
Raymond and I. 1956 (foreword by L. Woolf), New York 1956, Toronto [1956?]. Memoir.

Translations
Björnson, B. Mother's hands. New Rev 8 1893 (anon); rptd in Captain Mansana and Mother's hands (The novels of Björnstjerne Björnson 7), ed E. Gosse, 1897 (anon).
Björnson, B. Magnhild and Dust (The novels of Björnstjerne Björnson 6), ed E. Gosse, 1897 (anon).

Introductions
Uncle Tom's cabin, by H. B. Stowe. Bath c. 1909–10 (Bath Classics). First pbd in Author 20 1909. See Thomas, Bibliography, *above*.
Rebel women, by E. Sharp. 1915.
For Robins's contributions to anthologies and periodicals, reviews, radio broadcasts and letters to newspapers, see Thomas, Bibliography, above.

§2
Gates, J. E. Elizabeth Robins, 1862–1952: actress, novelist, feminist. Tuscaloosa AL 1994.
John, A. V. Elizabeth Robins: staging a life, 1862–1952. London and New York 1995.
Marcus, J. Elizabeth Robins. Ann Arbor MI 1973.
For reviews of and articles on Robins's books and plays, see Thomas, Bibliography, above. [ST]

Frances Mabel Robinson 1858–1956

Mr Butler's ward. 1885.
Disenchantment. 1886.
Irish history for English readers, from the earliest times to the close of the year 1885, by Wm Stephenson Gregg [pseud]. 1886.
The plan of campaign. 1888.
A woman of the world. 1890.
Hovenden, V. C.: the destiny of a man of action. 1891.
Chimera. 1895.

Translations
de Chateaubriant, A. The peat-cutters. 1888.
Tinayre, M. Priscilla Séverac. 1923.
Bourget, P. The gaol. 1924.
de Nolhac, P. The trianon of Marie-Antoinette. 1925. [MD]

James Runciman 1852–91

Mss located in Berg Collection, NYPL; Royal Literary Fund.

Bibliographies
See Wellesley *vol 5 1989.*

§1
The romance of the coast. 1883 (school edn).
Grace Balmaign's sweetheart. 1885.
School Board idylls. 1885.
Skippers and shellbacks. 1885, 1900.
Schools and scholars. 1887.
The Chequers: being the natural history of a public-house, set forth in a loafer's diary. 1888.
A dream of the North Sea. 1889.
Joints in our social armour. 1890, 1892 (as The ethics of drink and social questions; or joints in our social armour), 1902 (2nd edn), 1902 (as The ethics of drink and social questions; or joints in our social armour), 1893 (3rd edn).
Tales of the coast. 1890.
Side lights. 1893 (memoir by G. Allen, introd by W. T. Stead). REVIEW: Athenaeum 6 Jan 1894.

Contributions to periodicals
Runciman wrote for the Teacher, Schoolmaster, Family Herald, St James's Gazette *and in 1874 he became sub-editor of* Vanity Fair. *He also worked for W. E. Henley on the weekly* London *in 1878. For contributions to* Contemporary Rev, Cornhill Mag, Fortnightly Rev, Macmillan's Mag, *and* Nat Rev-II, *see* Wellesley *vol 5.*
English Illus Mag. English fishermen, 1878; Board school children, 1881.
Sunday Mag. Hob's Tommy: a story of fisher's life, 1882.
St James's Gazette. Sailors' songs and shanties, 4 Dec 1884.
Mag of Art. The unseen land, Dec 1892. Poem.

§2

Memoir by Grant Allen. In Runciman's Side lights, 1893 (introd by W. T. Stead). *See also* Nat Observer 9 Dec 1893.
Obits: Pall Mall Gazette 9 July 1891; Schoolmaster 11 July 1891; Illus London News 18 July 1891.
Boase, G. C. In DNB 1897.
Sutherland, J. In The Longman companion to Victorian fiction, 1988. [DA]

William Clark Russell 1844–1911

'Frà' Angelo: a tragedy in five acts. 1865.
The hunchback's charge: a romance. 3 vols 1867.
The book of authors. [1871.]
Is she a wife? 3 vols 1871. Pbd under the pseud 'Sydney Mostyn'.
Memoirs of Mrs Laetitia Boothby, written by herself; edited by Clark Russell. Written by Russell. 1872.
Perplexity. 3 vols 1872. Pbd under the pseud 'Sydney Mostyn'.
Representative actors .... [1872.]
The surgeon's secret: a novel by Sydney Mostyn. 1872.
Which sister?: a story by Sydney Mostyn. 2 vols 1873.
Kitty's rival: a story by Sydney Mostyn. 3 vols 1873.
The book of table talk: selections from the conversation of poets, philosophers, statesmen, divines, etc; with notes and memoirs by William Clark Russell. 1874.
John Holdsworth, Chief Mate: a story, in three vols. 3 vols 1875.
The mystery of Ashleigh Manor: a romance. 3 vols 1874. Pbd under the pseud 'Eliza Rhyl Davies'.
The deceased wife's sister; and, My beautiful neighbour. 3 vols 1874. Anon.
As innocent as a baby: a novel. 3 vols 1874. Anon.
Jilted! or my uncle's scheme: a novel in three vols. 3 vols 1875. Anon.
A dark secret. 3 vols 1875. Pbd under the pseud 'Eliza Rhyl Davies'.
Is he the man?: a novel. 3 vols 1876.
Captain Fanny. 3 vols 1876.
The wreck of the 'Grosvenor': an account of the mutiny of the crew and the loss of the ship when trying to make the Bermudas. 3 vols 1877.
Auld lang syne. 2 vols 1878.
The little Loo: a story of the South Sea, by Sydney Mostyn. 3 vols 1878, 1883 (as Little Loo). 'Little Loo' is the name both of a ship and of a personage; hence the slight change of title in 2nd edn.
A sailor's sweetheart: an account of the wreck of the sailing ship 'Waldershare', from the narrative of Mr William Lee, second mate. 3 vols 1880.
An ocean free-lance: from a privateersman's log, 1812. 3 vols 1881.
The 'Lady Maud', schooner yacht: a narrative of her loss on the Bahama Cays, from the account of a guest on board. 3 vols 1882.
My watch below; or yarns spun when off duty. By a seafarer. 1882. First pbd in Daily Telegraph.
Sailor's language: a collection of sea-terms and their definitions. 1883.
A sea queen. 3 vols 1883.
Round the galley fire. 1883. First pbd in Daily Telegraph.
On the fo'k'sle head. 1884.
English Channel ports and the estate of the East and West India Dock Co .... 1884. First pbd in Daily Telegraph.
Jack's courtship: a sailor's yarn of love and shipwreck. 3 vols 1884.
A strange voyage. 3 vols 1885.
In the middle watch. 1885.
A voyage to the Cape. 1886.
A book for the hammock. 1887. Tales.
The frozen pirate. 2 vols 1887.
The Golden Hope: a romance of the deep. 3 vols 1887.
The death ship: a strange story: an account of a cruise in 'The Flying Dutchman', collected from the papers of the late Mr Geoffrey Fenton, of Poplar, master mariner. 3 vols 1888.
The mystery of the 'Ocean Star': a collection of maritime sketches. 1888.
Betwixt the Forelands. [1889.]
Marooned. 3 vols 1889.
The romance of Jenny Harlowe; and sketches of maritime life. 1889.
William Dampier. 1889.
An ocean tragedy. 3 vols 1890.
Nelson and the naval supremacy of England. 1890. With W. H. Jacques.
Nelson's words and deeds. 1890. Ed Russell.
My shipmate Louise: the romance of a wreck. 3 vols 1890.
Collingwood. 1891.
Master Rockafellar's voyage. 1891.
My Danish sweetheart: a novel. 3 vols 1891.
A marriage at sea. 2 vols 1891.
A strange elopement. 1892.
Alone on a wide wide sea. 3 vols 1892.
The British seas: picturesque notes. 1892, 1894. By Russell et al.
Mrs Dines' jewels: a mid-Atlantic romance. 1892.
The emigrant ship. 3 vols 1893.
List, ye landsmen!: a romance of incident. 3 vols 1893, 1 vol 1893.
The tragedy of Ida Noble. 1893.
The good ship 'Mohock'. 2 vols 1894.
Miss Parson's adventure by W. Clark Russell and other stories by other writers. 1894.
The convict ship. 3 vols 1895.
Heart of oak: a three-stranded yarn. 3 vols 1895.
The phantom death and other stories. 1895.
The honour of the flag and other stories. 1896.
The tale of the ten: a salt-water romance. 3 vols 1896.
What cheer! 1896.
A noble haul. 1897.
Pictures from the life of Nelson. 1897.
The two captains. 1897.
The last entry. 1897.
A tale of two tunnels: a romance of the western waters. 1897.
Romance of a midshipman. 1898.
The ship: her story. 1899.
The Pretty Polly: a voyage of incident. 1900.
Rose Island: the strange story of a love adventure at sea. 1900.
A voyage at anchor. 1900.
The sequel. 1901. In Strange happenings.
The ship's adventure. 1901.
Overdue. 1903.
Abandoned. 1904.
Wrong side out. 1904.
An Atlantic tragedy and other stories. 1905.
His island Princess. 1905.
The life of Nelson in a series of episodes. 1905.
The yarn of Old Harbour Town. 1905.
The turnpike sailor: or rhymes on the road recited by buccaneers, privateers, slavers, and sailors of all degree. 1907.
The father of the sea and other legends of the deep. 1911.

'Mark Rutherford', William Hale White 1831–1913

Major collections of mss include the Colbeck Collection, Univ of British Columbia (notebooks, letters, the 'Groombridge Diary', 'Hale's Book' by Dorothy Vernon White, the 'Dorothy book', the '1910 manuscript'); the Bedford Public Lib (letters and miscellaneous mss); and the Bodleian Lib (letters).

Bibliographies

Stone, Wilfred H. Religion and art of William Hale White. 1954.
Davis, Eugene W. William Hale White, an annotated bibliography of writings about him. ELT 10 1967.

Nowell-Smith, S. Mark Rutherford: a short bibliography of the first editions. 1973. Reprint of a suppl to Bookman's Jnl, ser 3, vol 18 1930.

§1

Works published pseudonymously

The following appeared as 'by Mark Rutherford', the first 6 being 'edited by his friend Reuben Shapcott'.

The autobiography of Mark Rutherford, dissenting minister. 1881, 1884, 1892, 1893, 1896, 1900, 1903, 1904, 1905, 1913, 1923 (with memorial introd by W. H. Massingham), 1928, 1936, Oxford 1991 (WCp ed W. S. Peterson); New York 1881, 1889, 1916, 1923, 1929; tr Cz 1905. A novel.

Mark Rutherford's deliverance: being the second part of his autobiography. 1885, 1888 (rev and expanded with the Autobiography, *above*), 1892, 1904, 1913, 1923, 1927, 1936, Leicester 1969 (introd by B. Willey), London 1986, 1988 (introd by D. Cupitt); New York 1883, 1889, 1889, 1892, 1904, 1913, 1916, 1923, 1929, 1976.

The revolution in Tanner's Lane. 1887, 1893, 1904, 1913, 1923, 1927, 1936, 1971 (lst edn rptd, introd by S. Nowell-Smith), 1984 (introd by C. Tomalin); New York 1887, 1929, 1975 (with Miriam's schooling and other papers).

Miriam's schooling and other papers. 1890, 1892, 1904, 1905, 1923, 1936; New York 19??, 1975 (with The revolution, *above*).

Catharine Furze. 2 vols 1893, 1894, 1904, 1910, 1913, 1923, 1936, 1985 (introd by C. Tomalin); New York 1893, 1924, 1976 (with Clara Hopgood).

Clara Hopgood. 1896, 1907, 1913, 1923, 1936, 1985 (introd by C. Tomalin); New York 1896, 1976 (with Catharine Furze, *above*), 1996 ed L. Davies (ELp).

Other writings

An argument for an extension of the franchise: a letter addressed to G. J. Holyoake. 1866.

A letter written on the death of Mrs Elizabeth Street. 1877 (priv ptd and circulated).

A dream of two dimensions. 1884. Anon and priv ptd. Later included in Last pages from a journal, *below*.

The inner life of the House of Commons, by William White; preface by Justin McCarthy; introduction by the author's son [i.e. White]. 2 vols 1897.

A description of the Wordsworth and Coleridge manuscripts in the possession of Mr T. Norton Longman. 1897. Ed with notes by White.

An examination of the charge of apostasy against Wordsworth. 1898, 1976.

Coleridge's poems: a facsimile reproduction of the proofs and manuscripts of some of the poems; edited by the late James Dykes Campbell, with preface and notes by W. Hale White. 1899.

John Bunyan, by the author of 'Mark Rutherford'. 1895, 1905, 1922; New York 1904.

Selections from Dr Johnson's Rambler. 1907. Ed with preface and notes by White.

The life of John Sterling, by Thomas Carlyle. Oxford 1907 (WC). Introd by White.

The early life of Mark Rutherford (W. Hale White), by himself. 1913. Preface by White's son.

Reviews of individual works can be found in the Davis bibliography, above.

Contributions to periodicals

A comprehensive list of contributions to periodicals can be found in the Stone bibliography, above.

Published letters, journals, diaries

Pages from a journal, with other papers. 1900, 1910 (expanded), 1915, Oxford 1930 (WC).

More pages from a journal, with other papers. 1910.

Last pages from a journal, with other papers. Ed D. V. White 1915.

White, D. V. The Groombridge Diary. 1924.

Letters to three friends. Ed D. V. White 1924.

Translations

Benedict de Spinoza. Ethic. Tr White 1883, 1890, 1894 (rev and corrected with new preface), 1899 (rev and corrected), 1910 (rev and corrected), 1927, 1930.

Benedict de Spinoza. Tractatus de intellectus emendatione. Translation [by White] rev by Amelia H. Stirling. 1895.

§2

Nicoll, W. R. Memories of Mark Rutherford. 1924.

MacLean, C. M. Mark Rutherford: a biography of W. H. White. 1955.

Details of most of the secondary critical material relating to Rutherford can be found in the bibliographies of Davis and Stone, above. [LD]

Olive Schreiner 1855–1920

Important collections of letters and other mss are to be found in the Edward Carpenter Coll, Sheffield City Lib; Karl Pearson Coll, Univ Coll London; Cronwright-Schreiner Coll, Cradock Public Lib, South Africa; J. W. Jagger Lib, Univ of Cape Town; South African Lib, Cape Town; Havelock Ellis Coll, Univ of Texas, Austin.

Bibliographies

Verster, E. Olive Emilie Albertina Schreiner (1855–1920): a bibliography. Cape Town 1946.

Davis, R. Olive Schreiner 1920–1971: a bibliography. Johannesburg 1972.

Selection

Olive Schreiner: a selection. Ed U. Krige, Cape Town, London and New York 1968.

§1

The story of an African farm: a novel. 2 vols 1883. First pbd under the pseud 'Ralph Iron'.

Dreams. 1891.

Dream life and real life: a little African story. Pbd under the pseud 'Ralph Iron'. 1893. Also contains The woman's rose, and The policy in favour of protection —.

The political situation. 1896. With S. C. Cronwright-Schreiner.

Trooper Peter Halket of Mashonaland. 1897.

An English-South African's view of the situation: words in season. [1899.]

A letter on the Jew. Cape Town 1906. Priv ptd.

Closer union: a letter on the South African Union and the principles of government. 1909.

Woman and labour. 1911.

Stories, dreams and allegories. 1923, 1924 (with 1 additional item).

Thoughts on South Africa. 1923.

From man to man: or perhaps only –. 1926. With introd by S. C. Cronwright-Schreiner.

Undine. New York 1928, London 1929. With introd by S. C. Cronwright-Schreiner.

Diamond fields. Ed R. Rive. In English in Africa. Vol 1, Mar 1974. Fragment of an unpbd ms.

Letters

The letters of Olive Schreiner 1876–1920. Ed S. C. Cronwright-Schreiner 1924.

Rive, R. (ed). Olive Schreiner letters. Vol 1 Claremont, South Africa 1987, Oxford 1988.

'My other self': the letters of Olive Schreiner and Havelock Ellis 1884–1920, ed Y. C. Draznin. New York 1992.

§2

Cronwright-Schreiner, S. C. The life of Olive Schreiner. 1924.

Cazamian, M. L. In his Le roman et les idées en Angleterre vol 3, Paris 1955.

Gregg, L. Memories of Olive Schreiner. 1957.
Meintjes, J. Olive Schreiner: portrait of a South African woman. Johannesburg 1965.
Beeton, R. Olive Schreiner: a short guide to her writings. Cape Town 1974.
First, R. and A. Scott. Olive Schreiner. 1980, 1989.
Schoeman, K. Olive Schreiner: a woman in South Africa 1855–1881. Johannesburg 1991.
Clayton, C. Olive Schreiner. New York and London 1997. [EH]

Joseph Henry Shorthouse 1834–1903

Collections
Collected edition of the novels. 6 vols 1891–4.

§1

John Inglesant: a romance. Birmingham 1880 (priv ptd), 2 vols London 1881, 1881, 1882 (10 edns), 1 vol 1883 (3 edns) etc; ed M. Ramsey 1961 (abridged as John Inglesant in England).
The little schoolmaster Mark: a spiritual romance. 2 pts 1883–4.
Sir Percival: a story of the past and of the present. 1886.
A teacher of the violin and other tales. 1888.
The Countess Eve. 1888.
Blanche, Lady Falaise: a tale. 1891.
Life, letters and literary remains of J. H. Shorthouse, edited by his wife [Sarah]. With an introduction by John Hunter Smith. 2 vols 1905. Vol 1 Life and letters; vol 2 Literary remains.
Shorthouse also pbd a paper On the Platonism of Wordsworth, *1882, and wrote introds to George Herbert,* The Temple *and to several devotional works.*

§2

Gardiner, S. R. John Inglesant. Fraser's Mag May 1882.
John Inglesant. Dublin Rev Apr 1882.
'Lee, Vernon'. The little schoolmaster Mark. Acad 29 Dec 1883.
West, H. E. John Inglesant and Sartor resartus: two phases of religion. [1884.]
Wilson, H. S. The philosophy of John Inglesant. Modern Rev 5 1884.
Sir Percival. Blackwood's Mag Dec 1886.
Linnell, C. The true story of John Inglesant. Athenaeum 27 July, 17 Aug 1901.
Hutton, E. Shorthouse. Blackwood's Mag Apr 1903.
Montgomery, J. D. Personal recollections of Shorthouse. Temple Bar June 1903.
Acton, J. E. D. C., Baron. In his Letters to Mary Gladstone, 1904. Contains a discussion of Shorthouse's historical point of view.
Durham, J. Marius the Epicurean and John Inglesant. [1905.]
More, P. E. In his Shelburne essays ser 3, New York 1906.
Gosse, E. In his Portraits and sketches, 1912.
Coats, R. H. Birmingham mystics of the mid-Victorian era. Hibbert Jnl 16 1918.
Fleming, W. K. Some truths about John Inglesant. Quart Rev 245 1925.
Polak, M. The historical, philosophical and religious aspects of John Inglesant. Oxford 1934.
Thurmann, E. Der Niederschlag der evangelischen Bewegung in der englischen Literatur. Emsdetten 1938.
Anson, H. The Church in nineteenth-century fiction: Shorthouse. Listener 4 May 1939.
Hough, G. Books in general. New Statesman 3 Aug 1946.
Bishop, M. John Inglesant and its author. Essays by Divers Hands. 1958.
Wagner, F. J. J. H. Shorthouse. Boston 1979.

Henry Hawley Smart 1833–93

§1

Breezie Langton: a story of fifty-two to fifty-five. 3 vols 1869.
Bitter is the rind. 3 vols 1870, [1909] (as Bit and bridal).
A race for a wife: a novel. 1870.
Cecile: or modern idolaters. 3 vols 1871.
False cards. 3 vols 1873.
Broken bonds. 3 vols 1874.
Two kisses. 3 vols 1875.
Courtship in seventeen hundred and twenty, in eighteen hundred and sixty. 2 vols 1876.
Bound to win: a tale of the turf. 3 vols 1877.
Play or pay: a novelette. 1878.
Sunshine and snow: a novel. 3 vols 1878.
Social sinners: a novel. 3 vols 1880.
Belles and ringers: a novelette. 1880.
The Great Tontine: a novel. 3 vols 1881.
At fault: a novel. 3 vols 1883.
Hard lines: a novel. 3 vols 1883.
From post to finish: a novel. 3 vols 1884.
Salvage: a collection of stories. 1884.
Tie and trick: a melodramatic story. 3 vols 1885.
Lightly lost. 1885.
Struck down: 'a tale of Devon'. 1886.
Plucked: or a tale of a trap; and other contributions by Annie Thomas [... et al]. [1886.] Contains 3 additional stories by Smart.
Bad to beat: a novel. [1886.]
The outsider: a novel. 2 vols 1886.
A false start: a novel. 3 vols 1887.
Cleverly won: a romance of the Grand National – a novelette. 1887.
The pride of the paddock. 1888.
The master of Rathkelly: a novel. 2 vols 1888.
Saddle and sabre: a novel. 3 vols 1888.
The last coup: a novelette. 1889.
Long odds: a novel. 3 vols 1889.
A black business: a novelette. [1890.]
Without love or licence: a tale of South Devon. 3 vols 1890.
Thrice past the post: a novel. 1891.
Beatrice and Benedick: a romance of the Crimea. 2 vols 1891.
'The plunger': a turf tragedy of five-and-twenty years ago. 2 vols 1891.
A member of Tattersall's: a novel. 1892.
Vanity's daughter: a novel. 1893.
A racing rubber: a novel. 2 vols 1895.

Robert Louis Stevenson 1850–94

The Edwin J. Beinecke Collection at Yale has the largest collection of books, articles, portraits and photos, letters by Stevenson (and letters to and about him), drafts, notes and mss. Examples include juvenilia such as The sunbeam magazine, *many early essays and poems, journal for* An inland voyage, *mss of* Amateur emigrant, Body-snatcher, *poems including many in* A child's garden of verses, Underwoods, *and* Songs of travel, *intermediate version of* Dr Jekyll and Mr Hyde, *ms and proofs of* The wrong box, Records of a family of engineers, *intermediate version of* Catriona, The ebb-tide, *intermediate version of* St Ives, Weir of Hermiston. *Yale also has more than 1,000 Stevenson letters and his mother's diaries throughout his lifetime. The NLS has the business records of the Stevenson family of engineers, Graham Balfour's notes for his biography of Stevenson, juvenilia and essays by Stevenson, and letters notably to Mrs Sitwell and W. E. Henley. City of Edinburgh Writers' Museum (formerly Lady Stair's House Museum) has personal articles, photos throughout Stevenson's life and photo albums from his South Seas travels, also books, the Davos printing press, and letters. The Huntington has jnls for* Travels with a donkey *and* Silverado squatters, *final version of* Kidnapped, *the*

South Seas jnl, Beach of Falesá, *final version of* St Ives. *The Pierpont Morgan Lib has juvenilia, final version of* Dr Jekyll and Mr Hyde, *and draft of* Weir of Hermiston. *Harvard has letters,* Memoirs of himself, Markheim, *and final version of* Catriona. *Princeton has juvenile story* The plague cellar, *earliest ms of* St Ives, *correspondence with Scribner's, and books including variant bindings. The Mitchell Lib, Sydney, has ms of 1890 printing of* In the South Seas. *The Robert Louis Stevenson Silverado Museum, St Helena CA, has mss of poems and essays, letters, portraits, photos, and many personal articles, also letters and paintings by Stevenson's wife and others. Baker Cottage, Saranac Lake NY, has books and ms material originally from Stevenson Soc of America, personal articles, and two of RLS's mother's scrapbooks of reviews. Stevenson House, Monterey State Historic Park CA, has portraits of Stevenson by his wife, Joe Strong and A. J. Daplyn, furniture, personal articles, books, and four of Stevenson's mother's scrapbooks.*

Bibliographies

Prideaux, W. F. A bibliography of the works of Robert Louis Stevenson. 1903, 1917 (rev F. Livingston).

Rosenbach, A. S. W. A catalogue of the books and manuscripts of Robert Louis Stevenson in the library of the late Harry Elkins Widener. Philadelphia 1913. Collection now at Harvard.

Slater, J. H. Robert Louis Stevenson: a bibliography of his complete works. 1914. Earlier version 1894.

Autograph letters, original manuscripts, books, portraits, and curios ... of the late Robert Louis Stevenson. Anderson Auction Company 3-part sale, New York 1914–16. More than 1,300 lots, consigned by RLS's stepdaughter Isobel Field.

Grolier Club. First editions of the works of Robert Louis Stevenson, 1850–94, with other Stevensoniana exhibited Nov 5–28 1914. New York 1915 (illus edn).

Ehrsam, T. G. and R. H. Deily. In their Bibliographies of twelve Victorian authors, New York 1936.

Edinburgh Public Libraries. Robert Louis Stevenson 1850–1894. Catalogue. Edinburgh 1950; supplementary catalogue, Edinburgh 1978.

McKay, G. L. A Stevenson library: catalogue of a collection of writings by and about Robert Louis Stevenson formed by Edwin J. Beinecke. 6 vols New Haven CT 1951–64.

Edinburgh Libraries and Museums. Lady Stair's House Museum. Edinburgh 1966.

Wainwright, A. D. Robert Louis Stevenson: a catalogue. Princeton 1971.

Swearingen, R. G. The prose writings of RLS: a guide. Hamden CT 1980.

Collections

Many important works and fragments appeared or became widely known for the first time in the collected edns, in the Edinburgh and Vailima edns especially. As with edns of separate works, the hundreds of collections and reprints of stories, essays and fiction that appeared in the century since RLS's death in 1894 are omitted.

Edinburgh edition. Ed S. Colvin 28 vols 1894–8.

Thistle edition. 27 vols New York 1895–9, 1911–12.

Biographical edition. 31 vols New York 1905–12. Prefaces by Fanny Stevenson.

Household edition. Ed C. C. Bigelow and T. Scott 10 vols New York 1906. Also pbd as Bournemouth, Casco, Marquesan, Monterey, Ticonderoga, and no doubt other edns, each such 'Edition De Luxe' limited to 1,000 sets.

Pentland edition. Ed E. Gosse 20 vols 1906–7.

Swanston edition. Ed A. Lang 25 vols 1911–12.

Vailima edition. Ed L. Osbourne 26 vols 1922–3.

Tusitala edition. 35 vols 1924.

Skerryvore edition. 30 vols 1924–6.

South Seas edition. 32 vols New York 1925.

§1

First British and American edns are listed in order of publication date even when RLS himself worked only on a later edn. Examples include Dr Jekyll and Mr Hyde *(RLS saw and worked on the Longman edn),* The Master of Ballantrae *(he worked on the version in* Scribner's Mag*), and others. Englang edns and reprints before 1900 are listed only if possibly significant textually or authorised. Piracies, other reprints and the hundreds of edns, reprints and adaptations since 1900 are omitted. See also the separate sections on* Translations *and* Textual and bibliographical studies.

The Pentland rising: a page of history. Edinburgh 1866 (priv ptd pam).

An appeal to the clergy of the Church of Scotland. Edinburgh 1875.

The charity bazaar: an allegorical dialogue. Edinburgh [1875] (priv ptd folder).

An inland voyage. 1878, 1881 ('Second Edition', actually 2nd printing), 1887 (also 'Second Edition' but first by Chatto and Windus), Boston 1883, 1885, Leipzig 1886.

Edinburgh: picturesque notes, with etchings. '1879' [1878], '1889' [1888] (new edn, 8vo), New York 1889, London 1896. First pbd partially in Portfolio June–Dec 1878.

Travels with a donkey in the Cévennes. 1879 ('Second Edition' 1879 actually 2nd printing), Boston 1879 (additional printings as late as 1892), 1886 (first Chatto and Windus).

Deacon Brodie, or the double life: a melodrama founded on facts in four acts and ten tableaux. Edinburgh 1880 (priv ptd), 1888 (rev, priv ptd), 1892 (in Three plays), 1896 and 1907 (in The plays), '1897' [1896]. With W. E. Henley.

Virginibus puerisque and other papers. 1881, 1887 (2nd edn), New York 1887 (called 2nd edn but actually 1st). 15 essays, chiefly rptd from Cornhill Mag.

Familiar studies of men and books. 1882, 1886 (2nd edn), New York 1887 (Dodd, Mead edn), 1887 (Scribner's edn, from Dodd, Mead plates). 9 essays, chiefly rptd from Cornhill Mag.

New Arabian nights. 2 vols 1882 ('Second Edition', actually 2nd printing), New York 1882, 1 vol London 1882 ('A New Edition', Cheap Edition), Hamburg 1883, 1 vol London 1884 (Cheap Edition, illus covers), 1894 (illus). Vol 1 The suicide club, The rajah's diamond; vol 2 The pavilion on the links, The Sire de Malétroit's door, Providence and the guitar. The stories in vol 1 originally appeared in London 8 June–26 Oct 1878, as Latter-day Arabian nights; those in vol 2 were rptd from Cornhill Mag, Temple Bar and London.

The Silverado squatters. 1883, Boston 1884, London 1886 ('A New Edition'). First pbd in Century Mag Nov–Dec 1883.

Treasure Island. 1883, 1884 (2nd edn), Boston 1884 (illus; additional printings as late as 1895), Leipzig 1884, London 1885 ('Illustrated Edition'). First pbd as Treasure Island; or, the mutiny of the Hispaniola, by Captain George North in Young Folks 1 Oct 1881–22 Jan 1882.

Admiral Guinea: a melodrama in four acts. Edinburgh 1884 (priv ptd), 1892 (in Three plays), 1896 and 1907 (in The plays), 1897. With W. E. Henley.

Beau Austin: a play in four acts. Edinburgh 1884 (priv ptd), 1892 (in Three plays), 1896 and 1907 (in The plays), 1897. With W. E. Henley.

A child's garden of verses. 1885 ('Second Edition' 1885 actually 2nd printing), New York 1885, 1895 (illus), London 1896 (illus). Trial issue, 48 poems, ptd 1883 as Penny whistles (copies at Yale, Harvard, Princeton), much rev and augmented; 6 of the poems pbd 1884, Mag of Art; 9 poems in trial issue omitted by RLS from 1st edn; these were priv ptd from the trial issue by L. S. Livingston as Verses by RLS, 1912, also in Widener Collection catalogue, 1913; first pbd San Francisco 1978.

More new Arabian nights: the dynamiter. 1885, New York 1885. Except for Zero's tale of the explosive bomb, largely the work of Fanny Stevenson.

Prince Otto: a romance. 1885 ('Second Edition' 1885 and 'A New Edition' 1886 actually later printings), New York 1886. First pbd in Longman's Mag Apr–Oct 1885.

Macaire: a melodramatic farce in three acts. Edinburgh 1885 (priv ptd), Chicago 1895, London 1896 and 1907 (in The plays), 1897. With W. E. Henley.

Strange case of Dr Jekyll and Mr Hyde. New York 1886, 1886 ('Second Edition' 1886 actually 2nd printing; 40,000 copies total in 6 months), Leipzig 1886.

Kidnapped: being memoirs of the adventures of David Balfour in the year 1751 . . . . 1886 (2nd issue 1886 makes 3 small changes requested by RLS), New York 1886, London 1887 (illus), Leipzig 1888, London 1895 (includes corrections made by RLS in 1893). First pbd as Kidnapped; or, the lad with the silver button in Young Folks 1 May–31 July 1886.

The merry men and other tales and fables. 1887, New York 1887, Leipzig 1891. Contents: The merry men, Will o' the mill, Markheim, Thrawn Janet, Olalla, The treasure of Franchard. Rptd from Cornhill Mag and other periodicals.

Underwoods. 1887 ('Second Edition' 1887 and 'Third Edition' 1888 actually later printings), New York 1887. 38 poems in Eng, 16 in Scots; about one-quarter rptd from various sources.

Memories and portraits. 1887, New York 1887. 16 essays. Except for 'A college magazine', 'Memoirs of an islet', and 'A gossip on a novel of Dumas's', rptd from Cornhill Mag, Longman's Mag and other periodicals.

The hanging judge: a drama in three acts and six tableaux. Edinburgh 1887 (priv ptd); ed E. Gosse 1914 (priv ptd). With Fanny Stevenson.

The misadventures of John Nicholson: a Christmas story. New York [1887] and later. Rptd without authorisation from Yule-Tide: Cassell's Christmas annual for 1887.

Memoir of Fleeming Jenkin. New York 1887, 1912. First pbd in Papers literary, scientific, &c. by the late Fleeming Jenkin . . . with a memoir by Robert Louis Stevenson, 2 vols 1887.

The black arrow: a tale of the two roses. New York 1888 (illus), 1888, Leipzig 1888. First pbd as The black arrow, a tale of Tunstall Forest, by Captain George North in Young Folks 30 June–20 Oct 1883.

The wrong box. 1889 (3 printings); ed E. Mehew 1989; New York 1889. With Lloyd Osbourne. All edns before Mehew's lack corrections from proofs and ms.

The master of Ballantrae: a winter's tale. 1889, New York 1889 (illus), Leipzig 1889. First pbd in Scribner's Mag Nov 1888–Oct 1889.

Father Damien: an open letter to the Reverend Dr Hyde of Honolulu. Sydney 1890 (priv ptd), Honolulu [1890], Edinburgh 1890 (priv ptd), 1890. First pbd in Scots Observer 3, 10 May 1890.

Ballads. New York 1890, 1890. Contents: The song of Rahéro, The feast of famine, Ticonderoga (first pbd in Scribner's Mag Dec 1887), Heather ale, Christmas at sea (first pbd in Scots Observer 22 Dec 1888). Each poem except the last is followed by notes.

Across the plains: with other memories and essays. 1892, New York 1892, Leipzig 1892. 12 essays, all but 3 rptd from Scribner's Mag.

The wrecker. 1892 (illus), New York 1892 (illus). First pbd in Scribner's Mag Aug 1891–July 1892. With Lloyd Osbourne.

A footnote to history: eight years of trouble in Samoa. 1892 ('Third Thousand' is 2nd printing, Sep 1892), New York 1892.

Three plays: Deacon Brodie, Beau Austin, Admiral Guinea. 1892, New York 1892.

An object of pity; or, the man Haggard. 1892 (priv ptd, Sydney), 1898 (25 copies priv ptd uniform with Edinburgh edn of Works), New York 1900. Comic self-portraits by RLS and others, verses by RLS.

Island nights' entertainments: consisting of The beach of Falesá, The bottle imp, The isle of voices. New York 1893 (illus), London 1893 (illus), Leipzig 1893. The beach of Falesá first pbd in Illus London News 2 July–6 Aug 1892. The bottle imp first pbd in New York Herald 8 Feb–1 Mar 1891, and in Black and White 28 Mar–4 Apr 1891. The isle of voices first pbd in Nat Observer 4–25 Feb 1893.

Catriona: a sequel to Kidnapped. 1893, New York 1893 (titled David Balfour: being memoirs of his adventures at home and abroad: The second part . . .), Leipzig 1893. First pbd as David Balfour: memoirs of his adventures at home and abroad in Atalanta Dec 1892–Sep 1893.

The ebb-tide: a trio and a quartette. Chicago 1894 ('Second Edition' 20 Sep 1894 actually 2nd printing), London 1894; ed P. Hinchcliffe and C. Kerrigan, Edinburgh 1995. First pbd in Today 11 Nov 1893–3 Feb 1894 and in McClure's Mag Feb–July 1894. With Lloyd Osbourne.

The body-snatcher. New York 1895. First pbd in Pall Mall Christmas 'Extra' 1884.

The amateur emigrant: from the Clyde to Sandy Hook. Chicago 1895. First pbd in Edinburgh edn of Works vol 3, 1895.

The strange case of Dr Jekyll and Mr Hyde, with other fables. 1896, New York 1896. Fables first pbd in Longman's Mag Aug–Sep 1895.

Weir of Hermiston: an unfinished romance. 1896, New York 1896, Leipzig 1896; ed C. Kerrigan, Edinburgh 1995. Ed S. Colvin from RLS's unfinished ms (Yale); first pbd in Cosmopolis Jan–Apr 1896.

Poems and ballads. New York 1896, London 1913, New York 1913 ('Complete Edition'). First collected edn of RLS's poems. Contents first pbd together in Edinburgh edn of Works, 1895, and (two additional poems) Thistle edn, 1896. Most of the poems under the heading Songs of travel (separate edn 1896) were first pbd in these edns.

Songs of travel and other verses. 1896. First pbd in Edinburgh edn of Works vol 14, 1895, omitting additional 2 poems in Thistle edn. Of the 44 poems, only 13 had appeared previously and only 6 during RLS's lifetime.

In the South Seas. New York 1896, London 1900, Leipzig 2 vols 1901. Earliest version priv ptd as The South Seas: a record of three cruises, 1890; pbd, with additions, in the New York Sun, Black and White, and elsewhere, 1891; ed S. Colvin, Edinburgh edn of Works vol 20, 1896; additional material ed A. Lang, Swanston edn vol 18, 1911, and ed L. Osbourne, Vailima edn vol 25, 1923. Much material remains uncollected or unpbd in its original form.

A mountain town in France: a fragment. New York and London 1896 (printed in New York, possibly for US distribution only). First pbd in The Studio [London], Winter 1896–7, including 4 of the 5 pencil sketches in this edn.

The plays of W. E. Henley and R. L. Stevenson. 1896 (limited issue, 250 copies), 1907 (regular issue). Adds Macaire to contents of Three plays 1892.

St Ives: being the adventures of a French prisoner in England. 30 chs by Stevenson, left incomplete at his death. Version completed by A. T. Quiller-Couch first pbd in Pall Mall Mag Nov 1896–Nov 1897 and McClure's Mag Mar–Nov 1897; New York 1897, 1897, Leipzig 1898. Version completed by J. Calder, Glasgow 1990.

A Stevenson medley. Ed S. Colvin 1899. Various essays, also the private press woodcuts and poems from Davos, first rptd or pbd in Edinburgh edn of Works vol 28, 1898, with a few additions. Original woodblocks used for all but 3 of the items. Some of the Davos material had appeared in J. Pennell, Robert Louis Stevenson, illustrator, The Chap-Book [Chicago] 15 Nov 1896.

RLS Teuila. New York 1899 (priv ptd). 20 poems.

The morality of the profession of letters. New York 1899. First pbd in Fortnightly Rev Apr 1881; first collected in Edinburgh edn of Works vol 11, 1895.

Essays and criticisms. Boston 1903. Under the heading 'Swiss notes' first complete reprints of 4 of RLS's 5 essays on Davos first pbd in Pall Mall Gazette 17 Feb–5 Mar 1881. Other contents previously rptd in Edinburgh edn of Works.

The story of a lie and other tales. Boston 1904 (H. E. Turner & Co),

Boston 1907 (Small, Maynard & Co). The story of a lie, The misadventures of John Nicholson, and The body-snatcher. The first two had been rptd in the Edinburgh and Thistle edns of Works, the third was first rptd in Thistle edn of Works vol 8, 1895, and in Pentland edn of Works vol 3, 1906.

Prayers written at Vailima, with an introduction by Fanny Stevenson. New York 1904, 1905, 1910 (illus). First pbd in Edinburgh edn of Works vol 21, 1896.

Essays of travel. Boston 1904, 1905. The amateur emigrant and 9 essays, these rptd or first pbd in Edinburgh edn of Works, and the 4 essays on Davos first rptd in Essays and criticisms, Boston 1903.

Tales and fantasies. 1905. Same stories as in The story of a lie and other tales, Boston 1904.

Essays in the art of writing. 1905. 7 essays first rptd or pbd in Edinburgh edn of Works vols 11 and 21, 1895–6.

Lay morals and other papers. 1911. 17 essays and 3 unfinished works of fiction, all first rptd or pbd in Edinburgh edn of Works vols 21 and 26, 1896–7.

Records of a family of engineers. 1912. First pbd in Edinburgh edn of Works vol 18, 1898.

Memoirs of himself. Philadelphia 1912 (priv ptd).

The waif woman. 1916. First pbd in Scribner's Mag Dec 1914.

On the choice of a profession. 1916. First pbd in Scribner's Mag Jan 1915.

Poems hitherto unpublished. Ed G. S. Hellman 2 vols Boston 1916 (priv ptd Bibliophile Soc). Notebook drafts of poems on pages cut from various notebooks. Often erroneously transcribed, and advancing biographical speculations since disproved. Details in Collected poems, ed J. A. Smith, 2nd edn 1971, and in J. C. Furnas, Voyage to windward, 1951.

New poems and variant readings. 1918. Contents rptd from Poems hitherto unpublished, 1916, but without notes or other information.

The history of Moses. Daylesford PA 1919 (priv ptd).

Diogenes in London. San Francisco 1920 (priv ptd).

The bandbox. Cambridge MA 1921 (priv ptd).

Diogenes at the Savile Club. Chicago 1921 (priv ptd).

Poems hitherto unpublished. Ed G. S. Hellman and W. P. Trent, Boston 1921 (priv ptd, Bibliophile Soc). Additional notebook poems.

Hitherto unpublished prose writings. Ed H. H. Harper, Boston 1921 (priv ptd, Bibliophile Soc). Prose fragments from notebooks, including prefaces, essays, prayers. Also some letters.

Stevenson's workshop. Ed W. P. Trent, Boston 1921 (priv ptd, Bibliophile Soc). Facsimiles and transcriptions, often erroneous, of pages cut from various notebooks.

When the devil was well. Ed W. P. Trent, Boston 1921 (priv ptd, Bibliophile Soc). Long story drafted in early 1875, with comments by L. Stephen and S. Colvin (ms, Yale).

Confessions of a unionist: an unpublished talk on things current, written in 1888. Ed F. L[ivingston], Cambridge MA 1921 (priv ptd).

Moral emblems & other poems written and illustrated with woodcuts. 1921, New York 1921. Material from Davos first rptd or pbd in Edinburgh edn of Works vol 28, 1898.

The best thing in Edinburgh: an address by Robert Louis Stevenson to the Speculative Society of Edinburgh in March 1873. Ed K. D. Osbourne, San Francisco 1923. Inaccurately transcribed and mistitled version of RLS's valedictory address ending the 1872–3 session (ms, Speculative Soc). First pbd in The Outlook, 19 Feb 1898.

The complete poems of Robert Louis Stevenson. New York 1923. Contents adds to Poems and ballads 'Complete Edition' New York 1913 and New poems and variant readings 1918 the material in Bibliophile Soc Poems hitherto unpbd 1921 and a few items from other sources.

The castaways of Soledad: a manuscript by Robert Louis Stevenson hitherto unpublished. Ed G. S. Hellman, Buffalo NY 1928 (priv ptd).

Monmouth: a tragedy. Ed C. Vale, New York 1928 (priv ptd).

The manuscripts of Robert Louis Stevenson's Records of a family of engineers: the unfinished chapters. Ed J. C. Bay, Chicago 1930.

Collected poems. Ed J. A. Smith 1950, 1971 (2nd edn).

Robert Louis Stevenson's Silverado journal. Ed J. E. Jordan, San Francisco 1954.

From Scotland to Silverado. Ed J. D. Hart, Cambridge MA 1966. Contents: The amateur emigrant, adding to Edinburgh edn (1895) passages from RLS's ms (Yale); pbd periodical versions of Silverado squatters, essays on San Francisco and Monterey; uncollected essay San Carlos day; previously unpbd fragment on Simoneau's restaurant in Monterey (ms, Yale).

Letters from Hawaii. Ed A. G. Day, Honolulu 1973. Pbd letters, pbd material from In the South Seas, 'Kona Coast' (previously unpbd material for In the South Seas, not always accurately transcribed) (ms, Huntington).

The amateur emigrant. Ed R. G. Swearingen 2 vols Ashland OR 1976–7. First complete edn of RLS's ms (Yale).

The Cévennes journal. Ed G. Golding, Edinburgh 1978, Toulouse 1978 (French tr, with much additional annotation).

An old song and Edifying letters of the Rutherford family. Ed R. G. Swearingen, Paisley and Hamden CT 1982. RLS's first pbd story, previously unknown, and an unpbd early work of autobiographical fiction (ms, Yale). An old song first pbd anonymously in London 24 Feb–17 Mar 1877.

The lantern bearers and other essays. Ed J. Treglown 1988. First book-form pbn of 'Authors and publishers' (1890–1; first pbd TLS 15–21 Jan 1988; ms, Yale) and 'Confessions of a Unionist' (1888; priv ptd 1921). First book-form reprints of 'A ball at Mr Elsinare's' and 'A studio of ladies' (London 10, 17 Feb 1877), and 'The misgivings of convalescence' (Pall Mall Gazette 17 Mar 1881).

Plain John Wiltshire on the situation. Midland TX 1989. First pbn of mock letter by RLS on 1893 Samoan regulation; original typescript, Yale, is not used in this edn.

RLS: The Scottish stories and essays. Ed K. Gelder, Edinburgh 1989. First book-form pbn of juvenile story The plague-cellar (early 1860s); first pbd Weekend Scotsman 24 Aug 1985; ms, Princeton.

The enchantress. London and Rome 1990, includes Ital trn. First pbd Georgia Rev, Fall 1989. Story written during *Casco* voyage 1888; ms, Yale.

Tales from the prince of storytellers. Ed B. Menikoff, Evanston IL 1993. Uses ms versions for Markheim (Harvard) and The isle of voices (Rosenbach Collection, Philadelphia).

The letters of Robert Louis Stevenson. Ed B. A. Booth and E. Mehew. Appendix to vol 2, 1994, first book-form pbn of 6 prose poems written 1875, all but one previously unpbd.

The new lighthouse on the Dhu Heartach Rock, Argyllshire. Ed R. G. Swearingen, St Helena CA 1995. First pbn RLS's 1872 essay (ms Huntington) and sketches (Free Lib of Philadelphia) based on 1870 visit recalled in Kidnapped and Memoirs of an islet.

Forgeries by Thomas J. Wise

Among the forgeries by T. J. Wise and H. B. Forman are the following Stevenson items. Except for the genuine offprint of On the thermal influence of forests (the genuine version differs from the forgery in stating 'From the Proceedings of the Royal Society of Edinburgh . . .' on the cover), Scribner's sheets of Ticonderoga by F. Warne & Co (London 1887 for English copyright, Harvard), and a reprint of Ticonderoga that RLS had made for King Kalakaua of Hawaii in 1889 (printer's duplicate, Harvard), none of these items was ever issued separately during Stevenson's lifetime. See J. Carter and G. Pollard, An enquiry into the nature of certain nineteenth-century pamphlets, *1934, 2nd edn 1983, and N. Barker and J. Collins,* A sequel to an enquiry . . ., *1983.*

On the thermal influence of forests. 1873.
The story of a lie. 1882.
Some college memories. Edinburgh 1886.
Thomas Stevenson civil engineer. 1887.
Ticonderoga. Edinburgh 1887.
War in Samoa. 1893.

Translations

Entries are arranged by language in order of first trn. Dates indicate first and later new trns of all or part of the English vol, even if the trn is only one story or only excerpts.

An inland voyage. Fr 1900, 1919, 1925, 1951; Jap 1951; Swed 1953.
Travels with a donkey in the Cévennes. Fr 1901, 1925, 1951; Jap 1927, 1950, 1951, 1952 (2 trns); Irish 1937; Cz 1948; Finnish 1954.
Virginibus puerisque. Jap 1927, 1937; Danish 1950.
New Arabian nights. Fr 1885, 1947, 1954; Ger 1896, [1918], 1922, 1926, 1963; Finnish 1898; Du 1898–1900; Norwegian 1901; Rus 1901, 1946, 1960; Hungarian 1902; Jap 1910, 1924, 1935, 1950, 1952; Chinese 1914; Latin 1918; Ital 1920, 1944, 1953; Danish 1921; Cz 1922, 1948; Swed 1929, 1977, 1978, 1988, 1989; Serbo-Croat 1954; Sp 1958; Korean 1960.
The Silverado squatters. Danish 1922; Fr 1987.
Treasure Island. Fr 1884, 1885, 1924, 1926, 1934, 1939, 1946 (3 trns), 1947, 1948, 1950 (2 trns), 1951, [1960]; Du 1885, 1945, 1946, 1966; Ital 1886, 1934, 1947, 1963, 1967, 1968; Sp 1886, 1916, 1980; Danish 1887, 1923, 1929; Hungarian 1887; Swed 1887, 1976, 1979, 1982, 1983, 1986, 1989, 1990; Ger 1897, 1921, [1936], [1937], 1946, 1956, 1968; Finnish 1899, 1954, 1993; Norwegian 1900, 1990, 1993; Rus 1901, 1936, 1956, 1957; Cz 1902; Icelandic 1906 (pbd Winnipeg), 1992; Catalan 1915; Arabic 1921; Latin 1922; Polish 1925, 1947, 1953; Afrikaans 1925; Hebrew 1926, 1939, 1960s, 1974, 1991; Yiddish 1927; Chinese c. 1928, 1980; Jap 1928, 1930, 1933, 1935, 1937, 1948, 1949, 1951, 1952, 1954, 1976; Swahili 1928; Romanian 1935; Azerbaijani 1936; Armenian 1937; Portuguese 1940, 1955, 1959, 1964; Todzhik 1940; Turkmen 1941; Yakut 1941; Vietnamese 1944/5; Estonian 1949; Bulgarian 1950; Flemish 1950; Kazakh 1950; Moldavian 1950; Serbo-Croat 1950; Lithuanian 1951; Luganda 1951; Zulu 1953; Kamba 1958; Samoan 1958; Hindi 1959; Turkish 1959, 1975, 1985; Indonesian 1950s; Georgian 1960; Kirghiz 1960; Malay 1960; Korean 1961; Tamil 1962; Gujarati 1984; Persian [Iranian] 1986.
A child's garden of verses. Rus 1920; Jap 1922, [1936], 1950, 1952; Latin 1922; Hebrew 1944/45; Fr 1975; Finnish 1992.
More new Arabian nights: the dynamiter. Fr [1894]; Sp 1943.
Prince Otto. Fr 1896, 1897; Polish 1897; Hungarian 1898; Portuguese 1940; Swed 1945; Jap 1948, 1951, 1952; Sp 1958; Ital 1968.
Strange case of Dr Jekyll and Mr Hyde. Ger 1887, 1921, 1922, 1928, 1930, [1937], 1988; Danish 1889, 1990; Fr 1890, 1924, 1926, 1931, 1947, 1951, [1960], 1975; Sp 1891, 1920, 1921, 1981; Finnish 1897, 1921, 1945, 1953, 1960, 1974; Swed 1897, [1911], 1921, 1926, 1988; Hungarian 1899; Cz 1900; Rus 1901; Ital 1905, 1952, 1959, 1963, 1967, 1982, 1983, 1987; Du 1909, 1944, 1945, 1987; Esperanto 1909, 1980; Yiddish 1911; Norwegian 1917; Armenian 1923 (pbd Boston); Polish 1924, 1985; Slovak 1924 (pbd New York); Arabic 1927, 1978; Hebrew 1928, 1977, 1984; Irish 1929; Jap 1929, 1934, 1936, 1938, 1950 (2 trns), 1951, 1957; Icelandic 1943; Flemish 1944; Greek 1948; Afrikaans 1949; Thai 1949; Portuguese 1956, 1971; Vietnamese 1956; Chinese 1957; Hindi 1959; Gujarati 1962; Greenlandic 1967; Punjabi 1979.
Kidnapped. Ger c. 1889, 1924, 1962, 1979; Du 1892; Sp 1895; Danish 1900; Norwegian 1900; Rus 1901; Fr 1905; Ital 1906, 1945, 1958; Finnish 1910, 1937; Swed 1921, 1955, 1991; Cz 1922; Jap 1926, 1928, 1933, 1949, 1952; Hungarian 1927; Polish 1927; Irish 1931; Icelandic 1934; Greek 1950; Flemish 1954; Serbo-Croat 1954; Fijian 1959; Romanian 1960; Chinese 1961; Gujarati 1961; Hindi 1962; Scots Gaelic 1964; Hebrew 1963, 1970.
The merry men and other tales and fables. Swed 1897; Du 1905; Finnish 1917; Fr 1920, 1947; Danish 1921; Ger 1925; Cz 1928; Jap 1937, 1952; Swed 1977.
The misadventures of John Nicholson. Swed 1897; Cz 1919; Fr 1921; Hungarian 1921; Finnish 1933; Jap 1935; Sp 1955.
The black arrow. Fr 1901, 1947, 1948; Norwegian 1903; Swed 1905, 1985; Danish 1911; Finnish 1913, 1963; Ger 1922; Ital 1924, 1936, 1944, 1959; Sp 1925, 1949; Polish 1928; Du 1934; Jap 1948, 1950; Serbian 1951; Hebrew 1953, 1980; Portuguese 1942, 1953; Flemish 1954; Icelandic 1954; Cz 1957; Estonian 1957; Ukranian 1958; Bulgarian 1959; Lithuanian 1960; Rus 1960; Albanian 1961; Hindi 1961; Romanian 1961; Vietnamese 1961; Latvian 1964; Burmese nd; Arabic nd; Niuean 1970.
The wrong box. Du 1900; Fr 1905; Norwegian 1926; Cz 1928; Danish 1946; Serbo-Croat 1955.
The master of Ballantrae. Swed 1890; Fr 1893, 1920, 1966; Rus 1901, 1957; Danish 1908; Ger 1911, 1949; Finnish 1921; Cz 1925; Du 1929; Ital 1929, 1965, 1978; Hungarian 1930; Irish 1938; Jap 1940, 1953; Norwegian 1949; Polish 1949; Sp 1953, 1980; Chinese 1954; Flemish 1954; Serbo-Croat 1954; Portuguese 1956; Lithuanian 1959; Hebrew 1986.
The wrecker. Swed 1893, 1989; Cz 1905; Fr 1906, 1945, [1957]; Ital 1920, 1954; Norwegian 1949; Portuguese 1960; Rus 1960; Lithuanian 1964; Ger nd.
Island nights' entertainments. Samoan 1891, 1926; Swed [1897], 1909, 1984; Danish 1900; Rus 1901; Finnish 1917; Fr [1919], 1920, 1948, [1960]; Ger 1923, 1924, 1925, [1928], 1929, 1946 (2 trns), 1947, 1948; Hungarian 1926; Cz 1927; Chinese c. 1935; Ital 1939, 1952; Norwegian 1949; Polish 1949; Portuguese 1951; Jap 1947, 1949, 1950, 1955; Du 1955; Hebrew 1977; Esperanto 1982; Tahitian 1982.
Catriona [David Balfour]. Rus 1901, 1957; Fr 1907; Norwegian 1917; Swed 1917; Icelandic 1918; Danish 1921; Ger 1926; Cz 1927; Ital 1929; Irish 1933; Sp 1950; Serbo-Croat 1953; Flemish 1954; Finnish 1955; Portuguese 1955; Jap 1956; Polish 1956; Du 1957; Hungarian 1958.
The ebb-tide. Swed 1898; Fr 1905; Cz 1927; Ital 1930; Polish 1930; Danish 1946; Norwegian 1949; Portuguese 1956; Sp 1957.
The body-snatcher. Maltese 1986.
The amateur emigrant. Danish 1911, 1922; Finnish 1931; Fr 1931.
Fables. Swedish [1911]; Jap 1914, 1925.
Weir of Hermiston. Fr 1912; Ger [1927]; Ital 1945.
In the South Seas. Fr 1920; Ger 1927, [1928]; Ital 1944; Swed 1985.
St Ives. Swed 1898; Du 1904; Fr 1904; Danish 1909; Ital 1929; Polish 1929; Ger 1930; Cz 1948; Norwegian 1949; Flemish 1952; Portuguese 1961; Rus nd.
The story of a lie. Ger 1924; Cz 1927; Rus 1927.
An old song. Maltese 1986; Fr 1994.
The enchantress. Ital and Eng 1990.

Film versions

Entries give date, title if different from text, film company, director and principal actors. Includes major television productions after 1960. Additional details in D. F. Glut, Classic movie monsters, *1978, and S. A. Nollen,* Robert Louis Stevenson: life, literature, and the silver screen, *1994.*

New Arabian nights: The suicide club. 1909 (American Mutoscope-Biograph Co), 1914 (British and Colonial Kinematograph Co; dir M. Elvey), 1919 (title Unheimliche geschicten; dir R. Oswald; C. Veidt), 1932 (Universal), 1933 [USA, 1940] (title The living dead; J. H. Hoffberg, Germany; dir R. Oswald; P. Wegener), 1936 (USA title Trouble for two; MGM; dir J. W. Ruben; R. Montgomery, R. Russell), 1973 (Universal; J. Haskell, M. Kidder, J. Wiseman).
New Arabian nights: The pavilion on the links. 1920 (title The white circle; Paramount; dir M. Tourneur).
New Arabian nights: The Sire de Malétroit's door. 1951 (title The strange door; Universal; dir J. Pevney; C. Laughton, B. Karloff, S. Forrest).

The Silverado squatters. 1948 (title Adventures in Silverado; Columbia Pictures; E. Barrière).

Treasure Island. 1908 (Vitagraph), 1912 (Edison), 1918 (Fox), 1920 (Paramount; dir M. Tourneur; C. Ogle, S. Mason), 1934 (MGM; dir V. Fleming; W. Beery, J. Cooper, L. Barrymore), 1937 (USSR; dir Vaynstok), 1950 (RKO-Walt Disney; dir B. Haskin; R. Newton, B. Driscoll, B. Sidney; 1954 sequel titled Long John Silver), 1965 (UPA animation), 1969 (Franco London Films for Canadian Broadcasting Corp; 13-week serial), 1970 (produced and released in Australia; dir Z. Janzic), 1971 (produced and released in USSR; dir Bayslev), 1971 (Jap title Dobotsu Takarajima; Tokei, Japan; dir H. Ikeda; animation), 1971 (Nat General Pictures; dir J. Hough; screenplay W. Mankowitz and O. Welles; O. Welles, K. Burfield), 1977 (BBC1-TV; 4-pt serial by J. Lucarotti), 1990 (Turner Network Television; dir F. C. Heston; C. Heston, C. Bale).

Strange case of Dr Jekyll and Mr Hyde. 1897[?], 1908 (Kalem; dir S. Olcott), 1908 (alternative title The modern Dr Jekyll; Selig Polyscope, Chicago; dir O. Turner), 1909 (Nordisk, Copenhagen; dir A. Blom), 1910 (title The duality of man; Wrench Films, England), 1911 (Thanhouser, New York; dir L. Henderson; J. Cruze, H. Benham, M. Snow; earliest surviving print), 1913 (Imp; dir H. Brenon; K. Baggot), 1913 (British Kinemacolor Co; earliest colour version), 1915 (title Horrible Hyde; Lubin), 1915 (title Miss Jekyll and Madame Hyde; Vitagraph), 1920 (Paramount; dir J. S. Robertson; J. Barrymore, M. Mansfield, N. Naldi), 1920 (Pioneer Film Corp; prod L. B. Mayer; Sheldon Lewis), 1920 (title Der januskopf; Lipow, Germany; dir F. W. Murnau; C. Veidt), '1932' [1931] (Paramount; dir R. Mamoulian; F. March, M. Hopkins; earliest sound version; restored 1988, adding 17 mins censored originally), 1941 (MGM; dir V. Fleming; S. Tracy, I. Bergman, L. Turner), 1951 (title El Extraneo Caso del Hombre y la Bestia, also versions in Eng and Ital; prod and released in Argentina; dir M. Soffici), 1959 (title Le testament du docteur Cordelier, USA title Experiment in evil; Pathe; dir Jean Renoir; J.-L. Barrault), 1960 (British title The two faces of Dr Jekyll, USA title The house of fright; Hammer Productions; dir T. Fisher; P. Massie, D. Addams, C. Lee), 1968 (Canadian Broadcasting Corp; teleplay by I. M. Hunter), 1971 (title Dr Jekyll and sister Hyde; Hammer Productions; A. Bates, M. Beswick), 1971 (title I, Monster; Amicus-British Lion, 1971, Cannon Films, 1973; C. Lee, P. Cushing), 1973 (NBC-TV; dir D. Winters; K. Douglas, S. George; musical version), 1980 (BBC2-TV; dir J. Powell; D. Hemmings), 1990 (title Jekyll & Hyde; London Weekend TV; dir D. Wickes; M. Caine, C. Ladd).

Kidnapped. 1917 (Forum/Edison; dir A. Crosland), 1938 (Twentieth Century Fox; dir A. Werker; W. Baxter, F. Bartholomew), 1948 (Monogram Pictures; dir W. Beaudine; R. McDowell, S. England, D. O'Herlihy), 1960 (Walt Disney; dir R. Stevenson; P. Finch, J. MacArthur), 1968 (produced and released in E. Germany; dir Seemann), 1971 (Omnibus Productions; dir D. Mann; M. Caine, T. Howard), 1995 (CBS-TV; dir F. Coppola).

The treasure of Franchard. 1952 (title The treasure of lost canyon; Universal; dir T. Tetzlaff; W. Powell, J. Adams).

The black arrow. 1948 (British title The black arrow strikes; Columbia; dir G. Douglas; L. Hayward, J. Blair)

The wrong box. 1913 (Solax), 1966 (Salamander; dir B. Forbes; R. Richardson, M. Caine, P. Cook, D. Moore), 1971 (animation produced and released in Australia).

The master of Ballantrae. 1953 (Warner Brothers; dir W. Keighley; E. Flynn, R. Livesey, A. Steel), 1984 (CBS-TV; dir D. Hickox; R. Thomas, M. York, J. Gielgud).

The ebb-tide. 1922 (Famous Players-Lasky; dir G. Melford), 1937 (Paramount; dir J. Hogan; R. Milland, L. Nolan, B. Fitzgerald), 1947 (title Adventure Island; Paramount; R. Calhoun, R. Fleming. P. Kelly). 1997 (ITV; Robbie Coltrane).

The body-snatcher. 1945 (RKO; dir R. Wise; B. Karloff, B. Lugosi, H. Daniell).

Weir of Hermiston. 1972 (BBC2-TV serial; adapted T. Wright).

St Ives. 1949 (title The secret of St Ives; Columbia; dir P. Rosen; R. Ney, V. Brown).

Letters

Vailima letters: being correspondence addressed by Robert Louis Stevenson to Sidney Colvin, Nov 1890–Oct 1894. 1895.

The letters of Robert Louis Stevenson to his family and friends. Ed S. Colvin 2 vols 1899, 4 vols 1911 (enlarged).

Letters. Ed S. Colvin 5 vols 1924 (Tusitala edn).

Henry James and Robert Louis Stevenson: a record of friendship and criticism. Ed J. A. Smith 1948. Letters and essays.

RLS: Stevenson's letters to Charles Baxter. Ed D. Ferguson and M. Waingrow, New Haven CT 1956.

Dear Stevenson: letters from Andrew Lang to Robert Louis Stevenson. Ed M. Demoor, Louvain 1990.

The letters of Robert Louis Stevenson. Ed B. A. Booth and E. Mehew 8 vols New Haven CT and London 1994–5. Definitive edn of almost 3,000 letters.

§2

Memoirs, appreciations and landmark criticism

The Edwin J. Beinecke Collection at Yale has the largest collection of secondary materials on Stevenson. These are listed in vol 2 of the catalogue by G. L. McKay; see Bibliographies *above.*

Archer, W. Robert Louis Stevenson: his style and thought. Time Nov 1885.

Archer, W. Robert Louis Stevenson at 'Skerryvore'. Critic 5 Nov 1887.

Barrie, J. M. Robert Louis Stevenson. British Weekly 2 Nov 1888. Rptd in his An Edinburgh eleven, 1889.

James, H. In his Partial portraits, 1888. Rptd in Henry James and Robert Louis Stevenson: a record of friendship and criticism. Ed J. A. Smith 1948.

Doyle, A. C. Mr Stevenson's methods in fiction. Nat Rev Jan 1890.

Lang, A. In his Essays in little, 1891.

Walkley, A. B. In his Playhouse impressions, 1892.

Crockett, S. R. The apprenticeship of Robert Louis Stevenson. Bookman Mar 1893.

Gosse, E. In his Questions at issue, 1893.

Osbourne, L. A letter to Mr Stevenson's friends. [Apia, Samoa] 1894 (priv ptd).

Symons, A. In his Studies in prose and verse, [1894].

Archer, W. In memoriam R. L. S. New Rev Jan 1895.

Churchill, W. Stevenson in the South Sea. McClure's Mag Feb 1895.

Crockett, S. R. Mr Stevenson's Books. Bookman Jan 1895.

J. A., [Anne Jenkin]. Robert Louis Stevenson. Edinburgh Academy Chron Mar 1895.

Raleigh, W. Robert Louis Stevenson. 1895.

Schwob, M. R. L. S. New Rev Feb 1895; tr A. Lenalie, Portland ME 1920.

Shaw, G. B. Review: Macaire, Saturday Rev 8 June 1895. Review: Admiral Guinea, Saturday Rev 4 Dec 1897. Both rptd (with other comments) in his Our theatre in the nineties, 1932, vols 1 and 3.

Stevenson, M. I. Notes about Robert Louis Stevenson from his mother's diary. Vailima edn vol 26. Year-by-year summary 1850–88 from her own diaries prepared by Stevenson's mother in 1895–6.

Barrie, J. M. In his Margaret Ogilvy, 1896.

Gosse, E. In his Critical kit-kats, 1896.

Quiller-Couch, A. T. In his Adventures in criticism, 1896.

Shipman, L. E. Stevenson's first landing in New York. Book Buyer Feb 1896.

Symons, A. In his Studies in two literatures, 1897.

Black, M. M. Robert Louis Stevenson. [1898.]

Burgess, G. An interview with Mrs Robert Louis Stevenson. Bookman (New York) Sep 1898.

Simpson, E. B. Robert Louis Stevenson's Edinburgh days. 1898.

Balfour, J. C. and M. C. Robert Louis Stevenson. By two of his cousins. English Illus Mag May 1899.
Cornford, L. C. Robert Louis Stevenson. 1899.
Gosse, E. Stevenson's relations with children. Chambers's Jnl 1 July 1899.
Duncan, W. H. Jr. Stevenson's second visit to America. Bookman (New York) Jan 1900.
Baildon, H. B. Robert Louis Stevenson: a life study in criticism. 1901.
Vallings, H. Stevenson among the Philistines [at Davos]. Temple Bar Feb 1901.
Colvin, S. Robert Louis Stevenson at Hampstead. Hampstead Annual Dec 1902.
Stephen, L. In his Studies of a biographer vol 4, [1902].
Strong, I. and L. Osbourne. Memories of Vailima. New York 1902.
Pinero, A. W. Robert Louis Stevenson: the dramatist. 1903 (priv ptd), New York 1914. Also in Papers on playmaking, ed B. Matthews, New York 1957.
Stevenson, M. I. From Saranac to the Marquesas and beyond. 1903.
Stevensoniana. Ed J. A. Hammerton 1903, Edinburgh 1907 (enlarged).
Japp, A. H. Robert Louis Stevenson: a record, an estimate, and a memorial. 1905.
Johnstone, A. Recollections of Robert Louis Stevenson in the Pacific. 1905.
Lang, A. In his Adventures among books, 1905.
Simpson, E. B. Robert Louis Stevenson. 1906.
Stevenson, M. I. Letters from Samoa 1891–1895. 1906.
Hammerton, J. A. In the track of Robert Louis Stevenson and elsewhere in old France. [1907.]
Clarke, W. E. Personal recollections of Robert Louis Stevenson. Chron of the London Missionary Soc Apr–May 1908; rptd in Reminiscences of Robert Louis Stevenson [1908, facs 1974].
Claxton, A. E. Stevenson as I knew him. Chron of the London Missionary Soc May 1908; rptd in Reminiscences of Robert Louis Stevenson [1908, facs 1974].
Gosse, E. Biographical notes on the writings of Robert Louis Stevenson. 1908 [priv ptd]. Notes for the Pentland edn, rev.
Low, W. H. A chronicle of friendships. 1908.
Moors, H. J. With Stevenson in Samoa. 1910.
Beach, J. W. The sources of Stevenson's Bottle imp. MLN Jan 1910.
'Lee, Vernon' (Violet Paget). The handling of words: Stevenson. English Rev Oct 1911. Rptd with comments on Catriona from Contemporary Rev Sep 1895 in the The handling of words, 1923.
Osbourne, K. D. Robert Louis Stevenson in California. Chicago 1911. RLS's stepson Lloyd Osbourne's wife, whom he later divorced. She never met Stevenson. Yale also has first issue, withdrawn due to unauthorised pbn of some RLS letters.
Strong, I. Robert Louis Stevenson. New York 1911. RLS's step-daughter, later Mrs Isobel Field.
Chalmers, S. The penny piper of Saranac. The Outlook 12 Oct 1912; rptd in his The penny piper of Saranac an episode in Stevenson's life, New York 1916.
Simpson, E. B. The Robert Louis Stevenson originals. 1912.
Colvin, S. Robert Louis Stevenson. Proc Royal Institution of Great Britain July 1913.
Robert Louis Stevenson. Bookman Extra Number 1913.
Saint-Gaudens, A. In his Reminiscences, 2 vols New York 1913.
Watt, F. RLS. 1913.
James, H. In his Notes on novelists, 1914.
McClure, S. S. In his My autobiography, 1914.
Stevenson, F. The cruise of the 'Janet Nichol' among the South Sea islands. New York 1914. Diary by Fanny Stevenson.
Swinnerton, F. R. L. Stevenson: a critical study. 1914.
Hamilton, C. On the trail of Stevenson. New York 1915. Yale also has first version withdrawn before pbn.
Matthews, B. A moral from a toy theatre. Scribner's Mag Oct 1915.
Harrison, B. With Stevenson at Grez. Century Mag Dec 1916.
Knowlton, E. C. A Russian influence on Stevenson. MP Dec 1916.
Aydelotte, F. In his The Oxford stamp and other essays, New York 1917.
Daplyn, A. J. Robert Louis Stevenson at Barbizon. Chambers's Jnl 14 July 1917.
Rivenburgh, E. Stevenson in Hawaii. Bookman (New York) Oct–Dec 1917.
Sullivan, T. R. Robert Louis Stevenson at Saranac. Scribner's Mag Aug 1917; rptd in his Passages from the journal of Thomas Russell Sullivan 1891–1903, 1917.
Lansing, R. R. Robert Louis Stevenson's French reading as shown in his correspondence. Poet Lore Mar 1918.
Brown, G. E. A book of R. L. S.: works, travels, friends and commentators. [1919.]
Lysaght, S. R. A visit to Robert Louis Stevenson. TLS 4 Dec 1919; rptd in I can remember Robert Louis Stevenson, ed R. Masson, 1922.
Guthrie, C. J. Robert Louis Stevenson: some personal recollections. Edinburgh 1920.
Snyder, A. D. Paradox and antithesis in Stevenson's essays. JEGP 1920.
Clarke, W. E. Robert Louis Stevenson in Samoa. Yale Rev Jan 1921.
Colvin, S. In his Memories and notes of persons and places, 1921.
Eaton, C. Stevenson at Manasquan. Chicago 1921.
Robertson, S. Sir Thomas Browne and Robert Louis Stevenson. JEGP 1921.
Buell, L. M. Eilean Earraid: the beloved isle of Robert Louis Stevenson. Scribner's Mag Feb 1922.
Claxton, A. E. Stevenson as I knew him in Samoa. Chambers's Jnl 2 Sep 1922.
Hellman, G. S. The Stevenson myth. Century Mag Dec 1922.
I can remember Robert Louis Stevenson. Ed R. Masson 1922.
Snyder, A. D. Stevenson's conception of the fable. JEGP 1922.
Stevenson, M. I. Stevenson's baby book: being a record of the sayings and doings of Robert Louis Stevenson. San Francisco 1922.
Adcock, A. St J. Stevenson and the juvenile drama. Bookman Oct 1923.
Pears, E. R. Some recollections of Robert Louis Stevenson. Scribner's Mag Jan 1923.
Clark, E. M. The kinship of Hazlitt and Stevenson. SE 1924.
Osbourne, L. An intimate portrait of R. L. S. New York 1924. Pbd originally as prefaces in Tusitala edn. *See also* his general introd to Vailima edn.
Robert Louis Stevenson: his work and his personality. 1924. Rev edn of Bookman Extra 1913 with new material.
Taylor, U. In her Guests and memories: annals of a seaside villa, 1924.
Benson, E. F. The myth of Robert Louis Stevenson. London Mercury July–Aug 1925.
Burriss, E. E. The classical culture of Robert Louis Stevenson. Classical Jnl Feb 1925.
Hellman, G. S. 'Cue' stories of Stevenson. Bookman (New York) Oct 1925.
Hellman, G. S. Stevenson emerges. Bookman (New York) Jan 1925.
Hellman, G. S. The true Stevenson: a study in clarification. Boston 1925. Yale has galley proofs and other material.
Lipscomb, H. C. Stevenson and the classics. Classical Jnl June 1925.
Boodle, A. A. R. L. S. and his sine qua non: flashlights from Skerryvore. 1926.
Cunningham, A. Cummy's diary. Ed R. T. Skinner 1926. Account of 1863 travels chiefly in France and Italy with RLS and his family.
Hellman, G. S. Stevenson and Henry James. Century Mag Jan 1926.
Sherman, S. P. Robert Louis Stevenson encounters the 'modern' writers on their own ground. In his Critical woodcuts, New York 1926.
Chesterton, G. K. Robert Louis Stevenson. 1927.

MacCulloch, J. A. R. L. Stevenson and the Bridge of Allan, with other Stevenson essays. Glasgow 1927.
Lucas, E. V. The Colvins and their friends. 1928.
Garrod, H. W. In his The profession of poetry and other lectures, Oxford 1929.
Morris, D. B. Robert Louis Stevenson and the Scottish highlanders. Stirling 1929.
MacPherson, H. D. R. L. Stevenson: a study in French influence. New York 1930.
Charteris, E. The life and letters of Sir Edmund Gosse. [1931.]
Sherman, S. P. Who made the Stevenson myth? What is biographical truth? In his Emotional discovery of America, New York 1932, [rptd 1970].
Lockett, W. G. Robert Louis Stevenson at Davos. 1934.
MacCallum, T. M. Adrift in the South Seas including adventures with Robert Louis Stevenson. Los Angeles [1934].
Mackaness, G. Robert Louis Stevenson: his associations with Australia. Sydney 1935.
Hellman, G. S. R. L. S. and the streetwalker. Amer Mercury July 1936.
MacLean, C. La France dans l'oeuvre de R. L. S. Paris 1936.
Strong, I. This life I've loved. New York 1937.
Issler, A. R. Stevenson at Silverado. Caldwell ID 1939; rev and abridged as Our mountain hermitage: Silverado and Robert Louis Stevenson, Stanford CA [1950].
Vandiver, E. P. Jr. Stevenson and Shakspere, Shakespeare Assoc Bull Oct 1939.
Moore, J. R. Defoe, Stevenson, and the pirates. ELH Mar 1943.
Moore, J. R. Stevenson's source for The merry men. PQ Apr 1944.
Fisher, A. B. No more a stranger. Stanford CA [1946]. Semi-fictional but with good background on Stevenson in Monterey.
Parsons, C. O. Stevenson's use of witchcraft in Thrawn Janet. SP July 1946.
Daiches, D. Robert Louis Stevenson. Norfolk CT [1947].
Garrod, H. W. In Essays mainly on the nineteenth century presented to Sir Humphrey Milford, Oxford 1949.
Issler, A. R. Happier for his presence: San Francisco and Robert Louis Stevenson. Stanford CA [1949].
Green, R. L. Stevenson in search of a Madonna. E & S n.s. 1950.
McGaw, M. M. Stevenson in Hawaii. Honolulu 1950.
Daiches, D. Stevenson and the art of fiction. New York 1951.
Greene, G. In his The lost childhood and other essays, 1952.
Stevenson, F. Our Samoan adventure. Ed C. Neider, New York 1955. Diary by Fanny Stevenson, pbd letters by Robert Louis Stevenson.
Mackaness, G. In his The art of book-collecting in Australia. Sydney [1956].
McKay, G. L. Some notes on Robert Louis Stevenson, his finances and his agents and publishers. New Haven CT 1958.
Issler, A. R. Robert Louis Stevenson in Monterey. Pacific Historical Rev Aug 1965.
Daiches, D. Robert Louis Stevenson and his world. 1973.

Biographies

Colvin, S. In DNB, 1898.
Balfour, G. The life of Robert Louis Stevenson. 2 vols 1901.
Henley, W. E. 'R. L. S.' Pall Mall Mag Dec 1901. Review of Balfour.
Gosse, E. In Encyclopaedia Britannica, 1903.
Masson, R. O. The life of Robert Louis Stevenson. 1923. Expanded and rev from brief life pbd 1914.
Sanchez, N. V. The life of Mrs Robert Louis Stevenson. 1920.
Steuart, J. A. Robert Louis Stevenson, man and writer: a critical biography. 2 vols [1924].
Smith, J. A. R. L. Stevenson. 1937.
Furnas, J. C. Voyage to windward: the life of Robert Louis Stevenson. New York 1951, London 1952 (with corrections).
Balfour, M. How the biography of Robert Louis Stevenson came to be written. TLS 15 and 22 Jan 1960.
Pope Hennessy, J. Robert Louis Stevenson. 1974.
Calder, J. RLS: a life study. 1980.
Balfour, M. The first biography. In Stevenson and Victorian Scotland, ed J. Calder, 1981.
Lapierre, A. Fanny Stevenson: entre passion et liberté. Paris 1993, New York 1995 (tr Eng). Semi-fictional but with much good information.

Textual and bibliographical studies

Hills, G. Robert Louis Stevenson's handwriting. New York 1940.
Wilsey, M. Kidnapped, in manuscript. Amer Scholar, Spring 1948.
McCleary, G. F. Stevenson in Young Folks. Fortnightly Rev Feb 1949.
Hart, J. D. The private press ventures of Samuel Lloyd Osbourne and R. L. S. San Francisco 1966.
Robert Louis Stevenson: the critical heritage. Ed P. Maixner 1981. Contemporary reviews.
Menikoff, B. Robert Louis Stevenson and 'The beach of Falesá': a study in Victorian publishing. Stanford CA 1984. Commentary and complete edn of Robert Louis Stevenson's ms (Huntington).
Hardesty, P., W. Hardesty and D. Mann. 'Doctoring the doctor': how Stevenson altered the second narrator of Treasure Island. Stud in Scottish Lit 21 1986.
Hardesty, W. and D. Mann. Stevenson's revisions of Treasure Island: 'Writing down the whole particulars'. Text 3 1987.
Hardesty, W. and D. Mann. Robert Louis Stevenson's art of revision: 'The pavilion on the links' as rehearsal for Treasure Island. PBSA Sep 1988.
Dr Jekyll and Mr Hyde after one hundred years. Ed W. Veeder and G. Hirsch. Chicago 1988. First pbn of fragments from notebook versions (mss, Yale, Princeton).
Nollen, S. A. Robert Louis Stevenson: life, literature, and the silver screen. Jefferson NC 1994. Film adaptations. [RGS]

Bram Stoker, Abraham Stoker 1847–1912

Mss correspondence relating to Stoker's career as business manager of Sir Henry Irving is held at the Shakespeare Centre, Stratford-upon-Avon. The Brotherton Collection, Univ of Leeds, holds 5,000 letters to Stoker, and the Rosenbach Museum and Lib, Philadelphia, holds his working notes for Dracula.

Bibliographies

Dalby, R. Bram Stoker: a bibliography of first editions. 1983.
Bram Stoker: a bibliography ed W. Hughes. Victorian Fiction Research Guide 25 St Lucia, Queensland 1997.

Collections and selections

The Bram Stoker bedside companion. Ed Osborne 1973, New York 1973, 1974 (paperback).
Shades of Dracula. Ed I. Haining 1982.
Midnight tales. Ed I. Haining 1990.
Bram Stoker omnibus. 1992.

§1

Address delivered to the College Historical Soc, Univ of Dublin 1872 (as Abraham Stoker), entitled The necessity of political honesty.
The duties of clerks of Petty Sessions in Ireland. Dublin 1879.
Under the sunset. 1882, rptd North Hollywood CA 1978, rptd San Bernardino CA 1980. Children's stories.
A glimpse of America: a lecture given at the London Institution. 1885.
The Snake's Pass. 1890, New York 1890, London 1892, 1909, rptd Dingle, Co Kerry 1990. Serialised in The People 1889.
The Watter's Mou. 1895, New York 1895, rptd in The Bram Stoker bedside companion 1973. Novella.
The shoulder of Shasta. 1895. Romantic novel.

Dracula. 1897, New York 1899. First pbk London 1901. 8 edns in 11 years, reset when taken over by William Rider for 9th edn in 1912. Many US edns from 1902 onwards by Doubleday, and by Grosset and Dunlap from 1928 onwards. 1932 (Modern Lib edn); 1962, 1966, 1970, New York 1970 (ed J. Nelson), London 1973, 1974, 1974 (Dennis Wheatley Lib of the Occult, ed D. Wheatley), 1975, 1979, 1979, 1981, 1983, Oxford 1986 (Wcp, ed A. N. Wilson), New York 1988, London 1989, Dingle, Co Kerry 1992, London 1992, 1992, 1993 (ed M. Hindle) Pen Classics, 1993, 1993 (ed M. Howes) Everyman Classics, 1993, 1994. The annotated Dracula (ed L. Wolf) New York 1975. The essential Dracula (ed R. McNally and R. Florescu) New York 1979 annotated and illus. Tr Irish 1933; Rus nd (early 1930s).

ADAPTATIONS: Plays by: Hamilton Deane and J. L. Balderston 1933 (rptd New York 1971, 1993); Ted Tiller (New York 1972); Larry Ferguson (New York 1973); Crane Johnson (New York 1976); Gerald Savory (London 1976); Anne Pearson (1978); Bob Hall and David Richmond (New York 1979); Liz Lochhead (1989).

BALLET: Dracula 1991 (choreographed Stuart Sebastian for Dayton Ballet).

FILM VERSIONS INCLUDE: 1922 (dir F. W. Murnau); 1931 (dir Tod Browning); 1958 (dir Terence Fisher); 1970 (dir Jess Franco); 1979 (dir John Badham); 1992 (dir Francis Ford Coppola). The character of Dracula has taken on a life of its own and has been featured in many films and stories not directly adapted from Stoker.

Miss Betty. 1898, 1913, 1974. Romantic novel.

Sir Henry Irving and Miss Ellen Terry. 1899. Promotional pam for Irving–Terry Amer tour.

The mystery of the sea. 1902, 2 vols 1903, 1913, 1922, 1929 (abridged).

The jewel of Seven Stars. 1903, New York 1904. Rewritten (to give it a happy ending) and an entire ch omitted London 1912, 1919, 1962, 1966, 1975, New York 1972, North Hollywood CA 1974. Full text rptd with Dracula's guest as Dracula's curse and The jewel of Seven Stars 1968.

FILM VERSIONS: Blood from the mummy's tomb (dir Seth Holt and Michael Carreras) 1971, and The awakening (dir Mike Newell) 1980.

The man. 1905. Heavily abridged version as The gates of life, New York 1908, prepared by Stoker. Another abridged and rewritten Gates of life pbd in London nd (early 1920s); abridged by another unknown writer.

Personal reminiscences of Henry Irving. 2 vols 1906, New York 1906, 1 vol 1907 rev and abridged, rptd Westport CT 1970.

Lady Athlyne. 1908, New York 1909. Romantic novel.

Snowbound: the record of a theatrical touring party. 1908. Collection of short stories with theatrical background.

The lady of the shroud. 1909, 1914, 1920, 1934, 1962, 1966, 1974, 1994. (Contains only two-thirds of the original text.) The modern edns since 1962 are abridged.

Famous imposters. 1910, New York 1910, rptd 1967.

The lair of the White Worm. 1911, reprint of complete text as The garden of evil New York 1966. From 1925 on, edns heavily abridged: 1945, 1960, 1966, 1974, Dingle, Co Kerry 1991.

FILM VERSION: 1988 (dir Ken Russell).

Dracula's guest and other weird stories. 1914, New York 1937, 1966, 1974, 1974, Dingle, Co Kerry 1990. Collection of short stories.

§2

Ludlam, H. A biography of Dracula: the life story of Bram Stoker. 1962.

Farson, D. The man who wrote Dracula. 1975, New York 1976.

Frayling, C. Vampyres: Lord Byron to Dracula. 1991 (on the composition of Dracula).

Belford, B. Bram Stoker. 1996.

The Bram Stoker Soc was founded in Dublin in 1980 and distributes an annual jnl and 4 newsletters to members. [JR]

'Hesba Stretton', Sarah Smith 1832–1911

Stretton's ms logbooks of her life and literary career 1859–71 are held by Shropshire County Lib.

Collection

Victorian fiction: novels of faith and doubt, no 45. New York 1976. Includes Jessica's first prayer, Little Meg's children, Alone in London, Pilgrim Street.

§1

The dates of the many edns and reprints of Stretton's works are difficult to determine, since the publisher of most of them, the Religious Tract Soc (London), often did not supply dates. Most of her works after 1872 were first pbd in the Day of Rest *or the* Sunday Mag.

Fern's Hollow. [1864]; Boston 1865, with sub-title, a story of the English collieries; Philadelphia 1867; Philadelphia [1884?] as The collier boy: a story of Fern's Hollow, New York nd as The collier boy and his candle-box.

Enoch Roden's training. [1865]; as The young apprentice, Boston [1865]; tr Norwegian 1897.

The children of Cloverley. 1865 (sequel to Fern's Hollow); pbd New York [1880] in slightly abridged version as The children of Lake Huron; tr Swed 1875.

The fishers of Derby Haven. [1866]; Philadelphia nd; Boston [1880?] as Peter Killip's king, or the fishers of Derby Haven.

The Clives of Burcot. 3 vols '1867' [1866] (novel for adults); New York '1867' [1866].

REVIEW: Athenaeum, 12 Jan 1867.

Jessica's first prayer. First pbd in Sunday at Home 1866. 1867; Boston [c. 1867, 2 edns], New York [1867], 1901 as Jessica's first prayer and other stories; Philadelphia edn [c. 1903] (Altemus' Good Times Ser) rptd Saegertown PA 1993. Exists in over 40 printings and/or ser bindings, and sold over 1½ million copies; versions include penny pams, song services, lantern slides, and a film (1906). Abridged version pbd Chicago 1915 with abridgement of Charles Dickens's A Christmas carol. Modern edns: Grand Rapids MI 1955; St Catharine's, Ontario 1980; *see also under* Collection, *above*. Micros Cambridge MA [1970?] and NYPL [197?]. Tr all European languages, and some Asian and African languages.

Pilgrim Street: a story of Manchester life. [1867]; Philadelphia [1868] ('after revision by the Committee of Publication': the American Sunday School Union altered the story to strengthen its religious message). London edns 1880, 1886 (Religious Tract Soc Lib), 1883. Rptd in The ray of sunlight: or Jack Stafford's resolve. And other readings for working men's homes. By H. Stretton, R. Lamb, and other popular writers [1887] (Religious Tract Soc's Illus Penny Books for the People nos 13–24). Rptd Neerlandia, Alta, Canada and Pella, IA 1996. *See also under* Collection, *above*. Tr Du 1887.

Jessica's mother: a sequel to Jessica's first prayer. 1867. Edns of New York 1868, Philadelphia 1869 and [c. 1897] (Altemus' Devotional Ser no 30), Chicago [1897] (Colportage Lib vol 3 no 50) and New York 1903 all pbd with Jessica's first prayer. Jessica's first prayer and Jessica's mother also pbd together Neerlandia, Alta, Canada and Pella IA 1995. Tr Norwegian 1885.

Paul's courtship: a novel. 3 vols 1867 (for adults).

REVIEW: Athenaeum 15 June 1867.

Little Meg's children. 1868, rptd Wakefield NY 1970 (with new preface); New York 1868. Other London edns 1875, [1905] (Bouverie Ser of Penny Stories). Rptd with her Alone in London 1892. *See also under* Collection, *above*. Tr Welsh [c. 1905].

David Lloyd's last will. First pbd in Leisure Hour Jan–June 1869. 2 vols London and Edinburgh 1869 (novel for adults); New York [187?] (Household Tales for Week Day Hours). Other edns '1877' [1876], [1909] (Leisure Hour Monthly Lib no 42).

Alone in London. First pbd in Sunday at Home Aug–Sep 1869. [1869]

New York [1870]. Boston [1875]. Another edn 1880, rptd [1914] (Bouverie Ser of Penny Stories); New York [1883?] (Heart-Life Classics); Chicago 1898 (Colportage Lib vol 4 no 65); Philadelphia [191?] ('after revision by the Committee of Publication' of the American Sunday School Union); micro Cambridge MA [1970?]. *See also under* Collection, *above*. Tr Swed 1870; Ger, Milwaukee WI nd, New York 1885.

Nelly's dark days. Glasgow and New York 1870, Glasgow 1877, New York 1882 with Stretton's The worth of a baby, New York nd 'from 10th Glasgow edition' as Nelly Rodney's sorrows: the story of what a child suffered at the hands of a drunken father; tr Norwegian 1898.

Max Krömer: a story of the siege of Strasbourg. 1870 [1871]. First pbd in Leisure Hour Feb–Apr 1871 (text of book version altered by the Religious Tract Soc). New York 1871, [1913] (Bouverie Ser of Penny Books no 66).

Bede's charity. [1872]. First pbd in the Sunday at Home Jan–Apr 1872 (text of book version altered by Religious Tract Soc). New York 1872, 1879 (Seaside Lib vol 30 no 62).

The doctor's dilemma. 3 vols London and Manchester 1872 (novel for adults), 1 vol New York 1872, 1 vol Berlin 1873, 1 vol London 1897, 1901, 1908.
REVIEW: Athenaeum 15 Feb 1873.

Michel Lorio's cross. [1873]. First pbd in the Day of Rest, Christmas 1872. New York 1873 (with Ally Transome, from Stretton's The King's servants – *see below*). Another edn [1877]. Also pbd with Stretton's Left alone, 1876, and with her Lost Gip, New York 1873. Pbd also in Tales from many sources vol 2, New York 1885.

The King's servants. 1873 (stories), New York 1873, rptd [1879] with new title page. First story pbd as Ally Transome: or faithful in little, with Stretton's Michel Lorio's cross, New York 1873, and separately as Old Transome, London 1876, rptd [1879] with new title page. Tr Du 1913; Ger nd.

Lost Gip. 1873, 11th thousand 1873. Also presentation edn with engravings 1873, New York [1873?]. Other edns 1875 (41st thousand), [1879], [1891?] (Hesba Stretton Ser), [1907] (Bouverie Ser of Penny Stories no 30), [1914]. Also pbd with Stretton's Michel Lorio's cross, New York 1873. Tr Tamil 1890.

Hester Morley's promise. 3 vols 1873 (novel for adults), New York [1873], 1880 (Seaside Lib, vol 38 no 779), 1 vol London 1898.
REVIEW: Athenaeum 6 Sep 1873.

Cassy. [1874], rptd [1878] with new title page. New York [1874]. Other edns [1888] (Hesba Stretton Ser), [1908] (Bouverie Ser of Penny Stories no 36).

Brought home. Glasgow 1875, New York 1875, Glasgow 1879, Glasgow, Edinburgh and London 1880.

Friends till death and other stories. 1875, 10th thousand 1876, rptd [1879] minus half-title and with new title page, as Friends till death.

The wonderful life. 1875, New York [1875], London 1878, 1883. Pbd as The wonderful life of Christ [1899], rptd [1907], [1908], [1925], New York and Cincinnati 1908. Pbd in various works in US: Ingram Cobbin, The pictorial Bible and commentator, Philadelphia and Columbus OH 1878, rptd Philadelphia 1889 as The people's companion to the Bible; The beautiful life of Christ and the lives of the Apostles, Philadelphia 1896; The wonderful story of Christ and His Apostles, Philadelphia 1896, micro Washington nd (Lib of Congress); The child's life of Christ: or the wonderful life, Philadelphia and Chicago [1891]; The Gospel story for young people, Philadelphia [1896]; The new child's life of Christ . . . told in easy language, Philadelphia 1901; The child's story of the beautiful life of Jesus told in simple language . . . Hartford CT [1902]; The story of Jesus and the lives of His Apostles, Philadelphia [1902]; The young people's life of Christ, Philadelphia 1903. Tr Swed 1893.

Two secrets, and a man of his word. [1875?]. Rptd [1879] with new title page. New edn [1897]. A man of his word pbd separately 1878 and New York nd.

Two Christmas stories: Sam Franklin's savings-bank; A miserable Christmas and a happy New Year. [1876?] A miserable Christmas . . . first pbd in Leisure Hour 1870.

The worth of a baby, and How Apple-Tree Court was won. 1876, New York 1876 with Stretton's A night and a day. The worth of a baby pbd in Stretton's The Christmas child, and other stories 1888.

A night and a day. 1876, New York 1876, with Stretton's The worth of a baby, and How Apple-Tree Court was won. Another edn [1913] with her Left alone (Bouverie Ser of Penny Books no 65). Also pbd as A day and a night 1876.

The crew of the Dolphin. 1876, New York [1876] (micro New York 1988), London [1879], [1894], Chicago [1898] (Colportage Lib, vol 4 no 61).

The storm of life. London and Edinburgh 1876, 11th thousand 1876.

Mrs Burton's best bedroom. 1878 (Religious Tract Soc's Books for the People, nos 1–12). Pbd [188?] as Mrs Burton's best bedroom and other stories.

Through a needle's eye. 2 vols '1879' [1878], 1 vol New York 1878, 1 vol London 1880, [1907] (Leisure Hour Monthly Lib); tr Norwegian 1915; Ger nd. Novel for adults.
REVIEW: Athenaeum 9 Nov 1879.

A thorny path. [1879], New York [1879], London and Edinburgh [1890]. Pbd New York [1881] with Charlotte Mary Brame's The fatal lilies. Tr Ger [1890].

In prison and out: facts on a thread of fiction. First pbd in the Sunday Mag 1879. '1880' [1879], New York [1879]. Other edns New York [1879] (Seaside Lib vol 30 no 630), [1886] (Lovell's Lib vol 14 no 729), New York 1890, London [1906]. Tr Norwegian [1895].

Cobwebs and cables. [1881], New York [1881], Chicago [1883], London [1906] (Leisure Hour Monthly Lib), New York [1906].

No place like home. [1881]. Another edn [1905] (Bouverie Ser of Penny Stories no 6). Tr Norwegian 1897.

The Lord's purse-bearers. First pbd in the Day of Rest 1882. 1882, New York 1882 (Seaside Lib vol 68 no 1385), 2nd edn '1883' [1882], Boston 1882, micro Washington nd (Lib of Congress), New York 1900 (bound with The history of a threepenny bit).

Under the old roof. [1882], new edn [1913] (Bouverie Ser of Penny Stories).

Carola. [1884], New York 1884; tr Norwegian 1885.

Her only son. 1887, New York [1887].

The Christmas child, and other stories. 1888, [1908]. The Christmas child pbd separately, New York [1909].

Only a dog. [1888.]

An acrobat's girlhood. 1889. First pbd in the Sunday Mag 1889.

Half brothers. [1892], New York [1892], [1906] (Leisure Hour Monthly Lib).

In the hollow of His hand. [1897.]

The soul of honour. 1898.

The parables of our Lord. 1903.

Left alone, and other stories. [1905]. Left alone pbd with Stretton's A night and a day [1913] (Bouverie Ser of Penny Books no 65).

Contributions to periodicals

The lucky leg. Household Words, 19 Mar 1859.

Contributions to the Christmas numbers of All the Year Round, 1859–66.

Maurice Craven's madness. Temple Bar 19, Feb 1867.

Preface, collaborative work, editions

Pike, J. H. Children reclaimed for life: the story of Dr Barnardo's work in London. 1875 (Stretton wrote the preface).

The highway of sorrow at the close of the nineteenth century: a novel. 1894, New York 1894, [1908] (Leisure Hour Monthly Lib); tr Ger Halle 1895, Bremen 1896, Fr [1895]. With Sergei Kravchinskii.

Good words from the Apocrypha. Selected and arranged by Hesba Stretton. 1903.
Thoughts on old age: good words from many minds. Selected and arranged by Hesba Stretton. 1906.

§2

The Times 10 Oct 1911 (anon). Obituary.
Lee, Elizabeth. In DNB, 2nd suppl.
Bratton, J. S. The impact of Victorian children's fiction. 1981. Includes bibliographical information. [JW]

Anne Thackeray Ritchie, Anne Isabella Thackeray, later Lady Ritchie 1837–1919

The Univ of London houses the majority of ms material. Letters are widespread with major collections at Eton College (including journals) and Pierpont Morgan Lib, New York (including 2 journals).

Collections

Works of Miss Thackeray. 10 vols 1875–1903.
The writings of Anne Isabella Thackeray. New York 1876.

§1

The story of Elizabeth. First serialised in Cornhill Mag 6–7 1862–3. 1863, Philadelphia 1863, Leipzig 1863 (Tauchnitz); rptd with Two hours and From an island in Works vol 6, 1880, *above*, and in Writings, *above*; tr Fr 1883.
REVIEW: Athenaeum 25 Apr 1863.
The village on the cliff. First serialised in Cornhill Mag 14–15 1866–7. 1867, New York 1867, Leipzig 1867 (Tauchnitz); rptd in Works vol 2, 1875, *above*, and in Writings, *above*.
REVIEWS: The Times 24 Mar 1867; Fraser's Mag 5 Oct 1867.
Five old friends and a young prince. First serialised in Cornhill Mag 13–17 1866–8. 1868, Boston 1868 (as Fairy tales for grown folks), Leipzig 1868 (Tauchnitz); rptd in Works vol 3, 1876, *above*, and in Writings, *above*.
To Esther and other sketches. First serialised in Cornhill Mag 1862–5. 1869; rptd in Works vol 4, 1876, *above*.
Old Kensington. First serialised in Cornhill Mag Apr 1872–Apr 1873. 1873, New York 1873, Leipzig 1873 (Tauchnitz); rptd in Works vol 1, 1879, *above*; tr Du 1874.
REVIEW: [G. Barnett Smith] Edinburgh Rev 138, July 1873.
Bluebeard's keys and other stories. First serialised in Cornhill Mag 1871–4. 1874. 1874, Leipzig 1874 (Tauchnitz); rptd in Works vol 5, 1876, *above*.
Toilers and spinsters and other essays. Essays serialised in Pall Mall Gazette 1865–71 and Cornhill Mag 1860–74. 1874; rptd in Works vol 7, 1876, *above*.
Miss Angel. First serialised in Cornhill Mag 31 Jan–June 1875. 1875, New York 1875, Leipzig 1875 (Tauchnitz).
From an island and some essays. 1877, Leipzig 1877 (Tauchnitz), also Boston, nd. The story appeared previously in The story of Elizabeth, and 11 of the 12 essays first appeared in Pall Mall Gazette 1865–71; rptd in Toilers and spinsters.
Da Capo. New York 1878 (Harper's Half-Hour Ser); as Da Capo and other tales, Leipzig 1880 (Tauchnitz).
Madame de Sévigné. 1881; rptd in Foreign classics for English readers, ed Mrs Oliphant, vol 13, 1881.
Miss Williamson's divagations. 1881. 4 of the 6 stories pbd in Da Capo and other tales. First pbd in Cornhill Mag 1876–80.
A book of sibyls: Mrs Barbauld, Miss Edgeworth, Mrs Opie, Miss Austen. 1883. First pbd in Cornhill Mag 1881–3.
REVIEW: Saturday Rev 56, 27 Oct 1883.
Miss Angel and Fulham lawn. 1884. Reprint of Miss Angel with addition of Fulham lawn; in Works vol 8, 1880, *above*.
Mrs Dymond. 1885. First serialised in Macmillan's Mag 51–3, Mar–Dec 1885. Bk I first pbd in Cornhill Mag 39, May–June 1879.
REVIEW: Spectator 59, 16 Jan 1886.
Jack Frost's little prisoners. 1887.
Records of Tennyson, Ruskin and Robert and Elizabeth Browning. 1892, New York 1892. Essays first pbd in Harper's New Monthly Mag 1883–92.
REVIEWS: Athenaeum 100, 8 Oct 1892; Blackwood's Mag 152, Dec 1892.
Lord Amherst and the British advance eastwards to Burma. 1894. With R. Evans.
Chapters from some memoirs. 1894. Also pbd as Chapters from some unwritten memoirs New York 1894, Leipzig 1894 (Tauchnitz). First pbd in Macmillan's Mag 1890–4.
REVIEW: Athenaeum 104, 22 Dec 1894.
Blackstick papers. 1908, New York 1908. Essays first pbd in Cornhill Mag 1900–7, Macmillan's Mag 67, Jan 1893, New Quart Mag 1 Mar 1908.
REVIEW: Bookman 35, Dec 1908, suppl.
A discourse on modern sibyls. 1913 (Eng Assoc Pam No 24).
From the porch. 1913. Essays. First pbd Cornhill Mag 1886–1913; Macmillan's Mag 1893; Pall Mall Gazette 49, Mar 1912; Contemporary Rev 101, Apr 1912.
REVIEW: Bookman 45, Jan 1914.
From friend to friend. Ed Emily Ritchie 1919. Reminiscences and a short story, Binnie, first pbd as Willie, Illus London News 103, 28 Oct–9 Nov 1893. Essays first pbd Cornhill Mag 1916–17; The Sphere 1914–16.
REVIEW: Bookman 58, Apr 1920.

Contributions to periodicals

For contributions to Cornhill Mag *and* Macmillan's Mag *up to 1900, see* Wellesley *vol 5*.
Rome in the Holy Week. Letter I, Pall Mall Gazette 6 Apr 1869; Letter II, Pall Mall Gazette 7 Apr 1869; rptd in Toilers and spinsters.
Upstairs and downstairs. Mar 1882. Ptd as Pam for Council of the Metropolitan Assoc for Befriending Young Servants. Rptd from the porch.
Madame de Sévigné's grandmother. In The woman's world, ed Oscar Wilde, 1888; title changed to Sainte Jeanne Françoise de Chantal in From the porch.
The boyhood of Thackeray. St Nicholas Mag 17, Dec 1889.
Thackeray and his biographers. Illus London News 98, 20 June 1891.
Robert and Elizabeth Barrett Browning. Harper's New Monthly Mag 84, May 1892.
Comment on 'Lord Bateman': a ballad attributed to Thackeray. Harper's New Monthly Mag 86, Dec 1892.
A Frenchwoman's letter bag. Ed with Hester Ritchie. Cornhill Mag n.s. 39, Oct 1915.
Seagulls and white coiffes at Chelsea. Spectator 117, 26 Aug 1916.
An American lady. Spectator 119, 25 Aug 1917.

Letters and journals

Thackeray and his daughter: the letters and journals of Anne Thackeray Ritchie, with many letters of William Makepeace Thackeray. Ed H. T. Ritchie, New York 1924.
Thackeray's daughter: some recollections of Anne Thackeray Ritchie. Comp H. T. Fuller and V. Hammersley, Dublin 1951.
Anne Thackeray Ritchie: journals and letters. By L. Shankman, ed A. B. Bloom and J. Maynard, Columbus OH 1994.

Editions, introductions and reminiscences

Introduction to The orphan of Pimlico by W. M. Thackeray. 1876.
Memorial Preface to Poems and music by A. Evans. 1880.
Elizabeth Barrett Browning. In DNB, 1886.
Preface to Cranford by E. C. Gaskell. 1891.
Introduction to The fairy tales of Madame d'Aulnoy. 1892.

Reminiscences. Lord Tennyson and his friends: a collection of photographs by Julia Margaret Cameron and H. H. Cameron. London and New York 1893.
Introduction to Our village by M. R. Mitford. 1893.
Introductions to the following works by M. Edgeworth: Castle Rackrent and the absentee 1895; Ormond 1895; Popular tales 1895; Helen 1896; Belinda 1896; The Parents' Assistant 1897.
Reminiscence. Life and letters of Frederick Walker. Ed J. G. Marks 1896.
Biographical introductions to The works of William Makepeace Thackeray. Biographical Edn. 13 vols 1898–9.
Some recollections of Millais. Life and letters of Sir John Millais. Ed J. G. Millais. Vol 2 1899.
Preface to A week in a French country house by A. Sartoris. 1902.
Recollections of G. J. Cayley. The bridle roads of Spain by G. J. Cayley. 1908.
Biographical introductions to The works of William Makepeace Thackeray. Centenary Edn. 26 vols 1910–11.
Introduction to W. M. Thackeray and Edward FitzGerald, a literary friendship; unpublished letters and verses by W. M. Thackeray. 1916.

§2

Cornhill Mag 119, Apr 1919. Obituary.
Woolf, V. Lady Ritchie. TLS 6 Mar 1919; rptd in The essays of Virginia Woolf 3, ed A. McNeillie, 1988.
Sturgis, H. O. Anne Isabella Thackeray (Lady Ritchie). Cornhill Mag 120, Nov 1919.
Woolf, V. The enchanted organ: Anne Thackeray (1924). In The moment and other essays, 1947.
Gerin, W. Anne Thackeray Ritchie: a biography. Oxford 1981. [ABB]

Henry Duff Traill 1842–1900

See col 2397.

Katharine Tynan 1861–1931

See col 848.

Margaret Veley 1843–87

§1

'For Percival'. 3 vols 1878.
Damocles. 3 vols 1882.
Mitchelhurst Place: a novel. 2 vols 1884.
A garden of memories; Mrs Austin; Lizzie's bargain. 2 vols 1887.
A marriage of shadows and other poems; with biographical preface by Leslie Stephen. 1888. [EH]

Ethel Lillian Voynich, née Boole 1864–1960

Ms correspondence in Gurney Archive, Gloucester Public Lib; G. I. Taylor Archive, Cambridge Univ Lib. Yale Univ Lib contains c. 40 different edns and trns of The gadfly, *also 2 prints of the Russian 16mm colour film (music by Shostakovich) and a documentary film of Voynich viewing the earlier film.*

§1

The gadfly. New York 1897, London 1897, St Petersburg 1897, London 1898, 1905, New York 1906, London 1912, New York 1938 (Story Lib), Moscow 1955 (Foreign Languages Publishing House), London 1956, 4th edn Moscow 1958 (FLP), New York 1961 (Pyramid), Berlin 1967 (Seven Seas) (very slightly expurgated), St Albans 1973 (Granada/Mayflower).
REVIEWS: New York Times 26 June 1897; Dial 1 July 1897; Critic 7 Aug 1897; Acad Fiction Suppl 25 Sep 1897; Bookman (London) Oct 1897; Athenaeum 6 Nov 1897; Literature 13 Nov 1897; Spectator 8 Oct 1898.
Jack Raymond. 1901, Philadelphia 1901, (4th) new edn 1901, London 1910.
REVIEWS: Literature July 1901–Jan 1902; Acad 11 May 1901; Bookman (London) July 1901.
Olive Latham. 1904, Philadelphia 1904, London 1909.
REVIEWS: Acad June 1904; New York Times 4 June 1904; Athenaeum 11 June 1904; Outlook 18 June 1904; Bookman (London) Aug 1904; Dial 1 Oct 1904.
An interrupted friendship. 1910, New York 1910, 1928, London 1929, St Albans new edn 1974 (Granada/Mayflower).
REVIEWS: Athenaeum 19 Mar 1910; New York Times 26 Mar 1910; Bookman Apr 1910; Spectator 16 Apr 1910; Nation 16 June 1910; Bookman (London) July 1910.
Put off thy shoes. New York 1945, London 1946.
REVIEWS: New Yorker 26 May 1945; Saturday Rev Lit 26 May 1945; New York Times 27 May 1945; Book Week 10 June 1945.

Translations of Voynich's works

Izbrannye proizvedeniia [Selected works]. 2 vols Moscow 1960.
Sochineniia [Works]. 2 vols Moscow 1963.
Ovod [The gadfly]. 15 edns in 4 different Soviet languages before 1917. 90 printings in 18 languages after Revolution (including 700,000 copies in Chinese); St Petersburg/Moscow 1897, Moscow 1900, Moscow 1904, 1905, 1908, 1910, 1911, 1913, 1915, 1917, 1919, New York 1921, Moscow 1935, Moscow 1965, Leningrad 1970.
Di bihn [The gadfly]. Vilna 1907.
Dundurs [The gadfly]. 2 vols Riga 1928.
Marduth [The gadfly]. Tel Aviv 1932.
Obad [The gadfly]. Ljubljana 1951.
Der Sohn des Kardinals [The gadfly]. Berlin 1968.
Qai luap [The gadfly]. Bangkok 1969.
Yediduth she-nifsakah [An interrupted friendship]. Tel Aviv 1935/6.
Snimi obuv' tvoiu [Put off thy shoes]. Moscow 1965.

Translations by Voynich

Stories from Garshin. 1893.
REVIEW: Acad July–Dec 1893.
Nihilism as it is (pams by S. Stepniak). [1894.]
The humour of Russia. [nd], New York 1895.
REVIEWS: Bookman (London) May 1895; Nation 27 June 1895; Critic 18 Mar 1896.
Six lyrics from the Ruthenian of Tarás Shevchénko, also the Song of the Merchant Kaláshnikov, from the Russian of Mikhail Lérmontov. 1911.
Chopin's letters. New York 1931, London 1932, 1973, 1988.
The origin of the book, what is wanted?, and The agitation abroad (pams by S. M. Kravchinsky). [nd.]

§2

Courtney, W. L. The feminine note in fiction. 1904.
Kettle, A. E. L. Voynich: a forgotten English novelist. EIC 7 1957.
Kennedy, J. G. Voynich, Bennett, and Tressell: two alternatives for realism in the transition age. ELT 13 1970.
Fremantle, A. Return of the Gadfly. Commonweal 74 1961.
Fremantle, A. The Russian best seller. History Today Sep 1975. [BG]

Lucy Bethia Walford, née Colquhoun 1845–1915

§1

The merchant's sermon and other stories. Edinburgh 1870.
Mr Smith: a part of his life. 2 vols Edinburgh and London 1874, 1 vol Edinburgh and London 1875, Chicago 1875, New York 1875, 2 vols Leipzig 1876 (Tauchnitz), London and Sydney [188?], New York 1880, 1884, Edinburgh and London 1885, New York [1887],

Edinburgh and London [1888] (new edn), London 1889, 1890, 1897, London, New York and Bombay 1902, New York 1902.
REVIEWS: Athenaeum 2452 1874; Saturday Rev 38 1874; Nation 21 1875.

Pauline. Serialised in Blackwood's Mag Feb–Oct 1877. 2 vols Edinburgh and London 1877, 2 vols Leipzig 1877 (Tauchnitz), 1 vol Edinburgh and London 1878, 1878 (5th edn), 1885 (new edn), London 1890, 1892 (new edn), 1894.
REVIEWS: Athenaeum 2607 1877; Nation 26 1878; Spectator 51 1878.

Cousins. 3 vols Edinburgh and London 1879, 2 vols Leipzig 1879 (Tauchnitz), 1 vol Edinburgh and London 1879, New York 1879, [1884], Edinburgh and London 1885 (new edn), New York [1887], London 1889, [1891], 1894 (new edn), London and New York 1894 (new edn), London [1906].
REVIEW: Athenaeum 2700 1879.

Troublesome daughters. 3 vols Edinburgh 1880, 1 vol Edinburgh and London 1880, New York 1880, Leipzig 1881 (Tauchnitz), Edinburgh and London 1885 (new edn), New York [1887], London 1889 (new edn), 1890, 1892, 1903, [1909].
REVIEWS: Athenaeum 2752 1880; Spectator 53 1880.

Dick Netherby. Edinburgh 1881, New York 1881, 1882, London 1885 (new edn), 1890, 1892, London and New York 1894.
REVIEWS: Athenaeum 2826 1881; Nation 34 1882.

The baby's grandmother. Serialised in Blackwood's Mag Oct 1883–Aug 1884. 3 vols Edinburgh and London 1884, 1 vol 1884 (new edn), 1884 (4th edn), New York 1884, Edinburgh and London 1885, New York 1887, London 1889 (new edn), 2 vols Leipzig 1891 (Tauchnitz), London 1891, London, New York and Bombay 1897, 1901, London 1902, 1906.
REVIEWS: Athenaeum 2965 1884; Nation 39 1884; Spectator 57 1884.

Nan and other stories. 2 vols Edinburgh 1884, 2 vols Edinburgh and London 1885, London 1888, 1891.
REVIEWS: Athenaeum 2990 1885; Athenaeum 3192 1888.

Cheerful Christianity: brief essays dealing with the lesser beauties and blemishes of the Christian life. 1886 (SPCK).

The history of a week. Edinburgh and London 1886, New York 1886, [1887], London [1890], 1893.
REVIEW: Athenaeum 3050 1886.

Polly Spanker's green feathers. [1887] (anon) (SPCK).

Dinah's son. 1888.
REVIEW: Athenaeum 3177 1888.

Four biographies from Blackwood. Jane Taylor, Elizabeth Fry, Hannah More, Mary Somerville. Edinburgh and London 1888. First pbd in Blackwood's Mag Jan–June 1888.
REVIEW: Athenaeum 3173 1888.

Her great idea and other stories. 1888, New York 1888, London 1889 (new edn), 1889 (3rd edn), 1910 (new edn).
REVIEW: Athenaeum 3185 1888.

A mere child. 1888, New York 1888, 1889. Pbd with The havoc of a smile as Two stories, London 1892, *below*.
REVIEWS: Athenaeum 3177 1888; Nation 47 1888.

A stiff-necked generation. Serialised in Blackwood's Mag Apr 1888–Jan 1889. 3 vols Edinburgh and London 1889, 1 vol Edinburgh and London 1889, New York 1889, Edinburgh and London 1891, London 1891 (new edn), 1893, 1894.
REVIEW: Athenaeum 3196 1889.

A sage of sixteen. 1889 (illustr J. E. Goodall), New York 1889, London 1892, 1910, 1911 (new edn illustr J. Durden), [1913], 1914, [1915].
REVIEW: Athenaeum 3247 1890.

The havoc of a smile. 1890, New York [1890] (authorised edn). Pbd with A mere child as Two stories, London 1892. Review: Athenaeum 3280 1890.

The mischief of Monica. Serialised in Longman's Mag Nov 1890–Oct 1891. 3 vols 1891, 2 vols Leipzig 1891, 1 vol New York [1891], London 1892, London and New York 1893 (new edn).
REVIEWS: Athenaeum 3337 1891; Critic 19 1891; Spectator 67 1891; Dublin Rev 110 1892.

The jerry builder. [1891.]

A pinch of experience. 1891 (illustr G. Browne), New York [1891], London 1893.

Bertie boot-boy. [1892] (SPCK).

For grown-up children. 1892 (illustr J. Pym), New York 1892.
REVIEW: Nation 55 1892.

The little elevenpence halfpenny. [1892.]

The one good guest. 1892, New York 1892, Leipzig 1893, New York 1893, London 1894 (new edn).
REVIEWS: Athenaeum 3387 1892; Critic 21 1892.

Twelve English authoresses. 1892, London and New York 1892, 1893.
REVIEWS: Athenaeum 3402 1893; Critic 22 1893; Dial 14 1893.

Two stories: A mere child and The havoc of a smile. 1892. Previously pbd separately.

The last straw. [1893.]

Money: the boy and the man. [1893] (SPCK), [1902] (SPCK).

A question of penmanship. Stories. 1893, 1897.
REVIEW: Athenaeum 3454 1894.

The matchmaker. Serialised in Longman's Mag Nov 1893–Oct 1894. 3 vols 1894, 3 vols London and New York 1894, 1 vol New York 1894, 1 vol London 1895 (new edn), 1897.
REVIEWS: Athenaeum 3502 1894; Spectator 73 1894; Nation 60 1895.

The first cruise of the good ship 'Bethlehem'; and A woodland choir. [1894] (SPCK). Pbd separately [1902] (SPCK).

'Ploughed' and other stories. 1894, New York 1894, London 1897 (new edn).
REVIEWS: Athenaeum 3493 1894; Spectator 73 1894.

A bubble. 1895, New York [1895?].

Frederick. 1895, New York and London 1895.
REVIEWS: Athenaeum 3558 1896; London Quart Rev 86 1896.

Merrielands Farm. [1895] (SPCK).

Successors to the title. 1896, New York 1896, London 1902.
REVIEWS: Athenaeum 3585 1896; Spectator 76 1896.

Iva Kildare: a matrimonial problem. 1897, New York 1897 (new edn), London 1899.
REVIEWS: Athenaeum 3660 1897; Canadian 10 1897.

The archdeacon. 1898, 1899, New York 1899.
REVIEWS: Athenaeum 3720 1899; Bookman 15 1899.

The intruders. 1898, New York 1898, London 1900.
REVIEW: Athenaeum 3707 1898.

Leddy Marget. 1898, New York 1898, London 1899, Leipzig 1900 (Tauchnitz).
REVIEW: Athenaeum 3693 1898.

The little legacy and other stories. 1899, Chicago and New York 1899.
REVIEW: Athenaeum 3738 1899.

Sir Patrick: the puddock. 1899, New York 1899, Toronto 1899, London 1908.
REVIEWS: Athenaeum 3764 1899; London Quart Rev 93 1900.

One of ourselves. Serialised in Longman's Mag Nov 1899–Nov 1900. 1900, New York 1900, 1901.
REVIEW: Athenaeum 3815 1900.

Charlotte. 1902, New York 1902, London 1906.

A dream's fulfilment and other stories. 1902.

A woodland choir. [1902] (SPCK). First pbd with The first cruise of the good ship 'Bethlehem' [1894], *above*.

The black familiars. 1903, New York 1903, London 1905. Review: London Quart Rev 101 1904.

Stay-at-homes. 1903, New York 1903, London 1906.
REVIEW: Athenaeum 3945 1903.

A fair rebel and other stories. 1906.

The enlightenment of Olivia. 1907, New York, London, Bombay and Calcutta 1907. Rptd from the weekly edn of The Times.
REVIEWS: Athenaeum 4155 1907; London Quart Rev 108 1907; Punch 132 1907.

Leonore Stubbs. 1908, London, New York, Bombay and Calcutta 1908.
REVIEWS: Athenaeum 4228 1908; Bookman 35 1908; Nation 87 1908.

Celia: and the parents. [1910.]

Recollections of a Scottish novelist. 1910, Waddesdon 1984.
REVIEWS: Bookman 39 1910; Athenaeum 4342 1911; Dial 50 1911.

Star. 1911, [1922].

Memories of Victorian London. 1912, New York 1912.
REVIEW: Nation 96 1913.

David and Jonathan on the Riviera. 1914.

Contributions to periodicals and collaborative works

The fly's web. In Miss Parson's adventure and other stories by W. C. Russell etc, 1894.

The novel of manners. In On the art of writing fiction, [1894].

Sim, M. Margaret Sim's cookery. Introd by Walford. Helensburgh 1879, Edinburgh 1883.

Walford was the London correspondent for the New York Critic *from 1889 to 1893. She wrote stories, poems and articles for various periodicals, including* Atlanta, Blackwood's Mag, Sunday Mag *and* World. *See also* Wellesley *vol 5.*

§2

Mrs Walford at home. Critic 18 Feb 1891.

Black, H. C. In Notable women authors of the day, Glasgow 1893, rptd 1906, 1974.

Who was who 1897–1915.

Sutherland, J. The Longman companion to Victorian fiction. Harlow 1988.

Shattock, J. The Oxford guide to British women writers. Oxford and New York 1993.

Mrs Humphry Ward, Mary Augusta Ward, née Arnold 1851–1920

There is no central repository for Mrs Ward's letters and literary papers. Some are held in private collections. Some of the more important library holdings are: in the UK: The lib of Pusey House Oxford; Bodleian; the BL; the lib of Univ College London; the Brotherton Lib, Univ of Leeds; the Mary Ward Centre, London; the Borough of Hove Lib; in the US: the Honnold Lib, Claremont Univ, Claremont CA; Huntington; HRHRC, Univ of Texas; the Berg Collection, NYPL; Harvard; the Lib of Congress; The Alderman Lib, Univ of Virginia.

Bibliographies

Jones, E. In Mrs Humphry Ward, New York 1973.

Musil, C. In Art and ideology: the novels and times of Mrs Humphry Ward, Evanston IL 1974.

Peterson, W. In Victorian heretic: Mrs Humphry Ward's Robert Elsmere, Leicester 1976.

Smith, J. Mary Augusta Ward: an annotated bibliography of secondary writings, 1888–1985. Baton Rouge LA 1987.

Thesing, W. and S. Pulsford. Mrs Humphry Ward: a bibliography. Victorian Research Guide 13. St Lucia, Queensland 1987.

Sutherland, J. In Mrs Humphry Ward, Oxford 1990.

Collections

The writings of Mrs Humphry Ward. Westmoreland edn, introd by the author. 16 vols 1911–12.

The writings of Mrs Humphry Ward. Autograph edn. 16 vols Boston 1909–12 (750 sets, each signed and numbered in the 1st vol by Mrs Ward).

§1

Fiction

Milly and Olly or a holiday among the mountains: a story for children. 1881 (illustr Mrs A. Tadema), 1894 (new edn), New York 1907 (rev, illustr R. Hallock), London 1907 (new edn with a new preface and 48 illustrations by W. Pogany), New York 1913 (new edn).
REVIEW: Acad 24 Dec 1881.

Miss Bretherton. 1884, New York 1888 (Lovell's Lib), Chicago 1888 (Rand McNally edn), 1891 (new edn, cited in Nat Union Cat), Leipzig 1892 (Tauchnitz), London 1896 (new edn), New York [1897] (new edn, Munro's Lib of Popular Novels), London [1910] (new edn, Newnes' Sixpenny Copyright Novels), [1912] (new edn), New York nd (new edn, Seaside Lib, pocket edn no 369), nd (new edn, Famous Fiction Lib).
REVIEWS: Pall Mall Gazette 6 Dec 1884; The Times 12 Dec 1884; Graphic 31, 10 Jan 1885.

Robert Elsmere. 3 vols 1888, New York 1888, 3 vols Leipzig 1888 (Tauchnitz), 3 vols London 1888 (3rd, 5th and 9th edns), 1 vol London 1888 (new edn), 1 vol New York 1888 (new edn), 2 vols 1888 (new edn), 1888 (new edn, Lovell's Lib no 1188), Chicago 1888 (new edn), 2 vols in 1 New York 1888 (new edn, Seaside Lib, pocket edn no 1116), Chicago 1888 (new edn, Fireside ser no 62), New York 1888 (new edn), Albany NY 1888 (new edn), Boston 1888 (new edn), New York 1889 (new edn), Troy NY 1889 (new edn), New York 1889 (new edn), London 1899 (new edn, sixpenny edn), New York [1891?] (new edn), [189?] (new edn, Gladstone ser), 1 vol London [1899?] (cheap popular edn), New York (Nat Union Cat lists one copy, impossibly, as [1880?], and another as [18—]), 1902? (new edn, date is Nat Union Cat's speculation), 3 vols in 1 London 1904 (new edn with David Grieve and Marcella), 1907 (Nelson's Lib, reprint of 1888 1-vol Smith, Elder edn), 1909, 1912, 1914 (new edns), New York 1914 (new edn), London 1921 (new edn), 1952 (Nelson Classics no 405, reprint of 1907 edn), Lincoln NE 1967 (Bison Book ser 348, ed with introd by C. Ryals, text taken from 1888 1-vol London Macmillan edn), Bath 1974 (new edn), Louisville KY 1975 (micro edn), New York 1976 (new edn, Victorian fiction: novels of faith and doubt, reprint of 1888 Smith, Elder 1st edn), London 1987 (new edn, ed with introd and notes by R. Ashton, reprint of 1907 Nelson Lib edn), New York nd (new edn); tr Ger 1890.
REVIEWS: Nineteenth Cent 23, May 1888 (by W. E. Gladstone); Blackwood's Mag 146, July 1888; Unitarian Rev 3, Nov 1888; North Amer Rev 148, Jan 1889 (rev).

The history of David Grieve. 3 vols 1892, 1 vol New York 1892, 2 vols New York 1892, London 1892 ('with a prefatory note in answer to certain criticisms'), 1892, Toronto 1892 (new edn), London 1893 (new edn), London (before 1900, cheap popular edn), 3 vols in 1 London 1904 (with Robert Elsmere and Marcella), New York 1905 (new edn), 1906 (new edn), London 1907 (new edn), New York 1908 and 1913 (new edns), London 1925 (new edn), Cambridge MA 1967 (micro edn, copy of 1-vol 1892 Macmillan edn); tr Du 1892–3.

Marcella. 3 vols 1894 (1st Br edn), 2 vols New York 1894 (1st Amer edn, 1st ptd Mar 1894, rptd Apr twice, May, June, July, Aug 3 times, Sep), 3 vols Leipzig 1894 (Tauchnitz), 3 vols London 1894 (6th edn), New York 1895 (new edn, Macmillan's Novelists' Lib, vol 1, 1st ptd Mar 1895, rptd Apr, Oct 1895, Feb 1906, Sep 1907, Jan 1910, Aug 1914), London (before 1900, 16th edn), London 1900 (new edn, 'Sixpenny series of copyright books'), 3 vols in 1 1904 (new edn, with Robert Elsmere and David Grieve), 1908 (new edn, Nelson's Lib), 1909 and 1915 (new edns), 1919 (new edn), Harmondsworth 1984 (new edn, Virago Modern Classics), Cambridge MA 1967 (micro edn, copy of 1-vol Macmillan edn 1895); tr Du 1894, Swed 1910.
REVIEWS: Edinburgh Rev 180, July 1894; Sewanee Rev 3, Nov 1894.

The story of Bessie Costrell. Serialised in Cornhill Mag May–July

1895, Scribner's Mag May–July 1895. 1895 (1st Br edn), New York 1895 (1st Amer edn), London 1912 (new edn), Cambridge MA 1967 (micro edn).

Sir George Tressady. Serialised in Century Mag Nov 1895–Oct 1896. 1896 (1st Br edn), 2 vols New York 1896 (1st Amer edn), 2 vols London 1896 (private 1st edn; a limited edn of 6 copies bound in 2 vols for the author), 2 vols New York 1897 (new edn), London (before 1900, 4th edn), 2 vols in 1 New York 1909 (new edn), London 1909 and 1910 (new edns, Nelson's Lib), London 1919 (new edn).
REVIEW: Bookman 11, Nov 1896.

Helbeck of Bannisdale. 1898 (1st Br edn), 2 vols New York 1898 (1st Amer edn), London 1898 (new edn), 2 vols New York 1898 (new edn, Set up and electrotyped May 1898, rptd June, Aug, twice Sep, Oct, Nov, Dec 1898; Mar 1899), 2 vols Leipzig 1898 (Tauchnitz), London 1899 (5th edn), 1904 (new edn, Newnes Sixpenny Copyright Novels), 1911 (new edn), 1911 (new edn, Nelson's Lib), 1918 (new edn), New York 1975 (new edn, Victorian fiction: novels of faith and doubt, reprint of 1898 Smith, Elder 1st edn), Harmondsworth 1983 (new edn), Cambridge MA 1967 (micro edn, Victorian fiction and other nineteenth-century fiction, roll 21. Copy of 2-vol Macmillan 1st edn).
REVIEW: Nineteenth Cent 44, Oct 1898.

Eleanor. Serialised in Harper's Mag Jan–Dec 1900. 1900 (1st Br edn, illustr A. Sterner), New York 1900 (1st Amer edn, illustr A. Sterner), 2 vols Leipzig 1900 (Tauchnitz), 2 vols New York 1900 (new edn, paged continuously), London 1901 (new edn), New York 1901 (new edn), London 1904 (new edn), 1905 (new edn, Newnes' Sixpenny Novels, illus), 1912 (new edn, Nelson's Lib).

Lady Rose's daughter. Serialised in Harper's Mag May 1902–Apr 1903. 1903 (1st Br edn, illus), New York 1903 (1st Amer edn), 2 vols New York 1903 (special 1st edn, paged continuously, a limited edn of 350 copies bound in 2 vols, some or perhaps all signed by the author), 2 vols Leipzig 1903 (Tauchnitz), New York 1903 (new edn), London 1904 (new edn), 1906 (new edn, Newnes' Sixpenny Novels), 1909 (Nelson's Lib), 1914 (new edn), 1 vol 1914 (new edn), Cambridge MA 1967 (micro edn, Victorian fiction and other nineteenth-century fiction, roll 22. Copy of 1-vol Harper 1st edn).

Marriage of William Ashe. Serialised in Harper's Mag Dec 1904–May 1905. 1905 (1st Br edn, illustr A. Sterner), New York 1905 (1st Amer edn, illustr A. Sterner), 1 vol New York nd (special 1st edn, a reprint of the Harper's Mag format of the book), New York 1905 (special 1st edn, autograph edn limited to 972 copies), 2 vols Leipzig 1905 (Tauchnitz), New York 1906 (new edn), London 1907 (new edn, Nelson's Lib).

Fenwick's career. Serialised in Century Mag Nov 1905–June 1906. 1906 (1st Br edn, illustr A Sterner), New York 1906 (1st Amer edn, illustr A. Sterner), 2 vols London 1906 (special 1st edn, limited edn of 250 copies, each signed by the author), 1906 (new edn), Toronto 1906 (new edn), London 1910 (new edn, Daily Mail Sixpenny Novels no 111), Cambridge MA 1967 (micro edn, Victorian fiction and other nineteenth-century fiction, roll 21. Copy of Amer 1st edn); tr Swed 1906.

Diana Mallory (Amer title, The testing of Diana Mallory). Serialised in Harper's Mag Nov 1907–Oct 1908. 1908 (1st Br edn), New York 1908 (1st Amer edn, illustr W. Hatherell), London 1908 (2nd edn), 1908 (new edn), 1908 (new edn, Macmillan's Colonial Lib no 552), 1911 (new edn, Daily Mail Sixpenny Novels no 151), 1914 (new edn, Newnes Shilling Ser 14).
REVIEW: North Amer Rev 188, Nov 1908.

Daphne (1st Amer title, Marriage à la mode). Serialised in McClure's Mag Jan–June 1909. 1909 (1st Br edn, illustr F. Pegram), New York 1909 (1st Amer edn, illustr F. Pegram), Leipzig 1909 (Tauchnitz), London 1911 (new edn), New York 1911 (new edn), London 1912 (new edn); tr Ger 1910.

Canadian born (Amer title, Lady Merton, colonist). Serialised in Cornhill Mag Oct 1909–May 1910; Ladies Home Jnl Oct 1909–May 1910. 1910 (1st Br edn, frontispiece by A. Sterner), New York 1910 (1st Amer edn, frontispiece by A. Sterner), London 1910 (new edn), New York 1910 (new edn), London 1912 and 1914 (new edns); tr Ger 1912.

The case of Richard Meynell. Serialised in Cornhill Mag Jan–Dec 1911; McClure's Mag Jan–Dec 1911. 1911 (1st Br edn, illus), New York 1911 (1st Amer edn, illustr C. Brock), 2 vols Leipzig 1911 (Tauchnitz), New York 1911 (new edn), London 1912 and 1913 (new edns), 1913 (new edn, Newnes' Sixpenny Copyright Novels), 1918 (new condensed edn), Cambridge MA 1967 (micro edn, Victorian fiction and other nineteenth-century fiction, roll 21. Copy of 1st Amer edn).

The mating of Lydia. Serialised in Good Housekeeping Nov 1912–Nov 1913. 1913 (1st Br edn, illus), New York 1913 (1st Amer edn), 2 vols Leipzig 1913 (Tauchnitz), London 1913 (new edn), 1915 (Newnes' Sixpenny Copyright Novels).

The Coryston family. Serialised in Harper's Mag May–Nov 1913. 1913 (1st Br edn), New York 1913 (1st Amer edn, illustr E. Shippen), London 1919 (new edn).

Delia Blanchflower. 1915 (1st Br edn), New York 1914 (1st Amer edn), Toronto 1914 (new edn), London 1916 (new edn).
REVIEW: TLS 28 Jan 1915.

Eltham House. 1915 (1st Br edn), New York 1915 (1st Amer edn, frontispiece by F. Craig), 1915 (new edn, rptd from 1st Amer edn).
REVIEW: Boston Transcript 29 Sep 1915.

A great success. Serialised in Cornhill Mag May–July 1915. 1916 (1st Br edn), New York 1916 (1st Amer edn); tr Fr nd.

Lady Connie. Serialised in Cornhill Mag Dec 1915–June 1916, 1916 (1st Br edn), New York 1916 (1st Amer edn), 1916 (new edn), London 1918 (slightly condensed).

Missing. 1917 (1st Br edn), New York 1917 (1st Amer edn, frontispiece by C. Gilbert), Toronto 1917 (new edn), New York 1918 (new edn), 1918 (7th edn, illus with scenes from the photo-play of the same name); tr Sp nd.

The war and Elizabeth (Amer title, Elizabeth's campaign). 1918 (1st Br edn), New York 1918 (1st Amer edn, frontispiece by C. Gilbert), 1918 (2nd, 3rd and 4th edns), 1919 (5th edn); tr Fr 1920.

Cousin Philip (Amer title, Helena). 1919 (1st Br edn), New York 1919 (1st Amer edn, frontispiece by C. Gilbert), London 1919 (2nd impression).

Harvest (also pbd as Love's harvest). 1920 (1st British edn), New York 1920 (1st Amer edn), London 1929 (new edn, Novel Lib, as Love's harvest).

Non-fiction

A morning in the Bodleian. Windermere 1871 (priv ptd).

Unbelief and sin. A protest. Addressed to those who attended the Bampton lecture [by John Wordsworth] of Sunday, March 6th 1881. 1881 (ptd for the author).

Christianity and agnosticism; a controversy. New York 1889.

Address to mark the opening at University Hall. 1891.

The future of University Hall. 1892.

New forms of Christian education; an address to the University Hall Guild. 1892, New York 1898.

Unitarians and the future (the Essex Hall lecture). 1894.

Social ideals; an address delivered at the Passmore Edwards settlement. 1897.

Invalid children's schools (a paper read at the Nat Conference of Women Workers). 1900.

The play-time of the poor. 1906.

William Thomas Arnold, journalist and historian. Manchester 1907.

Women's national anti-suffrage league: speech. 1908 (Women's Suffrage Pams no 56).

Letters to my neighbours on the present election. 1910, 1910 (2nd edn, rev).

Sayings of Mrs Humphry Ward. 1915.
England's effort. 1916 (preface by the Earl of Rosebery), 1916 (3rd edn, with an epilogue bringing the story down to the middle of Aug), 1916 (4th edn), London 1916 and 1917 (4th edn and new edn), New York 1916 (1st Amer edn, preface by J. Choate), New York 1916 (2nd and 3rd edns), New York 1916 (4th edn, adds epilogue in the shape of a 7th letter), New York 1916 (5th edn), New York 1918 and 1919 (new edns); tr Fr 1916, Du 1916, Amsterdam 1917 (new edn), Swed 1917, Ital 1917.
Towards the goal. 1917 (introd by T. Roosevelt), New York 1917 (1st Amer edn, preface by T. Roosevelt), New York 1918 (new edn).
A writer's recollections. Serialised in Cornhill Mag Mar–May, July 1918; Harper's Mag Jan, Mar–Oct 1918. 1918 (1st Br edn), 2 vols New York 1918 (1st Amer edn).
Fields of victory. 1919 (1st Br edn, illus), New York 1919 (1st Amer edn, illus).

Prefaces, introductions and contributions to periodicals

For a nearly complete listing of items in this category, see William S. Peterson, Victorian heretic: Mrs Humphry Ward's 'Robert Elsmere' *(Leicester 1976) and Collister,* Some new items by Mrs Humphry Ward, *N & Q 25, Aug 1978, 309–11.*

Translations

Amiel's journal. 2 vols 1885 (1st Br edn), 2 vols New York 1885 (1st Amer edn), London 1887 (new edn), New York 1888 (2nd edn, rptd 1889; Jan and Oct 1890; Mar and Sep 1891, 1892; Jan and Apr 1893; Jan and Aug 1894; Aug 1895), London 1889 and 1891 (new edns), 2 vols London 1893 (new edn), 2 vols New York 1895 (new edn), 1900 (new edn).

Plays

Eleanor. 1903 (1st Br edn), 1905 (new edn).
Agatha. 1903 (private edn, B version).

§2

Copeland, C. George Eliot and Mrs Humphry Ward. In North Amer Rev 1892.
Y., G. The work of Mrs Humphry Ward. In Bookman 1892.
Stead, W. Mrs Humphry Ward: the art of marriage. 1896.
Traill, H. Sir George Tressady and the political novel. In Fortnightly Rev 1896.
Murray, D. In My contemporaries in fiction, 1897, ch 10.
Cross, W. In The development of the English novel, 1899, ch 8.
Wilson, S. In The theology of modern literature. Edinburgh 1899.
Curtis, A. The novels of Mrs Humphry Ward. In Kensington Mag 1901 (May, June and July).
Howells, W. In Heroines of fiction, 2 vols New York and London 1901.
Mabie, H. The work of Mrs Humphry Ward. In North Amer Rev 1903.
Courtney, W. Mrs Humphry Ward. In The feminine note in fiction, 1904.
Olcott, C. Mrs Humphry Ward and her work. In The Outlook, New York 1909.
Phelps, W. The novels of Mrs Humphry Ward. In Forum 1909.
Gwynn, S. Mrs Humphry Ward's novels. In Nineteenth Cent 1911.
Fawkes, A. The ideas of Mrs Humphry Ward. In London Quart Rev 1912.
Walters, J. Mrs Humphry Ward, her work and influence. 1912.
Courtney, W. The English girl in fiction. In North Amer Rev 1913.
Ward, W. Reduced Christianity: its advocates and its critics. In Men and matters, 1914.
Gwynn, S. Mrs Humphry Ward. New York 1915.
Bennett, A. Mrs Humphry Ward's heroines. In Books and persons, New York 1917.
Murry, J. The Victorian solitude. In Living Age 1918.
West, R. Mrs Humphry Ward again. In Bookman 1918.
Gilman, L. The mind of Mrs Humphry Ward. In North Amer Rev 1919.
Lovett, R. Mary in wonderland. In Dial 1919.
Scudder, V. The Victorian background. In Yale Rev 1919.
Obits: Mrs Humphry Ward, The Times 25 Mar 1920; Our booking office, Punch 1920; The gossip shop, Bookman 1920; Mrs Humphry Ward, Amer Monthly Rev of Revs 1920.
Trevelyan, J. The life of Mrs Humphry Ward. 1923.
Grey, R. The heroines of Mrs Humphry Ward. In Fortnightly Rev 1927.
Jones, E. Mrs Humphry Ward. 1973.
Peterson, W. Victorian heretic: Mrs Humphry Ward's Robert Elsmere. Leicester 1976.
Smith, E. Mrs Humphry Ward. 1980.
Smith, E. Mrs Humphry Ward. In Victorian novelists after 1885, 1983.
Sutherland, J. Mrs Humphry Ward. Oxford 1990. [WBT]

H. B. Marriott Watson, Henry Brereton Marriott Watson 1863–1921

Mss located in Berg Collection, NYPL; HRHRC, Austin TX; Pierpont Morgan Lib. See also LR.

Bibliographies

See Wellesley *vol 5 1989.*

§1

Marahuna. A romance. 1888, New York 1888.
REVIEWS: Literary World 20 Apr 1888; Athenaeum 19 May 1888; Dial July 1888.
Lady faint-heart: a novel. 3 vols 1890.
REVIEWS: Speaker 10 May 1890; Scots Observer 24 May 1890.
Prologue to Richard Savage: a play in four acts. 1891, New York 1891 (priv ptd).
The web of the spider. A tale of adventure. 1892, 1902, 1904, 1906, 1913, 1917.
REVIEWS: Literary Opinion Oct 1891; Literary World 2 Oct 1891; Athenaeum 3 Oct 1891; Acad 10 Oct 1891; Nat Observer 17 Oct 1891.
Diogenes of London and other fantasies and sketches. 1893.
REVIEWS: Literary World 3 Mar 1893; Nat Observer 11 Mar 1893; Athenaeum 18 Mar 1893.
At the first corner and other stories. 1895 (Keynote series), Boston 1895.
REVIEWS: Literary World 14 June 1895; Speaker 29 June 1895; Bookman (USA) July 1895; Athenaeum 13 July 1895.
Galloping Dick, being chapters from the life and fortunes of Richard Ryder, otherwise Galloping Dick, sometime gentleman of the road. 1896, Chicago 1896, London 1907, [1912].
REVIEWS: Athenaeum 11 Jan 1896; New York Times 26 Jan 1896: Bookman (USA) Mar 1896.
The adventurers: a tale of treasure trove. London and New York 1898, 1899, New York 1899, 1900, London [1912], [1920].
REVIEWS: Acad 7 Jan 1899; Speaker 7 Jan 1899; New York Times 21 Jan 1899; Literature 28 Jan 1899; Atlantic Feb 1899; Dial 16 Feb 1899.
The Princess Xenia. A romance. London and New York 1899, New York 1899, London [1912].
REVIEWS: Speaker 9 Dec 1899; Spectator 16 Dec 1899; Dial 1 Feb 1900; Acad 24 Feb 1900; Bookman (USA) Mar 1900.
The rebel. Being a memoir of Anthony, fourth Earl of Cherwell, including an account of the rising at Taunton in 1684, compiled and set forth by his cousin, Sir Henry Mace. 1900, New York and London 1900.
REVIEWS: Athenaeum 31 Mar 1900; Outlook 31 Mar 1900; Speaker 31 Mar 1900; Acad 7 Apr 1900; New York Times 28 Apr 1900; Literature 19 May 1900; Book Buyer June 1900; Dial 1 Sep 1900.

Chloris of the island: a novel. London and New York 1900, London [1912].
REVIEWS: New York Times 10 Nov 1900; Athenaeum 24 Nov 1900; Bookman Dec 1900; Spectator 15 Dec 1900; Dial 16 Dec 1900; Literature 23 Mar 1901.
The skirts of happy chances. Being some adventures of Francis, second son of the late Marquees of Auriol. 1901.
REVIEWS: Acad 3 Aug 1901; Acad 10 Aug 1901; Spectator 14 Aug 1901; Athenaeum 24 Aug 1901; Literary World 4 Oct 1901.
The house divided. London and New York 1901.
REVIEWS: New York Times 23 Nov 1901; Acad 7 Dec 1901; Pall Mall Gazette 10 Dec 1901; Spectator 14 Dec 1901; TLS 21 Dec 1901; Dial 1 Aug 1902.
Godfrey Merivale. Being a portion of his history. 1902, [1912].
REVIEWS: Literary World 13 June 1902; Athenaeum 21 June 1902; TLS 18 July 1902.
Alarums and excursions. 1903.
REVIEWS: Acad 29 Aug 1903; Acad 5 Sep 1903; Athenaeum 12 Sep 1903; Spectator 12 Sep 1903; Bookman Oct 1903; Literary World 2 Oct 1903; Outlook 10 Oct 1903.
Captain Fortune. 1904, 1912, 1913, [1920] (abridged).
REVIEWS: Athenaeum 30 July 1904; Acad 13 Aug 1904; Spectator 13 Aug 1904; Outlook 8 Oct 1904.
Hurricane island. 1904, New York 1904, London 1905, New York 1905, London 1911, [1915], [1917].
REVIEWS: Athenaeum 26 Nov 1904; T. P.'s Weekly 9 Dec 1904; Outlook 10 Dec 1904; New York Times 4 Mar 1905; Dial 1 June 1905.
Twisted eglantine. 1905, New York 1905.
REVIEWS: TLS 8 Sep 1905; Acad 9 Sep 1905; Athenaeum 9 Sep 1905; New York Times 18 Nov 1905; Dial 1 Jan 1906.
The high Toby. Being further chapters in the life and fortunes of Dick Ryder, otherwise Galloping Dick, sometime gentleman of the road. 1906, [1912].
REVIEWS: Athenaeum 10 Mar 1906; Spectator 5 May 1906.
A midsummer day's dream. New York 1906, London 1907, 1914.
REVIEWS: New York Times 22 Sep 1906; TLS 1 Feb 1907; Athenaeum 2 Feb 1907; Acad 9 Feb 1907; Dial 1 Apr 1907.
The privateers. 1907, New York 1907, London and Toronto [1915].
REVIEWS: New York Times 26 Jan 1907; Dial 1 Apr 1907; Athenaeum 31 Aug 1907; Outlook 31 Aug 1907; Acad 7 Sep 1907; TLS 13 Sep 1907.
A poppy show: being divers and diverse tales. 1908.
REVIEWS: Athenaeum 11 Apr 1908; Outlook 25 Apr 1908.
The devil's pulpit. New York 1908.
REVIEWS: New York Times 5 Dec 1908; Dial 1 Feb 1909.
The golden precipice. 1908, New York 1908.
REVIEWS: Athenaeum 14 Nov 1908; Bookman Dec 1908.
The flower of the heart. 1909 (3 edns).
REVIEWS: TLS 1 Jan 1909; Athenaeum 30 Jan 1909; Outlook 6 Feb 1909.
The castle by the sea. 1909, Boston 1909, New York 1909, London 1917, 1927.
REVIEWS: Athenaeum 4 Sep 1909; Bookman Oct 1909; New York Times 9 Oct 1909; Dial 16 Nov 1909.
Romance at random. 1909.
REVIEWS: Athenaeum 11 Dec 1909; Bookman Mar 1910.
The King's highway: being further episodes in the life of Richard Ryder. 1910.
REVIEWS: Outlook 23 Apr 1910; Athenaeum 30 Apr 1910.
Alise of Astra. 1910, Boston 1910, 1911.
REVIEWS: Athenaeum 13 Aug 1910; Outlook 13 Aug 1910.
At a venture. 1911 (2 edns).
REVIEW: Athenaeum 11 Mar 1911.
Couch fires and primrose ways. 1911.
REVIEW: Athenaeum 27 Jan 1912.
The tomboy and others. 1912, New York 1912.
REVIEWS: Acad 15 June 1912; Bookman Aug 1912; New York Times 4 Aug 1912.
The big fish. 1912 (2 edns), Boston 1912.
REVIEWS: New York Times 5 May 1912; Athenaeum 27 July 1912; Acad 24 Aug 1912; Bookman Sep 1912.
Ifs and ans. 1913.
REVIEW: Bookman June 1913.
Rosalind in Arden. London and Toronto 1913, [1914].
REVIEWS: Athenaeum 28 June 1913; Bookman Sep 1913.
Once upon a time. London and Toronto 1914, London [1915].
REVIEWS: TLS 5 Mar 1914; Athenaeum 7 Mar 1914; Bookman Apr 1914; Outlook 25 Apr 1914.
The house in the downs. London and Toronto 1914, London 1915, [1928].
REVIEWS: Athenaeum 21 Nov 1914; Spectator 26 Dec 1914; Outlook 25 Jan 1915; Bookman Sep 1915.
Chapman's wares. 1915.
REVIEWS: Athenaeum 24 Apr 1915; TLS 6 May 1915.
The affair on the island. 1916, Paris 1918.
As it chanced. 1916.
Mulberry warf. 1917.
The excelsior. 1918.
The pester finger. [1919.]
REVIEW: TLS 8 May 1919.
Aftermath: a garner of tales. 1919.
REVIEW: Athenaeum 19 Sep 1919.

Contributions to periodicals, collaborative works and anthologies

Watson was literary editor of Black and White *in the early 1890s and was a contributor to many jnls including the* St James's Gazette.

Nat Observer. 18 Apr 1891–31 Mar 1894.
Literary Opinion. July 1891–Jan 1892.
Black and White. The portrait in the inn, 29 Oct 1892; An honourable precedent, 17 Aug 1895.
Vanity Fair. That ruffian, the highwayman, 3 Dec 1892.
The Yellow Book. Jan 1895–Jan 1896.
Bookman. Aug 1895–June 1896.
The Chap-Book. 1 July–1 Nov 1895.
Bookman (USA). Feb–Mar 1896.
Pall Mall Mag. May 1896–Aug 1911.
Harper's Mag. The Lord Chief Justice, May 1897–Aug 1898; Princess Xenia, Apr–Nov 1899; Fairfax comedy, Sep 1910.
In By creek and gully: stories and sketches mostly of bush life. Told in prose and rhyme. By Australian writers in England, ed L. Fisher, 1899.
In Australian wilds, and other colonial tales and sketches, ed P. Mennell, 1899.
North Amer Rev. Thoughts on pain and death, Oct 1901; Intimations of immortality, Aug 1912; Orthodox science and psychical research, Aug 1917.
Outing. The alarm bell, Feb 1902.
Harmsworth's London Mag. Dec 1902–Aug 1909.
Cosmopolitan. Miss and my lady, Mar 1903; Romance at random, Sep 1910; Foundlings, Mar 1911.
T. P.'s Weekly. 19 Dec 1902–27 Jan 1905.
Cassell's Mag. The silent pool and its neighbour, June 1903.
Living Age. A vision of spring in winter, 3 Mar 1906.
Athenaeum. William Ernest Henley (obit), 18 July 1903; Frederick York Powell (obit), 14 May 1904; rev of Henley's Works, 25 July 1908.
Fortnightly Rev. Robert Louis Stevenson: an appreciation, Sep 1903; Orthodox science and psychical research, Sep 1917.
Monthly Rev. The old controversy, Oct 1903.
Nineteenth Cent. Deleterious effect of the Americanization upon women, Nov 1903; Analysis of American women, Sep 1904.

Daily Mail. 4–16 Dec 1903.
Sylvia's Jnl. The last of Blackbeard, Dec 1903.
Good Words. Hurricane Island, Jan–Oct 1904.
Windsor Mag. Feb 1904–Sep 1919.
Saturday Evening Post. 30 Apr 1904–9 Apr 1910.
Nat Rev. The Jew and his destiny, Dec 1905.
Independent Rev. The unknown God, Dec 1905.
Booklovers' Mag. The turtle-doves, 1905.
Strand. Her face, Aug 1905; July 1915–Nov 1916.
Outlook. 26 Aug 1905–23 Aug 1913.
Popular Mag. July 1907–15 Jan 1912.
Lady's Realm. Romance at random, Sep 1908–Aug 1909.
Harper's Weekly. 19 Mar 1910–15 July 1911.
Lippincott's Mag. Picaroon, Oct 1912; Girl at the ship, Nov 1913.
The Story-Teller. Quarantine, Mar 1915.
London Mag. Automatic writing, Oct 1915.
Country Life. Henry James, 11 Mar 1916.

Introductions

The poems of Rosamund Marriott Watson. Introd by Watson 1912, New York 1912.

Collaborative works

Dallas, H. A. Across the water. 1913 (additional chapter by Watson).

§2

Speaker 6 July 1895. Letter.
The Chap-Book 15 Mar 1896.
Acad 18 Dec 1897.
Books and their writers: our new serial. T. P.'s Weekly 31 July 1903.
Bookman (USA) Mar 1905. Portrait.
Obits: New York Times 31 Oct 1921; The Times 31 Oct 1921, 4 Nov 1921.
Hind, C. L. In his More Authors and I, 1922.
Rendall, V. The reminiscences of Marriott Watson. N & Q 6 July, 20 July, 3 Aug 1935.
Connell, J. (J. H. Robertson). In his W. E. Henley, 1949, rptd Port Washington NY 1972.
Mix, K. L. In her A study in yellow: the Yellow Book and its contributors, Lawrence KS 1960.
Sutherland, J. In The Longman companion to Victorian fiction, 1988.
Hughes, L. K. In The 1890s: an encyclopedia of British literature, art, and culture, ed G. A. Cevasco, 1993. [DA]

John Watson, 'Ian Maclaren', Rev John Watson

1850–1907

Mss located in: Harvard; Princeton. See also LR.

Bibliographies

In R. F. Sharp, A dictionary of English authors: biographical and bibliographical, 1904, rptd Detroit 1978.
See also Wellesley *vol 5 1989.*

Selections

The cunning speech of Drumtochty. In The Oxford book of Scottish short stories, ed D. Dunn, Oxford 1995.
In Stories by English authors: Scotland. New York 1896, 1899.

§1

Beside the bonnie brier bush. 1894, New York 1894, London 1895 (8th edn), New York 1895, Chicago 1895, Toronto [1895], Leipzig 1895 (Tauchnitz), London 1896 (illustr W. Hole), 1896 (11th edn), New York 1896, 1897 (illus), London 1898 (13th edn), Chicago 1898, 1900, New York 1902, 1904, London 1905 (15th edn), Chicago 1905, New York 1905, London 1907, Leipzig 1908 (Tauchnitz), London 1910, New York 1910, 1911 (illus), 1920, 1928 (illus), London 1935, Chicago 1950, 1976, New York 1981, 1983. Short stories.
REVIEWS: Bookman Oct 1894; Acad 24 Nov 1894.
A doctor of the old school. 1895 (illustr F. C. Gordon), New York 1895, Toronto 1895, London 1897 (illustr F. C. Gordon), New York 1897, London 1900, New York 1929, Louvain 1937 (4th edn, ed with preface and notes by F. A. Tasker); tr Welsh 1905.
The days of auld lang syne. 1895, New York 1895, Toronto [1895], Leipzig 1895, 1896 (Tauchnitz), London 1898 (4th edn), Leipzig 1898 (Tauchnitz), London 1902 (popular edn, illustr A. S. Boyd), Leipzig 1902, 1908 (Tauchnitz). Short stories.
REVIEW: Acad 18 Jan 1896.
Good news from a far country. 1895.
The mind of the master. New York 1895, London 1896, Cincinnatti 1896, New York 1896, Toronto 1896, London 1897 (3rd edn), New York 1897, 1899, London 1902 (7th edn), New York 1902, 1910, 1930. Theology.
REVIEWS: Expositor Sep 1896; Presbyterian and Reformed Rev Oct 1896.
The order of service for young people. 1895.
The upper room. (Little Books on Religion series.) 1895, New York 1895, London 1896, 1898, New York 1903, London 1909.
The cure of souls. Lyman Beecher lectures on preaching at Yale Univ, 1896. Cincinnatti 1896, New York 1896, Toronto 1896.
REVIEW: New York Times 28 Nov 1896.
Kate Carnegie and those ministers. Toronto 1896, London 1896 (2nd edn).
REVIEWS: Bookman Nov 1896; Acad 21 Nov 1896.
Rabbi Saunderson. New York 1896, London 1898, 1907. Short stories.
Named Ephemerides. The Ian Maclaren Kalendar, 1898. 1897 (decorative designs by W. S. Hadaway).
The potter's wheel. New York 1897, Toronto 1897, London 1899, New York 1906, London 1907 (4th edn). Religious essays.
The Ian Maclaren yearbook. 1897, New York 1897.
Afterwards, and other stories. 1898, New York 1898, Toronto [1898].
REVIEWS: Acad 17 Dec 1898; New York Times 24 Dec 1898.
Companions of the sorrowful way. New York 1898. Theology.
Church folks. 1900, New York 1900, London 1901 (3rd edn), 1907.
REVIEW: Acad 15 Dec 1900.
The doctrines of grace. 1900, New York 1900.
Life of the master. 1901, 1902. Religious.
Young barbarians. 1901, New York 1901, Toronto 1901 (illus), London '1906' [1907], New York 1906, London 1908, Edinburgh 1985. Short stories.
REVIEWS: Athenaeum 16 Nov 1901; New York Times 30 Nov 1901.
His majesty baby and some common people. 1902, Leipzig 1903 (Tauchnitz), 1904 (Tauchnitz), London 1907.
Homely virtues. New York 1902, 1903, 1904 (2nd edn).
The inspiration of our faith, and other sermons. 1905.
REVIEW: Athenaeum 10 Mar 1906.
The Scot of the eighteenth century: his religion and his life. Royal Institution lectures. 1907, Folcroft PA 1976, Norwood PA 1977, 1978.
St Jude's. 1907, Philadelphia 1907 (introd by R. Conner), London 1909.
REVIEW: Athenaeum 19 Oct 1907.
God's message to the human soul: the use of the Bible in the light of new knowledge. Cole lectures of Vanderbilt Univ for 1907. Nashville TN 1907, New York 1907. Maclaren died before giving his lecture.
REVIEW: New York Times 1 Feb 1908.
Graham of Claverhouse. New York 1907, Toronto 1907, London 1908, 1910.
Respectable sins. Ed his son, F. W. Watson. 1909, 1910, 1938.
Books and bookmen and other essays. 1912, Freeport NY 1971.

Contributions to periodicals and introductions

For Blackwood's Mag *and* Scottish Rev, *see* Wellesley *vol* 5 1989.

Scots Observer. 21 Dec 1889–25 Jan 1890.
Br Weekly. 2 Nov 1893–7 Mar 1895.
Introd to F. W. Robertson, Sermons preached at Brighton, 1898 (preface by C. B. Robertson).
Expositor. Feb 1894–Jan 1901.
Bookman. Feb 1895–Dec 1904 (sporadic).
Chapman's Mag. Past redemption, Aug 1895.
McClure's Mag. Feb 1896–Dec 1900.
Memorial sketches by W. R. Nicoll and Ian Maclaren. In H. Drummond, The ideal life and other unpublished addresses, 1897, 1898 (2nd edn), Toronto 1899, 1900 (5th edn).
Sunday Mag. Aug 1897–Aug 1901.
In Letters to ministers, 1898.
In memoriam, sermons and address, by the late J. D. Watters, with appreciations by Ian Maclaren et al. Swansea 1899.
Young Man. Feb–Oct 1899.
North Amer Rev. The restless energy of the American people – an impression, Oct 1899.
St Nicholas (USA). Nov–Dec 1899.
Sunday Strand. Life of Jesus Christ, Jan–Dec 1900.
Munsey's Mag. My favourite novelist and his best book, July 1900.
Windsor Mag. Mar–Dec 1901.
Sunday at Home. 1902–7.
Cassell's Mag. A successful deal, Dec 1902.
Young Woman. The service of womanhood: a Christmas message, Dec 1902.
Quiver. A beggar to cheer, June 1907.
In From a northern window. Papers critical and imaginative, ed F. Watson, 1911.

§2

Dryerre, J. M. Great Thoughts 1 Dec 1894.
Noble, J. A. Windsor Mag Mar 1895 (illus), rptd Bookman (USA) Dec 1895.
Millar, J. H. The literature of the kailyard. New Rev Apr 1895.
Phelphs, E. S. McClure's Mag Sep 1895.
Gordon, F. C. A visit to Drumtochty (Logiealmond?). Bookman (USA) Dec 1895.
Butchart, R. Canadian Mag Jan 1896.
Paton, D. Sunday Mag Jan 1896 (illus).
Lewins, G. Primitive Methodist Quart Rev July 1896.
Davidson, D. A visit to Drumtochty (Logiealmond). Sunday Mag Aug 1896.
Ross, Rev D. M. McClure's Mag Oct 1896.
Murray, D. C. My contemporary in fiction. Canadian Mag June 1897.
Butcher, Rev J. W. The fiction of the Scottish life and character. Great Thoughts Aug 1897.
Mellone, Rev S. H. New World Dec 1897.
In A wealth of laurel: being speeches on dramatic and kindred occasions. New York 1898.
Blathwayt, R. Interview. Great Thoughts Jan 1899.
Puritan May 1899.
Wills, E. Puritan May 1899.
Pond, Major J. B. In his Eccentricities of genius, 1901.
Bookman Apr 1901.
Pearson, C. B. Ian Maclaren: a study of the man and his works. Temple Mag May 1901.
Obits: Liverpool Post and Mercury 7 May 1907; Scotsman 7 May 1907; The Times 7 May 1907; Scottish Rev 9 May 1907; Br Weekly 16 May 1907; Bookman June 1907.
Moffatt, J. The stories of Ian Maclaren. Bookman June 1907.
Nicoll, W. R. 'Ian Maclaren': life of the Rev John Watson, D. D. 1908.
Gamble, W. F. In DNB 1901–1911.
Anderson, E. The kailyard revisited. In Nineteenth-century Scottish fiction: critical essays, ed I. Campbell, Totowa NJ 1979.
Sutherland, J. In The Longman companion to Victorian fiction, 1988.
Shepherd, G. The kailyard. In The history of Scottish literature, III: nineteenth century, Aberdeen 1988.
McLukie, C. W. In The 1890s: an encyclopedia of British literature, art, and culture, ed G. A. Cevasco, 1993.
Price, A. W. W. In his Robertson Nicoll and the genesis of the kailyard school. Durham Univ Jnl Jan 1994.
DLB vol 156 Detroit 1995. [DA]

Theodore Watts-Dunton 1832–1914

See col 2399.

Sir Frederick Wedmore 1844–1921

See col 2400.

Stanley John Weyman 1855–1928

Collections

The novels in thin paper and arranged chronologically, with an introduction in the first volume by the author. 21 vols 1911, 1922.

§1

The house of the wolf: a romance. 1890.
The new Rector. 2 vols 1891.
The story of Francis Cludde. 1891.
A gentleman of France: being the memoirs of Gaston de Bonne, Sieur de Marsac. 3 vols 1893.
The man in black. 1894.
My Lady Rotha: a romance. 1894 (limited edn of 20 copies), 1894.
Under the red robe. 2 vols 1894.
From the memoirs of a Minister of France. 1895.
The red cockade. 1895.
A little wizard. New York 1895.
The Castle Inn. 1898.
Shrewsbury: a romance. 1898.
Sophia. 1900.
Count Hannibal: a romance of the Court of France. 1901.
In Kings' byways: short stories. 1902.
The long night. 1903.
The Abbess of Vlaye. 1904.
Starvecrow Farm. 1905.
Chippinge. 1906.
Laid up in lavender. 1907. Stories.
The wild geese. [1908.]
The Great House. 1919.
Ovington's bank. 1922.
The traveller in the fur cloak. [1924.]
Queen's folly. 1925.
The lively Peggy. 1928.

Oscar Wilde 1854–1900

See col 2060.

Charles James Wills 1842–1912

In the land of the lion and sun, or modern Persia: being experiences of life in Persia during a residence of fifteen years in various parts of that country. 1883, 1891.
Persia as it is: being sketches of modern Persian life and character. 1886.

The Pit Town coronet: a family mystery. 3 vols 1888, 1 vol 1891.
The fatal Phryne. 2 vols 1889, 1 vol [1890]. With F. C. Philips.
The great Dorémi: being the life romance of Antonio Pisani, the last of his line. 1890.
The Scudamores: a novel. 2 vols 1890. With F. C. Philips.
Sybil Ross's marriage: the romance of an inexperienced girl. 1890. With F. C. Philips.
Jardyne's wife: a novel. 3 vols 1891.
John Squire's secret: a novel. 3 vols 1891, 1 vol 1893.
A maiden fair to see. 1891. With F. C. Philips.
Was he justified?: a novel. [1891.]
His sister's hand: a novel. 3 vols [1892], 1 vol [1906] (as Her dead hand).
In and about Bohemia: being forty-one short stories. [1892.]
Laura Ruthven's widowhood. 3 vols 1892. With J. Davidson.
Her portrait, or Phillida's fortunes: a story told in a novel way with pen and pencil. 1893.
Behind an eastern veil: a plain tale of events occurring in the experience of a lady who had a unique opportunity of observing the inner life of ladies of the upper class in Persia. Edinburgh 1894.
An easy-going fellow. 1896.
His dead past. 1897.
The yoke of steel: a novel. 1897. With G. Burchett.
The dean's apron. 1898. Beeton's Christmas annual. With G. Burchett. [EH]

Emma Caroline Wood, Lady Wood 1802–79

Rosewarn: a novel. 3 vols 1866. Pbd under the pseudonym 'C. Sylvester'.
Sorrow on the sea: a novel. 3 vols 1868.
Sabina: a novel. 3 vols 1868.
On credit. 2 vols 1870.
Seadrift: a novel. 3 vols 1871.
Cloth of frieze: a novel. 3 vols 1872.
Wild weather: a novel. 2 vols 1873.
Up hill: a novel. 3 vols 1873.
Ruling the roost: a novel. 3 vols 1874.
Below the salt: a novel. 3 vols 1876.
Through fire and water: a novel. 2 vols 1876.
Sheen's foreman: a novel. 3 vols 1877.
Youth on the prow: a novel. 3 vols 1879.
Lady Wood also pbd an anthology, Leaves from the poets' laurels, *1869.*

Margaret Louisa Woods, née Bradley 1856–1945

§1

A village tragedy. 1887.
Lyrics and ballads. 1889.
Esther Vanhomrigh. 3 vols 1891.
The vagabonds. 1894.
Songs. Oxford 1896 (priv ptd).
Aëromancy and other poems. 1896.
Wild justice. 1896.
Weeping ferry and other stories. 1898.
Sons of the sword: a romance of the Peninsular War. 1901.
The Princess of Hanover. 1902.
The King's revoke. 1905.
The invader. 1907.
Poems old and new. 1907.
Pastels under the southern cross. 1911. Essays of travel.
Collected poems. 1914.
Come unto these yellow sands. [1915.]
A poet's youth. 1923.
The Spanish lady. 1927.

§2

Courtney, W. L. In his Feminine note in fiction, 1904.

Edmund Hodgson Yates 1831–94

The Edmund Yates Papers in the Univ of Queensland Lib include many letters to and from Yates and his son Edmund Smedley Yates, and other mss. See catalogue, comp P. Edwards and A. Dowling (St Lucia, Queensland 1993). Yates's letters to T. H. S. Escott and William Archer, two members of the staff of his weekly The World, *are in the BL, which also holds his diary for 1885.*

Bibliographies

Edwards, P. (ed). Edmund Yates 1831–1894: a bibliography. St Lucia, Queensland 1980.

§1

My haunts and their frequenters. 1854.
Mirth and metre: by two merry men. 1855. With F. E. Smedley. Yates's contributions first pbd in the Keepsake 1854, Court Jnl 31 July–30 Oct 1852, George Cruikshank's Mag Feb 1854.
Our miscellany: which ought to have come out but didn't. 1856, 1857. With R. B. Brough. Parodies of Ainsworth, Tupper, Dickens, Macaulay, Longfellow, and others.
A night at Notting Hill: an original apropos sketch in one act. 1857, New York 1878–9. With N. H. Harrington. First performed Adelphi Theatre 5 Jan 1857.
REVIEWS: The Times 6 Jan 1857; Athenaeum 10 Jan 1857.
My friend from Leatherhead: a farce in one act. 1857. With N. H. Harrington. First performed Lyceum Theatre 25 Feb 1857.
REVIEWS: [J. Oxenford] The Times 24 Feb 1857; Athenaeum 28 Feb 1857.
Double dummy: a farce in one act. 1858. With N. H. Harrington. First performed Lyceum Theatre 3 Mar 1858.
REVIEWS: The Times 4 Mar 1858; Athenaeum 6 Mar 1858.
Your likeness – one shilling: a comic sketch in one act. 1858. With N. H. Harrington. First performed Strand Theatre 22 Apr 1858.
REVIEW: The Times 28 Apr 1858.
Mr Thackeray, Mr Yates, and the Garrick Club: the correspondence and facts stated by Edmund Yates. 1859 (priv ptd), c. 1890 (forged edn by T. J. Wise).
If the cap fits: a comedietta in one act. 1859. With N. H. Harrington. First performed Princess's Theatre 13 June 1859.
Hit him, he has no friends: a farce in one act. 1860, Boston 186?, London 186?, 188?, Boston 1889. With N. H. Harrington. First performed Strand Theatre 17 Sep 1860.
After office-hours. 1861, 1863 (with 5 sketches omitted and 1 added). First pbd in Court Jnl 25 Dec 1852, The Train July 1856, Household Words 17 May 1856–24 Jan 1859, Illus Times 11 Sep 1858, Welcome Guest 13 Nov 1858–1860, All the Year Round 21 May–30 July 1859.
Broken to harness: a story of English domestic life. 3 vols 1864, 1 vol 1864, 1865, 2 vols Leipzig 1866, 1 vol Boston 1866, London 1867, 1870, 1873, Boston 1873 (with A waiting race and The yellow flag), 187? ('9th edn'), London 187?, c. 1880, New York 188?, 1886, 1890. First pbd in Temple Bar Feb 1864–Jan 1865.
REVIEWS: [H. Dixon] Athenaeum 26 Nov 1864; Spectator 26 Nov 1864.
Pages in waiting. 1865, 1884. First pbd in Temple Bar Jan 1861–Mar 1864.
The business of pleasure. 2 vols 1865, 1 vol 1879, New York 1879. First pbd in All the Year Round 7 July 1860–21 Jan 1865.
Running the gauntlet: a novel. 3 vols 1865, 1 vol 1866, 1867, New York 1883, Boston 1886, New York 1886, 1891, London 1892.
REVIEW: Athenaeum 4 Nov 1865.
Kissing the rod: a novel. 3 vols 1866, 1 vol New York 1866, London '1867' [1866], 1867, 1892.
REVIEW: Athenaeum 23 June 1866.
Land at last: a novel in three books. 3 vols 1866, 2 vols Leipzig 1866, 1

vol London 1867, 1868, New York 1874, London 1881, New York 1883, 1886. First pbd in Temple Bar Apr 1865–Apr 1866.
REVIEWS: Spectator 10 Mar 1866; Athenaeum 17 Mar 1866.

The forlorn hope: a novel. 3 vols 1867, 2 vols Leipzig 1867, 1 vol London 1867, Boston 1867, London 187?, c. 1880, New York 1881.
REVIEW: Athenaeum 23 Feb 1867.

Black sheep: a novel. 3 vols 1867, 2 vols Leipzig 1867, 1 vol New York 1867, London 1869, New York 1877, London c. 1880, 1905 (with introd by E. A. Baker). First pbd in All the Year Round 25 Aug 1866–30 Mar 1867. Stage adaptation by Yates and J. Palgrave Simpson first performed at Olympic Theatre 25 Apr 1868, pbd by Lacy in the same year.
REVIEWS: Spectator 6 Apr 1867; Saturday Rev 10 Apr 1867; Athenaeum 13 Apr 1867; The Times 18 Oct 1867.

The rock ahead: a novel. 3 vols 1868, 1 vol 1869, 187?, c. 1880. First pbd Tinsley's Mag Aug 1867–Oct 1868.
REVIEW: Saturday Rev 16 May 1868.

Wrecked in port: a novel. 3 vols 1869, 1 vol New York 1869, London 1878, New York 1881. First pbd in All the Year Round 5 Dec 1868–7 Aug 1869.
REVIEWS: Spectator 14 Aug 1869; Athenaeum 28 Aug 1869; Saturday Rev 4 Sep 1869.

A righted wrong: a novel. 3 vols 1870, 1 vol 1871, c. 1880.
REVIEWS: Saturday Rev 12 Nov 1870; Athenaeum 15 Oct 1870.

Dr Wainwright's patient: a novel. 3 vols 1871, 1 vol New York 1873, London 1878.
REVIEWS: Saturday Rev 4 Feb 1871; Athenaeum 11 Feb 1871.

Nobody's fortune: a novel. 3 vols '1872' [1871?], 2 vols Leipzig 1871, 1 vol Boston 1871, Leipzig 1872, London 1877, 1886. First pbd in Every Saturday (Boston).
REVIEW: Athenaeum 2 Dec 1871.

Castaway: a novel. 3 vols 1872, 2 vols Leipzig 1872, 1 vol London 1872, 187?, 1882. First pbd in All the Year Round 8 July 1871–9 Mar 1872.
REVIEW: Athenaeum 13 Apr 1872.

A waiting race: a novel. 3 vols 1872, 1 vol New York 1872 (with The yellow flag), London 1873, Boston 1873 (with The yellow flag and Broken to harness), London c. 1880, 1892.
REVIEW: Athenaeum 24 Aug 1872.

The yellow flag: a novel. 3 vols 1872, 1 vol 1873, Boston 1873 (with Broken to harness and A waiting game), London c. 1880, New York 188?. First pbd in All the Year Round 27 Apr–7 Dec 1872.
REVIEW: Athenaeum 21 Dec 1872.

The impending sword: a novel. 3 vols 1874, 2 vols Leipzig 1874, London 1875, c. 1880. Rptd under the title A dangerous game Boston 1874, 1875. First pbd Home Jnl 20 Dec 1873–22 Aug 1874.
REVIEW: Athenaeum 30 May 1874.

Two, by tricks: a novel. 2 vols 1874, 1 vol 1875, 1892. First pbd, anonymously, in The World 8 July–11 Nov 1874.
REVIEW: Athenaeum 23 Jan 1875.

A silent witness: a novel. 3 vols 1875, 2 vols Leipzig 1875, Boston 1875, London 1877, New York 1879 (The silent witness and other stories), London [1892], [1894]. First pbd in All the Year Round 17 Oct 1874–29 May 1875.
REVIEW: Athenaeum 12 June 1875.

Going to the bad: a novel. Boston 1876, New York 1879, 1881, 1882. Probably first pbd, under the title A bad lot, in New York Fireside Companion 10 Feb–28 Apr 1873; if so there may have been an earlier Amer edn. No English edn has been found.

The wages of sin. Boston 1875. This too may have been first pbd in New York Fireside Companion.

Edmund Yates: his recollections and experiences. 2 vols 1884, 2 vols Leipzig 1884, 1 vol London 1885, 4th edn 1885 (with additional ch), New York 1884 and 1885 (under the title Fifty years of London life: memoirs of a man of the world), 1890 (2 edns under the title Man of the world).
REVIEWS: Athenaeum 22 Nov 1884; Saturday Rev 22 Nov 1884; Spectator 29 Nov 1884; [G. Archdale] Temple Bar Dec 1884; [C. Dawkins] Acad 6 Dec 1884; [T. Escott] Fortnightly Rev Dec 1884.

Contributions to periodicals

Yates edited and contributed to Comic Times *11 Aug–24 Nov 1855,* The Train *Jan 1856–June 1858,* Temple Bar *Feb 1863–July 1867,* Tinsley's Mag *Aug 1867–c. July 1869,* The World *8 July 1874–19 May 1894. Other jnls to which he contributed included* Court Jnl *Mar–Dec 1852,* Illus London Mag *July 1854–June 1855 (an unfinished serial story called* Arthur Hargrave, or the uniform of foolscap*),* Illus Times *(as the 'Lounger at the Clubs'), 30 June 1855–late 1863,* Inverness Courier *1855–early 1860s,* Daily News *1855–early 1860s, the* Northern Whig *(Belfast) c. Apr 1862–?early 1870s, the* Morning Star *(as the 'Flâneur') 4 Apr 1864–1867, the* Evening Star *(as 'Q') c. 1864–c. 1867,* Observer *1871–2,* Queen *(as 'Mrs Seaton') Feb 1872–Mar 1873, and the* New York Herald *1873–5. See also* After office-hours, Pages in waiting, *and* The business of pleasure, *above.*

Contributions to collaborative works

The life and correspondence of Charles Mathews the elder, comedian: by Mrs Mathews. 1860. 'Abridged and condensed' by Yates.

Mont Blanc: by Albert Smith. 1860. With a memoir of Smith by Yates.

For better, for worse: a romance of the affections. 2 vols 1864. 'Edited' by Yates.

Gathered leaves: being a collection of the poetical writings of the late Frank E. Smedley. 1865. With a 'memorial preface' by Yates.

Wit and pleasure: seven tales by seven authors. 1877. Includes Yates's Thoroughbred, a story in 4 chs.

Celebrities at home: reprinted from 'The World'. 3 ser 1877–8–9. Yates wrote the article on Henry Irving, ser 1.

Thoughts in my garden: by Mortimer Collins. 2 vols 1880. 'Edited' by Yates, with notes by him and by Mrs Mortimer Collins.

The struggles and adventures of Christopher Tadpole: by Albert Smith. 1897. With a 'biographical sketch' of Smith by Yates.

§2

Thackeray, W. M. The Virginians, ch 35. 1857–9. Contains a reference to Yates as 'Young Grub-street'.

Thackeray, W. M. On screens in dining rooms. Roundabout papers, Cornhill Mag Aug 1860.

A new type of journalist. Pall Mall Gazette 18 Feb 1865. Attacks Yates as 'Neddy Yapp'.

Hatton, J. Journalistic London. 1882.

Journalism in England: the London 'World'. New York Daily Tribune 2 Oct 1882.

Trollope, A. An autobiography. 1883.

Fox Bourne, H. English newspapers, vol 2. 1887.

Vizetelly, H. Glances back through seventy years. 1893.

Obits: Daily Telegraph [Clement Scott] 21 May 1894; The Times 24 May 1894; Truth (H. Labouchère) 24 May 1894; The World 23 May 1894.

Corelli, Marie. The last days of Edmund Yates. Temple Bar July 1894.

Escott, T. Edmund Yates: an appreciation and a retrospect. New Rev July 1894.

Hollingshead, J. My lifetime. 1895.

Tinsley, W. Random recollections of an old publisher. 1900.

Lucy, H. Nearing Babylon (vol 3 of his Sixty years in the wilderness). 1916.

Edwards, P. D. Dickens's 'young men': George Augustus Sala, Edmund Yates and the world of Victorian journalism. Aldershot 1997. [PDE]

Israel Zangwill 1864–1926

Bibliographies

Peterson, A. Zangwill: a selected bibliography. BB 23 1961.

Collections

Works. 14 vols 1925.

§1

The Premier and the painter. [1888.] With Louis Cowen. Pbd under the pseud J. Freeman Bell.
The Bachelors' Club. 1891, 1898 (with The Old Maids' Club as The Celibates' Club).
The big Bow mystery. 1892.
Children of the Ghetto. 3 vols 1892, 1 vol 1893.
The Old Maids' Club. 1892, 1898 (with The Bachelors' Club as The Celibates' Club).
Ghetto tragedies. 1893. Contents later pbd in They that walk in darkness, *below*, 1899.
'Merely Mary Ann'. [1893.]
The King of Schnorrers: grotesques and fantasies. 1894.
The master. 1895.
Without prejudice. 1896. Rptd articles.
Dreamers of the ghetto. 1898.
'They that walk in darkness': ghetto tragedies. 1899. Includes contents of Ghetto tragedies, *above*, 1893.
The mantle of Elijah. 1900.
Blind children. 1903. Poems.
The grey wig: stories and novelettes. 1903.
Ghetto comedies. 1907. The Jewish trinity also pbd separately.
The melting-pot: drama in four acts. 1909, 1914.
Italian fantasies. 1910.
The war god: a tragedy in five acts. 1911.
The hithertos. [1912.] Speech delivered at a meeting of the Women's Social and Political Union, Mar 1912.
The next religion: a play in three acts. 1912.
Plaster saints: a high comedy in three movements. 1914.
The war for the world. 1916.
The principles of nationalities. 1917 (Conway Memorial lecture).
Chosen peoples: the Hebraic ideal versus the Teutonic. With a foreword by H. Samuel. 1918 (Davis Memorial lecture).
Hands off Russia: a speech delivered at the Royal Albert Hall, February 8th 1919. 1919.
Jinny the carrier. 1919.
The voice of Jerusalem. 1920.
The cockpit: romantic drama in three acts. 1921.
The forcing house, or The cockpit continued: tragi-comedy in four acts. 1922.
Too much money: a farcical comedy in three acts. [1924.]
We moderns: a post-war comedy in three movements (allegro, andante, adagio). 1926.
Speeches, articles and letters of Israel Zangwill. Ed M. Simon 1937.

§2

Wells, H. G. Mr Zangwill's Master. Saturday Rev 18 May 1895.
Wells, H. G. Mr Zangwill's egoists. Saturday Rev 2 Jan 1897.
Oliphant, J. In his Victorian novelists, 1899.
Baron, A. and I. Finestein. The case of Zangwill. Jewish Quart 5 1957.
Leftwich, J. Israel Zangwill. 1957.
Wohlgelernter, M. Israel Zangwill: a study. 1964.
Adams, E. B. Israel Zangwill. New York 1971.
Udelson, J. H. Dreamer of the ghetto: the life and works of Israel Zangwill. Tuscaloosa 1990.

v. Children's books

The following are not included: (i) alphabets as such; (ii) didactic works of all kinds, including those meant merely to convey knowledge in a domestic or familiar way; (iii) works in which pictures purposely predominate over text; (iv) anthologies, with a few special exceptions, particularly in respect of fairy tales. The more voluminous writers are represented only by a typical selection.

(1) GENERAL WORKS

Trimmer, S. The guardian of education. 5 vols 1802–4.
[Kendrew, J. (publisher of York).] A collection of the publications of J. Kendrew. nd.
Titmarsh, Michael Angelo' (W. M. Thackeray). On some illustrated children's books. Fraser's Mag Apr 1846.
Yonge, C. M. Children's literature of the last century [1769–1869]. Macmillan's Mag July–Sep 1869.
Yonge, C. M. A storehouse of stories. 2 vols 1870–2. Selections from 18th and 19th centuries, with historical introd.
Mackarness, Mrs H. Children of the olden time. 1874.
Tytler, Sarah' (H. Keddie). Childhood a hundred years ago. 1877.
Tuer, A. W. 1,000 quaint cuts from books of other days. [1886.]
Molesworth, Mrs M. L. The best books for children. Pall Mall Gazette 29 Oct 1887.
Welsh, C. On coloured books for children. 1887. No 12 of priv ptd Opuscula of the sette of odd vols.
Yonge, C. M. What books to lend and what to give. [1887.]
Hewins, C. The history of children's books [early English and American]. Atlantic Monthly Jan 1888.
Salmon, E. Juvenile literature as it is. 1888.
Pearson, E. Banbury chapbooks and nursery toy book literature of the eighteenth and early nineteenth centuries. 1890 (priv ptd).
Field, Mrs E. N. The child and his book. 1891.
Molesworth, Mrs M. L. On the art of writing fiction for children. Atalanta 6 1893.
Anon. Children yesterday and today. Quart Rev 183 1896.
White, G. Children's books and their illustrators. Studio special no 1897–8.
Molesworth, Mrs M. L. Story-reading and story-writing. Chambers's Jnl 5 Nov 1898.
Tuer, A. W. Pages and pictures from forgotten children's books. 1898–9.
Tuer, A. W. Stories from old fashioned children's books. 1899–1900.
Tallentyre, S. G.' (E. B. Hall). The road to knowledge a hundred years ago. Cornhill Mag Dec 1900.
Lucas, E. V. Old fashioned tales. 1905. Selections with introd.
Lucas, E. V. Forgotten tales of long ago. 1906. Selections with introd.
Dodd, C. I. Some aspects of children's books. Nat Rev Jan 1905.
Moses, M. J. Children's books and reading. New York 1907.
H. M. Stationery Office. Catalogue of the British section of the international exhibition of the book industry and graphic arts, Leipzig. 1914. Special section devoted to children's books; introd by A. Rackham and F. J. H. Darton.
Barry, F. V. A century of children's books. 1922.
The Horn Book Magazine. Boston 1924– . In progress.
Andreae, G. The dawn of juvenile literature in England. Amsterdam 1925.
[Gumuchian et Cie.] Les livres de l'enfance du XVe au XIXe siècle. Préface de Paul Gavault. Paris [1930]. A bookseller's catalogue, virtually a bibliography.
Fulham Public Libraries. Catalogue of an exhibition of children's books of long ago; foreword by F. E. Hansford. [1931.]
Darton, F. J. H. Children's books in England: five centuries of social life. Cambridge 1932; ed K. M. Lines, Cambridge 1958 (rev); rev B. Alderson 1982.
Hazard, P. Les livres, les enfants et les hommes. Paris 1932; tr Boston 1944.
Ridding, L. E. A nursery library seventy-five years ago. Contemporary Rev Sep 1932.
Sayers, W. C. B. A manual of children's libraries. 1932.
James, P. Children's books of yesterday. Studio special no 1933.
Maxe, M. Children's books ancient and modern. Nat Rev Dec 1933.
Rosenbach, A. S. W. Early American children's books. Portland ME 1933 (priv ptd).

Junior Bookshelf. Huddersfield 1936– . In progress.
König, G. Der viktorianische Schulroman. Berlin 1937.
Osborne, E. Children's books in the nineteenth century. Junior Bookshelf 2 1937.
Smith, E. S. The history of children's literature: a syllabus with selected bibliographies. Chicago 1937, 1980 (rev M. Hodges and S. Steinfirst).
Osborne, E. From morality and instruction to Beatrix Potter. Eastbourne 1949.
Barnes, W. Children's literature past and present. Educational Forum 3 1939.
Moore, A. C. My roads to childhood. New York 1939.
Lines, K. M. Four to fourteen: a library of books for children. Cambridge 1940, 1950 (rev), 1956 (rev).
Morgan, P. E. A few notes on the production of children's books to 1860. N & Q 9–23 Mar 1943.
Morgan, P. E. Reward books. N & Q 31 July 1943.
Green, R. L. Tellers of tales. Leicester 1946, 1953 (rev), London 1965 (rewritten and expanded). A survey of children's books 1800–1964, with bibliographies.
Mahony, B. E. et al. Illustrators of children's books 1744–1945. Boston 1947.
Jordan, A. M. From Rollo to Tom Sawyer, and other papers. Boston 1948.
Milne, A. A. Books for children. Cambridge 1948.
Muir, P. H. Children's books of yesterday. 1948. Catalogue of Nat Book League exhibition.
Smith, J. A. Children's illustrated books. 1948.
Trease, G. Tales out of school. 1948, 1964 (rev).
Turner, E. S. Boys will be boys. 1948. Penny dreadfuls etc.
Partridge, C. Evangelical children's books 1828–59. N & Q 4 Feb 1950.
Egoff, S. A. Children's periodicals of the nineteenth century. 1951 (Lib Assoc pam).
Opie, I. and P. The Oxford dictionary of nursery rhymes. Oxford 1951, 1952 (corrected).
Lewis, C. S. On three ways of writing for children. Proc of Annual Conference, Lib Assoc 1952; rptd in his Of other worlds, 1966.
Smith, L. H. The unreluctant years: a critical approach to children's literature. Chicago 1953.
Meigs, C. et al. A critical history of children's literature. New York 1953, 1969.
Muir, P. H. English children's books 1600–1900. 1954.
Green, R. L. (ed). Modern fairy stories. 1955; Tales of make-believe, 1960. Selected nineteenth-century stories.
St John, J. The Osborne collection of early children's books 1566–1910. Toronto 1958, 1966 (corrected).
Hürlimann, B. Europäische Kinderbücher in drei Jahrhunderten. Zurich 1959, 1963 (rev); tr Oxford 1967.
Opie, I. and P. The lore and language of school-children. Oxford 1959.
Ford, B. (ed). Young writers, young readers. 1960. Articles by various authors from Jnl of Education, etc.
Fisher, M. Intent upon reading. Leicester 1961, 1964 (rev).
Crouch, M. Treasure seekers and borrowers. 1962.
Fisher, M. Growing point. Northampton 1962– . In progress.
Thwaite, M. F. From primer to pleasure: children's books in England to 1900. 1963.
Avery, G. and A. Bull. Nineteenth-century children. 1965.
De Vries, L. (ed). Flowers of delight [1765–1830]. 1965.
Townsend, J. R. Written for children: an outline of English language children's literature. 1965, 1974 (rev).
Ellis, A. How to find out about children's literature. Oxford 1966, 1968 (rev), 1973 (rev).
Boggis, D. H. (comp). Catalogue of the Hockcliffe collection of children's books. Bedford 1969.
Quayle, E. The collector's book of children's books. 1971.
Lanes, S. G. Down the rabbit hole: adventures and misadventure in the realm of children's literature. 1972.
Salway, L. (ed). Special collections in children's literature. A guide to collections in libraries and other organisations in London and the Home Counties. 1972.
The Wandsworth collection of early children's books. Wandsworth 1972, 1997.
Howarth, P. Play up and play the game: the heroes of popular fiction. 1973.
Quayle, E. The collector's book of boys' stories. 1973.
Hunt, P. An introduction to children's literature. Oxford 1974.
Whalley, J. I. Cobwebs to catch flies: illustrated books for the nursery and schoolroom 1700–1900. 1974.
Avery, G. Childhood's pattern: a study of the heroes and heroines of children's fiction 1770–1950. 1975.
Children's books in the Rare Books Division of the Library of Congress. 2 vols Towota NJ 1975.
Fisher, M. Who's who in children's books: a treasury of the familiar characters of childhood. 1975.
Bettelheim, B. The uses of enchantment: meaning and importance of fairy tales. 1976.
Cadogan, M. and P. Craig. You're a brick Angela: a new look at girls' fiction from 1839 to 1975. 1976.
Moon, M. John Harris's books for youth 1801–1843. Winchester and Detroit 1976. Suppl pbd 1983, repbd with suppl 1987.
Salway, L. (ed). A peculiar gift: nineteenth century writings on books for children. 1976.
Tucker, N. (ed). Suitable for children: controversies in children's literature. 1976.
After Alice: a hundred years of children's reading in Britain. 1977.
Commire, A. Yesterday's authors of books for children. Detroit 1977.
Feaver, W. When we were young: two centuries of children's book illustration. 1977.
Grylls, D. Guardians and angels, parents and children: an appraisal of children's classics in the Western tradition. 1978.
Schiller, J. G. Nursery rhymes and chapbooks 1805 and 1814. 1978.
Cutt, N. M. Ministering angels: a study of nineteenth century evangelical writing for children. Wormley, Herts 1979.
Alderson, B. Sing a song for sixpence: the English picture book tradition and R. Caldecott. 1980.
Index to the Baldwin Library of Books in English before 1800. Univ of Florida Lib, Gainesville. 3 vols Boston 1981.
Tucker, N. The child and the book: a psychological and literary exploration. Cambridge 1981.
Quigley, I. The heirs of Tom Brown: the English school story. 1982.
Demers, P. (ed). A garland from the golden age, an anthology of children's literature from 1850 to 1900. 1983.
Carpenter, H. and M. Prichard. The Oxford companion to children's literature. Oxford and New York 1984.
Musgrave, P. W. From Brown to Bunter: the life and death of the school story. 1985.
Barr, J. Illustrated children's books. 1986.
Carpenter, H. Secret gardens: a study of the golden age of children's literature. 1985.
Frey, C. and J. Griffith. The literary heritage of childhood: an appraisal of children's classics in the Western tradition. 1987.
Bingham, J. M. Writers for children: critical studies of major authors since the seventeenth century. New York 1988.
Cairns, E. M. (comp). Catalogue of the collection of children's books 1617–1939 in the library of the University of Reading. Reading 1988.
Clark, A. The children's annual. 1988.
Drotner, K. English children and their magazines. New Haven CT and London 1988.

Pyles, M. S. Death and dying in children's and young people's literature: a survey and bibliography. 1988.
Richards, J. Happiest days: the public schools in English fiction. 1988.
Sendak, M. Caldecott and Co: notes on books and pictures. 1988.
Sherclif, W. H. Morality to adventure: Manchester Polytechnic's collection of children's books. 1840–1939. Manchester 1988.
Whalley, J. and T. R. Chester. A history of children's book illustration. 1988.
Avery, G. and J. Briggs. Children and their books: a celebration of the work of Iona and Peter Opie. Oxford 1989.
Jackson, M. V. Engines of instruction, mischief and magic: children's literature in England from its beginnings to 1989. 1989.
Nodelman, P. Words about pictures: narrative art of children's picture books. 1989.
Rowbotham, J. Good girls make good wives. Oxford 1989.
Kirkpatrick, R. J. Bullies, beaks and flannelled fools: an annotated bibliography of boys' school fiction 1742–1990. 1990.
Moon, M. Benjamin Tabart's juvenile library: a bibliography of books for children published, written, edited and sold by Mr Tabart 1801–1820. Winchester and Detroit 1990.
Reynolds, K. Girls only? Gender and popular children's fiction in Britain 1880–1910. Hemel Hempstead 1990.
Bristow, J. Empire boys: adventures in a man's world. 1991.
Ward, E. H. Girl's own guide: an index to all the fiction in the Girl's Own Paper from 1880–1941. Colne 1992.
Watson, B. English schoolboy stories. Metuchen NJ 1992.
Wilkin, B. Survival themes in fiction for children and young people. 2nd edn 1993.
Alderson, B. Childhood re-collected: early children's books from the library of Marjorie Moon. 1994.
Lesnik-Oberstien, K. Children's literature: criticism and the fictional child. 1994.
Reynolds, K. Children's literature in the 1890s and the 1990s. Plymouth 1994.
Zaidman, L. M. (ed). British children's writers 1880–1914. Detroit and Washington 1994 (DLB vol 141).
Hunt, P. Children's literature: an illustrated history. 1995.
Hunt, P. International encyclopedia of children's literature. 1996.
Khorana, M. British children's writers 1800–1880. Detroit and Washington 1996 (DLB vol 163).
Zipes, J. Happily ever after: fairy tales, children and the culture industry. London and New York 1997.

(2) CHILDREN'S WRITERS

Cecil Adair

See Evelyn Everett Green.

Ellinor Davenport Adams

Wild raspberries: a tale of love and adventure. 1879.
Colonel Russell's baby. 1889.
Comrades true. 1891.
Robin's ride: a story for children. 1891 (illustr W. S. Stacey).
The disagreeable Duke. A Christmas whimsicality for holiday boys and girls. 1894.
The holiday prize. A modern fairy tale. 1896 (illustr K. M. Skeating).
Little Miss Conceit. [1896.]
The palace on the moor. 1896.
May, Guy and Jim; with other stories. 1897.
Miss Secretary Ethel: a story for girls of to-day. [1898] (illustr H. Furniss).
A girl of today. 1899.
Miss Mary's little maid. [1899.]
Betty the bold. [1900.]
Granny's coach and four. [1900.]
A queen among girls. 1900, [1935].
Little greycoat. [1901], [1929].
On honour. A home and school story. 1902, [1904].
Elsie wins. 1902 (rptd from Miss E. D. Adams's story).
Those twins! 1902.

Mrs Alfred W. Adams, Emma E. Adams

Crumbs from nature's table. 1878 (2nd edn).

Henry Cadwallader Adams

Capture of Tunis. nd.
Stories of the Kings: or tales for Sunday reading. nd (illus).
The first of June: or schoolboy rivalry. A second tale of Charlton School. 1856, 1892.
Sivan the sleeper. A tale of all time. 1857.
The twelve foundations, and other poems. 1859.
Schoolboy honour. A tale of Halminster College. 1861 (illus), 1891.
The Indian boy. 1865, [1893] (as Arthur's champion or the Indian boy. A tale of Brunswick House.)
The White Brunswickers: or reminiscences of schoolboy life. 1865.
Balderscourt: or holiday tales. 1866.
Sundays at Enscombe: or tales for Sunday reading. 1866.
The judges of Israel: or tales for Sunday reading. 1866.
Barford Bridge: or schoolboy trials. 1868.
The Enscombe stories: or tales for Sunday reading. 1868.
Tales for Sunday reading. [1868.]
The boy cavaliers: or the siege of Clidesford. 1869.
Falconhurst: or birthday tales. 1869.
Tales upon texts: or stories illustrative of scripture. 1870.
Friend or foe. A tale of Sedgmoor. 1871 (illus).
Tales of the Civil Wars. 2 vols 1871.
The Winborough boys: or Ellerslie Park. 1872 (illus).
The doctor's birthday: or the force of example. A third tale of Charlton School. 1873.
Tales of Walter's school-days: a sequel to tales of Charlton School. 1873 (illus).
Frank Lawrence: or a young man's fancy. 1873.
Walter's friend: or big boys and little ones. A fourth tale of Charlton School. 1873.
The Woodleigh stories: or tales for Sunday reading. 1873 (illus).
The chief of the school: or schoolboy ambition. A tale of Nethercourt. 1874 (illus), 1881.
The Falcon family: or Meta and Willy. A tale of two birthdays. [1874.]
Wroxby College: or the Luscombe prize. A tale of boy life. 1874.
Sunday evenings at home: being stories from history for every Sunday in the year. 1874, 1875, 1876, 1880–1.
Hair-breadth escapes: or the adventures of three boys in South Africa. 1876.
Tales of Nethercourt. 2 vols 1876.
The original Robinson Crusoe. [1877.]
The boys of Westonbury: or the monitorial system. 1878.
The lost rifle or schoolboy faction. A tale of Nethercourt. 1880.
Who did it?: or Holmwood Priory. A schoolboy's tale. 1882.
Traveller's tales. A book of marvels. 1883.
The mystery of Beechey Grange: or the missing host. A tale for boys. [1884.]
For James or George. A schoolboy's tale of 1745. 1886 (illus), 1892 (3rd edn), 1909.
Wilton of Cuthbert's. A tale of undergraduate life thirty years ago. 1886.
Who was Philip? A tale of public school life. 1886, 1910.

Charlie Lucken at school and college. 1887 (illustr J. Finnemore).
Ernest Hepburn: or revenge and forgiveness. [1888.]
Perils in the Transvaal and Zululand. [1888], 1917.
Hughie's mistake. Stories jolly: stories new. 1889.
In the fifteen. A tale of the first Jacobite insurrection. 1893 (illustr J. Fennimore).
Fighting the way: or Leslie Rice's first curacy. A tale of clerical life. 1895.

Also wrote guide bks, history bks and Latin and Greek grammars.

Henry Gardiner Adams, 'Nemo'

A story of the seasons. 1848.
The seaside lesson book. 1856.
The weaver boy who became a missionary: being the story of the life and labours of David Livingstone. 1867, 1873, 1874 (as David Livingstone: the weaver boy who became a missionary), 1881.
The life and adventures of Dr Livingstone: in the interior of South Africa. 1868 (illus).
The wonders and beauties of the year. [1878] (illus).

William Adams 1814–48

The cherry stones: or Charlton School: a tale for youth. Ed and partly rewritten by H. C. Adams 1851, 1853 (3rd edn). Partly from the mss of the Rev W. Adams.
Tales of Charlton School. Partly from the mss of the Rev W. Adams. Ed H. C. Adams. 1864.

William Henry Davenport Adams 1828–91

Heroes of the sea and their achievements. nd.
Neptune's heroes: or the sea-kings of England. 1861.
The steady aim: a book of examples and encouragements from modern biography. 1863, 1868, 1879.
The boy makes the man: a book of anecdotes and examples for the use of youth. 1867, 1872.
Truths and fancies from fairy land: or fairy stories with a purpose. [1867.]
Jessie Oglethorpe: or the story of a daughter's devotion. And other tales. 1868.
Scenes of the olden time. 1868.
Wonders of the vegetable world. 1869.
Before the conquest: or English worthies in the old English period. 1870.
The land of the Nile: or Egypt past and present. 1871.
The men at the helm: biographical sketches of great English statesmen. 1872.
The forest and the jungle and the prairie: or scenes with the trapper and hunter in many lands. 1873, 1882.
Animal life throughout the globe. An illustrated book of natural history. 1876.
The Arctic world: its plants, animals and natural phenomena. With a historical sketch of Arctic discovery, 1876.
Beneath the surface: or the wonders of the underground world. 1876.
The threshold of life: a book of illustrations and lessons for the encouragement and counsel of youth. 1876.
Scenes with the hunter and trapper in many lands: or stories of adventures with wild animals. 1877.
The bird world described with pen and pencil. 1878.
The Amazon and its wonders. 1879, 1894.
In the Far East: a narrative of exploration and adventures in Cochin-China, Cambodia, Laos and Siam. 1879, 1881.
The mariners of England. Stories of deeds of daring. 1879.
The eastern archipelago. A description of the scenery, animal and vegetable life, people and physical wonders of the islands in the eastern seas. 1880 (illus).
Eminent soldiers. A series of biographical sketches of great military commanders, English and foreign. [1880.]
Heroes of the cross: or studies in the biography of saints, martyrs and Christian pioneers. 1880.
Page, squire and knight: a romance of the days of chivalry. 1881, 1887.
Young Marmaduke. A story of the reign of terror. 1881.
Eminent sailors. 1882.
Heroes of maritime discovery. 1882.
Child life and girlhood of remarkable women. 1883, 1885.
Battle stories from British and European history. 1885, 10th edn 1902.
A book of earnest lives. 1885 (2nd edn), 1894 (7th edn).
The city of gold: or the wonderful story of Hernando Cortes and the conquest of Mexico. [1885.]
England on the sea: or the story of the British navy. 1885.
'In perils oft': romantic biographies illustrative of the adventurous life. [1885.]
The land of the Incas and the City of Sun: or the story of Franco Pizarro and the conquest of Peru. [1883], [1884], [1885].
England at war. 1886.
Master minds in art, science and letters. A book for boys. 1886.
Sunshine and shadow: or stories from Crayford for the young folk. 1888.
The maid of Orleans: and the great war of the English in France. 1889.
The wars of the cross: or the history of the crusades. 1891.
Warriors of the crescent. 1892.
Egypt past and present. Described and illustrated with a narrative of its occupation by the British and of recent events in the Soudan. 1894.
Under many flags: or stories of Scottish adventures. 1902.
English heroes in the reign of Elizabeth. [1902.]

Also wrote travel books, biographies, histories and geological texts and books of verse.

Eleanor C. Agnew

Geraldine: a tale of conscience. 1838 (2nd edn).
The young communicants. 1840.
Tales explanatory of the sacraments. 1846.
Rome and the abbey. 1849.
Saint Mary and her times. A poem. 1851.
The merchant prince and his heir: or the triumphs of duty, 1863.
The convent prize book. 1868.

Grace Aguilar

The days of Bruce: a story of Scottish history. Manchester 1852.
See also col 1089.

John Aikin, 'Uncle John' 1747–1822

England delineated: or a geographical description of every county in England and Wales with a description of its most important products, natural and artificial. For the use of young persons. 1788.
Letters from a father to his son, on various topics relevant to literature and the conduct of life. 1802 (2nd edn), 1806 (4th edn).
The calendar of nature: designed for the instruction and entertainment of young persons. New York 1815, 1822, 1835, New York and Baltimore nd, 1839.
The juvenile budget opened: being selections from the writings of Doctor John Aikin, with a sketch of his life by Mrs Sarah Hale. Boston 1840?, 1860.

The juvenile budget reopened: being further selections. Boston 1840, New York 1860.
Evening book: or fireside stories. 1852.

Lucy Aikin, 'Mary Godolphin' 1781–1864

Poetry for children. 1795, 1801, 1808 (5th edn), 1815 (6th edn), 1818 (7th edn), 1831, 1845.
Juvenile correspondence: or letters designed as examples of the epistolary style, for children of both sexes. 1811, 1816, 1826.
Evenings at home [retold] in words of one syllable. By Mary Godolphin. 1869.
See also col 2078.

William Harrison Ainsworth

Boscobel: or the Royal Oak, a tale of the year 1651. 1872.
See also col 1091.

Deborah Alcock 1835–1913

The cross and the crown. A tale of the revocation of the Edict of Nantes. nd.
Sunset in Provence and other tales of martyr times. 1864.
The Spanish brothers: a tale of the sixteenth century. 1871, 1888, 1900, 1903.
Under the Southern Cross: a tale of the new world. 1873, 1874, 1887.
She hath done what she could. A New Year's debate to older girls. 1880.
The Czar. 1882.
A tale of the time of the first Napoleon. 1883, 1906.
The Roman students on the wings of morning. A tale of the Renaissance. 1883.
Arthur Erskine's story. A tale of the days of Knox. London and Edinburgh 1884.
Archie's chances and the child's victory. 1886.
Genevieve: or the children of Port Royal. A story of old France. 1889.
Prisoners of hope: a story of the faith. 1894.
The well in the orchard. [1896.]
By far Euphrates. 1897.
Doctor Adrian: a story of old Holland. 1897.
The little captives and other stories. 1898, 1929.
The friends of Pascal: or the children of Port Royal. 1902.
Robert Musgrave's adventure. A story of old Geneva. 1909.
Wrote a number of bks on the history of the Protestant Church and hymn bks. See E. B. Bayly, The author of the Spanish brothers, Deborah Alcock, her life and works, *1914.*

'Isabella Alden'

Esther Reid yet speaking. [1890?]
Three people. [1890?]

Mrs Cecil Frances Alexander, née Humphreys 1818–95

The baron's little daughter and other tales. 1848, New York 1854, 1867. In prose and verse.
Hymns for little children. 1848 (many succeeding editions).
See also col 621.

Alexander Allardyce 1846–96

The city of sunshine. 1877.
Balmoral: a romance of the king's country. Edinburgh and London 1893, 1896.
Also pbd adult novels.

Phoebe Allen

The witch's den. nd (illustr F. Feller).
Asaph Wood: or little by little. 1882.
The black witch of Honeycritch. 1886 (illustr F. Dadd).
Minon: or the cat that the king looked at. 1887 (illustr F. Dadd), 1930.
Wanted a camel. 1888.
Match box Phil. 1890.
The boys of Priors Dean. 1891 (illustr H. W. Petherick).
Two little victims. 1891.
Jack and Jill's journey. A tour through the plant kingdom. 1899 (illustr H. Godfrey).
A pennyworth of kindness. 1900.
Playing at botany. 1901.
The pick of the basket. 1902.
As the twig is bent. 1903.
Bringing home the may. 1903.
Wrote numerous adult novels, as well as bks on botany, heraldry and architecture, and translated a number of works from French.

William Allingham 1824–88

In fairyland: a series of pictures from the elf world by Richard Doyle with a poem by William Allingham (A forest in fairyland). 1870.
The fairies: a child's song. (1st pbd in 1850 in Poems, which was withdrawn from circulation. Also appeared in the Music-makers.) 1883, 1912.
Rhymes for the young folk. [1887.]
See col 514.

'A. L. O. E.', 'A Lady of England', Charlotte Maria Tucker 1825–93

The Claremont tales: or illustrations of the beatitudes. [1854.]
Wings and strings: a tale for the young. 1855.
The giant killer: or the battle which all must fight. 1856, 1864, [1878?], 1894 (illustr Dalziel).
Upwards and downwards: or the sluggard and the diligent: a story for boys. 1856.
Daybreak in England. 1857 (illus).
The rambles of a rat. 1857, 1888 (illustr Dalziel).
The young pilgrim: a tale illustrative of 'The pilgrim's progress'. London and Edinburgh 1857.
The mine: or darkness and light. London and Edinburgh 1858.
Old friends with new faces. London and Edinburgh 1858.
The story of a needle. 1858.
My neighbour's shoes: or feeling for others. London and Edinburgh 1861.
Scripture picture puzzles, with single descriptive narratives and Bible questions. 1861?
The crown of success: or four heads to furnish. London and Edinburgh 1863.
Exiles in Babylon: or children of light. 1864.
The mine: or darkness and light. 1865, 1895.
Rescued from Egypt. London and Edinburgh 1865.
Fairy know-a-bit: or a nutshell of knowledge. 1866, 1868.
The triumph over Midian. London and Edinburgh 1866, 1871, [189?]
House beautiful: or the Bible museum. 1868.
The golden fleece: or who wins the prize? 1869.
The robbers' cave: a tale of Italy. 1870, 1883.
Flora: or self-deception. 1871, 1905.
A wreath of smoke. London and Edinburgh 1871.
A friend in need, and other stories. 1873.
The little maid. 1874.

The Spanish cavalier: a story of Seville. 1874.
A. L. O. E.'s picture story book. London and Edinburgh 1875.
The haunted room: a tale. 1875.
A wreath of Indian stories. 1876.
Harold Hartley: pictures of St Paul in an English home. [188?]
Idols in the hearth. [188?]
The lost jewel. [188?]
The lake of the woods. [1880?]
Pictures of St Paul in an English home. [188?]
Battling with the world. London and Edinburgh 1881.
Seven perils past: a series of stories. [1882.]
Life in the eagle's nest: a tale of Afghanistan. [1883.]
Rescued from Egypt. 1883 (illus).
Life in the white bear's den: a tale of Labrador. 1884.
Miracles of heavenly love in daily life. 1888.
Tales illustrative of the parables. London and Edinburgh 1891.
Driven into exile: a story of the Huguenots. 1892.
The iron chain and the golden. 1892.
The shepherd of Bethlehem, King of Israel. London and Edinburgh 1900.
Claudia. 1904.

Richard André

The butterfly and the toad. nd.
The oak and the nettle. nd.
The pebble in the brook. nd.
The children's menu; dished up by André to suit all tastes in blue and white and brown plates. 1881.
The cruise of the walnut shell. 1881.
Ada's birthday party. Pictures and a story. 1882.
The animated tea service. Pictures and a story. 1882.
Dottie's big bath: or the seaside. Pictures and words. 1882.
Georgie's money box. 1882.
Grandmother's thimble. 1882.
Jack's slate: scribbles and scratches. 1882.
Upstream: a journey from the present to the past. 1883.
Little blossom: a book of child fancies. 1884.
The magic ring. 1884.
May's muff: or rich and poor. 1884.
Tiny shoes. 1884.
The doormat and the scraper. 1885.
Every day fables. 1885.
The modern giant killer. 1885.
The oak and the nettle. 1885.
A patch-work quilt. 1885.
The outpost. A tale of the backwoods. 1886.
Ebb and Flo. A story of home and abroad. 1887.
Make believe: reality. 1888.
The king's bell tower. 1888.
Colonel Bogey's sketchbook. 1897.
Also illustrated children's books, including those by Mrs Ewing.

Marion Andrews

The quest of Jack Hazelwood. [1891.]
Cousin Isabel. A tale of the siege of Londonderry. 1892.
A loyal heart: a tale of the Cornish coast. 1895.
Countess Helena. 1896.
The child of the lighthouse: a tale of the Great War. 1898.
Cyril the foundling. 1899 (illustr W. H. C. Groome).
Sylvia's romance. 1900 (illustr W. H. C. Groome).

Mary H. Andrews

The story of a little crab. 1886.

'F. Anstey', Thomas A. Guthrie 1856–1934

Vice versa: or a lesson for fathers. 1882, 1883.
Voces populi. 1890.
The man from Blankley's. 1893.
Paleface and redskin, and other stories for boys and girls. 1898.
The brass bottle. 1900.
Only toys. 1903.
In brief authority. 1915.
See also col 1451.

'Henley I. Arden', Henrietta Knight

Aunt Bell, the good fairy of the family. 1890, [1904].
Elizabeth: or cloud and sunshine. London and Edinburgh 1891.
The leather mill farm. 1891 (rptd from Friendly leaves).
Aylmer Court. [1894], [1896].
The Indian chief. [1899.]

'Arabella Argus'

The juvenile spectator; being observations on the tempers, manners and foibles of various young persons. 1810, 1813, 1823, 1835.
The adventures of a donkey. 1814, 1815, 1823, 1860, 1864, 1872, 1878, 1971.
Further adventures of Jemmy Donkey; interspersed with biographical sketches of the horse. 1821, 1830, 1832.
Ostentation and liberality. A tale. 2 vols 1821, [1825?].

Annie E. Armstrong

Ethel's journey to strange lands in search of her doll. 1883.
Madge's mistake: a recollection of girlhood. London and Glasgow [1883].
Marion: or the Abbey Grange. 1892.
Three bright girls: a story of chance and mischance. 1892.
A very odd girl: or life at the gabled farm. 1893.
Spark and I: a story told by a cat. [1894.]
Mona St Clair. London and New York 1897.
Violet Vereker's vanity. '1897'. [1896.]
My ladies three. London and New York 1898.

Frances Charlotte Armstrong, 'F. C. A.'

Florence: or loyal quand même. 1873.
Looking up: or Nanny West and her grandson. [1874], London and New York [1881].
Dick Ford and his father. [1875.]
Phyllis Pengelley. [1875.]
Red herring: or Allie's little blue shoes. A tale for young readers. 1888 (illustr E. L. Thomas), 1893.
Her own way: or Kitty's promise. [1889.]
Noel and Geoff: or three Christmas days. A story for children. [1889.]
The fortunes of ruby, pearl and diamond. [1890.]
Under the walnut tree: stories told by the birds. 1890.
Changed lots: or nobody cares. [1891.]
Old Caleb's will: or the fortunes of the Cardew family. [1893], [1896].
A fair claimant: being a story for girls. 1894, 1900.
A girl's loyalty. 1897.
The general and his daughter. 1907.

Francis Claudius Armstrong

The two midshipmen: a tale of the sea. 1854.
The Battle of the Bosphorus. 1855.
The warhawk: a tale of the sea. 1855, 1858, 1859.

The young commander: a novel. 1856.
Bella Sandford: a tale. 1858.
The new buccaneers: a tale of the sea. 1858.
The young middy: or the perilous adventures of a boy officer among the royalists and republicans of the first French revolution. 1858, 1859, Boston 1867.
The cruise of the Daring: a tale of the sea. 1860.
The lion of war: or the pirates of Loo Chow: a tale of the China seas for youths. 1860.
The frigate and the lugger: a nautical romance. 1861.
The queen of the seas. 1864.
Our blue jackets, afloat and ashore. 1866.
Also wrote adult novels with a nautical theme.

James Leslie Armstrong

Beningborough Hall: a tale of the eighteenth century. 1836.
The heir of St Amerald: or the robber captain. 1845.
Life of Lord Byron. 1846.
Pretty tales for pretty people: or pictures of life. Designed chiefly for the perusal of young persons. 1848.

Jessie F. Armstrong

Birds and their ways. 1884 (illus).
There's a friend for little children. 1884.
Climbing higher. 1887.
Little Phil's Christmas gifts. 1887.
Ernest and Ida: or Christmas at Montague House. 1888.
Lost, stolen or strayed: a story of London life. 1888, 1905, [1907].
For the king and the cross: a story for girls. 1889, 1906.
A shadow on the threshold: or a little leaven. 1889.
Celestine and Sallie: or two dolls and two homes. 1890.
Frank Horton's heritage: or a yoke of bondage. [1890.]
Not like other folks: a city story. 1890, 1903.
Doris's little girl: a story. 1891.
Griggie's pilgrimage: or 'Heaven is my home'. 1891.
From out of the past: a story. 1892.
Westminster chimes. 1893.
St Mervyn's. 1894.
Mark Marksen's secret. A story. [1895.]
Benzoni's children. [1896.]
Kitty Landon's girlhood: a story. 1896.
Eva Chaloner's story: a temptation. [1897.]
Through Rosamund's eyes: a story of the seventeenth century. 1898.
No 6 Victoria Ward: a tale. London and New York 1901.
Zeph Miller: or a brother's love. [1906.]

Edwin Lester Linden Arnold

A summer holiday in Scandinavia. 1877.
England as she seems. Being selections from the notes of an Arab Hadji. 1888.
The wonderful adventures of Phra the Phoenician. 1891, 1898 (illustr H. M. Paget), 1910, 1936.
The constable of St Nicholas. 1894.
The story of Ulla and other tales. 1895.
Little Gullivar Jones: his vacation. 1901, 1905.
Lepidus the centurion. A Roman of to-day. 1901.
Also wrote a number of other bks, including some on coffee cultivation.

Rev John Christopher Atkinson 1814–1900

Walks, talks, travels and exploits of two schoolboys. A book for boys. 1859, 1892, 1898.
Playhours and half holidays: or further experiences of two schoolboys. 1860, 1862.
Lost: or what came from a slip from 'honour bright'. 1870.
The last of the giant killers: or the exploits of Sir Jack of Danby Dale. 1891, 1893 (illustr N. Ericksen).
Scenes in fairyland or Miss Mary's visits to the court of fairy realm. 1892 (illustr C. E. Brock).
Also wrote numerous other bks.

William Atkinson

Western stories. 1893 (illustr W. S. Stacey).

Helen Atteridge

Bunty and the boys. 1888.
Foremost if I can. 1891 (illustr G. Browne), 1891.
Butterfly ballads and stories in rhyme. 1898.
The bravest of the brave, and the story of a soldier, a donkey and a doll. 1900.
Fluffy and Jack. 1900.
The queer house next door. 1900.
To school and away. 1900.
The mystery of Master Max and the shrimps of Shrimpton. 1900.
Uncle Silvio's secret. 1900.

Madame Aublay

The young child's moralist: or the two little brothers. 1827.
The black aunt. Stories and legends for children. (Tr from Ger) Leipzig nd.

Adelaide Austen

Among the mountains: tales for the young. 1871.
Bible stories and their lessons. 1871.
Effie's Christmas and other stories. 1871.
The holidays at Wilton and other stories. Edinburgh 1871.
Noble Joe: or the boy that was washed ashore. Edinburgh 1871.
A book of favourite animals, domestic and wild. Edinburgh 1876, 1893.

Stella Austin d. 1893

Stumps: a story for children. 1873, 1885 (tr Fr).
Somebody. A story for children. 1875, 1883 (tr Fr), 1900.
Not a bit like mother. 1876.
Rags and tatters: a story for boys and girls. 1876.
For old sake's sake. 1877, 1882 (3rd edn), 1898 (4th edn).
Uncle Philip: a tale for boys and girls. 1877, 1903.
Ben Cramer, working jeweller: a tale for boys and girls. 1879.
Pat: a story for children. 1880, (as Pat: a story for boys and girls 1902, 1903).
Our next door neighbour. A story for children. 1881, 1898 (4th edn).
Great grandmother's shoes: a story for children. 1881, 1882 (2nd edn).
Other people. A story of modern chivalry. 1883, 1903.
Wings: a tale. 1883, 1904.
Kenneth's children. A story for boys and girls. 1884, 1903.
Mother Bunch: a story for boys and girls. 1884, 1905.
Two stories of two. Grandmother's darling and a faithful heart. 1885.
Jack Frost's little prisoners: a collection of stories for children from 4 to 12 years of age. 1887 (4th edn).
Tom the hero. 1887 (illus).
Paul's friend. A story for children and the childlike. 1889.
The little Princess Angle: a story for children of all ages. 1890, 1912.
Tib and Sib. A story for children. 1892.

E. L. Aveline

Simple ballads. Intended for the amusement of children. 1810.
The mother's fables in verse. 1812, 1814, 1818, 1824, 1835, 1865.

Charles Harold Avery 1867–1943

The orderly officer. A tale. 1894.
An old boy's yarns: or school tales for past and present boys. 1895.
The school's honour, and other stories. 1894, [1895], 1951.
Frank's first term: or making a man of him. 1896.
A boy all over. 1897.
The triple alliance. [1897?], 1899.
Soldiers of the Queen: or Jack Fenleigh's luck. A story of the dash to Khartoum. 1898.
The dormitory flag. 1899.
Stolen or strayed. 1899.
Mobsley's Mohicans. A tale of two terms. 1900.
Wrote numerous boys' and adult bks in the twentieth century. Many of his early stories appeared in Young England *and he was also a regular contributor to* Captain *and* Boy's Own Paper.

Mrs J. E. Aylmer

Distant homes: or the Graham family in New Zealand. 1862 (illus), 1881, 1888.

Matilda Chaplin Ayrton

Child life in Japan, and Japanese child stories. 1879 (illus), 1888.

John Thomas Watson Bacot

The Bahamas: a sketch. 1869.
Wrote for boys' magazines.

Mrs Clinton Baddeley

A little dog's diary. [1893.]
Also wrote poetry.

Charlotte Bain

Her Beau-Ideal. [1895.]
Ace o' hearts. 1898.
An echo of the spheres. 1919. Poems.

Maria Bainbridge

Rose of Woodlee. A tale. 1843.

Mrs Baker

The little traveller's wanderings in Europe. nd.
Pretty poetry for little children. [1840] (by Augusta and Mrs Sigourney and Mrs Baker).

Lady Amy Susan Baker, née Lady Amy Susan Marryat

Letters to my girl friends. [c. 1890.]
A chaplet of verse for children. 1904.

M. Baker

Emily and her cousins: a tale of real life for little girls. 1828.

Sir Samuel White Baker

Cast up by the sea. A boy's story. 1863 (illus and ed E. Rhys), 1869 (2nd edn), New York 1870, London and New York 1911.
True tales for my grandsons. 1883 (illus).
See also col 2718.

Mrs Alfred Baldwin

The pedlar's pack. nd (illus).
The shadow on the blind and other stories. 1895.
A chaplet of verse for children. 1904.

Clara Lucas Balfour, née Liddell 1808–78

All but lost. nd.
The garland of water flowers, a collection of poems and tales. 1841.
Moral heroism: or the trials and triumphs of the great and good. 1846.
The women of scripture. 1847.
The two Christmas days. [1852.]
Morning dew drops: or the juvenile abstainer. 1853, 1859 (4th edn).
The working women of the last half century: the lesson of their lives. 1854.
The Burnish family. 1857.
Dr Lignum's sliding scale: a story from real life. [1858.]
Glimpses of real life. 1859.
Frank's Sunday coat. 1860.
A peep out of the window: and what came of it. [1860?]
'Scrub': or the workhouse boy's first start in life. 1860.
Toil and trust: or the life-story of Patty, the workhouse girl. 1860, 1875 (4th edn).
Drift: a story of waifs and strays. Glasgow 1861.
Sunbeams for all seasons. 1861.
Uphill work. 1861.
The wanderings of a Bible. 1861.
Confessions of a decanter. 1862.
A mother's lessons on the Lord's prayer. [1862.]
Passages in the history of a shilling. [1862.]
A little voice and a sudden snarl. [1863.]
Cousin Bessie: a story of youthful earnestness. 1863, New York 1865, 1884.
Troubled waters. Glasgow 1864.
Cruelty and cowardice: a story for butchers and their boys. 1866.
One by herself. 1872.
The bond of kindness: a household record for the young. 1873.
Ethel's strange lodger. A story in four chapters. 1874, 1896.
Lame Duck's lantern: a story for children. 1874.
Two Christmas days; and the Christmas box. [188?] (illus).
Joe Tufton: a story of life struggles. [189?]
Also wrote many biographical sketches about contemporary women and tracts for the Scottish Temperance League.

Robert Michael Ballantyne 1825–94.

See col 1096.

Alice Banks

Cheep and chatter: or lessons from field and tree. 1884 (illus), 1888, 1904.

Isabella Banks, née Varley, Mrs G. Linneas Banks 1821–97

More than coronets. 1881 (illus).
See also col 1100.

George Nugent Bankes

A day of my life: or everyday experiences at Eton. 1877.

Helen Bannerman, née Watson, Brodie Cowan Watson 1862–1946

The story of little black Sambo. 1899, 1904, Chicago 1905, 1950, 1952.
The story of little black Mingo. [1901.]
The story of little black Quibba. 1902.
Pat and the spider: the biter bit. [1904.]
The story of little black Quasha. [1908.]
Pieces for the amusement and instruction of young people. Glasgow 1936.
The story of Sambo and the twins. 1937.

Margaret Fraser Barbour

The way home. 1856.
The child of the Kingdom. 1862.
The soul-gatherer. 1864.
The Irish orphan in a Scottish home. 1866.
The bottles broken and how the mischief was remedied. [1875.]
Also pbd evangelical books.

Sabine Baring-Gould 1834–1924

Grettir the outlaw: a story of Iceland. [1889], '1890'.
My Prague pig and other stories for children. 1890.
A book of fairy tales retold. 1894.
The crock of gold. [1899.] Fairy tales.
See also col 1452.

'Mrs Sale Barker', Lucy D. Sale

Puff the Pomeranian and other tales. 1855 (illustr A. W. Cooper).
With a stout heart. [1874.]
Routledge's holiday album for girls. 1877.
The holiday album for children. [1877.]
Little rosy cheek's story book. 1878.
Little rosy lips' story book. 1880.
Little silverlock's story book. 1880.
Pet's picture posies. 1880.
Tiny tots' treasure. 1880.
Little wide awake's pictures, described by Mrs Sale Barker.
Little wide awake's poetry book for children. 1881.
Some of my little friends. 1882.
Those boys. 1882.
Those girls. 1882.
Only a little child. 1883.
Some of my feathered and four footed friends. 1883.
Sunday talks with mama. 1884.
Our friends. A book of original verse. 1887 (illustr F. A. Fraser).
Sunny childhood. 1887 (illustr S. McCloy).
Also contributed to periodicals for children, including Routledge's Every Boy's Mag, *and to Kate Greenaway's* Birthday Book.

Lady Mary Anne Barker, later Broome

A Christmas cake in four quarters. 1871.
Spring comedies. 1871.
Ribbon stories. 1872.
Holiday stories for boys and girls. 1873.
Boys. 1874 (illus).
First lessons on the principles of cooking. 1874.
Sybil's book. 1874.
This troublesome world: or best of stories. 1875.
The white rat and other stories. 1880.
Also wrote books on her life in New Zealand.

Ellen Barlee

Helen Lindsay: or the trial of faith. 1863 (2nd edn).
Helen Macgregor: or conquest and sacrifice. Philadelphia 1865.
Stella Ashton: or conquered faults. Philadelphia 1868, 1871.
Effie's prayer: or 'Thy will be done'. 1871 (2nd edn).
Three paths in life. A tale for girls. 1872.
Good and bad manners. Three stories. 1874.
Locked out. A tale of the strike. 1874.
Life of the Prince Imperial. 1880.
Also pbd on social conditions and emigration.

Frances Catherine Barnard, Mrs Alfred Barnard

Embroidered facts. 1836.
The doleful death and flowery funeral of fancy. 1837. Verse.
The cottage and the hall: carelessness corrected. Yarmouth 1840.
The work-bag. In Mrs Bourne, Observation: or think a minute, 1844.
The schoolfellows: or holidays at the hall. 1845.

Caroline Barnard

The parent's offering: or tales for children. 1813, 1823.
The prize: or the lace makers of Missenden. 1817.
Dick's first school-days. 1875.

Emma J. Barnes

A needle and a thread: a tale for girls. 1873, 1882.
Faithful and true: or the mother's legacy. 1883.

John M. Barnford

Elias Power: or ease in Zion. 1891.

J. M. Barrie

See col 2029.

Fanny Barry

Stories jolly. Stories new. 1889–92.
Soap bubble stories. For children. 1892.
Now for a story. 1893.

Charles H. Barstow

Old Ransom: or light after darkness. A story of street life. [188?]

Dr Christian Gottlof Barth

The Huguenot galley slaves. nd (tr from Ger).
Stories for the young. nd.
Winter evening stories. 1840.
Examples and warnings. 1844.
The raven's feather: a story for children. [1847?], 1867, 1881.
René the young crusader. 1849 (tr from Ger).
Cuff, the negro boy. A story for Christian children. 1849 (tr from Ger by Rev R. Menzies), 1857.
The weaver of Quellbrun: or the roll of cloth. A story for Christian children. 1871 (tr from Ger).
Mick and Nick: or the power of conscience. 1873.

Poor Henry. 1877 (tr from Ger).
Natalie: or the broken spring. 1883 (tr from Ger).

Bernard Barton 1784–1849

Bible letters for children [by Lucy Barton], with introductory verses by B. Barton. 1831, 1862.
Fisher's juvenile scrapbook. 1836 (by A. Strickland and B. Barton).
Natural history of the Holy Land, and other places mentioned in the Bible. 1856.
Pbd numerous verses. See also col 229.

R. C. Barton

Chrysallina, or the butterfly's gala: an entertaining poem addressed to children. 1820.

Louisa Mary Barwell, née Bacon 1800–85

The value of money. 1834.
The value of time: a tale for children. 1834, Boston 1834, 1837.
Edward the Crusader's son. 2 vols 1836.
The elder brother. 1836 (illus).
The novel adventures of Tom Thumb the Great, showing how he visited the insect world, and learned much wisdom. 1838.
Sunday lessons for little children. 1838.
Trials of strength. 1839.
Little lessons for little learners in words of one syllable. Philadelphia 1846.
John Adams. [1850.]
The school. [1850?]
Childhood's hours. 1851 (illus).
Good in every thing: or the early history of Gilbert Harland. 1852, 1886.
Also pbd on infant welfare and child-care.

Mary Batchelor

Mary Chute: or incidents in the life of a village girl. 1885.
The tramp family: or Jack the tinker. 1887.

Mrs Battersby

The riband oath: an Irish story and the lighthouse keepers of Anticosti. 1886.

Diana Bayley, Mrs Henry Bayley

Employment: the true source of happiness: or the good uncle and aunt. 1825.
Tales of the heath for the improvement of the mind. 1825.
Scenes at home and abroad. 1827.
Improvement: or a visit to Grandmama. 1832.

Gertrude Beach

Her guardian ever. Being the story of a young girl's life. 1897.

Anne Beale

Poems. 1842.
The vale of the Towey: or sketches in South Wales. 1844, 1849 (as The vale of the Towey. Traits and stories of the Welsh peasantry).
The Baronet's family. 1852.
Simplicity and fascination: or guardians and wards. 1855, 1860, 1866, 1883.
Gladys the reaper. 1860.
Nothing venture, nothing have. A novel. 1864, 1887.
County courtships. A novel. 3 vols 1869.
Fay Arlington. 3 vols 1875.
The Pennant family. 1876.
The miller's daughter. 3 vols 1878, 1891, 1904.
Rose Mervyn of Whitelake. 3 vols 1879, 1889 (as Rose Mervyn: a tale of the Rebecca riots), 1916.
Idonea. 3 vols 1881.
The young refugee. 1882.
The Queen o' the May. 1883.
Squire Lisle's bequest. 3 vols 1883.
Seven years for Rachel: or Welsh pictures sketched from life. 1886 (an abridgement of The vale of the Towey).
Courtleroy. 3 vols 1887, 1892 (as The heiress of Courtleroy), 1893, 1905, 1906.
Restitution. 1889.
The farm on the down, and old Gwen. 1890.
The twin houses and other tales of real life. 1890.
Contributed extensively to periodicals, especially the Girl's Own Paper between 1880 and 1890.

H. Louisa Bedford

Enid's ugly duckling by H. Louisa Bedford and E. Everett Green. 1896.
The Deerhurst girls: or a triple alliance. 1905.

Catherine Douglas Bell d. 1861

Big Jane: or the disgrace to the school. New York nd.
An autumn at Karnford. 1847, 1866.
George and Lizzie. Edinburgh 1849.
Arnold Lee: or rich children and poor children. [1852], 1866.
Help in time of need: or the Lord careth for his own. 1856, 1866.
Self mastery: or Kenneth and Hugh. 1857.
The diary of three children: or fifty-two Saturdays. Edinburgh [1858], 1863.
The Douglas family. Edinburgh [1858], 1879.
Rest and unrest: or the story of a year. 1858, 1866.
The children's mirror: or which is my likeness? 1859.
The head or the heart: or knowledge puffethe up; charity edifieth. 1859.
Home sunshine. 1859, 1866.
Mike; the shop boy. 1859.
The way to be happy: or the story of Willie, the garden boy. 1859, 1871.
Aunt Ailie. Edinburgh 1861.
Rosa's wish and how she attained it. 1861.
Allen and Harry: or set about it at once. 1866.
The Grahams: or home life. 1866.
Hope Campbell: or know thyself. 1866.
Lily Gordon: or the young housekeeper. 1866.
Margaret Cecil: or I can because I ought. 1866.
We loved him because he first loved us: the story of Ned the shepherd boy. 1871.
Mary Elliott: or kindness of heart. 1876 (illus).
The amulet: or love thy neighbour as thyself. 1885.

Mary Bell

By northern seas. [1887.]
A book of counsel for girls. [1888.]
The lowly life: a simple book for girl workers. [1892.]
Denny Dick. [1894.]
Primroses. [1894.]
A work-a-day world: a Yorkshire story. [1900.]

Robert Stanley Warren Bell, 'Hawkesley Brett' 1871–1921

The refleckshuns of a kuntry pleeceman. 1892.
The papa papers and some stories. 1898.
The duffer. 1906.
Green at Greyhouse. A tale of adventure and mystery at a public school. 1908, 1911, 1924.
Black Evans: a school story. 1912, 1923.
Greyhouse days. 1918.
The three prefects. 1918.
Contributed to boys' mags, especially British Boys, *and became the first editor of* Captain. *He also wrote a number of adult novels.*

Hilaire Belloc 1870–1953

The bad child's book of beasts. 1896.
More beasts for worse children. 1897.
Most of Belloc's work was pbd post 1900.

Mary Belson

See Mary Elliott.

Charles Henry Bennett 1829–67

The frog, who would a-wooing go. 1851, 1864, 1867.
Old Nurse's book of rhymes, jingles and ditties. London and New York 1858 (illustr C. H. Bennett).
The sad history of greedy Jem and his little brother. 1858, 1867 (illustr C. H. Bennett).
The nine lives of a cat: a tale of wonder. 1860.
Oberon's horn. 1861 (illustr C. H. Bennett).
The book of blockheads: how and what they shot, got, and said. 1863.
The stories that little breeches told, and the pictures which Charles Bennett drew for them. 1863.
Mister Wind and Madam Rain. 1864.
Nursery nonsense. 1864.
Fun and earnest. 1865.
Jingles and jokes for little folks. 1865.
The sorrowful ending of Noodledoom with the fortunes and fate of his neighbours and friends. 1865.
The surprising, unheard of and never to be surpassed adventures of young Munchausen. London and New York 1865.
The attractive picture book. 1867.
Lightsome and the little golden lady. 1867 (illustr C. H. Bennett).
Birds, beasts and fishes. An alphabet for boys and girls. 1868.
The faithless parrot. 1870.
Also wrote verse and illustrated a number of fairy stories.

Mary Bennett

The cottage girl: or an account of Ann Edwards, a Sunday school scholar. 1820.
The gipsey bride: or the miser's daughter. 1840, 1841, 1855.
The rose of England: or the adventures of a prince. 1841.
Madge Gordon: or the mistletoe bough. 1843.
The boy's own book of stories from history. 1848, 1850.
Jane Shore: or the goldsmith's wife. [184?], [1850] (Tegg's juvenile series).
Don't tell: or mistaken kindness. 1858, 1861, 1870.
Martha Bell: or the old abbey farm. 1860.
Never mind: or the lost home. 1860, 1861, 1870.
The orphan sisters: or the lover's secret. [1860?]
The book of birthdays. 1868, 1870, 1872.
Edited the Boys' and girls' companion for leisure hours, *1857, 1858, 1860.*

Tertia Bennett

Tiptail: the adventures of a black kitten. 1900 (illus).

Edward White Benson

Education at home: or a father's instruction: miscellaneous pieces for the young. 1824.

Mrs Jane M. Besset

The black princess. A true story for young persons. 1854, 1870.
The lost child. A tale of London streets, and other stories in words of two syllables. 1854.
Memoirs of a doll, written by herself. 1854.

Mrs Best

The mother's jewels. Berwick 1833.
Fanny's birthday. Berwick 1839.

Matilda Barbara Betham-Edwards 1836–1919

Charles and Ernest, or play and work: a story of Hazlehurst school. Edinburgh 1859.
Ally and her school-fellow. A tale for the young. [1861].
Little bird red, and little bird blue. A tale of the woods. 1861 (illustr T. R. Macquoid).
Snowflakes and the stories they told the children. 1862 (illustr H. K. Browne).
Minna's holiday: or country cousins and other stories. London and Belfast 1875.
See also col 1461.

The Hon Augusta Bethell, later Parker

Eyebright: a tale from fairyland. 1863.
Maud Latimer; or patience and impatience: a tale for young people. 1863, 1868 (illus).
Echoes of an old bell, and other tales of fairy lore. [1865.]
Helen in Switzerland: a tale for young people. 1867 (illustr E. Whymper).
Millicent and her cousins. 1870, 1891 (illustr R. Paterson).
A village maiden. 1871.
Feathers and fairies: or stories from the realms of fancy. 1874.
Among the fairies. [1883.]
Also translated works from Norwegian and Spanish.

Favell Lee Bevan, later Mortimer, 'Mrs Mortimer' 1802–78

The peep of day. 1833, 1870, 1881, 1906, 1907. (Translated into several African languages.)
The history of Job in language adapted to children. 1842.
The English mother: or early lessons on the Church of England. 1842.
Tracts for children in streets and lanes, highways and hedges. 1848, 1849.
More about Jesus. 1859.
Lines left out. 1862; (as Children's stories from the Old Testament, 1901), 1915.
Latin without tears: or one word a day. 1871.
Kings of Israel and Judah: their history explained to children. 1872.
Fifty two Bible stories for children. 1892, 1914.

See L. C. Meyer, The author of the Peep of day. Being the life story of Mrs Mortimer, *1901, 1915; E. Bevan,* A law-giver in the nursery, The Times *27 June 1933. Mrs Mortimer also wrote a large number of travel bks, romantic novels and religious texts.*

Tom Bevan, 'Walter Bamfylde' 1868–193?

White ivory and black. A tale of the Zambesi and other stories by T. Bevan, E. Harcourt Burrage and John A. Higginson. 1899.
Also wrote numerous historical adventure stories and contributed to boys' mags.

Mrs M. E. Bewsher

The gypsy's secret: or Deb's revenge. [1871.]
Catherine's peril: or the little Russian girl lost in a forest. Edinburgh 1875.
The little ballet girl. Edinburgh 1875.
Nora and Mildred in the morning of life. [1876.]
Philip Stone and his companions. [1872.]
The young Muscovite. 1874.
Zipporah, the Jewish maiden. [1876], 1891.
Letty's romantic secret. 1902.

Emily Bickersteth, later Durrant

Plain Sunday reading for plough boys. 1857.
The children of long ago. 1863.
School and home: or leaves from a boy's journal. 1864 (2nd edn).
Tom Carter: or the ups and downs of life. A tale for boys going to service. [1865.]
Frances Leslie: or the prayer divinely taught. 1867, 1874, [1876].
Also wrote a number of devotional bks and works on women's rights.

Thomas Bingley

Stories illustrative of the instincts of animals. 1840.
Tales about birds. 1840, 1861 (4th edn), 1864.
Tales about travellers. 1840.
Stories about horses. 1858.
Stories about dogs. 1864.
Tales of shipwrecks and other disasters at sea. 1864.

William Bingley 1774–1823

Animal biography. 3 vols 1804, 4 vols 1820.
Useful knowledge. 3 vols 1816.
Travels in Africa. 1819.

Caroline Birley

We are seven. A tale for children. 1870 (2nd edn, illustr T. Pym), 1880 (3rd edn).
A heap of stones. 1881.
Eyes to the blind. 1886.
Gerald's rescue. 1886.
Jessamine and her lessons books, and how she missed the gipsey tea. 1886.
A Christmas wheatsheaf. 1887.

James Bishop, 'Uncle Know-all'

A visit to the farm. 1835.
Pretty little stories about the kitten, the bird, the myrtle, the lamb, the boat, mischievous habits, the dog, fishing, a visit to the farm, and the little watercress boy. [1838.]
The painted picture play-book. [1855] (illus), 1856 (2nd ser).
Animals (beasts and birds): their pictures, habits and uses. 1857 (illustr H. Weir).
Alphabets and anecdotes of animals. 1859.
Dean's delightful picture book of plain pictures for happy hours. 1860.
Pictures and knowledge. Pretty pages, to make all good little folks as wise as sages. By Uncle Know-All. 1862.
My own new coloured picture play book. 1864.

Thomas Bond Bishop

Walking in the light: or daily pasture for lambs of the flock. 1890.

'Miss Blackburne', Gertrude Mary Ireland

Algernon Sidney. 1885.
In opposition. 1888.
Zig zag. A quiet story. 1888.
A girl's difficulties. 1895.
How God is love. 1900.
In Sunday school. 1904.
Along the road. A book of verse for common days. 1907.
Also wrote a number of religious books.

'Martha Blackford', 'Mrs Blackford', Isabella Mary Stoddart

The Eskdale herd-boy, a Scottish tale for the amusement and instruction of young persons. 1819, 1824, 1828 (3rd edn), New York 1828, 1850, Boston 1853.
The Scottish orphans: a moral tale. Founded on historical fact: and calculated to improve the minds of young people. 1822, 1823, New York 1830, 1835, Paris 1839, Philadelphia 1843, 1857, London 1862.
Arthur Montieth: a moral tale calculated to improve the minds of young people. Being a continuation of The Scottish orphans. 1822, 1823, New York 1824, 1828.
Annals of the family of McRoy. 1823.
The young artist. 1825.
William Montgomery: or the young artist. 1829.

Richard Doddridge Blackmore 1825–1900

Lorna Doone: a romance of Exmoor. 3 vols 1869.
See also col 1103.

Mrs George Blagden

A little summer shower. 1887.
Trash: a tale of Brittany. 1891.
Pixie: or two little English girls in France. 1893 (illus).

Robert Bloomfield 1766–1823

The history of little Davy's new hat. 1815 (pbd anonymously), 1817, 1818, 1824, 1878.
The bird and insect's post office. 1880 (with a preface by Walter Bloomfield).
See also col 235.

Ellen M. Blunt

Twenty stories for the young. In prose and verse. [1876.]
Chats with my girls. 1894 (rptd from the Gospeller).
Thoughts by the way. Simple readings for all classes. 1895.

Just confirmed. 1896, 1904.
Carol, sweetly Carol. [1899.]
Jim's temptation. 1901.
As a sister, and the little white ball. 1904.
Brave Betty. 1904.
Archie's Christmas presents. 1913.
Also wrote religious bks.

Miss F. A. Blyth

The missing jug. 1896.
Mabel's white kitten and a discontented boy. 1896.

Harry Blyth, 'Hal Meredith' 1852–98

Eat, drink and be merry: or dainty bits from many tables. 1877.
The Old Bailey: an historical romance. 1879.
The secret of Sinclair's farm. 1887.
The black pirate. A stirring story of the sea. 1893.
Edited Marvel, *and contributed to many boys' periodicals.*

Jane Boden

Pleasant stories in prose and verse. 1881, 1889.
Little Toddles' story book. 1881.

Frederica Bodmer

Back to the Father's house. A parable. 1880.
The fairy cave. 1884.

Sybilla Mary Crawford Boevey

Topsy Turvey. [188?] (illus).
Also pbd adult novels.

Harriett Boultwood

Donald's charge. [1885.]
My lady May, and one other story. [1887.]
The adventures of a sixpence. [1888.]
Two little helpers and what they wrought. [1888.]
Up to the mark? A schoolboy's story. [1888.]
Brave and loyal: or lessons from the life of Joseph. 1890.
Clerk or carpenter? A story for boys. 1890.
Dot's scarlet geranium. 1890.
The dunce of the school. 1890.
Hero's story. The autobiography of a Newfoundland dog. Edinburgh 1890, [1906].
Little spangles: or trust in God. 1890.
Martin's mistake. [1890.]
Robbie's ambition. [1890.]
A sailor's darlings, and how they were cared for. [1890.]
All for himself. A story for boys. 1891.
As gold is tried: or through trial to triumph. [1893.]
Cecil Arlington's quest. A story. 1898 (3rd edn).

William St Hill Bourne

Taken home: a dream poem. [1873.]
Also wrote religious poems and contributed to boys' mags.

Mrs C. E. Bowen

The babes in the basket: or Daph and her charge. 1850, 1861, 1864, 1865, 1870, 1890.
Church Robin: or Christmas Eve. 1862.
Harry and the fourpenny piece: or honesty answers back. 1862.
Timid Lucy. 1862.
Dick and his donkey: or how to pay the rent. 1863, 1869, 1932.
Work for all and other stories. 1863.
Philip Markham's two lessons. 1864.
Sybil and her live snowball. 1865.
Ashgrove Farm: or a place for everyone. 1866.
Harry's monkey. How it saved the missionaries. 1866.
How Paul's penny became a pound. 1866.
How Peter's pound became a penny. 1866.
Faithful Bessie. 1867.
Farmer Ellicott: or begin and end with God. 1867.
Jack the conqueror: or difficulties overcome. 1868.
Christian Hatherley's childhood. 1869, 1872 (illus).
The young potato roasters. 1869.
The boy guardian. 1870.
Muftie's adventures in search of admiration. 1871.
Nobody's child. 1871.
Charley and son. 1872.
Johnnie's marketings. 1872.
New stories on an old subject. 1872.
Ben's boyhood. 1873.
Charlie Tyrell. 1873.
Grandmamma's relics and her stories about them. 1873.
Alice Neville: or a little child shall lead them. 1874 (illus).
Riversdale. 1874.
Among the brigands and other tales of adventure. 1875 (illus).
The brook's story. 1878.
The choristers of St Ethelberg. 1878.
How a farthing made a fortune: or honesty is the best policy. 1879, 1886.
Cared for: or the orphan wanderers. 1881.
The falcon's nest. 1882.
A winter night's adventure. 1882.
Harry's monkey: how it helped the missionaries by Mrs C. E. Bowen and How Sadie slipped by Jennie Chappell. [1890.]
Herbert's first year at Bramford. 1890.
Minnie's birthday story: or what the brook said. 1911.
Some works of Sarah Schoonmaker Baker were attributed to Mrs C. E. Bowen.

Anne Bowman

The castaways: or the adventures of a family in the wilds of Africa. 1837, 1857.
My mother's stories. 1838.
Laura Temple. 1853.
Travels of Rolando: or a tour round the world. 1853, 1854, 1857, 1859.
Esperanza: or the home of the wanderers. 1855.
The Norman invasion and the day of Rinrory. 1857. Poems.
The young exiles: or the wild tribes of the north. 1858.
The boy voyagers: or the pirates of the east. 1859 (illustr H. Weir).
The kangaroo hunters: or adventures in the bush. 1859, Philadelphia 1859.
Sunshine and clouds in the morning of life. 1860.
Among the tartar tents: or the lost fathers. 1861, 1875.
The bear hunters of the Rocky Mountains. 1861, Boston 1868, Philadelphia [187?].
How to make the best of it: a domestic tale for young ladies. 1862.
Clarissa: or the Mervyn inheritance. A tale for young ladies. 1863 (illustr J. A. Pasquier).
The rector's daughter. A tale for the young. 1864 (illus).
The young yachtsman: or the wreck of the Gypsy. London and New York 1865.

The boy pilgrims. 1866.
Tom and the crocodiles. 1867.
The boy foresters. A tale of the days of Robin Hood. [1868], 1869.
The young Nile voyagers. 1868 (illus).
Also wrote bks on acting, domestic economy and poetry. For other works, especially on domestic economy, see incomplete list at end of My mother's stories, *1838.*

Hetty Bowman, Henrietta Bowman 1838–72

Our village girls. 1863, 1886.
Evelyn Howard: a tale. [1865.]
Chapters in the life of Elsie Ellis. Edinburgh 1869, 1886.
Lily Hope and her friends: a tale. Edinburgh 1873, [1885].
Mary's work, and other tales for her young friends. Edinburgh 1874, 1886.
Also wrote a number of bks on moral theology.

Sir John Bowring 1792–1872

Minor morals for young people, illustrated in tales and travels. 3 pts 1834–9 (illustr G. Cruikshank and W. Heath).
Wrote on religion, politics, law and poetry. See also col 238.

Eleanor Vere Boyle, Mrs Boyle, the Hon Mrs Richard Cavendish Boyle 1825–1916

Seventeen drawings. [1852], [1859], [1869].
A children's summer. 1853 (illus).
Child's play. [1853.]
The May Queen. 1861 (illustr E. V. Boyle).
Waifs and strays from a scrap book. 1862.
In the fir-wood. 1866 (illus).
A dream book. 1870.
Beauty and the beast. 1873 (retold and illus).
A new child's play. 1877.
Days and hours in a garden. 1884, 1896.
A book of the heavenly birthdays. 1894 (2nd edn).
Seven gardens and a palace. 1900.
The peacock's pleasance. 1908.
Also wrote and illus bks on art and gardening and translated bks from Ger.

Mary Louisa Boyle 1819–90

Woodland gossip. 1864 (tr from Ger).
Also wrote dramatic verse and adult fiction.

E. C. Boyse

Murdered or . . . ? A tale. nd.
That most distressful country. 1886.

Elizabeth Jane Brabazon

Outlines of the history of Ireland for schools and families. 1844, 1847, 1865.
Historical tales from the history of the Muslims in Spain. 1853.
Home happiness: or three weeks in snow. 1855.
Also wrote travel guides.

Edward Bradley, 'Cuthbert Bede' 1827–89

Fairy fables. 1858 (illustr A. Crowquill).
Little Mr Bouncer and his friend. [1873].
Happy hours at Wynford Grange. A story for children. 1859.
See also col 1101.

Sheila E. Braine

Cynthia's holiday. 1896.
To tell the king the sky is falling. London and New York [1896] (illus).
The luck of the Eardleys. 1898.
Up the rainbow stairs. [1898.]
The Princess of hearts. [1899], 1934.
The Turkish automaton. 1899, 1912.
Pets and pastimes. 1900.
With Rupert the brave. [1900.]
A young crusader. 1901.
The King's blue boys. 1902.
Fifine and her friends. A story for girls. 1903.
Sparks from the nursery fire. 1903.
The little brown linnet. 1904.
Pleasant surprises. 1904.
Pip Pip. 1906.
Our happy holiday. 1907.
That lucky visit. 1913.
Also wrote a number of bks of verses.

Mary Eliza Bramston 1841–1912

The snowball society: a story for children. 1877.
Everingham girls. 1886.
Home and school. A story for girls. 189? (illustr A. Pearse). Sequel to The snowball society.
Rosamund's girls: a school story. [189?], 1905? (illustr H. Piffard).
The little treasure book of hymns and poems. [1891.]
Five victims. A schoolroom story. [1892.]
The story of a cat and a cake during the Thirty Years War. [1896.]
A girl's outlook. 1903.
The prince hereditary. A romance for boys. 1904.
Barbara's behaviour: a story for girls. 1907.
Also wrote numerous novels for adults.

Caroline Bray, Mrs Charles Bray, née Hennell 1814–1905

Paul Bradley. A village tale inculcating kindness to animals. 1876.
Little Mop and other stories. 1886.
Branded: or the sins of the Fathers shall be visited on the children. 1888.
Also wrote school textbooks.

'Brenda', Mrs G. Castle Smith

Froggy's little brother. [1875.]
Nothing to nobody. 1875.
Lotty's visits to Grandmama. 1877 (illus).
A Saturday's bairn. [1877.]
Victoria Bess: or the ups and downs of a doll's life. 1879 (illustr T. Pym).
Fynie's flower. 1880.
Little cousins: or Georgie's visits to Lotty. 1880.
Without a reference: a Christmas story. 1882.
Old England's story in little words for little children. 1884 (illustr S. P. Hall and others).
Five little partridges: or the pilot's house. 1885 (illus).
Dinah Mite. 1887.
The shepherd's darling. [1888], 1931.
Uncle Steve's locker. 1888 (illustr T. Pym).
The earl's granddaughter. 1896.
Wonderful mates. 1900.
A little brown tea-pot. [1902]; as Rosamund's home: or a little brown tea-pot, 1927.

The secret terror. 1909.
Mary Pillenger. 1912.
More about Froggy: a sequel to Froggy's little brother. [1914.]
Opened doors. The story of Sonny Baba. 1932, 1945.
Also wrote a number of religious bks.

E. J. Brett, Edwin John Brett 1828–95

Boys of England cricket guide. 1867.
Brett's illustrated naval history of Great Britain from the earliest period to the present time. 1871.
Brett's housekeeper and guide. 1872.
Edwin J. Brett's Harkaway series of stories. Vol 1 containing Jack Harkaway's schooldays, complete with numerous illustrations and coloured plates. 1877.
Edwin J. Brett's Jack Harkaway among the brigands. 1878?
Edwin J. Brett's Jack Harkaway's schooldays. 1880.
Edwin J. Brett's Jack Harkaway and his son's adventures in Australia. 1899.
Edwin J. Brett's Jack Harkaway and his son's adventures in Greece. 1899.
A pictorial and descriptive record of the origin and development of arms and armour. 1894.
Edwin J. Brett's adventures of Young Jack Harkaway and his boy tinker... sometimes attributed to Bracebridge Hemying. 1900.
Brett was a prolific author of sensational novels for adults, bks on armour and the editor of a number of boys' sensational weeklies.

C. E. Broad

Mary Lorn: the story of an ocean waif. A tale for the young. Glasgow 1879.

Janie Brockman

Bert. nd.
Buffer's best and his father's son. nd.
Scrap: or the mystery of Davington caves. A story for boys and girls. nd (illus).
Seven o'clock. A home story for home loving children. 1884.
Worth doing. 1890 (illus).
Right side up. [1895.]
The old tin box: or a missing legacy. 1900.

Frances Freeling Broderip, née Hood 1830–78

Way side fancies. 1857.
The orphans of Elfhold, and other stories. Containing the poor cousin, The young forester. [186?]
Funny fables for little folks. 1860 (illustr T. Hood).
Chrysal: or a story with an end. 1861 (illustr T. Hood).
Fairyland: or recreation for the rising generation by the late Thomas and Jane Hood, their son and daughter. 1861 (ed F. F. Broderip, illustr T. Hood).
Tiny tadpole, and other tales. 1862 (illustr T. Hood).
My grandmother's budget of stories and songs. 1863 (illustr T. Hood).
Peter Drake's dream. 1863, 1869.
The daisy and her friends: simple tales and stories for children. 1864 (illus), 1869.
Wee Maggie. 1864.
Crosspatch, the crickets and the counterpane: a patchwork of story and song. 1865 (illustr T. Hood).
Merry songs for little verses. 1865 (illus).
Mamma's morning gossips: or little bits for little birds. Being easy lessons for a month. 1866 (illustr T. Hood).
Wild roses: or simple stories of country life. 1867 (illus).
The daisy and her friends: simple tales and stories for children. 1869.
Tales of the toys, told by themselves. 1869 (illustr T. Hood).
The whispers of a shell: or stories from the sea. 1871 (illus).
Merry songs for little voices. 1864 (illus). With T. Hood.
Edited works by Tom Hood.

Emily Brodie

Rough the terrier: his life and adventures. 1879.
Lonely Jack and his friends at Sunnyside. 1882, [1893?].
Little Nell the flower seller. [1890.]
Old Christie's cabin. [1890.]
Right about face: or Ben the Gordon boy. 1891, 1896.
Norman and Elsie: or two little prisoners. [1894.]
Also pbd novels for adults.

Mary Isabella Irwin Brotherton

Poems. 1855, Brussels 1855 (2nd edn).
Arthur Brandon. 2 vols 1856.
Respectable sinners. 1863, 1865.
Old acquaintance. 1874.
Rosemary for remembrance. 1895. Poems.

Louisa Brown

The heathen mythology in easy and pleasing verses... intended for the instruction of young ladies. 1810.
Historical questions on the Kings of England in verse. Calculated to fix in the minds of children. 1815.

'Maggie Brown', Margaret Hamer, later Andrewes

Creatures tame. [1884.]
Little mothers and their children. [1884.]
Our schoolday hours. [1884.]
Our holiday hours. 1887.
Up and down the garden. [1887.]
Wandering ways. 1889.
Wanted a king: or how Merle set the nursery rhymes to rights. 1890.
Rub-a-dub tales – firelight stories. [1892.]
Sunday stories for small people. [1893.]
Bright tales and funny pictures. 1894.
Two old ladies, two foolish fairies and a tom cat. 1897.
Kurus: the King of the Cannibal islands. 1900.

Frances Browne 1816–79

The Ericksons. The clever boy: or consider another. Two stories for my young friends. 1852.
Granny's wonderful chair and its tales of fairy times. 1856, 1871 (illustr M. S. Lucas), 1906 (ed D. Radford, EL), 1963 (ed R. L. Green).
See also col 1144.

'A Nobody', Gordon Frederick Browne 1858–1932

Nonsense for somebody, anybody or everybody particularly the baby body. [1896.]
Some more nonsense for the same bodies as before. [1896.]

Jane Euphemia Browne, later Saxby 1811–98

The dove on the cross. 1849, 1853, 1859.
The child. From the Dove on the cross. 1862.
Sam Bolton's cottage: and what kept his wife from church. 1865.

'Carlton Bruce'

See George Mogridge.

Charles Bruce

Dick Barford: a boy who would go downhill. Edinburgh [1871].

Emily M. Bryant

'Jack'. The story of a scapegrace. 1897.
Norma: a school tale. 1897.
The doings of Denis and other stories. 1898.
Dolly and Syb at boarding school. 1898.
Kitty Lonsdale and some Rumsby folk. 1898.
A little pair and what they did. 1900.
The nine. A family history. 1900.
The North Sea, Lassie and other stories. 1900.

John Buchan 1875–1940

Sir Quixote of the moors. 1895.
John Burnet of Barns. 1897.
The one in the middle and other stories. 1903.
Prester John. 1910.
The thirty-nine steps. 1915.
The magic walking stick. 1932.
Most of Buchan's writing for adults was pbd in the twentieth century. See his Memory hold-the-door, *1940; J. A. Smith,* John Buchan, *1965.*

'Ruth Buck', Mrs Ruth Buck Lamb

Grateful Peter's new year gift. nd.
The longest way round for the shortest. nd.
Milly's mistakes and what she learned by them. nd.
How Charley helped his mother. 1850, [1861], Philadelphia 1870.
Old Cantanker: or what came of the flower show. nd.
Trials of a village artist. 1860, 1862 (as Dick Fraser, or the trials of a village artist), Philadelphia 1868.
Midsummer at Hay Lodge. London and Edinburgh 1861, 1870.
A little child's day and what she learned in it. [1862.]
The touch of the fairies. 1862.
It isn't right: or Frank Johnson's reason. 1863, 1878.
The experiences of Tom Neal and Sarah his wife. 1864.
Pleasant paths for little feet. [1864.]
The carpenter's family: a sketch of village life. 1865.
Master and servant: or Richard Owen's choice. 1865, [1882] (as Richard Owen's choice; being the history of one who would not work on Sundays).
Jem Morrison, the fisher boy. [1872.]
Sturdy Jack. [1877.]
Look on the sunny side, and other sketches. 1888.
Katie Brightside: or how she made the best of everything. 1895.
Joe's first earnings: or the wickedest weed of all. 1896.

Anna Jane Buckland b. 1827

The little Warringtons. [1860], [1961] (illustr E. Hall).
Twelve links of a golden chain. 1860, 1861.
Lily and Nannie at school. A story for little girls. London and New York 1868.
Noble rivers and stories concerning them. 1868.
The hillside farm. [1869] (illus).
The diary of Nanette Dampier during the years 1864–66. Edinburgh 1870.
Love and duty: or the happy life. 1870.
Stories about our pets by A. J. Buckland and H. Bowman. 1870.

Arabella Burton Buckley, later Mrs Fisher

The fairyland of science. 1879 (illus), 1906 (tr Danish), 1893 (tr Polish).
Life and her children. 1880, 1954.
Winners in life's great race: or the great backboned family. 1888 (illus).
Through magic glasses and other lectures. A sequel to The fairyland of science. 1890.
History of England for beginners. 1891, 1914.
History of England. 1892.
Cassell's Eyes and no eyes series. 1901, 1928.
Also wrote a number of bks on the history of science.

'A mother', Maria Elizabeth Budden, née Halsey

1780?–1832

Always happy!: or anecdotes of Felix and his sister Serena. A tale. 1814, 1815, 1818, 1820, 1823, 1824, [1828?], [1829?], 1833, 1840, 1847.
Right and wrong, exhibited in the history of Rosa and Agnes. 1815, 1818, 1822, 1829.
Nursery morals. 1818, 1837.
The pleasures of life. Written for her children. 1818.
Women: or minor maxims. A sketch. 1818.
Hints on the sources of happiness. Addressed to her children by a mother. 1819.
Nina, an Icelandic tale. Written for her children by a mother. 1819, [1845?] (3rd edn).
True stories from ancient history: chronologically arranged. 1819, 1821, 1825, 1830, 1835.
A key to knowledge: or things in common use simply and shortly explained. 1820 (3rd edn), 4th edn 1823, 1824, [1825?], [1827?], 1830; tr Sp [1829?].
Valdimar; or the career of falsehood: a tale for youth. 1820.
Claudine: or humility the basis of all the virtues. A Swiss tale. 1822, 1823, 1826, 1830, 1833, 1835, 1881.
True stories from modern history: chronologically arranged. 1824, 1825, 1834.
Women. Helen Egerton: or traits of female character. 1824.
Chit chat, or short tales in short words. 1825, 1831, 1859.
True stories from English history. 1825, 1831, 1834, 1852.
Thoughts on domestic education: the results of experience. By a mother. 1826.
Hoefer, the Tyrolese. [1828], [1829].
Nursery morals, chiefly in monosyllables. 1837.

Selina Bunbury 1802–82

Annot and her pupil: a simple story. 1827.
The triumphs of truth: or Henry and his sister. [1847.]
The blind clergyman and his little guide. 1850.
See also col 1161.

Florence E. Burch

Billy the acorn gatherer. [1886.]
No royal road: or the thing that lies the nearest. A story for girls. [1886.]
Joseph Adams: or two ways of facing life. [1886.]
How it came about. 1887.
Squirrel: or back from a far country. 1888.
Therefore: or Nessie's ideal. [1888.]
The broken strap: or her great reward. [1889.]

Farmer Bluff's dog Blazer: or at the eleventh hour. 1889.
Annie's 'Yes': the saving of him. 1890.
The cottage by the moor. 1890.
Farmer Hardy's watercress bed. 1890.
Two little fortune hunters: or where duty calls. [1890.]
Dick and Harry and Tom: or 'For our reaping by-and-by'. [1891], London and Edinburgh 1893.
Led by a little child: or the blind basket-maker. [1891], 1907.
Rollo and Tricksy: the story of a little boy and girl. 1891.
Ragged Simon: or Monkey's inheritance. [1892.]
Chris Willoughby: or against the current. A tale for boys. 1893.
Mrs Martin's little boy. [1893.]
Josh Jobson, or 'Pards'. [1894.]
Jack and Gill: or for his enemy. 1899, 1909.
Pete and his father. 1901, 1908.
Filling her place: or Nessie's ideal. 1913.
How Tilly found a friend. 1914.

Harriette E. Burch

More than conqueror: or a boy's temptation. [1888.]
'Sprats alive oh!' [1888].
Stella Rae: or the yoke of love. [1888.]
The avenger. [1889.]
Lally the hop-picker, or gathered in. [1890.]
Ivy's dream: or each one his brick. [1891.]
Jacko: a story for the young. 1891.
Jacob's sunbeam. 1891, 1907.
Ina and Kitty: or the little flower girl and her friend. 1892.
Bible Noel: or one step enough. [1893.]
Captain of the school. A story for boys. [1894.]
Bab: or tit for tat. [1895.]
The wind and wave: a story of the siege of Leyden. 1901.
Also worked as a translator.

Mrs Burden, née Corner

The three baskets: or how Henry, Richard and Charles were occupied while Papa was away. [1840?], [1850?].
The favourite dog and the idle cat. In words of one syllable. [1854], 1857.
James and Ann: or truth is best. By Miss Corner (or rather by Mrs Burden). In words of one syllable. [1854.]
The lame boy: or how he learned to read and write. [1854.]
Little Miss Fanny and her trip to the sea-shore. [1854], 1857.
The stray child. Mostly in words of one syllable. [1854], 1857.
Short stories in short world: about the lame boy; the sea shore; the cross boy; and the stray child. [1855?] (illus).
The faithful dog. [1857.]

Mrs C. B. Burkhardt

Fairy tales and legends of many nations. Dublin 1849.

'Darcy Burn', T. Sparrow

Tom in a tangle and other tales.

Mrs Burn

John Elton: or the results of anger, and Johnie the 'Bocher'. 1888.

Frances Eliza Hodgson Burnett

See col 1474.

Helen Marion Burnside 1844–1923

The little V. C. 1898.

Edwin Harcourt Burrage, 'Hal Strangeway'

The street waif. [1876?]
Gerard Mastyn, the son of a genius. 1877, 1895.
Crusoe Jack, the king of a thousand islands. 1880.
The King's hussars: a tale of India. 1880.
Tomahawk and rifle. 1880.
Broadarrow Jack. 1884, 1887, 1890.
For honour: or the young privateer. 1885.
Jack and Joe: or the troublesome twins. 1885.
Rags and riches. A story of three poor boys. 1885.
Daring Ching Ching. 1886.
Handsome Harry of the fighting Belvedere. 1886.
Wonderful Ching Ching. His further adventures. 1886.
Young Ching Ching. 1886, 1900.
Ching Ching on the trail. A new style of detective story. 1890.
Giant Jack: a story of the Red Mountains. 1890.
The wild adventures of Jam Josser and Edward Cutten at home and abroad. 1890, 1894.
Tom Tartar at school: or True friend and noble foe. 1891, 1892.
The brand of the black star. [1892?]
Dick Stornoway: or a hero in spite of his foes. 1892.
Donald Drew: or pressed for a privateer. 1892.
Giles Evergreen: or fresh from the country. 1892.
Hal o' the hearth: the wandering heir. 1892.
Lionel the bold: or the circus rider's revenge. 1892.
Boy of a thousand. 1893.
Daring Dave: or the treasures of the deep. 1893.
Football in Coketown: or who shall be captain? 1893.
Jack Coeur de Lion, outcast and hero. 1893.
Jack jaunty: or friend and foe. 1893.
The mutiny of the lapwing. [1893?]
Plucky Phil Farren: or the mystery of Brythewaite School. 1893.
Two gallant hearts: or bravery against knavery. 1893.
The veiled captain: or the hero of Eagle Craig. [1893?]
Will waif, boy of a thousand. 1893.
The school days of young Ching Ching. 1894.
The slapcrash boys. The liveliest of school stories. 1894, 1899.
The lambs of Littlecote. 1894, 1895.
Bob Hardy, agitator. A novel. 1895.
The five swordsmen, or the royal guard. 1895.
Hardiboy James: or chums and chappies. A sensational story of school life. 1895.
The island school. A story of school life and adventure. 1895.
Through perils dire: or gallant Willie Gray. 1895.
Tom Terrybell: the leader of Langton School. A splendid school story. 1895.
The slave raiders of Zanzibar, etc. 1896.
The missing million. 1897.
Out of the deep. A story of the Brays of Beachtown. 1898.
The vanished yacht. 1898.
The man who found Klondyke. 1899.
The slapcrash boys. The liveliest of school stories. 1899.
Cheerful-daring-wonderful Ching Ching. 1900.
Dick Strongbow, the diamond king. The wonder of the world. 1900.
The fatal nugget. 1900.
John Blessington's enemy. A story of life in South Africa. 1900.
The twin castaways. 1900.
Carbineer and spirit. A story of the great Boer war. 1901.
The Wurra Wurra boys. 1903.
A knowing dog. The story of a poodle, much loved and often lost. 1908.

Never beaten. The story of a boy's adventures in Canada. 1908.
Wrote extensively for boys' popular weekly periodicals, and wrote guidebooks and other bks.

Mrs E. Burrows

Sunlight through the mist: or practical lessons drawn from the lives of good men. 1854, 1855, 1860, 1864.
The triumphs of steam: or stories from the lives of Watt, Arkwright and Stephenson. 1859.
Tuppy: or the autobiography of a donkey. 1860 (illustr H. Weir).
The meadow lea: or the gipsy children. 1862.
Tiny stories for tiny children in tiny words. 1864.
Trottie's story book: or true tales in short words and large type. 1866.
Neptune: or the autobiography of a Newfoundland dog. 1869.

Annie Robina Butler

Little sufferers and little workers: or stories about medical missions. 1877.
Glimpses of Maori land. 1886.
Stories about China. 1887.
Stories about Japan. 1888.
In the beginning: or stories from the book of Genesis. 1889 (illus).
Little Kathleen: or sunny memories of a child worker. 1890.
The promised king: or the story of the children's saviour. 1890 (illus).
The children's king. The life of Jesus retold for young readers. 1900 (illus).
A gift for a pet. With verses by R. H. Butler. 1896.

Cecilia Mary Caddell d. 1877

Flower and fruit: or the use of tears. nd.
Blind Agnese: or the little spouse of the blessed sacrament. 1856 (2nd edn), 1861 (3rd edn).
The martyr maidens of Ostend. A legend of the eighteenth century. 1858.
Wild times: a tale of the days of Queen Elizabeth. 3 vols 1865.
The miner's daughter: a Catholic tale. 1866.
Also wrote adult fiction.

Oliver Vernon Caine b. 1862

Face to face with Napoleon: an English boy's adventures in the Great War. [1898.]

Randolph Caldecott 1846–86

R. Caldecott's collection of pictures and songs. 8 pts. [1881], [1886], London and New York 1906–7 (reissue of 14 pts).
The hey diddle diddle picture book. 4 pts. 1883.
A sketch book of R. Caldecott's. [1883.]
The Panjandrum picture book. 4 pts. 1885.
R. Caldecott's picture books. 16 pts. 1878–84 (1st 8 pts reissued 1879–81).
Illustrated numerous children's books.

Maria Hutchins Callcott, née Graham

Home among strangers: a tale. 1848.
The singer's alphabet: or hints on the English vowels. 1849.
The power of meekness. 1853.
Two firesides: or the mechanic and the tradesman. A tale of ninety years ago. 1859.
Also wrote on household management and philanthropy.

J. M. Callwell

Legends of olden times. Adapted from the German. 1880.
Little curiosity: the story of a German Christmas. 1884, 1887.
The squire's grandson: a Devonshire story. 1888.
Timothy tatters: a story for the young. 1890, 1900, [1909].
Town and country mice. 1891.
The rival princes. A story of the 14th century. 1893.
A champion of the faith. A tale of Prince Hal and the Lollards. 1894.
Dorothy Arden. A story of England and France two hundred years ago. 1897, 1904.
One summer by the sea. 1899.
A little Irish girl. 1902.
Old Irish life. 1912.

Maria Cambwell

Minnie Neilson's summer holidays and what came of them. 1889.

Charles Camden

The boys of Axelford. 1869 (illus), London and New York 1880.
When I was young: or Gideon and his grandchildren. 1872.
Hoity toity, the good little fellow. 1873, 1882, 1884. Rptd from Good Words for the Young.
The travelling menagerie. 1873 (illus). Rptd from Good Words for the Young.

Lucy Littleton Cameron, née Butt 1781–1858

The history of Margaret Whyte. nd. Written 1798 but not pbd until later.
The two lambs. 1821.
The polite little children. 1822 (6th edn).
See Life, *ed C. Cameron 1862, [1873] (rev G. T. Cameron).*

Verney Lovett Cameron, Commander V. L. Cameron

Our future highway. 1880.
Harry Raymond: his adventures among pirates, slavers and cannibals. 1886, 1887.
The queen's land: or Ard al Malakat. 1886.
In savage Africa: or the adventures of Frank Baldwin from the Gold Coast to Zanzibar. 1887 (illus), [1920].
Jack Hooper. His adventure at sea and in South Africa. 1887.
The adventures of Herbert Massey in Eastern Africa. 1888 (illus).
Among the Turks. 1890.
Three sailor boys: or adrift in the Pacific. 1901, [1926.]
Reverse the shield. 1926.
See W. R. Foran, African odyssey. The life of V. Lovett Cameron, *1957.*

Mrs C. C. Campbell

Natural history for young folks. 1884 (illus).
Home for the holidays. A tale. 1886 (illus).

E. A. Campbell

Miss Priss. [1888.]
The escape of the fugitives. A tale of Sedgmoor. [1895.]
Her soldier laddie. 1900.

Mrs Edmund Campbell

Buckets and spades, nursery rhymes, words. nd (illus).

Elizabeth Anne Campbell

Life unfolding: a poem for the young. [1862.]

Gertrude Elizabeth Campbell, née Blood, 'G. E. Brunefille', Lady Colin Campbell 1863–1911

The story of an apple. nd.
Topo: a tale about English children in Italy. 1881 (illustr K. Greenaway).
Also pbd other books on natural history and etiquette.

Sir Gilbert Edward Campbell

Prince Goldenblade: a rational fairy tale for big and little folks. 1889 (illustr R. André).
Also pbd numerous adult bks.

Mrs Graham Campbell

Louisa's metrical English grammar. Cheltenham and London 1861.
One hundred voices from nature: or apples of gold in a network of silver. 1861. Poems.
Christabelle and our little white rose. 1867.

John Campbell 1766–1840

A scripture catechism for the instruction of youth. 1801.
A picture of human life, drawn for the instruction and entertainment of youth. Edinburgh 1802.
Alfred and Galba: or the history of two brothers supposed to be written by themselves. For the use of young people. 1805, 1810, Boston 1812, Northampton 1817; as The two brothers or the history of Alfred and Galba 1822, 1831.
Worlds displayed for the benefit of young people. 1805, 1807, Catskill NY 1809, Boston 1811, 1815, 1819, Lewes, Sussex 1823.
Remarkable particulars in the life of Moses. 1808.
Voyages and travels of a Bible. 1814.
A recent instance of the Lord's goodness to children, exemplified in the happy death of J. Steven. [1815?]
Voyages to and from the Cape of Good Hope, in the years 1812 and 1814. 1816, 1819, 1840 (with An account of a journey into the interior of Africa).
The old world: or remarkable occurrences during the last 120 years before the flood, supposed to be taken from Noah's journal. Designed for young persons. 1818.
The journeys of Julius in North Africa. Part 1 written for the instruction and amusement of youth. 1824.
The juvenile cabinet of travels and narratives, for the amusement and instruction of young persons. London, Dublin and Edinburgh 1825, 1826, 1831.
Also wrote accounts of African tribes, travel and religious texts.

Lady Pamela Campbell

The story of an apple. 1853, 1856.
The cabin by the wayside: a tale for the young. 1854, 1855.
Martin Tobin: a novel. 3 vols 1864.

Walter Douglas Campbell

Beyond the border. 1898.
Auld Robin the farmer. A poem. 1894 (illustr Princess Louise).

William Canton

A child's book of saints. 1898 (illustr T. H. Robinson), 1902 (EL).
The reign of King Herla. 1900.
Little hands: a God's book. 1905.
A child's book of warriors. 1912 (illus).
Selections from a child's book of saints. [1920.]
Also wrote verse.

Harriet Capes, 'Magdalen Brooke'

Two little brothers. 1885.
The wise princess and other stories. 1887.
Sylvia Brooke. 1888, [1900?].
A change for the worse: or the lesson of a day. 1890.
Footsteps in the wood, and other stories. 1890.
Moved by example or strong as death. 1892.
Loyal to his trust. 1894.
The little runaways. 1896, 1899.
A lucky sovereign. 1899.
Also pbd trns and wrote bks on religious history.

'Maud Carew', Florence M. King

Peggy's little squire. 1890.
Miss Pussie. 1891.
Two little B's. 1891.
Stupid Chris. 1892.
Tom's trust. 1892 (illus).
Uncle Phil. 1894.
Pat. 1895.
Ralph Latimer. 1895.
Seaton Court. 1897.
The little King Richard. 1899 (illustr W. S. Stacey).
Pictorial church teaching. Short papers for young children. 1902. By E. Osborne, E. M. Blunt and M. Carew.

Elizabeth Sheridan Carey

Ivy leaves: or offerings in verse. Printed expressly for the use of young ladies. 1837.

John Carey 1756–1826

Learning better than house or land, as exemplified in the history of Harry Johnson and Dick Hobson. 1808, 1813 (3rd edn improved), 1824, 1864 (incomplete).
Also wrote Greek and Latin textbooks.

Rosa Nouchette Carey 1840–1909

Esther: a book for girls. [1887].
Little Miss Muffet. 1894 (illustr M. E. Edwards).
See also col 1489.

Edith Carrington 1840–1909

Nobody's business. 1891 (illustr E. E. Dell).
Stories for somebody. 1892 (illus).
Bread and butter stories. 1892.
Flower folk. Three tales. 1892.
The creatures delivered into our hands. 1893. Pams on kindness to animals.
Ten tales without a title. 1893 (illus).
Workers without wage. Short and simple lessons on natural history. 1893.
Five stars in a little pool. Tales. 1894.

A narrow, narrow world. 1894.
Dick and his cat, and other tales. 1895.
Old friends. 1895.
From many lands. 1895.
Man's helpers. 1895.
Rover and his friends, and other tales. 1895.
A story of wings. 1895.
Wild and tame. 1895.
Ages ago: the ancestry of animals. 1896.
The cat. Her place in society and treatment. 1896.
Cousin Catherine's servants. 1897, 1924. Illus.
The seven little baskets. 1897, Glasgow 1924.
The ugliest one. 1897.
The wise goose. 1897.
Wonderful tools. 1897 (illus).
Peeps into birdland. 1898.
Pretty Polly. A volume of pictures of birdland. 1899.
Round the farm. A picture book of pets. 1899.
Grandmother Pussy. 1904.
True stories about animals. 1904.
Nobody's dog. 1908.
The travels of a butterfly. 1924.
Untidy Mary. 1924.
Also wrote works on animal welfare.

'Lewis Carroll', Charles Lutwidge Dodgson 1832–98

Alice's adventures in Wonderland. 1865, 1886 (rev), 1897 (rev); ed E. Graham 1946, ed M. Gardner, New York 1960, ed R. L. Green 1965 (EL).
Through the looking glass, and what Alice found there. 1872, 1897 (rev).
See also col 1492.

Sabina Cecil

Little Ann: or the picture book. 1814.
Little John: or the picture book. 1815.
Little Mary: or the picture book. 1815.
Little Henry: or the picture book. 1817.
Little Sally: or the picture book. 1819.
Little Eliza: or the picture book. 1819, [1825].
Little William: or the picture book. 1820.
Little James: or the picture book. 1822.
Little Jane: or the picture book. 1822.
Little Thomas: or the picture book. 1822.
Little Edward: or the picture book. 1825.

Mrs Jessie Challacombe

Little Christopher's cross. nd.
The brother's promise. 1897.
Faithful Pollie. 1901.
How the fire spread. 1902.
Twilight stories. 1902.
Gilt and gold. 1910.
Jane Stiggins: a tale. 1910.
Wait and win. [1912.]
Tops: the story of a poor waif. [1913.]
Also wrote adult bks.

A. C. Chambers

Life in the walls, the hearth and the eaves. 4 pts 1871.
Life underground in the Church Tower, the woods and the old keep. [1873.]
The personal experience of Robin the Bold. [1874.]
Away on the moorland: a highland tale. 1875.
Annals of Hartfell Chase. [1879.]
Amid the greenwood. 1881, 1886.
Poor Miss Dick and her adventures in pursuit of happiness. 1898.

Julia Chandler

A night with a baby. nd.
Anybody's bundle. 1874.
Agatha's trust, and how she kept it. 1877, 1883.
Marion's revenge. 1882.

Jennie Chappell

Ruby Leighton's prize essay and other stories. 1879.
One Christmas: or how it came around and a happy disaster. [188?]
Oughts and crosses. 1886, 1888.
Two lilies and other stories. 1887, 1893, as Two lilies and Happy's guest 1894.
Little radiance: or a year in a child's life. 1889.
The Maltese Cross and other tales for girls. 1889.
Uncle Ray's choice and other stories for boys. 1889.
Terrie's travels: or the adventure of a small boy. 1891.
Who was the culprit? 1891.
Wild Bryonie: or bonds of steel and bands of love. 1891, 1897, 1904.
Ted's trust: or Aunt Elmerley's adventure. 1893.
Little Aunt Dorothy: being the experiences of a small girl. [1894.]
Those Barrington boys and a memorable adventure. [1894.]
Ronald and Chryssie: or the mystery of the Lady Tower. 1895.
My friend Kathleen. 1897.
The story of a Persian cat. 1898.
Top brick off the chimney. 1898.
Two girls and a dog. 1899.
Two little friends. 1899.
A little ray of sunshine. 1900.
Winnie's white frock. 1900.
The youngest princess: or little means to big ends. 1900.
Also wrote adult novels.

Maria Louisa Charlesworth 1819–90

Little Sue and her friends. nd.
Rose: or the little comforter. nd.
Ruth and little Jane: or blossoms of grace. nd.
Sunday afternoons in the nursery: or familiar narratives from the book of Genesis. 1853, 1855, 1859, 1866, 1874.
A letter to a child. 1849.
The light of life. Dedicated to the young. 1850.
Ministering children: a tale dedicated to childhood. 1854, 1855, 1857, New York 1859, Leipzig 1860, Boston [186?], New York 1867, London 1868, 1899, 1902; tr Fr 1862.
The Sabbath given: the Sabbath lost. 1856.
A book for the cottage: or the history of Mary and her children. 1863.
The sailor's chase: or little Lenny's friends on the shore. 1863.
Ministering children: a sequel. 1866.
The last command. 1870.
The blind man's child. 1873. Rptd from Ministering children.
Little Jane and other tales. 1873. Rptd from Ministering children.
Rose and the ministering child. 1873. Rptd from Ministering children.
Ruth and Patience. 1873. Rptd from Ministering children.
Oliver of the mill: a tale. 1876.
The old looking glass: or Mrs Dorothy Cope's recollections of service. 1877, 1881, 1880 (as The broken looking glass: or Mrs Dorothy Cope's recollections of service).
Also pbd religious and philanthropic texts.

'Charlton', Henry Emmet

Union Jack: the British boy sailor. 1870.

Algernon Stuart Mackenzie Chester

Up the chimney to ninnyland. A story for children. 1894.
Tommy at the zoo. London and Edinburgh 1895 (illustr J. A. Shepherd).

A. E. Cheyne

The story of Stella Peel. 1880.
Olive Smith: or an ugly duckling. 1883.
Dick Layard: or a schoolboy's trial. [189?]
Under the trees. A tale. 1891.
Fire and water. 1891 (illustr G. Browne).
Paid for. 1892.
Also wrote plays and poetry.

Lydia Maria Child, née Francis 1802–80

The girl's own book. 1869.
The girl's own book of amusements, studies and employment. [c. 1883.]

Alfred John Church, Rev Alfred John Church 1829–1910

Stories from Homer. 1878.
Stories of the old world. 1884.
The chantry priest of Barnet: a tale of the two roses. 1885.
Two thousand years ago: or the adventures of a Roman boy. 1886.
With the King at Oxford. A tale of the great rebellion. 1886.
The count of the Saxon shore: a tale of the departure of the Romans from Britain. 1887.
The three Greek children. A story of home in old time. 1889 (illus).
To the lions: a story of the early Christians. 1889.
Heroes of chivalry and romance. 1898.
Also pbd stories from classical literature, Latin grammars and sermons.

'Austin Clare', Wilhelmina Martha James

Davie Armstrong: a story of the fells. 1871, 1895.
The carved cartoon: a picture of the past. 1874, 1936, 1972.
The royal banner. A tale of life before and after confirmation. 1878.
A guiding star. 1880.
Left in charge; being the history of my great responsibility. 1884, 1888.
In the garden of Eden: an old story retold to children. 1888.
Foundation stones. Fifteen lessons, with story illustrations, on the founding of the Church in England. 1895.
Also wrote novels and devotional texts.

Benjamin Clark

Crocker the clown: a tale for boys. nd.
The life of Jesus for young people. 1867.
The first heroes of the cross. 1870 (illus).
The toll keepers and other stories for the young. Edinburgh 1872.
The land of the pigtail: its people and customs from a boy's point of view. 1876.
Pounceford Hall: a story of school life. 1877.
The infant zephyr: a tale of strolling life. 1881.
From tent to palace: or the story of Joseph. 1885.
My first voyage. 1893.
Also pbd adult religious texts.

Mrs C. M. Clark, Marion Clark

Oughts and crosses: a novel with a moral. 1872.
Anthony Ker: or living it down. A story for the young. 1882.
Cousin Dorry: or three measures of meal. 1883.
Con's acre: a tale of Gillcourt Farm. 1884.
Johnny's search. 1884, 1897.
The slippery ford: or how Tom was taught. 1885, 1889, 1903.
Out of step: or the broken crystal. 1886.
Among thorns. 1887.
More than truthful. 1887.

Emily Clark fl. 1796–1819

Ianthe: or the flower of Caernarvon, a novel. 2 vols 1798.
Ermina Montrose: or the cottage of the vale. 1800.
The banks of the Douro: or the maid of Portugal. A tale. 1805.
Poems consisting principally of ballads. 1810.
Tales at the fireside: or a father and mother's stories. 1817.
The esquimaux: or fidelity. A tale. 1819.

J. Erskine Clark

The children's picture book of scripture parables written in simple language. 1860.
The children's picture book of Bible miracles written in simple language. 1861.
Founder editor of Chatterbox *and also edited* Children's Prize *1863–75.*

Mary Senior Clark

The lost legends of the nursery songs. 1870, 1878 (illus).
Turnaside Cottage. London and Belfast 1870, 1875, 1920.
The professor's merry Christmas. 1871.

S. Dacre Clarke see 'Guy Rayner'

Charles Cowden Clarke 1787–1877

Adam the gardener. 1834.
Perserverence: or God helps them who help themselves. 1844 (illus).
The Princess Narina and her silver-feathered shoes. 1844 (illus).
See also col 2108.

Mary Victoria Cowden Clarke, née Novello 1809–98

The girlhood of Shakespeare's heroines in a series of fifteen tales. 3 vols 1851–2, 1879 (condensed by her sister), 1905 (EL).
The girlhood of Viola. 1924. From The girlhood of Shakespeare's heroines.
The girlhood of Beatrice and Hero. 1925. From The girlhood of Shakespeare's heroines.
See also col. 2221.

Lucy Clifford, née Lane, Mrs W. K. Clifford 1846–1929

Children busy, children glad, children naughty, children sad. [1881] (illustr T. Pym).
Anyhow stories for children. 1882 (illustr D. Tennant), 1885, 1899.
Under Mother's wing. London and New York 1885 (illustr T. Pym).
Very short stories and verses for children. 1886.
Children busy, children glad, children naughty, children sad. London and New York 1891.

Aunt Anne. 1893, 1901.
Dr Mr Ghost. A Christmas story. 1895.
See also col 1502.

James Francis Cobb b. 1829

A tale of two brothers. 1866.
Silent Jim: a Cornish story. 1871, 1872, [1880].
Stories of success as illustrated by the lives of humble men who have made themselves great. 1872 (illus).
The story of the great Czar. 1874.
Heroes of charity: records from the lives of merciful men. 1876.
The warden on the longships. A tale of Cornwall in the last century. [1878] (2nd edn illustr D. Knowles), 1882, 1883, 1886.
Workman and soldier: a tale of Paris life during the siege and the rule of the commune. 1880, 1883, 1911.
Off to California: a tale of the gold country. 1886.
Martin the skipper. A tale for boys and seafaring folk. [1888?]
A feast of stories from foreign lands. 1894.
Also wrote religious texts.

Thomas Cobb 1854–1932

The bountiful lady: or how May was changed from a very miserable little girl to a very happy one. 1900 (Dumpy Books for Children).
The little clown. 1901 (Dumpy Books for Children).
The treasure of Princegate Priory. 1902 (illus).
The lost ball. 1903.
Also wrote numerous adult novels, and works on philanthropy and women's rights.

Frances Power Cobbe 1822–1904

The confessions of a lost dog reported by her mistress. 1867.
False beasts and true. Essays on natural and unnatural history. 1879.
See also col 2222.

Mary Cockle

The juvenile journal: or tales of truth. 1807.
The fishes' grand gala. 1808 (illus).
Important studies for the female sex in relation to modern manners. 1809.
Moral truths, and studies from natural history: intended as a sequel to The juvenile journal. 1810.
Simple minstrelsy. 1812.
Lines to a boy chasing a butterfly. 1826.
An explanation of Dr Watt's hymns for children, in question and answer. 1829, 1836.
The banners of blue. An election song. 1835.
Also wrote elegiac verse.

Alfred Colbeck

The 'Petrel': a story of Cornish life. 1881.
John Shaw of Pudsey. 1890 (2nd edn).
The fall of the Staincliffes. 100 prize tales on the evils of gambling. 1891.
Scarletlea Grange: or a Luddite's daughter. 1893, reissued as In the toils of the Luddites 1910.
Dick of the 'Paradise'. 1894.
Cherton's work-people. 1894.
Saph's foster bairn: a true story. 1896.
The guardians of the 'Shield'. A story. 1920.
When the earth swung over. A strange story. 1926.
Also wrote travel bks.

Christabel Rose Coleridge 1843–1921

The girls of Flaxby. 1882.
Maud Florence Nellie or don't care. [188-?]
The green girls of Greythorpe. [1890.]
Fifty pounds. [1891.]
A pair of old shoes. [1892.]
Minstrel Dick: a tale of the XIVth century. 1896.
Helped edit Monthly Packet *and* Friendly Leaves *from 1890. Also wrote adult novels.*

Sara Coleridge 1802–52

Pretty lessons in verse, for good children; with some lessons in Latin, in easy rhyme. 1834, 1835, 1839, 1845 (4th edn), 1853, 1875, 1927.
Phantasmion: Prince of Palmland. 1837, 1839, 1874 (introd by Lord Coleridge).
See also col 602.

'Harry Collingwood', William Joseph Cosens Lancaster b. 1843

The secret of the sands: or the 'Water Lily' and her crew. A nautical novel. 1879.
The pirate island. A story from the South Pacific. New York 1884, 1885 (illustr C. J. Staniland and J. R. Wells).
Under the meteor flag. The log of a midshipman during the French Revolution. 1884.
The voyage of the Aurora. 1884 (illus).
The Congo rovers. A tale of the slave squadron. New York 1885.
The log of the flying fish. A story of ariel and submarine peril and adventure. 1887.
The rover's secret. A tale of the pirate caves and lagoons of Cuba. 1887.
The missing merchantman. [1888].
The doctor of the 'Juliet': a story of the sea. 1892.
Jack Beresford's yarn. 1896.
The homeward voyage: a book of adventure for boys. 1897.
For treasure bound. 1897, 1910.
An ocean chase. 1898.
A pirate of the Caribbees. 1898.
The castaways. 1899 (illus), 1912.
Also wrote other bks. See col 1820.

Emily H. Comyn

Rose Morrison: or sketches of home happiness. A tale for children. 1857.

L. N. Comyn

Ellice: a tale. 1862.
Atherstone Priory. 1864.
Harry and Phil: a tale. 1865.
Little Milly: or Aunt Eva's visit. 1866.
Elena: an Italian tale. 1873.
Christian Elliott: or Mrs Danver's prize. 1874 (illus).

Eustace Rogers Conder 1820–92

Tell it to your neighbour! A missionary address to the young. 1863.
The builders: a New Year's address to the young. Leeds 1871.
The child of prayer: a New Year's address to the young. Leeds 1872.
Sleepy forest and other stories for children. 1872.
Come! Follow! A New Year's address to the young. Leeds 1875.
The lamp that never goes out. A New Year's address to the young. Leeds 1876.

The marvellous meal. A New Year's address to the young. Leeds 1876.
Play: a New Year's address to the young. Leeds 1879.
Figs or thistles? A New Year's address to the young. Leeds 1880.
Drops and rocks, and other tales with the children. 1882.
Dust, and other short talks with children. Leeds 1882.
Leaves. A New Year's address to the young. Leeds 1892.
Also wrote nonconformist tracts.

Florence Coombe

A chum worth having. The story of Hector's friends. 1897 (illus).
That merry crew. A story for children of all sorts and sizes. 1897, 1915.
Her friend and mine: a story of two sisters. [1899.]
Islands of enchantment. Many sided Melanesia seen through many eyes, and recorded by F. Coombe. 1899.
Boys of the Priory School. 1900 (illus), 1934.
Jack of both sides: the story of a school war. 1900 (illus).
For the old school. 1901.
Two to one: the story of a holiday. 1902.
Comrades all. 1903.
Schooldays in Norfolk island. 1909.

Lina Orman Cooper

Charity Moore. The story of a stray. 1884.
Then and now: or Abe's temptation. 1885.
Aunt Tabitha's trial. 1886.
The cathedral cave: or the gate of heaven. 1886.
John Bunyan, the glorious dreamer. 1898 (illus), 1901 (4th edn), 1929.
Also wrote adult bks.

Esther Copley, née Hewlett (living in 1859)

The young reviewers: or the poems dissected. 1821.
The old man's head: or youthful recollections. [1824.]
The little cowslip gatherers: or what a penny will do. [1824?], [1830].
Early friendships: a tale for young people. 1842, 1859 (preface by L. Valentine).

Mary Corbet-Seymour

Brave Nora: or difficulty overcome. nd.
Nicola: or the career of a girl musician. 1894.
Only a shilling. 1894.
Long time ago. 1895.
Here, there and everywhere. [1896.]
The adventures of a leather purse. 1897.
Dulcie Smith. [1897.]
A girl's kingdom. [1897.]

Alice Abigail Corkran 1852–1916

Bessie Lang. 1876.
Latheby Towers. 1879.
The adventures of Mrs Wishing to-be; and other stories. 1883 (illus).
Down the snow stairs: or from goodnight to good morning. 1887 (illustr G. Browne), 1889.
The young Philistine: and other stories. [1887.]
Margery Merton's girlhood. 1888 (illustr G. Browne).
Meg's friend. 1888 (illustr R. Fowler), 1905, 1925.
Mischievous Jack and other stories. 1888.
The fatal house. 1889.
Joan's adventures at the North Pole and elsewhere. 1889.
Boppy's repentance and how it was brought to pass. 1896.
The dawn of British history. 1910 (illustr M. Lavars Harry).
The life of Queen Victoria for boys and girls. 1910.
Also wrote adult novels and contributed to girls' periodicals.

Julia Corner 1798–1875

The village school, with the history and what became of some of the scholars. [1848.]
The child's own Sunday book. 1850.
Squire Gray's fruit feast: with an account of how he entertained all his young friends; and some of the pretty tales he gave to them as prizes. [c. 1850] (illus).
The cow boy: or the reward of honesty. [1854.]
Little plays for little actors. [1854.]
Reward and gift books. [1855.]
The good children. In words of one syllable. 1857.
Also wrote historical novels and stories from biblical history.

George William Cox

The Crusades. 1874, 1887.
A history of Greece. 1874.
The Greeks and the Persians. 1876, 1889.
School history of Greece. 1877.
The little cyclopedia of common things. 1882, 1884, 1906.
A concise history of England and the English people. 1887 [1886].

Mrs M. B. Cox

Left on the prairie. 1896 (illustr A. Pearce).
Jack's mate. 1897 (illustr F. Feller).
The adventures of Tommy, Rosie and Spot. 1898.
The children of Swift Creek. 1898 (illustr A. Pearce).
The royal pardon. A tale for village lads. 1898.

Dinah Maria Craik, née Mulock 1826–87

Alice Learmont: a fairy tale. 1852, 1884 (rev).
A hero: Philip's book. 1853.
One year: a child's book. 1860.
The fairy book: the best popular fairy stories selected and rendered anew. 1863.
Little Sunshine's holiday: a picture from life. 1871.
The adventures of a Brownie as told to my child. 1872.
The little lame Prince and his travelling cloak: a parable for young and old. 1875.
Carlo Monti: a tale for boys. 1891.
See also col 1356.

Georgiana Marion Craik, later, Mrs A. W. May

Cousin Trix and her welcome tales. Leipzig 1868.
Twelve old friends: a book for boys and girls. 1885.

Augustine David Crake 1836–90

Simple prayers for schoolboys. 1867.
The first chronicle of Aescendune: a tale of the days of St Dunstan. 1874, 1880 (as Edwy the fair).
Alfgar the Dabe, or the second chronicle of Aescendune: a tale of the days of Edmund Ironside. 1875.
The rival heirs: being the third and last chronicle of Aescendune. 1882.
The last Abbot of Glastonbury: a tale of the dissolution of the monasteries. [1884.]

The doomed city, or the last days of Duroncina: a tale of the Anglo-Saxon conquest of Britain and mission of Saint Augustine. [1885.]

Lucy Crane

The baby's bouquet: a fresh bunch of old rhymes and tunes cut and printed in colour by Edmund Evans. nd.
The baby's opera: a book of old rhymes with new dresses by Walter Crane. 1876.

Beatrix (or Beatrice) Feodore Cresswell

The royal progress of King Pepito. [1889] (illustr K. Greenaway).
Alexis and his flowers. Flower lore for boys and girls. 1891 (illus).
Also wrote travel bks.

Jane Crewdson 1808–63

Aunt Jane's verses for children. 1851, 1855, 1871.
Also wrote poetry.

Arthur Crichton d. 1825

Juvenilia. (Unpbd 1812.)
The festival of Flora: a poem, with botanical notes. 1818 (2nd edn).
Also pubd sermons.

Samuel Rutherford Crockett 1860–1914

Blind mercy and other tales for the young. 1877.
The raiders. Being some passages in the life of John Faa, Lord and Earl of Little Egypt. [1893.]
Sweetheart travellers. A child's book for children, for women and for men. 1895 (illustr G. Browne and W. H. C. Groom).
The surprising adventures of Sir Toady Lion with those of General Napoleon Smith. An improving history for old boys, young boys, good boys, bad boys, big boys, little boys, cow boys, and tom-boys. 1897 (illustr G. Browne), New York 1897.
Joan of the sword hand. 1900.
Sir Toady Crusoe. 1905 (illustr G. Browne).
Sweethearts at home. [1912.]
See also col 1511.

Lily Croft

Our college theatricals. A story for big and little girls. [1889.]

Rev John Crofts

Flowers with roots, and other short sermons and allegories for children simply told. Chester 1883.
Effie and the strange acquaintances; a very curious story, almost true. Chester 1886.
Also pbd sermons.

Frances Eliza Crompton, later Walsh 1866–1952

Master Bartlemy. 1892.
The gentle heritage. 1893, 1920, 1964.
Messire. 1894 (with The wayfaring of Gluck, Pippo and Letty and I).
The green garland. 1895.
In the chimney corner. 1897.
The voyage of the 'Mary Adair'. London and New York 1899 (illustr E. Lance).
The rose carnation; and a leaf out of Master Harry's book. 1900 (illustr E. Lance).
The moorland brook. 1902.
The little swan maidens. 1903.
The children of Hermitage. 1970 (illustr A. Pendle).

J. Crompton

Robbie and the canary: a story for young folks. nd.

Sarah Crompton

Tales that are true in short words. [1853.], Birmingham 1879 (as A different selection of tales).
The scholar's book of birds, fishes, insects, etc. in short words. [1858.]
The scholar's book of beasts, in short words. 1858.
The life of Christopher Columbus in short words. 1860, 1868 (new edn, with an account of some of the followers of Columbus), 1875 (illus), 1888 (illus).
The life of Martin Luther, in short words. 1860.
The life of Robinson Crusoe, in short words. [1861.]
Tales of life in earnest. 1862.
Tales in short words. Written for the use of Sunday schools. [1870.]
Fairy tales and fables in short words, for young readers. [1872.]
A tale of the crusades. [1872.]

Mrs Newton Crosland, Constance Cross

No guiding star: a novel. 1868.
The children of Holy Baptism. A poem. 1877.
The coming of the Christ child: or the path of light. A legend. In verse. 1877.
Jimmy's lie. 1877.
Stanley's summer visit. 1882.
The river waif: or the 'Luck' of Godfrey's wharf. 1885.
Sailor Jack: a tale of the Southern seas. 1888.
Also wrote adult novels.

Rosalind Cross and Blanche Atkinson

Rosalinda and other fairy tales. 1890.
See Camilla Toulmin.

Catherine Crowe, née Stevens, Mrs Crowe [1800?–76]

Aristodemus: a tragedy. 1838.
The story of Martha Guinnis and her son. 1845.
Pippie's warning: or mind your temper. 1848.
The juvenile Uncle Tom's cabin arranged for young readers. 1853, [1879].
Ghosts and family legends. A volume for Christmas. 1859.
The story of Arthur Hunter and his first shilling. With other tales. 1861.
The adventures of a monkey. Little Tiny and blind Willie, being an interesting narrative of their extraordinary adventures. 1862.
See also col 1180.

'A. Crowquill', Alfred Henry Forester 1804–72

Crowquill's fairy book. Containing elegant poetical versions of Jack the giant killer, Little red riding hood, Blue beard, Beauty and the beast. nd.
Picture fables. 1854.
Aunt Mavor's fairy tales for good little people. 1855.
Little plays for little actors. 1855.
The giant hands: or the reward of industry. 1856.
The little pilgrim. 1856.

Tales of magic and of meaning. 1856.
Fairy tales, comprising Patty and her pitcher, Tiny and her vanity, The giant and the dwarf, The selfish man, Peter and his goose, The giant hands. 1857.
Patty and her pitcher: or kindness of heart. 1857.
The selfish man: or the world's teaching. 1857.
The giant and the dwarf: or strength and reason. 1857.
The good boy and the black book. 1858, 1859.
A new story book... comprising The good boy, and Simon and his great acquaintance. 1858.
Kindness and cruelty: or the grateful ogre. [1859.]
The red cap. 1859.
The two sparrows. 1859.
Fairy footsteps: or lessons from legends. [1861] (illus).
What Uncle told us. 1861.
The boys and the giant. 1870.
The cunning fox. 1870.
Dick doolittle. The idle sparrow. [1870] (illus).
The two puppies. 1870 (illus).
A prolific illustrator of bks of fables and nursery rhymes, who also wrote adult bks.

James Crowther

The five-barred gate: a story of the senses. 1881.
The unwritten record: a story of the world we live on. [1883.]
The starry cross: a story of dreamland. 1884.
Uncle James's sketchbook. 1884.
The horses of the sun: their mystery and their mission. 1886.
Solomon's little people: a story about the ants. 1886.
The autobiography of an acorn and other stories. 1887.
Lady Bird's tea party and other stories. 1888.
Across the channel: or picture stories of foreign lands. 1890.

Constance Cuming

Atid's friend. 1892.
In a stranger's garden. A story for boys and girls. 1895, 1926.

Maria Susanna Cummins, Miss Cummins

The lamplighter: or an orphan girl's struggles and triumphs. [1872], 1919.

Richenda Cunningham

Davy's schooldays: or deeds speak louder than words. 1862.
Also wrote hymnals and on natural history.

May Cunnington

The ogre: a story for children. [1885.]

Anne Jane Bertha Cupples, née Douglas; Mrs George Cupples 1839–98

Unexpected pleasures: or left alone in the holidays. 1868.
Alice Leighton: or a good name is rather to be chosen than riches. A tale for the young. 1869, Edinburgh and New York 1874.
Carry's rose: or the magic of kindness. 1869, Edinburgh and New York 1881.
Hugh Wellwood's success: or where there's a will there's a way. A tale for the young. 1869, 1875.
Norrie Seton: or driven to sea. Edinburgh 1869 (illus), Boston 1870 (as Driven to sea; or the adventures of Norrie Seton).
The story of the Miss Dollikins. 1870.
The story of our doll. '1871' [1870].
Grandpapa's presents: or take heed will surely speed. 1871.
The adventures of Mark Willis. 1872, Edinburgh and New York 1884.
Bertha Marchmont: or all is not gold that glitters. 1872, Edinburgh and New York 1879, as Marchmont: or all is not gold that glitters. A tale for the young, 1881.
Bluff Crag: or a good word costs nothing. 1872.
Fanny Silvester: or a merry heart doeth good like a medicine. 1872, 1879.
Grandpapa's pleasant companions and other stories with a picture on every page. 1872.
Tappy's chicks and other links between nature and human nature. 1872 (illus), Boston and New York 1872 (rptd as Singular creatures and how they were found: being stories and studies from the domestic zoology of a Scottish parish).
Vea and her cousins: or kind words awaken kind echoes. 1872.
The children's voyage: or a trip in the Water Fairy. [1873] (illustr E. Duncan).
Katty Lester. 1873 (illus after Harrison Weir).
Events in the life of Miss Dollikins. 1874.
Fables illustrated by stories from real life. [1874] (illus).
My pretty scrapbook: or picture pages and pleasant stories for little readers. 1874 (illus).
Shadows on the screen: or an evening with the children. [1874] (illus).
Sights at a peepshow: or pretty pictures and pleasing stories. 1874 (illus).
Edmund Darley: or one good turn deserves another. [1875.]
A kind action never thrown away: or the gypsy's gratitude. 1875.
The hidden talent: or use in everything. 1875.
The lost rabbit: or look at everything and touch nothing. 1875.
Tim Leeson's first shilling: or try again. 1875.
Uncle Dick's story: or what can't be cured must be endured. 1875.
Young bright-eye: or Charlie Harvey's first voyage. [1875.]
Clever little Madge, and other stories. 1876.
The happy family and other stories. 1876.
In the prairie and other stories. 1876.
Mama's stories about domestic pets. 1876.
Terrapin island; or adventures with the 'Gleam'. [1876.]
A nice secret and other stories. 1877.
Hard to win: or a yoke broken. 1878.
Hold firm please and other stories. 1878.
The cockatoo's story. 1881.
Our parlour panorama. 1882 (illus).
The shadows on the screen: or an evening with the children. 1883 (illus).
Hugh Wellwood's success: or where there's a will there's a way. 1884.
The little captain. 1885.
The old 'Dolphin'. 1885.
Aboard the Mersey: or our youngest passenger. [1886.]
Alf Jetsam: or found afloat. [1886.]
Hazelwood Farm. A country story. 1886.
Little Miss Matty: a tale of the sea. 1886.
The Redfords: an emigrant family. [1886.]
Our sailmaker's yarn. 1889.

George Cupples

The green hand: a sea story for boys. 1856, 1879, 1890, 1900, 1908.
Two frigates: or Captain Bisset's legacy. 1859.
The deserted ship: a story of the Atlantic. 1873.
The Ariadne and Le Harpagon. 1889.
Dick Webster: a yarn about pirates. 1889.
A spliced yarn. Some strands from the life cable of Bill Bullen. 1899 (illustr F. Brangwyn).
Also wrote other bks.

Edith E. Cuthell

In the sunny south. 1888 (illustr T. Pym).
Indian idylls. Tales. By an idle exile. 1890.
Indian pets and playmates. Tales. 1891.
In tent and bungalow. Tales. 1892.
Only a guard room dog. 1892.
By a Himalayan lake. 1893.
Indian memories. 1893. By W. S. Burrell and E. E. Cuthell.
Lady Lorrimer's scheme, and the story of a glamour. Tales. 1893.
A Baireuth pilgrimage. A novel. 1894.
Two little children and Ching. 1894.
Caught by a cook. 1895.
The wee widow's cruise in foreign waters. 1895.
The wee widow's cruise in quiet waters. 1895.
In camp and cantonment. Stories of foreign service. 1897.
Sweet Irish eyes. A novel. 1897.
A bad little girl and her good little brother. 1898 (SPCK).
The skipper, the story of an old sea dog. 1899 (illustr H. Copping), 1929.
My garden in the city of gardens. A memory. Reminiscences of life in Lucknow. 1905.
Wilhelmine, Margravine of Lucknow. 1905.
Comrades in camp and bungalow. 1907.
An imperial victim: Marie Louise, Archduchess of Austria, Empress of the French, Duchess of Parma, etc. 2 vols 1911.
A vagabond courtier. 1913.
The Scottish friend of Frederic the Great. 1915.
Reggy, Queenie and Blot. A story for children. 1920.
Stories of strange pets. 1933.
Contributed extensively to devotional periodicals for children.

Elizabeth Frances Dagley

Fairy favours, and other tales. 1825.
The birthday, with other tales. 1828.
The village nightingale, with other tales. 1829.
The young seer: or early searches into futurity. 1834.

Mrs Thomas Dalby

Dutch tiles: being narratives of Holy Scripture: with numerous appropriate engravings, for the use of children and young persons. 1842.

'Darley Dale', Francesca Maria Steele

The Jersey boys. [1878.]
A tearful victory. A story for children. 1880.
The black donkey: or the Guernsey boys, Fanny's king; and other stories. 1881.
Little bricks. 1882.
Cissy's troubles. 1883.
The family failing. 1883, 1896.
Helen's secret: or little by little. 1883.
Spoilt Guy: the story of a child. 1883.
Seven sons or the story of Malcolm and his brothers. 1884.
Fanny's king and other stories. 1885.
Fair Katherine. 1886.
Oughts and crosses: or Mr Holland's conquest. 1886.
Swallow tails and skippers. [1886.]
The glory of the sea. [1887] (illustr C. Whymper).
The wild marsh marigolds. 1887.
The shepherd fairy: a pastorale. 1888.
Mr Mygale's hobby, a story about spiders. 1889.
Noah's ark: a tale of the Norfolk broads. 1890.
Swallow tails and skippers. 1891.
The little doctor: or the magic of nature. 1892.
Stella's story. A Venetian tale. 1897 (illus).
Also wrote adult novels and bks on natural history.

William Dalton 1821–75

The wolf-boy of China: or incidents and adventures in the life of Lyu-Payo. Bath 1857, Boston 1859, Philadelphia 1883.
John Chinaman: or adventures in flowery land. [1858], Boston 1862.
The English boy in Japan: or the perils and adventures of Mark Raffles among princes, priests and people of that singular empire. 1858 (as The story of Mark Raffles: or an English boy's adventures among the Japanese), 1871 (illus).
The war tiger: or adventures and wonderful fortunes of the young sea chief and his lad Chow. A tale of the conquest of China. 1859 (illustr H. S. Melville), 1861, New York and Philadelphia 1881, 1888, 1911.
The white elephant: or the hunters of Ava and the King of the golden foot. 1860 (illustr H. Weir), [1888].
Lost in Ceylon: the story of a boy and girl's adventures in the woods and the wilds of the Lion King of Kandy. 1861 (illustr Harrison Weir), 1888, 1911.
Will Adams, the first Englishman in Japan. 1861, [1868].
Cortes and Pizarro. The stories of the conquests of Mexico and Peru, with a sketch of the early adventures of the Spaniards in the New World. 1862 (illus), [1872].
Phaulcon the adventurer: or the Europeans in the East. 1862.
The nest hunters: or adventures in the Indian archipelago. 1863 (illus).
The tiger prince: or adventures in the wilds of Abyssynia. Boston 1863, 1872.
The wasps of the ocean: or the little waif and the pirate of the eastern seas. A romance of travel in China and Siam. 1864, 1865.
Lost among the wild men: being incidents in the life of an old salt. 1868 (illus).
The powder monkey; or the adventures of two boy heroes in the Island of Madagascar. [1874.]
Also pbd on food technology.

Peter William Darnton

The story of James Brewster. 1883.
Lizzie Hurst: or the reward of truth and goodness. 1888.
The adventures of Jack Pomeroy. A book for boys. 1890, 1894.
Also wrote a number of religious texts.

G. E. Dartnell

Ella's locket and what it brought her. 1875.

Achilles Daunt

The three trappers: a story of adventure in the wilds of Canada. 1882, 1884 (illus), 1889, 1898, 1910.
Frank Redcliffe. A story of travel and adventure in the forest of Venezuela. A book for boys. 1883.
In the land of the moose, the bear and the beaver. Adventures in the forest of the Athabasca. 1885 (illus), 1909, 1928.
With pack and rifle in the far south-west. Adventures in New Mexico, Arizona and central America. 1886.
Our sea-coast heroes: or stories of wreck and of rescue by the lifeboat and rocket. 1887 (illus), 1910, 1927.
Crag, glacier and avalanches: narratives of daring and disaster. 1889.
Out on the Llanos. Adventures in the wilds of Columbia. [1901] (illus).

Frank Warleigh's holidays. [1903.]
The three trappers. [1909.]

Emma Anne Georgina Davenport

Kate and her cousins: or happy holidays. New York and Cincinatti nd.
Philip: or Content. A story of real life, written by a mother for her children. [1855.]
Jamie's questions. 1858.
Weak and wilful: a tale for children. 1858.
Live toys: or anecdotes of our four-legged and other pets. 1862 (illustr H. Weir).
Fickle Flora and her seaside friends. 1863 (illus), London and New York [1881].
Our birthdays; and how to improve them. 1864, 1867.
The happy holidays: or brothers and sisters at home. 1865, 1884.
The holidays abroad: or right at last. 1867, London and New York [1881].
Phillis: or the jealous one. 1867.
Grandmamma: a tale for children. 1868.
Constance and Nellie: or the lost will. 1869.
The author of adult fiction and religious tracts.

Gwendoline Davidson

Kitten goblins. [1889.]
A story of stops. [1890] (illustr G. Davidson).
The garden of time. A tale for children. [1896] (illustr J. J. Guthrie).
Also wrote poetry.

George Christopher Davies

Rambles and adventures of our school field club. 1875 (illus), 1881.
The Swan and her crew: or the adventures of three young naturalists and sportsmen on the rivers and broads of Norfolk. 1876 (illus), 1889 (6th edn), 1924, 1932.
Wildcat tower: or the adventures of four boys in pursuit of sport and natural history in the north countrie. 1877 (illus), 1889.
Peter Penniless, gamekeeper and gentleman. [1884.]
Also wrote on sailing and waterways.

Mary Davison

Lucille: or faithful in a few things. 1883 (illustr F. Dadd).

Isaac Day

Scenes for the young: or pleasing tales, designed to promote good manners and a love of virtue in children. 1807, 1809, 4th edn 1821.

Mary H. Debenham

The captain of five. 1885.
St Helen's well. London and New York [1888].
One red rose. 189? (illus).
Fairmeadows Farm. [1890.]
A little candle. 1890.
The princess of Penruth. 1890.
For king and home. [1891.]
Mistress Phil. 1891.
Moor and moss. 1892 (illustr W. S. Stacey).
Household troops. 1893.
My goddaughter. London and New York 1893 (illustr W. S. Stacey).
Three little maids from school. 1893.
The Mavis and the Merlin. London and New York 1895 (illustr W. S. Stacey).
Two maiden aunts. [1895.]
The whispering winds and the tales that they told. 1895.
Holiday tasks. A story for children. 1897 (illus).
The ruler of this house. London and New York 1898.
My lady's slippers. London and New York [1899] (illus).
Keepers of England. 1900.
Sowing and harvesting. London and New York 1900.
The roses of the red house. 1901.
The Waterloo lass. London and New York 1901 (illustr W. S. Stacey).
Lavender. 1906.
Also wrote religious bks and plays.

Clara de Chatelain, née de Poligny 1807–76

The captive sky lark: or do as you would be done by. A tale. nd, 1861.
The silver swan: a fairy tale. 1847 (illus).
Merry tales for little folk. 1851.
Naughty boys and girls. (Tr from Ger 1852.)
Cottage life: or tales at Dame Barbara's tea table. 1853 (illus).
Tony the sleepless. An original tale. 1854.
The girl's own book. 1856, 1858.
A laughter book for little folk. 1857.
The history of Tom Thumb. [186-?]
Finnikin and his golden pippins. An original tale. 1860.
Jocko: the Brazilian ape. [1860.]
Babyland: an original fairy tale. 1861.
Potluck: an original fairy tale. 1861.
The Lilliputian library. 1861[?]
The night laundress: an original fairy tale. 1861.
Up horsie: an original fairy tale. 1861.
Little Ada and her crinoline. A tale of the times for little folks. [1862.]
The story of Henrietta and the ayah: or do not trust to appearances. [1861.]
My little schoolfellow; or one good turn deserves another. 1864.
The sedan chair and Sir Wilfred's seven flights. 1866.
Dolly's picture book. (Tr from Ger 1870.)
Truly noble. 1873.
Also translated children's fiction and educational texts from Ger.

Mary Augusta de Morgan 1850–1907

On a pincushion and other tales. 1876, 1877 (illustr W. de Morgan).
The necklace of Princess Fiorimonde and other stories. 1880 (illustr W. Crane).
The French girl at our school, and other stories. 1887. By Mary Augusta de Morgan and Edith Dixon.
Nobody's pet. A story of brother and sister. [1894.]
The wind fairies and other tales. 1900.
See introd by R. L. Green to The necklace of Princess Fiorimonde and other stories: being the complete fairy tales of Mary de Morgan, *1963.*

Aimé de Ventoux

Dorothy's duck. [1888.]
Grandmother's forget-me-nots. A story for girls. 1894.
He, she and it. A story for younger children. 1894.

Charles Dickens 1812–70

The cricket on the hearth. A fairy tale of home. 1845 (20 edns were pbd in the first year of pbn).
A child's history of England. vol 1 1852, vol 2 1853, vol 3 1854.
Holiday romance. All the Year Round Jan–Mar 1868. (4 stories, 3 often rptd separately as Captain Boldheart, The magic fishbone, Mrs Orange and Mrs Alicumpaine).
See also col 1181.

Sarah Dixon, later Casterton

Fables for children. 1827.
The friends: or Edward and Joseph. 1827.
See The works of Mrs Casterton collected by N. Rogers, *1827.*

Catherine Anne Dorset, née Turner [1750?–1817?]

The peacock at home: a sequel to The butterfly's ball. 1807, 1809, 1810[?], 1812, 1849, 1851, 1883 (ed C. Welsh).
The lion's masquerade. 1807. By A lady.
The lioness's rout. [1808]. By A lady.
The peacock abroad: or visits returned. 1812.
See also William Roscoe.

David Alfred Doudney

Try: a book for boys. 1857.

Sarah Doudney 1842–1926

Grateful Annie: or the new skates. Wakefield nd.
Archie's old desk. 1872.
Loser and gainer. 1873.
Marion's three crowns. 1873.
Self-pleasing: a new year's address to senior scholars. 1873.
Wave upon wave. 1873, 1878.
Miss Irving's bible. 1875.
Nothing but leaves. 1875.
The pilot's daughters. 1875.
Brave Seth. 1877, 1892.
Stories of girlhood: or the brook and the river. 1877.
Monkesbury College: a tale of schoolgirl life. 1878.
The scarlet satin petticoat. 1879.
A story of Crossport, and other stories. 1879.
Stepping stones. A story of our inner life. 1880.
Anna Cavay: or the ugly princess. 1882.
Janet Darney. A tale of fisher-life in Chale Bay. 1882.
Michealmas daisy. A young girl's story. 1882.
The strength of her youth. 1884, 1887.
When we were girls together. 1886.
Old Anthony's secret and other stories. 1888.
Thy heart's desire. A story of girls' lives. 1888.
Under false colours. 1889, 1894.
Godiva Durleigh. A novel for girls. 1891.
A child of the precinct. 1892.
A romance of Lincoln's Inn. 1893.
Oliver's oath and how he kept it. 1896.
Wave upon wave and Under gray walls. 1898.
When my ship comes in. 1906.
Also wrote many other novels and contributed to girls' periodicals, especially Atalanta *and* Girl's Own Paper.

Lady Elizabeth K. Douglas

Truth: or great and little crosses. 1854.
The forest pony and other tales. Leamington 1856 (as The forest pony, The gipsy boy and other tales), 1870.
Alick and Janey: the shepherd's children. Leamington 1857, London 1870.
Earlscliff. A tale. 1871.

Elizabeth Ann Dove

Tales for my pupils: or an attempt to correct juvenile errors. 1823.

Richard Doyle

In fairyland. A series of pictures from the elf-world. With a poem by William Allingham. 1870.
Jack the giant killer. [1888] (illustr R. Doyle).

Alfred Wilks Drayson 1827–1901

The gentleman cadet: his career and adventures at the Royal Military Academy, Woolwich. 1857 (illustr C. J. Staniland).
Tales at the outspan: or adventures in the wild regions of Africa. 1862, 1865.
Among the Zulus: the adventures of Hans Sterk, the South African hunter and pioneer. 1869 (illustr J. B. Zwecker), 1879, 1891.
The young dragoon. 1870.
The white chief of the caffres. A story. 1897.
Also wrote on geology, astronomy, surveying and whist.

Mary Dring

Memory's review: or principles in practice. Bath 1847.
The child's poetical naturalist: with notes. 1848.
Sabbath recreations: or questions and answers for the young. 1848.
Infantine poems: or Aunt Mary's rhymes. 1854 (5th edn).

Henry Drummond 1851–97

Baxter's second innings: specially reported for the school eleven. 1892.

Mrs Drummond, Harriet Drummond

Glen Isla or the good and joyful thing. Edinburgh 1847, 1852, [1870].
Louisa Moreton: or children obey your parents in all things. 1848, London and Edinburgh 1870.
The Wilmot family; or 'They that deal truly are his delight'. Edinburgh 1848, Boston 1852, Edinburgh 1870.
Lucy Seymour: or it is more blessed to give than to receive. 1849, 1853.
Emily Vernon: or filial piety exemplified. [1855.]
Also pbd devotional texts.

Anna Harriet Drury

Annesley and other poems. 1847.
Friends and fortunes: a moral tale. 1848.
The blue ribbons: a story of the last century. 1855.
Misrepresentation. 2 vols 1859.
Deep waters. 3 vols 1863.
The three half crowns. A story for boys. 1866.
Richard Rowe's parcel. A story for boys. 1868.
Five pounds reward. 1871.
Called to the rescue. 1879.
Also wrote adult novels.

Henry William Dulcken 1832–94

The golden harp: hymns, rhymes and songs for the young. 1864 (illustr brothers Dalziel).
Domestic animals, familiar birds: their habits and history. 1865.
A picture history of England written for use of the young. 1866.
The child's popular fairy tales told for the hundredth time. 1869.
Good old stories and fairy tales told for the hundredth time. 1869.
Old nursery tales and famous histories. [1869.]
One by one: a child's book of tales and fables. 1869.
Rhyme and reason: a picture book of verses for little folks. 1869.

Animal life the world over. 1870.
A handy history of England for the young. London and New York 1875.
Happy day stories for the young. London and New York 1876 (illus).
The boy's handy book of natural history. London and Frome 1879.
Morning light . . . being scripture stories for the young. 1881.
Moral nursery tales for children. [c. 1885.]

Henry Duncan

The cottage friends. Edinburgh 1821.

Edith Dymond

Eight evenings at school. 1825.

Lina Eckenstein d. 1931

The little princess and the great plot. 1892 (illustr D. Heath).
Tulankh-aton. A story. 1924.
Also wrote about religious history.

Charles Henry Eden 1839–1900

Australia's heroes. 1875.
The home of the Wolverine and the Beaver: or fur hunting in the wilds of Canada. London and New York 1876.
In the Pacific Ocean. 1876.
Ralph Somerville: or a midshipman's adventures in the Pacific Ocean. 1876.
Coralie or the wreck of the Sybille. 1877.
Guinea gold: or the great barrier reef. 1879.
Africa seen through its explorers. [1880.]
Found though lost. 1881.
George Dorrington. 1885.
Queer chums: being a narrative of a midshipman's adventures and escapes in eighteen hundred and war time. 1887.
Jungle Jack: or to the east after elephants. 1889.
Prisoner of the Pampas; or the mysterious Seal Island. 1889.
Wronged: or Pedro the Torero. 1889.
In the bear's grip. 1892.
Afloat with Nelson or from Nile to Trafalgar. 1897.
At sea with Drake on the Spanish Main. 1899.

John George Edgar 1834–64

The boyhood of great men. Intended as an example to youth. 1853 (illus), 1862.
Footprints of famous men. New York 1854, 1856.
Boy princes: or the scions of royalty cut off in youth. 1857, 1863, 1865.
Heroes of England. Stories of the lives of England's warriors. 1858, 1861, 1884.
Stories of the struggle of York and Lancaster: or the Wars of the Roses. 1859, 1861.
The Wars of the Roses: or stories of the struggle of York and Lancaster. 1859, New York 1861, 1867.
The crusades and the crusaders: or stories of the struggle for the Holy Sepulchre. 1860, 1874.
History for boys: or annals of the nations of modern Europe. 1861.
Sea-kings and naval heroes. A book for boys. 1861, New York 1863, 1883.
Cavaliers and roundheads: or stories of the Great Civil War. 1862, 1866 (illus).
Danes, Saxons and Normans: or stories of our ancestors. 1863.
How I won my spurs: or a boy's adventures in the barons' war. 1863, [1870?] (as A boy's adventures in the barons' wars: or how I won my spurs).
Boy-princes. The story of their lives. 1864.
Noble dames of ancient story. 1864, 1870.
The boy crusaders. A story of the days of St Louis. 1865, Edinburgh 1870, 1871.
Cressy and Poictiers: or the story of the Black Prince's page. 1865, 1876 (illus).
Historical anecdotes of animals. 1865.
Runnymede and Lincoln Fair. A story of the Great Charter. 1866, 1867.
Great men and gallant deeds. 1868.
Found though lost. 1881.
The perils of a throne: or the lives of some boy princes. 1894.
Was the first editor of Every Boy's Mag.

Maria Edgeworth

See col 901.

Charles Edwardes

The new house-master: a school story. [1895.]
Dr Burleigh's boys: a tale of misrule. 1897.
Shadowed by the Gods: a tale of old Mexico. 1898.
Also wrote numerous travel bks.

Amelia Blandford Edwards 1831–92

The young marquis: or a story from a reign. 1857, 1859 (as The young marquis: or scenes from a reign).
The story of Cervantes; who was a scholar, poet, a soldier, a slave among the moors and the author of 'Don Quixote'. 1862.
See also col 1518.

Mrs Elizabeth Eiloart 1830–95

The young squire: or Peter and his friends. nd.
Ernie Elton, the lazy boy. 1865.
The curate's discipline. 3 vols 1867.
Johnny Jordan and his dog. 1867.
Ernie Elton at school and what came of his going there. 1867.
Archie Blake. A sea-side story. 1868.
The boys of Beechwood. 1868.
Chris Fairlie's boyhood. A tale of an old town. [1870.]
From thistles to grapes. 3 vols 1870.
Tom Dunstone's troubles and how he got over them. 1870.
Some of our girls. 3 vols 1875.
Boy with an idea. New York 1879.
My lady Clare. 3 vols 1882.
Also pbd novels for adults.

Mary Elliott, née Belson 1794–1870

Precept and example: or midsummer holidays. 1812.
The orphan boy: or a journey to Bath. [1814], New York 1816, 1819.
Simple truths in verse for the amusement and instruction of young children at an early age. 1816, 3rd edn 1822, 5th edn [1830?], New York [183?], [1840], [1845].
The history of Tommy Two-shoes own brother to Mrs Margery Two-shoes. [1818], Lancaster MA [1828].
Little lessons for little folks. 1818.
The modern goody two-shoes, exemplifying the good consequences of early attention to learning and virtue. 1819.
Peggy and her mummy. 1819.
The rambles of a butterfly. 1819, 1849.

William's secret. 1819.
Early seeds to produce spring flowers. [1820?]
Flowers of instruction: or familiar subjects in verse. [1820.]
The progress of the quartern loaf. A poem. 1820.
Rural employments: or a peep into village concerns. Designed to instruct the minds of young children. 1820.
The tell-tale. 1820.
Confidential memoirs: or the adventure of a parrot. 1821.
The history of Tommy Two-shoes, a greyhound, a cat and a monkey. 1821.
The book of birds, beautifully coloured, with a description of each, adapted to the capacities of infant minds, in words of two or three syllables. 1822, 1826.
The children in the wood. 1822, 1826.
The girl of friendship: or the riddle explained. 1822.
The sunflower. 1822. Verse.
Plain things for little folks. 1823.
The two Edwards: or pride and prejudice unmasked. 1823, Philadelphia 1827.
Gems in the mine: or traits and habits of childhood. 1824.
The rose. Containing original poems for young people. [1824.]
The bird's nest. [1825.]
Elliott's tales for boys and girls. 1825, 1829; tr Fr 1825 (by A. F. E. Lepée).
Innocent poetry, containing moral and religious truths for infant minds. [1825], 1828.
The little meddler: or one fault leads to many. 1825.
Mischief not fun. [1825?]
No time like the present. [1825.]
Precept and example: or midsummer holidays. [1825.]
The ramble: or more paths than one. [1825.]
The sailor boy. [1825.]
The little mimic. [1826.]
Grateful tributes: or recollections of infancy. [1830.]
Tales of truth. [1830?]
Amusement for little girls' leisure hours. [1831.]
Scripture sketches. 1835.
The aunt and niece. The double journal: or Christmas tidings. [1840.]
Bear and forbear and Pennywise and pound foolish. [1840.]
The contrast: or how to be happy. [1840.]
The cousins: or quality before quantity, conceit, not merit. [1840.]
Industry and idleness. [1840.]
Tales for girls. [1840.]
The truant reclaimed. [1840.]
Tales for boys. 1842.
Also pbd trns of moral theology from Fr. See also col 335.

Edwin John Ellis 1840–1916

Original nursery rhymes. 1865.
Doda's birthday: the faithful record of all that befell a little girl on a long eventful day. London and Belfast 1873.
Also wrote poetry.

Margaret Ellis

After the holidays: or Wynnie's work. nd.
What the children heard under the old oak tree: a story of Bradgate Park. London and Leicester 1858.

George Emmett

For valour: or how I won the Victoria Cross. 1860.
The boys of Bircham School. 1867, 1869 (as The boys of Bircham School and Out on the world).
Black-eyed Susan: or pirates ashore. 1868.
Robin Hood and the outlaws of Sherwood Forest. 1869, 1885.
Young Tom's schooldays. 1871 (illustr Phiz), 1885.
Young Tom Wildrake's adventures in Europe, Asia, Africa and America. 1871 (illus).
Adrift on the Spanish Main. 1875, 1885.
Crusoe Jack: the king of the thousand islands. 1875 (illus), 1890.
Charity Joe: or from street boy to Lord Mayor. 1880 (illus).
Sheet anchor Jack. 1880, 1885.
All's well. 1885.
Midshipman Tom. 1885.
The pirate's tale. 1885.
Shot and shell. A series of military stories. 1885.
Tomahawk and rifle. 1885.
The war cruise of the Mosca. 1885.
Whip-the-wind. A tale of the prairie. 1885.

Viscountess Enfield, Alice Harriet Frederica Byng, Viscountess Strafford 1830–1928

The Dayrells: a domestic story. 1866.
Blameless knights: or Lutzen and La Vendée. 1876.
Also edited biographical works and wrote devotional texts.

Alfred H. Engelbach

Lionel's revenge: or the young royalists. 1867.
The wreck of the Osprey. A story for boys. 1867.
Poor little Gaspard's drum. A tale of the French Revolution. 1868.
The Danes in England. A tale of the days of King Alfred. 1878.
Dick Darlington at home and abroad. 1878, 1881.
Kitty Bligh's birthday. 1879.
Monsieur Jack. A tale of the old war-time. 1879.
The three millstones. A story of the British Legion. 1880.
Bertie and his sister. A domestic story. 1881.
Ned Lyttleton's little one. A tale of a traveller. 1881.
Juanita: a peninsula story for young people. 1891.
Also wrote historical works and adult novels.

Clara English

The children in the wood: an instructive tale. 1801, 1807, 1814, 1818, 1820.
The affecting history of the children in the wood. 1813, 1816, 1817.

Evelyn Everett-Green, 'Cecil Adair', 'E. Ward' 1856–1932

By the sea: Frank Temple's last holiday. 1879.
Cuthbert Coningsby. A sequel to Maud Kingslake's collect. 1884.
Mr Hatherley's boys. 1885, 1908.
The cottage and the grange. 1885.
A child without a name. A tale. 1887, 1905.
Dulcie's little brother: or doings at Little Monksholm. 1887, 1903, 1920.
Our Winnie: or 'When the swallows go'. A story for children. 1887.
Barbara's brothers. 1888.
Dulcie and Tottie: the story of an old fashioned pair. 1888, 1889, 1911, 1923.
Sodo: an ugly little boy; or Handsome is that handsome does. 1888.
The little midshipman and other stories. 1889.
Marcus Stratford's charge: or Roy's temptation. A tale. 1889, 1911.
Miriam's ambition: a story for children. 1889.
Monica: a novel. 1889, 1900.
My black sheep. 1889.
My Boynie: the story of some motherless children. 1889.

Clive's conquest: a story for children. 1890.
Darling Doff: a story for children. 1890.
Dorothy's vocation. 1890.
Dulcie's love story. 1890, 1891, 1910.
Little Ruth's lady. 1890.
Loyal hearts: a story of good Queen Bess. 1890, 1891.
Mischievous Moncton; or jest turned to earnest. 1890.
Miss Meyrick's niece. 1890.
Oliver Langton's ward. 1890.
Dare Lorimer's heritage. 1891.
The Lord of Dynevor. A tale of Edward the first. 1891, 1892, 1905, 1920.
Bertie Clifton: or Paul's little schoolfellow. 1891.
Bridie's resolve and how it was accomplished. A tale for the young. 1891.
The church and the king. A tale of England in the days of Henry VIII. 1891.
Mrs Romaine's household. 1891.
Don Carlos, our childhood's hero. 1892.
Maud Melville's marriage. 1892, 1893, 1904.
Namesakes. The story of a secret. 1892.
Old Miss Audrey. 1892, 1902.
A pair of pickles. 1892.
Little Miss Vixen. 1893.
Over the sea wall. 1893.
Afterthought house. 1894.
Miss Uraca. 1894, 1934.
My cousin from Australia. 1894.
The phantom brother and the child. 1894.
Duff Darlington: or an unsuspected genius. 1895.
Pat, the lighthouse boy. 1895.
Olive Roscoe. 1895, 1896, 1906, 1920.
Ralph Roxburgh's revenge. 1895, 1931.
Arnold Inglehurst, the preacher. A story of the Fen country. 1896, 1927.
The Chatterton mystery. 1896.
Dominique's vengeance. A story of France and Florida. 1896, 1897.
A clerk of Oxford, and his adventures in the barons' war. 1897, 1898.
Molly Melville: a tale for girls. 1897.
Battledown boys: or an enemy overcome. 1898.
Esther's charge. 1898, 1899.
The mystery of Alton Grange. 1898, 1899, 1910.
Miss Marjorie of Silvermead. 1899.
The probation of Mervyn Castleton. 1899.
After Worcester. The story of a royal fugitive. 1900.
Bruno and Bimba: the story of some little people. 1900.
Eleanor's hero. 1900.
The King's butterfly. 1900.
The master of Fernhurst. 1900, 1927.
Odeyne's marriage. 1900.
Bob and Bill. 1901, 1919.
Olivia's experiment. A tale. 1901.
Princess Fairstar. 1901.
Alwyn Ravendale. 1902, 1913.
The boys of the red house. 1902.
My Lady Joanna: being a chronicle concerning the King's children. 1902.
A princess's token. 1902.
Audrey Marsh. 1903.
Called of her country: the story of Joan of Arc. 1903.
Cambria's chieftain. 1903.
The conscience of Roger Trehern. 1903.
The niece of Esther Lynne. 1903.
The castle of the white flag. A tale of the Franco-German war. 1904.
The children's crusade: a story of adventure. 1904, 1911.
Our Winnie, and the little match girl. 1904.
Aunt Patience: a story for girls. 1905, 1912, 1913.
Dufferin's Keep. 1905.
Madam of Clyst Peveril. 1905.
Miss Greyshott's girls. 1905, 1930.
The Percivals: or a house full of girls. 1905, 1907.
The defence of the rock. 1906, 1914.
The magic island. Being the story of a garden and its master. 1906.
The master of Marshlands. 1906, 1920.
A motherless maid. 1906.
Our great undertaking: a grandmother's story. 1906.
Percy Vere. 1906.
Carol Carew: or was it imprudent? 1907.
Clanrickard Court. 1907.
The Erincourts. 1907, 1912.
Married in haste. 1907, 1946.
Miss Lorimer of Chard. 1907.
The Cossart cousins: a story for girls. 1908, 1909.
The city of the golden gate. 1909.
Co-heiresses. 1909, 1920.
A pair of originals. 1909.
A queen of hearts. 1909.
Clive Lorimer's marriage. 1911.
Duckworth's diamonds. 1912.
Miss Malory of Mote. 1912.
Defiant Diana. 1913, 1925.
Loyal hearts and true. 1913.
Marcus Quayle, MD. 1913.
The price of friendship. 1913.
Barbed wire. 1914.
Blackladies. 1914.
The double house. 1914.
Confirmed bachelor. 1915.
Adventurous Anne. 1916.
Dashing Dick's daughter. 1916.
Mrs Desmond's daughter. 1919.
Monster's mistress. 1919, 1920.
Billy's bargain. 1920, 1923.
Lossie of the mill. 1920, 1926, 1939.
Magic emeralds. 1921.
Miss Anne Thrope. 1921, 1924.
Queen's Manor School. 1921.
Lynette Lynton. 1923.
The revolt of Waydolyn. 1924.
The back number. 1926.
Claud the charmer. 1927.
Miss Goshawk of Goshawk. 1929.
Quettendon's folly. 1929.
The curse of Carylon. 1931.
Monk Maltravers. 1931.
Daddy's ducklings. 1932.
An orchard idyll. 1933.
Contributed extensively to children's mags, especially Girls' Own Paper *and* Atalanta.

Juliana Horatia Ewing, née Gatty 1841–85

See col 1521.

Frederic William Farrar 1831–1903

Eric, or little by little: a tale of Rosslyn School. Edinburgh 1858, 1868, 1870, London 1887, New York 1887. (32 separate edns by 1902.)
St Winifred's: or the world of school. 1862 (anon).
See also col 1524.

George Edward Farrow 1866–1920

An ABC of everyday people. Good, bad and indifferent. nd.
Dick, Marjorie and Fidge. A search for the wonderful dodo. nd.
Wallypug at play. nd.
The Wallypug of Why. [1895], 1896. With 6 sequels. Illustr H. Furniss.
The missing prince. 1896.
The Wallypug in London. 1898 (illustr A. Wright).
The little Panjandrum's dodo. 1899 (illustr A. Wright).
The mandarin's kite. 1900.
Baker minor and the dragon. 1902.
The new Panjandrum. 1902.
The cinematograph train and other stories. 1904.
The mysterious Shin Shira. 1914.
See C. Scott-Sutherland, The great Panjandrum, Junior Bookshelf *29 1965.*

Annie S. Fenn

Little Dolly Forbes. [1885.]
Olive Mount. [1885.]
A year with Nellie. [1885], 1893.
A blind pupil. [1886.]
Jack's two sovereigns. 1886, 1893.
Ursula's Aunt. [1886], 1887.
Little neighbours. [1887], 1895.
The little cousin. [1888], 1890.
Their new home. [1888.]
The children of Haycombe. 1890.

Eleanor Fenn, Lady Frere, 'Mrs Teachwell', 'Mrs Lovechild', 'Solomon Lovechild' 1743–1813

School occurrences supposed to have arisen among a set of young ladies, under the tuition of Mrs Teachwell and to be recorded by one of them. [1782.]
Cobwebs to catch flies: or dialogues in short sentences adapted for children from the age of three to eight years. 2 vols 1783, 1815, 1817, 1822, 1829, 1833, New York 1851, London 1876.
School dialogues for boys. 2 vols [1783.]
The female guardian. Designed to correct some of the foibles incident to girls, and supply them with innocent amusement for their hours of leisure. 1784.
The juvenile Tatler. 1789.
The rational dame: or hints to supplying prattle to children. [179?], 1798 (4th edn).
The fairy spectator: or the invisible monitor. 1790. By Mrs Teachwell.
Sketches of little girls: the good natured little girl, the thoughtless, the vain, the orderly, the slovenly, the forward, the snappish, the persevering, the modest and the awkward little girl. [c. 1840] (3rd edn by 'Solomon Lovechild'), 7th edn [1850].
Sketches of little boys: the well behaved little boy, the covetous, the dilatory, the exact, the attentive, the inattentive, the quarrelsome and the good little boy. 5th edn 1845.
Little tales for the nursery. 1848 (by Solomon Lovechild), 1856.

George Manville Fenn 1831–1909

See col 1524.

William Wilthew Fenn

Half hours of blind man's holiday: or summer vacation sketches in black and white. 1878.
After sundown: or the palette and the pew. 1880.
A professional secret and other tales. 1880.
'Twixt the lights': or odd tales for odd times. [1894.]

Winifred Fenn

Edie's disobedience. 1899.
Aunt Emily's nieces. 1900.
Jack's story book. [1901.]

Eliza Fenwick, née Jaco, 'Rev David Blair' 1766?–1840

A visit to the juvenile library: or knowledge proved to be the source of happiness. 1805.
The class book: or three hundred and sixty five reading lessons adapted to the use of schools. 1806 (by the Rev David Blair), 1807 (3rd edn), 1858 (13th edn).
The life of the famous dog Carlo. 1809 (illus).
Infantine stories. 1810.
Lessons for children: or rudiments of good manners, morals and humanity. 1811, 1828; tr Fr 1820.
Rays from the rainbow. Being an easy method for perfecting children in the first principles of grammar. 1812 (2nd edn).
The bad family and other stories. Ed E. V. Lucas 1898 (selection).
See also col 907.

Jeanie Ferry

Maggie's life work. [189?]
Maggie's repentance. [189?]

Louise Frances Field, Mrs E. M. Field.

Bryda: a tale of the Indian Mutiny. [1890] (illus).
Bid me to live. 1891.
Master Magnus: or the Prince and the Princess and the dragon. [1895.]
Denis. 1896.

Lucy Field

Lucy Field and old Richard and his crown. 1853.
Hephzibah: a Christmas story for children. 1870.

Catherine Irene Finch

Noureddin: or the talisman of futurity. 1836.
Scripture history designed for the use of young people. 1846.
Juvenile dramas. 1849.

Percy Hetherington Fitzgerald 1834–1925

The autobiography of a small boy. 1867, 1869, 1907.
Schooldays at Saxonhurst. Edinburgh 1868 (2nd edn).
Stonyhurst memories: or six years at school. 1895.
Also wrote adult novels and bks on literary history and criticism.

Andrew Gibb Fleming

Peeps at Rome for young eyes. Paisley [1879].
Silver wings and other addresses to children. 1895.
Edited Children's Mag of the Presbyterian Church *and the* Golden Nails *series.*

Joseph Smith Fletcher 1863–1935

Alec's victory: or a brother's devotion rewarded. 1890.
The remarkable adventure of Walter Trelawney, parish 'prentice of Plymouth in the year of the great Armada. 1894.
Chrissie's faults: or fettered by a custom. 1896.
In the days of Drake. 1896.
The making of Mathias. 1898 (illustr Lucy Kemp Welsh).
Baden Powell of Mafeking. 1900.
Roberts of Pretoria. 1900.
Conquering: or Bernard's burden. A temperance tale. 1901.

William Fletcher 1794–1852

The deaf and dumb boy, a tale; with some account of the mode of educating the deaf and dumb. 1837.

Douglas Morey Ford

Kate Savage: a novel. 3 vols 1873.
A time of terror: the story of a great revenge. 1908.
Also wrote legal treatises.

H. A. Forde

The old ship: or better than strength. [1879] (illus).
Black and white mission stories. [1881.]
True gold. A tale of the diggings. [1884.]
Dust ho! and other pictures from troubled lives. 1885. By H. A. Forde and her sisters.
Straightforward. 1886.
Across two seas: a New Zealand tale. [1894.]
A difficult team: or one in a thousand. [1894.]
The fruit of the spirit. 1919. Poems.
The heroine of Lyme Regis. The story of Mary Anning, the celebrated geologist. [1925.]

The Hon John William Fortesque 1859–1933

The story of a red deer. 1898 (much rptd).
The drummer's coat. 1899 (illustr H. M. Brock).

William Foster

Follies, foibles and fancies of fish, flesh and fowl. [1889.]
A frog he would a-wooing go. [1890] (illustr W. Foster).
Keeper Jocks. [1904.]

Beata Francis

Fables and fancies. 1874 (illustr J. B. Zwecker).
Slyboots, and other farmyard chronicles. [1879], 1884.
The child's zoological garden. 1881.
The gentlemanly giant, and other denizens of the never, never forest. 1897 (illustr G. Strahan).
Also edited other bks.

Charles H. Frederick

Schoolboy courage and its reward. 1874.
The old brown book and its reward.
Under fire, being the story of a boy's battles against himself and other enemies. 1883.
Young Sir Richard. 1886.
Gentleman Jackson. 1889.
Jack: or the story of a pocket book. 1908.
Under fire. 1908.

James Hain Friswell 1825–78

Houses with the fronts off. 1854.
Out and about. A boy's adventures written for adventurous boys. 1860 (illustr G. Cruikshank), 1875, 1888.
Footsteps to fame. A book to open other books. 1875.
Also wrote adult novels.

Henry Frith b. 1840

Jack o' lanthorn: a tale of adventure. 1884.
The search for the talisman: a tale of adventure in Labrador. 1886 (illus).
The Saucy May: or the adventures of a stowaway. 1889 (illus).

Isabella Fyfie, later Mayo, 'Edward Garrett'

The crust and the cake. 1869.
Seen and heard. By the author of Occupations of a retired life. 1872.
Crooked places. 1873.
By still waters. A story for quiet hours. 1874.
The Capel girls. 1876.
Doing and dreaming: a tale for the young. 1877.
The magic flower pot, and other stories. [1878.]
The house by the works. 1881.
Mrs Rave's temptation. 1882.
Thoughts and stories for girls. 1884.
Her object in life. 1884.
At any cost. 1885.
The mystery of Allan Grale. 1885.
Equal to the occasion. 1887.
Ways and means or voices from the highways and hedges. 1889.
John Winter: a story of harvests. 1890.
Not by bread alone. 1890.
A black diamond. 1894.
Crooked places. A family chronicle. 1894.
Her day of service. 1897.
Other people's stairs. 1898.
Chrystal Joyce. The story of a golden life. 1899.
Recollections of what I saw, what I lived through, and what I learned, during more than fifty years of social and literary experience. 1910.
Stories and sayings from many lands. 1912.
Also wrote adult novels.

William Gardiner 1766–1825

The fortnight's visit concluded. [1820?]
Original tales from my landlord. London, Edinburgh and Dublin 1825.
The story of Pigou, a Malay boy, containing all the incidents and anecdotes of his life. 1825.
The shepherd's boy of Snowdon Hill. [1832.]

Alice Garland

Cousin Deb. A story for children. [1893.]

Elizabeth Garnett

Little rainbow. A story of navvy life. 1877.
Young six-foot and what became of him. [1882.]
Our navvies: a dozen years ago and today. 1885.
Her two sons, a story for young men and maidens. [1886.]
Loyally loved, and lost and found. Two tales. 1886.
Three little heroes. 1886.
Mad John Burleigh: a story of heroic self-sacrifice. [1882.]

'Edward Garrett'

See Isabella Fyfie.

Thomas Gaspey 1788–1871

Glory: a tale of morals drawn from history. 1844 (attributed).
See also col 916.

Margaret Gatty, née Scott 1809–73

Parables from nature. 1855.
'Worlds not realized'. 1856.
Proverbs illustrated. 1857.
Legendary tales. 1858 (illustr Phiz).
The fairy godmothers and other tales. 1859.
Aunt Judy's tales. 1859.
The human face divine and other tales. 1860.
Aunt Judy's letters. 1862 (illus).
Red snow and other parables from nature. 1862.
Aunt Sally's life. 1865.
Domestic pictures and tales. 1866.
A book of emblems, with interpretations thereof. 1872.
Founder editor of Aunt Judy's Mag. *See also col 1301.*

Emma Gellibrand

The story of Kitty and Harry: or disobedience. 1891.
Gerald and Max: or greediness. 1894.
J. Cole: the story of a boy. New York 1896, London 1907.

Mary E. Gellie

Louis Michaud: or the little French Protestant. [1868.]
Little Lisette. 1872.
Brave Nelly: or weak hands and a willing heart. [1875.]
Clement's trial and victory: or sowing and reaping. 1875.
The three wishes. 1878.
Stephen the schoolmaster. [1879.]
Old blind Ned. [1881.]
Dolly dear: or the story of a waxen beauty. 1883.
Nora's trust: or Uncle Ned's money. [1883.]
Fearless Frank: or the captain's children. A tale. 1885.
Roger Gildyke's secret. [1888.]
Ruby's choice: or the Brackenhurst girls. [1889.]
Raffan's folk. 1891.

H. F. Gethen

Nell's schooldays: a story of town and country. London and Glasgow 1898.

Edith A. Gibbs

Robert's trust, and other stories. 1894.
Joey and Louie: or the fairy's gift. [1900.]
A daughter in judgment. 1910.
A golden casket of stories. 1911.

Agnes Giberne 1845–1939

A visit to Aunt Agnes. 1864.
Linda. 1866.
Beechenhurst: a tale. 1867.
Willie and Lucy at the seaside. For very little children. 1868, 1907.
The curate's home. 1869.
Hungering and thirsting. [1869], 1882.
Charity's birthday text. 1870, 1888, 1905.
Detained in France. A tale of the French Empire. 1871.
The day-star: or the gospel story for the little ones. 1871.
Aimée: a tale of James the second. 1872.
Willie and Lucy at home. 1872.
Willie and Lucy abroad. 1873.
Drusie's own story. 1874.
Not forsaken: or the old house in the city. 1874.
Floss Silverthorn, or the Master's little handmaid. 1875, 1891.
Coulying Castle, or a knight of the olden days. 1875.
Will Foster of the Ferry. 1876, 1887.
The battlefield of life. 1877.
The hillside children. 1878, 1910.
Hohnfrida's Christmas cheer. 1879.
The upward gaze. 1879.
Duties and duties. A tale. 1881.
Through the Linn: or Miss Temple's wards. A tale. 1881.
Jacob Witherby: or need of patience. 1882.
Sweetbriar, or goings on in Priorsthorp Manor. A tale. 1882.
Decima's promise. 1882.
Trying to enter. 1882.
Twilight talks: or easy lessons on things around us. 1882.
The world's foundations, or geology for beginners. 1882, 1884, 1908.
Daily evening rest: or thoughts of peace about the master. 1883.
Five little birdies. 1883, 1905, 1908.
Beryl and Pearl. A novel. 1884.
Among the stars: or wonderful things in the sky. 1885.
Daisy of 'Old Meadow'. 1885.
Gwendoline. 1885, 1905.
Five thousand pounds. A tale. 1886.
The head of the house. 1886.
Lisa Baillie's story. 1886.
Father Aldur. A water story. 1887.
His adopted daughter: or a quiet valley. 1887.
The earls of the village. 1888.
Twilight verses. 1888.
Number three Winifred Place. [1889], [1905].
'Least said, soonest mended'. 1890.
The Dalrymples. 1891.
Tim Teddington's shoes, or who was the worst off? A second dream. 1891.
Besides the waters of comfort: thoughts from many minds. 1892.
Won at last, or Mrs Briscoe's nephews. A tale. 1892.
The Andersons, brother and sister. 1894.
The girl at the Dower House and afterward. 1896.
Molly Melville: a tale for girls. 1897.
This wonderful universe. 1897, 1920.
Everybody's business. 1898.
A modern Puck: a fairy story for children. 1898.
Easy lessons on things around us. 1899.
Anthony Cragg's tenant. 1901.
The family next door. 1908.
Sunday afternoons with Mamma. 1909.
Under Puritan rule. A tale of troublous days. 1909.
General John: a story for boy scouts. 1910.
Val and his friends. 1911.
Glimpses of Christ. 1912.
This wonder-world. 1913.
The doings of Doris. 1914.
The garden of earth or a little book on plant life. 1921.
The impudence of Carol Carew. 1933.
Also pbd adult novels.

Mrs Ann Gilbert, née Taylor

See col 474.

William Gilbert 1804–90

The magic mirror. A round of tales for young and old. 1866 (illustr W. S. Gilbert).
Indian fairy tales. 1892.
The book of wonder voyages. 1896.

Mrs Gilfin

Lucy: or the little Christian. [1877.]

A. H. Gilkes

Boys and masters: a story of school life. 1887.
The thing that hath been: or a young man's mistakes. 1894.
A day at Dulwich. 1905.
Four sons: a novel. 1916.

Mary Gillies

The voyage of the Constance: a tale of the polar seas. [1860.]
The Carewes: a tale of the civil wars. 1861.
My little Lizzie. 1861.
Great fun for our little friends. 1862.
More fun for our little friends. 1864.
Little Lizzie. [1866.]

Elizabeth Glaister

The Markhams of Ollerton: a tale of the Civil War 1642–1647. [1873.]

Geraldine Robertson Glasgow

True to the flag. 1891, [1898].
A nice game. [1895.]
The Christmas stocking and other stories. [1898.]
Doctor Dicky. [1898.]
Christabel's wish. [1899.]
Little Jack Hamilton. [1900.]

Isabella E. Glennie

Pictures and stories for little children. [1860], 1873.

Julia Bachope Goddard d. 1896

More stories. 1863.
The boy and the constellations. 1866.
Kaspar and the seven wonderful pigeons of Würzburg. London and Belfast 1876.
Worth more than gold: or Elsie's fortune. 1880.
The four cats of the Tippertons, and other stories about animals. [1881.]
Ursula's stumbling-block: or 'pride comes before a fall'. 1885, 1886.
Was he a fool? London and New York [1887].
Philip Danford: a story of school life. [1890.]
The golden weathercock. 1891.

'Mary Godolphin'

See Lucy Aikin.

George Laurence Gomme

The Queen's story book: being historical stories collected out of English romantic literature in illustrations of the reigns of English monarchs from the conquest to Queen Victoria. 1898 (illustr W. H. Robinson).

Samuel Goodrich

See Peter Parley.

Catherine Grace Frances Gore, née Moody 1799–1861

New Year's day: a winter's tale. London and Paris 1846.
See also col 919.

Francis Robert Goulding 1810–81

Robert and Harold: or the young marooners. 1853, [1882] (as The adventures of the young marooners: or Robert and Harold on the Florida coast).

Mina E. Goulding

Mother's place. Glasgow 1881.
Becky and Reubie, the little street singers. [1882.]
Little Sally. [1883.]

Jean Gow

Merry nights. A series of stories for boys and girls. [1896.]

Elizabeth Grant

Holiday rambles: or peeps into the book of nature. 1856.

Mrs G. Forsyth Grant

The boys at Penrohn. A story of English school life. Edinburgh [1893].
The heroes of Crampton School. Edinburgh 1895.
Burke's chum. A story of Thistleton School. Edinburgh 1896.

James Grant 1822–87

Jack Manly: his adventures by sea and land. 1861 (illus).
Dick Rodney: or the adventures of an Eton boy. 1863 (illus).
See also col 1302.

Ada J. Graves

The house by the railway. 1896.
Four little people and their year at Silverhaven. [1898.]

Ann Thomson Gray

The twin pupils: or education at home. A tale. 1853.

Anne Augusta Gray

Juvenile ballads and nursery rhymes. 1842.
Laura: or the only way to be happy is to be useful. 1848.
John's adventures: or the little knight errant. 1849.
Edward's dream: or good for evil. 1854.
The naughty little spider. 1854. Verse in phonetic characters.

Annie Gray

Ailie Stuart: a story of school life. [1873.]
Mary Mordaunt: or faithful in the least. [1878.]

Denny: or from haven to haven. [1883.]
The King's army. [1886.]
A blessing in disguise. [1887.]
The old lock farm. [1888.]
The King's diadem. [1890.]
Rosie Dale. [1890.]

E. M. Green

The child of the caravan: or the boy musician. [1889] (illus).

Kate Greenaway, Catherine Greenaway 1846–1901

Selection

The Kate Greenaway treasury: an anthology of the illustrations and writings of Kate Greenaway. Ed E. Ernest, introd by R. H. Viguers, London and Glasgow 1968.

§1

The little folks painting book with a series of 107 outline engravings for watercolour painting by Kate Greenaway, with verses and stories by George Weatherley. London, Paris and New York 1879.
Toyland, Trot's journey, and other poems and stories with illustrations by Kate Greenaway. New York 1879.
Trot's journey: pictures, rhymes and stories, with over sixty woodcut illustrations by Kate Greenaway. New York 1879. Originally pbd in Little folks.
Kate Greenaway's birthday book for children. 1880 (illus), reissued 1900.
The old farm gate, stories in prose and verse for little people. 1880 (illustr K. Greenaway, M. E. Edwards and M. Kerns).
Under the window. Pictures and rhymes for children. [1879] (illustr E. Evans); tr Ger Munich 1880.
Marigold garden: pictures and rhymes. [1879] (illus), 1885.
Almanack for 1883. 1882 (rptd with new text as Almanack for 1924), 1887, 1888, 1889, 1891.
Almanack for 1884. 1883.
Kate Greenaway's calendar for 1884 with coloured illustrations on four separate cards. 1883.
Almanack for 1885. 1884.
Baby's birthday book. 1884 (illustr K. Greenaway et al).
Kate Greenaway's carols. 1884. 4 pictorial cards.
A painting book by Kate Greenaway. With outlines from her various works. 1884, 1900 (reissued as Kate Greenaway's painting book).
The language of flowers. 1884 (illustr K. Greenaway); tr Fr 1884.
A summer at Aunt Helen's. 1884 (illustr K. Greenaway).
Almanack for 1886. 1885.
A apple pie. 1886 (illustr K. Greenaway), 1900 (reissued).
Kate Greenaway's album. 1885 (only 8 copies were ptd and the work was not pbd).
Kate Greenaway's alphabet. 1885 (illus), 1973.
Almanack for 1887. 1886 (reissued with new text as Almanack for 1925); tr Fr nd.
Almanack for 1888. 1887; tr Fr nd.
Queen Victoria's jubilee garland. 1887.
Around the house stories and poems. 1888 (illustr K. Greenaway taken from Little folks and Chatterbox).
Almanack for 1889. 1888; tr Fr nd.
Kate Greenaway's almanack for 1890. 1889; tr Fr nd.
Kate Greenaway's book of games. 1889 (illus), London and New York 1927 (reissued).
Kate Greenaway's almanack 1892. 1891; tr Fr nd.
Kate Greenaway's almanack 1893. 1892; tr Fr nd.
Kate Greenaway's almanack 1894. 1893 (illustr K. Greenaway taken from the English spelling book); tr Fr nd.
Kate Greenaway's almanack 1895 with coloured figures of childhood, youth and old age. London and New York 1894. Reissued with new text as Kate Greenaway's almanack for 1928.
Kate Greenaway's almanack and diary for 1897. London and New York 1896. Reissued with new text as Kate Greenaway's almanack and diary for 1929.
Catalogue of a collection of water colour drawings. 1898.
Kate Greenaway's calendar for 1899. 1898.
Pictures for painting. London and New York 1920.
Kate Greenaway pictures from originals presented by her to John Ruskin and other personal friends, hitherto unpublished. 1921 (introd by H. M. Cundall).
Kate Greenaway's birthday coloring book. With verses by Mrs Sale Barker. New York 1975.

Kate Greenaway illustrated numerous popular children's bks, a full listing of which can be found in R. Engen, Kate Greenaway: a biography. 1981. *Her illustrations also appeared in mags, including* Little Folks, Cassell's Mag, Graphic, Illus London News, Girls' Own Paper *and* Little Wide Awake.

The Hon Mrs Greene, née Plunkett, Louisa Lilias Plunkett d. 1891

Harry Galbraith: or the pierced eggs. nd. (As The pierced eggs and what came of them, 188?)
A winter and summer at Burton Hill: a children's tale. 1861 (illus).
Cushions and corners: or holidays at Old Orchard. 1864, Boston 1867, London 1891.
Filling up the chinks. 1869.
The schoolboy baronet. 1869, 1870.
The broken promise and other tales. 1870.
The grey house on the hill: or 'trust in God and do right'. 1870, 1891, 1903.
The little castle maiden: simple stories for young children. [1871] (illus).
Prince Croesus in search of a wife. 1873. Adapted from Ger of H. C. Anderson.
Gilbert's shadow: or the magic beads. 1875.
God's silver: or youthful days. 1877 (illus).
Dora's dolls' house: a story for the young. [1880], 1890.
On angel's wings: or the story of the little violet of Edelsheim. 1884, 1885, 1903.
The babe i' the mill, and Zanina, the flower girl of Florence. 1885.
Bound by a spell: or the hunted witch of the forest. 1885.
Whose hand: or the mystery of no man's heath. 1886.
The golden wrens. 1897, 1898.
The lost opal ring. 1897, 1898, 1905, 1919.
The lost telegram: or trust betrayed. 1897, 1898, 1908.
Jubilee Hall. 1906.

James Greenwood 1832–1929

Curiosities of savage life. 1864 (illustr H. S. Melville and F. W. Keyl).
The adventures of seven four-footed foresters, narrated by themselves. 1865 (illustr H. S. Melville).
The hatchet throwers. 1866 (illustr E. Griset).
The true history of a little ragamuffin. 1866, 1870.
Legends of savage life. 1867 (illustr E. Griset).
The bear king: a narrative confided to the marines. 1868 (illustr E. Griset).
The purgatory of Peter the Cruel. 1868 (illustr E. Griset).
The adventures of S. R. Davidger; seventeen years and four months captive among the Dyaks of Borneo. 1869 (illustr R. Hullula).
Savage habits and customs. 1869.

Rev William Gresley 1801–86

The baron's little daughter and other tales in prose and verse. 1848, 1850.
Frank's first trip to the Continent. 1854.
Colton Green: a tale of the Black Country. 1854.

Elizabeth Caroline Grey

The autobiography of Frank: the happiest little dog that ever lived. 1861.
Also pbd numerous religious texts.

Mrs Mary Grey

Memoirs of Dicky, a yellow canary. 1831.

Rosamond S. Grey

Summer clouds. A tale for the young. London and Dublin 1871.

Sidney Grey

Story-land. nd (illustr E. Evans).
The runaways. [1886.]

Miss Grierson

The visit: or Mamma and the children. Edinburgh 1824.
The student's walk: or a Sabbath in the country. 1825.
Also pbd historical and biographical works and evangelical fiction.

John Percy Groves

From cadet to captain. London and New York 1883.

Archibald Clavering Gunter

Small boys in big boots. A story for children of all ages. 1890.

John Habberton 1842–1921

Helen's babies. Glasgow 1877, 1911.
Other people's children. 1905.

Julia Hack

Kathleen: or a maiden's influence. [1899.]

Maria Hack, née Barton 1777–1844

Winter evenings: or tales of travellers. 4 vols 1818, 1823, 1840, 1853 (rev).
The winter scene. 1818.
Grecian stories. 1819.
English stories. 1820, 1839 (as English stories of the olden time).
Harry Beaufroy: or the pupil of nature. 1821, 1824.
Oriental fragments. 1828.
Stories of animals, intended for children between five and seven years old. 5th edn 1887. 2nd ser intended for children between seven and ten years old, 1831.
Adventures by land and sea. 1877.
Inland and ice deserts. 1877.
Travels in hot and cold lands. 1877.

Henry Rider Haggard 1856–1925

See also col 1557.

Anna Maria Hall

The Hartopp jubilee. [1840?]
See also col 1304.

Clara Hall

The juvenile mirror. 183?

Edith King Hall

My Aunt Nan. [1894.]
That little beggar. 1895.
The red umbrella and other stories. 1896.
Adventures in Toyland. [1897.]
Mig and her friends. 1897.
Mother's little lady. 1898.
Tales from a farmyard. 1898.
The Admiralty house: a story. 1899.
Andy's trust. 1899.
Irma's zither. 1899.
That examination paper! A story for girls. 1900.

Caroline M. Hallett

The upward path. A book for boys. 1883.
Every Sunday. A book for boys. [1889.]
With none to help. 1891.
Sunday evening. A book for girls. 1894.
Called to fight. A book for boys. 1900.

James Orchard Halliwell 1820–89

The nursery rhymes of England, obtained principally from oral tradition. 1842, 1843, 1844, 1846, 1853, 1860, 1863.
Popular rhymes and nursery tales of England: a sequel to The nursery rhymes of England. 1849.
Pbd extensively on literary history and biography.

Margaret Hamer *see* Maggie Brown

Sarah Sharp Hamer, 'Olive Patch', 'Phyllis Browne'

Happy little people. 1882.
A parcel of children, with some account of their doings. 1886.
Mrs Somerville and Mary Carpenter. 1887.

Mrs C. G. Hamilton

The unclaimed daughter. [1853.]

Catherine Jane Hamilton b. 1841

Rivals at school: or a lesson for life. [1888.]

S. L. Hands

Ben of Friar Alley: a story. 1898, 4th edn 1899.

Charles Henry Hanson

Stories of the days of King Arthur. 1882 (illustr G. Doré).

'Harriet'

See Lydia Falconer Miller.

Florence Harrington

Georgie Merton: or only a girl. 1877.

Lillie Harris

Mama's fairy tales. 1878.

Fanny Harrison

Our teacher's stories. [1888.]

Emily Hartley

Odd moments of the Willoughby boys. 1881, 1883.

Jane Harvey

The friends: or the history of Harcourt and Powlett. Derby [1820].
Poems, original and moral for the use of children. Derby [1820].
Also pbd historical works and verse.

Eleanor Luisa Haverfield b. 1870

The doctor's little dot. 1898.
Nancy's fancies. A story about children. 1899.
Our vow: a story for children. London and Edinburgh 1899, 1910.
Blind loyalty: a sequel to Our vow. 190?
Jim's sweethearts. The tale of a tiny lover. 1901, 1902.
Rhoda: a tale for girls. London and Edinburgh 1901.
Stanhope. A romance of the days of Cromwell. London and Edinburgh 1902, 1910, 1923.
The squire. 1903.
The sow's ear. 1904.
The twins and Sally. London and Edinburgh 1904, 1922.
The Mascotte of Sunnyside. 1906.
Queensland cousins. 1908, 1922.
Sylvia's victory. 1911, 1923.
An impossible friend. 1911.
The Ogilvie's adventures. 1913.
Joan Tudor's triumph. 1918.
Who are the Cromlyns? 1919.
The luck of Lois. A school story. 1921.
Just a jolly girl. 1922.
Audrey's awakening. 1924.
The discovery of Kate: a school story. 1925.
The mad cap trio. 1927, 1929.
The Scatterbrains and other stories. 1930.
Meriel's choice. 1933.
Through the green door. 1935.

Frances Ridley Havergal 1836–79

Bruey: a little worker for Christ. 1872, 2nd edn 1873, 1886.
Morning bells: or waking thoughts for the little ones. 1875, 1882, 1929.
My King: or daily thoughts for the King's children. 1877.
Morning stars: or names of Christ for his little ones. 1879.
Ben Brightboots, and other true stories, hymns and music. 1883.
Blessings for all. A religious poem. 1892 (illus).
Birthday hopes. 1895.
Birthday flowers: verses. 1898.
See also col 738.

Mrs Ann Hawkshaw, 'Aunt Effie'

Poems for my children. 1847.
Aunt Effie's rhymes for little children. [1852], 1854, 1858 (illustr H. K. Browne).
Aunt Effie's gift to the nursery. 1854.
Also pbd verse.

Margaret S. Haycraft

The children of Cherryholme. [1894.]

Herbert Hayens

Play up Lions. nd.
The British Legion: a tale of the Carlist war. 1898.
One of the red shirts: a story of Garibaldi's men. 1901 (illus), 1904.
Cleveley Sahib: a tale of the Khyber Pass. 1902.
The Gayton scholarship. 1904.
Stirring and true. 1920.

William Stephens Hayward

The cloud King: or up in the arie, and down on the sea. Being a history of the wonderful adventures of Victor Volans. [1865] (illus), 1866.
Also wrote numerous adult novels.

Arthur M. Heathcote

The magic umbrella. Bunny Princess Shockhead. 188?
Ragged robin, and other plays (in verse) for children. 1890.

Mary Margaret Heaton

Happy Spring-time. Rhymes for mothers and children. 1874.

Mary Ann Hedge, 'M. A. H.'

Affection's gift to a beloved godchild. 1819, 1821.
Letters on history addressed to a beloved godchild. 1819.
The retreat. 1820.
The flatterer; or false friendship. A tale. 1822.
Letters on profane history. 2nd edn 1822.
Life: or fashion and feeling. A novel. 1822.
Man: or anecdotes national and individual: an historic mélange for the amusement of youth. 1822.
Twilight's hours improved: or the visit to grandmama. 2nd edn 1822.
Samboe: or the African boy. 1823.
The orphan sailor boy: or young arctic voyager. 1824.
Radama: or the enlightened African. With sketches of Madagascar. 1826.

Cousin Helen

The children's party: or a day at Upland. [1863.] Prose and verse.

Nellie Hellis

Gypsy Tan. [1884], 1902.
Rob and Ralph: or a trust fulfilled. [1893.]

William Helme

Evenings rationally employed: or moral and entertaining incentives to virtue and improvement. Brentford and Richmond 1803.

Samuel Bracebridge Hemying 1841–1901

Jack Harkaway in America. 1880.
Jack Harkaway's after school days. His adventures afloat and ashore. 1891.

Jack Harkaway's schooldays. 1891. First pbd in Boys of England 1871.
Jack Harkaway among the brigands. 1892.
Jack Harkaway and his son's adventures in China. 1892.
Jack Harkaway and his son's adventures round the world. 1892.
Jack Harkaway at Oxford. 1892.
The rival schools: their fun, feuds and frolics. 1892.
Jack Harkaway and his son's adventures in Australia. 1893.
Jack Harkaway and his son's adventures in Greece. 1893.
Adventures of young Jack Harkaway. 1894.
Dick Lightheart, or the scapegrace at sea. 1895.
Jack o' lantern; or the imp of the school. 1895.
Contributed extensively to boys' periodicals.

Hamish Hendry

Red apple and silver bells. [1897], [1899]. Verse.

Thomas Heney

The history of Wilford and Moreton; or virtue the true nobility. An interesting tale designed to promote the love of mankind. 1827.

George Alfred Henty

See col 1576.

Jeanie Hering, later Acton 1846–1928

The child's delight. A picture book for little children. London, Manchester and New York nd.
Golden days. A tale of girls' school life in Germany. nd.
Honour and glory: or hard to win. A book for boys. nd.
Garry: a holiday story. 1868 (illus).
Little pickles. A tale for children. 1889.
Put to the test. 1889 (illus).
Rosebud. 1891 (illus).

Esther Hewlett

See Esther Copley.

Eva M. Hilder

Stories the sunflowers told. 1898.

Miranda Hill

The fairy spinner and 'out of date or not?'. London and New York [1875] (illustr K. Greenaway).

Edward Newenham Hoare 1802–77

Paths in the great waters. London and New York nd (illustr G. Browne).
Two voyages and what came of them. nd.
Between the locks: or the adventures of a water party. London and New York 1879.
Mike: a tale of the great Irish famine. 1880.
Percy Trevor's training. 1884.
A brave fight. Being a narrative of the many trials of Master William Lee, inventor. 189?

George Richard Hoare

The young traveller: or the adventures of Etienne in search of his father. 1812, New York 1815, 1837 (as Etienne in search of his father).

Mrs Carey Hobson

Old Greta's patchwork dress and stories told of some of the patches. nd.
South African stories. 1887.

Silas Kitto Hocking 1850–1935

Her Benny: a tale of street life. [1879], 1890, 1891, 1966.
Chips: a story of Manchester life. 1881.
His father: or a mother's legacy. [1882.]
Poor Mike: the story of a waif. [1882.]
Sea-waif: a tale of the Cornish cliffs. 1882, London and New York 1890.
Dick's fairy: a tale of the streets, and other stories. [1883.]
Our Joe. 1885.
Cricket: a tale of humble life. 1886.
Crookleigh: a village story. 1888 (illus).
Ivy: a tale of cottage life. 7th edn 1888.
Real Grit. 188?
Chips, Joe and Mike. 1890.
Tregeagle's head: a romance of the Cornish cliffs. 1890 (illus).
The blindness of Madge Tyndall. 1899.
The strange adventures of Israel Pendry. 1899.
Smugglers' Keep. 1913.
Also pbd numerous adult novels.

Mrs Edwin Hohler, née Goring, Agnes Venetia Goring 1870–1933

The bravest of them all. A story for young people. [187?], 1899.
The picture on the stairs. 1897.
For Peggy's sake. 1898.
The green toby jug, and the Princess who lived opposite. 1898, [1920] (as The green toby jug and other stories).

Ann Catherine Holbrook 1780–1837

Realities and reflections. [1834.]
Also pbd bks about the theatre.

Edward Holland

Mabel in rhymeland: or little Mabel's journey to Norwich and her wonderful adventures with the man in the moon and other heroes and heroines of nursery rhyme. 1885.

Frederick Morrell Holmes

Hugh Melville's quest: a boy's adventures in the days of the Armada. London and Edinburgh 1896.

Emily Sarah Holt b. 1836

At ye grene Griffin: or Mrs Treadwell's cook. nd.
King Alfred: the truth teller. nd.
King's daughters: or how two girls kept the faith. nd.
Through the storm: or the Lord's prisoners. nd.
The well in the desert. An old legend of the house of Arundel. nd.
Memoirs of royal ladies. 1861.
Mistress Margery: a tale of the Lollards. 1868.
Ashcliffe Hall: a tale of the last century. 1870.
Sister Rose: or Saint Bartholomew's eve. 1870, 1891, 1900.
For the master's sake. A story of the days of Queen Mary. 1877, [1883].
Out in the forty-five: or Duncan Keith's vow. 1888.
The slave girl of Pompeii: or by a way they knew not. 1888.
Our little lady: or six hundred years ago. 1891.

All for the best: or Bernard Gilpin's motto. 1898.
Margery's son: or how two girls kept the faith. 1905.

Thomas Hood ('Tom') 1835–74

The headlong career and woeful ending of precocious Piggy. 1864.
Fairy realm. 1865.
Upside down: or turnover traits. 1868.
Petsetilla's posy: a fairy tale for young and old. [1870] (illus).
The pleasant tale of Puss and Robin, and their friends Kitty and Bob. London and New York 1871.
Rainbows rest and other stories. 1872.
From nowhere to the North Pole: a Noah's arkaeological narrative. 1875 (for 1874).

Barbara Hoole, later Mrs Hofland, née Wreaks 1770–1844

The son of a genius. 1812.
Adelaide: or the intrepid daughter. 1823.
The young Crusoe. 1829.
See also col 933.

'Ascott R. Hope', Ascott Robert Hope-Moncrieff 1846–1927

The daughter of the regiment. A story from my grandmother's journal. nd.
'Dumps' and other stories. nd.
In forest and jungle: or adventures with wild beasts. nd.
On the warpath and other schoolboy stories. nd.
Tales of chivalry of the olden time. London and Edinburgh nd.
Wonders of electricity. nd.
Wonders of the volcano. nd.
A book about boys. 1869.
Stories of school life. 1870 (3rd edn).
Stories about boys. 1871 (illus).
Stories of Whitminster. 1873.
A pack of troubles. 1874.
George's enemies. 1875.
The pampas: a story of adventure in the Argentine Republic. 1876, 1878 (illustr Phiz junior).
The young rebels: a story of the battle of Lexington. 1879.
Spindle stories. New yarns from old wool. London and New York 1880.
Stories of long ago. 1881 (illus).
Young heads on old shoulders. 1881.
A book of boyhoods. 1882 (illus).
Our homemade stories. 1882.
The vulture's nest and other stories. 1883.
The wigwam and the warpath: or tales of the red Indians. 1884 (illustr G. Browne).
Boy's own stories. 1887.
The old tales of chivalry retold. Edinburgh 1888.
The seven wise scholars. [1888] (illustr G. Browne).
Youngster's yarns. 1888.
Dick's dog and other stories of country boys. 1891.
An emigrant boy's story. 1891.
A handful of stories. 1892.
The lost dog and other stories. 1892 (illus).
The ice world and its wonders. 1893.
Toby: his experiences and opinions. 1894.
Ups and downs. 1895.
Young traveller's tales. 1895 (illus).
Stories of long ago retold. 1897.
Stories of old renown: tales of knights and heroes. 1898.
Stories of the wild west. 1898.
With lance and sword: or old tales of chivalry retold. 1899.
A string of stories. 1902.

Catherine Cooper Hopley

Aunt Jenny's American pets. '1872' [1871].
Rambles and adventures in the wilds of the west. 1872.
Also wrote about the American Civil War.

Richard Henry Horne 1803–84

Memoirs of a London doll, written by herself. 1846 (illus).
See also col 618.

Mrs Hornibrook, Emma E. Hornibrook

One link in a chain. 188?
Worth the winning. 1885, 1899.

Isabel Hornibrook

Camp and trail. A story of the Maine woods. nd.
In the service. A story for boys. nd.
Luke: a story for boys. 1890.
Captain Curley's boy. London, Glasgow and Dublin 1900 (illus).

Caroline Horwood, later Baker fl. 1801–40

The deserted boy: or cruel parents. A tale of truth calculated to promote benevolence in children. Philadelphia 1817.
Original poetry for young minds. 1818, 1822, 1825, 1835.
Little Emma and her father. Philadelphia 1820?
Also pbd verse and adult fiction.

Lewis Hough

For fortune and glory: a story of the Soudan war. 1890 (illustr W. Paget).

Clemence Annie Housman 1861–1955

The were-wolf. 1896 (illustr L. Housman). First pbd in Atalanta.

Edward George Granville Howard 1792?–1841

Rattlin the reefer. 3 vols 1836 (ed and rev F. Marryat).
See also col 935.

Lady Harriet Howard 1823–65

The birthday: a tale for the young. 1844.
Also wrote religious texts.

Catherine Augusta Howell

Pages of child-life. [1860.]
Pictures of girl life. 1865.

Mary Howitt, née Botham 1799–1888

Sketches of natural history. 1834. This contains first pbn of The spider and the fly.
Tales in prose for young people. [1836.]
The children's year. 1847.

Our cousins in Ohio. 1849.
Tales for all seasons. 1881.
See also col 2156.

William Howitt 1792–1879

The boy's country book: being the real life of a country boy written by himself. 1839.
See also col 2157.

Maria A. Hoyer

Little Margit and other stories. 1887.
We four children. [1889.]
What happened at Morwyn. [1893.]
A forgotten link. [1899.]

Mary Hughes, née Robson

Aunt Mary's tales for the entertainment and improvement of little girls. 1811.
The ornaments discovered: a story in two parts. 1815, 1819.
The alchemist. 1818.
Metamorphoses: or effects of education. A tale. 1818.
The orphan girl: a moral story founded on fact. 1819.
Stories for children, chiefly confined to words of two syllables. 1819.
Something new from Aunt Mary. 1820.
Pleasing and instructive stories for young people. 1821.
The life of William Penn abridged and adapted for the use of young persons. 1822.
The good grandmother: or a visit to my uncle's. 1822.
Little Croppy and the May Queen. [1835.]
Also pbd educational texts.

Thomas Hughes 1822–96

Tom Brown's schooldays, by an old boy. Cambridge 1857, ed V. Rendall 1904, ed F. Sidgwick 1913.
See also col 1306.

Mary E. Hullah

A few words about music. 1851.
Hannah tame. 1883.
A little owl and other stories. 1883.
The lion battalion and other stories. 1885.
The gracious lady's ring. 1887.
Namesakes. 1887.
Philippa. 1887.
In hot haste. 1888.
As the tide turns. 1890.
Hans and his friends and other stories. 1893.
My aunt Constantia Jane: a story for children. 1893.

Fergus W. Hume 1859–1932

The chronicles of faeryland. Fantastic tales for old and young. [1982] (illustr M. Dunlop).

Madeline Bonavia Hunt

Maid Margery. nd.
Little hinges. [1879] (illustr M. Dunlop), London, Paris and New York 1883.
The magic mirror. London, Paris and New York 1883.
Little Empress Joan. 1885.
The two Hardcastles: or 'A friend in need is a friend indeed'. 1885.

Hurry, Mrs Ives, née Mitchell, Miss Mitchell

Tales of instruction and amusement. 1775, [c. 1803], 1807.
The faithful contrast: or virtue and vice accurately delineated in a series of moral and instructive tales. 1803.
National amusements for leisure hours. 1804.
Artless tales. 3 vols 1808.
Moral tales for young people. 1807, 2nd edn 1809.
Also wrote fiction for adults. See also col 1836.

John Conroy Hutcheson d. 1897

On board the 'Esmeralda': or Martin Leigh's log. 1885.
The wreck of the Nancy Bell: or cast away on Kerguelen Land. [1885] (illus), 1893.
Fritz and Eric: or the brother Crusoes. 1886.
The Penang pirate and the lost pinnacle. 1887 (illus).
Teddy: the story of a little pickle. 1888.
The black man's ghost: a story of the buccaneers' buried treasure of the Galapagos Islands. [1889] (illustr W. S. Stacey).
Afloat at last. A sailor boy's log of his life at sea. 1890.
The white squall: a story of the Sargasso Sea. 1893.
The pirate junk: a story of the Sooloo sea. 1896. (illustr J. B. Greene).
Tom Finch's monkey and how he dined with the admiral. 1896.
Young Tom Bowling: a story of the boys of the British navy. [1896] (illustr J. B. Greene).
Crown and anchor; or under the pen'ant. 1898 (illustr J. B. Greene).

John Robert Hutchinson b. 1858

Hal Hungerford: or the strange adventures of a boy emigrant. 1891, 1898.
The quest of the golden pearl. 1897 (illus).

Barbara Hutton, later Alexander

The fiery cross: or the vow of Montrose. nd.
Castles and their heroes. 1868 (illus), New York 1891.
Tales of the white cockade. 1870.
Heroes of the Crusades. New York 1891 (illus).
Tales of the Saracens. New York 1891.

Charles John Cutliffe Wright Hyne 1865-1944

The wild catters. A tale of the Pennsylvanian oil fields. nd.
Stimson's reef: a tale of adventure. 1892.
The captured cruiser: or two years from land. 1893.
The adventures of Captain Kettle. 1898. With several sequels.
See his My joyful life, *1935.*

Jean Ingelow 1820–97

Studies for stories from girls' lives. 1864, 1867, 1885? (illustr J. E. Millais et al).
Poor Matt: or the clouded intellect. 1866.
Stories told to a child. Boston 1865, 1867, [1891].
Deborah's book and The lonely rock. 1867.
The golden opportunity. 1867.
The grandmother's shoe. 1867.
Little Rie and the rosebuds, and Can and could. 1867.
The minnows with silver tales and Two ways of telling a story. 1867.
The moorish gold and The one-eyed servant. 1867.
The suspicious jackdaw and The life of John Smith. 1867.
The wild duck shooter; and I have a right. 1867.
A sister's bye-hours. 1868.

Mopsa the fairy. 1869, 1912 (EL), 1964 (Dent Illus Children's Classics).
The little wonder horn. [1872.]
The little wonder box. 6 vols [1887.] 6 booklets in a box, reprint of The little wonder horn [1872].
See also col 622.

Mary Inman

The leading hand: or Amy and Sybil. Manchester 1883.

'Isobel'

Lonely Queenie and the friends she made. 1873.

'Ita'

The fairy tree: or tales from far and near. 1861.
Far and near: or stories of a Christmas tree. London and New York 1864.

Raymond Jacberns

An uncut diamond and other stories. 1893.
Mists: fairy tales. 1895.
Witch demonia. A fairy tale. 1895.
Common chords: a story for girls. 1897.
The hobbledehoys. [1899.]
Four everyday girls. 1900.
Some ups and downs. 1900.
A handful of rebels: the escapades of five young pickles. [1901.]
Robin. [1901.]
A family of girls. 1902.
The new pupil: a school story. 1902.
Peggy Morton. [1902.]
A lonesome lassie. [1903.]
The Scaramouche club. 1903.
A family grievance. 1904.
The girls of Cromer Hall. [1904], [1920.]
A school champion. London and Edinburgh 1904.
Sunday talks with girls. 1904.
Crab cottage: a girl's story. 1905 (illus).
How things went wrong. 1905.
A bad three weeks. 1907 (illus).
A discontented schoolgirl. London and Edinburgh 1907.
That imp Marcella. London and Edinburgh 1907.
The truant five. [1907.]
A boy and a secret, a story for children. 1908.
A hard bit of road. [1908.]
The attic boarders. London and Edinburgh 1909 (illustr H. C. Earnshaw).
Becky Compton, ex-dux. London and Edinburgh 1909 (illus).
Poor Uncle Harry. 1910.
The record term: a school story for girls. 1910.
A school girl's battlefield. London and Edinburgh 1910 (illus).
An uncomfortable term. 1911 (illus).
That troublesome dog. London and Edinburgh 1911 (illustr M. L. Attwell).
Tabitha Smallways, schoolgirl. London and Edinburgh 1912.
The record term: a story for girls. 1922.

Alice F. Jackson

Mattie's mistake. 1888.
The choristers of Ravenswood. 1889.
Three little socialists. [1889.]
Fairy tales and true. Edinburgh 1890.
In the days of our childhood. 1890.
Toby and Tat. 1890.
Charlie: the story of a very little boy. [1891.]
The doll's dressmaker: a tale. [1891.]
Jack's little girls. [1892.]
Julie. 1892.
Miss Bright's guardian. 1894.
Our little sunbeams. Stories for the little ones. 1896.
Heroes of the Chitral seige. [1897], [1923].
A brave girl. A true story of the Indian mutiny. [1898.]
Over the garden gate. 1900.
Our jungle home. [1923.]
With Mahdi and Khalifa. [1930.]

'Catherine Jackson'

The storm's gift. A Lancashire story. 1891.

Edith Sophia Jacob

The gate of paradise: a dream of Easter eve. 1868, 1870, 1877.
The vision of the holy child. 1882.
Crump and smiles: the story of two bears. 1886.

George Payne Rainsford James 1799–1860

The last of the fairies. 1848.
See also col 936.

Mrs Jamieson, Frances Jamieson, née Thurtle

Ashford rectory: or the spoiled child reformed. 3rd edn 1820.
Popular voyages and travels throughout the continent and island of Europe. 1820.
The knight of the dove and his elfin page. 1826.

Annie M. L. Jarvis

Autobiography of a robin with his Christmas stories. 1885.
Rough: a clever dog. 1886.
A tame free robin. [1887.]

Mary Rowles Jarvis

The 'Bonny Susan'. 1883, 1912, 1919.
A bunch of seals. 1883.
The sliding panel: or the miser of Rayham Farm. 1890.
Sunshine and calm. [1895.]
The rescue on tempest reef. 1896.
Song of the kingdom. 1908.
Dick Lionheart. 1909 (illus).
The treasure finders. 1912.
Three girls and a garden. 1912.
Colin courageous. 1914.
Pleasing stories. 1916.
The fear. 1925.
Also pbd bks on natural history.

Richard Jefferies 1848–87

Bevis the story of a boy. 3 vols 1882; ed E. V. Lucas 1904, 1932.
See also col 1592.

Edward Jenkins 1838–1910

Little Hodge. 1872.
See also col 1601.

Annie Jenkyns

The wreckers of Laverock. 1885.

Jane Elizabeth Jerram, née Holmes

The little child's keepsake. nd.
The beautiful temple and other tales. [1830?]
My father's house. 1835.
Mamma's stories. [1843?]
The child's own story book. 1843, Philadelphia 1844, 12th edn 1864.
My three aunts; and other stories. 1838, [1845?], Manchester 1860.

Edward Jesse 1780–1868

Anecdotes of dogs. 1846.

Laura Jewry, later Valentine, Mrs R. Valentine, 'Aunt Louisa' d. 1899

The ransom. A tale of the thirteenth century. 1846, 1870 (as The knight's ransom, illus).
Kirkholme Priory: or modern heroism. A tale. 3 vols 1847.
The forest and the fortress: a romance of the nineteenth century. 1850.
The vassal: a story of old Normandy. 1850.
Harry Brightside: or the young traveller in Italy. 1852.
Beatrice: or six years of childhood and youth. 1859.
Baby Bianca: or the Venetians. 1861, 1881.
Burford Cottage and its robin redbreast. 1861, 1865.
The girl's own book. 1861, 1862, 1864, 1867, 1869.
Leighton Manor: or the orphan cousins. 1862.
No more, no less. 1864.
Honoria's Sunday book: being conversations on our Lord's miracles. 1865.
Aunt Louisa's book of animal stories. 1866, 1889. Illus.
Aunt Louisa's London toy books. 1866.
The language and sentiment of flowers. 1866 (illus).
Nursery tales: new version. 1869, 1878.
Warne's everlasting Victoria primer. 1869.
Heroism and adventure. A book for boys. 1871.
The Victoria picture reading book of original prose and selected poetry. 1872 (illus).
The brave days of old. A book for boys. 1874.
Daring and doing. A book for boys. 1874, [1877?].
The home book for young ladies. 1876.
Maidenhood: or the verge of the stream. 1876.
The girl's home book: or how to play and how to work. 1877.
The young women's book: a useful manual for everyday life. 1877.
Half hours of English history from James the first to Queen Victoria. 1881.
We three boys: or a year of adventure. 1884.
On honour's roll. Tales of heroism in the nineteenth century. 1885.
The day spring, a first Bible book for children. 1886.
The dawning. A first Bible book for children. 1886.
The Queen: her early life and reign. London and New York 1887.
Games for family parties and for children. 1888.
The old fairy tales. Collected and ed 1889 (illus).
Animal pictures. 4 pts 1892 (illus).
The life of Victoria, our Queen and Empress, simply told for children. 1897.
The girl's home companion. London and New York 1902, 1906 (rev edn).
Also wrote poetry and fiction for adults and primers and theological works.

Cecilia Anne Jones

Stories for Christmastide. London and Jersey 1861.
The sunbeam: or the misused gift. 1861.
Gertrude Dacre. 1862.
How Rachel Lee found the Christmas gift. 1867.
Three tales for an idle hour. 1867.
The story of Hermione. London and Frome 1868, 1870.
Our childhood's pattern: being tales based on incidents in the life of the Holy Child Jesus. [1870.]
Our childhood's prayer: or our Father's story. 1871.
A little life in a great city. 1873.
What the chums said. [1873.]
Poor Milly: a tale of London life. [1876.]
My Sunday friend: Bible stories. 1876.
Count up the sunny days. A story for boys and girls. 1882 (illus).
The foreign freaks of five friends. 1882.
Old Crumpet the shoemaker. 1885.
Little Jeanneton's work: a chronicle of Breton life. 1886.
Under the King's banner. 1888.
A modern red riding hood. 1889.
Little Sir Nicholas. A story for children. London and New York 1890 (illus).
Under the King's banner. Stories of the soldiers of Christ in all ages. 1891.
A new Dame Trot. A story for girls and boys. 1892 (illus).
Not quite a heroine. 1898.
Also pbd adult fiction and bks on religious history.

Dora M. Jones

The duke's ward: a romance of old Kent. Edinburgh 1896 (illus).

Harry Jones

Prince Boohoo and little Smuts. 1896 (illustr G. Browne).

Richard Kearton 1862–1928

Our bird friends: a book for all boys and girls. 1900.
Strange adventures in Dicky-bird land. Stories told by a mother to amuse her chicks. 1902.

Annie Keary 1825–79

Sidney Grey: or a year from home. 1856.
Father Phim. 1879, ed G. Avery 1962.
See also col 1310.

Annie Keary and Eliza Keary

The heroes of Asgard and the giants of Jotenheim. 1857, 1860.
Little Wanderlin and other fairy tales. 1865.
An early Egyptian history for the young. 1861.

Eliza Keary

At home again. nd.
The magic valley or patient Antoine. 1877 (illus).
Cat and dog life. Coloured and other pictures for children with stories. [1885?]

Mrs Henry Keary

Grandfather's sixpence. nd.
Hetty: or fresh watercresses. nd.

Sam: or a good name. 1871, 1881.
Phillis Phil: or alone in the world. London and New York 1874.
Hapless Harry: his own enemy. 1880.
A peep through the keyhole: or Mark Tuffin's troubles. 1890.

'Henrietta Keddie', Sarah Tytler 1829–1914

Papers for thoughtful girls with illustrative sketches of some girls' lives. Boston and New York 1865, Illustr J. E. Millais.
Sweet counsel: a book for girls. Boston 1866.
Vashti Savage. [1989].
The diamond rose. A life of love and duty. 1867.
Girl neighbors: or the old fashion and the new illustrated. 1888 [1887].
Girlhood and womanhood. The story of some fortunes and misfortunes. 1868.
Heroines in obscurity. A second series of 'Papers for thoughtful girls'. By the author of 'Papers for thoughtful girls'. 1871.
Musical composers and their works. For the use of schools and students in music. Boston 1875.
Childhood a hundred years ago. With six chromographs after paintings by Sir Joshua Reynolds. London and Belfast 1877.
Landseer's dogs and their stories. With six chromographs after paintings by Sir Edwin Landseer. London and Belfast 1877.
A lonely lassie. The Religious Tract Soc. (The Girl's Own Bookshelf.) [1889].
A young Oxford maid in the days of King and Parliament. [1890.]
A loyal little maid, a story of Mar's rebellion. 1899 (illus).
Mermaidens. A sea story for girls. nd (The Religious Tract Soc).

Frances Kelly

Domestic comforts. A tale founded on facts, for the use of young people. 1808, 1816.

Sophia Streeten Kelly, née Sherwood b. 1815

Edwin and Alicia: or the infant martyrs. 1834.

Mary Ann Kelty 1789–1873

The story of Isabel. 1826.
Biography for young ladies. 1839.
Mamma and Mary, discoursing upon good and evil, in six dialogues. 1840, 1844.
Gentle Gertrude: a tale for youth. 1843.
Visiting my relations and its results. 1851, 1852, 1853.
Alice Rivers. 1852.
Pbd numerous devotional bks.

Edward Augustus Kendall 1776?–1842

Little stories for pretty little birds. nd, [1856].
Keeper's travels in search of his master. 1798, 1803, 1807, Philadelphia 1808, London 1812, 1817, 1826, 1830, Boston 1833, London 1837, 1844, 1847, 1850, 1860, 1862, 1872.
The crested wren. 1799.
The canary bird: a moral story. 1799, 1801, Philadelphia 1814.
The stories of Senex: or little histories of little people. 1800.
The swallow: a fiction. 1800.
Lessons of virtue: or the book of happiness. 1801.
The sparrow. Philadelphia 1802.
Burford Cottage and its robin redbreast. 1824, 1835, 1861, 1865.
Also pbd travel bks.

Mrs Mary E. Kennard

Twilight tales. 1888.

Grace Kennedy 1782–1825

Jessy Allan, the lame girl. A story founded on facts. 1823, 6th edn Edinburgh 1828, 1831, 14th edn 1840, 187?
Anna Ross: a story for children. 1824, 3rd edn Edinburgh 1826 (anon), 1829, Oxford 1832, Edinburgh 1833, 1838, 9th edn London 1848, Philadelphia 185?, Edinburgh 1861 (as Annie Ross the orphan of Waterloo).
Philip Colville: or a covenanter's story. Edinburgh 1825 (anon unfinished), 1850, 1869.
Also pbd devotional fiction and tracts.

Jane Kennedy

Old maids and young maids in playful moods and mournful moods. 1851.
Sketches of character. 1851.
The bag of treasure. [1852.]
Light hearts and happy days: or tales of wisdom for children and youth. [1852.]
The strong bridle. 1852.
Young men and old men: or samples of life. 1852.
Mount Ephraim: or the change of profession, a tale for youth. Tunbridge Wells 1853.
Things new and old. 1854.
The balance of beauty: or the lost image restored. 1857.
The name. 1858.
Shreds and patches: or pathos and bathos. 1858.
Lionel Fitzgibbon and his parrot. 1858.
Also wrote evangelic tracts.

Edith C. Kenyon

Lost in the backwoods. [1899.]
Two girls in a siege: a tale of the great Civil War, founded on facts contained in old books relating to place and the period. [1908] (illus).

David Ker

The broken image, and other tales. 1870.
The boy slave in Bokhara. 1874, 1875.
On the road to Khiva. 1874.
The wild horsemen of the Pampas. 1875, 1876.
Cossack and star. 1892.
Prisoner among the pirates. 1893, 1894.
The wizard king. A story of the last invasion of Europe. 1895.
Vanished! Or the strange adventures of Arthur Hawksleigh. 1895.
Swept out to sea. A tale. 1896.
O'er Tartar deserts: or English and Russian in Central Asia. 1898.
A knight of honour. Historical and other stories. 1901.
Torn from its foundations: from Brazilian forests to inquisitions cells. 1902.
Ilderim the Afghan: a tale of the Indian border. 1903.
Among the dark mountains, or cast away in Sumatra. 1906, 1907.
Under the flag of France. 1907, 1908, 1912.
Rajah's legacy. 1910.
Blown away from the land. An adventure in the Mediterranean. 1911.
The last of the sea kings. 1913.
Over an unknown ocean. 1926.
In steel grey armour. 1927.

The hermit of Lihou. 1928.
The hidden face. 1928.
Where the Russian flag flew. 1928.
Up the rock! A story of the English in the Spanish War of Succession. 1929.
Cross and sword. 1930.
Fighting for freedom. A story of the Tirol. 1931.
A wave worn rock. A story of Russia. 1932.
In quest of the Upas. A tale of adventure in New Guinea. 1934.

Short stories
The biter bitten in 52 stories of pluck, peril and romance for girls. Ed Alfred H. Miles [1896].
The Czar's fish in 52 stories of pluck, peril and romance for girls. Ed Alfred H. Miles [1896].
Regularly contributed to boys' mags, especially Boy's Own Paper.

Margaret Keston

A girl's experiment. [1898.]

J. W. Keyworth

The golden shoemaker: or 'Cobbler's Horn'. [1899.]

Dorothy Kilner, 'M. Pelham' 1755–1836

Anecdotes of a boarding school. [1790], 1816.
The history of a great many little boys and girls, for the amusement of all good children of four and five years of age. [c. 1790.]
The rational brutes: or talking animals. 1799. By M. Pelham.
The holiday present. York 1803, 1831.
First going to school: or the story of Tom Brown and his sisters. 1804.

Charles Kingsley 1819–1875

Glaucus: or the wonders of the shore. Cambridge 1855.
Westward Ho! or the voyages and adventures of Sir Amyas Leigh. 3 vols Cambridge 1855.
The heroes: or Greek fairy tales for my children. Cambridge 1856.
The water babies: a fairy tale for a land baby. 1863.
Hereward the Wake: 'last of the English'. 2 vols 1866.
Madam How and Lady Why: or first lessons in earth lore for children. 1870.
See also col 1311.

Henry Kingsley 1830–76

The boy in grey. 1871.
The lost child. 1871.
Valentin: a French boy's story of Sedan. 2 vols 1872.
See also col 1318.

W. H. G. Kingston

See col 1319.

Rudyard Kipling 1865–1936

The jungle book. 1894.
The second jungle book. 1895.
'Captains Courageous': a story of the Grand Banks. 1897.
Stalky and Co. 1899.
Kim. 1901; ed C. E. Carrington, New York 1960; ed J. I. M. Stewart, New York 1962.
Just so stories for little children. 1902.
Puck of Pook's Hill. 1906.
Rewards and fairies. 1910.
Land and sea tales for scouts and guides. 1923.
See also col 1604.

Jane L. Kippen

Edith Oswald: or living for others. 1881.

Mary Kirby, afterwards Gregg 1817–1893 and Elizabeth Kirby 1823–73

The discontented children and how they were saved. 1855, 1859 (illustr Phiz).
The talking bird: or the little girl who knew what was going to happen. 1856.
Julia Maitland: or pride goes before a fall. 1857.
Truth is always best: or a fault confessed is half redressed. '1858' [1857].
Rose coloured spectacles. 1859.
Lucy Neville and her schoolfellows. 1860.
The sea and its wonders. A companion volume to the world at home. London, Edinburgh and New York 1871.

Marianne Kirlew

The red thread of honour. 1891.
Green Garry: a schoolboy's story. 1898.
The story of John Wesley told to girls and boys. nd.

Flora Klickman

At the seaside: or stories about ships and sailors. [1897.]
In make-believe land. [1899.]
In pinafore land. [1900.]
Contributed regularly to periodicals, including Alalanta *and* Girl's Own Paper, *which she edited.*

Edward Hugesson Knatchbull-Hugesson, Baron Brabourne 1829–93

Stories for my children. 1867, 1869.
Crackers for Christmas. 1870. By E. H. K.
The magic cake and Prince Filderkin. 1871.
Moonshine fairy stories. 1871.
Tales at tea-time. 1872.
Queer folk. 1874.
Higgledy piggledy: or stories for everybody and everybody's children. 1875, 1877.
Whispers from fairyland. 1875.
Uncle Joe's stories. 1879.
The mountain sprite's kingdom and other stories. 1881.
Ferdinand's adventure and other stories. 1882 (illustr E. Griset).
Friends and foes from fairyland. 1886 (illustr L. Sambourne).
Ella's fault. 1887.
Also pbd other works of fiction and bks on history and politics.

Eva Mary Knatchbull-Hugesson. d. 1895

A hit and a miss. [1893] (illustr L. L. Brooke).

Louisa Knatchbull-Hugesson

The history of Prince Perrypets. A fairy tale. 1872 (illustr W. Weigand).

Anne Knight

Mornings in the library. 1830 (introd by B. Barton).
Mary Gray: a tale for little girls. 1831.
Schoolroom lyrics. 1864.

Arthur Lee Knight

The young rajah. nd.
Dicky Beaumont: his perils and adventures. 1890.
The cruise of the Cormorant: or treasure seekers ahoy. 1893.
The brother middies and slavers ahoy. Edinburgh 1894.
Leaves from a middy's log. 1896.
The Rajah of Monkey Island. 1897 (illustr W. S. Stacey).
The gunman heroes: or adventures with Arabs, afloat and ashore. 1899.

Mrs Helen Cross Knight 1814–1906

Jane Hudson, the American girl: or exert yourself. 1848, 1855, 1868.
The valley of decision: or divine teachings in a boarding school. 1851.
The beautiful garment and other stories. 1856.
No gains without pains. A true life for boys. 6th edn [1856?]
Kitty King: or chapters for children. [1874], 1908 (illus).
Johnny: or how a little boy learned to be good. London, Edinburgh and New York 1881 (6th edn).
Also pbd tracts.

Kathleen Knox

Father Time's story book. 1873.
Fairy gifts: or a wallet of wonders. 1875.
Lily of the valley; a story for little boys. 1876.
Meadowleigh. A holiday history. 1876.
Seven birthdays: or the children of fortune. 1876.
Wildflower Win: the journal of a little girl. 1876.
Queen Dora: the life and lessons of a little girl. 1879.
Captain Eva. The story of a naughty girl. [1880.]
Cornertown chronicles: new legends of old lore. 1880.
The organist's baby: a story. '1895' [1894], [1927] (as Bab's two cousins).

Fanny Lablache

Starlight stories told to bright eyes. 1876, 1877.
A wayside posy. Gathered for girls. 1897.

Charles Lamb 1775–1834

The king and queen of hearts. 1805, 1902 (ed E. V. Lucas).
The adventures of Ulysses. 1808, 1890 (ed A. Lang).
Prince Dorus. 1811 (anon), 1889 (ed A. Tuer).
Beauty and the beast. [1811?] (anon), 1887 (ed A. Lang).

Charles and Mary Anne Lamb 1764–1847

Tales from Shakespear designed for the use of young persons. 2 vols 1807, 1899 (ed A. Lang), 2 vols 1901 (ed F. Furnivall), 1965 (ed J. C. Trewin).
Mrs Leicester's school: or the history of several young ladies related by themselves. 1809 (anon), 1885 (ed A. Ainger).
Poetry for children, entirely original, by the author of Mrs Leicester's school. 1809 (anon), 1872 (ed R. H. Shepherd).
See also col 2170.

'Ruth Buck', Mrs Ruth Buck Lamb

See Ruth Buck.

'Harry Collingwood', William Joseph Cosens Lancaster 1851–1922

The log of the 'Flying fish': a story of aerial and submarine peril and adventure. 1887 (illustr G. Browne), 1894.
The missing merchantman. 1889 (illustr W. H. Overend).
Harry Escombe: a tale of adventure in Peru. 1910.

Ebenezer Landells 1808–60

Home pastimes: or the child's own toymaker. 1858, 1859, New York 1860.
The boy's own toymaker: a practical illustrated guide to the useful employment of leisure hours. 4th edn 1860 (illus), 6th edn 1863, 1892.
The girl's own toymaker and book of recreations. 1860 (with A. Landells), 5th edn 1868.
An engraver who also wrote on shipwrecks.

Laura M. Lane

'A character': a story for girls. nd.
Ella's mistake. 1889.

Andrew Lang

See col 2362.

Elizabeth Lang

Jane and her family. A tale for the young. 1895.

Frederick Langbridge

Mysteriously missing: the strange adventures of two little pickles. 1881.
Shank's pony. 1886.
The happiest half hour. Sunday talks with children. 1888.
Scout's head: or St Nectan's ball. 1889.
Major Monk's motto: or look before you leap. 1892.

Edward Lear

See col 630.

Hilda Balfour Leatham

The King's castle: a story for children. 1895.
Big brother Dick. A story for boys and girls. [1896.]
Mother's ship. A story for boys and girls. [1897.]
The naughty little Newlands. [1898.]

Matilda Leathes, Mrs Stanley Leathes

Ruth Levison: or working and waiting. 1860.
Charity at home. 1863.
Soi même. 1869.
A story of a wilful life. 1869.
Penelope: or morning clouds dispersed. 1873.
Prue's babies. 1876.
The girls of Bredon, and manor house stories. [1877.]
On the doorsteps, or Crispin's story. [1880.]

Little pearl: or all among the daisies. nd. (As All among the daisies [1881].)
Jack and Jill of our own day. [1882.]
The caged linnet: or love's labour not lost. [1883.]
Inglenook stories. 1883.
Other lives than ours. [1884.]
Afloat. [1886.]
On the doorsteps: or Crispin's story. [1886.]
Over the hills and far away. [1887.]
Tomorrow. [1887.]
Dody and Joss: or all's well that ends well. [1889.]
Holidays in summer and winter. [1890.]
Zetty Craig: or no cross, no crown. 1898.

Mary Elizabeth Southwell Leathley 1818–99

Tales for children. nd.
The child's book of country things. 1840.
The cheerful companion, an easy story book for young children. 1850 (illustr G. Leighton).
The life of a dutiful son. 1854.
Little stories for little readers. 1855.
The children of Scripture. 1856, 1864.
Chick-seed without chick-weed: being very easy and entertaining lessons for little children. 1860.
Conquerors and captives: or from David to Daniel. 1873.
The star of promise: or from Bethlehem to Calvary. 1873.
The story of stories for little ones. 1875.
Requiescant: a little book of anniversaries. 1888, 1905.
Verses. 1896.

Elizabeth Lecky

Auntie's rhymes. nd (illus).
The story of Jack the cat. 1883.
The story of the good dog, Rover. 1883.
The little traveller. 1883.
Fairy folk. 1886. Verse.
Here, there and everywhere. [1890.]

Mary Lee and Catherine Lee

Lucy's campaign: a story of adventure. 1867.
Rosamund Fane: or the prisoners of St James's. 1870.
The oak staircase: or stories of Lord and Lady Desmond. 1872, [1911] illus.
Joachim's spectacles. 1876 (illus).
Goldhanger woods: a child's romance. 1887.
Mrs Dimsdale's grandchildren. [1888] (illus).
The family coach. [1890] (illus).
St Dunstan's fair. [1892.]
Told after tea. 1892.
Miss Coventry's maid: a story for girls. [1895.]
Kitty's birthday. [1897.]
Laurie's motto. [1897.]

Nelson Lee 1806–95

The life of a fairy. [1850] (illustr A. Crowquill).

Mrs R. Lee, Sarah Lee, née Bowdich 1791–1856

The juvenile album: or tales from far and near. 1841, [1845] illus.
Elements of natural history for the use of schools and young persons. 1844.
The farm and its scenes. 1852 (illustr H. Weir).
Twelve stories of the sayings and doings of animals. 1853 (illus).
Playing at settlers: or the fagott house. 1855 (illus).
Little Neddie's menagerie. [1880] (illustr H. Weir).
Little Nellie's birdcage. [1881] (illustr H. Weir).
Also pbd extensively on natural history and exploration.

Lady Maria Charlotte Lees d. 1881

Effie's and the doctor's tales: or visits from two spirits. A tale for girls of Effie's age. 1854.

Jane Eliza Leeson 1807–82

Hymns and scenes of childhood: or a sponsor's gift. 1842, 1848, 1850.
The lady Ella: or the story of Cinderella in verse. 1847.
The Christian child's book. 1848.
The child's book of ballads. 1849.
The orphan's home. 1849.
The child's new lesson book: or stories for little readers. [1850.]
Margaret: an olden tale. 1850.
The story of a dream: or a mother's version of an olden tale. 1850.
Also pbd religious books.

Mary Helena Cornwall Legh

Little orphans: or the story of Trudchen and Darling. 1894, 1894 (as Darling: or the little orphans).
How Dick and Molly went round the world. 1895.
My dog Plato. His adventures and impressions. [1895.]
An incorrigible girl. 1899.
At the foot of the rainbow. A tale of adventure. 1900.
Gold in the furnace. 1900.
Thorns and thistles. 1901.

Caroline Leicester

Fanny and her Mamma. 1848, 1872 (as Mamma's stories).
Susan and her doll: or do not be covetous. [1861.]
Juvenile poetry. 1863.

'Netta Leigh', Miss Whittemore?

Aline. 1892.
Patti Thorn. 1892.
The Somervilles. 1892.
Brave heart. 1893.
Busy bee: or the little watercress. 1899.

Robert Leighton 1859–1934

The pilots of Pomona: a story of the Orkney Islands. 1892, 1903.
In the grip of the Algerine. [1894.]
The wreck of the Golden Fleece. The story of a North Sea fisherboy. 1894 (illustr F. Brangwyn).
Olaf the glorious. 1895 (illustr R. Peacock).
Under the foeman's flag: a story of the Spanish Armada. 1896, 1930.
The golden galleon. 1898.
The splendid stranger: a story of the Monmouth rebellion. 1898.
The thirsty sword: a story of the Norse invasion of Scotland. 1900 (illus).
The boys of Waveney. 1902.
In the land of ju-ju: a tale of Benin, the city of blood. 1903 (illus).
The cleverest chap in the school. 1910.
The bravest boy in the camp. 1912.
The black prince of Africa: a story for boys. 1923.

Charles Godfrey Leland 1824–1903

Johnnykin and the goblins. 1877 (illus).

Mark Lemon 1809–70

The enchanted doll: a fairy tale for little people. 1849.
Fairy tales. 1868.
Tinykin's transformations: a child's story. 1869.
See also col 2006.

Eliza Lucy Leonard

The miller and his golden dream. In verse. 1816.
The ruby ring: or the transformation. In verse. 1816

Amélie Claire Le Roy, *see* Esmé Stuart

Emma Leslie

The two orphans. A tale for the young. 1863.
Trial and trust: or Ellen Morden's experience of life. 1864.
Teddy's dream: or a little sweep's mission. 1868.
Milly's errand: or saved to save. 1870.
Soldier Fritz and the enemies they fought: a story of the Reformation. 1871, 1914.
Maggie's message. 1872, 1890, 1906.
The orphan and the foundling: or alone in the world. 1872 (illus).
Percy Raydon: or self-conquest. 1872.
Myra's pink dress. 1873.
Peter the apprentice: a tale of the Reformation in England. 1873, 1905.
Hilda: or the golden age. [1874.]
Sunbeam Susette: a story of the siege of Paris. 1874.
Tom Perry's venture. 1874 (illus).
Lizzie's promise. 1875.
Out of the mouth of the Lion: or the Church in the catacombs. 1875.
Squire Lynne's will. 1875 (illus).
Before the dawn. A tale of Wycliffe and Bohemia. [188?]
Only a little fault. 1882.
Tom: the boater: a tale of English canal life. 1882.
The water waifs: a tale of barge life. 1882.
A slip at starting: or Johnny's first place. 1883.
Margaret's journal: or steps upward. 1884.
Marion and Augusta: or love and selfishness. 1884, 1890.
Saxby: a tale of old and new England. 1884, 1911.
Tom Watkin's mistake. A tale. 1885.
The martyr's victory. A tale of Danish England. 1886.
Stories from French history. 1886.
The life and reign of Queen Victoria. 1887, 1897 (illus).
That vulgar girl. 1887.
Through storm to calm: a tale of the last century. 1887.
How the strike began: a story for girls. 1888.
The magic runes: a tale of the times of Charlemagne. 1888.
The making of a hero. 1888.
Pretty Miss Hathaway. 1888.
A sailor's lass. 1888 (illus).
Shucks: a story for boys. 1888.
Saved by love. A story of London streets. 1889, 1904.
Arthur's temptation: or a brave beginning. [1890?]
Letty's Raymond training. A tale. 1890, 1893.
The story of a Christmas sixpence. 1890.
Tom Morris's error and other stories. 1890.
A London rose. A tale. 1891.
The seed she sowed: a tale of the great dock strike. 1891.
Lady Marjorie: a story of Methodist work a hundred years ago. 1892.
Our little lady. 1895.
Sowing beside all waters: a tale of the early church. 1895.
In the gipsies' van: or caught in a trap: a story for boys. 1896.
Lizzie's experiment. A story of London life. 1896.
The stolen rose. 1896.
Kate's ordeal. 1897.
Our little Nan: a story of twin sisters. London and Glasgow 1897, 1910.
A London rose and Kate's ordeal. 1898.
Leila's quest, and what came of it. 1900.
Lina's fortune. 1900.
The little gypsy. [1900?]
That scholarship boy. 1900.
On the Emperor's service: a story of the time of Constantine. 1905.
A young lady of quality: a story of the great Methodist revival in the eighteenth century. 1906.
The mystery of Rosabelle: or Lina's fortune. 1924.
Contributed to periodicals for the young, including Young England.

Mary E. Lester

Love's golden key: or the witch of Berryton. [189?]

Bitha Lloyd, née Fox 1811–84

The yews. [1859.]
Also pbd bks on the Lake District.

Hannah Jane Locker, née Lampson, Hannah Jane Locker-Lampson, Mrs Frederick Locker

The pedlar of Copthorne Common and other stories. 1879.
Shaw's farm. 1880.
What the blackbird said. A story in four chirps. 1881 (illustr R. Caldecott).

Hannah R. Lockwood, Miss Lockwood

Little May's mythology. A short account of the gods and goddesses of ancient Rome. 1869.
Progressive and classified spelling book. 1870.

Lady Julia Lockwood

Cyrus King of Persia and Media: his life and character for the use of the young. 1861.
Instinct or reason: being anecdotes of animal history. 1861 (illus), 1862, 1872.

Florence Lockyer

The garland alphabet. [1891.]

Agnes Loudon

Tales for young people. 1846.
Tales of school life. 1850.

'Solomon Lovechild'

See Lady Eleanor Fenn.

Charles Rathbone Low

The adventures of J. Hawsepipe, master mariner: a tale of the sea and land. 1868 (illus), 1869.

Tales of old ocean. 1869.
The land of the sun: sketches of travel, with memoranda, historical and geographical of places of interest in the East, visited during many years service in Indian waters. 1870.
Tales of the naval adventure. 1872 (illus).
The great battles of the British navy. 1873, 1885.
The letter of Marque and tales of the sea and land. 1873 (illus).
The life and correspondence of Field-Marshall Sir G. Pollock. 1873.
The autobiography of a man-o-war's bell: a tale of the sea. 1875 (illus).
History of the Indian navy, 1613–1863. 1877.
Maritime discovery: a history of nautical exploration from the earliest times. 1881.
Cyril Hamilton, his adventures by sea and land. 1885.
The great battles of the British army. 1885, 1890, 1908.
Memoir of Major-General J. T. Boileau. 1887.
Soldiers of the Victorian age. 1889.
Her Majesty's navy, including its deeds and battles. 1890–3.
Captain Cook's three voyages round the world. With a sketch of his life. 1891.
Old England's navy. 1891.
Cressy to Tel-el-Kebir. A narrative poem, descriptive of the deeds of the British army. 1892.
Major General Sir Frederick S. Roberts . . . a memoir. 1883.
England's sea victories. 1893.
Britannia's bulwarks: an historical poem, descriptive of the deeds of the British navy. 1895.
The epic of Olympus: a narrative poem descriptive of the deeds of the deities and heroes of the Greek mythology. 1897.
Famous frigate actions. 1898.
How we got to windward of the slave dealers: peril and prowess. 1899.
The Olympiad: classic tales in verse. 1903.

Frances H. Low

The air child, and other new fairy tales. 1896.
The little men in scarlet and other fairy tales. 1896.

Cecilia Selby Lowdnes

A lucky mistake. [188?]
A high resolve. [1891] (illus).

Constance M. Lowe

Children's pleasures. nd.

Edward Verall Lucas 1868–1938

The dumpy books for children. 1897–1900.
A book of verse for children. 1897. Ed Lucas.
The Flamp, The Ameliator and the schoolboy's apprentice. 1897.
Anne's terrible good nature and other stories. 1908.
The slowcoach. 1910.

Mary Elisabeth Lucy, M. E. L. d. 1890

Grandmamma's chapter of accidents. 1869.
Also wrote bks on history and travel.

William Luff

Our lifeboats. Pictures of peril and rescue. London and New York [1895].

Lady Henrietta Lushington, née Prescott d. 1875

Agnes Selby: a story for children. nd.
The happy home: or the children at the red house. 1864.
Littlehope Hall: a tale. 1864.
Hacco the dwarf, and other tales. 1865.
Almeira's castle: or my early life in India and in England. 1866 (illus).
The school for donkies and other stories. 1868.

Annette Lyster

The boy who never lost a chance: or Roger Read's history. [189?]
Dorothy the dictator. [189?]

George MacDonald 1824–1905

Dealings with the fairies. 1867.
At the back of the north wind. 1871.
Ranald Bannerman's boyhood. 1871.
The princess and the goblin. 1872.
The wise woman: a parable. 1875, New York 1876 (as A double story).
The princess and Curdie. 1882.
See also col 1332.

J. R. Macduff

The story of a dewdrop. 1881.

Herbert C. Macilwaine

The twilight reef, the poet of dead horse flat and the decivilisation of Mr Smyth. Tales. 1897.
Dinkinbar. A tale. 1899, 1908.
Fate the fiddler. A tale. 1900.
The white stone. The story of a boy from the bush. 1900.
The undersong. Short stories. 1903.
Anthony Britten constable. 1906.

Maria J. McIntosh

Juvenile tales for all seasons. 1858 (illus).

Robert Ellice Mack

Jack in the box. nd.
A Christmas tree fairy. nd. By Lizzie Mack and Robert Ellice Mack.
All around the clock. 1886.
Under the mistletoe. 1889. By Lizzie Lawson and Robert Ellice Mack.

Matilda Anne Mackarness, née Planché, 'Susie Sunbeam' 1826–81

Old Joliffe. 1845.
A trap to catch a sunbeam. 1849, Boston and Cambridge MA 1850.
The house on the rock. 1852.
Sunbeam stories. Boston and Cambridge MA 1856.
A ray of light to brighten cottage homes. 1857.
The golden rule: or stories illustrative of the ten commandments. 1859, 1867, 1869.
Helena's duties. 1860.
The picture alphabet with stories. 1860.
When we were young and other stories. 1860.
A guardian angel. 1864.
The children's Sunday album of short stories. 1870.
The young lady's book. A manual of amusements, exercises, stories and pursuits. 1876 (Routledge).
Also pbd other stories.

Minnie Mackean

The young naturalists: a book for boys. Paisley 1892.

Stephen J. MacKenna

Plucky fellows: being reminiscences from the notebook of Captain Fred: a book for boys. 1873, 1874.
Brave men in action. Thrilling stories of the British flag. 1878, 1890 (with Jack O'Shea), 1899.

Hannah B. Mackenzie

Kitty's cousin. London and Glasgow 1885.

Charles McKnight

Captain Jack; or old Fort Duquesne. A story of Indian adventure. 1874 (illus).
Our western border: its life one hundred years ago. Philadelphia 1876 (illus).

Mary Macleod

Robin Hood and his merry men. Stories from old ballads. nd, 1926.
Stories from the Faerie Queen. 1897, 1903 (introd by J. Hales).
The book of King Arthur and his noble knights. 1900, 1908, [1949].
Hilda at school. 1903.
The boys of Merlin's tower. 1908.
The house in the glen. 1909.
Franklin and his golden Pippins and other stories from the Charm. 1910.
Also edited ballads and other literary works.

Norman Macleod 1812–72

The gold thread. A story for the young. 1861, 1883, 1907 (ed D. McLeod), 1911 (as The gold thread and Wee Davie), 1920 (retold by A. Steedman), 1926, 1943.
Author of numerous devotional texts, lectures and novels, and editor of Good Words *and* Good Words for the Young. *See also col 2631.*

Katherine Sarah Macquoid 1824–1917

Too soon: a study of a girl's heart. 1873.
Little Fyfine and other tales. 1881.
The little vagabond: a story of Checo: a tale of Perugia. [1886.]
Puff: an autobiography. [1888.]
Pepin the dancing bear: a tale. 1889.
See also col 1340.

Catherine Mary MacSorley

His chosen work: or was it a failure. 1884.
Number one Brighton Street: or when we assemble and meet together. [1885.]
A few good women and what they teach us. Guildford 1886.
Exiled: or when grandmother was young. [1892.]
After many days. [1892.]
A dull life. [1892.]
The old house. 1893.
A steep road. 1894.
Aunt Dorothy's tea table. [1896.]
A seaside story. [1897.]
The dog and number twelve. [1898.]
The children's plan and what came of it. [1899.]
Rosie's friend. 1899.
The vicarage children. [1900.]
An Irish cousin. [1901.]
How the story ended. [1902.]
Goodbye summer: a story for girls. [1906.]
Nora: an Irish story. [1908] (illus).
The rectory family. [1910.]
Harold's mother: or the bugle call. [1914.]
Ireland and her Church: a simple history for children. 1915.
The road through the bog. 1918.

Maud Maddick

Mother's eyes: or 'faithful in the least'. 1891.

Julia Charlotte Maitland, née Barrett d. 1864

The dog and her friends: or the memoirs of the Lady Seraphina. 1853, 1854, 1858.
Cat and dog: or memoirs of Puss and the Captain. 1854, 1856, 1858 (5th edn) (illustr H. Weir); tr Fr 1863.
Also pbd charades and letters.

Muriel Maitland

Mrs Green's castle and other stories. [1892.]

Arthur Noel Malan

The young guard of the King's army: addresses to boys. 1885.
Ernest Fairfield: or two terms at St Andrews. 1888.
The cobbler of Cornikeranium. 1890.
Lost on Brown Willy: or the print of the cloven hoof. 1890.
Uncle Towser: a story for young and old. [1892.]
The Wallaby man. [1904.]
Schooldays at Highfield House. [1908] (illus).
Contributed to boys' periodicals, especially the Boy's Own Paper.

Hugh Poyntz Malet

Jack Nory: or courage and perseverance. 189?
A regular contributor to boys' periodicals, who also wrote on natural history, geology and India.

Lucas Malet 1852–1931

Little Peter: a Christmas morality for children of any age. 1888 (illus).
See also col 1626.

Rev Edward Mangin 1772–1852

Stories for short students: or light lore for little people. 1829.
Also pbd essays and novels.

Amy Manifold

For Hal's sake. 1892.
Bessie Drew: or the odd little girl. [1899.]

Anne Manning 1807–79

Jack and the tanner of Wymondham: a tale of the time of Edward the sixth. 1854.
See also col 1338.

Jessie Mansergh, later Mrs George de Horne Vaizey

Rose coloured thread. 1898.
About Peggy Saville. 1900, [1920?].
More about Peggy. 1901, 1908.
Tom and some other girls: a public school story. 1901.
More about Pixie. 1903, 1905, 1941.
Big game: a story for girls. [1905], [1908] (illus).
Ethelreda the ready: a school story. 1910.
Also pbd adult novels.

Charles Mansford

Under the naga banner. 1897 (illus).
A regular contributor to Chums *and* Boys' Friend.

Alicia Catherine Mant 1788?–1869

Ellen: or the young godmother. A tale for youth. 1812, 1814, 1815.
The canary bird. 1817.
Margaret Melville and the soldier's daughter: or juvenile memoirs. 1818, 1828.
The young naturalist: a tale. 1824 (2nd edn).
Also pbd adult novels.

Frederick Woods Mant

The young midshipman: or twelve years at sea. [189?]

M. B. Manwell

Gerty's triumph. A Cornish story. 1883, 1911, 1919.
Dad's Dorothy. The story of a Tuesday's bairn. 1889, 1908, 1922.
Crowded out: or the story of Lil's patience. [1890.]
The little house on the cliff. [1891.]
Geordie Stuart. A story of Waterloo. [1892.]
Niece Marjorie. A story for girls. [1892.]
Tony's neighbour. A story for boys. [1892.]
The Bents of Battersby. 1893.
Little Miss: or Leslie Underwood's fortune. 1895, 1910.
Mother's boy. 1895.
Nobly planned. [1896.]
The waif of bounder's tents. 1896.
The captain's bunk: a story for boys and girls. [1898.]
The white prince and Bobo link. [1898.]
Carol Adair. 1899 (illus).
Roy's sister: or 'this way and hers'. [1899.]
The other Carews. 1900.
The boys of Monk's Harold: a tale of adventure. [190?], 1907.
Daisy's knight. [1901.]
Kit and Co. [1901.]
The powder monkey's yarn. [1901.]
The wind that shakes the barley. [1901.]
The young knights of Gaddesdon. [1901.]
The girls of Dancy Dene. 1902.
Granny's girls. [1903.]
The doll, the Sprat and Peter. [1911.]
The crew of the rectory. [1912] (illus).
The girls of St Ursula's. 1912.

Grace Mara

Daisy's visit to Uncle Jack and what came of it. 1894.
The angel's charge: a story for children. 1898.

Jane Marcet, née Haldimand 1769–1858

Conversations for children on chemistry, in which the elements of science are familiarly explained and illustrated by experiment. 1806, 1809, 1814, 1817, 1819, 1824, 1853.
Conversations on the history of England for the use of children. 1829.
Bertha's visit to her uncle in England. 1830, 1831, 1836 (as Bertha's journal while on a visit to England), 1846 (6th edn).
The season's stories for very young children. 1832, 1854, 1861 (7th edn).
Mary's grammar interspersed with stories. 1833, 1885.
Willy's holidays: or conversations on different kinds of government. Intended for young children. 1836.
Conversations for children on land and water. 1838.
Conversations on language for children. 1844.
Lessons on animals, vegetables and minerals. 1844.
Willy's stories for young children. 1845.
Willy's travels on the railroad. 1847.
The heiress in her minority: or the progress of character. 1850.
Mary's grammar. 1851.
Rich and poor. 1851.
Also pbd numerous didactic bks. See also col 2494.

Clarice March

Marred by meddling. 1894.
Doris's high school days. 1899.

Bessie Marchant, later Mrs A. J. Comfort 1862–1941

The house at Brambling Minster. nd (illustr W. S. Stacey).
The Bessie Marchant omnibus book. [1892.]
The old house by the water. [1894.]
Weasel Tim. [1896.]
The Rajah's daughter: or the half-moon girl. 1899.
Winning his way: a story for boys. [1899.]
Also pbd over 100 adventure stories for girls in the twentieth century.

Augusta Marryat 1834–98

See col 1630.

Emilia Marryat, later Norris 1835–75

See col 1631.

'Captain Marryat', Frederick Marryat 1792–1848

Masterman ready: or the wreck of the Pacific, written for young people. 3 vols 1841–2.
The settlers in Canada, written for young people. 2 vols 1844.
The children of the New Forest. 2 vols [1847].
The little savage. 2 pts 1848–9. Ed F. S. Marryat; of pt 2 Frederick Marryat only wrote 2 chs.
See also col 953.

Beatrice Marshall

Nancy's nephew: or Mike's first campaign. [c. 1886–9.]

Charles Marshall, 'Heraclitus Gab'

King Gab's story bag and the wonderful stories it contained. London and New York [1869].

Emma Marshall, née Martin 1830–99

Happy days at Fernback. 1861.
Rainy days and how to meet them. 1863.
Roger's apprenticeship: or five years of a boy's life. [1865.]
Millicent Legh. 1866.
The old gateway: or the story of Agatha. 1867, [1900].
The dawn of life: or little Mildred's story, written by herself. [1867.]
Daisy Bright. 1868.
The little peat cutters: or the song of love. 1868.
Theodora's childhood: or the old house at Wynburn. 1868.
Violet Douglas: or the problems of life. 1868.
Grace Buxton: or the light of home. 1869.
Christabel Kingscote: or the patience of hope. 1870.
The lost lilies. New York [1870].
Primrose: or the bells of Old Effingham. 1870.
The story of the two Margarets. [1870.]
Three little sisters. 1871.
To-day and yesterday: or a story of summer and winter holidays. 1871.
Matthew Frost, carrier: or little snowdrop's mission. 1872.
Stellafont Abbey: or nothing new. 1872.
Between the cliffs: or Hal Forrester's anchor. 1873.
Mrs Mainwaring's journal. 1874.
Now-a-days: or King's daughters. 1875.
Three little brothers. 1875.
The errant boy and the shop woman: or want of consideration in little things. [1876.]
The governess: or pleading voices. 1876.
Life's aftermath. 1876.
Theodora's childhood: or the old house at Wynbourn. 1876.
Thoughtfulness for your mother. 1876.
Mrs Haycock's chronicles. [1877.]
A lily among thorns. 1878.
Marjory: or the gift of peace. 1878.
Enough and to spare. 1879.
Framilode Hall: or before honour is humility. 1879.
The Rochemonts. 1879.
The royal law: or the words of the King. [1879.]
A chip off the old block. 1880.
Memories of troublous times. 1880.
A rose without thorns. 1880.
A violet in the shade. 1880.
Dorothy's daughters. 1881.
Benvenuta: or rainbow colours. 1882.
Crusts and crumpets. 1882.
Dewdrops and diamonds. 1882.
Rex and Regina: or the song of the river. 1882.
Sir Christopher Crawley's crochets. [1882.]
The court and the cottage: a story for girls. 1883, 1898 (illus).
Dayspring. 1883.
Sir Valentine's victory, and other stories. 1883.
Mrs Willoughby's octave. 1884.
My Grandmother's pictures. 1884.
Silver chimes: or Olive. A story for children. 1884, [1904].
The two homes. [1884.]
Michael's treasure: or choice silver. 1885.
The mistress of Twain Court. 1885.
No. XIII: or the story of a lost vestal. 1885.
Over the down: or a chapter of accidents. 1885.
The story of the lost emerald. 1885.
Mistress Matchett's mistake. 1886.
Rhoda's reward. 1886.
Salome: or 'let Patience have her perfect work'. 1886, 1903.
The tower on the cliff. 1886.
Eaglehurst Towers. [1887.]
In four reigns: the recollections of Althea Allingham 1785–1842. 1887.
Mistress Matchett's mistake: or a very old story. 1887, [1905].
Only a bunch of cherries. [1887.]
Alma: or the story of a little music mistress. 1888.
Bristol diamonds. 1888.
Dulcibel's day-dreams. 1888.
Oliver's old pictures. 1888.
Golden silence: or annals of the Birkett family. 1889.
Chris and Tina: or the twins. 1890.
Curley's crystal: or a light heart lives long. [1890.]
Eastward ho! 1890.
The mother's chain: or the broken link. [1890.]
Robert's race: or more haste less speed. [1890.]
Under Salisbury's spire. 1890.
When I was young. 1890.
My lady bountiful. [1891.]
Those three: or little wings. 1891.
Little Miss Joy. [1892.]
Little Queenie. A story of child life sixty years ago. [1892.]
Pat's inheritance: a story of child life nowadays. 1892.
Bluebell. 1893.
Christopher's new home. 1893.
Nature's gentleman: or manners maketh man. 1893.
Peter's promises: or look before you leap. 1893.
The close of St Christopher's. 1894.
Mother and son: or 'I will'. [1894.]
Clement and Georgie: or manners makyth man. [1895], [1899?].
Lizette and her mission: or over the moors. 1895.
Abigail Templeton: or brave efforts. London and Edinburgh 1896.
An escape from the Tower. 1896.
A flight with the swallows: or little Dorothy's dream. [1896.]
A little curiosity. [1896.]
The master of the musicians. 1896.
Only Susan. [1896.]
Sir Benjamin's bounty. 1896.
The two Henriettas. 1896.
Better later than never. 1898.
Master Martin. 1898.
The young queen of hearts. 1898.
A good-hearted girl: or a present-day heroine. 1899.
The parson's daughter. 1899.
Rose Deane: or Christmas roses. Bristol [1899].
Time tries. 1899.
The thin edge of the wedge. [1900.]
Also pbd a number of historical romances and adult novels. See B. Marshall, Emma Marshall: a biographical sketch, *1900.*

Mrs Marshall

A sketch of my friend's family, intended to suggest some practical hints on religion and domestic manners. 1817, 1818, 1819, 1827.
Henwick tales: designed to amuse the mind ... of youth. 3rd edn 1818.
The child's guide to good breeding, founded on Christian principles, or seven chapters on politeness. 2nd edn 1839.
My first French book. 1851.
Mrs Profligate's dream. 1852, 1859.
Ida; or living for others. A story for the young. [1865], 1868.
Grannie's wardrobe: or the lost key. [1867.]

Louise Marston

Bennie: the King's little servant. 1882.
Cripple Jess: the hop-picker's daughter. 1882.
Blind Nettie: or seeking her future. 1883.

Rob and Mag: or a little light in a dark corner. 1886, New York nd.
Mr Bartholomew's little girl. 1887, 1894 (as Beckie's mission: or Mr Bartholomew's little girl).
Miss Mollie and her boys: or His great love. [1890.]
Two little boys: or I'd like to please him. [1890.]

Charles Martel

A better patrimony than gold: it is only a pin. A tale for youth. 1872 (illus), Philadelphia nd (as Henry Arden: or it is only a pin.)
Also translated from Fr and wrote on painting.

Mrs M. B. Martin

Our Tom: a story for little kittens. 1879.
Blinky and Onions: a ragged school reminiscence. [1881.]
A knight without spurs: or Judy's champions. 1892.
Also pbd devotional works for women.

Mary Emma Martin

An unknown girl. 2 vols 1881.
A country mouse: a story for girls. 1887.
Little great grandmother: a tale. 1896.
Uncle Jem's Stella: a story for girls. 1896.
Elsa's little boys. London and New York 1900.
Also pbd numerous adult novels.

Mary Kemble Martin

Our pets and companions: pictures and stories illustrating kindness to animals. [1886], [1889], [1906].
Fruits of Bible lands. 1891.
Archie's secret: or side by side. 1894.

Sarah Catherine Martin 1768–1826

The comic adventures of old Mother Hubbard and her dog. 1804, [1806], York 1820? (illus), 1938 (facs of 1804 edn).
Old Mother Hubbard and her dog. Banbury 1820.
Mother Hubbard and Cock Robin (verses). 1867.

William Martin, 'Peter Parley' 1801–67

Chimney corner stories, including the wonderful and extraordinary life and adventures of Neddy Bray. 1851.
The early educator: or the young inquirer answered. 1856.
The birthday gift for boys and girls. [1860], 1863.
Our boyish days and how we spent them: being tales of my schoolfellows. 1861.
Heroism of boyhood: or what boys have done. 1865 (illus).
Noble boys: their deeds of love and duty. 1870.
Jack Roden the sailor boy. 1889.
Spicklehurst and other stories. 1894.
Wrote numerous educational texts, edited the Educational Mag, *the* Boy's Own Annual *1861 and the* Boy's Own Lib *and* Peter Parley's Annual.
See also Peter Parley.

Harriet Martineau 1802–76

The playfellow. 1841. 4 pts frequently issued separately: Feats on the fiord, 1844; The settlers at home, 1856; The peasant and the Prince, 1856; The Crofton boys, 1856.
See also col 1344.

Clara L. Matéaux

Old proverbs with new pictures. nd.
The story of the Don rewritten for our young folks. 1870.
The wonderland of work. nd, New York 1884.
Home chat with our young folks on people and things they see or hear. 1870, London, Paris and New York 1881.
Raggles, baggles and the emperor. [1872], 1880.
Peeps abroad for folks at home. 1873, London, Paris and New York 1879.
Around and about old England. 1876.
Through picture land. [1876.]
Woodland romances: or fables and fancies. 1877, 1879.
Old folks at home. 1878.
Wee Willie Winkie: the story of a boy who was found. [1878.]
Tim Trumble's little mother. [1880.]
The wonderland of work. [1881.]
Brave lives and noble. 1883.
Rambles round London town. 1885.
In letters of flame: a tale of the Waldenses. [1886.]
George and Robert Stephenson. 1887.
Ups and downs of a donkey's life. 1889.
Noble lives and brave deeds. [1890?]

Mrs C. Mathews

Ellinor: or the young governess. A moral tale. York 1809.

Joanna Hooe Matthews 1849–1901

Little sunbeams. 1876.

Emily Juliana May

Louis's school days: a story of boys. [1851], Bath 1852, New York [1853], Bath [1854], 1855, [1876].
The sunshine of Greystone: a story for girls. Bath [1853], New York [1864], 1865.
Dashwood Priory: or Mortimer's college life. 1855.
Saxelford: a story for the young. 1857.
Bertram Noel: a story of youth. 1857, 1858.
The old coalpit: or the adventures of Richard Bentley in search of his own way. A story for boys. 1860.
The Stronge's of Netherstronge. 1864.
The broken balsam: or the story of a wreck. 1880.
Pansies: that's for thoughts. 1901.

Mrs Frank May

The witch of the Juniper Walk and other fairy tales. 1895 (illus).

L. T. Meade

See col 1635.

Mrs Meeke

The birthday present: or pleasing tales of amusement and instruction. 1829.

Anne Mercier

Only a girl's life. A story which is too true. 1871.
Pink ribbons: stories for our girls. 1876.
Edited Friendly Leaves. *Also pbd bks about the Church and adult novels.*

William Charles Metcalfe

Frank Weatherill: or life in the merchant marine. A sea story for youth. [1886], [1894], [1904].
Steady yur helm: or stowed away. 1892.
Rogues island. [1893.]
Watch and watch: or the 'Decoyed'. 1894.
The boy skipper. 1895.
Undaunted: a tale of the Solomon Islands. 1895, [1900].
On the face of the deep: or the bird borne missive. 1897.
On the other tack: a story of the sea. 1898.
All hands on deck. 1900.
Fetters of gold. 1900.
Billows and bergs. 1902.
Ocean chums. 1905.
Grit and pluck: or the young commander. [1906.]
Ice-gripped: or the memory of Moscow. 1907.
Blown out to sea. 1908.
Pigtails and pirates: a tale of the sea. 1908.
Dick Trawle: second mate. 1909.
The mystery of the 'Albatross'. 1911.
Junk ahoy!: a tale of the China seas. 1912.
Among Chinese pirates. 1929.

Anna Middleton

Tales for the young and the poor. 1863.

Arthur Henry Miles 1848–1929

Fifty two stories for boys. 1889.
Fifty two stories for girls. 1889.
Fifty two more stories for boys. 1890.
Fifty two more stories for girls. 1890.
Fifty two further stories for boys. 1891.
Fifty two further stories for girls. 1891.
Fifty two fairy tales. 1892.
Fifty two other stories for boys. 1892.
Fifty two other stories for girls. 1892.
Fifty two stories for boyhood and youth. 1893.
Fifty two stories for children. 1893.
Fifty two stories of girl life at home and abroad. 1894.
Fifty two stories of the British navy from Damme to Trafalgar. 1895.
Fifty two stories of the Indian mutiny. 1895.
Fifty two stories of the British army. 1897.
Fifty two stories of duty and daring for boys. [1897.]
Fifty two stories of heroism in life and action for boys. 1899.
Fifty two stories of heroism in life and action for girls. 1899.
Fifty two stories of the British Empire. [1900?]
Fifty two stories of courage and endeavour for boys. 1901 (illus).
Fifty two stories of courage and endeavour for girls. 1901.

'Harriet', 'Mrs Myrtle', 'Harriet Myrtle', Lydia Falconer Miller 1811?–1876

Little Amy's birthday, and other tales: a story book for autumn. 1846.
Home and its pleasures: simple stories for young people. 1852.
The ocean child: or showers and sunshine: a tale of girlhood. 1857.
Cats and dogs, nature's warriors and God's workers: or Mrs Myrtle's lessons in natural history. 1857, 1868, 1872.
The children's picture book of country scenes. 1860 (illus). By Harriet Myrtle.
Stories of the cat and her cousins, the lion and the tiger. [1877.]
The dog and his cousins, the wolf, the jackal and the hyena. 1876 (illus).
Also pbd bks on Scottish history and geology.

Olive Thorne Miller, 'Gwynfryn'

Friends in fur and feather. 1887 (illus).

Mary E. Mills

Simple stories for children. [1861], 1868 (illus).
Truth: or Frank's choice. 1866.
A troublesome godchild. [1902], [1911].

Helen Rose Anne Milman, later Crofton

Those children. [1891.]
Those little ladies. 1891.
Uncle Bill's children. [1892.]
Of high and low degree. [1893.]
In the garden of peace. 1896.
Little Ivan's hero: a story of child life. [1897.]
'Boy': word sketches of a child's life. [1902.]
The fairy of Inglewood Green. [1908.]
Also wrote about gardening.

Mary Mister

Mungo: or the little traveller. A work compiled for the instruction and amusement of youth. 1814, 1818, 1819, 1822, 1850.
Little anecdotes for little people. 1814, 1817, 1830.
Tales from the mountains. Intended for the instruction and amusement of youth. 1814.
The adventures of a doll. Compiled with the hope of affording instruction and amusement. 1816.
The friend of humble life. 1817.

Elizabeth Harcourt Mitchell, née Rolls

Hatherleigh Cross: a tale. 1865.
The little blue lady and other tales. 1881.
Her Majesty's bear: a tale. 1884.
Golden horseshoes: a tale of chivalry for young and old. 1885.
The King's stirrup: a tale of the forest. 1896.
Rachel's secret. 1905.
Also pbd numerous other religious bks, poetry and fiction.

Margaret Mitchell, later Hurry, Mrs Ives Hurry

The faithful contrast: or virtue and vice accurately delineated. 1804.
Rational amusement for leisure hours; consisting of interesting tales. 1804.
Moral tales for young people. 1807.
Tales of amusement and instruction. 1807.
Artless tales. 1808.

Ruth Mitchell

Aunt Lucia's locket, and other stories. [1881.]
Marion's two homes. [1882.]

Geraldine Mockler

Nell, Edie and Toby. Their strange adventures. [1891.]
The rambles of three children. [1892.]
A new friend. A story for boys and girls. [1895.]
The hollow tree. The story of a winter adventure. [1896.]
The little girl from next door. [1896.]
A long chase: the story of a seaside adventure. [1896.]
Proud Miss Sydney. '1896' [1895].

Her new kitten. A story for girls. [1897.]
Spring fairies and sea fairies. 1897.
Two children in black: a story for boys and girls. [1897.]
The best of intentions. A story. [1897], 1898.
A dreadful mistake. [1898.]
Jake's birthday present. [1898.]
Sir Wilfred's grandson and his strange adventures in a balloon. 1898.
The four Miss Whittingtons. [1899.]
The girls of St Bede's: a story. 1899.
A tale of the summer holidays. 1899.
A boy cousin. [1900.]
The travels of Fuzz and Buzz. [1900.]
Tony Maxwell's pluck. [1900], 1901.

Mrs A. F. Moffat

The ore seeker: a tale of the Harz. Cambridge 1860.

George Mogridge, 'Old Humphrey', 'Peter Parley', 'Carlton Bruce', 'Ephraim Holding', 'Uncle Adam' 1787–1854

A tale of wonder for the young. 1828.
Twelve moral maxims of my Uncle Newbury. 1828, 1832.
The juvenile culprits. 1829.
The juvenile moralists. 1829, New York 1838.
The moral budget of my Aunt Newbury. Wellington, Salop 1831, [1835], [1840?].
Mirth and morality: a collection of original tales. 1834 (illustr G. Cruikshank). 1834.
The encourager. [1835], [1864].
The boy's friend: or the maxims of a cheerful old man. 1837.
Aunt Upton and her nephews. [1841.]
Playhours: or the happy children. [1843?]
Learning to feel. [1844], [1845], [1855?].
Learning to think. [1844?]
Old Anthony's hints to young people. [1844?], [1864].
Alphabet of good and bad hearts. [1845?]
Learning to act. [1846.]
The balloon and other stories. [185?]
Things that have wings. 1851.
Aunt Rose and her nieces. [1852.]
Luke and little Lewis. [1852.]
The old sea captain. 1853.
Learning to converse. [1854.]
Memoir of old Humphrey; with Gleanings from his portfolio in prose and verse. 1855.
Sunny seasons of boyhood. 1859.
Aunt Mary's tales. 1867.
The little yearbook. [1867.]
Ephraim Holding's Sunday school illustrations. [1863], [1864].
Old Humphrey's fire-side tales. [1867.]
Old Humphrey's tales for all time. [1867.]
Frank's victory. [1868.]
Millie and her two friends. [1868.]
Susie's mistake and other stories. [1868.]
See also 'Peter Parley'.

John Edward Nassau Molesworth, 'John of Canterbury' 1790–1877

False impressions: or the rick burners. [1840?]

Mrs Molesworth 1839–1921

See col 1644.

M. Monget

Moral playthings: tales for children. 1806.

Edward Monro

Harry and Archie: or first and last communion. [1848], [1866?], 1881.
Edwin's fairing. 1867.

Florence Montgomery 1843–1923

A very simple story: being a chronicle of the thoughts and feelings of a child. 1867, 1870, 1878.
The children with the Indian-rubber ball. 1872.
The town crier, to which is added The children with the Indian-rubber ball. 1874.
Moral tales for children. 1886.
Tony; a sketch, being the account of a little incident on a short railway journey. 1898.
Behind the scenes in a schoolroom. 1914.
Also wrote adult novels.

Susannah Moodie, née Strickland

See Susannah Strickland.

Sophie Moody

The palm tree. 1864.
The fairy tree: or stories from far and near. 1872.
Also pbd bks about names.

Clara Moore d. 1849

Rhoda: or the excellence of charity. [1845.] By the author of The cottage on the common.

Clara Jessup Moore, 'H. O. Ward'

Gondaline's lesson, The warden's tale, Stories for children and other poems. 1881.
Also pbd poetry.

Emily Jane Moore

Dorothy Lavender: a temperance story. [1890.]
Grannie Goldenlocks. [1890.]
Little Bet: or the railway foundling. [1890.]
Little lads and lasses. [1890.]
Sunbeams and shadows: or pleasant half hour stories. [1890.]
Wilfred Mellice's children. [1890?]
Peter's idol: a domestic story. [1895.]

Georgina M. Moore

Mary with many friends. [1878.]
Mary's holiday task. [1879.]

Margaret Jane Moore, Countess of Cashel, née King

Stories of old Daniel: or tales of wonder and delight. 1808, 1810.
Continuation of the stories of old Daniel: or tales of wonder and delight. 1820.
Also pbd bks on physical education.

Sarah Mores

Pretty Polly, or the history of a cockatoo. [1877.]

Alice Talwyn Morris

The troubles of tatters and other stories. [1898.]
The elephant's apology. Glasgow and Dublin [1899.]
Our wonderful world: nature stories for children. 1907.
Out of doors: nature stories for children. 1908.
Tales and talks in nature's garden. 1908.
My book about the Empire. 1911.
Our holidays on a barge: nature stories for little folks. 1911.
More about the Empire. 1912.
A child's book of Empire. 1914.

Harriet Mozley, née Newman 1803–52

The fairy bower: or the history of a month. 1841.
The lost brooch. 1841.
Louisa. 1842.
Family adventures. 1852.
See C. R. Coleridge, C. M. Yonge, *1903; K. Tillotson,* Novels of the eighteen-forties, *Oxford 1954.*

Joyce Emmerson Muddock, later Preston, 'Donovan Dick'

Deare childe. A parish idyll. 1877 (illustr H. J. A. Miles).
Also wrote romantic novels.

Clara Mulholland

Linda's misfortunes and little Brian's trip to Dublin. 1885.
The strange adventures of little snowdrop and other tales. 1889.
Little merry face and his crown of content and other tales. [1895.]
Also pbd other bks.

Rosa Mulholland, later Gilbert

The wicked woods of Tobereevil. 1872.
The little flower seekers. London and Belfast [1873].
Five little farmers. 1876.
The wild birds of Kileevy. [1883.]
Hetty Gray: or nobody's bairn. 1884.
The walking trees and other stories. 1885.
Gianneta: a girl's story of herself. 1889.
Little witch and the misers. 1890.
Terry: or she ought to have been a boy. 1900.

Dinah Mulock, later Craik 1826–87

The fairy book: the best popular fairy stories selected and rendered anew. 1863.
See Dinah Maria Craik.

'Naomi', Mary E. Clements

The story of the beacon fire: or 'Trust in God and do the Right': a tale of the Cornish coast. 1887.

J. M. Neale 1818–1866

The farm of Aptonga: a story for children of the times of S. Cyprian. 1856, [1880].
The Egyptian wanderers: a story for children of the great tenth persecution. 1879 (3rd edn).
See also col 643.

E. Nesbit, Edith Nesbit, afterwards Bland and Tucker 1858–1924

The children's Shakespeare. London, Paris and New York 1897 (illus), Philadelphia [1900].
The story of the treasure seekers. 1899; ed E. Graham 1958.
The book of dragons. 1900.
Nine unlikely tales for children. 1901.
The would-be-goods. 1901.
Five children – and it. 1902.
The phoenix and the carpet. 1904.
The new treasure seekers. 1904.
Oswald Bastable – and others. 1905.
The story of the amulet. 1906.
The railway children. 1906.
The enchanted castle. 1907.
The house of Arden. 1908.
Harding's luck. 1909.
The magic city. 1910.
The wonderful garden: or the three C's. 1911.
The magic world. 1912.
Wet magic. 1913.
Five of us – and Madeline [stories linked by Rosamund Sharp]. 1925.
See also col 798.

'A. Nobody', Gordon Frederick Browne 1858–1932

Nonsense for somebody, anybody or everybody: written and illustrated by A. Nobody. [1895.]
Some more nonsense. 1896.
A Nobody's scrapbook. 1900.

Evelyn Nevinson, née Sharp

See Evelyn Sharp.

Sir Henry John Newbolt 1862–1937

Stories from Froissart. 1899.
Translator of chronicles and ballads, and wrote poetry. See also col 803.

Samuel Prout Newcombe

Pleasant pages: a journal of instruction for the family and the school. London, Edinburgh and Glasgow 1851.
Little Henry's Sunday book. 1852.
Pleasant pages for young people: or book of home education and entertainment. Boston 1853.
Also wrote religious texts.

William Newman

History of a quartern loaf. nd.

Rev Richard Newton

The five giants and other tales. nd.
Rills from the fountain of life: sermons to children. London and Philadelphia 1857, New York 1863.
The wonderful lamp. New York 1860.
The giants and how to fight them. 1862 (illustr J. Gilbert), New York

1864, London, Edinburgh and New York 1872, 1886, 1893, Edinburgh 1894.
The King's highway: or illustrations of the commandments. London, Edinburgh and New York 1864, 1879, 1880, Edinburgh 1892.
Rills from the fountain. 1866.
Bible wonders. 1869, 1870, 1877.
Bible blessings. 1870.
Bible jewels. 1870.
The safe compass and how it points. 1871, London and Edinburgh 1877, Edinburgh 1894.
The tables of stone: stories of the ten commandments. Edinburgh 1873, 1900.
The lessons of diligence. Edinburgh 1874.
Nature's mighty wonders. London, Edinburgh and New York 1877, 1880 (as Nature's wonders: or how God's works praise him).
Rays from the sun of righteousness. 1877.
The best things. London and Edinburgh 1878 (illus).
The life of Jesus Christ for the young. Philadelphia [1880].
Pebbles from the brook: a book for the young. Edinburgh and New York 1880.
The great pilot and his lessons. 1883.
Bible animals and the lessons taught by them. London, Edinburgh and New York 1889.

Hume Nisbet b. 1849

Eight bells. A tale of the sea and of the cannibals of New Guinea. 1889, 1900.
A colonial tramp: travels and adventures in Australia and New Guinea. 1891.
The divers: a romance of Corsica. 1892.
Valdemar the Viking: a romance of the eleventh century. 1893.
Hunting for gold: or adventures in Klondyke. 1894.
The great secret: a tale of tomorrow. 1895.
Kings of the sea: a story of the Spanish Main. 1896 (illus).
For liberty: the chronicles of a Jacobin. 1898.
The empire makers: a romance of adventure and war in South Africa. 1900.
Stories weird and wonderful. 1900.
Author of other bks and novels on travel and adventure and verse.

Lady Augusta May Noel 1838–1902

Effie's friends: or chronicles of the wood. 1865.
John Hatherton. 1865.
The story of wandering Willie. 1870.
The life and times of Conrad the squirrel. 1872.
Owen Gwynne's great work. 1875.
Hithersea Mere. 1887.
From generation to generation. 1879.
See also col 1665.

Maurice Noel

Under the water: a story for children. Bristol and London 1886.
Buz: or the life and adventures of a honey bee. Bristol and London 1898.

Cecil Marryat Norris

Captain Fortesque's handful. 1887 (illus).

George Norway

Adventures of Johnnie Pascoe. 1889.
A Roman household. 1889.
A true Cornish maid. A story of the last century. 1894, 1905.
Christiaan: the boy of Leyden: a story founded on fact. 1895.
Hussein the hostage: or a boy's adventures in Persia. 1896.
A dangerous conspirator. 1897.
The loss of John Humble, what led to it and what came of it. 1897.
Little Marjorie's secret. 1898.
Also wrote adult novels and contributed to boys' periodicals.

Charlotte Grace O'Brien 1845–1909

The coral necklace. 1855.
Lady Eva: or rich and poor. 1855.
Basil: or honesty and industry. 1856.
Midsummer holidays at Beechwood farm. 1856.
Primrose gathering. 1856.
The queen of the May. 1856, 1858.
Ernest's dream: a Christmas story. 1858.
Margaret and her friend. 1864.
Oliver Dale's decision. 1873, 1891.
The young folks of Hazelbrook. 1864.
George Wayland: the little medicine carrier. 1866.
Owen Netherby's choice. 1866.
Walter and Frank: or the two paths. 1871.
Gipsy Gem: or Willie's revenge. Philadelphia 1872.
Mother's warm shawl. A tale. 1894.
Gipsy Marion: a story of the New Forest. 1896.

Standish James O'Grady 1846–1928

Finn and his companions. 1892.
Lost on Du-Corrig: or 'twixt earth and ocean. 1894 (1st pbd in Chums 1893).
The chain of gold: or in crannied rocks. A boy's tale of adventure on the wild west coast of Ireland. 1895 (illus).
Wrote extensively on Ireland, and contributed regularly to boys' mags.

Adelaide O'Keeffe 1776–1855?

National characters exhibited in forty geographical poems. 1818.
A trip to the coast: or poems descriptive of various interesting objects on the sea shore. 1819.
Original poems calculated to improve the mind of youth and allure it to virtue. Philadelphia 1821.
Old Grandpapa and other poems. 1828.
Poems for young children. [1849.]
See also col 416.

Mrs William Olding

A Bible calendar for young people. 1857.
The young crossing sweepers: or wee Stan and little Llew. 1881.
Madeline: a novel. 1882.
All lost in the snow: a tale founded on fact. [1888?]

H. Oliver

Peter Parley's child's first step: or easy path to knowledge, in progressive lessons. 1839.

Mary Onley

Florrie Ros: or the voice of the snowdrops. [1873.]

Thomas Onwhyn

See 'Peter Palette'.

Amelia Opie, née Alderson 1769–1853

Tales of the Pemberton family for the use of children. 1825, 1844.
Tale of trials told to my children. 1845.
All is not gold that glitters. 1846.
See also col 965.

Eleanor Grace O'Reilly

Daisy's companions: or scenes from child life. A story for little girls. [1869], Boston 1872.
Deborah's drawer. 1871, New York 1875 (illus), Philadelphia 1881.
Little Grig and the tinker's letter. 1872.
Giles's minority: or scenes at the Red House. 1874.
Cicely's choice. 1875.
Little prescription and other tales. 1875.
The stories they tell me: or Sue and I. 1877.
The girls of the square and other tales. 1878.
Phoebe's fortunes. 1879.
Doll world: or play and earnest. 1888 (illustr M. E. Edwards).
Kitty Deane of Red Farm. 1894.
Also pbd novels and stories for adults.

Mrs Cuthbert Orlebar

Cinderella: a fairy tale in verse. 1848.
Harry and Walter: or the church spire. 1856.
The story of Hans Egede. 1864.

Mrs Alexandra S. Orr

Louis Belat: or the captives of Lake Leman. 1867.
Mountain patriots: a tale of the Reformation in Savoy. 1869.
The Roseville family. 1869.
The flower of the Ticino. 1872.
The twins of Saint Marcel. 1872.
Uline's escape: or hid with the nuns. 1877.
Leah: a tale of ancient Palestine. Illustrative of the story of Naaman the Syrian. 1893 (The Girls' Own Library) (illus).

Arthur William Edgar O'Shaughnessy 1844–81, and Eleanor O'Shaughnessy, née Martin d. 1871

Toyland. 1875.
See also col 804.

Yotty Osborn

Pickles: a funny little couple. [1878] (illustr T. Pym).
Judy: or only a little girl. [1880] (illustr T. Pym).

Emily Ospringe

Favouritism, virtue and contentment, instructive and entertaining stories for young people. [1840.]

'Ouida', Marie Louise de la Ramée

Bimbi. 1882, [1890].
See also col 1665.

Robert Overton

Bill Muggins. 1883.
Bob Scratchley's religion. 1883.
Jack's yarn or the three parsons. 1883.
Me and Bill. 1883.
Rummy fares: a cabman's story. 1883.
A round dozen: character sketches. 1884.
'20'. A volume of story and song. 1888.
Queer fish: character sketches. 1889, 1906.
The Overton reciter. Character sketches for recitation. 1889.
After school. 1893. Stories.
'Ten minutes'. Holiday yarns and recitations. 1893.
Far from home: or the fights and adventures of a runaway. 1895, 1896.
The King's pardon! or the boy who saved his father. A story of land and sea. 1895.
Waterworks: temperance readings and recitations for the platform, the library and the fireside. 1895, 1896.
Friend or fortune? The story of a strange year. 1896, 1897.
The record reciter and reader. 1897.
The son of a hundred fathers: or daring deeds in dangerous days. 1898, 1899.
A chase round the world. The following up of a chain of mystery. 1900.
Katie's uncle, or an artist's wife. 1900.
The Overton entertainer: a collection of old favourites and new aspirants. 1904.
Dangerous days. 1905.
The orphan of Tor College; a story for boys. 1905.
Decoyed across the seas: a tale of a tangle. 1907.
Nine and three: being nine recitations and three playlets. 1910.
The son of the school. A tale of daring deeds in dangerous days. 1913.
The story of the 'Broderick Castle' and of Captain David Mill Smith. 1914.
Saturday island: or fun, friendship and adventure at an elementary council school. 1915.
The three skippers and the secret of the caves. 1923.
Contributed extensively to boys' periodicals, especially Boys *and* Boy's Own Paper.

Fairleigh Owen

The Lathams. 1858.
Steyne's grief: or losing, seeking and finding. 1860.
Ritter Bell, the cripple. A tale for the young. 1861, Philadelphia 1868, Glasgow 1875.
Harty the wanderer: or conduct is fate. 1879.

Mrs M. C. Owen

What little hands can do: or the children of Beechgrove. 1874, 1898.

Harriet Packer

The twenty acres. 1862.
The hidden idol. 1863.
The two cottages. 1865.
Guilty or not guilty: the story of a token. 1865.
Agatha: or sketches of school life. 1868.
Grandfather's watch, and how it went at Eton and elsewhere. 1885.
Thoughts for my boys. 1888.

Frank Paddon

The school-boy days of Eustace Lambert. 5th edn 1896.

Jesse Page

The story of a yellow rose: told by itself. 1882, 1886.
That boy Bob and all about him. 1884.
A boy's friendship. 1889.
Bright Ben: the story of a mother's boy. 1893.

Harry the hero, or forgiveness wins. [189?]
Judson, the hero of Borneo: the stirring story of the first missionary to the Burmese, told to boys and girls. 1893.
Carrie and the cobbler. 1894.
Also pbd numerous bks about missionaries and religious martyrs.

Francis Edward Paget, 'William Churne' 1806–82

The bonfire. London and Rugeley 1844.
The hope of the Katzekopfs: or the sorrows of selfishness. 1844, 1846 (with new preface), 1874, 1885 (6th edn).
Tales of the village children. 2 sers 1844–5, 1847.
Luke Sharp. 1845.
The owlet of Owlstone Edge. 1856, 1857.
Tales of the village children. 1867.
The fairy godmother: or the adventures of Prince Eigenwillig. A tale for youth. New York 1867. By William Churne.
Edited Juvenile Englishman's Lib *and pbd numerous devotional texts. See also col 1376.*

'Peter Palette', Thomas Onwhyn d. 1886

Peter Palette's tales and pictures in short words for young folks. [1856].

Mary E. Palgrave

Marcel's duty: a story of war-time. 1881.
Under the blue flag. A story of Monmouth's rebellion. [1882.]
Miles Lambert's three chances. 1884.
A promise kept. 1887.
Driftwood. 1888.
In charge. A story of rough times. [1890.]
How Dick found his sea-legs: a story of a seaside holiday. 1896, 1917.
A child in Westminster Abbey and other stories. 1898.

Ellen Palmer

Helen Siddall: a story for children. [1871], Edinburgh 1887.
The standard bearer: a story of the fourth century. Edinburgh 1872.
Stories told in a fisherman's cottage. Edinburgh 1874.
Three wet Sundays. Edinburgh 1890.
Christmas day at the Beacon. [1893.]
Also pbd religious bks.

Frances Palmer

Dogged Jack. 1880 (illus).
Silent highways: a story of barge life. 1883.
True under trial: a tale for boys. 1888.
Twin brothers: the adventures of two little runaways. 1908 (illus).

Francis Paul Palmer

Puss in boots. 1844.
Old tales for the young, as newly retold. 1855.
The history of Mother Hubbard. Edinburgh [1880?]

Miss Pardoe, Julia Pardoe 1806–62

Lady Arabella: or the adventures of a doll. [1856].
See also col 1378.

Miss Marianne Parker

Birds on the wing: or pleasant tales and useful hints on the value and right use of time. 2nd edn 1824.

Bessie Rayner Parkes 1829–1925

Poems. 1852.
Summer sketches and other poems. 1852.
The history of our cat Aspasia [1856].
Gabriel. 1856. Verse.
Ballads and songs. 1863.
See also col 2264.

James Parkinson 1755–1824

Dangerous sports: a tale addressed to children, warning them against wanton, careless or mischievous exposure to situations from which alarming injuries so often proceed. 1800, 1803, 1808.
Also wrote bks on medicine and natural history.

'Peter Parley'

The inventor of this pseudonym was an American, Samuel Goodrich (1793–1860), but the name was at once adopted by English writers and publishers. Goodrich claimed in his Recollections of a lifetime, *1857, to have compiled 116 'Parley' books, but their titles were also used and their text often freely adapted in English edns by rivals. For a summary of the bks and authors, see F. J. H. Darton,* Children's books in England, *Cambridge 1932, and* Peter Parley and the battle of the children's books, *Cornhill Mag Nov 1932. Goodrich's first 'Parley' book was* Tales of Peter Parley about America, *Boston 1827. The writers who can certainly be identified as having produced original work under this pseudonym are: George Mogridge (1787–1854), also as 'Alan Gray', 'Aunt Mary', 'Aunt Newbury', 'Aunt Upton', 'Grandfather Gregory', 'Grandmamma Gilbert', 'Ephraim Holding', 'Old Humphrey', 'The Traveller', 'Uncle Adam', 'Uncle Newbury'. The juvenile moralists 1829; The juvenile culprits 1829. See C. Williams,* Life, character and writings, *1856; A. R. Buckland in* Mogridge, John Strong the boaster, *1904. William Martin (1801–67).* The parlour book, *[1835?].* The book of sports. *[1837?].* The hatchups of me and my schoolfellows, *1858.* Holiday tales, *1860. Samuel Clark (1810–75).* Peter Parley's wonders of earth, sea and sky, *[1837]. See his* Memorials from journals and letters, *ed his wife 1878.*

Harriet Parr, 'Holme Lee' 1828–1900

Legends from fairyland. 1860, 1862.
See also col 1322.

Miss Marianne Parrott

The naughty girl won. nd.
Rough rhymes for country boys. 1847.
Rough rhymes for farmers' boys. 1847, 1858.
Bible numbers: or scripture facts in rhyme. 1848.
Charlie Gilbert: or try again. Dublin 1851.
May Churnleigh and her friend conscience. 1857.
Weltheim's book of scripture stories for children. 1857.
Harry's mistakes and where they led him. 1860.
Little May and her friend conscience. 1872.
Tales of village school boys. 1874.
Little redcap: a tale for boys. 1888.
Also pbd other bks.

Sir Edward Abbott Parry 1863–1943

Katawampus: its treatment and cure. 1895 (illus), 1921 (illus).
Butterscotia: or a cheap trip to fairy land. 1896 (illus).
The first book of Krab: Christmas stories for young and old. 1897.
The scarlet herring and other stories. 1899 (illus).
Gamble gold. 1907.
Also pbd legal and historical works.

Sara Payson Parton 1811–72

Fern leaves from Fanny's portfolio. 2nd edn 1853, Buffalo and Cincinnati 1853, 1854.
Little ferns for Fanny's little friends. 1854.
Shadows and sunbeams: being a second series of fern leaves from Fanny's portfolio. 1854.
The play day-book: or new stories for little folks. 1857, New York 1857.
New story book for children. 1864.

James Kirke Paulding 1778–1860

A gift from fairy land. Tales and legends. 1840.

Mrs Henry H. B. Paull

Constance Somerville: a story. nd.
Horace Brereton's discovery. nd.
Lost half sovereign: or 'charity thinketh no evil'. nd.
Mabel's schooldays. nd.
School day memories: or 'charity envieth not'. nd.
Mary Elton: or self control. 1869, 1876.
Pride and principle: or the captain of Elvedon School. 1869.
Miss Herbert's keys: or honesty in little things. 1871.
Greatest is charity. 1872.
Margaret Ford: or what a young girl can do. 1872.
Dick the sailor: a tale of the days of Nelson and Wellington. 1875.
Evelyn Howard: or early friendships. 1875.
Dora's difficulty: or 'charity doth not behave itself unseemly'. 1876, 1885.
Frank Merton's conquest: or 'charity is not easily provoked'. 1876.
Englefield Grange or Mary Armstrong's troubles. 1878.
Harry Foster's rules. 1879.
Levelsie Manor. 1879.
Only a cat: the autobiography of Tom Blackman. 1880.
Robert Raikes and his scholars. 1880.
Horace Carleton's essay: 'charity vaunteth not itself: is not puffed up'. New York 1882.
Minatoo: or little Frankie's bearer. 1883.
Tom Fletcher's fortunes. 1885.
Ethel Seymour: or 'charity hopeth all things'. 1888.
Philip Thornton's legacy. 1888.
Breaking the rules: a tale of school-boy life. 1895.
Knowing and doing. Eight stories founded on Bible precepts. 1897.
Also pbd other stories.

Margaret Agnes Paull

Herbert's holiday: a tale for children. London and New York 1860.
Tim's troubles: or tried and true. 1870, London, Edinburgh and New York 1883, Edinburgh 1887.
Stories of the mountain and the forest. London, Edinburgh and New York 1882.
Willie's choice: or all is not gold that glitters. London, Edinburgh and New York 1882.
Sought and saved: a tale. London, Edinburgh and New York 1882.
May's sixpence: or waste not want not. London, Edinburgh and New York 1885.
True hearts make happy homes. London, Edinburgh and New York 1886.
The Vivians of Woodiford: or true hearts make happy homes. London, Edinburgh and New York 1886.
The children's tour: or everyday sights in a sunny land. London, Edinburgh and New York 1893.
Pretty pink's purpose: or the little street merchants. London, Paris and Melbourne 1894.

Lucy Peacock fl. 1786–1815

The rambles of fancy. 1786.
The adventures of the six princesses of Babylon in their travels to the temples of virtue: an allegory. 1788, 1820.
The visit for a week. 1794, 1795, 1804, 1806; tr Fr 1812.
The little emigrant. 1802, 1820.
Patty Primrose: or the parsonage house. 1813.
Emily: or the test of sincerity. 1816.
Friendly labours: or tales and dramas for the amusement and instruction of youth. Brentford 1819.
Ambrose and Eleanor: or the adventures of two children deserted on an uninhabited island. 1820.

Thomas Love Peacock 1785–1866

Sir Hornbrook, or Childe Launcelot's expedition: a gramatico-allegorical ballad. [1813.]
See also col 969.

Frances Mary Peard 1835–1923

Prentice Hugh. 1887.
The abbot's bridge. [1891.]
Jacob and the raven: with other stories for children. 1896.
See also col 1672.

Mark Guy Pearse

John Tregenoweth: his mark. 2nd edn 1876, 1878, 1885, 1891.
Mister Horn and his friends: or givers and giving. 1876, 1881, 1884.
Sermons for children. 1876.
Old Rosie: a story for the children. 1880.
Matt Stubb's dream: or Christmas Eve at the Blue Boar. 1881.
Simon Jasper. 1883.
Rob Rat: a tale of barge life. 1885.
Good will: a collection of Christmas stories. 1887.
Daniel Quorm: his religious notions. 1896.
Also wrote many devotional tracts and bks for adults.

Isabella Pearson

Summer fun and frolic: a tale for boys and girls. [1893.]
Pleasures and pranks: a story of holidays in the country. 1895 (illus).
Mischief and merry making. London, Edinburgh and Dublin 1896.

Miss Pearson

A few weeks at Clairmont Castle. 1828.
Tales of truth: containing the Woodville family, the Franks and Sir Francis Vanheson. 1828.

James Pedder 1775–1859

The yellow shoe-strings: or the good effects of obedience to parents. [1814], 1816, 1821.

Max Pemberton 1863–1950

The iron pirate. A plain tale of strange happenings on the sea. 1893.
The garden of swords. 1898.
Editor of Chums *and author of many adult novels.*

Sylvia Penn

The curse of the Fevrills. 1888.

Ethel Charlotte Penrose, née Coghill d. 1938

The fairy cobbler's gold. 1890.
Clear as the noon-day. [1893.]
Darby and Joan: being the adventures of two children. [1894.]

Eden Phillpotts 1862–1960

The human boy. 1899.

Anna Maria Diana Wilhelmina Pickering, later Stirling, Mrs A. M. W. Stirling 1865–1965

The adventures of Prince Almero: a tale of the windspirit. [1890.]
The queen of the goblins. 1892.
Author of numerous historical and topographical works.

Edgar Pickering

An old-time yarn: or with Hawkins and Drake. London and Glasgow 1893.

Mrs Pilkington, Mary Pilkington, née Hopkins 1766–1839

Obedience rewarded, and prejudice conquered: or the trials of Mortimer Lascells. Written for the instruction and amusement of young people. 1797.
Biography for girls: or moral and instructive examples for young ladies. 1799, 1806.
Henry: or the foundling. 1799.
A mirror for the female sex. Historical beauties for young ladies. 1799.
The spoiled child: or indulgence counteracted. 1799.
Biography for boys: or characteristic histories: calculated to impress the youthful mind with an admiration of virtuous principles and a detestation of vicious ones. 1800, 1815.
Edward: a tale for young persons. 1800.
Tales of the hermitage written for the instruction and amusement of the rising generation. 1800, 1815, New Haven CT 1820.
Marvellous adventures: or the vicissitudes of a cat. 1802.
Mentorial tales for the instruction of young ladies just leaving school and entering on the theatre of life. 1802, Philadelphia 1803.
The calendar: or monthly recreations chiefly consisting of dialogues between an aunt and her nieces, designed to improve the juvenile mind with a love of virtue and of the study of nature. 1807.
New tales of the castle: or the noble emigrants, a story of modern times. 1809.
A reward for attentive studies: or moral and entertaining stories. [c. 1815.]
The shipwreck: or misfortune the inspirer of virtuous sentiments. 1819.
Scripture histories: or interesting narratives extracted from the Old Testament for the instruction and amusement of youth. 1819.

Mrs Pinchard

The young countess: a tale for youth. 1820.

A. Pittis

Bright eyes: or Johnny's sacrifice. [189?]

James Robinson Planché 1796–1880

Four and twenty [French] fairy tales. 1858.
See also col 1976.

Matilda Anne Planché

See Matilda Anne Mackarness.

Annabella Plumptre, Bell Plumptre 1761–1838

Domestic stories, for the amusement and instruction of children. Taken from the German of different authors. 1800.
Stories for children. 1804, New York 1824.
Tales of wonder, of honour and of sentiment, original and translated. 1818.
Also pbd adult novels and translated works from Ger.

Hon Emmeline Plunket

Very short stories in short words. 1887 (illustr T. Pym).

Hon Isabel Plunket

The children's band: or the trial of Paul's faith. nd.
Hester's fortune; or pride and humility. 1871.

Elizabeth Plunkett, née Gunning, Miss Gunning 1769–1823

A sequel to family stories: or evenings at my grandmother's intended for young persons of eight years old. 1802.
The village library intended for the use of young persons. 1802.
See also col 983.

Mathilda Mary Pollard

Only me: an autobiography. nd.
The minister's daughter and old Anthony's will. Tales for the young. Edinburgh 1872, 1878.
An earl's daughter: a story for the young. 1873.
The old farm house: or Alice Morton's home. 1876.
Deborah's school: a village tale. 1882.
Rupert Deane's mission. A tale for the young. 1885.
Dorothy: or down at Polwin. 1888, [1902].
Cora: or three years of a girl's life. 1889.

Edith Caroline Pollock

See 'Ismay Thorn'.

Frederick Scarlett Potter b. 1834

Melcomb Manor: a family chronicle. London and Belfast 1875.
Erling; or the days of St Olaf. [1876.]
Cousin Flo. [1877.]
Marion and her cousins. 1877.
Princess Myra and her adventures among the fairy-folk. [1880.]
Paul and his troubles: a tale for country boys. 1883.
A venturesome voyage. [1898.]
Author of numerous other bks.

Rev Philip Bennett Power

The last shilling: or the selfish child. 1853, New York 1863, Philadelphia [1867].
Little Kitty's knitting needles. London and Edinburgh 1861, 1868, London, Edinburgh and New York 1883, 1889.
One moss rose. 1867, 1872.
A fagot of stories for little folks. New York 1868.
The oiled feather tracts. 1869, 1888.

The bag of blessings: or the singing tailor. 1872.
Stamp on it John and other narratives. New York 1872.
Truffle nephews and how they commenced. 1874.
The cup and the kiss and other sketches. 1894.
Also pbd numerous tracts.

Elizabeth Prentiss, née Payson, 'Aunt Susan' 1818–78

Only a dandelion and other stories. nd.
Little Susy's six birthdays. 1854.
Little threads: tangle thread, golden thread, silver thread. Edinburgh and New York 1864, 1865, New York 1873, 1876, 1881.
Little Lou's sayings and doings. 1868.
Nidworth and his three magic wands. [1869.]
The story Lizzie told. 1870.
Little Susy's little servants. 1871.
Little Susy's six teachers. 1871.
Stepping heavenward: a tale of home life. 1872.
Herman: or the little preacher. 1874.
Little Rosa: or the old brown pitcher. 1885.
Nidworth's choice; or the three wands. 1888.
See R. G. Prentiss, The life and letters of Elizabeth Prentiss, *1882.*

Annie Preston

Dame Durden's copper kettle. [1884.]
Uncle Jim. [1884.]

Alice Price

Miss Margaret's stories. 1880, [1884?].

Sophia Amelia Prosser, née Dibdin 1807–82

Cicely Brown's trials: how she got into them, how she got out of them and what they did for her. nd.
Golden, golden, all golden. nd.
How Jarvis got his house, an incident of life in the Black Country. nd.
Original fables. nd.
Tiger Jack. nd.
The wise man of Wittlebury: or 'charity begins at home'. nd.
Ludovic: or the boy's victory. [1867.]
Quality Fogg's old ledger. [1869.]
The cheery chime of Garth, and other stories. 1879.
Frog alley and what came out of it. 1879.
The light on the wall and other stories. 1881.
Fables for you. 1895.

S. S. Pugh

'Life's battle' lost and won. nd.
Our forest home: its inmates, and what became of them. [1871.]

Henry William Pullen 1836–1903

The house that Baby built. 1874, 1876.

Mabel Quiller Couch

Martha's trial, or truth will prevail. [1895.]
One good seed sown or old Jasper's protégé. [1896.]
The recovery of Jane Vercoe and other stories. [1896.]
The Carroll girls. 1906.
Kitty Trenire. 1909.

Mrs Milne Rae

Dan Stapleton's last race. [1881.]
A book for young women. 1887.

Mrs Herbert Railton

Lily and the lift and other stories. 1895.

Edgar Augustus Rand

Fighting the sea: or winter at the life saving station. 1887.
Making the best of it. 1888.
Margie at the harbour light: a story for the young. 1890, 1908, 1920.
Too late for the tide-mill. 1890.
Up north in a whaler: or would he keep his colours flying. 1891.
At the black rocks: a story for boys. 1892, 1903, 1927.
A candle in the sea: or winter at Seal's Head. 1892.
A knight that smote the dragon: or the young people's Gough. 1892.
The mill at Sandy Creek. 1894.
Our clerk from Barkton: or right rather than rich. 1894.
A salt-water hero. 1896.

William Brighty Rands 1823–82

Lilliput levee: poems of childhood, child fancy and child-like moods. 1864, 1867, 1868, London, New York and Philadelphia 1868.
Lilliput lectures. 1871.
Lilliput revels. London and New York 1871.
Lilliput legends. 1872.
Lilliput lyrics. 1899 (ed R. B. Johnson).
See also col 656.

'Guy Rayner', Samuel Dacre Clarke

Guy Rayner's adventures. 1889.
Guy Rayner's schooldays. 1889.
Guy Rayner's Boy's Hearts of Gold Library of complete stories. 1890.
'Guy Rayner' edited and contributed to a number of boys' short-lived popular weeklies in the 1870s and 1880s.

Mrs R. H. Read

Dora: a girl without a home. 1883.
Our Dolly: her words and ways. 1883.
Fairy fancy: what she saw and what she heard. 1883 (illus).
The goldsmith's ward: a tale of London city in the fifteenth century. 1891.
Silver Mill: a tale of the Don Valley. 1896 (illus), 1908.

Frances E. Reade

Tales for Sunday scholars. 1878.
How Willie became a hero. London and New York 1881, 1888.
Kate Temple's mate. 1883.
Black Jack and other temperance tales for boys and girls. 1884.
Chimney park: or Mrs Carter's 'Comings'. London and New York 1886.
Nell's bondage. 1887.
Aunt Edna. 1888.
Brave Tiny. 1888 (illus).
Polly Rivers: or what I must renounce. London and New York 1888.
Walter Morris. London and New York 1888 (illus).
How Sandy learned the creed. 1889, London and New York 1891.
Seven idols. A tale for girls. 1890.
Edith's charity. London and New York 1895 (illus).

Clary's confirmation: a tale for girls. London and New York 1896.
Mrs Heritage. 1898.

Mrs Isabel Reaney

Little Meggy's home: a Christmas story. 1874.
Waking and working: or from girlhood to womanhood. 1874.
Poor little me: or a little help is worth a great deal of pity. 1875.
Sunbeam Willie and other stories. 1875.
For Willie's sake. 1878.
Blessings and blessed: a sketch of girl life. 1878.
English girls: their place and power. 1879.
Rose Gurney's discovery: a story for girls. 1880.
Daisy Snowflake's secret: a story of home life. 1882.
Morning thoughts for our daughters. 1882, 1892, 1896.
Little Glory's mission. 1883, 1893 (as Little Glory's mission and Not alone in the world).
Number four: or making someone happy and other stories. 1883.
Willie Wills' wings. 1883.
Clovis and Madge: a story. 1884.
The angel baby: a tale. 1892.
Stella. 1893.
The face at the window. 1900.
Molly Brown: a girl in a thousand. 1909.
Also pbd adult novels and bks for mothers.

Mrs Andrew Reed

Mary and her mother: a sequel to scriptural stories for very young children. 1826, 1832, 1835.

Talbot Baines Reed 1852–93

The adventures of a three guinea watch. [1883.]
'Follow my leader': or the boys of Templeton. A school story. 1885.
The Willoughby captains: a school story. 1887, 1895 (illustr A. Pearse), 1908.
My friend Smith. A story of school and city life. [1889] (illustr G. Browne).
Sir Ludar: a story of the days of the great Queen Bess. 1889, 1892.
Master of the shell. [1890.]
The fifth form at St Dominics. [1890.]
The cock house at Fellsgarth. [1893] (illus).
Roger Ingleton minor. 1893.
A dog with a bad name. [1894] (illustr A. Pearse).
The master of the Shell. [1894.]
Tom, Dick and Harry. [1894.]
Parkhurst sketches and other stories. [1900] (ed G. Andrew Hutchison).
A regular contributor to the Boy's Own Paper.

Thomas Mayne Reid 1818–83

The bandolero: or a marriage among the mountains. 1866.
The castaways: a story of adventure in the wilds of Borneo. 1870.
The flag of distress. A story of the South Sea. 1879.
See also col 1389.

Miss B. Revell

Mary Ross. 1853.

Walter Rhoades

A houseful of rebels: being the story of three naughty girls and their adventures in fairyland. 1897 (illus).

For the sake of his chum: a school story. London, Glasgow and Dublin 1909.

Mrs Rice

The nabob. 1807.
Henry: or the secrets of the ruins: a moral tale. Coventry 1819 (2nd edn).

Mrs Richardson

The story of Bee and her friends. 1862.
Little Harry's troubles. A story of gipsy life. Edinburgh and London 1866.

D. Richmond

Amy Carlton: or first days at school. A tale for the young. London and New York 1856.
The four sisters: patience, humility, hope and love. London and New York 1858, 1862.
Accidents of childhood: or cautionary stories for heedless children. 1861.
Eildon Manor: a tale for girls. London and New York 1862.
The doctor's ward. London and New York 1868.
Harry and his homes: or the conquest of pride. 1879.
The children of blessing. London and New York 1886.

Legh Richmond, 'Simplex' 1772–1827

Collections

Annals of the poor (The young cottager; The negro servant; The dairyman's daughter; The negro's visit to the infirmary). 1828 (5th edn), 1831, 1850, 1851, 1858, 1866, 1869, 1871, 1875, 1878, 1879, 1883, 1908, 1970.
The dairyman's daughter and other annals of the poor. The landscape beauties of the Isle of Wight. 1843, 1860.
Annals of the poor. 1861, 1882, [189?].
Cottage annals. Comprising The dairyman's daughter, The young cottager and Robert Dawson, etc. 1877.

Individual works

The negro servant: an authentic narrative of a young negro. [1804?], [1810?], [1815?], 1820, 1825, 1838, 1860, 1869, 1876.
The fathers of the English church: or a selection from the writings of the reformers and early Protestant divines of the Church of England. With memorials of their lives from Fox and Bishop Bale. 1807–12.
A statement of facts relative to the supposed abstinence of Ann Moore of Tutbury, and a narrative of the facts which led to the recent detection of the imposture. 1813.
The young cottager Jane Squibb: a narrative from real life. 1815, 1817, 1820, 1826, 1830, 1834, 1860, 1863, 1866, 1868, 1876.
The dairyman's daughter: an authentic narrative. 1817, 1819, 1821, 1827, 1828, 1830, 1835, 1843, 1856, 1860, 1863, 1865, 1867, 1869, 1875, 1884, 1886, 1888, 1890. First pbd in 1809 in the Christian Guardian under the pseudonym 'Simplex', the work was translated into many languages and appeared in many edns.
The funeral of the dairyman's daughter; being the fifth part of her history. 1820.
Domestic portraiture: or the successful application of religious principle in the education of a family, exemplified in the memoirs of three of the deceased children of the Rev L. Richmond. 1833, 1834, 1835, 1843, 1847.
A visit to the infirmary. 1853.
A cottage conversation. A religious tract. [1855?]

The history of a poor black widow, etc. In verse. 1855.
Walk circumspectly: or rules for Christian conduct. 1855.
See also col 2634.

Rev C. J. Ridgway

Some sweet stories of old. London and Sydney 1891 (illus).

M. L. Ridley

Our captain: the heroes of Barton School. 1881, 1900.
The three chums. [1882.]
Walter Alison: his friend and foes. 1883, New York 1885.
King's scholars: or work and play at Eastbourne. 1884.
Sent to Coventry: or the boys of Highbeach. 1886.
Our soldier hero: the history of my brother. 1887.
Goldengates: or Rex Mortimer's friend. 1888, 1892.
Hillside Farm: or Marjorie's magic. 1888.

Rev William Henry Ridley

The two sailor boys: a tale for boys. 1869, London and New York 1876.

Mrs Caroline Rigg 1824–89

The pearly gates and almost a sacrifice. nd.
Lost in the snow: or the Kentish fisherman. 1886.
How Mrs Hewitt's house was turned out of window and other temperance tales. 1892.
Little black rover and other stories. [1892.]

E. Riley

Juvenile tales for boys and girls: designed to amuse, instruct and entertain those who are in the morning of life. Halifax 1849, 1851.

Abigail Roberts

The history of Tim Higgins, the cottage visitor. 1823, Dublin 1825.

Mrs Margaret Roberts

The telescope: or moral views for children. 1804, 1816 (as Moral views: or the telescope for children).
Rose and Emily: or sketches of youth. 1812, New York 1813.
Duty . . . a novel interspersed with poetry. [1814.]

Margaret Murray Robertson 1823–97

The orphans of Glen Elder: a tale of Scottish life. [1867], 1878.
Shenac's work at home: a story of Canadian life. [1868], 1893.
The bairns: or Janet's love and service. 1870.
Little Serena in a strange land. 1870.
The Inglises: or the way opened. 1872.
The perils of orphanhood: or Frederica and her guardians. 1874.
Chrissie Redfern's troubles. [1886], 1892.
A year and a day. [1886.]
Eunice. 1887.
By a way she knew not. 1888.
David Fleming's forgiveness. 1891.

Isabel Stuart Robson

Life in Malins Lea. 1891.
The odd little pair: or the doings of Molly and Larry. 1892 (illus).
Fabian and Phil: a story of two little boys. 1893, 1899.
Kavanagh major: a tale. 1894.
Uncle Jock's little girl. 1894.
The temperance cousins: the story of one year at Petravis. 1896.
Two little sisters and Humphrey. 1896.
Marjorie's stranger. 1897.
Master Piers: a tale. 1898.
Eelin's new home. 1899.
Nuttie: or the silver thread of love. 1900.
The girl without ambition. 1900, 1917.
Story weavers: or writers for the young. 1900.
Miss Pederson's niece: a tale. 1901.
The oddity: a tale of high school life. 1901.
The old house at Rungate. 1901.
What Gladys did. 1904.
The troublesome Bevans: or Laurence, the hero of Great Morvans. 1906.
The girl who was not clever. 1908.
Girls of the Red House. 1909.
The girls at the Stone House. 1912 (illus).
Also wrote adult novels.

Regina Maria Roche, née Dalton 1764?–1845

The children of the abbey. 3 vols Glasgow 1826, Exeter 1828, Charlestown MS 1829, 1840, Halifax 1854.
Morimer and Amanda: or the children of the abbey. Philadelphia and New York 1846, 1875.
See also col 989.

William Smyth Rockstro 1823–95

The choristers of St Mary's: a legend of Christmastide. 1858.

Mary Roding

Dollie's little niece: a story for children. 1890.
Tweedledum and Tweedledee: a story for children. 1891.
Paul's partner. 1894.
Sonny: a story for children. 1904.

Edward Payson Roe

Barriers burned away. 1873, 1874, 1877, 1878, 1881, 1894.
From jest to earnest. 1876, 1878, 1896.
A young girl's wooing: a love story. [1884], 1887, 1890, 1896.
Driven back to Eden. 1886, London and New York 1897 (illus).
A brave little Quakeress and other stories. New York 1892.
Also pbd numerous novels for adults.

Eva Rogers

The bear's kingdom: a fairy tale. 1897.
A tale of four foxes. 1900.
The magic wand and other Dartmoor legends. 1901, 1930.

Helen H. Rogers

That boy Jack!: a story for young folk. 1888, 1890 (illus).

Wilhelmina Lydia Rooper

Chats with the children. 1883, 1910.
The tree cake and other stories. 1886, 1892.
Delia's boots. 1887.
Papa's birthday. 1887.
The pic-nic. 1887 (illus).

The sand cave. 1887, 1891 (illus).
Sara: the woolgatherer. 1887.
A joke for a pic-nic. 1891.
Little tales for little folk. 1892.
Piecrust promises. 1893, 1905.
Ella's brown crown: a story of holiday adventure. 1895.
Wilful Joyce. 1896.
The blue bead. 1897.
The shoe black's cat. 1900.
Tony's pains and gains. 1900.
Cubie's adventure. 1907.
Also pbd plays and didactic bks.

Mary Emily Ropes b. 1842

Granny's darling. nd.
Springfield stories. 1873.
Only a beggar boy and other stories. 1875.
Caroline Street: or little homes and big hearts. 1877, 1903.
Finette, the Norman maiden and her English friends. 1877, 1882.
His little Hetty: or out of the dark. 1878.
Jock, the shrimper: or help yourself and God will help you. 1878.
Made clear at last: or the story of a ten pound note. [1879], 1884.
Till the sugar melts. [1879.]
Honesty the best policy and other stories. 1882.
My golden ship. 1882.
Only Milly: or a child's kingdom. [1882.]
Jim. 1883, 1896.
The story of Mary Jones and her Bible. 1883, 1891, Chicago 1892.
Prince and page: a story of Russia. 1884.
Ragged Robin. 1885, 1888.
Bob's trials and tests. 1887, 1893, 1907.
Out of Cabbage Court: a story of three waifs. 1887, 1897.
Lazy Laurie: or the mote and the beam. 1892.
Lily and her pony: or one too many. 1892.
Wild Meg and wee Dickie: a tale. 1892.
Bel's baby. 1893 (3rd edn).
Vassia: or a Russian boy's eventful journey. 1893.
Little Penny Wyse and nurse Priscilla's stories. 1893.
Tom's Bennie. 1894.
Seedy Mike. 1895.
Two little Finns. [1895.]
His Majesty's beggars. 1897.
The mystery of Hoyle's Mouth: or the adventures of two runaway boys. 1897, 1899.
Nat and his little heathen. [1899.]
Margie's venture: or when the ship comes home. 1908.
Two brave boys and the wrong twin. 1910.
What happened to Tad. 1913.
Also pbd other stories.

William Roscoe 1753–1831

The butterfly's ball and the grasshopper's feast. 1883 (ed C. Welsh), 1897. First pbd in GM Nov 1806.
The lion's masquerade. 1807.
The butterfly's birthday. 1809.
The butterfly's ball produced many imitations besides those by Mrs Dorset, such as The elephant's ball *by W. B., 1807;* The lion's parliament, *[1808?];* The rose's breakfast, *1808;* The horse's levée, *1808;* The fishes grand gala *by Mrs Cocke, 1808;* The tyger's theatre *by Samuel James Arnold (1774–1852), 1808;* Flora's gala, *1808;* The council of dogs, *1808;* The wedding among the flowers *by Ann Taylor, 1808;* The lobster's voyage, *1808;* La fête de la rose *by B. Hoole, later Mrs Hofland, [1809?].*
See A. W. Tuer, Pages and pictures from forgotten children's books, *1898–9. See also col 431.*

Christina Rossetti 1830–94

Sing-song: a nursery rhyme book. 1872, 1893 (with addns).
Speaking likenesses. 1874.
Maude: a story for girls. 1897. Introd by W. M. Rossetti.
See Not all roses in the Victorian nursery, TLS *29 May 1959; and also col 657.*

Emily Rottenslake

A tale of the Plaiting districts. [1873.]

Richard Rowe

A holiday book of stories for the young. 1877.
Famous British explorers and navigators from Drake to Franklin. 1892.
The history of a lifeboat. Edinburgh 1893.

Mary C. Rowsell

Hardy and foolhardy. nd.
Two blackbirds. nd.
Honor bright: a story of the days of King Charles. nd (illus).
Marion and Jessie: or children's influence. 1870.
Tom's opinion: a story of school life. Boston and Dover NH 1876, 1892.
Number Nip: or the spirit of the giant mountains. 1884.
The pedlar and his dog. 1885 (illustr G. Cruikshank), 1887, 1911, 1917.
Peasblossom. 1885.
Sepperl: the drummer boy. 1886.
One of a covey. 3rd edn 1888 (illus).
Robin and Linnet. 1888.
Gilly Flower. 1889.
Halt. 1890.
The story of a queen. 1890.
All's well! 1891.
Hatto's tower and other stories. 1892.
N or M. 1897 (illus).
Five, ten and fifteen. 1898.
Larry's luck. 1898.
Dick of Temple Bar. 1900.
Also pbd novels for adults.

John Ruskin 1819–1900

The king of the golden river: or the black brothers – a legend of Styria. 1851.
See also col 2275.

Fox Russell

The first cruise of the three middies. [189?].

H. Rutherfurd Russell

Tom, the history of a very little boy. 1873.
Tom, seven years old. 1876.
How Molly spent her Christmas. 1877.
Muriel. 1877.
My dolly. 1877.
Life's peepshow. 1899.

W. Clark Russell

The frozen pirate. 1892.

Annie Ryland

Alfred May. 1882, 1890.
Left to take care of themselves. 1883.

John Charles Ryle 1816–1900

Little and wise: being the substance of a sermon [on Prov. xx. 24–8] to children. Ipswich and London 1851, New York 1853, Ipswich and London 1856.
Sermons to children. New York 1856, 1857.
No more crying: an address to children. [1859.]
The bird's nest: missionary addresses to children. [1863.]
The two bears: an address to children. [1866], 1869.
Boys and girls playing and other addresses to children. 1880 (illus).

Ethel St Arthur

Astray and at home: or little Mollie and her brother. 1879.

'Alan St Aubyn', Francis Marshall

Little lady Maria. London and New York nd.
The dean's little daughter. London and New York 1890.
Jenny dear. London and New York 1894.
Joseph's little coat. 1900.

Percy Bolingbroke St John 1821–89

The young naturalist's book of birds: anecdotes of the feathered creation. nd.
The young naturalist's rambles through many lands. 1840.
The arctic Crusoe: a tale of the polar seas: or arctic adventures on the sea of ice. 1854, Boston and New York 1873.
The sea of ice: or the arctic adventurers. Boston 1859, 1863.
The backwood rangers. [1865?]
The sailor Crusoe. 1867.
The blue dwarf: a tale of love, mystery and crime. Introducing many startling incidents in the life of that celebrated highwayman Dick Turpin. 1880.
The snow ship: a tale of the arctic regions. 1891.
Contributed to popular penny weekly boys' mags.

Sergius St John

First impressions: or three tales of a grandfather addressed to the rising generation. Brentford 1805.

Vane Ireton Shaftesbury St John 1839–1911

Larry O'Calloran's school days: or the boys of Bally Botherum. nd.
The rightful heir. 1870, 1885.
The rival apprentice: a tale of the riots of 1780. 1870 (illus), 1880, 1905.
Rupert Dreadnought: or the secrets of the iron chest. [187?], 1891.
The night guard: or the secret of five masks. 1875, 1887.
The young apprentices; or the watch-words of old London. [1880] (illus).
Who shall be leader? 1882.
Unlucky Bob: or our boys at school. 1892.
The travelling schoolboys. 1895.
Who shall be leaders: the story of two boy's lives. 1896.
Also wrote adult novels and edited a number of popular boys' penny weeklies.

Alfred St Johnston

Camping among the cannibals. 1883.
In quest of gold: or under the Whanga Falls. 1885 (illustr G. Browne).
Twycross's redemption: a story of wild adventure. 1888.
Also wrote novels for adults.

Hugh St Leger

Sou'wester and sword: a story of struggle on sea and land. London, Glasgow and Dublin 1895.
'Halloween' ahoy: or lost on the Crozet Islands. 1896.
The 'Rover's' quest: a story of foam, fire and fight. 1897.

Mrs Hugh St Leger

Zillah, the little dancing girl: or 'One of Christ's lost little lambs'. nd.

Charlotte Elizabeth Sanders

Poems on various subjects. 1787.
The little family: written for the amusement and instruction of young persons. Bath 1797, Haverhill MA and Boston 1799, 1800.
Holidays at home: written for the amusement of young people. 1803, New York 1804, 3rd edn 1812.

Miss Sandham, Elizabeth Sandham

The happy family at Eason House. 1799.
Trifles: or friendly mites towards improving the rising generation. 1800.
The red book and the black one. 1802.
More trifles! For the benefit of the rising generation. 1804.
The twin sisters: or the advantages of religion. 1805, 1810.
The godmother's tales. 1808.
The adventures of poor Puss. 1809.
Alithea Woodley: or the adventures of an early friendship founded on virtue. [1810.]
A cup of sweets that can never cloy: or delightful tales for good children. 1810.
Pleasure and improvements blended: or an attempt to shew that knowledge can only be attained by early inquiry and judicious explanation. 1810.
Deaf and dumb. 1813.
Pleasing information. 1814.
The adopted daughter, a tale for young persons. 1815.
The history of William Selwyn. 1815.
The schoolfellows: a moral tale. 1818.
The boys' school: or traits of character in early life. [1821?]
Sketches of young people: or a visit to Brighton. 1822.
The bee and the butterfly: or industry and idleness. 1824.
The history and conversion of the Jewish boy. 1829.

J. Sands

Frank Powderhorn: a story of adventure in the Pampas of Buenos Ayres and in the wilds of Patagonia. London, Edinburgh and New York 1881.

Anna Maria Sargeant 1809?–52

Uncle William's birthday: or the children's choice. nd.
Blanche's one fault and other tales. nd.
Charlie and Bessie: or be honest and kind to all. nd.
Kate Ward: or home for the holidays. nd.

Mamma's stories: or strawberry gathering. nd.
A word in season: being a faithful and affectionate address to young people on leaving Sabbath and other schools connected with places of worship. 1849.
Short stories of easy reading; mostly in words of one syllable. 1853, 1890.
Progressive reward and gift books. [1855.]
Be just before you are generous. 1858.
Marion Lee and other tales. 1859.
Good and bad tales for twilight. 1860, [1889].
Frederick and Kate: or the little letter writers. 1861.
The school friends and other tales. [c. 1875.]
The sisters; or 'tis best to think before we act. 1880.

George Etell Sargent 1808?–83

Alice Barlow: or principle in everything. nd.
The English peasant girl. nd.
Frank Layton: an Australian story. nd.
Harry the whaler: what a young sailor saw and did in the North Sea. nd.
The little fish pedlar: or Mackerel Will and his friend Emma. nd.
My brother Ben. nd.
Nobody's own. nd.
An old sailor's story. nd.
Richard Hunne: a story of old London. nd.
The little sea bird. nd, 1876.
Stories for village lads. nd.
Stories of old England. nd.
The story of a child's companion. nd.
The story of a city Arab. nd.
The story of a pocket Bible. nd.
The story of Charles Ogilvie. nd.
The weed with an ill name. nd.
Without intending it: or John Tincroft, bachelor and Benedict. nd.
The Bedfordshire tinker: or the history of John Bunyan. 1848, 1849 (Biography for the Young).
The white slave: a life of John Newton written for young children. 1848.
Stories of schoolboys. 1849, Philadelphia 1850, 1871.
The turning point: a book for thinking boys and girls. 1849.
Charles Hamilton: or better rub than rust. [1851], [1853].
Egerton Roscoe: a story for the high spirited. 1851, 1853, 1876.
Frank Harrison. 1853.
Havering Hall and other stories. 1860, 1879.
Willy and Lucy. 1860.
Down in a mine: or buried alive. nd, 1864, 1886.
Lilian: a story of the days of martyrdom in England three hundred years ago. 1864, 1871, 1887.
Moncton Grange. 1865.
Harry, the sailor boy and his Uncle Gilbert. 1870.
Lucy the light bearer. 1874.
Ethel Rippon: or beware of idle words. 1875.
The poor clerk and his crooked sixpence. 1878.
Boys will be boys. [1879.]
The Grafton family and other tales. 1879.
My scarlet shawl: or 'Out of debt, out of danger'. 1881.
Basil Marsden: or struggles in life. [1885?]
The crooked sixpence. 1887 (illus).
The young Cumbrian and other stories. 1891.

Jane Alice Sarjant, née Smith 1789–1869

Rachel Johnson: a tale. nd.
Letters from a mother to her daughter at or going to school. 1821, 1844.
The broken arm: a National School story. 1841, 1851, 1856.
Charlie Burton: a tale. 1846, New York 1849, 1856, London and New York 1869; tr Ger 1854, Fr 1857.
The brothers: a seaside story. 1850.
Ann Ash; or the foundling. 1851.
The holiday week and other stories. London and New York 1851.
But once. 1853.
Home tales founded on fact. 1853.
No lie thrives: a tale. 1853.
Fireside tales. 1857.
Shades of character. 1858.
As the crystal ball: a child's book of fairy ballads. 1895 (illus).
Also pbd tracts, pams, poems and plays.

Emily Susan Goulding Saunders

The flower of grass: a story for children. 1865.
Missionary pictures. 1871.
Made for it: or the wild flower transplanted. 1874.
Also pbd poetry and bks about Italy.

Frances Maitland Savill

The flying postman and other stories. [1879.]
Jenny's journal: leaves from the diary of a young servant. 1880.
May's dream. 1882.
The beautiful house with its seven pillars. 1883.
Hettie: or not forsaken. 1883.

Elizabeth M. A. F. Saxby

Grandmother Owen. nd.
The parables of the kingdom: our Lord's story told for children. nd.
Earth's many voices. 1863, 1864, 1865.

Jane Euphemia Saxby

See Jane Euphemia Browne.

Jessie Margaret Saxby, née Edmonston 1842–1940

One wee lassie. 1875.
Geordie Roye: or a waif from the Greyfriars Wynd. Glasgow 1879.
Snow dreams: or funny fancies for little folks. Edinburgh 1882.
Breakers ahead: or Uncle Jack's stories of great shipwrecks of recent times. London, Edinburgh and New York 1883.
Ben Hansen. 1884.
The lads of Lunda: a tale. 1887.
Winnie's golden key: or the right of way. 1887.
Lindeman brothers: or shoulder to shoulder. 1888 (illus).
Kate and Jean: the story of two young and independent spinsters. 1889.
Crumbs from the children's table. 1890.
West nor' west. 1890.
Wrecked on the Shetlands: or the little sea king. 1890.
Viking boys. 1892.
Lucky lines: or won from the waves. 1893.
A Camersteria nacket: being the story of a contrary laddie ill to guide. 1894.
Brown Jack: a tale of north-west Canada. [1896.]
The saga book of Lunda, wherein is recorded some more of the notable adventures of Viking boys and their friends. 1896.
Also pbd bks about Shetland and adult novels, and contributed to the Boy's Own Paper.

Cecil Scott

Chrissie Lyle: a tale for the young. 1872.
Kate's new home. 1872, Edinburgh 1894, 1900.

Michael Scott

Tom Cringle's log. Edinburgh and London 1836, 1895.

Mrs Scott

Mary Mathieson: or duties and difficulties. 1856.
Joseph and the Jew: a story founded on fact. 1857.
Little tales on great truths: or six scripture warnings. 1860, 1881.
Witless Willie. [1864.]
Tom Ilderton and other stories. 1865.
Tales of my Sunday scholars. 1866.
Lame Allan: or cast thy burden on the Lord. Edinburgh and London 1868, 1871.

Mrs Emilie Searchfield

Claimed at last and Roy's reward. nd.
The secret cave: or the story of mistress Joan's ring. 1895.
Contributed to religious periodicals for the young.

'January Searle', George Searle Phillips 1815–89

Fell Farm: a country book for boys. 1851.
Contributed to girls' mags and pbd on christianity, religious architecture and literary history.

Mrs T. R. Seddon

The twining of the threads: the story of Simon Slade. London and New York nd.

Emma Louisa Seeley

Belt and spur: stories of the knights of the Middle Ages from old chronicles. 1883, New York 1883.
The city in the sea: stories of the deeds of the old Venetians from the chronicles. 1884.
Border lances. A romance of the northern marches in the reign of Edward the third. 1886.
Humble life: a tale for humble homes. [188?]

Angelica Selby

On duty. A story for children. London and New York 1889.
In the sunlight: a novel. 1890, 1912.

Gertrude Sellon

A man's boot and other tales. 1875, 1882 (as Short stories about animals).
Uncle Charlie's book of nursery rhymes. 1897.
Uncle Charlie's short stories about animals. nd (illus).

Patty Caroline Sellon d. 1887

The young governess: a tale for girls. nd.
Gerty and May. 1867 (illus), Boston 1890.
Granny's story box. 1873, 1889.
The new baby. 1873.
The children of the parsonage. 1875 (illustr K. Greenaway), London and New York 1884 (illus).
Our white violet. 1887.
Sunny days: or a month at the Great Stowe. 1887.

A. Selwyn

The little creoles: or the history of Francis and Blanche. [1820?]
Resignation: or memoirs of the Dufane family. 1824.
Tales at the vicarage. 1824.
A key; or familiar introduction to the science of botany. 1824.
The history of farmer Darwin and his family: a moral tale. [1825] (illus), [1840].
Montague Park: or family incidents. 1825.
A new year's gift: or domestic tales for children. 1825.
Revenge: or the young West Indian, and benevolence and little Agnes. 1825.
Tales for a winter's fireside. 2 vols 1828.
Moral fairy tales: containing Mary and Jane, Letitia and the fairy, Little Anna, History of farmer Darwin, and Flora and Edward. [1830?]
Youth's mirror: or tales adapted for the perusal of children. [1830], 1838.
Mary and Jane: or who would not be industrious. [1840?]

Emily Frances Adeline Sergeant 1851–1904

Reuben Touchett's granddaughter. nd.
Amy's Christmas. 1861.
Also pbd poetry and fiction.

Ernest Thompson Seton 1860–1946

Wild animals I have known. 1898, New York 1899.
The trail of the Sandhill stag. 1899, ed R. L. Green 1966 (with other stories).
The lives of the hunted. 1901.
Two little savages. 1903.
Wood myth and fable. 1905.
Animal heroes. New York 1905.
Rolf in the woods. 1911.

Harleigh Severne

Chums: a tale for the youngsters. [1878] (illustr H. Furniss].

Anna Sewell 1820–78

Black Beauty: the autobiography of a horse. 1877, 1950 (illustr L. Kemp-Welch] (Children's Illus Classics), 1954 (illustr C. Hough) (Puffin).
Black Beauty *has been in print continuously since the first edn. See M. J. Baker,* Anna Sewell and Black Beauty, *1956, and S. Chitty,* The woman who wrote Black Beauty, *1971.*

Elizabeth Missing Sewell 1815–1906

Amy Herbert, by a lady. 1844.
Laneton Parsonage: a tale for children on the practical use of a portion of the Church catechism. 3 pts 1846–8.
Stories illustrative of the Lord's prayer. 1851.
The castaways. 1857.
The boy voyagers: or the pirates of the East. 1859.
Among the Tartar tents. 1861.
The boy foresters. [1868.]
See also col 1399.

Mary Seymour

The children of Summerbrook. [1859.]
Happy schoolfellows and all about them. 1861.
Village children at home. 1861.
Patience Hart's first experience in service. [1862.]
Mother's last words: a ballad for boys. [1866.]
A little forester and his friend. [1866.]
Little Arthur at the zoo and the birds he saw there. London, Edinburgh and New York 1887.
Shakespeare's stories simply told by Mary Seamer. London, Edinburgh and New York 1887, 1889.
Also pbd verse.

Sydney Shadbolt

A moonbeam triangle. 1881 (illus).

Mrs Lucas Shadwell

Bible exercises for the family reading for the cottage meeting and the temperance Bible class. [1869.]
Only tell Jesus: or Naomi's secret and other life pages. [1884.]
Maggie's mistake: or bright light in the clouds. 1887.
Also pbd novels for adults.

Emily Mary Shapcote

Among the lilies and other tales. 1881.
The story of little Tina and other tales. 1881.

S. Russell Sharman

One of the least: a story founded on fact. 1882.

Evelyn Jane Sharp, later Nevinson 1869–1955

Fairy tales as they are and as they should be. 1893.
At the Ralton Arms. A novel. 1895.
The making of a prig. A tale. 1897.
The making of a school girl. 1897.
Wymps and other fairy tales. 1897.
All the way to fairyland. 1898, London and New York 1898.
The other side of the sun. Fairy stories. 1900.
The youngest girl in the school. 1901.
The other boy. 1902.
Round the world to Wympland. 1902.
The children who ran away. 1903.
The child's Christmas. 1905 (illustr C. Robinson).
Lessons, short stories. 1905.
Micky. 1905.
Niccolate: a novel. 1907.
The story of the weathercock. 1907.
The hill that fell down; a story of a large family. 1909.
Rebel women. 1910, 1915.
The victories of Olivia and other stories. 1912.
The war of all the ages. 1915.
What happened at Christmas. 1915.
A communion of sinners. 1917.
Somewhere in Christendom. 1919.
John's visit to the farm. 1920.
Who was Jane? 1922.
Young James. 1925.
The loafer and the loaf. An episode in one act. 1926.
The London child. 1927 (illustr E. Garnett).
Daily bread. 1928.
Here we go round. The story of the dance. 1928.
The child grows up. 1929.
Also pbd adult novels. See her autobiography, Unfinished adventure. Selected reminiscences from an Englishwoman's life, *1933.*

Catherine Shaw

Jack Forrester's fate. nd.
Sunday sunshine. nd.
Good night. 1892.
Half done: or Violet and Dorothy. 1893.

Flora Louise Shaw, later Lady Lugard 1852–1929

Castle Blair: a story of youthful days. 1878.
Hector: a story for young people. 1883 (illus).
Phyllis Browne. Boston 1883 (illus).
A sea change. Boston 1884 (illus), 1886.
A political journalist who also wrote biographical works.

Mrs Sherwood

See col 1072.

Mary Elizabeth Shipley b. 1842

First excercises in geography for the use of little children. [1865.]
Eye service: or schooldays at St Mary's. 1871.
The giant's grave. 1871.
Jessie's works: or faithfulness in little things. 1873.
Lofty aims and lowly efforts. A tale of Christian ministry. 1873.
A month at Brighton and what came of it. 1874.
Christmas at Annesley: or how the Grahams spent their holidays. London and Belfast 1875.
Little helpers: or what children may do for Jesus. 1876.
A desolate shore: a story for boys. 1884.
True to herself. 1891.
Granny's heroes: a tale of old Acton. 1895.
Also pbd verse.

Helen Shipton

Crooked. [189?] (illustr R. C. Woodville).

Louisa C. Silke

Dick's strength and how he gained it. [187?]
Bravely borne: or Archie's cross. [1882.]
Shag and doll and other stories. London and New York 1882.
Nora's surrender. 1884.
Turning point: or two years in Maud Vernon's life. [1885.]
Two little rooks. 1886.
Surly Bob. 1888.
A hero in the strife. 1892.
Tried in the fire. 1893.
Margaret Somerset: an historical tale. 1894.
School life at Bartrams. 1897.
Steadfast and true: a tale of the Huguenots. 1897.

'Silverpen', Eliza Meteyard

See col 1354.

Fanny Simon

Miss Blake's tinies. nd.

Catherine Sinclair 1800–64

Holiday house: a series of tales. Edinburgh 1839.
Frank Vansittart: or the model schoolboys. 1853.
Charlie Seymour: or the good and bad choice. 1856 (4th edn).
The first of April picture letter. Edinburgh 1864.
See E. V. Lucas, Introd to Old fashioned tales, [1905] *and col 1401.*

Dorothea S. Sinclair

Sugar plums for children. 1884.
Sayings and doings in fairyland: or old friends with new faces. 1890.
Strange adventures of some very old friends. 1896 (illus).
The enchanted princess. 1897.
The fairy prince and the goblin. 1897.

Jane Sinett, Mrs Percy Sinett

Hunters and fishers: or sketches of primitive races in lands beyond the sea. 1846.
A story about a Christmas in the seventeenth century. 1846.
Herdmen and tillers of the ground: or illustrations of early civilisation. 1847.
A child's history of the world. 1853.
Grandmother Katie: or trials and troubles and the way out of them. 1857.
A story about a Christmas in the olden time. 1858 (illus).
Also translated works from Fr and Ger, and pbd travel bks.

Sophia Sinnett

Lessons about God for very young children. London and Norwich [1863].

Florence A. Sitwell

Daybreak: a story for girls. nd.

Mrs Isla Sitwell, Sydney Mary Sitwell

Aunt Kezia's will. 1881.
The church farm. [1882.]
Born a soldier. 1884.
The dreadful cousin. 1884, 1887.
The one army. 1884.
Two friends. 1885.
Will Trahair's friends. London and New York [1888] (illustr A. Pearse).
Emmy's opportunity. [1889.]
Father's pet. [1889.]
A friend in need. [1889.]
The golden woof. A story of two girls' lives. 1890.
Farmer Goldsworthy's will. 1894.
The lady of St Ouen. 1895.
An innocent. 1895.
A bright farthing. 1896.
The hermit of Hillside Tower. 1900 (illus).
Also pbd numerous adult novels.

Kate Thomson Sizer

Hugh's ancestors: or English boys and girls in far-off times. 1895.
The four young musicians: or God's care is over all. [1899.]

William Skinner

The young Shetlander. nd.
Musical Andy: the story of a kidnapped boy. 1885.

Benjamin Smith

Vice royalty: or counsels respecting the government of the heart, addressed especially to young men. 1860.
Climbing: a manual for the young who desire to rise in both worlds. 1861, 5th edn 1873.
Also pbd other religious texts.

Catherine E. Smith

Enchanted ground. nd (illus).

Mrs Elizabeth Tomasina Smith, L. T. Meade

See col 1635.

Mrs G. Castle Smith, née Meyrick

See 'Brenda'.

Sarah Smith, 'Hesba Stretton'

See col 1704.

Mrs W. Glennie Smith

Little Lucy; what she thought and said and did. A story for young children. [1861.]
Sally Rainbow's stories, as she told them. A sequel to Little Lucy. [1863.]

Elizabeth Anne Smythe

The history of Tabby, a favourite cat. As related by herself to her kitten. 1809.
The history of Mary, the beggar girl. 1815.

Ruth E. Smythe

Wilful Peggy: a story for girls. [1892.]

Richard Gilbert Soans and Edith C. Kenyon

Brave all round: or Lionel's victory. [1893.]

Alice Somerton

Oeland: a thread of life. 1856.
Ida: or the last struggles of the Welsh for independence. 1858.
The torn Bible: or Hubert's best friend. 1862 (illus), 1900.
Also pbd other bks.

Elizabeth Somerville, née Townsend? c. 1776–1832

The history of little Charles and his friend Frank Wilful. nd.
The village maid: or Dame Burton's moral stories for the instruction and amusement of youth. 1801, Philadelphia 1802.
Mabel Woodbine and her sister Lydia, a tale. 1802.
My birthday: or moral dialogues and stories. 1802.
The birthday: or moral dialogues and stories for the instruction and amusement of juvenile readers. 1803.
Flora: or the deserted child. 1806, 1811.
The history of little Phoebe. 1808, 1814.
Aurora and Maria; or the advantage of adversity. 1809.
Maria: or the ever-blooming flower. New Haven CT 1818, 1819.

Florence Spenser

Lucy's temptation. 1896.
Three school girls: or Brenda's purpose. 1896.
John Fletcher, farmer. 1898.

Jane H. Spettigue

An Africander trio: a story of adventure for boys and girls. 1899 (illus).
An unappreciative aunt. 1899 (illus).
A pair of them. 1900.
A trek and a laager. 1901.

Elizabeth Spooner

Rose and Kate: or the little Howards. 1865.
Aunt Emma. 1866.
Minnie's legacy. 1867.

Emily Spratling

Out of the dark. 1893.
Sunshine after rain: or little Jim and his mother. [1894.]
A royal mandate. 1896.
Winsome Winnie. 1896.
The Morrison family. [1897.]
A heroine in the strife. 1898.

William Gordon Stables 1840–1910

Cats; their points and characteristics, with curiosities of cat life, and a chapter on feline ailments. 1876, 1877 (reissued as Friends in fur: true tales of cat life).
Jungle, peak and plain. A boy's book of adventure, etc. 1877.
Wild adventures in wild places. 1881.
The cruise of the Snowbird: story of Arctic adventure. 1882, 1910.
Our home in the silver west. A story of struggles and adventure. 1883, 1908.
Wild adventures around the pole. 1883, 1909.
Aileen Aroon: a memoir of a dog. With other tales of faithful friends and favourites, sketched from the life. 1884.
O'er many lands, on many seas. 1884.
Stanley Grahame, boy and man. A tale of the dark continent. 1884, 1889, 1909.
Kenneth McAlpine: a tale of mountain, moorland and sea. 1885.
The cruise of the land yacht Wanderer: or thirteen hundred miles in my caravan, etc. 1886.
Born to wander: a boy's book of nomadic adventures. 1887.
Harry Macilvaine: or the wanderings of a wayward boy. 1887, 1916.
From squire to squatter. A tale, etc. 1888.
In the dashing days of old: or the world wide adventures of Willie Grant, etc. 1888.
In touch with nature. Tales and sketches from the life. 1888.
Jack Locke: a tale of the war and the wave. 1888.
Harry Wilde: a tale of the brine and the breeze. 1889.
The hermit hunter of the wilds. 1890, 1925.
By sea and land. A tale of the blue and the scarlet. 1890.
The mystery of millionaire's grave. A novel. 1890.
Exiles of fortune. A tale of a far north land. 1890.
Rocked in the cradle of the deep. A tale of the salt, salt sea. 1890.
The Girl's Own book of health and beauty. 1891.
Leaves from the log of a gentleman gipsy in wayside camp and caravan, etc. 1891.
'Twixt school and college: a tale of self reliance. 1891, 1901, 1927.
The cruise of the Crystal Boat: the wild, the weird, the wonderful, etc. 1891.
Born to command. A tale of the sea and of sailors. 1892.
The Boy's Own book of health and strength. 1892.
Our humble friends and fellow mortals. 1892.
Two sailor lads. 1892, 1927.
Children of the mountains. A story of life in Scottish wilds. 1893.
Facing fearful odds: a tale of flood and field. 1893.
Hearts of oak. A story of Nelson and the navy. 1893.
Just like Jack. A story of the brine and the breeze. 1893.
As we sweep through the deep. 1894, 1905.
Westward with Columbus. 1894, 1925.
On to the rescue. A tale of the Indian mutiny. 1895.
A life on the ocean wave: or the cruise of the good ship 'Boreas'. 1895.
Shireen and her friends. Pages from the life of a Persian cat. 1895, 1918.
To Greenland and the Pole. A story of adventure, etc. 1895.
Born to be a sailor: or a home on the rolling deep. 1896.
The cruise of the Rover caravan. A story. 1896.
For honour, or honours: being the story of Gordon of Khartoum. 1896.
The pearl divers and crusoes of the Saragossa Sea. 1896.
The rose of Allandale: a sensational story of love and crime. 1896.
Shoulder to shoulder: a story of the stirring times of old. 1896, 1927.
Travels by the fireside: a book for the winter evenings. 1896 (illustr G. Browne).
For cross or crescent . . . a romance. 1897, 1927, 1936.
Every inch a sailor. 1897.
A fight for freedom. A story of the land of the Tsar. 1897.
In the land of the lion and the ostrich; a tale. 1897.
A girl from the States: a tale of love and intrigue. 1898.
The island of gold: a sailor's yarn. 1898.
The naval cadet. A story of adventure. 1898.
Off to Klondyke: or a cowboy's rush to the goldfield. 1898 (illustr C. Whymper).
'Twixt daydawn and light. A tale of the times of Alfred the Great. 1898.
Annie o' the banks o' Dee. 1899.
Courage, true hearts, the story of three boys. 1899, 1909.
A pirate's gold: a true story of buried treasure. 1899, 1904.
Remember the Maine: a story of the Spanish American war. 1899.
Allan Adair: or here and there in many lands. 1900.
England's hero prince: a story of the Black Prince. 1900.
Kidnapped by cannibals. 1900 (illustr J. Finnemore), 1925.
Old England on the sea: the story of Admiral Drake. 1900.
On war's red tide. A tale of the Boer War. 1900.
Valour and victory. 1900.
Cruises of the frozen north. 1901, 1920, 1933.
For England's flag. Stories by Gordon Stables and others. 1901.
With cutlass and torch. A story of the great slave coast. 1901.
The cruise of the Vengeful. A story of the Royal Navy. 1902, 1936.
In ships of steel. A tale of the navy to-day. 1902.
Rob Roy McGregor; highland chief and outlaw. 1902.
Sweeping the seas. 1902.
Chris Cunningham: a story of the stirring days of Nelson. 1903.
The cruise of the Arctic Fox in icy seas around the Pole. 1903.
In the great white land: a tale of the Antarctic Ocean. 1903.
An island afloat. By Silas Brigg, master mariner. 1903.
The shell hunters. 1903.
Young Peggy McQueen. 1903.
The meteor flag of England. The story of a coming conflict. 1905.
The sauciest boy in the service. 1905.
The city at the pole. 1906.
Leaves from the log of a sailor. 1906.
War on the world's roof. 1906.
Wild life in sunny lands: a romance of butterfly hunting. 1906.
A little gipsy lass. 1907.
The voyage of the Blue Vega. 1907, 1913.

From slum to quarter deck. 1908 (illustr A. Pearse).
A boy's book of battleships. 1909, 1915.
The ivory hunters: a story of wild adventure by land and sea. 1909.
On special service. 1910 (illustr S. H. Vedder).
Shadowed for life. 1914.
Regularly contributed to boys' mags, especially the Boy's Own Paper, *and pbd bks on animals and health.*

W. Edwards Staite

Fables for children, young and old. 1848, 1870.
Also pbd other bks.

Louisa Stanley

Children taught by experience: stories for the nursery. 1835.
The juvenile story book. [1840] (illus).
The little girl's keepsake: or pleasing stories for the home fireside. [1840.]
Original tales for boys and girls. [1840] (illus), 1854.

Henrietta Eliza Vaughan Stannard, née Palmer, 'John Strange Winter' 1856–1911

The child's gospel history. nd.
A Christmas fairy. [1897.]
Little Gervaise and other stories. [1898.]
Also pbd numerous adult novels.

Beatrice Stebbing, later Batty, 'Bee Bee'

An English girl's account of a Moravian settlement in the Black Forest. 1858.
The mill in the valley. A tale of German rural life. 1859.
Time answers best: or Jean and Nicotte. 1860.
Little Tija, or the new name, etc. [1870.]
Effie and her ayah. [1873.]
Matzchen and his mistresses. 1881.
Ernest Dacent. 1886.
Stories of my pets. 1886.
The life and adventures of a very little monkey and other tales. 1888.
Mrs Fauntleroy's nephew; an episode of Oxford history in eights week. 1912.
Strange but true: anecdotes of cats, dogs and birds. 1931.
Also pbd poetry, novels and travel bks.

Grace Stebbing

Denham Hall: a story of Wiclif's days. nd.
Fun and fairies: or those four little girls. nd.
Joe Underwood: or worth more than the sparrows. 1857.
Walter Benn, and how he stepped out of the gutter. 1877.
Gold and glory; or wild ways of other days. [1882.]
That aggravating schoolgirl. 1885.
That brother of a boy. 1890.
Lilla Thorn's voyage: or 'That for remembrance'. Boston 1892.
The Jessamines: a story of a country house. 1899.
Lost her shoe and a few little threads. 1900.
Also pbd numerous other bks.

Francesca Mary Steele *see* 'Darley Dale'

John Alexander Steuart 1861–1932

Self-exiled: a story of the high seas and East Africa. 1889 (illus).

Charles Stevens

Alone in the pirate's lair. 1870 (rptd from Boys of England).
Conducted and contributed to Boys of England *and other penny weekly mags for boys.*

Robert Louis Stevenson 1850–94

Treasure island. 1883.
A child's garden of verses. 1885.
Kidnapped: being memoirs of the adventures of David Balfour. 1886.
The black arrow: a tale of the two roses. 1888.
Catriona: a sequel to Kidnapped. 1893.
See also col 1688.

Mrs Stewart, Agnes M. Stewart

Brotherly love; or the sisters. 1848.
Chastity: or the sister of charity. 1848.
Diligence: or Ethel Villiers and her slothful friend. 1848.
Humility: or Blanche Neville and the fancy fair. 1848.
Meekness: or Emily Herbert and the victim of passion. 1848.
Stories of the seven virtues. 1848.
Temperance: or the broken glass. 1848.
The cousins: or pride and vanity. 1849.
Eustace: or self devotion. 1860.
Disappointed ambition. 1863.
The story of a boy's adventures and how he rose in the world. 1866 (illus).
Alone in the world. 1870.
Also wrote a number of devotional texts.

Caroline Stewart

A kitten's adventures. [1887.]
Lady Daisy and other stories. [1889.]
Glen Farm. A story of three children. [1896.]
Alice's teaparty. 1898.

Geraldine Stewart

The laird's return and what came of it. A story for young people. 1861 (illus).

Sarah Stickney, later Ellis 1799–1872

The young Hindoo. 1833.
Fireside tales for the young. 1849.
See also col 1284.

Catherine Mary Stirling

Prince Arthur: or the four trials. A fairy tale. 1861, 1874.

Walter Stirling

First impressions: or pleasing and instructive stories for children. nd.
Early impressions: or moral and instructive entertainment for children. [1820?], 1847.

Lady Isabella Stoddart, née Moncrieff Wellwood, 'Martha Blackford' d. 1846

The Eskdale herdboy, a Scottish tale. 1819, 1850.
Arthur Montieth: a moral tale. 1822.
The Scottish orphans. 1822, 1823, 1850.

The young artists. 1825.
William Montgomery. 1829.
The orphan of Waterloo. 1844.

Miss E. Strafford, Elizabeth Strafford 1828–68

The captain's little daughter and other tales. [1856.]
Hymns for the collects throughout the year for the use of children. 1857.
Enjoyment for all young readers. 1859.
Tales of delight for youthful readers. [1859.]

'Hesba Stretton'

See col 1704.

Agnes Strickland 1796–1874

The moss house. 1822.
The rival crusoes. 1826.
See also col 2199.

Susanna Strickland, later Moodie 1803–85

Little Downey: or the adventures of a field mouse. 1822, 1832, 1844 (as Adventures of little Downey, the field mouse and The little prisoner: or passion and patience).
The little prisoner: or passion and patience, and Amendment: or Charles Grant and his sister. 1828, [1850?].
Geoffrey Moncton: or the faithless guardian. New York 1855.

'Esmé Stuart', Amélie Claire Le Roy 1851–1934

The good old days, or Christmas under Queen Elizabeth. 1876 (illustr H. S. Marks).
A little brown girl: a story for children. 1877.
Master Trim's charge: a story. 1879.
Mimi: a story of peasant life in Normandy. 1879.
The belfry of St Jude. 1880.
How they were caught in a trap. A tale of France in 1802. 1880.
Overtaken by the tide: or holidays at Old Port. A story. 1881.
Vanda. A story. 1881.
The Vicar's trio: a story. 1881.
The white chapel. A story. 1881.
Ade: a story of German life. 1882.
Isabeau's hero. A story of the revolt of the Cevennes. 1882.
Lia: a tale of Nuremberg. 1883.
The fate of Castle Lowengard: a story of the days of Luther. [1884], 1890 (as In the days of Luther: or The fate of Castle Lowengard).
An out of the way place. A story. 1884, 1892 (as Through the flood).
The prisoner's daughter. A story of 1758. 1884.
A fair damzell. A novel. 1885.
Jesse Dearlove. A story. 1885.
The last hope: a tale. 1885.
A little place. A tale. 1885.
Married to order: a romance of modern days. 1885.
Miss Fenwick's failures; or Peggy Pepper Pot. 1885.
The unwelcome guest: a story for girls. 1886 (illustr M. E. Butler).
Ursula's fortune. 1886.
For half a crown. A story. [1887.]
The goldmakers. A tale. 1887.
In his grasp. A tale. 1887.
Muriel's marriage: a novel. 1887.
Carried off. A story of pirate times. 1888.
Daisy's king and How Mick Kevene won the race. Two tales. 1888.
An idle farthing. 1888.
Joan Vellacott. 1888.
Edgar's wife: a story. 1889.
One for the other: stories of French life. 1889.
By reeds and rushes. 1890.
Cast ashore. 1890.
Kestell of Greystone. 1891.
The silver mine. An underground story. 1891.
A brave fight, and other stories. 1892.
A nest of Royalists. (A tale of the second French revolution). 1892.
A small legacy: a story for children. 1892.
Through the flood. 1892.
Virginie's husband. A novel. 1892.
By right of succession. 1893.
Claudia's island. 1893.
A woman of forty. A monograph. 1893.
Inscrutable. 1894.
The power of the past. A novel. 1894.
Arrested: a novel. 1896.
The footsteps of fortune. 1896.
Harum Scarum: a poor relation. 1896, 1905, 1924.
A mine of wealth. 1896.
Tangled threads. 1897.
The knights of Rosemullion. 1898.
Sent to Coventry. 1898.
In the dark. 1899.
Christella: an unknown quantity. 1900.
The strength of straw: a novel. 1900.
For love and ransom. 1905.
Mona: a Manx idyll. 1905.
A charming girl. 1907.
Harum Scarum's fortune. [1909], 1915.
The culture of Chris. 1919.
The taming of Tamzin. 1920, 1931.
Two troubadours. A story. 1912 (illustr H. Holloway), 1912 (as Harum Scarum married).

Amelia Stubbs

Family tales for children. [1824.]

William Francis Sullivan 1756–1830

The flights of fancy, being a miscellaneous collection of original poems, epigrams, songs, etc. 1792.
The test of union and loyalty, or the long-threatened French invasion. A poem. 1803.
Early habits: or the effects of attention and neglect; exemplified by the history of Master Thomas Towardley and Lawrence Lacey, alias Lazy. 1816.
Emily and Henrietta: or a cure for idleness. 1816 (tr from Fr).
The history of Mr Rightway and his pupils. 1816.
Juvenile sketches: or the history of Mrs Barton and her little family. 1817.
Portraits from life; or the history of Charles and Charlotte. 1817.
Pleasant stories: or the history of Ben the sailor and Ned the soldier. 1818.
The recluse: or the hermit of Windermere. 1818, 1819.
The young truants; an interesting and instructive lesson .... 1818.
The young liar! A tale of truth and caution .... 1818.

'Mercie Sunshine'

Chats about animals. 1878.
Chats about birds. 1878.
The children's picture story book in prose and verse. 1881.
The child's pretty page picture book in prose and verse. 1881.

Little tales for little people. 1881.
The nursery treasure book of funny stories, good music and pretty rhymes for children. 1881.
Our baby's picture book. A volume of large type and large pictures for tiny trots. 1881.
Pretty pictures for little folks. 1881.
The young folks picture book of amusing and interesting tales. 1881.
Dottie and Tottie: or home for the holidays. [1882.]
The good sailor boy: or the adventures of Charley Morant. 1882.
Irene and the gypsies: or pray without ceasing. 1882.
Mercie Sunshine's new picture book of animals. 1882.
The sparrow's Christmas party, and other tales. [1882.]
Stirring scenes in English history for boys and girls. 1882.
The children's life of Jesus Christ. 1883.
Little Lily's large type picture book. 1883.
Little stories of famous places at home and abroad. 1887.
Chats about soldiers and sailors. 1892.
The cosy nook picture book of pictures and stories. 1895.
Cheery chats and pleasing pictures. 1897.
Little stories about famous places at home and abroad. 1898.
The sunny home: the story of a united family. 1899.

Elizabeth Surr

Stories about dogs. 1882.

Maggie Symington

The King's command: a story for girls. 1886.

Ann Taylor, née Martin

See col 473.

Ann Taylor, later Gilbert 1782–1866

See col 474.

Emily Taylor 1795–1872

Letters to a child on the subject of maritime discovery. 1820, 1828.
Letters to a very little girl from her aunt. 1820.
Historical prints representing some of the more memorable events in English history. 1821, 1844.
The vision of Las Casas, and the poems. 1825.
Poetical illustrations of passages of Scripture. 1826.
Sabbath recreations: or select poetry, of a religious kind, chiefly taken from the works of modern poets: with original pieces never before published. 1829.
Tales of the Saxons. 1832.
Tales of the English: William de Albini of Buckenham Castle. 1833.
A memoir of Sir Thomas More. 1834.
The boy and the birds. With designs by T. Landseer. 1835, 1840.
The Knevets. 1835, 1862.
Help to the schoolmistress: or village teaching. 1839.
The ball I live on: or sketches of the earth. 1845, 1846.
Chronicles of an old English oak: or sketches of English life and history. 1859, 1860.
England and its people or a familiar history ... of the country and the social and domestic manners of its inhabitants. 1859, 1860.
Ellis Gordeon: or Bolton Farm. 1860.
Purples and blues. 1860.
Flowers and fruit gathered by loving hands from old English gardens. 1864.
Memories of some contemporary poets with selections from their writings. 1868.
Dear Charlotte's boys. 1870.
Stories from history. 1876.

Isaac Taylor 1759–1829

See col 471.

Jane Taylor 1783–1824

See col 475.

Jefferys Taylor 1792–1853

See col 479.

Joseph Taylor

The general character of the dog, illustrated by a variety of anecdotes. 1804.
The wonders of the horse, recorded in anecdotes. 1813, New York 1836.
Tales of the robin, and other small birds. 1815.

Lucy Taylor

Fairy Phoebe: or facing the footlights. nd.
Led into light. 1886.
The children's champion and the victories to be won. London, Edinburgh and New York 1889.
Stories of noble lives. 1889.
Through peril, toil and pain. 1899.

Winifred Taylor

Rupert Rochester, the banker's son. Edinburgh 1870.
Violet Rivers: or loyal to duty. A tale for girls. 2nd edn Edinburgh 1871.
Labours of love: a tale for the young. 1876.

Crona Temple

About the feathered folk. nd.
Hill farm. Boston nd.
Kirsty's prince: a story of Holyrood. nd.
The old endeavour: a book for boys. nd.
Millicent's home. London and New York nd, 1882.
Little wave, the foundling of Glenderg. [1873.]
Royal captives. 1874.
Nobody cares. 1876.
The last of these. 1878.
Lady Rose. 1882.
Life at Hill Farm. 1883.
Bound with a chain. 1885.
John Denton's friends. 1885.
Etta's fairies: a little story for little folks. London, Edinburgh and New York 1887.
The ferryman's boy. 1887.
Knighted by the admiral: or the days of the Great Armada. 1889.
Dick's water lilies and other stories. 1894.
Sea larks: a tale of the Hebrides. 1898.

William Makepeace Thackeray 1811–63

The rose and the ring, or the history of Prince Giglio and Prince Bulbo: a fireside pantomime for great and small children, by Mr M. A. Titmarsh. 1855 (for 1854).
See also col 1406.

D'Arcy Wentworth Thompson

Fun and earnest: or rhymes with reason. 1865 (illus).
Nursery nonsense: or rhymes without reason. 1865 (illus).
Also pbd educational bks on the classics and natural history.

Louisa Thompson

The royal eagle: a story of Frederick the third of Germany. 1890.
Gladys Anstruther: or the young stepmother. 1892 (illustr F. H. Townsend), 1901.
The Christian's walk with God: or three invitations. 1893.
Rex: or winning the Victoria Cross. 1895.
Ivan Graham: a story of the medical mission to the Jews in Russia. 1896.

S. Emma Thomson

Mathilda's birthday: or the grand magic lantern. A tale for youth. nd.

'Ismay Thorn', Edith Caroline Pollock

All play. nd (illustr T. Pym).
Captain Geoff. nd.
Little sisters of pity. nd.
Quite unexpected. nd.
Tom tit: his sayings and doings. nd.
Pinafore days: the adventures of Fred and Dolly by wood and wave. 1879.
A six years' darling: or Trix in town. [1881.]
In and out. 1882 (illus).
Only five: or Pussie's frolics in farm and field. nd. (illustr T. Pym).
Geoff and Jim. [1891] (illus).
Phil and his father. [1893.]
Sam: the story of 'a little while'. 1895.
The Harringtons at home. [1898] (illustr G. Browne).
Courage. 1899.
Everybody's business: or a friend in need. 1899.
A flock of four: a story for young boys. 1899.
Geoff and Jim. 1900, New York nd.

'Eglanton Thorne', Elizabeth Emily Charlton

'It's all real true': the story of a child's difficulties. 1881, 1908.
As many as touched him. 1882.
The old Worcester jug: or John Griffin's little maid. 1882, 1911.
A tale of three week. 1883.
Caleb Gaye's success. 1884, 1887, 1914.
In London fields: a story of the lights and shadows of a child's life. [1884.]
A man of rock. [1884.]
Phil's mother. [1885.]
Caleb and Beryl: or children of the kingdom. [1886.]
Ida Nicolari. 1886.
The cottage by the Lynn. 1887.
The manse of Glen Cunie. [1888.]
My brother's friend. [1889.]
Nathan Quilter's fall. 1889.
The love that casteth out fear: or Muriel and her father. 1890.
Aldyth's inheritance. [1891.]
Rueben Toy's temptations. [1892.]
Worthy of his name. 1892.
Maud Marion artist: or the studio Mariano. [1894.]
An elder brother. 1895.
A sham princess. 1897.
Her own way. 1899.
A little Protestant in Rome. [1900.]
A girl of the name of Brown. 1901.
The blessedness of Irene Farquar. [1902.]
The widowhood of Gabrielle Grant. 1903.
A shop-girl's romance. [1906.]
Helena's dower: or a troublesome ward. 1907.
The wizard's cave. 1910.

Clara Thwaites

Songs for labour and leisure. [1885.]
Butterfly valley. 1903.

Lizzie Ellen Tiddeman

Toddy: a tale. 1888.
The twins. 1888.
Dr Rollison's dilemma. 1890, 1892.
From over the sea. 1890.
Kitty Carroll. 1891.
Grannie's treasures and how they helped her. 1892, 3rd edn 1903.
Daisy and her friends. 1894.
The doctor's lass. 1894.
Toby: what he said and what he did. 1894.
Bogie and Fluff: a story. [1896.]
A humble heroine. 1896, 1899.
A little ladybird: a story for girls. 1896.
Angelica's troubles. 1897.
A bright little pair: a story of brother and sister. 1897.
A fairygrandmother: or Madge Ridd, a little London waif. 1897.
Young Chris. 1897.
Rosa's repentance: a story for girls. 1898.
Daddy's darling. 1899.
Molly and mother. 1899.
Reine's kingdom. 1899.
Sahib's birthday. 1899, 1920.
The sea-bird. 1899.
What Mother said. 1899 (illus).
The apple of his eye: a story. 1900.
Celia's conquest. 1900.
Seeing is believing. 1900.
The colonel's boy and Roy's adventures. 1902.
Ray and Fairy. 1907.
When Bab was young. 1909 (illus).
The adventure of Jasmin. 1910.
All about me. 1910.
Aunt Pen: or roses and thorns. 1910.
The fortunes of Joyce. 1911.
Nancy and her cousins. 1911.
Trixi and her trio. 1913.
Uncle Sam's little lady. 1916.
Kitty Quick. 1923.
Three cheers for Aunt May. 1923.
The adventures of Jack Charrington: or the colonel's boy. 1925.
Ralph does his best. From 'What Mother said'. 1931.
Also pbd adult novels.

John Todd

Familiar lectures to children in which the important truths of the Gospel are engagingly set forth. 1835.
Truth made simple: being a system of theology for children. 1844.
The daughter at school. 1856.
The angel of the iceberg and other stories and parables illustrating great truths. 1860 (illus).
Todd's lectures to children. [1860], 1861, 1884.
Also pbd religious texts and bks about North America.

S. Grace Toplis

Charades and plays for school rooms and drawing rooms. 1889.
The girls of Cliff School. 1894.
Also pbd biographical and critical works on Richard Jefferies.

Mr Torkington

Christmas holidays: or the young visitants. 1806.

Camilla Toulmin, later Crosland, Mrs Newton Crosland 1812–95

The little Berlin woolworker: or cousin Caroline's visit. 1844.
Partners for life: a Christmas story. 1847.
Stratagems: a story. 1849.
The young lord and other tales. 1849, 1850.
The neglected child: a tale. 1858.
The island of the rainbow. A fairy tale and other fancies. '1866' [1865] (illus).
Stories of the City of London retold for youthful readers. 1880. Illus.
See also col 1417.

Isabella Jane Towers, née Clarke 1790–1867

The children's fireside: being a series of tales for winter evenings. 1828.
The wanderings of Tom Starboard: or the life of a sailor, his voyages and travels, perils and adventures, by sea and land. 1830.
The young wanderer's cave and other stories. 1830.
Perils in the woods: or an emigrant family's return. [1835.]

Elizabeth W. Townsend, Mrs Townsend

The white dove and other poems for children. New York 1855.

Mary Elizabeth Townsend

Walter and Lisette: a mountain story. 1875, 1893.
Aunt Margaret's story. 1876.
Daughters at home. 1876, 1881.
Rachel's resolution: a sketch from nature. 1876.
Steffan's angel: a Tyrolese story. 1876.
Stories for our girls. 1876.
Maidens of scripture. 1879.
Modest maidens. 1880.
Birdie's bonnet and other stories. 1884.
Little nurses. 1888.
Also contributed to Friendly Leaves *and wrote religious bks. Was a prominent writer on the* Girl's Friendly Soc.

Elizabeth C. Traice

Wee doggie. London, Edinburgh and New York 1898.

Catherine Parr Traill, née Strickland 1802–99

Little downy. 1822.
Fables for the nursery: original and select. 1825.
The keepsake guineas.
Young emigrants: or pictures of Canada.

Marie Trevelyan

Brave little women: stories of the heroism of girls founded on fact. [1888.]
From Snowdon to the sea: striking stories of North and South Wales. 1895.
Also wrote historical works.

Jane Trimmer

Miscellaneous stories for children. [1840.]

J. T. Trowbridge

His own master. 1879.

Charlotte Maria Tucker

See 'A. L. O. E.'

Miss E. Tuckett, Elizabeth Tuckett

Our children's story, by one of their gossips. 1870.
The children's journey, and other stories. 1872.
Baby and me. New York [1892].
Children of colonial days. New York [1894].
Rhymes and stories of olden days. New York [1894].
Tales and verses of long ago. [1894.]
Also pbd bks about the Dolomites and the Alps.

Andrew White Tuer

Pictures and pages from forgotten children's books. 1899.
Stories from old fashioned children's books. London and New York [1899].
Also pbd on bk history.

Elizabeth Turner d. 1846

The daisy: or cautionary stories in verse, adapted to the ideas of children from four to eight years old. 1806, 1807 (anon), 1810, 1816, [1840], [1849], [1855], [1860], 1885 (ed C. Welsh), [1899] (facs reprint of 1807 edn), 1900.
The cowslip: or more cautionary tales in verse. 1811, 1815, 1817, 1825, 1842, 1883 (ed C. Welsh), 1899, 1900 (facs reprint of 1911 edn).
The pink. 1811, 1823, 1835 (as The pink: or child's first book of poetry, ed M. Howitt, with addns).
The blue-bell: or tales and fables. Derby 1838.
The crocus: another series of cautionary tales in verse. [c. 1820?], 1844.
The rose. nd.
Short poems for young children. [1859.]
Little stories of famous places at home and abroad. 1887.
Mrs Turner's cautionary stories. 1897 (Dumpy Books for Children).
Grandmamma's book of rhymes for children. 1927 (introd G. K. Chesterton).
See R. G. Bulkeley, 'Suffer little children to come unto me'. A memoir of E. Turner, *1866.*

Ethel Sybil Turner, later Curlewis

The family at Misrule. London, New York and Melbourne 1895 (illus).
The little duchess and other stories. 1896.
The little larrikin. London, New York and Melbourne 1896.
Miss Bobbie. London, New York and Melbourne 1897.
Seven little Australians. London, New York and Melbourne 1897.
The camp at Wandinong. 1898.
Three little maids. 1900.

The story of a baby. 1901.
The wonder-child: an Australian story. 1901.
Betty and Co. 1903.
Mother's little girl. 1904.
Happy hearts: a picture book for boys and girls. London and Melbourne 1908.
That girl. 1908.
Fair Ines. 1910.
Apple of happiness. 1911.
Ogre up-to-date. 1911.
Captain Cub. 1917.
St Tom and the dragon. 1918.
Also pbd adult novels.

Lena Tyack

Brave Dick. [1883], [1895], [1912], [1919].
Christy's mission. [1883], [1895].
Poppy's holiday. 1892.
Don's two friends: a tale. 1895.
Fina's first fruits and other stories. 1897.
The fairy godmother. 1897.
The happiest thing. 1898.
Joyce Maxwell's mistakes. 1899.
Sybil's blue velvet bag. [1901.]
Betty Martindale's secret. 1911.
The feast of lanterns. 1911.
Audrey's offerings. [1913.]
The girl who lost things. 1913.
A sparrow on the housetop. [1920.]
Greenmeadows. 1926.
Also pbd other bks about missionary work.

Frances Isabelle Tylcoat

Elsie: or like a little candle. [1875.]
Truth speaking. [1876.]
Father Rutland: or the ban of St Peter. 1878.
Sunshine through the clouds: or the reward of gentleness. [1878], 4th edn 1897.
The adventures of Wouldn't Say Wee. [1881.]

Mrs George Tylee

Amy's wish and what came of it: a fairy tale. 1870.
Also pbd adult novels.

Ann Fraser Tytler

Leila: or the island. 1833, 1839, 1841, 1868 (14th edn).
Mary and Florence: or grave and gay. 1835.
Mary and Florence at sixteen. A continuation of Grave and gay. 1836, 1838.
Leila in England: a continuation of Leila: or the island. 1842, 1844, 1868, 1877, 1879, 1912.
Hymns and sketches in verse. 1840.
The deformed. 1845.
Leila at home. A continuation of Leila in England. 1852.
Common sense for housemaids. 1869.
Evan Lindsay. 1874.

Christina Catherine Fraser Tytler, later Liddell

Sweet violet and other stories. 1869.
Jasmine Leigh. 1871.
Also wrote adult novels and devotional texts.

Margaret Fraser Tytler

Tales of the great and brave. 1838, Edinburgh 1843, London and Edinburgh 1895.
Tales of many lands. 1839, 1861, 1863.
My boy's first book. 1840, Philadelphia 1845.
My boy's second book. 1841.
Tales of good and great kings. 1845.
The wonder seeker: or the history of Charles Douglas. 1846, Edinburgh 1859.
The wooden walls of old England: or the lives of celebrated admirals. 1847, 1864.
Little Fanny's journal: or my own child's book. Edinburgh 1851.
Also pbd bks of hymns, and novels.

Sarah Tytler

See 'Henrietta Keddie'.

Bertha Upton, née Hudson 1849–1912

The golliwog in Holland. 1894.
The adventures of two Dutch dolls and a golliwog: in verse. 1895, London and New York 1903.
The golliwog's bicycle club. 1896.
Little hearts. 1897.
The vege-man's revenge. 1897.
The golliwog at the seaside. 1898.
The golliwog in war. 1899.
The golliwog's polar adventures. 1900, 1967.
The golliwog's auto-go-cart. 1901.
The golliwog's air-ship. 1902.
The golliwog's circus. 1903.
The golliwog's desert island. 1905.
The golliwog's fox hunt. 1905.
The golliwog's Christmas. 1907.
The golliwog in the African jungle. 1909.

Elizabeth Boughton Upton, Lady Templetown

The birth-day gift: or the joy of a new doll. Toronto 1968 (facs reprint of 1786 edn).

Laura Belinda Valentine, née Jewry 1814–99

Aunt Louisa's Bible picture book. nd.
Aunt Louisa's book of nursery rhymes. nd (illus).
Aunt Louisa's book of wonder stories. nd (illus).
Aunt Louisa's nursery favourites. nd (illus).
Hector the dog. nd (Aunt Louisa's London toy books).
Home pets. nd (Aunt Louisa's London toy books).
Noted horses from paintings by 'Herring'. nd. (Aunt Louisa's London toy books).
Sea side. nd (Aunt Louisa's London toy books).
Sing a song of sixpence. nd (Aunt Louisa's London toy books).
The Zoological gardens. nd (Aunt Louisa's London toy books).
The girl's own book of amusements, studies, and employments. nd (illus).
Aunt Louisa's London picture book. 1867 (illus).
Hey diddle diddle. London and New York [c. 1870].
We three boys: or a year of adventure. [1884.]

Frances Bowyer Vaux

Henry: a story intended for little boys and girls. 1815, 1817, 1825.
The dew drop: or the summer morning's walk. 1816, 1818.

Domestic pleasures: or the happy fireside, illustrated by interesting conversations. 1816.
The happy travellers: or a trip to France. 1817.

E. Veale

Bonny birds. 1896 (illus).
Busy brownies. 1896 (illus).
Funny foxes. 1896 (illus).
The jolly chinee: interesting stories and sketches designed to please little people. 1897 (illus), Chicago 1900.
Merry mice. 1897.
The monkey's trick. 1897.

Mrs Agnes Veitch

Woodruff: or sweetest when crushed. nd, 1869.
Tom and his dog Towser. 1859.
Tinsel and gold: or what girls should learn. 1861.
Frank Fielding: or debts and difficulties. 1886.
The fairy ring and other stories. 1890.
Also pbd adult novels.

E. Velasco

The intelligent miscellany for the amusement and instruction of youth. 1815.

Ellen Velvin

Tales told at the zoo. nd (illus).
Martin Luther, the hero of the Reformation. [1897.]
More tales told at the zoo. 1899.
Our holiday in London. 1900.
More tales told at the zoo. [1900] (illus).
Rataplan, a rogue elephant and other stories. 1902, 1904, 1934 (as Animal stories).
Also wrote about wild animals.

Harriet Ventum, née Crossley or Crosley

Selima: or the village tale. 1798.
Justine: or the history of a young lady. 1801.
Surveys of nature: a sequel to Mrs Trimmer's Introduction: being familiar descriptions of some popular subjects in natural philosophy adapted to the capacities of children. 1802.
Interesting traits of character in youths of both sexes. 1804.
Tales for domestic instruction: containing the histories of Ben Hallyard, Hannah Jenkins, John Aplin, Edward Fletcher, or the memory of curbing our passions, Lucy and Jemima Meadows, and Mr Wilmot. 1806.
Charles Leeson: or the soldier. A tale. 1810.
The good aunt: including the story of Signior Aldersonini and his son. 1813.
The holiday reward; or tales to instruct and amuse good children, during the Christmas and midsummer vacations. 1814.

Katherine Elizabeth Vernham

Perry's pilgrimage. 1895.
A wonderful Christmas and other stories. 1896.
The tucker's turkey and other stories. 1898.
Jo: a stupid boy and other stories. [1899.]
Bab's bay and other stories. [1900.]
Bobby's forgetting and other stories for boys. [1900.]
Such a tomboy and other stories. [1900.]

Margaret Elizabeth Villiers, Countess of Jersey

Maurice: or the red jar: a tale of magic and adventure. 1894.
Eric, prince of Lorlonia, or the valley of wishes. 1895.

John Vincent

The pretty plate: or honesty is the best policy. 1854.

Louis Wain

Dogs in catland. nd.
Tinker, tailor, soldier, sailor. nd.
Three little kittens. nd.
Who said cats? nd.
Pussies and puppies. 1899.
The Louis Wain nursery book. 1902.
Louis Wain's baby's picture book. 1902.
Big dogs, little dogs, cats and kittens. 1903 (illustr L. Wain).
The Louis Wain kitten book. 1903.
A cat alphabet and picture book for little folk. 1904 (illustr L. Wain).
In animal land with Louis Wain. 1904.
Louis Wain's animal show with stories in prose and verse. 1905.
Daddy cat. 1915, 1925 (illustr L. Wain).
Cinderella and other fairy tales. 1917.
Louis Wain's children's book. 1923.
A prolific illustrator of cats in children's books and mags, including Boy's Own Paper, Girl's Own Paper *and* Our Darlings, *and founder of the* Louis Wain Annual.

George Walker 1772–1847

The adventures of Timothy Thoughtless: or the misfortunes of a little boy who ran away from boarding-school. 2nd edn 1813.
Also wrote poetry and adult novels.

John Alexander Walker

Jessie Dyson: a Christmas tale for the young. 1874, 1891, 1898.

J. G. Walker

Charley Ashley: or the adventures of an orphan boy. 1870.

George Henry Wall

The emigrant's lost son: or life alone in the forest. London and New York 1855 (illus), 1857.

Mrs Waller

The crosses of childhood: or Alice and her friends. [1864.]
All about the Marsdens: a chronicle of everyday life. 1865.
Maude's visit to Sandybeach. 1865 (illus), 1884.
Procrastinating Mary. 1865.

Hugh Mulleneux Walmsley

Wild sports and savage life in Zulu land. London and New York 1877 (illus).
Also wrote other tales of adventure, and bks about Africa.

Dorothy Walrond

These little ones. Glasgow 1881, 1885, 1886, London and New York 1896.

Mopsie: the story of a London waif. London, Edinburgh and New York 1894, 1909.

Elizabeth Hely Walshe

Cedar Creek from the shanty to the settlement: a story of Canadian life. 1863, 1902.
Also pbd historical bks, and stories about Ireland.

Amy Walton

Our Frank and other stories. 1886.
The Hawthorns: a story about children. 1887, 1905.
A pair of clogs, and other stories for children. 1888, 1890 (illus).
Susan: a story for children. 1888, 1897.
The kitchen cat and other stories for children. 1890 (illus), 1930, London and Glasgow 1937.
White lilac: or the Queen of the May. 1890, 1934.
Penelope and the others: a story of five country children. 1893 (illus), 1897.
Black, white and gray: a story of three homes. 1894.
Thistle and rose: a story for children. 1895.
Only twice: a tale. 1896.

Mrs O. F. Walton, Catherine Augusta Walton, née Deck 1849–1939

My little corner. A book for cottage homes. [1872], 1879, [1882], [1928].
Little Dot. [1873.]
Christie's old organ: or home sweet home. [c. 1875], [1882], [1883], 1890, 1913.
Angel's Christmas. 1877; as Angel's Christmas and Little Dot 1877, 1905, 1908.
A peep behind the scenes. [1877], [1882], 1903, [1909], [1918], [1940].
My mates and I, etc. 1878.
Saved at sea: a lighthouse story. [1879], [1885], [1905].
Was I right? 1879, Cambridge MA 1880, [1884].
Little Faith. [1880], [1905], 1906 (as Little Faith: or the children of the toy stall).
Olive's story. [1881], 1886, [1928].
Nobody loves me. [1883], [1905].
The four little preachers. A new year's address to Sunday Scholars. 1884.
Shadows and incidents in the life of an old armchair. [1884], [1892].
Taken or left. [1885], [1907].
Launch the lifeboat. 1886 (illustr H. J. Rhodes), 1910.
Our gracious Queen. Jubilee pictures and stories from her Majesty's life. 1886, [1887], 1897.
Poppy's presents. [1886], [1906].
Winter's folly. [1889.]
The mysterious house. [1890], [1909].
The King's cup-bearer. 1891.
Nemo: or the wonderful door. [1893], 1903 (as The wonderful door).
Audrey; or children of light. [1897], [1908].
Elisha, the man of Abel-Meholah. 1897.
Christie, the King's servant. A sequel to Christie's old organ. 1898, 1909.
Doctor Forrester. [1905], [1906].
The lost clue. 1905, 1907, 1909.
Golden threads for life's weaving. 1906.
Strange Diana. 1919.

Mrs Marshall Ward

Hardy and hunter: a boy's own story. 1858.
Gerry Ross and the little bluecoat boy. 1869.
Short stories for young people. 1870.

Davina Waterson

Malcolm and Doris: or learning to help. London and Edinburgh 1889.

E. M. Waterworth

Harry's holidays. 1883, 1919.
Joe Davy's trade mark: or where's the light? 1883.
Master Lionel: that tiresome child. 1885, 1894.
Listening to Jesus: or Sunday readings for the little ones. 1887.
Sunday afternoons at Rose Cottage. 1887.
Stories of Bible children. 1888.
Our Den. 1892.
The crab's umbrella and Ted's golden cloud. 1894.
Twice saved: or somebody's pet and nobody's darling. 1895, 1912.
Six in a doll's house. 1895.
Lady Betty's twins. 1896.
Dumpy Dolly. 1898.
Contributed to a number of children's mags, including Children's Friend, *and wrote several devotional texts.*

Rev J. B. Watkins

Anecdotes for youth, religious, moral and entertaining. 1822.
Scripture history, including the lives of the most celebrated apostles. Designed particularly for the improvement of youth. 2 vols 1823, 1828.
Anecdotes and tales for young people, moral and entertaining, forming an anecdote library for youth. 1849.

Jean L. Watson

Round the Grange Farm: or good old times. Edinburgh 1872.
Willie's upbringing and how he turned out. 1897.
Water-cress boy: or Johnnie Moreland. London and Edinburgh 1897.
Also pbd biographical texts.

Frederic Edward Weatherly 1848–1929

The cats' concert. nd.
Goosey gander. nd.
Holly boughs. nd.
Little Pickle. nd.
Little pussy-cat. nd.
Twilight land. nd.
Twilight tales. nd.
Two kittens: their true history. nd.
Nursery land. nd.
Our dear relations. nd.
Rhymes and roses. nd.
Sixes and sevens. nd.
Sunlight and song. nd.
Elsie in dreamland. 1879.
The maids of Lee. 1883.
Told in the twilight. 1883.
The men of Ware. [1883.]
The adventures of two children. [1884] (illus).
Little Miss Marigold. 1884, 1888.
Out of town. [1884.]
Punch and Judy and some of their friends. 1885.
The land of little people. London and New York 1886.
The star of Bethlehem. 1888.
Over the hills away. 1892.
The head boy of Wilton School. 1925.
A prolific writer of verse for children and adults.

Ellis H. Weaver

A line of light in the days of King Arthur. 1876.

Mrs J. B. Webb, Annie Webb, later Webb-Peploe

Blind Ursula. nd.
The travels and adventures of Charles Durand. 1839.
Naomi: or the last days of Jerusalem. 1841, 1853, 1854, 1861, 1865, 1870, 1877, 1886, 1894, 1895, 1898, 1899; tr Yiddish 1905, Ger 1928.
Tale of the Vaudois designed for young persons. 1842.
Loyal Charlie Betham. London and New York 1861.
Arthur Merton: a story for the young. 1863.
A stitch in time: or Ruthven Moore. 1866.
Julio Arnouf: a tale of the Vaudois. 1867.
The pilgrims of New England: a tale of the early American settlers. 1874.

Lucy L. Weedon

God with us: Bible stories for the little ones. nd.
Pets at the farm. nd.
Our playtime. nd.
Doggy and his doings. 1896.
Happy days and bright ways. London and New York 1896.
Pictureland stories. 1896.
Pretty and wise for sweet bright eyes. 1897.
Sunshiny stories for dull days. [1897.]
The children's guest. 1899.
Bright stories for dull days. 1900.
Dorry and the surrender of Uncle James. 1900.
A rebel's daughter: a tale of the Monmouth rebellion. 1900.
Twinkling pictures. 1901.
Yahie: a king's son. 1901.
Madcap Molly. 1902.
Rose or thistle: a romance of the border. 1903.
The story of a daisy. 1905.
Lamb tales. 1908.
The children's Sunday book. [1909.]
Our Sunday story book. 1910 (illus).
The children's farm. [1914] (illus).
Translated fairy stories and wrote other stories about the Bible.

Walter Wentworth

Swallow flights. nd.
Tens and elevens. nd.
There's many a slip 'twixt cup and lip. nd.
This little pig went to market. A tale in five curls. nd.
Through the meadows. nd (illus).
The drifting island: or the slave-hunters of the Congo. 1893.
Kibboo Ganey: or the lost chief of the copper mountain. Boston 1893.

Mrs F. West, Theresa Cornwallis J. West, née Whitby 1805?–86

All for an ideal: a girl's dream of a past period. 1876.
Frying pan alley: a story. 1880.
God's arithmetic, with other stories for the young. 1883.
Dora Maitland and other stories. 1884.
Stella's nosegay and other tales. 1884.
Unknown and yet well known: a tale of martyr times. 1884.
Live in the sunshine: or Constance Maxwell's choice. 1886.
Owen's fortune: or durable riches. 1886.
For the sake of a Crown: a tale of the Netherlands. London and Edinburgh 1889, 1903.

Sarah Wheatley

The Christmas fire-side: or the juvenile critics. 1806.

Frederick J. Whishaw

Lost in African jungles. The happy prince and other tales. London, Edinburgh and New York 1888, 1896.
Boris the bear hunter: a tale of Peter the Great and his times. 1895.
The adventures of a stowaway. 1897, 1916.
Gubbins minor, and some other fellows: a story of school life. [1897], 1913.
Harald the Norseman. 1897.
Bates and his bicycle. 1898.
Called back to Tsarland. 1899.
The three scouts: a story of the Boer War. 1900, 1914.
The lion cub: a story of Peter the Great. 1902, 1916.
The yellow satchel. 1903.
The boys of Brierley Grange. 1906 (illus).
The competitors: a tale of Upton House School. 1906.
Once bitten, twice shy: a tale of Peter the Great. [1910.]
Also pbd numerous other novels, many of which were about Russia.

Evelyn Whitaker 1857–1903

Miss Toosey's mission. 1878, 1884, 1893.
Laddie. 1880, 1894.
Tip cat. 1884.
Our little Ann. 1885.
Penn. 1888, 1891.
Lil. 1889, 1893.
Zoe. 1890.
Baby John. 1892.
Dear. 1892.
Pris. 1892, 1893.
Pomona. 1894.
Don. 1895.
Belle. 1898.
Tom's boy. 1900.
Lassie. 1901.

Eliza White

Gertrude: or thoughtlessness and inattention corrected. 1823.

Annie Whittem

Little Britannia: a story of Ben Rhydding. 1876.
Little May's friends: or country pets and pastimes. 1878 (illustr H. Weir).

Frances M. Wilbraham

Hal, the barge boy. A sketch from life. 1898.

E. G. Wilcox

Evie; or the visit to Orchard Farm. London and New York nd.

Oscar Fingall O'Flahertie Wills Wilde 1854–1900

The happy prince and other tales. 1888.
A house of pomegranates. 1891.
See also col 2060.

Anne Wilson, née Neville 1787–1859

A mother's stories for her children. 1838.

Charles Wilson

The amusing adventures of Mr Simon Snuff-box. 1861.

H. Mary Wilson

Crip: a story for Good Friday. nd.
Lance Henneley's holiday. nd.
Dew: a simple story for children. London, Edinburgh and Dublin 1889.
Storm tossed. 1899.

Lucy Sarah Wilson, née Atkins 1803–67

The India Cabinet opened: in which many natural curiosities are rendered a source of amusement to young minds. 1821, 1823.
A visit to Grove Cottage for the entertainment and instruction of children. 1823.
Juvenile rambler in a series of easy lessons. 1827, 1830.
The coral necklace; intended for the amusement of children. [1830?]
Grove Cottage and the India Cabinet opened. 1832.
Amusing anecdotes of various animals; intended for children. [c. 1835.]
Mamma's Bible stories for her little boys and girls. 1837, 1846, New York 1849, London 1850, New York 1851.
Sequel to Mamma's Bible stories for her little boys and girls. New York 1854, 5th edn 1859, 1865.

T. P. Wilson

Great heights gained by steady efforts; or perseverence and faithfulness triumphant. 1882.
A true hero; or the story of Amos Huntingdon: a tale of moral courage. 1889.

William Wilthew

Half hours of blind man's holiday; or summer and winter sketches in black and white. 1878.
After sundown, or the palette and the pew. 1880.
A professional secret and other tales. 1888.
'Twixt the lights, or odd tales for odd times. [1894.]

M. E. Winchester

A wayside snowdrop. 1883.
A nest of sparrows. 1893.

Marion Wingrave

The May blossom: or the princess and her people. 1881.

Jane Margaret Winnard, later Hooper, Miss Winnard

Arbell: a tale for young people. London and New York 1847, 1853 (illus), 1858.
Recollections of Mrs Anderson's school. A book for girls. 1851.
Little Maggie and her brother: a sketch for children. 1861.
Fanny and Arthur: or persevere and prosper. A tale of interest. [1862] (illus).
The little darling at the seaside. 1863.
The little darling at home. 1864.
Arbell's schooldays. London and New York 1865.

Beech Wood

Plucky Jim: or the gang of thieves. London and New York 1893.

Frances Hariott Wood

Headless and handless. 1889 (illus).
Ten minutes to spare: or short tales for a Bible class. 1893.
Heldai's treasure: a tale illustrating manners and customs of Bible lands. 1897.

H. J. Wood

Florence: or the orphan ward. 1868.

J. Claverdon Wood

The stolen grand lama: an English boy's adventures in wild Tibet. nd.

Rev John George Wood

Stories and anecdotes of dogs. 1856 (illus).
Sketches and anecdotes of animal life. 1861 (illus).
The boy's own book of natural history. London and New York 1871 (illus).
The boy's modern playmate: a book of sports, games and pastimes. 1891.
Author of numerous books on natural history.

Kate Wood

Waif of the sea. 1884 (illus).
Winnie's secret: a story of faith and patience. 1889 (illus).
Jack and the gypsies. 1891 (illus).

Sara Wood

Children of other lands. nd.
The town of toys, and other stories. nd.
The gift of life: a book for the young. 1872 (illus).
Dwellers in our gardens: their lives and works. 2nd edn 1877.

Mrs Arthur G. K. Woodgate

Jack and Floss at sea and at home. London, Edinburgh and New York 1891.

M. Woodland

Bear and forbear: or the history of Julia Marchmont: a moral tale for young ladies. 1809.
Rose and Agnes: or the dangers of partiality. 1809.
Mathilda Mortimer: or false pride: for the use of young ladies. 1810.

Sarah Woodward

Peter Noble, the Royalist: an historical tale of the seventeenth century. 1862.

Elizabeth Wordsworth

Snow garden and other fairy tales for children. London and New York 1895.

Sir C. F. Lascelles Wraxhall

The black panther: or a boy's adventures among the redskins. New York 1864.
Golden-hair: a tale of the pilgrim fathers. Boston 1865.

J. Jackson Wray

'A man every inch of him': or the story of Frank Fullerton's school-days. nd.
The man with the knapsack: or the miller of Burnham Lee. nd.
Peter Pengelly: or true as the clock. nd.
Chronicles of Capstan Cabin: or the children's hour. 1878, 1894.
Widow Winpenny's watchword. 1885.

Mrs Wright

The observing eye: or letters to children on the three lowest divisions of animal life. 1853, 1856, 1879.
Listen and learn: a short narrative of a three days ramble. [1856.]

G. E. Wyatt

Archie Digby: or an Eton boy's holidays. London and New York 1892.
Follow the right: a tale for boys. London, Edinburgh and New York 1893.

G. R. Wynne

Ralph Clifford: a tale of country life in Virginia after the Civil War. London and New York 1895.

John Huddlestone Wynne

Tales for youth in thirty poems. 1794.
Tales for youth. Pt 4 1802.
Choice emblems, natural, historical, fabulous, moral and divine for the improvement and pastime of youth. 1812, New York 1815, Hartford CT 1820.

May Wynne

The seven champions of Christendom: a tale for the nursery. London and New York 1806.

Rev M. S. B. Yates

Adventures in western Africa: a tale. Edinburgh 1880.

Katherine M. Yeo

Under the deep blue sea: a wonderful adventure in fish-land. A story for children. nd.

Charlotte Mary Yonge 1823–1901

The little duke. 1854.
The Lances of Linwood. 1855.
The daisy chain: or aspirations, a family chronicle. 2 vols 1856.
A book of golden deeds. 1864.
The dove in the eagle's nest. 2 vols 1866.
Unknown to history: a story of the captivity of Mary of Scotland. 2 vols 1882.
See also col 1443.

(3) ANONYMOUS

This section represents a selection of anonymous works written for children but is in no way comprehensive.
The child's hosanna in the house of God. [18?]
The entertaining history of Master Francis Murphy. [c. 1800.]
The heavenly messenger: or the child's plain pathway to eternal life. [c. 1800.]
Holiday amusements of children of the Vale. Coventry [1800].
Select and entertaining stories for the juvenile or child's library. [c. 1880.]
The village orphan: a tale for youth. [1800.]
Adventures of a Musul: or three gifts with other tales. 1800.
The child's first book. Improved with a preface addressed to all affectionate mothers. 1801.
The history of Jack and his eleven brothers, displaying the various adventures they encountered in their travels. 1801, 1815.
The dog of knowledge: or memoirs of Bob, the spotted terrier. 1801, 1821(rptd as Bob, the spotted terrier; or memoirs of the dog of knowledge by the author of Dick, the little pony), London and New York 1885.
The good child's cabinet of natural history. 1801.
The happy family: or winter evening's employment. By a friend of youth. York 1801.
Pleasant tales to improve the mind and correct the morals of youth. 1801.
Cabinet of Lilliput. Instructive stories. 12 vols 1802.
Stories of instruction and delight. 1802.
Biography of a spaniel. 1803, 1804, 1826 (to which is annexed The idiot: a tale).
Dame Partlett's farm: containing an account of the great riches she obtained by industry, the good life she led, and, alas, good reader, her sudden death; to which is added a hymn written by Dame Partlett just before her death as an epitaph for her tombstone. 1804, 1845.
A cup of sweets that can never cloy: or delightful tales for good children. By S. E. S. 1804.
Pleasing and instructive tales from nature. 1804.
The little islanders: or the blessings of industry. 1805.
The beautiful age: or child of romance, being the interesting history of a baronet's daughter. Intended as an instructive lesson for youth. [1805.]
Entertaining instructions, in a series of familiar dialogues between a parent and his children. 1805.
Presents for good boys in words of one or two syllables. 1805.
Charms for children. 1806.
Christmas holidays: or the young visitants. 1806.
The history of a goldfinch. 1806, 1807.
The life of Caro, the famous dog of Drury Lane Theatre. 1806.
Little Sophy: a true story for little children. 3rd edn 1806.
The magic lantern: or amusing and instructive exhibitions for young people. By S. E. S. 1806.
Memoirs of Dick the little pony supposed to be written by himself and published for the amusement of little masters and misses. 1806.
Amusing observations supposed to be made by children in early life which will enable them to read and converse with propriety. By S. E. S. 1808.
The castle on the rock: or a successful stratagem. 1808.
Juvenile dramas in three volumes. By S. E. S. Exeter 1808.
The rose's breakfast. 1808.
The pictures in the Hermitage: or the history of George Meadows. 1808.
Arabella, a tale. And the history of Prince Witty and Princess Astrea. 2nd edn 1809.
The child's new year's gift. A collection of riddles. 1809, 1820.

The island of slaves, and, the history of Bella and Monteserina. [1809.]
The little grey mouse: or the history of Rosabelle and Paridel. 1809.
The story of the unfortunate but heroic Highlander, narrated by himself. Wellington 1809.
The grey palfrey. [1810.]
The faithful greyhound: or treachery rewarded. An instance of filial affection. [1810.]
Paternal forgiveness, exemplified in the story of Emma Wallace. [c. 1810.]
Scenes at home: or a sketch of a plain family. By S. W. (possibly Sarah Wilkinson). 1810.
The masquerade. Indian superstition. The orphan. The birth of sensibility. [1810.]
The pranks of Robert Playfair and Alfred Briton, the juvenile sportsman. [1810.]
Aethelwold and Ethelinda. 1810.
Lucy, or the little enquirer: being the conversation of a mother with her infant daugher. 1810.
A puzzle for a curious girl. 3rd edn 1810, 4th edn 1814.
The recluse: or the old British officer and his faithful servant: an interesting tale for youth. 1810.
To a child. 1810.
True stories: or interesting anecdotes of children. 1810.
Wanton amusement and the swallows: or the natural consequences of theft. Otley 1810.
Felissa; or the life and opinions of a kitten of sentiment. 1811.
Modern Arabia displayed in four tales. 1811.
The Warren family: or scenes at home. By S. W. (possibly Sarah Wilkinson). 1813.
The child's instructor, from the earliest age, to riper years, in a short comprehensive view of this visible world. 1813.
A present for infants: or pictures from the nursery. 1814.
Arthur and the little wanderers. By S. E. S. 1815.
The adventures of a work-bag: in which is introduced the characters of several little folks. [1815.]
The assembly of little birds, an instructive tale for boys and girls. Chelmsford [c. 1815].
The casket: or memoirs of Miss Leonora Selwyn. 1815.
The child's instructor, or picture alphabet. 1815.
The cottage piper: or history of Edgar, the itinerant musician: an instructive tale. 1815.
Fat and lean: or the fairy queen, exhibiting the effects of moral magic, by the ring and three mirrors. Chelmsford 1815.
The history of the basket maker: or vanity reproved and industry rewarded. Chelmsford 1815.
The history of Jack and his eleven brothers. 1815.
The history of Master Watkins. 1815.
The little prattler: or Dame Teachwell's first picture book. 1815.
The little quaker: or the triumph of virtue. A tale for the instruction of youth. 1815.
The little Spanish piper: or the fortunate orphan. An authentic story. 1815.
Nurse Dandem's little repository of great instruction containing the surprising adventures of Little Wake Wilful and his deliverance from the Giant Grumbolumbo. [1815.]
Occurrences of Master Manley's journal to the metropolis. Chelmsford 1815.
The playmate: or pretty stories of young Towler and Dame Williams. [1815.]
Robin Goodfellow: a fairy tale written by a fairy. 1815.
The surprising adventures of a hen as related by herself to her family of chickens. 1815.
Virtue and vice: or the history of Charles Careful and Harry Heedless. 1815.
Walter and Herbert: or precipitation and slowness equally subversive of good intention. 1815.
The young sparrows: or little Robert taught humanity. Wellington 1815.
The young traveller's delight, continuing the lives of several noted characters likely to amuse all good children. Chelmsford 1815.
Cara: or interesting adventures of a dog of sentiment. 1816.
Cato, or interesting adventures of a dog; interspersed with many real anecdotes. 1816, 2nd edn 1823.
The little warbler of the cottage, and her dog Constant. 1816.
Motherless Mary, a tale. Shewing that goodness even in poverty is sure of meeting its proper reward. 1816.
My bird and my dog. A tale for youth. 1816.
The oracle: or the friend of youth. By S. E. S. 1816.
Aunt Mary's tales, for the entertainment and improvement of little boys. 1817.
Dame Truelove's tales, now first published as useful lessons for little misses and masters. 1817, 1833 (rev as Truelove's tales: a cup of sweets that can never cloy), 1833 (as Short stories written for children. By Dame Truelove and her friends).
The happy cottage children. Memoir of Mary Ann Harris. 1817.
The history of a tame robin supposed to be written by himself. 1817.
Improving tales. Containing The Storm, Beauty and deformity, The midshipman and Athlone Castle. 1817.
The child's preceptor; or a short and easy guide to spelling and reading the English language. Bury 1818.
Stories by a mother for the use of her children. 1818.
A visit to the manor house: or the twelve days of Christmas, with hints for improvement. 1818, 1819.
Whim and contradiction: or the party of pleasure: a tale for young people. By S. E. S. 1818.
The winter vacation: or holidays in the country. Intended for the amusement of children. 1818.
The advantages of education, elucidated in the history of the Wingfield family. 1819.
The child's new play-thing: or best amusement. 1819.
The history of little Lucy: or the birth-day present. 1819.
Julia and the pet lamb: or good temper rewarded. 4th edn 1819.
Juvenile friendship; the guide to virtue and happiness; in dialogues between two student friends. 1819.
The way to be happy: or the history of the family at Smiledale. 1819.
Albert the adventurer. To which is added The foster sisters: or early friendship. [c. 1820.]
The accidents of childhood, narrated in short stories, calculated to deter youth from similar actions. Edinburgh [c. 1820].
Cousrou the man: or no life pleasing to God that is not useful to mankind: an eastern story. [1820?]
The faithful greyhound. [c. 1820.]
Filial affection illustrated in the story of Bertha Harvey. Anecdote of Apelles, the famous painter. [1820?]
Buy a broom: an interesting moral tale for children, founded on fact. 1820.
The child's alphabet, emblematically described and embellished by twenty-four pictures brought into easy verse. 1820.
The child's amusing library. Natural history. Pictures with an alphabet. 1820.
Fun upon fun: or the humours of a fair. Glasgow 1820.
The history of little Lydia Somerville: an interesting story calculated for the instruction and entertainment of juvenile minds. 1820.
The history of William Tell, the Swiss patriot and saviour of his country. Plymouth [1820].
The history of Tommy and Harry. York 1820.
The juvenile fabulist. Selected from Esop and others, with suitable reflections, embellished with engravings on wood. [1820.]
The parental instructor: or a father's present to his children. Edinburgh 1820.

Pious Harriet Balduck: or the history of a young and devout Christian. 1820, 1821.
To a child. [1820?]
The interesting history of little Jack. A moral tale. 1821.
Little Abel; or the young orphan. An affecting tale. With the story of Amelia. 1821.
Mary and her cat in words not exceeding two syllables. 1821.
More minor words: or an introduction to the Winter family: with Aunt Eleanor's stories interspersed. 1821.
Tales of the academy. 1821.
The welcome visitor: or the good uncle, being a collection of original stories. 1821, 1824.
The little prisoner: or a visit to the island of Malta. 1822.
The adventures of Congo in search of his master; a tale. Containing a true account of a shipwreck. 1823, 1828.
The Buxton diamonds, or grateful Ellen. For the amusement and instruction of children. [1823.]
Constance and Caroline: a moral tale. By a young lady. 1823.
Harriet and her cousin; or prejudice overcome. Edinburgh, Glasgow and London 1823, 1839.
The life and adventures of Lady Anne, the little pedlar. 1823.
The peasants of Chamouni. 1823.
Rainsford villa: or juvenile independence. 1823.
Variety: or tales for children from seven years to twelve. 1823.
The literary box. 1824.
The vacation: or truth and falsehood: a tale for youth. Edinburgh [1824].
The widow of Roseneath: a lesson of piety affectionately dedicated to the young. Glasgow, Edinburgh and London 1824.
The advenures of Don Juan de Ulloa in a voyage to Calicut, soon after the discovery of India by Vasco da Gama. [1825.]
The child's sacred year: or thoughts in verse for the Sundays throughout the year. Written by the daughter of a deceased clergyman. [1825?]
The infant's toy book of pretty stories. [1825] (illus).
The child's and parent's monitor. By John Denman. 1825. Verse.
Christ the true Zion; or the perfection of beauty brought forth, and crowned with the crown of glory. 1825.
Emily: a tale for young persons. 1825.
The foundling: or the history of Lucius Stanhope. 1825.
The history and troubles of Peter Pliant. 1825.
The history of Fanny Thoughtless. [1825.]
Isabella: or the orphan cousin. A moral story for youth. By H. S. Bath. 1825.
The juvenile sketch book: or pictures of youth in a series of tales. 1825.
Little Peter Pry: or the danger of curiosity to which are added The three travelling cocks. [1825.]
Light reading for sober minds, a pretty present for good children. [1825.]
The child's instructor, or picture alphabet. Glasgow 1825.
The poor child's friend; consisting of narratives founded on fact and religious and moral subjects. 1825.
The little deserter: or holiday sports: an amusing tale dedicated to all good boys. 1825.
The Mirven family: or Christian principle developed in early life. 1825.
Prince Darling: a tale. 1825.
Tom of Bristol: or the green-haired monsters. 1825.
The veteran soldier: a narrative of the life and religious experience of the late Serjeant Greenleigh. [1825.]
Biography of a spaniel. To which is annexed: The idiot, a tale. 1826.
The contrast: or Caroline and Emma. Intended to convince little girls that perseverance is necessary to success. 1826.
Grandpapa's drawer opened. Wellington 1826.
Idle hours employed: or the new publication. A selection of moral tales. 1826.
In school and out of school: or the history of William and John. 1827.
The West Indian: or the happy effects of indulgence and self-control exemplified in the history of Philip Montague. 1827.
Early impressions: or moral and instructive entertainment for children. [1828.]
How to be happy: or fairy gifts proving the insufficiency of beauty and talent, fortune, rank and riches to secure contentment. [1828.]
The child's instructor, by a fellow of the Royal Society. 1828.
Familiar tales for young children. By M. A. W. Plymouth 1828.
Harriet and her scholars. A Sabbath school story. 1828.
The little dog Dash. 1828, 1865.
Midsummer holidays at Briar's Hall: or summer mornings improved. 1828.
The honest farmer and his good landlord. 1829.
The life of a midshipman: a tale founded on facts and intended to correct an injudicious predilection in boys for the life of a sailor. 1829.
Recollections of a Blue-coat boy: or a view of Christ's Hospital. Swaffham 1829.
The village bride. A simple statement of real events. By M. B. 1829.
A week at Christmas. Wellington 1829, 1835.
The adventures of a halfpenny: commonly called a Birmingham half-penny, or counterfeit, as related by itself. Banbury [c. 1830].
The benighted traveller: a tale of the Alps. Edinburgh [c. 1830].
The child's monitor: a collection of useful hints, both in verse and in prose. 1830.
The child's pleasing instructor: being a true guide to wisdom. York [1830?]
The good child; or sweet home embellished with fourteen neat coloured engravings. [1830?]
The good child's ménage and pretty picture book. [1830?]
The juvenile amulet: a pledge of affection. [1830?]
The child of disobedience, or the broken heart. A tale for youth. 1830.
The child's battledore. Alnwick 1830.
The history of a Banbury cake: an entertaining book for children. 1830.
Little Lucy Cary. 1830.
Lucy Newton: or an experiment in education. 1830.
The pretty portress of Windsor Lodge; filial affection rewarded. 1830.
Strawberry Hill and its inmates. Swaffham 1830.
The trial of an ox for killing a man. Banbury 1830.
The factory girl. London and Wellington 1831.
Idle hours employed: a selection of moral tales. 1831.
Pious William: a real character for the instruction and amusement of young persons. 1832.
The wet summer: a series of tales. 1833.
Christmas: or hunting Mrs P. 1834, 1835.
Daylight. 1835.
The month of adventures. 1835.
Not alone. 1835.
Progressive tales for little children. 1835.
The Polish exiles; and other tales by the Editor of the Juvenile cyclopedia. [1836.]
The child's own book. 1837.
The fallen horse and the Shetland pony. London and Wellington 1837.
Little Alfred of Anglesey. Edinburgh and Dublin 1837.
The picture shop for good children. 1837.
Are you happy when you are cross? 1838.
The child's guide to Christ: a scripture catechism for children, to which are added some questions without answers. Belfast 1838.
The child's own Bible: being a selection of narratives of the leading

events of revealed religion, in the language of Holy Writ. 1838 (Old Testament ser).
Little Annie and her sisters. By E. W. H. 1839.
The child's gift: or golden present. Devonport [1840?] In verse; a chapbook.
The child's own scrap book, with lessons not exceeding six letters. [1840?] (Part of Innes's Juvenile Lib).
John Williams: the sailor boy. [c. 1840?]
The magic lantern: or two Sunday school boys. [c. 1840.]
Recollections of childhood: or Sally the faithful nurse. By 'Primogenita'. [1840.]
The unfortunate shoemaker and the history of little Jack, his son. [c. 1840.]
The history of Peter Thomson in two parts. Birmingham 1840.
Lucy Motley: or a child's passage from death unto life. 1840.
The recovery: a tale. 1840.
Cousin Willy's holidays. 1841.
The child's guide to reading. Edinburgh 1842.
The young child's morning and evening prayers. 1842.
The children of Hazlewood School. Ill conduct at church. 1843.
The child's friend: a first book of lessons. Manchester 1843.
The child's own book for 1844. 1843.
Faith, hope and charity. 1843.
Sister Mary's recreations: tales for little girls. [1844.]
Norah Toole and other tales illustrative of national and domestic manners. 1844.
The child's illuminated prayer book. A first book of prayers for children. 1845.
The little basket maker and other tales. 1845.
Aunt Clara's stories for her nephews. [c. 1846.]
Lady Golightly and her cousins the grasshoppers; or make history while the sun shines. 1845.
The little child's tutor: or first book for children, in words not exceeding two syllables. Derby 1845.
The child's vision: or the angel and the oak. 1846.
The two dolls; a story. Edinburgh 1846. (Osborne attributes authorship to Lady Grey.)
The child's book of animals. 1847.
The child's illuminated fable book. 1847.
Dick and his mother. 1847.
The young drummer: or the affectionate son. A tale of the Russian campaign. London and Oxford 1847.
Clever boys and other stories. 1848, rptd 1873.
The little Robinson and other tales. 1848, 1874.
Moral courage and other tales. 1848, 1873.
Stories of the elements. 1848.
Truth and trust. 1848, London and Edinburgh 1874.
The two doves and other tales. A story book for holiday hours. 1848.
Aunt Anne's history of England on Christian principles for the use of young persons. 1849.
The child's book of birds. 1849.
Little stories of one and two syllables for little children. 1849.
The chilblain, a true story for the little ones, by one who loves them. [185?]
The child's guide to devotion. [1850.]
The child's own book of scripture pictures. Old Testament and New Testament. 1850.
Jane Hopkins. [1850.]
Lovely Harriet. The lowland queen of love. Nice young gel. [1850?]
The child's first step to learning. 1850.
Heedless Harry's day of disaster. 1850.
The child's own coloured picture reading book. [185?]
The child's month of May. 1851.
The comical creatures from Wurtemburg, including the story of Reynard the Fox. 1851.
The young child's own series of new threepenny coloured books. [1852.]
Buds and blossoms. 6 pts 1852–5.
The child's in-door companion. 1852.
Comical people. 1852 (illus).
Stories of Julian and his playfellows written by his mama. 1852.
The child's search for fairies. 1853 (Buds and Blossoms no 7).
The conceited pig. 1853 (illustr H. Weir).
The child and the sparrows. 1854.
The child's picture book of natural history. 1854.
Mamma's budget: or daily reading for little children. 3rd edn 1854.
The child's picture book [A religious tract]. [1855?]
Kitty the cat, and other stories. History of my pets. [1855.]
Little May and her brother. [1855.]
The angels and other stories. London and Edinburgh 1855.
The child's guide to the knowledge of God, in easy reading lessons. 1855.
The child's mission. 1855.
The frost-king: or the power of love and how it prevailed over fear and cruelty. 1855 (illus).
The good son. 1855.
Little Harriet, and other stories. 1855.
Questions on the Child's help to the knowledge of God. 1855.
Seven fairy tales. 1855.
The story of a promise that was kept. 1855.
The little child's book of divinity; or Grandmamma's stories about Bible doctrines. 1856.
The old Cornishwoman. [1856.]
Harriet and her sister. 3rd edn 1856.
Little Polly's doll's house. London and New York 1856.
Little Walter, the lame chorister. 1856.
Verses, sacred and miscellaneous. By Harriet. 1856.
The early dawn: or stories to think about. 1857 (illustr H. Weir).
Funny dogs wih funny tales. 1857 (illus).
Out-at-elbows and other tales. [1857.]
Grandmamma Wise, or visits to Rose Cottage. 1858.
Maud Summers, the sightless: a story for the young. 1858.
The child's horn book. 1858.
The child's own clock. To teach the time and strike the hours. [A mechanical contrivance.] 1858.
A child's walk through the year. 1858.
'Old Gingerbread' and the schoolboys. 1858.
The child's mass book. 1859.
Child's sketch book. Otley [1860?]
The good child's reading and spelling book. [1860?]
Katie Seymour: or how to make others happy. [1860.]
Nelly's experience: or try to be thankful. [1860.]
Alice Russell: or Grandmamma's stories. 1860.
The butterfly's ball. 1860.
The child's own prayer book; a help to nursery devotion. Glasgow 1860.
The child's own alphabet and object lessons. By the author of Plain stories for little folks. 1860.
Child's story book. Edinburgh 1860.
The child's own album, in pictures and verse, of favourite stories, which all may rehearse. With engravings by the brothers Dalziel. [1861.]
The child's own book. Revised and corrected with original tales translated from German. 1861 (illus).
The child's baptismal name, and the flower garden. By the author of The daily life of a Christian child. Derby 1862.
Ellen Mason: or principle and prejudice. Edinburgh and London 1862.
The history of a pin. Edinburgh 1862.
Susy's flowers: or 'blessed are the merciful, for they shall obtain mercy'. By F. M. S. 1862.

Pretty tales for the nursery. [1863.]
The child's scripture history. 1863.
The child's Sunday holiday. A true tale from the German. [1863.]
The little sea-bird. [1863.]
The child's own verse book. 1864.
The child's picture scrap book. 1864 (illustr G. J. D. Watson).
A child's Sunday at home; or the Sabbath a delight. [1865.]
The good child's ABC book. [1865?]
The idler cured: or Grandmother's lesson. [1865.]
The child's pictorial history of wild animals. 1865.
The good child's coloured book. [1866.]
Aunt Annie's stories: or the birthdays at Gordon Manor. 1866, 1868.
Bright thoughts for the little ones. By Grandmamma. 1866.
The child's month of the sacred heart. By the author of The child's book for Lent. 1866.
The child's pictorial museum of birds, beasts and fishes. 1866.
The child's sixpenny packet. 1866.
Tom Bryant: or the stolen mince-pie. Birmingham 1866.
Child's picture alphabet. [1867.]
Great riches. Nelly River's story by Aunt Fanny. Edinburgh [1867].
Aunt Annie's tales. 1867.
'Chains for the neck.' A textbook of heavenly truths for the young compiled by Aunt Harriet. 1867.
Grandmamma's nursery tales for all good boys and girls. [1867.]
The joy of well-doing. 1867.
Nursery times: or stories about the little ones. 1867 (illus).
For a good child. Containing the Alphabet of trades, The cat's tea-party, Cinderella. [1868], 1871 (as The cat's tea-party).
The chaffinch's nest: or be kind to the birds and other stories. [1868.]
William and Rupert: or the half holiday. [1868].
The history of Prince Perrypets: a fairy tale. By L. S. K. 1868 (illus).
The little child's fable book. 1868 (illustr Georgina Bowers).
My Sundays and what shall I do with them. Taken from life. 1868.
What makes me grow?: or walks and talks with Amy Dudley. 1868.
The young child's picture book, in words of one syllable. 1868.
The peasants of the Alps and Passe-tout, or the new fishing smack. [1869.]
Alice and Beatrice. 1869.
The child's picture book of domestic animals. 1869.
Little lasses and lads. 1869 (illustr O. Pletsch).
Aunt Louisa's Sunday picture book. [1870.]
The cottage on the cliffs. [1870.]
Dame Barton's party. [1870.]
Dr Savory's tongs and other tales. [1870.]
The life of a doll. [1870.]
Aunt Affable's book of tales. 1870.
The child's own book of country pleasures. 1870.
The child's own book of pictures, tales and poetry. 1870.
The secret drawer. 1870, 1886.
Alice Miles' Good Friday: a tale. 1871, [1882].
Merry, merry England and snug little Wales. By G. K. A governess. 1871.
Edith Hinton: or twice blessed. [1873.]
Broken bead: or the value of little gifts. London and Edinburgh 1873.
True heroism and other stories. 1873.
Mouse the door boy: a tale of the mining districts. [1874.]
The orphan boy: or from peasant to prince. By C. L. [1874.]
Pretty pictures. 1874.
The cottage on the shore: or little Gwen's story. [1875.]
The forest crossing: life in the Canadian backwoods. [1875.]
Childland: picture pages for the little ones. 1875 (illustr O. Pletsch).
The little snowdrop and her golden casket. 1875.
Grandmamma's nursery tales for all good boys and girls. [1876.]
True and false friendship and other stories. [1876.]
The boy artist: a tale for the young. By F. M. S. Edinburgh 1876.
Love sweetens truth: or how Caleb conquered. 1876.
Esther's journal: or a tale of Swiss pension life. 1876.
Once upon a time: or the boy's book of adventures. [1878.]
The children in the scrub. A story of Tasmania. [1878.]
Charley's rabbits. The little fisherman and other interesting tales. [1879.]
The little cripple and other tales for the young. 1879.
The story of Tommie Brown and the Queen of the fairies. [1879.]
Schoolboy life and incident. 1880.
Georgie's prayer and what came of it. [1881.]
Gerties' sunflower. By Mabel. [1881.]
The magic sunflower. By Mabel. [1881.]
Grannie's young days. By Mabel. 1881.
Mother's blessing and other stories. [1882.]
Nocholina: a story about an iceberg. And other tales of the far north. [1882.]
Pussy cat purr told in words and pictures. [1882.]
A bit of holly. 1882 (illustr J. Whymper).
The fool's paradise: mirth and fun for young and old. [1883] (illus).
From do nothing hall to happy-day house. 1883 (illustr J. A. Miles).
Our Ethel: a tale. By M. C. E. [1884] (illustr G. Browne).
The way to spend pocket money: or Johnny and his grandmother. 2nd edn 1884.
Childhood's joy: or to be good is to be happy. By Aunt Clara. 1886.
New fairy tales for children young and old. By Aunt Emmy. 1889.
Grandmamma's book of nursery rhymes for the nursery. [1894.]
Fluffy: or what a little dog did. By M. F. W. 1894.
Grandmamma's fireside stories. 1894.
Jem's wife: a story of life in London. Edinburgh 1894.
Uncle Will's heirs. By F. W. I. Edinburgh and London 1894.
Under the old oaks: or won by love. A tale. Edinburgh 1897.
Aunt Affable's two penny series of pretty play books. nd.

'Aunt Annie', pseud.

St Mary and her times. 1851.
The mountain refuge; or sure help in time of need. 1862.
The merchant prince and his heir; or the triumphs of duty. Dublin 1863.
Aunt Annie's stories; or the birthdays at Gordon Manor. 1866.
Aunt Annie's tales. 1867.
The convent prize book. '1868' [1867].
The white cat of York. [1879.]

'Aunt Charlotte', Charlotte M. Yonge.

See col 1443.

'Aunt Louisa'

See Laura Belinda Valentine.

'Harriet', pseud.

Harriet; or the innocent adultress. 1779.
Chains from the neck. A text-book of heavenly truths. 1867.
Harriet's mistakes. A story for servants. 1882.

'Margery Meanwell', pseud.

The new Tom Thumb with an account of his wonderful exploits. 1815 (illus).

'Billy Merrythought'

Juvenile dialogues and recreations for schoolboys during the leisure hours at boarding school. Chelmsford 1815.

'Mr Truelove'

The adventures of a silver three-pence. [1801.]

(4) FAIRY TALES AND LEGENDS

The stories already accumulated – traditional tales like Jack the giant-killer *and* Dick Whittington *existing in chapbook form, and the semi-traditional tales translated from Perrault, d'Aulnoy and the* Cabinet des fées *authors (see vol 2) – became a common repertory which editors and publishers varied and used at will. The chief collections made before fresh matter appeared with the impetus given to the study of Märchen by the brothers Grimm were:* Temple of the fairies, *2 vols 1804 (anon);* Popular stories for the nursery, *by Benjamin Tabart [4 vols?] 1809, [1818] (as* Popular fairy tales: or a Liliputian library). *One or more tales were issued separately at various dates. A great increase in the common stock was made by trns of Grimm, Andersen and others (see under Translations), by wider investigation of folklore, by the use of Edwin Lane's version of* The Arabian Nights, *and by the invention of new tales. Only the principal general collections are included here.*

Temple of the fairies. 2 vols 1804, 1823 (rev as The Court of Oberon: or temple of the fairies). Anon.
Mother Bunch's fairy tales. [c. 1814.] As The celebrated fairy tales of Mother Bunch, 1817. [1825].
'Robin Goodfellow'. The fairies' repository containing choice tales selected from Mother Bunch, Mother Grim and Mother Goose. Edinburgh [1820].
'Catherine Calico'. Fairy tales. 1826. From the Cabinet des fées.
Croker, Thomas Crofton. Fairy legends and traditions of the south of Ireland. 3 pts 1825–8; ed T. Wright 1882.
Chambers, Robert. The popular rhymes of Scotland. 1826, 1842 (rev with addns).
Keightley, Thomas. Fairy mythology. 1828, 1847 (enlarged).
Southey, Robert. The three bears. In The doctor, 1835. Previously thought to be Southey's own invention, but a version in verse by Eleanor Mure, written 1831, apparently not pbd, was discovered about 1950. *See* The Times 7, 9 Aug 1951; TLS 23 Nov 1951. Included in The book of verse for children, ed R. L. Green, 1962.
'Felix Summerly' (Sir Henry Cole). The home treasury. 1841–9. Original edn 12 vols, afterwards regrouped into 5; included ballads and other matter. For contents, *see* F. J. H. Darton, Children's books in England, Cambridge 1932, ch 13.
Comic nursery tales with illustrations humorous and numerous. 1844.
The book of nursery tales. A keepsake for the young. 1845.
'Ambrose Merton' (William John Thoms). Gammer Gurton's famous histories, newly revised and amended. [1846.] Guy of Warwick and other romances.
'Ambrose Merton' (William John Thoms). Gammer Gurton's famous stories, newly revised and amended. [1846.] A miscellany of fairy tales and ballads.
Montalba, Anthony. Fairy tales of all nations. 1849.
[Cundall, Joseph.] A treasury of pleasure books for young and old. 1849.
Burkhardt, C. B. Fairy tales and legends of many nations. Dublin 1849.
Halliwell, James Orchard. Popular rhymes and nursery tales of England. 1849.
Palmer, F. P. Old tales for the young, as newly retold. 1855.
Kingsley, Charles. The heroes: or Greek fairy tales for my children. 1856.
Keary, Annie and Eliza. The heroes of Asgard, and the giants of Jotenheim. 1857.
[Maclaren, A.] The fairy family: a series of ballads and metrical tales illustrating the fairy mythology of Europe. 1857.
Planché, James Robinson. Four and twenty [French] fairy tales. 1858.
The fairy album for good little folk. [1859.]
Cox, Sir George. Tales of ancient Greece. 1861.
Knowles, Sir James. The story of King Arthur and his knights of the Round Table. 1862.
Mulock, Dinah Maria, later Mrs Craik. The fairy book: the best popular fairy stories selected and rendered anew. 1863.
Hood, Tom. Fairy realm. A collection of the old favourite tales. [1865.]
The enchanted crow and other famous fairy tales. 1871 (illustr R. Doyle).
Fairy tales told again. 1872 (illustr B. Doie).
Mason, J. The old fairy tales: collected and edited. [1873.]
Household tales and fairy stories: a collection of the most popular favourites. 1877.
Church, Alfred John. Stories from Homer. 1878.
Fryer, Alfred Cooper. Book of fairy tales from the north country. 1884.
Harrison, Constance Clay. Folk and fairy tales. 1885.
Fairy and folk tales of the Irish peasantry. 1888.
Lang, Andrew. The blue fairy book. 1889. Special introd in large paper edn only.
Further collections under colours: Red, 1890; Green, 1892; Yellow, 1894; Pink, 1897; Grey, 1900; Violet, 1901; Crimson, 1903; Brown, 1904; Orange, 1906; Olive, 1907; Lilac, 1910. *All rptd with illustrations, New York 1966–7. Selections include* Old friends among the fairies, *1926;* The rose fairy book, *1951; and* Fifty favourite fairy tales, *ed K. M. Lines 1963;* More favourite fairy tales, *ed Lines 1967. See also col 2365.*
Lang, Andrew. The Arabian nights entertainments. Ed A. Lang 1898.
Lang, Andrew. The book of romance. 1902.
Lang, Andrew. The red romance book. 1905.
Jacobs, Joseph. English fairy tales. 1890, [sequel] 1894.
Jacobs, Joseph. Celtic fairy tales. 1891, [sequel] 1894.
Jacobs, Joseph. Indian fairy tales. 1892.
Jacobs, Joseph. The book of wonder voyages. 1896.
Milne Holme, Mary Pamela, née Ellis. Mamma's black nurse stories: West Indian folklore. Edinburgh and London 1890.
Montalba, Anthony R. The Doyle fairy book. 1890, 1895. Illustr R. Doyle.
Wilde, Constance, née Lloyd. A long time ago. Favourite stories retold by Mrs Oscar Wilde and others. London and New York [1891].
Miles, Arthur Henry. Fifty two fairy tales. [1892] (illus).
Molesworth, Mary Louisa, née Stewart. Stories of the saints for children. 1892.
Yeats, William Butler. Irish fairy tales. 1892.
Old Mother Hubbard's fairy tale book. [1892.]
Polevoi, P. N. Russian fairy tales. Tr Nisbet Bain 1892.
Cossack fairy tales and folk tales. Tr Nisbet Bain 1894.
The golden fairy book. 1894. An imitation of Andrew Lang's fairy books.
Sargant, Alice. The crystal ball: a child's book of fairy ballads. 1894.
Steel, Flora Annie, née Webster. Tales of the Punjab told by the people. 1894.
Quiller Couch, Sir Arthur T. Fairy tales far and near. 1895 (illus).
'Carmen Sylva', (H. M. The Queen of Romania) and Alma Strettell. Legends from river and mountain. 1896 (illustr T. H. Robinson).
Parker, Catherine, née Kield. Australian legendary tales: folklore of the Noongahburras as told to the piccaninies. Introd A. Lang. London and Melbourne 1896.
Macleod, Mary. Stories from the Faerie Queene. 1897.
Macleod, Mary. The book of King Arthur and his noble knights. 1900.
Canton, William. A child's book of saints. 1898.
Newbolt, Sir Henry. Stories from Froissart. 1899.
An extensive bibliography of the literature of fairy tales appears in J. Zipes,

Happily ever after: fairy tales, children and the culture industry, *London and New York 1997.*

(5) TRANSLATIONS

Andersen, Hans Christian. Eventyr og historier. 5 sers 1835–72. Select tales tr Mary Howitt, 1846; Charles Boner, 1846; Caroline Peachey, 1846; Catherine de Chatelain, 1852; H. W. Dulcken, 1866; Plesner and S. Rugeley-Powers, 1867; Mrs H. B. Paull, 1867; A. Wehnert, 1869; H. L. D. Ward and A. Plesner, 1872; Mrs E. Lucas, 1899; H. L. Braekstad, ed E. Gosse 1900.

Arabian nights entertainments. From E. W. Lane's version 3 vols 1839–41 derive the Dalziel edn 1863–5, and one 'revised and emendated throughout' by H. W. Dulcken, nd; A. Lang, 1898, translated from A. Galland's Fr version 12 vols 1704–17. *See also vol 2.*

Asbjörnsen, Peter Christian and Joergen Moe. Norske folkeeventyr. 2 sers 1842–71. Tr Sir George Webbe Dasent as Popular tales from the Norse, 1859, and Tales from the Fjeld, 1874; also by H. L. Braekstad in Round the Yule log, 1881. Dasent also translated, from the Icelandic, The saga of burnt Njal, 1861. Tr H. L. Braekstad as Fairy tales from the far north, 1897.

d'Aulnoy, Marie Catherine la Mothe, Countess. Les contes des fées. [1700?] For eighteenth-century trns, *see vol 2.* Besides many miscellaneous fairy tale collections that include one or more of her stories, *see* Fairy tales and novels by the Countess D'Anois, 2 vols 1817 (anon); J. R. Planché, 1855; A. Macdonald and Miss Lee, 1892 (with introd by A. T. Ritchie).

Bechstein, Ludwig. Deutsches Märchenbuch. 1845. Tr in part as The old story-teller, 1854.

Brentano, Clemens. Geschichte vom braven Kasperl und dem schönen Annerl. 1838. Also other stories, such as Gockel, Hinkel und Gackeleia, tr K. Freiligrath-Kroeker as Fairy tales from Brentano, 1884, and New fairy tales from Brentano, 1887.

Chamisso, Adelbert von. Peter Schlemihl. 1813. Various trns, usually as The shadowless man, by William Howitt (c. 1850) and others anon and nd.

'C. Collodi' (Carlo Lorenzini). Pinocchio: la storia di un burratino. 1881. First tr as The story of a puppet, 1891 (anon).

Cottin, Sophie. Élizabeth: ou les exilés de Sibérie. 1806. Tr (anon, attributed to Fanny Burney) as Elizabeth: or the exiles of Siberia, 1807; tr Mary Meeke 1817.

Fouqué, Friedrich Heinrich Karl de la Motte, Baron. Aslauga's knight, tr T. Carlyle 1827; Sintram and his companions, tr J. C. Hare 1820; with Undine, 1896, introd by C. M. Yonge; Undine, tr G. Soane 1818; T. Tracy 1841; E. Gosse 1896.

Grimm, Jakob Ludwig and Wilhelm Carl. Kinder und Hausmärchen. 3 vols 1819–22. Anon trns by Edgar Taylor, 2 vols 1823–6, 1839 (2nd edn as Gammer Grethel); ed J. Ruskin 1869, 1876 (as Grimm's goblins); tr Mrs H. B. Paull [1872]; L. Crane 1882; M. Hunt 1884 (introd by A. Lang); Mrs E. Lucas 1884; B. Marshall 1900.

Hoffmann, E. T. A. Nussknacker und Mausekönig. 1816. Tr Mrs St Simon, New York 1853. Adapted by Alexandre Dumas as Les aventures d'un casse-noisette, 1845; tr C. Bertall 1875; included in the anon A picture story book [1880?]. Version from Hoffman as Nutcracker and mouse-king, 1893.

Hoffmann, Heinrich. Lustige Geschichten und drollige Bilder. 1845. Tr (J. R. Planché?) as The English Struwwelpeter: or pretty stories and funny pictures for little children, Leipzig 1848; *see* I. and P. Opie, TLS 25 Nov 1955.

König Nussknacker und der arme Reinhold. 1851. Tr J. R. Planché as King Nut-cracker: or the dream of poor Reinhold – a fairy tale for children, Leipzig 1853; 'A. H.' as King Nutcracker and the poor boy, 1854; anon as The wondrous tale of King Nutcracker and poor Richard, 1860.

Lie, Ionas Lauritz Idemil. Weird tales from the northern seas. Tr from Danish by N. Bain, 1893.

Lossius, Caspar Freidrich. Gumal und Lina. Tr from a Fr version by S. B. Moens as Gumal and Lina: or the African children, 1817.

de Musset, Paul. Monsieur le Vent et Madame la Pluie. 1846. Tr Emily Makepeace as Mr Wind and Madam Rain, 1864.

von Schmid, Christoph. Die Ostereier. 1816; Das Blumenkörbchen, 1825. Tr 'G. T. B.' as The basket of flowers, and other tales [Lewis, the little emigrant; Christmas Eve; The diamond ring; The gold snuffbox], Halifax 1857. Many edns of these and other stories in separate vols preceded it, from the same publisher. See A. Renier, The basket of flowers by Christoph von Schmid: a checklist of copies in the Renier collection. Stroud 1972.

Spyri, Johanna. Heidi. 1880; tr 1884.

Verne, Jules. Cinq semaines en ballon. 1863; tr 1870 (anon).

Verne, Jules. Voyage au centre de la terre. 1864. Tr J. V. 1872; F. A. Malleson 1876, 1970 (Children's Illus Classics).

Verne, Jules. De la terre à la Lune. 1865; with sequel, Autour de la lune, 1870. Tr Q. Mercier and E. G. King as From the earth to the moon, and a trip round it, 1873, 1970 (Children's Illus Classics).

Verne, Jules. Vingt milles lieues sous les mers. 1870. Tr anon 1873; H. Frith 1876.

Verne, Jules. Le tour du monde en quatre-vingts jours. 1873. Tr G. M. Towle and N. D'Anvers 1874; H. Frith 1879, 1966 (reprint of 1873 edn, Children's Illus Classics).

Verne, Jules. L'île mystérieuse. 1875. Tr W. H. G. Kingston 1875.

Verne, Jules. Les Indes noires. 1877. Tr W. H. G. Kingston as The child of the cavern, 1875.

Verne, Jules. Hector Servadoc. 1877. Tr E. Frewer 1878.

Also many others. See K. Allott, Jules Verne, *1940, and the list of trns in EL edns of* Five weeks in a balloon, *etc.*

Wyss, Johann David Rudolf. Der schweizerische Robinson. 2 pts 1812–13. English versions: The family Robinson Crusoe, chiefly from the French trns by Mme de Montholieu (1814), who expanded the original, anon 1814 (apparently 2 issues, 1 vol and 2 vols, containing Wyss's 1st pt only); complete version 1816 (anon). Tr, with revisions and abridgements, W. H. Davenport Adams 1869–70; W. H. G. Kingston 1879; A. Clark 1957.

(6) CHILDREN'S MAGAZINES

Ackermann's Juvenile Forget-me-not. 1830–2. Ed F. Shobbert. Annual.

African Tidings. *See* Children's Paper.

After School Hours. 1–11, Apr 1883–4. Props Lile & Fawcett.

Aldine Cheerful Library: a weekly of stirring stories of real life and adventure. 1894–1911. Props Aldine Pub Co. Weekly. Absorbed Aldine Garfield Boy's Jnl.

Aldine Garfield Boy's Journal. Sep 1894–July 1895. Incorporated with the Cheerful Library. Props Aldine Pub Co.

The Aldine Half Holiday Library: a complete story of adventure. Weekly. 1– 904, [1893]–1901. Props Aldine Printing & Pub Co.

The Ark: good words for the young. 1863.

Arrows from the Quiver for Girls. 1–24, 1877. Prop Cassell.

Atalanta. 1–11, Oct 1887–Sep 1898. Props Marshall Bros Hatchards. Ed L. T. Meade. Monthly.

At Home and Abroad. *See* Wesleyan Juvenile Offering.

Aunt Judy's Mag. 1–19, 1866–81, n.s. 1–4, Nov 1881–5. Prop Bell & Daldy. Eds H. K. F. Gatty, J. H. Ewing. Monthly.

The Bad Boys' Paper. 1889–90. Ed G. Rayner.

Bairns Annual. 1–5, 1885–90. Prop Field & Ther. Ed Alice Corkran. Annual.

Band of Hope Boy's Reciter. [1900?] Prop J. Brook & Co. Weekly.

Band of Hope Chronicle. 1877–? Prop Band of Hope Union.

Band of Hope Pioneer. 1, Oct 1892. Prop Gee Bros.

Band of Hope Review and Sunday Scholars and Children's Friend.

1851–1902. Continued as Band of Hope Review, 1903–37. Prop S. W. Partridge for Religious Tract Soc.
Band of Mercy Advocate. 1879–83. Continued as Band of Mercy, 1883–1934. Props S. W. Partridge & Co. Monthly.
Baptists' Children's Magazine and Juvenile Missionary Record. 1851–8. Continued as Baptist Youth's Mag, 1859–61. Ed J. Winks.
Baptist Messenger. *See* Messenger.
Beautiful Valley. 1890. Prop Houlston & Sons. Monthly.
Beeton's Annual: a book for boys: a volume of fact, fiction etc. 1870. Ed S. O. Beeton.
Beeton's Boy's Own Magazine: an illustrated journal of fact, fiction, history and adventure. 1888–90. Prop Ward Lock. Ed G. A. Henty.
Bethel Juvenile Magazine. 1894–1900? Hull. Prop M. Waller.
Bible Class Mag. 1–13, 1848–67. Continued as Bible Class and Youth's Mag, 8–14, 1868–74. Prop Sunday School Union. Monthly.
Bible Society Gleanings for the Young. *See* Gleanings for the Young.
Bits for Boys: a journal for young Britons. 1–12, June–Sep 1893. Prop Sully & Ford. Weekly.
Bonnie Boys of Britain. 1–26, Oct 1884–Apr 1885. Prop H. J. Brandon. Ed Guy Rayner. Weekly.
Bo-Peep: a magazine for the nursery. 1882–1924. Prop Cassell.
Boy: an illustrated paper for school and home. 1, 3 Jan 1891. Prop Iliffe & Sons.
Boyhood. Mar–June 1890. Ed G. Rayner. Weekly. Incorporated with Boy's Graphic.
Boys. 1–2104, July 1892–1894. Prop Sampson, Low, Marston & Co. Monthly. Merged in Boy's Own Paper.
Boys and Girls. 1–16, July–Nov 1887. Continued as the Boys of the United Kingdom, Nov 1887–Apr 1888. Prop J. S. Turner. Ed G. Rayner. Weekly.
Boys' and Girls' Almanack. 1887–1936. Glasgow. Prop Pickering & Inglis. Annual.
Boys' and Girls' Companion for Leisure Hours. 1857–8. Continued as The Companion for Youth, 1858–60; n.s. 1860–1. Props. J. & M. Bennett.
The Boys' and Girls' Companion: an illustrated mag for boys and girls. [1886.] *See* Sunday Scholar's Companion.
Boys' and Girls' Illustrated Gospel Mag. 1–3, 1888–90. Glasgow. Prop Henry Pickering. Monthly.
Boys' and Girls' Magazine. 1886–19? Prop Pickering and Inglis.
Boys' and Girls' Penny Mag. 1832–3.
Boys' and Girls' Refuge.
Boys' and Girls' Story Newspaper. [1850?] Prop George Holt.
Boys' Atheneum: a weekly illustrated journal of fact, fiction, science and instruction. 1–2, Jan–Feb 1875. Prop Ward Lock & Tyler. Weekly.
B. B. (Boy's Brigade): an illustrated monthly for boys. 1–5, 1895–1900. Incorporated with Young England. Monthly.
Boy's Brigade Gazette. 1, 1889. Prop Glasgow Boy's Brigade. Bi-monthly.
Boy's Brigade Magazine. 1–3, May 1892–Apr 1894.
The Boy's Champion Journal. 1–12, Apr 1889–92. Prop C. Fox. Weekly. Incorporated with Boy's Standard, 1892.
The Boy's Champion Paper. 1–5, Sep–Oct 1885. Ed Guy Rayner. Weekly.
Boy's Comic Journal: stories, fun and adventure. 1–181, Mar 1883–98. Prop and ed E. J. Brett. Weekly.
Boy's Companion and British Traveller. 1865–6. Incorporated with Boy's Own Reader. Weekly.
Boy's Favourite. 1871. Prop and ed E. J. Brett. Weekly. Incorporates Boys of the World.
Boy's Friend: a mag of literature and science. 1864–7.
The Boys' Friend. 1–1385, Jan 1895–1927. Prop Harmsworth. Ed Hamilton Edwards. Weekly.
Boy's Graphic. 1–2, 26 Mar 1890–Feb 1891. Ed Guy Rayner. Weekly.
The Boys' Guide, Philosopher and Friend. 1–19, Oct 1888–Mar 1889. Prop Sterne & Co. Weekly.
Boys' Halfpenny Journal of Miscellaneous and Entertaining Literature. 1–24, Oct 1878–Sep 1879. Weekly. Incorporated with Every Week.
The Boy's Half Holiday. 1–12, Apr–July 1887. Prop C. Fox. Ed Philander Jackson. Weekly. Incorporated with Boys' Leisure Hour.
Boy's Herald. 1866.
Boy's Herald: entertaining, instructive and useful. 1–4, 10 Jan 1877–1878. Props J. Beveridge and John Dicks. Weekly.
Boys' Home Journal. 1–5, Apr–May 1895. Continued as the Comic Home Journal 1–488, May 1895–Sep 1904, then the Butterfly 1–655, Sep 1904–Mar 1917. Prop Harmsworth. Weekly.
Boyhood. 188? Ed Guy Rayner.
Boy's Illustrated Annual.
Boys' Illustrated News. 1–61, Apr 1881–May 1882. Prop Illus London News. Eds Captain Mayne Reed and John Latley. Incorporated in Boy's Newspaper.
The Boy's Journal: a magazine of literature, science, adventure and amusement. 1–12, 1863–Feb 1871. Incorporated with Youth's Play Hour. Prop Henry Vickers. Monthly.
The Boy's Jubilee Journal. 1–61, Apr 1887–June 1888. Prop Popular Publishing Co. Ed G. Rayner. Weekly. Continued as Young Briton's Journal.
Boys' Leader: a library of fact and fiction. 1895–Feb 1900. Prop H. W. Jackson. Incorporated with Boys of London and New York. Weekly.
Boys' Leisure Hour: a reissue of the favourite journal The Boy's Standard. 1–13, 1884–91. Prop C. Fox. Weekly.
The Boy's Library. Feb–May 1879. Prop and ed E. J. Brett. Weekly.
Boy's Magazine. *See* Our Boy's Magazine.
Boy's Mail Bag or The Messenger's Mail Bag. 1–17, 81. Oct 1892–Oct 1909. Prop S. W. Partridge. Ed Miss A. F. Syne. Quart.
The Boy's Miscellany: an illustrated magazine of useful and entertaining literature for youth. Mar 1863–Feb 1864.
Boys' Monster Monthly Magazine. Apr 1899–1900? Prop C. Shurey?
The Boy's Monster Weekly. 1–2, 45. Feb 1899–Jan 1900. Prop C. Shurey.
Boy's Monthly Magazine. 1863–7. Ward Lock & Co.
The Boy's Newspaper. 1–98, 1880–2. Continued as Youth, 1–450, Aug 1882–Apr 1888. Casell Petter and Galpin. Weekly.
Boys of Albion. 1888. Prop F. E. Palmer. Ed G. Rayner. Weekly.
Boys of the British Empire. May 1882–4. Prop E. J. Brett. Weekly.
The Boys of the Empire: a magazine for British boys all over the world. 1–366, Feb 1888–Sep 1889. Continued as Boys of the Empire and Young Men of Great Britain, June 1888–1901. Prop E. J. Brett. Weekly.
Boys of the Empire. Oct 1900–June 1901. Continued as Boys of Our Empire, July 1901–3. Alexander and Shepheard Sunday School Union. Weekly.
Boys of England: a young gentleman's journal of sport, sensation, fun and instruction. Nov 1866–Feb 1899; Sep–Dec 1906. Ed E. J. Brett, C. Stevens and E. Brett. Weekly.
Boys of England Pocket Novelette, containing an original and complete story each week. 1880–3.
Boys of the Isles. *See* Boys' Popular Weekly.
The Boys of London and the Boys of New York. 1–12, 19 Jan 1879–Sep 1900. Prop H. W. Jackson. Weekly.
The Boys of the Nation. 1–12, 13 Sep–Nov 1895. Prop C. Fox. Weekly.
Boys of Our Empire. *See* Boys of the Empire.
Boys of the United Kingdom. *See* Boys and Girls.
Boys of the World: a journal for prince and peasant. 1–2, 52. Sep 1869–Aug 1870. Prop E. J. Brett. Weekly. Incorporated with Boy's Favourite.
Boy's Own Annual. *See* Boy's Own Paper.

The Boy's Own Journal and Youth's Miscellany. 1856–97. Incorporated in Boy's Own Paper.
Boy's Own Journal. May–Dec 1883. Ed G. Rayner. Weekly.
The Boy's Own Magazine. 1–8, 1855–62. Continued as the Boy's Own Volume, 1–8, 1863–8. Continued as Beeton's Boy's Annual, 9–11, 1869–70. Continued as the Boy's Own Magazine (Beeton's fact, fiction etc), 1–7, 1870–4. Ward Lock & Co. Weekly.
Boy's Own Paper. 1879–1967. RTS. Ed J. Macaulay. Weekly. Also sold as Boy's Own Annual.
Boy's Own Picture Gallery, or The Young Artist's Journal. 1–10, Sep–Nov 1872. Prop F. Farrah, ed A. Ellison.
Boy's Penny Magazine. 1864–8.
The Boys' Popular Weekly. 1–2, 41. Apr 1888–Jan 1889. Prop Popular Publishing Co. Ed G. Rayner. Weekly. Continued as Boys of the Isles: Guy Rayner's popular weekly, Jan–Sep 1889. Prop Popular Publishing Co. Ed Guy Rayner. Weekly.
Boy's Protestant Union. *See* Our Juniors.
Boy's Own Reader and Companion: a mag of instruction and recreation for the young. Jan–June 1866. Incorporated with The Boy's Herald. 1866. Ed G. Darcy Irvine.
The Boy's Standard, 1–9, 1875–6; n.s. 1–56, 1881–92. Props Brooke & Ford for Charles Fox Weekly.
Boys' Stories of Adventure and Daring. 1–26, 1898–9. Prop T. Harrison Roberts.
Boy's Story Teller. 1–6, May–June 1897. Family Herald for W. Stevens Ltd. Weekly.
Boys' Sunday Reader: a mag of pure literature. 1879–81. Continued as the Boy's Weekly Reader Novelette: containing an original and complete story every week, 1881–3. Prop and ed E. J. Brett. Weekly.
Boys' Telegram: a journal devoted to the instruction and amusement of youth in all parts of the world. 15 Sep 1866.
The Boy's War News. 1–2, Dec 1899.
Boys' Weekly Novelette. 1–169, June 1892–Sep 1895. C. Fox. Weekly.
Boys' Weekly Reader: a mag of pure literature devoted to the intellectual recreation and instruction of the home circle. Mar 1880. Prop and ed E. J. Brett.
Boys' Weekly Reader Novelette. *See* Boys' Sunday Reader.
The Boy's Welcome. 21 July 1897. Aldine Pub Co.
Boy's World. 1–299, Apr 1879–Mar 1883. Continued as The Boy's World and Our Boys' Paper. 5, 16–8, 58. Apr 1883–Dec 1886. Ed R. Rollington. Incorporated Champion Journal, 1884.
Brave Lads and True. *See* Our Juniors.
Bright Eyes: an annual for little folks. 1893–1900. Prop G. Stoneman. Annual.
British Boy in Sport and in Earnest, at Home, at School and Abroad. 1866–7.
British Boys. 1883. Prop Emmett Bros.
British Boys. 1–104, Dec 1896–Dec 1898. Prop Newnes. Weekly.
British Boys' Paper. 1–52, Mar 1888–Feb 1889. Prop Aldine Publishing Co. Weekly.
The British Juvenile at Home, at Work, at Play. July 1866–Nov 1899. Prop R. Willoughby. Monthly.
Bubbles. *See* Our Bubble.
The Bull's Eye: novels founded mainly on the annals of Scotland Yard. 1–4, 94. 1898–1900. Aldine Publishing Co. Weekly.
Cadet's Own: a monthly magazine. 1, 1894. Props Order of the Sons of the Temperance.
Camps and Quarters: an annual. 1889. Ward Lock.
Captain: a magazine for boys and old boys. 1–50, 1899–1924. Prop G. Newnes. Ed R. S. W. Bell. Monthly.
Catholic Child's Magazine of Religious and Entertaining Instruction. 1857–63. Ed Iskander A. Gertsen.
The Catholic Children's Mag: a fortnightly journal of instructive amusement for our little ones. 1878–81. Props Duffy & Sons. Monthly.
Catholic Girls' Magazine. *See* Children's Corner.
Catholic Progress: the journal of the Young Men's Catholic Association. 1–14, 158. Jan 1872–Apr 1885. Prop R. Washbourne for the Young Men's Catholic Assoc. Monthly.
Catholic Tales and Tit-bits. [1875–8.] Ed F. J. O'Connor?
The Champion Journal for Boys of the United Kingdom. Sep 1877–July 1880. Prop Ritchie & Co for the Useful Lit Soc. Ed H. C. Emmett. Weekly.
The Chap-book. Jan 1876–June 1879. John Lane, the Bodley Head. Monthly.
The Charm: a book for boys and girls. 1853–5.
Chatterbox. Dec 1866–1956. Wells, Gardner & Darton. Founder ed J. E. Clarke. Weekly.
Chatterbox Christmas Box. 1898–9.
Child at Home: an illustrated magazine for the young, 1842–3. Continued as Children's Bethel Flag or the Star of Hope, 1843–4. Continued as the Juvenile Bethel Flag Magazine, 1844–8.
Childhood: a monthly magazine for little folks. Jan–Aug 1892. Issues for Sep and Oct 1892 merged with Home Life and Childhood; discontinued Nov 1892–Dec 1895. Revived as Childhood, 2–6, 1896–1900. Prop G. Stoneman. Monthly.
Children. *See* Children's Advocate.
Children: pictures and stories for little ones. 1–7, June–July 1899. Marshall & Brooks. Weekly.
Children: a quarterly magazine. 1 Apr 1886–Oct 1897. Prop Wells, Gardner & Darton.
Children's Advocate. 1872–3. Ed T. B. Stephenson.
Children's Annual. 1869–71. Book Soc.
Children's Corner: a magazine for the young. Dec 1890–Mar 1893. Continued as Catholic Girls' Magazine and Children's Corner, Apr 1893–Feb 1894. Continued as the Chimney Corner, Mar–Sep 1894. Ed Henry Potter, Father Fletcher. Weekly.
Children's Friend. Jan 1824–1930. Seeley Jackson & Halliday, then S. W. Partridge. Ed W. Carus Wilson. Monthly.
Children's Gospel Magazine. *See* The Little Messenger.
Children's Guide. 1–6, Jan–June 1890. Edinburgh. D. Balsillie. Monthly.
The Children's Hour: a magazine for the young of the fold. 1865–71. Edinburgh. Props Johnstone, Hunter & Co and Groombridge. Monthly.
The Children's Hour from the Children's Home. 1–132, Jan 1889–99. Ed M. Bateman and T. B. Stephenson.
Children's Illustrated Magazine. 1–2, 1888–9. Props Seeley & Co. Monthly.
Children's Jewish Advocate. *See* Jewish Advocate for the Young.
Children's Journal. 1863.
The Children's Journal: for schools and Bands of Hope. 1, [1878].
The Children's League of Pity Paper for the Child Members of the NSPCC. 1–14, 2. Aug 1893–1916. Bi-monthly.
Children's Magazine of General Knowledge. 1–7, 1838–44. Continued as Children's Magazine and Missionary Repository, 8–28, 1845–65. Continued as the Children's Picture Magazine 1866–8. Continued as the Picture Magazine, 1869–71. Simpkin & Co.
Children's Magazine of the United Presbyterian Church. 1887. Edinburgh and London. Prop J. Cochrane & Co.
Children's Messenger. *See* Sabbath School Messenger.
Children's Messenger of the Presbyterian Church in England. 1–2, 1876–7. Continued as the Messenger for the Children of the Presbyterian Church in England, 3–5, 1878–80, n.s. 1881–1919. Glasgow. T. Downie.
The Children's Missionary Magazine. 1–8, n.s. 1–3, n.s. 1–9, 1838–59. Continued as Coral Missionary Magazine 1860–94. Props Nisbet & Co. Ed J. M. Randall and Miss M. A. S. Barber. Monthly.
Children's Missionary Magazine of the United Presbyterian Church. 1–8, 1838–45; n.s. 1848–? Edinburgh. Prop J. Cochrane & Co.

Children's Missionary Newspaper. nd. Ed C. H. Bateman.
Children's Missionary Record. 1–19, 1845–63. Edinburgh. Hodder & Stoughton for Free Church of Scotland. Continued as Children's Record, 20–86, 1864–1900. James Nisbet & Co. Incorporated with Juvenile Missionary Magazine of the United Secession Church. Monthly.
Children's Monthly Garden of True Wisdom and Sound Knowledge. 1847. Continued as Children's Guide and Garden of Wisdom and Knowledge, Jan–Mar 1848. Ed A. W. Brown.
Children's Own Paper. 1–230, Aug 1882–95. Manchester. Prop Frances Street and S. W. Partridge. Ed 'Uncle Gilbert'. Weekly.
The Children's Paper. July 1855–1925. T. Nelson.
The Children's Paper. July–Oct 1885. Continued as Children's Tidings, Oct 1885–1892; continued as African Tidings. Props Wells, Gardner & Darton. Monthly.
Children's Picture Annual. 1877–1904. Ward Lock. Ed Mercie Sunshine.
Children's Prize. 1863–75. Continued as Prize for Boys and Girls 1876–1931. Prop W. M. Mackintosh. Monthly.
Children's Record of the Free Church of Scotland. *See* Children's Missionary Record.
Children's Record of the Presbyterian Church in England. 1868–75. T. Nelson. Monthly.
Children's Round World. *See* Church Missionary Juvenile Instructor.
The Children's Sunbeam: a monthly magazine for the young folks. 1–54, 1880–4. Prop F. E. Longley. Ed Rev W. Newton. Monthly.
Children's Tidings. *See* Children's paper.
Children's Treasure. *See* Father William's Stories.
Children's Treasure. 1–43, 1870–3. Prop Graphotyping Co and Simpkin & Marshall. Monthly.
Children's Treasury and Advocate of the Homeless and Destitute. An illustrated magazine for boys and girls. 1879. Haughton & Co. Ed Dr Barnardo.
Children's Visitor. 1–12, 1877. Prop F. E. Longley.
Children's Weekly Visitor. 1833.
Children's World. *See* Church Missionary Juvenile Instructor.
Child's Bible Companion. nd. Prop W. B. Horner.
Child's Champion. *See* Messenger for the Children of the Presbyterian Church.
Child's Companion and Juvenile Companion or Sunday Scholar's Reward. 1824–1922. Prop Religious Tract Soc. Monthly.
Child's Friend. 1865–1916. Ed W. Lister, E. Lamb, J. Toulson, T. Mitchell. Monthly.
Child's Magazine and Sunday Scholar's Companion. 1824–1938.
Child's Own Annual. 1843–4. Annual.
Child's Own Annual. 1886. Prop Sunday School Union. Annual.
Child's Own Book. 1, 1842–9, n.s. 1850–1.
Child's Own Daily Text Book and Birthday Register. Sep 1876. Ward Lock. Ed G. T. Bellamy. Weekly.
Child's Own Magazine. 1852–1938. Prop Sunday School Union. Monthly.
The Child's Pictorial: a monthly pictorial paper. 1–11, 1886–96. SPCK. Monthly.
Child's Visitor and Pleasing Instructor. Jan–Aug 1854.
Chimney Corner. *See* Children's Corner.
Ching Ching's Own. 1–218, June 1888–Aug 1892. Continued as Merry Boys: Ching Ching's Own, 219–61, Aug 1892–June 1893. Ed E. Harcourt Burrage.
Christmas Box: an annual present for children. 1828–9. Ed T. C. Croker.
Christmas Box: or a New Year's Gift. 1889–1900. Props Religious Tract Soc and Simpkin Marshall & Co. Annual.
Christmas Tree: a book of instruction and amusement for all young people. 1856–60. Ed George Frederick Pardon.
City Sparrows: the monthly magazine of the Scottish Children's League of Pity. 1894. Edinburgh. Prop Scottish Children's League of Pity.
Choice Chips. 1–60. June 1884–Aug 1885.
Chums: an illustrated paper for boys. 1892–1934. Continued as Chums' Annual 1934–1939. Prop Cassell. Founder ed Max Pemberton. Weekly.
The Church Missionary Juvenile Instructor. 1842–90. Continued as Children's World and Church, 1891–1900; continued as Round World and They That Dwell Therein, 1901. Prop Seeley for Church Missionary Soc. Monthly.
Church of England Sunday Scholar's Magazine. 1847–53. Continued as Church Scholar's Magazine, 1854–60.
The Companion for Youth. *See* Boys' and Girls' Companion for Leisure Hours.
Comrades. Jan 1893–Oct 1895. Continued as Pals: a boy's story paper. 1–31, 1895–6. Prop C. Shurey. Ed G. Rayner and Vane St John. Weekly.
Coral Missionary Magazine. *See* Children's Missionary Magazine.
Crumbs for the Lord's Little Ones. 1855–7.
Crystal Stories. 1–16, 18. 1881–96. Ed Richard Willoughby. Monthly.
Daisy Family Story Paper. 1882. Ed F. Bordon Hunt. Contains a children's section.
The Daisy Basket for Children. 1893–4. Prop Manchester Vegetarian Soc. Quart.
Darton's Leading Strings. 1891–1929. Continued as Leading Strings, 1929–35. Props Wells Gardner & Darton.
Dayspring and Children's Messenger. 1872–1939. Paisley. Houlston. Monthly.
Dean's Magazine. *See* Little One's Own Coloured Picture Paper.
Dew Drop and Young Herald. 1848–1904. Glasgow. Prop T. Morison. Monthly.
Diamonds from South Africa for the Young. 1–23. 1898–1919. Prop Marshall Bros for Cape General Mission. Monthly.
Eagle's Wings. 1899–1900. Reading. Prop Dr Luxmore. Monthly.
Early Days: or the Wesleyan Scholar's Guide. 1846–1916. Continued as the Kiddies' Magazine, 1916–48. Prop C. H. Kelly for Wesleyan Conference Office. Monthly.
Erin's Hope: Irish Church mission's juvenile magazine. 1883–94. Dublin. Prop George Herbert. Ed Miss Sarah Davies. Monthly.
Every Boy's Favourite Journal. 1–39, Feb–Sep 1892. Prop Charles Fox. Weekly.
Every Boy's Journal. Apr–June 1884. Continued as Every Boys Paper, June–Aug 1884. Prop E. Maurice. Weekly.
Every Boy's Magazine. 1862–4. Continued as Routledge's Magazine for Boys, 1865–8. Continued as Young Gentleman's Magazine, 1869–73. Continued as Every Boy's Magazine 1874–89. Incorporated in Boy's Own Paper. G. Routledge. Monthly.
Every Boy's Paper. *See* Every Boy's Journal.
Every Child's Friend or The Infant's Guide. 1–5, 1870. Birmingham.
Every Girl's Magazine. *See* Routledge's Every Girl's Annual.
Excelsior. *See* Morning of Life.
Faith of our Fathers and the Net of St Peter. 1–3, 7 July 1889–May 1900. Continued as St Peter's Net, 3, 8, 1900. Prop St Vincent's Press. Monthly.
Father Christmas: our little one's budget. 1877–99.
Father Tuck's Annual. 1897. Prop R. Tuck.
Father William's Stories. 1–2, 1866–7. Continued as Children's Treasury, 1, 5, 1868–81. Continued as Our Darlings, 1881. Prop J. Shaw. Monthly.
Fisher's Juvenile Scrap Book. 1836–50. Ed B. Barton, A. Strickland, Mrs Ellis, J. Strickland, Mrs Milner.
Folks at Home. *See* Our Young Folks Weekly Budget.
For His Sake. 1899–1901. Continued as The Children's Quarterly, 1901. Prop Church Pastoral Aid Soc. Quart.
Forward: official journal of the Church of England Young Men's Society. Apr 1887–Aug 1890. Church of England Young Men's Soc.

The Friend of Youth: a child's magazine. 1852–65.
Friendly Companion and Illustrated Instructor. 1857–1946.
Friendly Leaves. 1–43, 7, 1876–1917. Prop Wells Gardner & Darton for Girls' Friendly Soc. Monthly.
Friendly Work. 1–12, 1883–94. Continued as Girl's Quarterly, 1–28, 1894–1901. Continued as Friendly Work for Friendly Workers, 1902. Props Wells, Gardner & Darton for Girls' Friendly Soc. Monthly.
Friends Society. Ed G. H. Tucker. Monthly.
GFS Advertiser. Jan 1880–Dec 1882. Continued as Girls Friendly Society Associates and Advertiser, Jan 1883–1919. Props Wells, Gardner & Darton for Girls Friendly Soc. Monthly.
Garfield Boys Journal. *See* Aldine Garfield Boy's Journal.
Gentleman's Journal and Youth's Miscellany. 1869–72.
Girls. 1, 9 Dec 1893 [registration issue].
Girls. May 1897. Prop C. A. Pearson. Weekly.
Girls and Boys Penny Magazine. 1832–3.
Girl's Best Friend. Feb 1898–June 1899. Continued as Girl's Friend, 1899–1931. Prop Harmsworth. Weekly.
Girl's Friend. *See* Girl's Best Friend.
Girls Friendly Society Reporter. 1–2, 1875. Prop Girls Friendly Soc. Incorporated with Friendly Leaves.
Girls Home. 1–261, Mar 1900–Feb 1915. Prop Fleetway. Incorporated with Our Girls.
The Girl's Own Paper. 1880–1927. Religious Tract Soc. Ed Flora Klickmann. Weekly.
Girls Quarterly. *See* Friendly Work.
Girl's Realm. 1–17, Nov 1898–Feb 1915. Prop Hutchinson then Bousfield & Sons.
Girls Own Messenger. 1892. Ed Ymal Oswin.
The Girl's School Magazine. 1–2, 12, Mar 1892–3.
Gleaner. 1–12, 1887–96. Continued as Gleaner's Magazine, 1897. Continued as Gleaners, 3–5, 12, 1898–1900. Prop Church Extension Assoc. Weekly.
Gleanings for the Young. 1–10, 1869–88. Continued as Bible Society Gleanings for the Young, 1889–1922. Prop Br and Foreign Bible Soc. Monthly.
Golden Childhood: or the child's own annual of pictures, poetry and music. [187?]. Continued as Merry Sunbeams, 1876. Continued as Golden Childhood: the little people's magazine, 1877–80. Ward Lock. Monthly.
Golden Cords: a magazine for young people of all ages. [1889]–1891. Prop Christian Million Newspaper. Ed Uncle Mark and Aunt Nora Loveall. Monthly.
Golden Hours: a magazine for Sunday reading. 1–4, 1864–84. Prop Lile & Fawcett. Ed W. M. Whittemore.
Golden Leaves Annual: for home and school. 1899–1900. Prop G. Stoneman. Annual.
Golden Link Between Church and Home. *See* Juvenile Instructor and Companion.
Golden Story Book. *See* Golden Childhood.
Golden Sunbeams: a church magazine for children. 1–20, Dec 1896–Mar 1916. SPCK. Monthly.
Good Bits. *See* Young Christian's Goodbits.
Good News for the Little Ones. 1–18, 1859–61. Continued as Good News for Young People, 1862. Continued as Good News for Young and Old, 1877–83. Props W. H. Broom and Good Rouse. Monthly.
Good Things. *See* Good Words for the Young.
Good Words for the Young. 1868–72. Continued as Good Things for the Young of all Ages, 1872–7. Prop Strahan. Ed G. Macdonald. Monthly.
Gospel Stories for the Young. 1876–1946. Prop G. Morrish. Monthly.
Green's Nursery Annual. 1847–8.
Grip: a weekly journal for British boys. 1–13, Nov 1883–Feb 1884. Incorporated with Our Boys.
Guy Rayner's Boys Novelette. 1–26, 1889. Prop Popular Publishing Co. Weekly.
Halfpenny Marvel Library. 1–3, 1893. Continued as the Halfpenny Marvel, 1893–98. Continued as the Marvel, 1898–1922. Weekly.
Halfpenny Picture Magazine for Little Children. 1854. Continued as the Pictorial Magazine for Little Children, 2–5, 1855–8. Continued as The Little Child's Picture Magazine in Easy Words, 1859–62. Continued as Picture Magazine, 1863–5. Ed J. Winks.
Halfpenny Standard Journal. 1896. A reissue of The Boy's Standard.
The Halfpenny Surprise. 1–23, Nov 1894–Apr 1906. Continued as Surprise, May–Sep 1906. Prop E. J. Brett. Weekly.
Harper's Round Table: a magazine for young people. 1–2, 24, Nov 1897–9. Prop Harper Bros. Monthly.
Harper's Young People: an illustrated weekly. 1885–91. Prop Sampson & Low.
Home and Fatherland: a magazine for boys and girls. 1887–9. Prop James Clarke. Ed Rev A. Mearns. Monthly.
Home Tidings of the Young Men's Christian Institute. 1880–6. Continued as Polytechnic Magazine 1888– . Prop Polytechnic Young Men's Christian Institute.
Home Word. *See* Sunday school world.
The Homely Friend for Young Women and Girls. 1–36, Jan 1877–Dec 1879. Continued as the Home Friend, 1880–1925. Prop S. W. Partridge for Scottish Girls Friendly Soc. Monthly.
Horae Juveniles. 23 Apr–23 June 1830. Prop Blemmel House, Brompton.
Illustrated Juvenile Miscellany. 1847–8. Continued as the Playmate, 1848–9.
Infant Annual. 1833–5. Edinburgh. Ed H. M. Marshall.
The Infant's Magazine. 1866–1931. Props Seeley & Co then S. W. Partridge. Ed W. C. Wilson. Monthly.
Infant Scholar's Magazine. 1827–8. Continued as the Child's Repository and Infant Scholar's Magazine, 1829.
Israel: a magazine for Jewish youth. *See* Young Israel.
The Jabberwock: a monthly magazine for boys and girls. 1887. Continued as Jack's Journal: a weekly illustrated miscellany for everybody, 115–21, May–June 1887. Prop W. Long. Weekly.
Jack Harkaway's Journal for Boys. 1–4, Apr–Sep 1893. Prop E. J. Brett. Incorporated with Boys of England.
Jewish Advocate for the Young. 1–10, 1846–54. Continued as the Children's Jewish Advocate, 1855–79. Continued as Jewish Advocate: a quarterly paper for the young, n.s. 1–15, 1880–92. Continued as Jewish Missionary Advocate, 1893–1908. Continued as Beehive, 1910– . Prop Nisbet & Co for London Soc for Promoting Christianity Among Jews. Monthly.
Joyful Hours: an illustrated monthly magazine for boys and girls. 1897. Prop George Newnes.
Joyful News. Feb 1883–8. Continued as Joyful News Banner of Hope, 1–45, 1889–92. Continued as Banner of Hope, 1893–1910. Bacup & Stockport. Prop W. J. Tyne. Monthly.
Junior Quarterly Review. 1883. Prop H. W. Guest.
Junior Review: a monthly journal of science, literature and art. 1888. Ed N. Lynn. Monthly.
The Juvenile: an illustrated penny magazine for children. 1853–4.
The Juvenile. 1894. Prop John Snow & Co for Children's Missionary Selections.
Juvenile Christian's Remembrancer. 1845.
The Juvenile Companion and Sunday School Hive. 1854–71. Continued as Sunday School Hive and Juvenile Companion, 1882–91. Prop W. Reed.
The Juvenile Forget Me Not. 1829–37. Ed Mrs S. C. Hall.
Juvenile Instructor and Companion. 1–44, 1850–93. Continued as The Golden Link Between Church and Home, 45–9, 1894–8. Continued as Young People, 50–8, 1899–1907. Prop J. Hudson for Methodist New Connection.
Juvenile Journal. Jersey. 1839.

The Juvenile Library. 1800–3.
Juvenile Magazine and Young People's Record. 1861–1901. Continued as New Church People's Magazine, 1901–?. Prop Manchester New Church Sunday School Union. Continued as James Spiers London Juvenile Magazine, 1890. Ed J. Toulson.
Juvenile Magazine. 1894. Prop J. B. Knapp.
Juvenile Messenger of the Presbyterian Church in England. 1855–67.
Juvenile Messenger. 1873. Prop James Nisbet & Co.
The Juvenile Miscellany: or Magazine of knowledge and entertainment for young persons of both sexes. 1–12, Oct 1808–Sep 1809. B. Tabart. Monthly.
The Juvenile Missionary Herald. 1–31, n.s. 1–16, Jan 1845–1908. Continued as Wonderlands: the young folks' magazine of the Baptist Missionary Society 1909–46. Prop Alexander & Shepheard. Monthly.
Juvenile Missionary Magazine. 1–23, 24 June 1844–Dec 1887. Continued as The Juvenile: a magazine for the young, 1–7, 1888–94. Continued as News from Afar, 1895–1946. Prop John Snow & Co. Ed J. J. Freeman.
Juvenile Missionary Magazine. 1–3, 1845–6. Continued as Juvenile of the United Presbyterian Church, 4–22, 1846–77. Continued as Children's Magazine (Missionary Magazine) of the United Presbyterian Church, 1880–1911. Continued as Greatheart.
Juvenile Missionary News. 1884. *See* Missionary News for the Young.
Juvenile Offering. 1848. London and Leicester.
Juvenile Photographer. 1894–1900. Prop Bradford Percy Lund & Co.
The Juvenile Rechabite. 1880–1946. Manchester. Prop R. Campbell. Organ of the Independent Order of the Rechabites Friendly Soc. Monthly.
Juvenile Review. 1817.
Juvenilia. 1833. Ed E. Canton.
Kate Greenaway's Almanack. *See col 1799.*
Kind Words for Boys and Girls. 1866–70, n.s. 1871–9. Continued as Young England, 1880–1935. Prop Sunday School Union. Monthly.
Kingston's Magazine for Boys. 1859–63. Ed W. H. G. Kingston.
Lads and Lasses. 1–26, 6 Mar–25 Aug 1894. Prop E. J. Brett.
The Lads of the Village: a magazine of universal recreation. 1874. Prop Curtice & Co. Ed W. Watkins.
Leaves of Learning: a monthly journal of instruction and recreation for pupils in public and private schools. 1852. Ed R. Wilkinson and C. M. Collins.
The Liberal World: a monthly journal and review for young men. 1–23, 1880. Prop E. W. Allen.
The Little Boy's Friend. 1874–7, n.s. 1–24, 1876–7. Ed A. O. Charles.
Little Christian 1. 1886. Prop Haughton & Son. Ed L. Hastings.
Little England's Illustrated Newspaper. 1856–7. Continued as Young England's Illustrated Newspaper, 1858–61. Continued as Young England, 1862–5.
Little Folks. 1871–1931.
Little Gleaner: a monthly magazine for children. 1854–94. Continued as Young People's Treasury and Little Gleaner, 1895–1908. Continued as Little Gleaner and Young People's Treasury, 1909–46. Prop Houlston. Ed S. Sears.
Little Frolic. 1893–1935. Prop John F. Shaw. Annual.
Little Girl's Treasure. 1–8, [1875]. Prop Simpkin & Marshall.
Little Hearts and Little Hands. 1, 1882.
Little Learner: a monthly educational magazine. 1–2, 9, Dec 1882–Oct 1884. Prop J. Hughes.
Little Magazine of Useful and Entertaining Knowledge. 1842–4. Continued as Bradshaw's Little Magazine of Interesting and Entertaining Knowlege.
Little Messenger for the Young. 1–48, 1873–83.
The Little Messenger. 1896–1904. Continued as Children's Gospel Magazine, 1905– . Prop James Carter. Monthly.
Little Missionary. 1–205, 1870–87.
Little Ones at Home: an illustrated monthly magazine for children. 1–2, Jan–Feb 1877. Ed C. A. Jones.
Little One's Own Coloured Picture Paper. 1885–92. Continued as The Little One's Own, 1892–3. Continued as Dean's Magazine, June 1893–Jan 1893. PropsDean & Son. Ed Mrs E. Day.
Little One's (Our Little One's) Treasury. 1–18, 1894. Kilmarnock. Prop J. Ritchie.
The Little Learner: a monthly educational magazine. 1–29, 1882–3. Ed J. Hughes.
Little Messenger. 1896–1904. Continued as Children's Gospel Magazine, 1905.
Little Soldier of the Salvation Army: our children's war cry. 1–332, Aug 1881–7.
Little Standard Bearer: an illustrated Protestant magazine for the young. 1–3, 1854. Continued as Little Standard Bearer and Children's Treasury, 4–9, 1854.
Little Star: a monthly magazine for children. 1886–9. Prop George Stoneman. Ed W. M. Whittemore.
Little Times. 1–22, Apr–May 1867. Ed C. Mayne Reid.
Little Wide Awake: an illustrated magazine for good children. 1875–1892. Routledge, Mrs D. Sale Barker.
Longman's School Magazine. 1892–1903. Longman. Ed D. Salmon.
Lyceum Banner: a monthly journal for conductors, leaders and members of the children's progressive lyceum. 1–50, Nov 1890–1949. Liverpool. J. J. Morse for Spiritualists Sunday School Union.
Magazine for the Young. 1–408, 1842–75. J & C Mozley. Monthly.
Marvel. Sep–Oct 1890?
Merry and Wise: a magazine for young people. 1–4, 1865–8. Monthly. Continued as Old Merry's Annual, 5–7, 1869–71. Continued as Old Merry's Monthly, 8, 1872. Continued as Round Robin. Hodder & Stoughton.
Merry and Wise: a magazine for children. 1–24, 1886–7. Burnes & Oates Ltd. Monthly.
Merry Boys. *See* Ching Ching's own.
Merry Sunbeams. *See* Golden Childhood.
Messenger for the Children of the Presbyterian Church. 1876–1921. Presbyterian Church in England.
Missionary Juvenile and Illustrated Missionary News for Young People. 1–4 May, 1880–3. Continued as Juvenile Missionary News, 1884. Elliot Stock. Monthly.
Missionary Pages for the Young. 1–24, n.s. 1–12, 1879–Oct 1887. Shaw & Co for the Society for Promoting Female Education in the East.
Monthly Packet of Evening Readings for Younger Members of the English Church. 1 n.s. 30, 1851–65; n.s. 1866–80, 3rd ser 1881–90; 1891. Ed C. M. Yonge, R. Coleridge and A. Nines.
The Monthly Preceptor: or Juvenile Library. c. 1800.
Monthly Preceptor and Youth's Annual. 1–10, 1831–2.
The Monthly Rosebud: a children's magazine. 1872–7. Christian Book Society. Continued as Rosebud: a monthly magazine of nursery, nurture and amusement, 1–34, Apr 1881–Dec 1914. J. Clarke.
Monthly School Reader: an abridged edition of the School and Home Magazine. 1–2, 11, May 1893–Nov 1894.
Morning: tales and sketches for children. *See* Primitive Methodist Children's Magazine.
Morning of Life: a treasury of counsel, information and entertainment for young people. 1–4, 1875–89. Continued as Excelsior: helps to progress in thought and action, 1879–82. Sunday School Union.
Morning Rays: Church of Scotland's sabbath scholar's treasury and juvenile mission record. 1896–1917. R. & R. Clark.
My Little Friend. 1–12, 1876. George Cooper. Monthly.
My Own Annual: an illustrated gift book for boys and girls. 1847–8. Ed Mark Merriwell.

My Sunday Friend: an illustrated magazine for children. 1–5, 1870–4; n.s. 1875–86. Griffith & Farran. Monthly.
National School Magazine. 1–3, 1824–5.
New Juvenile Keepsake. nd.
New Year's Gift and Juvenile Souvenir. 1829–35. Ed Mrs A. Watts.
New Year's Token or Christmas Present. 1835–6.
New Youth's Magazine. 1824.
Nuggets. 1892–1906. James Henderson.
The Nursery: a magazine for the little ones. Written chiefly in works of one or two syllables. 1–12, 1880. Moffat & Paige.
Nursery and Infant's School Magazine. 1831–2. Continued as Nursery Magazine, 1833. Ed Mrs L. Cameron.
Nursery Offering or Children's Gift. 1835–60.
On Service: the children's magazine of the church pastoral. 1896–1922. Church Pastoral Aid Soc. Monthly.
Our Boys. 1–2, 13, Nov 1883–Aug 1884.
Our Boys. July 1897. Aldine Publishing Co.
Our Boys and The Boy's Companion. July 1892.
Our Boys and Girls: a monthly magazine. 1877–1910. Methodist Sunday School Union. Ed R. Culley and J. W. Baker. Incorporated the Children's Advocate.
Our Boys and Girls Band of Hope Journal. 1–12, Oct 1886–Sep 1897. UK Band of Hope Union. Ed S. Knowles.
Our Boys Holiday Book. 9, 1867–8.
Our Boys Journal: a weekly magazine for every home. Aug 1876–Aug 1877. Prop E. J. Brett.
Our Boy's Magazine. 1–40, Aug 1886–1926. Continued as Boy's Magazine, 1927. Children's Special Service Mission. Monthly.
Our Boys Paper. 1880–3. Prop and ed R. Rollington.
Our Boy's Wideawake Library. 1884. V. T. Denny. Weekly.
Our Bubble: a coloured magazine for girls and boys. Aug 1–19, 123, 1894–1904. Ed Dr Barnardo. Weekly.
Our Children. *See* Sunday School World.
Our Children's Weekly Pulpit and Talk with the Little Folk. 1–20, Feb–June 1873. Christian Age. Ed J. Edward.
Our Darlings. *See* Father William's stories.
Our Highways and Byways: the Church Pastoral Aid society's home mission record for the young. July 1883–Jan 1891. Church Pastoral Aid Soc. Q.
Our Juniors: the monthly paper of the Boy's Protestant Union. 1–12, 1899. Continued as Brave Lads and True, Jan–Dec 1900. Boys Protestant Union.
Our Little Dots: pretty pictures and stories for little boys and girls. 1–36, 1887–1922. Continued as The Little Dots, 37–53, 1923–40. Continued as Little Dots Playways. Religious Track Society. Monthly.
Our Little Ones: illustrated stories and poems for little people. 1–3, Nov 1880–3. Griffith & Farran. Ed William T. Adams. Monthly.
Our Little One's Treasury. *See* Little One's Treasury.
Our Magazine. 1853.
Our Own: a monthly magazine for boys and girls. 1–4, 1877. W. Stewart & Co. Monthly.
Our Own Illustrated Monthly. 1888–Sep 1899. James Sears.
Our Own Magazine. 1873. Gall & Ingles.
Our Own Magazine: a monthly paper for children and young people. 1879–1946. Children's Special Service Mission. Ed T. Bishop.
Our Young Folk's Weekly Budget. 1–288, 1871–June 1876. Continued as Young Folk's Weekly Budget, 289–431, July 1876–Mar 1879. Continued as Young Folk's Budget, 432–7, Mar–June 1879. Continued as Young Folks, 448–733, July 1879–Dec 1884. Continued as Young Folk's Paper, 734–1074, Dec 1884–June 1891. Continued as Old and Young, 1891–6. Continued as The Folks at Home, 1–27, Sep 1896–Apr 1897. J. Henderson. Monthly.
Our Young People's Treasury: a collection of interesting narratives. 1885.
Pals. *See* Comrades.
The Parade: an illustrated gift book for boys and girls. 1896–7. H. Henry & Co. Ed Gleeson White.
Pearls from the Golden Stream. 1–19, 1861–79. Houlston & Wright.
Peter Parley's Annual: a Christmas and New Year present for young people. 1–54, 1839–92. Simpkin Marshall & Co. [Peter Parley's Magazine 1840–63.]
The Picture Magazine: or monthly exhibition for young people. 1800–1.
Picture Magazine. 1863–5; *see* Halfpenny Picture Magazine.
Picture Magazine. 1869–71; *see* Children's Magazine of General Knowledge.
Pictorial Juvenile Penny Magazine. 1855.
Pictorial Magazine for Children. *See* Halfpenny Picture Magazine.
The Playhour: a paper for children. 1857–8.
Playmate. *See* Illustrated Juvenile Miscellany.
Pleasant Hours for Church Scholars. 1861–73. Continued as Pleasant hours, 1874. Nat Soc. Monthly.
Pleasant Words: talks with the younger ones. 1–5, 1883–4. F. E. Longley.
Pleasure: Catholic Boys Journal. Mar–Oct 1893. Continued as Pleasure: boy's half holiday journal, 1, 4, Nov 1893–4. Arundel Press. Weekly.
Polytechnic Magazine. *See* Home Tidings of the Young Men's Christian Institute.
Pluck. *See* Stories of Pluck.
Primitive Methodist Children's Magazine. 1851. Continued as Primitive Methodist Juvenile Magazine, 4–19, 1855–70. Continued as Juvenile & Bible Class Magazine, 20–21, 1871–2. Continued as Juvenile Magazine, 22–5, 1873–6, n.s. 1–34, 1877–1900. Continued as Morning: a magazine for our young folk, n.s. 581–90, Jan 1901–Dec 1932. G. Lamb.
Prince. Sep 1–12 1893. Best for Boys Pub Co for Sully & Co.
Prize. *See* Children's Prize.
Protestant Girl. 1–5, 12, 1893–1900. Marshall Bros for Girls Protestant Union. Monthly.
Quarterly Juvenile Review. 1827–.
Ragged School Children's Magazine. 1850–1. Continued as Our Children's Magazine, 1852–6.
Red Berries. *See* Sunshine for the Home.
Rosebud. *See* Monthly Rosebud.
Routledge's Christmas Annual. 1866.
Routledge's Every Girls Annual. 1878–88.
Rover's Log. 1–59, Mar 1872–Apr 1873. Prop C. Fox & Emmett Bros.
Rovers of the Sea. Mar 1872–Apr 1873. Prop E. J. Brett.
Sabbath School Messenger. 1857–73. Continued as the Children's Messenger, 1874–1928. Houlston & Sons.
The Safeguard: a monthly magazine devoted to religious and temperance principles for the young. 15 Jan 1887. Exeter. W. J. Southwood. Monthly.
St Anthony's Journal for the Young. 1–10, June 1900–Mar 1901. Continued as Young Catholic. Balham. Ed Henry Potter.
St Nicholas: Scribner's illustrated magazine for girls and boys. 1872–1940. T. Fisher. Unwin & Sampson Low.
The Scholar: a monthly educational paper for school and home. 1–4, Mar 1882–Mar 1885. Ed J. Hughes.
The Scholars Magazine. 1–16, 1891–Sep 1906. Manchester. John Heywood.
The Scholar's Own: a magazine for boys and girls. Sep 1893–Oct 1914. Continued as Work and Play: the scholar's own, Sep 1914–17. W. S. Latham. Monthly.
The School and Home Magazine. 1–2, 1892–3. Continued as School and Home, 3–15, 1894–1906.
The School Magazine. 1876–9. Continued as School and University Magazine, 1–3, 1880–3. Ed J. D. Morrell. Stewart & Co.
The School Monthly: a magazine for scholars and teachers. 1892–4. Ed Andrew Brown. Monthly.

School Newspaper. Jan 1894–July 1923. William Collins. Weekly.
School of Authors: a journal devoted to the interests of the young. 1–28, Dec 1891–May 1893.
The School Review: an illustrated literary monthly. 1–18, May 1891–Sep 1908. Leicester. Thornley & Waddington.
The Schoolboy's Journal: a magazine of amusing and instructive literature. 1873. Ed W. E. Waller.
Schooldays. Mar 1896–May 1905. Homewood & Co.
Schoolgirls. 1, 1–6, June 1894–June 1895. Marshall Bros. Ed Olivia Langdale. Weekly.
The Scottish Girl: homely friend for young women and girls. 1880–1944. Edinburgh. Monthly.
Scottish Instructor: designed for the moral, religious and intellectual improvement of youth. 1847. Edinburgh.
Select Magazine for the Instruction and Amusement of Young People. 1822–4. Wellington.
The Silver Link: an illustrated monthly magazine. 1–96, 1892–9. Continued as the Golden Rule: an illustrated magazine for Sunday scholars, 1900. Sunday School Union.
Sons of Britannia. Mar 1870–7. Emmett.
Sons of Old England. 1883–4. Emmett.
South American Missionary Society's Juvenile Gift. 1872–9.
Springtide: an illustrated magazine for girls and boys. 1, 1890. Elliot Stock. Monthly.
Springtime (and Christian Endeavour): a magazine for our young men and maidens. 1–47, Jan 1886–Dec 1932. Merged with Primitive Methodist Children's Magazine. E. Dalton. Monthly.
Spy. 1–295, Apr 1891–May 1898. Manchester. Ed J. B. Knapp. Monthly.
Standard Journal: complete stories of romance and adventure and fun. 1, 1, 18 Mar 1896. C. Fox.
The Star of Hope, or Band of Hope Journal. 1860–4. Ed G. S. Dowling.
Stories of Pluck: a high class weekly library of adventure at home and abroad on land and sea. 1–2, 46, 1895. Continued as Pluck, 1896–1916. Prop Harmsworth. Weekly.
Strahan's Boys and Girls Annual. 1876–7. Continued as the Strahan's Grand Annual for the Young, 1879.
The Student. 1, 10, Mar–Dec 1898. Colchester.
The Student Movement. 1, 1898. Prop S. C. M.
Sun Children's Budget: a botanical quarterly. 1–7, 8, Mar 1897–Feb 1905. Wells, Gardner & Darton. Weekly.
Sunbeam: a little luminary to guide the young to glory. 1–3, 1858–61.
The Sunbeam. 1–22, 1869–87. Manchester and Birmingham. J. Fisher. Monthly.
Sunbeam Penny Stories. 1–4, 1896. Continued as Sunbeam stories, 5–11, 1896.
Sunbeams: a journal for Sunday reading. 1–72, Nov 1897– Mar 1899.
Sunbeams for Every Household. 1–7, 1886.
The Sunday Friend. 1–27, 1887–1900. Prop G. H. Curtice then Simpkin Marshall.
Sunday Hours for Boys and Girls. 1–2, 1896–7.
Sunday Reading for the Young. 1872–1917. Continued as Sunday and Everyday, 1917–25. Prop Wells Gardner & Darton. Weekly.
Sunday Scholar. 1843–4.
Sunday Scholar's Annual. 1–3, 1866–8.
Sunday Scholars Companion: an illustrated magazine for the young of all ages and ranks. 1855–82. Continued as The Boys and Girls Companion: an illustrated magazine for boys and girls, 1883–1903. Prop Sunday School Institute. Monthly.
Sunday Scholar's Magazine; or Monthly Record Book. 1821.
Sunday Scholar's Magazine and Juvenile Miscellany. 1842–9.
Sunday School. Dec 1892–4.
Sunday School Chronicle. 1–58, Oct 1874–Oct 1928.
Sunday School Hive and Juvenile Companion. *See* Juvenile Companion.
Sunday School Penny Magazine. 1848–67.
Sunday School World. 1874–8. Continued as Our children, 1878–9. Continued as the Home Word, 1879–83.
Sunday Sunshine for Children. 1893–1934. J. Shaw.
Sunny Hours for Children. 1–4, Jan–Apr 1892. James E. Hawkins. Monthly.
The Sunrise: a magazine for young folks. 1878–1919. Kempster & Co. Ed J. Yeames. Monthly.
Sunshine for the Home, the School and the World: a monthly magazine for young people, family reading and readers in general. 1862–82. Continued as Christmas Sunshine, 1883. Continued as Red Berries, 1884–91. Continued as Sunshine, 1895–1921. Prop G. Stoneman. Ed W. M. Whittemore.
Sweethearts. 1–17, Feb–June 1898. Continued as Girl's Favourite: a weekly story paper of wholesome reading for young women. June–Dec 1898. Prop Harmsworth.
Tiny Library: a weekly journal for young persons. 1846–7.
Tiny Tots: a magazine for very little folks. 1899–1948. Cassell. Monthly.
Tiny Trots: an annual for very little people. 1894. Prop G. Stoneman.
Toddles: pictures, stories, recitations. 1900. Prop G. Stoneman.
True Blue. 1898–1900. Prop Aldine Pub Co.
Uncle Ben's Budget: a monthly magazine for young Christians. 1–3, Mar 1897–1916. Prop G. Stoneman. Weekly.
The Union Jack: tales for British boys. 1–3, 1880–3. Prop Griffith & Farran. Ed W. H. G. Kingston and G. A. Henty. Monthly.
United Presbyterian Juvenile Missionary Magazine. 1870. Edinburgh. W. Oliphant & Co. Weekly.
The Wesleyan Juvenile Magazine. 1852–3.
Wesleyan Juvenile Offering: a miscellany of missionary information for young persons. 1–23, n.s. 1–12, 1844–78. Continued as At Home and Abroad, 1879. Prop Wesleyan Missionary Society.
Wide Awake Temperance Reciter for Girls and Boys. 1–14, 1895–1905. Maidstone. Prop G. Graham. Monthly.
Winning Words: a lamp of love for the young folks at home. 1–8, 1865–72. Edinburgh. Gall & Inglis.
Winsome Words: the help one another magazine for boys and girls. 1–66, 1879–84. Prop F. E. Longley. Ed Grandfather Goodheart. Monthly.
You and I: a weekly periodical for young men and women. 1–27, Mar–Aug 1894.
Young Britannia. nd. Ed and prop Guy Rayner.
Young Briton: a young gentleman's journal of amusement, adventure and instruction. 1869–77. Emmett. Weekly. Incorporated in Young Gentlemen of Britain.
Young Briton's Journal. 1–2, 38, June 1888–Mar 1889. Prop Popular Publishing Co. Ed Guy Rayner. Weekly. Incorporated in Boy's Jubilee Journal.
Young Christian. 1, 16 Nov 1893. Registration issue.
Young Christian's Goodbits. 1–2, 17, 1885–6. Prop W. M. Carey. Ed T. Eyres. Monthly.
Young Churchman. 1891–1914.
Young Churchman: a monthly religious and literary journal. Jan–Mar 1872. Prop Bemrose. Monthly.
Young Churchmen. 1–4, Sep–Dec 1896.
Young Crusader. 1891–1915. Monthly.
Young Days: a monthly illustrated magazine for the young. 1–42, 1876–1917. Prop Sunday School Association. Monthly.
Young England. 1–14, Jan–Apr 1845. *See also* Kind Words.
Young Englishman. 1–13, 313, n.s. 1–56. 1872?–Aug 1883. Prop G. Emmett. Ed A. Burrage. Weekly.
Young Englishwoman. 1–4, n.s. 1–3, 1–8. 1865–77. Continued as Sylvia's Home Journal, 1–14, 1878–91. Continued as Sylvia's Journal, 1–2, 24, 1892–4.
Young Folks Weekly Budget. *See* Our Young Folks Weekly Budget.
Young Gentleman's Journal. 1867– ?

Young Gentleman's Magazine. *See* Every Boy's Magazine.
Young Gentlemen of Britain. 1868–70. Prop Emmett Bros. Weekly. Incorporated in Young Britain.
Young Gentlewoman. Dec 1892–Jan 1921. Monthly.
Young Herald: the children's magazine of the Congregational churches. 1896–1904. Edinburgh.
Young Israel: a magazine for Jewish youth. 1–2, Mar 1897–8. Continued as Israel. 3–5, 1899–1900. Prop Greenberg & Co. Monthly.
Young Ladies Journal: an illustrated magazine. Apr 1864–Feb 1920. Harrison & Howard Wiles. Monthly.
Young Ladies of Great Britain. 1–4, 1868–Aug 1871. Continued as Young Ladies of Great Britain Dress and Fashion, Sep 1871–2. Continues as the Month's Dress and Fashion, 1872–4. Prop Emmett Bros. Weekly.
The Young Man: monthly journal and review. 1–35, 1887–1915. Continued as Young Man and Woman, 1915–19. Continued as British Man and Woman, Jan–June 1920. S. W. Partridge. Monthly.
Young Man's Monthly Magazine. 1, 1853.
Young Men: a journal specially devoted to the interests of young men. 1–55, Jan–Apr 1888.
Young Men of Great Britain: a journal of amusing and instructive literature. 1–9, 1868–72. E. J. Brett. Weekly.
Young Men's Magazine and Monthly Record of Christian Young Men's Associations. 1875–9. Elliot Stock.
Young Methodism. Dec 1893–Nov 1894. Ed Elliot Stock, A. G. Cargill-Gentry and E. G. Dixon. Monthly. [Originally Methodist Family, 1870–93.]
Young Mineralogist and Antiquarian. 1–9, 1884–5.
Young Naturalist: an illustrated magazine on natural history. 1–11, Nov 1879–1890. Continued as The British Naturalist: an illustrated magazine of natural history, 1891–4. Schwann Sonneschein. Ed J. E. Ronson and S. L. Mosley. Quart.
Young Men: a journal specially devoted to the interests of young men. Jan–Apr 1888.
Young People. *See* Harper's Young People.
Young People. *See* the Juvenile Instructor.
Young People: an illustrated weekly. 1–2, 19, July 1890–Feb 1892. Continued as Young People Illustrated Monthly, 2, 20–59, Mar 1892–June 1895 . Christian Herald Weekly.
Young People's Letter: organ of the Bible Reading Band. 1–3, 1890. Rev H. F. Kelvey.
Young People's Paper. W. Stewart & Co.
Young People's Treasury. *See* Little Gleaner.
Young People's Section of the Monthly Journal. 1, 1–8, Oct 1889–May 1890. Continued as Young People's Magazine, 2–59, 1890–4. Continued as merged in General Reader's Magazine: young people's section, Oct 1894–June 1905. Continued as Young People's Magazine, 17–25, Sep 1905–1914. National Home Reading Union. Monthly.
Young Pilgrim: a book for Sunday schools, 1867–1903.
The Young Scholar: a monthly magazine for schoolboys. 1–2, 1872–3. Manchester.
Young Scientist. 1, 1887.
Young Stamp Collector. 1–4, Mar–June 1900. Ed F. J. Melville.
Young Standard Bearer. 1–30, 1880–1910. Wells Gardner, Darton & Co for Church of England Temperance Soc. Monthly.
Young Templar. 1–4, 1873–6. Continued as The Juvenile Templar, an illustrated magazine for the young, 1877. Birmingham and London. Kempster & Co. J. Yeames. Monthly.
The Young Watchman. Kilmarnock 1883–1946. Ed J. Ritchie. Monthly.
Young Woman. 1–32, Oct 1892–Apr 1915. Merged with Young Man. Ed S. W. Partridge and F. A. Atkins. Monthly.
Youth. *See* The Boy's Newspaper.
Youth: a magazine for church and home. 1–9. Edinburgh.
Youth and Age. 1890–1. Continued as Home Life, 1892–5. Merged with Childhood, 1892 as Home Life and Childhood.
Youth's Biblical Cabinet. 1843–4. Leicester.
Youth's Gazette and Advertiser: a magazine and review for the rising generation. 1–3, 1869–70. F. May. Monthly.
Youth's Institute Magazine. 1, 1882. Ed G. Day.
Youth's Instructor. 1–9, 1858.
The Youth's Instructor and Guardian. 1817–55.
The Youth's Magazine: or Evangelical Miscellany. 1805–67.
Youth's Monthly Visitor. 1832. Continued as Youth's Miscellany of Knowledge and Entertainment.
Youth's Penny Miscellany. 1870? G. J. Stevenson.
Youth's Pictorial Treasurer. 1–2. Birmingham 1870–1.
Youth's Play Hour. 1–3, 1870–2. [DD]

5 Drama

i. General introduction

Mss of plays submitted to the Lord Chamberlain in the first quarter of the century are in the Larpent Collection in the Huntington; those of plays submitted during the rest of the century, from 1824 have now been deposited by the Lord Chamberlain in the BL. See below, D. MacMillan (1939) and British Museum (1964). *The remainder of the plays are in the process of formal cataloguing.*

(1) BIBLIOGRAPHIES ETC

Baker, D. E., I. Reed and S. Jones. Biographia dramatica. 3 vols in 4 1812.

[Genest, J.] Some account of the English stage from 1660 to 1830. 10 vols Bath 1832, rptd New York [1965].

Ledger, E. et al. The Era Almanack. 1868–1917. Annual.

Pascoe, C. E. Our actors and actresses: the dramatic list, a record of the performances of living actors and actresses of the British stage. 1879, 1880 (enlarged edn), rptd New York 1969.

Lowe, R. W. A bibliographical account of English theatrical literature from the earliest times to the present. 1888, rptd Detroit 1966.

Archer, W. The theatrical 'world' for 1893–1897. 5 vols [1894]–8.

Cameron, J. A bibliography of Scottish theatrical literature. Trans Edinburgh Bibl Soc I 1896; suppl ibid.

Adams, W. D. A dictionary of the drama: a guide to the plays, playwrights, players, and playhouses of the United Kingdom and America, from the earliest times to the present. Vol 1 (A–G) 1904, Philadelphia 1904, rptd New York nd. Only 1 vol issued.

Hunt, B. et al. (ed). The green room book. 4 edns 1906–9. Ed J. Parker from 1907 and continued as Who's who in the theatre, *below.*

'Clarence, Reginald' (H. J. Eldridge). 'The stage' cyclopaedia: a bibliography of plays. 1909, rptd New York 1970. An alphabetical list of plays with dates of first London productions.

Parker, J. (ed). Who's who in the theatre: a biographical record of the contemporary stage. 1912 etc; 1967 (14th edn, ed F. Gaye), 1977 (16th edn, ed I. Herbert with C. Baxter), 1978 (concise 16th edn). Contains lists of casts, long 'runs' and much other valuable information.

Dramatic compositions copyrighted in the United States 1870 to 1916. 2 vols Washington 1918.

O'Neill, J. J. A bibliographical account of Irish theatrical literature. Dublin 1920.

Firkins, I. T. E. Index to plays 1800–1926. New York 1927; suppl New York 1935.

Kent, V. (comp). The player's library and bibliography of the theatre. 1930. Reissued 1950, with suppls 1951, 1954, 1956, as The player's library: the catalogue of the library of the British Drama League.

Gilder, R. and G. Freedley. Theatre collections in libraries and museums: an international hand book. New York 1936.

Rhodes, R. C. The early nineteenth-century drama. Library 4th ser 16 1936. Two articles. On play series.

Sper, F. The periodical press of London: theatrical and literary, excluding the daily newspaper 1800–30. Boston 1938.

Macmillan, D. Catalogue of the Larpent plays in the Huntington Library. San Marino CA 1939.

Pearce, E. The Larpent plays: additions and corrections. HLQ 6 1943. Corrections to Macmillan, *above.*

Stone, M. W. Unrecorded plays published by William West. TN 1 1946.

Forsyth, G. Notes on pantomime with a list of Drury Lane pantomimes 1879–1914. TN 2 1947.

Loewenberg, A. The theatre of the British Isles excluding London: a bibliography. 1950.

The player's library: the catalogue of the library of the British Drama League. 1950; suppls 1951, 1954, 1956.

Hartnoll, P. (ed). The Oxford companion to the theatre. Oxford 1951, 1957, 1967, 1983 (4th edn).

Nicoll, A. A history of English drama 1660–1900. 6 vols Cambridge 1952–9. Vol 4 Early nineteenth-century drama 1800–1850, Cambridge 1955 (2nd edn); vol 5 Late nineteenth-century drama 1850–1900, Cambridge 1959 (2nd edn). Rev edn in 6 vols Cambridge 1965–7. Originally pbd as A history of early nineteenth century drama 1800–1850, 2 vols Cambridge 1930 and A history of late nineteenth century drama, 2 vols Cambridge 1946. Cited throughout this section as Nicoll.

Enciclopedia dello spettaculo. 9 vols Rome 1954–62.

Townsend, F. G. et al. Victorian bibliography. VS 1 1957–8 to date. Annual.

Youngs, O. E. B. Important articles on the theatre in the Times Literary Supplement, 1902–1956. Theatre Research 1 1958.

Stratman, C. J. Additions to Allardyce Nicoll's handlist of plays 1800–18. N & Q 206, June 1961.

Stratman, C. J. A bibliography of British dramatic periodicals. New York 1962.

Stratman, C. J. English tragedy 1819–23. PQ 41 1962.

British Museum. Catalogue of additions to the manuscripts: plays submitted to the Lord Chamberlain 1824–51, Additional manuscripts 42865–43038. 1964.

Stratman, C. J. Bibliography of English printed tragedy 1565–1900. Carbondale IL 1966.

Taylor, J. R. The Penguin dictionary of the theatre. 1967.

Levitt, P. M. The well-made problem play: a selective bibliography. ELT 11 1968.

Gassner, J. and E. Quinn (ed). The reader's encyclopedia of world drama. New York 1969, London 1970.
Watson, G. (ed). The new Cambridge bibliography of English literature: vol 3 1800–1900. Cambridge 1969.
Arnott, J. F. and J. W. Robinson. English theatrical literature 1559–1900: a bibliography. 1970. Incorporates Lowe, *above*. Cited throughout this section as Arnott and Robinson.
Young, W. C. (ed). American theatrical arts: a guide to manuscripts and special collections in the United States and Canada. Chicago 1971.
Hartnoll, P. (ed). The concise Oxford companion to the theatre. Oxford 1972, 1992 (new edn, ed P. Founds).
Mikhail, E. H. A bibliography of modern Irish drama 1899–1970. London and Seattle 1972.
McGraw-Hill encyclopedia of world drama: an international reference work. 4 vols New York 1972.
Nicoll, A. English drama, 1900–1930: the beginnings of the modern period. Cambridge 1973.
Conolly, L. W. and J. P. Wearing. Nineteenth century theatre research: a bibliography. Nineteenth Century Theatre Research 1973–82. 1973–82. Annual.
Du Bois, W. R. English and American stage productions, an annotated checklist of promptbooks 1800–1900, from the Nisbet-Snyder drama collection, Northern Illinois University Library. Boston 1973.
Wells, S. (ed). English drama (excluding Shakespeare); select bibliographical guides. Oxford 1975.
Wearing, J. P. The London stage 1890–1899: a calendar of plays and players. 2 vols Metuchen NJ 1976.
Hixon, D. L. and D. A. Hennessee. Nineteenth-century American drama: a finding guide. Metuchen NJ and London 1977. An index to the Readex micro collection.
Mikhail, E. K. English drama, 1900–1950: a guide to information sources. Detroit 1977.
Conolly, L. W. and J. P. Wearing. English drama and theatre, 1800–1900: a guide to information sources. Detroit 1978.
Who was who in the theatre [1912–76]. 4 vols Detroit 1978.
Boyer, R. D. Realism in European theatre and drama, 1870–1920: a bibliography. Westport CT 1979.
Vison, J. (ed). Great writers of the English language: dramatists. 1979.
Wearing, J. P. American and British theatrical biography: a directory. Metuchen NJ and London 1979.
Kent, C. Periodical critics of drama, music & art, 1830–1914: a preliminary list. Victorian Periodicals Rev 13 1980.
Meserve, W. J. American drama to 1900: a guide to information sources. Detroit 1980.
Senelick, L., D. F. Cheshire and U. Schneider. British music-hall 1840–1923: a bibliography and guide to sources, with a supplement on European music-hall. Hamden CT 1981.
Wearing, J. P. The London stage 1900–1909: a calendar of plays and players. 2 vols Metuchen NJ 1981.
Johnson, C. D. and V. E. Nineteenth-century theatrical memoirs. 1982.
Bordman, G. (ed). The Oxford companion to American theatre. New York and Oxford 1984.
Ellis, J., with J. Donohue. English drama of the nineteenth century: an index and finding guide. New Canaan CT 1985. An index to the Readex micro collection 1965–81.
Howard, D. Directory of theatre resources: a guide to research collections and information services. 1986 (2nd edn).
Mullin, D. Victorian plays: a record of significant productions on the London stage, 1837–1901. Westport CT 1987.
Banham, M. (ed). The Cambridge guide to world theatre. Cambridge 1988; as The Cambridge guide to theatre 1992 (rev pbk edn), 1995 (new edn).
Bordman, G. The concise Oxford companion to American theatre. Oxford 1988.
Youngs, O. Forty years of books: the publications of the Society for Theatre Research. TN 42 1988.
Cavanagh, J. British theatre: a bibliography 1901–1985. Romsey, Hants 1989. Lists books pbd on theatre since 1901.
Corvin, M. (ed). Dictionnaire encylopédique du théâtre. Paris 1991.
Mikotowicz, T. J. (ed). Theatrical designers: an international biographical dictionary. 1992.
Hawkins-Dady, M. (ed). The reader's guide to literature in English. 1996.
Stanton, S. and M. Banham (ed). Cambridge paperback guide to theatre. Cambridge 1996. Condensed version of The Cambridge guide to theatre, *above*. [JRS]

(2) GENERAL HISTORIES

Archer, William. English dramatists of to-day. 1882.
About the theatre: essays and studies. 1886.
Arthur, G. From Phelps to Gielgud: reminiscences of the stage through sixty-five years. 1936.
Axton, Marie and R. Williams (ed). English drama: forms and development: essays in honour of Muriel Clara Bradbrook. Cambridge 1977.
Baker, Henry Barton. The London stage 1576–1888. 2 vols 1889, 2nd edn 1904.
Baker, M. The rise of the Victorian actor. 1978.
Barish, J. A. Antitheatrical prejudice in the 19th century. UTQ 40 1971.
Bergholz, H. Die Neugestaltung des modernen englischen Theaters 1870–1930. Berlin 1933.
Bernard, John. Retrospections of the stage. 2 vols 1812.
Block, A. The changing world in plays and theatre. Boston 1939.
Booth, M. R. English melodrama. 1965.
et al. In The revels history of drama in English, ed C. Leech and T. W. Craik, vol 6 1750–1880, 1975.
Shakespeare as spectacle and history: the Victorian period. ThR 1 1976.
East End melodrama. ThS 17 1976.
East End and West End: class and audience in Victorian London. ThR 2 1977.
Theatre history and the literary critic. YES 9 1979.
Victorian spectacular theatre 1850–1910. 1981.
(ed). Victorian theatrical trades: articles from The Stage 1883–1884. 1981.
The Meininger Company and English Shakespeare. ShS 35 1982.
Theatre in the Victorian age. Cambridge 1991.
Borsa, M. The English stage of today. 1908.
Bradby, D. et al. (ed). Performances and politics in popular drama: aspects of popular entertainment in theatre, film, and television 1800–1976. Cambridge 1980.
Brayley, Edward W. Historical and descriptive account of the theatres of London. 1826.
Broadbent, R. J. A history of pantomime. [1901], rptd New York 1964.
Stage whispers. [1901.]
Annals of the Liverpool stage. 1908.
Brook, D. The romance of the English theatre. 1952.
Bunn, A. The stage: both before and behind the curtain, from 'observations taken on the spot'. 3 vols 1840, Philadelphia 1840.
Burton, E. J. The British theatre: its repertory and practice. 1960.
Byrne, Muriel St Clare. What we said about the Meiningers in 1881. E & S 18 1965.
[Carlisle, Frederick H.] Thoughts upon the present condition of the stage. 1809.
Cheshire, D. F. Music hall in Britain. Newton Abbot, Devon 1974.
Child, H. Nineteenth-century drama. CHEL vol 13 1916.

Clinton-Baddeley, V. C. The burlesque tradition in the English theatre after 1660. 1952, rptd 1973.
All right on the night. 1954.
Clunes, A. The British theatre. 1964.
Coleman, J. Players and playwrights I have known. 2 vols 1888, 1889, Philadelphia 1890.
Colman, George the younger. Random records. 2 vols 1830.
Considerations on the past and present state of the stage. 1809.
Cook, [Edward] Dutton. On the stage: studies of theatrical history and the actor's art. 1883.
Cooke, James. The stage: its present state and prospects for the future. [nd.]
Crane, Harvey. Playbill – a history of the theatre in the West Country. 1980.
Cunliffe, J. W. Modern English playwrights: a short history of the English drama from 1825. New York 1927.
Darton, F. J. Harvey. Vincent Crummles: his theatre and his times. 1926.
Davison, Peter. Popular appeal in English drama to 1850. Totowa NJ 1982.
Dibdin, Charles I. History and illustrations of the London theatres. 1826.
Dibdin, J. C. The annals of the Edinburgh stage. 1888.
Dickens, C. The amusements of the people. Household Words 30 Mar, 30 Apr 1850. A vivid picture of the early Victorian cheap theatres in London: *see* Great expectations chs 31 and 47, and, for its provincial parallel, Nicholas Nickleby chs 20–5, 29, 48.
The guild of literature and art. Household Words 10 May 1851.
Gaslight fairies. Household Words 10 Feb 1855. All 3 articles rptd in Miscellaneous papers in the Gadshill edn of the Works.
Disher, M. W. Clowns and pantomimes. 1925, rptd New York 1968.
Winkles and champagne: comedies and tragedies of the music hall. 1938.
Fairs, circuses and music halls. 1942.
Blood and thunder: mid-Victorian melodrama and its origins. 1949.
Melodrama: plots that thrilled. 1954.
Dixon, Peter and Rodney Hayley. The provoked husband on the 19th century stage. NCTR 8 1980.
Donaldson, F. The actor managers. Chicago 1970.
Donne, William Bodham. Essays on the drama. 1858.
Donohue, Joseph W. Dramatic character in the English romantic age. Princeton 1970.
(ed). The theatrical manager in England and America: player of a perilous game. Princeton 1971.
and James Ellis. The London stage 1800–1900: a proposal for a calendar of performances. VS 16 1973.
Theatre in the age of Kean. Oxford 1975.
Doran, J. 'The Majesties' servants': annals of the English stage, from Betterton to Kean. 2 vols 1864, 1865, New York 1865; ed R. H. Stoddard 1880; rev R. W. Lowe 3 vols 1888.
In and about Drury Lane and other papers. 2 vols 1881, Boston [19??].
Downer, A. S. Players and painted-stage: nineteenth-century acting. PMLA 61 1946.
Mr Dangle's defense: acting and stage history. English Institute Essays. 1946.
Dramaticus. The stage as it is. 1847.
Driver, Tom F. Romantic quest and modern query: a history of the modern theatre. New York 1970.
Dye, William S. A study of melodrama in England from 1800–1840. State College PA 1919.
Eastman, Arthur M. A short history of Shakespearean criticism. New York 1968.
Ebers, J. Seven years of the King's Theatre. 1823.
The eighteen-seventies. 1929 (Royal Soc of Lit). Includes Sir A. Pinero, The theatre in the seventies; and H. Granville-Barker, Tennyson, Swinburne, Meredith and the theatre.
Ellis, J. Critics of the mid-Victorian London theatre. London Jnl 2 1976.
The counterfeit presentment: nineteenth century burlesques of Hamlet. NCTR 5 1977.
A great reckoning in a little room: English plays of the nineteenth century. NCTR 5 1977.
Elton, O. A survey of English literature 1780–1830. Vol 2 1912.
Evans, Bertrand. Gothic drama from Walpole to Shelley. Berkeley and Los Angeles 1947.
Favorini, Attilio. The old school of acting and the English provinces. Quart Jnl of Speech 58 1972.
Filon, A. The English stage: being an account of the Victorian drama. Tr Frederick Whyte 1897, New York 1970.
Findlater, Richard. Banned! a review of theatrical censorship in Britain. 1967.
The player kings. 1968.
Fitzball, E. Thirty-five years of a dramatic author's life. 2 vols 1859.
Fitzgerald, P. H. The book of theatrical anecdotes. 2 vols 1874.
The romance of the English stage. 2 vols 1874.
The world behind the scenes. 1881.
A new history of the English stage from the Restoration to the liberty of the theatres. 2 vols 1882.
Music Hall land: an account of the natives, male and female, pastimes, songs, antics and general oddities of that strange country. 1890.
Fitz-simon, Christopher. The Irish theatre. 1983.
Fletcher, Richard M. English romantic drama 1795–1843: a critical history. New York 1966.
Foote, Horace. A companion to the theatres. 1829.
Foulkes, Richard. The Shakespeare tercentenary of 1864. 1984.
Frenz, H. Die Entwicklung des sozialen Dramas in England vor Galsworthy. Bleicherode-am-Harz 1941.
[Frere, B.] The adventures of a dramatist on a journey to the London managers. 2 vols 1813, 1813, 1832.
Fricker, R. Das historische Drama in English von der Romantik vis zur Gegenwart. Berne 1940.
Frohman, D. Memories of a manager: reminiscences of the old Lyceum and of some players of the last quarter century. 1911.
G., G. M. The stage censor: an historical sketch 1544–1907. 1908.
Gaiety theatre, Dublin 1871–1971: one hundred years of Gaiety. Dublin 1971.
Genest, John. Some account of the English stage. 10 vols Bath 1832.
Goddard, Arthur. Players of the period. 1891.
Godwin, George. On the desirability of obtaining a national theatre not wholly controlled by the prevailing popular taste. 1878.
Grebanier, Bernard. Then came each actor: Shakespearean actors great and otherwise. New York 1975.
Grice, Elizabeth. Rogues and vagabonds: or the actors' road to respectability. Lavenham, Suffolk 1977.
Grimsted, David. Melodrama unveiled. Chicago 1968.
Grube, M. The story of the Meininger. Tr Ann Marie Koller, Coral Gables FL 1963.
Guest, Ivor. The romantic ballet in England: its development, fulfilment and decline. 1972.
Halliday, Andrew. Comical fellows: or the history and mystery of the pantomime. 1863.
Hamilton, Walter. A sketch of the drama in England during the last three centuries. 1890 (priv ptd).
Hanger, George. English musical theatre 1830–1900. TN 36 1982.
Hanley, P. Random recollections of the stage. [1883] (priv ptd), [1884], 1887 (as A jubilee of playgoing).
Hanratty, J. Melodrama – then and now. REL 4 1963.
Hartnoll, Phyllis. A concise history of the theatre. 1968.
Headlam, S. D. The function of the stage. 1889.

Herford, C. H. A sketch of the history of the English drama in its social aspects: being the essay which obtained the Le Bas prize, 1880. Cambridge 1881.
Herring, Paul D. Nineteenth-century drama. MP 68 1970.
Hogan, Robert and James Kilroy. The Irish literary theatre 1899–1901. Atlantic Highlands NJ 1978.
Hogarth, G. Memoirs of the musical drama. 1838, [1851] (as Memoirs of the opera).
Holbrook, A. C. The dramatist: or memoirs of the stage. Birmingham 1809.
Holcroft, T. Memoirs of the late Thomas Holcroft, written by himself and continued to the time of his death [by William Hazlitt]. 3 vols 1816, 1852; ed Eldridge Colby 1925.
Holingshead, J. My lifetime. 2 vols 1895, 1895.
Howard, Diana. London theatres and music halls, 1850–1950. 1970.
Howard, Frederick. Thoughts upon the present condition of the stage and upon the construction of a new theatre. 1809.
Hudson, L. The English stage 1850–1950. 1951.
Hyman, Alan. Sullivan and his satellites: a survey of English operettas, 1860–1914. 1978.
Jackson, H. The eighteen-nineties. 1923.
Jackson, Russell. Before the Shakespeare revolution: developments in the study of nineteenth-century Shakespeare production. ShS 35 1982.
(ed). Victorian theatre. 1989.
James, Louis. Taking melodrama seriously: theatre, and nineteenth-century studies. History Workshop 3 1977.
Johnson, Claudia D. and Vernon E. Johnson. Nineteenth-century theatrical memoirs. Westport CT 1982.
Jones, Stanley. The actor and his art: some considerations of the present state of the stage. 1899.
Joseph, B. L. The tragic actor. 1959.
Kelly, Linda. The Kemble era: John Philip Kemble, Sarah Siddons and the London stage. 1979.
Kernodle, George R. Stage spectacle and Victorian society. Quart Jnl Speech 40 1954.
Klemm, W. Die englische Farce im 19 Jahrhundert. Berne 1946.
Knight, J. The history of the English stage during the reign of Victoria. 1901.
Lacey, Alexander. Pixérécourt and the French romantic drama. Toronto 1928.
Lawrence, James. Dramatic emancipation. 1813.
Lawrence, W. J. Old theatre days and ways. 1935.
Leacroft, Richard. The development of the English playhouse. 1973.
Lee, Henry. Memoirs of a manager. 2 vols Taunton 1830.
Lennox, Lord William Pitt. Plays, players and playhouses. 2 vols 1881.
Lumley, Benjamin. Reminiscences of the opera. 1864.
Lunari, G. Henry Irving e il teatro inglese dell'1800, documenti di teatro 22. Bologna 1962.
McInnes, Edward. Naturalism and the English theatre. Forum for Modern Language Stud 1 1965.
Mackechnie, Samuel. Popular entertainment through the ages. [1931.]
Mackintosh, Matthew. Stage reminiscences: being recollections chiefly personal of celebrated theatrical and musical performers during the last forty years. Glasgow 1866, 1870.
Macqueen-Pope, W. Carriages at eleven. 1947.
The melodies linger on: the story of music hall. 1950.
Mander, Raymond and Joe Mitchenson. The artist and the theatre. 1955.
A picture history of the British theatre. 1957.
The lost theatres of London. New York 1968.
Pantomime: a story in pictures. 1973.
Mantzius, K. In Skuespilkunstens historie. 5 vols Copenhagen 1897–1907; tr 6 vols 1903–21.
Mayer, David. Harlequin in his element: the English pantomime 1806–1836. Cambridge MA 1969.
Meeks, L. H. Sheridan Knowles and the theatre of his time. Bloomington IN 1933.
Meisel, M. Political extravaganza: a phase of nineteenth-century British theatre. TS 3 1962.
Shaw and the nineteenth-century theatre. Princeton 1963.
Merchant, W. Moelwyn. Shakespeare and the artist. 1959.
Miller, A. I. The independent theatre in Europe. 1931.
Molloy, J. F. The romance of the Irish stage. 2 vols 1897, 1897, New York 1897.
Morgan, A. E. Tendencies of modern English drama. 1923.
Morley, Henry. Journal of a London playgoer from 1851 to 1866. 1891.
Nag, U. C. The English theatre of the romantic period. Nineteenth Century and After 104 1928.
Neville, Henry. The stage: its past and present relations to fine art. 1875.
Nicholson, Watson. The struggle for a free stage in London. 1906, rptd New York 1966.
Nicoll, Allardyce. British drama. 1925.
The English theatre: a short history. 1936.
A history of the English drama 1660–1900. Vol 4 Early nineteenth-century drama 1800–50, 2nd edn Cambridge 1955. Vol 5 Late nineteenth-century drama 1850–1900, 2nd edn Cambridge 1959. Cited throughout this section as Nicoll.
Odell, G. C. D. Shakespeare from Betterton to Irving. 2 vols New York 1920, 1964.
Oliver, D. E. The English stage: its origins and modern developments. [1912.]
Otten, Terry. The deserted stage: the search for dramatic form in the nineteenth-century. Athens OH 1972.
Oulton, W. C. A history of the theatres of London. 3 vols 1818.
Palmer, J. The censor and the theatres. 1912.
Pellizzi, C. Il teatro inglese. Milan 1934; tr 1935 (as English drama: the last great phase). Vol 3 of Il teatro del Novecento.
Penley, Belville S. The Bath stage. 1892.
Perugini, M. E. The omnibus book: being digressions and asides on social and theatrical life in London and Paris 1830–50. 1933.
Planche, J. R. Suggestions for establishing an English art theatre. 1879.
Poel, W. William Poel and his stage productions. 1933 (priv ptd).
Pulling, C. They were singing and what they sang about. 1952.
Rahill, Frank. The world of melodrama. Univ Park PA 1967.
Reade, C. The eighth commandment. 1860.
Report from the Select Committee on Dramatic Literature. 1832. On theatrical licences and regulations 1866; On theatres and places of entertainment 1892. Rptd in British parliamentary papers: stage and theate 1 and 2, Shannon, Eire 1968.
Reynolds, E. Early Victorian drama 1830–70. Cambridge 1936, rptd New York 1956.
Rice, C. The London theatre in the eighteen-thirties. Ed A. C. Sprague and B. Shuttleworth 1950.
Richards, E. and P. Thomson (ed). Nineteenth century British theatre: the proceedings of a symposium sponsored by the Manchester University Department of Drama. 1971.
Richardson, J. Recollections political, literary, dramatic and miscellaneous of the last half century. 2 vols 1856.
Robinson, Henry Crabb. The London theatre 1811–1866. Ed Eluned Brown 1966.
Rosenfeld, S. Pictorial records of provincial theatres. TN 2 1948.
Theatrical history: bills of the play. N & Q 21 July 1951.
Rowell, G. The Victorian theatre: a survey. 1956, 2nd edn Cambridge 1978.
and A. Jackson. The repertory movement: a history of regional theatre in Britain. Cambridge 1984.
Rubinstein, H. F. The English drama. 1928.

Russell, W. Clark. Representative actors. 1888.
[Ryan, Richard.] Dramatic table talk. 3 vols 1825–30.
Ryley, S. W. The itinerant. 9 vols 1808–27, [1860] (abridged), 1880; 1817 (vols 1–3 of original edn only).
Saxon, A. H. Enter foot and horse: a history of hippodrama in England and France. New Haven CT and London 1968.
Schelling, F. E. English drama. 1914.
Scott, Clement. The drama of yesterday and today. 2 vols 1899.
Scott, Harold. The early doors: origins of the music hall. 1946.
Sharp, R. F. A short history of the English stage to 1908. 1909.
Shattuck, Charles H. (ed). Bulwer and Macready: a chronicle of the early Victorian theatre. Urbana IL 1958.
Sherson, Errol. London's lost theatres of the nineteenth century. 1925.
Short, E. Theatrical cavalcade. 1942.
Fifty years of vaudeville. 1946.
Sixty years of theatre. 1951.
The British drama grows up. Quart Rev 295 1957.
Simpson, J. Bell. Literary and dramatic sketches. Glasgow 1872.
Smith, James L. Melodrama. 1973.
Southern, Richard. The Victorian theatre: a pictorial survey. 1970.
Speaight, G. The juvenile drama. [1946.]
(ed). Professional and literary memoirs of Charles Dibdin the younger. 1956.
Pantomime. TN 5 1951.
The history of the English toy theatre. Boston 1969.
Sprague, Arthur C. and B. Shuttleworth (ed). The London theatre in the eighteen-thirties. 1950.
Stahl, E. Das englische Theater im 19 Jahrhundert. Munich 1914.
Stephens, J. R. The censorship of English drama 1824–1901. Cambridge 1980.
The profession of the playwright: British theatre 1800–1900. Cambridge 1992.
Stokes, John. Resistible theatres: enterprise and experiment in the late nineteenth century. 1972.
Stokoe, F. W. German influence in the English romantic period 1788–1818. Cambridge 1926.
Stone, M. W. William Blake and the juvenile drama. TN 1 1945.
Stuart, Charles Douglas and A. J. Park. The variety stage: a history of the music halls from the earliest period to the present time. [1895.]
Studies in English theatre history in memory of Gabrielle Enthoven. 1952.
Taylor, John Russell. The rise and fall of the well-made play. 1967.
Taylor, Tom. The theatre in England: some of its shortcomings and possibilities. 1871.
Thompson, Alan Reynolds. Melodrama and tragedy. PMLA 43 1928.
Thompson, L. F. Kotzebue: a survey of his progress in England and France. Paris 1928.
Thorndike, A. H. English comedy. New York 1929.
Thorp, W. The stage adventures of some Gothic novels. PMLA 63 1928.
Tomlins, Frederick G. A brief view of the English drama, from the earliest to the present time .... 1840.
The nature and state of the English drama: a lecture. 1841.
Remarks on the present state of the English drama. 1851.
Trewin, J. C. Verse drama since 1800. Cambridge 1956.
The pomping folk in the nineteenth-century theatre. 1968.
Troubridge, St Vincent. The benefit system in the British Isles. 1967.
Walkley, A. B. Playhouse impressions. 1892.
Drama and life [1907], rptd Freeport NY 1967.
Watson, Ernest B. Sheridan to Robertson: a study of the early nineteenth-century London stage. Cambridge MA 1926, rptd New York 1963.
Watts, G. T. Theatrical Bristol. 1915.
West, E. J. From a player's to a playwright's theatre: the London stage 1870–90. Quart Jnl of Speech 28 1942.
White, Eric W. The rise of English opera. New York 1951.
White, H. A. Sir Walter Scott's novels on the stage. New Haven CT 1927.
Wilson, A. E. Penny plain twopence coloured: a history of the juvenile drama. 1931, rptd New York 1969.
Pantomime pageant. [1945.]
King Panto: the story of pantomime. New York 1935.
East end entertainment. 1954.
[Winston, James.] The theatric tourist. 1805.
Wolcott, J. R. The genesis of gas lights. ThR 12 1972.
Wray, E. English adaptations of French drama between 1780 and 1815. MLN 43 1928.
Wyndham, H. Saxe. The annals of Covent Garden Theatre. 2 vols 1906.
Wynne, A. The growth of English drama. Oxford 1914. [BJO'C]

(3) HISTORIES OF INDIVIDUAL THEATRES

Anderson, D. Theatres in Totnes. TN 44 1990.
Angus, J. K. A Scotch playhouse: being the historical records of the old Theatre Royal, Marischal Street Aberdeen. Aberdeen 1878, 1878.
Arundell, D. The story of Sadler's Wells 1683–1964. 1965; as The story of Sadler's Wells 1683–1977, Newton Abbot 1978.
Baily, L. J. R. The Royal West London Theatre in the nineteenth century. N & Q 21 Oct 1944. Further note by G. Morice 16 June 1945.
Baker, H. B. History of the London stage 1576–1903. 1904.
Baker, W. T. The Manchester stage 1800–1900. 1903.
Barker, C. The audience of the Britannia Theatre, Hoxton. TQ 9 Summer 1979.
Barker, K. The Lyric Theatre, Hammersmith. TN 24 1970.
Theatre Royal Bristol 1766–1966. 1974.
The decline and rise of the Brighton Theatre 1840–1860. NCTR 8 1980.
Barrell, D. John Hare's Court Theatre 1875–79. NCTR 8 1980.
Barry, E. M. On the construction and rebuilding of the Italian Opera House, Covent Garden. Royal Insitute Br Architects Trans 1859–60.
Baynham, W. The Glasgow stage. [1892.]
Betjeman, J. The Criterion Theatre. Connoisseur 185 1974.
Blanchard, E. L. Some managerial memories. Theatre Annual 1885.
Bloore, C. The Bournemouth theatres 1882–1908. Bournemouth 1980.
Board, M. E. The story of the Bristol stage 1490–1925. Bristol 1925.
Brayley, E. W. Historical and descriptive accounts of the theatres of London. 1826.
Brereton, A. Theatrical Richmond. Theatre Sep 1885. Refers to the Richmond Theatre, Surrey.
The Lyceum and Henry Irving. 1903.
Brereton, C. The Hippodrome. Theatrephile 1 1983.
Britton, J. and A. Pugin. Illustrations of the public buildings of London. 2 vols 1825–8. Refers to Covent Garden, Drury Lane, Haymarket and Astley's theatres.
Broadbent, R. J. Annals of the Liverpool stage. Liverpool 1908.
Burley, T. L. G. Playhouses and players of East Anglia. Norwich 1928.
Butler, N. Theatre in Colchester. Colchester 1981.
'C. H.' The Hare and Kendal management at the St James's. The Theatre Sep 1888.
Carter, R. The Drury Lane theatres of Henry Holland and Benjamin Dean Wyatt. Jnl Soc Architectural Historians Oct 1967.
Cotton, W. The story of the drama in Exeter. Exeter 1887.
Crump, J. Patronage, pleasure and profit: a study of the Theatre Royal, Leicester 1847–1900. TN 38 1984.
Cunningham, J. E. Theatre Royal, Birmingham. 1950.
Dale, A. The Theatre Royal Brighton. Stocksfield 1980.

Davis, J. Stage-managing the Brit: the diaries of F. C. Wilton. TN 42 1988.
The Britannia diaries, 1863–1875: selections from the diaries of Frederick C. Wilton. 1992. On the Britannia theatre, Hoxton.
Delderfield, E. R. Cavalcade by candlelight: the story of Exeter's five theatres 1725–1950. Exmouth 1950.
Dibdin, C. History and illustrations of the London theatres. 1826.
Dibdin, J. C. The annals of the Edinburgh stage. 1888.
Disher, M. W. Greatest show on earth: Astley's. 1937.
Dobbs, B. Drury Lane: three centuries of the Theatre Royal 1663–1971. 1972.
Donohue, J. (ed). The Empire Theatre of Varieties licensing controversy of 1894. NCTR 15 1987.
Drogheda, G. M. The Covent Garden album: 250 years of theatre, opera and ballet. 1984.
Duncan, B. The St James' Theatre: its strange and complete history. 1964.
East, J. 'Neath the mask. 1967. Chapters on the Lyric Theatre, Hammersmith, the Elephant and Castle, the Britannia.
Ebers, J. Seven years of the King's Theatre. 1828, New York 1969.
Eddison, R. Capon and Goodman's Fields Theatre. TN 18 1964.
Eshleman, D. H. (ed). Committee Books of the Theatre Royal, Norwich 1768–1825. 1970.
Fagg, E. The old 'Old Vic'. 1936.
Fahrner, R. The second Sans Souci Theatre 1796–1835. TN 29 1975.
Field, M. The lamplit stage: the Fisher theatre circuit 1792–1844. Norwich 1985.
Findlater, R. Lilian Baylis: the lady of the Old Vic. 1975.
Fitzgerald, P. The Drury Lane managers: from Killigrew to Augustus Harris. Theatre Jan, Feb, Mar, May, June 1887.
F[letcher], I. K. The Royal Marylebone Theatre. TN 17 1962.
Foulston, J. The public buildings in the west of England. 1830. Refers to the Theatre Royal, Plymouth.
Gibbon, W. M. A change of scene: a nostalgic appreciation of Barrow's theatres and cinemas. Kendal 1986.
Gilliland, T. The dramatic mirror. 2 vols 1808. Refers to Covent Garden, Drury Lane, Haymarket and Theatre Royal, Birmingham, Norwich circuit.
Glasstone, V. Victorian and Edwardian theatres. 1975. Refers to the Garrick, Covent Garden, Grand (Leeds), Richmond (Surrey) Theatres.
Hamilton, C and L. Baylis. The Old Vic. 1926.
Hannam-Clark, T. Drama in Gloucestershire. 1928.
Harcourt, B. The Theatre Royal, Norwich. 1903.
Hinton, P. The dramatic library of the old Theatre Royal, Birmingham. TN 1 1945.
Hodgkinson, J. L. and R. Pogson. The early Manchester theatre. 1960.
Hollingshead, J. Gaiety chronicles. 1890.
Howard, D. London theatres and music halls 1850–1950. 1970.
Howard, V. The show must go on: the story of the Theatre Royal, Norwich. Norwich 1977.
[Howe, H.] Recollections of the Haymarket Theatre. Theatre Feb 1880.
Howell, M. A. The theatre at Richmond, Yorkshire: new evidence and conjectures. TN 46 1992.
Hughes, A. The Lyceum staff: a Victorian theatrical organisation. TN 23 1974.
Hyman, A. The Gaiety years. 1975.
Jackson, A. S. The Standard Theatre of Victorian England. 1993, Toronto 1993.
Jackson, R. The Lyceum in Irving's absence: G. E. Terry's letters to Bram Stoker. NCTR 6 1978.
King, R. North Shields theatres. Gateshead 1948.
Knight, W. C. A major London 'minor': the Surrey Theatre 1805–1865. 1997.
Knowlson, J. Red plush and gilt, the heyday of Manchester theatre during the Victorian and Edwardian periods. Manchester 1986.
Langford, J. M. Some Olympic reminiscences. Era Almanack 1870.
Lawson, R. The story of the Scottish stage. Glasgow 1917.
Leacroft, R. Remains of the theatres at Ashby de la Zouch and Loughborough. TN 4 1950.
Remains of the Fisher theatres at Beccles, Bungay, Lowestoft and North Walsham. TN 5 1951.
The development of the English playhouse. 1973. For detailed references to The Builder and Building News articles on Covent Garden, Drury Lane, New English Opera House, Her Majesty's, Daly's, Theatre Royal, Birmingham, esp p. 339.
The Theatre Royal Leicester. TN 40 1986.
Levey, R. M. and J. O'Rorke. Annals of the Theatre Royal, Dublin. Dublin 1880.
Lingwood, H. R. Ipswich playhouse: chapters of local theatrical history. [Ipswich 1936.]
Lorenzen, R. L. The old Prince of Wales's Theatre: a view of the physical structure. TN 25 1971.
Lowndes, W. The Theatre Royal at Bath. Bristol 1982.
McCoola, R. Theatre in the hills: two centuries of the theatre in Buxton. Chapel-en-le-Frith 1984.
Mackintosh, I. and G. Ashton. Royal Opera House retrospective 1732–1982. 1982.
[Mackintosh, M.] Stage reminiscences . . . by an old stager. Glasgow 1866. On the Olympic Theatre, London and Scottish theatres.
Macqueen-Pope, W. J. Theatre Royal, Drury Lane. 1945.
Haymarket: theatre of perfection. 1948.
Gaiety: theatre of enchantment. 1949.
St James': theatre of distinction. 1957.
Maguire, H. F. B. The architect of the Garrick Theatre, London. TN 42 1988.
The Manchester stage 1880–1900. [1900.] Criticisms rptd from Manchester Guardian.
Mander, R. and J. Mitchenson. London's lost theatres. 1968.
Theatres of London. 1961, 1975.
The Old Vic: a pictorial history. Theatrephile 1 1983.
Maude, C. The Haymarket Theatre. 1903.
Morice, G. A record of some nineteenth century London theatres. N & Q 9 Oct 1934, 26 Feb 1944, 30 Mar 1945. Notes by H. Harting 8 Apr 1944, C. D. Williams 22 Apr 1944.
Morley, M. The first Strand Theatre. TN 18 1964.
Margate and its theatres 1730–1965. 1966.
Nalbach, D. The King's Theatre 1704–1867: London's first Italian opera house. 1972.
Newton, C. The Old Vic and its associations. 1923.
Nikolopoulou, A. Panopticism and the politics of the proscenium frame theatre: Benjamin Wyatt's Drury Lane, 1812. ET 12 1994.
Odell, M. T. The Old Theatre, Worthing, 1807–55. Aylesbury 1938.
Mr Trotter of Worthing and the Brighton Theatre. 1944.
More about the Old Theatre, Worthing. Worthing 1945.
Oswald, H. The Theatres Royal in Newcastle-upon-Tyne. Newcastle 1936.
Oulton, W. C. History of the theatres of London. 3 vols 1818.
Pemberton, T. E. The Birmingham theatres [1862–79]. Birmingham [1889.]
The Theatre Royal, Birmingham 1774–1901. Birmingham 1901.
The Criterion Theatre 1875–1903. 1903.
Penley, B. S. The Bath stage. 1892.
Porter, H. C. A history of the theatres of Brighton from 1774 to 1855. Brighton 1886.
Powell, G. R. The Bristol stage. 1919.
Ranger, P. A matter of choice: a comparison of locations and repertoire in some English provincial theatres. NCTR 10 1982.
Rhodes, R. C. The Theatre Royal, Birmingham 1774–1924. 1924.
Richards, J. The Lyceum Theatre, London. History Today Oct 1988.

Roberts, P. The Old Vic story. 1976.
Rosenfeld, S. The Georgian theatre of Richmond, Yorkshire. 1984.
Rowell, G. A Lyceum sketchbook. NCTR 6 1978.
The Old Vic Theatre. 1993.
Sachs, E. O. Modern opera houses and theatres. 3 vols 1896–9, New York 1968. Refers to the Savoy, Her Majesty's, Garrick, Daly's, Lyric, Grand (Islington), Grand (Leeds).
Sandoe, J. Private theatricals and private theatres. Colorado-Wyoming Jnl of Letters 1939.
Sawyer, P. The New Theatre in Lincoln's Inn Fields. 1979.
Scharf, G. Recollections of the scenic effects of the Covent Garden Theatre. [1838–9.]
[Scott, C.] Some old Olympians. Theatre Apr 1886. Refers to the Olympic Theatre after Vestris.
Senior, W. The old Wakefield Theatre. Wakefield 1894.
Shawe-Taylor, D. Covent Garden. 1948.
Sheppard, F. H. W. (gen ed). Survey of London. Vol 23 South Bank and Vauxhall, 1951, refers to the Old Vic, Royal Coburg and Surrey Theatres.
Vol 29 St James Westminster, 1961, refers to Haymarket Opera House (King's, Queen's, His Majesty's, Her Majesty's Theatres).
Vol 35 The Theatre Royal Drury Lane and the Royal Opera House Covent Garden 1970.
Sheppard, T. Evolution of the drama in Hull and district. Hull 1917.
Sheridan, P. Late and early joys at the Players' Theatre. 1953.
Penny theatres of Victorian London. 1981.
Sherson, E. London's lost theatres of the nineteenth century. 1925.
Southern, R. Interesting matter relating to the scenery, decorations etc of the Theatre Royal, Tackett Street, Ipswich. Architectural Rev Aug 1946.
The Georgian playhouse. 1948.
Stirling, E. Old Drury Lane: fifty years' recollections. 2 vols 1881.
Stockwell, L. T. Dublin theatres and theatre customs 1637–1820. 1968.
Thorne, R. The Princess's Theatre, Oxford Street. Theatrephile 2 1985.
Troubridge, St V. Victorian playhouses. N & Q 17 Aug 1940. Note by G. Morice 14 Sep 1940.
Adelphi advertising in 1862. TN 7 1953.
Turner, H. Reminiscences of the Royalty Theatre. Theatre June 1883.
Wade, A. Royal Clarence Theatre. TLS 6 July 1933.
Watts, G. T. Theatrical Bristol. Bristol 1915.
Webster, B. The series of dramatic entertainments performed by Royal Command at Windsor Castle 1848–9. [1849.]
Wellwarth, G. E. The disappearance of the New Royal Brunswick Theatre: or the mystery of the iron roof. TN 22 1967.
Williams, M. Some London theatres past and present. 1883.
Wilson, A. E. The Lyceum. 1952.
Winslow, D. F. Daly's: the biography of a theatre. 1944.
Wyatt, B. Observations on the design of the Theatre Royal, Drury Lane. 1813.
Wyndham, H. S. The annals of Covent Garden Theatre 1732–1897. 2 vols 1906.
See also Arnott and Robinson: for London theatres pp. 113–50; for provincial theatres pp. 151–92. See also Nicoll vol 4 pp. 222–44 and vol 5 pp. 214–28. [VE]

(4) CRITICISM

Agate, J. (ed). These were actors: extracts from a newspaper cutting book 1811–33. 1943.
Those were the nights. [1946.]
Archer, C. William Archer: life, work and friendships. [1931.]
Archer, W. English dramatists of today. 1882.
About the theatre. 1886.
The theatrical 'World'. 5 vols 1893–7.
Study and stage: a yearbook of criticism. 1899.
Play-making. 1912, 1913, 1926, 1930.
The old drama and the new. 1923.
William Archer on Ibsen: the major essays 1889–1919. Ed T. Postlewait, Westport CT 1984.
Arnold, M. Letters of an old playgoer. Ed B. Matthews, New York 1919.
Baylen, J. O. A note on William Archer and the Pall Mall Gazette. 1888. Univ of Mississippi Stud in Eng 4 1963.
William Archer, W. T. Stead and the theatre; some unpublished letters. Univ of Mississippi Stud in Eng 5 1964.
Beerbohm, M. Around theatres. 2 vols 1924, New York 1930, London 1953.
Borsa, M. Il teatro inglese contemporaneo. Milan 1906; tr 1908.
Brereton, A. Some famous Hamlets. 1884.
Carter, H. The new spirit in drama and art. 1912.
Chandler, F. W. Aspects of modern drama. New York 1914.
Clapp, H. A. Reminiscences of a dramatic critic; with an essay on the art of Henry Irving. 1902.
Cook, D. A book of the play. 2 vols 1876, 1876, 1881, 1882.
Hours with the players. 2 vols 1881.
Nights at the play. 2 vols 1883.
On the stage. 2 vols 1883.
Cooke, J. The stage. [1840.]
Courtney, W. L. The idea of tragedy in ancient and modern drama, with a prefatory note by Sir A. W. Pinero. 1900.
Craig, E. G. The art of the theatre. Edinburgh 1905.
On the art of the theatre. 1911, Chicago [1911].
Davies, R. In A voice from the attic, Toronto 1960.
Dickinson, T. H. The contemporary drama of England. 1920.
Dimmick, R. C. Our theatres today and yesterday. 1913.
Donne, W. B. Essays of the drama. 1858.
A new drama: or we faint!!! decline of the drama!!! review of the actors!!! reprinted from Bentley's Monthly Review. 1853.
'Dramaticus'. An impartial view of the stage. 1816.
The stage as it is. 1847.
Dukes, A. Modern dramatists. [1911.]
Ellehauge, M. Striking figures among modern English dramatists. Copenhagen 1931.
Ervine, St J. The Victorian theatre. Fortnightly Rev Nov 1946.
Filon, A. Le Théâtre anglais. Paris 1896; tr 1897.
Fitzgerald, P. H. Principles of comedy and dramatic effect. 1870.
Fornelli, G. Tendenze e motivi nel dramma inglese moderno e contemporaneo. Florence [1930].
Forster, J. S. and G. H. Lewes. Dramatic essays with notes and an introduction by W. Archer and R. W. Lowe. 1896.
Goldman, E. The social significance of the modern drama. Boston 1914.
Grau, R. Forty years' observation of music and drama. New York 1909.
Grein, J. T. Dramatic criticism. 5 vols 1899–1905.
Hadow, W. H. The use of comic episodes in tragedy. Oxford 1915.
Hale, E. E. Dramatists of today. 1906.
Hamilton, C. The theory of the theatre. 1910.
Hastings, C. Le Théâtre français et anglais. Paris 1900; tr 1901.
Hazlitt, W. A view of the English stage. 1818, 1821, 1851, 1854, 1895; ed W. Archer and R. W. Lowe 1906, 1957; and in Collected works 1902–4, 1936.
Henderson, A. The changing drama. 1914.
Hobson, H. Verdict at midnight: sixty years of dramatic criticism. 1952.
Horne, R. H. A new spirit of the age. 2 vols 1844.
Howe, P. P. Dramatic portraits. 1913.
Huneker, J. G. Iconoclasts: a book of dramatists. 1905.
Hunt, Leigh. Critical essays on the performers of the London theatres. 1807.
Dramatic essays. Ed W. Archer and R. W. Lowe 1894.
Dramatic criticism 1808–31. Ed L. H. and C. W. Houtchens 1950.

Innes, F. M. On the causes of the decline of the drama. Edinburgh 1834.
Jackson, R. Shakespeare in the theatrical criticism of Henry Morley. ShS 38 1985.
Jones, H. A. The renascence of the English drama. 1895.
Foundations of a national drama. 1913.
Kendal, Madge. The drama. [1884] (4 edns).
Dramatic opinions. 1890.
Knight, J. Theatrical notes. 1893.
Knowles, J. S. Lectures on dramatic literature delivered by James Sheridan Knowles during the years 1820–1850. 1875.
Lamb, C. The art of the stage. Ed P. Fitzgerald 1885.
Dramatic essays. Ed B. Matthews 1891, New York 1893.
Lewes, G. H. On actors and the art of acting. 1875, 1875, rptd New York 1957.
Martin, Sir T. Essays on the drama: first series. 1874; second series, 1879.
Mayhew, E. Stage effect: or the principles which command dramatic success in the theatre. 1840.
Meredith, G. On the idea of comedy and the uses of the comic spirit. 1897. First pbd 1877 in New Quart Rev.
Morley, H. The journal of a London playgoer 1851–66. 1866, 1891.
Morris, M. Essays in theatrical criticism. 1882.
Nag, U. C. The English theatre of the Romantic Revival. Nineteenth Cent Sep 1928.
Neville, H. The stage: its past and present in relation to fine art. 1871, 1875.
Parlby, S. Desultory thoughts on the national drama, past and present. By an old playgoer. 1850.
Pascoe, C. E. Dramatic notes. 1870.
[Purnell, T.] Dramatists of the present day, by 'Q'. 1871.
Quinlan, M. A. Poetic justice in the drama; the history of an ethical principle in literary criticism. Notre Dame IN 1912.
Rowell, G. (ed). Victorian dramatic criticism. 1971.
Russell, E. R. The theatre and things said about it. Liverpool 1911.
Schmid, H. The dramatic criticism of William Archer. Berne 1964.
Schoonderwoerd, N. H. G. J. T. Grein: ambassador of the theatre 1862–1935. Assen 1963.
Scott, C. W. Thirty years at the play, and dramatic table talk. 1891.
From The bells to King Arthur: a critical record of the first-night productions at the Lyceum Theatre from 1871 to 1895. 1896, 1897.
The drama of yesterday and to-day. 2 vols 1899.
Some notable Hamlets of the present time. 1900, 1905.
Shaw, G. B. The quintessence of Ibsenism. 1891, 1913 (rev).
Dramatic opinions and essays. 2 vols 1907.
Our theatres in the nineties. 3 vols 1932.
Simpson, E. The dramatic unities in the present day. 1874.
Spence, E. F. Our stage and its critics. 1910.
Syles, L. D. Essays in dramatic criticism. 1898.
Taylor, T. The theatre in England. 1871.
Thouless, P. Modern poetic drama. Oxford 1934.
Tomlins, F. G. A brief view of the English drama. 1840.
Van Dijk, M. John Phillip Kemble and the critics. TN 36 1982.
Walbrook, H. M. Nights at the play. 1911.
Walkley, A. B. Playhouse impressions. 1892.
Frames of mind. 1899.
Drama and life. 1907.
Wilson, M. G. jr. George Henry Lewes as critic of Charles Kean's acting. Educational Theatre Jnl 16 1964.
Ziegler, G. The actress as Shakespearean critic: three nineteenth-century Portias. ThS 30, May–Nov 1989. [HH]

(5) ACTORS AND ACTING

À Beckett, A. W. Green room recollections of Fechter. Theatre Sep 1894.
'An Actor'. The stage with the curtain raised. 1881.
Adams, W. D. 'Stock' versus 'star' companies. Theatre Nov 1878.
Miss Ellen Terry as Beatrice. Theatre Oct 1880.
Edward S. Willard: a biographical and critical sketch. Theatre Oct 1890.
Ada Rehan: her life and work. Theatre Apr 1891.
Adolphus, J. Memoirs of John Bannister, comedian. 1839, 1839.
Aidé Hamilton. A dramatic school. Theatre Feb 1882.
Allen, P. The stage life of Mrs Stirling. 1922.
Allen, S. S. Samuel Phelps and the Sadler's Wells Theatre. Middletown CT 1971.
Anderson, Mary (Mme de Navarro). Girlhood of an actress. New York 1895.
Appleton, W. W. Madame Vestris and the London stage. New York 1974.
'Archer, Frank' (F. B. Arnold). An actor's note-books. [1912.]
Archer, W. Henry Irving, actor and manager: a critical study. 1883, 1883, [1884].
Masks or faces? 1888.
William Charles Macready. 1890.
[Archer, W. and R. W. Lowe.] The fashionable tragedian. Edinburgh 1877, 1877 (with postscript). On Irving.
Arliss, G. On the stage. 1928.
Armstrong, C. F. A century of great actors 1750–1850. 1912.
Armstrong, M. Fanny Kemble: a passionate Victorian. New York 1938.
Asche, O. Oscar Asche: his life. 1929.
Auerbach, N. Ellen Terry: player in her time. 1987, New York 1987.
Baker, H. B. Our old actors. 1878, 1881, New York 1879.
Baker, M. The rise of the Victorian actor. 1978.
[Ballantyne, J.] Dramatic characters of Mrs Siddons. Edinburgh 1812.
Bancroft, Lady (M. E.) and Sir S. Mr and Mrs Bancroft on and off the stage, written by themselves. 2 vols 1888 (6 edns), 1889, 1891.
The Bancrofts: recollections of sixty years. 1909.
Empty chairs. 1925.
Barclay, G. I. The life and remarkable career of Adah Isaacs Menken. Philadelphia 1868.
Barker, K. The first English performance of Byron's Werner. MP 66 1969.
A provincial tragedian abroad. ThR 11 Spring 1986. Refers to Charles Dillon.
Barnes, J. H. Forty years on the stage. 1914.
Barrett, D. Refined vivacity: the acting of Leigh Murray. TN 38 1984.
Bedford, P. J. Recollections and wanderings. 1864.
Beerbohm, M. Herbert Beerbohm Tree. 1921.
Belton, F. Random recollections of an actor. 1880.
Benson, C. Mainly players: Bensonian memories. 1926.
Benson, F. My memoirs. 1930.
Bernard, J. Retrospections of the stage. 1830, Boston 1832.
Bettany, W. A. L. Miss Winifred Emery, an appreciation and a forecast. Theatre Dec 1893.
Bingham, M. Henry Irving and the Victorian theatre. 1978, New York 1978.
The great lover: the life and art of Herbert Beerbohm Tree. 1979, New York 1979.
Boaden, J. Memoirs of the life of John Philip Kemble. 2 vols 1825, Philadelphia and New York 1825, 1969.
Memoirs of Mrs Siddons. 2 vols 1827, Philadelphia 1827, London 1831, 1893.
Life of Mrs Jordan. 2 vols 1831 (3 edns).
Booth, A. From Miranda to Prospero: the works of Fanny Kemble. VS 38 1995.
Booth, J. B. Memoirs of Junius Brutus Booth. 1817.
Booth, M., J. Stokes and S. Bassnett. Three tragic actresses: Siddons, Rachel, Ristori. Cambridge 1996, New York 1996.

'Boz' (Charles Dickens). Memoirs of Joseph Grimaldi, with illustrations by G. Cruikshank. 2 vols 1838; ed C. Whitehead 1846; ed P. Fitzgerald 1903; ed R. Findlater [1968], Cambridge 1978.
Macready as Benedict. Examiner 4 Mar 1843.
On Mr Fechter's acting. Atlantic Monthly Aug 1869.
Both the above articles are rptd in Miscellaneous papers *in the Gadshill edn of the* Works.
Bratton, J. Music Hall: performance and style. 1986, Philadelphia 1986.
Brereton, A. Wilson Barrett. Theatre Sep 1882 and Jan 1883.
Henry Irving. 1883, 1884, 1885.
Reminiscences of Joseph Shepherd Munden. Theatre Sep 1884.
The life of Henry Irving. 1905, 1908, New York 1969.
H. B. and Laurence Irving. 1922.
Bright, A. Mr William Barrett's revival of Othello. Theatre Dec 1891.
George Alexander, actor and manager. Theatre May 1892.
Brook, D. A pageant of English actors. [1950.]
Butler, N. John Martin-Harvey. Colchester 1998.
Byron, H. J. Going on the stage. Theatre Oct 1879.
Calvert, A. H. Sixty-eight years on the stage. 1911.
Calvert, W. Souvenir of Sir Henry Irving. 1895.
Campbell, H., R. F. Brewer and Henry G. Neville. Voice, speech and gesture. 1895, 1897 (new and enlarged), New York 1895, 1904 (new and enlarged).
Campbell, Mrs P. My life and some letters. 1922.
Campbell, T. Life of Mrs Siddons. 2 vols 1834, New York 1834, London 1839.
Carlisle, C. J. Two notes on Helen Faucit. TN 30 1976.
Helen Faucit's acting style. ThS 17 1976.
The other Miss Faucit. NCTR 6 1978.
Cheshire, D. Portrait of Ellen Terry. 1990.
Chevalier, Albert and Brian Daly. Albert Chevalier. 1895.
Cima, G. G. Elizabeth Robins: the genesis of an independent manageress. ThS 21 1980.
Claris, L. J. Henry Irving, actor and artist. Theatre Mar 1882.
Clarke, A. B. The elder and the younger Booth by Asia Booth Clarke. Boston 1882.
Cole, J. W. The life and theatrical times of Charles Kean. 2 vols 1859, 1859.
Cole, T. and H. K. Chinoy (ed). Actors on acting. New York 1949, 1970 (rev).
Coleman, J. Memoir of Samuel Phelps. 1886.
Players and playwrights I have known. 2 vols 1888.
In memoriam Barry Sullivan. Theatre June 1891.
In memoriam Carlotta Leclercq. Theatre Sep 1893.
Fifty years of an actor's life. 2 vols 1904.
Compton, C. and E. Memoir of Henry Compton. 1879.
Cook, E. Dutton. Ellen Terry. Theatre June 1880.
The art of acting. Theatre Sep 1882.
Hours with the players. 2 vols 1881; 1 vol 1883.
'Cornwall, Barry' (B. W. Procter). The life of Edmund Kean. 2 vols 1835, New York 1969.
Courtneidge, R. 'I was an actor once'. 1930.
'Cowell, Joe' (Hawkins Witchett). Thirty years passed among the players of England and America. New York 1844, Hamden CT 1979.
Craig, E. G. Henry Irving, Ellen Terry: a book of portraits. [Chicago 1899.]
Henry Irving. 1930, New York 1969.
Ellen Terry and her secret self. [nd.]
Cran, Mrs G. Herbert Beerbohm Tree. 1907.
Crauford, R. Ramblings of an old mummer. 1909.
Darlington, W. A. The actor and his audience. 1949.
Davis, J. John Liston, comedian. 1985.
Colonial experience: English comedians in Australia in the nineteenth century. NCTR 16 1988. Refers to Toole and Charles Mathews.
Davis, T. Acting in Ibsen. TN 39 1985.
Actresses as working women: their social identity in Victorian culture. 1991.
Dawson, J. The autobiography of James Dawson. Truro 1865.
Day, W. C. Behind the footlights. 1885.
[Deans, Mrs C.] Memoirs of the life of Mrs Charlotte Deans. 1837; ed F. Marshall, Kendal 1984 as Charlotte Deans (1768–1859). A commentary on the story of a travelling player.
Decastro, J. The memoirs of J. Decastro, comedian. Ed R. Humphreys 1824.
De Felice, J. The London theatrical agent. TN 23 1969.
Dent, A. Mrs Patrick Campbell. 1961.
Dickens, C. (ed). The life of Charles James Mathews. 2 vols 1879, New York 1879. *See also* 'Boz', *above.*
Disher, M. W. The last romantic: the authorized biography of Sir John Martin-Harvey. 1948.
Mad genius: a biography of Edmund Kean. 1950.
Donaldson, F. The actor-managers. 1970.
Donaldson, W. A. Recollections of an actor. 1865; rptd as Fifty years of green-room gossip, [1881].
Donohue, J. W. (ed). The theatrical manager in England and America. Princeton 1971.
Doran, J. Annals of the English stage from Thomas Betterton to Edmund Kean. 2 vols 1864, New York 1865, London 1865, New York 1880, Philadelphia 1890, 1897; 3 vols 1888. Ed. R. W. Lowe. Vol 3 discusses Siddons, Cooke, John Kemble, Master Betty, Kean and 'the new actors'.
Downer, A. Players and the painted stage: nineteenth century acting. PMLA 61, June 1946.
The eminent tragedian: William Charles Macready. Cambridge MA 1966.
The dramatic peerage. Ed. E. Reid and H. Compton [1892].
Drew, E. Henry Irving, on and off the stage. 1889.
Driver, L. S. Fanny Kemble. Chapel Hill NC 1933.
Dunkel, W. Kean's portrayal of Cardinal Wolsey. TN 6 1952.
Dunlap, W. Memoirs of George Frederick Cooke. 2 vols 1813, New York 1813, London 1815.
Dyer, R. Nine years of an actor's life. 1833.
[Ellerslie, A.] The diary of an actress. 1885.
Ellis, S. M. The life of Michael Kelly: musician, actor and bon viveur 1762–1826. 1930.
Everard, E. C. Memoirs of an unfortunate son of Thespis. Edinburgh 1818.
Faucit, H. (Lady Martin). On some of Shakespeare's female characters. Edinburgh 1885. Discusses Ophelia, Portia, Desdemona, Juliet, Imogen, Rosalind, Beatrice.
Fawkes, R. Dion Boucicault: a biography. 1979.
Fecher, C. Bright star: a portrait of Ellen Terry. New York 1970.
Field, K. Adelaide Ristori: a biography. 1867.
Charles Albert Fechter. 1882, New York 1969.
Findlater, R. The player kings. 1968.
The player queens. 1976.
Joe Grimaldi: his life and theatre. 1978, New York 1978; pbd as Grimaldi: king of clowns 1955.
Findon, B. L. The amateur club as a stepping stone to the stage. Theatre Aug 1890. On the absence of actor training.
[Fitzgerald, E.] Letters of Edward FitzGerald to Fanny Kemble 1871–83. Ed W. A. Wright 1895, New York 1895.
Fitzgerald, P. H. The Kembles. 2 vols [1871].
First appearances: Kean, Macready, Miss O'Neill. Theatre Oct 1886.
The art of acting. 1892.
Henry Irving: a record of twenty years at the Lyceum. 1893, 1895 (rev).
Sir Henry Irving. 1906, Philadelphia 1906.
Fitzsimons, R. Edmund Kean: fire from heaven. 1976, New York 1976.

Fleetwood, F. Conquest, the story of a theatre family. 1953.
Fletcher, K. Planche, Vestris, and the transvestite role: sexuality and gender in Victorian popular theatre. NCTR 15 1987.
Forbes-Robertson, J. A player under three reigns. 1925.
Fothergill, B. Mrs Jordan: portrait of an actress. 1965.
Foulkes, R. Henry Irving and Laurence Olivier as Shylock. TN 27 1972.
Two notes on Helen Faucit. TN 30 1976.
Helen Faucit and Ellen Terry as Portia. TN 31 1977.
The Calverts: actors of some importance. 1992.
Francis, B. Fanny Kelly of Drury Lane. New York 1950.
Franklyn, C. W. Isabel Dallas Glyn. Theatre July 1889.
Frenz, H. and L. W. Campbell. William Gillette on the London stage. Queen's Quart 3 1945.
Furnas, J. C. Fanny Kemble: leading lady of the nineteenth century stage: a biography. New York 1982.
Fyvie, J. Tragedy queens of the Georgian era. 1903.
Comedy queens of the Georgian era. 1906.
Galt, J. The lives of the players. 2 vols 1831, Boston 1831, London 1886.
Garcia, Gustave. The actor's art. 1882.
Genest, John. Some account of the English stage. 10 vols Bath 1832.
Gerson, N. Lillie Langtry. 1972.
Gibbs, H. Affectionately yours: Fanny Kemble and the theatre. 1947.
Glover, J. M. Jimmy Glover his book. 1911.
Jimmy Glover and his friends. 1913.
Goddard, A. Players of the period: a series of anecdotal, biographical and critical monographs of the leading English actors of the day. 2 vols 1891.
Goodman, W. The Keeleys: on stage and at home. 1895.
Gordon, W. Recollections of Mr W. H. Chippendale. Theatre Feb 1888.
Graham, J. An old stock-actor's memories. 1930.
Grant, G. The science of acting. 1826.
Grice, E. Rogues and vagabonds, or the actors' road to respectability. Lavenham, Suffolk 1977.
Grossmith, Weedon. From studio to stage. 1913.
Guerbel, Countess de (Genevieve Ward) and Richard Whiteing. Both sides of the curtain. 1918.
Gustafson, Z. B. Genevieve Ward. [1881], Boston 1882.
Hammerton, J. A. The actor's art. 1897.
Hardwick, J. M. D. (ed). Emigrant in motley. 1954. Refers to Charles and Ellen Kean.
Hare, A. George Frederick Cooke: the actor and the man. 1980.
Harley, G. D. An authentic biographical sketch of William Henry West Betty, the celebrated young Roscius. 1804, 1804, 1805.
Hatton, J. Reminiscences of Mark Lemon. 1872.
Hawkins, F. W. The life of Edmund Kean. 2 vols 1869.
Hazlitt, W. View of the English stage. 1818.
Criticisms and dramatic essays of the English stage. 1851.
Henley, W. E. A corporation of actors. Theatre Nov 1880.
Hervey, C. Louisa Nisbett. Theatre Nov 1886.
Hiatt, C. Ellen Terry and her impersonations. 1898, 1900.
Hicks, S. Between ourselves. 1930.
Acting. 1931.
Hillebrand, H. N. Edmund Kean. New York 1933.
Hingston, E. P. The Siddons of modern Italy: Adelaide Ristori. 1856.
Hodgson, N. Sarah Baker, governess-general of the Kentish drama. Stud in Eng Theatre Hist 1952.
Holloway, D. Playing the Empire. 1979. On the Holloway company of touring actors.
Holman, L. E. Lamb's 'Barbara S—': the life of Frances Maria Kelly, actress. 1935.
Houtchens L. H. and C. W. Leigh Hunt's dramatic criticism. 1950.
Hubert, P. G. The stage as a career. 1900, New York 1900. With opinions by Irving, Modjeska, Boucicault, Jefferson and others.
Hughes, A. Henry Irving: Shakespearean. Cambridge 1981.
Hunt, L. Critical essays on the performers of the London theatres. 1807.
Irving, H. The art of acting. Chicago [1887] (authorised edn), Edinburgh 1891.
The drama: addresses. New York [1892], London 1893, 1893, New York 1893, 1969.
The theatre in its relation to the stage. Boston 1898.
Irving, L. Henry Irving: the actor and his world. 1951, Columbus OH 1989.
Jackson, J. Strictures upon the merits of young Roscius. Glasgow 1804, London 1804, 1804.
Jackson, R. Cleopatra 'Lilyised': Antony and Cleopatra at the Princess's 1890. Theatrephile 2 1985. Refers to Lily Langtry.
James, Henry. The scenic art, notes on acting and the drama 1872–1901. Ed A. Wade 1949.
Jefferson, Joseph. The autobiography of Joseph Jefferson. [1890]; as Rip Van Winkle. 1949, New York 1890, 1897, 1950, 1964.
Jerome, Jerome K. On the stage – and off. 1885.
John, A. Elizabeth Robins: staging a life 1862–1952. 1995.
Jones, C. I. Memoirs of Miss O'Neill. 1816, 1818.
Joseph, B. The tragic actor. 1959.
Kelly, L. The Kemble era: John Philip Kemble, Sarah Siddons and the London stage. 1980.
Kelly, Michael. Reminiscences of Michael Kelly. Ed T. Hook 2 vols 1826, 1826, New York 1826; ed R. Fiske, Oxford 1975.
Kemble, F. A. Record of a girlhood. 3 vols 1878, 1878, New York 1879.
Notes upon some of Shakespeare's plays. 1882.
Further records 1843–83. 2 vols 1890, New York 1891.
Kendal, M. Dame Madge Kendal, by herself. 1933.
Kennard, Mrs A. Mrs Siddons. 1887.
Lang, M. Mr Wu looks back: thoughts and memories. 1940.
Lawrence, W. J. Barry Sullivan: a biographical sketch. 1893.
The life of Gustavus Vaughan Brooke. Belfast 1892.
Lee, R. Samuel Phelps, a biographical sketch. Theatre Aug, Sep 1886.
Leman, W. Memories of an old actor. San Francisco 1886, New York 1969.
Lewes, C. Lee. Memoirs of Charles Lee Lewes. Ed John Lee Lewes 4 vols 1805.
Lewes, G. H. On actors and the art of acting. 1875, New York 1957, 1968.
Lowhig, R. M. Ira Aldridge in Manchester. ThR 11 Autumn 1986.
McDonald, J. Lesser ladies of the Victorian stage. ThR 13 Autumn 1988. Refers to Charlotte Dean, Alma Ellerslie, Ann Holbrook.
Macready, W. C. Reminiscences. Ed Sir F. Pollock 2 vols 1875, 1876, 1912.
The diaries of William Charles Macready 1833–51. Ed W. Toynbee 2 vols 1912, New York 1969.
Mankowitz, W. Mazeppa: the lives, loves and legends of Adah Isaacs Menken. 1982.
Manvell, R. Ellen Terry. 1968, New York 1968.
Sarah Siddons: portrait of an actress. 1976.
Marshall, D. Fanny Kemble. 1977, New York 1977.
Marshall, H. and Mildred Stock. Ira Aldridge. 1958, rptd Washington 1993.
Marshall, T. Lives of the most celebrated actors and actresses. [1848.]
Marston, J. W. Our recent actors. 2 vols 1888, Boston 1888, 1 vol London 1890.
Martin, T. An eye-witness of John Kemble. Nineteenth Cent Feb 1880.
Helen Faucit Lady Martin. 1900, 1900.
Martin-Harvey, J. The autobiography of Sir John Martin-Harvey. 1933.
Mason, A. E. W. Sir George Alexander and the St James's Theatre. 1935, New York 1969.
Mason, E. T. The Othello of Tomasso Salvini. New York 1890.

Mathews, Mrs A. Memoirs of Charles Mathews. 4 vols 1838–9, 1839, Philadelphia 1839.
Matthews, J. B. and L. Hutton. Actors and actresses of Great Britain and the United States. 5 vols New York [1886].
Meisel, M. Perspectives on Victorian and other acting: the actor's last call, or no curtain like the shroud. VS 6 1963.
Melville, J. Ellen and Edy: a biography of Ellen Terry and her daughter, Edith Craig 1847–1947. 1988, New York 1988.
Modjeska, H. Memories and impressions of Helena Modjeska. 1910, New York 1969.
Molloy, J. F. The life and adventures of Edmund Kean. 2 vols 1888, 1897.
Mosely, B. L. Miss Alma Murray as Beatrice Cenci. 1887.
Munden, T. S. Memoirs of Joseph Shepherd Munden, by his son. 1844, 1846.
Murray, C. Robert William Elliston manager: a theatrical biography. 1975.
Neilson, J. Time for remembrance. 1941.
Northcott, R. Adah Isaac Menken. 1921.
'An Old Playgoer'. William Terriss. Theatre Dec 1882.
'An Old Stager' (J. S. Hodson). A complete guide to the stage and manual for amateurs and actors. [1851.]
'An Old Stager' (Matthew Mackintosh). Stage reminiscences. Glasgow 1866.
Oxberry, W. Oxberry's dramatic biography. 7 vols 1825–7.
Parsons, Mrs Clement. The incomparable Siddons. 1909.
Pascoe, C. E. The dramatic list. 1879, 1880 (rev and enlarged), 1969, New York 1969.
'Paterson, Peter' (J. G. Bertram). The confessions of a strolling player. 1852; as Behind the scenes 1858, 1859; as Glimpses of real life 1864, Hamden CT 1979.
Paulus, G. Beerbohm Tree and the 'new drama'. UTQ 27 1957.
Peake, R. B. Memoirs of the Colman family. 2 vols 1841.
Pearce, C. E. Madame Vestris and her times. 1923.
Pearson, H. The last actor-managers. 1950.
Beerbohm Tree: his life and laughter. 1955, 1971.
Pemberton, T. E. A memoir of Edward Askew Sothern. 1889, 1889, 1890.
John Hare, comedian 1865–95. 1895.
The Kendals. 1900.
Ellen Terry and her sisters. 1902.
Sir Charles Wyndham. 1904.
Percy, E. Remember Ellen Terry and Edith Craig. 1948.
Peters, M. Mrs Pat: the life of Mrs Patrick Campbell. 1984, New York 1984.
Phelps, W. M. and J. Forbes-Robertson. The life and life-work of Samuel Phelps. 1886.
Playfair, G. W. Kean. 1939.
The prodigy. 1967. On Master Betty.
The flash of lightning: a portrait of Edmund Kean. 1983.
Pollock, Lady J. Macready as I knew him. 1884.
Pollock, W. H. Mr E. A. Sothern. Theatre Mar 1880.
Henry Irving, on and off the stage. 1908.
Prideaux, T. Love or nothing: the life and times of Ellen Terry. New York 1975.
Raby, P. 'Fair Ophelia': a life of Harriet Smithson Berlioz. Cambridge 1982.
Raymond, G. The life and enterprises of Robert William Elliston, comedian. 2 vols 1842–3, 1 vol 1844, 1845, 2 vols 1846, 1851, 1857, New York 1969.
Rede, L. T. The road to the stage. 1827, 1835, 1836, 1868, 1871; New York 1863, 1864, 1872.
Reed, J. W. jr. Browning and Macready: the final quarrel. PMLA 75 1960.
Reid, E. and Herbert Compton. The dramatic peerage. [1890.]
Richardson, J. The Kemble dynasty. History Today 24 1974.
Rinear, D. Alfred Wigan: Victorian realist. ThS 13 1972.
From the artificial towards the real: the acting of William Farren. TN 31 1977.
To submit and patiently to wait: the career of Mrs Stirling. ThS 35 1993.
Ritchie, H. M. Kean versus Macready: Sheridan Knowles's Virginius. ThS 17 1976.
Roberts, Arthur. The adventures of Arthur Roberts. 1895.
Robins, E. Both sides of the curtain. 1940.
Robinson, H. C. Selections from the diary of Henry Crabb Robinson – the London theatre 1811–66. Ed Eluned Brown 1966.
Robinson, J. R and H. H. The life of Robert Coates. 1891. Refers to 'Romeo' Coates.
Robson, W. The old playgoer. 1845, Fontwell, Sussex 1969. Discusses the Kembles, Mrs Jordan, Charles Mathews, Edmund Kean and their contemporaries.
Roston, D. John Philip Kemble's Coriolanus and Julius Caesar: an examination of the prompt copies. TN 23 1968.
Rowell, G. William Terriss and Richard Prince: two players in an Adelphi melodrama. 1987.
Rushmore, R. Fanny Kemble. New York 1970.
Russell, E. R. Irving as Hamlet. 1875, 1875.
Russell, W. C. Representative actors. [1872], 1875, 1883, 1888.
Ryley, S. M. The itinerant, or memoirs of an actor. Vol 1 1808; vols 2, 3, 1809; vol 4 1816; vols 5, 6 1817; vols 7, 8, 9 (as The itinerant in Scotland) 1827; [1860], 1880, vol 1 New York 1810.
St Clare Byrne, M. Charles Kean and the Meininger myth, ThR 6 1964.
St John, C. (ed). Ellen Terry and Bernard Shaw: a correspondence. [1949.]
Saintsbury, H. A. and C. Palmer (ed). We saw him act: a symposium on the art of Sir Henry Irving. 1939, New York 1969.
Salvini, T. Leaves from the autobiography of Tomasso Salvini. 1893.
Sanderson, M. Adam Smith, Sir Herbert Tree and the wages of actors 1890–1914. Business History 27 1985.
Sands, Mollie. Robson of the Olympic. 1979.
Saxon, A. H. The life and art of Andrew Ducrow and the romantic age of the English circus. 1978.
Schultz, S. C. Towards an Irvingesque theory of Shakespearian acting. Quart Jnl of Speech 61 1975.
Scott, C. Kyrle Bellew. Theatre Nov 1882.
John Clayton. Theatre Apr 1888. Further note on Clayton by 'A. C.', The private life of John Clayton, Theatre Apr 1888.
Ellen Terry. New York 1900 (rev).
Shaffer, B. Henry Irving's theories of drama. Ohio State Univ Theatre Coll Bull 15 1968.
Shattuck, C. H. The dramatic collaborations of William Charles Macready. Urbana IL 1938.
(ed). Bulwer and Macready: a chronicle of the early Victorian theatre. Urbana IL 1958.
Macready prompt-books. TN 4 1961.
Mr Macready produces As you like it: a prompt-book study. Urbana IL 1962.
(ed). William Charles Macready's King John: a facsimile prompt-book. Urbana IL 1963.
Shore, F. T. Sir Charles Wyndham. 1908.
Shuttleworth, B. Irving's Macbeth. TN 5 1951.
Shuttleworth, H. C. (ed). The diary of an actress, or the realities of stage life. 1885. Refers to Alma Ellerslie.
Siddons, H. Practical illustrations of rhetorical gesture and action. 1807, 1822, New York 1969.
Sillard, R. S. Barry Sullivan and his contemporaries. 1901.
Simpson, H. and Mrs C. Brown. A century of famous actresses 1750–1850. [1913.]
[Smith, C. W.] The art of acting. [1855], New York 1855, Boston [1856].

Smythe, A. J. The life of William Terriss. 1898.
Soldene, E. My theatrical and musical recollections. 1897, 1897, 1898, 1906.
Sothern, E. H. The melancholy tale of me: my remembrances.... New York 1916.
Sprague, A. C. Shakespeare and the actors: the stage business in his plays 1660–1905. Cambridge MA 1944.
Shakespearian players and performances. Cambridge MA 1953.
Stedman, J. W. General utility: Victorian actor-authors from Knowles to Pinero. Educational Theatre 24 1972.
Stebbins, E. Charlotte Cushman. Boston 1878.
Steen, M. A pride of Terrys: family saga. [1962.]
Stoker, B. Personal reminiscences of Henry Irving. 2 vols New York 1906.
Actor managers. Nineteenth Cen June 1890.
Stokes, J., M. Booth and S. Bassnett. Bernhardt, Terry, Duse. Cambridge 1988.
Stuart, C. Clara Morris. Theatre Mar 1881.
Symons, A. Plays, acting and music. 1903.
Taylor, G. Players and performances in the Victorian theatre. Manchester 1989, New York 1989. Discusses the major performance styles and their exponents.
Templeton, W. The strolling player. 1802.
Terriss, Ellaline. By herself and with others. 1928.
Just a little bit of string. 1955.
Terry, Ellen. The story of my life. 1908, Woodbridge CT 1982.
Memoirs, with additional chapters by E. Craig and C. St John. 1933, New York 1969.
Thomas, J. The art of the actor-manager: Wilson Barrett and the Victorian theatre. Ann Arbor MI 1984.
Thomas, J. B. Charley's aunt's father: a life of Brandon Thomas. 1955.
Tomalin, C. Mrs Jordan's profession: the story of a great actress and a future king. 1994.
Toole, J. L. Reminiscences of J. L. Toole, related by himself and chronicled by J. Hatton. 2 vols 1889 (3 edns), 1890, 1892 (abbreviated).
Tree, Herbert Beerbohm. Hamlet, from an actor's prompt book. 1897.
Thoughts and afterthoughts. 1913, 1915.
Nothing matters. 1917.
Trewin, J. C. Mr Macready: a nineteenth-century tragedian and his theatre. [1955.]
Benson and the Bensonians. 1960.
Turner, H. Recollections of Ryder. Theatre May 1885. Refers to John Ryder. With a further note by A Correspondent in Our Omnibus-box, Theatre June 1885.
Vandenhoff, G. Leaves from an actor's notebook. New York 1860, London 1860 (as Dramatic reminiscences), 1865 (as An actor's notebooks); tr Ger 1860.
'Veteran Stager' (G. Grant). An essay on the science of acting. 1828.
Vincent, W. T. Recollections of Fred Leslie. 1893.
Wagner, L. How to get on the stage. 1899.
Waitzkin, L. The witch of Wych Street: a study of the theatrical reforms of Madame Vestris. Cambridge MA 1933.
Wallack, L. Memories of fifty years. New York 1889, 1969.
Walsh, Townsend. The career of Dion Boucicault. New York 1915.
Watson, E. B. From Sheridan to Robertson. Cambridge MA 1926, New York 1963.
[Wemyss, F. C.] Twenty-six years of the life of an actor and manager. New York 1847, Glasgow 1848 (as Theatrical biography or the life of an actor and manager).
West, E. T. The London stage 1870–90: a study of the old and new schools of acting. Univ of Colorado Stud ser B 2 1943.
Whyte, F. Actors of the century. 1898.
Williams, C. J. Madame Vestris: a theatrical biography. 1973.
Williams, J. A. Memoirs of John Philip Kemble, Esq. 1817.
Williamson, J. Charles Kemble, man of the theatre. 1970.
Wilmeth, D. B. George Frederick Cooke, Machiavel of the stage. 1980, Westport CT 1980.
Winter, W. Henry Irving. New York 1885.
Ada Rehan. 1898, 1969, New York 1969.
The Jeffersons. 1881, 1969, New York 1969.
The life and art of Edwin Booth. 1894, 1973, New York 1973.
Shakespeare on stage. 3 vols 1911–16. New York 1969. Discusses all the major Eng and Amer performers of the nineteenth century.
Yates, E. H. (ed). The life and correspondence of Charles Mathews the elder. 1860.
Young, J. C. A memoir of Charles Mayne Young. 2 vols 1871.
Ziegler, G. The actress as Shakespearian critic: three nineteenth century portraits. ThS 30 1989. Refers to Fanny Kemble, Helen Faucit, Ellen Terry. [VE]

(6) DESIGN

Ainger, A. On the illumination of theatres. Jnl of the Royal Institution of Great Britain 2 1831.
Bean, A. W. Artistic stage interiors. Theatre July 1891.
Blanchard, E. L. Scenery and scene-painters. Era Almanack 1871.
Booth, M. R. Victorian spectacular theatre 1850–1910. 1981.
(ed). Victorian theatrical trades: articles from The Stage 1883–84. 1981.
Campbell, L. B. A history of costuming on the English stage between 1660 and 1823. Wisconsin Univ Stud 2 1918.
Fitzgerald, P. The world behind the scenes. 1881.
On scenic illusion and stage appliances. Jnl of the Soc of the Arts 1887.
Harris, A. Art in the theatre: spectacle. Mag of Art 12 1889.
Hunter, J. W. Some research problems in a study of the Corsican brothers. Ohio State Univ Theatre Bull 9 1962.
Jackson, A. S. and J. C. Morrow. Aqua scenes at Sadler's Wells Theatre. Ohio State Univ Theatre Bull 9 1962.
Jackson, R. Alfred Thompson 1831–1894: a forgotton talent. TN 36 1982.
(ed). Victorian theatre: the theatre in its time. 1989.
Lawrence, W. J. Some famous scene painters. Mag of Art Dec 1888.
William Roxby Beverley. DNB Suppl 1 1901.
Lloyds, F. Practical guide to scene painting and painting in distemper. [1875.]
Meisel, M. Realizations: narrative, pictorial, and theatrical arts in nineteenth-century England. Princeton 1983.
Monkhouse, C. Clarkson Stanfield. DNB vol 3 1898.
Nicoll, A. The development of the theatre. 1927, 1937 (rev).
Norris, H. A directory of Victorian scene painters. Theatrephile Mar 1984.
Redgrave, S. Dictionary of artists of the English school. 1878.
Rosenfeld, S. A short history of British scene design. Oxford 1973.
S[charf], G. Jr. Recollections of the scenic effects of Covent Garden Theatre during the season 1838–9. 1839.
Southern, R. Trickwork in the English nineteenth-century theatre. Life & Letters May 1939.
Benwell on Victorian scene-painting. TN 1 1946.
Théodore de Banville and the Hanlon Lees troupe. TN 2 1948.
The picture-frame proscenium of 1880. TN 5 1951.
Changeable scenery: its origins and development in the British theatre. 1952.
Stoker, B. Irving and stage lighting. Nineteenth Cent May 1911.
Strange, E. F. Scenery of Charles Kean's plays. Mag of Art 1902.
Telbin, W. The painting of scenery. Mag of Art 12 1889.
Art in the theatre: scenery. Mag of Art 12 1889.
Van der Merwe, P. The spectacular career of Clarkson Stanfield 1793–1867. Tyne and Wear County Council Museums 1978.

Wilde, O. Shakespeare and stage costume. Nineteenth Cent May 1885.
The truth of masks. Intentions. 1891. [HH]

(7) THEATRICAL PERIODICALS

The dramatic censor: or weekly theatrical report. Vols 1–2 1800. Weekly. Continued as The dramatic censor: or monthly epitome of taste, fashion and manners, vols 3–4 1800–1, monthly. Continued as The dramatic and literary censor, vol 4 monthly, vol 5 weekly 1801.
Authentic memoirs of the green room. Vols 1–4 [1801]–4. Annually.
The theatrical repertory. Nos 1–24 1801–2. Weekly. Nos 25–8 1802. Irregularly.
The Glasgow theatrical register. Vols 1–4 Glasgow 1803. Weekly.
The pic nic. Nos 1–14 1803. Weekly. [Ed W. Combe.] Later incorporated in The cabinet, 1803.
The Edinburgh theatrical censor. Nos 1–12 Edinburgh 1803. Irregularly, nos 10–12 weekly.
The man in the moon. Nos 1–21 1803–4. Bi-weekly. Nos 22– 1804. Weekly.
The townsman: addressed to the inhabitants of Manchester on the-atricals. Nos 1–24 Manchester 1803–5. Weekly until no 17, then irregularly.
Argus: or the theatrical observer. Nos 1–7 Manchester 1804–5. Irregularly.
Stage: or theatrical touchstone. [Nos 1–4] 1805. Fortnightly but irregular.
The theatrical recorder. Nos 1–12 1805–6. Monthly. Ed Thomas Holcroft.
The thespian review. Nos 1–7 Manchester 1806. Weekly.
The Liverpool dramatic censor: or theatrical recorder. Nos 1–4 Liverpool 1806. Weekly.
The theatrical review. Nos [1–3] 1807. Monthly.
The Lincoln dramatic censor. Nos 1–4 Lincoln 1809. Weekly.
The dramatic censor: or critical and biographical illustration of the British stage. Nos [1–3] 4–6 1811. Irregularly.
The Irish dramatic censor. Nos [1–2] 3–6 Dublin 1811–12.
The scourge: or monthly expositor of imposture and folly. [Nos 1–40] 1811–14. Continued as The scourge: or literary, theatrical and miscellaneous magazine, [nos 1–26] 1814–16. Continued as The scourge and satirist, [nos 1–4] 1816, monthly.
The theatrical inquisitor: or literary mirror. Vol 1 1812–13. Monthly. Continued as The theatrical inquisitor and monthly mirror, vols 2–14 1813–19. Continued as The theatrical inquisitor, vols 15–16; n.s. vol 1 1819–20. Monthly.
Theatre. Nos 1–[8] Edinburgh 1813–[14]. Weekly.
Dramatic review and register of fine arts. Nos 1–3 1814. Weekly.
The monthly theatrical reporter: or literary mirror. Nos 1–4 [5–10] 1814–15. Monthly.
The stage. Vols 1–3 1814–15; n.s. vol 1 1815–16. Weekly.
The prompter: or theatrical investigator. Nos 1–19 Manchester 1815–16. Weekly.
Theatrical gazette. No 1 1815. Daily.
The Covent-Garden theatrical gazette. Nos 1–148 1816–17. Nos 1–11 tri-weekly; nos 12–13 daily; nos 14–22 five days a week; nos 23–148 six days a week. Ed W. Leggett.
Drury-Lane theatrical gazette. Nos 1–148 [1816–17]. 1816 three days a week; 1817 six days a week.
The prompter prompted: or the theatrical investigator dissected. Nos 1–5 Manchester 1816. [Undated.]
The thespian critique: or theatrical censor. Nos 1–5 Edinburgh 1816. Weekly.
The British stage and literary cabinet. Vols 1–6 1817–22. Monthly. [Vol 5] ed T. Kenrick.
The theatrical gazette: or nightly reflector of the theatres royal Covent Garden and Drury Lane. No 1 1818. Daily.
The thespian censor: or weekly dramatic journal. Nos 1–3 Edinburgh 1818. Weekly.
Grim typo, the Tyne demon. Nos 1–3 Newcastle upon Tyne 1818. Monthly.
The inspector: a weekly dramatic paper. Nos 1–4 1819. Ed J. B. Collis.
The theatre: or dramatic and literary mirror. Nos 1–9 1819. Weekly. Nos 10–23 1819. Fortnightly.
Keene's theatrical evening mirror. Nos 1–25 [1820]. Tri-weekly, later daily.
The London magazine and monthly critical and dramatic review. Nos 1–12 1820. Continued as The London magazine and theatrical inquisitor, nos [13]–18 1821, monthly. Continued as The London magazine, no 19 1821.
The new dramatic censor: or monthly epitome of taste, fashion and manners. No 1 1820.
The theatrical observer: or thespian critique. No 1 [Glasgow] 1820.
The stage. Nos 1–30 Dublin 1821. Daily. Ed F. W. Conway and J. T. Haydn.
The drama: or theatrical pocket magazine. Vols 1–7 1821–5, monthly. n.s. vol 1 1825, fortnightly (weekly from no 11).
Thalia's tablet and Melpomene's memorandum-book: or Orpheus's olio: or the album of all sorts. No 1 1821. Weekly.
The theatrical observer. Nos 1–35 1821. Daily. Continued as The theatrical observer and daily bills of the play, nos 1–16,950 1821–76, daily.
The theatrical observer. Vols 1–16 Dublin 1821–3. Daily. From vol 9 called Nolan's theatrical observer, the longest lived of several competing periodicals of this title.
The independent theatrical observer. Vols 10–11 Dublin 1822. Daily. This was intended as a continuation of The original theatrical observer, which was in fact continued.
The theatrical looker-on. Nos 1–25 Birmingham 1822–3. Weekly.
The mirror of the stage: or the new dramatic censor. Nos 1–24 1822–4. Fortnightly to no 22, then every three weeks. n.s. nos 1–12 1823–4, every three weeks to no 2, then fortnightly to nos 10–11, then every three weeks. Continued as The mirror of the stage and new theatrical inquisitor, nos 13–24 1824, every three weeks to no 16, then mostly monthly.
The thespian. Nos 1–15 Bristol 1823. Weekly.
The Birmingham reporter: and theatrical review. Nos 1–14 Birmingham 1823. Weekly.
The dramatic observer and musical review. No 1 1823. Daily.
The literary humbug: or weekly take-in. Nos 1–6 1823. Weekly.
The Edinburgh theatrical observer and musical review. Nos 1–155 Edinburgh 1823–4. Daily.
The Newcastle theatrical observer. Nos 1–6 Newcastle 1824. Bi-weekly.
The Glasgow theatrical observer. Nos 1–6 Glasgow 1824. Weekly. Nos 7–12 1824, irregularly. Nos 13–16 1824, weekly.
The Birmingham spectator. Nos 1–24 Birmingham 1824. Weekly.
The theatrical John Bull. Nos 1–21 [Birmingham] 1824–[5]. Weekly.
The theatrical note-book. No 1 Birmingham 1824.
The Edinburgh dramatic recorder. Nos 1–12 Edinburgh 1825. Weekly.
The Glasgow dramatic review. Nos 1–14 [Glasgow] 1825. Daily.
Oxberry's dramatic biography and histrionic anecdotes. Nos 1–108 1825–7. Weekly. Ed William and Mrs C. Oxberry. Continued as Oxberry's dramatic biography or the green room spy. n.s. nos 1–16; 17–25 1827, weekly.
The Roscius: consisting of original memoirs .... Nos 1–7 1825. Nos 1–4 fortnightly, then irregularly.
The theatrical mince pie. Nos 1–8 1825. Weekly.
The Norwich theatrical observer. Nos 1–42 Norwich 1827. Ed A. T. Fayerman.

The theatrical mirror: or daily record. Nos 1–31 1827. Daily. Continued as The theatrical mirror: or daily bills of the performances, nos 32–6 1827, daily.
The theatrical examiner. Nos 1–5 Newcastle 1827. Weekly.
The Edinburgh dramatic and musical magazine. Nos 1–3 [Edinburgh] [1827]. Weekly.
The Edinburgh dramatic review. Nos 1–50[i.e. 49] Edinburgh 1827. Weekly.
Stratford theatrical review. Nos 1–10 Stratford-on-Avon 1827–8. Weekly.
The Plymouth theatrical spy: or a pair of spectacles for the manager. Nos 1–8 Plymouth 1828. Weekly.
The Manchester theatrical censor. Nos 1–6 Manchester 1828. Continued as The theatrical censor, no 7 1828, monthly.
The Edinburgh dramatic journal: or theatrical observer. Nos 1–11 Edinburgh 1828. Weekly to no 3, then bi-weekly.
The Edinburgh dramatic tête-à-tête. Nos 1–42 Edinburgh 1828. Daily.
The weekly dramatic review. Nos 1–6 Edinburgh 1828. Weekly.
The censor. Nos 1–16 1828–9. Bi-weekly.
The stage: or theatrical inquisitor. Nos 1–13 1828. Monthly. Nos 4–11 1828–9, fortnightly.
The dramatic register. Nos 1–10 Newcastle 1828–9. Weekly.
The monthly theatrical review. Nos 1–4 [1829]. Monthly.
The dramatic censor. Nos 1–79[i.e. 78] Edinburgh 1829. Daily, nos 28–38 bi-weekly.
The opera glass. Nos 1–27 Glasgow 1829–30. Weekly.
The thistle: or literary, theatrical and police reporter. Vols 1–3 Glasgow 1829–32. Weekly.
The theatrical Argus. No 1 [Birmingham] 1830.
The theatrical tattler. Nos 2–3 Birmingham 1830.
The new opera glass: or theatrical tribunal. Nos 1–7 Glasgow 1830–1. Weekly.
The tatler: a daily journal of literature and the stage. Nos 1–493 1830–2. n.s. nos 1–592 1832. Daily. Ed Leigh Hunt et al.
The British stage: or dramatic censor. Nos 1–3 1831. Monthly.
The theatre: containing a review of the performances at the Theatre Royal, &c. No 1 Edinburgh 1831.
The theatrical speculum and musical review. Nos 1–9 Edinburgh 1831. Weekly.
The theatrical rod! Nos 1–2 [1831?]. Weekly.
The Edinburgh theatrical casket. No 1 Edinburgh 1831.
The Liverpool dramatic journal. No 1 Liverpool [1832].
The theatrical record. No 1 Edinburgh 1833. Weekly.
The theatrical Athenaeum. No 1 1833.
The theatrical examiner. Nos 1–10 Glasgow 1833–4.
The prompter: or theatrical and concert guide. No 1 1834. Weekly.
The Liverpool dramatic censor. No 1 Liverpool 1834.
Paul Pry in Liverpool. No 1 Liverpool [1834].
The Edinburgh theatrical and musical review. Nos 1–34 Edinburgh 1835. Weekly.
The theatrical visitor. Nos 1–6 Glasgow [1835]. Weekly.
The London amusement guide and theatrical reporter. Nos 1–56 1835–6. Weekly.
Liverpool thespian register and mirror of the stage. No 1 Liverpool [1836].
The dramatic spectator. Nos 1–10 Edinburgh 1837. Weekly.
Actors by daylight: or pencilings in the pit. Nos 1–43 1838. Continued as Actors by daylight and miscellany of the drama, music and literature, nos 44–55 1838–9, weekly.
Actors by Gaslight: or 'Boz' in the boxes. Nos 1–37 1838. Weekly.
The era. Vols 1–103 1838–1939. Weekly.
The theatrical register and general amusement guide. Nos 1–5 1838. Mostly weekly.
The theatrical journal and stranger's guide. Nos 1–159 1839–42. Weekly. Continued as The theatrical journal, nos 160–263 1843–4. Continued as The theatrical journal: a weekly review of the drama, music &c, nos 264–315 1845. Continued as The theatrical journal: a weekly review . . . , nos 316–420 1846–8. Continued as The theatrical review: a weekly review of amusements by gentlemen of acknowledged talent, nos 528–1098 1850–60; nos 1099–1516 1861–8; nos 1517–1672 1869–71; nos 1673–1747 1872–3.
The pepper-box: containing criticisms on theatricals and other amusements. Nos 1–21 [Glasgow] 1840. Weekly.
The opera-glass. Nos 1–29 Edinburgh 1840–1. Weekly.
The lyre: a musical and theatrical register. Nos 1–22 1841. Weekly.
The Edinburgh dramatic censor. Nos 1–3 Edinburgh 1842. Weekly.
The Cicerone: a record of the drama, music and fine arts. Nos 1–24 [1843–4]. Weekly.
The critic: a journal of theatricals, music and exhibitions. No 1 1843. Continued as The critic, nos 2–19 1843–4, weekly.
Oxberry's weekly budget of plays and magazine of romance . . . . Nos 1–52 1843–4. Weekly. Continued as Oxberry's weekly budget of plays and dramatic recorder . . . , nos 53–79 1844.
The stage: a weekly magazine of plays and players. Nos 1–14 1844–5.
The Glasgow dramatic review. Nos 1–54 Glasgow 1844–6. Fortnightly, occasionally weekly.
The theatrical critic. Nos 1–2 [Glasgow] 1845. Fortnightly.
The Birmingham musical examiner and dramatic review. Nos 1–19 Birmingham 1845–6. Weekly.
The Liverpool dramatic Argus. Nos 1–6 Liverpool 1846. Weekly.
The drama: a companion to the stage and concert room. Nos 1–22 1846. Continued as The drama, nos 3–4 1846. Continued as The drama: a companion to the theatre and concert room, nos 5–7 1846. Weekly.
The drama. Nos 1–3 Glasgow 1847. Weekly.
The dramatic review. Nos 1–2 Glasgow 1847. Every Wednesday.
The dramatic mirror and review of music and fine arts. Nos 1–137 1847–8. Weekly.
Dramatic review. Nos 1–8 [1848]. Weekly.
The opera-glass: a weekly public amusement guide. Nos 1–9 Glasgow 1848. Weekly.
The stage and literary and musical review. [No 1] Glasgow 1848. Weekly.
The scene shifter: or dramatic indicator and panorama of life as it is. Nos 1–3 1848. Weekly.
Theatrical Paul Pry. Vol 1 1848. Weekly.
The Glasgow dramatic review. Nos 1–54 Glasgow 1844–8. Fortnightly.
The Manchester dramatic and musical review. Nos 1–43 Manchester 1846–7. Weekly.
The Euterpean: a critical review of music and the drama . . . . Nos 1–14 1849. Weekly.
The stage: a weekly magazine of generalities . . . . Nos 1–[2–14] 1849. Weekly [from no 2].
The stage-manager: a journal of dramatic literature and criticism. Nos 1–20 1849. Weekly [from no 4]. N.s. nos 1–14 1849–50. Continued as The literary review and stage manager, n.s. nos 1–11 1850.
The theatrical programme and entr'acte. Nos 1–12 1849. Weekly. Continued as the theatrical mirror and playgoer's companion, nos 13[i.e. 1], 2–6 1849. Weekly.
The printer's devil. Nos 1–4 [Edinburgh] 1850. Continued as The Edinburgh general review, no 5 1850. Continued as The London and Edinburgh general review, nos 6–14 1850. Weekly.
The playgoer and public amusement guide. Nos 1–7 [Glasgow] 1850. Weekly.
Tallis's dramatic magazine and general theatrical and musical review. 1850–1. Monthly. Continued as Tallis's drawing room table book of theatrical portraits, memoirs and anecdotes 1851. Continued as Tallis's Shakspere [*sic*] gallery of engravings 1851–2.

The manager's circular: or general theatrical directory. No 1 1851. [Ed Henry Butler.]

Dramatic register. [Nos 1–3] 1851–4. Annually.

The dramatic review. Nos 1–10 Edinburgh 1851–2. Weekly.

The weekly review and dramatic critic. Nos 1–45 Edinburgh 1852–3. Weekly.

Dramatic spectator and Glasgow musical and public amusement guide. Nos 1–7 Glasgow 1853. Fortnightly.

The entr'acte: a daily programme of theatrical and other public entertainments. Nos 1–120 1859–60. Daily. Continued as The daily director and entr'acte, nos 121–432 1859–60.

The evening programme: a programme of theatrical and other public entertainments. No 181 1859. Continued as The evening programme and entr'acte: a journal of the drama, music, fine arts &c, no 222 1860.

Illustrated sporting news and theatrical and musical review. Nos 1–186 1862–5. Weekly. Continued as Illustrated sporting news theatrical review, nos 187–93 1865, weekly. Continued as Illustrated sporting and theatrical news, nos 194–364 1865–9, weekly. n.s. nos 1–44 1869–70, weekly.

The orchestra: a weekly journal of music and the drama. Nos 1–52 1863–4. Continued as The orchestra: a weekly review of music and the drama, nos 53–260 1864–8. Continued as The orchestra: a weekly review: musical, dramatic, literary, nos 261–561 1869–74. Continued as The orchestra: a monthly review: musical, dramatic, literary, n.s. nos 1–72 1874–80. Continued as The orchestra and the choir: a monthly review: musical, dramatic and literary, n.s. nos 73–98 1880–2. Continued as The orchestra, choir, and musical education: a monthly review: musical, educational, dramatic and literary, n.s. nos 99–122 1882–4. Continued as The orchestra musical review: a weekly record of art, education and the drama, &c, n.s. nos 123–213 1884–6. Continued as Orchestra musical review: a record of musical art, education, the drama, &c, n.s. nos 214–30 1886–7, monthly.

Boosey's musical and dramatic review. Nos 1–9 1864. Weekly. Continued as The musical and dramatic review, nos 10–14 1864, weekly.

The prompter (of Liverpool): theatrical and universal advertiser. No 18 Liverpool 1865.

The dramatic telegram music and the drama. Nos 1–14 [1865–6]. Fortnightly.

The era almanack. 1868–9. Annually. Continued as The era almanack and annual, 1870–1905. Continued as The era almanack and annual, 1906–13. Continued as The era annual, 1914–19. Annually.

The music halls' gazette: a journal of intercommunication between music hall managers, their artistes at home and abroad, and the public. Nos 1–36 1868. Weekly.

Pictorial sporting and theatrical guide and record of music, literature and fine arts. Nos 1041–4 1868. Weekly.

The London entr'acte: illustrated theatrical and musical critic and advertiser. Nos 1–137 1870–2. Weekly. Continued as The entr'acte theatrical and musical critic and advertiser, nos 138–306 1872–5. Continued as The entr'acte and limelight, nos 307–1,974 1875–1907, weekly.

The vaudeville magazine. Nos 1–5 1871–2. Monthly.

The wandering thespian annual. No [2] 1871. Ed Walter Stephens.

Figaro-programme. n.s. nos 1–49 1874–5. Weekly. Continued as The London programme and sketch book, nos 50–1 1875. Continued as The Saturday programme and sketch book, nos 52–181 1875. Weekly.

The illustrated sporting and dramatic news. Nos 1–3,587 1874–1943. Weekly then fortnightly.

The lorgnette programme. Nos 1–2 1874. Continued as The lorgnette programme dramatic and musical critic, nos 3–5 1874. Weekly.

The dramatic art circular. No 1 1875. Monthly. Ed Charles Sleigh.

The programme and dramatic review. Nos 1–2 1875.

The theatre: a weekly critical review. Vols 1–3 1877–8. Continued as The theatre: a monthly review and magazine, n.s. vols 1–3 1878–9. Continued as The theatre: a monthly review of the drama, music, and the fine arts, n.s. vols 1–6 1880–2. Ed Clement Scott. n.s. vols 1–30 1883–97.

The curtain: a weekly programme and review of the drama. Nos 1–2 1878. Continued as The curtain: a programme and review of the drama. Nos 3–10 1878. Weekly.

The manager's guide and artistes' advertiser. Nos 1–23 Manchester 1878. Weekly.

Dramatic notes: an illustrated handbook of the London theatres. 1879. Continued as Dramatic notes: an illustrated year-book of the London stage, 1880–1. Continued as Dramatic notes: an illustrated year-book of the stage, 1881–2. Ed A. Brereton 1882–7. Annually until 1893.

The Saturday musical review. Nos 1–42 1879. Weekly.

The green room. Nos 1–2 1880. Weekly.

The prompter: a journal for amateur actors and authors. Nos 1–4 1880. Weekly.

The stage directory. Nos 1–14 1880–1. Monthly. Continued as The stage No 1–   1881– , weekly.

The actor and the elocutionist: a journal of elocutionary, literary, dramatic, musical and general interest. No 1 1881.

The play: a chronicle of the London stage. Nos 1–119 1881–4. Weekly.

The theatrical world. Vol 1 nos 1–23; vol 2 nos 1–3 1881–2. Weekly.

The dramatic album of 'Quiz' for 1882. Glasgow [1883]. Continued as Quiz album for 1883, [1883].

The general theatrical programme. Nos 1–52 1883–4. Weekly. Continued as The theatrical programme, nos 53–113 1884–6, weekly.

The theatrical times. Nos 1–22 1883–4. Weekly [from no 3].

The Birmingham and Midlands musical journal and dramatic news. Nos 1–18 [Birmingham] 1884–5. Weekly.

The fly paper: a satirical, dramatic, musical and sporting journal. No 1 [1884].

The theatrical and musical guide. Nos [1–15] [1884–6]. Monthly.

The theatrical managers' register. Nos 1–2 1884.

Walter's theatrical and sporting directory. [Vols 1–5] [1884–8]. Annually.

The wings: a monthly record of general theatrical and musical information and events. No 1 1884. Monthly. Ed Charles Sleigh.

The Birmingham dramatic news: an illustrated record of the Midland stage. Nos 1–12 [Birmingham] 1885. Weekly.

The bat. Nos 1–153 1885–8. Weekly. Ed James Davis.

The dramatic review. Vols 1–17 1885–94. Weekly.

Interlude: the organ of the variety profession. Nos 1–25 1885–6. Weekly.

Sock and buskin. Nos 1–2 1885.

M.H.A.A. [music hall artistes' association] gazette. Nos 1–42 1886–7. Weekly.

The artiste: music hall gossip, theatrical and general news. Nos 1–18 1887. Weekly.

Entertainment gazette and guide to London. Nos 1–41 1887–8. Fortnightly until 12, then weekly.

The playgoers' pocket book. Vols [1–2] [1887–8]. Annually.

Murray's entertainment guide. [Nos 1–?] [188?–?]. Monthly. Continued as The entertainment guide, nos 19–? 1890–?, monthly. Continued as Reid's London entertainment guide, nos 45–503 1892–1931, monthly.

The playgoer: a leaflet for playgoers. Nos 1–27 1888–90. Mostly monthly.

The playgoers' magazine. Nos 1–3 [1888]. Monthly. Ed Paul Vedder.

The music hall. Nos 1–1,229 1889–1912. Weekly.

The prompter and the footlights: a music hall and theatrical review. No 1 [1889].
The weekly comedy: a review of the drama, music and literature. Nos 1–11 1889. Ed J. T. Grein and C. W. Jarvis.
The foot-lights. Nos 1–11 1890.
The actor. No 1 1891.
Dramatic opinions: an impartial weekly leaflet for players and play-goers. Nos 1–28 1891–2. Weekly, nos 26–8 monthly.
The encore: a music hall and theatrical review. Nos 1–1,972 1892–1930. Weekly.
The sporting and dramatic mirror. n.s. no 1 1892. Continued as The sporting mirror and dramatic and music hall record, n.s. nos 2–441 1892–1900, weekly.
The prompter: the organ of the Scottish amateur dramatic and musical federation. Nos 1–5 Glasgow 1892–3. Monthly. Continued as The prompter: an illustrated dramatic and musical record, n.s. nos 1–21 1893, monthly until end July, then weekly.
Birmingham amusements and souvenir of the stage. Nos 2–65 [Manchester and Birmingham] 1893–4.
The theatrical 'world' for 1893. 1893–7. Annually. By W. Archer 1893–4.
Paisley society and dramatic mirror. Nos 1–3 Paisley [1894]. Weekly.
The Glasgow pantomime annual and theatrical review. Glasgow 1894–5. Continued as The Glasgow theatrical annual, 1895–1901, annually.
The dramatic world: a monthly epitome of the stage. Vols 1–3 1894–7. Continued as The dramatic illustrated world, vols 3–9 1897–1902, monthly. Ed E. and H. Gordon-Clifford.
The graphic guide to the London theatres. Nos 1–7 1894.
Pearson's photographic portfolio of footlight favourites by eminent photographers. Nos 1–8 1894–5; n.s. nos 1–5 1895–6. Monthly.
Boorman's theatrical directory of the United Kingdom, 1895. Vol 1 1895.
The dramatic times: the only organ devoted to amateur theatricals. Nos 1–13 1895. Fortnightly.
The London Bridge theatre diary and amusement list. Nos 2–7 1895. Monthly.
The Glasgow harlequin. Nos 1–5 Glasgow [1895–6]. Weekly.
The stage news: the new theatrical paper. Nos 1–2 Glasgow 1897. Weekly. Continued as The stage news and musical notes, nos 3–8 1897.
The playgoer: a journal of amusement. Nos 1–14 1897–8. Weekly.
The programme and playbill. Nos 1–197 1898–9. Daily.
Theatrical and music hall life. No 1 1898.
The theatrical public guide. Nos 1–7 1898. Monthly.
Theatrical and public life. Nos 1–8 1898–9. Monthly, weekly in Mar.
Variety and 'variety critic'. Nos 1–13 1898. Weekly. Ed Bernard Hounsell.
The Anglo-French stage chronicle. Nos 1–2 1899. Every Friday. Continued as The Anglo-French chronicle: political, literary and theatrical, no 3 1899, every Saturday, bilingual.
Beltaine: the organ of the Irish literary theatre. No 1–3 1899–1900. Ed W. B. Yeats.
Footlights: the bulletin of the London and New York dramatic exchange. No 1 1899.
The Irish playgoer. Nos 1–30 Dublin 1899–1900.
The London theatre, entertainment and concert guide. Nos [1]–16 1900–1. Continued as The London theatre, concert and fine art guide, nos 17–623, weekly from no 2.

For further titles to this summary list, see C. J. Stratman, A bibliography of British dramatic periodicals *1962; and J. F. Arnott and J. W. Robinson,* English theatrical literature 1559–1900; a bibliography, *1969.* [BJO'C]

(8) COLLECTIONS OF PLAYS

The plays to be found in many of the early collections listed were usually sold individually as well as in bound vols. In the larger edns there are occasional discrepancies between extant bound sets. For more information on some principal British nineteenth-century acting edns and the problems of bibliographical description, see two articles by R. C. Rhodes, Library *4th ser 16 1936. See also* Nicoll *7, pp. 357–64, and* Readex Index, *pp. 314–36. The short titles given at the end of entries are used throughout the Drama section.*

The British drama: comprehending the best plays in the English language. 3 vols London and Edinburgh 1804.
The English and American stage. 35 vols New York 1807.
The British theatre: or a collection of plays, which are acted at the theatres royal, Drury Lane, Covent Garden, and Haymarket. Ed E. Inchbald 25 vols 1808; 20 vols 1824 (new edn). *Inchbald.*
A collection of farces and other afterpieces which are acted at the theatres royal, Drury-Lane, Covent-Garden and Haymarket. Ed E. Inchbald 7 vols 1809, 1815. *Inchbald Farces.*
The modern theatre: a collection of successful modern plays, as acted at the theatres royal, London. Ed E. Inchbald 10 vols 1811. *Inchbald Mod Th.*
The rejected theatre: or a collection of dramas which have been offered for representation but declined by the managers of the playhouses. [c. 15 nos] 1814.
The new British theatre: a selection of original dramas, not yet acted; some of which have been offered for representation, but not accepted; with critical remarks by the editor [John Galt]. 4 vols 1814–15. An expanded version of The rejected theatre, *above.*
The London theatre. Ed T. J. Dibdin 12 vols 1815.
The London theatre: a collection of the most celebrated dramatic pieces, correctly given, from copies used in the theatres. Ed T. Dibdin 26 vols 1815–18. An expanded version of The London theatre, *above.*
The British drama: a collection of the most esteemed dramatic productions, with biography of the respective authors, and critique on each play. Ed R. Cumberland 14 vols 1817.
The new English drama. Ed W. Oxberry; with prefatory remarks, stage business and stage directions. Issued as separate plays, two per month, with dated title pages, 1818–24, 20 vols (also 21, 22-vol sets) 1818–25; (as Oxberry's edition and in different vol configuration) Boston 1819–26?. *Oxberry.*
[John] Duncombe's new acting drama. 12 nos [one play each] 1821–5.
[Thomas] Dolby's British theatre. 12 vols 1823–5. Contains 84 plays, each with separate title page. Continued as Cumberland, *below,* with same vol nos. *Dolby.*
The British drama: a collection of the most approved tragedies, comedies, operas, and farces. 2 vols 1824.
The British drama: a collection of the most esteemed tragedies, comedies, operas and farces in the English language. 2 vols 1824–6, 1828–9, 1831; Philadelphia 1832, 1833, 1837, 1838, 1842, 1850, 1854, 1859. A variant of the above. *BD.*
The London stage: a collection of the most reputed tragedies, comedies, operas, melo-dramas, farces, and interludes. 4 vols [1824–7]. *LSt.*
[John] Cumberland's British theatre, with remarks, biographical and critical, by D.–G. [i.e. George Daniel]. 48 vols 1826–[55?]. Contains 398 plays, each with separate title page, but including many originally issued in Dolby, *above,* and several in Cumberland Minor, *below.* From c. 1849 pbd as Davidson's shilling volume of Cumberland's plays by G. H. Davidson, who amalgamated Cumberland and Cumberland Minor, and assigned new vol nos. Absorbed by Lacy, *below. Cumberland.*
The acting American theatre. [Ed M. Lopez] Philadelphia 1826–?.
British theatre: comprising tragedies, comedies, operas and farces; with biography, critical account and explanatory notes by an Englishman [Owen Williams]. Leipzig 1828; London 1830, 1831 (2nd edn).
Ames series of standard and minor drama. Compiled and pbd by A. D. Ames, Clyde OH. 18o?–.

[John] Duncombe's [acting] edition [of the British theatre]. 67 vols? [1828–52]. *Duncombe.*

[Thomas] Richardson's new minor drama; with remarks, biographical and critical, by W. T. Moncrieff. 4 vols 1828–31. All plays later appeared in Cumberland Minor, *below*, sometimes still under Richardson imprint. *Richardson.*

[John] Cumberland's minor theatre; with remarks biographical and critical, by D.–G. [i.e. George Daniel]. c. 17 vols [1828–43]. *Cumberland Minor.*

[John] Miller's modern acting drama. 1833–7. Noted on several title pages as agent for the Dramatic Authors' Soc. *Miller.*

The acting drama: containing all the popular plays, standard and modern. 1834.

[John] Duncombe's minor theatre. 24 nos [one play each] [1834]. Variant title Duncombe's minor British drama. *Duncombe Minor.*

[Strange's] London acting drama. c. 31 nos 1837–8.

[Webster's] acting national drama; under the auspices of the Dramatic Authors' Society. Ed B. N. Webster 18 vols 1837–[59]. Variant title The acting national drama, comprising every popular new play, farce, melo-drama, opera, burletta, etc, carefully printed from the acting copies. *Webster.*

[James] Pattie's penny play: or weekly acting drama. At least 45 nos [often several plays to each no] [1838–9]. Later pbd as Pattie's modern stage.

[James] Pattie's universal stage: or theatrical prompt book. More than 100 nos [one play each] [1839–45]. From no 33 onwards pbd by William Barth as Barth's universal stage etc. Absorbed by Lacy, *below*. *Pattie; Barth.*

S[amuel] G[lover] Fairbrother's edition [of plays]. [c. 1842–54.] Absorbed by Lacy, *below.*

The British and American theatre: a choice collection of the most favorite dramatic pieces of both nations. Ed H. Croll 12 nos Stuttgart 1842. With notes in Ger.

The modern English comic theatre. Ed L. Hilsenberg, J. A. Diezemann and C. Albrecht 6 ser Leipzig 1843–[90?]. With notes in Ger. *Mod Eng Com Th.*

Modern standard drama: a collection of the most popular acting plays, with critical remarks, also the stage business, costumes, etc. Ed Epes Sargent 21 [at least] vols New York and Baltimore 1846–[56?]. Absorbed by French NY, *below.*

The series of dramatic entertainments performed by royal command... at Windsor Castle 1848–9. Ed B. N. Webster 1849, [1849]. *Dram Ents.*

Pownceby's new acting drama. 1854–5.

Spencer's Boston theatre. [More than?] 24 vols Boston 1855–8. Absorbed by French NY, *below. Boston Th.*

The new British theatre (late Duncombe's). [c. 1860.] Reprint of Duncombe's British theatre by T. H. Lacy, *below. New BT.*

Sergel's acting drama. [More than 500 plays] Chicago c. 1860–99 [or later]. *Sergel.*

[Thomas Hailes] Lacy's acting edition of plays, dramas, extravaganzas, farces etc. Includes sub-series Lacy's home plays, Lacy's home plays for ladies, Sensation series, Anglo-American edn of standard plays etc. 165 vols [1850–1917]. Pbd as single plays. Bought by French (London and New York) in 1872 and continued as French's acting edition (late Lacy's). Later pbd variously as French's acting edition, French's standard drama, French's international copyrighted edition of the best authors, French's standard library edition etc and sub-series Sensation dramas, Temperance dramas, Fairy plays etc. At least 2 ser were pbd in New York (French's American drama, French's minor drama). For contents, *see* Lacy, List of plays wholly or partially the property of T. H. Lacy, 1864, and Samuel French, Descriptive catalogue of plays and dramatic works, from c. 1891 etc.... French's [acting] edition in progress. *Lacy; French; French Int Copyr Edn; French NY; French Minor NY.*

[John Dicks.] The British drama, illustrated. 4 vols 1864–5.

[John Dicks.] The British drama, illustrated. 12 vols 1864–72. A fuller version of The British drama, *above*. Contains 240 plays. *Dicks' BD.*

Selections from the modern British dramatists. 2 vols Leipzig 1867.

Drawing-room plays and parlour pantomimes. Ed C. Scott 1870.

De Witt's acting plays. 21 vols New York [1873?]–84. *De Witt.*

[John] Dicks' standard plays, and free acting drama. 1074 nos [some containing more than one play] [1875–1908]. Mainly comprises reprints of out-of-copyright plays. *Dicks.*

The New York drama. 5 vols New York 1875–[80].

Short plays for drawing-room performance. 1890.

Lynn's acting edition. [At least] 32 nos [1893–6?].

The later English drama. Ed C. S. Brown New York 1898.

Dickinson, T. H. (ed). Chief contemporary dramatists: twenty plays from the recent drama. Boston and New York 1915, [1921] (2nd ser), [1930] (3rd ser).

Quinn, A. H. (ed). Representative American plays. New York 1917, 1938 (6th edn).

Moses, M. J. (ed). Representative British drama, Victorian and modern. Boston 1918 etc, 1931 (new, rev edn). *Moses, Boston.*

Marriott, J. W. (ed). Great modern British plays. 1929.

Morgan, A. E. (ed). English plays, 1660–1820. New York and London 1935.

Rowell, G. (ed). Nineteenth-century plays. Oxford 1953, London 1972 (2nd edn) (WC). *Rowell.*

Brings, L. M. (ed). Gay nineties melodramas. Minneapolis 1963.

Booth, M. (ed). Hiss the villain: six English and American melodramas. 1964. *Booth melodramas.*

Freedley, G. and A. Nicoll (ed). Nineteenth century English and American plays. New Canaan CT 1965– . Micro edn. Since 1975 ed J. Ellis and J. Donohue. Their Readex index catalogues plays issued 1965–81 inclusive. In progress. *Readex micro.*

Bailey, J. O. (ed). British plays of the nineteenth century: an anthology to illustrate the evolution of the drama. New York 1966. *Bailey.*

Ashley, L. R. N. (ed). Nineteenth-century British drama: an anthology of representative plays. Glenville IL 1967.

Corrigan, R. (ed). Laurel British drama: the nineteenth century. New York 1967.

Rowell, G. (ed). Late Victorian plays, 1890–1914. Oxford 1968, London 1972 (2nd edn). *Rowell WC2.*

Salerno, H. (ed). English drama in transition: 1880–1914. New York 1968.

Booth, M. (ed). English plays of the nineteenth century. 5 vols Oxford 1969–76. With substantial introds, rptd separately as Prefaces to English nineteenth-century theatre, Manchester [1980]. *Booth 1 etc.*

Kauvar, G. B. et al. (ed). Nineteenth-century verse drama. Rutherford, Madison, Teaneck NJ 1973.

Booth, M. (ed). The magistrate and other nineteenth-century plays. Oxford 1974. Reprints 9 plays from vols 1–4 of his edn above. *Booth.*

Kilgarriff, M. (ed). The golden age of melodrama: twelve 19th century melodramas. 1974. Some texts abridged. *Kilgarriff.*

Wischhusen, S. (ed). The hour of one: six Gothic melodramas. 1975.

Smith, J. L. (ed). Victorian melodramas: seven English, French and American melodramas. 1976. *Smith.*

Lorenzen, R. (ed). Nineteenth-century popular British drama acting editions. Seattle and London 1977. Micro edn, containing 87 plays from Univ of Washington Lib. *Lorenzen micro.*

Wells, S. (ed). Nineteenth-century Shakespeare burlesques. 5 vols 1977–8. *Shakesp bsqs.*

Banham, M. and P. Thomson (gen eds). British and American playwrights 1750–1920. [16 vols] Cambridge 1982–7. Individual vols devoted to selected works by one or, occasionally, two authors.

Gerould, D. C. (ed). American melodramas. New York 1983.

Cox, J. N. (ed). Seven Gothic melodramas, 1789–1825. Athens OH 1992.
Mayer, D. (ed). Playing out the [Roman] empire: Ben Hur and other toga plays and films. Oxford 1994. *Mayer.*
Booth, M. R. (ed). The lights of London and other Victorian plays. Oxford and New York 1995 (WC). *Booth WC.*
Scullion, A. (ed). Female playwrights of the nineteenth century. 1996.
Taylor, G. (ed). Trilby and other plays. Oxford and New York 1996 (WC). *Taylor WC.* [JRS]

ii. Early nineteenth-century drama 1800–1835

This section has been restricted, with a few exceptions, to writers born between 1760 and 1800. Moreover, here, and in the following sections, cross-references have not usually been included to the unacted poetic dramas of the period, which will be found under Poetry, col 207, above. Plays are listed in order of production, not of pbn and, for the most part, unpbd plays are not included. The following abbreviations have been adopted:

Ba burletta, Bal ballet, Bsq burlesque, C comedy, Ca comedietta, CD comic drama, CO comic opera, D drama, DO dramatic opera, DSk dramatic sketch, Duol duologue, Ent entertainment, Ext extravaganza, F farce, FC farcical comedy, Int interlude, Mat matinée, MD melodrama, Monol monologue, MF musical farce, O opera, Oa operetta, OF operatic farce, P pantomime, Rev Revue, RD romantic drama, Sk sketch, Spec spectacle, T tragedy, TC tragi-comedy, TF tragic farce, Vaud vaudeville *and for theatres, the word 'theatre' being omitted:* Adel Adelphi, Aven Avenue, Brit Brittania, CG Covent Garden, CL Royal City of London, Cob Royal Coburg, Com Comedy, Crit Criterion, DL Drury Lane, DofY Duke of York's, EOH English Opera House, Gai Gaiety, Gar Garrick, Glo Globe, Grec Grecian, H Haymarket, HM Her Majesty's, K Kings, Lyc Lyceum, M'bone Marylebone, NT New Theatre, OH Opera House, Olym Olympic, Pav Pavilion, P'cess Princess's, PW Prince of Wales's, Roy Royalty, RA Royal Amphitheatre, RC Royal Circus, Sav Savoy, StJ St James's, Shaft Shaftesbury, Str Strand, Sur Surrey, SW Sadler's Wells, TR Theatre Royal, Vaud Vaudeville, Vic Victoria. Cumberland, Dicks *etc refer to their collections of plays (listed in full cols 1951–1955, above). References to vols 4, 5 and 7 of A. Nicoll,* A history of English drama, *Cambridge 1955, 1959, 1973, have been abbreviated to* Nicoll; *to C. J. Stratman (ed),* Bibliography of English printed tragedy, *1966, to* Stratman; *to J. P. Wearing,* The London stage 1890–99: a calendar of plays and players, *2 vols Metuchen NJ 1976, and* The London stage 1900–1909, *2 vols 1981, as* Wearing; *to L. W. Conolly and J. P. Wearing,* English drama and theatre, 1800–1900, *Detroit 1978, as* Conolly English drama; *and to J. Ellis, J. Donohue and L. A. Zak (ed),* English drama of the nineteenth century: an index and finding guide. *New Canaan CT 1995 as* Readex Index.

Samuel James Arnold 1774–1852

Auld Robin Gray: a pastoral entertainment, in two acts. CO. (H 26 July 1794). 1794.
The shipwreck: a comic opera, in two acts. (DL 10 Dec 1796). 1796, 1797, 1807 (2 edns), 1820 (2 edns); New York 1805, 1882; Oxberry 9; Cawthorn 29.
The songs, duetts [*sic*], chorusses [*sic*] &c in The shipwreck. 1796.
The Creole: or the haunted island. 3 vols 1796 (Novel).
The veteran tar: or a chip off the old block, a comic opera, in two acts. (DL 29 Jan 1801). 1801. From Pigault-Lebrun's Le petit matelot.
The songs, choruses, &c in The veteran tar. 1801.
'Foul deeds will rise': a musical drama. (H 18 July 1804). 1804. From The traveller's story, in Miss Lee's Canterbury tales.
A prior claim: a comedy, in five acts. (DL 29 Oct 1805). 1805. With Henry J. Pye.
The tyger's theatre. [1808.] (Verse.)
Man and wife: or more secrets than one, a comedy in five acts. (DL 5 Jan 1809). 1809 (8 edns); New York 1809, Philadelphia 1810, Boston 1855; Dicks 575.
Songs, duetts [*sic*], &c chorusses [*sic*] and finales of Up all night! or the smuggler's cave, a comic opera, in three acts. (Lyc 26 June 1809). 1809.
Songs, duetts [*sic*], choruses, finales, &c of The maniac! or the Swiss banditti, a serio comic-opera. (Lyc 13 Mar 1810). [1810].
Songs, duetts [*sic*], chorusses [*sic*] &c in Plots: or the north tower, a melo-dramatic opera in three acts. MD. (L 3 Sep 1810). [1810?]
Songs, duets, trios, chorusses [*sic*] &c in The Americans: a comic opera in three acts. (EOH 27 Mar 1811). [1811?], 1818.
Free and easy: a musical farce in two acts. (Lyc 16 Sep 1816). 1812; Cumberland 42.
Songs, duets, choruses in the operatic romance of The Devil's bridge. (See performance date below.) 1812, 1815, 1818.
Illusion: or the trances of Nourjahad, an oriental romance in three acts. Spec. (DL 25 Nov 1813). 1813.
The jovial crew: or the merry beggars, a comick opera. (Lyc 7 Sep 1815). 1813. Based on The beggar's bush?
The woodman's hut: a melo-dramatic romance, in three acts. (DL 12 Apr 1814). 1814, 1814 [2 edns], 1818; Oxberry 4; [1822], Hodgdon's juvenile drama 1; [1859]. Sub-titled as: or the burning forest, a melodrama in two acts. [1859]. Lacy 36; Dicks 935.
Songs, duetts [*sic*], chorusses [*sic*] in the new operatick anecdote called Frederick the Great: or the heart of a soldier. (Lyc 4 Aug 1814). [1814?], 1815.
Jean de Paris: a comic drama in two acts. F. (DL 1 Nov 1814). 1814. From C. Godard d'Ancour de Saint Just, Jean de Paris.
My aunt: a petite comedy, in two acts. OF. (Lyc 1 Aug 1815). [1815]; Boston 1820, London 1855, New York 1828, Philadelphia 1829; French's Minor Drama 302.
Songs, &c in the musical farce of My aunt. 1815.
Songs, duets, chorusses [*sic*], &c in The King's proxy: a comick opera, in three acts. (Lyc 19 Aug 1815). 1815.
The maid and the magpye: or which is the thief? A musical entertainment, in two acts. (Lyc 21 Aug 1815). 1815. From Caigniez and D'Aubigny, La pie voleuse.
The Devil's bridge: an opera in three acts. (Lyc 6 May 1812). New York 1817; Dublin 1820, London [1825?], [1842]; Cumberland 42.
A letter to all the proprietors of Drury-Lane Theatre, excepting Peter Moore esq. 1818. Letters.
Songs, recitative and duetts [*sic*], trios, chorusses [*sic*] &c in the new grand opera Tarrare: the Tartar Chief. (EOH 15 Aug 1825). [1825.]
Marian: or the prisoner of Elville Castle, a drama in three acts. ([Never performed?]). 1825.
Recitative, songs, duets, chorusses [*sic*] in Tit for tat: or the tables turned, a grand comic opera. (EOH 29 July 1828) [nd.] Adapted from Mozart's Cosé fan tutte.
Forgotten facts in the Memoirs of Charles Mathews, comedian, recalled in a letter to Mrs Mathews, his biographer. [1839.] (Letters).
The sergeant's wife: a drama in two acts. (DL 8 June 1835). Boston 1855.
See also Nicoll *3, pp. 234, 377; 4, pp. 255–6, 569.* [BJO'C]

Joanna Baillie 1762–1851

See col 226.

John Banim 1798–1842

See col 883.

William Barrymore d. 1845

§1

The dog of Montargis: or the Forest of Bondy. D. (CG 30 Sep 1814). Dicks 163. From Pixérécourt, Le chien de Montargis.
Trial by battle: or Heaven defend the right. Spec. (Cob 11 May 1818). Duncombe 8; [1854]; New BT 62.
Wallace, the hero of Scotland. MD. (RA 6 Oct 1817). Duncombe Minor 1; Boston [1856?]; Lacy 73; Dicks 953.
El Hyder, the chief of the Ghaut Mountains. MD. (Cob 7 Dec 1818). Lacy 6; Dicks 140.
Gilderoy: or the bonnie boy. MD. (Cob 25 June 1822). Richardson 2; Cumberland Minor 8.
The secret. Ba. (RA 11 May 1824). [1854]; Lacy 48; New BT 478.
The two sisters. D. Duncombe 66.
The fatal snowstorm. D. (Astley's). Cumberland Minor 13; Richardson 4.
See also Nicoll, *4, pp. 261–2, 570.*

Thomas Haynes Bayly 1797–1839

See col 231.

Samuel Beazley, Junior 1786–1851

The boarding-house; or five hours at Brighton. MF. (EOH, TR, Lyc 26 Aug 1811). 1811 (3 edns), 1816; Cumberland Minor 15.
Is he jealous? Oa. (EOH 2 July 1816). 1816, 1818; New York 1857; Oxberry 3; Dicks 774; French 741; New British Theatre 72; Cumberland 34.
My uncle. Oa. (EOH 23 June 1817). 1817.
Jealous on all sides: or the landlord in jeopardy! CO. (EOH 19 Aug 1818). 1818.
The steward: or fashion and feeling, from Thomas Holcroft, Deserted daughter. C. (CG 15 Sep 1819). 1819. Dicks 539; Cumberland 34.
Love's dream, from Scribe, La somnambule. O. (EOH 5 July 1821). 1821; Duncombe 8 and 64.
The lottery ticket: or the lawyer's clerk [alternative title: The lottery ticket and the lawyer's clerk]. F. (DL 13 Dec 1826). 1827; Lacy 68; Dicks 226; Cumberland 35.
The roué: or the hazards of women. 3 vols 1828; 2 vols New York 1828. A novel. [Often attributed to Sir Edward Bulwer Lytton.]
The Oxonians: a glance at society. 3 vols 1830; 2 vols New York 1830. A novel. [Often attributed to Sir Edward Bulwer Lytton.]
Hints for husbands. C. (Theatre Royal, Haymarket 29 Aug 1835). 1835.
You know what. F. (SW 28 Nov 1842). Dicks 653.
See also Nicoll *4, pp. 263–4, 571.* [DS]

James Boaden 1762–1839

Mss, including some correspondence, agreements with publishers, and letters of application to the Royal Literary Fund, are located in BL. Licensing copies of the plays are in the Huntington.

Collection

The plays of James Boaden. Introd by S. Cohan, New York 1980. Contains facs of plays, *below*, ptd 1793–1803.

§1

Songs and choruses in Ozmyn and Daraxa, a musical romance. (K 7 Mar 1793). [1793.]
Fontainville Forest. MD. (CG 25 Mar 1794). 1794 (2 edns); Dublin 1794. From A. Radcliffe, The romance of the forest.
The secret tribunal. MD. (CG 3 June 1795). 1795; Philadelphia 1797.
A letter to George Steevens, esq, containing a critical examination of the papers of Shakspeare; published by Mr Samuel Ireland. To which are added, extracts from Vortigern [by Samuel Ireland]. 1796 (2 edns); New York 1972 (facs reprint).
The Italian monk. D. (H 15 Aug 1797). 1797 (2 edns). From A. Radcliffe, The Italian.
Cambro-Britons: an historical play. (H 21 July 1798). 1798.
Aurelio and Miranda. (DL 29 Dec 1798). 1799 (3 edns). From M. G. Lewis, The monk.
A rainy day: or poetical impressions during a stay at Brighthelmstone, in the month of July 1801. 1801.
The voice of nature. MD. (H 31 July 1802). 1803; Readex micro. From L. C. Caigniez, Le jugement de Salomon.
The maid of Bristol. D. (H 24 Aug 1803). 1803 (3 edns); New York 1803; Readex micro.
An inquiry into the authenticity of various pictures and prints, which, from the decease of the poet to our own times, have been offered to the public as portraits of Shakespeare. 1824, 1824; New York 1975 (facs reprint).
Memoirs of the life of John Philip Kemble, esq., including a history of the stage, from the time of Garrick to the present period. 2 vols 1825; Philadelphia and New York 1825; New York 1979 (facs reprint).
Memoirs of Mrs Siddons, interspersed with anecdotes of authors and actors. 2 vols 1827; 1831 (2nd edn); 1893 (1 vol), 1896, [190?] (limited edn), Philadelphia and New York [1907?] (limited edn).
The man of two lives. 2 vols 1828; Boston 1829. A novel [signed by 'Edward Sydenham'].
The life of Mrs Jordan, including original private correspondence and numerous anecdotes of her contemporaries. 2 vols 1831; 1831 (2nd edn); 1831 (3rd edn, 1 vol); [190?] (limited edn); New York [1907?] (limited edn).
The private correspondence of David Garrick, with the most celebrated persons of his time, now first published from the originals with notes and a new biographical memoir of Garrick. [Ed James Boaden.] 1831; 1835 (2nd edn).
Memoirs of Mrs Inchbald: including her familiar correspondence with the most distinguished persons of her time. To which are added The massacre, and A case of conscience, now first published from her autograph copies. 2 vols 1833.
REVIEWS: North Amer Rev 37 1833; Tait's Edinburgh Mag 3 1833.
The doom of Giallo: or the vision of judgment. 2 vols 1835. A novel.
On the sonnets of Shakespeare. Identifying the person to whom they are addressed; and elucidating several points in the poet's history. 1837; New York 1972 (facs reprint). First pbd GM, *see below*.
To what person the sonnets of Shakespeare were actually addressed. 2 pts GM, vol 102 pt 2, Sep–Oct 1832. *See also* letter ibid. (1 Nov 1832) asserting the independence and early date of Boaden's conclusions.

§2

Biographia Dramatica 1812, vol 1 pt 2.
GM Mar 1839, pp. 437–8.
For performance data to 1800, see Hogan *pt 5 vol 3. See also* Nicoll *3, pp. 238–9, 378; 4, p. 269;* Stratman, *pp. 52–3;* Readex Index, *p. 30.* [JRS]

Alfred Bunn 1796–1860

Poems. 1816.
Tancred: a tale, and other poems. By the author of Conrad: a tragedy. 1819. Anon.
Kenilworth: an historical drama. (CG 8 Mar 1831). [1821]; Duncombe

10; Lacy 98; Dicks 334. Adapted from T. J. Dibdin's dramatisation of Scott.
Conrad: or, the usurper: a tragedy. T. 1821. Anon.
The kinsmen of Naples. T. 1821. Anon.
A monody. Birmingham 1822.
Address recited at the theatre in Stratford-on-Avon. Birmingham [1823].
A letter to the Rev J. A. James, with notes critical, religious and moral. Birmingham 1824.
My neighbour's wife. F. (CG 7 Oct 1833). Lacy, 18; Dicks, 316.
The minister and the mercer. C. (DL 8 Feb 1824). 1834. From Scribe, Bertrand et Raton.
Songs, duets etc. In the opera The bronze horse, adapted from Scribe's drama Le cheval de bronze, [1836].
The stage: both before and behind the curtain. 3 vols 1840.
The Bohemian girl. O. (DL 27 Nov 1843). [1843]. From St Georges, La gipsey; music by M. W. Balfe.
The brides of Venice. O. (DL 22 Apr 1844). [1844]. Music by Benedict.
The daughter of St Mark. O. (DL 27 Nov 1844). [1845]. Tr Bunn; music by Balfe.
The enchantress. O. (DL 14 May 1845). [1845]. Tr Bunn; music by Balfe.
Loretta, a tale of Seville. D. (DL 9 Nov 1846). 1846. Music by Ann Bishop.
The maid of Artois. O. (DL 26 May 1836). 1846. Music by Balfe.
The bondman. O. (DL 11 Dec 1846). [1847]. Tr Bunn; music by Balfe.
Matilda of Hungary. O. (DL 22 Feb 1847). 1847. Music by Wallace.
A word with Punch. No I (all pbd) [1847]. A satire upon G. A. à Beckett, D. W. Jerrold and M. Lemon, with extracts from their writings.
Old England and New England, in a series of views taken on the spot. 2 vols 1853.
See also Nicoll *4, pp. 276, 575; 5, p. 287.*

§2

Era 23 Dec 1860. Obituary.
J. K. [Joseph Knight]. In DNB.
Urwin, G. G. Alfred Bunn 1786–1860: a revaluation. TN 11 1956–7.
[VE]

John C. Cross d. 1810

Collections

Circusiana: or a collection of the most favourite ballets, spectacles, melodramas etc performed at the Royal Circus, St George's Fields. 2 vols 1809, 1812 (as The dramatic works of Cross).

§1

The insolvent debtor: a simple pathetic tale [in verse], founded on facts; to which is added a small collection of miscellaneous poetry. Salisbury 1793.
The purse: or benevolent tar: a musical drama. (H 8 Feb 1794). 1794, 1794, Dublin 1794, London 1797.
The apparition! a musical dramatic romance. (CG 29 Apr 1794). 1794; Songs and choruses, 1794.
Parnassian bagatelles: being a miscellaneous collection of poetical attempts. 1796. Contains 2 plays, both acted 1796.
The raft, or both sides of the water: a musical drama. (CG 17 Mar 1798). 1798; Songs, 1798.
The songs in the new splendid serious spectacle called Cora: or the virgin of the sun. (RC July 1799). [1799.]
The enchanted harp: or harlequin for Ireland. P. (RC 22 Apr 1802). 1802.
The rival statues: or harlequin humourist. P. (RC 11 Apr 1803). 1803.
John Bull and Buonaparte: or a meeting at Dover. Spec. (RC 8 Aug 1803).
Pedlar's acre: or harlequin mendicant. P. (RC 2 July 1804). 1804.
The false friend: or assassin of the rocks. MD. (RC 25 Aug 1806).
See also Nicoll *3, pp. 249–51, 380; 4, pp. 286–7, 578.*

Charles Dance 1794–1863

Licensing copies of the plays are located in BL.

§1

All the plays listed below are also issued in one or more Readex micro *edns.*
The water party. Ba. (Olym 1 Oct 1832). 1836; Dicks 563.
Kill or cure. F. (Olym 29 Oct 1832). French Minor NY 48; Dicks 366.
A match in the dark. Ca. (Olym 21 Feb 1833). 1836; Dicks 852.
The Beulah spa. Ba. (Olym 18 Nov 1833). 1833; Dicks 446.
Hush money. Ba. (Olym 28 Nov 1833). Duncombe 13; Dicks 330. Also attributed to G. Dance.
Pleasant dreams. F. (CG 24 May 1834). 1834; Lacy 80; Dicks 590.
The country squire: or two days at the hall. C. (CG 19 Jan 1837). Webster 1 (3 edns); Dicks 326.
Advice gratis. F. (Olym 29 Sep 1837). Webster 2; Mod Eng Com Th 2 (dated 1845); French 141; Dicks 590.
A dream of the future. C. (Olym 6 Nov 1837). 1853; Lacy 21; Dicks 359.
The Bengal tiger. F. (Olym 18 Dec 1837). 1838; Webster 2 (dated 1838); Mod Eng Com Th ser 2; Dicks 366.
Puss in boots. Ba. (Olym 26 Dec 1837). Webster 3. With J. R. Planché.
Naval engagements. C. (Olym 3 May 1838). 1838; Webster 4; French Minor 32; Dicks 351; Lorenzen micro.
Sons and systems. Ba. (Olym 29 Sep 1838). Webster 5; Dicks 580.
The Burlington Arcade. Ba. (Olym 17 Dec 1838). Webster 6.
Izaak Walton. D. (Olym 1 Apr 1839). 1839; Webster 6; Dicks 566.
Alive and merry. F. (CG 30 Sep 1839). Duncombe 38; Dicks 927.
A close seige. Ba. (St J 25 Nov 1839). Duncombe 40; Dicks 709. Also attributed to G. Dance.
Lucky stars: or the cobbler of Cripplegate! Ba. (Str July 1842). Duncombe 45; Lacy 94; Dicks 564. Also attributed to G. Dance.
Hasty conclusions. C. (Lyc 8 Apr 1844). Barth nd; Dicks 858. Also attributed to G. Dance.
The magic horn. Ext. (Lyc 24 Aug 1844). [1844?]
The dustman's belle. C. (Lyc 1 June 1846). [1846.]
The enchanted forest: or the bear! the eagle! and the dolphin! Bsq. (Lyc 22 Feb 1847). 1847.
Who speaks first? C. (Lyc 11 Jan 1849). [1849]; Lacy 23.
A wonderful woman. C. (Lyc 24 May 1849). [1849]; Lacy 18; Dicks 1038.
Delicate ground: or Paris in 1793. C. (Lyc 27 Nov 1849). [1850?]; Lacy 18; Lacy no 268; Dicks 1008.
A morning call. Ca. (DL 17 Mar 1851). [1851]; Lacy 22; French Minor 57.
The victor vanquished. Ca. (P'cess 25 Mar 1856). Lacy 26.
The Stock Exchange: or the green business. F. (P'cess 5 Apr 1858). Lacy 36.
Marriage a lottery. C. (Str 20 May 1858). Lacy 36; De Witt 249.
The two b'hoys: or the Beulah spa. Ba. French Minor NY no 288; Lorenzen micro.
Dance collaborated on a number of other plays with J. R. Planché. See also Nicoll *4, pp. 288–9, 578–9; 5, p. 335; Conolly,* English drama, *pp. 144–5;* Readex Index *pp. 68–9.*

§2

Obits: The Times 9 Jan 1863; Era 11 Jan 1863; GM ser 3 vol 14 1863.
[JRS]

Charles Isaac Mungo Dibdin, known as Charles Dibdin, C. I. Pitt 1768–1833

§1

The age: a satire, in six cantos. By C. I. Pitt. 1795. Anon.
Wizard's wake: or harlequin's regeneration. P. (SW 23 Aug 1802). [1803].

The little gipsies. O. (SW 2 Apr 1804). [1804.]
Harlequin and the water kelpe. P. (SW 14 Apr 1806). 1806.
Mirth and metre: consisting of poems, serious, humorous and satirical. 1807.
The wild man: or the water pageant. O. (SW 22 May 1809). 1809, 1814; Cumberland Minor 96.
The council of ten: or the lake of the grotto. MD. (SW 3 June 1811). 1811.
The farmer's wife. CO. (CG 1 Feb 1814). 1814; Dicks 110; Dibdin's London Theatre 17.
My spouse and I. CO. (DL 7 Dec 1815). 1815, 1816; Cumberland 41; Dicks 180.
Young Arthur, or the child of mystery: a metrical romance. 1819.
Life in London: or the day and night adventures of Logic, Tom and Jerry. Ext. (Olym 12 Nov 1821). 1821.
Comic tales and lyrical fancies: including the Chessiad, a mock heroic in five cantos; and the wreath of love in four cantos. 1825.
History and illustrations of the London theatres: comprising an account of the origin and progress of the drama in England. 1826.
The high-mettled racer. 1831.
Dibdin was enormously productive. Most of his pieces were pantomimes, operatic farces and melodramas, and only a few were ever pbd. See also Nicoll *4, pp. 290–6, 580.*

§2

Memoirs of Charles Dibdin the younger. Ed G. Speaight 1955.

Thomas John Dibdin 1771–1841

§1

The mouth of the Nile, or the glorious first of August: a musical entertainment. (CG 25 Oct 1798). 1798.
The Jew and the doctor. F. (CG 23 Nov 1798). 1800, 1809 (in Mrs Inchbald's Collection of farces, vol 2); Cumberland 34.
Il Bondocani: or the caliph robber. CO. (CG 15 Nov 1800). 1801, 1801 (songs and choruses).
Valentine and Orson. MD. (CG 3 Apr 1804). 1804; Cumberland 27.
The cabinet. O. (CG 9 Feb 1802). Dublin 1802 (pirated), London 1805, New York 1809, 1810, 1811; London 1802, 1803 (songs and duets); Cumberland 21.
Two faces under a hood. O. (CG 17 Nov 1807). [1807], 1807 (songs and duets).
Harlequin harper: or a jump from Japan. P. (DL 27 Dec 1813). 1813.
A metrical history of England: or recollections in rhyme of some of the most prominent features in our national chronology. 2 vols 1813.
Invanhoe: or the Jew's daughter. D. (Sur 20 Jan 1820). 1820; Cumberland Minor 2; Lacy 92. From Scott.
The fate of Calais. D. (Sur 3 Apr 1820). 1820, nd; Cumberland Minor 8.
The lady of the lake: a drama. After W. Scott. Dublin 1822; London [1830], [1835?] (in Cumberland's minor theatre vol 3); New York [185?] (anon) (in French's standard drama no 275); Boston [1856?] (in Spencer's Boston theatre).
The reminiscences of Thomas Dibdin. 2 vols 1827, 1837.
A ryghte sorroweful tragyke lamentacyonne. [1830.]
Thomas Dibdin's penny trumpet. 1832. A periodical of which only 4 nos appeared.
The last lays of the last of the three Dibdins. 1833 (2 issues).
Bunyan's Pilgrim's progress metrically condensed. 1834.
Harlequin and mother goose: or the golden egg! A comic pantomime. [1862] (in Lacy's acting edn vol 54).
Dibdin also wrote many songs, and several collections were pbd. For numerous other works, see Nicoll *3, pp. 256, 382–3, and 4, pp. 296–305, 580–1. They include dramatic versions of several of Scott's novels.*

§2

Sandoe, J. Some notes on the plays of Dibdin. Univ of Colorado Stud 8th ser 1 1940.
Master of melodrama. TLS 20 Sep 1941.

William Dimond [1780?–1836?]

Petrarchal sonnets and miscellaneous poems. 1800. Verse.
The sea-side story: an operatic drama, in two acts. CO. (CG 12 May 1801). 1801 (2 edns), 1806.
Airs, duets, choruses in The sea-side story. 1801.
Poetry of the songs, chorusses … in The hero of the north: an historical play. MD. (DL 19 Feb 1803). 1803 (7 edns). Anon.
Songs and choruses in The hero of the north. 1803.
The hunter of the Alps: a drama in one act. MD. (H 3 July 1804). 1804 (4 edns); New York 1804 (3 edns). Sub-titled: in two acts, [1838]; Cumberland 39; Lacy's 91; Dicks 961; Ames 26.
Youth, love, and folly: or the little jockey, a comic opera. (DL 24 May 1805). 1805; Cumberland 39; Dicks 427.
Songs, duetts [*sic*], trios, &c in the new comic opera called Youth and folly. 1805.
Adrian and Orrila: or a mother's vengeance, a play in five acts. D. (CG 15 Nov 1806). 1806; New York 1807, 1811.
The young hussar: or love and mercy, an operatic drama, in two acts. CO. (DL 12 Mar 1807). 1807; Cumberland 41.
The foundling of the forest: a play in three acts. MD. (H 10 July 1809). 1809, 1814; New York 1809; Philadelphia 1809; Boston 1810; Dublin 1818; Cumberland 40; Lacy 99; French 17; Dicks 74.
The doubtful son: or secrets of a palace, a play in five acts. D. (H 3 July 1810). 1810 (3 edns); New York 1810.
Gustavus Vasa: the hero of the north. O. (CG 29 Nov 1810). 1811. From his own melodrama, The hero of the north, *see above*.
The peasant boy: an opera in three acts. (L 31 Jan 1811). 1811, 1812; Cumberland 40.
The royal oak: an historical play. (H 10 June 1811). 1811 (2 edns); New York 1812; Dicks 688. Based on Charles the Second.
The Aethiop: or the child of the desart [*sic*], a romantic play, in three acts. (CG 6 Oct 1812). 1812, 1813 (2nd edn); New York 1813; Philadelphia 1816; French 136; French's American drama 40.
The broken sword: or the torrent of the valley, a grand melo-drama, in two acts, interspersed with songs, chorusses [*sic*], &c. (CG 7 Oct 1816). 1816; New York 1817; Philadelphia 1826; Cumberland 41; Lacy 85; Dicks 272; French 173. From Fré dé ric [i.e. Dupetit-Méré] La vallé e du torrent: ou L'orphelin et le meurtrier.
The conquest of Taranto: or St Clara's Eve, a play. MD. (CG 15 Feb 1817). 1817; New York 1817.
The bride of Abydos: a tragick play, in three acts. MD [Lacy has 'romantic drama']. (DL 5 Feb 1818). 1818; Baltimore 1818, 1831; New York 1818; London [nd]; Lacy 70. Based on Byron's poem.
The songs, duets, chorusses [*sic*], &c in The bride of Abydos. [1818?]
The lady and the devil: a romantic drama, in two acts. CO. (DL 3 May 1820). 1820; Cumberland 45; Lacy 90; Dicks 435. From Calderón, La dama duende.
Brother and sister: a comic opera in two acts. (CG 1 Feb 1815). New York 1822; 1829; Lacy 46; with the sub-title: a comic operatic drama in one act, [1860?]; French 684.
Native land: or the return from slavery, an opera in three acts. DO. (CG 10 Feb 1824). 1824; New York 1824.
Airs, duets, songs in the Native land. 1824.
Abou Hassan: a comic drama in two acts. C. (DL 4 Apr 1825). 1825. Adaptation of the opera by F. K. Hiemer.
Englishmen in India: a comic opera, in three acts. (DL 27 Jan 1827). [1827?], [c. 1840]; Duncombe 42.
Songs, duets, chorusses [*sic*] in Englishmen in India. 1827.
The seraglio: an opera, in three acts. (CG 24 Nov 1827). 1828.

The nymph of the grotto: or a daughter's vow, an opera in three acts. (CG 15 Jan 1829). 1829.
Songs, duetts [*sic*], chorusses [*sic*], &c in The nymph of the grotto. 1829.
The carnival at Naples: a play in five acts. (CG 30 Oct 1831). 1831.
Stage struck: or the loves of Augustus Portarlington and Celestina Beverley, a farce in one act. (EOH 12 Nov 1835). [18??]; Lacy 10; Dicks 324; French 142. From James Cobb's Love in the east.
Sketches in India; a farce in one act. (SW 18 Mar 1846). New York [18??]; French 90. Adapted from the Englishmen in India (*see above*).
See also Nicoll *4, pp. 306–7, 581.* [BJO'C]

Charles Farley 1771–1859

Actor, dancer, choreographer, and pantomime 'arranger'. Along with T. J. Dibdin, with whom he initially collaborated, Farley is responsible for developing pantomime, with its extended harlequinade, as the principle nineteenth-century theatrical genre to express topical satire. His manuscript work, before 1824, is in the Larpent Collection (Huntington), and thereafter in the Lord Chamberlain's Collection, BL. Abbreviated printed libretti are in BL, Kemble-Devonshire Collection (Huntington), in the Theatre Collection, Harvard, and the Theatre Museum, London.

§1

The magic oak; or, Harlequin woodcutter. (CG 29 Jan 1799).
The corsair; or, The Italian nuptials. (H 29 July 1801).
Harlequin's magnet; or, The Scandinavian sorcerer. (CG 30 Dec 1805). With T. J. Dibdin.
Harlequin and Mother Goose; or, The golden egg. (CG 29 Dec 1806). With T. J. Dibdin. (Fairburn's description of the new pantomime called Harlequin and mother goose; or, The golden egg, now performing with unbounded applause at the Theatre Royal Covent Garden, wherein is fully described the transformations, scenes &c, also the songs, London, published by John Fairburn, Price Sixpence. n.d. This is the first of only two full contemporary texts describing an entire pantomime. See Niklaus, *below*).
Harlequin in his element; or, Fire, water, earth, and air. (CG 26 Dec 1807). With T. J. Dibdin. (Scale's edn. A description of Harlequin in his element; or, Fire, water, earth, and air, a popular pantomime, performing with universal applause at Covent-Garden Theatre. London. Printed for J. Scales, No. 26 Green-Walk, Holland Street, Blackfriar's Road; and sold by all other booksellers. Price six-pence. n.d. This is the second of only two full contemporary texts describing an entire pantomime. See Booth and Niklaus, *below*).
Harlequin pedlar; or, The haunted well. (CG 26 Dec 1809). With T. J. Dibdin.
Harlequin and Asmodeus; or Cupid on crutches. (CG 26 Dec 1810). Licensed as Harlequin Zambullo; or, The devil on two sticks.
Harlequin and Padmanaba; or, The golden fish. (CG 26 Dec 1811).
Harlequin and the red dwarf; or, The adamant rock. (CG 26 Dec 1812).
Harlequin and the swans; or, The bath of beauty. (CG 27 Dec 1813).
Harlequin Whittington; or Lord mayor of London. (CG 26 Dec 1814).
Harlequin and Fortunio; or, Shing-Moo and Thun-Ton. (CG 26 Dec 1815).
Harlequin and the sylph of the oak; or, The blind beggar of Bethnal Green. (CG 26 Dec 1816).
Harlequin Gulliver; or, The flying island. (CG 26 Dec 1817).
Harlequin Munchausen; or, The fountain of love. (CG 26 Dec 1818).
Harlequin and Don Quixote; or, Sancho Panza in his Glory!!! (CG 27 Dec 1819).
Harlequin and Cinderella; or, The little glass slipper. (CG 3 Apr 1820).
The battle of Bothwell Brigg. (CG 22 May 1820). With H. Bishop from Scott's Old Mortality.
Harlequin and Friar Bacon; or, The brazen head. (CG 26 Dec 1820).
Harlequin and Mother Bunch; or, The yellow dwarf. (CG 26 Dec 1821).
Harlequin and the ogress; or, The sleeping beauty of the wood. (CG 26 Dec 1822).
Harlequin and poor Robin; or, The house that Jack built. (CG 26 Dec 1823).
Harlequin and the dragon of Wantley; or, More of More Hall. (CG 27 Dec 1824).
Harlequin and the magic rose; or, Beauty and the beast. (CG 26 Dec 1825).
Harlequin and Mother Shipton; or, Riquet with the tuft. (CG 26 Dec 1826).
Harlequin and Number Nip; or, The giant mountain. (CG 26 Dec 1827).
Harlequin and Red Riding Hood, or, The wizard and the wolf. (CG 26 Dec 1828).
Harlequin and Cock Robin; or, Vulcan and Venus. (CG 26 Dec 1829).
Harlequin Pat and Harlequin Bat; or, The Giant's Causeway. (CG 27 Dec 1830).
Hop o' my Thumb and his brothers; or, Harlequin and the Ogre. (CG 26 Dec 1831).
Puss in Boots; or, Harlequin and the miller's son. (CG 26 Dec 1832). Licensed as Harlequin Puss in Boots.
Old Mother Hubbard and her dog; or, Harlequin and the tales of the nursery. (CG 26 Dec 1833). Licensed as Old Mother Hubbard; or Harlequin and the magic pie; or, The island of flatheads.

§2

P. Highfill et al, A biographical dictionary of actors. Vol 5, Carbondale IL 1978 pp. 152–7
Niklaus, T. Harlequin. New York 1956.
Booth, M. English plays of the 19th century. Vol 5, Pantomimes, extravaganzas and burlesques, Oxford 1976.
Mayer, D. Harlequin in his element: the English pantomime 1806–1836. Cambridge MA 1969. [DM]

Edward Fitzball, originally Edward Ball 1793–1873

§1

Bertha; or, The assassins of Istria. T. (Norwich 8 Mar 1819). 1819.
The innkeeper of Abbeville; or, The ostler and the robber. MD. (Norwich 6 Mar 1822). J. Lowndes 1822; Cumberland Minor vol 3 no 3; Lacy 90; French's standard no 198.
The fortune's of Nigel; or, King James I and his times. MD. (Sur 25 June 1822). J. Lowndes 1822; Cumberland Minor vol 4 no 5.
Joan of Arc; or, The maid of Orleans. MD. (SW 12 Aug 1822). French's standard no 103.
The barber; or, The mill of Bagdad. Ba. (Sur 21 Oct 1822). J. Lowndes 182?; Dicks 975.
The treadmill; or Tom and Jerry at Brixton. Ba. (Sur ? 1822). J. Lowndes nd.
Peveril of the Peak; or, The days of King Charles II. MD. (Sur 6 Feb 1823). J. Lowndes 1823; J. L. Huie 1823; Cumberland Minor vol 5 no 6.
Waverley; or, Sixty years since. MD. (Adel 8 Mar 1824). J. Lowndes 1824; Cumberland Minor vol 5 no 8.
The floating beacon; or, The Norwegian wreckers. MD. (Sur 19 Apr 1824). Cumberland Minor vol 2 no 9; Lacy 75; French's standard no 178.
Der Freischutz; or, The demon of the wolf's glen and the seven charmed bullets. MD. (Sur 6 Sep 1824). nd.
The Koeuba; or, The pirate vessel. D. (Sur 4 Oct 1824). Cumberland Minor 12.

Wardock Kennilson; or, The wild woman of the village. MD. (Sur 25 Oct 1824). Cumberland Minor vol 8 no 2. Dicks 376.
Father and son; or, The rock of La Charbonniere. MD. (CG 28 Feb 1825). Cumberland Minor vol 11 no 4; French's standard no 193.
Omala; or, settlers in America. MD. (Sur 6 June 1825). J. Lowndes 1826.
The pilot; or, A storm at sea. Ba. (Adel 31 Oct 1825). 1825. Cumberland Minor vol 1 no 1; French's American drama 41.
The three hunchbacks; or, The sabre grinders of Damascus. MD. (Str 5 July 1847). J. Lowndes 1823; Cumberland Minor vol 6.
The flying dutchman; or, The phantom ship. MD. (Adel 1 Jan 1827). Cumberland Minor vol 2 no 5; Lacy 71; French's American drama 6.
The libertine's lesson. Ba. (Adel 8 Oct 1827). Dicks 598.
Nelson; or, The life of a sailor. Ba. (Adel 19 Nov 1827). Dicks 760.
The Inchcape bell; or The dumb sailor boy. MD. (Sur 26 May 1828). G. H. Davidson, nd; Cumberland Minor vol 1 no 3; Lacy 71; Oxford 1995 (WC).
The earthquake; or, The spectre of the Nile. MD. (Adel 15 Dec 1828). Cumberland Minor vol 1.
The red rover; or, The mutiny of the dolphin. MD. (Adel 9 Feb 1829). Cumberland Minor vol 6 no 8; Dicks 450.
The devil's elixir; or, The shadowless man. MD. (CG 20 Apr 1829). Cumberland's British theatre vol 22 no 4.
Die Rauberbraut; or, The robber's bride. O. (EOH 15 July 1829). Music by F. Ries. W. Hawes nd.
Ninetta; or, The maid of Palaiseau. O. (CG 4 Feb 1830). Music by Bishop. Based on Rossini's La Gazza Ladra. J. Ebers 1830, also W. Wright nd.
The haunted hulk. MD. (Adel 12 July 1831 and Sur 21 Jan 1833). Cumberland Minor nd.
Andreas Hofer, the tell of the Tyrol. MD. (Sur 11 June 1832). Cumberland Minor vol 6 no 1; French's standard no 162.
Jonathan Bradford; or, The murder at the roadside inn. MD. (Sur 12 June 1833). Dicks 370; Duncombe 12; Lacy 55.
Mary Glastonbury; or, The dream girl of the Devil-Holl. MD. (Sur 28 Sep 1833). Cumberland Minor vol 6 no 7.
Walter Brand; or, The duel in the mist. D. (Sur 26 Dec 1833). Duncombe 13.
Esmeralda; or, the deformed of Notre Dame. MD. (Sur 14 Apr 1834). Dicks 346; Lacy 18; French's standard 110.
Tom Cringle; or, The man with the iron hand. D. (Sur 26 May 1834). Duncombe 14; Lacy 41; French's Amer drama 140.
The note forger. D. (DL 21 Apr 1835). Duncombe 17; Lacy 38; French's standard 115.
Carlmilhan; or, The drowned crew. D. (CG 21 Apr 1835). Duncombe 131.
Paul Clifford. MD. (CG 28 Oct 1835). Dicks 367; Duncombe 20; Lacy nd.
The siege of Rochelle. O. (DL 29 Oct 1835). Duncombe 47; Lacy 95. Music by M. W. Balfe. Boosey nd.
The Carmelites; or, The convent belles. D. (CG 3 Dec 1835). Duncombe nd.
The bronze horse; or, The spell of the cloud king. MD. (CG 14 Dec 1835). Duncombe 151.
Quasimodo; or, The gypsy girl of Notre Dame. D. (CG 4 Feb 1836). Duncombe 25.
False colours; or, The free trader. D. (CG 4 Mar 1836). Duncombe 201; Lacy 110.
Za-ze-zi-zo-zu; or, Dominoes! chess! and cards! Bsq. (CG 4 Apr 1836). Duncombe 21.
Thalaba the destroyer; or, The burning sword. MD. (CG 21 Nov 1836). Cumberland Minor vol 5 no 7.
Walter Tyrrel. D. (CG 16 May 1837). Dicks 565; Acting nat drama vol 1 no 4; Webster's acting drama no 7.
Joan of Arc; or, The maid of Orleans. O. (DL 30 Nov 1837). Cumberland Minor vol 4; Lacy 103. Music by M. W. Balfe.
The negro of Wapping; or, The boat-builder's hovel. MD. (Gar 16 Apr 1838). Duncombe 29.
The king of the mist; or, The miller of Hartz mountains. MD. (DL 1 Apr 1839). Duncombe 36.
Scaramuccia; or, The villagers of San Quintino. CO. (EOH 23 Aug 1839). E. H. Tornour nd.
Hans of Iceland. Bal. (CG 27 Sep 1841). nd.
Mary Melvyn; or, The marriage of interest. MD. (Adel 20 Feb 1843). Dicks 622.
The queen of the Thames; or, The anglers. Oa. (DL 25 Feb 1843). G. Berger 1843. Music by Hatton.
Ondine; or, The naid. Bal. (Queen's 9 Nov 1843). Dicks 746.
The daughter of the regiment. D. (DL 30 Nov 1843). Duncombe 52.
The momentous question. D. (Lyc 17 June 1844). Lacy 30; New British theatre vol 25 no 399.
Home again; or, The lieutenant's daughters. D. (Lyc 28 Nov 1844). Dicks 820; Duncombe 51; Lacy 30.
Maritana. O. (DL 15 Nov 1845). W. S. Johnson nd. Music by W. V. Wallace. Hutchings and Romer nd (vocal score).
The crown jewels. O. (DL 16 Apr 1846). W. S. Johnson nd.
The traveller's room. D. (Sur 1 Nov 1847). Duncombe 60.
The maid of honour. O. (DL 20 Dec 1847). Chappell nd. Music by M. W. Balfe. Chappell 1847 (vocal score).
The daughter of the regiment. O. (Sur 21 Dec 1847). Dicks 761. (New version for the Surrey.)
The Lancashire witches. A romance of Pendle Forest. MD. (Adel 3 Jan 1848). Dicks 1036.
The crock of gold; or, The murder at the hall. D. (CL May 1848). Duncombe nd.
Marmion; or, The battle of Flodden Field. Spec. (RA 12 June 1848). Duncombe 63.
Quentin Durward. O. (CG 6 Dec 1848). 1848. Music by H. R. Laurent.
Hans von Stein; or, The robber knight. MD. (Marylebone 11 Aug 1851). French 104.
Azael; or, The prodigal of Memphis. Spec. (Astleys 3 Nov 1851). Duncombe nd; Lacy 56.
The Greek slave; or, The spectre gambler. MD. (Marylebone 20 Nov 1851). Lacy nd; French nd.
The last of the fairies. D. (Olym 4 Mar 1852). Duncombe 537.
Alice May; or, The last appeal. D. (Sur 23 June 1852). Duncombe nd; Lacy nd.
Peter the Great. MD. (Astleys 26 July 1852). Dicks nd; Duncombe 541; Lacy nd.
Uncle Tom's cabin; or, The horrors of slavery. MD. (Olym 20 Sep 1852). Duncombe nd. There were also separate versions produced at Grec (25 Oct 1852) and DL (27 Dec 1852). *See* Thirty-five years of a dramatic author's life, *below*, vol 2, p. 261.
The miller of Derwent Water. D. (Olym 2 May 1853). Ames' Standard 36; Lacy 12.
The children of the castle. D. (M'bone 23 Nov 1853). Lacy 35.
Pierette; or, The village rivals. CO. (Hull 6 Mar 1858). Lacy 36. Music by W. H. Montgomery.
Lurline. O. (CG 23 Feb 1860). Covent Garden nd; William Hall and Sons 1868. Music by W. V. Wallace.
Christmas eve; or, The duel in the snow. D. (DL 12 Feb 1860; SW 4 June 1862 as The duel in the snow). Lacy 45.
Robin Hood; or, The merry outlaws of Sherwood. D. (Astleys 8 Oct 1860). Lacy 48.

Non-dramatic works

The ideot boy: a Spanish tale of pity. Norwich 1814; Nottingham 1815 (as The idiot boy: a tale).
Serena of Oakwood, and other poems. 2nd edn. C. N. Wright 1815.
The black robber, a romance. 3 vols A. K. Newman 1815.
The revenge of Taran, a poem. 1821, 1922.
The sibyl's warning. 2 vols 1822.

The house to let. 1857. Poetry.
Bahanavar, a romantic poem and The story of Fadleen, a prose tale. 1858.
Michael Schwartz; or, The two runaway apprentices. 1858.
Thirty-five years of a dramatic author's life. 2 vols 1859.
A leaf from creation. 1867. Poem.
To an early daisy. 1867. Poem.
My angel. 1868. Poem.
The 'wee craft'. Red, white and blue. Broadsheet. 1886.
My pretty Jane. London and New York (ptd in Germany) 1891.

Plays of unknown date and performance

Margaret's ghost; or, The libertine's ship. MD. Duncombe nd.

§2

Clifton, L. The terrible Fitzball. The melodramatist of the macabre. Athens OH 1993.
Winn, P. C. The 'terrible' Fitzball. The work of a hack dramatist, 1817–1873. Ithaca NY 1979. [BY]

John Thomas Haines 1799?–1843

Licensing copies of the later plays are located in BL.

§1

The idiot witness: or a tale of blood. MD. (Cob 6 Oct 1823). Duncombe 5; Lacy 46; Philadelphia and New York [c. 1844]; Boston Th 4 (dated 1856); Lorenzen micro; Readex micro.
The wraith of the lake: or the brownie's brig! MD. (Cob 26 Oct 1829). Duncombe nd; Readex micro.
Austerlitz: or the soldier's bride. MD. (Queen's 26 Sep 1831). Cumberland Minor 14; Dicks 479; Readex micro.
Jacob Faithful: or the life of a Thames waterman! D. (Vic 16 Dec 1834 as Jacob Faithful, the lighter-boy: a tale of the Thames). Duncombe 16; Dicks 507; Readex micro. From Marryat.
My Poll and my partner Joe. MD. (Sur 31 Aug 1835). Cumberland Minor 9; Lacy 71; French no 1058; Dicks 500; Booth melodramas; Readex micro.
The ocean of life: or every inch a sailor. D. (Sur 4 Apr 1836). Cumberland Minor 11; Lacy 69; Dicks 634; Kilgarriff; Readex micro.
Rattlin the reefer: or the tiger of the sea! MD. (Vic 22 Aug 1836). Duncombe 24; French no 2008; Readex micro.
Richard Plantagenet. D. (Vic 1 Dec 1836). Cumberland Minor 14; Dicks 449. Variant title A legend of Walworth; Readex micro.
Maidens beware! Ba. (Vic 6 Dec 1836). Duncombe 25; Dicks 772; Readex micro.
Breakers ahead: or a seaman's log. D. (Vic 27 Mar 1837). Duncombe 27; Readex micro.
Angeline. D. (StJ 29 Sep 1837). Webster 3; Dicks 669. Variant title Angeline le Lis; Readex micro.
Amilie: or the love test. D. (CG 2 Dec 1837). [1837] (songs, duets etc); 1862; Baltimore nd; Readex micro.
The French spy: or the siege of Constantina. D. (Adel 4 Dec 1837). French NY 153; Dicks 680; Readex micro.
The Rye house plot: or the maltster's daughter. D. (SW 4 June 1838). Dicks 426.
The charming Polly: or lucky or unlucky days. D. (Sur 2 July 1838). Duncombe 30; Dicks 600; Readex micro.
Alice Grey, the suspected one: or the moral brand. D. (Sur 1 Apr 1839). Pattie 1; Lacy 44; Dicks 354; Readex micro.
Jack Sheppard. MD. (Sur 21 Oct 1839). Pattie 1. From Ainsworth.
Nick of the woods: or the altar of revenge! MD. (Vic 1839). Duncombe 44; Lacy nd; Readex micro.
The life of a woman: or the curate's daughter. T. (Sur 20 Apr 1840). Pattie 2; Dicks 468; Readex micro. From Hogarth, Harlot's progress.
The factory boy. D. (Sur 8 June 1840). Pattie 2; Dicks 641; Readex micro.
The wizard of the wave: or the ship of the avenger. D. (Vic 7 Sep 1840). Pattie 2; Lacy 46; Dicks 921; Readex micro.
The yew tree ruins: or the wreck, the miser, and the mines. D. (Vic 11 Jan 1841). Lacy 74; Dicks 485; Readex micro.
A queen of a day. D. (Sur 14 June 1841). [1841]; [1841] (songs); Readex micro. From Scribe.
Ruth: or the lass that loves a sailor. D. (Vic 23 Jan 1843). Lacy 44; Readex micro; Dicks 925 (as The lass that loves a sailor).
Uncle Oliver: or a house divided. D. (EOH 20 Mar 1843). Pattie 3; Readex micro; Dicks 576 (as A house divided).
See also Nicoll *4, pp. 322–3, 586–7; Conolly,* English drama, *pp. 188–9;* Readex Index, *pp. 114–15.*

§2

GM July 1843. Obituary.
Wewiara, G. E. J. T. Haines in Manchester, 1828–29. ThN 27 1972–3. [JRS]

James Haynes 1788–1851

Except for Mary Stuart, *which is located in BL, licensing copies of the plays are in the Huntington.*

§1

All plays listed below are available in one or more Readex micro *edns.*
Conscience: or the bridal night. T. (DL 21 Feb 1821). 1821; New York 1821.
REVIEW: London Mag Mar 1821.
Durazzo. T. (Park, New York 18 Oct 1823). 1823; New York 1823. Withdrawn by author from production in London in 1823.
Mary Stuart. T. (DL 22 Jan 1840). 1840 (3 edns); Dicks 749.

§2

James Haynes's Conscience: or the bridal night. London Mag Mar 1821.
See also Nicoll *4, p. 314; Conolly,* English drama, *p. 189;* Stratman, *pp. 236–7;* Readex Index, *p. 122.* [JRS]

Charles Kemble 1775–1854

Mss are located in BL, Folger, Harvard Theatre Collection, Garrick Club, Shakespeare Memorial Theatre Lib, and the Theatre Museum, London. Except for the revised version of The wanderer, *which is in BL, licensing copies of the plays are in the Huntington.*

Bibliography

In J. Williamson, *below.*

§1

The point of honour. C. (H 15 July 1800). 1800, 1801, 1805; Baltimore 1830; Inchbald 24; Cumberland 28; Dicks 791; Readex micro. From L. S. Mercier, Le déserteur.
The wanderer; or the rights of hospitality. D. (CG 12 Jan 1808). 1808; [1808] (as A sketch of the wanderer); New York 1808; Readex micro. From Kotzebue, Eduard in Schottland. Revived as The royal fugitive CG 26 Nov 1829.
Plot and counterplot; or the portrait of Michael Cervantes. F. (H 30 June 1808). 1808, 1812 (2nd edn); Cumberland 41; Lacy 90; Dicks 503; Readex micro. From Dieulafoi, Le portrait de Michel Cervantes.
REVIEW: Br Critic Dec 1809.
C. Kemble's Shakespere readings. Ed R. J. Lane 3 vols 1870, 1879.
Henry VI: a tragedy . . . condensed [by C. Kemble] from Shakespeare. In The works of William Shakespeare, ed Henry Irving and F. A. Marshall, 1890.

Attributed or spurious works

A budget of blunders. F. (CG 16 Feb 1810). Philadelphia 1811, 1823. Spurious.

See also Nicoll *4, pp. 334, 591; Conolly,* English drama, *p. 203;* Readex Index, *p. 144.*

§2

Donne, W. B. Charles Kemble. In Essays on the drama, and on popular amusements, 1858, 1863 (2nd edn). Rptd from Fraser's Mag Dec 1854.
Kemble (afterwards Butler), F. A. Records of a girlhood: an autobiography. 1878.
Kemble (afterwards Butler), F. A. Records of later life. 3 vols 1882.
Williamson, J. Charles Kemble: man of the theater. Lincoln NE 1970. [JRS]

James Kenney 1780–1849

Licensing copies of the plays to 1824 are located in the Huntington; later plays are in BL.

§1

All plays listed below are also issued in one or more Readex micro *edns.*
Society: a poem in two parts; with other poems. 1803.
Raising the wind. F. (CG 5 Nov 1803). 1803, 1804 (2 edns), [1804], New York 1804, London 1805; Stuttgart 1842; Inchbald Farces 1; Cumberland 19 (dated 1828); Lacy suppl 2; Paris 1861; Dicks 208; Booth 4.
REVIEW: Br Critic Dec 1804.
Matrimony. CO. (DL 20 Nov 1804). 1804 (3 edns), 1804 (songs, duets etc); [1810]; Inchbald Farces 1; Cumberland 26; Lacy 37; Dicks 906. From B. J. Marsollier des Vivetières, Adolphe et Clare.
Too many cooks. F. (CG 12 Feb 1805). 1805, 1805 (songs, duets etc); New York 1813.
False alarms: or my cousin. CO. (DL 12 Jan 1807). 1807 (2 edns), 1807 (airs, duets, trios etc); New York 1807; Cumberland 39. Music by Braham and M. P. King.
Ella Rosenberg. MD. (DL 19 Nov 1807). 1807, [1807]; Inchbald Farces 1; Cumberland 27; Boston Th 14; Dicks 216.
REVIEW: Monthly Rev Sep 1808.
The blind boy. MD. (CG 1 Dec 1807). 1807 (synopsis), 1808; Cumberland 25; Lacy 58; Dicks 753. From Caigniez, L'illustre aveugle.
The world! C. (DL 31 Mar 1808). 1808; New York 1808.
Turn out! F. (Lyc 7 Mar 1812). 1812 (2 edns); Cumberland 45.
Love, law, and physic. F. (CG 20 Nov 1812). [Dublin] 1821; Cumberland 24; Lacy suppl 1; Stuttgart 1842; Dicks 673.
Debtor and creditor. C. (CG 20 Apr 1814). 1814; New York 1816.
The portfolio; or the family of Anglade. D. (CG 1 Feb 1816). 1816.
The fortune of war. C. (CG 17 May 1815). New York 1816.
The touchstone: or the world as it goes. C. (DL 3 May 1817). 1817; New York 1817.
A house out at windows. F. (DL 10 May 1817). 1817.
Valdi, or the libertine's son: a poem. 1820.
Match breaking: or the prince's present. F. (H 20 Sep 1821). 1821. From Decomberouse and Baudoin, Le présent du prince.
John Buzzby: or a day's pleasure. C. (H 3 July 1822). 1822; New York 1822.
Sweethearts and wives. CO. (H 7 July 1823). 1823 (songs, duets, choruses); Philadelphia [1827]; Webster 15; Dram Ents; Dicks 228.
The Alcaid: or the secrets of office. CO. (H 10 Aug 1824). [1824], Dolby 8 (dated 1825); Cumberland 8.
Benyowsky: or the exiles of Kamschatka. D. (DL 16 Mar 1826). 1826. From Kotzebue.
Spring and autumn; or married for money. C. (H 6 Sep 1827 subtitled The bride at fifty). Lacy 24; Boston Th 2 (dated 1855); Dicks 708. From the Fr.
The illustrious stranger: or married and buried. F. (DL 1 Oct 1827). 1827; Cumberland 23; Lacy 52; Lacy home plays, pt 1; Dicks 254; Lorenzen micro. With J. Millingen.
Masaniello. O. (DL 4 May 1829). 1831; 1850; Lacy dated 1871; Lacy 93; Lorenzen micro. With C. Kenney. Music by Auber. From Scribe, La muette de Portici.
The pledge: or Castillian honour. T. (DL 8 Apr 1831). 1831; Lacy 77 (as Hernani: or the pledge of honour). From Hugo, Hernani.
The Irish ambassador. F. (CG 17 Nov 1831). Minor Drama NY no 37; Dicks 920.
A good-looking fellow. F. (CG 17 Apr 1834). 1834. With A. Bunn.
The king's seal. C. (DL 10 Jan 1835). 1835. With Mrs C. Gore.
Fighting by proxy. Ba. (Olym 9 Dec 1835). 1835; Lacy 74; Boston Th 16.
The Sicilian vespers. T. (Sur 21 Sep 1840). 1840. From Delavigne, Les vêpres Siciliennes.
See also Nicoll *4, pp. 336–8, 591–2; 5, p. 443;* NSTC, *ser 1, 3, pp. 87–8; Conolly,* English drama, *pp. 203–5;* Readex Index, *pp. 146–7.*

§2

GM Jan 1850. Obituary.
C[ole], J. W. In The dramatic writers of Ireland, pt 10, Dublin Univ Mag Jan 1856.
Clayden, P. W. Rogers and his contemporaries. 2 vols 1889. [JRS]

James Sheridan Knowles 1784–1862

Collections

The dramatic works of Knowles, with a memoir by R. Shelton Mackenzie. Baltimore 1835, Calcutta 1838.
Plays: The hunchback, The wife, The beggar of Bethnal Green, The daughter. 1838. Separate plays bound together, with a general title.
The dramatic works. 2 vols 1841, 3 vols 1841–3, 1847, 2 vols 1856, [1883].
Various dramatic works of Knowles. 2 vols 1874 (priv ptd).

§1

The Welch harper: a ballad. 1796.
Fugitive pieces. 1810.
Brian Boroihme: or the maid of Erin. D. (Belfast 2 Mar 1812; CG 20 Apr 1837). Webster 8; French 109; Dicks 670. From D. O'Meara.
Caius Gracchus. T. (Belfast 13 Feb 1815; DL 18 Nov 1823). Glasgow 1823; Cumberland 6; Dicks 298.
Virginius: or the liberation of Rome. T. (TR Glasgow 1820; CG 17 May 1820). 1820, 1820, 1823 (5th edn); Dolby 12; Cumberland 38; French's standard 25; Dicks 246; Moses, Boston 1918. Anthologised in Booth vol 1.
The elocutionist: a collection of pieces in prose and verse, peculiarly adapted to display the art of reading. Belfast [1823]?, 1831 (7th edn), New York 1844, [1883] (28th edn).
William Tell. D. (DL 11 May 1825). 1825; Cumberland 22; Lacy 83; French's standard 39; Dicks 238.
The beggar's daughter of Bethnal Green. C. (DL 22 Nov 1828). 1828. Rev as The beggar of Bethnal Green (Vic 1834), 1834; Dicks 695.
The hunchback. D. (CG 5 Apr 1832). 1832, 1832, 1836 (9th edn); Cumberland 13 (336); Lacy 67 (1000); Dicks 206; New York [1876?]; tr Ger 1838.
The wife: a tale of Mantua. D. (CG 24 Apr 1833). 1833 (6 edns); French's standard 5; French 109; Dicks 288. Charles Lamb wrote a prologue and an epilogue to the play.
The love-chase. C. (H 9 Oct 1837). 1837; Cumberland 41 (326); Lacy 68 (1007); French's standard 22; Dicks 322.
Old maids. C. (CG 12 Oct 1841). 1841; Dicks 629.
Fortescue: a novel. 1846 (priv ptd); New York 1846; 3 vols 1847.
George Lovell: a novel. 3 vols 1847.
The rock of Rome: or the arch heresy. 1849.
The idol demolished by its own priest: an answer to Cardinal Wiseman's lectures on transubstantiation. Edinburgh 1851.
The gospel attributed to Matthew is the record of the whole original apostlehood. 1855.

Old adventures. In The tale book by Knowles et al., Königsberg 1859.
Lectures on dramatic literature etc: lectures on oratory, gesture and poetry; to which is added a correspondence with four clergymen in defence of the stage. Ed S. W. Abbott and F. Harvey 2 vols 1873 (priv ptd).
Lectures on dramatic literature: Macbeth. 1875.
Tales and novelettes. Rev and ed F. Harvey 1874 (priv ptd).
For other plays, see Nicoll *4, pp. 338–9; 5, p. 445.*

§2

Hazlitt, W. In his Spirit of the age, 1825.
Horne, R. H. In his A new spirit of the age vol 2, 1844.
Knowles. Blackwood's Mag Oct 1863.
Knowles, R. B. The life of Knowles. Rev and ed F. Harvey 1872 (priv ptd).
Maginn, W. A gallery of illustrious characters. Ed W. Bates [1873], 1883. Essay on Knowles first pbd, with drawing by Maclise, in Fraser's Mag Sep 1836.
Hasberg, L. Knowles Leben und dramatische Werke. Lingen 1883.
Klapp, W. Knowles Virginius und sein angebliches französisches Gegenstück. Rostock 1904.
Meeks, L. H. Knowles and the theatre of his time. Bloomington IN 1933. With bibliography.
Ritchie, H. M. Kean versus Macready: Sheridan Knowles's Virginius. ThS 17 1976. [PT]

Michael Rophino Lacy 1795–1867

Love and reason. C. (CG 22 May 1827). 1827. From Scribe, Bertrand et Suzette.
The two friends. C. (H 11 July 1828). Cumberland 37; Dicks 679. From Scribe, Rodolphe.
The maid of Judah: or the Knights Templars. O. (CG 7 Mar 1829). Cumberland 25. From Scott, Ivanhoe.
Robert the devil: or the fiend father. O. (CG 2 Feb 1830). Lacy 31. From A. E. Scribe and G. Delavigne.
Cinderella: or the fairy-queen and the glass slipper. CO. (CG 13 Apr 1830). 1830, 1840 (songs and duets); Lacy 18; Dicks 1060.
Fra Diavolo: or the inn of Terracina. O. (CG 3 Nov 1831). 1831, 1833. From Scribe, Fra Diavolo, with music by Auber.
Doing for the best. D. (SW 13 Nov 1861). Lacy 55.
Doing my uncle. F. (Sur 8 Sep 1866). Lacy 72.
See also Nicoll *4, pp. 340, 592; 5, pp. 446, 801. According to* DNB, *provided the first English adaptations of* Semiramide, Cinderella, William Tell, Fra Diavolo, *and others less famous. He wrote an oratorio,* The Israelites in Egypt, *for music by Handel and Rossini, and collaborated in Schälcher's* Life of Handel.

Matthew Gregory Lewis 1775–1818

See col 947.

Samuel Lover 1797–1868

See col 951.

Charles Robert Maturin 1782–1824

See col 956.

Henry M. Milner

Barmecide: or the fatal offspring. D. (DL 3 Nov 1818). 1818.
The bandit of the blind mine. D. (Cob 15 Oct 1821). [1821.]
Frankenstein: or the demon of Switzerland. MD. (Cob 18 Aug 1823). Duncombe 2; Lacy 75. From Mrs Shelley.
Alonzo the brave and the fair Imogene: or the spectre bride. MD. (Cob 19 June 1826). Duncombe 2.
The gambler's fate: or a lapse of twenty years. MD. (DL 15 Oct 1827). 1827; Dicks 308. From V. Ducange, Trente ans.
Mazeppa: or the wild horse of Tartary. D. (RA 4 Apr 1831). Philadelphia nd, New York nd; Cumberland Minor 5; Dicks 620. From Byron.
Gustavus of Sweden: or the masked ball. D. (Vic 8 Nov 1833). Duncombe 13; Dicks 630.
Dick Turpin's ride to York. D. (Sur 30 Aug 1841). Dicks 632.
See also Nicoll *4, pp. 356–7, 599.*

Mary Russell Mitford 1787–1855

See col 960.

'William Thomas Moncrieff', William Thomas Thomas 1794–1857

Collections

Selections from the dramatic works. 3 vols 1851.

§1

All at Coventry: or love and laugh. Ba. (Olym 8 Jan 1816). [1816]; Richardson 2; Lacy 59.
Giovanni in London: or the libertine reclaimed. CO. (Olym 26 Dec 1817). 1825, 1818 (songs, duets, choruses); LSt 3; Cumberland 17; BD 3; Dicks 104.
Wanted a wife: or a cheque on my banker's. C. (DL 3 May 1819). 1819.
The Lear of private life. D. (Cob 27 Apr 1820). Dicks 924; Richardson 1; Cumberland Minor 7. From Mrs Opie, Father and daughter.
Prison-thoughts: elegy written in the King's Bench ... By a collegian. 1821 (anon).
The spectre bridegroom: or a ghost in spite of himself. F. (DL 2 July 1821). 1821, New York 1821; Cumberland 16; Lacy 35; Dicks 353.
Tom and Jerry: or life in London. Ba. (Adel 26 Nov 1821). 1826; Cumberland 33; Lacy 88; Dicks 82; French Minor NY. From Egan, Life in London.
The cataract of the Ganges: or the Rajah's daughter. MD. (DL 27 Oct 1823). 1823; Richardson 3; Cumberland 33; French NY.
The new guide to the Spa of Leamington Priors; to which is added historical notices of Warwick and its castle. 1822, 1824.
Excursion to Stratford upon Avon; with a compendious life of Shakespeare, account of the Jubilee, catalogue of the Shakespeare relics. Leamington 1824.
William's visits. 1825 (in Duncombe's British theatre vol 3). Prose and verse.
Songs, duets and glees sung at the Royal Gardens Vauxhall. [1827.]
The somnambulist: or the phantom of the village. MD. (CG 19 Feb 1828). 1828; Cumberland 18; Lacy 86; Dicks 224. From Scribe, La somnambule.
Poems. 1829 (priv ptd at the author's press).
The march of intellect: a comic poem. 1830, 1831 (in Facetiae vol 1).
Old Booty: serio-comic sailor's tale. 1830, 1831, 1832 (in Facetiae vol 2). In verse.
The triumph of reform: a comic poem with six plates by R. Seymour. [1832.]
Eugene Aram: or St Robert's cave. MD. (Sur 8 Feb 1832). Cumberland Minor 10; Lacy 103; Dicks 312.
The scamps of London: or the cross roads of life. D. (SW 13 Nov 1843). 1851; Lacy 81; Dicks 472; French 1213.
An original collection of songs, sung at the Theatres Royal etc. [1850.]
Moncrieff also edited Richardson's new minor drama, *4 vols 1828–31. For other plays, see* Nicoll *4, pp. 358–61, 600.*

Frederic Coleman Nantz [1810?]–44

Nantz claimed to have written seven plays. None were published, and copies of only three have been traced. The most extensive collection of reviews and playbills is in the Eyre mss, Ipswich Record Office.

§1

Woman. Censor 20 Sep 1828. Poem.
Stanzas ('Why dost thou sit'). Censor 1 Nov 1828. Poem.
Elegy to the memory of Harry Kay. Censor 27 Dec 1828. Poem.
The accursed. Censor 24 Jan, 7 Feb 1829. Tale.
The brown devil; or Chi Chue Ali, the charmed pirate. B. (Olym 16 Jan 1830). Adapted from Poor Jack, by Charles Dibdin. LC.
Dennis, or the gibbet law of Halifax. D. (Halifax 11 Feb 1833). Ms dated 28 Jan 1833 in Birmingham Public Lib.
St Ann's well; or 'Tis ninety years since [later: St Ann's well; or a century gone]. D. (Nottingham 30 Dec 1833; SW 20 Jan 1840). Based on the exploits of a celebrated Nottingham poacher. No copy traced.
L'Ecart. D. (Derby circuit, 1834). No copy traced.
John Doe. D. (Derby circuit, 1834). No copy traced.
Blue eyed Mary; or the lily of the village [alternative title Blue eyed Mary; or wrecked in sight of port]. D. (Pavilion 17 June 1835). No copy traced.
An actor's vindication of his profession, in reply to a sermon preached by the Reverend John McCrea, on Sunday evening, Mar 19th 1837, at St Margaret's Church, King's Lynn. Lynn 1837.
Pickwick; or the sayings and doings of Sam Weller (Colchester 18 Dec 1837). D. Adapted from other dramatisations of The Pickwick Papers by Charles Dickens. LC.

§2

Bentley, William. Hallifax and its gibbet law placed in a true light. Ed J. Horsfall Turner, Bradford 1886.
McGowan, M. T. Pickwick and the pirates: a study of some early imitations, dramatizations, and plagiarisms of Pickwick Papers. Unpbd PhD thesis, Univ of London 1975.
Schlicke, P. The life of a strolling player: Frederic Coleman Nantz (1810–1844). Theatre Annual 34 1979. [PS]

John Howard Payne 1791–1852

Mss, including plays, letters and accounts, are located in Columbia Univ Libs.

Bibliography

Heartman, C. F. and H. B. Weiss. Payne: a bibliography. In Amer Book Collector 1933.

Selections

Hislop, C. and W. R. Richardson (ed). Trial without jury and other plays. America's lost plays vol 5. Princeton 1940; rptd Bloomington IN 1964. Also includes Mount Savage, The boarding schools, The two sons-in-law, Mazeppa, The Spanish husband.
Hislop, C. and W. R. Richardson (ed). The last duel in Spain and other plays. America's lost plays vol 6. Princeton 1940; rptd Bloomington IN 1964. Also includes Woman's revenge, The Italian bride, Romulus, The shepherd king, The black man: or the spleen.

§1

Julia: or the wanderer. C. (Park, New York, 7 Feb 1806). New York 1806.
Essays of Howard: or tales of the prison. 1811.
Juvenile poems. Baltimore 1813 (priv ptd?).
Lispings of the muse: a selection from Juvenile poems, chiefly written at and before the age of sixteen. 1815 (priv ptd).
Accusation: or the family of d'Anglade. D. (DL 1 Feb 1816). 1817; Boston 1818. From Frédéric du Petit-Méré. Revised by T. J. Dibdin.
Brutus: or the fall of Tarquin. T. (DL 3 Dec 1818). 1818 (5 edns); 1819 (6th edn); Baltimore 1819; New York 1821; Baltimore 1827; New York 1848; New York [1868], [1873] (adapted by Henry L. Hinton); Albany NY 1875; New York 1878, [1878?]; Dolby 11 (dated 1825); Cumberland 11; Dicks' BD 3; Dicks 31; Lorenzen micro; Readex micro.
Therese, the orphan of Geneva. M. (DL 2 Feb 1821). 1821 (2 edns); Cumberland 40; Duncombe 39; New BT 306; Dicks' BD 5; Readex micro. From V. Ducange.
Love in a humble life. A petite comedy. (DL 14 Feb 1822). Dolby 10 (dated 1825); Cumberland 11; Lacy suppl 1; Dicks 358; Readex micro. From Scribe and Dupin, Michael et Christine.
Peter Smink: or the armistice. C. (Sur July 1822; rev H 26 Sep 1826 as Peter Smink: or which is the miller?). Lacy 75; Dicks 683; Readex micro. From the Fr.
Ali Pacha: or the signet ring. MD (CG 19 Oct 1822). 1822; New York 1823; Dolby 11 (dated 1825); Cumberland 11; Readex micro. Also attributed to, or altered by, J. R. Planché.
The two galley slaves: or the mill of St Aldervon. MD. (CG 6 Nov 1822). Dolby 10 (dated 1825); Cumberland 10; Lacy 72; Readex micro. From the Fr. Music by T. Cooke and C. E. Horne.
Clari: or the maid of Milan. O. (CG 8 May 1823). 1823; Philadelphia [1836?]; Boston Th 6 (dated 1856); Cumberland 24; Lacy 95; Dicks 406; Readex micro. Altered by J. R. Planché. Music by Sir H. Bishop.
Mrs Smith: or the wife and the widow. F. (H 18 June 1823). 1823; Lacy 84; Dicks 683; Readex micro.
Charles the Second: or the merry monarch. C. (CG 27 May 1824). 1824; 1825; Philadelphia 1848; Dolby 9 (dated 1825); Cumberland 9; Lacy 30; reissue Lacy no 447; Dicks 244; in Representative American plays, ed A. H. Quinn, 1917; Readex micro. With Washington Irving. From A. V. Pineux-Duval, La jeuness de Henri V.
The fall of Algiers. O. (DL 19 Jan 1825). Dolby 9 (dated 1825); Cumberland 9; Readex micro. Music by Sir H. Bishop. Also attributed to C. E. Walker.
'Twas I: or the truth a lie. OF. (CG 3 Dec 1825). 1827; Lacy 9; Dicks 405; Readex micro. From La rose et le baiser: ou la servante justifiée.
Richelieu: a domestic tragedy. D. (CG 11 Feb 1826 as The French libertine). New York 1826; Readex micro. From A. V. P. Duval. With Washington Irving.
The lancers: an interlude. F. (DL 1 Dec 1827). Cumberland 19 (dated 1828); Dicks 517; Readex micro.

Born in the USA, Payne spent the middle part of his theatrical career in London and Paris. He also edited in New York The Thespian Mirror *1805–6,* The Pastime *1807–8, the monthly* Ladies' Companion *1834–44 (with others); and in London the weekly* Opera Glass *1826–7. For other dramatic works, see* Nicoll 4, *pp. 368–9, 603. For further bibliographical details, see Conolly,* English drama, *pp. 231–2;* Stratman, *pp. 516–18 and* Readex Index, *p 209.*

§2

Harrison, G. Life and writings of John Howard Payne. New York 1875; Philadelphia 1885 (rev edn as John Howard Payne, dramatist, poet, actor, and author of Home sweet home!); New York [1969].
Miller, W. C. The author of 'Home, sweet home'. Theatre n.s. 6, June–Dec 1885.
Gilbert, V. M. The stage career of John Howard Payne, author of Home, sweet home. Northwest Ohio Quart 1950–1.
Overmyer, G. America's first Hamlet. New York 1957.
Saxon, A. H. John Howard Payne, playwright with a system. TN 24 1969–70. [JRS]

Richard Brinsley Peake 1792–1847

Licensing copies of the plays to 1824 are located in the Huntington; playscripts from 1824 (including some partly autograph), letters, and accounts are in BL.

§1

All plays listed below are also issued in one or more Readex micro *edns.*
French characteristic costumes. 1816.
Wanted, a governess. F. (Lyc 15 Sep 1817). 1817.
Amateurs and actors. F. (EOH 29 Aug 1818). 1818; Cumberland 16; Dicks 962.
A walk for a wager: or a bailiff's bet. F. (EOH 2 Aug 1819). 1819.
The duel: or my two nephews. F. (CG 18 Feb 1823 as My two nephews). 1823; Cumberland 22.
Frankenstein. D. (EOH 28 July 1823 as Presumption: or the fate of Frankenstein). Dicks 431. From Mary Shelley.
Americans abroad: or notes and notions. F. (EOH 3 Sep 1824 as Jonathan in England). Dicks 589.
The life of an actor. F. (Adel 2 Dec 1824). Dicks 582.
The £100 note. F. (CG 7 Feb 1827). 1827; New York 1828; Cumberland 34; Dicks 640.
Comfortable lodgings: or Paris in 1750. F. (DL 10 Mar 1827). Cumberland 29; Lacy 82; Dicks 678.
The haunted inn. F. (DL 31 Jan 1828). Cumberland 30; Lacy Suppl 1; Dicks 677.
The bottle imp. D. (EOH 7 July 1828). 1838; Webster 2; Dicks 593. Music by G. H. Rodwell.
The Noyades: or love and gratitude. D. (EOH 14 July 1828). Dicks 671.
Master's rival: or a day at Boulogne. F. (DL 12 Feb 1829). Cumberland 22; Lacy 94. From Le Sage, Crispin, rival de son maître.
The Middle Temple: or which is my son? F. (EOH 27 June 1829). 1837; Webster 1; Dicks 692. Music by G. H. Rodwell.
The spring lock. Musical Ent. (EOH 18 Aug 1829). 1838; Webster 4. Music by G. H. Rodwell.
The Chancery suit! C. (CG 30 Nov 1830). 1831; Baltimore 1831; Dicks 583.
The evil eye. D. (Adel 18 Aug 1831). [1831]; Lacy 43; Dicks 540.
The climbing boy: or the little sweep. D. (Olym 13 July 1832). 1834; Dicks 675.
In the wrong box. F. (Olym 3 Feb 1834). Dicks 737.
The chain of gold: or a daughter's devotion. D. (Adel 29 Sep 1834). Dicks 694.
House room: or the dishonoured bill. F. (EOH 8 Aug 1836). 1836. From the Fr.
A quarter to nine. F. (Lyc 27 July 1837). 1838; Webster 2; Mod Eng Com Th ser 2; Dicks 946.
Blanche of Jersey. D. (EOH 9 Aug 1837). 1838; Webster 2; Dicks 557. Music by J. Barnett.
The Meltonians. Ext. (DL 16 Apr 1838). 1838; Webster 4.
Lying in ordinary. F. (EOH 28 June 1838). 1838; Webster 4; Dicks 768.
Gemini. F. (EOH 2 July 1838). 1838; Webster 5; Dicks 768.
Snobson's seasons, being annals of Cockney sports. [1838?]; 1846 (as An evening's announcement: or the adventures of a Cockney sportsman).
H. B. F. (Adel 9 Dec 1839). 1840; Webster 8; Dicks 703.
The devil in London: or sketches in 1840. Ext. (Adel 20 Apr 1840). Dicks 718. With J. B. Buckstone.
Memoirs of the Colman family, including their correspondence with the most distinguished personages of their time. 2 vols 1841, [1841] (2 vols in 1).
Court and city. C. (CG 17 Nov 1841). Cumberland 42; Dicks 655. From Steele, The tender husband, and Frances Sheridan, The discovery.
Uncle Rip. F. (Lyc 13 June 1842). Cumberland 42; Mod Eng Com Th 3. From L. B. Picard, Les deux Philibert.
Ten thousand a year. D. (Adel 29 Mar 1844). Cumberland Minor 16; Dicks 445. From S. Warren, Diary of a physician.
Cartouche, the celebrated French robber. 3 vols 1844.
The three wives of Madrid: or the diamond ring. F. (Lyc 25 Apr 1844). Barth [1844?].
The sheriff of the county. C. (H 24 Feb 1845). 1845; Webster 11; Dicks 843.
The devil of Marseilles: or the spirit of avarice. MD. (Adel 1 July 1846). Barth [1846?]. Music by A. Mellon.
The title deeds. C. (Adel 21 June 1847). [1847]; Webster 14; Dicks 1013.
The bequeathed heart. D. (Adel 18 Nov 1847 as Gabrielli: or the bequeathed heart). Dicks 584.

Contributions to Periodicals

The Toledo rapier. 2 pts. Bentley's Misc Nov–Dec 1839.
The portfolio of Peter Popkin. 4 pts. Bentley's Misc Feb–Sep 1840.
Journal of Old Barnes. 4 pts. Bentley's Misc May–Aug 1840.
The cobbler physician. Bentley's Misc Aug 1840.
The Transylvanian anatomie! Bentley's Misc Sep 1840.
The bequeathed heart. NMM May 1841.
Pope Joan. Bentley's Misc Aug 1842.
Story-tellers and street music. Ainsworth's Mag Oct 1842.
The haunted mine. Bentley's Misc Nov 1842.
The Prussian paddy grenadier. 2 pts. Ainsworth's Mag July–Aug 1844.
Anticipations of 1860. Ainsworth's Mag Dec 1844.
The post-bag. 3 pts. Bentley's Misc Dec 1844–Feb 1845.
Anecdotical gatherings. Bentley's Misc Mar 1845.
See also Nicoll *4, pp. 369–71, 603; Conolly,* English drama, *pp. 232–3;* Readex Index, *p. 210.*

§2

The Times 7 Oct 1847. Obituary.
Era 10 Oct 1847. Obituary. [JRS]

James Robinson Planché 1796–1880

Ms copies of most of the dramatic works listed below are held in the Lord Chamberlain's Collection at the BL. Of more than 50 other pieces written by Planché but not extant in printed form, the majority can also be found in ms either in this collection or in the Larpent Collection at the Huntington.

Collections

The extravaganzas of Planché 1825–71. Ed T. F. D. Croker and S. Tucker 5 vols 1879.
Songs and poems, from 1819 to 1879. Ed M. A. Mackarness 1881.
Plays by James Robinson Planché. Ed D. Roy 1986.

Selections

Booth, M. (ed). English plays of the nineteenth century. Vol 5 1976.

§1

Amoroso, king of Little Britain. Bsq. (DL 21 Apr 1818). 1818; 1829; Cumberland 43; 1862.
Rodolph, the wolf: or Columbine Red Riding-Hood. P. (Olym 21 Dec 1818). 1818, 1819.
The troubadours: or jealousy outwitted. DO. (Olym 9 Feb 1819). 1819 [Songs, duets, trios, choruses, &c].
The vampire: or the bride of the Isles. MD. (EOH 9 Aug 1820). 1820; Baltimore 1820; Hodgson's juvenile drama [1822]; Cumberland 27; Lacy 107; Dicks 875. From P. F. A. Carmouche, J. E. C. Nodier and A. F. L. de Jouffroy d'Abbans, Le vampire.
A burletta of errors: or Jupiter and Alcmena. Ba. (Adel 6 Nov 1820). 1820 [Songs, duets, glees, choruses, &c]. From Dryden, Amphitryon.
Giovanni, the vampire: or how shall we get rid of him? Bsq Ba. (Adel 15 Jan 1821). 1821 [Songs, duets, glees, choruses, &c].
Peter and Paul: or love in the vineyards. Vaud. (H 4 July 1821). Dicks 898.
The pirate. MD. (Olym 14 Jan 1822). 1822. From Scott.
[Henri Quatre and] the fair Gabrielle. Oa. (EOH 19 June 1822). 1822.

All in the dark: or the banks of the Elbe. CO. (EOH 10 July 1822). 1822; Dicks 896. From H. J. B. D. Victor, Hasard et folie.
Ali Pacha: or the signet ring. MD. (CG 19 Oct 1822). Dolby's British Theatre, 1823-25; Cumberland 11. From J. H. Payne, with additional songs.
Maid Marian: or the huntress of Arlingford. O. (CG 3 Dec 1822). [1822]; New York 1823. From Peacock.
[Hernando] Cortez: or the conquest of Mexico. MD. (CG 13 Oct 1823). [1823]; 1823 [Songs, duets, glees, choruses, &c]; New York 1824.
Shere Afkun, the first husband of Nourmahal: a legend of Hindoostan. 2 pts [1823]. A poem.
Costume of Shakespeare's King John [etc] selected from the best authorities with biographical, critical and explanatory notices by J. R. Planché. 5 pts 1823–5.
Der Freischütz: or the black huntsman of Bohemia. O. (CG 14 Oct 1824). 1824 [Songs, duets, choruses, incantations, &c]; 1825. From J. F. Kind.
A woman never vext: or the widow of Cornhill. C. (CG 9 Nov 1824). [1824]; New York 1827; Cumberland 8; Dicks 880. From Rowley.
Success: or a hit if you like it. Ba. (Adel 12 Dec 1825). Extravaganzas vol 1 1879.
Oberon: or the elf-king's oath. O. (CG 12 Apr 1826). 1826; [1826: Songs, duets, choruses]; 1827; Lacy 59; [1865?]. From W. Sotheby and C. M. Wieland.
Returned killed. F. (CG 31 Oct 1826). 1826; Dicks 894. From Le mort dans l'embarras.
The rencontre: or love will find out the way. CO. (H 12 July 1827). Philadelphia 1835.
Descent of the Danube from Ratisbon to Vienna, during the autumn of 1827; with anecdotes and recollections, historical and legendary. 1828, 1836.
Paris and London: or a trip across the herring pond. Ba. (Adel 21 Jan 1828). Cumberland Minor 3; Hallberger Lib, Stuttgart 1842; Dicks 886.
The merchant's wedding: or London frolics in 1638. C. (CG 5 Feb 1828). 1828; 1829 (in Cumberland 19); [1887] (in Dicks 879). From J. Mayne, The City match, and Rowley, Match me at midnight.
A daughter to marry. F. (H 16 June 1828). From Scribe and Mélesville, Une demoiselle à marier. [See My daughter, sir (1832).]
The green-eyed monster. CO. (H 18 Aug 1828). Cumberland 21; Lacy 101; Dicks 891. From Les deux jaloux.
The mason of Buda. Ba. (Adel 21 Oct 1828). [1828?]; Cumberland Minor 1. From Scribe, Le maçon.
Charles XII: or the siege of Stralsund. D. (DL 11 Dec 1828). Cumberland 25; New York 1848; Hallberger Lib, Stuttgart 1855; Lacy 67; Dicks 871. From Voltaire.
Thierna-na-oge: or the prince of the lakes. MD. (DL 20 Apr 1829). 1829 [Songs, choruses, &c]. With W. Barrymore.
Manoeuvring. Int. (H 1 July 1829). 1829. With C. Dance, from Scribe and Mélesville, L'ambassadeur.
The brigand [chief]. D. (DL 18 Nov 1829). Cumberland 24; Baltimore 1830; Lacy suppl vol 1; Dicks 876. From M. E. G. M. Théaulon C. Nombret Saint-Laurent and T. Anne, Le bandit.
The national guard: or bride and no bride. CO. (DL 4 Feb 1830). 1830 [Songs, duets, &c]. From Scribe, La fiancée.
Hofer: or the Tell of the Tyrol. O. (DL 1 May 1830). [1830]; 1830 [Songs, duets, choruses]. From V. J. E. de Jouy and H. L. F. Bis, Guillaume Tell.
The Jenkinses: or boarded and done for. F. (DL 9 Dec 1830). Lacy 8; Dicks 899.
Olympic revels: or Prometheus and Pandora. Ba. (Olym 3 Jan 1831). 1834; Lacy 41. With C. Dance.
The romance of a day. O. (CG 3 Feb 1831). [1831.]
My great aunt: or where there's a will. F. (Olym 5 Mar 1831). 1846; Lacy 20; Dicks 897.
Olympic devils: or Orpheus and Eurydice. Ba. (Olym 26 Dec 1831). 1836; Lacy 41. With C. Dance.
My daughter, sir: or a daughter to marry. F. (Olym 9 Oct 1832). Cumberland 37; Lacy 74; Dicks 897. [Another version of A daughter to marry (1828).]
The Paphian bower: or Venus and Adonis. Ba. (Olym 26 Dec 1832). [1832]; 1866; Lacy 44. With C. Dance.
Promotion: or a morning at Versailles in 1750. Vaud. (Olym 18 Feb 1833). 1852; Lacy 21; French NY 161; Dicks 893.
Reputation: or the court secret. D. (CG 4 Mar 1833). [1833]; [1887] (in Dicks 892).
High, low, jack and the game: or the card party. Ext. (Olym 30 Sep 1833). 1833; New York 1834 [Songs, duets and concerted pieces]; New York 1838; French NY 155. With C. Dance.
Gustavus III: or the masked ball. O. (CG 13 Nov 1833). 1833; [1833: Songs, duets, choruses]. From Scribe.
The deep, deep sea: or Perseus and Andromeda. Ba. (Olym 26 Dec 1833). [1833: Songs, duets, choruses]; 1834; Philadelphia 1835; New York [18–?]; London [1859] (in Lacy 41). With C. Dance.
Secret service. CD. (DL 29 Apr 1834). 1834; Dicks 870. From Mélesville and C. Duveyrier, Michel Perrin.
The loan of a lover. Vaud. (Olym 29 Sep 1834). 1834; Lacy 9; New York 1847; Dicks 895.
My friend, the governor. Vaud. (Olym 29 Sep 1834). 1834; Dicks 899.
The regent. D. (DL 18 Oct 1834). 1834; Dicks 884. From Scribe and Mélesville, Le moulin de Javelle.
The red mask: or the council of three. O. (DL 15 Nov 1834). [1834]. From A. Berretoni, Il bravo.
Telemachus: or the island of Calypso. Ext. (Olym 26 Dec 1834). [1834: Songs, duets, choruses, &c]; Lacy 51. With C. Dance.
History of British costume to the close of the 18th century. 1834, 1847, 1874.
The court beauties. Ba. (Olym 12 Mar 1835). 1835; [1850?]; Lacy 21; Dicks 898.
The jewess. OD. (DL 16 Nov 1835). 1835. From Scribe, La juive.
Chevy Chase. MD. (DL 3 Mar 1836). 1836 [Songs, choruses].
Court favour: or private and confidential. C. (Olym 29 Sep 1836). [1837]; Webster 2, 16; Dicks 883. From P. F. A. Carmouche.
The siege of Corinth. O. (DL 8 Nov 1836). [1836: Songs, duets, trios, choruses]. From Byron and L. Balocchi and A. Soumet.
The two Figaros. Vaud. (Olym 30 Nov 1836). [1837]; Webster 1; Dicks 888. From H. A. Richaud-Martelly, Les deux Figaro: ou le sujet de comédie.
Riquet with the tuft. Ba. (Olym 26 Dec 1836). [1837]; Webster 1. With C. Dance, from C. A. Sewrin and N. Brazier, Riquet à la houppe.
A peculiar position. F. (Olym 3 May 1837). [1837]; Webster 1; Dicks 878. From Scribe and J. F. A. Bayard, La frontière de Savoie.
Norma. O. (DL 24 June 1837). [1841]; 1848; Lacy 32. From F. Romani.
The child of the wreck. MD. (DL 7 Oct 1837). Lacy 39; Dicks 877.
Puss in boots. Ba. (Olym 26 Dec 1837). 1838; Webster 3. With C. Dance.
The magic flute. O. (DL 10 Mar 1838). [1838: Songs]. From J. E. Schikaneder.
The drama's levée: or a peep at the past. Dramatic Review. (Olym 16 Apr 1838). 1879 [in Extravaganzas 2].
The printer's devil. F. (Olym 11 Oct 1838). [1838]; Webster 5; Hilsenberg, Leipzig 1843; Dicks 889.
The Queen's horse: or the brewer of Preston. Ba. (Olym 3 Dec 1838). [1839]; Webster 6. With M. B. Honan.
Regal records: or a chronicle of the coronation of the Queens Regnant of England. 1838.
Blue Beard. Ba. (Olym 2 Jan 1839). [1839]; [1839: Songs, duets and choruses]; Lacy 19. With C. Dance.
Faint heart ne'er won fair lady. F. (Olym 28 Feb 1839). Duncombe 39; New York 1847; Lacy 35; Dicks 878.

The Garrick fever. F. (Olym 1 Apr 1839). Lacy 22; New York [1870]; Dicks 881.
The fortunate isles: or the triumphs of Britannia. Masque. (CG 12 Feb 1840). 1840.
The sleeping beauty in the wood. Ext. (CG 20 Apr 1840). [1840]; 1840 [Songs, duets, choruses]; [1852?]; Lacy 19.
The Spanish curate. C. (CG 13 Oct 1840). [1840]; Dicks 874. From Fletcher and Massinger.
The captain of the watch. C. (CG 25 Feb 1841). [1841]; Lacy [nd]; Dicks 893; French 270. From Lockroy, Le chevalier du guet.
Beauty and the beast: a . . . fairy extravaganza. Ext. (CG 12 Apr 1841). 1841 [Songs, duets, choruses]; [1841]; New York 1847; 1848; London [1849], [1857]; Lacy 19; Dicks 1017.
The marriage of Figaro. CO. (CG 15 Mar 1842). 1842 [Songs, duets, choruses]. From L. Da Ponte.
The white cat. Ext. (CG 28 Mar 1842). 1842; 1842 [Songs, duets, choruses]; 1856; Lacy 24.
The follies of a night. Vaud. (DL 5 Oct 1842). 1842; New York 1847; Lacy 14; Dicks 869. From Lockroy, A. A. Bourgeois and E. L. Vanderburch, Charlot.
Fortunio and his seven gifted servants. Ext. (DL 17 Apr 1843). 1843; 1843 [Songs, duets, choruses, &c]; Boston 1844; G. H. Lewes, Selections from the modern British dramatists 2 (1867); Lacy 19; French 276.
Who's your friend?: or the Queensberry fête. C. (H 22 Aug 1843). [1843]; Webster 10; Lacy suppl vol 3; Dicks 882. From J. F. A. Bayard and L. B. Picard, Trianon.
The fair one with the golden locks. Ext. (H 26 Dec 1843). 1844; 1852; Lacy 19. See Queen Lucidora. 1868.
Grist to the mill. C. (H 22 Feb 1844). 1844; Lacy 20; Dicks 890. From J. F. A. Bayard and P. F. Pinel-Dumanoir, La marquise de Carabas.
The drama at home: or an evening with Puff. Dramatic Review (H 8 Apr 1844). 1844; Lacy 20.
Somebody else. Vaud. (H 4 Dec 1844). 1845; Lacy 11; French NY [1880?]; Dicks 895.
Graciosa and Percinet. Ext. (H 26 Dec 1844). 1845; 1845 [Songs, duets, choruses, &c]; Lacy 20.
The golden fleece: or Jason in Colchis and Medea in Corinth. Ext. (H 24 Mar 1845). 1845; Lacy 20.
A cabinet question. F. (H 23 Sep 1845). 1845; Lacy 20; Dicks 889.
The bee and the orange tree: or the four wishes. Ext. (H 26 Dec 1845). 1846; Lacy 20.
The Irish post. F. (H 28 Feb 1846). 1846; Lacy 20; Dicks 937.
'The Birds' of Aristophanes. Bsq. (H 13 Apr 1846). 1846; 1846 [Songs, duets, choruses, &c]; Lacy 20.
Queen Mary's bower. C. (H 10 Oct 1846). [1846?]; 1847; Lacy 20; Dicks 996. From J. H. Vernoy de St Georges, Les mousquetaires de la reine.
Spring Gardens. F. (H 15 Oct 1846). [1846]; Dicks 997.
The invisible prince: or the island of tranquil delights. Ext. (H 26 Dec 1846). [1846: Songs, duets, choruses]; 1847; New York 1848; [1852]; Lacy 19.
The new planet: or Harlequin out of place. Ext. (H 5 Apr 1847). 1847.
The Jacobite. D. (H 12 June 1847). [1847]; 1852; Lacy 14; Dicks 1015.
The pride of the market. D. (Lyc 18 Oct 1847). 1847; New York 1848; Lacy 20; French NY 9; Dicks 999.
The golden branch. Ext. (Lyc 27 Dec 1847). 1847 [Songs, duets, choruses]; [1848]; Lacy 19.
Lavater the physiognomist: or Not a bad judge. D. (Lyc 2 Mar 1848). 1848; New York [1856?]; Boston [1858?]; Lacy 8; Dicks 1016.
Theseus and Ariadne: or the marriage of Bacchus. Ext. (Lyc 24 Apr 1848). 1848, 1849; Lacy 19.
The king of the peacocks. Ext. (Lyc 26 Dec 1848). [1849]; 1849 [Songs, duets, choruses, &c]; Lacy 19.
A romantic idea. D. (Lyc 8 Mar 1849). 1849, 1855; Lacy 21; Dicks 1010.
Hold your tongue. C. (Lyc 22 Mar 1849). [1849]; Lacy 20; Dicks 1010.
The seven champions of Christendom. Ext. (Lyc 9 Apr 1849). [1849]; [1849: Songs, duets, choruses, &c]; Lacy 21.
A lady in difficulties. C. (Lyc 15 Oct 1849). [1849]; Lacy 21.
The island of jewels. Ext. (Lyc 26 Dec 1849). [1850]; [1850: Songs, duets, choruses, &c]; Lacy 19.
Fiesco: or the revolt of Genoa. D. (DL 4 Feb 1850). 1850. From Schiller.
Cymon and Iphigenia. Ext. (Lyc 1 Apr 1850). 1850; [1875]. From D. Garrick, Cymon.
My heart's idol: or a desperate remedy. C. (Lyc 16 Oct 1850). [1850]; Lacy 274.
Rise gentle moon. A song. [1850?]
A/The day of reckoning. MD. (Lyc 4 Dec 1850). 1852; Lacy 21.
King Charming: or the blue bird of paradise. Ext. (Lyc 26 Dec 1850). [1851]; Lacy 19.
The queen of the frogs. Ext. (Lyc 21 Apr 1851). [1851]; 1851 [Songs, duets, choruses, &c]; Lacy 19.
The prince of Happy Land: or the fawn in the forest. Ext. (Lyc 26 Dec 1851). [1852.]
The mysterious lady: or worth makes the man. C. (Lyc 18 Oct 1852). [1853]; Lacy 8.
The good woman in the wood. Ext. (Lyc 27 Dec 1852). 1853 [Songs, duets, &c]; Lacy 9.
The Pursuivant of Arms: or heraldry founded upon facts. 1852, [1859] (rev), [1874].
Mr Buckstone's ascent of Mount Parnassus. Dramatic Review (H 28 Mar 1853). Lacy 10.
The camp at the Olympic. Dramatic Review (Olym 17 Oct 1853). [1853: Songs, duets]; Lacy 12, 18.
Once upon a time there were two kings. Ext. (Lyc 26 Dec 1853). [1853?: Songs, duets, &c]; Lacy 13.
Mr Buckstone's voyage round the globe (in Leicester Square). Dramatic Review (H 12 Apr 1854). Lacy 15.
The knights of the round table. C. (H 20 May 1854). Lacy 15. From E. Grangé and X. de Montépin, Les chevaliers du Lansquenet.
The yellow dwarf and the king of the gold mines. Ext. (Olym 26 Dec 1854). Lacy 17.
The new Haymarket spring meeting. Dramatic Review (H 9 Apr 1855). 1855 [Songs, duets, &c]; Lacy 22.
The discreet princess: or the three glass distaffs. Ext. (Olym 26 Dec 1855). Lacy 24.
Young and handsome. Ext. (Olym 26 Dec 1856). 1857; Lacy 29.
An old offender. CD. (Adel 22 July 1859). Lacy 41.
Love and fortune. C. (P'cess 24 Sep 1859). Lacy 42. From A. H. de La Motte, La ceinture de Vénus.
My lord and my lady: or it might have been worse. C. (H 12 July 1861). Lacy 52. From A. Dumas, Un mariage sous Louis XV.
Love's triumph. O. (CG 3 Nov 1862). 1862.
A corner of Kent: or some account of the parish of Ash-next-Sandwich, its historical sites and existing antiquities. 1864.
Orpheus in the Haymarket. Bsq. (H 26 Dec 1865). 1865; Lacy 68. From H. Crémieux, Orphée aux enfers.
Pieces of pleasantry for private performance during the Christmas holidays. [1868.]
Queen Lucidora, the fair one with the golden locks; Harlequin Prince Graceful: or the carp, the crow, and the owl. P. (SW [26?] Dec 1868). [1869]. Another version of The fair one with the golden locks. 1843.
King Christmas. Masque. (Gallery of Illus, 26 Dec 1871). Lacy 95.
William with the ring: a romance in rhyme. 1873.
The Conqueror and his companions. 2 vols 1874.
A cyclopaedia of costume: or dictionary of dress; including notices of contemporaneous fashions on the Continent and a general chronological history of the costumes of the principal countries of Europe. 2 vols 1876–9.
Suggestions for a national theatre. 1879.

Contributions to collaborative works

Songs in Clari: or the maid of Milan [by J. H. Payne]. O. (CG 8 May 1823). 1823; Cumberland 24; Boston 1856; Lacy 95; Dicks 406.

Lays and legends of the Rhine [with music by H. R. Bishop]. 2 vols 1827, 1832; Frankfurt 1830, London 1832, Frankfurt 1836 (with Legends of the Rhine by T. C. Grattan), 1837 (as The Rhenish keepsake).

Twelve designs for the costume of Shakespeare's Richard the Third [with drawings by C. F. Tomkins]. 1830.

Continental gleanings of unpublished scenery [with drawings by C. F. Tomkins, executed on stone by J. S. Cooper]. [1836?]

Souvenir of the bal costumé given by Queen Victoria at Buckingham Palace, May 12, 1842 [with drawings by C. Smyth]. 1843.

Extravaganza and spectacle. Temple Bar 1861.

An old fairy tale [The sleeping beauty] told anew in pictures and verse [with drawings by R. Doyle, engraved by the brothers Dalziel]. [1865.]

An introduction to heraldry [by H. Clark, revised and corrected by J. R. Planché]. 1866, 1892.

Songs in Babil and Bijou: or the lost regalia [by D. Boucicault]. Spectacle (CG 29 Aug 1872). [1882?] (rev).

Journals

The recollections and reflections of J. R. Planché: a professional autobiography. 2 vols 1872, 1901.

Translations

King Nut-Cracker: or the dream of poor Reinhold. A fairy tale. [1853], [1927]. From H. Hoffmann.

Fairy tales by the Countess d'Aulnoy. 1855, 1888.

Four and twenty fairy tales: selected from those of Perrault and other popular writers. 1858.

Planché also edited or annotated several other works on costume, armoury and antiquities.

§2

J. R. Planché. Critic 5 Nov 1859. Anon.

Athenaeum 5 June 1880. Obituary.

Jnl of Br Archaeological Assoc 36 1880. Obituary.

Simpson, J. P. J. R. Planché. Theatre Aug 1880.

A theatrical reformer (J. R. Planché). Stage 16, 23 Sep 1915. Anon. [DR]

Isaac Pocock 1782–1835

Hit or miss! O. (Lyc 26 Feb 1810). 1810 (3 edns), 1811, 1816 (Dibdin's London Theatre 6), 1818; Cumberland 34.

The miller and his men. MD. (CG 21 Oct 1813). 1813, 1816, 1820; Cumberland 26; Dicks 28; Dicks' BD; Lacy suppl vol 1; Boston 1856.

The magpie or the maid? MD. (CG 15 Sep 1815). [1815], 1816; Cumberland 28; Lacy 87; Dicks 948. First produced as The daughter (DL 7 Sep 1815). From Caigniez, La pie voleuse.

Robinson Crusoe: or the bold bucaniers. MD. (CG 7 Apr 1817). 1817; Cumberland 28; Lacy 89; [1871]; Dicks 214. From Pixérécourt, Robinson Crusoe.

Rob Roy Macgregor: or auld lang syne! MD. (CG 12 Mar 1818). 1818, 1818; Oxberry 10; Lacy 3; Dicks 70; BD 2; Dicks' BD [1867]; Waverley dramas [1845]. From Scott.

Montrose: or the children of the mist. MD. (CG 14 Feb 1822). 1822, Baltimore 1822. From Scott, The legend of Montrose.

Nigel: or the crown jewels. MD. (CG 28 Jan 1823). 1923. From Scott, The fortunes of Nigel.

The robber's bride. MD. (CG 22 Oct 1829). Cumberland Minor 2; Boston 1856; Dicks 362; Cumberland 28; Lacy 69.

See also Nicoll *4, pp. 383–5, 606.*

John Poole 1786–1872

§1

Byzantium: a dramatic poem. nd.

Hamlet travestie. Bsq. (NT 24 Jan 1811). 1810 (anon), 1810 (authorship acknowledged), 1811 (2nd–3rd edns), New York 1811, London [1812], 1816, 1817, New York 1820, 1837, Oxford 1849, London 1853 (in Lacy 10), New York 1866, London [187-?] (reprint of 1811).

The hole in the wall. F. (DL 23 June 1813). 1813, New York 1813.

A short reign and a merry one. F. (CG 19 Nov 1819). 1819.

Simpson and Co. C. (DL 5 Dec 1822). New York 1823, 1827; Cumberland 43; Lacy 74; Dicks 336.

'Twould puzzle a conjuror. F. (H 11 Sep 1824). Lacy 14; Dicks 648.

Paul Pry. C. (H 13 Sep 1825). Duncombe 1; New York 1826; Lacy 15; Dicks 321; tr Ger 1854, Hungarian 1882.

Lodgings for single gentlemen. F. (H 15 June 1829). Lacy 115; Dicks 403; Duncombe 54.

Patrician and parvenu: or confusion worse confounded. C. (DL 21 Mar 1835). 1835.

Crotchets in the air: or an [un]scientific account of a balloon-trip in a familiar letter to a friend. 1838, 1838.

Little Pedlington and the Pedlingtonians. 2 vols 1839, 1860.

Phineas Quiddy: or sheer industry. 3 vols 1843.

Christmas festivities: tales, sketches and characters, with beauties of the modern drama in four specimens. 4 vols 1845–8.

The comic miscellany for 1845. 1845. Ed Poole.

The comic sketch-book or sketches and recollections. 1859 ('new edn').

For other dramatic pieces, see Nicoll *4, pp. 386–7, 606.*

§2

Fitzgerald, P. The author of Paul Pry. GM Sep 1874.

Richard John Raymond

The castle of Paluzzi: or the extorted oath. MD. (CG 27 May 1818). 1818.

Cherry bounce. F. (SW 27 Aug 1821). Lacy 69; Dicks 360; Duncombe 9.

Robert the devil: or the wizard's ring. MD. (Cob 21 June 1830). 1830; Cumberland 33.

The deuce is in her. F. (Adel 28 Aug 1830). Duncombe 7; Dicks 993.

The farmer's daughter of the Severnside: or the broken heart. D. (Cob 11 Apr 1831). Lacy 26.

The old oak tree. MD. (EOH 24 Aug 1835). Duncombe 18.

Mrs White. Oa. (EOH 23 June 1836). Duncombe 22; Lacy 55; Dicks 360.

The discarded daughter. (Sur 5 Apr 1847). Duncombe 59.

See also Nicoll *4, pp. 388–9, 606.*

William Barnes Rhodes 1772–1826

§1

The satires of Juvenal translated into English verse. 1801.

Epigrams, in two books. 1803.

Eccentric tales in verse, by Cornelius Crambo. 1808.

Bombastes furioso: a burlesque tragic opera. (H 7 Aug 1810). [Dublin] 1813, London 1822 (pirated), 1822 (first authorised edn), 1830; Duncombe 48; Cumberland 43; Lacy 3; Dicks 222.

§2

Bibliotheca dramatica: a catalogue of the dramatic library of W. B. Rhodes esq, which will be sold by auction by Mr Sotheby. [1825.]

GM Nov 1826. Obituary.

Lord John Russell, 1st Earl Russell 1792–1878

Don Carlos: or persecution. D. (Sur 8 June 1848). 1822 (6 edns). From Schiller.

Caius Gracchus. [1830.] From Monti.

For Russell's other writings, biographical, political, historical and miscellaneous (including the suppressed story The nun of Arouca *1822), see S. Walpole,* The life of Lord John Russell, *2 vols 1889.*

Thomas James Serle 1798–1889

Ms letters and licensing copies of the plays (one partly autograph) from 1832 onwards are located in BL.

§1

All plays listed below are also issued in Readex micro *edn.*

Raffaelle Cimaro. T. (Unacted). 1819.
 REVIEW: Br Stage and Literary Cabinet June 1819.
Fulvius Valens: or the martyr of Caesarea. D. (Unacted). 1823; nd.
The victim of St Vincent: or the horrors of an assault. MD. (Cob 22 Aug 1831). Duncombe Minor 10; Dicks nd.
The man in the iron mask: or the secrets of the Bastille. D. (Cob 16 Jan 1832). Duncombe Minor 22; Dicks 428; Dicks 1030 (reissue).
The merchant of London. D. (DL 26 Apr 1832). 1832; Dicks 1033.
The house of Colberg. T. (DL 1 Oct 1832). 1833.
The yeoman's daughter. D. (Adel 17 July 1833). Duncombe 12; New BT 91.
The gamester of Milan. D. (Vic 21 Apr 1834). Duncombe 14.
The shadow on the wall. MD. (EOH 20 Apr 1835). [1835.]
A ghost story. D. (Adel 4 Jan 1836). 1836.
The parole of honour. D. (CG 4 Nov 1837). 1837; Duncombe 34; Dicks 543; Dicks 1032 (reissue).
Joan of Arc, the maid of Orleans. D. (CG 28 Nov 1837). 1837; Duncombe 34; Dicks 347; Dicks 1029 (reissue).
Windsor Castle: or the prisoner-king. Oa. (CG 7 Apr 1838). 1838 (libretto).
Master Clarke. D. (H 26 Sep 1840). 1840, [1840]; Dicks 537; Dicks 1031 (reissue).
Joan of Arc, the maid of Orleans. 3 vols 1841.
Sappho. O. (DL 1 Apr 1843). [1843] (libretto).
The players: or the stage of life. 3 vols 1847.
Waltheof. T. (Sur 17 Mar 1851). 1851. Also attributed to W. J. Robson.
Tender precautions: or the romance of marriage. C. (P'cess 24 Nov 1851). Lacy 5.

For other dramatic pieces see Nicoll *4, pp. 399–400, 610; 5, p. 561. See also Conolly,* English drama, *p. 269,* Stratman, *p. 572;* Readex Index, *p. 244.*

§2

Era Almanack 1869.
The Biograph and Rev Nov 1879.

Founder secretary of the Dramatic Authors' Soc, Serle also wrote political commentary for (and was sometime editor of) The Weekly Dispatch. [JRS]

Sir Martin Archer Shee, RA 1769–1850

Correspondence with Sir Robert Peel and others is located in BL.

§1

Rhymes on art: or the remonstrance of a painter; with notes and a preface, including strictures on the state of the arts, criticism, patronage, and public taste. 1805, 1805 (with additional preface and notes); 1806 (3rd edn), 1809 (reissue); Philadelphia 1811.
A letter to the President and directors of the British Institution; containing the outlines of a plan for the national encouragement of historical painting in the United Kingdom. 1809.
Elements of art, a poem: in six cantos; with notes and a preface; including strictures on the state of the arts, criticism, patronage and public taste. 1809.
The commemoration of Reynolds, in two parts, with notes and other poems. 1814.
Alasco ... Excluded from the stage, by authority of the Lord Chamberlain. T. (Sur 5 Apr 1824). 1824; New York 1825; New York, Philadelphia and Boston 1825; Readex micro. First performance arranged outside the Lord Chamberlain's jurisdiction.
Oldcourt. 3 vols 1829. A novel.
Cecil Hyde. 2 vols 1834. A novel.
Harry Calverley. 3 vols 1835. A novel.
A letter to Lord John Russell ... on the alleged claim of the public to be admitted gratis to the exhibition of the Royal Academy. 1837.
A letter to Joseph Hume, Esq, M. P., in reply to his aspersions on the character and proceedings of the Royal Academy. 1838.

See also Nicoll *4, p. 400; Conolly,* English drama, *p. 270;* Stratman, *pp. 580–1;* NCSTC *ser 1, 4, pp. 156–7.*

§2

Shee, M. A. The life of Sir Martin Archer Shee, President of the Royal Academy ... by his son. 2 vols 1860. [JRS]

Richard Lalor Sheil 1791–1851

Mss of two unpbd plays and licensing copies of the acted plays are in the Huntington; political correspondence is located in BL.

§1

All plays listed below are issued in one or more Readex micro *edns.*

Adelaide: or the emigrants. T. (Crow St, Dublin 19 Feb 1814; CG 23 May 1816). Dublin 1814, 1816 (2nd edn).
The apostate. T. (CG 3 May 1817). 1817 (4 edns), 1818 (5th edn); New York 1817, 1819; Baltimore 1827; Philadelphia 1828; New York 1835; Philadelphia and New York [1844?]; New York 1848; French NY nd.
 REVIEW: [C. Maturin and W. Gifford] Quart Rev 17 1817.
Bellamira: or the fall of Tunis. T. (CG 22 Apr 1818). 1818 (4 edns); New York 1818; Baltimore 1818.
Evadne: or the statue. T. (CG 10 Feb 1819). 1819 (5 edns); New York 1819, 1824; Oxberry 14; New York 1847, [1847?], 1848, [1848?]; Lacy 24; French NY nd; BD 4 (dated 1865); Dicks 25; New York drama 4 [1876–80]. Based on Shirley, The traitor.
Damon and Pythias. T. (CG 28 May 1821). 1821 (2 edns); Philadelphia 1829; Duncombe 61; BD 3 (dated 1865); Dicks 19. By J. Banim, altered and rev for the stage by Sheil.
An irregular ode for the drawing-room ... Written at the command of his Ex——y, by Richard Sh—l, Esq. [1825?]
The speeches of the Right Honourable Richard Lalor Sheil, M. P. Ed T. MacNevin, Dublin 1845; London 1847; Dublin 1853; Dublin and London 1872.
Sketches of the Irish Bar. With memoir and notes by R. S. Mackenzie. 2 vols New York 1854, 1858; Chicago 1882. With W. H. Curran. Sheil's own contributions, mainly comprising papers from the NMM Oct 1822–Mar 1829, were rptd as Sketches, legal and political, ed with notes by M. W. Savage, 2 vols 1855.

Sheil wrote two unpbd plays, Montoni: or the phantom *(CG 3 May 1820) and* The Huguenot *(CG 11 Dec 1822). He adapted Massinger,* The fatal dowry *(DL 5 Jan 1825). See also* Nicoll *4, pp. 400–1, 610; Nicoll,* English drama 1900–30, *pp. 270–1;* Stratman, *pp. 581–4;* Readex Index, *p. 248.*

Contributions to periodicals

Talma. NMM July 1822.
Sketches of the Irish Bar. NMM 14 pts Oct 1822–Mar 1829.
Les vêpres Siciliennes: a tragedy [by C. Delavigne]. NMM 2 pts Nov–Dec 1822.
Conversations of Maturin. NMM 4 pts May–Oct 1827. Attributed.
Schoolboy recollections of the Jesuits. NMM 2 pts Aug–Oct 1829.
Moore's Lord Edward Fitzgerald. ER Sep 1831.

For list of other periodical articles, mainly on political topics, in NMM *and* Br and Foreign Rev, *see* Wellesley *vol 5. 1989.*

§2

Fraser's Mag June 1846.
GM July 1852. Obituary.

MacCullagh, W. T., afterwards MacCullagh Torrens. Memoirs of Richard Lalor Sheil. 2 vols 1855. [JRS]

George Soane 1790–1860

§1

Knight Damon and a robber chief. 1812.
The eve of St Marco. 1813. A novel.
The peasant of Lucern: a melo-drama. 1815.
The innkeeper's daughter. MD. (DL 7 Apr 1817). 1817; Duncombe 43; Lacy 114.
The falls of Clyde. MD. (DL 29 Oct 1817). 1817, 1818; French 1894; Cumberland 31.
Self-sacrifice: or the maid of the cottage. D. (EOH 19 July 1819). 1819.
Extracts from Göethe's tragedy of Faustus. Tr 1820.
The Hebrew. D. (DL 2 Mar 1820). 1820. From Scott, Ivanhoe.
Faustus. MD. (DL 16 May 1825). 1825. 1825; Cumberland 33.
Masaniello, the fisherman of Naples. 1825. Anon.
Specimens of German romance, selected and translated from various authors. 1826.
Pride shall have a fall: or the ladder of life. MD. (Cob 30 July 1832). 1824.
The frolics of Puck. 1834.
Zarah. MD. (Queen's 7 Sep 1835). Cumberland 35; Lacy 92; Dicks 357.
Life of the Duke of Wellington, compiled from his Grace's despatches, and other authentic records and original documents. 2 vols 1839–40.
The last ball, and other tales. 3 vols 1843.
The syren. CO. (P'cess 14 Oct 1844). [1844]. From Scribe, La sirène.
January Eve: a tale of the times. 1847.
New curiosities of literature, and book of the months. 2 vols 1847.
Haydée: or the secret. O. (Str 3 Apr 1848). 1848. From Scribe, Haydée.
For other dramatic works, see Nicoll *4, pp. 403–4, 612.*

§2

Bowman, W. P. Some plays by Soane. MLN 54 1939.

Charles A. Somerset

Crazy Jane. MD. (Sur 19 June 1827). Cumberland Minor 2.
The roebuck: or guilty and not guilty. D. (Sur 1 Oct 1827). Duncombe 2; Dicks 544. From Kotzebue.
A day after the fair: or the roadside cottage. F. (Olym 5 Jan 1829). Cumberland Minor 3; New York 1828 (for 1829?); Lacy 76; Dicks 415.
Home sweet home!: or the ranz des vaches. MD. (CG 19 Mar 1829); 1829; Duncombe 3; Dicks 296. Adapted from the Ger.
Shakespeare's early days. Ba. (CG 29 Oct 1829). Cumberland 28; Lacy 93; Dicks 792. First called The life of William Shakespeare.
The female Mascaroni: or the fair brigands. Oa. (Sur 12 Feb 1821). Cumberland Minor 13.
The mistletoe bough: or the fatal chest. (Garrick's Subscription Theatre 1834). Cumberland Minor 12 (as The mistletoe bough: or young Lovel's bride); Lacy 100.
The sea. D. (Queen's 1834). Cumberland Minor 7; Lacy 105.
See also Nicoll *4, pp. 404–5, 612; 5, pp. 574, 817.*

Sir Thomas Noon Talfourd 1795–1854

Collections

In Miles, A. H. et al. The poets and poetry of the century 10 vols [1891–7], 12 vols [1905–7].
Ion. The Athenian captive. Glencoe 1840.
Tragedies; to which are added a few sonnets and verses. 1844, New York and Boston 1846, London 1848, New York and Boston 1849, London 1850, Boston and New York 1865, London and New York 1889.

§1

Poems on various subjects, including a poem on the education of the poor; an Indian tale; and the offering of Isaac: a sacred drama. 1811.
Hazlitt's lectures on drama. Edinburgh Rev 34 1820.
The Athenian captive. T. (CG 4 Aug 1835). 1838, Berlin 1838, New York 1838, New York and Philadelphia 1838, Philadelphia 1838, London [188-?] (in Dicks 327).
Ion. T. (CG 26 May 1836). [1835] (2 edns priv ptd), [1835] (priv ptd, with a few sonnets), 1836 (3 edns), Berlin 1836, New York 1836, London 1837 (4 edns), New York 1837, Philadelphia [1840]; Providence RI 1840, New York 1844 [1845], New York, Baltimore and Washington 1846, New York [186?], London [1880] (in Dicks 319); tr Ger by P. Kühles, Neustadt a. S. [1873].
The letters of Charles Lamb, with a sketch of his life by T. N. Talfourd. 1837, 1849.
Speech delivered in the House of Commons on moving for leave to bring in a Bill to consolidate the law relating to copyright and to extend the term of its duration. 1837.
Glencoe: or the fate of the Macdonalds. T. (H 23 May 1840). 1839 (priv ptd), 1840; Dicks 323.
Three speeches in favour of a measure for an extension of copyright. 1840.
Speech for the defendant in the prosecution of the Queen v. Moxon for the publication of Shelley's works. 1841.
Recollections of a first visit to the Alps, in August and September 1841. [1842?] (priv ptd).
The legend of St Bernard: a poem. Norwich [1844] (not pbd, anon).
Vacation rambles and thoughts. 2 vols 1845, 1851 (3rd edn).
Address written for the occasion of the amateur performance at Manchester on July 26 1847, for the benefit of Mr Leigh Hunt... spoken by Mr Charles Dickens. 1847.
Final memorials of Charles Lamb, consisting chiefly of his letters not before published. 1848, 1850.
Encyclopaedia metropolitana. Ed E. Smedley c. 1848–50. Contributions to the history of Greece and of Rome, and on early Greek poetry.
The importance of literature to men of business: an address delivered to members of the Manchester Athenaeum. 1852.
The Castilian. T. (unacted?). 1853.
Supplement to Vacation rambles, consisting of recollections of a tour through France to Italy, and homewards by Switzerland, in the vacation of 1846. 1854.
Talfourd also contributed important reviews and critical essays to Pamphleteer, NMM *and* Retrospective Rev *1816–25, and later to other periodicals.*

§2

Gallery of literary characters no. 74: Mr Serjeant Talfourd (with portrait). Fraser's Mag 14 1836.
Modern English dramatists: Mr Serjeant Talfourd. Bentley's Misc 9 1841. Anon.
Horne, R. H. In his A new spirit of the age vol 1, 1844.
Dickens, C. The late Mr Justice Talfourd. Household Words 25 Mar 1854.
A memoir of the late Mr Justice Talfourd, by a member of the Oxford Circuit. 1854.
The life and writings of the late Mr Justice Talfourd. North Br Rev 43 1856. Anon.
Brain, J. A. An evening with Talfourd. Reading [1889]. A lecture.
Garnett, R. In DNB.
Clark, B. H. Contemporary English dramatists. Eng Jnl 15 1926.
Merriam, H. G. Edward Moxon: publisher of poets. New York 1939.

Newdick, R. S. A Victorian Demosthenes. Quart Jnl of Speech 25 1939.
Harrocks, S. H. Talfourd. N & Q June 1949. Further notes by F. Taylor 6 Aug 1949 and J. M. T. 7 Jan 1950.
McCormick, J. P. An early champion of Wordsworth: Talfourd. PMLA 68 1953.
Sutherland, J. A. Thackeray's Before the curtain. N & Q 217 1972.
Feather, J. Publishers and politicians: the remaking of the law of copyright in Britain 1775–1842: the rights of authors. Publishing History 25 1989. [VE]

Benjamin Thompson 1776?–1816

Mss of two unacted trns are located in BL; licensing copies of the acted plays are in the Huntington.

Collections

The German theatre. 6 vols 1800, 1801, 1805, 1811 (4th edn). Contains trns of 19 plays by Babo, Goethe, Iffland, Kotzebue, Lessing, Reitzenstein, Schiller and Schroeder. Except for The stranger, all unacted.

§1

The dramatic works of Baron von Kotzebue. 3 vols 1802. Contains 10 trns. Except for The stranger, all unacted.
A biographical account of Baron Augustus von Kotzebue, to which is added a brief statement of his dramatic works. 1801; Kotzebue Works 1.
The Florentines: or secret memoirs of the noble family De C**. 1808.
The recal of Momus: a bagatelle. 1809 (2nd edn).
Godolphin, the lion of the north. MD. (DL 12 Oct 1813). Unpbd; Readex micro.
Oberon's oath: or the paladin and the princess. MD. (DL 21 May 1816). 1816 [posthumous]; Readex micro. With a memoir.
REVIEW: Theatrical Inquisitor July 1816.

Translations

The stranger. D. (DL 24 Mar 1798). 1800, 1801, 1802, 1806; in German Theatre 1; Kotzebue Works 2; Inchbald 24; LSt 3; Oxberry 22; Cumberland 14 (dated 1826); Penny Nat Lib [c. 1830]; Webster 15; Dram Ents; Lacy 22; Dicks' BD 1; Dicks 12; Readex micro (4 edns). From Kotzebue, Menschenhass und Reue. Performance review with other trns of Kotzebue in Monthly Mag 6 1799; Anti-Jacobin 1 1798, 3 1799.
The happy family. D. (Unacted). 1799, 1801; in German Theatre 5; Kotzebue Works 2. From Kotzebue.
REVIEW: Br Critic Apr 1800.
Count Benyowsky: or the conspiracy of Kamtschatka. D. (Unacted). 1800; in German Theatre 2; Kotzebue Works 1. From Kotzebue.
Ignes de Castro. T. (Unacted). 1800. From D. Quita.
Lovers' vows: or the natural son. D. (Unacted). 1800; in German Theatre 3; Kotzebue Works 2; Baltimore 1802. From Kotzebue.
An account of the introduction of Merino sheep into the different states of Europe and at the Cape of Good Hope. 1810. From C. P. Lasteyrie.
See also Nicoll *3, pp. 311, 397; 4, pp. 412;* NSTC, *ser 1, 4, pp. 308–9;* Readex Index, *p. 270.*

§2

Some account of the late Mr Benjamin Thompson. In his Oberon's oath, 1816. [JRS]

John Tobin 1770–1804

§1

The honey moon. C. (DL 31 Jan 1805). 1805 (2 edns), ed Mrs Inchbald 1807, New York 1807, London 1808 (in The British theatre vol 25), [1810] (in London stage vol 4), Philadelphia 1823, London [1824] (in The British theatre vol 17), New York [184?] (in French), New York, Baltimore and Washington 1846, New York 1847, London [1850] (in Lacy 16), ed [G. Daniel] (1850), [1864] (in The British drama vol 2), [1874] (in Dicks 14); tr Fr by C. Nodier 1822.
The curfew. D. (DL 19 Feb 1807). 1807 (7 edns), [1824] (in London stage vol 4), Philadelphia 1826, London [1829] (in Cumberland 43), [1864] (in The British drama vol 4), [1875] (in Dicks 102). Verse and prose.
The school for authors. C. (CG 5 Dec 1808). 1808.
The faro table: or the guardians. C. (DL 5 Nov 1816). 1816.
The farce All's fair in love *(CG 29 Apr 1803) is unpbd. The operatic farce* Yours or mine? *(CG 23 Sep 1816) was pbd with Benger's* Memoirs, *below. See also* Nicoll *4, pp. 413, 614.*

§2

Benger, E. O. Memoirs of Tobin, with a selection from his unpublished writings. 1820.

Benjamin Nottingham Webster 1797–1882

High ways and by ways. F. (DL 15 Mar 1831). Cumberland 28. From Monsieur Rigaud and Partie et revanche.
Paul Clifford, the highwayman of 1770: or crime and ambition. D. (Cob 12 Mar 1832). Cumberland Minor 6. From Lytton.
The modern Orpheus: or music the food of love. F. (CG 15 Apr 1837). Webster 1.
The village doctor: or the hind's disease. C. (H 24 July 1839). Webster 7.
Caught in a trap. F. (H 25 Nov 1843). Webster 10.
Pierrot (the married man) and Polichinello (the gay single fellow). Ba (Adel 27 Dec 1847). Webster 14.
Belphegor, the mountebank: or pride of Bath. D. (Adel 13 Jan 1851). Webster 17.
The man of law. D. (H 9 Dec 1851). Webster 17.
Webster wrote, adapted or translated about a hundred plays. See Nicoll *4, pp. 417–18, 616; 5, pp. 618, 823. A memoir will be found in Webster's* Acting national drama *vol 4, 1838.*

iii. Mid-nineteenth-century drama 1835–1870

For an explanation of the abbreviations used see under Early Nineteenth-Century Drama, col 1955.

Gilbert Abbott À Beckett 1811–56

Many of À Beckett's plays were unpbd. 37 are lodged in the Lord Chamberlain's Collection in the BL; a further 8 are listed by Nicoll. 36 letters to Frederick Evans dated 1844–53 are in the Punch *archives. The À Beckett family papers were lost or destroyed during World War II.*

§1

The king incog. F. (Fitzroy 9 Jan 1834). Miller.
The son of the sun; or the fate of Phaeton. Bsq. (Fitzroy 13 Feb 1834). Miller 3.
The revolt of the workhouse. Bsq. (Fitzroy 24 Feb 1834; City 1835). Miller 20; Cumberland 8. A travestie of The revolt of the harem, an English version of Labarre's ballet, then appearing at Covent Garden.
The Siamese twins. D. (Fitzroy 14 Apr 1834). Cumberland 14; French; Boston Th 14; Dicks 338.
The turned head. F. (Vic 3 Nov 1834). Cumberland 13; French 220; Boston Th 13; Lacy 67; Dicks 338.
Figaro in London. F. (Str 24 Nov 1834). Cumberland 45.

Man Fred. B. (Str 26 Dec 1834; Vic 1835). Cumberland 9.
Love is blind; or manners make the man. D. (StJ 5 Jan 1835). Duncombe 25.
Unfortunate Miss Bailey. Ba. (Str 2 Feb 1835). Cumberland 11.
The roof scrambler. Bsq. (Vic 15 June 1835). Cumberland 10, 32.
The man with the carpet bag. F. (Str 19 Jan 1835; Vic 20 Sep 1835; StJ 1836). Cumberland 13; Leipzig 1845; Mo Eng Com Th 3; Lacy 1018; French 1018; French's minor drama 319; Dicks 959; Cumberland acting plays 47; Music Publishing Co nd.
A clear case. F. (StJ 14 Dec 1835). Cumberland 44.
The mendicant. B. (StJ 2 Feb 1836). Cumberland 37.
The tradesman's ball. F. (StJ 29 Sep 1836). Duncombe 23. Dicks 1040; in Alphons J. Middel, Sammlung englischer komödien und schauspiele; original areiten aus der feder erster englischer autoren 1923.
The postilion. Ba. (StJ 13 Mar 1837). Cumberland 43. Adapted from Le postillon de Lonjumeau by Adolphe de Leuven and Léon Lhérie.
Jack Brag; or a chandler's chances. F. (StJ 23 May 1837). Leipzig; Hartung; Mod Eng Com Th ser 3, vol 8; Cumberland 37; Dicks 534. Adapted from Theodore Hook's novel.
The assignation; or, what will my wife say? C. (StJ 29 Sep 1837). Duncombe 34; Dicks 452; French 1800; Lacy.
King John (with the benefit of the act). B. (StJ 16 Oct 1837). Duncombe 34; Cumberland.
Wanted, a brigand; or a visit from Fra Diavolo. Ba. (StJ 6 Dec 1837). Duncombe 35; Dicks 613.
Pascal Bruno, the brigand chief. B. (StJ 26 Dec 1837). Duncombe 35; New York and Philadelphia 1838; Dicks 559. Adapted from Alexander Dumas's novel.
The black domino [alternative title: The queen's ball; or the black domino]. B. (StJ 29 Jan 1838). Duncombe 29, 35; Dicks 443. English version of Le domino noir by A. E. Scribe.
The ambassadress. CO. (StJ 5 Mar 1838). Duncombe 32. A version of L'ambassadrice by A. E. Scribe.
The artist's wife. C. (H 28 July 1838). Webster 5; Dicks 442; French.
Oliver Twiss, the workhouse boy. Imitation. (By 'Poz'). 1838.
Posthumous papers of the Wonderful Discovery Club, formerly of Camden Town, established by Peter Patron. Imitation. (By 'Poz'). [1838.]
The yellow dwarf; or the king of the gold mines. Bsq. (P'cess 26 Dec 1842). Barth; Lacy 17; French.
The liberal candidate. F. (P'cess 16 Jan 1843). Barth 7.
The three graces. Bsq. (P'cess 17 Apr 1843). Barth 3.
The magic mirror; or the hall of statues [alternative title: The magic mirror; or, the ninth statue]. B. (P'cess 26 Dec 1843). W. S. Johnson 1843.
Open sesame; or a night with the forty thieves [alternative title: The thorough bred Arabian]. Ext. (Lyc 8 Apr 1844). W. S. Johnson 1844. In collaboration with Mark Lemon.
The wonderful lamp in a new light. Bsq. (P'cess 4 July 1844). W. S. Johnson [18??]. Adapted from Aladdin.
Don Caesar de Bazan. (P'cess 8 Oct 1844). New York and Baltimore 1846; Lacy 12; New York 1878; Dicks 800. Translated and adapted from the Fr play by Dumanoir and Dennery; in collaboration with Mark Lemon.
The knight and the sprite! or the cold water cure. (Str 11 Nov 1844). Barth. In collaboration with Mark Lemon.
The chimes: a goblin story of some bells that rang an old year out and a new year in [alternative title: The chimes; or a goblin tale]. D. (Adel 19 Dec 1844). Webster 11; Dicks 819. Adapted from Dickens's Christmas book; in collaboration with Mark Lemon.
Joe Miller and his men. Ext. (P'cess 24 Dec 1844). Barth.
The comic Blackstone. Humour. 1844 (illustr George Cruikshank). Widely rptd throughout the nineteenth century.
Scenes from the rejected comedies by some of the competitors for the prize of £500 offered by Mr B. Webster, lessee of the Haymarket Theatre, for the best original comedy illustrative of English manners. 1844. Also ptd as pt 3 of Quizziology, 1846.
Hop o' My Thumb. 1844. (illustr John Leech). Children's book.
St George and the dragon. Bsq. (Adel 24 Mar 1845). Webster 11. In collaboration with Mark Lemon.
Timour; or the cream of Tartar [alternatived title: Timour, the cream of all the Tartars]. Ext. (P'cess 24 Mar 1845). W. S. Johnson 1845. Altered from Timour the Tartar by Matthew Lewis.
Heathen mythology (as 'Punch'). Humour. Philadelphia 1845.
The small debts act [An Act for the better securing the payment of small debts, 9 Aug 1845], with annotations and explanations critical and analytical. 1845. Pam.
Peter Wilkins; or the loadstone rock and the flying Indians. Ext. (Adel 9 Apr 1846). Webster 14; French 148. In collaboration with Mark Lemon.
The quizziology of the British drama, comprising I Stage passions; II Stage characters; III Stage plays. 1846. Essay.
The comic history of England. Humour. 1847–8 (illustr John Leech). Widely rptd into the twentieth century.
The castle of Otronto. Ext. (H 24 Apr 1848). Webster 150.
The comic history of Rome. Humour. 1848 (illustr John Leech). Widely rptd throughout the nineteenth century.
The debts and funds of England. (By 'Poz'). 1850. Pam.
O Gemini! or the brothers of Co(u)rse. B. (H 12 Apr 1852). Webster 17. In collaboration with Mark Lemon.
Angelo; or the actress of Padua. D. (1852). French 177. Altered and translated from Victor Hugo.
Sardanapalus; or the 'fast' king of Assyria. Bsq. (Adel 20 July 1853). Webster 17. In collaboration with Mark Lemon.
The fiddle faddle fashion book. Humour. nd. Illustr John Leech.

Contributions to periodicals

À Beckett was a founding contributor to Punch *and a leader writer for* The Times, Morning Chron, Morning Advertiser, Morning Herald, Globe, Sun, Standard, *and* Daily News. *As 'The Perambulating Philosopher' he contributed to* Illus London News. *According to Bunn, below, he also founded some 11 further short-lived periodicals.*

The Censor. An entirely original work devoted to literature, poetry and the drama. (By Gilbert Abbott À Beckett, assisted by his brothers Thomas Turner and William À Beckett). Nos 1–16, 6 Sep 1828–4 Apr 1829. Bi-weekly.
Figaro in London. 8 vols. 1832–9. Weekly. [No 1 dated 10 Dec 1831.]
The Comic Almanack. An ephemeris in jest and earnest, containing merry tales, humorous poetry, quips and oddities. Edited by [William Makepeace] Thackeray, Albert Smith, Gilbert [Abbott] À Beckett, and the brothers Mayhew. Illustr George Cruikshank. 1st ser 1835–43. 2nd ser 1844–53.
Dramatic Spectator. Ed by Poz, Quiz and Co. 1837.
The Almanack of the Month. A review of everything and everybody. 2 vols 1846.
George Cruikshank's Table Book. 1856, 1869.

Unpublished works

The frolics of the fairies; or Puck in a pucker. Spec. (Fitzroy 31 Mar 1834). Nicoll.
Wagustavus; or the barn ball. Bsq. (Fitzroy 19 May 1834). Nicoll.
Caught courting; or, Juno, by Jove! Ba. (Vic 2 Aug 1834). Nicoll.
The twelve months. Ba. (Str 18 Dec 1834). Nicoll.
St Mark's Eve. Ba. (Olym 19 Dec 1834).
The echoes of Westminster Bridge (Vic 6 July 1835). Attributed to À Beckett by his widow in her petition to the Royal Literary Fund, 5 December 1859.
Agnes Sorel. O. (StJ 14 Dec 1835).
A French company. F. (StJ 14 Dec 1835).
Browne's horse. (StJ 18 Jan 1836). Altered from Tin donkey.
The Parish Revolution. Bsq. (StJ 26 Dec 1836).

Temptation; or, the Vale of Sarnam [alternative title; Sarnem]. Bt. (StJ 1837). By Gilbert Abbot À Beckett or C. Millingen.
Oliver Twist. B. (StJ 27 Mar 1838). Adapted from Dickens's novel.
Punch's pantomime; or Harlequin and Magna Charta [alternative title: Punch's pantomime; or Harlequin, King John and Magna Charta]. P. (CG 26 Dec 1842). In collaboration with Mark Lemon, Albert Smith, D. W. Jerrold et al.
Little Red Riding Hood. O. (P'cess 5 Feb 1843). Nicoll.
I puritani. Bsq. (P'cess 16 Mar 1843). Nicoll. An English version of Pepoli's opera.
Geraldine; or, the lovers' well. CO. (P'cess 14 Aug 1843). Nicoll. Adapted from Le puits d'amour by A. E. Scribe and A. de Leuvin.
The gaming table. D. (Fitzroy 3 Feb 1844). Nicoll.
Prologue for Mary A. Keeley. Verse. 1844.
The world underground, etc, etc [alternative title: The world underground; or, the golden flute and the brazen waters]. Ext. (H 27 Dec 1847).
Charles II; or, something like history. B. J. W. Last 1872. Presumably misattributed by Nat Union Cat, mistaking Gilbert Abbott À Beckett for Gilbert Arthur À Beckett.
Christabel; or, the bard bewitched. B. J. W. Last 1872. Misattributed by Nat Union Cat, mistaking Gilbert Abbott À Beckett for Gilbert Arthur À Beckett.
An utter perversion of the brigand; or, new lines to an old banditty. Bsq. (H 26 Dec 1867). Phillips [1878]. Misattributed by Nat Union Cat, mistaking Gilbert Abbott À Beckett for Gilbert Arthur À Beckett.
Happy Arcadia. In collaboration with William Schwenk Gilbert. Court 3 Mar 1873. Misattribution by Nicoll; by Gilbert Arthur À Beckett.
The Sleeping Beauty; or Harlequin and the spiteful fairy. P. (CG 26 Dec 1870). In collaboration with Charles Henry Ross. Misattributed by Nat Union Cat, mistaking Gilbert Abbott À Beckett for Gilbert Arthur À Beckett.
A morning call. Ms, with alterations in another hand. Lib of Congress.

§2

Bunn, Alfred. A word with Punch. [1847.]
À Beckett, Arthur William. The À Becketts of Punch: memoirs of father and sons. 1903.
Burnand, F. C. Mr Punch: some precursors and competitors. Pall Mall Mag 1904.
Boyd, Martin. Day of my delight. Melbourne 1965. [PS]

Henry Robert Addison, Lt-Col. 1805–76

Licensing copies of the plays are located in BL.

§1

All plays listed below are also issued in one or more Readex micro *edns.*
Lo Zingaro. MD. (Adel 3 Aug 1833). Duncombe 12.
Jessie, the flower of Dumblaine: or weel may the keel row! Oa. (Adel 26 Aug 1833). Duncombe 13.
Tam O'Shanter. F. (DL 25 Nov 1834). 1834; Dicks 532. In verse.
The king's word. Int. (DL 20 Jan 1835). 1835.
Marie: a tale of the Pont Neuf. Ca. (CG 27 Feb 1836). Duncombe 21; Dicks 991.
Handbook for residents and tourists in Belgium. Brussels 1838.
The Rhine and it's [*sic*] banks and environs etc. Brussels 1839.
Belgium as she is. Brussels and Leipzig 1843.
Sophia's supper. OF. (Sur 21 May 1849). Lacy 16; Boston Th 1 (dated 1855).
Traits and stories of Anglo-Indian life. 1858.
Diary of a judge: being trials of life compiled from the note-books of a recently deceased judge etc. 1860.
No 117, Arundel Street, Strand. F. (Lyc 24 Mar 1860). Lacy 48.
Recollections of an Irish police magistrate, and other reminiscences of the south of Ireland. 1862.
Locked in with a lady. F. (Roy 2 Feb 1863). Lacy nd; Sergel 85; De Witt 85.
'All at sea': or recollections of a half-pay officer. 1864.
Behind the curtain: a novel. 3 vols 1865.
Paris social: a sketch of every-day life in the French metropolis. 1866.
Forty-eight hours in Paris, amidst the ruins. [1871].
The blue-faced baboon: or the man-monkey. (No performance details). Dicks 606.

Contributions to periodicals

For Addison's contributions to Dublin Univ Mag, Bentley's Misc *and* Ainsworth's Mag, *see* Wellesley *vol 5 1989.*
Addison edited the first edn of Who's who *1849. See also* Nicoll *4, pp. 251, 567; 5, pp. 235–6, 777;* Readex Index, *p. 3*

§2

Dublin Univ Mag Oct 1841. Attributed to C. Lever.
Era Almanack. 1868. [JRS]

George Almar

The rover's bride: or the bittern's swamp. MD. (Sur 30 Aug 1830). Cumberland Minor 11.
Pedlar's acre: or the wife of seven husbands. D. (Sur 22 Aug 1831). Cumberland Minor 5; Lacy 84; Dicks 280.
The tower of Nesle. MD. (Sur 17 Sep 1832). Cumberland Minor 6; Lacy 91; Dicks 234.
The knights of St John: or the fire banner. MD. (SW 26 Aug 1833). Duncombe 12; Lacy 56.
The clerk of Clerkenwell: or the three black bottles. MD. (SW 27 Jan 1834). Cumberland Minor 7.
The bull-fighter: or the bridal ring. MD. (Sur 8 Oct 1838). Cumberland Minor 14.
Oliver Twist: or the parish boy's progress. D. (Sur 19 Nov 1838). Webster 6; Dicks 293; Mod Eng Com Th 1. From Dickens.
Jane of the Hatchet: or the siege of Beauvais. Spec. (Sur 20 July 1840). Duncombe 41.
See also Nicoll *4, pp. 252–3, 568; 5, pp. 239–40, 777.*

Morris Barnett 1800–56

The bold dragoons. Ba. (Adel 9 Feb 1820). Lacy 19; Dicks 509.
Tact: or the wrong box. F. (Queen's 21 Feb 1831). Duncombe 13.
Mrs G. of the golden pippin: a musical entertainment. (Queen's 14 Mar 1831). Duncombe 8.
The spirit of the Rhine. D. (Queen's 22 Sep 1835). Duncombe 29.
The yellow kids. Ba. (Adel 19 Oct 1835). Duncombe 18; Dicks 967.
Monsieur Jacques. Ba. (StJ 13 Jan 1836). Lacy 28; Dicks 503. From Cogniard, Le pauvre Jacques.
The serious family. F. (H 30 Oct 1849). Dicks 1007. From Le mari à la campagne.
Sarah Blange. D. (Olym 27 Oct 1852). Lacy 31 (as Sarah the Creole).
See also Nicoll *4, pp. 261, 510; 5, pp. 249–50.*

Thomas Lovell Beddoes 1803–49

See col 535.

William Bayle (Baile) Bernard 1807–75

Letters, accounts and licensing copies of the plays are located in BL.

§1

All plays listed below are also issued in one or more Readex micro *edns.*
The freebooter's bride: or the black pirate of the Mediterranean: including the mystery of the Morescoes. A romance. 5 vols 1829.

The old regimentals. D. (Adel 21 Nov 1831). Cumberland 33.
The wept of the wish-ton-wish. D. (Adel 21 Nov 1831). 1831; French NY 154; Dicks 546. From Fennimore Cooper.
The dumb belle. Ca. (Olym 14 Dec 1831). Lacy 23; Dicks 522; Boston Th 2; Mod Eng Com Th ser 2.
The four sisters. F. (Str 3 May 1832). Lacy 23; Dicks 411.
The conquering game. C. (Olym 28 Nov 1832). Duncombe 36; New BT 284; Dicks 676.
The nervous man and the man of nerve. F. (DL 26 Jan 1833). Duncombe 27; Lacy 39; Dicks 458; New York, Baltimore and Boston nd.
The mummy. F. (Adel 4 June 1833). Duncombe 24; Lacy 48; Boston Th 11.
Woman's faith. D. (EOH 2 Nov 1835). 1835; Dicks 536.
Lucille: or the story of a heart. D. (EOH 4 Apr 1836). 1836; Lacy 28; Philadelphia and New York nd; Dicks 410. From Lytton, Maid of Malines (in Pilgrims of the Rhine).
The man about town. F. (EOH 5 May 1836). Duncombe 22; French 118; Dicks 740.
The middy ashore. F. (EOH 23 May 1836). Duncombe 22; New BT 177; Dicks 349.
The farmer's story. D. (EOH 13 June 1836). Duncombe 22; New BT 174; Lacy 44; Dicks 434.
Paulina: or the passage of the Beresina. D. (Adel 5 Dec 1836). Lacy; Dicks 516.
St Mary's Eve: or a Solway story. D. (Adel 1 Jan 1838 with sub-title The story of the Solway). Lacy 33; Dicks 382.
A maiden's fame: or a legend of Lisbon! D. (Adel 12 Feb 1838). Duncombe 28; Dicks 735.
His last legs. F. (H 15 Oct 1839). Webster 7; Dicks 439; French Minor NY 6; tr Esperanto, London 1915.
The happiest man alive. F. (Olym 21 Mar 1840). Duncombe 41; Lacy nd; Dicks 965.
The Irish attorney: or Galway practice in 1770. F. (H 6 May 1840). Webster 9; New York 1847; Dicks 463.
Robespierre: or two days of the Revolution. D. (Adel 5 Oct 1840 with sub-title The fete day). Duncombe 42; French 144; Dicks 610.
The philosophers of Berlin. C. (Lyc 20 May 1841). Dicks 779.
Marie Ducange. D. (Lyc 29 May 1841). Lacy 32; Dicks 475.
The boarding school. F. (H 1 Sep 1841). Webster 9; Dicks 409.
The woman hater. C. (H 22 Feb 1842). Webster 9; Dicks 526.
Louison, the angel of the attic: or the recompense. C. (H 29 May 1843). Dicks 710. From Scribe, Louise: ou la réparation.
The round of wrong: or a fireside story. D. (H 19 Dec 1846). Webster 13; Dicks 1000.
A practical man. F. (Lyc 20 Oct 1849). Lacy 1.
Trevanion: or the false position. D. (Sur 22 Oct 1849). [1849]. With J. W. Marston.
The passing cloud. D. (DL 8 Apr 1850). Lacy 1; New York nd.
Platonic attachments. F. (P'cess 28 Sep 1850). Lacy 2; Mod Eng Com Th ser 4; tr Hungarian, Budapest 1888.
A storm in a tea cup. Ca. (P'cess 20 Mar 1854). Lacy 14; Mod Eng Com Th ser 5.
The balance of comfort. F. (H 23 Nov 1854). Lacy 17.
Charlotte Corday. D. (Adel 10 Oct 1855). Dicks 1042.
The evil genius. C. (H 8 Mar 1856). Lacy 26.
A splendid investment. F. (Olym 11 Feb 1857). Lacy 30.
A life's trial. D. (H 19 Mar 1857). Lacy 30.
The tide of time. C. (H 13 Dec 1858). Lacy 38.
No name. D. (Unacted). 1863. From Wilkie Collins' novel. Commissioned by Collins to secure copyright on dramatisations of the novel.
Faust: or the fate of Margaret. D. (DL 20 Oct 1866). Lacy 83. From Goethe.
The man of two lives. D. (DL 29 Mar 1869). Lacy 85. From Hugo, Les misérables.
The life of Samuel Lover, R. H. A., artistic, literary and musical, with selections from his unpublished papers and correspondence. 2 vols 1874; New York 1874 (1 vol).

Edited works

Retrospections of the stage. By the late John Bernard, manager of the American theatres, and formerly secretary to the Beef-steak Club. [Ed W. Baile Bernard] 2 vols 1830; Boston 1832.

See also Nicoll *4, pp. 265–6, 572; 5, p. 259; Conolly,* English drama, *pp. 81–2;* Readex index, *pp. 24–5.*

§2

Era Almanack 1868. [JRS]

Edward Litt Leman (Laman) Blanchard, Brothers Grinn, with T. L. Greenwood, 'Francisco Frost' 1820–89

§1

The artful dodge. F. (Olym 21 Feb 1841). Lacy 602.
Pork chops: or a dream at home. Ext. (Olym 13 Feb 1843). Lacy 605.
Faith, hope and charity! Or chance and change. D. (Sur 7 July 1845). [1845?], Duncombe vol 54.
Adam's illustrated descriptive guide to the watering-places of England and companion to the coast. 2 vols 1848.
The stranger's and visitor's conductor through London. 1851. As Bradshaw's Guide through London and its environs 1857, (corrected and rev) 1859.
The carpet bag, crammed full of light articles, for shortening long faces and long journeys, and forming a pleasant companion for the road[,] the rail, and the steamer. [1852.]
Peter Wilkins: or Harlequin and the flying women, of the Loadstone Rock. P. (DL 26 Dec 1860). 1860.
Tom Thumb: or Merlin the magician, and the good fairies of the court of King Arthur. P. (Her Majesty's 26 Dec 1860). [1860.]
Cherry and fair star: or the singing apple, the talking bird and the dancing waters. P. (SW 26 Dec 1861). [1862.]
Number Nip: or Harlequin and the Gnome King of the Giant Mountain. P. (DL 26 Dec 1866). 1866.
Faw! Fee! Fo!!! Fum!!!! or Harlequin Jack, the giant killer. (DL 26 Dec 1867). 1867.
The three temptations. In Drawing-room plays and parlour pantomimes, ed C. Scott '1870' [1869].
Flights of fancy: a medley of quips and cranks in prose and verse. 1882. Includes selections from Fun in the 1860s.
The life and reminiscences of E. L. Blanchard. Ed C. Scott and C. Howard 2 vols 1891. (Mainly diaries kept by Blanchard.)

Blanchard also wrote many other pieces, mainly pantomimes. For DL and other theatres, see Nicoll *4, pp. 268–9, 573; 5, pp. 262–5, 779. He reviewed plays for many periodicals, including the* Daily Telegraph, *and edited* Chambers's London Jnl (1841), The Astrologer *and* Oracle of Destiny *(1845), and others.*

§2

Obits: Athenaeum 7 Sep 1889; Era 7 and 14 Sep 1889; The Times 6 Sep 1889.
Knight, Joseph. In DNB suppl 1. [JWS]

Dionysius Lardner Boucicault 1822–90

There is a Boucicault collection of ms and ptd material at the Univ of South Florida.

Collections

Nicoll, A. and T. Cloak (ed). Forbidden fruit and other plays. Princeton 1940. Contains Forbidden fruit, Louis XI, Dot, The flying scud, Mercy Dodd, Robert Emmet.
Krause, D. (ed). The Dolmen Boucicault; with an essay by the editor.

Dublin 1964. Contains The colleen bawn, Arrah-na-Pogue, The shaughraun.
Thomson, P. (ed). Plays by Dion Boucicault; with an essay by the editor. Cambridge 1984. Contains Used up, Old heads and young hearts, Jessie Brown, The octoroon, The shaughraun.
Parkin, A. (ed). Selected plays of Dion Boucicault; with an essay by the editor. Gerrards Cross 1987. Contains London assurance, The Corsican brothers, The octoroon, The colleen bawn, The shaughraun, Robert Emmet.
The Drama on Microfilm series of the Univ of Kent at Canterbury contains 35 plays by Boucicault (from the Frank Pettingell Collection).

§1

London assurance. C. (CG 4 Mar 1841). 1841, 1841; Lacy 34; French 500; Dicks 1044; Moses, Boston 1918; ed R. Eyre London 1971; ed J. L. Smith 1984. Anthologised in Bailey 1966, and Corrigan 1967. *See* Parkin, Collections, *above*.
Used up. C. (H 6 Feb 1844). Webster's Acting National Drama 15; Dicks 1047; French's minor NY; Mod Eng Com Th 5; Kent microfilm. Authorship disputed by Charles Mathews. *See* Thomson, Collections, *above*.
Old heads and young hearts. C. (H 18 Nov 1844). [1845], [1845]; Webster 138; French's standard 62; Mod Eng Com Th 3; Kent microfilm. *See* Thomson, Collections, *above*.
Love in a maze. C. (P'cess 6 Mar 1851). 1851.
The Corsican brothers. D. (P'cess 24 Feb 1852). [Lacy 6 is not Boucicault's]; Kent microfilm. Anthologised in Booth vol 2 and Smith 1976. *See* Parkin, Collections, *above*.
Andy Blake: or The Irish diamond. C. (Boston 20 Nov 1854). Dicks 556; French 110. From Bayard, Le gamin de Paris.
The poor of New York. D. (Wallack's New York 8 Dec 1857). French 189; Dicks 381; Kent microfilm. Anthologised in Gerould 1983.
Jessie Brown: or The relief of Lucknow. D. (Wallack's New York 22 Feb 1858). Lacy 38; French 558; French's standard 203; Dicks 473; Kent microfilm. *See* Thomson, Collections, *above*.
The octoroon: or Life in Louisiana. D. (Winter Garden New York 6 Dec 1859). Lacy/French 963; Dicks 391; Kent microfilm. Anthologised in Quinn 1953, Gassner 1967 and Rogers 1979. Ending revised for performance in England. *See* Thomson and Parkin, Collections, *above*.
The colleen bawn: or The brides of Garryowen. D. (Keene's New York 29 Mar 1860). Lacy/French 932; French's standard 366; Dicks 389; Kent microfilm. Anthologised in Rowell 1953. From Griffin, The collegians. *See* Krause and Parkin, Collections, *above*.
Arragh-na-Pogue: or The Wicklow wedding. D. (Dublin 7 Nov 1864). French 945; Kent microfilm. *See* Krause, Collections, *above*.
Rip Van Winkle. D. (Adel 4 Sep 1865). New York 1895. Anthologised in Quinn 1953. Anon text reworked with and for Joseph Jefferson.
The long strike. D. (Lyc 15 Sep 1866). French's standard 360.
Formosa; or The railroad to ruin. D. (DL 5 Oct 1869). [1869]; Chicago 1869; Kent microfilm.
The rapparee: or The treaty of Limerick. D. (P'cess 9 Sep 1870). [1870]; Chicago 1870; Kent microfilm.
The shaughraun. D. (Wallack's New York 14 Nov 1874). Lacy/French 123; Webster; Dicks 390; New York [1885?]; Kent microfilm. Anthologised in Booth vol 2. *See* Krause, Thomson and Parkin, Collections, *above*.
For other plays, see Fawkes, *below, pp. 260–6;* Thomson, *pp. 228–35;* Nicoll *4, pp. 267–70, 573; 5, pp. 267–9, 779.*
Ireland's story. New York 1881.
The art of acting. New York 1926.

Contributions to periodicals

The art of dramatic composition. North Amer Rev 126, Jan 1878.
Parnell and the times. North Amer Rev 144, June 1887.
The debut of a dramatist. North Amer Rev 148, Apr 1889.
The early days of a dramatist. North Amer Rev 148, May 1889.
Leaves from a dramatist's diary. North Amer Rev 149, Aug 1889.

§2

Kenney, C. The life and career of Dion Boucicault. New York 1883. Probably written by Boucicault himself.
Obits: Athenaeum 27 Sep 1890; The Spirit of the Times 27 Sep 1890.
Fiske, H. G. Boucicault: a memory. Dramatic Mirror Sep 1890.
Walsh, T. The career of Dion Boucicault. New York [1915].
Duggan, G. C. The stage Irishman. Dublin 1937.
Downer, A. S. The case of Mr Lee Moreton. TN 4 1950.
Johnson, A. E. Dion Boucicault: man and fable. Educational Theatre Jnl 6 1954.
McMahon, S. The wearing of the green: the Irish plays of Dion Boucicault. Eire-Ireland 2 1957.
McMahon, S. The great train scene robbery. Quart Jnl of Speech 50 1963.
Johnson, A. E. The birth of Dion Boucicault. Modern Drama 11 1968.
Folland, H. F. Lee Moreton: the debut of a theatre man. TN 23 1969.
Hogan, R. Dion Boucicault. New York 1969.
Degan, J. A. How to end The octoroon. Educational Theatre Jnl 27 1975.
Fawkes, R. Dion Boucicault: a biography. 1979.
Molin, S. E. and R. Goodfellowe. Dion Boucicault, the shaughraun: a documentary life. Pt 1 1979; pt 2 1982.
Richardson, G. A. Boucicault's The octoroon and American law. Educational Theatre Jnl 34 1982.
Cave, R. A. Staging the Irishman. In Acts of supremacy, ed J. S. Bratton et al, Manchester 1991. [PT]

Charles William Shirley Brooks 1816–74

Licensing copies of the plays are located in BL.

§1

All the plays listed below are also issued in one or more Readex micro *edns.*
Our new governess. C. (Lyc 1 May 1845). Barth nd; Dicks 855.
The wigwam. Ba. (Lyc 25 Jan 1847). Dicks 1004.
The Creole: or love's fetters. D. (Lyc 8 Apr 1847). [1847] (priv ptd); Lacy nd [1850?]; Lacy 1; Dicks 1009.
Anything for a change. Ca. (Lyc 7 June 1848). Lacy 4; French 43; De Witt 114.
The opera; The coulisses; Foreign gentlemen in London. In A. R. Smith, Gavarni in London, 1849, [1859] (as Sketches of London life and characters).
The guardian angel. F. (H 5 Oct 1849). Lacy 5.
The daughter of the stars. D. (Str 5 Aug 1850). Lacy 2.
The exposition: a Scandinavian sketch. Ext. (Str 28 Apr 1851). Lacy 3.
A story with a vengeance: or how many joints may go to a tale. [1852], [1853]. With A. B. Reach.
The Russians of the south [Egypt and Syria]. 1854. Rptd from the Morning Chron.
Aspen Court: a story of our times. 3 vols 1855; 1857 (1 vol), 1869. First pbd in Bentley's Misc, *see below*.
The Gordian knot: a story of good and of evil; with illustrations by J. Tenniel. 1860. First pbd in pts 1858–9.
Timour the Tartar: or the iron master of Samarkand-by-Oxus. Ext. (Olym 26 Dec 1860). Lacy 49. With J. Oxenford.
The silver cord: a story. 3 vols 1861; New York 1861; Leipzig 1862; London 1865.
Sooner or later, with illustrations by G. du Maurier. 2 vols 1868. First pbd in pts 1866–8.
The Naggletons, and Miss Violet and her 'offers'. 1875.
Wit and humour: poems from Punch. Ed R. S. Brooks 1875.
The Naggletons. New York 1883.

Contributions to periodicals

The gentleman's tiger. Ainsworth's Mag May 1842.
An evening with Nell Gwynne. Ainsworth's Mag June 1842.
The lounge in the Oeil du Boeuf. Ainsworth's Mag July 1842.
The shrift on the raft. Ainsworth's Mag Aug 1842.
The walls of Famagusta. Ainsworth's Mag Sep 1842.
The guerillas of Leon. Ainsworth's Mag Nov 1842.
A fool's advice: Feste. Ainsworth's Mag Dec 1842.
State and prospects of the legitimate drama in China: a letter from the manager of the Imperial Theatre, and Chinese Opera-House, Pekin, to Charles W. Brooks. Ainsworth's Mag Jan 1843.
'What became of the executioner?' Ainsworth's Mag Mar 1843.
Cousin Emily. Ainsworth's Mag 2 pts May–June 1843.
The mysteries of Beechingthorpe: a true history. Ainsworth's Mag Sep 1843.
A demon's mirror. Ainsworth's Mag Mar 1844.
The country editor: a sketch. Ainsworth's Mag July 1845.
How Miss Mountmorris got a husband. Ainsworth's Mag Jan 1846.
How Mrs Malmsey managed her uncle. Ainsworth's Mag Feb 1846.
A charade solved by a codicil. Ainsworth's Mag Mar 1846.
Aspen Court, and who lost and who won it: a story of our own time. Bentley's Misc 22 pts Jan 1853–Nov 1855.
The House of Commons. Quart Rev June 1854.
The partners. Dublin Univ Mag 6 pts June 1857–Jan 1858.
Brooks contributed regularly to Punch *from 1851, becoming editor in 1870. He also wrote for the* Morning Chron *and* Illus London News. *He edited the* Literary Gazette *from 1858 to 1859 and* Home *in 1867. See also* Nicoll *4, pp. 271, 574; 5, p. 277; Conolly,* English drama, *pp. 92–3;* Readex Index, *p. 36.*

Edition

Amusing poetry. 1857, 1874. Ed Shirley Brooks.

§2

Era Almanack 1868.
Jerrold, B. Shirley Brooks. GM May 1874.
Layard, G. S. A great Punch editor: being the life, letters and diaries of Shirley Brooks. 1907. [JRS]

Robert Barnabas Brough 1828–60

§1

The enchanted isle, or 'raising the wind' on the most approved principles: a drama without the smallest claim to legitimacy, consistency, probability, or anything else but absurdity, in which will be found much that is unaccountably coincident with Shakespeare's Tempest. (Amphitheatre, Liverpool 1848; Adel 20 Nov 1848). [1848]; Webster 14. With W. Brough.
Camaralzaman and Badoura: or the peri who loved the Prince. Ext. (H 26 Dec 1848). Webster 15. With W. Brough.
The sphinx. Ext. (H 9 Apr 1849). Webster 15. With W. Brough.
The second calendar: extravaganza. (H 26 Dec 1850). Webster 15. With W. Brough.
A cracker bon-bon for Christmas parties. 1852. Includes 3 short plays (unacted) and Christmas miscellanies in prose and verse.
The Alain family: a tale. 1853. Tr Brough from the Fr of J. B. A. Karr.
Songs of the governing classes and other lyrics. 1855, 1890.
Béranger's songs translated into English verse. 1856.
The life of Sir John Falstaff; with a biography of the knight, from authentic sources. 1858. First pbd in 10 pts 1857–8. Illustr George Cruikshank.
The siege of Troy: a burlesque. (Lyc 27 Dec 1858). 1858.
Alfred the Great: or the minstrel king. Ext. (Olym 26 Dec 1859). Lacy 43. With W. Brough.
Alf the minstrel, or the Princess Diamonducky and the hazel fairy: a dragon story for Christmas. 1859.
Miss Brown: a romance; and other tales in prose and verse. 1860. Rptd from Welcome Guest, a periodical briefly ed Brough.
Which is which? or Miles Cassidy's contract. 2 vols 1860.
Marston Lynch: a personal biography; with a memoir of the author by G. A. Sala. 1860. First pbd in Train 1856–7.
Shadow and substance, by C. H. Bennett and R. B. Brough. 1860.
Character sketches by C. H. Bennett and R. B. Brough. [1872.]
Other extravaganzas by the brothers Brough will be found in Lacy *6, 14, 15, 27, 29, 32, 52, 88 and Suppl 2. See also* Nicoll *4, p. 271; 5, pp. 277–8.*

§2

Archer, W. In Poets and the poetry of the century, ed A. H. Miles, vol 5 1893.

John Baldwin Buckstone 1802–79

§1

Luke the labourer: or the lost son. D. (Adel 17 Oct 1826). 1826; Cumberland Minor 2; Lacy 69; Dicks 830; ed A. E. Morgan 1935 (in English plays 1660–1820).
The May queen: or Sampson the serjeant. Ba. (Adel 9 Oct 1828). 1834; Dicks 818.
Ellen Wareham. D. (H 24 Apr 1833). Dicks 837.
Agnes de Vere. D. (Adel 10 Nov 1834). 1836; Lacy 106; Dicks 805; Boston 1885.
Isabelle: or a woman's life. D. (Adel 27 Jan 1834). 1835; Dicks 817; Webster's Acting Nat Drama 8. Also called Thirty years of a woman's life.
Jack Sheppard. D. (Adel 28 Oct 1839). Webster 7.
The green bushes: or a hundred years ago. D. (Adel 27 Jan 1845). Webster 11; Boston [1857?]; Dicks 827.
The flowers of the forest: a gipsy story. MD. (Adel 11 Mar 1847). Webster 13; Boston [1857?]; Dicks 1002.
Nine too many. Ba. (Adel 11 Mar 1847). Dicks 1004.
An alarming sacrifice. F. (H 12 July 1849). Boston [1885?]; Dicks 1012.
See also Nicoll *4, pp. 272–5, 574–5; 5, pp. 286–7, 781.*

§2

John Baldwin Buckstone. Once a Week Nov 1872.
Maginn, W. A. In his Gallery of illustrious characters, ed W. Bates [1873], 1883. The essay on Buckstone was first pbd, with a drawing by Maclise, in Fraser's Mag Dec 1836.
Taylor, T. Impressions of Buckstone. Theatre Dec 1879.

Frederick Fox Cooper 1806–79

Licensing copies of the plays are located in BL.

§1

The elbow-shakers: or thirty years of a rattler's life. Bsq. (Adel 3 Dec 1827). Richardson 1; Readex micro.
Black-eyed Sukey: or all in the dumps. Bsq. (Olym 30 Nov 1829). 1830, [1830]; Richardson 3; Cumberland Minor 14; Readex micro.
The spare bed: or the shower bath. (Vic 8 July 1833). Cumberland Minor 7; Dicks 786; Readex micro.
The deserted village. Ba. (Adel 28 Oct 1833). Duncombe 15; Dicks 727; Readex micro. From Goldsmith.
Hercules, king of clubs! F. (Str 7 July 1836). Cumberland Minor 13; Lacy 89; Dicks 387; Readex micro.
Ion. Bsq. (Gar 9 Nov 1836). Cumberland Minor 12; Readex micro.
The queen's visit. Ca. (CL 6 Nov 1837 as The queen's visit to the city). Pattie's penny play 1; Readex micro.
Ivanhoe. D. (Astley's 27 Mar 1837 as The lists of Ashby). Dicks 385; Readex micro. From Scott.
Jenny Jones. Oa. (StJ 1 Mar 1838). Pattie's penny play 1; Readex micro.
Master Humphrey's clock. D. (Vic 26 May 1840). Duncombe 41; Dicks 724; Readex micro. From Dickens.
Shooting the moon: or the cove of Cork. Ca. (Str 29 Oct 1850). New BT 548; French 135; Readex micro.

Ovingdean Grange: or a tale of the South Downs. D. Dicks 1019; Readex micro. From Ainsworth.
Hard times. D. (Str 14 Aug 1854). 1854; Dicks 785; Readex micro. From Dickens.
Who's a traveller? F. (Str 30 Oct 1854). 1855; Readex micro.
Little Dorrit. D. (Str 10 Nov 1856). [1856?] From Dickens.
The tale of two cities: or the incarcerated victim of the Bastille. D. (Vic 7 July 1860). Dicks 780; Readex micro. From Dickens.
Under the earth: or the sons of toil. D. (Astley's 22 Apr 1867). Dicks' BD 6. Also attributed to W. H. C. Nation.
For other dramatic works, including other adaptations of Dickens, see Nicoll *4, pp. 283, 577; 5, pp. 324, 786. See also* Readex Index, *pp. 60–1.*

Contributions to periodicals

Cooper was editor of, or contributor to, a number of short-lived newspapers and periodicals, including Drama: or the theatrical pocket mag *(Nov 1821–May 1822),* Paul Pry *(1830),* Cerebus *(1834), and* Theatrical Chron *(Sep 1848–Mar 1849).*

§2

Era 19 Jan 1879. Obituary.
Glasgow News Jan 1879, rptd Entr'acte no 500. By E. L. Blanchard. Obituary.
Cooper, F. R. Nothing extenuate: the life of Frederick Fox Cooper. 1964. [JRS]

Joseph Stirling Coyne 1803–68

Licensing copies of the plays, including several autographs, are located in BL.

§1

All the plays listed below are also issued in one or more Readex micro *edns.*
The queer subject. F. (Adel 28 Nov 1836). 1837; Webster 1; Dicks 782.
Valsha: or the slave queen. D. (Adel 30 Oct 1837). Webster 2; Dicks 702. From La guerre des servantes.
All for love: or the lost pleiad. D. (Adel 16 Jan 1838). Webster 3.
Arajoon: or the conquest of Mysore. Ba. (Adel 22 Oct 1838). Dicks 700.
Helen Oakleigh: or the wife's stratagem. MD. (EOH 9 June 1840). Duncombe 42; Dicks 605.
Satanas and the spirit of beauty. Spec. (Adel 11 Feb 1841). Lacy 39. From the ballet Le diable amoureux.
My friend the capt. F. (H 20 July 1841). Barth nd; Dicks 740.
The scenery and antiquities of Ireland, illustrated from drawings by W. H. Bartlett: the literary portion of the work by N. P. Willis and J. Stirling Coyne. 2 vols [1842], [1875?].
The water witches. F. (EOH 6 June 1842). Lacy 41; Lorenzen micro.
The merchant and his clerks. D. (Adel 12 Dec 1842). Barth nd; Dicks 642.
Binks the bagman. F. (Adel 13 Feb 1843). Lacy 7; Dicks 624.
The trumpeter's daughter. F. (H 7 Dec 1843). French Minor NY 276.
The signal. D. (Olym 8 Apr 1844). Duncombe 49; French 110; Dicks 741.
Richard III. Bsq. (Adel 1844?). 1844; Barth nd.
Railway bubbles. F. (H 29 Nov 1845). Barth nd.
Did you ever send your wife to Camberwell? F. (Adel 16 Mar 1846). Webster 12; Dicks 955; Booth WC; New York nd (as Did you ever send your wife to Brooklyn?); Oxford 1995 (WC).
The queen of the Abruzzi. Spec. (Adel 8 June 1846). Duncombe 58.
How to settle accounts with your laundress. F. (Adel 26 July 1847). Webster 14; Dicks 1006; Booth 4; Booth.
This house to be sold (the property of the late William Shakespeare) – inquire within. Ext. (Adel 9 Sep 1847). Webster 14. Music by A. Mackenzie.
The Tipperary legacy. F. (Adel 6 Dec 1847). Webster 14; New York nd. With H. Hamilton.
Our national defences: or the Cockshot yeomanry. F. (Adel 27 Jan 1848). Webster 14.
Pas de fascination: or catching a governor. F. (H 26 Apr 1848 as Lola Montes: or a countess for an hour). Webster 14; Boston Th 24; French Minor NY 270.
The barmaid; The potato can. In A. R. Smith, Gavarni in London, 1849; rptd in his Sketches of London life, [1859].
Cocknies in California. F. (Adel 26 Feb 1849). Webster 15; French Minor NY 33 (as Cockneys in California).
Separate maintenance. F. (H 12 Mar 1849). Duncombe 64; New BT 506; Lacy 94.
Mrs Bunbury's spoons. Sk. (Adel 15 Oct 1849). Webster 15.
A scene in the life of an unprotected female. F. (Str 4 Feb 1850 as An unprotected female). Duncombe 64; Boston Th 16; French 111; French Minor NY 233.
My wife's daughter. C. (Olym 14 Oct 1850). Lacy 2.
The vicar of Wakefield: or the pastor's fireside. D. (H 1850?). Webster 16. From Goldsmith.
Presented at court. C. (H 6 Feb 1851). Webster 16.
A duel in the dark. F. (H 31 Jan 1852). Lacy 6.
Wanted, 1000 spirited young milliners for the gold diggings. F. (Olym 2 Oct 1852). Lacy 8; Boston Th 10.
Box and Cox married and settled. F. (H 15 Oct 1852). Lacy 8; French Minor NY 49.
Leo the terrible. Bsq. (H 27 Dec 1852). Lacy 9. With F. Talfourd.
The hope of the family. C. (H 3 Dec 1853). Lacy 13.
Willikind and hys Dinah. D. (H 16 Mar 1854). Lacy 14.
The old chateau: or a night of peril. MD. (H 24 July 1854). Lacy 15.
Pippins and pies: or sketches out of school. Being the adventures and misadventures of Master Frank Pickleberry during that month he was home for the holidays. 1855.
The secret agent. C. (H 10 Mar 1855). Lacy 18. From F. W. Hackländer, Der geheime agent.
The man of many friends. C. (H 1 Sep 1855). Lacy 23; Boston Th 11 (dated 1855).
Catching a mermaid. Ext. (Olym 20 Oct 1855). Lacy 24.
Urgent private affairs. F. (Adel 7 Jan 1856). Lacy 24.
Angel or devil. D. (Lyc 2 Mar 1857). Lacy 29.
Fraud and its victims. D. (Sur 2 Mar 1857). Lacy 29; Boston Th 20.
What will they say at Brompton? Ca. (Olym 23 Nov 1857). Lacy 34.
The love-knot. C. (DL 8 Mar 1858). Lacy 35; Boston Th 21.
Nothing venture, nothing win. C. (Str 5 Apr 1858). Lacy 35.
Samuel in search of himself. F. (P'cess 5 Apr 1858). Lacy 36. With H. C. Coape.
Everybody's friend. C. (H 2 Apr 1859). Lacy 40; De Witt 135.
The pets of the parterre: or love in a garden. Ca. (Lyc 5 Nov 1860). Lacy 48.
The little rebel. F. (Olym 1 Apr 1861). Lacy 50; De Witt 32.
Black sheep. C. (H 22 Apr 1861). Lacy 51.
That affair at Finchley. Ca. (Str 14 Oct 1861). Lacy 52.
A terrible secret. F. (DL 28 Oct 1861). Lacy 53.
Duck hunting. F. (H 29 Sep 1862). Lacy 56.
Buckstone at home: or the manager and his friends. Sk. (H 6 Apr 1863). Lacy 58.
The woman in red. D. (Vic 28 Mar 1864). Lacy 92; Sergel 136. From V. Séjour, La tireuse des cartes.
Dark doings in the cupboard. F. (Adel 29 Dec 1864). Lacy 64.
Sam Spangles: or the history of a harlequin. 1866.
'Oil is better for a wig than vinegar': a dramatic proverb. In Mixed sweets from Routledge's annual, [1867].
The broken-hearted club. Ca. (H 16 Jan 1868). Sergel 25.
The woman of the world. C. (Olym 17 Feb 1868). Lacy 81.
The home wreck. D. (Sur 8 Feb 1869). Lacy 85. Completed by J. Denis Coyne. From Tennyson, Enoch Arden.

Contributions to periodicals

Tim Hogan's ghost. Bentley's Misc July 1841.
Phil Flannigan's adventures. Bentley's Misc Feb 1842.

The guard-room alarm. Bentley's Misc Apr 1842.

Coyne was an early contributor to Punch *and dramatic critic of* The Sunday Times. *From 1856 until his death he was secretary of the Dramatic Authors' Soc. See also* Nicoll *4, pp. 284–5, 578; 5, pp. 327–8, 786; Conolly,* English drama, *pp. 140–2;* Readex Index, *pp. 63–4.*

§2

Obits: Sunday Times 26 July 1868; GM Aug 1868.

In H. T. M. Bell, Half hours with representative novelists of the nineteenth century; being passages from their works with brief biographies, and a critical essay. 3 vols 1927. [JRS]

'Henry Thornton Craven', Henry Thornton 1818–1905

Done Brown! F [also called a vaudeville]. (Adelphi, Edinburgh 1845). Duncombe 56; Lacy 81; Duncombe's British theatre 442.

Bletchington House: or the surrender! D. (CL 20 Apr 1846). Duncombe 56; New BT 447.

The village nightingale: or the spider, the fly and the butterfly. Ba. (Str 23 June 1851). French 108.

Bowl'd out: or a bit of brummagem. F. (P'cess 9 July 1860). Boston 1868; Lacy 47 and 694.

The post-boy. D. (Str 31 Oct 1860). 1860. Lacy 720; French 720.

The chimney corner. D. (Olym 21 Feb 1861). Lacy 50; French 346 and 742.

Miriam's crime. D. (Royal Str 9 Oct 1863). Lacy 60; De Witt 46.

Milky white: an original serio-comic drama. (PW, Liverpool 20 June 1864; Str 28 Sep 1864). 189?. Lacy 85 and 1264; French 1264.

Meg's diversion[s]. C. or D. ([New] Royalty 17 Oct 1866). Lacy 73; French 341 and 1082.

See also Nicoll *4, p. 285; 5, pp. 328–9, 786.* [DS]

Charles Dickens 1812–70

See col 1181.

Colin Henry Fleetwood Hazlewood 1819–75

Mss are located in Hackney archives, Rose Lipman Lib, London, and in BL, where licensing copies of the plays are to be found.

§1

All plays listed below are also issued in Readex micro *edns.*

Going to Chobham: or the petticoat captains. F. (CL 30 July 1853). Lacy 11.

Jenny Foster, the sailor's child: or the winter robin. D. (Brit Oct 1855). Lacy 32.

Jessy Vere: or the return of the wanderer. D. (Brit Feb 1856). Lacy 25.

The marble bride: or the elves of the forest. D. (Brit Mar 1857). Lacy 32. From Les elves.

Never too late to mend. D. (M'bone 1859). French 370; Lorenzen micro. From C. Reade.

Waiting for the verdict: or falsely accused. D. (CL 29 Jan 1859). Lacy 99.

Capitola: or the masked mother and the hidden hand. D. (Sur 4 July 1859). Lacy 70.

The chevalier of the maison rouge: or the days of terror! D. (Acton 1 Aug 1859). Lacy 42. From A. Dumas.

The staff of diamonds. D. (Sur 14 Jan 1861). French 104.

The bridal wreath. D. (CL 1861). French 107.

The dragon of Wantley: or Harlequin Moore, of Moore Hall, and his fayre Margery. (No performance details). Sheffield 1861. With W. Reeve.

The house on the bridge of Notre Dame. (M'bone 1 Apr 1861). Lacy 50. From T. Barrière & H. de Kock, La maison du pont Notre Dame.

The clock on the stairs. D. (Brit 3 Feb 1862). Lacy 70.

The harvest storm. D. (Brit June 1862?). Lacy 55.

Mary Edmonstone. D. (Brit 22 Dec 1862). French 103.

Aurora Floyd: or the dark duel in the wood. D. (Brit 20 Apr 1863). Lacy 58. Also as Aurora Floyd: or the first and second marriage. From M. E. Braddon.

Lady Audley's secret. D. (Vic 25 May 1863; new version Olym 25 June 1877). Lacy 57; Lacy Suppl 2; (new Amer edn) New York 1889; Rowell. From M. E. Braddon.

Ashore and afloat. D. (Sur 15 Feb 1864). French 106.

The mother's dying child. D. (Brit 5 Oct 1864). Lacy 64.

The female detective: or the mother's dying child. D. (21 June 1865?). De Witt 128.

Poul a Dhoil: or the fairy man. D. (Brit 4 Oct 1865). Lacy 77.

The headless horseman: or the ride of death. D. (Brit Nov 1868). French 107. From Capt M. Reid.

Hop-pickers and gipsies: or the lost daughter. D. (Brit 17 May 1869). Lacy 85.

Lizzie Lyle: or the flower makers of Finsbury. D. (Grec 7 Oct 1869 as Flower makers and heart breakers: or the tale of trials and temptations). Lacy 87.

Taking the veil: or the harsh step-father. D. (Brit 30 July 1870). French 106.

Leave it to me. F. (Sur 26 Dec 1870). Lacy 96. With A. Williams.

The bitter reckoning. D. (Brit 19 June 1871). French 107.

The lost wife: or a husband's confession. D. (Brit 7 Aug 1871). Lacy 93 (dated 1871).

The stolen Jewess: or the two children of Israel. D. (Brit 1 Apr 1872). French 105.

For honour's sake. D. (Brit 1 Oct 1873). French 108.

Jessamy's courtship. D. (Philharmonic 12 Apr 1875). French 109.

Splendid misery. Dicks' English novels 83 nd.

§2

Era almanack 1869.

J. Davis (ed). The Britannia diaries 1863–1875: selections from the diaries of Frederick C. Wilton. 1992.

Hazlewood was an extremely prolific author, providing the Britannia with two-thirds of its new melodramas in the 1860s and early 1870s, though he was not, as often supposed, its official house dramatist. See also Nicoll *5, 412–15, 796–7; Conolly,* English drama, *pp. 189–90;* Readex Index, *p. 122.* [JRS]

Richard Hengist Horne 1803–84

See col 618.

Douglas Jerrold, Douglas William Jerrold 1803–57

There are substantial collections of Jerrold letters in the following libs: Brotherton, Leeds; Berg Collection, NYPL; Chicago Univ Lib; New York Univ (De Coursey Fales Collection); Pierpont Morgan, New York (Gordon N. Ray Collection); Victoria and Albert Museum (Forster Collection; this also contains mss of two plays by Jerrold and four mag articles). The Lord Chamberlain's Collection in the BL contains mss of all plays first performed at the patent theatres and some others. Copies of the sale-catalogue of his lib are in the Bodleian and the BL.

Collections

Writings of Douglas Jerrold. 8 vols 1851–4. Also issued in weekly and monthly pts.

Works with introductory memoir by W. B. Jerrold. 4 vols [1863–4]. Also issued in 5 vols without introductory memoir but with 2nd edn of W. B. Jerrold's life and remains (*see §2, below*) as vol 5.

Selections

Wit and opinions of Douglas Jerrold. Ed B. Jerrold 1859.

The Brownrigg papers. Ed B. Jerrold, illustr G. Cruikshank 1860, 1874.

Other times, being Liberal leaders contributed to Lloyd's Weekly Newspaper by Douglas Jerrold and Blanchard Jerrold. Pt 1 1852–4 [1868].
Mrs Caudle's curtain lectures; Mrs Bib's baby. Ed B. Jerrold 1873.
Fireside saints: Mr Caudle's breakfast talk, and other papers. Boston 1873.
The barber's chair and the Hedgehog letters. Ed B. Jerrold 1874; 1890.
The popular tales of Douglas William Jerrold. Illustr G. Cruikshank [c. 1890].
The handbook of swindling, and other papers. Ed W. Jerrold [1891].
Tales of Douglas Jerrold, now first collected. Ed J. L. Robertson 1891.
Mrs Caudle's curtain lectures and other stories. [1892].
Bon-mots of Charles Lamb and Douglas Jerrold. Ed W. Jerrold, illustr A. Beardsley 1893, 1904.
Essays of Douglas Jerrold. Ed W. Jerrold, illustr H. M. Brock 1903.
Fireside saints. Ed W. Jerrold, illustr C. Robinson 1904. Rptd from Punch Almanack for 1857.
Mrs Caudle's curtain lectures, and other stories and essays. Ed W. Jerrold, illustr J. Leech, R. Doyle and C. Keene 1907 (WC).
Douglas Jerrold and Punch. Ed W. Jerrold 1910.
Mrs Caudle's curtain lectures, and other stories. Nottingham [c. 1920].
The whimsical tales of Douglas Jerrold. Illustr L. Daniel, Allentown PA 1949.
The best of Mr Punch. The humorous writings of Douglas Jerrold. Ed R. M. Kelly, Knoxville TN 1970.

§1

More frightened than hurt. F. (SW 30 Apr 1821). Duncombe's new acting drama 1; Dicks 992.
The gipsy of Derncleugh. MD. (SW 27 Aug 1821). Duncombe's new acting drama.
Dolly and the rat; or, the Brisket family. Bsq. (Olym 6 Jan 1823; ? rev version of The Brisket family; or the running of the rat! Olym 9 Jan 1822). Duncombe's new acting drama.
The smoked miser; or, the benefit of hanging. Int. (SW 23 June 1823). Duncombe's new acting drama; Duncombe 52; Dicks 360; Lacy 58.
Paul Pry. C. (Cob 27 Nov 1827). Dicks 928; Lacy 47; Mod Eng Com Th 67; Booth 4.
The statue lover; or, music in marble. Vaud. (Vauxhall Gdns 2 June 1828). Duncombe 2.
Descart, the French buccaneer; or, the rock of Annaboa. MD. (Cob 1 Sep 1828). Duncombe 3; Dicks 258.
The tower of Lochlain; or, the idiot son. MD. (Cob 1 Sep 1828). Duncombe 8; Lacy 110.
Wives by advertisement; or, courting in the newspapers. Dramatic Satire. (Cob 8 Sep 1828). Duncombe 2; Dicks 971.
Ambrose Gwinnett; or, a sea-side story. MD. (Cob 6 Oct 1828). Dicks 637; Cumberland Minor 8; Richardson 2; Lacy 86; Turner's American Stage, Philadelphia 1833.
Two eyes between two; or, pay me for my eye. Ext. (Cob 13 Oct 1828). Dicks 975; Duncombe 6.
Fifteen years of a drunkard's life. MD. (Cob 24 Nov 1828). Dicks 220; Duncombe 3; Clayton, New York 1830.
Bamfylde Moore Carew. MD. (Sur 13 Feb 1829). Duncombe 5.
John Overy, the miser; or, the Southwark ferry. MD. (Sur 20 Apr 1829). Dicks 796; Cumberland Minor 7; Richardson 2; Lacy 86.
Law and lions! F. (Sur 21 May 1829). Dicks 964; Duncombe 4.
Black Eyed Susan; or, all in the downs. MD. (Sur 8 June 1829). 1829; Dicks 230; Lacy 23; Duncombe 4; Spencer, Boston 1855 [2-act version based on E. L. Davenport's acting adaptation]; Moses, Boston 1918; Rowell. Emmett, G. Black Eyed Susan . . . illustrated by eminent artists based on the drama by Douglas Jerrold [c. 1885]; issued in 13 pts.
Vidocq! the French police spy. MD. (Sur 15 Oct 1829). Duncombe 4.
The flying Dutchman. MD. (Sur 15 Oct 1829). Richardson 3 [with interesting preface by Elliotson].
Thomas à Beckett. T. (Sur 30 Nov 1829). 1829; Dicks 219; Cumberland Minor 11; Richardson.
Sally in our alley. MD. (Sur 11 Jan 1830). Dicks 934; Cumberland Minor 16.
The mutiny at the Nore; or, British sailors in 1797. MD. (Royal Pavilion 31 May 1830). Dicks 795; Lacy 78; Cumberland Minor 5.
The devil's ducat; or, the gift of Mammon. MD. (Adel 16 Dec 1830). Dicks 933; Cumberland Minor 5; Lacy 107.
Martha Willis the servant maid; or, service in London. D. (Royal Pavilion 4 Apr 1831). Dicks 420; Lacy 33.
The bride of Ludgate. C. (DL 8 Dec 1831). Dicks 530; Cumberland 30; Lacy 93.
The rent day. D. (DL 25 Jan 1832). 1832; Dicks 210; Duncombe 25; Lacy 15; Mod Standard Drama 4, New York 1846; G. H. Lewes, Selections from Modern British drama, 1867; J. O. Bailey, British plays of the 19th century, New York 1966; C. Worth, Monash 19th century drama 6, Australia nd.
The golden calf. C. (Str 30 June 1832). Dicks 529; Cumberland Minor 9.
Nell Gwynne; or, the prologue. C. (CG 9 Jan 1833). 1833; Dicks 274; Lacy 37; Duncombe 65.
The housekeeper; or, the white rose. C. (H 17 July 1833). 1833; Dicks 294; Duncombe 16; Lacy 29.
The wedding gown. C. (DL 2 Jan 1834). 1834; Dicks 591; Duncombe 37.
Beau Nash, the king of Bath. C. (H 16 July 1834). 1834; Dicks 554.
The hazard of the die. T. (DL 16 Feb 1835). 1835; Dicks 638; Duncombe 18.
The school fellows. C. (Queens 16 Feb 1835). Dicks 525; Duncombe 16.
Doves in a cage. C. (Adel 21 Dec 1835). 1835; Dicks 633; Duncombe 20; Lacy 99.
The painter of Ghent. T. (Str 25 Apr 1836). 1836; Dicks 651; Duncombe 21; Lacy 29.
The man for the ladies. F. (Str 9 May 1836). Dicks 652.
The perils of Pippins; or, the man who 'couldn't help it'. Ba. (Str 8 Sep 1836). 1836; Dicks 447; Duncombe 23.
Men of character. 3 vols illustr (anon) Thackeray 1838. Rptd from Blackwood's and other jnls. Tauchnitz edn Leipzig 1852.
The handbook of swindling by Captain Barabbas Whitefeather. Illustr H. K. Browne (Phiz) 1839.
Heads of the people: or, portraits of the English. Drawn by Kenny Meadows, described by Douglas Jerrold [et al]. 2 vols 1840–1. Originally issued in 13 (as 12) pts entitled Heads of the people taken off by Quizzfizz [i.e. Meadows] 1838, followed by a second ser, also 13 (as 12) [1839], and a composite ser in 20 pts [1839–40].
The white milliner. C. (CG 9 Feb 1841). Dicks 607; Duncombe 43; Lacy 72.
The prisoner of war. D. (DL 8 Feb 1842). 1842; Dicks 521; Duncombe 58; Lacy 27; G. H. Lewes, Selections from Modern British drama, 1867.
Bubbles of the day. C. (CG 25 Feb 1842). 1842; 1845; Dicks 553.
Cakes and ale. 2 vols illustr G. Cruikshank 1842 (original sketches in Beinecke Lib, Yale). Tales and sketches rptd from NMM.
Gertrude's cherries; or, Waterloo in 1835. C. (CG 30 Aug 1842). 1842; Dicks 656; Lacy 88.
Punch's letters to his son. 1843. Rptd from Punch.
The story of a feather. Novel. 1844; illustr G. du Maurier 1867. Rptd from Punch.
Time works wonders. C. (H 26 Apr 1845; Boston 1845; Dicks 851; Lacy 92; Mod Eng Com Th ser 3. *See* E. Dutton Cook, review of 1873 revival in Nights at the play, 1883.
Punch's complete letter-writer. 1845. Rptd from Punch.

Mrs Caudle's curtain lectures. 1846 (rptd from Punch; review by Thackeray in Morning Chron 26 Dec 1845); 1856 etc; illustr C. Keene 1866; centenary edn with bibliography by W. Jerrold, 1902; illustr MacKay, Edinburgh 1950; introd by A. Burgess 1974 (review by M. Slater in TLS Dec 1974; Robertson Davies Victorian Periodicals Rev 9 1976); tr Hungarian 1860, Fr 1865, 1890, Ger 1869, 1870, Swed 1872, Ital 1885.
The chronicles of Clovernook; with some account of the hermit of Bellyfulle. Rptd with other essays from the Illuminated Mag 1846; rptd 1996 in Modern British Utopias, ed G. Claeys, vol 8; tr Ger 1847.
A man made of money. Novel. Illustr J. Leech 1849; 1892. Originally issued in 6 pts.
REVIEW: Br Quart Rev 10 1849.
Retired from business. C. (H 3 May 1851). Mod Eng Com Th.
St Cupid; or Dorothy's fortune. C. (P'cess 2 Jan 1853). 1853; ed F. C. Wemyss, New York (the Minor drama no 50), nd; Mod Eng Com Th; French's acting edn.
A heart of gold. D. (P'cess 9 Oct 1854). 1854.

Contributions to periodicals

Throughout his career Jerrold wrote extensively for numerous jnls, notably the following:
Mirror of the Stage 1823–4.
Weekly Times 1826–7.
Monthly Mag 1826–32.
Ballot 1831.
Examiner 1831–4(?).
Athenaeum 1832–4.
Morning Herald 1832–40.
Cambridge Quart Rev 1833–4.
Freemason's Quart 1834–8.
Blackwood's Mag 1835–8 (*see* Wellesley vol 5).
NMM 1837–41 (*see* Wellesley vol 5).
Punch 1841–57. (*See* B. Jerrold, Douglas Jerrold and Punch, for full listing of contribution to end 1848 – from 1849 contributions are very scantily noted; also B. A. White, Douglas Jerrold's 'Q' papers in Punch, Victorian Periodicals Rev 15 1982.)
Daily News 1846.
Illust London News (Christmas suppl 1850: 'The sick giant and the doctor dwarf').
Jerrold also edited the following jnls:
The Illuminated Mag 1843–4.
Contributed The chronicles of Clovernook (Utopian fantasy), etc.
Douglas Jerrold's Shilling Mag 1845–8.
Contributed The history of St Giles and St James (novel), The Hedgehog letters, etc; *see* M. Fryckstedt, in Victorian Periodicals Rev 19 1986.
Douglas Jerrold's Weekly Newspaper 1846–8.
Contributed The barber's chair (satiric drama sketches), etc.
Lloyd's Weekly Newspaper 1852–7.

§2

Powell, T. In his Pictures of the living authors of Britain, 1851.
Saturday Rev Dec 1855. Anon.
[Dixon, J. H.] Athenaeum 1857. Obituary.
Hannay, J. Douglas Jerrold. Personal reminiscences. Atlantic Monthly 1 1857.
[Sinnet, J.] NMM 110 1857.
North Br Rev 30 1859. Anon.
Jerrold, W. B. The life and remains of Douglas Jerrold 1859. 2nd edn as vol 5 of re-issued Works (*see* §1, *above*).
Stirling, J. H. Jerrold, Tennyson and Macaulay. Edinburgh 1868.
Collins, W. My miscellanies. 1875.
Clarke, C. and M. Recollections of writers. 1878.
Copping, E. Douglas Jerrold. New Rev 7 1892.
Jerrold, W. Douglas Jerrold, dramatist and wit. 2 vols [1914].
Jerrold, W. Douglas Jerrold's facts and fancies. Fortnightly Rev 124 1928.
Kelly, R. M. Douglas Jerrold. New York 1972.
Emeljanov, V. Victorian popular dramatists. Boston 1987. [MS]

Mark Lemon 1809–70

§1

P. L.: or 30 Strand. MF. (Str 25 Apr 1836). Duncombe 22; Dicks 977.
Arnold of Winkelreid: or the flight of the Sempach. D. (Sur 25 July 1836). Duncombe 22.
The MP for the rotten borough. MF. (EOH 27 July 1838). Dicks 719.
A familiar friend. Ba. (Olym 8 Feb 1840). [1840]; Dicks 981.
The gentleman in black: or the loves of the devils. (Olym 9 Dec 1840). [1840?]; Dicks 776.
What will the world say? (CG 25 Sep 1841). 1841.
Grandfather Whitehead. C. (H 31 Sep 1842). Webster 10; Dicks 505.
Hearts are trumps. F. (Str 30 July 1849). [1863]; Dicks 1058.
The enchanted doll: a fairy tale for little people; the illustrations by R. Doyle. 1849.
Prose and verse. 1852.
The railway belle. F. (Adel 20 Nov 1854). Lacy 17.
A Christmas hamper. 1860. Tales.
Wait for the end: a story. 3 vols 1863.
Legends of number nip. 1864. From the Ger of J. C. A. Musaeus.
The jest book: the choicest anecdotes and sayings, selected and arranged by Mark Lemon. Cambridge 1864.
Loved at last: a story. 3 vols 1864.
Tom Moody's tales, edited [or rather written] by Mark Lemon; illustrated by H. K. Browne. 1864.
Falkner Lyle: or the story of two wives. 3 vols 1866.
Leyton Hall and other tales. 3 vols 1867.
Golden fetters. 3 vols 1867. A novel.
Up and down the London streets. 1867. Historical and descriptive lectures.
Fairy tales; with illustrations by R. Doyle and C. H. Bennett. 1868.
Tinykin's transformations: a child's story. 1869.
The small house over the water, and other stories; with portrait and illustrations by G. Cruikshank. 1888.
Lemon, with Henry Mayhew, founded Punch, *the first number of which appeared on 17 July 1841. He remained editor until his death.*
For other dramatic works, see Nicoll *4, pp. 343–5, 594–5; 5, pp. 455, 803.*

§2

Friswell, J. H. In his Modern men of letters, 1870.
Hatton, J. Reminiscences of Lemon. GM July–Dec 1870.
Hatton, J. The true story of Punch. London Soc 28, 30 1875–6.
Spielmann, M. H. The history of Punch. 1895.
Adrian, A. A. Lemon: first editor of Punch. 1966.

Leopold David Lewis 1828–90

The mask: a humorous and fantastic review, edited by Lewis and Alfred Thompson [and entirely written by them]. Feb–Dec 1868.
The bells. D. (Lyc 25 Nov 1871). Lacy 97; New York 1872. From Erckmann-Chatrian, Le juif polonais.
A peal of merry bells. 3 vols [1880]. A novel.
For other dramatic works, see Nicoll *5, p. 459.*

George William Lovell 1804–78

§1

The provost of Bruges. T. (DL 10 Feb 1836). 1837; Dicks 681. From Leitch Ritchie, The serf, in his Romance of history.
Love's sacrifice: or the rival merchants. D. (CG 12 Sep 1842). Lacy 67; Dicks 650.

The wife's secret. D. (Park Theatre, New York 12 Oct 1846; H 17 Jan 1848). Lacy 82; Dicks 1005.
Look before you leap: or wooings and weddings. C. (H 29 Oct 1846). Webster 13; Dicks 998.
See also Nicoll *4, pp. 347, 596; 5, p. 463.*

§2

Dunkel, W. D. The career of Lovell. TN 5 1951.

E. G. E. L. Bulwer-Lytton, 1st Baron Lytton 1803–73

See col 1144.

W. R. S. Markwell

Louis XI: an historical drama. (DL 14 Feb 1835). Lacy 9. From Delavigne.
The prophet's curse. D. (Unacted?) 1862.
See also Nicoll *5, p. 477.*

John Westland Marston 1819–90

Some letters and licensing copies of the plays are located in BL.

Collections

Dramatic and poetical works. 2 vols 1876. Includes all plays below, except The heart and the world (fragments only) and Trevanion. Some of the texts are much rev.

§1

All the plays listed below are also issued in one or more Readex micro *edns.*
Poetry as an universal nature: a lecture; to which is added The poet: an ode. 1838.
Poetic culture: an appeal to those interested in human destiny. 1839.
The patrician's daughter. T. (DL 10 Dec 1842). 1841, 1842 (2nd edn rev for performance), 1842 (3rd edn), 1843 (4th edn), 1843 (5th edn); Boston Th 5 (dated 1856); Lacy 43; Bailey.
Gerald: a dramatic poem, and other poems. 1842.
Borough politics. C. (H 27 June 1846). Webster 12.
The heart and the world. D. (H 4 Oct 1847). 1847.
Strathmore. T. (H 20 June 1849). 1849 (2 edns); Lacy 56 (with sub-title Love and duty); Lorenzen micro. From Scott, Old Mortality.
Trevanion: or the false position. D. (Sur 22 Oct 1849). [1849]. With W. B. Bernard.
Philip of France and Marie de Méranie. T. (Olym 4 Nov 1850). 1850 (2 edns). From G. P. R. James, Philip Augustus.
Anne Blake. D. (P'cess 28 Oct 1852). 1852; Boston Th 8; Lacy 49.
The death-ride: a tale of the light brigade. 1855.
A life's ransom. D. (Lyc 16 Feb 1857). 1857 (with preface on the principles of poetic drama); Lacy 54; Boston Th 14.
A hard struggle. D. (Lyc 1 Feb 1858). Lacy 48; Boston Th 21.
A lady in her own right: a novel. 1860.
The wife's portrait: a household picture under two lights. D. (H 10 Mar 1862). Lacy 54.
The family credit and other tales. 1862.
Pure gold. D. (SW 9 Nov 1863). Lacy 61.
Donna Diana. C. (P'cess 2 Jan 1864).
The favourite of fortune. C. (H 2 Apr 1866).
Life for life. D. (Lyc 6 Mar 1869). 1869.
Address ... on the inauguration of the Shakespeare memorial theatre at Stratford-upon-Avon, Apr 23rd, 1879. Delivered by Miss Kate Field. [1879.]
John Baldwin Buckstone. In DNB 7, 1886.
Oliver Madox Brown. In DNB 7, 1886.
Our recent actors: being recollections, critical, and in many cases, personal, of late distinguished performers of both sexes, with some incidental notices of living actors. 2 vols 1888.

Contributions to periodicals

Realism in dramatic art. New Quart Mag Apr 1876.
Marston also edited the Nat Mag, *with J. Saunders, 1857–64. For unpbd dramatic works, see* Nicoll *4, p. 353; 5, pp. 478–9. See also Conolly,* English drama, *pp. 216–18;* Stratman, *pp. 402–3;* Readex Index, *pp. 174–5.*

§2

Horne, R. H. In his A new spirit of the age vol 2, 1844.
The late Westland Marston: recollections by a friend. Pall Mall Gazette 10 Jan 1890.
Dr Westland Marston. Athenaeum 11 May 1890.
Clarke, H. E. In The poets and poetry of the century, ed A. H. Miles, vol 4 [1891]. [JRS]

Charles James Mathews 1803–78

§1

My wife's mother. C. (H 3 July 1833). Lacy 23; Dicks 659.
Truth: or a glass too much. Ba. (Adel 10 Mar 1834). Webster 3.
The hump-backed lover. F. (Olym 7 Dec 1835). Cumberland Minor 12; Dicks 660.
Why did you die? Ba. (Olym 20 Nov 1837). Webster 2; Dicks 662.
The black domino. B. (Olym 18 Jan 1838). Webster 3. From Scribe, Le domino noir.
Patter versus clatter. F. (Olym 21 May 1838). Lacy 118; Dicks 660.
Lettre aux auteurs dramatiques de la France. 1852; tr Mathews 1852.
Married for money. F. (DL 10 Oct 1815). French 117.
My awful dad. C. (Ga 13 Sep 1875). French 117.
The life of Mathews [chiefly autobiographical]. Ed C. Dickens 2 vols 1879.
For other dramatic works, see Nicoll *4, pp. 353–4, 597–8; 5, pp. 480, 806.*

§2

Mathews, A. Memoirs of Charles Mathews, comedian. 4 vols 1838–9; abridged E. Yates 1860. On early years.
Biographical sketch. Webster 3 [1838].

John Maddison Morton 1811–91

Collections

Comediettas and farces. New York, 1886.
Plays for home performance. 1889.

§1

All the plays listed below are issued in a Readex micro *edn.*
My first fit of the gout. F. (Queen's 9 Mar 1835). Lacy 11.
My husband's ghost. F. (H 26 Apr 1836). Boston [1857?]; Cumberland 35; Lacy 93; French's minor drama 230; Spencer's Boston Th 124.
The sentinel. Ba. (Olym 23 Feb 1837). Webster 4; [1852].
The spitfire. F. (EOH 13 Sep 1837). Webster 17; Lacy 62 (as Alabama); Turner 42, Philadelphia.
The barbers of Bassora. OF. (CG 11 Nov 1837). Webster 2; [1837?].
The original. Int. (CG 13 Nov 1837). [1837]; Webster 20.
Chaos is come again; or, The race ball. F. (CG 19 Nov 1838). Webster 65; [1838].
Sayings and doings; or, The rule of contrary. F. (CG 18 Apr 1839). Webster 77; Acting Drama 30, New York.
Brother Ben. F. (CG 9 Dec 1840). Lacy 34; Spencer's Boston Th 40.
The wrong man. F. (CG 6 Nov 1841). Dicks 433.
The attic story. F. (DL 19 May 1842). Cumberland 42; Mod Eng Com Th 3.
Cousin Lambkin. F. (CG 8 Oct 1842). Duncombe 45.
Guy, Earl of Warwick or, Harlequin and the dun cow. P. [1842?].
The highwayman. F. [1843.] CG?
A thumping legacy. F. (DL 11 Feb 1843). [1843]; Lacy 15; French's minor drama 102.

The double-bedded room. F. (H 3 July 1843). Duncombe 47; Lacy 887; French's minor drama 171.
My wife's second floor. F. (P'cess 22 July 1843). Duncombe 74; Lacy 44; French 659.
The wedding breakfast. F. (H 24 Aug 1843). Duncombe 48; French 2193.
My wife's come! F. (DL 18 Oct 1843). Duncombe 48.
The railroad trip, or London, Birmingham & Bristol!! F. (H 23 Oct 1843). Duncombe 38. Written with Thomas Morton Jr.
The milliner's holiday. F. (H 29 June 1844). Duncombe 1; Lacy 38.
Young England. F. (H 30 Nov 1844). Duncombe 51; Lacy 408.
The corporal's wedding, or A kiss from the bride. F. (Adel 20 Jan 1845). Duncombe 52.
The mother and child are doing well. F. (Adel 24 Feb 1845). Webster 117; New York. [1845?].
Who's the composer? CD. (H 28 Oct 1845). Duncombe 54; French 1845.
Lend me five shillings. F. (H 19 Feb 1846). Lacy 30; Duncombe 55; French 24; Spencer's Boston Th.
The Irish tiger. F. (H 2 May 1846). Lacy 34; Duncombe 56; French's minor drama 84.
The king and I! F. (H 4 June 1846). Duncombe 53; Lacy 40.
Done on both sides. F. (Lyc 24 Feb 1847). Lacy 26; Duncombe 61.
Who do they take me for? F. (H 1 June 1847). Cumberland 473; Lacy 111; Duncombe 59; French 111.
Who's my husband? F. (H 16 Oct 1847). Lacy 80; Duncombe 60; French 1194.
Box and Cox, a romance of real life. F. (Lyc 1 Nov 1847). Dicks 1059; Lacy 5; Duncombe 60; Heywood 190; French's minor drama 21; Mod Eng Com Th 4; Booth 4. Micro. From Une chambre pour deux and Une chambre à deux lits. An Ethiopian version Africanised expressly for George Christy by E. B. Christy, New York [1856] (Brady's Ethiopian drama 2). Cox and Box, or The long-lost brothers: triumviretta in 1 act adapted by F. C. Burnand; music by Arthur S. Sullivan [1866]; French's minor drama 324.
Old Honesty. CD. (H 6 Apr 1848). Duncombe 61; Lacy 38; Spencer's Boston Th 7.
Going to the Derby. F. (Adel 22 May 1848). Duncombe 62; Lacy 37; New Br Th 42.
Poor Pillicoddy. F. (Lyc 12 July 1848). Lacy 38; Duncombe 62; French's minor drama 209; Spencer's Boston Th 79; The acting drama, New York.
The midnight watch. D. (M'bone 5 Oct 1848). Lacy 39; Duncombe 62; De Witt 49.
Slasher and Crasher. F. (Adel 13 Nov 1848). Duncombe 62; Lacy 8; French's minor drama 31.
Your life's in danger. F. (H 20 Dec 1848). Duncombe 63; Lacy 9; French 131; Spencer's Boston Th 34.
John Dobbs; or, A dab at anything. F. (Str 23 Apr 1849). Duncombe 54; Lacy 7; French 5; Spencer 11, Boston.
A most unwarrantable intrusion. F. (Adel 11 June 1849). Duncombe 64; Lacy 7; French's minor drama 238; Spencer's Boston Th 135.
Where there's a will there's a way. CD. (Str 6 Sep 1849). Duncombe 64; Lacy 9; French 129.
My precious Betsy! F. (Adel 18 Feb 1850). Duncombe; Lacy 115; Spencer's Boston Th 19.
The three cuckoos; or Ticklish times. F. (H 13 Mar 1850). Duncombe 518; Lacy 35 [as Ticklish times].
Friend Waggles. F. (H 15 Apr 1850). Duncombe; Lacy; French 482.
Sent to the Tower! F. (P'cess 24 Oct 1850). Duncombe 526; Lacy; French's minor drama 224; Spencer's Boston Th 109.
Betsey Baker; or, Too attentive by half. F. (P'cess 13 Nov 1850). Lacy; French's minor drama 192; Spencer's Boston Th 50, as Betsy Baker.
All that glitters is not gold. CD. (Olym 13 Jan 1851). Lacy; French's minor drama 40. Written in collaboration with Thomas Morton Jr.
Grimshaw, Bagshaw and Bradshaw. F. (H 1 July 1851). Lacy 54; French's minor drama 42.
A hopeless passion. F. (Str 15 Sep 1851). Lacy 5.
The two Bonnycastles. F. (H 25 Nov 1851). Lacy; French's minor drama 44.
Harlequin Hogarth, or The two London 'prentices. P. (DL 26 Dec 1851). Lacy 5. Written in collaboration with Nelson Lee.
Who stole the pocketbook? or A dinner for six. F. (Adel 29 Mar 1852; H 23 June 1851 as Dinner for six). Lacy 84; French's minor drama 236.
The writing on the wall. D. (H 9 Aug 1852). [1852] New York; Lacy. Written in collaboration with Thomas Morton Jr.
The woman I adore! F. (H 9 Oct 1852). Lacy 112; French 112.
A capital match! F. (H 4 Nov 1852). Lacy 116; French 116.
To Paris and back for five pounds. F. (H 5 Feb 1853). Lacy; French 43.
A desperate game. F. (Adel 9 Apr 1853). Lacy; Ames 2.
Whitebait at Greenwich. F. (Adel 14 Nov 1853). Lacy; French's minor drama 90; Spencer's Boston Th 38, as The two Buzzards; or, Whitebait at Greenwich.
Away with melancholy. F. (P'cess 13 Mar 1854). Lacy 14.
From village to court. CD. (P'cess 5 June 1854). Lacy 15.
Waiting for an omnibus in the Lowther Arcade on a rainy day. F. (Adel 26 June 1854). Lacy 15.
Harlequin Bluebeard, the great bashaw; or, The good fairy triumphant over the demon of discord. P. (P'cess 26 Dec 1854). Lacy 243; French's minor drama 146.
A game of romps. F. (P'cess 12 Mar 1855). Lacy 260; French 260.
The muleteer of Toledo; or King, queen and knave. CD. (P'cess 9 Apr 1855). Lacy 264; French.
How stout you're getting. F. (P'cess 16 July 1855). Lacy 22.
Don't judge by appearances. F. (P'cess 22 Oct 1855); [c. 1884] Lacy 346; Spencer's Boston Th 51.
A prince for an hour. CD. (P'cess 24 Mar 1856). Lacy 25.
The rights and wrongs of women. F. (H 24 May 1856). Lacy 26.
Our wife, or, The rose of Amiens. CD. (P'cess 18 Nov 1856). Lacy 417; French's minor drama 200; Spencer's Boston Th 67.
Aladdin and the wonderful lamp. P. (P'cess 25 Dec 1856). Lacy; French.
An Englishman's home is his castle. F. (P'cess 11 May 1857). Lacy 31.
'Take care of Dowb'. F. (H 23 Nov 1857). Lacy 34.
Aunt Charlotte's maid. F. (Adel 1858). Lacy; Spencer's Boston Th 13.
Thirty-three next birthday. F. (P'cess 22 Nov 1858). Lacy 560; Ames 28, Clyde, Ohio.
Dying for love. C. (P'cess 25 June 1858) [1858?]; French 536.
Which of the two? F. (Str 25 Apr 1859). Lacy; French 589; World acting drama, Chicago.
Love and hunger. F. (Adel 26 Sep 1859). Lacy 42; French 624.
A husband to order. Serio-comic D. (Olym 17 Oct 1859). Lacy 632; French 632; Spencer's Boston Th 69, New York.
FitzSmythe of FitzSmythe Hall. F. (H 26 May 1860). Lacy 46; French 688.
A regular fix! F. (Olym 11 Oct 1860). Lacy 714; French 282.
The pacha of Pimlico. Ext. (StJ 15 Apr 1861). Lacy.
Wooing one's wife. F. (Olym 21 Oct 1861). Lacy 52.
Margery Daw; or, The two bumpkins. F. (Adel 16 Dec 1861). Lacy 52.
Catch a weazel. F. (Str 17 Mar 1862). Lacy 54.
She would and he wouldn't. C. (StJ 6 Sep 1862). Lacy 56.
Lad from the country. F. (Olym 5 June 1863) [1878?]; French 1736.
The 'Alabama': altered from H. M. Sloop 'Spitfire'. Ext. (DL 7 Mar 1864). Lacy 920.
Drawing rooms, second floor and attics. F. (P'cess 28 Mar 1864). Lacy.
Woodcock's little game. CF. (StJ 6 Oct 1864). Lacy 945; De Witt 11.
My wife's bonnet. F. (Olym 2 Nov 1864). Lacy 949.
The steeple-chase; or, In the pigskin. F. (Adel 22 Mar 1865). Lacy 66; French 982.
Pouter's wedding. F. (StJ 19 June 1865). Lacy 67.

Newington Butts! F. (StJ 2 Nov 1866). Lacy 1088; French 1088.
A slice of luck. F. (Adel 17 June 1867). Lacy 76; Spencer's Boston Th 24.
The two Puddifoots. F. (Olym 14 Oct 1867) [Boston 1869]. French; Spencer's Boston Th 6.
If I had a thousand a year. F. (Olym 21 Oct 1867). Lacy; World acting drama, Chicago.
Master Jones's birthday. F. (P'cess 24 Aug 1868). Lacy; De Witt 39.
A day's fishing. F. (Adel 8 Mar 1869). Lacy; French's minor drama 311.
'Little mother'. Ca. (Roy 21 Apr 1870). Lacy 91; French 1363.
Maggie's situation. Ca. (Court 27 Jan 1875). Lacy 83; French 1797.
My bachelor days. (Wynd 1 Aug 1901). From Célimare le bïen-aimé.
Sea-bathing at home; and The wrong man. [1883?]; Dicks' 433.
Something to do. (Hay as News from China) rev and adapted 1 Apr 1884.
Going it! Another lesson to fathers. FC. (Roy Glasgow 13 Nov 1885). French. Micro. Written with W. A. Vicars.
After a storm, comes a calm. Ca. [c. 1886]; Lacy 134; De Witt 340; Sergel 340.
Declined with thanks. FCa. [c. 1886]; French; Sergel 342. Adapted by H. L. Williams.
The auctioneer. C. (Bournemouth 30 May 1898). Written with Robert Reece. Revised as The highest bidder by David Belasco and E. H. Sothern. C. New York [1887].
At sixes and sevens. Ca. French 1848; Roorbach's acting drama 188?, New York.
Atchi! Ca. (POW 21 Sep 1868). Lacy; Roorbach's acting plays 20, New York.
Change partners. Ca. French 1850. Micro. Written with T. J. Williams.
Eight hours at the seaside. F. French 1849.
Express! A railway romance in 1 compartment. F. French 2000.
First come, first served. Ca. French.
Harlequin and William Tell, or The genius of the ribstone pippin. P. [18??]
Kiss and be friends. F. [188?] Lacy 124; French.
The little savage. F. (Str Nov 1858). Lacy 557.
Love and rain. F. Lacy 61.
A narrow squeak. F. French 1839.
Not if I know it! F. World acting drama, Chicago. From Le supplice d'un homme.
Old Gossett. FC. [18??]. Written with W. A. Vicars.
On the sly. F. (H. 24 Oct 1864). Lacy 944; Ames 33, Clyde, Ohio.
Pepperpot's little pets! F. French 1998.
Slight mistakes. F. (CG 1 Jan 1884). French 1810.
Taken from the French. Ca. French 2001.
Ticklish times. F. (Olym 8 Mar 1858). Lacy 513; French's minor drama 256; Spencer's Boston Th 187.
Trade. C. New York. Written with Robert Reece.
The trumpeter's wedding. F. Duncombe; Lacy.
See also Nicoll *4, pp. 361–3, 600–1; 5, pp. 495–7, 807.*

§2

Knight, J. In DNB.
Scott, C. John Maddison Morton. London Soc 49 [1886].
Scott, C. Memoir. In Plays for home performance, 1889.
Theatre 14 1889.
London Figaro 23 Dec 1891.
Black and White 2 Jan 1892. [LS]

John Oxenford 1812–77

Collections

Catalogue of a collection of books, including the library of the late John Oxenford, Esq. [...]. Which will be sold by auction by Messrs. Puttic and Simpson [...] on Tuesday, July 31st, 1877. 1877.
A clearance sale. A miscellaneous collection of old and new books from the libraries of John Oxenford, Esq. Dramatic critic, [...] which will be sold by auction by Bernard Quaritch [...] on Tuesday, June 25, 1878. 1878.
Catalogue of a collection of books, including a portion of the library of the late John Oxenford, Esq, [...]. To be sold by auction by Messrs. Puttic and Simpson [...]. On Wednesday May 26, 1880. 1880.

§1

My fellow clerk. F. (Lyc 20 Apr 1835). Dicks 558; Duncombe 264; French 196; Lacy 48; J. Miller 1835; Mod Eng Com Th 1.
I and my double. F. (Lyc 16 June 1835). Dicks 579; Duncombe 280.
The dice of death. MD. (Lyc 14 Sep 1835). Dicks 592; Duncombe 218; Lacy 10. Revived as Apollyon the great fiend! or The love token. (Lyc 12 Apr 1841).
Twice killed. F. (Olym 26 Nov 1835). Dicks 531; Duncombe 166; Lacy 24; in B. N. Webster, The series of dramatic entertainments performed [...] at Windsor Castle, [1849]; Selections from the modern British dramatists. With introduction and biographical notes, ed G. H. Lewes, 2 vols Leipzig 1867, vol 2, pp. 369–91.
A day well spent. F. (Lyc 4 Apr 1836). Dicks 531; Duncombe 247; Lacy 34; Mod Eng Com Th 2; 1836; Leipzig 1839 (Wunder); Breslau 1855.
The rape of the lock. Bsq. (Olym 27 Mar 1837). Duncombe 261; Dicks 1021.
No followers. F. (Str 4 Sep 1837); Dicks 987; Duncombe 267; Mod Eng Com Th 1.
A quiet day. F. (Olym 12 Oct 1837). Dicks 987; Duncombe 270; Mod Eng Com Th 1.
What have I done?. F. (Olym 12 Mar 1838). Duncombe 255.
Dr Dilworth. F. (Olym 15 Apr 1839). Dicks 558; National Acting Drama 7; Chapman & Hall 1839; Boston 1857.
English etiquette. F. (Olym 2 Nov 1840). Dicks 658.
Legerdemain or The conjurer's wife. Ca. (Str 5 Oct 1842). Dicks 657.
Dearest Elizabeth. F. (H 22 Jan 1848). Webster's National acting drama 14.
The reigning favourite. D. (Str 9 Oct 1849). Lacy n.s. 1.
The sleeper awakened. O. (H 15 Nov 1850). Music by G. A. Macfarren. 1850.
Aminta. CO. (H 26 Jan 1852). Music by W. H. Glover. Webster's National acting drama 182.
Only a half-penny. F. (Olym 30 May 1855). Lacy 22.
Five pounds reward. F. (Olym 3 Dec 1855). Lacy 24.
A family failing. F. (H 17 Nov 1856). Lacy 29.
A doubtful victory. Ca. (Olym 26 Apr 1858). French 531; Lacy 36; Spencer, Boston 1871.
The porter's knot. MD. (Olym 2 Dec 1858). Lacy 38.
Retained for the defence. F. (Olym 25 May 1859). Lacy 41.
The magic toys. Ext. (StJ 24 Oct 1859). Lacy 42.
Uncle Zachary. D. (Olym 8 Mar 1860). Lacy 45.
Robin Hood. O. (H 11 Oct 1860). Music by G. A. Macfarren. Cramer, Beak and Chappell 1860, rptd 1865.
Timour the Tartar or The Iron Master of Samarkand by Oxus. Bsq. (Olym 26 Dec 1860). Lacy 49. With C. W. S. Brooks.
A legal impediment. F. (Lyc 28 Oct 1861). Lacy 53.
The lily of Killarney. O. (CG 10 Feb 1862). Music by J. Benedict. 1862; Boosey [1910]. With D. Boucicault.
The world of fashion. C. (Olym 17 Mar 1862). Lacy 55.
I couldn't help it. F. (Lyc 19 Apr 1862). French 816; Lacy 55.
Bristol diamonds. F. (StJ 11 Aug 1862). Lacy 56.
Sam's arrival. F. (Str 8 Sep 1862). Lacy 56.
Freya's gift; An allegorical masque in honour of the nuptials of H. R. H. the Prince of Wales and H. R. H. the Princess Alexandra. Bal. (CG 10 Mar 1863). 1863.
Beauty or the beast. F. (DL 2 Nov 1863). Lacy 60.

Jessy Lea. O. (Gallery of Illustration 2 Nov 1863). Music by G. A. Macfarren. Novello, Ewer and Co [nd].
The monastery of St Just. D. (P'cess 27 June 1864). Lacy 63.
A young lad from the country. F. (DL 21 Nov 1864). Lacy 64.
Billing and cooing. Ca. (Roy 16 Jan 1865). Lacy 65.
Felix or The festival of roses. O. (Roy 23 Oct 1865). Music by Meyer-Lutz. [1865].
A cleft stick. C. (Olym 8 Nov 1865). Lacy 68.
Please to remember the grotto or The manageress in a fix. Bsq. (StJ 26 Dec 1865). Lacy 70. With W. S. Emden.
East Lynne. MD. (Sur 5 Feb 1866). Kilgariff.
The life chase. D. (Gai 11 Oct 1869). T. H. Lacy [1869].
Down in a balloon. F. (Adel 10 Apr 1871). Lacy 92.
A waltz by Arditi. F. (Adel 7 Mar 1874). Lacy 101.
The two orphans. D. (Olym 14 Sep 1874). 1874; Lacy 106.

Contributions to periodicals

For Oxenford's contributions to the Athenaeum, *see the* Athenaeum Index, *City Univ, London. For contributions to other periodicals, see* Wellesley *vol* 5.
Molière. In The Penny Cyclopaedia, 1839.
A bundle of German legends. Ainsworth's Mag 2 1842.
Cibber detected. Punch 6 1844.
Physiology of an 'occasional correspondent'. Punch 6 1844.
The seven wise men. Punch 7 1844.
The bubble of life. Cruikshank's Table Book 1845.
The demon of 1845. By a dreamer of realities. Cruikshank's Table Book 1845.
Selections from Jean Paul Friedrich Richter. Ainsworth's Mag 7 1845; NMM 74 1845.
Tales from the Spanish dramatists. NMM 78 1846; 79 1847; 81 1847.
Sonnet [by 'N. D.']. Musical World 21, Sep 1846–25, Jan 1850 [173 sonnets]. Identification of Oxenford's authorship based on Music during the Victorian era … being the memoirs of J. W. Davison, ed H. Davison, 1912.
Viennese legends. NMM 81 1847.
Legends of Gastein. NMM 82 1848.
Legends of Salzburg. NMM 82 1848.
Austrian legends. NMM 83 1848.
Castle Schildheiss. NMM 84 1848.
The giants' invasion. NMM 85 1849.
Legends of Breslau. NMM 86 1849.
Legends of Leubus. NMM 86 1849.
Legends of Trachenberg. NMM 87 1849.
A French audience. Household Words 7 1853.
Iconoclasm in German philosophy. Westminster Rev 59 1853.
The dwarf's bubble. A fantasia. The Train 1 1856.
Touching the Lord Hamlet. Household Words 16 1857.
Popular music of the olden times. Quart Rev 106 1859.
Stage adaptations of Shakespeare. Cornhill Mag 8 1863.
Faust dramatic and legendary. Belgravia 1 1867.
The present aspect of the London stage. Temple Bar 40 1874.
Stage decorum. Theatre 1 1877.
The toy theatre. Era Almanack 1871.
Lord Dundreary. Theatre n.s. 1 1878.

Translations

Oxenford's numerous translations of individual poems, mainly from the German, have not been included here.
Calderón. Life is a dream. Tr from the Sp. NMM 96 1842.
Tales from the German. Tr Oxenford and C. A. Feiling. 1844.
Spanish ballads. Tr and ed Oxenford, NMM 76 1846; 77 1846.
Goethe, J. W. von. Affinities. Musical World 21–2 1846–7.
Aristotle on poetry. Musical World 23 1848.
Winckelmann's history of ancient art. Musical World 23 1848; 24 1849.
Goethe, J. W. von. The autobiography. 1848; ed E. Bell, 1888; ed W. Knoblauch 1904; introd by G. Sebba 1969, 1971.
Göthe's [*sic*] epigrams from Venice. Musical World 23 1848; 24 1849.
The Enterpe of Herodotus. Musical World 24 1849; 25 1850.
Epigrams from the Greek. Musical World 24 1849; 25 1850.
Boiardo. Musical World 25 1850 [discontinued].
Eckermann, J. P. Conversations of Goethe with Eckermann and Soret. Tr from the Ger 2 vols 1850, 1874, 1930 (EL abridged).
Molière. Tartuffe. C. Tr Oxenford. (H 25 Mar 1851). Webster's National acting drama 17.
Callery, J. M. and M. Yvan. History of the insurrection in China. Tr from the Fr 1853, 1853, 1854.
Bürger, G. A. Lenora. Birmingham 1855.
The illustrated book of French songs from the sixteenth to the nineteenth century. 1855, 1868.
Jacobs, F. C. W. Hellas or The home, history, literature and art of the Greeks. Tr from the Ger 1855.
Fischer, K. Francis Bacon of Verulam. Realistic philosophy and its age. 1857.
Fluegel, J. G. Flugel's Complete dictionary of the German and English languages. Adapted to the English student by C. A. Fielding, A. Heinemann, J. Oxenford. 1857, 1861, 1880.
Weber, C. M. von. Der Freischütz. O. Tr Oxenford. (Astleys 2 Apr 1866). Lacy 69.
Wagner, R. Lohengrin. 1872.
Bach, J. S. The passion (according to St Matthew). [1877].
Wagner festival, Royal Albert Hall, May 1877. With English versions by Dr Hueffer and J. Oxenford. 1877, 1877.

§2

Hawkins, F. John Oxenford. Theatre 30 1897.
Stierstorfer, K. John Oxenford (1812–1877) as farceur and critic of comedy. Frankfurt am Main 1996. [KS]

Watts Phillips 1825–74

§1

The model republic: or Cato Potts in Paris. [1848?] Etchings.
A case in bankruptcy. [1850.] Etchings.
Showing how the Honourable Mr Teddington Locke MP was not returned for the incorruptible borough of Bubengrub; drawn and etched by Watts Phillips, from notions by Edward Grant. [1850?]
The wild tribes of London. 1855. On the slums.
The dead heart. D. (Adel 21 Nov 1859). Lacy 82. This play had considerable renown, and was revived by Irving at the Lyceum in 1889. 2 novels were founded on it: C. Gibbon, The dead heart: a tale of the Bastille, 1865; and A. R. Phillips, Love in death, 1889.
The hooded snake: a story of the secret police. [1860.]
Amos Clark, or the poor dependent: a story of country life in the seventeenth century. 1862.
Canary bird, a story of town life in the seventeenth century: a sequel to Amos Clark. 1862.
His last victory. D. (StJ 21 June 1862). Lacy 59.
Camilla's husband. D. (Olym 22 Nov 1862). Lacy 59.
Paul's return. C. (P'cess 15 Feb 1864). Lacy 62.
Theodora, actress and empress. Historical Romance (New Sur 9 Apr 1866). Lacy 74.
Lost in London. D. (Adel 16 Mar 1867). Lacy 80; Bailey.
Nobody's child. D. (Sur 14 Sep 1867). French 1155.
Maud's peril. D. (Adel 23 Oct 1867). Lacy 80.
Not guilty. D. (Queen's 13 Feb 1869). Lacy 84.
On the jury. D. (P'cess 16 Dec 1871). Lacy 1137.
Who will save her? 3 vols 1874. Novel.
For other dramatic works, see Nicoll *5, p. 523.*

§2

Era Almanack. 1863.
Cook, D. Nights at the play. 2 vols 1883.

Phillips, E. W. Phillips: artist and playwright. 1891.
Knight, J. Watts Phillips. DNB 45 1896. [HH]

George Dibdin Pitt 1799–1855

The last man: or the miser of Eltham Green. D. (Sur 22 July 1833). Duncombe 24.
The monster of the Eddystone: or the lighthouse keepers. MD. (SW 7 Apr 1834). Cumberland Minor 10; Lacy 69.
The Jersey girl: or the red robbers. MD (Sur 9 Feb 1835). Lacy 26; Dicks 512.
The twins, Paul and Philip. Ba. (Queen's 21 Jan 1836). Dicks 419.
Simon Lee: or the murder of the Five Fields Copse. D. (CL 1 Apr 1839). Lacy 78.
Susan Hopley: or the vicissitudes of a servant girl. (Vic 31 May 1841). Lacy 69; Cumberland Minor 145.
The beggar's petition: or a father's love and a mother's care. D. (CL 18 Oct 1841). Lacy 97; Dicks 514.
Marianne, the child of charity: or the head of a lawyer. (Vic 30 Dec 1844). French 119; Dicks 825.

Charles Reade 1814–84

See col 1385.

William Leman Rede 1802–47

Licensing copies of most of the plays are located in BL.

§1

All the plays listed below are also issued in one or more Readex micro *edns.*
The wedded wanderer: or the soldier's fate. A novel. 1827.
The rake's progress. MD. (City ? Feb 1832). Duncombe 12; Boston Th 10; Lacy 32; Dicks 240; Boston Th 1856.
His first champagne. F. (Str 7 Oct 1833). [1839?]; Webster 6; Lacy 73; Dicks 212.
Faith and falsehood: or the fate of the bushranger. D. (Queen's 22 Sep 1834). Duncombe 33; New BT 263; Dicks 548.
An affair of honour. F. (Olym 12 Mar 1835). 1835; Cumberland 44; Lacy 78; Dicks 517.
The skeleton witness: or murder at the mound. D. (Sur 27 Apr 1835 with sub-title The king's evidence). 1835; Cumberland 47; French NY 197.
Cupid in London: or some passages in the life of love. Ext. (Queen's 18 June 1835). Duncombe 17.
The old and young stager. Ba (Olym 7 Dec 1835). Duncombe 20; Dicks 728; Lorenzen micro.
Come to town: or next door neighbours. Ba. (Str 25 Apr 1836). Duncombe 21.
The Gaberlunzie man. MD. (EOH 26 Sep 1836). Duncombe 23.
The flight to America: or ten hours in New York. D. (Adel 7 Nov 1836). Duncombe 24; Philadelphia and New York [1840?].
Douglas travestie. Bsq. (Adel 13 Feb 1837). 1837; Duncombe 25; Lacy 46; Lorenzen micro.
The peregrinations of Pickwick: or Boz-i-a-na. F. (Adel 3 Apr 1837). 1837; Duncombe 33.
The two greens. Ba. (Olym 20 Feb 1840). Pattie 1.
The devil and Dr Faustus. Ba. (Str 31 May 1841). Cumberland 45.
Sixteen string Jack: or Ravin the reefer. D. (Olym 15 Nov 1841). Cumberland Minor no 152; Dicks 392. Rev of Cob 18 Feb 1832 version.
Jack in the water: or the ladder of life. D. (Olym 25 Apr 1842). Cumberland Minor 16; Dicks 574.
The royal rake [George IV], and the adventures of Alfred Chesterton. [A satirical romance.] 1842 (priv ptd). Serialised in The Sunday Times 1846.
Life's a lottery: or Jolly Dick the lamplighter. D. (Olym 14 Nov 1842). Cumberland 47; Dicks 601.
Our village: or lost and found. D. (Olym 17 Apr 1843). Lacy 88 (with sub-title The lost ship); Dicks 711.
The queen's bench. F. (Str 13 Nov 1848). Cumberland 44.
La somnambula: or the somnambulist. CO. (CG 1848). [1848].
Pickwick. (No performance details). Dicks 1065. From Dickens.

Contributions to periodicals

Early days of Edmund Kean. NMM Apr 1834.
Recollections of Kean, 1814 to his death. NMM May 1834.
Records of a stage veteran. (13 pts). NMM Aug 1834–Oct 1837.
Peeping Tom and Lady Godiva. NMM Jan 1838.
John Reeve. NMM Mar 1838.

Editions

Preface to Hannah Maria Jones (afterwards Lowndes), The strangers of the glen: or the travellers benighted. A tale of mystery. 1827.
[Ed W. L. Rede.] The road to the stage: contains clear and ample instructions for obtaining theatrical engagements . . . To which is added a list of the London theatres . . . an account of the Dramatic Authors' Society . . . and a copy of the Dramatic Copyright Act. By the late Leman Thomas Rede. 1836 (new edn). First pbd under his brother's name in 1827.
Rede started Judy *in 1842 as a rival to* Punch, *but only 2 issues appeared. For other dramatic works, see* Nicoll *4, pp. 389–91, 607. See also Conolly,* English drama, *pp. 258–9;* Readex Index, *p. 228.*

§2

Era 11 Apr 1847. Obituary.
Recollections of Rede. NMM May 1847.
GM June 1847. Obituary. [JRS]

Thomas William Robertson 1829–1871

Collections

Principal dramatic works, with a memoir by his son [T. W. S. Robertson]. 2 vols 1889.
Society and Caste. Ed T. Edgar Pemberton, Boston and London 1905.
T. W. Robertson: six plays, with an introduction by M. R. Booth. 1980.
Plays by Tom Robertson. Ed with an introd by W. Tydeman. British and American Playwrights Series 1750–1920. Cambridge 1982.

§1

The chevalier de St George. D. (P'cess 20 May 1845). [1870?]; Lacy 25. From the Fr of M. Mélesville and R. de Beauvoir.
Noémie. Also Ernestine. Also Clarisse; or, The foster sister. Also The foster sisters. D. (P'cess 14 Apr 1846). Lacy 23. From the Fr of A. D'Ennery and Clément.
The ladies' battle. C. (H 18 Nov 1851). Boston [1856?]; Lacy suppl 1. From the Fr of A. E. Scribe and Legouvé.
Faust and Marguerite. D. (P'cess Apr 1854). Lacy 15. From the Fr of M. Carré. Also attrib to Boucicault.
My wife's diary. Also A wife's journal. F. (Olym 18 Dec 1854). Lacy 18. Adapted from Les memoires de deux jeunes mariées by A. D'Ennery and Clairville.
The star of the north. D. (SW 5 Mar 1855, as The northern star). Lacy 93. From the Fr?
The clockmaker's hat. Also Betty Martin. C. (Adelphi 7 Mar 1855). Lacy 266. Also attrib to H. G. Harris.
Peace at any price. F. (Str 13 Feb 1856). Lacy 95; De Witt 156.
The half caste; or, The poisoned pearl. D. (Sur 8 Sep 1856). Lacy 97.
Two gay deceivers; or, Black, white and grey. F. (Str 1858). Lacy 23: Dramatic Publishing Co nd; Sergel 56. With T. H. Lacy. From Deux profonds scélérats by E. M. Labiche.
The Cantab. Also The young collegian. F. (Str 14 Feb 1861). Lacy 50.

Jocrisse the juggler. Also Magloire the prestigitator. [?]. (Adel 1 Apr 1861). French nd. Adapted from the play by Dennery and Bresil.
David Garrick. C. (PW Birmingham Apr 1864; H 30 Apr 1864). French 117. Adapted from the play Sullivan by 'M. Mélesville' (Anne H. J. Duveyrier).
Society. C. (PW Liverpool 1865; PW 11 Nov 1865). Lacy 71.
Robinson Crusoe. B. (Unacted?). [1865?]; Lacy nd. After A. E. Scribe, Un verre d'eau.
David Garrick: a love story. 1865. A novel.
The ring. In A bunch of keys, ed T. Hood, 1865.
Ours. C. (PW Liverpool 23 Aug 1866; PW 16 Sep 1866). French 384.
The poor-rate. In Rates and taxes, ed T. Hood, 1866.
Caste. C. (PW 6 Apr 1867). De Witt; French 131; Boston 1918; ed M. Slater 1951; Rowell.
The sea of ice; or, The prayer of the wrecked and the gold-seeker of Mexico. Also The thirst of gold; or, The lost ship and the wild flowers of Mexico. Also The struggle for gold. Also The struggle for gold and the orphan of the frozen sea. M. (Colosseum (?) Glasgow nd). Lacy nd; French nd.
Play. C. (PW 15 Feb 1868). French 132.
Home. C. (H 14 Jan 1869). New York [1879]; French 131; De Witt. Based on G. V. E Augier, L'aventurière.
School. C. (PW 16 Jan 1869). De Witt; French 133; Philadelphia 1903. Based on the theme of the play Aschenbrodel by Roderick Benedix.
My Lady Clara. Also Dreams. D. (Alexandra, Liverpool 22 Feb 1869; Gai 27 Mar 1869, as Dreams). New York [1875]; French 131 (as Dreams).
A breach of promise. C. (Glo 10 Apr 1869). French 128, De Witt 179.
Progress. C. (Glo 18 Sep 1869). French 133. Based on V. Sardou, Les Ganches.
The nightingale. D. (Adel 15 Jan 1870). French 132.
M. P. C. (PW 23 Apr 1870). French 131.
Birth. [D] (TR Bristol 5 Oct 1870). French nd.
War. D. (StJ 16 Jan 1871). French 133; French's standard drama 407.
Birds of prey; or, A duel in the dark. (Not performed?). Lacy 93.
Not at all jealous. F. (Court 29 May 1871). Lacy 91.
A row in the house. F. (Toole's 30 Aug 1883). French 128.
Dazzled not blinded. nd. A novel.
Stephen Caldrick. nd. A novel.

§2

The comedies of Robertson. Broadway 6 1870.
Friswell, J. H. In his Modern men of letters, 1870.
Robertson and the modern theatre. Temple Bar 44, June 1875.
Jones, W. W. Robertson as dramatist. Theatre 1 1879.
Pemberton, T. E. The life and writings of Robertson. 1893.
Hawkins, F. Acad 3 June 1893. Review of preceeding.
Shaw, G. B. Robertson's Caste. Sat Rev June 1897.
Beerbohm, Max. 'More in sorrow –' Sat Rev 85, 14 Jan 1899. Rptd in Around theatres, 1953.
Montefiore, E. Robertsoniana. 1910.
Grein, K. Robertson 1829–71; ein Beitrag zur Geschichte des neueren englischen Dramas. Marburg 1911.
Armstrong, C. F. Shakespeare to Shaw: studies in the life's work of six dramatists of the English stage. 1913.
Watson, E. B. Sheridan to Robertson: a study of the nineteenth-century London stage. Cambridge MA 1926.
Harrison, D. Tom Robertson: a century of criticism. Contemporary Rev Apr 1929.
Rahill, F. A mid-Victorian regisseur. Theatre Arts Nov 1929.
Bulloch, J. M. Dame Madge Kendal's Robertson Ancestors. N & Q 3–17 Dec 1932.
Reynolds, E. Early Victorian drama (1830–1870). Cambridge 1936.
Miestinger, G. Die Dramentechnik des Thomas William Robertson. Vienna 1939.
Savin, M. Robertson: his plays and stagecraft. Providence RI 1950.
Lorenzen, R. L. The dramaturgy of Thomas William Robertson. A study of six plays produced at the Prince of Wales's Theatre 1865–70. Columbus OH 1965.
Meier, E. Realism and reality. Berne 1967.
Taylor, J. R. The rise and fall of the well-made play. 1967.
Booth, M. Introduction to English plays of the nineteenth century vol 3. Oxford 1973.
Willems, S. L. The emergence of the modern British director. Thomas William Robertson. Madison WI 1976.
Rouyer, P. T. W. Robertson (1829–1871) et le Prince of Wales's Theatre. Paris 1977.
Barret, J. D. The plays of Tom Robertson. Colchester 1978.
Jenkins, A. The making of Victorian drama. Cambridge 1991. [BY]

George Herbert Buonaparte Rodwell 1800–52

Where shall I dine? F. (Olym 12 Feb 1819). [1819]; Dicks 973.
Freaks and follies: or a match for the old one. F. (Adel 5 Nov 1827). Dicks 988.
Teddy the tiler. F. (CG 8 Feb 1830). Cumberland 25; Dicks 784. From Pierre le couvreur.
Was I to blame? Ba. (Adel 13 Dec 1830). Lacy 32.
I'll be your second. F. (Olym 10 Oct 1831). Lacy 3.
The first rudiments of harmony. 1831.
A letter to the musicians of Great Britain, containing a prospectus of proposed plans for the better encouragement of native musical talent, and for the erection and management of a grand national opera in London. 1833.
A catechism of music. [1840?] (21st edn).
A catechism on harmony. [1841?]
My wife's out. F. (CG 2 Oct 1843). Lacy 45; Dicks 699.
The picnic: or husbands, wives and lovers. F. (Adel 4 Dec 1843). Dicks 561.
Memoirs of an umbrella. [1845.] A novel.
Woman's love: a romance of smiles and tears. [1846.]
The seven maids of Munich: or the ghost's tower. MD. (P'cess 19 Dec 1846). 1846 (songs, duets, choruses only).
Old London Bridge: a romance of the sixteenth century. [1848–9.]
The devil's ring, or fire, water, earth and air: a grand musical fairy romance in three acts and four elements. [1850.] In verse.
For other dramatic works, see Nicoll *4, pp. 395, 608.*

Charles Selby 1801–63

§1

Licensing copies of some plays are located in BL. All plays listed below are also issued in one or more Readex micro *edns.*
One fault. Ba. (CL 11 July 1831). [1831?]; Dicks 551. From Scribe, Une faute.
A day in Paris. F. (Str 18 July 1832). Duncombe 16; Lacy no 1025; Dicks 425; Philadelphia nd.
Captain Stevens. (CL 31 Dec 1832). F. Duncombe 11; Dicks 957.
Frank Fox Phipps, Esq. F. (Vic 18 Feb 1834). Duncombe 14; Lacy no 1492; Dicks 959.
The heiress of Bruges. D. (Vic 4 Aug 1834). Duncombe 15; Dicks 674.
The unfinished gentleman. Ba. (Adel 1 Dec 1834). Duncombe 15; Lacy no 502; Dicks 417; Philadelphia and New York nd.
The married rake. F. (Queen's 9 Feb 1835). [1835]; Duncombe 16; Lacy 71; Philadelphia [1840?]; Dicks 676; French NY no 71.
Robert Macaire or les [*sic*] auberge des Adrets! MD. (Vic 3 Dec 1834?). Duncombe no 123; Duncombe 16 (as The two murderers: or the auberge des Adrets! City 1835); Lacy 30; Dicks 325. Also as Robert Macaire: or the two murderers, (Adel 2 Mar 1835?), Brit and Amer Theatre 8, Stuttgart 1842, [1890]. From Benjamin, Saint-Amand and Ployanthe, L'auberge des Adrets.

Catching an heiress. F. (Queen's 15 July 1835). Duncombe 18; Lacy no 582; Dicks 402.
The guardian sylph: or the magic rose. Oa. (Queen's 3 Aug 1835). Duncombe 50.
Hunting a turtle. F. (Queen's 14 Sep 1835). Duncombe 19; Lacy 40; Dicks 402; Philadelphia [1836?].
The rival pages. C. (Queen's 8 Oct 1835). Duncombe 25; Lacy no 1400; Dicks 926.
The widow's victim. F. (Adel 17 Dec 1835). Duncombe no 153; Lacy no 930; Dicks 415.
Little sins and pretty sinners. Ba. (Queen's 12 Jan 1836). Duncombe 30; Lacy no 281; Dicks 957.
Frederick of Prussia: or the monarch and the mimic. Ba. (Queen's 24 July 1837 as The king of Prussia). Duncombe 27; Lacy no 478; Dicks 423.
The dancing barber. Ba. (Adel 8 Jan 1838). 1838; Webster 3; Mod Eng Com Th ser 2; Dicks 380.
The rifle brigade. F. (Adel 19 Feb 1838 as Rifle manoeuvres). Webster 3; Dicks 757.
The valet de sham. Ba (StJ 29 Mar 1838). Webster 4; Dicks 770; Boston Th 23.
Jacques Strop: or a few more passages in the life of the renowned and illustrious Robert Macaire. D. (Str 24 Sep 1838). Duncombe 31; Lacy no 1516; Dicks 599.
Ask no questions. Ba. (Olym 24 Oct 1838). Webster 5; Dicks 454. From Bayard and Pickard, Mathias l'invalide.
The king's gardener: or nipped in the bud. Ba. (Str 1 Apr 1839). Duncombe 36; New BT 286; Dicks 535.
The fairy lake: or the magic veil. Ba. (Str 13 May 1839). Duncombe 37. From Le lac des fées.
The loves of Lord Bateman and the fair Sophia. Bsq. (Str 3 July 1839). Duncombe 37.
Marceline: or the soldier's legacy. D. (Str 9 Sep 1839). Duncombe 41; Dicks 568.
Behind the scenes: or actors by lamplight. Ba. (Str 12 Sep 1839). Duncombe 38; Lacy no 1702; Dicks 703.
The pink of politeness. Ba. (Olym 8 Feb 1840). Duncombe 41; Dicks 772.
Maximums and specimens of William Muggins, natural philosopher and citizen of the world. 1841, 1859 (new edn). First pbd in The Sunday Times.
The handsel penny. F. (Lyc 13 May 1841). Pattie no 32.
Barnaby Rudge. D. (EOH 28 June 1841). Duncombe 43; Mod Eng Com Th ser 1; Lacy no 1511; Dicks 393. With C. Melville. From Dickens.
A lady and gentleman in a peculiarly perplexing predicament. Ba. (EOH 9 Aug 1841). Duncombe 44; Lacy no 1031; Dicks 425; Boston Th 19; New York and Philadelphia nd.
Punch. Ext. (Str 18 Sep 1841). Dicks 618.
The new footman. Ba. (Str 28 Mar 1842). Duncombe 45; New BT 353; Lacy no 1595; Dicks 535.
The boots at the Swan. F. (Str 8 June 1842). Duncombe 45; Lacy no 503; Dicks 564. Baltimore and New York 1847; French Minor NY no 2.
Antony and Cleopatra. Ba. (Adel 7 Nov 1842). Duncombe 46; Boston Th 11; Dicks 602.
The moral philosopher. Ba. (Adel 9 Oct 1843). Duncombe 48.
Antony and Cleopatra married and settled. Bsq. (Adel 4 Dec 1843). Dicks 748.
Dissolving views: or lights and shadows of life. F. (Str 22 Jan 1844). Barth nd.
King Richard ye Third: or ye battel of Bosworth. Bsq. (Str 26 Feb 1844). Duncombe 49; Lacy no 587; Shakesp bsqs 2.
The mysterious stranger. D. (Adel 30 Oct 1844). Webster 10; Boston Th 2 1855 (dated) (as Satan in Paris: or the mysterious stranger); Dicks 798. From M. Clarville et Damarin, Satan: ou le diable à Paris.
London by night. D. (Str 12 May 1845). Dicks 721; Smith.
Powder and ball: or St Tibb's Eve. F. (Adel 16 June 1845). Duncombe 53.
Taming a Tartar: or magic and mazourkaphobia. F. (Adel 20 Oct 1845). Webster no 126.
The lioness of the north: or the prisoner of Schlusselbourg. D. (Adel 22 Dec 1845). Webster 12; Dicks 929.
The Irish Dragoon: or wards in Chancery. F. (Adel 1845?). Webster 11; Dicks 952.
The phantom breakfast. F. (Adel 15 Jan 1846). Bsq. Duncombe 55; Lacy no 1511; Dicks 955. From L'omelette fantastique.
Out on the sly: or a fête at Rosherville. F. (Adel 12 July 1847). Duncombe 60; New BT 475.
Peggy Green. C. (Lyc 1 Dec 1847). Duncombe 61; Lacy 42; Sergel 127; Dicks 1012.
The tutor's assistant. C. (Lyc 3 July 1848 as The court guide). Duncombe 62.
The witch of Windermere. C. (M'bone 4 Dec 1848). Lacy no 36, no 1249 (reissue).
Taken in and done for. F. (Str 10 May 1849). 1849; Lacy 3.
Chamber practice: or life in the Temple. F. (Str 25 June 1849). Duncombe 64; Cumberland no 510.
The white serjeants: or the buttermilk volunteers. C. (Adel 6 May 1850). Webster 16.
The husband of my heart. C. (H 23 Oct 1850). Lacy no 30.
My friend in the straps. F. (H 24 Oct 1850). Webster 16; Mod Eng Com Th ser 4.
Events to be remembered in the history of England; forming a series of interesting narratives of the most remarkable occurrences in each reign. [1851], 1860 (25th edn), 1891 (28th edn). A history for school use.
The fire eater. F. (Olym 30 June 1851). Lacy no 52.
My sister from India: or the mystical milkman. F. (Str 5 Jan 1852). Lacy no 1612.
Hotel charges: or how to cook a biffin. F. (Adel 13 Oct 1853). Lacy no 169.
The marble heart: or the sculptor's dream. D. (Adel 22 May 1854). Lacy no 214; Boston Th 8. From Barrière and Thiboust, Les filles de marbre.
My friend the major. F. (StJ 2 Oct 1854). Lacy no 231.
The Spanish dancers: or fans and fandangoes. Ba. (StJ 18 Oct 1854). Lacy no 735.
Fearful tragedy in the Seven Dials. F. (Adel 4 May 1857). Lacy no 452.
The drapery question: or who's for India. F. (Adel 28 Oct 1857). Lacy no 489.
The last of the pigtails. Ca. (Str 6 Sep 1858). Lacy no 545; Boston Th 24.
The bonnie fish wife. F. (Str 20 Sep 1858). Lacy no 551; De Witt 70.
Harold Hawk: or the convict's vengeance. D. (Sur 27 Sep 1858). Lacy no 559.
My aunt's husband. F. (Str 27 Sep 1858). Lacy no 554.
The young mother. CD. (H 28 Feb 1859). Lacy no 574.
Caught by the ears. F. (Str 30 May 1859). Lacy no 604.
Paris and pleasure: or home and happiness. D. (Lyc 28 Nov 1859). Lacy no 725.
The pet lamb. Ca. (Str 10 Sep 1860). Lacy no 702.
The dinner question, by Tabitha Tickletooth. 1860.
The poor nobleman. D. (StJ 14 Nov 1861). Lacy no 787. From P. F. Pinel Dumanoir and P. Lafargue.
The pirates of Putney. Ext. (Roy 31 Aug 1863). Lacy no 890.
For other dramatic works see Nicoll *4, pp. 397–9, 610; 5, pp. 560, 815; see also Conolly,* English drama, *pp. 266–8;* Readex Index, *pp. 243–4.*

§2

Era 22 Mar 1863. Obituary. [JRS]

John Palgrave Simpson 1807–87

Licensing copies of the plays are located in BL.

§1

All plays listed below are also issued in one or more Readex micro *edns.*

Second love, and other tales, from the notebook of a traveller. 3 vols 1846.

Gisella. 3 vols 1847.

Pictures from revolutionary Paris, sketched during the first phasis of the revolution of 1848. Edinburgh and London 1848. Rptd from Blackwood's Mag, Bentley's Misc, The Times.

The lily of Paris: or the king's nurse. 3 vols 1849.

Poor Cousin Walter. D. (Str 8 Apr 1850). Lacy 2.

Without incumbrances. F. (Str 12 Aug 1850). [1850]; Lacy 2.

That odious Captain Cutter! F. (Olym 24 Feb 1851). Lacy 3.

Only a clod. F. (Olym 20 May 1851). [1851]; Lacy 21; Boston nd (Spencer's universal stage 41).

Matrimonial prospectuses. F. (Str 4 Mar 1852). Lacy 6.

Very suspicious! F. (Lyc 12 June 1852). Lacy 6.

Marco Spada. D. (P'cess 28 Mar 1853). Lacy 10; French NY no 99. From Scribe.

Ranelagh. CD. (H 11 Feb 1854). Lacy 13. With C. Wray.

Heads or tails? Ca. (Olym 29 June 1854). Mod Eng Com Th ser 5; Lacy 15; Boston Th 22.

Second love. C. (H 23 July 1856). Lacy 28; Boston Th 9.

Daddy Hardacre. D. (Olym 26 Mar 1857). Lacy 100.

World and stage. C. (H 12 Mar 1859). Lacy 97.

A school for coquettes. Ca. (Str 4 July 1859). Lacy 41.

Romance! Oa. (CG 2 Feb 1860). 1860, [1860]. Music by H. Leslie.

First affections. C. (StJ 13 Feb 1860). Lacy 52.

Appearances. C. (Str 28 May 1860). Lacy 47.

Bianca, the bravo's bride. O. (CG 6 Dec 1860). [1860.] Music by M. W. Balfe.

A scrap of paper. C. (StJ 22 Apr 1861). Lacy 51. From Sardou, Les pattes de mouches.

Court cards. Ca. (Olym 25 Nov 1861). Lacy 53. From J. Barbier and M. Carré, La fileuse.

Dreams of delusion. D. (Sur 11 Apr 1862). Boston Th 21. From Elle est folle.

Sybilla: or step by step. Ca. (StJ 29 Oct 1864). Lacy 64.

A fair pretender. D. (PW 10 May 1865). Lacy 66.

Jack in a box! Ca. (StJ 11 June 1866). Lacy 71.

An atrocious criminal. F. (Olym 18 Feb 1867). Lacy 74.

Shadows of the past. D. (TR Brighton 1 Nov 1867). Lacy 97.

Black sheep. D. (Olym 25 Apr 1868). Lacy 81. With E. H. Yates, based on his novel.

Time and the hour. D. (Queens 29 June 1868). Lacy 81; De Witt 42. With H. C. Merivale.

The serpent on the hearth. D. (Adel 2 Aug 1869). Lacy 85.

The watch dog of the Walsinghams. RD. (Liverpool 28 Aug 1869). Lacy 92.

Two gentlemen at Mivart's. Duol. In Scott, Drawing room plays, 1870.

Broken ties. D. (Olym 8 June 1872). Lacy 96. From M. Uchard, La fiammina.

Alone. C. (Crit 25 Oct 1873). French 103. With H. C. Merivale.

Lady Dedlock's secret. D. (Aberdeen 3 Apr 1874). French no 1822. From Dickens, Bleak House.

Alarmingly suspicious. [No performance details.] Clyde, Ohio nd (Ames' Standard & Minor Drama 80).

For ever and never: a novel. 2 vols 1884.

A cloud in the honeymoon. [No performance details.] Sergel 326 (dated Chicago 1884).

My mysterious rival. [No performance details.] De Witt 324 (dated New York 1884).

See also Nicoll 5, *pp. 567–8, 816; Conolly,* English drama, *pp. 282–3;* Readex Index, *p. 251.*

Contributions to periodicals

The witchfinder. Blackwood's Mag 2 pts Sep–Oct 1844.

The midnight watch. Blackwood's Mag Apr 1845.

The last hours of a reign. Blackwood's Mag 2 pts Dec 1845–Jan 1846.

The flaneur in Paris: from the notebook of a traveller. Bentley's Misc 11 pts Aug 1846–Nov 1847.

'Moriamur pro rege nostro'. Blackwood's Mag Aug 1846.

The King of Bavaria and Lola Montez. Fraser's Mag Jan 1848. Attributed.

The witches' stone. Fraser's Mag Feb 1848. Attributed.

Scenes from the last French republic. Bentley's Misc Apr 1848.

Republican clubs in Paris. Bentley's Misc May 1848.

Republican Paris, Mar, Apr 1848. Blackwood's Mag May 1848.

Republican manners. Bentley's Misc June 1848.

Sentiments and symbols of the French Revolution. Blackwood's Mag June 1848.

The French National Assembly. Bentley's Misc July 1848.

Republican France. Blackwood's Mag July 1848.

The Republican newspapers of Paris. Bentley's Misc Aug 1848.

Sketches in Paris. Blackwood's Mag Aug 1848.

What would revolutionising Germany be at? Blackwood's Mag Sep 1848.

A morning in the German National Assembly. Bentley's Misc Oct 1848.

Prophecies for the present. Blackwood's Mag Dec 1848.

Hans Michel: or a few old German proverbs applied to new German politics. Bentley's Misc Jan 1849.

After a year's republicanism. Blackwood's Mag Mar 1849.

The mirror of the French republic: or the Parisian theatres. Bentley's Misc Apr 1849.

Legitimacy in France. Blackwood's Mag May 1849.

What has revolutionising Germany attained? Blackwood's Mag Oct 1849.

A revolutionary ramble on the Rhine. Bentley's Misc Dec 1849.

New Year's Day adventures of a box of bonbons. Bentley's Misc Jan 1855.

Letters

Letters from the Danube. 2 vols 1847.

Translations

Carl Maria von Weber: the life of an artist; from the German by J. P. Simpson. 2 vols 1865.
REVIEW: Edinburgh Rev Oct 1865.

§2

Era Almanack 1868. [JRS]

Edward Stirling 1809?–94

§1

Licensing copies of the plays, some autograph, are located in BL.

The lucky hit: or railroads for ever. Ba. (Licensed 23 Apr 1836; no performance details). Lacy 3.

Carline, the female brigand. D. (Pav 16 Jan 1837). Duncombe 26.

The Pickwick Club: or the age we live in. Ba. (CL 27 Mar 1837). Duncombe 26; Philadelphia and New York nd. From Dickens.

Bachelor's buttons. F. (Str 29 May 1837). Duncombe 26; French nd.

The rose of Corbeil: or the forest of Senart. MD. (CL 13 Nov 1837). Duncombe 29; French 111.

Dandolo: or the last of the Doges. F. (CL 8 Jan 1838). 1838; Duncombe 35.

The blue jackets: or her majesty's service. F. (Adel 5 Oct 1838). Duncombe 31; Lacy 47.

Nicholas Nickleby. F. (Adel 19 Nov 1838). Webster 5; Mod Eng Com Th ser 2; Boston Th 23.

Grace Darling: or the wreck at sea. D. (Adel 3 Dec 1838). Webster 6; French 105. Also as The wreck at sea: or The fern light.
Jane Lomas: or a mother's crime. MD. (Adel 4 Feb 1839). Webster 6.
The little back parlour. F. (EOH 17 Aug 1839). Duncombe 38; French 111.
The devil's daughters: or hell's belles. Ba. (Sur 4 Nov 1839). Duncombe 39; New BT 313 as The devil's daughters: or h—l upon earth!
The dragon knight: or the queen of beauty! D. (Adel 18 Nov 1839 as The knight of the dragon). Duncombe 39; New BT 311. From Ainsworth's Crichton.
The fortunes of Smike: or a sequel to Nicholas Nickleby. D. (Adel 2 Mar 1840). Webster 9; Mod Eng Com Th ser 1.
The serpent of the Nile: or the battle of Actium. MD. (Adel 20 Apr 1840). Duncombe 41.
Guido Fawkes: or the prophetess of Ordsall Cave! MD. (Queen's Manchester June 1840; EOH 24 Aug 1840). Duncombe 42. From Ainsworth, Guy Fawkes: or the gunpowder treason.
The old curiosity shop. Ba. (Adel 9 Nov 1840). Duncombe 48; Lacy 77; Lorenzen micro. From Dickens.
Teddy Roe. F. (Str 19 Apr 1841). Duncombe 43; Mod Eng Com Th 7; Boston Th 7; French Minor NY 194.
The rubber of life: or St James's and St Giles's. D. (Str 10 May 1841). Duncombe 43.
The miser's daughter. Spec. (Adel 21 Oct 1842). Duncombe 45; New BT 361; Lacy 99. From Ainsworth.
Yankee notes for English circulation. F. (Adel 24 Dec 1842). Duncombe 46; New BT 367.
Captain Charlotte. F. (Adel 6 Mar 1843). Duncombe 46; Lacy 39.
Ondine: or the water sprite and the fire fiend. Spec. (CL 17 Apr 1843). Duncombe 46.
Aline, the rose of Killarney. D. (Str 10 July 1843). Duncombe 47; Lacy 94.
Wanted a wife: or London, Liverpool, and Bristol. Ba (Adel 23 Oct 1843). Barth nd.
The Bohemians: or the rogues of Paris. D. (Adel 6 Nov 1843). Dicks' BD 10. From Sue, Les mystères de Paris.
The young scamp: or my grandmother's pet! Ba. (P'cess 27 Feb 1844). Duncombe 49.
Martin Chuzzlewit. D. (Lyc 9 July 1844). Duncombe 50. From Dickens.
The seven castles of the passions. D. (Lyc 21 Oct 1844). Barth nd.
Margaret Catchpole, the heroine of Suffolk: or the vicissitudes of real life. D. (Sur 24 Mar 1845). Duncombe 52; Lacy 3. From R. Cobbold, The history of Margaret Catchpole, a Suffolk girl.
The secret foe. D. (Sur 12 May 1845). Duncombe 53.
Mrs Caudle's curtain lecture. Sk. (Lyc 10 July 1845). Duncombe 53.
Lestelle: or the wrecker's bride. D. (Sur 21 Aug 1845). Cumberland no 427; Duncombe 54.
By royal command. Ca. (Lyc 25 Aug 1845). French 106; Dicks' BD 11.
Clarisse: or the merchant's daughter. D. (Adel 1 Sep 1845). Webster 11.
The cricket on the hearth. D. (Adel 31 Dec 1845). Webster 12. From Dickens.
The sea king's vow: or a struggle for liberty. D. (Sur 16 Feb 1846). Duncombe 55; New BT 441.
The cabin boy. D. (Adel 9 Mar 1846). Webster 12; French 104.
Industry and indolence: or the orphan's legacy. D. (Adel 9 Apr 1846). Duncombe no 476.
On the tiles. F. (Sur 13 Apr 1846). Duncombe 56; Lacy no 1874.
The last kiss: or the soldier's grave. D. (Sur 30 Apr 1846). Duncombe 56; New BT 444.
Above and below. C. (Lyc 16 July 1846). Duncombe 57.
The jockey club. Ext. (Adel 19 Oct 1846). Webster 13.
Mrs Harris. F. (Lyc 22 Oct 1846). Duncombe 57.
The hand of cards. D. (Sur 30 Dec 1846). Duncombe 57.
The battle of life. D. (Sur Jan 1847). Duncombe 57. From Dickens.
Raby Rattler: or the progress of a scamp. D. (Sur 3 Feb 1847). Duncombe 58.
Lilly Dawson: or a poor girl's story. D. (Sur 8 Mar 1847). Duncombe 58; Lacy no 1909.
Kissing goes by favour. F. (Sur 5 Apr 1847). Duncombe 58; Lacy no 2019.
The buffalo girls: or the female serenaders. F. (Sur 17 Apr 1847). Duncombe 59.
The anchor of hope: or the seaman's star. D. (Sur 19 Apr 1847). Duncombe 59; French 111.
The rag-picker of Paris and the dress-maker of St Antoine. D. (Sur 24 June 1847). Duncombe 59; Lacy 81; French NY 108.
The idiot of the mill. D. (CL 10 Aug 1848). Duncombe 63; French nd.
Nora Creina. D. (Sur 11 Sep 1848). Duncombe 55; New BT 439; Mod Eng Com Th 9; Boston Th 9.
Jeanette & Jeannot [*sic*]: or the village pride. D. (Olym 26 Oct 1848). French 106.
The bould soger boy. F. (Olym 6 Nov 1848). Duncombe no 533; French 111.
The lost diamonds. D. (Olym 12 Feb 1849). Duncombe 63; Lacy nd.
Family pictures. F. (M'bone 11 Mar 1849). [1849]; French 106.
Clarence Clevedon, his struggle for life or death. D. (Vic 9 Apr 1849). Duncombe 64.
The mother's bequest. D. (Str 7 May 1849). Duncombe 64.
The lilly of the desert. D. (Sur 28 May 1849). Dicks' BD 3.
The white slave. F. (Vic 10 Aug 1849). Duncombe 66; Lacy no 1948.
The teacher taught. F. (SW 17 Oct 1850). Duncombe 66; Mod Eng Com Th ser 4; Lacy 48.
A figure of fun: or the bloomer costume. F. (Str 26 Dec 1851). 1852, [1852?].
The ragged school. D. (Str 15 Mar 1852). Duncombe nd.
A pet of the public. F. (Str 7 Nov 1853). Lacy no 180.
A struggle for gold: or the orphan of the frozen sea. D. (CL Jan 1854). 1854. Also as A struggle for gold: or a mother's prayer.
The courier of Lyons. D. (CL July 1854). 1854; Dicks' BD 4.
The three black seals. D. (Astley's 25 Apr 1864). Dicks' BD 3.
The dark glen of Ballyfoill. D. (Ipswich 28 Oct 1871). Dicks' BD 9 (dated 1871).
Old Drury Lane: fifty years' recollections of author, actor, and manager. 2 vols 1881.

Attributed works

The roving tragedian. In Era Almanack for 1886.
My first engagement. In Era Almanack for 1888.
Stirling was a very prolific author; many plays are unpbd including adaptations of Dickens's novels. See also Nicoll *4, pp. 406–9, 612–13; 5, pp. 584, 818; Conolly,* English drama, *pp. 292–3;* Readex Index, *pp. 259–61.*

§2

Theatrical Times 3 1848; 4 1849. [JRS]

Tom Taylor 1817–80

There is a large collection of Taylor mss in the BL and the Br Theatre Museum.

§1

A trip to Kissingen. F. (Lyc 14 Nov 1844). Dicks 881.
Masks and faces: or before and behind the curtain. C. (H 20 Nov 1852). 1854; Dicks; Lacy; Rowell. With C. Reade. Played also as Peg Woffington.
Plot and passion. D. (Olym 17 Oct 1853). Lacy 13; Dicks 1048; New York [1869?]. With J. Lang.
Three dramas, 1854. (Masks and faces; The king's rival; Two loves and a life). 1854. With C. Reade.
Still waters run deep. C. (Olym 14 May 1855). Lacy 22; Dicks 1049; Banham (1985); Boston [1856?].

Going to the bad. C. (Olym 5 June 1858). Lacy 37.
Our American cousin. C. (Laura Keene's, New York 18 Oct 1858, H 11 Nov 1861). 1869; Lacy.
The contested election. C. (H 29 June 1859). Chambers (Manchester 1868); Banham (1985).
The fool's revenge. D. (SW 18 Oct 1859). Lacy 43; New York [1863?]. From Victor Hugo, Le roi s'amuse.
The overland route. C. (H 23 Feb 1860). Lacy 1853; Banham (1985).
Up at the hills. C. (StJ 29 Oct 1860). Lacy 50.
Handbook of the pictures in the International Exhibition of 1862. 1862.
The railway station, painted by W. P. Frith, described by Tom Taylor. 1862.
The Ticket-of-Leave Man. D. (Olym 27 May 1863). Lacy 59, Rowell; Banham; Booth 2. From Brisebane and Nus, Le retour du Melun.
Birket Foster's pictures of English landscape; with pictures in words by Tom Taylor. 1863 (for 1862).
A marriage memorial: verse and prose, commemorative of the wedding of the Prince and Princess of Wales, Mar 10 1863. [1863.]
Life and times of Sir Joshua Reynolds, commenced by C. R. Leslie, continued by Tom Taylor. 2 vols 1865.
New men and old acres. C. (H 25 Oct 1869). Lacy 90; Booth 3. With A. W. Dubourg.
English painters of the present day: essays by J. B. Atkinson [etc] and Tom Taylor. 1871.
The theatre in England: some of its shortcomings and possibilities. 1871.
English artists of the present day: essays by J. B. Atkinson [et al] and Tom Taylor. 1872.
Leicester Square: its associations and its worthies; with a sketch of Hunter's scientific character and works by Richard Owen. 1874.
Historical dramas. (The fool's revenge; Jeanne D'arc; 'Twixt axe and crown; Lady Clancarty; Arkwright's wife; Anne Boleyn; Plot and passion.) 1877.
Storm at midnight, and other poems. Ed J. H. Burn, 1893.
Taylor edited Punch *from 1874 until his death in 1880. Besides the above works, he edited* C. R. Leslie, Autobiographical recollections, *1860;* B. R. Haydon, Life, *1853; and* Mortimer Collins, Pen sketches by a vanished hand, *2 vols 1879. For other dramatic works, see* Nicoll *4, pp. 411, 614; 5, pp. 592–9, 820.*

§2

Sheehan, J. Tom Taylor. Dublin Univ Mag Aug 1877.
Hughes, T. In memoriam Tom Taylor. Macmillan's Mag Aug 1880.
Tolles, W. Taylor and the Victorian drama. New York 1940.
Banham, M. Plays by Tom Taylor. Cambridge 1985. [MB]

Alfred, Baron Tennyson 1809–92

See col 675.

Charles Whitehead 1804–62

See col 692.

Alfred Sydney Wigan 1814–78

A model of a wife. F. (Lyc 27 Jan 1845). Lacy 61 and 914; Dicks 1008.
The loan of a wife, from the French. F. (Lyc 29 June 1846). Duncombe's British Theatre 56; French 2007.
Five hundred pounds reward: or Dick Turpin the second. F. or C. (Lyc 28 Jan 1847). Duncombe 58; Dicks 1003; Cumberland 459.
Tit for tat. F. (Olym 22 [or 23] Jan 1855). Lacy 17. With F. Talfourd (sometimes attributed solely to Talfourd).
See also Nicoll *4, pp. 419, 617; 5, p. 621.* [DS]

Thomas Egerton Wilks 1812–54

Licensing copies of the plays, including some autograph, are located in BL. All plays listed below are also issued in one or more Readex micro *edns.*
The brothers: or the wolf and the lamb. C. (H 23 June 1832 as sub-title). [1834?] (London Acting Drama 31); Duncombe 32; Dicks 968.
The red crow: or the archers of Islington and the fayre maid of West Cheap. MD. (SW 30 June 1834 with sub-title The archers of Islington and the hog of Highbury). Duncombe 14; Dicks 270.
Wenlock of Wenlock: or the spirit of the black mantle. MD. (SW 30 June 1834). Duncombe 17; New BT 132.
The seven clerks: or the three thieves and the denouncer. D. (Sur 3 Nov 1834). Duncombe 15; Lacy 40; French American drama 115; Dicks 923; Philadelphia and New York [1844?] (as The denouncer: or the seven clerks and the three thieves).
Rinaldo Rinaldini: or the brigand and the blacksmith. D. (SW 7 Jan 1836). Duncombe 20.
The captain's not a-miss. OF. (EOH 18 Apr 1836). Duncombe 21; Lacy 29; Dicks 417; French Minor NY 159.
State secrets: or the tailor of Tamworth. Ba. (Sur 12 Sep 1836). Duncombe 23; Lacy 53; Dicks 914.
The death token! D. (Sur 15 May 1837). Duncombe 26.
Lord Darnley: or the keep of Castle Hill! D. (Sur 11 Sep 1837). 1837; Duncombe 32; Lacy 78; Dicks 715.
Sudden thoughts. F. (City 21 Oct 1837). 1837; Duncombe 34; Mod Eng Comic Th ser 1; New BT 271; Lacy 33; Boston Th 18; Dicks 407.
The king's wager: or the cottage and the court. Ba. (Vic 5 Dec 1837). [1837]; Duncombe 35; Lacy 62; Dicks 501. An earlier version probably staged as The golden cornet: or the king's wager (SW 15 Sep 1834).
Letter to the Rev T. Binney, in defence of the drama; showing the futility of the objections made by him against theatrical amusements, in his lecture recently delivered in Wells Street Chapel. 1838, 1838 (2nd edn enlarged).
The black domino: or the masked ball. C. (SW 6 Feb 1838). Duncombe 28; Lacy 88. From Scribe, Le domino noir.
'Tis she!: or the maid, the wife, and the widow. Ba. (StJ 6 Feb 1838). 1838; Duncombe 35; Dicks 750.
The jacket of blue. OF. (Royal Pavilion 14 Feb 1838). Duncombe 28; French 108; Dicks 552.
The crown prince: or the buckle of brilliants. Ba. (SW 16 July 1838). Duncombe 30; Lacy 26; Dicks 484; French Minor NY 100.
The Wren boys: or the moment of peril. F. (CL 8 Oct 1838). Duncombe 32; Lacy 52; Dicks 404.
My wife's dentist. F. (H 4 May 1839). Duncombe 43; Lacy 35; Dicks 524.
The ladye of Lambythe: or a bridal three centuries back! D. (Sur 5 Aug 1839). Duncombe 38.
Ben the boatswain. D. (Sur 19 Aug 1839). Duncombe 38; Lacy 28; Dicks 752.
Michael Erle the maniac lover: or the fayre lass of Lichfield! RD. (Sur 26 Nov 1839). Duncombe 40; Lacy 33; Boston Th 26 (dated 1856).
The ruby ring: or the murder at Sadler's Wells! MD. (SW 22 June 1840). Duncombe 41.
The railroad station. Ba. (Olym 3 Oct 1840). Duncombe 42; Lacy 47; Dicks 524.
The sergeant's wedding. CD. (Prince's 17 Nov 1840). Duncombe 43; Lacy 91; Dicks 627.
Cousin Peter. CD. (Olym 11 Oct 1841). Duncombe 44; French 117; Dicks 552.
Raffaelle the reprobate: or the secret mission and the signet ring. D. (Vic 3 Nov 1841). Lacy 10; Boston Th 13; Dicks 401.
Bamboozling. F. (Olym 16 May 1842). Duncombe 41; Lacy 28; Dicks 627.
My valet and I. F. (Olym 31 Oct 1842). Duncombe 46; Dicks 770.

Sixteen string Jack: or the knaves of Knaves' Acre. MD. (SW 28 Nov 1842). Duncombe 63; New BT 505; French 105.
The devil's in it. C. (P'cess 9 May 1843). Dicks 649.
Halvei the Unknown. D. (SW 12 June 1843). Lacy 42; Dicks 690.
The dream spectre. RD. (Vic 24 July 1843). Lacy 40; Dicks 913.
The ambassador's lady: or the rose and the ring! RD. (Str 7 Aug 1843). Duncombe 47; New BT 374; Dicks 707.
The roll of the drum. MD. (Adel 16 Oct 1843). Duncombe 49; French 103; De Witt 77; Dicks 706.
A mistaken story. F. (P'cess 1 Nov 1843). Duncombe 49; New BT 38; Lacy 20; Dicks 736.
Woman's love: or Kate Wynsley, the cottage girl. D. (Vic 22 Apr 1845). [1840]; Lacy 4; Dicks 414.
Kennyngton Crosse: or the old house on the common. D. (Sur 12 June 1848). Lacy 75.
How's your uncle? : or the ladies of the court. F. (Adel 27 Aug 1855). Lacy 41; Dicks 736.
The miller of Whetstone: or the cross-bow letter. Ba. (Standard 1 Aug 1857). Lacy 7.
Eily O'Connor. D. (Brit 22 Oct 1860). Duncombe 10, Lacy 47.
Scarlet mantle: or the robbers' hold and the bandit's bride. (No performance details.) New BT 538.
See also Nicoll *4, pp. 420–1, 617; 5, pp. 623, 823; Conolly,* English drama, *pp. 334–6;* Readex Index, *p. 292.*

§2

Era Almanack 1872. [JRS]

William Gorman Wills 1828–91

Licensing copies of the acted plays are located in BL.

§1

Old times: a novel... with illustrations by the author. 1857. First pbd in pts Waterford [1856]–7.
Life's foreshadowings: a novel. 3 vols 1859.
Notice to quit. 3 vols 1861.
The wife's evidence. 3 vols 1864, 1 vol 1876.
David Chantry. 3 vols 1865, 1 vol 1877. First pbd in Temple Bar Dec 1864–Dec 1865.
The three watches. 3 vols 1865.
The love that kills: a novel. 3 vols 1867.
Hinko: or the headsman's bond. D. (Queens 9 Sep 1871 as Hinko: or the headsman's daughter). 1871; De Witt 301; Readex micro.
Charles the First. T. (Lyc 28 Sep 1872). Edinburgh and London 1873; French nd; French NY [1912]; Readex micro. In verse.
Drawing room dramas. Edinburgh and London 1873. In verse; with the Hon Mrs Greene.
Eugene Aram. D. (Lyc 19 Apr 1873). Not pbd; Kilgarriff.
Marie Stuart. D. (P'cess 23 Feb 1874 as Mary Queen of Scots). French nd; Readex micro.
Olivia. D. (Court 28 Mar 1878). 1878 (priv ptd). From Goldsmith, The vicar of Wakefield.
Juanna. T. (Crit 7 May 1881). 1881.
Claudian. D. (P'cess 6 Dec 1883). Mayer. With H. Herman.
A little tramp: or landlords and tenants. C. (P'cess, Bristol 12 Sep 1885 as A young tramp). 1884.
Melchior. 1884 (priv ptd), 1885. A poem in blank verse.
Faust. (Lyc 19 Dec 1885). [1886?] (priv ptd), 1887. From Goethe.
See also Nicoll *5, pp. 627–8, 824;* Stratman, *p. 689;* Readex Index, *p. 294.*

§2

Wills, Freeman. W. G. Wills: dramatist and painter. 1898.
Stottlar, J. F. A Victorian stage adapter at work: W. G. Wills 'rehabilitates' the classics. VS 16 1973. [JRS]

iv. Late nineteenth-century drama 1870–1900

For an explanation of abbreviations used, see under Early Nineteenth-Century Drama, col 1955.

James Albery 1838–89

Collections

Dramatic works. Ed W. Albery 2 vols 1939. Includes memoir, chronological table, correspondence and newspaper reports in full.

§1

Two roses. C. (Vaud 27 Aug 1870). French c. 1871; W. Albery vol 1; Rowell.
Two thorns. C. (StJ 4 Mar 1871). W. Albery vol 1.
Tweedie's rights. CD. (Vaud 27 May 1871). W. Albery vol 1.
Apple blossoms. C. (Vaud 9 Sep 1871). French c. 1872; W. Albery vol 1.
Forgiven. C. (Glo 9 Mar 1872). W. Albery vol 1.
Oriana. Fairy C. (Glo 15 Feb 1873). W. Albery vol 1.
Married. C. (Roy 29 Nov 1873). W. Albery vol 1.
Fortune. C. (5th Ave, New York 3 Dec 1873). W. Albery vol 1.
Wig and gown. CD. (Glo 6 Apr 1874). W. Albery vol 1.
Pride. C. (Vaud 22 Apr 1874). W. Albery vol 1.
The spendthrift. C. (Olym 24 May 1875). W. Albery vol 2.
The man in possession. D. (Gai 4 Dec 1876). W. Albery vol 2.
The pink dominos. FC. (Crit 31 Mar 1877). [1878]. W. Albery vol 2. From Hennequin and Delacour.
The spectre knight. Oa (O. C. 9 Feb 1878). W. Albery vol 2. Music by A. Cellier.
The crisis. C. (H 2 Dec 1878). W. Albery vol 2. From Augier, revised as The Denhams (Court 21 Feb 1885).
Duty. C. (PW 27 Sep 1879). French c. 1880; W. Albery vol 2.
Where's the cat? C. (Crit 20 Nov 1880). W. Albery vol 2.

Letters

Numerous letters to and from Albery rptd in W. Albery (see Collections, above). Also in W. Trewin, All on stage: Charles Wyndham and the Alberys, *1980.*

§2

Knight, J. In DNB Suppl 1 1904.
See also M. Moore, Charles Wyndham and Mary Moore, *1925 (priv ptd); W. Albery and W. Trewin above.* [GR]

Wilson (William Henry) Barrett 1846–1904

Barrett's personal papers are held in the HRHRC. Ms scripts are in the Lord Chamberlain's Collection, BL, and the Lib of Congress.

§1

Plays

Twilight. (Lyc Sunderland 20 Oct 1871).
Moro. (H 28 Jan 1882). With M. W. Balfe.
Hoodman blind. (P'cess 18 Aug 1885). With H. A. Jones.
The Lord Harry. (P'cess 18 Feb 1886). With H. A. Jones.
Sister Mary. (Brighton 8 Mar 1886; Com 11 Oct 1886). With C. Scott. Title altered to Captain Leigh, VC, June 1900.
Clito. (P'cess 1 May 1886). With S. Grundy.
The golden ladder. (Glo 22 Dec 1887). With G. R. Sims.
Ben-my-Chree. (P'cess 17 May 1888). With H. Caine.
The good old times. (P'cess 12 Feb 1889). With H. Caine.
Nowadays: a tale of the turf. (P'cess 28 Feb 1889).
The people's idol. (Olym 4 Dec 1890). With V. Widnell.
The acrobat. (Olym 21 Apr 1891).

Jenny the barber. (P'cess Bristol 10 Dec 1891).
Pharaoh. (Grand Leeds 29 Oct 1892).
Our pleasant sins. (Grand Leeds 13 Feb 1893). With C. Hannan.
The Manxman. (Grand Leeds 22 Sep 1894; Shaftesbury 18 Nov 1895).
The sign of the cross. (St Louis 27 Mar 1894; Grand Leeds 26 Sep 1895; Lyr 4 Nov 1896). *See* Mayer, *below.*
The daughters of Babylon. (Lyric 6 Feb 1897).
The sledgehammer. (Kilburn 22 Feb 1897).
Man and his makers. (Lyc 7 Oct 1899). With L. N. Parker.
Quo Vadis? (Lyc Edinburgh 29 May 1900; P'cess W. Kennington 18 June 1900). From the novel by H. Sienkiewicz.
The never-never land. (Vic Broughton 9 Apr 1902; Grand Hull 1 Feb 1904; K Hammersmith 21 Mar 1904).
The Christian king; or, Alfred of Engleland. (P'cess Bristol 6 Nov 1902; Adel 18 Dec 1902; originally titled The king).
In the middle of June. (Middlesbrough 11 June 1903).
Lucky Durham. (Shakespeare L'pool 9 June 1904; K Hammersmith 28 Aug 1905).
The last moment. (Hippodrome Crouch End 18 Apr 1910).
The Jew of Prague. (Colchester 29 Apr 1912; Whitney 8 May 1912).

Novels
The sign of the cross. Preston 1896.
The daughters of Babylon. 1899. With R. Hitchens.

Souvenir
Souvenir of The sign of the cross. Octavo 1896.
Souvenir of The Daughters of Babylon. Octavo 1897.
The Wilson Barrett Birthday Book. nd [1898?].
Barrett's The sign of the cross *may have been the most widely seen play of the late nineteenth century and was twice made into a motion picture (1914 and 1932). None of Barrett's plays was published in his lifetime.*

§2
Brereton, A. Wilson Barrett. Theatre Jan 1883.
Shaw, G. B. Our theatres in the nineties, 1895–1898. 3 vols 1932.
Archer, W. (ed). The theatrical world for 1895, 1896, 1897.
Thomas, J. The art of the actor manager: Wilson Barrett and the Victorian theatre. Ann Arbor MI 1984.
Mayer, D. Playing out the empire: Ben-Hur and other 'toga' plays and films. Oxford 1994. [DM]

Sir James Matthew Barrie, 'McConnachie'
1860–1937

The largest holding of mss is in the Beinecke Lib, Yale. Other Amer collections are found in Boston Public Lib, Huntington Lib, Houghton Lib (Harvard), HRHRC, Lilly Lib Indiana Univ, Berg Collection (NYPL), Princeton, Pierpont Morgan Lib (New York), Queen's Univ Archives (Kingston, Ontario). For smaller Br holdings, see LR.

Bibliographies
Garland, H. A bibliography of the writings of Barrie. 1928.
Cutler, B. D. Barrie: a bibliography, with full collations of the American unauthorised editions. [1931.]
Block, A. Barrie: his first editions, points and values. 1933.
Wynne, M. G. The Barrie collection. YULG 23 1949.
Beinecke, W. jr. Barrie in the Parrish Collection. Princeton Univ Lib Chron 17 1956.
Mott, H. S. Beinecke Collection of Barrie. YULG 1965.
Nicoll, A. In A history of English drama, 1600–1900 vol 5 (2nd edn), Cambridge 1959.
Nicoll, A. In English drama: 1900–30, Cambridge 1973.
Rudolph, V. C. James M. Barrie. In Dictionary of literary biography vol 10, Modern British dramatists 1900–1945, part 1a–l, ed S. Weintraub, Detroit 1982.
Markgraf, C. J. M. Barrie: an annotated secondary bibliography. Greenboro NC 1989 (vol 4 1880–1920, British Authors ser).

Collections
Novels, tales and sketches. 12 vols New York 1896–1902. Thistle edn.
The Kirriemuir edition of the works (novels, short stories). 10 vols 1913, 1922.
Uniform edition of the works (novels, short stories). 11 vols 1913–32.
Half hours. [1914], New York 1914, 1919 (with Der Tag Coliseum 21 Dec 1914). Contains the following plays, all produced at DofY; Pantaloon (5 Apr 1905); The twelve-pound look (1 Mar 1910); Rosalind (14 Oct 1912); The will (4 Sep 1913).
Uniform edition of the plays. 12 vols 1918–38. Includes the following 1st edns: What every woman knows (DofY 3 Sep 1908), 1918; Alice sit-by-the-fire (DofY 5 Apr 1905), 1919; A kiss for Cinderella (Wyndham's 3 Mar 1916), 1920; Dear Brutus (Wyndham's 17 Oct 1917), 1922; Mary Rose (H 22 Apr 1920), 1924; Peter Pan: or the boy who would not grow up (DofY 27 Dec 1904), 1928; The boy David (King's Edinburgh 21 Nov 1936 , His Majesty's Dec 1936), 1938 (preface by H. G[ranville]-B[arker]).
Works (novels, short stories). 10 vols New York 1918.
Echoes of the war. [1918], New York [1918]. Contains The old lady shows her medals (NT 7 Apr 1917); The new word (DofY 22 Mar 1915); Barbara's wedding (Apollo 23 Aug 1927); A well-remembered voice (Wyndham's 28 June 1918).
Representative plays. Ed W. L. Phelps, New York 1926.
Plays. 1928, rptd 1929, 1930, 1931, 1933, 1936, 1939. Collected edn. Includes first pbn of Old friends (DofY 1 Mar 1910); Half an hour (Hippodrome 29 Sep 1913); Seven women (NT 7 Apr 1917), being the first act of The adored one with altered ending.
Selections from the plays. 1929.
Selections from the prose works. 1929.
Works: Peter Pan edition. 16 vols New York 1929–40.
Plays. New York 1930.
McConnachie and JMB. Preface by Hugh Walpole. 1938. Speeches.
Plays. Ed A. E. Wilson 1942, rptd 1943, 1945. Definitive edn with first pbn of The professor's love story (Star, New York 19 Dec 1892, Com 25 June 1894); Little Mary (Wyndham's 24 Sep 1903), a dramatic version of The little minister (H 6 Nov 1897).
Plays and stories. Ed R. L. Green 1962.
Peter Pan and other plays, ed P. Hollindale. Oxford 1995 (WCp).

§1
There were numerous Amer pirated edns of many of the works of fiction; as a rule these are not noted. See Cutler, Barrie: a bibliography, *above.*
For a full list of early reviews, see C. J. M. Markgraf, Barrie: an annotated secondary bibliography, *above.*
Better dead. '1888' [1887], 1888, New York [1890] (with My Lady Nicotine, *below*), 1891, London 1891 (3 edns), 1896, 1903, 1925. Novel.
REVIEW: [G. B. Shaw] Pall Mall Gazette 47, 27 Mar 1888.
Auld licht idylls. 1888, 1895, 1898 (11th edn), New York 1897. Based on articles first pbd in St James's Gazette and in Home Chimes 1884–5. Short stories.
REVIEWS: Acad 26 May 1888; Critic (NY) 20 [n.s. 17] 1892.
When a man's single: a tale of literary life. 1888, New York 1896. First pbd in Br Weekly 1867–8. Novel.
An Edinburgh eleven: pencil portraits from college life. 1889, New York 1889, 1892. First pbd in Br Weekly 1888, gathered Jan 1889 Br Weekly extra.
A window in Thrums. 1889, 1892, 1898 (16th edn), New York 1897. Ch I separately rptd as The sabbath day, 1895. Short stories.
REVIEW: Athenaeum 20 July 1889.
Richard Savage. (Crit 16 Apr 1890). 1891 (priv ptd). With H. B. Marriott Watson.
My Lady Nicotine. 1890, New York 1896. Essays.
Ibsen's ghost: or Toole up-to-date. (Toole's 30 May 1891). 1939 (priv ptd).
The little minister. 3 vols 1891, 1891, New York 1891, 1891, 2 vols

Leipzig 1891, London 1892, New York 1892, London 1897, 1898, 1903, 1905, 1907. First pbd in Good Words Jan–Dec 1891; dramatic version (H 6 Nov 1897); 1942 (in Plays, *above*). Novel.
REVIEWS: Bookman (London) 1 1891; Fortnightly Rev 58 1892; Critic (NY) 20 n.s. 1892.

Walker, London: a farcical comedy. (Toole's 25 Feb 1892). 1907.

A holiday in bed, and other sketches; with a short biographical sketch of the author. New York 1892. Unauthorised collection of contributions to periodicals.

Jane Annie, or the good conduct prize: a new and original English comic opera. (Sav 13 May 1893). 1893. With A. Conan Doyle.

A lady's shoe. New York [1893] (unauthorised 1st edn, with The inconsiderate waiter), London 1894 (in Miss Parson's adventure by W. C. Russell, and other stories by other writers), New York 1898.

Two of them. New York [1893]. Unauthorised collection of contributions to periodicals.

An Auld Licht manse, and other sketches. New York [1893]. Unauthorised collection of contributions to periodicals.

A Tillyloss scandal. New York [1893], [1893], 1894, 1915? Unauthorised collection of contributions to periodicals.

A powerful drug; and other stories. New York [1893]. Unauthorised collection of contributions to periodicals.

Allahakbarries C[ricket] C[lub]. 1893 (priv ptd), 1950.

Scotland's lament: a poem on the death of Robert Louis Stevenson, December 3rd 1894. 1895 (priv ptd), 1918 (priv ptd). First pbd in Bookman Jan 1895.

Sentimental Tommy: the story of his boyhood. 1896, 1896, 1897, New York 1897, 1900, 1909; tr Cz 1902.
REVIEWS: [A. Quiller Couch] Contemporary Rev 70 1896; Blackwood's Mag 160, Dec 1896.

Margaret Ogilvy: by her son J. M. Barrie. 1896, 1896, New York 1896. Autobiographical novel.
REVIEWS: Athenaeum 9 Jan 1897; Blackwood's Mag 161, Apr 1897.

Jess. Boston [1898]. Unauthorised collection of the first 16 stories in A window in Thrums.

The Allahakbarrie book of Broadway cricket for 1899. 1899 (priv ptd), 1950.

Life in a country manse. New York 1899. Unauthorised; first pbd in Br Weekly July–Aug 1891; rptd in A holiday in bed and other sketches, 1892, and A Tillyloss scandal, [1893].

The wedding guest. C. (Gar 27 Sep 1900). 1900 (pbd as a suppl to Fortnightly Rev), New York 1900.

Tommy and Grizel. 1900, New York [1900], Toronto 1900. First pbd in Scribner's Mag Jan–Nov 1900. Novel.
REVIEWS: Athenaeum 27 Nov 1900; [Henry Van Dyke] Book Buyer 21 1900; Sewanee Rev 9 Jan 1901.

The boy castaways of Black Lake Island. 1901 (priv ptd). Photographic tale.

Quality Street. C. (Toledo OH 14 Oct 1901, Vaud 17 Sep 1902). 1913, 1913, New York 1918.
REVIEWS: [William Archer] The World (London) 24 Sep 1902; [E. K. Chambers] Acad 63, Sep 1902.

The Admirable Crichton. (DofY 4 Nov 1902). 1914, New York 1918; tr Fr 1920.
REVIEWS: [William Archer] The World (London) 12 Nov 1902; [Max Beerbohm] Saturday Rev 25 July 1903.

The little white bird. 1902, New York 1902, Toronto 1902. First pbd in Scribner's Mag Aug–Nov 1902.
REVIEWS: Acad 63 1902; [A. Quiller-Couch] Bookman 23 Nov 1902; Nation (NY) 76 1903.

Peter Pan in Kensington Gardens; from The little white bird; with drawings by Arthur Rackham. 1906, New York 1906, 1921; tr Fr 1917.
REVIEW: TLS 14 Dec 1906.

When Wendy grew up: an afterthought. (DofY 3 Sep 1908). 1957.

George Meredith. 1909, Chicago 1910 (as Neither Dorking nor the Abbey), Portland ME 1911, 1912, 1914 (all 4 pirated). First pbd in Westminster Gazette 26 May 1909 as Neither Dorking nor the Abbey.

Peter and Wendy. 1911, New York 1911, London 1915, 1921 (as Peter Pan and Wendy), New York 1921; tr Sp 1925. Many adaptations of Peter Pan for young children pbd.
REVIEW: [Alfred Noyes] Bookman (London) 41, Dec 1911.

Shakespear's legacy. F. (14 Apr 1916). [1916] (priv ptd).

Who was Sarah Findlay? by Mark Twain; with a suggested solution of the mystery by Barrie. 1917 (priv ptd).

The truth about the Russian dancers. Ballet-fantasy. (Coliseum 16 Mar 1920). New York 1962. With Arnold Bax.
REVIEW: [Ezra Pound] Athenaeum 2 Apr 1920.

Shall we join the ladies? (Royal Dramatic Academy's Theatre 27 Mar 1921). In The black mask, ed C. Asquith, 1927.

Courage: the Rectorial Address delivered at St Andrews University, May 3rd 1922. [1922], [1922], New York 1922. First pbd in St Andrews Univ Mag 17 1922.

Neil and Tintinnabulum. In The flying carpet, ed C. Asquith, 1925. Short story.

The blot on Peter Pan. In The treasure ship, ed C. Asquith, 1927. Short story.

Peter Pan. 1928 (in Uniform edn), 1939, 1942, 1964, 1967, 1973.
REVIEWS: *See* Markgraf, Bibliographies, *above*.

The entrancing life: speech at Edinburgh. October 28th 1930. 1930.

The Greenwood hat. 1930 (priv ptd), 1937. Essays.
REVIEWS: TLS 4 Dec 1937; Quart Rev 270, Jan 1938.

Farewell, Miss Julie Logan. 1932 (in uniform edn), Edinburgh 1989. First pbd in Christmas suppl to The Times 24 Dec 1931. Short story.
REVIEW: Saturday Rev 26 Nov 1932; Bookman (London) 29 Jan 1933.

Mrs Lapraik. YULG 67 1992. Short story.

The house of fear. Stud in Scottish Lit 27 1992.

For Dear Brutus, Mary Rose, Peter Pan, The boy David, What every woman knows, *and other plays first pbd in Uniform edn; for* Pantaloon, The twelve-pound look, Rosalind, *and* The will, *first pbd in* Half hours; *for* The old lady shows her medals, *first pbd in* Echoes of the war; *for* Old friends, Half an hour *and* Seven women, *first pbd in* Plays, 1928; *for* The professor's love story *and* Little Mary, *first pbd in* Plays, 1942; *see under Collections, above. The following have not been pbd:* The adored one *(DofY 4 Sep 1913), as* Legend of Leonora *(Empire, New York 5 Jan 1914);* Rosy rapture: or the pride of the beauty chorus *(DofY 22 Mar 1915). For other dramatic works, see* Nicoll *5, pp. 251, 778 and* R. L. Green, Barrie, *1960.*

Contributions to periodicals

For Barrie's numerous contributions to periodicals, see Wellesley *vol 5.*

Letters

Letters. Ed V. Maynell 1942.

Malany, M. H. Letters by Barrie to the Duchess of Sutherland. Boston Public Lib Quart 5 1953.

Introductions and prefaces

These include:

G. W. Cable, The Grandissimes. 1898.

M. Oliphant, A widow's tale. 1898.

R. M. Ballantyne, The coral island. 1913.

I. F. Marcosson and D. Frohman, Charles Frohman. 1916.

L. Merrick, Conrad in quest of his youth. 1918.

D. Ashford, The young visiters. 1919.

§2

Bookman (London) Oct 1910. Autumn double number.

Howe, P. P. In his Dramatic portraits, 1913.

Bookman Dec 1920. Christmas suppl.

Walbrook, H. M. Barrie and the theatre. 1922.

Moult, T. Barrie. 1928.

Hammerton, J. A. J. M. Barrie: the story of a genius. 1929.
Mackail, D. J. M. B. 1942.
Asquith, C. Portrait of Barrie. 1954.
Green, R. L. Fifty years of Peter Pan. 1954.
Birkin, A. J. M. Barrie and the lost boys. 1979, rptd 1980.
Ormond, L. J. M. Barrie's Mary Rose. YULG 1983.
Rose, J. The case of Peter Pan. 1984.
Jack, R. D. S. The road to the never land. 1991. [RDSJ]

Charles Hallam Elton Brookfield 1857–1913

Licensing copies of the plays are located in BL.

§1

The illustrated sporting glossary. [1881.]
Nearly seven. Monol. (H 7 Oct 1882). French 124.
The poet and the puppets. Bsq. (Com 19 May 1892). [1892?]; New York and London 1978 (facs reprint).
The burglar and the judge. F. (H 5 Nov 1892). French 136. With F. C. Philips.
The twilight of love. Being four studies of the artistic temperament. 1893.
A woman's reason. D. (Shaft 27 Dec 1895). Typescript. Readex micro. With F. C. Philips.
The Grand Duchess of Gerolstein. O. (Sav 4 Dec 1897). 1897. With A. Ross. Music by Offenbach.
The cuckoo. C. (Aven 23 Sep 1899). Typescript. Readex micro.
Poor Jonathan. C. (PW 15 June 1893). [1900?] With H. Greenbank. From H. Wittman and J. Bauer, Der arme Jonathan.
Random reminiscences. 1902, [1911].
Mrs Brookfield and her circle. 2 vols 1905, 1 vol 1906. With F. M. Brookfield.
Jack Goldie: or the boy who knew best. A story. 1911.
See also Nicoll 5, *pp. 276–7, 780; Nicoll,* English drama 1900–30, *pp. 533–4;* Readex Index, *pp. 35–6.* [JRS]

Robert Buchanan 1841–1901

See col 722.

Sir Francis Cowley Burnand 1836–1917

Some autograph letters and licensing copies of the plays are located in BL.

§1

All plays listed below are issued in one or more Readex micro *edns.*
Villikins and his Dinah: or the cup of cold poison. Bsq. (Sur 27 Feb 1854). Lacy 54.
Alonzo the brave: or Faust and the fair Imogene. Bsq. (Str 5 Feb 1855). Lacy 58; Lorenzen micro. First produced Amateur Dramatic Club Cambridge? Variant title Faust and Mephistopheles: or Alonzo the brave and the fair Imogene.
Lord Lovel and Lady Nancy Bell: or the bounding brigade of Bakumboilum. Bsq. (ADC Cambridge Nov 1856). Lacy 30.
Romance under difficulties. F. (ADC Cambridge 1856). Lacy 26.
In for a holyday. F. (ADC Cambridge? 1856?). Lacy 26. Variant title In for a holiday.
Dido. Bsq. (StJ 11 Feb 1860). Lacy 44.
B. B. F. (Olym 22 Mar 1860). Lacy 45. With M. Williams.
The isle of St Tropez. D. (StJ 20 Dec 1860). Lacy 52. With M. Williams.
The Turkish bath. F. (Adel 29 Mar 1861). Lacy 51; Boston [1862?]. With M. Williams.
Deerfoot. F. (Olym 16 Dec 1861). De Witt 125.
The king of the Merrows: or the prince and the piper. Ext. (Olym 26 Dec 1861). Lacy 53. With J. P. Simpson.
Fair Rosamond: or the maze, the maid and the monarch. Ext. (Olym 21 Apr 1862). Lacy 55.
Robin Hood: or the forester's fate. Ext. (Olym 26 Dec 1862). Lacy 57.
Carte de visite. F. (StJ 26 Dec 1862). Lacy 57. With M. Williams.
Bishop Colenso, utterly refuted by Lord Dundreary. 1862. Pam.
Acis and Galatea: or the nimble nymph and the terrible troglodyte. Ext. (Olym 6 Apr 1863). Lacy 58.
Easy shaving. F. (H 11 June 1863). Lacy 60; De Witt 47. With M. Williams.
The Deal boatman. D. (DL 21 Sep 1863). Lacy 60.
Ixion: or the man at the wheel. Ext. (Roy 28 Sep 1863). Lacy 60.
Patient Penelope: or the return of Ulysses. Bsq. (Str 25 Nov 1863). Lacy 61. With M. Williams.
Madame Berliot's ball: or the chalet in the valley. Ca. (Roy 26 Dec 1863). Lacy 61.
Rumplestiltskin and the maid: or the woman at the wheel. Ext. (Roy 28 Mar 1864). Lacy 62.
Venus and Adonis: or the two rivals and the small boar. Bsq. (H 28 Mar 1864). Lacy 62.
Faust and Marguerite: an 'im-morality'. Ext. (StJ 9 July 1864). Lacy 63.
Snowdrop: or the seven mannikins and the magic mirror. Ext. (Roy 21 Nov 1864). Lacy 64.
Cupid and Psyche: or beautiful as a butterfly. Bsq. (Olym 26 Dec 1864). Lacy 64.
Tracks for tourists: or the continental companion, being a handbook with foot-notes for pedestrians, and a guide to the principal mounts for equestrians ... Reprinted from ... Punch. 1864.
Pirithous, the son of Ixion. Bsq. (Roy 13 Apr 1865). Lacy 65.
Ulysses: or the iron-clad warrior and the little tug of war. Bsq. (StJ 17 Apr 1865). Lacy 66.
Windsor Castle. Bsq. (Str 5 June 1865). Lacy 67. With M. Williams. Music by F. Musgrave.
L'Africaine: or the Queen of the Cannibal Islands. Bsq. (Str 18 Nov 1865). 1865. With M. Williams. Music by F. Musgrave.
Beeton's book of burlesques. 1865. With W. Brough. Includes Boadicea the beautiful: or harlequin Julius Caesar and the delightful druid; Orpheus: or the magic lyre; and Sappho: or look before you leap.
Paris: or vive Lemprière. Bsq. (Str 2 Apr 1866). 1866; Lacy 84.
Antony and Cleopatra: or his-story and her-story in a modern Nilometre. Bsq. (H 21 Nov 1866). 1866; Shakesp bsqs 3.
The latest edition of Black-eyed Susan: or the little bill that was taken up. Bsq. (Roy 29 Nov 1866). 1866; Lacy 77.
Guy Fawkes: or the ugly mug and the couple of spoons. Bsq. (Str 26 Dec 1866). 1866.
Happy thoughts. 1866, 1868 (10th thousand); Boston 1869, 1872, London 1904, [1915], 1930, 1954.
Olympic games: or the major, the miner, and the cock-a-doodle-do. Bsq. (Olym 22 Apr 1867). 1867.
Cox and Box: or the long lost brothers. MF. (Adel May 1867). [1867?]; Lacy nd. With J. M. Morton. Music by Sir A. Sullivan.
Mary Turner: or the wicious willin and wictorious wirtue. Bsq. (Holborn 25 Oct 1867). Lacy 78.
Humbug. C. (Roy 19 Dec 1867). Lacy 79.
Hit and miss: or all my eye and Betty Martyn. Ext. (Olym 13 Apr 1868). [1868.]
Fowl play: or a story of chikkin hazard. Bsq. (Queen's 20 June 1868). [1868.]
The very little Faust and more Mephistopheles. Bsq. (Charing Cross 18 Aug 1868). [1868.]
The rise and fall of Richard III: or a new front to an old dicky. Bsq. (Roy 24 Sep 1868). [1868.]
The frightful hair: or who shot the dog. Bsq. (H 26 Dec 1868). [1869?]
Claude du Val: or the highwayman for the ladies. Bsq. (Roy 22 Jan 1869). [1869.]
The military Billy Taylor: or the war in Carriboo. Ca. (Roy 22 Apr 1869). 1869.
The turn of the tide. D. (Queen's 29 May 1869). 1869 (priv ptd).

The beast and the beauty: or no rose without a thorn. (Roy 4 Oct 1869). [1869.]
Dead Man's Point: or the lighthouse on the Carn Ruth. D. (Adel 4 Feb 1871). Lacy 92.
Poll and Partner Joe: or the pride of Putney and the pressing pirate. Bsq. (StJ 6 May 1871). 1871.
Arion: or the story of a lyre. Ext. (Str 20 Dec 1871). 1872.
The new history of Sandford and Merton. 1872, [1892], New York [1900].
Kissi-kissi. Bsq. (Opéra Comique 12 July 1873 as Kissi-kissi: or the pa, the ma, and the padishah). [1873.] Revised version of King Kokatoo (Leeds 4 Mar 1872). Music by Offenbach.
La belle Hélène. Ext. (Alhambra 16 Aug 1873). [1873.] Revised version of Helen (Adel 30 June 1866).
Mokeanna! a treble temptation. 1873.
My time and what I've done with it: an autobiography compiled from the diary, notes, and personal recollections of Cecil Colvin. [A novel.] 1874 (2 edns), New York [1890], 1976. First pbd in Macmillan's Mag, *see below*.
The doom of St Querec: a[n] Xmas legend. [1875.] With A. W. À Beckett.
The shadow witness. [1877.] With A. W. À Beckett.
Betsy. C. (Crit 6 Aug 1879). French 128; New York nd. From E. de Najac and A. Hennequin, Bébé.
The A. D. C. Being personal reminiscences of the University Amateur Dramatic Club, Cambridge. '1880' [1879].
No rose without a thorn. In Society novelettes vol 1, 1883.
Paw Clawdian: or the Roman awry. Bsq. (Toole's 14 Feb 1884). 1884.
Mazeppa: or 'bound' to win. Bsq. (Gai 12 Mar 1885). 1885.
Faust and loose. Bsq. (Toole's 4 Feb 1886). [1886.]
The incompleat angler: after Master Izaak Walton. 1887.
Airey Annie: travestie on Mrs Campbell Praed's play of Arcaine. Bsq. (Str 4 Apr 1888). [1888.]
Pickwick. MF. (mat Com 7 Feb 1889; Trafalgar Square 13 Dec 1893). [1889.] Music by E. Solomon.
Sir Dagobert and the dragon: or how to run through the scales. In Short plays for drawing-room performance, 1890.
Helen. In Short plays for drawing-room performance, 1890.
Quiet at home ... with illustrations from Punch. 1890.
Rather at sea ... with illustrations from Punch. 1890.
Captain Thérèse. CO. (PW 25 Aug 1890). [1890.] With G. A. À Beckett. Music by R. Planquette.
La cigale. CO. (Lyr 9 Oct 1890). [1890.] From H. C. Chivet and A. Duru, La cigale et le fourmie. Music by E. Audran.
The real adventures of Robinson Crusoe. 1893. Bsq of Defoe.
The chieftain. O. (Sav 12 Dec 1894). 1894 (libretto), 1895 (vocal score) (2 edns), [1895]. Music by Sir A. Sullivan. A revised version of The contrabandista (St George's 18 Dec 1867).
The Z. Z. G.: or zig zag guide round and about the bold and beautiful Kentish coast. 1897.
Records and reminiscences, personal and general. 2 vols '1904' [1903]; 1905 (4th edn, 1 vol); 1917 (abridged by E. V. Lucas).
Penelope Anne. F. (No performance details). nd; in Additional adventures of Messrs Box and Cox, comp R. Macphail, Bridgewater VA 1974. From J. M. Morton's Box and Cox.
Burnand wrote over 200 plays. See also Nicoll *5, pp. 287–92, 781–2;* Readex Index, *pp. 42–4; and, for performance details, casts and reviews, see Wearing,* London stage 1890–9.

Contributions to periodicals
My time: what I've done with it. 13 pts. Macmillan's Mag Apr 1873–Apr 1874.
Authors and managers. Theatre Feb 1879.
Something about a little theatre out of Tottenham Court Road. Era Almanack 1879.
A school for dramatic art. Nineteenth Cent May 1882.
An autobiography. Theatre Feb 1883.
Behind the scenes. Fortnightly Rev Jan 1885.
Councils and comedians. Fortnightly Rev Sep 1885.
History in Punch. 3 pts. Fortnightly Rev July 1886–Apr 1887. With A. W. À Beckett.
Burnand was a regular contributor to early issues of Fun *and* Punch; *and was editor of the latter from 1880 to 1906. He also edited* The Catholic Who's who & year-book, *1908 etc.*

Introductions, prefaces etc
Poems of Thomas Hood. 1907.
Poems from Punch. 1908.

§2
'Q' [T. Purnell]. Dramatists of the present day. 1871.
Adams, W. D. A book of burlesque. Sketches of English stage travestie and parody. 1891.
The Times 23 Apr 1917. Obituary.
Two Victorian humorists: Burnand and the mask of Gilbert. TLS 21 Nov 1936. [JRS]

Henry James Byron 1834–84

Collections
Davis, J. (ed). Plays by H. J. Byron with an essay by the editor. Cambridge 1984. Contains The babes in the wood, The Lancashire lass, Our boys, The Gaiety Gulliver.

§1
Fra Diavolo. Bsq. (Str 5 Apr 1858). Lacy 522.
The babes in the wood. Bsq. (Adel 18 July 1859). Lacy 612. *See* Davis, Collections, *above.*
Robinson Crusoe. P. (P'cess 26 Dec 1860). Lacy 727. Anthologised in Booth 5.
George de Barnwell. Bsq. (Adel 26 Dec 1862). Lacy 57.
War to the knife. C. (PW 10 June 1865). Lacy 67.
Paid in full: a novel. 3 vols 1865. First pbd in Temple Bar.
A hundred thousand pounds. C. (PW 5 May 1866). Lacy 1154.
The Lancashire lass. D. (Liverpool 28 Oct 1867). French 1721. *See* Davis, Collections, *above.*
Blow for blow. D. (TR Holborn 5 Sep 1868). French 1501.
Cyril's success. C. (Glo 28 Nov 1868). Lacy 1321.
Partners for life. C. (Glo 7 Oct 1871). Lacy/French 1620.
Old soldiers. C. (Str 25 Jan 1873). Lacy/French 1691.
Our boys. C. (Vaud 16 Jan 1875). Lib of Eng Lit 2 1885; Lacy/French 1728. *See* Davis, Collections, *above.*
The Gaiety Gulliver. P. (Gai 26 Dec 1879). 1879–80; [1880?]. *See* Davis, Collections, *above.*
For other dramatic works, see Davis *pp. 216–20;* Nicoll *5, pp. 295–9, 782.*

§2
Wrey, P. Byron. London Soc Aug 1874.
Archer, W. In his Dramatists of to-day, 1882.
Era 19 Apr 1884. Obituary. [PT]

'R. C. Carton', Richard Claude Critchett 1856–1928

Some typescripts of unpbd plays are available in the Lord Chamberlain's Collection, BL, and in the NYPL Readex Collection of English and American drama of the 19th century. A short bibliography is listed in The Player's Library: the catalogue of the library of the British Drama League, *1950.*

§1
Sunlight and shadow. C. (Aven 1 Nov 1890). French 1900.
Liberty Hall. C. (StJ 3 Dec 1892). [priv ptd 1892]; French 1900.
Dinner for two. C. (Brighton 9 Mar 1893). French [1903]. Lacy 151.
Lady Huntsworth's experiment. C. (Crit 26 Apr 1900). French 1904.
REVIEW: Beerbohm, M. More theatres, 1969.

The ninth waltz. C. (Gar 11 Dec 1900). French [1904]; Lacy 151.
See also Nicholl 5, *p. 305 and D. Mullin,* Victorian plays, *Westport CT 1987. For later plays, see* Who's who in the theatre, *1925. Earlier (unpbd) plays, dating from 1885 to 1888, were written in collaboration with Cecil Raleigh.*

§2
Biography. Theatre 1 Jan 1893.
Mr R. C. at home. Era 4 Feb 1893.
Who's who in the theatre. 1925. Biography.
The Times 2 Apr 1928. Obituary.
Tarpey, W. K. Work as dramatist. Critic Aug 1900.
Rowell, George. The Victorian theatre. 1956. [DHT]

Charles Haddon Chambers 1860–1921

Licensing copies of the plays are located in BL.

§1
The open gate. D. (Com 28 Mar 1887). French no 1902; Chicago [1887]; Sergel 426; Readex micro.
The pipe of peace. In Oak boughs and wattle blossom, ed A. P. Martin, 1888.
Captain Swift. C. (mat H 20 June 1888; H 1 Sep 1888). French copyr 1902 (French Int Copyr Edn 55); Readex micro.
An underground tragedy. In In Australian wilds, and other colonial tales and sketches, ed P. Mennell, 1889.
In a thirsty land. In In Australian wilds etc, ed P. Mennell, 1889.
The 'ne'er-do-weel': a doctor's story. In In Australian wilds etc, ed P. Mennell, 1889; another edn in Fifty-two stories of the British empire, ed A. H. Miles [1900].
The idler. D. (Lyc New York 11 Nov 1890; StJ 26 Feb 1891). French copyr 1902 (French Int Copyr Edn 52); Readex micro.
REVIEW: A. B. Walkley, The new melodrama, in Playhouse impressions, 1892.
Thumb-nail sketches of Australian life. New York [1891].
The collaborators. F. (Vaud 7 Jan 1892). French nd.
John-a-dreams. D. (H 8 Nov 1894). Np.
The tyranny of tears. C. (Crit 6 Apr 1899). 1900; Boston 1902; Booth 3; Readex micro. Also in Masterpieces of modern drama, ed J. A. Pierce and B. Matthews, Garden City NY 1915.
The upturned faces of the roses. In Souvenir of the Charing Cross hospital bazaar, ed H. Beerbohm Tree, 1899.
The awakening. D. (StJ 6 Feb 1901). 1902, Boston 1903.
REVIEW: M. Beerbohm, More theatres, 1969.
Passer-by. D. (Wyndham's 29 Mar 1911). 1913.
For other dramatic pieces, see Nicoll 5, *p. 307; Nicoll,* English drama 1900–30, *p. 555, Conolly,* English drama, *pp. 134–5;* Readex Index, *p. 51. For performance details, casts and reviews, see Wearing,* London Stage 1890–9; 1900–9; 1910–19. [JRS AND DHT]

'Henry Vernon Esmond', Henry Vernon Jack 1869–1922

In and out of a punt. C. (StJ 9 May 1896). French 148.
One summer's day. C. (Com 16 Sep 1897). New York [1901?].
Grierson's way. D. (H 7 Feb 1899). 1899 (priv ptd).
The wilderness. C. (StJ 11 Apr 1901). New York 1901.
When we were twenty-one. C. (Com 2 Sep 1901). New York 1901.
Imprudence. C. (NY Empire 17 Nov 1902). [1902.]
Billy's little love affair. C. (Crit 2 Sep 1903). [1904?]
Her vote. C. (Playhouse 18 May 1909). French 158.
Eliza comes to stay. F. (Crit 12 Feb 1913). French 2510.
The law divine. C. (Wyndham's 29 Aug 1918). French 1035.
Birds of a feather. C. (Glo 9 Apr 1920). 1920.
The woman in chains. (Lyceum Club 26 Feb 1926). [1926]; French 1831.
See also Nicoll 5, *pp. 359, 700, and Nicoll,* English drama 1900–30, *p. 633.*

§2
Our portraits and biographies no 287: Mr Henry V. Esmond. Theatre Apr 1892.
[Bright, Addison]. Mr and Mrs H. V. Esmond. Theatre Jan 1896.
The Times 18 Apr 1922. Obituary.
Moore, E. Exits and entrances. 1923.
Mason, A. E. W. Sir George Alexander and the St James's Theatre. 1935, New York 1969.
Child, H. H. In DNB Suppl 1922–30.
See also Max Beerbohm's review articles in the Saturday Rev, *rptd in* Around theatres, *1953, and* More theatres, *1969.* [VE]

'Michael Field'

See col 735.

'George Fleming', Julia Constance Fletcher 1858–1938

Some unpbd plays are available in the Lord Chamberlain's Collection, BL, in the Library of Congress (Nat Union Cat pre-1956 imprints), and in the NYPL Readex Collection of English and American drama of the 19th century.

§1
Kismet. Boston 1877; 1901; Freeport NY 1971. Novel.
A Nile novel. 1877; 2nd edn Oxford 1877. (Running title reads 'Kismet'.)
Kismet, a Nile novel. Leipzig 1884 (Tauchnitz). Collection of British authors, ed Tauchnitz, vol 2294.
Mirage. 1877; Sydenham 1878; Boston 1878. Novel.
The head of Medusa. 1880, Boston 1880. Novel.
Notes by G. F. on a collection of pictures by ... Costa exhibited at the Fine Art Society's ... New Bond Street, 1882. [1882.]
Vestigia. 1884, Boston 1884. Novel.
Andromeda. 2 vols 1885, Boston 1885, Leipzig 1885 (Tauchnitz). Collection of British authors, ed Tauchnitz, vols 2366–7. Novel.
REVIEW: Lit World (Boston) 16 1885.
The truth about Clement Ker .... [1888] (Arrowsmith's two-shilling ser vol 3). Boston 1889. Novel.
Prince of Morocco. Living Age 190, 5 Sep 1891. Short story.
Mrs Lessingham. D. (Gar 7 Apr 1894). 1894 (priv ptd).
REVIEWS: Archer, W. Theatrical 'world' of 1894; Archer, W. Some recent plays, Fortnightly Rev n.s. 55, May 1894.
For plain women only. New York 1896. The Mayfair set IV. Appeared originally in Pall Mall Gazette.
Little stories about women. 1897.
The fantasticks. C. (Roy 29 May 1900). New York 1900. From Edmond Rostand, Les romanesques.
M. Rostand and the literary prospects of the drama. Anon article. Edinburgh Rev 192, Oct 1900.
See also Nicoll 5, *p. 369 and D. Mullin,* Victorian plays, *Westport CT 1987. For later plays, see* Who's who in the theatre, *1936.*

Translations

Gaspara stampa. Sonnets. By Eugene Benson. Tr George Fleming, Boston 1881.

§2
Who's who in the theatre, 1936. Biography. [DHT]

Sir William Schwenck Gilbert, 'F. Latour Tomline' 1836–1911

Major collections of mss, holograph letters, photographs, journals, etc are in the BL and in the Pierpont Morgan Lib, New York. See K. W. Gransden and P. J. Willetts, Papers of W. S. Gilbert, Br Museum Quart *21, 1958.*

Bibliographies

Searle, T. A bibliography of Sir William Schwenck Gilbert with bibliographical adventures in the Gilbert and Sullivan operas; introduction by R. E. Swartwout. [1931] (priv ptd); 1931 (as William Schwenck Gilbert: a topsy-turvy adventure).

Dubois, A. E. Additions to the bibliography of Gilbert's contributions to magazines. MLN 47 1932.

Allen, R. W. S. Gilbert: an anniversary survey and exhibition check-list with thirty-five illustrations. Charlottesville VA 1963.

Jones, J. B. W. S. Gilbert's contributions to Fun, 1865–1874. BNYPL 73, Apr 1969.

Ellis, J. The unsung W. S. Gilbert. HLB 18 [1970].

Jones, J. B. Gilbert and his ballads: problems in the bibliography and attribution of Victorian comic journalism. SB 25 1972.

Dillard, P. H. How quaint the ways of paradox! an annotated Gilbert and Sullivan bibliography. Metuchen NJ 1991. Also contains secondary material.

Collections

Original plays. 1876. Contains The wicked world, Pygmalion and Galatea, Charity, The palace of truth, The princess, Trial by jury. Reissued as Original plays, first ser 1881. Iolanthe added 1905.

Original plays. Second ser 1881. Contains Broken hearts, Engaged, Sweethearts, Dan'l Druce, Gretchen, Tom Cobb, The sorcerer, HMS Pinafore, The pirates of Penzance.

Original plays. Third ser 1895. Contains Comedy and tragedy, Foggerty's fairy, Rosencrantz and Guildenstern, Patience, Princess Ida, The Mikado, Ruddigore, The Yeomen of the Guard, The mountebanks, The gondoliers, Utopia limited.

Original plays. Fourth ser 1911. The fairy's dilemma, The Grand Duke, His Excellency, Haste to the wedding, Fallen fairies, The gentleman in black, Brantinghame Hall, Creatures of impulse, Randall's thumb, The fortune hunter, Thespis. The hooligan and Trying a dramatist added 1920.

Original comic operas; containing The sorcerer; Patience; HMS Pinafore; Princess Ida; The pirates of Penzance; The Mikado; Iolanthe; Trial by jury. [1890.]

Original comic operas, second series: containing The gondoliers, The Grand Duke; The Yeomen of the Guard; His Excellency; Utopia limited; Ruddigore; The mountebanks; Haste to the wedding. [1896?]

The Mikado and other plays. Introd by C. Day jr, New York 1917. Contains The Mikado, The pirates of Penzance, Iolanthe, The gondoliers.

The Savoy operas: being the complete text of the Gilbert and Sullivan operas. 1926.

Goldberg, I. (ed). New and original extravaganzas. Boston 1931. Contains Dulcamara, La viviandière, Merry zingara, The pretty druidess, Robert the devil.

Allen, R. (ed). The first night Gilbert and Sullivan. Containing complete librettos of the fourteen operas, exactly as presented at their première performances: together with facsimiles of the first-night programmes. Foreword by Bridget D'Oyly Carte. Illus with contemporary drawings. New York 1958.

The Savoy operas. St Martin's Lib 1962.

The Savoy operas. Introd by D. Cecil. WC 1962, 1963. 2 vols.

Stedman, J. W.(ed). Gilbert before Sullivan. Chicago 1967, London 1969. Contains the texts of Gilbert's German Reed entertainments: No cards, Ages ago, Our island home, A sensation novel, Happy Arcadia, Eyes and no eyes.

Ellis, J. (ed). The Bab ballads. Cambridge MA 1970.

Selections

The Gilbert and Sullivan birthday book, compiled by A. Watson. 1888.

Savoy operas. Illustr W. R. Flint 1909.

Iolanthe, and other operas. Illustr W. R. Flint. Also issued in separate vols 1911–12.

Lost Bab ballads: collected and illustrated by T. A. Searle. 1932.

A treasury of Gilbert and Sullivan: the words and music of one hundred and two songs from eleven operettas. New York 1941.

Engaged. In English plays of the nineteenth century, ed M. R. Booth, vol 4, Oxford 1973. Including 'Criticism of Engaged'.

Tom Cobb. In English plays of the nineteenth century, ed M. R. Booth, vol 4, Oxford 1973.

Plays by W. S. Gilbert. Ed and introd by G. Rowell, Cambridge 1982. Contains Palace of truth, Princess Toto, Engaged, Rosencrantz and Guildenstern, Sweethearts.

The lost stories of W. S. Gilbert. Ed P. Haining 1982.

Wilson, F. W. The Gilbert and Sullivan birthday book. Dobbs Ferry NY 1983.

Dixon, G. The Gilbert and Sullivan concordance. New York 1987.

Benford, H. The Gilbert and Sullivan lexicon in which is gilded the philosophic pill. Illus. Ann Arbor MI 1991 (2nd edn), 1999 (3rd edn).

The complete annotated Gilbert and Sullivan, ed and introd by I. Bradley. Oxford 1996.

Other selections, mainly from the Savoy operas, have been pbd, but they are of little editorial significance.

§1

Newspaper reviews of Thespis, Trial by jury, and all works performed at the Opéra Comique and the Savoy theatres, except Fallen fairies, are rptd in Allen, The first night Gilbert and Sullivan, *above. Joseph Knight's Athenaeum reviews from Nov 1874 to Dec 1879 are rptd in his* Theatrical notes *1893. Reviews of Gilbert's later libretti are rptd in William Archer,* The theatrical 'World' for 1893 [1894]: for 1894 [1895]: for 1895 [1896]: for 1896 [1897].

Only a representative sample of Gilbert's many stories and articles is included here. Note that Lacy nos refer to vols; French's to individual plays.

Uncle Baby. Ca (Lyc 31 Oct 1863). Ed and introd by Terence Rees 1968 (priv ptd).

My maiden brief. Cornhill Mag Dec 1863 (pbd anon). Story.

A colossal idea. F. (Unacted). c. 1862; ed T. A. Searle 1932.

The key of the strong room. ('Johnny Pounce'.) In T. Hood, A bunch of keys, 1865.

The income-tax. ('Maxwell and I'.) In T. Hood, Rates and taxes, 1866.

The lawyer's story. ('I plead for all'.) In T. Hood, The five alls. Warne's Christmas annual 1866. Reissued 1868.

Ruy Blas. Bsq. In Warne's Christmas annual 1866, illustr Gilbert.

Dulcamara! or, the little duck and the great quack. Ext. (StJ 29 Dec 1866). 1866. From Donizetti, L'elisir d'amore.

La vivandière, or true to the corps. Ext. (St James's Hall, Liverpool 15 June 1867; Queen's 22 Jan 1868). Liverpool 1867, London 1868. From Donizetti, La figlia del regimento.

Robinson Crusoe; or, the Injun bride & the injured wife. Bsq. (H 6 July 1867). 1867. With H. J. Byron, T. Hood, H. S. Leigh, A. Sketchley and 'Nicholas' [W. J. Prowse].

Harlequin cock-robin and jenny wren, or Fortunatus and the water of life, the three bears, the three gifts, the three wishes, and the little man who woo'd the little maid. P. (Lyc 26 Dec 1867). 1867.

The merry zingara; or, the tipsy gipsy and the pipsy wipsy. Bsq. (Roy 21 Mar 1868). [1868.] From Bunn and Balfe, The 'Bohemian girl'.

Robert the devil; or, the nun, the dun and the son of a gun. Ext. (Gai 21 Dec 1868). 1868. From Meyerbeer, Robert le diable.

The triumph of vice. In The Savage Club papers, 1867. Story.

The 'Bab' ballads: much sound and little sense, with illustrations by the author. '1869', [1868], 1870 (Cheap edn, omits 10 ballads).

Chap. 2. In Two 'pon ten: a novel in a nutshell. In Tom Hood's Comic annual for 1869, [1868]. Story.

No cards: a musical piece in one act for four characters. Music by German Reed. (Gallery of Illus 29 Mar 1869). [1869.] Re-set by L. Elliott (1901).

The pretty druidess; or the mother, the maid, and the mistletoe

bough. Ext. (Charing Cross 19 June 1869). [1869]. From Bellini's Norma.
An old score. CD. (Gai 26 July 1869). Returned to pre-production title, Quits, in Autumn 1869. Lacy 85; French 1610.
Ages ago. Oa. Music by F. Clay. (Gallery of Illus 22 Nov 1869). [1869], 1895.
The Princess: a whimsical allegory: being a respectful perversion of Mr Tennyson's poem. Bsq. (Olym 8 Jan 1870). Lacy 87; French 1291.
The gentleman in black: an original musical legend. Music by F. Clay. (Charing Cross 26 May 1870). Lacy 88.
Our island home. Oa. Music by German Reed. (Gallery of Illus 20 June 1870). 1967. *See* Stedman, *above*. Songs in addition J. W. Stedman, 'Three new Gilbert lyrics', BNYPL 74, Dec 1970.
The palace of truth. Fairy C. (H 19 Nov 1870). Lacy 89; French 1332.
A medical man: a comedietta. (St George's Hall 24 Oct 1870). In C. Scott, Drawing-room plays and parlour pantomimes, 1870.
Randall's thumb. C. (Court 25 Jan 1871). Lacy 91. First pbd as a story in Tom Hood's Comic annual for 1870, [1869].
A sensation novel, in three volumes. Oa. Music by German Reed. (Gallery of Illus 30 Jan 1871). [1871.] Re-set by Florian Pascal 1897.
Creatures of impulse: a musical fairy tale; music by A. Randegger. (Court 15 Apr 1871). [1871]; Lacy 91; French 1364. Originally story of same name.
Les brigands: opéra bouffe en trois actes, par H. Meilhac et L. Halévy; musique de J. Offenbach; l'adaptation anglaise par Gilbert. Text in Fr and Eng. 1871. Undated edn. Eng only without Gilbert's name; The brigands undated with Gilbert's name. (TR Plymouth 2 Sep 1889; Ave 16 Sep 1889).
On guard. C. (Court 28 Oct 1871). Lacy 98.
Pygmalion and Galatea. Mythological C. (H 9 Dec 1871). 1873; French 1545.
Thespis, or the gods grown old: a grotesque opera. Music by Arthur Sullivan. (Gai 26 Dec 1871). 1871. Full musical score never pbd. Reconstructed libretto in Terence Rees, Thespis: a Gilbert and Sullivan enigma, 1964 (priv ptd).
The finger of fate. In Tom Hood's Comic annual for 1872, [1871]. Story.
Happy Arcadia. Oa. Music by F. Clay. (Gallery of Illus 28 Oct 1872). [1872]; 1896.
More 'Bab' ballads; with illustrations by the author. 1873.
The wicked world. A fairy comedy. (H 4 Jan 1873). 1873; Lacy 126; French 1883. First pbd as story in Tom Hood's Comic annual for 1871, [1870].
The happy land: a burlesque version of The wicked world, by 'F. Tomline' and G. À Beckett. (Court 3 Mar 1873; prohibited by the Lord Chamberlain 7 Mar 1873, but re-opened thereafter). 1873.
The realm of joy. F. (Royalty 18 Oct 1873). By 'F. Latour Tomline'. A free and easy version of Le roi candaule by H. Meilhac and L. Halévy. Ed T. Rees 1969 (priv ptd). Title later changed to Realms of joy.
The wedding march. An eccentricity. (Court 15 Nov 1873). Lacy 114; French 1703. Adaptation of Labiche and Marc-Michel, Le chapeau de paille d'Italie.
A stage play. In Tom Hood's Comic annual 1873, [1872]. Pbd with introd by W. Archer, New York 1916.
Charity. D. (H 3 Jan 1874). Lacy 123; French 1844.
Ought we to visit her? C. (Roy 17 Jan 1874). [1874]. Ptd as ms.
Committed for trial. FC. (Glo 24 Jan 1874). By 'F. Latour Tomline'. *See* On bail, *below*.
The blue-legged lady. F. (Court 4 Mar 1874). By 'F. L. Tomline'. In J. W. Stedman, A new absurdity from Tomline: W. S. Gilbert's 'Dramatic Sell', NCTR 3 Spring 1975.
Topsy-Turvydom. Ext. (Crit 21 Mar 1874). Oxford 1931 (priv ptd).
Sweethearts. Dramatic contrast. (PW 7 Nov 1874). Lacy 111; French 1655.
The 'Bab' ballads and more 'Bab' ballads: much sound and little sense; with illustrations by the author. [1874.]
The story of a twelfth cake. In Christmas no of the Graphic, 1874. Story.
Trial by jury. Dramatic cantata. Music by Arthur Sullivan. (Roy 25 Mar 1875). 1875. From Closet O. Fun 11 Apr 1968.
Tom Cobb, or fortune's toy. FC. (StJ 24 Apr 1875). Lacy 117; French 1752.
A proposal for elevating the position of the modern drama. Era Almanack 1875. Article.
Eyes and no eyes: or the art of seeing. Oa. Music by German Reed. (St George's Hall 5 July 1875). [1875.] Re-set by Florian Pascal 1896. Suggested by Hans Christian Andersen, The emperor's new clothes.
Broken hearts. Fairy D. (Court 9 Dec 1875). French 1765.
Princess Toto. CO. Music by F. Clay. (ThR Nottingham 1 July 1876; Alexandra Liverpool 24 July 1876; Str 2 Oct 1876). [1876.]
Dan'l Druce, blacksmith. D. (H 11 Sep 1876). Lacy 118. French 1759. Suggested by George Eliot, Silas Marner.
Fifty 'Bab' ballads. '1877' [1876].
On bail. FC. (Crit 3 Feb 1877). French 1750. From H. Meilhac and L. Halévy, Le Reveillon. Expanded version of Committed for trial, *above*.
A letter addressed to the members of the dramatic profession in reply to Miss Henrietta Hodson's pamphlet. (18 May 1877.) (Priv ptd.) Prose.
Engaged. FC. (H 3 Oct 1877). [1877]; Lacy 117; French 1748.
The sorcerer. CO. (Opéra Comique 17 Nov 1877). [1877]; (Sav 11 Oct 1884 with addns and deletions); [1898]. Founded on story An elixir of love, Christmas no of the Graphic 1876.
The forty thieves. P. (Gai 13 Feb 1878). 1878. With H. J. Byron, F. C. Burnand and R. Reece.
The ne'er-do-well. D. (Olym 25 Feb 1878). [1878] (priv ptd). Revised as The vagabond (Olym 25 Mar 1878).
HMS Pinafore, or the lass that loved a sailor. CO. Music by Arthur Sullivan. (Opéra Comique 25 May 1878). [1878.]
Gretchen. D. (Olym 24 May 1879). 1879; Lacy 125.
The pirates of Penzance, or the slave of duty. CO. Music by Arthur Sullivan. (Bijou, Paignton, 30 Dec 1879; Fifth Avenue, New York 31 Dec 1879; Opéra Comique 3 Apr 1880). 1880.
A hornpipe in fetters. Era Almanack and Annual 1879. Article.
Actors, authors and audiences – A trial by Jury. In Christmas no of Illus Sporting and Dramatic News. 1880 DSK. Rev version Trying a dramatist pbd in Century Mag Dec 1911.
Patience: or Bunthorne's bride! Aesthetic opera. Music by Arthur Sullivan. (Opéra Comique 23 Apr 1881). [1881.]
Foggerty's fairy. C. (Crit 15 Dec 1881). [1881] (ptd as ms). Based on story of same name.
Iolanthe: or the peer and the peri. Fairy opera. Music by Arthur Sullivan. (Sav 25 Nov 1882). [1882.]
The 'Bab' ballads with 215 illustrations by the author. [1882.]
An autobiography. Theatre n.s. 1, Apr 1883.
Princess Ida: or Castle Adamant. A respectful operatic per-version of Tennyson's Princess. Music by Arthur Sullivan. (Sav 5 Jan 1884). [1884.]
Comedy and tragedy. D. (Lyc 26 Jan 1884). [1884]; Lacy 139; French 2072. First pbd as story in C. Scott, The stage door, Routledge's Christmas annual ['1880'] [1879].
My pantomime. Era Almanack 1884. Article.
The Mikado: or the town of Titipu. CO. Music by Arthur Sullivan. (Sav 14 Mar 1885). [1885]; tr Danish 1887, Ger [1887]; Ital 1899.
Ruddygore: or the witch's curse! CO. Music by Arthur Sullivan. (Sav 22 Jan 1887). [1887]. Spelling of title altered to Ruddigore and textual changes made during week after production because of audience response.
The Yeomen of the Guard: or the merryman and his maid. CO. Music by Arthur Sullivan. (Sav 3 Oct 1888). [1888]; tr Ger nd.
Brantinghame Hall. D. (StJ 29 Nov 1888). 1888 (priv ptd).

The Gondoliers: or the King of Barataria. CO. Music by Arthur Sullivan. (Sav 7 Dec 1889). [1889.]

Songs of a Savoyard, illustrated by the author. 1890. Selected lyrics from the operas set by Arthur Sullivan.

Foggerty's fairy and other tales. '1890', [1889].

Rosencrantz and Guildenstern: a tragic episode in three tableaux, founded on an old Danish legend. Travesty. (Vaud 3 June 1891). Lacy 133; French 1989. Enlarged from verses of same name in Fun, Dec 1874.

The Mountebanks. CO. Music by A. Cellier. (Lyric 4 Jan 1892). 1891 (as 'Proof', containing songs and dialogue deleted in rehearsal), 1892.

Haste to the wedding. CO. Music by G. Grossmith. (Crit 27 July 1892). 1892. A musical version of Le chapeau de paille d'Italie. *See* The wedding march, *above.*

Songs of two Savoyards. 1892.

Utopia (limited): or the flowers of progress. CO. Music by Arthur Sullivan. (Sav 7 Oct 1893). 1893.

His Excellency. CO. Music by O. Carr. (Lyric 27 Oct 1894). 1894.

The Grand Duke, or the statutory duel. CO. Music by Arthur Sullivan. (Sav 7 Mar 1896). 1896.

The fortune hunter. D. (TR Birmingham 27 Sep 1897). [1897] (priv ptd).

The Bab ballads, with which are included Songs of a Savoyard; with 350 illustrations by the author. 1898.

The fairy's dilemma: a domestic pantomime. (Gar 3 May 1904). [1904] (priv ptd). First pbd as story in Graphic Christmas no 1900.

The lady in the plaid shawl. The Flag 1908.

My case against the Rev J. Pullein Thompson. [1908] (priv ptd). Prose.

The Pinafore picture book. 1908. Children's fiction.

Preface to Rutland Barrington . . . by himself. 1908.

Fallen fairies: or the wicked world. CO. Music by E. German. (Sav 15 Dec 1909). 1909.

The hooligan. D. (Coliseum 27 Feb 1911). Pbd in Century Mag Nov 1911.

The story of the Mikado. 1921. Children's fiction.

The following plays were performed but never printed: Allow me to explain. F. *(PW 4 Nov 1867)*; Highly improbable. F. *(Roy 5 Dec 1867)*; Great expectations. D. *(Court 27 May 1871), adapted from Dickens's novel;* Committed for trial. C. *(Glo 24 Jan 1874).*

Gilbert wrote the words for 6 songs in addition to those pbd from his plays and libretti: Thady O'Flinn (Molloy) [1868]; Corisande (Molloy) [1870]; Eily's reason (Molloy) [1871]; The distant short (Sullivan) [1874]; Sweethearts (Sullivan) [1875]; The love that loves me not (Sullivan) [1875]. *He also illustrated books and stories, chiefly those written by his father, William Gilbert, including* The magic mirror, *'1866' [1865], and* King George's middy, *1868–9.*

Contributions to periodicals

In addition to the periodicals referred to under §1, above, Gilbert contributed to Belgravia, Broadway Annual, Comic News, Cornhill, The Dark Blue, Fun, London Soc, Graphic, Illus Sporting and Dramatic News, Mirth, Once a Week, Punch, *etc. His chief connection was with* Fun, *beginning in 1861, for which he wrote prose and verse of all kinds and contributed many illustrations. He reviewed plays for* Fun, Illus Times, Daily News, *and the* Observer.

Letters

Gilbert wrote many sporadic letters to The Times, Era *and other newspapers, from the 1860s to 1911.*

Brown, H. R. and R. Grey. The W. S. Gilbert of his own letters. Cornhill Mag 52, Feb 1922.

Dark, S. and R. Grey. W. S. Gilbert: his life and letters. 1923.

Barnby, M. My letters from Gilbert and Sullivan. Strand Mag 72, Dec 1926, Jan 1927.

Allen, R. and G. R. D'Luhy. Sir Arthur Sullivan: composer & personage. New York 1975.

Jacobs, A. Arthur Sullivan: a Victorian musician. 2nd edn 1992.

§2

Adams, W. D. Mr Gilbert as a dramatist. Belgravia 45, Oct 1881.

Archer, W. In his English dramatists of to-day, 1882.

Howe, H. Illustrated interviews. 1893.

Fitzgerald, P. H. The Savoy opera and the Savoyards. 1894.

Righton, E. A suppressed burlesque: the happy land. Theatre 28 Aug 1896.

Filon, A. In his The English stage, 1897. Trns by F. Whyte.

Archer, W. In his Real conversations, 1904.

Beerbohm, M. Gilbert as humorist. Saturday Rev 14 May 1904.

St John-Brenon, E. Mr W. S. Gilbert's original comedy. Grand Mag Apr–May 1905.

Browne, E. A. W. S. Gilbert. 1907. In Stars of the stage ser.

Valentine, E. S. Sir W. S. Gilbert as an artist. Illus Strand 37, Feb 1909.

Obits. The Times 30 May 1911; Manchester Guardian 30 May 1911.

Cellier, F. A. and C. Bridgeman. Gilbert, Sullivan and D'Oyly Carte: reminiscences of the Savoy and the Savoyards. 1914.

Goldberg, I. The story of Gilbert and Sullivan: or the 'Compleat' Savoyard. New York 1928, (rev edn) 1935.

Granville-Barker, H. Exit Planché – enter Gilbert. London Mercury 25, Mar–Apr 1932.

Ellehauge, M. Initial stages in the development of the English problem-play: the Savoy opera. EStudien 66 1932.

Two Victorian humorists: Burnand and the mask of Gilbert. TLS 21 Nov 1936.

Troubridge, St V. Gilbert's sources. N & Q 29 Mar 1941.

Darlington, W. S. The world of Gilbert and Sullivan. New York [1950], London 1951, New York 1952 (2nd edn).

James, P. A note on Gilbert as an illustrator. In Selected Bab ballads with introd by H. Pearson, Oxford 1955 (priv ptd).

Williamson, A. Gilbert and Sullivan opera. 1955, (rev edn) 1982.

Pearson, H. Gilbert: his life and strife. 1957.

Cox-Ife, W. How to sing both Gilbert and Sullivan. 1961.

Rollins, C. and R. J. Witts. The D'Oyly Carte company in Gilbert and Sullivan operas. A record of productions 1875–1961. 1962. Supplements.

Mander, R. and J. Mitchenson. A picture history of Gilbert and Sullivan. 1962.

Meisel, M. In his Shaw and the nineteenth-century theatre, Princeton 1963.

Baily, L. The Gilbert and Sullivan book. Revised edn 1966.

Jones, J. B. (ed). W. S. Gilbert: a century of scholarship and commentary. New York 1970.

Helyar, J. (ed). Gilbert and Sullivan papers presented at the international conference held at the University of Kansas in May 1970. Lawrence KS 1971.

Bargainnier, E. Gilbert and pantomime. Panto! The jnl of the Br Pantomime Assoc 4 Christmas 1975.

Wolfson, J. Final curtain: the last Gilbert and Sullivan operas. 1976.

Cox-Ife, W. W. S. Gilbert: stage director. 1977.

Goodman, A. Gilbert and Sullivan at law. 1983.

McElroy, G. Whose zoo; or when did the Trial begin? NCTR 12 Dec 1984.

Stedman, J. W. S. Gilbert: a classic Victorian and his theatre. Oxford 1996.

Eden, D. A tale of two kidnaps. Coventry 1988.

Periodicals devoted to Gilbert

The Gilbert and Sullivan Jnl. 1925–81.

The Savoyard. Apr 1962–Sep 1982.

Jnl of the W. S. Gilbert Soc. Spring 1985– .

Regional Amer jnls such as Gasbag (Univ of Michigan). 5 Mar 1969– . [JWS]

Clothilde Inez Mary Graves, 'Richard Dehan'
1863–1932

Unpbd plays are available in the Lord Chamberlain's Collection, BL and in the NYPL Readex Collection of English and American drama of the 19th century. A short list of novels appears in Diva Daims and Janet Grimes, Toward a feminist tradition: an annotated bibliography of novels in English by women 1891–1920, *New York 1982.*

§1
The Belle of Rock Harbour. 'Judy' Office [1887]. Short story.
The pirate's hand. 'Judy' Office [1889]. Parody of style of R. L. Stevenson.
Dragon's teeth. 1891, [1916]. Novel.
A field of tares. New York 1891. Novel.
Maids in a market garden. Illustr M. Greiffenhagen. 1894, New York 1912, London [1914]. Novel.
Seven Xmas eves, being the romance of a social evolution. Illustr D. Hardy [1894]. Short stories.
A mother of three. F. (Com 8 Apr 1896). French no 1909; French's acting edn vol 157.
REVIEW: Archer, W. Theatrical 'world' of 1896, [1895].
A well-meaning woman. 1896. Novel.
The lovers' battle: a heroical comedy in rhyme. Founded upon Alexander Pope's 'Rape of the lock'. 1902, New York 1902.
See also Nicoll *5, pp. 389, 794 and D. Mullin,* Victorian plays, *Westport CT 1987. For later works see Nat Union Cat (pre-1956 imprints).*

§2
Who's who in the theatre. 1930. Biography.
Obits: The Times 5 Dec 1932; Publishers World 17 Dec 1932.
Murray, D. L. 'Richard Dehan'. The Times 12 Dec 1932.
Catholic authors. Ed M. Hoehn, St Mary's Abbey 1948. [DHT]

Sydney Grundy 1848–1914

Licensing copies of the plays are located in BL.

§1
A little change. F. (H 13 July 1872). Lacy 95; Readex micro.
The days of his vanity: a passage in the life of a young man. 3 vols London and Guildford 1876, 1894 (new edn).
Man proposes. Ca. (Duke's 18 Mar 1878). French no 1837; Readex micro.
The snowball. FC. (Str 2 Feb 1879). French 131; Hong Kong 1891; Readex micro.
In honour bound. C. (PW 25 Sep 1880). [1880] (as A debt of honour) (priv ptd); French no 1838; New York nd; Readex micro. From Scribe, Une chaîne.
The vicar of Bray. CO. (Glo 22 July 1882; Sav 28 Jan 1892). [1882], [1892]; Readex micro. Music by E. Solomon.
The glass of fashion. C. (Glasgow 26 Mar 1883; Glo 8 Sep 1883). French 142; French Int Copyr Edn 3, 1898; Readex micro.
The silver shield. C. (Mat Str 19 May 1885; Com 20 June 1885). French 142; French 1898; French Int Copyr Edn 2, 1898; Readex micro.
A fool's paradise. D. (copyr performance PW Greenwich 7 Oct 1887 as The mousetrap; mat Gai 12 Feb 1889; Gar 2 Jan 1892). French 142 (copyr 1898); French Int Copyr Edn 1, 1898; Readex micro.
The Arabian nights. C. (Glo 5 Nov 1887). French no 2004; New York nd; Readex micro. From von Moser, Haroun al Rashid.
The dean's daughter. CD. (StJ 13 Oct 1888). 1891. With F. C. Philips.
A pair of spectacles. C. (Gar 22 Feb 1890). French 142 (copyr 1898); French Int Copyr Edn 4, 1898; Rowell; Readex micro. From Labiche and Delacour, Les petits oiseaux.
Haddon Hall. O. (Sav 24 Sep 1892). 1892 (libretto), 1892 (vocal score). Music by Sir A. Sullivan.
Sowing the wind. D. (Com 30 Sep 1893). 1893 (priv ptd); French 148; French Int Copyr Edn 45, 1901; Readex micro.
An old jew. C. (Gar 6 Jan 1894). New York 1894; Readex micro.
A bunch of violets. D. (H 25 Apr 1894). French 148 (copyr 1901); French Int Copyr Edn 47, 1901; Readex micro. From Geuillet, Montjoye.
The new woman. C. (Com 1 Sep 1894). 1894 (priv ptd); Readex micro.
Slaves of the ring. C. (Gar 29 Dec 1894). 1894 (priv ptd).
The greatest of these –. D. (Grand Hull 13 Sep 1895; Gar 10 June 1896). 1896 (priv ptd).
The late Mr Costello. F. (Com 28 Dec 1895). French 148 (copyr 1898); French Int Copyr Edn 46, 1901; Readex micro.
A son of Israel. (Unacted?). 1896 (priv ptd).
A marriage of convenience. D. (H 5 June 1897). French 144; Readex micro. From A. Dumas, Un mariage sous Louis XV.
The musketeers. MD. (Her Majesty's 3 Nov 1898). 1899; Readex micro (typescript). From A. Dumas.
Sympathetic souls. D. (Kennington 26 Feb 1900). French 146; French Int Copyr Edn 33, 1900; Readex micro. From Scribe, Les inconsolables.
The head of Romulus. Ca. (10 May 1900). French 146; French Int Copyr Edn 34, 1900; Readex micro. From Scribe.
A debt of honour. D. (StJ 1 Sep 1900). [1900?] (priv ptd); Readex micro.
A Napoleon of finance. C. (Unacted). 1903 (priv ptd).
The play of the future, by a playwright of the past; [and] a glance at the future of the theatre by John Palmer. 1914.

Contributions to periodicals
The dearth of originality. Theatre Nov 1878.
The dramatic ring. Theatre Dec 1879.
The science of the drama. New Rev July 1891.
See also Nicoll *5, pp. 396–7, 795; Nicoll,* English drama 1900–30, *pp. 692–3; Conolly,* English drama, *pp. 186–7;* Readex Index *(including typescripts of other unpbd plays), p. 113. For performance details and reviews, see Wearing,* London stage 1890–99; 1900–09.

§2
In W. Archer, English dramatists of to-day, 1882.
A gossip with Sydney Grundy. Era 8 Oct 1892.
Watson, M. Mr Grundy and the critics. Theatre Oct 1894.
Beerbohm, M. Degenerates. Saturday Rev 4 Nov 1899.
The Times 6 July 1914. Obituary.
In T. H. Dickinson, The contemporary drama of England, 1920. [JRS]

John Oliver Hobbes 1867–1906

See col 1579.

Henry Arthur Jones 1851–1929

Mss of Jones's plays and letters are to be found in the BL, Yale, the Bodleian, the Theatre Museum (London), London Univ Lib and Chicago Univ Lib.

Bibliographies
Jones, D. A. Appendices A–B. In Life and letters of Henry Arthur Jones, 1930. As Taking the curtain call: the life and letters of Henry Arthur Jones, New York 1930.
Wisenthal, J. L. Henry Arthur Jones. In DLB: vol 10: Modern British dramatists, 1900–1945: part 1: A–L, ed S. Weintraub, Detroit 1982.

Collections
Representative plays. Ed C. Hamilton (with historical, biographical and critical introd) 4 vols New York 1925, London 1926. Vol 1 The silver king, The middleman, Judah, The dancing girl; vol 2 The crusaders, The tempter, The masqueraders, The case of rebellious Susan; vol 3 Michael and his lost angel, The liars, Mrs Dane's defence, The hypocrites; vol 4 Dolly reforming herself, The divine gift, Mary goes first, The goal, Grace Mary.
Plays by Henry Arthur Jones. Ed R. Jackson (with critical introd),

Cambridge 1982. The silver king, The case of rebellious Susan, and The liars.

There is a Uniform (but not complete) demy 8vo edn of 24 of Jones's plays pbd by Samuel French, nd.

§1

Hearts of oak: or, a chip off the old block: a domestic drama. (TR Exeter 29 May 1879). Lacy 122. Rewritten with fuller dialogue as Honour bright, 1879, but unacted in this form. Both versions priv ptd Ilfracombe 1879.

Harmony: a domestic drama. (Grand Leeds 13 Aug 1879 as Harmony restored; TR Exeter 11 Dec 1879 as It's only round the corner; Str 14 Jan 1884 as Harmony). Lacy 119. Performed as The organist, Lyc New York 9 May 1892; Royalty 25 Sep 1895 (as Harmony).

Elopement: a comedy. (TR Oxford 19 Aug 1879). Lacy 122; [Ilfracombe] 1879 (priv ptd).

A clerical error: a comedy. (Court 13 Oct 1879). [Ilfracombe] 1879 (priv ptd); Lacy 152.

A drive in June. D. (Unacted). [Ilfracombe] 1879 (priv ptd).

An old master: a comedy. (P'cess 6 Nov 1880). Lacy 119; Ilfracombe 1880 (priv ptd).

A garden party. C. (Unacted). [Ilfracombe] 1880 (priv ptd).

Lady Caprice: a comedy. (Unacted). [Ilfracombe] 1880 (priv ptd).

Humbug. G. (Unacted). [Ilfracombe] 1881 (priv ptd).

A bed of roses: a comedy. (Glo 26 Jan 1882). Lacy 119; Ilfracombe 1882 (priv ptd).

The silver king. D. (P'cess 16 Nov 1882). [1907]; French 1675. With H. A. Herman.

REVIEWS: The theatres, Saturday Rev 54 Nov 1882; Our play-box, Theatre n.s. 6 Dec 1882.

The wedding guest. C. (Unacted). [Ilfracombe] 1882 (priv ptd).

Breaking a butterfly. D. (Prince's 3 Mar 1884). [1884] (priv ptd). With H. A. Herman. Founded on Ibsen, A doll's house.

REVIEW: [W. Archer], Our play-box: breaking a butterfly, Theatre n.s. 3 Apr 1884.

Saints and sinners. D. (PW Greenwich 17 Sep 1884, Vaud 25 Sep 1884). 1891.

REVIEW: Our play-box, Theatre n.s. 4 Oct 1884.

Hoodman blind. D. (P'cess 18 Aug 1885). [Lacy nd.] With W. Barrett.

Sweet Will: a comedy. (New Club, CG 5 Mar 1887; Shaftesbury 27 July 1893). Lacy 131.

REVIEWS: The theatres, Saturday Rev 70, 2 Aug 1890; Our play-box. Theatre n.s. 16 Sep 1890.

The middleman. D. (Shaftesbury 27 Aug 1889). [1907.]

REVIEW: Our play-box, Theatre n.s. 14 Oct 1889.

Judah. D. (Shaftesbury 21 May 1890). New York 1894 (with a preface by Joseph Knight).

REVIEW: Mr H. A. Jones's new play, Saturday Rev 69, 24 May 1890.

The deacon: a comedy sketch. (Shaftesbury 27 Aug 1890). Lacy 133.

REVIEW: Our play-box, Theatre n.s. 16 Oct 1890.

The dancing girl: a drama. (H 15 Jan 1891). [1907.]

REVIEW: Our play-box, Theatre n.s. 17 Feb 1891.

The crusaders: an original comedy of modern London life. (Aven 2 Nov 1891). 1893 (with a preface by W. Archer).

REVIEW: Our play-box, Theatre n.s. 18 1891.

The bauble shop. D. (Crit 26 Jan 1893). [1893.]

REVIEW: The theatres, Saturday Rev 75, 4 Feb 1893.

The tempter: a tragedy in verse. (H 30 Sep 1893). [1893] (priv ptd), 1898.

REVIEWS: The theatres, Saturday Rev 76, 23 Sep 1893; Plays of the month, Theatre n.s. 22 Nov 1893.

A lay sermon to preachers. In A. Reid, Vox clamantium: the gospel of the people, 1894.

The masqueraders. C. (StJ 28 Apr 1894). [1894] (priv ptd), 1899.

REVIEW: Saturday Rev 77, 5 May 1894.

The case of rebellious Susan. C. (Crit 3 Oct 1894). 1894 (priv ptd), 1897.

REVIEW: At the play, Theatre n.s. 24 Nov 1894.

The triumph of the Philistines, and how Mr Jorgan preserved the morals of Market Pewbury under very trying circumstances: a comedy. (StJ 11 May 1895). 1895 (priv ptd), 1899.

REVIEW: Theatre n.s. 25 June 1895.

Grace Mary. T. (Unacted). [1895] (priv ptd); rptd in The theatre of ideas, 1915.

The renascence of the English drama: essays, lectures and fragments relating to the modern English stage 1883–94. 1895.

Michael and his lost angel. D. (Lyc 15 Jan 1896). [1896] (priv ptd), 1896 (with preface by Joseph Knight).

REVIEW: At the play, Theatre n.s. 27 Feb 1896.

The rogue's comedy. D. (Gar 21 Apr 1896). [1896] (priv ptd), 1898.

REVIEW: At the play, Theatre n.s. 27 May 1896.

The physician. D. (Crit 25 Mar 1897). [1897] (priv ptd), 1899.

REVIEW: At the play, Theatre n.s. 29 May 1897.

The liars: an original comedy. (Crit 6 Oct 1897). [1897] (priv ptd), New York 1901; French 2519.

REVIEWS: Shaw, G. B. At several theatres, Saturday Rev 84, 9 Oct 1897; At the play, Theatre n.s. 30 Nov 1897.

The manoeuvres of Jane: an original comedy. (H 29 Oct 1898). [1898] (priv ptd), 1904.

REVIEW: [M. Beerbohm] Saturday Rev 86, 5 Nov 1898.

Carnac Sahib. D. (Her Majesty's 12 Apr 1899). 1899 (priv ptd), 1899.

REVIEW: [M. Beerbohm] Background in foreground, Saturday Rev 87, 22 Apr 1899.

James the fogey. D. (Unacted). 1900 (priv ptd).

The lackey's carnival. C. (DofY 26 Sep 1900). 1900 (priv ptd).

REVIEW: [M. Beerbohm] Mr Jones below stairs, Saturday Rev 90, 6 Oct 1900.

Mrs Dane's defence. D. (Wyndham's 9 Oct 1900). [1900] (priv ptd), 1905.

REVIEW: [M. Beerbohm] This inimpedible Mr Jones, Saturday Rev 90, 13 Oct 1900.

The Princess's nose: a comedy. (DofY 11 Mar 1902). [1902] (priv ptd).

REVIEW: [M. Beerbohm] An indiscreet play, Saturday Rev 93, 22 Mar 1902.

Chance, the idol. D. (Wyndham's 9 Sep 1902). [1902] (priv ptd).

REVIEW: [M. Beerbohm] Saturday Rev 94, 13 Sep 1902.

Whitewashing Julia: a comedy. (Gar 2 Mar 1903). [1903] (priv ptd), 1905.

REVIEW: [M. Beerbohm] At the Garrick theatre, Saturday Rev 95, 7 Mar 1903.

Joseph entangled: a comedy. (H 19 Jan 1904). [1904] (priv ptd), 1906.

The chevaleer: a comedy. (Gar 27 Aug 1904). [1904] (priv ptd), [1905?].

REVIEW: [M. Beerbohm] Saturday Rev 98, 10 Sep 1904.

Chrysold. D. (Unacted). [1904] (priv ptd).

The sword of Gideon. D. (Unacted). [1905] (priv ptd).

The corner stones of modern drama. 1906 (priv ptd).

The heroic Stubbs: a comedy. (Terry's 24 Jan 1906). [1906] (priv ptd).

REVIEW: [M. Beerbohm] Saturday Rev 101, 27 Jan 1906.

The hypocrites. D. (Hudson New York 30 Aug 1906; Hicks's London 27 Aug 1907). [1907] (priv ptd), [1908].

REVIEW: [M. Beerbohm] Re-enter Mr Jones, Saturday Rev 104, 7 Sep 1907.

The evangelist: a tragi-comedy. (Knickerbocker New York 30 Sep 1907). 1907 (priv ptd) (as The Galilean's victory).

Literature and the modern drama. 1907 (priv ptd).

Dolly reforming herself: a comedy (H 3 Nov 1908). [1908] (priv ptd), [1913]. Samuel French & Co also pbd in New York a one-act version called Dolly's little bills (Hippodrome 8 July 1912).

REVIEW: [M. Beerbohm] Saturday Rev 106, 7 Nov 1908.

The censorship muddle and a way out of it. 1909.

The knife. D. (Palace 20 Dec 1909). [New York 1925?]

REVIEW: [M. Beerbohm] Mr Henry Arthur Jones' sketch, Saturday Rev 1 Jan 1910.
Fall in, rookies! D. (Alhambra 24 Oct 1910). [1910] (priv ptd).
An open letter to the right honble Winston Churchill, MP. [1910] (priv ptd). On legalising plays at music halls.
On reading modern plays. In The amateur's hand-book: a guide to home or drawing room theatricals, [1910].
We can't be as bad as all that. C. (Nazimova New York 30 Dec 1910; Croydon Hippodrome 4 Sep 1916). New York 1910 (priv ptd).
Mary goes first: a comedy. (Playhouse 18 Sep 1913). 1913.
The divine gift. D. (Unacted). 1913.
The foundations of a national drama: a collection of lectures, essays and speeches, delivered and written in the years 1896–1912, revised and corrected, with additions. 1913.
Municipal and repertory theatres. 1913 (priv ptd).
The goal. D. (Chicago 1907; P'cess New York 26 Oct 1914; Palace London 20 May 1919). 1898 (priv ptd); in The theatre of ideas, 1915.
The lie. D. (Harris New York 24 Dec 1914; NT London 13 Oct 1923). London and New York [1915], London 1923.
The theatre of ideas: a burlesque allegory; and three one-act plays: The goal; Her tongue; Grace Mary. 1915.
Shakespeare and Germany. 1916.
The pacifists: a parable. (Southport Opera House 27 Aug 1917; StJ 4 Sep 1917). [1917] (priv ptd), London and Glasgow [1955].
Last word on the drama. 1919.
Patriotism and popular education. 1919, 1919.
My dear Wells: a manual for the haters of England; being a series of letters upon Bolshevism, collectivism, internationalism and the distribution of wealth, addressed to Mr H. G. Wells. 1921, 1922, New York 1921, 1921.
Mr Mayor of Shakespeare's town. 1925.
What is capital? an inquiry into the meaning of the words 'capital' and 'labour'. 1925.

The following were also produced but remain unpbd: It's only round the corner. C. (TR Exeter 11 Dec 1879); His wife. D. (SW 16 Apr 1881); Home again. C. (TR Oxford 7 Sep 1881); Chatterton. D. (P'cess 22 May 1884). *With H. A. Herman,* The Lord Harry. Romance. (P'cess 18 Feb 1886). *With W. Barrett,* The noble vagabond. Romance. (P'cess 22 Dec 1886); Heart of hearts. D. (Vaud 3 Nov 1887); Wealth. D. (H 27 Apr 1889); The princess's nose. C. (DofY 11 Mar 1902); The ogre. D. (StJ 11 Sep 1911); Lydia Gilmore. (Lyc New York 1 Feb 1912); Cock o' the walk. F. (Cohan New York 27 Dec 1915).

D. A. Jones's bibliography, above, records 4 film scenarios, written in 1920, which were neither used nor ptd. It also records, in Appendix 6, all Jones's letters to the press, articles, lectures, speeches etc.

Introductions and prefaces

Filon, A. The English stage. 1897.
Brunetière, F. The law of the drama. 1914.

§2

Archer, W. In his About the theatre: essays and studies, 1886.
Walkley, A. B. In his Playhouse impressions, 1892.
Bettany, W. A. L. The drama of modern England, as viewed by Mr H. A. Jones. Theatre 31 1893.
Blathwayt, R. Lions in their dens: Henry Arthur Jones. Idler 4 Aug 1893.
Archer, W. In his Theatrical 'world', 5 vols 1894–8.
Hamilton, J. A. Henry Arthur Jones. Munsey's Mag 9 1894.
Newton, H. C. Jones. Theatre 36 Mar 1896.
Filon, A. In his The English stage: being an account of the Victorian drama, 1897.
Bulloch, J. M. Henry Arthur Jones (with bibliography of his plays). Book Buyer 16 1898.
Archer, W. In his Study and stage: a year-book of criticism, 1899.
Grein, J. T. In his Dramatic criticism, 5 vols 1899–1905.
Scott, C. In his The drama of yesterday & to-day, 2 vols 1899.
Tarpey, W. K. English dramatists of to-day. Critic 37 1900.
Maude, C. In his The Haymarket theatre, 1903.
Beers, H. A. The English drama to-day. North Amer Rev 180 1905.
Howells, W. D. On reading the plays of Mr Henry Arthur Jones. North Amer Rev 186 1907.
Shaw, G. B. In his Dramatic opinions and essays, 2 vols New York 1906, London 1907.
Walkley, A. B. In his Drama and life, [1907].
Borsa, M. In his The English stage of to-day, 1908.
Archer, W. In his Play-making: a manual of craftsmanship, 1912.
Howe, P. P. In his Dramatic portraits, 1913.
Winter, W. In his Wallet of time, 2 vols 1913.
Chandler, F. W. In his Aspects of modern drama, New York 1914.
Dickinson, T. H. Henry Arthur Jones and the dramatic renascence. North Amer Rev 202, Nov 1915.
Dickinson, T. H. In his The contemporary drama of England, Boston 1917.
Wauchope, G. A. Henry Arthur Jones and the social drama. Sewanee Rev 29 1921.
Henry Arthur Jones, dramatist: self-revealed; a conversation on the art of writing plays with Archibald Henderson. Nation (London) 38 Dec 1925.
Shorey, P. Henry Arthur Jones. New York 1925.
The Times 8 Jan 1929. Obituary.
Shelley, H. C. Jones. Bookman (London) 75, Feb 1929.
Henry Arthur Jones. London Mercury 19 Feb 1929. Obituary.
Allen, P. Henry Arthur Jones. Fortnightly Rev 125, May 1929.
Jones, D. A. The life and letters of Henry Arthur Jones. 1930. As Taking the curtain call: the life and letters of Henry Arthur Jones, New York 1930. [JPW]

Arthur William Law 1844–1913

Licensing copies of the plays are located in BL.

Collections

[Dramatic works.] 19 pts 1904.

§1

Castle Botherem. Ca. (St George's Hall 13 Jan 1880). 1904; Readex micro. With H. Clarke.
All at sea. Musical Sk. (St George's Hall 28 Feb 1881). 1904; Readex micro. Music by C. Grain.
A bright idea. Ca. (St George's Hall 30 May 1881). [1881?] (libretto); French nd; Readex micro. Music by A. Cecil.
Cherry Tree farm. Ca. (St George's Hall 30 May 1881). [1881?] (libretto); French nd; Readex micro. Music by H. Clarke.
The head of the poll. Ca. (St George's Hall 28 Feb 1882). 1904; Readex micro. Music by E. Fanning.
Nobody's fault. Ca. (St George's Hall 5 June 1882). [1882?] (priv ptd), 1904; Readex micro. Music by H. Clarke.
The happy return. Ca. (Court 9 Jan 1883). French no 1888; Readex micro.
The moss-rose rent. Vaud. (St George's Hall 17 Dec 1883). 1904; Readex micro. Music by A. J. Caldicott.
Old Knockles. Ca. (St George's Hall 24 Nov 1884). [1884?] (priv ptd); London and New York 1894; Readex micro. Music by A. J. Caldicott.
A peculiar case. Ca. (St Leonard's 2 Dec 1884). [1884?] (libretto) (priv ptd); Readex micro. Music by G. Grossmith.
The magic opal. Oa. (Lyr 19 Jan 1893). 1911; Readex micro. Music by Albeniz.
The new boy. F. (Devonshire Park Eastbourne 1 Feb 1894 as The boy; Terry's 21 Feb 1894). French copyr 1904; Readex micro.
A country mouse. D. (Worthing 24 Feb 1902; PW 27 Feb 1902). French nd.
Three blind mice: or Marjorie's lovers. C. (TR Margate 30 June 1906; Crit 14 Feb 1907). French 159 (copyr 1910).

Contributions to periodicals

Hamlet's father. Era Almanack 1879.
A property supper. Era Almanack 1881. Short story.
A great draw. Era Almanack 1882. Short story.
A dreadful story. Era Almanack 1883.
A domestic drama. Era Almanack 1884.
An old playhouse. Era Almanack 1885.
The wrong play. Era Almanack 1887.
See also Nicoll 5, *pp. 449–50, 802; Nicoll,* English drama 1900–30, *p. 775; and for performance details and cast lists, see Wearing,* London stage 1890–99; 1900–09.

§2

The Times 7 Apr 1913. Obituary. [JRS]

'Paul Meritt', R. Maetzger 1848–95

§1

Glin Gath: or the man in the cleft. D. (Grecian 1 Apr 1872). French 99.
Thad: or linked by love. C. (Grecian 29 July 1872). French 128.
'British born'. D. (Grecian 17 Oct 1873). French 109. With H. Pettitt.
Velvet and rags: a Spanish romance of the present day. D. (Grecian 6 Apr 1874). French 112. With G. Conquest.
Hand and glove. D. (Grecian 25 May 1874). French 109. With G. Conquest.
Chopstick and spikins. F. (Grecian 23 Sep 1874). French 109.
The word of honour. D. (Grecian 22 Oct 1874). French 113.
Stolen kisses. C. (Glo 2 July 1877). French 2078.
The golden plough. MD. (Adel 11 Aug 1877). French 111. Revised from his Grace royal (P'cess Edinburgh 31 May 1876).
New Babylon: or daughters of Eve, by Merritt and W. H. Poole. 3 vols 1882.
'The hidden million': a sensational story. New York 1883. Short story.
Pleasure: by Merritt and A. Harris. Theatre Oct 1887.
Loaded dice: a story of modern life. Round Table Annual 1891.
See also Nicoll 5, *pp. 485–7, 806.*

§2

Archer, W. In his English dramatists of today, 1882.
The bill of the play: an illustrated record of the drama for 1881. 1882.
Death of Paul Meritt. Era 13 July 1895.
Era Almanack 1895. [HH]

Herman Charles Merivale, 'Felix Dale' 1839–1906

A son of the soil, from François Ponsard, Le lion amoureux. D. (Court 4 Sep 1872). 187?; Lacy 97; French 1445.
A husband in clover, from Thiboust, Un mari dans du coton. F. (Lyc 26 Dec 1873). French 100; Lacy 100; New York Drama 1.
The white pilgrim: or Earl Olaf's vow, from the legend by Gilbert Abbott À Beckett. T. (Court 14 Feb 1874). 1874 (priv ptd), 1883 (with other poems); French 113 and 1687.
Peacock's holiday, from Labiche and Martin, Le voyage de Monsieur Perrichon. F. (Court 16 Apr 1874). 187?; French 115 and 1718; Lacy 115.
The lady of Lyons[,] married and settled. F. [also called a vaud]. (Gai 5 Oct 1878). French 115; Lacy 115.
Stage-English. Theatre n.s. 2 (1 June 1879).
Faucit of Balliol: a story in two parts. 3 vols 1882.
Florien: a tragedy in five acts[,] and other poems. (Unacted). 1884.
Binko's blues: a tale for children of all growth. 1884.
Ravenswood, from Scott, The bride of Lammermoor. (Lyc 20 Sep 1890). 1890 (priv ptd).
Life of W. M. Thackeray. 1891. Completed by Sir Frank T. Marzials.
Bar, stage & platform: autobiographic memories. 1902.
See also Nicoll 5, *pp. 487, 806.*

§2

Adams, William Davenport. 'Herman Merivale'. Theatre n.s. 15 (May 1890), [233]–8. [DS]

Henry Chance Newton, 'Richard Henry' 1854–1931

§1

The penny showman, and other poems ... reprinted from The Referee. 1886, [1896].
Sixty years' stage service; being a record of the life of Charles Morton, the 'father of the halls'. 1905. With W. H. Morton.
The Old Vic and its associations. 1920, [1923].
Crime and the drama: or dark deeds dramatized. 1927.
Cues and curtain calls; being the theatrical reminiscences of H. Chance Newton ('Carados' of The Referee). 1927.
Idols of the 'halls'; being my music hall memories. 1928.

Contributions to periodicals

Tales of the old Brit[annia]. In The Referee 27 Jan, 3 Feb 1924.

Collaborative works (under pseud Richard Henry, with R. W. Butler)

Licensing copies of the plays are located in BL.
Fast friends. C. (Steinway Hall 14 June 1878). French.
A happy day. F. (Gai 6 Oct 1886). Lynn's acting edn 23, [1894]; Readex micro.
First mate. D. (Gai 31 Dec 1888). French; Readex micro.
Adoption. Sk. (Toole's 26 May 1890). French; Readex micro.
Queer street. D. (Gai 21 Mar 1892). French; Readex micro.
Under the pseudonym 'Carados', Newton contributed dramatic anecdote and criticism to The Referee *from first issue in Aug 1877 until near his death. For other dramatic pieces, see* Nicoll 5, *pp. 503, 808; Nicoll,* English drama 1900–30, *p. 856. See also* Readex Index, *p. 124.* [JRS]

T. A. Palmer 1838–1905

Too late to save: or doomed to die. D. (TR Exeter 1861). 1878.
Among the relics. C. (TR Plymouth 22 Nov 1869). French 108.
Rely on my discretion. F. (Roy 17 Jan 1870). French 106.
Insured at Lloyd's. D. (New Queen's Manchester 5 Nov 1870). French 110.
A dodge for a dinner. F. (Str 28 Dec 1872). French 100.
The last life. D. (Greenwich 9 Feb 1874). French 103. From Mrs S. C. Hall, Stories of Irish life.
East Lynne. D. (Nottingham 19 Nov 1874). French 103. From Mrs Henry Wood.
Woman's rights. Ca. (Grand Douglas Aug 1882). French 121.

Harry Major Paull, 'Paul Blake' 1854–1934

Licensing copies of the acted plays are located in BL.

§1

The Felicidad. C. (mat Gai 24 Mar 1887 as The great Felicidad). [1928.]
A dangerous experiment. C. 1887; Readex micro.
A deed of gift. C. 1887.
His son and heir. C. 1888.
The gentleman whip. C. (Devonshire Park Eastbourne 1 Feb 1894; Terry's 21 Feb 1894). French 138; Readex micro.
Hal, the highwayman. C. (Vaud 15 Dec 1894). French 151 (copyr 1904); Readex micro.
In Nelson's days. D. (Lyr Ealing 23 Apr 1896 as The spy). French 140; Readex micro.
Merrifield's ghost. C. (Vaud 13 Nov 1895). French 139; Readex micro.
My lord from town. D. (Worcester College Oxford 18 June 1904). French 163.

The anti-suffragist; or the other side. Monol. [1913.]
The last day of term. French's Plays for Schoolgirls 1, [1922].
Back to college. French's Plays for Schoolgirls 8, [1923].
Chums. French's Plays for Schoolgirls 11, [1925].
The last train up. French's Plays for Boys 13, [1927].
Literary ethics: a study in the growth of the literary conscience. 1928.
Bluff! a detective story. [1928.]
Supper for two. C. (No performance details). [1928.]

Contributions to periodicals

The National Gallery and common sense. Fortnightly Rev Apr 1898.
Dramatic convention: the soliloquy. Fortnightly Rev May 1899.
The personal element in fiction: a question of technique. Nineteenth Cent Dec 1916.
A forgotten immortal: Vincent Voiture. Nineteenth Cent July 1919.
The unknown star: a Christmas mystery play. Nineteenth Cent Dec 1919. With L. Housman.

Pseudonymous Works (as 'Paul Blake')

My friend & my enemy. 1887. Boy's story.
Phil and I. 1900; reissued [1904], [1923]. Boy's story.
Expelled. A story of Eastgate school. [1922.] Short story.
See also Nicoll 5, *pp. 516, 809; Nicoll,* English drama 1900–30, *pp. 876–7;* Readex Index, *p. 209; and for performance details, casts and reviews, see Wearing,* London stage 1890–99; 1900–09.

§2

The Times 3 Dec 1934. Obituary. [JRS]

Stephen Phillips 1864–1915

§1

Orestes and other poems. 1884 (priv ptd).
Primavera: poems by four authors. Oxford 1890. 16 poems, 4 by Phillips.
Eremus: a poem. 1890.
Christ in Hades. 1896; ed C. L. Hind 1917.
Poems. 1897, 1898 (enlarged and rev).
Herod. T. (Her Majesty's 31 Oct 1900). 1901.
Marpessa: a poem. 1900, 1928.
Ulysses. D. (His Majesty's 1 Feb 1902). 1902.
Paolo and Francesca. T. (StJ 6 Mar 1902). 1899.
The sin of David. D. (Stadttheater Düsseldorf 30 Sep 1905; Sav July 1914). 1904, 1912 (rev).
Nero. T. (His Majesty's 25 Jan 1906). 1906. Part omitted appears as one-act play, Nero's mother, in Lyrics and dramas, *below*.
Faust. T. (His Majesty's 5 Sep 1908). 1908. With J. Comyns Carr.
Iole. D. (Cosmopolis June 1913). 1908 (in New poems, *below*).
New poems. 1907.
Pietro of Siena. D. (Studio 10 Oct 1911). 1910.
The new Inferno. 1910.
The King. D. (Unacted). 1912, 1913 (in Lyrics and dramas, *below*).
Lyrics and dramas. 1913.
Armageddon: a modern epic drama. (NT 1 Jan 1915). 1915; rptd from Lyrics and dramas, *above*. Partly in verse and partly in prose.
Panama and other poems, narrative and occasional. 1915.
Harold: a chronicle play. (Unacted). Poetry Rev Jan, Mar 1916; ed A. Symons 1927.
The last heir, *also called* The bride of Lammermoor, *though acted was never pbd.* The adversary, *included in* Lyrics and dramas, *1913, was never acted.*

§2

Acad 1 Jan 1898. Review of Poems 1897.
Farrer, R. J. Herod through the opera glass. 1901. A parody of Phillips's Herod.
Streatfield, R. A. Two poets of the new century: Phillips and Laurence Binyon. 1901. Rptd from Monthly Rev.
Archer, W. In his Poets of the younger generation, 1902.
Real conversations. 1904.
Hale, E. E. In his Dramatists of to-day, 1906.
Kyle, G. Edited by Phillips. Poetry Rev Jan–Feb 1916.
Meynell, A. Phillips. Poetry Rev Jan–Feb 1916.
Waugh, A. Phillips. Fortnightly Rev Jan 1916, rptd in his Tradition and change, 1919.
Kernahan, C. In good company. 1917.
Colvin, S. In English poets, ed T. H. Ward, vol 5, 1918.
Celebrities. 1923.
Benson, C. Bensonian memories: mainly players. 1926.
Thouless, P. Modern poetic drama. Oxford 1934.
Mason, A. E. W. Sir George Alexander and the St. James's Theatre. 1935. [HH]

Sir Arthur Wing Pinero 1855–1934

Mss of Pinero's plays and letters are located in the BL, the Theatre Collection in the Houghton Lib of Harvard Univ, the Brotherton Collection of the Univ of Leeds, the Berg Collection of NYPL, the Fales Collection of New York Univ Lib, the Univ of Rochester Lib, HRHRC, the Theatre Museum, London, and Yale.

Bibliography

Wearing, J. P. Arthur Wing Pinero. In DLB. Vol 10: Modern British dramatists 1900–1945, pt 2: M–Z, ed S. Weintraub, Detroit 1982.

Collections

The social plays of Pinero. Ed C. Hamilton (with general introd and critical preface to each play) 4 vols New York 1917–22. Vol 1 The second Mrs Tanqueray, The notorious Mrs Ebbsmith; vol 2 The gay Lord Quex, Iris; vol 3 Letty, His house in order; vol 4 The thunderbolt, Mid-channel.
Arthur Wing Pinero: three plays. With introds by S. Wyatt, 1985. Reprints French's acting edns of The magistrate, The second Mrs Tanqueray, and Trelawny of the 'Wells'.
Plays by A. W. Pinero: The schoolmistress, The second Mrs Tanqueray, Trelawny of the 'Wells', The thunderbolt. Ed G. Rowell (with introd, notes and bibliography), Cambridge 1986.

§1

*The plays marked * constitute a uniform (but not complete) edn in 29 vols, the first 11 with introductory notes by M. C. Salaman.*
Hester's mystery: a comedy. (Folly 5 June 1880). [1893]; Lacy 136.
The money spinner: an original comedy. (Prince's Manchester 5 Nov 1880; StJ 8 Jan 1881). 1900; Lacy 146.
The squire: an original comedy. (StJ 29 Dec 1881). 1881 (priv ptd); 1905.
The rocket: an original comedy. (PW Liverpool 30 July 1883; Gai 10 Dec 1883). 1905.
In chancery: an original fantastic comedy. (Lyc Edinburgh 19 Sep 1884; Gai 24 Dec 1884). 1905.
*The magistrate: a farce. (Court 23 Jan 1885). 1892.
*The schoolmistress: a farce. (Court 27 Mar 1886). 1894.
*The hobby-horse: a comedy. (StJ 23 Oct 1886). 1892.
*Dandy Dick: a farce. (Court 27 Jan 1887). 1893.
REVIEW: [M. Beerbohm] Saturday Rev 89, Feb 1900.
*Sweet Lavender: a domestic drama. (Terry's 21 Mar 1888). 1893.
*The weaker sex: a comedy. (TR Manchester 28 Sep 1888; Court 16 Mar 1889). 1894.
REVIEW: [C. Howard] Theatre n.s. 13 Apr 1889.
*The profligate. D. (Gar 24 Apr 1889). 1892.
*The Cabinet Minister: a farce. (Court 23 Apr 1890). 1892.
*Lady Bountiful: a story of years. D. (Gar 7 Mar 1891). 1892.
REVIEW: Saturday Rev 71, Mar 1891.
*The Times: a comedy. (Terry's 24 Oct 1891). 1891.

*The Amazons: a farcical romance. (Court 7 Mar 1893). 1895.
*The second Mrs Tanqueray. D. (StJ 27 May 1893). 1892 (priv ptd); 1895.
REVIEWS: [W. Archer] Plays and acting of the season, Fortune n.s. 54, Aug 1893; [G. B. Shaw] An old new play and a new old one, Saturday Rev 79, Feb 1895.
*The notorious Mrs Ebbsmith: a drama. (Gar 13 Mar 1895). 1895 (priv ptd); 1895.
REVIEWS: [G. B. Shaw] Mr Pinero's new play, Saturday Rev 79, Mar 1895; [G. B. Shaw] A new Lady Macbeth and a new Mrs Ebbsmith, Saturday Rev 79, May 1895; [M. Beerbohm] The notorious Mrs Ebbsmith. Saturday Rev 91, Mar 1901.
*The benefit of the doubt: a comedy. (Com 16 Oct 1895). 1895 (priv ptd), 1896.
REVIEW: [G. B. Shaw] Pinero as he is acted, Saturday Rev 80, Oct 1895.
*The Princess and the butterfly, or the fantastics: a comedy. (StJ 29 Mar 1897). 1896 (priv ptd), 1898.
REVIEW: [W. L. Courtney] The idea of comedy and Mr Pinero's new play. Fortnightly Rev n.s. 61, May 1897.
*Trelawny of the 'Wells': a comedietta. (Court 20 Jan 1898). 1897 (priv ptd), New York 1898, London 1899.
REVIEW: [G. B. Shaw] Mr Pinero's past, Saturday Rev 85, Feb 1898.
The beauty stone: an original romantic musical drama. (Sav 28 May 1898). With J. C. Carr, music by Arthur Sullivan. [1898].
*The gay Lord Quex. C. (Glo 8 Apr 1899). 1899 (priv ptd), 1900.
REVIEWS: [W. Archer] Plays of the season, Fortune n.s. 66, July 1899; [M. Beerbohm] The gay Lord Quex, Saturday Rev 87, Apr 1899.
*Iris. D. (Gar 21 Sep 1901). 1901 (priv ptd), 1902.
Robert Louis Stevenson the dramatist: a lecture. 1903 (priv ptd). 1909 (in Critic 42), New York 1914 (with introd and biographical appendix by C. Hamilton).
*Letty. D. (DofY 8 Oct 1903). 1903 (priv ptd), 1904.
REVIEW: [M. Beerbohm] Saturday Rev 96, Oct 1903.
*A wife without a smile: a comedy in disguise. (Wyndham's 12 Oct 1904). 1904 (priv ptd), 1905.
REVIEW: [M. Beerbohm] Mr Pinero's doll, Saturday Rev 98, Oct 1904.
*His house in order. C. (StJ 1 Feb 1906). 1905 (priv ptd), 1906.
REVIEWS: [M. Beerbohm] Mr Pinero's new play, Saturday Rev 101, Feb 1906; Drama and music, Nation (London) 83, Sep 1906.
*The thunderbolt. C. (StJ 9 May 1908). [1907] (priv ptd), 1909.
*Mid-channel. D. (StJ 2 Sep 1909). [1908] (priv ptd), 1910.
*Preserving Mr Panmure: a comic play. (Com 19 Jan 1911). 1910 (priv ptd), 1912.
*The 'mind the paint' girl: a comedy. (DofY 17 Feb 1912). 1912 (priv ptd), 1913.
The widow of Wasdale Head: a fantasy. (DofY 14 Oct 1912). 1912 (priv ptd).
Playgoers: a domestic episode. (StJ 31 Mar 1913). 1913; French 2507.
The Bulkeley peerage. (Unacted). Pearson's Mag 37, Dec 1914.
*The big drum: a comedy. (StJ 1 Sep 1915). 1915 (priv ptd), 1915.
REVIEW: [W. Archer] Pinero's new satire, The big drum, Nation (London) 101, Sep 1915.
*The freaks, an idyll of suburbia: a comedy. (NT 14 Feb 1918). 1917 (priv ptd), 1922.
Quick work. (Stamford CT 14 Nov 1919). 1918 (priv ptd).
A seat in the park. C. (Winter Garden 21 Feb 1922). 1922 (priv ptd), 1922. French 2618.
*The enchanted cottage: a fable. (DofY 1 Mar 1922). 1922.
A private room. D. (Little 14 May 1928). London and New York 1928. French 852.
*Dr Harmer's holidays: a contrast in nine scenes. (Shubert-Belasco Washington 16 Mar 1931). 1930. Pbd with Child man: a sedate farce (unacted) in Two plays, 1930 (with preface).
A cold June. C. (Duchess 20 May 1932). 1931 (priv ptd).
The following were also produced but remain unpbd: Two hundred a year. F. (Glo 6 Oct 1877); La comète, or two hearts. D. (TR Croydon 22 Apr 1878); Two can play at that game. C. (Lyc 20 May 1878); Daisy's escape. C. (Lyc 20 Sep 1879); Bygones. C. (Lyc 18 Sep 1880); Imprudence. C. (Folly 27 July 1881); Girls and boys: a nursery tale. C. (Toole's 1 Nov 1882); The rector; the story of four friends. D. (Court 24 Mar 1883); Lords and commons. C. (H 24 Nov 1883); Low water. C. (Glo 12 Jan 1884); The iron-master. D. (SJ 17 Apr 1884); Mayfair. C. (SJ 31 Oct 1885); Mr Livermore's dream. (Coliseum 15 Jan 1917); Monica's blue boy. Mime. (NT 8 Apr 1918).

Contributions to periodicals and collaborative works

A theatrical art union. Era Almanack and Annual 1879.
Theatrical byways. Theatre n.s. 2 May 1879.
Capel and Capello. Era Almanack and Annual 1880.
The Inverness cape. Theatre n.s. 2 Aug 1880. Story.
How actors draw. Era Almanack and Annual 1881.
A fallen star. Era Almanack and Annual 1881; rptd in Leopold Wagner, XX stories by xx tellers, 1895. Story.
A fairy. Era Almanack and Annual 1883. Poem.
Felicity's song. Theatre n.s. 1 Jan 1883. Poem.
The riddle. Theatre n.s. 2 Sep 1883. Poem.
The whirlpool. Theatre n.s. 2 July 1883. Poem.
Mathews and Sothern. Era Almanack and Annual 1884.
One day. Theatre n.s. 3 Jan 1884. Poem.
Consulting the oracle. Era Almanack and Annual 1886.
The man who gave a matinee. Era Almanack and Annual 1888. Story.
From the Dianthus to the Edelweiss. Theatre n.s. 24 Oct 1894. Poem.
The modern British drama. Theatre n.s. 25 June 1895.
Robert Browning as a dramatist. Trans of the Royal Soc of Lit. 2nd ser 31, 1912.
The theatre in the 'seventies. In The eighteen-seventies, ed Harley Granville-Barker, 1929.
Tom Robertson's pals. Theatre Guild Mag 6 1929.
J. L. Toole: a great comic actor: the natural man. The Times 12 Mar 1932.
The theatre in transition. In Fifty years: memories and contrasts: a composite picture of the period 1882–1932. 1932.

Letters

The collected letters of Sir Arthur Pinero. Ed J. P. Wearing, Minneapolis 1974.

Prefaces and introductions

L. N. Tolstoi. The fruits of enlightenment. 1891.
W. Archer. The theatrical 'world' of 1893. 1894.
W. L. Courtney. The idea of tragedy in ancient and modern drama. 1900.
L. Merrick. Works. [1918.]

Pinero-iana

The Pinero birthday book. 1898. Selected and arranged by M. Hamilton.

§2

Archer, W. In his English dramatists of to-day, 1882.
Cook, D. Plays, plagiarisms and Mr Pinero. Theatre 5 Jan 1882.
Cook, D. The case of Mr Pinero. Theatre 5 Feb–Apr 1882.
Moore, G. In his Impressions and opinions, 1891; rev 1913.
Sharp, R. F. Pinero and farce. Theatre 29 Oct 1892.
Walkley, A. B. In his Playhouse impressions, 1892.
Mr Pinero and the literary drama. Theatre 31 July 1893.
Archer, W. In his Theatrical 'World', 5 vols 1894–8.
Hamilton, J. A. Pinero. Munsey's Mag 10 July 1894.
Lund, T. W. M. The second Mrs Tanqueray: what? and why? Liverpool 1894.
Fyfe, H. H. Mr Pinero's plays as literature. Theatre 35, June 1895.

Sichel, W. S. The new drama. Quart Rev 182, Oct 1895.
Wilson, H. S. The notorious Mrs Ebbsmith. 1895.
Archer, W. In his Study and stage, 1899.
Kobbé, G. The plays of Arthur Wing Pinero. Forum 26 1899.
Walkley, A. B. In his Frames of mind, 1899.
Hamelius, J. P. A. W. Pinero und das englische Drama der Jetztzeit, Brussels 1900.
Tarpey, W. K. English dramatists of to-day. Critic 37 1900.
Fyfe, H. H. Arthur Wing Pinero playwright: a study. 1902. With casts.
Archer, W. In his Real conversations, 1904.
Beers, H. A. The English drama of to-day. North Amer Rev 180 1905.
Massee, Will W. Arthur Wing Pinero. In Living dramatists, ed Oscar Hermann, New York 1905.
Hale, E. E. In his Dramatists of to-day, New York 1906.
Shaw, G. B. In his Dramatic opinions and essays, 2 vols, New York 1906, London 1907.
Walkley, A. B. In his Drama and life, [1907].
Rideing, W. H. Some women of Pinero's. North Amer Rev 188, July 1908.
Frohman, D. In his Memories of a manager, 1911.
Stocker, W. Pineros Dramen. Marburg 1911.
Walbrook, H. H. In his Nights at the play, 1911.
Archer, W. In his Play-making: a manual of craftsmanship, 1912.
Armstrong, C. F. In his Shakespeare to Shaw, 1913.
Clark, B. H. Realistic drama, part II. Fortune 99 1913.
Courtney, W. L. Realistic drama. Fortnightly Rev n.s. 93–4, June 1913.
Howe, P. P. In his Dramatic portraits, 1913.
Chandler, F. W. In his Aspects of modern drama, New York 1914.
After the play. New Republic 13 1917.
Dickinson, T. H. In his Contemporary drama of England, 1917.
Courtney, W. L. In his Old saws and modern instances, 1918.
Phelps, W. L. Sir Arthur Pinero. Bookman (New York) 47, Apr 1918.
Jameson, Storm. In her Modern drama in Europe, London and New York, 1920.
Clark, B. H. In his British and American drama of to-day, Cincinnati OH 1921.
Archer, W. In his Old drama and the new, 1923.
The Times 24 Nov 1934. Obituary. [JPW]

Robert Reece, 'E. G. Lankester' 1838–91

Licensing copies of the plays are located in BL.

§1

All plays listed below are also issued in one or more Readex micro *edns.*
Prometheus: or the man on the rock. Ext. (Roy 23 Dec 1865). Lacy 68.
The lady of the lake, plaid in a tartan. Bsq. (Roy 8 Sep 1866). Lacy 71. From Scott.
The stranger – stranger than ever. Ext. (Queen's 4 Nov 1868). Lacy 82.
The ambassadress. CO. (St George Dec 1868). [1868?]. With T. G. Reed. Music by Auber.
Brown and the Brahmins: or Captain Pop and the Princess Pretty-eyes. Bsq. (Glo 23 Jan 1869). Lacy 82.
Ingomar: or the noble savage. In Drawing-room plays, ed Scott, 1870.
Whittington, Junior, and his sensation cat. Bsq. (Roy 23 Nov 1870). Lacy 89.
Dora's device. C. (Roy 11 Jan 1871). Lacy 90.
Perfect love: or the triumph of Oberon. Fairy D. (Olym 25 Feb 1871). Lacy 90.
Little Robin Hood: or quite a new beau! Bsq. (Roy 19 Apr 1871). Lacy 91.
Paquita: or love in a frame. CO. (Roy 21 Oct 1871). Lacy 94 (libretto).
The very last days of Pompeii: or a complete Bulwer-sement of the classical drama. Bsq. (Vaud 13 Feb 1872). Lacy 95; Lorenzen micro.
Romulus and Remus. Bsq. (Vaud 23 Dec 1872). Lacy 97.
Don Giovanni in Venice. Bsq. (Gai 17 Feb 1873). [1873.]
Martha, or a fair take-in. Bsq. (Gai 14 Apr 1873). [1873.]
Ruy Blas righted: or the lover, the lugger, and the lacquey. Bsq. (Vaud 3 Jan 1874). Lacy 100.
May: or Dolly's delusion. D. (Str 4 Apr 1874). French 126.
Green old age. Musical Sk. (Vaud 31 Oct 1874). French 103 (libretto).
An old man. D. (Duke's 25 Mar 1876). French 108.
A young Rip van Winkle. Bsq. (Charing Cross 17 Apr 1876). [1876.]
The creole. CO. (Brighton 3 Sep 1877). [1877.] With H. B. Farnie. Music by Offenbach.
The forty thieves. Bsq. (Gai 23 Dec 1880). [1881?]
Jeanne, Jeannette and Jeanneton. CO. (Alhambra 28 Mar 1881). [1881.] Music by P. Lacome.
Valentine and Orson. Bsq. (Gai 23 Dec 1882). 1882.
Our Helen. Bsq. (Gai 8 Apr 1884). 1884.
The commodore. Bsq. (Ave 10 May 1886). [1886]; New York nd. With H. B. Farnie. Music by Offenbach.

Contributions to periodicals
Sheridan Knowles at Eastbourne. Era Almanack 1869.
The refractory 'super'. Era Almanack 1875.
A bed of roses. Theatre Aug 1879.
Stage management. Theatre Nov 1879.
How he dined with a clown. Era Almanack 1884.

Pseudonymous works (as 'E. G. Lankester')
Warranted! F. (Str 4 May 1875). [1875?] (priv ptd).
The guv'nor. F. (Vaud 23 June 1880). French Int Copyr Edn 39, 1900.
See also Nicoll 5, *pp. 537–9, 812–13: Conolly,* English drama, *pp. 259–60;* Readex Index, *pp. 228–9.*

§2

Era Almanack 1868.
Archer, W. In his English dramatists of to-day, 1882.
Era 11 July 1891. Obituary.
Illus London News 18 July 1891. Obituary. [JRS]

George Robert Sims 1847–1922

§1

The merry duchess. CO. (Roy 23 Apr 1883). nd. Music by F. Clay.
In the ranks; or A soldier's wife. D. (Adel Oct 1883). Written with H. A. Pettitt. Home Lib of Powerful Dramatic Tales 4. Novelisation by Henry Llewellyn Williams.
Faust up to date. Bsq. (Gai 30 Oct 1888). 1889. Written with H. A. Pettitt. Music by Lutz, Meyer.
Blue-eyed Susan. CO. (PW 6 Feb 1892). Written with H. A. Pettitt. Music by Carr, F. Osmond, E. Ascherberg 1892.
Little Christopher Columbus. CO. (Lyr 10 Oct 1893). nd. Written with C. Raleigh. Music by I. Caryl.
Dandy Dick Whittington. Bsq. (Aven 2 Mar 1895). c. 1895. Music by I. Caryl.
The Dandy fifth. CO. (PW Birmingham 11 Apr 1898; DofY 16 Aug 1899). nd. Music by C. C. Corri.
The sleeping beauty. P. (DL 26 Dec 1913). 1913–14. Written with A. Collins. Music by J. M. Glover.
The sleeping beauty beautified. P. (DL 26 Dec 1914). 1914–15. Written with A. Collins. Music by J. M. Glover.
Puss in boots. P. (DL 26 Dec 1915). 1915–16. Written with F. Dix and A. Collins. Music by J. M. Glover.

Non-dramatic works
Dragonet ballads. 1881.
Ballads and poems: The Dragonet ballads; The ballads of Babylon; The lifeboat and other poems. 1883.

How the poor live and horrible London. 1889; rptd New York 1984.
Living London. 1903; rptd as Edwardian London 4 vols New York 1990.
Among my autographs. 1904.
My life. Sixty years' recollections of Bohemian London. 1917.
Prepare to shed them now: the ballads of George R. Sims. 1968. [BY]

Robert Louis Stevenson 1850–94

See col 1688.

(Walter) Brandon Thomas 1848–1914

Licensing copies of the plays are located in BL.

§1

The colour-sergeant. C. (P'cess 26 Feb 1885). French 153 (copyr 1905); Readex micro.
A Highland legacy. F. (Str 17 Nov 1888). French 143 (copyr 1898); Readex micro.
The Lancashire sailor. C. (Terry's 6 June 1891). French 142 (copyr 1898); Readex micro.
Charley's aunt. F. (Bury St Edmund's 29 Feb 1892; Roy 21 Dec 1892). French no 470 (copyr 1935) (modernised 1933 by J. Brandon-Thomas and W. D. Barnes-Brand); ed E. R. Wood 1969.
The queen of brilliants. O. (Lyc 8 Sep 1894). [1894] (lyrics); Readex micro. From the Ger of T. Taube and L. Tuchs. Music by E. Jakobowski.
See also Nicoll 5, *pp.* 595–6; *Nicoll,* English drama 1900–30, *p.* 985; *and* Readex Index, *p.* 270. *For performance details and casts, see Wearing,* London stage 1890–9; 1900–9; 1910–19.

§2

The Times 20 June 1914. Obituary.
Hibbert, H. G. A playgoer's memories. 1920.
Brandon-Thomas, J. Charley's aunt's father: a life of Brandon Thomas. 1955.
Stedman, J. General utility: Victorian author-actors from Knowles to Pinero. Educational Theatre Jnl 24 1972. [JRS]

John Todhunter 1839–1916

Some playscripts are available in the Lord Chamberlain's Collection, BL.

Collections

Essays by the late John Todhunter, with a foreword by Standish O'Grady. 1920. Includes The thoery of the beautiful; Essays read before 'The sette of odd volumes'; An essay on essays; A riverside walk; An essay in search of a subject; Murmurs from the Hesperides; An unconsidered trifle; Some old singers.

Selections

The poets and poetry of the century. Ed. A. H. Miles 10 vols [1891–7].
Selected poems. Ed D. L. Todhunter and A. P. Graves 1929.

§1

The theory of the beautiful. A 'Saturday lecture' delivered in the Museum building, Trinity College, Dublin. Dublin 1872. Pam.
Alcestis. New York 1874; London 1879. Poem.
Laurella and other poems. 1876.
A study of Shelley. 1880.
Forest songs and other poems. 1881.
The true tragedy of Rienzi, tribune of Rome [in 5 acts and in prose and verse]. 1881.
Prologue to 'The Cenci', a tragedy in 5 acts by Percy Bysshe Shelley. (Grand 7 May 1886). 1886; Shelley Soc pbns, ser 4, vol 3. Pam.
Helena in Troas. T. (Hengler's 17 May 1886). 1886, 1886. Prepared in collaboration with E. W. Godwin.
REVIEW: Theatre 1 June 1886.
Notes on Shelley's unfinished poem, 'The triumph of life'. 1887 (priv ptd).
The banshee and other poems. 1888; 2nd edn Dublin 1891.
Shelley and the marriage question. 1889 (priv ptd).
A Sicilian idyll. Pastoral play. (Club theatre, Bedford Park 5 May 1890). 1890, 1891.
REVIEW: Athenaeum 26 Sep 1891.
How dreams come true. DSk. (Grosvenor Gallery 17 July 1890). Bemrose [1890] (priv ptd).
The legend of Stauffenberg, a dramatic cantata by J. C. Culwick: the poem by J. Todhunter. Dublin 1890.
The poison flower. DSk. (Vaud 15 June 1891). Based on Hawthorne's Rappacini's daughter. 1891, 1927 (with Isolt of Ireland, by John Todhunter, a legend in a prologue and three acts).
Cäcilchen at the piano: music as of the winds when they awake. Poem. Spectator 10 June 1893.
The black cat. D. (OC 8 Dec 1893). 1895. Independent Theatre ser 4.
REVIEW: Archer, W. Theatrical 'world' for 1893.
An essay upon essays. Sette of odd vols, no 36. Folkard 1896 (priv ptd).
The life of Patrick Sarsfield, earl of Lucan; with a short narrative of the principal events of the Jacobite war in Ireland. 1896. New Irish lib vol 7; Dublin 1901.
REVIEW: Nation 62, 23 Jan 1896.
Maureen. Atheneaum 108, 29 Aug 1896. Poem.
Three Irish bardic tales. 1896, Chicago 1896, rptd New York 1978.
A riverside walk. 1898. Essay.
John Ruskin. Cornhill Mag 81, Mar 1900. Poem.
Blank-verse on the stage. Fortnightly Rev 77, Feb 1902.
Poetic drama and its prospects on the stage. Fortnightly Rev 77, Apr 1902.

Translations

Heine's Book of songs. Tr Todhunter 1907.
Goethe's Faust first part. Tr Todhunter, Oxford 1924.

§2

Obituary. The Times 27 Oct 1916.
Kunitz, S. J. British authors of the nineteenth century. New York 1936.
Moriarty, D. J. John Todhunter: child of the coming century. Unpbd diss Univ of Wisconsin 1979. Contains bibliography and unpbd works.
Woodfield, J. English Theatre in transition, 1881–1914. 1984. [DHT]

Oscar Fingal O'Flahertie Wills Wilde, 'Sebastian Melmoth' 1854–1900

Wilde's mss, notebooks and letters as well as corrected proofs and prompt copies of some of his plays are scattered in a variety of public and private collections, principally in England and the US. Among important institutional holdings are those at Bristol Univ (Tree), BL (including the licensing copies of Wilde's plays in Lord Chamberlain's Collection), Oxford (Ross), Harvard, HRHRC, Lib of Congress, NYPL (including Arents, Berg and Billy Rose Collections), Princeton, Pierpont Morgan, Rosenbach, Texas Christian Univ, Yale, the William Andrews Clark Memorial Lib at UCLA, Trinity College Dublin, and the Bodmer Lib in Geneva. Guides to a number of these collections are listed in the following section.

Bibliographies, catalogues, reviews of research and general reference

R., W. Notes for a bibliography of Oscar Wilde. Books and Book-plates 5 1904–5.
Glaenzer, R. B. Catalogue of the library of Richard Butler Glaenzer. New York 1905.
Mason, S. [C. S. Millard]. A bibliography of the poems of Oscar Wilde. 1907.

Mason, S. [C. S. Millard]. A bibliography of Oscar Wilde. [Edinburgh 1908], London 1914. Reissue, introd by T. d'Arch Smith 1967; rptd Boston 1972.
Haber, L. J. The library of Louis J. Haber [sale catalogue]. New York [1909].
Ledger, W. Bibliography [of early Salomé edns]. In Works 1909–11.
Glaenzer, R. B. Two hundred books from the library of Richard Butler Glaenzer [sale catalogue]. New York 1911.
Stetson, J. B. The Oscar Wilde collection of John B. Stetson, Jr [sale catalogue]. New York 1920. See S. Mason [C. S. Millard], TLS 13 May 1920.
Cowan, R. E. and W. A. Clark, Jr. The library of William Andrews Clark, Jr: Wilde and Wildeiana. 5 vols San Francisco 1922–31.
Complete catalogue of the library of John Quinn [sale catalogue]. New York 1924.
Dulau, A. B. and Co Ltd. A collection of original manuscripts, letters and books ... formerly in the possession of Robert Ross, C. S. Millard [Stuart Mason] and the younger son of Oscar Wilde [sale catalogue]. 1928.
Handlist of the Ross Memorial Collection, bequeathed by Mr Walter E. Ledger to University College, and placed in the Bodleian on permanent deposit. Apr 1932.
Guillot de Saix, L. G. M. Bibliographie. In Le chant du cygne: contes parlés d'Oscar Wilde, Paris 1942; rptd 1979.
Dickson, S. A. The Arents Tobacco Collection. BNYPL 54 1950.
Wing, D. G. The Katherine S. Dreier Collection of Oscar Wilde. YULG 28 1953.
Trinity College, Dublin. Catalogue of an exhibition of books and manuscripts in commemoration of the centenary of the birth of Oscar Wilde. Dublin 1954.
Finzi, J. C. Oscar Wilde and his literary circle: a catalogue of manuscripts and letters in the William Andrews Clark Memorial Library. Berkeley and Los Angeles 1957.
Ryskamp, C. (ed). Wilde and the nineties: an essay and an exhibition by Richard Ellmann, E. D. H. Johnson, and Alfred L. Bush. Princeton 1966.
Hyde, H. M. Oscar Wilde in Four Oaks Library. Ed G. Austin, Somerville NJ 1967.
Stevenson, L. Oscar Wilde. In The Victorian poets: a guide to research, ed F. E. Faverty, Cambridge MA 1968.
Munby, A. N. L. Sale catalogues of libraries of eminent persons. Vol 1 Poets and men of letters [sale of Wilde's Tite Street library 24 Apr 1895], 1971.
Harris, W. V. Oscar Wilde. In Victorian prose: a guide to research, ed D. J. DeLaura, New York 1973.
Lawler, D. E. Oscar Wilde in the NCBEL. PBSA 67 1973.
Fletcher, I. and J. Stokes. Oscar Wilde. In Anglo-Irish literature: a review of research, ed R. J. Finneran, New York 1976.
Dowling, L. Aestheticism and decadence: a selective annotated bibliography. 1977.
Johnson, E. D. H. Romantic, Victorian, and Edwardian (items in the collection of Robert H. Taylor at Princeton Univ). Princeton Univ Lib Chron 38 1977.
Conolly, L. W. and J. P. Wearing. Oscar Wilde. In English drama and theatre 1800–1900, Detroit 1978.
Mikhail, E. H. Oscar Wilde: an annotated bibliography of criticism. 1978.
Kohl, N. Bibliographie. In Oscar Wilde: das literarische werke zwischen provokation und anpassung, Heidelberg 1980.
The Prescott Collection: printed books and manuscripts sold at [Christie's] New York on Friday 6 Feb 1981. New York 1981.
Fletcher, I. and J. Stokes. Oscar Wilde. In Recent research on Anglo-Irish writers, ed R. J. Finneran, New York 1983.
Woudhuysen, H. R. Sales of books and manuscripts [at Sotheby's 10–11 July 1986]. TLS 4 July 1986.
Donohue, J. Recent studies of Oscar Wilde. NCTR 16 1988.
Oscar Wilde. B. Shapero [sale catalogue]. Introd by M. Holland 1989.
Morgan, M. (comp). File on Wilde. 1990.
Page, N. (comp). An Oscar Wilde chronology. 1991.
Donohue, J. Oscar Wilde refashioned: a review of recent scholarship. NCTR 21 1993.
Small, I. Oscar Wilde revalued: an essay on new materials and methods of research. Greensboro NC 1993.
Wilde, Beardsley and the eighteen-nineties: the collection of Giles Gordon. R. Gekoski [sale catalogue]. Introd by P. Ackroyd 1994.
Beckson, K. Wilde encyclopedia. New York 1998.
Raby, P. (ed). The Cambridge companion to Oscar Wilde. Cambridge 1997.

Complete works

Complete editions

Werke. Tr O. Hauser. 10 vols Vienna and Leipzig 1906–8; 12 vols in 4 Berlin 1906–9.
Writings. Florentine uniform edn [unauthorised]. 15 vols (with introd by R. Le Gallienne), London and New York 1907; rptd Boston 1909. See R. Ross TLS 28 June 1907; R. Le Gallienne TLS 3 Oct 1907; R. Ross TLS 10 Oct 1907.
[Collected works.] Ed R. Ross. First [authorised] collected edn. 14 vols [unnumbered], 1908. 13 vols ptd in London; the remaining vol, The Picture of Dorian Gray, ptd in Paris. In 1922 a parallel 15th vol was issued containing the spurious For love of the king: a Burmese masque. The entire edn was reissued in facs 1969.
REVIEWS: Nation 21 Mar 1908; Pall Mall Gazette 25 Mar 1908; [Spender, J. A.] Westminster Gazette 28 Mar and 8 Aug 1908; Sunday Times 29 Mar 1908; Standard 30 Mar 1908; Onlooker 4 Apr 1908; [Thomas, Edward] Daily Chron 13 Apr 1908; [M[ontague], C. E. M.] Manchester Guardian 13 Apr 1908; Birmingham Daily Post 24 Apr 1908; [Symons, A.] Athenaeum 16 May 1908; [Child, H.] TLS 18 June 1908; [Turner, R.] Daily Telegraph 8 July 1908; [D[ouglas], [Lord] A.] Acad 11 July 1908; Saturday Rev 8 Aug 1908.
REVIEW (of play vols only): [Hankin, St J.] Fortnightly Rev 1 May 1908.
REVIEWS (of Reviews and Miscellanies vols only): Glasgow Herald 16 Oct 1908; Manchester Courier 16 Oct 1908; Pall Mall Gazette 16 Oct 1908; Outlook 17 Oct 1908; [Chesterton, G. K.] Daily News 19 Oct 1908; [Turner, R.] Daily Telegraph 23 Oct 1908; New Age 24 Oct 1908; Manchester Guardian 26 Oct 1908; Bookman Nov 1908; TLS 5 Nov 1908; Acad 7 Nov 1908; Daily Mail 7 Nov 1908; Daily Graphic 13 Nov 1908; Morning Leader 4 Dec 1908; Literary World 15 Dec 1908; [S., D.] Liverpool Daily Courier 18 Dec 1908.
Works. Tauchnitz edn. 11 vols Leipzig 1908–11.
Works. Ed R. Ross. Authorised [Amer] edn. 14 vols Boston 1910; rptd 1911.
Works. Ed R. Ross. Second collected edn. 14 vols 1909–11. 12 vols ptd in London 1909; a 13th vol, The Picture of Dorian Gray, ptd in Paris 1910; a 14th vol, Salome [English text with note by R. Ross, bibliography by W. Ledger, and 16 illus by A. Beardsley] issued in 1911 but dated '1912'; entire edn rptd Boston 1911.
Complete works. 12 vols Garden City NY 1923 [with introds by R. Le Gallienne; J. Forbes-Robertson; W. B. Yeats; A. B. Walkley; J. Drinkwater; A. Symons; and others]. Rptd as Writings 1925 and Complete works 1927.
Works. (with 15 original drawings by D. Nachshen). London and Glasgow [1931].
Obras completas. Tr R. Baeza. Madrid 1917– ; 1929.
Obras completas. Tr J. Gómez de la Serna. Madrid 1943.
Complete works. Ed with introd by G. F. Maine, London and Glasgow 1948; rev with introd by V. Holland 1966; rev with introd by M. Holland 1994.
Sämtliche werke. Ed N. Kohl 10 vols Frankfurt 1982.

Oeuvres complètes. Tr A. Delahaye et al 2 vols Paris. Vol 1, 1992; vol 2 forthcoming.
[Works.] Ed with introd by M. Holland 3 vols 1993.
Oeuvres complètes. Ed J. Gattégno, Paris forthcoming.
Complete works. Oxford English Text Edition. General eds R. Jackson and I. Small, 8 vols Oxford. In progress.

Complete plays

Plays. 4 vols Boston and London 1905–8.
The complete plays. Introd by H. M. Hyde 1988.
The plays of Oscar Wilde. Ed with introd by R. Cave. Harmondsworth. Forthcoming.

Selections and anthologies

Poems by Oscar Wilde, also his lecture on the English renaissance. New York 1882.
Echoes. Ed G. Enthoven [1890?].
Oscariana. Epigrams [chosen by Mrs O. Wilde]. 1895; 1910 [new selection from Sebastian Melmoth, *see below*], 1912.
The George Alexander birthday book. 1903.
Sebastian Melmoth [Oscar Wilde]. 1904, 1905, 1908, 1911.
Epigrams and aphorisms by Oscar Wilde. Boston 1905.
The best of Oscar Wilde . . . collected by Oscar Hermann. Ed W. W. Massee, New York [1905].
Decorative art in America . . . together with letters, reviews, and interviews. Ed R. B. Glaenzer, New York 1906.
The wisdom of Oscar Wilde. Ed T. Scott, New York 1906, 1908.
Poems . . . with The ballad of Reading gaol. With note by R. Ross 1909.
The Oscar Wilde calendar. Ed S. Mason [C. S. Millard] 1910; rev 1911, 1914.
Selected poems, including The ballad of Reading gaol. Ed R. Ross 1911 (4 edns); 1925 (13th edn).
Great thoughts from Oscar Wilde. 1912.
Charmides and other poems. 1913, 1914.
Selected prose. Ed R. Sherard [with introd by R. Ross] 1914.
Aphorisms of Oscar Wilde. Ed G. N. Sutton 1914.
Poems in prose and private letters [with introd by F. Harris]. 1919.
A critic in Pall Mall (collected reviews). 1919.
Art and decoration. 1920.
The picture of Dorian Gray, The importance of being earnest, The ballad of Reading gaol and other works of Oscar Wilde. Ed H. Pearson 1930 (EL); reissued 1955 as Plays, prose writings and poems; rev with introd by I. Murray 1975.
Les songes merveilleux du dormeur eveille. Le chant du cygne: contes parlés d'Oscar Wilde. Ed G. de Saix, Paris 1942.
The portable Oscar Wilde. Ed R. Aldington, New York 1946; rptd Harmondsworth 1977; rev with introd by S. Weintraub 1981.
Essays. Ed H. Pearson 1950.
Five famous plays. Ed A. Harris 1952.
The epigrams of Oscar Wilde. Ed A. Redman [with introd by V. Holland] 1952.
Selected essays and poems. Ed H. Pearson, Harmondsworth 1954; reissued as De profundis and other writings 1973.
Plays. Harmondsworth 1954; reissued as The importance of being earnest and other plays 1986.
Poems and essays [with introd by K. Amis]. 1956.
Selections from the work. Ed G. Hough, New York 1960.
The wit and wisdom of Oscar Wilde. Ed C. Hewetson 1960, 1967.
Five plays. Ed H. Pearson, New York 1961.
Selected writings. Ed with introd by R. Ellmann, Oxford 1961 (WC).
Lady Windermere's fan and The importance of being earnest. Introd by L. Kronenberger 1962.
The artist as critic: critical writings of Oscar Wilde. Ed with introd by R. Ellmann, New York 1968.
The literary criticism of Oscar Wilde. Ed with introd by S. Weintraub, Lincoln NE 1968.
The wit of Oscar Wilde. Ed S. McCann 1969.
The witticisms of Oscar Wilde. Ed D. Stanford 1971.
Some early poems and fragments. [Ed A. Anderson], Edinburgh 1974.
The illustrated Oscar Wilde. Introd by R. Gasson 1977.
The complete shorter fiction. Ed with introd by I. Murray, Oxford 1979.
Extracts from the poems of Oscar Wilde with sixteen illustrations by Mervyn Peake. Ed M. Gilmore 1980.
The annotated Oscar Wilde. Introd by H. M. Hyde 1982.
Two society comedies: A woman of no importance and An ideal husband. Ed with introd by I. Small and R. Jackson 1983; rev and reissued as separate vols 1993.
The writings of Oscar Wilde. Ed with introd by I. Murray, Oxford 1989 (OSA).
The fireworks of Oscar Wilde. Ed O. D. Edwards 1989.
The sayings of Oscar Wilde. Ed H. Russell [with introd by J. Bayley] 1989.
The soul of man and prison writings. Ed with introd by I. Murray, Oxford 1990 (WC).
Oscar Wilde: plays, prose writings and poems. Introd by T. Eagleton 1991.
Aristotle at afternoon tea: the rare Oscar Wilde [reviews]. Ed J. W. Jackson 1991.
The importance of being earnest and related writings. Ed with introd by J. Bristow 1992.
The importance of being earnest and other plays. Ed with introd by P. Raby, Oxford 1995 (WCp).

§1

Individual works and premières

Most of the following works appear in the collected edns (including trns) listed above. In view of the vast number of texts available this section has been limited to items of bibliographical or historical significance.

Newdigate prize poem. Ravenna. Recited in the [Sheldonian] theatre, Oxford, June 26, 1878. Oxford 1878. Rptd in all Complete works noted above.

Vera; or, the nihilists. A drama in four acts. T. 1880; Vera; or, the nihilists. A drama in a prologue and four acts, [New York] 1882; Vera; or, the nihilists. A drama in a prologue and four acts with 'corrections and additions made by the author in his original copy', 1902; rptd in all Complete works and Complete plays noted above; ed F. M. Reed as Vera; or, the nihilist [*sic*], Lampeter, Dyfed 1989. First performed as Vera, or the nihilist [*sic*], New York Union Sq 20 Aug 1883.
REVIEWS: New York Herald 12 and 21 Aug 1883; New York Times 21 Aug 1883; [New York] World 21 Aug 1883; [New York] Evening Post 21 Aug 1883; New York Daily Tribune 21, 26 and 27 Aug 1883; New York Mirror 25 Aug 1883; Spirit of the Times 25 Aug 1883; Punch 1 Sep 1883.

Poems. 1881 (3 edns); rev 1882 (4th–5th edns); Boston 1881, 1882; 5th edn reissued with designs by C. Ricketts, 1892. Rptd in all Complete edns noted *above*.
REVIEWS: [M., E. A.] Lady's Pictorial 9 July 1881; Athenaeum 23 July 1881; Punch 23 July 1881, 12 Nov 1881; Sat Rev 23 July 1881; [Browning, O.] Acad 30 July 1881; [Browne, F. F.] Dial (Chicago) Aug 1881; [Yates, E.] World 3 Aug 1881; Brownell, W. C. Nation (New York) 4 Aug 1881; Spectator 13 Aug 1881; Century (New York) Nov 1881; New York Times 7 Dec 1881; Higginson, T. W. Woman's Jnl (Boston) 4 Feb 1882; Musical and Literary Times (Halifax, Nova Scotia) Feb 1882; [Bierce, A.] Wasp (San Francisco) 31 Mar 1882.

L'envoi. Introd to R. Rodd, Rose leaf and apple leaf, Philadelphia 1882.

The Duchess of Padua: a [verse] tragedy of the XVI century . . . written in Paris in the XIX century. [New York 1883?]; tr Ger (by M. Meyerfeld), Berlin [1904]; The Duchess of Padua: a tragedy of the sixteenth century [English prose text from Ger trn], 'New

York' [Paris 1905]; The Duchess of Padua: a play with preface by R. Ross, 1907; 1908; rptd in all Complete edns and Complete plays noted above. First performed as Guido Ferranti. (New York Broadway 26 Jan 1891).

REVIEWS (of Ross 1907 edn): Manchester Courier 13 Feb 1908; [Scott-James, R. A.] Daily News 13 Feb 1908; [Thomas, E.] Daily Chron 13 Feb 1908; Birmingham Daily Post 14 Feb 1908; [C., B.] Morning Leader 14 Feb 1908; Daily Graphic 14 Feb 1908; [Courtney, W. L.] Daily Telegraph 19 Feb 1908; [M[ontague], C. E.] Manchester Guardian 20 Feb 1908; Glasgow Herald 24 Feb 1908; Evening Standard and St James's Gazette 27 Feb 1908; [S., D.] Liverpool Daily Courier 28 Feb 1908; Globe 27 Mar 1908; New Age 4 Apr 1908; Literary World 15 Apr 1908.

REVIEWS (of first performance): New York Daily Tribune 27 Jan 1891; New York Sun 27 Jan 1891; New York Times 27 Jan 1891; [New York] World 27 Jan 1891; New York Dramatic Mirror 31 Jan 1891; Critic (New York) 7 Feb 1891.

The happy prince and other tales. Contains The happy prince; The nightingale and the rose; The selfish giant; The devoted friend; The remarkable rocket [illustr W. Crane and J. Hood]. 1888 (2 edns) (facs with introd by J. Espey 1977), 1902, 1905, 1907, 1908, 1910, illustr C. Robinson 1913. Boston 1888, 1890, 1894. Rptd in all Complete edns noted above.

REVIEWS: [Quilter, H.] Universal Rev 15 June 1888; Athenaeum 1 Sep 1888; [Ross, A. G.] Saturday Rev 20 Oct 1888.

The picture of Dorian Gray. Novel. New York 1890; London, New York and Melbourne 1891, 1895; Paris 1901, 1905; 1st pbd (in earlier form) in Lippincott's Monthly Mag July [20 June] 1890; preface 1st pbd in Fortnightly Rev Mar 1891; rptd in all Complete edns noted above; dramatised by G. C. Lounsbury (Vaud 28 Aug 1913); ed W. Edener [Lippincott text] Nürnberg 1964; ed I. Murray 1974 (Oxford Eng Novels); ed D. L. Lawler, New York 1988 (The picture of Dorian Gray: authoritative texts, backgrounds, reviews and reactions, criticism); tr Du 1893, Fr 1895, Ger 1901, Cz, Danish, Rus, Swed 1905, Finnish, Ital, Polish 1906, Magyar 1907, Greek, Yiddish 1912.

REVIEWS (of 1890 Lippincott text): [Jeyes, S. H.] St James's Gazette 24 June 1890 (see also Wilde's letters to the editor (26, 27, 28 and 30 June), letter from A London Editor (28 June), and Notes (2 July)); St James's Budget 27 June 1890 (see also Mr Oscar Wilde and the St James's Gazette (4 July)); Daily Chron 30 June 1890 (see also Wilde's letter 2 July); Christian Leader (Glasgow) 3 July 1890; Scottish Leader (Edinburgh) 3 July 1890; Scots Observer (Edinburgh) 5 July 1890 (see also Wilde's letters to the editor (12 July, 2 and 16 Aug)); Speaker 5 July 1890; Christian World 10 July 1890; Light 12 July 1890; Punch 19 July 1890; [Hawthorne, J.] Lippincott's Monthly Mag (Philadelphia and London) Sep 1890; [Wharton, A.] Lippincott's Monthly Mag (Philadelphia and London) Sep 1890.

REVIEWS: (of 1891 text): Pall Mall Gazette 3 Mar 1891; Punch 14 Mar 1891; Glasgow Herald 30 Apr 1891; Manchester Guardian 5 May 1891; Theatre 1 June 1891; Athenaeum 27 June 1891; [Pater, Walter] Bookman Nov 1891.

REVIEWS (of Lounsbury dramatisation): World 2 Sep 1913; Era 3 Sep 1913; Sketch 3 and 10 Sep 1913; Stage 4 Sep 1913; Illus London News 6 Sep 1913; The Times 29 Aug 1913.

Intentions (essays). The decay of lying first pbd Nineteenth Cent Jan 1889; Pen pencil and poison first pbd Fortnightly Rev Jan 1889; The critic as artist first pbd as The true function and value of criticism; with some remarks on the importance of doing nothing Nineteenth Cent July and Sep 1890; The truth of masks first pbd as Shakespeare and stage costume Nineteenth Cent May 1885. 1891, 1894, New York 1891, 1894. Rptd in all Complete edns above; tr Fr (J. J. Reynaud) 1905.

REVIEWS: The Times 7 May 1891; Pall Mall Gazette 12 May 1891; Speaker 16 May 1891; Punch 30 May 1891; Photo Amer Rev June 1891; Athenaeum 6 June 1891; Observer 14 June 1891; [Le Gallienne, R.] Acad 4 July 1891; [Symons, A.] Speaker 4 July 1891; Birmingham Daily Post 6 July 1891; Nation (New York) 9 July 1891; Spectator 11 July 1891; Literary Opinion July 1891; Newcastle Daily Chron 22 Sep 1891; [Middleman, J.] London Figaro 10 Oct 1891; Yorkshire Post 14 Oct 1891; [Carpenter, G. R.] Andover Rev (Boston) Dec 1891; Graphic 12 Dec 1891; [Repplier, A.] North Amer Rev (Cedar Falls IA) Jan 1892.

Lord Arthur Savile's crime and other stories. Lord Arthur Savile's crime first pbd Court and Soc Rev May 1887; The model millionaire first pbd World June 1887; The sphinx without a secret first pbd as Lady Alroy World May 1887; The Canterville ghost first pbd Court and Soc Rev Feb and Mar 1887. 1891; New York 1891; Rptd in all Complete edns noted above.

REVIEWS: Graphic 22 Aug 1891; [Sharp, W.] Acad 5 Sep 1891; [Yeats, W. B.] United Ireland 26 Sep 1891; Athenaeum 23 Jan 1892; Nation (New York) 11 Feb 1892.

A house of pomegranates. The young king first pbd Lady's Pictorial Dec 1888; The birthday of the infanta first pbd as The birthday of the little princess Paris Illustré Mar 1889; The fisherman and his soul; The star-child. Stories. Illustr C. Ricketts and C. Shannon 1891 (facs with introd by J. Espey 1977); 6th edn illustr J. King 1915; New York 1918 with introd by H. L. Mencken; rptd in all Complete edns noted above.

REVIEWS: Speaker 28 Nov 1891 (see also Wilde's letter 5 Dec); Pall Mall Gazette 30 Nov 1891 (see also Wilde's letter 11 Dec); Liverpool Daily Courier 16 Dec 1891; Lady's Pictorial 19 Dec 1891; [Saintsbury, G.] New Rev Jan 1892; Speaker 2 Jan 1892; Mag of Art Jan 1892; Athenaeum 6 Feb 1892; Saturday Rev 6 Feb 1892; Nation (New York) 16 June 1892; Spectator 14 Apr 1894.

Salomé. Drame en un acte [Fr text]. T. Paris 1893, 1907; London 1893. Salome. A tragedy in one act: translated from the French of Oscar Wilde [by Wilde and Lord A. Douglas]. Pictured by Aubrey Beardsley. London and Boston 1894; rptd in all Complete edns and Complete plays noted above; Salome ... with sixteen drawings by Aubrey Beardsley [and a note by R. Ross] '1907' [1906]; with introd by H. Jackson 1938; tr R. A. Walker [1st edn with unexpurgated Beardsley plates] 1957; tr V. Holland 1957; with introd by S. Berkoff 1989. First performed Paris, Théâtre de l'Oeuvre 11 Feb 1896; Berlin Kleines Theater 22 Feb 1902; London Bijou 10 May 1905; with A Florentine tragedy London King's Hall, CG 10 June 1906. Tr Du 1893; Swed 1895; Ger (H. Lachman) 1903, (F. Uhl) 1908; Polish 1904; Rus 1904; Cz 1905; Ital 1906; Greek 1907; Magyar 1908; Catalan 1908; Yiddish 1909; Sp nd.

REVIEWS (of text): The Times 23 Jan 1893 (see also Wilde's letter 2 Mar); [Le Gallienne, R.] Star 22 Feb 1893; Pall Mall Gazette 27 Feb 1893; Westminster Budget 10 Mar 1893; [Archer, W.] Black and White 11 May 1893; [Douglas, Lord Alfred] Spirit Lamp May 1893.

REVIEWS (of first Eng performances (a press boycott restricted coverage of the first London stagings. Max Beerbohm of the Saturday Rev was an important exception)): [Beerbohm, M.] Saturday Rev 13 May 1905; [Beerbohm, M.] Saturday Rev 6 June 1906; Speaker 14 July 1906.

Lady Windermere's fan: a play about a good woman. C. 1893; [Acting edn] London and New York [nd]; rptd in all Complete edns and Complete plays noted above; Paris [London] 1903, 1911, New York and London [1921], ed I. Small 1980. First performed StJ 20 Feb 1892.

REVIEWS: [McC[arthy], J. H.] Sunday Sun 21 Feb 1892; Observer 21 Feb 1892; Referee 21 Feb 1892; Reynolds's Newspaper 21 Feb 1892; Sunday Times 21 Feb 1892; Daily Chron 22 Feb 1892; Daily Graphic 22 Feb 1892; Daily News 22 Feb 1892; Daily Telegraph 22 Feb 1892; Morning Advertiser 22 Feb 1892; Morning Post 22 Feb 1892; [Scott, C.] Daily Telegraph 22 and 26 Feb 1892; Standard 22 Feb 1892; The Times 22 Feb 1892; Echo 22 Feb 1892; Evening News and Post 22 Feb 1892; Players 23 Feb and 8 Mar 1892; Truth 25 Feb

1892; St James's Gazette 26 Feb 1892 (see also Wilde's letter 27 Feb, and reply by 'Tame' 29 Feb); Athenaeum 27 Feb 1892; Black and White 27 Feb 1892; Era 27 Feb 1892; Lady's Pictorial 27 Feb 1892; [Moy, T.] Graphic 27 Feb 1892; Queen 27 Feb 1892; [Scott, C.] Illus London News 27 Feb 1892; Vanity Fair 27 Feb 1892; [W[alkley], A. B.] Speaker 27 Feb 1892; Moonshine 5 Mar 1892; Punch 5 and 12 Mar 1892; [Wedmore, F.] Acad 5 Mar 1892; [Scott, C.] Players 8 Mar 1892; Lady 10 Mar 1892; [Watson, W.] Spectator 26 Mar 1892; Illustrated Sporting and Dramatic News 9 Apr and 5 May 1892; Pick-Me-Up 16 Apr 1892; Modern Soc 27 Apr 1892; [McCarthy, J. H.] GM Apr 1892; Theatre Apr 1892; Westminster Rev Apr 1892; Spectator 26 Nov? 1892.

The sphinx. (Poem) illustr C. Ricketts. 1894; Boston 1894; rptd in all Complete edns noted above; with note by R. Ross London and New York 1910; illustr Alastair 1920.
REVIEWS: Daily News 11 June 1894; Pall Mall Budget 21 June 1894; [Henley, W. E.] Pall Mall Gazette 9 July 1894; [Leverson, A.] Punch 21 July 1894; Athenaeum 25 Aug 1894.

A few maxims for the instruction of the over-educated. Saturday Rev Nov 1894; rptd Letters.

Phrases and philosophies for the use of the young. Chameleon Dec 1894.

A woman of no importance. 1894; New York 1894; Paris 1903; rptd in all Complete works and Complete plays noted above; adapted P. Dehn 1954; ed I. Small 1983, rev 1993.
REVIEW: [Yeats, W. B.] Bookman Mar 1895. First performed H 19 Apr 1893.
REVIEWS (of first performance): Mother 18 and 25 Apr 1893; [Gielgud, K. T.] 19 Apr 1893 in A Victorian playgoer 1980; Daily Chron 20 Apr 1893; Daily Graphic 20 Apr 1893; Daily News 20 Apr 1893; Daily Telegraph 20 Apr 1893; Echo 20 Apr 1893; Evening News 20 Apr 1893; Morning Post 20 Apr 1893; St James's Gazette 20 Apr 1893; Stage 20 Apr 1893; Standard 20 Apr 1893; The Times 20 Apr 1893; Athenaeum 22 Apr 1893; Era 22 Apr 1893; Queen 22 and 29 Apr 1893; Observer 23 Apr 1893; People 23 Apr 1893; Sunday Times 23 Apr 1893; Weekly Sun 23 Apr 1893; [A[rcher], W.] World 26 Apr 1893; Lady's World 26 Apr 1893; Sketch 26 Apr 1893; Smart Soc 26 Apr 1893; Vanity Fair 27 Apr 1893; Westminster Budget 28 Apr 1893; Black and White 29 Apr 1893; Illus London News 29 Apr 1893; Lady's Pictorial 29 Apr 1893; Modern Soc 29 Apr 1893; [Thomas, M.] Graphic 29 Apr 1893; [W[alkley], A. B.] Speaker 29 Apr 1893; Illustrated Sporting and Dramatic News 29 Apr and 6 May 1893; Punch 6, 13, 26 May and 3 June 1893; Saturday Rev 6 May 1893; Pick-Me-Up 20 May 1893; Illus Church News 27 May 1893; Theatre June 1893; Westminster Rev June 1893.

The soul of man. First pbd as The soul of man under socialism, Fortnightly Rev Feb 1891. Essay. 1895; 1907, 1909, introd by R. Ross 1912; rptd in all Complete edns noted above.
REVIEW: Spectator 7 Feb 1891.

The ballad of Reading gaol by C.3.3. Poem. 1898 (6 edns), Wilde's name first appears on title page of 7th edn 1899; rptd in all Complete edns noted above; 1910 [shorter version based on original draft]. With woodcuts by F. Masereel 1924. Introd by B. Rascoe and lithographs by Z. Gay, New York 1937; tr Fr 1898, Swed 1907, Ger [1907], Magyar 1912, Norwegian [1915], Rus 1919.
REVIEWS: Sunday Special 13 Feb 1898; [B., N. O.] Echo 19 Feb 1898; Acad 26 Feb 1898; [B[ooth], W. B.] War Cry 26 Feb 1898; [Henley, W. E.] Outlook 5 Mar 1898; Referee 6 Mar 1898; [Symons, A.] Saturday Rev 12 Mar 1898; [G., S.] Pall Mall Gazette 19 Mar 1898; Literature 26 Mar 1898; [Jerrold, L.] Revue Blanche (Paris) 15 Apr 1898; [Davray, H.-D.] Mercure de France (Paris) Apr 1898.

The importance of being earnest: a trivial comedy for serious people by the author of Lady Windermere's fan [3 acts]. 1899; London and New York [1903]; rptd in all Complete edns and Complete plays noted above, with exception of V. Holland 1966 (revision of Maine 1948) which uses a composite 4-act text; tr Ger as Bunbury (1902) and Ernst sein! (1903); ed S. A. Dickson as The importance of being earnest ... in four acts as originally written, 2 vols New York 1956; ed V. Holland as The original four-act version of The importance of being earnest, 1957; ed R. Jackson 1980; ed R. Berggren as The definitive four-act version of The importance of being earnest [C. Frohman's New York prompt book], New York 1987; ed J. Donohue as Oscar Wilde's The importance of being earnest: a reconstructive critical edition of the text of the first production ..., 1895, Gerrards Cross 1995. First performed (3 acts) StJ 14 Feb 1895.
REVIEW (of text): Outlook 18 Mar 1899.
REVIEWS (of first performance): St James's Gazette 18 Jan 1895; Daily Chron 15 Feb 1895; Daily Graphic 15 Feb 1895; Daily News 15 Feb 1895; Daily Telegraph 15 Feb 1895; Evening News 15 Feb 1895; Evening Standard 15 Feb 1895; Morning Advertiser 15 Feb 1895; Morning Post 15 Feb 1895; Standard 15 Feb 1895; The Times 15 Feb 1895; [Wells, H. G.] Pall Mall Gazette 15 Feb 1895; Black and White 16 Feb 1895; Observer 17 Feb 1895; People 17 Feb 1895; Reynolds's Newspaper 17 Feb 1895; Sunday Times 17 Feb 1895; Weekly Sun 17 Feb 1895; [A[rcher], W.] World 20 Feb 1895; Sketch 20 Feb and 20 Mar 1895; Stage 21 Feb 1895; Truth 21 Feb 1895; Realm 22 Feb 1895; Athenaeum 23 Feb 1895; Black and White 23 Feb 1895; Graphic 23 Feb 1895; Illus London News 23 Feb 1895; Lika Joko 23 Feb 1895; Punch 23 Feb 1895; [S[haw], G. B.] Saturday Rev 23 Feb 1895; W[alkley], A. B. Speaker 23 Feb 1895; Theatre 1 Mar 1895; [Leverson, A.] Punch 2 Mar 1895.

An ideal husband: by the author of Lady Windermere's fan. C. 1899; rptd in all Complete edns and Complete plays noted above; new acting version [R. Ross] 1914; ed R. Jackson 1983, rev 1993. First performed H 3 Jan 1895.
REVIEWS: [Gielgud, K. T.] 3 Jan 1895 (in A Victorian playgoer 1980); Daily Chron 4 Jan 1895; Daily Graphic 4 Jan 1895; Daily News 4 Jan 1895; Daily Telegraph 4 Jan 1895; Echo 4 Jan 1895; Evening News 4 Jan 1895; Evening Standard 4 Jan 1895; Morning Advertiser 4 Jan 1895; Morning Post 4 Jan 1895; St James's Gazette 4 Jan 1895; Standard 4 Jan 1895; The Times 4 Jan 1895; [Wells, H. G.] Pall Mall Gazette 4 Jan 1895; Era 5 Jan 1895; Observer 6 Jan 1895; People 6 Jan 1895; Reynolds's Newspaper 6 Jan 1895; Sunday Times 6 Jan 1895; Weekly Sun 6 Jan 1895; [A[rcher], W.] World 9 Jan 1895; [Burgess, G.] Sketch 9 Jan 1895; Stage 10 Jan 1895; Realm 11 Jan 1895; Athenaeum 12 Jan 1895; Black and White 12 Jan 1895; Gentlewoman 12 Jan 1895; Illustrated Sporting and Dramatic News 12, 19 and 26 Jan 1895; Lady's Pictorial 12 Jan 1895; [Leverson, A.] Punch 12 Jan 1895; Lika Joko 12 Jan 1895; Modern Soc 12 Jan 1895; Queen 12 Jan 1895; [Scott, C.] Illus London News 12 Jan 1895; [S[haw], G. B.] Saturday Rev 12 Jan 1895; [W[alkley], A. B.] Speaker 12 Jan 1895; [Ross, R.] St James's Gazette 18 Jan 1895; Pick-Me-Up 19 Jan 1895; Critic (New York) 26 Jan 1895; Punch 2 Feb 1895; Sketch 13 Feb 1895; Theatre Feb 1895.

Essays, criticisms, and reviews. 1901.

De profundis. Autobiography. Berlin (tr M. Meyerfeld) 1905; German tr tr into Fr, Ital and Sp 1905; 1st Eng text New York and London 1905; with additional matter and preface by R. Ross '1908' [1909]; The suppressed portion of De profundis ... now for the first time published, New York 1913; ed V. Holland as De profundis. Being the first complete and accurate version of Epistola: in carcere et vinculis, 1949; ed R. Hart-Davis, To Lord Alfred Douglas in Letters 1962, pp. 423–511 [most complete text]; ed J. Barzun, De profundis [unexpurgated], New York 1964.
REVIEWS: [Walker, H.] Hibbert Jnl Jan 1905; [B., W. F.] Echo 23 Feb 1905; [Courtney, W. L.] Daily Telegraph 23 Feb 1905 (see also letter 24 Feb); [Douglas, J.] Star 23 Feb 1905; [Fyfe, H. H.] Daily Mail 23 Feb 1905 (see also letter 13 Mar); North Mail (Newcastle-upon-Tyne) 23 Feb 1905; [Robinson, B. F.] Daily Express 23 Feb 1905; [Thomas, E.] Daily Chron 23 Feb 1905; [Lucas, E. V.] TLS 24 Feb

1905; [Berlyn, A.] World 28 Feb 1905; [B., W. T. A.] Birmingham Gazette and Express 1 Mar 1905; [D[ouglas], [Lord] A.] Motorist and Traveller 1 Mar 1905; [Beerbohm, M.] Vanity Fair 2 Mar 1905; [S., E. W.] Sunday School Chron 2 Mar 1905; [Cunningham Graham, R. B.] Saturday Rev 4 Mar 1905; [Northcroft, G. H.] London Opinion 4 Mar 1905; [Street, G. S.] Outlook 4 Mar 1905; [Murray, H.] Sunday Sun 5 Mar 1905; [Montefiore, D. B.] New Age 9 Mar 1905; ['W.'] Christian Leader (Glasgow) 9 and 23 Mar 1905; ['Viator'] Church Times 10 Mar 1905; [Archer, W.] Morning Leader 11 Mar 1905; [S[cott], N. C.] Free Lance 11 Mar 1905; [Kerr, A.] Der Tag 12 Mar 1905; [Dawson, W. J.] Essex County Chron 24 Mar 1905; ['S.'] New Age 30 Mar 1905; [Stead, W. T.] Rev of Revs Mar 1905; [Barry, Rev. W.] Bookman Apr 1905; [Dickinson, G. L.] Independent Rev Apr 1905; [Petre, M. D.] Month Apr 1905; [Lord, W. F.] Nineteenth Cent May 1905; Theatre Mag (New York) May 1905; [Tyssul-Davis, J.] Inquirer 12 Aug 1905; [Gorton, Rev C.] Manchester Courier 16 Aug 1905; [B., C.] N & Q 26 Aug 1905 (see also letters by W. F. Prideaux, Stuart Mason, and E. Menken 16 Sep); [Ryan, F.] Free Thinker 3 Sep 1905; [Bartlett, V.] Examiner 7 Dec 1905; Manchester Courier 20 Mar 1908; Outlook 21 Mar 1908; Pall Mall Gazette 25 Mar 1908; Daily Graphic 27 Mar 1908; Globe 27 Mar 1908; Literary World 15 Apr 1908; Morning Leader 12 June 1908; New Age 27 June 1908; [S., D.] Liverpool Daily Courier 21 Aug 1908.

The rise of historical criticism. Essay. Hartford CT 1905.

A Florentine tragedy [with additional first scene by T. Sturge Moore]. In Complete plays 1905–8. Rptd in all Complete edns and Complete plays noted above. First performed Berlin Deutsches Theater 12 Jan 1906; London, Kings Hall, CG 10 June 1906 (on double bill with Salome).

REVIEW: [Beerbohm, M.] Saturday Rev 6 June 1906.

Impressions of America. Lecture. Ed S. Mason [C. S. Millard] Sunderland 1906.

La sainte courtisane. Unacted verse fragment. First pbd Works 1909.

The cardinal of Avignon. Unacted verse fragment. First pbd Mason, Bibliography of Oscar Wilde, 1914. *See* Bibliographies, *above.*

To M[argaret]. B[urne-]. J[ones]. Poem. With note by S. Mason. 1920.

The portrait of Mr W. H. New York 1921. Story. First pbd (in earlier form) in Blackwood's Mag July 1890; rptd in all Complete edns noted above; with introd by V. Holland 1958.

Mr and Mrs Daventry. D. [Play by Frank Harris from a scenario by Wilde.] Ed H. M. Hyde 1956. First performed Roy 25 Oct 1900.

REVIEWS: Daily Telegraph 26 Oct 1900; The Times 26 Oct 1900; Era 27 Oct 1900; [Grein, J. T.] Sunday Suppl 28 Oct 1900; Athenaeum 3 Nov 1900; [Beerbohm, M.] Saturday Rev 3 Nov 1900.

Irish poets and the poetry of the nineteenth century. Lecture. Ed R. D. Pepper, San Francisco 1972.

The house beautiful: a reconstruction of Oscar Wilde's American lecture. Ed K. H. F. O'Brien, VS June 1974.

Hellenism. Essay. Edinburgh 1979.

A wife's tragedy. Unfinished prose play. Ed R. Shewan, ThR 7 1982; see also ThR 8 1983.

Oscar Wilde's Oxford notebooks. Ed P. E. Smith II and M. Helfand, New York 1989.

Further reviews of Wilde's publications and plays in performance may be located using Mason and Mikhail, under Bibliographies, above, and Wearing, London stage. *Reprints or summaries of contemporary notices are provided in the following collections:*

Beckson, K. (ed). Oscar Wilde: the critical heritage. 1970.

Tydeman, W. (ed). Wilde: comedies, a casebook. 1982.

Nelson, W. W. Oscar Wilde from Ravenna to Salomé: a survey of contemporary English criticism. Dublin 1987.

Nelson, W. W. Oscar Wilde and the dramatic critics: a study in Victorian theatre. Lund, Sweden 1989.

Morgan, M. (comp). File on Wilde. 1990.

Contributions to periodicals

In addition to the items already listed, Wilde contributed poems, poems in prose, letters, and reviews (signed and unsigned) to a variety of periodicals, including Woman's World, *which he edited from 1887 to 1889,* Art and Letters, Burlington Mag, Centenial Mag, Daily Chron, Daily Telegraph, Dramatic Rev, Dublin Univ Mag, English Illus Mag, Idler, Illus Monitor, Irish Monthly, Kottabos, Macmillan's Mag, [New York] Herald, [New York] World, Our Continent, Pall Mall Budget, Pall Mall Gazette, Pan, Picture Mag, Queen, La Revue Blanche, Routledge's Christmas Annual, St James's Budget, St James's Gazette, St Moritz Post, Saturday Rev, Saunders' Irish Daily News, Scots Observer, Speaker, Spirit Lamp, Sunday Times, Time, The Times, Truth, *and* Waifs and Strays. *See Mason,* Bibliography of Oscar Wilde, *pp. 3–237.*

Letters

Most of Wilde's letters pbd before 1960 are included in Hart-Davis's Letters of Oscar Wilde *(1962). Those listed below are of interest for historical reasons and/or for their accompanying introductions and reminiscences.*

Children in prison and other cruelties of prison life. 1898.

Four letters by Oscar Wilde [to Robert Ross]. 1906.

Wilde v. Whistler; being an acrimonious correspondence on art between Oscar Wilde and James A. McNeill Whistler. 1906.

Resurgam: [six] unpublished letters [to Dalhousie Young, 1897]. Ed C. Shorter 1917.

After Reading: letters of Oscar Wilde to Robert Ross [1897]. [Introd by S. Mason (C. S. Millard)] 1921.

After Berneval: letters of Oscar Wilde to Robert Ross [1897–8]. Introd by M. Adey 1922.

Oscar Wilde's letters to Sarah Bernhardt. Ed S. Dorian, Girard KS 1924.

Some letters from Oscar Wilde to Lord Alfred Douglas, 1892–1897, heretofore unpublished. San Francisco 1924.

Letters to the sphinx from Oscar Wilde [1893–7], with reminiscences of the author by Ada Leverson. 1930.

Sixteen letters from Oscar Wilde [to William Rothenstein]. Ed J. Rothenstein 1930.

Thirty-three letters from Oscar Wilde to Reginald Richard ('Kitten') Harding and William Welsford ('Bouncer') Ward, 1876–1878. In V. Holland, Son of Oscar Wilde, 1954, pp. 209–49.

The letters of Oscar Wilde. Ed R. Hart-Davis 1962.

Gollin, R. M. Beerbohm, Wilde, Shaw, and The good-natured critic: some new letters. BNYPL 68 1964.

Green, D. B. Oscar Wilde and Gabriel Sarrazin: a new Wilde letter. EA 13 1965.

Beckson, K. A new Oscar Wilde letter [to Wilde's American agent E. Marbury]. ELN 8 1971.

Walker, J. Oscar Wilde and Cunningham Graham. N & Q 221 1976.

Oscar Wilde: letters to Graham Hill. [Edinburgh] 1978.

Selected letters of Oscar Wilde. Ed R. Hart-Davis, Oxford 1979.

Berneval: an unpublished letter by Oscar Wilde. Ed J. Mason, Edinburgh 1981.

Oscar Wilde: Graham Hill. A brief friendship. Ed J. Mason, Edinburgh 1982.

More letters of Oscar Wilde. Ed R. Hart-Davis, 1985.

Gatton, J. S. Informal wind-like music: two unpublished letters from Oscar Wilde. ELN 27 1989.

Oscar Wilde on vegetarianism: an unpublished letter to Violet Fane. Ed J. Mason [Edinburgh] 1991.

Wilde letters. In I. Small, Oscar Wilde revalued, Greensboro NC 1993, pp. 27–97.

Attributed or spurious works

Teleny: or, the reverse of the medal: a physiological romance. 2 vols 1893; rptd 1906; ed C. Hirsch, Paris 1934; Paris [1958]; [expurgated] with introd by H. M. Hyde 1966; introd by J. Hirschman, North Hollywood CA 1967; introd by D. Gamlin, San

Diego 1967; introd by W. Leyland, San Francisco 1984; New York 1984; ed J. McRae 1986.
[Bloxam, J. F.] The priest and the acolyte. In The Chameleon 1:1 Dec 1894, pp. 29–47; rptd [1894]; in Writings, New York 1907; The priest and the acolyte with an introductory protest by Stuart Mason [C. S. Millard]. 1907.
[Allinson, A. R.] The Satyricon of Petronius Arbiter ... a new translation ... from the original Latin by Sebastian Melmoth (Oscar Wilde). Paris 1902, New York 1934.
Barbey d'Aurevilly, J. A. What never dies [Ce qui ne meurt pas]. A romance ... translated ... by Sebastian Melmoth, O[scar]. W[ilde]. Paris 1902. In Writings, New York 1907.
[Toon, Mrs C.] For love of the king: a Burmese masque. '1923' [1922]. In Collected works (ed Ross 1908) as added parallel vol 1922.
Smith, H. T. (ed). Psychic messages from Oscar Wilde. 1924; New York 1926 as Oscar Wilde from purgatory: psychic messages from Oscar Wilde.
The ghost-epigrams of Oscar Wilde as taken down through automatic writing by Lazar. 1928.
Constance. Comédie en quatre actes reconstitution inédite par Henri de Briel et Guillot de Saix. In Les Oeuvres Libres n.s. 101, Paris Oct 1954.

§2

Text and theatre history

Much essential bibliographical information is contained in the introductions to and apparatuses accompanying recent texts of single works. See especially the edns of The picture of Dorian Gray *by Murray (1974) and Lawler (1988),* Vera *by Reed (1989),* Lady Windermere's fan *(1980) and* A woman of no importance *(1983; 1993) by Small,* An ideal husband *(1983; 1993) by Jackson, and* The importance of being earnest *by Dickson (1956), Jackson (1980), Berggren (1987), and Donohue (1995).*

Meyerfeld, M. [on first German edn of De Profundis]. New York Times Book Review 21 Dec 1924.
Mason, S. [C. S. Millard]. Who wrote For love of the king? Birmingham [1926].
Bell, T. H. Oscar Wilde's unwritten play [Mr and Mrs Daventry]. Bookman (New York) 71 1930.
Guillot de Saix, L. G. M. Une tragédie de femme [A wife's tragedy] par Oscar Wilde. Mercure 286 1938.
Agate, J. An unwise forgery. Princeton Univ Lib Chron 8 1947.
Thomas, J. D. The composition of Wilde's The harlot's house. MLN 65 1950.
Horodisch, A. Oscar Wilde's Ballad of Reading gaol: a bibliographical study. New York 1954.
Hyde, H. M. The importance of being earnest: the 'lost' scene from Oscar Wilde's play. Listener 4 Nov 1954.
O'Neill, M. J. Unpublished lecture notes of a speech by Oscar Wilde at San Francisco. Univ Rev (Dublin) 1 1955.
Bolton, T. The importance of being earnest. PBSA 50 1956.
E., D. V. The importance of publishing Earnest [in four-act version]. BNYPL 60 1956; also Penultimate Earnest, BNYPL 60 1956.
Wilde's comedy in its first version [review of Dickson's four-act Earnest]. TLS 1 Mar 1957.
Sims, G. Who wrote For love of the king, Oscar Wilde or Mrs Chan Toon? BC 7 1958.
Ms of De profundis made available at British Museum. The Times 2 Jan 1960.
Hyde, H. M. The De profundis affair. Sunday Times 3 Jan 1960.
Harrod, R. Wilde's De profundis. TLS 30 Aug 1963. Replies by J. Lees-Milne 6 Sep; M. Seeker 13 Sep; H. M. Hyde 13 and 20 Sep, 4 Oct, 14 Nov; B. Bridgewater 27 Sep; C. H. Norman 27 Sep, 14 Nov.
Mikhail, E. H. The four-act version of The importance of being earnest. Modern Drama 11 1968.
Donohue, J. W. The first production of The importance of being earnest: a proposal for a reconstructive study. In Essays on nineteenth century British theatre, ed K. Richards and P. Thomson, 1971.
Lawler, D. L. Oscar Wilde's first manuscript of The picture of Dorian Gray. SB 25 1972.
Murray, I. Some elements in the composition of The picture of Dorian Gray. Durham Univ Jnl 33 1972.
Not so fond after all [review of Murray's Dorian Gray]. TLS 26 July 1974; replies: H. M. Hyde 9 Aug and 13 Sep; O. D. Edwards 23 Aug; K. Beckson 30 Aug.
Lawler, D. L. The revisions of Dorian Gray. Victorian Inst Jnl 3 1974.
Espey, J. Resources for Wilde studies at the Clark Library. In Oscar Wilde: two approaches, Los Angeles 1977.
Fong, B. Oscar Wilde: five fugitive poems [from mss in Clark, Beinecke, and Berg Collections]. ELT 22 1979.
Stokes, J. Wilde on Dostoevsky [Wilde's review of Crime and punishment]. N & Q 225 1980.
Andrews, A. Horrible flesh and blood [Wilde's stage directions]. TN 36 1982. *See* R. Jackson, Horrible flesh and blood – a rejoinder, TN 37 1983.
Shewan, R. (ed). A wife's tragedy: an unpublished sketch for a play by Oscar Wilde. ThR 7 1982.
Good, G. Early productions of Oscar Wilde's Salomé. NCTR 11 1983.
Hyde, H. M. The riddle of De profundis: who owns the manuscript? Antigonish Rev 54 1983.
O'Brien, K. H. F. Oscar Wilde: an unsigned book review. N & Q 228 1983.
Shewan, R. Oscar Wilde and A wife's tragedy: facts and conjectures. ThR 8 1983.
Schroeder, H. Oscar Wilde, The portait of Mr W. H. – its composition, publication, and reception. Braunschweig 1984.
Reed, F. M. Oscar Wilde's Vera; or, the nihilist: the history of a failed play. ThS 26 1985.
Gagnier, R. Idylls of the marketplace: Oscar Wilde and the Victorian public. Stanford CA 1986.
Lich, G. E. Anything but a misprint: comments on an Oscar Wilde typescript [of An ideal husband]. South Central Rev 3 1986.
Schroeder, H. Annotations to Oscar Wilde: The portrait of Mr W. H. Braunschweig 1986.
Glavin, J. Deadly earnest and earnest revised: Oscar Wilde's four-act play. Nineteenth-Century Stud 1 1987.
Small, I. and R. Jackson. Some new drafts of a Wilde play [A woman of no importance]. ELT 30 1987.
Lawler, D. L. An inquiry into Oscar Wilde's revisions of The picture of Dorian Gray. New York 1988.
Lewis, R. C. A misattribution: Oscar Wilde's unpublished sonnet on Chatterton. VP 28 1990.
Murray, I. Some problems of editing Wilde's poem The sphinx. Durham Univ Jnl 51 1990.
Powell, K. Oscar Wilde and the theatre of the 1890s. Cambridge 1990.
Raby, P. The making of The importance of being earnest. TLS 20 Dec 1991.
Schroeder, H. Two cruces in Intentions: a source analysis. N & Q 236 1991.
Kaplan, J. H. A puppet's power: George Alexander, Clement Scott, and the replotting of Lady Windermere's fan. TN 46 1992.
Stephens, J. R. The profession of the playwright: British theatre 1800–1900. Cambridge 1992.
Rowell, G. The truth about Vera. NCTR 1993.
Small, I. Oscar Wilde revalued: an essay on new materials and methods of research. Greensboro NC 1993.
Cave, R. A. Wilde designs: some thoughts about recent British productions of his plays. Modern Drama 37 1994.
Danson, L. Wilde in Arden, or the masks of truth [Wilde's revision of The truth of masks]. Modern Drama 37 1994.

Kaplan, J. H. Oscar Wilde's contract for A woman of no importance. TN 48 1994.
Kaplan, J. H. and S. Stowell. Theatre and fashion: Oscar Wilde to the suffragettes. Cambridge 1994.
Raby, P. The origins of The importance of being earnest. Modern Drama 37 1994.
Stokes, J. Wilde interpretations. Modern Drama 37 1994.
Gordon, R. Wilde's plays of modern life on the contemporary British stage. In Rediscovering Oscar Wilde, ed C. G. Sandulescue, Gerrards Cross 1994.
Kaplan, J. H. Wilde in the Gorbals: society drama and citizens theatre. In Rediscovering Oscar Wilde, ed C. G. Sandulescue, Gerrards Cross 1994.
Raby, P. The importance of being earnest: a reader's companion. New York and Oxford 1995.
Jackson, R. Oscar Wilde's contract for a new play, 1900. TN 50 1996.
Tydeman, W. and S. Price. Wilde: Salome. Cambridge 1996 (Plays in Production ser).

Selected criticism (up to 1920), including obituaries

See K. Beckson, Oscar Wilde: the critical heritage *for a survey and discussion of pre–1920 Wilde criticism.*

Hamilton, W. The aesthetic movement in England. 1882.
Gómez Carillo, E. Esquisses: siluetas de escritores y artistas. Madrid 1892.
Nordau, M. Entartung. 2 vols Berlin 1892–3, rev 1896; tr Eng as Degeneration 1895.
Repplier, A. Essays in miniature. 1893.
Symons, A. The decadent movement in literature. Harper's New Monthly Mag 87 1893.
Newman, E. Oscar Wilde: a literary appreciation. Free Rev 4 1895.
Filon, A. Le théâtre anglais. Paris 1896. (Material on Wilde removed from Eng trn.)
Obits: New York Times 1 Dec 1900; Pall Mall Gazette 1 Dec 1900; The Times 1 Dec 1900; [Beerbohm, M.] Saturday Rev 8 Dec 1900; [Davray, H.-D.] Mercure de France 27 Feb 1901.
Grein, J. T. Dramatic criticism: 1900–1. Vol 3 1902.
Greve, F. P. Oscar Wilde. Berlin 1903.
Greve, F. P. Randarabesken zu Wilde. Minden 1903.
Hagemann, C. Oscar Wilde: studien zur modernen welt-literatur. Minden 1904; 1925.
Meyerfeld, M. Wilde in Deutschland. Literarische Echo 15 Jan 1904.
Symons, A. Studies in prose and verse. 1904.
Hofmannsthall, H. von. Sebastian Melmoth. From Der Tag 1905; rptd in Gesammelte werke. Prose 2. Frankfurt 1951. Trn in Selected prose 1952.
Meyerfeld, M. Wilde, Wilde, Wilde. Literarische Echo 15 Apr 1905.
Sewett, A. Oscar Wildes seelische kämpfe. Die nation 1905.
Shaw, G. B. From Neue Freie Presse 1905; rptd as The matter with Ireland, ed D. H. Greene and D. H. Laurence, 1962.
Leadman, W. M. The literary position of Wilde. Westminster Rev 166 1906.
Vickery, W. Oscar Wilde. Cedar Rapids IA 1906.
Woodbridge, H. E. Oscar Wilde: a study in decadent romanticism. Harvard Monthly 41 1906.
Henderson, A. The dramas of Oscar Wilde. Arena [Boston] 37, Aug 1907.
Shaw, B. Dramatic opinions and essays. 1907; rptd in Our theatres in the nineties, 1932.
Borsa, M. Il teatro inglese contemporanea. Milan 1906; tr as The English stage of today, 1908.
Greve, F. Wilde und das drama. Vienna 1908.
Mason, S. [C. S. Millard]. Oscar Wilde: art and morality: a defence of The picture of Dorian Gray. 1908; rev as Oscar Wilde: art and morality; a record of the discussion which followed the publication of Dorian Gray, 1912.
Weisz, E. Psychologische streifzüge Über Oscar Wilde. Leipzig 1908.
Woodbridge, H. E. Wilde as a poet. Poet Lore 19 1908.
Scott-James, R. A. Modernism and Romance. 1908.
Gómez-Carillo, E. El libro de los mujeros. Paris 1909.
Mason, S. [C. S. Millard] and R. Ross. In memoriam Oscar Wilde. 1909.
Pollard, P. Their day in court. 1909.
Joyce, J. Oscar Wilde: il poeta di Salomé. Il piccolo della sera. 24 Mar 1909; rptd in The critical writings of James Joyce, ed E. Mason and R. Ellmann, New York 1959.
Esdaile, A. J. K. The new Hellenism. Fortnightly Rev n.s. 88 1910.
Laurent, R. Études anglaises. Paris 1910.
Piaget, L. Oscar Wilde's place in literature. Dial [Chicago] 48 1910.
Bendz, E. Some stray notes on the personality and writings of Oscar Wilde. Göteborg 1911.
Bennett, A. Suppressions in De profundis. In Books and persons: being comments on a past epoch, 1908–1911, 1911.
Glaenzer, R. B. The story of The ballad of Reading gaol. Bookman [New York] 33 1911.
Henderson, A. Interpreters of life and the modern spirit. 1911.
Montague, C. E. Dramatic values. 1911.
Archer, W. Playmaking: a manual of craftsmanship. 1912.
Crosland, T. W. H. The first stone: on reading the unpublished portions of Oscar Wilde's De profundis. 1912.
Daffner, H. Salome: ihre gestalt in geschichte und kunst. Munich 1912.
Kennedy, J. M. English literature 1880–1905. 1912.
Kenilworth, W. W. A study of Oscar Wilde. New York 1912.
Newton, A. E. Oscar Wilde. Philadelphia 1912.
Ransome, A. Oscar Wilde: a critical study. London and New York 1912, rev edn 1913 [expurgated], rptd New York 1971.
Bock, E. J. Walter Paters einfluss auf Oscar Wilde. Bonn 1913.
Brass, F. K. Oscar Wildes Salome: eine kritische quellenstudie. Munich 1913.
Hopkins, R. T. Oscar Wilde: a study of the man and his work. 1913, rptd 1970.
Jackson, H. The eighteen nineties: a review of art and ideas at the close of the nineteenth century. 1913, 1922.
Turquet-Milnes, G. The influence of Baudelaire in France and England. 1913.
Bendz, E. The influence of Pater and Matthew Arnold in the prose writings of Oscar Wilde. Göteborg and London 1914.
Henderson, A. European dramatists. 1914.
Huneker, J. G. The seven arts. Puck [New York] 76 1914.
Mason, S. [C. S. Millard]. An Oscar Wilde dictionary. 1914.
Chislett, W. The new Hellenism of Oscar Wilde. Sewanee Rev 23 1915.
Throop, G. R. A classical romanticist. Mid-West Quart 2 1915.
Wood, A. Oscar Wilde as a critic. North Amer Rev 202 1915.
Bendz, E. Lord Alfred Douglas's apologia. EStudien 46 1916; rptd in Oscar Wilde, Vienna 1921.
Fehr, B. Oscar Wilde's The harlot's house. Archiv 134 1916.
Powys, J. C. Suspended judgments. New York 1916.
Gargiles, Lady. Petit essai sur Portrait de Dorian Gray d'Oscar Wilde. Paris 1917.
Beerbohm, M. A note on Patience. 1918.
Fehr, B. Studien zu Oscar Wilde's gedichten. Berlin 1918.
Moore, G. Pearson's Mag [New York] 38 1918. Letter to Frank Harris.
Newton, A. E. The amenities of book-collecting and kindred affections. Boston 1918.
O'Sullivan, V. Pearson's Mag [New York] 38 1918. Letter to Frank Harris.
Sinclair, U. Pearson's Mag [New York] 39 1918. Letter to Frank Harris.
Félipe, L. El renacimiento del arte ingles y otros ensayos. Madrid 1920.
Hutchinson, H. G. Portraits of the eighties. 1920.

Mason, S. [C. S. Millard]. Oscar Wilde and the aesthetic movement. Dublin [1920].
Muddimen, B. The men of the nineties. 1920.
Murry, J. M. Oscar Wilde as a tragic hero [response to F. Harris Oscar Wilde]. Athenaeum 1920.
Richter, H. Oscar Wilde's persönlichkeit in seinen gedichten. EStudien 54 1920.
Symons, A. A jester with genius. Bookman 51 1920.
Thomas, L. L'esprit d'Oscar Wilde. Paris 1920.

Biography, reminiscences, contemporary portraits

With Wilde there is not always a clear line between biography and criticism. Some items listed under §2, above, could just as easily have appeared below, and vice versa. In the following section post–1920 biographies are limited to essential works.

Gilbert, W. S. and A. Sullivan. An entirely new and original aesthetic opera . . . entitled Patience; or Bunthorne's bride. (Opéra Comique 23 Apr 1881). [1881].
Ye soul agonies in ye life of Oscar Wilde. Illustr C. Kendrick, New York 1882. Anon.
Whistler, J. A. McNeill. The gentle art of making enemies. London 1890.
Brookfield, C. The poet and the puppets: a travestie suggested by Lady Windermere's fan. (Comedy 19 May 1892). [1892?]; rptd 1979.
Hichens, R. S. The green carnation. 1894, New York 1895; rptd 1949, 1970.
Y. T. O. [L. C. Amery, F. W. Hirst and H. A. Cruso]. Aristophanes at Oxford. Oxford 1894, rptd 1979.
Young, D. Apologia pro Oscar Wilde. [1895.]
Raffalovich, M.-A. Uranisme et unisexualité: étude sur différentes manifestations de l'instinct sexuel. Lyons and Paris 1896.
Sherard, R. H. Oscar Wilde: the story of an unhappy friendship. 1902, 1905; also The life of Oscar Wilde, 1906; The real Oscar Wilde, [1915]; Oscar Wilde 'drunkard and swindler': a reply to George Bernard Shaw, G. J. Renier, Frank Harris, Calvi, Corsica 1933; André Gide's wicked lies about the late Mr Oscar Wilde in Algiers in January, 1895, as translated from the French and broadcast by Dr G. J. Renier, Calvi, Corsica 1933; Oscar Wilde twice defended from André Gide's wicked lies and Frank Harris's cruel libels, Chicago 1934; Bernard Shaw, Frank Harris, and Oscar Wilde, 1937; TLS 1 and 15 Oct 1938.
Blei, F. In memoriam Oscar Wilde. Leipzig 1905.
Gide, A. Oscar Wilde: a study from the French of André Gide, introd by S. Mason [C. S. Millard]. Oxford 1905.
Young, J. M. S. Osrac, the self-sufficient, and other poems, with a memoir of the late Oscar Wilde. 1905.
La Jeunesse, E., A. Gide and F. Blei. Recollections of Oscar Wilde. Tr and introd by P. Pollard, Boston and London 1906.
The trial of Oscar Wilde from the shorthand reports. (In US, The shame of Oscar Wilde.) Paris 1906.
Ingleby, L. C. Oscar Wilde. [1907]; also Oscar Wilde: some reminiscences, [1912].
Terry, E. The story of my life. 1908.
Balen, C. van. Oscar Wilde. Haarlem 1910.
Brémont, A. Comtesse de. Oscar Wilde and his mother: a memoir. 1911.
Ford, F. M. Ancient lights. 1911.
[Millard, C. S.] Oscar Wilde: three times tried. 1912.
Newton, A. Oscar Wilde. 1912.
Howe, P. P. Dramatic portraits. 1913.
Birnbaum, M. Oscar Wilde: fragments and memories. 1914.
Douglas, Lord A. Oscar Wilde and myself. 1914, tr Fr 1917, rptd 1919; also Autobiography, 1929 (in US, My friendship with Oscar Wilde, New York 1932); A letter from Lord Alfred Douglas on André Gide's lies about himself and Oscar Wilde, Calvi, Corsica 1933; Without apology, 1938; Oscar Wilde: a summing-up, 1940.
Harris, F. Oscar Wilde, his life and confessions. 2 vols 1916; rptd with B. Shaw, Memories of Oscar Wilde, New York [1918], rev New York 1930, London 1938, 1965, New York 1974; also with Lord A. Douglas, New preface to The life and confessions of Oscar Wilde, 1925; tr Fr 1928.
Gosse, E. The life of Algernon Charles Swinburne. 1917.
Kernahan, C. In good company. 1917.
Saltus, E. Oscar Wilde: an idler's impression. Chicago 1917.
Epstein, M. Max Reinhardt. Berlin 1918.
Le Gallienne, R. Coming back of Wilde. Munsey's Mag 66 1919.
Aldrich, L. Crowding memories. Boston 1920.
Pearson, H. The life of Oscar Wilde. 1946; US as Oscar Wilde: his life and wit, rev 1954, rptd 1975, Harmondsworth 1985.
Hyde, H. M. (ed). The trials of Oscar Wilde. 1948 (Notable British trials series). (US as The three trials of Oscar Wilde, New York 1956); enlarged edn Harmondsworth 1962. Also Oscar Wilde: the aftermath, 1963; Oscar Wilde, New York 1975, London 1976.
Holland, V. Son of Oscar Wilde. 1954. With foreword by M. Holland, 1987; also Oscar Wilde: a pictorial biography, 1960 (US as Oscar Wilde and his world, New York 1960).
Jullian, P. Oscar Wilde. Paris 1967; tr V. Wyndham 1967.
Kohl, N. (ed). Oscar Wilde: leben und werk in daten und bildern. Frankfurt 1976; rev 1986.
Mikhail, E. H. (ed). Oscar Wilde: interviews and recollections. 2 vols 1979.
Ellmann, R. Oscar Wilde. 1987. *See also* H. Schroeder, Additions and corrections to Richard Ellmann's Oscar Wilde, Braunschweig 1989; J. Stokes, Wilde shot; London Rev of Books 27 Feb 1992; and M. Holland, What killed Oscar Wilde? Spectator 24 Dec 1988 and Wilde as Salomé, TLS 22 July 1994.
Vickers, J. and P. Copeland. The voice of Oscar Wilde: an investigation. B[r] A[ssoc of] S[ound] C[ollections] News 2 1987.
Symons, J. Oscar Wilde: a problem in biography. Council Bluffs IA 1988.
Small, I. Biography reconsidered. In Oscar Wilde revalued, Greensboro NC 1993; also with R. Jackson, Oscar Wilde: a 'writerly' life, Modern Drama 37 1994. [JK]

6
Prose

i. Early nineteenth-century prose 1800–1835

This section has been restricted, with one or two exceptions, to critics, essayists and miscellaneous writers born between 1765 and 1800. Cross-references have been included to critical writings appearing elsewhere. For other nineteenth-century prose writers, see under Religion, English Studies, Political Economy, and Philosophy and Science.

Eliza Acton 1799–1859

Two letters and ms of her poem 'The reception' are in the BL.

§1

Poems. Ipswich 1826, 1827 (2nd edn).
The two portraits. Sudbury Pocket Book 1835. Poem. Anon.
Original poetry by Miss Acton, author of The two portraits. Sudbury Pocket Book 1836.
Chronicles of Castel-Framlingham. Fulcher's Sudbury Journal 1838.
The voice of the north. 1842. Poem.
Modern cookery. 1845, Philadelphia 1845 (ed S. J. Hale), London 1845 (2nd edn), 1845 (4th edn illus), 1846 (5th edn to which is added Directions for carving), 1847 (7th edn), 1849, Philadelphia 1849 (rev and prepared for American housekeepers from the 2nd London edn by S. J. Hale), London 1850, 1853 (13th edn), 1854 (14th edn), 1855 (newly rev and much enlarged), Philadelphia 1858, 1860, London 1861, Philadelphia 1861, London 1864, Philadelphia 1864, London 1865, 1868, Philadelphia 1868, London 1882, 1887 (new edn), London and Glasgow [c. 1905] (35th edn rev and enlarged); The people's book of modern cookery, 1914; [1966] (with an introduction for the modern reader by Penelope Farmer, facs of 1865 edn); The best of Eliza Acton. Recipes from her classic modern cookery, London and Harlow 1968 (selected and ed E. Ray etc, with an introduction by E. David), Harmondsworth 1974; Southover 1993.
The English bread-book. 1857, Southover 1990.

§2

In DNB.

Lucy Aikin, 'Mary Godolphin' 1781–1864

§1

Epistles on women exemplifying their character and condition in various ages and nations. 1810, Boston 1810.
Juvenile correspondence: examples of epistolatory style for children of both sexes. 1811, 1816 (2nd edn), Boston 1822, London 1826 (3rd edn), Paris 1837.
Lorimer: a tale. 1814 (anon), Philadelphia 1816.
Memoirs of the court of Queen Elizabeth. 2 vols 1818 (illus), 1818 (2nd edn), 1819 (3rd edn), 1819 (4th edn rev and corrected), Boston 1821, Boston and Philadelphia 1823, London 1823 (5th edn rev and corrected), 1826 (6th edn rev and corrected), 1869 (reprint of 6th edn), New York 1870, London [1872], [1875]; tr Ger 1819.
Memoirs of the court of King James I. 2 vols 1822, 2 vols Boston 1822, London 1822 (2nd edn), 1823 (3rd edn).
REVIEW: Edinburgh Rev 37 1822.
Memoir of John Aikin MD. 2 vols 1823, Philadelphia 1824.
An English lesson book for the junior classes. 1828, 1833.
Memoirs of the court of King Charles I. 2 vols 1833, 1833 (2nd edn), Philadelphia 1833.
REVIEW: Edinburgh Rev 58 1834.
The life of Joseph Addison. 2 vols 1834, Philadelphia 1846.
REVIEWS: Spectator 16 1843; North Amer Rev 64 1847.
Holiday stories for young readers. 1858.
Correspondence of W. E. Channing and Lucy Aikin from 1826–42. Ed A. L. le Breton, Boston 1874.

Anthologies, editions, translations

Poetry for children. Selected by Lucy Aikin. 1801, 1803 (2nd edn with additions and corrections), 1804, 1805 (3rd edn), 1815 (6th edn), 1818 (7th edn), 1820 (new edn), 1822, 1825, 1826 (new edn considerably improved), 1828, 1834, 1836, [1840?].
Hess, J. G. The life of Ulrich Zwingli. Tr Aikin 1812.
Jauffret, L. F. The travels of Rolando. Tr Aikin 1822, 1823, 1852.
The works of Anna Laetitia Barbauld. Ed with a memoir by Aikin. 2 vols 1825, Boston 1826.
A legacy for young ladies. Ed Aikin 1826.
Selected works of the British poets by John Aikin. With a supplement by Lucy Aikin. 1845, 1852.
The arts of life by John Aikin. A new edn with additions and alterations by Lucy Aikin. 1858.

By 'Mary Godolphin'

Robinson Crusoe in words of one syllable. By Mary Godolphin. London and New York '1868' [1867], New York 1882, London and New York '1884' [1883], Chicago [1931] (as Young Folks' Robinson Crusoe).
Aesop's fables in words of one syllable. By Mary Godolphin. [1868] (illus), New York [1897], London 1908; Bath 1884 (printed in the learners' style of phonography ... by Isaac Pitman), London 1891, [1913].
Sandford and Merton in words of one syllable. By Mary Godolphin. [1868] (illus), New York 1868.

Evenings at home in words of one syllable. By Mary Godolphin. 1869.
The Pilgrim's Progress in words of one syllable. By Mary Godolphin. 1869 (illus), New York [1884], 1939.
The Swiss Family Robinson in words of one syllable. By Mary Godolphin. 1869, Boston and New York [1914].
The one-syllable Sunday book. By Mary Godolphin. [1870.]

§2

le Breton, P. H. (ed). Memoirs, miscellanies and letters of the late Lucy Aikin. 1864.
REVIEW: London Quart Rev 24 1865.
Boase, F. In Modern English biography, 1892.
In DNB.

Archibald Alison 1792–1867

§1

Travels in France during the years 1814–15: comprising a residence at Paris during the stay of the allied armies and at Aix at the period of the landing of Bonaparte. 2 vols Edinburgh 1815, Edinburgh 1816 (rev and enlarged edn). Anon; in collaboration with W. P. Alison, J. Hope and A. F. Tytler.
Remarks on the administration of criminal justice in Scotland, and the dangers proposed to be introduced into it, by a member of the faculty of advocates. Edinburgh 1825.
Principles of the criminal law of Scotland. Edinburgh 1832.
Practice of the criminal law of Scotland. Edinburgh 1833.
History of Europe from the commencement of the French revolution in 1789 to the restoration of the Bourbons in 1815. 10 vols Edinburgh 1833–42, Paris 1841–2, New York 1842–3, Edinburgh 1844 (6th edn), 20 vols Edinburgh 1848 (7th edn), 14 vols Edinburgh 1849–50 (8th edn), 12 vols Edinburgh 1853–6 (9th edn), 14 vols Edinburgh 1860 (10th edn).
The principles of population and their connection with human happiness. 2 vols Edinburgh 1840, 1860.
Free trade and protection. Edinburgh 1844. Rptd from a chapter in The principles of population and 2 articles in Blackwood's.
England in 1815 and 1845, or a sufficient and a contracted currency. Edinburgh 1845, 1845 (rev edn), 1846, 1847.
Miscellaneous essays. Philadelphia 1845, other edns pbd Philadelphia 1846–53, Boston 1854, 1856, 1857, 1859, New York 1860, other edns pbd New York 1863–81.
Free trade and a fettered currency. Edinburgh 1847.
Suggestions for a domestic currency founded upon philosophic and unerring principles .... New York 1847.
The military life of John Duke of Marlborough. Edinburgh 1848, New York 1848 etc, 2 vols Edinburgh 1852 (2nd edn, enlarged, as The life of John Duke of Marlborough), Edinburgh 1853; tr Ger 1852, 1865 (new edn).
Essays, political, historical, and miscellaneous. 3 vols Edinburgh 1850.
Inaugural address delivered ... on his installation as Lord Rector of the University of Glasgow ... 1851. Edinburgh [1851].
History of Europe from the fall of Napoleon in 1815 to the accession of Louis Napoleon in 1852. 9 vols Edinburgh 1853–9, 4 vols New York 1853–60 etc.
A lecture on the currency, delivered in the City Hall, Glasgow, on Tuesday, March 15, 1859. Birmingham [1859], Glasgow [1859]. Rptd from Glasgow Morning Jnl.
The currency laws: their effect on the profits of trade and wages of labour. Glasgow 1859.
Lives of Lord Castlereagh and Sir Charles Stewart, the second and third Marquesses of Londonderry, with annals of contemporary events in which they bore a part. 3 vols Edinburgh 1861.
For Alison's contributions to Blackwood's Mag, Edinburgh Rev, Foreign Quarterly Rev, *and the* Dublin Univ Mag, *see* Wellesley *vol 5, 1989.*

§2

Alison, Lady [Jane] (ed). Some account of my life and writings: an autobiography by the late Sir Archibald Alison ... edited by his daughter-in-law. 2 vols Edinburgh 1883. [GW]

John Anster 1793–1867

See col 224.

Sarah Austin, née Taylor 1793–1867

For locations of the mss of Austin's extensive correspondence, see L. and J. Hamburger's Contemplating adultery: the secret life of a Victorian woman, *New York 1991, London 1992.*

§1

Life of Carsten Niebuhr. 1833 (anon). (Biographies of Eminent Men ser; also issued as part of Library of Useful Knowledge: Lives of Eminent Persons).
On national education. First pbd in Foreign Quart Rev 12, Oct 1833.
Germany from 1760 to 1814: or sketches of German life, from the decay of the empire to the expulsion of the French. 1854, micros New Haven CT [1978] and Cambridge MA [198?]. Partly rptd from articles in Edinburgh Rev 77 (Feb 1843), 78 (Oct 1843), and 86 (Oct 1846), and Br and Foreign Rev 26 (June 1842).
Two letters on girls' schools, and on the training of working women: with additions. 1857, micro Glen Rock NJ 1975.

Contributions to periodicals

For Austin's contributions to the Foreign Quart Rev, Br and Foreign Rev, Edinburgh Rev *and* Fraser's Mag, *see* Wellesley *vol 5.*
Reports to the Athenaeum from the Continent, on various aspects of life and culture there, 1842–5.
The grave of Locke. Athenaeum 5 Oct 1850.
Industrial girls' schools. Athenaeum 22 Nov 1856 and 24 Jan 1857.

Collaborative work (with Edgar Taylor)

Lays of the Minnesingers or German troubadours of the twelfth and thirteenth centuries. 1825. Anon.

Translations

Foscolo, Ugo. History of the democratical constitution of Venice. Edinburgh Rev 46, June 1827.
[Pückler-Muskau, H. L. H., Fürst von]. Tour in England, Ireland and France, in the years 1828 and 1829. Tr from Ger 2 vols 1831, 1 vol Philadelphia 1833.
[Pückler-Muskau, H. L. H., Fürst von]. Tour in Germany, Holland and England, in the years 1826, 1827, and 1828. Tr from Ger 2 vols 1832. This and the preceding title were pbd in 2 vols in London in 1832 and in 1 vol in Philadelphia 1833 as Tour in England, Ireland and France in the years 1826, 1827, 1828, and 1829; new 8-vol edn Philadelphia 1835, new edn Zurich 1940 (rev). The sections of the Tour relating to England were partly rptd in A Regency visitor: the English tour of Prince Pückler-Muskau described in his letters, ed and introd by E. M. Butler 1957. Sarah Austin's trns of the Tour involved significant censorship and rewording of the original.
Sismondi, Leonard Simond de. A history of the Italian Republics. Tr from Fr 1832 (anon).
On the recent attempts to revolutionise Germany. Tr from Ger, from the 1832 issue of Bibliothek der Neuesten Weltkunde, in NMM 37, Jan 1833.
Characteristics of Goethe from the German of Falk, von Muller &c. 3 vols 1833, Philadelphia 1841, micro Washington [19–?] (Lib of Congress).
REVIEW: Edinburgh Rev 57, July 1833 by Herman Merivale.
Sismondi, Leonard Simond de. A history of the fall of the Roman Empire. Tr from Fr 2 vols 1834. Anon.

Cousin, Victor. Report on the state of public instruction in Prussia. Tr from Fr 1834, New York 1835. Selections rptd 1930.
REVIEWS: Athenaeum 26 Apr 1834; Westminster Rev 34, June 1840.
Carové, Friedrich Wilhelm. The story without an end. Tr from Ger 1834, rptd Columbia NY 1995. Boston and New York 1836 with preface by A. Bronson Alcott (new edn 1848, rptd New York 1876 and [1888?]). Other edns Paris 1837, London [1840], 1856, [1864] ('new and improved'), 1868 (rptd 1872, 1874, 1879), New York 1868, London 1889, Portland ME 1897, London 1899, Portland ME 1900, Boston 1902 (with preface by T. W. Higginson, rptd 1909), London, Philadelphia and Portland ME 1904, Portland ME 1907, London 1909, Chelsea 1910, London 1912, New York 1912, Boston 1934. Micro Ann Arbor MI 1991.
von Räumer, Friedrich Ludwig Georg. England in 1835. Tr from Ger 3 vols 1836. 1 vol Philadelphia 1836, micro Woodbridge CT 1980. Partly rptd from the Athenaeum 6, 13 and 20 Feb 1836.
REVIEWS: (Merivale, Herman) Athenaeum 26 Mar 1836; Edinburgh Rev 63, Apr 1836; (Quin, M. J.) Dublin Rev 1, May 1836.
von Ranke, Leopold. The ecclesiastical and political history of the Popes of Rome during the sixteenth and seventeenth centuries. Tr from Ger 3 vols 1840, 2 vols Philadelphia 1841; 2nd edn 3 vols London 1841, 3 vols Philadelphia 1841; new edn, as The Popes of Rome: their ecclesiastical and political history during the sixteenth and seventeenth centuries, 3 vols 1847; 4th edn 1866 under same title and with preface by H. H. Milman.
REVIEWS: Extensively reviewed, including (Macaulay, T. B.) Edinburgh Rev 72, Oct 1840.
Fragments from German prose writers. 1841 (illus), New York 1841. Rptd from NMM 1830–3.
REVIEW: Athenaeum 29 May 1841.
von Ranke, Leopold. History of the Reformation in Germany. Tr from Ger of 3 of Ranke's 5 vols 1845, 1 vol Philadelphia 1845 (micro Cleveland OH [1975?]); 2nd edn 3 vols 1845–7; new edn, ed Robert A. Johnson, London and New York 1905, rptd New York 1966, micros Ann Arbor MI 1960, Wooster OH [19–?], Washington [19–?] (Lib of Congress).
REVIEWS: Athenaeum 18 and 25 Jan 1845.
Travels and travellers in Italy ['from a German journal']. Bentley's Misc 20, Sep 1846.
Guizot, François Pierre Guillaume. On the state of religion in France. Quart Rev 83, June 1848.
Guizot, François Pierre Guillaume. On the causes of the success of the English Revolution of 1640–1688. Tr from Fr 1850. Cheap rev edn 1850.
REVIEWS: Athenaeum 12 Feb 1850; Fraser's Mag 41, Mar 1850.
D'Harcourt, Paule (Marchioness). The Duchess of Orleans (Helen of Mecklenburgh-Schwerin): a memoir. With a preface by the translator. Tr from Fr 1859; 2nd edn 1860 (with additions).

Editions

Selections from the Old Testament. 1833.
Letters of the Rev Sydney Smith. Vol 2 of A memoir of the Reverend Sydney Smith, by his daughter, Lady Holland. 1854 (priv ptd); 4 edns 1855 (micro of 3rd edn Chicago 1978); New York 1855 (micros Louisville KY [1979?] and Evanston IL 1993); London 1856, New York 1856, London 1869, New York 1880 (abridged and rearranged).
REVIEWS: Extensively reviewed, including (Charles Kingsley) Fraser's Mag 52, July 1855.
Austin, John. The province of jurisprudence determined and lectures on jurisprudence. Vol 1 prefaced by memoir of John Austin by Sarah Austin, his wife. 3 vols 1861–3; 2nd edn 1863; 3rd edn, rev and ed Robert Campbell, under title, Lectures on jurisprudence, 2 vols 1869 (micro Ann Arbor MI [19–?]); 4th edn 2 vols 1879; 5th edn 2 vols 1885, rptd 1911, 1929, micros Littleton CO [1985] and Woodbridge CT [1986].
Duff Gordon, Lucie (Austin's daughter). Letters from Egypt, 1863–65. 1866. *See* Lucie Duff Gordon, *col 2229*.

Spurious work

Niebuhr, Barthold. Stories of the gods and heroes of Greece. Ed S. Austin 1843. Tr and ed Lucie Duff Gordon; wrongly attributed to Sarah Austin.

§2

The Times, 12 Aug 1867. Obituary.
Ross, Janet (Austin's granddaughter). Three generations of Englishwomen: memoirs and correspondence of Mrs John Taylor, Mrs Sarah Austin, and Lady Duff Gordon. 2 vols 1888, rptd 1892.
Erskine, Mrs Steuart (ed). Anna Jameson: letters and friendships (1812–1860). 1915.
MacDonell, Sir John. In DNB.
Hamburger, L. and J. Hamburger. Troubled lives: John and Sarah Austin. 1985.
Hamburger, L. and J. Hamburger. Contemplating adultery: the secret life of a Victorian woman. New York 1991, London 1992. Focussed on Sarah Austin's correspondence with Pückler-Muskau, this book also discusses the alterations to his works she made in translating them. [JW]

John Barrow 1764–1848

Bibliography

Cutmore, J. Sir John Barrow's contributions to the Quarterly Review 1809–24. N & Q 239 1994.

§1

An account of travels into the interior of Southern Africa, in the years 1797 and 1798. 2 vols 1801–4, New York 1802, London 1806 (2nd edn with addns and alterations); tr Ger 1801, Fr 1806.
Travels in China. 1804, Philadelphia 1805, London 1806 (2nd edn), 1807 (abridged), Taipei China 1982 (reprint of 2nd edn); tr Ger 1804, Fr [1805], [1896].
A voyage to Cochinchina, in the years 1792 and 1793. 2 vols 1806, Kuala Lumpur and New York '1975' [1976] (facs with introd by M. Osborne); tr Fr 1807 (spurious); Ger 1808.
Some account of the public life, and a selection from the unpublished writings, of the Earl of Macartney. 2 vols 1807.
A chronological history of voyages into the Arctic regions. 1818, Newton Abbot and New York 1971 (facs with introd by C. Lloyd); tr Fr 1819.
The eventful history of the mutiny and piratical seizure of H. M. S. Bounty; its causes and consequences. 1831 (anon), New York 1832 etc (Amer title: A description of Pitcairn's island and its inhabitants. With an authentic account of the mutiny of the ship Bounty, and of the subsequent fortunes of the mutineers), London 1835 (2nd edn), 1839 (3rd edn), 1847 (4th edn), 1885 (as The mutiny of the Bounty, abridged, together with W. Bligh's account), 1914 etc (WC as The eventful history . . .), London and Glasgow 1961 (as The mutiny of the 'Bounty', illustr N. Lambourne); ed S. W. Roskill 1976 (Folio Soc reprint of lst edn); ed G. Kennedy, Boston 1980 (as Mutiny of the Bounty).
A memoir of the life of Peter the Great. 1832 (anon), New York 1834 etc, London 1839 (3rd edn), 1845, [1874] (with notes), [1881?] (with additions and notes), New York 1903 (with notes).
Life of Richard Earl Howe. 1838.
The life of George, Lord Anson. 1839.
Voyages of discovery and research within the Arctic regions, from the year 1818 to the present time. 1846, New York 1846 etc, 1859 (abridged).

An auto-biographical memoir of Sir John Barrow. 1847.
Sketches of the Royal Society and the Royal Society club. 1849, [1971] (new impression).
Facsimile copy of letter dated 5th Aug 1816. [1881?]
Barrow also edited J. H. Tuckey, Narrative *1818; S. Daniell,* Sketches *1820 (with notes); H. Clapperton* Journal *1826, 1829 (with introd), 1831.*

Contributions to periodicals

Various anon articles in the Quart Rev 1809–24. *See* H. and H. Chadwick Shine, The Quarterly Review under Gifford 1949; Wellesley vol 5; Cutmore, Bibliography, *above*; §2, *below*.
Twelve articles in the Encyclopaedia Britannica 5th edn suppl 1–4 (1824); 3 articles in the Jnl of the Royal Geographical Soc 1830, 1833, 1836; 5 articles in the Edinburgh Rev 1841–44. *See* Wellesley vol 5.

§2

[Staunton, G. T.] Memoir of Sir John Barrow. [1852.]
Lloyd, C. Mr Barrow of the Admiralty. 1970.
Cutmore, J. The Quarterly Review under Gifford: some new attributions. Victorian Periodicals Rev 24 1991.
Cutmore, J. The early Quarterly Review: new attributions of authorship. Victorian Periodicals Rev 28 1995. [JC]

Mary Matilda Betham 1776–1852

§1

In memory of Mr Agostina Isola of Cambridge who died on the 5th of June 1797. Poem signed M. M. Betham, copied 19 June 1833. Ms in the possession of Harvard Univ Lib.
Elegies. 1797, Ipswich 1797; rptd in Poems and elegies, *below*.
A biographical dictionary of celebrated women of every age and country. 1804.
Poems. 1808; Poems and elegies, London and New York 1928 (facs reprint with introd by D. H. Reiman).
The lay of Marie: a poem. 1816, Poole 1996 (facs reprint).
Vignettes: in verse. 1818.

§2

Betham-Edwards, M. In her Six life studies of famous women, 1880. In DNB.
Betham, E. (ed). A house of letters. Being excerpts from the correspondence of Miss Charlotte Jerningham ... and others, with Matilda Betham. [1905.]

James Boaden 1762–1839

See col 1957.

Sir John Bowring 1792–1872

See col 238.

Sir Samuel Egerton Brydges 1762–1837

Bibliography

Woodworth, M. K. The literary career of Brydges. Oxford 1935. Bibliography, pp. 167–88, includes mss, books written or edited by Brydges, some of his contributions to periodicals, and books about Brydges. Some minor addns in TLS 16 Nov 1935.

§1

Sonnets and other poems, with a versification of the six bards of Ossian. 1785 (anon), 1785 (signed and expanded), 1789, 1795, 1807 (further expanded as Poems).
The topographer: containing a variety of original articles, illustrative of the local history and antiquities of England. 4 vols 1789–91. With Lawrence Stebbing Shaw.
Topographical miscellanies. 1792.
Mary de Clifford: a story; interspersed with many poems. 1792 (anon), 1800.
Verses on the late unanimous resolutions to support the Constitution [with] some other poems. Canterbury 1794.
Arthur Fitz Albini: a novel. 2 vols 1798, 1799, 1810.
Le Forester: a novel. 3 vols 1802.
Censura literaria: containing titles, abstracts and opinions of old English books, with original disquisitions, articles of biography and other literary antiquities. 10 vols 1805–9, 1815 (articles rearranged chronologically).
The British bibliographer. 4 vols 1810–14.
The sylvan wanderer: consisting of a series of moral, sentimental and critical essays. 4 pts Lee Priory 1813–21 (priv ptd).
The ruminator: containing a series of moral, critical and sentimental essays. 2 vols 1813.
Hasty lines on the words 'this beautiful creation'. 1813.
Occasional poems, written in the year 1811. Lee Priory 1814 (priv ptd).
Select poems. Lee Priory 1814 (priv ptd).
Bertram: a poetical tale. Lee Priory 1814 (priv ptd), London 1816.
Restituta: or titles, extracts and characters of old books in English literature revived. 4 vols 1814–16.
Excerpta Tudoriana: or extracts from Elizabethan literature, with a critical preface. 2 vols Lee Priory 1814–18 (priv ptd).
Archaica: containing a reprint of scarce old English tracts, with prefaces, critical and biographical. 2 vols 1815 (priv ptd).
Desultoria: or comments of a South-Briton on books and men. Lee Priory 1815 (priv ptd).
Fragment of a poem occasioned by ... visit to ... old mansion. By [S. E. B.]. Lee Priory 1815 (priv ptd).
Verses written as a preface to The sylvan wanderer. Lee Priory 1815 (priv ptd).
To a lady. 1817. Broadsheet. Anon.
May-day: a song. [1817.] Broadsheet. Anon.
The muse of Lough Corrib. 1817. Broadsheet. Anon.
Five sonnets, addressed to Wootton. Lee Priory 1819. Anon.
Lord Brokenhurst: or a fragment of winter leaves. Geneva 1819; rptd in his Tragic tales, 1820.
Coningsby. Paris 1819; rptd in his Tragic tales, 1820.
Sir Ralph Willoughby: an historical tale of the sixteenth century. Florence 1820.
Res literariae: bibliographical and critical. 3 nos Naples, Rome, Geneva 1820–2.
The hall of Hellingsley: a tale. 3 vols 1821.
Odo, Count of Lingen: a poetical tale in six cantos. Geneva 1824, Paris 1826.
Gnomica: detached thought, sententious, axiomatic, moral and critical. Geneva 1824.
Letters on the character and poetical genius of Lord Byron. 1824.
An impartial portrait of Lord Byron as a poet and a man. Paris 1825.
Recollections of foreign travel on life, literature and self-knowledge. 2 vols 1825.
Modern aristocracy: or the bard's reception. Geneva 1831. Poem on Byron.
A poem on birth. By [S. E. B.]. [n.p.] 1831.
The lake of Geneva: a poem moral and descriptive. 2 vols Geneva 1832.
Darkness: an ode. Written 6 January 1832. By [S. E. B.]. 1832.
Elegiac lines on ... Bostetten. By [S. E. B.]. [1832.] Broadsheet.
Imaginative biography. 2 vols 1834.
The autobiography, time, opinions and contemporaries of Sir Egerton Brydges. 2 vols 1834.
Moral axioms in single couplets for the use of the young. 1837.
Human fate, and an address to the poets Wordsworth and Southey: poems. Great Totham 1846 (priv ptd), 1848, 1850.
Also a large number of genealogical works. Brydges edited (with matter

included in the above) one or more works by the following: Edward Phillips (Theatrum poetarum anglicanorum), *Duchess of Newcastle, Greene, Ralegh, Thomas Stanley, Breton, Drayton, Henry Wotton, William Browne, Wither, Brathwait, William Hammond, John Hall (of Durham), Chapman, William Collins, Milton, several minor seventeenth-century poets and some Latin and Italian writers; also a number of books on economic and social questions (summarised by M. K. Woodworth, Bibliography above, Appendix) and numerous pams.*

§2

Woodworth, M. K. The literary career of Brydges. Oxford 1935.
Sadleir, M. Archdeacon Francis Wrangham: a supplement. Library 4th ser 19 1939.
Jones, W. P. Brydges on Lord Byron. HLQ 13 1950.
Jones, W. P. New light on Brydges. HLB 11 1957.

Charles Bucke 1781–1846

§1

The philosophy of nature: or the influence of scenery on the mind and heart. 2 vols 1813, 4 vols 1821 (as On the beauties, harmonies and sublimities of nature; with occasional remarks on the laws, customs, manners and opinions of various nations), 3 vols 1837 (enlarged), New York 1843 (with notes, commentaries and illustrations, selected and rev W. P. Page).
Amusements in retirement. 1816.
The fall of the leaf, and other poems. 1819 (4 edns).
The Italians, or the fatal accusation: a tragedy. 1819 (7 edns) (anon), 1820 (with the prefaces to the 1st, 3rd, 6th, 7th and 8th edns). Produced Drury Lane 3 Apr 1819.
A classical grammar of the English language; with a short history of its origin and formation. 1829.
Julio Romano, or the force of the passions: an epic drama in six books. 1830.
On the life, writings and genius of Akenside; with some account of his friends. 1832.
The book of human character. 2 vols 1837.
A letter intended (one day) as a supplement to Lockhart's Life of Sir Walter Scott. 1838 (priv ptd). On Scott's mention of Bucke's dispute with Kean.
The life of John, Duke of Marlborough. 1839.
Ruins of ancient cities: with general and particular accounts of their rise, fall and present condition. 2 vols 1840, New York 1845.

§2

The assailant assailed: being a vindication of Mr Kean. 1819. On his conduct in connection with The Italians.
A defence of Edmund Kean Esq: being a reply to Mr Bucke's preface, and remarks on his tragedy of The Italians. [1819.]
Bucke's Julio Romano. Monthly Rev May 1830.

Thomas Campbell 1777–1844

See col 283.

Richard Carlile 1790–1843

Selections

Simon, B. (ed). The radical tradition in education in Britain: a compilation of writings by William Godwin, Thomas Paine, Robert Owen, Richard Carlile, Robert Dale Owen, William Thompson, William Lovett and William Morris. 1971.

§1

The order for the administration of the loaves and fishes: or the communion of corruption's host, to be read at the Treasury the day preceding all Cabinet dinners. 1817.
Life of Thomas Paine. In Political and miscellaneous writings of Paine vol 1, 1819; 1821 (separately).
The deist: or moral philosopher. 2 vols 1819–20. Selections from writers ancient and modern.
An address to men of science, calling upon them to stand forward and vindicate the truth from the foul grasp and persecution of superstition. 1821.
The reformers of Great Britain. 6 pts [1821]. Letters from Dorchester gaol.
Observations on Letters to a friend on the evidences, doctrines and duties of the Christian religion, by Olinthus Gregory. 1821.
Every man's book: or what is God? 1826.
Richard Carlile's first sermon upon the mount: a sermon upon the subject of deity. 1827.
The gospel according to Richard Carlile, shewing the true parentage, birth and life of our allegorical Lord and Saviour Jesus Christ. 1827.
A new view of insanity: in which is set forth the mismanagement of public and private madhouses. 1831.
Church reform: the only means to that end, stated in a letter to Sir Robert Peel. 1835.
Carlile also edited various periodicals including Republican, *1820;* Lion, *1828;* Prompter, *1831;* Gauntlet, *1834.*

§2

Vice versus reason: a copy of the bill of indictment against Carlile for publishing Paine's Age of reason. 1819.
Holyoake, G. J. The life and character of Carlile. 1870.
Campbell, T. C. The battle of the press. 1899.
Aldred, G. A. Carlile, agitator: his life and times. 1923.
Nott, J. W. Richard Carlile 1816–1843. 1970.
Wiener, J. H. Radicalism and free thought in nineteenth century Britain: the life of Richard Carlile. 1987.

Thomas Carlyle 1795–1881

Bowdoin College, Bodleian Lib, BL, Harvard Univ, NLS, Univ of California (Santa Cruz) and Yale Univ hold substantial collections. These and other more minor collections are documented in IELM *vol 4 pt 1 1982.*

Bibliographies

Primary

Lane, W. C. The Carlyle collection: a catalogue of books on Oliver Cromwell and Frederick the Great bequeathed to Harvard College Library. Cambridge MA 1888.
Wead, M. E. A catalogue of the Dr Samuel A. Jones Carlyle collection. Ann Arbor MI 1919.
Dyer, I. W. A bibliography of Thomas Carlyle's writings and ana. Portland ME 1928.
James, J. D. and C. S. Fineman. Carlyle: book and margins. Santa Cruz CA 1980. Catalogue of the Strouse Collection. Suppls to this catalogue were issued in 1982 and 1985 under the title Lectures on Carlyle & his era. 1985 suppl ed J. D. James and R. B. Bottoms.
Tarr, R. L. Thomas Carlyle: a descriptive bibliography. Pittsburgh 1989. The standard primary bibliography. Supersedes Dyer.

Secondary

Moore, C. In The English romantic poets and essayists. A review of research and criticism, rev edn ed C. W. Houtchens and L. H. Houtchens, New York 1966.
Tennyson, G. B. In Victorian prose: a guide to research, ed D. J. DeLaura, New York 1973.
Tarr, R. L. Thomas Carlyle: a bibliography of English-language criticism 1824–1974. Charlottesville VA 1976.

Collections

Thomas Carlyle's Ausgewählte Schriften. Ed A. Kretzschmar. 6 vols Leipzig 1855–6 (Wigand).

Uniform Edition. 16 vols 1857–8 (Chapman and Hall).
Cheap Edition. 23 vols 1864–9 (Chapman and Hall).
Library Edition. 34 vols 1869–75 (Chapman and Hall).
People's Edition. 39 vols 1871–8 (Chapman and Hall).
Cabinet Edition. 21 vols 1874 (Chapman and Hall).
Edition De Luxe. 20 vols Boston 1884 (Estes and Lauriat).
Sterling Edition. 20 vols Boston 1885 (Estes and Lauriat).
Alden Edition. 12 vols New York 1885 (Alden).
Ashburton Edition. 30 vols 1885–8 (Chapman and Hall).
Copyright Edition. 37 vols 1888 (Chapman and Hall).
Centennial Edition. Ed W. J. Rolfe 26 vols Boston [1892].
Centenary Edition. Ed H. D. Traill 30 vols 1896–9 (Chapman and Hall).
Chelsea Edition. 11 vols [1900] (Chapman and Hall).
Edinburgh Edition. 30 vols 1903 (Chapman and Hall).
Standard Edition. 18 vols New York 1905 (Funk and Wagnalls).
California Edition. Berkeley CA 1993– . Heroes and hero-worship pbd 1993. Sartor Resartus, The French Revolution, Past and present, Essays (3 vols) are projected. The California Edn is the first scholarly critical edn of Carlyle's works.
The collected poems of Thomas and Jane Welsh Carlyle. Ed R. L. Tarr and F. McClelland, Greenwood FL 1986.

Selections

Ballantyne, T. (ed). Passages selected from the writings of Carlyle, with a biographical memoir [by the editor]. 1855.
REVIEWS: Rambler n.s. 4 1855; New Quart Rev 5 1856.
Dawson, C. C. Pictures of the modern intellect. East Saginaw MI 1870.
Barrett, E. (ed). The Carlyle anthology. New York 1876.
Williamson, C. N. (ed). Carlyle birthday-book. [1879.]
Oswald, E. (ed and tr). Carlyle: ein Lebensbild, und Goldkörner aus Seinen Werken. Leipzig 1882.
Lewin, W. (ed). Cope's smoke-room booklets. No 5. Liverpool [1891].
The socialism and unsocialism of Carlyle. 2 vols New York [1891].
Last words of Carlyle: Wotton Reinfred, a romance; Excursion (futile enough) to Paris; Letters. 1892, New York 1892 (with introd on Wotton Reinfred), ed K. J. Fielding New York 1892, Farnborough Hants 1971.
REVIEWS: Critic (New York) 21 1892; Popular Science Monthly 41 1892.
Rescued essays of Carlyle. Ed P. Newberry [1892]. Contains Louis-Philippe; The repeal of the Union; Legislation for Ireland; Ireland for the British Chief Governor; Irish regiments of the new era; Trees of liberty; Death of Charles Buller.
Leask, W. K. (ed). Readings from Carlyle. 1894.
Hensel, P. (ed). Sozialpolitische Schriften. Tr E. von Pfannkuche 3 vols Göttingen 1894–8.
Duncan, R. (ed). Thoughts on life. 1895.
Wood, J. (ed). The Carlyle reader. Edinburgh 1895.
Boynton, H. W. (ed). Selections from Carlyle. Boston 1896.
Johnson, R. B. (ed). Pen portraits. 1896 (Allen).
An outline of the doctrines of Thomas Carlyle. 1896.
Montaigne and other essays chiefly biographical. Ed S. R. Crockett 1897, Philadelphia 1897.
Bachelor, A. (ed). Carlyle year-book. Boston [1900].
Kretschmar, A., and M. Kühn (ed and tr). Arbeiten und Nicht Verzweifein, Düsseldorf 1902.
Collectanea 1821–55. Ed S. A. Jones, Canton PA 1903. Contains Metrical legends of exalted characters; Faustus; Faust's curse; Heintze's German translation of Burns; Indian meal; A letter to the editor of the London Times [concerning the Misses Lowe].
Fischer, T. A. (ed and tr). Zerstreute Historische Aufsätze. Leipzig 1905.
Masson, É. (ed and tr). Pages choisies des grands écrivains: Carlyle. Paris 1905.
Ryding, E. (ed and tr). Arbeta och Förtvifla Icke: Lefvande ord ur Thomas Carlyle. Stockholm 1906.
Barthélemy, E. (ed and tr). Essais choisies de critique et de morale. Paris 1907.
Stones from Carlyle. 1907.
Wolf, G. J. (ed). Worte Carlyles. Minden 1907.
Gardner, R. (ed). Pocket Carlyle. 1908.
Spencer, S. (ed). Short passages from the works of Thomas Carlyle. 1908.
Barthélemy, E. (ed and tr). Nouveaux essais choisis de critique et de morale. Paris 1909.
Evans, A. W. (ed). Masters of literature: Carlyle. 1909.
Pringle-Pattison, A. S. (ed). Selected essays of Thomas Carlyle. 1909.
Thoughts from Carlyle. [1909.]
Ford, D. M. (ed). Stories from Carlyle. nd.
Dircks, R. (ed). The sayings of Carlyle. 1910.
Lee, E. (ed). Selections from Carlyle. 1910.
Marsh, E. C. The wisdom of Thomas Carlyle. New York 1910.
Morali, V. (ed and tr). Lavora, non disperarti: brani scelti delle sue opere. Turin 1910.
Wisdom and humour of Thomas Carlyle. Philadelphia [1910].
Ayres, L. C. (ed). Selections from Carlyle. Cincinnati 1911.
Hemingway, S. B. and C. Seymour (ed). Selections from Carlyle. Boston [1915].
Bube, J. (ed). Carlyle a faithful friend of Germany: Eine Auswahl. Leipzig 1919.
Woods, E. C. (ed). A Carlyle calendar. Portland ME 1919.
Valori, G. (ed and tr). Pagine Scelte. Milan 1920.
Glencross, T. O. (ed). The best of Carlyle. 1923.
Benham, A. R. (ed). Selections from the writings of Thomas Carlyle. New York 1928.
Ball, A. H. R. (ed). Selections from Carlyle. Cambridge 1929.
Trevelyan, G. M. (ed). Carlyle: an anthology. 1953.
Hughes, A. M. D. (ed). Selections. Oxford 1957.
Symons, J. (ed). Selected works, reminiscences and letters. Cambridge MA 1967.
Tennyson, G. B. (ed). A Carlyle reader. New York 1969.
Sussman, H. (ed). Thomas Carlyle: Sartor resartus and selected prose. New York 1970.

§1

For details of first pbn in periodical form of items listed, see Contributions to periodicals, *below.*

Elements of geometry and plane trigonometry. Ed J. Leslie, Edinburgh 1817 (3rd edn). Solution to a mathematical problem.
Elements of geometry and trigonometry with notes, translated from the French of A. M. Legendre. Edinburgh 1822, 1824, New York 1828, 1830. Tr and introductory ch on Proportion by Carlyle (anon).
Wilhelm Meister's apprenticeship: a novel from the German of Goethe. 3 vols Edinburgh 1824 (anon), Boston 1828, London 1839, Philadelphia 1840, London 1842, Boston 1851, London 1858, Boston 1865; ed E. Dowden, 1890; ed N. H. Dole, Boston 1901, Columbia SC 1991.
REVIEWS: Blackwood's Mag 16 1824; [De Quincey, T.] London Mag 10 1824; [Q.] Examiner 858 1824; [Jeffrey, F.] Edinburgh Rev 42 1825; [Lockhart, J. G.] Quart Rev 34 1826; North Amer Rev 28 1829; Southern Rev 3 1829; [Willis, N. P.] Amer Monthly Mag 1 1829; Amer Monthly Mag 2 1830; Monthly Mag 91 1840.
Life of Friedrich Schiller. 1825, Frankfurt 1830 (tr Goethe), Boston 1833, New York 1837, London 1845, New York 1846, Philadelphia 1859, Boston 1860, Leipzig 1869 (Tauchnitz), London 1873, Boston 1877, Columbia SC 1992.
REVIEWS: Amer Quart Rev 13 1833; Amer Quart Observer 2 1834; Knickerbocker Mag 3 1834; New England Mag 6 1834; [Calvert, G?] North Amer Rev 39 1834; [Hedge, F. H.] Christian Examiner 16

1834; Knickerbocker Mag 9 1837; Amer Whig Rev 2 1845; Broadway Jnl 2 1845; Richmond Enquirer 1 Dec 1845; Amer Whig Rev 3 1846; Methodist Quart Rev 28 1846; Southern Quart Rev 9 1846.

German romance: specimens of its chief authors with biographical and critical notices, by the translator of Wilhelm Meister, and the author of The life of Schiller. 4 vols Edinburgh 1827. (Vol 1 Musaeus and Fouqué; vol 2 Tieck and Hoffman; vol 3 Richter; vol 4 Goethe (Wilhelm Meister), 2 vols Boston 1841; (rptd as Tales by Musaeus, Tieck, Richter, London 1858; 2 vols as Stories by Musäus and Fouqué, Columbia SC 1991; as Schmelzle's journey to Flaetz and Quintus Fixlein, Columbia SC 1991.
REVIEWS: [Q.] Examiner 992 1827; J., Arcturus 2 1841.

Sartor resartus. 1834 (priv ptd, 50 copies from Fraser's Mag bound with new title page, 1834, for distribution to friends), Boston 1836, 1837 (with preface by R. W. Emerson), London 1838 (with added title: The life and opinions of Herr Teufelsdröckh), Boston 1840, London 1841, New York 1844, 1846, 1848, London 1849, Leipzig 1855 (tr A. Kretzschmar), Amsterdam 1880 (tr J. W. C. A. Zurcher); ed E. Dowden 1896; ed A. MacMechan, Boston 1896; ed J. A. S. Barrett 1897, 1905 (rev); ed J. Wood 1902; ed P. C. Parr 1913; ed C. S. Northup, New York 1921; ed A. Thorndike, New York [1921]; ed W. D. Johnson, Boston 1924; ed F. W. Roe, New York 1927; ed C. F. Harrold, New York 1937; ed G. B. Tennyson, New York 1969; ed H. Sussman, New York, 1970; ed K. McSweeney and P. Sabor, Oxford 1987; tr Du 1880, Ger 1882, Fr 1899, 1973.
REVIEWS: Sun 1 Apr 1834; Athenaeum 424 1835; [F[rothingham], N[athaniel] L.] Christian Examiner 21 1836; Knickerbocker Mag 9 1837; Southern Literary Jnl 1 1837; Metropolitan Mag 23 1838; Monthly Rev 147 1838; Tait's Edinburgh Mag 5 1838; Democratic Rev 23 1848; [Barrett, Joseph H.] Amer Whig Rev 9 1849.

Memoirs of Mirabeau. 1837 (priv ptd, 38 copies).

The diamond necklace. 1837 (priv ptd, 24 copies).

The French Revolution: a history. 3 vols. 1837, Boston 1838, London 1839, Boston 1839, New York 1841, London 1842, Leipzig and Paris 1844 (Ger tr P. Feddersen), New York 1846, London 1848, Maarssen 1851 (tr F. F. W. Koch), Leipzig 1851 (Tauchnitz), Paris 1865–7 (tr M. M. É. Regnault and O. Barot); ed C. R. L. Fletcher 3 vols 1902; ed J. H. Rose 3 vols 1902; tr Ger 1844, Fr 1865, 1888.
REVIEWS: Examiner 1546–8 1837; Literary Gazette 1062 1837; Monthly Repository 11 1837; Monthly Rev 11 1837; Southern Rose 6 1837; [A. [John S. Mill]] London and Westminster Rev 27 1837; [Morgan, Lady Sydney] Athenaeum 499 1837; [Thackeray, W. M.] The Times 3 Aug 1837; [Wilson, J.] Blackwood's Mag 42 1837; Amer Monthly Mag 5 1838; Christian Examiner 23 1838; New Yorker 4 1838; Southern Rose 6 1838; [B[artol], C. A.] Christian Examiner 24 1838; [Channing, W. H.] Boston Quart Rev 1 1838; New York Rev 5 1839; [Prescott, W. H.] North Amer Rev 49 1839; Little's Museum of Foreign Literature 90 1840; M[azzini], J[oseph] Monthly Chron 5 1840; [Merivale, H.] Edinburgh Rev 71 1840; Amer Biblical Repository 7 1842; Democratic Rev 19 1846; Graham's Mag 30 1847.

Goethe's novel. 1837. Tr of Goethe's The tale.

Lectures on German literature. 1837. Not pbd; *see* Spectator 6 May 1837 for concise report.

Critical and miscellaneous essays. 4 vols Boston 1838–9, New York 1839, London 1839, 1840 (5 vols), Philadelphia 1845, London 1847, Boston 1860.
REVIEWS: Christian Register 17 1838; Literary Examiner and Western Monthly Rev 1 1839; [D[eLeon], E.] Magnolia; or, Southern Appalachian 2 1843.

Six lectures on revolutions in Modern Europe. 1839. Not pbd.

Chartism. '1840' [1839], Boston 1840, London 1842, New York 1847, 1848.
REVIEWS: Br and Foreign Rev 11 1840; Christian Examiner 29 1840; Democratic Rev 8 1840; Monthly Chron 5 1840; Monthly Mag 91 1840; Monthly Rev 41 1840; NMM 58 1840; Tait's Edinburgh Mag 7 1840; [Brownson, Orestes A.] Boston Quart Rev 3 1840; [Morgan, Lady Sidney] Athenaeum 637 1840; [N.] Western Messenger 8 1840; Br and Foreign Rev 12 1841; Eclectic Rev 75 1842.

On heroes, hero-worship, and the heroic in history: six lectures [delivered May 1840]. 1841, New York 1841, London 1842, New York 1842, Cincinnati 1842, London 1846, New York 1846, London 1852, Berlin 1853 (tr J. Neuberg), New York 1865; ed A. MacMechan, Boston 1901; ed J. C. Adams, Boston 1907; ed P. C. Parr 1910; ed H. M. Buller 2 vols 1926; ed M. Goldberg 1993 (critical edn); tr Fr 1888, Sp 1893, Ger 1895, Ital 1897.
REVIEWS: [Barrett, J. H.] Monthly Rev 155 1841; [D.] Arcturus 1 1841; [Fuller, M.] Dial 2 1841; [H., J. A.] Monthly Mag 93 1841; [Thomson, W.] Christian Remembrancer 3 1842; [Thomson, W.] Christian Remembrancer 6 1843; Democratic Rev 19 1846; Biblical Rev 3 1847; Amer Whig Rev 9 1849.

Essays by R. W. Emerson. 1841. Preface.

Past and present. 1843, Boston 1843, New York 1843, London 1845, New York 1847, 1848; ed O. Smeaton 1902 (Temple Classics); ed F. Harrison [1903]; ed E. Mims, New York 1918; ed A. M. D. Hughes, Oxford 1921; ed J. Paton, New York 1927; ed E. Rhys nd (with Emerson's review) (EL); ed R. D. Altick, Boston 1965. *See* R. B. E., Thoughts on Carlyle: or a commentary on past and present, 1843; Dial 4, July 1843 (Emerson's review); W. H. Smith, Blackwood's Mag July 1843; F. Schneider, Carlyle's Past and present und der Chronica Jocelini de Brakelonda, Halle 1911; S. T. Williams, South Atlantic Quart 21 1922; G. J. Calder, The writing of past and present: a study of Carlyle's manuscripts, New Haven CT 1949.
REVIEWS: Examiner 1839 1843; Graham's Mag 23 1843; Mag of Domestic Economy and Family Rev 1 1843; Monthly Rev 161 1843; Tait's Edinburgh Mag 10 1843; The Times 6 Oct 1843; [Emerson, R. W.] Dial 4 1843; [Morgan, Lady Sydney] Athenaeum 811–12 1843; [Renouf, P. L.] Dublin Rev 15 1843; [Smith, W. H.] Blackwood's Mag 54 1843; [Richardson, M.] New Englander 2 1844; Smith, J. T., Amer Biblical Repository 12 1844.

Essays. Second ser. By R. W. Emerson. 1844. Notice.

Oliver Cromwell's letters and speeches, with elucidations. 2 vols. 1845, New York 1845, London 1846 (3 vols, expanded preface and additional materials), Paris 1847 (tr M. Philarète), London '1850' [1849] (4 vols, expanded to include the Squire Papers), Leipzig 1861 (Tauchnitz); ed S. C. Lomas 1904; ed W. A. Shaw [1907] (EL); ed E. Sanderson, New York [1924] (abridged).
REVIEWS: Critic 2 1845; Examiner 1976 1845; [Fuller, M.] New York Tribune 19 Dec 1845; [Heraud, A.] Athenaeum 945–7 1845; Amer Whig Rev 3 1846; Athenaeum 973 1846; Democratic Rev 18 1846; Douglas Jerrold's Shilling Mag 3 1846; Knickerbocker Mag 27 1846; Knight's Penny Mag 15 (1846): 81–96; Littell's Living Age 8 1846; Metropolitan Mag 41 1846; Peterson's Mag 9 1846; Southern Quart Rev 10 1846; Tait's Edinburgh Mag 13 1846; The Times 17 Apr, 4 May 1846; [Felton, C. C.]. North Amer Rev 62 1846; L., W. P. [Edwin P. Whipple?] Christian Examiner 40 1846; [Mozley, J. B.] Christian Remembrancer 11 1846; [Richardson, M.] New Englander 4 1846; [Taylor, J. J.] Prospective Rev 2 1846; [Vaughan, R.] Br Quart Rev 3 1846; [Bain, A.] Westminster Rev 44 1847; [Smith, W. H.] Blackwood's Mag 61 1847; Elephant 1 1848; [Smith, G.] Carlyle's and Guizot's Cromwell, Littell's Living Age 44 1855; [Venables, G. S.] Saturday Rev 3 1857.

Oliver Cromwell's letters and speeches: with elucidations. 1846. Suppl to 1st edn.

Ireland and Sir Robert Peel. Bungay 1849. Broadsheet.

Legislation for Ireland. Bungay 1849. Broadsheet.

Ireland and the British Chief Governor. Bungay 1849. Broadsheet.

The Squire Papers: List of the Long Parliament; and Lists of the Eastern-Association Committees. 1849.

Occasional discourse on the negro question. 1849, 1853 (priv ptd). 1st pam edn.
REVIEW: D. [John Stuart Mill] Fraser's Mag 41 1850.

Report of the Commissioners appointed to inquire into the constitution and government of the British Museum; with minutes and evidence. 1850. Evidence.

Latter-day pamphlets. 1850, Boston 1850, New York 1850, London 1855. 8 pams: 1 (Feb) The present time; 2 (Mar) Model prisons; 3 (Apr) Downing Street; 4 (Apr) The new Downing Street; 5 (May) Stump-orator; 6 (June) Parliaments; 7 (July) Hudson's statue; 8 (Aug) Jesuitism. Ed M. K. Goldberg and J. P. Seigel, Ontario Canada 1983 (facs).
REVIEWS: [J. Hanay] Blackwood v. Carlyle: a vindication by a Carlylian, 1850; Amer Whig Rev 11 1850; Chamber's Edinburgh Jnl 14 1850; Christian Observatory 4 1850; Christian Observer 50 1850; Christian Register 29 1850; Eclectic Rev 102 1850; Eliza Cook's Jnl 2 1850; Examiner 2213 1850; Fraser's Mag 62 1850; Harper's Mag 1 1850; Holden's Dollar Mag 6 1850; Independent 2 1850; Leader 1 1850; Literary World 6 1850; Literary World 7 1850; Methodist Quart Rev 32 1850; Palladium 1 1850; Peterson's Mag 17–18 1850; Rambler 5 1850; Sartain's Union Mag 6 1850; Southern Quart Rev 17 1850; The Times 25, 31 Dec 1850; [Aytoun, W. E.] Blackwood's Mag 67 1850; [C., E. W.] Critic 9 1850; [Cooke, J. E.] Southern Literary Messenger 16 1850; [Dixon, H.] Athenaeum 1162–91 1850; [H., G. F.] Southern Quart Rev 18 1850; [Hervey, T. K.] Athenaeum 1166 1850; [M., W.] Christian Register 29 1850; [Masson, D.] North Br Rev 14 1850; [P., N. E.] Truth-Seeker 1 1850; [Spring-Rice, T.] Edinburgh Rev 91 1850; [Wicksteed, C.] Prospective Rev 6 1850; The Times 13 Jan 1851; English Rev 16 1852; Critic 12 1853; Eclectic Rev 17 1855; [Ware, M. [J. E. Cooke]] Southern Literary Messenger 27 1858.

Life of John Sterling. 1851, Boston 1851, London 1852, Boston 1852; ed W. H. White 1907 (WC).
REVIEWS: Critic 10 1851; Examiner 2281–2 1851; International Monthly Mag 4 1851; Leader 2 1851; Literary World 9 1851; Princeton Rev 23 1851; Tait's Edinburgh Mag 18 1851; The Times 13 Jan, 1 Nov 1851; [Brimley, G.] Spectator 24 1851; [Dixon, H.] Athenaeum 1251 1851; [Gilfillian, G.] Eclectic Rev 104 1851; Br Quart Rev 15 1852; Christian Observer 52 1852; Christian Remembrancer 23 1852; Democratic Rev 30 1852; Dublin Univ Mag 39 1852; Leader 3 1852; Nat Mag 1 1852; Sharpe's London Mag 15 1852; [Eliot, George] Westminter Rev 57 1852; [Newman, F. W.] Prospective Rev 8 1852; [Tullock, J.] North Br Rev 16 1852.

The keepsake 1852. Ed F. A. Heath 1852. 1st printing of The opera.

Samuel Johnson. 1853. 1st pam edn.

Burns. 1854, Boston 1877. 1st pam edn.

The history of Friedrich II of Prussia, called Frederick the Great. 6 vols 1858–65, 6 vols New York 1858–66, 6 vols Berlin 1858–69 (tr J. Neuberg), 13 vols Leipzig 1858–65 (Tauchnitz); ed C. Ransome, New York 1892 (abridged); ed E. Sanderson 1909 (abridged); ed A. M. D. Hughes, Oxford 1916 (abridged); tr Ger 1858–69.
REVIEWS: Albion 36 1858; Athenaeum 1612–13 1858; Critic 17 1858; GM 5 1858; Leader 9 1858; Nat Rev 7 1858; Russell's Mag 4 1858; Tait's Edinburgh Mag 25 1858; The Times 12, 19, 26 Oct 1858; [Acton, J. E., Lord] Rambler 10 1858; [Guernsey, A. H.] Harper's Mag 18 1858; [L[ewes], G[eorge] H. Fraser's Mag 58 1858; [Nathaniel, Sir [pseud]] NMM 114 1858; [Venables, G. S.] Saturday Rev 6 1858; Br Quart Rev 29 1859; Chamber's Jnl 31 1859; Dublin Univ Mag 53 1859; Methodist Quart Rev 41 1859; Nat Mag 5 1859; Peterson's Mag 35 1859; Tait's Edinburgh Mag 26 1859; [Bucker, L.] Westminster Rev 71 1859; [Gilfillian, G.] Scottish Rev 9 1859; [Hale, E. E.] Christian Examiner 66 1859; [Hamley, E. B.] Blackwood's Mag 85 1859; [Kelton, Mrs] North Br Rev 30 1859; [Pollock, W. F.] Quart Rev 105 1859; [Russell, C. W.] Dublin Rev 42 1859; [Stigand, W.] Edinburgh Rev 110 1859; [Tiffany, O.] North Amer Rev 88 1859; [Fitzhugh, G.] De Bow's Rev 29 1860; Calcutta Rev 36 1861; NMM 121 1861; Amer Presbyterian Rev 4 1862; Atlantic Monthly 10 1862; Christian Rev 28 1862; Critic 24 1862; Dublin Univ Mag 60 1862; London Rev 4 1862; Peterson's Mag 42 1862; The Times 14 Aug 1862; Westminster Rev 78 1862; [Abraham, G. W.] Dublin Rev 51 1862; [Guernsey, A. H.] Harper's Mag 35 1862; [Hood, E. P.] Eclectic Rev 115 1862; [L., S.] Weldon's Register 2nd ser 1862; [Lewes, G. H. and F. Greenwood] Cornhill Mag 6 1862; [St John, H.] Athenaeum 1801 1862; Amer Presbyterian Rev 2 1864; Eclectic Rev 119 1864; Examiner 2928–30 1864; London Rev 8 1864; New York Times 18 July 1864; Peterson's Mag 46 1864; The Times 23 Mar 1864; Westminster Rev 82 1864; [Doran, J.] Athenaeum 1898 1864; [Lowell, J. R.] North Amer Rev 99 1864; [Stephen, J. F.] Fraser's Mag 69 1864; [Stephen, J. F.] Saturday Rev 17 1864; Eclectic Rev 122 1865; Examiner 2982–5 1865; London Rev 10 1865; The Times 18 Apr 1865; Westminster Rev 84 1865; [Doran, J.] Athenaeum 1952 1865; [Hamley, E. B.] Blackwood's Mag 98 1865; [Lancaster, H. H.] North Br Rev 43 1865; [Merivale, H.] Quart Rev 118 1865; [Stephen, J. F.] Fraser's Mag 72 1865; [Stephen, J. F.] Saturday Rev 19 1865; Amer Presbyterian Rev 4 1866; Harper's Weekly 10 1866; [Lowell, J. R.] North Amer Rev 102 1866; Nation 5 1867; A wandering Englishman [W. G. Hamley] Blackwood's Mag 118 1875.

Inaugural address at Edinburgh, April 2nd 1866. Edinburgh 1866. 1st pamp edn. On the choice of books, 1866 (1st book edn), 1869 ('With a new life of the author'); On the choice of books, Melbourne 1866.
REVIEWS: London Rev 22 1866; [Alden, H.] Harper's Mag 33 1866; [Smith, A.] Argosy 1 1866; N & Q 9 1866; Punch 50 1866; Saturday Rev 21 1866; The Times 4 Apr 1866;

Shooting Niagara: and after? 1867.
REVIEWS: Harper's Weekly 11 1867; New York Tribune 16 Aug 1867; Saturday Rev 24 1867; [Parsons, R.] Catholic World 6 1867.

Memoir of Sir William Hamilton, Bart. Ed J. Veitch, Edinburgh 1869. Reminiscence.

Early kings of Norway: also an essay on the portraits of John Knox. 1875, New York 1875.
REVIEWS: Examiner 3515 1875; Literary World 6 1875; Methodist Quart Rev 57 1875; Saturday Rev 39 1875; The Times 23 Dec 1875; [Dasent, G. W.] Edinburgh Rev 142 1875; [Gosse, E.] Athenaeum 2476 1875; [Drummond, J.] Proc of the Soc of Antiquaries of Scotland 11 1875; [Smith, G.] Nation 23 1876.

Characteristics. Boston 1877.

Goethe. Boston 1877.

Work about the Five Dials. Ed M. A. Stanley 1878. Prefatory note.

Reminiscences. Ed J. A. Froude 2 vols 1881, New York 1881, 1881.
REVIEWS: American 1 1881; Athenaeum 2785–6 1881; Atlantic Monthly 47 1881; Br Quart Rev 63 1881; Churchman 4 1881; Critic (New York) 1 1881; Graphic 23 1881; Inquirer 2020–4 1881; Lippincott's Mag 1 1881; Literary World 12, 23 1881; Methodist Quart Rev 63 1881; Month 41 1881; New York Times 5 May 1881; N & Q 3 1881; Saturday Rev 51 1881; The Times 3, 7 Mar 1881; [Alden, H.] Harper's Mag 62 1881; B[entley], G[eorge] Temple Bar 62 1881; [Brownell, W. C.] Nation 32 1881; [Bryce, J.] Nation 32 1881; [Carlyle, M.] The Times 5, 7 May 1881; [Dorling, W.] Christian World Mag 17 1881; [Dorling, W.] Sunday Mag 17 1881; [Froude, J. A.] The Times 6, 9 May 1881; The Times 24 Mar 1881; [Hayward, A.] Quart Rev 151 1881; [Keeling, A. E.] Wesleyan Methodist Mag 104 1881; [Lang, A.] Fraser's Mag 103 1881; [Morison, J. C.] Fortnightly Rev 35 1881; [Reeve, H.] Edinburgh Rev 43 1881; [Taylor, H.] Nineteenth Cent 9 1881; [W., G.] Churchman's Shilling Mag 29 1881.

Reminiscences of my Irish journey in 1849. Century Mag 24 1882; London 1882 (with revisions), New York 1882.
REVIEWS: Athenaeum 2853 1882; Critic (New York) 2 1882; Saturday Rev 54 1882; Spectator 55 1882; [Heaton, M. M.] Academy 22 1882.

Last words of Carlyle on trades-unions, promoterism and signs of the times. Ed J. C. Aitkin, Edinburgh 1882.
REVIEW: N & Q 6 1882.
Reminiscences. Ed C. E. Norton 2 vols 1887, 2 vols in 1 1887; ed K. J. Fielding and I. Campbell, Oxford 1997.
Thomas Carlyle on the repeal of the union. Ed P. E. N[ewberry] 1889.
The nibelungen lied: an essay. New York and London 1890.
Lectures on the history of literature, delivered April to July 1838. Ed J. Reay Greene 1892, New York 1892; ed R. P. Karkaria 1892.
REVIEWS: Athenaeum 3358 1892; Bookman (50) 1 1892; Critic (New York) 20 1892; Nation 54 1892; New York Times 31 Jan 1892; Saturday Rev 73 1892; Spectator 67 1892; Westminster Rev 137 1892; Westminster Rev 139 1893.
El Doctor Francia. Ed Luis M. Drago, Buenos Aires [1893?].
Scott Walter [*sic*]. Tr Baráth Ferencz, Budapest 1895.
Abhandlung über Goethes Faust. Tr R. Schröder, Braunschweig 1896.
Historical sketches of notable persons and events in the reigns of James I and Charles I. Ed Alexander Carlyle 1898. Written 1842–3.
Journey to Germany: Autumn 1858. Ed R. A. E. Brooks, New Haven CT 1940.
Le Comte Cagliostro. Tr G. A. Garnier, Fribourg 1944, 1945.
Carlyle's unfinished history of German literature. Ed Hill Shine, Lexington KY 1951.
To Day. West Linton, Scotland 1973. Poem.
Two Reminiscences. Ed J. Clubbe, Durham NC 1974.
Wooden-headed publishers and locust-swarms authors. Ed H. Henderson. Edinburgh 1979. From ms Victoria and Albert museum.
The guises. Ed R. L. Tarr, Special issue VS 25 1981.

Contributions to periodicals

Works rptd in vol form following first pbn in periodicals are listed in §1, above.

On the phenomenon of thunder. Dumfries and Galloway Courier 6 June 1815. Signed 'Ichneretes'.
Examination of some compounds which depend on very weak affinities, by Jacob Berzelius. Edinburgh Philosophical Jnl 1 1819. Tr Carlyle.
Remarks upon Professor Hansteen's inquiries concerning the magnetism of the Earth. Edinburgh Philosophical Jnl 3–4 1819. Tr Carlyle.
Outlines of Professor Moh's new system of crystallography and mineralogy. Edinburgh Philosophical Jnl 3–4 1820–1. Tr Carlyle.
[Articles in Brewster's Edinburgh Encyclopaedia]. 14 1820: Montaigne; Lady Montagu; Montesquieu; Montfaucon; Montucla; Dr John Moore; Sir John Moore; Persia; Quakers. 15 1822: Necker; Nelson; Netherlands; Newfoundland; Pascal; William Pitt, Earl of Chatham; William Pitt the Younger. 17 1824: Sismondi, 'Political economy', tr Carlyle. Rptd, except for Persia, Quakers and Pascal, and trn of Sismondi, in Montaigne and other essays chiefly biographical, ed S. R. Crocket 1897.
Joanna Baillie's metrical legends. New Edinburgh Rev 1 1821.
Goethe's Faust. New Edinburgh Rev 2 1822; ed R. Garnett, Pbns of the New England Goethe Soc 4 1888.
Schiller's life and writings. London Mag 8, 9, 10 1823, Oct, Jan, July–Sep 1823–4.
Jean Paul Friedrich Richter. Edinburgh Rev 46 1827.
State of German literature. Edinburgh Rev 46 1827.
Life and writings of Werner. Foreign Rev 1 1828.
Goethe's Helena. Foreign Rev 1 1828.
Goethe. Foreign Rev 2 1828.
Life of Heyne. Foreign Rev 2 1828.
Burns. Edinburgh Rev 48 1828.
German playwrights. Foreign Rev 3 1829.
Voltaire. Foreign Rev 3 1829.
Signs of the times. Edinburgh Rev 49 1829.
Novalis. Foreign Rev 4 1829.
Jean Paul Friedrich Richter [again]. Foreign Rev 5 1830.
Jean Paul Richter's review of Madame de Staël's 'De l'Allemange'. Fraser's Mag 1 1830.
Cui bono? and Four fables by Pilpay Junior. Fraser's Mag 2 1830.
Thoughts on History. Fraser's Mag 2 1830.
Luther's Psalm. Fraser's Mag 2 1831.
Cruthers and Jonson. Fraser's Mag 2 1831.
'Peter Nimmo'. Fraser's Mag 3 1831.
The beetle. Fraser's Mag 3 1831.
Taylor's historic survey of German poetry. Edinburgh Rev 53 1831.
Schiller. Fraser's Mag 3 1831.
The sower's song. Fraser's Mag 3 1831.
The Niebelungen Lied. Westminster Rev 15 1831.
'Tragedy of the night-moth'. Fraser's Mag 4 1831.
German literature of the fourteenth and fifteenth centuries. Foreign Quart Rev 8 1831.
Characteristics. Edinburgh Rev 54 1831.
Faust's curse. Athenaeum 219 1832.
Schiller, Goethe and Madame de Staël, and Goethe's portrait. Fraser's Mag 5 1832.
Biography. Fraser's Mag 5 1832.
Boswell's Life of Johnson. Fraser's Mag 5 1832.
Death of Goethe. NMM 34 1832.
Corn law rhymes. Edinburgh Rev 55 1832.
Goethe's Works. Foreign Quart Rev 10 1832.
The tale, by Goethe. Fraser's Mag 6 1832.
Novelle, by Goethe. Fraser's Mag 6 1832.
Diderot. Foreign Quart Rev 11 1833.
Quae cogitavit. Fraser's Mag 7 1833.
Count Cagliostro. Fraser's Mag 8 1833.
Sartor resartus. Fraser's Mag 8, 9, 10 1833–4.
Death of Edward Irving. Fraser's Mag 11 1835.
Memoirs of Mirabeau. London and Westminster Rev 26 1837.
The diamond necklace. Fraser's Mag 15 1837.
Parliamentary history of the French Revolution. London and Westminster Rev 27 1837.
Sir Walter Scott. London and Westminster Rev 28 1838.
Varnhagen von Ense's memoirs. London and Westminster Rev 32 1838.
Appeal for London Library. Examiner 1617 1839.
Petition on the Copyright Bill. Examiner 1627 1839.
On the sinking of the Vengeur. Fraser's Mag 20 1839.
Baillie the Covenanter. Westminster Rev 37 1842.
Dr Francia. Foreign Quart Rev 31 1843.
On the opening of Mazzini's letters. The Times 19 June 1844.
An election to the Long Parliament. Fraser's Mag 30 1844.
Thirty-five unpublished letters of Oliver Cromwell. Fraser's Mag 36 1847.
Louis Philippe. Examiner 2092 1848.
Repeal of the Union. Examiner 2100 1848.
Legislation for Ireland. Examiner 2102 1848.
Ireland and the British Chief Governor: Irish regiments of the new era. Spectator 21 1848.
Death of Charles Buller. Examiner 2131 1848.
Indian meal. Fraser's Mag 39 1849.
Ireland and Sir Robert Peel. Spectator 22 1849.
Trees of liberty, from Mr Bramble's unpublished Arboretum Hibericum. Nation (Dublin) 7 1849.
Occasional discourse on the negro question. Fraser's Mag 40 1849. Pbd 1853 (separately), *see* §1, *above*.
Two hundred and fifty years ago: a fragment about duels. Leigh Hunt's Jnl nos 1–6 1850–1.
The Prinzenraub. Westminster Rev 63 1855.

Suggestions for a national exhibition of Scottish portraits. Proc of the Soc of Antiquaries of Scotland 1 1855.
State and appeal for Miss Lowe and her sister. The Times 1 Nov 1855.
[Inspector Braidwood]. The Times 2 July 1861.
Memoranda concerning Mr Leigh Hunt. Macmillan's Mag 6 1862.
'Ilias (Americana) in Nuce' [The American Iliad in a nutshell]. Macmillan's Mag 8 1863.
Shooting Niagara: and after? Macmillan's Mag 16 1867.
On the French–German War. The Times 18 Nov 1870.
Early Kings of Norway. Fraser's Mag 11 1875.
On the eastern question. The Times 28 Nov 1876.
On the crisis. The Times 5 May 1877. On Disraeli's foreign policy.

Letters and journals

Sanders, C. R., K. J. Fielding, C. de L. Ryals et al (ed). The collected letters of Thomas and Jane Welsh Carlyle. Duke–Edinburgh edn, 24 vols to date, Durham NC 1970– . The standard edn of letters.
The following contain one or more letters.
Paul, L. [Francis Epinasse]. Thomas Carlyle. Critic 10 1851.
Correspondence, Carlyle's gift of books on Cromwell and Frederick the Great to Harvard College. Harvard Univ Bull 2 1881. Anon.
Carlyle, T. Letters addressed to Mrs Basil Montagu and B. W. Procter. 1881 (priv circulation); rptd Lakeland MI 1907.
Conway, M. D. Thomas Carlyle: a memorial discourse. 1881. Contains many letters and excerpts from letters.
Shepherd, R. H. Memoirs of the life and writings of Carlyle. 2 vols 1881. Contains many letters.
Hewlett, H. G. [Carlyle letter to H. F. Chorley]. Athenaeum 2875 1882.
[Inglis, H.] Some early letters of Mr Carlyle. Glasgow Herald 16 Feb 1882.
Skinner, C. M. An unpublished letter from Carlyle. Critic (New York) 2 1882.
One of Carlyle's letters. New York Times 22 Apr 1883. Anon.
Hewlett, H. J. Two letters from Thomas Carlyle to the Chorleys. Athenaeum 2887 1883.
Norton, C. E. (ed). The correspondence of Thomas Carlyle and Ralph Waldo Emerson. 2 vols Boston 1883, 1883, 1886 (with addns), 1888; ed J. Slater, New York 1964 (with addns and notes).
REVIEWS: Athenaeum 2890 1883; Manhattan 1 1883; Spectator 56 1883; [Alden, H.] Harper's Mag 66 1883; [Burroughs, J.] Emerson and Carlyle again, Critic (New York) 3 1883; [Ireland, A.] Acad 23 1883; [James, H., jun.] Century Mag 26 1883; [Schuyler, M.] Atlantic Monthly 51 1883; [Whipple, E. P.] North Amer Rev 136 1883.
[Carlyle letters to Judge Beverly Tucker]. Harper's Mag 71 1885. Anon.
A letter by Carlyle. The Times 13 Aug 1885. Anon.
An unpublished letter of Carlyle's [to Gavan Duffy]. Irish Monthly 13 1885. Anon.
Five letters of Carlyle's. Athenaeum 3064 1886. Anon. Letters to Coventry Patmore.
Norton, C. E. (ed). Early letters of Carlyle 1814–26. 2 vols 1886, 2 vols in 1 1886.
REVIEWS: Athenaeum 3080 1886; Critic (New York) 9 1886; New York Times 13 Nov 1886; Saturday Rev 62 1886; The Times 6 Nov 1886; [Wallace, W.] Acad 30 1886; Literary World 18 1887; [Woodberry, G. E.] Nation 44 1887; Literary World 20 1889.
Stirling, J. H. (ed). Thomas Carlyle's counsels to a literary aspirant. Edinburgh 1886.
Norton, C. E. (ed). Correspondence between Goethe and Carlyle. 1887; ed H. Oldenberg, Berlin 1887; ed G. Hecht, Dachau [1913].
REVIEWS: All the Year Round 40 1887; Atlantic Monthly 59 1887; Blackwood's Mag 142 1887; Critic (New York) 10 1887; Literary World 18 1887; New Princeton Rev 4 1887; Saturday Rev 63 1887; [H. Grimm] Deutsche Rundschau 53 1887.
Norton, C. E. (ed). Letters of Carlyle 1826–36. 2 vols 1888, 2 vols in 1 1889.
REVIEWS: Athenaeum 3204 1889; Atlantic Monthly 64 1889; New York Times 31 Mar 1889; [Harrison, F.] Nineteenth Cent 25 1889.
[Carlyle letter to John L. Motley]. Critic (New York) 14 1889.
[Carlyle letter]. Critic (New York) 15 1889.
Carlyle and Ruskin (two letters). English Illus Mag 9 1891.
[Carlyle letter to Dr Hanna]. Critic (New York) 19 1891.
[Carlyle letter to Emerson]. Critic (New York) 18 1891.
Carlyle, Thomas. Excursion (futile enough) to Paris, Autumn 1851. New Rev 5 1891; rptd in Last words, 1892, *above*.
[Kingsland, W. G.] Letter of advice to a young man, 1 April 1870. Poet-Lore 3 1891.
Murray, P. Dr Murray as an Edinburgh reviewer, with an unpublished letter of Thomas Carlyle. Irish Monthly 19 1891.
Atkinson, B. My four letters from Carlyle. Good Words 33 1892.
Duffy, C. G. Conversations and correspondence with Thomas Carlyle. Contemporary Rev 61 1892.
Duffy, C. G. Conversations with Carlyle. 1892. Records much conversation, with many letters.
Preuss, R. (ed). Briefe Carlyles an Varnhagen von Ense. Berlin 1892. Letters from Carlyle to Varnhagen von Ense in Last words, 1892, *above*.
[Preuss, R.] Letters of Carlyle to Varnhagen von Ense. New Rev 6 1892.
Unpublished letters of Carlyle. Scribner's Mag 13 1893.
Strachey, G. Reminiscences of Carlyle, with some unpublished letters. New Rev 9 1893.
Strachey, E. Some letters and conversations of Thomas Carlyle. Atlantic Monthly 73 1894.
Letters from Carlyle. New York Times 8 May 1897.
[Sale of Carlyle letters at Sotheby's]. Critic (New York) 30 1897.
Copeland, C. T. Unpublished letters of Carlyle. Atlantic Monthly 82 1898.
Norton, C. E. (ed). Two note books of Carlyle from 23 March 1822 to 16 May 1832. New York 1898.
Copeland, C. T. (ed). Letters of Thomas Carlyle to his youngest sister. Boston 1899, London 1899.
Garnett, R. Eight unpublished letters of Thomas Carlyle. Archiv für das Studium der Neueren Sprachen und Literaturen 102 1899.
C., E. S. C. Carlyle and Robert Chambers: unpublished letters. Chambers's Jnl 77 1900.
Literature portraits, XIV. Thomas Carlyle; also bibliography of Thomas Carlyle, an unpublished letter from Carlyle, and Carlyle as schoolmaster. Literature, suppl to The Times 199 1901.
D'Eichthal, E. (ed). Carlyle et le Saint-Simonisme: lettres à Gustave D'Eichthal. Paris 1903.
Carlyle, A. (ed). New letters of Thomas Carlyle. 2 vols 1904.
Harrison, F. Carlyle and the London Library . . . together with unpublished letters of Thomas Carlyle. 1906.
An unpublished Carlyle letter. Scottish Rev 5 1907.
Masson, É. (ed). Lettres de Thomas Carlyle à sa mère. Paris 1907.
Pitollet, C. Quelques lettres inédites de Carlyle. Revue Germanique 4 1908.
Carlyle, A. (ed). Love letters of Carlyle and Jane Welsh. 2 vols 1909.
Cook, E. T. and A. D. O. Wedderburn (ed). Works of Ruskin. 39 vols 1909. Vols 36–7 contain letters. *See* Carlyle's letters to Ruskin, ed C. R. Sanders, BJRL 41 1958.
[McCarthy, D.?]. Carlyle's letters to the Socialists of 1830. New Quart Rev 2 1909.
Strachey, Lytton. Some new Carlyle letters. Spectator 102 1909.
[Wilberforce, W.] More Carlyle letters. Nation 88 1909.
Allingham, H. and E. Baumer Williams, (ed). Letters to William Allingham. 1911.
Carré, J.-M. Quelques lettres inédites de William Taylor, Coleridge

et Carlyle à Henry Crabbe Robinson sur la littérature allemande. Revue Germanique 8 1912.
Gorrie, D. Letters by Carlyle to a fellow student. Fortnightly Rev 101 1914.
Carlyle, A. Correspondence between Carlyle and Browning. Cornhill Mag 111 1915.
Shorter, C. (ed). Letter to a young man. 1915 (priv ptd, 20 copies).
Dickens letter to Carlyle. Dickensian 12 1916.
Cook, D. A strange old brown manuscript. The story of an Anglo-American Franklin relic, with some hitherto unpublished Carlyle letters. Bookman 56 1919.
Brand, C. N. A letter of Carlyle's. TLS 10 June 1920.
Bathurst, K. Carlyle's unpublished letters to Miss Wilson. Nineteenth Cent and After 89 1921.
Carlyle, A. Thomas Carlyle and Thomas Spedding: their friendship and correspondence. Cornhill Mag 123 1921.
Gorrie, D. More letters by Carlyle to a fellow student. Fortnightly Rev 96 1921.
Carlyle, A. Notes of a three-days' tour to the Netherlands, August 1842. Cornhill Mag 126 1922.
Carlyle, A. (ed). Letters of Carlyle to John Stuart Mill, John Sterling and Robert Browning. 1923, New York 1923.
Meunier, P. Lettres inédites de Carlyle et de George Eliot à Emile Montégut. Revue de Littérature Comparée 5 1925.
Speck, W. A. New letters of Carlyle to Eckerman. Yale Rev 15 1926.
Peel, A. A new Carlyle letter. Yale Rev 16 1927.
Morris, R. Thomas Carlyle: an unpublished letter. Spectator 140 1928.
An original letter of Thomas Carlyle. Jnl of the Friends Historical Soc 27 1930.
Sotheby. Catalogue of printed books, autograph letters, literary manuscripts . . . formerly the property of Thomas Carlyle. 1932.
Shine, H. Carlyle and Fraser's letter on the Doctrine of St Simon. N & Q 171 1936.
Flower, R. Letters of William Somerville and Thomas Carlyle. Br Museum Quart 11 1937.
Gray, W. F. Carlyle and John Forster: an unpublished correspondence. Quart Rev 268 1937.
Reilly, J. J. Some immortal letters. Catholic World 153 1941.
Roberts, W. W. English autograph letters in the John Rylands Library. BJRL 25 1941.
Fiedler, H. G. The friendship of Thomas Carlyle and Varnhagen von Ense, with a letter hitherto unknown. MLR 38 1943.
Strout, A. L. Some unpublished letters of John Gibson Lockhart to John Wilson Croker. N & Q 187 1944.
Ethlinger, L. Carlyle on the portraits of Frederick the Great. An unpublished letter. MLR 40 1945.
Altick, R. D. Dickens and America: some unpublished letters. Pennsylvania Mag of History and Biography 73 1949.
Gallup, D. Two old letters. YULG 24 1949.
Graham, J., jun. (ed). Letters of Carlyle to William Graham. Princeton 1950.
Bliss, T. (ed). Carlyle: letters to his wife. 1953, Cambridge MA 1953.
Calder, G. J. Carlyle and 'Irving's London Circle': some unpublished letters by Thomas Carlyle and Mrs Edward Strachey. PMLA 69 1954.
[Carlyle letter]. N & Q 199 1954.
Sanders, C. R. Carlyle's letters. Victorian Newsletter 5 1954.
Nobbe, S. H. Four unpublished letters of Thomas Carlyle. PMLA 70 1955.
Sanders, C. R. Carlyle's letters. BJRL 38 1955.
Allott, K. An Arnold–Clough letter: references to Carlyle and Tennyson. N & Q 201 1956.
Dunn, W. H. Carlyle's last letter to Froude. Twentieth Cent 159 1956.
Letters of Ruskin and Carlyle. BJRL 40 1957.
Mulhauser, F. L. (ed). Correspondence of Arthur H. Clough. 2 vols Oxford 1957. Carlyle's letters to Clough.
Sanders, C. R. Carlyle's letters to Ruskin: a finding list with some unpublished letters and comments. BJRL 41 1958.
Marrs, E. W. Discovery of some new Carlyle letters. Thoth 3 1962.
Sanders, C. R. The correspondence and friendship of Thomas Carlyle and Leigh Hunt: the early years. BJRL 46 1963.
Sanders, C. R. The correspondence and friendship of Thomas Carlyle and Leigh Hunt: the later years. BJRL 46 1963.
Sanders, C. R. Some lost and unpublished Carlyle–Browning correspondence. JEGP 62 1963.
Sanders, C. R. Carlyle as editor and critic of Literary Letter. Emory Univ Quart 20 1964.
Sanders, C. R. Editing the Carlyle letters: problems and opportunities. In editing nineteenth-cent texts, ed J. M. Robson, Toronto 1967.
Marrs, E. W., jun. (ed). The letters of Thomas Carlyle to his brother Alexander, with related family matters. Cambridge MA 1968.
Shipley, J. B. A new Carlyle letter. Eng Stud 49 1968.
Tarr, R. L. Thomas Carlyle and Henry M'Cormac: two letters on the condition of Ireland in 1848. Stud in Scottish Lit 5 1968.
Campbell, I. James Barrett and Carlyle's journal. N & Q 17 1970.
Tarr, R. L. Emerson's transcendentalism in L. M. Child's Letter to Carlyle. Emerson Soc Quart 58 1970.
Tarr, R. L. A sentimental journey: Carlyle's final visit to the Grange. N & Q 215 1970.
Campbell, I. The Duke and Edinburgh Edition of the Carlyle letters. Scottish Literary News 1 1971.
Tarr, R. L. Mary Aitken Carlyle: an unpublished letter to her son. ELN 8 1971.
Faulkner, P. Carlyle's letter to Charles Redwood. YES 2 1972.
Tarr, R. L. Some unpublished letters of Varnhagen von Ense to Thomas Carlyle. MLR 68 1973.
Küster, B. Lettres inédites de Carlyle et de George Henry Lewes à Emile Montègut. Revue de Littérature Comparée 49 1975.
Sanders, C. R. The Carlyle–Browning correspondence and relationship. BJRL 57 1975.
Campbell, I. (ed). Thomas and Jane: selected letters from the Edinburgh University Library Collection. Edinburgh 1980.
DeBruyn, John R. Thomas Carlyle and Sir Arthur Helps. BJRL 64 1981.
Cate, G. A. (ed). The correspondence of Thomas Carlyle and John Ruskin. Stanford CA 1982.
DeBruyn, J. R. Thomas Carlyle and Sir Arthur Helps: II. BJRL 64 1982.
Sanders, Charles R. A brief history of the Duke–Edinburgh Edition of the Carlyle letters. Stud in Scottish Lit 17 1982.
Trela, D. J. FitzGerald to Carlyle to FitzGerald: two unpublished letters. N & Q 224.4 1984.
Campbell, I. Conversations with Carlyle: the Monckton Milnes diaries. Prose Stud 8.1 1985.
Campbell, I. More conversations with Carlyle: the Monckton Milnes diaries, II. Prose Stud 9.1 1986.
Campbell, I. Thomas Carlyle: Borderer [Border Mag]. Carlyle Newsletter 7 1986.
Fielding, K. J. Carlyle and the Speddings: new letters. Carlyle Newsletter 7 1986.
Richardson, T. Carlyle and John Lockhart: some unpublished letters. Carlyle Newsletter 7 1986.
Tarr, R. L. Carlyle on Field Marshal James Keith: a new impression. Carlyle Newsletter 7 1986.
Campbell, I. Letters from home: the Carlyle family correspondence. Prose Stud 10.3 1987.
Campbell, I. and K. J. Fielding. New Carlyle letters. Carlyle Newsletter 8 1987.
Fielding, K. J. Carlyle and the Speddings – new letters II. Carlyle Newsletter 8 1987.
Fielding, K. J. Vernon Lushington: Carlyle's friend and editor. Carlyle Newsletter 8 1987.

Küster, B. Unveröffentlichte Briefe von Carlyle und E. F. S. Pigott an Emile Montégut. Archiv 224.1 1987.

Ryals, C. de L. Thomas Carlyle and John Childs: a forgotten friendship. Prose Stud 10.3 1987.

Tarr, R. L. Let us burn our ships: Carlyle, Sarah Austin, and house-hunting in London. Stud in Scottish Lit 22 1987.

Fielding, K. J. Editing the Carlyle letters: 1966–1991. Carlyle Annual 11 1990.

Campbell, I. Henry Larkin and the Carlyles. Huntington Lib Quart 54 1991.

Campbell, I. Carlyle House. Carlyle Annual 12 1991.

Fielding, K. J. Carlyle writes local history: Dumfries-shire three hundred years ago. Carlyle Annual 12 1991.

§2

For a more comprehensive list of pbns, see R. L. Tarr, Thomas Carlyle: a bibliography of English-language criticism, 1824–1974. *See also J. P. Seigel,* Thomas Carlyle: the critical heritage, *1971.*

[Maginn, W.] Thomas Carlyle. Fraser's Mag 7 1833.

[Everett, A. H.] Thomas Carlyle. North Amer Rev 41 1835.

[Anstey, T. C.] Carlyle's works. Dublin Rev 5 1838.

J., J. J. [Isaac Jewett]. Thomas Carlyle. Hesperian 2 1838.

[Henry, C. S.?] Writings of Thomas Carlyle. New York Rev 4 1839.

[Sterling, J.] Carlyle's works. London and Westminster Rev 33 1839.

[Porter, O.] Hints for a critical estimate of the writings of Thomas Carlyle. Yale Literary Mag 5 1840.

[Sewell, W.] Carlyle's works. Quart Rev 66 1840.

Richardson, M. The religious sentiments of Thomas Carlyle. Amer Biblical Repository 8 1842.

Foster, J. K. On Thomas Carlyle's writings. Congregational Mag 26 1843.

Maurice, F[rederick D.] On the tendency of Mr Carlyle's writings. Christian Remembrancer 6 1843.

Horne, R. H. Thomas Carlyle. In his A new spirit of the age vol 2, 1844.

[Mazzini, J.] The works of Thomas Carlyle. Br and Foreign Rev 16 1844.

[Thackeray, W. M.] Carlyle, Dickens, and Christmas. Fraser's Mag 29 1844.

Hudson, T. B. Thomas Carlyle. Oberlin Quart Rev 1 1845.

The works of Thomas Carlyle. Eclectic Rev 81 1845.

[Moncrieff, J.] Carlyle's works. North Br Rev 4 1846.

[Donaldson, J. W.] Pantagruelism. Quart Rev 81 1847.

Fuller, [M.] Miss. A picture of Thomas Carlyle. Littell's Living Age 21 1847.

Lester, J. W. In his Criticisms. 1847.

Thoreau, H. D. Carlyle and his works. Graham's Mag 30 1847.

Carlyle's works. Southern Quart Rev 14 1848.

[Lewes, G. H.] Thomas Carlyle. Br Quart Rev 10 1849.

Montégut, É. Carlyle: sa vie et ses écrits. Revue des Deux Mondes 19 1849.

Moore, T. V. Thomas Carlyle. Methodist Quart Rev 31 1849.

Caliban [J. H. Sterling]. Letters on Carlyle. Truth-Seeker 1 1850.

Carlyle on West India emancipation. De Bow's Rev 8 1850.

Carlylian [J. Hannay]. Blackwood versus Carlyle: a vindication. 1850.

D. [John S. Mill]. The negro question. Fraser's Mag 41 1850.

[Field, H. M.] Writing and opinions of Thomas Carlyle. New Englander 8 1850.

Gilfillan, G. Thomas Carlyle. Harper's Mag 1 1850.

Montégut, É. Littérature américaine: du culte des héros, Carlyle et Emerson. Revue des Deux Mondes 20 1850.

[O'Hagan, J.] Carlyle's works. Dublin Rev 29 1850.

Poe, E. A. Carlyle's style. Graham's Mag 36 1850.

Wright, E. Perforations in the Latter-day pamphlets by one of the 'Eighteen Millions of Bores'. Boston 1850.

Paul, L. [Francis Epinasse]. Thomas Carlyle. Critic 10 1851.

Fuller, M. [Ossoli]. In her Memoirs vol 2, Boston 1852.

[McNicoll, T.] Writings of Thomas Carlyle. Wesleyan Methodist Mag 75 1852.

Montégut, É. Carlyle et John Sterling. Revue des Deux Mondes 22 1852.

Writings of Thomas Carlyle. Chamber's Repository of Tracts 5 1853.

[Eliot, G.] Thomas Carlyle. Leader 6 1855.

[Martineau, J.] Personal influences on our present theology: Newman – Coleridge – Carlyle. Nat Rev 3 1856.

[Philips, G. S.] Thomas Carlyle. Atlantic Monthly 1 1857.

[Stephen, J. F.] Mr Carlyle. Saturday Rev 5 1858.

Carlyle and his writings. Meloria 1 1859.

Häusser, L. Macaulay's Friedrich der Grosse mit einem Nachtrag über Carlyle. Historische Zeitshrift 1 1859.

Newcomb, H. O. Carlyle's philosophy. Univ Quart Rev 4 1861.

Dillard, A. W. Thomas Carlyle – his philosophy and style. Southern Literary Messenger 34 1862.

H[arte], F. B[ret]. 'Peter of the North' to Thomas Carlyle. San Francisco Evening Bull 8 Sep 1863.

[Clarke, J. F.] The two Carlyles, or Carlyle Past and present. Christian Examiner 77 1864.

Taine, H. A. L'idéalisme anglais: étude sur Carlyle. Paris 1864.

Taine, H. A. Philosophy and history – Carlyle. In Histoire de la littérature anglaise vol 4, Paris 1864.

Blair, D. Carlylism and Christianity. Melbourne 1865.

Japp, A. H. Three great teachers of our own times: Carlyle, Tennyson and Ruskin. 1865.

Mr Carlyle on natural history. The Times 10 Oct 1865.

Alexander, P. P. Mill and Carlyle: an examination of Mr John Stuart Mill's doctrine of causation in relation to moral freedom, with an occasional discourse on Sauertag, by Smelfungus. Edinburgh 1866.

Althaus, F. Carlyle: eine biografisch-literarische Characteristik. Unsere Zeit n.s. 2 1866.

Smith, A. Mr Carlyle at Edinburgh. Argosy 1 1866.

Three cynical observers: Gulliver – Candide – Teufelsdröckh. Dublin Univ Mag 67 1866.

Whitman, W. Democracy. Galaxy 4 1867.

Thomas Carlyle as a practical guide. Putnam's Monthly Mag 13 1869.

Morley, J. Carlyle. Fortnightly Rev 14 1870.

C., T. L. The philosopher of Chelsea. GM 231 1871.

[Dwinell, I. E.] Religion according to Carlyle. Congregational Rev 11 1871.

Lowell, J. R. My study windows. Boston 1871.

Mozley, J. B. Thomas Carlyle's Collected Works. Quart Rev 132 1872.

Routledge, J. Thomas Carlyle. Mookerjee's Mag 1 1872.

Towle, G. M. Carlyle as historian. Penn Monthly 3 1872.

Hodge, D. Thomas Carlyle: the man and the teacher. Edinburgh [1873].

Stephen, L. Hours in a library. 1874.

Drummond, J. Notes upon some Scottish historical portraits – John Knox and George Buchanan. Proc of the Soc of Antiquaries of Scotland 11 1875.

Hood, E. P. Thomas Carlyle: philosophic thinker, theologian, historian, poet. 1875.

McCrie, G. Religion of our literature: essays upon Carlyle, Browning, Tennyson. 1875.

Guernsey, A. H. Thomas Carlyle. Appleton's Jnl 15 1876.

Mr Carlyle. Dublin Rev 78 1876.

Martin, F. Thomas Carlyle: a biography, with autobiographical notes. Biographical Mag 1 1877.

Bayne, P. Lessons from my masters: Carlyle, Tennyson and Ruskin. 1879.

Courtney, W. L. Carlyle's political doctrines. Fortnightly Rev 32 1879.

Guernsey, A. H. Carlyle: his life, his books, and his theories. New York 1879.

Spalding, J. L. Theories of education and life: Thomas Carlyle. Amer Catholic Quart 4 1879.
Grant, C. Carlyle als Moralist. Deutsche Rundschau 24 1880.
Alexander, P. P. Carlyle redivivus. Glasgow 1881.
A[llen], G[rant]. The Carlyle controversy. Temple Bar 63 1881.
Althaus, F. Erinnerungen an Thomas Carlyle. Unsere Zeit n.s. 1 1881.
[Barbour, W. M.] Thomas Carlyle. New Englander 40 1881.
Bell, C. D. Thomas Carlyle. Churchman 4 1881.
Boglietti, G. Tommaso Carlyle. Nuova Antologia 66 1881.
C., J. [J. C. Manchester]. Thomas Carlyle: a study. Manchester 1881.
[Call, W. M. W.] Thomas Carlyle: his life and writings. Westminster Rev 115 1881.
Carlyle's lost manuscript. The Times 16 Jan 1881.
Carlyle's will. The Times 9 Apr 1881.
Chadwick, J. W. Thomas Carlyle. Unitarian Rev 15 1881.
Coffey, R. S. Thomas Carlyle and some of the lessons of his career. Bradford [1881].
Conway, M. D. Thomas Carlyle. New York 1881.
Conway, M. D. Thomas Carlyle: a memorial discourse. South Place Chapel, Finsbury, London, 1881.
[D., H. W.] The life of Thomas Carlyle. [1881].
Dowden, E. Carlyle's lectures on the periods of European culture, from Homer to Goethe. Nineteenth Cent 9 1881.
Emerson, R. W. Impressions of Thomas Carlyle in 1848. Scribner's Monthly Mag 22 1881.
Froude, J. A. Mr Carlyle's papers. The Times 14 Feb 1881.
Gostwick, J. Thomas Carlyle. Wesleyan Methodist Mag 104 1881.
Hale, E. Thomas Carlyle. Boston 1881 (priv ptd).
Howe, J. W. A meeting with Thomas Carlyle. Critic (New York) 1 1881.
James, H. Some personal recollections of Carlyle. Atlantic Monthly 48 1881.
Jones, P. L. Thomas Carlyle. Baptist Rev 3 1881.
Knighton, W. Conversations with Carlyle. Contemporary Rev 39 1881.
Larkin, H. Carlyle and Mrs Carlyle: a ten years' reminiscence. Br Quart Rev 74 1881.
Mead, E. D. The philosophy of Carlyle. Boston 1881.
Murray, L. A defense of Carlyle's Reminiscences, partly written by himself. Canadian Monthly 20 1881.
[O'Conor, J. V.] Thomas Carlyle. Catholic World 33 1881.
O[liphant], M. O. W. Thomas Carlyle. Macmillan's Mag 43 1881.
Reid, S. J. Thomas Carlyle: his work and worth. Manchester [1881].
S., F. Carlyle on music. N & Q 3 1881.
[Saintsbury, G.] The literary work of Thomas Carlyle. Scribner's Monthly Mag 22 1881.
Sarson, G. George Eliot and Thomas Carlyle. Modern Rev 2 1881.
Scribner. The Carlyle Reminiscences. New York 1881.
Shepherd, R. H. Memoirs of the life and writings of Thomas Carlyle. 2 vols 1881.
[Statue and bust of Carlyle]. The Times 25 Feb 1881.
[Stephen, L.] Carlyle's ethics. Cornhill Mag 44 1881.
[Stephen, L.] Thomas Carlyle. Cornhill Mag 43 1881.
Swinburne, A. C. The deaths of Thomas Carlyle and George Eliot. Athenaeum 2792 1881.
Thomas, David. Thomas Carlyle: the cedar is fallen. 1881.
Thompson, R. E. Thomas Carlyle. Penn Monthly 12 1881.
'Valbert, G.' (C. V. Cherbuliez). Carlyle. Revue des Deux Mondes 44 1881.
[Wedgwood, J.] Mr Froude as a biographer. Contemporary Rev 39 1881.
[Wedgwood, J.] A study of Carlyle. Contemporary Rev 39 1881.
Williamson, C. N. The late Thomas Carlyle: a biographical and critical sketch. Graphic 23 1881.
Wilson, J. Thomas Carlyle: the iconoclast of modern shams. Paisley 1881.
Wylie, W. H. Thomas Carlyle: the man and his books. 1881.
Arden, C. The philosophy of Thomas Carlyle. Jnl of Science 19 1882.
[Brown, J.] Thomas Carlyle's apprenticeship. Scottish Rev 1 1882.
Fischer, E. L. [Thomas A. Fischer]. Thomas Carlyle. Leipzig 1882.
Fox-Bourne, H. R. Carlyle and his wife. GM 252 1882.
Froude, J. A. Thomas Carlyle: a history of the first forty years of his life, 1795–1835. 2 vols 1882.
Scherer, E. Études critiques de littérature. Paris 1882.
Watt, F. Thomas Carlyle and religious thoughts. St James's Mag 42 1882.
Burroughs, J. Carlyle. Century Mag 26 1883.
Burroughs, J. In Carlyle's country. Atlantic Monthly 51 1883.
[Lyttleton, A. T.] Carlyle's life and works. Church Quart Rev 15 1883.
Krummacher, M. Notizen über den Sprachgebrauch Carlyles. EStudien 6 1883.
Morison, J. C. Thomas Carlyle. Macmillan's Mag 47 1883.
Oliphant, M. O. W. The ethics of biography. Contemporary Rev 44 1883.
Wise, D. Thomas Carlyle. New York 1883.
Austin, A. Some lessons from Carlyle's life. Nat Rev 4 1884.
Beveridge, H. Some thoughts of Thomas Carlyle. Calcutta Rev 79 1884.
[Birrell, A.] Obiter dicta. 1884.
Froude, J. A. Thomas Carlyle: a history of his life in London, 1834–1881. 2 vols 1884.
Hannay, D. Some portraits of Carlyle. Mag of Art 7 1884.
Harris, J. Wales as Carlyle saw it forty years ago. Red Dragon Mag 6 1884.
Howells, J. Carlyle's holidays in Wales. Red Dragon Mag 5 1884.
[Morley, J.] The man of letters as hero. Macmillan's Mag 51 1884.
Saladin [W. S. Ross]. A visit to Carlyle's grave. [1884.]
Seaton, R. C. The attitude of Carlyle and Emerson towards Christianity. Nat Rev 3 1884.
West, H. E. John Inglesant and Sartor resartus. [1884.]
Barry, W. F. Carlyle. Dublin Rev 96 1885.
Chamberlain, D. H. The man, Thomas Carlyle, at last. Andover Rev 3 1885.
Emerson, G. H. Thomas Carlyle. Universalist Quart Rev 42 1885.
F., A. [A. F. Hewitt]. Carlyle as prophet. Catholic World 40–1 1885.
Masson, D. Carlyle: personally and in his writings. 1885.
Obiter dicta [Augustine Birrell]. Views of Carlyle. Bookworm 2 1885.
Thomas Carlyle. London Quart Rev 64 1885.
Browning, O. The flight of Louis XVI to Varennes. A criticism of Carlyle. Trans of the Royal Historical Soc 3 1886.
Francison, A. National lessons from the life and works of Carlyle. [1886.]
Froude, J. A. Carlyle's letters. The Times 2 Nov 1886.
Larkin, H. Carlyle and the open secret of his life. 1886.
Müller, F. M. Goethe and Carlyle. Contemporary Rev 49 1886.
Norton, C. E. Recollections of Carlyle, with notes concerning his Reminiscences. New Princeton Rev 2 1886.
O'Donoghue, T. G. Carlyle's Irish tours. Irish Monthly 14 1886.
Stephen, J. F. The late Mr Carlyle's papers. 1886 (priv ptd).
Symington, A. J. Some personal reminiscences of Carlyle. Paisley 1886.
Wright, W. A. The Squire Papers. English Historical Rev 1 1886.
Flügel, E. Carlyle religiöse und sittliche Entwicklung und Weltanschauung. Leipzig 1887.
Garnett, R. Life of Thomas Carlyle. Bibliography by J. P. Anderson. 1887.
Kerr, J. Carlyle as seen in his works. 1887.
Palgrave, R. Carlyle, the 'Pious Editor' of Cromwell's speeches. Nat Rev 8 1887.
Parkes, W. K. Thomas Carlyle: an essay. 1887.
Pollock, F. Personal remembrances. 2 vols 1887, vol 2.
Arnold, A. S. The story of Thomas Carlyle. 1888.
Jenks, E. Thomas Carlyle and John Stuart Mill. Orpington 1888.

Krummacher, M. Sprache und Stil in Carlyles Friedrich II. EStudien 11 1888.
Winsor, J. Bibliographical contributions. The Carlyle Collection. Cambridge MA 1888.
Gibbs, W. E. Thomas Carlyle. Universalist Quart Rev 46 1889.
James, L. G. Carlyle's philosophy of history. Westminster Rev 132 1889.
Troye, V. Carlyle hans liv og hans vaerk. Bergen 1889.
Lewin, W. Thomas Carlyle. Liverpool 1890.
Martin, W. Thomas Carlyle: his life and work. Glasgow [1890].
Tyndall, J. Personal recollections of Carlyle. Fortnightly Rev 53 1890.
Venturi, E. A. A memory of Thomas Carlyle. Paternoster Rev 1890.
C[ather], W[illa]. Concerning Thomas Carlyle. Nebraska State Jnl 21 1891.
Dilthey, W. Thomas Carlyle. Archiv für Geschichte der Philosophie 4 1891.
[Espinasse, F.] The Carlyles and a segment of their circle: recollections and reflections. Bookman 50 1891.
Flügel, E. Thomas Carlyle's moral and religious development. Tr J. G. Tyler, New York 1891.
Lecky, W[illiam] E. H. Carlyle's message to his age. Contemporary Rev 60 1891.
Martin, E. C. Carlyle's politics. Scribner's Monthly Mag 10 1891.
Masson, D. Carlyle. Glasgow 1891.
Duffy, C. G. Conversations and correspondence with Thomas Carlyle. Contemporary Rev 61 1892.
Masson, D. Edinburgh sketches and memories. 1892.
[Nichol, J.] Thomas Carlyle. 1892.
Smith, W. Ruskin and Carlyle on 'Sir Walter Scott'. Igdrasil 3 1892.
Strachey, G. Carlyle and the 'Rose Goddess'. Nineteenth Cent 32 1892.
Espinasse, F. Literary recollections and sketches. 1893.
Muir, J. Thomas Carlyle's apprenticeship. Glasgow 1893.
Strachey, G. Reminiscences of Carlyle, with some unpublished letters. New Rev 9 1893.
von Schultz-Gaevernitz, G. Carlyles Welt und Gesellschafts-anschauung. Dresden 1893.
Harrison, F. Carlyle's place in literature. Forum 17 1894.
Strachey, E. Some letters and conversations of Thomas Carlyle. Atlantic Monthly 73 1894.
Blunt, R. The Carlyles' Chelsea home. 1895.
[Cochrane, R. and M. Cochrane]. Thomas Carlyle: the story of his life and writings. 1895.
Horsley, R. Thomas Carlyle. Edinburgh 1895.
[Shelley, H. C.] The homes and haunts of Thomas Carlyle. 1895.
Thayer, W. R. Thomas Carlyle: his work and influence. Forum 20 1895.
Alger, J. G. Corrigenda in Carlyle's French Revolution. Westminster Rev 145 1896.
Aronstein, P. Dickens and Carlyle. Anglia 18 1896.
Illustrated memorial volume of the Carlyles, House Purchase Fund Committee with catalogue of Carlyle's books, manuscripts, pictures, and furniture exhibited therein. 1896.
[Henshaw, M.] Recollections of Thomas Carlyle. Blackwood's Mag 159 1896.
[Carlyle's windowpane verse]. Critic (New York) 28 1896.
Macpherson, H. C. Thomas Carlyle. Edinburgh 1896.
Schröder, R. Carlyles Abhandlung über den Goetheschen Faust. Archiv 96 1896.
Smithers, C. G., F. W. Jackson and E. P. Belben. Carlyle's window-pane verse. N & Q 10 1896.
Forster, J. Four great teachers. 1897.
Graham, P. A. Thomas Carlyle. Academy 51 1897.
Schmidt, F. J. Thomas Carlyle. Preussische Jahrbücher 89 1897.
Wilhelmi, J. H. Carlyle und Nietzsche: wie sie Gott suchten und was für einen Gott sie fanden. Göttingen 1897.
[Browning, E. B.] Mrs Browning's opinion of Carlyle. Poet-Lore 10 1898.
Copeland, C. T. Carlyle as a letter writer. Atlantic Monthly 82 1898.
Kraeger, H. Carlyles deutsche Studien und der Wotton Reinfred. Anglia Beiblatt 9 1898.
Muir, J. Carlyle on Burns. Glasgow 1898.
Wilson, D. A. Mr Froude and Carlyle. 1898.
Kraeger, H. Carlyles Stellung zur deutschen Sprache und Literatur. Anglia 22 1899.
Malsby, D. L. The growth of Sartor resartus. Malden MA 1899.
Stephen, L. Historians and essayists. New York 1899.
Trevelyan, G. M. Carlyle as historian. Nineteenth Cent 46 1899.
Wells, J. T. Thomas Carlyle: his religious experience as reflected in Sartor resartus. Edinburgh 1899.
Barthélemy, E. Carlyle: essai biographique et critique. Paris 1900.
Schmeding, O. Über Wortbildung bei Carlyle. Halle 1900.
von Gildermeester, F. Thomas Carlyle. Nijkerk [1900].
Brownell, W. C. Thomas Carlyle. Scribner's Mag 30 1901.
Hensel, P. Thomas Carlyle. Stuttgart 1901.
Chesterton, G. K. Twelve types. 1902.
'du Bos, Charles' (H. Boeuf). Le Kantisme de Carlyle. Archiv für Geschichte der Philosophie 15 1902.
Heggie, D. How I read Carlyle's French Revolution. Toronto 1902.
Matz, B. W. Thomas Carlyle: a brief account of his life and writings. 1902.
Chesterton, G. K. Varied types. New York 1903.
d'Eichthal, E. Carlyle et la Saint-Simonisme. Revue Historique 82 1903.
Duffy, C. G. The real Carlyle. Contemporary Rev 84 1903.
Froude, J. A. My relations with Carlyle. 1903.
Jones, S. A. Carlyle's apprenticeship. In Collectanea Thomas Carlyle, Canton PA 1903.
Cazamian, L. Le roman social en Angleterre 1830–50. Paris 1904.
Lee, V. [Violet Paget]. Studies in literary psychology: Carlyle and the present tense. Contemporary Rev 85 1904.
Lincke, O. Über die Wortzusammensetzung in Sartor resartus. Berlin 1904.
Sloan, J. M. The Carlyle country with a study of Carlyle's life. 1904.
Vandyopādyāya, H. Notes on Thomas Carlyle's Heroes and hero-worship. Lahore 1904.
Warner, P. Thomas Carlyle: the man and his influence. 1904.
Brown, J. M. The Sartor resartus of Carlyle. Christchurch [1905].
Cosh, T. R. The ethical teaching of Thomas Carlyle in Sartor resartus. Greenock 1905.
Goodwin, C. J. Carlyle's ethics. International Jnl of Ethics 15 1905.
More, P. E. The spirit of Carlyle. In Shelburne essays, 1905.
Baumgarten, O. Carlyle und Goethe. Tübingen 1906.
Harrison, F. Carlyle and the London Library. 1906.
Allingham, W. A diary. Ed H. Allingham and D. Radford 1907.
Durand, W. Y. De Quincey and Carlyle in their relation to the Germans. PMLA 22 1907.
Giles, E. Carlyle's Heroes and hero-worship. Jnl of Education 66–8 1907–8.
MacCunn, J. Six radical thinkers: Bentham, Mill, Cobden, Carlyle, Mazzini, T. H. Green. 1907.
Craig, R. S. The making of Carlyle. 1908.
Masson, D. Memories of London in the 'forties. Edinburgh 1908.
Archibald, R. C. Carlyle's first love: Margaret Gordon, Lady Bannerman. 1909.
Krauske, O. Macauley and Carlyle. Berlin 1909.
[Wilberforce, W.] Froude and Carlyle. Catholic World 90 1909.
Miller, F. The poets of Dumfriesshire. Glasgow 1910.
Roe, F. Thomas Carlyle as a critic of literature. New York 1910.
Stephen, L. Thomas Carlyle. Encyclopaedia Britannica, 11th edn, Cambridge 1910, vol 5.
Vaughan, C. E. Carlyle and his german masters. E & S 1 1910.

Carlyle, A. Frank Harris and his (imaginary) 'Talks with Carlyle'; a reply by Frank Harris. English Rev 9 1911.

Carlyle's birthplace: the arched house, Ecclefechan. 1911.

Harris, F. Talks with Carlyle. English Rev 7 1911.

Johnson, W. S. Thomas Carlyle: a study of his literary apprenticeship, 1814–1831. New Haven CT 1911.

Moisant, X. L'optimisme au xixe siècle. Beauchesne 1911.

Orr, L. Famous affinities of history: the story of the Carlyles. Munsey's Mag 45 1911.

Watt, L. M. Thomas Carlyle. [1912.]

Cazamian, L. Carlyle. Paris 1913; tr 1932.

Clare, M. [M. C. Byron]. A day with Thomas Carlyle. [1913.]

Wilson, D. A. The truth about Carlyle. 1913.

Crichton-Browne, J. Thomas Carlyle. In Famous Edinburgh students, Edinburgh 1914.

Meyer, M. Carlyles Einfluss auf Kingsley in sozial-politischer und religiös-ethischer Hinsicht. Weimar 1914.

Perry, B. Thomas Carlyle: how to know him. Indianapolis [1915].

Sloan, J. M. Carlyle's Germans. Hibbert Jnl 13 1915.

Guthrie, Lord. Thomas Carlyle: an appreciation. Glasgow 1916.

Morgan, W. Carlyle and German thought. Queen's Quart 23 1916.

Robertson, J. G. Carlyle. In Cambridge history of English literature, ed A. W. Ward and A. R. Waller, vol 13, Cambridge 1916.

Stewart, H. L. Carlyle's conception of history. Political Science Quart 32 1917.

Stewart, H. L. Carlyle's conception of religion. American Jnl of Theology 21 1917.

[Gunn, S.] Carlyle and Kultur. Unpopular Rev 10 1918.

Millar, M. I. S. Carlyle and the nineteenth century. Catholic World 16 1918.

Stewart, H. L. The alleged Prussianism of Thomas Carlyle. International Jnl of Ethics 28 1918.

Trevelyan, G. M. The two Carlyles. Cornhill Mag 44 1918.

Besch, J. Sprecher Gottes in unserer Zeit: Schleiermacher, Carlyle, Tolstoi. Stuttgart 1919.

Hunter, J. Thomas Carlyle. Modern Churchman 9 1919.

Jones, S. A. A catalogue of the Dr Samuel A. Jones Carlyle Collection. Ed M. E. Wead, Ann Arbor MI 1919.

Stewart, H. L. Carlyle's place in philosophy. Monist 29 1919.

Ralli, A. Guide to Carlyle. 2 vols [1920].

Hohfeld, A. R. The poems in Carlyle's translation of Wilhelm Meister. MLN 36 1921.

Carlyle, A. Notes on a three days' tour to the Netherlands: August, 1842 – T. Carlyle. Cornhill Mag 126 1922.

[Carlyle's Will]. Harvard Lib Notes 10 1923.

Marx, O. Carlyle's translation of 'Wilhelm Meister'. Baltimore 1925.

Barrett, J. A. S. The principle portraits and statues of Thomas Carlyle. [1928.]

Harrold, C. F. The translated passages in Carlyle's French Revolution. JEGP 27 1928.

[Wells, Gabriel] Gives Carlyle draft to British Museum. New York Times 20 July 1928.

Carlyle, A. The Carlyle myth refuted. Edinburgh 1930.

Dunn, W. Froude and Carlyle. 1930.

Mabbott, T. O. Carlyle: a bibliographical item. N & Q 160 1931.

Thrall, M. M. Two articles attributed to Carlyle. MLN 46 1931.

Neff, E. Carlyle. 1932.

Sotheby. Catalogue of printed books, autograph letters, literary manuscripts … formerly the property of Thomas Carlyle. 1932.

Coffin, E. F. American first editions of Carlyle. Amer Book Collector 4 1933.

Parsons, C. O. A Goethe poem and Carlyle's translation. Archiv für das Studium der Neueren Sprachen und Literaturen 164 1933.

Brooks, R. Manuscripts pertaining to Carlyle's Frederick the Great. YULG 9 1934.

Shine, Hill. Articles in Fraser's Magazine attributed to Carlyle. MLN 51 1936.

Hirst, W. A. The manuscript of Carlyle's French Revolution. Nineteenth Cent and After 123 1938.

Tuell, A. K. Carlyle's marginalia in Sterling's Essays and tales. PMLA 54 1939.

Salomon, R. Notes and Carlyle's journey to Germany, Autumn 1858. MLN 58 1943.

Blackburn, W. Carlyle and the composition of The life of John Sterling. SP 44 1947.

Carr, C. T. Carlyle's translations from German. MLR 42 1947.

Calder, G. The writing of Past and present. New Haven CT 1949.

Stark, L. M. and R. W. Hill. The bequest of Mary Stillman Harkness. BNYPL 55 1951.

King, Marjorie P. 'Illudo Chartis': an initial study in Carlyle's mode of composition. MLR 49 1954.

Worth, G. C. Three Carlyle documents. PMLA 71 1956.

Clark, A. The manuscript collections of the Princeton University Library. Princeton Univ Lib Chron 19 1958.

Finlayson, C. P. Thomas Carlyle's borrowings from Edinburgh University Library, 1819–1820. Bibliotheck 3 1961.

Brown, T. J. English Literary Autographs 47: Thomas Carlyle, 1795–1881. BC 12 1963.

Tennyson, G. B. Carlyle's poetry to 1840: a checklist and discussion, a new attribution, and six unpublished poems. VP 1 1963.

Tennyson, G. B. Unnoted encyclopaedia articles by Carlyle. ELN 1 1963.

Cameron, K. W. New Japanese translations of Carlyle's works. Emerson Soc Quart 35 1964.

Tennyson, G. B. Carlyle's earliest German translation. American N & Q 3 1964.

Waller, J. O. Thomas Carlyle and his Nutshell Iliad. BNYPL 69 1965.

Marrs, E. W. Dating the writings of Past and present. N & Q 212 1967.

Clarke, A. F. [Alexander the Great Ms]. Manuscripts 20 1968.

Curran, E. M. Carlyle's first contribution to the Foreign Quarterly Review: a small identification. Victorian Periodicals Newsletter 2 1968.

Alexander, E. Mill's marginal notes on Carlyle's 'Hudson Statue'. ELN 7 1969.

Campbell, I. Carlyle's borrowings from the Theological Library of Edinburgh University. Bibliotheck 5 1969

Sharples, E. Carlyle's 'Christopher North'. N & Q 16 1969.

Campbell, Ian. James Barrett and Carlyle's Journal. N & Q 17 1970.

Tarr, R. L. Carlyle's answer to the 'Libussa Riddle'. Amer N & Q 9 1971.

Tarr, R. L. Thomas Carlyle's libraries at Chelsea and Ecclefechan. Stud in Bibliography 27 1974.

Tennyson, G. B. The Carlyles. In A guide to the year's work in Victorian poetry and prose, 1973. VP suppl 1974.

Tennyson, G. B. The Carlyles. VP 13 1975.

Tarr, R. L. A new Carlyle manuscript. Victorian Newsletter 54 1978.

Bell, A. Some Carlyle acquisitions of the National Library of Scotland, 1972–1978. Carlyle Newsletter 1 1979.

Fielding, K. J. Unpublished manuscripts I: Carlyle among the Cannibals. Carlyle Newsletter 1 1979.

Henderson, H. Carlyle and the book clubs: a new approach to publishing. Publishing History 6 1979.

Skabarnicki, A. M. The manuscripts of Carlyle's Reminiscences in the National Library of Scotland. Carlyle Newsletter 1 1979.

Baumgarten, M. (ed). In the margins: Carlyle's markings and annotations in his gift copy of Mill's Principles of political economy, first edition, London: J. W. Parker, 1848, Two Volumes. Carlyle: books and margins. Santa Cruz CA 1980.

Fielding, K. J. Unpublished manuscripts II: Carlyle's Scenario for Cromwell. Carlyle Newsletter 2 1980.

Kaplan, F. 'Phallus-Worship' (1848): unpublished manuscripts III: a response to the Revolution of 1848. Carlyle Newsletter 2 1980.
Skarbarnicki, A. M. The Strouse Collection at Santa Cruz. Carlyle Newsletter 2 1980.
Tarr, R. L. Emendation as challenge: Carlyle's 'Negro Question' from journal to pamphlet. PBSA 75:3 1981.
Seigel, J. Carlyle and Peel: the prophet's search for a heroic politician and an unpublished fragment. VS 26.2 1983.
Trela, D. J. The lasses of the Canongate: an unknown poem of Carlyle's. Carlyle Newsletter 7 1986.
Campbell, I. Froude, Moncure Conway and the American edition of the Reminiscences. Carlyle Newsletter 8 1987.
Tarr, R. L. 'For My Mother': Carlyle's poem on his sister Margaret. Carlyle Newsletter 8 1987.
Campbell, Ian. The Patrick photographs of Carlyle. Carlyle Newsletter 9 1988.
Fielding, K. J. 'George Selwyn' by Thomas Carlyle. Carlyle Newsletter 9 1988.
Nye, E. W. An edition of John Sterling uncovers new Carlyle letters. Carlyle Newsletter 9 1988.
Tarr, R. L. Carlyle's The French Revolution: a hitherto unavailable manuscript fragment. Carlyle Newsletter 9 1988.
Campbell, I. Carlyle's Death mask of Goethe rediscovered. Carlyle Annual 10 1989.
Fielding, K. J. Carlyle makes his Will (1865–1871): new documents discovered. Carlyle Annual 10 1989.
Fielding, K. J. Carlyle's unpublished comments on the Northcote–Trevelyan Report. Carlyle Annual 10 1989.
Myerson, J. and P. Scott. Moncure Conway and Carlyle: a bibliographical addendum. Carlyle Annual 10 1989.
Tarr, R. L. Carlyle's Past and present: a hitherto unavailable manuscript fragment. Carlyle Annual 10 1989.
Trela, D. J. An unpublished Cromwellian draft on usurpation. Carlyle Annual 10 1989.
Vanden Bossche, C. R. Carlyle's Faereyinga Saga translation. Carlyle Annual 10 1989.
Fielding, K. J. Carlyle writes local history: 'Dumfries-shire three hundred years ago'. Carlyle Annual 12 1991.
Hardin, J. (ed). Goethe's Wilhelm Meister's travels: translation of the first edition by Thomas Carlyle. Columbia SC 1991.
Koepke, Wulf, (ed). Army Chaplain Schmelzle's journey to Flaetz and Life of Quintus Fixlein: translated by Thomas Carlyle. Columbia SC 1991.
Scheck, U. (ed). Stories by Musaus and Fouqué translated by Thomas Carlyle. Stud in German Lit, Linguistics, and Culture 61, Columbia SC 1991.
Fielding, K. J. New notes for The letters: I Carlyle's sketch of Joseph Neuberg; II. 'Leave it alone; time will mend it'. Carlyle Annual 13 1992–3.
Oakman, R. L. Carlyle and the computer: putting together a new edition without reinventing the wheel. Literatur im Kontext – Literature in Context: Festschrift für Horst W. Drescher, ed J. Schwend, S. Hagemann and H. Volkel, Scottish Stud 14, Frankfurt am Main 1992.
Trela, D. J. A history of Oliver Cromwell's letters and speeches. Lewiston NY 1992.
Trela, D. J. Carlyle and the periodical press: unused manuscripts for the revision of Shooting Niagara: and after? Stud in Scottish Lit 27 1992.
Trela, D. J. Carlyle's Shooting Niagara: the writing and revising of an article and pamphlet. Victorian Periodicals Rev 25 1992.
Brown, M. Thomas Carlyle 1795–1881. Research guide to European historical biography 1450–present. Washington 1993.
Trela, D. J. The writing of 'An election to the Long Parliament': Carlyle, primary research and the book clubs. Carlyle Stud Annual 14 1994.
Heffer, S. Moral desperado: the life of Thomas Carlyle. 1995.
Ryals, C. de L. Thomas Carlyle on the Mormons: an unpublished essay. Carlyle Stud Annual 15 1995.
Scott, P. and J. Hansen. Thomas Carlyle: 1795–1881. Columbia SC 1995. An exhibit catalogue of the Rodger L. Tarr Carlyle Collection.

Biographies

Froude, J. A. Thomas Carlyle: a history of the first forty years of his life, 1795–1835. 2 vols 1882.
REVIEWS: [Dodds, J.] Christian Monthly 4 1881; All the Year Round n.s. 29 1882; Athenaeum 2841–2 1882; Atlantic Monthly 50 1882; Century Mag 24 1882; Modern Rev 3 1882; Month 46 1882; N & Q 5 1882; Temple Bar 65 1882; [Alden, H.] Harper's Mag 65 1882; [Cowell, H.] Blackwood's Mag 132 1882; [Dickens, J.] Catholic World 35 1882; [Sedgwick, A. G.] Nation 34 1882; [William, W.] Acad 21 1882.
Froude, J. A. Thomas Carlyle: a history of his life in London, 1834–1881. 2 vols 1884.
REVIEWS: Bookbuyer 1 1884; Critic (New York) 5 1884; Literary World 15 1884; [Sedgwick, A. G.] Nation 39 1884; [Venables, G. S.] Fortnightly Rev 42 1884; [Wallace, W.] Acad 26 1884; Atlantic Monthly 55 1885; Br Quart Rev 81 1885; Methodist Quart Rev 67 1885; [Harrison, F.] North Amer Rev 140 1885; [Hedge, F. H.] Unitarian Rev 23 1885; [Metcalfe, W. M.] Scottish Rev 5 1885; [Morris, M.] Quart Rev 159 1885.
Wilson, D. A. Life of Thomas Carlyle [vols variously titled]. 6 vols 1923–9. Vol 6 completed by D. W. MacArthur.
Kaplan, F. Thomas Carlyle: a biography. Ithaca NY 1983.

Obituaries

American 1 1881; Harper's Weekly 25 1881; Illus London News 78 1881; Literary World 12, 23 1881; New York Times 27 Feb 1881; Pall Mall Gazette 5 Feb 1881; Punch 80 1881; Saturday Rev 51 1881; Tablet 25 1881; The Times 7, 8, 11, 22 Feb, 28 Mar 1881; [Whitman, W.] Critic (New York) 1 1881; [Whitman, W.] Literary World 12 1881. [RLT]

Robert Carruthers 1799–1878

§1

The history of Huntingdon. 1824.
The poetry of Milton's prose: selected from his various writings, with notes and an introductory essay. 1827.
The Highland note-book: or sketches and anecdotes. Edinburgh 1843.
Chambers's cyclopaedia of English literature. [1857], [1876] (rev Carruthers).
The life of Alexander Pope; including extracts from his correspondence. 1857 (rev and enlarged from memoir in edn of Pope's Poetical works, 1853).
Carruthers edited the following: Pope, Poetical works, *4 vols 1853, 1853–4, 1858 (rev); Boswell,* Tour to the Hebrides, *1851; Falconer,* Shipwreck, *1858; James Montgomery,* Poetical works, *1860;* Chambers's Household edition of Shakespeare, *1861–3 (with W. Chambers); R. Chambers,* Life of Sir W. Scott, *1871; Gray's* Select poems, *1876.*

§2

Scotsman 28 May 1878. Obituary.

Henry Francis Cary 1772–1844

See col 291.

Charles Cowden Clarke 1787–1877

§1

Readings in natural philosophy: or a popular display of the wonders of nature etc. 1828.

Tales from Chaucer in prose: designed chiefly for the use of young persons. 1833, 1870 (carefully rev).
Adam the gardener. 1834. A boys' book.
The riches of Chaucer. 1835, 1870.
Carmina minima. 1859.
Shakespeare characters: chiefly those subordinate. 1863.
Molière-characters. Edinburgh 1865.
On the comic writers of England. GM Apr–Dec 1871. On Chaucer; Jonson; Beaumont and Fletcher; Butler; Addison and Steele; Swift; Burlesque writers; English satirists: Wycherley and Congreve.
Clarke also edited Nyren, Young cricketers' tutor, *1833, and the text of most of the vols in Gilfillan's Lib Edn of the* British poets. *For his collaborations with his wife Mary Cowden Clarke and for her biographical sketch of him, see col 2221.*

§2

Altick, R. D. The Cowden Clarkes. New York 1948. Contains a list of writings of Charles and Mary Cowden Clarke.
Blunden, E. Letters from Charles and Mary Cowden Clarke to Alexander Main 1864–86. Keats–Shelley Memorial Bull 3 1951.

William Cobbett, 'Peter Porcupine' 1763–1835

Cobbett's mss and correspondence are widely scattered both in Britain and the USA. A series of six letters to Sir Francis Burdett dated 1815–17 has also recently come to light in the Russian Centre for the Preservation and Study of Modern Historical Documents, Moscow. Details of mss held at British locations are available in LR. Locations of mss in the USA are listed in G. Spater, William Cobbett: the poor man's friend *(see below). For further details of Cobbett's publication history in America, see the authoritative bibliography by Gaines (below).*

Bibliographies

Muirhead, A. M. An introduction to a bibliography of Cobbett. Library 4th ser 20 1939.
Pearl, M. L. Cobbett: a bibliographical account of his life and times. Oxford 1953.
Gaines, P. W. William Cobbett and the United States 1792–1835: a bibliography. Worcester MA 1971.
The William Cobbett collection at Adelphi University. New York 1982.

Selections

The works of Peter Porcupine. Philadelphia 1795, 1796 (variously collected). Also as Porcupine's political tracts, Philadelphia 1797, and Porcupine's works, 2 vols Philadelphia [1797] (variously collected).
Porcupine's works. 12 vols 1801, Dayton OH 1970 (microform edn).
Porcupine revived. New York 1813. 'By William Cobbett'; anon editor.
The life of William Cobbett, dedicated to his sons. 1835, 1835, Philadelphia 1835.
Selections from Cobbett's political works. Ed J. M. and J. P. Cobbett 1835–7 (weekly pts and 6 vols). Selections from Porcupine's works and political register.
The beauties of Cobbett. [Ed J. Oldfield] 1836 (monthly pts and 1 vol). Selections from Porcupine's works.
The last of the Saxons. Ed E. P. Hood 1854. Autobiographical selections.
Mr Cobbett's remarks on our Indian empire. 1857. Selections from Political Register 1804–22; perhaps ed J. M. Cobbett.
The days of good Queen Bess; Social effects of the Reformation; The suppression of the English monasteries. 1917. 3 booklet selections by the Catholic Truth Soc from History of the Protestant Reformation 1917; Social effects rptd 1929; tr Polish 1947.
A history of the last hundred days of English freedom. Ed J. L. Hammond 1921, rptd Westport CT 1971. Selections from Political Register 1817.
Selections, with Hazlitt's essay. Ed A. M. D. Hughes, Oxford 1923, rptd 1925, 1935, 1951, 1961.
Life and adventures of Peter Porcupine, with other records of his early career. Ed G. D. H. Cole 1927, rptd New York 1970. Autobiographical selections to 1800.
The progress of a ploughboy. Ed W. Reitzel 1933; 1947 (rev as The autobiography of Cobbett), rptd 1967. Autobiographical selections to 1835.
The opinions of William Cobbett. Ed G. D. H. and M. Cole 1944, rptd Kettering 1977. Selections from Political Register 1802–35.
Cobbett and Lamb. Ed W. V. Aughterson, Melbourne 1958.
Cobbett's England. Ed J. Derry 1968.
Cobbett's country book. Ed R. Ingrams, Newton Abbott 1974.
Cobbett in Ireland: a warning to England. Ed D. Knight 1984.
Cobbett's America. Ed J. E. Morpurgo 1985.
Peter Porcupine in America. Ed D. A. Wilson 1994.
Collected social and political works. Ed N. Thompson and D. Eastwood 1998.
William Cobbett: selected writings. Ed L. Nattrass 1998.

Hostile selections

The cameleon. 1807.
Cobbett against himself. 1808.
Elements of reform. 1809; rev as Parliamentary reform, Manchester and Bolton 1816.
The friend of the people. [1816–17.]
The beauties of Cobbett. 3 pts [1819–20], Dublin 1820; rev as Politics for the people, Birmingham [1819–20] (2 edns).
Cobbett's reflections on religion, no 1; on politics, no 2, Sunderland [1819], Manchester no 2 1832; and Life of Thomas Paine, Durham 1819 (*see below*).
The book of wonders. 2 pts 1821 (selections: Cobbett versus Wright).
Cobbett's gridiron. 1822; rev as Cobbett's cardinal virtues, Manchester 1832.
Cobbett's book of the Roman Catholic Church. 1825.
The Political Mountebank. 11 nos Preston 1826.
The poor man's friend. 1826.
Cobbett's Penny Trash. 3 nos 1831 (no 1 also as Cobbett's Genuine Penny Trash).

§1

The soldier's friend. 1792, 1793. Anon; written with or by Cobbett.
Le nomenclature anglais. Philadelphia 1794.
Observations on the emigration of Dr Priestley. Philadelphia 1794, 1794 (author and publisher anon), New York 1794, London 1794 (3 edns), [Liverpool?] 1794, Birmingham 1794, Bath 1794, Bristol 1794, Philadelphia 1795 ('3rd edn' naming publisher with Story of a farmer's bull, Address), 1796 ('4th edn' naming Peter Porcupine as author), 1796, 1797, 1798, London 1798, 1974, Philadelphia 1974.
A bone to gnaw for the Democrats. Pt 1 Philadelphia 1795 (3 edns; anon in 1st), 1796 ('4th edn' by 'Peter Porcupine'), 1797 ('3rd edn' pbd by Cobbett); pt 2 Philadelphia 1795, 1795, 1797, 1797; pts 1–2 London 1797 (with A rod for the backs of the critics by 'Humphrey Hedgehog' [J. Gifford]).
A kick for a bite. By 'Peter Porcupine'. Philadelphia 1795, 1796.
A little plain English. By 'Peter Porcupine'. Philadelphia 1795, Boston 1795, London 1795, Philadelphia 1796.
Le tuteur anglais. Philadelphia 1795, Paris 1801 ('Le Maître d'anglais', '2ème' edn), 1803 ('3ème' edn), Philadelphia 1805 ('2nd edn'), Paris 1810 ('4ème' edn), 1815, 1816 ('5ème' edn), 1817 ('new edn'), 1819, 1823 (new edn rev J. Perrin), 1827, 1830, 1832, 1850, 1854, 1861 ('35ème' edn); also numerous pirated edns.
The bloody buoy. By 'Peter Porcupine'. Philadelphia 1796, 1796, Reading PA 1797 (Ger trn as Die Blut-Fahne), (facs and English

trn of extracts of this trn, Description of an old book, ed J. A. Donahoe, Wilmington DE [c. 1958]); London [1796], 1797 ('3rd edn'), Cambridge 1797 (as Annals of blood by an American), London 1798 (11 abridged edns), Paradise PA 1823 ('2nd edn'), Philadelphia 1823 ('3rd edn'), Woodbridge CT 1983 (microform edn).

History of the American Jacobins. By 'Peter Porcupine'. Philadelphia 1796, 1796, Edinburgh 1797.

The life and adventures of Peter Porcupine. By 'Peter Porcupine'. Philadelphia 1796, 1796, 1797 ('2nd edn'), London 1797, Glasgow 1797, 1798, London 1809 ('2nd edn'); rev as The life of William Cobbett 1809; 1816 ('2nd', '7th', '8th', '9th' edns); New York 1970; ed G. D. H. Cole 1927 ('with other records of his early career').

The life of Thomas Paine. By 'Peter Porcupine'. Philadelphia 1796, London 1797, 1797 (as Cobbett's review of The life). Hostile edns, Sunderland 1819, Durham 1819, New York 1892, London 1892. Rptd from the Political Censor, 1796, *below*, ed Cobbett from Lives of Paine by H. Mackenzie and 'F. Oldys' [G. Chalmers].

A new year's gift to the Democrats. By 'Peter Porcupine'. Philadelphia 1796, 1796, 1798.

The Political Censor. Also Porcupine's Political Censor. Philadelphia 1796–7. A monthly periodical, ed Cobbett, nos 2–9, a continuation of A prospect from the Congress gallery (*below*) and continued as Porcupine's Gazette.

A prospect from the Congress gallery. By 'Peter Porcupine'. Philadelphia 1796, 1796. Continued as monthly periodical The Political Censor 1796–7.

The scare-crow. By 'Peter Porcupine'. Philadelphia 1796, 1796, 1797. Rptd from Political Censor 1796, *above*.

The carriers of Porcupine's Gazette. [Philadelphia 1797.] Poem.

Democratic principles illustrated by example. By 'Peter Porcupine'. 2 pts (pt 1 extracted from pt 2 of A bone to gnaw 1795; pt 2 extracted from The bloody buoy 1796). [Manchester 1797], Dublin [1797] (5th edn), 1798, London 1798 ('2nd'–'18th' edns), London, Edinburgh, Glasgow and Aberdeen 1798 ('7th' edn); Birmingham [1798] (shortened (unauthorised?) rev pt 1 as Read and reflect: a faint picture of the horrors); Quebec 1799 ('16th edn').

A letter to the infamous Tom Paine. By 'Peter Porcupine'. [Philadelphia 1797], New York 1797, London 1797, Glasgow 1797, Edinburgh 1797, [1798?]. Rptd from Political Censor 1796, *above*.

Observations on the debates of the American Congress. By 'Peter Porcupine'. [Philadelphia 1797?], London 1797. Rptd from Political Censor 1796, *above*.

Porcupine's Gazette and United States Daily Advertiser. Daily evening periodical, ed Cobbett, Philadelphia 4 Mar 1797–28 Aug 1799; title changed to Porcupine's Gazette 24 Apr 1799; weekly, Bustleton 6 Sep–11 Oct 1799 and 19–26 Oct 1799; New York, final no, 13 Jan 1800; another tri-weekly edn Philadelphia 3 Mar 1798–28 Aug 1799, extracts pbd as The country porcupine, 5 Mar 1798–26 Aug 1799. Porcupine's Gazette inspired a Pennsylvanian Ger imitation and partial trn: Der deutsche Porcupein und Lancaster Anzeigs Nachrichten, weekly, Lancaster PA 3 Jan 1798–25 Dec 1799, later Der Americanische Staatsbothe.

The democratic judge. By 'Peter Porcupine'. Philadelphia 1798; pbd in England as The republican judge 1798 (3 edns), New York 1970, Ann Arbor MI 1973 (microform edn).

Detection of a conspiracy. By 'Peter Porcupine'. Philadelphia 1798, London 1799, Dublin 1799.

The detection of Bache. By 'Peter Porcupine'. [Philadelphia 1798.] Broadside, rptd from Porcupine's Gazette 20 June 1798, *above*.

French arrogance. By 'Peter Porcupine'. Philadelphia 1798, New York 1915 (in Magazine of History, no 44). Poem.

Remarks on the insidious letter [The antidote]. By 'Peter Porcupine'. [Philadelphia 1798.] Broadside, rptd from Porcupine's Gazette 16 June 1798, *above*.

Proposals for publishing Porcupine's works. [Philadelphia] 1799.

Remarks on the explanation lately published by Dr Priestley. By 'Peter Porcupine'. 1799 (rptd from Porcupine's Gazette, *above*, Sep 1798–Jan 1799); tr Fr 1798 (ed Cobbett as Lettres au Docteur Priestley).

The trial of republicanism. Philadelphia 1799 (no known copy), London 1801 (with postscript).

An address to the people of England. London and New York 1800, Philadelphia 1812, London 1830. From The Rush-Light, *below*.

A brief statement of opinions. Philadelphia 1800. Written with Cobbett?

Cobbett's advice. [1800.] Broadside, rev and repbd as Prospectus of a new daily paper, 1800, 1800; rptd as A refutation of the present political sentiments, as appendix to The British treaty, by Governor Morris 1808, 1808.

The Porcupine. Daily periodical, ed Cobbett 30 Oct 1800–31 Dec 1801, nos 1–3 (another edn); from no 299 as The Porcupine and Anti-Gallican Monitor; from 1 Jan 1802 absorbed by True Briton.

The Rush-Light. Fortnightly periodical, ed 'Peter Porcupine', New York 15 Feb–30 Apr 1800 nos 1–5; London 30 Aug 1800 no 6 repbd as An address to the people of England, London and New York 1800, Philadelphia 1812, London 1830; nos 1–4 repbd as The American Rush-Light, 1800. The Republican Rush-Light 30 Aug 1800 no 7 is a forgery.

A collection of facts. 1801, Philadelphia 1802. Rptd mainly from Porcupine, 1801, *above*.

Cobbett's Political Register. Weekly periodical, ed Cobbett as Cobbett's Annual Register, Jan 1802–Dec 1803; as Cobbett's Weekly Political Register, 7 Jan 1804–5 Apr 1817 (none issued in England 12 Apr–5 July 1817, but twice weekly edn 12 Sep 1810–22 June 1811); as Cobbett's Weekly Political Pamphlet, July–Dec 1817; as Cobbett's Weekly Political Register, Jan 1818–7 Apr 1821 (none issued 21 Mar, 2 May, 27 June–15 Aug, 17 Oct–14 Nov 1818, 29 May–14 Aug, 16 Oct, 20, 27 Nov 1819, or 26 Feb–18 Mar 1820); as Cobbett's Weekly Register, 14 Apr–Dec 1827; as Cobbett's Weekly Political Register, Jan 1828–12 Sep 1835 (no 11); extracts 1830–2 pbd as Cobbett's Two-Penny Trash, 1831, 1832; [from 20 June 1835 (no 12) ed W. Cobbett jr]; as Renewal of Cobbett's Register, Jan 1836 (unnumbered) and 20 Feb 1836 ('no 2'); full run rptd Westport CT 1971 (including microform edn). Many pam reprints of articles in Political Register were issued, particularly after 1810 (*see below*); periodicals borrowing largely from it, or derived from it, or influenced by it, are: Le Mercure Anglais (ed Cobbett, monthly Fr trn of a part, 16 Feb–? May 1803, no known copies); cheap weekly edns 12 Oct 1816 (first no pbd 2 Nov)–6 Jan 1820 (none pbd in England 12 Apr–5 July 1817), unstamped twopenny edns (pbd mainly alongside the stamped); Cobbett's American Political Register, New York 6 Jan–29 June 1816, May 1817–Jan 1818; Ulster Register, Belfast? 1817 (pbd J. Lawless with Cobbett's agreement, no known copy); Weekly Register, Dublin (unauthorised imitation 1822–4, no known copy); hostile imitations of the Political Register pbd 1816–17 with Government aid at Romsey (Romsey Political Register, c. Nov 1816); Detector c. Jan 1817; Friend of the People Dec 1816–Jan 1817; Anti-Cobbett Mar–Apr 1817; Norwich (Brunswick Weekly Political Register, Feb–Mar 1817); Oxford; and other places (see Home Office Papers 41/1/490, 42/158/160).

Letters to the Right Honourable Henry Addington. 1802.

Letters to the Right Honourable Lord Hawkesbury and the Right Honourable Henry Addington. 1802, 1802. Rptd mainly from A collection of facts 1801, and from Letters to Addington 1802, *above*. The ninth letter to Lord Hawkesbury pbd separately, Philadelphia 1802.

Four letters to the Chancellor of the Exchequer. 1803. Rptd from Political Register 9, 16, 23, 30 Apr 1803.

Important considerations for the people of this Kingdom. 1803 (7 edns), Edinburgh 1803. Anon. Rptd (anon) in Political Register 30 July 1803.

Letter to Lord Auckland on the Post Office. 1803. Rptd from Political Register 27 Nov 1803.

Narrative of the taking of the invincible standard. 1803. Rptd from Political Register 25 Dec 1802.

The political Proteus. 1804. Rptd largely from Political Register 1803.

Cobbett's remarks on Sir F. Burdett's letter. 1810. Rptd from Political Register 24 Mar 1810.

Letters to the Prince Regent. 1812 (no known copy). Rptd from Political Register 1812.

Three letters to the electors of Bristol. Bath 1812. Rptd from Political Register 4 July, 1, 15 Aug 1812.

Letter to the inhabitants of Southampton on the Corn Bill. 1814. Rptd from Political Register 4 June 1814.

Five letters to Lord Sheffield. 1815. Rptd from Political Register 26 Aug 1815.

Letters on the late war between the United States and Great Britain. New York 1815, Philadelphia 1815, Ann Arbor MI 1965 (microform edn). One letter rptd as An address to the clergy of Massachusetts, Boston 1815, 1815. Rptd, except for one letter, from Political Register 1811–15.

Paper against gold. 2 vols 1815, 15 pts 1817 (24 Feb–29 Mar), 1 vol 1821 and 1822 ('4th edn') (accompanied by separately pbd Preliminary part of Paper against gold, 1821), 1828 (omits last 3 of a total of 32 articles or 'letters'), New York 1834, Manchester 1841 ('condensed' by M. Chappelsmith), London 1841 (no known copy), New York 1846, London 1917. Paper against gold rptd from Political Register 1810–15; Preliminary part of Paper against gold rptd from Political Register 1803–6.

The pride of Britannia humbled. Ed T. Branagan, New York 1815, 1815, Philadelphia 1815, Baltimore 1815, New York 1817, Cincinnatti 1817, Ann Arbor MI 1966 (microform edn).

Cobbett's American Political Register. 1816–17. *See* Cobbett's Political Register, *above*.

A letter addressed to Mr Jabet of Birmingham. Coventry 1816. Rptd from Political Register 9 Nov 1816.

To the journeymen and labourers. Manchester 1816, Coventry 1816. Rptd from Political Register 2 Nov 1816 and also issued as unstamped Political Register by Cobbett in London. Reproduced in G. Saintsbury, Political pamphlets, New York 1892.

Two letters addressed to Sir F. Burdett, bart. Coventry 1816. Rptd from Political Register 12, 19 Oct 1816.

Cobbett's address to the Americans. [1817], 1817.

Cobbett's new year's gift to old George Rose. Nottingham 1817. Rptd from Political Register 4 Jan 1817.

Mr Cobbett's address to his countrymen. [1817.]

Mr Cobbett's taking leave of his countrymen. 1817. Rptd from Political Register 5 Apr 1817.

A grammar of the English language. New York 1818, London '1819' (for 1818), 1819 (3 edns), 1820 ('4th edn'), 1823 (with additional 'six lessons'), Madras 1823 (no known copy), London 1824, Berlin 1824, Jena 1825, London 1826, 1829, 1831, 1832, New York 1832, 1833, London 1833, 1836, New York 1837, London 1838, Madras 1839, London 1840, 1842, 1844, New York 1846, London 1847, 1850, 1852, Philadelphia 1854, London 1856, 1859, 1860 (as An abridgement), 1863, 1863, 1865, 1866 (2 edns, one with ch on pronunciation by J. P. Cobbett), 1868, 1870, 1875, [1880], 1882 (as Grammar for the million); ed R. Waters, New York 1883 (as How to get on in the world), 1901 ('10th edn'); New York 1884, 1886, London 1889, 1906, 1923 (as Cobbett's easy grammar); Amsterdam 1983, Oxford 1984, New York 1986; tr Ger 1839.

Our anti-neutral conduct reviewed. [New York 1818.] Rptd mainly from American Political Register 1817.

A year's residence in the United States of America. New York 1818–19, London 1818–19, Belfast 1818, London 1819, 1822 ('3rd edn'), 1822, 1828 (another '3rd edn'); Paris 1834 (partial trn in Fr as De la culture des betteraves); Boston 1918, London 1922, Louisville KY 1959, Carbondale IL and Fontwell 1964, New York 1969, Dayton OH 1970 (microform edn), New York 1978, Gloucester 1983.

Correspondence between Mr Cobbett, Mr Tipper and Sir Francis Burdett. 1819.

A full report of a public meeting [with a speech by Cobbett]. 1819.

An answer to the speech of the Attorney-General against her Majesty the Queen. 1820, New York 1820. Rptd from Political Register 26 Aug 1820.

Cobbett's Evening Post. Daily periodical, ed Cobbett, 29 Jan–1 Apr 1820.

Cobbett's Parliamentary Register. Weekly periodical, ed Cobbett, 6 May–Dec 1820.

A letter from the Queen to the King. By 'Queen Caroline', actually by Cobbett. 1820, Philadelphia 1821 ('5th edn'). Rptd from Political Register 19 Aug 1820.

A ptd circular letter inviting subscriptions in support of Cobbett's candidature at Coventry, 25 Feb 1820, beginning 'Sir, You have already heard that I am a candidate.'

The American gardener. 1821, Baltimore 1823, 1829 (rev as The English gardener), New York 1835, 1841, Claremont NH 1835, Concord NH and Boston 1842, New York 1844, 1846, Philadelphia 1851, New York 1852, Philadelphia 1854, New York 1856, 1865; tr Ital 1826.

Cobbett's sermons. 12 monthly pts 1821–2 (nos 1–3 as Cobbett's monthly religious tracts, nos 4–12 as Cobbett's monthly sermons), 1822 ('stereotype' edn), London 1823, France and Italy 1822 (no known copies), London 1823 (Andover ptd, as Twelve sermons), 1828 (as 'new edn'), New York 1834 (as Thirteen sermons with 'address', an additional sermon, and Good Friday, which was also pbd separately, London 1830), Philadelphia [183?], New York 1846.

Cottage economy. 7 monthly pts Aug 1821–Mar 1822; 1 vol 1822, 1823 ('new edn'), 1824 ('6th edn'), New York 1824, London 1826, 1828, Frome 1829 (as Cottage domestic economy [extracts from Cobbett et al ed 'I. B.' – Marchioness of Bath]), London 1831 ('new edn'), New York 1833 (with The poor man's friend), London 1835 ('new edn'), 1838 ('15th edn'), 1843 ('16th edn'), 1850 ('17th edn'), Hartford CT 1848, 1854, London [1865] ('19th edn'), 1867 ('18th edn'); preface by G. K. Chesterton 1916, 1926; New York 1970, Bromyard, Herefordshire 1975, Bath 1975, Shrewsbury 1978, Oxford 1979; tr Greek 1829 (no known copy).

Preliminary part of Paper against gold. 1821. *See* Paper against gold, 1815, *above*.

The Queen's answer to the letter from the King to his people. 1821, Philadelphia 1821. Rptd from Political Register 27 Jan 1821.

Speech of Mr Cobbett delivered at a public meeting at Huntingdon. Holt? 1821.

Cobbett's collective commentaries. 1822. Mainly rptd from Statesman 1822, *below*.

The farmer's friend. 1822. Rptd from Political Register 15 Dec 1821, 5 Jan 1822.

The farmer's wife's friend. 1822. Rptd from Political Register 23 Mar 1822.

[Long Island prophecies] Cobbett's too long petition; Letter to Tierney; Letter to the Regent. 1822 (5 issues including caption title Long Island prophecies). Rptd from Political Register 7 Feb, 1 July 1818, 30 Oct 1819.

Mr Cobbett's publications. A descriptive catalogue frequently rptd from Political Register and advertisements in Cobbett's books 1822–4; later versions as List of Mr Cobbett's publications, c. 1824; List of Mr Cobbett's books, 1828–32, 1834, 1842; and The Cobbett library, 1830, 1835.

[Proceedings at the dinner:] Cobbett's warnings to Norfolk farmers. 1822. Rptd from Political Register 29 Dec 1821, 5 Jan 1822.
Reduction no robbery. 1822. Rptd from Political Register 22 June 1822.
The Statesman. Daily evening periodical 1806–24, incorporated in the Globe and Traveller, 1824, part owned by Cobbett Mar 1822–May 1823, when he wrote articles for it, some rptd in Cobbett's collective commentaries 1822, *above*.
Narrative. London? 1823 (no known copy). Rptd from Political Register 11 Jan 1823.
The Norfolk Yeoman's Gazette. Weekly periodical, ed Cobbett, Norwich 8 Feb–3 May 1823.
To Lord Suffield. 1823. Rptd from Political Register 1 Feb 1823.
A French grammar. 1824, New York 1824, Paris 1825, London 1829, New York 1832, London 1832, New York 1837, London 1838 ('7th edn'), 1840, New York 1841, London 1842, 1844 ('9th edn'), New York 1848, London 1849 ('10th edn'), 1851 ('11th edn'), 1861 ('11th edn' rev J. P. Cobbett), [1862?] ('15th edn'), 1867 ('12th edn'), 1875 ('14th edn'), [1882] ('new edn'), New York 1884; *see also* J. P. Cobbett, Practical exercises, 1834.
A history of the Protestant Reformation in England and Ireland. 16 nos 1824–6, many nos rptd and bound together; nos 1–3 tr Fr in pts, nos 1–16 ('17') tr Ital in pts.
[pt 1]. 1824, 1824 (for 1826), Baltimore 1824 (for 1826), Philadelphia [1824], London 1825 (for 1826) (Fr trn), New York 1825 (Sp trn), Pittsburgh 1825 (for 1826) (3rd Amer edn), Philadelphia 1825, 1825 (for 1826), Baltimore 1826 ('4th American' edn, incl letter to Earl of Rodan), New York 1826, Philadelphia 1826 (as A history of the Reformation), Louvain 1826, Paris 1826, 1826, 1827, Baltimore 1827, Lisbon 1827 (Ital trn), [Netherlands (no known copies) 1828], Philadelphia 1828, London 1829, Aschaffenberg 1832, New York 1832, Aschaffenberg 1833, New York 1834, Paris 1836 ('5ème edn'), Aschaffenberg 1839, Naples 1841, Philadelphia [1843], Sydney 1844, 1846, Baltimore 1849, London 1850, [1850], Barcelona 1850, Philadelphia [1850?], Baltimore 1852, Pittsburg 1852, Philadelphia 1853, Baltimore 1855, Valparaiso 1858, Baltimore 1866, Dublin 1868, [186?–7?], Baltimore [187?], [1881?], [1895?], Dublin [189?]; ed F. A. Gasquet, London 1896 (abridged), 1899, 1905, New York 1897, 1899, 1905, Cincinnati 1905; London 1917 (3 booklet extracts); ed F. A. Gasquet, London 1925 (abridged), 1929, New York [1938], Cincinnati [1938]; tr Polish 1947 (abstract); ed F. A. Gasquet, Illinois 1988 (abridged); ed Hugh Arnold, Sevenoaks 1994 (abridged).
[pt 2]. A list of the abbeys confiscated, 1827, 1829, 1868.
[pts 1–2]. 2 vols 1827, 1827, Baltimore [1827?], Madrid 1827, tr Ger 1827–8, Fr 1827, 1829, Caracas 1830, New York 1832, 1832–4, Boston 1834, Hungarian 1834, Paris 1836, 1836 ('6ème' edn), 1841, New York 1842, London 1847, New York 1849, Barcelona 1850, London [1853–7], Montreal [1860?], New York 1861, 1864, Dublin 1867, London 1868, New York [1886], 1895, London 1905, Santo Domingo 1913.
Big O and Sir Glory. 1825. Rptd from Political Register 24 Sep 1825. Play.
Gold for ever. 1825; rptd in Political Register 10 Sep 1825.
Cobbett at the King's cottage. [1826.] Rptd from Political Register 5 Aug 1826.
Cobbett's poor man's friend. 4 nos Aug–Nov 1826. Hostile imitation, The poor man's friend, 1826. No 5 Oct 1827, nos 2–4 pbd as 'new edn' Oct 1830, 1833 (rev as Cobbett's poor man's friend, in Cottage economy, *above*), 1826, 1829, [1830] ('new edn'), [1832], [1836–4?], Fairfield NJ 1977.
Mr Cobbett's petition to the King. 1826. A broadside.
American trees and shrubs. [1827?] Rptd from Political Register 25 Nov 1826.
Bank circular. 1827. Rptd from Political Register 16 June 1827.
Noble nonsense. [1828.] Rptd from Political Register 3 May 1828.
The woodlands. 7 nos Dec 1825–Mar 1828, 1 vol 1825 (for 1828).
The English gardener. 1829 (for 1828) (2 edns), 1833, 1838, 1845, Oxford 1980, London 1996. Rev from American gardener, *above*.
Facts for the men of Kent. [1828.] Rptd from Political Register 25 Oct 1828.
A letter from Mr William Cobbett to Mr Huskisson. [1828] (no known copy), Philadelphia [1828]. Rptd from Political Register 2 Aug 1828.
A letter to His Holiness the Pope. 1828. Rptd from Political Register 15 Nov 1828.
A treatise on Cobbett's corn. 1828, 1831 ('with an addition').
The emigrant's guide. 1829, 1830, 1830, Ann Arbor MI 1972 and 1976 (microform edns).
Englishmen, hear me. 1829. A placard; no known copy. Rptd from Political Register 21 Feb 1829.
Mr Cobbett's ... lecture. 5 pts 1829–30. 5 lectures; third lecture also pbd Birmingham [1830] as broadside, A summary report.
Advice to young men. 14 pts June 1829–Sep 1830; 1 vol London (Andover ptd) '1829' (for 1830) (2 edns), 'London 1829' (for 1830), Paris 1830 (no known copy), New York 1831, 1833, Claremont NH [183?], London 1837, Huntsville AL 1840, London 1842, New York 1844, 1846, 1846, [1847] (extract, as Advice to lovers), Philadelphia 1851, London 1861, 1866, 1868, [1874], [1876], 1880, Philadelphia 1881, London 1885, 1886 (abridged), 1887, [1892], [London 1900?], 1906, New York 1911, Allahabad 1914 (extract, as Advice to a youth), London 1926, 1930, 1937 (extract, as Advice to a lover), New York 1938 (extract, as Advice to a lover), London 1972, Farnborough 1972, Oxford 1980; tr Fr 1842, 1889.
A Talleyrand Perigord. [Paris? 1830] (no known copy). Fr trn from Political Register 16 Oct 1830.
Aux braves ouvriers de Paris. [Paris? 1830] (no known copy). Fr trn from Political Register 30 Oct 1830.
Cobbett's exposure of the practices of the pretended friends of the blacks. 1830, Louisville KY 1971 (microform edn). Rptd from Political Register 26 June 1830.
Cobbett's plan of parliamentary reform. 1830. Rptd from Political Register 30 Oct 1830.
Cobbett's twopenny trash. 24 pts July 1830–July 1832; 2 vols 1831–2, 1832; one pt (Tithes) tr Welsh 1831 (no known copy). Rptd from Political Register 1830–2, except for vol 1 nos 1–6 and vol 2 nos 4, 10; Cobbett's penny trash, nos 1–3; no 1 also issued as Cobbett's genuine twopenny trash, is a hostile imitation.
Eleven lectures on the French and Belgian revolutions. 11 pts Sep–Oct 1830; 1 vol 1830.
French Revolution: an address to the people of Paris. Birmingham 1830. Rptd from Political Register 21 Aug 1830.
Mr Cobbett's address to the tax-payers. [1830] ('new edn' enlarged). Rptd from Political Register 10 Apr 1830, with addns.
Good Friday. 1830; rptd in Thirteen sermons, New York 1834, *above*, and in Political Register 9 Mar 1833.
History of the regency and reign of King George the Fourth. ? pts 1830–4; 2 vols 1830–4, 1834; rptd in Political Register 1830–4.
A letter to the King. [1830.]
Report of a lecture-speech, Halifax. Halifax 1830, 1830.
Rural rides. 1830, 1830. Rptd from Political Register 1821–6; later edns from Political Register 1821–34; rptd 1833 (as Cobbett's tour in Scotland and the northern counties of England in 1832); ed J. P. Cobbett 1853; ed Pitt Cobbett 1885, 1886, rptd 1893, 1908, Cambridge 1908 (abridged for schools), London 1910; London and New York [1912], rptd 1934, 1953; London 1914 [1914], 1923 (abridged for schools), 1926 (abridged); ed G. D. H. and M. Cole 1930 (with addns not previously rptd from Political Register), 1932 (abridged), London and New York 1932 (abridged), London 1948 (abridged), 1950 (abridged), 1957, 1958, Harmondsworth 1967, London and New York 1973, London 1975, 1977 (abridged), 1982 (abridged), Exeter 1984, Abingdon 1992.

Tableau de l'Angleterre. 3 nos 1830. Fr trn from Political Register 14–21 Aug 1830.
Three lectures, Sheffield. Sheffield 1830.
Cobbett's letter on the abolition of tithes. Dublin [1831?]. Rptd from Political Register 10 Sep 1831. Rptd as Mr Cobbett's propositions, Manchester 1831.
Cobbett's opinions on the great question of parliamentary reform. Warrington 1831. Rptd from Twopenny Trash Apr 1831.
Evils of emigration. Manchester 1831. Rptd from Political Register 5 Apr 1831.
A full and accurate report of the trial of William Cobbett. 1831 (5 edns), New York 1831. Ed anon; not by Cobbett.
Mr Cobbett's answer to the address of his committee in Manchester. Manchester 1831. Rptd from Political Register 22 Aug 1831.
A spelling book. 1831, 1831, 1832, 1834, 1843 ('7th edn'), 1845 ('9th edn').
Surplus population. [1831?], [1835?]; rptd from Political Register 28 May 1831 and Cobbett's Twopenny Trash June 1831. Ed Steve Bushell as Surplus population and the poor law bill, 1994. Play.
Cobbett's advice to the chopsticks of Kent, Sussex. 1832.
Cobbett's Manchester lectures. 1832.
Extracts from Cobbett's Register, and Mr Cobbett's remarks. Birmingham [1832].
Mansell & Co's report of the important discussion held in Birmingham. Birmingham [1832], [1832]. Ed anon; not by Cobbett.
Cobbett's Magazine. Monthly periodical Feb 1833–Apr 1834; title changed to Shilling Magazine, Apr 1834. Ed J. M. and J. P. Cobbett with some articles by Cobbett.
Cobbett's poor man's friend. [1833.] Rev from Poor man's friend, 1826–7, *above*. Rptd from Political Register 5 Jan 1833.
Disgraceful squandering of the public money. Glasgow 1833. Rptd from Political Register 15 June 1831.
The flash in the pan. 1833. Rptd from Political Register 18–25 May 1833.
Mr Cobbett's answer to Mr Stanley's manifesto. [1833], [1833]. Rptd from Political Register 29 Dec 1832.
A new French and English dictionary. 1833.
Popay the police spy. 1833. Rptd from Political Register 17 Aug 1833.
Rights of industry. 1833. By Cobbett and J. Fielden. Rptd from Political Register 14 Dec 1833.
The speeches of W. Cobbett MP. 2 nos 1833. Rptd from True Sun 1833.
Cobbett's legacy to labourers. 1834 (for 1835), 1835, 1835, New York 1835, 1844, 1847 (with Cobbett's legacy to parsons) rptd 1860, London 1872. Dedication rptd as Mr Cobbett and the new poor law act, [1838?].
Four letters to the Hon John Stuart Wortley. 1834. Rptd from Political Register 31 Aug–19 Oct 1833.
Get gold! get gold! Leeds 1834. Rptd from Political Register 16 Aug 1834.
[Five] Letters to the Earl of Radnor. 1834. Rptd from Political Register 9, 23 Aug, 20 Sep, 18, 25 Oct 1834.
Mr Cobbett's speech for an abolition of the malt tax. 1834. Rptd from Political Register 22 Mar 1834.
Three lectures on the political state of Ireland. Dublin 1834. First lecture in another version in Political Register 4 Oct 1834.
Cobbett's legacy to parsons. 1835 (6 edns), New York 1835, 1844, 1860, London 1868, 1869, Croydon 1876 (as There being no gospel for tithes), London 1947; tr Welsh 1835.
The malt tax. 1835. Rptd from Political Register 24 Mar 1835.
Cobbett's legacy to Peel. 1836. Rptd from Political Register 24 Jan–18 Apr 1835.
The right of the poor to the suffrage of the people's charter. Leeds 1841. 'Together with Mr Cobbett's address to the farmers and tradesmen . . . on their treatment of the poor'. Rptd from Cobbett's Twopenny Trash.
Cobbett's reasons for war against Russia. 1854. Ed anon; extracts rptd from Political Register 1822, 1826, 1829, 1833, 1834.
Mr Cobbett's remarks on our Indian empire. 1857. By Cobbett and J. Fielden, ed anon. Extracts rptd from Political Register 1804–22.
A letter from London. Philadelphia 1958.
Cobbett's tour in Scotland. Ed D. Green, Aberdeen 1984.

Letters

'Melville, Lewis' (L. S. Benjamin). In Life and letters of Cobbett, 2 vols 1913.
Countryman 4 1931, 6 1932, 10–11 1935, 12 1936, 16 1938.
Cole, G. D. H. Letters from Cobbett to Edward Thornton 1797–1800. Oxford 1937.
Pearl, M. L. Cobbett at Botley, Cobbett and his men, Cobbett and his family, Cobbett and the 'Chop-sticks'. Countryman 153–4 1951, 157 1953.
Davis, C. R. Cobbett letters in the library. Jnl Rutgers Univ Lib 17 1954.
Fontinelles, A. Un inédit de Cobbett: lettre à Thomas Hulme. Études Anglaises 15 1962.
Duff, G. Letters of William Cobbett. Salzburg 1974.

Translations, editions, prefaces and appendices

Impeachment of Mr Lafayette. Philadelphia 1793, Hagerstown MD 1794. Tr Cobbett.
Summary of the law of nations. Philadelphia 1795, London 1802 (as A compendium of the law of nations), 1829 ('4th edn'). By G. F. von Martens, tr Cobbett.
An answer to Paine's Rights of man. Philadelphia 1796. By H. Mackenzie, ed Cobbett with A letter from Peter Porcupine to citizen John Swanwick.
A topographical and political description of the Spanish port of St Domingo. Philadelphia 1796, Boston 1808. By M. L. E. Moreau de St Mery, tr Cobbett.
The gros mousqueton diplomatique: or diplomatic blunderbuss. Philadelphia 1796. By P. A. Adet, tr and ed Cobbett, rptd from Political Censor 1796, *above*.
The history of Jacobinism. 2 vols Philadelphia 1796, London 1798. By W. Playfair, ed Cobbett with his own appendix, History of the American Jacobins, *above*.
A letter to a noble lord. Philadelphia 1796. By Edmund Burke, ed Cobbett, with preface.
An answer to Paine's letter to Washington. 1797, Glasgow 1797, Philadelphia 1798. By P. Kennedy, brief 'advertisement' by 'P. P.' (Cobbett) and pbd by him.
The anti-Gallican. Philadelphia 1797. By 'A citizen of New England', 'Leonidas', 'Philo-Leonidas', 'Ascanius', 'Impartial', brief dedication by Cobbett and pbd by him.
A view of the causes and consequences of the present war with France. Philadelphia 1797. By T. Erskine et al, ed 'Peter Porcupine' (Cobbett), with 'dedication' and 'appendix'.
The cannibal's progress. 1798, Philadelphia 1798, 1798 (as Introductory address to the people of America). Numerous edns of this and other trns from the Ger pbd Albany, Amherst, Boston, Charleston, Hartford, Newburyport, New Hampshire, New Haven, New London, Northampton, Portsmouth, Savannah, Vergennes, Walpole 1798; Cobbett inspired many of these Amer edns including Ger edns Der Fortgang der Menschenfresser; [1798] (rev as A warning to Britons), 1801 (as The cannibal's progress, with an introductory address to the subjects of the British Empire), 1803. Tr A. Aufrère, ed Cobbett with 'introductory address'.
Observations on the dispute between the United States and France. Philadelphia 1798. By R. G. Harper et al, ed Cobbett with 'preface' and appendix; '3rd' Amer edn pbd and ed Cobbett.
History of the campaigns of Prince Alexander Suworow Rymnikski. New York 1800. By J. F. Anthing, ed and pbd Cobbett with additional trn, A history of his Italian campaign, by Cobbett.

The unsex'd females. New York 1800. By Rev Richard Polwhele, preface by Cobbett.

A treatise on the culture and management of fruit trees. Philadelphia 1802, New York 1802, Albany NY 1803, Philadelphia 1803, 1804 (by 'an American farmer', as An epitome of Mr Forsyth's treatise). By W. Forsyth, ed Cobbett with introd and notes, 'adapting ... the treatise to ... America'.

The empire of Germany. 1803. By J. G. Peltier, tr Cobbett with a trn of a memoir by Peltier rptd from Political Register 1802.

Cobbett's parliamentary debates. 1804– . Ed Cobbett with J. Wright until 1811, then by Wright only. From 1813 (vol 24) as The parliamentary debates; supplemented by Cobbett's parliamentary history, similarly edited, 36 vols 1806–20, which also passed out of his hands in 1812 and entitled The parliamentary history from vol 13. Repbd New York 1966. The parliamentary debates became Hansard's parliamentary debates in 1818 and eventually the present Hansard.

Cobbett's Spirit of the Public Journals. Weekly periodical, ed Cobbett, 2 Jan–26 Dec 1804; 1 vol 1805.

Cobbett's complete collection of state trials. 33 vols 1809–26, 1972, Wilmington DE 1979. Cobbett with J. Wright and T. B. Howell until 1811, then by T. B. Howell; from 1812 dissociated from Cobbett as Howell's state trials.

An essay on sheep. 1811, New Haven CT 1813. By R. R. Livingston, ed Cobbett from 1st edn New York 1809, with his preface and notes.

The trial of Miss Mary Ann Tocker. New York 1818 (3 edns), Boston 1818 (as the Triumph of virtue). Ed Cobbett with 'letter' and 'address'.

American slave trade. 1822. By J. Torrey jr, ed Cobbett with preface from 1st Amer edn, Portraiture of domestic slavery, Philadelphia 1822.

The horse hoeing husbandry. 1822, 1829. Ed Cobbett with introd from A specimen etc by J. Tull, 1731.

Elements of the Roman history. 1828, 1829 (rev as An abridged history of the Emperors, 1829). By J. H. Sievrac, tr Cobbett.

Usury. [1824?], 1828, 1834, 1856. By J. O'Callaghan, ed Cobbett from 1st edn New York 1824, with dedication.

A geographical dictionary. 1832, 1854. Ed Cobbett et al.

The curse of paper money. 1833, New York 1968. By W. M. Gouge, ed Cobbett with preface and introd rptd from Political Register 20 July 1833, the rest from Philadelphia 1833 edn.

Life of Andrew Jackson. 1834, New York 1834, 1834, Baltimore 1834, [another Amer edn 1834], New York [1837]. Ed Cobbett from the Life by J. H. Eaton, Philadelphia 1824.

Doom of the tithes. 1836. Introd by Cobbett to a trn from a Sp work, Historia y origen de las rentas de la Iglesia de España, 1793.

Works written under the pseudonym 'Peter Porcupine'
See under individual works, above.

§2

Hazlitt, W. Character of Cobbett. In his Table talk, vol 1, 1821, and Spirit of the age, 1825 (2nd edn), 1835.

Obituary. The Times 20 June 1835.

The life of William Cobbett, esq. late MP for Oldham. 1835.

Chesterton, G. K. William Cobbett. 1925.

Clark, M. E. Peter Porcupine in America. Philadelphia 1939.

Cole, G. D. H. The life of William Cobbett. 1947.

Spater, G. William Cobbett: the poor man's friend. 2 vols Cambridge 1982.

Green, D. Great Cobbett: the noblest agitator. 1983.

Cobbett's New Register *(jnl of the William Cobbett Soc) is pbd annually.* [LN]

Hartley Coleridge 1796–1849

See col 297.

Henry Nelson Coleridge 1798–1843

§1

Poetry of the College Magazine. Windsor 1819 (with J. Moultrie).

Six months in the West Indies in 1825. 1826 (anon), 1832 (with addns), 1841 (with addns); rptd New York 1970; tr Du 1826.

The young logicians ... with particular reference to 'Six months ...'. 1827.

Introductions to the study of the Greek classic poets. Pt 1 (all pbd) 1830, 1834. On Homer.

The genuine life of Mr Francis Swing. 1831.

Specimens of the table-talk of the late Samuel Taylor Coleridge. 2 vols 1835, 1836 (with slight alterations), 1851 etc.

Table talk, recorded by Henry Nelson Coleridge (and John Taylor Coleridge), edited by C. Woodring. 2 vols 1990 (Collected works of S. T. Coleridge vol 14).

For H. N. Coleridge's edns of his uncle's Literary remains, Aids to reflection, Confessions of an inquiring spirit, Biographia literaria *etc, see under S. T. Coleridge, col 298, above. His pseudonymous and anon critical essays and reviews in* Etonian, Br Critic *and* Quart Rev *are summarised in W. Graham,* Henry Nelson Coleridge: expositor of romantic criticism, PQ 4 1925.

§2

Coleridge, E. Some recollections of Henry Nelson Coleridge and his family. 1910. [PL]

Edward Copleston 1776–1849

§1

Advice to a young reviewer, with a specimen of the art. Oxford 1807 (anon); ed J. C. Collins 1903 (in Critical essays and literary fragments); ed G. S. Gordon 1927 (in Three Oxford ironies; with bibliographical notes) (with note on the author by V. M. D.).

The Examiner examined: or logic vindicated. 1809. Anon.

A reply to the calumnies of the Edinburgh Review against Oxford: containing an account of the studies pursued in that university. Oxford 1810; A second reply, Oxford 1810; A third reply, Oxford 1811.

Praelectiones academicae Oxonii habitae. Oxford 1813. 35 Latin lectures on poetry.

Remains of the late Edward Copleston, with an introduction containing some reminiscences of his life. Ed R. Whately 1854.

Copleston also pbd An inquiry into the doctrines of necessity and predestination, in four discourses, *1831, and a number of sermons, charges and pams.*

§2

Copleston, W. J. Memoir of Copleston with selections from his diary and correspondence. 1851. Includes bibliography.

Tuckwell, W. In his Pre-Tractarian Oxford: a reminiscence of the Oriel Noetics, 1909.

George Lillie Craik 1798–1866

The New Zealanders. 1830. Anon.

The pursuit of knowledge under difficulties, illustrated by anecdotes. 2 vols 1830–1 (anon), 1844, 3 vols 1845, 2 vols 1858 (rev and enlarged), 1 vol 1865 (rev and enlarged), Edinburgh 1881, London 1906 (rev and enlarged).

Paris and its historical scenes. 2 vols 1831–2. Anon.

The pictorial history of England: being a history of the people as well as a history of the Kingdom. 4 vols 1837–41 (to the accession of George III), 1841–4 (during the reign of George III), 9 vols 1850 (vol 9 with index by H. C. Hamilton). With C. MacFarlane.

The history of British commerce from the earliest times. 3 vols 1844. Rptd from The pictorial history of England by Craik and MacFarlane.

Sketches of the history of literature and learning in England from the Norman Conquest. 6 vols 1844–5, 2 vols 1861 (much enlarged, as A compendious history of English literature and language from the Conquest), 1 vol 1862 (abridged); ed H. Craik [1883] (abridged edn, with ch on recent lit by Craik, as A manual of English literature and of the history of the English language).
Spenser and his poetry. 3 vols 1845.
Bacon: his writings and his philosophy. 3 vols 1846–7, 1 vol 1860 ('corrected').
The pursuit of knowledge under difficulties, illustrated by female examples. 1847. A suppl to the first work of the same title.
The romance of the peerage: or curiosities of family history. 4 vols 1848–50.
Paris and its historical buildings. 1849.
Outlines of the history of the English language for the use of junior classes. 1851, 1864 (5th edn, rev and improved).
The English of Shakespeare illustrated by a philological commentary on Julius Caesar. 1857.
For Craik's contributions to periodicals, see Wellesley *vol 5.*

John Wilson Croker 1780–1857

Bibliography
Brightfield, M. F. In his Croker, Berkeley 1940.

Selections
The Croker papers 1808–57. Ed B. Pool 1967.
Reiman, D. H. (ed). Familiar epistles to Frederick J(ones) esq. on the present state of the Irish stage. Reprint of 1804 edn with Amazoniad, Histrionic epistles and Battles of Talavera. New York 1978 (Romantic Context ser).

§1

Familiar epistles on the state of the Irish stage. [By T. C. D.] Dublin 1804 (2 edns), 1805 (2 edns), London 1805 (2 edns), Dublin 1806; ed W. Donaldson 1875 (attributed). Letters in verse addressed to F. Jones.
An intercepted letter from Canton. Dublin 1804 (3 edns) (anon), 1805 (3 edns). A satire on Dublin society.
The amazoniad, or figure and fashion: a scuffle in high life. Cantos 1–3 Dublin 1806 (2 edns); cantos 4–5 Dublin 1806 (anon). A satirical poem.
Histrionic epistles. Dublin 1807. Anon.
A sketch of the state of Ireland. 1808. Anon.
The battles of Talavera. 2nd edn anon, 1809 (authorship acknowledged), 1810 (4 edns) anon, Philadelphia 1811, London 1812, London, Edinburgh and Dublin 1812, London 1816 (9th edn, as Talavera; to which are added other poems).
A key to the orders in council. 1812. Anon.
The letters on the subject of the naval war with America. 1813.
Ode to be sung at the dinner given by the gentlemen from India ... to Wellington. [1814.] Anon.
A letter on the fittest style and situation for the Wellington testimonial about to be erected in Dublin. 1815.
Stories for children from the history of England. 1817.
Keats's Endymion. Quart Rev 19 1818.
Substance of the speech in the House of Commons on the Roman Catholic question. 1819.
An answer to O'Meara's Napoleon in exile. New York 1823. Rptd from Quart Rev.
Royal memoirs on the French Revolution, with historical and biographical illustrations. 1823. Trns of 2 memoirs by Madame Royale, Duchess of Angoulême, and the Narrative of a journey to Brussels and Coblenz by Louis XVIII.
Progressive geography for children. 1828.
The life of Samuel Johnson LLD by James Boswell. 5 vols 1831, 1835, 1848 ('thoroughly revised with much additional matter').
Speech on the reform question. 1831.
Speech on the question that 'The reform bill do pass'. 1831.
Resolutions moved by Mr Croker on the report of the reform bill. 1832.
Poems by Alfred Tennyson. Quart Rev 49 1833.
Johnsoniana: or supplement to Boswell. 2 vols 1835, 1859 (with much new material).
Robespierre. 1835. Rptd from Quart Rev 54 1835.
Memoirs of the reign of George the Second by John, Lord Hervey. 2 vols 1848.
Macaulay's History of England. Quart Rev 84 1849.
History of the guillotine. 1853. Rev from Quart Rev.
Correspondence with the Right Honourable Lord John Russell on some passages of Moore's diary; with a postscript by Mr Croker explanatory of Mr Moore's acquaintance and correspondence with him. 1854.
Essays on the early period of the French Revolution. 1857. Rptd with addns and corrections from Quart Rev.
An essay towards a new edition of Pope's works. 1871 (priv ptd).
The Croker papers: the correspondence and diaries of Croker. Ed L. J. Jennings 3 vols 1884 (with memoir), 1885 (rev).
For details of Croker's contributions to periodicals, particularly the Quart Review, *see* Wellesley *vol 5 1989. See also Brightfield, Bibliography, above.*

§2

Macaulay, T. B. The life of Johnson. Edinburgh Rev 54 1831; rptd in his Critical and historical essays contributed to the Edinburgh Review, 3 vols 1843.
Answers to Mr Macaulay's criticism on Mr Croker's edition of Boswell's Life of Johnson. 1856. Selected from Blackwood's Mag.
Maginn, W. A gallery of illustrious characters. Ed W. Bates [1873].
Quart Rev 158 1884.
Brightfield, M. F. Croker. Berkeley 1940.
Strout, A. L. Croker and the Noctes ambrosianae. TLS 9 Mar 1940.
Lucas, F. L. Croker and Tennyson. TLS 30 Nov 1946. Further correspondence by J. Murray 14 Dec 1946, 18 Jan 1947; C. P. Hsu 21 Dec 1946.
Strout, A. L. Croker and Tennyson again. N & Q 26 July, 15 Nov 1947.
Staniforth, J. H. M. Croker's pettifoggery. TLS 25 Aug 1950.
de Beer, E. S. Macaulay and Croker: the reviewer of Croker's Boswell. RES 10 1959.
Broadhurst, A. C. The French revolution collections in the British Library. BLJ 2, Autumn 1976.
Morgan, P. F. Croker as literary critic in the Quarterly Review. TWC 8 1977.
Richardson, T. C. Carlyle's Chartism and the Quarterly Review. Carlyle Annual 10 1989.
Shattock, J. Politics and reviewers: the Edinburgh and the Quarterly in the early Victorian age. Leicester 1989.
See also under John Gibson Lockhart, below.

Allan Cunningham 1785–1842

See col 327.

George Daniel 1789–1864

§1

Stanzas on Lord Nelson's death and victory, by G. D. and E[dwin] B[entley]. 1806. Anon.
The times: a poem. 1810 (anon), 1811 (as The times: or the prophecy: a poem), 1813 (acknowledged).
Miscellaneous poems. 1812. Includes Woman, and other poems rptd from Ackermann's Mag, mostly satirical.
The r---l first born. By P- P-, poet laureate. 1812. Anon.
R-y-l stripes, or a kick from Yar-th to Wa-s: a poem by P- P-, poet

laureate. 1812. Suppressed and bought up by order of the Prince Regent. Only 6 copies known to exist.
The ghost of R-L stripes: a poem by P- P-, poet laureate. 1812.
Sophia's letters to the B-r-n Ger--ub: or Whiskers in the dumps, by P- P-, poet laureate. 1812 (anon).
The r-l first born, by P- P-, poet laureate. 1812.
Suppressed evidence: or royal intriguing. 1813. By P- P-, poet laureate (anon).
Virgil in London: or town eclogues. 1814 (anon).
The modern Dunciad: a satire; with notes biographical and critical. 1814 (anon), 1815, 1816, 1835 (with Virgil in London, and other poems).
London and Dublin: an heroic epistle to Counsellor Phillips, the celebrated Irish orator. 1817. Anon; probably by Daniel.
Doctor Bolus: a serio-comick-bombastick-operatick interlude. 1818. Anon.
An assified mare: a poem. By Peter Pindar, Jr. 1818. Anon.
Cumberland's British theatre; with remarks biographical and critical by D. G. 48 vols 1826–[61]. Daniel contributed a critical preface to each play.
Cumberland's minor theatre: with remarks biographical and critical by D. G. 17 vols 1828–43. Daniel contributed a critical preface to each farce etc.
Garrick in the green room. 1829. A biographical and critical analysis of a picture painted by Hogarth and engraved by W. Ward.
The disagreeable surprise: a farce. In Cumberland's British theatre vol 14, 1829.
Ophelia Keen! a dramatic legendary tale. 1829. Anon; an attack on Charles Kean's private life, suppressed.
Sworn at Highgate: a farce. In Cumberland's minor theatre vol 6, [1833].
Merrie England in the olden time. 2 vols 1842, [1873]. Illustr Leech and Cruikshank, rptd from Bentley's Misc.
The missionary: a religious poem. 1847.
Democritus in London: with the mad pranks and comical conceits of Motley and Robin Good-Fellow, to which are added notes festivous [etc]. 1852. A verse continuation of Merrie England, *above*, with The stranger guest: a religious poem.
An Elizabethan garland: a descriptive catalogue of seventy black-letter ballads printed between 1559 and 1597. 1856 (priv ptd).
Love's last labour not lost. 1863. Includes Recollections of Charles Lamb, Robert Cruikshank, a Reply to Macaulay's essay on Dr Johnson and other essays in prose and verse.
Recollections of Charles Lamb. 1927. Rptd from Love's last labour not lost.
Daniel also pbd a novel, The adventures of Dick Distich, *3 vols 1812 (anon).*

§2

Athenaeum 9 Apr 1864. Obituary.
Catalogue of the most valuable, interesting and highly important library of the late George Daniel esq. 1864.

George Darley 1795–1846

See col 328.

Thomas de Quincey 1785–1859

De Quincey sometimes altered the titles of his essays when he reprinted them, as did D. Masson, editor of what has been the standard collected edn. Here the first published titles of works by De Quincey are used, but any significant changes to titles in later eds are noted.

Manuscripts

The Wordsworth Trust, Dove Cottage, holds the most complete ms of Confessions of an English opium-eater, as pbd in the London Mag 1821, in addition to other De Quincey mss. *See* IELM 4 1982.

Bibliographies

Lowndes, W. T. In The bibliographer's manual of English literature, vol 3 1861.
Masson, D. Appendix chronological and bibliographical. In his edn of The collected writings of Thomas De Quincey, vol 14 1890.
Axon, W. E. A. The De Quincey collection at Moss Side. Lib Assoc Record 2, Aug 1900.
Green, J. A. De Quincey; a bibliography based upon the Thomas De Quincey collection in the Moss Side Library, Manchester 1908.
Axon, W. E. A. The canon of De Quincey's writings, with references to some of his unidentified articles. Trans Royal Soc of Lit 2nd ser 32 1914.
Jones, C. E. Some De Quincey manuscripts. ELH 8, Mar 1941.
Byrns, R. H. Some unpublished works of De Quincey. PMLA 71, Dec 1956.
Jordon, J. E. In The English romantic poets and essayists; a review of research and criticism, ed C. W. and L. H. Houtchens, New York 1957; rptd and rev 1966.
Moreux, F. In Thomas De Quincey; la vie – l'homme – l'oeuvre, Paris 1964.
Tave, S. M. In New essays by De Quincey; his contributions to the Edinburgh Saturday Post and the Edinburgh Evening Post, 1827–8, Princeton 1966.
Janzow, F. S. In The English opium-eater as editor. Costerus n.s. 1 1974. Articles by De Quincey in The Westmorland Gazette including attributions.
Dendurent, H. O. Thomas De Quincey: a reference guide. Boston 1978. (Secondary.)
Baxter, E. In De Quincey's art of autobiography, Edinburgh 1990. Includes some newly attributed items.

Collections

De Quincey's writings. Ed J. T. Fields, with the consent of De Quincey, 22 vols, Boston 1851–9 (vol 12 is a revised version of vol 5 and supersedes it. Intermediate vols were renumbered accordingly. Counting both the original and the new vol 5, there are 23 vols); 22 vols in 11, Boston 1873.
Selections grave and gay; from writings, published and unpublished, of De Quincey, revised and arranged by himself. 14 vols, Edinburgh 1853–60.
De Quincey's works. 17 vols, Edinburgh 1862–3 (this edn is in part a reissue of Selections grave and gay. To have been completed in 15 vols; 2 vols added in course of pbn); 16 vols, Edinburgh 1871 (vols retain earlier dates, 1862–3, and there are addns to last 4); 16 vols, Edinburgh 1878 (all vols save 1st are dated 1862 or 1863 and 3 essays added).
The works of Thomas De Quincey. 12 vols New York 1877 (Riverside edn). A reissue, with alterations, of the stereotyped edn pbd by Ticknor and Fields, Boston. With notes and general index; several times rptd.
The collected writings of Thomas De Quincey. New and enlarged edn by D. Masson, 14 vols, Edinburgh 1889–90. With introds and notes; considerable new material now first collected. Standard edn, several times rptd.
The uncollected writings of Thomas De Quincey, with a preface and annotations by James Hogg. 2 vols 1890.
The posthumous works of Thomas De Quincey. Edited from the original mss with introds and notes by A. H. Japp, 2 vols 1891–3. Vol 1 Suspiria de profundis, with other essays, critical, historical, biographical, philosophical, imaginative and humorous; vol 2 Conversation and Coleridge, with other essays, critical, historical, biographical, philosophical, imaginative and humorous.
REVIEWS: Noble, J. A., Acad 40, Aug 1891; Saturday Rev 71, 1891; Noble, J. A., Acad 44, Dec 1893; Athenaeum Dec 1893.
New essays by De Quincey: his contributions to the Edinburgh

Saturday Post and the Edinburgh Evening Post 1827–8. Ed S. M. Tave, Princeton 1966.
The works of Thomas De Quincey. 16 vols forthcoming (gen ed G. Lindop).

Selections

Eds of Confessions with other writings have been placed under subsequent edns of Confessions. See §1, below.

Letters to a young man; and other papers. Boston 1858.
Letters on self-education; with hints on style, and dialogues on political economy. [1861].
Beauties; selected from the writings of Thomas De Quincey. New York 1862. *See also* edns of 1866 and 1876.
Notes from the pocket-book of an opium-eater; with anecdotes etc. Ed S. O. Beeton [1878].
Romances and extravagances. Nashville TN [1882].
Select essays of Thomas De Quincey, narrative and imaginative. Ed D. Masson, 2 vols, Edinburgh 1888.
De Quincey; a selection of his best works. Ed W. H. Bennett, 2 vols 1889.
Joan of Arc and other selections from Thomas De Quincey. Ed H. H. Belfield, Boston [1892].
Essays on style, rhetoric, and language. Ed F. N. Scott, Boston 1893.
Joan of Arc; The English mail-coach. Ed J. M. Hart, New York 1893.
Thomas De Quincey's Glory of motion and The vision of sudden death. Ed E. E. Kellett, Madras 1894.
De Quincey's Revolt of the Tartars and The English mail-coach. Ed C. M. Barrow and M. Hunter 1895.
Selected essays of De Quincey. Ed W. Sharp, with introd by Sir G. Douglas, [1895].
Lyrics in prose by De Quincey. Ed R. B. Johnson, New York '1897' [1896].
Murder as a fine art, and The English mail-coach. 1899.
Essays from De Quincey. Ed J. H. Fowler 1900.
A dream of infinity by De Quincey; and other selected dreams and legends. Ed L. Capel [1902].
Selections from De Quincey. Ed M. H. Turk, Boston 1902.
Essays by Thomas De Quincey. Ed C. Whibley [1903].
Essays. Ed T. Bayne [1903].
De Quincey's English mail-coach and Joan of Arc. Ed M. H. Turk, Boston [1905].
Joan of Arc, and The English mail-coach. Ed R. A. Witham, Boston 1905.
Joan of Arc, and The English mail-coach. Ed C. S. Baldwin 1906.
Reminiscences of the English Lake poets. [1907].
Joan of Arc and The English mail-coach. Ed C. M. Stebbins 1908.
De Quincey's Literary criticism, ed H. Darbishire, Oxford 1909.
Joan of Arc, The English mail-coach, and The Spanish military nun, ed C. M. Newman, New York 1909.
The Spanish military nun and Revolt of the Tartars. Ed V. H. Collins, Oxford 1909.
Selections from De Quincey. Ed E. B. Collins, Cambridge 1910.
De Quincey (selections). Ed S. Low 1911 (Masters of Lit).
The English mail-coach and other essays. Ed J. H. Burton [1912].
The early life of Thomas De Quincey from his own writings. [1914] (English literature for schools no 30).
The English mail-coach and other essays. 1914 (EL); ed J. E. Jordan 1961 (EL).
De Quincey; reminiscences of his boyhood. First pbd 1834–52; ed H. E. Icely 1926.
De Quincey selections. Ed M. R. Ridley, with essays by L. Stephen and F. Thompson, Oxford 1927.
The ecstasies of Thomas De Quincey. Ed T. Burke 1928.
Selections from De Quincey. Ed A. H. R. Ball [1932].
Selected writings of Thomas De Quincey. Ed P. Van D. Stern, New York 1937.
Thomas De Quincey's Joan of Arc, and The English mail-coach. Ed A. A. Purcell, New York [1938].
Recollections of the Lake Poets. Ed E. Sackville-West 1948. Rev text supplemented from Tait's Mag 1839–40.
Selected writings of Thomas De Quincey. Ed P. V. D. Stern [1959].
Reminiscences of the English Lake poets. Ed J. E. Jordan 1961 (EL). Rev text with notes on 1839–40 mag text.
Thomas De Quincey. Ed B. Dobrée 1965.
Selected essays on rhetoric. Ed F. Burwick, Carbondale IL 1967.
Recollections of the Lakes and the Lake poets. Ed D. Wright, Harmondsworth 1970.
De Quincey as critic. Ed J. E. Jordan 1973.
On murder and On war; two essays by Thomas De Quincey 1980.

§1

Translation from Horace, ode 22 lib 1 (third prize translation). Juvenile Lib 1 1800; rptd in Confessions of an English opium-eater, ed R. Garnett 1885 and in The collected writings of Thomas De Quincey, ed D. Masson, vol 14 1890.
Concerning the relations of Great Britain, Spain and Portugal, as affected by the convention of Cintra, by William Wordsworth, appendix on the letters of Sir J. Moore by De Quincey. 1809. For subsequent edns and further details, *see* William Wordsworth, *col 492 above*.
Close comments upon a straggling speech. Kendal 1818; rptd PMLA 55 1940.
Confessions of an English opium-eater. London Mag 4, Sep–Oct 1821, and London Mag 5, Dec 1822 (appendix); 1822, 1823, 1826, 1845; in De Quincey's writings, ed J. T. Fields, vol 1 1851; 1853 (new edn); in Selections grave and gay, vol 5 Edinburgh 1856 (greatly enlarged); [1867] (new edn, with Notes from the pocket-book of a late opium-eater, World-wide Lib); 1867 (new edn, with Analects from John Paul Richter); ed S. O. Beeton [1874] and [1878] (with Essays on men of letters); in The works of Thomas De Quincey, Riverside edn, vol 1 1877 (from 1822 edn); [1881] (new edn, Familiar Quotation ser 17); ed R. Garnett 1885 (from 1822 edn with De Quincey's Conversations with R. Woodhouse, a note on De Quincey and Musset); ed H. Morley 1886 (with The lives of Shakespeare and Goethe); ed W. Sharp 1886 (with Levana, The Rosecrucians and freemasons and Notes from the pocket-book of a late opium-eater); in The collected writings of Thomas De Quincey, ed D. Masson, vol 3 1890; ed M. Hunter 1896 (from 1856 edn); ed R. Le Gallienne 1898; ed W. Jerrold 1899; 1901 (Library of English Classics); ed J. Downie 1901 (with D. Masson's notes and J. R. Findlay's Life of De Quincey); 1902 (WC); Ann; a memory. The Bibelot 9, Portland ME 1903 (extracted from Confessions); ed D. Masson 1904 (from 1856 edn); ed C. Whibley [1904]; ed W. Sharp [1905]; [1905] (New Universal Lib); 1905 (Little Masterpieces); ed T. Hopkins [1906] (with Autobiography); ed A. Beatty 1907 (from 1821 edn); introd H. Bennett 1907 (from 1821 edn); ed G. Douglas 1907 (EL); 1908 (The People's Lib); ed G. Saintsbury 1927 (from 1822 edn); ed W. Bolitho with lithographs by Zhenya Gay, Oxford 1930; illustr S. Woolf, New York 1930 (from 1856 edn); with wood engravings by B. Hughes-Stanton 1948, 1963; Ann of Oxford Street, illustr P. Jullian 1948 (from Confessions); ed E. Sackville-West 1950 (from 1822 edn with selections from Autobiography); ed M. Elwin 1956 (both 1822 and 1856 edns with Suspiria); ed J. E. Jordan 1960 (EL); ed A. Ward, New York 1966 (with other writings); ed A. Hayter, Harmondsworth 1971 (from 1821 edn); ed G. Lindop, Oxford 1985 (from 1821 edn and with other writings); tr Fr 1828 (adaptation by Musset), 1860 (in part by C. Baudelaire), 1890 ('première traduction intégrale'), 1962; Swed 1869, 1926; Norwegian 1878; Ger 1886, 1888, 1928, 1947; Ital 1889, 1956; Danish 1921; Sp 1927, 1936; Jap 1950, 1951, 1952; Du 1953; Polish 1980.
REVIEWS: Montgomery, J., Sheffield Iris Dec 1821; The Album 2,

Nov 1822; The British Critic n.s. 18, Nov 1822; European Mag and London Rev 82, Nov 1822; GM 92, Nov 1822; London Museum Nov 1822; British Rev and London Critical Jnl 20, Dec 1822; Monthly Mag 54, Dec 1822; Imperial Mag 5, Jan 1823; New Edinburgh Rev 4, Jan 1823; Monthly Censor 2, Mar 1823; Monthly Rev 100, Mar 1823; Eclectic Rev n.s. 19, Apr 1823; [Phillips, W.] North American Rev Jan 1824; [Maginn, W.] The John Bull Mag and Literary Recorder 1, July 1824; United States Literary Gazette 1, 1825.

Popular tales and romances of the northern nations. 3 vols 1823. De Quincey contributed anon an unidentified trn from the German of J. A. Apel, The fatal marksman; rptd in Selections grave and gay vol 12 1859; in The works of Thomas De Quincey, Riverside edn, vol 11 1877; in The collected writings of Thomas De Quincey, ed D. Masson, vol 12 1890.

Walladmor; freely translated into German from the English of Sir Walter Scott, and now freely translated from the German into English. 2 vols 1825 (a German forgery by G. W. H. Haering, freely adapted in English; *see* De Quincey's papers on Walladmor, London Mag 1824 and Tait's Mag 1838).

Klosterheim; or the masque. Edinburgh 1832; ed R. Shelton-Mackenzie, Boston 1855; rptd in De Quincey's writings, ed J. T. Fields, vol 20 1856; in The works of Thomas De Quincey, Riverside edn, vol 11 1877; in The collected writings of Thomas De Quincey, ed D. Masson, vol 12 1890; rptd in penny edn as The mystery of the masque 1898; Santa Barbara 1982 (Banquo books).

The gallery of portraits; with memoirs. Ed A. T. Malkin, 7 vols 1833–7. De Quincey contributed anon a Life of Milton to vol 1; rptd in Distinguished men of modern times, ed A. T. Malkin, 4 vols 1838; in Selections grave and gay, vol 11 1859; in The works of Thomas De Quincey, Riverside edn, vol 6 1877; in The collected writings of Thomas De Quincey, ed D. Masson, vol 4 1890.

Encyclopaedia Britannica, 7th edn 1827–42. De Quincey contributed articles on Goethe, 1835; Pope, 1837–8; Schiller, 1838; Shakespeare, 1838. All 4 articles rptd in De Quincey's writings, ed J. T. Fields, vol 2 1851; in The works of Thomas De Quincey, Riverside edn, vol 5 1877 (Pope) and vol 6 1877 (Shakespeare, Goethe and Schiller); in The collected writings of Thomas De Quincey, ed D. Masson, vol 4 1890; Shakespeare and Goethe rptd in Confessions of an English opium-eater; also the lives of Shakespeare and Goethe, ed H. Morley 1883.
REVIEWS: Fraser's Mag 24, July 1841 (Shakespeare); [Brown, G. W.] North American Rev 74, Apr 1852 (all 4 articles); H. Morley, in introd to his edn of Confessions of an English opium-eater; also the lives of Shakespeare and Goethe, 1883 (Shakespeare and Goethe).

The logic of political economy. Edinburgh 1844; rptd in De Quincey's writings, ed J. T. Fields, vol 22 1859; in The works of Thomas De Quincey, Riverside edn, vol 10 1877; in The collected writings of Thomas De Quincey, ed D. Masson, vol 9 1890. *See also* Chapters on political economy; adapted from Mr. De Quincey's essay, ed J. R. Ballantyne, Allahabad 1854.
REVIEWS: [Mill, J. S.] Westminster Rev 43, Apr 1845; J. R. McCulloch, in his The literature of political economy; a classified catalogue, 1845; Hogg's Instructor 9, 1852; S. H. Hodgson in Outcast essays and verse translations, 1881.

The Glasgow Athenaeum album. Glasgow 1848. De Quincey contributed an essay: Sortilege on behalf of the Glasgow Athenaeum; rptd (as Sortilege and astrology) in Selections grave and gay, vol 9 1858; in The works of Thomas De Quincey, Riverside edn, vol 8 1877; in The collected writings of Thomas De Quincey, ed D. Masson, vol 13 1890.

China. 1857 (rev from articles in Titan, with preface and addns); rptd in De Quincey's works (2nd edn) vol 16 1871; in The works of Thomas De Quincey, Riverside edn, vol 12 1877; and as The Chinese question in 1857 in The collected writings of Thomas De Quincey, ed D. Masson, vol 14 1890.

The wider hope; essays and strictures on the doctrine and literature of future punishment. Ed J. Hogg 1890. De Quincey contributed an essay: On the supposed scriptural expression for eternity; rptd from Hogg's Instructor Jan 1853. De Quincey's essay rptd in De Quincey and his friends; personal recollections, souvenirs, and anecdotes of Thomas De Quincey, his friends and associates, ed J. Hogg 1895.
REVIEWS: Athenaeum Jan 1896 (review of Hogg's edn with esp mention of De Quincey's essay).

Dr Johnson and Lord Chesterfield. New York 1945 (priv ptd with facs of the ms).

Niels Klim, by Ludvig Holberg. Tr De Quincey, ed S. Musgrove, Auckland Univ College Bull 42 1953.
REVIEWS: Koefoed, H. A., MLR 50 1955; Margoliouth, H. M., RES n.s. 6 1956.

Contributions to periodicals

The majority of De Quincey's periodical contributions were first published either anonymously or pseudonymously. His most common pseudonyms were The English opium-eater and X. Y. Z. Periodical contributions pre-1824 are listed below under title of periodical.

The Westmorland Gazette: (De Quincey was editor 11 July 1818–5 Nov 1819). For a list of De Quincey's contributions 1818–19 (including attributions), *see* F. S. Janzow, The English opium-eater as editor, Costerus n.s. 1 1974.

Blackwood's Mag: The sport of fortune (trans from Schiller). Blackwood's Mag Jan 1821.

London Mag: For a list of De Quincey's contributions 1821–4, *see* The collected writings of Thomas De Quincey, ed. D. Masson, vol 14 1890, appendix 1.

See also Walladmor; Sir Walter Scott's German novel. London Mag Oct 1824.

Knight's Quart Mag: The incognito; or Count Fitz-Hum (from the German of Schultz, alias F. Laun). Knight's Quart Mag 3 1824.

Periodical contributions 1824– are listed in Wellesley *vol* 5. Wellesley *covers De Quincey's contributions, from 1824 onwards, to the following periodicals:* Blackwood's Mag, New Rev, North Br Rev *and* Tait's Edinburgh Mag. *The following periodical contributions 1824– are not listed in* Wellesley.

The Edinburgh Saturday Post and its continuation, from May 1828, The Edinburgh Evening Post: De Quincey's contributions (including attributions) are listed in New essays by De Quincey; his contributions to the Edinburgh Saturday Post 1827–8 and the Edinburgh Evening Post 1828, ed S. M. Tave, Princeton 1966.

Macphail's Edinburgh Ecclesiastical Jnl: War, Macphail's Edinburgh Ecclesiastical Jnl 5, Feb 1848.

Hogg's Instructor: Letter to the editor of the Instructor (dated 21 Sep 1850), Hogg's Instructor n.s. 6 1851.

Titan (the continuation, from 1856, of Hogg's Instructor): Shakespeare's text – Suetonius unravelled, Titan 22, July 1856 (presented as a letter); rptd as Aelius Lamia in Selections grave and gay vol 10 1859. Storms in English history; a glance at the reign of Henry VIII, Titan 23, Sep 1856. The Lake dialect; a letter from Thomas De Quincey, Titan 24, Jan 1857. China, Titan 24, Feb–Apr 1857; rptd together as a pam: China 1857; in De Quincey's works, 2nd edn, vol 16 1871; in The works of Thomas De Quincey, Riverside edn, vol 12 1877; and as The Chinese question in 1857 in The collected writings of Thomas De Quincey, ed D. Masson, vol 14 1890. Hints towards an appreciation of the coming war in China, Titan 25, July 1857. Hurried notes of Indian affairs, Titan 25, Sep 1857. Passing notes on Indian affairs, Titan 25, Oct 1857. Suggestions upon the secret of the mutiny, Titan 26, Jan 1858.

Archivist and Autograph Rev: An essay on novels (in the form of a letter), Archivist and Autograph Rev 1, June 1888.

Manchester Quart: Testimonial for J. F. Ferrier, in W. E. A. Axon, De Quincey and J. F. Ferrier, Manchester Quart 17, 1898.

Letters and papers

Gordon, M. In Christopher North; a memoir of John Wilson, 2 vols, Edinburgh 1862. One letter to Wilson.

Knight, C. In Passages of a working life during half a century; with a prelude of early reminiscences, 3 vols 1864–5. Quotes several letters to Knight.

Curwen, H. In A history of booksellers, 1873.

Davenport-Hill, R. and F. In The Recorder of Birmingham; a memoir of Matthew Davenport-Hill, 1878. One letter to M. D. Hill.

Findlay, J. R. In Personal recollections of Thomas De Quincey, Edinburgh 1886.

Japp, A. H. Some unconscious confessions of De Quincey. GM 261, Aug 1886. Extracts from mss.

Japp, A. H. In Thomas De Quincey; his life and writings, with unpublished correspondence, 1890. 60 letters.

The collected writings of Thomas De Quincey, ed D. Masson, vol 14 1890. A letter of 1847 to De Quincey's son Francis, printed as On the religious objections to the use of chloroform.

Japp, A. H. In his edn of De Quincey memorials; being letters and other records here first published, with communications from Coleridge, the Wordsworths, Hannah More, Professor Wilson and others, 2 vols, New York 1891.

Japp, A. H. Early intercourse of the Wordsworths and De Quincey. Century Mag 41 1891.

Clowes, A. A. In Charles Knight; a sketch, 1892.

The uncollected writings of Thomas De Quincey. Ed J. Hogg, 2 vols 1892. See preface.

Fields, Mrs J. T. In A shelf of old books, 1894. Facs of letter to Fields.

Hill, G. B. In Talks about autographs, Boston 1896. One letter to Mrs Hill.

Lang, A. In The life and letters of John Gibson Lockhart, 2 vols 1897. One letter.

In Some early contributors to Chambers's journal. Chambers's Jnl 5th ser 14, Nov 1897. One letter.

Oliphant, M. O. W. and Mrs G. Porter. In Annals of a publishing house; William Blackwood and his sons, 3 vols, Edinburgh 1897–8. 6 letters to Blackwood.

[Axon, W. E. A.] Some De Quincey documents. Manchester Guardian Dec 1900. 2 letters.

Axon, W. E. A. De Quincey and T. F. Dibdin. Library n.s. 8, July 1907.

Axon, W. E. A. Thomas De Quincey. Bookman 31, Feb 1907.

Priestley, E. In The story of a lifetime, 1908. One letter to Chambers and an extract of a letter to Mrs Chambers.

Fairbrother, E. H. Lieut Horatio De Quincey. N & Q 12, Oct 1915. One letter to War Office.

Armitt, M. L. In Rydal, Kendal 1916. 5 letters to W. A. Duckworth.

Gray, W. F. De Quincey as Lady Nairne's tenant. Chambers's Jnl Mar 1926. One letter to Lady Nairne's lawyers, one to J. H. Burton.

A diary of Thomas De Quincey 1803, here reproduced in replica as well as in print from the original manuscript in the possession of the Rev C. H. Steel. Ed H. A. Eaton [1927].

Moore, E. H. Some unpublished letters of Thomas De Quincey. RES 9 1933. 4 letters to rental agents.

Parsons, C. O. The woes of Thomas De Quincey. RES 10 1934. 3 letters.

De Quincey at work: as seen in one hundred and thirty new and newly edited letters. Ed W. H. Bonner, Buffalo NY 1936.

Eaton, H. A. In Thomas De Quincey; a biography, New York 1936.

McCusker, H. De Quincey and the landlord. More Books 14, Feb 1939.

De Quincey on French drama. More Books 14, Feb 1939. 7 fragments.

Wells, J. E. Wordsworth and De Quincey in Westmorland politics, 1818. PMLA 55 1940. 8 letters.

Brockway, W. and B. K. Winer. In A second treasury of the world's great letters, New York 1941. One letter to William Tait.

Broughton, L. N. Wordsworth and De Quincey in Westmorland politics, 1818; addendum. PMLA 56 1941. One letter.

Jones, C. E. Some De Quincey manuscripts. ELH 8 1941.

Grantham, E. De Quincey to his publisher. More Books 20, Dec 1945 One letter to J. A. Hessey.

Unpublished letters of Thomas De Quincey and Elizabeth Barrett Browning. Ed S. Musgrove, Auckland Univ College Bull 44 1954. 7 letters, 2 to Southey.

Green, D. B. A Thomas De Quincey letter. N & Q 5, Sep 1958.

De Quincey to Wordsworth; a biography of a relationship, with the letters of De Quincey to the Wordsworth family. Ed J. E. Jordan, Berkeley CA 1962.

Vann, J. D. An unpublished De Quincey letter. PQ 50 1971.

Lindop, G. In The opium-eater; a life of Thomas De Quincey, 1981.

Finkelstein, D. Thomas De Quincey and Robert Blackwood; an unpublished letter. N & Q 237, June 1992.

Translations

Some of the following are arguably adaptations rather than trns, and Walladmor is arguably an original. However, every work by De Quincey which has some claim to being categorised as a trns is included.

Translation from Horace. 1800. *See* §1, *above.*

The happy life of a parish priest in Sweden; from Richter. London Mag 4 1821.

The sport of fortune (from Schiller). Blackwood's Mag Jan 1821.

Mr Schnackenburger; or two masters for one dog (from the German). London Mag 7 1823.

The dice (from the German). London Mag 8 1823.

The fatal marksman (from J. A. Apel). In Popular tales and romances of the northern nations, 3 vols 1823.

The king of Hayti (from the German). London Mag 8 1823.

Abstract of Swedenborgianism; by Immanuel Kant. London Mag 9 1824.

Analects from John Paul Richter; by the author of the Confessions of an English opium-eater. London Mag 9 1824.

Dream upon the universe; by John Paul Richter. London Mag 9 1824.

Historico-critical inquiry into the origin of the Rosecrucians and Free-Masons (from the German). London Mag 9 1824.

Idea of a universal history on a cosmo-political plan; by Immanuel Kant. London Mag 10 1824.

Kant on national character in relation to the sense of the sublime and beautiful. London Mag 9 1824.

The incognito; or Count Fitz-Hum (from Friedrich Laun [Schultz]). Knight's Quart Mag 3 1824.

Walladmor. 1825. *See above.*

Gallery of the German prose classics; by the English opium-eater, no 1. Blackwood's Mag 20–1 1826–7. Includes a trn from Lessing's Laocoon.

Gallery of the German prose classics; by the English opium-eater, no 3. Blackwood's Mag 21 1827; rptd as The last days of Immanuel Kant in Selections grave and gay vol 3 1854 (from Wasianski).

Klopstock; from the Danish. Edinburgh Saturday Post Aug 1827.

Toilette of the Hebrew lady; exhibited in six scenes (from Hartmann). Blackwood's Mag 23 1828.

Age of the earth (from Kant). Tait's Edinburgh Mag 4 1833.

The nautico-military nun of Spain (from Alexis de Valon). Tait's Edinburgh Mag May–July 1847 (rptd as The Spanish military nun in Selections grave and gay vol 3 1854).

Neils Klim (from Ludwig Holberg). 1953. *See above.*

Edition

Selections grave and gay. 1853–60. *See* Collections, *above.*

Attributed works

Letter. The Times 6 Jan 1809 (attrib G. Lindop 1981).

Letter (signed One of the old school). The Carlisle Patriot 25 Apr 1818 (attrib Lindop 1981).

The Westmorland gazette 1818–19. Over 100 essays and articles attributed by F. S. Janzow, Costerus n.s. 1 1974.

Review of Guide to the English Lakes by Green. Blackwood's Mag 12, July 1822 (attrib W. E. A. Axon, Bookman 1907).

The street companion; or the young man's guide and the old man's comfort in the choice of shoes; ne sutor ultra crepidam; by the Rev Tom Foggy Dribble. London Mag 10, Jan 1825 (attrib W. E. A. Axon, The Library 1907).

The New Times Jan–May 1825. 15 unsigned or pseudonymous articles (*see* G. Lindop 1981, *below*).

Review of Michael Scott; a romance by A. Cunningham. Edinburgh Saturday Post Dec 1827 (attrib D. Groves, RES n.s. vol 41 May 1990).

The peasant of Portugal. In The literary souvenir; or cabinet of poetry and romance, ed A. Watts 1827; ed E. Baxter 1985.

The Cacadore; a story of the peninsular war. 1828; ed E. Baxter 1988.

Edinburgh Literary Gazette May–Oct 1829. 86 anon paragraphs on German and Danish literature (attrib Groves, N & Q 235, Mar 1990).

Review of Exodus; or the curse of Egypt, a sketch from scripture, and other poems by T. B. J. Edinburgh Evening Post Jan 1830 (attrib Groves, N & Q 232, Dec 1987).

Lessons of the French Revolution. The Independent 77 1914 (supposedly written 1848 but unpbd).

Spuriously attributed works

The stranger's grave 1823 (attrib W. E. A. Axon, Nation 1907); ed E. Baxter 1988. Now known to be by the Rev G. Gleig.

The love-charm. Knight's Quart Mag 1825. Now known to be from the German of Teick by J. Hare. *See* H. K. Galinsky, *§2, below*.

Traditions of the Rabbins. By G. Croly but included as De Quincey's in De Quincey's writings, ed J. T. Fields 1851–9; and in Selections grave and gay vol 14 1860. Continued to be rptd as De Quincey's up to 2nd Amer edn of 1873 and 4th Edinburgh edn of 1878.

Parodies

North, C. [John Wilson]. In Noctes ambrosianae. Blackwood's Mag 14, Oct 1823 and 27, Apr–Aug 1830; rptd as Noctes ambrosianae, 4 vols 1864.

Moir, D. M. De Quincey's revenge; a ballad in three fittes. Blackwood's Mag 48, Nov 1840.

[Hamley, E. B.] A recent confession of an opium-eater. Blackwood's Mag 80, Dec 1856.

§2

See also §1, above, especially contemporary reviews of individual works and letters and papers (articles containing letters are there and not below). Material included in introductions to eds has not been included here, nor have several articles of minor biographical interest. A comprehensive bibliography of secondary material on De Quincey 1821–1975 is provided by H. O. Dendurent, Thomas De Quincey; a reference guide, *Boston 1978.*

Biographies

Knight, C. In Passages of a working life during half a century; with a prelude of early reminiscences, ed J. Thorne, 3 vols 1864.

'Page, H. A.' [A. H. Japp]. Thomas De Quincey; his life and writings; with unpublished correspondence. 2 vols 1877; rptd in 1 vol 1890 (rev with omissions and addns). With appendix by W. C. B. Eatwell, A medical view of Mr De Quincey's case, and Reminiscences by J. Hogg.

Masson, D. De Quincey. London and New York 1881 (EML).

Findlay, J. R. Personal recollections of Thomas De Quincey. Edinburgh 1886.

Hogg, J. De Quincey and his friends; personal recollections, souvenirs and anecdotes of Thomas De Quincey, his friends and associates. 1895.

Eaton, H. A. Thomas De Quincey; a biography. Oxford 1936, New York 1936; rptd New York 1972. 1936 edn rev as introd to Elwin's edn of Confessions of an English opium-eater, 1956.

Sackville-West, E. A flame in sunlight; the life and works of Thomas De Quincey. 1936 (pbd in USA as Thomas De Quincey; his life and work).

Metcalf, J. C. De Quincey; a portrait. 1940, rptd New York 1963.

Jordan, J. E. De Quincey to Wordsworth; a biography of a relationship. Berkeley CA 1962.

Moreux, F. Thomas De Quincey; la vie – l'homme – l'oeuvre. Paris 1964.

Lindop, G. The opium-eater; a life of Thomas De Quincey. 1981.

Textual/bibliographical criticism

Useful bibliographical and textual criticism may often be found in edns of De Quincey's works, see section §1, above.

Rowan, A. B. N & Q 2nd ser 7 1859.

D., E. Curious error in De Quincey. N & Q 3rd ser 4 1863.

Curwen, H. In A history of booksellers, 1873.

Watts, T. The fatal marksman. Athenaeum no 2830, Jan 1882.

Japp, A. H. Some unconscious confessions of De Quincey. GM 261 1886.

Fields, J. T. A shelf of old books. 1894.

Axon, W. E. A. De Quincey and the Blackwoods. Manchester Guardian 12 Oct 1897.

Axon, W. E. A. De Quincey and J. F. Ferrier. Manchester Quart 17 1898.

Axon, W. E. A. The De Quincey collection at Moss Side. Manchester Herald 16 Sep 1899, rptd Library Assoc Record 2, Aug 1900.

Axon, W. E. A. De Quincey and Kant. Manchester Guardian 30 Oct 1906.

Axon, W. E. A. Thomas De Quincey. Bookman (London) 31, Feb 1907.

Axon, W. E. A. De Quincey and T. F. Dibdin. Library 2nd ser 8, July 1907.

Axon, W. E. A. De Quincey and the stranger's grave. Nation (London) 85, Dec 1907.

Axon, W. E. A. Some De Quincey proof sheets. Scottish Rev Nov 1908.

Axon, W. E. A. The canon of De Quincey's writings; with references to some of his unidentified articles. Trans of the Royal Society of Lit of the UK 32 1914.

Wells, J. E. The story of Wordsworth's Cintra. SP 18 1921.

Wells, J. E. De Quincey's punctuation of Wordsworth's Cintra. TLS 3 Nov 1932.

Wells, J. E. Wordsworth and De Quincey in Westmorland politics 1818. PMLA 55 1940; addn by L. N. Broughton, PMLA 56 1941.

Wells, J. E. De Quincey and the Prelude in 1839. PQ 20, Jan 1941.

Burke, T. The obsequies of Mr Williams; new light on De Quincey's famous tale of murder. Bookman (New York) 68 1928.

Meyerstein, E. H. W. De Quincey's copy of Chatterton's miscellanies. TLS 8 May 1930.

Super, R. H. De Quincey and a murderer's conscience. TLS 5 Dec 1936.

Forward, K. Libellous attack on De Quincey. PMLA 52 1937.

Galinsky, H. K. Is Thomas De Quincey author of The love charm? MLN 52 1937.

De Quincey on French drama. More Books 14 1939.

Musgrove, S. and M. K. Joseph. A De Quincey manuscript. TLS 30 Mar 1951.

Byrns, R. H. De Quincey's first article in Blackwood's Magazine. BNYPL 60 1956.

Byrns, R. H. Some unpublished works of De Quincey. PMLA 71 1956.

Mixon, P. L. The nature and origin of modifications in the text of De Quincey's writings published in collective editions. Unpbd PhD diss, Univ of Florida, 1956.

Jack, I. De Quincey revises his Confessions. PMLA 72 1957.

Byrns, R. H. De Quincey's revisions in the Dream Fugue. PMLA 77 1962.

Byrns, R. H. A note on De Quincey's The vision of sudden death. N & Q 207, May 1962.

Jack, I. De Quincey's revisions in The dream-fugue. PMLA 77 1962.

Goldman, A. The mine and the mint; sources for the writings of Thomas De Quincey. Carbondale IL 1965.
Michelsen, P. Thomas De Quincey als verdichter; seine ubersetzung der Luise von J. H. Voss. Archiv 202 1965.
Janzow, F. S. De Quincey's Danish origin of the Lake country dialect republished. Costerus 1 1972.
Chilcott, T. De Quincey and The London Magazine. Charles Lamb Bull n.s. 1 1973.
Janzow, F. S. Philadelphus; a new essay by De Quincey. Costerus 9 1973.
Janzow, F. S. The English opium-eater as editor. Costerus n.s. 1 1974.
Byrns, R. H. Some unrepublished articles of De Quincey's in Blackwood's Magazine. BRH 85 1982.
Groves, D. Thomas De Quincey and the ditch-water school of poetry. N & Q 232, Dec 1987.
Groves, D. De Quincey and Danish poetry. N & Q 233, Sep 1988.
Groves, D. De Quincey, Friedrich Schlegel and Victor Cousin. N & Q 235, Mar 1990.
Groves, D. De Quincey; a lost passage from the Edinburgh Evening Post. N & Q 235, Dec 1990.
Groves, D. De Quincey, David Robinson and the Edinburgh Post. N & Q 235, Dec 1990.
Finkelstein, D. Thomas De Quincey and Robert Blackwood; an unpublished letter. N & Q 237, June 1992.

Landmark criticism and obituaries

Death of Thomas De Quincey. The Scotsman 10 Dec 1859.
Thomas De Quincey. Athenaeum 17 Dec 1859.
Miller, J. H. In The disappearance of God; five nineteenth-century writers, Cambridge MA 1963.
Barrell, J. The infection of Thomas De Quincey; A psychopathology of imperialism. 1991.

Other criticism to 1920

Macnish, R. Modified by opium. In Anatomy of drunkenness, Glasgow 1827; rptd New York 1835.
H[are], J. C. Samuel Taylor Coleridge and the English opium-eater. Br Mag 7 1835.
Cottle, J. In Early recollections; chiefly relating to the late Samuel Taylor Coleridge, 2 vols 1837–9.
Gillman, J. In The life of Samuel Taylor Coleridge, 1838.
M., E. D. Use and abuse of opium. The Mirror; or Monthly Mag Nov 1839.
Gilfillan, G. Thomas De Quincey. In A gallery of literary portraits, Edinburgh 1845; rptd in Sketches of modern literature, 2 vols New York 1846.
[Jacox, F.] The English opium-eater. People's and Howitt's Jnl 8 1849.
[Gilfillan, G.] Thomas De Quincey. Eclectic Rev 27, Apr 1850; rptd Eclectic Mag 20, July 1850 and Harper's New Monthly Mag 1, July 1850.
Gillies, R. P. In Memoirs of a literary veteran including sketches and anecdotes, 3 vols 1851; rptd in De Quincey and his friends, ed J. Hogg, 1895.
'Peregrine.' Lord Carlisle, Pope and Mr De Quincey. Tait's Edinburgh Mag Aug 1851.
[Brown, G. W.] De Quincey's writings. North Amer Rev 74, Apr 1852. Review of Ticknor and Fields.
Der Englisch opiumesser; a fragment from a German. Hogg's Instructor 9 1852.
Jacox, F. The humour of Thomas De Quincey. Colburn's New Monthly Mag 96, Oct 1852; rptd in Littell's Living Age 36, Jan 1853.
Thomas De Quincey. Eclectic Mag 27, Dec 1852.
Ford, R. T. The British essayists; De Quincey. New York Quart 2 1853.
[Gilfillan, G.] De Quincey. The Critic June 1853.
Jacox, F. Thomas De Quincey's autobiographic sketches. Colburn's New Monthly Mag 98, June 1853.
Jacox, F. The pathos of Thomas De Quincey. Colburn's New Monthly Mag 98, Aug 1853.
T., H. T. [H. Tuckerman]. De Quincey's writings. Christian Examiner 4th ser 19, May 1853.
De Quincey and his works. Westminster Rev 61, Apr 1854; rptd in Littell's Living Age 41, June 1854 and Eclectic Mag 32, July 1854.
De Quincey and his works. Hogg's Instructor 3, July 1854.
De Quincey's miscellanies. Colburn's New Monthly Mag 101, July 1854.
Eclectic Rev n.s. 8, Oct 1854. Review of Selections grave and gay.
[Giles, H.] Thomas De Quincey. Christian Rev 19 1854; rptd in Illustrations of genius; in some of its relations to culture and society, Boston 1854.
[Gilfillan, G.] Miscellaneous. The Critic Mar, July, Dec 1854.
Life and adventures of an opium-eater. Dublin Univ Mag 43, Apr, Sep 1854.
Masson, D. Review of Selections grave and gay. Br Quart Rev 20, July 1854; rptd in Essays biographical and critical; chiefly on English poets, Cambridge 1856; and in Wordsworth, Shelley, Keats and other essays, 1874.
Autobiographical sketches. Christian Remembrancer 29, Jan 1855; rptd as De Quincey's autobiographical sketches, Littell's Living Age 57, June 1858.
De Quincey's miscellanies. Colburn's New Monthly Mag 105 1855.
Jacox, F. Thomas De Quincey. Bentley's Misc 37, Mar 1855.
[Landreth, P.] Review of Selections grave and gay. The Scottish Rev 3, Apr 1855; rptd in Studies and sketches in modern literature periodical publications, Edinburgh 1861.
Gilfillan, G. Thomas De Quincey – first sitting and second sitting. In Gallery of literary portraits, vol 2, Edinburgh 1856 (rptd from Gilfillan 1845 and 1850).
[Gilfillan, G.] The Critic Oct 1857. Review of Sketches biographical and critical.
Thomas De Quincey. London Quart Rev 8, Apr 1857.
Thomas De Quincey. GM 96, Aug 1857.
Bayne, P. Thomas De Quincey and his works. In Essays in biography and criticism, 2 vols, Boston 1857–8.
[Gilfillan, G.] De Quincey's new volume. The Critic Nov 1858.
[Phillips, G. S.] Life and writings of De Quincey. North Amer Rev 88, Jan 1859. Review of Fields.
Baudelaire, C. Les paradis artificiels; opium et hachisch. Paris 1860.
Littell's Living Age 66, July 1860. Review of The works of Thomas De Quincey.
P., H. W. Leigh Hunt, De Quincey, Macaulay. Christian Spectator n.s. 1, Mar 1860.
S., H. W. Life and writings of Thomas De Quincey. Fraser's Mag 62, Dec 1860–Jan 1861; rptd, with 1860 essay, in Littell's Living Age 68, Feb 1861.
[Kebbel, T. E.] Quart Rev 110, July 1861. Review of Selections grave and gay.
Hood, T. In Literary reminiscences, 1861; rptd in De Quincey and his friends, ed J. Hogg 1895.
Minto, W. A. Thomas De Quincey. In A manual of English prose literature, biographical and critical, Boston 1861; rptd Edinburgh 1872; rev 1881.
Burton, J. H. Thomas Papaverins. In The book-hunter, 1862.
[Cheever, D. W.] Narcotics. North Amer Rev 95, Oct 1862.
Gordon, M. In Christopher North; a memoir of John Wilson, 1862.
A., J. Thomas De Quincey. Sharpe's London Mag 38 1863.
N[ichol], J. De Quincey, Thomas. Imperial Dictionary of Universal Biography, ed J. F. Waller, 3 vols 1863.
[Cheever, G. B.] De Quincey. Christian Examiner 74, Jan 1863.
Br Quart Rev 38, July 1863. Review of The works of Thomas De Quincey.

[Massey, G.] Thomas De Quincey – grave and gay. North Br Rev 39, Aug 1863; rptd Eclectic Mag 60, Dec 1863.
Alden, H. M. Thomas De Quincey. Atlantic Monthly 12, Sep 1863.
Spring, L. W. Thomas De Quincey and his writings. Continental Monthly 5, June 1864.
Charles Knight's personal recollections. Br Quart Rev Oct 1864.
Masson, D. Dead men whom I have known, or recollections of three cities. Macmillan's Mag 12, May 1865.
De Quincey and the religion of the Greeks. Christian Examiner 80, Mar 1866.
Cleveland, C. D. Thomas De Quincey, 1785–1859. In English literature of the nineteenth century, 1867.
Stirling, J. H. De Quincey and Coleridge upon Kant. Fortnightly Rev n.s. 10, Oct 1867; rptd in Jerrold, Tennyson and Macaulay; with other critical essays, Edinburgh 1868.
Day, H. B. Thomas De Quincey's Confessions of an English opium-eater. In The opium habit, New York 1868.
Smith, J. F. The admission register of the Manchester school, vol 2, Manchester 1868 (Chetham Soc 73).
Martineau, H. Thomas De Quincey. In Biographical sketches, London and New York 1869.
Thomas De Quincey. Eclectic Rev 15, Aug 1868; rptd Eclectic Mag 8, Oct 1868.
Robinson, H. C. In Diary, reminiscences and correspondence, 1869; rptd Boston 1871.
Robinson, H. C. In Correspondence with the Wordsworth circle 1808–66, ed E. J. Morley, 2 vols Oxford 1927.
Robinson, H. C. In Crabb Robinson on books and their writers, ed E. J. Morley, 3 vols 1938.
Thomas De Quincey. Sharpe's London Mag 49 1869.
[Alden, H. M.] De Quincey. Every Saturday 9, Feb 1870.
Review of The works of Thomas De Quincey. National Quart Rev 22, Dec 1870.
Stephen, L. De Quincey. Fortnightly Rev 15, Mar 1871; rptd as On the writings of De Quincey in Littell's Living Age 109 1871; and in Stephen's Hours in a library, 1874.
Fields, J. T. In Yesterdays with authors, Boston 1872.
Jacox, F. In Aspects of authorship; or book marks and book makers, 1872.
Espinasse, F. In Lancashire worthies, 2 vols 1874–7.
Davey, S. Thomas De Quincey. In Darwin, Carlyle and Dickens; with other essays, 1875.
De Quincey. New Quart Mag July 1875.
Thomas De Quincey. The Saturday Rev June 1877.
Davies, J. The Academy n.s. 272, July 1877. Review of H. A. Page, Thomas De Quincey; his life and writings.
[Ingram, J. H.] Review of H. A. Page, Thomas De Quincey; his life and writings. International Rev 4, Sep 1877.
Review of H. A. Page's Thomas De Quincey; his life and writings. Br Quart Rev 66, Oct 1877.
Thomas De Quincey. London Quart and Holborn Rev 49, Oct 1877.
Lathrop, G. P. Some aspects of De Quincey. Atlantic Monthly 40, Nov 1877.
[Oliphant, M. O. W.] The opium-eater. Blackwood's Mag 122, Dec 1877.
F[indlay], J. R. Thomas De Quincey. Encyclopaedia Britannica, 9th edn 1877.
Mackay, C. Professor J. P. Nichol and Thomas De Quincey. In Forty years' recollections of life, literature and public affairs from 1830 to 1870, 2 vols 1877.
Mathews, W. Thomas De Quincey. In Hours with men and books, 13th edn Chicago 1877.
Proctor, B. W. ('Barry Cornwall'). An autobiographical fragment, and biographical notes. 1877.
Drury, B. P. Thomas De Quincey. The Western 4 1878.
St. Quentin. Three friends of mine; De Quincey, Coleridge and Poe. Canadian Monthly and National Rev 13 1878.
[Conway, M. D.] In The English Lakes and their genii. Harper's New Monthly Mag Dec 1880–Feb 1881.
Carlyle, T. In Reminiscences, ed. J. A. Froude, 2 vols 1881.
Gilfillan, G. De Quincey. In Sketches, literary and philosophical, ed F. Henderson, Edinburgh 1881.
Hodgson, S. H. The genius of De Quincey, and De Quincey as political economist; or De Quincey and Mill on supply and demand. In Outcast essays and verse translations, 1881.
Troup, G. E. Life of George Troup, journalist. Edinburgh 1881.
De Quincey. The Literary World, Dec 1881.
Leighton, R. Acad 21, Jan 1882. Review of D. Masson, De Quincey.
Oliphant, M. O. W. In The literary history of England in the end of the eighteenth and beginning of the nineteenth century, vol 2 1882.
Froude, J. A. In Thomas Carlyle; a history of the first forty years of his life, 1795–1835, 4 vols, London and New York 1882–4.
Anton, P. De Quincey. In England's essayists; Addison, Bacon, De Quincey, Lamb, Edinburgh 1883.
Nicoll, H. J. In Landmarks of English literature, 1883.
Cranbrook, Lord. Christopher North. Nat Rev 3 1884.
Payn, J. In Some literary recollections, New York 1884; rptd in De Quincey and his friends, ed J. Hogg 1895.
Mason, E. T. Thomas De Quincey. In Personal traits of British authors, 2 vols 1885.
Woodhouse, R. Notes of conversations with Thomas De Quincey. In Confessions, ed R. Garnett 1885; rptd in De Quincey and his friends, ed J. Hogg 1895.
Brandl, A. In Samuel Taylor Coleridge und die englische Romantik, Berlin 1886; tr Eng 1887.
Cook, A. S. Native and foreign words in De Quincey. MLN 1 1886.
Japp, A. H. Some unconscious confessions of De Quincey. GM 261, 1886; rptd Eclectic Mag n.s. 44 1886; and Littell's Living Age 170 1886.
Hunt, T. W. The prose style of Thomas De Quincey. In Representative English prose and prose writers, New York 1887.
Salt, H. S. Some thoughts on De Quincey. Time 17 1887; rptd in Literary sketches, 1888.
Brown, J. In Life of William B. Robertson DD, Glasgow 1888.
Carlyle, T. In Letters 1826–36, ed C. E. Norton, 2 vols 1888.
Ingleby, C. M. Thomas De Quincey. In Essays edited by his son, 1888.
Sandford, Mrs H. In Thomas Poole and his friends, 2 vols 1888.
Stephen, L. Thomas De Quincey. DNB 14 1888.
Dove, C. C. Thomas De Quincey. N & Q 7th ser 7 Apr 1889.
Rae-Brown, C. A reminiscence of De Quincey. Universal Rev 5, Nov 1889.
Bourget, P. C. J. Les lacs anglais. In Etudes et portraits, 2 vols, Paris 1889.
Stuart, M. In Letters from the Lake poets, S. T. Coleridge, Wordsworth, Southey to Daniel Stuart, 1889 (priv ptd).
Hogg, J. Nights and days with De Quincey. Harper's Monthly Mag 80, Feb 1890; rptd in De Quincey and his friends, 1895.
Thomas De Quincey. Saturday Rev 69, Feb 1890.
[Dennis, J.] De Quincey and his editors. The Spectator 64, May 1890.
Anderson, M. B. Masson's edition of De Quincey. Dial 11, June 1890.
Saintsbury, G. De Quincey. Macmillan's Mag 62, June 1890; rptd in Eclectic Mag n.s. 52, Aug 1890; in Essays in English literature 1780–1860, 1890.
Bain, J. De Quincey and his supposed descent from the Earls of Winchester. Genealogist n.s. 7, July 1890.
Japp, A. H. Thomas De Quincey. Sun Mag Nov 1890.
Pollitt, C. De Quincey's editorship of the Westmorland Gazette, with selections from his work on that journal from July 1818 to November 1819. Kendal 1890.
Dennis, J. De Quincey. The Leisure Hour 40, Feb 1891.
Japp, A. H. Early intercourse of the Wordsworths and De Quincey. Century Mag 41, Apr 1891.

Axon, W. E. A. De Quincey's highwayman. Manchester Guardian 31 Aug 1891; rptd in Echoes of old Lancashire, 1899.
De Quincey memorials. Saturday Rev 71 1891.
Saintsbury, G. The style of De Quincey. Dial 12, Aug 1891.
Nisbet, J. F. In The insanity of genius, 1891.
The religion of letters, 1750–1850. Blackwood's Mag 154, July 1892.
Stansfield, A. Thomas De Quincey. Manchester Quart 2, Oct 1892.
Opium in literature. The daily picayune (New Orleans) Dec 1892.
Oliphant, M. O. W. In The Victorian age of English literature, New York 1892.
Bayne, T. De Quincey and Charlotte Brontë, N & Q 8th ser 4, Sep 1893.
Bertram, J. G. Thomas De Quincey. In Some memories of books, authors and events, 1893.
Campbell, J. D. In Samuel Taylor Coleridge; a narrative of the events of his life, 1893.
de Contades, G. La Jeanne d'Arc de Thomas De Quincey. Revue des Deux Mondes 115, Feb 1893.
C., A. T. Q. A literary causerie; the utilisation of waste products in literature. The Speaker Feb 1894.
L[andreth], P. Emerson's meeting with De Quincey. Blackwood's Mag 155, Apr 1894.
Birrell, A. Alexander Knox and Thomas De Quincey. In Essays about men, women and books, 1894; rptd 1912.
[Dowden, E.] How De Quincey worked. Saturday Rev 79, Feb 1895.
Chancellor, E. B. Thomas De Quincey – man of letters. In Literary types, 1895.
Athenaeum Jan 1896. Review of De Quincey and his friends, ed J. Hogg.
New York Daily Tribune Jan 1896. Review of De Quincey and his friends, ed J. Hogg.
Barine, A. [C. Vincens] L'Opium – Thomas De Quincey. Revue des Deux Mondes 138 1896.
de Wyzewa, T. Thomas De Quincey. In Ecrivains étrangers, Paris 1896.
Johnson, R. B. Thomas De Quincey. In English prose, ed H. Craik, 5 vols, New York 1896.
Saintsbury, G. Thomas De Quincey. In A history of nineteenth-century literature 1780–1895, New York 1896.
Thomas De Quincey. Acad 51, Jan 1897.
The Unitarian 12, Sep 1897. Review of Flight of a Tartar tribe.
Herford, C. H. In The age of Wordsworth, 1897; rptd 1925.
Lang, A. In Life and letters of John Gibson Lockhart, 2 vols 1897.
Stansfield, A. A neglected Manchester man; Thomas De Quincey. In Essays and sketches, Manchester 1897.
Slatterlee, J. S. Thomas De Quincey. The New York Times 9 July 1898.
Barine, A. [C. Vincens]. In Poètes et Névrosés: Hoffmann, Quincey [*sic*], Edgar Poe, G. de Nerval, Paris 1898 (rev from Barine 1896); rptd as Névrosés, 1936.
Clark, J. S. De Quincey, 1785–1859. In A study of English prose writers; a laboratory method, New York 1898.
Christoph, F. Über den Einfluss Jean Paul Friedrich Richters auf Thomas De Quincey. Hof 1899.
[Thompson, F.] A monument of personality. Acad 56, Apr 1899.
Swindells, T. Thomas De Quincey and Wordsworth. Manchester Guardian 4 Sep 1899.
Dawson, W. J. Thomas De Quincey. In Makers of modern prose, New York 1899.
Hitchcock, R. Thomas De Quincey; a study. New York 1899.
Mortimer, J. Some notes of Thomas De Quincey. Manchester Quart Apr 1900.
Stout, J. F. De Quincey's Confessions of an English opium-eater. Univ Correspondent 26 May 1900.
Axon, W. E. A. De Quincey and the story of Aladdin. N & Q 9th ser 6, Dec 1900.
Axon, W. E. A. A. De Quincey and Hugo Grotius. N & Q 9th ser 6 1900.
Dunn, W. A. Thomas De Quincey's relation to German literature and philosophy. Strasbourg 1900.
Knight, W. In Dove cottage, Grasmere, from 1800 to 1900, Ambleside 1900.
[Axon, W. E. A.] The Manchester grammar school a century ago. Manchester Guardian 11 Feb 1901.
Fowler, J. H. Poetic prose. The Guardian 5 June 1901.
Shaylor, J. Thomas De Quincey. In Some favourite books and their authors, 1901.
[Symons, A.] De Quincey. Saturday Rev 91 1901.
Cooper, L. The prose poetry of Thomas De Quincey. Leipzig 1902.
Axon, W. E. A. De Quincey on animal magnetism. Manchester Guardian 1 Aug 1903.
Lee, V. [V. Paget]. Studies on literary psychology; part I – The syntax of De Quincey. Contemporary Rev 84, Nov 1903; rptd in The Living Age 239 1903; and in Eclectic Mag 142 1904.
Axon, W. E. A. A daughter of Thomas De Quincey. Manchester Guardian 16 Dec 1903.
Axon, W. E. A. A. The portraits of De Quincey. Manchester Guardian 24 Dec 1903.
Gould, G. M. De Quincey. In Biographic clinics; the origin of the ill-health of De Quincey, Carlyle, Darwin, Huxley and Browning, Philadelphia 1903.
Smith, G. G. Thomas De Quincey. Chambers's Cyclopaedia of Eng lit, ed R. Chambers, 3 vols 1903.
Clay, L. De Quincey as self-pourtrayed [*sic*]. Manchester Quart 23, Jan 1904.
Japp, A. H. Opium in literature. East and West (Bombay) Feb 1904.
Salt, H. S. De Quincey and Wordsworth. Manchester Guardian 20 Aug 1904.
Bailey-Kempling, W. B. De Quincey's editorship of the Westmorland Gazette. N & Q 10th ser 2 6 Aug 1904.
Saintsbury, G. In A history of criticism and literary taste in Europe from the earlier texts to the present day, vol 3 (modern criticism), New York 1904.
Salt, H. S. De Quincey. 1904.
Symons, A. A word on De Quincey. In Studies in prose and verse, 1904.
De Quincey and his critics. Humane Rev 5 1905.
Frisby, E. Notes on De Quincey's Confessions of an English opium-eater. 1905.
Gosse, E. Thomas De Quincey. In Modern English literature; a short history, 1905.
Sessions, F. The English opium-eater; Thomas De Quincey. In Literary celebrities of the English Lake-district, 1905.
Axon, W. E. A. Millgate memories; Part I – Thomas De Quincey. Millgate Monthly Feb 1906.
Robinson, H. P. De Quincey and the 'grand style'. Acad 70, Feb 1906.
Thomas, E. Thomas De Quincey. Temple Bar 133, Apr 1906.
Kidd, H. C. De Quincey's grammar. Saturday Rev 102, Aug 1906.
Jarvis, J. B. The neglect shown to De Quincey. Month 108, Nov 1906.
Compton-Rickett, A. Thomas De Quincey. In Personal forces in modern literature, 1906; rptd Freeport NY 1968.
Compton-Rickett, A. Thomas De Quincey. In Vagabond in literature, Port Washington, NY 1906.
Axon, W. E. A. De Quincey as electioneer. Manchester Guardian 28 Sep 1907.
Durand, W. Y. De Quincey and Carlyle in their relation to the Germans. PMLA 22, Sep 1907.
A note on Thomas De Quincey. T. P.'s Weekly 8 Nov 1907.
Emerson, R. W. In Journals of Ralph Waldo Emerson, ed E. W. Emerson and W. E. Forbes, vol 2, Boston 1907.
Guerrier, P. Etude médico-psychologique sur Thomas De Quincey. Lyons 1907.
Lombroso, C. Quincey [*sic*]. In Genio e degenerazione, Milan 1907.
Rannie, D. W. Thomas De Quincey. In Wordsworth and his circle, 1907.

Sellar, E. M. In Recollections and impressions, Edinburgh 1907.
Salt, H. S. De Quincey the defaulter. Saturday Rev 30 May 1908.
Winchester, C. T. Thomas De Quincey. In A group of English essayists of the early nineteenth century, Freeport NY 1910.
Shelly, J. In Rhythmical prose in Latin and English. Church Quart Rev 74, Apr 1912.
Dupouy, R. Thomas De Quincey. In Opiomanes, mangeurs, buveurs, fumeurs d'opium; étude clinique et médico-littéraire, Paris 1912.
Elton, O. In A survey of English literature, 1780–1830, 2 vols 1912.
Fitch, G. H. De Quincey as a master of style. In Modern English books of power, New York 1912.
Saintsbury, G. In A history of English prose rhythm, 1912.
Stekel, W. Die Traüme der Dichter; eine vergleichende Untersuchung der unbewussten Triebkräfte bei Dichtern, Neurotikern, und Verbrechern. Wiesbaden 1912.
Green, J. A. Notes on the portraits of Thomas De Quincey. Manchester Quart 32, July 1913.
Clark, A. C. In Prose rhythm in English, Oxford 1913.
Meynell, E. In The life of Francis Thompson, New York 1913.
Eaton, H. A. De Quincey's love of music. JEGP 13 1914.
Saintsbury, G. The Landors, Leigh Hunt, De Quincey. In The Cambridge history of English literature, ed A. W. Ward and A. R. Waller, vol 12 1914; rptd New York 1916.
Jaeck, E. G. Thomas De Quincey, 1785–1859. In Madame de Stael and the spread of German literature, New York 1915.
Walker, H. In The English essay and essayists, 1915.
Bartholomew, A. T. Thomas De Quincey. In Chambers's history of English literature, vol 12 1916.
Patterson, W. H. In Rhythm of prose. New York 1916.
Leonard, L. P. De Quincey's Dream-fugue. Poet Lore 28, Nov 1917.
Gay, F. R. De Quincey as a student of Greek and a writer on Greek literature and history. Unpbd MA thesis, Univ of Chicago 1917.
MacFarlane, C. Thomas De Quincey. In Reminiscences of a literary life, 1917.
Peltier, P. Musset et Baudelaire à propos des Confessions d'un mangeur d'opium. Mercure de France 16 Dec 1918.
Pace, R. B. Thomas De Quincey, 1785–1859. In his English literature, Boston 1918.
Hussey, D. De Quincey's mother. Athenaeum 12–19 Mar 1920; rptd as The trials of a great man's mother; the true story of Mrs De Quincey in Living Age 8th ser 17, Apr 1920.
Duckers, J. S. The De Quincey family. TLS 21 Oct 1920.
S[teel], C. H. A De Quincey relic. Bookman's Jnl and Print Collector Oct 1920. [JRN]

Charles Wentworth Dilke 1789–1864

Old English plays: being a selection from the early dramatic writers. 6 vols 1814–15. Ed Dilke to supplement Dodsley's collection.
The papers of a critic: selected from the writings of Dilke, with a biographical sketch by his grandson, Sir Charles Wentworth Dilke. 2 vols 1875. Essays on Pope, Lady M. W. Montagu, 'Junius', Wilkes, 'Peter Pindar' et al, rptd from Athenaeum.
Dilke was for many years editor of Athenaeum *and contributed regularly 1848–64; his best earlier writing was for* Retrospective Rev *1820–5.*

Isaac D'Israeli 1766–1848

Collections

Miscellanies of literature. 1840, [1882–3] (monthly pts), [1884], [1886]. Includes Miscellanies of literature; Quarrels of authors; Calamities of authors; The literary character; Character of James I; Literary miscellanies (not the same as earlier work of this title); Goldsmith and Johnson; Molière; Racine; Sterne; Hume etc.
Works. Ed B. Disraeli 7 vols 1858–9 (with memoir), 1863, 1866, [1881].

§1

A defence of poetry. 1790, 1791.
Curiosities of literature: consisting of anecdotes, characters, sketches and dissertations literary, critical and historical. Ser 1 1791, 3 vols 1793–1817 (with addns), 5 vols 1823; ser 2 3 vols 1834 (containing the Secret histories); both ser 6 vols 1834, 3 vols 1849 (with memoir by B. Disraeli), 1858, 1866, 1881; ed E. V. Mitchell 1932 (abridged); ed E. Bleiler 1964 (abridged).
A dissertation on anecdotes. 1793, 1801 (with Literary miscellanies).
Domestic anecdotes of the French nation. 1794, 1800.
An essay on the manners and genius of the literary character. 1795, 1818 (rev and enlarged as The literary character), 2 vols 1822 (rev and enlarged), 1828 (rev and enlarged), 1 vol 1840 (rev as part of Miscellanies of literature); ed B. Disraeli 1927.
Miscellanies: or literary recreations. 1796, 1801 (as Literary miscellanies; adds A dissertation on anecdotes).
Vaurien: or sketches of the times. 2 vols 1797.
Mejnoun and Leila: the Arabian Petrarch and Laura. 1797, 1799 (adds Love and humility, The lovers, and a Poetical essay on romance), 1801 (adds The daughter).
Romances. 1799 (Mejnoun and Leila, Love and humility, The lovers), 1801 (adds The daughter), 1803, 1807 (omits The daughter).
The loves of Mejnoun and Leila. 1800; tr Ger 1803.
Narrative poems. 1803, Philadelphia, Baltimore, Washington, Petersburg and Norfolk VA 1803.
Flim-flams! or the life and errors of my uncle, and the amours of my aunt! with an illuminating index! 3 vols 1805, 1806 (rev and enlarged).
Despotism: or the fall of the Jesuits. 2 vols 1811.
Calamities of authors: including some inquiries respecting their moral and literary characters. 2 vols 1812; ed B. Disraeli 1859, [1881].
Quarrels of authors: or some memoirs for our literary history. 3 vols 1814; ed B. Disraeli [1881] (with Calamities of authors). Includes Warburton; Pope and Curll; Pope and Cibber; Addison; Lintot's account book; Boyle; Bentley; Jonson; Dekker etc.
Inquiry into the literary and political character of James I. 1816.
Psyche. [1823?]
Commentaries on the life and reign of Charles the First, King of England. 5 vols 1828–31; ed B. Disraeli 2 vols 1851 (rev).
Eliot, Hampden and Pym. 1832.
Genius of Judaism. 1833; tr Ger 1836.
Amenities of literature: consisting of sketches and characters of English literature. 2 vols 1841, 1 vol 1842, [1884]. A history of English literature from the beginnings to Bacon, with some chapters on contemporary literary affairs.

§2

Biographical sketch of D'Israeli. Monthly Mirror Dec 1796.
Corney, B. Curiosities of literature. 1837, 1838 (rev 'and acuminated', adding Ideas on controversy deduced from the practice of a veteran). An attack on D'Israeli.
Taylor, W. C. The late Isaac D'Israeli, Esq and the genius of Judaism. Bentley's Misc 23 1848.
Disraeli, B. The life and writings of Mr Disraeli by his son. Prefixed to Curiosities of literature, 1849.
Maginn, W. In his A gallery of illustrious characters, ed W. Bates, [1873].
Axon, W. E. A. D'Israeli the novelist. GM Aug 1889.
Monypenny, W. F. and G. E. Buckle. The life of Benjamin Disraeli. 2 vols 1929 (rev). Vol 1 has a ch on Isaac D'Israeli.
Kipstein, S. D'Israeli. Jerusalem 1939.
Cline, C. L. The correspondence of Robert Southey and D'Israeli. RES 17 1941.
Cline, C. L. Unpublished notes on romantic poets by D'Israeli. SE 1941.

Anderson, G. K. D'Israeli's Amenities of literature: a centennial review. PQ 22 1943.
Samuel, W. S. D'Israeli: first published writings. N & Q 30 Apr 1949.

Nathan Drake 1766–1836

The speculator. 26 nos 27 Mar–22 June 1790; 1791, Dublin 1791. By Drake and an unidentified collaborator.
Literary hours: or sketches critical and narrative. Sudbury 1798, 2 vols Sudbury 1800 (enlarged), 3 vols 1804, 1820.
The old abbey tale. In Canterbury tales, by C. F. Barrett, Drake and others, 1802.
Essays biographical, critical and historical; illustrative of the Tatler, Spectator and Guardian. 3 vols 1805, 1814.
The gleaner: a series of periodical essays, selected and arranged from scarce and neglected volumes. 4 vols 1811.
Shakespeare and his times. 2 vols 1817, 1 vol Paris 1843.
Winter nights: or fire-side lucubrations. 2 vols 1820.
Evenings in autumn: a series of essays. 2 vols 1822.
Noontide leisure: or sketches in summer, including a tale of the days of Shakespeare. 2 vols 1824.
Mornings in spring: or retrospections biographical, critical and historical. 2 vols 1828.
Memorials of Shakespeare: or sketches of his character and genius by various writers. 1828.
The harp of Judah: or songs of Sion, being a metrical translation of the Psalms. 1837.

John Colin Dunlop d. 1842

The history of fiction: being a critical account of the most celebrated prose works of fiction from the earliest Greek romances to the novels of the present age. 3 vols 1814, Edinburgh 1816, London 1845; ed H. Wilson 2 vols 1888 (rev); tr Ger 1851.
REVIEW: Hazlitt, Edinburgh Rev 24 1814.
History of Roman literature from its earliest period to the Augustan age. 3 vols 1823–8.
Memoirs of Spain during the reigns of Philip IV and Charles II from 1621 to 1700. 2 vols Edinburgh 1834.
Selections from the Latin anthology translated into English verse. Edinburgh 1838.

George Dyer 1775–1841

See col 332.

Pierce Egan 1775–1849

Many of Pierce Egan's works went through several edns, with minor changes in the titles.

§1

Boxiana: sketches of antient and modern pugilism. Vol 1 1812, vol 2 1818, vol 3 1821, (vol 4 1824 was not by Egan but probably by John Badcock); n.s. vol 1 1828, vol 2 1829.
The mistress of royalty: or the loves of Florizel and Perdita. 1814. Anon; (attack on the Prince Regent and Mrs Robinson).
Walks through Bath. 1819.
A key to the picture of the fancy (on a panorama by George Cruikshank). 1819.
A concise biographical memoir of his late majesty George the Third, by E. Pierce [Pierce Egan]. 1820.
Life in London: or the day and night scenes of Jerry Hawthorn esq and his elegant friend Corinthian Tom ... with thirty-six scenes from real life, designed and etched by I. R. and G. Cruikshank. 1820–1; ed J. C. Hotten 1870.
The songs, parodies etc introduced in the comic burletta called Tom and Jerry or Life in London. [1822.]
The life and adventures of Samuel Denmore Hayward, the modern Macheath. 1822.
Pierce Egan's account of the trial of John Thurtell and Joseph Hunt; with an appendix; with portraits and many other illustrative engravings. 1824.
Recollections of John Thurtell. 1825.
The life of an actor. 1825, 1892.
Pierce Egan's anecdotes of the turf, the chase, the ring and the stage, embellished with thirteen coloured plates by T. Lane. 1827.
The finish to the adventures of Tom, Jerry and Logic in their pursuits through life in and out of London; with coloured illustrations by R. Cruikshank. [1828]; ed J. C. Hotten [1871].
The show folks, with nine designs on wood by Mr Theodore Lane; to which is added a sketch of the life of Mr Theodore Lane. 1831. A poem.
Pierce Egan's account of the trial of Bishop, Williams and May for murder. 1831.
Matthews's comic annual: or the snuff-box and the leetel bird, an original humorous poem. 1831, 1832, London and Edinburgh 1832.
Pierce Egan's book of sports and mirror of life. 1832. Periodical.
Epsom races. The Derby day: a (crambo) sporting poem. 1835.
The pilgrims of the Thames in search of the National! Illustrations on wood by Pierce Egan the younger. 1838.
Captain Macheath. 1842.
Every gentleman's manual. A lecture on the art of self-defence. 1845.
Pierce Egan edited and expanded Grose's classical dictionary of the vulgar tongue *[1822?] 1823. He also edited* Pierce Egan's Life in London and Sporting Guide, *1 Feb 1824–4 Nov 1827;* Pierce Egan's Weekly Courier, *1 Jan 1832–25 Mar 1855.*
Pierce Egan also wrote several locally successful plays, all unpbd:
Tom and Jerry, or Life in London. Adelphi Theatre 1822.
Life in Dublin. Theatre Royal, Dublin, 1834. BM Add mss 42964.
Tom, Jerry and Logic's Hop at Brighton. Theatre Royal, Brighton, 1834. BM Add mss 42928.
Life in Liverpool. Liver Theatre, Liverpool, 1835.
There were numerous imitations, dramatic versions and parodies of Life in London. *The most popular included:*
Real life in London. 1821. Anon.
Real life in Ireland. 1821. Anon.
Carey, David. Life in Paris. 1822.
Moncreiff, W. T. Tom and Jerry, or Life in London. (Play, Adelphi Theatre 1821) nd.

§2

The one full-length study of Pierce Egan and his work is J. C. Reid, Bucks and bruisers, *1971.*
In DNB.
Review of Life in London. European Mag Nov 1820. Anon.
(Christopher North.) Boxiana, or Sketches of pugilism. Blackwood's Mag July 1819–Oct 1820.
GM vol 32, Nov 1849. Obituary.
Hindley, Charles. The true history of Tom and Jerry. 1890.
Child, Harold. Caricature and the literature of sport. Cambridge History of Eng Lit vol 14, 1932.
Kolb, E. Pierce Egan. TLS 27 Aug 1938.
Darwin, Bernard. Sporting writers of the 19th century. Essays ... presented to Sir Humphrey Milford. 1948. [WLGJ]

Thomas Erskine, 1st Baron Erskine 1750–1823

Collections

The speeches (at length) of the Rt Hon C. J. Fox, T. Erskine [etc]. 1797.
Speeches of J. P. Curran; with the speeches of Grattan, Erskine and Burke. 2 vols New York 1809.

The speeches of the Hon Thomas Erskine, when at the bar, on subjects connected with the liberty of the press, and against constructive treasons; collected by J. Ridgway. 4 vols 1810, 1812, Georgetown 1813, 4 vols London 1813–16, 1847 (with prefatory memoir by Lord Brougham), 2 vols 1870 (with memoir by E. Walford).
The beauties of Erskine: consisting of selections from his prose and poetry, by A. Howard. [1834?]
The modern orator: the most celebrated speeches of the Earl of Chatham, R. B. Sheridan, Lord Erskine and Edmund Burke. 1847.

§1

Plain thoughts of a plain man addressed to the common sense of the people of Great Britain. 1797.
A view of the causes and consequences of the present war with France. 1797 (35 edns); tr Fr [1797] (23 edns at least).
Cruelty to animals: the speech of Lord Erskine in the House of Peers on the second reading of the bill for preventing malicious and wanton cruelty to animals. 1809, 1824.
Armata: a fragment. 1817 (anon, 4 edns); The second part of Armata, 1817 (3 edns). A political romance.
A short defence of the Whigs against the imputations attempted to be cast upon them during the late election for Westminster. 1819, 1819.
A letter to An elector of Westminster, author of A reply to the short defence of the Whigs. 1819.
The defences of the Whigs. 1819. Rptd from the 2 preceding.
The farmer's vision, by E. 1819 (priv ptd).
A letter to the Earl of Liverpool on the subject of the Greeks. 1822 (2nd edn).
The poetical works; with a biographical memoir. 1823.
Age of reason: Erskine's defence of the cause of Newton, Boyle, Locke, Hale and Milton, versus T. Paine. [1831.]
Erskine's opinion of Paine's Age of reason. [1831.]
The speeches above constitute only a representative selection from a considerable body of pbd speeches and pams.

§2

A sketch of the character of Erskine. Pamphleteer 23 1823.
Campbell, J. In his Lives of the Lord Chancellors ser 3, 6 1847.
Duméril, H. Erskine: étude sur le barreau anglais à la fin du XVIIIe siècle. Paris 1883.
Fraser, J. A. L. Erskine. Cambridge 1932.

John Foster 1770–1843

§1

Essays in a series of letters to a friend. 2 vols 1805, 1806 (rev), 1806, 1 vol 1830 (9th edn, embodying final revisions); ed J. M. 1876 (as Decision of character and other essays). On a man's writing memoirs of himself; On decision of character; On the application of the epithet romantic; On some of the causes by which evangelical religion has been rendered less acceptable to persons of cultivated taste.
Discourse on missions. 1818.
An essay on the evils of popular ignorance. 1820, 1821 (with a Discourse on the communication of Christianity to the people of Hindoostan), 1846 (rev and enlarged).
Contributions biographical, literary and philosophical to the Eclectic Review. 2 vols 1844; ed J. E. Ryland 1856.
Lectures delivered at Broadmead Chapel, Bristol. Ed J. E. Ryland 2 ser 1844–7, 2 vols 1853 (with addns).
The life and correspondence of John Foster. Ed J. E. Ryland, with notices of Mr Foster as a preacher and a companion by John Sheppard 2 vols 1846.
A brief memoir of Miss Sarah Saunders, with nine letters addressed to her during her last illness. [1847.]
Fosteriana: consisting of thoughts, reflections and criticisms of John Foster, selected from periodical papers not hitherto published in a collected form. Ed H. G. Bohn 1858.
An essay on the improvement of time and other literary remains; with a preface by John Sheppard. Ed J. E. Ryland 1863, 1886 (with Notes of sermons and other pieces).
Letters from Foster to Thomas Coles MA, now first published with an appendix by Henry Coles. 1864.
An important introductory essay by Foster is prefixed to the 1825 and later edns of Doddridge, The rise and progress of religion. *Foster also pbd various sermons, religious discourses and controversial works. He was a regular contributor to the* Eclectic Rev *1806–39.*

§2

Hall, R. Reviews. 1825. Includes a review of Foster's Essays, *above.*
Gilfillan, G. In his Galleries of literary portraits vol 2, Edinburgh 1856.
Whately, E. Life and writings of Foster the essayist. In his Afternoon lectures on English literature, Dublin 1863.
Everts, W. W. Life and thoughts of Foster. 1868.
Bayne, P. In his Six Christian biographies, 1887.
Kaufman, P. Foster's pioneer interpretation of the romantic. MLN 38 1923.

Basil Hall 1788–1844

Account of a voyage of discovery to the west coast of Corea and the Great Loo-Choo Island; with an appendix and a vocabulary of the Loo-Choo language by H. I. Clifford. 1818, 1820 (with plates), Edinburgh 1826, London 1840 (with an interview with Napoleon Bonaparte at St Helena).
Extracts from a journal written on the coasts of Chili, Peru and Mexico, in the years 1820, 1821, 1822. 2 vols 1823, Edinburgh 1824, London 1825 (4th edn); tr Portuguese 1906, Sp 1920.
Hall's voyages. 4 vols Edinburgh 1826–7.
Travels in North America in the years 1827 and 1828. 3 vols Edinburgh 1829, 2 vols Philadelphia 1829; tr Fr [1841?].
Fragments of voyages and travels. Ser 1 3 vols 1831; ser 2 3 vols Edinburgh 1832; ser 3 3 vols Edinburgh 1833, 1834; tr Fr 1858. Autobiographical sketches from this work were separately pbd as The midshipman and The lieutenant and commander, 1862.
Schloss Hainfeld: or a winter in Lower Styria. Edinburgh 1836, 1836.
Patchwork. 3 vols 1841.
Voyages and travels. 1895. With biographical preface.
Travels in India, Ceylon and Borneo, selected and edited with biographical introduction by H. G. Rawlinson. 1931.

Henry Hallam 1777–1859

See col 2430.

Julius Charles Hare 1795–1855

Bibliographies

GM Apr 1855. Incomplete but accurate bibliography with much information unobtainable elsewhere.

§1

La Motte Fouqué's Sintram and his companions. 1820.
Guesses at truth, by two brothers. Ser 1 1827, 1838 (with addns), 1840 (rev); ser 2 1848 (title page states '2nd edn with large addns', but preface explains that '2nd edn' means that part of ser 1 is included); both ser, 1866, 1871 (with memoir of J. C. Hare by E. H. Plumptre), 1905. With A. W. Hare, until his death; essays, epigrams etc.
Niebuhr's The history of Rome. 3 vols 1828–42. Vols 1–2 by Hare and

Connop Thirlwall. Vol 3 by W. Smith and L. Schmitz; a 2nd edn of vols 1–2, rev and rearranged by Hare, appeared 1829–32.
A vindication of Niebuhr's History of Rome. Cambridge 1829.
The old man of the mountain; The lovecharm; and Pietro of Abano: tales from the German of Tieck. 1831.
The victory of faith and other sermons. Cambridge 1840; ed E. H. Plumptre 1874 (introductory notices by J. F. D. Maurice and A. P. Stanley, the later rptd from Quart Rev 97 1855).
The mission of the Comforter and other sermons, with notes. 2 vols 1846, Cambridge 1850 (rev); ed E. H. Plumptre 1876. Vindication of Luther ptd separately, 1855.
Schiller's poems. 1847. Tr with some poems by Goethe into English hexameters.
Memoir of John Sterling. Prefixed to Essays and tales of John Sterling, collected and ed Hare 2 vols 1848.
Thou shalt not bear false witness against thy neighbour: a letter to the editor of the English Review, with a letter from Professor Maurice to the author. 1849.
The life of Luther in forty-eight historical engravings by G. Koenig. 1855. Text by Hare, continued by S. Winkworth.
Charges to the clergy of the archdeaconry of Lewes 1840–54, with notes on events affecting the Church during that period; with a memoir of the author by F. D. Maurice. 3 vols 1856.
Fragments of two essays in English philology. Ed J. E. B. Mayor 1873.
Hare also pbd a number of sermons, charges and tracts on ecclesiastical subjects.

§2
Rigg, J. H. Modern Anglican theology. 1857.
Hare, A. J. C. Memorials of a quiet life. 1872.
Galinsky, H. K. Is Thomas De Quincey the author of The love-charm? MLN 52 1937. By Hare?
Sanders, C. R. Coleridge and the Broad Church movement. Durham NC 1942.

Benjamin Robert Haydon 1786–1846

§1
The judgment of connoisseurs upon works of art compared with that of professional men, in reference more particularly to the Elgin Marbles. 1816.
New churches considered with respect to the opportunities they afford for the encouragement of painting. 1818.
Some enquiry into the causes which have obstructed the advance of historical painting for the last seventy years in England. 1829.
On academies of art (more particularly the Royal Academy) and their pernicious effect on the genius of Europe: lecture xiii. 1839.
Thoughts on the relative value of fresco and oil painting, as applied to the architectural decorations of the Houses of Parliament. 1842.

Letters, diaries etc
The life of Haydon, from his autobiography and journals. Ed T. Taylor 3 vols 1853, 1853 (with additional appendix and index by W. R. S. Ralston); ed A. Huxley 2 vols 1926; ed A. P. D. Penrose 1927; ed E. Blunden, Oxford 1927 (WC); ed M. Elwin 1950.
Correspondence and table-talk: with a memoir by his son F. W. Haydon; with facsimile illustrations from his journals. 2 vols 1876.
The diary of Haydon. Ed W. B. Pope 5 vols Cambridge MA 1960–3.
Savage, B. The immortal dinner: a photo-facsimile of pages from Haydon's diary. CLB 10–11 1975.
Jones, S. B. R. Haydon on some contemporaries: a new letter. RES 26 1975.
Neglected genius: the diaries of Benjamin Robert Haydon 1808–1846. Ed J. Jolliffe 1990.

§2
Haydon and Wilkie. Fraser's Mag July 1847.
The autobiography of Haydon. Fraser's Mag Sep 1853.
The life of Haydon. Edinburgh Rev 98 1853.
Taylor's life of Haydon. Quart Rev 93 1853.
Haydon. Temple Bar Feb, Apr 1891.
'Paston, George' (E. M. Symonds). Little memoirs of the nineteenth century. 1902.
Forman, H. B. Keats and Haydon. Athenaeum 21 May 1904.
Haydon and his friends. 1905.
Sargant, F. W. Haydon, forerunner. Nineteenth Cent Feb 1923.
Woolf, V. The genius of Haydon. Nation 18 Dec 1926; rptd in her Moment and other essays, 1947.
Walker, F. R. The diary of a defeated painter. Independent 118 1927.
Blunden, E. Haydon outside his autobiography. Nation 7 Apr 1928.
Wagner, I. Das literarische Werk des Malers Haydon. Göttingen 1934.
Sewter, A. C. A revaluation of Haydon. Art Quart 5 1942.
Lang, V. Haydon. PQ 26 1947.
George, E. The life and death of Haydon. Oxford 1948.
Cohen, B. B. Haydon, Hunt, Scott and Six sonnets (1816) by Wordsworth. PQ 29 1950.
Olney, C. Haydon: historical painter. Athens GA 1953.
Gray, D. and V. W. Walker. Haydon on Byron and others. Keats–Shelley Memorial Bull 7 1956.
Brooks, E. L. An unidentified article by Haydon. KSJ 6 1957.
Gaunt, W. A book of drawings by Haydon. Connoisseur June 1963.
Hayter, A. In her Sultry month, 1964, rptd 1992.
Kearney, C. B. R. Haydon and The Examiner. KSJ 27 1978. Checklist of contributions.
Brown, D. B., R. Woof and S. Hebron. Benjamin Robert Haydon 1786–1846: painter and writer, friend of Wordsworth and Keats. Grasmere 1996.

William Hazlitt 1778–1830

For the location of mss, including those of letters and journals, see IELM 4 1800-1900, pt 2 Hardy-Lamb. 1990.

Bibliographies
Hazlitt, W. C. Chronological catalogue. In Memoirs of William Hazlitt, 2 vols 1867.
Ireland, A. List of the writings of William Hazlitt and Leigh Hunt. 1868.
Douady, J. Liste chronologique des oeuvres de William Hazlitt. Paris 1906.
Keynes, G. L. Bibliography of Hazlitt. 1931, 1981 (rev).
Schneider, E. W. In English romantic poets and essayists: a review of research and criticism, ed C. W. and L. H. Houtchens, New York 1957, 1966 (rev).
Houck, J. A. William Hazlitt: a reference guide. Boston 1977.

Collections
The 12 vols ed Hazlitt's son 1838–58, under §1, below, were part of a projected collected edn in 34 vols intended to include all the ptd works with contents rearranged and addns from ms and other sources. The 7 vols ed W. C. Hazlitt 1869–86, under §1, below, represented part of a similar project, and together with an 8th, A view of the English stage, ed W. S. Jackson 1906, *constituted the Bohn Standard Lib edn of Hazlitt's* Works.
The collected works. Ed A. R. Waller and A. Glover 13 vols 1902–6. Introd by W. E. Henley.
The complete works. Ed P. P. Howe 21 vols 1930–4; rptd New York 1967. Based on the Waller and Glover edn, *above*, with additional notes, Life of Napoleon and other uncollected matter.

Selections
For a comprehensive list of selections pbd before 1930, see Keynes, Bibliographies, *above.*

Hazlitt: essayist and critic. Ed A. Ireland 1889.
Hazlitt: essays on poetry. Ed D. Nichol Smith, Edinburgh and London 1901.
Selections. Ed W. D. Howe, Boston 1913.
Hazlitt on English literature. Ed J. Zeitlin, New York 1913.
Selected essays. Ed G. Sampson, Cambridge 1917.
Twenty selected essays. Ed A. J. Wyatt 1925.
Selected essays. Ed G. L. Keynes 1930 (Nonesuch Lib) (defective text).
Essays and characters. Ed S. Williams 1937.
Selections from Lamb and Hazlitt. Ed R. W. Jepson 1940.
Selected essays. Ed R. Wilson 1942.
Hazlitt painted by himself. Ed C. M. Maclean 1948. An 'autobiography' compiled and paraphrased from the essays.
The essays: a selection. Ed C. M. Maclean 1949.
The Hazlitt sampler. Ed H. M. Sikes, Greenwich CT 1961.
Selected essays. Ed L. Bonnerot, Paris 1961.
Essays. Ed R. Vallance and J. Hampden 1964 (Folio Soc).
On the love of life, On the fear of death. Ed J. Voisine, Paris 1966.
Selected writings. Ed R. Blythe, Harmondsworth 1970 (Pen).
Selected writings. Ed C. Salvesen, New York 1972.
Selected writings. Ed J. Cook, Oxford 1991 (WCp).
Selected writings. Ed D. Wu 9 vols 1998.

§1

An essay on the principles of human action: being an argument in favour of the natural disinterestedness of the human mind, to which are added some remarks on the systems of Hartley and Helvetius. 1805 (anon); ed W. Hazlitt jr [1836] (with marginal corrections from the author's copy and an additional essay on abstract ideas).
REVIEWS: Annual Rev, 1805; (attributed to Christopher Wordsworth) Br Critic Nov 1805; General Rev, Mar 1806; Critical Rev, Dec 1806; Anti-Jacobin Rev, Jan 1807; Monthly Rev, Apr 1807; Eclectic Rev, Aug 1807.

Free thoughts on public affairs: or advice to a patriot in a letter addressed to a member of the old opposition. 1806 (anon); ed W. C. Hazlitt 1886 (with Spirit of the age, Letter to William Gifford).

An abridgement of the Light of nature pursued, by Abraham Tucker. 1807. Anon.
REVIEWS: Br Critic, Nov 1807; Cabinet, Jan–Feb 1808.

The eloquence of the British senate; or select specimens from the speeches of the most distinguished parliamentary speakers from the beginning of the reign of Charles I to the present time. With biographical, critical and explanatory notes. 2 vols 1807 (anon), 1808, Brooklyn NY 1809–10, New York 1810, London 1812, Brooklyn NY 1840.
REVIEWS: Annual Rev, 1807; Critical Rev, Mar 1808; Monthly Rev, June 1809; Br Critic, Aug 1810.

A reply to the Essay on population by the Rev T. R. Malthus, in a series of letters. 1807 (anon), New York 1967. Letters 1–3 1st pbd in Cobbett's Political Register, 14 Mar, 16–23 May 1807.
REVIEWS: Annual Rev, 1807; Monthly Rev, May 1808; (H. Twiss) London Rev, May 1809; Edinburgh Rev, Aug 1810.

A new and improved grammar of the English tongue for the use of schools; to which is added a New guide to the English tongue [by Godwin]. 1810. Rptd only in The complete works, ed P. P. Howe. Outlines of English grammar, 1810, 1824 is a partial abridgement by Godwin.
REVIEWS: Critical Rev, Dec 1809; Anti-Jacobin Rev, Apr 1810; Monthly Rev, Oct 1812.

Memoirs of the late Thomas Holcroft, written by himself and continued to the time of his death [by Hazlitt]. 3 vols 1816, 1 vol 1852; ed E. Colby 2 vols 1925; Oxford 1926 (WC).
REVIEWS 1816: GM, Apr; Critical Rev, May; European Mag, July; Morning Chron, 14 Nov.

The round table: a collection of essays on literature, men and manners. 2 vols Edinburgh 1817 (includes 12 essays by Leigh Hunt); ed W. Hazlitt jr, London 1841 (retains Hunt's essays, omits 12 of Hazlitt's, adds 3 uncollected from Liberal, 1822–3); ed W. C. Hazlitt 1871 (Hazlitt's essays only, with Northcote's conversations, Characteristics, Common-places (from Literary Examiner), Trifles light as air (from Atlas)); 1936 (EL) (with Characters of Shakespear's plays).
REVIEWS 1817: Scots Mag, Feb; Critical Rev, Mar; Eclectic Rev, Apr; Monthly Mag, Apr; (attributed to J. Russell) Quart Rev, Apr; Br Lady's Mag, May; Literary Gazette, 3, 17 May, 7 June; Br Critic, June; NMM, July; Edinburgh Mag, Nov (with Characters of Shakespear's plays); Literary and Statistical Mag, Nov.

Characters of Shakespear's plays. 1817, 1818, Boston 1818; New York 1836; ed W. Hazlitt jr, London 1838, 1848, 1854; Philadelphia 1838; New York 1859; ed W. C. Hazlitt, London 1869 (with Lectures on the dramatic literature of the age of Elizabeth); 1903 (with Lectures on the English poets); 1905; 1906 (EL) (with Round table, rptd 1936); ed J. H. Lobban, Cambridge 1908; Oxford 1917 (WC); ed C. Morgan, London 1948 (as Liber amoris and dramatic criticisms). Tr Ger 1838.
REVIEWS: (attributed to J. H. Reynolds) Champion, 20-7 July 1817; [F. Jeffrey] Edinburgh Rev, Aug 1817; NMM, Aug 1817; [L. Hunt] Examiner, 26 Oct, 2, 23 Nov 1817; Edinburgh Mag, Nov 1817 (with Round table); Literary Gazette, 20 Dec 1817; Br Critic, Jan 1818, Analectic Mag, Sep 1818; Br Rev, May 1819; [W. Taylor] Monthly Rev, May 1820 (with Lectures on the English poets, Lectures on the English comic writers); Revue Britannique (Paris), May 1829.

A view of the English stage: or a series of dramatic criticisms. 1818, 1821; ed W. Hazlitt jr 1851 (selection pbd as Criticisms and dramatic essays, of the English stage); ed W. Archer and R. W. Lowe 1895 (as Dramatic essays), New York 1957 (as Hazlitt on theatre); ed W. S. Jackson, London 1906 (text from original articles, with 3 uncollected contributions from Examiner). Originally contributed to Morning Chron, Champion, Examiner and The Times 1814–18.
REVIEWS: Br Stage, May 1818; Champion, 24 May 1818; Analectic Mag, Sep 1818; Monthly Mag, Sep 1818; Br Critic, Oct 1818; Inspector, 23 Jan 1819; Br Rev, May 1819.

Lectures on the English poets, delivered at the Surrey Institution. 1818, Philadelphia 1818, London 1819; ed W. Hazlitt jr 1841 (further matter in 4 appendixes); ed W. C. Hazlitt 1869 (with Lectures on the English comic writers); 1903 (with Characters of Shakespear's plays); 1908; 1910 (EL) (with Spirit of the age); Oxford 1924 (WC); 1929.
REVIEWS 1818 (and 2 later): Scotsman, 16 May, 27 June; Champion, 24 May; Edinburgh Mag, July; Edinburgh Reflector, 1 July; Literary Jnl, 25, 30 July; Monthly Mag, July, Sep; [E. S. Barrett] Quarterly Rev, July; Analectic Mag, Sep; Literary Panorama, Sep; NMM, Oct–Nov; Br Critic, Dec; [R. H. Dana] North Amer Rev, Mar 1819; [W. Taylor] Monthly Rev, May 1820.

A letter to William Gifford esq. 1819, 1820; ed W. C. Hazlitt 1886 (with Spirit of the age, Free thoughts). 1st draft in Examiner, 15 June 1818.
REVIEW: Examiner, 7–14 Mar 1819.

Lectures on the English comic writers, delivered at the Surrey Institution. 1819, Philadelphia 1819; ed W. C. Hazlitt jr, London 1841 (expanded, mainly from prefaces originally contributed to Oxberry's New English drama 1818–19); New York 1845; ed W. C. Hazlitt, London 1869 (with Lectures on the English poets); ed A. Dobson 1900; ed R. B. Johnson, Oxford 1907 (WC); ed W. E. Henley, London 1910 (EL) (with essays from Monthly Mag and New Monthly Mag); ed A. Johnson 1965 (EL).
REVIEWS: Scotsman, 17 Apr 1819, rptd Examiner, 6 June; [L. Hunt] Examiner, 18 Apr 1819; Literary and Statistical Mag, May 1819; Br Stage, June 1819; [W. Taylor] Monthly Rev, May 1820.

Political essays, with sketches of public characters. 1819, 1822. Mainly rptd from articles in various periodicals 1813–18 but including extracts from The eloquence of the British senate, A reply to Malthus.
REVIEWS: (attributed to Gifford) Quart Rev, July 1819; The Times, 14 Aug 1819; Literary Chron, 21 Aug 1819; Monthly Mag, Sep 1819; Champion, 7 Nov 1819; Anti-Jacobin Rev, Dec 1819; Edinburgh Monthly Rev, Mar 1820; Monthly Rev, Nov 1820; Revue Encyclopédique (Paris), Feb 1821.

Lectures chiefly on the dramatic literature of the age of Elizabeth, delivered at the Surrey Institution. 1820, 1821; ed W. Hazlitt jr 1840; New York 1845; Philadelphia 1854; ed W. C. Hazlitt, London 1869 (with Characters of Shakespear's plays).
REVIEWS: [J. Scott] London Mag, Feb 1820; Gold's London Mag, Mar 1820; [L. Hunt] Examiner, 19 Mar 1820; Monthly Mag, May 1820; [W. Taylor] Monthly Rev, Sep 1820; [T. N. Talfourd] Edinburgh Rev, Nov 1820.

Table-talk: or original essays. 2 vols 1821–2, 1824, Paris 1825 (contents taken from Table-talk, Plain speaker, Political essays, with 1 unpbd essay), New York 1845–6 (same contents); ed W. Hazlitt jr, 2 vols London 1845–6 (largely based like all succeeding edns on 1st edn); ed W. C. Hazlitt 1869; 1901 (WC); 1908 (EL); 1909.
REVIEWS 1821 (of vol 1): London Mag, Apr; Literary Chron, 14–21 Apr; Beacon, 21 Apr; Monthly Mag, May; Monthly Rev, May; Br Critic, June; Gold's London Mag, June; Literary Museum, 13–20 July; Examiner, 8 Sep; Quart Rev, Oct; GM, Nov; (of vol 2): Literary Register, 27 July, 3 Aug 1822; Blackwood's Mag, Aug 1822 (vols 1–2); Br Critic, Aug 1822; Examiner, 8 Sep 1822; Monthly Censor, Dec 1822; [W. Taylor] Monthly Rev, May 1823 (vols 1–2); (attributed to J. H. Reynolds) London Mag, June 1823.

Liber amoris: or the new Pygmalion. 1823 (anon), 1884; ed R. Le Gallienne 1893; ed (with much additional matter) R. Le Gallienne [and W. C. Hazlitt] 1894 (priv ptd); 1907; Portland ME 1908; ed C. Morgan, London 1948 (as Liber amoris and dramatic criticisms, introd rptd in his Writer and his world, 1960); ed G. Lahey, New York 1980; ed M. Neve 1985.
REVIEWS 1823: Examiner, 11 May; Literary Register, 17–24 May; Br Luminary, 18 May; The Times, 30 May; Literary Gazette, 31 May; Literary Museum, 31 May; (attributed to J. G. Lockhart) Blackwood's Mag, June; New European Mag, June; Globe, 7 June; John Bull, 15–22 June; Literary Chron, 28 June; Edinburgh Gazette, 2 July.

Characteristics, in the manner of Rochefoucault's Maxims. 1823 (anon); ed R. H. Horne 1837, 1927; ed W. C. Hazlitt 1871 (with Round table, Northcote's conversations).
REVIEWS 1823 (and 1 later): Literary Examiner, 12 July; Literary Gazette, 12 July; Literary Register, 19 July; NMM, Aug; Literary Chron, 9 Aug; Edinburgh Literary Gazette, 27 Aug; Monthly Mag, Sep; Monthly Rev, Feb 1824.

Sketches of the principal picture-galleries in England, with a criticism of Marriage à-la-mode. 1824 (anon); ed W. Hazlitt jr 1843 (as part of Criticisms on art ser 1). Originally contributed to London Mag, 1822–3. Hogarth essay rptd from Round table 1817.
REVIEW: Eclectic Rev, Mar 1825.

Select British poets: or new elegant extracts from Chaucer to the present time, with critical remarks. 1824 (withdrawn owing to infringements of copyright), 1825 (omitting contemporary section, as Select poets of Great Britain).

The spirit of the age: or contemporary portraits. 1825 (anon), 1825 (enlarges Coleridge, adds Cobbett from Table-talk), Paris 1825 (rearranged; omits Moore and Irving, adds Canning and Knowles); ed W. Hazlitt jr, London 1858; ed W. C. Hazlitt 1886 (with Letter to William Gifford, Free thoughts); ed R. B. Johnson 1893 (selection); Oxford 1904 (WC); London 1910 (EL) (with Lectures on English poets); ed E. D. Mackerness 1969. Partly rptd from London Mag and New Monthly Mag.
REVIEWS 1825: Examiner, 9 Jan; Iris 15–22–29 Jan; Le Globe (Paris) 29 Jan, 8 Feb; Eclectic Rev, Feb; [J. Wilson] Blackwood's Mag, Mar; GM, Mar; [F. Jeffrey] Edinburgh Rev, Apr; European Mag, Apr; [W. Taylor] Monthly Rev, May; Scotsman, 28 May; London Mag, June; Oxford Quart Mag, June; Literary Gazette 11 June.

The plain speaker: opinions on books, men and things. 2 vols 1826 (anon); ed W. Hazlitt jr 2 vols 1851–2 (1 essay omitted); ed W. C. Hazlitt 1870; 1928 (EL).
REVIEWS: Star Chamber, 17 May 1826; Atlas, 28 May 1826; Monthly Rev, June 1826; Monthly Mag, Aug 1826; Literary Chron, 26 Aug 1826; [L. Hunt] Companion, 12–19 Mar 1828.

Notes of a journey through France and Italy. 1826, Philadelphia 1833. Rptd from Morning Chron.
REVIEWS: Atlas, 28 May 1826; Monthly Rev, Aug 1826; Monthly Mag, Oct 1826.

The life of Napoleon Buonaparte. 4 vols 1828–30 (vols 1–2 reissued 1830), 3 vols New York 1847–8; Philadelphia 1848, New York 1849; rev W. Hazlitt jr 4 vols London 1852; 3 vols Philadelphia 1875; c. 1885, 1894, 6 vols Paris and Boston 1895 (Napoleon Soc); 6 vols London [1910] (Grolier Soc). Tr Ger, 1835.
REVIEWS: London Weekly Rev, 5–12 Jan 1828; Companion, 20 Feb 1828; Examiner, 9 Mar 1828; Monthly Mag, June 1828; Monthly Rev, June 1828; Morning Chron, 11, 15, 18 Sep 1828; Literary Gazette, 8 Nov 1828; Atlas, 2 May 1830; Court Jnl, 13 Nov 1830; Athenaeum, 25 Dec 1830.

Conversations of James Northcote esq RA. 1830; ed W. C. Hazlitt 1871 (with Round table, Characteristics); ed E. Gosse 1894; ed F. Swinnerton 1949. Rptd from NMM, Aug 1826–Mar 1827, London Weekly Rev, 1829, Atlas, Mar–Nov 1829, Court Jnl, 1830.
REVIEWS: Literary Gazette, 25 Sep 1830; Br Mag, Oct 1830; Monthly Rev, Oct 1830; Court Jnl, 2 Oct 1830; Athenaeum, 2 Oct 1830; Edinburgh Literary Journal, 9 Oct 1830; Monthly Mag, Jan 1831.

Literary remains of the late William Hazlitt, with a notice of his life by his son, and thoughts on his genius and writings by E. L. Bulwer esq MP and Mr Sergeant Talfourd MP. 2 vols 1836, 1 vol New York 1836. 22 essays mainly rptd from periodicals.

Painting [by B. R. Haydon] and the fine arts [by Hazlitt]. Edinburgh 1838. Rptd from Encyclopaedia Britannica, 7th edn suppl vol 1 1816.

Sketches and essays, now first collected by his son. 1839, 1852 (as Men and manners); ed W. C. Hazlitt 1872 (with Winterslow); 1902 (WC); 1970. 18 essays rptd from periodicals.

Criticisms on art, and sketches of the picture galleries of England. Ed W. Hazlitt jr 2 sers 1843–4; ed W. C. Hazlitt 1873 (expanded as Essays on the fine arts).

Winterslow: essays and characters written there, collected by his son. 1850; ed W. C. Hazlitt 1872 (with Sketches and essays); 1902 (WC). Partly rptd from Literary remains, mainly from periodicals.

A reply to Z. Ed C. Whibley 1923. Unpbd reply to article signed 'Z' in Blackwood's Mag, Aug 1818.

New writings by Hazlitt. Ed P. P. Howe 2 ser 1925–7. Articles rptd from periodicals and Oxberry's New English drama 1818–9.

Contributions to periodicals

Contributions not collected by Hazlitt himself in A view of the English stage, Political essays *etc. were rptd in* The complete works, vols 16 Contributions to the Edinburgh Review, 17 Uncollected essays, 18 Art and dramatic criticism, 19 Literary and political criticism, 20 Miscellaneous writings. *The following have since been identified.*

A proposal for the basis of a new system of metaphysical philosophy. Monthly Mag, Feb 1809. 1st rptd in G. Carnall. A Hazlitt contribution, TLS, 19 June 1953.

Letter to the editor signed 'Philo' on Malthus's Essay on population. Monthly Mag, Apr 1809. 1st rptd in J. Kinnaird. 'Philo' and prudence, BNYPL, Mar 1965.

Theatrical examiner no 244. Examiner, 14 July 1816. 1st rptd in S. Jones, Hazlitt and the Theatrical examiner: two additions to the canon, EA, Dec 1985.

Theatrical examiner no 254. Examiner, 29 Sep 1816. 1st rptd by Jones in EA, Dec 1985.

The Editor of the Times. Examiner, 8 Dec 1816. 1st rptd in S. Jones, Three additions to the canon of Hazlitt's political writings, RES, Aug 1987.

[The Plymouth bell-ringer]. Examiner, 11 May 1817. 1st rptd by Jones in RES, Aug 1987.

Notices of curious and highly finished cabinet-pictures at Fonthill abbey. Morning Chron, 20, 22, 25 Aug, 1 Sep 1823. 1st rptd in S. Jones, The Fonthill abbey pictures: two additions to the Hazlitt canon, Jnl of the Warburg and Courtauld Insts, 1978.

The science of a connoisseur. Morning Chron, 30 Sep 1823. 1st rptd by Jones in Jnl of the Warburg and Courtauld Insts, 1978.

A half-length. Examiner, 1 Aug 1824. 1st rptd in S. Jones, Three additions to the canon of Hazlitt's political writings, RES, Aug 1987.

Bad English in the Scotch novels. Morning Chron, 9, 16 Oct 1825. 1st rptd by S. Jones under that title, Library 6th ser 3, 1981.

Letters and journals

Hazlitt, W. C. Memoirs of Hazlitt, with portions of his correspondence. 2 vols 1867.

Hazlitt, W. C. Unpublished correspondence of William Hazlitt. Atlantic Monthly, Apr 1873.

Hazlitt, W. C. Four generations of a literary family. 2 vols 1897.

Lamb and Hazlitt: further letters and records. 1900.

Howe, P. P. Unpublished letters. Athenaeum, 8–15 Aug 1919.

Howe, P. P. New Hazlitt letters. London Mercury, Mar 1923, May 1924, Aug 1925.

Howe, P. P. Three Hazlitt letters. TLS, 21 March 1936.

Bonner, W. H. The journals of Sarah and William Hazlitt 1822–31. Univ of Buffalo Stud 24, 1959.

Barker, J. R. Some early correspondence of Sarah Stoddart and the Lambs. HLQ 24, 1960.

Moyne, E. J. An unpublished letter of Hazlitt. PMLA 77, 1962.

Jones, S. Hazlitt and John Bull: a neglected letter. RES new ser 17, 1966.

Jones, S. Nine new Hazlitt letters and some others. EA 19, 1966.

Jones, S. Some new Hazlitt letters. N & Q new ser 24, 1977.

The letters of William Hazlitt. Ed H. M. Sikes, W. H. Bonner and G. Lahey 1978.

Robinson, C. E. William Hazlitt to his publishers, friends and creditors: twenty-seven new holograph letters. Keats–Shelley Rev 2, 1987.

Jones, S. Hazlitt: a life. 1989. Contains 4 new letters.

Gates, E. M. Leigh Hunt: a life in letters together with correspondence of William Hazlitt. 1999.

§2

Mr Hazlitt's lectures. The Times 23 Jan, 13 Feb, 2 May 1812. Reports of unpbd philosophy lectures.

[Patmore, P. G.]. Notice of a course of lectures on English poetry now delivering at the Surrey Institution London by William Hazlitt esq. Blackwood's Mag, Feb–Apr 1818.

Kenrick, T. Oxberry's New English drama nos 1 and 2. Br Stage 2 14, Feb 1818. Review of Hazlitt's prefaces.

Mr Hazlitt's lectures on poetry. Examiner, 1 Feb, 8 Mar 1818.

Jeffrey and Hazlitt. Blackwood's Mag, June 1818.

Hazlitt cross-questioned. Blackwood's Mag, Aug 1818. Attributed to Lockhart or Wilson.

On the Cockney school of prose writers. NMM, Oct–Nov 1818.

Surrey Institution. Examiner, 8–22 Nov, 20 Dec 1818. Reports of lectures on English comic writers.

[Reynolds, J. H.]. Mr Hazlitt's lectures on the comic genius of England. Edinburgh Mag, Dec 1818–Feb 1819. Based on a ms copy given to Reynolds by Hazlitt before publication. *See* Letters of John Keats, ed H. E. Rollins 2 vols 1958, vol 2, p. 24n.

Hazlitt's essays, criticisms and lectures. Br Rev, May 1819.

Surrey Institution. Examiner, 7, 21 Nov, 5, 19–26 Dec 1819. Reports of lectures on the age of Elizabeth.

Strictures on Mr Hazlitt's remarks on certain presumed inconsistencies in Sir Joshua Reynolds's Discourses. Mag of the Fine Arts, Jan 1821.

Defence of Mr Hazlitt against the misrepresentations of the Quarterly Review. Academic 1 June 1821.

On the writings of Hazlitt. Literary Speculum 2, 1822.

Specimens of modern prose writers, no 1: the author of Table-talk. European Mag 86, 1824.

[Forbes, W. H.]. Hunt and Hazlitt. Blackwood's Mag, June 1824.

[Patmore, P. G.]. Memoir of William Hazlitt. Literary Chron, 26 Aug 1826.

Obituaries (all 1830): [L. Hunt] Tatler, 20 Sep; The Times, 20 Sep; Court Jnl, 25 Sep; GM, Oct; Monthly Mag, Oct; NMM, Oct; Atlas, 17 Oct; Blackwood's Mag, Nov; Mercure de France au Dix-neuvième Siècle, Nov; New York Mirror, 13 Nov; La Belle Assemblée, Dec; Annual biography and obituary, 1830.

[L. Hunt]. Mr Hazlitt and the utilitarians. Tatler, 28 Sep 1830.

[Procter, B. W.]. My recollections of the late William Hazlitt. NMM, Nov 1830.

[Haydon, B. R.]. Hazlitt and Northcote. Athenaeum, 4 May 1833.

[Horne, R. H.]. Hazlitt's first essay. Monthly Repository, June 1835.

[Christian Johnstone]. Writings of Hazlitt. Tait's Edinburgh Mag, Nov–Dec 1836.

[Christian Johnstone]. Hazlitt as a critic of the drama and the fine arts. Ibid, Oct 1837.

[Darley, G.]. Painting and the fine arts. Athenaeum, 14–28 July 1838.

[Egerton, F.]. Painting and the fine arts. Quart Rev 62, 1838.

[R. H. Horne]. British artists and writers on art. Br & Foreign Rev 6, 1838.

Medwin, T. Hazlitt in Switzerland. Fraser's Mag, Mar 1839.

Gilfillan, G. Hazlitt. In his Galleries of literary portraits vol 2 Edinburgh 1845.

DeQuincey, T. Notes on Gilfillan's Gallery of literary portraits: William Hazlitt. Tait's Edinburgh Mag, Dec 1845.

[Whipple, E. P.]. The British critics. North Amer Rev 61, 1845.

Haydon, B. R. Autobiography and memoirs. Ed T. Taylor 3 vols 1853.

[Patmore, P. G.]. My friends and acquaintance. 3 vols 1854.

Etienne, L. Hazlitt, artiste, métaphysician, critique. Revue des Deux Mondes 84, 1869.

Stephen, L. In his Hours in a library ser 2 1876.

Cross, L. Hazlitt. NMM, Mar 1880.

[Noble, J. A.]. Hazlitt's Liber amoris. Temple Bar, Mar 1881.

Saintsbury, G. In his Essays in English literature 1780–1860 ser 1 1890.

Birrell, A. Hazlitt. 1902 (EML).

More, P. E. The first complete edition of Hazlitt. In his Shelburne essays ser 2 1905.

Irwin, S. T. Hazlitt and Lamb. Quart Rev 204, Jan 1906.

Wright, E. Hazlitt and Sainte-Beuve. Acad, 25 Aug 1906.

Douady, J. Vie de William Hazlitt l'essayiste. Paris 1907.

Hazlitt, W. C. The Hazlitts: an account of their origin and descent, with autobiographical particulars of Hazlitt. 2 vols Edinburgh 1911–12 (priv ptd).

Zeitlin, J. A letter of Hazlitt's. Nation, 19 Oct 1911.

Sichel, W. Hazlitt: romantic and amorist. Fortnightly Rev, Jan 1914.

Howe, P. P. Hazlitt and Liber amoris. Ibid, Feb 1916.

Howe, P. P. Hazlitt's second marriage. Ibid, Aug 1916.

Zeitlin, J. Philosophy for schoolboys. Nation, 22 Mar 1917.

Howe, P. P. Hazlitt and Blackwood's. Fortnightly Rev, Oct 1919.

Howe, P. P. Life of Hazlitt. 1922, 1928 (rev); ed F. Swinnerton 1947, Harmondsworth 1949 (Pen).

Carver, P. L. Hazlitt's contributions to the Edinburgh Review. RES, Oct 1928.
Carver, P. L. The authorship of a review of Christabel attributed to Hazlitt. JEGP, Oct 1930.
Keynes, G. L. Hazlitt's Grammar abridged. Library 4th ser vol 13, 1932.
Nowell-Smith, S. H. Hazlitt's essay on the principles of human action. Bibl N & Q, Oct 1936.
Vigneron, R. Stendhal et Hazlitt. MP 35, 1938.
Wilcox, S. C. A manuscript addition to Hazlitt's On the fear of death. MLN, Jan 1940.
Maclean, C. M. Born under Saturn. 1943.
Wilcox, S. C. Hazlitt in the workshop: the manuscript of The fight. Baltimore 1943.
Poston, M. L. Hazlitt's Liber amoris. TLS, 14 Aug 1943.
Gates, P. G. Bacon, Keats and Hazlitt. SAQ, Apr 1947.
Fitzgerald, M. A. et al. The text of Hazlitt. TLS, 27 Feb, 2–27 Mar, 3–17 Apr, 8 May, 5–12 June 1953. A correspondence on the initials in the essay Of persons one would wish to have seen.
Stallbaumer, V. S. S. Hazlitt's Life of Thomas Holcroft. Amer Benedictine Rev 5, 1954.
Schneider, E. W. The unknown reviewer of Christabel: Jeffrey, Hazlitt, Tom Moore. PMLA 70, 1955. Replies by H. H. Jordan, MP 54, 1956; E. W. Schneider, PMLA 77, 1962; W. S. Dowden, MP 60, 1962; K. Coburn, TLS, 20 May 1965; J. Beer, RES new ser 37, 1986. *See* Carver 1930, *above*.
Marshall, W. H. An addition to the Hazlitt canon. PBSA 55, 1961.
Sikes, H. M. Hazlitt, the London Magazine and the 'anonymous reviewer'. BNYPL 65, 1961.
Baker, H. William Hazlitt. Cambridge MA and London 1962.
Jones, S. Hazlitt as lecturer: three unnoticed contemporary accounts. EA 15, 1962.
Marshall, W. H. Pulpit oratory, I–III: essays by J. H. Reynolds in imitation of Hazlitt. Lib Chron 28, 1962.
Sikes, H. M. The infernal Hazlitt. In Essays in history and literature presented to Stanley Pargellis, Chicago 1965.
Jones, S. Isabella Bridgewater: a charade by Hazlitt? REL 7, 1967.
Jones. S. Dating Hazlitt's essay On taste. EA 22, 1969.
Jones, S. Hazlitt, Cobbett and the Edinburgh Review. Neophilologus 53, 1969.
Story, P. L. Byron's death and Hazlitt's Spirit of the age. ELN 7, 1969.
Jones, S. Hazlitt's journal of 1823: some notes and emendations. Library 5th ser 26, 1971.
Kinnaird, J. Hazlitt as poet: the probable authorship of some anonymous verses on Wordsworth's appointment as stamp-distributor. SiR 12, 1973.
Jones, S. Hazlitt's missing essay On individuality. RES new ser 28, 1977. *See also* Letter to the editor, ibid, 32, 1981.
Jones, S. Regency newspaper verse: an anonymous squib on Wordsworth. KSJ, 1978.
Jones, S. A Hazlitt corruption. Library 5th ser 33, 1978.
McCracken, D. Hazlitt: a case of charitable journalism. KSJ, 1979.
Lamb, C. Table-talk: an unpublished review [c. June 1821]. In R. Park, Lamb as critic, 1980.
Jones, S. Dating Hazlitt's essay On reading new books: bibliography and biography. EA 33, 1980.
Jones, S. Bibliography of William Hazlitt by Sir Geoffrey Keynes. Analytical and Enumerative Bibliography (DeKalb IL) 6, 1982.
Jones, S. Some notes on the Letters of Hazlitt. Library 6th ser 5, 1983.
Rosa, G. M. Un emprunt possible de Hazlitt à Stendhal. Revue de Littérature Comparée no 4, 1984.
Jones, S. A Hazlitt anomaly. Library 6th ser 7, 1985
Gates, P. G. Hazlitt's Select British poets: an American publication. KSJ, 1986.
Jones, S. The 'suppression' of Hazlitt's English grammar: a reconstruction of events. Library 6th ser 9, 1987.
Jones, S. Hazlitt: a life, from Winterslow to Frith street. Oxford 1989.
Mulvihill, J. William Hazlitt and the 'impressions' of print culture. KSJ, 1991.
Gates, E. M. Leigh Hunt's marginal comments on Hazlitt's Literary remains. KSJ, 1993.
Gates, E. M. John Bowring, a nineteenth century Kilroy. Wordsworth Circle 26, 1995. *See* Kinnaird 1973 *and* Jones, KSJ, 1978, *above*.
Freeman, A. and G. I. The report of the illustrious obscure: Hazlitt, rackets and the coronation. BC 44 1995.
Edwards, G. William Hazlitt and the case of the initial letter. Text (Ann Arbor) 9 1996. [SJ]

John Abraham Heraud 1799–1887

See col 360.

William Hone 1780–1842

Bibliographies

Jerrold, W. B. Life of G. Cruikshank. 2 vols 1882. Includes list of Hone's works illustr Cruikshank.
Stephens, F. G. Memoir of G. Cruikshank. 1891. Also includes list of Hone's works illustr Cruikshank.

Collections

Facetiae and miscellanies with one hundred and twenty engravings drawn by George Cruikshank. 1827 (2 edns). 12 of Hone's most successful political pams including The political house that Jack built, The queen's matrimonial ladder, The political showman.
Radical squibs and loyal ripostes. Ed E. Rickwood 1971.

§1

The rules and regulations of an institution called tranquillity commenced as an economical bank. 1807.
The King's statue at Guildhall. 1815. A broadside.
Report of the coroner's inquest on Jane Watson. 1815.
The case of Elizabeth Fenning. 1815.
Appearance of an apparition to James Sympson commanding him to do strange things in Pall Mall, and what he did: with coloured illustrations by G. Cruikshank. 1816.
View of the Regent's bomb, now uncovered in St James's Park. 1816. A broadside.
An authentic account of the royal marriage, containing memoirs of Prince Leopold and Princess Charlotte. 1816.
Four trials at Kingston, with 13 questions to Mr Espinasse respecting Elizabeth Fenning. 1816.
An account of Christian slavery in Algiers. 1816.
An account of the riots in London, Dec 2 1816. 3 pts [1816].
The Reformists' Register and Weekly Commentary. Issued from 1 Feb 1816 to 25 Oct 1817; ed and owned by Hone, who was the largest contributor.
The life of William Cobbett, written by himself. 1816. Cobbett indignantly denied authorship; little doubt that Hone was responsible.
Another ministerial defeat: the trial of the dog for biting the noble lord [Castlereagh]. 1817. With woodcut by G. Cruikshank.
Official account of the noble lord's bite! and his dangerous condition. 1817. With woodcut by G. Cruikshank.
Bag Nodle's feast: or the partition and re-union of Turkey. 1817. A ballad on the alleged meanness of Lord and Lady Eldon.
The late John Wilkes's catechism. 1817.
The bullet Te Deum with the canticle of the stone. 1817 (2 edns). Anon.
The political litany. 1817. For this and the 2 following parodies Hone was prosecuted, but defended himself successfully and was acquitted; *see* The trials of William Hone, *below*.

The sinecurist's creed. 1817.
A political catechism, dedicated without permission to His Most Serene Highness Omar, Bashan Day etc, etc of Algiers, by an Englishman. 1817.
The political house that Jack built. 1819 (42 edns) (anon), 1820 (8 edns), 1821 (3 edns), 1827 (in Facetiae and miscellanies). With 13 cuts by George Cruikshank.
The radical house that Jack built. 1819.
Dance in chains. 1819.
The Englishman's mentor: a picture of the Palais Royal. [1819?]
The Queen's matrimonial ladder: a national toy. 1819. With 14 'step-scenes' and illustrations in verse, with 18 other cuts by G. Cruikshank.
Caroline: a poem in blank verse. 1820. Anon.
Buonepartephobia. The origin of Dr Slop's name. 1820 (10 edns) (anon), 1827 (in Facetiae and miscellanies).
The green bag: ... a ballad. By the author of The political 'a, apple pie'. 1820 (9 edns). Anon.
The Queen's budget opened. 1820.
The man in the moon. 1820 (25 edns) (anon), 1821, 1827 (in Facetiae and miscellanies). With 15 illustrations by Cruikshank.
The midnight intruder: or Old Nick at Carlton House. 3 pts 1820. A poem.
'Non mi ricordo'. 1820 (31 edns). Anon. Satire on George IV.
A political lecture on heads. 1820.
A political Christmas carol. 1820.
Plenipo and the devil: or the upshot of the plot: an infernal poem. By the author of The house that Jack built. 1820 (3 edns). Anon.
The political 'a, apple pie': or the 'extraordinary red book' versified. By the author of The house that Jack built. 1820 (20 edns). Anon.
The political queen that Jack loves. 1820 (10 edns). Anon.
The queen and magna charta: or the thing that Jack signed. 1820 (3 edns) anon: authorship uncertain.
The queen that Jack found. 1820 (10 edns). Anon: authorship uncertain.
The queen's matrimonial ladder ... illustrations in verse. 1820 (44 edns) (anon), 1827 (in Facetiae and miscellanies).
The form of prayer, with thanksgiving to Almighty God, to be used daily for the happy deliverance of Queen Caroline from the late most traitorous conspiracy. 1820.
The bank-restriction barometer. 1820. Originally ptd as a large open half-sheet, as an envelope for Cruikshank's 'Banknote not to be imitated'.
The apocryphal New Testament: being all the gospels, epistles and other pieces now extant, attributed in the first four centuries to Jesus Christ, his apostles and companions, and not included in the New Testament. 1820. Fiercely attacked in Quart Rev and furiously defended by Hone.
The political showman – at home! [1821.]
A slap at Slop and the Bridge St gang. 1821. A burlesque on Stoddart's New Times, illustr Cruikshank, who inspired it.
The right divine of kings to govern wrong. 1821 (8 edns) (anon), 1827 (in Facetiae and miscellanies). An adaptation, with addns and alterations, of Defoe's Jure divino, 1706, with a preface by Hone and 2 woodcuts by G. Cruikshank.
An imaginary interview between W. Hone and a lady. 1822.
The northern excursion of Geordie, emperor of Gotham. [1822.] Anon.
Ancient mysteries described. 1823. Old English miracle plays and other early dramas found by Hone in ms in BM and pbd with notes and illustrations, the latter by G. Cruikshank.
The every-day book: or everlasting calendar of popular amusements; with four hundred and ninety engravings [by G. Cruikshank and others]. 2 vols 1826–7, introd by L. Shepard, Detroit 1967.
The table book. 2 vols 1827–8, Detroit 1966. With 116 engravings by Cruikshank and others.
Full annals of the revolution in France. 1830.
The year-book of daily recreation and information concerning remarkable men and manners, times and seasons. 1832, rptd 1967. Illustr George Cruikshank and others.
The early life and conversion of William Hone by himself, edited by his son. 1841.
Some account of the conversion of the late W. Hone, with further particulars of his life and extracts from his correspondence. 1853.

§2

The three trials of Hone, for publishing three parodies. 1818; ed W. Tegg 1876. The Trials were pbd separately in 1817.
Hackwood, F. W. Hone: his life and times. 1912.
Herd, H. In his Seven editors, 1955.
Sikes, H. M. Hone: Regency patriot, parodist and pamphleteer. Newberry Lib Bull 5 1961.
Regency radicalism and antiquarianism: William Hone's Ancient mysteries described (1823). Leeds Stud in English 10 1978.
Robinson, D. L. Hawthorne's April fools: sources and significance. American Transcendental Quart 53, Winter 1982.
Vitale, M. The domesticated heroine in Byron's Corsair and William Hone's prose adaptation. Literature and History 10, Spring 1984.
Manning, P. J. The Hone-ing of Byron's Corsair. In Textual criticism and literary interpretation, ed J. J. McGann, Chicago 1985.

Mary Howitt, née Botham 1799–1888

For works written in collaboration with her husband, see William Howitt, below.

Bibliographies

Woodring, C. R. William and Mary Howitt: bibliographical notes. HLB 5 1951.

Collections

Complete poetical works. Boston 1858, 1859.
In Miles, The poets and poetry of the century 10 vols [1891–7].
The poetical works of Howitt, Milman and Keats. Philadelphia 1840, 1845, 1846, 1847, 1849, 1852, 1853, [c. 1855].
The poetical works of Mary Howitt, Eliza Cook and L. E. L. Boston 1849, 1850, 1852, 1853, 1855, 1856, 1857, 1859, 1860, 1866.

§1

The forest minstrel, and other poems. 1823. With William Howitt.
The desolation of Eyam, the emigrant: a tale of the American woods and other poems. London, Edinburgh and Dublin 1827, 1828. With William Howitt.
The seven temptations. 1834.
Sketches of natural history. 1834, Philadelphia 1834, London [1839], Boston 1842, London [1851] (7th edn, enlarged), [1864], [1872].
Wood Leighton: or a year in the country. 3 vols 1836.
Tales in verse. [1836], New York [1836], Boston 1839, 1842, 1843, London [1850?] (as Mary Howitt's Tales in verse for the young), [1857?], London and Edinburgh [1865].
Hymns and fireside verses. 1839 (2 edns), [1845?].
Hope on, hope ever! 1840.
Strive and thrive: a tale. 1840.
Sowing and reaping: or what will come of it? 1841, 1841.
Work and wages: or life in service. [1842.]
Little coin, much care. 1842.
Love and money: an every day tale. [1843.]
No sense like common sense: or some passages in the life of Charles Middleton. 1843. Probably by William Howitt.
The child's poetry book. New York 1844.
Marien's pilgrimage: a fire-side story, and other poems. [New York 1844]; [n.p. 1845], London [1859].

The poems. New York 1844, Philadelphia 1844, 1846, New York 1851, 1854, London and New York [1872].
Fireside verses. [1845.]
Ballads and other poems. 1847, New York 1847, 1848, 1849, 1854, London 1856.
Floral gems. With others. New York 1847, 1848, 1849, 1851.
Poetical tales for good boys and girls. Worcester MA 1847, 1850.
The children's year. 1847.
The heir of Wast-Waylan. 1847.
Our cousins in Ohio. 1849.
Pictures and verses. For young people. New York 1853.
Songs and stories for mother's darling. Philadelphia 1854. Anon.
The picture book for the young. 1855.
Birds and flowers and other country things. [1855], London and Edinburgh 1871.
Stories in rhyme. Boston 1855.
Marion's pilgrimage: a fire-side story; and other poems. [1859.]
A popular history of the United States of America, from the discovery of the American continent to the present time. 2 vols 1859.
Lillieslea: or lost and found. 1861.
The cost of Caergwyn. 3 vols 1864.
Stories of Stapleford. 2 pts [1864].
Tales in prose for young people. [1864.]
Tales in verse for young people. [1865.]
Our four-footed friends. [1867.]
Vignettes of American history. [1869], [1876].
Birds and their nests. [1872.]
Tales for all seasons. [1881.]
Mrs Howitt wrote, edited and translated some 110 works. Among her more notable trns are various tales from the Danish of Hans Andersen, and the novels of Fredrika Bremer from the Swed in 18 vols.

§2

[Wilson, J.] Noctes ambrosianae. Blackwood's Mag Nov 1828, Apr 1831.
Mary Howitt: an autobiography. Ed Margaret Howitt 1889, [1891].
Britten, J. Mary Howitt. [1890.] A biography.
Woodring, C. R. Victorian samplers: William and Mary Howitt. Lawrence KS 1952.
Lee, A. Laurels and rosemary: the life of William and Mary Howitt. Oxford 1955.
Dunicliff, J. Mary Howitt: another lost Victorian writer. 1992.

William Howitt 1792–1879

Bibliographies

Woodring, C. R. William and Mary Howitt: bibliographical notes. HLB 5 1951.

§1

The influence of nature and poetry on a national spirit. 1814. Anon.
Commemorative verses, addressed to the friends of Richard Leaver. Mansfield [1818]. Anon.
A poet's thoughts at the interment of Lord Byron. 1824.
The book of the seasons: or the calendar of nature. 1831.
A popular history of priestcraft in all ages and nations. 1833, 1834 (4th edn, enlarged), [1834] (abridged).
Pantika: or traditions of the most ancient times. 2 vols 1835.
Colonization and Christianity: a popular history of the treatment of the natives by the Europeans in all their colonies. 1838.
The rural life of England. 2 vols 1838.
The boy's country-book: being the real life of a country boy. 1839.
Visits to remarkable places, old halls, battlefields and scenes illustrative of striking passages in English history and poetry. 1840; ser 2 'chiefly in the counties of Durham and Northumberland', 1842.
The student-life of Germany, by Dr Cornelius. 1841.
The rural and domestic life of Germany; with characteristic sketches of its cities and scenery, collected in a general tour, and during a residence in the country in 1840, 41 and 42. 1842.
German experiences, addressed to the English, both stayers at home and goers abroad. 1844.
The life and adventures of Jack of the mill, commonly called Lord Othmill: a fire-side story. 2 vols 1844.
Homes and haunts of the eminent British poets. 2 vols 1847, 1857 (3rd edn).
The hall and the hamlet: or scenes and characters of country life. 2 vols 1848.
The year-book of the country: or the field, the forest and the fireside. 1850.
Madam Dorrington of the dene: the story of a life. 3 vols 1851.
A boy's adventures in the wilds of Australia: or Herbert's note-book. 1854.
Land, labour and gold: or two years in Victoria; with visits to Sydney and Van Diemen's Land. 2 vols 1855.
Cassell's illustrated history of England: the text to Edward I by J. F. Smith and [thence] by W. Howitt. 8 vols [1856]–64.
Tallangetta, the squatter's home: a story of Australian life. 2 vols 1857.
The man of the people. 3 vols 1860.
The history of the supernatural in all ages and nations, and in all churches, christian and pagan, demonstrating a universal faith. 2 vols 1863.
The history of discovery in Australia, Tasmania and New Zealand from the earliest date to the present day. 1865.
Woodburn Grange: a story of English country life. 3 vols 1867.
The northern heights of London: or historical associations of Hampstead, Highgate, Muswell Hill, Hornsey and Islington. 1869.
The mad war-planet: and other poems. London and Guildford 1871.
The religion of Rome described by a Roman. 1873.

Works written with Mary Howitt

The forest minstrel and other poems. 1823. With notes.
The desolation of Eyam, the emigrant: a tale of the American woods; and other poems. 1827.
Howitt's journal of literature and popular progress. 1847–9.
Stories of English and foreign life. 1849.
The literature and romance of Northern Europe: constituting a complete history of the literature of Sweden, Denmark, Norway and Iceland. 2 vols 1852.
Ruined abbeys and castles of Great Britain. 2 ser 1862–4. Separate extracts from the above were brought out – Yorkshire, 1863; the Wye, 1863; the Border, 1865.
Howitt also pbd some shorter tales and a number of trns, including von Chamisso de Boncourt, History of Peter Schlemihl, *1843, and J. Ennemoser,* History of magic, *1854; he wrote a number of minor works and many contributions to periodicals, including about 100 articles on spiritualism in* Spiritual Mag.

§2

Horne, R. H. William and Mary Howitt. In his A new spirit of the age vol 1, 1844.
Brown, Cornelius. The worthies of Nottinghamshire. 1883.
Hall, S. C. Retrospect of a long life. 2 vols 1883.
Howitt (later Watts), A. M. The pioneers of the spiritual reformation: life and works of D. J. Kerner; Howitt and his work for spiritualism: biographical sketches. 1883.
Mary Howitt: an autobiography. Ed Margaret Howitt 1889. With ch describing his youth by W. Howitt.
Woodring, C. R. Charles Reade's debt to William Howitt. Nineteenth-Cent Fiction 5 1951.
Woodring, C. R. Victorian samplers: William and Mary Howitt. Lawrence KS 1952.

Lee, A. Laurels and rosemary: the life of William and Mary Howitt. Oxford 1955.

Leigh Hunt 1784–1859

The most noteworthy collection of Hunt mss is the Brewer Collection at the Univ of Iowa, Iowa City: over 100 literary mss and more than 650 letters from Hunt. Bodleian MS Eng Poet e 38 is a notebook containing unptd draft poems by Hunt. Other mss can be found at the Pierpont Morgan Lib, New York, and in the Berg Collection at the New York Public Lib (see TLS 22 Nov 1957). Letters are widely scattered, but over 100 can be found in the Brotherton Library at the Univ of Leeds; significant smaller groups can be found at Princeton Univ and Lib of Congress. For further details, see Commentary, BC 3 1954.

Bibliographies

Ireland, A. List of the writings of William Hazlitt and Leigh Hunt. 1868, New York 1970.

Swann, J. H. Catalogue of the Alexander Ireland collection in the Free Reference Library. Manchester 1898.

Mitchell, A. A bibliography of the writings of Hunt. Bookman's Jnl (London) 15 1927; rptd in Bibliographies of modern authors, 3rd ser, 1931.

Brewer, L. A. My Leigh Hunt library: the first editions. Cedar Rapids IA 1932.

Bay, J. C. The Leigh Hunt collection of Luther Albertus Brewer. Cedar Rapids IA 1933.

Landré, L. In Leigh Hunt, vol 2, Paris 1936.

Bernbaum, E. Keats, Shelley, Byron, Hunt: a critical sketch of important books and articles concerning them published in 1940–1950. KSJ 1 1952.

Hanlin, F. S. The Brewer–Leigh Hunt collection at the State University of Iowa. KSJ 8 1959.

Green, D. B. and E. G. Wilson (ed). Keats, Shelley, Byron, Hunt and their circles: a bibliography July 1 1950–June 30 1962. Lincoln NE 1964.

Lulofs, T. J. Leigh Hunt: a reference guide. 1985.

Waltman, J. L. and G. G. McDaniel. Leigh Hunt. A comprehensive bibliography. New York 1985.

Collections

Poetical works. 3 vols 1819. Five separate pbns bound together with collective title pages.

Poetical works. 1832. A cautious selection.

Poetical works. 1844, 1846, 1849. Another selective edn.

Poetical works. Ed S. Adams Lee 2 vols Boston 1857.

Poetical works. Ed his son, Thornton Hunt, 1860. Collected and arranged with 'his own final judgment'.

In 1870 Smith, Elder pbd a Uniform reprint in 7 vols of some of Hunt's prose works. There has been no full collected edn of the prose, though substantial parts have been completed.

A tale for a chimney corner, and other essays. Ed E. Ollier [1869], 1879.

Favorite poems. Boston MA 1877.

Poetical works. 1883.

Essays. Ed A. Symons 1887, 1888, 1892, 1903, 1905, 1908, 1910.

Leigh Hunt as poet and essayist. Ed C. Kent 1889, London and New York 1891.

Poetical works of L. Hunt and T. Hood. Ed J. H. Panting [1889]. A selection.

Essays. Ed E. Ollier 1890.

Essays and poems. Ed R. B. Johnson 2 vols 1891.

Tales. Ed W. Knight 1891.

Dramatic essays. Ed W. Archer and R. W. Lowe 1894.

Selections. 1905.

Essays. Ed Hannaford Bennett 1907, 1924.

Selections in prose and verse. Ed J. H. Lobban 1909.

Leigh Hunt. Ed E. Storer [1911].

Essays and sketches. Ed R. B. Johnson 1912.

Poetical works. Ed H. S. Milford 1923, New York 1978. The definitive edn; a few pieces remain uncollected; to some Milford provides references; he omits juvenilia and the trn Amyntas.

Prefaces by Leigh Hunt, mainly to his periodicals. Ed R. B. Johnson 1927, Chicago 1927, Port Washington NY 1967.

Essays. Ed J. B. Priestley 1929 (EL). A selection.

Leigh Hunt's dramatic criticism 1808–31. Ed L. H. and C. W. Houtchens, New York 1950, New York 1976.

Leigh Hunt's literary criticism. Ed L. H. and C. W. Houtchens, with an essay, Leigh Hunt as man of letters, by C. D. Thorpe, New York 1956, London 1976.

Political and occasional essays. Ed L. H. and C. W. Houtchens, with an essay, Leigh Hunt as political essayist, by C. R. Woodring, New York 1962.

Selected writings. Manchester 1990.

§1

Juvenilia written between the ages of twelve and sixteen. 1801, 1801, 1802, 1803, Philadelphia 1804.

Critical essays on the performers of the London theatres. 1807.

An attempt to shew the folly and danger of Methodism. 1809.

The reformist's answer to the article entitled 'State of parties' in the last Edinburgh Review (no 30). 1810.

The Prince of Wales v the Examiner. A full report of the trial of John and Leigh Hunt . . ., to which are added, observations on the trial, by the editor of the Examiner. 1812.

The feast of the poets, with notes, and other pieces in verse. Boston 1813, London 1814 (2 issues, different imprints), New York 1814, London 1815 ('amended and enlarged'), Oxford 1989.

The descent of liberty: a mask. 1815, 1816, Philadelphia 1816.

The story of Rimini. 1816, Boston 1816, London 1817, 1819, Boston 1844.

Musical copyright: Whitaker versus Hime: to which are subjoined, observations on the extraordinary defence made by Mr Sergeant Joy, by Leigh Hunt. 1816.

The round table: a collection of essays. 1817, 1841. The round table in the Examiner was principally by Hazlitt, but of the 52 papers collected in vol form, 10 are by Hunt.

Foliage: or poems original and translated. 1818, Philadelphia 1818.

Hero and Leander, and Bacchus and Ariadne. 1819.

Amyntas, a tale of the woods. 1820. Trn from Tasso; dedicated to Keats.

The months, descriptive of the successive beauties of the year. 1821; ed W. Andrews 1897; ed R. H. Bath 1929, 1936. Founded on articles in the Literary pocket-book.

Ultra-Crepidarius: a satire on William Gifford. 1823.

Bacchus in Tuscany, from the Italian of F. Redi. 1825.

The keepsake for 1828. 1828. Hunt contributed anon Dreams on the borders of the land of poetry and Pocket-books and keepsakes.

Lord Byron and some of his contemporaries. 1828, 2 vols 1828, 2 vols Philadelphia 1828, New York 1966, New York 1976, 3 vols Paris 1828 (with addns). The autobiography, 1850, *below*, was partly a reconstruction of this work.

Sir Ralph Esher: or, adventures of a gentleman of the Court of Charles II. 3 vols 1832 (anon), 1835, 1850 (3rd edn, with preface). A novel; some copies dated 1830.

Christianism: or belief and unbelief reconciled. 1832. Expanded for general circulation into The religion of the heart, 1853, *below*.

The indicator, and the companion; a miscellany for the fields and the fire-side. 2 vols 1834, 1835, 1840, 1845, New York 1845. Hunt's selections from the periodicals named.

Captain sword and captain pen. 1835, 1839, 1849 (with new preface); Iowa City 1984 (with introd by R. Dunlop).

A legend of Florence. A play. 1840, 1840 (with added preface); rptd in G. H. Lewes, Modern British dramatists, 1867, 1885.

The seer; or, common-places refreshed. 1840, 2 pts 1840–1, 1850, Boston 1864, Boston 1878.
Heads of the people drawn by Kenny Meadows, with original essays. 1840. Hunt's contributions are The monthly nurse and The omnibus conductor.
Notice of the late Mr Egerton Webbe. 1840. Rptd from Morning Chron.
The poems of Geoffrey Chaucer, modernized. 1841. Ed R. H. Horne and Hunt, who modernized the Tales of the Squire, the Friar, and the Manciple.
The palfrey; a love-story of old times. 1842.
Imagination and fancy; and an essay in answer to the question 'What is poetry?' 1844, 1845, New York 1845, London 1846, New York 1850, New York 1852, London 1870, New York 1875, London 1891; ed E. Gosse 1907, 1910, 1995.
Wit and humour, with an illustrative essay. 1846, New York 1846, Paris 1846, 3 vols New York 1846, London 1848, 1890, Folcroft PA 1972.
Stories from the Italian poets. 2 vols 1846, 1854. An excerpt entitled Dante's Divine comedy: the book and its story, 1903.
Men, women, and books, 2 vols 1847, 2 vols New York 1847, London 1852, New York 1855, London 1876, 1943.
A jar of honey from Mount Hybla. 1848, 1852, 1870, 1897.
The town; its memorable characters and events. 2 vols 1848, 1859, 1870, 1889, 1893, 1902, 1903, 1906; ed A. Dobson 1907 (WC).
The autobiography. 3 vols 1850, 2 vols New York 1850, London 1859, 1860, 1872, 1878, 1885, 1891; ('revised by the author; with further revision, and an introduction by his eldest son'); ed R. Ingpen 2 vols 1903, New York 1903; ed E. Blunden, London 1928 (WC); ed J. E. Morpurgo 1949; ed from the ms in the Brewer Col by S. F. Fogle as Leigh Hunt's autobiography: the earliest sketches, Gainesville FL 1959; New York 1965; in Italy and the English Romantics, ed Ferruccio Terrani, Rimini 1984, 1985.
Table talk. 1851, New York 1879, 1882.
The religion of the heart. 1853, New York 1857. *See* Christianism, *above.*
The old court suburb; or, memorials of Kensington. 2 vols 1855, 2 vols 1855 (enlarged), 1860; ed A. Dobson 2 vols 1902.
Stories in verse. Now first collected. 1855.
A saunter through the West End. 1861.
A day by the fire; and other papers hitherto uncollected. Ed J. E. Babson 1870, Boston 1870.
The wishing-cap papers. Now first collected [by J. E. Babson]. Boston 1873, Boston 1874.
An answer to the question 'What is Poetry' including remarks on versification. Ed Albert S. Cook 1893.
Coaches and coaching. 1908.
My books, an essay. Cambridge MA 1910, San Francisco 1949.
Ballads of Robin Hood. Ed L. A. Brewer, Cedar Rapids IA 1922.
The love of books. Ed L. A. and E. T. Brewer, Cedar Rapids IA 1923. Rptd from Hunt's My books, *above.*
Marginalia. Ed L. A. Brewer, Cedar Rapids IA 1926.
The old lady and the maid-servant. 1929.
Leigh Hunt's 'Rules for newspaper editors', Wisdom for the wicked. 1930.
The inexhaustibility of the subject of Christmas. New York 1937.
Musical evenings or selections, vocal and instrumental. Ed D. R. Cheney, Columbia MO 1964.
Leigh Hunt on eight sonnets of Dante. Ed R. Dunlop, Iowa City IA 1965.
A copy of verses written for the Bellmen. Oxford 1970.
Rondeau; Abou ben Adhem. Iowa City IA 1984.

Contributions to periodicals

No register has yet been made of Hunt's very numerous and often anon contributions to periodicals other than those which he edited. The following references may be found useful so far as uncollected writings are concerned: papers signed 'Mr Town, Junior' *in* Traveller (before 1805); *theatre articles in* News *(1805–7); papers in* Statesman (1806); *notices of plays in* The Times *(Aug 1807); essays and verses in* NMM (particularly 1825–37, and occasionally until 1850), Atlas (c. 1828–30), True Sun, *and* Weekly True Sun (c. 1833–4), Spectator 1858–9), Ainsworth Mag (1844), Bentley's Misc (1838), Edinburgh Rev (1816, 1841–51), Fraser's Mag (1832, 1858–9), London and Westminster Rev (1837–9), Monthly Chron (1838–9), *and at intervals throughout his life* Tait's Edinburgh Mag (1832–7); *see* Wellesley *5, 1989. See also the article in* DNB, *which points out some of Hunt's contributions to musical criticism.*
The examiner: a Sunday paper. 1808–21. Hunt's editorial work ended in 1821, but he contributed until 1825.
The reflector: a quarterly magazine. 1810–11. Reissued as Reflector: a collection of essays, 2 vols 1812.
The literary pocket-book: or, companion for the lover of nature and art. 1818–22 (for 1819–23).
The indicator. 76 nos 13 Oct 1819–21 Mar 1821; 2 vols in 1 1822. Other Indicators appeared in Literary Examiner 1823; no 89 and last in NMM May 1832.
The liberal: verse and prose from the south. 1822–3 (4 nos, 2 vols); rptd New York 1967.
The literary examiner. 1823. Probably ed John Hunt.
The companion. 9 Jan–23 July 1828 (nos 1–28); rptd New York 1967.
The chat of the week. 28 June–28 Aug 1830.
The tatler: a daily journal of literature and the stage. 4 Sep 1830–13 Feb 1832.
Leigh Hunt's London journal. 2 vols 2 Apr 1834–26 Dec 1835; rptd New York 1967.
The monthly repository. July 1837–Apr 1838; ed F. E. Mineka as The dissidence of dissent, Chapel Hill NC 1944.
Leigh Hunt's journal. 7 Dec 1850–29 Mar 1851. Weekly.

Anthologies etc

Classic tales, serious and lively; with critical essays. 5 vols 1806–7, 5 vols New York 1810, London 1895. Critical papers by Hunt on Henry Mackenzie, Goldsmith, Henry Brooke, Voltaire and Dr Johnson.
The masque of anarchy. A poem by Percy Bysshe Shelley: now first published, with a preface by Hunt. 1832.
The dramatic works of Richard Brinsley Sheridan. 1840, 1846, 1855, 1865.
The dramatic works of Wycherley, Congreve, Vanbrugh, and Farquhar. 1840, 1855.
One hundred romances of real life. 1843, 1846, 1888, Boston 1889 as Romances of real life.
The foster brother: a tale of the war of Chiozza. 3 vols 1845, New York 1864. By Thornton Hunt; ed Leigh Hunt.
A book for a corner. 2 vols 1849, 2 vols New York 1852, New York 1857, London 1858.
Readings for railways. 1849; ser 2, 1853 (with J. B. Syme).
Beaumont and Fletcher. 1855. A selection.
The book of the sonnet. Ed Hunt and S. Adams Lee 2 vols Boston 1867, 2 vols London 1867, 2 vols New York 1885. Includes Hunt's essay on the sonnet.

Letters

Correspondence. Ed his eldest son 2 vols 1862, New York 1973.
Selections from Hunt's correspondence with B. R. Haydon, Charles Ollier and Southwood Smith. Ed S. R. T. Mayer, St James's Mag 1874–5.
Mayer, S. R. T. Hunt and Lord Brougham; with original letters. Temple Bar June 1876.
Six letters of Leigh Hunt addressed to W. W. Story, 1850–6. 1913.
Leigh Hunt's letter on Hogg's Life of Shelley. Ed L. A. Brewer, Cedar Rapids IA 1927.

Brewer, L. A. Some letters from my Leigh Hunt portfolios. Cedar Rapids IA 1929.
My Leigh Hunt library: the holograph letters. Ed L. A. Brewer, Iowa City 1938. Nine hundred letters and ms scraps, most unpbd.
Gates, P. G. A Hunt–Byron letter. KSJ 2 1953.
Kaser, D. E. Two new Hunt letters. N & Q Mar 1955.
Barnett, G. L. Hunt revises a letter. HLQ 20 1957.
Marshall, W. H. Hunt on Walt Whitman: a new letter. N & Q Sep 1957.
Green, D. B. Some new Hunt letters. N & Q Aug 1958.
Marshall, W. H. Three new Hunt letters. KSJ 9 1960.
Sanders, C. R. The correspondence and friendship of Carlyle and Hunt: the early years. Bull of John Rylands Lib 45 1963.
Sanders, C. R. The correspondence and friendship of Carlyle and Hunt: the later years. Bull of John Rylands Lib 46 1963.
Enkvist, N. E. In his British and American literary letters in Scandinavian public collections, Abo 1964.
Barnes, W. Hunt's letters in the Luther Brewer collections: plans for a new edition. Books at Iowa no 3 1965.
The correspondence of Leigh Hunt and Charles Ollier in the winter of 1853–4. Ed D. R. Cheney 1976.

Dubious ascriptions

Among the pbns sometimes attributed to Hunt, Reminiscences of Michael Kelly the singer (2 vols 1826) *should not stand: it was prepared by Theodore Hook.* The rebellion of the beasts: or the ass is dead! Long live the ass! (1825) *by 'a late Fellow of St John's College, Cambridge' may or may not be Hunt's; it is nowhere mentioned in his available letters.* Dictionary of anonymous and pseudonymous English literature, ed J. Kennedy, W. A. Smith and A. F. Johnson, *describes* Florentine tales (1847), *as* 'largely by Thomas Powell, but after his death by J. H. Leigh Hunt.' *Powell, however, was sufficiently alive in 1849 to emigrate to New York, pursued by the execrations of Browning. A poem in* Ollier's Literary miscellany 1820 – The universal Pan – *signed L., is more the fault of 'Barry Cornwall' than of Hunt.*
Marshall, W. H. An early misattribution to Byron: Hunt's The feast of the poets. N & Q May 1962.

§2

Numerous references to Hunt will also be found in the standard edns of the works and in letters of Byron, Hazlitt, Keats and Shelley.
Hunt, Leigh. Autobiographical paper. Monthly Mirror Apr 1810.
Keats, J. In Poems, 1817.
'Z'. The cockney school of poetry. Blackwood's Mag Oct 1817–Jan 1818.
'A'. Mr Hunt's Hero and Leander. London Mag July 1820.
Shelley, P. B. The Cenci. 1821. Dedication.
[Kent, E.] Flora domestica. 1823.
Lamb, C. Letter of Elia to Robert Southey esq. London Mag Oct 1823.
Hazlitt, W. In Spirit of the age, 1825.
Kent, E. Sylvan sketches. 1825.
[Lytton, E. B.] Sir Ralph Esher. NMM Mar 1832.
Brougham, H. P. (Baron Brougham and Vaux). In Speeches, 4 vols 1838.
Hall, S. C. In Book of gems 1836–1838, 1838. A notice of Hunt; also memoranda by Hunt and Shelley, Keats and Tennyson.
[Macaulay, T. B.] Comic dramatists of the Restoration. Edinburgh Rev 72 1841.
Horne, R. H. In his A new spirit of the age, vol 1, 1844.
Howitt, W. In his Homes and haunts of the most eminent British poets, 2 vols 1847.
[Ireland, A.] The genius and writings of Hunt. Manchester Examiner July 1847.
Dickens, C. In Bleak house, 1853. The character Harold Skimpole.
Haydon, B. R. In Autobiography and journals, 3 vols 1853.
Moore, T. In his Memoirs, journal and correspondence vol 8, 1856.
[Ollier, E.] The occasional. Spectator 3 Sep 1859.
Dickens, C. Hunt: a remonstrance. All the Year Round 24 Dec 1859.
[Hunt, T. L.] A man of letters of the last generation. Cornhill Mag Jan 1860.
Collier, J. P. The late Duke of Devonshire and Hunt. Athenaeum 8 Mar 1862.
Ollier, E. Correspondence of Hunt. Spectator 22 Mar 1862.
Ollier, E. A literary life. All the Year Round 12 Apr 1862.
[Carlyle, T.] Memoranda concerning Mr Leigh Hunt. Macmillan's Mag July 1862.
Hawthorne, N. In Our old home, 1863.
Kent, C. Footprints on the road. 1864.
Bates, W. (ed). A gallery of illustrious literary characters 1830–8 drawn by the late Daniel Maclise RA and accompanied by notices chiefly by the late William Maginn LL D. [1876].
Hall, S. C. In A book of memories, [1876].
Horne, R. H. (ed). Letters of E. B. Browning. 2 vols 1877.
Proctor, B. W. An autobiographical fragment. 1877.
Cowden Clarke, C. and M. In Recollections of writers, 1878.
Dickens, C. In Letters, 3 vols 1880–2.
Dowden, E. In Life of Percy Bysshe Shelley, 2 vols 1886.
Saintsbury, G. In Essays in English literature 1780–1860, 1890.
Monkhouse, W. C. Life of Leigh Hunt. 1893.
Shelley, P. B. Letters to Hunt. Ed T. J. Wise 2 vols 1894.
Johnson, R. B. Leigh Hunt. 1896.
Punchard, C. D. Helps to the study of Leigh Hunt's essays. 1899.
Allingham, W. A diary. 1907, 1967.
Adams, M. Some Hampstead memories. Illustr F. Adcock 1909.
Miller, B. Leigh Hunt's relations with Byron, Shelley and Keats. 1910.
Moebus, O. Leigh Hunts Kritik der Entwicklung der englischen Literatur bis zum Ende des 18. Jahrhunderts. Strasbourg 1916.
Howe, P. P. In Life of William Hazlitt, 1922, 1928 (rev).
Gosse, E. In More books on the table, 1923.
Brewer, L. A. Some Lamb and Browning letters to Leigh Hunt. Cedar Rapids IA 1924.
Forman, M. B. Hunt: some unfamiliar apologists. London Mercury June 1926.
Brewer, L. A. The joys and sorrows of a book collector. Cedar Rapids IA 1928.
Johnson, R. B. Shelley–Leigh Hunt. 1928, New York 1972. [RM]

Catherine Hutton 1756–1846

§1

The miser married: a novel. 1813.
The life of William Hutton, by himself; conclusion by Catherine Hutton. 1816, 1817, 1841.
The Welsh mountaineer: a novel. 3 vols 1817.
The history of Birmingham by William Hutton; continued to the present time by Catherine Hutton. 1819.
Oakwood Hall: a novel. 3 vols 1819.
The tour of Africa: containing a concise account of all the countries in that quarter of the globe hitherto visited by Europeans, selected from the best authors and arranged by C[atherine] H[utton]. 3 vols 1819–21.

Letters

Reminiscences of a gentlewoman of the last century: letters of Catherine Hutton. Ed C. H. Beale, Birmingham 1891.
Catherine Hutton and her friends. Ed C. H. Beale, Birmingham 1895.

§2

Miss Catherine Hutton. GM Apr–May 1846.
Colvile, F. L. The worthies of Warwickshire who lived between 1500 and 1800. Warwick [1870].
Jewitt, Ll. F. W. The life of William Hutton. [1872.]

Anna Brownell Jameson, née Murphy 1794–1860

No extant mss of pbd work have been located but there are substantial collections of private correspondence in the following institutions: Goethe and Schiller Archives, Weimar (most of Jameson's letters are in English); The Lovelace Papers, Western Mss, Bodleian; Wellesley College Lib, Wellesley MA; Beinecke Rare Book and Ms Lib, Yale; Houghton Lib, Harvard; Girton College Lib, Cambridge.

Bibliographies

Dictionary of British women writers. Ed J. Todd 1989.

Collections

Mrs Jameson's works. 10 vols Boston 1866.
Jameson's works. 10 vols Boston 1885, 1899–1911.

§1

A first or mother's dictionary for children: containing upwards of 3,800 words. [1825?]

The diary of an ennuyée. First issued anonymously as A lady's diary. 1826, 1826 (new edn), Philadelphia 1826, Boston 1833, New York 1834, Paris 1836 (in English) (Baudry's European Lib), 1838 (3rd edn), (numerous edns pbd Boston 1857–94), Boston and New York 1885, 1899.
REVIEWS: Monthly Rev 1 1826; NMM 18 1826; [Shelley, M.] Westminster Rev 6 1826.

The beauties of the court of King Charles the Second; a series of portraits, illuminating the diaries of Pepys, Evelyn, Clarendon, and other contemporary writers. With memoirs biographical and critical. (From 2nd edn pbd as Memoirs of the beauties of the court of King Charles the Second.) Partially serialised in NMM 16 and 17 1826 as The Windsor beauties and The Hampton Court beauties, [1827?], 1833, Philadelphia 1834, 2 vols London 1838 (2nd edn), 1851 (3rd edn), New York 1852, London 1859, 1861 (4th edn), 1872, 1881, Boston 1884.
REVIEWS: NMM 19 1827 and 33 1831; Blackwood's Mag 33 1833; The Times 16 Oct 1838; NMM 52 and 53 1838; Tait's Edinburgh Mag 5 1838.

The loves of the poets. (Sometimes titled Memoirs of the loves of the poets.) 2 vols 1829, 1831 (2nd edn), Boston and New York 1833, London 1837 (3rd edn as The romance of biography; or, memoirs of women loved and celebrated by poets), Philadelphia 1844, (numerous edns pbd Boston 1857–94), Boston and New York 1888, 1889, 1892, 1898, 1900, New York 1972.
REVIEWS: Blackwood's Mag 26 1829; Monthly Rev 120 1829; Spectator 2 1829; [Shelley, M.] Westminster Rev 11 1829; Literary Gazette 11 July 1829; Quart Rev 75 1844–5.

Memoirs of celebrated female sovereigns. 2 vols 1831, New York 1832 (Harper's Family Lib), London 1834 (2nd edn), (numerous edns pbd New York 1836–58), London 1840 (3rd edn), London and New York 1869, Philadelphia 1870 (as Lives of celebrated female sovereigns and illustrious women, ed M. E. Hewitt), New York 1900 (Criterion Lib), 1910 (as Memoirs of famous female sovereigns).
REVIEWS: GM 101 1831; NMM 33 1831; Spectator 4 1831; Literary Gazette 22 Oct 1831; [Jewsbury, J.] Athenaeum 12 Nov 1831.

Characteristics of women, moral, poetical and historical. 2 vols 1832, New York 1832, Annapolis MD 1833, London 1833 (new edn), 1833 (2nd edn), Philadelphia 1833, London 1836 (3rd edn), New York 1837, London 1846 (4th edn), (numerous edns pbd Boston 1846–1900), New York 1847, 1848, 1850, 1854, London 1858 (new edn), London and New York 1870, Boston and New York 1885, London 1889 (Bohn's Standard Lib), 1893, London and New York 1893, Boston and New York 1898, 1899, 1911, New York 1967, 1971. As The heroines of Shakespeare, New York 1845, 1848. As Heroines of history, ed M. E. Hewitt, New York 1852, 1862. As Shakespeare's heroines: characteristics of women moral, poetical, and historical 1879, 1879 (new edn), 1886 (2nd edn), 1889, 1891, 1893, 1897, 1897 (New Lib), 1898, Philadelphia c. 1899, London 1900 with 26 portraits of famous players in character, London and New York 1901 illustr R. A. Bell (Miranda's Lib), London 1903 (Bohn's Standard Lib), 1905 (York Lib), London and New York 1905 illustr R. A. Bell (Miranda's Lib), New York 1905, London 1908, 1909 (York Lib), 1911 (Bohn's Standard Lib), 1913 (Bohn's Popular Lib), 1916 (Bohn's Standard Lib), 192–? (Burt's Home Lib), 1924 (Bohn's Popular Lib), 1930, New York 1967; tr Ger Leipzig 1834 as Frauenbilder: oden Charakteristik der vorzüglichsten frauen in Shakspeares dramen, Stuttgart 1840, Stuttgart 1843 as Shakspeare's weibliche charakters.
REVIEWS: Monthly Rev 128 1832; NMM 36 1832; Spectator 5 1832; Literary Gazette 28 July 1832; [Wilson, J.] Blackwood's Mag 33 1833; Edinburgh Rev 60 1834–5; Spectator 8 1835.

Visits and sketches at home and abroad, with tales and miscellanies now first collected, and a new edition of The diary of an ennuyée. (Subsequent edns dropped the diary.) 4 vols 1834, New York 1834, 3 vols London 1835 (2nd edn), Frankfurt 1837 (as Sketches of Germany: art, literature, character), 2 vols London 1839 (3rd edn). Numerous edns pbd as Sketches of art, literature and character, Boston 1857–1911.
REVIEWS: NMM 41 1834; Spectator 7 1834; Athenaeum 28 June, 12 and 26 July 1834; Westminster Rev 22 1835.

Winter studies and summer rambles in Canada. 3 vols 1838, New York 1839, 184–?, Toronto 1923 (introd by P. A. W. Wallace), ed J. J. Talman and E. McMurray 1943, 1965 (introd by C. Thomas, abridged), 1972, 1990 (New Canadian Lib). As Sketches in Canada and rambles among the redmen, London 1852 (new edn), 1856 (Traveller's Lib); tr Ger Braunschweig 1839.
REVIEWS: Metropolitan Mag 23 1838; Spectator 11 1838; Athenaeum 8 and 29 Dec 1838; [Chorley, H.] British and Foreign Rev 8 1839; GM 11 1839; [Johnstone, C. I.] Tait's Edinburgh Mag 6 1839; Monthly Rev 148 1839; Westminster Rev 35 1841; Eclectic Rev 4 1852; Tait's Edinburgh Mag 19 1852.

A handbook to the public galleries of art in and near London, with catalogues of the pictures, accompanied by critical, historical and biographical notices, and copious indexes to facilitate reference. 1842, 1845.
REVIEWS: Fraser's Mag 26 1842; GM 18 1842; Monthly Rev 157 1842; Spectator 15 1842; Athenaeum 12 Feb 1842; Art Union 1 Mar 1842; British & Foreign Quart Rev 14 1843.

Companion to the most celebrated private galleries of art in London; with a prefatory essay on art, artists, collectors and connoisseurs. 1844.
REVIEWS: Metropolitan Mag 40 1844; Spectator 17 1844; Athenaeum 27 July, 3 and 10 Aug 1844.

Memoirs of the early Italian painters, and of the progress of painting in Italy. From Cimabue to Bassano. Serialised in the Penny Mag Jan 1843–Aug 1845 as Essays on the lives of remarkable painters. 2 vols 1845, 1858 (new edn), 1859 (new edn), (numerous edns pbd Boston 1859–98), 1868 (new edn), 1874, 1880 (new edn), 1891 (new edn), Boston and New York 1894, [1911?]. Rev and in part rewritten by E. M. Hurll, Boston c. 1895, 1896, 1899; tr Fr Paris 1862 as La peinture et les peintres Italien.
REVIEWS: Westminster Rev 44 1845; [Darley, G.] Athenaeum 16 Aug 1845; North Amer Rev 87 1858; Saturday Rev 5 1858; Illus London News 10 Apr 1858; Art Jnl 22 1860; GM 8 1860.

Memoirs and essays illustrative of art, literature and social morals. 1846, New York 1846, London 1860 (new edn) (Bentley's Family ser), (numerous edns pbd as Studies, stories and memoirs, Boston 1859–93), Boston and New York 1911.
REVIEWS: [Fuller, M.] New York Tribune 1846 (rptd in Woman in the nineteenth century, and kindred papers 1874); Spectator 19 1846 and 33 1860; [Chorley, H.] Athenaeum 27 June 1846.

The relative position of mothers and governesses. 1848 (2nd edn). [Essay rptd from Memoirs and essays for the benefit of the Asylum for Aged Governesses.]

The poetry of sacred and legendary art. (From 3rd edn 'The poetry of' omitted from the title.) Serialised in Athenaeum 11 Jan 1845–21 Feb 1846 as Sacred and legendary art. 2 vols 1848, 1850 (2nd edn), 1857 (3rd edn), (numerous edns pbd Boston 1857–98), 1863 (4th edn), 1866 (5th edn), 1870 (6th edn), 1874 (7th edn), 1879 (8th edn), 1883 (9th edn), Boston and New York 1885, London 1888 (10th edn), 1890 (new edn), 1891 (new edn), Boston and New York 1898, vol 1 London 1900, 1905, vol 2 1911, London and New York 1905, Boston and New York 1911, London and New York 1911, 1911 (new impression), New York 1970. Ed with additional notes E. M. Hurll, Boston and New York 1895, London 1896, 1897, 1899, 1900, 1904, St Clair Shores MI 1972; tr Polish Wilno Poland 1848 as Ziota legenda Artystów (extracts from Sacred and legendary art).
REVIEWS: Art Union 10 1848; Spectator 21 1848; [Hart, S. A.] Athenaeum 30 Dec 1848; Blackwood's Mag 65 1849; British Quart Rev 10 1849; Edinburgh Rev 89 1849; [Kingsley, C.] Fraser's Mag 39 1849 (rptd in Works vol 20 1880); GM 31 1849; Blackwood's Mag 78 1855.

Legends of the monastic orders as represented in the fine arts, forming the second series of Sacred and legendary art. 1850, 1852 (2nd edn), 1862, 1863 (3rd edn), (numerous edns pbd Boston 1865–92), 1867 (4th edn), 1872 (5th edn), 1880 (6th edn), 1888 (7th edn), 1890 (new edn), 1891, Boston and New York 1894, 1898, London 1900, London and New York 1905, Boston and New York 1911. Ed with additional notes E. M. Hurll, Boston and New York 1896, 1898, 1901.
REVIEWS: Art Jnl 12 1850; Br Quart Rev 12 1850; GM 34 1850; Spectator 23 1850; Blackwood's Mag 69 1851; Dublin Rev 30 1851.

Legends of the Madonna as represented in the fine arts: forming the third series of Sacred and legendary art. 1852, (numerous edns pbd Boston 1853–1906), 1857 (2nd edn), 1864 (3rd edn), [1866?], 1867 (4th edn), 1872 (5th edn), 1873, 1879 (6th edn), 1885 (7th edn), 1890 (new edn), Boston and New York 1891, 1892, 1897, London 1899 (new impression), 1902 (new impression), 1903 (Unit Lib), 1907, 1909, Boston and New York [1911?], Detroit 1972. Ed with additional notes by E. M. Hurll, Boston and New York 1895, 1896, 1897, 1898.
REVIEWS: Spectator 25 1852; Art Jnl 5 1853; Blackwood's Mag 74 1853; Dublin Rev 34 1853; Edinburgh Rev 97 1853; GM 39 1853.

A commonplace book of thoughts, memories and fancies, original and selected. 1854, New York 1855, London 1855 (2nd edn), New York 1856, 1877 (new edn).
REVIEWS: Leader 5 1854; Spectator 27 1854; [Chorley, H.] Athenaeum 18 Nov 1854; Literary Gazette 30 Dec 1854; Art Jnl 1 1855; GM 43 1855; NMM 103 1855; Littell's Living Age 44 1855 (rptd from NMM).

A handbook to the courts of modern sculpture. (No 12 of a ser of pams bound together in a book titled Guide to the Crystal Palace and park, ed S. Phillips, illustr P. H. Delamotte, 1854). 1854.
REVIEWS: The Times 15 June 1854; Literary Gazette 9 Sep 1854; Art Jnl 1 1855.

Sisters of charity, Catholic and Protestant, abroad and at home. 1855, 1855 (2nd edn enlarged), Boston 1857, London 1859 (pbd with The communion of labour and a letter to Lord John Russell), Westport CT 1976.
REVIEWS: Br Quart Rev 22 1855; Dublin Rev 38 1855; Spectator 28 1855; [Jewsbury, G.] Athenaeum 7 Apr 1855; Literary Gazette 15 Sep 1855; Quart Rev 108 1860.

The communion of labour: a second lecture on the social employments of women. 1856, 1859 (pbd with Sisters of charity and a letter to Lord John Russell), Westport CT 1976.
REVIEWS: Literary Gazette 13 Sep 1856; [St John, H.] Athenaeum 20 Sep 1856; Br Quart Rev 25 1857; Dublin Rev 42 1857; Westminster Rev 67 1857.

The history of our Lord as exemplified in works of art: with that of His types; St John the Baptist; and other persons of the Old and New Testament. Commenced by Anna Jameson, completed by Elizabeth, Lady Eastlake (née Rigby). 2 vols 1864, 1865 (2nd edn), 1872 (3rd edn), 1881 (4th edn), 1888, 1890 (new edn), New York 1890, 1892 (new edn), Detroit 1976.
REVIEWS: Art Jnl 3 1864; Blackwood's Mag 96 1864; Dublin Rev 3 1864; Edinburgh Rev 120 1864; GM 17 1864; London Quart Rev 23 1864–5; Quart Rev 116 1864; Spectator 37 1864; Athenaeum 14 May 1864; The Times 19 May 1864.

Contributions to periodicals

Farewell to Italy. London Mag 6 1822.

Halloran the pedlar. Bijou Annual 1828.

Much coin, much care. Christmas Box Annual 1828.

Althorpe (no 1 pbd only). NMM 25 1829.

Mrs Siddons, NMM 32 1831.

The exhibition of the Royal Academy. English art and artists, Monthly Chron 1 1838.

On Albert Durer, and the modern German and English schools of painting. Monthly Chron 3 1839.

Sculpture in England. Monthly Chron 3 1839.

Court of the Commissioners on the employment of Children etc; with appendices etc. Condition of the women and the female children. Athenaeum 18 Mar 1843. (Pt 3. Pts 1 and 2 written by others appear on 4 and 11 Mar 1843.)

Washington Allston. Athenaeum 6 and 13 Jan 1844.

The Spanish school of painting. Athenaeum 13 Apr 1844.

The Dutch landscape painters. Athenaeum 27 Apr 1844.

The Xanthian marbles. Athenaeum 24 Aug 1844.

Some thoughts on art, addressed to the uninitiated parts I and II. Art Jnl 2 1849.

John Gibson. Art Jnl 2 1849.

Review of Specimens of ornamental art, in eighty plates by Lewis Gruner. Art Jnl 12 1850.

The Nuremberg Madonnas, Art Jnl 14 1852.

Review of Life of Benjamin Robert Haydon, historical painter, with his autobiography and journals by Tom Taylor. Edinburgh Rev 98 1853.

Letters

Anna Jameson: letters and friendships (1812–1860). Ed Mrs Steuart Erskine 1915.

Letters of Anna Jameson to Ottilie Von Goethe. Ed G. H. Needler 1939.

Boyce, G. K. From Paris to Pisa with the Brownings. New Colophon 3 1950.

Translations, introductions, prefaces

Fantasien. Fancies; a series of subjects in outline, now first published from the original plates, designed and etched by Moritz Retzsch. Introd by Jameson 1834.

Collection of pictures of W. G. Coesvelt Esq., of London. Introd by Jameson 1836.
REVIEW: Literary Gazette 21 May 1836.

Social life in Germany illustrated in the acted dramas of Her Royal Highness the Princess Amelia of Saxony. Tr from the Ger with introd and notes by Jameson 2 vols 1840.
REVIEWS: Metropolitan Mag 27 1840; Monthly Rev 151 1840; Spectator 13 1840; Westminster Rev 34 1840; Athenaeum 15 Feb 1840; North Amer Rev 52 1841.

Peter Paul Rubens, his life and genius. Tr from the Ger of Dr Waagen by R. R. Noel, ed Jameson 1840.
REVIEWS: Edinburgh Rev 72 1840; Literary World 3 1840; Monthly Rev 152 1840; Spectator 13 1840; Tait's Edinburgh Mag 7 1840; [Cunningham, A.] Athenaeum 2 May 1840; GM 17 1842.

The decorations of the garden-pavilion in the grounds of Buckingham Palace. Engraved under the superintendence of L. Gruner. Introd by Jameson 1846.

REVIEWS: The Times 20 Jan 1846; Illus London News 21 Feb and 7 Mar 1846.

Spurious works

Sketches on the road, a series appearing in London Magazine 5 and 6 1822 once attributed to Jameson but now thought to be by Charles Macfarlane. *See* Index to the London Mag, ed F. P. Riga and C. A. Prance, 1978.

Cadijah; or The black palace. A tragedy. 1825.

§2

Horne, R. H. In his A new spirit of the age vol 2, 1844.

Literary leaflets by Sir Nathanial. No 14 – Mrs Jameson. NMM 99 1853.

Macpherson, G. Memoirs of the life of Anna Jameson, with a postscript by Margaret Oliphant. 1878.

Two ladies [Anna Jameson and Fanny Kemble]. Blackwood's Mag Feb 1879.

Hamilton, C. J. In her Women writers vol 2, 1893.

Thomas, C. Love and work enough. The life of Anna Jameson. Toronto 1967. [JJ]

Francis, Lord Jeffrey 1773–1850

Selections

Morgan P. (ed). Jeffrey's criticism: a selection. 1983.

§1

Observations on Mr Thelwall's letter to the editor of the Edinburgh Review. 1804.

Wordsworth's Poems. Edinburgh Rev 11 1807.

A summary view of the rights and claims of the Roman Catholics of Ireland. Edinburgh 1808. Rptd from Edinburgh Rev 11 1807.

Byron's Childe Harold. Edinburgh Rev 19 1812; Scott's Waverley, 24 1814; Byron's poetry, 27 1816; Keats's Poems, 34 1820; Byron's tragedies, 36 1822.

Essay on beauty. Rptd from Edinburgh Rev with addns in Encyclopaedia Britannica supplement, 1824, 1841; rptd in Contributions to the Edinburgh Rev vol 1, 1844.

Combinations of workmen: a speech. Edinburgh 1825.

Corrected report of the speech of the Lord Advocate of Scotland upon the motion of Lord John Russell, in the House of Commons, for reform of Parliament. 1831.

Eulogium of James Watt. 1839. Rptd from Encyclopaedia Britannica and included in the Life of Watt by D. F. J. Arago, 1839.

Two inaugural addresses and a parting address delivered at Glasgow University. First 3 addresses in Inaugural addresses by Lords Rectors of the University of Glasgow, ed J. B. Hay, Glasgow 1839.

Contributions to the Edinburgh Review. 4 vols 1844, 3 vols 1846, Philadelphia 1848, 1 vol 1853.

Samuel Richardson. 1852. Pam.

Jonathan Swift. 1853. Pam.

Peter and his enemies. Edinburgh 1859 (2nd edn). A story exposing abuses in the law.

Jeffrey's literary criticism. Ed D. N. Smith 1910. With list of Jeffrey's articles in Edinburgh Rev.

Contemporary reviews of romantic poetry. Ed J. Wain 1953.

For a full list of Jeffrey's contributions to Edinburgh Rev, *see* Wellesley *vol 5 1989.*

Letters

The letters of Jeffrey to Ugo Foscolo. Ed J. Purves, Edinburgh 1934.

Albrecht, W. P. A letter by Jeffrey. N & Q 5 Mar 1958.

Brand, C. P. Ugo Foscolo and the Edinburgh Review: unpublished letters to Francis Jeffrey. MLR 70 1975.

Portsch, S. R. The odd man out: an unpublished letter from Jeffrey to Malthus. Victorian Periodicals Newsletter 11 1978.

Coleman, D. Jeffrey and Coleridge: four unpublished letters. TWC 18 1987.

§2

Cockburn, H. T. Life of Jeffrey; with a selection from his correspondence. 2 vols Edinburgh 1852, 1852, 1872 (Works of Cockburn, vol 1). With list of Jeffrey's articles in Edinburgh Rev.

Gilfillan, G. In his Galleries of literary portraits vol 2, Edinburgh 1856.

Carlyle, T. In his Reminiscences, ed J. A. Froude 2 vols 1881.

Taylor, James. Jeffrey and Craigcrook. Edinburgh 1892. With a sketch of Jeffrey's character and Craigcrook life by Moncreif.

Gates, L. E. In his Three studies in literature, New York 1899.

Elsner, R. Jeffrey und seine kritischen Prinzipien. Berlin [1908].

Hughes, M. Y. The humanism of Jeffrey. MLR 16 1921.

Beatty, J. M. Jeffrey and Wordsworth. PMLA 38 1923.

Bald, R. C. Jeffrey as a literary critic. Nineteenth Cent Feb 1925.

Charvat, W. Jeffrey in America. New Eng Quart 14 1941.

Goldberg, M. H. Jeffrey: mutilator of Carlyle's Burns. PMLA 56 1941.

Noyes, R. Wordsworth and Jeffrey in controversy. Bloomington IN 1941.

Daniel, R. Jeffrey and Wordsworth: the shape of persecution. Sewanee Rev 50 1942.

Derby, R. The paradox of Jeffrey: reason versus sensibility. MLQ 7 1946.

Goldberg, M. H. Carlyle, Pictet and Jeffrey. MLQ 7 1946.

Greig, J. A. Jeffrey of the Edinburgh Review. 1948.

Guyer, B. Jeffrey's Essay on beauty. HLQ 13 1950.

Guyer, B. The philosophy of Jeffrey. MLQ 11 1950.

Schneider, E. The unknown reviewer of Christabel: Jeffrey, Hazlitt, Tom Moore. PMLA 70 1955.

Clive, J. Scotch reviewers: the Edinburgh Review 1802–15. Cambridge MA 1957.

Dwyer, J. T. Check list of primary sources of the Byron–Jeffrey relationship. N & Q 205 1960.

Thomson, D. C. Jeffrey: Charles Dickens' friend and critic. REL 2 1961.

Erdman, D. V. and P. M. Zall. Coleridge and Jeffrey in controversy. SiR 14 1975.

Cook, P. A. Chronology of the 'Lake School' argument: some revisions. RES 28 1977.

Flynn, P. Francis Jeffrey. Newark DE 1977.

Bell, A. (ed). Lord Cockburn: a bicentenary commemoration 1779–1979. Edinburgh 1979.

Morgan, P. Francis Jeffrey as epistolary critic. Stud in Scottish Lit 17 1982.

Pitre, D. W. Francis Jeffrey and religion: excerpts from his 1799–1800 commonplace book. Eighteenth-Century Life 8, Oct 1982.

Shattock, J. Politics and reviewers: the Edinburgh and the Quarterly in the early Victorian age. Leicester 1989.

Christie, W. H. Francis Jeffrey's Associationist aesthetics. British Jnl of Aesthetics 33, July 1993.

Charles Lamb 1775–1834

For the location of Lamb's mss, see IELM IV pt 2 1990.

§1

Bibliographies of primary material

North, E. D. In B. E. Martin, In the footprints of Lamb, 1891.

Dodd, Mead and Co. Descriptions of a few books from Lamb's library, and of some presentation copies and first editions of his rarer books. New York [1899]. A sale catalogue.

Livingston, L. S. Some notes on three of Lamb's juveniles. Bibliographer 1 1902.

Livingston, L. S. A bibliography of the first editions in book form of

the writings of C. and Mary Lamb, published prior to C. Lamb's death in 1834. New York 1903.
Hutchinson, T. In his Works in prose and verse of C. and Mary Lamb vol 1, Oxford [1908].
Thomson, J. C. Bibliography of the writings of C. and Mary Lamb. Hull 1908.
American Art Association. The literary treasures of W. T. Wallace. New York 1920. A sale catalogue, nos 755–804.
Wise, T. J. In his Ashley library: a catalogue vol 3, 1923. Describes more than 40 Lamb items.
Tregaskis, J. An important collection of some of the rarer works of Lamb, together with some 'Lambiana'. 1927. A bookseller's catalogue with facs.
Griffith, R. H. Lamb: an exhibition of books and manuscripts in the library of the University of Texas. Austin 1935.
Finch, J. S. The Scribner Lamb collection. Princeton Univ Lib Chron 7 1946.
Woodring, C. R. Lamb in the Harvard library. Harvard Lib Bull 10 1956.
Barnett, G. L. and S. M. Tave. In English romantic poets and essayists: a review of research and criticism, ed C. W. and L. H. Houtchens, New York 1957, 1966 (rev).
Woodring, C. R. Lamb's hoaxes and the Lamb canon. Charles Lamb Bull n.s. 2, Apr/July 1975.
Wilson, D. G. Chronological list of editions of Tales from Shakespear. Charles Lamb Bull n.s. 7, Jan 1985.

Collections

Works [with 6 poems by Mary Lamb]. 2 vols 1818.
REVIEWS: [Wilson, J.] Blackwood's Mag 3 Aug 1818; Br Critic 11, Feb 1819; [Hunt, L.] Examiner 586, 21–8 Mar 1819; European Mag Apr 1819; [Talfourd, T. N.] Champion 16 May 1819; [Dyer, G.] GM 89, July and Aug 1819; Literary Gazette 14 Aug 1819; Monthly Rev 90, Nov 1819. [Hunt, L.] Indicator 31 Jan–7 Feb 1821.
Poetical works of Rogers, Lamb [et al]. Paris 1829. Unauthorised.
Prose works. 3 vols 1835.
Poetical works [with 6 poems by Mary Lamb]. 1836, 1848.
Works. [Ed T. N. Talfourd] 1840 (includes Letters with a sketch of his life), 2 vols New York 1852, 4 vols London 1855 (vols 1–2 new edns of Letters and Final memorials), 1859, 1 vol 1865.
Complete correspondence and works. Vol 1 (no more pbd) 1868. Introd by G. A. Sala.
Complete correspondence and works. Ed T. Purnell 4 vols 1870. Vol 1 re-issue of incomplete 1868 edn.
Complete works in prose and verse. Ed R. H. Shepherd '1875' [1874].
Life, letters and writings. Ed P. Fitzgerald 6 vols 1876, Edinburgh 6 vols 1882–4, London 1895 (Temple edn).
Works. Ed C. Kent [1876], Routledge's Popular Lib 1889.
Life and works. Ed A. Ainger 7 vols 1883–8, 12 vols 1899–1900.
Works. Ed E. V. Lucas 7 vols 1903–5, 6 vols 1912. Includes rev edn of Letters in 2 vols but omits Dramatic specimens.
Works. Ed W. Macdonald 12 vols 1903.
Works. Ed T. Hutchinson 2 vols Oxford [1908] (OSA).

Selections

The dramatic essays of Lamb. Ed J. B. Matthews 1891.
The best of Lamb. Ed E. V. Lucas 1914.
Lamb: prose and poetry. Ed G. S. Gordon, Oxford 1921.
Lamb's criticism: a selection. Ed E. M. W. Tillyard, Cambridge 1923.
The Elian miscellany: a Charles Lamb anthology. Ed S. M. Rich 1931.
Everybody's Lamb. Ed A. C. Ward 1933.
Essays and letters. Ed J. M. French, New York 1937.
Selections from Lamb and Hazlitt. Ed R. W. Jepson 1940.
The portable Lamb. Ed J. M. Brown, New York 1949, London 1964 (Pen).
Lamb and Elia. Ed J. E. Morpurgo 1949 (Pen), Manchester 1993.
Selected essays, letters, poems. Ed J. L. May 1953.
Essays. Ed R. Vallance and J. Hampden 1963 (Folio Soc).
A Lamb selection. Ed F. B. Pinion 1965.
Lamb on Shakespeare. Ed J. Coldwell 1978.
Lamb as critic. Ed R. Park 1980.
Selected prose. Ed A. Phillips 1985 (Pen).

§1

Blank verse by Charles Lloyd and Charles Lamb. 1798. With 7 poems by Lamb, including The old familiar faces.
REVIEWS: Analytical Rev 1, May 1798; Br Critic 9, June 1798; Monthly Mag 6, July 1798.
A tale of Rosamund Gray and old blind Margaret. Birmingham 1798, London 1798, 1835 (with Recollections of Christ's Hospital); ed R. B. Johnson 1928 (Golden Cockerel Press), Oxford 1991 (facs of London 1798 edn).
REVIEWS: Analytical Rev 1, Feb 1799; Monthly Rev 138, Sep 1835.
John Woodvil: a tragedy; to which are added Fragments of Burton [with 1 poem by Mary Lamb]. 1802.
REVIEWS: Annual Rev 1, Jan 1803; [Brown, T.] Edinburgh Rev 2, Apr 1803; [Ferrier, J.] Monthly Rev 40, Apr 1803; Retrospective Rev 1, 1820.
The king and queen of hearts. 1805 (anon), 1806, 1808, 1809; ed E. V. Lucas 1902 (facs of 1806 edn). *See* Tregaskis catalogue, *above*.
Tales from Shakespear, designed for the use of young persons. 2 vols 1807 (14 of the tales were by Mary Lamb; only the 6 tragedies were by Charles Lamb), 1809, 1810, Philadelphia 1813 (unauthorised), London 1816, 1822, 1 vol 1831; ed F. J. Furnivall 2 vols 1901; 1906 (EL); ed G. Tillotson 1962 (EL); ed J. C. Trewin 1964 (Nonesuch Lib); 1987 (Pen). Some of the tales were issued separately as well as in pairs, triads and quartets. Mary Lamb's name first appeared on the title page in 1838 (6th edn); tr Ger 1842, 1843, Fr 1847, 1884, Sp 1847, 1893, Swed 1851, 1947; Polish 1893, 1947, Jap 1923, Ital 1929, Chinese 1953, Serbo-Croat 1959.
REVIEWS: Critical Rev 11, May 1807; Portfolio (Dennie's, Philadelphia) 10, 1813; Spectator 58, 5 Dec 1885.
Adventures of Ulysses. 1808, 1819, 1827; ed A. Lang 1890; ed J. Cooke 1892; ed E. A. Gardner, Cambridge 1921; Edinburgh 1992 (facs of 1892 edn).
Specimens of English dramatic poets who lived about the time of Shakespeare, with notes. 1808, 1813, 2 vols 1835 (with Extracts from the Garrick plays), 1 vol 1854; ed I. Gollancz 2 vols 1893; ed J. D. Campbell 1907.
REVIEWS: Annual Rev 7, 1808; Monthly Rev 58, Apr 1809; Critical Rev May 1810; [Dilke, C. W.] Athenaeum 8, Aug 1835; GM n.s. 4, Sep 1835.
Mrs Leicester's school: or the history of several young ladies, related by themselves. 1809 (anon) (7 of the stories were by Mary Lamb; only The witch aunt, First time of going to church, and The sea voyage, were by Charles Lamb), 1809 (preface signed by Charles and Mary Lamb), 1810, Georgetown DC 1811, London 1814, 1828 (10th edn); ed A. Ainger 1885; 1899 (Dent); Woodstock 1995 (facs of 2nd edn 1809); tr Fr 1923. *See* Woodring bibliography, *above*.
Poetry for children, entirely original, by the author of Mrs Leicester's school. 2 vols 1809 (anon) (about two-thirds of the poems were by Mary Lamb: poems known to be Charles Lamb's are Chusing a name, To a river in which a child was drowned, The three friends, and Queen Oriana's dream), 1 vol Boston 1812, New Haven CT 1820; ed R. H. Shepherd, London 1872; New York 1878; ed A. W. T[uer] 2 vols London 1892 (facs of 1809 edn); 1898 (Dent).
Prince Dorus, or flattery put out of countenance: a poetical version of an ancient tale. 1811 (anon), 1818; ed A. W. T[uer] 1889 (facs of 1811 edn); ed J. P. Briscoe, Nottingham 1896 (facs of 1811 edn).
Mr H: or beware a bad name. Philadelphia 1813 (anon), and 1825. Farce.
Elia: essays which have appeared under that signature in the

London Magazine. 1823 (anon), ed O. C. Williams, Oxford 1911, 1991 (facs of 1823 edn).
REVIEWS: Monthly Mag 55, Feb 1823; Monthly Rev 101, June 1823; Br Critic 20, July 1823; [Wilson, J.] Blackwood's Mag Oct 1823.
Elia: second series. Philadelphia 1828 (anon). Unauthorised (with 3 spurious pieces and 4 from Works 1818).
Album verses. 1830.
REVIEWS: [Jerdan, W.] Literary Gazette 10 July 1830; Br Mag Aug 1830; Monthly Rev Aug 1830.
Satan in search of a wife, with the whole process of his courtship and marriage, and who danced at the wedding. By an eyewitness. 1831 (anon).
The last essays of Elia: being a sequel to essays published under that name. 1833 (anon); ed F. Page, Oxford 1929 (introd by E. Blunden).
REVIEWS: [Jerdan, W.] Literary Gazette 2 Mar 1833; [Coleridge, H. N.] Quart Rev 54, July 1835.
Elia. 2 vols 1835. Ed E. Moxon (first collected edn of both series) 1849, 1853; ed N. L. Hallward and S. C. Hill 2 vols 1895–1900; 1901 (WC); 1906 (EL); ed A. H. Thompson 2 vols Cambridge 1913; ed W. Macdonald 2 vols London 1929; 2 vols Newtown 1929–30 (Gregynog Press); ed M. Elwin 1952; ed J. Bate 1987 (WC).
REVIEW: Methodist Rev 69, 1887.
Essays of Elia [both ser]; to which are added Letters, and Rosamund: a tale. Paris 1835. Unauthorised.
Recollections of Christ's Hospital. 1835 (with Rosamund Gray and other pieces).
Eliana: being the hitherto uncollected writings. [Ed J. E. Babson] 1864.
Mary and C. Lamb: poems, letters and remains. Ed W. C. Hazlitt 1874.
Table talk; or original essays. By William Hazlitt. 1821. Unpbd review. In Lamb as critic, ed R. Park, 1980.

Contributions to periodicals

To Mrs Siddons. Signed S. T. C. Morning Chron 29 Dec 1794. Rptd signed C. L. in Coleridge's Poems on various subjects, 1796, and Poems, 1797.
Sonnet [We were two pretty babes]. Monthly Mag 1, July 1796. Rptd in Coleridge, Sonnets from various authors, 1796, and Works, 1818.
To the poet Cowper. Monthly Mag Dec 1796. Poem.
Lines, addressed from London .... Monthly Mag Jan 1797.
To a young lady. Monthly Mag Mar 1797. Poem.
Sonnet to a friend. Monthly Mag Oct 1797.
To a friend. Monthly Mag Oct 1797. Rptd as To Charles Lloyd in Blank verse 1798. Poem.
Sonnet [The lord of life shakes off his drowsihead]. Monthly Mag Dec 1797.
Living without God in the world. Annual Anthology Sep 1799. Poem.
From an unpublished drama. Recreations in Agriculture, Natural History, Arts and Miscellaneous History Nov 1800. Rptd in John Woodvil 1802.
To Sir James Mackintosh. The Albion July 1801. Poem.
G. F. Cooke in Richard the Third. Anon. Morning Post 4 Jan 1802.
Grand state bed. Anon. Morning Post 4 Jan 1802.
Dick Strype. Anon. Morning Post 6 Jan 1802. Poem.
Fable for twelfth day. Anon. Morning Post 6 Jan 1802.
Twelfth-night characters. Morning Post 8 Jan 1802. Poem.
The Londoner. Anon. Morning Post 1 Feb 1802. Rptd with changes in Works 1818.
Epitaph on a young lady .... Morning Post 7 Feb 1804.
On the ambiguities arising from proper names. Anon. The Reflector no 2 1811.
On the danger of confounding moral with personal deformity. Anon. The Reflector no 2 1811. Rptd in Works 1818.
On the inconveniences resulting from being hanged. Anon. The Reflector no 2 1811. Rptd in Works 1818.
On the probable effects of the gunpowder treason .... Signed 'Speculator'. The Reflector no 2 1811. Rptd with addns as 'Guy Faux', signed 'Elia', in London Mag Nov 1823.
Memoir of Robert Lloyd. Anon. GM Nov 1811.
The triumph of the whale. The Examiner 15 Mar 1812. Poem.
Two epigrams. The Examiner 22 Mar 1812.
On burial societies; and the character of an undertaker. Anon. The Reflector no 3 1812. Rptd in Works 1818.
On the custom of hissing at the theatres. Anon. The Reflector no 3 1812.
On the genius and character of Hogarth. Anon. The Reflector no 3 1812. Rptd in Works 1818.
A bachelor's complaint of the behaviour of married people. Signed Innuptus. The Reflector no 4 1812. Rptd in London Mag Sep 1812 signed Elia, and in Elia 1823.
Edax on appetite. Anon. The Reflector no 4 1812. Rptd in Works 1818.
A farewell to tobacco. The Reflector no 4 1812. Rptd in Works 1818. Poem.
The good clerk, a character. Signed L. B. The Reflector no 4 1812.
Hospita on the immoderate indulgence of the pleasures of the palate. Anon. The Reflector no 4 1812. Rptd in Works 1818.
Specimens from the writings of Fuller. Anon. The Reflector no 4 1812. Rptd in Works 1818.
Theatralia, No 1. On Garrick and acting; and the plays of Shakespeare, considered with reference to their fitness for stage-representation. Anon. The Reflector no 4 1812. Rptd as On the tragedies of Shakspeare in Works 1818.
On Christ's Hospital and the character of the Christ's Hospital boys. Anon. GM June 1813. Rptd minus introductory paragraphs as Recollections of Christ's Hospital in Works 1818.
Table talk. The Examiner 6 June, 18 July (2 entries), 12 Sep (4 entries), 26 Sep (2 entries), 19 Dec 1813. 5 of the pieces were rptd in The Indicator 13 Dec 1820–3 Jan 1821.
Confessions of a drunkard. Anon. The Philanthropist 3, Sep 1813. Rptd in Some enquiries into the effects of fermented liquors, by a water drinker 1814; and with introductory note and emendments in London Mag Aug 1822; and in Last essays of Elia, 1835 (2nd edn).
Wordsworth's excursion. Quart Rev Oct 1814.
On the melancholy of tailors. Signed Burton Junior. The Champion 4 Dec 1814. Rptd in Works 1818.
To T. L. H. The Examiner 1 Jan 1815. Poem.
Mrs Gould (Miss Burrell) in 'Don Giovanni in London'. Anon. The Examiner 12 Nov 1818.
Miss Kelly at Bath. Anon. Felix Farley's Bristol Jnl 30 Jan 1819. Rptd in The Examiner 7 and 8 Feb 1819.
St Valentine's day. Anon. The Examiner 14 and 15 Feb 1819. Rptd in The Indicator 14 Feb 1821 and in Elia 1823.
Sonnet. The Examiner 20 and 21 June 1819. Rptd as Work in Album verses 1830.
Richard Brome's 'Jovial crew'. Anon. The Examiner 4 and 5 July 1819.
Isaac Bickerstaff's Hypocrite. Anon. The Examiner 1 and 2 Aug 1819.
New pieces at the Lyceum. Anon. The Examiner 8 and 9 Aug 1819.
Written at Cambridge. The Examiner 29 and 30 Aug 1819. Rptd in Album verses 1830. Poem.
Falstaff's letters [review of Original letters of Sir John Falstaff ...]. Anon. The Examiner 5 and 6 Sep 1819. Rptd in The Indicator 24 Jan 1821.
St Crispin to Mr Gifford. The Examiner 3 and 4 Oct 1819. Poem.
Review of Charles Lloyd's poems. Anon. The Examiner 24 and 25 Oct 1819.

[On the acting of Munden.] The Examiner 7 and 8 Nov 1819. Rptd with some changes as The old actors in London Mag Oct 1822 and as On the acting of Munden in Elia 1823.
On a celebrated female performer in the 'Blind Boy'. Morning Chron 10 Nov 1819. Rptd as Sonnet to Miss Kelly... in Table Bk 1827, and in Album verses 1830. Poem.
First fruits of Australian poetry. Anon. The Examiner 16 and 17 Jan 1820.
The godlike. The Champion 18 and 19 Mar 1820. Poem.
Sonnet to Mathew Wood, esq. The Champion 13 and 14 May 1820.
In Tabulam Eximii.... The Champion 6 and 7 May 1820. Latin poem and trn.
The three graves. Signed Dante. The Champion 13 and 14 May 1820. Rptd in London Mag May 1825. Poem.
On a late empiric of 'balmy' morning. The Champion 15 and 16 June 1820. Poem.
Sonnet to Miss Burney. Morning Chron 13 July 1820.
On a projected journey. The Champion 15 and 16 July 1820. Poem.
Song for the C—n. The Champion 15 and 16 July 1820.
Keats's 'Lamia'. Anon. The New Times 19 July 1820.
The South-Sea House. London Mag Aug 1820. Rptd in Elia 1823.
To the author of poems, published under the name of Barry Cornwall. London Mag Sep 1820. Rptd in Album verses 1830. Poem.
To R. S. Knowles, esq.... London Mag Sep 1820. Rptd in Album verses 1830. Poem.
The unbeloved. The Champion 23 and 24 Sep 1820. Poem.
To my friend the Indicator. The Indicator 27 Sep 1820. Poem.
The ape. London Mag Oct 1820. Poem.
Oxford in the vacation. London Mag Oct 1820. Rptd in Elia 1823.
Christ's Hospital five and thirty years ago. London Mag Nov 1820. Rptd in Elia 1823.
The two races of men. London Mag Dec 1820. Rptd in Elia 1823.
Sir Thomas More. Anon. The Indicator 20 Dec 1820.
New Year's Eve. London Mag Jan 1821. Rptd in Elia 1823.
Mrs Battle's opinions on whist. London Mag Feb 1821. Rptd in Elia 1823.
A chapter on ears. London Mag Mar 1821. Rptd with changes in Elia 1823.
All Fool's Day. London Mag Apr 1821. Rptd in Elia 1823.
The confessions of H. F. V. H. Delamore, esq. Anon. London Mag Apr 1821.
A Quaker's meeting. London Mag Apr 1821. Rptd in Elia 1823.
They talk of time.... London Mag Apr 1821. Rptd as Leisure in Album verses 1830. Poem.
The old and the new schoolmaster. London Mag May 1821. Rptd in Elia 1823.
My relations. London Mag June 1821. Rptd in Elia 1823.
Mackery End, in Hertfordshire. London Mag July 1821. Rptd in Elia 1823.
Jews, Quakers, Scotchmen, and other imperfect sympathies. London Mag Aug 1821. Rptd as Imperfect sympathies in Elia 1823.
The old benchers of the Inner Temple. London Mag Sep 1821. Rptd in Elia 1823.
Witches, and other night-fears. London Mag Oct 1821. Rptd in Elia 1823.
Grace before meat. London Mag Nov 1821. Rptd in Elia 1823.
My first play. London Mag Dec 1821. Rptd in Elia 1823.
Dream-children; a reverie. London Mag Jan 1822. Rptd in Elia 1823.
On some of the old actors. London Mag Feb 1822. Rptd with addns and omissions in Elia 1823.
Distant correspondents. London Mag Mar 1822. Rptd in Elia 1823.
The old actors. London Mag Apr 1822. Rptd without final pages as On the artificial comedy of the last century in Elia 1823.
The praise of chimney-sweepers: a May-day effusion. London Mag May 1822. Rptd without sub-title in Elia 1823.
A complaint of the decay of beggars in the metropolis. London Mag June 1822. Rptd in Elia 1823.
Detached thoughts on books and reading. London Mag July 1822. Rptd in Last essays of Elia 1833.
A dissertation upon roast pig. London Mag Sep 1822. Rptd in Elia 1823.
Modern gallantry. London Mag Nov 1822. Rptd in Elia 1823.
The gentle giantess. Signed 'Elia'. London Mag Dec 1822.
A character of the late Elia. By a friend. London Mag Jan 1823. Rptd as Preface in Last essays of Elia 1833.
Rejoicings upon the New Year's coming of age. Signed Elia's ghost. London Mag Jan 1823. Rptd in Last essays of Elia 1833.
Old china. London Mag Mar 1823. Rptd in Last essays of Elia 1833.
Ritson versus John Scott, the Quaker. Signed Elia. London Mag Apr 1823.
Poor relations. London Mag May 1823. Rptd in Last essays of Elia 1833.
The child angel: a dream. London Mag June 1823. Rptd in Last essays of Elia 1833.
The old Margate Hoy. London Mag July 1823. Rptd in Last essays of Elia 1833.
Nugae criticae. By the author of Elia. No I. Defence of the sonnets of Sir Philip Sidney. London Mag Sep 1823. Rptd as Some sonnets of Sir Philip Sidney in Last essays of Elia 1833.
Letter of Elia to Robert Southey. London Mag Oct 1823. Last few pages only rptd as The tombs in the abbey in Last essays of Elia 1833.
Nugae criticae. By the author of Elia. No II. On a passage in 'The Tempest'. London Mag Nov 1823.
Amicus redivivius. London Mag Dec 1823. Rptd in Last essays of Elia 1833.
Blakesmoor in H—shire. London Mag Sep 1824. Rptd in Last essays of Elia 1833.
Captain Jackson. London Mag Nov 1824. Rptd in Last essays of Elia 1833.
Biographical memoir of Mr Liston. Anon. London Mag Jan 1825.
The illustrious defunct. Anon. NMM Jan 1825.
Letter to an old gentleman whose education has been neglected. Signed 'Elia'. London Mag Jan 1825.
A vision of horns. Signed Elia. London Mag Jan 1825.
Many friends. Signed Lepus. New Times 8 Jan 1825.
Readers against the grain. Signed Lepus. New Times 13 Jan 1825.
Mortifications of an author. Signed Lepus. New Times 31 Jan 1825.
Autobiography of Mr Munden. Signed Joseph Munden. London Mag Feb 1825.
Unitarian protests. Signed Elia. London Mag Feb 1825.
Tom Pry. Signed Lepus. New Times 8 Feb 1825.
Tom Pry's wife. Signed Lepus. New Times 28 Feb 1825.
Reflections in the pillory. Anon. London Mag Mar 1825.
Barbara S—. London Mag Apr 1825. Rptd in Last essays of Elia 1833.
The last peach. Signed Suspensurus. London Mag Apr 1825.
[Review of T. Hood's] Odes and addresses to great people. Anon. New Times 12 Apr 1825.
The superannuated man. London Mag May 1825. Rptd in Last essays of Elia 1833.
Quatrains to the editor of the 'Every-Day Book'. London Mag May 1825. Rptd in Album verses 1830.
Remarkable correspondent. Anon. Hone's Every-day Bk 1 May 1825.
The wedding. London Mag June 1825. Rptd in Last essays of Elia 1833.
The convalescent. London Mag July 1825. Rptd in Last essays of Elia 1833.
Dog days. Signed Pompey. Hone's Every-day Bk 14 July 1825.
Captain Starkey. Signed C. L. Hone's Every-day Bk 21 July 1825.
Imperfect dramatic illusion. London Mag Aug 1825. Rptd as Stage illusion in Last essays of Elia 1833.

Twelfth of August. Anon. Hone's Every-day Bk, 12 Aug 1825.
A character. Signed 'Lepus'. New Times 25 Aug 1825.
The ass. Signed C. L. Hone's Every-day Bk 5 Oct 1825.
In re squirrels. Signed C. L. Hone's Every-day Bk 18 Oct 1825.
Pindaric ode to the treadmill. New Times 24 Oct 1825. Rptd with changes in Album verses 1830.
The poetical cask. New Times 24 Oct 1825. Poem.
Popular fallacies. NMM Jan, Feb, Mar, Apr and Sep 1826. Rptd in Last essays of Elia 1833.
An appearance of the seasons. Anon. Hone's Every-day Bk 28 Jan 1826.
Popular fallacy: that my Lord Shaftesbury and Sir William Temple are models of the genteel style in writing.... NMM Mar 1826. Rptd as The genteel style in writing in Last essays of Elia 1833.
The religion of actors. Anon. NMM Apr 1826.
The months. Signed C. L. Hone's Every-day Bk 16 Apr 1826.
Popular fallacy: that great wit is allied to madness. NMM May 1826. Rptd as Sanity of true genius in Last essays of Elia 1833.
Popular fallacy: that a deformed person is a lord. NMM June 1826.
Reminiscences of Juke Judkins, esq. Signed Elia. NMM June 1826.
Reminiscences of Sir Jeffery Dunstan. Signed C. L. Hone's Every-day Bk 22 June 1826.
The defeat of time. Signed Elia. Hone's Table Bk 1827.
A death-bed. Signed L. Hone's Table Bk 1827. Rptd in Last essays of Elia 1833, but not in subsequent edns.
Extracts from the Garrick plays. Hone's Table Bk 1827.
Mrs Gilpin riding to Edmonton. Anon. Hone's Table Bk 1827.
Gone or going. Hone's Table Bk 1827. Rptd with deletions as Going or gone in Album verses 1830. Poem
Angel help. NMM 1827. Rptd in Album verses 1830. Poem.
Verses for an album. The Bijou 1828. Rptd as In my own album in Album verses 1830.
Shakespeare's improvers. Signed C. L. Spectator 22 Nov 1828.
The wife's trial. Blackwood's Mag Dec 1828. Play
On an infant dying as soon as born. The Gem 1829. Rptd in Album verses 1830. Poem.
The gipsy's malison. Blackwood's Mag Jan 1829. Rptd in Album verses 1830. Poem.
The christening. Blackwood's Mag May 1829. Rptd in Album verses 1830. Poem.
For a young lady's album. Blackwood's Mag May 1829. Rptd as In the album of Miss — in Album verses 1830. Poem.
For the album of Miss —.... Blackwood's Mag June 1829. Rptd as In the album of a French teacher in Album verses 1830.
To Emma, learning Latin, and desponding. Blackwood's Mag June 1829. Poem.
Saturday night. Signed Nepos. The Gem 1830.
The pawnbroker's daughter: a farce. Anon. Blackwood's Mag Jan 1830.
Clarence songs. Signed C. L. Spectator 24 July 1830.
The royal wonders. The Times 10 Aug 1830. Poem.
A true story. The Talisman 1831.
To C. Aders, esq. Hone's Year Bk 19 Mar 1831. Poem.
Hercules pacificatus. Englishman's Mag Aug 1831.
Reminiscences of Elliston. Signed Mr H. Englishman's Mag Aug 1831. Rptd with slight changes as To the shade of Elliston and Ellistoniana in Last essays of Elia 1833.
Lines suggested by a sight of Waltham Cross. Englishman's Mag Sep 1831.
Peter's net... No I. Recollections of a late Royal Academician. Englishman's Mag Sep 1831.
Peter's net... No II. On the total defect of the faculty of imagination observable in the works of modern British artists. Englishman's Mag Oct 1831. Rptd as Newspapers thirty-five years ago in Last essays of Elia 1833.
The change. Hone's Year Bk 30 Dec 1831. Rptd as To Louisa M—... in Poetical works 1836. Poem.
The self-enchanted. Athenaeum 7 Jan 1832. Rptd in Poetical works 1836.
Munden, the comedian. Athenaeum 11 Feb 1832.
The parting speech of the celestial messenger to the poet. Athenaeum 25 Feb 1832.
Existence, considered in itself, no blessing. Athenaeum 7 July 1832. Poem.
On the total defects of the quality of imagination, observable in the works of modern British artists. Moxon's Reflector no 2 Dec 1832. Rptd and completed in Athenaeum 12, 19, 26 Jan and 2 Feb 1833; rptd as Barrenness of the imaginative faculty in the productions of modern art in Last essays of Elia 1833.
In the album of Edith S—. Athenaeum 9 Mar 1833. Rptd in Poetical works 1836.
Thoughts on presents of game, etc. Signed Elia. Athenaeum 30 Nov 1833.
To a friend on his marriage. Athenaeum 7 Dec 1833. Rptd in Poetical works 1836. Poem.
To Samuel Rogers.... The Times 13 Dec 1833. Poem.
To T. Stothard, esq. Athenaeum 21 Dec 1833. Rptd in Poetical works 1836. Poem.
Cheap gifts: a sonnet. Athenaeum 15 Feb 1834. Rptd in Poetical works 1836.

Posthumous publications

Table-talk by the late Elia. Athenaeum 4 Jan, 31 May, 7 June, 19 July 1834.
To Clara N—. Athenaeum 26 July 1834. Poem.
[Forster, J.] Lamb: his last words on Coleridge; Lamb: an autobiographical sketch. NMM Feb and Apr 1835.
To Margaret W—. Athenaeum 14 Mar 1835. Poem.
The first leaf of spring. Athenaeum 10 Jan 1846 (probably contributed by T. Westwood). Poem.
Lines addressed to Lieut R. W. H. Hardy.... Athenaeum 10 Jan 1846 (probably contributed by T. Westwood). Poem.
On being asked to write in Miss Westwood's album. Athenaeum 10 Jan 1846 (probably contributed by T. Westwood). Poem.
Cupid's revenge. Harper's Mag Dec 1858. From T. Allsop's collection of Lamb's mss.
What is an album? N & Q 11 Oct 1856 (contributed by J. M. Gutch). Poem.
The sisters. N & Q 4 June 1870 (contributed by T. Westwood). Poem.
[Five comic epitaphs.] New York Tribune 22 Feb 1879 (contributed by J. H. Siddons).
Brevis Esse Laboro 'One Dip' and Suum Cuique. The Taylorian Mar 1884 (contributed by J. A. Hessey). Poems, the second in Latin.
Barnett, G. L. An unpublished poem by Charles Lamb. HLQ May 1943.
Turnbull, J. M. Two Lamb poems. TLS 5 Feb 1949.
Prance, C. A. A forgotten skit by Lamb. TLS 9 Feb 1951.
Barnett, G. L. Lamb and the Button family: an unpublished poem and letter. HLQ Feb 1956.
Barnett, G. L. An unpublished review by Charles Lamb. MLQ Dec 1956.
Schwartz, L. M. A new review of Coleridge's 'Christabel'. SiR 9 1970.
James, L. The Lambs' story of revolutionary France: a newly discovered fragment. Charles Lamb Bull Apr 1973.
Wills, J. T. New Lamb material in the Aders album: Jacob Götzenberger and two versions of 'Angel Help'. HLB 22 1974.
Courtney, W. F. New Lamb texts from The Albion? Charles Lamb Bull Jan, Apr, Oct 1977.

Contributions to collaborative works

Gory, J. C. Sentimental tablets of the good Pamphile. Tr P. S. Dupuy 1795. Rev for pbn by Lamb.
Coleridge, S. T. Poems on various subjects. 1796, Oxford 1990 (facs). Includes 4 sonnets by Lamb.

Lloyd, C. Poems on the death of Priscilla Farmer. Bristol 1796. Includes Lamb's The grandame.

[Selected sonnets from Bowles, Bamfylde and others, with some original sonnets by STC . . . ed S. T. Coleridge.] Bristol 1796 (priv ptd), ed P. M. Zall, Berkeley CA 1968 (facs). Includes 4 sonnets by Lamb.

Poems by S. T. Coleridge, second edition, to which are now added poems by Charles Lamb and Charles Lloyd. Bristol 1797. Includes 16 poems by Lamb.

Godwin, W. Faulkener: a tragedy. 1807. Includes prologue by Lamb.

Siddons, H. Time's a tell-tale: a comedy. 1807. Includes epilogue by Lamb.

Coleridge, S. T. Remorse. 1813. Includes prologue by Lamb.

Kenny, J. Debtor and creditor. 1814. Includes epilogue by Lamb.

Knowles, J. S. The wife. 1833. Includes epilogue by Lamb. For Lamb's prologue, *see* Works, ed Lucas, vol 5.

The poetical recreations of the Champion 1822. Ed and pbd by J. Thelwall. Includes 10 poems by Lamb.

Wilson, W. Memoirs of the life and times of Daniel de Foe. 1830. Includes Estimate of de Foe's secondary novels by Lamb.

Letters

Letters of Charles Lamb, with a sketch of his life. Ed T. N. Talfourd 2 vols 1837, 1849.
REVIEWS: [Talfourd, T. N.] Br & Foreign Rev 5 1837; [Empson, W.] Edinburgh Rev 66 1837; [Bulwer-Lytton, E. G.] Westminster Rev 27 1837; Literary Gazette 8, 15 July 1837; Tait's Mag Sep 1837; [Felton, C. C.] North Amer Rev 46 1838; Dublin Univ Mag Feb 1838.

Final memorials of Lamb consisting chiefly of his letters not before published, with sketches of some of his companions. Ed T. N. Talfourd 2 vols 1848, New York 1848, London 1850.
REVIEWS: [Lewes, G. H.] Br Quart Rev 7 1848; Christian Remembrancer 16 1848; Eclectic Rev n.s. 24 1848; Westminster Rev 50 1849; [Smith, W. H.] Blackwood's Mag Aug 1849.

Letters of Charles Lamb. Ed W. C. Hazlitt 2 vols 1886.

Letters of Charles Lamb. Ed A. Ainger 2 vols London and New York 1888, London 4 vols 1900, 2 vols 1904.

Hazlitt, W. C. The Lambs: their lives, their friends and their correspondence. 1897.

Lucas, E. V. Lamb and the Lloyds. 1898.

Hazlitt, W. C. Lamb and Hazlitt: further letters and records. 1900.

Letters of Charles Lamb. Ed H. H. Harper and R. Garnett 5 vols Boston 1905 (priv ptd). Vol 1 contains facs.

Letters. Ed W. Macdonald 2 vols 1906 (EL); ed E. V. Lucas, selected and arranged by G. Pocock 2 vols 1945 (EL).

Letters. Ed R. D. Gillman 1907.

Some Lamb and Browning letters to Leigh Hunt. Ed A. L. Brewer, Cedar Rapids IA 1924. With facs.

The letters of Lamb to which are added those of his sister Mary Lamb. Ed E. V. Lucas 3 vols 1935. Incorporates projected edn by Mrs G. A. Anderson.

Lucas, E. V. An unpublished letter of Lamb. TLS 13 Feb 1937.

Birss, J. H. Lamb on revisions: an uncollected letter. N & Q 183 1942.

Finch, J. S. Lamb's companionship . . . in almost solitude. Princeton Univ Lib Chron 6 1945.

Letters. Ed G. Woodcock 1950. A selection.

Barnett, G. L. Lamb to John Britton: an unpublished letter. MLQ 13 1952.

Selected letters. Ed T. S. Matthews. New York 1956.

Watson, V. T. N. Talfourd and his friends. TLS 20–7 Apr 1956.

Klingopulos, G. D. Lamb and John Chambers. TLS 5 Sep 1958.

Woodring, C. R. Lamb takes a holiday. HLB 14 1960.

Skeat, T. C. Letters of C. and Mary Lamb and Coleridge. BM Quart 26 1962.

Green, D. B. Three new letters of Lamb. HLQ 27 1963.

The letters of Charles and Mary Anne Lamb 1796–1817. Ed E. W. Marrs, jr, 3 vols Ithaca NY and London 1975–8. *See* vol 1, pp. lxii–xcii, for full listing of all pbns related to Lamb's correspondence.

Marginalia

Marginalia on the fly-leaf of Samuel Johnson's Works. In Eliana, ed J. E. Babson, 1864.

London fogs. In ms, bound by W. Ayrton with Works 1818. Pbd in Works vol 1, ed E. V. Lucas, 1903.

Smith, H. B. Lamb's Album. Scribner's Mag Oct 1923.

Finch, J. S. Lamb's copy of the History of Philip de Commines, with autograph notes by Lamb and Coleridge. Princeton Univ Lib Chron 9 1947.

Translations, editions, introductions, prefaces, etc

Coleridge, S. T. The Piccolomini, or the first part of Wallenstein . . . . Tr from the German of Frederick Schiller. 1800. Includes 1 poem by Lamb, rptd as Ballad, from the German in John Woodvil 1802.

Attributed or spurious works

Original letters etc of Sir John Falstaff and his friends. 1796, 1797, 2 vols Philadelphia 1813; ed R. H. Shepherd London 1877; ed I. Gollancz 1907. Lamb's assistance to the author J. White is purely conjectural.

Beauty and the Beast: or a rough outside with a gentle heart; a poetical version of an ancient tale. [1811] (anon), 1825; ed R. H. Shepherd 1886; ed A. Lang, London and New York [1887]; 1955.

§2

Textual/bibliographical criticism

[Hill, A. S.] Lamb and his biographers. North Amer Rev 104 1867.

C. and Mary Lamb: their editors and biographers. Westminster rev n.s. 45 1874.

Russell, J. F. Lamb's notes on a metrical novel. N & Q 17 Sep, 5 Nov 1881.

Barnett, G. L. Dating Lamb's contributions to the Table book. PMLA 60 1945.

Barnett, G. L. Corrections in the text of Lamb's letters. HLQ 18 1955.

Foxon, D. The chapbook editions of the Lambs' Tales from Shakespear. BC 6 1957.

Barnett, G. L. Lamb's part in an edition of Hogarth. MLQ 20 1959.

Nethery, W. Charles Lamb in America to 1848. Worcester MA 1963.

Barnett, G. L. Lamb: the evolution of Elia. Bloomington IN 1964.

Meserole, H. T. Charles Lamb's reputation and influence in America to 1835. Jnl of General Education 16 Jan 1965.

Tillotson, G. The historical importance of certain Essays of Elia. In Some British Romantics, ed J. V. Logan et al, Columbus OH 1966.

Nethery, W. Eliana Americana: Charles Lamb in the United States 1849–1866. Los Angeles 1971.

Marrs, Edwin J. Some account of the publishing history of the Lambs' letters with notes of a new edition in progress. Charles Lamb Bull n.s. 1, Apr 1973.

Riga, F. P. and C. A. Prance. Index to the London Mag. New York 1978.

Prance, C. A. Companion to Charles Lamb: a guide to people and places 1760–1847. 1983. Entries on Lamb's editors, publishers, illustrators, etc.

Bate, J. Elia: restoring the London connection, Charles Lamb Bull 8, Apr 1988.

Russell, G. Lamb's Specimens of English dramatic poets: the publishing context and the principles of selection. Charles Lamb Bull n.s. 9, Jan 1989.

Wu, D. Unpublished drafts of sonnets by Lamb and Favell. Charles Lamb Bull n.s. 10, July 1991.

Wu, D. Lamb's dream-children: the manuscript text. Charles Lamb Bull n.s. 10, July 1992.

Ozawa, Y. Bibliography of reviews of the works of Charles Lamb in the British and American periodicals (1) 1798–1934. Stud in the Humanities 45, July 1994.

Landmark works of criticism (and obituaries) up to 1920

[Coleridge, H. N.] On Lamb's Poetry. Etonian Mar 1821.
Hazlitt, W. In his Table-talk, 2 vols 1821–2; Lectures on the dramatic literature of the age of Elizabeth 1820; The spirit of the age, 1825; The plain speaker, 2 vols 1826. Rptd in Complete works, ed P. P. Howe, vols 8 and 11–12 1930–4.
[Lockhart, J. G.] Letter of Timothy Tickler to Christopher North. Blackwood's Mag Sep 1823.
[Wilson, J.] Manifesto. Blackwood's Mag Oct 1823.
[Jerdan, W.] Literary Gazette 8 Dec 1832. Review of Tennyson's poems mocking the Baa-Lamb school.
[Adams, S. F.] An evening with Charles Lamb and Coleridge. Monthly Repository 9 1835.
[Moxon, E.] Lamb. 1835 (priv ptd).
[Hunt, L.] Lamb. Leigh Hunt's London Jnl 7 Jan 1835.
[Procter, B. W.] Recollections of Charles Lamb. Athenaeum 3, 24 Jan, 7 Feb 1835.
[Maginn, W.] Lamb. Fraser's Mag Feb 1835.
[Dyer, G.] Memoir of Lamb. GM Mar 1835.
[Patmore, P. G.] Personal recollections of the late C. Lamb, with original letters. Court Mag Mar–Apr, Dec 1835.
F[ield], B. Lamb. Annual Biography & Obituary 20 1836.
Characteristics of Lamb. Amer Quart Rev 19 1836.
Monthly Rev Feb 1836.
Life and writings of Lamb. Amer Quart Rev 122 1837.
British artists and writers on art. Br & Foreign Rev 6 1838.
Hood, T. Hood's own. 1839. Rptd in Thomas Hood and Lamb; being the literary reminiscences of Hood, ed W. Jerrold, 1930.
Tuckerman, H. T. Characteristics of Lamb. Southern Literary Messenger 6 Sep 1840.
[Macaulay, T. B.] Comic dramatists of the Restoration. Edinburgh Rev 72 1841.
Chasles, P. Le dernier humoriste anglais. Revue des Deux Mondes 15 Nov 1842.
Gilfillan, G. Lamb. In his A gallery of literary portraits vol 1, Edinburgh 1845.
[Lewes, G. H.] Br Quart Rev 7 1848. Review of 1848 edn of Works.
[Lewes, G. H.] Lamb and his friends. Br Quart Rev 8 1848.
De Quincey, T. Charles Lamb and his friends. North Br Rev 10 Nov 1848; rptd in Collected writings, ed D. Masson, Edinburgh 1889–90, vol 3.
Tuckerman, H. T. In his Characteristics of literature, New York 1849.
De Quincey, T. Charles Lamb. In his Biographical essays, 1851; reptd in Collected writings, ed D. Masson, Edinburgh 1889–90, vol 5.
Patmore, P. G. My friends and acquaintance. 3 vols 1854.
Fitzgerald, P. Two English essayists: Lamb and Dickens. 1863.
Fitzgerald, P. Lamb: his friends, his haunts and his books. 1866.
[Procter, B. W.] Lamb: a memoir. 1866.
[Bulwer-Lytton, E. G.] Charles Lamb and some of his companions. Quart Rev 122 1867.
Massey, G. Lamb. Fraser's Mag May 1867.
Robinson, H. C. Diary reminiscences and correspondence. Ed T. Sadler 3 vols 1869.
Robinson, H. C. The correspondence of Robinson with the Wordsworth circle 1808–66. Ed E. J. Morley 2 vols Oxford 1927.
Robinson, H. C. Robinson on books and their writers. Ed E. J. Morley 3 vols 1938.
Clarke, C. C. and M. C. Recollections of writers. 1878.
Ainger, A. Lamb. 1882 (EML).
Swinburne, A. C. Lamb and George Wither. Nineteenth Cent 17 Jan 1885. Rptd in his Miscellanies, 1886.
Birrell, A. C. Lamb. Macmillan's Mag 54 1886. Rptd in his Obiter Dicta ser 2 1887.
Pater, W. In his Appreciations, 1889.
Martin, B. E. In the footprints of Lamb. 1891.
Lucas, E. V. Bernard Barton and his friends. 1893.
[Gosse, E.] Lamb. Quart Rev 192 1900.
Dobell, B. Sidelights on Lamb. 1903.
Lake, B. A general introduction to Lamb, together with a special study of his relation to Robert Burton. Leipzig 1903.
Derocquigny, J. Lamb: sa vie et ses oeuvres. Lille 1904.
Jerrold, W. Lamb. 1905.
More, P. E. In his Shelburne essays ser 2 1905; ser 4 1906.
Symons, A. Charles Lamb. Monthly Rev 21 1905.
Irwin, S. T. Hazlitt and Lamb. Quart Rev 204 1906.
Masson, F. Lamb. 1913.
Symons, A. In his Figures of several centuries, 1916.

Biographies

Lucas, E. V. The life of Charles Lamb. 2 vols 1905.
Blunden, E. Lamb: his life recorded by his contemporaries. 1934.
Courtney, W. F. Young Charles Lamb. 1982.
Aaron, J. A double singleness: gender and the writings of Charles and Mary Lamb. Oxford 1991.
See Charles Lamb Soc Bull 1935–72 and Charles Lamb Bull n.s. 1973– for regular biographical, bibliographical and critical articles and notes on Lamb.
[JA]

Mary Anne Lamb 1764–1847

Mss of letters widely scattered, but there are small collections in Berg Collection, NYPL; Harvard; Lockwood Lib, SUNY at Buffalo; Pierpont Morgan Lib, New York; Univ of Texas Lib.

§1

Bibliographies

See L. S. Livingston 1903, J. C. Thomson 1908, and C. R. Woodring 1956, under Charles Lamb, col 2170.

Collections

Works of Charles and Mary Lamb. Ed E. V. Lucas 7 vols 1903–5, 6 vols 1912.
Works in prose and verse of Charles and Mary Lamb. Ed T. Hutchinson 2 vols Oxford [1908].

Selections

Hazlitt, W. C. Mary and Charles Lamb: poems, letters, and remains; now first collected with reminiscences and notes. 1874.

§1

Helen. In John Woodvil: a tragedy; to which are added Fragments of Burton. By Charles Lamb. 1802. Rptd in Works 1818. Poem.
Tales from Shakespear, designed for the use of young persons. By Charles Lamb. 2 vols 1807 [14 of the tales were by Mary Lamb; only the 6 tragedies were by Charles Lamb], 1809, 1810, Philadelphia 1813 (unauthorised), London 1816, 1822, 1 vol 1831; ed F. J. Furnivall 2 vols 1901; 1906 (EL); ed G. Tillotson 1962 (EL); ed J. C. Trewin 1964 (Nonesuch Lib); 1987 (Pen). Some of the tales were issued separately as well as in pairs, triads and quartets. Mary Lamb's name first appeared on the title page in 1838 (6th edn). TRANSLATIONS: Ger 1842, 1843; Fr 1847, 1884; Sp 1847, 1893; Swed 1851, 1947; Polish 1893, 1947; Jap 1923; Ital 1929; Serbo-Croat 1959. REVIEWS: Critical Rev 11, May 1807; Portfolio (Dennie's), Philadelphia 10, 1813; Spectator 58, 5 Dec 1885.
Mrs Leicester's school: or the history of several young ladies, related by themselves. 1809 (anon) [7 of the stories were by Mary Lamb; only The witch aunt, First time of going to church, The sea voyage, were by Charles Lamb], 1809 (preface signed by Charles and Mary Lamb), 1810, Georgetown DC 1811, London 1814, 1828

(10th edn); ed A. Ainger 1885; 1899 (Dent); Woodstock 1995 (facs of 2nd edn 1809); tr Fr 1923. *See* Woodring bibliography, *above.*

Poetry for children, entirely original, by the author of Mrs Leicester's school. 2 vols 1809 (anon) [about two-thirds of the poems were by Mary Lamb: poems known to be hers are Choosing a profession, Breakfast, The two boys, David in the cave of Adullam], 1 vol Boston 1812, New Haven CT 1820; ed R. H. Shepherd 1872; New York 1878; ed A. W. T[uer] 2 vols 1892 (facs of 1809 edn); 1898 (Dent).

On needle-work. By 'Sempronia'. Br Lady's Mag and Monthly Misc Apr 1815.

Works of Charles Lamb. 2 vols 1818 [contains 6 poems by Mary Lamb].

In Miss Westwood's album. N & Q 4 June 1870. Dated 17 May 1828. Poem.

Summer friends. In Works of Charles and Mary Lamb, ed E. V. Lucas, vol 3 1903. Dated 1809. Poem.

Letters

Hazlitt, W. C. The Lambs: their lives, their friends, and their correspondence. 1897.

The letters of Charles Lamb to which are added those of his sister Mary Lamb. Ed E. V. Lucas 3 vols 1935. Incorporates projected edn by Mrs G. A. Anderson.

Skeat, T. C. Letters of Charles and Mary Lamb and Coleridge. BM Quart 26 1962.

The letters of Charles and Mary Anne Lamb 1796–1817. Ed E. W. Marrs Jr, 3 vols Ithaca NY and London 1975–8. See vol 1, pp. lxii–xcii, for full listing of all pbns related to the Lambs' correspondence.

§2

Talfourd, T. N. in Final memorials of Charles Lamb, consisting chiefly of his letters not before published, with sketches of some of his companions. 2 vols 1848.

Clarke, M. C. Mary Lamb. Nat Mag 1858. Rptd in C. and M. C. Clarke, Recollections of writers, 1878.

Gray, J. M. Mary Lamb. Acad 24 1883.

Gilchrist, A. Mary Lamb. 1883.

Ross, E. C. The ordeal of Bridget Elia. 1940.

Aaron, J. A double singleness: gender and the writings of Charles and Mary Lamb. Oxford 1991.

See Charles Lamb Soc Bull 1935–72 and Charles Lamb Bull n.s. 1973– for regular biographical, bibliographical and critical articles and notes on Charles and Mary Lamb. [JA]

Walter Savage Landor 1775–1864

Landor mss are held by a number of Br and Amer libs. The only major poetic ms to survive – that of 'Count Julian' – is in the Forster Col at the Lib of the Victoria and Albert Museum, together with letters from Landor to Forster (mostly pbd in Forster's Walter Savage Landor. A biography). *The BL has various mss for prose and verse compositions, including the sonnet 'To Robert Browning', and letters to a variety of correspondents, including Charles Lamb, Swinburne and the Countess of Blessington. The Bodleian, Edinburgh Univ Lib and John Rylands Univ Lib, Manchester, also have significant ms cols of correspondence. The Huntington holds many items, including literary mss, correspondence and private papers. The Baylor Univ Browning Col has many letters from Landor to Browning (unreliable texts of these letters are published in Minchin's* Landor: last days, letters and conversations). *Arkansas Univ Lib has correspondence with Elizabeth Barrett Browning; the Beinecke Rare Book and Manuscript Lib at Yale holds a col of mostly unpbd letters to Kenneth Robert Henderson Mackenzie; the Chicago Univ Lib holds letters, including some to John Forster on literary topics; the HRHRC at the Univ of Texas at Austin has correspondence with Dickens. Other items are in the Berg Col, New York Public Lib; the Houghton Lib, Harvard; Iowa Univ Lib, Knox College Archives; the Carl H. Pforzheimer Lib, New York; the Pierpont Morgan Lib, New York; the Univ of Virginia Lib; and the Swann archive, Univ of Sunderland. See the IELM for further information.*

Bibliographies

Forster collection, South Kensington Museum: catalogue of the printed books. 1888; catalogue of the paintings, manuscripts, autograph letters, pamphlets etc, 1893.

The Browning collections: catalogue of autograph letters and manuscripts, [and] books, the property of R. W. Barrett Browning, sold by Sotheby. 1–8 May 1913.

Wise, T. J. and S. Wheeler. A bibliography of the writings in prose and verse of Landor. 1919.

Wise, T. J. A Landor library. 1928 (priv ptd).

Super, R. H. The publication of Landor's early works. PMLA 63 1948; rptd in his Publication of Landor's works, *below.*

Super, R. H. Notes on some obscure Landor editions. PBSA 46 1952.

Super, R. H. Landor's unrecorded contributions to periodicals. N & Q 197, Nov 1952.

Karlson, M. The Landor collection. YULG 27 1953.

Super, R. H. Landor's American publications. MLQ 14 1953.

Super, R. H. The publication of Landor's works. 1954.

Brumbaugh, T. B. On collecting Landor. Emory Univ Quart 12 1956.

Super, R. H. In The English romantic poets and essayists: a review of research and criticism, ed C. W. and L. H. Houtchens, New York 1957, 1966 (rev).

Metzdorf, R. F. The Tinker library. New Haven CT 1959.

Lyde, R. G. A Landor gift. BM Quart 22 1960.

Nowell-Smith, S. Gebir: a poem (1798). Library 5th ser 17 1962.

Lohrli, A. The first publication of Landor's Diana de Poictiers. N & Q 208, Jan 1963.

Brumbaugh, T. B. A Landor collection. Lib Chron 8 1966.

Collections

Gebir, Count Julian and other poems. 1831.

The works of Landor. 2 vols 1846, 1853, 1868, 1895.

Poemata et inscriptiones. 1847.

The works and life of Landor. Ed J. Forster 8 vols 1876. Vol 1 is an abridgement of Forster's Landor, 1869.

Imaginary conversations. Ed C. G. Crump 6 vols 1891; Poems, dialogues in verse and epigrams, 2 vols 1892; Longer prose works, 2 vols 1892–3.

The complete works: prose. Ed T. E. Welby 12 vols 1927–31; Poetry, ed S. Wheeler 4 vols 1933–6; 3 vols Oxford 1937.

Selections

Selections from the [prose] writings. Ed G. S. Hillard, Boston 1856.

Cameos selected from the works of Landor by E. C. Stedman and T. B. Aldrich. Boston 1874.

Selections from the writings of Landor. Ed S. Colvin 1882.

Poems. Ed E. Radford [1889].

Aphorisms. Ed R. B. Johnson 1897.

Selections. Ed W. B. S. Clymer, Boston 1898.

Love poems. Ed 'F. C.' 1901.

Shorter works. 1904.

A day-book. Ed J. Bailey, Oxford 1919.

Imaginary conversations and poems. Ed H. Ellis 1933 (EL).

Brevities, epigrammi. Tr and ed A. Obertello, Florence [1946].

Poetry and prose, with Swinburne's poem and essays by E. de Selincourt, W. Raleigh and O. Elton. Ed E. K. Chambers, Oxford 1946.

Shorter poems. Ed J. B. Sidgwick, Cambridge 1946.

The sculptured garland: a selection from the lyrical poems. Ed R. Buxton 1948.

Poems. Ed G. Grigson, Fontwell and London 1964.

A biographical anthology. Ed H. van Thal 1973.

Landor as critic. Ed C. L. Proudfit 1979.

Selected poetry and prose. Ed K. Hanley, Manchester 1981.

§1

Poems. 1795.

REVIEWS: Analytical Rev 22, Aug 1795; Br Critic 6, Sep 1795; Monthly Rev n.s. 21, Nov 1796; Critical Rev n.s. 19, Apr 1797.

Moral epistle respectfully dedicated to Earl Stanhope. 1795.

REVIEW: Critical Rev n.s. 19, Apr 1797.

To the burgesses of Warwick. [Warwick 1797]; ed R. H. Super, Oxford 1949 (Luttrell Soc).

Gebir: a poem in seven books. 1798 (facs Oxford 1993). Oxford 1803; Gebirus poema, Oxford 1803 (Latin trn by Landor); Gebir and Count Julian, ed H. Morley, London 1887.

REVIEWS: [Southey, R.] Critical Rev Sep 1799; Gentleman's Mag suppl 1799; Br Critic Feb 1800; Monthly Rev n.s. 31, Feb 1800.

Poems from the Arabic and Persian with notes by the author of Gebir. Warwick 1800 (1st issue, with Fr preface); Warwick and London 1800 (2nd issue), London 1927 (facs).

REVIEW: Monthly Rev n.s. 44, July 1804.

Poetry by the author of Gebir. Warwick 1800 (1st issue, with An address to the fellows of Trinity College Oxford, Postscript to Gebir etc), 1802 (2nd issue).

REVIEWS: [Southey, R.] Annual Rev 1 1802; Br Critic 20, Oct 1802; Anti-Jacobin Rev 13, Nov 1802; Poetical Register for 1802; Critical Rev n.s. 38, June 1803.

Iambi incerto auctore. [Oxford? 1802?].

Simonidea. Bath [1806].

REVIEW: Anti-Jacobin Rev 26, Apr 1807.

Three letters written in Spain to D. Francisco Riquelme [Riguelme]. 1809.

Ode ad Gustavum regem; ode ad Gustavum exulem. 1810.

Count Julian: a tragedy. 1812.

REVIEW: [Southey, R.] Quart Rev 8, 1812.

Commentary on memoirs of Mr Fox. 1812 (ptd but not pbd); rptd as Charles James Fox: a commentary on his life and character, ed S. Wheeler 1907.

Letters addressed to Lord Liverpool and the Parliament on the preliminaries of peace by Calvus. 1814.

Letter from Mr Landor to Mr Jervis. Bath 1814, Gloucester Jnl 23 May 1814.

Idyllia nova quinque heroum atque heroidum. Oxford 1815.

Sponsalia Polyxenae. Pistoia 1819.

Idyllia heroica decem librum phaleuciorum unum. Pisa 1820.

Poche osservazioni sullo stato attuale di que' popoli che vogliono governarsi per mezzo delle rappresentanze. [Naples?] 1821.

Imaginary conversations of literary men and statesmen. Vols 1–2 1824, 1826; vol 3 1828; vols 4–5 1829; 5 vols Boston 1882, London 1883; [selections] ed H. Ellis 1886, [1895]; ed A. G. Newcomer, New York 1899; [selections] ed C. L. Proudfit, Lincoln NE 1969; Classical (imaginary) conversations Greek, Roman, modern, ed G. M. Adam, Washington [1901]; ed J. P. Mahaffy [London 1910, 1925]; ed F. A. Cavenagh, Oxford 1914; ed E. de Selincourt, Oxford 1915 (WC); ed T. E. Welby, Oxford 1934 (introd by C. Williams, notes by F. A. Cavenagh and A. C. Ward); ed R. H. Boothroyd 1936 (Limited Edns Club); tr Ger 1878, 1919, 1923, Süddeutsche Monatshefte Sep 1932.

Reviews (of vols 1–2): [Taylor, H.] Quart Rev 30, Jan 1824; [Hazlitt, W.] Edinburgh Rev 40, Mar 1824; [Wilson, J.?] Blackwood's Mag 15, Apr 1824; [Hare, J. C.] London Mag May 1824; (of vol 3): [Hazlitt, W.] London Weekly Rev June 1828.

Citation and examination of William Shakspeare before the worshipful Sir Thomas Lucy Knight touching deer stealing, to which is added a conference of Master Edmund Spenser, a gentleman of note, with the Earl of Essex touching the state of Ireland. 1834, 1891; ed H. W. Mabie, New York [1891].

Pericles and Aspasia. 2 vols 1836, Philadelphia 1839, 1 vol Boston 1871; ed C. G. Crump 2 vols London 1890 (Temple Lib); ed H. Ellis [1892]; ed G. R. Dennis 1903.

REVIEWS: Examiner 27 Mar 1836; [Forster, J.] Examiner 3 Apr 1836.

The letters of a conservative, in which are shown the only means of saving what is left of the English Church. 1836.

Terry Hogan: an eclogue. 1836. Anon, probably Landor's.

A satire on satirists and admonition to detractors. 1836.

Literary hours by various friends. Ed J. Ablett, Liverpool 1837 (priv ptd). Contains prose and verse by Landor.

The pentameron and pentalogia. 1837, Boston 1888 (with Citation and examination of William Shakspeare, minor prose pieces and criticisms); ed H. Ellis 1889; ed D. Pettoello, Turin 1954. A poet's dream (from The pentameron), Edinburgh 1928 (priv ptd).

Andrea of Hungary and Giovanna of Naples. 1839.

Fra Rupert. 1840.

To Robert Browning. [1845]. Rptd from Morning Chron 22 Nov 1845.

The hellenics enlarged and completed. 1847; The hellenics, comprising heroic idyls &c, Edinburgh 1859 (enlarged); with Gebir, ed A. Symons 1907 (Temple Classics); tr Ital, 1908; Fr by B. Buisson, Paris 1916.

The Italics of Landor. 1848.

Savagius Landor Lamartino. [Bath? 1848].

Imaginary conversation of King Carlo-Alberto and the Duchess Belgioioso on the affairs and prospects of Italy. [1848].

Carmen ad heroinam. [Bath? 1848].

Epistola ad Pium IX pontificem. [Bath? 1849].

Epistola ad Romanos. [Bath? 1849].

Ad Cossuthum et Bemum. [Bath? 1849].

Statement of occurrences at Llanbedr. Bath [1849].

Popery, British and foreign. 1851, Boston 1851.

On Kossuth's voyage to America. [Birmingham? 1851].

Tyrannicide, published for the benefit of the Hungarians in America. [Bath 1851].

Imaginary conversations of Greeks and Romans. 1853; Epicurus Leontion and Ternissa [1896].

The last fruit off an old tree. 1853.

Letters of an American mainly on Russia and revolution. 1854.

Antony and Octavius: scenes for the study. 1856.

Letter from Landor to R. W. Emerson. Bath [1856]; rptd with Emerson's paper on Landor from Dial, ed S. A. Jones, Cleveland OH 1895.

Landor and the Honorable Mrs Yescombe. [Bath 1857].

Mr Landor threatened. Bath [1857], [1857].

Dry sticks fagoted by Landor. Edinburgh 1858.

Mr Landor's remarks on a suit preferred against him at the summer assizes in Taunton 1858. 1859.

Savonarola e il priore di San Marco. Florence 1860.

Heroic idyls with additional poems. 1863.

An address to the Fellows of Trinity College Oxford on the alarm of invasion. 1917 (priv ptd).

Garibaldi and the President of the Sicilian Senate (an Imaginary conversation). 1917 (priv ptd).

A modern Greek idyl. 1917 (priv ptd).

To Elizabeth Barrett Browning and other verses. 1917 (priv ptd).

See also vols ed S. Wheeler and H. C. Minchin under Letters and papers, *below.*

Contributions to periodicals

See R. H. Super, Landor's unrecorded contributions to periodicals *under* Bibliographies, *above, and* Wellesley *5, 1989.*

Letters and papers

Madden, R. R. The literary life and correspondence of the Countess of Blessington, 3 vols 1855.

Lowell, J. R. Some letters of Landor. Century Mag Feb 1888. To Mary Boyle.

Morrison, A. Collection of autograph letters and historical

documents: the Blessington papers. 1895 (priv ptd). Ninety letters and mss of Landor.

Wheeler, S. Letters and other unpublished writings of Landor. 1897.

Wheeler, S. Letters of Landor private and public. 1899.

Layard, G. S. Mrs Lynn Linton, her life, letters, and opinions. 1901.

Tatham, E. H. R. Some unpublished letters of Landor. Fortnightly Rev Feb 1910. To Walter Birch.

Boselli, A. Una lettera di Landor a Margherita Bodoni; Landor e G. B. Bodoni. Aurea Parma 2 1913.

Blakeney, E. H. A letter believed to be hitherto unpublished. Winchester 1929 (priv ptd). To Caroline Southey.

Mason, A. H. Landor and Lady Blessington. Howard College Bull 87 1929.

Armstrong, A. J. Unpublished letters of Landor. Baylor Bull 35 1932.

Minchin, H. C. Landor: last days, letters and conversations. 1934. Not quite a duplicate of Armstrong, Unpublished letters, *above*.

Bagnall, A. G. Some Landor letters to J. E. Fitzgerald. Turnbull Lib Record 2 1940.

Pfeiffer, K. G. Landor's critique of the Cenci. SP 39 1942. Letter to Leigh Hunt. Reply by R. H. Super, SP 40 1943.

Hubbell, J. B. Some new letters of Landor. Virginia Mag of History & Biography 51 1943. To G. P. R. James.

Super, R. H. Landor's 'Dear Daughter,' Eliza Lynn Linton. PMLA 59 1944.

Super, R. H. Landor's letters to Wordsworth and Coleridge, MP 55 1957.

Brumbaugh, T. B. A Landor letter. N & Q 208, Jan 1963. To Lady Blessington.

Ruoff, A. L. and E. B. Levine, Landor's letters to the reverend Walter Birch. Bull of John Rylands Lib 51 1968.

Ruoff, A. L. Landor's letters to his family: 1802–25. Bull of John Rylands Lib 53 1971.

Ruoff, A. L. Landor's letters to his family: 1826–29. Bull of John Rylands Lib 54 1972.

Mariani, J. F. The letters of Walter Savage Landor to Marguerite Countess of Blessington. Unpd PhD diss, Columbia Univ 1973.

Ruoff, A. L. Walter Savage Landor's letters to his family, 1830–32. Bull of John Rylands Lib 58 1976.

Attributed or spurious works

Two anon works sometimes attributed to Landor, The dun cow (1808) *and* A reply from the den (after 1858) *are probably not his.*

§2

Biographies

Forster, J. Landor: a biography. 2 vols. 1869, 1 vol Boston 1869; London 1876 (abridged), 1895.

Elwin, M. Savage Landor. 1941, 1958 (rev and enlarged as Landor: a replevin).

Super, R. H. Walter Savage Landor: a biography. New York 1954.

Textual/bibliographical criticism

[Linton, E. L.] An unpublished fragment by Landor. Athenaeum 23 Nov 1889.

Tatham, E. H. R. Unpublished Latin verse by Landor. Athenaeum 22 June 1907.

Schlaak, R. Entstehungs-und textgeschichte von Gebir. Halle 1909.

Carré, J. M. Two unpublished poems of Landor. MLR 7 1912.

Browning, R. Some records of Landor. Ed T. J. Wise 1919 (priv ptd). Three letters to I. Blagden.

Ashley-Montagu, M. F. Three unpublished 'Imaginary Conversations' by Walter Savage Landor. Nineteenth Century 107 1930.

Ashley-Montagu, M. F. An unpublished poem by Landor. Nineteenth Century Jan 1939.

McKinnon, B. Three Latin poems by W. S. Landor. Durham Univ Jnl 72 1979.

Landmark criticism

[De Quincey, T.] On Goethe and Landor. Westmorland Gazette 8 May 1819.

[Forster, J.] Evidences of genius for dramatic poetry: Landor. NMM Oct 1836.

Smith, W. H. Works of Mr W. S. Landor. Quart Rev Feb 1837.

Emerson, R. W. Walter Savage Landor. Dial Oct 1841.

Quillinan, E. Imaginary conversation between Mr Landor and the editor of Blackwood's Magazine. Blackwood's Mag Apr 1843; rptd in Eclectic Museum 2 1843.

Horne, R. H. Landor. In New spirit of the age, 1844. Written chiefly by Elizabeth Barrett.

Smith, W. H. Edinburgh Rev 83 1846; ptd in Eclectic Mag June 1846. Review of The works of Landor.

De Quincey, T. Notes on Landor. Tait's Mag Jan–Feb 1847; rptd in Collected writings, ed D. Masson, Edinburgh 1890.

De Quincey, T. Orthographic mutineers (with special reference to the Works of Landor). Tait's Mag Mar 1847; rptd in Collected writings, ed D. Masson, Edinburgh 1890.

De Quincey, T. Milton versus Southey and Landor. Tait's Mag Apr 1847; rptd in Collected writings, ed D. Masson, Edinburgh 1890.

[De Vere, A.] Edinburgh Rev 91 1850; rptd in his Essays chiefly on poetry, 1887. Review of The works of Landor etc.

Emerson, R. W. English traits, 1856.

[Spender, E.] Life and opinions of Landor. London Quart Rev 24 1865.

Field, K. Last days of Landor. Atlantic Monthly Apr–June 1866.

[Houghton, Baron (R. M. Milnes).] Forster's Life of Landor. Edinburgh Rev 130 1869; rptd in Living Age 4 Sep 1869 and in his Monographs personal and social 1873.

[Linton, E. L.] Walter Savage Landor. North Br Rev 50 1869; rptd in Living Age 21 Aug 1869.

[Dickens, C.] Landor's life. All the Year Round 24 July 1869; rptd in Every Sat 14 Aug 1869.

Linton, E. L. Walter Savage Landor. Broadway Aug 1869.

Linton, E. L. Reminiscences of Landor. Fraser's Mag July 1870.

Trollope, T. A. Some recollections of Landor. Lippincott's Mag Apr 1874.

Stephen, L. Landor's Imaginary conversations. Cornhill Mag Dec 1878; rptd in Living Age 4 Jan 1879 and in Hours in a library, 1879.

Colvin, S. Landor. 1881 (EML).

Swinburne, A. C. Landor. Encyclopaedia Britannica 1882 (9th edn); rptd in Miscellanies, 1886.

Lytton, R. Lady. Reminiscences of Landor. Tinsleys' Mag June 1883; rptd in Living Age 21 July 1883.

Linton, E. L. The autobiography of Christopher Kirkland. 1885. Deals with her friendship with Landor.

Sarrazin, G. In Poètes modernes de l'Angleterre, Paris 1885.

Trollope, T. A. What I remember. 1887.

Crosse, Mrs A. Walter Savage Landor. Temple Bar June 1891; rptd in Living Age 11 July 1891.

Evans, E. W. Landor: a critical study. New York 1892.

Benson, A. C. Llanthony Abbey and two of its priors. Nat Rev 28 1896; rptd in Eclectic Mag Feb 1897.

Linton, E. L. Landor, Dickens, Thackeray. Bookman (New York) Apr 1896; rptd in her My literary life, 1899.

Thompson, F. Walter Savage Landor. Acad 27 Feb 1897.

Holyoake, M. Q. The last writings of Landor. GM Jan 1899.

White, W. H. The editing of a classic. Athenaeum 22 Dec 1900.

Wall, G. E. Stray words from Landor. Critic Mar 1901.

Duke, R. E. H. Notes on the family of Savage of Warwickshire. Miscellanea Genealogica et Heraldica 3rd ser 4–5 1901–2.

Auer, J. Landor in seinen Beziehungen zu den Dichtern des Trecento: Dante, Boccaccio, Petrarca. Rheydt 1903.

Betham, E. The Llanthony maze. In his House of letters: being excerpts from the correspondence of Matilda Betham, 1905.

Thompson, E. N. S. Dante and Landor. MLN 20 1905.
Schwichtenberg, O. E. Southey's Roderick the last of the Goths and Landor's Count Julian. Königsberg 1906.
Symons, A. The poetry of Landor. Atlantic Monthly June 1906; rptd in his Romantic movement in English poetry, 1909.
Beckh, G. F. Landor und die englische Literatur von 1798–1836. Marburg 1911.
Cory, H. E. Landor and the academic attitude in poetry. Univ of California Chron 14 1912.
Duke, R. E. H. A pedigree of the paternal ancestry of Landor. Miscellanea Genealogica et Heraldica 4th ser 5 1912.
Bradley, W. A. The early poems of Landor: a study of his development and debt to Milton. 1914.
Peruzzi de' Medici, E. Walter Savage Landor. Cornhill Mag Apr 1915; rptd in Living Age 29 May 1915.
Borenius, T. Pictures by the old masters in the library of Christ Church Oxford. Oxford 1916. The Landor–Duke bequest.
Wheeler, S. Landor: his early life and lost writings. Bookman (London) July 1916.
Goldmark, R. I. The influence of Greek literature on Landor. In her Studies in the influence of the classics on English literature, New York 1918.
Henderson, W. B. D. Swinburne and Landor: a study of their spiritual relationship and its effect on Swinburne's moral and poetic development. 1918.
Nitchie, E. The classicism of Landor. Classical Jnl Dec 1919.
Wheeler, S. Landor's Llanthony. Nineteenth Century Mar 1921.
Wheeler, S. Landor: the man and the poet. Nineteenth Century Feb 1922. [KH]

Charles Lloyd 1775–1839

See col 401.

John Gibson Lockhart 1794–1854

§1

Peter's letters to his kinsfolk, by Peter Morris the odontist. Assisted by 'Christopher North' (J. Wilson). 3 vols Edinburgh 1819, 1 vol 1952 (abridged); ed W. Ruddick, Edinburgh 1977.
Valerius: a Roman story. 3 vols Edinburgh 1821 (anon), 1 vol 1842 (rev).
Some passages in the life of Mr Adam Blair, minister of the gospel at Cross Meikle: a novel. Edinburgh 1822 (anon), 1843 (with Matthew Wald); ed D. Craig, Edinburgh 1963.
Reginald Dalton: a story of English university life. 3 vols Edinburgh 1823, 1 vol 1842, [1880].
Ancient Spanish ballads, historical and romantic: translated with notes. Edinburgh 1823, London 1841 (rev), 1842, New York 1842, London 1853, 1854, 1856 (rev with memoir), Boston and Milwaukee 1856, New York 1856, Boston 1857, London 1859, Boston 1861, London 1868 (Chandos Classics), 1870, New York 1877, London 1883 (Morley's Universal Lib), New York [1889?], London and New York 1890 (Routledge's Pocket Lib), 1895, New York [1900?], [1912?].
The history of Matthew Wald: a novel. Edinburgh 1824 (anon), 1843 (with Adam Blair).
Janus: or the Edinburgh literary almanack. Edinburgh 1826. With John Wilson.
Life of Robert Burns. Edinburgh 1828, 1828, 1830, New York 1831, London 1838, 1847, 1871, 1872 etc; ed W. S. Douglas 1882, 1890 (rev J. H. Ingram); ed E. Rhys 1907 (EL); ed J. Kinsley 1959 (EL).
The history of Napoleon Buonaparte. 1829 (anon), 2 vols New York 1843, London 1867, 1878 (abridged by W. Tegg), Edinburgh 1885 (abridged), London 1889, 1906 (EL); ed J. H. Rose, Oxford 1916.
The history of the late war: including sketches of Buonaparte, Nelson and Wellington: for children. 1832. Preface signed 'J. G. L.'.
Memoirs of the life of Sir Walter Scott Bart. 7 vols Edinburgh 1837–8, 4 vols Paris 1838, 10 vols Edinburgh 1839, 1902–3 (with addns from Narrative, *below*), 1 vol 1842, 1845, 2 vols 1848 (rev and abridged as Narrative of the life of Sir Walter Scott), 1 vol 1850, 1853, 1871 (abridged with letter by J. R. H. Scott), 5 vols 1900; ed J. M. Sloan 1904 (abridged), 1906 (EL); 1912 (abridged); ed O. L. Reid 1914 (abridged); tr Ger 1839–41.
The Ballantyne-humbug handled. Edinburgh 1839. Reply to criticisms of the Life of Scott made by James Ballantyne's trustees and son.
The noctes ambrosianae of Blackwood. 4 vols Philadelphia 1843, Edinburgh 1863; ed R. S. Mackenzie 5 vols New York 1866, 1 vol 1904 (abridged). First pbd in Blackwood's Mag 1822–35. Mainly by John Wilson, but Lockhart wrote several of the earlier papers.
Lockhart's literary criticism: with introduction and bibliography by M. C. Hildyard. Oxford 1931.
John Bull's letter to Lord Byron (1821). Ed A. L. Strout, Norman OK 1947.
Theodore Hook: a sketch. 1953. First pbd in Quart Rev 72 1843.
Lockhart also supplied copious notes and an essay on the life and writings of Cervantes to the reprint of Motteux's Don Quixote, *5 vols 1822. For a list of his contributions to* Blackwood's Mag, *Apr 1817–May 1846, and* Quart Rev *(which he edited), Mar 1826–June 1852, see M. C. Hildyard's selection, above.*

§2

Gleig, G. R. Quart Rev 116 1864.
Maginn, W. In his A gallery of illustrious characters, ed W. Bates [1873].
Croker, J. W. The Croker papers. Ed L. J. Jennings 3 vols 1884.
Smiles, S. A publisher and his friends. 2 vols 1891.
Land, A. The life and letters of Lockhart. 2 vols [1897].
Birrell, A. The biographer of Sir Walter Scott. In his Et cetera: a collection, 1930.
Hildyard, M. C. Lockhart. Cornhill Mag Sep 1932.
Rait, R. Boswell and Lockhart. Essays by Divers Hands n.s. 12 1933.
Ewen, F. Lockhart, propagandist of German literature. MLN 49 1934.
Swann, E. In his Christopher North (John Wilson), Edinburgh 1934.
Macbeth, G. Lockhart: a critical study. Urbana IL 1935. With bibliography.
MacCurdy, E. A literary enigma: the Canadian boatsong. Stirling 1936.
MacCurdy, E. Lockhart. N & Q 15–29 Oct, 3 Dec 1938, 11, 25 Sep, 9 Oct 1943, 9, 23 Sep, 7, 21 Oct, 4, 18 Nov 1944, 30 June, 14, 28 July, 11, 25 Aug, 8, 22 Sep, 6, 20 Oct, 3 Nov 1945, 9, 23 Mar, 20 Apr, 4, 18 May, 1, 15 June 1946.
Parker, W. M. Lockhart and Scott. TLS 1 Oct 1938.
MacCurdy, E. Lockhart on Don Juan. TLS 30 Nov 1940.
MacCurdy, E. An unpublished letter of Lockhart. TLS 16 Mar 1940.
Parker, W. M. Peter's letters to his kinsfolk. TLS 22–29 June 1940. *See* 6–20 July 1940.
Cline, C. L. D'Israeli and Lockhart. MLN 56 1941.
F., L. Lockhart's novels. N & Q 15 Mar, 5 Apr 1941.
MacCurdy, E. Blackwood's Magazine, Lockhart and John Scott. N & Q 11 Jan 1941.
MacCurdy, E. Lockhart and Croker. TLS 30 Aug, 13 Sep 1941.
MacCurdy, E. Lockhart as gossip. TLS 17, 31 Oct 1942.
Brightfield, M. F. Lockhart's Quarterly contributions. PMLA 59 1944.
Gordon, G. S. Lockhart: commemorative address, delivered 1930. Glasgow 1944.
Parker, W. M. Lockhart's obiter dicta. TLS 5–12 Feb 1944.
MacCurdy, E. Lockhart as ogre. N & Q 2 June 1945.
Parsons, C. O. The possible origin of Lockhart's Adam Blair. N & Q 17 Nov 1945.
MacCurdy, E. Lockhart's quotations. N & Q 7 Sep 1946.

Woolf, V. Lockhart's criticism. In her Moment and other essays, 1947.
Cowley, J. Lockhart and the publication of Marmion. PQ 32 1953.
Lochhead, M. Lockhart. 1954.
MacCurdy, E. Lockhart, champion of Shelley. TLS 12 Aug 1955.
Parker, W. M. Lockhart's notes on Paradise lost. English 12 1958.
Hart, F. R. Proofreading Lockhart's 'Scott': the dynamics of biographical reticence. SB 14 1961.
Corson, J. C. Lockhart the scorpion: an unpublished manuscript. Stud in Scottish Lit 1 1964.
Shattock, J. In her Politics and reviewers: the Edinburgh and the Quarterly in the early Victorian age, Leicester 1989.
See also under Sir Walter Scott, col 992.

William Maginn 1793–1842

For a bibliography see Sadleir, below.

Collections

Miscellaneous writings. Ed R. S. Mackenzie 5 vols New York 1855–7. Vols 1–2 The Odoherty papers; vol 3 Shakespeare papers; vol 4 Homeric ballads and comedies of Lucian; vol 5 The Fraserian papers, with a life of the author.
Miscellanies, prose and verse. Ed R. W. Montagu [Johnson] 2 vols 1885. With memoir.
Ten tales. 1933. Preface signed W. B.

§1

Whitehall: or the days of George IV. [1827.] Anon.
The city of demons. In A. A. Watts, The literary souvenir, 1828.
Memoirs of Vidocq, translated from the French [of E. Morice and L. F. L'Héritier]. 4 vols 1828–9; Memoirs of Madame Du Barri: translated from the French [of E. L. de La Mothe Langon], by the translator of 'Vidocq', 4 vols 1830–1. Respectively vols 25–8 and 29–32 of Autobiography: a collection of the most instructive and amusing lives ever published. Vol 4 of Memoirs of Vidocq has a sequel appended (apparently by the translator) signed H. T. R. Both trns are conjecturally attributed to Maginn by Halkett and Laing; they have also been assigned to George Borrow.
Magazine miscellanies. [1841.] Tales, verses, maxims etc.
The noctes ambrosianae of Blackwood. 4 vols Philadelphia 1843, Edinburgh 1863; ed R. S. Mackenzie 5 vols New York 1866, 1 vol 1904 (abridged). First pbd in Blackwood's Mag 1822–35. Mainly by John Wilson, but some papers by Maginn, J. G. Lockhart, James Hogg et al.
John Manesty, the Liverpool merchant; with illustrations by George Cruikshank. 2 vols 1844.
Maxims of Sir Morgan O'Doherty. Edinburgh 1849. A parody of La Rochefoucauld.
Homeric ballads; with translations and notes. 1850; ed S. Mackenzie, New York 1856. Verse.
Jochonan in the city of demons. In Light from the East, ed G. Measom, 1856.
A story without a tail. 1858. In Tales from Blackwood vol 2, ed G. Saintsbury, 1928. First pbd in Blackwood's Mag 1834.
Shakespeare papers: pictures grave and gay. 1859, 1860 (adds paper on Hamlet and a sketch of Maginn signed B.).
A gallery of illustrious literary characters (1830–8) drawn by Daniel Maclise and accompanied by notices, chiefly by William Maginn; republished from Fraser's Magazine. Ed W. Bates [1873].
Maginn also wrote a great deal in Blackwood's Mag, Fraser's Mag *and other jnls. The anon* The military sketch book, *2 vols 1827, and* Tales of military life by the author of the Military sketch book, *3 vols 1829, have also been implausibly attributed to Maginn.*

§2

[Lockhart, J. G.] The doctor. Fraser's Mag Jan 1831; rptd in A gallery of illustrious characters, ed W. Bates, [1873].
[Kenealy, E. V. and D. M. Moir.] William Maginn. Dublin Univ Mag Jan 1844.
Hall, S. C. A book of memories of great men and women of the age, from personal acquaintance. 1871.
Sadleir, M. Bulwer: a panorama 1803–36. 1931. Appendix 4 consists of a bibliography of Maginn.
Elwin, M. Victorian wallflowers. 1934.
Thrall, M. Rebellious Fraser's. New York 1934.
Tragedy of a writer: Maginn. TLS 22 Aug 1942.
Wardle, R. M. Outwitting Hazlitt. MLN 57 1942.
Wardle, R. M. 'Timothy Tickler's' Irish blood. RES 18 1942.
MacCarthy, B. G. Centenary of Maginn. Stud 32 1943.
Herd, H. In his Seven editors, 1955.
Strout, A. L. Maginn as gossip. N & Q 2 June 1955.
Cooke, A. K. Maginn on John Keats. N & Q 3 Mar 1956.

Thomas Robert Malthus 1766–1834

See col 2491.

John Mitford 1781–1859

See col 408.

George Moir 1800–70

§1

Wallenstein, by F. Schiller, tr G. Moir. Edinburgh 1827.
Table-talk, or selections from the ana: containing extracts from the different collections of ana, French, English, Italian, and German. Edinburgh 1827.
The historical works of Friedrich Schiller, tr G. Moir. Edinburgh 1828.
Notes on Mr Bannerman's 'Inquiry into the rights of the guildry of Aberdeen' by a burgess. Aberdeen 1834.
Fragments from the history of John Bull. Edinburgh 1835.
Wallenstein's camp, by F. Schiller, tr G. Moir. Boston 1837.
Treatises on poetry, modern romance, and rhetoric, being the articles under those heads contributed to the Encyclopaedia Britannica 7th edn. Edinburgh 1839.
Poetry, modern romance and rhetoric. Edinburgh 1851. Poetry and modern romance by G. Moir, Rhetoric by W. Spalding.
The appellate jurisdiction of Scotch appeals. Edinburgh 1851.
Magic and witchcraft. 1852.
Extracts from lectures in J. Erskine, The principles of the law of Scotland. Edinburgh 1870 (14th edn), 1874 (15th edn), 1881 (16th edn), 1886 (17th edn) etc.
For Moir's contributions to Blackwood's Mag, Edinburgh Rev *and* Quart Rev, *see* Wellesley *vol 1, Toronto 1966; for his contributions to* Foreign Quart Rev, *see* Wellesley *vol 5, 1989; for his contributions to* NMM *see* Wellesley *vol 3, Toronto 1979.*

§2

Scotsman 21 Oct 1870. Obituary. [GW]

James Montgomery 1771–1854

See col 408.

William Mudford 1782–1848

See col 965.

Robert Owen 1771–1858

See col 2498.

Robert Dale Owen 1801–77

Selections

Simon, B. (ed). The radical tradition in education in Britain: a compilation of writings by William Godwin, Thomas Paine, Robert Owen, Richard Carlile, Robert Dale Owen, William Thompson, William Lovett and William Morris. 1971.

§1

An outline of the system of education at New Lanark. Glasgow 1824.
Moral physiology: or a brief and plain treatise on the population question. 1831, 1833 (10th edn), [1870] (new edn).
Pocahontas: a historical drama. New York 1837.
Situations: lawyers, clergy, physicians, men and women. 1839.
Address on free inquiry: on fear as a motive of action. 1840.
Address on the hopes and destinies of the human species. [1840?]
An address on the influence of the clerical profession; to which is added a trace and a warning: Truth and error; On the fear of God. 1840, [1845?].
Darby and Susan: a tale of Old England. [1840?]
A sermon on loyalty; a remonstrance to God; and a sermon on free inquiry. [1840.]
Wealth and misery. [1840?]
A lecture on consistency. 1841.
Popular tracts. 1841.
Prossimo's experience; On the study of theology; Safest to believe. [1841.]
Annexation of Texas: speech delivered in the House of Representatives on the right and duty of the United States now to accept the offer made by Texas of annexation. [Washington 1844.]
Occupation of Oregon: speech delivered in the House of Representatives. [Washington 1844.]
Labour: its history and its progress. Cincinnati 1848.
Hints in public architecture. New York 1849.
A brief practical treatise on the construction and management of plank roads. New Albany 1850.
Footfalls on the boundary of another world. 1860.
The policy of emancipation: in three letters. Philadelphia 1862.
The future of the north-west: in connection with the scheme of reconstruction without New England. Philadelphia 1863.
The wrong of slavery, the right of emancipation and the future of the African race in the United States. Philadelphia 1864.
Beyond the breakers. New York 1870. A novel.
The debatable land between this world and the next. 1871.
Threading my way: twenty-seven years of autobiography. New York 1874.
Looking back across the war-gulf, originally printed in Old and New Boston, May 1870. In The magazine of history, New York 1915.
Owen collaborated in a Discussion on the existence of God and the authenticity of the bible, *1832 with Origen Bacheler, and in a correspondence on* Divorce, *1860 with H. Greeley: and edited the* Crisis *1832 (with Robert Owen) and the* New Harmony Gazette, *1825.*

§2

Leopold, R. W. Owen: a biography. 1940.

Henry John Temple, 3rd Viscount Palmerston 1784–1865

§1

The new Whig guide. 1819, 1824. By Palmerston and others; ed 'E'.
Speech in the House of Commons on 1 June 1829, upon the motion of Sir J. Macintosh respecting the relations of England with Portugal. [1829.]
Speech in the House of Commons on 16 February 1842, on Lord John Russell's motion against a sliding scale of duties on the importation of foreign corn. 1842.
Speech to the electors of Tiverton 31 July 1847. 1847.
Speech in the House of Commons on 25 June 1850, on Mr Roebuck's motion on the foreign policy of the government. 1850; tr Fr 1850.
Opinions and policy of Viscount Palmerston; with a memoir by G. H. Francis. 1852. Selections from speeches.
Many further speeches pbd.

Letters and diaries

Selections from [Palmerston's] diaries and correspondence. In H. L. E. Bulwer, Life, 5 vols 1871–6; tr Fr 1878–9.
Selection from private journals of tours in France in 1815 and 1818. 1871.
The Palmerston papers: Gladstone and Palmerston – being the correspondence of Lord Palmerston with Mr Gladstone 1851–65. Ed P. Guedalla 1928.
Regina v. Palmerston: the correspondence between Queen Victoria and her Prime Minister 1837–65. Ed B. Connell 1962.

§2

[Francis, G. H.] The oratory of Lord Palmerston. Fraser's Mag Mar 1846.
Bulwer, H. L. E. The life of Palmerston, with selections from his diaries and correspondence. 5 vols 1871–6. With A. E. M. Ashley, who wrote part of vol 3 and the whole of vols 4–5; the whole rev and abridged by A. E. M. Ashley 2 vols 1879.
Trollope, A. Lord Palmerston. 1882.
Bell, H. C. F. Lord Palmerston. 2 vols 1936.
Pemberton, N. W. B. Lord Palmerston. 1954.

Peter George Patmore 1786–1855

§1

Letters on England by Victoire, Count de Soligny. 1823. By Patmore.
British galleries of art. 1824. Anon.
Mirror of the month. 1826. Anon; a novel.
Rejected articles. 1826, 1826 (both anon), 1844 (4th edn, as Imitations of celebrated authors, or imaginary rejected articles). Parodies.
Sir Thomas Lawrence's cabinet of gems; with biographical and descriptive memorials by Patmore. 1837.
Finden's gallary of beauty: or Court of Queen Victoria. Ed P. G. Patmore [1841].
Chatsworth: or the romance of a week. Ed R. P. Ward 1844. Anon.
Marriage in May Fair: a comedy in five acts. 1854 (2nd edn).
My friends and acquaintances: being memorials, mind-portraits and personal recollections of deceased celebrities of the nineteenth century. 3 vols 1854.
REVIEW: New Quart Rev 3 1854.
Patmore edited NMM, *1841–53.*

§2

Richardson, J. Patmore on Lamb and Hazlitt. TLS 19 June 1953.

Francis Place 1771–1854

§1

The mystery of the sinking fund explained. 1821.
Illustrations and proofs of the principle of population. 1822; ed N. E. Himes 1930.
On the law of libel. 1823.
Observations on Mr Huskisson's speech on the laws relating to combinations of workmen. [1825.]
An essay on the state of the country in respect to the condition and conduct of the husbandry labourers and to the consequences likely to result therefrom. [1831.]

A letter to a Minister of State respecting taxes on knowledge. [1831], 1835 (3rd edn).
Improvement of the working people: drunkenness – education etc. 1834.
Observations on a pamphlet relating to the Corn Laws. [1840.]

§2

Wallas, G. Place. 1898.
Ervine, St J. G. Place. 1912.
See also col 2500.

Bryan Waller Procter 1787–1874

See col 422.

David Ricardo 1772–1823

See col 2502.

Henry Crabb Robinson 1775–1867

Selections

The London theatre 1811–1866: selections from the Diary of Henry Crabb Robinson. 1966.

§1

Strictures [by T. Clarkson] on a Life of W. Wilberforce by the Rev W. Wilberforce and the Rev S. Wilberforce; with a correspondence between Lord Brougham and Mr Clarkson; also a supplement. 1838. Ed Robinson.
Exposure of misrepresentations contained in the preface to the correspondence of William Wilberforce. 1840.
The diary, reminiscences and correspondence of Crabb Robinson. Ed T. Sadler 3 vols 1869, 2 vols 1872 (with Augustus De Morgan's Recollections of Robinson).
Blake, Coleridge, Wordsworth etc: being selections from the remains of Crabb Robinson. Ed E. J. Morley, Manchester 1922.
The correspondence of Crabb Robinson with the Wordsworth circle 1808–66. Ed E. J. Morley 2 vols Oxford 1927.
Crabb Robinson in Germany 1800–5: extracts from his correspondence. Ed E. J. Morley, Oxford 1929.
Crabb Robinson on books and their writers. Ed E. J. Morley 3 vols 1938.
The diary of Henry Crabb Robinson: an abridgement. Ed D. Hudson, New York 1966.

Contributions to periodicals

Wellens, O. Henry Crabb Robinson, reviewer of Wordsworth, Coleridge and Byron in the Critical Review: some new attributions. BRH 84 1981.

§2

Bagehot, W. In his Literary studies vol 2, 1879.
Wright, H. G. Crabb Robinson's Essay on Blake. MLR 22 1927.
King, R. W. Crabb Robinson's opinion of Shelley. RES 4 1928.
Larg, D. G. Mme de Staël et Crabb Robinson. Revue de Littérature Comparée 8 1928.
Larg, D. G. Crabb Robinson and Madame de Staël. RES 5 1929.
Norman, P. Crabb Robinson and Goethe. 2 pts Pbns of Eng Goethe Soc 1930–1.
Morse, B. J. Crabb Robinson and Goethe in England. EStudien 67 1932.
Morley, E. J. The life and times of Crabb Robinson. 1935.
Baker, J. M. Crabb Robinson of Bury, Jena, The Times and Russell Square. 1937.
Gilbert, M. E. Two little-known references to Crabb Robinson. MLR 33 1938.
Brown, E. A note on Crabb Robinson's reactions to J. P. Kemble and Edmund Kean. Theatre Notebook 13 1958.
Elliott, I. Index to the Crabb Robinson letters in Dr Williams's Library. 1960.
Singh, G. Henry Crabb Robinson on Italian literature. Italica 43 1966.
Reed, M. Blake, Wordsworth, Lamb etc: further information from Henry Crabb Robinson. Blake Newsletter 3 1970.
Behler, D. I. Henry Crabb Robinson as a mediator of early German romanticisim to England. Arcadia 12 1977.
Corfield, P. J. and C. Evans (ed). Youth and revolution in the 1790s. 1996. Letters of W. Pattison, T. Amyot and H. C. Robinson.

Samuel Romilly 1757–1818

§1

Thoughts on the probable influence of the French Revolution on Great Britain. 1790.
Observations on the criminal law of England as it relates to capital punishments. 1810, 1811, 1813.
Speeches in the House of Commons. 1820.
Memoirs of the life written by himself; with a selection of his correspondence edited by his sons. 1840.

§2

Collins, W. J. Life and work of Romilly. 1908.
Atkinson, C. M. Account of the life and principles of Romilly. 1920.
Phillipson, C. Three critical law reformers. 1923.
Oakes, C. G. Romilly. 1935.
Romilly, S. H. Romilly–Edgeworth letters 1813–18. 1936.
Shientag, B. L. Romilly. [1936.]

Thomas Roscoe 1791–1871

Gonzalo the traitor: a tragedy in five acts. 1820. Verse.
Benvenuto Cellini, Memoirs; with the notes and observations of G. P. Carpani. 1822, 1847; ed L. Ricci 1904 (rev), [1906] (EL).
The king of the peak. 3 vols 1823. Anon.
J. C. L. Simonde de Sismondi, Historical view of the literature of the south of Europe, with notes. 4 vols 1823, 2 vols 1846.
The Italian novelists: selected from the most approved authors, from the earliest period down to the close of the eighteenth century, translated from the original Italian; accompanied with notes critical and biographical. 4 vols 1825, 1 vol 1880.
The German novelists: tales selected from ancient and modern authors in that language; translated with critical and biographical notices. 4 vols 1826, 1 vol [1880].
Owain Goch: a tale of the revolution. 3 vols 1827. Anon.
L. A. Lanzi, The history of painting in Italy. 6 vols 1828, 1 vol 1852.
L. J. A. de Potter, Memoirs of S. de Ricci. 2 vols 1829.
The tourist in Switzerland and Italy. 1830. The 1st pt of his Landscape annual, in which the following subsequently appeared: Italy 1831–3; France 1834; Spain 3 vols 1835–7; Spain and Morocco [1838].
The remembrance. 1831. Ed Roscoe.
The Spanish novelists: a series of tales, from the earliest period to the close of the seventeenth century, translated [by Roscoe] with critical and biographical notices. 3 vols 1832.
The life of Michael Angelo Buonaroti. In Lives of eminent persons, 1833.
Silvio Pellico. My imprisonments. 1833.
Silvio Pellico. The duties of men. 1834.
Wanderings and excursions in North Wales. 1836, 1853. Illustrations after Cox et al.
Wanderings and excursions in South Wales, including the scenery

of the river Wye. [1837.] With L. A. Twamley, later Meredith; illustrations after Cox et al.
Windsor Castle and its environs; illustrated with historical sketches by Thomas Roscoe and engravings by J. Carter. Pt 1 (all pbd) 1838.
The London and Birmingham railway; with the home and country scenes on each side of the line; historical details by P. Lecount. [1839.]
The book of the Grand Junction Railway: being a history and description of the line from Birmingham to Liverpool and Manchester. 1839. Later issued with the preceding as Illustrated history of the London and North-Western Railway.
M. Fernandez de Navarett. The life and writings of Miguel de Cervantes Saavedra. 1839.
Legends of Venice. 1841.
Belgium in a picturesque tour. 1843.
Summer tour to the Isle of Wight, including Portsmouth, Southampton, Winchester etc. 1843.
J. G. Kohl, Travels in England and Wales. 1845.
Lives of the kings of England, from the Norman Conquest. Vol 1 (all pbd) 1846. On William I.
The last of the Abencerrages, or the fall of Granada with other poems. 1850.
Roscoe also revised his father William's Leo X and Lorenzo de' Medici, *and contributed memoirs of the following authors to edns of their works: Fielding, Hurtado de Mendoza, Cervantes, Swift. He edited* The Juvenile Keepsake, *1828–30, and the* Novelists' Lib *12 vols 1831–2.*

Nassau William Senior 1790–1864

See col 2505.

Sydney Smith 1771–1845

Collections

Works. 4 vols 1839–40, 1839–40, 3 vols 1840, New York 1844, London 1850, 3 vols 1854, 2 vols 1859, 1 vol 1869.
Sermons preached at St Paul's Cathedral, the Foundling Hospital, and several churches in London, together with others addressed to a country congregation. 1846.
Selections from the writings of Smith. 2 vols 1855.
Wit and wisdom of Smith; with a biographical memoir and notes by E. A. Duyckinck. New York 1858. Long extracts almost forming an abridgment of the Works.
The wit and wisdom of Smith. 1860. A different selection from the American, *above*; short complete extracts.
Selections. Ed E. Rhys 1892.
Bon-mots of Smith and R. Brinsley Sheridan. Ed W. Jerrold 1893.
The letters of Peter Plymley, with other selected writings, sermons and speeches. Ed G. C. Heseltine 1929.
Bullett, G. Smith: a biography and a selection. 1951.
Selected writings. Ed W. H. Auden, New York 1956.
Selected letters. Ed N. C. Smith, Oxford 1956 (WC, introd A. Waugh), 1981.
The sayings of Sydney Smith. Ed A. Bell 1993.
Twelve miles from a lemon: selected writings of Sydney Smith. Ed N. Taylor and A. Hankinson, Cambridge 1996.

§1

Six sermons. Edinburgh 1800, 2 vols 1801 (enlarged).
Elementary sketches of moral philosophy. 1804, 1805, 1806 (priv ptd), 1850 (public issue). Lectures at the Royal Institution 1804–6.
The letters of Peter Plymley on the subject of the Catholics to my brother Abraham who lives in the country. 1807–8, 1808 (the 9 letters collected); ed H. Morley 1886 (with Selected essays); ed G. C. Heseltine 1929 (with other selected writings).
A sermon upon the conduct to be observed by the Established Church towards Catholics and other dissenters. 1807.
Extracts from the Edinburgh Review. [1810?] On Methodism; Indian missions; Proc of the Soc for the suppression of vice.
The lawyer that tempted Christ: a sermon. York [1824] (priv ptd).
Catholic claims: a speech. 1825.
A sermon on religious charity. York 1825.
A letter to the electors upon the Catholic question. York 1826.
Mr Dyson's speech to the freeholders on reform. 1831. 'Dyson' was Smith.
Speech at the Taunton reform meeting. [1831.]
The new reign: the duties of Queen Victoria – a sermon. 1837.
A letter to Archdeacon Singleton on the ecclesiastical commission. 1837.
A letter to Lord John Russell on the Church bills. 1838.
Second letter to Archdeacon Singleton: being the third of the cathedral letters. 1838.
Third letter to Archdeacon Singleton. 1839.
Ballot. 1839. Against the secret ballot.
Letters on American debts. 1844 (2nd edn). Rptd from Morning Chron.
A fragment on the Irish Roman Catholic Church. 1845 (7 edns).
Essays 1802–[27]. 2 vols 1874–80. Rptd from Edinburgh Rev.
Essays social and political 1802–25. [1874], [1877] (adds Essays from Edinburgh Rev and Letters of Peter Plymley, with a brief memoir by S. O. Beeton). Necker; Suppression of vice; Bentham; Education; English public schools; C. J. Fox; Poor-laws; Prisons; Reviews, etc.

Letters

Nine letters. Ed E. Cheney, Philobiblon Soc Miscellany 15 1877–84.
Letters. Ed N. C. Smith 2 vols Oxford 1953.
Lane, W. G. Additional letters of Smith. Harvard Lib Bull 9 1955.
Green, D. B. Letters to Samuel Rogers from Tom Moore and Sydney Smith. N & Q 2 Dec 1955.
Dilworth, E. Letters of Sydney Smith. N & Q 209 1964.
Schneider, D. B. Unpublished letters of Sydney Smith. N & Q 212 1967.
Bell, A. The letters of Sydney Smith. BJRL 59 1976.

§2

Horne, R. H. In his A new spirit of the age vol 1, 1844.
Holland, S. A memoir of Smith by his daughter; with a selection from his letters. Ed Mrs Austin 1855. With list of his articles in 1856.
Gilfillan, G. In his Galleries of literary portraits vol 2, Edinburgh 1856.
Vaughan, R. A. In his Essays and remains, 2 vols 1858.
Maginn, W. In his A gallery of illustrious characters, ed W. Bates [1873].
Milnes, R. M. In his Monographs, 1873.
Hayward, A. In his Selected essays vol 1, 1878.
Reid, S. J. A sketch of the life and times of Smith. 1884.
Chevrillon, A. Smith et la renaissance des idées libérales en Angleterre au XIXe siècle. Paris 1894.
Russell, G. W. E. Sydney Smith. 1905 (EML).
St Clair, O. Smith: a biographical sketch. 1913.
Biron, H. C. A Victorian prophet. Fortnightly Rev Jan 1921.
Williams, S. T. The literary criticism of Smith. MLN 38 1923.
Burdett, O. The Rev Smith. 1934.
Pearson, H. The Smith of Smiths. 1934.
Murphy, J. Some plagiarisms of Smith. RES 14 1938.
The Smith of Smiths. TLS 24 Feb 1945.
Auden, W. H. Portrait of a Whig. Eng Misc 3 1952.
Smith, N. C. Letters of Smith. N & Q 1 Sep 1954.
Sparrow, J. Jane Austen and Smith. TLS 2 July 1954; *see* 16 July–6 Aug, 15 Oct 1954.

Halpern, S. Smith in the Edinburgh Review. BNYPL Nov 1962.
Schneider, D. G. Sydney Smith in America to 1900: Two checklists. BNYPL 70 1966.
Halpern, S. Sydney Smith. Boston 1967.
Mackey, Howard. Verse and nonsense: the rhymes of Sydney Smith. Research Stud 39 1971.
Bell, A. Sydney Smith. Oxford 1980, rptd 1982.

John Sterling 1806–44

Collections

Poetical works. Ed R. W. Griswold, Philadelphia 1842.

§1

Thoughts on the foreign policy of England by Jacob Sternwall. 1827.
FitzGeorge: a novel. 3 vols 1832. Anon.
Arthur Coningsby: a novel. 3 vols 1833. Anon.
Poems. 1839.
The election: a poem in seven books. 1841. Anon.
Strafford: a tragedy. 1843.
Essays and tales: collected and edited with a memoir of his life by Julius Charles Hare. 2 vols 1848. Vol 1 historical and critical essays (Christabel, Napier's War in the Peninsula, Montaigne, Carlyle, Tennyson etc); vol 2 aphorisms, apologues etc.

Letters

Letters to a friend [William Coningham]. Brighton [1848] (priv ptd), 1851 (as Twelve letters), Bath [1872].
A correspondence between Sterling and Ralph Waldo Emerson. Ed E. W. Emerson, Boston 1897.

§2

Carlyle, T. The life of Sterling. 1851, 1852; ed W. H. White, Oxford 1907 (WC).
Gilfillan, G. In his Galleries of literary portraits vol 2, Edinburgh 1856.
Ince, R. B. Calverley and some Cambridge wits of the nineteenth century. 1929. Includes a study of Sterling's career.
Tuell, A. K. Sterling: a representative Victorian. New York 1941.
Burchell, S. C. The approaching darkness: a Victorian father to his son. YULG 28 1953.

Agnes Strickland 1796–1874 and Elizabeth Strickland 1794–1875

All works by Agnes unless otherwise indicated; the sisters' collaborations are listed under Collaborative works.

See U. Pope-Hennessy, Agnes Strickland, biographer of the Queens of England, 1796–1874, *1940. BL holds mss of Agnes's sketches and essays pbd in the* Album *1827–8, and her agreements with the publishers R. Bentley. The revised proofs of* Lives of Queens of Scotland *are in the Nat Lib of Scotland. See also LR 2, pp. 907–9.*

All works by Agnes unless otherwise indicated; the sisters' collaborations are listed under Collaborative works.

§1

Agnes Strickland's early works, for children, are variously difficult to find, date and attribute with confidence: see U. Pope-Hennessy, Agnes Strickland, *which also attributes to Elizabeth a children's tale called* Disobedience *(1818).*

Nursery fables. [1817–21.]
Guthred: the widow's slave. The Druid's retreat. 1821. Another edn London and Norwich 1876. Guthred rptd in Historical tales of illustrious British children, 1833.
The moss house: in which many of the works of nature are rendered a source of amusement to children. '1822' [1823].
The tell tale: an original collection of moral and amusing stories. 1823.
The aviary: or an agreeable visit. Intended for children. 1824.
The little tradesman: or a peep into English industry. 1824.
The use of sight: or I wish I were Julia. Intended for the amusement and instruction of children. 1824.
Prejudice reproved. 1826.
The rival Crusoes: or the shipwreck. Also, A voyage to Norway: and The fisherman's cottage. Founded on facts. [1826], [1830] (2nd and 3rd edns), 1836 (4th edn), 1845 (5th edn), 1851 (6th edn), rptd New York 1861, 1881; tr Fr 1834. Later rewritten with same title by W. H. G. Kingston.
The young emigrants: or pictures of Canada. 1826.
Worcester Field or the Cavalier: a poem in four cantos, with historical notes. 1827.
The seven ages of woman, and other poems. 1827, 1833, 1847.
The keepsake guineas: or the best use of money. 1828.
Sketches from nature: or hints to juvenile naturalists. 1830.
Rally round your colours and Banners of blue. 1832. Tory election songs.
Demetrius: a tale of modern Greece: in three cantos. With other poems. 1833.
A visit to the banks of Jordan: designed for children . . . showing how they may pass over 'on dry ground'. 1834.
The broken heart: and the bridal. [1835.]
The pilgrims of Walsingham: or tales of the Middles Ages. An historical romance. 3 vols 1835, 1 vol New York [1854]. The royal sisters rptd Boston 1845. Don Froila and his ten daughters rptd Boston 1845.
Tales of the school-room. 1835, Providence RI 1839, 1842.
Floral sketches, fables, and other poems. [1836.] New edn [1861] with coloured illustrations (pbd without Agnes's permission).
Thoughts for the sea: designed as a companion for a voyage. [183?] Anthology.
Queen Victoria from her birth to her bridal. 2 vols 1840.
Alda: the British captive. 1841; tr Fr 1892.
Narratives of nature, and history book for young naturalists. [1845.]
Historic scenes and poetic fancies. [1850.] Includes some poems from earlier publications.
The birthday gift: a Christmas and New Year's present. [1852.]
The sea-side offering. Edinburgh 1856 (priv ptd).
Old friends and new acquaintances. 2 vols 1860, 2nd ser 1861. Contributions to annuals and anecdotes of rural life.
How will it end? 3 vols 1865, 1865 (2nd edn). Novel.
The royal Christian martyr: St Edmund, the last King of East Anglia. 1870.
Lives of the last four princesses of the Royal House of Stuart. 1872.

Contributions to periodicals

Monody on the death of Princess Charlotte. Norwich Mercury 1817.
Essays and sketches in the Album, 1827–8.
Fisher's juvenile scrap-book. 1837–9. With Bernard Barton.
Jackson's juvenile scrap-book. 1849. With her sister Jane Margaret Strickland.

For Agnes's contributions to the NMM *and* Macmillan's Mag, *see* Wellesley *vol 5. Elizabeth edited the* Court Jnl *for several years from 1830, and Agnes sometimes contributed to it stories on English history. For Agnes's contributions to annuals, see A. Boyle,* An index to the annuals vol 1, 1967.

Collaborative works

Poems by the Rev J. Mitford, Miss Agnes Strickland and others, extracted from J. Raw's pocket book. 1830.
Pic-nic papers. Ed Charles Dickens 1841. Agnes contributed two tales.

All the following works were collaborations between Agnes and Elizabeth Strickland, but Elizabeth's name never appeared on the title pages.

Historical tales of illustrious British children. 1833, Boston [184?] with title Historical tales of illustrious children, 1847, new edn [1858] illustr G. Measom. Various US edns up to 1890s with title

Tales from English history: for children. Last edn Philadelphia 1899 with title Illustrious British children: a story of their childhood. The royal brothers rptd separately 1876.

Tales and stories from history. 2 vols 1836, 1 vol Philadelphia 1848, London 1855, 1859 (8th edn, 1 vol), 1870 (1 vol). US edns with title Stories from history, New York and Boston 1854, New York 1860, Philadelphia 1876. US edn with title True stories from modern history . . . revised and amended, New York 1853, Philadelphia [188?] and 1900. Tr Fr 1836.

Lives of the Queens of England, from the Norman Conquest; with anecdotes of their courts, now first published from official records and other authentic documents, private as well as public. 12 vols 1840–8, 12 vols Philadelphia 1840–8, 12 vols with corrections to first 3 vols, 1841–8. First 3 vols pbd with corrections and additions, Philadelphia 1841. Another 12-vol edn with corrections and additions to first 7 vols, Philadelphia 1844–8, rptd in 5 vols New York 1885, and micro Emporia KS 1969. 12 vols in 6 Philadelphia 1848, rptd many times up to 1859. New 8-vol edn 1851–2 ('revised and greatly augmented', with new preface by Agnes acknowledging Elizabeth's contribution), rptd Bath 1972 (introd Antonia Fraser). New 8-vol edn 1854 ('embellished with portraits of every queen', micro Ottawa 1985); this edn reissued 1857, rptd 1871, 1882–5. 6-vol edn 1864 (rev, minus portraits), rptd many times, lastly in 1912–16. Limited edns, with biographical introd by J. F. Kirk, 8 vols Philadelphia 1892, 16 vols Philadelphia 1902–3 (priv ptd). 1 vol abridgement by Agnes Strickland, 1867, New York 1867 (rev and ed C. G. Parker). 3-vol abridgement by R. Kaufman, Boston [1882] (with new sections on queens up to Victoria), Chicago and New York [1895], Akron OH 1895.

Lives of the Queens of England was often issued in sets comprising vols from more than one edn. Extracts were also pbd in the following:

Elizabeth, second Queen Regnant of England and Ireland. 2 vols in 1 Philadelphia 1849. Includes Anne of Denmark.

The Queens of England: a series of portraits of distinguished female sovereigns, with biographical and historical sketches. 1 vol New York 1851, 1852 (new edn).

Memoirs of the Queens of Henry VIII, and of his mother Elizabeth of York. 1 vol Philadelphia 1853.

Biographical sketches of the Queens of England, from the Norman Conquest to the reign of Victoria: or Royal book of beauty. Ed Mary Howitt 1868.

Life of Elizabeth, Queen of England . . . . New York [1880?].

The life of Queen Elizabeth. 1905 (abridged and ed I. A. Taylor). New York [190?], rptd [193-?].

The life of Queen Elizabeth. 1906 (EL), rptd [1915], [1924].

In Lives of the Queens of England, *Agnes covered the following queens: Matilda of Flanders, Matilda of Scotland, Matilda of Boulogne, Eleanor of Provence, Isabella of France, Joanna of Navarre, Margaret of Anjou, Anne Boleyn, Anne of Cleves, Katharine Howard, Katharine Parr, Elizabeth I, Catherine of Braganza, Mary Beatrice of Modena.*

Elizabeth covered: Adelicia of Louvaine, Eleanora of Aquitaine, Berengaria of Navarre, Isabella of Angouleme, Eleanora of Castile, Marguerite of France, Philippa of Hainault, Anne of Bohemia, Isabella of Valois, Katherine of Valois, Elizabeth Woodville, Anne of Warwick, Elizabeth of York, Katharine of Aragon, Jane Seymour, Mary I, Anne of Denmark, Henrietta Maria of France, Mary II, Anne.

Lives of the Queens of Scotland and English princesses connected with the regal succession of Great Britain. 8 vols Edinburgh and London 1850–9; 8 vols New York 1851–9; 2nd edn of first 2 vols 1854; 3rd edn of vol 1 1859 (with new preface). A 2-vol abridgement and adaptation by R. Kaufman pbd Boston '1887' [1886] with title The Queens of Scotland, rptd [1894], Chicago and New York [1895]; vol 2 of this was reissued separately in 1887 as The life of Mary Stuart, Queen of Scotland. Like Lives of the Queens of England, Lives of the Queens of Scotland was often issued in sets comprising vols from more than one edn.

Agnes covered Magdalen of France, Mary of Lorraine, Mary, Queen of Scots, and Lady Margaret Douglas; Elizabeth covered Margaret Tudor, Elizabeth of Bohemia, and Sophia, Electress of Hanover.

Agnes's abridgement of the vols on Mary, Queen of Scots was pbd as Life of Mary, Queen of Scots, *2 vols 1873, rptd several times up to 1913, New York 1893.*

Lives of the bachelor Kings of England. 1861. Agnes covered William Rufus and Edward VI; Elizabeth covered Edward V.

The lives of the seven bishops committed to the Tower in 1688. Enriched and illustrated with personal letters, now first published, from the Bodleian Library. 1866. Agnes covered Sancroft, Ken, Lake, White and Turner; Elizabeth covered Lloyd and Trelawney.

Lives of the Tudor princesses, including Lady Jane Grey and her sisters. 1868. Another edn 1888. Agnes covered Lady Eleanor Brandon, Lady Frances Brandon, Lady Margaret Clifford and Lady Arabella Stuart; Elizabeth covered Mary Tudor and Ladies Jane, Katharine and Mary Grey. The book was repbd with Agnes's Lives of the last four princesses of the Royal House of Stuart, 1888, with the title Lives of the Tudor and Stuart princesses, 1888.

Editions

Letters of Mary, Queen of Scots. Now first published from the originals, from various sources, private as well as public, with an historical introduction and notes. 3 vols 1842, 2 vols 1843, micro New Haven CT 1975. New 2-vol edn 1844, micro Ann Arbor MI 1975; this edn rptd 1848.

The writers of the following works were all siblings of Agnes and Elizabeth Strickland:

Traill, Catherine Parr. Canadian Crusoes: a tale of the Rice Lake Plains. 1852, 1869 (2nd edn), rptd [1923].

Strickland, Samuel. Twenty-seven years in Canada West: or the experience of an early settler. 1853.

Strickland, Jane Margaret. Rome, regal and republican: a family history of Rome. 1854.

§2

Strickland, Jane Margaret. Life of Agnes Strickland, by her sister. Edinburgh and London 1887.

Pope-Hennessy, U. Agnes Strickland, biographer of the Queens of England, 1796–1874. 1940. [JW]

William Taylor 1765–1836

§1

Lessing, Nathan the wise, written originally in German. Norwich 1791 (priv ptd), London 1805; ed H. Morley 1886.

Goethe, Iphigenia in Tauris: a tragedy. 1793 (priv ptd), 1794.

Wieland. Dialogues of the gods. 1795.

Bürger, Ellenore. 1796. Rptd with some alterations from Monthly Mag Mar 1796.

Select fairy tales from the German of Wieland. 1796.

Tales of yore. 3 vols 1810. From Fr to Ger.

A letter concerning the two first chapters of Luke. 1810. Anon.

English synonyms discriminated. 1813, 1850; tr Ger 1851.

Some biographic particulars of the late Dr Sayers. Prefixed to Frank Sayers, Collective works, Norwich 1823.

Historic survey of German poetry: interspersed with various translations. 3 vols 1828–30.

A memoir of the late Philip Meadows Martineau, surgeon. 1831. With F. Elwin.

Taylor's 1,754 articles and reviews were largely pbd in Monthly Rev *1793–1824.*

§2

Carlyle, T. Taylor's historic survey of German poetry. Edinburgh Rev 53 1831.

Robberds, J. W. A memoir of the life and writings of Taylor of Norwich, containing his correspondence. 2 vols 1843.

Herzfeld, G. Taylor von Norwich: eine Studie über den Einfluss der neueren deutschen Literatur in England. Halle 1897.

Christensen, M. A. Taylor of Norwich and the higher criticism. JHI 20 1959.

Edward John Trelawny 1792–1881

§1

The adventures of a younger son. 3 vols 1831, 1 vol 1835, 1848; ed E. Garnett 1890; ed H. N. Brailsford 2 vols 1914; ed E. C. Mayne, Oxford 1925 (WC).

Recollections of the last days of Shelley and Byron. 1858, 2 vols 1878 (with addns, as Records of Shelley, Byron and the author); ed E. Dowden 1906; ed J. E. Morpurgo 1952.

The relations of Percy Bysshe Shelley with his two wives Harriet and Mary, and a comment on the character of Lady Byron. 1920 (priv ptd).

Letters

Letters. Ed H. Buxton Forman 1910.

The relations of Lord Byron and Augusta Leigh; with a comparison of the characters of Byron and Shelley, and a rebuke to Jane Clairmont on her hatred of the former. 1920 (priv ptd). 4 letters.

§2

Garnett, R. Shelley's last days. Fortnightly Rev June 1878.

Mathilde Blind. Whitehall Rev 10 Jan 1880. Record of conversation.

Rossetti, W. M. Talks with Trelawny 1879–80. Athenaeum 15, 29 July, 5 Aug 1882.

Edgcumbe, R. Trelawny: a biographical sketch. Plymouth 1882.

Sharp, W. The life and letters of Joseph Severn. 1892.

Miller, J. Trelawny with Shelley and Byron. 1922.

Massingham, H. J. The friend of Shelley: a memoir of Trelawny. 1930.

Armstrong, M. Trelawny: a man's life. New York 1940.

Grylls, R. G. Trelawny. 1950.

Richard Whately 1787–1863

Bibliographies

Kane, P. E. Whately in the United States: a partial bibliography. BB 23 1961.

Selections

Detached thoughts and apophthegms, extracted from some of the writings of Archbishop Whately. Ser 1 1854.

Selections from the writings of Dr Whately. 1856 (for 1855).

Miscellaneous remains from the common-place book of Whately: being a collection of notes and essays made during the preparation of his various works. Ed E. J. Whately 1864, 1865 (with addns).

§1

Historic doubts relative to Napoleon Bonaparte. 1819 (anon), 1821 etc. A travesty of the higher criticism.

Essays on some of the peculiarities of the Christian religion. Oxford 1825, 1846 (5th edn rev).

Elements of logic: comprising the substance of the article in the Encyclopaedia metropolitana, with additions. 1826, 1832 (4th edn rev), 1836 (6th edn rev), 1840 (rev), 1844 (rev), 1848 (rev).

Elements of rhetoric. 1828, 1836 (5th edn rev), 1846 (7th edn rev); ed D. Ehninger, Carbondale IL 1963. Rptd from Encyclopaedia metropolitana.

Introductory lectures on political economy. 2 ptd 1831–2, 1847 (3rd edn rev), 1855 (rev and enlarged).

Sermons on various subjects. 1835, 1849 (adds 4 sermons), 1854–62 (enlarged, as Sermons on the principal Christian festivals and other occasions).

The Kingdom of Christ delineated. 1841, 1842, 1877 (abridged as Apostolical succession considered).

Historic certainties respecting the early history of America, by Rev Aristarchus Newlight [i.e. Whately]. 1851.

Miscellaneous lectures and reviews. 1861.

Whately also edited Thomas Whately, Remarks on some of the characters of Shakespeare, *1839; E. Copleston,* Remains, *1854; Francis Bacon,* Essays, *1856; W. Paley,* Moral philosophy, *and* Evidences, *1859. For many other works, see BM catalogue and col 2512.*

§2

Blanco (afterwards White), J. M. The life of the Rev Blanco White, written by himself; with portions of his correspondence. Ed J. H. Thom 3 vols 1845.

'An old Oxonian'. Recollections of Archbishop Whately. Christian Observer Nov 1863.

Fitzpatrick, W. J. Memoirs of Archbishop Whately of Dublin; with a glance at his contemporaries and times. 2 vols 1864.

Archbishop Whately. Eclectic Rev Sep 1864.

Memoirs of Whately. Blackwood's Mag Oct 1864.

Whately, E. J. Life and correspondence of Whately. 2 vols 1866, 1868, 1875 (enlarged).

Parrish, W. M. Whately and his rhetoric. Quart Jnl of Speech 15 1929.

See also col 2512.

Thomas Dunham Whitaker 1759–1821

§1

A history of the original parish of Whalley and Honor of Clitheroe, in the counties of Lancaster and York. Blackburn 1801 (illus), Blackburn and London 1806 (called 2nd edn, but lst edn with new title page, addenda and suppls, some cancelled matter and 4 new engravings), 1818 (3rd edn rev and enlarged), 2 vols London and Manchester 1872–6 (4th edn, rev and enlarged by J. G. Nichols; vol 2 completed by P. A. Lyons).

The history and antiquities of the deanery of Craven in the county of York. 1805, 1812 (2nd edn with addns and corrections, some copies in folio); ed A. W. Morant, London and Leeds 1878 (3rd edn with corrections and addenda by L. C. Miall), 2 vols Manchester and Skipton 1973 (reprint of 3rd edn, introd by R. G. Rowley).

De motu per Britanniam civico, annis 1745 et 1746. 1809.

The life and original correspondence of Sir G. Radcliffe. 1810.

Loidis and Elmete: or, an attempt to illustrate the districts described in those words by Bede. A history of Leeds vol 2. Leeds and London 1816 (folio), 1820 (with appendix). An excerpt, 'Parish of Dewsebury', is rptd in J. B. Greenwood, The early ecclesiastical history of Dewesbury, 1859. A history of Leeds vol 1 is Whitaker's edn of R. Thoresby's Ducatus leodiensis.

A series of views of the abbeys and castles in Yorkshire. 1820 (folio, illustr W. Westall and F. Mackenzie).

An history of Richmondshire, in the North Riding of the County of York. 2 vols 1823 (folio, illustr J. W. Turner and J. Buckler), 1843 (folio, excerpts Turner's illustrations and parts of Whitaker's text).

Whitaker also pbd separately a number of sermons and speeches and an edn of Piers Ploughman *(1813).*

Contributions to periodicals

Various anon articles in the Quart Rev *1809–21. See H. Shine and H. Chadwick Shine,* The Quarterly Review under Gifford, *1949.*

§2

Nichols, J. G. Biographical memoirs of T. D. Whitaker. In An history of the original parish of Whalley vol 1, 1872. [JC]

John Wilson, 'Christopher North' 1785–1854

Collections

The works of Professor Wilson of the University of Edinburgh. Ed his son-in-law Professor Ferrier 12 vols Edinburgh 1855–8. Vols 5–8: Essays critical and imaginative, rptd 4 vols Edinburgh 1866.
British poets of the nineteenth century. Ed [J. W. Lake], Paris 1828 (includes selections from Wilson).
The poetical works of Milman, Bowles, Wilson and Barry Cornwall. Paris 1829.
The poetical works. Edinburgh 1858, Edinburgh and London 1865, 1868; ed J. F. Ferrier 1874, 1896.
Lakeland poems. Ed. W. Bailey-Kempling, Ambleside 1902.

§1

A recommendation of the study of the remains of ancient Grecian and Roman architecture, sculpture and painting: a prize poem. Oxford 1807.
Lines sacred to the memory of the Rev James Grahame. Glasgow 1811. Anon.
The isle of palms and other poems. Edinburgh, London and Glasgow 1812, New York 1812.
The magic mirror, addressed to Walter Scott esq. Edinburgh 1812.
The city of the plague and other poems. Edinburgh, Glasgow and London 1816, New York 1816.
Translation from an ancient Chaldee manuscript, from no vii of Blackwood's Magazine. [Edinburgh 1817.]
Lights and shadows of Scottish life: a selection from the papers of the late Arthur Austin. Edinburgh 1822, 1853; tr Fr 1826.
Little Hannah Lee: a winter's story. 1823. From Lights and shadows, *above*.
The trials of Margaret Lyndsay, by the author of Lights and shadows of Scottish life. Edinburgh 1823, 1854, Glasgow [1879], [1886].
The foresters, by the author of Lights and shadows of Scottish life and the Trials of Margaret Lyndsay. Edinburgh 1825, 1852.
Poems: a new edition. 2 vols Edinburgh and London 1825.
Janus: or the Edinburgh literary almanack. Edinburgh 1826. With Lockhart.
Some illustrations of Mr McCullogh's Principles of political economy by Mordecai Mullion, private secretary to Christopher North. Edinburgh 1826.
The poetical works of Milman, Bowles, Wilson and Barry Cornwall. Paris 1829.
The land of Burns: a series of landscapes and portraits, illustrative of the life and writings of the Scottish poet. 2 vols Glasgow 1840. Illustr D. O. Hill with letterpress by Robert Chambers and Wilson.
Blind Allan: a tale. [1840?], [Falkirk? 1850?]. From Lights and shadows, *above*.
The recreations of Christopher North. 3 vols Edinburgh 1842, Philadelphia 1850, 2 vols London 1864.
The Noctes ambrosianae of Blackwood. 4 vols Philadelphia 1843, Edinburgh 1863; ed R. S. Mackenzie 5 vols New York 1866 (Best edn), 4 vols 1868, 1 vol 1904. Mainly by Wilson, but some papers by J. Hogg, J. G. Lockhart, W. Maginn et al; first pbd in Blackwood's Mag 1822–35. Selections: ed J. Skelton, Edinburgh 1876; ed J. S. Moncrieff and J. H. Millar 1904.
The works of Robert Burns; with Dr Currie's memoir of the poet, and an essay on his genius and character by Professor Wilson. Vol 1 Glasgow 1843. Wilson's essay was rptd separately New York 1845, Philadelphia 1854, New York 1861.
Scotland illustrated by John C. Brown and other Scottish artists; with letter-press descriptions and an essay on the scenery of the Highlands by Professor Wilson. 1845. Wilson's essay is rptd in A history of the Scottish highlands, ed J. S. Keltie, vol 1, Edinburgh 1875.
Specimens of the British critics by Christopher North. Philadelphia 1846, facs reprint 1979.
The poetical works of Professor Wilson. Edinburgh 1865, 1874.
Tales by Professor Wilson: Lights and shadows, Margaret Lyndsay, The foresters. Edinburgh 1865.
Essays critical and imaginative. 4 vols Edinburgh 1866.
Letters from the Lakes by Professor Wilson. Ambleside 1889.
Lakeland poems by Professor Wilson. Ed W. Bailey-Kempling, Ambleside 1902.
Contemporary reviews of romantic poetry. Ed J. Wain 1953.
For a list of Wilson's extensive contributions to Blackwood's Mag *see also* Wellesley *vol* 5.

§2

Lockhart, J. G. Peter's letters to his kinsfolk. 3 vols Edinburgh 1819.
Professor Wilson: a memorial and estimate by one of his students. Edinburgh 1854.
Gilfillan, G. In his Galleries of literary portraits vol 2, Edinburgh 1856.
Heart-break: the trials of literary life, or recollections of Christopher North. 1859. A story introducing recollections of Wilson.
Gordon, Mary. Christopher North: a memoir of Wilson, compiled from family papers and other sources. 2 vols Edinburgh 1862.
Hannay, J. Professor Wilson. In his Characters and criticisms, Edinburgh 1865.
Maginn, W. In his A gallery of illustrious characters, ed W. Bates [1873].
Saintsbury, G. In his Essays in English literature 1780–1860, 1890.
Oliphant, M. O. W. In his Annals of a publishing house: William Blackwood and his sons, 3 vols 1897–8.
Douglas, G. In his Blackwood group, 1897.
Masson, D. In his Memoirs of two cities, Edinburgh 1911.
von Struve, H. Wilson (Christopher North) als Kritiker. Leipzig 1922.
Elwin, M. In his Victorian wall-flowers, 1934.
Strout, A. L. Wilson, 'champion' of Wordsworth. MP 31 1934.
Swann, E. Christopher North (John Wilson). Edinburgh 1934. Includes lists of Wilson's works and of books and articles about him.
Strout, A. L. Purple patches in the Noctes Ambrosianae. ELH 2 1935.
Strout, A. L. Concerning the Noctes Ambrosianae. MLN 51 1935. *See also* RES 13 1937, pp. 46–63, 177–89.
Strout, A. L. Wilson as a Shakespeare critic: a study of Shakespeare and the English romantic movement. Sh Jb 72 1936.
Strout, A. L. Unidentified quotations in the Noctes Ambrosianae. N & Q 25 Jan 1936. *See also* 8–15 Feb 1936.
Strout, A. L. Christopher North on Tennyson. RES 14 1938.
Strout, A. L. Wilson as a professor. N & Q 11 Mar 1939.
Strout, A. L. Wilson and the chair of modern philosophy at the University of Edinburgh. N & Q 1 Apr 1939.
Strout, A. L. Wilson and the Orphan-maid: some unpublished letters. PMLA 55 1940.
Strout, A. L. The recreations of Christopher North 1842. N & Q 6 June, 1 Aug 1942.
Strout, A. L. A study in periodical patchwork: Wilson's Recreations of Christopher North, 1842. MLR 38 1943.
Wardle, R. M. The authorship of the Noctes Ambrosianae. MP 42 1944.
Aurnor, N. S. An unknown castigator of Christopher North. In If by your art: testament to Percival Hunt, Pittsburgh 1948.
Gravely, W. H. Christopher North and the genesis of the Raven. PMLA 66 1951.
Strout, A. L. The first twenty-three numbers of the Noctes Ambrosianae: excerpts from the Blackwood papers in the National Library of Scotland. Library 5th ser 12 1957.

Dorothy Wordsworth 1771–1855

All literary mss are at the Wordsworth Lib, Grasmere; summary account given in Siemens, The Wordsworth collection, *1971, pp. 101–10, though it should be borne in mind that it has been superseded in certain cases by the more detailed treatment provided in individual vols of the Cornell Wordsworth Series. See also* The Grasmere journals, *ed P. Woof, Oxford 1991, pp. 143–4, 180–1, 205–6, 225.*

Bibliographies

Siemens, R. The Wordsworth collection. Edmonton, Alberta 1971. Contains facsimile pages from mss of Grasmere journals and poems.

Siemens, R. The writings of Dorothy Wordsworth; the mss journals, Dove Cottage papers facsimiles, University of Alberta. TWC 2 1971.

Taylor, E. R. Dorothy Wordsworth: primary and secondary sources. BB 40 1983.

Collections

Journals of Dorothy Wordsworth. Ed W. Knight 2 vols 1897; ed E. de Selincourt 2 vols Oxford 1941; ed H. Darbishire, Oxford 1958 (WC), 1971 (rev M. Moorman).

The early letters of William and Dorothy Wordsworth. Ed E. de Selincourt, Oxford 1935, 1967 (rev C. L. Shaver).

The letters of William and Dorothy Wordsworth: the middle years. Ed E. de Selincourt 2 vols Oxford 1937; ed M. Moorman and A. G. Hill 2 vols Oxford 1969–70.

The letters of William and Dorothy Wordsworth: the later years. Ed E. de Selincourt 3 vols Oxford 1939; ed A. G. Hill 4 vols Oxford 1978–88.

The Grasmere journal: the revised complete text. Ed P. Woof, introd by J. Wordsworth 1987.

Journal of my second tour in Scotland, 1822. Ed J. Nagasawa, Tokyo 1989. Dorothy Wordsworth's text in English, introd and notes in Japanese.

The Grasmere journals. Ed P. Woof, Oxford 1991.

The letters of William and Dorothy Wordsworth: a supplement of new letters. Ed A. G. Hill, Oxford 1993.

Selections

Address to a child during a boisterous winter evening, The mother's return, and The cottager to her infant. First pbd in William Wordsworth, Poems, 2 vols 1815. Rptd in subsequent edns of his collected works including 1820, Boston 1824, Paris 1828 (pirated); Loving and liking and The floating island added 1836 onwards.

Select poetry for children. Ed J. Payne. 1854 (11th edn). Contains Loving and liking.

The songs and ballads of Cumberland. Ed S. Gilpin. London, Edinburgh and Carlisle 1866. Contains The mother's return and The cottager to her infant.

Peaceful our valley, fair and green, Lines addressed to Joanna H. from Gwerndwffnant in June 1826, Holiday at Gwerndwffnant, May 1826: irregular stanzas, To my niece Dora, and The worship of this Sabbath morn. Pbd in William Wordsworth, Poems, ed W. Knight 8 vols 1896.

The poetry of Dorothy Wordsworth. Ed from the journals by H. Eigerman, New York 1940. Not the poems, but brief extracts from the journals arranged on the page as vers libre.

Journals of Dorothy Wordsworth. Ed Mary Moorman, Oxford 1971. Contains two poems, including A winter's ramble in Grasmere vale, hitherto unpbd.

Levin, S. and R. Ready. Unpublished poems from Dorothy Wordsworth's commonplace book. TWC 9 1978. Six poems either previously unpbd or only partially pbd.

Levin, S. M. Dorothy Wordsworth and Romanticism. Rutgers NJ 1987. Fullest collection of Dorothy Wordsworth's poetry thus far pbd; includes some hitherto unpbd works.

Romanticism: an anthology. Ed D. Wu, Oxford 1994. Contains 8 poems edited from mss.

§1

George and Sarah Green: a narrative by Dorothy Wordsworth. Ed E. de Selincourt, Oxford 1936; ed H. Clark, Wolverhampton 1987.

Contributions to periodicals

The Monthly Packet. The worship of this Sabbath morn, July 1891; Grasmere: a fragment, Feb 1892.

Letters, journals etc

The following publications contain texts of letters and/or journals, or extracts from them:

Wilkinson, J. Select views in Cumberland, Westmoreland and Lancashire. 1810. Contains description of Wastwater attributed to Dorothy Wordsworth by Owen and Smyser, Prose works of William Wordsworth, 3 vols Oxford 1974.

Wordsworth, W. Description of the scenery of the Lakes in the north of England. 1822 (3rd edn). Dorothy Wordsworth's account of a climb of Scawfell appears here from this edn onwards.

Wordsworth, C. Memoirs of William Wordsworth. 2 vols 1851.

Pearson, W. Papers letters and journals of William Pearson. [Ed A. Pearson] 1863 (priv ptd).

Robinson, H. C. Diary, reminiscences, and correspondence. Ed T. Sadler 3 vols 1869.

Recollections of a tour made in Scotland AD 1803. Ed J. C. Shairp, Edinburgh 1874, 1874, 1894; Edinburgh 1981 (photo facs).

Myers, F. W. H. Wordsworth. 1881.

Wordsworth, W. Poetical works. Ed W. Knight 11 vols Edinburgh 1882–9.

Graves, R. P. The life of Sir William Rowan Hamilton. 3 vols 1882–9.

Lee, E. Dorothy Wordsworth: the story of a sister's love. 1886, 1894 (rev).

Knight, W. Letters from Wordsworth, his wife, and sister to Henry Crabb Robinson, and others. Trans of the Wordsworth Soc 8 1886.

Knight, W. Memorials of Coleorton. 2 vols 1887. Letters to Sir George and Lady Beaumont.

Rogers and his contemporaries. Ed P. W. Clayden 2 vols 1889.

Knight, W. The Life of William Wordsworth. 3 vols Edinburgh 1889.

Letters of the Wordsworth family from 1787 to 1855. Ed W. Knight 3 vols Boston and London 1907.

Knight, W. Coleridge and Wordsworth in the west country. 1913.

Correspondence of Henry Crabb Robinson with the Wordsworth circle. Ed E. J. Morley 2 vols Oxford 1927.

Maclean, C. Letters of Dorothy Wordsworth. TLS 12 Sep 1935.

Some letters of the Wordsworth family. Ed L. N. Broughton, Ithaca NY 1942.

Letters of Dora Wordsworth. Ed H. P. Vincent, Chicago 1944.

Bullough, G. The Wordsworth–Laing letters. MLR 46 1951.

The letters of Sara Hutchinson. Ed K. Coburn 1954.

The letters of Mary Wordsworth 1800–1855. Ed M. E. Burton, Oxford 1958. Letter of 16 Mar jointly written with Dorothy Wordsworth.

Home at Grasmere: extracts from the journal of Dorothy Wordsworth. Ed C. Clark, Harmondsworth 1960.

A Dorothy Wordsworth selection. Ed M. M. Barber, London and New York 1965.

Romantic poetry and prose. Ed H. Bloom and L. Trilling, Oxford and New York 1969.

Reed, M. L. Wordsworth letters: new items. N & Q 217 1972.

Tetreault, R. Wordsworth on enthusiasm: a new letter to Thomas Clarkson on the slavery question. MP 75 1977.

Letters of Dorothy Wordsworth: a selection. Ed A. G. Hill, Oxford 1981.

The love letters of William and Mary Wordsworth. Ed B. Darlington, Ithaca NY 1982. Contains one letter from Dorothy Wordsworth.

Dorothy Wordsworth's illustrated Lakeland journals. Introd by R. Trickett 1987.
Selections from the journals of Dorothy Wordsworth. Ed P. Hamilton 1992.
Betz, Paul F. Romantic archaeologies. 1995. Contains a letter and a poem, both hitherto unpbd.

Translations

Journals. Tr Jap Yasuko Fujii, Tokyo 1989. Trn of Moorman, 1971.

§2

Pre-1920 criticism

Review of Recollections of a tour made in Scotland. Athenaeum 11 July 1874.
Miss Wordsworth's Tour in Scotland. Saturday Rev 22 Aug 1874.
Review of Recollections of a tour made in Scotland. Christian Observer 73 1874.
Contemporary literature. Westminster Rev 46 1874.
C[hambers], W. William and Dorothy Wordsworth. Chambers's Jnl 4th ser 11 1874.
Hutton, R. H. Dorothy Wordsworth's Scotch journal. Spectator 47 1874.
Dowden, E. Wordsworth's 'Glowworm'; Lucy; and Miss Wordsworth. Acad 14 1878.
Gilchrist, A. Mary Lamb. 1883.
Lee, E. Dorothy Wordsworth. Christian World Mag 21 1885.
Review of Lee, Dorothy Wordsworth. Athenaeum 28 Aug 1886.
Dorothy Wordsworth. Saturday Rev 62 1886.
Fawcett, Mrs H. Dorothy Wordsworth. Mothers' Companion 2 1888.
Tourists in Scotland before Scott: Dorothy Wordsworth. Scots Observer 2 1889.
Dennis, J. Dorothy Wordsworth. Leisure Hour 39 1889.
Review of Lyrical ballads [ed Dowden]. Athenaeum 10 May 1890.
Lee, E. Some noble sisters. 1892.
The Wordsworths in Scotland. Spectator 72 1894.
Small, A. Dorothy Wordsworth. Great Thoughts 3rd ser 5 1895.
Dorothy Wordsworth. Saturday Rev 84 1897.
Review of Journals of Dorothy Wordsworth. Spectator 80 1897.
Review of Journals of Dorothy Wordsworth. Speaker 17 1898.
Kirlew, M. Famous sisters of great men. 1905.
Corkran, A. The romance of woman's influence. 1906.

Textual criticism

Bateson, F. W. Wordsworth. TLS 9 Apr 1976; J. Wordsworth, TLS 30 Apr 1976; Bateson, TLS 7 May 1976; J. Wordsworth, TLS 21 May 1976; R. S. Woof, TLS 28 May 1976. Cancellations in the journals.
Ketcham, C. H. Dorothy Wordsworth's journals, 1824–1835. TWC 9 1978.
Nagasawa, J. Dove Cottage MSS 98, 99 to the Forth and Clyde Canal. Eibungaku Kenkyu 63 1986.
Nagasawa, J. Dove Cottage Manuscripts, 98, 99. Eigo Seinen 133 1987.
Woof, P. Dorothy Wordsworth's Grasmere journals: readings in a familiar text. TWC 20 1989.
Woof, P. Dorothy Wordsworth's Grasmere journals: the patterns and pressures of composition. In Romantic revisions, ed. R. Brinkley and K. Hanley, Cambridge 1992. Includes four facsimile pages.
Tomlinson, B. Editing Dorothy Wordsworth. Contemporary Rev 262 Jan 1993.
Woof, P. The Alfoxden Journal and its mysteries. TWC 26 1995.
Butler, James A. William and Dorothy Wordsworth, 'Emma', and a German translation in the Alfoxden notebook. SiR 36 1997.

Biographies

De Quincey, T. Lake reminiscences. Tait's Edinburgh Mag 1839. 5 articles.
Maclean, C. M. Dorothy and William Wordsworth. 1927.
McLean, C. M. Dorothy Wordsworth: the early years. 1932. With a bibliography.
De Selincourt, E. Dorothy Wordsworth: a biography. Oxford 1933.
Gittings, R. and J. Manton. Dorothy Wordsworth. Oxford 1985.
[DW]

ii. Mid-nineteenth-century prose 1835–1870

In general, this section has been restricted to writers born after 1799 and before 1830.

William Davenport Adams 1851–1904

Famous books: sketches in the highways and byeways of English literature. 1875.
Dictionary of English literature: being a comprehensive guide to English authors and their works. [1878], [1880] (rev).
The witty and humorous side of the English poets, by Arthur H. Elliott [i.e. Adams]. 1880.
By-ways in book-land: short essays on literary subjects. 1888.
Rambles in book-land: short essays on literary subjects. 1889.
A book of burlesque: sketches of English stage travestie and parody. 1891.
With poet and player: essays on literature and the stage. 1891.
A dictionary of the drama: a guide to the plays, playwrights, players and play-houses of the United Kingdom and America, from the earliest times to the present. Vol 1 (all pbd) 1904.
Adams also compiled 9 anthologies of anecdote, epigram, verse etc, and edited A. C. Calmour, Practical playwriting, *[1891], and Disraeli,* The revolutionary epick, *1904.*

Walter Bagehot 1826–77

See col 2468.

Mrs Beeton, Isabella Mary Beeton, née Mayson 1836–65

Mrs Beeton's title as Editor concealed the elements of her own writing in The book of household mangagement. *During her lifetime several new edns and derivatives of the book were pbd by her husband, Samuel Orchart Beeton. After her death he sold his publishing house and titles to Ward, Lock and Tyler (later Ward and Lock) who produced a large number of such works, all carrying her name but with revised or abbreviated contents and sometimes new titles. Numbers in brackets indicate probable minimum number of reissues.*

§1

Beeton's book of household management. 1859–61 (pt-issue), rptd 1 vol 1861 as The book of household management. (1,982 impressions + 12 edns); Beeton's book of household management 1915 (1,950 impressions + 3 edns).
The Englishwoman's cookery book, being a collection of economical receipts taken from her Book of household management. '1863' [1862]; Mrs Beeton's shilling cookery book 1882 (155,000 impressions + 5[?] edns).
Mrs Beeton's dictionary of everyday cookery. 1865; All about cookery: a collection of practical recipes. (Mrs Beeton's all about cookery.) 1871 (1,963 impressions + 16 edns)
Beeton's house and home books. 1866–7.
How to manage house and servants and make the most of your means. [1866.]

The management of children in health and sickness. [1866.]
Beeton's penny cookery book. [c. 1870?] (1,908? impressions + 5? edns).
Beeton's everyday cookery and housekeeping book. (Beeton's everyday cookery.) 1872 (1,963 impressions + 7 edns), facs edn 1984.
Mrs Beeton's cookery and household guide. (Mrs Beeton's cookery book.) 1890 (1,960? impressions + 21 edns).
Mrs Beeton's family cookery and housekeeping book. (Mrs Beeton's family cookery.) 1893 (1,972 impressions + 7 edns).
Mrs Beeton's sixpenny cookery. [1910?].
Extensive variations of these titles also occurred in the twentieth century, including Mrs Beeton's cake-making *1924, 1952;* Mrs Beeton's jam making *1924;* Mrs Beeton's cold sweets *1925;* Mrs Beeton's hors d'oeuvres and salads *1925;* Mrs Beeton's meat dishes *1925;* Mrs Beeton's puddings and pies *1925;* Mrs Beeton's sauces and soups *1925;* Mrs Beeton's fish recipes *1926;* Mrs Beeton's poultry and game *1926, 1963;* Mrs Beeton's hints to housewives *1928;* Cakes and pastries *1963;* Mrs Beeton's preserves *1963;* Continental cookery *1964;* Mrs Beeton's favourite recipes *1972;* Mrs Beeton's easy-to-cook book *1973.*

Contributions to periodicals
Mrs Beeton also contributed to some of the periodical publications of S. O. Beeton, in particular the Englishwoman's Domestic Mag *(monthly) n.s. 1 1860–4, which she co-edited;* Queen *(weekly), ed F. Greenwood 1861–3; and* Young Englishwoman *(monthly) 1863– .*

§2
Athenaeum 19 July 1862.
Spectator 72, 27 Jan 1894.
Spain, N. Mrs Beeton and her husband. 1948, rev edn The Beeton story 1956.
Hyde, M. Mr and Mrs Beeton. 1951.
Freeman, S. Isabella and Sam: the story of Mrs Beeton. 1977.
See also Household Books, col 2735. [MB]

Samuel Orchart Beeton S. O. B 1831–77

The extent of Beeton's personal involvement in the range of works attributed to him and which he published is impossible to disentangle. In most cases he was editor, or editor and compiler, rather than sole author. In 1866 Ward, Lock and Tyler (later Ward and Lock) took over his publishing house with the right to all existing and future Beeton titles. Disagreements over their use of his name were only resolved after a lawsuit. Beeton then left Ward and Lock (1875) but they continued to use his name for works he originated. See also Mrs (Isabella Mary) Beeton, above.

§1
Beeton's dictionary of universal information I. 1858–62. With John Sherer.
Beeton's dictionary of universal information II. 1861–5. With John Sherer.
Beeton's historian. 1858–60.
Beeton's book of home pets. 1860.
Beeton's book of garden management. 1861, 1870.
Beeton's dictionary of universal biography. 1863.
Beeton's guide to journalism. 1863.
Beeton's book of birds. 1864.
All about it books. (Cookery, Everything, Gardening, Country life, Mothers' handbook.) 1865–79.
Beeton's book of anecdote, wit and humour. 1865 (3rd edn?).
Beeton's book of chemistry with experiments. 1865.
Beeton's riddle book: a collection of upwards of 500. 1865.
Beeton's book of jokes and jests and good things said and sung. 1865.
Beeton's book of songs: being a collection of national and popular songs. 1865.
Beeton's book of acting charades. 1866.
Beeton's book of anecdote, jokes and jests: or good things said and sung. 1866.
Beeton's book of games (backgammon, croquet etc). 1866.
Beeton's sixpenny book of songs: being a collection of the national and popular songs of England, Scotland and Ireland. 1866.
Our soldiers and the Victoria Cross. 1867.
Beeton's dictionary of geography and universal gazeteer. 1868.
Beeton's great book of poetry: from Caedmon and King Alfred's Boethius to Browning and Tennyson. 1868–70.
Beeton's Bible dictionary. 1870.
Beeton's book of needlework consisting of instructions with engravings. 1870.
Beeton's book of poultry and domestic animals. 1870.
Beeton's British biography from the earliest times to present day. 1870.
Beeton's British gazeteer: being a topographical and historical guide to the United Kingdom. 1870.
Beeton's fact, fiction, history and adventure. 1870.
Beeton's guide book to the stock exchange and money market. 1870.
Beeton's guide to investing money with safety and profit. 1870.
Beeton's modern men and women: British biography from the accession of George III to the present time. 1870.
Beeton's book of the laundry: or the art of washing and bleaching. 1871.
Beeton's book of the war: being a narrative of the most striking military and romantic incidents which occurred during the time from the declaration of war to the capitulation of Paris. 1871.
Beeton's British biography: from the earliest times to the accession of George III. 1871.
Beeton's classical dictionary: a cyclopedia of Greek and Roman biography. 1871.
Beeton's dictionary of practical recipes and everyday information. 1871.
Beeton's historical romances, daring deeds and animal stories. 1871.
Beeton's law books: Property, Women and children, Divorce and matrimonial causes, Wills, executors and trustees. 1871–2.
Beeton's medical dictionary. 1871.
Beeton's ready reckoner etc. 1871.
Beeton's book of games. 1872.
Beeton's brave tales, bold ballads, travels and perils (ed S. O. B.). 1872. Illus.
Beeton's datebook: a British chronology from the earliest times. 1872.
Beeton's humorous books. 1872–8.
Beeton's nine hour wages books. 1872.
Beeton's penny books. 1872–4.
The coming K . . . i.e. Edward, Prince of Wales: a satire in verse. 1872. With A. Dowty and E. D. Jerrold.
Livingstone and Stanley: an account of Dr Livingstone's early career, his travels and discoveries. Also a sketch of modern explorations of the Nile etc. 1872. With R. M. Smith.
Beeton's book of cottage management. 1873.
Beeton's complete letter writer for ladies: a useful compendium. 1873.
Beeton's complete letter writer for ladies and gentlemen. 1873.
Beeton's family register to record important family events. 1873.
Beeton's famous voyages, brigand adventures, tales of the battlefield, life and nature. 1873.
Beeton's good aim series. 1873–6.
Beeton's penny children's books. 1873.
Beeton's pictorial speller. 1873.
The Siliad: or the siege of the seats. 1873. With A. Dowty and E. D. Jerrold.
Beeton's books for all time. 1874–8.
Beeton's dictionary of everyday gardening. 1874.
Beeton's gardening book. 1874. Illus.
Beeton's men of the age and annals of the time. 1874.

Beeton's modern European celebrities: a biography of continental men and women. 1874.
Jon Duan: a twofold journey with manifold purposes in verse on past and present time with a view to the future. 1874. With A. Dowty and E. D. Jerrold.
Beeton's counting house book and ready reckoner. 1875.
Beeton's public speaker: a collection of specimens of British and foreign eloquence political, ecclesiastical and miscellaneous. 1875.
Beeton's complete etiquette for gentlemen. 1876.
Beeton's complete etiquette for ladies. 1876.
Beeton's manners of polite society: or etiquette for ladies, gentlemen and families. (Containing memoir signed S. O. B.) 1876.
Edward the Seventh: a play in seven acts. 1876. With A. Dowty and E. D. Jerrold.
Family etiquette: a complete guide. 1876.
Bacon, Francis, Viscount of St Albans. 1877.

Introductions, memoirs and prefaces

Preface in P. V. Nasby, Nasby papers, 1865.
Boisnormand de Bonnechose. History of France. Ed S. O. B. 1868.
London's great outing: the Derby Carnival. Illustr Phiz. Ed S. O. B. 1868.
Preface in J. G. Holland, Arthur Bonnicastle, 1874.
Sidney Smith, Canon of St Paul's. Essays political and social. With a brief memoir by S. O. B. 1877.

Periodicals

Beeton founded, edited and wrote regularly in the following periodicals:
Englishwoman's Domestic Mag. (Monthly) 1852–9, n.s. 1860–4, n.s. 2 1865–77.
Boys' Own Mag. (Monthly) 1855–63, n.s. 1863–8?
Boys' Own Jnl. (Monthly) 1856–7.
Beeton's Christmas annual. 1860–73. (See above, The coming K . . ., Siliad, Jon Duan, and Edward the Seventh, which were all Christmas annuals.)
Queen. (Weekly) Ed F. Greenwood. 1861–3.
Beeton's Illuminated Almanac. 1862.
Boys' Penny Mag. (Monthly) 1863–4.
Young Englishwoman. (Monthly) 1864–77.
Beeton's Jnl of Travel, Sport, History and Romance. (Weekly) 7 Dec 1867–22 Feb 1868.
Beeton's Englishwoman's Almanac. 1869–72, 1873; Beeton's Almanac and Ladies' Annual. 1874– .
Beeton's Boys' Annual. 1870.

§2

Spain, N. Mrs Beeton and her husband. 1948; rev edn The Beeton story, 1956.
Hyde, M. Mr and Mrs Beeton. 1951.
Freeman, S. Isabella and Sam: the story of Mrs Beeton. 1977. [MB]

John Stuart Blackie 1809–95

See col 540.

Barbara Leigh Bodichon, née Smith 1827–91

Bodichon's letters and notebooks are held at Girton College, Cambridge; letters and diaries at the Beinecke Lib, Yale Univ. There are also collections of her letters at Columbia Univ; in the MacCrimmon Collection, Tallahassee FL; and in the Fawcett Lib, Guildhall Univ, London. Her letters to Emily Davies pbd Harvester Microform, Brighton 1984.

§1

A brief summary in plain language of the most important laws concerning women. 1854 (anon), 1856 (2nd edn with additions), 1869 (3rd edn rev with additions).
Women and work by B. L. Smith. 1857, New York 1859 (with introd by C. M. Sedgwick).
Objections to the enfranchisement of women considered. 1866, 1867. Pam.
Reasons for the enfranchisement of women. 1866, 1867.
Reasons for and against the enfranchisement of women. [np] 1869, 1872 (2nd edn). Pam.
An American diary 1857–58. 1972 (ed J. W. Reed).
Australian forests and Algerian deserts. Pall Mall Gazette 8 1868.
Bodichon, E. Guide book. Algeria considered as a winter residence for the English. 1858. Ed Smith.
Her articles for the English Woman's Jnl *(which she helped to found) are listed in Herstein, below. She also wrote for* Macmillan's Mag *and* Temple Bar Mag. *See* Wellesley *vol 5.*

§2

Hays, F. In her Women of the day, 1885.
Belloc, B. R. P. Madame Bodichon. Englishwoman's Rev 15 July 1891.
Betham-Edwards, M. B. Madame Bodichon: a reminiscence. Fortnightly Rev 57 (n.s. 51) 1892.
In DNB 1901–1911.
Burton, H. Barbara Bodichon 1827–1891. 1949.
Banks, O. The biographical dictionary of British feminists, vol 1 1800–1930. Brighton 1985.
Herstein, S. R. A mid-Victorian feminist. Barbara Leigh Smith Bodichon. New Haven CT and London 1985.

Emilia Jessie Boucherett 1825–1905

§1

Female industry. Edinburgh Rev Apr 1859.
Hints on self-help. A book for young women. 1863, 1866.
The conditions of women in France. First pbd in Contemporary Rev May 1867. 1867. Pam.
How to provide for superfluous women. In Woman's work and woman's culture, ed J. Butler, 1869.
The industrial movement. In The woman question in Europe, ed T. Stanton, New York 1884.
The condition of working women and the factory acts. 1896. With H. Blackburn and others.
Boucherett wrote for the Englishwoman's Rev *and was its editor from 1866 to Jan 1871.*

§2

In DNB 1901–1911.
Banks, O. The biographical dictionary of British feminists, vol 1 1800–1930. Brighton 1985.

Andrew Kennedy Hutchinson Boyd 1825–99

Selections

A. K. H. B.: a volume of selections. Ed C. Boyd [1914].

§1

The recreations of a country parson. 3 ser 1859–78.
The commonplace philosopher in town and country. 1862.
Leisure hours in town. 1862.
Counsel and comfort spoken from a city pulpit. 1863.
The graver thoughts of a country parson. 3 ser 1863–76.
The autumn holidays of a country parson. 1864.
The critical essays of a country parson. 1865.
Sunday afternoons at the parish church of a university city. 1866.
Lessons of middle age. 1868.
Changed aspects of unchanged truths. 1869.
Present-day thoughts. 1871.
Seaside musings on Sundays and weekdays. 1872.
A Scotch communion Sunday. 1873.

Landscapes, churches and moralities. 1874.
From a quiet place: discourses. 1879.
East coast days and memories. 1881.
Our little life: essays consolatory. 2 ser 1882–4.
Towards the sunset: teachings after thirty years. 1883.
A young man, his home and friends. 1884.
What set him right; with other chapters to help. 1885–8.
Our homely comedy and tragedy. 1887.
The best last, with other papers. 1888.
To meet the day through the Christian year. 1889.
Twenty-five years of St Andrews, September 1865 to September 1890. 2 vols 1892.
St Andrews and elsewhere: glimpses of some gone and of things left. 1894.
Occasional and immemorial days. 1895. Sermons.
The last years of St Andrews, September 1890 to September 1895. 1896.
Sermons and stray papers: with a biographical sketch by W. W. Tulloch. 1907.
Boyd also pbd several lectures and sermons.

§2

Story, R. H. A. K. H. B. Guild Life & Work (Edinburgh) 13 May 1899.
The true significance of Boyd. Eclectic Mag 132 1899.

George Brimley 1819–57

Essays. Ed W. G. Clark, Cambridge 1858 (with memoir), 1860, 1882, [1905].
For appreciations of Brimley, see G. Saintsbury, A history of criticism *vol 3, 1904, pp. 504–8; S. T. Williams,* A mid-Victorian critic, Sewanee Rev *30 1922.*

John Brown 1810–82

§1

Horae subsecivae: Locke and Sydenham, with other occasional papers. Vol 1 Edinburgh 1858; vol 2 Edinburgh 1861. Vols 1–2, 2 vols 1862; ed A. Dobson, Oxford 1907 (WC); vol 3 Edinburgh 1882.
Rab and his friends. Edinburgh 1859, London 1901 ('and other papers'), [1905] (with Our dogs, and notes), 1906 (EL) (with other papers and essays, and bibliography), 1908 (with character sketches of the author by A. C. Brown and E. T. Maclaren), 1931. From Horae subsecivae, *above.*
'With brains, Sir'. Edinburgh 1860. An essay on education extracted from Horae subsecivae vol 1, *above.*
On the deaths of Rev John M'Gilchrist, John Brown and John Henderson. Edinburgh 1860.
Letter to Rev Dr Cairns. Edinburgh 1860, 1861 (in Horae subsecivae vol 2, *above*). Contains Domestic and personal details of the life of John Brown DD (the elder).
Health: five lay sermons to working people. Edinburgh 1862.
Our dogs. Edinburgh 1862. From Horae subsecivae vol 2, *above.*
Marjorie Fleming: a sketch. Edinburgh 1863. Rptd from North Br Rev; included in Horae subsecivae vol 3, *above.*
Jeems the doorkeeper: a lay sermon. Edinburgh 1864, 1912 ('and other stories', viz Her last half crown, Landseer's picture, In clear dream and solemn vision, The black dwarf's bones). Subsequently included in Horae subsecivae vol 3, *above.*
Minchmoor. Edinburgh 1864, 1912 (with Enterkin, Biggar and the house of Fleming). Included in Horae subsecivae vol 3, *above.*
Locke and Sydenham. Edinburgh 1866. Originally in Horae subsecivae vol 1, *above,* but not included in later edns.
Sir Henry Raeburn and his works. Edinburgh 1876 (priv ptd). Included in Horae subsecivae vol 3, *above.*
John Leech. Edinburgh 1877, 1882. In Horae subsecivae vol 3, *above.*
Thackeray: his literary career. Boston 1877.
Something about a well; with more of Our dogs. Edinburgh 1882.

Letters

Letters; with letters from Ruskin, Thackeray and others. Ed J. Brown and D. W. Forrest 1907.

§2

Lang, A. Rab's friend. Cent Illus Monthly Mag Feb 1883.
Maclaren, E. T. Brown and his sister Isabella. 1889, 1896 (as Brown and his sisters Isabella and Jane), 1901 (with introductory note by A. C. Brown).
Masson, D. In his Edinburgh sketches and memories, 1892.
Peddie, A. Recollections of Brown, with a selection from his correspondence. 1893.
Brown, J. T. Brown: a biography and a criticism. 1903.

Josephine Elizabeth Butler, née Grey 1828–1906

The Josephine Butler Soc Lib containing letters, papers and pams, is in the Fawcett Lib, Guildhall Univ, London. There is also a collection of her letters in Josephine Butler House, Liverpool Univ.

Bibliographies

Johnson, G. W. and L. A. (ed). In their Josephine E. Butler, 1909.
Petrie, G. In his A singular iniquity. The campaigns of Josephine Butler, 1971.

§1

The education and employment of women. Liverpool 1868, London 1868.
Letter to Mr Boyce on examination for governesses. Liverpool [1868].
Memoir of John Grey of Dilston. Edinburgh 1869, London 1874 (rev edn); tr Ital 1871.
REVIEWS: Fortnightly Rev 12 1869; Spectator 42 1869.
An appeal to the people of England on the recognition and superintendence of prostitution by government. Nottingham 1870 (anon). Pam.
The duty of women. Address at Carlisle. Carlisle 1870.
On the moral reclaimability of prostitutes. 1870; tr Ital 1875. Pam.
Address delivered at Craigie Hall, Edinburgh, 24 Feb 1871. Manchester 1871. Pam.
Address delivered at Croydon, 3 July 1871. 1871. Pam.
The constitutional iniquity of the contagious diseases acts. Bradford 1871. Pam.
The constitution violated. Edinburgh 1871. Anon.
Letter to the Order of Good Templars. Liverpool 1871. Pam.
Sursum corda: annual address delivered to the Ladies' National Association. Liverpool 1871. Pam.
Vox populi. Liverpool 1871.
A few words addressed to true-hearted women. 1872. Pam.
A letter on the subject of Mr Bruce's bill, addressed to the repealers of the contagious diseases act. [Liverpool] 1872.
The new era: containing a retrospect of the history of the regulation system in Berlin.... Liverpool 1872.
Letter to a friend on recent divisions in the House of Commons. Liverpool 1873. Pam.
Some thoughts on the present aspect of the crusade against the state regulation of vice. Liverpool 1874.
Speech delivered ... at the 4th annual meeting of the Vigilance Association ... Bristol, 15 Oct 1874. [1874.] Pam.
A letter to the members of the Ladies' National Association. [Liverpool 1875.] Pam.
Une voix dans le desert. [1875], Geneva 1905, Bristol 1913 (as A voice of one crying in the wilderness; tr O. Airy, with an introd by J. Stuart).

The hour before the dawn. An appeal to men. 1876 (anon), 1882 (2nd edn); tr Fr 1876.
State regulation of vice. np 1876. Pam.
The Paris of regulated vice. 1877. Pam.
Catharine of Siena: a biography. 1878, 1879 (2nd edn), 1881 (3rd edn), 1885 (4th edn), 1894, 1895; tr Fr 1887.
REVIEW: Spectator 52 1879.
Government by police. 1879, 1880 (2nd edn), 1888 (new edn).
Social purity. An address given at Cambridge in May 1879. [1879], 1881 (2nd edn), 1882; tr Du 1884.
Deposition regarding treatment of English girls in immoral houses in Brussels. 1880 (priv ptd).
Address at the tenth anniversary of the Ladies' National Association. Liverpool 1880. Pam.
A call to action. Birmingham 1881. Pam.
A letter to the mothers of England. Liverpool 1881; tr Fr 1882.
Address at the conference of women at Geneva. 1881. Pam.
The life of Jean-Frédéric Oberlin, pastor of the Ban de la Roche. [1882] (illus), 1886.
REVIEW: London Quart Rev 60 1883.
The bright side of the question. Bristol 1883.
The dangers of constructive legislation in matters of purity. Bristol 1883, 1914. Pam.
The Salvation Army in Switzerland. 1883, 1884.
The principles of the abolitionists. An address delivered at Exeter Hall, 20 Feb 1885. [1885]; tr Fr nd, Ger nd.
Mrs Rebecca Jarrett. 1885. Biography.
The work of the Federation. 1885.
A grave question ... that needs answering by the churches of Great Britain. [1886.]
Simple words for simple folk about the repeal of the C. D. acts. Bristol [1886].
Our Christianity tested by the Irish question. [1887.] Pam.
The revival and extension of the abolitionist cause. A letter. Winchester 1887.
A letter to the international convention of women at Washington. 1888. Pam.
Mrs Butler's appeal to the women of America. New York 1888.
Recollections of George Butler. Bristol [1892] (illus).
A letter to the world's women's Christian temperance union. Bristol 1892. Pam.
The present aspect of the abolitionist cause in relation to British India. [1893]; tr Fr 1894.
St Agnes. 1893.
The lady of Shunem. [1894], 1895. Religious writings.
Two letters of earnest appeal and warning. 1895. Pam.
A doomed iniquity. 1896.
Address to the ladies' National Association. Bristol 1896. Pam.
Personal reminiscences of a great crusade. 1896, 1898 (new edn), 1899, 1910 (new edn), 1911, 1913, [1935]; tr Fr 1900, Ger 1904, Polish 1904, Rus 1904.
Truth before everything. 1897.
Some lessons from contemporary history. 1898.
Prophets and prophetesses. Newcastle 1898; tr Fr 1898.
Native races and the war. 1900.
Silent victories. 1900.
In memoriam, Harriet Meuricoffre. [1901.]
The morning cometh. Newcastle 1903. Anon. Pam.
The voice of one crying in the wilderness. Bristol 1913. Eng trn of Une voix dans le desert, 1875, *above*.
The social purity movement. nd.

Articles, letters etc.

Legislative restrictions on the industry of women considered from the women's point of view. By Butler and others. 1873. Pam.
The Paris of regulated vice. Methodist Protest. 1877.
Women's place in church work. Rev of the Churches 1892.
A letter to conference in London. Shield. 1897.
Receiving, Wings. 1900.
Burton, M. Josephine Butler has her say about her contemporaries. Selected from the letters of Josephine Butler. 1972.
Woman's work and woman's culture. Ed and introd by Butler. 1896.
REVIEWS: Edinburgh Rev 266 1869; Nation (New York) 9 1869; London Quart Rev 33 1870.
Thomas, H. E. The martyrs of hell's highway. Preface and appendix by Butler. 1896.
Butler edited and wrote for the periodicals the Dawn *(1888–96) and the* Storm-Bell *(1898–1900). See also* Wellesley *vol 5.*

§2

Stead, W. T. Josephine Butler. A life sketch. 1887.
Dawson, A. A noble woman and her work. A talk with Mrs Josephine Butler. Young Woman 1 1892–3.
In DNB 1901–1911.
Johnson, G. W. and L. A. (ed). Josephine E. Butler. An autobiographical memoir, with an introd by J. Stuart. Bristol 1909, 1911 (2nd edn), Bristol and London 1928 (3rd edn rev and enlarged).
REVIEW: Bookman 36 1909.
Petrie, G. A singular iniquity. The campaigns of Josephine Butler. 1971.
Banks, O. The biographical dictionary of British feminists, vol 1 1800–1930. Brighton 1985.

Jane Welsh Carlyle 1801–66

Bowdoin College, Bodleian Lib, BL, Harvard, Nat Lib of Scotland, Univ of California (Santa Cruz), and Yale contain substantial collections of mss. More minor collections are documented in IELM vol 4 pt 1 1982.

Bibliographies

Tennyson, G. B. Jane Welsh Carlyle. In Victorian prose: a guide to research, ed D. J. DeLaura, New York 1973.
Tennyson, G. B. The Carlyles. In A guide to the year's work in Victorian poetry and prose, 1973. Victorian Poetry (suppl). Ed R. Tobias Autumn 1974.
Tarr, R. L. A bibliography of English language articles on Thomas Carlyle, 1824–1974. Charlottesville VA 1974.
Tarr, R. L. Thomas Carlyle: a descriptive bibliography. Pittsburgh 1989.

§1

Budget of a femme incomprise. In J. A. Froude, Thomas Carlyle: a history of the first forty years of his life vol 2, 1884. Full text in Mrs A. Ireland, Jane Welsh Carlyle, 1892.
The simple story of my own first-love. In New letters and memorials of Jane Welsh Carlyle vol 2, ed A. Carlyle, 1903.
Poems: 'I Love the mountain torrent', 'The wish,' 'Lines to Lord Byron', 'Verses written at midnight'; poetic translations: 'The fisher', 'An Indian mother's lament', 'A love song', 'A Sirvente'. In Love letters of Thomas and Jane Welsh Carlyle vol 2, ed A. Carlyle, 1909 (John Lane). Corrected texts in The collected poems of Thomas and Jane Welsh Carlyle, ed R. L. Tarr and F. McClelland, Greenwood FL 1986.
A story from real life. By Jane Welsh Carlyle. Cornhill Mag 121 1920. Ed A. Carlyle. Story.
The rival brothers. In Collected letters of Thomas and Jane Welsh Carlyle vol 7, ed C. R. Sanders and K. J. Fielding, Durham NC 1977. Play.
My loved minstrel. In Thomas and Jane: selected letters, ed I. M. Campbell, Edinburgh 1980. Poem.
Poems: 'Lines on – I don't know what', ['The setting sun'], ['With song and dance grotesque'], ['Dark chain']. In The collected poems.

Letters and journals

Froude, J. A. (ed). Letters and memorials of Jane Welsh Carlyle. 3 vols 1883.

REVIEWS: Wallace, W. Acad 23 1883; [Jenkins, M.] American 6 1883; [Skelton, J.] Blackwood's Edinburgh Mag 133 1883; [Browne, F. F.] Dial 4 1883; Good Words 24 1883; Hibernia 2 1883; Literary World 14 1883; Saturday Rev 55 1883; [Metcalfe, W. M.] Scottish Rev 2 1883; The Times 31 Mar 1883; Callaway, M. Methodist Quart Rev 66 1884.

Letters of William Maccall and Jane Welsh Carlyle. Pall Mall Gazette 26 1884.

Jane Welsh Carlyle letter to Mrs Daubeny. Critic (NY) 13 1888.

Early letters of Jane Welsh Carlyle. Ed D. G. Ritchie 1889.

REVIEWS: Athenaeum 3218 1889; N & Q 8 1889; Saturday Rev 48 1889; Spectator 63 1889.

Letters of Jane Welsh Carlyle to Amely Bölte. New Rev 6 1892.

New letters and memorials of Jane Welsh Carlyle. Ed A. Carlyle 2 vols 1903. Vol 2 contains a part of the journal which she kept 21 Oct 1855–5 July 1856.

Love letters of Thomas Carlyle and Jane Welsh. Ed A. Carlyle 2 vols 1909.

Carlyle, A. Eight new love letters of Jane Welsh. Nineteenth Cent and After 75 1914.

Carlyle, A. More new letters of Jane Welsh Carlyle. Nineteenth Cent and After 76 1914.

Blunt, R. Jane Carlyle's unpublished letters. Forum 66 1921.

Huxley, L. Family letters of Jane Welsh Carlyle. Cent Mag 17 1924.

Jane Welsh Carlyle: letters to her family, 1839–1863. Ed L. Huxley 1924.

Huxley, L. A sheaf of letters from Jane Welsh Carlyle. Cornhill Mag 124 1926.

Letters of Jane Welsh Carlyle to Joseph Neuberg 1848–62. Ed. T. Scudder 1931.

Meikle, H. W. Two letters of Jane Welsh Carlyle. Scottish Historical Rev 28 1949.

Jane Welsh Carlyle: a new selection of her letters. Ed T. Bliss 1949.

Reynolds, M. M. A new letter of Jane Welsh Carlyle. TLS 28 Mar 1952.

Chalmers, E. B. Mrs Carlyle's letters to John Stodart. TLS 25 June 1971.

I too am here: selections from the letters of Jane Welsh Carlyle. Ed A. and M. McQueen Simpson, Cambridge 1977.

§2

The late Mrs Carlyle. The Times 23 June 1866.

Jane Welsh Carlyle. Chambers's Jnl 58 1881.

Larkin, H. Carlyle and Mrs Carlyle: a ten years' reminiscence. Br Quart Rev 74 1881.

Tabor, M. C. Young Mrs Carlyle: a life study. Good Words 22 1881.

Jane Welsh Carlyle. Atlantic Monthly 51 1883.

Mrs Carlyle. Spectator 56 1883.

Some reminiscences of Jane Welsh Carlyle. Temple Bar 69 1883.

Oliphant, M. O. W. Mrs. Carlyle. Contemporary Rev 43 1883.

Dowden, E. George Eliot and Jane Carlyle. Critic NY 6 1885.

Mackintosh, E. J. Carlyle and Carlyle's wife. Peterson's Mag 87 1885.

[Leigh Hunt, Jane Welsh Carlyle, and 'Jenny kissed me']. Dial 10 1889.

Ireland, Mrs A. Life of Jane Welsh Carlyle. 1891.

A Scotchwoman a week with Mrs Carlyle. Independent NY 50 1898.

Blunt, R. Mrs. Carlyle and her housemaid. Cornhill Mag 84 1901.

Hogben, J. Jane Welsh Carlyle. Scotia 5 1911.

Blunt, R. Mrs Carlyle and her little Charlotte. Strand Mag 49 1915.

Drew, E. A. Jane Welsh and Jane Carlyle. [1928.]

Woolf, V. Geraldine and Jane. TLS 28 Feb 1929.

Wilson, G. Temperamental Jane: the strange story of Carlyle's wife. New York 1931.

Thornton-Cook, E. P. Speaking dust: Thomas and Jane Carlyle. A biographical novel. 1938.

Scudder, T. Jane Welsh Carlyle. New York 1939.

Hughes, G. Mrs Carlyle: a historical play. Seattle 1950.

Hanson, L. and E. Hanson. Necessary evil: the life of Jane Carlyle. 1952.

Morrison, N. Brysson. When Thomas Carlyle met Jane Welsh. Scots Mag 56 1952.

Stebbens, L. P. Friendship and love: Jane Welsh, Carlyle and Edward Irving. London Ladies. New York 1952.

Morrison, N. Brysson. True minds: the marriage of Thomas and Jane Carlyle. 1974.

Disch, T. M. and C. Naylor. Neighboring lives. New York 1981.

Rose, P. Parallel lives: five victorian marriages. New York 1983.

Surtees, V. Jane Welsh Carlyle. Salisbury 1986.

Bloom, A. B. Jane Welsh Carlyle: review of recent research 1974–1987. Carlyle Annual 10 1989.

Campbell, Ian. Jane Welsh Carlyle. In Dictionary of literary biography, vol 55 Victorian prose writers before 1867, ed W. B. Thesing, Detroit 1987.

Clarke, N. Ambitious heights: writing, friendship, love – The Jewsbury sisters, Felicia Hemans, and Jane Welsh Carlyle. 1990.

[RLT]

Robert Chambers 1802–71

See col 2528.

William Chappell 1809–88

A collection of national English airs: consisting of ancient song, ballad and dance tunes, interspersed with remarks and anecdote, and preceded by an essay on English minstrelsy. 2 pts 1838–40.

Popular music of the olden time: a collection of ancient songs, ballads and dance tunes, illustrative of the national music of England; with short introductions to the different reigns, and notices of the airs from writers of the sixteenth and seventeenth centuries; also a short account of the minstrels. 2 vols [1855–9]; rev H. E. Wooldridge 2 vols 1893.

The Roxburghe ballads; with short notes by William Chappell, and copies of the original woodcuts. 3 vols 1869–75 (Ballad Soc).

The history of music. Vol 1 (all pbd) [1874].

Chappell founded the Musical Antiquarian Soc, 1841, and edited one of its pbns as well as several other works.

Henry Fothergill Chorley 1808–72

§1

Sketches of a sea port town. 3 vols 1834.

Conti the discarded; with other tales and fancies. 3 vols 1835.

Memorials of Mrs Hemans; with illustrations of her literary character from her private correspondence. 2 vols 1836.

The authors of England: a series of medallion portraits of modern literary characters, engraved from the works of British artists by A. Collas; with illustrative notices by H. F. Chorley. 1838; rev G. B. 1861.

The lion: a tale of the coteries. 3 vols 1839. Anon.

Music and manners in France and Germany: a series of travelling sketches of art and society. 3 vols 1841.

Pomfret: or public opinion and private judgment. 3 vols 1845.

Old love and new fortune: a play [in verse]. 1850.

Modern German music: recollections and criticisms. 2 vols 1854.

Duchess Eleanour: a tragedy by H. F. C[horley]. [1854.]

The may-queen: a pastoral. [1858.]

Roccabella: a tale of a woman's life by Paul Bell. 2 vols [1859].

The amber witch: a romantic opera, in four acts [and in verse]. [1861.]

The prodigy: a tale of music. 3 vols 1866. Anon.
Thirty years' recollections. 2 vols 1862; ed E. Newman, New York 1926.
Mendelssohn's letters from Italy and Switzerland [with biographical sketch by Chorley]. 1864.
Life of F. Mendelssohn Bartholdy, by W. A. Lampadius; with supplementary sketches by H. F. Chorley. 1865.
The national music of the world. Ed H. G. Hewlett 1880.
Chorley also edited several works and arranged Scribe's Black domino *for the English stage.*

§2

Linley, G. Musical cynics of London: a satire. 1862.
Chorley: autobiography, memoir and letters compiled by H. G. Hewlett. 2 vols 1873.
Chorley and his contemporaries. Temple Bar Dec 1873.
Marshall, J. In G. Grove, Dictionary of music and musicians vol 1, 1879.

Mary Victoria Cowden Clarke, née Novello 1809–98

§1

The complete concordance to Shakespeare: being a verbal index to all the passages in the dramatic works of the poet. 18 monthly pts 1844–5, 1845, 1847, [1855] (rev).
A book of stories for young people. [1847.] By Mrs Howitt, Mrs S. C. Hall and Mrs Clarke (2 stories).
Shakespeare proverbs: or the wise saws of our wisest poet. 1848; ed W. J. Rolfe, New York 1908.
Kit Bam's adventures: or the yarns of an old mariner. 1849.
The girlhood of Shakespeare's heroines in a series of fifteen tales. 3 vols 1851–2, 1 vol 1879 (condensed by S. Novello), 5 vols [1892] (with new preface), 3 vols [1906] (EL).
The iron cousin: or mutual influence. 2 vols 1854, 1 vol 1862.
The song of a drop o' wather, by Harry Wandsworth Shortfellow. 1856.
World-noted women: or types of womanly attributes. New York 1858.
The life and labours of Vincent Novello. [1864.]
The trust and the remittance: two love stories. 1873.
Short stories in metrical prose. 1873.
A rambling story. 2 vols 1874.
An idyl of London streets. Rome 1875.
Recollections of writers. 1878. With Charles Cowden Clarke.
The Shakespeare key: unlocking the treasures of his style. 1879. Selections; with Charles Cowden Clarke.
Honey from the weed: verses. 1881; Verse-waifs: forming an appendix to Honey from the weed, 1883.
A score of sonnets to one object. 1884.
Uncle, Peep and I: a child's novel. 1886.
Centennial biographic sketch of Charles Cowden Clarke. 1887 (priv ptd).
Memorial sonnets. 1888.
My long life. 1896, 1896.

Letters

Letters to an enthusiast: being a series of letters addressed to Robert Balmanno esq of New York 1850–61. Ed A. U. Nettleton, Chicago 1902.
Mary Cowden Clarke also pbd several edns of Shakespeare, the most elaborate being Cassell's Illustrated Shakespeare, *with Charles Cowden Clarke. She translated Berlioz,* Treatise upon modern instrumentation, *and edited the* Musical Times *1853–6.*

§2

Blos, H. Die Auffassung der Frauengestalten Shakespeares in dem Werke der Mrs Cowden Clarke The Girlhood of Shakespeare's heroines. Würzburg 1936.
Altick, R. D. The Cowden Clarkes. New York 1948.
B., E. Cowden Clarke and Chaucer. N & Q 6 Aug 1949.
Black, M. W. The Cowden Clarkes and the Furnesses. Univ of Pennsylvania Lib Chron 18 1952.
The Novello–Cowden Clarke collection. Leeds 1955.
Falk, D. V. Mary Cowden Clarke and her East End Injun. Jnl Rutgers Univ Lib 24 1961.

Frances Power Cobbe 1822–1904

§1

An essay on intuitive morals: being an attempt to popularise ethical science. 2 vols 1855, 1857.
Female education and how it would be affected by university examinations. 1862.
Essays on the pursuits of women. 1863.
Thanksgiving: a chapter of religious duty. 1863.
Broken lights: an inquiry into the present condition and future prospects of religious faith. 1864, 1865.
The cities of the past. 1864.
Italics: brief notes on politics, people and places in Italy in 1864. 1864.
Religious duty. 1864, Boston 1883, London 1894.
Studies new and old of ethical and social subjects. 1865.
Hours of work and play. 1867.
The confessions of a lost dog. 1867.
Dawning lights: an inquiry concerning the secular results of the new reformation. 1868, 1894.
Criminals, idiots, women and minors? Is the classification sound? Manchester 1869. On married women's property laws.
Auricular confession in the Church of England. 1872, [1898] (4th edn rev).
Darwinism in morals and other essays. 1872.
Doomed to be saved. 1874.
The hopes of the human race hereafter and here. 1874, 1894.
Re-echoes. 1876, 1877.
False beasts and true: essays on natural and unnatural history. [1876.]
The duties of women. 1881, Boston 1881, 1888 (8th Amer edn); ed B. Atkinson 1905.
The peak in Darien, with some other inquiries touching concerns of the soul and body. 1882, Boston 1882, London 1894.
A faithless world. 1885, 1891, 1894 (with Health and holiness, *below*).
Rest in the Lord, and other small pieces. 1887 (priv ptd).
The scientific spirit of the age, and other pleas and discussions. 1888.
The friend of man; and his friends – the poets. 1889.
The modern rack: papers on vivisection. 1889.
Health and holiness. 1891.
Miss Cobbe also wrote a large number of pams against vivisection.

§2

Life: by herself. 2 vols 1894, 1904 (with addns and introd by B. Atkinson).
Chappell, J. Women of worth. [1908.]

John Conington 1825–69

See col 602.

Eneas Sweetland Dallas 1828–79

§1

Poetics: an essay on poetry. 1852.
Curren Bell. Blackwood's Mag July 1857; Blake, Macmillan's Mag July 1864.

The gay science. 2 vols 1866.
The Stowe–Byron controversy: a complete résumé of all that has been written and said upon the subject, together with an impartial review of the merits of the case. [1869.]
Kettner's Book of the table: a manual of cookery. 1877.
Dallas also edited an abridgement of Richardson's Clarissa, *1868. He was editor of* Once a Week, *1868, and on the staff of* The Times.

§2

Drinkwater, J. In The eighteen-sixties, Cambridge 1932.
Roberts, M. The dream and the poet. TLS 18 Jan 1936.
Roellinger, F. X. A note on Kettner's Book of the table. MLN 54 1939.
Roellinger, F. X. Dallas in Trollope's Autobiography. MLN 55 1940.
Roellinger, F. X. Dallas: a mid-Victorian critic of individualism. PQ 20 1941.
Roellinger, F. X. Dallas on imagination. SP 38 1941.
Buckler, W. E. William Shenstone and Dallas: an identification. N & Q 18 Mar 1950.
Buckler, W. E. Dallas's appointment as editor of Once a Week. N & Q 24 June 1950.
Warren, A. H. Poetics: an essay on poetry, 1852. In his English poetic theory 1825–65, Princeton 1950.
Forsyth, R. A. The onward march of thought and the poetic theory of Dallas. Br Jnl of Aesthetics 3 1963.
For some of Dallas's periodial contributions, see Wellesley *vol 5.*

Charles Robert Darwin 1809–82

See col 2537.

James William Davison 1813–85

Chopin. [1843.]
Music during the Victorian era, from Mendelssohn to Wagner: being the memoirs of J. W. Davison, compiled by his son Henry Davison from memoranda and documents; with numerous portraits of musicians, and important letters (previously unpublished) of Mendelssohn, Berlioz, Gounod, Jullien, Macfarren, Sterndale Bennett etc. 1912.
Davison was editor of the Musical World *from about 1844 until his death. He became musical critic of* The Times *c. 1846.*

Aubrey Thomas de Vere 1814–1902

See col 605.

John Doran 1807–78

§1

Sketches and reminiscences [from Paris]. 1828.
The history and antiquities of the town and borough of Reading. Reading 1835. Anon.
Filia dolorosa: memoirs of Marie Thérèse Charlotte, Duchess of Angoulême. 1852. The first 115 pp. by Mrs I. F. Romer; completed by Doran.
Habits and men; with remnants of record touching the makers of both. 1854.
Table traits; with something on them. 1854.
Lives of the queens of England of the house of Hanover. 2 vols 1855, 1874 (rev and enlarged).
Knights and their days. 1856.
Monarchs retired from business. 2 vols 1857.
The history of Court fools. 1858.
New pictures and old panels. 1859.
The book of the Princes of Wales, heirs to the Crown of England. 1860.
Memoir of Queen Adelaide, Consort of King William IV. 1861.
'Their Majesties' servants': annals of the English stage from Thomas Betterton to Edward Kean: actors – authors – audiences. 2 vols 1864, 1865 (rev and enlarged); rev R. W. Lowe 3 vols 1888.
Saints and sinners; or in church and about it. 2 vols 1868.
A lady of the last century (Mrs E. Montagu), illustrated in her unpublished letters; collected and arranged, with a biographical sketch and a chapter on Blue Stockings. 1873.
London in the Jacobite times. 2 vols 1877.
Memoirs of our great towns; with anecdotic gleanings concerning their worthies and their oddities 1860–77. 1878.
In and about Drury Lane and other papers, reprinted from Temple Bar etc. [Ed G. B., i.e. G. Bentley?] 2 vols 1881.
Doran also edited or wrote introds for 10 other works.

§2

Jeaffreson, J. C. The life and writings of Doran. Temple Bar Apr 1878.
Jowitt, J. Some departed contributors and literary friends. Reliquary 18 1878.
Doran. London Soc July 1882.

Sir Francis Hastings Charles Doyle 1810–88

See col 608.

Elizabeth, Lady Eastlake, née Rigby 1809–93

§1

A residence on the shores of the Baltic. 2 vols 1841, 1842 (as Letters from the shores of the Baltic). Anon.
The Jewess: a tale from the shores of the Baltic. 1843.
Livonian tales. 1846. The disponent; The wolves; The Jewess.
Vanity fair and Jane Eyre. Quart Rev 84 1848.
Music and the art of dress: two essays. 1852. Anon; rptd from Quart Rev.
Treasures of art in Great Britain. 4 vols 1845–7. Tr from G. F. Waagen.
The history of our Lord as exemplified in works of art. 1864. Begun by Mrs A. Jameson; completed by Lady Eastlake.
Fellowship: letters addressed to my sister mourners. 1868. 7 letters written on the death of her husband.
Memoir of Sir C. L. Eastlake. Prefixed to Sir C. L. Eastlake, Contributions to the literature of the fine arts ser 2, 1870.
Life of John Gibson RA. 1870.
The schools of painting in Italy. 2 pts 1874. Tr from F. T. Kugler. First pbd in 1842, with Sir Charles Eastlake as editor, and in charge of the trn. There were two new edns before this, which is entirely tr Lady Eastlake and rev and remodelled from the latest researches.
Mrs Grote: a sketch. 1880.
Five great painters. 2 vols 1883. Essays rptd from Edinburgh Rev and Quart Rev: Leonardo da Vinci, Michael Angelo, Titian, Raphael, Dürer.
S. T. Coleridge and the English romantic school. 1887. Tr from the Ger of A. Brandl.

Letters

Journals and correspondence of Lady Eastlake, edited by her nephew C. E. Smith. 2 vols 1895. Forms a memoir of Lady Eastlake.

§2

Kugler, F. T. The schools of painting in Italy, edited and in part rewritten by A. H. Layard. 2 vols 1887. The introd gives an account of Lady Eastlake.
The Times 3 Oct 1893. Obituary.

Whitwell Elwin 1816–1900

§1

The complete works of Alexander Pope. Vols 1, 2, 6, 8, 1871–2; vols 3–5, 9, 10, ed W. J. Courthope 1881–9.
John Forster. Prefixed to the catalogue of the Dyce and Forster Library, 1888.
Some eighteenth century men of letters. Ed Warwick Elwin 2 vols 1902. Rptd from Quart Rev: Cowper, Sterne, Fielding, Goldsmith, Boswell and Dr Johnson. Includes anon memoir.
For Elwin's contributions to Quart Rev, *see* Wellesley *vol 5.*

§2

Williams, S. T. A critic of eighteenth-century literature. Texas Rev 8 1922.
Some letters of Elwin. TLS 18–25 Sep 1953.

John Forster 1812–76

§1

The cabinet cyclopaedia. Ed D. Lardner. To the section Lives of eminent British statesmen, Forster contributed the following biographies: vol 2 1836, Sir John Eliot (rptd enlarged 2 vols 1864) and Thomas Wentworth, Earl of Strafford; vol 3 1837, John Pym and John Hampden; vol 4 1838, Sir Henry Vane and Henry Marten; vols 6–7 1839, Oliver Cromwell. Forster's contributions were rptd 5 vols 1840 as Statesmen of the Commonwealth.
A treatise on the popular progress in English history. Introd to Statesmen of the Commonwealth, 1840.
The life and adventures of Oliver Goldsmith. 1848, 2 vols 1854 (enlarged as The life and times of Goldsmith); ed R. Ingpen 1903 (abridged).
Daniel De Foe and Charles Churchill. 2 vols 1855. Rptd from Edinburgh Rev; later included in Historical and biographical essays, vol 2, *below*.
Historical and biographical essays. 2 vols 1858, 1860 (with rev and enlarged edn of vol 2). Vol 1 The debates on the Grand Remonstrance, The Plantagenets and the Tudors, The Civil Wars and Oliver Cromwell; vol 2 Defoe, Steele, Churchill, Foote.
The arrest of the five members by Charles the First; a chapter of history re-written. 1860.
The debates on the Grand Remonstrance, November and December 1641; with an introductory essay on English freedom under the Plantagenet and Tudor sovereigns. 1860. Rptd with addns from Historical and biographical essays vol 1, *above*.
Walter Savage Landor: a biography. 2 vols 1869, 1876 (rev and abridged as vol 1 of The works of Landor).
The life of Charles Dickens. 3 vols 1872–4; ed G. Gissing 1903 (rev and abridged); ed G. K. Chesterton 2 vols 1927 (EL); ed J. W. T. Ley [1928] (rev).
Alexander Dyce: a biographical sketch. Prefixed to vol 1 of catalogue of the Dyce collection in the South Kensington Museum, 1875.
The life of Jonathan Swift. Vol 1 (all pbd) 1875. Completed by Sir H. Craik.
Dramatic essays by John Forster and G. H. Lewes. Ed W. Archer and R. W. Lowe 1896. 11 essays by Forster rptd from Examiner, 6 on Macready as actor and as producer, 4 on Forster and one on Charles Kean as Hamlet.

§2

Powell, T. Pictures of the living authors of Britain. 1851.
Morley, H. Sketch of Forster. Prefixed to the Handbook of the Forster and Dyce collections, 1877.
Elwin, W. Biographical notice. Prefixed to catalogue of the Dyce and Forster Library, 1888.
Renton, R. Forster and his friendships. 1912.
S[awyer], C. J. and F. J. H. D[arton]. Dickens v. Barabbas, Forster intervening. 1930. A study of Dickens's relations with his publishers and with Forster.
Elwin, M. Forster. In his Victorian wallflowers, 1934.
Grubb, G. G. New letters from Dickens to Forster. Boston Univ Stud in Eng 2 1956.
Davies, J. A. John Forster: a literary life. Leicester 1983.

William Forsyth 1812–99

Hortensius: or the advocate; an historical essay. 1849, 1874 (illus).
Fides laici. 1850. Anon; a long religious poem.
The great fair of Nijni Novogorod and how we got there. 1850 (priv ptd). Later included in Essays critical and narrative, 1874.
History of trial by jury. 1852.
History of the captivity of Napoleon at St Helena, from the letters and journals of the late Lieut-Gen Sir H. Lowe, and official documents not before made public. 3 vols 1853.
The life of M. T. Cicero. 2 vols 1864, 1867.
Rome and its ruins. [1865.]
Marie Antoinette in the Conciergerie: a lecture. [1867.]
The novels and novelists of the eighteenth century, in illustration of the manners and morals of the age. 1871.
History of ancient manuscripts: a lecture. 1872.
Hannibal in Italy: an historical drama. 1872.
Essays critical and narrative. 1874. Literary style; William Cobbett; Eugénie de Guérin etc.
The rules of evidence as applicable to the credibility of history; with the discussion thereon from the Journal of the Victoria Institute. 1874.
The Slavonic provinces south of the Danube: a sketch of their history and present state in relation to the Ottoman Porte. 1876.
Forsyth also pbd several legal works.

Sir Francis Galton 1822–1911

See col 2543.

Anne Gilchrist, née Burrows 1828–85

For mss of Gilchrist's letters, including those to Alfred and Emily Tennyson, Lord Houghton, Francis Palgrave, D. G. Rossetti and publishers Macmillan and Blackwood, see LR I, 398.

§1

Mary Lamb. 1883. Eminent Women Ser, ed John H. Ingram, micro Chicago 1978. Boston 1883 with ser title Famous Women, rptd New York 1972, and micros Louisville KY [19?] and New Haven CT 1977; 1889 (new edn), Boston 1898, 1909 (3rd edn).

Contributions to periodicals

A glance at the vegetable kingdom. Chambers's Jnl 8, 10 Oct 1857.
Our nearest relation. All the Year Round 1, 28 May 1859.
The indestructibility of force. Macmillan's Mag 6, Aug 1862.
A neglected art. Macmillan's Mag 12, Oct 1865.
A woman's estimate of Walt Whitman (from late letters by an English lady to William Michael Rossetti). Radical 7, May 1870.
Three glimpses of a New England village. Blackwood's Mag 136, Nov 1884. Rptd in Anne Gilchrist: her life and writings, ed H. H. Gilchrist, 1887.
A confession of faith. Today n.s. 3 no 6, June 1885. On Whitman.
Both articles on Whitman are rptd in Anne Gilchrist: her life and writings, *ed H. H. Gilchrist, 1887, and in* The letters of Anne Gilchrist and Walt Whitman, *ed with an introd by T. B. Harned, New York 1918.* A woman's estimate of Walt Whitman *has also been rptd in* In re Walt Whitman, *ed H. L. Traubel, R. M. Bucke and T. B. Harned, Philadelphia 1893. Abridgements of it have been pbd in R. M. Bucke,* Walt Whitman, *Philadelphia 1883,* A century of Whitman criticism, *ed E. H. Miller,*

Bloomington IN 1969, and in Walt Whitman: the critical heritage, *ed M. Hindus, 1971.* A confession of faith *has been rptd in E. P. Gould,* Anne Gilchrist and Walt Whitman, *Philadelphia 1900, rptd Folcroft PA 1974 and Norwood PA 1976.*

Collaborative works

Life of William Blake, 'pictor ignotus', with selections from his poems and other writings, by the late Alexander Gilchrist. Illustrated from Blake's own works ... with a few of Blake's original plates. 2 vols 1863. (Alexander Gilchrist was Anne's husband; she edited the work after his death, in collaboration with Dante Gabriel and William Michael Rossetti, and wrote the preface. In the new and enlarged edn, 2 vols 1880, she added a memoir of her husband.)

Entry on William Blake in DNB (with W. M. Rossetti).

Published letters

The letters of Anne Gilchrist and Walt Whitman. Ed with an introd by T. B. Harned, New York 1918, London 1919, rptd New York 1973 and micro New Haven CT 1977.

§2

Anne Gilchrist: her life and writings. Ed H. H. Gilchrist (Anne's son). With a prefatory notice by William Michael Rossetti. 1887 (2 edns); 1st edn micro New Haven CT 1977; 2nd edn rptd New York 1973.

Gould, E. P. Anne Gilchrist and Walt Whitman. Philadelphia 1900. Rptd Folcroft PA 1974 and Norwood PA 1976.

Alcaro, M. W. Walt Whitman's Mrs G: a biography of Anne Gilchrist. 1991. [JW]

George Gilfillan 1813–78

§1

Hades, or the unseen. Dundee 1842.

A gallery of literary portraits. Ser 1, Edinburgh 1845; ser 2, Edinburgh 1850; ser 3, Edinburgh 1854; 2 vols Edinburgh 1856–7 (complete); ed (in part) W. R. Nicoll [1909] (EL). Short essays on poets, French revolutionaries, novelists, critics etc.

The Christian bearings of astronomy. Edinburgh 1848.

The connection between science, literature and religion: a lecture. 1849, 1856.

The bards of the Bible. Edinburgh 1851.

The apocalypse of Jesus Christ. Aberdeen 1851.

Lord Byron: a lecture. 1852. In Lectures delivered before the Young Men's Christian Association in Exeter Hall 1851–2.

The martyrs, heroes and bards of the Scottish Covenant. 1852. Appendix on the Massacre of Glencoe, rptd enlarged, with D. Campbell and J. S. Blackie, as The Campbells of Glenlyon, Stirling 1912.

The poets and poetry of the Bible. New York 1853.

Rosaline's dream, in four duans: and other poems. 1853.

The grand discovery; or the Fatherhood of God. 1854.

The influence of Burns on Scottish poetry and song; an essay. In The modern Scottish minstrel, ed C. Rogers, vol 4 Edinburgh 1855.

Library edition of poets of Britain. 48 vols 1853–60. Ed Gilfillan, with short memoirs and notes.

The genesis; a poem. 1856.

The history of a man, edited [in fact written] by Gilfillan. 1856. Autobiography.

Christianity and our era: a book for the times. Edinburgh 1857.

The age of lead; a satire. 1858.

Thoughts in rhyme. 1859.

Alpha and omega: or a series of scripture studies. 2 vols 1860.

Specimens, with memoirs, of the less-known British poets. 3 vols Edinburgh 1860. With a long introductory essay; the work amounts to a richly illustrated history of minor British poetry.

Young's night thoughts. 1861, 1868. For Charles Cowden edn.

Reliques of ancient English poetry. 1864.

Hours of quiet thought. 1865. Introductory essay.

Remoter stars in the church sky: being a gallery of uncelebrated divines. 1867. W. Anderson, J. Everett, Samuel Gilfillan, G. Croley, J. Bruce, T. Spencer, J. Jamieson, G. Steward, H. Stewart, F. W. Robertson etc.

Night: a poem. 1867.

Poems and ballads. 1868.

Modern Christian heroes: a gallery of protesting and reforming men. 1869. Cromwell, Milton, Owen and Howe, Baxter and Bunyan, Scottish Covenanters, Secession and Relief Churches in their cradles, Wesley, Whitfield, Liberty of conscience.

Auld Yule and other poems. 1869.

The life of Sir Walter Scott. Edinburgh 1870.

Comrie and its environs ... the scenery by the Rev George Gilfillan ... the geology and botany by James Bryce. 1870.

The life of the Rev W. Anderson. 1873.

Life of Burns. In the Works of Burns: national edition, 1878.

Sketches literary and theological. Ed F. Henderson, Edinburgh 1881. Selections from an unpbd ms, critical and religious.

Gilfillan also pbd numerous single sermons and lectures. See Wellesley *vol 5.*

Letters

Watson, R. A. and E. S. Gilfillan: letters and journals, with memoir. 1892. Includes list of his contributions to periodicals and his introductory essays.

§2

Livingston, P. In Livingston's Poems and songs, Aberdeen 1855 (9th edn).

In memoriam. Dundee 1878. Rptd from Dundee Advertiser.

Macrae, D. Gilfillan: anecdotes and reminiscences. 1891.

Aubin, R. A. Three notes on 'graveyard' poetry. SP 32 1935.

Scudder, T. Emerson in Dundee. Amer Scholar 4 1935; rptd rev as A harmless stranger: son of genius, in his Lonely wayfaring man: Emerson and some Englishmen, New York 1936.

Westwater, M. In her Spasmodic career of Sydney Dobell. 1992. [MW]

William Ewart Gladstone 1809–98

Bibliographies

The British Museum Catalogue of additions to the manuscripts: the Gladstone papers, additional manuscripts 44,086–835. 1935.

Contributions to a bibliography of Gladstone. N & Q 10 Dec 1892, 7, 21 Jan 1893. Addns 18 Feb, 18 Mar, 10 June 1893.

§1

The State in its relations with the Church. 1838, 1841 (rev and enlarged); tr Ger 1843.

Church principles considered in their results. 1840.

A manual of prayers from the liturgy, arranged for family use. 1845.

Studies on Homer and the Homeric age. 3 vols Oxford 1858; tr Ger 1863.

Speeches on parliamentary reform in 1866; with an appendix. 1866.

A chapter of autobiography. 1868.

Juventus mundi: the gods and men of the heroic age. 1869.

Speeches on great questions of the day. 1870.

Rome and the newest fashions in religion: three tracts – the Vatican decrees; Vaticanism; Speeches of the Pope. 1875; tr Danish 1876, Ger 1875–6. Vatican decrees, originally pbd alone 1874, was tr Fr 1875.

Homeric synchronism: an enquiry into the time and place of Homer. 1876; tr Ger 1877.

Bulgarian horrors and the question of the East. 1876; tr Du 1876, Rus 1876.

The Church of England and ritualism. [1876.]
Gleanings of past years 1843–78. 7 vols 1879. Miscellaneous papers and reviews.
Speeches of the Rt Hon W. E. Gladstone; with a sketch of his life. Ed H. W. Lucy 1885.
Speeches on the Irish question in 1886; with an appendix containing the full text of the Government of Ireland and the Sale and Purchase of Land Bills of 1886. [Ed P. W. Clayden], Edinburgh 1886.
Landmarks of Homeric study; together with an essay on the points of contact between the Assyrian tablets and the Homeric text. 1890.
The impregnable rock of Holy Scripture. 1890, 1892 (rev).
The speeches and public addresses of the Right Hon W. E. Gladstone MP; with notes and introductions. Ed A. W. Hutton and H. J. Cohen 2 vols 1892. This edn was projected in 10 vols, but only 2 appeared.
The odes of Horace. 1894, 1895.
The psalter; with a concordance and other auxiliary matter. 1895.
On the condition of man in a future life. 3 pts 1896.
Studies subsidiary to the works of Bishop Butler: additional volume uniform with the works. 1896.
Later gleanings, theological and ecclesiastical. 1897.
Gladstone's speeches: descriptive index and bibliography by A. T. Bassett; with a preface by Viscount Bryce OM and introductions to the selection speeches by Herbert Paul. 1916.
Two hymns translated into Latin verse by Gladstone. Winchester 1951.
Essay on public speaking. Ed L. D. Reid, Quart Jnl of Speech 39 1953.
For Gladstone's reviews see Wellesley *vol 5.*

Letters and diaries

Correspondence on church and religion. Ed D. C. Lathbury 2 vols 1910.
The Queen and Mr Gladstone. Ed P. Guedalla 1933. A selection from their correspondence.
Gladstone to his wife. Ed A. T. Bassett 1936.
Brush, E. P. Seven letters from Gladstone to Guizot. Jnl of Mod History 11 1939.
Knaplund, P. Extracts from Gladstone's private political diary, touching Canadian questions in 1840. Canadian Historical Rev 20 1939.
The political correspondence of Mr Gladstone and Lord Granville 1868–76. Ed A. Ramm 1952.
Knaplund, P. Gladstone–Gordon correspondence 1851–96: selections from the private correspondence of a British Prime Minister and a colonial governor. Philadelphia 1961.

§2

[Francis, G. H.] The oratory of Gladstone. Fraser's Mag Dec 1846.
Gladstone as a man of letters. Fraser's Mag Nov 1879.
Smith, G. B. The life of Gladstone. 1879.
Laing, S. Gladstone as a theologian. Fortnightly Rev July 1886.
von Bunsen, T. A German view of Gladstone. Nineteenth Cent Sep 1887.
Russell, G. W. E. Gladstone. 1891, 1913 (EL).
Gladstone as reader and critic. Acad 28 May, 2–9 July 1898.
Hamilton, E. W. Mr Gladstone: a monograph. 1898.
Paul, H. W. The life of Gladstone. 1901.
Morley, J. The life of Gladstone. 3 vols 1903; ed C. F. G. Masterman [1927] (abridged).
Zumbini, B. Gladstone nelle sue relazioni con l'Italia. Bari 1914.

Lucie Duff Gordon, née Austin 1821–69

For sources of mss of Duff Gordon's letters and of other material relating to her, see K. Frank, Lucie Duff Gordon: a passage to Egypt, *1994.*

§1

Letters from the Cape. 1864. First pbd in Vacation tourists and other notes of travel, ed Francis Galton 1862–3. Rptd with her Last letters from Egypt, 1875, *below*; ed J. Purves 1921; ed H. J. Anderson for school use, Cape Town [1925]; annotated by D. Fairbridge with an introd by Janet Ross (Duff Gordon's daughter), 1927.
Letters from Egypt, 1863–65. Ed and preface by Sarah Austin (Duff Gordon's mother). 1865; New York 1865 as Lady Duff Gordon's letters . . .; 1865 (2nd edn), rptd New York 1972 (facs); 1866 (3rd edn); micros Ann Arbor MI [19–?] Wooster OH [19–?], and Woodbridge CT 1995; tr Fr [1869] by Janet Ross, Arabic 1976. Partly pbd in Macmillan's Mag 11–13, 1865.
REVIEWS: (Poole, E. Stanley) Edinburgh Rev 122, July 1865; Fraser's Mag 72, Nov 1865.
Last letters from Egypt. To which are added Letters from the Cape. . . . 1875 (includes memoir by Janet Ross) (micro Woodbridge CT 1995); 1876 (2nd edn) (micro Evanston IL 1987), rptd 1886. Partly pbd Macmillan's Mag 13, 15, 16, 18, 1866–8.
REVIEW: (James, Henry) Nation 17 June 1875.
Letters from Egypt *and* Last letters from Egypt *were expanded and collected under the title* Lady Duff Gordon's letters from Egypt: *rev with memoir by her daughter Janet Ross, new introd by George Meredith 1902, New York 1902. This edn was rptd under the title* Letters from Egypt, *introd by Sarah Searight 1983 (Virago Travellers). The letters were further expanded and pbd under the title* Letters from Egypt (1862–1869) . . . *ed with introd by Gordon Waterfield, 1969.*

Collaborative work (with her husband Sir Alexander Duff Gordon)

von Ranke, Leopold. Memoirs of the House of Brandenburg, and history of Prussia. Tr from Ger. 3 vols 1849, micro Washington 1970 (Lib of Congress).
REVIEW: Athenaeum 27 Jan 1849.

Translations

Niebuhr, Barthold. Stories of the gods and heroes of Greece. Ed Sarah Austin. Tr from Ger 1842.
Meinhold, Wilhelm. Mary Schweidler, the amber witch. Tr from Ger 1844 (micro Cambridge MA 1989), New York 1845 (micro Littleton CO [1989]). New edns 1846, New York 1848 (Lib of Choice Reading), 1861, London and New York 1888 (Cassell's Nat Lib 150, micro Urbana IL 1995), London 1894 (pbd with Sidonia the sorceress . . ., tr Lady Wilde, micro Berkeley CA 1990), London and New York 1903. Also pbd with title The amber witch, New York [1888], London [1894] and 1928 (WC); included under this title in Five Victorian ghost novels, ed E. F. Bleiler, New York 1971.
REVIEW: (Milman, H. H.) Quart Rev 74, June 1844.
The French in Algiers. I The soldier of the Foreign Legion (by Clemens Lamping). II The prisoners of Abd-el-Kader (by F. A. Alby). Comp and tr from Ger and Fr 1845, New York 1845 (2 edns, one bound with A. W. Kinglake's Eothen). New edns 1855, New York 1880 (with Charles Dickens's Pictures from Italy).
von Feuerbach, Anselm. Narratives of remarkable criminal trials. Tr from Ger 1846. New York 1846, 1855.
REVIEWS: Athenaeum 21 and 28 Mar 1846.
The mermaid; from the Danish of H. C. Andersen. Bentley's Misc 19, Apr 1846.
The apprenticeship of Raphael Santi of Urbino – a tale of painting; from the Ger. Bentley's Misc 19, May 1846.
Jacques Bonhomme; from the Fr. Bentley's Misc 20, July 1846.
Auerbach, Berthold. The forester's son. Tr from Ger. Bentley's Misc 22, Aug 1847.
de Wailly, A. F. L. Stella and Vanessa: a romance. Tr from Fr 1850. 1853 (new edn), micro New York 1988 (Lib of Congress).
von Ranke, Leopold. Ferdinand I and Maximilian II of Austria, an essay. Tr from Ger 1853. 1856 (new edn) (The Traveller's Lib vol 15).

D'Arbouville, Sophie, Countess. The village doctor. Tr from Fr 1853.
von Moltke, H. C. B., Count. The Russians in Bulgaria and Rumelia in 1828 and 1829. Tr from Ger 1854.
von Sybel, Heinrich. The history and literature of the Crusades. Ed and tr from Ger 1861 (micro Woodbridge CT 1995). 1905 (new edn) (micro Ann Arbor MI 1985).

§2

Norton, the Hon Mrs (Caroline). Lady Duff Gordon and her works. Macmillan's Mag 20, Oct 1869.
Ross, J. Three generations of Englishwomen: memoirs and correspondence of Mrs John Taylor, Mrs Sarah Austin, and Lady Duff Gordon. 1888, rptd 1892.
Waterfield, G. Lucie Duff Gordon in England, South Africa, and Egypt. 1937.
Frank, K. Lucie Duff Gordon: a passage to Egypt. 1994. Includes correct transcriptions of letters altered by Janet Ross for her Three generations of Englishwomen. [JW]

Maria Georgina Grey, née Shirreff 1816–1906

Ms material by Grey is held in Cambridge Univ Lib, the George Baily Lib of the Univ of Vermont, LSE, and the archives of the Girls' Public Day School Trust, the Maria Grey Training College, and the North London Collegiate School.

§1

Love's sacrifice: a novel. 3 vols 1868.
Is the exercise of the suffrage unfeminine? 1870. Pbd by the London Nat Soc for Women's Suffrage.
On the education of women: a paper read by Mrs William Grey at the meeting of the Society of Arts, May 31st, 1871. 1871. First pbd in Jnl of the Soc of Arts 19 1871.
The School Board of London: three addresses of Mrs William Grey. 1871.
On the special requirements for improving the education of girls: paper read at the Social Science Congress, October 1871. 1872.
The National Union for Improving the Education of Women: a letter to the editor of The Times, May 22, 1872. 1872.
Paper on the study of education as a science . . ., read at the meeting of the British Association at Belfast. 1874. Pbd by the Nat Union for Improving the Education of Women. Micro New Haven CT 1977.
Paper on the standard of national education . . ., read at the meeting of the British Association, Bristol, August, 1875. 1875. First pbd in the Jnl of the Women's Education Union.
Old maids: a lecture. 1875, micro New Haven CT 1977.
Last words to girls on life in school and after school. 1889, micro Woodbridge CT 1988.
Memorials of Emily Anne Eliza Shirreff, with a sketch of her life. 1897 (priv ptd).

Contributions to periodicals

For Grey's contributions to Fraser's Mag *and the* Fortnightly Rev, *see* Wellesley *vol 5.*
The physical force objection to women's suffrage. Women's Suffrage Jnl July 1877, micro Woodbridge CT [1977].
'God, duty and immortality', a reply. Theological Rev 16, Apr 1879. Response to article by F. W. Newman in Jan no.
Things new and old in Italy. Modern Rev 1, Oct 1880.
Educational principles of the kindergarten. Education 1, 1881.
Theism and atheism as moral influences. Modern Rev 2, July 1881.
Law and lawlessness. Modern Rev 5, July 1884.

Collaborative works (with her sister Emily Shirreff)

Letters from Spain and Barbary. 1835.
Thoughts on self-culture, addressed to women. 1850 (micro New Haven CT 1975), Boston 1851 (micro Glen Rock NJ 1976); 1854 (2nd edn).
Passion and principle: a novel. 1853; 1854 (new edn) (Routledge's Railway Lib).

Translation and edition

Rosmini Serbati, A. The ruling principle of method applied to education. Tr from Ital 1887, Boston 1887 (micro Ann Arbor MI [1983]); last rptd London 1903, Boston 1903.
Fouché, Catharina, Duchesse d'Otrante. Journal of a visit to Egypt, Constantinople, the Crimea, Greece, &c in the suite of the Prince and Princess of Wales. 1869, New York 1870; 1870 (2nd and 3rd edns); tr Swed 1870.

§2

The Times 21 and 24 Sep 1906. Obituary.
Lee, Elizabeth In DNB.
Ellsworth, E. W. Liberators of the female mind: the Shirreff sisters, educational reform, and the women's movement. 1979. [JW]

Sir George Grove 1820–1900

§1

Beethoven's nine symphonies: analytical essays, with a preface by G. Henschel. Boston 1884, London 1896 (rev as Beethoven and his nine Symphonies); tr Ger [1906].
A dictionary of music and musicians AD 1450–1880, by eminent writers. Ed Grove 4 vols 1879–89; ed J. A. F. Maitland 4 vols 1900, 5 vols 1904–10; ed N. C. Colles 6 vols 1927–40; ed E. Blom 9 vols 1954; Amer suppl ed W. S. Pratt and C. N. Boyd, Philadelphia 1920.
A short history of cheap music as exemplified in the records of the house of Novello, Ewer & Co, with especial reference to the first fifty years of the reign of Queen Victoria; with portraits, and a preface by Grove. 1887.
Beethoven, Schubert, Mendelssohn. Ed E. Blom 1951.
Grove's wide literary activities including the writing of a large portion of Sir William Smith's Dictionary of the Bible, *1860–3, other biblical works and a primer of geography. He edited various works on music, and was for some years editor of* Macmillan's Mag.

§2

E[dwards], F. G. A biographical sketch of Grove. [1897.]
Groves, C. L. The life and letters of Grove. 1903.

Arthur Henry Hallam 1811–33

Bibliographies

Motter, T. H. V. Hallam's centenary: a bibliographical note. YULG 8 1934.
Motter, T. H. V. Hallam's Poems of 1830: a census of copies. PBSA 35 1941. *See also* M. V. Bowman, SB 1 1948.

Collections

Remains, in verse and prose. Ed with a prefatory memoir by Henry Hallam. 1834 (priv ptd), 1853, Boston 1853, London 1862, Boston 1863, London 1863, 1896.
Remains in verse and prose, originally printed in 1834. 1852. This edn was never issued.
Remains in verse and prose, originally printed in 1834. 1853 (priv ptd), 1862, 1863, Boston 1863, London 1869. *See also* Motter, *above*, for variations in contents.
Poems, together with his essay on the lyrical poems of Alfred Tennyson. Ed R. Le Gallienne, London and New York 1893, London 1898.
Poetical remains. Appendix to Temple Classics edn of In Memoriam, 1899.
Writings. Ed T. H. V. Motter, New York 1943.

§1

On names; Remarks on Gifford's Ford; Two letters to Bartholomew Bouverie Esq; The battle of the Boyne; The bride of the lake. Eton Misc 1 1827.
[Review of Tennyson's Timbuctoo.] Athenaeum 22 July 1829. Anon. By Hallam?
Timbuctoo. [Cambridge 1829] (priv ptd).
Adonais: an elegy on the death of John Keats, author of Endymion, Hyperion etc, by Percy B. Shelley. Cambridge 1829. Unsigned note p. iii by Hallam, who arranged pbn.
Poems by A. H. Hallam Esq. [1830] (priv ptd).
Stanzas. Englishman's Mag Aug 1831.
On some of the characteristics of modern poetry, and on the lyrical poems of Alfred Tennyson. Englishman's Mag Aug 1831.
Essay on the philosophical writings of Cicero. Cambridge 1832 (priv ptd).
Oration on the influence of Italian works of imagination on the same class of compositions in England, delivered in Trinity College Chapel, December 16 1831. Cambridge 1832 (priv ptd).
Remarks on Professor Rossetti's Disquisizioni sullo spirito antipapale. 1832.
[Unsigned review of Sorelli, Il paradiso perduto di Milton, 1832 (3rd edn).] Foreign Quart Rev Oct 1832.
[Biographical sketches of Voltaire, Petrarch and Burke.] The gallery of portraits; with memoirs. 5 vols 1833–5. First issued monthly from June 1832; rptd 7 vols 1833–7, 3 vols 1853.
On hearing Miss Emily — play. Metropolitan Mag Jan 1833. Anon. By Hallam?
Some unpublished poems. Ed C. Tennyson and F. T. Baker, VP 3 1965.

Letters

Gaskell, C. M. Records of an Eton schoolboy [James Milnes Gaskell]. 1883 (priv ptd), 1939 (as An Eton boy 1820–30).
[Trench, M.] Richard Chevenix Trench, Archbishop: letters and memorial. 2 vols 1888.
Nicoll, W. R. and T. J. Wise. In their Literary anecdotes of the nineteenth century, 1895.
Tennyson, H. Alfred Lord Tennyson: a memoir. 2 vols 1897.
Brookfield, A. M. Some letters from Hallam. Fortnightly Rev July 1903. 6 letters, 3 rptd in whole or in part in F. M. Brookfield, The Cambridge 'Apostles', 1906.
Zamick, M. Unpublished letters of Hallam from Eton, now in the John Rylands Library. BJRL 18 1934.

§2

Brown, J. Hallam. North Br Rev Feb 1851; rptd in his Horae subsecivae, Edinburgh 1858; separately pbd Edinburgh 1862; rptd in Tennyson and his friends, ed Hallam Lord Tennyson, 1911.
Gladstone, W. E. On Tennyson. Quart Rev 106 1859; rptd in his Gleanings of past years vol 2, 1879; separately pbd in Gladstone on Tennyson, Old South Leaflets no 193 [Boston 1908].
[Field, A.?] Memoir of Hallam. In In memoriam, Boston 1861.
[Alford, F.] Life, journals and letters of Henry Alford. 1873.
Ritchie, A. T. Tennyson. Harper's Mag Dec 1883; rptd in Complete poetical works of Tennyson, New York 1884.
Maurice, J. F. The life of Frederick Denison Maurice, chiefly told in his own letters. 2 vols 1884.
Reminiscences and opinions of Francis Hastings Doyle. New York 1887.
[C. J. C.] Hallam's Remains. N & Q 27 Sep 1890.
Gladstone, W. E. Personal recollections of Hallam. Daily Telegraph 5 Jan 1898, Youth's Companion (Boston) 6 Jan 1898; separately pbd, Companion Classics (Boston) 1 [1898].
Weld, A. G. Glimpses of Tennyson and of some of his relations and friends. 1903.
Brookfield, C. and F. Mrs Brookfield and her circle. 2 vols 1905.
Brookfield, F. M. The Cambridge 'Apostles'. 1906.
[Collins, C. W.] The Cambridge Apostles. Blackwood's Mag Mar 1907.
Toynbee, P. J. Dante in English literature. 2 vols 1909, vol 2.
Thwing, F. B. Hallam. North Amer Rev Feb 1911.
Lounsbury, T. R. The life and times of Tennyson. New Haven CT 1915.
Shorter, C. K. The love-story of In memoriam. 1916 (priv ptd).
Cornish, Mrs W. Memories of Tennyson. London Mercury Dec 1921–Jan 1922.
Bassett, A. T. (ed). The Gladstone papers. [1930.]
Motter, T. H. V. A 'lost' poem by Hallam. PMLA 50 1935.
Tennyson, C. Tennyson papers, 2: J. M. Heath's commonplace book. Cornhill Mag Apr 1936.

James Hannay 1827–73

Bibliography

Worth, G. J. James Hannay: his life and works. Lawrence KS 1964. See pp. 177–84.

§1

Biscuits and grog: personal reminiscences and sketches by Percival Plug RN. 1848.
REVIEW: Athenaeum 4 Mar 1848.
A claret-cup: further reminiscences and sketches of Percival Plug RN. 1848.
Hearts are trumps: an amphibious story. [1848.]
King Dobbs: sketches in ultra-marine. 1849.
Singleton Fontenoy RN. 3 vols 1850, 1 vol 1850.
REVIEW: Critic 15 Nov 1850.
Blackwood v. Carlyle, by a Carlylian. 1850.
Sketches in ultra-marine. 2 vols 1853. Biscuits and grog, A claret-cup, and King Dobbs, rev and abridged; fiction from United Service Mag.
REVIEW: Examiner 3 Sep 1853.
Edgar Allan Poe. Prefixed to Poe, Poetical works, 1853.
Satire and satirists: six lectures. 1854.
REVIEW: Athenaeum 29 July 1854.
Sand and shells: nautical sketches. 1854. Short stories rptd from United Service Mag.
Eustace Conyers: a novel. 3 vols 1855, 1 vol 1857; tr Ger 1856.
REVIEW: Athenaeum 26 May 1855.
Essays from the Quarterly Review. 1861.
REVIEW: Spectator 13 Apr 1861.
Hogarth as a satirist. Prefixed to The complete works of William Hogarth, with descriptive letterpress by J. Trusler and E. F. Roberts. [1861.]
A brief memoir of the late Mr Thackeray. Edinburgh 1864. Rptd from Edinburgh Courant.
Characters and criticisms: a book of miscellanies. Edinburgh 1865.
REVIEW: [Trollope, A.] Fortnightly Rev 2 1865.
A course of English literature. 1866. Rptd from Welcome Guest.
REVIEW: Saturday Rev 14 July 1866.
Memoir of Churchill. Prefixed to Churchill, Poetical works, 1866.
Three hundred years of a Norman house: the barons of Gournay from the tenth to the thirteenth century, with genealogical miscellanies. '1867' [1866.]
REVIEW: Spectator 24 Nov 1866.
Studies on Thackeray. [1869.]

For Hannay's contributions to Cornhill Mag, North Br Rev *and* Quart Rev, *see* Wellesley *vol 1; for his contributions to* Temple Bar *and* Westminster Rev *see* Wellesley *vol 3. For Hannay's contributions to* All the Year Round, Athenaeum, Atlantic Monthly, Dumfries and Galloway Courier, Household Words, Idler, Illustrated London News, Imperial Rev, Leader, Nat Mag, New Quarterly Rev, New York Tribune, Pall Mall Gazette, Press, United Service Mag, Universal Rev *and* Welcome Guest *see Bibliography in Worth, above.*

§2

[Cudlip, A. Thomas.] James Hannay. Temple Bar 38 1873.
Espinasse, F. Literary recollections and sketches. 1893.
Jeaffreson, J. C. A book of recollections. 1894.
Worth, G. J. James Hannay: his life and works. Lawrence KS 1964. [GW]

Abraham Hayward 1801–84

The statutes founded on the common law reports, with observations and notes. 1832.
Faust. 1833 (priv ptd), 1833, 1834 (adds summary of pt 2 and account of Faust story). A prose trn of Goethe's pt 1, with notes on former versions.
Some account of a journey across the Alps in a letter to a friend. [1834] (priv ptd); rptd in Selections from the correspondence of Abraham Hayward, 1886.
Verses of other days. 1847 (priv ptd) (anon), 1878 (enlarged).
The art of dining. 1852 (anon); ed with addns C. Sayle 1899. Based on 2 articles in Quart Rev.
Lord Chesterfield: his life, character and opinions; and George Selwyn: his life and times. 1854.
Juridical tracts. Pt 1 (all pbd) 1856.
Biographical and critical essays. 5 vols 1858–74. Sydney Smith, S. Rogers, J. Smith, Lord Melbourne, Stendhal, Lord Eldon, British field sports, Dumas, Maria Edgeworth, Canning, H. Holland etc.
The life and writings of Mrs Piozzi (Mrs Thrale). Prefixed to the Autobiography, letters and literary remains of Mrs Piozzi, ed Hayward, 2 vols 1861, 1861 (rearranged and expanded).
Mr Kinglake and the Quarterlys, by an old reviewer. 1863.
More about Junius: the Franciscan theory unsound. 1868. Rptd with addns from Fraser's Mag.
The second armada: a chapter of future history. 1871. Anon. Rptd with addns from The Times. An account of an imaginary invasion of England by Germany.
John Stuart Mill. 1873 (priv ptd). Rptd from The Times. An account of the life and work of Mill which became the subject of an acute controversy.
Goethe. 1877.
Selected essays. 2 vols 1878 (from Biographical and critical essays).
Short rules for modern whist. [1878.]
Sketches of eminent statesmen and writers. 2 vols 1880. Rptd with addns from Quart Rev: Thiers, Bismarck, Cavour, Metternich, Montalembert, Melbourne, Wellesley, Sévigné, Byron, Tennyson, du Deffand etc.
Hayward translated F. C. von Savigny, On the vocation of our age for legislation, *[1831] (priv ptd) and also pbd other legal and controversial works. He also reviewed extensively for* Edinburgh Rev *and* Quart Rev; *see* Wellesley *vol 5.*

Letters

A selection from the correspondence of Hayward from 1834 to 1884, with an account of his early life. Ed H. E. Carlisle 2 vols 1886.

Sir Arthur Helps 1813–75

Selections

Essays and aphorisms. Ed E. A. Helps 1892.

§1

Thoughts in the cloister and the crowd. 1835 (anon), 1901. Aphorisms.
Essays written in the intervals of business. 1841 (anon); ed F. J. Rowe and W. T. Webb 1889.
King Henry the Second: an historical drama. 1843. Anon.
Catherine Douglas: a tragedy. 1843. Anon.
The claims of labour: an essay on the duties of the employers to the employed. 1844 (anon), [1907].
Friends in council. 4 ser 1847–59 (anon); ser 1 ed E. A. Helps [1907]. Dialogues on social and intellectual subjects.
The conquerors of the new world and their bondsmen: the events which led to negro slavery. 2 vols 1848–52. Anon.
A letter from one of the special constables in London on the late occasion of their being called out to keep the peace. 1848. Anon.
On the responsibilities of employers. 1849.
Companions of my solitude. 1851 (anon); ed E. A. Helps [1907]. Chiefly on social questions.
A letter on Uncle Tom's cabin. Cambridge 1852.
The Spanish conquest in America and its relation to the history of slavery. 4 vols 1855–61; ed M. Oppenheim 4 vols 1900–4 (with maps and introd).
Oulita the serf: a tragedy. 1858. Anon.
Organization in daily life: an essay. 1862. Anon.
The life of Las Casas: the apostle of the Indians. 1868. Rptd from Spanish conquest, *above*.
Realmah. 2 vols 1868. Serialised in Macmillan's Mag Nov 1867–Nov 1868.
The life of Columbus. 1869; ed E. A. Helps [1910] (EL). Rptd from Spanish conquest, *above*.
The life of Pizarro. 1869. Rptd from Spanish conquest, *above*.
Casimir Maremma. 2 vols 1870, 1873.
Brevia: short essays and aphorisms. 1871.
Conversations on war and general culture. 1871.
The life of Hernando Cortes. 2 vols 1871. Rptd from Spanish conquest, *above*.
The life and labours of Mr [Thomas] Brassey 1805–70. 1872, 1888 (7th edn). Helps also edited Brassey, On work and wages, 1872.
Thoughts upon government. 1872.
Some talk about animals and their masters. 1873. Dialogues.
Ivan de Biron: a Russian story. 3 vols 1874.
Social pressure. 1875.
Helps also edited the speeches of Prince Albert, 1892, and Queen Victoria, Leaves from the journal of our life in Highlands, *1868, and her* Mountain, loch and glen, *1869.*

Letters

Correspondence. Ed E. A. Helps 1917.

Edwin Paxton Hood 1820–85

§1

Fragments of thought and composition. 1846.
An encycopaedia of facts, anecdotes, and illustrations in support of the principles of permanent and universal peace. 1847.
The ideals of civilization. 1847.
The age and its architects. 1851.
Genius and industry: the achievements of mind among the cottages. 1851.
The literature of labour: illustrations of the education of poetry in poverty. 1851.
Self-education: twelve chapters for young thinkers. 1851.
The dark days of Queen Mary. 1851.
The bright days of Queen Bess. 1851.
Old England: scenes from life in the hall and hamlet, by the forest and fireside. 1851.
The uses of biography: romantic, philosophic, and didactic. 1852.
John Milton: illustrations of the model man. 1852.
The mental and moral philosophy of laughter. 1852.
Dream land and ghost land. 1852.
Andrew Marvell: the wit, statesman and poet. 1853.
Swedenborg: a biography and an exposition. 1854.

The last of the Saxons: light and fire from the writings of William Cobbett. 1854.
William Wordsworth. 1856.
The peerage of poverty: learners and workers in fields, factories and farms. 1st ser 1859, 2nd ser 1861, 5th edn enlarged 1870. This work is a rewritten and extended version of The literature of labour.
The world of anecdote. 1870, Cheap edn 1876.
Lamps, pitchers and trumpets: lectures on the vocation of the preacher. 1870.
Thomas Binney: his mind, life and opinions. 1874.
Isaac Watts: his life and writing. 1875.
The maid of Nurenberg and other voluntaries. 1878.
Vignettes of the great revival of the eighteenth century. 1880.
Robert Hall. 1881.
Scottish characteristics. 1883.
The throne of eloquence: great preachers, ancient and modern. 1885.
The vocation of the preacher. 1886.
Paxton Hood wrote many other educational works aimed at children and artisans, most of which were published anonymously by William Tweedie or Partridge and Oakey. He also edited the Eclectic and Congregational Rev *and the* Argonaut.

§2

In DNB.
Maidment, B. Popular exemplary biography in the nineteenth century: Edwin Paxton Hood and his books. Prose Stud 7 1984.
[BM]

Richard Henry Horne 1803–84

See col 618.

Richard Holt Hutton 1826–97

Collections and selections

Aspects of religious and scientific thought. Ed E. M. Roscoe 1899. Selection from contributions to Spectator.
Brief literary criticisms selected from the Spectator. Ed E. M. Roscoe 1906.
Woodfield, M. (ed). A Victorian spectator: uncollected writings of R. H. Hutton. 1989, 1991.

§1

The incarnation and principles of evidence. [1862.]
The relative value of studies and accomplishments in the education of women. 1862.
Studies in parliament. 1866. Rptd from Pall Mall Gazette: Disraeli, Cobden, Palmerston, Bright, Earl Grey etc.
The political character of the working class. 1867.
Essays theological and literary. 2 vols 1871. Vol 1 theological; vol 2 Goethe, Wordsworth, Shelley, Browning, George Eliot, Clough, Hawthorne.
Sir Walter Scott. 1878 (EML).
Essays on some of the modern guides of English thought in matters of faith. 1887.
Cardinal Newman. 1891.
Criticisms on contemporary thought and thinkers. 2 vols 1894. Carlyle, Emerson, Poe, Longfellow, Dickens, Leslie Stephen, J. S. Mill, Arnold, Clough, Renan, Huxley, Bagehot, Ruskin, Wordsworth, Darwin etc.

§2

Watson, W. Excursions in criticism. [1893.]
Wedgwood, J. Hutton. Contemporary Rev Oct 1897.
Escott, T. H. S. Hutton: an estimate of his life and work. Bookman (London) Oct 1897.
Hogben, J. Hutton of the Spectator. Edinburgh 1899.
Boas, F. S. Critics and criticism in the 'seventies. In The eighteen-seventies, 1929 (Royal Soc of Lit).
LeRoy, G. C. Hutton. PMLA 56 1941.
Thomas, G. N. Hutton. TLS 24 Apr 1948.
Colby, R. A. 'How it strikes a contemporary': the Spectator as critic. Nineteenth-Cent Fiction 11 1957.
Mackerness, E. D. Hutton and the Victorian lay sermon. Dalhousie Rev 37 1957; rptd in his Heeded voice, Cambridge 1959.
Tener, R. H. Clough, Hutton and University Hall. N & Q 205, Dec 1960.
Tener, R. H. Hutton's Essays theological and literary: a bibliographical note. N & Q 205, May 1960.
Tener, R. H. More articles by Hutton. BNYPL Jan 1962.
Tener, R. H. Sources of Hutton's Modern Guides essay on Carlyle. N & Q 208, Dec 1963.
Tener, R. H. Hutton and 'agnostic'. N & Q 209, Nov 1964.
Woodfield, M. R. H. Hutton, critic and theologian: the writings of R. H. Hutton on Newman, Arnold, Tennyson, Wordsworth and George Eliot. 1986.

Joseph Knight 1829–1907

§1

Life of D. G. Rossetti. 1887.
Theatrical notes. 1893.
David Garrick. 1894.
A history of the stage during the Victorian era. 1901.
Knight contributed more than 500 lives (mainly of dramatists) to DNB. In 1886 he wrote an historical preface to J. Downes, Roscius anglicanus, *and he wrote prefaces to plays by Sheridan and Henry Arthur Jones. From 1883 until his death he edited* N & Q.

§2

Francis, J. C. Notes by the way; with memoirs of Knight. 1909.
Rendall, V. H. Some reminiscences of Knight. Nineteenth Cent Dec 1911.

Percival Leigh 1813–89

§1

Stories and poems. In The fiddle-faddle fashion book, 1840.
The comic Latin grammar. 1840 (anon); ed C. E. Smith, New York 1930.
The comic English grammar. 1840. Anon.
Portraits of children of the nobility: with memoirs and characteristic sketches. 1841. Illustr J. Leech.
Jack the giant killer. [1843.] Anon; verse. Illustr J. Leech.
Ye manners and customs of ye Englyshe, drawn from ye quick by Rychard Doyle; to which be added some extracts from Mr Pips hys diary contrybuted by P[ercival] L[eigh]. [1849], 1876 (extended).
Paul Predergast: or the comic schoolmaster. 3 ptd [1859]. Anon. Illustr J. Leech, A. Crowquill et al. Contains the two comic grammars and The comic Cocker on arithmetic.

§2

Athenaeum 2 Nov 1889. Obituary.
Frith, W. P. John Leech. Vol 1, 1891.

George Henry Lewes 1817–78

See col 2550.

John Ferguson McLennan 1827–81

Primitive marriage: an inquiry into the origin of the form of capture in marriage ceremonies. Edinburgh 1865, London 1876 (as Studies in ancient history), 1886; 2nd ser ed E. A. McLennan 1896.

Memoir of Thomas Drummond. Edinburgh 1867.
The patriarchal theory. Ed D. McLennan 1885.

Francis Sylvester Mahony 1804–66

§1

The reliques of Father Prout, late P. P. of Watergrasshill in the county of Cork, collected and arranged by Oliver Yorke esq. 2 vols 1836, 1 vol 1859. Illustr 'Alfred Croquis esq' (Daniel Maclise). Rptd from Fraser's Mag 1834–6.
Facts and figures from Italy by Don Jeremy Savonarola, Benedictine monk, addressed during the last two winters to Charles Dickens, being an appendix to his Pictures [from Italy]. 1847.
The final reliques of Father Prout. Ed D. Jerrold 1876.
The works of Father Prout. Ed C. Kent 1881 (with memoir).
Mahony was the Paris correspondent of the Globe *1858–66.*

§2

Athenaeum 26 May 1866. Obituary.
Hannay, J. Aytoun, Peacock and Prout. North Br Rev Sep 1866.
Bates, W. The Maclise portrait-gallery. 1883.

David Masson 1822–1907

§1

College-education and self-education: a lecture. [1854.]
Essays biographical and critical, chiefly on English poets. Cambridge 1856. Shakespeare and Goethe, Milton's youth, The three devils, Dryden, Swift, Chatterton, Wordsworth, Scottish influence in British literature, Theories of poetry, De Quincey.
British novelists and their styles: being a critical sketch of the history of British prose fiction. Cambridge 1859, Boston 1859, Folcroft PA 1969, Freeport NY 1975.
The life of John Milton, narrated in connexion with the political, ecclesiastical and literary history of his time. 7 vols 1859–94, Boston 1859–80, London 1881–96 (rev edn), New York 1946, Gloucester MA 1965.
Recent British philosophy: a review, with criticisms; including some comments on Mr Mill's answer to Sir William Hamilton. Cambridge 1865, New York 1866, London 1867 (2nd edn), 1877 (3rd edn adds ch). British Comtism, Bain and Herbert Spencer, Ferrier and a British Hegelian, J. S. Mill on Sir William Hamilton, Swedenborgianism and 'Spiritualism', etc.
The state of learning in Scotland: a lecture. Edinburgh 1866.
University teaching for women. Edinburgh 1868; in Introductory lectures of the second series of lectures in Shandwick Place, 1868.
Oliver Goldsmith. Memoir prefixed to The miscellaneous works of Oliver Goldsmith, Globe edn 1868, 1871, 1874, 1878, 1881, 1884, 1889; rptd in The Vicar of Wakefield 1883, 1889.
Drummond of Hawthornden: the story of his life and writings. 1873.
Chatterton: a story of the year 1770. 1874, 1899 (rev and enlarged), New York 1899. Rptd from Essays biographical and critical, *above*.
The three devils: Luther's, Milton's and Goethe's. 1874. 5 essays rptd from Essays biographical and critical, *above*, with How literature may illustrate history.
Wordsworth, Shelley, Keats and other essays. 1874, 1875. 4 essays rptd from Essays biographical and critical, *above*, with Shelley and Keats.
De Quincey. 1881, New York 1882, London 1885 (rev) (EML).
Carlyle, personally and in his writings: two Edinburgh lectures. 1885.
Carlyle: the address delivered by David Masson on unveiling a bust of Thomas Carlyle. Glasgow 1891.
Edinburgh sketches and memories. 1892. Queen Mary, R. Rollock, King James, Drummond of Hawthornden, Allan Ramsay, Lady Wardlaw and Baroness Nairne, the Dundas despotism, Sir Walter Scott, Carlyle, C. K. Sharpe, J. H. Burton, Dr John Brown, Literary history of Edinburgh.
Milton. In In the footsteps of the poets, [1893], New York [1894].
James Melvin, rector of the grammar school of Aberdeen: a sketch. Aberdeen 1895.
Memories of London in the 'forties: arranged and annotated by F. Masson. Edinburgh 1908. Carlyle, Down Street Piccadilly, Mazzini, A London club.
Memories of two cities: Edinburgh and Aberdeen. Ed F. Masson, Edinburgh 1911. Papers rptd from Macmillan's Mag: Dr Chalmers, David Welsh, 'Christopher North', Hugh Miller, De Quincey, W. Hamilton etc.
Shakespeare personally. Ed R. Masson 1914. Lectures delivered 1865–95 at Edinburgh Univ.
To Chambers's Educational Course, Masson contributed: Ancient history *and* History of Rome, *1848;* Mediaeval history, *1855, and* Modern history from the Restoration to the present time, *1856; for the same publishers he wrote an account of the British Museum, 1848. He also edited the poetry of Milton, 1874, and the works of De Quincey, 1889–90. For Masson's contributions to* Blackwood's Mag, Contemporary Rev, Edinburgh Rev, Macmillan's Mag, North Br Rev, Quart Rev, Fraser's Mag, Nineteenth Cent, Nat Rev, Westminster Rev, Br Quart Rev *and* Dublin Univ Mag, *see* Wellesley *vol 5. Masson edited* Macmillan's Mag *1859–67 and the* Reader *1863–4.*

Letters

Macmillan, A. Letters. 1908.

§2

Barrie, J. M. An Edinburgh eleven. 1889.
Obits: Scotsman 8 Oct 1907, The Times 8 Oct 1907.
Masson, F. Masson. Cornhill Mag Nov 1910, June 1911. [GW]

John Frederick Denison Maurice 1805–72

Bibliographies

Gray, G. J. Bibliography of the writings of Maurice. In J. F. Maurice, Life of Maurice vol 1, 1884.

§1

Eustace Conway, or the brother and sister: a novel. 1834. Anon.
The Kingdom of Christ: or hints on the principles, ordinances and constitution of the Catholic Church. 3 vols 1837. *See col 2655.*
Moral and metaphysical philosophy. 1845, 2 vols 1872. A selection of Encyclopaedia metropolitana, ed E. Smedley. Later expanded into 4 separate works: Ancient philosophy, 1850; Philosophy of the first six centuries, 1853; Mediaeval philosophy, 1857; Modern philosophy, 1862.
The religions of the world, and their relation to Christianity. 1847 (Boyle Lectures).
Theological essays. Cambridge 1853, 1853 (with addns), London 1871; ed E. F. Carpenter 1958.
Sermons. 6 vols [1857–9], 1860.
The workman and the franchise: chapters from English history on the representation and education of the people. 1866.
The conscience: lectures on casuistry. 1868, 1872.
Social morality: twenty-one lectures. 1869.
The friendship of books and other lectures. Ed T. Hughes 1874.
Maurice also pbd numerous sermons, tracts etc, as well as contributing prefaces to works by others. He edited, at different periods, Athenaeum, Christian Socialist *and* Educational Mag. *For his reviews, see* Wellesley *vol 5.*

§2

Maurice and his writings. London Quart Rev 3 1855.
Rigg, J. H. Modern Anglican theology: chapters on Coleridge, Maurice [et al]. 1857.
Kingsley, C. Memorial of Maurice. Macmillan's Mag May 1872.
Stephen, L. The theology of Maurice. Fortnightly Rev May 1874.

Davies, J. L. Secularism and Mr Maurice's theology. Contemporary Rev June 1874.
A modern prophet. Atlantic Monthly Aug 1884.
Maurice, J. F. The life of Maurice, chiefly told in his own letters. 2 vols 1884.
Hutton, R. H. Essays on some of the modern guides of English thought in matters of faith. 1887.
von Dungern, H. Führer der christlichsozialen Bewegung Englands von 1848–66: Maurice. Göttingen 1900.
Masterman, C. F. G. Maurice. 1907.
Sanders, C. R. Coleridge, Maurice and the distinction between the reason and the understanding. PMLA 51 1936.
Jenkins, C. Maurice and the new reformation. 1938.
Sanders, C. R. Maurice as a commentator on Coleridge. PMLA 53 1938.
Sanders, C. R. Sir Leslie Stephen, Coleridge and two Coleridgeans. PMLA 55 1940.
Sanders, C. R. Coleridge, Maurice and the church universal. Jnl of Religion 21 1941.
Gloyn, C. K. The Church in the social order: a study of Anglican social theory from Coleridge to Maurice. Forest Grove OR 1942.
Sanders, C. R. A major outlet: Maurice. In his Coleridge and the Broad Church movement, Durham NC 1942.
Higham, F. Maurice. 1947.
Reckitt, M. B. Maurice to Temple: a century of the social movement in the Church of England. 1947.
Dring, T. Maurice: the greatest prophet of the nineteenth century. London Quart 173 1948.
Grylls, R. G. Queen's College 1848–1948, founded by Maurice. 1948.
Vidler, A. R. Witness to the light: Maurice's message for today. New York 1948.
Vidler, A. R. The theology of Maurice. 1948.
Wood, H. G. Maurice. 1950.
Ramsey, A. M. Maurice and the conflicts of modern theology. Cambridge 1951.
Ranson, G. H. The kingdom of God as the design of society. Church History 30 1961.
Dring, T. The philosophy of Maurice. London Quart 187 1962.
Vidler, A. R. F. D. Maurice and company. 1967.

Henry Mayhew 1812–87

Selections

The street trader's lot. 1851; ed S. Rubenstein 1947 (with introd by M. D. George).
Mayhew's London. Ed P. C. Quennell 1949, 1951.
London's underworld. Ed P. C. Quennell 1950. Selections from London labour and the London poor vol 4.
Mayhew's characters. Ed P. C. Quennell 1951.
Selections from London labour and the London poor. Ed J. Bradley 1965.
The unknown Mayhew. Ed E. Yeo and E. P. Thompson 1971. Selections from Mayhew letters to Morning Chron and Low wages.
Voices of the poor. Ed Anne Humpherys 1972. Selections from Mayhew letters to Morning Chron.
The Morning Chronicle survey of labour and the poor. Vol 1 The metropolitan districts. Sussex 1980.
London labour and the London poor. Ed V. Neuberg 1986 (Pen).

§1

The wandering minstrel. 1834, Philadelphia 1836, London 1850, Boston 1856, [1880] (with Intrigue), [1897] (with The tradesman's ball). A one-act farce.
But, however–. 1838, 1843, [1883]. A one-act farce. With Henry Baylis.
What to teach and how to teach it. Pt 1 1842. No more pbd.
The Prince of Wales's library: no 1 – the primer. 1844.
The good genius that turned everything into gold. 1847, 1879, New York 1890. Fairy tale. With Augustus Mayhew.
The greatest plague of life: or the adventures of a lady in search of a servant. Illustr G. Cruikshank 1847, [1892]. With his brother Augustus Mayhew.
Whom to marry and how to get married. [1848], 1854, 1872. With Augustus Mayhew.
The image of his father. Illustr 'Phiz' 1848, 1850, 1859. With Augustus Mayhew.
The magic of kindness. Illustr G. Cruikshank and K. Meadows 1849, [1869], Manchester [1879]. With Augustus Mayhew.
Labour and the poor. Letters I–LXXXII. Morning Chron 1849–50.
REVIEWS: Morning Chron on the state of the poor, Spectator 27 Oct 1849; [Ludlow, J. M.] Labour and the poor, Fraser's Mag 41, Jan 1850; Labour and the poor, Eclectic 11, May 1850; Distressed populations, Economist 16 Nov 1850.
Acting charades. 1850, [1852]. With Augustus Mayhew.
The comic almanack. 2 vols 1850–1, 1871. With Augustus Mayhew, Thackeray et al.
The fear of the world. 1850, [1855]. With Augustus Mayhew. Also titled Living for appearances.
1851: or the adventures of Mr and Mrs Sandboys. 1851.
The great exhibition. Nos 1–9. Edinburgh News and Literary Chron 1851.
Home is home, be it never so homely. In Meliora, ed Earl of Shrewsbury, 1851.
London labour and the London poor. Nos 1–63. Vol 1 and pts of vols 2–3, 1851–2; vol 3, 1856; expanded as 4 vols 1861–2; 1864; rptd 1967, New York 1968. Some of the material first appeared in Labour and the poor, *above*.
Low wages, their causes, consequences and remedies. Pts 1–4. 1851.
The story of the peasant-boy philosopher. 1854, 1855, New York 1856, London 1857.
The wonders of science: or young Humphry Davy. 1855, 1856, New York 1856.
The great world of London. Pts 1–9 1856. Pp. 498–634 by John Binny. Whole pbd as The criminal prisons of London and scenes of prison life, 1862.
REVIEW: New serial, The great world of London, Spectator 8 Mar 1856.
On capital punishments. Three papers on capital punishment. 1856.
The Rhine and its picturesque scenery. Illustr B. Foster 1856; 1860 (as The lower Rhine).
The upper Rhine. Illustr B. Foster 1858.
Young Benjamin Franklin: or the right road through life. 1861, New York 1862, London [1870].
The boyhood of Martin Luther. 1863, [1879].
German life and manners as seen in Saxony at the present day. 2 vols 1864, 1 vol 1865.
The shops and companies of London and the trades and manufactories of Great Britain. Pts 1–7 1865.
Report concerning the trade and hours of closing usual among the unlicensed victualling establishments . . . at certain so-called 'Working Men's Clubs'. 1871.
London characters. Illustr W. S. Gilbert et al 1874, 1881. With others.
Mont Blanc. 1874. For private circulation. A comedy, with Athol Mayhew.

Mayhew edited Figaro in London, *1835–9 (with Gilbert à Beckett). He was one of the originators in 1841 and for a short time joint editor of* Punch. *He also edited the* Morning News, *1859, and* Only Once a Year, *1871.*

§2

Obits: The Times 27 July 1887; Punch 6 Aug 1887.
Humpherys, Anne. Travels into the poor man's country. Athens GA 1977. [AH]

Horace Mayhew 1816–72

Change for a chilling. [1848.] Illustr H. G. Hine.
The comic almanac for 1848. 1848. Ed Mayhew.
Model men, modelled by Mayhew, sculptured by H. G. Hine. 1848.
Model women and children, modelled by Mayhew, sculptured by H. G. Hine. 1848.
Guy Faux: a squib manufactured by Mayhew and Percy Cruikshank. [1849.]
The tooth-ache, imagined by Mayhew and realized by George Cruikshank. [1849.]
Letters left at the pastrycook's: being the clandestine correspondence between Kitty Clover at school, and her 'dear, dear friend' in town. 1853.
In Dec 1847 Mayhew brought out a Plum pudding pantomime *at the Olympic Theatre, apparently unpbd. See obituary,* Athenaeum *4 May 1872.*

John Stuart Mill 1806–73

See col 2558.

Hugh Miller 1802–56

Selections

Selections. Ed W. M. Mackenzie, Paisley 1908.

§1

Letters on the herring fishery. Inverness 1829. Rptd from Inverness Courier.
Poems written in the leisure hours of a journeyman mason. Inverness 1829.
Scenes and legends of the north of Scotland: or the traditional history of Cromarty. 1835.
Memoir of William Forsyth. 1839.
The Whiggism of the old school. Edinburgh 1839.
A letter to Lord Brougham. Edinburgh 1839.
The two parties in the Church of Scotland exhibited as missionary and anti-missionary. Edinburgh 1841.
The old red sandstone: or new walks in an old field. Edinburgh 1841, Glasgow 1858 (adds a series of geological papers), London 1906 (EL). Rptd from Witness.
Sutherland as it was and is: or how a country may be ruined. 1843. Anon.
Words of warning to the people of Scotland on Sir Robert Peel's Scotch currency scheme. Edinburgh 1844.
First impressions of England and its people. 1847.
The Sites Bill and the Toleration Laws. Edinburgh 1848.
Geology of the Bass. In T. MacCrie, The Bass Rock: its civil and ecclesiastical history, 1848.
Footprints of the Creator: or the asterolepsis of Stromness. 1849 (anon); ed L. F. F. Miller, Edinburgh 1861 (with memoir by L. Agassiz). A reply to Vestiges of creation, 1844.
Thoughts on the educational question. 1850. Rptd from Witness.
My school and schoolmasters: or the story of my education. Edinburgh 1854; ed A. M. Mackenzie, Edinburgh 1905.
The fossiliferous deposits of Scotland. Edinburgh 1854.
The two records – mosaic and geological: a lecture. 1854.
Geology versus astronomy: a view of the modifying effects of geologic discovery on the old astronomic inferences respecting the plurality of inhabited worlds. Glasgow [1855].
Strange but true: incidents in the life of J. Kitto. Edinburgh 1856.
The testimony of the rocks. Edinburgh 1857.
Voices from the rocks: or proofs of the existence of man during the palaeozoic period. 1857.
The cruise of the Betsy: or a summer ramble among the fossiliferous deposits of the Hebrides; with rambles of a geologist. Ed W. S. Symonds, Edinburgh 1858.
Sketch-book of popular geology: a series of lectures; with a preface by Mrs Miller. Edinburgh 1859.
The headship of Christ and the rights of the Christian people; with a preface by P. Bayne. Edinburgh 1861.
Essays historical and biographical, political and social, literary and scientific. Ed P. Bayne, Edinburgh 1862. Rptd from Witness.
Tales and sketches. Ed L. F. F. Miller, Edinburgh 1863.
Edinburgh and its neighbourhood, geological and historical; with the geology of the Bass Rock. Ed L. F. F. Miller, Edinburgh 1864.
Leading articles on various subjects. Ed J. Davidson, Edinburgh 1870.
Geology of the country around Otterburn and Elsdon. 1887.

§2

Brown, T. N. Labour and triumph: the life and times of Miller. 1858.
Bingham, W. The life and writings of Miller: an oration. 1859.
Allibone's Dictionary of authors vol 2. 1859–71. Includes biography, bibliography, references to and extracts from reviews and articles on Miller.
The life of Miller: a sketch for working men. 1862. Rptd from Northern Daily Express.
Bayne, P. The life and letters of Miller. 1871.
Watson, T. L. Life of Miller. Edinburgh 1880.
Leask, W. K. Miller. Edinburgh [1896].
Mackenzie, W. M. Miller: a critical study. 1905.
Masson, D. Miller. In his Memories of two cities: Edinburgh and Aberdeen, Edinburgh 1911.

Richard Monckton Milnes, 1st Baron Houghton 1809–85

See col 640.

Susanna Moodie, née Strickland 1803–85

The Susanna Moodie Collection of letters and papers is in the Nat Lib of Canada, Ottawa.

Bibliography

Ballstadt, C. P. A. In his The literary history of the Strickland family, unpbd PhD thesis, Univ of London 1965.

Selection

Voyages, short narratives of Susanna Moodie. Ed J. Thurston, Ottawa 1991.

§1

Little Downey: or the history of a field mouse. A moral tale. 1822 (anon), [1832] (as The adventures of little Downey); 1844 (with The little prisoner: or passion and patience), [1887].
Spartacus, a Roman story. 1822.
The little Quaker: or the triumph of virtue. 1825.
Hugh Latimer: or the school-boys' friendship. 1828, 1834, [1853] (as The soldier's orphan: or Hugh Latimer).
The little prisoner: or passion and patience, and Amendment: or Charles Grant and his sister. 1828 (anon), [c. 1850]. With C. P. Traill.
Patriotic songs. 1830. With A. Strickland.
Enthusiasm and other poems. 1831.
The history of Mary Prince, a West Indian slave. 1831.
Negro slavery described by a negro. 1831.
Profession and principle: tales. 1833.
Roland Massingham. 1837.
The little black pony and other stories. Philadelphia 1850.
Roughing it in the bush: or life in Canada. 2 vols 1852, 2 vols New York 1852, London 1854 (3rd edn with addns), 2 vols New York 1854, London 1857 (new edn), 1986 (facs reprint of 1852 edn introd by M. Atwood), Ottawa 1988 (introd by C. Ballstadt); Toronto 1871

(new and rev edn with an introductory chapter in which Canada of the present is contrasted with Canada of 40 years ago), New York [1877], 1887, Toronto, London and Edinburgh 1913, New York [1913], Toronto 1913, 1923; London 1932 (abridged and ed F. W. Tickner), London and New York [1938]; Toronto 1962 (ed and introd by C. F. Klinck), 1970.
Life in the clearings versus the bush. 1853, New York [1854?], [1875?], 1887, [1892?]; Toronto 1959 (to which is added Moodie's introd to Mark Hurdlestone, ed and introd by R. McDougall), 1976.
Mark Hurdlestone, the gold worshipper. 2 vols 1853, New York [1853] (3rd edn), 1855.
Flora Lyndsay: or passages in an eventful life. 2 vols 1854, New York [1854], [188?], [1887], [1891].
Matrimonial speculations. 1854. Contains Waiting for dead men's shoes, The Miss Greens, Richard Redpath, The voluntary slave.
The Monctons: a novel. 2 vols 1854, 2 vols 1856; 1 vol New York 1855, 1 vol London 1856, 1 vol New York 1887 (all 3 pbd as Geoffrey Moncton: or the faithless guardian).
Happy because good, The tame peasant and The blind brother and kind sister. [1859.]
The world before them: a novel. 3 vols 1868.
George Leatrim: or the mother's test. Edinburgh 1875.

Letters

Ballstadt, C., E. Hopkins and M. Peterman (ed). Letters of a lifetime. Toronto 1985.
Ballstadt, C., E. Hopkins and M. Peterman (ed). Letters of love and duty: the correspondence of Susanna and John Moodie. Toronto, Buffalo and London 1993.

Moodie contributed poems, sketches and stories to a range of periodicals including Athenaeum, La Belle Assemblée, The Lady's Mag. *She contributed prolifically to the* Literary Garland *(Montreal) and to the* Victoria Mag, *of which she was co-editor. For details, see Ballstadt, bibliography, above.*

§2

Boase, F. Modern English biography. 1897.
Ballstadt, C. P. A. The literary history of the Srickland family. Unpbd PhD thesis, Univ of London 1965.
Morris, A. Y. Gentle pioneers: five nineteenth-century Canadians. Toronto and London 1968.
Dictionary of Canadian biography, 1881–1890. Toronto 1982.
The Oxford companion to Canadian literature. Ed W. Toye, Toronto, Oxford and New York 1983.

Henry Morley 1822–94

§1

The dream of the Lilybell: tales and poems, with translations of the Hymns to night from the German of Novalis and Jean Paul's Death of an angel. 1845.
A tract upon health for cottage circulation. 1847.
Sunrise in Italy. 1848. A poem.
How to make home unhealthy. 1850. Anon. Rptd from Examiner; afterwards included in Early papers and some memories, 1891.
A defence of ignorance. 1851. A satirical essay on education.
Palissy the potter. 2 vols 1852.
The life of Geronimo Cardano of Milan, Physician. 2 vols 1854.
Cornelius Agrippa von Nettesheim. 2 vols 1856.
Gossip. 1857. Tales, papers and verses rptd from Household Words.
Memoirs of Bartholomew Fair. 1859.
Fables and fairy tales. 1860.
Oberon's horn: a book of fairy tales. 1861.
English writers. Vol 1, 1864 (subsequently divided into 2 half vols); vol 2, 1867 (half vol only; 2nd half never pbd, and all 3 half vols allowed to go out of print). Vols 1–11, 1887–95. 20 vols intended, but Morley only lived to write 10, vol 11 being completed by W. Hall Griffin.
The journal of a London playgoer from 1851 to 1866. 1866.
Fairy tales. 1867, [1877] (as The chicken market and other fairy tales). Tales previously pbd in Fables and fairy tales and Oberon's horn, *above.*
Tables of English literature. 1870, 1870 (with index).
Clement Marot and other studies. 2 vols 1871. Marot, Vesalius, Gesner, Cyrano de Bergerac, Gabriel Harvey, Caedmon's Paraphrase, Influence of the Celt on English literature etc.
A first sketch of English literature. [1873], 1886 (enlarged).
Cassell's library of English literature. 5 vols 1875–81. Extracts from and summaries of the greatest English classics, with notes and explanatory text by Morley.
University College London 1827–78: a lecture. 1878.
An account of the new north wing and recent additions to University College London. 1881. Anon.
Of English literature in the reign of Victoria, with a glance at the past. Leipzig 1881.
Morley's universal library. 6 vols 1883–8, 1891. Every vol with critical and biographical introd, by Morley.
Candide, by F. A. M. de Voltaire. 1884; [1922]. Trn by Morley; originally ptd with Johnson's Rasselas as Morley's universal library vol 19, *above.*
Cassell's national library. 213 vols 1886–92. A wide selection from the English classics with introd to each vol by Morley.
The Carisbrooke library. 14 vols 1889–92. Ed Morley.
Memoir of Thomas Sadler. [1891.]
Early papers and some memories. 1891. Short autobiographical ch followed by How to make home unhealthy, A defence of ignorance, Dream of the Lilybell, and 16 other papers, largely rptd from Household Words and All the Year Round.

§2

Solly, H. S. The life of Morley. 1898.

John Henry Newman 1801–90

The Newman letters, diaries, correspondence and mss have been collected and catalogued at the Birmingham Oratory of St Phillip Neri. Copies of his letters to E. B. Pusey and others can be found at Pusey House, Oxford, which also has a vast collection of mss and letters about Newman and others in the Catholic revival (Anglican and Roman), as well as an extensive collection of pams about Newman and his writings. The letters of John Keble to Newman and much of Keble's other correspondence are in the Bodleian rare books collection (Coleridge Collection); other Keble letters and mss are at Keble College, Oxford; Henry Manning's papers are stored and partially catalogued at St Mary's College, Bayswater, London. The papers of Nicholas Wiseman are catalogued and stored at Ushaw College, Durham.

Bibliographies

Lenz, M. Bibliography. In Newman's Apologia: a classic reconsidered, ed V. Blehl, New York 1964.
Dessain, C. S. Newman's philosophy and theology. In Victorian prose: a guide to research, ed D. DeLaura, New York 1973.
Svaglic, M. Newman: man and humanist. In Victorian prose: a guide to research, ed D. DeLaura, New York 1973.
Blehl, V. John Henry Newman: a bibliographical catalogue of his writings. Charlottesville VA 1978.
Griffin, J. Newman: a bibliography of secondary writings. Front Royal VA 1980.
Crumb, L. The Oxford Movement and its leaders: a bibliography of secondary and lesser primary sources. London 1988; suppl 1993.
Clavel, P. Essai de bibliographie chronologique des écrits en française sur Newman. Bulletin de l'Association Française des Amis de J. H. Newman 6 1990.
Simon, A. A list of works written and edited by Cardinal Newman in the library of St Mary College, Moraga. Moraga CA [1990].

Clavel, P. Complement de bibliographie Newmanienne. Bulletin des Amis de J. H. Newman 7 1991.
Biemer, G. John Henry Newman (1801–1890) nach einhundert jahren ein literatur beit. Theologische Revue 89 1993.
Kenis, L. Studies on Newman, 1990–1995. In J. Boudens, Two cardinals: J. H. Newman and D. J. Mercier, Louvain 1995.

Collections

[Collected works.] 36 vols 1868–81. The first systematic re-issue, described as the 'Uniform edition of Dr Newman's works', began with the pbn of Parochial and plain sermons and closed with his trn of the Select treatises of St Athanasius against the Arians. Some vols contain specially written prefaces and notes by the author. This edn was issued by Rivingtons, Burns & Oates, Pickering, and Longmans, Green & Co. From 1886 all the vols were pbd by Longmans.
37 vols 1870–7, 40 vols 1874–1921 (with index by J. Rickaby), 38 vols 1890–7, 34 vols 1898, 41 vols 1908–18 (the fullest Uniform edn), 38 vols 1917.
Ausgewählte Werke. Ed M. Laros 8 vols Mainz 1922–40. Several of the vols have been rptd.
Gesammelte Werke. Ed D. Feuling, E. Przywara, P. Simon 2 vols Munich 1924–8. A projected edn of the collected works abandoned after the second vol.
A new edition of the [selected] works. Ed C. F. Harrold 9 vols New York 1947–9. Projected in 12 vols and halted by the death of the editor.
Werken. Ed A. Pompen 7 vols Bussum 1946–58.
Gesamtausgabe seiner Predigten. 11 vols Stuttgart 1950– .
Textes Newmaniens. Ed H. Tristram, L. Bouyer, M. Nédoncelle 3 vols Paris 1955– .
The works of Cardinal Newman. Christian classics edn Westminster MD 1968– (9 vols only).
Newman: Opere. Ed G. Velocci et al, Milan 1988– .

Selections

Miscellanies from the Oxford sermons and other writings. 1870.
Six selections from the writings by a late member of Oriel College, Oxford [W. S. Lilly]. 1874.
Characteristics from the writings: being selections, personal, historical, philosophical and religious, from his various works, arranged by W. S. Lilly. 1875, 1876, 1880, 1882 (6th edn), 1949 (as A Newman anthology), 1977.
Selection adapted to the seasons of the ecclesiastical year from the Parochial and plain sermons. Ed W. J. C[opeland] 1870, 1878, 1882, 1890 (5th edn), nd (7th edn), 1908, 1915 (10th edn); tr Ger 1907.
Echoes from the oratory: selections from the poems. New York 1884.
Sayings of Cardinal Newman. [1890.]
Select essays. Ed G. Sampson [1903].
Le chrétien: choix de discours extraits des sermons de Newman – traduction et préface par R. Saleilles. Paris 1906.
Cardinal Newman. Ed W. Meynell [1907].
Literary selections. Ed Sister of Notre Dame 1913.
The spirit of Cardinal Newman. Ed C. C. Martindale 1914.
Le pensée de Newman: extraits choisis et traduits par F. Delattre, avec une introduction, une bibliographie et le texte anglais correspondant. Paris [1920].
Readings from Newman. Ed G. O'Neill 1923.
A Newman synthesis, arranged by E. Przywara. 1930, 1963 (as The heart of Newman). An abridgement, in the original Eng, of the Ger arrangement entitled Christentum: ein Aufbau, vol 4.
The fine gold of Newman. Ed J. J. Reilly, New York 1931.
According to Cardinal Newman: the life of Christ and the mission of his Church. Ed A. K. Maxwell, New York 1932.
Favorite Newman sermons. Ed D. M. O'Connell, Milwaukee 1932.
The Newman book of religion. Ed A. Ambruzzi 1937.
Heart to heart; Kindly light; And with the morn. Ed D. M. O'Connell, New York 1938–41, Paterson NJ 1947. 3 Newman prayer-books.
A Newman treasury: selections from the prose works. Ed C. F. Harrold, New York 1943.
Newman on university education. Ed R. J. McHugh, Dublin 1944.
Die Kirche: Übertragung und Einführung von O. Karrer. 2 vols Einsiedeln and Cologne 1946.
Essays and sketches. Ed C. F. Harrold 3 vols New York 1948.
The living thoughts of Cardinal Newman. Ed H. Tristram 1948.
Sermons and discourses 1825–39. Ed C. F. Harrold, New York 1949; Sermons and discourses 1839–57, ed Harrold, New York 1949.
The idea of a liberal education: a selection from the works. Ed H. Tristram 1952.
Newman 1845–52, the honeymoon years: an anthology. Ed J. Bradley, Bradford 1953.
The mystical rose: thoughts on the Blessed Virgin from the writings of Newman. Ed J. Regina [1955].
Pensées sur l'église, traduit par A. Roucou-Barthélémy. Paris 1956.
Prose and poetry. Ed G. Tillotson 1957 (Reynard Lib).
Realizations: Newman's selections of his Parochial and plain sermons. Ed V. F. Blehl 1964. Foreword by M. Spark.
A Newman prayer book. Ed R. Myers, Colorado Springs 1966.
A Newman reader. Ed F. X. Connolly, New York 1968.
The mind of Cardinal Newman. Ed C. S. Dessain 1974; rptd 1994.
The theological papers of John Henry Newman on faith and certainty. Ed H. de Achaval and J. D. Holmes 1976.
John Henry Newman: the theological papers on biblical inspiration and infallibility. Ed J. D. Holmes 1978.
The genius of John Henry Newman: selections from the writings. Ed I. Ker, Oxford 1989.
Newman the theologian. Ed I. Ker 1990.
Reasons for faith: nine sermons. San Francisco CA 1990.
Straight from the heart: thoughts of John Henry Newman. Ed K. and G. Dean, Chicago 1990.
Sermons 1824: sermons on the liturgy and sacraments and on Christ the mediator. Ed P. Murray, Oxford 1991.
Conscience, consensus, and the development of doctrine: revolutionary texts. Ed J. Gaffney, New York 1992.
Sermons 1824–1843: sermons on biblical history, sin and justification. Ed V. Blehl, Oxford 1993.
Selected sermons. Ed I. Ker, New York 1994.
The Newman correspondence for Sundays and feastdays. Ed J. Tolhurst, Birmingham 1995.

§1

St Bartholomew's eve: a tale of the sixteenth century in two cantos. 1821. Anon. With J. W. Bowden. The copy in the BM contains ms notes by J. R. Bloxam, assigning the separate parts to their authors.
Parish of St Clement Oxon. Dec 1 1824. Oxford 1824. A letter, signed by Newman, calling a meeting in aid of a fund for building a new church at Littlemore. Copy in Bodleian.
The life of Apollonius Tyanaeus; with a comparison between the miracles of Scriptures and those elsewhere related, as regards their respective object, nature and evidence. 1824 and 1853 (in Encyclopaedia metropolitana), 1825, 1853 (separately). The Life only was rptd in Historical sketches vol 1, 1872 etc (as Apollonius of Tyana), and the Miracles of Scripture in Two essays on Scripture miracles and on ecclesiastical, 1870 etc.
Suggestions respectfully offered to certain resident clergymen of the University in behalf of the Church Missionary Society, by a Master of Arts. Oxford 1830; rptd in The via media of the Anglican Church vol 2, 1877 etc.
Memorials of the past. Oxford 1832. Poems; prefatory verse signed J. H. N. Many are included in Verses on various occasions, *below*.
The Arians of the fourth century: their doctrine, temper and

conduct, chiefly as exhibited in the councils of the Church, between AD 325 and AD 381. 1833; ed G. H. Forbes 1854; 1871 (rev), 1876 (rev), 1888, 1890, 1890, 1895, 1901, 1908, 1919, 1968.

Price, B. Newman's history of the Arians. Edinburgh Rev 63 1836.

Tracts for the times, by members of the University of Oxford. [Ed Newman] 6 vols 1833–41; rptd New York 1974. 90 tracts were issued anon between 9 Sep 1833 (3 tracts) and 27 Feb 1841 (no 90). 5 lists of the tracts and their authors are extant: (1) appendix to H. P. Liddon, Life of Pusey vol 3, 1897, pp. 473–80; (2) Sir G. Prevost, Whitaker's almanack, 1883; (3) F. H. Rivington [based on information supplied by Newman in 1869], John Bull Sep 1890; (4) J. R. Bloxam, ms at Magdalen College, Oxford; (5) W. J. Copeland, revision of list in Whitaker's almanack, 1883. In the case of 2 tracts, further evidence has come to light. The following are by Newman: vol 1 nos 1–3, 6–7, 8 (with R. H. Froude), 10–11, 15 (with Sir W. Palmer), 19–21, 31, 33–4, 38, 41, 45; vol 2 no 47; vol 3 nos 71, 73, 74 (with B. Harrison), 75–6; vol 4 nos 79, 82; vol 5 nos 83, 85, 88; vol 6 no 90 (remarks on certain passages in the Thirty-nine Articles). Nos 83 and 85 were rptd in Discussions and arguments on various subjects, 1872 etc, *below*; no 73 was rptd in Essays, critical and historical vol 1, 1872 etc, *below*; and nos 38, 41, 71, 82 and 90 were rptd in The via media of the Anglican Church vol 2, 1877 etc, *below*. No 90 has been frequently rptd separately: ed J. J. Frew 1855; ed E. B. Pusey (with appendix by J. Keble) 1865, 1866, 1893; ed A. W. Evans 1933; tr Ger 1844.

Maurice, P. In his Popery of Oxford confronted, disavowed and repudiated, 2 pts 1837–51.

Froude, R. H. In his Remains of the Rev R. Hurrell Froude, [ed J. H. Newman and J. Keble] 2 pts 1838–9.

Nevile, C. A review of Mr Newman's Lectures on Romanism; with general observations on the Oxford tracts and Dr Pusey's Letter to the Bishop of Oxford. 1839.

Bennett, J. Justification as revealed in Scripture: in opposition to the Council of Trent and Mr Newman's Lectures. 1840.

Golightly, C. P. Brief remarks upon no 90 [of Tracts for the times]. Oxford 1841.

Pusey, E. B. The articles treated on in Tract 90 reconsidered and their interpretation vindicated in a letter to R. W. Jelf. 1841.

Pusey, E. B. In his Holy eucharist, a comfort to the penitent: a sermon, Oxford 1843.

Pusey, E. B. First letter to Newman in explanation chiefly in regard to the reverential love due to the ever-blessed Theotokos, and the doctrine of her immaculate conception etc. 1869. Pt 2 of his Eirenicon 1865–70.

Ward, W. G. A few more words in support of no 90 of the Tracts for the times. 1841.

Abeken, H. In his Das englische Bistum in Jerusalem, Berlin 1842.

Harper, F. W. A few observations on the teaching of Mr Newman concerning justification. 1842.

Illustration of the actual state of Oxford and of the attempts of Mr Newman to unprotestantize the National Church. Oxford 1842.

Wiseman, N. P. S. A letter respectfully addressed to the Rev Newman upon some passages in his letter to the Rev Dr Jelf. 1842.

Buchanan, J. On the Tracts for the times. Edinburgh 1843.

de Mestral, A. In his L'école théologique d'Oxford, Lausanne 1843.

Palmer, W. A narrative of events connected with the publication of the Tracts for the times. Oxford 1843.

Palmer, W. The doctrine of development and conscience, considered in relation to the evidences of Christianity and of the Catholic system. 1846.

Perceval, A. A collection of papers connected with the theological revival of 1833. 1843.

Unden, H. F. In his Die Zustände der anglikanischen Kirche, Leipzig 1843.

Bricknell, W. S. Oxford: tract no 90 and Ward's Ideal of a Christian church: a practical suggestion respectfully submitted to members of Convocation; with an appendix containing the testimonies of twenty-four prelates against tract no 90, and a series of extracts from Ward's Ideal. Oxford 1844.

Bricknell, W. S. The judgement of the bishops upon tractarian theology: a complete analytical arrangement of the charges delivered by the prelates of the Anglican Church, from 1837 to 1842 inclusive, so far as they relate to the tractarian movement. Oxford 1845.

Goode, W. Tract XC historically refuted: or a reply to a work by the Rev F. Oakeley entitled The subject of tract XC historically examined. 1845, 1866.

Rogers, F. A short appeal to the members of Convocation upon the proposed censure of tract 90. 1845.

von Gerlach, O. In his Über den religiösen Zustand der anglikanischen Kirche in ihren verschiedenen Gliederungen im Jahre 1842, Potsdam 1845.

Parochial sermons. 3 vols 1834–6, 6 vols (2–3 are of the 2nd edn) 1834–42, 1837–42, 1838–44; ed W. J. Copeland 8 vols 1868 (including Plain sermons by contributors to the tracts for the times, vol 5, as Parochial and plain sermons), 1872–3, 1875–80, 1877, 1879, 1881–4, 1886, 1900–2, 1924. Selection from the First four volumes of Parochial sermons, 1841. Selection adapted to the seasons of the ecclesiastical year from the Parochial and plain sermons, ed W. J. C[opeland] 1870, 1878, 1882, 1890 (5th edn), nd (7th edn), 1908, 1915 (10th edn); tr Ger 1907. Twelve sermons selected from the Parochial and plain sermons [1908].

To my parishioners, on occasion of laying of the first stone of the church at Littlemore. Oxford 1835. A letter by Newman. Copy in Bodleian.

The restoration of suffragan bishops recommended, as a means of effecting a more equal distribution of episcopal duties, as contemplated by His Majesty's recent Ecclesiastical Commission. 1835; rptd in The via media of the Anglican Church vol 2, 1877 etc, *below*.

Elucidations of Dr Hampden's theological statements. Oxford 1836. Signed J. H. N. [With E. B. Pusey].

Arnold, T. The Oxford malignants and Dr Hampden. Edinburgh Rev 63 1836.

Wiseman, N. The Oxford controversy. Dublin Rev 1 1836.

Make ventures for Christ's sake: a sermon. Oxford 1836 (anon); 1839 etc (in Parochial sermons vol 4, *above*).

Lectures on the prophetical office of the Church, viewed relatively to Romanism and popular Protestantism. 1837; rptd, with additional matter, in The via media of the Anglican Church vol 1, 1877 etc, *below*.

A letter to the Rev Godfrey Faussett DD, Margaret Professor of Divinity, on certain points of faith and practice. Oxford 1838; rptd in The via media of the Anglican Church vol 2, 1877 etc, *below*.

Lectures on justification. 1838, 1840, 1874 (as Lectures on the doctrine of justification), 1885, 1890, 1892, 1900, 1924.

The Church of the Fathers. Dublin [1839] (anon), London 1840 (anon), 1842, 1857, 1868, 1872 (in Historical sketches vol 3; material omitted from the 1857 and 1868 edns rptd rev in Historical sketches vol 2, *below*), 1900, 1908, 1931; tr Fr 1908.

The Tamworth reading room: letters on an address delivered by Sir Robert Peel Bart MP on the establishment of a reading room at Tamworth, by Catholicus, originally published in The Times, and since revised and corrected by the author. 1841; rptd in Discussions and arguments, 1872, *below*; Washington DC 1946.

A letter addressed to the Rev R. W. Jelf DD, Canon of Christ Church, in explanation of no 90 in the series called the Tracts for the times, by the author. Oxford 1841 (3 edns), 1877 (in The via media of the Anglican Church vol 2, 1877 etc, *below*). Signed J. H. N.

A letter to the Right Reverend Father in God, Richard [Bagot], Lord

Bishop of Oxford, on occasion of no 90 in the series called the Tracts for the times. 1841, 1877 (in The via media of the Anglican Church vol 2, 1877 etc, *below*).

Mr Vice-Chancellor, I write this respectfully to inform you... Oxford 1841; rptd in R. D. Middleton, Newman at Oxford, 1950. Ptd broadside letter acknowledging the authorship of Tract 90. Copy in Library of Congress.

An essay on the miracles recorded in the ecclesiastical history of the early ages. In Fleury's Ecclesiastical history, 1842; Oxford 1843, 1870 (in Two essays on Scripture miracles and on ecclesiastical), 1870, 1873 (in Two essays on biblical and ecclesiastical miracles), 1881, 1885, 1890, 1890, 1901, 1924.

Sermons, bearing on subjects of the day. 1843, 1844; ed W. J. Copeland 1869, 1873, 1879, 1885, 1902, 1902, 1917; tr Ger 1925 (selection), 1958 (complete).

Sermons, chiefly on the theory of religious belief, preached before the University of Oxford. 1843, 1844, 1872 (as Fifteen sermons preached before the University of Oxford), 1880, 1884, 1890, 1900, 1906, 1918; ed J. D. Holmes, Oxford 1978; tr Fr 1850, 1905 (6 sermons only), 1955 (complete), Sp 1993.

The Cistercian saints of England, [continued as] Lives of the English saints. 4 vols 1844–5 (vols 1–2 ed Newman, who wrote the prose portions of St Bettelin, St Edilwald and St Gundleas); ed A. W. Hutton 6 vols 1900–1.

Ecclesiastical miracles. North Br Rev 4 1846.

Lives of the saints. Dolman's Quart Rev 6 1846.

Lyra Innocentium, by the author of The Christian year. Dublin Rev 20 1846; rptd as John Keble in Essays critical and historical, 1871.

Whately, R. Tendencies of Puseyism. Westminster Rev 45 1846. On Lives.

An essay on the development of Christian doctrine. [The Advertisement contains Newman's Retraction of anti-Catholic statements.] 1845, 1846, 1878, 1885, 1890, 1894, 1903, 1920, 1927; ed C. F. Harrold, New York 1949 (with appendix on Newman's textual changes by O. I. Schreiber); ed G. Weigel 1960; 1960; ed J. Cameron, 1976 (Pen); 1989. Tr Fr 1846, 1848, 1905 (with trn of The theory of developments in Christian doctrine: a sermon by Newman), Ger 1846, 1922, Du 1957, Polish 1957. Newman's Retraction was tr Fr in J. Gondon, Motifs de conversion de dix ministres anglicans, Paris 1847.

Barter, W. B. A postscript to The English church not in schism: containing a few words on Mr Newman's Essay on development. 1846.

[Brownson, O. A.?] An essay on the Development of Christian doctrine by Newman, by an English Churchman. Brownson's Quart Rev 3 1846.

[Brownson, O. A.?] The fourfold difficulty of Anglicanism by J. Spencer Northcote. Brownson's Quart Rev n.s. 1 1847.

Faber, G. S. Letters on tractarian secession to popery; with remarks on Mr Newman's principle of development etc. 1846.

A few words to the author of An essay on the development of Christian doctrine. 1846.

Fry, H. P. Sermons on the nature and design of heresy: on the defection of the Rev Newman from the Church of England and on other subjects. Hobart 1846.

Gillis, J. Lectures on the Essay on development. Edinburgh 1846.

Irons, W. J. The theory of development examined with reference specially to Mr Newman's Essay. 1846.

Irvine, A. Romanism briefly considered, as represented by the Rev Newman. 1846.

Maurice, J. F. D. The Epistle to the Hebrews: with a preface containing a review of Mr Newman's Theory of developments. 1846.

Mithridates: or Mr Newman's Essay on development its own confutation, by a quondam disciple. 1846.

Moberly, G. The sayings of the great forty days, with an examination of Mr Newman's theory of developments. 1846.

Newman on the development of Christian doctrine. North Br Rev 5 1846.

A review of Mr Newman's Essay on the development of Christian doctrine, by an English churchman. 1846.

Doctrinal developments. Dublin Rev 22 1847.

Mozley, J. B. The theory of the development: a criticism of Dr Newman's Essay on the development of Christian doctrine. Christian Remembrancer Jan 1847; rptd 1878 (separately).

Butler, W. A. Letters on the development of Christian doctrine, in reply to Mr Newman's Essay. Ed Rev T. Woodward, Dublin 1850.

Maguire, R. The Oxford movement: strictures on the personal reminiscences and revelations of Dr Newman, Mr Oakeley and others; with special reference to the Essay on development. 1855.

Dissertatiunculae quaedam critico-theologicae (ex nupera Oxoniensi Biblioteca Patrum maxima ex parte desumpta; Latine autem liberius reddita etc). Rome 1847, London 1874 etc (in Tracts theological and ecclesiastical).

Loss and gain. 1848 (anon), 1853 (signed; with subtitle The story of a convert), Dublin 1853, London 1858, 1874, 1881, 1891, 1896, 1903, 1904, 1919, 1934; ed M. Trevor 1962; tr Ital 1857, Fr 1859, 1945 (extracts), 1949 (complete), Ger 1861, 1924. A novel.

Discourses addressed to mixed congregations. 1849, 1850, 1880, 1881, 1886, 1891, 1892, 1902, 1921; tr Fr 1850, 1853, Ger 1851, 1924 (selection), Du 1947, Ital 1955, Sp 1994.

Lectures on certain difficulties felt by Anglicans in submitting to the Catholic Church. 1850, 1850, Dublin 1857 (rev), London 1872 (as Difficulties felt by Anglicans in Catholic teaching considered, I, In twelve lectures addressed to the party of the religious movement in 1833; II, In a letter addressed to the Rev E. B. Pusey &c), 1876 (as Certain difficulties felt by Anglicans in Catholic teaching considered in a letter addressed to the Rev E. B. Pusey and in a letter addressed to the Duke of Norfolk &c), 2 vols 1876–9, 1885 (as Difficulties felt by Anglicans in Catholic teaching), 1891, 1894 (as Certain difficulties felt by Anglicans in Catholic teaching considered), 1897, 1901, 1918–20; tr Fr 1851; Ger 1949 (selection), 1951.

Christ upon the waters: a sermon preached on occasion of the establishment of the Catholic hierarchy in this country. Birmingham 1850 (3 edns), [1852], London 1857 etc (in Sermons preached on various occasions, *below*), Birmingham [1898].

Lectures on the present position of Catholics in England, addressed to the Brothers of the Oratory. 1851, 1851, Birmingham 1851 (as Lectures on Catholicism in England), Dublin nd (as Lectures on Catholicism in England), 1872, 1880, 1889, 1890 (pt 5 omitted), 1892 (Silver Lib, with subtitle Addressed to the Brothers of the Oratory in the summer of 1851), 1903, 1908, 1913, 1924; ed D. M. O'Connell SJ, Chicago 1925 (school edn); ed J. J. Daly, Beirut 1942; tr Ger 1853, Du 1958.

Capes, J. Newman's Lectures on the present position of Catholics in England. Rambler 8 1851.

Capes, J. Protestant justice and royal clemency. Rambler 9 1852.

Minton, S. An exposure of the inconsistencies, fictions and fallacies of Dr Newman's lectures at Birmingham [on the position of Catholics in England]. 1851.

Minton, S. Facts and figures: three letters to Dr Newman, in reply to some of his lectures recently delivered at Birmingham. Liverpool [1851].

Achilli versus Newman. Christian Remembrancer 24 1852.

Achilli v. Newman: a full and authentic report of the prosecution for libel tried before Lord Campbell and a special jury, June 1852; with introductory remarks by the editor of the Confessional unmasked. [1852.]

Finlaison, W. Achilli versus Newman. Rambler 10 1852.

Ward, W. Newman's Lectures on the present position of Catholics in England. Dublin Rev 32 1852.

Dr Achilli. Bulwark 11 1853.

Discourses on the scope and nature of university education,

addressed to the Catholics of Dublin. Dublin 1852, London 1859 (rev and altered, and with new titles to several of the discourses, as The scope and nature of university education), 1873 (with some titles of discourses again altered, and with the addn of 10 pieces pbd in 1859 as Lectures and essays on university subjects, as The idea of a university defined and illustrated, I: In nine discourses addressed to the Catholics of Dublin; II: In occasional lectures and essays addressed to the members of the Catholic University), 1875, 1885, 1889, 1891, 1893, 1896 (2 discourses only, in My campaign in Ireland), 1898 (as The idea of a university etc), 1902; ed A. R. Waller 1903 (Cloister Lib; as The scope and nature of university education); ed J. Norris 1908 (Longman's Pocket Lib; as University teaching considered in nine discourses: being the first part of The idea of a university defined and illustrated etc), 1910 (as The idea of a university defined and illustrated etc), 1912; ed W. Ward 1915 (EL; as On the scope and nature of university education), 1923 (as The idea of a university defined and illustrated etc); ed D. M. O'Connell SJ, Chicago 1927, 1929, 1931 (as University teaching considered in nine discourses: being the first part of The idea of a university defined and illustrated); ed M. Yardley, Cambridge 1931 (Landmarks in the History of Education: as Select discourses from The idea of a university); ed D. M. O'Connell, New York 1941 (as The idea of a university defined and illustrated); ed R. J. McHugh, Dublin 1944 (nos 5–6, 7, 9, with part of the preface to Discourses on the scope and nature of university education, with excerpts from the second part of The idea of a university defined and illustrated, as Newman on university education); ed C. F. Harrold, New York 1947 (as The idea of a university defined and illustrated); ed L. L. Ward, New York 1948 (as The uses of knowledge; selections from The idea of a university); 1955 (EL; as On the scope and nature of university education); ed M. Yardley, Cambridge 1956 (as Select discourses from The idea of a university); ed G. N. Shuster, New York 1959 (as The idea of a university); ed M. J. Svaglic, New York 1960 (as The idea of a university defined and illustrated), 1979; ed I. Ker, Oxford 1971; ed F. Turner, New Haven CT 1996; tr Ger 1927 (selection), 1957 (selection), Du 1946. Many of the discourses have been rptd separately at various dates.

Newman's Discourses on the scope and nature of university education. Christian Observer 11 1853.

Ward, W. Father Newman, The idea of a university. Dublin Rev 21 1873, 22 1874.

The second spring: a sermon preached in the synod of Oscott, on Tuesday July 13th 1852. 1852, 1857 etc (in Sermons preached on various occasions, *below*); ed F. P. Donnolly, New York 1911.

Verses on religious subjects. Dublin 1853. Anon. Most of the poems in this coll are rptd in Verses on various occasions, 1868 etc, *below*.

Lectures on the history of the Turks in its relation to Christianity, by the author of Loss and gain. Dublin 1854 (anon), 1872 etc (in Historical sketches vol 2); tr Ger 1854.

Callista: a sketch of the third century. 1856 (anon), Leipzig [c. 1865] (Tauchnitz), London 1873, 1876, 1881, 1889 (with subtitle A tale of the third century), 1890, 1898, 1901, 1904 (with subtitle A tale of the third century), 1910 (with subtitle A tale of the third century), 1923, 1928, 1934; ed A. Duggan 1962; dramatised version by F. C. Husenbeth, entitled The convert martyr, 1857; tr Ger 1856, 1860, 1862, 1885, 1890, 1893, 1895, 1900, 1903, 1908, 1910, [1920], [1926], Fr 1857, 1859, 1867, 1868, 1867 (for 1869), 1873, 1875, 1877, 1880, 1881, 1884, 1885, 1888, 1890, 1891, 1894, 1896, 1908, dramatised version in Fr 1874, 1993, nd, Polish 1858, Ital 1859, 1928, Cz 1887, Serbo-Croat [1926], Sp 1948, 1993. A novel.

The office and work of universities [articles rptd from Catholic Univ Gazette]. 1856, 1859, 1872 etc (as The rise and progress of universities, in Historical sketches vol 2); ed G. Sampson [1902] (as University sketches); ed C. F. Harrold 1948 (selection of 8 of the 20 articles, in Essays and sketches vol 2); ed M. Tierney, Dublin 1952 (as University sketches); ed Tierney, New York 1964; tr Ger 1949, 1958.

Sermons preached on various occasions. 1857, 1870, 1874, 1881, 1887, 1891, 1900, 1921; tr Fr 1860, Ger 1924 (selection). The mission of St Philip Neri was rptd separately, Rome 1901, *below*.

Lectures and essays on university subjects. 1859, 1873 etc (as pt 2 of The idea of a university defined and illustrated). *See also under* Discourses on the scope and nature of university education, *above*.

The tree beside the waters: a sermon preached in the chapel of St Mary's College Oscott on Friday November 11 1859, at the funeral of the Right Rev Henry Weedall DD. [1859], 1870 etc (in Sermons preached on various occasions, *above*).

Mr Kingsley and Dr Newman: a correspondence on the question whether Dr Newman teaches that truth is no virtue? 1864, 1913, 1931 (both with Apologia pro vita sua); tr Ger 1865.

Apologia pro vita sua: being a reply to a pamphlet [by Charles Kingsley] entitled What, then, does Dr Newman mean? 7 pts, with appendix issued on successive Thursdays 21 Apr–2 June 1864; the appendix pbd a fortnight later. Pts 1–2 and appendix were omitted by Newman from later edns. 1864, 1865 (as History of my religious opinions), 1865 (as Apologia pro vita sua: being a reply to a pamphlet entitled What, then, does Dr Newman mean?), 1865, 1865, 1869 (as History of my religious opinions), 1873 (as Apologia pro vita sua: being a history of his religious opinions), 1878, 1879, 1882 (as A history of his religious opinions), 1885 (as Apologia pro vita sua: history of his religious opinions), 1887 (as Apologia pro vita sua: being a history of his religious opinions), 1890; ed A. H. Barton 1891, 1892, 1897, 1902; ed W. P. Neville 1904; 1907 (Longman's Pocket Lib); ed W. Meynell [1907] (an abridgement entitled Newman: the story of his religious opinions, abstracted in his own words from the Apologia pro vita sua); [1907], 1908; ed C. Sarolea [1912] (EL); ed W. Ward, Oxford 1913 (the 2 versions of 1864 and 1865, preceded by Newman's and Kingsley's pams); ed J. Gamble 2 vols [1913] (Scott Lib) (text of 1864 with supplementary matter included in 1865 and Newman's and Kingsley's pams); 1920 (Longman's Pocket Lib); [1921] (EL); 1924; ed D. M. O'Connell SJ with foreword by H. Belloc, Chicago 1930 (text of 1865); ed A. B. G. Hart, New York 1931; ed W. Ward, Oxford 1931 (the 2 versions of 1864 and 1865, preceded by Newman's and Kingsley's pams); arranged by M. R. Grennan, with introd by J. J. Reilly, New York 1934 (as The heart of Newman's Apologia); ed M. Ward 1946; ed C. F. Harrold, New York 1947; ed A. C. Pegis, New York 1950 (Modern Lib); ed S. Leslie 1955 (EL); ed P. Hughes, New York 1956; ed A. D. Culler, New York 1956; 1959 (Fontana); ed B. Willey, Oxford 1964 (WC); ed M. J. Svaglic, Oxford 1967, 1990 (rptd); ed P. Hughes, New York 1971, 1989 (rptd); ed W. Oddie, 1993 (EL); ed I. T. Ker 1994 (Pen); tr Fr 1866, 1939, 1951, 1963, 1984, 1990, Ger 1913, 1920, 1922, 1968, 1982, 1990, Sp 1934, 1961, 1989, 1992, Du 1946, 1949, 1956, Polish 1948, 1988, Ital 1956, 1971, 1995, Swed 1960, 1993.

Coleridge, H. Newman's Apologia. Dublin Rev 3 1864.

Cox, G. Newman's Apologia. Westminster Rev 82 1864.

Stephen, L. Dr Newman's Apologia. Fortnightly Rev 70 1864.

Whately, R. Newman and phenakism. Macmillan's Mag 10 1864.

Wilberforce, S. Dr Newman's Apologia. Quart Rev 116 1864.

Dr Newman and Mr Kingsley. London Quart Rev 23 1865.

Oakeley, F. Historical notes on the Oxford movement. 1865.

Colette, C. Dr Newman and his opinions. 1866.

D[arcy], J. N. Analysis of Dr Newman's Apologia pro vita sua. 1866.

The dream of Gerontius. Month 12 May–June 1865, 1866 (dedication signed J. H. N.), 1868 etc (in Verses on various occasions, *below*); 1886 (22nd edn), 1888, 1897 (30th edn), 1898, 1900; set to music by E. Elgar, 1900; 1903 (34th edn); ed M. F. Egan 1903; ed Egan 1906; ed E. B. [L.] 1907 (illus); illustr 'Ryl' 1907; illustr M. P. Webb 1907; ed E. Bellasis 1909 (with ms facs); illustr R. T. Rose 1910; illustr F.

E. Hiley 1911; illustr R. T. Rose 1911; ed M. F. Egan 1912; Oxford 1914 (together with Verses on various occasions, *below*, and some poems from Lyra apostolica not included in Verses, 1868); ed G. Tidy, illustr S. Langdale 1916; ed J. Gliebe, New York 1916 (college edn); ed J. J. Clifford, Chicago 1917 (school edn); ed W. F. P. Stockley 1923; ed with concordance and chronicle by 'Anglican' (A. F. Dauglish) 1928; ed H. Tristram [1933]; ed M. Sargent, illustr M. P. Webb 1937; tr Fr 1869, 1869, 1882, 1889, 1912, 1926, 1944, 1960, Ger 1885, 1923, 1923 (in Der Gral vol 17), 1925, 1939, 1939, [1946] (Eng and Ger), 1952, 1959, 1960, Du 1947.

A letter to the Rev E. B. Pusey DD on his recent Eirenicon. 1866 (3 edns), 1872 etc (in Difficulties felt by Anglicans in Catholic teaching); tr Ger 1866, 1911, 1953 (selection), Fr 1867 (in J. Gondon, De la réunion de l'église d'Angleterre protestante à l'église catholique).

The Pope and the revolution: a sermon preached in the Oratory Church Birmingham on Sunday October 7 1866. 1866, 1870 etc (in Sermons preached on various occasions, *above*); tr Fr 1867, Ger 1867.

Verses on various occasions. 1868 (dedication signed J. H. N.), 1869, 1874, 1880, 1883, 1888, 1890, 1903, 1912 (Longman's Pocket Lib), Oxford 1914 (in The dream of Gerontius and other poems), 1918.

An essay in aid of a grammar of assent. 1870, 1870, 1874, 1881, 1885, 1891, 1892, 1901, 1903, 1909, 1924, 1930; ed C. F. Harrold, New York 1947; ed E. Gilson 1955, 1958, 1979; ed I. Ker, Oxford 1985; tr Fr 1907, 1972, 1988, Ger 1921, 1936–40, 1978, Polish 1956, Sp 1960, 1983.

Brownson, O. The Grammar. Catholic World 12 1870.

Dr Newman's Grammar of assent. Christian Observer 70 1870.

Dr Newman's Grammar of assent. Edinburgh Rev 132 1870.

Dr Newman's Grammar of assent. Theologische Rev 7 1870.

Harper, T. Dr Newman's Essay in aid of a grammar of assent. Month 12 1870.

Maurice, F. Dr Newman's Grammar of assent. Contemporary Rev 14 1870.

Certitude in religious assent. Dublin Rev 16 1871.

Two essays on Scripture miracles and on ecclesiastical. 1870, 1873 (as Two essays on biblical and on ecclesiastical miracles), 1881, 1885, 1890, 1890, 1901, 1924. Rptd respectively from the Encyclopaedia metropolitana, 1824 etc, and from Newman's trn of a portion of Fleury's Ecclesiastical history.

Essays critical and historical. 2 vols 1872, 1877, 1885, 1890, 1895, 1901, 1910, 1919. Essays and periodical articles rptd. Poetry with reference to Aristotle's Poetics rptd separately, ed A. S. Cook, Boston 1891.

Historical sketches [i.e. The office and work of universities, 1856, rptd as The rise and progress of universities; Lectures on the history of the Turks, 1854; Personal and literary character of Cicero, 1824; Apollonius of Tyana, 1824; Primitive Christianity (from the 1840 and 1842 edns of The Church of the Fathers); The Church of the Fathers (text of 1857 and 1868 edns) and various shorter pieces]. 3 vols 1872–3, 1873, 1876, 1878–81, 1891, 1901–3, 1920; tr Ger 1948 (selection), 1949 (selection). The mission of St Benedict and The Benedictine schools only were rptd in 1908, ed H. Bennett, as The mission of the Benedictine order, and in 1914, ed H. N. Birt, as Cardinal Newman on the Benedictine order; the same 2 essays were tr Ger 1926. The mission of St Benedict was tr Fr 1909. St Crysostom and The trials of Theodoret were tr Ger, 1923.

Discussions and arguments on various subjects. 1872, 1873, 1878, 1899, 1907, 1924. The Tamworth reading room, 1841, nos 82 and 85 of the Tracts for the times, 1838, and various periodical articles rptd.

Orate pro anima Jacobi Roberti Hope Scott [a sermon]. [1873] (advertisement and text signed J. H. N.), 1874 etc (as In the world but not of the world, in Sermons on various occasions, *above*); rptd in Memoirs of James Robert Hope-Scott, ed R. Ormsby, 1884.

The idea of a university. 1873 etc. *See also* Discourses on the scope and nature of university education, *above*.

Tracts theological and ecclesiastical. 1874, 1891, 1895, 1899, 1902, 1924. Collects Dissertatiunculae quaedam critico-theologicae, 1847, and other uncollected pieces.

A letter addressed to his Grace the Duke of Norfolk on occasion of Mr Gladstone's recent expostulations. 1875, 1875 (with Postscript on Mr Gladstone's Vaticanism), 1875 (4th edn, with Postscript), New York 1875, London 1876 etc (appended to Certain difficulties felt by Anglicans in Catholic teaching, *above*); ed A. S. Ryan, Notre Dame IN 1962 (as Letter to his Grace the Duke of Norfolk, in Newman and Gladstone); tr Ger 1875.

Dr John Henry Newman and Mr Gladstone. Literary Churchman 21 1875.

Father Newman on ecclesiastical prudence. Dublin Rev 25 1875.

Newman's reply to Gladstone. Brownson's Quart Rev 24 1875.

Ultramontanism and civil allegiance. Br Quart Rev 61 1875.

Newman and Dr Dollinger. Month 36 1879.

The via media of the Anglican Church, illustrated in lectures, letters, and tracts written between 1830 and 1841; with a preface and notes. 2 vols 1877, 1885, 1891, 1891 (Silver Lib), 1891–8, 1901, 1918–23; ed H. Widener, Oxford 1990; tr Ger 1938 (preface to Lectures on the prophetical office only, vol 1), 1947; Sp 1995. Reprints Lectures on the prophetical office of the Church, viewed relatively to Romanism and popular Protestantism, 1837; Suggestions in behalf of the Church Missionary Society, 1830; nos 38, 41, 71, 82 and 90 of the Tracts for the times, 1833–41; The restoration of suffragan bishops recommended, 1835; A letter addressed to the Rev Godfrey Faussett, 1838; A letter addressed to the Rev R. W. Jelf, 1841; A letter to the Bishop of Oxford, 1841; and Retraction of anti-Catholic statements, 1843.

Biglietto speech. 1879 (priv ptd); rptd in A Newman reader, ed F. X. Connolly, New York 1968.

The cardinal. The Times 13 May 1879.

England's cardinal. Guardian 13 May 879.

Pusey, E. B. Letter to Mr Belaney. Weekly Register 20 May 1879.

Two sermons preached in the Church of S Aloysius, Oxford on Trinity Sunday 1880. [Oxford 1880] (priv ptd).

Prologue on the Andria of Terence. 1882 (ptd for priv circulation). Copy of this work, written in 1820, in BM.

What is of obligation for a Catholic to believe concerning the inspiration of the canonical scriptures: being a postscript to an article in the February no of the Nineteenth Century Review in answer to Professor Healy. [1884], 1890 (as Further illustrations, in Stray essays on controversial points variously illustrated).

The development of religious error. Contemporary Rev 48 1885; rptd in The theological papers of John Henry Newman on faith and certainty, 1976.

Fairbairn, A. M. Reason and religion: a reply to Cardinal Newman. Contemporary Rev 48 1885.

Fairbairn, A. M. Catholicism: Roman and Anglican. 1899.

Stray essays on controversial points variously illustrated. Birmingham 1890 (priv ptd). Reprints What is of obligation for a Catholic to believe, 1884, and 2 other periodical articles.

Poetry with reference to Aristotle's Poetics. Ed A. S. Cook, Boston 1891. *See also* Essays critical and historical, *above*.

Meditations and devotions of the late Cardinal Newman. Ed W. P. Neville 1893, 1903, 1908, 1914, 1923, 1932, 1953; ed M. Trevor 1964; tr Fr 1906, Ital 1906, 1907, 1926, Ger 1919, 1922, 1930, [1939], 1946, 1949, 1952, 1953, 1954, 1960, 1960, Sp 1952, Du 1955.

My campaign in Ireland, part 1: Catholic University reports and other papers. Ed W. P. Neville, Aberdeen 1896 (priv ptd). Part 2, Note on Cardinal Newman's preaching and influence at Oxford, by J. C. Shairp.

The mission of St Philip Neri: an instruction delivered in substance in the Birmingham Oratory, January 1850, and at subsequent times. Rome 1901. *See also* Sermons preached on various occasions, *above*.

Addresses to Cardinal Newman, with his replies etc. 1879–81. Ed W. P. Neville 1905; Dublin 1976.

The mission of the Benedictine order. Ed H. Bennett 1908 etc. *See also* Historical sketches, *above*.

Sermon notes 1849–78. Ed Fathers of the Birmingham Oratory 1913; tr Fr 1914.

Autobiographical writings. Ed H. Tristram 1956; tr Fr 1956 (with Eng text), Ger 1959, Sp 1963.

Faith and prejudice and other unpublished sermons. Ed C. S. Dessain, New York 1956, London 1957 (as Catholic sermons); tr Sp 1959.

On consulting the faithful in matters of doctrine. Ed J. Coulson 1961, 1985; tr Ger 1940. Originally pbd in Rambler July 1859, rptd 1871, with addns and amendments, as an appendix to the 3rd edn of The Arians of the fourth century.

The argument from conscience to the existence of God, according to Newman, by A. J. Boekraad and H. Tristram. Louvain 1961. Among the unpbd writings by Newman, the paper entitled Proof of theism.

The philosophical notebook. Ed E. Sillem, Louvain 1970.

Works edited, translated, or with contributions by Newman

Newman edited Br Critic July 1838–July 1841 and, in May and July 1859, two nos of Rambler, both of which jnls contain articles by him. He also contributed to the following periodicals: London Rev, Br Mag, Dublin Rev, Catholic Univ Gazette (Dublin), Atlantis, Month, Nineteenth Cent; and in the Conservative Jnl Feb 1843 he pbd his Retraction of anti-Catholic statements.

Encyclopaedia metropolitana. Ed E. Smedley, Hugh J. Rose and Henry J. Rose 29 vols 1817–45, 40 vols 1848–58. Newman contributed articles on Cicero, 1824, Apollonius Tyanaeus, 1824, and the Miracles of scripture, 1826. The essay on Cicero was rptd in Historical sketches vol 1, 1872; that on Apollonius Tyanaeus was rptd separately, 1828, and included in Historical sketches vol 1, 1872; the essay on Miracles was rptd as pt 1 of Two essays on Scripture miracles and on ecclesiastical, 1870.

Elements of logic, by R. Whately. 1826, 1827, 1832 (4th edn, rev), 1836 (6th edn, rev), 1840 (rev), 1844 (rev), 1848 (rev). Newman had a large share in the composition.

Tracts for the times, by members of the University of Oxford. 6 vols 1833–41. Ed Newman. For a list of tracts contributed by Newman, *see above*.

Lyra apostolica. Derby 1836, 1837, 1838, 1840, 1843 (6th edn), 1864 (13th edn), 1866, London 1879, 1897; ed H. S. Holland and H. C. Beeching [1901]. Most of the poems by Newman, but not all, were included in Verses on various occasions, 1868 etc. The hymn known as Lead, kindly light was first pbd anon in Br Mag, 1 Feb 1834, under the title of Faith; it was rptd without title as no 25 in the Lyra apostolica, and later in Verses on various occasions as The pillar of the cloud. Probably one of the most popular English hymns, it has been frequently rptd both in separate form and in anthologies and hymnals. Poems originally pbd in Br Mag. Of the 179 pieces, Newman wrote 109; his contributions are signed δ.

A library of the Fathers of the Holy Catholic Church, anterior to the division of the East and West. Ed J. Keble, Newman, E. B. Pusey and [1843–57] C. Marriott. 48 vols Oxford 1838–85. Newman translated and annotated Select treaties of S Athanasius in controversy with the Arians, 2 vols 1842–4, 1881; rptd in part in A select library of Nicene and post-Nicene Fathers of the Christian Church, 2nd ser vol 4 ed A. Robinson, Oxford 1892. Newman also contributed prefaces to the following vols in A library of the Fathers: S Cyril's Catechetical lectures, 1838; S Cyprian's treatises, 1839; S Chrysostom on Galatians and Ephesians, 1840; and S Athanasius's historical tracts, 1843.

Godly meditations upon the Lord's supper, by C. Sutton. Oxford 1838. Preface by Newman.

Hymni ecclesiae: excerpti e breviariis Romano, Sarisburiensi, Eboracensi et aliunde. Oxford 1838 (preface by Newman), 1865 (with Newman's edn of Hymni ecclesiae e breviario Parisiensi).

Hymni ecclesiae e breviario Parisiensi. Oxford 1838 (preface by Newman), 1865 (with Newman's edn of Hymni excerpti e breviariis Romano, Sarisburiensi, Eboracensi et aliunde).

Remains of the late Rev R. H. Froude. 4 vols 1838–9. Ed Newman and J. Keble.

Stephen, J. Lives of Whitfield and Froude – Oxford Catholicism. Edinburgh Rev 67 1838.

Froude's Remains. Dublin Rev 6 1839.

Disce vivere: learn to live, by C. Sutton. Oxford 1839. Preface by Newman.

A rationale upon the Book of Common Prayer of the Church of England, by A. Sparrow. Oxford 1839. Preface by Newman.

The rich man's duty to contribute liberally to the building, rebuilding, repairing, beautifying and adorning of churches: to which is added the journal of William Dowsing etc, by E. Wells. Oxford 1840. Preface by Newman.

The life of George Bull, Bishop of St Davids, by R. Nelson. Oxford 1840. Preface by Newman.

Sacra privata: the private meditations, devotions and prayers of the Right Rev T. Wilson, reprinted entire. Oxford 1840. Preface by Newman.

Catena aurea: commentary on the four Gospels. 1841. Preface by Newman.

The devotions of Bishop [Lancelot] Andrewes. 2 pts Oxford 1842–4. Pt 1 tr from the Greek and arranged by Newman; pt 2 tr from the Latin by J. M. Neale. Pt 1 had appeared in 1840 as no 88 of Tracts for the times, *above*. Rptd Oxford 1867; ed and rev E. Venables 1883, 1883; Newman's trn rptd verbatim, ed H. B. Swete, 1920; New York 1897 (250 copies); Nashville TN 1950 (photo facs of 1897 edn).

The ecclesiastical history of M. l'Abbé [Claude] Fleury, from the second Ecumenical Council to the end of the fourth century: translated, with notes and an essay on the miracles of the period. Oxford 1842; The ecclesiastical history from AD 400 to AD 429, Oxford 1843; The ecclesiastical history from AD 429 to AD 456, Oxford 1844. Newman's introd to vol 1 was rptd separately as An essay on the miracles recorded in the ecclesiastical history of the early ages, 1843, and in 1870 as pt 2 of Two essays on Scripture miracles and on ecclesiastical.

Thoughts on the work of the six days of creation, by J. W. Bowden. Oxford 1845. Ed Newman.

Maxims of the kingdom of heaven. 1860, 1867, 1873 (enlarged and rearranged), 1887. A coll of passages from the Scriptures with a preface by Newman.

P. Terentius Phormio, expurgatus in usum puerorum; with English notes and translations [by Newman]. 1864, 1883, 1889.

Pincerna ex Terentio [i.e. the Eunuchus], expurgatus in usum puerorum; with English notes and translations [by Newman]. 1866, 1880, 1883, 1887.

Aulularia Plauti, expurgatus in usum puerorum; with English notes and translations [by Newman]. 1866, 1883, 1888.

Andria Terentii, expurgatus in usum puerorum; with English notes and translations [by Newman]. 1870, 1883, 1889.

The Church and the empires, preceded by a memoir of the author [by Newman], by H. W. Wilberforce. 1874.

The Anglican ministry, with a preface by Cardinal Newman, by A. W. Hutton. 1879.

Notes of a visit by the Russian Church in the years 1840, 1841, by W. Palmer, selected and arranged by Cardinal Newman. 1882.

Letters

Letters and correspondence of Newman during his life in the English Church; with a brief autobiography. Ed A. Mozley 2 vols 1891.

Ward, W. P. The life of Newman based on his private journals and correspondence. 2 vols 1912, 1913, 2 vols in 1 1927.

Correspondence of Newman with John Keble and others 1839–45. Ed at Birmingham Oratory [by J. Bacchus] 1917.

Selections from the correspondence of the first Lord Acton, vol 1: Correspondence with Cardinal Newman, Lady Blennerhassett, W. E. Gladstone and others. Ed J. N. Figgis and R. V. Laurence 1917.

Cross, F. L. John Henry Newman. 1933. Contains a set of unpbd letters to Alfred Plummer.

Cardinal Newman and William Froude FRS: a correspondence. Ed G. H. Harper, Baltimore 1933.

Mossner, E. C. Newman on Bishop Butler: an unpublished letter. Theology 32 1936.

Stephenson, G. Edward Stuart Talbot 1844–1934. 1936.

The Acland family: letters 1829–1901. Bodleian Lib Record 1 1940.

De correspondentie tussen Newman en [Charles] Meynell over de Grammar of assent. In O. M. Zeno, Newman's leer over het menselijk denken: inleiding op Newman's Grammar of assent etc, Utrecht and Nijmegen 1943; tr Leiden 1957.

Newman's letters and poems from Malta 1832–3. Ed H. Galea [Malta 1945].

Letters of Newman. Bodleian Lib Record 2 1949.

Tristram, H. The correspondence between Newman and the Comte de Montalembert. Dublin Rev 232 1949.

McGrath, F. Newman's university: idea and reality. 1951.

Letters of Newman: a selection. Ed D. Stanford and M. Spark. 1957.

The edn of The letters and diaries of Newman 1961– *supersedes all earlier edns of Newman's correspondence.*

The letters and diaries of Newman. Ed C. S. Dessain. Vol 11, Littlemore to Rome, October 1845 to December 1846, 1961; vol 12, Rome to Birmingham, January 1847 to December 1848, 1962; vol 13, Birmingham and London, January 1849 to June 1850, 1963; vol 14, ed C. S. Dessain and V. F. Blehl, Papal aggression, July 1850 to December 1851, 1963; vol 15, ed Dessain and Blehl, The Achilli trial, January 1852 to December 1853, 1964; vol 16, ed Dessain, Founding of a university, January 1854 to September 1855, 1965; vol 17, ed Dessain, Opposition in Dublin and London, October 1855 to March 1857, 1966; vol 18, ed Dessain, New beginnings in England, April 1857 to December 1858, 1968; vol 19, ed Dessain, Consulting the laity, January 1859 to June 1861, 1969; vol 20, ed Dessain, Standing firm among trials, July 1861 to December 1863, 1970; vol 21, ed Dessain and E. E. Kelly, The Apologia, January 1864 to June 1865, 1971; vol 22, Between Pusey and the extremists, July 1865 to December 1866, 1972; vol 23, ed Dessain, Defeat at Oxford, Defence at Rome, January to December 1867, 1972; vol 24, ed Dessain and T. Gornall, A Grammar of assent, January 1868 to December 1869, Oxford 1973; vol 25, ed Dessain and Gornall, The Vatican council, January 1870 to December 1871, Oxford 1973; vol 26, ed Dessain and Gornall, Aftermaths, January 1872 to December 1873, Oxford 1974; vol 27, ed Dessain and Gornall, Controversy with Gladstone, January 1874 to December 1875, Oxford 1975; vol 28, ed Dessain and Gornall, Fellow of Trinity, January 1876 to December 1878, Oxford 1975; vol 29, ed Dessain and Gornall, The cardinalate, January 1879 to September 1881, Oxford 1976; vol 30, ed Dessain and Gornall, A cardinal's apostolate, October 1881 to December 1884, Oxford 1976; vol 31, ed Dessain and Gornall, The last years, January 1885 to August 1890, Oxford 1977 with suppl to vols 11–30; (Anglican) vol 1, ed I. Ker and T. Gornall, Ealing, Trinity, Oriel, February 1801 to December 1826, Oxford 1978; vol 2, ed Ker and Gornall, Tutor of Oriel, January 1827 to December 1831, Oxford 1979; vol 3, ed Ker and Gornall, New bearings, January 1832 to December 1834, Oxford 1980; vol 4, ed Ker and Gornall, The Oxford movement, July 1833 to December 1834, Oxford 1981; vol 5, ed Gornall, Liberalism in Oxford, January 1835 to December 1836, Oxford 1984; vol 6, ed G. Tracey, The via media and Froude's Remains, January 1837 to December 1838, Oxford 1984; vol 7, ed Tracey, Editing the British Critic, January 1839 to December 1840, Oxford 1995.

Newman family letters. Ed D. Mozley 1962.

A packet of letters. Ed J. Sugg, Oxford 1983; tr Fr 1985.

§2

Jager, J.-N. In his Le protestantisme aux prises avec la doctrine catholique: ou controverses avec plusieurs ministres anglicans, Paris 1836. Ed and tr by L. Allen in Newman and Abbé Jager, Durham 1976.

Barberi, D. The conversion. Tablet Nov 1845.

Froude, J. A. Nemesis of Faith. 1845.

Pusey, E. B. A letter to the Rev John Keble. Eng Churchman Nov 1845; rptd in H. P. Liddon, Life of E. B. Pusey, vol 4 (*see* Liddon, *below*).

White, J. B. The life of the Rev Joseph Blanco White, written by himself, with portions of his correspondence. Ed J. H. Thom 3 vols 1845.

Mozley, J. A. The recent schism. Christian Remembrancer 11 1846.

Capes, J. Rise, progress and results of Puseyism. Rambler 6–7 1850–1.

Newman, F. W. Phases of Faith. 1850.

Oakeley, F. Personal reminiscences of the Oxford movement; with illustrations from Dr Newman's Loss and gain. In his Popular lectures [on Church questions], 1855.

[Martineau, J.] Personal influences on our present theology: Newman. Nat Rev 3 1856.

Davis, C. H. Romanism and romanizingism, revived galatianism and perverted judaism: a sermon with copious notes and appendices on Dr J. H. Newman's assertion of a better 'hope in death' of a profane and 'bad Catholic' than of 'the most virtuous of protestants' and discussional memoranda. [1860.]

Du Boulay, J. English common sense versus foreign fallacies in questions of religion. 1864. Remarks on Renan's Vie de Jésus and Newman's Essay on the development of Christian doctrine etc.

Kingsley, C. Mr Kingsley and Dr Newman: a correspondence on the question whether Dr Newman teaches that truth is no virtue? 1864.

Kingsley, C. 'What, then, does Dr Newman mean?' A reply to a pamphlet lately published by Dr Newman. 1864.

Meyrick, F. But isn't Kingsley right after all? A letter to Dr Newman. 1864.

Meyrick, F. On Dr Newman's rejection of Ligouri's doctrine of equivocation. 1864.

[Renouf, P. le P.] University education for English Catholics: a letter to the Very Rev Dr Newman by a Catholic layman. 1864.

Stephen, L. The theory of belief of Dr Newman. Fortnightly Rev Nov–Dec 1877; rptd in An agnostic's apology, 1880.

Burgon, J. W. Lives of twelve good men. 2 vols 1880, 1898.

Connelly, P. Cardinal Newman versus the Apostles' Creed. 1880.

Dr Newman and Mr Froude. Month May 1881.

Shairp, J. C. In his Aspects of poetry, Oxford 1881.

Mozley, J. A. Letters of J. B. Mozley. Ed A. Mozley 1882.

Mozley, T. Reminiscences chiefly of Oriel College and the Oxford movement. 2 vols 1882, 1966.

Pattison, M. In his Memoirs, 1885, 1984.

Hutton, R. H. In his Essays on some of the modern guides of English thought in matters of faith, 1887.

A study on Cardinal Newman's Grammar of assent. 1889.

Ward, W. P. William George Ward and the Oxford movement. 1889.

[Church, R. W.] Cardinal Newman's course. Guardian 13 Aug 1890.

[Church, R. W.] Cardinal Newman's naturalness. Guardian 20 Aug 1890.

Clement, W. Newman, Sibthorp and Lockhart: converts to the church of Rome. 2 pts [1890?].
Hutton, R. H. J. H. Newman. Expositor n.s. 2 1890.
Meynell, W. Newman: the founder of modern Anglicanism and a Cardinal of the Roman Church. 1890, 1907 (rev).
Abbott, E. A. Philomythus: an antidote against credulity – a discussion of Cardinal Newman's Essay on ecclesiastical miracles. 1891.
Church, R. W. The Oxford movement: twelve years 1833–45. 1891; ed G. Best, Chicago 1970.
Hutton, R. H. Cardinal Newman. 1891.
Jacobs, J. George Eliot, Matthew Arnold, Browning, Newman: essays and reviews from the Athenaeum. 1891.
[Kraus, F. X.] Newman: in memoriam. Deutsche Rundschau 17 1891.
Lockhart, W. Cardinal Newman: reminiscences of fifty years since. 1891.
Williams, I. Autobiography. Ed G. Prevost 1891.
Abbott, E. A. The Anglican career of Cardinal Newman. 2 vols 1892.
Bellasis, E. Cardinal Newman as a musician. 1892.
Birrell, A. In his Res judicatae: papers and essays, 1892.
Newman, F. W. Contributions to the early life of Cardinal Newman. 1892.
Preston, J. W. Cardinal Newman: or catholicity down to date. Lyme Regis 1892.
Sanday, W. England's debt to Newman. Oxford 1892.
What then did Dr Newman do? Being an inquiry into his share in the Catholic revival. Oxford 1892.
Bellasis, E. Memorials of Mr Serjeant Bellasis 1800–73. 1893.
Caird, E. The evolution of religion. 2 vols Glasgow 1893.
Grabinski, G. La renaissance catholique en Angleterre et le Cardinal Newman, d'après une étude du Cardinal Capecelatro. Lyons 1893.
Liddon, H. P. In his Life of E. B. Pusey, 4 vols 1893–7.
Ward, W. P. In his William George Ward and the Catholic revival, 1893.
Ward, W. P. In his Witnesses to the unseen and other essays, 1893.
Overton, J. H. In his English Church in the nineteenth century 1800–33, 1894.
Purcell, E. S. In his Life of Cardinal Manning, 2 vols 1895.
Hort, A. F. In his Life and letters of Fenton John Anthony Hort, 2 vols 1896.
Joye, D. Théorie du Cardinal Newman sur le développement du dogme chrétien. Paris 1896.
Rivington, L. The conversion of Cardinal Newman. 1896.
Barry, W. F. Cardinal Newman and Renan. Nat Rev 29 1897.
Brémond, H. Les sermons de Newman. Études 72 1897.
Church, R. W. In his Occasional papers vol 2, 1897.
de Vere, A. In his Recollections, 1897.
Hemmer, H. Manning, Newman et la question de l'éducation des catholiques à Oxford. Revue d'Histoire et de Littérature Religieuse 2 1897.
Mignot, E.-I. L'évolutionnisme religieux. Correspondant 186 1897.
Walsh, W. The secret history of the Oxford movement. 1897, 1977, rptd 1977.
Ward, W. P. The life and times of Cardinal Newman. 2 vols 1897.
Firmin, A. (A. Loisy). Le développement chrétien d'après le Cardinal Newman. Revue du Clergé Français 17 1898.
MacRae, A. Die religiöse Gewissheit bei Newman. Jena 1898.
Thureau-Dangin, P. La renaissance catholique en Angleterre au XIXe siècle. 3 vols Paris 1899–1906; tr 2 vols 1914.
Firmin, A. (A. Loisy). Les preuves et l'économie de la révélation. Revue du Clergé Français 21 1900.
Walsh, W. History of the Romeward movement in the Church of England 1833–64. 1900.
Ward, W. P. Newman and Sabatier. Fortnightly Rev May 1901.
Grappe, G. Newman: essai de psychologie religieuse; préface de P. Bourget. Paris 1902.
Semeria, G. Il Cardinale Newman. Rome 1902.
Dimnet, E. Quelques aspects du Cardinal Newman. Revue du Clergé Français 34 1903.
Fletcher, G. The Month and Newman. Month Jan–Apr 1903.
Grabinski, G. La conversione di Newman e il rinascimento cattolico in Inghilterra. 1903.
Ward, W. P. In his Problems and persons, 1903.
Barry, W. F. Newman. 1904, [1927] (rev).
Blennerhassett, C. J. Newman: ein Beitrag zur religiösen Entwicklungsgeschichte der Gegenwart. Berlin 1904.
Gout, R. Du Protestantisme au Catholicisme: Newman. Anduze 1904.
Guiney, L. I. Hurrell Froude: memoranda and comments. 1904.
Jörimann, A.-Pl. Exposé critique de la doctrine de Newman. Geneva 1904.
Lilly, W. S. Cardinal Newman and the new generation. Fortnightly Rev Aug 1904.
Mounier, J. L'essai sur le développement de la doctrine chrétienne de Newman. Paris 1904.
Aveling, F. Universals and the illative sense. Dublin Rev 137 1905.
Fletcher, J. B. Newman and Carlyle: an unrecognized affinity. Atlantic Monthly May 1905.
Gerrard, T. J. The Grammar of assent and the Sure future. Dublin Rev 137 1905.
Neville, W. P. (ed). Addresses to Cardinal Newman, with his replies. 1905.
Brémond, H. Newman: le développement du dogme chrétien. Paris 1906.
Brémond, H. Newman: essai de biographie psychologique. Paris [1906]; tr Eng 1907.
Cardinal Newman and creative theology. Dublin Rev 138 1906.
Dawson, W. J. In his Makers of English prose, New York 1906.
de Grandmaison, L. Le développement du dogme chrétien. Revue Pratique d'Apologétique 3 1906.
de Grandmaison, L. Newman considéré comme maître. Études 109–10 1906–7.
Dimnet, E. La pensée catholique dans l'Angleterre contemporaine. Paris 1906.
Gasquet, A. (ed). Lord Acton and his circle. 1906.
Hutton, R. H. Pilgrims in the region of faith: Amiel, Tolstoy, Pater, Newman. 1906.
Lebreton, J. Le primat de la conscience d'après Newman. Revue Pratique d'Apologétique 3 1906.
Toohey, J. J. An indexed synopsis of An essay in aid of a grammar of assent. 1906.
Dimnet, E. Newman et l'intellectualisme. Annales de Philosophie Chrétienne June, Aug 1907.
Guibert, J. Le réveil du Catholicisme en Angleterre au XIX siècle: conférences prêchées dans l'église Saint-Sulpice 1901–6. Paris 1907.
Lebreton, J. Autour de Newman. Revue Pratique d'Apologétique 3 1907.
Tyrrell, G. The condemnation of Newman. Guardian 20 Nov 1907.
Brémond, H. Autour de Newman. Annales de Philosophie Chrétienne Jan 1908.
Morley, J. In his Miscellanies ser 4, 1908.
O'Dwyer, E. T. Cardinal Newman and the encyclical Pascendi dominici gregis: an essay. 1908.
Pius X, Pope. [Brief to Bishop O'Dwyer, of Limerick]. In Acta Sanctae Sedis vol 41, 1908.
Sarolea, C. Cardinal Newman and his influence on religious life and thought. Edinburgh 1908.
Ward, W. P. In his Ten personal studies, 1908.
Brémond, H. L'inquiétude religieuse: aubes et lendemains de conversion. 2 vols 1909.
Cecil, A. In his Six Oxford thinkers, 1909.
Carey, W. H. The story of the Oxford movement. 1910.

Cornish, F. W. In his The English church in the nineteenth century, 2 pts 1910.
Rickaby, J. Newman memorial sermons. 1910.
Stock, E. In his The English church in the nineteenth century, 1910.
Bucaille, V. Newman: histoire d'une âme. Paris 1912.
Cardinal Newman. Edinburgh Rev 215 1912.
Corcoran, T. Newman's ideals and Irish realities. Studies Mar 1912.
Thureau-Dangin, P. Newman catholique, d'après des documents nouveaux. Paris 1912.
Tyrrell, G. Die Oxfordbewegung und die Wiedergeburt des Katholizismus in England. Akademische Bonifatiuskorrespondenz 1912.
Ward, W. P. The life of Newman based on his private journals and correspondence. 2 vols 1912, 1913, 2 vols in 1 1927.
Gerrard, T. J. Bergson, Newman and Aquinas. Catholic World Mar 1913.
More, P. E. In his Shelburne essays ser 8, New York 1913.
Storr, V. F. In his Development of English theology in the nineteenth century 1800–60, 1913.
Fecker, F. Kardinal Newman und sein Weg Zur Kirche. Munich 1914.
Rickaby, J. Index to the works of Newman. 1914.
Ward, W. P. In his Men and matters, 1914.
Ollard, S. L. In his A short history of the Oxford movement, 1915.
Ryan, E. Brownson and Newman. Ecclesiastical Rev 52 1915.
Ward, B. In his Sequel to Catholic emancipation [1830–50], 2 vols 1915.
Bellasis, E. Coram cardinali. 1916.
Cadman, S. P. The three religious leaders of Oxford and their movements. New York 1916.
Cecil, A. Wycliffe, Wesley, Newman: a study in contrasts. Dublin Rev 160 1917.
Figgis, J. N. and R. V. Laurence. In their Selections from the correspondence of the first Lord Acton vol 1, 1917.
Laski, H. J. In his Studies in the problem of sovereignty, New Haven CT 1917.
Tyrrell, G. Newman. Akademische Bonifatiuskorrespondenz 1917.
Brickel, A. G. Cardinal Newman's theory of knowledge. Amer Catholic Quart Rev 43 1918.
Lilly, W. S. A last word on Newman. Fortnightly Rev June 1918.
Strachey, L. Cardinal Manning. In his Eminent Victorians, 1918.
Ward, W. P. In his Last lectures, 1918.
Barry, W. F. The Turks, Cardinal Newman and the Council of Ten. 1919, 1920.
Tyrrell, G. In S. Merkle and B. Besz, Religiöse Erzieher der Katholischen Kirsche, Leipzig [1920].
Brémond, H. La vision et le rêve. Études June 1936.
Middleton, E. Tract 90. Jnl Ecclesiastical History 2 1951.
Svaglic, M. Revisions of Newman's Apologia. MP 50 1952.
Culler, A. The imperial intellect: a study of Newman's educational ideal. New Haven CT 1955.
Trevor, M. Newman: Light in Winter. 1962.
Trevor, M. Newman: The pillar of the cloud. 1962.
Blehl, V. The Apologia: reactions, 1864–5. Month 31 1964.
Holmes, J. D. Newman's reputation and the Lives of the English saints. Catholic History Rev 51 1966.
Lawler, J. Newman's Apologia and the burthens of editing. MLQ 32 1971.
Henry, L. The genesis of John Henry Newman's theory of development and the reception of his Essay on the development of Christian doctrine. Unpbd PhD thesis, Univ of Texas 1973.
Griffin, J. The Anglican response to Newman's conversion. Faith and Reason 3 1977.
Wolff, R. Gains and losses: novels of faith and doubt in Victorian England. New York 1977.
Gilley, S. Newman and his age. 1990.
Ker, I. T. John Henry Newman: a biography. Oxford 1990.

Jnls and mags devoted to publishing material on Newman include:
International Centre of Newman Friends, Newsletter. Rome.
Bulletin de l'Association Française des Amis de J. H. Newman. Lyons, France.
Newman Newsletter, cor ad cor loquitur. Rensselaer IN.
Friends of Cardinal Newman, Newsletter. Birmingham.
Newmania. Argentina. [JG]

Francis Turner Palgrave 1824–97

See col 649.

Bessie Rayner Parkes, later Belloc 1829–1925

§1

Poems. 1852, 1855 (2nd edn).
REVIEWS: [Lewes, G. H.] Leader 8 Jan 1852; Westminster Rev 59, Jan 1853.
Summer sketches and other poems. 1853, 1854.
REVIEWS: Athenaeum 1373 1854; London Quart and Holborn Rev 2 1854.
Remarks on the education of girls. 1854 (anon), 1856 (2nd edn), 1856 (3rd edn), 1865.
Gabriel. 1856. Poem.
REVIEWS: Athenaeum 1494 1856; [Eliot, G.] Westminster Rev 66, July 1856.
The history of our cat Aspasia. [1856] (priv ptd), 1856 (2nd edn illustr A. L. Smith).
REVIEW: Athenaeum 1520 1856.
Ballads and songs. 1863.
Essays on woman's work. 1865, 1865 (2nd edn), 1866.
REVIEWS: Fortnightly Rev 1 1865; Saturday Rev 20 1865; London Quart and Holborn Rev 26 1866.
Vignettes. Twelve biographical sketches. 1866, London and New York 1866.
REVIEWS: Athenaeum 2019 1866; Spectator 39 1866; Nation 4 1867.
La belle France. 1868, 1877.
REVIEW: Athenaeum 2119 1868.
Peoples of the world. [1870] (illus), London and New York [1870], [187?] (3rd edn).
In a walled garden. 1895, New York 1895, London 1896 (3rd edn).
REVIEWS: Spectator 75 1895; Athenaeum 3569 1896; Dial 20 1896; Nation 62 1896; Outlook 54 1896.
Historical nuns. 1896, 1898, New York 1899, St Louis 1911.
REVIEWS: Catholic World 69 1899; Dial 26 1899; Dublin Rev 125 1899.
A passing world. 1897.
REVIEWS: Academy 51 1897; Nation 65 1897.
The flowing tide. (A record of the religious revival in the nineteenth century.) 1900, St Louis 1900.
REVIEWS: Athenaeum 3786 1900; Dublin Rev 128 1901.
In fifty years. 1904. Poems.

Contributions to periodicals and collaborative works
Madame Bodichon. Englishwoman's Rev July 1891.
Dorothea Casaubon and George Eliot. Contemporary Rev 65 1894.
Joseph Priestly in domestic life. Contemporary Rev 66 1894.
Merryweather, M. Experience of factory life. 1862 (3rd edn, much enlarged). Preface by Parkes.
Parkes also wrote for the Englishwoman's Jnl *which she helped to found with B. Bodichon in 1858.*

§2

Belloc-Lowndes, M. I, too have lived in Arcadia. 1941.
Banks, O. The biographical dictionary of British feminists, vol 1 1800–1930. Brighton 1985.

Blain, V., P. Clements and I. Grundy. The feminist companion to literature in English. 1990.

Mark Pattison 1813–84

§1

The lives of the English saints. Ed J. H. Newman 4 vols 1844–5; rev A. W. Hutton 6 vols 1901. Pattison contributed anon lives of Stephen Langton and St Edmund.

Oxford studies. In Oxford essays, 1855. On university reform.

Report on elementary education in Protestant Germany. 1859; in the Report of the Assistant Commissioners on the state of popular education in Continental Europe vol 4, 1861.

Tendencies of religious thought in England 1688–1750. In Essays and reviews, 1860; enlarged in Essays, 1889, *below*. *See col 2655*.

Suggestions on academical organisation, with special reference to Oxford. Edinburgh 1868.

Isaac Casaubon 1559–1614. 1875; ed H. Nettleship, Oxford 1892 (with index).

Encyclopaedia Britannica. 1875–89 (9th edn). Pattison wrote articles on Bentley, Erasmus, Grotius, Sir Thomas More, Lipsius and Lord Macaulay; the last is rptd prefixed to Macauley's Life of Pitt, 1902.

Review of the situation. In Essays on the endowment of research, 1876.

Milton. 1879, 1880 (rev) (EML).

Memoirs. Ed Mrs Pattison 1885; ed V. H. H. Green 1988.

Essays. Ed H. Nettleship 2 vols Oxford 1889, London [1908] (5 essays omitted). The 1889 edn contains (with dated list of other essays appearing in periodicals) Muretus, Life of Scaliger, University history, Oxford studies, Pope and his editors, and (in this edn only) Montaigne, P. D. Huet, Calvin at Geneva etc.

The Estiennes: a biographical essay, illustrated with original leaves from books printed by the three greatest members of that distinguished family. San Francisco 1949.

Pattison also edited Pope, Essay on man, *1869 and his* Satires and epistles, *1872, with notes.*

Letters

Montague, F. C. Some early letters of Pattison. BJRL 18 1934.

Letters of Pattison to Gertrude M. Tuckwell. BM Quart 11 1937.

§2

Nettleship, H. Obituary. Academy 9 Aug 1884.

Althaus, T. F. Recollections of Pattison. 1885. Rptd from Temple Bar.

Tollemache, L. A. Recollections of Pattison. 1885. Rptd with addns from Jnl of Education.

Morley, J. In his Critical miscellanies vol 3, 1886.

Badger, K. Pattison and the Victorian scholar. MLQ 4 1945.

Emden, C. S. Pattison (1813–84) and J. A. Froude (1818–94): an appropriate friendship. In his Oriel papers, Oxford 1948.

Strachan, L. R. M. The Cambridge history of English literature on Mark Pattison. N & Q 24 Jan 1948.

Green, V. H. H. Oxford common room: a study of Lincoln College and Pattison. 1957.

Sparrow, J. Pattison and the idea of a university. Cambridge 1967.

Augustus Welby Northmore Pugin 1812–52

Deposits of more than 50 ms letters are held by the Birmingham City Archives, Chester Diocesan Record Office, Guildford Muniment Room, Magdalen College, Oxford, Duke of Northumberland at Alnwick Castle, Royal Inst of Br Architects (see A. Wedgwood, Catalogue of the drawings collection of the RIBA: The Pugin family, 1977, *for description of the collection), Southwark Archdiocesan Archives and Victoria and Albert Museum, where Pugin's diaries are also preserved.*

Bibliographies

Belcher, M. A. W. N. Pugin: an annotated critical bibliography. 1987.

Collections and selections

Ancient timber houses, Gothic furniture, Designs for gold and silversmiths and Designs for iron and brass work collected as Ornaments of the XVth and XVIth centuries, [1840?]; Fifteenth and sixteenth century ornaments, Edinburgh 1904; A. W. N. Pugin, Gothic furniture 1835 . . . 1972.

§1

Gothic furniture in the style of the 15th century, designed and etched by A. W. N. Pugin. 1835.

Ameublement gothique. Paris nd. Meubles dans le style gothique. Paris 1844 (and later; apparently pirated). Plates only. *See also* Collections.

A letter to A. W. Hakewill, architect, in answer to his reflections on the style for rebuilding the Houses of Parliament. 1835.

Designs for iron and brass work in the style of the xv and xvi centuries drawn and etched by A. W. N. Pugin. 1 Feb 1836; Modèles de ferronnerie, serrurerie et bronzerie . . . Paris nd; Dessins pour fer et bronze . . . Paris 1844. Dessins de Fer et Bronze . . . Paris 1849 (apparently pirated). Plates only. *See also* Collections.

Designs for gold and silversmiths. 4 April 1836; Modèles d'orfèvrerie argenterie etc. Art chrétien. Paris and Liège nd. Plates only. *See also* Collections.

Contrasts; or a parallel between the noble edifices of the fourteenth and fifteenth centuries, and similar buildings of the present day, shewing the present decay of taste. [Aug] 1836; Contrasts: or a parallel between the noble edifices of the middle ages, and corresponding buildings of the present day; shewing the present decay of taste, 1841 (rev and enlarged), Edinburgh 1898, Leicester and New York 1969.
REVIEWS (1st edn): M. Habershon, in his The ancient half-timbered houses of England, 1836; Athenaeum, 14 Jan 1837; [Loudon's] Architectural Mag, Mar 1837; Fraser's Mag, Mar 1837; GM, Mar 1837; Edinburgh Catholic Mag, May 1837; Dublin Rev, Oct 1837; Reply to 'Contrasts', by A. Welby Pugin, by an architect, 1837; Br Critic and Quart Theological Rev, Apr 1839; (2nd edn): Tablet, 25 Dec 1841; Catholic Mag, Jan 1842; Dublin Rev, Aug 1842. *See also* An apology for a work entitled Contrasts *and* A reply to observations which appeared in Fraser's Magazine, *below*.

Details of antient timber houses of the 15th and 16th centuries selected from those existing at Rouen, Caen, Beauvais, Gisors, Abbeville, Strasbourg, etc drawn on the spot and etched by A. Welby Pugin. 1836 [Feb 1837]. Plates only. *See also* Collections.

A reply to observations which appeared in Fraser's Magazine, for March 1837, on a work entitled Contrasts. By the author of that publication. [Not later than May 1837].

An apology for a work entitled Contrasts; being a defence of the assertions advanced in that publication, against the various attacks lately made upon it. Birmingham [Aug?] 1837. Followed by Some observations on the state of the arts in England: shewing that the degraded condition to which art has fallen is owing to the absence of Catholic feeling among its professors, the loss of all ecclesiastical patronage owing to a Protestant church establishment, and the apathy with which a Protestant nation treats the higher branches of art.

A letter on the proposed Protestant memorial to Cranmer, Ridley, and Latymer, addressed to the subscribers to and promoters of that undertaking, by A. Welby Pugin, Professor of Ecclesiastical Antiquities at St Mary's College, Oscott. 1839.

The true principles of pointed or Christian architecture. 1841, 1853, rptd in instalments in Architect and Contract Reporter, Jul, Aug 1894, Edinburgh 1895, Oxford 1969 [facs of 1853 edn], London and New York 1973.
REVIEWS: Atlas, 17 July 1841; Monthly Rev, Aug 1841; Tablet, 7 Aug 1841; Archaeologist, Oct 1841; Polytechnic Jnl, Oct 1841; Quart Rev, Dec 1841; GM, Jan 1842; Christian Remembrancer, Mar 1842.

Les vrais principes de l'architecture ogivale ou chrétienne, avec des remarques sur leur renaissance au temps actuel, remanié et développé d'après le texte anglais de A. W. Pugin, par T. H. King, et traduit en français, par P. Lebrocquy. Bruges 1850. Substantially altered version of Pugin's book.

The present state of ecclesiastical architecture in England. 1843, Oxford 1969 (facs). 2 articles 1st pbd in Dublin Rev, May 1841, Feb 1842.
REVIEWS (1st article): London and Dublin Orthodox Jnl of Useful Knowledge 3 Jul 1841; Christian Remembrancer, Aug 1841; (2nd article): Civil Engineer and Architect's Jnl, Apr 1842; (complete work): Builder, 18 Mar, 1 Apr 1843; Westminster Rev, Mar 1844.

An apology for the revival of Christian architecture in England. 1843, Edinburgh 1895, Oxford 1969 (facs).
REVIEWS: Artizan, 30 Apr 1843; Civil Engineer and Architect's Jnl, May 1843; Athenaeum, 15 July 1843; Weekly Dispatch, 20 Aug 1843; Fraser's Mag, Nov 1843.

Glossary of ecclesiastical ornament and costume, compiled and illustrated from antient authorities and examples. With trns by B. Smith. 1844, 1846 (enlarged), 1868.
REVIEW: Ecclesiologist, Aug 1844.

[Open letter to] The Rev Pelham Maitland, curate of Broadstairs. 1847.

A statement of facts relative to the engagement of marriage between Miss Selina Helen Sandys Lumsdaine, of Upper Hardres, Kent, and Augustus Welby Pugin, Esq. of S. Augustins, Isle of Thanet. 1848 (priv ptd).

Floriated ornament. 1849, 1875.
REVIEW: Ecclesiologist, Feb 1850.

Some remarks on the articles which have recently appeared in the Rambler, relative to ecclesiastical architecture and decoration. 1850.
REVIEWS: Ecclesiologist, Apr 1850; Rambler, Apr 1850.

An earnest appeal for the revival of the ancient plain song. 1850; New-York Ecclesiologist, Jan 1853; London and New York [1905]; Liturgical Arts, 1933.
REVIEWS: Eng Churchman, 24 Oct 1850; Catholic Standard, 26 Oct 1850; Tablet, 9 Nov 1850; Dublin Rev, Mar 1851.

An address to the inhabitants of Ramsgate. 1850.
REVIEW: Tablet, 4 Jan 1851.

An earnest address, on the establishment of the hierarchy. 1851, rptd with modifications by Pugin's son Edward Welby Pugin as Church and state; or Christian liberty. 4 edns 1875.
REVIEWS: Globe, 28 Feb 1851; Morning Post, 5 Mar 1851; Eng Churchman, 6 Mar 1851; Tablet, 8 Mar 1851.

A treatise on chancel screens and rood lofts, their antiquity, use, and symbolic signification. 1851.
REVIEWS: Tablet, 17 May 1851; Ecclesiologist, June 1851; Lamp, 7 June 1851; Annales Archéologiques Sep–Oct 1851; New-York Ecclesiologist, Jan, Mar 1852.

Pugin supplied illustrations for the works of other writers. For a full list see Belcher, Bibliographies, *above. Engravings of Pugin's designs were also pbd.*

Contributions to periodicals

To the editor of the Salisbury & Winchester Journal. Salisbury and Winchester Jnl 116, 26 Sep 1836.

To Mr Arthur Fane. Ibid, 17 Oct 1836.

London and Dublin Orthodox Jnl of Useful Knowledge: West front of Rouen cathedral, 17 Feb 1838; Jubé of St Ouen, 3 Mar 1838; Doorway of cloister, abbey of St. Wandrille, 17 Mar 1838; Fire-place in the abbey of St Amand, Rouen, 31 Mar 1838; Chasuble of cloth of gold, embroidered, 14 Apr 1838; Monumental brass of the fifteenth century, 12 May 1838; West front of St Lawrence's church, Nuremberg, 26 May 1838; Ancient style of family portraits, 14 July 1838; Cover of an ancient book of the Gospels, 21 July 1838; Chancel of St Marie's, Uttoxeter, 20 July 1839; New church at Hereford, 24 Aug 1839; On the erection and adornment of Catholic churches, 31 Aug 1839; Catholic surplices, 22 Feb 1840.

Catholic Magazine: Lectures on ecclesiastical architecture... Lecture the first, ns 2, Apr 1838, rptd Catholic Weekly Instructor 3, 31 Jan, 7 Feb 1846; Catholic Herald 14, 21, 28 May 1846; Merry England 24, Dec 1894; Lecture the second, ns 2, June 1838, rptd Catholic Weekly Instructor 3, 14, 21 Feb 1846; Catholic Herald 14, 25 June, 2 July 1846; Lecture the third, ns 3, Jan, Feb 1839.

Mouvement archéologique. Bulletin Archéologique 2, 1842–3.

Pugin's letter on spires. Proc of the Oxford Soc for Promoting the Study of Gothic Architecture, Easter, Trinity terms 1843, rptd with omissions restored Architectural Rev 23, Jan 1908.

Mr Pugin on the school of design. Tablet 6, 14 Jun 1845.

St Mary's Catholic church, Edmund-street. Liverpool Mercury 35, 1 Aug 1845, rptd Tablet 6, 9 Aug 1845.

Mr Pugin on Christian art. Builder 3, 2 Aug 1845.

Decorations of the new House of Lords. Builder 3, 6 Sep 1845.

Catholic intelligence: Letter from Mr Pugin. Tablet 7, 3 Jan 1846.

Catholic intelligence: Letter of A. W. Pugin, Esq. to the editor of the Ecclesiologist. Ibid, 31 Jan 1846.

Opening of a Catholic chapel at Cheadle, Staffordshire. Morning Post, 3 Sep 1846, rptd Tablet 7, 5 Sep 1846; Builder 4, 19 Sep 1846; GM 180, Dec 1846.

Penzance. – New Catholic church. Tablet 9, 8 Jan 1848.

Church of St Thomas of Canterbury, Fulham. Ibid, 1 July 1848.

Opening of the new Roman Catholic church of St George's in-the-fields. Morning Post, 5 July 1848, rptd Tablet 9, 8 July 1848; Dolman's Mag 8, Aug 1848.

The pictures at St George's. Tablet 9, 29 July 1848.

Catholic intelligence: Catholic church architecture. Ibid, 2 Sep 1848.

A defence of the revival of pointed ecclesiastical architecture, in reply to some recent attacks, by A. Welby Pugin: 'Why this waste!' Weekly Register 1, 6 Oct 1849, rptd Merry England 7, Jun 1886.

How shall we build our churches? Builder 8, 23 Mar 1850, rptd Tablet 11, 30 Mar 1850.

Ireland: Catholic intelligence: The Killarney cathedral. Tablet 11, 23 Mar 1850.

Mr Pugin and the Rambler. Ibid, 20 Apr 1850.

Mr Pugin. Eng Churchman 8, 4 Jul 1850.

The Gothic and Italian schools. Catholic Standard 2, 7 Sep 1850.

The earl of Shrewsbury – Mr Pugin. Freeman's Jnl 83, 20 Dec 1850, rptd Morning Herald, 21 Dec 1850; Standard, 21 Dec 1850; The Times, 21 Dec 1850.

To the editor of the Catholic Standard. Catholic Standard 2, 28 Dec 1850.

To the editor of the Catholic Standard. Ibid 3, 22 Feb 1851, rptd Tablet 12, 8 Mar 1851.

[Untitled letter to the editor]. Globe, 5 Mar 1851.

Mr Pugin's pamphlet. Morning Post, 10 Mar 1851.

Reply of Mr Pugin to the letter of 'A Catholic priest'. Tablet 12, 15 Mar 1851; copy Catholic Standard 3, 15 Mar 1851.

Mr Pugin's pamphlet. Catholic Standard 3, 29 Mar 1851.

The devotion to St Joseph – letter of Mr Pugin. Tablet 12, 24 May 1851.

To the editor of the Morning Chronicle. Morning Chron, 6 Sep 1851.

Diaries and letters

Wedgwood, A. In her A. W. N. Pugin and the Pugin family, 1985.

The collected letters of A. W. N. Pugin. Ed M. Belcher 5 vols Oxford 2000– . Vol 1 1830–42.

§2

Selected obituaries

Morning Chron, 17 Sep 1852; Athenaeum, 18 Sep 1852; Builder 10, 25 Sep 1852; Tablet 13, 25 Sep 1852; Civil Engineer and Architect's Jnl, 15 Oct 1852; Ecclesiologist, 13 Oct 1852, rptd New York

Ecclesiologist, 5 Jan 1853; Illus London News 21, 2 Oct 1852; Lamp 4, 2 Oct 1852.
Ferrey, B. Recollections of A. N. Welby Pugin and his father, Augustus Pugin: with notices of their works. 1861, rptd as Recollections of A. W. N. Pugin and his father Augustus Pugin, 1978.
Pugin, E. W. Who was the art architect of the Houses of Parliament? 1867.
Barry, A. The architect of the new palace at Westminster. 1868.
Pugin, E. W. Notes on the reply of the Rev Alfred Barry ... 1868.
Eastlake, C. L. A history of the Gothic revival. 1872.
Waterhouse, P. Architectural Rev 3, Dec 1897–May 1898; 4, June–Nov 1898.
Wickham, W. A. Trans of the Historic Soc of Lancashire and Cheshire 59, 1907.
Trappes-Lomax, M. Pugin: a mediaeval Victorian. 1932.
Stanton, P. Pugin. 1971. [MB]

Angus Bethune Reach 1821–56

§1

The natural history of 'bores'. 1847.
The natural history of humbugs. 1847.
The natural history of tuft-hunters and toadies. 1848.
The comic Bradshaw: or bubbles from the boiler. 1848.
The natural history of the 'hawk' tribe. 1848.
A romance of a mince-pice: an incident in the life of John Chirrup. 1848, [1850?]. Illustr 'Phiz'.
Clement Lorimer: or the book with the iron clasps: a romance. 1849, 1856. Illustr G. Cruikshank.
Leonard Linsay: or the story of a buccaneer. 2 vols 1850.
Claret and olives, from the Garonne to the Rhone: or notes social, picturesque and legendary, by the way. 1852, New York 1852.
A story with a vengeance: or how many joints go to a tale? [1852], [1853] (rev). With C. W. S. Brooks.
Men of the hour. 1856.
Christmas cheer. 1856. With J. Hannay and Albert R. Smith.
Sketches of London life and character. 1858. With Albert R. Smith et al.

Reach was for some time on the staff of Punch *and wrote many contributions to periodicals.*

§2

Athenaeum 29 Nov 1856. Obituary.
Mackay, C. Forty years' recollections of life, literature and public affairs 1830–70. 2 vols 1877.
Spielmann, M. H. History of Punch. 1895.

William Winwood Reade 1838–75

Charlotte and Myra: a puzzle in six bits. 1859.
Liberty Hall, Oxon. 3 vols 1860.
The veil of Isis: or the mysteries of the druids. 1861.
Savage Africa: being the narrative of a tour. 1863.
See-saw: a novel, edited by Reade. 1865. Written by Reade.
The martyrdom of man. 1872, 1877 (4th edn); ed F. Legge 1910.
The African sketch-book. 2 vols 1873.
The story of the Ashantee campaign. 1874.
The outcast. 1875, 1933.

Henry Reeve 1813–95

Correspondence to and from Reeve can be found in BL Ms Collection; Blackwood Papers, Nat Lib of Scotland; Kings College Modern Record Centre, Cambridge Univ; Cambridge Univ Lib Department of Mss; William L. Clements Lib, Univ of Michigan; Bodleian; All Souls College, Oxford Univ; St Andrews Univ Lib; and the Public Record Office, Kew.

§1

Graphidae, or Characteristics of painters. Priv ptd 1838, 1842.
The military resources of Prussia and France, and recent changes in the art of war, with Charles Cornwallis Chesney. 1870.
Royal and republican France. 2 vols 1872. Rptd from the Edinburgh, Quart and Foreign Revs.
Petrarch. 1878, 1905.

Reeve was foreign affairs editor of The Times *1840–55, and editor and contributor to the* Edinburgh Rev *1855–95. For a full list of periodical contributions, see* Wellesley *vol 5, 1989.*

Letters

Correspondence de Sigismond Krasinski et de Henry Reeve. Preface by Joseph Kallenbach. Paris 1902.
The letters of Charles Greville and Henry Reeve, 1836–1865. Ed Rev A. H. Johnston, 1924.
Letters to C. A. H. M. Clerel de Tocqueville. In Count Clerel de Tocqueville, Works, vol 1 1954.

Translations and editions

Alexis Tocqueville. Democracy in America. Tr Henry Reeve. 1840, abridged with an introd by Henry Steel Commager, New York and Oxford 1947, 1961, 1974.
F. P. G. Guizot. Washington. Tr Reeve. 1840.
Translations from the German. Prose and verse. Tr Reeve and J. E. Taylor. 1842.
Alexis Tocqueville. The republic of the United States of America, and its political institutions. Reviewed and examined. Tr Reeve. New York 1851.
Sir Bulstrode Whitelocke. A journal of the Swedish Embassy in the years 1653 and 1654. New edn rev by H. Reeve. 1855.
Alexis Tocqueville. On the state of society in France before the revolution of 1789, and on the causes which led to that event. Tr Reeve. 1856.
Memorandum on the diaries of the late Mr Charles Greville. Ed H. Reeve. 1865. First pbd in Philobiblon Soc – Bibliographical and Historical Miscs 9 1854.
Edward John Lyttleton, First Lord Atherton. Memoir and correspondence relating to political occurrences in June and July 1834. Ed H. Reeve. 1872.
Charles Cavendish F. Greville. The Greville memoirs. Ed Reeve. 8 vols 1874–87, 2 vols New York 1887, 2 vols London 1888.
Henry Reeve sr. Journal of a residence at Vienna and Berlin in the eventful winter 1805–1806. Ed H. Reeve. 1877.
Charles Cavendish F. Greville. A visit to Paris in 1855. Communicated by Henry Reeve. 1884. First pbd in Philobiblon Soc – Bibliographical and Historical Miscs 15 1854.
St Petersburg and London in the years 1852–1864. Reminiscences of Count Charles Frederick Vizthum von Eckstaedt. Ed with preface by H. Reeve. 1887.

§2

Athenaeum 26 Oct 1895. Obituary.
Lecky, W. E. H. Henry Reeve. Edinburgh Rev Jan 1896.
Elliott, A. R. D. Memoirs of Henry Reeve. Edinburgh Rev Oct 1898.
Escott, T. H. S. Mr Henry Reeve. Fortnightly Rev Nov 1898.
Laughton, John Knox. Memoirs of the life and correspondence of Henry Reeve, C. B., D. C. L. 2 vols 1898.
Millar, J. H. Old Whig and new: Henry Reeve and Sir Frank Lockwood. Blackwood's Mag Nov 1898. [DF]

William Michael Rossetti 1829–1919

Univ of Br Columbia Lib is the principal repository of mss, diaries and correspondence by or relating to Rossetti. Substantial collections of mss and correspondence are held at BL, Bodleian, HRHRC, Harvard, the John Rylands Lib of the Univ of Manchester and the Library of Congress.

Bibliographies

William Michael Rossetti. In W. E. Fredeman, Pre-Raphaelitism: a bibliocritical study, Cambridge MA 1965.

Bibliography. In R. W. Peattie, William Michael Rossetti as critic and editor, together with a consideration of his life and character, unpbd PhD thesis, Univ of London 1966. Includes lists of Rossetti ms material in 45 repositories, and his 604 contributions to periodicals and encyclopaedias.

Peattie, R. W. William Michael Rossetti's art notices in the periodicals, 1850–1878: an annotated checklist. VPN 8, June 1975.

Peattie, R. W. W. M. Rossetti's contributions to the Edinburgh Weekly Review. VPR 19, Fall 1986.

Peattie, R. W. William Michael Rossetti's contributions to the Athenaeum. VPR 23, Winter 1990.

§1

For a fuller list of reviews of individual works, see Peattie, Bibliographies, above.

Swinburne's poems and ballads: a criticism. 1866.
REVIEWS: Saturday Rev 17 Nov 1866; Spectator 24 Nov 1866; London Rev 1 Dec 1866; London Quart Rev 31, Oct 1868.

Fine art, chiefly contemporary: notices re-printed, with revisions. 1867. Notices originally appeared in periodicals.
REVIEWS: Chronicle 13 July 1867; Westminster Rev n.s. 32, Oct 1867; London Rev 26 Oct 1867; Saturday Rev 16 May 1868.

Notes on the Royal Academy exhibition. 1868. With A. C. Swinburne.
REVIEWS: Morning Star 15 June 1868; London Rev 18 July 1868; London Quart Rev 31, Jan 1869.

Lives of famous poets: a companion volume to the series Moxon's Popular Poets. 1878. Essays originally written as introd to edns in the ser.
REVIEWS: Examiner 16 Mar 1878; Athenaeum 13 Apr 1878; Acad 8 June 1878; Fortnightly Rev n.s. 28, Dec 1880 (by Swinburne, A. C.).

Catalogue of the remaining works of Dante Gabriel Rossetti, which will be sold by Christie, Manson & Woods, May 12, 1883. 1883.

Memoir of Shelley (with a fresh preface). 1886 (Shelley Soc Pbns 4th ser no 2), rptd 1886 (with index). Rptd from Rossetti's edn of Shelley, 1870. Edn with index rptd as Memoir of Percy Bysshe Shelley (with new preface), 1886 (John Slark).

Shelley's Prometheus unbound: a study of its meaning and personages. 1886 (priv ptd, 25 copies), pbd in Shelley Soc Papers, pt 1, 1888 (Shelley Soc Pbns 1st ser no 1).

Life of John Keats. 1887 (Great Writers ser).
REVIEWS: Pall Mall Gazette 27 Sep 1887 (by Wilde, O.); Athenaeum 1 Oct 1887; Saturday Rev 26 Nov 1887.

Shelley's Prometheus unbound considered as a poem [pt 1]. 1887 (priv ptd, 25 copies), pbd in Shelley Soc Papers, pt 1, 1888 (Shelley Soc Pbns 1st ser no 1). Pt 2 pbd only in Shelley Soc Papers, pt 1.

Dante Gabriel Rossetti as designer and writer. 1889.
REVIEWS: Acad 7 Dec 1889; Mag of Art 13 1890; Saturday Rev 25 Jan 1890; Spectator 19 Apr 1890; Athenaeum 28 June 1890 (by Watts-Dunton, T.).

Dante Gabriel Rossetti: his family-letters, with a memoir. 2 vols 1895.
REVIEWS: Daily News 2 Dec 1895; Manchester Guardian 6 Dec 1895; Saturday Rev 21 Dec 1895; The Times 24 Dec 1895; Longman's Mag 27, Mar 1896 (by Hueffer, F. M. [Ford]); Acad 14 Mar 1896; Spectator 18 Apr 1896; Quart Rev 184, July 1896; Edinburgh Rev 185, Apr 1897.

Bibliography of the works of Dante Gabriel Rossetti. 1905.

Dante Gabriel Rossetti: classified lists of his writings with the dates. 1906 (priv ptd, 100 copies).

Some reminiscences. 2 vols 1906.
REVIEWS: Athenaeum 3 Nov 1906; Acad 10 Nov 1906; Bookman 31, Dec 1906; Spectator 26 Jan 1907.

Democratic sonnets. 2 vols 1907 (Contemporary Poets Ser ed F. M. Hueffer [Ford]).
REVIEWS: Athenaeum 16 Mar 1907; Bookman 32, Apr 1907 (by Thomas, E.).

Dante and his Convito: a study with translations. 1910.
REVIEWS: MLR 6, Jan 1910; Athenaeum 10 Sep 1910.

Contributions to periodicals

Only articles, reviews and poems of substantial length or exceptional interest are listed. Articles and reviews on art are excluded. For a complete listing, see Peattie, Bibliographies, above.

Review of A. H. Clough, The bothie of Toper-na-fuosich. Germ Jan 1850.

Review of M. Arnold, The strayed reveller and other poems. Germ Feb 1850.

Review of R. Browning, Christmas eve and Easter day. Germ May 1850.

Review of G. Meredith, Poems. Critic 15 Nov 1851.

English opinion on the American war. Atlantic Monthly 17, Feb 1866.

Review of A. C. Swinburne, A song of Italy. Chron, 18 May 1867.

Review of W. Morris. The life and death of Jason. Chron, 29 June 1867.

Walt Whitman's poems. Chron, 6 July 1867.

Review of The divine comedy of Dante, trans H. W. Longfellow. Chron, 27 July 1867.

Mrs Holmes Grey. Broadway Annual 1868. Poetry.
REVIEW: Tinsley's Mag 5, Oct 1869 by H. B. Forman.

Emendations of Shelley. N & Q 28 Mar, 11, 18, 25 Apr 1868.

Shelley in 1812–13: an unpublished poem, and other particulars. Fortnightly Rev n.s. 9, Jan 1871.

Review of Poems of William Blake, ed R. H. Shepherd. Acad 5 Sep 1874.

William Bell Scott and modern British poetry. Macmillan's Mag 33, Mar 1876.

Review of Poetical works of Shelley, ed H. B. Forman. Acad 13 Oct 1877.

Shelley's life and writings: two lectures. Dublin Univ Mag n.s. 1, Feb, Mar 1878.

Obituary of Claire Clairmont. Athenaeum 29 Mar 1879.

The wives of poets. Atlantic Monthly 47, Jan, Feb, Mar, Apr 1881.

Obituary of E. J. Trelawny. Athenaeum 20 Aug 1881.

Obituary of H. W. Longfellow. Athenaeum 1 Apr 1882.

Talks with Trelawny. Athenaeum 15, 29 July, 5 Aug 1882.

Notes on [D. G.] Rossetti and his works. Art Jnl 46, May, June, July 1884.

Portraits of Dante Gabriel Rossetti. Mag of Art 12 1889 (3 pts).

Portraits of Robert Browning. Mag of Art 13 1890 (3 pts).

Some scraps of verse and prose by Dante Gabriel Rossetti. Pall Mall Mag 16, Dec 1898.

Bibliography of the works of Dante Gabriel Rossetti. Bibliographer (NY) 1, Dec 1902, 2, Jan 1903.

Dante Rossetti and Elizabeth Siddal. Burlington Mag 1, May 1903.

Swinburne. Bookman 36, June 1909.

Personal reminiscences of George Meredith. African Monthly 7, Feb 1910.

Contributions to collaborative works

Annotated catalogue of Blake's pictures and drawings. In A. Gilchrist, Life of William Blake, 2 vols 1863, rev 1880.

Notes on the stacyons of Rome. In Political, religious and love poems from Lambeth ms no 36, ed F. J. Furnivall, 1866 (EETS no 15).

Italian courtesy-books: Fra Bonvicino da Riva's Fifty courtesies for the table, with other translations and elucidations. In Queene Elizabethes achademy: a book of precedence, &c, ed F. J. Furnivall, 1869 (EETS extra ser 8).

Oliver Madox Brown, The dwale bluth, Hebditch's legacy, and other literary remains. 2 vols 1876. Ed with F. Hueffer, memoir by F. M. Brown.
Taurello Salinguerra: historical details illustrative of Browning's Sordello. Muratori and Browning compared. In Browning Soc Papers 3 1889–90.
Chaucer's Saint Loy. In Essays on Chaucer, ed F. J. Furnivall, 1892 (Chaucer Soc 2nd ser 29).
Shelley at Cwm Elan and Nantgwilt. In R. E. Tickell, The vale of Nantgwilt: a submerged valley, 1894.
Letters from Percy Bysshe Shelley to Thomas Jefferson Hogg. 1897 (priv ptd, 30 copies). Notes by Rossetti.
Leopardi. In Studies in European literature, being the Taylorian lectures 1889–1899, Oxford 1900. Lecture delivered in 1891.
Gabriele Rossetti e i suoi parenti. In Opere inedite e rare di Gabriele Rossetti, ed D. Ciàmpoli, Lanciano 1910.

Letters and diaries

Letters about Shelley interchanged by Edward Dowden, Richard Garnett and Wm Michael Rossetti. Ed R. S. Garnett 1917.
Letters of William Michael Rossetti concerning Whitman, Blake and Shelley to Anne and Herbert Gilchrist. Ed C. Gohdes and P. F. Baum, Durham NC 1934.
Three Rossettis: unpublished letters to and from Dante Gabriel, Christina, William. Ed J. C. Troxell, Cambridge MA 1937.
The Rossetti–Macmillan letters. Ed L. M. Packer, Berkeley CA 1963.
P. R. B. journal: William Michael Rossetti's diary of the Pre-Raphaelite brotherhood, 1849–1853. Ed W. E. Fredeman, Oxford 1975.
Diary of W. M. Rossetti, 1870–1873. Ed O. Bornand, Oxford 1977.
The owl and the Rossettis: letters of Charles A. Howell and Dante Gabriel, Christina and William Michael Rossetti. Ed C. L. Cline, Univ Park PA 1978.
A shadow of Dante: [D. G.] Rossetti in the final years (extracts from W. M. Rossetti's unpublished diaries, 1876–1882). Ed W. E. Fredeman in VP 20 Autumn–Winter 1982.
Selected letters of William Michael Rossetti. Ed R. W. Peattie, Univ Park PA 1990.

Translations

The comedy of Dante: the hell. 1865.
REVIEWS: Westminster Rev n.s. 27, Apr 1865; Athenaeum 1 Apr 1865; Spectator 6 May 1865.
Gabriele Rossetti: a versified autobiography, translated and supplemented. 1901.

Editions

The Germ: thoughts towards nature in poetry, literature and art. 4 nos 1850. Rossetti pbd a facs with introd, 1901.
Poems by Walt Whitman. 1868, rptd 1886 (in larger format), 1892, 1895, 1910, 1911, 1920, New York 1925.
REVIEWS: Academia 21 Mar 1868; London Rev 21 Mar 1868; Express 26 Mar 1868; Sunday Times 29 Mar 1868; Morning Star 6 Apr 1868; Sun 17 Apr 1868; Examiner 18 Apr 1868; Lloyd's Weekly London Newspaper 19 Apr 1868; Athenaeum 25 Apr 1868; Saturday Rev 2 May 1868; Westminster Rev 34, July 1868; Chambers's Jnl, 4 July 1868.
Poetical works of Percy Bysshe Shelley: the text carefully revised, with notes and a memoir. 2 vols 1870, rev 3 vols 1878.
REVIEWS: Athenaeum 29 Jan 1870 (by Buchanan, R.); Examiner 5 Feb 1870; Daily News 23 Feb 1870; Pall Mall Gazette 14 Mar 1870; Acad 9 Apr 1870 (by Symonds, J. A.); Westminster Rev n.s. 38, July 1870 (by Blind, M.); North Br Rev 53, Oct 1870; Edinburgh Rev 133, Apr 1871.
Poetical works of Henry W. Longfellow: edited, with a critical memoir. [1870] (Moxon's Popular Poets). Rossetti added another 20 edns to the ser, 1870–8: Burns, Byron, Campbell, Coleridge, Cowper, Hemans, Hood (2 ser), Keats, Lowell, Milton, Moore, Pope, Scott, Shelley, Thompson, Whittier, Wordsworth, American poems, Humorous poems. Numerous reprints through early 1900s.
Chaucer's Troylus and Cryseyde compared with Boccaccio's Filostrato. 2 pts 1873, 1883 (Chaucer Soc ser 1 nos 44, 65). Filostrato trans by Rossetti.
Poetical works of William Blake, with a memoir. 1874. Rptd 1875, 1879, 1882, 1883, 1885, 1888, May and Oct 1890, 1891, 1893, 1913, 1914.
REVIEWS: Examiner 14, 21 Nov 1874 (by Gosse, E.); Sunday Times 22 Nov 1874; Acad 5 Dec 1874 (by Saintsbury, G.); Daily News 5 Dec 1874; Spectator 2 Jan 1875; Nat Reformer 14, 21, 28 Feb, 21 Mar 1875 (by Foote, G. W.); Cornhill Mag 31, June 1875 (by Collins, J. C.).
Collected works of Dante Gabriel Rossetti, with preface and notes. 2 vols 1886. Formed the basis of Poetical works of Dante Gabriel Rossetti, with preface, 1891; Dante and his circle, trans Dante Gabriel Rossetti, with preface, 1892; Siddal edition [of the works of Dante Gabriel Rossetti], with prefatory notes, 7 vols 1899–1901; Poems of Dante Gabriel Rossetti, with illustrations from his own pictures and designs, introd and notes, 2 vols 1904; Poems of Dante Gabriel Rossetti, with prefatory note, 1907 (Pocket ed); Works of Dante Gabriel Rossetti, rev and enlarged, 1911.
REVIEWS: St James's Gazette 20 Jan 1887 (by Patmore, C.); Pall Mall Gazette 22 Jan 1887; Saturday Rev 29 Jan 1887; Acad 5 Feb 1887 (by Dowden, E.); Nat Rev 9, Mar 1887 (by Sharp, W.); Athenaeum 12 Mar 1887.
Shelley, Adonais, with introd and notes. Oxford 1891, rev with A. O. Prickard 1903.
Tiberius: a drama by Francis Adams, with introd. 1894.
New poems by Christina Rossetti. 1896.
REVIEWS: Br Weekly 23 Jan 1896 (by Nicoll, W. R.); Athenaeum 15 Feb 1896 (by Watts-Dunton, T.); Spectator 29 Feb 1896; Blackwood's Mag 159, June 1896; Acad 25 July 1896 (by Johnson, L.); Westminster Rev 145, Apr 1896.
Maude: a story for girls by Christina Rossetti, with introd. 1897.
Poems by the late John Lucas Tupper. 1897.
Ruskin: Rossetti: Preraphaelitism; papers 1854 to 1862. 1899.
Lenore by G. A. Bürger, translated by D. G. Rossetti. 1900.
Preraphaelite diaries and letters. 1900.
Rossetti papers, 1862 to 1870. 1903.
Poetical works of Christina Georgina Rossetti, with memoir and notes. 1904. Formed the basis of Poems of Christina Rossetti, 1904 (Golden Treasury ser).
REVIEWS: Fortnightly Rev n.s. 75, Mar 1904 (by Hueffer, F. M. [Ford]); Athenaeum 2 Apr 1904; Spectator 9 July 1904.
Family letters of Christina Georgina Rossetti. 1908.
REVIEWS: Athenaeum 14 Nov 1908; Saturday Rev 21 Nov 1908; Bookman 35, Dec 1908.
Diary of John William Polidori. 1911.

Introductions and prefaces

Works of Shakespeare. [1880.] Moxon's Popular Poets. Memoir rptd from Rossetti's Lives of famous poets.
Gilchrist, Herbert. Anne Gilchrist: her life and writings. 1887.
Webster, Augusta. Mother and daughter. 1895.
Proctor, Ellen A. A brief memoir of Christina G. Rossetti. 1895.
A Pre-Raphaelite collection (Goupil Gallery, London 1896). Exhibition catalogue of James Leathart collection.
Rossetti, Dante Gabriel. The blessed damozel (decorations by W. B. Macdougall). 1898.
Permanent photographs after the works of Dante Gabriel Rossetti, with explanatory text. 1900.
Permanent photographs after the works of the Pre-Raphaelite school, with an explanatory note. 1900.

Loan exhibition of pictures [by the Pre-Raphaelites] (Leighton House, London 1902). 1902. Family note.

Dunn, Henry Treffry. Recollections of Dante Gabriel Rossetti and his circle. Ed G. Pedrick 1904.

§2

Obits: The Times 6 Feb 1919; Westminster Gazette 6 Feb 1919; Manchester Guardian 7 Feb 1919; Paton, J. L. Some memories [of W. M. Rossetti], Manchester Guardian 7 Feb 1919; Eagle, S. [J. C. Squire], New Statesman 8 Feb 1919.

William Michael Rossetti. In H. Blodgett, Walt Whitman in England, Ithaca NY 1934.

Chewning, L. H. William Michael Rossetti and the Shelley renaissance. KSJ 4 1955.

Arinshtein, L. M. and W. E. Fredeman. William Michael Rossetti's Democratic sonnets. VS 14, Mar 1971.

Peattie, R. W. William Michael Rossetti and the defence of Swinburne's poems and ballads. HLB 19, Oct 1971.

Fredeman, W. E. A key poem of the Pre-Raphaelite movement: W. M. Rossetti's Mrs Holmes Grey. In Nineteenth-century literary perspectives: essays in honor of Lionel Stevenson, ed C. de L. Ryals, Durham NC 1974.

Peattie, R. W. William Michael Rossetti's Aldine edition of Blake. Blake: an Illus Quart 12 Summer 1978.

Paley, M. D. John Camden Hotten and the first British editions of Walt Whitman. Publishing History 6 1979.

Peattie, R. W. W. M. Rossetti as reluctant biographer: the genesis of Dante Gabriel Rossetti, his family letters, with a memoir. Nineteenth-Cent Prose 22 Spring 1995. [RWP]

John Ruskin 1819–1900

The works of Ruskin pbd before 1868 went out of copyright in 1907, and all edns since then, except those issued by Ruskin's publisher, George Allen (or by arrangement with him, as WC and Tauchnitz edns) are based on the early and in many cases unrevised text. There were no copyright edns of Ruskin ptd in America before the Brantwood edn of the Collected works 1891 *(ed C. E. Norton), except the New York edn of the* Lectures on art 1870. *An attempt has been made to list here all non-copyright edns to 1900; it is, however, certain that a number have been overlooked.*

Among repositories of Ruskin mss, the Ruskin Lib, Lancaster Univ, is of central importance, holding autographs and/or proofs of some thirty of Ruskin's works, the ms of his Diaries and many thousands of letters. (The Ruskin Lib now holds the collections formerly housed at the Ruskin Galleries, Bembridge School, Bembridge, Isle of Wight.)

In the British Isles there are also very significant holdings of mss and correspondence at the Bodleian, Oxford Univ, in the BL and at John Rylands Univ Lib, Manchester, while there are significant holdings also at the Fitzwilliam Museum, Cambridge, and a large collection of letters at Brantwood, Coniston, Cumbria. Detailed information on these collections, and on the very many smaller holdings of Ruskin material in the British Isles is available in LR vol 2, 1988.

In the United States, there are very important collections at the Bienecke Lib, Yale; at the Pierpont Morgan Lib, New York; at the Huntington; and at the Univ of Texas at Austin. There are significant collections also at Princeton, Columbia Univ Lib, at the Houghton Lib, Harvard, and at the Univ of North Carolina. See also:

Thorpe, W. The Ruskin mss. Princeton Univ Lib Chron 1 1940.

Hogan, C. B. The Yale collection of the mss of Ruskin. Yale Gazette 16 1942.

Dearden, J. S. The Ruskin Galleries at Bembridge school. BJRL 51 1968–9.

Dearden, J. S. The Ruskin Galleries, Bembridge school. In his Facets of Ruskin, 1970. Rptd from Apollo 1961.

Dearden, J. S. The Haddon C. Adams Ruskin collection at Bembridge. BJRL 55 1972–3.

Taylor, F. and G. A. Matheson. Handlist of additions to the collections of English mss in the John Rylands Library, 1952–70. BJRL 60 1978–9.

Dearden, J. S. Ruskin, Bembridge and Brantwood. Keele 1994.

Bibliographies

Allibone, S. A. A critical dictionary of English literature, and British and American authors. Philadelphia 1870, vol 2 pp. 1894–6. Useful for contemporary reviews and Amer edns.

[Shepherd, R. H.] The bibliography of Ruskin from 1834 to the present time. [1878], New York 1878, London [1879], 1881 (5th edn).

Axon, W. E. A. Ruskin: a bibliographical biography. Manchester 1879, 1881 (enlarged). Rptd from Papers of Manchester Lib Club vol 5.

Kennedy, W. S. A bibliography of Ruskin. Literary World (Boston) 13 June 1885.

Wise, T. J. and J. P. Smart. A bibliography of the writings in prose and verse of Ruskin, with a list of the more important Ruskiniana. 19 pts 1889–93 (priv ptd), 2 vols 1964. The most minute account of the earlier edns of each text, listing also works ed or contributed to by Ruskin, and most early reviews.

Jameson, M. E. A bibliographical contribution to the study of Ruskin. Cambridge MA 1901. The fullest list of Amer edns, but at second hand and unreliable.

Copyright and copy-wrong: the authentic and the unauthentic Ruskin. 1907. Not a bibliography, but a summary of the controversy arising when Ruskin's works printed before 1865 went out of copyright in 1907, and were rptd in large numbers in their unrevised form.

Cook, E. T. and A. D. O. Wedderburn. The works of Ruskin. Library edition 1912, vol 38: Bibliography. By far the most comprehensive and reliable bibliography, including references to the detailed bibliographies prefixed to each work separately in the earlier vols of the set.

Carter, J. and H. G. Pollard. An enquiry into the nature of certain nineteenth-century pamphlets. 1934. 8 of the pams discussed are by Ruskin.

Dearden, J. S. Wise and Ruskin, 1–3. BC 18 Spring, Summer, Autumn 1969 (with a note under same title in BC 20 1971). Further and very full discussion of the forgeries dealt with by Carter and Pollard in their Enquiry, *above*.

Beetz, K. H. Ruskin: a bibliography 1900–74. Metuchen NJ 1976. A listing of later edns, along with a bibliography of criticism.

Cate, G. A. John Ruskin, a reference guide: a selective guide to significant and representative works about him. Boston 1988. Lists and annotates important reviews, criticism and biography from 1843 to 1987.

Garbutt, J. Ruskin index: the works and associated items of John Ruskin held at the Armitt Library, Ambleside. Ambleside 1993.

Collections

Collected works. 15 vols New York 1861–3, 13 vols New York 1866–7.

Collected works. 11 vols 1871–80. Vol 1 Sesame and lilies, 1871; vol 2 Munera pulveris, Keston 1872; vol 3 Aratra Pentelici, Keston 1872; vol 4 The eagle's nest, Keston 1872; vol 5 Time and tide, Keston 1872; vol 6 The crown of wild olive, Keston 1873; vol 7 Ariadne Florentina, Orpington 1876; vol 8 Val d'Arno, Orpington 1874; vol 9 The queen of the air, Orpington 1874; vol 10 The two paths, Orpington 1878; vol 11 A joy for ever, Orpington 1880.

Collected works. 30 vols New York 1876, 25 vols New York 1884 (Library edn), 12 vols New York 1885 (Popular edn), 14 vols New York 1885, 26 vols New York 1885–90, 13 vols New York 1887, 26 vols New York 1887, 26 vols Boston 1887, 26 vols New York 1890, 26 vols Philadelphia 1891, 10 vols New York 1895, 13 vols New York 1895, 27 vols Boston 1898 (St Mark's edn) (including study by J. A. Hobson), 13 vols Boston 1900, 30 vols New York 1905.

Poems. Ed J. O. Wright, New York 1882.
Selected works. 8 vols New York 1885, 4 vols Chicago 1900.
Collected works. Brantwood edition, with introductions by C. E. Norton, 22 vols New York 1891–2. First authorised Amer edn.
The poems of Ruskin: now first collected from original manuscript and printed sources, and edited in chronological order, with notes, biographical and critical, by W. G. Collingwood. 2 vols Orpington 1891.
Ausgewählte Werke von Ruskin. Ed C. Broicher and W. Schoelermann 15 vols Leipzig and Jena 1900–4.
The works of Ruskin. Library edition, ed E. T. Cook and A. D. O. Wedderburn 39 vols 1902–12. The only complete edn, reprinting almost every word Ruskin is known to have written and edited with meticulous care. The following works were first ptd here: Ascent of the St Bernard, 1835–6; Reply to Blackwood's criticism of Turner, 1836; the first draft of Modern painters; Marcolini, 1836; On the relative dignity of the studies of painting and music, 1838; Letters on painted glass, 1844; Notes on the Louvre, 1844, 1849, 1854; An essay on baptism, 1850–1; Letters on politics, 1852; Notes on German galleries, 1859; The Rede Lecture at Cambridge, 1867; The flamboyant architecture of the valley of the Somme, 1869; The aesthetic and mathematical schools of art in Florence, 1874; Studies in the discourse of Sir Joshua Reynolds, 1875; Final lectures at Oxford, 1884; The grammar of Silica, nd. Important addns or projected continuations to the following works were also included: Modern painters; The seven lamps of architecture; The stones of Venice; The queen of the air; Fors clavigera; Aratra pentelici; Love's meinie; Mornings in Florence; Proserpina; Deucalion; Bibliotheca pastorum; Fiction, fair and foul; 'Our fathers have told us' (pt iii, Ara coeli); The pleasures of England; Praeterita; Dilecta.
The works of Ruskin. Library edition, ed E. T. Cook and A. D. O. Wedderburn 39 vols 1902–12 on CD-ROM. Introd by M. Wheeler, with a History of the Library edition by J. S. Dearden, Cambridge 1996.
Collected works. Routledge's New Universal edition. 15 vols 1907. Non-copyright; works as pbd before 1865.
The Ruskin House edition. 4 vols 1907 (WC).
Poems, with an essay on the author by G. K. Chesterton. [1908] (ML).
A walk in Chamouni and other poems. [Ed J. R. Tutin] Hull 1908.

Selections and extracts

The true and the beautiful in nature, art, morals and religion, selected from the writings of Ruskin with a notice of the author. Ed L. C. Tuthill, New York 1858 etc, 1890 (2 vols), Chicago 1902.
Selections from the writings of Ruskin. [Ed W. S. Williams] 1861 etc, New York 1868, London 1869 etc, Edinburgh 1907 (with biographical introd by W. Sinclair).
Art culture: a hand-book of art technicalities and criticisms selected from the works of Ruskin. Ed W. H. Platt, New York 1873 etc.
Pearls for young ladies. Ed L. C. Tuthill, New York 1878 etc.
The Ruskin birthday book. [Ed M. A. Bateman and G. Allen] Orpington 1883, New York 1884.
Art and life: a Ruskin anthology. Ed W. S. Kennedy, New York 1886 etc. Pt 3, The conduct of life, and pt 5, Nature and literature, also pbd separately, New York 1886.
Selections from Ruskin on reading and other subjects. Ed E. Ginn, Boston 1888 etc.
An introduction to the writings of John Ruskin. Ed V. D. Scudder, Boston 1890, 1901 (rev).
The communism of John Ruskin. Ed W. D. P. Bliss, New York 1891.
Selections from the writings of Ruskin. Ed W. G. Collingwood 2 vols Orpington 1893 etc. Vol 1 is practically identical with Selections, ed W. S. Williams, *above*.
Essays and letters selected from the writings of Ruskin. Ed L. G. Hufford, Boston 1894.
Ruskin on education. Ed W. Jolly, Orpington 1894 etc.
Ruskin on music. Ed A. M. Wakefield, Orpington 1894 etc.
The Ruskin reader. [Ed W. G. Collingwood,] Orpington 1895 etc.
Studies in both arts: being ten subjects drawn and described by Ruskin. [Ed W. G. Collingwood,] Orpington 1895.
Was wir lieben und pflegen müssen: eine Sammlung Natur-Ansichten und Schilderungen aus den Werken Ruskins. Ed J. Feis, Strasburg 1895, 1898 (2 vols), 1900 (rev).
Wie wir arbeiten und wirthschaften müssen: eine Gedankenlese aus den Werken Ruskins. Ed J. Feis, Strasburg 1896.
The Bible references of Ruskin. Ed M. and E. Gibbs 1898, New York 1898 etc, London 1905.
The two boyhoods etc. New York 1898 etc, London [1914] (EL).
Wege zur Kunst: eine Gedankenlese aus den Werken Ruskins. Ed J. Feis 4 vols Strasburg 1898. Vols 1–2 rev Strasburg 1898–1900.
Huru vi rätt skola försten Konsten. Ed O. H. Dumrath, Stockholm 1900. Adapted from Wege zur Kunst, ed Feis, *above*.
Nature studies. Ed R. Porter, Boston 1900.
Thoughts from Ruskin. Ed H. Atwell 1900, New York 1901.
Turner and Ruskin: an exposition of Turner from the writings of Ruskin. Ed F. Wedmore 2 vols 1900.
Pen pictures from Ruskin. Ed C. A. Wurtzburg 2 vols 1901–2 etc.
Ruskin's principles of art criticism. Ed I. M. Street, Chicago 1901.
Ruskin on pictures: a collection of criticism by Ruskin not heretofore reprinted. Ed E. T. Cook 2 vols 1902.
Dante references: comments of Ruskin on the Divina Commedia. Ed G. P. Huntington, introd by C. E. Norton, Boston 1903.
Obras escogidas. Ed E. Gonzalez-Blanco 2 vols Madrid [1906].
Huru vi skola arbeta och hushålla. Ed O. H. Dumrath, Stockholm 1907. Adapted from Wie wir arbeiten, ed Feis, *above*.
The pocket Ruskin. Ed R. Gardner 1907, New York 1907.
The pocket Ruskin: being aphorisms and passages from the works of Ruskin. Ed A. H. Hyatt 1907.
Out in the open: extracts from Ruskin. Ed R. M. Lawton, Springfield MA 1908.
A Ruskin calendar. Ed A. E. Sims 1908, New York 1912.
Selections and essays. Ed F. W. Roe, Philadelphia 1908, New York 1918 etc.
Selections from the works of Ruskin. Ed C. B. Tinker, Boston 1908 etc.
Ruskin: pages choisies. Ed R. de la Sizeranne, Paris 1909.
Selections from Ruskin. Ed H. Hampshire 1909.
Readings from Ruskin. Ed S. Cunnington 1921.
Selections from Ruskin. Ed A. C. Benson, Cambridge 1923 etc.
Selections from the prose of Ruskin. Ed C. I. Thomson [1925].
Views of social justice. Ed J. Fuchs, New York 1926.
Ruskin as literary critic. Ed A. H. R. Ball, Cambridge 1928, New York 1969.
Selected writings. Ed P. Quennell 1952.
The lamp of beauty. Ed J. Evans 1959, Oxford 1980, Ithaca NY 1980.
The genius of Ruskin. Ed J. D. Rosenberg, New York 1963, London 1964, Boston 1979.
Ruskin today. Ed K. Clark 1964, New York 1965, Harmondsworth 1967 etc; as Selected writings, London 1991.
The art criticism of Ruskin. Ed R. L. Herbert, Gloucester MA 1964 etc, New York 1964, 1987.
The literary criticism of Ruskin. Ed H. Bloom, Garden City NY 1965, Gloucester MA 1969, New York 1972 (abridged), 1986, 1987.
Selected prose of Ruskin. Ed M. Hodgart, New York 1972.
Opere. Ed G. Leoni, Rome 1987. Excerpts from selected essays.
Ruskin on Turner. Ed D. Birch, Boston and London 1990.
Selected writings. Ed P. Davis 1995.

§1

Ruskin's catalogues of drawings, minerals etc, 1857–89, and his St George's Guild pbns, 1878–85, have not been included. For them and for such

Ruskiniana as catalogues of St George's Museum, the bibliographies of T. J. Wise and J. P. Smart and of E. T. Cook and A. D. O. Wedderburn, above, should be consulted.

Salsette and Elephanta: a prize poem. Oxford 1839, Orpington 1879; rptd in Oxford prize poems, Oxford 1839, 1846.

The Scythian guest: a poem. 1849. A forgery executed 1880–90; *see* The works of Ruskin, ed E. T. Cook and A. D. O. Wedderburn, vol 2 pp. 101–2; J. Carter and H. G. Pollard, An enquiry into the nature of certain nineteenth-century pamphlets, 1934, pp. 225–6, and J. S. Dearden, BC 18 Summer 1969, pp. 176–8. The poem was first pbd in Friendship's offering, 1840, pp. 52–60.

Modern painters: their superiority in the art of landscape painting to all the ancient masters proved by examples of the true, the beautiful and the intellectual, from the works of modern artists, especially from those of J. M. W. Turner, by a graduate of Oxford. 1843, 1844 (with new preface), 1846 (with new preface), New York 1847 etc, London 1848, 1851 (with Ruskin's name for the first time), 1857, 1867; vol 2, 1846 (anon), 1848, New York 1848 etc, London 1851 (with Ruskin's name for the first time), 1856, 1867; 2 vols Orpington 1883 (rev and rearranged), New York 1883, Orpington 1885, 1888, 1891; ed C. E. Norton, New York 1891, Orpington 1893, 1896; vol 3, 1856, New York 1856 etc, London 1867; vol 4, 1856, New York 1856 etc, London 1868; vol 5, 1860, New York 1860; 5 vols New York 1865 etc, London 1873 (Autograph edn), New York 1873 (5 edns), 3 vols New York 1873, 5 vols New York 1875, 1876 etc, 4 vols New York 1883, 3 vols New York 1885, 4 vols New York 1885 etc, 5 vols New York 1885, Orpington 1888, 1892, 2 vols Boston 1894, New York 1894, 1895 etc, Orpington 1897, New York 1897, Boston 1897 etc, Orpington 1898 etc; ed L. Cust 5 vols 1907 (EL; text from 1st edns); tr Ger 1902–4.

GM 20 1843.

Nature in art. Foreign Quart Rev 37 1846.

Brown, J. North Br Rev 6 1847.

[Chorley, H. F.] Ruskinism. Edinburgh Rev 103 1856.

[Eastlake, E.] Quart Rev 98 1856.

[Eliot, G.] Westminster Rev n.s. 9 1856.

[Morris, W. and E. Burne-Jones]. Ruskin and the Quarterly. Oxford & Cambridge Mag June 1856.

[Richmond, G.?] Pictures and picture criticism. Nat Rev 3 1856.

Frondes agrestes: readings in Modern painters. Orpington 1875, New York 1875 etc, Orpington 1876, 1878, 1879, 1880, 1883, 1884, New York 1885, Orpington 1886, 1889, 1890, New York 1890, Orpington 1891, 1893, 1895, 1896, 1898, 1899, New York 1900, London 1900, 1902, 1904.

Ruskin on painting, with a biographical sketch. New York 1879.

In montibus sanctis: studies of mountain form and of its visible causes, collected and completed out of Modern painters. 2 pts Orpington 1884–5, New York 1894 (with Hortus inclusus).

Modern painters: selections. Ed J. W. Abernethy, New York 1884.

Coeli enarrant: studies of cloud form and of its visible causes, collected and completed out of Modern painters. Pt 1 (all pbd) Orpington 1885, New York 1894 (with Hortus inclusus).

Wedderburn, A. D. O. Modern painters: general index, bibliography and notes. Orpington 1888.

Modern painters: a volume of selections. 1909.

Modern painters. Abridged and ed A. J. Finsberg 1927.

Dolk, L. The reception of Modern painters. MLN 57 1942.

Modern painters. Abridged and ed D. Barrie 1987.

Ali, K. I. The reception of the third volume of Ruskin's Modern painters. Explorations 12 1988–9.

The seven lamps of architecture, with illustrations drawn and etched by the author. 1849, New York 1849 etc, London 1855 (with additional preface), New York 1876, 1880, Orpington 1880 (with new preface and notes), New York 1880 (text from 3rd Eng edn), Orpington 1883, New York 1884 etc, 1885 (2 edns), Orpington 1886, New York 1889, Orpington 1890, 1891, New York 1891; ed C. E. Norton, New York 1891; Orpington 1894, 1895, New York 1895, Orpington 1897, 1898, 1899; ed R. Sturgis, New York 1899; London 1900, 1901, 1903; ed S. Image 1907 etc (EL) (text from 1st edn); Leipzig 1907 (text from 1880 edn); ed A. Meynell 1910 (text from 1st edn); ed A. Lunn 1956 etc (EL); New York 1961 etc; tr Fr 1900 (rptd 1916; 1987 with John Ruskin by Marcel Proust), Ger 1900, 1994, Sp 1913, Jap 1930.

[Capes, J. M.] Rambler 4 1849.

[Ferguson, S.] Dublin Univ Mag 34 1849.

Patmore, C. North Br Rev 12 1850.

Wedderburn, A. D. O. Ruskin: Seven lamps of architecture: general index. 1891 (priv ptd).

The King of the Golden River, or the black brothers: a legend of Stiria. Illustr Richard Doyle 1851 (3 edns), 1856, Boston 1856 (in Curious stories), London 1859, Boston 1860, New York 1860 etc, London 1863, Boston 1863 etc, London [1867], Boston 1875 (in Little classics, ed R. Johnson, vol 10), Chicago 1876 etc, New York 1876, Orpington [1882], New York 1882, London 1885, Boston 1885 etc, New York 1885, Orpington 1886, New York 1886 etc, Orpington 1888, New York 1890, 1890 (in Miscellanea: minor writings of Ruskin, vol 1), Orpington 1892, Boston 1893 etc, 1895, New York 1895 (2 edns), New York 1898 (in King of the Golden River and other wonder stories), Orpington 1899, New York 1900, Chicago 1900 etc; ed H. Bates 1900 (with Sesame and lilies); ed M. V. O'Shea, Boston 1900 etc; ed E. Hubbard, East Aurora NY 1900; Orpington 1901; ed K. L. Bates, Chicago 1903; Toronto 1905; ed O. Lodge 1907 etc (EL) (with Sesame and lilies and The two paths); ed A. G. Schmidt, Chicago 1918; ed E. A. Noble, New York 1930; illustr A. Rackham 1932; Philadelphia 1932; London 1939 (with The magic fishbone by Dickens); ed A. B. Allen 1946; ed M. L. Becker, Cleveland OH 1946; ed M. W. and G. Thomas London 1961; ed E. Bowen, New York 1962; ed J. Brydson London 1970 (EL); illustr J. Vylethal 1973; illustr K. Turska 1978; illustr E. Breccia 1979; tr Ger 1861, 1861, Ital 1891, 1963, Rus 1894, 1904, Welsh 1909, Jap 1921, 1928, Afrikaans 1936 (abridged, with Swift's Gulliver's travels), Polish 1969.

The stones of Venice, vol 1; The foundations, with illustrations drawn by the author. 1851, New York 1851 etc, London 1858; vol 2 The sea stories, with illustrations drawn by the author, 1853, 1867; vol 3: The fall, with illustrations drawn by the author, 1853, 1867; 3 vols New York 1860 etc, London 1874 (with new signed preface), New York 1884 etc (in 2 vols), 1885 (2 edns), Orpington 1886, New York 1889; ed C. E. Norton, New York 1891; Orpington 1893 (adds index), Boston 1894, New York 1894, 1897, Orpington 1898, 1900, 1902, London 1905, 1907 etc; ed L. M. Phillips 3 vols 1907 etc (EL); ed and abridged J. G. Links 1960 etc; tr Ger 1903, 1994, Fr 1906, Hungarian 1907.

Examples of the architecture of Venice, selected and drawn to measurement from the edifices by John Ruskin. 1851, Orpington 1887.

[Patmore, C.] Br Quart Rev 13 1851.

Something on Ruskinism; with a 'vestibule' in rhyme. By an architect. 1851. Parody.

[Meredith, G.] The Times 24 Sep, 1 Oct, 12 Nov 1853.

Fraser's Mag 49 Feb, Apr 1854.

On the nature of Gothic: and herein of the true functions of the workman in art. Being the greater part of the sixth chapter of the second volume of Mr Ruskin's Stones of Venice. 1854, 1854, 1892 (Kelmscott Press), Orpington 1899, 1900, Paris 1908 (with preface by W. Morris); tr Fr 1907, Swed 1909, Danish 1917.

Notice of the paintings by Tintoretto in the Scuola di San Rocco at Venice. Extracted from Mr Ruskin's Stones of Venice, vol 3. Arundel Soc [1857].

The stones of Venice: introductory chapters and local indices for the use of travellers, while staying in Venice and Verona. 2 vols

Orpington 1879–81, 1881–5, 1884–8, 1888–90, New York 1890 (in 1 vol); ed C. E. Norton, New York 1891; Orpington 1892, 1894, 1896, 1897, 1900, 1902, 1904, 1905, Leipzig 1906; tr Fr 1906 (with preface, also ptd separately, by R. de la Sizeranne).

[Wedderburn, A. D. O.] The stones of Venice: index. 1886 (priv ptd).

Selections from The stones of Venice. Ed E. A. Parker 1925.

The stones of Venice (text in English and Italian). Ed and abridged D. Gazzoni-Pisani, Rome 1975.

Ruskin's Venice. Ed A. Whittick 1976.

The stones of Venice: selections. Ed J. Morris 1981.

Notes on the construction of sheepfolds. 1851, 1851, New York 1851 etc (with Pre-Raphaelitism), Orpington 1875, New York 1876, Orpington 1879, New York 1885 (2 edns), London 1910 (EL); rptd in On the old road vol 2, 1885.

Dyce, W. Notes on shepherds and sheep. 1851.

A reply to Notes on the construction of sheepfolds by a graduate of the University of Cambridge. 1851, Prospective Rev 7 1851.

Two letters concerning Notes on the construction of sheepfolds addressed to the Rev F. D. Maurice by John Ruskin in 1851. Ed F. J. Furnivall 1890 (priv ptd).

John Ruskin and F. D. Maurice on Notes on the construction of sheepfolds. Ed T. J. Wise 1896 (priv ptd). *See also* F. D. Maurice, Three letters concerning Ruskin's Notes on the construction of sheepfolds, in Literary anecdotes of the nineteenth century, ed W. R. Nicoll and T. J. Wise, vol 2 1896.

Pre-Raphaelitism, by the author of Modern painters. 1851, New York 1851 etc, London 1862 (with Ruskin's name), New York 1876 (with other essays), Chicago 1876, New York 1885, 1891, 1895; ed W. M. Rossetti, Boston 1899; ed L. Binyon 1907 etc (EL) (with other essays by Ruskin); also rptd in On the old road vol 1, 1885.

Art Jnl n.s. 3 Nov 1851.

Irish Quart Rev 1 Dec 1851.

Rippingille, E. V. A reply to the author of Modern painters in his defence of Pre-Raphaelitism. 1852.

Young, E. Art, its constitution and capacities. Bristol 1854.

Ballantyne, J. What is Pre-Raphaelitism? Edinburgh 1856.

Young, E. Pre-Raphaelitism: or a popular enquiry into some newly-asserted principles of art. 1857.

Thomas, W. C. Pre-Raphaelitism tested by the principles of Christianity. 1860 (priv ptd).

National Gallery. Two letters to the Editor of The Times by the author of Modern painters. 1852. A forgery executed 1880–90; *see* The works of Ruskin, ed E. T. Cook and A. D. O. Wedderburn, vol 12 p. 396; J. Carter and H. G. Pollard, An enquiry into the nature of certain nineteenth-century pamphlets, 1934, pp. 227–9, and J. S. Dearden, BC 18 Summer 1969, pp. 171–2. The letters appeared in The Times 7 Jan 1847, 29 Dec 1852; rptd in Arrows of the chace vol 1, 1880.

'Verax'. The abuses of the National Gallery. 1847. Includes Ruskin's first letter.

Moore, M. Revival of vandalism at the National Gallery: a reply to Messrs Ruskin, Heaphy and Wornum's letters in The Times. 1853.

Giotto and his works in Padua: being an explanatory notice of the series of woodcuts executed for the Arundel Society after the frescoes in the Arena Chapel. 1854. Really 3 pts 1853, 1854, 1860, bound up as 1 vol 1877; New York 1872 (in Miscellanea: minor writings of Ruskin, vol 1), 1885 (2 edns), 1886, 1887 etc (with Poetry of architecture and Poems), 1890, 1899, Orpington 1900, 1905.

Lectures on architecture and painting delivered at Edinburgh in November 1853, with illustrations drawn by the author. 1854, New York 1854 etc, London 1855, New York 1885 (2 edns), Orpington 1891; ed C. E. Norton, New York 1892; Orpington 1899, London 1902 etc; ed L. Binyon 1907 etc (EL) (with other essays by Ruskin).

The opening of the Crystal Palace considered in some of its relations to the prospects of art. 1854, New York 1885; rptd in On the old road vol 1, 1885.

Notes on some of the principal pictures exhibited in the rooms of the Royal Academy, 1855. 1855, 1855 (anon), 1855 (with suppl); ed E. T. Cook in Ruskin on pictures vol 2, 1902; ed L. Binyon 1907 etc (EL). Modern painters vol 2 (2nd edn) had included as Addendum: Notes on pictures exhibited in the Royal Academy, 1848. The later notes below are also included in Ruskin on pictures (1902), and EL 1907.

Notes on so much of the catalogue of the present exhibition of the Royal Academy as relates to the works of the members. 1855 (priv ptd). A reply to Ruskin.

Notes on some of the principal pictures exhibited in the rooms of the Royal Academy, and the Society of Painters in Water Colours, no 2, 1856. 1856, 1856, 1856 (adds Postscript; 4 edns).

Notes on some of the principal pictures exhibited in the rooms of the Royal Academy, and the Society of Painters in Water Colours, no 3, 1857. 1857, 1857.

Notes on some of the principal pictures exhibited in the rooms of the Royal Academy, the Old and New Societies of Painters in Water Colours, the Society of British Artists and the French Exhibition, no 4, 1858. 1858.

Hamley, Sir Edward. Mr Dusky's opinions on art. Blackwood's Mag 84 July 1858.

Notes on some of the principal pictures exhibited in the rooms of the Royal Academy, the Old and New Societies of Painters in Water Colours, the Society of British Artists, and the French Exhibition, no 5, 1859. 1859.

Notes on some of the principal pictures exhibited in the rooms of the Royal Academy, 1875. Orpington 1875 (4 edns).

[Morgan, J.] [Index to Notes on the Royal Academy.] Aberdeen 1888 (priv ptd), 1890.

The harbours of England, engraved by Thomas Lupton, from original drawings made expressly for the work by J. M. W. Turner, with illustrative text by J. Ruskin. 1856, [1857?], [1859?], 1872, 1877; [ed T. J. Wise] Orpington 1895, London 1902, 1905, 1907.

Notes on the Turner Gallery at Marlborough House, 1856. 1857 (5 edns, 4th adds Preface, 5th rev); ed E. T. Cook in Ruskin on pictures vol 1, 1902; ed L. Binyon 1907 etc (EL) (with other essays by Ruskin).

The elements of drawing in three letters to beginners, with illustrations drawn by the author. 1857, New York 1857, 1857 etc, London 1857 (adds second appendix), 1859, 1860, 1861, New York 1876, 1885 (2 edns), 1885 (with Aratra pentelici), London 1887, Orpington 1892; ed C. E. Norton, New York 1893; Orpington 1895, 1898, 1900, 1901, 1904, London 1904, 1907 (EL) (with The elements of perspective); ed B. Dunstan, London 1991; tr Ital 1898 etc, Ger [1901] (abridged). Partly rptd in R. St J. Tyrwhitt, Our sketching club: letters and studies in landscape art, with an authorised reproduction of the lessons and woodcuts in Professor Ruskin's Elements of drawing, 1874, 1875, Boston 1875, London 1882, 1886, 1896.

Br Quart Rev 26, Oct 1857.

The political economy of art: being the substance (with additions) of two lectures delivered at Manchester, July 10th and 13th 1857. 1857, New York 1858 etc, London 1867, 1868, New York 1876, 1895; ed O. Lodge 1907 etc (EL) (with Unto this last); ed C. F. G. Masterman 1907. Rptd with 3 supplementary papers: (1) Education in art (first pbd in Trans Nat Assoc for Promotion of Social Science, 1858, pp. 311–16); (2) Remarks addressed to the Mansfield art night class, Oct 14th [1873] (priv ptd [1873]); (3) Social policy must be based on the scientific principle of natural selection (read before Metaphysical Soc 11 May 1875; priv ptd 1875), in Collected works vol 11, Orpington 1880 as A joy for ever. Later rptd in this form New York 1885, 1886 etc, Orpington 1887, 1889; ed C. E. Norton, New York 1891, Orpington 1893 (adds index), 1895, 1897, 1899, New York 1899, London 1901, 1904, 1904, 1905, 1928 (WC) (with The two paths); tr Jap 1927.

Cambridge School of Art: Mr Ruskin's inaugural address, delivered at Cambridge, Oct 29 1858. Cambridge 1858, Orpington 1879, New York 1885 (2 edns) (with other works), London [1910] etc (with Time and tide). Also ptd in Cambridge School of Art, inaugural soirée, Cambridge 1858. Rptd in On the old road vol 1, 1885.

The Oxford Museum, by Henry W. Acland and John Ruskin. 1859, 1860, 1866, 1867 (both the latter omitting Ruskin's contribution), 1893 (adds new preface by Ruskin). Ruskin's original contributions are rptd in Arrows of the chace vol 1, 1880.

The unity of art, delivered at the annual meeting of the Manchester School of Art, Feb 22nd 1859. Manchester 1859. Largely rptd in The two paths, 1859, *below*.

The two paths: being lectures on art and its application to decoration and manufacture, delivered in 1858–9. 1859, New York 1859 etc, Orpington 1878 (with new preface) (as Collected works vol 10), 1884, New York 1885 (2 edns), Orpington 1887, New York 1889; ed C. E. Norton, New York 1891; Orpington 1891, New York 1894, 1895, Orpington 1896 (adds index), 1898, 1900, 1901, London 1904; ed G. Wallas 1907; ed O. Lodge 1907 etc (EL) (with Sesame and lilies etc); 1928 (WC) (with A joy for ever); ed H. Bloom, New York 1983; tr Cz 1909.

The elements of perspective arranged for the use of schools and intended to be read in connexion with the first three books of Euclid. 1859, New York 1860 etc, 1876, 1885 (with other works by Ruskin), 1895, London 1907 etc (EL) (with The elements of drawing), 1910 (rev).

'Unto this last': four essays on the first principles of political economy. 1862, New York 1866 etc, London 1876, Orpington 1877, 1882, 1884, New York 1885 (2 edns), Orpington 1887, 1888, 1890, 1892, 1893 (adds index), 1895, New York 1895, Orpington 1896, 1898, 1899, 1900 etc, Leipzig 1906 (with Munera pulveris); ed J. A. Hobson 1907; ed O. Lodge 1907 etc (EL) (with The political economy of art and Munera pulveris); 1911 (WC) (with Munera pulveris); ed S. Cunnington 1920; ed J. D. C. Monfries and G. E. Hollingworth 1931; ed L. J. Hubenka, Lincoln NE 1967; ed J. L. Bradley, New York 1967 (with Traffic from The crown of wild olive); ed J. Bryson 1979 (EL) (with other essays by Ruskin); ed H. Bloom, New York 1983; ed C. Wilmer, Harmondsworth 1985 (with extracts from The stones of Venice etc); tr Fr 1902, Ger 1902, Ital 1902, 1946, Danish 1917. First pbd in Cornhill Mag Aug–Nov 1860 and Harper's Mag Sep–Dec 1860.

Manchester Rev 18 Aug 1860.

Mr Ruskin again. Saturday Rev 10 Nov 1860.

Press 28 June 1862.

The rights of labour according to John Ruskin, arranged by Thomas Barclay. Leicester [1887], [1888?], London 1889.

Papjewski, H. Zur Erkenntniss des Gehalts von Ruskins Unto this last. Breslau 1930.

Unto this last; a paraphrase by M. K. Gandhi. Tr from the Gujerati by V. J. Desai, Ahmadabad 1951.

Hendrick, G. The influence of Ruskin's Unto this last on Gandhi. Ball State Teachers College Forum 1 1960.

Sesame and lilies: two lectures delivered at Manchester in 1864: 1, Of kings' treasuries; 2, Of queens' gardens. 1865, New York 1865 etc, London 1865 (adds preface), 1866, 1867, Orpington 1882 (with new preface), New York 1883, Orpington 1884, New York 1885, Orpington 1886, 1887, 1888, New York 1888, Chicago 1889, Orpington 1889, 1890, New York 1890, Orpington 1891; ed C. E. Norton, New York 1891; ed R. K. Root, New York 1891 etc; Orpington 1892, London 1894, 1896, 1897, 1898, 1898, 1900 etc, New York 1900, Boston 1900 etc, Portland ME 1900; ed J. E. Keysor, Boston 1903 etc; ed O. Lodge 1907 etc (EL) (with The two paths etc); ed T. Cartwright 1908; ed A. E. Roberts 1910; ed G. G. Whiskard 1912; tr Ger 1900, Swed 1900, Fr 1906 (by Marcel Proust), Ital 1907, Sp 1907, Hungarian 1911. Also rev and enlarged with new preface and a third lecture, The mystery of life and its arts; as Collected works vol 1, Keston 1871; rptd in this form New York 1875 etc, Orpington 1876, 1880, 1883; ed C. A. R[and] and E. R. W[ebster], New York 1883 etc; New York 1884, 1885 (2 edns), 1885 etc, Orpington 1887, New York 1888, 1889 etc, Chicago 1889 etc, New York 1890, Toronto 1890 etc (as New York 1883), Orpington 1891, Philadelphia 1892, Orpington 1893, 1894, New York 1894, Orpington 1895, 1896, 1897, Boston 1897, Toronto 1897, Orpington 1898, 1898, New York 1898, Boston 1898, Orpington 1899, 1900 etc, New York 1900, Leipzig 1906; ed G. Buck, New York 1906 etc; ed J. W. Linn, Chicago 1906 etc; ed A. H. Bates, New York 1907 etc; ed C. R. Gaston, Boston 1909; ed C. R. Rounds, New York 1916 etc; ed S. Wragge [1920]; ed J. W. Bartram 1925; ed G. E. Hollingworth 1932.

The queens' gardens: a lecture delivered at the Town Hall, Manchester on Wednesday Dec 14 1864. Manchester 1864. A forgery executed 1880–90, *see* The works of Ruskin, ed E. T. Cook and A. D. O. Wedderburn, vol 18, pp. 13–15; J. Carter and H. G. Pollard, An enquiry into the nature of certain nineteenth-century pamphlets, 1934, pp. 232–5; and J. S. Dearden, BC 18 Summer 1969, pp. 178–81.

[Trollope, A.] Fortnightly Rev 15 July 1865.

[Wise, J. de C.] Westminster Rev 28 Oct 1865.

The mystery of life and its arts. New York 1869, 1907, 1909. First pbd in The afternoon lectures on literature and art ser 5, Dublin 1869.

Sykes, F. H. Commentary to Sesame and lilies of John Ruskin. Toronto 1891.

Of kings' treasuries. New York [1895], 1899, London 1902; ed E. D. Jones 1907.

Of queens' gardens. New York [1896], 1899, London 1902.

Warren, P. W. T. Notes on Ruskin's Sesame and lilies. Cape Town 1898.

Warren, P. W. T. Reader's companion to Sesame and lilies. 1899.

Booth, J. B. Notes on Sesame and lilies. St George 4–5 1901–2.

An inquiry into some of the conditions at present affecting the study of architecture in our schools. New York 1866 etc, 1872 etc, 1885, Philadelphia 1891, Boston 1894, New York 1894, 1895. First pbd in The sessional papers of the Royal Inst of Br Architects pt 3 1864–5; rptd in On the old road vol 1, 1885.

The ethics of the dust: ten lectures to little housewives on the elements of crystallisation. 1866, New York 1866 etc, 1876, Orpington 1877 (with new preface), New York 1878 etc, Orpington 1883, New York 1884, 1885, Orpington 1886, 1888, 1890, New York 1890; ed C. E. Norton, New York 1891; Orpington 1892, Philadelphia 1893 etc, Orpington 1894 (adds index), 1896, 1898, 1900, Chicago 1900, Orpington 1901, 1902, 1903, London 1904; ed G. Rhys 1908 etc (EL); ed R. O. Morris 1914; London 1916 (WC) (with Sesame and lilies).

Saturday Rev 30 Dec 1865.

Guardian 21 Feb 1866.

The crown of wild olive: three lectures on work, traffic and war. 1866, 1866, New York 1866 etc, London 1867, New York 1876, 1885 (2 edns), 1888 (2 edns), 1890, 1893 etc, 1898. Also rev and enlarged with a 4th lecture, The future of England, and an appendix, Notes on the political economy of Prussia, as Collected works vol 6, Keston 1873; rptd in this form Orpington 1882, 1886, 1888, 1889, New York 1890, 1890 etc, 1891 etc; ed C. E. Norton, New York 1891; Orpington 1892, Chicago 1892 etc, New York 1894 etc, Orpington 1894 (adds index), 1895, Philadelphia 1895, Orpington 1897; ed J. C. Saul and D. M. Duncan, Toronto 1897; Orpington 1898, 1899, 1900, 1900, Chicago 1900, Orpington 1901, 1902, 1902, London 1904 etc; ed C. Bax 1908 etc (EL) (with The cestus of Aglaia); ed F. W. Melton, New York 1910 etc (with The queen of the air); ed J. H. Fowler 1962; tr Fr 1900, Polish [1900], Ger 1901, Sp 1901, Ital 1923.

War: a lecture delivered at the Royal Military Academy, Woolwich. 1866 (priv ptd).

[The future of England.] A paper read at the Royal Artillery Institution, Woolwich, Dec 14 1869. Woolwich 1870. This title appears on the wrapper; an unauthorised type facs without wrappers is discussed in J. Carter and H. G. Pollard, An enquiry into the nature of certain nineteenth-century pamphlets, 1934, pp. 238–9, and in J. S. Dearden, BC 18 Summer 1969, pp. 181–6.

Time and tide by Weare and Tyne: twenty-five letters to a working man of Sunderland on the laws of work. 1867, 1868, New York 1868 etc, Keston 1872 (as Collected works vol 5), New York 1876, Orpington 1882, New York 1885, 1885 etc, Orpington 1886, 1891; ed C. E. Norton, New York 1891, London 1894 (adds index), New York 1895, London 1897, 1899, 1900, 1901, 1903, 1904 etc, 1907 (WC) (with The crown of wild olive), 1910 etc (EL) (with other Ruskin essays); ed P. Kaufman, New York 1928 (with Munera pulveris); tr Swed 1903. First pbd in Leeds Mercury 1 Mar–4 May 1867; Manchester Daily Examiner & Times 1 Mar–7 May 1867; Letters i–ii, Scotsman 27 Feb, 4 Mar 1867; Letter v, Pall Mall Gazette 1 Mar 1867.

The latest lawgiver. Blackwood's Mag 103 June 1868.

Leoni: a legend of Italy, by J. R. 1868. A forgery executed 1880–90; *see* The works of Ruskin, ed E. T. Cook and A. D. O. Wedderburn, vol 1, p. 288; J. Carter and H. G. Pollard, An enquiry into the nature of certain nineteenth-century pamphlets, 1934, pp. 236–7; and J. S. Dearden, BC 18 Summer 1969, pp. 170–1.

First notes on the general principles of employment for the destitute and criminal classes. 1868 (priv ptd), 1868 (enlarged with 'First' omitted from title); rptd with further addns in The queen of the air, 1869. Portions of the 2nd edn were ptd in Daily Telegraph 26 Dec 1868, together with a letter from Ruskin. The letter together with the complete text of the pam rptd in Arrows of the chace vol 2, 1880.

The queen of the air: being a study of the Greek myths of cloud and storm. 1869, 1869, New York 1869 etc, Philadelphia 1869, Orpington 1874 (as Collected works vol 9), New York 1876, 1882, Orpington 1883 (Collected works rev edn; rev J. P. Faunthorpe), New York 1885 (2 edns), Orpington 1887, 1890, New York 1890 (2 edns); ed C. E. Norton, New York 1891; New York 1891, Orpington 1892, 1895 (adds index), New York 1895, Orpington 1898, 1899, 1899, 1900, Chicago 1900, Orpington 1901, 1903, London 1904; ed W. F. Melton, New York 1910 etc (with The crown of wild olive); tr Ger 1905. Rptd in part from the preceding item, and from passages in The cestus of Aglaia, *below*.

Spectator 17 July 1869.

Saturday Rev 21 Aug 1869.

Bond, R. W. St George 6 Jan 1903.

Samuel Prout. Oxford 1870 (priv ptd). A probable forgery. *See* J. Carter and H. G. Pollard, An enquiry into the nature of certain nineteenth-century pamphlets, 1934, pp. 240–1, and J. S. Dearden, BC 18 Summer 1969, pp. 172–4. First pbd in Art Jnl Mar 1849; rptd in On the old road vol 1, 1885, and in Ruskin on pictures, 1902.

Lectures on art delivered before the University of Oxford in Hilary Term 1870. Oxford 1870, London 1870, New York 1870, 1870 etc, Oxford 1875, New York 1876, Oxford 1880, New York 1885, Orpington 1887 (rev), 1890; ed C. E. Norton, New York 1891; Orpington 1891, London 1894 (adds index), 1898, 1901, 1903, 1904 etc; tr Ger 1901, 1903 (partial).

Brooke, S. Macmillan's Mag 22 Oct 1870.

[Day, H. N.] New Englander (New Haven CT) 29 Oct 1870.

The range of intellectual conception is proportioned to the rank in animated life. Metaphysical Soc Papers no 16 [1871] (priv ptd); rptd in Contemporary Rev June 1871, and in On the old road vol 1, 1885.

Fors clavigera: letters to the workmen and labourers of Great Britain. 8 vols Keston and Orpington 1871–84, New York 1876 (vols 1–5); New York 1880, 1884 (vols 1–7); New York 1886 (vols 1–8); 3 vols New York 1888 etc; 4 vols New York 1890, Philadelphia 1891, New York 1894, Boston 1897; 4 vols London 1906. Vols 1–7 appeared each year 1871–7, every vol being originally issued in 12 pts on the 1st or 2nd of each month; the 12 pts of vol 8 were issued irregularly Jan 1878–Xmas 1884. Most of the pts were rptd two or three times between 1872 and 1900; tr Jap 1991 (Bk 1).

Letter to young girls. [Orpington 1876], [1890] (18th edn) etc.

Faunthorpe, J. P. Index to Fors clavigera. Orpington 1887. Contains an appendix not included in Fors. The indexes to vols 1, 2 and 3, 4 appeared in 1873 and 1875 respectively, both rptd once.

Fors clavigera: a new edition. Ed W. G. Collingwood 4 vols Orpington 1896, 1899–1902 etc. Though professing to omit only the letters to Ruskin, this abridgement actually omits some of Ruskin's own words.

Readings in John Ruskin's Fors clavigera. [Ed C. A. Wurtzburg] Orpington 1899.

Munera pulveris: six essays on the elements of political economy. Keston 1872 (as Collected works vol 2), New York 1872 etc, Orpington 1880, New York 1885, Orpington 1886, New York 1889; ed C. E. Norton, New York 1891; Orpington 1894, New York 1895, Orpington 1898, 1899, 1904, London 1904 etc; ed O. Lodge 1907 etc (EL) (with Unto this last and The political economy of art); London 1911 (WC) (with Unto this last); ed P. Kaufman, New York 1928 (with Time and tide); tr Sp 1907. First pbd in Fraser's Mag June 1862–Apr 1863.

Gold: a dialogue connected with the subject of Munera pulveris. Ed H. B. Forman 1891 (priv ptd). A reply to criticism by J. E. Cairnes, Macmillan's Mag Nov 1863. *See* J. S. Dearden, BC 18 Spring 1969, pp. 52–5.

Aratra pentelici: six lectures on the elements of sculpture, given before the University of Oxford in Michaelmas Term 1870. Keston 1872 (as Collected works vol 3), New York 1872 etc, 1876, Orpington 1879, New York 1885, Orpington 1890 (adds next item); ed C. E. Norton, New York 1891; New York 1895, Orpington 1899 (adds index), London 1901, 1907; tr Ger [1903] (5 lectures).

The relation between Michael Angelo and Tintoret: seventh of the course of lectures on sculpture delivered at Oxford 1870–1. Keston 1872, Orpington 1879, New York 1885 (with other Ruskin essays), 1885 (with Stones of Venice), Orpington 1887; rptd in 1890 and subsequent edns of Aratra pentelici.

The eagle's nest: ten lectures on the relation of natural science to art, given before the University of Oxford in Lent Term 1872. Keston 1872 (as Collected works vol 4), New York 1873 etc, 1876, Orpington 1880, New York 1885, 1886, Orpington 1887, 1890; ed C. E. Norton, New York 1891, 1892; London 1894 (adds index), 1897, 1899, 1900, 1902, 1904; tr Ger [1902] (5 lectures).

The sepulchral monuments of Italy: monuments of the Cavalli family in the Church of Santa Anastasia, Verona. 1872 (Arundel Soc); rptd in On the old road vol 1, 1885.

The nature and authority of miracle. Metaphysical Soc Papers no 32 1873 (priv ptd). Another edn dated 1873 is a forgery; *see* J. Carter and H. G. Pollard, An enquiry into the nature of certain nineteenth-century pamphlets, 1934, pp. 242–3, and J. S. Dearden, BC 18 Summer 1969, pp. 174–6. First pbd in Contemporary Rev Mar 1873; rptd in On the old road vol 2, 1885.

Love's meinie: lectures on Greek and English birds given before the University of Oxford. Lecture 1: The robin, Keston 1873; Lecture 2: The swallow, Keston 1873; Lecture 3: The dabchicks, Orpington 1881. Lectures 1–2, New York 1873, 1876, Orpington 1883, New York 1885 (2 edns), Orpington 1892. Collected edns: Orpington 1881, New York 1885, Orpington 1893, 1897 (adds index) etc. Lecture 4 (The chough) first pbd in The works of Ruskin, ed E. T. Cook and A. D. O. Wedderburn, vol 25.

The poetry of architecture: or the architecture of the nations of

Europe considered in its association with natural scenery and national character. New York 1873 etc, 1876, 1885, 1890, Orpington 1893 (1st authorised edn), New York 1895, Boston 1897, London 1905 etc. First pbd in Architectural Mag Nov 1837–Dec 1838, and rptd in Crayon (New York) 1 1855.

Val d'Arno: ten lectures on the Tuscan art directly antecedent to the Florentine Year of Victories, given before the University of Oxford in Michaelmas Term 1874. Orpington 1874 (as Collected works vol 8), 1882, New York 1885, 1885 (with Mornings in Florence and other works), 1886, 1889, 1890, Orpington 1890; ed C. E. Norton, New York 1891; New York 1895, Orpington 1900 (adds index) etc.

Mornings in Florence: being simple studies of Christian art for English travellers. 6 pts Orpington 1875–7, New York 1875 (pts 1–2), 1875 (pt 3; with Deucalion, pts 1, 2), 1876 (pts 1–5), Orpington 1881–3, 1889–92 (pt 1 rptd 1894). Collected edns: New York 1877 etc, Orpington 1885, New York 1885, 1889 etc, Orpington 1889, London 1894 (adds index), New York 1895 (2 edns), London 1899, 1901; ed M. Baker, New York [1902]; London 1903, 1904 etc, Leipzig 1907; tr Ger [1901], Fr 1906, Ital 1908.

Ariadne Florentina: six lectures on wood and metal engraving, with appendix, given before the University of Oxford in Michaelmas Term 1872. Orpington 1876 (as Collected works vol 7), New York 1876, 1878 etc, Orpington 1890, 1891; ed C. E. Norton, New York 1891; New York 1895, London 1907. Originally issued in 7 pts: pts 1–2, 1873; pts 3–4, 1874; pts 5–6, 1875; appendix, 1876; a 2-vol unauthorised edn lacking appendix pbd New York 1874–5.

The shepherd's tower: a series of photographs of the sculptures of Giotto's tower, to illustrate part 6 of Mornings in Florence. 1881.

Proserpina: studies of wayside flowers, while the air was yet pure among the Alps, and in the Scotland and England which my father knew. Vol 1 (all collected) Orpington 1879, Chicago 1880, Orpington 1882, New York 1885, 1886 etc, Boston 1887. Originally issued in 6 pts: pt 1 Orpington 1875, New York 1875, Orpington 1878, 1883, 1884; pt 2 Orpington 1875, New York 1875, Orpington 1879, 1886; pt 3 Orpington 1876, New York 1876, Orpington 1879, 1889; pt 4 Orpington 1876, New York 1877, Orpington 1880, 1889; pt 5 Orpington 1878, New York 1879, Orpington 1881, 1896; pt 6 Orpington 1879, New York 1879, Orpington 1882, 1897. Only 4 pts of vol 2 were pbd: pt 7 1882; pt 8 1882; pt 9 1885; pt 10 1886 (all Orpington).

Deucalion: collected studies of the lapse of waves and life of stones. Vol 1 (all collected) Orpington 1879, 1882, New York 1885 (2 edns), 1886, 1886 etc, Boston 1886, Philadelphia 1891, Orpington 1894, New York 1895, Boston 1897 etc. Originally issued in 6 pts: pt 1 Orpington 1875, New York 1875, Orpington 1883; pt 2 Orpington 1875, New York 1875, Orpington 1883; pt 3 Orpington 1876, New York 1877, Orpington 1883; pt 4 Orpington 1876, New York 1877, Orpington 1883; pt 5 Orpington 1878, 1888; pt 6 Orpington 1879. Only 2 pts of vol 2 were pbd: pt 7 Orpington 1880; pt 8 Orpington 1883.

Yewdale and its streamlets: report of a lecture delivered in connection with the Kendal Literary and Scientific Institution. Kendal 1877. First pbd in Kendal Mercury 6 Oct 1877 and Kendal Times 6 Oct 1877. The lecture forms ch 12 in Deucalion pt 5.

Collingwood, W. G. Deucalion, first supplement: the limestone Alps of Savoy. Orpington 1884. With an introd by Ruskin.

Letters to The Times on the principal Pre-Raphaelite pictures in the Exhibition of 1854, from the author of Modern painters. 1876 (priv ptd). Originally pbd in The Times 5, 25 May 1854; rptd in Arrows of the chace vol 1, 1880, and 'A. G. Crawford' (i.e. A. G. Wise), Notes on the pictures of Mr Holman Hunt exhibited at the rooms of the Fine Art Society, 1886.

Guide to the principal pictures in the Academy of Fine Arts at Venice, arranged for English travellers. 2 pts Venice 1877, Orpington 1882–3, Orpington 1891 (rev); tr Ital 1901, Fr 1908.

Notes by Mr Ruskin on his drawings by the late J. M. W. Turner, exhibited at the Fine Art Society's Galleries, March 1878: also an appendix containing a list of the engraved works of Turner exhibited at the same time. [1878], [1878], 1878 (adds addenda and the epilogue in incomplete form) (4 edns), 1878 (rev with completed epilogue and appendix by W. Kingsley), 1878, 1878 (adds pt 2, On his own handiwork illustrative of Turner), 1878 (pt 2 rev) (4 edns), 1900 (with catalogue of the drawings first exhibited in 1900); rptd in Ruskin on pictures vol 1, 1902.

St Mark's rest: the history of Venice written for the help of the few travellers who still care for her monuments. New York 1879, Orpington 1884 (1st complete and authorised collection), New York 1884, 1885 (2 edns), 1886 etc, 1889, Orpington 1894, New York 1895, Boston 1897 etc, Boston 1900, Chicago 1900, Orpington 1902, London 1904, Leipzig 1910; tr Ital 1901, Fr 1908, Sp 1910. Originally issued in 6 sections: pt 1 Orpington 1877, New York 1877, Orpington 1884, 1889, 1894; pt 2 Orpington 1877, New York 1877, Orpington 1889; 1st suppl Orpington 1877, 1887, 1889, 1894, tr Ital 1885 (priv ptd); pt 3 Orpington 1879, 1887, 1889, 1894; 2nd suppl Orpington 1879, 1889; appendix Orpington 1884, 1894.

The laws of Fésole: a familiar treatise on the elementary principles and practice of drawing and painting, as determined by the Tuscan masters, arranged for the use of schools. Vol 1 (all pbd) Orpington 1879, New York 1879 etc, Chicago 1880, Orpington 1882, New York 1885 (2 edns), Orpington 1890, New York 1897, Boston 1897 etc, London 1907; ed B. Beckley, New York 1996. Originally issued in 4 pts: pt 1 Orpington 1877, New York 1877, Orpington 1879, 1885; pt 2 Orpington 1878, 1880, 1889; pt 3 Orpington 1878, 1881, 1889; pt 4 Orpington 1879, 1882, 1891.

Notes on Samuel Prout and William Hunt, illustrated by a loan collection of drawings, exhibited at the Fine Art Society's Galleries. 1879–80 (4 edns), 1880, 1904 (with Academy notes); rptd in Ruskin on pictures vol 2, 1902.

Circular respecting memorial studies of St Mark's Venice, now in progress under Mr Ruskin's direction. 1879, 1879 (adds postscript), 1880.

Letters addressed by Prof Ruskin to the clergy on the Lord's Prayer and the Church. Ed F. A. Malleson 1879 (priv ptd), [1880] (adds Replies from clergy and laity, and an epilogue by Mr Ruskin), [1880], 1883, 1896 (rev and with additional letters), New York 1896. Ruskin's letters rptd in Contemporary Rev 36 Dec 1879, and in The Lib Mag (New York) 3 1880; also in On the old road vol 1, 1885, and ed T. J. Wise 1896 (priv ptd).

Sillar, W. C. A defence of the Church of England against the accusations contained in the letters of Mr Ruskin in the Contemporary Review. 1880.

Elements of English prosody for use in St George's schools, explanatory of the various terms used in Rock honeycomb. Orpington 1880.

Arrows of the chace: being a collection of scattered letters published chiefly in the daily newspapers 1840–80, and now edited by an Oxford pupil [A. D. O. Wedderburn] with a preface by the author. 2 vols Orpington 1880, New York 1881, 1885 (2 edns), 1890, Boston 1897 etc, 1900. Vol 1 Letters on art and science; vol 2 Letters on politics, economy and miscellaneous matters.

[Wedderburn, A. D. O.] The public letters of John Ruskin. Contemporary Rev June, July 1880. Contains many extracts from the above in preparation.

'Our fathers have told us': sketches of the history of Christendom for boys and girls who have been held at its fonts: pt 1 The Bible of Amiens. Orpington 1884, New York 1885 (2 edns), 1886 etc, 1895 etc, Orpington 1897, 1902, London 1907; tr Fr 1903 (by Marcel Proust), Sp 1907, Ital [1946]. Originally issued in 4 chs and an appendix: ch 1 Orpington 1880, 1883, 1893; ch 2 Orpington 1881, 1885; ch 3 Orpington 1882, 1885; ch 4 Orpington 1883, 1893; appendix Orpington 1885. Ch 4 had been previously pbd in a separate travellers' edition to serve as a guide to the Cathedral, Orpington 1881, 1886, 1897, 1898, 1909. Ruskin projected a 6th pt entitled Valle crucis, 2 chs of which were first pbd in Verona and other lectures, 1894. An intended 3rd pt, entitled Ara coeli, was first pbd in The works of Ruskin, ed E. T. Cook and A. D. O. Wedderburn, vol 33.

The art of England: lectures given in Oxford. New York 1883–4 (in successive pts), Orpington 1884, New York 1885, 1885 etc, 1886, Orpington 1887, 1893, Boston 1897 etc, Orpington 1898 (with The pleasures of England), 1900, Boston 1900, Orpington 1904, London 1907. Originally issued in 7 pts: pt 1 1883, 1883, 1890; pt 2 1883, 1883, 1893; pt 3 1883, 1884, 1898; pt 4 1883, 1884, 1898; pt 5 1883, 1885; pt 6 1883, 1885; pt 7 1884, 1887, 1893.

Materialism in modern art. Church Quart Rev 22, Apr 1886.

The pleasures of England: lectures given in Oxford. Orpington 1884, New York 1885 (pts 1–3), 1885 (complete) (3 edns), 1895, Boston 1897 etc, Orpington 1898 (with The art of England), 1900, New York 1900 etc, Orpington 1904, London 1907. Originally issued in 4 pts: pts 1–2 Orpington 1884; pts 3–4 Orpington 1885.

The storm cloud of the nineteenth century: two lectures delivered at the London Institution, Feb 4 and 11 1884. 2 pts Orpington 1884, 1884 (complete), New York 1884, 1885, London 1885, New York 1895; tr Jap 1994. First lecture fully reported in The Times 5 Feb 1884, Pall Mall Gazette 5 Feb 1884 (by E. T. Cook), and Art Jnl Apr 1884 (by A. D. O. Wedderburn).

On the old road: a collection of miscellaneous essays, pamphlets &c &c published 1834–85. [Ed A. D. O. Wedderburn] 2 vols Orpington 1885, 3 vols Orpington 1899 (rev), 3 vols London 1905.

Praeterita: outlines of scenes and thoughts perhaps worthy of memory in my past life, volume 1. Orpington 1886, 1886, New York 1886, 1886 etc, Boston 1889, 3 vols New York 1890 (with vol 2), Philadelphia 1891, New York 1892, Orpington 1899, 1900, 1905, London 1907, ed A. O. J. Cockshut, Keele 1994; tr Ger 1903, 1903. The first two pts largely from Fors clavigera, *above*. Originally issued in 12 pts: pts 1–7 1885; pts 8–12 1886; rptd New York 1885–6.

Praeterita: volume 2. Orpington 1887, New York 1887 etc, Boston 1889, 3 vols New York 1890 (with vol 1), Philadelphia 1891, Orpington 1899, 1900, 1906, London 1907; tr Ger 1903, 1903. Originally issued in 12 pts: pts 13–20 1886; pts 21–4 1887; New York 1886–7.

Praeterita: volume 3. 4 pts Orpington 1888–9, New York 1888–9, Orpington 1900 (with index and Dilecta, *below*), 1900, London 1907. Pts 25–6 1888; pts 27–8 1889.

Praeterita. Ed and abridged K. Clark 1949, Oxford 1978 etc.

Dilecta: correspondence, diary notes and extracts from books, illustrating Praeterita. 3 pts Orpington 1886–1900. Pt 2 1887; pt 3 first issued with reprint of pts 1–2 and Praeterita vol 3, 1900.

Hortus inclusus: messages from the wood to the garden, sent in happy days to the sister ladies of the Thwaite, Coniston [Mary and Susie Beever]. [Ed A. Fleming] Orpington 1887, New York 1887, Orpington 1888, New York 1892, 1894, 1900, London 1902.

Ruskiniana, part 1: letters published in, and collected from various sources, and mostly reprinted in Igdrasil, 1890. [Ed A. D. O. Wedderburn] 1890 (priv ptd).

Ruskiniana, part 2: lectures and addresses reported in the press, but not reprinted in collected works. [Ed A. D. O. Wedderburn] 1892 (priv ptd).

Verona and other lectures. [Ed W. G. Collingwood] Orpington 1894, New York and London 1894; tr (of the title lecture) Ital 1981. The title lecture was delivered at the Royal Institution 4 Feb 1870; a partial report appeared in Pall Mall Gazette 5 Feb 1870; rptd in Igdrasil Mar 1892 vol 3, and in Ruskiniana pt 2, 1892. 2 of the other lectures were for an intended continuation of Our fathers have told us, *above*.

Lectures on landscape delivered at Oxford in Lent term, 1871. Orpington 1897.

The cestus of Aglaia. 1905 (with The queen of the air); ed C. Bax 1908 etc (EL) (with The crown of wild olive). Originally appeared in Art Jnl Jan–July 1865, Jan–Feb, Apr 1866. Chs 2, 6 were incorporated in The queen of the air, 1869, and a small portion in Ariadne Florentina, 1876; the rest was rptd in On the old road vol 1, 1885.

Contributions to periodicals

Ruskin's longer contributions to periodicals were partly collected in On the old road, 2 vols 1885. *A complete list of those pbd in his lifetime is in* T. J. Wise and J. P. Smart, A bibliography of Ruskin, vol 2 pp. 111–22. *A complete list of Ruskin's letters to newspapers is in* The works, ed E. T. Cook and A. D. O. Wedderburn, vol 38 pp. 48–55. *They were largely collected in* Arrows of the chace, 2 vols 1880, *and in* Ruskiniana pt 1, 1890. *Only those not rptd are listed here.*

On the convergence of perpendiculars. [Loudon's] Architectural Mag Feb 1838–Jan 1839.

On the propriety of combining works of art with the sublimity of nature. [Loudon's] Architectural Mag Jan 1839.

Notice respecting some artificial sections illustrating the geology of Chamouni, communicated in a letter to Prof Forbes. Proc Royal Soc of Edinburgh 4 1857–8. There is also a separate offprint.

Notes on the shape and structure of some parts of the Alps with reference to denudation. Geological Mag Feb–May 1865.

On banded and brecciated concretions. Geological Mag Aug 1867–Jan 1870. There was also a separate offprint of each article.

Notes on Bewick's birds. Art Jnl Oct, Dec 1886.

Arthur Burgess. Century Guild Hobby Horse Apr 1887.

Books which have influenced me. Br Weekly Extra 1887.

Books edited by Ruskin, or for which he supplied prefaces, notes or appendices

Repton, Humphrey. Landscape gardening. 1840. Footnote on the proper shapes of pictures and engravings, pp. 32–8.

Handbook for travellers in Northern Italy. 1847 (3rd edn). Notes. Also in 4th (1852), 5th (1854) and 6th edns; incorporated in the text in subsequent edns.

The report of the National Gallery Site Commission. 1857. Evidence, pp. 92–7; rptd in Literary Gazette 22 Aug 1857, and in On the old road vol 1, 1885.

The report of the Director of the National Gallery to the Lords Commissioners of Her Majesty's Treasury. 1858. Appendix 7, pp. 67–9.

The report from the Select Committee [of the House of Commons] on Public Institutions. 1860. Evidence, pp. 113–23; rptd in On the old road vol 1, 1885.

The report of the Royal Academy Commission. 1863. Evidence, pp. 546–55; rptd in On the old road vol 1, 1885.

Grimm Jacob. German popular stories. Ed E. Taylor 1868. Introd.

Tyrwhitt, R. St John. Christian art and symbolism. 1872. Preface; rptd in On the old road vol 1, 1885.

Catalogue of an exhibition of outlines by the late John Leech, at the Gallery, 9 Conduit Street. 1872. Preface; rptd in The Times 8 May 1872; in Percival Leigh, Portraits of children of the nobility illustrated by John Leech, 1875 (first pbd 1841); in Arrows of the chace vol 1, 1880.

Derby Central School of Art: report for the year 1872–3. Derby [1873]. Remarks addressed to students of the school; rptd in Arrows of the chace vol 2, 1880 and Bookman Mar 1900.

Rendu, Louis. Theory of the glaciers of Savoy, tr Alfred Wills. Ed G. Forbes 1874. Supplementary articles, pp. 205–7; rptd in Arrows of the chace vol 1, 1880.

Corporation of Brighton. The exhibition of pictures lent by Prof Ruskin and the Arundel Society opened April 6 1876, the Royal Pavilion Gallery. [Brighton 1876]. Note on Botticelli's Zipporah.

Owen, A. C. The art schools of medieval Christendom. 1876. Preface and footnotes; rptd in On the old road vol 1, 1885.

Somervell, R. A protest against the extension of railways in the Lake

District. Windermere [1876]. Preface; rptd in On the old road vol 1, 1885.

Bibliotheca pastorum, edited by John Ruskin. Vol 1: The economist of Xenophon, tr A. D. O. Wedderburn, and W. G. Collingwood, Orpington 1876. Vol 2: Rock honeycomb: broken pieces of Sir Philip Sidney's Psalter, laid up in store for English homes, 2 pts Orpington 1877. [No vol 3.] Vol 4: A knight's faith: passages in the life of Sir Herbert Edwardes collated by John Ruskin, Orpington 1885.

The science of life: a pamphlet addressed to all members of the universities of Oxford and Cambridge, and all who are, or who will be, teachers, clergymen, fathers. 1877, 1878. 5 letters: letters 1–4 in 1st edn; 1, 5 in 2nd edn. Rptd in Arrows of the chace vol 2, 1885.

Zorzi, A. P. Osservazioni intorno ai ristauri interni ed esterni della Basilica di San Marco. Venice 1877. Letter, pp. 11–22; rptd in Igdrasil May 1890, and Ruskiniana pt 1, 1890.

Swan, H. Collected notes on some of the pictures in the St George's Museum, Sheffield. [Sheffield 1879.] Note on Fra Filippi and Carpaccio.

Notes on drawings by Mr Ruskin, placed on exhibition by Prof Norton, Boston, Oct 1879. Cambridge MA 1879. Notes on his own drawings.

Catalogue of the first exhibition of pictures and water colour drawings &c at Douglas, Isle of Man, with original notes by Prof Ruskin. Douglas 1880.

The Ruskin cabinet at Whitelands College: notes on the sixty pictures by Prof Ruskin. 1883.

[Alexander, Francesca.] The story of Ida: epitaph on an Etrurian tomb, edited with a preface by John Ruskin. Orpington 1883.

Horsfall, T. C. The study of beauty and art in large towns. 1883. Introd; rptd in On the old road vol 1, 1885.

Smart, W. A disciple of Plato: a critical study of John Ruskin, with a note by Mr Ruskin. Glasgow 1883.

Reid, S. J. Sketch of the life and times of Sydney Smith. 1884. Letter to the author.

Collingwood, W. G. Deucalion – first supplement: the limestone Alps of Savoy, a study in physical geology. Orpington 1884. Preface.

The Bishop of Oxford and Prof Ruskin on vivisection. Victoria Soc for Protection of Animals from Vivisection 1885.

Alexander, Francesca. Roadside songs of Tuscany, translated and illustrated by Francesca Alexander, and edited by John Ruskin. Orpington 1885. Originally issued in 10 pts from Apr 1884–Aug 1885.

Chesneau, E. The English school of painting, translated by L. N. Etherington. 1885. Preface.

[Sillar, R. G.] Usury: its pernicious effects on English agriculture and commerce; an allegory dedicated, without permission, to the Bishops of Manchester, Peterborough and Rochester. 1885. Introd; rptd in On the old road vol 2, 1885.

Dame Wiggins of Lee and her seven wonderful cats, edited with additional verses by John Ruskin. Orpington 1885.

[Wise, A. G.] Notes on some of the principal pictures of Sir John Everett Millais at the Grosvenor Gallery by A. Gordon Crawford, with a preface and original and selected criticisms by John Ruskin. 1886.

A catalogue of the exhibition of water colour drawings by deceased masters of the British School at the Royal Institute. 1886. Appendix; rptd in Ruskiniana pt 1, 1890.

Turner's rivers of France. 2 vols 1887. The introd consists of unauthorised extracts from Modern painters.

[Bitzius, A.] Ulric the farm servant: a story of the Bernese Lowland, by Jeremias Gotthelf, translated into English by Julia Firth. Orpington 1888. Issued in 9 pts from July 1886–Oct 1888. Preface and notes.

Cook, Sir E. T. A popular handbook to the National Gallery including, by special permission, notes collected from the works of Mr Ruskin. 1888 etc. Also preface.

Alexander, Francesca. Christ's folk in the Apennine: reminiscences of her friends among the Tuscan peasantry. Orpington 1889. Issued in pts 1887–9. Preface etc.

White, W. The principles of art as illustrated in the Ruskin Museum, Sheffield, with passages from the writings of John Ruskin. 1895.

Letters and diaries

There is a long list of Ruskin's private letters and notebooks in The works of Ruskin, ed E. T. Cook and A. D. O. Wedderburn, vol 38 pp. 56–93. *See also:*

Sotheby & Co. Catalogue of the mss and remaining library of Ruskin, removed from his residence Brantwood. 24 July 1930; final portion 18 May 1931.

Thorpe, W. The Ruskin mss. Princeton Univ Lib Chron 1 1940.

Hogan, C. B. The Yale collection of the mss of Ruskin. Yale Lib Gazette 16 1942. *See also* 27 1952.

Skelton, R. Ruskin: the final years – a survey of the Ruskin correspondence in the John Rylands Library. BJRL 37 1955.

Letters upon subjects of general interest from Ruskin to various correspondents. Ed T. J. Wise 1892 (priv ptd).

Stray letters from Prof Ruskin to a London bibliophile [F. S. Ellis]. Ed T. J. Wise 1892 (priv ptd).

Letters from Ruskin to William Ward. Ed T. J. Wise 2 vols 1892 (priv ptd), Boston 1922 (with a biography of Ward by William C. Ward, introd by A. M. Brook).

Letters of Ruskin to his secretary [C. A. Howell]. New Rev Mar 1892.

Three letters and an essay by Ruskin 1836–41 found in his tutor's [Canon Dale's] desk. [Ed H. P. Dale] Orpington 1893.

Letters addressed to a college friend [Edward Clayton] 1840–5. Orpington 1894, New York 1894.

Letters on art and literature. Ed T. J. Wise 1894 (priv ptd).

Letters to Ernest Chesneau. Ed T. J. Wise 1894 (priv ptd).

Stronach, G. Some Ruskin letters to J. J. Laing. Westminster Gazette 27 Aug 1894.

Letters to Rev F. J. Faunthorpe. Ed T. J. Wise 1895, 1896 (priv ptd).

Letters to Rev F. A. Malleson. Ed T. J. Wise 1896 (priv ptd).

Letters to F. J. Furnivall. Ed T. J. Wise 1897 (priv ptd).

[14 letters to Miss Adelaide Ironside.] Catholic Press (Sydney) 3 Feb 1900.

The letters of Ruskin to C. E. Norton. [Ed C. E. Norton] 2 vols Boston 1903.

Letters to M. G. & H. G. [Mary and Hellen Gladstone]. Edinburgh 1903 (priv ptd), New York 1903; rptd in North Amer Rev July 1903.

Spielman, M. H. and G. S. Layard. Kate Greenaway. 1905.

The letters of Dr John Brown. Ed his son and D. W. Forrest 1907.

Young, M. F. Letters of a noble woman [Mrs La Touche]. 1908.

Life of Octavia Hill, as told in her letters. Ed C. E. Maurice 1913.

An ill assorted marriage. Ed C. K. Shorter 1915 (priv ptd). Letter to F. J. Furnivall.

Ruskin in old age: some unpublished letters. Ed J. H. Whitehouse, Scribner's Mag 62, Dec 1917.

Ruskin and an early friendship, with many unpublished letters. In Ruskin the prophet and other centenary studies, ed J. H. Whitehouse, 1920.

Ruskin to Rawdon Brown. Ed P. Kaufmann, North Amer Rev Sep–Dec 1925.

From a Victorian post-bag: being letters addressed to J. L. Davies. 1926.

A girl's [Jessie Leete's] friendship with Ruskin. Ed L. Huxley, Cornhill Mag Dec 1926–Jan 1927; Atlantic Monthly Dec 1926–Jan 1927.

The Giustani memoirs. Ed P. Dearmer, London Mercury Oct 1927.

The solitary warrior. Ed J. H. Whitehouse 1929.

Letters to Francesca, and memoirs of the Alexanders. Ed L. G. Swett, Boston 1931.
Macdonald, G. Reminiscences of a specialist. 1932. *See also* TLS 14 Mar 1935.
Letters to Bernard Quaritch 1867–88. Ed C. Q. Wrentmore 1938.
Davis, C. R. A Ruskin letter. Jnl Rutgers Univ Lib 2 1939.
M., M. 22 Ruskin letters. More Books 14 Nov 1939.
Friends of a lifetime: letters to S. C. C[ockerell]. Ed V. Meynell 1940.
Ruskin at the Lyceum. Letter to Thornton Leigh Hunt. TLS 8 June 1946.
James, W. The order of release. 1947.
[Letter to Sir J. T. Coleridge, 1866.] Jnl Rutgers Univ Lib 12 1948. On Swinburne.
Two unpublished letters. N & Q 12 Nov 1949.
Ferguson, O. W. Ruskin's continental letters to Mrs Severn. JEGP 51 1952.
Häusermann, H. W. The Genevese background. 1952.
The gulf of years: letters to Kathleen Olander. Ed R. Unwin [1953].
Letters of Ruskin. BJRL 26 1953.
Ruskin's letters from Venice 1851–2. Ed J. L. Bradley, New Haven CT 1955.
The diaries of Ruskin. Ed J. Evans and J. H. Whitehouse 3 vols Oxford 1956–9.
An unpublished Ruskin letter. Ed J. L. Bradley, Burlington Mag 100 1958.
A Ruskin letter. Ed D. V. Rexford, Jnl Rutgers Univ Lib 2 1959.
Spence, M. E. Ruskin's correspondence with Miss Blanche Atkinson. BJRL 42 1959.
Spence, M. E. Ruskin's friendship with Mrs Fanny Talbot. BJRL 42 1959.
Ruskin's advice to an amateur artist, Louisa Marchioness of Waterford. Ed J. L. Bradley, SEL 1 1961.
Spence, M. E. Ruskin's correspondence with his god-daughter, Constance Oldham. BJRL 43 1961.
Strouse, N. H. The contemptible horse: text of Ruskin's letter, with an introductory essay. New York 1962.
Two unpublished letters to Edward Clayton. Ed S. M. B. Coulling, HLQ 27 1963.
Three Ruskin letters [to E. L. Tarbuck]. Ed R. E. T. Williams, N & Q 208, 1963.
Letters of Ruskin to Lord and Lady Mount-Temple. Ed J. L. Bradley, Columbus OH 1964.
Godfather to Venice. TLS 28 Jan 1965. Letters to Mr and Mrs A. W. Hunt 1864–73.
Dougherty, C. T. Ruskin and Manning. Manuscripta 10 1966.
The Froude-Ruskin friendship. Ed H. G. Viljoen, New York 1966.
Spence, M. E. Dearest Mama Talbot. 1966. Letters to Mrs Talbot 1874–89.
Two secretaries: letters of Ruskin to C. A. Howell and R. St J. Tyrwhitt. Ed J. W. Claiborne, Unpbd thesis, Univ of Texas at Austin 1969.
The Winnington letters. Ed V. A. Burd, Cambridge MA 1969.
The Brantwood diary. Ed H. G. Viljoen, New Haven CT 1971.
Ruskin and the Brownings: 25 unpublished letters. Ed D. J. DeLaura, BJRL 54 1971.
Four letters to two young ladies [Mary Sophia and Sarah Emily Crosfield]. Bembridge 1972.
Kimball, J. C. A Ruskin letter to Mrs Browning. Browning Newsletter 8 1972.
Landow, G. P. Another Ruskin letter [to J. I. Smith]. N & Q 217 1972.
Landow, G. P. Ruskin and W. J. Linton: a new letter. ELN 10 1972.
Mahl, M. R. A letter from Ruskin to Jean Ingelow. N & Q 217 1972.
Maidment, B. E. A new Ruskin letter. N & Q 217 1972.
Ruskin in Italy: letters to his parents 1845. Ed H. I. Shapiro, Oxford 1972.
Sublime and instructive: letters to Louisa, Marchioness of Waterford, Anna Blunden and Ellen Heaton. Ed V. Surtees 1972.
Claiborne, J. W. Ruskin and C. A. Howell: some new letters. TSLL 15 1973.
Landow, G. P. I heard of a delightful ghost: a new Ruskin letter. PQ 52 1973.
The Ruskin family letters. Ed V. A. Burd 3 vols Ithaca NY 1973.
Shapiro, H. L. Another Ruskin letter. N & Q 218 1973.
Burd, V. A. A week at Winnington: two new letters of 1864. ELN 12 1974.
Hayman, J. Ruskin and his Oxford tutor: an unpublished letter from Venice. RES 27 1976.
Landow, G. P. Your good influence on me: the correspondence of John Ruskin and William Holman Hunt. BJRL 59 1976.
Clegg, J. Ruskin's correspondence with Angelo Alessandri. BJRL 60 1977.
Hayman, J. John Ruskin's unpublished letters to his Oxford tutors on theology. Études Anglaises 30 1977.
Ruskin's letters from Venice, 1851–2. Ed J. L. Bradley, Westport CT 1978.
Spear, J. L. Ruskin on his marriage: the Acland letter. TLS 10 Feb 1978.
Reflections of a friendship: Ruskin's letters to Pauline Trevelyan 1848–66. Ed V. Surtees 1979.
Maidment, B. E. The stones of Gt Russell Street: some unpublished Ruskin letters. Ruskin Newsletter 25 1981.
The correspondence of Thomas Carlyle and John Ruskin. Ed G. A. Cate, Stanford CA 1982.
John Ruskin: letters from the Continent 1858. Ed J. Hayman, Toronto 1982.
My darling Charles: selections from the Ruskin–Norton correspondence. Ed J. L. Spear, in The Ruskin polygon, ed J. D. Hunt and F. M. Holland, Manchester 1982.
Ruskin and Alfred Hunt: new letters and the record of a friendship. Ed R. Secor, Victoria BC 1982.
Miles, F. Two unpublished Ruskin letters. Jnl Pre-Raphaelite Stud 3 1983.
Dearden, J. S. John Ruskin and Bernard Quaritch. BLR 11 1984.
My dearest Dora: letters to Dora Livesey, her family and friends 1860–1900. Windermere 1984.
Levinger, M. No old man's sorrow: a new Ruskin letter. Burlington Mag 960 1986.
Peattie, R. W. Ruskin's August 1870 letter to D. G. Rossetti. N & Q 231 1986.
The correspondence of Ruskin and Charles Eliot Norton. Ed J. L. Bradley and I. Ousby, Cambridge 1987.
Christmas story: Ruskin's Venetian letters of 1876–77. Ed V. A. Burd 1990.
Dwyer, W. Ruskin to the elusive Horn: an unpublished letter. Victorian Newsletter no 78 1990.
A tour to the Lakes in Cumberland: Ruskin's diary for 1830. Ed J. S. Dearden and V. A. Burd, Aldershot 1990.
Ruskin's letters in the Mikimoto collection. Ed M. Sumiya, Tokyo 1994.

Ruskin periodicals

The Ruskin Reading Guild Journal. Arbroath Jan–Dec 1889. Monthly; originally, from Nov 1887 to Dec 1888, circulated in ms form, ed W. Marwick.
[Continued as] Igdrasil: journal of the Ruskin reading guild – a magazine of literature, art and social philosophy. Vol 1 Orpington Jan–Sep 1890, vol 2 Orpington Oct–Dec 1890, vol 3 Edinburgh June 1891–Mar 1892. Monthly, ed W. Marwick and K. Parkes.
[Continued as] World-Literature; the journal of the reading guild and kindred societies, and supplement to Igdrasil. Vol 1 15

Sep–Mar 1892, vol 2 Edinburgh May–Sep 1892. Monthly, ed W. Marwick.

Saint George: the journal of the Ruskin Society of Birmingham (the Society of the Rose). Vols 1–13 Birmingham Mar 1898–May 1911. Quarterly, ed J. H. Whitehouse et al.

The Ruskin Union Journal. No 1 Mar 1900. No other no issued; Saint George became thenceforth the organ of the Ruskin Union as well.

The Ruskin Gazette: the journal of the Ruskin Society of London. Vol 1– Oxford 1987– (continuing).

Time and Tide. Vol 1 1996. Annual, ed M. Wheeler.

§2

Criticism to 1920

The following list does not include review articles; certain selected reviews have been noticed after the individual titles with which they deal. For notices and discussion of the contemporary reception of Ruskin, see also:

Wise, T. J. and J. P. Smart. Pt 3: Ruskiniana. In their Complete bibliography of the writings in prose and verse of Ruskin, 1889–93, 2 vols 1964.

The works of Ruskin (library edn). Ed E. T. Cook and A. D. O. Wedderburn 1902–12. Notices in the introds, and bibliographical notes to his individual works, and especially in vol 38, bibliography.

Jump, J. D. Ruskin's reputation in the eighteen-fifties: the evidence of the three principal weeklies. PMLA 63 1948.

Townsend, F. G. The American estimate of Ruskin 1847–60. PQ 32 1953.

Halladay, J. Ruskin's reputation as seen in various British literary periodicals 1837–55. Unpbd doctoral diss, Univ of Kentucky 1963.

Autret, J. Ruskin and the French before Marcel Proust. Geneva 1965.

Stein, R. B. Ruskin and aesthetic thought in America 1840–1900. Cambridge MA 1967.

Kacher, R. E. Ruskin and the reviewers: studies in the social and economic criticism 1857–1866. Unpbd doctoral diss, Univ of Maryland 1974.

Ali, K. I. Some notes on the bibliography of John Ruskin. PBSA 73 1979.

Maidment, B. E. Ruskin and Punch 1870–1900. Victorian Periodicals Rev 12 1979.

Ruskin: the critical heritage. Ed J. L. Bradley 1984.

Cate, G. A. Ruskin: a reference guide. Boston 1988.

[Smith, W. H.] Mr Ruskin's works. Blackwood's Mag 70, Sep 1851.

[Patmore, C.] Sources of expression in architecture. Edinburgh Rev 94, Oct 1851.

[Bayne, P.] John Ruskin. Eclectic Mag 31 1854.

Leslie, C. R. A. A handbook for young painters. 1855.

Mitford, M. R. Recollections of a literary life. Vol 3, 1855.

[Oliphant, M. O.] Modern light literature: art. Blackwood's Mag 78, Dec 1855.

B., A. Notes on some of the critics of Ruskin. 1856.

Gaskell, E. C. In her Life of Charlotte Brontë, 2 vols 1857.

Gladstone, W. E. In his Studies on Homer and the Homeric age vol 3, Oxford 1858.

[Bayne, P.] Essays, biographical, critical and miscellaneous. Edinburgh 1859.

Brown, J. In his Horae Subsecivae: a second series, Edinburgh 1861.

Hamerton, P. G. A painter's camp and thoughts on art. 2 vols 1862.

[Lancaster, H. H.] The writings of Mr Ruskin. North Br Rev 36 1862; rptd in his Essays and reviews, 1876.

Patterson, R. H. Essays in history and art. Edinburgh 1862.

Ruskin's literary spirit. Boston Rev 2 1862.

Ruskin as a religious writer. Christian Observer 62 1862.

Thornbury, G. W. The life of J. M. W. Turner. 2 vols 1862.

Marsh, G. P. Lectures on the English language. New York 1863 (4th edn).

Milsand, J. L'ésthétique anglaise. Paris 1864, Lausanne 1906.

Arnold, M. In his Essays in criticism, 1865.

Japp, A. H. In his Three great teachers of our own time, 1865.

Noel, R. On the use of metaphor and 'pathetic fallacy' in poetry. Fortnightly Rev 1 Aug 1866; rptd in his Essays on poetry and poets, 1886.

Rossetti, W. M. Fine art, chiefly contemporary. 1867.

Hamerton, P. G. Etching and etchers. 1868.

Cook, D. Art in England. 1869.

Green, B. H. Mr Ruskin: his opinions and comparisons of painters – a few remarks dedicated to the shades of Raphael, Correggio and Murillo. 1869.

Rossetti, W. M. Ruskin as a writer on art. Broadway 2 1869.

Friswell, J. H. Modern men of letters honestly criticised. 1870.

Bedford, H. Mr Ruskin as an art-critic. Month July–Aug 1871.

Eastlake, C. L. A history of the Gothic revival. 1872.

McCarthy, J. In his Modern leaders, New York 1872.

Mitford, M. R. Letters. Ed H. F. Chorley 2 vols 1872.

Taine, H. In his Notes sur l'Angleterre, Paris 1872; tr 1872.

Kidd, G. B. Mr Ruskin and political economy. Derby 1873.

Jarves, J. J. Ruskin the art-seer. Art Jnl 13, Jan 1874.

Stephen, L. Mr Ruskin's recent writings. Fraser's Mag 89, June 1874.

Saintsbury, G. In his Modern English prose, Fortnightly Rev Feb 1876.

Mallock, W. H. The new Republic. 1877. Ruskin as Mr Herbert.

Whistler v. Ruskin. The Times 26 Nov 1878.

Whistler, J. A. Mc'N. Whistler v. Ruskin: art and art critics. 1878; rptd in his Gentle art of making enemies, 1890.

[Bayne, P.] Lessons from my masters, Carlyle, Tennyson and Ruskin. 1879.

Mr Ruskin's society. Spectator 15, 22 Mar 1879.

Poynter, E. J. In his Lectures on art, 1879.

Walker, R. B. John Ruskin. Manchester 1879.

Nisbet, H. The practical in painting. Edinburgh 1880.

Smart, W. Ruskin: his life and work. Manchester 1880.

Watt, P. B. The educational value of art. Glasgow 1880.

Watt, P. B. The progress of taste. Quart Rev 149 1880.

Cooke, B. John Ruskin. Birkenhead 1881.

Baillie, E. J. Ruskin: aspects of his thought and teaching. 1882.

[Cassels, W.] Wealth: definitions by Ruskin and Mill compared. Glasgow 1882.

Hamilton, W. The aesthetic movement in England. 1882.

Watt, F. Mr Ruskin and political economy. St James's Mag 42 1882.

Froude, J. A. (ed). Letters and memorials of Jane Welsh Carlyle. 1883.

Geddes, P. The Round Table series iii: Ruskin, economist. Edinburgh 1883.

'Lee, Vernon' (Violet Paget). Belcaro. [1883.]

Mather, J. M. Life and teaching of Ruskin. Manchester 1883.

Smart, W. A disciple of Plato: a critical study of Ruskin. Manchester 1883.

Ruskin as a teacher. Catholic World Aug 1884.

[Cassels, W.] The social problem. Glasgow 1885. Anon.

Froude, J. A. Thomas Carlyle: a history of his life in London. 1885.

Hamerton, P. G. Landscape. 1885.

Wilson, D. M. Ruskin, economist. Unitarian Rev (Boston) 23 1885.

Cooke, G. W. Ruskin. In his Poets and problems, Boston 1886.

Holman Hunt, W. The Pre-Raphaelite Brotherhood: a fight for art. Contemporary Rev 49 1886.

Holmes, J. Two papers on Ruskin. Sheffield 1886.

Royce, G. M. Ruskin v. Gibbon and Grote. New Englander 43 1886.

Martin, W. Aspects of nature in relation to individual and national life. Glasgow 1887.

Van Dyke, J. C. Principles of art. New York 1887.

Hubert, P. G. Mr Ruskin's Guild of St George. Lippincott's Mag 41, June 1888.
Mr Ruskin and the Edinburgh Review. Spectator 28 Jan 1888.
Moreton, W. T. The religious teachings of Ruskin. Christian World Pulpit 18, 25 Apr, 2 May 1888.
Stillman, W. J. John Ruskin. Century Mag 35 1888; rptd in his Old Rome and the new, 1897.
Stimson, F. J. Ruskin as a political economist. Quart Jnl of Economics 2 1888.
The works of Mr Ruskin. Edinburgh Rev 147 1888.
Clayden, P. W. Samuel Rogers and his contemporaries. 1889.
Collingwood, W. G. Ruskin: a biographical outline. 1889.
Dyer, H. The foundation of social politics. Glasgow 1889.
Cook, E. T. Studies in Ruskin. Orpington 1890.
Downes, R. P. Ruskin: a study. 1890.
Foster, J. Four great teachers: Ruskin, Carlyle, Emerson and Browning. 1890.
Collingwood, W. The art teaching of Ruskin. 1891.
Robertson, J. M. In his Modern humanists, 1891.
Rose, H. The new political economy: the social teaching of Carlyle, Ruskin and George. 1891.
Symonds, J. A. A morning at San Rocco. Nat Observer 1 Aug 1891.
Bosanquet, B. In his History of aesthetic, 1892.
Gibbins, H. de B. English social reformers. 1892.
Morris, W. Preface to Ruskin's The nature of Gothic (Kelmscott edn) 1892.
Oliphant, M. O. and F. R. In their Victorian age of English literature, 1892.
Sharp, W. Life and letters of Joseph Severn. 1892.
Waldstein, C. The work of Ruskin. New York 1893, London 1894.
Cook, E. T. Mr Ruskin in relation to modern problems. Nat Rev 23 1894.
de Reul, P. L'ésthéthique en Angleterre. Brussels 1894.
Marks, H. S. Pen and pencil sketches. 2 vols 1894.
Ruskin: a study in development. London Quart Rev 81 1894.
Harrison, F. Ruskin as master of prose. 1895; rptd in his Tennyson, Ruskin, Mill and other literary estimates, 1900.
Rossetti, W. M. Dante Gabriel Rossetti. 2 vols 1895.
Saintsbury, G. In his Corrected impressions, 1895.
Smith, C. E. Journals and correspondence of Lady Eastlake. 2 vols 1895.
Middlemiss, J. T. A modern prophet and his message. 1896.
Browning, E. B. Letters. Ed F. G. Kenyon 2 vols 1897.
de la Sizeranne, R. Ruskin et la religion de la beauté. Paris 1897; tr Vera Monckton Milnes, Countess Galway, Orpington 1899 (with 2 appendices by G. Allen).
Fowler, J. H. In his Nineteenth-century prose, Edinburgh 1897.
Muir, R. J. Ruskin revisited, and other papers on education. Edinburgh 1897.
Sulman, T. A memorable art class. Good Words Aug 1897.
Bruce, J. M. Ruskin as an Oxford lecturer. Century Mag 33, Feb 1898.
Fechheimer, S. S. Ueber die Bedeutung Ruskins für das Leben und die Erziehung in England. Jena 1898.
Hobson, J. A. Ruskin, social reformer. 1898.
Muller, F. M. Auld Lang Syne. 2 vols 1898.
Signac, P. L'éducation de l'oeil. Revue Blanche 1 July 1898.
Spurgeon, C. H. In his Autobiography, 3 vols 1898.
Marius, G. H. Een inleiding tot zijn werken. The Hague 1899.
Millais, J. G. The life of Sir J. E. Millais. 2 vols 1899.
Rossetti, W. M. Ruskin, Rossetti and Pre-Raphaelitism. 1899.
Bardoux, J. Le mouvement idéaliste et social dans la littérature anglaise: Ruskin. [Paris 1900.]
Bookman. Ruskin memorial number. Mar 1900.
Champneys, B. In his Memoirs and correspondence of Coventry Patmore, 2 vols 1900.
Cook, E. T. Ruskin and modern business. Spectator 17 Feb 1900.
Cook, E. T. Ruskin as an artist and art critic. Studio Mar 1900.
Dodd, L. T. and J. A. Dale. The Ruskin Hall movement. Fortnightly Rev Feb 1900.
Geddes, P. Ruskin as economist. International Monthly 1 Mar 1900.
Hocart, J. Ruskin: le prophète du Beau. Brussels 1900.
John Ruskin. Quart Rev 191 1900.
Meynell, A. John Ruskin. Edinburgh 1900.
Morton, E. P. Ruskin's pathetic fallacy and Keats's treatment of nature. Poet Lore 12 1900.
Pengelly, R. E. Ruskin; A biographical sketch. 1900.
Proust, M. Ruskin à Notre-Dame d'Amiens. Mercure de France Apr 1900.
Proust, M. Sur Ruskin. Gazette des Beaux-Arts Apr, Aug 1900.
Rossetti, W. M. Pre-Raphaelite diaries and letters. 1900.
Ruskin Exhibition, Coniston. Catalogue. Ed W. G. Collingwood, Ulverston 1900, 1906 (rev).
Scalinger, G. M. L'estetica di Ruskin. Naples 1900.
Stephen, L. John Ruskin. Nat Rev Apr 1900.
Ward, M. A. Prophets of the nineteenth century: Carlyle, Ruskin, Tolstoi. 1900.
Brunhes, H. J. Ruskin et la Bible. Paris 1901.
Shaw, W. H. Ruskin: ethical and religious teacher. Oxford 1901.
Stillman, W. J. In his Autobiography of a journalist, 2 vols 1901.
Broicher, C. Ruskin und sein Werk. 3 vols Leipzig 1902–8.
Harrison, F. John Ruskin. 1902 (EML).
Hobson, J. A. Ruskin and democracy. Contemporary Rev 81, Jan 1902.
Sänger, S. Ruskin: sein Leben und Lebenswerk. Strasburg 1902.
Gladden, W. Witnesses of the light. 1903.
McCarthy, J. In his Portraits of the sixties, 1903.
Pollock, M. Light and water. 1903.
Rossetti, W. M. Rossetti papers. 1903.
Von Bunsen, M. Ruskin: sein Leben und seine Werke. Leipzig 1903.
Farrar, F. W. Ruskin as a religious teacher. 1904.
Kitchin, G. W. Ruskin in Oxford, and other studies. 1904.
Proust, M. [Translator's preface to] La Bible d'Amiens. Paris 1904; tr J. Autret, W. Burford and P. Wolfe in On reading Ruskin, 1987.
Sieper, E. Das Evangelium der Schönheit in der englischen Literatur und Kunst des xix Jahrhunderts. Dortmund [1904].
Hunt, H. Pre-Raphaelitism and the Pre-Raphaelite Brotherhood. 2 vols 1905.
Powell, F. Y. Ruskin and thoughts on democracy. 1905.
Vitali, G. Le idee fondamentali di Ruskin. Rivista d'Italia Dec 1905.
Cherfils, C. Canon de Turner: essai de synthèse critique des théories picturales de Ruskin. Paris 1906.
Clayden, P. W. John Ruskin. Temple Bar n.s. 6 1906.
de la Sizeranne, R. Ruskin at Venice. A lecture at the Ruskin commemoration, Venice. Tr Mrs F. Harrison 1906.
Proust, M. [Translator's preface to] Sésame et les lys. Paris 1906; tr J. Autret, W. Burford and P. Wolfe in On reading Ruskin, 1987.
Zorzi, A. Ruskin in Venice. Cornhill Mag Aug–Sep 1906.
Herford, C. H. Ruskin and the Gothic revival. Quart Rev 207 1907.
Stephen, L. In his Studies of a biographer, 1907.
Hall Caine, T. H. In his My story, 1908.
Ruskin Double Number. Bookman (London) Oct 1908.
Rainero, C. Il pensiero di Ruskin e sua influenza sui contemporanei. Turin 1909.
Catalogue of Ruskin Exhibition in memory of Charles Eliot Norton. Boston 1909.
Chevrillon, A. La pensée de Ruskin. Paris 1909.
Earland, A. Ruskin and his circle. 1910.
Durrant, W. S. From art to social reform: Ruskin's nature of Gothic. Nineteenth Cent May 1910.
Guillon, C. Le christianisme de Ruskin. Cahors 1910.
Benson, A. C. Ruskin: a study in personality. 1911.
Scott, W. T. Chesterton and other essays. Cincinnati 1912

Vetter, T. Ruskin und William Morris: Feinde und Förderer der Technik. Zurich 1912.
Danel, J. Les idées sociales de Ruskin. Paris 1913.
Gale, C. F. At Canterbury and Amiens with John Ruskin. Cornhill Mag Feb 1913.
Maurice, F. D. In his Life of Octavia Hill, 1913.
Mitford, M. R. Correspondence with C. Boner and Ruskin. Ed E. Lee 1914.
Moreley, E. J. Ruskin and social ethics. 1917 (Fabian Soc).
Devereux, A. F. X. John Ruskin: economist. Catholic World 108 1919.
Mumm, A. L. Ruskin and the Alps. Alpine Jnl 32 1919.
Proust, M. In his Pastiches et mélanges. Paris 1919; tr Gerard Hopkins as Marcel Proust: a selection from his miscellaneous writings, 1948.
Whitehouse, J. H. (ed). Ruskin centenary addresses. 1919.
Graham, J. W. The harvest of Ruskin. 1920.
Masefield, J. John Ruskin. Bembridge 1920.
Whitehouse, J. H. Ruskin the prophet. 1920.

Biographies

Collingwood, W. G. The life and work of John Ruskin. 2 vols 1893. With biographical addns in 1 vol, as The life of Ruskin, 1900.
Cook, E. T. The life of John Ruskin. 2 vols 1911.
Wilenski, R. H. John Ruskin: an introduction to further study of his life and work. 1933.
Leon, D. John Ruskin: the great Victorian. 1949.
Quennell, P. John Ruskin: the portrait of a prophet. 1949.
Evans, J. John Ruskin. 1954.
Hunt, J. D. The wider sea: a life of John Ruskin. 1982.
Kemp, W. John Ruskin: Leben und Werk, 1819–1900. Munich 1983; tr 1990 as The desire of mine eyes: the life and work of John Ruskin.
Hilton, T. John Ruskin: the early years, 1819–1900. New Haven CT 1985, London 1985.

Reminiscences

Cowper-Temple, G. (Lady Mount-Temple). Memorials. 1890 (priv ptd).
Ritchie, A. T. Records of Tennyson, Ruskin, Browning. 1892.
Spielman, M. H. John Ruskin: a sketch of his life, his work and his opinions with personal reminiscences. 1900.
Tuckwell, W. Reminiscences of Oxford. 1900.
Rawnsley, H. D. Ruskin and the English lakes. Glasgow 1902.
Atlay, J. B. Henry Wentworth Acland: a memoir. 1903.
Collingwood, W. G. Ruskin relics. 1903.
Burne-Jones, G. Memorials of Edward Burne-Jones. 2 vols 1904.
Emslie, J. P. Recollections of Ruskin. Working Men's College Jnl 10 1908.
Cook, E. T. Homes and haunts of Ruskin. 1912.
[Burdon, J.] Reminiscences of Ruskin by a St George's Companion. 1919.
MacDonald, G. Reminiscences of a specialist. 1932.
Cockerell, S. C. Friends of a lifetime. Ed V. Meynell 1940.
The professor: Arthur Severn's memoir of John Ruskin. Ed J. S. Dearden 1967.

Textual and bibliographical criticism

Is it true that Mr Ruskin's books are 'scarce, dear and difficult to obtain'? [Manchester 1880].
The American trade in 'Ruskins': an interview at Mr Wiley's. New York Pall Mall Gazette 21 Dec 1887.
Schooling, J. H. The handwriting of Ruskin 1828–84. Strand Mag Dec 1895.
Cook, E. T. Ruskin and his books: an interview with his publisher. Strand Mag Dec 1902.
Cook, E. T. Book wars! Ruskin as the father of the Net system. Book Monthly May 1907.
Roche, A. J. Proust as translator of Ruskin. PMLA 45 1930.
Keefe, H. J. A. A century in print: the story of Hazell's. 1939.
Burd, V. A. Another light on the writing of Modern painters. PMLA 68 1953.
Mumby, F. A. and F. H. S. Stallybrass. From Swan Sonnenschein to George Allen & Unwin Ltd. 1955.
Brown, S. E. The published passages in the manuscript of Ruskin's autobiography. Victorian Newsletter no 16 1959.
Burd, V. A. Background to Modern painters. PMLA 74 1959.
Brown, T. J. English literary autographs 38: John Ruskin. BC 10 1961.
Stein, R. B. Appendix on the American publication of Ruskin. In his John Ruskin and aesthetic thought in America 1840–1900, Cambridge MA 1967.
Dearden, J. S. The production and distribution of Ruskin's Poems, 1850. BC 17 1968.
Landow, G. P. Ruskin's revisions of the third edition of Modern painters vol 3. Victorian Newsletter no 33 1968.
Dearden, J. S. Edward Burne-Jones: designer to John Ruskin. Connoisseur 170 1969.
Dearden, J. S. Ruskin's typography. In his Facets of Ruskin, 1970.
Maidment, B. E. Only print: Ruskin and the publishers. Durham Univ Jnl 63 1971.
Maidment, B. E. Author and publisher: Ruskin and George Allen 1890–1900. Business Archives no 36, June 1972.
Maidment, B. E. Ruskin and George Allen. Unpbd PhD thesis, Leicester Univ 1973.
Maidment, B. E. Ruskin, George Allen, and American printed books. Publishing History 9 1981.
Dearden, J. S. King of the golden river; a bio-bibliographical study. In Studies in Ruskin, ed R. Rhodes and D. I. Janik, Athens OH 1982.
Spear, J. L. and J. D. Hunt. An unused preface by Ruskin for St Mark's rest. Princeton Univ Lib Chron 44 1983.
Beatty, M. Ruskin and the context of Modern painters. Eng Stud in Africa 27 1984.
Dearden, J. S. Nineteenth-century galley proofs. Library 6th ser 7 1985.
Dearden, J. S. Ruskin's Salsette and Elephanta. BC 34 1985.
Rahn, S. The sources of Ruskin's King of the golden river. Victorian Newsletter no 68 1985.
Finley, C. S. The structure of Ruskin's Fors clavigera. Prose Stud 9 1986.
Glynn, J. Prince of publishers: a biography of George Smith. 1986.
Harrod, T. John Ruskin and the Arundel Society. Apollo 127 1988.
Dearden, J. S. Ruskin's Poems, 1850. BC 38 1989.
Garrigan, K. O. Bearding the competition: Ruskin's Academy notes. Victorian Periodicals Rev 22 1989.
Hayman, J. Ruskin's Hortus inclusus: the ms sources and publication history. HLQ 52 1989.
Richards, B. The authorship of Something on Ruskinism. Ruskin Gazette 1 1990.
Davis, A. Job's iron pen: Ruskin's use of engraved illustration in Modern painters. Time and Tide 1 1996. [DJB]

William Bell Scott 1811–90

See col 669.

John Campbell Shairp 1918–85

§1

Charles the twelfth: a prize poem recited in the Theatre, Oxford. Oxford 1842.
Kilmahoe: a highland pastoral, with other poems. 1864.
John Keble: an essay. Edinburgh 1866.
Studies in poetry and philosophy. Edinburgh 1868, 1886 (with preface by G. D. Boyle). Wordsworth, Coleridge, Keble, The moral dynamic.

A. H. Clough: a sketch. Included in the anon memoir prefixed to Poems and prose remains of A. H. Clough, 2 vols 1869.
Culture and religion. 1870.
The life and letters of J. D. Forbes. 1873. With P. G. Tait and A. A. Reilly.
Recollections of a tour made in Scotland, 1803, by Dorothy Wordsworth. 1874. Ed Shairp.
On poetic interpretation of nature. Edinburgh 1877.
Robert Burns. 1879 (EML).
Aspects of poetry: being lectures delivered at Oxford. Oxford 1881. Virgil, Burns, Shelley, Ossian, Duncan MacIntyre, Wordsworth, Scott, Carlyle, Newman, and Five essays on poetry.
Sketches in history and poetry: collected and edited by Professor Veitch. Edinburgh 1887. Henry Vaughan, The Ettrick shepherd, Early poetry of Scotland, Songs of Scotland before Burns, Queen Margaret of Scotland etc.
Glen Desseray, and other poems. Ed F. T. Palgrave 1888.
Shairp also pbd The wants of Scottish universities and some of the remedies, *Edinburgh 1856, and an* Address on missions, *Edinburgh 1874. For his reviews, see* Wellesley *vol 5.*

§2
Rodger, M. Shairp: an address. Edinburgh 1885.
Knight, W. A. Shairp and his friends. 1888.
Sellar, W. Y. Portraits of friends. Boston 1889.

Emily Anne Eliza Shirreff 1814–97

Ms material by Shirreff is held in Cambridge Univ Lib, the George Baily Lib of the Univ of Vermont, LSE, and the archives of the Girls' Public Day School Trust, the Maria Grey Training College, and the North London Collegiate School.

Collection
Essays and lectures on the kindergarten . . . with an appendix by E. P. Peabody. New York 1883.

§1
Intellectual education, and its influence on the character and happiness of women. 1858 (micros Woodbridge CT 1975 and Cambridge MA [19–?]; new edn 1862; abridged edn Chicago [19–?]; tr Du 1864.
The chivalry of the South. 1864 (Ladies London Emancipation Soc Tract no 6, micro Sanford NC 1980).
A few more words on the chivalry of the South. 1864 (Ladies London Emancipation Soc Tract no 11, micro Sanford NC 1980).
The work of the National Union. 1872, 1873 (2nd edn).
Why should we learn? Short lectures addressed to schools. 1872.
The enjoyment of life: a lecture by E. A. E. Shirreff. 1875.
Kindergarten: principles of Froebel's system and their bearing on the education of women, also remarks on the higher education of women. 1876, 1880 (2nd edn), rptd London and Syracuse 1889; 1882 (3rd edn), 1897 (6th edn).
The claim of Froebel's system to be called the new education. 1877, New York 1877 (micro Ann Arbor MI [1983]).
The kindergarten in relation to schools: paper read before the Society of Arts, December 12th, 1877. Reading 1877.
A sketch of the life of Friedrich Fröbel: together with a notice of Madame von Marenholtz-Bülow's 'Personal recollections of Friedrich Fröbel'. 1877, Boston and New York 1877, micro Ann Arbor MI 1993. Amer edn pbd with Bertha von Marenholtz-Bülow's Reminiscences of Friedrich Fröbel, and rptd many times until 1905, with micros of reprints of 1889 (Chicago 1986) and 1897 (Woodbridge CT 1988). Also pbd 1887 (micro Ann Arbor MI [198?]), with title A short sketch of the life of Friedrich Froebel: new edn including Froebel's letters from Dresden and Leipzig to his wife, now first translated into English.
The kinder-garten in relation to family life. [1878], New York 1883.
On the connection between the kindergarten and the school: a lecture on Mdme Portugall's synoptical table. 1880. Froebel Soc's Kindergarten Tract no 1.
Wasted forces. 1880. Froebel Soc's Kindergarten Tract no 5.
Home education in relation to the kindergarten: two lectures. 1884 (micro Ann Arbor MI 1968).
The kindergarten at home. 1884 (Hughes's Teachers' Lib). [1889] (2nd edn) (rev and illus), [1895] (4th edn), [1903] (6th edn).
Kindergarten teachers and their qualification: the annual address delivered before the Froebel Society. 1885. 1885.
Moral training: Froebel and Herbert Spencer. 1892, New York 1892.

Contributions to periodicals
See Wellesley *vol 5 1989.*

Collaborative works (with her sister Maria Grey)
Letters from Spain and Barbary. 1835.
Thoughts on self-culture, addressed to women. 1850 (micro New Haven CT 1975), Boston 1851 (micro Glen Rock NJ 1976), 1854 (2nd edn).
Passion and principle: a novel. 1853; 1854 (new edn) (Routledge's Railway Lib).

§2
The Times 24 Mar 1897. Obituary.
Grey, Maria Georgina. Memorials of Emily Anne Eliza Shirreff. 1897 (priv ptd).
Lee, Elizabeth. In DNB.
Ellsworth, E. W. Liberators of the female mind: the Shirreff sisters, educational reform, and the women's movement. 1979. [JW]

James Smetham 1821–89

See col 670.

Goldwin Smith 1823–1910

See col 2450.

William Spalding 1809–59

§1
A letter on Shakespeare's authorship of the two noble kinsmen: a drama. 1833, 1876 (New Shakespeare Soc) (with life of Spalding by J. H. Burton).
Italy and the Italian islands from the earliest ages to the present time. 3 vols Edinburgh 1841, New York 1843.
The history of English literature with an outline of the origin and growth of the English language. Edinburgh 1853, London 1870 (11th edn, continued to 1870), Edinburgh 1877 (continued to 1876); tr Ger 1854.
The British Empire. Glasgow 1856. With 19 other contributors Spalding assisted in compiling an encyclopaedic vol on the British Empire. He wrote a large number of memoirs for the biographical section and helped to prepare the historical section.
An introduction to logical science. Edinburgh 1857. Rptd from Encyclopaedia Britannica (8th edn).

§2
Gilfillan, G. In his Galleries of literary portraits vol 2, Edinburgh 1857.
Scotsman 19 Nov 1859. Obituary.

James Spedding 1808–81

Evenings with a reviewer, or a free and particular examination of Mr Macaulay's article on Lord Bacon, in a series of dialogues. 2

vols 1848 (priv ptd), 1881 (with prefatory notice by G. S. Venables).
Companion to the railway edition of Lord Campbell's Life of Bacon, by a railway reader. 1853. Rptd from Examiner.
The works of Francis Bacon. Ed Spedding, R. L. Ellis and D. D. Heath 7 vols 1857–9.
The letters and the life of Francis Bacon, set forth in chronological order, with a commentary. 7 vols 1861–72.
Publishers and authors. 1867.
A conference of pleasure, composed about 1592 by Francis Bacon. 1870. Ed Spedding.
An account of the life and times of Francis Bacon. 2 vols Boston 1878. An abridged version of the American edn of the Works of Bacon in 15 vols. Consists mainly of Spedding's original commentary and constitutes a complete short biography of Bacon.
Reviews and discussions, literary, political and historical, not relating to Bacon. 1879. Dickens, Tennyson, English hexameters, Twelfth Night etc.
Studies in English history by James Gairdner and James Spedding. Edinburgh 1881. Contains 2 historical essays by Spedding.
Charles Tennyson, afterwards Turner. In Turner's Collected sonnets, old and new, 1898.
For Spedding's reviews, see Wellesley *vol* 5.

Sir James Fitzjames Stephen 1829–94

Bibliographies

Stephen, L. The life of Sir James Fitzjames Stephen. 1895. *See* pp. 483–6.
Radzinowicz, L. Sir James Fitzjames Stephen and his contributions to criminal law. 1957. *See* pp. 49–66.

§1

The relation of novels to life. In Cambridge essays, 1855.
The characteristics of English criminal law. In Cambridge essays, 1857.
Essays by a barrister. 1862. Anon. 33 articles rptd from the Saturday Rev.
Defence of the Rev Rowland Williams. 1862.
A general view of the criminal law of England. 1863, 1890 (2nd edn); tr Rus 1865.
The definition of murder considered in relation to the report of the capital punishment commissioners. 1866. Rptd from Fraser's Mag Feb 1866.
The Indian Evidence Act of 1872. 1872, Calcutta 1904 (as Introduction to the Indian Evidence Act).
Liberty, equality, fraternity. 1873, New York 1873, London 1874 (2nd edn).
REVIEWS: Athenaeum 17 May 1873; Spectator 7, 14 June 1873.
A digest of the law of evidence. 1876, 1876, St Louis 1876, London 1877 (3rd edn); ed J. W. May, Boston 1877, 1886; St Louis 1879; ed W. Reynolds, Chicago 1879, 1888, 1896, 1905, London 1881 (4th edn); ed G. Chase, New York 1885, 1886, 1887, 1890, 1892, 1898, 1907, 1912; ed H. and H. L. Stephen 1899 (5th edn), 1904 (6th edn), 1914, 1922 (10th edn), 1925 (11th edn); ed G. E. Beers, Hartford CT 1901, 1902, 1903, 1904, 1907; ed G. S. Berry, Denver 1918; ed H. L. Stephen and L. F. Sturge 1936 (12th edn), 1946 (12th edn rev), 1948 (12th edn rev with addns); tr Rus 1912.
A digest of the criminal law (crimes and punishments). 1877, St Louis 1877, 1878, London 1879, 1883 (3rd edn), 1887 (4th edn); ed H. and H. L. Stephen 1894 (5th edn), 1904 (6th edn), 1926 (7th edn); ed L. F. Sturge 1947 (8th edn), 1950 (9th edn).
A digest of the law of criminal procedure in indictable offences. 1883. With H. Stephen.
A history of the criminal law of England. 3 vols 1883.
Letters on the Ilbert Bill: reprinted from The Times. 1883.
The story of Nuncomar and the impeachment of Sir Elijah Impey. 2 vols 1885.
The late Mr Carlyle's papers. 1886 (priv ptd). Defends Froude's conduct as Carlyle's literary executor.
Horae sabbaticae. 3 ser 1892. 55 articles rptd from Saturday Rev.
REVIEW: Athenaeum 6 Feb, 12 Nov 1892.
For Stephen's contributions to Contemporary Rev, Cornhill Mag, Edinburgh Rev, Macmillan's Mag, Fortnightly Rev, Fraser's Mag, Nat Rev (founded 1883), Nineteenth Cent, Nat Rev (founded 1855), *see* Wellesley *vol* 5; *for his contributions to* Law Mag and Rev, Law Quarterly Rev *and* Saturday Rev, *see Bibliographies, above.*

§2

Harrison, F. The religion of inhumanity. Fortnightly Rev June 1873.
Morley, J. Mr Mill's doctrine of liberty. Fortnightly Rev Aug 1873.
Stephen, L. The life of Sir James Fitzjames Stephen. 1895.
Pollock, F. Sir J. F. Stephen. Nat Rev Aug 1895.
[Roscoe, E. S.] Sir J. F. Stephen. Edinburgh Rev Oct 1895.
Smith, K. J. M. James Fitzjames Stephen: portrait of a Victorian rationalist. Cambridge 1988. [GW]

Frederic George Stephens 1828–1907

§1

William Holman Hunt and his works. 1860. Anon.
Normandy, its Gothic architecture and history: a sketch. 1865.
Flemish relics: architectural, legendary and pictorial. 1866.
English children as painted by Sir Joshua Reynolds: an essay on some of the characteristics of Reynolds as a painter. 1867.
Masterpieces of Mulready: memorials of William Mulready. 1867.
The early works of Sir Edwin Landseer: a brief sketch of the life of the artist. 1869 (anon), 1874 (as Memoirs of Landseer), 1880 (extended as Sir Edwin Landseer).
Catalogue of prints and drawings in the British Museum: division 1, political and personal satires prepared by F. G. Stephens, and containing many descriptions by E. Hawkins. 4 vols 1870–83. Vols 5–11 by M. D. George, 1954.
A history of Gibraltar and its sieges. 1870. Anon.
English artists of the present day: essays by J. B. Atkinson, Sidney Colvin, F. G. Stephens, T. Taylor and J. L. Tupper. 1872.
Flemish and French pictures, with notes concerning the painters and their works. 1875.
Notes on Thomas Bewick, illustrating a loan collection of his drawings and woodcuts. 1880.
Notes on a collection of drawings and woodcuts by Thomas Bewick exhibited at the Fine Art Society's rooms 1880; also a complete list of all works illustrated by T. and J. Bewick. 2 pts 1881.
Notes on a collection of drawings, paintings and etchings by Samuel Palmer; with an account of the Milton series of drawings by L. R. Valpy. 1881.
Artists at home: photographed by J. P. Mayall and reproduced in facsimile. Ed with biographical notices and descriptions by F. G. Stephens 6 pts 1884.
Catalogue of the works of Sir Joshua Reynolds exhibited at the Grosvenor Gallery 1883–4. 1884.
J. C. Hook. 1884, [1888].
Memorials of William Mulready. 1890.
A memoir of George Cruikshank by F. G. Stephens and an essay on the genius of George Cruikshank by W. M. Thackeray. 1891.
Dante Gabriel Rossetti. 1894, 1908.
Lawrence Alma Tadema RA: a sketch of his life and work. 1895.
Sir Frederic Leighton: an illustrated chronicle by E. Rhys, with prefatory essay by F. G. Stephens. 1895, 1898 (rev G. White as Frederic Lord Leighton).
Stephens also wrote Notes to the Grosvenor Gallery catalogues of works by Reynolds [1884] Gainsborough [1885], Millais [1886] and

Van Dyck [1887]. *He was art-critic to* Athenaeum *from 1861 to 1901, contributing to every issue but two in those 40 years. His articles on the private collections of England are important.*

§2

Rossetti, W. M. Obituary. Athenaeum 16 Mar 1907.
Stephens and the Pre-Raphaelite brothers; with reproduction of twenty-four pictures from his collection, and notes by J. B. Manson. [1920] (priv ptd).
Grylls, R. G. The correspondence of F. G. Stephens. TLS 5–12 Apr 1957.

James Hutchison Stirling 1820–1909

See col 2611.

Sir Henry Taylor 1800–86

See col 674.

Tom Taylor 1817–80

See col 2024.

William Thomas Thornton 1813–80

See col 2508.

Richard Chenevix Trench 1807–86

See col 687.

Robert Alfred Vaughan 1823–57

The witch of Endor and other poems. 1844.
Hours with the mystics: a contribution to the history of religious opinion. 2 vols 1856; ed R. Vaughan 2 vols 1860; ed W. Vaughan 2 vols [1880].
Essays and remains. Ed R. Vaughan 2 vols 1858 (with memoir). Largely rptd from Br Quart Rev; the elder Vaughan's memoir was enlarged and pbd separately, 1864.

Bartholomew Eliot George Warburton 1810–52

The crescent and the cross: or romance and realities of Eastern travel. 2 vols 1845.
Zoë: an episode of the Greek war. 1847.
Memoirs of Prince Rupert and the Cavaliers: including their private correspondence, now first published from the original manuscripts. 3 vols 1849; tr Fr 1851.
Reginald Hastings: or a tale of the troubles in 164–. 3 vols 1850.
Darien: or the merchant prince, a historical romance. 3 vols 1852.
Warburton also edited G. D. Warburton, Hochelaga, *1846, and R. F. Williams,* Memoirs of Horace Walpole and his contemporaries, *1851. For appreciations, see* The late Eliot Warburton, Dublin Univ Mag *Feb 1852, and* Works of Eliot Warburton, *Eng Rev 17 1852.*

Sir William Wilde 1815–76

The beauties of the Boyne and the Blackwater. Dublin 1849.
Catalogue of the contents of the museum of the Royal Irish Academy. 3 vols 1857–62.
Lough Corrib and Lough Mask. Dublin 1867, 1872, 1936 (rev C. O. Lochlainn), 1955.
The ancient races of Ireland. 1874; rptd in Lady Wilde, Ancient legends of Ireland vol 2, 1887.

Robert Eldridge Aris Willmott 1809–63

Lives of sacred poets. 2 ser 1834–8.
Conversations at Cambridge. 1836. Anon.
Letters of eminent persons, selected and illustrated. 1839.
Parlour table book: extracts from various authors. 1840.
Pictures of Christian life. 1841.
Poems. 1841, 1848 (rev and expanded).
Bishop Jeremy Taylor: his predecessors, contemporaries and successors. 1847, 1848 (rev).
A journal of summer time in the country. 1849, 1858, 1864 (4th edn, with memoir by C. Willmott), 1928 (with biographical note by E. P[artridge]).
Precious stones, aids to reflection, from prose writers of the sixteenth, seventeenth and eighteenth centuries. 1850.
Pleasures, objects and advantages of literature. 1851, 1852, 1856, 1860 (5th edn, enlarged); ed C. Metcalfe 1906.
The poets of the nineteenth century. 1857.
English sacred poetry. 1862, 1883. An anthology.
In addn to numerous sermons (of some literary distinction), Willmott also produced edns of Gray, Herbert, Akenside, Fairfax's Tasso, *Wordsworth, James Montgomery and other English poets, mainly in Routledge's British Poets ser.*

Christopher Wordsworth 1807–85

See col 697.

Dora Wordsworth, later Quillinan 1804–47

Most of Dora's extant letters are at the Wordsworth Lib, Grasmere, along with her autograph book and letters to her by Edward Quillinan. Letters to her also appear in The letters of William and Dorothy Wordsworth: the middle years; the later years; a supplement, *ed E. de Selincourt, M. Moorman, A. G. Hill, Oxford 1969–93.*

§1

Letters, journals, etc.

Journal of a few months' residence in Portugal, and glimpses of the south of Spain, by Mrs Quillinan. 2 vols 1847, ed Edmund Lee 1895 (2nd edn with memoir).
Collyer, R. The Wordsworths. N & Q ser 5, 21 Feb 1874. Prints letter by Dora Wordsworth.
Dora Wordsworth her book. Ed F. V. Morley 1924.
Letters of Dora Wordsworth. Ed H. P. Vincent, Chicago 1944.
The letters of Dora Wordsworth to Maria Kinnaird. Ed J. O. Hayden, TWC 15 1984. Texts of letters retained at the Univ of California at Davis.
Page, J. W. Wordsworth and the cultivation of women. 1994. Contains hitherto unpbd material. [DW]

iii. Late nineteenth-century prose 1870–1900

This section has been restricted to writers born after 1829 whose more important writings fall within the nineteenth century.

Edwin Abbott, Edwin Abbott Abbott, A. Square 1838–1926

Collected works

Diatessarica: a series dealing with the interpretation of the Gospels. 15 vols 1900–15.

§1

A second Latin book. 1858.
The church and the congregation. 1868.
A Shakespearian grammar. 1869, rev and enlarged 1870.
Bible lessons: part 1: Old Testament, part 2: New Testament. 1870.
The good voices: a child's guide to the Bible. 1872.
How to write clearly: rules and exercises on English composition. 1872.
On teaching the English language. 1872.
The proposed examination of first-grade schools by the universities. 1872.
Latin prose through English idiom. 1873.
Parables for children. 1873. Illus.
Cambridge sermons preached before the University. 1875.
How to parse. 1875.
How to tell the parts of speech. 1875 (2 edns).
Hand-book of arithmetic, and first steps in algebra. 1876 (7 edns).
Bacon and Essex: a sketch of Bacon's earlier life. 1877.
Through nature to Christ: or, the ascent of worship through illusion to the truth. 1877.
Philochristus: memoirs of a disciple of the Lord. 1878 (2 edns).
Handbook of English grammar. 1879 (3 edns).
Oxford sermons preached before the University. 1879.
Via Latina: a first Latin book. 1880.
On the teaching of Latin. 1881.
Onesimus: memoirs of a disciple of St Paul. 1882.
Hints on home teaching. 1883.
On the teaching of Latin verse composition. 1883.
Flatland: a romance of many dimensions. By A. Square. 1884 (novel, mathematics); (rev) 1884, Boston 1915, New York 1927, Boston 1928; (5th edn) introd by W. Garnett, Oxford 1944, 1950; (6th edn) introd by B. Hoffman, New York 1952; introd by W. Garnett 1963, Cutchogue NY 1976; notes by D. Davies, Pasadena CA 1978, San Francisco 1980; introd by K. Freiden, Verplanck NY 1982; introd by W. Garnett, foreword by Issac Asimov, New York 1983, 1984, 1987; introd by Thomas Banchoff, Princeton 1991; introd by Banesh Hoffman, New York 1992, 1994.
Francis Bacon: an account of his life and works. 1885.
The kernel and the husk: letters on spiritual Christianity. 1886.
The Latin gate: a first Latin translation book. 1889.
Philomythus: an antidote against credulity. A discussion of Cardinal Newman's essay on ecclesiastical miracles. 1891 (2 edns).
The Anglican career of Cardinal Newman. 2 vols 1892.
Dux Latinus: a first Latin construing book. 1893.
The spirit on the waters: the evolution of the divine from the human. 1897.
St Thomas of Canterbury: his death and miracles. 2 vols 1898, rptd New York 1980.
Contrast: or, a prophet and a forger. 1903.
Silanus the Christian. 1906.
Apologia: an explanation and defence. 1907.
Miscellanea evangelica. 2 vols 1913–15.
'Righteousness' in the Gospels: from the proceedings of the British Academy. 1918.

Collaborative works

English lessons for English people. 1871. With John Robert Seeley.
The common tradition of the synoptic gospels in the text of the revised version. 1884. With William George Rushbrooke. [LA]

Alfred Ainger 1837–1904

See LR *and* NRA *for mss and letters. Notable collections in BL and Bodleian.*

§1

Sermons preached in the Temple Church. 1870.
Charles Lamb. 1882 (EML).
Crabbe. 1903 (EML).
The gospel and human life: sermons. Ed H. C. Beeching 1904.
Lectures and essays. Ed H. C. Beeching 2 vols 1905. Miscellaneous studies of English writers.

Contributions to periodicals

See Wellesley *5 1989 for Ainger's contributions to* Macmillan's Mag.

Editions and introductions

Ainger edited the writings and letters of Charles and Mary Lamb (1879–99), as well as the poems of Thomas Hood (1893–7). He also prepared an edn of Tennyson for the young *(1891), and wrote an introduction to John Galt's* Annals of the parish and the Ayrshire legatees *(1895). In addition, he contributed articles on Lamb, Tennyson et al to* DNB.

§2

The Times 9 Feb 1904. Obituary.
Monthly Rev Mar 1904.
Ward, A. W. Macmillan's Mag Apr 1904.
Quart Rev Jan 1905.
The life and letters of Alfred Ainger. Ed E. Sichel 1906. [OD]

William Archer 1856–1924

See LR *and* NRA *for mss and letters. Notable collections in BL, Bodleian, Br Theatre Assoc Lib, Folger, Nat Lib of Scotland, Regent's College London.*

Bibliographies

Archer, C. William Archer: his life, work and friendships. 1931. Contains bibliography.
Whitebrook, P. William Archer: a biography. 1993. Contains select bibliography.

Collections and selections

William Archer as rationalist: a collection of his heterodox writings. Ed J. M. Robertson 1925.
Three plays; with a personal note by Bernard Shaw. 1927. Contains Martha Washington, Beatriz Juana, Lidia.
On dreams. Ed T. Besterman 1935. Anthology of Archer's notes on dreams.

§1

The fashionable tragedian: a criticism. Edinburgh 1877. With R. W. Lowe. An essay on H. Irving.
English analyses of the French plays represented at the Gaiety Theatre London, June and July 1879. 1879. Rptd from London Figaro.
English dramatists of today. 1882. Includes Playwrights of yesterday, F. W. Broughton, H. J. Byron, W. S. Gilbert, P. Merritt, A. W. Pinero etc.
Henry Irving, actor and manager: a critical study. 1883.
About the theatre: essays and studies. 1886. Mainly rptd from Theatre.
Masks or faces? a study in the psychology of acting. 1888.
William Charles Macready. 1890.
The theatrical 'world'. 5 vols 1893–7. Archer's dramatic criticism rptd from Athenaeum, Pall Mall Budget, Sketch, World, etc. Vol 1 prefaced by Letter from Archer to R. W. Lowe; vol 2 introd by G. B. Shaw; vol 3 with prefatory letter from A. W. Pinero; vol 4 prefaced by Archer's essay On the need for an endowed theatre; vol 5 introd by S. Grundy.
Study and stage: a year-book of criticism. 1899.
America to-day: observations and reflections. 1900.
Real conversations. 1904. Dialogues with A. W. Pinero, T. Hardy, S. Phillips, G. Moore, W. S. Gilbert et al.
Scheme and estimate for a national theatre. 1904 (priv ptd), 1907 (as A national theatre: scheme and estimates). With H. Granville-Barker.
Let youth but know: a plea for reason in education, by 'Kappa' [pseud]. 1905.
Through Afro-America: an English reading of the race problem. 1910.

The life, trial and death of Francisco Ferrer. 1911.
The great analysis: a plea for a rational world-order, with an introduction by Gilbert Murray. 1912 (anon).
Play-making: a manual of craftsmanship. 1912.
The thirteen days, July 23–August 4, 1914: a chronicle and interpretation. Oxford 1915.
God and Mr Wells: a critical examination of God, the invisible king. 1917.
India and the future. 1917.
A letter on the debt of European literature to Russia. 1917.
The peace-president: a brief appreciation. 1918. On T. Woodrow-Wilson.
The pirate's progress: a short history of the U-boat. 1918.
War is war, or the Germans in Belgium: a drama of 1914. New York 1919.
The green goddess: a play in four acts. New York 1921.
The old drama and the new: an essay in re-valuation. 1923.
In addition, Archer wrote over 20 unpbd plays, of which only a few have survived in ms. The following plays were performed in his lifetime: Mesmerism or quits *(1876)*, Rosalind *(1878)*, Australia or the bushrangers *(1881)*, The joy-ride *(1923)*, The samurai *(1923)*. *Archer also pbd many lectures and pams, mostly of a polemical nature.*

Contributions to periodicals and collaborative works
Archer wrote for a great number of periodicals on a wide variety of subjects; see Wellesley *5 1989 for his contributions to* Br Quart Rev, Contemporary Rev, Fortnightly Rev, Longman's Mag, Macmillan's Mag, Nat Rev, New Rev *and* Westminster Rev. *He also contributed articles to such collaborative works as B. Matthews and L. Hutton (ed),* Actors and actresses of Great Britain and Ireland *(New York 1886) and* Shakespeare's England *(Oxford 1916).*

Letters
The religion of tomorrow: a friendly correspondence between H. H. Powers . . . and W. Archer. 1925.
Tourist to the Antipodes: William Archer's Australian journey 1876–77. Ed R. Stanley, St Lucia, Queensland 1977.
Ibseniana: letters from Archer to Charles Archer [1881–3]. London Mercury Oct 1937.

Editions, introductions and translations
Archer made a notable contribution to Ibsen's reception in England by translating into prose all Ibsen's more important plays, occasionally in collaboration with Charles Archer or Edmund Gosse, 1888–1913; he also translated plays by Hauptmann, Maeterlinck and Brandes, and essays etc by Brandes and other Scandinavian writers. He edited and introduced a number of miscellaneous works, among which are plays by Congreve, Farquhar, Gilbert and Shakespeare.

§2
Aas, L. William Archer. Kristiania 1920.
Hind, C. L. William Archer. In his More authors and I, 1922.
Obits: Manchester Guardian 29 Dec 1924; The Times 29 Dec 1924; Observer 4 Jan 1925.
Granville-Barker, H. Archer. Drama Nov 1926.
Archer, C. William Archer: his life, work and friendships. 1931.
Woodbridge, H. E. William Archer: prophet of modern drama. Sewanee Rev 44 1936.
Gebauer, E. L. The theatrical criticism of William Archer. Quart Rev of Speech 24 1938.
Postlewait, T. Prophet of the new drama: William Archer and the Ibsen campaign. Westport CT 1986.
Whitebrook, P. William Archer: a biography. 1993. [OD]

Sir Walter Armstrong 1850–1918

§1
Alfred Stevens: a biographical study. 1881.
Sir J. E. Millais: his life and work. [1885.]
The Thames from its source to the sea. 2 vols [1886–7.]
Notes on the National Gallery. 1887.
Celebrated pictures exhibited at the Glasgow International Exhibition, Fine Arts section: a series of engravings, with notes and criticisms. 1888.
Celebrated pictures exhibited at the Manchester Royal Jubilee Exhibition, Fine Arts section: a series of engravings, with notes and criticisms. [1888.]
Memoir of Peter De Wint. 1888.
Scottish painters: a critical study. 1888.
Briton Riviere: his life and work. [1891.]
Thomas Gainsborough. 1894, 1905 (rev).
The art of W. A. Orchardson. 1895.
The art of Velazquez. 1896.
The life of Velazquez. 1896.
Gainsborough and his place in English art. 1898.
Sir Joshua Reynolds. 1900.
Sir Henry Raeburn; with an introduction by R. A. M. Stevenson and a bibliographical and descriptive catalogue by J. L. Caw. 1901.
Turner. 1902; tr Fr 1902.
The Peel collection and the Dutch school of painting. 1904.
Art in Great Britain and Ireland. 1909; tr Ger 1909, Fr and Ital 1910.
Lawrence. 1913.

Editions, introductions and translations
Véron, E. Aesthetics. Tr Armstrong 1877.
Müntz, E. Raphael: his life, work and times. Ed Armstrong 1881, 1896 (abridged).
Perrot, G. and C. Chipiez. A history of art in ancient Egypt. Tr and ed Armstrong 2 vols 1883.
Perrot, G. and C. Chipiez. A history of art in Chaldaea and Assyria. Tr and ed Armstrong 2 vols 1884.
Perrot, G. and C. Chipiez. History of art in Phoenicia and its dependencies. Tr and ed Armstrong 2 vols 1885.
Lacroix, P. The arts in the Middle Ages and at the period of the Renaissance. Tr and ed J. Dafforne 1875, 1886 (rev Armstrong).
Bryan, M. A biographical and critical dictionary of painters and engravers. 2 vols 1889 (vol 2 ed Armstrong and R. E. Graves).
Exhibition of pictures by masters of the Netherlandish and allied schools of xv and early xvi centuries. Introd by Armstrong 1892.
Corroyer, É. J. Gothic architecture. Ed Armstrong 1893.
Exhibition of pictures by Dutch masters of the seventeenth century. Introd by Armstrong 1900.
Dobson, H. A. William Hogarth. Introd by Armstrong 1902.
Wölfflin, H. The art of the Italian Renaissance: a handbook for students and travellers. Introd by Armstrong 1903.
Geffroy, G. The National Gallery. Introd by Armstrong 1904.
Sir Joshua Reynolds at Althorp House. Introd by Armstrong [1905].

Contributions to periodicals and collaborative works
See Wellesley *5 1989 for Amstrong's contributions to* Fortnightly Rev, Nat Rev *and* Nineteenth Cent. *Armstrong also wrote over 30 articles in* DNB.

§2
Spielman, M. H. Sir Walter Armstrong. 1918. Rptd from Fortnightly Rev. [OD]

Alfred Austin 1835–1913

See col 699.

Peter Bayne 1830–96

See NRA *for letters from Ruskin to Bayne.*

§1
Nineveh, a prize poem, and other pieces. Aberdeen 185?
The Christian life, social and individual. Edinburgh 1855, 1859 (rev edn).

Essays in biography and criticism. 2 vols Boston 1857–8, Edinburgh 1859 (as Essays biographical, critical and miscellaneous).
The testimony of Christ to Christianity. 1862, New York [1904] (ed and introd by G. C. Morgan).
The days of Jezebel: an historical drama. 1872.
The national history of England. 1873. Vol 4 by Bayne.
Emma Cheyne: a prose idyll of English life by Ellis Brandt [pseud]. 1875.
The chief actors in the Puritan revolution. 1878. Largely rptd from Contemporary Rev.
Lessons from my masters: Carlyle, Tennyson and Ruskin. 1879. Pbd originally in Literary World.
Two great Englishwomen: Mrs Browning and Charlotte Brontë; with an essay on poetry, illustrated from Wordsworth, Burns and Byron. '1881' [1880].
Martin Luther: his life and work. 2 vols 1887.
Six Christian biographies: John Howard. William Wilberforce. Thomas Chalmers. Thomas Arnold. Samuel Budgett. John Foster. 1887, 1890 (as Men worthy to lead).
The Free Church of Scotland: her origin, founders and testimony. Edinburgh 1893.
Bayne also pbd several theological and political pams. He contributed numerous articles to Blackwood's Mag, Br Quart Rev, Contemporary Rev, Fortnightly Rev, Fraser's Mag, Literary World, St Paul's Mag, *and* Tait's Edinburgh Mag *(see also* Wellesley *5 1989).*

Editions and introductions

Miller, H. The headship of Christ. Ed and introd by Bayne 1861, Boston 1872 (as The witness papers).
Gould, G. (ed). Documents relating to the settlement of the Church of England by the Act of Uniformity of 1662. Historical introd (English Puritanism, its character and history) by Bayne. 1862.
Miller, H. Essays, historical and biographical. Ed and introd by Bayne 1862.
The life and letters of Hugh Miller. Ed Bayne 2 vols 1871.

§2

Taylor, A. The geological difficulty of the age theory: an examination of Mr P. Bayne's defence of The testimony of the rocks [i.e. the work by H. Miller]. 1858. A reaction to A defence of The testimony of the rocks: rptd from Witness in reply to an article in North Br Rev, Edinburgh 1858.
[Brownell, W. C.] Bayne's Lessons from my masters. Nation (New York) 20 Nov 1879.
Bayne. Acad 15 Feb 1896. Obituary. [JMB]

Henry Charles Beeching 1859–1919

See col 711.

Gertrude Bell, Gertrude Margaret Lowthian Bell 1868–1926

The Univ of Newcastle-upon-Tyne Lib is the principal repository of letters, diaries and papers of Bell. See bibliographies, below.

Bibliographies

Catalogue of the Gertrude Bell collection in the library of King's College, Newcastle-upon-Tyne. Newcastle-upon-Tyne 1960.
The letters and papers of Gertrude Bell: a list compiled and edited by W. C. Donkin. Newcastle-upon-Tyne 1966 (Newcastle-upon-Tyne Univ Lib pbn).
Winstone, H. V. F. In his Gertrude Bell, 1978.

§1

Safar nameh. Persian pictures; a book of travel. 1894 (anon); 2nd edn pbd as Persian pictures, [1928] (with preface by Sir E. D. Ross), New York 1928; London [1937] (with an introd by V. Sackville-West), [1940]; [1947] (3rd edn with a preface by A. J. Arberry).
REVIEWS: Athenaeum 3507 1895; Bookman 75 1928; Life and Letters 1 1928; London Quart and Holborn Rev 150 1928; Punch 174 1928.
Notes on a journey through Cilicia and Lycaonia. Angers, Burgin 1906. Rptd from Revue Archéologique 1906.
The desert and the sown. 1907 (illus), New York 1907 (illus), London 1908 (new edn), 1919, 1928 (new edn pbd as Syria. The desert and the sown), 1985 (facs of 1907 edn), 1985 (introd by S. Graham-Brown); tr Ger 1908.
REVIEWS: Bookman 31 1907; Dial 42 1907; Nation 84 1907; Fortnightly Rev 95 1911.
The thousand and one churches. 1909. With Sir W. Ramsay.
The churches and monasteries of the Tur Abdin. Heidelberg 1910, 1913, Nendeln/Liechtenstein 1978 (facs of 1913 edn); London 1982 (introd and notes by M. M. Mango).
Amureth to Amureth. 1911 (illus), New York 1911, London 1924 (2nd edn), 1929.
REVIEWS: Bookman 40 1911; Dial 50 1911; Fortnightly Rev 95 1911; Nation 93 1911; Bookman 66 1924.
Palace and mosque at Ukhaidir: a study in early Mohammadan architecture. Oxford 1914.
The Arabs of Mesopotamia. Basrah [1917?], 1918 (anon).
Asiatic Turkey. Basrah 1917.
Iraq. Review of the civil administration of Mesopotamia. 1920 (HMSO).
The Arab war: confidential information for general headquarters from Gertrude Bell, being despatches from the secret Arab Bulletin. Introd by Sir K. Cornwallis [1940] (limited edn, 500 copies only).

Contributions to periodicals

The Alps of Dauphiné. Nineteenth Cent Feb 1900.
The ruins of the Hauran. Monthly Rev 3 1900.
Islam in India. Nineteenth Cent and After 60 1906.
The vaulting system at Ukhaidir. Jnl of Hellenic Stud 30 1910.
Damascus. Blackwood's Mag 189 1911.
Postroad through the Syrian desert. Blackwood's Mag 190 1911.
Great Britain and Iraq: an experiment in Anglo-Asiatic relations. Round Table 1924 (anon).
Iraq: political history. Encyclopaedia Britannica 1926 (13th edn).

Letters

The letters of Gertrude Bell. Selected and edited by Lady Bell. 2 vols 1927, New York [1927], 2 vols London [1928], 2 vols New York [1928], 1 vol London [1930], 2 vols 1931 (illus), 2 vols Harmondsworth [1939], 1 vol London 1947, 1950; Harmondsworth 1987 (with a new introd by Jan Morris).
REVIEWS: Bookman 73 1927; London Mercury 17 1927; Punch 173 1927; Dalhousie 7 1927–8; Canadian Forum 8 1928; London Quart and Holborn Rev 149 1928.
The earlier letters of Gertrude Bell. Collected and ed by E. Richmond 1937, New York [1937].
REVIEWS: London Mercury 35 1937; Punch 192 1937; Spectator 158 1937.
The letters of Gertrude Bell. Selected by Lady Richmond from Lady Bell's standard edition. London and Baltimore 1953, Melbourne [1953].
Poems from the Divan of Hafiz. Tr Bell 1897, 1928 (with a preface by Sir E. D. Ross); Teachings of Hafiz, tr Bell, Tihran 1986 (with a preface by Sir E. D. Ross and introd by I. Shah); The Hafiz poems of Gertrude Bell (with a preface by Sir E. D. Ross), Bethesda MD 1994.
REVIEWS: Bookman 74 1928; Life and Letters 1 1928.

§2

The Times 13, 14, 15 July 1926.
Hogarth, D. G. Gertrude Bell's journey to Hayil. Geographical Jnl 70 1927.
In DNB 1922–30.
Burgoyne, E. (ed). Gertrude Bell. From her personal papers 1889–1914. With biographical contributions. 2 vols 1958. Illus. REVIEWS: Spectator 201 1958, 207 1961.
Gertrude Bell 1868–1926; a selection from the photographic archive of an archaeologist and traveller [compiled] by S. Hill. Newcastle-upon-Tyne 1976 (Dept of archaeology, Univ of Newcastle-upon-Tyne). Pam.
Winstone, H. V. F. Gertrude Bell. 1978.
Catalogue of the Gertrude Bell photographic archive, compiled by S. Hill, L. Ritchie and B. Hathaway. Newcastle-upon-Tyne 1982 (Dept of archaeology, Univ of Newcastle-upon-Tyne).
Goodman, S. Gertrude Bell. Leamington Spa and Dover NH 1985.

Joseph Bennett 1831–1911

§1

Letters from Bayreuth descriptive and critical of Wagner's Der Ring des Nibelungen, with an appendix. 1877. Most of these letters first appeared in the Daily Telegraph in 1876.
The musical year 1883: a record of noteworthy musical events in the United Kingdom, with a reprint of criticisms on many of them. [1884.] The 'criticisms' first appeared in the Daily Telegraph.
Novello's primers of musical biography. 5 vols [1884–5]. Chopin, Meyerbeer, Rossini, Berlioz, Cherubini.
A short history of cheap music, as exemplified in the records of the house of Novello, Ewer & Co. 1887. Anon; preface by G. Grove.
A story of ten hundred concerts, being a short account of the origin and progress of the Monday popular concerts, St James's Hall London. 1887.
History of the Leeds musical festivals 1858–89, with portraits and facsimiles. Leeds 1892. With F. R. Spark.
Forty years of music 1865–1905. 1908.

Editions and introductions

Leeds triennial musical festival (Leeds musical festival): analytical programmes for the festivals of 1880, 1883, 1886, 1889, 1892, 1898, 1913. Compiled by Bennett. 1880–92, Leeds [1880–1913].
Berlioz, L. H. A treatise upon modern instrumentation and orchestration. First pbd 1856, rev and ed Bennett 1882.
Warriner, J. National portrait gallery of British musicians. Introd by Bennett [1896].
Cherubini, L. A treatise on counterpoint and fugue. Tr M. C. Clarke, rev and ed Bennett [190–?].
Bennett provided the books of words and analytical notes for numerous musical compositions (F. H. Cowen, A. Dvořák, E. Elgar, C. F. Gounod, A. C. Mackenzie, C. H. H. Parry, etc).

Contributions to periodicals

Bennett was music critic for the Daily Telegraph, *and contributed articles to* Macmillan's Mag *(see* Wellesley *5 1989). He was editor of* Concordia: a weekly journal of music and the sister arts, *May 1875–Apr 1876.* [FJMK]

Arthur Christopher Benson 1862–1925

See LR *and* NRA *for mss and letters. Notable collections in Bodleian, Magdalene College Cambridge (180 vols of diaries), Harvard, Univ of British Columbia, Univ of Iowa, HRHRC.*

Bibliographies

Newsome, D. On the edge of paradise: A. C. Benson, the diarist. 1980. Contains bibliography.
See also DLB *vol 98 1990, below.*

Collections and selections

The beauty of life: being selections from the writings of A. C. Benson. Ed C. Abbot, Derby [1912].
The thread of gold: compiled from the books of A. C. Benson. 1914.
Thoughts from A. C. Benson. Compiled by H. B. Elliott [1917].
A little anthology from A. C. Benson. Compiled by A. Patterson Webb 1925.
A thought for every day. Selected by M. A. Stanton 1925.

§1

Memoirs of Arthur Hamilton, B. A., of Trinity College Cambridge, extracted from his letters and diaries, with reminiscences of his conversation. By Christopher Carr [pseud]. 1886.
William Laud, sometime Archbishop of Canterbury: a study. 1887.
Le cahier jaune: poems. Eton 1892 (priv ptd).
Men of might: studies of great characters. 1892, 1921 (new illustr edn). With H. F. W. Tatham.
Poems. 1893.
Babylonica. Eton 1895.
Genealogy of the family of Benson, of Banger House and Northwoods in the parish of Ripon and chapelry of Pately Bridge: with biographical and illustrative notes. Eton 1895 (priv ptd).
Lyrics. 1895.
The professor. Eton 1895 (priv ptd). Poem.
Thomas Gray. Eton 1895 (priv ptd). Poem.
Essays. '1896' [1895].
Monnow: an ode. Eton 1896.
Lord Vyet, and other poems. 1897.
Ode in memory of the Rt Honble William Ewart Gladstone. Eton 1898 (priv ptd). Contains Latin version by W. Durnford.
Fasti Etonenses: a biographical history of Eton selected from the lives of celebrated Etonians. Eton 1899.
The life of Edward White Benson, sometime Archbishop of Canterbury. 2 vols 1899, 1 vol 1901 (abridged).
Mac: an ode . . . with prefatory memoir. Eton 1899 (priv ptd).
The professor, and other poems. 1900.
Coronation ode [1902]. Music by E. Elgar, notes by J. Bennett.
Ode to Japan. 1902 (priv ptd). Rptd from Macmillan's Mag.
The schoolmaster: a commentary upon the aims and methods of an assistant-master in a public school. 1902, 1908 (Popular edn); tr Ger 1904.
The hill of trouble, and other stories. 1903. *See also* Paul the minstrel, *below.*
The myrtle bough: a vale. Eton 1903 (priv ptd).
Alfred Tennyson. 1904.
The house of quiet: an autobiography. Ed J. T. 1904 (anon), 1906 (with author's name).
The isles of sunset. 1904. Stories. *See also* Paul the minstrel, *below.*
The olive bough. Eton 1904 (priv ptd).
Rossetti. 1904 (EML).
Edward Fitzgerald. 1905 (EML).
Peace, and other poems. 1905.
The thread of gold, by the author of The house of quiet. 1905.
The Upton letters, by T. B. 1905, 1906 (with new preface). Numerous later edns.
From a college window. 1906. Numerous later edns. 12 of these essays rptd from Cornhill Mag.
Walter Pater. 1906 (EML).
The altar fire. 1907.
Beside still waters. 1907.
Hymns and carols. Eton 1907 (priv ptd).
The letters of one: a study in limitations, by Charles Hare Plunkett [pseud]. 1907.
At large. 1908. Some of these essays rptd from Putnam's Monthly.
The church and literature. 1908.
The poems of A. C. Benson. 1909.

The silent isle. 1910.
The leaves of the tree: studies in biography. 1911. Rptd from Cornhill Mag.
Paul the minstrel, and other stories. 1911. Rptd from The hill of trouble and The isles of sunset, *above*.
Ruskin: a study in personality. 1911.
The child of dawn. 1912.
Thy rod and thy staff. 1912.
Along the road. 1913. Essays contributed week by week to the Church Family Newspaper under the head of Along the road.
Joyous Gard. 1913.
Watersprings. 1913.
The orchard pavilion. 1914.
Where no fear was: a book about fear. 1914.
Escape, and other essays. 1915.
Father Payne. 1915. Anon.
Hugh: memoirs of a brother. 1915. On R. H. Benson.
Life and letters of Maggie Benson. 1917.
Magdalene College, Cambridge: a little view of its buildings and history. Cambridge 1923.
The trefoil: Wellington College, Lincoln, and Truro. 1923. On the early life of Archbishop Benson.
Chris Gascoyne: an experiment in solitude. 1924. From the diaries of John Trevor.
Selected poems. 1924.
Memories and friends. 1924.
The house of Menerdue. 1925.
The canon. 1926.
Essays of to-day and yesterday. 1926.
Rambles and reflections. 1926.
Basil Netherby. [1927].
Cressage. 1927.
Benson also produced several works of pam length. He contributed to composite works, such as W. H. Tucker (ed), Eton of old, *1892;* Windsor & Eton: an illustrated invitation, *Windsor [1905] and to* Royal society of literature of the United Kingdom. Essays by divers hands, being the transactions, *1926. Many of Benson's essays were later included in collections of essays, such as E. Rhys (ed),* Modern English essays, *New York 1922. He contributed to* Atlantic Monthly, Church Family Newspaper, Contemporary Rev, Cornhill Mag, Fortnightly Rev, Macmillan's Mag, Monthly Rev, Nat Rev, New Rev, Poetry Rev, Teachers' Guild Quart, Temple Bar, Thrush *and* Yellow Book *(see also* Wellesley *5 1989).*

Editions, introductions and translations

Benson, M. E. At sundry times and in divers manners. 1891. A novel with a memoir by Benson.
Benson, E. W. Cyprian: his life, his times, his work. Introd by Benson 1897.
Arnold, M. Poems. Introd by Benson '1900' [1899].
Cory, W. Johnson. Ionica. Biographical introd and notes by Benson 1905.
Whittier, J. G. Poems of Whittier. Selected and introd by Benson [1906].
Victoria. The letters of Queen Victoria: a selection from her Majesty's correspondence between the years 1837 and 1861. Ed Benson and Viscount Esher 3 vols 1907; tr Ger 1908.
Edward Fitzgerald: 1809–1909: centenary celebrations souvenir. Ed Benson, Ipswich 1909.
Francis of Assisi. The little flowers of St Francis. Introd by Benson 1909.
Tatham, H. F. W. The footprints in the snow. Memoir by Benson 1910.
Acorn, G. One of the multitude. Introd by Benson 1911.
'Umar Khàiyam. Rubaiyat of Omar Khayyam. Tr E. Fitzgerald, introd by Benson [1911].
Westcott, B. F. Daily readings from the works of Bishop Westcott. Introd by Benson 1911.
Dickens, C. The adventures of Oliver Twist. Introd by Benson 1913.
Brontë, C., E., A. and B. Selections from the poetry. Ed and introd by Benson 1915.
Keable, R. A city of the dawn. Introd by Benson 1915.
Cambridge essays on education. Ed Benson, introd by Viscount Bryce, Cambridge 1917. Benson's own contribution was The training of the imagination.
The reed of Pan: English renderings of Greek epigrams [from the Greek Anthology] and lyrics. Tr Benson 1922.
Ruskin, John. Selections. Ed Benson 1923.
Mary, Queen consort of George V. The book of the queen's dolls' house. Vol 1 ed Benson and Sir L. Weaver 1924, vol 2 ed E. V. Lucas [1924], [1924] (abbreviated as Souvenir book of the queen's dolls' house), [1924] (abbreviated again by F. V. Morley as Everybody's book of the queen's dolls' house).

Letters and diaries

The gate of death: a diary. 1906. Anon.
Meanwhile: a packet of war letters, by H. L. G. [pseud]. With a foreword by K. W. 1916.
The diary of Arthur Christopher Benson: a selection by P. Lubbock. [1926.]
Extracts from the letters of Dr A. C. Benson to M. E. A[llen]. 1926. Selected by M. E. Allen.
Newsome, D. (ed). Edwardian excursions: from the diaries of A. C. Benson 1899–1904. 1981.

§2

Archer, W. Poets of the younger generation. 1902.
Weygandt, C. The poetry of Benson. Sewanee Rev 14 1906.
Martindale, C. C. The life of Monsignor Robert Hugh Benson. 1916.
Benson, E. F. Our family affairs, 1867–1896. 1920.
Turner, F. A. C. Benson. Cambridge 1922.
Macnaghten, H. Benson. Spectator 27 June 1925.
Collins, J. P. Benson. Bookman (London) Aug 1925.
Arthur Christopher Benson as seen by some friends. Ed E. H. Ryle 1925. Includes Benson's An account of visits to pensioners in London and vicinity.
Benson, E. F. Mother. 1925.
James, M. R. Eton and King's: recollections, mostly trivial, 1875–1925. 1926.
Benson, E. F. As we were: a Victorian peep-show. 1930.
Weygandt, C. The time of Yeats: English poetry of today against an American background. New York 1937.
Benson, E. F. Final edition: an autobiography. 1940.
Poisel, C. Die Brüder Benson. Unpbd diss, Vienna 1944.
Newsome, D. Godliness and good learning: four studies on a Victorian ideal. 1961.
Howarth, T. E. B. Cambridge between two wars. 1970.
Warren, A. A. C. Benson & his friends. In Connections, Univ of Michigan 1970.
Newsome, D. On the edge of paradise: A. C. Benson, the diarist. 1980.
Wormleighton, S., Wilfred Owen and A. C. Benson. N & Q vol 37 no 4 Dec 1990.
Wilson, K. A. C. Benson. In DLB vol 98 1990. [JMB]

Annie Besant, née Wood 1847–1933

Besant papers are in the ms collections of the Theosophical Soc, Adyar, Madras, India; Theosophical Soc Lib, London; BL; Univ of Chicago Lib; Churchill College, Cambridge; Dickinson College Lib, Carlisle PA; with lesser holdings in other libraries.

Bibliographies

Besterman, T. Bibliography of Annie Besant. 1924.
Theosophist (Besant centenary issue 1847–1947) 69 1947.

Selections

My path to atheism. 1877. Pams written 1873–7.
Essays political and social. [1882.]
Legends and tales. 1885. Rptd from Our Corner 1883–4.
Essays and addresses. 4 vols 1911–13. Vol 1 Psychology 1911; vol 2 The spiritual life 1912; vol 3 Evolution and occultism 1913; vol 4 India 1913.
For India's uplift: a collection of speeches and writings on Indian questions. Madras [1913]; rev edn entitled Speeches and writings of Annie Besant, Madras [1923].
India and the empire. 1914. Articles rptd from newspapers, a lecture, and 2 letters.
War articles and notes. 1915. Rptd from New India, Commonweal, and Theosophist.
The coming of the world-teacher, war and evolution. Extracts from lectures and writings of C. W. Leadbeater, A. Besant, and others. [1917.]
The birth of new India: a collection of writings and speeches on Indian affairs. Adyar 1917.
Congress speeches. Adyar 1917. 6 speeches delivered to the Indian Nat Congress.
Besant spirit series. 10 vols Adyar 1938–43. Compiled from the writings of Besant.
A selection of the political and social pamphlets of Annie Besant. Ed J. Saville, New York 1970.
The origin of theosophy: Annie Besant – the atheist years. Ed J. G. Melton, New York 1990.

§1

On the deity of Jesus of Nazareth. By the wife of a beneficed clergyman. Ed and with preface by C. Voysey 1873. Pam.
On the nature and the existence of god. 1875. Pam. Anon.
History of the great French revolution. 1876, rptd 1879, 1893 (2nd edn), rptd Madras 1931.
Is the Bible indictable? 1877, rptd 1884.
The law of population: its consequences, and its bearing upon human conduct and morals. 1877, rptd 1881 with new preface, New York 1878, London 1887, San Francisco 1893; tr Ital 1879, Ger 1881, and other languages.
Marriage: as it was, as it is, and as it should be. With a sketch of the life of Mrs Besant. Ed A. K. Butts, New York [1879], 1882, Seattle 1919. Sketch rptd from Secular Chron.
The story of Afghanistan: or, why the Tory government gags the Indian press. 1879, rptd Madras 1931. Rptd from Nat Reformer. Pam.
Light, heat and sound. 1881.
Physiology of the home. 1882.
The Christian creed; or, what it is blasphemy to deny. 1883.
Auguste Comte: his philosophy, his religion, and his sociology. [1885.] Anon.
Autobiographical sketches. 1885. Rptd from Our Corner 1884–5.
The sins of the church. 1886.
Why I do not believe in God. 1887. Pam.
Why I became a Theosophist. 1890, 1912 (new edn), New York 1896. Pam.
Theosophy and the law of population. 1891. Rptd from Lucifer July 1891.
The seven principles of man. 1892, New York 1896, London [1897] (rev edn), 1909; tr Ger 1899.
Reincarnation. 1892, 1905 (4th edn), rptd 1985.
Annie Besant: an autobiography. 1893, Philadelphia 1893; 3rd edn with an additional survey of her life by G. S. Arundale and biographical notes compiled mainly from her own writings. Adyar 1939, rptd.1984.
REVIEWS: Athenaeum 103 1894; London Quart Rev 83 1894; [W. E. Gladstone] True and false conceptions of the atonement, Nineteenth Cent 36 1894; Spectator 72 1894.
The building of the kosmos and other lectures. 1894.
Death – and after? 1894, rptd Adyar 1952.
In the outer court. 1895, Adyar 1955 (5th edn) (rptd 1983), Chicago 1923.
Karma. 1895, 1905 (3rd edn) (rptd 1947), New York 1897, Krotona CA 1918; tr Finnish 1907, Ger 1910, Polish 1936.
The means of India's regeneration. Benares 1895. Pam.
The place of politics in the life of a nation. Benares 1895. Pam.
The self and its sheathes. Benares 1895, Adyar 1948.
Disestablish the Church: or, sins of the Church of England. 1896. Reprint of The sins of the Church 1886 and additional essays.
Man and his bodies. 1896, Chicago 1923; Adyar 1952 (10th edn); tr Portuguese 1925.
The path of discipleship. 1896, 1980 (11th reprint).
The ancient wisdom: an outline of Theosophical teachings. 1897.
Four great religions. [1897], Chicago 1897, Madras 1949.
The three paths to union with God. 1897, Chicago 1923, Adyar 1925.
Dharma. 1899, 1986 (9th reprint).
Evolution of life and form. Madras 1899, 1909 (3rd edn).
The story of the great war: some lessons from the Mahabharata for the use of the Hindu students in the schools of India. 1899, rptd 1919.
Avataras. 1900, Chicago 1923, Adyar 1925 (3rd edn).
Some problems of life. 1900, rptd 1904, Krotona CA 1919.
Ancient ideals in modern life. 1901, Adyar 1925 (2nd edn).
Esoteric Christianity or the lesser mysteries. 1901, New York 1902, Adyar 1953.
Shri Rama Chandra, the ideal king: some lessons for the use of Hindu students in the schools of India. 1901.
Thought power: its control and culture. 1901, Adyar 1952 (18th reprint), Wheaton IL 1953.
Theosophy and imperialism. 1902.
The laws of the higher life. 1903.
The education of Indian girls. 1904. Pam.
Hindu ideals. 1904.
The pedigree of man. 1904, 2nd edn with tables and charts 1908.
A study in consciousness: a contribution to the science of psychology. 1904, Madras 1954; tr Ger 1904, Du 1905, Ital 1911.
Theosophy and the new psychology. 1904.
The value of Theosophy in the raising of India. 1904.
Theosophy in relation to human life. 1905.
Hints on the study of the Bhagavad-Gita. 1906, 1925 (3rd edn).
India's awakening. [1906.]
Children of the motherland. Benares 1906.
East and West and the destinies of nations: 2 lectures. Benares 1906.
England and India. 1906, rptd Adyar 1921. Pam.
H. P. Blavatsky and the masters of wisdom. 1907, Krotona CA 1918, Chicago 1962.
London lectures of 1907. 1907.
The wisdom of the upanishads. 1907, 1919 (2nd edn).
Australian lectures 1908. Sydney 1908.
Buddhist popular lectures. Adyar 1908.
An introduction to yoga. 1908, Adyar 1920; tr Fr 1912, Portuguese 1922.
REVIEW: Athenaeum 27 Sep 1913.
The changing world and lectures to Theosophical students. 1909; tr Portuguese 1926.
Questions on Hinduism, with answers. Benares [1909?]. Rptd from Central Hindu Mag 1901–8.
The religious problem in India. Madras 1909.
Popular lectures on Theosophy. [1910], Chicago 1910, Adyar 1948; tr Ger 1911, with a new foreword.
The immediate future and other lectures. 1911, Chicago 1922; tr Fr 1912 with a new preface.
The ideals of Theosophy. Adyar 1912; tr Portuguese 1925.

Initiation: the perfecting of man. 1912.
An introduction to the science of peace. Adyar 1912.
A study in Karma. Adyar [1912], 1917 (2nd edn).
Theosophy. 1912.
Giordano Bruno: Theosophy's apostle in the sixteenth century. Adyar 1913. Includes reprint of 1877 essay on Bruno.
An introduction to Theosophy. Adyar 1913.
Man's life in this and other worlds. 1913.
Superhuman men in history and religion. 1913.
Theosophy and the Theosophical Society. Adyar 1913, Chicago 1913.
Wake up, India: a plea for social reform. 1913.
REVIEW: Athenaeum 27 Sep 1913; *see also* M. V. Srinivasa Aiyangar, An open letter to Mrs Annie Besant, being a reply to her attacks on Hinduism, Madras 1915.
Mysticism. 1914.
India and the empire. 1914.
How India wrought for freedom: the story of the National Congress told from official records. Adyar 1915.
REVIEW: South Asia Rev 9 1916.
War articles and notes. 1915.
India: a nation. A plea for Indian self-government. Foreword by C. P. Ramaswami Aiyar. [1916], 1923 (3rd and enlarged edn), 1930 (4th edn).
REVIEW: South Asia Rev 9 1916.
Theosophy and life's deeper problems. Adyar 1916.
Duties of the Theosophist. Adyar 1917.
In defence of Hinduism: a booklet written for Hindu boys. 1919.
Lectures on political science. Adyar 1919, 1920 (2nd edn).
Man's life in three worlds: a booklet for beginners. Adyar 1919.
The war and its lessons on fraternity. 1919.
Problems of reconstruction. Adyar 1919.
The inner government of the world. Adyar 1920, 1930 (4th edn).
Britain's place in the great plan. 1921.
The great plan. Adyar 1921.
Talks with a class. 1921.
The future of Indian politics: a contribution to the understanding of present-day problems. 1922.
Brahmavidya-divine wisdom. Adyar 1923.
Indian ideals in education, philosophy and religion, and art. Calcutta 1925.
India: bond or free? 1926.
REVIEW: Sociological Rev 19 1927.
How a world teacher comes. 1926.
A new civilization. 1927.
In addition to those listed above, Besant wrote hundreds of other pams.

Contributions to periodicals

The socialist movement. Westminster Rev 126 1886.
Charles Bradlaugh. Rev of Revs 3 1891.
What Theosophy is. Outlook 14 Oct 1893. Reply: A. P. Atterbury, What Theosophy is, Outlook 28 Oct 1893.
'True and false conceptions of the atonement'. Nineteenth Cent 37 1895. Reply to W. E. Gladstone's review of Annie Besant: an autobiography (1894) in Nineteenth Cent 36 1893.
The conditions of life after death. Nineteenth Cent 40 1896.
Besant frequently contributed to Nat Reformer, Malthusian, Our Corner, Link, Lucifer, Theosophist, Theosophical Rev, Vahan, Adyar Bull, Young Citizen, Commonweal, New India *and* Herald of the Star.

Collaborative works

The freethinker's text-book. Ed C. Bradlaugh, A. Besant, and C. Watts 1876–8.
Fabian essays in socialism. Ed G. B. Shaw 1889, 6th edn with introd by A. Briggs 1962. Besant's essay entitled Industry under socialism.
The Theosophical Society and H. P. B. By A. Besant and H. Burrows. 1891.
Thought-forms. By A. Besant and C. W. Leadbeater. 1905, Wheaton IL 1969; tr Du 1905, Fr 1925.
Occult chemistry: a series of clairvoyant observations on the chemical elements. By A. Besant and C. W. Leadbeater. Adyar [1909], rev edn by A. P. Sinnett 1919, 3rd edn Adyar 1951.
Man: whence, how and whither. A record of clairvoyant investigation. By A. Besant and C. Bradlaugh. Adyar 1913, 1922, Chicago 1922.
The origin and history of reincarnation. [1921.] Includes writings of A. Besant and others.
Theosophy and world-problems. By A. Besant, C. Jinarajadasa, J. Krishnamurti and G. S. Arundale. Adyar 1922.
The real and the unreal. By A. Besant, C. Jinarajadasa and G. S. Arundale. Adyar 1923.
The lives of Alcyone. By A. Besant and C. W. Leadbeater. 2 vols Adyar 1924.

Letters

Bright, Esther. Old memories and letters of Annie Besant. 1936.
Jinarajadasa, C. (ed). Extracts from letters of C. W. Leadbeater to Annie Besant, 1916–1923. Adyar 1952.
Ross, J. E. Krotona of old Hollywood. Montecito CA 1989. Includes many verbatim letters of Besant.

Translations

The idea of God in the revolution. By E. Acollas. [1877.]
The influence of heredity on free will. By L. Büchner. 1880.
Mind in animals. By L. Büchner. 1880.
The religion of Israel: a study in comparative mythology. By J. Soury. [1881.]
The Bhagavad Gita or the lord's song. 1895, Adyar 1953 (3rd edn).
The Bhagavad-Gita. With Sanskrit text, free translation into English, literal translation, and an introduction on Sanskrit grammar. 1905, rptd 1924, 1927.

Editions

The secular song and hymn book. 1876.
The fruits of philosophy. By C. Knowlton. Ed C. Bradlaugh and A. Besant. 1878, Chicago 1878.
What is Theosophy? A handbook for inquirers into the wisdom-religion. By W. R. Old. 1891.
The secret doctrine: the synthesis of science, religion, and philosophy. By H. P. Blavatsky. 3rd edn ed A. Besant and G. R. S. Mead 1893.
First steps in occultism. By H. P. Blavatsky and M. Collins. 1895.
The doctrine of the heart: extracts from Hindu letters. 1899, rptd 1903.
The universal text book of religion and morals. 3 pts Adyar 1911–15; pt 1 tr Fr 1911.
Gandhian non-co-operation, or shall India commit suicide? A vademecum against non-co-operation for all Indian patriots. Madras 1920.
Work of the Indian legislatures. Compiled under the order of the national conference. Madras 1923.

§2

West, G. The life of Annie Besant. 1929.
Obits: The Times 21 Sep 1933; Vote 29 Sep 1933; Modern Rev (Calcutta) 74 1933; Indian Rev (Madras) 34 1933; Hindu (Madras) 23 Sep 1933; Indian Ladies Mag 6 1933; Theosophy in India. Special memorial vol Oct 1933.
The Annie Besant centenary book 1847–1947. Adyar 1947. Essays by colleagues and friends.
Nethercot, A. The first five lives of Annie Besant. 1960. The last four lives of Annie Besant. 1963.
Taylor, A. Annie Besant: a biography. 1992. [NFA]

Isabella Bird, Isabella Lucy Bird, later Bishop

1831–1904

Selections

The grand beyond. The travels of Isabella Bird Bishop. Selected and introduced by C. P. Haveley. 1984.

§1

The Englishwoman in America. 1856 (anon), 1856 (2nd edn); London and Madison WI 1966 (foreword and notes by A. H. Clark).
REVIEWS: Athenaeum 1473 1856; Saturday Rev 1 1856.
The revival in America, by an English eye-witness. 1858. Anon.
The aspects of religion in the United States of America. 1859. Anon.
Notes on old Edinburgh. Edinburgh 1869. Anon.
The Hawaiian archipelago: or six months among the ... Sandwich Islands. 1875, 1876 (2nd edn), 1880 (3rd edn), 1881 (4th edn), New York 1881, 1882, London 1886, 1890 (7th edn), New York 1893, 1894, London 1905; Honolulu 1964 (pbd as Six months on the Sandwich Islands); London 1986 (pbd as Six months in Hawaii. Facs of 1875 edn with an introd by P. Barr).
REVIEWS: Athenaeum 2474 1875; Spectator 48 1875; Dial 18 1895.
A lady's life in the Rocky Mountains. First pbd in Leisure Hour 27 1879 (illus), 1879 (2nd edn), New York 1879, London 1880 (3rd edn), New York 1880, London 1881 (4th edn), New York 1881, 1882, 1883, London 1885, London and New York 1885, New York 1886, 1887, 1888, London and New York 1893, London 1894, New York 1894, London and New York 1900, London 1910 (7th edn), 1924; Berkeley CA 1945 (pbd as Journey to Truckee; 175 copies printed); Norman OK [1960] (new edn with an introd by D. J. Boorstin); 1982 (facs of 1880 edn with an introd by P. Barr); 1988 (with an introd by D. Murphy).
REVIEWS: Athenaeum 2722 1879; Spectator 52 1879; Nation (New York) 30 1880.
Selections from A lady's life in the Rocky Mountains. 1923 (Blackie's English Texts).
Unbeaten tracks in Japan. 2 vols 1880, 1880 (2nd edn), 1880 (3rd edn), 1 vol New York [1880?], London 1881 (4th edn), New York 1881, 1883, London 1886, 1888, New York 1888, London 1893, 1900 (new edn), 1905, 1911, New York [1916], Geneva [1971]; London 1984 (introd by P. Barr), Boston 1987; London 1885 (abridged edn), 1911 (reissue of abridged edn); tr Fr 1888.
REVIEWS: Nation (New York) 31 1880; Quart Rev 150 1880; Spectator 53 1880; Edinburgh Rev 315 1881; London Quart and Holborn Rev 55 1881.
The golden Chersonese and the way thither. 1883 (illus), New York 1883, 1884, 1885, 1886, London and New York 1892; Kuala Lumpur 1967 (introd by W. Gungwu), Kuala Lumpur and Oxford 1980, Singapore and Oxford 1990; 1983 (introd by R. Hanbury-Tenison); tr Ger 1884.
REVIEWS: Dial 4 1883; Edinburgh Rev 323 1883; Fortnightly Rev 40 1883; Nation (New York) 36 1883; Spectator 56 1883.
Journeys in Persia and Kurdistan. 2 vols 1891 (illus), New York 1891 (illus); vol 1 1988 (introd by P. Barr), vol 2 1989 (introd by S. Guppy).
REVIEWS: Athenaeum 3351 1892; Atlantic Monthly 69 1892; Blackwood's Mag 151 1892; Critic 20 (n.s. 17) 1892; Nation (New York) 54 1892.
Heathen claims and Christian duty. New York [1893], [1894].
Among the Tibetans. 1894 (illustr E. Whymper), New York and Chicago 1894, 1904 (new edn).
REVIEWS: London Quart and Holborn Rev 83 1894; Nation (New York) 59 1894; Spectator 73 1894; Westminster Rev 142 1894.
Korea and her neighbours. 2 vols 1898 (illus with a preface by Sir W. C. Hillier), New York and Chicago 1898, New York 1898 (3rd edn), 1905; 1985 (introd by P. Barr).
REVIEWS: Athenaeum 3664 1898; Blackwood's Mag 163 1898; Bookman 13 1898; Critic 32 (n.s. 29) 1898; Dial 24 1898; London Quart and Holborn Rev 90 1898; Nation (New York) 66 1898; Spectator 80 1898.
The Yangtze valley and beyond. 2 vols 1899, New York 1899, 1900; 1985 (facs of 1899 edn with an introd by P. Barr), Boston 1987.
REVIEWS: Dial 28 1900; Nation 70 1900; Nat Geographic Mag 11 1900.
Chinese pictures. Notes on photographs made in China. 1900, New York [1900?], London 1904, New York 1904.
A traveller's testimony. 1905.

Contributions to periodicals

Victoria, Australia. Leisure Hour 26 1877.
Malay peninsula. Leisure Hour 32 1883.
A lady's winter holiday in Ireland. Murray's Mag 3 1888.
Journey in western Sze-Chuan. Geographical Jnl 10 1897.
Education in China: an elementary school. Critic 35 1899.
Notes on Morocco. Monthly Rev 5 1901.

Preface

Ballard, S. Fairy tales from far Japan. With a prefatory note by Bishop [1898].
Bird wrote for numerous mags and periodicals including Family Treasury, Good Words, Leisure Hour, Monthly Rev, Patriot, Quart Rev, St James's Gazette *and* Sunday Mag. *See also* Wellesley *5 1989*.

§2

Stoddart, A. M. The life of Isabella Bird. 1906.
Chappell, J. In her Women of worth, [1908].
In DNB 1901–1911.
Williams, C. The story of Isabella Bird Bishop. 1909.
Barr, P. M. A curious life for a lady: the story of Isabella Bird. 1970.
Kaye, E. Amazing traveller. Isabella Bird. Boulder CO 1994.

Augustine Birrell 1850–1933

See LR *and* NRA *for mss and letters; notable collections in BL, Bodleian, Leeds Univ Lib, Liverpool Univ Lib and Westfield College Lib (London).*

Collections and selections

Collected essays. 2 vols 1899. Contains Obiter dicta (2 ser), Res judicatae, Essays about men, women and books.
Selected essays 1884–1907. [1909.]
Thoughts from Augustine Birrell. Selected by E. E. Morton 1913.
Self-selected essays: a second series. 1916.
Collected essays and addresses 1880–1920. 3 vols 1922. Includes 5 uncollected essays.
Essays of to-day and yesterday. Ed F. H. Pritchard 1926.

§1

Obiter dicta. Ser 1 1884 (anon and priv ptd), 1885, numerous edns; ser 2 1887; 2 ser London 1910. Ser 1 includes an essay on Falstaff by G. Radford.
Thomas Carlyle. 1885.
The life of Charlotte Brontë. 1887.
Res judicatae. 1892.
Essays about men, women and books. 1894.
The Liberal Magazine. [1894.]
The duties and liabilities of trustees: six lectures. 1896.
Four lectures on the law of employers' liability at home and abroad. 1897.
The ideal university: a lecture. [1898.]
Sir Frank Lockwood: a biographical sketch. 1898.
Seven lectures on the law and history of copyright in books. 1899.
Essays and addresses. New York 1901.
Miscellanies. 1901.
An appreciation of John Wesley's Journal. 1902.
William Hazlitt. 1902 (EML).
Emerson: a lecture. 1903.

In the name of the Bodleian and other essays. 1905.
Andrew Marvell. 1905 (EML).
Essays. 1912. On Carlyle, Milton, Pope, Johnson, Gibbon.
On a dictum of Mr Disraeli's and other matters: an address. 1912.
A rogue's memoirs. 1912. Three essays extracted from Obiter dicta.
Frederick Locker-Lampson. 1920.
More obiter dicta. 1924.
Three essays. New York 1924.
Some early recollections of Liverpool. Liverpool 1924.
Et cetera. 1930.
Things past redress. [1937.] Autobiographical.
John Wesley: some aspects. 1938.
Burke's speech on conciliation with America, and America, and Edmund Burke, an essay by Augustine Birrell. Ed C. R. Morris, New York [1945].

Editions, introductions and translations

Lamb, C. The essays of Elia. Ed Birrell 1888. Numerous edns.
Uzanne, O. The book-hunter in Paris. Preface by Birrell 1893.
Boswell, W. Life of Johnson. Ed Birrell 1896.
Locker-Lampson, F. My confidences. Ed Birrell 1896.
Browning, R. The poetical works. Ed Birrell and F. G. Kenyon 1896, New York 1907.
Sheridan, R. B. B. The school for scandal. Introd by Birrell 1896.
Five years of Tory government, 1895–1900. 1900. Eight years of Tory government, 1895–1903. 1903. Ten years of Tory government, 1895–1905. Ed and preface by Birrell 1905.
Locker-Lampson, F. An appendix to the Rowfant library. Preface by Birrell 1900.
Broadhurst, H. The story of his life. Introd by Birrell 1901.
Hugo, V. The story of the bold Pécopin. Tr E. and A. Birrell 1902.
Johnson, S. Prayers and meditations. Preface by Birrell [1904].
Shakespeare, W. The complete works. Introd by Birrell 1906.
Watson, R. S. The national liberal federation. Introd by Birrell 1907.
Browning, R. Poems. Selected and introd by Birrell. [1908.]
Brewer, D. J. Crowned masterpieces of eloquence. Introd by Birrell 1910.
O'Brien, R. John Bright. Preface by Birrell 1910.
Lampson, S. A quaker post-bag. Introd by Birrell 1910.
Aphorisms on authors and their ways: with some general observations on the humours, habits, and methods of composition of poets – good, bad, and indifferent, diligently collected from Johnson's 'Lives'. Ed Birrell 1917.
Concerning solicitors, by one of them. Preface by Birrell 1920.
Locker-Lampson, F. Patchwork. With a note by Birrell 1927.
Disraeli, B. Home letters. Introd by Birrell 1928.

Contributions to periodicals and collaborative works

For Birrell's contributions to Contemporary Rev, Cornhill Mag, Edinburgh Rev, Fortnightly Rev, Macmillan's Mag, New Rev *and* Nineteenth Cent, *see* Wellesley *vol 5. He also contributed an entry to the* DNB.

The transmission of Dr Johnson's personality portrait. Modern Eloquence Dec 1884.
Barristers. In Pitcairn, Unwritten laws and ideals, 1899.
Changes in equity, procedure, and principles: a lecture on the changes in the law of England during the nineteenth century. In A century of law reform, 1901.
An appreciation of John Wesley's Journal. In J. Wesley, The heart of John Wesley's Journal, [1903].
John Wesley, his times and work. In G. Eayrs, Letters of John Wesley, 1915, ch 2.
Truth-hunting. In L. W. Smith (ed), Mechanism of English style, 1916.
Carlyle. In Modern English essays, 1922.
Introduction. In T. J. Wise (ed), Catalogue of the Ashley Lib collection, New York 1934.

§2

Gallwey, P. Mr Birrell's Education Bill. Selections from the objections raised against it. 1906.
Harding, C. Under the papal crown: or 'Birrellism' in Ireland. [1915.]
Gaines, C. H. The good taste of Birrell. North Amer Rev June 1923.
Kernahan, C. In Celebrities, 1923.
Pritchard, F. H. (ed). In Essays of Today and Yesterday, no 14 1926.
[MD]

Stopford Augustus Brooke 1832–1916

See LR *and* NRA *for Brooke's mss and letters. Notable collections in BL, Castle Howard, Nat Lib of Wales, Pierpont Morgan Lib.*

Bibliographies

Standley, F. L. Stopford Augustus Brooke, 1832–1916: a primary bibliography. BB 24 no 4 1964; *see also* under §2, *below*.

Collections and selections

Brilliants: selected from the writings of Stopford A. Brooke, by Mrs A. Williams. New York [1893].
'Die to live': selections from Stopford Brooke, arranged by Mrs O. Jacks. [1924.]

§1

Sermons preached in St James's Chapel. 1869. Numerous later edns.
Freedom in the Church of England: six sermons. 1871.
Christ in modern life: sermons preached in St James's Chapel. 1872. Numerous later edns.
Some philosophical aspects of poetry. Edinburgh 1872. An address.
Theology in the English poets: Cowper, Coleridge, Wordsworth and Burns. 1874, [1910] (EL, with a note by E. Rhys).
English literature. 1876; tr Fr [1892]. Numerous other edns, often extensively rev and enlarged by, among others, F. Gilbert, C. F. Johnson and G. Sampson, and supplemented with accounts of Amer lit by, among others, J. Harris Patton and G. R. Carpenter.
The fight of faith: sermons. 1877.
Milton. 1879.
Riquet of the tuft: a love drama. 1880.
Faith and freedom. Boston 1881.
Sermons . . . preached in Bedford Chapel. 1881–5 (31 pts, priv ptd).
The spirit of the Christian life: sermons. 1881.
The story of Nain. 1885.
The inaugural address to the Shelley Society. 1886 (priv ptd), rptd in Studies in poetry 1907, *below*.
Sunshine and shadow: meditations from the sermons of S. A. Brooke. 1886.
The unity of God and man, and other sermons. 1886.
The early life of Jesus: sermons. 1888.
Poems. 1888.
Dove cottage: Wordsworth's home from 1800–1808. 1890.
Reasons for secession from the Church of England. 2 pts 1891.
The history of early English literature: being the history of English poetry from its beginning to the accession of King Ælfred. 2 vols 1892, 1 vol edn New York 1892.
Short sermons. 1892.
The development of theology as illustrated in English poetry from 1780–1830. 1893. The Essex Hall lecture.
The need and use of getting Irish literature into the English tongue: an address. 1893.
God and Christ: sermons. 1894.
Jesus and modern thought: discourses. 1894.
Tennyson: his art and relation to modern life. 1894 (the Introduction appeared originally in Contemporary Rev Dec 1892). Numerous later 1-vol and 2-vol edns.
The Old Testament and modern life. 1896. Sermons.

English literature, from the beginning to the Norman Conquest. New York 1898. Numerous later edns.
The gospel of joy. 1898.
The ship of the soul, and other papers. 1898.
Religion in literature and religion in life: two lectures. 1900.
King Alfred, as educator of his people and man of letters ... With an appendix of passages from the writings of Alfred, selected and translated from the Old English by Kate M. Warren. 1901.
The poetry of Robert Browning. 1902, 2 vols 1905.
The kingship of love. 1903.
On ten plays of Shakespeare. 1905.
The life superlative. 1906.
The sea-charm of Venice. 1907.
Studies in poetry. 1907. On Blake, Scott, Shelley, Keats. Contains also The inaugural address, *above*.
A study of Clough, Arnold, Rossetti and Morris: with an introduction on the course of poetry from 1822 to 1852. 1908, New York 1908 (as Four Victorian poets), 1910 (as Clough, Arnold, Rossetti and Morris), 1913 (as Four poets: Clough, Arnold, Rossetti, Morris).
The onward cry, and other sermons. 1911.
Ten more plays of Shakespeare. 1913.
The spikenard, and other sermons. 1919. Introd by J. H. Weatherall.
Naturalism in English poetry. New York 1920, London 1922 (omitting some essays). On Dryden, Pope, Young, Thomson, Collins, Gray, Crabbe, Cowper, Burns, Wordsworth, Shelley, Byron.
Various sermons by Brooke appeared separately and in collections, such as Modern sermons *1883. He contributed to composite works, such as* Chambers' Cyclopedia of English Literature, *ed D. Patrick, 3 vols, 1902–4. He wrote reviews and articles for* Century Mag, Contemporary Rev, Dublin Univ Mag, Hibbert Jnl, Living Age, Macmillan's Mag, New England Mag, Nineteenth Cent *and* Popular Mag *(see also* Wellesley *5 1989).*

Editions and introductions

The life and letters of the Rev F. W. Robertson. Ed Brooke 1865, 2 vols Boston 1866, 1876 (as Frederick W. Robertson. Lectures, addresses and other literary remains), New York 1903 (as Life, letters, lectures and addresses of Fredk. W. Robertson); tr Ger 1888.
Shelley, P. B. Poems from Shelley. Selected and arranged by Brooke 1880. Numerous later edns.
Christian hymns. Ed Brooke 1881.
Turner, J. M. W. The liber studiorum. Ed Brooke 1882, 1885 (as Notes on the liber studiorum), [1890] (abbreviated edn as A selection from the liber studiorum).
Méyron, C. Old Paris: ten etchings ... reproduced in copper and accompanied with preface and notes by Brooke. 1887.
Shelley, P. B. Epipsychidion. Introd by Brooke and a note by A. C. Swinburne, ed R. A. Potts 1887.
Coleridge, S. T. The golden book of Coleridge. Ed Brooke 1895.
Crackanthorpe, H. Last studies ... with a poem by Brooke. 1897.
Wordsworth, W. Poems dedicated to national independence and liberty. Introd by Brooke 1897.
A treasury of Irish poetry in the English tongue. Ed Brooke and T. W. Rolleston 1900, 1932 (rev and enlarged).
Lawless, E. With the wild geese. Introd by Brooke 1902.
Warren, K. M. A treasury of English literature. Introd by Brooke 1906.
Wordsworth, W. Poems. Selected and introd by Brooke 1907.
Rolleston, T. W. H. The high deeds of Finn, and other bardic romances of ancient Ireland. Introd by Brooke 1910.

§2

Reverend Stopford A. Brooke, M. A. Dublin Univ Mag vol 62, Sep 1878.
Fay, E. The Rev Stopford Brooke's reason for his total abandonment of orthodoxy. Sheffield 1880.
Matthews, W. The London pulpit. In Men, places, and things, Chicago 1887.
Clarke, W. Stopford Brooke. New England Mag vol 3, Oct 1890.
Molloy, J. F. The Unitarians: Sunday morning with the Rev Stopford Brooke. In The faiths of the people, 1892.
Stopford Brooke. Outlook vol 70, 5 Apr 1902.
Clegg, S. The library of the Rev Stopford Augustus Brooke, M. A. Bibliophile vol 3, June 1909.
Carpenter, J. E. The theology of the Rev Stopford Brooke. Hibbert Jnl vol 15, Oct 1916.
Hull, E. Stopford Augustus Brooke. Fortnightly Rev vol 106, Sep 1916.
Stopford, F. The late Mr Stopford Brooke. Spectator vol 116, 1 and 8 Apr 1916, vol 117, 29 July 1916.
Jacks, L. P. The life and letters of Stopford Brooke. 2 vols New York 1917.
Chesterton, G. K. Stopford Brooke. Hibbert Jnl vol 16, Apr 1918.
Drinkwater, J. Stopford Brooke. Quart Rev vol 229, Apr 1918.
Lovett, R. M. The real Stopford Brooke. Dial vol 65, 16 Nov 1918.
Stevenson, G. H. The elementals and a popular teacher. Fortnightly Rev vol 118, Oct 1922.
Standley, F. L. Stopford Augustus Brooke: studies toward a biography. Evanston IL 1961. Unpbd diss.
Standley, F. L. Stopford Brooke. New York [1972]. Twayne's English Authors ser; contains bibliography.
Crook, K. Matthew Arnold and Stopford Brooke. Nineteenth Cent Prose 16 1989. [JMB]

Robert Williams Buchanan 1841–1901

See col 722.

Arthur John Butler 1844–1910

§1

Dante: his times and his work. 1894.
Life and letters of W. J. Butler, Dean of Lincoln. 1897. Preface signed A. J. B.
Some Elizabethan cipher-books. 1901.
Dante and the renaissance. [1909.]

Editions, introductions and translations

Dante Alighieri. The purgatory. Tr and ed Butler 1880.
Dante Alighieri. The paradise. Tr and ed Butler 1885.
Dante Alighieri. La commedia. Ed Butler 1890.
Dante Alighieri. The hell. Tr and ed Butler 1892.
De Marbot, Baron. The memoirs. Tr Butler 1892.
Scartazzini, G. A. A companion to Dante. Tr Butler 1893.
Count Cavour and Madame de Circourt. Ed Count Nigra, tr Butler 1894.
Sainte-Beuve, C. A. Select essays chiefly bearing on English literature. Tr Butler [1895].
Ratzel, Prof Friedrich. The history of mankind. Tr from the 2nd edn by Butler 1896–8.
Thiébault, Baron. The memoirs. Tr and condensed by Butler 1896.
Bismarck, the man and the statesman. Tr from Ger under supervision of Butler 1898.
Calendar of state papers, foreign series, of Elizabeth 1577–83. Ed Butler 6 vols 1901–13. Vol 6 completed by S. C. Lomas.
Federn, C. Dante and his time. Introd by Butler 1902.
Plumptre, E. H. The life of Dante. Ed Butler 1903.
The forerunners of Dante. Ed Butler 1910.

Contributions to periodicals

Arthur John Butler contributed to Cornhill Mag *and* Nat Rev *(see* Wellesley *vol 5). He also wrote for the* Athenaeum. *For Butler's contributions to* The Cambridge modern history *etc, see bibliography in A. T. Quiller-Couch,* Memoir of Butler, *1917.*

§2

Quiller-Couch, A. T. Memoir of Arthur John Butler. 1917. [MD]

Samuel Butler 1835–1902

Major collections of Butler mss are in the BL, Williams College MA, and St John's College Cambridge. See IELM *vol 4 pt 1 1982. There is also a considerable number of letters in Italian by Butler; some were exhibited at the Samuel Butler Exhibition held at the Biblioteca Civica 'Farinone-Centa', Varallo-Sesia, as part of the five hundredth anniversary of the Sacro Monte, Varallo, in 1986. These are for the most part in the possession of the descendants of Butler's Italian correspondents.*

Bibliographies

Jones, H. F. In his Butler: a memoir, 2 vols 1919.

The Samuel Butler collection at St John's College, Cambridge; a catalogue and a commentary by H. F. Jones and A. T. Bartholomew. Cambridge 1921.

Hoppé, A. J. A bibliography of the writings of Butler and of writings about him, with some letters from Butler to F. G. Fleay now first published. [1925.] For addns, *see* J. B. Fort, Samuel Butler, Bordeaux 1934.

Catalogue of the collection of Butler in the Chapin Library, Williams College, Williamstown, MA. Portland ME 1945.

Harkness, S. B. The career of Butler: a bibliography. 1955.

Gerber, H. E. Bibliography [of Butler]. Eng Fiction in Transition 1 1957.

Howard, D. F. Butler manuscripts. Eng Fiction in Transition 1 1957.

Davies, D. The Butler collection of the Honnold Library. Claremont Quart 7 1960.

Howard, D. F. In G. H. Ford (ed), Victorian fiction: a second guide to research, New York 1978.

Collections

The Shrewsbury edition of the works. Ed H. F. Jones and A. T. Bartholomew 20 vols 1923–6.

The essential Butler. Ed G. D. H. Cole 1950, 1961 (rev).

§1

For music, see A. J. Hoppé, Bibliographies, above. For paintings, drawings and photography, see Butler collection at St John's College, *and* Catalogue of the collection of Butler in the Chapin Library *(above) and E. S. Shaffer,* Erewhons of the eye. Samuel Butler as painter, photographer, and art critic, *1988, for 100 illustrations and bibliography of exhibitions and exhibition catalogues.*

A first year in Canterbury settlement. 1863; ed R. A. Streatfeild 1914 (with other early essays); ed A. C. Brassington and P. B. Maling, Auckland and Hamilton 1964.

The evidence for the resurrection of Jesus Christ, as given by the four evangelists, critically examined. 1865. Anon.

Erewhon: or over the range. 1872 (anon), 1872 (rev and corrected), 1901 (rev); ed F. N. Hackett, New York 1917; ed L. Mumford, New York 1927; ed H. M. Tomlinson, New York 1931; ed A. Huxley, New York 1934; 1935 (Pen); ed D. McCarthy 1960; ed K. Amis, New York 1961; ed with an introd by P. Mudford, Harmondsworth 1970 (Pen, rptd 1974 and 1976); ed H.-P. Breuer and D. F. Howard, Newark DE 1981; tr Du 1873, Ger 1879, Fr 1920, Sp 1926, Ital 1945.

The fair haven: a work in defence of the miraculous element in our Lord's ministry upon earth, both as against rationalistic impugners and certain orthodox defenders, by the late J. P. Owen, edited by W. B. Owen, with a memoir of the author. 1873; ed R. A. Streatfeild 1913; ed A. T. Bartholomew 1929; ed G. Bullett 1938.

Life and habit: an essay after a completer view of evolution. 1878; ed R. A. Streatfeild 1910 (with addns), rptd London, Wildwood House, 1981.

Evolution, old and new: or the theories of Buffon, Dr Erasmus Darwin and Lamarck, as compared with that of Mr Charles Darwin. 1879, 1882 (with appendix and index); ed R. A. Streatfeild 1911.

Unconscious memory: a comparison between the theory of Dr Ewald Hering, professor of physiology at Prague, and the philosophy of the unconscious of Dr Edward von Hartmann; with translations from these authors. 1880; [ed R. A. Streatfeild] 1910 (with introd by M. Hartog).

Alps and sanctuaries of Piedmont and the Canton Ticino. 1882; ed R. A. Streatfeild 1913 (with author's revisions and index, and introd); Gloucester 1986.

Selections from previous works, with remarks on Mr G. J. Romanes' Mental evolution in animals, and A psalm of Montreal. 1884.

Luck or cunning as the main means of organic modification? an attempt to throw additional light upon the late Mr Charles Darwin's theory of natural selection. 1887, ed H. F. Jones 1920.

Ex voto: an account of the Sacro Monte or New Jerusalem at Varallo-Sesia, with some notice of Tabachetti's remaining work at the sanctuary of Crea. 1888, 1889 (rev and enlarged); New York and London 1890; reprint of Shrewsbury edn Ex voto, ed H. Festing Jones and A. T. Bartholomew, 1928; tr Ital by A. Rizzetti, Novara 1894.

A lecture on the humour of Homer, Jan 30, 1892; reprinted with preface and additional matter from the Eagle. Cambridge 1892.

'L'Origine Siciliana dell'Odissea', Rassegna della Letteratura Siciliana, anno I, 3–4, Acireale, 1893.

'On the Trapanese origin of the Odyssey', Cambridge 1893. Pam.

'Ancora sull'origine dell'Odissea', Rassegna della Letteratura Siciliana, anno II, 3–4, Acireale, 1894.

The life and letters of Dr Samuel Butler, headmaster of Shrewsbury School 1798–1836, and afterwards Bishop of Lichfield. 2 vols 1896.

The authoress of the Odyssey, where and when she wrote, who she was, the use she made of the Iliad, and how the poem grew under her hands. 1897; ed H. F. Jones 1922; 1922 (2nd edn); rptd with an introd by D. Grene, Chicago and London 1967. Butler's theory about the Odyssey was first announced in several articles written by him in Sicilian and English papers.

The Iliad of Homer, rendered into English prose. 1898; ed L. R. Loomis, New York 1942.

Shakespeare's sonnets reconsidered, and in part rearranged, with introductory chapters by Butler. 1899.

The Odyssey, rendered into English prose. 1900; ed L. R. Loomis, New York 1942.

The Iliad of Homer and The Odyssey, rendered into English prose by Samuel Butler. Chicago 1952.

Erewhon revisited twenty years later, both by the original discoverer of the country and by his son. 1901; ed G. M. Acklom, New York 1920.

The way of all flesh. [Ed R. A. Streatfeild] 1903; ed W. L. Phelps, New York 1916; ed T. Dreiser, New York 1936; ed G. B. Shaw 1936; ed J. Cochrane, with an introd and notes by R. Hoggart, 1947 (Pen); ed R. A. Gettmann, New York 1948; ed W. Y. Tindall, New York 1950; ed M. D. Zabel, New York 1950; ed G. M. Acklom, New York 1952; ed A. C. Ward 1953; ed L. B. Salomon, New York 1957; ed D. F. Howard, Boston 1964; 1966 (Pen) (7 reprints to 1980).

Essays on life, art and science. Ed R. A. Streatfeild 1904.

Seven sonnets and A psalm of Montreal. [Ed R. A. Streatfeild] Cambridge 1904 (priv ptd).

God the known and God the unknown. [Ed R. A. Streatfeild] 1909.

The humour of Homer, and other essays. Ed R. A. Streatfeild 1913. With a biographical sketch by H. F. Jones.

Hesiod's works and days: a translation. Central School of Arts and Crafts, London 1924.

Letters and notebooks

Note-books: Selections, ed H. F. Jones [1912], rptd 1985; Further extracts from the note-books, ed A. T. Bartholomew 1914; Further extracts, ed A. T. Bartholomew 1930; Further extracts from the

note-books, ed A. T. Bartholomew 1934; Selections, ed G. Keynes and B. Hill 1951; The note-books, vol 1 (1874–83), ed H.-P. Breuer 1984.
Butleriana. 1932 (Nonesuch); ed A. C. Bartholomew 1932. Compiled mainly from previously unpbd portions of the note-books by A. T. Bartholomew.
Letters between Butler and Miss E. M. A. Savage. Ed G. L. Keynes and B. Hill 1935.
Correspondence of Butler with his sister May. Ed D. F. Howard, Berkeley CA 1962.
The family letters of Butler 1841–86. Ed A. Silver, Stanford CA 1962.

§2

Sugameli, P. Origine trapanese dell' Odissea secondo Butler. Trapani 1892.
Streatfeild, R. A. Butler: a critical study. 1902.
Streatfeild, R. A. Samuel Butler. Monthly Rev Sep 1902.
Streatfeild, R. A. Butler: records and memorials. 1903.
Jones, H. F. Diary of a journey through North Italy to Sicily for the purpose of leaving the manuscripts of three books by Butler at Varallo-Sesia, Aci-Reale and Trapani. 1904.
MacCarthy, D. Samuel Butler. Independent Rev 3 1904.
Shaw, G. B. John Bull's other island and Major Barbara. 1907. Preface to Major Barbara.
Blum, J. Samuel Butler. [1910.]
Jones, H. F. Charles Darwin and Butler: a step towards reconciliation. 1911.
Salter, W. H. Essays on two moderns: Euripides; Butler. 1911.
Kellogg, V. L. Butler and biological memory. Science (Garrison NY) 35 1912.
H[arris], J. F. Butler and his note-books. 1913.
Jourdain, P. E. B. Aspects of Butler. Open Court 27 1913.
Barry, W. Butler of Erewhon. Dublin Rev 155 1914.
Hartog, M. M. Butler and recent mnemic biological theories. 1914.
Pestalozzi, G. Butler der jüngere: Versuch einer Darstellung seiner Gedankenwelt. Zurich 1914.
Rattray, R. F. The philosophy of Butler. Mind 23 1914.
Cannan, G. Butler: a critical study. 1915.
H[arris], J. F. Butler, author of Erewhon: the man and his work. 1916.
Heitland, W. E. A 'few earnest words' on Butler. [1916.]
Russell, E. S. Butler and the memory theories of heredity. In his Form and function, 1916.
Stillman, C. G. The literary and scientific work of Butler. North Amer Rev 204 1916.
Sincalie, M. The pan-psychism of Butler. In her A defence of idealism, 1917.
MacCarthy, D. Butler: an impression. In his Remnants, 1918.
Yeats, J. B. Recollections of Butler. In his Essays Irish and American, 1918.
Jones, H. F. Butler: a memoir. 2 vols 1919.
Clutton-Brock, A. In his Essays on books, 1920. 2 essays on Butler.
Duffin, H. C. Of Samuel Butler. In his Quintessence of Bernard Shaw, 1920.
Jones, H. F. Butler as a musical critic. Chesterton May 1920.
Larbaud, V. Butler (étude et fragments traduits d'Erewhon). Nouvelle Revue Française Jan 1920.
Larbaud, V. Préface, Erewhon. [1920], Paris 1961 [Fr trn].
Larbaud, V. Samuel Butler: conférence. Paris 1920.
Blum, J. ('Jean Florence'). Le litre et l'amphore. Paris 1924.
MacCarthy, D. Samuel Butler. Life & Letters Oct 1931.
Furbank, P. N. Samuel Butler. Cambridge 1948.
Shaw, G. B. Butler when I was a nobody. Saturday Rev of Lit 29 Apr 1950.
Jones, J. J. The cradle of Erewhon. Austin TX 1959.
Holt, L. J. Samuel Butler. Boston 1964 (Twayne English Authors ser), rev 1989.
Shaffer, E. S. Erewhons of the Eye. Samuel Butler as painter, photographer, and art critic. 1988. [ESS]

Edward Carpenter 1844–1929

See LR *and* NRA *for Carpenter's letters. Notable collections in Manchester UL, Sheffield Archives, Univ of Br Columbia, HRHRC.*

Bibliographies

A bibliography of the writings of Carpenter. 1916. Apparently by Carpenter himself; forms appendix to My days and dreams, *below*; also pbd separately.
A bibliography of Edward Carpenter. Sheffield 1949. Anon.
Delavenay, E. D. H. Lawrence and Edward Carpenter. 1971. Contains bibliography; *see under* §2, *below*.
Rowbotham, S. and J. Weeks. Socialism and the new life. 1977. Contains bibliography; *see under* §2, *below*.
Khan, S. A. Edward Carpenter (man and work). Aurangabad 1979. Contains bibliography; *see under* §2, *below*.
Tsuzuki, C. Edward Carpenter, 1844–1929. Cambridge 1980. Contains bibliography; *see under* §2, *below*.
Brown, T. Edward Carpenter: an annotated secondary bibliography. ELT 32 1989.

Selections

The simplification of life. Selected by H. Roberts 1905.
Selected writings. 1984. Introd by N. Greig (Gay Modern Classics).

§1

The religious influence of art. Cambridge 1870. Burney Prize essay for 1869.
Narcissus and other poems. 1873.
Moses: a drama in five acts. [1875], 1910 (rev as The promised land).
Desirable mansions. 1883. Rptd from Progress June 1883.
Towards democracy. Pt 1 Manchester 1883; 2 pts Manchester 1885; 3 pts 1892; pt 4 (Who shall command the heart?) 1902; 4 pts 1905; 1 vol 1980 (Gay Modern Classics); 1985 with foreword by G. Beith; numerous other edns; tr Ger [1903–9], Ital 1912 (pt 1), Fr 1914, Jap [1915], Rus nd, Ital c. 1980.
Modern science: a criticism. Manchester 1885; tr Rus 1898 with preface by L. N. Tolstoi.
England arise: socialist marching song. Words and music by Carpenter 1886.
England's ideal and other papers on social subjects. 1887, 1895 (rev); tr Ger [1912]. England's ideal rptd from To-day; other essays, such as The enchanted ticket, were subsequently pbd separately.
Socialism & religion: or, thoughts after reading Mr Carpenter's Ideal England. By An onlooker [pseud]. 1890.
Civilization: its cause and cure, and other essays. 1889, New York 1891 (abbreviated), 1919 (enlarged); numerous other edns; tr Du 1899, Ger 1903, Cz 1910.
From Adam's Peak to Elephanta: sketches in Ceylon and India. 1892, 1903 (rev), 1911 (chs 8–11 pbd separately as A visit to a gñáni).
Vivisection. 1893, 1905 (rev). With E. Maitland.
Homogenic love: and its place in a free society. Manchester 1894 (priv ptd); tr Ger 1895, 1979 (rev), Du nd.
Marriage in a free society. Manchester 1894; tr Ger [1895], Du 1898.
Sex-love: and its place in a free society. Manchester 1894; tr Ger 1895, Du c. 1920.
Woman and her place in a free society. Manchester 1894; tr Ger [1895], Du [1899].
St George and the dragon. Manchester 1895. A children's play.
Love's coming-of-age: a series of papers on the relations of the sexes. Manchester 1896, 1906 (5th edn enlarged), [1914] (omits Note on preventive checks), 1923 (12th edn further enlarged); numerous subsequent edns; tr Ger 1902, Du 1904, Ital 1909, Fr 1917. Collects earlier 1894 pams.

An unknown people. 1897.
Angels' wings: a series of essays on art and its relation to life. 1898.
Apuleius, L. The story of Eros and Psyche from Apuleius and the first book of the Iliad of Homer done into English. 1900 (verse, with Eros & Psyche in prose); 1923 (as Eros & Psyche ... together with some early verses). Partly rptd from Narcissus, 1873, *above*.
The art of creation: essays on the self and its powers. 1903, 1907 (enlarged); tr Ger 1908, Ital 1909, Fr 1923. Ch 2 of this book, entitled The art of creation, was pbd separately in 1903.
Prisons, police and punishment: an inquiry into the causes and treatment of crime and criminals. 1905; tr Fr 1907.
Days with Walt Whitman: with some notes on his life and work. 1906.
The intermediate sex: a study of some transitional types of men and women. [1908]; tr Ger 1907, Rus 1915.
Sketches from life in town and country, and some verses. 1908.
The drama of love and death: a study of human evolution and transfiguration. 1912; tr Ger 1924.
In thanking my friends on the occasion of my seventieth birthday. [1914.] An open letter.
Intermediate types among primitive folk: a study in social evolution. 1914. Originally pbd in the Amer Jnl of Religious Psychology, 1911, and the Revue d'Ethnographie et de Sociologie, 1911.
The healing of nations and the hidden sources of their strife. 1915.
My days and dreams: being autobiographical notes. 1916; Nottingham 1993 (as Sheffield and socialism; introd by D. Blunkett). Contains bibliography.
Never again! A protest and a warning addressed to the people of Europe. 1916; tr Danish 1916, Norwegian 1917.
Three ballads (an intermezzo in war time). Manchester 1917.
Towards industrial freedom. 1917.
Pagan & Christian creeds: their origin and meaning. 1920; tr Du 1925.
The teaching of the Upanishads ... Two lectures to popular audiences. 1920. Rptd from Pagan & Christian creeds.
A song of freedom and joy. [c. 1920.] Score by E. G. Bainton, words by Carpenter.
Some friends of Walt Whitman. 1924 (Br Soc for the Study of Sex Psychology Pbn no 13). Comments on Leaves of grass.
The psychology of the poet Shelley. 1925. With G. Barnefield.
Several of Carpenter's social and economic essays were pbd separately as tracts, some of them as Fabian Tracts. He wrote articles and reviews for Albany Rev, Amer Jnl of Religious Psychology, Clarion, Eng Rev, Fortnightly Rev, Humane Rev, International Jnl of Ethics, Macmillan's Mag, Progress, Reformer, Revue d'Ethnographie et de Sociologie, Savoy *and* To-Day *(see also* Wellesley *5 1989). He also contributed to composite works, such as* Cruelties of civilisation, *1895,* Humane science lectures by various authors, *1897,* Hand and Brain: a symposium of essays on socialism, *New York 1898, and É. Armand's* Les différents visages de l'anarchisme, *Paris 1927. Several of Carpenter's essays were later collected in anthologies, such as R. L. Woods (ed),* World of dreams, *New York 1947.*

Editions and introductions

Chants of labour: a song-book of the people with music. Ed Carpenter 1888.
Brown, J. M. Verses. Introd by Carpenter 1893.
Forecasts of the coming century, by a decade of writers. Ed Carpenter 1897.
Ioläus: an anthology of friendship. Ed Carpenter 1902, 1906 (enlarged), 1915 (as Anthology of friendship).
Rolland, R. E. P. E. Beethoven. Tr from Fr by C. Hull. Introd by Carpenter 1917.
Ellis, E. M. O. The new horizon in love and life. Introd by Carpenter 1921.
A ruṇāchalam. Light from the east. Ed Carpenter 1927.

§2

Crosby, E. H. Edward Carpenter, poet and prophet. Philadelphia 1901.
Swan, T. Carpenter: the man and his message. Manchester 1901, 1922 (rev).
Ellis, E. M. O. In Three modern seers, [1910]. On J. Hinton, F. Nietzsche and Carpenter.
Jackson, H. In All manner of folk, 1912.
Senard, M. Carpenter et sa philosophie. Paris 1914.
Lewis, E. Carpenter: an exposition and an appreciation. 1915.
Sime, A. H. M. Carpenter: his ideas and ideals. 1916.
Ellis, E. M. O. Personal impressions of Edward Carpenter. Berkeley Heights NJ [1922].
Willcocks, M. P. Walt Whitman and Edward Carpenter. In Between the old world and the new, 1926.
Edward Carpenter: in appreciation. Ed G. Beith 1931. Contributions by E. J. Dent, G. L. Dickinson, H. and E. Ellis, L. Housman, H. W. Nevinson et al.
Bell, T. H. Edward Carpenter: the English Tolstoi. Los Angeles 1932.
Bienert, G. Die Weltanschauung ECs. Unpbd diss, Vienna 1936.
Poets of democracy: Carpenter. Aeons of peace and progress. TLS 2 Sep 1944.
Forster, E. M. Edward Carpenter. Tribune 22 Sep 1944; later included in Two cheers for democracy, 1951.
Vanson, F. Carpenter: the English Whitman. Contemporary Rev June 1958.
Carpenter, E. F. Edward Carpenter 1844–1929: democratic author and poet, a restatement and reappraisal. 1970 (Friends of Dr Williams's Lib, lecture no 24).
Delavenay, E. D. H. Lawrence and Edward Carpenter: a study in Edwardian transition. 1971.
Rowbotham, S. and J. Weeks. Socialism and the new life: the personal and sexual politics of Edward Carpenter and Havelock Ellis. 1977.
Weeks, J. In Coming out: homosexual politics in Britain from the 19th century to the present. 1978.
Hartley, E. Edward Carpenter, 1844–1929. Sheffield 1979.
Khan, S. A. Edward Carpenter (man and work): with special reference to the influence of Walt Whitman on his life and art. Aurangabad 1979.
Tsuzuki, C. Edward Carpenter, 1844–1929: prophet of human fellowship. Cambridge 1980.
Brown, T. Edward Carpenter, Forster and the evolution of A room with a view. English Lit in Transition vol 30 1987.
Rahman, T. An alienated prophet: the relationship between Edward Carpenter's Psyche and the development of his metaphysic. Forum for Mod Lang Stud vol 23 1987.
Brown, T. (ed). Edward Carpenter and late Victorian radicalism. 1990.
Barna, D. K. Edward Carpenter, 1844–1929: an apostle of freedom. Burdwan 1991.
Buckton, O. S. In Closet dramas: strategies of secrecy and disclosure in four Victorian autobiographies, Unpbd PhD diss, Cornell Univ 1993.
Martin, R. K. Edward Carpenter and the double structure of Maurice. In E. M. Forster, ed J. Tambling, New York 1995. [JMB]

John Churton Collins 1848–1908

See LR *and* NRA *for mss and letters. Notable collections in Birmingham Univ Lib and BL.*

Collections and selections

Greek influence on English poetry. Ed and introd by M. Macmillan 1910. 5 lectures.
The posthumous essays of John Churton Collins. Ed L. C. Collins 1912. Shakespeare, Johnson, Burke, Arnold, Browning etc.

§1

Sir Joshua Reynolds as a portrait painter. 1874.
Bolingbroke: a historical study, and Voltaire in England. 1886.
Illustrations of Tennyson. 1891.
The study of English literature: a plea for its recognition and organization at the universities. 1891.
Jonathan Swift: a biographical and critical study. 1893.
Essays and studies. 1895.
Ephemera critica: or plain truths about current literature. 1901.
Studies in Shakespeare. 1904.
Studies in poetry and criticism. 1905.
Voltaire, Montesquieu and Rousseau in England. 1908; tr Fr 1911.

Contributions to periodicals and collaborative works

Collins wrote for a large number of literary periodicals. For his contributions to Contemporary Rev, Cornhill Mag, Macmillan's Mag, Nineteenth Cent, Quart Rev *and* Temple Bar, *see* Wellesley *5 1989. He also contributed to Andrew Lang's* Poet's country, *1907.*

Letters

Letters from Algernon Charles Swinburne to Collins 1873–86. 1910 (priv ptd).

Editions and introductions

Collins pbd edns of Br authors like Arnold, Dryden, Milton, Pope, Shakespeare, Tennyson, Tourneur et al, as well as of the Greek dramatists Aeschylus, Euripides and Sophocles. He was general editor of Arnold's British Classics for Schools *(7 vols), Arnold's* School Shakespeare, *and the Renaissance edn of Shakespeare's complete works.*

§2

Luce, M. E. Collins. 1908.
The Times 16–18 Sep 1908. Obituary.
Collins, L. C. Life and memoirs of John Churton Collins. 1912.
Kearney, A. The louse on the locks of literature. Edinburgh 1986.
[OD]

Sir Sidney Colvin 1845–1927

See LR *for letters. Notable collections in BL, Keats House, Univ of Delaware Lib.*

§1

Notes on the exhibitions of the Royal Academy and Old Water-Colour Society. 1869.
A word for Germany, from an English republican: being a letter to Professor Beesly. 1870. A reply to Beesly's A word for France.
Children in Italian and English design. 1872.
English artists of the present day. 1872.
A selection from occasional writings on fine art. 1873 (priv ptd).
Albert Duerer, his teachers, his rivals, and his scholars. 1877.
Landor. 1881 (EML).
Guide to drawings, prints and illustrative works exhibited in the second Northern Gallery. 1885.
A guide to the historical collection of prints in the second Northern Gallery of the British Museum. 1887.
Keats. 1887 (EML).
Guide to the exhibition of Chinese and Japanese paintings. 1888.
Richard Steele. 1888.
Guide to the exhibition of drawings and sketches by continental and British masters. 1892.
Selected poems. 1892.
Guide to an exhibition of drawings and engravings by the old masters, principally from the Malcolm Collection, and of engravings of the early German and Italian schools. 1894, 1895 (pt 1).
Ninety three drawings by Albert Dürer reproduced in facsimile from originals in the British Museum, accompanied with descriptive text by Sidney Colvin. 1894.
A Florentine picture chronicle. 1898. Illustr T. di Finiguerra.
Guide to an exhibition of drawing and etchings by Rembrandt. 1899.
A brief catalogue of the pictures in the Fitzwilliam Museum. 1901.
Samuel Richardson. 1902.
Early engravings and engravers in England 1545–1695: a critical and historical essay. 1905.
On concentration and suggestion in poetry. 1905.
Drawings of the old masters in the university galleries and in the library of Christ Church, Oxford. 1907.
Catalogue of early Italian engravings preserved in the department of prints and drawings in the British Museum. 1910.
Guide to an exhibition of drawings and sketches by old masters and artists of the English school. 1912.
Rosalba's journal. 1915.
John Keats: his life and poetry, his friends, critics and after-fame. 1917.
Memories and notes of persons and places. 1921.

Editions and introductions

Palma di Cesnola, L. The antiquities of Cyprus. Introd by Colvin 1873.
Flaxman, J. The catalogue of Flaxman drawings in the gallery of University College London. Preface by Colvin 1876.
Woltmann, A. F. G. A. History of painting. Ed Colvin 1880.
Landor, W. S. Selections from the writings. Ed Colvin 1882.
Jenkin, H. C. F. Papers. Ed Colvin 1887.
Original drawings by Rembrandt H. van Rijn. Ed Colvin et al, Berlin 1888–92.
Stevenson, R. L. Across the plains. Ed Colvin 1892.
Stevenson, R. L. Songs of travel. Ed Colvin 1895.
Stevenson, R. L. Vailima letters. Ed Colvin 1895.
Stevenson, R. L. The strange case of Dr Jekyll and Mr Hyde. Ed Colvin 1896.
Stevenson, R. L. Weir of Hermiston. Ed Colvin 1896.
Stevenson, R. L. Correspondence addressed to Sidney Colvin. Ed Colvin, New York 1896.
Stevenson, R. L. St Ives. Ed Colvin 1897.
Stevenson, R. L. Novels and tales. Ed Colvin, New York 1897–1919.
Cust, L. H. History of the Society of Dilettanti. Ed Colvin 1898.
di Finguerra, T. A Florentine picture-chronicle. Critical and descriptive text by Colvin 1898.
The letters of Robert Louis Stevenson to his family and friends. Selected and ed Colvin 1899, New York 1907, 1911 (enlarged with 150 new letters).
A Stevenson medley. Ed Colvin 1899.
Petrarca, F. The triumphs of Petrarca. With a note on the engravings by Colvin 1906.
Keats, J. The poems arranged in chronological order. Preface by Colvin 1915.
Keats, J. Letters to his family and friends. Ed Colvin 1921.
Stevenson, R. L. Fables. Ed Colvin 1923.
The works of Robert Louis Stevenson. Ed Colvin 1925 (South Sea edn).

Contributions to periodicals and collaborative works

For Colvin's contributions to Cornhill Mag, Edinburgh Rev, Macmillan's Mag, Fortnightly Rev, New Quart Mag, Nineteenth Cent, *and* Westminster Rev, *see* Wellesley *5 1989. He also contributed 4* DNB *entries.*

E. J. Poynter; Albert Moore; E. Burne-Jones; Simeon Solomon; Frederick Walker; Ford Madox Brown. In English painters of the present day, 1871.
Millais; George Mason; Thomas Armstrong; G. H. Boughton. In English artists of the present day, 1872.
Florence. In A complete collection of the English poems which have obtained the Chancellor's Gold Medal in the University of

Cambridge vol 2, 1894. Colvin's was the prize-winning poem in 1865.

Adventus Augusti. In British school at Rome, 1913.

Robert Louis Stevenson: his work and his personality, by Sidney Colvin, Edmund Gosse, Neil Munro, et al. 1924.

§2

Garvin, J. L. A perfect friend. Observer 15 May 1927.

Lucas, E. V. The Colvins and their friends. 1928. [MD]

William John Courthope 1842–1917

See LR *and* NRA *for letters. Notable collections in Bodleian and Reading Univ Lib.*

Bibliographies

Herford, C. H. Eng Illus Mag n.s. no 31 1904.

§1

Essay on chivalry. 1860 (priv ptd). Harrow prize essay.

The tercentenary of Corydon: a bucolic drama in three acts by 'Novus Homo' [pseud]. Oxford 1864.

The three hundredth anniversary of Shakespeare's death: a prize poem recited in the Theatre, Oxford, June 8, 1864. Oxford 1864.

Poems by 'Novus Homo' [pseud]. Oxford 1865.

The genius of Spenser: an English prize essay read in the Theatre, Oxford, June 17, 1868. 1868.

Ludibria lunae, or the wars of the women and the gods: an allegorical burlesque. 1869.

The paradise of birds: an old extravaganza in a modern dress. Edinburgh 1870.

Addison. 1884 (EML).

The liberal movement in English literature. 1885. The conservatism of eighteenth century poetry; Wordsworth's theory of poetry; The revival of romance: Scott, Byron, Shelley; Poetry, music and painting: Coleridge and Keats; Conclusion: the prospects of poetry.

The life of Alexander Pope. 1889. Vol 5 of The works of Alexander Pope, begun in 1871 by Whitwell Elwin, continued from 1881 and completed by Courthope, 10 vols 1871–89.

A history of English poetry. 6 vols 1895–1910.

Liberty and authority in matters of taste: an inaugural lecture delivered in the Sheldonian Theatre on the 15th of February 1896. 1896, rptd in Life in poetry: law in taste, 1901, *below*.

The longest reign: an ode on the completion of the sixtieth year of the reign of Her Majesty Queen Victoria. Oxford 1897.

Life in poetry: law in taste. 1901. 2 ser of lectures delivered in Oxford, 1895–1900.

A consideration of Macaulay's comparison of Dante and Milton. [1908.] Also in PBA 3 1908; rptd in Essays on Milton, Folcroft PA 1970.

The connexion between ancient and modern romance. [1911.] Also in PBA 5 1914.

Selections from the epigrams of M. Valerius Martialis: translated or imitated in English verse. 1914.

The country town and other poems. 1920. With a memoir by A. O. Prickard.

Contributions to periodicals and collaborative works

Courthope was, with Alfred Austin, editor of the Nat Rev *1883–7. He wrote articles and reviews for* Quart Rev, Nat Rev *and* Nineteenth Cent *(see* Wellesley *5 1989). He contributed to* Cambridge modern history *vol 10,* CHEL *vol 3,* Trans of the Royal Soc of Lit of the UK *vols 29 and 31.*

§2

Mackail, J. W. W. J. Courthope 1842–1917. [1919.] Also in PBA 9 1919. [FJMK]

Sir Henry Craik 1846–1927

See NRA *for Craik's letters. Notable collections in BL, Nat Lib of Scotland, Scottish Record Office.*

The English citizen: his rights and responsibilities. Ed Craik 30 vols 1881–1914.

The life of Jonathan Swift, Dean of St Patrick's, Dublin. 1882, 2 vols 1894.

Craik, G. L. A manual of English literature. 9th edn with an additional ch on recent lit by H. Craik [1883].

The State in its relation to education. 1884, 1896 (rev), 1914 (rev). (The English citizen.)

Swift, Jonathan. Swift: selections from his works. Ed with life, introd and notes by Craik 1892, 1912 (abbrev as The battle of the books).

English prose: selections with critical introductions by various writers and general introductions to each period. Ed Craik 5 vols 1893–6. Numerous later edns.

A century of Scottish history: from the days before the '45 to those within living memory. 2 vols 1901, 1 vol 1911.

Impressions of India. 1908.

Traill, H. D. Central government. Rev and corrected by Craik 1908. (The English citizen.)

The life of Edward, Earl of Clarendon, Lord High Chancellor of England. 2 vols 1911.

Swift, Jonathan. Travels ... by Lemuel Gulliver. Preface by Craik 1912.

Craik contributed to Blackwood's Mag, Fortnightly Rev, Glasgow Herald, Macmillan's Mag *and* Quart Rev *(see also* Wellesley *5 1989). Craik also pbd reports for the Scottish Education Department as chairman of various committees.* [JMB]

Henry Harry Cust, Henry John Cockayne Cust 1861–1917

Mss located in Princeton.

Bibliographies

See Wellesley *5 1989.*

Selections

Occasional poems. Chosen by N. C. and R. S. (E. M. E. Cust and Sir R. Storrs), Jerusalem 1918.
REVIEW: New York Times 7 Dec 1919.

§1

The small holdings bill. Debate in the House of Commons on the second reading. Grantham [1891].

Contributions to periodicals

Cust edited the Pall Mall Gazette *1892–6. For the* Nat Rev *and* New Rev, *see* Wellesley *5 1989.*

North Amer Rev. Feb 1900; July 1902.

Introductions and prefaces

Introd to Machiavelli's The art of war, and Florentine history, Tudor translations vols 39 and 40, 1905.

The Henley Memorial: an account of the inaugural ceremony in St Paul's Cathedral July 11th 1907. 1908. Speech.

Preface to G. de Wesselitsky, Russia and democracy: the German canker in Russia, 1915.

§2

Obits: Daily Telegraph 3 Mar 1917; The Times 3 Mar 1917.

Whibley, C. Musings without method. Blackwood's Mag Apr 1917.

Scott, J. W. R. In The story of the Pall Mall Gazette, 1950.

Scott, J. W. R. In The life and death of a newspaper (Pall Mall Gazette), 1952.

Guillaume, A. In William Ernest Henley et son groupe: néo-romantisme et impérialisme à fin du XIX siècle, Paris 1973.

Egremont, E. In The cousins: the friendship, opinions and activities of Wilfrid Scawen Blunt and George Wyndham, 1977.
Lambert, A. In Unquiet souls, New York 1984.
Abdy, J. and C. Gere. In The souls, 1984.
Ridley J. and C. Percy (ed). The letters of Arthur Balfour and Lady Elcho 1885–1917. 1992. [DA]

Henry Austin Dobson 1840–1921

For mss and letters, see LR *and* NRA. *There is an Austin Dobson Collection at the Univ of London Lib. Other notable collections in the BL, Leeds Univ Lib, and the Univ of Reading Lib.*

Bibliographies

Murray, F. E. A bibliography of Dobson. Derby 1900.
Murdoch, W. G. B. Eng Illus Mag Dec 1903–Jan 1904.
Dobson's library: notes on sales. TLS 23 Mar 1922.
Dobson, A. T. A. A bibliography of the first editions of published and privately printed books and pamphlets by Dobson. With a preface by E. Gosse 1925.
Dobson, A. T. A. In his Dobson: some notes, 1928. With chs by E. Gosse and G. Saintsbury.
Dobson, A. T. A. Catalogue of the collection of the works of Dobson, London University Library. 1960.

Collections and selections

Selected poems. 1892, 1924 (rev and enlarged).
Collected poems. New York [1895], 1902 (adds selection from Carmina votiva, 1901), 1909 (enlarged), 1913 (adds 27 pieces), Oxford 1923. Numerous edns.
Poems (selected). 1905.
An anthology of prose and verse. Foreword by E. Gosse, ed A. T. A. Dobson 1922, 1924 (rev).
Complete poetical works. Ed A. T. A. Dobson 1923, 1924 (rev and enlarged).
The WC reprints of Dobson's essays form a virtually complete edn, 9 vols Oxford 1923–6.

§1

Vignettes in rhyme. 1873, 1874 (with omissions and addns).
The civil service handbook of English literature. 1874.
Proverbs in porcelain. 1877, 1878 (enlarged), 1893 (as Proverbs in porcelain, to which is added Au revoir, the latter rptd from At the sign of the lyre; only retains the 6 proverbs from 1877 edn), Portland ME 1909.
Hogarth. 1879.
A handbook of English literature. 1880, 1896 (enlarged by W. H. Griffin), New York 1897.
Vignettes in rhyme and other verses. New York 1880, London 1883 (with addns and omissions as Old world idylls), 1906 (with further notes). Contents mainly a selection from Vignettes in rhyme and Proverbs in porcelain. Numerous edns.
Fielding. 1883 (EML).
Thomas Bewick and his pupils. 1884.
A calendar of the year, with verses by Austin Dobson. Troy NY [1885].
At the sign of the lyre. 1885, New York 1885 (with addns and omissions), London 1889 (enlarged). Numerous edns.
Richard Steele. 1885.
Life of Oliver Goldsmith. 1888.
Poems on several occasions. 2 vols 1889, 1895 (rev with 12 poems), New York 1895 (rev and enlarged). Contents mainly as in Old world idylls and At the sign of the lyre.
The sundial: a poem. New York 1890.
Four Frenchwomen. 1890, Toronto 1900, Oxford 1923 (WC).
Horace Walpole. 1890, 1927 (enlarged P. Toynbee).
William Hogarth. 1891, 1898 (enlarged), London 1900 (enlarged); ed W. Armstrong 1902, 1907 (enlarged); tr Fr 1904.
Alfred Lord Tennyson. 1892. Poem.
The ballad of Beau Brocade and other poems of the xviiith century. 1892, 1903 (with hand-coloured illustrations by H. Thomas).
Eighteenth century vignettes. Ser 1 1892, 1897 (At Leicester Fields added); ser 2 1894; ser 3 1896, New York 1896.
The story of Rosina and other verses. 1895, New York 1895.
Verses read at the dinner of the Omar Khayyám Club. 1897 (priv ptd).
Miscellanies. Ser 1, New York 1898, London 1899 (with addns and omissions as A paladin of philanthropy), Oxford 1925 (WC); ser 2 1901.
Oliver Goldsmith. New York 1899, Philadelphia 1902.
A paladin of philanthropy and other papers. 1899.
A paper of verses (selections from At the sign of the lyre). Boston 1899.
A Whitehall eclogue. [1899] (priv ptd).
Carmina votiva and other occasional verses. 1901 (priv ptd).
Samuel Richardson. 1902 (EML).
Side-walk studies. 1902, Oxford 1924 (WC).
To William John Courthope on his dining with the Johnson Club. [1902] (priv ptd).
Fanny Burney. 1903 (EML).
De libris: prose and verse. 1908, 1911 (adds 2 essays).
Lyrics by Austin Dobson. 1908.
Old Kensington Palace and other papers. 1910, Oxford 1926, 1939 (WC).
At Prior Park and other papers. 1912.
Eighteenth century studies. 1912.
Poems on the war. 1915.
Rosalba's journal, and other papers. 1915.
A bookman's budget. 1917. A collection of extracts from the works of English prose writers with numerous contributions from Dobson.
Later essays 1917–20. Oxford 1921.
Life and writings of Oliver Goldsmith. 1921.
An anthology of prose and verse. Ed A. T. A. Dobson with a foreword by E. Gosse 1922.
Side-walk studies. 1924.
Three unpublished poems. 1930 (priv ptd).

Editions, introductions and translations

L'Epine, E. L. V. J. The authentic story of Captain Castagnette. Tr Dobson 1866.
Whit, F. A. The civil service history of England. Rev Dobson 1870. Numerous edns.
Lang, A. The library. With a chapter on modern, Eng illus books by Dobson 1881.
Eighteenth century essays. Selected and annotated by Dobson 1882, New York 1882. Numerous edns.
Gay, J. Fables. With a memoir by Dobson 1882.
Defoe, D. The life and strange surprising adventures of Robinson Crusoe. Introd by Dobson 1883.
Goldsmith, O. The vicar of Wakefield. Preface and notes by Dobson 1883.
Herrick, R. Selections from the poetry. Ed Dobson 1883.
De Beaumarchais, P. A. C. Le barbier de Séville. Ed and notes by Dobson 1884.
Lang, A. Ballades and verses vain. Selected by Dobson 1884.
Steele, R. Selections from the Tatler, Spectator and Guardian. Introd by Dobson 1885, 1896 (rev).
Bewick, T. A memoir. Ed and annotated by Dobson 1887.
Goldsmith, O. She stoops to conquer. Introd by Dobson 1887.
Goldsmith, O. Poems and plays. Ed Dobson 1889.
Prior, M. Selected poems of Matthew Prior. Introd by Dobson 1889.
The quiet life: certain verses by various hands. Prologue and epilogue by Dobson, New York 1890.
Goldsmith, O. The citizen of the world. Ed Dobson 1891.

Fielding, H. The journal of a voyage to Lisbon. Introd and notes by Dobson 1892.
Goldsmith, O. The plays. Ed Dobson 1893.
Goldsmith, O. The poems. Ed Dobson 1893.
Chelidonius, B. The little passion of Albert Dürer. Introd by Dobson 1894.
Coridon's songs and other verses from various sources. Introd by Dobson 1894.
Old English songs. Introd by Dobson. 1894.
Austen, J. Pride and prejudice. Introd by Dobson 1895.
Marteilhe, J. Memoirs of a protestant. Introd by Dobson 1895.
Austen, J. Emma. Introd by Dobson 1896.
Austen, J. Sense and sensibility. Introd by Dobson 1896.
Hood, T. The haunted house. Introd by Dobson 1896.
Puckle, J. Puckle's club. Introd by Dobson 1896.
Austen, J. Mansfield Park. Introd by Dobson 1897.
Austen, J. Northanger Abbey and Persuasion. Introd by Dobson 1897.
The Spectator. Introd by Dobson 1897–8.
Walton, I. Lives of John Donne. Ed Dobson 1898.
Reade, C. Peg Woffington. Introd by Dobson 1899.
Walton, I. The compleat angler. Ed Dobson 1899.
Hazlitt, W. Lectures on the English comic writers. Under the editorial care of Dobson 1900.
Hogarth, W. The works. Ed Dobson 1900.
Boswell, J. The life of Samuel Johnson. Introd by Dobson 1901.
Monkhouse, W. C. Pasiteles the elder. Preface by Dobson 1901.
Hunt, J. H. L. The old court suburb. Ed Dobson 1902.
Burney, Fanny. Evelina. Introd by Dobson 1903.
Carroll, L. Alice's adventures in Wonderland. Proem by Dobson 1903.
Edgeworth, M. Tales. Introd by Dobson 1903.
Goldsmith, O. The bee and other essays. Introd by Dobson 1903.
Goldsmith, O. A good natur'd man and She stoops to conquer. Introd by Dobson 1903.
Thackeray, W. M. The history of Henry Esmond. Introd by Dobson 1903.
Barbeau, A. Life and Letters at Bath in the xviiith century. Ed Dobson 1904.
Evelyn, J. The diary. Introd by Dobson 1904.
Locker-Lampson, F. London lyrics. Introd and notes by Dobson 1904.
Burney, Fanny. Diary & letters (1778–1840) as edited by her niece C. Barrett. Preface and notes by Dobson 1904–5.
Addison, J. Selected essays. Introd by Dobson 1906.
Evelyn, J. The diary. Ed Dobson 3 vols 1906.
Goldsmith, O. The complete poetical works. Ed, introd and notes by Dobson 1906.
Scott, W. Lives of the novelists. Introd by Dobson 1906.
Shakespeare, W. The complete works. Introd by Dobson 1906.
Brown, J. Horae subsecivae. Introd by Dobson 1907.
Hunt, J. H. L. The old town. Ed, introd and notes by Dobson 1907.
Reynolds, J. The discourses. Introd by Dobson 1907.
Edgeworth, M. Tales. Introd by Dobson 1908.
Rose of my life. Prefatory poem by Dobson 1916.
Goldsmith, O. The poetical works. Ed Dobson 1927.
Goldsmith, O. The citizen of the world and The bee. Ed Dobson 1934.

Contributions to periodicals and collaborative works

Dobson's contributions to Fortnightly Rev, Nat Rev, Temple Bar *and* Contemporary Rev *are recorded in* Wellesley 5 *1989. He also contributed to* The poets and poetry of the century, *ed A. H. Miles, 1891, and* Cassell's little classics, *1909. He wrote 41 entries to the* DNB.

Letters

Dobson, A. T. A. (ed). Dobson: some letters from his friends. Cornhill Mag Aug–Oct 1927, May 1928.
Dobson, A. T. A. (ed). An Austin Dobson letter book. Introd by E. V. Lucas, Cleveland OH 1935.

§2

Watson, W. In his Excursions in criticism, 1893.
Ellis, S. M. Dobson. Fortnightly Rev Oct 1921; rptd in his Mainly Victorian, 1925.
Gosse, E. Dobson. Quart Rev vol 237 1922.
Kernahan, C. In Celebrities, 1923.
Noyes, A. The poems of Dobson. Bookman (London) Apr 1924.
Dobson, A. T. A. An Austin Dobson causerie. Cornhill Mag Feb 1925.
Dobson, A. T. A. Dobson: some notes; with chapters by Edmund Gosse and George Saintsbury. 1928.
Weygandt, C. Dobson Augustan. In his Tuesdays at ten, Philadelphia 1928.
Rawson, C. J. Dobson. N & Q Dec 1960. [MD]

Edward Dowden 1843–1913

See LR *and* NRA *for mss and letters. Notable collections in BL and Trinity College, Dublin.*

Bibliographies

Shorter, C. K. Eng Illustr Mag 29 May 1903.
Bayard, E. J. Irish Book Lover 4 June 1913.

§1

Considerations on the criticism of literature: an address. Dublin 1864.
Mr Tennyson and Mr Browning. In Afternoon lectures on English literature, Dublin 1869.
Shakspere: a critical study of his mind and art. 1875; tr Ger 1879, Ital 1895.
Poems. 1876, 1914 (ed E. D. Dowden 2 vols, with addns).
Shakspere. 1877.
Studies in literature 1789–1877. 1878. The French Revolution; The transcendental movement; The scientific movement and literature; Wordsworth; Landor; Tennyson; Browning; George Eliot; Hugo; Whitman etc.
Southey. 1879 (EML).
Spenser, the poet and teacher. 1882. Vol 1 of The complete works of Edmund Spenser, ed A. B. Grosart.
The life of Percy Bysshe Shelley. 2 vols 1886, 1 vol 1896.
Transcripts and studies. 1888. Carlyle, Shelley, Wordsworth, Spenser, Shakespeare, Marlowe, Milton, Browning.
Introduction to Shakespeare. 1893.
New studies in literature. 1895. Meredith, Bridges, Donne, Goethe, Coleridge, E. Scherer etc.
The French Revolution and English literature: lectures. 1897.
A history of French literature. 1897. Vol 2 of Short histories, ed E. Gosse.
Literary criticism in France. In Studies in European literature, being the Taylorian lectures 1889–1899, Oxford 1900.
Puritan and Anglican: studies in literature. 1900. Puritanism and English literature, Thomas Browne, Hooker, Herbert, Vaughan, Milton, Jeremy Taylor, Baxter, Bunyan, Butler, Transition to the eighteenth century.
William Shakespeare as a comic dramatist: a monograph. In Representative English comedies, ed C. M. Gayley, vol 1 1903.
Michel de Montaigne. 1905.
Robert Browning. 1905, 1915 (EL).
Essays, modern and Elizabethan. 1910. Pater, Ibsen, Heine, Goethe, Cowper and William Hayley, Shakespeare etc.
A woman's reliquary. Dundrum 1913.

Contributions to periodicals

Dowden contributed to a large number of periodicals. See Wellesley 5 *1989 for his contributions to* Blackwood's Edinburgh Mag, Contemporary Rev, Cornhill Mag, New Rev, Temple Bar *and* Westminster Rev.

Letters

Fragments from old letters: E. D. to E. D. W. 1869–92. [Ed E. D. Dowden] 1914.

Letters of Dowden and his correspondents. [Ed E. D. Dowden and H. M. Dowden, introd by J. Eglinton] 1914.

Letters about Shelley interchanged by Dowden, Richard Garnett and Wm Michael Rossetti. Ed R. S. Garnett 1917.

Editions, introductions and translations

For Dowden's edns of Shakespeare, see vol 1. He also edited works of Coleridge, Shelley, Southey, Wordsworth et al, and wrote introductions to edns of Browning, Carlyle, Goethe, Scott et al. In addition, he translated Goethe's Iphigineia in Tauris *and* West-Eastern Divan.

§2

The poems of Dowden. Irish Monthly Aug 1881.

Yeats, J. B. Edward Dowden. Nation Apr 1913.

Fiske, H. S. Recollections of Edward Dowden. Nation May 1913.

Irish Book Lover May 1913. Obituary.

Rolleston, T. W. Recollections of Dowden. Irish Book Lover Apr 1914.

Gerotwohl, M. A. Edward Dowden. Fortnightly Rev June 1914.

A catalogue of mss and autograph letters from the collection of the late Edward Dowden. 1914.

Sampson, M. W. The poetry of Edward Dowden. Nation Mar 1915.

Boyd, E. A. A lonely Irishman: Edward Dowden. In his Appreciations and depreciations, 1917.

Ludwigson, K. R. Edward Dowden. New York 1973.

Edward Dowden. In DLB vols 135 and 149. [OD]

Henry Havelock Ellis 1859–1939

See LR *and* NRA *for mss and letters. Notable collections in BL, Bristol Univ Lib, Harvard, HRHRC, Sheffield City Libs, UCLA, Yale.*

Bibliographies

Peterson, H. Havelock Ellis: philosopher of love. 1928. Contains bibliography.

Burne, G. S. Havelock Ellis: an annotated selected bibliography of primary and secondary works. Eng Lit in Transition vol 9 no 2 1966.

Walton, A. H. Bibliography. In Ellis, My life, 1967 (not in 1939 edn).

Collections and selections

The art of life: gleanings from the works of Ellis. Ed Mrs S. Herbert [1929].

Selected essays. Ed J. S. Collis 1936 (EL).

Poems. Ed J. Gawsworth [1937].

Morals, manners, and men. Ed A. G. W. 1939.

From Marlowe to Shaw: the studies, 1876–1936, in English literature of Havelock Ellis. Ed and introd by J. Gawsworth 1950. With prefatory letter by T. Hardy.

The genius of Europe. Ed F. Delisle 1950.

Sex and marriage: Eros in contemporary life. Ed J. Gawsworth 1951.

§1

The criminal. New York 1890 (Contemporary Science Ser VII), 1900 (rev and enlarged).

The new spirit. 1890, 1892 (with new preface), 1926 (with new preface), New York 1930 (Mod Lib, with preface and introd), Washington 1935 (Nat Home Lib, with 2 prefaces and introductions).

The nationalisation of health. 1892.

Man and woman: a study of human secondary sexual characters. 1894, 1904 (rev), 1914 (rev and enlarged).

Studies in the psychology of sex. 7 vols Philadelphia 1897–1928, 4 vols New York 1936 (with new preface).

Sexual inversion. 1897 (vol 1 of Studies in the psychology of sex), Philadelphia 1901 (renumbered as vol 2 of Studies in the psychology of sex), 1915 (rev and enlarged). The original version of this work was written in cooperation with J. A. Symonds, but withdrawn from pbn after Symonds's death at the request of his executors. Ger trn of this version 1896.

Affirmations. 1898, Boston and New York 1915 (with new preface).

A note on the Bedborough trial. 1898 (priv ptd).

The evolution of modesty. 1899 (vol 2 of Studies in the psychology of sex), Philadelphia 1903 (rev and renumbered as vol 1 of Studies in the psychology of sex), 1910 (rev and enlarged).

The nineteenth century: a dialogue in Utopia. 1900.

The analysis of the sexual impulse. Philadelphia 1903 (vol 3 of Studies in the psychology of sex), 1913 (rev and enlarged).

A study of British genius. 1904, 1926 (rev and enlarged).

Sexual selection in man. Philadelphia 1905 (vol 4 of Studies in the psychology of sex).

Erotic symbolism. Philadelphia 1906 (vol 5 of Studies in the psychology of sex).

The soul of Spain. 1908, 1937 (with new preface).

Sex in relation to society. Philadelphia 1910 (vol 6 of Studies in the psychology of sex), London 1926 (rev and abridged).

The problems of race regeneration. 1911.

The world of dreams. 1911.

The task of social hygiene. 1912.

Impressions and comments. 3 ser 1914–24, 1 vol Boston and New York 1930 (as Fountain of life).

Essays in war-time. 1917.

The philosophy of conflict and other essays in war-time. 1919.

Kanga Creek: an Australian idyll. Waltham St Lawrence 1922, Berkeley Heights NJ 1938 (with new introduction).

Little essays of love and virtue. 1922.

The dance of life. 1923.

Sonnets, with folk songs from the Spanish. Waltham St Lawrence 1925.

Eonism and other supplementary studies. Philadelphia 1928 (vol 7 of Studies in the psychology of sex).

The colour-sense in literature. 1931. Rptd from Contemporary Rev May 1896.

Concerning Jude the obscure. 1931. Rptd from Savoy Oct 1896.

More essays of love and virtue. 1931. Combined with Little essays of love and virtue, *above*, and enlarged as On life and sex, Garden City NY 1937, London 1945 (rev and enlarged).

An open letter to biographers. Introd by J. Ishill, Berkeley Heights NJ 1931.

Views and reviews: a selection of uncollected articles, 1884–1932. 2 vols 1932.

Psychology of sex: a manual for students. 1933.

Chapman, with illustrative passages. 1934.

My confessional: questions of our day. 1934.

From Rousseau to Proust. Boston and New York 1935.

Questions of our day. 1936.

On life and sex: essays of love and virtue. Garden City NY 1937 (Little essays of love and virtue and More Essays of love and virtue in 1 vol), London 1945 (enlarged with 3 additional essays).

My life: the autobiography of Havelock Ellis. Boston 1939.

Contributions to periodicals and collaborative works

Ellis contributed several hundred articles on literary, political, medical, psychological and anthropological subjects to well over 50 European and Amer periodicals. See Wellesley 5 *1989 for his contributions to* Contemporary Rev, Fortnightly Rev, Modern Rev, Nineteenth Cent *and* Westminster Rev. *Ellis also contributed widely to collaborative works and wrote numerous pams, particularly on sexual psychology.*

Letters

Letters to an American. Virginia Quart Rev Apr 1940.

The unpublished letters of Havelock Ellis to Joseph Ishill. Ed and introd by J. Ishill, Berkeley Heights NJ 1954 (priv ptd).

Editions, introductions and translations
From 1887 to 1889 Ellis was editor of the Mermaid Series of Old Dramatists, *and edited plays by Marlowe, Middleton, Porter and Ford, to which he also wrote introductions. From 1889 to 1914 he was editor of the* Contemporary Science Ser. *In addition, Ellis wrote a great many introductions to literary works as well as to works in the field of psychology, sociology etc; he edited writings of (among others) Chapman, Heine, Ibsen and Landor, and translated work by Lombroso, Renan, Zola et al.*

§2

Hundreds of reviews of Ellis's works were written in his lifetime, and at his death obituaries and appreciations were pbd in a great many European and Amer jnls. Listed below are a number of full-length secondary works which have been important in the establishment of Ellis's reputation or which emphasise his accomplishments in the field of lit. For an extensive list of further secondary material, see in particular the bibliography by G. S. Burne, above.

Goldberg, I. Havelock Ellis: a biographical and critical survey. 1926.
Peterson, H. Havelock Ellis: philosopher of love. Boston 1928.
Calder-Marshall, A. The sage of sex: a life of Havelock Ellis. New York 1959.
Collis, J. S. Havelock Ellis, artist of life: a study of his life. 1959.
Mittleman, L. Havelock Ellis: literary critic of the nineties. Unpbd diss, Univ of Chicago 1968.
Sprich, C. R. Energetic movement and well-balanced grace: the literary criticism of Havelock Ellis. Unpbd diss, Tufts Univ 1971.
Brome, V. Havelock Ellis: philosopher of love. 1979.
Grosskurth, P. Havelock Ellis: a biography. 1980. [OD]

Percy Hetherington Fitzgerald 1834–1925

See col 1530.

Richard Garnett 1835–1906

For mss and letters, see LR *and* NRA. *Notable collection in HRHRC.*

Bibliographies
Catalogue of the library of the late Dr Richard Garnett. 1906.

§1

Primula: a book of lyrics. 1858 (anon), 1859 (signed, as Io in Egypt and other poems), 1893 (as Poems, rev and enlarged edn).
Poems from the German. 1862.
Idylls and epigrams, chiefly from the Greek anthology. 1869, 1892 (as A chaplet from the Greek anthology).
Life of Thomas Carlyle. 1887.
Shelley and Lord Beaconsfield. 1887 (priv ptd).
Life of Ralph Waldo Emerson. 1888.
The twilight of the gods and other tales. 1888, 1903 (augmented), New York 1926 (introd by T. E. Lawrence). Numerous edns.
Life of John Milton. 1890.
Poems. 1893.
The soul and the stars, by A. G. Trent [pseud]. 1893, 1903 (expanded). First pbd in a more primitive form in Univ Mag Mar 1880; tr Ger 1894.
The age of Dryden. 1895. Numerous edns.
William Blake: painter and poet. 1895.
Edward Gibbon Wakefield: the colonization of South Australia and New Zealand. 1898.
Essays in librarianship and bibliography. 1899.
Historians and essayists. 1899.
Essays of an ex-librarian. 1901.
The queen and other poems. 1901.
English literature: an illustrated record by Richard Garnett and Edmund Gosse. 4 vols 1903–4, New York 1904–5. Vol 1 by Garnett, vol 2 by Garnett and Gosse, vols 3–4 by Gosse. Numerous edns.
Tennyson. 1903. With G. K. Chesterton.
Coleridge. 1904.
William Shakespeare, pedagogue and preacher: a drama. 1905.
De flagello myrteo: thoughts and fancies on love. 1905, 1906 (rev and augmented).
The life of William Johnson Fox, public teacher and social reformer 1786–1864. 1910. Completed by E. Garnett.
Garnett also pbd several tracts on lib problems; he was keeper of BM ptd bks 1890–9.

Translations
Poems from the German. 1862.
Selections from the Greek anthology. Ed Graham Tomson 1889. Tr Garnett, A. Lang et al.
Iphigenia in Delphi: a dramatic poem, with Homer's 'Shield of Achilles' and other trns from the Greek. 1890.
The accession of Queen Mary: being the contemporary narrative of Antonio de Guaras. 1892.
Dante, Petrarch, Camoens: CXXIV sonnets. 1896.

Editions, introductions
Garnett, R. The philological essays. Ed, with a memoir by Garnett 1859.
Relics of Shelley. Ed Garnett 1862.
Coleridge, S. T. Notes on Stillingfleet. Ed Garnett 1875.
Patmore, C. K. D. Florilegium amantis. Ed Garnett 1879.
Shelley, P. B. Select letters. Introd by Garnett 1882.
De Quincey, T. Confessions of an English opium-eater. Ed Garnett 1885 (rptd from the 1st edn).
Pérès, Jean Baptiste. Historic and other doubts: or the non-existence of Napoléon. Introd by Garnett 1885.
Shelley, P. B. Prologue to Hellas. Introd by Garnett 1886.
Warter, J. W. An old Shropshire oak. Ed Garnett 4 vols 1886–91.
Lowell, J. R. My study windows. Introd by Garnett 1887.
Peacock, T. L. Calidore & miscellanea. Ed Garnett 1891.
Shelley, M. Tales and stories. Collected and introd by Garnett 1891.
At Shakespeare's shrine: a poetical anthology. Ed C. S. Forshaw, introd by A. B. Fraser with Plays partly written by Shakespeare by Garnett 1893.
Beckford, W. T. Vathek. Ed Garnett 1893.
Drayton, M. The bataille of Agincourt. Introd and notes by Garnett 1893.
Milton, J. Prose. Selected, ed Garnett 1894.
Arnold, M. Alaric at Rome. Introd by Garnett 1896.
Blades, W. The enemies of books. Preface by Garnett 1896.
Porphyry, the philosopher to his wife, Marcella. Tr A. Zimmern, preface by Garnett, 1896.
Browning, R. Poems. Introd by Garnett 1897.
The library series. Ed Garnett 5 vols 1897–9.
Coleridge, S. T. The poetry. Ed Garnett 1898.
Shelley, P. B. and E. Shelley. Original poetry by Victor and Cazire. Ed Garnett 1898.
Khayam, Omar. The Ruba'yat. Introd by Garnett 1899.
Moore, T. Anecdotes. Introd by Garnett 1899.
Blind, M. The poetical works. With a memoir by Garnett, 1900.
Dickens, C. The complete works. Ed Garnett 1900.
Orations of British orators. Introd by Garnett, New York and London 1900.
Streamer, V. What makes a friend. Introd by Garnett 1900.
Wilde, G. Chaldean astrology up to date. Preface, notes, comments by A. G. Trent (pseud) 1901.
Dumas, A. The black tulip. Introd by Garnett 1902.
Nelson's literature readers. Selected and annotated by Garnett 2 pts 1902–4.
Williams, E. E. Journal. Introd by Garnett 1902.
Dibdin, T. F. The bibliomania. Introd by Garnett, Boston 1903.
Goldsmith, O. Letters from a citizen of the world. Introd by Garnett 1904.

Eliot, G. Silas Marner. Introd by Garnett 1905.
Pollard, A. W. An essay on colophone. Introd by Garnett 1905.
Reade, C. Peg Woffington. Introd by Garnett 1905.
Travers, R. The two Arcadias. Introd by Garnett 1905.
Goldsmith, O. The vicar of Wakefield. Introd by Garnett 1906.
Plato. The republic. Tr H. Spens, introd by Garnett 1906 (EL).
Shakespeare, W. Complete works. Introd by Garnett 1906.
Lamb, C. The letters. Ed Garnett 1907.
Peacock, T. L. Headlong Hall and Nightmare Abbey. Introd by Garnett 1908.
Pepys, S. Diary and correspondence. Introd by Garnett 1908 (EL).
Manning, A. The household of Sir Thomas More. Introd by Garnett 1909.
Peacock, T. L. Letters to Edward Hookham and Percy B. Shelley. Ed Garnett, Boston 1910.
Shelley, P. B. Poetical works. Introd by Garnett 1911.
The book of literature: a comprehensive anthology of the best literature. Ed with biographical and explanatory notes by Garnett et al, 1922.
Richard Garnett was general editor of the International Lib of Famous Lit 20 vols 1899.

Contributions to periodicals and collaborative works

Garnett wrote for Macmillan's Mag, Fortnightly Rev, Fraser's Mag, Nat Rev, New Quart Mag, New Rev, Temple Bar *and* Dublin Univ Mag *(see* Wellesley *5 1989). He contributed 196 articles to* DNB.
Literature 1837–87. In T. H. Ward, Reign of Queen Victoria vol 2, 1887.
A history of Italian literature. 1898. Vol 4 of E. Gosse, Short histories of the literatures of the world.
The universal anthology. Ed Garnett, Léon Vallée and Alois Brandl 1899–1902. Numerous edns.

Letters

Letters about Shelley, interchanged by three friends – Edward Dowden, Richard Garnett and Wm Michael Rossetti. Ed Garnett 1917.

§2

Cordier, H. Le docteur Richard Garnett. 1906.
McCrimmon, B. Richard Garnett, the scholar as librarian. 1989.
[MD]

Sir William Edmund Gosse 1849–1928

For mss and letters, see LR. *Notable collections of Gosse mss in BL, Leeds Univ Lib, Cambridge Univ Lib and in several libs in the US.*

Bibliographies

Lister, R. J. A catalogue of a portion of the library of Edmund Gosse. 1893.
Garnett, R. Eng Illus Mag Sep 1903. Includes articles by and on Gosse.
Cox, E. H. M. The library of Edmund Gosse. 1924.
Catalogue of the library of the late Edmund Gosse. 1928–9.
Gullick, N. In E. Charteris, The life and letters of Gosse, 1931, *below*.
A catalogue of the Gosse correspondence in the Brotherton collection consisting mainly of letters written to Gosse 1867–1928. Ed P. Gosse, Leeds 1950.

Collections

Collected poems. 1911.
Portraits and sketches. 1912.
Collected essays. 12 vols 1912–27.
Selected poems. [1926.]
Selected essays. 2 vols 1928.

§1

Madrigals, songs and sonnets. 1870. 32 by Gosse and 30 by J. A. Blaikie.
Two visits to Denmark. 1872; tr Danish 1912.
On viol and flute. 1873, 1883 (author's edn), 1890 (33 poems from the original edn and 36 poems drawn from other vols including New poems, 1879).
The ethical condition of the early Scandinavian peoples. 1875. Rptd from the Jnl of the Trans of the Victoria Philosophical Inst.
King Erik. 1876, 1893 (with introductory essay by T. Watts [-Dunton]). A tragedy in verse.
The unknown lover. 1878. A play for private performance with an essay on the Chamber drama in England.
New poems. 1879.
Studies in the literature of Northern Europe. 1879, 1883 (new and cheaper edn).
Gray. 1882 (EML), 1889 (rev).
Cecil Lawson: a memoir. 1883.
Lawrence Alma Tadema. 1883.
Seventeenth-century studies: a contribution to the history of English poetry. 1883. Rptd for the most part from Cornhill Mag.
A critical essay on the life and works of George Tinworth. 1883.
Notes on the pictures and drawings of Mr Alfred W. Hunt. 1884.
An epistle to Dr Oliver Wendell Holmes on his seventy-fifth birthday. 1884 (priv ptd).
Firdausi in exile and other poems. 1885.
The masque of painters. 1885 (priv ptd).
From Shakespeare to Pope: an inquiry into the causes and phenomena of the rise of classical poetry in England. Cambridge 1885.
Raleigh. 1886.
The life of William Congreve. 1888, 1924 (rev and enlarged).
A history of eighteenth century literature 1660–1780. 1889.
Robert Browning: personalia. 1890.
Heinemann's international library. 21 vols 1890–4. With special introd by Gosse to each vol.
The life of Philip Henry Gosse. 1890.
Northern studies. 1890.
Gossip in a library. 1891. Rptd from Saturday Rev, St James's Gazette, and Black and White.
The Shelley centenary address at Horsham, August 4th, 1892. Arundel 1892 (priv ptd). Includes address by Gosse.
Wolcott Balestier: a portrait sketch. 1892 (priv ptd). Rptd from Century Mag.
The secret of Narcisse: a romance. 1892.
The rose of Omar: inscription for the rose-tree brought from Omar's tomb and planted on the grave of Edward FitzGerald. 1893, [1893] (priv ptd).
Questions at issue. 1893.
In russet and silver. 1894, Chicago 1895.
The Jacobean poets. 1894.
Critical kit-kats. 1896; the essay on Walt Whitman tr Ger 1902.
A short history of modern English literature. 1897, 1924 (with 2 further chs).
The life and letters of John Donne, Dean of St Paul's. 2 vols 1899.
Hypolympia, or the gods in the island: an ironic fantasy. 1901.
The challenge of the Brontës. 1903 (priv ptd). Also in Pbns of Brontë Soc Feb 1904.
Jeremy Taylor. 1903 (EML).
English literature: an illustrated record by Richard Garnett and Edmund Gosse. 4 vols 1903–4, New York 1904–5. Vol 1 by Garnett, vol 2 by Garnett and Gosse, vols 3–4 by Gosse. Numerous edns.
British portrait painters and engravers of the eighteenth century – Kneller to Reynolds; with an introductory essay and biographical notes. 2 vols 1905.
Coventry Patmore. 1905.
French profiles. 1905.

Modern English literature, a short history. 1905, New York 1906 (new edn rev), 1928.
Sir Thomas Browne. 1905 (EML).
Father and son: a study of two temperaments. 1907 (anon), 1949 (Pen); tr Fr 1912, Du 1993.
Ibsen. New York 1907; tr Finnish 1909.
Biographical notes on the writings of Robert Louis Stevenson. 1908 (priv ptd).
Catalogue of the library of the House of Lords. 1908 (priv ptd).
Swinburne: personal recollections. 1909 (priv ptd). Rptd from Fortnightly Rev.
A paradox on beauty. 1909. Priv ptd offprint from Fasciculus Joanni Willis Clark dicatus.
The autumn garden. 1909.
The future of English poetry. [Oxford] 1913.
Lady Dorothy Nevill: an open letter. 1913 (priv ptd).
Sir Alfred East. 1914.
Two pioneers of Romanticism: Joseph and Thomas Warton. [1915.] Lecture Brit Acad.
Catherine Trotter: the precursor of the Blue-stockings. 1916 (priv ptd).
Inter arma: being essays written in time of war. 1916. Rptd from Edinburgh Rev.
Reims revisited. 1916 (priv ptd). Rptd from Fortnightly Rev.
The life of Algernon Charles Swinburne. 1917.
Lord Cromer as a man of letters. 1917 (priv ptd). Rptd from Fortnightly Rev.
The novels of Benjamin Disraeli. 1918 (priv ptd). Also in Trans Royal Soc Lit 36.
France et Angleterre: l'avenir de leurs relations intellectuelles. 1918. Rptd from Revue des Deux Mondes.
Three French moralists, and the gallantry of France. [1918.] On La Bruyère, La Rochefoucauld, Vauvenargues.
A visit to the friends of Ibsen. 1918.
A catalogue of the works of A. C. Swinburne in the library of Gosse. 1919 (priv ptd).
Some diversions of a man of letters. 1919.
Some literary aspects of France in the war. 1919. Rptd from the Trans Royal Soc of Lit.
The first draft of Swinburne's Anactoria. Cambridge [1919] (priv ptd). A short critical essay.
Malherbe and the classical reaction in the seventeenth century. Oxford 1920.
Books on the table. 1921.
The continuity of literature: presidential address, 1922. [Oxford] 1922.
Byways round Helicon. 1922.
Aspects and impressions. 1922.
More books on the table. 1923. Miniature monographs on literary subjects rptd from Sunday Times.
Swinburne: an essay written in 1875 and now first printed. Edinburgh 1925 (priv ptd).
Tallement des Réaux or the art of miniature biography: the Zaharoff lecture. Oxford 1925.
Silhouettes. 1925. Revs rptd from Sunday Times.
The earliest Charles Lamb dinner. In Cambridge and Charles Lamb, Cambridge 1925.
Leaves and fruit. 1927.
Austin Dobson. In A. T. A. Dobson, Austin Dobson: some notes, 1928.
A memoir of Thomas Lovell Beddoes. Prefixed to Complete works of Beddoes, 2 vols 1928.
Two unpublished poems. Winchester 1929 (priv ptd).
Studies in European literature, being the Taylorian lectures, second ser 1920–30. 1930.
An address to the Fountain Club, 1923. 1931 (priv ptd).
America: the diary of a visit, winter 1884–1885. Ed R. L. Peters and D. G. Halliburton, West Lafayette IN 1966.
A Norwegian ghost story. Ed W. M. Parker, St Peter Port 1967. Gosse's earliest work of fiction.
Thomas Hardy. From a lecture given in March 1928. Ed R. Knight, Bulphan 1968.
Sir Henry Doulton: the man of business as a man of imagination. Ed D. Eyles 1970.

Translations

Jaeger, Henrik. The life of Henrik Ibsen. Tr C. Bell with the verse tr E. Gosse. 1890.
Ibsen, Henrik. Hedda Gabler. New York 1891.
Ibsen, Henrik. The master builder. New York 1893. With W. Archer.
La Motte-Fouqué, F. H. C. de. Undine. 1912.
Clémenceau, G. E. B. Europe's liberation speech. 1918.
Dumas, Alexandre. Camille. 1937.

Editions and introductions

Rowlands, S. The complete works. Memoir by Gosse 1880.
Asbjörnsen, P. C. Round the yule log. Introd by Gosse 1881.
English odes. Selected by Gosse 1881.
Firdausi. The epic of kings. Prefatory poem by Gosse 1882.
Datta, Tarulatā. Ancient ballads. Introductory memoir by Gosse 1882.
Lodge, T. The complete works. Memoir by Gosse 1883.
Gray, T. The works. Ed Gosse 1884.
Reynolds, Sir J. The discourses. Ed and annotated by Gosse 1884.
Gray, T. Selected poems. Ed Gosse 1885.
Webster, J. Love's graduate. Prefatory essay by Gosse 1885.
Shirley, J. Plays. Introd by Gosse 1888.
Ibsen, H. The lady of the sea. Tr E. Marx-Aveling, introd by Gosse 1890.
Beddoes, T. L. The poetical works. Ed Gosse 1890.
Ibsen, H. The prose dramas. Biographical introd by Gosse, New York 1890–1.
Couperus, L. Eline Vere. Tr J. T. Grein, introd by Gosse 1892, New York 1892.
Nash, T. The unfortunate traveller. With an essay on his life and writings by Gosse 1892.
Zola, E. The attack on the mill. With an essay on the short stories of M. Zola by Gosse 1892.
Browning, E. Barrett. Sonnets from the Portuguese. Introd by Gosse 1894.
Beddoes, L. The letters. Ed Gosse 1894.
Björnson, B. The novels. Ed Gosse 1894.
Northcote, J. Conversations. Ed Gosse 1894.
Smith, J. T. Nollekens and his times. Ed with an essay on Georgian sculpture by Gosse 1894.
Björnson, Björnstjerne. The novels. Ed Gosse 1895–1909.
Victorian songs. Collected by E. H. Garrett, introd by Gosse 1895.
Carlyle, T. On heroes. Introd by Gosse 1896.
La Motte Fouqué, F. H. C. de. Undine. Introd by Gosse 1896.
The tavern of the three virtues. Tr from the original of Saint-Juirs, with a critical essay by Gosse 1896.
Fielding, H. The works. Introd by Gosse 1898.
Andersen, H. C. Fairy tales. Introd by Gosse 1900, 1909 (a new trn by H. L. Braekstad).
Penn, W. Some fruits of solitude. Introd by Gosse 1900.
A century of French romance. Ed Gosse 1901–2.
Cawein, M. J. Kentucky poems. Introd by Gosse 1902.
Dumas, A. The lady of the camellias. Introd by Gosse 1902.
Disraeli, B. The works. Critical introd by Gosse 1904–5.
Shirley, J. James Shirley. Introd by Gosse 1904.
Disraeli, B. Endymion. Critical introd by Gosse 1905.
Sheridan, R. B. B. The plays. Introd by Gosse 1905.

British portrait painters and engravers of the eighteenth century. Introd and biographical notes by Gosse 1906; tr Fr 1906.
Shakespeare, W. The complete works. Introd by Gosse 1906.
Stevenson, R. L. Works. With bibliographical notes by Gosse 1906.
Thomson, J. The seasons. Biographical note by Gosse 1906.
Carlyle, T. Letters addressed to Mrs B. Montagu and B. W. Procter. Preface by Gosse 1907.
Hunt, J. H. Leigh. Imagination and fancy. Introd by Gosse 1907.
Brightwen, E. The life and thoughts of a naturalist. Ed W. H. Chesson, introd and epilogue by Gosse 1909.
Milton, J. Les petits poèmes. Tr F. Henry, introd by Gosse 1909.
Swinburne, A. C. Of liberty and loyalty. Preface by Gosse 1909.
Swinburne, A. C. M. Prudhomme at the international exhibition. Preface by Gosse 1909.
Swinburne, A. C. The worm of Spindlestonheugh. Preface by Gosse 1909.
Milton, J. Poetical works. Introd by Gosse 1911.
Shelley, P. B. The sensitive plant. Introd by Gosse 1911.
Under the Swedish colours, an anthology of modern Swedish poets. Tr F. A. Judd, preface by Gosse 1911.
Nayadu, Sarojini. The bird of time. Introd by Gosse 1912.
Restoration plays from Dryden to Farquhar. Introd by Gosse 1912.
Vazoff, Y. Under the yoke. Introd by Gosse 1912.
Browning, E. Barrett. Epistle to a canary. Ed Gosse 1913.
Coleridge, T. S. Two addresses on Sir Robert Peel's bill. Ed Gosse 1913.
Ohlenschläger, A. G. The gold horns. Tr G. Borrow, ed and introd by Gosse 1913.
Swinburne, A. C. Les fleurs du mal. Ed and introd by Gosse 1913.
East, Sir A. Memorial exhibition. Prefatory note by Gosse 1914.
Swinburne, A. C. Letters to John Morley. Ed Gosse 1914.
Swinburne, A. C. A study of Victor Hugo's Les misérables. Ed and introd by Gosse 1914.
Nyström, A. K. Before, during, and after 1914. Introd by Gosse 1915.
Swinburne, A. C. Félicien Cossu. Ed Gosse 1915.
Swinburne, A. C. Théophile. Ed Gosse 1915.
The Allies' fairy book (illustr Arthur Rackham). Introd by Gosse 1916.
Turquet-Milnes, G. (Mrs Gladys Rosaleen). Some modern Belgian writers. Prefatory note by Gosse 1916.
Swinburne, A. C. The death of Sir John Franklin. Ed and preface by Gosse 1916.
Swinburne, A. C. Ernest Clouët. Ed Gosse 1916.
Swinburne, A. C. The triumph of Gloriana. Ed Gosse 1916.
Swinburne, A. C. A vision of bags. Ed Gosse 1916.
Mitford, A. B. F. Further memories. Introd by Gosse 1917.
Swinburne, A. C. Posthumous poems. Ed Gosse 1917.
Vernède, R. E. War poems. Introd by Gosse 1917.
Gray, T. Notes on Churchill. Introd by Gosse 1918.
Hutchinson, W. The splendour of France. Introd by Gosse 1918.
Swinburne, A. C. A letter to R. W. Emerson. Ed Gosse 1918.
Swinburne, A. C. Queen Yseult. Introd by Gosse 1918.
Swinburne, A. C. The springtide of life. Ed and preface by Gosse 1918.
Browning, R. Letters from Le Croisic. Introd by Gosse 1919.
Swinburne, A. C. Contemporaries of Shakespeare. Ed Gosse 1919.
Swinburne, A. C. The first draft of Swinburne's Anactoria. Ed Gosse 1919.
Swinburne, A. C. The letters. Ed Gosse 1919.
Swinburne, A. C. Selections. Ed Gosse and T. J. Wise 1919.
Masterpieces of French romance. Ed Gosse 1923.
The Oxford Book of Scandinavian verse, XVII century–XX century. Chosen by Gosse and W. A. Craigie 1925.
Swinburne, A. C. The complete works. Ed Gosse and T. J. Wise 1925–7.
Bocaric, S. Twenty-five caricatures. Introd by Gosse 1926.
Farquhar, G. The recruiting officer. Note by Gosse 1926.
Beddoes, T. L. The complete works. Ed Gosse 1928.
Dobson, Alban. Austin Dobson. With a ch by Gosse. 1928.
Lapthorne, R. The Portland papers. Preface by Gosse 1928.

Contributions to periodicals and collaborative works

Gosse also contributed to many periodicals and composite works. For his contributions to Fortnightly Rev, Fraser's Mag, Nat Rev, New Quart Mag, Nineteenth Cent, Contemporary Rev, Cornhill Mag, Macmillan's Mag, Quart Rev, New Rev, Temple Bar, Westminster Rev *and* Longman's Mag, *see* Wellesley *5 1989. He wrote 16 articles for the* DNB. *He contributed the entry on poetry to* Chambers' Encyclopadia, *and entries on Scandinavia 1815–70 and Dano-Norwegian literature 1815–65 to* The Cambridge modern history *vol 11, 1908.*

The garland of Rachel. 1881. Poems addressed to Rachel Daniel on her first birthday.
Lawrence Alma-Tadema. In Modern Artists section 4 [1882].
Miles, A. H. The poets and the poetry of the century. 1891.
Short histories of the literature of the world. 15 vols 1897–1915. Vol 3 on modern English literature entirely by Gosse, who was also general editor.
English literature: an illustrated record by Richard Garnett and Edmund Gosse. 4 vols 1903–4, New York 1904–5. Vol 1 by Garnett, vol 2 by Garnett and Gosse, vols 3–4 by Gosse. Numerous edns.
Browning's centenary. 1912. Addresses by Gosse, A. Pinero and H. James.

Letters

Brugmans, Linette F. (ed). The correspondence of André Gide and Edmund Gosse 1904–1928. 1959.
Bredsdorff, E. (ed). Sir Edmund Gosse's correspondence with Scandinavian writers. Copenhagen, etc, London 1960.
Mattheisen, P. F. and M. Millgate. (ed). Transatlantic dialogue: selected American correspondence of Edmund Gosse. 1966.
Moore, Rayburn S. Selected letters of Henry James to Edmund Gosse, 1882–1915, a literary friendship. 1988.

§2

Williams, S. T. Two Victorian boyhoods. North Amer Rev June 1921.
Braybrooke, P. Considerations on Edmund. 1925.
Bellows, W. Edmund Gosse. 1929.
Charteris, E. E. Life and letters. 1931.
Woolf, James D. Sir Edmund Gosse. 1972.
Thwaite, Ann. Edmund Gosse: a literary landscape. 1985. [MD]

P. Anderson Graham, Peter Anderson Graham

1853–1925

Bibliographies

In R. F. A. Sharp, A dictionary of English authors: biographical and bibliographical, 1904, rptd Detroit 1978.
In Nineteenth century readers' guide to periodical literature 1890–1899, ed H. G. Cushing and A. V. Morriss, 2 vols New York 1944.
See also Wellesley *vol 5, 1989.*

§1

Nature in books: some studies in biography. 1891.
REVIEW: Nat Observer 9 Jan 1892.
The rural exodus: the problem of the village and the town. 1892.
REVIEW: Nat Observer 11 June 1892.
All the year with nature. 1893.
REVIEWS: Nat Observer 23 Dec 1893; Athenaeum 27 Jan 1894.
Country pastimes for boys. 1895.
REVIEW: Spectator 10 Aug 1895.
The red scaur: a novel of manners. '1897' [1896].
REVIEWS: Athenaeum 2 Jan 1897; Spectator 30 Jan 1897; Acad 6 Feb 1897.

The Victorian era. 1897.
REVIEWS: Acad 12 June 1897; Bookman (USA) Sep 1897.
The revival of English agriculture. [1899.]
REVIEW: Acad 25 Nov 1899.
Reclaiming the waste. 1916 (Increased productivity series).
Highways and byways in Northumbria. 1920 (illustr H. Thomson), Manchester 1973, Stocksfield 1988 (also pbk edn).
REVIEWS: TLS 16 Dec 1920; New York Times 19 June 1921.
Lindisfarne or Holy Island: its cathedral, priory & castle, A. D. 635–1920. 1920 (folio).
The collapse of homo sapiens. London and New York 1923. Novel.

Contributions to periodicals

Graham was editor of the Edinburgh Courant *and contributed to many jnls and newspapers, especially the* St James's Gazette, Acad *and the* Pall Mall Gazette, *for which he wrote the Country notes. He was also editor of* Country Life *for 22 years.*
Scots Observer. 1 June 1889–18 Oct 1890.
Living Age. Rooks and farmers, 4 Jan 1890; Bondager, 9 May 1896.
Nat Observer. 25 Apr 1891–22 Oct 1892.
Art Jnl. Jan 1891–Jan 1893.
Atlanta. The last Lady Cressbrook, Jan 1895.
Chambers's Jnl. 1895–6.
Country Life. 1902–1923?
For contributions to Contemporary Rev, Longman's Mag, Macmillan's Mag, Nat Rev *and* New Rev, *see* Wellesley *vol 5.*

Introductions and editions

Mr Blackburne's games at chess. Ed Graham 1899, New York 1979 (as Blackburne's chess games, introd by D. Hooper).
The Country Life anthology of verse. Ed Graham 1915.
The increased productivity series. General ed Graham 1916–19.
Iwerne minster before, during, and after the Great War. Ed Graham 1923 (priv ptd).

§2

Bookman Aug 1923. Portrait.
Country notes. Country Life 31 Oct 1925.
The Times 27 Oct 1925. Obituary.
Graham, S. Country Life 31 Oct 1925. [DA]

Francis Hindes Groome 1851–1902

See NRA *for mss and letters. Collections in BL and Boston Athenaeum.*

§1

In gipsy tents. Edinburgh 1880, rptd with a new foreword by A. J. Clinch, Norwood PA 1973.
A short border history. Kelso 1887.
The gypsies. In Eiríkr Magnússon, National life and thought of the various nations throughout the world, 1891.
Two Suffolk friends. Edinburgh 1895. Recollections of R. H. Groome and Edward FitzGerald.
Kriegspiel: the war-game. 1896. Novel.
Gypsy folk-tales. 1899, rptd with a foreword by W. Starkie, Hatboro and London 1963.
Edward FitzGerald: an aftermath. In Edward FitzGerald: an aftermath by Francis Hindes Groome, with miscellanies in verse and prose, Portland ME 1902.

Editions and introductions

Ordnance gazetteer of Scotland: a survey of Scottish topography, statistical, biographical and historical. Ed Groome 6 vols Edinburgh 1884–5; frequently reissued in a varying number of vols.
Chambers's biographical dictionary. Ed D. Patrick and Groome 1897.
Borrow, G. H. Lavengro: the scholar, the gypsy, the priest. Ed and introd by Groome 2 vols 1901.

Contributions to periodicals

Groome wrote articles for Blackwood's Mag *and the* Nat Rev *(see* Wellesley *5 1989). He contributed 15 entries to* DNB.

§2

Watts-Dunton, T. The Tarno rye (Francis Hindes Groome). Athenaeum 22 Feb 1902, rptd in Edward FitzGerald: an aftermath, 1902, *above.* [FJMK]

Edmund Gurney 1847–88

§1

The power of sound. 1880. On music.
Phantasms of the living. 2 vols 1886, 1 vol 1918 (abridged by Mrs H. Sidgwick); tr Fr 1891, Ger 1897. With F. W. H. Myers and F. Podmore.
Tertium quid: chapters on various disputed questions. 2 vols 1887.

Contributions to periodicals

Gurney's contributions to the Cornhill Mag, Macmillan's Mag, Dublin Rev, Fortnightly Rev, Fraser's Mag, Nat Rev *and* Nineteenth Cent *are listed in* Wellesley *5 1989. He also contributed to* Mind *and* Jnl of Soc for Psychical Research. *See F. W. H. Myers,* The work of Gurney in experimental psychology, Proc Soc for Psychical Research *5 1888.*

Editions

Art and literature. Ed Titus Munson Coan [pseud], New York 1883.

§2

Hall, T. H. The strange case of Edmund Gurney. 1964, 1980 (new introd).
Gauld, A. In The founders of psychical research, 1968. [MD]

Sir William Henry Hadow 1859–1937

See NRA *for letters, diaries and ms music. Notable collections in BL and Worcester College, Oxford.*

§1

Studies in modern music: Hector Berlioz, Robert Schumann, Richard Wagner [ser 1]; Frederick Chopin, Antonin Dvořák, Johannes Brahms [ser 2]. 2 ser 1892–5. Numerous later edns.
Sonata form. [1896.]
A Croatian composer: notes towards the study of Joseph Haydn. 1897. Based on notes by F. S. Kuhak.
The Oxford history of music. Ed Hadow who himself wrote vol 5 (The Viennese period) 6 vols Oxford 1901–5, 8 vols 1929–38.
A course of lectures on the history of instrumental form. 1906.
Hymn tunes. [1914.]
The use of comic episodes in tragedy. 1915.
British music: a report upon the history and present prospects in the United Kingdom. 1921.
Citizenship. Oxford 1923.
Music. [1924], 1925 (rev), 1949 (3rd edn rev G. Dyson).
A comparison of poetry and music. Cambridge 1926.
Beethoven's Op. 18 quartets. 1926.
Church music. 1926.
Collected essays. Oxford 1928.
English music. 1931.
Richard Wagner. 1934; tr Sp [1951].
Hadow contributed to Contemporary Rev, Living Age, Macmillan's Mag, Musical Quart *and* Quart Rev *(see also* Wellesley *5 1989); he also contributed to composite works, such as* Milton memorial lectures *1909,* PBA *vol 11 1923, H. Foss's* The heritage of music, *1934, English Assoc London,* English essays of to-day, *Oxford 1936, and* Bibliography of social studies *1936. Hadow pbd a number of governmental reports, pams and lectures on music; he also pbd songs and music scores. Several of Hadow's*

essays were collected in anthologies, such as D. Ewen (ed), From Bach to Stravinsky, *1933 and E. Vivas and M. Krieger (ed),* Problems of aesthetics, *New York 1953.*

Editions and introductions

Poems of English country life. Selected by and ed Hadow and H. B. George 1902.
Songs of the British islands. Selected by and ed Hadow 1903.
Tennyson, A. Select poems of Tennyson. Introd and notes for the use of schools by Hadow 1903.
Bridges, R. Demeter: a mask. Lyrics and incidental music by Hadow, Oxford 1905.
The Oxford treasury of English literature. Ed Hadow and G. E. Hadow 3 vols Oxford 1906–8.
Shakespeare, W. Shakespeare's sonnets and A lover's complaint. Introd by Hadow 1907.
Schumann, C. An artist's life. 2 vols 1913. Tr and abridged by G. E. Hadow; preface by Hadow.
Bain, A. W. The modern teacher. Introd by Hadow 1921.
Brenet, M. (pseud of Marie Bobillier). Haydn. 1926. Tr from Fr by C. Leonard Leese. Commentary by Hadow 1926.
Fisher, L. The citizen. Preface by Hadow 1927.
Essays and studies by members of the English Association vol 17. Ed Hadow, Oxford 1932.

§2

Obits. The Times 10 Apr 1937; Musical Times May 1937; Music and Letters July 1937.
Sheffield Univ Mag June 1938. [JMB]

Philip Gilbert Hamerton 1834–94.

See NRA *for Hamerton's correspondence with Macmillan's in BL.*

§1

Observations on heraldry. 1851.
The isles of Loch Awe and other poems of my youth. 1855.
A painter's camp in the Highlands and Thoughts about art. 2 vols Cambridge 1862, 1866 (rev). Thoughts about art rptd separately Boston 1871.
Contemporary French painters: an essay. 1868, Boston 1895 (enlarged).
Etching and etchers. 1868, 1876 (enlarged). Numerous later edns and reprints.
Painting in France after the decline of classicism. 1869.
Wenderholme: a story of Lancashire and Yorkshire. 3 vols 1869.
The etcher's handbook. 1871.
The unknown river: an etcher's voyage of discovery. 1871.
The intellectual life. 1873. Numerous later edns and reprints.
Chapters on animals. 1874.
Harry Blount: passages in a boy's life on land and sea. 1875.
Round my house: notes of rural life in France in peace and war. 1876.
The sylvan year: leaves from the notebook of Raoul Dubois. 1876.
Marmorne: the story is told by Adolphus Segrave, the youngest of three brothers [pseud]. 1878.
Modern Frenchmen: five biographies. 1878. V. Jacquemont, H. Perreyve, F. Rude, J. J. A. Ampère, H. Regnault.
The life of J. M. W. Turner. 1879.
Hart, C. H. Hamerton's Life of Turner: a review. Philadelphia 1879.
Art essays. 2 vols New York [c. 1880]. Rptd from International Rev and Princeton Rev.
The graphic arts: a treatise on the varieties of drawing, painting and engraving. 1882, Boston 1882 (enlarged).
... Her picture. Boston 1882.
Human intercourse. 1884, ed R. Ishikawa, Tokyo 1928 (selected). Numerous other edns and reprints.
Landscape. 1885.
Paris in old and present times, with especial reference to changes in its architecture and topography. 1885.
Exploration of the Arroux, a canoe voyage: etchings in 4 monthly parts. 1887.
Imagination in landscape painting. 1887, Boston 1895 (enlarged).
The Saône: a summer voyage. 1887, Boston 1889 (as A summer voyage on the river Saone).
French & English: a comparison. 1889; tr Fr 1891. Largely rptd from the Atlantic Monthly.
Portfolio papers. 1889. Rptd from Portfolio.
Turner. Paris [1889]. Written in Fr and distinct from the Eng work above.
Drawing and engraving: a brief exposition of technical principles and practice. 1892.
Man in art: studies in religious and historical art, portrait and genre. 1892.
The present state of the fine arts in France. 1892.
The art of the American wood-engraver. 2 vols New York 1894. With a bibliography by J. B. Carrington in vol 1.
The etchings of Rembrandt. 1894, 1896 (together with L. Binyon's Dutch etchings of the seventeenth century), 1905 (with an annotated catalogue of all Rembrandt's etchings by Campbell Dodgson).
The mount: narrative of a visit to the site of a Gaulish city on Mont Beuvray, with a description of the neighbouring city of Autun. Ed Mrs E. Hamerton 1897.
Philip Gilbert Hamerton: an autobiography 1834–1858, and a memoir by his wife 1858–94. 1897.
The quest of happiness. Ed M. R. F. Gilman, Boston 1897.
Armorial bearings, their use and inheritance. nd.

Editions, introductions and translations

Twelve etchings by French and English artists. With notes by Hamerton 1874.
Examples of modern etching. With notes by Hamerton 1875.
Hamerton, E. The mirror of truth and other marvellous stories. Introd by Hamerton 1875.
Ménard, R. Entretiens sur la peinture. (Chapters on painting ... translated under the superintendence of Hamerton.) Paris 1875 (Fr and Eng).
Eighteen etchings by English, French and German artists. With notes by Hamerton 1877.
Keppel, F. & Co. The print-collector's bulletin: an illustrated catalogue of painter-etchings for sale by Frederick Keppel & Co New York 1908. Three catalogues of etchings with notices of the etchers by Hamerton and others.
Méryon, C. Old Paris: twenty etchings by Charles Méryon with an essay on the etcher by Hamerton. Liverpool 1914.

Contributions to periodicals and collaborative works

Hamerton was editor of Portfolio: an artistic periodical, *Jan 1870–Dec 1893, and he started the series* Portfolio: Monographs on Artistic Subjects, *1894–1907. He wrote articles for* Atlantic Monthly, Contemporary Rev, Cornhill Mag, Fortnightly Rev, International Rev, Longman's Mag, Princeton Rev *(see also* Wellesley *5 1989). He contributed to various collective works such as* English painters of the present day, *1871; A. T. J. M. Potémont's* Nouveau traité de la gravure, *1873;* Encyclopaedia Britannica, *9th edn 1875 etc;* Higher education and a common language, *1879; R. Johnson's* Little classics, *[1880];* Irving classics, *1885.*

§2

Benson, E. Philip Gilbert Hamerton as an art critic. Atlantic Monthly 16 1865.
Powers, H. N. Philip Gilbert Hamerton. Old and New 8 1873.
Philip Gilbert Hamerton and his works. International Rev 21 1877.
Philip Gilbert Hamerton as an artist. Southern Rev n.s. 21 1877.

Kissane, J. Art historians and art critics – IX: P. G. Hamerton, Victorian art critic. Burlington Mag 114 1972, pp. 22–30.
Marandon, S. Figures d'agnostiques victoriens. Cahiers d'Études Victoriens et Edouardiens Apr 1982, pp. 15–28. On J. Morley, Hamerton and F. Harrison.
Hamerton's library was sold by auction on 26 Nov 1895 (auction-sale catalogue reference: S.-C. S. 1092(3)). [FJMK]

Augustus John Cuthbert Hare 1834–1903

See LR *and* NRA *for Hare's correspondence and sketch books. Notable collections in West Sussex Record Office and York Univ Lib.*

Selections

Augustus Hare in Italy. Ed G. Henderson, introd by S. Sitwell, Salisbury 1977.

§1

A handbook for travellers in Berks, Bucks and Oxfordshire. 1860, 1894 (abbreviated as A handbook for travellers in Oxfordshire).
A winter at Mentone. [1862.]
A handbook for travellers to Durham and Northumberland. 1864.
Walks in Rome. 2 vols 1871, 1893 (13th edn rev), 1903 (16th edn rev St Clair Baddeley), 1 vol 1905. Numerous later edns.
Memorials of a quiet life. 2 vols 1872, 3 vols 1873–6, 1 vol 1873 (rev W. L. Cage as Records of a quiet life). Memoir of Maria Hare. Numerous later edns.
Wanderings in Spain. 1873.
Days near Rome. 2 vols 1875, 1906 (4th edn rev St Clair Baddeley).
Cities of Northern and Central Italy. 3 vols 1876.
Walks in London. 2 vols 1878, 1 vol 1878, 1883 (5th edn rev), 1894 (abbreviated as Westminster). Numerous later edns.
The life and letters of Frances, Baroness Bunsen. 2 vols '1879' [1878], 1 vol New York 1880; rev and tr Ger (as Freifrau von Bunsen: ein Lebensbild aus ihren Briefen zusammengestellt), Gotha 1881.
Cities of Southern Italy and Sicily. 1883, 1905 (abbreviated as Sicily by St Clair Baddeley), 1911 (new edn by St Clair Baddeley).
Cities of Central Italy. 2 vols 1884.
Cities of Northern Italy. 2 vols 1884.
Florence. 1884, 1900 (combined with Venice, *below*), 1904 (6th edn rev St Clair Baddeley). Numerous later edns.
Venice. 1884, 1904 (6th edn partly by St Clair Baddeley). Numerous later edns.
Sketches in Holland and Scandinavia. 1885.
Studies in Russia. 1885.
Days near Paris. 1887. Numerous later edns.
Paris. 1887, New York 1888 (as Walks in Paris), 2 vols 1900.
North-eastern France. 1890.
South-eastern France. 1890.
South-western France. 1890.
The story of two noble lives: being memorials of Charlotte, Countess Canning, and Louisa, Marchioness of Waterford. 3 vols 1893.
Sussex. 1894.
Biographical sketches. Being memorials of A. P. Stanley, H. Alford, Mrs Duncan Steward, Paray Le Monial. 1895.
The Gurneys of Earlham. 2 vols 1895.
North-western France. 1895.
The Rivieras. 1896.
The story of my life. 6 vols 1896–1900, 1952 (ed M. Barnes as The years with mother: being an abridgement of the first three volumes of The story of my life), 1953 (ed M. Barnes as In my solitary life: being an abridgement of the last three volumes of The story of my life).
Shropshire. 1898.
The wooden legs. 1974 (10 copies ptd).
Hare contributed to Edinburgh Rev *and* Macmillan's Mag *(see* Wellesley 5 1989*). Hare also contributed 4 entries to* DNB *1885–1901. An essay by Hare was included in* More chapters from the Kilvert saga, *Hereford [1977].*

Editions and introductions

Epitaphs for country churchyards. Ed Hare, Oxford 1856.
von Lasaulx, A. Sister Augustine. Preface by Hare 1880.
The life and letters of Maria Edgeworth. Ed Hare 2 vols 1894.
Stanley, A. P. Thoughts that breathe. Selected by E. E. Brown. Includes biographical sketch by Hare, Boston nd.

§2

Athenaeum 24 Nov 1900.
Obits: The Times 23, 27 and 28 Jan 1903; Athenaeum, 31 Jan 1903.
Leslie, J. R. S. Men were different . . . Five studies in late Victorian biography . . . Augustus Hare. 1937.
Maugham, W. S. Vagrant mood: six essays. New York 1953. [JMB]

Frederic Harrison 1831–1923

See LR *and* NRA *for mss and letters. Notable collections in BL, Bodleian, London Univ, Maison d'Auguste Comte Paris.*

Bibliographies

Farquharson, S. English Illus Mag Oct 1903.
Bibliography of Frederic Harrison. Hawkhurst 1908.
Autobiographic memoirs. 2 vols 1911. Vol 2 includes a bibliography and a comprehensive list of Harrison's contributions to periodicals.
DLB vol 57 1987 (*see below*).

Collections and selections

The insuppressible book: a controversy between Herbert Spencer and Frederic Harrison. From the Nineteenth Cent and Pall Mall Gazette. Ed M. A. Dodge, Boston 1885, New York 1885 (as The nature and reality of religion).
Selected essays, literary and historical. Ed A. Jha 1925.

§1

The meaning of history: two lectures. 1862.
Order and progress. 2 pts 1875, Hassocks 1975 (ed and introd M. S. Vogeler).
The present and the future: a positivist address. 1880.
The choice of books and other literary pieces. 1886, New York 1886 (abridged). Numerous later edns and reprints of both versions.
Oliver Cromwell. 1888.
  Hoare, W. E. Notes on Frederic Harrison's Oliver Cromwell. Madras 1890.
  Sena, V. and S. Maulika. A key to Frederic Harrison's Life of Cromwell. Calcutta 1894.
Annals of an old manor house, Sutton Place, Guildford. 1893, 1899 (abridged).
The meaning of history and other historical pieces. 1894.
Studies in early Victorian literature. 1895.
William the Silent. 1897, New York 1902 (enlarged); tr Du [1898].
Tennyson, Ruskin, Mill and other literary estimates. 1899.
Byzantine history in the early Middle Ages: the Rede Lecture delivered in the Senate House Cambridge, June 12, 1900. 1900.
George Washington and other American addresses. 1901.
John Ruskin. 1902 (EML).
Theophano: the crusade of the tenth century: a romantic monograph. 1904, New York 1904 (enlarged).
Chatham. 1905.
Memories and thoughts: men, books, cities, art. 1906.
Nicephorus: a tragedy of new Rome. 1906. A verse drama on the same subject as Theophano.
Carlyle and the London Library: account of its foundation. 1907.
The creed of a layman: apologia pro fide mea. 1907.
The philosophy of common sense. 1907.

Collected essays. 4 pts 1907–8.
My alpine jubilee 1851–1907. 1908.
National and social problems. 1908.
Realities and ideals social, political, literary and artistic. 1908.
Autobiographic memoirs: I. 1831–1870. II. 1870–1910. 2 vols 1911.
Among my books: centenaries, reviews, memoirs. 1912.
The positive evolution of religion: its moral and social reaction. 1913.
The German peril: forecasts 1864–1914, realities 1915, hopes 191–. 1915.
On society. 1918. Lectures given to several positivist societies.
Obiter scripta 1918. 1919.
On jurisprudence and the conflict of laws; revised and annotated by A. H. F. Lefroy. Oxford 1919. Rptd from Fortnightly Rev.
Novissima verba: last words 1920. 1921.
De senectute: more last words. 1923.

Editions, introductions and translations

Comte, A. System of positive polity. Tr J. H. Bridges, Harrison and others 4 vols 1875–7.
Fleay, F. G. Three lectures on education. With a preface by Harrison. 1883.
Comte, A. The positivist library of Auguste Comte. Tr and ed Harrison 1886.
The new calendar of great men: biographies of the 558 worthies in the positivist calendar of Auguste Comte. Ed Harrison '1892' [1891], 1920 (rev and enlarged).
Comte, A. The positive philosophy of Auguste Comte. Introd by Harrison 3 vols 1896 (originally, in 1853, tr H. Martineau).
Carlyle, T. Past and present. Introd by Harrison 1897.
Shore, L. C. Poems: with a memoir by Arabella Shore and an appreciation by Harrison. 1897.
Levy-Bruhl, L. The philosophy of Auguste Comte. Tr K. de Beaumont-Klein, introd by Harrison 1903.
Carlyle, T. Essays. Introd by Harrison [1904].
Gissing, G. Veranilda: a romance. Introd by Harrison 1904.
Bacon, F. Essays. Introd by Harrison 1905.
Trollope, A. The Barsetshire novels. Introd by Harrison 8 vols 1906.
Bridges, J. H. Essays and addresses. Ed L. T. Hobhouse, introd by Harrison 1907.
Comte, A. A general view of positivism. Tr J. H. Bridges, introd by Harrison [1908].
Comte, A. Early essays on social philosophy. Tr by H. Dix Hutton from vol 4 of Comte's Système de politique positive, ed and introd Harrison [1911].
Trollope, A. Phineas Finn and Phineas Redux. Introd by Harrison 2 vols 1911.
Russell, M. A. Golden grain: thoughts of many minds. Compiled by A. Russell, introd by Harrison 1912.
Edwards, M. B. B. The lord of the harvest. Introd by Harrison 1913. Novel (WC).
Harrison, A. The Kaiser's war. Introd by Harrison [1914].

Letters

Letters to Eugen Oswald. BLR 2 1941.

Contributions to periodicals and collaborative works

Harrison contributed numerous reviews, notes and articles to periodicals, notably Contemporary Rev, Fortnightly Rev, Forum, Literature, Nineteenth Cent *and* Positivist Rev *(see also* Wellesley 5 1989 *and vol 2 of* Autobiographic memoirs). *Many of Harrison's notes and articles were rptd in collections such as* Trans of the Royal Historical Soc, *or separately; his articles in* Forum *on the major nineteenth-century English prose-writers and novelists were first pbd separately by Edward Arnold in 1894 and 1895, and together in 1895 as* Studies in early Victorian literature. *Harrison also contributed to the* Encyclopaedia Britannnica *and to collective works such as* International policy: essays on the foreign relations of England, *1866; A. Bowker's* Alfred the Great, *1899, and* Great religions of the world, *1901.*

§2

Harris, M. Two Victorian portraits. North Amer Rev Sep 1920. On J. Morley and Harrison.
Frederic Harrison, the writer as man of action: an unabashed Victorian. The Times 15 Jan 1923.
Luce, M. Harrison. Nineteenth Cent Mar 1923.
Saintsbury, G. Harrison. Fortnightly Rev Mar 1923.
Harrison, A. Frederic Harrison: thoughts and memories. 1926.
Bicknell, J. W. Frederic Harrison. In Victorian prose: a guide to research, ed D. J. DeLaura, New York 1973.
Marandon, S. Figures d'agnostiques victoriens. Cahiers d'Études Victoriens et Edouardiens 15 Apr 1982. On J. Morley, P. G. Hamerton and Harrison.
Sullivan, H. R. Frederic Harrison. Boston 1983.
Vogeler, M. S. Frederic Harrison: the vocations of a positivist. Oxford 1984.
Coustillas, P. Frederic Harrison ou l'art d'être positiviste. Études Anglaises 40 1987.
Sullivan, H. R. Frederic Harrison. DLB vol 57 1987. [FJMK]

Elizabeth Julia Hasell 1830–87

The rock: and other short lectures on passages of Holy Scripture. 1867.
Calderon. Edinburgh and London 1879, Philadelphia 1879. Foreign classics for English readers, ed Margaret Oliphant.
Short family prayers. 1879.
Tasso. Edinburgh 1882, Philadelphia 1882.
Bible partings. 1883. [MD]

William Ernest Henley 1849–1903

See col 741.

Auberon Edward William Herbert 1838–1906

§1

The Danes in camp: letters from Sönderborg. 1864.
A politician in trouble about his soul. 1884. Rptd with alterations and additions from the Fortnightly Rev.
Anti-force papers, nos 1–3. [1885.] Rptd with alterations and additions from the Newcastle Weekly Chron. Partly tr Ger 1892.
Windfall and waterdrift. 1894. Poems.
The voluntaryist creed: being the Herbert Spencer lecture delivered at Oxford June 7 1906, and a plea for voluntaryism. 1908.
Taxation and anarchism: a discussion between the Hon Auberon Herbert and J. H. Levy. [1912.]

Editions, contributions to periodicals and collaborative works

Herbert edited a series of letters, The sacrifice of education to examination, *1889. He collaborated with J. H. Levy et al in* A symposium on the land question, *1890, with H. Wager in* Bad air and bad health, *1894, and with F. Harrison in* Two open letters to Lord Salisbury on the iniquity of a war against the Transvaal, *[1899]. Herbert wrote articles for* Contemporary Rev, Daily News, Fortnightly Rev, Newcastle Weekly Chron, New Rev *and* Nineteenth Cent *(see also* Wellesley 5 1989). *Essays and articles by Herbert were included in several works such as T. Mackay,* A plea for liberty: an argument against socialism and socialistic legislation, *1891, T. Thatcher,* Common sense health reform, *[1899], and E. Mack,* The right and wrong of compulsion by the state, *Indianapolis 1978.*

§2

Harris, S. H. Auberon Herbert: crusader for liberty. 1943. [FJMK]

Charles Harold Herford 1853–1931

See NRA *for letters. Notable collections in BL and Nat Lib of Scotland.*

Bibliography

Owen, W. Charles Harold Herford. DLB vol 149 1995.

§1

The essential characteristics of the romantic and classical styles: with illustrations from English literature. Cambridge 1880.

The first quarto edition of Hamlet 1603: two essays, to which the Harness prize was awarded .... I. by C. H. Herford; II. by W. H. Widgery, 1880.

A sketch of the history of the English drama in its social aspects: being the essay which obtained the Le Bas prize, 1880. Cambridge 1881.

The stoics as teachers: the Hare prize essay for 1881. Cambridge 1882.

Studies in the literary relations of England and Germany in the sixteenth century. Cambridge 1886.

The age of Wordsworth. 1897, 1899 (3rd edn rev). Numerous later edns.

Goethe's Italian journey: studies in European literature. Oxford 1900.

The permanent power of English poetry. Manchester 1902.

Robert Browning. 1905.

Literature and ethics: an inaugural lecture. Aberystwyth 1907.

The bearing of English studies upon the national life. 1910.

Shakespeare. 1912; tr Hungarian [1919], Norwegian 1926.

Goethe. 1913.

Is there a poetic view of the world? British Academy: Wharton lecture on British poetry 7. [1917].

The normality of Shakespeare illustrated in his treatment of love and marriage. 1920.

Shakespeare's treatment of love & marriage, and other essays. 1921.

A sketch of recent Shakespearian investigation 1893–1923. 1923.

English literature. 1927; tr Portuguese 1941.

The post-war mind of Germany, and other European studies. Oxford 1927.

Wordsworth. 1930.

Philip Henry Wicksteed: his life and work ... With foreword and appreciation by Joseph H. Wicksteed and a chapter on The economic works by Lionel Robbins. 1931.

The significance of Dante for the modern world. A lecture. Manchester [1933].

Herford also contributed largely to composite works, such as DNB 1885–1900 *(4 entries);* Studies in European literature: being the Taylorian lectures 1889–1899; *A. W. Ward and A. R. Waller (ed),* The Cambridge history of English literature, *15 vols 1907–27; F. S. Marvin (ed),* Recent developments in European thought, *Oxford 1920;* Essays and studies by members of the English Association, *vol 8 Oxford 1922; and* English Goethe Society Publications, *1930. He wrote articles and reviews for* Bookman, Contemporary Rev, Cornhill Mag, English Illus Mag, Fortnightly Rev, Macmillan's Mag, Manchester Guardian, Nation, Neue Freie Presse, New Shakespeare Soc *(1888) and* PBA *(1919) (see also* Wellesley 5 1989*). A number of his articles in* BJRL *1918–28, were rptd separately as pams.*

Editions, introductions and translations

Jonson, B. Ben Jonson [Works]. Ed B. Nicholson, introd by Herford [1893–1894], 2 vols New York 1957.

Ibsen, H. Brand. Tr Herford 1894, 1910 (as vol 3 of The collected works of Henrik Ibsen).

Spenser, E. Shepheard's calender. Ed, introd and notes by Herford 1895.

Fletcher, J. and W. Shakespeare. The two noble kinsmen. Ed, introd, notes and glossary by Herford 1897.

Ibsen, H. Love's comedy. Tr Herford 1900.

English tales in verse. Ed and introd by Herford [1902].

Browne, Sir T. Browne's Religio medici. Introd by Herford [1906].

Herford, W. H. The student's Froebel. Rev and ed Herford and D. B. Herford, introd by M. E. Sadler, memoir by Herford 2pts 1911–15.

Germany in the nineteenth century. Ed Herford, who also contributed The intellectual and literary history, Manchester 1912; tr Ger 1913.

Jonson, B. Every man in his humour. Critical essay and notes by Herford 1913.

Essays and studies by members of the English Association. Vol 4 collected by Herford 1913.

Wedgwood, F. J. The personal life of Josiah Wedgwood the potter. Rev, ed, introd and memoir by Herford 1915.

Shelley, P. B. The lyrical poems and translations (The dramatic poems). Ed and preface by Herford [1917].

Vasil'evsky, I. Chassidism. Introd by Herford [1918].

The year's work in English studies. Vol 5. Ed Herford 1921.

Jonson, B. Ben Jonson. Ed Herford and P. and E. Simpson, 11 vols 1925–52 (vols 1 and 2 The man and his work were by Herford), Oxford 1954–65 (corrected), New York 1957 (abbreviated), Oxford 1981–3 (a 3-vol edn of The complete plays of Ben Jonson, ed G. A. Wilkes, based on the edn by Herford and P. and E. Simpson), Oxford 1986 (vols 3–9).

Fingeller, H. The case of German South Tyrol against Italy. Tr and ed Herford 1927.

Herbert, E. The autobiography of Edward, Lord Herbert of Cherbury. Introd by Herford 1928.

Carpenter, J. E. Joseph Eslin Carpenter. Ed and memoir by Herford 1929.

Southey, R. Journal of a tour in Scotland in 1819. Introd and notes by Herford 1929.

Herford was general editor of a number of different Shakespeare edns, such as The Warwick Shakespeare, The Aldus Shakespeare, The Arden Shakespeare, and Heath's Shakespeare. He himself edited Richard II *(1893),* Othello *(1920) and* The Winter's Tale *(1926), which were individually rptd.*

§2

Obits: Manchester Guardian 27 Apr 1931; The Times 27 Apr 1931.

Gardner, J. E. G. Professor Herford as an Italian scholar. Oxford 1932.

Simpson, P. In memoriam: Charles Harold Herford. In Ben Jonson vol 4 1932, *above.*

Robertson, J. G. Charles Harold Herford 1853–1931. [1933.] Rptd from PBA vol 17 1931.

Abercrombie, L. Herford and international literature. The fourth Herford memorial lecture (rptd from BJRL 1935). [JMB]

Lionel Johnson 1867–1902

See col 758.

Denham Jordan ('A Son of the marshes') 1836–1920

§1

All of Jordan's works were written in collaboration with J. A. Owen and were edited by her.

Woodland, moor and stream: being the notes of a naturalist. 1889.

Annals of a fishing village. 1891.

On Surrey hills. Edinburgh 1891.

Within an hour of London town among wild birds and their haunts. 1892.

Forest tithes and other studies from nature. 1893.

With the woodlanders and by the tide. 1893.

From spring to fall: or when life stirs. 1894.

The wild-fowl and sea-fowl of Great Britain. 1895.

In the green leaf and the sere. 1896.

Drift from longshore. 1898.

Contributions to periodicals

In collaboration with J. A. Owen, Jordan wrote notes and articles for Blackwood's Mag, Cornhill Mag *(most of them rptd in* Woodland, moor and stream, *above),* Fortnightly Rev, Macmilllan's Mag *(partly rptd in* With the woodlanders and by the tide, *above),* Nat Rev. *See* Wellesley 5 *1989*. [FJMK]

William Paton Ker 1855–1923

For mss and letters, see NRA. *Notable collections in Glasgow Univ Lib and Univ College London.*

Bibliographies

Pafford, J. H. P. W. P. Ker 1855–1923: a bibliography. 1950.

Collections

Collected essays. Ed C. Whibley 2 vols 1925. Uncollected essays rptd from single pams, periodicals and composite works.
On modern literature: lectures and addresses. Ed T. Spencer and J. R. Sutherland, Oxford 1955.

§1

Epic and romance: essays on mediaeval literature. 1897.
Boccaccio. 1900.
An English miscellany. 1901.
The dark ages. Edinburgh 1904, 1955 (with a foreword by B. I. Evans).
Essays on mediaeval literature. 1905.
Sturia the historian. Oxford 1906.
On the philosophy of history. Glasgow 1909.
Romance. 1909.
Tennyson: the Leslie Stephen lecture. Cambridge 1909.
Thomas Wharton. 1911.
English literature: medieval. [1912.]
Medieval English literature. 1912.
Jacob Grimm: an address. 1915.
The eighteenth century. 1916.
Two essays. Glasgow 1918.
Joseph Ritson. Cambridge 1922. Presidential address.
The art of poetry: seven lectures 1920–2. Oxford 1923.
Form and style in poetry: lectures and notes. Ed R. W. Chambers 1928.

Editions and introductions

Sellar, W. Y. The Roman poets of the Augustan age. Ed Ker 1892.
Notes and materials for the history of University College. Ed Ker 1898.
Dryden, J. Essays. Selected by and ed Ker 1900.
Froissart, J. The chronicle of Froissart. Tr J. Bourchier, introd by Ker 1901–3.
Essays and studies. Vol 3 collected by Ker (English Assoc) 1910 etc.
Doyle, J. Essays on various subjects. Ed Ker 1911.
Low, S. Samuel Henry Jeyes. With a selection of his fugitive writings by Ker 1915.
Modern language texts. Ed Ker 1918.
Fleurs de France. Introd by Ker 1921.

Contributions to periodicals and collaborative works

For Ker's contributions to Contemporary Rev, Edinburgh Rev *and* Quart Rev, *see* Wellesley 5 *1989*.
The philosophy of art. In Essays in philosophical criticism, ed A. Seth and R. B. Haldane, 1883.
Studies in European literature, being the Taylorian lectures 1889–1899 delivered by S. Mallarmé, W. Pater, E. Dowden et al. Oxford 1900.
Metrical romances. In CHEL vol 1 1907.
The literary influence of the Middle Ages. In CHEL vol 10 1913.
The humanist ideal. Vol 6 in Essays and studies (English Assoc) 1920.
Hazlitt. Vol 8 in Essays and studies (English Assoc) 1922.
Scott centenary articles. 1932. Essays by T. Seccombe, W. P. Ker and others.

§2

de Arteaga y Pereira, F. To the memory of W. P. Ker. 1925.
Chambers, R. W. W. P. Ker. 1925.
Pafford, J. H. P. W. P. Ker: a biography. 1950.
Barker, E. W. P. Ker. 1953.
Evans, B. I. W. P. Ker as a critic of literature. 1955. [MD]

Robert Francis Kilvert 1840–79

The Nat Lib of Wales and Durham Univ Lib have surviving vols of the ms diaries. The Herefordshire Record Office has archives of the Kilvert Soc.

§1

Musings in verse. Oxford 1882 (poems priv ptd).
Selections from the diary of the Rev Francis Kilvert. Ed W. Plomer 3 vols 1938, 1939, 1940, 1960 (rev), 1961 (index).
Collected verse. Ed O. Prosser, Hereford 1962.
Kilvert's diary, 1870–79: selections. Ed and introd by W. Plomer 1944, 1977 (Pen).
Ardizzone's Kilvert: selections from the diary of the Rev Francis Kilvert, 1970–79. Ed W. Plomer, abridged E. Divine, illustr E. Ardizzone 1976.
Journal of a country curate: selections from the diary of Francis Kilvert, 1870–79. Ed and introd by Peter Wait 1977 (Folio Soc).
The diary of Francis Kilvert, April–June 1870. Ed K. Hughes and D. Ifans, Aberystwyth 1982.
The diary of Francis Kilvert, June–July 1870. Ed D. Ifans, Aberystwyth 1989.
Kilvert's Cornish diary. Journal no 4, from July 19th to August 6th. Ed R. Maber and A. Tregoning, Penryn 1989.
Kilvert the Victorian: a new selection from Kilvert's diaries [by] D. Lockwood. Bridgend 1992.

§2

Mayhew, A. L. Some Radnorshire words. N & Q 10 Aug 1878 (based on material provided by Kilvert).
Hereford Times 4 Oct 1879. Obituary.
Hope, E. Radnorshire legends and superstitions. Occult Rev Sep 1921. Based on ms notes left by Kilvert now lost.
Pritchett, V. S. In my good books. 1942.
O'Brien, K. English diaries and journals. 1943.
Plomer, W. At home. 1958. [PL]

Andrew Lang 1844–1912

For mss, letters, page proofs and typescripts see LR *and* NRA. *Notable collections of mss in St Andrews Univ Lib, Beinecke Lib (Yale), BL, Brotherton Lib (Leeds), Harvard College Lib, Houghton Lib (Yale), Lockwood Lib (Buffalo), Nat Lib of Scotland, Senate House (London), Univ of Texas Lib (Austin). For more detailed information, see Marysa Demoor,* Andrew Lang's letters; a descriptive checklist, *unpbd PhD thesis, 2 vols Gent 1983.*

Bibliographies

Falconer, C. M. Specimens of a bibliography of the works of Andrew Lang. Dundee 1889 (priv ptd).
Falconer, C. M. The writings of Andrew Lang. Dundee 1894.
Falconer, C. M. Catalogue of a library, chiefly the writings of Lang. Dundee 1898 (priv ptd).
Courtney, W. L. Eng Illustr Mag Mar 1904.
Catalogue of the library formed by the late Andrew Lang. 1912 (sold at auction by Sotheby, Wilkinson and Hodge, 5–6 Dec 1912).
Green, R. L. Descriptions from the Darlington collection of Lang. Indiana Univ Bookman 7 1965. A full bibliography.

Collections

Ballades and verses vain. New York 1884. Selected by A. Dobson.
Poetical works. Ed Mrs Lang 4 vols 1923.
The Augustan books of modern poetry: Lang. [1926.]
Essays of to-day and yesterday: Lang. 1926.
The Iliad and the Odyssey. Extracts from the translations by Lang, Leaf and Myers, and Butcher and Lang. 1935.
Lang and St Andrews: a centenary anthology. Ed J. B. Salmond, St Andrews 1944.

§1

Ballads and lyrics of old France; with other poems. 1872.
The folklore of France. 1878 (priv ptd). Pam.
XXII Ballades in blue china. 1880.
Oxford: brief historical and descriptive notes. 1880. Numerous edns.
XXII and X: XXXII Ballades in blue china. 1881.
The library. 1881.
Notes on a collection of pictures by J. E. Millais. 1881.
The black thief: a play. 1882 (priv ptd).
Helen of Troy. 1882.
Ballades and verses vain. New York 1884. Pbd in UK as Rhymes à la mode, 1885.
Custom and myth. 1884, 1885 (rev).
Much darker days, by 'A Huge Longway'. 1884, 1885 (rev). Parodies Hugh Conway, Dark days.
The Princess Nobody: a tale of fairy land. [1884.] Rptd as In fairy-land: a series of pictures from the elfworld by Richard Doyle with a poem by William Allingham and The Princess Nobody: a tale of fairyland by Andrew Lang, introd Brian Holme, biographical note by Patricia Thomson, 1979.
That very Mab. 1885 (anon). With May Kendall.
Books and bookmen. 1886.
A cheap nigger. 1886.
In the wrong paradise and other stories. 1886.
Letters to dead authors. 1886, New York 1893 (with addns), London 1906 (with addns as New and old letters to dead authors), 1907 (Pocket edn).
Lines on the inaugural meeting of the Shelley Society. 1886 (priv ptd). Anon. First pbd in Saturday Rev 13 Mar 1886.
The mark of Cain. Bristol 1886.
La mythologie. Paris 1886 (tr from Encyclopaedia Britannica).
Almae matres. 1887. Poem.
He, by the authors of It, King Solomon's wives and Bess. 1887 (anon). With W. H. Pollock. Parodies H. R. Haggard, King Solomon's mines.
Myth, ritual and religion. 2 vols 1887, 1899 (rev).
The gold of Fairnilee. Bristol 1888. Children's book.
Grass of Parnassus: rhymes old and new. 1888, 1892 (with addns).
Pictures at play or dialogues of the galleries: by two art-critics. 1888 (anon). With W. E. Henley.
Letters on literature. 1889.
Lost leaders. 1889. Rptd from Daily News.
Ode to golf. 1889 (priv ptd).
Prince Prigio. Bristol 1889. Children's book.
Études traditionnistes. Paris 1890. Essays from Sat Rev, tr H. Carnoy.
How to fail in literature: a lecture. 1890.
Life, letters and diaries of Sir Stafford Northcote, first Earl of Iddesleigh. 2 vols Edinburgh 1890.
Old friends: essays in epistolary parody. 1890.
The world's desire. 1890. With Sir H. Rider Haggard.
Angling sketches. 1891.
Essays in little. 1891.
On Calais sands. 1891. Poem with music by J. More Smieton.
Homer and the epic. 1893.
Prince Ricardo of Pantouflia. Bristol [1893], 1932 (with Prince Prigio as Chronicles of Pantouflia), 1961 (Children's Illus Classics).
St Andrews. 1893. Ed G. H. Bushnell, St Andrews 1951.
The tercentenary of Izaak Walton. 1893 (priv ptd).
Ban and arrière ban: a rally of fugitive rhymes. 1894.
Cock Lane and common-sense. 1894.
My own fairy book. Bristol 1895. Collected fairy tales.
The voices of Jeanne d'Arc. 1895 (priv ptd).
A monk of Fife. 1896.
The book of dreams and ghosts. 1897.
The life and letters of J. G. Lockhart. 2 vols 1897.
Modern mythology: a reply to Max Müller. 1897.
Pickle the spy: or the incognito of Prince Charles. 1897.
The companions of Pickle. 1898.
The making of religion. 1898.
Waiting on the Glesca train. 1898. Poem set to music by R. T. Boothby.
Parson Kelly. New York 1899, London 1900. With A. E. W. Mason.
A history of Scotland from the Roman occupation. 4 vols Edinburgh 1900–7.
Notes and names in books. Chicago 1900 (priv ptd).
Prince Charles Edward. 1900.
Alfred Tennyson. Edinburgh 1901.
Magic and religion. 1901.
The mystery of Mary Stuart. 1901, 1904 (rev).
Psychical research of the century. In The 19th century: a review of progress, 1901.
Adventures among books. Cleveland OH 1901 (priv ptd), London 1905.
The disentanglers. 1902.
James VI and the Gowrie mystery. 1902.
The young Ruthven. 1902 (priv ptd). Ballad.
Social origins, by Lang; Primal Law, by J. J. Atkinson. 1903.
The story of the golden fleece. 1903.
The valet's tragedy, and other studies. 1903.
Historical mysteries. 1904.
The Clyde mystery: a study in forgeries and folklore. Glasgow 1905.
John Knox and the reformation. 1905.
New collected rhymes. 1905.
The puzzle of Dickens's last plot. 1905.
The secret of the totem. 1905.
Homer and his age. 1906.
Portraits and jewels of Mary Stuart. 1906.
Sir Walter Scott. 1906.
The story of Joan of Arc. [1906.]
The King over the water. 1907. Mainly by A. Shield.
Tales of a fairy court. [1907.]
The maid of France: the life and death of Jeanne d'Arc. 1908; tr Fr [1911], Portuguese 1940. A reply to Anatole France, Vie de Jeanne d'Arc, 1908.
The origins of religion and other essays. 1908. Reprints from earlier vols, with one new essay on Theories of the origins of religion.
The origin of terms of human relationship. [1909.] From PBA 3 1909.
La Jeanne d'Arc de M. Anatole France. Paris 1909.
Sir George Mackenzie, King's Advocate: his life and times. 1909.
Sir Walter Scott and the Border minstrelsy. 1910.
The world of Homer. 1910.
Ballades and rhymes: from Ballades and rhymes à la mode. 1911.
Method in the study of totemism. Glasgow 1911.
A short history of Scotland. Edinburgh 1911.
History of English literature from Beowulf to Swinburne. 1912, 1912 (rev).
In praise of frugality. 1912 (priv ptd). Poem tr from Pope Leo XII.
Ode on a distant memory of Jane Eyre. [1912.]
Ode to the opening century. 1912 (priv ptd). Poem tr from Pope Leo XII.

Shakespeare, Bacon and the great unknown. 1912.
Highways and byways on the Border. 1913. With John Lang.
Bibliomania. 1914 (priv ptd).
The paradise of poets. 1929 (priv ptd).
The new Pygmalion. 1962 (priv ptd). Poems.
Most of Lang's important pbns were rptd by AMS Press Inc.

Children's books
The black thief: a new and original drama. 1882 (priv ptd).
The princess Nobody: a tale of fairyland. 1884, 1955 (in Modern fairy stories, ed R. L. Green).
The gold of Fairnilee. 1888; ed G. Avery 1967 (as The gold of Fairnilee and other stories)(with Princess Nobody, *above*, and Tales of a fairy court, *below*).
Prince Prigio. 1889; ed R. L. Green 1961 (with Prince Ricardo, *below*), 1962, 1982 (with Prince Ricardo as Chronicles of Pantouflia).
Prince Ricardo of Pantouflia. 1893.
The story of the Golden Fleece. 1903.
The story of Joan of Arc. 1906.
Tales of a fairy court. 1906.
Tales of Troy and Greece. 1907, rptd 1978; selection rptd as Tales of the Greek seas, 1909; selection rptd as Tales of Troy, 1909.
See R. L. Green, Andrew Lang, *1962; and below under Fairy tales.*

Fairy tales and legends
Blue fairy book. 1889, rptd 1975; ed Brian Alderson 1987.
Further collections under colours: Red, 1890; Green, 1892; Yellow, 1894, rptd 1976 ed Brian Alderson; Pink, 1897, rptd 1982 ed Brian Alderson; Grey, 1900; Violet, 1901; Crimson, 1903; Brown, 1904; Orange, 1906; Olive, 1907; Lilac, 1910. Numerous edns. All rptd with illus, New York 1966–7. Selections include Old friends among the fairies, 1926; The rose fairy book, 1951; Fifty favourite fairy books, ed K. M. Lines 1963; More favourite fairy tales, ed K. M. Lines 1967.
The Arabian nights entertainments. 1898. Rptd as Sinbad the Sailor and other stories, 1986.
The book of romance. 1902.
The red romance book. 1905.
Aladdin and the wonderful lamp, retold by Andrew Lang. 1981.

Translations
The Odyssey of Homer, book vi. 1877 (priv ptd).
Specimens of a translation of Theocritus. 1879 (priv ptd).
The Odyssey of Homer, done into English prose by S. H. Butcher and Lang. 1879, 1935 (with the Iliad as The complete works of Homer).
Theocritus, Bion and Moschus. 1880.
The Iliad of Homer, done into English prose by Lang, Walter Leaf and Ernest Myers. 1883.
Aucassin and Nicolete. 1887.
Deulin, Charles. Johnny Nut and the golden goose. 1887.
The dead leman and other tales from the French. 1889. With P. Sylvester.
The miracles of Madame Saint Katherine of Fierbois, translated from the edition of the Abbé J. J. Bowrassé, Tours 1858. Chicago 1897.
The Homeric hymns: a new prose translation and essays. 1899.
Ballades and lyrics of François Villon. Mount Vernon 1940.

Introductions and editions
Aristotle's politics. Tr W. E. Bolland, introd by Lang 1877. Rptd as The politics of Aristotle: introductory essays by Lang, 1886.
Poe, E. A. The poems. With an essay on his poetry by Lang 1881.
Grimm's household tales. Tr Margaret Hunt, introd by Lang 1884.
Molière. Les précieuses ridicules. Ed, introd and notes by Lang 1884.
Apuleius, L. The marriage of Cupid and Psyche. Tr W. Adlington with a discourse on the fable by Lang. 1887.
Lamb, C. Beauty and the beast. Introd by Lang 1887.
Ballads of books. Ed Lang 1888.
Border ballads. Introd by Lang 1888.
Herodotus. Euterpe. Ed Lang 1888.
Perrault's popular tales. Ed and introd by Lang 1888.
The blue fairy book. Ed Lang 1889. For other coloured vols, *see* Children's books, *above*.
Romilly, H. H. From my verandah in New Guinea. Introd by Lang 1889.
Colonna, Francesco. The strife of love in a dream. Ed Lang 1890.
Kipling, R. The courting of Dinah Shadd, etc. Biographical and critical sketch by Lang 1890.
Lamb, C. Adventures of Ulysses. Introd by Lang 1890.
Longinus on the sublime. Tr H. L. Havell, introd by Lang 1890.
Rae, T. Songs and verses. Introd by Lang 1890.
Blue poetry book. Ed Lang 1891.
Garrett, E. H. Elizabethan songs in honour of love and beautie. Introd by Lang 1891.
Malory, Sir T. Morte d'Arthur. Ed H. O. Somer, essay on Malory's prose by Lang 1891.
Selected poems of Robert Burns. Introd by Lang 1891.
Sellar, W. Y. The Roman poets of the Augustan age. With a memoir of the author by Lang. Oxford 1892.
Scott, Sir W. The Waverley novels. Introd and notes by Lang, 1892–4 (Border edn), Boston 1892–4.
Cox, M. Cinderella. Introd by Lang 1893.
Daft, R. Kings of cricket. Introd by Lang 1893.
Du Camp, M. Theophile Gautier. Tr J. E. Gordon, preface by Lang 1893.
Kirk, R. The secret commonwealth of elves, fauns and fairies. Comment by Lang 1893.
Lever, C. J. The confessions of Harry Lorrequer. Introd by Lang [New York] 1894.
Robert F. Murray: his poems; with a memoir by Lang. 1894.
Scott, Sir Walter. The lyrics and ballads. Ed and introd by Lang 1894.
Van Eeden, F. Little Johannes. Tr Clara Bell, introd by Lang 1894.
Border ballads. Introd by Lang 1895.
Scott, Sir Walter. Poetical works. Selected, ed and introd by Lang 1895, etc.
Stoddart, T. T. The death wake. Introd by Lang 1895.
The animal story book. Ed Lang 1896.
Burns, R. The poems and songs. 1896. Introd, notes and glossary by Lang and W. A. Craigie.
Parker, C. Langloh. Australian legendary tales. Introd by Lang 1896.
Poems and songs of Burns. Ed and introd by Lang 1896.
Roth, H. Ling. The natives of Sarawak and British North Borneo. Preface by Lang 1896.
Walton, I. The complete angler. Introd by Lang 1896.
About, E. The king of the mountains. Introd by Lang 1897.
A collection of ballads. Ed Lang 1897.
Corbet, S. Animal land. Introd by Lang 1897.
Dickens, C. Gadshill edition of Dickens's works. Introd and notes by Lang 1897.
The highlands of Scotland in 1750. Introd by Lang 1897.
The nursery rhyme book. Ed Lang 1897.
Scott, Sir Walter. The lady of the lake. Introd by Lang 1897.
Selections from Wordsworth. Ed Lang 1897.
Arabian nights' entertainments. Selected by and ed Lang 1898, 1951 (as Arabian nights), 1986 (as Sinbad the sailor and other stories).
Holmes, O. W. The autocrat at the breakfast table. Introd by Lang 1898.
Parker, C. L. More Australian legendary tales. Introd by Lang 1898, 1978.
Selections from Coleridge. Ed Lang 1898.
Shaylor, J. Pleasures of literature. Introd by Lang 1898.
Comparetti, Domenico. Traditional poetry of the Finns. Tr Isabella M. Anderton, introd by Lang 1899.

De Saint-Pierre, Henri Bernardin. Paul and Virginia. Introd by Lang 1899.
Lamb, C. and Mary Ann. Tales from Shakespeare. Introd by Lang 1899.
Mackenzie, A. Prophecies of the Braham seer. Introd by Lang 1899.
Brown, J. Rab and his friends. Introd by Lang 1900.
Low, J. L. F. G. Tait. Introd by Lang 1900.
Scott, Sir W. The poems and ballads. Introd and notes by Lang, Boston 1900.
Oliphant, N. A diary of the siege of the legations in Peking. Preface by Lang 1901.
The Gowrie conspiracy: confessions of Sprott. Ed Lang 1902.
Hugo, V. Notre-Dame of Paris, with a critical introd by Lang. 1902.
Social England illustrated. Introd by Lang, ed Thomas Seccombe 1903. Rptd and selected from E. Arbor, An English garner, 8 vols 1877–90.
Brown, G. D. The house with the green shutters. Introd by Lang 1903.
Lennox, C. George Douglas Brown. Introd by Lang 1903.
Barclay, R. Memories. Preface by Lang 1904.
Elton, C. I. In C. I. Elton, William Shakespeare, his family and friends, ed A. H. Thompson, memoir of the author by Lang, 1904.
Maitland, J. The apology for William Maitland of Lethington. Ed Lang 1904.
Parker, C. L. The Eahlayi tribe: a study of aboriginal life in Australia. Introd by Lang 1905.
Thomas, N. W. Crystal gazing. Introd by Lang 1905.
Dumas, A. My memoirs. Tr E. M. Waller, introd by Lang 1907.
Farrer, J. A. Literary forgeries. Introd by Lang 1907.
Poet's country. Ed Lang 1907.
Shakespeare, W. All's well that ends well. Introd by Lang 1907.
Stevenson, R. L. A child's garden. Introd by Lang 1907.
Ingelow, J. Poems. Selected by Lang 1908.
Shield, A. Henry Stuart, Cardinal of York. Introd by Lang 1908.
Murray, C. Hamewith. Introd by Lang 1909.
Murray, R. F. The scarlet gown. Introd by Lang 1909.
Dayrell, Elphinstone. Folk stories from southern Nigeria, West Africa.... Introd by Lang 1910.
Reade, C. A good fight. Introd by Lang 1910.
Morgan, J. V. A study in nationality. Introd by Lang 1911.
Scott, Sir Walter. Poems and plays. Introd by Lang 1911.
Stevenson, R. L. Swanston edition of the works. Introd by Lang 1911.
The Annesley case. Ed Lang 1912.
Lang, Leonora B. Men, women and minxes. Preface by Lang 1912.
Barnett, A. and L. Dale. An anthology of English prose (1332–1740). Preface by Lang 1912.
The Waverley edition of the works of Charles Dickens. Introd by Lang 1913.
Shaylor, J. The pleasures of bookland. Introd by Lang 1914.
Dumas, A. The three musketeers. Tr A. Allison, introd by Lang 1928.
Khaiyam, Umar. The Andrew Lang edition of the Rubaiyat. 1935.

Contributions to periodicals and collaborative works

Lang was a prolific contributor to Blackwood's Mag, Dark Blue, Contemporary Rev, Cornhill Mag, Edinburgh Rev, Longman's Mag, Macmillan's Mag, North Br Rev, Quart Rev, Fortnightly Rev, Fraser's Mag, Nat Rev, New Quart Mag, Nineteenth Cent, New Rev *and* Westminster Rev, *as listed in* Wellesley 5 1989, *besides contributing signed and anonymous essays to numerous other jnls such as* Athenaeum, Spectator, Saturday Rev, *etc.*

On Dogs. The new Amphion 1886.
Old St Leonards days, The grave of Orpheus, almae matres mirror. 1887.
The history of cricket. In Cricket, 1888 (Badminton Lib).
History of golf. In Golf, ed H. G. Hutchinson, 1890 (Badminton Lib).
Famous golf links. With H. G. Hutchinson et al, 1891.
[Selected poems.] *See* The poets and poetry of the century, ed A. H. Miles, vol 8, 1891, etc.
A batch of golfing papers. Ed R. Barclay [1892]. By Lang et al.
Piccadilly. The great streets of the world. 1892.
Classical sport. In Hedley Peek, The poetry of sport, 1896 (Badminton Lib).
Scott. In Homes and haunts of famous authors, 1906.
Australian problems. In Anthropological essays presented to Edward Burnett Tylor, Oxford 1907. With notice of Tylor's work by Lang.
'The end of an auld sang': a romantic plot against the Union. The union of 1707. Ed Peter H. Brown 1907.
Homer and anthropology. In R. R. Marett, Anthropology and the classics, Oxford 1908.
Presidential addresses to the Society for Psychical Research. 1912.

Lang contributed the following articles to the 11th edn of the Encyclopaedia Britannica *1910–11 (some from the 9th):* Apparitions, Ballads, Casket letters, Crystal gazing, Fairy, Family, Edmund Gurney, Hauntings, James de la Cloche, Molière, Mythology, Names, Poltergeist, Prometheus, Psychical Research, Scotland (History), Second sight, Tale and Totem. *He also contributed articles on Burns and Scott to* Chambers' encyclopedia *and on ballads to* Chambers' cyclopedia of English literature.

Published letters

Friends over the ocean: Andrew Lang's letters to J. B. Matthews, H. H. Furness, F. J. Child, William James, and J. R. Lowell 1881–1912. Ed Marysa Demoor, Ghent 1989.
Dear Stevenson: Andrew Lang's letters to Robert Louis Stevenson with five letters from Stevenson to Lang. Ed Marysa Demoor, Leuven '1990' [1991].

§2

Pennell, Elizabeth. Andrew Lang as a lecturer. The Critic Dec 1888.
To an old humourist. Bookman Nov 1891.
Austin, L. F. The modern Pan. Bookman Mar 1892.
Matthews, Brander. Andrew Lang. Century Jan 1894.
Matthews, Brander. Andrew Lang. Critic Jan 1894.
Canton, William. Mr Lang as a poet. Bookman 8 Aug 1895.
Moore, George. Mr Andrew Lang as critic. Sat Rev Dec 1897.
Brown, R. Semitic influence in Hellenic mythology, with special reference to works of Max Müller and Lang. 1898.
Falconer, C. M. A new friendship's garland. 1898.
Ridge, W. Pett. Mr Andrew Lang. Bookman Oct 1900.
Courtney, W. L. Andrew Lang. Eng Illus Mag Mar 1904.
Wanliss, T. D. Scotland and Presbyterianism vindicated: being a critical review of the third volume of Mr Lang's history. Edinburgh 1905.
Wanliss, T. D. The muckrake in Scottish history: or Mr Lang recriticised. Edinburgh 1906.
Lang, Patrick Sellar. The Langs of Selkirk. Melbourne 1910.
Chesterton, G. K. Andrew Lang. Illus London News 27 July 1912.
Marett, Robert Ranulph. The late Andrew Lang. Athenaeum Aug 1912.
Gordon, G. S. TLS 5 Sep 1912 (anon); rptd in his Lives of authors, 1950. Obituary.
Gosse, E. W. Andrew Lang. Bookman Sep 1912; rptd in Portraits and sketches 1913.
Henry, Stuart. Andrew Lang – an old-fashioned memory. Bookman Sep 1912.
In memoriam Andrew Lang. Bk Sep 1912.
Saintsbury, G. Oxford Mag 17 Oct 1912. Obituary.
Menzies, Allan. Andrew Lang as student. College Echoes 25 Oct 1912.
Salmond, James B. The man of letters. College Echoes 25 Oct 1912.
Anderson, James Maitland. Andrew Lang. St Andrews Lib Bull 5 1912.
Repplier, Agnes. Andrew Lang. Catholic World Dec 1912.

Brown, P. H. Andrew Lang. PBA 5 1912.
Clodd, Edward. In memoriam: Andrew Lang (1844–1912). Folk Lore 1912.
Van Gennep, Arnold, Wilhelm Schmidt and W. H. R. Rivers. Andrew Lang: folklorist and critic. Folk Lore 1912.
Ker, W. P. Commemorative address. Proc Academic Committee, Royal Soc of Lit 1913.
Rait, R. S., Gilbert Murray, Salomon Reinach and J. H. Millar. Andrew Lang. Quart Rev Apr 1913.
Greenwood, G. G. Is there a Shakespeare problem? with a reply to Mr J. M. Robertson and Mr Lang. 1916.
Green, Roger Lancelyn. Andrew Lang: a critical biography. Leicester 1946.
Langstaff, Eleanor de Selms. Andrew Lang. Boston 1978. [MD]

'Vernon Lee', Violet Paget 1856–1935

Lee's mss are at Colby College, Waterville ME.

Bibliographies

Mannocchi, P. F. 'Vernon Lee': a reintroduction and primary bibliography. ELT 26 1983.
Markgraf, C. 'Vernon Lee': a commentary and an annotated bibliography of writings about her. ELT 26 1983.

Collections

A Vernon Lee anthology: selections from the earlier works. Ed I. C. Willis 1929.
The snake lady and other stories. Ed H. Gregory, New York 1954.
Supernatural tales: excursions into fantasy. Ed I. C. Willis 1955.
Pope Jacynth and more supernatural tales: excursions into fantasy. 1956.

§1

Studies of the eighteenth century in Italy. 1880, 1887, 1907 (2nd edn, illus, with new preface), Chicago 1908, New York 1978; tr Ital 2 vols 1881, 1 vol 1932.
Tuscan fairy tales, taken down from the mouths of the people. 1880. Ed Vernon Lee.
Belcaro: being essays on sundry aesthetical questions. 1881, 1883, 1887 (new edn).
The prince of the hundred soups: a puppet-show in narrative, edited [i.e. written] with an introduction by Vernon Lee. Illustr S. Birch 1883, New York 1886.
Ottilie: an eighteenth-century idyl. 1883, New York 1886 (includes The prince of the hundred soups), London 1893, 1913; tr Sp 1937.
Miss Brown: a novel. 3 vols Edinburgh 1884, New York 1885; tr Fr 1889.
The Countess of Albany. 1884, Boston 1884 etc, London 1909 (2nd edn), 1910 (2nd edn with portraits).
Euphorion: being studies of the antique and the mediaeval in the Renaissance. 2 vols 1884, 2 vols Boston 1884, 1 vol London 1885 (rev), 1894 (3rd edn), 1899.
Baldwin: being dialogues on views and aspirations. 1886, Boston 1886.
A phantom lover: a fantastic story. Edinburgh 1886, Boston 1886, New York 1886; tr Sp 1936.
Juvenilia: being a second series of essays on sundry aesthetical questions. 2 vols 1887, 1 vol Boston 1887.
Hauntings: fantastic stories. 1890, New York 1890, London 1896 (2nd edn).
Vanitas: polite stories. 1892, New York 1892, London 1911 (2nd edn, adds A frivolous conversion), Leipzig 1911.
Althea: a second book of dialogues on aspirations and duties. 1894, 1910 (new edn).
Au pays de Vénus. Paris [1894]. Tales tr Fr, rptd from Les lettres et les arts.
Renaissance fancies and studies: a sequel to Euphorion. 1895, New York 1896.
An essay on art and life. East Aurora NY 1896.
Limbo and other essays. 1897, 1908 (adds Ariadne in Mantua).
Genius loci: notes on places. 1899, Leipzig 1906 (Genius loci and The enchanted woods), London 1907 (2nd edn), 1908 (3rd edn); tr Ger 1905.
Le rôle de l'élément moteur dans la perception esthétique visuelle: mémoire et questionnaire soumis au quatrième Congrès de psychologie. Paris 1900. With C. Anstruther-Thomson.
Ariadne in Mantua: a romance in five acts. Oxford 1903, Portland ME 1912, 1930 (adds Limbo and other essays); tr Ital 1907, Ger 1909, Fr 1910.
Penelope Brandling: a tale of the Welsh coast in the eighteenth century. 1903.
Hortus vitae: essays on the gardening of life. 1903, 1904 (2nd edn), Leipzig 1907 (Hortus vitae and Limbo), London 1928.
Pope Jacynth and other fantastic tales. 1904, Leipzig 1906 (adds Ariadne in Mantua etc), London 1907 (2nd edn).
The enchanted woods and other essays on the genius of places. 1905, Leipzig 1906, London 1910 (2nd edn).
Sister Benvenuta and the Christ child: an eighteenth century legend. New York 1905, 1906.
The spirit of Rome: leaves from a diary. 1906, 1906 (2nd edn), Leipzig 1910 (The spirit of Rome and Laurus nobilis).
The sentimental traveller: notes on places. 1908, Leipzig 1921.
Gospels of anarchy and other contemporary studies. 1908, New York 1909.
Laurus nobilis: chapters on art and life. 1909.
Vital lies: studies of some varieties of recent obscurantism. 2 vols 1912; tr Fr 1921.
Beauty and ugliness and other studies in psychological aesthetics. 1912. With C. Anstruther-Thomson.
The beautiful: an introduction to psychological aesthetics. Cambridge 1913, New York 1913.
The tower of the mirrors and other essays on the spirit of places. 1914, Leipzig 1922.
Louis Norbert: a two-fold romance. 1914, Leipzig 1920.
Peace with honour: controversial notes on the settlement. 1915.
The ballet of the nations: a present-day morality; with a pictorial commentary by M. Armfield. 1915, New York 1915.
Satan the waster: a philosophic war trilogy, with notes and introduction. 1920, 1930 (adds new preface).
The handling of words and other studies in literary psychology. 1923, New York 1923, 1927.
The golden keys and other essays on the genius loci. 1925, New York 1925, Leipzig 1925.
Proteus: or the future of intelligence. 1925, New York 1925.
The poet's eye: some notes on the differences between verse and prose. 1926.
For Maurice: five unlikely stories. 1927.
Music and its lovers: an empirical study of emotion and imaginative responses to music. Ed I. C. Willis 1932, New York 1933.

'Vernon Lee' also wrote introductions to C. Anstruther-Thomson, Art and man; *E. E. Charteris,* John Sargent; *R. W. Semon,* Mnemic psychology; *I. Forbes-Mosse,* Don Juan's daughters, *etc.*

For Lee's contributions to periodicals and newspapers, see the Primary bibliography *in* ELT 26 1983.

Letters

Vernon Lee's letters. Ed I. C. Willis 1937.

§2

The literary life of Vernon Lee. Literary World (Boston) 1 Nov 1884.
Preston, H. W. Vernon Lee. Atlantic Monthly Feb 1885.
Brooks, V. W. Notes on Vernon Lee. Forum Apr 1911.
Shaw, G. B. Satan the Waster. Nation 18 Sep 1920.

MacCarthy, D. Vernon Lee. Bookman (London) Oct 1931.
'Vernon Lee' – the Renaissance in Italy. The Times 14 Feb 1935. Obituary.
Miss Violet Paget, British author, dies. New York Times 14 Feb 1935. Obituary.
Vernon Lee: an appreciation. The Times 15 Feb 1935. Obituary.
Gunn, P. Vernon Lee: Violet Paget, 1856–1935. 1964. [GW]

Richard Le Gallienne 1866–1947

See col 1622.

Sir Alfred Comyns Lyall 1835–1911

See col 764.

Alice Meynell 1847–1922

See col 766.

William Minto 1845–93

See NRA *for mss and letters. Notable collections in Aberdeen Univ Lib, Nat Lib of Scotland.*

Bibliography

MacDonald, K. I. William Minto; 1845–1893: a checklist. Bibliotheck vol 5 no 5 1964.

§1

The claims of classical studies whether as information or as training, by a Scotch graduate. Aberdeen 1869.
A manual of English prose literature, biographical and critical, designed mainly to show characteristics of style. Edinburgh 1872. Essay on style; Biographies of De Quincey, Macaulay and Carlyle; History of English prose writers.
Characteristics of English poets from Chaucer to Shirley. Edinburgh 1874.
The colorado beetle: a farce, in one act. 1877.
Daniel Defoe. 1879 (EML).
The crack of doom: a novel. 3 vols Edinburgh 1886. Rptd from Blackwood's Mag.
The mediation of Ralph Hardelot. 3 vols 1888. Novel.
Was she good or bad? A holiday episode. 1889.
Logic inductive and deductive. 1893.
Plain principles of prose composition. 1893.
The literature of the Georgian era. Ed with biographical introd by W. Knight, Edinburgh 1894. Chaucer, Spenser, Renaissance, Shakespeare, Pope and the eighteenth century, The Novel, Wordsworth, Coleridge, Shelley, Keats etc.

Editions and introductions

Scott, W. Lay of the last minstrel, introduction and canto I. Ed Minto, Oxford 1882.
Scott, W. Lay of the last minstrel. Ed and introd by Minto, Oxford 1886.
Scott, W. Poetical works. Ed Minto 2 vols Edinburgh 1888.
Scott, W. Lady of the lake. Ed and introd by Minto, Oxford 1891.
Scott, W. B. Autobiographical notes of the life of William Bell Scott and notices of his artistic and poetical circle of friends. Ed Minto 2 vols 1892.

Contributions to periodicals

Minto contributed to over a dozen periodicals; see Wellesley 5 *1989 for Minto's contributions to* Blackwood's Mag, Fortnightly Rev, Fraser's Mag, *and* Macmillan's Mag. *Minto also contributed articles on literary subjects to the* Encyclopaedia Britannica, *and he was (co-)editor of the* Examiner, a Political, Social and Literary Review, *from 1874 to 1878.*

§2

Obits: Acad 11 Mar 1893; Bookman (London) Apr 1893. [OD]

Cosmo Monkhouse, William Cosmo Monkhouse 1840–1901

Mss located in Berg Collection, NYPL; Colby College Lib; Harvard Univ Lib; Huntington; Pierpont Morgan Lib; Princeton; Univ of British Columbia Lib. See also LR.

Bibliographies

In R. F. Sharp, A dictionary of English authors: biographical and bibliographical, 1904, rptd Detroit 1978.
In Nineteenth century readers' guide to periodical literature 1890–1899, ed H. G. Cushing and A. V. Morris, 2 vols New York 1944.
See also Wellesley 5 *1989.*

Selections

In Ballades and rondeaus, chants royal, sestinas, villanelles, &c., ed G. White, London and Newcastle-on-Tyne 1887, New York 1888, 1892, 1893, 1897, London 1900, 1905, 1909.
In The poets and poetry of the century, ed A. H. Miles, vol 6 1891–7.
Lyrics. The Bibelot 6 (3) 1900, Portland ME 1900.

§1

A dream of idleness, and other poems. 1865.
A question of honour. 3 vols 1868. Novel.
Joseph Mallord Turner. 1879, [1929] (Great Artists ser).
Corn and poppies. 1890, 1890. Poems.
REVIEWS: Scots Observer 14 June 1890; Acad 28 June 1890; Athenaeum 9 Aug 1890.
Life of Leigh Hunt. 1893 (Great Writers ser).
REVIEWS: Acad 13 May 1893; Athenaeum 10 June 1893; Spectator 30 Sep 1893.
The Christ upon the hill. A ballad. Etched by W. Strang. 1895.
REVIEW: Athenaeum 25 Jan 1896.
In the National Gallery. 1895, [1900?].
To Our Sovereign Lady Queen Victoria. June 22, 1897. [1897.] Poems.
British contemporary artists. 1899, New York 1899, 1901.
REVIEW: New York Times 16 Dec 1899.
Pasiteles the elder, and other poems. 1901 (preface A. Dobson).
Nonsense rhymes. [1902] (illustr G. K. Chesterton).

Contributions to periodicals, collaborative works and anthologies

Acad. 24 Jan 1880–15 Oct 1887.
Art Jnl. Apr 1881–Feb 1901.
Mag of Art. Jan 1882–July 1900.
Blackwood's Mag. Under the oak and True lover, 8 Feb 1890. Poems.
Portfolio. July 1884–Dec 1892.
Scots Observer. 20 Apr 1889–16 Nov 1889.
The Critic. O love, no skill can move thy will, 6 Sep 1890. Poem.
Spectator. Secret, 11 Oct 1890; On one not beautiful, 11 Oct 1890. Poems.
Art Jnl Easter Annual. 1897–1901.
Art Jnl Jubilee. 1899.
DNB. Monkhouse contributed 137 articles to the DNB, among them those on Landseer, Millais, Reynolds and Turner: *see* G. Fenwick, The contributors' index to the National Dictionary of Biography 1885–1901, Winchester 1989.
Scribner's Mag. Dec 1894–19 Dec 1897.
Parents' Rev. Art in education, Sep 1898.
For contributions to Nat Rev-II *and* St Paul's Mag, *see* Wellesley 5 *1989.*

Editions, introductions, etc

Masterpieces of English art. 1869 (illus). Text by Monkhouse.
A few words about Hogarth. In The works of W[illiam] H[ogarth], 2 vols 1872.

Pictures by W. Etty. With descriptions and a biographical sketch of the painter by W[illiam] C[osmo] M[onkhouse]. 1874.
Pictures by Sir C. Eastlake. With a sketch of the artist by W[illiam] C[osmo] M[onkhouse]. 1875 (folio).
The works of J. H. Foley, R. A. Sculptor. With notes by W. C. M[onkhouse]. 1875 (folio).
The studies of Sir Edwin Landseer. With a history of his art-life by W. C. M[onkhouse]. [1877] (folio).
Pictures of Sir Edwin Landseer. A new series with descriptions by W. C. M[onkhouse]. [1877.]
The Turner Gallery. Descriptive text by W. C. M[onkhouse]. 3 vols [1878] (folio), 1 vol New York 1879.
The works of Sir Edwin Landseer. With a history of his art-life by W[illiam] C[osmo] M[onkhouse]. [1879 (folio), 1880 (folio)], Alton 1990 (facs of 1879 edn, ed J. Batty).
Preface. In The life and works of Joseph Wright, A. R. A., ed W. Bemrose, 1885.
The National Gallery. The Pre-Raphaelites. 1887.
Heaton, Mrs C. A concise history of painting. Rev edn by Monkhouse 1888, 1917.
The earlier English water-colour painters, etc. 1890 (folio), 1890, 1897 (folio, 2nd edn).
Introd to the Exhibition illustrative of the French revival of etching, 1891.
In The child set in the midst: by modern poets, ed W. Meynell, 1892.
Historical catalogue of the collection of water-colour drawings by deceased artists. Ed and introd by Monkhouse, 1894.
Introd to R. Mills, Catalogue of blue and white oriental porcelain exhibited in 1895, 1895.
Introd to Catalogue of coloured Chinese porcelain exhibited in 1896, 1896.
Introd to the Exhibition of drawings in water colour by A. W. Hunt, 1897.
Introd to the Exhibition of drawings and studies by Sir Edward Burne-Jones, Bart, 1899.

§2

Obits: The Times 22 July 1901; A[dams], W. A. W. Acad 27 July 1901; Lee, Sir S. Athenaeum 27 July 1901; Bond, R. W. Letter, Acad 3 Aug 1901.
Dobson, A. In DNB 1901–1911.
Gosse, E. W. Art Jnl Mar 1902.
Buckley, J. H. In William Ernest Henley: a study in the 'counter-decadence' of the nineties, Princeton 1945, rptd New York 1971.
Connell, J. (J. H. Robertson). In W. E. Henley, 1949, rptd Port Washington NY 1972. [DA]

George Moore 1857–1933

See col 1647.

John Morley, Viscount Morley 1838–1923

See LR *and* NRA *for mss and letters. Notable collections in BL, Bodleian, Cambridge Univ Lib, House of Lords Record Office, London Univ and Nat Lib of Scotland.*

Bibliographies

Stead, W. T. English Illus Mag Dec 1903.
DLB vols 57 and 144, 1987 and 1995 (*see below*).

Collections and selections

Select essays. Ed and introd by H. G. Rawlinson 1923.

§1

Modern characteristics: a series of short essays from the Saturday Review. 1865. Anon.
Edmund Burke: a historical study. 1867.
Studies in conduct: short essays from the Saturday Review. 1867. Anon.
Critical miscellanies. 2 ser 1871–7, 3 vols 1886 (with addns and omissions), ser 4 1908, numerous later edns and reprints in a varying number of vols.
Voltaire. 1872, 1872 (rev); tr Rus 1889. Numerous later edns and reprints.
Rousseau. 2 vols 1873, 1 vol New York 1878. Numerous later edns and reprints.
The struggle for national education. 1873, rptd in Francis Adams, History of the elementary school contest in England, Brighton 1972.
On compromise. 1874, 1877 (rev), 1886 (enlarged); tr Ger 1879, Rus 1881. Numerous later edns and reprints.
Diderot and the encyclopaedists. 2 vols 1878, 1 vol New York 1878. Numerous later edns and reprints.
Burke. 1879, 1888 (enlarged) (EML).
The life of Richard Cobden. 2 vols 1881, 1 vol 1882; tr Fr 1885. Numerous later edns and reprints.
Ralph Waldo Emerson: an essay. New York 1884.
On the study of literature. 1887.
Walpole. 1889. Numerous later edns and reprints.
Studies in literature. 1891. Several essays from this collection appeared in a Fr trn in 1895 as Essais critiques.
Machiavelli: the Romanes lecture delivered in the Sheldonian Theatre June 2 1897. 1897.
Oliver Cromwell. 1900.
The life of William Ewart Gladstone. 3 vols 1903, 2 vols 1905–7, 1 vol introd by C. F. G. Masterman 1927. Numerous later edns and reprints.
  Bigelow, J. Lest we forget. Gladstone, Morley and the confederate loan of 1863: a rectification [of certain statements in Morley's Life of Gladstone]. New York 1905.
Literary essays. 1906. Byron, Carlyle, Macaulay, On the study of literature, Wordsworth.
Speeches on Indian affairs: with an appreciation [signed: P. N. R. P.]. Madras 1908, 1917 (rev and enlarged).
Indian speeches 1907–1909. 1909.
Science and literature: presidential address delivered at the annual general meeting of the English Association Jan 28 1911. [Oxford] 1911 (priv ptd).
Notes on politics and history: a university address. 1913.
Recollections. 2 vols 1917.
Memorandum on resignation – August 1914. Introd by F. W. Hirst 1928; tr Ger 1929.
The works of John Morley. 15 vols 1921, 12 vols 1923.
Oracles on man and government. Freeport NY 1968. Reprint of one of the 12 vols of the collected works, *above*.
Biographical studies. Freeport NY 1969. Reprint of one of the 12 vols of the collected works, *above*.

Editions and introductions

Emerson, R. W. The works. Ed Morley 6 vols 1883.
Wordsworth, W. The complete poetical works. Introd by Morley 1888.
Voltaire. The works. With notes by Tobias Smollett; revised and modernised by W. F. Fleming; introd by O. H. G. Leigh; with a critique and biography by Morley. Paris and New York [1901].
Morley was general editor of both the Original Series *(1878–92) and the* New Series *(1902–19) of the* English Men of Letters. *Three vols of this ser (Defoe, Goldsmith and Thackeray) were translated into Ger in 1880.*

Contributions to periodicals and collaborative works

Morley was editor of the Literary Gazette *1861,* Fortnightly Rev, *1867–82,* Morning Star, *June–Oct 1869,* Light, *Apr–Oct 1876,* Pall Mall Gazette, *1881–3,* Macmillan's Mag, *1883–5. He also contributed to several other periodicals such as* Nineteenth Cent, New Rev *and* Saturday Rev *(see also*

Wellesley 5 1989). *Essays and articles by Morley appeared in collective works such as* G. H. P. Prose masterpieces from modern essayists *1886,* Books and how to read them, *1905,* Nineteenth century essays, *introd by P. Stansky, Chicago 1970. Morley contributed one entry to* DNB.

§2

Letters addressed to the Right Hon John Morley M. P. By an Irish Liberal. Dublin 1888.

Quill, W. A. Mr John Morley and Home Rule. Dublin 1888.

Robinson, G. F. S. Proceedings in connection with the visit to Dublin of the Marquis of Ripon and the Right Hon J. Morley. Dublin 1888.

Filon, A. Profils Anglais: Randolph Churchill, Joseph Chamberlain, John Morley, Parnell. Paris 1893.

Cecil, A. In his Six Oxford thinkers, 1909.

Major, E. Viscount Morley and Indian reform. 1910.

Hyndman, H. M. The emancipation of India: a reply to the article of the Right Hon Viscount Morley. [1911.]

Harper, G. M. In his John Morley and other essays, Princeton 1920.

Harris, M. Two Victorian portraits. North Amer Rev Sep 1920.

Morison, J. L. John Morley: a study in Victorianism. Kingston, Ontario 1920.

MacCallum, J. D. Lord Morley's criticism of English poetry and prose. Princeton [1921].

Khan, S. A. The life of Lord Morley. 1923.

Massingham, H. W. Morley the humanist. Fortnightly Rev Nov 1923.

Braybrooke, P. Lord Morley, writer and thinker. [1924.]

Morgan, J. H. John, Viscount Morley: an appreciation and some reminiscences. 1924.

Hirst, F. W. Early life and letters of John Morley. 2 vols 1927.

Meredith, G. George Meredith on John Morley: Glasgow Univ Rectorial election 1902. Winchester 1936 (priv ptd; letter addressed to John Bain).

Hamer, D. A. John Morley: liberal intellectual in politics. Oxford 1968.

Koss, S. E. John Morley at the India Office 1905–1910. New Haven CT 1969.

Alexander, E. John Morley. New York 1972.

Bicknell, J. W. John Morley. In Victorian prose: a guide to research, ed D. DeLaura, New York 1973.

Plybon, I. F. John Morley: the Victorian rationalist as literary critic. Unpbd diss, Univ of Maryland 1974.

Marandon, S. Figures d'agnostiques victoriens. Cahiers d'Études Victoriens et Edouardiens 15 Apr 1982. On Morley, P. G. Hamerton and F. Harrison.

Elliott, P. L. John Morley. DLB 57 1987.

Kijinski, J. L. John Morley's 'English Men of Letters' series and the politics of reading. VS Winter 1991.

Korsten, F. J. M. The 'English Men of Letters' Series: a monument of late-Victorian literary criticism. ES vol 73 Dec 1992.

Hopkinson, D. John Morley. DLB 144 1995. [FJMK]

Sir Henry Newbolt 1862–1937

See col 803.

John Owen 1836–96

§1

Evenings with the skeptics: or, free discussion on free thinkers. 2 vols 1881.

Glanvill, J. Scepsis scientifica. Ed and introd by Owen 1885.

Verse-musings on nature, faith, and freedom. 1889, 1894 (enlarged).

The skeptics of the French renaissance. 1893.

The skeptics of the Italian renaissance. 1893.

von Harnack, C. G. A. Sources of the apostolic canons; with a treatise on the origin of the readership and other lower orders. Tr L. A. Wheatley, introd by Owen 1895.

The five great skeptical dramas of history. 1896. The Prometheus vinctus of Aeschylus; the Book of Job; Goethe's Faust; Shakespeare's Hamlet; 'El magico prodigioso'.

Owen contributed to Acad, Contemporary Rev, Edinburgh Rev, Fraser's Mag, Mod Rev *and* Theological Rev *(see also* Wellesley 5 1989*). A number of his sermons and theological lectures were pbd separately.*

§2

C[otton], J. S. Owen. Acad 15 Feb 1896. Obituary. [JMB]

Sir Charles Hubert Hastings Parry 1848–1918

See NRA *for letters. Notable collections in BL, Bodleian, McMaster Univ Lib and privately owned, Broadheath, Worcester.*

Bibliographies

Daymond, E. Complete catalogue of Parry's published and unpublished works. In Grove's Dictionary of music and musicians, 1940 (4th edn).

§1

Studies of great composers. 1887.

The art of music. 1893. Appeared from 1896 as The evolution of the art of music, *below*.

Summary of the history and development of mediaeval and modern European music. [1893?], 1905 (rev) (Novello, Ewer & Co's Music Primers no 42).

The evolution of the art of music. 1896, New York 1930 (ed and with additional chs by H. C. Colles). Numerous other edns and reprints.

Style in musical art: an inaugural lecture delivered at Oxford on March 7 1900. Oxford 1900.

The music of the seventeenth century. Oxford 1902, 1938 (rev and introd by E. J. Dent). Oxford history of music vol 3.

Johann Sebastian Bach: the story of the development of a great personality. 1909, 1934 (rev and introd by E. Daymond).

Style in musical art. 1911.

College addresses delivered to pupils of the Royal College of Music. Ed with memoir by H. C. Colles 1920.

Apart from being a prolific composer, Parry also wrote the books of words for numerous musical compositions, such as Job: an oratorio *[1893] and* War and peace: a symphonic ode *[1905], and he edited several musical works such as* Arion: a collection of madrigals, glees, part-songs etc. by ancient composers, *2 vols [1895?–7?] (with L. S. Benson and W. B. Squire).*

Contributions to periodicals and collaborative works

Parry wrote an article on Purcell for Nat Rev. *See* Wellesley *vol 5. He edited, together with J. Staines, the series of* Novello, Ewer & Co's Music Primers *[1877 etc], and he contributed articles to* Grove's Dictionary of music and musicians.

§2

Maitland, J. A. F. The life and work of Parry. Musical Quart 5 1919.

Colles, H. C. Parry as a song-writer. Musical Times 1921.

Graves, C. L. Hubert Parry: his life and works. 2 vols 1926.

Greene, G. M. Two witnesses: a personal recollection of Hubert Parry and Friedrich von Hügel. 1930.

Maitland, J. A. F. The music of Parry and Stanford: an essay in comparative criticism. Cambridge 1934.

Dibble, J. C. Hubert H. Parry: his life and music. Oxford 1992. [FJMK]

Walter Pater, Walter Horatio Pater 1839–94

Surviving mss *of Pater's works published during his lifetime and posthumously by C. L. Shadwell are* Demeter and Persephone *at Brasenose,* Pascal *at Bodleian,* Gaston de Latour, chs 1–5, 7, *Berg Collection at* NYPL,

Measure for measure *at Folger,* Samuel Taylor Coleridge (in part) *at Houghton, Harvard,* Sir Thomas Browne and Dante Gabriel Rossetti *at Pierpont Morgan NYC. The ms of* Diaphaneitè *at King's School Canterbury, signed W. H. P. July 1864, is written on Oriel College stationery and is apparently a transcription in the hand of Shadwell. Brasenose has* Gaston de Latour, *chs 10–13 left unpbd; Houghton, c. 600 pp. of works and fragments left unpbd. For detail see* L. Evans, Walter Pater, in Victorian prose: a guide to research, ed D. J. DeLaura, New York 1973; B. Rosenbaum, Walter Horatio Pater, in IELM vol 4 pt 3. *Letters are scattered; see* Letters of Walter Pater, ed L. Evans, Oxford 1970 *and* IELM.

Bibliographies and reference works

Shadwell, C. L. A brief chronological list of his published writings. In Preface, Miscellaneous studies by Walter Pater, 1895. Includes major periodical pbns.

Wright, T. Appendix VI: bibliography of Walter Pater. In his Life of Walter Pater, 2 vols 1907. Includes poems and most reviews.

Stonehill, C. A. and H. W. Stonehill. Walter Pater. New York 1925 ([Descriptive] Bibliographies of Modern Authors 2nd ser).

d'Hangest, G. Appendice bibliographique. In his Walter Pater: l'homme et l'oeuvre, 2 vols Paris 1961. Primary and secondary works.

Evans, L. Walter Pater: bibliography, manuscripts, editions. In Victorian prose: a guide to research, ed D. J. De Laura, New York 1973.

Wright, S. A bibliography of the writings of Walter H. Pater. New York 1975.

Court, F. E. Walter Pater: an annotated bibliography of writings about him. Dekalb IL 1980.

Recent publications (annotated list). Pater Newsletter. Ed J. Losey, Baylor U., Waco TX twice annually, from no 4, Summer 1979 to present.

Inman, B. A. Walter Pater's reading: a bibliography of his library borrowings and literary references, 1858–1873. New York 1981.

Wright, S. An informative index to the writings of Walter H. Pater. West Cornwall CT 1987.

Inman, B. A. Walter Pater and his reading, 1874–1877, with a bibliography of his library borrowings, 1878–1894. New York 1990.

Collections

Works. 8 vols 1900–1. Deluxe edn.
REVIEW: ([Johnson, L.], J.) Acad 58, 13 Oct 1900, rptd rev as Mr Pater and his public, in Post liminium: essays and critical papers by Lionel Johnson, ed T. Whittemore, New York 1912.

Works. Lib edn 10 vols 1910, rptd Oxford and New York 1967, 1973. (Essays, fiction, reviews from Guardian).
REVIEWS: Spectator 104, 25 June 1910; [Bailey, J. C.] TLS, 1 Sep 1910, rptd in Poets and poetry, Oxford 1911; (P. E. More) Nation (New York) 92, 13 Apr 1911, rptd in Evening Post (New York), 15 Apr 1911, rptd rev in Shelbourne essays: the drift of romanticism, Boston 1913; (L. P. Shanks) Dial 50, 16 Apr 1911; (W. M. Reedy) St Louis Mirror, 20 Apr 1911; (R. D. Burchard) Evening Post (New York), 21 Apr 1911; (J. L. Hervey) St Louis Mirror, 25 May 1911; Pater reread, Sun (New York), 11 June 1911; Is Walter Pater demoralizing? Current Lit (New York) 50, June 1911; The alleged corrupting influence of Walter Pater, Current Lit (New York) 51, Aug 1911.

Works of Walter Pater. Ed Yoshiyuki Fujikawa (various translators) 3 vols Tokyo 1995. In Jap. Major works and selected reviews, with notes.

Selections

Selections from Walter Pater. Ed with notes E. E. Hale, jr, New York 1901.

Sketches and reviews by Walter Pater. Foreword A. Mordell, New York 1919.

Selections from Walter Pater. Ed A. L. F. Snell, Boston 1924.

Selected essays of Walter Pater. Ed with notes H. G. Rawlinson 1927.

Walter Pater. Ed and tr M. Praz, Milan 1944. In Ital.

Walter Pater: selected works. Ed R. Aldington, New York 1948.

Selected writings: Walter Pater. Ed D. Patmore 1949.

Walter Pater: essays on literature and art. Ed with notes J. Uglow 1973, 1991.

Selected writings of Walter Pater. Ed with notes H. Bloom, New York 1974.

Walter Pater: three major texts. Ed W. E. Buckler, New York 1986.

§1

Studies in the history of the Renaissance. 1873, 2nd edn 1877 as The Renaissance: studies in art and poetry (rev, conclusion omitted, Aucassin and Nicolette replaced by Two early French stories), 3rd 1888 (rev, conclusion restored and The school of Giorgione added), 4th 1893 (rev), Deluxe edn 1900, 5th 1901 (resembling 3rd), Lib edn 1910; The Renaissance, with Raphael (1892) included, introd by K. Clark, London and New York 1961; The Renaissance: studies in art and poetry, the 1893 text, ed D. L. Hill, Berkeley CA 1980 (var edn with notes). Tr Ger 1902, 1906, Hungarian 1913, Jap 1915, 1929, 1948, 1977, Fr 1917, Ital 1925, 1946, 1965, Sp 1938.
REVIEWS: [S. Colvin] Pall Mall Gazette, 1 Mar 1873; (J. A. Symonds), Acad 4, 15 Mar 1873; (Z.) Modern Cyrenaicism, Examiner, 12 Apr 1873; Br Quart Rev 57, Apr 1873; [J. Morley] Fortnightly Rev n.s. 13, Apr 1873; [E. F. S. Pattison] Westminster Rev n.s. 43, Apr 1873; (H. R.) Penn Monthly (Philadelphia) 4, June 1873; [R. H. Hutton] Spectator 46, 14 June 1873; Athenaeum, 28 June 1873; London Quart Rev 40, July 1873; Sat Rev 36, 26 July 1873; Scribner's Monthly 6, Aug 1873; [W. D. Howells] Atlantic Monthly 32, Oct 1873; [W. J. Stillman] Nation 17, 9 Oct 1873; [M. Oliphant] Blackwood's Mag 114, Nov 1873; (S. B. Wister) North Amer Rev 121, July 1975; 2nd edn: Art Jnl, 1877; 3rd edn: Oxford Mag, 16 Oct 1889.

Marius the Epicurean: his sensations and ideas. 2 vols 1885 (Mar), 2nd edn 1885 (Nov, rev), 3rd 1892 (extensively rev), 4th 1898, Deluxe edn 1900, 5th 1902, Lib edn 1910; annotated printings: ed A. K. Tuell, New York 1926; ed J. Sagmaster, Garden City NY 1935; ed Sir Michael Levey 1985 (Pen); text of 3rd edn, ed I. Small 1986 (WCp); notes: R. G. Frean, Walter Pater's Marius the Epicurean: notes and commentary preliminary to a critical edn (without text), unpbd diss, Univ of Toronto 1961. Tr Ger 1908, Fr 1922, Jap 1926, 1950, Ital 1939, 1970.
REVIEWS: [Sharp, W.] Athenaeum, 28 Feb 1885; (W. Sharp) Time 12, Mar 1885; Pall Mall Gazette, 18 Mar 1885; (J. M. Gray) Acad 27, 21 Mar 1885; The Times, 9 Apr 1885; (Julia Wedgwood) Contemporary Rev 47, May 1885; (M. A. W. [Mary Augusta Ward]) Macmillan's Mag 42, June 1885; (A. Goodwin) Mind 10, July 1885; Atlantic Monthly 56, Aug 1885; (H. N. Powers) Dial 6, Aug 1885; Br Quart Rev 81, Sep 1885; [G. E. Woodberry] Nation 41, 10 Sep 1885; Westminister Rev n.s. 69, Apr 1886; [A. Repplier] Catholic World (New York) 43, May 1886; Two Roman novels, Edinburgh Rev 165, Jan 1887; (G. Bradford, jr) Andover (MA) Rev 10, Aug 1888; 3rd edn rev: (R. Le Gallienne), 1892, rptd Retrospective Rev 1 1896.

Imaginary portraits. 1887, 2nd edn 1890 (rev), 3rd 1896; Deluxe edn (with Gaston de Latour in vol 4) 1900; Lib edn 1910; Imaginary portraits: a new collection, ed E. J. Brzenk 1964 (contains 9 portraits). Tr Fr (introd by A. Symons) 1899, (introd by P. Neel) 1930 Ger 1903, 1946 (7 portraits), Cz 1907, Jap 1930, 1981, 1984, Ital 1913, 1944, 1980, 1994.
REVIEWS: [O. Wilde] Pall Mall Gazette, 11 June 1887; (T. W. Lyster) Acad 31, 18 June 1887; [E. F. S. Pattison] Athenaeum, 25 June 1887; Sat Rev 63, 25 June 1887; Westminster Rev n.s. 62, July 1887; Spectator 60, 16 July 1887; [G. E. Woodberry] Nation 45, 28 July 1887; (A. Symons) Time 17, Aug 1887; Dial 8, Sep 1887; Critic (New York) n.s. 8, 24 Sep 1887; (S. Image) Cent Guild Hobby Horse 3, 1888; Oxford Mag, 25 Jan 1888; (G. Bradford, jr) Andover (MA) Rev 10, Aug 1888.

Appreciations, with an essay on style. 1889, 2nd edn 1890 (rev, with Aesthetic poetry replaced by Feuillet's La morte), 3rd 1895, Deluxe edn 1900, 4th 1901, Lib edn 1910; facs (photo) of Lib edn text, introd by L. Evans, Evanston IL 1987.
REVIEWS: [C. K. Shorter] Star, 21 Nov 1889; [W. Sharp] Glasgow Herald, 28 Nov 1889; Pall Mall Gazette, 10 Dec 1889; [A. Symons] Athenaeum, 14 Dec 1889; (W. Watson) Acad 36, 21 Dec 1889; Spectator 63, 21 Dec 1889; Nation 49, 26 Dec 1889; [M. Oliphant] Blackwood's Mag 147, Jan 1890; (L. Johnson) Cent Guild Hobby Horse 5, 1890; (L. C. Moulton) Boston Sunday Herald, 5 Jan 1890; [A. Repplier] Catholic World (New York) 50, Feb 1890; Critic (New York) n.s. 13, 8 Feb 1890; (E. Nencioni) Nuova Antologia, 16 Feb 1890, rptd in Saggi critici di letteratura inglese, Firenze 1897, 1910; Atlantic Monthly 65, Mar 1890; (O. Wilde) Speaker 1, 22 Mar 1890; (W. J. Courthope) Nineteenth Cent 27, Apr 1890; (C. A. L. Richards) Dial 11, June 1890.

Plato and Platonism: a series of lectures. London and New York 1893, 2nd edn 1895, Deluxe edn 1901, 3rd 1901, Lib edn London 1910. Tr Fr 1923, Ger 1904, Jap 1931, 1933 (with Greek studies).
REVIEWS: [J. R. Thursfield] The Times, 16 Feb 1893; ('Logroller' [R. Le Gallienne]) Star, 23 Feb 1893; (E. J. Ellis) Bookman 3, Mar 1893; [L. Johnson] Westminster Gazette, 3 Mar 1893, extracts rptd in Post liminium 1912; Athenaeum, 18 Mar 1893; (A. Waugh in London letter). Critic (New York) n.s. 20, 25 Mar 1893; Catholic World (New York) 57, Apr 1893; (P. Shorey) Dial 14, Apr 1893; Mind 2, Apr 1893; (E. Gosse) New Rev 8, Apr 1893; Westminster Rev n.s. 83, Apr 1893; Artist and Journal of Home Culture, 1 Apr 1893; [R. H. Hutton] Spectator 70, 1 Apr 1893; (C. Dodgson) Acad 43, 15 Apr 1893; (L. Campbell) Classical Rev 7, June 1893; Critic (New York) n.s. 20, 1 July 1893; (T. D. Seymour) Educational Rev (New York) 6, Sep 1893; (H. W. Mabie) Outlook (New York) 48, 9 Sep 1893; [L. Johnson] Speaker 8, 28 Oct 1893, extracts rptd in Post liminium 1912; [J. H. McDaniels] Nation 57, 30 Nov 1893; (W. Hammond) Philosophical Rev (Ithaca NY) 3, Jan 1894; (J. T. S. [Joseph Trumbell Stickney]) Harvard Monthly 19, May 1894; Popular Science Monthly (New York) 45, May 1894; (B. L. Gildersleeve) Amer Jnl of Philology 15, Winter 1894.

An imaginary portrait by Walter Pater: the child in the house. Oxford 1894 (Daniel Press, limited edn), pbd in this separate vol after appearance in Macmillan's Mag, Aug 1878, rptd in Miscellaneous studies (*see below*), rptd by T. B. Mosher, Portland ME 1895, 1896, 1898, 1900, 1902, 1903, 1906, 1910 – an example of Mosher's many reprints from Pater's pbns (*others are not listed*). Worcester College Oxford has sheets from the Macmillan's Mag pbn rev Pater for Daniel Press.
REVIEW: (The Crier) Pall Mall Budget, 12 July 1894 (review of Daniel Press edn).

Greek studies: a series of essays. Prepared for press, with preface, C. L. Shadwell (essays previously pbd in periodicals), London and New York 1895, Deluxe edn 1900, 2nd 1901, Lib edn London 1910. Tr Ger 1904, Jap 1933 (with Plato and Platonism), Ital 1994.
REVIEWS: Realm, 25 Jan 1895; Sat Rev 79, 9 Feb 1895; Athenaeum, 23 Feb 1895; (A. Lang) Illus London News 106, 9 Mar 1895; (C. Dodgson) Acad 47, 16 Mar 1895; (W. M. Ramsay) Bookman 8, Apr 1895; (A. W. Verrall) Classical Rev 9, May 1895; (A. Repellier) Cosmopolitan (Rochester NY), May 1895; [J. H. McDaniels] Nation 60, 13 June 1895; (E. E. Hale, jr). Dial 19, 16 Nov 1895; Spectator 76, 20 June 1896.

Miscellaneous studies: a series of essays. Prepared for press, with preface including list of Pater's pbns, C. L. Shadwell (essays and stories previously pbd plus Diaphaneitè), London and New York 1895, Deluxe edn 1901, 2nd 1904, Lib edn London 1910.
REVIEWS: The Times, 25 Oct 1895; (A. M[acdonell].) Bookman 9, Nov 1895; Athenaeum, 7 Dec 1895; Spectator 75, 28 Dec 1895; Outlook (New York) 53, 25 Jan 1896; (C. Dodgson) Acad 49, 8 Feb 1896; Nation 62, 9 Apr 1896; [H. Horne Sat Rev 82, 1 Aug 1896.

Gaston de Latour: an unfinished romance. Prepared for press, with preface, C. L. Shadwell, London and New York 1896, Deluxe edn 1900 (with Imaginary portraits), 2nd 1904, Lib edn London 1910; Gaston de Latour (chs 1–13), ed G. Monsman, Greensboro NC 1995. Tr Ital 1995.
REVIEWS: (G. S. Street) Pall Mall Gazette, 12 Oct 1896; Athenaeum, 17 Oct 1896; Sat Rev 82, 17 Oct 1896; (A. M[acdonell].) Bookman 11, Nov 1896; (T. de Wyzewa) Revue des Deux Mondes 4th ser, 15 Nov 1896; Catholic World (New York) 64, Dec 1896; Critic (New York) n.s. 26, 5 Dec 1896; Spectator 78, 30 Jan 1897 suppl; (E. E. Hale, jr) Dial 22, 1 Feb 1897; [J. H. McDaniels] Nation 64, 4 Mar 1897; Outlook (New York) 55, 27 Mar 1897; Atlantic Monthly 79, May 1897.

Essays from the Guardian. Priv pbd Chiswick Press 1896, rptd T. B. Mosher, Portland ME 1897, rptd Macmillan 1901, Lib edn 1910.
REVIEWS: (L. Johnson) Acad 51, 16 Jan 1897; [A. Symons] Athenaeum, 12 June 1897; (A. Symons) Athenaeum, 21 Sep, 5 Oct 1901; (D. Stott) Athenaeum, 28 Sep 1901; (F. W. Bourdillon) Athenaeum, 28 Sep, 12 Oct 1901; Contemporary Rev 80, Oct 1901; Acad 60, 19 Oct 1901; (R. Garnett) Bookman 22, Apr 1902

Uncollected essays. Collected T. B. Mosher, Portland ME 1903. Mainly reviews not from Guardian.

The chant of the celestial sailors. Priv ptd E. H. Blakeney, Winchester 1928. Poem.

Imaginary portraits 2: an English poet. Ed M. Ottley, Fortnightly Rev n.s. 129, 1 Apr 1931; pbd separately by Chapman Hall 1931.

Walter Pater's portrait of Marguerite of Valois, Queen of Navarre: the hitherto unpubd chs IX and X of Gaston de Latour. Ed G. Monsman, Victorians Inst Jnl, 1992.

Most of Pater's essays and all of his fiction besides Marius the Epicurean *appeared first in periodical form, primarily in* Fortnightly Rev *and* Macmillan's Mag, *but also in* Contemporary Rev, Harper's New Monthly Mag, New Rev, Nineteenth Cent, Scribner's Mag and Westminster Rev; *2 essays appeared first in* The English poets, ed T. H. Ward 1880, 2nd edn rev 1883. *He reviewed primarily in Guardian and also in Acad, Athenaeum, Bookman, Daily Chron, Nineteenth Cent, Oxford Mag and Pall Mall Gazette. These and other occasional pubns are listed in S. Wright 1975, Bibliographies, above.*

Introductions, notes

English at the universities. Pall Mall Gazette, 27 Nov 1886.

Introduction. In The Purgatory of Dante Alighieri, tr C. L. Shadwell 1892. Review: L. Johnson, Spirit Lamp (Oxford), 6 Dec 1892.

Note on F. W. Bussell. In Sir William Rothenstein, Oxford characters, vol 6 1893, rptd in S. Wright 1975 (Bibliographies, *above*).

§2

Obituary notices and essays

The Times, 31 July 1894.

New York Times, 1 Aug 1894.

Pall Mall Gazette, 2 Aug 1894.

Sat Rev 78, 4 Aug 1894.

T. B. S. Athenaeum, 4 Aug 1894.

J. S. C[otton], Acad 46, 11 Aug 1894.

'Field, Michael'. July 30, 1894. Acad 46, 11 Aug 1894. Sonnet.

Dial 17, 16 Aug 1894.

Johnson, L. Fortnightly Rev n.s. 62, Sep 1894, rptd in Post liminium, 1912.

Bookman 6, Sep 1894.

Waugh, A. London letter. Critic (New York) n.s. 25, 1 Sep 1894.

Escott, T. H. S. Some Oxford memories of the prae-aesthetic age. Nat Rev 24, Oct 1894.

Bussell, F. W. Oxford Mag 13, 17 Oct 1894, rptd as In memoriam: W. H. P., Oxford 1894 (pamphlet).

A. A tribute to Pater in an obituary on J. A. Froude. Chameleon (Oxford), ed J. F. Bloxam, Nov 1894.

O'Hagan, A. [Hugo von Hofmannsthal]. Walter Pater. Die Zeit

(Vienna), 17 Nov 1894, rptd rev in Hofmannsthal, Gesammelte Werke in Einzelausgaben, prosa 1 1950.
In Memoriam. In the Cantaurian (King's School Canterbury), Dec 1894.
Gosse, E. Contemporary Rev 66, Dec 1894, rptd in his Critical kit-kats 1896.
Sharp, W. Atlantic Monthly 74, Dec 1894, rptd rev in his Papers critical and reminiscent, ed Mrs William Sharp 1912.
Obituaries, foreign. Appleton's annual encyclopedia . . . 1894. New York 1895.
Lee, V. [Violet Paget]. Valedictory. In her Renaissance fancies and studies, 1895.
Le Gallienne, R. Walter Pater (1894). In his Retrospective reviews: literary log, vol 2 1896.
Wyzewa, T de. Deux morts: Pater et Froude [dated Jan 1895]. In his Ecrivains étrangers, Paris 1896.

Pre-1920 criticism and reminiscences

Capes, W. W. University sermon. Oxford Undergraduates' Jnl 27, Nov 1873.
[Courthope, W. J.]. Modern culture. Quart Rev 137, Oct 1874.
Mackarness, J. F. A charge delivered to the clergy of the diocese of Oxford. In Charges and visitation sermons 1872–75, Oxford 1875.
[Courthope, W. J.]. Wordsworth and Gray. Quart Rev 141, Jan 1876.
Saintsbury, G. Modern English prose. Fortnightly Rev n.s. 19, Feb 1876, rptd in his Miscellaneous essays, New York 1892.
[Mallock, W. H.]. The new republic. Belgravia 29, 30 June–Dec 1876, rptd anon rev as The new republic: or culture, faith and philosophy in an English country house, 1877.
[Hutchinson, C. E.]. Boy-worship. Oxford 1880.
Ellis, H. Present position of English criticism. Time 13, Dec 1885.
Symonds, J. A. Is music the type or measure of all art? Cent Guild Hobby Horse 3, 1888; rptd in his Essays speculative and suggestive, vol 2 1890.
[Barry, W. F.]. Neo-paganism. Quart Rev 172, Apr 1891, rptd in his Heralds of revolt, 1904.
A High street reverie. Spirit Lamp (Oxford), ed Lord A. Douglas, 13 May 1892.
Symons, A. In The decadent movement in literature. Harper's New Monthly Mag 77, Nov 1893.
Lewis, E. H. Walter Pater. In his history of the English paragraph, Chicago 1894.
Letters from C. Pater to E. Gosse on 'Pascal', 1895. With Pascal ms at Bodleian.
[Barry, W. F.]. Latter-day pagans (Symonds and Pater). Quart Rev 182, July 1895, rptd in his Heralds of revolt, 1904.
Beerbohm, M. Be it cosiness. Pageant 1, Dec 1895 (dated Jan 1896), rptd as Diminuendo in Works of Max Beerbohm, 1896.
Mabie, H. W. By way of introduction. In his Books and culture, New York 1896, 1900.
Saintsbury, G. Walter Pater. In English prose selections, ed H. Craik 1896.
Jacobus, R. P. The blessedness of egoism: Maurice Barrès and Walter Pater, parts 1st and 2nd. Fortnightly Rev n.s. 65, Jan, Mar 1896.
Symons, A. Walter Pater: some characteristics. Savoy, Dec 1896.
Gosse. E. In his Short history of modern English literature, 1897.
Pater, Walter. In New Amer suppl to the latest (9th) edn of Encylopaedia Britannica, 5 vols New York 1897.
Sholl, A. McClure. Introd. Walter Pater. In Library of the world's best literature: ancient and modern, 46 vols. New York 1897. vol 28.
Buchan, J. Its famous men. In Brasenose College, Oxford 1898.
P. Reputations reconsidered, II: Walter Pater. Acad 53, 1 Jan 1898.
Reedy, W. M. Foreword: A golden book. In Pater, Marius the Epicurean, Portland ME 1900.
Malley, the Rev. A. D. A study of Pater. Catholic World (New York) 50, Feb 1900.
Mosher, T. B. Introd to Leonardo da Vinci. Bibelot 6, 1900.
F. E. H. Pater's philosophy of life. Macmillan's Mag 39, Jan 1902.
Wa[ugh], A. Pater, Walter Horatio. In Encyclopaedia Britannica, 10th edn 1902, rptd 11th edn 1910.
Dowden, E. Walter Pater. Atlantic Monthly 90, July 1902, rptd in his Essays modern and Elizabethan, London and New York 1910.
Greenslet, F. Walter Pater. New York 1903.
Pater, Walter Horatio. In Encyclopaedia Americana, New York 1903–6.
Pater, Walter Horatio. In Library of literary criticism of English and American authors, ed C. W. Moulton vol 8. Buffalo NY 1901–5.
[Creighton, L.]. Life and letters of Mandell Creighton by his wife, vol 1 (passim) 1904.
Moore, G. Avowals, VI: Walter Pater. Pall Mall Mag 33, Aug 1904, rptd rev in his Avowals, 1919.
Wilde, O. In his De profundis, 1905.
Hutton, J. A. Walter Pater in Marius the Epicurean. In his Pilgrims in the region of faith: Amiel, Tolstoy, Pater, Newman, Edinburgh 1906.
Walter Pater. In English literary criticism, introd by C. E. Vaughan 1906.
Anon. Literature: Walter Pater by A. C. Benson. Athenaeum, 2 June 1906.
Saintsbury, G. Walter Pater. Bookman 30, Aug 1906, rptd in his Prefaces and essays, 1933.
Symons, A. Walter Pater. Monthly Rev 24, Sep 1906, rptd slightly rev in his Figures of several centuries, 1916.
Harris, F. Walter Pater: the pagan. John Bull, 8 Sep 1906. Review of Benson's Walter Pater.
Manson, E. Recollections of Walter Pater. Oxford Mag 25, 7 Nov 1906.
Wright, T. John Payne and Walter Pater. Acad 72, 6 Apr 1907. Letter dated 29 Mar 1907.
The aesthetic outlook. Edinburgh Rev 206, July 1907.
Orton, W. A. Walter Pater. Westminister Rev 170, Nov 1908.
Buchan, J. Nine Brasenose worthies, IX: Walter Horatio Pater. Oxford 1909 (Brasenose College Quatercentenary Monographs II pt 2).
Ward, T. H. Reminiscences: Brasenose, 1864–72. Oxford 1909 (Brasenose College Quatercentenary Monographs II pt 2).
Cecil, A. Walter Pater. In his Six Oxford thinkers, 1909.
Ross, R. Mr Benson's Pater (dated 1906, but not pbd in Athenaeum 2 June). In Masques and phases, 1909.
Browning, O. In his Memories of sixty years at Eton, Cambridge and elsewhere, 1910.
Laurent, R. In his Études anglaises. Introd by R. J. E. Tiddy, Paris 1910.
Sharp, E. A. In William Sharp (Fiona Macleod): a memoir, New York 1910.
Binyon, L. A postscript to Pater's Renaissance. Sat Rev 110, 15 Oct 1910.
Christian, I. Pater's philosophy. Evening Post (New York), 27 Apr 1912.
Fehr, B. Der ästhetische Impressionismus von Walter Pater. In his Streifzüge durch die neueste englische Literatur. Strasburg 1912.
Saintsbury, G. In his A history of prose rhythm, 1912.
Wedmore, F. Walter Pater. In his Memories, 1912.
Le Gallienne, R. On re-reading Pater. North Amer Rev 195, Feb 1912.
Bendz, E. Notes on the literary relationship between Walter Pater and Oscar Wilde. Neuphilogische Mitteilungen 14, May–June 1912, rptd rev in his The influence of Pater and Matthew Arnold in the prose writings of Oscar Wilde, Gothenburg 1914.
Bock, E. J. Walter Paters einfluss auf Oscar Wilde. Vol 8 of Bonner Studien zur Englischen Philologie. Bonn 1913.
Olivero, F. Marius the Epicurean e gli Imaginary portraits di Walter Pater. In Saggi di letteratura inglese, Bari 1913.

Ransome, A. Walter Pater (1912). In his Portraits and speculations, 1913.
Thomas, P. E. Walter Pater: a critical study. 1913.
Mobbs, R. Étude comparée des jugements de Mme Humphry Ward, de Matthew Arnold et de Walter Pater sur le Journal intime de H. F. Amiel. Geneva 1913. Pbd thesis.
Chew, S. C. Pater's quotations. Nation 99, 1 Oct 1914.
Harris. F. Walter Pater. In his Contemporary portraits, 2nd ser New York 1915.
Powys, J. C. Walter Pater. In his Visions and revisions: a book of literary devotions, 1915.
Ralli, A. Pater the humanist. North Amer Rev 201, Feb 1915, rptd in his Critiques, 1927.
Fehr, B. Walter Paters beschreibung der Mona Lisa und Théophile Gautiers romantischer Orientalismus. Archiv für das Studium der neuren Sprachen und Literaturen 135, 1916.
Fehr, B. Walter Pater und Hegel. EStudien 50, 1916.
Jackson, W. W. In his Ingram Bywater: the memoir of an Oxford scholar 1840–1914, Oxford 1917.
Proesler, H. Walter Pater und sein verhältnis zur deutschen literatur. Freiburg im Breisgau 1917. Pbd thesis.
Michaud, R. Un païen mystique: Walter Pater. In his Mystiques et réalistes: Anglo-Saxons d'Emerson à Bernard Shaw, Paris 1918.
Ward, M. A. In her A writer's recollections, 1918.

Textual and bibliographical criticism

Law, H. H. Pater's use of Greek quotations. MLN 58, Dec 1943.
Chandler, E. Pater on style: an examination of the essay On style and the textual history of Marius the Epicurean. Vol 2 of Anglistica, Copenhagen 1958.
Inman, B. A. Tracing the Pater legacy (mss). Pater Newsletter no 11, Spring 1983; pt II: manuscripts and copyrights no 32, Winter 1995.
Falsey, E. A. The Pater manuscripts at Houghton, Harvard University. Pater Newsletter no 24, Spring 1990. Mss nos 1–35 listed.
Shuter, W. F. The Houghton Pater manuscripts, bMS Eng 1150: notes. Pater Newsletter no 24, Spring 1990. Concerned with dating.
Bassett, S. Dating the Pater manuscripts at the Houghton Library. Pater Newsletter no 25, Fall 1990.
Small, I. Intertextuality in Pater and Wilde. English Lit in Transition, special ser no 4, 1990.
Seiler, R. M. The book beautiful: Walter Pater and the house of Macmillan. 1999.

Information on pbn and transmission of Pater's texts, much of it unassimilated, can be found at the BL in Macmillan letterbooks – letters from Macmillan & Co to Walter Pater and surrogates; correspondence between Macmillan & Co and G. P. Brett, Macmillan New York; letters from C. A. Pater, H. M. Pater and C. L. Shadwell to Macmillan & Co (pbd in Hiroko Hagiwara, Walter Pater and his circle *[text in Jap, letters in Eng],* Toyko 1984*); letters from Macmillan & Co to R & R Clark, printer, Edinburgh – and at Univ of Reading in archives: letters to Macmillan & Co from R. L. Ottley and M. Ottley, named by H. M. Pater as heirs.*

Biographical works

There is no definitive biography of Pater. Each of the following contains information not to be found elsewhere.

Madan, F. Private account of college matters, 16 Jan 1877–4 Dec 1895. In archives at Brasenose; selections ptd in Walter Pater, ed R. M. Seiler 1987, *below*. Pater passim.
[T.] Wright ms correspondence, 1878–1907 (including letters from J. R. McQueen). In Lilly Lib Indiana Univ; selections ptd in Walter Pater, ed R. M. Seiler 1987, *below*.
Letters of Vernon Lee (Violet Paget). BL and Miller Lib, Colby College Waterville ME; some priv ptd as Vernon Lee's letters, ed I. C. Willis 1937; selections ptd in Walter Pater, ed R. M. Seiler 1987, *below*.
Gosse, E. Walter Pater. In DNB 44 1895; rev 1908–9 (see L. Brake, Problems in Victorian biography: the DNB and the DNB Pater, MLR 70, Oct 1975).
Benson, A. C. Walter Pater. EML 1906.
Wright, T. The life of Walter Pater. 2 vols 1907.
d'Hangest, G. Walter Pater: l'homme et l'oeuvre. 2 vols Paris 1961.
Fletcher, I. Review of d'Hangest's biography. MLR 58, July 1963.
Evans, L. Introd to Letters of Walter Pater. Oxford 1970.
Levey, Sir Michael. The case of Walter Pater. 1978.
Walter Pater: a life remembered (reminiscences, 1851–1907), ed R. M. Seiler, Calgary 1987.
Shuter, W. F. Pater as don. Prose Stud 11, May 1988.
Inman, B. A. Estrangement and connection: Walter Pater, Benjamin Jowett and William M. Hardinge. In Pater in the 1990s, ed L. Brake and I. Small, Greensboro NC 1991.
Rosenbaum. B. Introd to Walter Horatio Pater. IELM 4 iii, 1993.
Brake, L. Judas and the widow. In her Subjugated knowledges, London and New York 1994. On Benson's and Wright's biographies.
Donoghue, D. Brief life. In Walter Pater: lover of strange souls, New York 1995. [BAI]

Emilia Frances Pattison, née Strong, later Dilke

1840–1904

§1

The renaissance of art in France. 2 vols 1879.
Claude Lorrain, sa vie et ses oeuvres. Paris 1884 (Bibliothèque internationale de l'art).
The shrine of death, and other stories. London and New York 1886.
Art in the modern state. 1888. Partly pbd in Fortnightly Rev n.s. 38, Dec 1885 and n.s. 39, Feb 1886.
The shrine of love, and other stories. New York 1891.
Benefit societies and trade unions for women . . . reprinted from The Fortnightly Review (n.s. 45, June 1889). [1893.] Pam pbd by the Women's Trades Union League.
Trades Unions for women . . . reprinted from The North American Review. [1893?] Pam pbd by the Women's Trades Union League.
The industrial position of women. [1895?] First pbd in Fortnightly Rev n.s. 54, Oct 1893, rptd as pam by the Women's Trades Union League.
French painters of the XVIIIth century. 1899.
French architects and sculptors of the XVIIIth century. 1900.
Les Coustou; les chevaux de Marly et le tombeau du dauphin. Paris 1901. First pbd in the Gazette des beaux-arts, 3rd ser vol 25.
French furniture and decoration in the XVIIIth century. 1901.
The shrine of death and the shrine of love. Boston 1901.
French engravers and draughtsmen of the XVIIIth century. 1902.
The book of the spiritual life . . . With a memoir of the author by the Rt Hon Sir C. W. Dilke. 1905, New York 1905. Also contains stories, 'The mirror of the soul' and 'The last hour'. 1911 (new edn without memoir or stories).

Contributions to periodicals

See Wellesley *5 1989 for contributions to the* Contemporary Rev, Fortnightly Rev, New Rev *and* Westminster Rev. *See* Poole's index to periodical literature *for contributions to* Acad, Art Jnl, Athenaeum, Cosmopolitan (New York), Eclectic Mag (New York), Mag of Art, North Amer Rev, Portfolio, *and the* Universal Rev.

Collaborative works

Sir Frederick Leighton, F. R. A. In Illustrated biographies of modern artists, ed François Guillaume Dumas, Paris 1882.
Trades unionism among women. I. By Lady Dilke. II. By Florence Routledge. [1893]. Rptd from the Fortnightly Rev n.s. 49 May 1891. Pam pbd by the Women's Trade Union League.

Edition and Introductions

Pattison, Mark. Memoirs. 1885, rptd Farnborough and London 1969. Many reviews, including those by Henry Nettleship in Acad 28 Mar 1885, John Morley in Macmillan's Mag 51, Apr 1885, and Eliza Lynn Linton in Temple Bar 74, June 1885.

Bulley, A. A. and M. Whitley. Women's work . . . with a preface by Lady Dilke. 1894 (Gibbin's Social Questions no 13).

Molinier, E. The Wallace Collection (objets d'art) at Hertford House . . . With an introduction by Lady Dilke. 1903.

§2

Obits: The Times, 25 Oct 1904; Athenaeum 30 Oct 1904.

Dilke, Sir C. W. Memoir. In 1905 edn of The book of the spiritual life.

Askwith, The Hon B. E. Lady Dilke: a biography. 1969.

Israel, K. Names and stories: Emilia Dilke and Victorian culture. New York and Oxford 1998. [JW]

Sir Arthur Thomas Quiller-Couch 1863–1944

See col 1677.

Sir Walter Alexander Raleigh 1861–1922

See LR *and* NRA *for mss and letters. Notable collections in BL, Bodleian, Cambridge Univ: King's College, Glasgow Univ Lib, Liverpool Univ: Sidney Jones Lib.*

Bibliographies

Bibliography of Raleigh's works 1883–1922. Periodical, 8 Sep 1922, rptd in abstract in the Letters vol 2, *below*.

§1

Poetry and fact: an inaugural address delivered at University College, Liverpool 13 March 1890. Liverpool 1890.

The English novel: being a short sketch of its history from the earliest times to the appearance of Waverley. 1894.

The riddle: a pleasant pastoral comedy adapted from the Wife of Bath's tale as it is set forth in the works of Master Geoffrey Chaucer, presented at Otterspool on Midsummers Eve 1895. Liverpool 1895.

Robert Louis Stevenson. 1895.

Style. 1897.

The study of arts in a modern university. Liverpool 1899.

Milton. 1900.

The study of English literature: being the inaugural lecture delivered at the University of Glasgow on Thursday October 18 1900. Glasgow 1900.

Mackay in 'Egitto: a cantata in two inundations. 1901. Rptd from A miscellany: presented to J. M. Mackay.

Wordsworth. 1903.

The English voyages of the sixteenth century. Vol 12 of Hakluyt's The principal navigations. Glasgow 1903–5, 1906 (rev and reissued separately).

In memoriam: James McNeill Whistler. 1905.

Some thoughts on examinations: by an examiner. 1906 (priv ptd).

Samuel Johnson: the Leslie Stephen lecture delivered in the Senate House, Cambridge 22 February 1907. Oxford 1907.

Shakespeare. 1907 (EML).

Vandyopadhyana, J. Notes on Raleigh's life of Shakespeare. Calcutta 1917.

Six essays on Johnson. Oxford 1910.

The meaning of a university: an inaugural address delivered to the students of University College Aberystwyth. 1911.

Richard who would not be king: a puppet play in three acts. Oxford 1911.

James: a comedy in one act. [Oxford] 1913.

The age of Elizabeth. Oxford 1916. In Shakespeare's England: an account of the life and manners of his age, 2 vols Oxford 1916 (planned by W. Raleigh and ed S. Lee and C. T. Onions).

Romance: two lectures. Princeton 1916. Lectures delivered at Princeton Univ 4 & 5 May 1915.

England and the war: being sundry addresses delivered during the war. Oxford 1918.

Shakespeare and England. 1918. Annual Shakespeare lecture for the Br Acad, also in PBA 1917–18, 1921.

The war in the air: being the story of the part played in the Great War by the Royal Air Force. 6 vols Oxford 1922–37 (vol 1 by Raleigh, vols 2–6 by H. A. Jones).

Laughter from a cloud. Introd by H. Raleigh 1923. Humorous sketches and poems.

Some authors: a collection of literary essays 1896–1916. Oxford 1923.

On writing and writers: being extracts from his notebooks. Selected and ed by G. Gordon. 1926.

Editions, introductions, contributions to periodicals and collaborative works

Raleigh edited and wrote introductions for numerous authors such as Matthew Arnold, Blake, Baldassare Castiglione, Samuel Johnson, Keats, Milton, Shakespeare and Shelley. He edited the Cambridge Rev, *1883–4, and made contributions to* Fortnightly Rev, New Rev *(see* Wellesley 5 *1989),* Thrush, TLS *and the* Yellow Book. *His* Address of reception to John Masefield *appeared in* Royal Society of Literature of the United Kingdom, London: addresses of reception, *1914.*

Letters

The letters of Sir Walter Raleigh 1879–1922. Ed Lady Raleigh 2 vols 1926, 1928 (enlarged).

A selection from the letters of Sir Walter Raleigh 1880–1922. Ed Lady Raleigh, preface D. Nichol Smith, introd by R. Bridges. 1928.

§2

Raleigh. Acad 18 Dec 1897.

Obituary notices on Raleigh appeared in May and June 1922, in the Liverpool Post (O. Elton), Oxford Chron (H. W. Garrod), Oxford Mag (T. H. Warren), TLS (G. S. Gordon, rptd in his Lives of authors, 1950).

Chapman, R. W. Raleigh. London Mercury July 1922.

Jones, H. A. Sir Walter Raleigh and the air history: a personal recollection. 1922.

Crum, V. Sir Walter Alexander Raleigh. Oxford 1923.

Gordon, G. S. Raleigh in his letters. London Mercury 13 Apr 1926 (rptd in his Discipline of letters, Oxford 1949).

Legouis, E. Raleigh d'après ses lettres. Revue Anglo-Américaine 4 1926.

Hart, H. L. A. The position of Raleigh among literary critics. Nineteenth Cent Oct 1927.

Garrod, H. W. Walter Raleigh. In his The profession of poetry, 1929.

Palmer, D. J. Walter Raleigh and the years of the English Fund. In his The rise of English studies, 1965.

Kelly, T. Some thoughts of Sir Walter Raleigh. In KM80: a birthday album for Kenneth Muir, Tuesday 5 May 1987. Liverpool nd.

Ansari, A. A. Essays on Sir Walter Raleigh 1988. Aligarh 1988. [FJMK]

John Mackinnon Robertson 1856–1933

See NRA *for mss and letters. Notable collections in BL, Bodleian, Durham Univ Lib, Lib of the International Inst for Social History at Amsterdam, Lilly Lib Indiana.*

Bibliography

Bibliography of the works by J. M. Robertson. In J. M. Robertson (1856–1933), liberal, rationalist, and scholar, ed G. A. Wells, 1987.

§1

Walt Whitman, poet and democrat. Edinburgh 1884.
The religion of Shakspere: two discourses. [1887.]
Christ and Krishna. 1889, 1900 (rev and enlarged as Christianity and mythology). Rptd from Nat Reformer.
Essays towards a critical method. 1889.
Essays in history and politics. 1891.
Modern humanists. 1891. Carlyle, Mill, Emerson, Arnold, Ruskin, Spencer.
The fallacy of saving. 1892.
The eight hours question. 1893.
Buckle and his critics: a study in sociology. 1895.
The dynamics of religion: an essay in English culture history. 1897, 1926 (rev). Originally pbd under pseud of M. W. Wiseman.
Montaigne and Shakespeare. 1897, 1909 (adds 2 essays on the Originality and Learning of Shakespeare).
New essays towards a critical method. 1897.
The Saxon and the Celt: a study in sociology. 1897.
Essays and discourses. 1898.
Miscellanies. 1898.
Patriotism and empire. 1899.
A short history of freethought, ancient and modern. 1899, 2 vols 1906 (rewritten and greatly enlarged), 1915 (rev and enlarged).
Christianity and mythology. 1900, 1910 (rev and enlarged); tr Ger 1910.
An introduction to English politics. 1900, 1912 (rev and enlarged as The evolution of states: an introduction to English politics).
Studies in religious fallacy. 1900.
Wrecking the empire. 1901.
Letters on reasoning. 1902, 1905 (rev and enlarged), [1935] (abridged).
A short history of Christianity. 1902, 1913 (rev and enlarged), 1931 (rev and condensed).
Criticisms. 2 vols 1902–3.
Browning and Tennyson as teachers: two studies. 1903.
Essays in ethics. 1903.
Pagan christs: studies in comparative hierology. 1903, 1911 (rev and expanded).
Studies in practical politics. 1903.
Courses of study. 1904, 1908 (rev and enlarged), 1932 (enlarged).
Essays in sociology. 2 vols 1904.
What to read: suggestions for the better utilisation of public libraries. 1904.
Did Shakespeare write 'Titus Andronicus'? a study in Elizabethan literature. 1905, 1924 (rev and expanded as Introduction to the study of the Shakespeare canon).
Rudyard Kipling: a criticism. Madras [1905].
Pioneer humanists. 1907. Machiavelli, Bacon, Hobbes, Spinoza, Shaftesbury, Mandeville, Gibbon, Mary Wollstonecraft.
Trade and tariffs. 1908.
The evolution of states: an introduction to English politics. 1912.
The meaning of Liberalism. 1912, 1925 (rev and enlarged).
Rationalism. 1912, 1945 (abridged).
The Baconian heresy: a confutation. 1913.
Elizabethan literature. 1914.
The future of militarism, by 'Roland' [pseud]. 1916.
The Germans. 1916.
The historical Jesus: a survey of positions. 1916.
The Jesus problem: a re-statement of the myth theory. 1917.
Shakespeare and Chapman: a thesis of Chapman's authorship of A lover's complaint, and his origination of Timon of Athens, with indications of future problems. 1917.
The economics of progress. 1918.
The problem of The merry wives of Windsor. [1918.]
Bolingbroke and Walpole. 1919.
Free trade. 1919.
The problem of Hamlet. 1919.
Charles Bradlaugh. 1920.
A short history of morals. 1920.
Croce as Shakespearean critic. 1922.
Voltaire. 1922.
The Shakespeare canon. 5 vols 1922–32.
Explorations. 1923.
Hamlet once more. 1923.
Ernest Renan. 1924.
Gibbon. 1925.
Mr Shaw and 'the Maid'. [1925.]
Spoken essays. 1925.
The problems of the Shakespeare sonnets. 1926.
Jesus and Judas: a textual and historical investigation. 1927.
Modern humanists reconsidered. 1927.
The political economy of free trade. 1928.
A history of free thought in the nineteenth century. 1929, 2 vols 1936 (rev and enlarged).
The genuine in Shakespeare: a conspectus. 1930.
Electoral justice: a survey of the theory and practice of electoral representation. [1931.]
Fiscal fraud and folly. 1931.
Literary detection: a symposium on Macbeth. 1931.
Marlow: a conspectus. 1931.
The state of Shakespeare study: a critical conspectus. 1931.
Robertson also pbd many rationalist, sociological and political tracts and lectures.

Contributions to periodicals and collaborative works

Robertson wrote many hundreds of articles for the periodical press on a wide variety of subjects. His main output may be found in periodicals of an outspokenly rationalist signature, such as the Nat Reformer *and the* Literary Guide, *but he also contributed to periodicals like the* Criterion *and the* Yellow Book. *For his contributions to* Fortnightly Rev *and* Westminster Rev *see Wellesley 5 1989. Robertson was editor of the* Nat Reformer *from 1891 to 1893, and of the* Free Rev *from 1893 to 1897. He contributed to many collaborative works, such as H. B. Bonner (ed),* Essays towards peace *(1913), and* Essays in Liberalism *(1922).*

Editions and introductions

Robertson edited edns of Bacon's Philosophical works, *Buckle's* Introduction to the history of civilization, *Shaftesbury's* Characteristics of men, manners, opinions, times etc. *He also contributed introductions to works such as E. J. Trechmann's translation of Montaigne's* Essays.

§2

Obits: Morning Post 7 Jan 1933; Manchester Guardian 7 Jan 1933.
Obituaries and tributes by J. P. Gilmour, E. Phillpotts, J. A. Hobson et al. Literary Guide Feb and Mar 1933.
Gilmour, J. P. et al. Appreciations of J. M. Robertson. In A history of Freethought, ed J. M. Robertson, 4 vols 1936.
Kaczkowski, C. J. John Mackinnon Robertson: freethinker and radical. Unpbd diss, St Louis Univ 1964.
Page, M. Britain's unknown genius: an introduction to the life-work of John Mackinnon Robertson. 1984.
J. M. Robertson (1856–1933), liberal, rationalist, & scholar. Ed G. A. Wells 1987.
Dekkers, O. J. M. Robertson: Rationalist and literary critic. Aldershot 1998. [OD]

George Edward Bateman Saintsbury 1845–1933

See LR and NRA for mss and letters. Notable collections in BL, London Univ Lib, Nat Lib of Scotland, Oxford Univ: Merton College Lib, Queens Univ of Belfast.

Bibliographies

James, W. P. English Illus Mag Oct 1903. Lists reviews and articles on and by Saintsbury.
Leuba, W. Bibliography of Saintsbury. Book-Collector's Quart 12 1933.
Parker, W. M. A Saintsbury bibliography. In A last vintage: essays and papers, ed J. W. Oliver, A. M. Clark and A. Muir, 1950.
Brown, C. C. and W. B. Thesing. George Saintsbury. In their English prose and criticism 1900–1950: a guide to information sources, Detroit 1983.
DLB vols 57 and 149, 1987 and 1995 (*below*).
Jones, D. R. Bibliography. In her 'King of Critics': George Saintsbury 1845–1933, critic, journalist, historian, professor. Ann Arbor MI 1992.

Collections and selections

Prefaces and essays. Ed O. Elton 1933.
George Saintsbury: the memorial volume – a new collection of his essays and papers: personal portraits by O. Elton, H. Grierson, J. W. Oliver, J. Purves with a biographical memoir by A. B. Webster. Ed A. Muir et al 1945, New York 1946 (as A Saintsbury miscellany).
French literature and its masters. Ed H. Cairns, New York 1946.
A last vintage: essays and papers. Ed J. W. Oliver, A. M. Clark and A. Muir 1950.

§1

A primer of French literature. Oxford 1880, rev edns 1884, 1891, 1896, 1912, 1925 (with supplementary ch The present day by T. B. Rudmose-Brown).
Dryden. 1881 (EML).
A short history of the life and writings of A. R. Le Sage. [1881] (priv ptd).
A short history of French literature. Oxford 1882, 1897 (rev and enlarged).
Marlborough. 1885.
A history of Elizabethan literature. 1887. Numerous later edns and reprints.
Manchester. 1887. A history of the town.
Essays in English literature 1780–1860. 2 ser 1890–5.
Essays on French novelists. 1891.
The Earl of Derby. 1892.
Miscellaneous essays. 1892.
Corrected impressions: essays on Victorian writers. 1895.
Inaugural address delivered at Edinburgh Univ 15 October 1895. Edinburgh 1895.
A history of nineteenth century literature 1780–1895. 1896, 1901 (extended edn covering period 1780–1900). Numerous later edns and reprints of both versions.
The flourishing of romance and the rise of allegory. Edinburgh 1897 (Periods of European literature, ed Saintsbury, vol 2).
Sir Walter Scott. 1897.
A short history of English literature. 1898. Numerous later edns and reprints.
Matthew Arnold. 1899.
A history of criticism and literary taste in Europe. 3 vols Edinburgh 1900–4.
The earlier Renaissance. Edinburgh 1901 (Periods of European literature vol 5).
A history of English prosody from the twelfth century to the present day. 3 vols 1906–10.
The later nineteenth century. Edinburgh 1907 (Periods of European literature vol 12).
A historical manual of English prosody. 1910, New York 1966 (introd by H. Gross).
A history of English criticism: being the English chapters of A history of criticism and literary taste in Europe, revised, adapted and supplemented. Edinburgh 1911.
A history of English prose rhythm. 1912.
The English novel. 1913.
A first book of English literature. 1914.
The peace of the Augustans. 1916, 1946 (introd by H. Grierson) (WC).
A history of the French novel to the close of the nineteenth century. 2 vols 1917–19.
Notes on a cellar-book. 1920, 1962 (introd by A. Graham), 1978 (with a new preface by H. W. Yoxall).
A scrap book. 1922.
A second scrap book. 1923.
The collected essays and papers of George Saintsbury 1875–1920. 4 vols 1923–4.
A last scrap book. 1924.
A consideration of Thackeray. 1931.
Shakespeare. Cambridge 1934. Rptd from CHEL vol 5 1910, with an appreciation of Saintsbury by H. Waddell.

Editions, introductions and translations

Saintsbury pbd edns of and introductions to the works of numerous English and several French authors, the chief of which are Balzac, Dryden, Fielding, Flaubert, Montaigne, Peacock, Smollett, Thackeray and Voltaire. He also edited collective works such as The pocket library of English literature, *6 vols 1891–2,* Periods of European literature, *12 vols Edinburgh 1899–1923 and* Minor poets of the Caroline period, *3 vols Oxford 1905–21. He translated works by Balzac, Marmontel, Mérimée, Scherer and Madame de Stael.*

Contributions to periodicals and collaborative works

Saintsbury was subeditor of the Saturday Rev *from 1880 to 1894. He wrote thousands of articles, reviews and obituaries for more than 50 periodicals and newspapers in Britain and the United States (see also* Wellesley 5 1989*). He also contributed widely to composite works like* CHEL, *Craik's* English prose, Encyclopaedia Britannica, Essays and studies by members of the English Assoc, PBA *and Ward's* English poets.

§2

Watson, W. In his Excursions in criticism, 1893.
Collins, J. C. Saturday Rev 23 Feb and 30 Nov 1895.
Chambers, E. K. Acad 1 June 1895.
Waugh, A. Bookman (London) Aug 1896.
Duncanson, R. University Mag & Free Rev June 1897.
Craik, H. Blackwood's Edinburgh Mag Sep 1897.
Greenslet, F. Atlantic Monthly July 1905.
Dobson, A. In his Old Kensington Palace, 1910.
Babbitt, I. Nation 16 May 1912.
Steinberg, T. MLN 41, Dec 1912.
George Saintsbury. Student (Univ of Edinburgh) 21 and 26 Jan 1916.
Bennett, A. In his Books and persons, 1917.
Hewlett, M. In his Extempore essays, 1922.
Priestley, J. B. London Mercury vol 6 Sep 1922. Rptd in his Figures in modern literature, 1924.
Guedalla, P. In his Masters and men, 1923.
Lewisohn, L. Nation 5 Dec 1923. Rptd in his Cities and men, 1929.
Williams, O. In his Contemporary criticism of literature, 1924.
Gosse, E. In his Silhouettes, 1925.
Roberts, R. E. Bookman (London) Oct 1925.
A great reader at eighty. Living Age 5 Dec 1925.
O'Leary, J. G. In his English literary history, 1928.
Swinnerton, F. In his A London Bookman, 1928.
Chapman, J. A. In his Papers on Shelley, Wordsworth and others, 1929.
George Saintsbury. The Times 26 June 1931.
Garnett, R. Blackwood's Mag Dec 1931.
Ralli, A. In his A history of Shakespearian criticism vol 2, Oxford 1932.
In 1933 numerous obituaries appeared in American, British and French periodicals and newspapers.
Webster, A. B. George Saintsbury. Edinburgh 1933.
Leuba, W. George Saintsbury. New York 1967.

Harris, W. V. George Saintsbury and Edmund Gosse. In Victorian prose: a guide to research, ed D. J. DeLaura, New York 1973.
Lindenberger, H. S. In his Profession, 1984.
Orel, H. In his Victorian literary critics, 1984.
Oram, R. W. George Saintsbury. DLB 57 1987.
Jones, D. R. 'King of critics': George Saintsbury, 1845–1933, critic, journalist, historian, professor. Ann Arbor MI 1992.
Maertz, G. Papers on Language and Literature vol 30 no 2, Spring 1994.
Hewison, P. E. George Saintsbury. DLB 149 1995. [FJMK]

Edith Simcox, Edith Jemima Simcox 1844–1901

Ms Autobiography of a shirt maker, *Bodleian.*

§1

Natural law: an essay in ethics. 1877, Boston 1877, London 1878 (2nd edn), Boston 1879 (2nd edn).
Episodes in the lives of men, women, and lovers. 1882, Boston 1882, New York [1885] as Men, women and lovers.
REVIEWS: Acad Apr 1882; Pall Mall Gazette May 1882.
Primitive civilizations; or, outlines of the history of ownership of archaic communities. 2 vols London and New York 1894, London and New York 1897.
Simcox contributed articles and reviews to various periodicals and newspapers, initially under the pseudonym 'H. Lawrenny', including Acad, Co-operative News, Fortnightly Rev, Fraser's Mag, Labour Tribune, Nineteenth Cent *and* Women's Union Jnl. *Some of these are listed in* Wellesley *5 1989.*

§2

The Times 18 Sep 1901.
McKenzie, K. A. Edith Simcox and George Eliot. 1961.

Sir John Skelton 1831–97

See NRA *for letters. Notable collection in the Nat Lib of Scotland.*

§1

Nugae criticae: occasional papers written at the seaside. By Shirley [pseud]. Edinburgh 1862.
Thalatta! or the great commoner: a political romance. Edinburgh 1862. Preface signed 'S'.
A campaigner at home. By Shirley [pseud]. 1865. A novel, rptd from Fraser's Mag.
John Dryden: 'in defence'. 1865. Rptd from Fraser's Mag.
Spring songs, by a western Highlander. Ed and partly written by Skelton 1865.
Benjamin Disraeli: the past and the future. By A democratic Tory [pseud]. 1868.
The great Lord Bolingbroke, Henry St John. An address. Edinburgh 1868.
The boarding-out of pauper children in Scotland. Edinburgh 1876.
The impeachment of Mary Stuart. Edinburgh 1876.
Essays in romance and studies from life. Edinburgh 1878. Sketches and short stories.
The crookit Meg: a story of the year one. 1880. Rptd from Fraser's Mag.
Essays of Shirley. Edinburgh 1882, 2 vols 1883.
Essays in history and biography, including the defence of Mary Stuart. Edinburgh 1883.
Maitland of Lethington and the Scotland of Mary Stuart. 2 vols Edinburgh 1887–8.
The handbook of public health: a complete edition of the Public Health and other sanitary acts relating to Scotland. Edinburgh 1890, suppl Edinburgh 1891, Edinburgh 1898 (rev by J. P. MacDougall and A. Murray).
The Local Government (Scotland) Act in relation to public health. Edinburgh 1890, 1890 (enlarged).
Mary Stuart. 1893.
The table-talk of Shirley. Edinburgh 1895. Reminiscences of and letters from Froude, Thackeray, Disraeli, Browning, Rossetti, Kingsley, Baynes, Huxley, Tyndall et al.
Summers and winters at Balmawhapple. 2 vols Edinburgh 1896. Ser 2 of The table-talk of Shirley, *above*; appeared originally in Blackwood's Mag.
Charles I. Edinburgh 1898.

Editions and introductions

Dickson, W. G. A treatise on the law of evidence in Scotland. 1864 (2nd edn 2 vols). Ed Skelton, together with W. Ellis Cloag.
Wilson, J. The comedy of the noctes ambrosiana. Selected by Skelton 1876, New York 1884 (as Noctes Ambrosiana).
The royal house of Stuart: illustrated by a series of forty plates in colours drawn from relics of the Stuarts by W. Gibb. Introd by Skelton, notes by W. H. St J. Hops 1890.
Skelton wrote numerous reviews and articles, especially for Blackwood's Mag *and* Fraser's Mag; *for his contributions to these periodicals and to* Contemporary Rev, Cornhill Mag, Guardian, Macmillan's Mag, North Br Rev *and* St Paul's Mag, *see* Wellesley *5 1989. He also contributed to* Edinburgh essays, by members of the university, *Edinburgh 1857. Some of his essays were collected in anthologies, such as* Great English essayists, *ed W. J. Dawson and C. W. Dawson, 1909.*

§2

Henderson, T. F. The casket letters and Mary, Queen of Scots . . . With reply to objections [urged by Skelton]. 1890 (2nd edn).
Obits: Scotsman 21 July 1897; The Times 21 July 1897; Daily Chron 22 July 1897. [JMB]

G. W. Steevens, George Warrington Steevens 1869–1900

Mss located in Berg Collection, NYPL; King's College, Cambridge; Nat Lib of Scotland.

Bibliographies

See Wellesley *vol 5 1989.*

Collections and selections

The works of George Warrington Steevens. Ed G. S. Street 7 vols Edinburgh and London 1900–2 (Memorial edn with memoir by W. E. Henley in vol 1).
Chapters from 'In India'. 1927 (Readers of Today ser).

§1

Naval policy: with some account of the warships of the principal powers. 1896, New York 1896.
REVIEWS: Athenaeum 24 Oct 1896; Literary World 20 Nov 1896; Spectator 28 Nov 1896; Speaker 13 Feb 1897.
Monologues of the dead. Edinburgh and London 1896, 1902.
REVIEWS: Acad 26 Sep 1896, 30 Jan 1897; Literary World 4 Apr 1902.
The land of the dollar. Edinburgh 1897 (3 edns), New York 1897, 1898, 1900 (4th & 5th edns), Freeport NY 1971.
REVIEWS: Br Weekly 28 Jan 1897; Acad 6 Feb 1897; Athenaeum 6 Feb 1897; New York Times 13 Feb 1897; Spectator 13 Feb 1897; Literary World 26 Feb 1897; Blackwood's Mag Apr 1897; Living Age May 1897; Chap-Book 1 Aug 1897; Bookman (USA) Sep 1897; Dial 1 Oct 1897; Nation 28 Oct 1897; New York Times 30 Oct 1897.
With the conquering Turk: confessions of a Bashi-Bazouk. Edinburgh and London 1897, New York 1897, 1901.
REVIEWS: Athenaeum 20 Nov 1897; Literary World 24 Dec 1897; Literature 25 Dec 1897; Westminster Rev Feb 1898; New York

Times 9 Apr 1898; Chap-Book 1 May 1898; Nation 19 May 1898; Dial 1 July 1898.
The downfall of Mahadism. 1898.
Egypt in 1898. Edinburgh 1898, New York 1898, 1899.
REVIEWS: Acad 11 June 1898; Literature 11 June 1898; New York Times 3 Sep 1898; Speaker 17 Sep 1898; Nation 29 Sep 1898; Dial 1 Oct 1898; Spectator 15 Oct 1898; Literary World 21 Oct 1898.
With Kitchener to Khartoum. Edinburgh and London 1898 (15 edns), New York 1898, Toronto 1898, Edinburgh and London 1899, New York 1899, 1900, 1908, London [1909], New York 1911, 1915, London [1919] (school edn with ch on Egypt), [1925?] Glasgow (school edn), 1987, 1990.
REVIEWS: Acad 8 Oct 1898; Literature 8 Oct 1898; Spectator 15 Oct 1898; Speaker 29 Oct 1898; Bookman Nov 1898; Dial 16 Feb 1899; New York Times 25 Feb 1899; Nation 22 June 1899.
The tragedy of Dreyfus. 1899, New York 1899.
REVIEWS: Acad 23 Sep 1899; Athenaeum 30 Sep 1899; Bookman Oct 1899; New York Times 21 Oct 1899; Spectator suppl 4 Nov 1899; Nation 23 Nov 1899; Harper's Mag suppl 30 Dec 1899.
In India. Edinburgh and London 1899 (3 edns), 1899 (Nelson Lib of Notable Books), New York 1899, London 1900, 1901, New York 1905, London [1910], 1927, Delhi 1984 (as India of yesteryears. Cambridge 1992 (as In the India of the Raj).
REVIEWS: Speaker 4 Feb 1899; Spectator 4 Feb 1899; Athenaeum 7 Oct 1899; Literary World 13 Oct 1899; Outlook 14 Oct 1899; Acad 11 Nov 1899; Nation 14 Dec 1899; Critic Feb 1900.
From Capetown to Ladysmith. An unfinished record of the South African war. Ed V. Blackburn, Edinburgh and London 1900 (2 edns), Leipzig 1900 (Tauchnitz), New York 1900, Toronto [1900], New York 1969.
REVIEWS: Acad 3 Mar 1900; Athenaeum 3 Mar 1900; Literature 3 Mar 1900; The Times 8 Mar 1900; Literary World 9 Mar 1900; Dial 1 Apr 1900; American Historical Rev Oct 1900; Spectator 9 Feb 1901.
Glimpses of three nations. Ed V. Blackburn, New York 1900, Edinburgh 1901.
REVIEWS: Dial 16 Feb 1901; Athenaeum 25 May 1901; Acad 1 June 1901; Literature 1 June 1901; Spectator suppl 2 Nov 1901.
Things seen. Ed G. S. Street, memoir by W. E. Henley, Edinburgh and London 1900, Indianapolis 1900, Toledo OH 1902.
REVIEWS: Spectator 23 June 1900; Athenaeum 30 June 1900; Acad 7 July 1900; New York Times 25 May 1901.
Chicago. New York 1907 (Historic landmarks of America).
Denver. New York 1907 (Historic landmarks of America).

Contributions to periodicals and collaborative works

Steevens, sometime Fellow of Pembroke College, Oxford, was editor of the Cambridge Observer *1893, on the staff of the* Pall Mall Gazette *1893–5, and the* Daily Mail *from 1896. During the siege of Ladysmith he was editor of the* Ladysmith Lyre *from 27 Nov 1899 until his death.*
Nat Observer. 2 May 1891–26 Aug 1893.
Daily Mail. June 1897–8 Dec 1903. Rptd as Foreign affairs. In Politics in 1896, ed F. Whelen, 1897.
Scribner's Mag. Installation of Lord Curzon as Viceroy of India, May 1899.
McClure's Mag. Scenes and actors in the Dreyfus case, Oct 1899.
Living Age. New humanitarianism, 12 Mar 1898.
Harper's Mag. France as affected by the Dreyfus case, Oct 1899.
Windsor Mag. England's free hand on the Nile, Feb 1901.

§2

Acad 4 Dec 1897.
Notes and news. Acad 25 Dec 1897.
(Note re his unfinished novel John King.) Literature 7 Oct 1899.
Chronicle and comment. Bookman (USA) Nov 1899.
Obituaries: St James's Gazette 20 Jan 1900; New York Times 21 Jan 1900; Daily Mail 22 Jan 1900; The Times 22 Jan 1900; Natal Mercury 22 Jan 1900; St James's Gazette 22 Jan 1900; Lee, S., Letter, Daily Mail 23 Jan 1900; Natal Witness 23 Jan 1900; Politics and persons, St James's Gazette 25 Jan 1900; The literary world, Acad 27 Jan 1900; Literary gossip, Athenaeum 27 Jan 1900; (Photo & short note), Graphic 27 Jan 1900; Personal (photo), Illustr London News 27 Jan 1900; Literature 27 Jan 1900; Natal Witness 27 Jan 1900; Outlook 27 Jan 1900; News of the week, Spectator 27 Jan 1900; Sphere 27 Jan 1900.
The siege of Ladysmith. St James's Gazette 29 Jan 1900.
Authors and publishers. Literature 10 Feb 1900.
Abrahams, B. A. City of London School Mag Mar 1900.
Chronicle and comment. Bookman (USA) Mar 1900.
The lounger. The Critic Mar 1900.
Many inventions (photo). Illus London News 14 Apr 1900.
The literary world. Acad 3 Mar 1900, 23 June 1900.
Chronicle and comment. Bookman (USA) June 1900.
Letter re memorial to G. W. S. The Times 2 July 1900.
G. W. Steevens. Literary World 6 July 1900.
Sphere 4 Aug 1900. Photo.
Lee, S. DNB (22 suppl) 1901.
The literary week. Acad 3 May 1902.
Browning, O. In his Memories of sixty years, 1910.
Bullard, F. L. In his Famous war correspondents, 1914.
Stearn, R. T. Steevens and the message of Empire. Jnl of Imperial and Commonwealth History Jan 1989. [DAPA]

Leslie Stephen 1832–1904

Principal repositories of mss and correspondence: BL; Cambridge Univ Lib, Trinity Hall, Cambridge; Duke Univ; Harvard Univ; Nat Lib of Scotland; HRHRC. Smaller collections at the Univ of Leeds; Pierpont Morgan Lib; NYPL; Bodleian; Yale. See also Fenwick, Bibliographies, below. The archives of John Murray Publishers and the collections of publishers' archives at the Univ of Reading and the Nat Lib of Scotland contain relevant materials. Washington State Univ at Pullman has inscribed and annotated books from Stephen's library.

Bibliographies

Fenwick, G. Leslie Stephen's life in letters: a bibliographical study. Aldershot 1993.
Bicknell, J. The unbelievers. In Victorian prose: a guide to research, ed. D. DeLaura, New York 1973.

Collections and selections

A defense of philosophical skepticism and other essays. 1941.
Men, books and mountains: essays. Ed S. O. A. Ullmann, Minneapolis 1956.
Leslie Stephen: selected writings in British intellectual history. Ed N. Annan 1979.

§1

Stephen's works were variously rptd during his life and after. As most of the reprints have little textual authority they are not listed below.
The poll degree from a third point of view. 1863.
The Times on the American war: an historical study by L. S. 1865, rptd 1915.
Sketches from Cambridge, by a don. 1865; ed with a foreword by G. M. Trevelyan, Oxford 1932. Rptd from Pall Mall Gazette.
The playground of Europe. 1871, 1894 (rev edn), Oxford 1936; tr Fr 1935.
Essays on freethinking and plainspeaking. 1873, 1905 rev edn (with introductory essays by J. Bryce and H. Paul).
Hours in a library. 3 vols 1874, 1876, 1879, rev edns 1892, 1907.
History of English thought in the eighteenth century. 2 vols 1876.
Belief and evidence. A paper read before the Metaphysical Society. 1877.
Samuel Johnson. 1878. (EML)

The uniformity of nature. A paper read before the Metaphysical Society. 1879.
Alexander Pope. 1880 (EML).
The science of ethics. 1882.
Swift. 1882 (EML).
Life of Henry Fawcett. 1885.
What is materialism? A discourse delivered in South Place Chapel 1886.
An agnostic's apology, and other essays. 1893, 1903 (rev edn).
The life of Sir James Fitzjames Stephen. 1895.
Social rights and duties. 2 vols 1896.
Studies of a biographer. 2 vols 1898, 2 vols 1902.
The English Utilitarians. 3 vols 1900.
Henry Sidgwick. 1901.
Robert Louis Stevenson: an essay. 1902.
George Eliot. 1902 (EML).
English literature and society in the eighteenth century. 1904.
Hobbes. 1904 (EML).
Some early impressions. 1924. Rptd from Nat Rev.
Sir Leslie Stephen's mausoleum book. Oxford 1977. Introd by A. Bell.

Translation

The Alps or sketches of life and nature in the mountains. 1981. Tr of Berlepsch's Die Alpen.

Contributions to periodicals

Stephen edited the Alpine Jnl *1868–72 and the* Cornhill Mag *1871–82. He wrote 462 signed newspaper and mag articles, listed in Fenwick, bibliographies, above. Periodicals to which he contributed include* Macmillan's Mag, Alpine Jnl, the Pall Mall Gazette, Saturday Rev, Cornhill Mag, Nation, Chambers' Jnl, St Paul's, Fraser's Mag, North Amer Rev, Fortnightly Rev, Nineteenth Cent, Mind, English Historical Rev, International Jnl of Ethics, Contemporary Rev, Nat Rev, Athenaeum, Quart Rev *and* Monthly Rev. Wellesley *5 1989 includes some of these titles.*

Letters

Bickwell, J. W. Selected letters of Leslie Stephen. Vol 1 (1864–1882), vol 2 (1882–1904) 1996.

Editions, introductions, prefaces and contributions to collaborative works

Stephen edited the DNB, *1882–91 and contributed 283 signed biographies, listed in Fenwick, bibliographies, above. For Stephen's 43 contributions to books, including chapters and essays not previously pbd, introductions and books edited, see Fenwick.*

§2

Maitland, F. W. The Life and letters of Leslie Stephen. 1906.
Lee, S. DNB article on Stephen in the 1901–11 Second Suppl 1912.
Annan, N. Leslie Stephen: his thought and character in relation to his time. 1951.
Annan, N. Leslie Stephen the godless Victorian. 1984.
Bicknell, J. Leslie Stephen. In DLB vol 57 1987.
Fenwick, G. The contributors' index to the Dictionary of national biography 1885–1901, Winchester 1989.
Fenwick, G. Women and the Dictionary of national biography: a guide to DNB volumes 1885–1985 and Missing Persons. Aldershot 1994. [GF]

Robert Alan Mowbray Stevenson 1847–1900

Engraving: its origin, processes, and history. 1886. Trn of H. Delaborde, La gravure.
The devils of Notre Dame. 1894. Illustr Joseph Pennell.
The art of Velasquez. 1895, 1899 (rev and expanded), 1962 ('New Revised Edition' ed D. Sutton and T. Crombie).
Peter Paul Rubens. 1898 (The portfolio monographs no 38), 1909, 1939.
Uncollected reviews and criticism in Mag of Art (from 1885), Art Jnl, Studio, Pall Mall Gazette (1893–9).
Introduction. In W. Armstrong, Sir Henry Raeburn, 1901.
Isaacs, J. R. A. M. Stevenson. Listener 27 Nov 1947.
Sutton, D. Biographical study: R. A. M. Stevenson: art critic. In Velasquez, 1962, *above*.
Mehew, E. Robert Alan Mowbray (Bob) Stevenson. In The letters of Robert Louis Stevenson, vol 1, New Haven CT and London 1994. [RGS]

Robert Louis Stevenson 1850–94

See col 1688.

Algernon Charles Swinburne 1837–1909

See col 817.

John Addington Symonds 1840–93

See col 2454.

Arthur Symons 1865–1945

See col 837.

Helen Taylor 1831–1907

Taylor's papers are in the John Stuart Mill/Taylor Collection in the lib of the London School of Economics.

§1

The claims of Englishwomen to the suffrage constitutionally considered. 1867. Rptd from Westminster Rev 87, Jan 1867, *below*.
Nationalisation of the land. [1890] (Tract no 19 of the Land Nationalisation Soc). Rptd from the Liberal and Radical Year Book.
The restoration of their homes to the people: an appeal to women. [1890?]

Contributions to periodicals.

Greece and the Greeks. Westminster Rev 79, Jan 1863.
Personal representation. Westminster Rev 84, Oct 1865.
Women and criticism. Macmillan's Mag 14 Sep 1866. Rptd in Robson, 1994, *below*.
The ladies' petition. Westminster Rev 87, Jan 1867.
Fragment on the reign of Elizabeth. From the posthumous papers of Mr Buckle, ed Taylor. Fraser's Mag 75, Feb 1867: 76, Aug and Sep 1867.
A few words on Mr Trollope's defence of fox-hunting. Fortnightly Rev n.s. 7, Jan 1870.
Sir Thomas More on the politics of today. Fortnightly Rev n.s. 8, Aug 1870.
Paris and France. Fortnightly Rev n.s. 9, Apr 1871.
A new attack on toleration. Fortnightly Rev n.s. 10, Dec 1871.
Chapters on Socialism. J. S. Mill. Introd note by H. Taylor. Fortnightly Rev n.s. 25, Feb 1879.
Women's rights as preached by women. Westminster Rev 116, Oct 1881. Rptd in Robson, 1994, *below*.
Robson, A. P. and Robson, J. M. (ed). Sexual equality. Writings by J. S. Mill, H. Taylor Mill and H. Taylor. Toronto, Buffalo and London 1994. Includes unpbd papers and speeches of Taylor.
Miscellaneous and posthumous works of H. T. Buckle. Ed with a biographical notice by Taylor. 3 vols 1872.
Autobiography of J. S. Mill. Ed Taylor 1873, 1885.

Three essays on religion: nature, the utility of religion and theism. By J. S. Mill. Ed Taylor 1874.

§2

DNB 1901–1911.

The biographical dictionary of modern British radicals. Ed J. Baylen and N. Gossman. Vol 3 Hemel Hempstead 1988.

Henry Duff Traill 1842–1900

See LR *and* NRA *for letters. Notable collections in BL and Leeds Univ Lib, Brotherton Collection.*

§1

Glaucus: a tale of a fish – a new and original extravaganza, performed July 1865. [1865.]

Who is the guide of nature, but only the God of nature? Oxford 1868. Ellerton theological essay.

Present versus past, performed June 1869. [1869.]

The battle of the professors, performed June 1874. [1874.]

The Israelitish question and the comments of the Canaan journals thereon. 1876. Burlesque of leading London newspapers. Anon.

Central government. 1881, 1908 (rev H. Craik). Account of the English constitution.

Sterne. 1882 (EML).

Recaptured rhymes: being a batch of political and other fugitives arrested and brought to book. Edinburgh 1882.

Coleridge. 1884 (EML).

The new Lucian: being a series of dialogues of the dead. 1884, 1900 (rev and enlarged).

Shaftesbury. 1886. A memoir of Anthony Ashley Cooper, first Earl of Shaftesbury.

William the Third. 1888.

Lord Strafford. 1889.

Saturday songs. 1890. Satirical verses largely rptd from the Saturday Rev.

The Marquis of Salisbury. New York 1891.

Number twenty: fables and fantasies. [1892.] Chiefly in prose, with some in verse.

Two proper prides [A tale]. In Lucy Clifford, A grey romance . . . And stories by H. D. Traill, W. E. Hodgson. 1894.

The barbarous Britishers: a tip-top novel. [1896.] A parody of Grant Allen's The British barbarians.

From Cairo to the Soudan frontier. 1896. Letters rptd from the Daily Telegraph.

The life of Sir John Franklin, R. N. 1896.

Lord Cromer: a biography. 1897.

The new fiction and other essays on literary subjects. 1897.

The medicine man, performed May 1898. [1898.] With R. Hichens.

The unflinching realist. The Anglo-Saxon Rev 3 Dec 1899. Short story.

England, Egypt and the Sudan. 1900.

The baby of the future. [1911.] Parodies of nursery rhymes rptd from Punch.

Editions and introductions

The capitals of the world. Tr from Fr. Ed N. Bell and Traill 1892.

Perl, H. Venezia. Adapted from the German by Mrs A. Bell. Introd by Traill 1892.

Social England. Ed Traill and J. S. Mann 6 vols 1893–7. Numerous later edns and reprints. Appeared as The building of Britain and the empire, 1909, and as Our country: its story from the earliest days, New York nd. Tr Rus 1896–9.

Disraeli, B. Sybil. Introd by Traill 1895.

Barrett, C. R. B. Battles and battlefields in England. Introd by Traill 1896.

Carlyle, T. The works of Thomas Carlyle (Centenary edition). Ed and introd by Traill 30 vols 1896–9.

Among my books: papers on literary subjects. Introd by Traill [1898]. Rptd from Literature.

Contributions to periodicals and collaborative works

Traill edited the Observer, *1889–91 and* Literature, *1897–1900. He wrote numerous articles and reviews for* Contemporary Rev, Daily Telegraph, Dark Blue, Fortnightly Rev, Macmillan's Mag, Nat Rev, New Rev, Nineteenth Cent, Pall Mall Gazette, St James's Gazette, Saturday Rev, Yellow Book *and* Yorkshire Post *(see also* Wellesley 5 *1989). He also contributed to such collective works as T. M. Coan (ed),* Studies in biography, *New York 1883 and to T. G. Bonney et al,* The Mediterranean, its storied cities and venerable ruins, *New York 1902.*

§2

Obits: The Times 22 Feb 1900; Observer 25 Feb 1900.

Traill's library was sold by auction on 12 July 1900 (auction-sale catalogue reference: S. – C. S. 1187(4)).

Beeching, H. C. In his Conferences on books and men, 1900.

Tennyson, G. B. Introduction to the reprint of Traill's edition of The works of Thomas Carlyle, New York 1980.

Trela, D. J. In G. A. Cevasco, The 1890s: an encyclopedia of British Literature, art and culture, New York 1993. [FJMK]

Arthur Bingham Walkley 1855–1926

See NRA *for his correspondence with William Archer.*

§1

Playhouse impressions. 1892. Rptd from his dramatic criticism in Speaker, Nat Observer and other periodicals.

Frames of mind. 1899. Essays rptd from various periodicals.

Dramatic criticism: three lectures delivered at the Royal Institution. 1903.

Drama and life. 1907. Essays rptd from The Times and Edinburgh Rev.

Pastiche and prejudice. 1921. Essays rptd from The Times.

More prejudice. 1923. Articles rptd from The Times.

Still more prejudice. 1925. Articles rptd from The Times.

He contributed to Arts and Decoration, Cosmopolis, Fortnightly Rev, Literature, Nat Observer, New Rev, Speaker, Star, Temple Bar, The Times *and* TLS *(see also* Wellesley 5 *1989). Some of Walkley's essays were included in anthologies, such as R. M. Gay (ed),* Facts, fancy and opinion, *1923; F. H. Pritchard (ed),* Essays of to-day, *1924; W. T. Hastings (ed),* Contemporary essays, *1928; C. H. Slover and W. T. De Starnes (ed),* Types of prose writing, *1933 and G. J. Nathan (ed),* The magic mirror: selected writings on the theatre, *New York 1960.*

Editions and introductions

Maeterlinck, M. P. M. B. The treasure of the humble. Tr from Fr by A. Sutro. Introd by Walkley 1897.

de Voltaire, F. M. A. The history of Candide. Introd by Walkley [1922].

Austen, J. The Watsons. Introd by Walkley 1923.

Morand, P. Green shoots. Tr from Fr. Introd by Walkley, preface by M. Proust 1923.

§2

Bennet, A. Things that interested me. 1921–6.

Hind, C. L. More authors and I. 1922.

Agate, J. E. Fantasies and impromptus. 1925.

The Times 9 Oct 1926. Obituary.

Memorial Service in St Bride's Church, Fleet Street [1926].

Child, H. N. The post-Victorians. 1933.

Beerbohm, M. Around theatres. 1953.

Bushko, D. A. Arthur Bingham Walkley's theory and practice of dramatic criticism. Unpbd diss, Columbia Univ 1976. [JMB]

Thomas Humphry Ward 1845–1926

Humphry Sandwith: a memoir. 1884.
Oxford. Illustr J. Fulleylove, notes by Ward 1889.
Romney: a biographical and critical essay, with a catalogue raisonné of his works. 2 vols 1904. With W. Roberts.
History of the Athenaeum [Club] 1824–1925, based on materials collected by the late H. R. Tedder. 1926.

Editions and introductions

Brasenose ale: a collection of verses annually presented on Shrove Tuesday. Ed Ward 1878.
The English poets: selection with critical introductions by various writers and a general introduction by Matthew Arnold. Ed Ward 4 vols 1880–1. Numerous edns.
Men of the reign: a biographical dictionary of eminent persons of British and colonial birth who have died during the reign of Queen Victoria. Ed Ward 1885.
The reign of Queen Victoria: a survey of fifty years of progress. Ed Ward 2 vols 1887.
English art in the public galleries of London, published under the direction of Ward, with the assistance of W. Armstrong and others. 1888.
Pictures in the collection of J. Pierpont Morgan. Introd by Ward 1907.

Contributions to periodicals

For Ward's contributions to Edinburgh Rev, Macmillan's Mag *and* Quart Rev, *see* Wellesley 5 *1989*. [MD]

Theodore Watts-Dunton, earlier Watts 1832–1914

For mss and letters, see LR *and* NRA. *Notable collections in BL, Leeds Univ Lib and Rutgers Univ Lib.*

Bibliographies

Catalogue of the library of Walter Theodore Watts-Dunton. 1917. Poem.
Truss, T. J. Watts-Dunton: a primary bibliography. BB 23 1961.

§1

Jubilee greeting at Spithead to the men of Greater Britain. 1897.
The coming of love and other poems. 1898, 1899 (includes Rhona Boswell's story and adds long prefatory note), 1906 (rev and enlarged), 1907 (with introductory note and portrait by D. G. Rossetti).
Aylwin: a novel. 1899, [1900] (adds further introd), 1901 (with 2 appendices), 1902 (illus), 1904 (WC), 1906 (illus with a note on the Renascence of wonder and postscript), 1929 (with a note on the character of D'Arcy and a key to the story).
Christmas at the Mermaid. 1902. First pbd in The coming of love and other poems.
The Rhodes memorial at Oxford: the work of Cecil Rhodes – a sonnet sequence. [1907.]
Rossetti and Charles Wells: a reminiscence of Kelmscott Manor. In Joseph and his brethren by Charles Wells, Oxford 1908 (WC).
Henry Thoreau and other children of the open air. 1910.
Old familiar faces. 1916. Sketches rptd from Athenaeum: Borrow, Rossetti, Tennyson, Christina Rossetti, Gordon Hake, de Tabley, Morris and Groome.
Poetry and the renascence of wonder: with a preface by Thomas Hake. 1916. Article on Poetry rptd from Encyclopaedia Britannica 1885 (9th edn), on Renascence of wonder from Chambers' Cyclopaedia of English literature vol 3, 1901.
Vesprie Towers: a novel. 1916.

Editions and introductions

Borrow, G. H. Lavengro. Introd by Watts-Dunton 1893.
Gosse, E. W. King Erik. Introductory essay by Watts-Dunton 1893.
Borrow, G. H. The romany rye. Introd by Watts-Dunton 1900.
Brontë, C., E. and A. The novels and poems. Introd by Watts-Dunton to vol 6 1901 (WC).
Borrow, G. H. Wild Wales. Introd by Watts-Dunton 1906.
Shakespeare, W. The complete works. Notes and introd by Sidney Lee, special introd by Watts-Dunton. 1906, 1910 (WC).
Thoreau, H. D. The works. Introd by Watts-Dunton 1906.
Johnson, E. P. Flint and feather. Introd by Watts-Dunton 1913.
Swinburne, A. C. Charles Dickens. Preface and illustrative notes by Watts-Dunton 1913.
The Keats letters. 1914.
Swinburne, A. C. Selections. Ed Watts-Dunton 1915.

Contributions to periodicals and collaborative works

Watts-Dunton's contributions to Fortnightly Rev, New Quart Mag *and* Nineteenth Cent *are listed in* Wellesley 5 *1989. He also contributed to such composite works as* The poets and poetry of the century, *ed A. H. Miles, 1891.*

§2

Hamelius, J. P. Theodore Watts. 1899.
Douglas, J. Theodore Watts-Dunton. 1904.
Hake, T. S. E. and A. Compton-Rickett. The life and letters of Theodore Watts-Dunton. 1916.
Panter-Downes, M. At the Pines: Swinburne and Watts-Dunton on Putney. 1971. [MD]

Sir Frederick Wedmore 1844–1921

See LR *and* NRA *for letters to Clement Shorter.*

§1

The two lives of Wilfrid Harris. 1868.
A snapt gold ring. 2 vols 1871.
Two girls. 2 vols 1873.
Studies in English art. 2 ser 1876–80.
Pastorals of France: A last love at Pornic – Yvonne of Croisic – The four bells of Chartres. 1877, 1893 (with Renunciations, *below*).
The masters of genre painting: being an introductory handbook to the study of genre painting. [1879.]
Meryon and Meryon's Paris; with a descriptive catalogue of the artist's work. 1879, 1892 (2nd edn rev and enlarged).
Four masters of etching ... with original etchings by Haden, Jacquemart, Whistler and Legros. 1883.
The pictures of the season. 1883.
Notes ... on French eighteenth century art. 1885.
Whistler's etchings: a study and a catalogue. 1886, 1899 (rev and enlarged). A supplement by An amateur, New York 1902.
Notes on Velasquez and Titian in the etchings of R. W. Macbeth. 1888.
A chemist in the suburbs. [1890] (priv ptd). Later included in Renunciations, *below*.
Fontainebleau. Fifteen photogravures after the pictures by J. Haynes-Williams. 1890.
Life of Honoré de Balzac. 1890.
A descriptive catalogue of drawings, prints, pictures and porcelain collected by James Pyke Thompson. 1891 (priv ptd).
Renunciations: A chemist in the suburbs – A confidence at the Savile – The north coast and Eleanor. 1893, 1893 (with Pastorals of France).
English episodes: The vicar of Pimlico – Justice Wilkinshaw's attentions – The fitting obsequies – Katherine in the Temple – The new 'Marienbad-elegy'. 1894.
Etching in England. 1895, New York 1895 (partly rptd as Dry-points of Paul Helleu).
Orgeas and Miradou. [Grasse? 1895] (priv ptd). Also included in Orgeas and Miradou, with other pieces: To Nancy; The poet on

the wolds, 1896. Partly rptd 1905 as Dreams of Provence. To Nancy rptd separately in 1905.
Fine prints. 1897, 1905 (enlarged).
On books and arts. 1899.
The collapse of the penitent. 1900.
The poet's chronicle. 1902 (priv ptd).
Cameron's etchings: a study and a catalogue. 1903. Partly rptd in A. H. Hahlo & Co's Catalogue of etchings by D. Y. Cameron, New York 1912.
Constable – Lucas: with a descriptive catalogue of the prints they did between them. 1904.
To Nancy. 1905.
Whistler and others. 1906.
Some of the moderns. 1909.
Hercules Brabazon Brabazon. An essay. [1910?]
Etchings. 1911.
Catalogue of an exhibition of the etchings of the late Alphonse Legros. [1912.]
Memories. 1912.
Pages assembled: a selection from the writings imaginative and critical of Frederick Wedmore. 1913.
Painters and paintings. [1913.]
Brenda walks on. 1916.
Certain comments, with introductory essays by Sir George Douglas and George C. Williamson. [1925.]
Wedmore contributed to Acad, Anglo-Saxon Rev, Bentley's Misc, Contemporary Rev, Fortnightly Rev, Macmillan's Mag, New Rev, Nineteenth Cent, Print-collector's Bull *and* Savoy *(see also* Wellesley 5 *1989). He also contributed to* DNB *(2 entries) and to* Art and literature, *ed F. M. Coan, 2 vols New York 1883.*

Editions and introductions
Burlington Fine Arts Club: exhibition of drawings by Dutch masters. Note by Wedmore 1875.
Burlington Fine Arts Club: exhibition of drawings in water colour ... by John Sell Cotman. Biographical note by Wedmore 1888.
A selection from the Liber studiorum of J. M. W. Turner. Introd by Wedmore. In Sir E. J. Poynter, The South Kensington drawing-book, [1890].
Michel, É. Rembrandt: his life, his work and his time. From the Fr by F. Simmonds. Ed Wedmore 3 vols 1894.
Rembrandt: seventeen of his masterpieces from the collection of his pictures in the Cassel Gallery ... with an essay by Wedmore [1894].
Poems of the love and pride of England. Ed Wedmore and M. Wedmore 1897.
Ruskin, J. Turner and Ruskin: an exposition of the work of Turner from the writings of Ruskin. Ed with biographical note on Turner by Wedmore 2 vols 1900.
Hardie, M. The etched work. Appreciation by Wedmore 19??
A catalogue of etchings by Méryon as exhibited at no. 168 New Bond Street, Nov–Dec, 1902. Introd by Wedmore 1902.
Burlington Fine Arts Club: exhibition of English mezzotint portraits from circa 1750 to circa 1830. Introd by Wedmore 1902.
Holme, C. English water-colour: with reproductions of drawings by eminent painters. Introd by Wedmore 1902.
Rimington, A. W. England and Spain contrasted in landscape and architecture. Introd by Wedmore [1902].
Exhibition of etchings by J. McNeill Whistler. Note by Wedmore [1903].
Bayliss, W. Olives. The reminiscences of a president. Introd by Wedmore 1906.
The National Gallery – London. The Flemish School. Introd by Wedmore [1906].
Helleu, P. A gallery of portraits: reproduced from original etchings by P. Helleu. Introd by Wedmore 1907.

§2
Duffy, J. J. The stories of Frederick Wedmore: some correspondences with Dubliners. James Joyce Quart vol 5 1968.
Stanford, D. (ed). Critics of the nineties. 1970. [JMB]

Charles Whibley 1865–1930

Mss located in Berg Collection, NYPL; Indiana Univ Lib; Pierpont Morgan Lib; Princeton; HRHRC. See also LR.

Bibliographies
In Nineteenth century readers' guide to periodical literature 1890–1899, New York 1944.
See also Wellesley *5 1989.*
In An index to Blackwood's Magazine 1901–1980, ed D. Finkelstein, Aldershot 1995.

§1
The cathedrals of England and Wales. 1888 (preface by A. W. Thorold), New York 1888, Woodbridge CT 1973.
A book of scoundrels. New York 1896, London 1897, 1910, 1911, New York 1912, London 1921, New York 1971. Literary criticism.
REVIEWS: Dial 1 Feb 1896; Acad 21 Nov 1896; Blackwood's Mag Dec 1896; Speaker 30 Jan 1897; Athenaeum 3 Dec 1910; TLS 15 Dec 1910; New York Times 5 May 1912.
Studies in frankness. 1898, 1910, New York 1912, 1926, Port Washington NY 1970. Literary criticism.
REVIEWS: Westminster Gazette 24 Nov 1897; Acad 27 Nov 1897; Athenaeum 11 Dec 1897; Speaker 11 Dec 1897; Literature 15 Jan 1898; Literary World 18 Feb 1898; TLS 15 Dec 1910; Spectator 18 Feb 1911; New York Times 5 May 1912; Dial 16 Sep 1912.
The pageantry of life. 1900, New York 1900, London 1901 (2nd edn), 1910, New York 1912, 1921. Essays.
REVIEWS: Acad 6 Oct 1900; Outlook 6 Oct 1900; Athenaeum 20 Oct 1900; Spectator 20 Oct 1900; Outlook 3 Nov 1900; Dial 16 Dec 1900; New York Times 29 Dec 1900; Athenaeum 3 Dec 1910; TLS 15 Dec 1910; New York Times 5 May 1912.
The jubilee of printing. [1900?]
Musings without method: a record of 1900–1 by Annalist. Edinburgh and London 1902. Mainly political commentary.
William Makepeace Thackeray. Edinburgh and London 1903 (Modern English Writers ser), New York 1903, Folcroft PA 1973.
REVIEWS: Bookman Oct 1903; TLS 2 Oct 1903; Acad 10 Oct 1903; Speaker 17 Oct 1903; Athenaeum 24 Oct 1903; Literary World 30 Oct 1903; New York Times 7 Nov 1903; Spectator 7 Nov 1903; Critic Dec 1903; Dial 1 Apr 1904.
Literary portraits. 1904, New York 1905, 1920. Literary criticism.
REVIEWS: Outlook 31 Dec 1904; Bookman Jan 1905; TLS 6 Jan 1905; Acad 7 Jan 1905; Athenaeum 21 Jan 1905; Spectator 21 Jan 1905; Dial 1 May 1905.
William Pitt. Edinburgh and London 1906.
REVIEWS: TLS 26 Jan 1906; Acad 27 Jan 1906; New York Times 3 Feb 1906; Athenaeum 10 Feb 1906; Spectator 3 Mar 1906.
Musings without method: The Times and the publisher – the real object of The Times. [n.p.] Nov 1906. Rptd from Blackwood's Mag.
American sketches. Edinburgh and London 1908.
REVIEWS: TLS 25 June 1908; Spectator 25 July 1908; Bookman Oct 1908.
The letters of an Englishman. 2 vols 1911, 1912 (2nd ser), 1915, 1917. Rptd from the Daily Mail.
Essays in biography. 1913, New York 1913, 1918, Freeport NY 1968.
REVIEWS: Athenaeum 29 Mar 1913; TLS 10 Apr 1913; Bookman May 1913.
Political portraits (1st ser). 1917, Freeport NY 1970, Port Washington NY 1970.
REVIEWS: Athenaeum Dec 1917; TLS 6 Dec 1917; New York Times 3 Mar 1918; Dial 11 Apr 1918.

Jonathan Swift. (The Leslie Stephen lecture). Cambridge 1917, Folcroft PA 1969, Norwood PA 1977, London 1978.
Literary studies. 1919, 1925, Freeport NY 1969.
REVIEWS: Athenaeum 12 Dec 1919; TLS 12 Dec 1919.
Political portraits (2nd ser). 1923, 1924, Freeport NY 1970, Port Washington NY 1970.
REVIEW: TLS 6 Dec 1923.
Lord Manners and his friends. 2 vols 1925.
REVIEW: TLS 2 Apr 1925.

Contributions to periodicals, collaborative works and anthologies

Whibley acted as W. E. Henley's second in command on the Scots Observer, *later the* Nat Observer, *from Jan 1889 to 10 Mar 1894.*
Chambers's Encyclopaedia. Michelangelo, 1888–1892 edn, 1901 edn, 1923 edn; Sculpture, 1888–1892 edn, 1901 edn, 1923 edn.
Art Jnl. A Bavarian caricaturist, May 1889; Michelangelo, Oct 1893.
Scots Observer. 26 Jan 1889–25 Oct 1890.
Nat Observer. 29 Nov 1890–31 Mar 1894.
Mag of Art. Dec 1887–Oct 1893.
Literary Opinion. W. E. Henley, Nov 1891, rptd Bookman (USA) Nov 1895.
North Amer Rev. The tercentenary of Velasquez, July 1899; Jubilee of the printing press, Dec 1900; Jubilee of Ivan Turgenev, Feb 1902.
Living Age. 22 Dec 1906–3 Aug 1918.
Pall Mall Mag. Is anonymity in journalism desirable? Jan 1894; Piètro Mascagni of Livorno, May 1894.
Mercure de France. L'art et L'industrie dans la littérature Anglais, Mar 1895.
Bookman (USA). Nov 1895–Jan 1917.
Daily Mail. An election in France, 11 May 1898.
Blackwood's Mag. As well as irregular contributions, Whibley contributed a monthly article, Musings without method, to Blackwood's from Feb 1900 to Dec 1929. (*See also* Wellesley 5 1989 and An index to Blackwood's Mag 1900–80, ed D. Finkelstein, Aldershot 1995.
Literature. Slang and its uses, 2 Mar 1901.
McClure's Mag. George Douglas Brown, Nov 1902.
The fortunate youth. In A volunteer haversack containing contributions of certain writers to the Queen's Rifle Volunteer Brigade: The Royal Scots, ed A. S. Walker, Edinburgh 1902.
Cornhill Mag. Literary forgers, May 1902, rptd Bookman (USA) May 1902.
Acad. Marcel Schwob, 18 May 1905.
Outlook. 28 Jan 1905–31 Mar 1906.
Harper's Monthly Mag. Jeffreys of the Bloody Assizes, Dec 1906.
In Cambridge history of English literature, vols 3, 4, 8 and 9, 1909–12.
Pall Mall Gazette. Pall Mall papers, 8 Jan 1913–7 July 1914. Literary criticism.
Rouges and vagabonds. In Shakespeare's England, ed Sir S. Lee and C. T. Onions, Oxford 1916.
The Strand. Who is the worst man who ever lived? Ä. Ä. Joseph Le Bon, Apr 1916.
Nineteenth Cent. A wanderer and novels (rev of C. F. Keary's novel), June 1918.
Country Life. 16 Nov 1918–7 June 1919.
Henry John Cockayne Cust. DNB 1912–1921.
Criterion. Bolingbroke, Apr 1923; July 1923.

Editions and introductions

In cap and gown: three centuries of Cambridge wit. Ed Whibley 1889, 1890 (2nd edn), 1898 (3rd edn, new preface).
Introd to J. Nyren, The young cricketer's tutor, 1893.
Introds to Tudor translations (1st ser): IV. The golden ass of Apuleius, 1893; V. An Æthiopian history written in Greek by Heliodorus, 1895, New York 1967; XVII–XVIII. The history of Comines, 1897, New York 1897; XXI–XXII. Seutonius. History of twelve Caesars, 1899, New York 1899; XXIV–XXVI. Rabelais. Gargantua and Pantagruel, 1900, New York 1967. Whibley was general editor of the 2nd series.
A book of English prose, character and incident, 1387–1649. 1894, Philadelphia 1894. Co-ed Whibley with W. E. Henley.
Introd to L. Sterne, Tristram Shandy, 2 vols 1894 (English Classics).
Lucian's true history. Ed Whibley, tr F. Hicks, illustr Beardsley among others, 1894 (priv ptd), 1902.
Lover, S. Handy Andy: a tale of Irish life. Ed Whibley 1896 (illustr H. M. Brock).
Essays of De Quincey. Ed with introd by Whibley 1903 (Red Letter Lib).
De Quincey, T. Confessions of an opium-eater. Ed Whibley 1904 (Red Letter Lib).
Introd to E. Hall, The lives of the kings: Henry VIII. Ed Whibley 2 vols London and Edinburgh 1904, New York 1911.
Introd to B. Disraeli, Lord George Bentinck, 1905.
Introd to Essays of William Hazlitt, 1906 (Red Letter Lib), 1925.
Introd to Sir T. Browne, Religio Medici, and other essays, 1906.
Poems of Lord Byron. Ed and introd by Whibley 1907.
Introd to Poems of Arthur Hugh Clough, 1913, 1920, 1973 (6th edn).
G. Wyndham's Essays in romantic literature. Ed with introd by Whibley 1919.
Introd to W. Hazlitt, A reply to Z, 1923.
Introd to Twenty select colloquies of Erasmus. Tr Sir R. L'Estrange 1680. [1923], Boston 1985.
Tudor translations (general editor 2nd ser). 12 vols. Vol I. Sallust. The conspiracy of Catiline and the war of Jugurtha, ed Whibley 1924.
Collected essays of W. P. Ker. Ed Whibley 2 vols 1925.
Introd to Letters of the King of Hanover to Viscount Strangford, 1925.
Introd to D. Defoe, The life and strange surprising adventures of Robinson Crusoe of York, mariner, 3 vols 1925.
The works of William Shakespeare chronologically arranged. Ed with introds by Whibley 3 vols 1925.
Bunyan, J. The pilgrim's progress. Ed Whibley 1926, Boston 1926, 1930.
Introd to R. Graves, The spiritual Quixote: or the summer's ramble of Mr Geoffrey Wildgoose, 2 vols 1926.
Introd to Voltaire, Lettres philosophiques: letters concerning the English nation, 1926.
The golden ass, being the metamorphoses of Lucius Apuleius. Ed Whibley, tr W. Adlington, New York 1927, London 1943.
Sir Matthew Hale's Discourse touching provision for the poor. Ed Whibley 1927.
Introd to The satyricon of Petronius Arbiter. New York 1927, 1943.
Little books. Ed Whibley 6 vols 1927.
A facsimile reproduction of a unique catalogue of Laurence Sterne's library. 1930, New York 1930.

§2

Acad 4 Dec 1897.
Londoner's diary. Evening Standard 5 Mar 1930.
Obits: The Times 5 Mar 1930; New York Times 6 Mar 1930; Blackwood's Mag Apr 1930; London Mercury Apr 1930.
A catalogue of the valuable and extensive library of the late Charles Whibley. 1930.
The Charles Whibley library. TLS 10 July 1930.
The Whibley library at Hodgson's. Bookman's Jnl 18 (4) 1930.
Malcolm, D. O. In DNB 1922–1933.
Eliot, T. S. Charles Whibley: a memoir. 1931; rptd in his Selected essays, 1932.

Altick, R. D. Toryism's last stand: Charles Whibley and his Musings without method. South Atlantic Quart July 1942.
Ellenberger, N. In The 1890s: an encyclopedia of British literature, art, and culture, ed G. A. Cevasco, New York 1993. [DA]

Oscar Wilde 1854–1900

See col 2060.

George Wyndham 1863–1913

Mss located in BL; Berg Collection, NYPL; Harvard Univ Lib; Public Record Office, Kew.

Bibliographies

See Wellesley 5 *1989*.

§1

A short criticism of a lecture delivered by Mr S. Halifax (on behalf of the National Reform Union) with a note of introduction. Dover [1890].
Lies and replies: an exposure of some of the commoner Gladstone fallacies. Westminster 1892.
Speech delivered on behalf of the South African Association by Mr George Wyndham. 1898.
Debate on the Queen's Speech. The war in the Transvaal. 1 Feb 1900. Rptd from Parliamentary Debates, [1900].
The ballad of Mr Rook. By G. W[yndham]. 1901 (illustr Hon Mrs P. Wyndham).
The development of the state: being an address delivered to the students of the University of Glasgow, Nov 1904. 1904.
Sir Walter Scott. (Speech to the Edinburgh Sir Walter Scott Club 29 Nov 1907.) 1908.
The springs of romance in the literature of Europe. An address delivered to the students of the University of Edinburgh, Oct 1910. 1910, Folcroft PA 1973, Norwood PA 1978.
Essays in romantic literature. Ed and introd C. Whibley 1919.
REVIEW: New Statesman 26 Apr 1919.

Contributions to periodicals and collaborative works

For contributions to Contemporary Rev, Fortnightly Rev *and* New Rev, *see* Wellesley 5 *1989*.
Nat Observer. 22 Oct 1892–4 Mar 1893.
In Lights on home rule, 1893. Rptd from Nat Observer.
New Rev. A remarkable book. Review of Stephen Crane's A red badge of courage, Jan 1896; rptd in Critical essays on American literature, Boston, 1990.
The poetry of Wilfrid Blunt. 1898. Co-ed Wyndham with W. E. Henley.
Dublin Rev. Review of A. Meynell's Poems, Oct 1913.

Letters

Gatty, C. T. George Wyndham. Recognita. 1917.
Letters of George Wyndham, 1877–1913. Ed Guy Wyndham 2 vols Edinburgh 1915 (priv ptd).
Mackail, J. W. and G. Wyndham (ed). Life and letters of George Wyndham. 2 vols [1925].

Editions and introductions

The poems of Shakespeare. Ed Wyndham 1898, New York 1899, London 1910, 1994 (facs of 1899 edn).
REVIEWS: Bookman May 1898; New York Times 11 June 1898; Sewanee Rev July 1898.
Ronsard & La Pléiade: with selections from their poetry and some translations in the original metres. Ed Wyndham 1906, rptd 1983.
REVIEW: Bookman Dec 1906.
In The Henley Memorial: an account of the inaugural ceremony in St Paul's Cathedral July 11th, 1907, 1908. Speech.

§2

'Spy cartoon'. Vanity Fair 20 Sep 1900.
Kelly, R. J. New Ireland Rev Jan 1901.
Boland, P. J. Dana Jan 1905.
Obits: The Times 10 June 1913; New York Times 11 June 1913.
Ward, W. Dublin Rev July 1913.
Boyd, C. Cornhill Mag Oct 1913.
Boyd, C. George Wyndham. 1913.
Gatty, C. T. George Wyndham. Recognita. 1917.
Blunt, W. S. In My diaries, 1919, 1920.
Chesterton, G. K. In his The uses of diversity, 1920 (2 edns), 1927 (5th edn).
Sykes, E. Ireland: a contrast. Dublin Rev Apr 1921.
Eliot, T. S. In The sacred wood, 1921, [New York] 1921, rptd 1991; tr Ital 1946.
Harris, F. In his Contemporary portraits (4th ser), New York 1923, London 1924.
Long, Viscount. In his Memories, 1923.
Baumann, A. A. In his The last Victorians, Philadelphia 1927.
Milne, J. In his Pages in waiting, 1927.
Kent, M. George Wyndham: portrait of a romantic. Calcutta Rev June 1927.
Kent, M. George Wyndham: romantic statesman. Eng Rev Sep 1927.
Raymond, E. T. In his Portraits of the new century (The first ten years), 1928.
Hagberg, K. In his personalities and powers, 1930. Tr from the Swed Medmänniskor.
Shane, L. In his Men were different: five studies in late Victorian biography. [Toronto] 1937.
Connell, J. New light on George Wyndham: a selection of unpublished letters to W. E. Henley. Nat and Eng Rev May 1951, June 1951.
Biggs-Davison, J. George Wyndham. 1951.
Ferrell, W. R. George Wyndham at the Irish Office, 1990–1905. 1974.
Egremont, M. The cousins: the friendship, opinions and activities of Wilfrid Scawen Blunt and George Wyndham. 1977.
Lambert, A. In her Unquiet souls, New York 1984.
Abdy, J. and C. Gere. In The souls, 1984.
Thompson, J. A. and A. Mejia (ed) Edwardian conservatism: five studies in adaptation. 1988.
Ridley, J and C. Percy (ed). The letters of Arthur Balfour and Lady Elcho 1885–1917. 1992.
Gilmour, D. Curzon. 1994. [DA]

Alice Zimmern 1855–1939

Half-hours with foreign novelists. 1880. With Helen Zimmern.
Exercises to accompany the school German grammar. 1889. With H. W. Eve.
Methods of education in the United States. 1894.
Old tales from Greece. 1897.
The renaissance of girls' education in England: a record of fifty years' progress. 1898.
Greek history for young readers. 1903.
Old tales from Rome. 1906.
Gods and heroes of the north. 1907.
Women's suffrage in many lands. With a foreword by Mrs Chapman Catt. 1909; tr Fr 1911.
Demand and achievement. The international women's suffrage movement. 1912.

Translations

The meditations of Marcus Aurelius. Tr Jeremy Collier, rev A. Zimmern, 1891.

Bluemner, H. The home life of the ancient Greeks. 1893.
Porphyry, the philosopher to his wife Marcella. Preface by Garnett 1896.
von Hoensbroech, P. K. Fourteen years a Jesuit. 1911.
Ionescu, T. The origins of the war. 1917. [MD]

Helen Zimmern 1846–1934

Stories in precious stones. 1873.
Told by the waves: stories in nature. 1874.
Schopenhauer, Arthur. His life and his philosophy. 1876; tr Ital 1887, 1932 (rev).
G. E. Lessing, his life and his work. 1878; tr Ger 1880.
Half-hours with foreign novelists. 1880. With Alice Zimmern.
Maria Edgeworth. 1883, Boston 1883.
Tales from the Edda. Illustr K. Greenaway 1883.
Sir L. Alma Tadema: his life and works. 1886.
The Hansa towns. 1889.
Sir Lawrence Alma Tadema. 1902.
The Brownings. 1906.
The Italy of the Italians. 1906, 1914 (rev).
Tripoli and young Italy. 1912. With C. Lapworth.
Italian leaders of today. 1915.
New Italy. 1918, Chautauqua NY 1920. With A. Agresti.

Translations

Benrath, C. Bernardino Ochino of Siena. 1876.
Heroic tales retold from Firdausi. With a prefatory poem by E. W. Gosse 1882.
Paulina Elizabeth Ottilia Louisa [of Wied]. Pilgrim sorrow. 1884.
Basile, G. B. The pentamerone. 1893.
de Amicis, Edmondo. Holland. Tr from the 13th edn, 1894.
Lewes, L. The women of Shakespeare. 1894.
Ferruggia, G. Woman's folly. 1895.
Selected prose works of G. E. Lessing. Tr E. C. Beasley and H. Zimmern, ed Edward Bell 1900.
Nietzsche, F. W. Beyond good and evil. 1907.
de Cesare, R. The last days of papal Rome, 1850–1870. Abridged and tr H. Zimmern 1909.
Nietzsche, F. W. The complete works. Tr H. Zimmern and others, ed O. Levy 1909–13.
Levi Catellani, Enrico. Italy and Austria at war. 1918. With A. McCaskill.
Motta, Luigi. Flames on the Bosphorus. 1920.

Editions

The dramatic works of G. E. Lessing. With a short memoir by H. Zimmern. [18–?]
Sir Joshua Reynolds' discourses. Ed H. Zimmern 1887.
The comedies of Goldoni. 1892. [MD]

7
History

John Emerich Edward Dalberg Acton, 1st Baron Acton 1834–1902

Acton's papers are in the Acton Collection, Cambridge Univ Lib.

Bibliographies

Shaw, W. A. A bibliography of the historical works of Dr Creighton, Dr Stubbs, Dr S. R. Gardiner and Lord Acton. 1903.

Conzemius, V. (ed). Ignaz von Döllinger: Lord Acton Briefwechsel. 3 vols Munich 1963–71, vol 1 pp. xxv–xlv.

McElrath, D. Lord Acton: the decisive decade. Louvain 1970, pp. xi–xvi.

The library of Lord Acton. Ed G. Watson, Cambridge 1992.

Selections

Selected writings of Lord Acton. Ed J. R. Fears, Indianapolis 1985.

§1

Römische Briefe vom Concil, von Quirinus. Munich 1870: tr 1870 (as Letters from Rome on the Council). By Acton et al; rptd from Allgemeine Zeitung 1869.

Sendschreiben an einen deutschen Bischof des vaticanischen Concils. Nördlingen [1870].

Zur Geschichte des vaticanischen Concils. Munich 1871.

The war of 1870: a lecture. 1871.

The history of freedom in antiquity: an address. Bridgnorth [1877]; tr Fr 1878.

The history of freedom in Christianity: an address. Bridgnorth [1877]; tr Fr 1878.

A lecture on the study of history. 1895, 1896, 1905, 1906 (in Lectures on modern history), 1911; tr Ger 1897. Acton's inaugural lecture at Cambridge.

Lectures on modern history. Ed J. N. Figgis and R. V. Laurence 1906, 1952, 1956, New York 1959; ed H. R. Trevor-Roper 1961; ed H. Kohn, New York 1961 (as Renaissance to revolution: the rise of the free state).

Historical essays and studies. Ed J. N. Figgis and R. V. Laurence 1907.

The history of freedom and other essays. Ed J. N. Figgis and R. V. Laurence 1907.

Lectures on the French revolution. Ed J. N. Figgis and R. V. Laurence 1910.

Essays on freedom and power. Ed G. Himmelfarb, Boston 1948, London 1956.

Essays on church and state. Ed D. Woodruff 1952.

Lord Acton's History of liberty: a study of his library with an edited text of his History of liberty notes. Ed G. Watson, Aldershot 1994.

Contributions to periodicals

For a list of Acton's periodical reviews and articles, see Wellesley, *and the index to vols 1–20 of* EHR.

Letters and journals

Letters of Lord Acton to Mary, daughter of W. E. Gladstone; with a memoir. Ed H. Paul 1904, 1913.

Gasquet, F. A. Lord Acton and his circle. 1906.

Selections from the correspondence of the first Lord Acton. Ed J. N. Figgis and R. V. Laurence 1917.

de Janösi, F. E. The correspondence between Acton and Bishop Creighton. Cambridge Historical Jnl 6 1940.

Knaplund, P. The Poet-Laureateship in 1892: some Acton–Gladstone letters. Quart Rev 288 1950.

von Döllinger, I. Briefwechsel mit Lord Acton 1850–69. Ed V. Conzemius, Munich 1963.

von Döllinger, I. Briefwechsel mit Lord Acton 1869–70. Ed V. Conzemius, Munich 1966.

The correspondence of Lord Acton and Richard Simpson. Ed J. Altholz, D. McElrath and J. C. Holland 3 vols Cambridge 1971–5.

Jackman, S. W. (ed). Acton in America. The American Journal of Sir John Acton. Shepherdstown WV 1979.

§2

Biographies and evaluations

Poole, R. Lord Acton. EHR 17 1902.

Bryce, J. In his Studies in contemporary biography, 1903.

Bryce, J. Lord Acton. Proc Br Acad 1 1904.

Himmelfarb, G. Lord Acton: a study in conscience and politics. Chicago 1962.

Lucy Aikin 1781–1864

See col 2078.

Archibald Alison 1792–1867

See col 2079.

Thomas Arnold 1795–1842

Collections

Miscellaneous works. Ed A. P. Stanley 1845, New York 1845 (with 9 essays added), 1858 (2nd edn).

§1

Thirteen letters on our social condition. 1822.

Sermons. 3 vols 1829–34; rev J. A. Forster 6 vols 1878.

Thucydides, The history of the Peloponnesian war. 3 vols Oxford 1830–5, 1840–2, 4 vols Oxford 1847–54. Ed Arnold.

Principles of Church reform. 1833 (3 edns), 1833 (4th edn with post-

script); ed A. P. Stanley 1845 (in Miscellaneous works, *above*); ed M. J. Jackson and J. Rogan 1962.
The Oxford malignants and Dr Hampden. Edinburgh Rev 63 1836.
History of Rome. 3 vols 1838–42, Philadelphia 1846, 2 vols New York 1851, Cambridge 1857; vol 3 chs 42–7 ed W. T. Arnold 1886 (as The second Punic war).
REVIEW: [A. Alison] Blackwood's Mag 44 1838.
Two sermons on the interpretation of prophecy. 1839.
The Christian life: its course, its hindrances and its helps. 1841; ed J. A. Forster 1878 (as vol 4 of Sermons).
REVIEW: [W. G. Ward] Br Critic 30 1841.
Introductory lectures on modern history: with the inaugural lecture. Oxford 1842, 1843, New York 1845, London 1849 (4th edn).
REVIEWS: [J. G. Phillimore] Blackwood's Mag 53 1843; [W. B. Greg] Westminster Rev 39 1843.
The Christian life: its hopes, its fears and its close. Ed M. Arnold 1842, 1845 (3rd edn); ed J. A. Forster 1878 (as vol 5 of Sermons).
Fragment of the Church. 1844.
Sermons chiefly on the interpretation of scripture. Ed M. Arnold 1845; ed J. A. Forster 1878 (as vol 6 of Sermons).
Sermons preached in the chapel of Rugby School: with an address before confirmation. 1845, New York 1846; ed J. A. Forster London 1878 (as vol 2 of Sermons).
History of the later Roman commonwealth. 2 vols 1845, New York 1846, London 1857. Rptd from Encyclopaedia metropolitana, ed E. Smedley 1845.

Journals

Arnold's travelling journals, with extracts from the Life and letters. Ed A. P. Stanley 1852.

§2

Stanley, A. P. A sermon preached in the chapel of Rugby School on the death of the Rev Thomas Arnold. Rugby 1842.
Stanley, A. P. Life and correspondence of Arnold. Edinburgh Rev 81 1843.
Mozley, J. B. In his Essays historical and theological, 1878.
Martineau, J. In his Essays, reviews and addresses, 1890.
[Hutton, R. H.] Dr Arnold after fifty years. Spectator 18 June 1892.
Fitch, J. Thomas and Matthew Arnold and their influence on English education. New York 1899.
Strachey, L. In his Eminent Victorians, 1918.

Biographies

Stanley, A. P. The life and correspondence of Thomas Arnold. 2 vols 1844.
Wymer, N. Dr Arnold of Rugby. 1953.
Bamford, T. W. Thomas Arnold. 1960.
McCrum, M. Thomas Arnold, headmaster. Oxford 1989.

Mary Berry 1763–1852

§1

The fashionable friends: a comedy in five acts. [By M. Berry]. 1802.
REVIEWS: Br Critic 20 1802; Critical Rev 36 1802; New Annual Register 23 1802; Poetical Register 2 1802; Monthly Mag suppl vol 14 1803.
Some account of the life of the Marquise du Deffand. In Letters of the Marquise du Deffand to Horace Walpole vol 1, 1810.
REVIEW: [J. Playfair] Edinburgh Rev 17 1811.
A comparative view of the social life of England and France from the Restoration of Charles the Second to the French Revolution. By the editor of Madame du Deffand's letters. Pt 1 1828, pt 2 1831, 2 vols 1834 (new edn titled England and France: a comparative view of the social condition of both countries from the Restoration of Charles the Second to the present time), 2 vols 1844.

Letters and journals

Extracts of the journals and correspondence of Miss Berry from the year 1783 to 1852. Ed Lady Theresa Lewis 1865, 1866.
The Berry papers: being the correspondence hitherto unpublished of Mary and Agnes Berry. Ed L. Melville 1914.

Editions

The works of Horatio Walpole. Ed R. Berry with the assistance of M. Berry [in fact by M. Berry alone] 5 vols 1798.
Letters of the Marquise du Deffand to the Hon Horace Walpole. [Ed M. Berry] 1810.
Some account of the life of Rachel Wriothesley, Lady Russell. Followed by a series of letters from Lady Russell to her husband, William Lord Russell. 1819.

Biographical notice

Lawrance, Hannah. Mary Berry, her friends and her times. Br Quart Rev 43 1866.

George Brodie 1786?–1867

§1

A history of the British Empire from the accession of Charles I to the Restoration. 4 vols Edinburgh 1822, 3 vols London 1866 (as A constitutional history of the British Empire).
REVIEW: [F. Jeffrey] Edinburgh Rev 40 1824.
Strictures on the appellate jurisdiction of the House of Lords. Edinburgh 1856.

Editions and commentaries

Stair, James Dalrymple, Viscount. The institutions of the laws of Scotland. With commentary and a suppl by G. Brodie. 2 vols Edinburgh 1826–31.
Faculty of Advocates. Report by the committee upon the privileges of the College of Justice in regard to exemptions from local taxes. Dissent [by G. Brodie]. Edinburgh 1834.

Henry Peter Brougham, 1st Baron Brougham and Vaux 1778–1868

The Brougham papers are at Univ College, London.

Bibliographies

Thomas, R. Bibliography of Brougham's works. In Works of Brougham, *below*, vol 11, Edinburgh 1873.

Collections

Selections from the speeches and writings. 1832.
Opinions of Lord Brougham on politics, theology, law, science, education &c &c. 1837, 2 vols Philadelphia 1839, 1 vol Paris 1841.
Speeches upon questions relating to public rights. 4 vols Edinburgh 1838, 2 vols Philadelphia 1841.
The critical and miscellaneous writings. 2 vols Philadelphia 1841.
Works. 11 vols 1855–61, Edinburgh 1872–3.
Contributions to the Edinburgh Review. 3 vols 1856.
Brougham's acts and bills from 1811 to the present time now first collected. Ed J. E. Eardley-Wilmot 1857, 1860 (as Brougham's law reforms).

§1

An inquiry into the colonial policy of the European powers. 2 vols Edinburgh 1803.
An inquiry into the state of the nation at the commencement of the present administration. 1806, 1806 (6th edn), 1806 (7th edn rev).
Practical observations upon the education of the people. 1825, 1825 (11th edn), 1825 (17th edn), 1825 (20th edn), Boston 1826; tr Ger 1827.

Inaugural discourse on being installed Lord Rector of the University of Glasgow. Glasgow 1825.
Thoughts upon the aristocracy of England, by Isaac Tomkins, Gent. 1835, 1835 (6th edn), 1835 (11th edn).
'We can't afford it!': being thoughts upon the aristocracy of England part 2, by Isaac Tomkins, Gent. 1835, 1835 (4th edn), 1835 (6th edn).
A discourse of natural theology. Brussels 1835, London 1835 (4th edn), Philadelphia 1835; tr Fr 1835.
Dissertations on subjects of science connected with natural theology. 2 vols 1839.
Historical sketches of statesmen who flourished in the time of George III. 2 vols 1839, Philadelphia 1839; second ser, 2 vols London 1839, Philadelphia 1839; third ser, 2 vols London 1842, Philadelphia 1842; collected 3 vols London 1845–53, 2 vols Philadelphia 1854, 3 vols London 1855–6, 1856–8; tr Fr 1847.
Sketches of public characters. 2 vols Philadelphia 1839.
Political philosophy. 3 vols 1842–3, 1 vol Paris 1845, 3 vols London 1846, 1853, 1855, 1861.
REVIEW: [Senior, N. W.] Edinburgh Rev 81 1845.
The British constitution. 1844, 1861 (3 edns).
Dialogues on instinct. 1844, Philadelphia 1845.
Albert Lunel: or the chateau of Languedoc. 3 vols 1844 (anon), 1872. A novel.
Lives of men of letters and science in the time of George III. 2 vols 1845–6, 3 vols 1845–7.
REVIEW: [Lockhart, J. G.] Quart Rev 76 1845.
Masters and workmen: a tale illustrative of the social and moral condition of the people, by Lord B—. 3 vols 1851. A novel attributed to Brougham.
History of England and France under the house of Lancaster. 1852 (anon), 1855, 1861.
Analytical view of Sir Isaac Newton's Principia. 1855. With E. J. Routh.
Addresses on popular literature. 1858.
Tracts: mathematical and physical. 1860.

Contributions to periodicals

For a list of Brougham's many contributions to the Edinburgh Rev *and other periodicals, see* Wellesley.

Letters and autobiography

The life and times of Lord Brougham written by himself. 3 vols Edinburgh 1871, 1872 (3rd edn).
Selections from the correspondence of Macvey Napier: edited by his son. 1879. Includes letters from Brougham to the editor of the Edinburgh Rev.
Brougham and his early friends: letters to James Loch 1798–1809. Ed R. H. M. Buddle-Atkinson and G. A. Jackson 3 vols Edinburgh 1908 (priv ptd).
Bourne, K. (ed). The blackmailing of the chancellor: some intimate ... letters from Harriette Wilson to Brougham. 1975.

§2

Gilfillan, G. In his A gallery of literary portraits, Edinburgh 1845.
Bagehot, W. Brougham. Nat Rev 5 1857; rptd in his Biographical studies, 1881.
Campbell, J. C. Lives of Lyndhurst and Brougham. 1869.
Mignet, F. A. M. In his Nouveaux éloges historiques, Paris 1877.
Retournay, H. Brougham et le centenaire. Paris 1878.
Atlay, J. B. In his Victorian Chancellors, 1906.

Biographies

New, C. W. The life of Brougham to 1830. Oxford 1961.
Huch, R. K. Henry, Lord Brougham: the later years 1830–68. Lampeter 1993.
Ford, T. H. Henry Lord Brougham and his world: a biography. Chichester 1995.

James Bryce, 1st Viscount Bryce of Dechmont

1838–1922

§1

The flora of the island of Arran. 1859.
The Holy Roman Empire. Arnold prize essay 1864. Oxford 1864, London 1871 (3rd edn rev), 1886 (8th edn), New York 1886, London 1892, 1896, 1904 (rev), 1906, 1919, New York 1921, London 1922 (enlarged); ed H. Kohn, New York 1961; tr Ger 1873; Fr 1890; Rus 1891.
REVIEW: [Freeman, E. A.] Saturday Rev 29 Oct 1864; North Br Rev 42 1865.
Report on the condition of education in Lancashire. 1867.
The academic study of the civil law: an inaugural lecture delivered at Oxford. 1871.
Trans-Caucasia and Ararat: being notes of a vacation tour in the autumn of 1876. 1877, 1877, 1896 (4th edn rev).
The trade marks registration act. 1877.
The predictions of Hamilton and de Tocqueville. Baltimore 1887.
Handbook of home rule: being articles on the Irish question. 1887. Ed Bryce.
The American commonwealth. 3 vols 1888, 2 vols 1888, 1889 (2nd edn rev), 1891, 1893–5 (3rd edn rev), 1895–6, 1 vol New York 1896 (abridged), 2 vols London 1899, 1 vol New York 1899, London 1906, 1934, 1958; 2 vols New York 1908 (with ch on the Tweed ring by R. R. Wilson), 2 vols New York 1910 (new edn rev), London 1914–15, 1918–19, 1922–3, 1924, 1926–7, 1931–3; ed L. M. Hacker 2 vols New York 1959; tr Rus 1889–90, Fr 1900–2, Croatian 1905–7, Sp 1912–14, Ital 1913. Selections: Chautauqua NY 1891 (as Social institutions of the United States); ed M. G. Fulton, New York 1918 (as Bryce on American democracy); ed H. S. Commager, New York 1961 (as Reflections on American institutions).
REVIEWS: [Dicey, A. V.] Edinburgh Rev 169 1889; [Acton, J. E. D.] EHR 4 1889; [Smith, Rev G.] Macmillan's Mag 59 1889; [Harrison, F.] Nineteenth Cent 25 1889.
The migrations of the races of men considered historically. 1893.
Legal studies in the University of Oxford: a valedictory lecture. 1893.
Impressions of South Africa. 1897, New York 1897, London 1898, 1900 (3rd edn); tr Ger 1900.
William Ewart Gladstone: his characteristics as man and statesman. 1898, New York 1898.
Studies in history and jurisprudence. 2 vols Oxford 1901, New York 1901.
Studies in contemporary biography. 1903, 1911, 1927.
The relations between the advanced and the backward races of mankind. Oxford 1903.
Constitutions. New York 1905; tr Sp 1952.
Marriage and divorce. New York 1905.
The hindrances to good citizenship. New Haven CT 1909.
South America: observations and impressions. 1912, New York 1912, 1913, London 1914 (rev), Detroit 1914, London 1916, New York 1917; tr Sp 1914, Portuguese 1920.
University and historical addresses delivered during a residence in the United States. New York 1913.
The ancient Roman Empire and the British Empire in India; the diffusion of Roman and English law throughout the world – two essays. Oxford 1914.
Neutral nations and the war. 1914; tr Sp 1914, Ger 1914.
The attitude of Great Britain in the present war. 1916; tr Fr 1916.
Proposals for the prevention of future wars. 1917.
Essays and addresses in war time. New York 1918.
Modern democracies. 2 vols 1921, New York 1921, London 1929, New York 1931; tr Cz 1927.
Canada: an actual democracy. Toronto 1921.
The study of American history. Cambridge 1921, New York 1922.

International relations: eight lectures. New York 1922.
Memories of travel. Ed Lady Bryce 1923, New York 1923.

Contributions to periodicals

For Bryce's contributions to periodicals, see Wellesley.

§2

McCarthy, J. In his British political portraits, 1903.
Morley, J. In his Recollections, 1917.
Fisher, H. A. L. Viscount Bryce. Proc Br Acad 12 1926.
Fisher, H. A. L. James Bryce. 2 vols 1927.
Bryce's American commonwealth: fiftieth anniversary. Ed R. C. Brooks, New York 1939. Includes reviews by Acton, Woodrow Wilson et al.
Toynbee, A. J. In his Acquaintances, 1967.

Henry Thomas Buckle 1821–62

Collected works

The works of Thomas Buckle. Ed H. Taylor 3 vols Bristol 1995.

§1

History of civilization in England. 2 vols 1857–61, 1858–64, New York 1860–2, 3 vols London 1866, 1867, 1868, 1869, 1871, 1873, 2 vols New York 1876, 3 vols London 1876, 3 vols London 1878, 2 vols New York 1883, 3 vols London 1885, 2 vols New York 1897, 3 vols 1903–4, Oxford 1931 (WC); ed J. M. Robertson 1904, 1925; ed A. Brisbane 4 vols New York 1913; tr Ger 1860, Rus 1862–4, 1895, Sp 1862, Fr 1865, Hungarian 1873–5; Hebrew 1901.
REVIEWS: Droysen, J. G., Grundiss der Historik, Berlin 1857, tr 1895; [Pattison, M.] Westminster Rev 68 1857; T. C. S[anders] Fraser's Mag Oct 1857; [Sanders, T. C.] Saturday Rev 11 July 1857; [Stephen, J. F.] Edinburgh Rev 107 1858; [Pollock, W. F.] Quart Rev 104 1858; [Smith, W. H.] Blackwood's Mag 84 1858; [Dallas, E. S.] The Times 20, 22–3 Aug 1861; G. H. L[ewes] Blackwood's Mag 90 1861; [McCarthy, J.] Westminster Rev July 1861; [Reeve, H.] Edinburgh Rev 114 1861.
The influence of women on the progress of knowledge. Fraser's Mag Apr 1858; tr Du 1872.
Mill on liberty. Fraser's Mag May 1859.
A letter to a gentleman respecting Pooley's case. 1859.
Essays; with a biographical sketch of the author. Leipzig 1867, New York 1877; tr Rus 1867.
Fragment on the reign of Elizabeth. Fraser's Mag Feb–Sep 1867.
Miscellaneous and posthumous works. Ed H. Taylor 3 vols 1872, 2 vols New York 1873; ed G. Allen 2 vols 1885 (abridged); ed J. M. Robertson 1904.

§2

Coleridge, J. D. Mr Buckle and Sir John Coleridge. Fraser's Mag June 1859.
Froude, J. A. The science of history. In his Short studies, 1867.
[Macdonell, J.] The natural history of morals. North Br Rev 47 1867.
Étienne, L. Le positivisme dans l'histoire. Revue des Deux Mondes 15 Mar 1868.
Stirling, J. H. Buckle: his problem and his metaphysics. North Amer Rev 115 1872.
[Dicey, A. V.] Buckle. Nation (New York) 17 Apr 1873.
Stirling, J. H. Mr Buckle and the Aufklärung. Jnl of Speculative Philosophy 9 1875.
[Wedgwood, J.] Buckle. Spectator 30 Oct 1875.
Huth, A. H. The life and writings of Buckle. 2 vols 1880, New York 1880.
Simcox, G. A. Buckle. Fortnightly Rev Feb 1880.
Stephen, L. An attempted philosophy of history. Fortnightly Rev May 1880.
Benn, A. W. Buckle and the economics of knowledge. Mind 6 1881.
Robertson, J. M. Buckle and his critics. 1895.
Clarke, J. F. In his Nineteenth-century questions, Boston 1900.
Fraenkel, F. Buckle und seine Geschichtsphilosophie. Berner Studien zur Philosophie 50 1906.
St Aubyn, G. A Victorian eminence: the life and works of Buckle. 1958.

Edward Bulwer-Lytton 1802–73

See col 1144.

Thomas Carlyle 1795–1881

See col 2086.

Julia Cartwright, later Mrs Henry Ady 1851–1924

§1

Mantegna and Francia. 1881, New York 1881, London 1896.
Francesca da Rimini. 1884.
The pilgrims' way from Winchester to Canterbury. 1893, 1895 (new edn), 1901, 1911, New York 1911, 1982.
Sacharissa. Some account of Dorothy Sidney, Countess of Sunderland. '1893' [1894], 1901 (3rd edn), New York 1901, 1926. Extracts originally appeared in Macmillan's Mag 55 1886, 57 1888.
Madame. A life of Henrietta, daughter of Charles I and Duchess of Orleans. '1894' [1893], New York 1894, London 1900, New York 1901 (3rd edn), 1907. Extracts originally appeared in Macmillan's Mag 62 1890.
Jules Bastien-Lepage. 1894.
Sir Edward Burne-Jones, Bart. His life and work. 1894.
The early work of Raphael. 1895, 1905, 1907 (rev), New York 1907.
Raphael. 1895, 1900, London and New York 1905, London 1907 (rev), 1914, Chicago 1915.
Raphael in Rome. 1895, 1896, 1907 (rev).
G. F. Watts, Royal Academician. His life and work. 1896.
Jean-François Millet. His life and letters. 1896, New York 1902, 1910; tr Ger 1903.
Beatrice d'Este, Duchess of Milan, 1475–1497. 1899, 1903.
The painters of Florence from the thirteenth to the sixteenth century. 1901, New York 1901, London 1910, New York 1911.
Sandro Botticelli. [1903], New York [1903], London 1904, 1914, New York 1915, London 1920.
Isabella d'Este, Marchioness of Mantua, 1474–1539. 2 vols 1903, New York 1903, London 1904 (2nd edn), New York 1904, 1905 (3rd edn), London 1907, New York 1910, London 1911, New York 1914, London 1915, New York 1923, 1926, London 1932; tr Fr 1912.
Baldassare Castiglione, the perfect courtier: his life and letters. 2 vols 1908, 1927, New York 1927.
Hampton Court. 1910.
Christina of Denmark, Duchess of Milan and Lorraine, 1522–1590. 1913, New York 1913.
Italian gardens of the Renaissance and other studies. 1914, New York 1914.

Diaries

A bright remembrance: the diaries of Julia Cartwright 1851–1924. Ed A. Emanuel, Foreword Sir John Hale, 1989.

Editions and introductions

de La Motte-Fouqué, F. H. C. Undine. Introd by J. Cartwright 1888.
Christ and his mother in Italian art. Ed J. Cartwright, introd by R. Eyton, 1897.
Howell, A. S. Bernardino of Siena. With a chapter on S. Bernardino in art by Julia Cartwright. 1913.
The journals of Lady Knightley. Ed J. Cartwright 1915.

Contributions to periodicals

For Julia Cartwright's contributions to the Nineteenth Cent, Macmillan's Mag, *the* Quart Rev, *the* National Rev, *and the* New Quart Mag, *see* Wellesley *vol 5 1989*.

Thomas Clarkson 1760–1846

Collections of Clarkson's papers are to be found in the BL, St John's College Cambridge, Atlanta Univ, Howard Univ (Washington DC) and the Huntington.

Bibliographies

Griggs, E. L. Clarkson: the friend of slaves. 1936. *See* pp. 199–204.

§1

An essay on the slavery and commerce of the human species. 1786, Philadelphia 1786, London 1788, Georgetown KY 1816.

An essay on the impolicy of the African slave trade. 1788, 1788 (rev).

A portraiture of Quakerism, as taken from a view of the moral education, discipline, peculiar customs, religious principles, political and civil œconomy and character of the Society of Friends. 3 vols 1806, New York 1806, London 1807 (3rd edn), Philadelphia 1808; ed R. Smeal, Glasgow 1869 (as A portraiture of the Christian profession and practice of the Society of Friends); tr Fr 1820.

The history of the rise, progress and accomplishment of the abolition of the African slave-trade. 2 vols 1808, Philadelphia 1808, 1 vol Wilmington DE 1816, 2 vols Augusta ME 1830, New York 1836, London 1839.
REVIEW: [Coleridge, S. T.] Edinburgh Rev 12 1808.

Memoirs of the private and public life of William Penn. 2 vols 1813, Philadelphia 1813, London 1814, Dover NH 1827; ed W. E. Forster London 1849, New York 1849.
REVIEW: [Jeffrey, F.] Edinburgh Rev 21 1813.

An essay on the doctrines and practice of the early Christians as they relate to war. 1817, 1818 (3rd edn).

The cries of Africa to the inhabitants of Europe. [1822]; tr Fr 1822, Sp 1823, Portuguese 1823.

Thoughts on the necessity for improving the condition of the slaves in the British colonies with a view to their ultimate emancipation. 1823, 1823 (rev), 1824 (4th edn).

Researches antediluvian, patriarchal and historical. 1836.

Strictures on a life of William Wilberforce; with a correspondence between Lord Brougham and Mr Clarkson. Ed H. C. Robinson 1838.
REVIEW: [Brougham, Rev H.] Edinburgh Rev 68 1838.

Henry Christophe and Clarkson: a correspondence. Ed E. L. Griggs and C. H. Prater, Berkeley 1952.

§2

Stephen, J. Life of William Wilberforce. Edinburgh Rev 67 1838.

Wilberforce, R. I. and S. In their Life of William Wilberforce, 1838.

Wilberforce, R. I. and S. The correspondence of William Wilberforce. 1840.

Elmes, J. Clarkson: a monograph. 1854.

Griggs, E. L. Clarkson: the friend of slaves. 1936.

Wilson, E. G. Thomas Clarkson: a biography. 1989.

Mandell Creighton 1843–1901

Bibliographies

Shaw, W. A. A bibliography of the historical works of Dr Creighton, Dr Stubbs, Dr S. R. Gardiner and Lord Acton. 1903.

Creighton, L. Life and letters of Creighton. 2 vols 1904. *See* vol 2 pp. 517–22.

§1

History of Rome. 1875, 1877 (3rd edn), 1885 (10th edn), Toronto 1899, London 1912; tr Sp 1881; Fr 1885.

The Tudors and the Reformation. 1876, New York 1877.

The age of Elizabeth. 1876, Boston 1876, New York 1887, London 1890, 1892 (9th edn), 1899, New York 1928, London 1930.

Epochs of English history. 10 vols 1876–95. Ed Creighton.

Historical biographies. 9 vols 1876–93. Ed Creighton.

The shilling history of England: being an introductory volume to Epochs of English history. 1879, New York 1879 (as The half-hour history of England); ed L. Creighton 1904.

A history of the Papacy during the period of the Reformation. 5 vols 1882–94, 1887–94 (rev), 6 vols 1897 (as History of the Papacy from the Great Schism to the sack of Rome), New York 1902–4, London 1919.
REVIEW: [Lord Acton] EHR 2 1887.

Memoir of Sir George Grey. Newcastle upon Tyne 1884 (priv ptd); ed E. Grey 1901.

Epochs of church history. 16 vols 1886–98. Ed Creighton.

Cardinal Wolsey. 1888; ed H. Ketcham, New York 1903; London 1904.

Carlisle. 1889, 1889 (Historic Towns ser).

Persecution and tolerance. Hulsean lectures 1893–4. 1895.

The early renaissance in England. Rede lecture 1895. Cambridge 1895.

Queen Elizabeth. 1896, Paris 1896, 1899, New York 1899, London 1920, 1927, Leipzig 1943.

The heritage of the spirit and other sermons. 1896, 1913.

The story of some English shires. 1898.

Lessons from the cross: addresses. 1898.

The abolition of the Roman jurisdiction. 1899, 1899, New York 1899.

The Church and the nation: charges and addresses. Ed L. Creighton 1901.

Counsels of churchpeople. Ed J. H. Burn 1901.

Historical essays and reviews. Ed L. Creighton 1902, 1902.

Thoughts on education: speeches and sermons. Ed L. Creighton 1902; ed E. A. Knox 1906 (abridged).

Historical lectures and addresses. Ed L. Creighton 1903.

University and other sermons. Ed L. Creighton 1903.

The mind of St Peter and other sermons. Ed L. Creighton 1904.

Counsel for the young: extracts from letters. Ed L. Creighton 1905.

Life of Simon de Montfort. 1905.

The claims of the common life: sermons preached in Merton College chapel 1871–4. 1905.

Contributions to periodicals

For a list of Creighton's periodical articles and reviews, see Wellesley. *Creighton also edited the* EHR *1886–91.*

Letters

Creighton, L. Life and letters of Creighton. 2 vols 1904.

de Janösi, F. E. Correspondence between Acton and Creighton. Cambridge Historical Jnl 6 1940.

§2

Creighton and Stubbs. Church Quart Rev 61 1905.

Paul, H. In his Stray leaves, 1906.

Strachey, L. In his Portraits in miniature, 1931.

Albert Venn Dicey 1835–1922

§1

The Privy Council. Arnold prize essay 1860. Oxford 1860, London 1887.

A treatise on the rules for the selection of parties in an action. 1870; ed J. H. Truman, New York 1876; London 1886; ed J. B. Moore, New York 1896.

The law of domicil. 1879; tr Fr 1887–8.

Can English law be taught at the universities? An inaugural lecture (Oxford 1883). 1883.

Lectures introductory to the study of the law of the constitution. 1885, 1889 (3rd edn rev as Introduction to the study of the law of the constitution), 1893, 1897, 1902, 1908, 1915 (8th edn), 1923, 1931; ed C. S. Wade 1939, 1959 (10th edn), 1960; introd by E. Wade 1985; tr Fr 1902, Rus 1905–7, Chinese 1930.
England's case against Home Rule. 1886, 1887 (3rd edn), 1887 (as Why England maintains the union).
Letters on unionist delusions. 1887.
The verdict: a trace on the political significance of the report of the Parnell Commission. 1890.
A leap in the dark: or our new constitution. 1893, 1911.
A digest of the laws of England with reference to the conflict of laws. 1896, Boston 1896, London 1908; ed A. B. Keith 1922 (3rd edn), 1927, 1932; ed J. H. C. Morris 1949 (6th edn as Conflict of laws), 1958, 1987 (11th edn).
Lectures on the relation between law and public opinion in England during the nineteenth century. 1905, 1914, 1920, 1924, 1930; ed E. C. S. Wade 1962; tr Fr 1906.
Letters to a friend on votes for women. 1909, 1912.
A fool's paradise: being a constitutionalist's criticism of the Home Rule Bill of 1912. 1913.
The statesmanship of Wordsworth. Oxford 1917.
Thoughts on the union between England and Scotland. 1920. With R. S. Rait.

Contributions to periodicals

For a list of Dicey's periodical reviews and articles, see Wellesley.

§2

Rait, R. S. Memorials of Dicey. 1925.
Holdsworth, W. S. In his Historians of Anglo-American law, New York 1928.
Lawson, F. H. Dicey revisited. Political Stud 7 1959.
Ford, T. Albert Venn Dicey: the man and his times. Chichester 1985.

Isaac D'Israeli 1766–1848

See col 2139.

Hon Mountstuart Elphinstone 1779–1859

Elphinstone's jnls, letters and dispatches are in the India Office lib.

§1

An account of the kingdom of Caubul and its dependencies in Persia, Tartary and India. 1815, 2 vols 1819, 2 vols 1839 (rev); tr Fr 1817, Ger 1817.
Report on the territories conquered from the Paishwa. Submitted to the supreme government of British India. Calcutta 1821, Bombay 1838 (rptd).
Opinions of the Hon Mountstuart Elphinstone upon some of the leading questions connected with the government of British India. Ed by the author of An enquiry into the causes of the stationary condition of India. 1831.
The history of India. 2 vols 1841, 1843, 1849, 1857 (4th edn), Bombay 1861, London 1866 (5th edn with notes and additions by E. B. Cowell), 1889 (7th edn), 1905 (9th edn); tr Gujarati 1851, Urdu 1866; 1847 Biographical extracts ed Krishnamohana Vandyopadhyaya.
REVIEW: [H. H. Milman] Quart Rev 68 1841.
Selected minutes by the Hon Mountstuart Elphinstone, in the Military department, 1820–1827. In Selections from the records of the Bombay government n.s. 104 1867.
Selections from the minutes and other official writings of M. E., governor of Bombay. With an introductory memoir. Ed G. W. Forrest 1884.
The rise of British power in the East by the late Hon M. Elphinstone, being a continuation of his history of India. Ed E. Colebrooke 1887.

§2

Colebrooke, E. Life of the Honourable Mountstuart Elphinstone. 2 vols 1884.
Strachey, E. Mountstuart Elphinstone. Quart Rev 157 1884.
Choskey, R. D. Mountstuart Elphinstone: the Indian years 1796–1827. Bombay 1971.
Varma, Sushma J. Mountstuart Elphinstone in Maharaschtra 1801–26. Calcutta 1981.

George Finlay 1799–1875

Bibliographies

Miller, W. The Finlay papers. EHR 39 1924.

§1

The Hellenic kingdom and the Greek nation. 1836; ed S. G. Howe, Boston 1837.
Remarks on the topography of Oropia and Diacria. Athens 1838; tr Ger 1842.
Greece under the Romans. Edinburgh 1844, 1857; ed V. R. Reynolds 1907, 1927 (EL).
ΕΠΙΣΤΟΛΗ ΠΡΟΣ ΤΟΥΣ ΑΘΗΝΑΙΟΥΣ. Athens 1844. On the site of the Holy Sepulchre. 1847.
The history of Greece from its conquest by the Crusaders to its conquest by the Turks, and of the empire of Trebizond 1204–1461. Edinburgh 1851.
History of the Byzantine and Greek empires 716–1453. 2 vols Edinburgh 1853–4, London 1855, 1 vol Edinburgh 1856 (2nd edn: 716–1507); Byzantine empire, ed V. R. Reynolds 1906, 1935 (EL).
REVIEW: [Freeman, E. A.] North Br Rev 21 1854.
The history of Greece under Ottoman and Venetian domination. Edinburgh 1856; tr Greek 1958.
REVIEW: [Freeman, E. A.] Edinburgh Rev 103 1856.
History of the Greek revolution. 2 vols Edinburgh 1861.
Objects found in Greece in the collection of G. Finlay. Athens 1869.
A history of Greece from its conquest by the Romans to the present time BC 146 to AD 1864. Ed H. F. Tozer 7 vols Oxford 1877. Includes Greece under the Romans, Byzantine and Greek empires, and Greece under Othoman and Venetian domination.
REVIEWS: [Freeman, E. A.] Br Quart Rev 68 1878; [Mahaffy, J. P.] Contemporary Rev Mar 1878; [Hodgkin, T.] Edinburgh Rev 148 1878.

Finlay also contributed letters from Greece to The Times *1864–70, and to* Blackwood's Mag *1842–63 (see* Wellesley*).*

§2

Autobiography. In his History of Greece vol 1, ed H. F. Tozer, Oxford 1877.
Miller, W. Finlay as a journalist. EHR 39 1924.

William Warde Fowler 1847–1921

Col Barrow's ms log-book in the Bodleian contains many entries by Fowler.

Bibliography

Coon, R. H. William Warde Fowler. 1934.

§1

Home and college: two lectures on education. 1882 (priv ptd).
Historical study in Oxford: its progress and value. 1885 (priv ptd).
A year with the birds. By an Oxford tutor. Oxford 1886, 1886 (2nd edn enlarged), 1889 (3rd edn enlarged), 1925.
Tales of the birds. 1888, 1889 (2nd edn), 1901 (school edn), 1909.
Julius Caesar and the foundation of the Roman imperial system.

New York 1891, London 1892, New York 1907 (2nd edn), London 1928 (new edn), 1931; tr Fr 1931.
The city-state of the Greeks and Romans. A survey introductory to the study of ancient history. 1893, New York 1893, London 1910 (Macmillan's manuals for students), 1952 (rptd).
The marsh warbler in Oxfordshire and Switzerland. Oxford 1893.
Summer studies of birds and books. 1895.
The Roman festivals of the period of the Republic. An introduction to the study of the religion of the Romans. 1899, 1916, 1925.
A brief memoir of John Cooke Fowler. By W. W. F. Oxford 1901 (priv ptd).
The museum and the park: a letter to the Rev Vice-Chancellor. Oxford 1901.
More tales of the birds. 1902.
Social life at Rome in the age of Cicero. 1908, New York 1909, London 1937 (rptd).
Theodor Mommsen, his life and work. Edinburgh 1909.
Stray notes on Mozart and his music. 1910 (priv ptd).
The religious experience of the Roman people from the earliest times to the age of Augustus. The Gifford lectures for 1909–10. 1911, 1922, 1933.
Rome. In Home univ lib of modern knowledge, 1911, 1912, New York 1912, 1921, London 1947 (2nd edn rev M. P. Charlesworth), 1952.
A concluding lecture on the Roman revolution. 1912(?) (priv ptd).
Kingham old and new: studies in a rural parish. Oxford 1913.
Roman ideas of deity in the last century before the Christian era. 1914.
Virgil's gathering of the clans: being observations on Aeneid VII, 601–817. 1916, 1918 (rev).
Essays in brief for war time. Oxford 1916, 1917.
Aeneas at the site of Rome: observations on the eighth book of the Aeneid. Oxford 1917, 1918 (2nd edn rev), 1931.
The death of Turnus. Observations on the twelfth book of the Aeneid. Oxford 1919, 1927.
Roman essays and interpretations. Oxford 1920.
Reminiscences. 1921 (priv ptd).

Contributions to periodicals and collaborative works

The matriculation examination of the University of London. In Essays on secondary education, ed Christopher Cookson, 1898.
For Fowler's numerous ornithological contributions to Macmillan's Mag, *see* Wellesley. *For articles in the* Classical Rev, EHR, Oxford Mag *and other academic and ornithological articles, see Coon's biography, below.*

Editions, prefaces, introductions

White, Gilbert. The natural history and antiquities of Selbourne. 1901. Ed Fowler with L. C. Miall.
An Oxford correspondence of 1903. Oxford 1904. Ed Fowler.
Irwin, S. T. Clifton school addresses. With an introduction by W. W. Fowler. 1912.
Royds, T. F. The beasts, birds and bees of Virgil. With a preface by W. W. Fowler. Oxford 1914.
Eliot, George. Scenes of clerical life. 1916. Ed Fowler and E. Limouzin.

§2

Coon, R. H. William Warde Fowler. 1934.

Sir James George Frazer 1854–1941

The Frazer collection of mss is in the BL.

Bibliographies

Besterman, T. A bibliography of Frazer. 1934.

§1

C. Sallusti Crispi Catalina et Jugurtha. 1884. Ed Frazer.
Totemism. Edinburgh 1887; tr Fr 1898.
The golden bough: a study in comparative religion. 2 vols 1890, New York 1890, 3 vols London 1900 (rev), New York 1900, 12 vols London 1906–15 (as The golden bough: a study in magic and religion: vols 1–2 The magic art and the evolution of kings, 1911; vol 3 Taboo and the perils of the soul, 1911; vol 4 The dying god, 1911; vols 5–6 Adonis, Attis, Osiris, 1914; vols 7–8 Spirits of the corn and the wild, 1912; vol 9 The scapegoat, 1913; vols 10–11 Balder the beautiful, 1913; vol 12 Bibliography and general index, 1915), 1914–17, 1925–30, New York 1935, London 1936–7, New York 1951, 13 vols London 1955 (with Aftermath – *see below*); 1 vol 1922 (abridged by Lady Frazer with Frazer's assistance), New York 1922, London 1923, 1924, 1925, New York 1927, London 1929, 2 vols New York 1929, 1 vol London 1932, 1940, New York 1951, London 1959, 1975 (reprint of 1929), illus 1978, now abridged and ed R. Frazer 1994 (WC); chs 1–7 ed G. M. Trevelyan 1944 (as Magic and religion); ed T. H. Gaster, New York 1959, 1965 (as The new Golden bough); tr Fr 1903–11, 1923, Ital 1925, Swed 1925, Ger 1928. REVIEWS: [Lyall, A.] Edinburgh Rev 172 1890; [Marindin, G. E.] Quart Rev 172 1891; [Jevons, F. B.] Edinburgh Rev 194 1901; [Lang, A.] Fortnightly Rev Feb 1901, Apr 1901.
Leaves from The golden bough culled by Lady Frazer. 1924, New York 1924; tr Fr 1925.
Passages of the Bible chosen for their literary beauty and interest. 1895, 1909, 1927. Ed Frazer.
Pausanias, Description of Greece. 6 vols 1898. Tr and ed Frazer.
The origin of totemism. Fortnightly Rev Apr–May 1899. Reply by A. Lang, Mr Frazer's theory of totemism, June 1899.
Pausanias and other Greek sketches. 1900, 1917 (as Studies in Greek scenery, legend and history); tr Fr 1922.
Lectures on the early history of the kingship. 1905, 1920 (as The magical origin of kings); tr Fr 1920.
Adonis, Attis, Osiris: studies in the history of oriental religion. 1906, 1907, 1914 (as vols 5–6 of Golden bough, *above*), New York 1962; Adonis, 1932; tr Fr 1921, 1926.
Questions on the customs, briefs and languages of savages. Cambridge 1907.
The scope of social anthropology. 1908, 1927 (with The devil's advocate, *below*).
Psyche's task: a discourse concerning the influence of superstitions as the growth of institutions. 1909, 1913, 1920, 1927 (as The devil's advocate: a plea for superstition), 1928.
Totemism and exogamy: a treatise on certain early forms of superstition and society. 4 vols 1910; tr Fr 1923.
The letters of William Cowper. 2 vols 1912. Ed Frazer.
The belief in immorality and the worship of the dead. Vol 1 (Gifford lectures 1911–12), 1913; vol 2, 1922; vol 3, 1924.
Essays of Joseph Addison. 2 vols 1915. Ed Frazer.
Folk-lore in the Old Testament: studies in comparative religion, legend and law. 3 vols 1918, 1919, 1919, 1 vol 1923 (abridged), New York 1923, London 1927, New York 1927; tr Fr 1924, Ger 1960.
Sir Roger de Coverley and other literary pieces. 1920, 1927 (as The gorgon's head); tr Fr 1922.
Apollodorus, The library. 2 vols 1921 (Loeb Lib). Tr and ed Frazer.
Sur Ernest Renan. Paris 1923.
Frazer: selected passages from his works. Ed G. Roth, Paris 1924.
The worship of nature. 1926, New York 1926; tr Fr 1927.
The gorgon's head and other literary pieces. 1927.
Man, god and immortality: passages chosen by Pierre Sayn from the writings of Frazer, revised and edited by the author. 1927, New York 1927; tr Fr 1928, Du 1929, Ger 1932.
Publii Ovidii Nasonis Fastorum libri sex. 5 vols 1929, 1 vol 1931 (Loeb Lib).
Myths of the origin of fire. 1930, 1930, New York 1942; tr Sp 1942, New York 1974.
The growth of Plato's ideal theory. 1930.
Garnered sheaves: essays, addresses and reviews. 1931.

The fear of the dead in primitive religion. 3 vols 1933–6.
Condorcet on the progress of the human mind. Zaharoff lecture 1933. Oxford 1933.
Creation and evolution in primitive cosmogonies, and other pieces. 1935.
Aftermath: a supplement to The golden bough. 1936, New York 1937, London 1951, 1955 (as vol 12 of Golden bough).
Totemica: a supplement to Totemism and exogamy. 1937.
Greece and Rome: a selection from the works of Frazer. Ed S. G. Owen 1937.
Pasha the pom: the story of a little dog. Philadelphia 1937. With Lady Frazer.
Anthologia anthropologica. Ed R. A. Downie 4 vols 1938, 1939. Extracts from Frazer's notebooks.
Frazer and the age of science. 1992. Extracts.

§2

Downie, R. A. James George Frazer: the portrait of a scholar. 1940.
Malinowski, B. A scientific theory of culture and other essays. Chapel Hill NC 1944.
Wittgenstein, L. Remarks on Frazer's The golden bough. Ed and tr R. Rhees and A. C. Miles, Retford, Nottinghamshire 1979.
Ackerman, R. J. G. Frazer: his life and work. Cambridge 1987, 1990.

Edward Augustus Freeman 1823–92

Letters and drafts by Freeman are in the Bodleian.

Bibliographies

Stephens, W. R. W. The life and letters of Freeman. 2 vols 1895. *See* vol 2 pp. 481–91.

§1

Principles of church restoration. 1846.
Thoughts on the study of history with reference to the proposed changes in the public examinations. Oxford 1849.
Remarks on the nomenclature of Gothic architecture. Oxford 1849.
A history of architecture. 1849.
Poems: legendary and historical. 1850. With G. W. Cox.
On Anglo-Saxon remains in Iver church, Bucks. Archaeological Jnl [1850].
Remarks on the architecture of Llandaff Cathedral, with an essay towards the history of the fabric. 1850.
Notes on the archaeological antiquities of the district of Gower. [From the Archaeologica Cambriensis] 1850.
An essay on the origin and development of window tracery in England. Oxford 1850–1.
The preservation and restoration of ancient monuments. Oxford 1852.
Suggestions with regard to certain proposed changes in the University and colleges of Oxford. Oxford 1854. With F. H. Dickinson.
The history and antiquities of St David's. 1856. With W. B. Jones.
The history and conquests of the Saracens. Six lectures. Oxford 1856.
Ancient Greece and mediaeval Italy. In Oxford essays by members of the University, Oxford 1857.
Parliamentary reform. Cardiff 1859.
The parish church and priory. In G. F. Townsend, The town and borough of Leominster, Leominster [1863].
The new examination statute. [Signed E. A. F.] Oxford 1863.
History of federal government: general introduction; history of the Greek federations. London and Cambridge 1863; ed J. B. Bury 1893 (as History of federal government in Greece and Italy).
The history of the Norman Conquest of England; its causes and its results. 6 vols Oxford 1867–79, vols 1–3 1870–5 (2nd edn), 6 vols New York 1873–80, vols 1–2 Oxford 1877 (3rd edn).
REVIEWS: [Norton, C. E.] North Amer Rev 105 1867; [Lord Carnarvon] Quart Rev 123 1867; [Green, J. R.] Saturday Rev 13, 27 Apr 1867, 15–29 Aug 1868, 3–10 Feb 1872; [Fann, J. H. C.] Edinburgh Rev 130 1869; [Bryce, J.] Bentley's Quart Rev July 1870.
Old English history for children. 1869, 1881, 1892 (9th edn), 1911 (EL).
Old English history for younger students. 1870.
History of the Cathedral Church of Wells. 1870.
Owens College extension. 1870. Speech.
Historical essays. 1871, 1896 (5th edn); Historical essays: second ser, 1873, 1880, 1889; Historical essays: third ser, 1879; Historical essays: fourth ser, 1892.
The growth of the English constitution from the earliest times. 1872, Leipzig 1872, London 1894, 1898; tr Fr 1877, Hungarian 1893.
General sketch of European history. 1872, 1873 (3rd edn), New York 1874, London 1905 (5th edn), 1910; tr Sp 1885.
The unity of history. Rede lecture 1872. 1872, 1873 (with Comparative politics, *below*).
The cathedral churches of the old foundation. In Essays on cathedrals, ed J. S. Howson, 1872.
Comparative politics. 1873 (with The unity of history, *above*), 1896.
Disestablishment and disendowment: what are they? 1874, 1885.
History of Europe. 1876, 1877, 1884, New York 1884; ed F. J. C. Hearnshaw 1926; tr Fr 1929.
Historical and architectural sketches, chiefly Italian. 1876.
The eastern question in its historical bearings: an address. Manchester 1876.
The Ottoman power in Europe. 1877, New York 1877.
The Turks in Europe. 1877, New York 1877.
The origin of the English nation. New York 1879.
How the study of history is let and hindered: an address. [1879.]
A short history of the Norman Conquest of England. Oxford 1880, 1896, 1901.
Sketches from the subject and neighbour lands of Venice. 1881.
The historical geography of Europe. 2 vols 1881, 1882; ed J. B. Bury 2 vols 1903.
Lectures to American audiences. Philadelphia 1882.
The reign of William Rufus and the accession of Henry the First. 2 vols Oxford 1882.
Some impressions of the United States. 1883.
An introduction to American institutional history. Johns Hopkins Univ Stud in Historical & Political Science 1 1883.
English towns and districts: addresses and sketches. 1883.
Farren, R. Cathedral cities: Ely and Norwich. Cambridge 1883. Introds by Freeman.
The office of the historical professor: inaugural lecture. 1884, 1886 (with The methods of historical study, *below*).
The methods of historical study. 1886; tr Rus 1893, Hungarian 1895.
The chief periods of European history: six lectures with an essay on Greek cities under Roman rule. 1886.
Greater Greece and greater Britain; George Washington the expander of England: two lectures. 1886.
Exeter. 1887 (Historic Towns ser).
Four Oxford lectures 1887: Fifty years of European history; Teutonic conquest in Gaul and Britain. 1888.
William the Conqueror. 1888, 1894; ed H. Ketcham, New York 1902.
Sketches from French travel. Leipzig 1891.
The history of Sicily from the earliest times. 4 vols Oxford 1891–4; tr Ger 1895–1901. Vol 4 ed A. J. Evans.
Sicily: Phoenician, Greek and Roman. 1892.
The physical and political bases of national unity. In Brittannic Confederation, ed A. S. White, 1892.
Studies of travel: Greece, Italy. 2 vols New York [1893].
Farren, R. Cathedral cities: York, Lincoln and Beverley. Cambridge 1896. Introds by Freeman.
Sketches of travel in Normandy and Maine. Ed W. H. Hutton 1897.
Western Europe in the fifth century: an aftermath. 1904.

Western Europe in the eighth century and onward: an aftermath. 1904.

Contributions to periodicals

For a list of Freeman's reviews, see Wellesley. *Also see* Waybourne church, Norfolk, *rptd from* GM 1860; Froude's History of England, Saturday Rev 16–30 Jan 1864, 27 Oct, 3, 24 Nov, 1 Dec 1866, 22–9 Jan, 5–12 Feb 1870, 8, 29 Sep 1877 *(all anon)*; Mr Froude's Life and times of Thomas Becket, Contemporary Rev 31–2 June 1878; *reply by Froude*, Nineteenth Century 5 1879; *rejoinder by Freeman*, Contemporary Rev 35 1879; Pearson's Early and Middle Ages of England, Fortnightly Rev 9 1868; *reply by Pearson entitled* A short answer to Mr Freeman's strictures 1868. *For further attributed* Saturday Rev *articles, see* M. M. Bevington, The Saturday Review, New York 1941.

§2

Bryce, J. Freeman as a historian. Nation 12 May 1892.
[Bryce, J.] The late Professor Freeman. Nation 5 May 1892.
[Doyle, J. A.] Freeman, Froude and Seeley. Quart Rev 182 1895.
Stephens, W. R. W. The life and letters of Freeman. 2 vols 1895.
Harrison, F. The historical method of Freeman. Nineteenth Cent Nov 1898; rptd in his Tennyson, Ruskin, Mill and other literary estimates, 1899.
Friske, J. In his A century of science and other essays, Boston 1899.
Bryce, J. In his Studies in contemporary biography, 1903.
Cronne, H. A. Freeman 1823–92. History 28 1943.
Norton, B. Freeman's life, highlights, chronology, letters and works. Farnborough 1990.

James Anthony Froude 1818–94

Bibliographies

Goetzman, R. James Anthony Froude: a bibliography of studies. New York and London 1977.

§1

The influence of the science of political economy on the moral and social welfare of a nation, a prize essay. Oxford 1842.
St Neot. In Lives of the English saints, 4 vols 1844–5; ed A. W. Hutton 6 vols 1900–1. Ser suggested by J. H. Newman.
Shadows of the clouds, by Zeta. 1847.
A sermon preached at St Mary Church on the death of the Rev George May Coleridge. Torquay 1847.
The nemesis of faith. 1848, 1849, New York 1879, London 1892, 1903; introd by R. Ashton 1988.
The book of Job. 1854. Rptd from Westminster Rev 60 1853.
Goethe, J. W. Novels and tales. 1854. Tr Froude.
Suggestions on the best means of teaching English History. In Oxford essays by members of the University, Oxford 1855.
History of England from the fall of Wolsey to the death of Elizabeth. 12 vols 1856–70 (vols 1–2 rev 1858; vols 1–4, 7–8 rev 1862–4), 12 vols New York 1865–70, 2 vols New York 1867–8, London 1870 (as History of England from the fall of Wolsey to the defeat of the Spanish Armada), New York 1870, London 1875, 1881, 1893, New York 1899; ed W. L. Williams 10 vols London 1909–12 (EL).
REVIEWS: [Kingsley, C.] North Br Rev 26 1856; [Goldwin Smith] Edinburgh Rev July 1858; Maurice, F. D., Macmillan's Mag 2 1860; [Dallas, E. S.] The Times 31 Aug–1 Sep 1860; [Goldwin Smith] Edin Rev 119 1864; [Kingsley, C.] Macmillan's May 9 1864; [Freeman, E. A.] Saturday Rev 16–30 Jan 1864, 27 Oct, 3, 24 Nov, 1 Dec 1866, 22–9 Jan, 5–12 Feb 1870, 8, 29 Sep 1877. Attacks on Froude's History: [Burrows, M.] Quart Rev 128 1870; [Reeve, H.] Edinburgh Rev 131 1870; [Freeman, E. A.] Mr Froude's Life and times of Thomas Becket, Contemporary Rev 31–2 1878; reply by Froude, A few words on Mr Freeman, Nineteenth Cent Apr 1879; rejoinder by Freeman, Last words on Mr Froude, Contemporary Rev 35 1879; [Oliphant, M. W.] Mr Froude and Queen Mary, Blackwood's Mag 107 1870.
Thomas, W. The pilgrim: a dialogue on the life and actions of King Henry the eighth. 1861. Ed Froude.
The influence of the Reformation on the Scottish character. Address delivered before the Philosophical Institution of Edinburgh. 1865.
Short studies on great subjects. 2 vols 1867, New York 1868, London 1872; ed H. Belloc 1915 (EL); Oxford 1924 (WC); Second ser 1871, New York 1872; Third ser 1877, New York 1882; Fourth ser 1883, New York 1883. Collected 3 vols London 1877 (with preface), New York 1878, 4 vols London 1883, New York 1883, 5 vols London 1907.
Inaugural address delivered to the University of St Andrews 19 March 1869. 1869.
The cat's pilgrimage. Edinburgh 1870; ed O. Maurer, New Haven CT 1949.
Calvinism: an address delivered to the University of St Andrews 17 March 1871. 1871.
The English in Ireland in the eighteenth century. 3 vols 1872–4, New York 1873–4, London 1881, New York 1888.
REVIEWS: [Croskerry, T.] Edinburgh Rev 139 1874; [Cairns, J. E.] Fortnightly Rev Aug 1874.
The life and times of Thomas Becket. New York 1878. Rptd from Nineteenth Cent June–Nov 1877.
REVIEW: [Freeman, E. A.] Contemporary Rev 31–2 1878.
Caesar: a sketch. 1879, New York 1879, London 1880, New York 1884, London 1894, New York 1895, London 1903, 1937; tr Cz 1884.
Science and theology ancient and modern. Toronto 1879, New York 1880 (in Theological unrest: discussions in science and religion).
Bunyan. 1880 (EML), New York 1880, London 1884, New York 1887, London 1894, New York 1895, London 1905.
Two lectures on South Africa delivered before the Philosophical Institute. Edinburgh 1880; ed M. Froude 1900.
Carlyle, Thomas. Reminiscences. 2 vols 1881. Ed Froude.
Thomas Carlyle: a history of the first forty years of his life 1795–1835. 2 vols 1882, 1882, New York 1882, 1 vol New York 1882, 2 vols London 1890, 1891; tr Ger 1886.
Luther: a short biography. 1883, 1884, New York 1884.
Memorials of Jane Welsh Carlyle, prepared for publication by Thomas Carlyle. 3 vols 1883. Ed Froude.
Historical and other sketches. Ed D. H. Wheeler, New York 1883.
Thomas Carlyle: a history of his life in London 1834–81. 2 vols 1884, 1884, New York 1884, London 1890, 1979 (abridged); tr Ger 1886.
REVIEW: [Harrison, F.] North Amer Rev 140 1885.
Oceana: or England and her colonies. 1886, 1887, New York 1887.
The Knights Templars. New York 1886.
My relations with Carlyle: together with a letter from the late Sir James Stephen. 1886; ed A. A. Froude and M. Froude 1903, 1903, New York 1903.
The English in the West Indies: or the bow of Ulysses. 1888, 1900, New York 1900.
Liberty and property: an address to the Liberty and Property Defence. 1888.
The two chiefs of Dunboy: or an Irish romance of the last century. 1889, New York 1889.
Lord Beaconsfield. 1890, New York 1890, London 1905 (9th edn), 1906, 1931 (EL).
The divorce of Catherine of Aragon: being a supplement to the History of England. 1891, New York 1891.
REVIEW: [Jessopp, A.] EHR 7 1892.
The Spanish story of the Armada and other essays. 1892, Leipzig 1892, New York 1892, London 1896; ed A. L. Rowse, Gloucester 1988.
Life and letters of Erasmus. 1893, 1894, New York 1894; tr Du 1896.
Lectures on the Council of Trent. 1893, 1896, New York 1896.

English seamen in the sixteenth century. 1895, New York 1895, London 1901; ed A. A. Froude 1923, 1925.
Selected essays. Ed H. G. Rawlinson 1900.
The dissolution of the monasteries and other essays. 1905.
A siding at a railway station: an allegory. 1905.

Contributions to periodicals

For a list of Froude's reviews and articles, see Wellesley, *vol 5 1989.*

Letters

Letters of J. A. Froude. Ed R. M. Bennett, Jnl Rutgers Univ Lib 11–12 1947–8, 25–6 1961–2.

§2

Meline, J. F. Mary Queen of Scots and her latest English historian. New York 1872.
Thumping English lies: Froude's slanders on Ireland and Irishmen. New York 1872.
Fisher, H. A. L. Modern historians and their methods. Fortnightly Rev Dec 1894.
Skelton, J. Reminiscences of Froude. Blackwood's Mag Dec 1894–Jan 1895; rptd in his Table talk of Shirley: reminiscences of and letters from Froude, Edinburgh 1895.
Smith, Goldwin. Froude. North Amer Rev 159 1894.
Strachey, St Loe. Mr Froude. Spectator 27 Oct 1894.
[Doyle, J. A.] Freeman, Froude and Seeley. Quart Rev 182 1895.
Harrison, F. The historical method of Froude. Nineteenth Cent Sep 1898; rptd in his Tennyson, Ruskin, Mill and other literary estimates, 1899.
Wilson, D. A. Mr Froude and Carlyle. 1898.
Stephen, L. In his Studies of a biographer, 1902.
Crichton-Browne, J. The nemesis of Froude. 1903. A reply to Froude's My relations with Carlyle, *above.*
Paul, H. The life of Froude. 1905.
Dawson, W. J. In his Makers of English prose, New York 1906.
McNeill, R. Froude and Freeman. Monthly Rev Feb 1906.
Smith, Goldwin. Froude as a historian. Atlantic Monthly May 1906.
Cecil, A. In his Six Oxford thinkers, 1909.
Wilson, D. A. The truth about Carlyle. 1913.
Hone, J. M. The imperialisation of Froude. New Statesman 1 June 1918.
Stewart, H. L. Froude and Anglo-Catholicism. Amer Jnl of Theology 22 1918.
Dunn, W. H. James Anthony Froude: a biography. Oxford 1961.

Samuel Rawson Gardiner 1829–1902

Gardiner's letters and notebooks are in the Bodleian.

Bibliographies

Shaw, W. A. A bibliography of the historical works of Dr Creighton, Dr Stubbs, Dr S. R. Gardiner and Lord Acton. 1903.

§1

History of England from the accession of James I to the disgrace of Chief-Justice Coke 1603–16. 2 vols 1863.
Prince Charles and the Spanish marriage 1617–23. 2 vols 1869.
A history of England under the Duke of Buckingham and Charles I 1624–28. 2 vols 1875.
The personal government of Charles I: a history of England from the assassination of the Duke of Buckingham to the declaration of the judges on ship-money 1628–37. 2 vols 1877.
The fall of the monarchy of Charles I 1637–49 [–42]. 2 vols 1882.
REVIEW: [Seeley, J. R.] Academy 21 1882.
History of England from the accession of James I to the outbreak of the Civil War 1603–42. 10 vols 1883–4, 1883–6, 1894–6, 1900–8. A collected edn of the 5 works listed above.
REVIEW: [Seeley, J. R.] Academy 31 1887.
The Thirty Years' War. 1874, 1886 (7th edn), New York 1889, London 1903 (13th edn).
The first two Stuarts and the Puritan revolution 1603–60. 1876, Boston 1876, New York 1886, London 1888 (8th edn), New York 1890, London 1902 (15th edn), 1928 (23rd edn), 1930.
REVIEW: [Cordery, B. M.] Edinburgh Rev 143 1876.
English history for students. 1881, New York 1881. With J. B. Mullingar.
Introduction to the study of English history. 1881, 1882, 1894, 1903. With J. B. Mullingar.
Outline of English history. 2 vols 1881, 1896, 1901, 1912; ed D. Salmon 1919, 1927.
Illustrated English history. 3 vols 1883, vol 1 1887 (5th edn); vol 3 1902 (continued to 1901), 1912 (continued to 1910).
Historical biographies. 1884, 1906.
An easy history of England. 1887–8.
The constitutional documents of the Puritan revolution 1628–60. Oxford 1889, 1899, 1906, 1958 (3rd edn rev), 1979. Ed Gardiner.
REVIEW: [Prothero, G. W.] EHR 6 1891.
A student's history of England from the earliest times to 1885. 3 vols 1890–1, 1892, 1897, 1898, 1899; vol 3 (with continuations) 1902, 1907, 1910, 1920, 1922; ed A. H. Shearer, New York 1906, 1913, 1938, 1939 (as England).
A school atlas of English history. 1892, 1895, 1899, 1905, 1922, 1928, 1936.
Browning, R. Strafford: a tragedy. 1892, 1915. Ed Gardiner.
The Tudor period. 1893.
The Stuart period. 1894.
History of the Commonwealth and Protectorate 1649–60. 3 vols 1894–1901, 4 vols 1894–1903. Unfinished at Gardiner's death; completed by C. H. Firth, The last years of the Protectorate, 2 vols 1909, rptd 1979, 4 vols Adlestrop 1988–9.
REVIEW: [Firth, C. H.] EHR 3 1888.
Cromwell's place in history. Ford lectures 1896. 1897, 1897 (3rd edn).
What Gunpowder Plot was. 1897.
Oliver Cromwell. 1899, 1901, 1909, rptd Wakefield 1976; ed M. Ashley, New York 1962; tr Ger 1903.
REVIEW: [Firth, C. H.] EHR 15 1900.

Gardiner also edited seventeenth-century documents for the Camden Soc and contributed to DNB *(21 articles) and* Encyclopaedia Britannica *9th edn (17 articles).*

Contributions to periodicals

For a list of Gardiner's periodical reviews, see Wellesley, *and index to vols 1–20 of* EHR *(which he edited 1891–1901).*

§2

Seeley, J. R. History of the great Civil War. Academy 21 May 1887.
[Dicey, A. V.] Gardiner's History. Nation (New York) 20 Mar 1890, 12–19 May 1892, 11 Apr 1895, 6–13 Jan 1898.
Beer, G. L. Gardiner: an appreciation. Critic June 1901.
Learned, H. B. Gardiner. Yale Scientific Monthly June 1902.
Powell, F. Y. Gardiner. EHR 17 1902.
Powell, F. Y. Two Oxford historians. Quart Rev 195 1902. With C. H. Firth; on Gardiner and J. R. Green.
Rhodes, J. F. Gardiner. Atlantic Monthly June 1902; rptd in his Historical essays, New York 1909.
Firth, C. H. Gardiner. Proc Br Acad 1 1904.

John Richard Green 1837–83

Green's ms material is at Jesus College, Oxford.

Bibliographies

Letters of J. R. Green. Ed L. Stephen 1901. *See* pp. 497–503.

§1

Oxford during the last century: being two series of papers published in the Oxford Chronicle and Bucks and Berks Gazette

during 1859. Oxford 1859 (anon); ed C. L. Stainer 1901 (as Studies in Oxford history); ed A. S. Green and K. Norgate 1901 (Green's ser only, in Oxford studies, *below*). With G. Roberson.
A short history of the English people. 1874, 1875, 1876, New York 1876, London 1877, 1878, 1880, New York 1880, London 1881, 1881, 1882, 1884, 1885, 1886; ed A. S. Green (with memoir) 1888; 4 vols 1889–91 (with tables and analysis by C. W. A. Tait); ed A. S. Green and K. Norgate 4 vols 1892–4 (illus edn), New York 1893–5, 1 vol London 1894, 4 vols 1895, 1907–8; ed G. B. Adams 2 vols New York 1898; ed A. S. Cook 3 vols New York 1900; 1 vol 1911 (rev), New York 1911, London 1915 (with Epilogue 1815–1914 by A. S. Green), New York 1916, London 1921; ed L. C. Jane 2 vols 1915 (with survey 1815–1914 by R. F. Farley), 1916, 1940 (EL), introd by A. Cook, New York 1990; ed R. Hudson 1992, 2 vols 1960 (with survey 1815–1960); tr Ital 1884, Fr 1888, Ger 1889, Rus 1891–2, Chinese 1898.
REVIEWS: [Gairdner, J.] Academy 6 1874; Fraser's Mag 92 1875; [Rowley, J.] Fraser's Mag 92 1875; [Brewer, J. S.] Quart Rev 141 1876.
Stray studies from England and Italy. 1876, New York 1876; Stray studies: second ser, ed Mrs J. R. Green 1903.
History of the English people. 4 vols 1877–80, New York 1878–80, London 1881, 1882, 5 vols New York 1882, 4 vols London 1886, 1890, 8 vols 1895–6 (Eversley edn); 4 vols New York 1898 (as England, with suppl by J. Hawthorne), London 1902; 4 vols 1901–3, 8 vols 1905–8, 10 vols New York 1910.
REVIEW: [Gairdner, J.] Academy 13 1878, 18 1880.
Readings from English history. 1879, New York 1879, London 1880, 1883, 1898. Ed Green.
A short geography of the British islands. 1879, 1884, 1893, 1896 (rev). With A. S. Green.
Essays of Joseph Addison. 1880, 1882, 1892, 1899, 1956 (with notes by G. St Quintin). Ed Green.
The making of England. 1881, 1882, New York 1882, London 1885 (3rd edn), 2 vols 1897, 1900.
The conquest of England. 1883, New York 1883, London 1884, 2 vols 1899 (3rd edn).
Oxford studies. Ed A. S. Green and K. Norgate 1901.
Historical studies. Ed A. S. Green 1903.

Contributions to periodicals
See Wellesley.

Letters
Letters of J. R. Green. Ed L. Stephen 1901.

§2
Bryce, J. Green: in memoriam. Macmillan's Mag May 1883.
Creighton, M. J. R. Green. British Quart Rev 155 1883.
Maitland, F. W. Mr J. R. Green. Saturday Rev 55 1883.
Green, A. S. Green the historian. London Quart Rev 63 1884.
Powell, F. Y. Two Oxford historians. Quart Rev 195 1902. With C. H. Firth; on Green and S. R. Gardiner.
Bryce, J. In his Studies in contemporary biography, 1903.
Creighton, L. In her Life and letters of Mandel Creighton, 2 vols 1905.
Rhodes, J. F. In his Historical essays, New York 1909.
Brundage, A. The people's historian: John Richard Green and the writing of history in Victorian England. Westport CT 1994.

George Grote 1794–1871

§1
Statement of the question of parliamentary reform. 1821.
Analysis of the influence of natural religion on the temporal happiness of mankind, by Philip Beauchamp. 1822, 1875; tr Fr 1875. Based on notes by Jeremy Bentham.
Institutions of ancient Greece. Westminster Rev 5 1826. A critique of W. Mitford, History of Greece.
Essentials of parliamentary reform. 1831, 1873 (in Minor works, *below*).
Grecian legends and early history. Westminster Rev 39 1843. On B. G. Niebuhr, Griechische Herrengeschichten.
A history of Greece. 12 vols 1845–56, 1854–7 (4th edn), 8 vols 1862, 12 vols 1869, 10 vols 1872, 1888, 12 vols New York 1900; ed A. D. Lindsay 12 vols 1906, 1934 (EL); ed J. M. Mitchell and M. O. B. Caspari 1907 (condensed); tr Ger 1850–5, Fr 1864–7.
REVIEWS: [J. S. Mill] Edinburgh Rev 84 1846, 98 1853; [H. H. Milman] Quart Rev 78 1846; [J. S. Mill] Spectator 4 Apr 1846, 5 June 1847, 3 Mar 1849; [W. H. Smith] Blackwood's Mag 62 1847; [A. P. Stanley] Quart Rev 86 1850; Quart Rev 88 1850; [W. Smith] Quart Rev 99 1856; [E. A. Freeman] North Br Rev 25 1856; Edinburgh Rev 105 1857.
Seven letters on the recent politics of Switzerland. 1847, 1876 (with Letter to A. de Tocqueville).
REVIEW: [G. C. Lewis] Credibility of early Roman history, Edinburgh Rev 104 1856; rptd in Minor works, *below.*
Plato's doctrine respecting the rotation of the earth and Aristotle's comments upon that doctrine. 1860, 1873 (in Minor works, *below*).
Plato and the other companions of Sokrates. 3 vols 1865, 1867, 1874, 4 vols 1885, 1888.
Review of the works of Mr J. S. Mill entitled Examination of Sir William Hamilton's philosophy. 1868 (for 1867), 1873 (in Minor works, *below*). Rptd from Westminster Rev 85 1866.
Aristotle. Ed A. Bain and G. C. Robertson 2 vols 1872, 1880 (for 1879).
REVIEW: [J. S. Mill] Fortnightly Rev Jan 1873.
Poems 1815–23. [1872] (priv ptd).
The minor works of George Grote; with remarks on his intellectual character, writings and speeches by A. Bain. 1873.
Posthumous papers. Ed Mrs Grote 1874 (priv ptd).
Fragments on ethical subjects. Ed A. Bain 1876.

§2
Sully, J. Professor Grote and the Utilitarian philosophy. Westminster Rev 95 1871.
George Grote. Quart Rev 135 1873.
Grote, H. The personal life of Grote. 1873; tr Ger 1874.
Clarke, M. L. Grote: a biography. 1962.

Henry Hallam 1777–1859

§1
View of the state of Europe during the Middle Ages. 2 vols 1818, 3 vols 1819, 4 vols Philadelphia 1821, 2 vols Paris 1835, 3 vols London 1837 (7th edn), 2 vols Paris 1840, 2 vols London 1846 (9th edn), 3 vols 1853, 1855; ed W. Smith, New York 1871, 1880; ed G. L. Burr, 2 vols New York 1899; ed A. R. Marsh, New York 1900 (as History of Europe during the Middle Ages, introd by A. R. Marsh); tr Fr 1820–2, Ger 1820–1, Ital 1874. Hallam's Supplemental notes, 1848, were incorporated in 1853 and later edns.
REVIEW: [R. Southey] Quart Rev 30 1818.
The constitutional history of England from the accession of Henry VII to the death of George I. 2 vols 1827, 3 vols 1829, Boston 1829, 3 vols London 1832, 2 vols 1846 (5th edn), New York 1847, 3 vols London 1854 (7th edn), 1855, 5 vols New York 1865–6 (continued T. Erskine May), London 1866 (11th edn); ed W. Smith, New York 1896; ed J. H. Morgan, 3 vols London 1912, 1930 (EL); tr Ger 1828, Fr 1832, Ital 1854.
REVIEWS: [T. B. Macaulay] Edinburgh Rev 48 1828; [R. Southey] Quart Rev 37 1828.
Survey of the principal repositories of the public records: extracted from the proceedings of the commissioners on the public records. 1833. With R. H. Inglis.

Memoirs of A. H. Hallam. In Remains in verse and prose of A. H. Hallam, 1834 (priv ptd), 1862, Boston 1863.
Introduction to the literature of Europe in the fifteenth, sixteenth and seventeenth centuries. 4 vols 1837–9, Paris 1839, 2 vols New York 1841, 3 vols London 1854 (4th edn), 4 vols 1855, 3 vols 1882; tr Fr 1839–40.
REVIEWS: [J. Smith] Blackwood's Mag 41 1837; [C. Merivale] Edinburgh Rev 72 1840; [H. H. Milman] Quart Rev 65 1840.
Letters addressed to Lord Ashley... on the importance of a Slavonic chair at Oxford. 1844.

Contributions to periodicals

For a list of Hallam's reviews, see Wellesley. *See also review of Elton's classic poets,* Quart Rev 13 1815.

§2

Wordsworth, C. King Charles the First, the author of Icon Basilike: in reply to Mr Hallam. 1828.

Thomas Hodgkin 1831–1913

Bibliography

Creighton, L. Life and letters of T. Hodgkin. 1917, 1918 (2nd edn), pp 419–27.

§1

Thoughts on the inspiration of the scriptures. 1865.
Christus iudex: a poem. 1871.
The duties of neutrality: a plea for the prohibition of the export of arms to belligerents. 1871. Rptd from The Friend.
Claudian: the last of the Roman poets. Two lectures. Newcastle upon Tyne and London 1875.
A parallel case or the straits of Dover question. 1896.
Italy and her invaders. 8 vols Oxford 1880–99, 1899 (extracts as The walls, gates and aqueducts of Rome), 4 vols Oxford 1931 (centenary re-issue).
REVIEWS: Edinburgh Rev 152 1880; Creighton, M., The Times 1880.
The pfahlgraben: an essay towards a description of the barrier of the Roman empire between the Danube and the Rhine. Newcastle upon Tyne 1882.
Jordanes [Jornandes]. 1882. Rptd from Encyclopaedia Britannica.
Battle of the Apennines: Totila and Narses, AD 552. Newcastle upon Tyne 1883. Rptd from Encyclopaedia Britannica.
The letters of Cassiodorus. Oxford 1886.
Think it out. A lecture on the question of home rule for Ireland. 1887.
Emigration and colonial railways. 1887.
The dynasty of Theodosius or eighty years' struggle with the barbarians. Oxford 1889.
Theodoric the Goth. 1890, New York and London 1891, London 1893, 1923 (2nd edn).
Balfour's land purchase bill. An address delivered at Falmouth, April 1890. 1890.
The two rules: home rule and the golden rule. 1893.
George Fox. 1896, Boston 1898, London 1906.
Charles the Great. 1897, 1899, New York 1902 (as Charlemagne, with notes by H. Ketcham), London 1903, 1908, 1921.
Roman occupation of Northumberland. Lectures delivered to the Literary and Philosophical Society, Newcastle upon Tyne, on Northumbrian history. By T. Hodgkin and others. Newcastle upon Tyne 1898.
Sulla relazione etnologica fra i Langobardi egli Angli. Cividale 1899.
Origins of barbarian history. 1902. Rptd from Hermathena vol 12.
Ernst Curtius. 1905. Rptd from Proc Br Acad 2 1905.
The history of England from the earliest times to the Norman conquest. 1905, 1906, 1914, 1920, 1931.
National education. A retrospect and a prospect. 1906.
Hodgkin pedigree book: or dates of births, marriages and deaths of the Hodgkin family 1644–1906. Darlington 1907 (priv ptd).
The wardens of the northern marches. The Creighton memorial lecture, Univ of London. 1908.
Cornwall and Brittany: presidential address before the Royal Cornwall Polytechnic Society. 1910.
Western Europe in the Middle Ages. 1910 (Harmsworth's History of the world pt 27).
Southward ho! Being a plea for a greatly extended and scientific system of emigration to Australia. Contemporary Rev 1910, 1912 (abridged and separately ptd).
Human progress and the inward light. Swarthmore lecture. 1911.
The trial of our faith and other papers. 1911.
Sacerdotalism. 1911 (priv ptd).
The fellowship of silence: being experiences in the common use of prayer without words narrated and interpreted by T. Hodgkin et al. Ed C. Hepher 1915.
The young Suplicius. Lecture delivered 1871. nd (priv ptd).

Prefaces and introductions

Von Cohausen, A. and L. Jacobi. The Roman castellum Saalburg. Tr F. C. Fischer, preface by T. Hodgkin, Homburg v.d., Hohe 1882.
Backhouse, E. Early church history. 1892, 1899. Preface by Hodgkin.
Bennett, A. W. Pre-Foxite Quakerism by A. W. Bennett. 1894. Prefatory note by Hodgkin.
Rendel, Hon Grace D. Newcastle upon Tyne. 1898. Preface by Hodgkin.
Scarborough summer school. Echoes from Scarborough. 1898. Preface by Hodgkin.
Friends historical society. The first publishers of truth. 1904, 1907 (as suppl to the Jnl of the Friends' Historical Soc 1–5). Introd by Hodgkin.
Stephen, C. The vision of faith. 1911. Introductory note by Hodgkin.

Contributions to periodicals

For reviews, addresses, archaeological items and articles in Quaker pbns, see Creighton's bibliography, above.

The Roman camp of the Saalburg. Macmillan's Mag 46 1882.
Creighton's history of the Papacy. Macmillan's Mag 48 1883.
Law reform in the days of Justinian. Contemporary Rev 39 1886.
The Roman province of Dacia. EHR 2 1887.
Theon and son: Egyptian bankers of the second century. Contemporary Rev 75 1899.

§2

Creighton, L. Life and letters of T. Hodgkin. 1917, 1918 (2nd edn).

Anna Brownell Jameson 1794–1860

See col 2165.

Alexander William Kinglake 1809–91

§1

Eothen: or traces of travel brought home from the East. 1844 (anon), 1844, 1845, New York 1845, 1845 (2nd edn), Leipzig 1846, London 1847 (5th edn), 1849, New York 1849, London 1850, 1856, 1859, New York 1859, London 1864, 1878, Edinburgh 1879, New York 1879, 1891; ed A. I. Shand, Edinburgh 1896; ed W. Tuckwell 1898; ed J. W. Redway, New York 1898; ed J. Bryce, New York 1900; ed W. H. D. Rouse 1901; ed J. C. Hogarth, Oxford 1906; ed A. T. Quiller-Couch 1907; ed J. Spender 1908, 1931, 1954 (EL); illustr F. Brangwyn 1913; ed H. G. Smith 1927; ed B. J. Hayes 1931; ed G. Boas 1932; ed R. W. Jepson 1935; ed C. H. Hopkins, Edinburgh 1935; ed J. W. Oliver, Edinburgh 1941; ed R. Fedden 1948; ed P. H. Newby

1949, 1952; ed F. Baker 1964, 1987 (selections); introd by J. Morris, Oxford 1982; ed J. Raban 1982.
REVIEW: [Warburton, E.] Quart Rev 75 1845.
Milner on the hareem: the rights of women. Quart Rev 75 1844.
The French lake. Quart Rev 75 1845.
Summer in Russia. NMM July–Sep 1846.
Victor Hugo on the great French puzzle. Blackwood's Mag Dec 1862. On Hugo's account of Waterloo in Les misérables.
The invasion of the Crimea: its origin and an account of its progress down to the death of Lord Raglan. Vols 1–2 Edinburgh 1863 (4 edns), 2 vols New York 1863–8, 8 vols Edinburgh 1863–87, 7 vols Leipzig 1863–89, 9 vols Edinburgh 1877–8 (6th edn); ed G. S. Clarke, Edinburgh 1899 (abridged); tr Fr 1864, Rus 1890.
REVIEWS: [Hamley, E. B.] Blackwood's Mag 93 1863; [Reeve, H.] Edinburgh Rev 117 1863; [Layard, A. H.] Quart Rev 113 1863; [Shand, A. Innes] Blackwood's Mag 143 1888; [Maurice, J. F.] Macmillan's Mag 57 1888.
Life of Madame de Lafayette. Blackwood's Mag 112 1872.
The Slavonic menace to Europe. Quart Rev 149 1880. With A. Austin.
Memoir of Hayward. Fortnightly Rev 41 1884.
Bernal Osborne. Fortnightly Rev 42 1884. Collaboration.

§2

Hayward, A. Mr Kinglake and the quarterlys, by an old reviewer. 1863 (3 edns).
Gregory, I. Eothen and the Athenaeum Club. Blackwood's Mag 158 1895.
Tuckwell, W. Kinglake: a biographical and literary study. 1902.

Charles Kingsley 1819–75

See col 1311.

Malcolm Laing 1762–1818

A number of Laing's letters are in the NLS.

§1

Henry, R. The history of Great Britain. 1793. Appendix to vol 6 by Laing.
The history of Scotland from the union of the crowns to ... the reign of Queen Anne. 2 vols 1800, Edinburgh 1804 (2nd edn corrected), 4 vols London 1804, 4 vols 1819.
The historie and life of King James the Sext. Edinburgh 1804. Ed Laing.
The poems of Ossian. Edinburgh 1805. With notes and illustr by Laing.
Report by the committee of the Faculty of Advocates appointed to consider the bill intituled An act for better regulating the courts of justice in Scotland. Edinburgh 1807. Ascribed in ms note to Laing.

Contributions to periodicals

Clerk's naval tactics. Edinburgh Rev 6 1805.
Roscoe's Leo X. Edinburgh Rev 7 1806.

§2

Cockburn, H. Memoirs of his time. Edinburgh 1856.

Hannah Lawrance 1785–1875

§1

Historical memoirs of the queens of England from the commencement of the twelfth century. 2 vols 1838–40.
The history of woman in England and her influence on society and literature. To the year 1200. 1843.
The treasure-seeker's daughter: a tale of the days of James the First. 1852.

Contributions to periodicals

For Lawrance's large number of reviews and articles in the Br Quart Rev *(including items on medieval poetry and architecture, and reviews of Tennyson, Dickens and E. B. Browning) and also in* Blackwood's Mag, *see* Wellesley.

William Edward Hartpole Lecky 1838–1903

The Lecky papers are in Trinity College, Dublin.

Bibliography

McCartney, D. W. E. H. Lecky: historian and politician. Dublin 1994.

§1

Friendship and other poems, by Hibernicus. 1859.
The religious tendencies of the age. 1860. Anon.
The leaders of public opinion in Ireland. 1861 (anon), 1871 (rev, omitting Clerical influences), New York 1872, London 1882, 2 vols 1903 (omitting Life of Swift), 1912; tr Ger 1873; Life of Swift rev as introd to Prose works of Jonathan Swift, ed T. Scott 1901; Clerical influences, ed W. E. G. Lloyd and F. C. O'Brien, Dublin 1911.
On the declining sense of the miraculous. Dublin 1863.
History of the rise of the spirit of rationalism in Europe. 2 vols 1865, 1865, 1866, 2 vols New York 1866, London 1869 (4th edn), 1872, 1873, 1875, 1877, 1880, 1882, New York 1882, London 1884, 1887, 1890, 1892, 1897, 1898, 1900, New York 1903, London 1904, 1910, 1914 (rev), 1925, New York 1925; ed C. W. Mills, New York 1955; tr Ger 1868, 1873, Du 1894.
REVIEWS: [Eliot, George] Fortnightly Rev 15 May 1865; [Stephen, J. F.] Fraser's Mag Nov 1865.
History of European morals from Augustus to Charlemagne. 2 vols 1869, New York 1869, London 1877 (3rd edn), 1886 (7th edn rev), 1897 (12th edn), 1903, 1905, 1911, 1929, New York 1929; ed C. Wood, New York 1926 (abridged); ed C. W. Mills, New York 1955; tr Ger 1870. Ch 1 ed W. A. Hiest 1903 (as A survey of English ethics).
REVIEWS: [Morley, J.] Fortnightly Rev May 1869; [Church, R. W.] Saturday Rev 1 May 1869; [Appleton, C. E.] Contemporary Rev June 1869; [Stephen, L.] Nation (New York) 17 June 1869; [Bryce, J.] Quart Rev 128 1870.
A history of England in the eighteenth century. 8 vols 1878–90, New York 1878–90, London 1883–90 (vols 1–2 3rd edn, vols 3–4 2nd edn), 1891, New York 1891, 12 vols London 1892 (as A history of England 7 vols, A history of Ireland 5 vols), New York 1892–3, London 1908–12; chs on The religious revival tr Ger 1880.
REVIEWS: [Reeve, H.] Edinburgh Rev 148 1878; [Dicey, A. V.] Nation (New York) 18–25 Apr 1878; [Hayward, A.] Quart Rev 145 1879, 153 1882; [Gladstone, W. E.] Nineteenth Cent June 1887; [McCarthy, J.] Contemporary Rev Nov 1890.
The history of Ireland in the eighteenth century. 5 vols 1892.
The American revolution: chapters and passages relating to America from History of England in the eighteenth century. Ed J. A. Woodburn, New York 1898.
The French Revolution: chapters from History of England during the eighteenth century. Ed H. E. Bourne, New York 1904, 1928.
Poems. 1891, New York 1891.
The political value of history. Birmingham 1892, London 1892 (rev), 1908 (in Historical and political essays, *below*).
The Empire, its value and growth: an inaugural address. 1893, 1908 (in Historical and political essays, *below*).
Speeches and addresses of Edward Henry 16th Earl of Derby. Ed T. H. Sanderson and E. S. Roscoe, 2 vols 1894. Memoir by Lecky.
Democracy and liberty. 2 vols 1896, 1896, New York 1896, London 1899 (rev), 1900.
The map of life: conduct and character. 1899, New York 1899, London 1901, New York 1901, London 1913.
Historical and political essays. 1908, New York 1908, London 1910.

Memorandum on the proposed abolition of the viceroyalty in Ireland. nd.

Contributions to periodicals

See McCartney, W. E. H. Lecky, *pp. 253–6, and N. Pilling,* The reception of the major works of W. E. H. Lecky., unpbd M. Phil diss, Univ of London 1978.

Letters

Hyde, H. M. A Victorian historian: private letters of Lecky 1859–78. 1947.

The Lecky–Lea correspondence in the Henry Charles Lea Library of the University of Pennsylvania. Hermathena 92 1958.

§2

Daubeny, C. Christianity and rationalism . . . being a protest against certain principles advocated in Mr Lecky's History. 1867.

Reid, M. Our young historians: account of lectures on history by W. E. H. Lecky and J. A. Froude. Living Age Mar 1893.

Morley, J. Lecky on democracy. Nineteenth Cent May 1896; rptd in his Oracles on man and government, 1923.

Walker, H. The Rt Hon W. E. H. Lecky. Good Words 40 1899.

Walpole, S. Mr Lecky. Proc Br Acad 1 1904.

Lecky, E. van D. A memoir of Lecky by his wife. 1909.

Rhodes, J. F. In his Historical essays, New York 1909.

Roome, H. D. Two historians of the eighteenth century. Fortnightly Rev Nov 1909. On Macaulay and Lecky.

Franqueville, A. C. Notice sur la vie et les travaux du très-honorable W. E. H. Lecky. Paris 1910.

Gooch, G. P. History and historians in the nineteenth century. 1913.

McCartney, D. W. E. H. Lecky. Dublin 1994.

John Lingard 1771–1851

Bibliographies

Gillow, J. Bibliographical dictionary of the English Catholics. 5 vols 1885–1902. *See* vol 4 pp. 254–78.

Haile, M. and E. Bonney. Life and letters of Lingard. 1911. *See* pp. 383–8.

§1

Catholic loyalty vindicated. 1805.

The antiquities of the Anglo-Saxon Church. 2 vols Newcastle upon Tyne 1806, 1810, Philadelphia 1841, London 1845 (rev as The history and antiquities of the Anglo-Saxon Church), 1858 (4th edn); tr Fr 1828, Ger 1847.

Letters on Catholic loyalty. Newcastle upon Tyne 1807.

Observations on the laws and ordinances which exist in foreign states relative to the religious concerns of their Roman Catholic subjects. 1817, 1851.

The history of England from the first invasion by the Romans to the accession of Henry VIII. 3 vols 1819, 8 vols 1819–30 (as History of England from the first invasion by the Romans to the accession of William and Mary in 1688), 14 vols 1825 (3rd edn), 13 vols 1837–9 (rev), 10 vols 1849, 1854 (6th edn with memoir by M. A. Tierney), 1883, Dublin 1888, Edinburgh 1902, 11 vols London 1912–15 (supplementary vol by H. Belloc); ed P. Sadler, Paris 1836 (abridged); ed J. Burke 1855 (abridged); ed M. J. Kerney, Baltimore 1855, 1875; ed H. Mensch, Berlin 1863; ed T. Young, Dublin 1867; ed H. N. Birt 1903, 1912; selections ed J. A. Hilton 1981; tr Fr 1825–31, 1833–5, Ital [1835].

REVIEWS: [Allen, J.] Edinburgh Rev 42 1825; [Milman, H. H.] Quart Rev 33 1825; [Hallam, H.] Edinburgh Rev 53 1831.

A collection of tracts on several subjects connected with the civil and religious principles of Catholics. 1826.

A new version of the four Gospels with notes critical and explanatory, by a Catholic. 1836, 1846, 1851.

Dodd's Church history of England. Dublin Rev 6 1839.

Did the Church of England reform herself? Dublin Rev 9 1840.

The ancient church of England and the liturgy of the Anglican Church. Dublin Rev 11 1841.

Lingard also pbd a number of pams defending the Catholic position against Anglican attacks.

§2

Phillpotts, H. Letter to Charles Butler . . . with remarks on certain works of Dr Milner and Dr Lingard. 1825.

[Allen, J.] The massacre of St Bartholomew. Edinburgh Rev 44 1826. Reply by Lingard, A vindication of certain passages in the fourth and fifth volumes of The history of England, 1826 (3 edns), 1827 (rev), 1827; tr Fr 1827.

Todd, H. J. A vindication of Cranmer against some of the allegations of Dr Lingard. 1826.

[Wiseman, N. P.] Dr Lingard. Dublin Rev 35 1854.

Tierney, M. A. Memoir of Lingard. 1855.

Haile, M. and E. Bonney. Life and letters of Lingard. 1911, St Louis 1911.

Fletcher, J. Lingard 1771–1851. 1925.

Thomas Babington Macaulay, 1st Baron Macaulay 1800–59

The mss of the diary etc are in the lib of Trinity College Cambridge, with annotated edns of the classics and the corrected proofs of the Life of Pitt.

Bibliographies etc.

Catalogue of a portion of the library of Macaulay. 1863 (Sotheby's). About 470 other vols, many annotated, are at Wallington Hall, Northumberland.

Pinney, T. (ed). The letters of T. B. Macaulay. 6 vols Cambridge 1974–81. See vol 6 pp. 289–302 for a list of Macaulay's pbd writings.

Collections

Scenes and characters from the writings of Macaulay. New York 1846.

Selections from Macaulay's essays and speeches. 2 vols 1856.

Biographical and historical sketches. New York 1857.

Biographical essays. Leipzig 1857.

The miscellaneous writings of Lord Macaulay. Ed T. F. Ellis 2 vols 1860, 1865, 1871 (with Speeches), 4 vols 1880 (with Poems), 1 vol 1910, 1958 (EL) (with Lays); tr Fr 1860.

Biographies by Lord Macaulay contributed to the Encyclopaedia Britannica: with extracts from his letters and speeches. Edinburgh 1860. With a memoir by A. Black.

Oeuvres: traduites par M. G. Guizot. 6 vols Paris 1862–5.

The works of Lord Macaulay, edited by his sister Lady Trevelyan. 8 vols 1866, New York 1866, London 1897.

Speeches and poems, with the report and notes on the Indian Criminal Code. 2 vols Boston [1874].

Selections from the writings. Ed G. O. Trevelyan 1876.

Morceaux choisis de l'histoire d'Angleterre et des chants de l'ancienne Rome. Ed W. Battier, Paris 1892.

Works. Albany edition 12 vols 1898; Whitehall edition 20 vols New York 1898–1900.

Works. New Cambridge edition (with 3 more speeches) 10 vols Cambridge 1900.

Works. 9 vols 1905–7 (vols 4–8, The history of England, ed T. F. Henderson).

The reader's Macaulay. Ed W. H. French and G. D. Sanders, New York 1936.

Prose and poetry. Ed G. M. Young 1953 (Reynard Lib).

§1

Pompeii: a poem which obtained the Chancellor's Medal 1819. [Cambridge 1819.]

Evening: a poem which obtained the Chancellor's Medal 1821. Cambridge 1821.

Ivry. Knight's Quart Mag 1 1823; rptd in Lays, *below.*

A speech in the House of Commons, March 2 1831, on a bill to amend the representation of the people in England and Wales. 1831.

The speech of T. B. Macaulay on the second reading of the third Reform Bill, 16 December 1831. 1831.

A speech on the second reading of the East India Bill, 10 July 1833. 1833.

The Armada. Friendship's Offering 1833; rptd in Lays, *below.*

A Penal Code prepared by the Indian Law Commissioners and published by command of the Governor General of India in Council. Calcutta 1837. Compiled by Macaulay with the assistance of C. H. Cameron, J. M. Macleod, G. W. Anderson and F. Millett.

Edinburgh election speech of Mr Macaulay. 1839.

Critical and miscellaneous essays. 3 vols Boston and Philadelphia 1840–1, 5 vols Philadelphia 1841–4. Unauthorised.

Speech ... on Mr Sergeant Talford's bill for the extension of copyright. 1841.

Lays of ancient Rome. 1842, Philadelphia 1843, London 1846 (7th edn), 1847, 1848 (with Ivry and The Armada, *above*), Leipzig 1851, Boston 1853, New York 1862, London 1882, 1884 (3 edns), 1886, 1887, 1888; ed W. J. Rolfe, New York 1888; Glasgow 1889, London 1902, Oxford 1903 (WC), London 1910 (EL); ed G. M. Trevelyan 1928; many school edns London and New York 1899–1929; tr Ger 1853, Ital 1869, 1918, Fr 1892.
REVIEWS: [J. Wilson] Blackwood's Mag 52 1842; [J. S. Mill] Westminster Rev 39 1843.

Critical and historical essays contributed to the Edinburgh Review. 3 vols 1843, New York 1843, Philadelphia 1843–4, London 1848, 1849 (containing all the essays Macaulay wished to preserve), 1850, 5 vols Leipzig 1850, 3 vols London 1853, 2 vols London 1854, 5 vols New York 1857, 7 vols New York 1859–61, London 1872; ed G. T. Bettany 1892; 5 vols 1900; ed F. C. Montague 3 vols 1903; ed A. J. Grieve 2 vols 1907 (EL), 2 vols Oxford 1913; ed H. Trevor-Roper 1965; many school edns of one or more essays; tr Ital 1859–66, Fr 1860, Du 1865, Sp 1880, 1886–1903, Hebrew 1944.

Speech in the House of Commons, February 26 1845, on the proposed duties on sugar. Edinburgh 1845.

Speech in the House of Commons, July 9 1845, on the bill for the abolition of Scottish university tests. Edinburgh 1845; Government plan of education: speech in the House of Commons, April 19 1847, [1847].

City election. Addresses by T. B. Macaulay and W. Gibson-Greg at a meeting of electors of the city. [Edinburgh 1847].

The history of England from the accession of James II. Vols 1–2 1849, 5 vols Philadelphia 1849–51, 5 vols New York 1849–61; vols 3–4 1855; vol 5 ed Lady Trevelyan 1861; 10 vols Leipzig 1849–61; 8 vols 1858–62 (with memoir by H. H. Milman); ed S. A. Allibone 5 vols Philadelphia 1875; ed H. D. Sedgwick 10 vols Boston 1899; ed D. Jerrold 3 vols 1906; ed T. F. Henderson 1907; 1934 (EL); ed C. H. Firth 6 vols 1913–15; ed T. F. Henderson 5 vols Oxford 1931 (WC); many school edns of ch 3; selected and abridged by H. Trevor-Roper 1979 (Pen), facs of 1913–15 edn with an introd by P. Rowlandson 2 vols 1985, vol 4 ed P. Rowlandson 1986, illus abridgement with introd by Lord Home of Hirsel 1988, selections on Ireland ed G. Lucy, Lurgan 1989; tr Du 1851–3, 1868, Danish 1852–8, Ital 1852–3, Hungarian 1853, Polish 1854–61, Fr 1857–61, 1858, 1989, Cz 1862–5, Ger 1863 (5th edn), Finnish 1866, Greek 1897–1902, Sp 1905–6.
REVIEWS: [A. Alison] Blackwood's Mag 65 1849; [James Moncreiff] Edinburgh Rev 90 1849; [J. W. Croker] Quart Rev 84 1849; Westminster Rev 50 1849 (as part of an article by W. E. Hickson); [E. S. Dallas] The Times 17–18 Dec 1855, 11 Jan 1856; [J. Moncreiff] Edinburgh Rev 114 1861.

Inaugural address delivered on his installation as Lord Rector of the University of Glasgow. Glasgow 1849, Edinburgh 1849.

Speech ... delivered in the music hall in Manchester. [1852.]

Speeches, parliamentary and miscellaneous. 2 vols 1853, 2 vols New York 1853. Unauthorised.

Speeches corrected by himself. 1854, New York 1854, Leipzig 1860, London 1866; ed W. E. Gladstone 1909, 1924 (EL); ed G. M. Young, Oxford 1935 (WC); tr Ger 1854, Sp 1885–1902.

The Indian Civil Service. 1855. A report by Macaulay, Ashburton, Jowett et al.

Minutes on education in India. Ed H. Woodrow, Calcutta 1862.

Hymn by Lord Macaulay: an effort of his early childhood. Ed L. Horton-Smith, Cambridge 1902.

Marginal notes. Ed G. O. Trevelyan 1907.

Essays and speech on Jewish disabilities. Ed I. Abrahams and S. Levy, Edinburgh 1910, 1920.

Lord Macaulay's legislative minutes. Ed C. D. Dharker, Madras 1946.

The life and character of King William III. TLS 1 May 1969. University prize essay.

Hamburger, J. (ed). Napoleon and the restoration of the Bourbons. 1977. Surviving fragment of The history of France.

Contributions to periodicals

For a list of Macaulay's separate articles, see Wellesley.

Letters

Were human sacrifices in use among the Romans? Correspondence between Mr Macaulay, Sir Robert Peel and Lord Mahon. 1860 (priv ptd); in Earl Stanhope, Miscellanies, 2 vols 1863–72; ed T. Thayer 1878 (priv ptd) (as Some inquiries concerning human sacrifice among the Romans).

Correspondence between the Bishop of Exeter and T. B. Macaulay in January 1849 on certain statements respecting the Church of England. 1860.

Selection from the correspondence of Macvey Napier, edited by his son. 1879. Letters to the editor of the Edinburgh Rev.

What did Macaulay say about America? Ed H. M. Lydenberg, New York 1925. 4 letters to H. S. Randall.

The letters of Thomas Babington Macaulay. Ed T. Pinney 6 vols Cambridge 1974–81.

Selected letters. Ed T. Pinney, Cambridge 1982.

See also G. O. Trevelyan, 1876, below.

§2

Early criticism

[Croker, J. W.] Noctes ambrosiana. Blackwood's Mag 30 1831. A defence of Croker's edn of Boswell against Macaulay, the material supplied by Croker.

[Croker, J. W.] The French Revolution. Quart Rev 46 1832. An attack on Macaulay's speeches.

Mahon, Lord (later Earl Stanhope). Lord John Russell and Mr Macaulay on the French Revolution. 1833. Rptd from Quart Rev 49 1833.

Montagu, B. Letters to Macaulay upon the review of the life of Lord Bacon. 1841.

Horne, R. H. In his A new spirit of the age, 1844.

Spedding, J. Evenings with a reviewer: or a free and particular examination of Mr Macaulay's article on Lord Bacon. 2 vols 1848 (priv ptd); ed G. S. Venables 2 vols 1881.

Babington, C. Macaulay's character of the clergy in the seventeenth century considered. Cambridge 1849.

Forster, W. E. William Penn and Macaulay. Philadelphia 1850. Originally pbd as preface to T. Clarkson, Memoirs of William Penn, 1849.

Fairbairn, H. A defence of William Penn from the charges contained in The history of England by Macaulay. 1849.

Dixon, W. H. William Penn: an historical biography with an extra chapter on the Macaulay charges. 1851, 1856 (rev).
Bagehot, W. Macaulay. Nat Rev 2 1856; rptd in his Literary studies, ed R. H. Hutton, 1879.
[Dallas, E. S.] Macaulay. The Times 1 Sep 1856.
Devon, F. Vindication of the first Lord Dartmouth from the charge of conspiracy or high treason revived by Macaulay. 1856.
Miller, H. Macaulay on Scotland: a critique. 1857.
Lancaster, H. H. Macaulay's place in English literature. North Br Rev 33 1860; rptd in his Essays and reviews, 1876.
Thackeray, W. M. nil nisi bonum. Cornhill Mag Feb 1860; rptd in his Roundabout papers, 1863.
Paget, J. The new examen: or an inquiry into the evidence relating to certain passages in Macaulay's History. Edinburgh 1861, 1934; rptd in his Paradoxes and puzzles, Edinburgh 1874.
Rowntree, J. S. An inquiry into the truthfulness of Lord Macaulay's portraiture of George Fox, in two lectures. York 1861.
Mignet, F. A. M. In his Éloges historiques, Paris 1864.
Trevelyan, G. O. The competition wallah. 1864.
Stirling, J. H. Jerrold, Tennyson and Macaulay: with other critical essays. Edinburgh 1868.
Freeman, E. A. Macaulay. International Rev 3 1876.
Froude, J. A. Macaulay. Fraser's Mag June 1876.
Gladstone, W. E. Macaulay. Quart Rev 142 1876; rptd in his Gleanings of past years, 1879.
Morley, J. Macaulay. Fortnightly Rev Apr 1876; rptd in his Critical miscellanies, 1877.
Punshon, W. M. Macaulay. 1876.
Kinkel, J. G. Macaulay: sein Leben und sein Geschictswerk. Basle 1879.
Stephen, L. In his Hours in a library ser 3, 1879.
Jones, C. H. Macaulay. New York [1880], 1901.
Canning, A. S. G. Macaulay: essayist and historian. 1882, [1913] (rev).
Morison, J. C. Macaulay. 1882 (EML).
Parnell, A. Macaulay and the assault of Namur. EHR 2 1883.
Barbey d'Aurevilly, J. In his Littérature étrangère, Paris 1891.
Harrison, F. Macaulay's place in literature. Forum Sep 1894; rptd in his Studies in early Victorian literature, 1895.
Saintsbury, G. In his Corrected impressions, 1895.
Sedgwick, H. D. The vitality of Macaulay. Atlantic Monthly Aug 1899; rptd in his Essays on great writers, Boston 1903.
Jebb, R. C. Macaulay: a lecture. Cambridge 1900; rptd in his Essays and addresses, Cambridge 1907.
Paul, H. Macaulay and his critics. Anglo-Saxon Rev 4 1900; rptd in his Men and letters, 1901.
Brownell, W. C. In his Victorian prose masters, New York 1901.
Bülow, G. Macaulay: sein Leben und seine Werke. Schweidnitz 1901.
Macgregor, D. H. Lord Macaulay. 1901.
[Dicey, A. V.] Macaulay and his critics. Nation (New York) 15 May 1902.
Dawson, W. J. In his Makers of English prose, New York 1906.
Strachey, L. Macaulay's marginalia. Spectator 16 Nov 1907; rptd in his Spectatorial essays, 1964.
Courthope, W. J. A consideration of Macaulay's comparison of Dante and Milton. Proc Br Acad 3 1908.
Roome, H. D. Two historians of the eighteenth century. Fortnightly Rev Nov 1909. On Macaulay and Lecky.
Thayer, W. R. Macaulay fifty years after. North Amer Rev 190 1909.
Trevelyan, G. M. In his Clio: a muse, 1913.
Kellett, E. E. Macaulay's lay figures. Br Rev May 1914; rptd in his Suggestions, Cambridge 1923.
Chesterton, C. The art of controversy: Macaulay, Huxley and Newman. Catholic World July 1917.
Hassard, A. R. A new light on Lord Macaulay. Toronto 1918.
Williams, S. T. Macaulay's reading and literary criticism. PQ 3 1924.
Sampson, G. Macaulay and Milton. Edinburgh Rev 242 1925.
Strachey, L. In his Portraits in miniature, 1931.
Kellett, E. E. Macaulay's History. London Quart Rev 163 1938.

Memoirs, biographies and obituaries

[Dallas, E. S.] The late Lord Macaulay. The Times 31 Dec 1859.
Letters of Hannah More to Zachary Macaulay containing notice of Lord Macaulay's youth. Ed A. Roberts 1860.
Maurice, F. D. Macaulay. Macmillan's Mag 1 1860.
[Stephen, J. F.] Macaulay. Saturday Rev 7 Jan 1860.
Arnold, F. The public life of Macaulay. 1862.
Milman, H. H. Memoir of Macaulay. 1862. First pbd in Proc Royal Soc 11 1862.
Macaulay, M. Recollections by a sister of T. B. Macaulay. Priv ptd 1864, 1881.
Martineau, H. In her Biographical sketches, 1869.
Trevelyan, G. O. The life and letters of Macaulay. 2 vols 1876, New York 1876 (with appendix, Macaulay on American institutions), Leipzig 1876, London 1877 (rev), New York 1877, London 1878, 1 vol 1881, 2 vols Chicago 1885, 1 vol London 1889, 1908 ('enlarged'), 1913; ed G. M. Trevelyan 2 vols Oxford 1932 (WC); 1 vol 1959; 2 vols Oxford 1961; ed G. M. Trevelyan London 1978; tr Sp (in part) 1899; P. Clarke, Index to Trevelyan's Life and letters of Macaulay, 1881.
Clive, J. Macaulay: the shaping of the historian. Cambridge MA 1973.

Justin McCarthy 1830–1912

§1

Paul Massie. A romance. 1866.
The Waterdale neighbours. 1867.
Con amore: or critical chapters. 1868.
My enemy's daughter. A novel. 3 vols 1869.
The settlement of the Alabama question. 1871.
Modern leaders: biographical sketches. New York 1872.
A fair Saxon. A novel. 3 vols 1873, 1878.
Linley Rochford. A novel. 3 vols 1874.
Dear Lady Disdain. 1875, New York 1876, London 1878, 1887. A novel.
Miss Misanthrope. 2 vols 1878.
Donna Quixote. 1879.
A history of our own times from the accession of Queen Victoria to the Berlin Congress. Vols 1–2 1879, vols 3–4 1880 (as History of our own times from the accession of Queen Victoria to the general election of 1880), 5 vols Leipzig 1879–80, 4 vols London 1880, 2 vols New York 1880, 1 vol New York 1880, 4 vols Chicago 1887, 5 vols London 1889–97 (with continuation to the Diamond Jubilee), 7 vols 1897–1905 (with continuation to the accession of Edward VII), 5 vols New York 1897–1905, 7 vols London 1908; ed G. M. Adam 2 vols New York 1900; tr Ger 1881, Fr 1885–7.
REVIEW: [Craile, H.] Quart Rev 151 1881.
The comet of a season. A novel. 3 vols 1881.
The epoch of reform 1830–50. 1882, New York 1882, London 1888.
Maid of Athens. A novel. 3 vols 1883.
A history of the four Georges. 2 vols 1884, New York 1884, London 1884, Leipzig 1885, 4 vols London 1901 (as A history of the four Georges and of William IV, vols 3–4 completed by J. H. McCarthy), 2 vols London 1905.
A short history of our own times. New York 1884, London 1888, 2 vols New York 1893, 1 vol London 1907, New York 1908, Leipzig 1990. *See* English literature in the reign of Queen Victoria, *below*.
The Right Honourable: a romance of society and politics. 3 vols 1886. With R. Praed.
The ladies gallery. A novel. 3 vols 1888. With R. Praed.
The rebel rose. A novel. 1888. With R. Praed. Pirate edn as The rival princess, Edinburgh and London 1890.
Ireland's cause in England's parliament. Ed J. B. O'Reilly, Boston 1888.

The Grey river. 1889. With Mrs Campbell Praed and M. Menpes.
Roland Oliver. A novel. 1889.
Charing Cross to St Paul's. Illustr J. Pennell 1891, 1893, New York 1893.
Sir Robert Peel. 1891, New York 1891, London 1906 (4th edn).
The dictator. A novel. 3 vols 1893.
Pope Leo XIII. 1896, 1899, New York 1899.
The riddle ring. A novel. 3 vols 1896.
The Daily News jubilee: a political and social retrospect. 1896. With J. R. Robinson.
The story of Mr Gladstone's life. 1897, 1898 (rev), 1898.
White, W. The inner life of the House of Commons. 2 vols 1897. Ed McCarthy.
Modern England. 2 vols 1899, New York 1899 (as The story of the people of England in the nineteenth century).
Reminiscences. 2 vols 1899, New York 1899.
English literature in the reign of Queen Victoria. Ed R. Ackermann, Dresden 1899. Selected from A short history of our own times, *above*.
Mononia, a love story of Forty-Eight. 1901.
The reign of Queen Anne. 2 vols 1902, New York 1902, London 1905.
Portraits of the sixties. 1903, New York 1903.
Ireland and her story. 1903.
British political portraits. 1903.
Irish literature. 10 vols Chicago 1904. Ed McCarthy, Lady Gregory et al.
The story of an Irishman. 1904, New York 1904 (as An Irishman's story). Autobiography.
Julian Revelstone: a romance. 1909.
Irish recollections. 1911, New York 1912.
Our book of memories: letters of Justin McCarthy to Mrs Campbell Praed. 1912.

Contributions to periodicals
See Wellesley. *McCarthy also wrote leader articles for the Daily News in 1871.*

§2
O'Connor, T. P. In his Parnell movement, 1889.
The Times 26 Apr 1912.

Sir James Mackintosh 1765–1832

§1
Vindiciae gallicae. Dublin 1791, London 1791 (rev), 1791 (3rd edn), Philadelphia 1792, London 1838, Oxford 1989; tr Fr 1792. A reply to Burke's Reflections on the revolution in France.
A discourse on the study of the law of nature and of nations. 1799, Dublin 1799, London 1828, 1835, Edinburgh 1835; ed J. G. Marvin, Boston 1843; tr Fr 1830.
Mélanges philosophiques. Paris 1829.
Dissertation on the progress of philosophy chiefly during the seventeenth and eighteenth centuries. 1830 (as suppl to Encyclopaedia Britannica 7th edn), Edinburgh 1830 (priv ptd), Philadelphia 1832, 1834; ed W. Whewell, Edinburgh 1836 (as A general view of the progress of ethical philosophy), 1862, 1872 (4th edn).
The history of England. 3 vols 1830–2 (in Cabinet cyclopaedia, ed D. Lardner, 1830–40), 3 vols Philadelphia 1830–3, 10 vols London 1850 (completed by W. Wallace and R. Bell); ed R. J. Mackintosh 2 vols 1853.
The life of Sir Thomas More. 1831 (in Cabinet cyclopaedia), 1844.
History of the revolution in England in 1688 completed to the settlement of the crown by the editor William Wallace. 1834 (with memoir), Philadelphia 1835; London 1835 (Mackintosh's portion only, as A view of the reign of James II).
Tracts and speeches. 5 pts Edinburgh 1840 (25 copies).
Miscellaneous works. Ed R. J. Mackintosh 3 vols 1846, Philadelphia 1848, 1 vol London 1851, Boston 1854, 3 vols London 1854, 1 vol New York 1871, London 1878.

Contributions to periodicals
For a list of Mackintosh's reviews for the Edinburgh Rev, *see* Wellesley.

§2
Memoirs of the life of Mackintosh. Ed R. J. Mackintosh 2 vols 1835, Philadelphia 1835, London 1853, Boston 1853.
[Croker, J. W.] Life of Mackintosh. Quart Rev 54 1835.
Macaulay, T. B. Sir James Mackintosh. Edinburgh Rev 61 1835; rptd in his Critical and historical essays vol 2, 1843.
Mill, James. A fragment on Mackintosh. 1835.
De Quincey, T. A glance at the works of Mackintosh. Tait's Mag June 1846; rptd in his Works, ed D. Masson, 1897.
[MacDowall, A.] Miscellaneous works of Mackintosh. North Br Rev 5 1846.
Bulwer, H. In his Historical characters, 1868.
O'Leary, P. Sir James Mackintosh, the Whig Cicero. Aberdeen 1989.

Sir Henry James Sumner Maine 1822–88

§1
Memoir of Henry Fitzmaurice Hallam. [1851], 1862 (in Remains in verse and prose of A. H. Hallam). With F. Lushington.
Roman law and legal education. 1856 (in Cambridge essays), 1876 (in Village-communities, *below*, 3rd edn).
Ancient law: its connection with the early history of society and its relation to modern ideas. 1861, New York 1864, London 1885 (10th edn); ed T. W. Dwight, New York 1888; 1894 (15th edn), 1897 (16th edn); ed F. Pollock 1906, 1907, 1930; ed J. H. Morgan 1917 (EL); 1930; ed C. K. Allen, Oxford 1931 (WC); EL reprint New York 1977, Tucson AZ 1986; tr Rus 1873, Hungarian 1875, Chinese 1959.
Village-communities in the east and west. 1871, 1876 (3rd edn with lectures, addresses, essays), 1895 (7th edn).
REVIEW: [Mill, J. S.] Fortnightly Rev May 1871.
The early history of the property of married women: a lecture. [1873.]
Lectures on the early history of institutions. 1875, 1880 (3rd edn), New York 1888, London 1893 (6th edn), 1897 (7th edn).
The effects of observation of India on modern European thought. Rede lecture 1875. 1875, 1876 (in Village-communities, *above*, 3rd edn).
The King in his relation to early civil justice. Proc Royal Inst 9 1882.
Dissertations on early law and custom. 1883, 1890; tr Fr 1884, Rus 1884, Sp c. 1885.
Popular government: four essays. 1885, 1886, New York 1888, London 1909; tr Sp 1888.
REVIEWS: [Benn, A. W.] Academy 7 Nov 1885; [Morley, J.] Fortnightly Rev Feb 1886; [Dicey, A. V.] Nation (New York) 25 Mar–1 Apr 1886.
India. In The reign of Queen Victoria, ed T. H. Ward, 1887.
International law. Whewell lectures 1888. 1888, New York 1889, London 1894; tr Fr 1890.
Minutes 1862–9: with a note on Indian codification. Calcutta 1892.

Contributions to periodicals
For a list, see Wellesley.

§2
[Stephen, J. F.] Sir Henry Maine. Saturday Rev 11 Feb 1888.
Pollock, F. Maine and his work. Contemporary Rev Feb 1889; rptd in his Oxford lectures, 1890.
Duff, M. R. Grant. Maine: a brief memoir with some of his Indian speeches and minutes. Ed W. Stokes 1892.
[Lyall, A.] Sir Henry Maine. Quart Rev 176 1893.
Wilson, Woodrow. A lawyer with a style. Atlantic Monthly Sep 1898.
Vinogradoff, P. The teaching of Maine. 1904.

Frederic William Maitland 1850–1906

Bibliographies

Smith, A. L. Maitland: two lectures and a bibliography. Oxford 1908.
Cameron, J. R. Maitland and the history of English law. Norman OK 1961. *See* pp. 168–94.

§1

Laws of real property. Westminster Rev 112 1879; rptd in Collected papers, *below*.
Justice and police. 1885.
Why the history of English law is not written: an inaugural lecture. Cambridge 1888.
The history of English law before the time of Edward I. 2 vols Cambridge 1895, Boston 1895, Cambridge 1898, Boston 1898, Cambridge 1911 (2nd edn), 1 vol Washington 1959. With F. Pollock.
REVIEW: [Roscoe, E. S.] Edinburgh Rev 183 1896.
Domesday book and beyond: three essays. Cambridge 1897, Boston 1897, Cambridge 1907; ed E. Miller 1960, 1987.
Roman canon law in the Church of England: six essays. Cambridge 1898.
Township and borough: being the Ford lectures 1897 with notes relating to the history of Cambridge. Cambridge 1898, 1965.
Canon MacColl's new convocation. Fortnightly Rev Dec 1899.
Political theories of the middle age, by Otto Gierke. Cambridge 1900, 1913, 1922, 1951. Tr Maitland.
English law and the Renaissance. Rede lecture 1901. Cambridge 1901.
Essays on the teaching of history. Ed W. A. J. Archbold, Cambridge 1901. With H. M. Gwatkin et al.
The life and letters of Leslie Stephen. 1906, New York 1906, London 1907, 1910, Bristol 1991 (facs of 1906 edn).
The constitutional history of England. Ed H. A. L. Fisher, Cambridge 1908, 1909, 1920, 1948, 1961. Lectures delivered 1887–8.
Equity: also the forms of action at common law. Ed A. H. Chaytor and W. J. Whittaker, Cambridge 1909, 1916, 1929, 1932; Equity, ed J. Brunyate, Cambridge 1936, 1949; Forms of action, ed Chaytor and J. Whittaker, Cambridge 1936, 1941, 1958.
Collected papers. Ed H. A. L. Fisher 3 vols Cambridge 1911.
A sketch of English legal history. Ed J. F. Colby, New York [1915]. Rptd from Social England, ed H. D. Traill 6 vols 1893–7. With F. C. Montague.
Selected essays. Ed J. D. Hazeltine, G. Lapsley and P. H. Winfield, Cambridge 1936.
Selected historical essays. Ed H. M. Cam, Cambridge 1957.
F. W. Maitland, historian: selections from his writings. Ed R. L. Schuyler, Berkeley 1960.

Contributions to periodicals

Maitland's EHR *articles are indexed in the first* EHR *index.*

Letters

The letters of F. W. Maitland. Ed C. H. S. Fifoot, Cambridge 1965.
Letters to George Neilson. Ed E. L. G. Stones, Glasgow 1976.
Letters of F. W. Maitland. Ed P. N. R. Zutshi, Cambridge 1995. Supplements Fifoot's edn.
Maitland also edited medieval legal documents (chiefly for the Selden Soc) 1884–1907.

§2

Pollock, F. Maitland. Quart Rev 206 1907.
Vinogradoff, P. Maitland. EHR 22 1907.
Smith, A. L. Maitland: two lectures and a bibliography. Oxford 1908.
Fisher, H. A. L. Maitland: a biographical sketch. Cambridge 1910.
Liebermann, F. Maitland's collected papers. Historische Zeitschrift 3rd ser 18 1915.
White, R. J. Maitland 1850–1950. Cambridge Jnl 4 1950.
Hollond, H. A. Maitland. 1953. A memorial address.
Maitland, E. Maitland: a child's eye view. 1957.

Harriet Martineau 1802–76

See col 1344.

Sir Thomas Erskine May, 1st Baron Farnborough 1815–86

§1

The Imperial Parliament. 1840 (anon in Penny cyclopaedia vol 17), 1841 (in Knight's Store of knowledge for all readers).
A treatise on the law, privileges, proceedings and usage of Parliament. 1844, 1851 (rev), 1859 (4th edn), 1868 (6th edn), 1879 (8th edn), 1883; ed R. R. D. Palgrave and A. B. Carter 1893; ed T. L. Webster and W. R. Grey 1906, 1924 (13th edn); ed G. Campion and T. G. B. Cocks 1950 (15th edn); ed E. Fellowes and T. G. B. Cocks 1957 (16th edn); ed B. Cocks 1965 (17th edn); ed D. Lidderdale 1976 (19th edn); ed C. Gordon 1983 (20th edn); ed C. J. Boulton 1989 (21st edn); tr Ger 1888, Ital 1888, Fr 1909.
Remarks and suggestions with a view to facilitating the dispatch of public business in Parliament. 1849, 1849 (2nd edn).
On the consolidation of the election laws. 1850.
The constitutional history of England since the accession of George II. 2 vols 1861–3, 1863–5, Boston 1862–3, 3 vols London 1871, 2 vols New York 1876–7, 3 vols London 1878 (6th edn), 1896 (11th edn); ed F. Holland 3 vols 1912; tr Fr 1865–6, Sp 1883–4.
REVIEWS: [Massey, W. N.] Edinburgh Rev 115 1862; [Smith, C. C.] North Amer Rev 97 1863.
Democracy in Europe: a history. 2 vols 1877, New York 1878; tr Fr 1879, Ital 1883.
REVIEWS: [Rogers, F.] Edinburgh Rev 147 1878; [Acton, J. D.] Quart Rev 145 1878.
The machinery of parliamentary legislation. 1881. Rptd from Edinburgh Rev 99 1854.
Erskine May's private journal. Ed D. Holland and D. Menhennet 1972; ed W. R. McKay 1984.

Contributions to periodicals

For Erskine May's contributions to the Edinburgh Rev, *see* Wellesley.

§2

Arnold, M. In his Equality, Fortnightly Rev Mar 1878; rptd in his Mixed essays, 1879.
The Times 18, 25, 27 May 1886.

Charles Merivale 1808–93

§1

History of Rome under the Emperors: the Augustan age. 1843.
A history of the Romans under the Empire. 7 vols 1850–62, 1862, New York 1864–79, 8 vols London 1865, 1890; tr Fr 1865–7, Ital 1865, Ger 1866–72.
C. Sallustii Crispi Catilina et Jugurtha. 1852; Jugurtha, 1884; Catilina, 1888. Ed Merivale.
The fall of the Roman Republic: a short history of the last century of the commonwealth. 1853, 1853 (2nd edn). An abridgement of vols 1–3 of History of the Romans, *above*.
An account of the life and letters of Cicero, by B. R. Abeken. 1854. Tr Merivale.
Keatsii Hyperionis libri tres. Cambridge 1863, 1882 (rev). Tr Merivale.
The conversion of the Roman Empire. Boyle lectures 1864. 1865, 1865, New York 1865.
The conversion of the northern nations. Boyle lectures 1865. 1866, New York 1866.

Homer's Iliad in English rhymed verse. 2 vols 1869.
The contrast between pagan and Christian society: a lecture. 1872, 1880.
A general history of Rome from the foundation of the city to the fall of Augustulus BC 753–AD 476. 1875, 1875, 1876, 1877, New York 1877, London 1891; ed C. Puller 1877, New York 1878 (abridged); ed O. Smeaton 2 vols 1910 (as History of Rome to the reign of Trajan), 1928 (EL).
The Roman triumvirates. 1876, 1883 (3rd edn), 1887 (5th edn), New York 1889.
The heathen world and St Paul. 1877.
The continental Teutons. In The conversion of the west, 5 vols 1878–9.
Four lectures on some epochs of early church history. 1879.
Autobiography and letters. Ed J. A. Merivale, Oxford 1898 (priv ptd), London 1899 (as Autobiography of Merivale with selections from his correspondence).

Contributions to periodicals
For a list of Merivale's periodical articles, see Wellesley.

§2
The Times 28 Dec 1893.
Watkins, H. W. In his Churchmen, scholars and gentlemen, Quart Rev 191 1900.

James Mill 1773–1836
See col 2556.

Henry Hart Milman 1791–1868

Collected works
The poetical works. 3 vols 1839.

§1
The Belvedere Apollo: a prize poem. [Oxford 1812], London 1821. Anon.
Alexander tumulus Achillis invisens ... Oxford 1813.
Fazio: a tragedy. Oxford and London 1815, 1816, London 1818 (4 edns), New York 1818, Philadelphia 1819, London 1821, Baltimore 1833, New York [1846], 1847, 1854, [1878?]; tr Ital by F. dall'Ongaro, London 1857, Sp by J. d'Araujo, Madrid 1857.
Samor, lord of the bright city: an heroic poem. 1818 (2 edns), New York 1818.
The fall of Jerusalem: a dramatic poem. 1820 (2 edns), New York 1820, London 1821, 1822, 1825, 1831, 1853, 1865, 1977.
Belshazzar: a dramatic poem. 1822, Boston 1822, New York 1822, 1977.
The martyr of Antioch: a dramatic poem. 1822, New York 1822, London 1823.
Anne Boleyn: a dramatic poem. 1826, 1827.
The character and conduct of the Apostles. Bampton lectures. Oxford 1827.
The history of the Jews. 3 vols 1829 (anon), 1830, New York 1832, 1841, London 1843, 1863, New York 1864, London 1866 (4th edn); ed A. P. Hayes, Philadelphia 1871; 3 vols 1878, 1880, 1892; ed G. H. Jones 2 vols 1909, 1923, 1930 (EL), 1986.
Poetical works of Milman, Bowles, Wilson and 'Barry Cornwall'. Paris 1829.
The history of Christianity from the birth of Christ to the abolition of paganism in the Roman Empire. 3 vols 1840, New York 1841, London 1863 (rev), 1867, New York 1894, 1978 (rptd).
REVIEW: [J. Newman] Br Critic 60 1841.
The poetical works of Howitt, Milman and Keats. Philadelphia 1840.
History of Latin Christianity, including that of the Popes to Nicolas V. 6 vols 1854–5, 1857, 9 vols 1864, 1867, 4 vols New York 1889–92, London 1903.
Life of Thomas à Becket. New York 1860.
Memoir of Lord Macaulay. 1862, 1862, 1862 (in Macaulay's History of England vol 8). Rptd from Proc Royal Soc 11 1862.
Annals of St Paul's Cathedral. Ed A. Milman 1868, 1869.

Editions and translations
Mahabharata. Nala and Damayanti ... Tr Milman, Oxford 1835, 1860, 1914; ed M. Williams, Oxford 1879 (Nala alone).
The history of the decline and fall of the Roman Empire, by Edward Gibbon. 12 vols 1838–9. Ed Milman.
The life of Edward Gibbon with selections from his correspondence. 1839, 1840. Ed Milman.
The Agamemnon of Aeschylus and the Bacchanals of Euripides. 1865, Bacchanals (only) 1888, rptd in The plays of Euripides, ed V. R. Reynolds 2 vols 1906, 1911, 1934 (EL). Tr Milman.
Savonarola, Erasmus and other essays reprinted from the Quarterly Review. Ed A. Milman 1870.

Contributions to periodicals
For a list of Milman's reviews, see Wellesley. *See also* New churches: progress of dissent, Quart Rev 31 1824.

§2
[Smith, W. H.] Dean Milman. Blackwood's Mag 104 1868.
Stanley, A. P. The late Dean of St Paul's. Macmillan's Mag 19 1869.
Green, J. R. Milman's Annals of St Paul's. Saturday Rev 2 Jan 1869; rptd in his Stray studies 2nd ser, 1903.
Milman, A. Milman, Dean of St Paul's, a biographical sketch. 1900.

Mrs Moore fl. 1819–29
Some information can be found in Hedva Ben-Israel, English historians on the French Revolution, Cambridge 1968.

§1
A short history of France from the foundation of the Empire to the Restoration of Louis XVIII. Intended as a continuator of a series of historical books for children of the late Mrs Trimmer by her daughter Mrs Moore. 1819, 1829 (3rd edn augmented).

Frances Moore, 'Madame Panache' 1789[90]–1881

§1
Manners: a novel. By Miss F. Moore. 3 vols 1817, 2 vols New York 1818.
REVIEW: Monthly Rev 85 1818.
A year and a day: a novel in two volumes by Madame Panache, author of Manners. 2 vols 1818, 1819, in The Novelist's Mag vol 1, Philadelphia 1833.
REVIEWS: Fireside Mag 1 1819; Literary Panorama 9 1819; Monthly Rev 88 1819.
Historical life of Joanna of Sicily, Queen of Naples. 2 vols 1824.
REVIEW: Quarterly Rev 31 1824.
Botta, C. History of Italy during the Consultate and Empire of Napoleon Buonaparte. Tr by the author of The life of Joanna Queen of Naples. 1828, 1829.

Sir William Francis Patrick Napier 1785–1860

§1
The art of war. Edinburgh Rev 35 1821.
History of the war in the Peninsula and the south of France from the year 1807 to the year 1814. 6 vols 1828–40, 4 vols Paris 1839–40, Philadelphia 1842, 6 vols London 1851 (rev), 5 vols 1856, New York 1856, 3 vols London 1876–82, 6 vols 1882, 1900; ed R. W. O'Byrne 1889; ed W. T. Dobson 1889; ed E. A. Arnold 1905; ed A. T. Quiller-Couch, Oxford 1908; ed M. Fanshawe 1911; ed H. Strang 1913,

Chicago 1979 (abridged); 6 vols 1992–3 (facs of 1st edn); tr Fr 1828–44. Abridged by Napier as English battles, *below.*
REVIEWS: [Murray, G.] Quart Rev 56 1836 (2 articles); reply by Napier, Westminster Rev 26 1837; [Roebuck, J. A.] Edinburgh Rev 72 1841.

A reply to various opponents. 1832 (in History of the war in the Peninsula vol 1, 2nd edn), 1833, 1833.

Colonel Napier's justification of his third volume. 1833.

The conquest of Scinde; with some introductory passages in the life of Major-General Sir Charles James Napier. 1845, 1845 (2nd edn).

History of General Sir Charles James Napier's administration of Scinde and campaign in the Cutchee Hills. 1851, 1857, 1858 (3rd edn).

English battles and sieges in the Peninsula. 1852, 1855, 1866, 1904, 1910; ed W. H. D. Rouse 2 vols 1905, 1990 (facs of 1855 edn). Abridgement by Napier of History of the war in the Peninsula, *above.*

The life and opinions of General Sir Charles James Napier. 4 vols 1857, 1857 (2nd edn).

Contributions to periodicals

For a list of Napier's other articles and reviews, see Wellesley.

§2

Outram, J. The conquest of Scinde: a commentary. 1846.

[Dallas, E. S.] General Sir Charles Napier. The Times 8, 10 Apr, 25 May, 24 July 1857.

[Hamley, E. B.] Life of Napier. Blackwood's Mag 95 1864.

Holmes, T. R. W. In his Four famous soldiers, 1889.

Gwynn, S. L. A brotherhood of heroes: being memorials of Charles, George and William Napier. 1910.

The life of Napier. Ed H. A. Bruce 2 vols 1864.

Edward Nares 1762–1841

Nares's ms autobiography is in the lib of Merton College, Oxford. Oxford Univ archives contain material relating to Nares's tenure of the Regius Chair of history.

§1

A preface to the iron chest. A satirical poem. Written by Thinks-I-to-myself. [1796.]

A sermon preached at the parish church of Shobdon, Hertfordshire. 1798.

A sermon [on Matt v 21–2]. 1799.

Εἲς θεος εἲς μεσιτης: or an attempt to shew how far the philosophical notion of a plurality of worlds is consistent ... with holy scripture. 1801.
REVIEW: [S. Smith] Edinburgh Rev 1 1802.

View of the evidences of Christianity. Bampton lectures. 1805.

A letter to F. Stone in reply to his sermon. 1807.

A sermon [on Acts ii 7–11]. Oxford 1808.

Jubilee. A sermon [on Ezra vi 10]. Cranbrook [1809].

Remarks on the version of the New Testament lately edited by the Unitarians. 1810, 1814.

Thinks-I-to-myself: a serio-ludicro tragico-comico tale written by Thinks-I-to-myself, who? [By E. Nares]. 1811, 2 vols 1811 (2nd edn with additions, limited circulation), 2 vols 1811 (3rd edn), 1812 (8th edn), Baltimore 1812, Boston 1812, Philadelphia 1812, 2 vols London 1816, 1823 (embellished), 1826 (to which is added a preface concerning the author), 1829; tr Ger 1827.
REVIEWS: Br Critic 38 1811, 42 1813; Critical Rev 24 1811; GM 81 1811; Monthly Rev 66 1811; New Annual Register 32 1811; Universal Mag 16 1811.

I says, says I: a novel. By Thinks-I-to-myself. 2 vols 1812, 1812 (2nd edn).
REVIEWS: Br Critic 39 1812; Universal Mag 17 1812.

A sermon [on 1 Cor i 20]. 1814.

A sermon [on Heb xiii 16] preached July 11 1816. 1816.

Syllabus for a course of lectures on modern history. Oxford 1816–17.

Syllabus of lectures on political economy. Oxford 1817.

Discourses on the three creeds ... preached before the University of Oxford. 1819.

Heraldic anomalies: or rank confusion in our orders of precedence. 2 vols 1823, 1824.

Memoirs of the life and administration of William Cecil, Lord Burghley. 3 vols 1828–31.
REVIEW: [T. B. Macaulay] Edinburgh Rev 54 1832.

A few observations on the Edinburgh review of Dr Nares's Memoir of Lord Burghley. [E. Nares]. 1832.

Man as known to us theologically and geologically. 1834.

Continuations

Tytler, A. Elements of general history. Vol 3, being a continuation terminating at the demise of King George III. By E. Nares. 1822, 1823 (to which is added A view of the state of arts, sciences, religion), 1825 (corrected with additions), 1827, 1837, 1839, 1840, 1855 (with additions and a continuation).

Prefaces

The Holy Bible with historical prefaces by the Rev E. Nares. 3 vols 1816–24.

Burnet, G. The history of the Reformation. Preface E. Nares. 1829, 1833 (rev and corrected with additional notes), 1837.

§2

White, G. C. A versatile professor. Reminiscences of the Rev E. Nares. 1903.

Black, J. A Regency Regius: the historian Edward Nares. Oxoniensa 52 1987.

Kate Norgate 1853–1935

§1

England under the Angevin kings. 2 vols 1887.
REVIEW: [E. A. Freeman] EHR 2 1887.

Green, J. R. A short history of the English people. Ed Mrs J. R. Green and K. Norgate 1892–4, 1902, 1907.

Green, J. R. Oxford studies. Ed Mrs J. R. Green and K. Norgate 1901.

John Lackland. London and New York 1902.

The minority of Henry the Third. 1912.

Richard the Lion Heart. 1924.

Contributions to periodicals and collaborative works

Carucage. EHR 3 1888.

Ode of Champagne, Count of Blois and tyrant of Burgundy. EHR 5 1890.

The bull laudabiliter. EHR 8 1893.

The battle of Hastings. EHR 9 1894. With J. A. Archer.

The alledged condemnation of King John by the court of France in 1202. Royal Historical Soc Trans n.s. 4 1900.

Julia Pardoe 1806–62

See col 1378.

Frederick York Powell 1850–1904

Bibliographies

Elton, O. Powell: his life and a selection from his letters. 2 vols Oxford 1906. *See* vol 2 pp. vii–xvi.

§1

Early England up to the Norman Conquest. 1876, New York 1877, 1895 (11th edn).

An Icelandic prose reader. Oxford 1879. With G. Vigfússon.
Alfred the Great and William the Conqueror. 1881.
Old stories from British history. 1882, 1885 (3rd edn).
Corpus poeticum boreale: the poetry of the old northern tongues. 2 vols Oxford 1883; ed L. Thompson 1974. Ed and tr with G. Vigfússon.
History of England. 3 vols 1885–90, 1898–1900, 1 vol 1904. With J. M. Mackay and T. F. Tout.
English history by contemporary writers. 1887. Ed Powell.
Sketches from British history. 1888, 1889.
The first nine books of the Danish history of Saxo Grammaticus translated by Oliver Elton. 1894. Ed Powell.
Some words on allegory in England. 1895 (priv ptd); ed E. Clarke and J. Todhunter 1910.
The tale of Thrond of Gate: commonly called Faereyinga saga. 1896. Tr Powell.
XXIV quatrains from Omar. New York 1900. Tr Powell.
Two Oxford historians. Quart Rev 195 1902. With C. H. Firth; on S. R. Gardiner and J. R. Green.
John Ruskin and thoughts on democracy. 1905.
Origines Islandicae: a collection of the more important sagas. 2 vols Oxford 1905. Ed and tr with G. Vigfússon.
Collingwood, W. G. Scandinavian Britain; with chapters introductory to the subject by F. York Powell. 1908.

§2

Cook, T. A. F. York Powell. Monthly Rev June 1904.
Rait, R. S. F. York Powell. EHR 19 1904.
Watson, H. B. M. Professor Powell. Athenaeum 14 May 1904.
Elton, O. Powell: his life and a selection from his letters and occasional writings. 2 vols Oxford 1906.

Sir John Robert Seeley 1834–95

Bibliography

Wormell, D. Sir John Seeley and the uses of history. Cambridge 1980. *See* pp. 211–16 (includes details of the Seeley papers and other ms sources).

§1

Prize essay on the Greek tragedians and Shakespeare. City of London School. 1850.
A parallel between Shakespeare's King Lear and the Oedipus in Colono of Sophocles. In Three essays on King Lear by pupils of the City of London School, 1851.
David and Samuel, with other poems, by John Robertson. 1859.
The student's guide to the University of Cambridge. Cambridge 1863, 1866; rev R. B. Somerset 1874. Ed Seeley.
Classical studies as an introduction to the moral sciences: an introductory lecture. 1864.
Ecce homo: a survey of the life and work of Jesus Christ. 1866 (for 1865) (anon), 1866 (5th edn), Boston 1866, 1867, London 1867, 1895, Boston 1903, London 1905, 1914; ed O. Lodge 1908, 1923 (EL), 1969 (new EL edn); ed J. E. Odgers 1910; tr Ger 1867, Danish 1874, Ital nd.
REVIEWS: [Sidgwick, H.] Westminster Rev 86 1866; The Reader Jan 1866; [Stephen, J. F.] Fraser's Mag 73 1866; [Stanley, A. P.] Macmillan's Mag 14 1866; Month June 1866; Dublin Rev 59 1866; London Quart Rev 27 1866; [Connington, J.] Contemporary Rev 7 1868; [Gladstone, W. E.] Good Words Jan–Mar 1868.
Lectures and essays. 1870; ed M. Seeley 1895.
Livy, Book 1. Oxford 1871, 1881 (3rd edn). Ed Seeley.
English lessons for English people. 1871. With E. A. Abbott.
Life and times of Stein: or Germany and Prussia in the Napoleonic age. 3 vols Cambridge 1878, 2 vols Boston 1879; tr Ger 1883–7.
REVIEWS: [Gardiner, S. R.] Contemporary Rev 34 1879; International Rev 6 1879; [Duff, M. E. Grant] Macmillan's Mag 40 1879; [Dicey, A. V.] The Nation 29 1879; Saturday Rev 47 1879.
Natural religion, by the author of Ecce homo. 1882, Boston 1882, London 1891 (3rd edn), 1895.
REVIEWS: [Davies, J. L.] Contemporary Rev 42 1882; [Bradley, A. C.] Macmillan's Mag 47 1882.
The expansion of England. 1883, Boston 1883, Leipzig 1884, London 1888, 1895, 1898, Boston 1900, London 1911, Chicago 1971 (introd by J. Gross); abridged 1887 (as Our colonial expansion); tr Fr 1885, Portuguese 1891, Ital 1897, Ger 1954.
REVIEWS: [Creighton, M.] Contemporary Rev 45 1884; [Smith, G.] Contemporary Rev 45 1884. [Morley, J.] Macmillan's Mag 49 1884; [Solly, H.] Modern Rev 5 1884.
A short history of Napoleon the First. 1886, Boston 1886, London 1900, Boston 1901; tr Fr 1887.
REVIEWS: [Gardiner, B. M.] Academy 29 1886; The house of Bourbon, EHR 1 1886; Paul Ewald and Pope Gregory, EHR 1 1886; [Acton, J. E.] EHR 2 1887; [Dicey, A. V.] The Nation 44 1887.
Roman imperialism and other lectures and essays. Boston 1889.
Goethe reviewed after sixty years. Boston 1893, London 1894, Leipzig 1894.
The growth of British policy: an historical essay. 2 vols Cambridge 1895, 1903, 1 vol Cambridge 1921, 1922. Memoir by G. W. Prothero.
REVIEWS: Athenaeum 1895 pt ii; [Rannie, D. W.] Academy 49 1896; [Gardiner, S. R.] EHR 11 1896.
Introduction to political science. Ed H. Sidgwick 1896, 1901.

Contributions to periodicals

For a list of Seeley's periodical articles, see Wellesley *vol 5 1989. Other articles and papers are listed in Wormell's bibliography.*

§2

Newman, J. H. An internal argument for Christianity. Month June 1866; rptd in his Discussions and arguments, 1872.
[Parker, J.] Ecce deus. 1867, New York 1867, London 1868 (3rd edn).
Stedefeld, G. F. Über die naturalistische Auffassung der Engländer. Berlin 1869.
Myers, F. W. H. A new eirenicon. In his Essays modern, 1883.
[Doyle, J. A.] Freeman, Froude and Seeley. Quart Rev 182 1895.
Jacobs, J. In his Literary studies, 1895.
Gazeau, J. L'impérialisme anglais, son évolution: Carlyle, Seeley, Chamberlain. Paris 1903.
Benn, A. W. In his History of English rationalism in the nineteenth century, 1906.
Rein, A. Seeley: eine Studie über den Historiker. Langensalza 1912; tr as Sir John Robert Seeley: a study of the historian, 1987.

Goldwin Smith 1823–1910

§1

The war passages in Maud. Saturday Rev 3 Nov 1855.
Oxford university reform. In Oxford essays by members of the University, Oxford 1858.
Lectures on modern history. Oxford 1861, 1865 (as Lectures on the study of history), New York 1866, Toronto 1873.
Irish history and Irish character. Oxford 1861, 1862.
Rational religion and the rationalistic objections of the Bampton lectures for 1858. Oxford 1861. On H. L. Mansel, Limits of religious thought.
Does the Bible sanction American slavery? Oxford 1863, Cambridge MA 1863.
The Empire: a series of letters published in the Daily News. Oxford 1863.
England and America: a lecture. Atlantic Monthly Dec 1864; rptd Boston 1865, Manchester 1865.
A letter to a Whig member of the Southern Independence Association. Boston 1864.
A plea for the abolition of tests in the University of Oxford. Oxford 1864.

The civil war in America: an address. 1866.
Three English statesmen: a course of lectures. 1867, New York 1867. On Pym, Cromwell and Pitt.
The reorganization of the University of Oxford. 1868.
The political destiny of Canada. Toronto 1877, 1878, New York 1878.
Cowper. 1880, New York 1880, 1884, London 1888, 1898, 1904 (EML).
Lectures and essays. Toronto 1881 (priv ptd).
False hopes: or fallacies socialistic and semi-socialistic briefly answered. New York 1883, London 1886.
Life of Jane Austen. 1890.
Loyalty, aristocracy and jingoism: three lectures. Toronto 1891.
Canada and the Canadian question. 1891, Toronto 1891.
A trip to England. Toronto 1891, 1892, New York 1892, London 1895.
The moral crusader: William Lloyd Garrison. Toronto 1892, New York 1892.
The United States: an outline of political history 1492–1871. 1893, New York 1893, 1899.
Bay leaves: translations from the Latin poets. New York 1893.
Specimens of Greek tragedy. 2 vols New York 1893. Tr Smith.
Essays on questions of the day: political and social. New York 1893, 1894 (rev), Boston 1894.
Oxford and her colleges. 1894, New York 1895, 1906.
Guesses at the riddle of existence. New York 1897, 1898.
Shakespeare the man. Toronto 1899, New York 1900.
The United Kingdom: a political history. 2 vols 1899, Toronto 1899, New York 1899.
Commonwealth or empire? A bystander's view of the question. New York 1902.
In the court of history: an apology for Canadians who were opposed to the South African War. Toronto 1902.
The founder of Christendom. Boston 1903.
My memory of Gladstone. 1904, 1904, Toronto 1904.
Irish history and the Irish question. 1905, Toronto 1905, New York 1905.
In quest of light. New York 1906.
No refuge but in truth. Toronto 1908, London 1909, New York 1909.
Reminiscences. Ed A. Haultain, New York 1910, 1911.
A selection from Smith's correspondence. Ed A. Haultain 1913, New York 1913.

Contributions to periodicals

For Smith's many articles and reviews, see Wellesley.

§2

Andrews, C. M. Goldwin Smith. Amer Historical Rev 5 1900.
McCarthy, J. In his Portraits of the sixties, 1903.
Haultain, A. Smith: his life and opinions. 1913.
Wallace, E. Goldwin Smith: Victorian liberal. Toronto 1957.
Steffe, N. Goldwin Smith. 1986.

Lucy Toulmin Smith 1838–1911

See col 2707.

Robert Southey 1774–1843

See col 457.

Philip Henry Stanhope, 5th Earl Stanhope, called Viscount Mahon 1821–55 1805–75

§1

The life of Belisarius. 1829, 1848.
History of the war of the succession in Spain. 1832–3, 1836.
Lord John Russell and Mr Macaulay on the French Revolution. 1833. Rptd from Quart Rev 49 1833.
Letters from the Earl of Peterborough to General Stanhope in Spain. 1834. Ed Stanhope.
History of England from the Peace of Utrecht to the Peace of Aix-la-Chapelle. 7 vols 1836–54, 1839–54 (as History of England from the Peace of Utrecht to the Peace of Versailles 1713–83); ed H. Reed 2 vols New York 1849 (as History of England from the Peace of Utrecht to the Peace of Paris); 7 vols 1853–4, (3rd edn rev), Boston 1853–4, 4 vols Leipzig 1853–4, 7 vols London 1858 (5th edn rev). For extracts, *see below.*
The rise of our Indian Empire. 1838, 1876 (3rd edn). Extracted from History of England, *above.*
Spain under Charles the second: extracts from the correspondence of the honourable Alexander Stanhope. 1840. Ed Stanhope.
Essai sur la vie du grand Condé. 1842 (priv ptd); tr 1845 (as The life of Louis Prince of Condé), New York 1845.
Correspondence between William Pitt and Charles Duke of Rutland. 1842 (priv ptd), 1890. Ed Stanhope.
The decline of the last Stuarts: extracts from despatches. 1843. Ed Stanhope.
The letters of Philip Dormer Stanhope, Earl of Chesterfield. 5 vols 1845–53. Ed Stanhope.
Historical essays contributed to the Quarterly Review. 1849, 1861. *See* Joan of Arc, *below.*
The Forty-Five. 1851, 1851. Extracted from History of England, *above.*
Secret correspondence connected with Mr Pitt's return to office in 1804. 1852 (priv ptd). Ed Stanhope.
Joan of Arc. 1854. Rptd from Historical essays, *above.*
Lord Chatham at Chevening 1769. 1855, 1859.
Addresses delivered at Manchester, Leeds and Birmingham. 1856.
Memoirs of Sir Robert Peel. 2 vols 1856–7. Ed Stanhope and E. Cardwell.
Were human sacrifices in use among the Romans? Correspondence between Mr Macaulay, Sir Robert Peel and Lord Mahon. 1860 (priv ptd); in Miscellanies, *below*; ed T. Thayer 1878 (priv ptd) (as Some inquiries concerning human sacrifice among the Romans).
Life of William Pitt. 4 vols 1861–2, 1862, 1867 (3rd edn), 3 vols 1879; tr Fr 1862–3, Ital 1864.
REVIEWS: [Cecil, R.] Quart Rev 109 1861; [Dallas, E. S.] The Times 21 May 1861, 25 Apr 1862.
Miscellanies. 1863, 1863 (rev); second ser, 1872.
REVIEW: [Macpherson, W.] Quart Rev 113 1863.
History of England comprising the reign of Queen Anne until the Peace of Utrecht. 1870, 1870, Leipzig 1870, 2 vols London 1872 (4th edn).
Notes of conversation with Louis-Philippe at Claremont. 1873 (priv ptd).
The French retreat from Moscow and other historical essays. 1876.
Notes of conversations with the Duke of Wellington. 1888, 1889 (3rd edn); ed P. Guedella, Oxford 1938 (WC).

Contributions to periodicals

See Wellesley.

§2

Macaulay, T. B. Lord Mahon's War of the Succession. Edinburgh Rev 56 1833; rptd in his Critical and historical essays, 1843.
The Times 25 Dec 1875.
Mayer, J. Philip H. Lord Stanhope. Stuttgart 1988.

Sir James Stephen 1789–1859

§1

Critical and miscellaneous essays. Philadelphia 1843, 1846, 1848, Boston 1854, 1856, New York 1873.
Essays in ecclesiastical biography. 2 vols 1849, 1853 (3rd edn); ed J. F. Stephen 1860, 1872, 1907.

Lectures on the history of France. 2 vols 1851, 1852, 1 vol New York 1852, London 1855, 2 vols 1857 (3rd edn rev).
Letters; with biographical notes by his daughter C. E. Stephen. Gloucester 1906 (priv ptd).

Contributions to periodicals
See Wellesley.

§2

Stephen, J. F. Biographical notice. In Essays in ecclesiastical biography, *above*, 1860.
Stephen, L. In his Life of Sir James Fitzjames Stephen, 1895.
Maitland, F. W. In his Life and letters of Leslie Stephen, 1906.
Russell, G. W. E. In his Short history of the Evangelical Movement, 1915.
Stephen, L. In his Some early impressions, 1924.
Foden, N. A. Stephen: architect of empire. Auckland 1938.

Sir James Fitzjames Stephen 1829–94

See col 2303.

Elizabeth Wheeler Stone 1803–61

See col 1403.

Agnes Strickland 1796–1874

See col 2199.

Elizabeth Strickland 1794–1875

See col 2199.

William Stubbs 1825–1901

Stubbs's papers are in the Bodleian.

Bibliographies
Shaw, W. A. A bibliography of the historical works of Dr Creighton, Dr Stubbs, Dr S. R. Gardiner and Lord Acton. 1903.
Letters of Stubbs. Ed W. H. Hutton 1904. *See* pp. 409–15.

§1

Registrum sacrum anglicanum: an attempt to exhibit the course of episcopal succession in England. Oxford 1858; ed S. E. Holmes, Oxford 1897.
Select charters and other illustrations of English constitutional history. Oxford 1866, 1870, 1874, 1884 (6th edn), 1895 (8th edn), 1900; ed H. W. C. Davis, Oxford 1913 (9th edn), 1921, 1929.
An address delivered by way of inaugural lecture. 1867, Oxford 1867 (rev).
The historical works of Gervase of Canterbury. 2 vols 1870–80. Ed Stubbs.
Memorials of St Dunstan. 1874. Ed Stubbs.
The constitutional history of England in its origin and development. 3 vols Oxford 1874–8, 1877–80, 1896–7, 1926–9; preface, ed C. Morley, Madison NJ 1950 (as Kettel Hall Christmas 1873).
REVIEWS: [Adams, H.] North Amer Rev 119 1874; [Dicey, A. V.] Nation (New York) 4 Mar 1875; [Stebbing, W.] Edinburgh Rev 150 1879.
The early Plantagenets. 1876, Boston 1876, London 1886 (5th edn), New York 1887, London 1889, New York 1889, London 1901 (10th edn).
Two lectures on the present state and prospects of historical study. Oxford 1876 (priv ptd).
The mediaeval kingdoms of Cyprus and Armenia: two lectures. Oxford 1878.
Chronicles of the reigns of Edward I and Edward II. 2 vols 1882–3. Ed Stubbs.
Origines Celticae. 2 vols 1883. Ed Stubbs and C. Deedes.
An address delivered by way of a last statutory lecture. Oxford 1884.
Seventeen lectures on the study of mediaeval and modern history. Oxford 1886, 1887, 1900.
Wilhelmi Malmesbiriensis de gestis regum Anglorum. 1887. Ed Stubbs.
Ordination addresses. Ed E. E. Holmes 1901.
Historical introductions to the Rolls Series. Ed A. Hassall 1902.
Lectures on European history. Ed A. Hassall 1904.
Letters of Stubbs. Ed W. H. Hutton 1904, 1906 (abridged).
Visitation charges. Ed E. E. Holmes 1904.
Lectures on early English history. Ed A. Hassall 1906.
Germany in the early Middle Ages 476–1250. Ed A. Hassall 1908.
Germany in the later Middle Ages 1200–1500. Ed A. Hassall 1908.
Genealogical history of the family of Bishop Stubbs, compiled by himself. Ed F. Collins 1915.
On convocation. Ed W. H. Hutton 1917.

§2

Maitland, F. W. Stubbs: Bishop of Oxford. EHR 16 1901; rptd in his Collected papers, ed H. A. L. Fisher, 1911.
Green, J. R. Stubbs's inaugural lecture. In his Stray studies 2nd ser, 1903.
Paul, H. In his Stray leaves, 1906.
Petit-Dutaillis, C. Studies and notes supplementary to Stubbs's Constitutional history. 3 vols Manchester 1908–29. With G. Lefebvre.
Edwards, J. G. William Stubbs. 1952.

John Addington Symonds 1840–93

Most of Symonds's papers are in Bristol Univ lib.

Bibliographies
Brown, H. F. In his Symonds: a biography vol 2, 1895.
Babington, P. L. Bibliography of the writings of Symonds. 1925.

§1

The Escorial: a prize poem. Oxford 1860.
The Renaissance: an essay. Oxford 1863.
The ring and the book. Macmillan's Mag 19 1869.
Miscellanies, by J. A. Symonds M. D. 1871. Ed Symonds.
An introduction to the study of Dante. 1872, Edinburgh 1890; ed H. F. Brown 1899 (4th edn).
The Renaissance of modern Europe: a lecture. 1872.
Studies of the Greek poets. 2 vols 1873–6, New York 1880, 1893 (3rd edn), 1902, 1920.
REVIEW: [Strachey, E.] Spectator 29 July 1876.
Sketches in Italy and Greece. 1874, 1879.
The Renaissance in Italy. Vol 1 The age of the despots, 1875, 1876, New York 1881, 1883, London 1884, New York 1918, London 1923, New York 1960, tr Ital 1900; vol 2 The revival of learning, 1877, 1880, New York 1883, 1888, London 1906, New York 1908, 1960; vol 3 The fine arts, 1870, 1877, New York 1883, London 1901, New York 1961, tr Ital 1879; vols 4–5 Italian literature, 1881, New York 1882, London 1888, New York 1888; vols 6–7 The Catholic reaction, 1886, New York 1887, London 1909; collected 7 vols 1875–86, New York 1881–7, 5 vols 1900; ed A. Pearson 2 vols 1893, New York 1893, 1893, London 1904, 1935 (as A short history of the Renaissance in Italy).
REVIEWS: [Strachey, E.] Spectator 24 July 1875, 27 Oct, 3 Nov 1877; [Courthope, W. J.] Quart Rev 145 1878; [Hueffer, F.] The Times 7 Apr 1882.
Shelley. 1878, New York 1879, London 1887, New York 1894, 1901, London 1902, New York 1902 (EML).

Many moods: a volume of verse. 1878.
The sonnets of Michelangelo Buonarroti and Tommaso Companella. 1878; Michelangelo, New York and London 1950, 1989. Tr Symonds.
Sketches and studies in Italy. 1879, Leipzig 1883; tr Ger 1912.
New and old: a volume of verse. 1880, Boston 1880.
Sketches and studies in southern Europe. 2 vols New York 1880.
Animi figura. 1882. Verse.
Notes on Mr D. G. Rossetti's new poems. Macmillan's Mag 45 1882.
Italian byways. 1883, New York 1883, Leipzig 1884 (as New Italian sketches).
A problem in Greek ethics. 1883, 1901, 1908 (all priv ptd), 1928 (in Studies in sexual inversion).
Fragilia labilia. 1884 (priv ptd), Portland ME 1902.
Vagabunduli libellus. 1884. Verse.
Shakespere's predecessors in the English drama. 1884, 1900.
Wine, women and song: mediaeval Latin students' songs. 1884, Portland ME 1899, 1918, London 1907, 1925, 1931, San Francisco 1928 (as Medieval latin students' songs). Tr Symonds.
Life of Ben Jonson. 1886.
Sir Philip Sidney. 1886, New York 1887, 1894, 1901, 1902, London 1902, 1906 (EML).
The life of Benevenuto Cellini. 1888, 1889, 1896, 1901, New York 1942; ed J. Pope-Hennessy, New York 1949. Tr Symonds.
Webster and Tourneur. 1888 (Mermaid ser), 1903, New York 1948, 1956, London 1954, 1959. Ed Symonds.
Essays speculative and suggestive. 2 vols 1890, 1 vol 1894, New York 1894; ed H. F. Brown 1907 (3rd edn).
The memoirs of Count Carlo Gozzi. 2 vols 1890; ed P. Horne, Oxford 1962. Tr Symonds.
A problem in modern ethics. 1891 (priv ptd) (anon), 1896, 1897 (in Sexual inversion by H. Ellis and Symonds), 1928 (in Studies in sexual inversion); ed J. Lauriston as Male love, New York 1983.
Our life in the Swiss highlands. 1892, 1907. With his daughter M. Symonds.
Midnight in Baiae. 1893.
In the key of blue and other prose essays. 1893, 1896 (3rd edn).
The life of Michelangelo Buonarroti. 2 vols 1893, 1893, 1911 (3rd edn), 1925, 1 vol New York 1928, 1936; tr Ital 1943, Sp 1943.
Walt Whitman: a study. 1893, 1893, 1896, 1906.
Blank verse. Ed H. F. Brown 1894, 1895, New York 1895.
Giovanni Boccaccio as man and author. 1895.
Sketches and studies in Italy and Greece. Ed H. F. Brown 3 vols 1898, 1900. Includes Sketches in Italy and Greece, Sketches and studies in Italy, Italian byways.
Last and first: two essays. New York 1919.
Letters and papers. Ed H. F. Brown 1923.
The letters of John Addington Symonds. Ed H. M. Schueller and R. L. Peters 3 vols Detroit 1967–9.

Contributions to periodicals

For further items, see Wellesley. *Symonds also contributed to the* Pall Mall Gazette *and* Saturday Review.

§2

Brown, H. F. Symonds: a biography. 2 vols 1895, New York 1895, London 1903.
Harrison, F. J. A. Symonds. 1896.
Symonds, A. In his Studies in two literatures, 1897.
Harrison, F. J. A. In his Tennyson, Ruskin, Mill and other literary estimates, 1899.
Symonds, M. Last days of Symonds. 1906.
Brooks, Van W. Symonds: a biographical study. 1914.
Symonds, A. A study of Symonds. Fortnightly Rev Feb 1924.
Symonds, M. Out of the past. 1925.
Grantham, E. Letters from Symonds to Swinburne. More Books 21 1946.
Grosskurth, P. M. Symonds: a biography. 1964.
Grosskurth, P. M. (ed). Memoirs of J. A. Symonds. 1984.

Connop Thirlwall 1797–1875

§1

Primitiae: or essays and poems. 1809 (priv ptd).
A critical essay on the gospel of Luke, by Dr F. Schleiermacher. 1825. Tr and ed Thirlwall, amended T. Tice, Lampeter 1993.
The history of Rome, by B. G. Niebuhr. 3 vols Cambridge 1828–42, 1847–51 (3rd edn). Vols 1–2 tr Thirlwall and J. C. Hare.
A vindication of Niebuhr's History of Rome from the charges of the Quarterly Review, by J. C. Hare. Cambridge 1829. Postscript by Thirlwall.
The irony of Sophocles. Philological Museum 2 1833; rptd in Remains, *below*, 1877.
A letter to the Rev T. Turton on the admission of Dissenters to academical degrees. Cambridge 1834, 1834 (rev).
A history of Greece. 8 vols 1835–44 (in Cabinet cyclopaedia, ed D. Lardner), 1839–44, 1845–52, 2 vols New York 1845, 1848–51; tr Ger (in part) 1839–40, Fr 1852.
Schleiermacher on the worth of Socrates as a philosopher. In A life of Socrates by G. Wiggers, 1840. Tr Thirlwall.
The centre of unity: a sermon. 1850; ed J. E. B. Mayor, Cambridge 1901.
The present state of the relations between science and literature. 1867.
Notes on contemporary questions. Contemporary Rev 26 1875.
Remains, literary and theological. Ed J. J. S. Perowne 3 vols 1877, 1878.
Essays, speeches and sermons. 1880.
Letters literary and theological. Ed J. J. S. Perowne and L. Stokes 1881.
Letters to a friend. Ed A. P. Stanley 1881, 1882, Boston 1883.

§2

Freeman, E. A. Greece during the Macedonian period. North Br Rev 21 1854; rptd in his Historical essays, 1879.
Plumptree, E. H. Connop Thirlwall, Bishop of St David's. Edinburgh Rev 143 1876.
[Beard, C.] Thirlwall's Remains. Theological Rev 15 1878.
[Dicey, A. V.] Bishop Thirlwall. Nation 28 Feb 1878.
Clark, J. W. In his Old friends at Cambridge and elsewhere, 1900.
Thirlwall, J. C. Thirlwall: historian and theologian. 1936.

Sir George Otto Trevelyan 1838–1928

The G. O. Trevelyan papers are at the Univ of Newcastle upon Tyne.

§1

The Cambridge Dionysia: a classic dream by the editor of the Bear. Cambridge 1858.
Horace at the University of Athens: a dramatic sketch. Cambridge 1861 (anon), 1862.
The Pope and his patron. 1862.
The dawk bungalow: or 'Is his appointment pucka?' by H. Broughton. 1863. A comedy.
Letters from a competition wallah. Macmillan's Mag 8 1863–10 1864; rptd 1864 (as The competition wallah), 1866, 1895.
Cawnpore. 1865, 1866, 1886 (new edn), 1894, 1910, Brentwood 1986.
The ladies in Parliament and other pieces. Cambridge 1869, London 1888.
The life and letters of Lord Macaulay. 2 vols 1876, New York 1876 (with appendix, Macaulay on American institutions), Leipzig 1876, London 1877 (rev), New York 1877, London 1878, 1 vol 1881, 2 vols Chicago 1885, 1 vol London 1889, 1908 ('enlarged'), 1913; ed G. M. Trevelyan 2 vols Oxford 1932 (WC); 1 vol 1959, 2 vols Oxford

1961, 1976; ed G. M. Trevelyan 1978; tr Sp (in part) 1899. P. Clarke, Index to Trevelyan's Life and letters of Macauley, 1881.
REVIEWS: [Froude, Rev J. A.] Fraser's Mag 93 1876; [Gladstone, W. E.] Quart Rev 142 1876.
Selections from the writings of Lord Macaulay. 1876. Ed Trevelyan.
The early history of Charles James Fox. 1880, 1880, New York 1880, London 1881 (3rd edn), New York 1881, 1900, London 1901, 1905, 1908, 1911.
The American Revolution. 4 vols London and New York 1899–1907, 1899–1913, 1905–12, 1917–18, 1926–9; ed R. B. Morris, New York 1964 (abridged), London 1966.
REVIEWS: [Elliot, A. R. D.] Edinburgh Rev 189 1899; [Walpole, S.] Edinburgh Rev 199 1904.
Interludes in verse and prose. 1905, 1924.
Marginal notes by Lord Macaulay. 1907. Ed Trevelyan.
George the Third and Charles Fox: the concluding part of The American Revolution. 2 vols 1912–14, New York 1912–14, 1915–16, London 1921–7.

Contributions to periodicals

For a list of Trevelyan's reviews and articles, see Wellesley.

§2

[Dallas, E. S.] Cawnpore. The Times 31 May 1865.
[Griffin, M. J.] Trevelyan as a historian. Blackwood's Mag 165 1899.
Trevelyan, G. M. Sir G. O. Trevelyan: a memoir by his son. 1932.
Trevelyan, G. M. Sir G. O. Trevelyan. DNB 1937.
Trevelyan, G. M. In his Autobiography and other essays, 1949.
Cowboys and kings: three great letters. Ed C. E. Morrison, Cambridge MA 1954.
Bratcher, J. T. G. M. Trevelyan's copy of Horace at Athens. LCUT 8 1966.

Sharon Turner 1768–1847

Turner's ms letters to H. Coburn are in the BL.

§1

The history of the Anglo-Saxons . . . to the Norman Conquest. 4 vols 1799–1805, 2 vols 1807 (2nd edn enlarged), 4 vols 1820 (3rd edn), 3 vols 1823 (4th edn), 3 vols 1828, 3 vols 1836 (6th edn as vols 1–3 of The history of England from the earliest period), 3 vols Paris 1840, 2 vols Philadelphia 1841, London 1852 (7th edn revised by his son Sydney Turner).
An enquiry respecting the early use of rhyme. 1803 (first ptd 1802 in an unidentified periodical).
A vindication of the genuineness of the ancient British poems of Anuerin, Taliesin, Llywarch Hen and Merdhin. 1803.
A brief epitome of the history of England from 1066. 2 vols 1807.
Reasons for the modification of the act of Anne respecting the delivery of books and copyright. 1813.
The history of England from the Norman Conquest to the accession of Edward I, and continued to the death of Henry VII. 3 vols 1814–23; retitled The history of England during the Middle Ages from the reign of William the Conqueror to the accession of Henry VIII, 5 vols 1825 (2nd edn), 5 vols 1830 (3rd edn as vols 4–8 of The history of England from the earliest period), 4 vols 1853 (5th edn).
To the chairman of the committee upon the copyright laws. 1818.
Prolusions on the present greatness of Britain: on modern poetry: and on the present aspect of the world. 1819. Poem.
History of the reign of Henry VIII. 1826, 1827, 1828 (3rd edn).
Registrum Wiltunese. Ed Turner et al 1827.
The history of the reigns of Edward VI, Mary and Elizabeth. 2 vols 1829. Also issued with the History of Henry VIII as The modern history of England, 4 vols 1827–9.
The sacred history of the world. 3 vols 1832–7, 3 vols 1833–7 (3rd and 4th edns), 3 vols New York 1832–8 (Harper's Family Lib), 3 vols 1840–4 (new edn); ed Sydney Turner 3 vols 1848 (8th edn).
The history of England from the earliest period to the death of Elizabeth. 12 vols 1839. Brings together the 4 histories of England from the Anglo-Saxons to Elizabeth.
Richard III: a poem. 1845.

Contributions to periodicals

Review of Grammar of the Sanscrita language. Quart Rev 1 1809.
Review of Austrian state papers. Quart Rev 1 1809.
Letter on the terms used by different nations to express mother. Essays by Divers Hands 1 1829.
On the classification and affinities of the words in various languages for father. Essays by Divers Hands 1 1829.
On the elementary compound terms and their classifications and affinities for the numeral two. Essays by Divers Hands 1 1829.
On the affinities and diversities in all the languages of the world. Essays by Divers Hands 1 1829.
Further illustrations of the primeval cause of affinities and diversities of language. Essays by Divers Hands 1 1829.
Further illustrations of the preceeding principles. Essays by Divers Hands 1 1829.
On the Asiatic origins of the Anglo-Saxons. Essays by Divers Hands 2 1834.

Alexander Fraser Tytler, Lord Woodhouselee

1747–1813

Ms works can be found in the Laing Collection at Edinburgh Univ Lib. Letters and the draft of the Memoirs of Kames are in the NLS.

§1

The decisions of the court of session. [Vol supplementary to Lord Kames's Dictionary of decisions.] Edinburgh 1778.
Plan and outlines of a course of lectures on universal history. Edinburgh 1783.
Essay on the life and character of Petrarch. 1784.
Essay on the principles of translation. 1791, 1797, Edinburgh 1813 (3rd edn enlarged), London 1907 (EL); ed J. Huntsman 1978.
A critical examination of Mr Whitaker's course of Hannibal over the Alps. Edinburgh 1798.
Ireland profiting by example, or the question considered whether Scotland has gained or lost by the union. Edinburgh 1799.
Essay on military law and the practice of courts martial. Edinburgh 1800, 1806, 1814 (3rd edn).
Elements of general history ancient and modern. 2 vols 1801, 3 vols Edinburgh 1801–22 (vol 3 a continuation by E. Nares), 2 vols Edinburgh 1803 (2nd edn), 1805 (3rd edn), Philadelphia 1809, 2 vols Edinburgh 1812 (5th edn corrected and improved), 2 vols Edinburgh 1813 (6th edn), New York 1817, Hartford CT 1818 (continued by T. Robbins), Concord NH 1823 (adapted for schools), 2 vols London 1825 (9th edn with addns), 1839 (new edn continued to the death of William IV), 1844 (continued to the present time by T. E. Tomlins), ed B. Turner 1846, Concord NH 1851 (195th edn), 1855 (rev and continued to the present by J. H. Burton), Edinburgh 1857 (new edn brought down to conclusion of war with Russia), ed E. Bell 1875 (continued to the present by C. J. Smith; tr Hindi 1829; abridged Cork 1824; abstracts for school use 1832, 1843; ancient history pt ptd separately Edinburgh 1850, 1851; modern history pt ptd Edinburgh 1850 (continued to 1850), 1856 (continued by J. Campbell Smith).
Memoirs of the life and writings of the Hon Henry Home of Kames. 2 vols Edinburgh 1807, 3 vols Edinburgh 1814.
An historical and critical essay on the life and character of Petrarch. Edinburgh 1810, 1812.
Travels in France during the year 1814–15. [Vol 1 by A. Alison, W.

Alison and J. Hope; vol 2 by A. Tytler.] 2 vols 1815, 2 vols 1816 (enlarged).

Considerations on the present political state of India. 2 vols 1815, 2 vols 1816.

Contributions to periodicals

Tytler wrote pieces for Henry Mackenzie's Mirror *nos 17, 37, 59, 79 (1779–80) and* Lounger *nos 7, 19, 24, 44, 63, 70, 79 (1785–6).*

History of the Royal Society of Edinburgh. Trans of the Royal Soc of Edinburgh 1 1787.

Life of Lord Dundas. Trans of the Royal Soc of Edinburgh 2 1790.

An account of some extraordinary structures on the tops of hills in the Highlands. Trans of the Royal Soc of Edinburgh 2 1790.

Remarks on a mixed species of evidence in matters of history. Trans of the Royal Soc of Edinburgh 5 1805.

Prefaces, translations, editions

Fletcher, P. Piscatory eclogues. Edinburgh 1771. Ed Tytler.

Gregory, J. Works. 4 vols Edinburgh 1788. Preface by Tytler.

von Schiller, J. C. F. The robbers. 1792, 1795, 1800. Tr Tytler.

Derham, W. Physico-Theology: or a demonstration of the being and attributes of God. Account of the author and a dissertation on final causes by A. Tytler. 2 vols Edinburgh 1798.

The works of Allan Ramsay. To which are prefixed remarks on his poems [by Tytler]. 1800, 1848, 1851, 1853, 1866, 1877.

Universal history from the creation to the beginning of the eighteenth century. 6 vols 1834, 6 vols 1835 (2nd edn), 2 vols Boston 1835, 6 vols London 1839 (3rd edn), ed An American 6 vols New York 1839–40 (continued by Tytler and E. Nares to 1820), 2 vols Philadelphia 1860; adapted as A Course of historical and chronological instruction by W. E. Bickmore, 1836. Ed Tytler.

Attributed works

Considerations on the game law. 1772.

§2

Alison, A. Memoir of the life and writings of the Hon Alexander Fraser Tytler. 1818.

Sir Spencer Walpole 1839–1907

§1

The life of Spencer Perceval by his grandson. 2 vols 1874.

A manual of the law of salmon fisheries in England and Wales. 1877.

A history of England from the conclusion of the great war in 1815. 2 vols 1879–80, 5 vols 1879–86 (2nd edn), 6 vols 1890 (rev), 1902–5, 1912.

REVIEWS: [Dicey, A. V.] Nation (New York) 30 Oct 1879; [Fytte, C. A.] EHR 2 1887.

The electorate and the legislature. 1881, 1892.

Foreign relations. 1882.

The British fish trade. 1883.

The life of Lord John Russell. 2 vols 1889, 1889, 1891.

Todd, A. On parliamentary government in England. 2 vols 1892; tr Fr 1900. Ed Walpole.

The land of home rule: an essay on the history and constitution of the Isle of Man. 1893.

Some unpublished letters of Horace Walpole. 1902. Ed Walpole.

The history of twenty-five years 1856–1880. 2 vols 1904, 4 vols 1904–8. Vols 3–4 completed by A. C. Lyall.

Studies in biography. 1907, 1907, New York 1907.

Essays political and biographical. Ed F. Holland 1908.

Contributions to periodicals

For a list of Walpole's reviews and articles, see Wellesley.

§2

Gladstone, W. E. The Melbourne government. Nineteenth Cent Jan 1890.

[Roscoe, E. S.] Walpole's Life of Russell. Edinburgh Rev 171 1890.

[Roscoe, E. S.] The land of home rule. Edinburgh Rev 178 1893.

Hutchinson, H. G. Sir Spencer Walpole. Cornhill Mag Sep 1907.

Holland, F. Memoir of Walpole. In Essays political and biographical, 1908.

Mary Anne Everett Wood, later Green 1818–95

§1

Lives of the princesses of England from the Norman Conquest. 6 vols 1849–55; extract from Life of Elizabeth of Bohemia rev S. C. Lomas, ed A. W. Ward 1909.

Editions

Letters of royal and illustrious ladies of Great Britain. 3 vols 1846.

Diary of John Rous. 1856 (Camden Soc no 66).

Letters of Queen Henrietta Maria. '1857' [1856].

Calendar of state papers, domestic series: addenda for the volume 1547–65. 1870. The reign of James I, ed Wood 5 vols 1857–9; vols for 1649–59, ed Wood 13 vols 1875–86; Calendar of the proceedings of the committee for advance of money 1642–56, ed Wood 3 vols 1888; vol for 1659–60, ed Wood 1888; Calendar of the proceedings of the committee for compounding 1643–60, ed Wood 7 pts 1889–93; vols 1–10 for the reign of Charles II, ed Wood 10 vols 1860–6; added vol for the years 1660–70, ed Wood 1895.

Life of Mr William Whittingham, Dean of Durham. Ed from ms 1871 (Camden Misc vol 6).

Extracts from pedigrees of the Sydenham family. Ed M. Green and F. Brown 1884.

Wood also contributed to the Athenaeum *and the* Gentleman's London Rev.

Thomas Wright 1810–77

§1

The history and topography of the County of Essex. 2 vols 1836.

Coup-d'œil sur les progrès et sur l'état actuel de la littérature anglo-saxonne en Angleterre: traduction de [P.-F.] de Larenaudière. Paris 1836. For English version, *see* Biographia britannica, *below.*

The history and antiquities of London, Westminster, Southward and parts adjacent. 5 vols 1837. Vols 1–4 by T. Allen; vol 5 by Wright.

The universities: Le Keux's Memorials of Cambridge; with historical and descriptive accounts by Thomas Wright and H. Longueville Jones. 2 vols 1841–2; ed C. H. Cooper 2 vols Cambridge 1860, 3 vols Cambridge [1880].

The history of Ludlow and its neighbourhood. Ludlow 1852 (for 1841–52).

Biographia britannica literaria: or biography of literary characters of Great Britain and Ireland. Anglo-Saxon period, 1842. Anglo-Norman period, 1846; Introduction also separately pbd as An essay on the state of literature and learning under the Anglo-Saxons, introductory to the Biographia britannica literaria, 1839.

St Patrick's purgatory: an essay on the legends of Purgatory, Hell and Paradise current during the Middle Ages. 1844.

Essays on subjects connected with the literature, popular superstitions and history of England in the Middle Ages. 2 vols 1846. Rptd from periodicals.

England under the House of Hanover: its history during the reigns of the three Georges, illustrated from the caricatures and satires of the day. 2 vols 1848, [1868], 1876 (as Caricature history of the Georges).

The history of Ireland. 3 vols [1848–52].

Narratives of sorcery and magic. 2 vols 1851.

Historical and descriptive account of the caricatures of James

Gillray. 1851, [1873] (expanded as The works of James Gillray, with the history of his life and times). With R. H. Evans.
The Celt, the Roman and the Saxon: a history of the early inhabitants of Britain, down to the conversion of the Anglo-Saxons. 1852, 1861 (rev), 1875, 1885.
The history of Scotland. 3 vols [1852–5], [1873–4], 1888.
Wanderings of an antiquary, chiefly upon the traces of the Romans in Britain. 1854.
A lecture on the antiquities of the Anglo-Saxon cemeteries of the ages of paganism, illustrative of the Faussett Collection. Liverpool 1854.
Guide to the Caterham railway, and to the country around it. 1856.
The history of France. 3 vols [1856–62], 3 vols [1871–2] (including A faithful account of the war with Germany by Lt-Col Williams).
Miscellanea graphica: representations of remains in the possession of Lord Londesborough. Drawn by F. W. Fairholt; the historical introduction by Thomas Wright. 1857.
Dictionary of obsolete and provincial English. 2 vols 1857.
Guide to the ruins of the Roman city of Uriconium at Wroxeter near Shrewsbury. Shrewsbury 1859, 1859 (as The ruins of the Roman city of Uriconium), 1860, 1868, 1877 (6th edn).
History and antiquities of Cumberland and Westmoreland. In W. Whellan, The history and topography of Cumberland and Westmoreland, Pontefract 1860.
Essays on archaeological subjects and on various questions connected with the Middle Ages. 2 vols 1861.
A history of domestic manners and sentiments in England during the Middle Ages. 1862, 1871 (expanded as The homes of other days).
Historical and descriptive sketch of Ludlow Castle. [1862?], Ludlow 1869 (4th edn rev), 1909 (13th edn) etc.
A history of caricature and grotesque in literature and art. 1865; tr Fr 1867.
Ludlow sketches: a series of papers. Ludlow 1867.
Historical cartoons. By Gustav Doré. With descriptive text by Wright. [1868.]
Womankind in Western Europe from the earliest times to the seventeenth century. 1869.
Uriconium: a historical account of the ancient Roman city. 1872.
Historical sketch of Stokesay Castle, Salop. Ludlow 1921, 1924.

Editions

Early English poetry. 4 vols 1836. Anthology.
The tour of the French traveller, M. de la Boullaye le Gouz, in Ireland, AD 1644. Ed T. C. Croker 1837. With notes by Wright.
Anglo-Norman poem on the conquest of Ireland by Henry the Second. Ed F. Michel 1837. With an introductory essay on the conquest by Wright.
Galfridi de Monemuta Vita Merlini. Vie de Merlin, attribuée à Geoffroy de Monmouth. Paris 1837. Ed Wright with F. Michel.
Early mysteries, and other Latin poems of the twelfth and thirteenth centuries. 1838.
Alliterative poem on the deposition of King Richard II. 1838 (Camden Soc).
Queen Elizabeth and her times. A series of original letters, selected from the unedited private correspondence of Lord Burghley, the Earl of Leicester etc. 2 vols 1838.
The political songs of England, from John to Edward II. 1839 (Camden Soc), ed E. Goldsmid 4 vols 1884.
Relations des voyages de Guillaume de Rubruk, Jean de Plan Carpin, Bernard, Saewulf etc. Ed F. Michel and Wright, in Recueil de Voyages et de Mémoires, publié par la Société de Géographie 4 Paris 1839.
The history of English poetry. By Thomas Warton. 3 vols 1840. Corrections and addns by Wright et al.
Popular treatises on science written during the Middle Ages, in Anglo-Saxon, Anglo-Norman and English. 1841 (Historical Soc of Science).
The Latin poems attributed to Walter Mapes. 1841 (Camden Soc).
Political ballads published in England during the Commonwealth. 1841 (Percy Soc).
Specimens of old Christmas carols. 1841 (Percy Soc).
The Archaeologist and Journal of Antiquarian Science. Sep 1841–June 1842. Ed J. O. Halliwell and Wright.
Reliquiae antiquae. Scraps from ancient manuscripts, illustrating Early English literature and the English language. 2 vols 1841–3, 2 vols 1845. Ed J. O. Halliwell and Wright.
A dialogue concerning witches and witchcrafts. By G. Gifford. 1842 (Percy Soc).
Specimens of lyric poetry, composed in England in the reign of Edward the First. 1842 (Percy Soc).
A selection of Latin stories. A contribution to the history of fiction during the Middle Ages. 1842 (Percy Soc).
The autobiography of Joseph Lister, of Bradford in Yorkshire. 1842.
The vision and the creed of Piers Ploughman. 1842, 2 vols 1856. With introd, notes and glossary. Anon.
A contemporary narrative of the proceedings against Dame Alice Kyteler. 1843 (Camden Soc).
Three chapters of letters relating to the suppression of the monasteries. 1843 (Camden Soc).
The owl and the nightingale: attributed to Nicholas de Guildford, with some shorter poems. 1843 (Percy Soc).
The Chester plays. 2 vols 1843–7 (Shakespeare Soc).
St Brandan. A medieval legend of the sea. 1844 (Percy Soc).
Anecdota literaria. A collection of short poems in English, Latin and French, illustrative of the literature and history of England in the thirteenth century. 1844.
The archaeological album, or Museum of national antiquities. 1845.
The pastime of pleasure. By Stephen Hawes. 1845 (Percy Soc).
The seven sages in English verse. 1845 (Percy Soc); introd 1846.
Songs and carols from a manuscript of the fifteenth century. 1847 (Percy Soc).
The Canterbury tales of Geoffrey Chaucer: a new text. 3 vols 1847–51 (Percy Soc), 1853.
Early travels in Palestine, comprising the narratives of Arculf, Willibald, Bernard etc. 1848.
A new general biographical dictionary, projected and partly arranged by H. J. Rose. 12 vols 1848. Vols 2–12 ed Wright.
The religious poems of William de Shoreham. 1849 (Percy Soc).
Gualteri Mapes De nugis curialium. 1850 (Camden Soc).
The Anglo-Norman metrical chronicle of Geoffrey Gaimar. 1850 (Caxton Soc).
The ancient laws of the fifteenth century, for King's College Cambridge and Eton College, collected by J. Heywood and T. Wright. 1850.
The life of King Alfred, by R. Pauli. 1852.
The universal pronouncing dictionary. Compiled under the direction of Thomas Wright. 6 vols 1852–6.
Cambridge universal transactions during the Puritan controversies of the 16th and 17th centuries. Collected by J. Heywood and Wright. 2 vols 1854.
The travels of Marco Polo, the Venetian. The translation of Marsden revised. 1854, 1904.
The history of Fulke Warine, with an English translation and notes. 1855 (Warton Club).
Songs and carols from a manuscript of the fifteenth century. 1856 (Warton Club). Distinct from Percy Soc vol 1847.
Johannis de Garlandia De triumphis ecclesiæ. 1856 (Roxburghe Club).
A volume of vocabularies, illustrating the condition and manners of our forefathers, from the tenth century to the fifteenth. 2 vols 1857–73 (priv ptd) (J. Mayer's Library of National Antiquities); ed R. P. Wülcker 2 vols 1884.

Les cent nouvelles nouvelles, publiées d'après le seul manuscrit connu, avec introduction et notes. 2 vols Paris 1857–8.
La morte d'Arthure: the history of King Arthur and of the Knights of the Round Table, compiled by Sir Thomas Malory. 3 vols 1858, 3 vols 1866 (rev), 1893. Ed from 1634 edn.
Manual of ethnology, by J. C. Prichard, revised by Wright and Monsieur d'Avezac, extracted from Admiralty Manual of scientific enquiry. 1859 (3rd edn).
A glossary by Robert Nares: a new edition by J. O. Halliwell and T. Wright. 2 vols 1859, 1888, 1905.
Political poems and songs relating to English history, composed during the period from the accession of Edw III to that of Ric III. 2 vols 1859–61 (Rerum Britannicarum Medii Ævi Scriptores).
Songs and ballads, with other short poems, chiefly of the reign of Philip and Mary. 1860 (Roxburghe Club).
Fairy legends and traditions of the South of Ireland, by T. C. Croker. [1862], [1870], [1882], 1902.
The Royal dictionary-cyclopaedia, compiled under the direction of Wright. 5 vols [1862–7].
Alexandri Neckam De naturis rerum. 1863 (Rerum Britannicarum Medii Ævi Scriptores).
The historical works of Giraldus Cambrensis. 1863. Tr T. Forester and Sir R. Colt Hoare.
The roll of arms of the princes, barons and knights who attended Edward I to the siege of Caerlaverock in 1300. 1864. With trn and notes.
Autobiography of Thomas Wright of Birkenshaw 1736–97. 1864.
History of Julius Caesar, by Napoleon III. 2 vols [1865–6]. Tr Wright.
The chronicle of Pierre de Langtoft. 2 vols 1866–8 (Rerum Britannicarum Medii Ævi Scriptores).
The book of the Knight of La Tour-Landry, translated from the French into English in the reign of Henry VI. 1868, 1906 (rev) (EETS).
Churchwardens' accounts of the town of Ludlow. 1869 (Camden Soc).
Feudal manuals of English history: a series of popular sketches of our national history, compiled from the thirteenth century to the fifteenth. 1872.
The Anglo-Latin satirical poets and epigrammatists of the twelfth century. 2 vols 1872 (Rerum Britannicarum Medii Ævi Scriptores).
The Decameron of Boccaccio. 1874.
Killarney legends. By T. C. Croker. [1876.]

Contributions to periodicals

See Wellesley *vol 5 1989*.

§2

Academy 29 Dec 1877.
Athenaeum 29 Dec 1877.
Garnett, R. Antiquarian club books. Quart Rev 82 1878.
Jewitt, L. Some departed contributors and literary friends. Reliquary 18 1878.
Fitch, E. A. Historians of Essex: Wright. Essex Rev 9 1900. [KO]

8 Political Economy

Bibliographic sources

The nineteenth century is less well served than its predecessor by the available bibliographies dealing with primary printed sources. The only work that covers the entire century has the minor regional limitation indicated in its subtitle: A catalogue of pamphlets on economic subjects, published between 1750 and 1900, and now housed in Irish libraries by R. D. Collison Black, *Belfast 1969. The second vol of* The catalogue of the Goldsmiths' Library of Economic Literature *(comp M. Canney, D. Knott and J. M Gibbs with an introd by J. H. P. Pafford, 2 vols Cambridge, vol 1 1970, vol 2 1975) covers the period from 1801–50, using a chronological arrangement supplemented by subject divisions within each year. The second and third vols of* The catalogue of the Kress Library of Business and Economics *(5 vols plus supplementary vols, Harvard 1940, 1956, 1957, 1964, 1967) only cover the period up to 1848, though a consolidated bibliography for the Goldsmith and Kress Collections, now available in microform, is promised.*

The following useful sources are more partial in their coverage for the reasons indicated in their titles, dates of publication, and supplementary comments.

McCulloch, J. R. The literature of political economy. 1845, rptd New York 1964.

McCulloch, J. R. A catalogue of books, the property of a political economist. 1862.

Palgrave, R. H. I. Dictionary of political economy. 3 vols 1894, rptd 1987, now updated as The new Palgrave: a dictionary of economics, ed J. Eatwell, M. Milgate and P. Newman 4 vols 1987. Provides two additional bibliographic sources for individual authors. (Cited respectively as DPE and NPDE, *below*.)

Williams, J. B. A guide to the printed materials for English social and economic history 1750–1850. 2 vols New York 1926.

Batson, H. E. A select bibliography of modern economic theory 1870–1929. 1930.

Amano, K. Bibliography of the classical economists. Pbd by The Science Council of Japan; Division of Economics, Commerce and Business Administration, Economic ser nos 27, 30, 31, 32 and 33, Tokyo 1961–4. The sequence covers primary and secondary sources for Adam Smith and T. R. Malthus (Pts I and II), David Ricardo (Pt III), John Stuart Mill (Pt IV) and shorter bibliographies in Pt V on the following authors: S. Bailey, J. Bentham, T. Chalmers, R. Jones, J. R. McCulloch, J. Maitland, James Mill, S. Mountifield Longfield, N. W. Senior, D. Stewart, T. Tooke, R. Torrens, E. G. Wakefield and E. West. (Cited as Amano, *below*.)

Black, R. D. C. The Statistical and Social Inquiry Society of Ireland: centenary volume 1847–1947. Dublin 1947. This contains indexes to the transactions of the Society identifying contributors. Together with the same author's Select bibliography of economic writings by members of Trinity College Dublin, Hermathena 66 1945, it provides a guide to work by Irish authors connected with Trinity College, without attempting to be comprehensive.

Sturges, R. Economists' papers 1750–1950: a guide to archive and other manuscript sources for the history of British and Irish economic thought. 1975. (Cited as Sturges, *below*.)

The pioneering work in identifying the authors of anonymous articles in some leading periodicals was done by Frank W. Fetter: see The authorship of economic articles in the Edinburgh Rev 1802–47, *Jnl of Political Economy 61 1953;* The economic articles in the Quarterly Review and their authors 1809–52, *Jnl of Political Economy 66 1958;* Economic articles in Blackwood's, *Scottish Jnl of Political Economy 7 1960;* The economic articles in the Westminster Review and their authors, 1824–51, *Jnl of Political Economy 70 1962. These articles still contain valuable material on authorship, despite the fact that in terms of coverage they have been superseded by* Wellesley.

Sir William James Ashley 1860–1927

For information on the location of papers and correspondence, see Sturges.

Collections and selections

Ashley, W. J. Surveys historic and economic. 1900, rptd New York 1966. Articles and reviews pbd outside Britain.

§1

Edward III and his wars. 1887.

The early history of the English woollen industry. 1887.

An introduction to English economic history and theory. 2 vols 1888, 1892, 1893, 1894, 1966.

What is political science? Toronto 1888.

The character of villein tenure. 1891.

The Anglo-Saxon township. 1894.

The railroad strike of 1894. 1895.

The beginnings of town life in the Middle Ages. 1896.

The tariff problem. 1903, 1904, 1911, 1920, 1968.

The adjustment of wages; a study of the coal and iron industries of Great Britain and America. 1903.

Social legislation. 1909.

The faculty of commerce and the University of Birmingham. Birmingham 1912.

The economic organisation of England. 1914, 1926.

Scientific management and the engineering situation. Oxford 1922.

The Christian outlook. 1925.

Business economics. 1926.

Contributions to periodicals and collaborative works

Feudalism. In H. O. Wakeman and A. Hassal, Essays introductory to the study of the English constitutional history, 1880, 1887, 1891.

Introductory chapter on the English manor. In The origin of property in land, ed F. de Coulanges, 1891.
The rehabilitation of Ricardo. Economic Jnl Sep 1891.
The destruction of the village community. Economic Rev July 1891.
Methods of industrial peace. Economic Rev July 1892.
On the study of economic history. Quart Jnl of Economics Jan 1893.
The history of English serfdom. Economic Rev Apr 1893.
The tory origins of free trade policy. Quart Jnl of Economics 1897.
The present position of political economy in England. Economic Jnl Dec 1907.
The enlargement of economics. Economic Jnl June 1908.
The place of economic history in university studies. Economic History Rev Jan 1927.

Editions and translations

Economic classics. 8 vols 1895–8.
Schmoller, G. The mercantile system and its historical significance. New York 1896. Tr and introd by Ashley.
Mill, J. S. Principles of political economy. Ed Ashley 1909.

§2

Clapham, J. H. Sir William Ashley. Economic Jnl Dec 1927.
Ashley, A. William James Ashley: a life. 1932.
Kadish, A. The Oxford economists in the late nineteenth century. Oxford 1982.

Thomas Attwood 1783–1856

For information on the location of papers and correspondence, see Sturges.

Bibliography

Fetter, F. W. (ed). Selected economic writings of Thomas Attwood. 1964. Primary.

Selections

See Fetter,, above.

§1

The remedy, or thoughts on the present distress. 1816 (in Fetter, *above*).
A letter to the Rt Hon Nicholas Vansittart on the creation of money. 1817.
Prosperity restored. 1817.
Observations on currency, population, and pauperism. 1818.
A letter to the Earl of Liverpool . . . on the questions of the Bank Restriction Act. 1819 (in Fetter, *above*).
A second letter to the Earl of Liverpool on the bank reports. 1819.
State of Ireland. 1820.
Thoughts on the report of the committee appointed by the House of Commons to inquire into agricultural distress. 1821, rptd as An exposition of the causes and remedy of the agricultural distress, 1828.
Mr Attwood's letter and table, shewing the unjust payment from the landed to the monied interest. 1822.
The late prosperity and the adversity of the country explained. 1826 (in Fetter, *above*).
The Scotch banker. 1828, 1832.
Proposed remedy for the distresses of the country. 1829.
Distressed state of the country. 1829.
Causes of the present distress. 1829.
On circulating credit. Edinburgh 1832.
Letter to Sir Robert Peel on the currency. 1837, 1843 (in Fetter, *above*).
Exportation of gold. 1839.

§2

Wakefield, C. M. Life of Thomas Attwood. 1885.
Checkland, S. G. The Birmingham economists, 1815–50. Economic History Rev 1 1948.

Charles Babbage 1792–1871

For information on the location of papers and correspondence, see Sturges.

Bibliography

Babbage, C. Passages from the life of a philosopher. 1864, 1969. Primary.
Morrison, P. and E. (ed). Charles Babbage and his calculating engine; selected writings. New York 1961. Primary and secondary.

Selections

See Morrison, above.
Mathematical and scientific library of the late Charles Babbage. 1872.
Babbage's calculating engine. Ed H. P. Babbage 1889, 1907.
How to invent machinery. Ed W. H. Atherton 1897.

§1

Examples of the solutions of functional equations. 1820.
A comparative view of the various institutions for the assurance of lives. 1826.
Table of logarithms of the natural numbers. 1827, 1844, 1915; tr Ger 1834, Hungarian 1834.
Reflections on the decline of science in England. 1830, 1969.
On the advantage of a collection of numbers. 1832.
A word to the wise. 1833, 1856.
On the economy of machinery and manufactures. 1832, Philadelphia 1832, London 1833, 1835 (4th edn enlarged), 1846; tr Fr 1833.
On currency, on a new system of manufacturing, and on the effect of machinery on human labour. Three chs from 3rd edn of On the economy of machinery, 1833.
The ninth Bridgewater treatise. 1835, 1837, 1841, 1967.
Observations on the temple of Serapis. 1847.
Thoughts on the principles of taxation, with reference to a property tax and its exceptions. 1848, 1851, 1852.
The exposition of 1851; or, views of the industry, the science, and the government of England. 1851, 1851, 1968, 1969.
Laws of mechanical notation. 1851.
Notes respecting lighthouses. 1852.
A letter to the Board of Visitors. 1854.
Observations . . . to the President and Fellows of the Royal Society. 1856.
An analysis of the statistics of the clearing house during the year 1839. 1856.
Observations on the discovery . . . of remains of human art. 1859.
Thoughts upon an extension of the franchise. 1865.
A letter from John Davy. 1865.

§2

Moseley, M. Irascible genius. 1964.
Hyman, A. Charles Babbage: pioneer of the computer. Oxford 1982.

Walter Bagehot 1826–77

Collections

The works, with memoirs by R. H. Hutton. Ed F. Morgan 5 vols Hartford CT 1889.
The works and life. Ed E. I. Barrington 10 vols 1915.
Collected works. Ed N. St John-Stevas 15 vols 1965–86. Literary essays vols 1–2, 1965; Historical writings vols 3–4, 1968; Political writings vols 5–8, 1974; Economic writings vols 9–11, 1978; Letters vols 12–13, 1986; Miscellaneous vols 14–15, 1986.

§1

Estimates of some Englishmen and Scotchmen. 1858. Rptd from Nat Rev.
Parliamentary reform: an essay reprinted, with considerable additions, from the National Review. 1859.

The history of the unreformed Parliament and its lessons: an essay reprinted from the National Review. 1860.
Memoir of the Rt Hon J. Wilson. 1861. Rptd from Economist.
Count your enemies and economise your expenditure. 1862.
The English constitution, reprinted from the Fortnightly Review. 1867, 1872 (adds one ch); ed A. J. Balfour, Oxford 1928 (WC); ed R. H. S. Crossman 1964 (with bibliography on government and politics).
A practical plan for assimilating the English and American money, reprinted from the Economist with additions. 1869.
Physics and politics: or thoughts on the application of the principles of 'natural selection' and 'inheritance' to political society. 1872; ed J. Barzun, New York 1948.
Lombard Street: a description of the money market. 1873; ed E. Johnstone 1892 (brought up to date); 1900; ed H. Withers 1910; ed A. W. Wright 1915 (notes rev); ed F. C. Genovese, Homewood IL 1962.
Some articles on the depreciation of silver and on topics connected with it, reprinted from the Economist. 1877.
Literary studies. Ed R. H. Hutton 2 vols 1879 (with memoir), 3 vols 1895, 1906 (reissue of vol 3 with addns); ed G. Sampson 2 vols 1906 (EL). Rptd in part from Estimates, *above.*
Economic studies. Ed R. H. Hutton 1879, 1888; first 2 chs pbd as The postulates of English political economy, preface by A. Marshall 1885.
Biographical studies. Ed R. H. Hutton 1881, 1907 (adds index).
Essays on parliamentary reform. 1883.
The postulates of English political economy: student's edition with a preface by A. Marshall. 1885. Rptd from Economic studies, *above.*
Estimations in criticism. Ed C. Lennox 2 vols 1908. Rptd from Literary studies, *above.*

Letters

The love-letters of Bagehot and Eliza Wilson. Ed E. I. Barrington 1933.
Letters. In Collected works vols 12–13, ed N. St John-Stevas, 1986.

Contributions to periodicals

See Wellesley *5 1989 and* Collected works, *ed N. St John-Stevas, above.*

§2

Bagehot: in memoriam. 1878 (priv ptd). A collection of obituary notices.
Giffen, R. Bagehot as an economist. Fortnightly Rev n.s. 27 Apr 1880. Rptd in Collected works vol 10, 1978.
Hutton, R. H. In his Criticisms on contemporary thought and thinkers, 2 vols 1894.
Stephen, L. In his Studies of a biographer vol 3, 1902.
Barrington, E. I. Life of Bagehot. 1914, 1915 (as vol 10 of Works and life of Bagehot, *above*).
Irvine, W. Walter Bagehot. New York 1939.
The Economist 1843–1943: a centenary volume. 1943.
Chapman, R. W. The text of Bagehot's Constitution. PQ 31 1952.
Sayers, R. S. Central banking after Bagehot. Oxford 1957.
Buchan, A. The spare Chancellor: the life of Bagehot. 1959.
St John-Stevas, N. Walter Bagehot. 1959. With selected writings and bibliography.
St John-Stevas, N. Walter Bagehot. 1963 (Br Council pam).
Sayers, R. S. Bagehot as an economist. In Collected works vol 9, 1978.

Samuel Bailey 1791–1870

Bibliographies

Ireland, A. Bailey of Sheffield. N & Q 9 Mar 1878. *See also* 16 Mar, 27 Apr 1878, 21 June 1879.
Rauner, R. M. Samuel Bailey and the classical theory of value. 1961 (primary).

§1

Essays on the formation and publication of opinions and on other subjects. 1821, 1826 (rev and enlarged), Philadelphia 1831, London 1837 (3rd edn), Boston 1854.
Observations on certain verbal disputes in political economy. 1821.
Questions in political economy, morals, metaphysics, polite literature, etc. 1823.
A critical dissertation on the nature, measures, and causes of value. 1825, rptd 1931 (London School of Economics); tr Ital 1856.
A letter to a political economist, occasioned by an article in the Westminster Review. 1826.
Essays on the pursuit of truth. 1829, Philadelphia 1831 (2nd edn), 1844 (rev and enlarged), 1854.
A discussion of parliamentary reform. 1831.
An essay on the standard measure of value. 1832.
Currency fallacies refuted. 1833.
The rationale of political representation. 1835.
Money and its vicissitudes in value. 1837.
The right of primogeniture examined. 1837.
Letters of an Egyptian Kafir on a visit to England. 1839.
A defence of joint stock banks. 1840.
A review of Berkeley's theory of vision. 1842.
A letter to a philosopher in reply to some recent attempts to vindicate Berkeley's theory of vision. 1842.
Maro; or poetic irritability. 1845. Poem.
Letters on the philosophy of the human mind. Ser 1 1846; 3 vols 1855, 1858, 1862.
The theory of reasoning. 1851, 1852.
Discourses on various subjects. 1852.
On free public libraries. 1853.
On the received text of Shakespeare's dramatic writings. Vol 1 1862, vol 2 1866.
A glance at some points in education. Sheffield 1865.

§2

[James Mill?] Review of A critical dissertation. Westminster Rev 6, Jan 1826.
Cotterill, C. F. An examination of the doctrines of value. 1826.
Thompson, T. P. Essays on the pursuit of truth. Westminster Rev 11 1829.
Wardlaw, R. Four sermons, with an appendix on an article in the Westminster Review. 1830.
Empson, W. Principles of belief and expectation as applied to miracles. Edinburgh Rev 52 1831.
Mill, J. S. Rationale of representation. London Rev 1 1835.
Mill, J. S. Mr Bailey's reply to the Westminster Review. Westminster Rev 39 1843.
Mill, J. S. Bailey on Berkeley's Theory of vision (1842). In his Dissertations and discussions vol 2, 1859.
Ferrier, J. F. Berkeley's Theory of vision (1843). In his Lectures on Greek philosophy and other philosophical remains, Edinburgh 1866.
Ribot, T. A. La psychologie anglaise contemporaine. Paris 1870; tr 1873.
Seligman, E. R. A. On some neglected British economists. Economic Jnl 13 1903.
Rauner, R. M. Samuel Bailey and the classical theory of value. 1963.
Amano, K. In his Bibliography of the classical economists vol 4 pt V, Tokyo 1964.

Thomas Charles Banfield 1800–82?

§1

The progress of the Prussian nation 1805. 1831, 1842, 1847.
Six letters to Sir Robert Peel on the dangerous tendency of the theory of rent advocated by Ricardo. 1843.

Four lectures on the organization of industry. 1845, 1848.
Industry of the Rhine: agriculture 1846; manufactures 1848.
Free production having freed trade! 1852.
A letter to William Brown on the advantages of his proposed system of decimal coinage. 1855.

§2
See NPDE.

John Barton 1789–1852

For information on the location of papers and correspondence, see Sturges.

Bibliography
Sotiroff, G. (ed). John Barton: economic writings. Regina, Saskatchewan 1962.

Selections
See Sotiroff, above.

§1
Observations on the circumstances which influence the condition of the labouring classes of society. 1817.
An inquiry into the causes of the progressive depreciation of agricultural labour in modern times. 1820.
A statement of the consequences likely to ensue from our growing excess of population. 1830.
An inquiry into the expediency of the existing restriction on the importation of foreign corn. 1833.
The monetary crisis of 1847. 1847.

§2
See NPDE.

Charles Francis Bastable 1855–1945

For information on the location of papers and correspondence, see Sturges.

Bibliography
Black, R. D. C. A select bibliography of economic writings by members of Trinity College Dublin. Hermathena 66 1945. Primary.

§1
An examination of some current objections to the state of political economy. 1884, Dublin 1884.
The theory of international trade. Dublin 1887, 2nd edn 1897, 3rd edn 1900, 4th edn 1903, with further edns 1897–1903.
The commerce of nations. 1891; subsequent edns 1899, 1904, 1907, 1911, 1912, 1917; rev T. E. Gregory 1923.
Public finance. 1892, 2nd edn 1895, 3rd edn 1903.

Contributions to periodicals and chapters
See Black, above.

§2
See NPDE.

Jeremy Bentham 1748–1832

See also vol 3 of CBEL.

Collections
The works of Jeremy Bentham. Ed J. Bowring 11 vols Edinburgh 1838–43.
Jeremy Bentham's economic writings. Ed W. Stark 3 vols 1952–4.
The collected works of Jeremy Bentham. Ed J. H. Burns et al 1968– .

§1
Defence of usury. 1787; in Stark, *above*, vol 1.
Supply without burden, or escheat vice taxation. 1793; in Stark, *above*, vol 1.
Pauper management improved. 1798; in Bowring, *above*, vol 8.
Circulating annuities. 1801; in Stark, *above*, vol. 2.

§2
Hutchison, T. W. Bentham as an economist. Economic Jnl June 1956.
Black, R. D. C. Bentham and the political economists of the nineteenth century. Bentham Newsletter 12 1988.

William Blake 1774–1852

§1
Observations on the principles which regulate the course of exchange. 1810.
Observations on the effects produced by the expenditure of government during the restriction of cash payments. 1823.
Observations in reply to the Rev Richard Jones . . . on the assessment of tithes to the poor rate. 1839, 2nd edn 1839.

Letters
Blake's letters to Ricardo are in D. Ricardo, Works and correspondence, below, vols 6–9.

§2
McCulloch, J. R. Review of Blake's Observations. The Scotsman, 12 Apr 1823.
Ricardo, D. Works and correspondence. Ed P. Sraffa and M. H. Dobb 11 vols Cambridge 1951–73. Vols 3 and 4 contain Ricardo's notes on Blake with Blake's replies.
Corry, B. A. The theory of economic effects of government expenditure in English classical political economy. Economica 25 1958.
See also NPDE.

James Bonar 1852–1941

For information on the location of papers and correspondence, see Sturges.

§1
Parson Malthus. Glasgow 1881.
Malthus and his work. 1885, 1924.
Philosophy and political economy. 1893, 1909, 1922, rptd 1967.
The tables turned. 1926.
Theories of population from Raleigh to Arthur Young. 1931.

Contributions to periodicals
A peep at French schools. Macmillan's Mag July 1881.
Austrian economists and their view of value. Quart Jnl of Economics Oct 1888–9.
Knapp's theory of money. Economic Jnl 32 1922.
Memories of F. Y. Edgworth. Economic Jnl 36 1926.
Ricardo on Malthus. Economic Jnl 39 1929.

Editions
Letters of David Ricardo to Thomas Robert Malthus. 1887.
A catalogue of the library of Adam Smith. 1894.
Letters of David Ricardo to Hutches Trower. Oxford 1899. With J. H. Hollander.

§2
Keynes, J. M. Essays in biography. 1933, 1972.
Shirras, G. F. James Bonar. Proc of the Br Acad 28 1942.

John Francis Bray 1809–97

For information on the location of papers and correspondence, see Sturges.

Bibliography
See NPDE *(secondary).*

§1

Labour's wrongs and labour's remedy. Leeds 1839, 1842 (abridged version), New York 1968.

An essay upon the union of agriculture and manufacturing. 1844.

The industrial employment of women. 1857.

American destiny. New York 1864.

§2

Foxwell, H. S. Introd to English trn of A. Menger, The right to the whole produce of labour, 1899.

Thompson, N. W. The people's science. Cambridge 1984.

Henderson, J. P. An English communist. History of Political Economy 17 1985.

David Buchanan 1779–1848

§1

Inquiry into the taxation and commercial policy of Great Britain. Edinburgh 1844.

Contributions to periodicals

Buchanan edited the Caledonian Mercury *1810–27 and the* Daily Courant *(Edinburgh) 1827–48. See also* Wellesley *vol 5.*

Editions

Adam Smith's Wealth of nations, 4 vols, with Observations on the subjects treated of in Dr Smith's inquiry in 4th vol. Edinburgh 1814, 1817; tr Fr 1844.

§2

Anderson, W. The Scottish nation. Edinburgh 1863.

See also NPDE.

Isaac Butt 1813–79

For information on the location of papers and correspondence, see Sturges.

Bibliography

See R. D. C. Black, A select bibliography of economic writings by members of Trinity College Dublin, Hermathena 66 1945.

§1

Introductory lecture. Dublin 1837.

Rent, profits and labour. Dublin 1838.

Protection to home industry. Dublin 1846.

Land tenure in Ireland. Dublin 1866.

The Irish querist. Dublin 1867.

The Irish deep sea fisheries. Dublin 1874.

Contributions to periodicals

Butt edited the Dublin Univ Mag *Aug 1834–Nov 1838. See* Wellesley *vol 5.*

§2

Thornely, D. Isaac Butt and Home Rule. 1964.

See also NPDE.

John Elliot Cairnes 1823–75

For information on the location of papers and correspondence, see Sturges.

§1

The character and logical method of political economy. 1857, 2nd edn 1875, rptd 1888, New York 1965.

An examination into the principles of currency. 1859.

Political economy as a branch of general education. 1860.

The slave power. 1862, 2nd edn 1863, rptd 1969.

The revolution in America. 1863.

The southern confederacy. 1863.

Colonization and colonial government. 1864.

England's neutrality in the American contest. 1864.

Essay in political economy. 1873.

Political essays. 1873.

Some leading principles of political economy. 1874, 1875, 1884.

University education in Ireland. 1886, 1873.

Woman suffrage. 1874.

Contributions to periodicals

See Wellesley *vol 5 and R. D. C. Black,* Statistical and Social Inquiry Society of Ireland: centenary volume, *Dublin 1947, for other contributions.*

Letters

Letters to J. S. Mill. In The later letters of John Stuart Mill vols 2–4, 1972.

§2

Mill, J. S. The slave power. Westminster Rev n.s. 22, Oct 1862.

Macdevitt, J. University education in Ireland. 1866.

Obituary by H. Fawcett. Fortnightly Rev n.s. 18, Aug 1875.

Black, R. D. C. Jevons and Cairnes. Economica 27 1960.

Weinberg, A. John Elliot Cairnes and the American Civil War. 1970.

Boylan, T. A. and T. P. Foley. John Elliot Cairnes, John Stuart Mill and Ireland. In Economists and the Irish economy, ed A. E. Murphy, Dublin 1984.

Thomas Chalmers 1780–1847

See col 2626, above.

For information on the location of papers and correspondence, see Sturges.

Collected works and selections

The works of Thomas Chalmers. Philadelphia 1833.

The works of Thomas Chalmers. 25 vols Glasgow 1836–42.

Posthumous works. Ed W. Hanna 9 vols Edinburgh 1848–9.

Select works of Thomas Chalmers. 4 vols New York 1850.

Select works of Thomas Chalmers. 12 vols Edinburgh 1854–79.

§1

An enquiry into the nature and stability of national resources. Edinburgh 1808.

The influence of bible societies on the temporal necessities of the poor. Cupar 1814.

Thoughts on universal peace. 1816, New York 1819.

The importance of civil government to society. Glasgow 1820.

The application of Christianity to the commercial and ordinary affairs of life. Glasgow 1820, rptd 1881, New York 1821; tr Fr 1824.

The Christian and civic economy of large towns. 3 vols Glasgow 1821–6, abridged New York 1900; tr Ger 1847.

A few thoughts on the abolition of colonial slavery. Glasgow 1826.

On political economy in connexion with the moral state and moral prospects of society. Glasgow 1832, 2nd edn 1832, New York 1832; tr Ital 1855.

The supreme importance of a right moral to the right economical state. Glasgow 1832.

Tracts on pauperism. 1833.

On the sufficiency of a parochial system. 1841.

Contributions to periodicals

See Wellesley *vol 5.*

Letters

A selection from the correspondence. Ed W. Hanna, Edinburgh 1853.

The correspondence between Dr Chalmers and the Earl of Aberdeen. Edinburgh 1893.

§2

McCulloch, J. R. Edinburgh Rev 56, Oct 1832.

Scrope, G. P. Dr Chalmers on political economy. Quart Rev 48, Oct 1832.

Memoirs of the life and writings. Ed W. Hanna 4 vols Edinburgh 1849–52.
Brown, J. Stewart. Thomas Chalmers. 1982.
Hilton, A. J. B. Age of atonement. 1988.
Waterman, A. M. C. Revolution, economics and religion. 1991.

Richard Cobden 1804–65

For information on the location of papers and correspondence, see Sturges; see also F. W. Steer, The Cobden papers; a catalogue, *Chichester 1964.*

Collections

The political writings of Richard Cobden. 2 vols 1867.
Speeches on questions of public policy. Ed J. Bright and J. E. T. Rogers 2 vols Oxford 1868.

§1

England, Ireland and America, by a Manchester manufacturer. 1835.
Russia. Edinburgh 1836.
Speeches on peace, financial reform and other subjects. 1849.

Letters and journals

The American diaries of Richard Cobden. Ed E. H. Crawley, Princeton 1952.

§2

Rogers, J. E. T. Cobden and modern political opinions. 1873.
Morley, J. The life of Richard Cobden. 1879, 1881, 1882, 1883, 1896, 1902, 1903, 1905, 1906, 1919.
Read, D. Cobden and Bright; a Victorian partnership. 1967.

Patrick Colquhoun 1745–1820

§1

Considerations relative to a plan of relief for the cotton industry. 1788.
A presentation of facts relative to the rise and progress of the cotton industry. 1789.
A treatise on the police of the metropolis. 1796, 5th edn 1798, 7th edn 1806.
The state of indigence. 1799.
A general view of the national police system. 1799, 2nd edn in 2 vols 1790–2, 3rd edn 1896, 4th edn in 3 vols 1907, 5th edn 1910–12.
A treatise on the commerce and police of the river Thames. 1800.
A treatise on the functions and duties of a constable. 1803.
A new and appropriate system of education for the labouring people. 1806.
A treatise on indigence. 1806.
A treatise on the wealth, power and resources of the British empire. 1814, 1815.

§2

McCulloch, J. R. State and defects of British statistics. Edinburgh Rev 61, Apr 1835.
Deane, P. Contemporary estimates of national income in the first half of the nineteenth century. Economic History Rev 8 1956.

Edward Copleston 1776–1849

§1

Advice to a young reviewer, with a specimen of the art. Oxford 1807 (anon); ed J. C. Collins 1903 (in Critical essays and literary fragments); ed G. S. Gordon 1927 (in Three Oxford ironies; with bibliographical notes) (with note on the author by V. M. D.).
The Examiner examined: or logic vindicated. 1809 (anon).
A reply to the calumnies of the Edinburgh Review against Oxford: containing an account of the studies pursued in that university. Oxford 1810. A second reply, Oxford 1810. A third reply, Oxford 1811.
Praelectiones academicae Oxonii habitae. Oxford 1813. 35 Latin lectures on poetry.
A letter to the Rt Hon Robert Peel... on the pernicious effects of a variable standard of value. Oxford 1814.
Cursory hints on the application of public subscription in providing employment and relief for the labouring classes. 1817.
A second letter to the Rt Hon Robert Peel... on the causes of the increase in pauperism and on the poor laws. Oxford 1819.
Inquiry into the doctrines of necessity and predestination. 1821.
An examination of the currency question. 1830.
Remains of the late Edward Copleston, with an introduction containing some reminiscences of his life. Ed R. Whateley 1854.

Contributions to periodicals

See Wellesley *vol 5 1989.*

§2

Copleston, W. J. Memoir of Edward Copleston, with selections from his diary and correspondence. 1851.
Tuckwell, W. Pre-tractarian Oxford. 1909.
Waterman, A. M. C. Revolution, economics and religion. Cambridge 1991.

William Cunningham 1849–1919

Bibliography

See Maloney, below.

§1

Syllabus of twelve lectures on England during the Reformation. Liverpool 1877.
The growth of English industry and commerce. Cambridge 1882.
Politics and economics. 1885.
Political economy treated as an empirical science. Cambridge 1887.
Strikes. Boston 1895.
Modern civilisation in some of its economic aspects. 1896.
The rise and decline of the free trade movement. Cambridge 1904.
The wisdom of the wise. Cambridge 1906.
Christianity and social questions. 1910.
The case against free trade. 1911.
The causes of the labour unrest. 1912.
Christianity and economic science. 1914.
Christianity and politics. 1916.

Contributions to periodicals

See Wellesley *vol 5.*
On the Comtist criticism of economic science. Proc of the Br Assoc for the Advancement of Science 1889.
Nationalism and cosmopolitanism in economics. Proc of the Br Assoc for the Advancement of Science 1891.
A plea for pure theory. Economic Rev Jan 1892.
The relativity of economic doctrines. Economic Jnl 2 1892.
The perversion of economic history. Economic Jnl 2 1892.
Political economy in relation to practical life. International Jnl of Ethics Jan 1893.
Economists as mischief makers. Economic Rev Jan 1894.
The failure of free traders to realise their ideal. Economic Rev Jan 1904.
Unconscious assumptions in economics. Proc of the Br Assoc for the Advancement of Science 1906.

§2

Scott, W. R. William Cunningham. Proc of the Br Acad 9 1920.
Maloney, J. Marshall, orthodoxy, and the professionalisation of economics. 1985.

Thomas De Quincey 1785–1859

See col 2123, above.

§1

The logic of political economy. 1844.

Contributions to periodicals

Notes from the pocket-book of a late opium-eater, Malthus. London Mag Oct–Dec 1823.

Dialogues of the three templars on political economy. London Mag Mar–Oct 1824.

Ricardo made easy; or what is the radical difference between Ricardo and Adam Smith. Blackwood's Mag 52, Sep–Dec 1842.

§2

Ricardo, D. On the principles of political economy. 1817.

Mill, J. S. Review of Logic of political economy. Westminster Rev 43, June 1845.

Sir Frederick Morton Eden 1766–1809

For information on the location of papers and correspondence, see Sturges.

§1

The state of the poor; or an history of the labouring classes in England from the Conquest to the present period. 3 vols 1797, abridged 1928, rptd New York 1966.

Porto-bello. 1798.

Estimate of the number of inhabitants of Great Britain and Ireland. 1800.

Observations on friendly societies. 1801.

Eight letters on the peace. 1802.

Brontës: a cento to the memory of the late Viscount Nelson. 1806.

On the policy and expediency of granting insurance charters. 1806.

Address on the maritime rights of Great Britain. 1808.

Letters

Letters to J. Bentham. In The collected works of Jeremy Bentham vols 6 and 7, ed J. R. Dinwiddy, Oxford 1984.

§2

Poynter, J. R. Society and pauperism. 1969.

Supple, B. The Royal Exchange Assurance; a history of British insurance 1720–1970. Cambridge 1970.

Francis Ysidro Edgeworth 1845–1926

For information on the location of papers and correspondence, see Sturges.

Bibliographies

See NPDE. Primary and secondary.

Johnson, H. G. F. Y. Edgeworth: a select bibliography. 1955. Primary.

Newman, P. Reviews by Edgeworth. In A century of economics, ed J. Hey and D. Winch, 1990. Primary and secondary.

Collections and selections

Papers relating to political economy. Ed F. Y. Edgeworth 3 vols 1925, rptd New York in 1 vol.

F. Y. Edgeworth: writings in probability, statistics and economics. Ed C. R. McCann Jr 3 vols 1996.

§1

New and old methods of ethics. Oxford 1876, 1877.

Mathematical psychics. 1881.

Metretike, or the method of measuring probability and utility. 1887.

Contributions to periodicals

See Newman and Johnson, above, and Wellesley *vol 5.*

§2

Bowley, A. L. F. Y. Edgeworth's contribution to mathematical statistics. 1928.

Keynes, J. M. Essays in biography. 1933, 1972.

William Ellis 1800–81

For information on the location of papers and correspondence, see Sturges.

Bibliography

Primary sources identified in Blyth, below.

§1

Outlines of social economy. 1846, 1850.

Questions and answers suggested by a consideration of some of the arrangements and relations of social life. 1849.

Education as a means of preventing destitution. 1851.

Lessons on the phenomena of industrial life. 1855.

A layman's contribution to the knowledge and practice of religion in common life. 1857.

Progressive lessons in social science: philosocrates. 4 vols 1861–4.

Introduction in elementary social science. 1863.

Three letters from a London merchant on the late monetary crisis. 1866.

What stops the way? 1868.

A chart of industrial life. 1869.

Contributions to periodicals

See Wellesley *vol 5.*

Letters

Letters to J. S. Mill. In The later letters of J. S. Mill, ed F. E. Mineka and D. N. Lindley, 4 vols 1972.

See also Ellis, below.

§2

Ellis, E. Memoirs of William Ellis. 1888.

Blyth, E. K. Life of William Ellis. 1889.

Henry Fawcett 1833–84

For information on the location of papers and correspondence, see Sturges, above, and Goldman, below.

Bibliography

Goldman, L. (ed). The blind Victorian. 1989. Primary.

§1

Mr Hare's reform bill. 1860.

The leading clauses of a new reform bill. 1860.

Manual of political economy. 1863, 6th edn 1883.

The economic position of the British labourer. 1865.

Pauperism: its causes and remedies. 1871.

Essays and lectures on social and political subjects. 1872.

The present position of the government. 1872.

Speeches on some current political questions. 1873.

Free trade and protection. 1878.

Indian finance. 1880.

The post office and aids to thrift. 1881.

State socialism and the nationalisation of land. 1883.

Labour and wages. 1884.

Contributions to periodicals

See Goldman, above, and Wellesley *vol 5.*

§2

Stephen, L. Life of Henry Fawcett. 1885.

Fawcett, M. G. What I remember. 1925.

Goldman, L. (ed). The blind Victorian. 1989.

Herbert Somerton Foxwell 1849–1936

For information on the location of papers and correspondence, see Sturges.

Bibliography
See Keynes, below, for primary sources.

§1
The claims of labour. 1886.
Papers on current finance. 1919.

Contributions to periodicals
See Wellesley *vol 5.*
The economic movement in England. Quart Jnl of Economics Oct 1887.
Mr Goschen's currency proposals. Economic Jnl Mar 1892.
The international monetary conference. Contemporary Rev 62, Dec 1892.
For other contributions, see Keynes, below.

Editions and translations
Jevons, W. S. Investigations in currency and finance. Ed and introd by Foxwell 1884, 1909.
Menger, A. The right to the whole produce of labour. Tr and introd by Foxwell 1889.

§2
Keynes, J. M. Essays in biography. 1933, 1972.
Koot, G. M. H. S. Foxwell and English historical economics. Jnl of Economic Issues 2 1977.

Sir Robert Giffen 1837–1910

For information on the location of papers and correspondence, see Sturges.

Collections (of contributions to periodicals)
Economic inquiries and studies. 2 vols 1904.
Essays in finance. Vol 1 1880, vol 2 1886.

§1
American railways as investment. In B. Cracroft, Investment tracts, 1872, 1873; tr Fr 1873. With B. Cracroft.
The production and movement of gold since 1848. 1873.
Stock exchange securities. 1877.
The Statist on Ireland. 1881.
The progress of the working class in the last half century. 1884.
The growth of capital. 1889.
The case against bimetallism. 1892.

Contributions to collaborative works
Growth and distribution of wealth 1837–1887. In T. H. Ward, Reign of Queen Victoria vol 2, 1887.

Editions
Jnl of the [Royal] Statistical Society 1876–91.
Giffen was proprietor of The Statist *1878–1910.*

§2
See NPDE and DNB.

Edward Carter Kersey Gonner 1862–1922

§1
The socialist state; its nature, aims and conditions. 1895.
The social philosophy of Rodbertus. 1899.
Interest and saving. 1906.
Common land and inclosure. 1912.

Contributions to periodicals and collaborative works
Ricardo and his critics. Quart Jnl of Economics 4 1890.
The economic history. In J. H. Rose et al, Germany in the nineteenth century, 1912.

Editions
Ricardo, D. Principles of political economy. 1891.
Ricardo, D. Economic essays. 1923.

George Goschen, Viscount Goschen 1831–1907

For information on the location of papers and correspondence, see Sturges.

Collections
Goschen's political speeches. Edinburgh 1886.
Essays and addresses on economic questions. 1905.

§1
The theory of foreign exchanges. 1861.
Life and times of George Joachim Goschen. 1903.

Contributions to periodicals
See Wellesley *vol 5.*

Letters
Colson, P. Lord Goschen and his friends. 1946.

§2
Elliott, A. R. D. Life of Lord Goschen. 2 vols 1911.
See also DNB.

John Gray 1799–1883

Bibliography
Dictionary of labour history. Ed J. M. Bellamy and J. Saville, vol 6 1982.

§1
A lecture on human happiness. 1825, rptd 1831; tr Ger 1907.
A word of advice to the Orbistonians on the principles which ought to regulate their present proceedings. Edinburgh 1826.
An address to the printers of Edinburgh. Edinburgh 1830.
The social system: a treatise on the principle of exchange. Edinburgh 1831, rptd Clifton NJ 1973.
An efficient remedy for the distress of nations. Edinburgh 1842.
The currency question. Edinburgh 1847.
Lectures on the nature and use of money. Edinburgh 1848.

§2
Foxwell, H. S. Introd to English trn of A. Menger, The right to the whole produce of labour, 1899.
Kimball, J. The economic doctrines of John Gray. Washington 1946.
Thompson, N. W. The people's science. Cambridge 1984.

Simon Gray, 'George Purves' fl. 1795–1840

Bibliography
See NPDE.

§1
The essential principles of the wealth of nations, illustrated, in opposition to some false doctrines of Dr Adam Smith, and others. 1797.
The happiness of states. 1815, 1819.
All classes productive of national wealth. 1817, 1840. [As G. Purves.]
Gray versus Malthus. 1818. [As G. Purves.]
Remarks on the production of wealth. 1820.
The grazier's ready reckoner. 1823. [As G. Purves.]
The Spaniard . . . a tragedy in five acts. 1839.
The Messiad. 1842.

§2
Masuda, E. and S. Newman. Gray and Giffen goods. Economic Jnl 91 1981.
See also NPDE.

William Rathbone Greg 1809–81

Collections
Literary and social judgements. 1869, 2 vols 1877 (4th edn).
Miscellaneous essays. 1882, 2nd ser 2 vols 1882.

§1
Observations on a late pamphlet . . . on the phrenological development of Burke, Hare, etc. Edinburgh 1829.
An enquiry into the state of the manufacturing population. 1831.
Social statistics of the Netherlands. 1835.
Past and present efforts for the extinction of the African slave trade. 1840.
Agriculture and the Corn Law. 1842.
Not over-production, but deficient consumption the source of our suffering. 1842.
The German schism and the Irish priests. Manchester 1845.
The creed of Christendom. 1851, 2 vols 1877 (8th edn), rptd 1905.
Sketches in Greece and Turkey. 1853.
The great sin of great cities. 1853.
The one thing needful. 1855.
The way out. 1855.
Truth versus edification. 1869.
Why are women redundant? 1869.
Political problems for our age and country. 1870.
The great duel. 1871.
Enigmas of life. 1872, 15th edn 1883.
Rocks ahead. 1874.
Mistaken aims and attainable ideals of the working classes. 1876.

Contributions to periodicals
See Wellesley *vol 5*.

§2
See DNB.
See also col 2672.

Charles Hall c. 1731–1825

Bibliography
Dictionary of modern British radicals. Vol 1, ed J. O. Baylen and N. J. Gossman, Brighton 1988.

§1
The effects of civilization on the peoples in European states. 1805, rptd 1805 as Observations on the principal conclusions of Mr Malthus's essay on population.

Contributions to periodicals
On Whitbread's proposals for reform of the poor laws. Monthly Mag 23 1807.
Thoughts on corruption and on the defects of the representation of the people in parliament. Monthly Mag 32 1811.

Letters
Claeys, G. Four letters between Thomas Spence and Charles Hall. N & Q Aug 1981.

§2
Dinwiddy, J. R. Charles Hall, early English socialist. International Rev of Social History 21 1976.

William Edward Hearn 1826–88

Bibliography
Copland, D. B. W. E. Hearn: first Australian economist. Melbourne 1935.

Collections
Essays on political and social subjects. 1853.

§1
The Cassell prize essay on the condition of Ireland. 1851, Dublin 1851.
Plutology: or the theory of the efforts to satisfy human wants. Melbourne 1864.
The government of England. 1867, 1887.
Payment by results. 1872.
The Aryan household. 1879.
The theory of legal duties and rights. 1883.

§2
Morley, J. Memoir in Macmillan's Mag 48 1889.
See also Copland, above.

Thomas Hodgskin 1787–1869

For information on the location of papers and correspondence, see Sturges.

Bibliography
Halévy, E. Thomas Hodgskin. Ed in trn with an introd by A. J. Taylor. 1956.
Dictionary of labour biography. Ed J. M. Bellamy and J. Saville, vol 9 1993.

§1
An essay on naval discipline. 1814.
Travels in the north of Germany. 2 vols Edinburgh 1820.
Labour defended against the claims of capital. 1825, 1831, rptd with introd by G. D. H. Cole 1922.
Popular political economy. 1827, New York 1966.
Natural and artificial rights of property contrasted. 1832.
Peace, law and order. 1842.
A lecture on free trade. 1843, rptd New York 1966 with Popular political economy.
What shall we do with criminals? 1857.

Contributions to periodicals
See Wellesley *vol 5*.

§2
Halévy, E. Thomas Hodgskin. Ed A. J. Taylor 1956.
Stack, D. Nature and artifice: the life and thought of Thomas Hodgskin. 1997.

Francis Horner 1778–1817

Letters in Horner Collection, London School of Economics, NLS, and Kinnordy mss now pbd in The Horner papers, ed K. Bourne and W. B. Taylor, below.

Selections
The economic writings of Francis Horner in the Edinburgh Review 1802–6. Ed F. W. Fetter 1957.

Contributions to periodicals
See Wellesley *vol 5*.

Letters
Memoirs and correspondence of Francis Horner. Ed E. L. J. Horner 2 vols 1843, Boston 1853.
Memoir of Francis Horner with selections from his correspondence. Edinburgh 1849.

§2
Bourne, K. and W. B. Taylor. The Horner papers. Edinburgh 1994.

William Huskisson 1770–1830

For information on the location of papers and correspondence, see Sturges.

Collections
The speeches of William Huskisson. Ed J. Wright 3 vols 1831.
The Huskisson papers. Ed L. Melville 1931.

§1

The question concerning the depreciation of our currency stated and examined. 1810, 1811, 1812, 1819, 1857.

Equitable adjustment: speech on resumption of cash payments. 1823.

Free trade: speech in House of Commons. 1826.

A letter on the corn law in 1814. 1826.

Navigation laws: speech in House of Commons. 1826.

Essays in political economy. 1830.

§2

Wright, J. A biographical memoir of William Huskisson. 1831. Also in The speeches, *above*.

Brady, A. William Huskisson and liberal reform. 1928, 1967.

John Kells Ingram 1823–1907

Ingram papers, Public Record Office, Northern Ireland; see also Sturges for letters.

Bibliographies

Lyster, T. W. Bibliography of the writings of John Kells Ingram, 1823–1907, with a brief chronology. Dublin 1909.

Black, R. D. C. A select bibliography of economic writings by members of Trinity College Dublin. Hermathena 66 1945.

§1

Who fears to speak of ninety-eight? Nation (Dublin) 1 Apr 1843; rptd in The spirit of the nation, 1843, and in his Sonnets and other poems, 1900, *below*.

On the 'Opus majus' of Roger Bacon. From the Nat History Rev and Quart Jnl Science, Dublin 1858.

Considerations on the state of Ireland: an address. Dublin 1863, 2nd edn 1864.

Shakespeare. 1863. Lecture.

Tennyson's works. 1863. Lecture.

A comparison between the English and Irish poor laws, with respect to the conditions of relief. [Dublin 1864.]

The present position and prospects of political economy. 1878.

Work and the workman. 1880, Dublin 1880, 1884, rptd with an introd by R. T. Ely, Dublin 1928.

A history of political economy. Edinburgh 1888, new edn with introd by R. T. Ely 1915, 1923.

A history of slavery and serfdom. 1895.

Outlines of the history of religion. 1900.

Sonnets and other poems. 1900.

Human nature and morals according to Auguste Comte. 1901.

Passages from the letters of Auguste Comte. 1901.

Practical morals. 1904.

Contributions to periodicals

Considerations on the state of Ireland. Jnl of the Statistical and Social Inquiry Soc of Ireland 26 1864–5.

The organization of charity and the education of the children of the state. Jnl of the Statistical and Social Inquiry Soc of Ireland Dec 1875.

The present position and prospects of political economy. Proc of the Br Assoc for the Advancement of Science 1878.

§2

Falkiner, C. L. Litton. Memoir of John Kells Ingram. Dublin 1907, rptd Jnl of the Statistical and Social Inquiry Soc of Ireland 12 1908.

Abstract of Minutes. Proc of the Royal Irish Acad 1907–8.

Koot, G. M. English historical economics, 1870–1926. Cambridge 1987.

Henry Charles Fleeming Jenkin 1833–85

For information on the location of papers and correspondence, see Sturges.

Bibliography

Brownlie, A. D. and M. F. Lloyd Prichard. Professor Fleeming Jenkin, 1833–1885, pioneer in engineering and political economy. Oxford Economic Papers 15 1963.

Collections

Papers, literary, scientific, etc. Ed S. C. Colvin and J. A. Ewing 2 vols 1887, vol 2 rptd 1931.

Contributions to periodicals

See Wellesley *vol 5 1989*.

§1

The graphic representation of the laws of supply and demand. In Recess studies, ed A. Grant, Edinburgh 1870. In vol 2 of Colvin and Ewing, *above*.

On the principles which regulate the incidence of taxes. Proc of the Royal Soc of Edinburgh 1871–2. In vol 2 of Colvin and Ewing, *above*.

§2

See memoir by R. L. Stevenson in Brownlie and Prichard, above.

William Stanley Jevons 1835–82

Main collection of letters and papers at Manchester Univ Lib. Letters to J. E. Cairnes in Nat Lib of Ireland. Letters to his brother in Seton-Jevons Collection, Seton Hall Univ, South Orange NJ; see guide compiled by R. D. C. Black, History of Economic Thought Newsletter *no 29 Autumn 1982.*

Bibliography

Inoue, T. and M. V. White. Bibliography of published works by W. S. Jevons. Jnl of the History of Economic Thought 15 1993. *See also* Black and Koenekamp, *below*.

Collections

Methods of social reform. Ed H. A. Jevons 1883, 1886, 1904, New York 1965.

Investigations in currency and finance. Ed H. S. Foxwell 1884.

Pure logic and other minor works. Ed H. A. Jevons and R. Adamson 1890, rptd New York 1971.

Principles of economics. Ed H. Higgs 1905.

§1

A serious fall in the value of gold ascertained, and its social effects set forth. 1863, rptd in Investigations, *above*.

Pure logic: or the science of quality apart from quantity. 1864.

The coal question. 1865, 1866, ed A. W. Flux 1906, 1956, New York 1962.

An introductory lecture on the importance of diffusing a knowledge of political economy. Manchester 1866, rptd in Black and Koenekamp, *below*, vol 7.

The state in relation to labour. 1866.

A lecture on trades' societies. Manchester 1868, rptd in Methods, *above*.

The substitution of similars. 1869, rptd in Pure logic, *above*.

Elementary lessons in logic. 1870, 1884, 1891, 1905, 1957.

The mechanical performance of logical interference. Philosophical Trans 1870.

The match tax. 1871.

The theory of political economy. 1871, enlarged 2nd edn 1879, ed H. A. Jevons 1888, 1909, ed H. S. Jevons 1911, 1924, 1931, 1957, New York 1965 (Pen), ed with introd by R. D. C. Black 1970 (Pen); tr Fr 1879, Sp 1879, Ital 1947.

Logic. 1872, 1876, 1880, 1889; tr Ital 1878, Sp 1885, 1941.

The principles of science; a treatise on logic and scientific method.

2 vols 1874, New York 1877, 1879, 1883, 1887, 1892, 1900, 1905, 1913, 1920, 1924; introd by E. Nagel, New York 1958; tr Polish 1960.
Money and the mechanism of exchange. 1875, 1876, 3rd edn 1877, 25th edn 1923.
Primer of logic. 1876, 2nd edn 1876, rptd 15 times up to 1931.
Primer of political economy. 1878, 2nd edn 1878, 10th edn 1907, rptd 1917, 1926.
Studies in deductive logic. 1880, 2nd edn 1884, 1896, 1904, 1908.
The state in relation to labour. 1882, 1887; introd by M. Bababe 1894; introd by F. W. Hirst 1910; 1914, New York 1968.
The principles of economics. 1905, New York 1905.

Contributions to periodicals
See Wellesley *vol 5, and Inoue and White, above.*

Letters
Letters and journal of W. Stanley Jevons edited by his wife. 1886.
Black, R. D. C. and R. Koenekamp (ed). The papers and correspondence of W. S. Jevons. 7 vols 1972–81.

§2
Young, A. A. Jevons's Theory of political economy. Amer Economic Rev 2 1912.
Keynes, J. M. Essays in biography. 1933, 1972.
Black, R. D. C. Introd to Pen edn of Theory of political economy, 1970.
Koenekamp, R. In Papers and correspondence, *above*, vol 1, 1972.
Schabas, M. A world ruled by number: William Stanley Jevons and the rise of mathematical economics. Princeton 1990.

Richard Jones 1790–1855

For information on the location of papers and correspondence, see Sturges.

Collections
Literary remains, consisting of lectures and tracts on political economy of the late Rev Richard Jones. Ed W. Whewell 1859, New York 1956, 1958, 1964.

§1
An essay on the distribution of wealth and on the sources of taxation. 1831, 1844, New York 1964.
Peasant rents [first half of An essay]. 1831, ed W. J. Ashley 1895 (Economic Classics), New York 1914.

Contributions to periodicals
See Wellesley *vol 5 1989.*

§2
McCulloch, J. R. Review of Essay on distribution. Edinburgh Rev 54 1831.
Scrope, G. P. Jones on the doctrine of rent. Quart Rev 46 1831.
Whewell, W. Introduction to Literary remains, *above.*
Edgeworth, F. Y. On Richard Jones in PDPE.
Miller, W. L. Two articles in History of Political Economy 3 1971 and 9 1977.

Thomas Joplin c. 1790–1847

For information on the location of papers and correspondence, see Sturges.

§1
An essay on the general principles and present practice of banking in England and Scotland. 1813, 1822.
Outlines of a system of political economy. 1823.
Views on the subject of corn and currency. 1826.
Views on the corn bill of 1827. 1828.
Views on the currency. 1828.
An analysis and history of the currency question. 1832.
A letter to the directors of the National Provincial Bank of England. 1834.
On our monetary system. 1839.
An essay on the condition of the National Provincial Bank of England. 1843.
Currency reform. 1844.
An examination of Sir Robert Peel's currency bill of 1844. 1845.
Mr Joplin's circular to the directors and management of the joint-stock banks. 1845.

§2
Ellis, A. Bold adventure; the pioneering story of a great enterprise. 1953.
O'Brien, D. P. Thomas Joplin and classical macroeconomics. Aldershot. 1993.

John Neville Keynes 1852–1949

Diaries and letters held in Cambridge UL. For other letters, see Sturges.

§1
Studies and exercises in formal logic. 1884, 1889 (enlarged), 1894 (enlarged), 1906 (rewritten and enlarged), 1928.
The scope and method of political economy. 1891, 1897 (rev), 1930, New York 1955, 1963.

§2
Bonar, J. Review of Scope and method. Acad Mar 1891.
See also NPDE.

Samuel Laing 1812–97

§1
National distress; its causes and remedies. 1844.
Observations on Mr Strutt's amended railway regulation bill. 1847.
Railway taxation. 1849.
Observations on the social and political standards of the European peoples in 1848 and 1849. 1850.

John Lalor 1814–56

§1
The expediency and means of elevating the profession of educator in society. 1839.
Money and morals: a book for the times. 1852, partly rptd 1864 as England among the nations.

§2
See DNB, PDPE.

Dionysius Lardner 1793–1859

§1
An elementary treatise on calculus. 1825.
An analytical treatise on plane and spherical trigonometry. 1828.
A discourse on natural philosophy. 1828.
The first six books of Euclid. 1828, 1838, 1843, 1846.
A treatise on mechanics. 1829, 1830, 1836. With H. Kater.
A manual of electricity, magnetism and meteorology. 2 vols 1830.
A letter to the shareholders of the University of London. 1830.
The steam engine. 1836, 1840, 1851.
Course of lectures on the sun. 1842.
The great exhibition. 1850.
Railway economy; a treatise on the new art of transport. 1850, New York 1855, 1968.
The electrical telegraph. 1855, 1863, 1874.
Common things explained. 1855.

Handbook of astronomy. 2 vols 1855, 1860, 1867, 1875.
Animal physiology. 1856.
The bee and white ants. 1856.
Natural philosophy for schools. 1857.
Animal physics. 1857, 1873.
Chemistry for schools. 1859.

Editions

The museum of science and art. 12 vols 1854–6.
The cabinet cyclopaedia. 133 vols 1830–49.

§2

Ekelund, R. B., E. G. Furubotn and W. P. Gramm. The evolution of modern demand theory. Lexington MA 1972.

Thomas Edward Cliffe Leslie 1825–82

For information on the location of papers and correspondence, see Sturges.

Bibliography

See R. D. C. Black, Statistical and Social Inquiry Society of Ireland: centenary volume, *Dublin 1947. Primary.*

Collections

Essays in political and moral philosophy. Dublin 1878, 2nd edn by J. K. Ingram and C. F. Bastable entitled Essays in political economy, Dublin 1888.

§1

The military systems of Europe economically considered. Belfast 1856.
Land systems and the industrial economy of England, Ireland and continental countries. 1870, New York 1968.

Contributions to periodicals

See Wellesley *vol 5, and Black, above.*

Letters

Letters to J. S. Mill. In The later letters of J. S. Mill, ed F. E. Mineka and D. N. Lindley, 4 vols 1972.

§2

Mill, J. S. Leslie on the land question. 1870, in Collected Works of John Stuart Mill, ed J. M. Robson, vol 5 1967.
Political and economical heterodoxy: Cliffe Leslie. Westminster Rev n.s. 64, Oct 1883.
Ingram, J. K. Biographical notice in posthumous edition of Essays in political economy.
Koot, G. English historical economics. Cambridge 1987.

Francis David Longe 1802–c. 1905

Bibliography

Hollander, J. H. Introd to F. D. Longe, The wages fund theory, Baltimore 1903.

§1

A refutation on the wage-fund theory of modern political economy. 1866.
A critical examination of Mr George's 'progress and poverty' and Mr Mill's theory of wages. 1883.

Contributions to periodicals

The law of trade combinations in France. Fortnightly Rev n.s. 2, Aug 1867.

§2

See Hollander, above.
McNulty, P. J. The origins and development of labour economics. Cambridge MA 1980.

Samuel Mountifort Longfield 1802–84

Bibliography

The economic writings of Mountifort Longfield. Ed with introd by R. D. C. Black, New York 1971.

Collections

See Black, above.

§1

Lectures on political economy. 1834, rptd 1931, also rptd in Black, *above.*
Four lectures on poor laws. 1834, Dublin 1834, rptd in Black, *above.*
Three lectures on commerce and one on absenteeism. Dublin 1835, rptd 1938 and in Black, *above.*
An elementary treatise on series. 1872.
The tenure of land in Ireland. In Systems of land tenure, ed J. W. Probyn, 1876.

Contributions to periodicals

See Wellesley *vol 5.*
Banking and currency. Dublin Univ Mag 15 and 16 1840, rptd in Black, *above.*
Tenure of land in Ireland. In Systems of land tenure, Cobden Club 1870.
The limits of state interference with the distribution of wealth. Jnl of the Statistical and Social Inquiry Soc of Ireland 6 1872.

§2

See Black, above.

Robert Lowe, Viscount Sherbrooke 1811–92

Lowe papers, NRA; see Sturges for other letters.

§1

The utilitarian argument against reform. 1867.
Primary and classical education. 1867.
Speeches and letters on reform. 1867.
Middle class and primary education. 1868.
Middle class education. 1868.
The new law courts. 1869.
The national debt. 1869.
A defence of the British currency. 1870.
Budget speeches. 1870.
Poems of a life. 1885.

Contributions to periodicals

See Wellesley *vol 5.*

§2

Almond, H. H. Mr Lowe's educational theories examined. 1868.
Chamberlain, J. Speeches and other works in reply to Robert Lowe. 1877.
Cobbe, F. P. Mr Lowe and the vivisection act. 1877.
Cashin, T. F. The inutility of bankruptcy laws, Lord Sherbrooke's remedy. 1883.
Hogan, J. F. Robert Lowe. 1893.
Martin, A. P. O. Life and letters. 2 vols 1893.
Knight, R. A. Illiberal Liberal: Robert Lowe in New South Wales 1842–1883. Melbourne 1966.
Sylvester, D. W. Robert Lowe and education. 1974.

Samuel Jones Loyd [sic], Lord Overstone 1796–1883

Overstone papers, London Univ Lib. See Sturges for location of other letters.

§1

Reflections suggested by a perusal of Mr J. Horsley Palmer's pamphlet on the causes and consequences of the pressure on the money market. 1837.

Tracts and other publications on metallic and paper currency. 1857.
The evidence given by Lord Overstone before the select committee of the House of Commons of 1857 on bank acts. 1858.

Letters

O'Brien, D. P. The correspondence of Lord Overstone. 3 vols Cambridge 1971.

§2

See D. P. O'Brien, Correspondence, *above.*

John Ramsay McCulloch 1789–1864

For information on the location of papers and correspondence, see Sturges.

Bibliography

O'Brien, D. P. J. R. McCulloch: a study in classical economics. 1970. Primary and secondary.

Collections

Essays on exchange, interest, money, etc. Boston 1850. Reprint of McCulloch's articles for the Encyclopaedia Britannica.
J. R. McCulloch: works on economic theory and policy. 8 vols, introd by D. P. O'Brien, Bristol 1994.

§1

An essay on the question of reducing the interest of the national debt. 1816.
An essay on a reduction of the interest on the national debt. 1817.
Treatise on the circumstances which determine the course of exchange. 1820.
A discourse on the rise, progress, and peculiar objects and importance of political economy. 1824, 1825; tr Fr 1825.
Memoir of François Quesnay. 1824.
Syllabus of course of lectures on political economy. 1825.
The principles of political economy. 1825, enlarged 1830, 1843, 1849, 1864, 1872, 1886; tr Sp 1830, Ger 1831, Fr 1851, 1924, Ital 1853.
An essay on the circumstances which determine the rate of wages and the condition of labouring classes. Edinburgh 1826, rev 1851 as A treatise on . . ., 1854; tr Du 1853, Ital 1863.
Historical sketch of the rise and progress of the science of political economy. Edinburgh 1826.
Letter to the shareholders of the University of London. 1830.
Remarks on the coal trade. 1830.
Observations on the influence of the East India Company's monopoly. 1831.
Historical sketch of the Bank of England. 1831.
A treatise on the principles, practice and history of commerce. 1831.
A dictionary, practical, theoretical and historical of commerce and commercial navigation. 1832, 1834, enlarged 1837, 1839, 1840, 1846, 1847, 1850, 1852, 1854, 1856, 1859, 1860, 1871, 1877, 1882; Philadelphia 1840, 1849, 1852; tr Ger 1834; Fr 1837–9.
On commerce. 1833.
A statistical account of the British empire. 1837, 1839, 1847, 1854.
A dictionary, geographical, statistical, and historical. 2 vols 1841, 1846–9, 1851–2, 1854, 1866; New York 1843–4, 1852.
A treatise on the principles and practical influence of taxation and the funding system. 1845, 1852, 1863, rptd with an introd by D. P. O'Brien, Edinburgh 1974; tr Ital 1868.
The literature of political economy. 1845.
A treatise on the succession of property vacant by death. 1848; tr Ital 1852.
Treatises on . . . economical policy. Edinburgh 1853.
A catalogue of books, the property of a political economist. 1856, 1862.
Considerations on partnerships. 1856; tr Ital 1859.
A treatise on metallic and paper money. 1858, 1859.

Contributions to periodicals

See Wellesley *vol 5, and D. P. O'Brien, above.*

Editions

Smith, Adam. Wealth of nations. Edinburgh 1828, 1838, 1849, 1855, 1859.
The works of David Ricardo. 1846, 1852.
A select collection of early English tracts on commerce. 1856.
A select collection of scarce and valuable tracts on money. 1856.
A select collection of scarce and valuable tracts on paper currency and banking. 1857.
A select collection of scarce and valuable tracts on the national debt and the sinking fund. 1857.
A select collection of scarce and valuable tracts on commerce. 1859.
All these collections are now rptd as Classical writings on economics, 6 vols with introd by D. P. O'Brien, 1996.

Letters

Letters to David Ricardo. In D. Ricardo, Works and correspondence, ed P. Sraffa and M. H. Dobb 11 vols Cambridge 1951–73, vols 6–9.

§2

Malthus, T. R. Political economy. Quart Rev Jan 1826.
Ingram, J. K. J. R. McCulloch. Encyclopaedia Britannica 9th edn, Edinburgh 33, 1883.
For biography and assessment, see D. P. O'Brien, Works, *above.*

Henry Dunning Macleod 1821–1902

For information on the location of papers and correspondence, see Sturges.

§1

The results of the operation of the poorhouse system in Ross, Inverness. 1851.
The theory and practice of banking. 2 vols 1855–6.
The elements of political economy. 1858.
A dictionary of political economy. 1863.
The theory of credit. 2 vols 1889–91.
Bimetallism. 1894.
A history of banking. 1896.
The history of economics. 1896.
Indian currency. 1898.

Contributions to periodicals

See Wellesley *vol 5.*

§2

Article on Macleod in International Encyclopedia of the Social Sciences. New York 1933.
See also NPDE.

James Maitland, Earl of Lauderdale 1759–1839

For information on the location of papers and correspondence, see Sturges.

§1

Letters to the peers of Scotland. 1794.
Speech on . . . national finances. 1796.
Thoughts on finance. 1797.
A letter on the present measures of finance. 1798.
Inquiry into the nature and origin of public wealth. Edinburgh 1804, enlarged 1819, New York 1964; tr Fr 1808, Ger 1809, 1914, 1923, Ital 1859.
Observations on the review of his Inquiry. Edinburgh Rev 1804.
Hints to the manufacturers of Great Britain. 1805.
Thoughts on the alarming state of the circulation. 1805.
An inquiry into the practical merits of the system for the government of India. 1809.
The depreciation of paper currency. 1812.

Further considerations on the state of currency. 1813.
A letter on the corn laws. 1814.
Three letters on the causes of the present state of the exchanges. 1819.
Sinking fund. 1820.
Three letters to the Duke of Wellington. 1829.
National savings bank. 1834.

§2

Brougham, H. Review of Lauderdale's Inquiry. Edinburgh Rev July 1804.
Paglin, M. Malthus and Lauderdale. 1961.

(Thomas) Robert Malthus 1766–1834

Cambridge UL holds copies of a travel journal, parts of the ms of Principles of political economy, with addns intended for a later edn, and some letters from David Ricardo. Letters to Napier are in the BL; to Francis Horner in London School of Economics Lib; to Robert Wilmot Horton in Derbyshire Record Office; and to his publisher, John Murray, Albermarle Street, London. Kanto Gakuen Univ in Ohta City, Japan, holds a collection of family and other letters, together with sermons, now published in 2 vols as T. R. Malthus, The unpublished papers, ed J. Pullen and T. Hughes-Parry, Cambridge 1997.

Bibliographies

Glass, D. V. (ed). Introduction to Malthus. 1953, 1959. Primary and secondary.
Wrigley, E. A. and D. Souden (ed). Works of Thomas Robert Malthus. 8 vols 1986, vol 1. Primary and secondary.
Thweatt, W. O. (ed). Classical political economy; a survey of recent literature. Lancaster 1988. Secondary.

Collected works

Five papers on political economy. Ed C. Renwick, Sydney 1953.
Introduction to Malthus. Ed D. V. Glass 1953. A summary view of The principle of population and A letter to Samuel Whitbread.
Occasional papers of T. R. Malthus. Ed B. Semmel, New York 1963. Selected articles in contemporary reviews.
The pamphlets of T. R. Malthus. New York 1970.
Works. Ed E. A. Wrigley and D. Souden 8 vols 1986. Texts of last edns compared with first, where necessary; *see below* for variorum edns of Essay on population and Principles of political economy.

§1

An essay on the principle of population, as it affects the future improvement of society, with remarks on the speculations of Mr Godwin, M. Condorcet, and other writers. 1798 (octavo); rptd with introd by J. Bonar 1926; with introd by K. Boulding, Ann Arbor MI 1959; with introd by A. Flew 1970 (Pen); with introd by G. Gilbert, Oxford 1995 (WCp).
An essay on the principle of population, or, a view of its past and present effects on human happiness, with an inquiry into our prospects respecting the future removal or mitigation of the evils which it occasions. 1803 (quarto), 2 vols 1806 (with appendix answering critics), 2 vols 1807, 3 vols 1817 (5th edn with addns and another appendix), 2 vols 1826, 1 vol 1872, 1888, 1890, 2 vols with introd by W. T. Layton 1914 (EL, with omissions); M. P. Fogarty 1958, New York 1976 (selections with introd by P. Appleman); 1986 (Works vols 1–3, 1798 and 1826 edns with introd by E. A. Wrigley); Cambridge 1989 variorum (ed and introd by P. James), Cambridge 1992 (abbreviated version of James, introd by D. Winch); tr Ger 1807, 1879, Fr 1809, 1821, 1823, 1853, Ital 1867, Jap 1876, Rus 1895.
An investigation of the causes of the present high price of provisions. 1800, 1800; in Works vol 7.
A letter to Samuel Whitbread on his proposed bill for the amendment of the poor laws. 1807, 1807; rptd in Glass, *above*, and Works vol 4.
A letter to Lord Grenville occasioned by some observations of His Lordship on the East India Company's establishment for the education of their civil servants. 1813; in Works vol 4.
Observations on the effects of the corn laws on the agricultural and general wealth of the country. 1814, 1814, 1815; in Works vol 7; tr Ger 1896.
An inquiry into the nature and progress of rent. 1815, ed J. H. Hollander, Baltimore 1903, rptd 1935 and in Works vol 7; tr Ger 1896, Rus 1908.
The grounds of an opinion on the policy of restricting the importation of foreign corn. 1815; in Works vol 7; tr Ger 1896.
Statements respecting the East India College. 1817; in Works vol 4.
Principles of political economy considered with a view to their practical application. 1820, Boston 1829, 2nd edn 1836 (probably by J. Cazenove, with memoir of author by W. Otter), rptd with introd by J. H. Hollander and T. E. Gregory 1928, 1936 (London School of Economics), New York 1951, 1964; in Works vols 5–6; tr Fr 1820, 1847, Ital 1854, Ger 1910. Variorum edn in 2 vols Cambridge 1989 (ed and introd by J. M. Pullen).
The measure of value stated and illustrated, with an application of it to the alteration in the value of the English currency since 1790. 1823; in Works vol 7.
Definitions in political economy. 1827, 1853, rptd New York 1954; in Works vol 8; tr Ital 1854.
A summary view of the principle of population. 1830, reprint of article on Population in Encyclopaedia Britannica, 1824; in Works vol 4, also in D. V. Glass, *above*.

Contributions to periodicals and collaborative works

See Wellesley *vol 5*.
Article on Population in Supplement to 4th, 5th and 6th edns of Encyclopaedia Britannica, 1824.
On the measure of the conditions necessary to the supply of commodities. Trans of the Royal Soc of Lit 1825.
On the meaning which is most usually and most correctly attached to the term value of a commodity. Trans of the Royal Soc of Lit 1827.

Letters and journals

For Malthus's correspondence with Nassau Senior, see Senior, Two lectures on population, *1829; and with D. Ricardo, see* The works and correspondence of David Ricardo, *ed P. Sraffa and M. H. Dobb 11 vols Cambridge 1951–73, vols 6–9; and with Francis Horner, see Horner,* The Horner papers, *ed K. Bourne and W. B. Taylor, Edinburgh 1994. Many letters located and cited in P. James,* Population Malthus, *1979.*
Travel diaries. Ed P. James, Cambridge 1966.
T. R. Malthus, The unpublished papers. Ed J. M. Pullen, T. Hughes-Parry et al, Cambridge 1997. Family letters, sermons and journals.

§2

Godwin, W. Thoughts occasioned by the perusal of Dr Parr's spital sermon, preached at Christ Church, April 15 1800, being a reply to the attacks of Dr Parr, Mr Mackintosh, the author of an essay on population, and others. 1801; rev [by Sydney Smith] in Edinburgh Rev Oct 1802.
Cobbett, William. Cobbett's Political Register 8 Dec 1804, 16 Feb 1805, 18 Jan 1806, 21 Mar 1807, 8 May 1819.
Hall, Charles. The effects of civilization on the people in European states, with an appendix containing observations on the principal conclusion in Mr Malthus's 'Essay on population'. 1805 (appendix pbd separately), 2nd edn 1813; the whole rptd 1850.
Jarrold, Thomas. Dissertations on man, philosophical, physiological and political, in answer to Mr Malthus's essay on the principle of population. 1806.
[Hazlitt, William]. Reply to the 'Essay on population' by the Rev T. R. Malthus, in a series of letters to which are added extracts from the essay with notes. 1807. Originally pbd as letters, signed A. O., in Cobbett's Political Register 11, Jan–June 1807.

Ingram, R. A. Disquisitions on population in which the principles of the essay on population by the Rev T. R. Malthus are examined and refuted. 1808.
Grahame, James. An inquiry into the principle of population. Edinburgh 1816.
Sumner, John Bird. A treatise on the records of the Creation. 1816, 2nd edn 1818, 3rd edn corrected 1825, 5th edn 1833. Reviewed [by G. D'Oyly] in Quart Rev Oct 1816.
Weyland, John. The principles of population and production. 1816.
Ensor, George. An inquiry concerning the population of nations, containing a refutation of Mr Malthus's 'Essay on population'. 1818.
Godwin, W. Of population. An enquiry concerning the power of increase in the numbers of mankind, being an answer to Mr Malthus' essay on that subject. 1820. Reviewed [by T. R. Malthus] Edinburgh Rev July 1821.
Gray, Simon. Remarks on the production of wealth . . . in a letter to the Rev T. R. Malthus. 1820. [The Pamphleteer vol 17 no 34.]
Chalmers, Thomas. The Christian and civic economy of large towns. 3 vols Glasgow: vol 1 1821; vol 2 1823; vol 3 1826. Vol 10 of his Select works, ed Rev W. Hanna, as Christian and economic polity of a nation with special reference to large towns, Edinburgh 1856.
Ravenstone, Piercy. A few doubts as to the correctness of some opinions generally entertained on the subject of population and political economy. 1821.
Read, Samuel. General statement of an argument on the subject of population. 1821.
Place, Francis. Illustrations and proofs of the principle of population, including an examination of the proposed remedies of Mr Malthus and a reply to the objections of Mr Godwin and others. 1822.
Chalmers, Thomas. Statement in regard to the pauperism of Glasgow. Glasgow 1823; rptd as Tract on pauperism no 2 Glasgow 1833. Reviewed in Edinburgh Rev Oct 1824.
[De Quincey, Thomas]. 'Malthus on population', London Mag Oct 1823; [Reply to Hazlitt on Malthus], London Mag Dec 1823; 'Malthus on the measure of value', London Mag Dec 1823.
De Quincey, Thomas. Notes from the pocket book of a late opium eater, no 11 'Malthus'. London 1823, 1867, 1874. Rptd from London Mag 1823.
Hazlitt, William. The spirit of the age, or contemporary portraits. 1825, 2nd edn 1825, 3rd edn 1858.
McCulloch, John Ramsay. The principles of political economy: with a sketch of the rise and the progress of the sciences. Edinburgh and London 1825.
Senior, Nassau William. Two lectures on population, delivered before the University of Oxford in Easter term 1828 to which is added a correspondence between the author and the Rev T. R. Malthus. 1829, 2nd edn 1831.
Sadler, Michael Thomas. The law of population: a treatise, in six books; in disproof of the superfecundity of human beings, and developing the real principle of their increase. 1830. Reviewed [by T. B. Macaulay] in Edinburgh Rev July 1830; and in Quart Rev Apr 1831.
Chalmers, Thomas. On political economy, in connexion with the moral state, and moral prospects of society. Glasgow 1832, 2nd edn Glasgow 1832. Vol 9 of his Select works, ed Rev W. Hanna, Edinburgh 1856. Reviewed in Edinburgh Rev Oct 1832; Quart Rev Oct 1832; Westminster Rev July 1832.
Edmonds, Thomas Rowe. Enquiry into the principles of population. 1832.
Martineau, Harriet. Illustrations of political economy, nos 1–13. 1832. No 6, Weal and woe in Garvelock, A tale . . ., 2nd edn 1832. Reviewed in Quart Rev Apr 1832; [W. Empson] Edinburgh Rev Apr 1833.
Chalmers, Thomas. On the power, wisdom and goodness of God as manifested in the adaptation of external nature to the moral and intellectual constitution of man. 1833. The first of the Bridgewater Treatises.
Lloyd, William Forster. Two lectures on the checks to population, delivered before the University of Oxford in Michaelmas term 1832. Oxford 1833.
Mill, John Stuart. Principles of political economy, with some of their applications to social philosophy. 1848, 2nd edn 1849, 3rd edn 1852, 4th edn 1857, 5th edn 1862, 6th edn 1865, 7th edn 1871. Reviewed in Edinburgh Rev Oct 1848.
Scrope, George Poulett. Some notes of a tour in England, Scotland and Ireland made with a view to the inquiry whether our labouring population be really redundant. 1849.
[Spencer, Herbert]. A theory of population deduced from the general law of animal fertility. Westminster Rev Apr 1852.

Biographies

Otter, W. Memoir of Robert Malthus. Introd to Principles of political economy, 1836.
Life, writings and character of Mr Malthus. Edinburgh Rev Jan 1837.
Bonar, J. Malthus and his work. 1885, 1924.
Keynes, J. M. In Essays in biography, 1933, 1972.
James, P. Population Malthus. 1979.

Jane Marcet 1769–1858

§1

Conversations on chemistry. 1806.
Conversations on political economy. 1816.
John Hopkins' notions on political economy. Boston 1833.
Rich and poor. 1851.

§2

Thomson, D. L. Adam Smith's daughters. 1973.
See also col 1830.

Alfred Marshall 1842–1924

For information on the location of papers and correspondence, see Sturges.

Bibliographies

Memorials of Alfred Marshall. Ed A. C. Pigou 1925.
The early economic writings of Alfred Marshall, 1867–1890. Ed J. K. Whitaker 2 vols 1975.
See also NPDE.

Collections

See Memorials, *above.*
Official papers by Alfred Marshall. 1926. Memoranda and evidence to official inquiries.
Official papers of Alfred Marshall: a supplement. Ed P. Groenewegen, Cambridge 1996.

§1

The pure theory of foreign trade. The pure theory of domestic values. 1879, rptd 1930.
The economics of industry. 1879, rev edn 1881, rptd 10 times. With M. P. Marshall.
The present position of political economy; an inaugural lecture. 1885; in Memorials, *above.*
Principles of economics. 1890, 1891, rev 1895, 1898, rev 1907, 1910, 1916, 1920, 1920, rptd 1922. Variorum edn, ed C. W. Guillebaud 2 vols 1961; tr Ital 1905, Sp 1931, Fr 1971.
Elements of economics of industry. 1892, rptd 1893, 1894, 2nd edn 1896, rptd 1898, 1899, 3rd edn 1899, rptd 8 times, 4th edn 1913, rptd 7 times.
A plea for the creation of a curriculum in economics. 1902.
Industry and trade. 1919, 1919, 1920, 1921, 1923.
Money, credit and commerce. 1923.

Contributions to periodicals
See listings in Memorials, *above.*

Letters
The correspondence of Alfred Marshall, economist. Ed J. K. Whitaker 3 vols Cambridge 1996.

§2
Keynes, J. M. Essays in biography. 1933, 1972.
Groenewegen, P. The soaring eagle. Cambridge 1995.
Centenary essays on Alfred Marshall. Ed J. K. Whitaker, Cambridge 1990.

Mary Paley Marshall 1850–1944

§1
The economics of industry. 1879. With A. Marshall.

§2
Keynes, J. M. Essays in biography. 1933, 1972.
Marshall, M. P. What I remember. Cambridge 1947.

Harriet Martineau 1802–76

See col 1344, above.

Bibliography
Rivlin, J. B. Harriet Martineau; a bibliography of her separately printed books. 1946.

§1
Illustrations of political economy. 1832–4, 1845; tr Sp 1836.
The tendency of charitable institutions. 1833.
Poor laws and paupers illustrated. 1833.
Illustrations of taxation. 1834.
Society in America. 1837, 1968.
History of the thirty years' peace. 1849–50.
Letters on the laws of man's nature and development. 1851. With H. G. Atkinson.
Half a century of the British empire. 1851.
British rule in India. 1857.
Corporate traditions and national rights. 1857.
Biographical sketches. 1869, 1876.
Autobiography. 2 vols 1877, 1969, 1983.

Contributions to periodicals
See Wellesley *vol* 5.

Editions and translations
Comte, A. Cours de philosophie positive. 1896.

§2
Blaug, M. Ricardian economics. 1958.
Thomson, D. L. Adam Smith's daughters. 1973.

Herman Merivale 1806–74

For information on the location of papers and correspondence, see Sturges.

Collections
Historical studies. 1865. Contributions to periodicals.

§1
The character of Socrates. 1830.
An introductory lecture on the study of political economy. 1837.
Five lectures on the principles of legislative provision for the poor in Ireland. 1838.
Lectures on colonisation and colonies delivered before the University of Oxford in 1839. 1840, 1841, 1841, 1861, 1928, New York 1967.
Life of Sir Henry Lawrence 1872. Vol 2 by Herman Merivale.

Contributions to periodicals
See Wellesley *vol* 5.

Editions and translations
Translation of Bacon's Essays, ed B. Montagu, 1836.

§2
Merivale, C. Herman Merivale; a brief memoir. Trans of Devonshire Assoc 1884.
Merivale, A. Family memorials. 1884.

James Mill 1773–1836

See col 2556, above. For information on the location of papers and correspondence, see Sturges.

Bibliography
Fenn, R. Concise list of the works of James Mill. In his James Mill's political thought, 1987.

Collections
See Winch, below.

§1
An essay on the impolicy of a bounty on the exportation of grain. 1804; in Winch, *below.*
Commerce defended. 1808; in Winch, *below.*
History of British India. 3 vols 1817–18, 6 vols 1820, ed H. H. Wilson 9 vols 1840–8, 10 vols 1856; tr Ger 1872.
Elements of political economy. 1821, 1824, 1826, 1844; in Winch, *below*; tr Fr 1823, Ger 1824, 1921, Sp 1827, Ital 1854.

Contributions to periodicals
See Wellesley *vol* 5; *Fenn, above; and Winch, below.*

§2
Spence, W. Agriculture the source of the wealth of Britain. 1808.
Thompson, T. P. An exposition of the fallacies on rent. 1826.
Bain, A. James Mill; a biography. 1882, 1889.
Winch, D. James Mill: selected economic writings. Edinburgh 1966.
De Marchi, N. B. The case for James Mill. In Methodological controversy in economics, ed A. W. Coats, Connecticut 1983.

John Stuart Mill 1806–73

See col 2558.

Bibliographies
The collected works of John Stuart Mill. Ed J. M. Robson 33 vols Toronto 1963–91. Includes all primary sources.
Laine, M. Bibliography of works on John Stuart Mill. Toronto 1982. Mill Newsletter and now Utilitas, a journal of utilitarian studies. Secondary sources.

Collections
See Robson, above. Economic writings to be found in vols 2–5.

§1
A system of logic. 1843, 8th edn 1872; in Robson, *above*, vols 7 and 8.
Essays on some unsettled questions in political economy. 1844; in Robson, *above*, vol 4.
Principles of political economy. 2 vols 1848, 7th edn 1870, 1878, 1885; 1 vol People's edn 1865, 17th reprint 1891; Silver Lib 1892, 7th reprint 1909; ed W. J. Ashley 1909; ed D. Winch, Harmondsworth 1970 (Pen, abridged); ed J. Riley, Oxford 1994 (WC, abridged); also in Robson, *above*, vols 2 and 3.

Contributions to periodicals
See Wellesley *vol* 5 *and Robson, above, especially vols 4 and 5.*

§2
Marshall, A. Mr Mill's theory of value. Fortnightly Rev 19 1876.
Schwartz, P. The new political economy of John Stuart Mill. 1968.

Whitaker, J. K. John Stuart Mill's methodology. Jnl of Political Economy Oct 1975.
Hollander, S. The economics of John Stuart Mill. 2 vols Oxford 1985.
De Marchi, N. B. John Stuart Mill interpretation since Schumpeter. In Classical political economy: a survey of recent literature, ed W. O. Thweatt, Boston 1988.

Simon Newcomb 1835–1909

Bibliography

Archibald, R. C. Simon Newcomb 1835–1909. Bibliography of his life and work. In Memoirs of the National Academy of Sciences, Washington 1924.

§1

A critical examination of our financial policy during the Southern rebellion. 1865.
The ABC of finance. 1877.
Principles of political economy. 1885.
A plain man's talk on the labour question. 1886.
Reminiscences of an astronomer. 1903.

§2

Fisher, I. Obituary. Economic Jnl 19 1909.
See also Archibald, above.

William Newmarch 1820–82

For information on the location of papers and correspondence, see Sturges.

§1

New supplies of gold. 1853.
On the loans raised by Mr Pitt during the first French war. 1855.
Money. 1855.
A history of prices and of the state of the circulation. 1857. With T. Tooke.

Contributions to periodicals

See Wellesley *vol 5.*

§2

In memoriam: William Newmarch. 1882.
Fitzpatrick, P. J. Leading British statisticians of the nineteenth century. Jnl of the Amer Statistical Assoc 55 1960.
Ashbee, R. A. William Newmarch and Glyns. Three Banks Rev 12 1979.

Joseph Shield Nicholson 1850–1927

For information on the location of papers and correspondence, see Sturges.

§1

Effects of machinery on wages. 1878, 1892.
Political economy as a branch of education. 1881.
Tenants gain not landlord's loss. 1883.
Bimetallism for practical men. 1887.
A treatise on money. 1888, 1893, 1895, 1901; tr Ital 1905.
Tariffs and international commerce. 1891.
A dreamer of dreams: a modern romance. 1892.
Principles of political economy. 3 vols 1893, 1902.
Historical progress and ideal socialism. 1894.
Strikes and social problems. 1896.
The relations of rents, wages, and profits in agriculture. 1896.
Banker's money. 1902.
Elements of political economy. 1903, 1906.
The tariff question, with special reference to wages and employment. 1903.
History of the English corn laws. 1904.
Rates and taxes. 1905.
The British economists. 1907.
A project of empire. 1909.
Life and genius of Ariosto. 1914.
The neutrality of the United States in relation to the British and German empires. 1915.
War finance. 1917, 1918.
Inflation. 1919.
The revival of Marxism. 1920.

Contributions to periodicals

See Wellesley *vol 5 and H. E. Batson,* A select bibliography of modern economic theory 1870–1929, *1930.*

Editions

Smith, Adam. Wealth of nations. 1884, 1901.
List, F. National system of political economy. 1904.
The opinions of Dr Chalmers. 1912.

§2

Scott, W. R. John Shield Nicholson. Proc of the Br Acad 14 1928.
Maloney, J. Marshall, orthodoxy and the professionalisation of economics. 1985.

Robert Owen 1771–1858

For information on the location of papers and correspondence, see Sturges.

Bibliographies

A bibliography of Robert Owen, the Socialist 1771–1858. Aberystwyth 1914, 1925.
Dictionary of labour biography. Ed J. M. Bellamy and J. Saville, vol 6 1982.

Collections

Addresses. 1830.
A new view of society and other writings. Ed G. D. H. Cole 1927 (EL).

§1

A statement regarding the New Lanark establishment. 1812.
A new view of society: or essays on the principle of the formation of human character. 1813, 1816, 1817, New York 1825, Edinburgh 1826, London 1927 (EL); abridged L. D. Abbott 1946, 1970 (Pen).
Observations on the effect of the manufacturing system. 1815, 1817, 1818.
An address to the inhabitants of New Lanark at the opening of the New Institution established for the formation of character. 1816 (2nd edn), 1817.
Peace on earth: development of the plan for the relief of the poor and the emancipation of mankind. [1817.]
Two memorials on behalf of the working classes: the first presented to the governments of Europe and America, the second to the Allied Powers assembled at Aix-la-Chapelle. 1818.
An address to the master manufacturers of Great Britain. Boston 1819.
Lectures on an entire new state of society: comprehending an analysis of British society relative to the production and distribution of wealth. 1820.
Report to the county of Lanark of a plan for relieving public distress and removing discontent by giving employment to the poor and working classes. Glasgow 1821, London 1832.
An exploration of the cause of the distress which pervades the civilised parts of the world and of the means whereby it may be removed. 1823.
Discourses on a new system of society as delivered in the Hall of Representatives of the United States. Louisville KY 1825.
Address at a public meeting in Philadelphia, to which is added an exposition of the pecuniary transactions between [Owen] and W. McClure. Philadelphia 1827.
Memorial to the Mexican Republic. Philadelphia 1827.

Debate on the evidences of Christianity between Owen and A. Campbell. Ed A. Campbell 2 vols Bethany VA 1829, London 1839.
An address to all classes in the state. 1832.
Six lectures on charity at New Lanark. 1833–4.
Lectures on the marriages of the priesthood of the old immoral world. Leeds 1835.
The book of the new moral world concerning the rational system of society. Pt 1 1836, Glasgow 1837.
Public discussion between Owen and J. H. Roebuck. Manchester 1837, 1837.
A development of the origin and effects of moral good and of the principles and practices of moral good. Manchester 1838.
The marriage system of the new world. Leeds 1838.
Six lectures delivered in Manchester previously to the discussion between Owen and J. H. Roebuck. Manchester [1839].
The catechism of the new moral world. Manchester [1840?].
Manifesto of Owen. 1840, 1841 (8th edn).
An outline of the rational system of society. Manchester [1840?], Leeds 1840 (6th edn).
Social hymns. 1840, 1841.
The social Bible, being an outline of the rational system of society. [1840?]
The signs of the times: or the approach of the millenium. 1841 (2nd edn).
An address to the Socialists on the present position of the rational system of society, May 1841. 1841.
Lectures on the rational system of society versus Socialism as explained by the Bishop of Exeter and others. 1841.
What is Socialism? 1841. Discussion between Owen and J. Brindley.
A development of the principles and plans on which to establish home colonies. 1841.
Address to the ministers of all religions, 21 Dec 1845. Philadelphia 1845.
On the employment of children in manufactories. [New Lanark 1848.]
The revolution in the mind and practice of the human race. 1849. A supplement to The revolution in the mind and practice of the human race, 1849.
Letters on education. 1849.
The future of the human race. 1853, 1854.
Address to the human race on his eighty-fourth birthday. 1854.
The new existence of man upon the earth. 8 pts 1854–5.
Address in St Martin's Hall on 1 Jan 1855. 1855.
Tracts on the coming millenium. 1855.
Papers sent to the National Association for Promoting Social Sciences at its first meeting, 1857. [1857.]
Life written by himself; with selections from his writings and correspondence. Vol 1 (2 pts) 1857–8; ed M. Beer 1920.
Owen also edited the following periodicals: Economist, *1821;* Crisis, *1832–4;* New Moral World, *1835–45;* Weekly Letters to the Human Race, *1850; his* Journal, *1851–2;* Rational Quart Rev, *1853; and his* Millennial Gazette, *1856–8.*

§2

Reybaud, M. R. L. In his Étude sur les réformateurs contemporaires, Paris 1840.
The life of Robert Owen written by himself. 2 vols 1857–8.
Holyoake, G. J. Life and last days of Owen. 1859.
Sargent, W. L. Owen and his social philosophy. 1860.
Martineau, H. In her Biographical sketches, 1869.
Owen, R. D. Threading my way. 1874.
Seligman, E. R. A. Owen and the Christian Socialists. Boston 1886.
Holyoake, G. J. History of co-operation in England. 2 vols 1875–9.
Jones, L. Life, times and labour of Owen. 2 vols 1889–90.
Dolléans, E. Owen 1771–1858. Paris 1905.
Simon, H. Owen: sein Leben und seine Bedeutung. Jena 1905.
Podmore, F. Owen: a biography. 1906.
Sadler, M. E. Owen, Lovatt, Maurice and Toynbee. 1907.
Davies, R. E. Life of Owen. 1907.
Clayton, J. Owen, pioneer of social reforms. 1908.
Hutchins, B. L. Owen, social reformer. 1912.
Joad, C. E. M. Owen, idealist. 1917.
McCabe, J. Owen. 1920.
Cole, G. D. H. Life of Owen. 1930; ed M. Cole 1865 (3rd edn).
Rennard, T. A. Owen. 1937.
Davies, A. T. Owen 1771–1858: pioneer social reformer and philanthropist. 1948.
Cole, M. In her Makers of the labour movement, 1948.
Cole, M. Owen of New Lanark. 1953.
House, H. New Lanark. In his All in due time, 1955.
Harrison, J. F. C. Owen and the Owenites in Britain and America. 1969.

Henry Brooke Parnell, Lord Congleton 1776–1842

For information on the location of papers and correspondence, see Sturges.

§1

Observations upon the state of the currency of Ireland. 1804.
The principles of currency and exchange. 1805.
Treatise on the corn trade and agriculture. 1809.
The substance of the speeches of Sir Henry Parnell in the House of Commons. 1814.
Observations on paper money. 1827, 1829.
On financial reform. 1830, 1832.
A plain statement of the power of the Bank of England. 1832.
A treatise on roads. 1833, 1838.

Contributions to periodicals

See Wellesley *vol 5.*

§2

Hilton, A. J. B. Corn, cash, commerce. Oxford 1977.

Francis Place 1771–1854

For information on the location of papers and correspondence, see Sturges. Mss in BL; London Univ Lib; Ely Collection, Louisiana State Univ Lib, Baton Rouge; Seligman Collection, Columbia Univ Lib. The papers of Francis Place, 1791–1854, are available in microform, 54 reels, Brighton 1978.

§1

The mystery of the sinking fund explained. 1821.
Illustrations and proofs of the principle of population, including an examination of the proposed remedies of Mr Malthus, and a reply to the objections of Mr Godwin. 1822; ed N. E. Himes with introd and appendices on Place as advocate of birth control 1930, 1960.
On the law of libel. 1823.
Observations on Mr Huskisson's speech on the laws relating to combinations of workmen. 1825.
An essay on the state of the country in respect to the condition and conduct of the husbandry labourers and to the consequences likely to result therefrom. 1831.
A letter to a Minister of State respecting taxes on knowledge. 1831, 3rd edn 1835.
Improvement of the working people: drunkenness, education etc. 1834.
Observations on a pamphlet relating to the corn laws. 1840.

§2

Wallas, G. Life of Francis Place. 1898, rev 1918, 3rd edn 1919, 4th edn 1925.
Ervine, St J. G. Place. 1912.

Miles, D. Francis Place: the life of a remarkable radical. Brighton 1988.

William Playfair 1759–1823

Bibliography
Gentleman's Mag, Part 1. 1823.

§1
The increase of manufactures. 1785.
The commercial and political atlas. 1785, 1787, 1801.
An essay on the national debt. 1787.
Lineal arithmetic applied to shew the progress of the commerce and revenue of England. 1789, 1798.
Inevitable consequences of a reform in parliament. 1792.
Thoughts on the present state of French politics. 1793.
A general view of the actual force and resources of France. 1793.
Better prospects to the merchants and manufacturers of Great Britain. 1793.
For the use of the enemies of England; a real statement of the finances and resources of Great Britain. 1796.
A letter to Sir William Pulteney. 1797.
The history of jacobinism. 1798.
Strictures on the Asiatic establishments of Great Britain. 1799.
Statistical tables, from the German of Boetticher. 1800.
The statistical breviary. 1801.
An inquiry into the permanent causes of the decline and fall of powerful and wealthy nations. 1805, 1807.
Statistical account of the US from the French. 1807.
A fair and candid address to the nobility. 1809.
A second address to the nobility. 1810.
Outlines of a plan for a new and solid balance of power in Europe. 1813.
A letter on the advantages of apprenticeship. 1814.
A letter on our agricultural discontents. 1821, 1822.

Editions
Smith, Adam. Wealth of nations. 1805.

§2
See PDPE.

George Richardson Porter 1792–1855

For information on the location of papers and correspondence, see Sturges.

§1
On the nature and properties of sugar cane. 1830, 1843.
A treatise on the origin, progressive improvement, and present state of the manufacture of porcelain and glass. 1830.
The progress of the nation, in the various social and economic relations from the beginning of the nineteenth century to the present time. 1836, 1838, 1846, 1851, rev edn introd by F. W. Hirst 1912, rptd New York 1970.
The effect of restriction on the importation of corn. 1839.
Result of an enquiry into the condition of the labouring classes in five parishes in Norfolk. 1839.
The many sacrificed to the few, proved by the effects of the sugar monopoly. 1841.
The geography of Great Britain. 1850.
Statistics. 1851, 1859.

Contributions to periodicals
See Wellesley *vol 5.*

Translation
Bastiat, F. Popular fallacies regarding general interests. 1846.

§2
See DNB and PDPE.

John Rae 1796–1872

§1
Statement of some new principles on the subject of political economy. Boston 1834, rptd as The sociological theory of capital, with a biography and notes, by C. W. Mixter, New York 1905.

§2
Senior, N. W. An outline of the science of political economy. 1836.
Mill, J. S. Principles of political economy. 1848.
Hearn, W. E. Plutology. Melbourne 1863.
Mixter, C. W. A forerunner of Böhm-Bawerk. Quart Jnl of Economics 11 1897.
Veblen, T. The theory of the leisure class. New York 1899.
Fisher, I. The rate of interest. New York 1907.
James, R. W. John Rae, political economist; an account of his life and a compilation of his main writings. 2 vols Toronto 1965.
James, R. W. and A. Brewer. In The Scottish contribution to modern economic thought, ed D. Mair, Aberdeen 1990.

John Rae 1845–1915

§1
Contemporary socialism. 1884, 1891, 1901, 1908.
Eight hours for work. 1894.
Life of Adam Smith. 1895.

Contributions to periodicals
See Wellesley *vol 5.*

§2
See NPDE.

Piercy Ravenstone, Richard Puller? fl. 1789–1831

§1
A few doubts as to the correctness of some opinions generally entertained on the subject of population and political economy. 1821.
Thoughts on the funding system. 1824.

§2
See NPDE.

Samuel Read fl. 1816–29

§1
On money and the bank restriction laws. Edinburgh 1816.
The problem solved: an explication of a plan of a safe, steady, and secure government paper currency. Edinburgh 1818.
Exposure of certain plagiarisms of J. R. McCulloch. Edinburgh 1819.
General statement of an argument on the subject of population in answer to Mr Malthus's theory. Edinburgh 1819.
Political economy, an inquiry into the natural grounds of right to vendible property or wealth. Edinburgh 1829.

§2
Bailey, S. A critical dissertation. 1825.
Senior, N. W. An outline of the science of political economy. 1836.
See also PDPE.

David Ricardo 1772–1823

For information on the location of papers and correspondence, see Sturges.

Bibliographies
Franklin, B. and G. Legman. David Ricardo and Ricardian theory: a bibliographical check-list. New York 1949 (primary and secondary).

Works, ed Sraffa and Dobb, *below*, vol 10. Primary and secondary.
See also Amano. Primary and secondary.

Collections

McCulloch, J. R. The works of David Ricardo. 1846, 1852, 1862, 1871, 1876, 1881, 1884; tr Fr 1847, 2nd edn 1882, Rus 1875, 1882, 1897.
Essays on currency and finance. Ed C. S. Griffin, Tokyo 1901.
Economic essays. Ed E. C. K. Gonner 1923, rptd 1966.
Notes on Malthus. Ed J. H. Hollander and T. E. Gregory, Baltimore 1928.
Minor papers on the currency question. Ed J. H. Hollander, Baltimore 1932.
Hollander, J. H. Minor papers on the currency question. 1932.
The works and correspondence of David Ricardo. Ed P. Sraffa and M. H. Dobb 11 vols Cambridge 1951–73.

§1

The price of gold, three contributions to the Morning Chronicle. 1809.
The high price of bullion. 1810–11; tr Fr 1810, 1847, Ital 1846, 1852, Rus 1882, 1926, 1955, Ger 1905, 1923.
Three letters to the Morning Chronicle on the bullion report. 1810.
Reply to Mr Bosanquet's practical observations on the report of the bullion committee. 1811; tr Fr 1847, Ital 1857, 1948, Rus 1882, 1955.
The above 4 items are in Sraffa, above, vol 3.
An essay on the influence of a low price of corn on the profits of stock. 1815; tr Fr 1847, Ital 1860, 1948, Rus 1882, 1955, Ger 1905.
Proposals for an economical and secure currency. 1816, 1819; tr Fr 1847, Ital 1857, Ger 1925, 1927.
Funding system. In Supplement to the 4th, 5th and 6th edns of Encyclopaedia Britannica. 1820; tr Fr 1847, Ital 1866, 1948, Ger 1923.
On protection of agriculture. 1822; tr Fr 1847, Ger 1905.
Plan for the establishment of a national bank. 1824.
The above 5 items are in Sraffa, above, vol 4.
On the principles of political economy and taxation. 1817, corrected 1819, rev 1821, Washington 1819, London 1830; ed E. C. K. Gonner 1882, 1891, 1903, 1911, 1929; ed F. W. Kolthammer 1911 (EL), 1912, 1926, 1929, 1933, 1943; ed M. J. Fogarty 1955; ed D. Winch 1973, 1992. Tr Fr 1819, 1835, 1847, 1882, 1891, 1933; Ger 1821, 1837, 1877, 1905, 1959; Ital 1856, 1948; Rus 1882, 1895, 1910; Jap 1921, 1928, 1930, 1937; Sp 1932, 1941, 1955. First six chs in Economic classics, ed Ashley, New York 1895; Masterworks of economics, ed Ashley 1946. In Sraffa, *above*, vol 1, 1951, 1953, 1962, 1966, 1970, 1975, 1981, 1986, 1990, 1995, 1996.

Letters

Letters to T. R. Malthus. Ed J. Bonar, Oxford 1887.
Letters to J. R. McCulloch. Ed J. H. Hollander 1895.
Letters to Hutches Trower. Ed J. Bonar and J. H. Hollander, Oxford 1899.
For complete correspondence, see Sraffa, above, vols 6–10.

§2

McCulloch, J. R. On Ricardo's Principles of political economy. Edinburgh Rev June 1818.
Mill, James. Elements of political economy. 1821.
Malthus, T. R. Political economy. Quart Rev Jan 1824.
De Quincey, T. Dialogue of three templars on political economy. London Mag Mar–Oct 1824.
Bailey, S. A critical dissertation on the nature, measure and causes of value. 1825, rptd 1931.
Hodgskin, T. Labour defended. 1825.
Jones, R. An essay on the distribution of wealth. 1831.
Scrope, G. P. Principles of political economy. 1833.
Banfield, T. C. Six letters to the Right Honourable Sir Robert Peel, being an attempt to expose the dangerous tendencies of the theory of rent advocated by Mr Ricardo. 1853.
Marx, K. Capital. 1867–94.
Bagehot, Walter. Economic studies. 1879, 1888.
Toynbee, A. Lectures on the industrial revolution in England. 1884, 1890, 1913, 1929.
Patten, S. N. The interpretation of Ricardo. Quart Jnl of Economics 7 1889.
Ashley, W. J. The rehabilitation of Ricardo. Economic Jnl 1 1891.
Cannan, E. A history of the theories of production and distribution from 1776 to 1848. 1898.
Hollander, J. H. David Ricardo: a centenary estimate. Baltimore 1910.
Blaug, M. Ricardian economics. New Haven CT 1958.
Weatherall, D. David Ricardo: a biography. The Hague 1976.
Peach, T. Interpreting Ricardo. Cambridge 1993.

J. E. Thorold Rogers 1823–90

For information on the location of papers and correspondence, see Sturges.

§1

The law of settlement. 1861.
Education in Oxford: its method, its aids, and its rewards. Oxford 1861.
A history of agriculture and prices in England from the year after the Oxford parliament to the commencement of the continental war. 7 vols Oxford 1866–1902.
A manual of political economy. 1868.
The free trade policy of the Liberal party. 1868.
Cobden and modern political opinion. 1873.
Epistles, satires and epigrams. 1876.
Six centuries of work and wages: the history of English labour. 1884. Ed with introd by G. D. H. Cole 1949.
The economic interpretation of history. 1888.
The relations of economic science to social and political action. 1888.
The industrial and commercial history of England. Ed A. G. L. Rogers, New York 1892.

Contributions to periodicals

See Wellesley *vol 5.*
On a continuous price of wheat for 105 years. Jnl of the Statistical Soc 27, Mar 1864.
The colonial question. Cobden Club Essay 1871–2.
Review of Cliffe Leslie's Essays in philosophy. Acad June 1879.
Review of William Cunningham's The growth of English industry and commerce. Acad May 1882.
Lessons from the Dutch republic. In National life and thought, ed Magnuason et al, New York 1891.

Editions

Aristotle. Nicomachean ethics. 1865.
Smith, Adam. Wealth of nations. 2 vols Oxford 1869.

§2

Ashley, W. J. James E. Thorold Rogers. Political Science Quart 4, 1889.
Kadish, A. Historians, economists, and economic history. 1989.
See also DNB.

George Poulet Scrope 1797–1876

For information on the location of papers and correspondence, see Sturges.

Bibliography

Sturges, P. A bibliography of George Poulet Scrope: geologist, economist and local historian. Boston 1984 (Kress Lib).

§1

Considerations on volcanos. 1825; tr Fr 1864.
Memoir on the geology of central France. 1827, 1858; tr Fr 1866.
A letter to the magistrates of the south and west of England. 1828, 1831.

Plea for the abolition of slavery in England. 1829.
The common cause of the landlord, tenant, and labour. 1830.
The currency question freed from mystery. 1830.
On credit currency and its superiority to coin. 1830.
Extracts of letters from poor persons who emigrated to Canada and the United States. 1831, 1832.
An examination of the bank charter question. 1833.
Principles of political economy. 1833; tr Ital 1855. 2nd edn pbd as Political economy for plain people, 1873, New York 1969.
Plan of a poor law for Ireland. 1834.
How is Ireland to be governed? 1834, 1846.
Letters to Lord Russell on the expediency of enlarging the Irish poor law. 1846.
A letter to the landed proprietors of Ireland. 1847.
Remarks on the Irish poor law relief bill. 1847.
Memoir of the life of Lord Sydenham. 1847.
Letters to Lord Russell on the further measures needed for the social amelioration of Ireland. 1847.
Plea for the rights of industry in Ireland. 1848.
How to make Ireland self-supporting. 1848.
The Irish relief measures. 1848.
A labour rate recommended. 1849.
The Irish poor law. 1849.
Some notes on a tour in England, Scotland, and Ireland. 1849.
Suggested legislation [on] dwellings of the poor. 1849.
The savings bank bill. 1850.
History of the manor of Castle Combe. 1852.
On the mode of formation of volcanic cones and craters. 1859; tr Fr 1860.
No vote, no rate. 1867.
Remarks and suggestions on friendly societies. 1874.

Contributions to periodicals
See Wellesley *vol 5*.

§2
Opie, R. A neglected English economist: George Poulet Scrope. Quart Jnl of Economics 44 1928.
See also NPDE.

Nassau William Senior 1790–1864

For information on the location of papers and correspondence, see Sturges.

Bibliography
See Bowley, below (primary), and Amano.

Selections
Selected writings on economics, a volume of pamphlets, 1827–1852. New York 1965.

§1
An introductory lecture on political economy. 1827, 1828, 1831.
Three lectures on the transmission of the precious metals. 1828, 1830, rptd 1931 (London School of Economics).
Two lectures on population. 1829.
Three lectures on the rate of wages. 1830, rptd 1931 (London School of Economics); tr Ger 1921.
Three lectures on the cost of obtaining money. 1830, 1931.
A letter to Lord Howick on a legal provision for the Irish poor. 1831, 1832.
Report from His Majesty's Commissioners on the administration of the poor laws. British Parliamentary Papers 1834, 1974 (Pen).
Outline of the poor law amendment act. 1834.
Statement of the provision for the poor and of the condition of the labouring classes in a considerable portion of America and Europe. 1835.
On national property, and on the prospects of the present administration. 1835.
An outline of the science of political economy. 1836, 1850, 1858, 1863, 1872, rptd 1938, New York 1965; tr Ger 1923.
Letters on the factory act as it affects the cotton manufacture. 1837, 1844.
Three lectures on the value of money. 1840, rptd 1931 (London School of Economics); tr Ger 1925.
On the improvement of design and patterns, and extension of copyright (from the Report of the Commissioners on Hand-Loom Weaving). 1841. With S. J. Loyd, W. E. Hicks and J. Leslie.
Remarks on the opposition to the poor law amendment bill. 1841.
A letter on the production of wealth. 1849.
Four introductory lectures on political economy. 1852.
A journal kept in Turkey and Greece in the autumn of 1857 and the beginning of 1858. 1859; tr Fr 1861.
Resolutions and head of a report [on elementary education]. 1860, rptd as Suggestions on popular education, 1861.
American slavery. 1862.
Address on education. 1863
Biographical sketches. 1863.
Essays on fiction. 1864.
Historical and philosophical essays. Ed M. C. M. Senior 2 vols 1865.
Journals, conversations and essays relating to Ireland. 2 vols 1868.
Journals kept in France and Italy, 1848–52. Ed M. C. M. Simpson 2 vols 1871; tr Ital 1937.
Correspondence and conversations of Alexis de Toqueville with Nassau William Senior from 1834 to 1859. Ed M. C. M. Simpson 2 vols 1872; tr Fr 1877.
Conversations with Thiers, Guizot, etc. Ed M. C. M. Simpson 2 vols 1878.
Conversations with distinguished persons during the Second Empire from 1860 to 1863. Ed M. C. M. Simpson 2 vols 1880.
Conversations and journals in Egypt and Malta. Ed M. C. M. Simpson 2 vols 1882.
Industrial efficiency and social economy. Ed S. L. Levy 2 vols 1929.

Contributions to periodicals
See Wellesley *vol 5*.

Letters
See vols ed by Simpson, above.
Tennant, C. Letters forming part of a correspondence with N. W. Senior concerning systematic colonization. 1831.
Torrens, R. A letter to N. W. Senior. 1843.

§2
Bowley, M. Nassau Senior and classical economics. 1937.
See also NPDE.

Henry Sidgwick 1838–1900

For information on the location of papers and correspondence, see Sturges, and J. B. Schneewind, Sidgwick's ethics and Victorian moral philosophy, *Oxford 1977.*
See col 2587 above.

Bibliography
See Schneewind, above.

§1
The principles of political economy. 1883, 1887, 1901.
The elements of politics. 1891, 1897, 1908, 1919.
The development of European polity. Ed E. M. Sidgwick 1903.

Contributions to periodicals
See Wellesley *vol 5*.
The scope and method of economic science. Proc of the British Assoc for the Advancement of Science 1885.

§2
Ritchie, D. G. Review of Elements of politics. International Jnl of Ethics 2 1891.
Keynes, J. N. Henry Sidgwick. Economic Jnl 10 1900.
Sidgwick, A. and E. M. Henry Sidgwick: a memoir. 1906.

Sir John Sinclair 1754–1835

For information on the location of papers and correspondence, see Sturges.

Collections
Essays on miscellaneous subjects. 1802.
A collection of papers on political subjects. 1813.

§1
Report of Committee on the Highlands. 1790.
The statistical account of Scotland. 21 vols Edinburgh 1791–9, 1925, rptd 1976–.
Account of the origin of the Board of Agriculture. 1796.
The consequences of the redemption of the land tax. 1798.
The history of the public revenue of the British empire 1795–1890. 3rd edn 1803–4.
A dissertation on the authenticity of the poems of Ossian. 1806, 1807.
An account of the systems of husbandry adopted in . . . Scotland. Edinburgh 1809, 1813.
Observations on the report of the bullion committee. 1810.
An account of the Highland Society of London. 1813.
The code of agriculture. 1817, 1832.
The code of health and longevity. 1815, 3rd edn 1816.
General report of the agricultural state and political circumstances of Scotland. 10 vols 1812, 1813.
The late prosperity. 1826.

Editions
A letter on the principles of the Christian faith. 1818, 1823.

Letters
Washington, G. Letters to Sir John Sinclair on agricutural and other topics. 1800.
The correspondence of Sir John Sinclair. 2 vols 1831.

§2
Memoirs of the life of Sir John Sinclair. Edinburgh 1837.
Mitchison, R. Agricultural Sir John. 1962.

William Spence 1783–1860

Collections
Tracts on political economy. 1822.

§1
Britain independent of commerce. 1807, 3rd edn 1808.
Radical causes of the distresses of the West Indian planters. 1807, 1818.
Agriculture the source of the wealth of Britain. 1808.
The objections against the corn bill refuted. 1815.
Introduction to Entomology. 4 vols 1815–26, 7th edn 1856. With W. Kirby.

§2
Mill, J. Commerce defended. 1807.
Torrens, R. The economists refuted. 1808.
Meek, R. L. The economics of physiocracy. 1962.

T. Perronet Thompson 1783–1869

For information on the location of papers and correspondence, see Sturges.

§1
An exposition of fallacies on rent, tithes, etc. 1826. 2nd edn entitled The true theory of rent in opposition to Mr Ricardo and others, 1826, 1829, 1830, 1832.
A catechism on the corn laws. 1827, 1829, 1831, 1834, 1940.
Corn-law fallacies, with the answers. 1839.
Exercises, political and other. 6 vols 1842.
A catechism on the currency. 1848.
A catechism on the ballot. 1859, 1864.

Contributions to periodicals
See Wellesley *vol 5.*

§2
Mill, J. S. Review of Catechism on the corn laws. Westminster Rev 13 1828.
Johnson, L. G. General T. Perronet Thompson, 1783–1869: his military, literary and political campaigns. 1957.

William Thompson 1785–1833

§1
An inquiry into the principles of the distribution of wealth most conducive to human happiness. 1824.
Labour rewarded, the claims of labour and capital conciliated, by one of the idle classes. 1827.
Practical directions for the speedy and economical establishment of communities. 1830.

§2
Foxwell, W. S. Introduction. In A. Menger, The right to the whole produce of labour, 1899.
Thompson, N. W. The people's science. 1984.

Henry Thornton 1760–1815

For information on the location of papers and correspondence, see Sturges.

Bibliography
Hayek, F. A. Introd to reprint of Enquiry into paper credit. 1939. Primary and secondary.

Collections
Works of the late Henry Thornton. Ed R. H. Inglis 1854. Reprint of Family prayers, Family commentary upon the sermon of the mount, and Family commentary on portions of the Pentateuch by the late Henry Thornton.
Three female characters. 1846. Reprints articles from Christian Observer.

§1
On the probable effects of the peace with respect to the commercial interests of Great Britain. 1802.
An enquiry into the nature and effects of the paper credit of Great Britain. 1802, 1807; tr Fr and Ger 1803. Rptd in Select collection of scarce and valuable tracts, ed J. R. McCulloch, 1857. Ed with introd by F. A. Hayek 1939, New York 1962.
The substance of two speeches of Henry Thornton. 1811.

§2
Hollander, J. H. The development of the theory of money from Adam Smith to David Ricardo. Quart Jnl of Economics 25 1911.
Cannan, E. The paper pound of 1797–1821. 1919, 1921, 1925, New York 1969.
Viner, J. Studies in the theory of international trade. 1937.
Meacham, S. Henry Thornton of Clapham. 1964.
See also col 2636.

William Thomas Thornton 1813–80

For information on the location of papers and correspondence, see Sturges.

§1
Over-population and its remedy. 1846.
A plea for peasant proprietors. 1848.

The siege of Silistria. 1854. Poem.
Zohrab; or a midsummer day's dream, and other poems. 1854.
Modern Manicheism, Labour's Utopia and other poems. 1857.
On labour: its wrongful claims and rightful duties, its actual present and possible future. 1869, 1870, rptd Shannon 1971.
Old fashioned ethics and common-sense metaphysics. 1873.
Indian public works. 1875.
Horatius Flaccus, word for word from Horace. 1878.

Contributions to periodicals
See Wellesley *vol 5 1989.*

§2

Mill, J. S. Thornton on Labour and its claims. Fortnightly Rev May and June 1869, rptd in Mill's Collected works vol 5, 1967.
Walker, F. A. The wage-fund theory. North Amer Rev 99 1875.
Taussig, F. W. Wages and capital. New York 1896, 1968.
Hollander, J. H. Introd to F. D. Longe, The wages fund theory, Baltimore 1903.

Thomas Tooke 1774–1858

For information on the location of papers and correspondence, see Sturges.

Bibliography
See Amano. Primary and secondary.

§1

Free trade: some account of the free trade movement as it originated with the petition of the merchants of London. 1820, 1853.
Thoughts and details on the high and low prices of the last thirty years. 1823, 1824.
Considerations on the state of the currency. 1826.
On currency in connexion with the corn trade. 1829.
A letter to Lord Grenville on the effects ascribed to the resumption of cash payments on the value of the currency. 1829.
A history of prices and of the state of the circulation from 1793 to 1837. 2 vols 1838, 1840.
An inquiry into the currency principle. 1844, rptd 1959 (London School of Economics).
A history of prices and of the state of the currency from 1839 to 1847. 1848.
On the bank charter act of 1844. 1856.
A history of prices and of the state of the circulation during the nine years 1848–1856. 2 vols 1857, rptd with introd by T. E. Gregory, 6 vols 1928; tr Ger 1862, Ital 1918. With W. Newmarch.

Contributions to periodicals
See Wellesley *vol 5.*

§2

Malthus, T. R. Review of Thoughts and details. Quart Rev 29, Apr 1823.
Torrens, R. A letter to Thomas Tooke. 1840.
Mill, J. S. Review of Inquiry into the currency principle. Westminster Rev Mar 1844.
Torrens, R. An inquiry into the renewal of the charter of the Bank of England. 1844.
Fitzpatrick, P. J. Leading British statisticians of the nineteenth century. Jnl of the Amer Statistical Assoc 55 1960.

Robert Torrens 1780–1864

For information on the location of papers and correspondence, see Sturges.

Bibliography
Robbins, L. Robert Torrens and the evolution of classical economics. 1958. Primary.
See also Amano. Primary and secondary.

§1

The economists refuted. 1808.
Thoughts on the catholic question. 1808, 1813.
Coelibia choosing a husband. 2 vols 1809. Novel.
An essay on money and paper currency. 1812.
The victim of intolerance. 3 vols 1814. Novel.
An essay on the external corn trade. 1815, 1820, 1827, 1829, 1832.
A letter to the Earl of Liverpool on the state of agriculture. 1816.
National currency: Major Torrens to the Earl of Lauderdale. 1816.
A paper on the means of reducing the poor's rages. 1817.
A letter to the independent freemen of the City of Rochester. 1819.
A comparative estimate of the effects which a continuance and a removal of the restriction upon cash payments are respectively calculated to produce. 1819.
An essay on the production of wealth. 1821; tr Ital 1856.
The crisis and the remedies. 1830.
A letter to the Right Honourable Sir George Murray on systematic colonization. 1830.
Address to the farmers ... on low rates of profit. 1831.
Letters on commercial policy. 1833.
On wages and combination. 1834, 1838.
Colonization of South Australia. 1835.
A letter to Viscount Melbourne on the causes of the recent derangement in the money market. 1837.
A letter to Lord John Russell on ... establishing poor laws in Ireland. 1837, 1838.
Plan of an association in aid of the Irish poor law. 1838.
Three letters to the Marquis of Chandos on the effects of the corn laws. 1839.
A letter to Thomas Tooke. 1840.
A letter to Lord John Russell. 1842.
A letter to Nassau William Senior. 1843.
The budget; a series of letters on financial, commercial and colonial policy. 1841–3, 1844.
On the operation of the bank charter act of 1844. 1847.
A letter to Lord Ashley on the principles which regulate wages. 1844.
An inquiry into the practical workings of ... the Charter of the Bank of England. 1844.
Reply to the objections of the Westminster Review. 1844.
Self-supporting colonization. 1847.
On the operation of the Bank Charter Act of 1844. 1847, rptd as The currency question made easy, 1847.
The petition of the merchants, bankers and traders of London. 1847. With S. J. Loyd.
The principles ... of Sir Robert Peel's bill of 1844 explained. 1848, 1857, 1858.
Systematic colonization. 1849.
Tracts on finance and trade. 1852.
Political economy and representative government in Australia. 1855.

Contributions to periodicals
See Wellesley *vol 5 1989, and Robbins, above.*

§2

Robbins, L. Robert Torrens and the evolution of classical economics. 1958.

Arnold Toynbee 1852–83

Bibliography
See Kadish, below.

§1

Lectures on the industrial revolution of the eighteenth century in England, popular addresses, notes and other fragments. 1884, new edn with appendix including Progress and poverty, a criticism of Mr Henry George 1894 (appendix omitted in 1908 edn, and Lord Milner's Arnold Toynbee, a reminiscence, added), 7th reprint 1923.

§2

Montague, F. C. Arnold Toynbee. Baltimore 1889.
Kadish, A. Apostle Arnold. Durham NC 1986.

Edward Wakefield 1774–1854

For information on the location of papers and correspondence, see Sturges.

§1

A letter to the landowners and other contributors to the poor rates. 1802.
An account of Ireland, statistical and political. 2 vols 1812.

§2

See DPE.

Edward Gibbon Wakefield 1796–1862

For information on the location of papers and correspondence, see Sturges.

Bibliography
See Amano.

Collections
Collected works of Edward Gibbon Wakefield. Ed M. F. Lloyd Prichard 1968.

§1

A letter from Sydney. 1829, 1929 (EL).
Sketches of a proposal for colonising Australasia. 1829.
A statement of the principles and objects of a proposed national society for the cure and prevention of pauperism. 1830.
Facts relating to the punishment of death in the metropolis. 1831, 1832.
Swing unmasked. 1831.
Plan of company to be established for the purpose of founding a colony in Southern Australia. 1831.
Householders in danger. 1832.
The hangman and the judge. 1833.
The terrorstruck town. 1833.
England and America. 2 vols 1833, New York 1834.
Outlines of the plan of a proposed colony to be founded on the south coast of Australia. 1834.
The new British province of South Australia. 1834.
The British colony of New Zealand. 1837.
Popular politics. 1837.
A view of Sir Charles Metcalf's Government of Canada. 1844.
A view of the art of colonization. 1849, 1914.

Editions
Smith, Adam. Wealth of nations. 4 vols 1835–9, 1843.

Letters
The founders of Canterbury, letters from the late EGW to the late J. R. Godley. 1868, 1973.

§2

The trial of Edward Gibbon Wakefield. 1827.
Marx, K. Capital. 1867–94, vol 1 ch 23.
Siegried, A. Edward Gibbon Wakefield et sa doctrine de colonisation systematique. 1904.
Macdonell, U. N. Gibbon Wakefield and Canada. 1928.
Bloomfield, P. Edward Gibbon Wakefield. 1961.
Norman, J. Edward Gibbon Wakefield, a political appraisal. 1963.
Stuart, P. A. Edward Gibbon Wakefield in New Zealand. 1971.

Sir Edward West 1782–1828

§1

Essay on the application of capital to land, with observations shewing the impolicy of any great restriction of the importation of corn. 1815, rptd Baltimore 1903, 1935.
A treatise of the law and practice of extents. 1817.
Price of corn and wages of labour, with observations upon Dr Smith's, Mr Ricardo's and Mr Malthus's doctrines upon those subjects. 1826.

§2

Grampp. W. D. Edward West reconsidered. History of Political Economy 2 1970.

Richard Whately, Archbishop of Dublin 1787–1863

See col 2203.
For information on the location of papers and correspondence, see Sturges.

§1

Elements of logic: comprising the substance of the article in the Encyclopaedia Metropolitana, with additions. 1826, 1827, 1832 (14th edn), 1836 (16th edn), 1840 (rev), 1848 (rev), 1874, 1975.
Introductory lectures on political economy. 1831, expanded 1832, 1847 (3rd edn rev) 1855, New York 1966.
Thoughts on secondary punishments. 1832.
Easy lessons on money matters. 1833, with 15 more edns and trns into 3 languages.
Remarks on transportation. 1834.
Easy lessons on reasoning. 1843, 1848.
Speeches on transportation. 1840.
Speeches on the Irish poor laws. 1847.
A few words of remonstrance and advice addressed to the farming and labouring classes of Ireland. 1848.

Contributions to periodicals
See Wellesley *vol* 5.
Secondary punishment. Jnl of Dublin Statistical Soc 52, Apr 1863.

§2

Lewis, G. C. An examination of Dr Whately's elements of logic. 1829.
Bentham, G. Outline of new system of logic, with a critical examination of Dr Whately's elements of logic. 1827.
Arthur, G. Defence of transportation in reply to the Archbishop of Dublin. 1835.
Scrope, G. P. Reply to speech of the Archbishop of Dublin. 1847.
Forsythe, J. Questions on Archbishop Whately's Elements of logic. 1849.
Bayes, W. Remarks on Archbishop Whately's letter on medical trades-unions. 1863.
Miscellaneous remains. Ed E. J. Whately 1861.
Fraser, A. C. Archbishop Whately and the restoration of the study of logic. 1864.
Life and correspondence. Ed E. J. Whately 2 vols 1866, 1868, 1875 enlarged.
Goldstrom, J. M. Richard Whately and political economy in school books 1833–80. Irish Historical Stud 15 1966.
Hilton, A. J. B. Age of atonement. 1988.
Waterman, A. M. C. Revolution, economics and religion. 1991.

John Wheatley 1772–1830

Letters to Lord Grey in Howick Papers, Durham Univ; to Charles Wynn, Nat Lib of Wales.

Bibliography
Fetter, F. W. The life and writings of John Wheatley. Jnl of Political Economy June 1942. Primary.

§1

Remarks on currency and commerce. 1803.
Thoughts on the object of a foreign subsidy. 1805.
An essay on the theory of money. Vol 1 1807, vol 2 1822.
A letter to Lord Grenville on the distress of the country. 1807.
A report on the reports of the bank committee. Shrewsbury 1819.
A plan to relieve the country from its difficulties. Shrewsbury 1821.
Letter to the Right Hon Charles Watkin Williams Wynn. Calcutta 1823.
A letter to the Duke of Devonshire on the state of Ireland. Calcutta 1824.
Tempora praeterita, or more currency and more corn. Cape Town 1828.

§2

Fetter, F. W. The life and writings of John Wheatley. Jnl of Political Economy June 1942.

William Whewell 1799–1866

For information on the location of papers and correspondence, see Sturges. See also col 2616.

§1

Mathematical exposition of some doctrines of political economy. Cambridge 1829, 1831, 1850, rptd as Mathematical exposition of certain doctrines of political economy, New York 1971.
Six lectures on political economy. Cambridge 1862, New York 1967.

§2

See NPDE. [DNW]

9
Philosophy and Science

GENERAL STUDIES TO 1920

Deucher, R. A brief review of ancient and modern philosophy. 1864.
Masson, D. Recent British philosophy. 1865.
Laurie, S. S. Notes on certain British theories of morals. 1868.
McCosh, J. The present state of moral philosophy in England. 1868.
Ribot, T. La psychologie anglaise contemporaine. Paris 1870; tr 1873.
Renouvier, C. B. De l'esprit de la philosophie anglaise contemporaine. In his La critique philosophique vol 1, Paris 1872.
McCosh, J. Scottish philosophy from Hutcheson to Hamilton. 1874.
Überweg, F. History of philosophy from Thales to the present time. Vol 2, tr New York 1874 (from 4th Ger edn).
Liard, L. Les logiciens anglais contemporains. Paris 1878.
Morris, G. S. British thought and thinkers. 1880.
Höffding, H. Die englische Philosophie unserer Zeit. Tr Ger (from Danish), Berlin 1889.
Hutton, R. H. Criticisms on contemporary thought and thinkers. 2 vols 1894.
Merz, J. T. A history of European thought in the nineteenth century. 4 vols Edinburgh 1896–1914.
Bigge, S. British moralists. 2 vols 1897.
Höffding, H. A history of modern philosophy. Tr 2 vols 1900.
Stephen, L. The English Utilitarians. 3 vols 1900.
Halévy, E. La formation du radicalisme philosophique. 3 vols Paris 1901–4; tr 1928, 1952.
Sturt, H. (ed). Personal idealism: philosophical essays by eight members of the University of Oxford. 1902.
Dicey, A. V. Lectures on the relation between law and public opinion in England during the nineteenth century. 1905.
Ladd, G. T. The development of philosophy in the nineteenth century. Philosophical Rev 14 1905.
Rand, B. Bibliography of philosophy, psychology and cognate subjects. In Dictionary of philosophy and psychology, ed J. M. Baldwin, vol 3, New York 1905, 1949.
Benn, A. W. English rationalism in the nineteenth century. 1906.
Forsyth, J. M. English philosophy. 1910.
Jones, H. (ed). The schools of philosophy. 1912, 1914.
Perry, R. B. Present philosophical tendencies. 1912.
Seth, J. English philosophers and schools of philosophy. 1912.
Thilly, F. A history of philosophy. New York 1914, 1957 (3rd edn rev).
Davidson, W. L. Political thought in England: the Utilitarians from Bentham to J. S. Mill. 1915 (Home Univ Lib).
Barker, E. Political thought in England 1848–1914. [1915] (Home Univ Lib).
Tufts, J. H. Ethics in the last twenty-five years. Philosophical Rev 26 1917.
Sorley, W. R. A history of English philosophy. Cambridge 1920.
Taylor, A. E. Philosophy. In Recent developments in European thought, ed F. S. Marvin, 1920.
Sorley, W. R. Fifty years of Mind. Mind n.s. 35 1926.

Thomas Kingsmill Abbott 1829–1913

Smith and touch: an attempt to disprove the received (or Berkeleian) theory of vision. 1864.
Logic versus Murray's Logic. Dublin 1881.
Elements of Logic. Dublin 1883.
Also works on religion.

John Abercrombie 1780–1884

§1

Inquiries concerning the intellectual powers and the investigation of truth. Edinburgh 1830, 1854 (15th edn).
The philosophy of the moral feelings. Edinburgh 1833, 1836 (4th edn), London 1841 (6th edn).
Address on the occasion of his installation as Lord Rector of the University of Aberdeen. Aberdeen 1835.
The culture and discipline of the mind. Edinburgh 1837, 1862 (enlarged).
Essays and tracts. Edinburgh 1847.
Also works on religion.

§2

MacLagan, D. Sketch of the life and character of Dr Abercrombie. 1854.

Robert Adamson 1852–1902

§1

Roger Bacon: the philosophy of science in the Middle Ages. Manchester 1876.
On the philosophy of Kant. Edinburgh 1879; tr Ger 1880.
Fichte. 1881.
Moral theory and moral practice. In Ethical democracy, ed S. Coit, 1900.
The development of modern philosophy, with other lectures and essays. Ed W. R. Sorley 2 vols 1903, 1930 (vol 1).
The development of Greek philosophy. Ed W. R. Sorley and R. P. Hardie 1908.
A short history of logic. Ed W. R. Sorley 1911.

§2

Jones, H. Adamson. Mind n.s. 11 1902.
Hicks, G. D. Adamson's philosophical lectures. Mind n.s. 13 1904.
Rees, D. A. Adamson. Philosophical Quart 2 1952.

Grant Allen 1848–99

See col 1449.

George Douglas Campbell, 8th Duke of Argyll 1823–1900

§1

Address delivered to the members of the Glasgow Athenaeum. Glasgow 1852.
Inaugural address as Chancellor of the University of St Andrews. Edinburgh 1852.
Phrenology. North Br Rev 17 1852.
Inaugural address as Rector of the University of Glasgow. 1855.
Address of the Duke of Argyll, before the British Association for the Advancement of Science. Glasgow 1855.
Address to the Royal Society of Edinburgh. Edinburgh 1864.
The reign of law. 1867, 1890 (19th edn).
Primeval man. 1869.
Iona. 1870, Edinburgh 1889.
On variety as an aim in nature. 1871.
On Hibernicisms in philosophy. Contemporary Rev Jan 1872.
On animal instinct. Contemporary Rev July 1875.
Morality in politics. Contemporary Rev July 1877.
The unity of nature. 1884.
The prophet of San Francisco. 1884. Reply by Henry George in his The peer and the prophet, 1884.
Scotland as it was and as it is. 2 vols Edinburgh 1887.
The identity of thought and language. Contemporary Rev Dec 1888.
What is truth? Edinburgh 1889.
The Highland nurse: a tale. 1892.
The unseen foundations of society. 1893.
The application of the historical method to economic science. 1894.
The burdens of belief and other poems. 1894.
Lord Bacon versus Professor Huxley. Nineteenth Cent Dec 1894.
The philosophy of belief: or law in Christian theology. 1896.
Organic evolution cross-examined. 1898.
What is science? Edinburgh 1898.
Autobiography and memoirs. Ed Dowager Duchess of Argyll 2 vols 1906.
Also works on economics, religious affairs, geology and current politics.

§2

English, W. W. An essay on moral philosophy. 1869.
Bacon, T. S. The reign of God not the Reign of law. 1878.
Bain, F. W. The unseen foundation of The unseen foundations of society. 1893.
'Goth Amos'. The reign of lust, by the Duke of Oatmeal. 1895.
Knox, H. V. Argyll on purpose in nature. Philosophical Rev 7 1898.

John Austin 1790–1859

§1

The province of jurisprudence determined. 1832.
Centralisation. Edinburgh Rev 85 1847.
A plea for the Constitution. 1859.
Lectures on jurisprudence: or the philosophy of positive law. Ed S. Austin 3 vols 1861–3, 1885 (5th edn); tr Fr 1894. Also referred to as 2nd edn of The province of jurisprudence determined, *above*.
The province of jurisprudence determined, and The uses of the study of jurisprudence. Ed H. L. A. Hart 1954.

§2

Mill, J. S. Austin on jurisprudence. In his Dissertations and discussions vol 3, 1867.
Campbell, F. G. B. An analysis of Austin's Lectures on jurisprudence. 1877.
Clark, E. C. Practical jurisprudence. 1883.
Purnalingam, P. An epitome of Maine's Ancient law and Austin's Jurisprudence. 1915.
Eastwood, R. A. A brief introduction to Austin's theory of positive law and sovereignty. 1916.
Eastwood, R. A. and G. W. Keeton. The Austinian theories of law and sovereignty. 1929.

Charles Babbage 1792–1871

See col 2468.

Samuel Bailey 1791–1870

See col 2469.

Alexander Bain 1818–1903

§1

On the applications of science to human health and well-being. 1848.
The senses and the intellect. 1855, 1864 (rev and enlarged), 1868 (enlarged), 1894; tr Fr 1873, 1889, 1895; Rus 1887.
The emotions and the will. 1859, 1865 (rev), 1875 (rev), New York 1876, 1899 (with addns); tr Fr 1885; Rus 1887.
On the study of character, including an estimate of phrenology. 1861.
An English grammar. 1863, 1872 (rev as A higher English grammar), 1879 (rev), 1904 (rev and enlarged). Also A first English grammar, with key, 1872, 1882.
The methods of debate: an address delivered to the Aberdeen University Debating Society. Aberdeen 1863.
A letter to Westerton, chairman of Mill's [election] committee. [1865.]
English composition and rhetoric. 1866, 1869, 2 vols 1887–8 (enlarged).
Mental and moral science. 1868, 2 vols 1872 (enlarged), New York 1880; tr Rus 1881.
Logic: deductive and inductive. 2 vols 1870, 1873, 1879, New York 1887 (rev); tr Fr 1875; Sp 1881.
Mind and body: the theories of their relation. 1873, 1910 (11th edn); tr Fr 1874; Ger 1874; Rus 1880; Sp 1881.
Education as a science. 1879 (7 edns), New York 1879, 1884, 1897; tr Fr 1879; Ger 1879; Ital 1885; Sp 1888.
Presidential address to the Society for the development of the science of education. 1879.
James Mill. 1882. Enlarged from Mind 1–2 1876–7.
John Stuart Mill. 1882. Rptd from Mind 4–5 1879–80.
Practical essays. 1884.
On teaching English, with an enquiry into the definition of poetry. 1887. Auxiliary to enlarged edn of English composition and rhetoric, above.
Dissertations on leading philosophical topics. 1903.
Autobiography. Ed W. L. Davidson 1904. With bibliography.

Articles

Many of Bain's articles are rptd in Practical essays, Dissertations on leading philosophical topics, *and* On the study of character, *above*. *For additional periodical contributions see* Wellesley *vol 5 1989*.
Constitution of matter. Westminster Rev 36 1841.
On toys. Westminster Rev 37 1842.
Mill's Logic. Westminster Rev 39 1843.
Carlyle's Cromwell. Westminster Rev 46 1847.

On the abuse of language in science and in common life. Fraser's Mag Feb 1847.
Oken's physiophilosophy. Chambers's Jnl 5 Feb 1848.
The scholastic logic. Chambers's Jnl 11 Mar 1848.
Wit and humour. Westminster Rev 48 1848.
Of a liberal education in general. Westminster Rev 49 1848.
Sydney Smith's moral philosophy. Chambers's Jnl 15 June 1850.
Reichenbach's researches. Chambers's Jnl 20 July 1850.
Grote's Plato. Macmillan's Mag July, Oct 1865.
The feelings and the will physiologically considered. Fortnightly Rev 15 Jan 1866.
The intellect viewed physiologically. Fortnightly Rev 1 Feb 1866.
A historical view of the theories of the soul. Fortnightly Rev 15 May 1866.
On early philosophy. Macmillan's Mag June 1866.
On the correlation of force in its bearing on mind. Macmillan's Mag Sep 1867.
The retentive power of the mind in its bearing on education. Fortnightly Rev Sep 1868.
Memoir of Clark. Jnl of Chemical Soc of London n.s. 6 1868.
Notes on Bastian's paper. Fortnightly Rev Apr 1869.
On teaching English. Fortnightly Rev Aug 1869.
Darwinism and religion. Macmillan's Mag May 1871.
On Sully's Essays. Fortnightly Rev July 1874.
Sidgwick's Methods of ethics. Mind 1 1876.
Alexander's Moral causation. Mind 1 1876.
Spencer's Principles of sociology. Mind 1 1876.
Lewes on the postulates of experience. Mind 1 1876.
The gratification derived from the infliction of pain. Mind 1 1876.
Education as a science. Mind 2–3 1877–8.
Sully's Pessimism. Mind 2 1877.
The growth of the will. Popular Science Monthly May 1879.
Spencer's Data of ethics. Mind 4 1879.
Ward on free-will. Mind 5 1880. Reply by W. G. Ward, ibid.
Galton's statistics of mental imagery. Mind 5 1880.
Spencer's psychological congruities. Mind 6 1881.
Mind and body. Mind 8 1883.
Biographical memoirs of Clark, Shier and Arnott. Trans Aberdeen Philosophical Soc 1 1884.
Ward's Psychology. Mind 11 1886.
On feeling as indifference. Mind 12, 14 1887, 1889.
On Ward's Psychological principles. Mind 12 1887.
The distinction between will and desire (Symposium). Proc Aristotelian Soc 1 1888.
The nature of force (Symposium). Proc Aristotelian Soc 1 1888.
Is the distinction of feeling, cognition and conation valid as an ultimate distinction of the mental functions? (Symposium). Proc Aristotelian Soc 1 1888.
Notes on volition. Mind 16 1891.
Biographical notice of Robertson. Mind n.s. 2 1893.
Ethics from a purely practical standpoint. International Jnl of Ethics 10 1900.

§2

Mill, J. S. Bain's psychology. In his Dissertations and discussions vol 3, 1867.
Ribot, T. A. English psychology. 1873.
Hyde, T. A. How to study character, including a review of Bain's criticisms of the phrenological system. 1884.
'Psychosis'. Our modern philosophers, Darwin, Bain and Spencer: a rhyme. 1884.
Davidson, W. L. Bain's philosophy. Mind n.s. 13 1904.
MacKenzie, W. L. Bain's autobiography. Mind n.s. 14 1905.
Schiller, F. C. S. Bradley, Bain and pragmatism. Jnl of Philosophy 14 1917.

Arthur James Balfour, 1st Earl of Balfour

1848–1930

§1

A defence of philosophic doubt. 1879, 1921.
Handel. [1887?]
The pleasures of reading: inaugural address as Rector of St Andrews University. 1888.
The religion of humanity. Edinburgh 1888.
A fragment of progress: inaugural address as Rector of the University of Glasgow. Edinburgh 1892.
Essays and addresses. Edinburgh 1893, 1905 (3rd edn enlarged).
The foundations of belief. 1895, 1901 (8th edn); tr Fr 1896; Ger 1896; Ital 1906.
The nineteenth century: inaugural address at Cambridge. Cambridge 1900.
Reflections suggested by the new theory of matter: presidential address to the British Association for the Advancement of Science. 1904; tr Ger 1905.
Decadence. Cambridge 1908.
Questionings on criticism and beauty. 1909, Oxford 1910 (rev as Criticism and beauty).
Francis Bacon. 1913.
Theism and humanism: Gifford lectures. 1915.
Essays speculative and political. 1920.
Theism and thought. [1923.]
Familiar beliefs and transcendent reason. 1927.
Chapters of autobiography. Ed Mrs E. Dugdale 1930.

Articles

The philosophy of ethics. Mind 3 1878.
Transcendentalism. Mind 3 1878. Replies by E. Caird, H. Sidgwick and Balfour, 4 1879; by Sidgwick and Caird, 5 1880.
Watson on transcendentalism. Mind 6 1881.
Green's metaphysics of knowledge. Mind 9 1884.
Naturalism and ethics. International Jnl of Ethics 4 1894.
Creative evolution and philosophic doubt. Hibbert Jnl 10 1912. Reply by A. Wolf, ibid.
Also works on current affairs.

§2

Beesley, E. S. Positivism before the Church Congress: a reply to Balfour. 1889.
Martineau, J. Balfour's Foundations of belief. Nineteenth Cent Apr 1895.
Wallace, W. Balfour's Foundations of belief. Fortnightly Rev Apr 1895.
Shurman, J. G. The rebound from agnosticism. Forum May 1895.
Mivart, St G. Spencer versus Balfour. Nineteenth Cent Aug 1895.
Pearson, K. Reaction: a criticism of Balfour's attacks on rationalism. 1895.
Daniels, W. M. Balfour's criticism of transcendental idealism. Philosophic Rev 5 1896. Reply by R. B. Johnson, ibid.
Nicholson, J. A. The immorality of naturalism. 1896.
Cecil, H. M. Pseudo-philosophy at the end of the nineteenth century. 1897.
Rey, J. La philosophie de Balfour. Paris [1897].
Alderson, B. Balfour: the man and his work. 1903.
Jones, H. Balfour as sophist. Hibbert Jnl 3 1905.
Brown, F. The doings of Arthur. 1905.
Lobley, J. L. Positive knowledge: a reply to the Cambridge address. [1905.]
Lodge, O. Balfour and Bergson. Hibbert Jnl 10 1912.
Seth, A. Balfour's Theism and humanism. Hibbert Jnl 14, 1916.
'Raymond, E. T.' (E. R. Thompson). Balfour: a biography. 1920.

Alfred Barratt 1844–81

Physical ethics: or the science of action. 1869.
Physical metempiric; with a memoir by Dorothea Barratt. 1883.

Thomas Spencer Baynes 1823–87

§1

An essay on the new analytic of logical forms. Edinburgh 1850.
Sir William Hamilton. 1857.
The Song of Solomon in the Somerset dialect. [1860.]
Somerset dialect: its pronunciation. 1861.
Shakespeare studies and other essays; with biographical preface by Lewis Campbell. 1894, 1896.

§2

Skelton, J. In his Table-talk of Shirley: reminiscences of Froude, Baynes, Tyndall and others, 1895.

Edward Spencer Beesly 1831–1915

§1

The social future of the working class. 1869.
Letters to the working classes. [1870.]
Cataline, Clodius and Tiberius (Necker and Calonne: an old story). 1878.
Some public aspects of positivism. 1881.
Comte as a moral type. 1885.
Positivism before the Church Congress: a reply to Mr Balfour. 1889.

§2

Harrison, R. In his Before the Socialists, 1965.

George Bentham 1800–84

§1

An outline of a new system of logic. 1827.
The classification of fictions. Psyche 33 1928.
Also works on botany.

§2

Liard, L. In his Les logiciens anglais, Paris 1878.
Jackson, B. D. George Bentham. 1906.

George Boole 1815–64

§1

Address on the genius and discoveries of Sir Isaac Newton. Lincoln 1835.
The mathematical analysis of logic. Cambridge 1847; tr Sp 1960.
The right use of leisure. 1847.
The claims of science, especially as founded in its relations to human nature. 1851.
An investigation of the laws of thought on which are founded the mathematical theories of logic and probabilities. 1854; ed P. E. B. Jourdain 1916 (as Boole's Collected logical works vol 2); New York 1961 (corrected).
Studies in logic and probability. Ed R. Rhees 1952.

§2

Jevons, W. S. Pure logic, with remarks on Boole's system. 1864.
Hughlings, I. P. The logic of names: an introduction to Boole's laws of thought. 1869.
Liard, L. In his Les logiciens anglais, Paris 1878.
Boole, M. E. The mathematical philosophy of Gratry and Boole. 1897.

Bernard Bosanquet 1848–1923

§1

Knowledge and reality. 1885.
Introduction to Hegel's philosophy of the fine arts. 1886.
Logic: or the morphology of knowledge. 2 vols Oxford 1888, 1911.
Essays and addresses. 1889, 1899 (3rd edn).
'In darkest England': on the wrong track. 1891.
A history of aesthetic. 1892, 1917 (4th edn).
The civilisation of Christendom and other studies. 1893, 1899 (2nd edn).
Aspects of the social problem. 1895. Ed Bosanquet.
The essentials of logic. 1895; tr Hebrew 1952.
Companion to Plato's Republic. 1895.
Rousseau's Social contract. 1895.
Psychology of the moral self. 1897.
The philosophical theory of the state. 1899, 1923 (4th edn).
The communication of moral ideas as a function of an ethical society. 1900.
Education of the young in Plato. Cambridge 1900.
The social criterion. 1907.
Truth and coherence. St Andrews 1911.
The principle of individuality and value. 1912.
The value and destiny of the individual. 1913.
The distinction between mind and its objects. Manchester 1913.
Germany in the nineteenth century. Manchester 1915.
Three lectures on aesthetic. 1915, ed R. Ross, Indianapolis 1963.
Social and international ideals. 1917.
Some suggestions in ethics. 1918.
Implication and linear inference. 1920.
What religion is. 1920.
Meeting of extremes in contemporary philosophy. 1921.
Three chapters on the nature of mind. Ed H. Bosanquet 1923.
Science and philosophy and other essays. Ed J. H. Muirhead and R. C. Bosanquet 1927.

Articles

Logic as the science of knowledge. In A. Seth and R. B. Haldane, Essays in philosophical criticism, 1883.
Our right to regard evil as a mystery. Mind 8 1883. Reply to F. H. Bradley, ibid.
Bradley on fact and inference. Mind 10 1885.
Comparison in psychology and in logic. Mind 11 1886.
Is mind synonymous with consciousness? (symposium). Proc Aristotelian Soc 1 1888.
The philosophical importance of a true theory of identity. Mind 13 1888.
Hegel's Correspondence. Mind 13 1888.
The part played by aesthetic in the growth of modern philosophy. Proc Aristotelian Soc 1 1889.
What takes place in voluntary action? (symposium). Proc Aristotelian Soc 1 1889.
The aesthetic theory of ugliness. Proc Aristotelian Soc 1 1889.
The relation of the fine arts to one another (symposium). Proc Aristotelian Soc 1 1889.
Booth's Labour and life of the people. International Jnl of Ethics 2 1891.
Origin of the perception of an external world (symposium). Proc Aristotelian Soc 2 1892.
The permanent meaning of the argument from design. Proc Aristotelian Soc 2 1892
Will and reason. Monist 2 1892.
The principles and chief dangers of the administration of charity. In Philanthropy and social progress, [1893].
On the nature of aesthetic emotion. Mind n.s. 3 1894.
The reality of the general will. International Jnl of Ethics 4 1894.

On an essential distinction in theories of experience. Proc Aristotelian Soc 3 1895.
The evolution of religion. International Jnl of Ethics 5 1895.
Are character and circumstances co-ordinate factors in human life, or is either subordinate to the other? Proc Aristotelian Soc 3 1896.
Time and the absolute. Proc Aristotelian Soc 3 1896.
Charity organisation. Contemporary Rev Jan 1897. With H. Bosanquet.
In what sense, if any, do past and future time exist? Mind n.s. 6 1897. Replies by S. H. Hodgson and G. E. Moore, ibid.
The relation of sociology to philosophy. Mind n.s. 6 1897.
Hegel's theory of the political organism. Mind n.s. 7 1898.
A moral from Athenian history. International Jnl of Ethics 9 1898.
Social automatism and the imitation theory. Mind n.s. 8 1899.
'Ladies and Gentlemen'. International Jnl of Ethics 10 1900.
The meaning of social work. International Jnl of Ethics 11 1901.
Recent criticism of Green's ethics. Proc Aristotelian Soc n.s. 2 1902.
The Dark Ages and the Renaissance. International Jnl of Ethics 12 1902.
Hedonism among idealists. Mind n.s. 12 1903.
Imitation and selective thinking. Psychological Rev 10 1903.
Plato's conception of death. Hibbert Jnl 2 1904.
Xenophon's Memorabilia of Socrates. International Jnl of Ethics 15 1905.
Can logic abstract from the psychological conditions of thinking? Proc Aristotelian Soc n.s. 6 1906.
The meaning of teleology. Proc Br Acad 2 1906.
Contradiction and reality. Mind n.s. 15 1906.
The place of experts in democracy (symposium). Proc Aristotelian Soc n.s. 9 1909.
Cause and ground. Jnl of Philosophy 7 1910. Reply to H. S. Shelton, Jnl of Philosophy 7 1910. Replies by Shelton and Bosanquet, Jnl of Philosophy 8 1911.
Charity organization and the majority report. International Jnl of Ethics 20 1910. Reply to T. Jones, ibid.
On a defect in the customary logical formulation of inductive reasoning. Proc Aristotelian Soc n.s. 11 1911.
The place of leisure in life. International Jnl of Ethics 21 1911.
The prediction of human conduct: a study in Bergson. International Jnl of Ethics 21 1911.
Purpose and mechanism (symposium). Proc Aristotelian Soc n.s. 12 1912.
The analysis of categorical propositions. Mind n.s. 23 1914.
Idealism and the reality of time. Mind n.s. 23 1914.
The import of propositions (symposium). Proc Aristotelian Soc n.s. 15 1915.
Note on G. D. H. Cole's paper on Conflicting social obligations. Proc Aristotelian Soc n.s. 15 1915.
Science and philosophy. Proc Aristotelian Soc n.s. 15 1915.
Patriotism in the perfect state. In The international crisis in its ethical and psychological aspects, 1915.
Causality and the implication. Mind n.s. 25–6 1916–17. Reply by C. A. Mercier 26 1917.
The function of the state in promoting the unity of mankind. Proc Aristotelian Soc n.s. 17 1917.
Realism and metaphysics. Philosophical Rev 26 1917.
The relation of coherence to immediacy and specific purpose. Philosophical Rev 26 1917.
Do finite individuals possess a substantive or an adjectival mode of being? (symposium). Proc Aristotelian Soc n.s. 18 1918; Supplement 1 1918.
Appearance and reality, and the solution of problems. Philosophical Rev 28 1919. Replies by W. P. Montague and K. E. Gilbert, ibid.
The basis of Bosanquet's logic. Mind n.s. 28 1919. Reply to L. J. Russell 27 1918.
The state and the individual. Mind n.s. 28 1919. Reply to C. D. Broad 27 1918.
Croc's Aesthetic. Proc Br Acad 9 1920. Replies by H. W. Carr and Bosanquet, Mind n.s. 29 1920.
Appearances and the absolute. Philosophical Rev 29 1920.
The notion of a general will. Mind n.s. 29 1920. Reply to C. D. Broad, ibid.
Implication and linear inference. Jnl of Philosophy 19 1922.
7 + 5 = 12. Philosophical Rev 31 1922. Reply to G. W. Cunningham, ibid.
A word about 'coherence'. Mind n.s. 31 1922.
Life and philosophy [of Bosanquet]. In J. H. Muirhead, Contemporary British philosophy, 1924. A self-evaluation, with bibliography of books.

§2

Johnson, W. E. Bosanquet's Logic. Mind 14 1889.
Ball, S. The moral aspects of Socialism. International Jnl of Ethics 6 1896. Replies by Bosanquet, ibid; by Ball and S. Webb, 7 1897; by Bosanquet, Ball, J. S. Mackenzie and F. Brocklehurst, ibid.
Robins, E. P. Bosanquet's theory of judgment. Philosophical Rev 7 1898.
Gibson, W. R. B. The relation of logic to psychology, with special reference to the views of Bosanquet. Proc Aristotelian Soc n.s. 3 1903. Reply by Bosanquet, ibid.
Sabine, G. H. Bosanquet's logic and the concrete universal. Philosophical Rev 21 1912.
Sabine, G. H. Liberty and the social system. Philosophical Rev 25 1916.
Bussey, G. C. Bosanquet's doctrine of freedom. Philosophical Rev 25 1916. Replies by M. D. Crane and Bussey, ibid.
Cuming, A. Lotze, Bradley and Bosanquet. Mind n.s. 26 1917.
Russel, L. J. The basis of Bosanquet's logic. Mind n.s. 27 1918. Replies by Bosanquet, 28 1919; Russell, 29 1920; Bosanquet, 30 1921.
Turner, J. E. Bosanquet's theory of mental states. Mind n.s. 27 1918.
Broad, C. D. Bosanquet's Implication and linear inference. Mind n.s. 29 1920. Reply by Bosanquet, 31 1922.
Carroll, M. C. Method in the metaphysics of Bosanquet. Philosophical Rev 29 1920.
Tsanoff, R. A. The destiny of the self in Bosanquet's theory. Philosophical Rev 29 1920.
Carroll, M. C. The nature of the absolute in the metaphysics of Bosanquet. Philosophical Rev 30 1921.
Carroll, M. C. The principle of individuality in the metaphysics of Bosanquet. Philosophical Rev 30 1921.

Francis Herbert Bradley 1846–1924

§1

The presuppositions of critical history. Oxford 1874.
Ethical studies. Oxford 1876, 1927 (rev), 1959; ed R. G. Ross, New York 1951.
Mr Sedgwick's hedonism. 1877.
The principles of logic. 1883, 1922 (rev edn with commentary and terminal essays), 1958.
Appearance and reality. 1893, 1897 (rev), Oxford 1959; tr Ital 1947.
Essays on truth and reality. Oxford 1914, 1962.
Aphorisms. Oxford 1930.
Collected essays. 2 vols Oxford 1935.

Articles

Most of Bradley's many articles, including those listed with replies below, are rptd in his Appearance and reality, Essays on truth and reality *or* Collected essays *(with bibliography), above.*

Is self-sacrifice an enigma? Mind 8 1883. Reply by B. Bosanquet, ibid.

Is there such a thing as pure malevolence? Mind 8 1883. Reply by A. Bain, ibid.
Jones' Browning as a philosophical and religious teacher. International Jnl of Ethics 2 1892.
Consciousness and experience. Mind n.s. 2 1893.
On Jones' doctrine of simple resemblance. Mind n.s. 2 1893. Reply by W. James, ibid.
A personal explanation. International Jnl of Ethics 4 1894. Reply to A. L. Hodder, 3 1892.
A reply to criticism by J. Ward. Mind n.s. 3 1894. Reply by Ward, ibid.
Some remarks on punishment. International Jnl of Ethics 4 1894. Reply by H. Rashdall, 5 1895.
Rational hedonism. International Jnl of Ethics 5 1895. Reply to E. E. C. Jones and J. S. Mackenzie, ibid; reply by E. E. C. Jones, ibid.
Note. Mind n.s. 14 1905. Reply to A. Sidgwick, 13 1904.
On truth and copying. Mind n.s. 16 1907. Reply by H. Sturt, ibid.
On the ambiguity of pragmatism. Mind n.s. 17 1908. Replies by A. Sidgwick and F. C. S. Schiller, ibid.
On appearance, error and contradiction. Mind n.s. 19 1910. Reply by F. C. S. Schiller, ibid.

§2

Sidgwick, H. Bradley's Ethical studies. Mind 1 1876. Replies by Bradley and Sidgwick 2 1877.
Dyde, S. W. Bradley's Principles of logic. Jnl of Speculative Philosophy 18–19 1884–5.
Bosanquet, B. Knowledge and reality. 1885.
Ward, J. Bradley's analysis of mind. Mind 12 1887.
Carr, H. W. Bradley's Appearance and reality. Proc Aristotelian Soc 2 1894.
Mackenzie, J. L. Bradley's view of the self. Mind n.s. 3 1894.
Sidgwick, A. Bradley and the sceptics. Mind n.s. 3 1894.
Seth, A. A new theory of the absolute. Contemporary Rev Nov–Dec 1894.
Robins, E. P. Bradley's theory of judgment. Philosophic Rev 7 1898.
Carr, H. W. Bradley's theory of appearance. Proc Aristotelian Soc n.s. 2 1902.
Seth, A. In his Man's place in the cosmos, 1902 (2nd edn).
Stout, G. F. Alleged self-contradictions in the concept of relation: a criticism of Bradley. Proc Artistotelian Soc n.s. 2 1902. Replies by H. W. Carr, S. H. Hodgson, J. Lindsay, ibid; by A. J. Finberg and Carr 3 1903.
Stout, G. F. Bradley's theory of judgment. Proc Aristotelian Soc n.s. 3 1903.
Knox, H. Bradley's 'absolute criterion'. Mind n.s. 14 1905. Replies by Bradley, ibid; Knox 16 1907.
Schiller, F. C. S. Bradley's theory of truth. Mind n.s. 16 1907.
Sidgwick, A. Notes on a note. Mind n.s. 18 1909.
James, W. Bradley or Bergson? Jnl of Philosophy 7 1910. Reply by Bradley, ibid.
Russell, B. Some explanations in reply to Bradley. Mind n.s. 19 1910. Reply by Bradley 20 1911.
Rashdall, H. The metaphysics of Bradley. Proc Br Acad 5 1912.
Broad, C. D. Bradley on truth and reality. Mind n.s. 23 1914.
Strange, E. H. Bradley's doctrine of knowledge. Mind n.s. 23 1914.
Schiller, F. C. S. The new developments of Bradley's philosophy. Mind n.s. 24 1915.
Eliot, T. S. Leibnitz's monads and Bradley's finite centers. Monist 26 1916.
Eliot, T. S. Knowledge and experience in the philosophy of Bradley. Ed A. Bolgan 1964. A Harvard PhD thesis, written 1916.
Cuming, A. Bradley, Lotze and Bosanquet. Mind n.s. 26 1917.
Schiller, F. C. S. Bradley, Bain and pragmatism. Jnl of Philosophy 14 1917.
Kenna, J. C. Ten unpublished letters from W. James to Bradley. Mind n.s. 75 1966.

John Henry Bridges 1832–1906

§1

The unity of Comte's life and doctrine: a reply to J. S. Mill. 1866, 1910.
Religion and progress. 1879.
Five discourses on positive religion. 1882.
Comte: the successor to Aristotle and St Paul. 1883.
Positivism and the Bible. 1885.
Roger Bacon's Opus majus edited. 1897; ed H. G. Jones 1914 (as The life and work of Roger Bacon).
Some guiding principles in the philosophy of history. 1906.
Essays and addresses. Ed L. T. Hobhouse 1907.
Illustrations of positivism. Ed E. S. Beesly 1907; ed H. G. Jones 1915 (enlarged).

§2

Bridges, M. A. (ed). Recollections of J. H. Bridges [by various authors]. 1908.
Torlesse, F. H. Some account of Bridges and his family. 1912.
Liveing, S. A nineteenth-century teacher. 1926.

Thomas Brown 1778–1820

§1

Observations on the Zoonomia of Erasmus Darwin. Edinburgh 1798.
Observations on the nature and tendency of the doctrine of Hume concerning the relations of cause and effect. Edinburgh 1805, 1806 (enlarged), 1818 (enlarged as Inquiry into the relation of cause and effect), 1835 (4th edn).
An examination of some remarks in the reply of Inglis to Playfair. Edinburgh 1806.
Lectures on the philosophy of the human mind. 4 vols Edinburgh 1820, 1834 (8th edn with memoir by D. Welsh), 1860 (20th edn).
Poetical works. 4 vols Edinburgh 1820.
Sketch of a system of philosophy of the human mind, part 1. Edinburgh 1820. No more pbd.
Lectures on ethics. Edinburgh 1846, London 1860.

§2

Shepherd, M. An essay upon the relation of cause and effect, with observations upon the opinions of Brown. 1824.
Welsh, D. Account of the life and writings of Brown. Edinburgh 1825.
Payne, G. Elements of mental and moral science. 1828.
Crybbace, T. T. An essay on moral freedom; to which is attached a review of Brown's theory of causation and agency. Edinburgh 1829.
Mill, J. In his Analysis of the phenomena of the human mind, 1829.
Wainwright, L. A vindication of Paley's theory of morals from the principal objects of Stewart and Brown. 1830.
Reid, T. An examination of the article entitled Philosophy of perception—Reid and Brown. Edinburgh 1831.
Young, J. Lectures on intellectual philosophy. Glasgow 1835.
Upham, T. C. Elements of mental philosophy. Portland ME 1839.
Carson, A. History of providence as manifested in Scripture, and an examination of the philosophy of Brown. Edinburgh 1840.
Hamilton, W. In his Discussions, 1852.
Milsand, J. Brown, le médecin philosophe. Revue des Deux Mondes Apr 1858.
Réthoré, F. Critique de la philosophie de Brown. Paris 1863.
Bain, A. In his Senses and the intellect, 1865.
McCosh, J. In his Scottish philosophy, 1875.
Dobrzyňska-Rybicka, L. Die Ethik von Brown. Poznan 1909.
Landes, M. W. Brown: associationist. Philosophical Rev 35 1926.

Samuel Butler 1835–1902

See col 2327.

Edward Caird 1835–1908

§1

A critical account of the philosophy of Kant. Glasgow 1877.
The problem of philosophy at the present time. Glasgow 1881.
Hegel. Edinburgh 1883.
The social philosophy and religion of Comte. Glasgow 1885; tr Fr 1907.
The critical philosophy of Kant. 2 vols Glasgow 1889, 1909.
Essays on literature and philosophy. 2 vols Glasgow 1892. Vol 1 rptd as Essays on literature, 1909.
The evolution of religion. 2 vols Glasgow 1893, 1899 (3rd edn).
Individualism and Socialism. Glasgow 1897.
The evolution of theology in the Greek philosophers. 2 vols Glasgow 1904, 1923.
Lay sermons and addresses. Glasgow 1907.

Articles

Reply to Stirling. Jnl of Speculative Philosophy 13 1879.
Kant's deduction of the categories, with relation to the views of Stirling. Jnl of Speculative Philosophy 14 1880.
The problem of philosophy at the present time. Jnl of Speculative Philosophy 16 1882.
Green's last work. Mind 8 1883.
The modern conception of the science of religion. International Jnl of Ethics 1 1891.
Jowett. International Jnl of Ethics 8 1897.
Anselm's argument for the being of God. Jnl of Theological Stud 1 1899.
Idealism and the theory of knowledge. Proc Br Acad 1 1904.
St Paul and the idea of evolution. Hibbert Jnl 2 1904. Reply by H. G. Smith, ibid.
The influence of Kant on modern thought. Quart Rev 200 1904.

§2

Stirling, J. H. Caird on Kant. Jnl of Speculative Philosophy 16 1882.
Blakeney, E. H. Caird's Essays. [1893.]
Bosanquet, B. Caird. Proc Br Acad 3 1908.
MacVannel, J. A. Caird. Jnl of Philosophy 5 1908.
Mackenzie, J. S. Caird. International Jnl of Ethics 19 1909.
Mackenzie, J. S. Caird as a philosophical teacher. Mind n.s. 18 1909.
Watson, J. The idealism of Caird. Philosophical Rev 18 1909.
Jones, H. and J. H. Muirhead. The life and philosophy of Caird. 1921.

John Caird 1820–98

The unity of the sciences. Glasgow 1874.
An introduction to the philosophy of religion. Glasgow 1880, 1901.
Spinoza. Edinburgh 1888.
University addresses. Glasgow 1898.
The fundamental ideas of Christianity. 2 vols Glasgow 1899. With memoir by E. Caird.
Also works on religion.

Henry Calderwood 1830–97

§1

The philosophy of the infinite. Edinburgh 1854, Cambridge 1861 (enlarged).
Moral philosophy as a science and as a discipline. Edinburgh 1868.
Handbook of moral philosophy. 1872, 1888 (14th edn, rewritten).
On teaching: its ends and means. Edinburgh 1874, 1881 (3rd edn).
The relations of mind and brain. 1877, 1884 (enlarged), 1892.
The relations of science and religion. New York 1881.
Evolution and man's place in nature. 1893, 1896.
The vocabulary of philosophy and student's book of reference. 1894.
Hume. Edinburgh 1898.
Also works on religion.

§2

Vera, A. An inquiry into speculative and experimental science, with special reference to Calderwood and Ferrier. 1856.
Calderwood, W. and D. Woodside. Life of Calderwood. 1900.

Thomas Carlyle 1795–1881

See col 2086.

William Benjamin Carpenter 1813–85

§1

Principles of mental physiology. 1874, 1896 (7th edn).
Is man an automaton? 1875.
Mesmerism and spiritualism. 1877.
Nature and man: essays scientific and philosophical. Ed J. E. Carpenter 1888 (with memoir).
Also works on science.

§2

Lingard, J. T. Carpenter's theory of attention. Mind 2 1872.
Gill, W. L. Evolution and progress, with a review of quasi opponents, as Le Conte and Carpenter. 1875.
Guthrie, M. The causational and free-will theories of volition: being a review of Carpenter's Mental physiology. 1877.

Thomas Chalmers 1780–1847

See col 2626.

Robert Chambers 1802–71

A large collection of mss, including letters, account bks and diaries, is on deposit in the Nat Lib of Scotland.

Bibliographies

Chambers, C. E. S. A catalogue of some of the rarer books, also manuscripts and autograph letters in the collection of C. E. S. Chambers; with a bibliography of the works of William and Robert Chambers. Edinburgh 1891 (priv ptd).
Most of Chambers's vast output was pbd anonymously in periodicals and reference bks and is not listed in this or any other bibliography.
Catalogue of scientific papers (1800–1863). Compiled and pbd by the Royal Soc of London, 1867, vol 1 p 868; (1864–1873), 1877, vol 7 p 366. Lists articles by R. Chambers in scientific periodicals.

Selections

Select writings. 7 vols Edinburgh 1847. Vol 1–2, Essays familiar and humorous; vol 3, Essays moral and economic; vol 4, Essays philosophical, sentimental and historical sketches; vol 5, History of the rebellion of 1745–6; vol 6, Traditions of Edinburgh; vol 7, Popular rhymes of Scotland.
Essays familiar and humorous. 2 vols [1866], 1884.
Vestiges of the natural history of creation and other evolutionary writings. Chicago 1994 (ed and introd by J. A. Secord). Vestiges (rpt of 1844 1st edn) and Explanations (rpt of 1845 1st edn), together with autobiographical preface to 1853 10th edn of Vestiges and reactions to C. Darwin.

§1

Illustrations of the author of Waverley: being notices and anecdotes of real characters, scenes and incidents supposed to be described in his works. Edinburgh 1822 (anon), 1825 (enlarged), 1884.

Traditions of Edinburgh. Edinburgh 1824–5 (anon) 7 pts, 1824–5 (anon) 2 vols, 1828, 1869 (rev); ed C. E. S. Chambers 1912; 1967.

Walks in Edinburgh. Edinburgh 1825, 1829 ('with an improved plan, and a view of the city'). A sequel to Traditions of Edinburgh, above.

Notices of the most remarkable fires in Edinburgh from 1385 to 1824. Edinburgh 1825.

The popular rhymes of Scotland; with illustrations, chiefly collected from oral sources. Edinburgh 1826, 1840 (rev with addns), also later edns.

History of the rebellion in Scotland in 1745, 1746. 2 vols Edinburgh 1827, 1840 (greatly enlarged), 1869 (with appendix), 1934.

The picture of Scotland. 2 vols Edinburgh 1827, 1828, 1830, 1837, 1840. A topographical account of Scotland.

History of the rebellions in Scotland under the Marquis of Montrose and others, from 1638 till 1660. 2 vols Edinburgh 1828.

History of the rebellions in Scotland, under the Viscount of Dundee and the Earl of Mar, in 1689 and 1715. Edinburgh 1829.

The Scottish ballads. Edinburgh 1829.

The Scottish songs. 2 vols Edinburgh 1829.

The life of King James the First. 2 vols Edinburgh 1830.

Picture of Stirling: a series of eight views, engraved by J. Gellatly from drawings by A. S. Masson. Stirling 1830. Historical and descriptive notes by Chambers.

Life of Sir Walter Scott. Edinburgh 1832; rev W. Chambers 1871, 1894 (rev with addns). First pbd in Chambers's Edinburgh Jnl 1832.

The history of Scotland, from the earliest period to the present time. 2 vols Edinburgh 1832, 1849.

Scottish jests and anecdotes. To which are added a selection of choice English and Irish jests. Edinburgh 1832 (anon); also later edns.

Gazetteer of Scotland. Edinburgh 1832; further edns in 1830s and 1840s. Comp with W. Chambers.

A biographical dictionary of eminent Scotsmen. 4 vols Glasgow 1832–5, 5 vols Glasgow 1855 (rev with supplemental vol by T. Thomson), 3 vols 1870 (rev T. Thomson), 1875 (with suppl of biographies to date of pbn).

Reekiana: or minor antiquities of Edinburgh. Edinburgh 1833. Rptd in 1869 edn of Traditions of Edinburgh, above.

Forbes, R. Jacobite memoirs of the Rebellion of 1745. Edinburgh 1834, ed R. Chambers.

Poems. Edinburgh 1835 (priv ptd). Rptd with some omissions with Popular rhymes of Scotland, to form vol of the Select writings, above.

History of the English language and literature. Edinburgh 1835. Numerous edns, also in US as Historical sketches of English and American literature, addns by R. Robbins, Hartfort CT 1837 and later edns. A vol in Chambers's Educational course.

Introduction to the sciences. For use in schools and for private instruction. Edinburgh 1836 (anon). Numerous edns, also in US. A vol in Chambers's Educational course.

The life of Robert Burns with a criticism of his writings. Edinburgh 1838. By James Currie. Expanded by Chambers.

The poetical works of Robert Burns; to which are now added notes illustrating historical, personal and local allusions. Edinburgh 1838.

The prose works of Robert Burns; with the notes of Currie and Cromek, and many by the present editor. Edinburgh 1839.

Cyclopaedia of English literature. 2 vols Edinburgh 1840–4. With R. Carruthers. Numerous later edns, also in US. 1857–60 rev R. Carruthers, 1876, 1892, 3 vols 1901–3 ed D. Patrick. 1922 new edn vol 3, 1938.

The land of Burns. Glasgow 1844. With J. Wilson.

Twelve romantic Scottish ballads. With the original airs, arranged for the pianoforte. Edinburgh 1844. Comp R. Chambers.

Vestiges of the natural history of creation. 1844 (anon), 1844 (2nd edn rev, anon), New York 1845 (anon, with at least fifteen further edns by various Amer publishers), 1845 (3rd edn rev, anon), 1845 (4th edn rev, anon), 1846 (5th edn rev, anon), 1847 (6th edn rev, anon), 1847 (cheap reissue of 6th edn text, anon), 1850 (8th edn rev, anon), 1851 (9th edn rev, anon), 1853 (10th edn, illus and rev, anon), 1884 (12th edn, introd by A. Ireland), 1887 (text of 2nd edn, introd by H. Morley), rptd 1890, Leicester 1969 (rpt of 1st edn, introd by G. de Beer), Chicago 1994 (rpt of 1st edn in Vestiges of the natural history of creation and other evolutionary writings, Selections, *above*; this also lists all known reviews and foreign edns); tr Du 1849, 1866; Ger 1846, 1851.

Explanations: a sequel to Vestiges of the natural history of creation. 1845 (anon), New York 1846 (anon, with further Amer edns), 1846 (2nd edn rev, anon), Chicago 1994 (see above; rpt of 1st edn, with full listing of reviews and foreign edns).

Ancient sea-margins, as memorials of changes in the relative level of sea and land. Edinburgh 1848.

Tracings of the North of Europe. 1851 (priv ptd). Rptd from Chambers's Edinburgh Jnl. An account of voyagings in the Baltic.

Life and works of Robert Burns. 4 vols Edinburgh 1851. Numerous edns in 1800s.

Tracings of Iceland and the Faröe Islands. Edinburgh 1856.

Domestic annals of Scotland from the Reformation to the Revolution. 2 vols Edinburgh 1858, 1859, 1861, 1 vol Edinburgh 1885 (abridged).

Edinburgh papers. 5 pts Edinburgh 1859–61, 1861.

Sketch of the history of the Edinburgh Theatre Royal. Edinburgh 1859 (priv ptd).

William Forbes, memoirs of a banking house. Edinburgh 1860. Introd signed R. C.

Domestic annals of Scotland from the Revolution to the Rebellion of 1745. 1861. Intended to form vol 3 to Domestic annals of Scotland from the Reformation to the Revolution.

The songs of Scotland prior to Burns, with the tunes. 1862, 1880, 1890.

The book of days: a miscellany of popular antiquities in connection with the calendar. 2 vols 1862–4. Numerous later edns in US and UK.

Introduction to D. D. Home. Incidents in my life. First ser 1863 (anon). Supports Home and the reality of spiritualism.

Smollett: his life and a selection of his writings. Edinburgh 1867.

The Threiplands of Fingask: a family memoir. Edinburgh 1880. Written in 1852. Also contains Life in a Scottish country mansion; Two days on the moors of Perthshire.

Poetical remains. Edinburgh 1883 (limited edn).

Contributions to periodicals and series

The patriot. Edinburgh 1819. Joint proprietor and (possibly) contributor. Copy in Mitchell Lib, Glasgow.

The kaleidoscope: or Edinburgh literary amusement. A periodical miscellany, chiefly humorous. Edinburgh 1821–2. Proprietor and principal contributor. Marked copy in Edinburgh City Lib.

Edinburgh advertiser. Edinburgh 1830–2. Editor.

Chambers's Edinburgh Jnl. Edinburgh 1832–71. Joint proprietor (from May 1832) and principal contributor, especially in 1830s and 1840s. Most of Chambers's writings appeared as essays in this weekly periodical; for a sampling, see Essays familiar and humorous, Selections, *above*.

Chambers's information for the people. Edinburgh 1833–71. Editor and occasional contributor.

Chambers's educational course. Edinburgh 1835–71. Editor and occasional contributor.

Chambers's historical newspaper. Edinburgh 1836. Proprietor and contributor.

§2

Chambers, W. Memoir of Robert Chambers with autobiographical reminiscences of William Chambers. Edinburgh 1872, 1884 (enlarged).

Catalogue of the very valuable library of the late Robert Chambers ... which will be sold by auction by Mr T. Chapman. Edinburgh 1873. Copy in Nat Lib of Scotland.
Parsons, C. O. Serial publication of Traditions of Edinburgh. Library 4th ser 14 1934.
Millhauser, M. Just before Darwin: Robert Chambers and Vestiges. Middletown CT 1959.
Cooney, S. M. Publishers for the people: W. and R. Chambers: the early years, 1832–1850. PhD dissertation Ohio State Univ 1970.
Ogilvie, M. B. Robert Chambers and the successive revisions of the Vestiges of the natural history of creation. PhD dissertation Univ of Oklahoma 1973.
Bennett, S. Revolutions in thought: serial publication and the mass market for reading. In The Victorian periodical press: samplings and soundings, ed J. Shattock and M. Wolff, Leicester 1982.
Secord, J. Behind the veil: Robert Chambers and Vestiges. In History, humanity and evolution, ed J. R. Moore, Cambridge 1989.
Layman, C. H. ed. Man of letters: the early life and love-letters of Robert Chambers. Edinburgh 1990. Prints part of an early autobiography together with early letters to his fiancée. [JAS]

William Kingdon Clifford 1845–79

Notebooks, mss and correspondence by and relating to Clifford are mainly held in a private collection of his descendants. Original ms for Mathematical fragments and some letters from period 1871–4 held at Univ College, London.

Bibliographies

Bibliographical introduction in vol I, Lectures and essays by the late William Kingdon Clifford, FRS, ed L. Stephen and F. Pollock, 1879.
Bibliographical preface in Mathematical papers of W. K. Clifford, ed R. Tucker, 1882.

Collections and selections

Lectures and essays by the late William Kingdon Clifford, FRS. 2 vols, ed L. Stephen and F. Pollock. Vol 1 with an introd by F. Pollock (biographical, selections from letters, etc and bibliographical) 1879, London and New York 1886 (1 vol with two essays removed which were pbd in Mathematical papers), New York 1901 (2 vols), 1918 (Rationalist Press Assoc cheap rpt 52).
Mathematical fragments (facs of unfinished papers on the theory of graphs). 1881.
Mathematical papers. Ed and preface by R. Tucker (biographical and bibliographical), introd by H. J. S. Smith. 51 mathematical research papers and appendix containing notes on mathematical topics, lecture notes, syllabuses of lectures, reviews, answers to problems. 1882, New York 1968; tr Ger by H. Klemperer, Leipzig 1913.
The scientific basis of morals, and other essays. New York 1884.
Conditions of mental development, and other essays. New York 1885.
The unseen universe and philosophy of the pure sciences. New York 1886.
Select works of William Kingdon Clifford (including Seeing and thinking and other essays from Lectures and essays). New York 1889.
The ethics of belief and other essays. Ed L. Stephen and F. Pollock 1947.
Three lectures on psychology. Rpt of three essays from Lectures and essays (History of British psychology series, the emergence of psychology with an introduction by R. Thomson), 1993.

§1

Elements of dynamic: an introduction to the study of motion and rest in solid and fluid bodies. Part 1 kinematic: Book 1 translations, Book 2 rotations, Book 3 strains. 1878.
Seeing and thinking: transcript of a series of lectures given in the Town Hall, Shoreditch. (Diagrams by M. Foster.) 1879, rptd 1880, New York 1881 (Humboldt Library of Popular Science Literature), London and New York 1890, Cincinatti OH 1891.
Elements of dynamic: an introduction to the study of motion and rest in solid and fluid bodies. Part 1 (as above). Part 2: Book 4 masses, appendix. (ed posthumously, with a preface, by R. Tucker). 1886.
The common sense of the exact sciences. Entrusted to R. C. Rowe then ed and completed with preface by K. Pearson. London and New York 1885, 2nd edn London 1886, New York 1888, 1894, London 1898, New York 1899, 1903, 5th edn London 1907, New York 1946 (new edn with preface by B. Russell and introd by J. R. Newman), London 1947, New York 1955.
Body and mind, with other essays. New York 1891 (Humboldt Lib of Science 145).
Von der natur der singe an sich. Ans dem englischen ubersetztund hrsg. von Hans Kleinpeter. Mit einer ein leitung das heransgebersuber Clifford's leben und werken. (Trn into German of On the nature of things-in-themselves with an account of Clifford's life and work.) Leipzig 1903.
The ethics of religion. New York 1917 (Truth Seeker tracts 130).

Contributions to periodicals

On some of the conditions of mental development. Proc Royal Institution 6 Mar 1868, rptd Lectures and essays Vol 1 1879, rptd Lectures and essays second edn 1886. (With subsequent letter pbd in Pall Mall Gazette 24 June 1868.)
On theories of the physical forces. Proc Royal Institution 18 Feb 1870, rptd Lectures and essays Vol 1 1879, rptd Lectures and essays 2nd edn 1886.
On the aims and instruments of scientific thought. Lecture to the British Assoc at Brighton 10 Aug 1872. Reported and rptd in Macmillan's Mag Oct 1872, rptd Lectures and essays Vol 1 1879, rptd Lectures and essays 2nd edn 1886.
Atoms. Sunday Lecture Soc 7 Jan 1872, repeated Manchester 20 Nov 1872, ptd in Manchester Science Lectures for the People ser 4 no 4 1872, rptd Lectures and essays Vol 1 1879, rptd Lectures and essays 2nd edn 1886.
The unreasonable. Nature 7, 13 Feb 1873. (Debate with C. M. Ingleby, Nature 7, 6 Feb, 13 Feb, 20 Feb 1873.)
Rev of Volume 1 of G. H. Lewes, Problems of life and mind. Academy, 7 Feb 1874.
Atoms. In D. Estes ed, Half hour recreations in popular science, Boston 1874.
The first and the last catastrophe. Sunday Lecture Soc 12 Apr 1874. Ptd (rev) in Fortnightly Rev Apr 1875, rptd Lectures and essays Vol 1 1879, rptd Lectures and essays 2nd edn 1886.
The philosophy of the pure sciences. Part 1: The statement of the question. Afternoon lectures at the Royal Institution 1 Mar 1873, pbd in Contemporary Rev 24, Oct 1874.
Body and mind. Sunday Lecture Soc 1 Nov 1874, Fortnightly Rev Dec 1874, rptd Lectures and essays Vol 2 1879, rptd Lectures and essays 2nd edn 1886.
The philosophy of the pure sciences. Part 2: The postulates of the science of space. Afternoon lectures at the Royal Institution 8 Mar 1873, Contemporary Rev 25, Feb 1875.
The unseen universe or Physical speculations on a future state. 1875, Fortnightly Rev June 1875, rptd Lectures and essays Vol 1 1879, rptd Lectures and essays 2nd edn 1886.
On the scientific basis of morals. Paper read to Metaphysical Soc 1875, Contemporary Rev Sep 1875, rptd Lectures and essays Vol 2 1879, rptd Lectures and essays 2nd edn 1886.
Right and wrong: the scientific ground of their distinction. Sunday Lecture Soc 7 Nov 1875, Fortnightly Rev Dec 1875, rptd Lectures and essays Vol 2 1879, rptd Lectures and essays 2nd edn 1886.

Instruments used in measurement: instruments illustrating kinematics, statics and dynamics. South Kensington handbook to loan collection of scientific apparatus 1876, rptd Lectures and essays Vol 2 1879, rptd Mathematical papers 1882.
The ethics of belief. Paper read to Metaphysical Soc, pbd (with considerable addns) in Contemporary Rev Jan 1877, rptd Lectures and essays Vol 2 1879, rptd Lectures and essays 2nd edn 1886.
On the types of compound statement involving four classes. Memoirs of the Literary and Philosophical Soc of Manchester, Session 1876–7, Vol 16, rptd Lectures and essays Vol 2 1879, rptd Mathematical papers 1882.
The influence upon morality of a decline in religious belief. Pbd in A modern symposium in Nineteenth Century, Apr 1877, rptd Lectures and essays Vol 2 1879, rptd Lectures and essays 2nd edn 1886, extracts in Nineteenth century opinion, comp and ed M. Goodwin, Harmondsworth 1951.
The ethics of religion. Sunday Lecture Soc (with title The bearings of Morals on Religion) 4 Mar 1877, Fortnightly Rev July 1877, rptd Lectures and essays Vol 2 1879, rptd Lectures and essays 2nd edn 1886.
Cosmic emotion. Nineteenth Century Oct 1877, rptd Lectures and essays Vol 2 1879, rptd Lectures and essays 2nd edn 1886.
On the nature of things-in-themselves. Paper read to Metaphysical Soc 1874. Mind Jan 1878, rptd Lectures and essays Vol 2 1879, rptd Lectures and essays 2nd edn 1886.
Virchow on the teaching of science. Nineteenth Cent Apr 1878, rptd Lectures and essays Vol 2 1879, rptd Lectures and essays 2nd edn 1886.
Childhood and ignorance. Nineteenth Cent May 1878.
The philosophy of the pure sciences. Part 3: The universal statements of arithmetic. Afternoon lectures at the Royal Institution 15 Mar 1873, pbd in Nineteenth Cent 5, Mar 1879.
The philosophy of the pure sciences. Afternoon lectures at the Royal Institution 1, 8, 15 Mar 1873, with fragment Knowledge and feeling, pbd in Lectures and essays Vol 1 1879, rptd Lectures and essays 2nd edn 1886.

Contributions to collaborative works

The little people. Stories by Lady Pollock, W. K. Clifford and W. H. Pollock, with illustrations by J. Collier. Two stories by W. K. Clifford: The new crown, The giant's shoes. 1874.
A modern symposium. Ed J. Martineau. Essay by W. K. Clifford: The influence upon morality of a decline in religious belief. 1877.
Cosmic emotion. (With The teaching of science by R. Virchow.) New York 1888.

Letters

Lectures and essays. Ed L. Stephen and F. Pollock (as above), contains a selection from letters written by W. K. Clifford. 1879.
Smith, D. E. Clifford's genius shown as a boy. Amer Mathematical Monthly 29 1922.

Translations

Riemann, G. F. B. On the hypotheses which lie at the bases of geometry being Ueber die hypothesen, welche der geometrie zu gründe liegen (Habilitationsvortrag, 1854). Nature 3 1873.

§2

Tait, P. G. Clifford's dynamic. (Review of pt 1.) Nature 18, 23 May 1878.
Anon. Professor Clifford's Elements of dynamic. Saturday Rev 45, 22 June 1878.
Pollock, F. Report on Friday evening discourse Force and energy by W. K. Clifford at Royal Institution 28 Mar 1873. Nature 22 1880.
Chrystal, G. Rev of Mathematical papers and mathematical fragments. Nature 26, 6 July 1882.
Tait, P. G. Clifford's Exact sciences. Nature 32, 11 June 1885 (with responses in defence of Clifford by R. Tucker Nature 32, 18 June 1885, 'R' Nature 32, 25 June 1885, K. Pearson Nature 32, 2 July 1885).
Pearson, K. Elements of dynamic: Part 1, Book 4 and Appendix. Athenaeum 16 July 1887.
Pollock, F. (ed with L. Stephen). Introduction in Lectures and essays by the late William Kingdon Clifford, FRS. 1879 and other edns above.
Newman, J. R. William Kingdon Clifford. Scientific American 188, Feb 1953.
Power, E. A. Exeter's Mathematician—W. K. Clifford, FRS, 1845–1879. Advancement of Science 26 1970. [JSRC and RSF]

Stanton Coit 1857–1944

Ethical culture as a religion for the people. 1888; tr Fr 1891.
The ethical movement defined. [1898?]; rptd in The ethical movement, ed H. J. Bridges 1911.
Ethical democracy: essays in social dynamics. 1900.
Humanity and God. International Jnl of Ethics 16 1906.
Ethical mysticism. In Aspects of ethical religion: essays in honour of Felix Adler, 1926.
Spinoza's moral insight. In Spinoza: tercentenary addresses, ed I. Maltuck, 1932.
Also works on religion and current events.

Samuel Taylor Coleridge 1772–1834

See col 298.

George Combe 1788–1858

The Nat Lib of Scotland is the repository of the Combe mss (letters and diaries).

Bibliographies

Cooter, R. J. Phrenology in the British Isles: an annotated, historical biobibliography and index. Metuchen NJ and London 1989. Pp 68–81 provides a complete list of Combe's pbns.
Sait, J. E. The Combe collection in the National Library of Scotland. Bibliotheck 8 1976, pp 53–4.

Collection

Select works. 5 vols 1893–4.

§1

Essays on phrenology. 1819. Edinburgh 1825 (as System of phrenology), 2 vols 1836 (4th edn), 1843 (5th edn), 1853 (rev), 1863 (10th edn, rev).
Elements of phrenology. Edinburgh 1824, 1850 (7th edn enlarged).
Letter to Francis Jeffrey in answer to his criticism on phrenology in the Edinburgh Review. 1826.
The constitution of man considered in relation to external objects. Edinburgh 1828, 1835 (4th edn rev and enlarged), 1866 (9th edn). Reviews and critiques: Educational Mag 1835; Medico-Chirurgical Jnl 1835; Analyst 1836; Monthly Repository 1836; Presbyterian Mag 1836; [Wm Gillespie] An Exposure, Edinburgh 1836; British and Foreign Medical Rev 1840; British and Foreign Rev 1841; tr Ger (S. E. Hirschfeld) 1836; Swed 1833; Polish 1843.
Letter on the prejudices of the great in science and philosophy against phrenology. Edinburgh 1829.
Lectures on popular education. Edinburgh 1833, 1837 (enlarged), 1848 (enlarged). Amer edns from 1836.
Lectures on moral philosophy. 1836, 1846 (3rd edn enlarged). Also pbd as Moral philosophy. Edinburgh 1840.
Lectures on Phrenology. New York 1839, 1871 (3rd edn).
Notes on the United States of America. 3 vols Edinburgh 1841, 2 vols Philadelphia 1841.

On the relation between religion and science. Edinburgh 1847, 1857 (4th edn enlarged), 1893 (as Science and religion).
Remarks on national education. Edinburgh 1847, 1848 (5th edn).
The life and correspondence of Andrew Combe, MD. Edinburgh 1850.
Remarks on the principles of criminal legislation. 1854. Review: The Leader 1854.
Phrenology applied to painting and sculpture. 1855. Review: Athenaeum 1855.

Translations

On the functions of the cerebellum, by Drs Gall, Vimont and Broussais. Edinburgh 1838. By G.C.
Also works on phrenology.

§2

Gibbon, C. Life of Combe. 1878.
Capen, N. Reminiscences of Spurzheim and Combe. 1881.
Grant, A. C. George Combe and his circle. Unpbd PhD thesis, Univ of Edinburgh 1960.
DeGiustino, D. Phrenology in Britain, 1815–1855: a study of George Combe and his circle. Unpbd PhD thesis, Univ of Wisconsin 1969. [RC]

Richard Congreve 1818–99

§1

Pilgrimage: a prize poem recited in Rugby School. 1837.
The new religion in its attitude to the old. 1859.
The propagation of the religion of humanity. 1860.
Religion de l'humanité. Paris 1864.
Two addresses: systematic policy, education. 1870.
Essays political, social and religious. 3 vols 1874, 1900.
Human catholicism. 2 nos 1876–7.
The religion of humanity [annual addresses]. 1878, 1881, 1882, 1894.
Also works on historical and contemporary questions.

§2

Thomas, P. Comte and Congreve. 1910.

Thomas Cooper 1805–92

See col 603.

Caroline Frances Cornwallis 1786–1858

§1

The following works are part of a series of 24 called Small books on great subjects, all pbd anon. Cornwallis was responsible for 17 of them, and contributed to a further 4. Her authorship was revealed posthumously by M. C. Power in her Selections from the letters of Caroline Frances Cornwallis, *1865.*
No 1: Philosophical theories and philosophical experience. 1841. 'By a Pariah' (ie a woman). 2nd edn 1845 (enlarged). Philadelphia 1846 (from 2nd edn). 3rd edn 1854, rptd in Appendix to Selections from the letters of Caroline Frances Cornwallis, 1865.
No 2: On the connection between physiology and intellectual philosophy. 1842. 3rd edn 1857 (enlarged).
REVIEW: British and Foreign Medical Rev 15, Apr 1843, attributed to the Rev John Barlow.
No 3: On man's power over himself to prevent or control insanity. 1843, 3rd edn 1855.
No 4: An introduction to practical organic chemistry, with reference to the works of Davy, Brande, Liebig, etc. 1843, Philadelphia 1846, 2nd edn 1854 (rev).
No 5: A brief view of Greek philosophy up to the age of Pericles. 1844, Philadelphia 1846 (with no 6), Philadelphia 1846 (with nos 6–8), 2nd edn 1850.
REVIEW: Athenaeum 9 Nov 1844 (with number 6).
No 6: A brief view of Greek philosophy from the age of Socrates to the coming of Christ. 1844, Philadelphia 1846 (with no 5), Philadelphia 1846 (with nos 5, 7, 8), 2nd edn 1850.
REVIEW: Athenaeum, 9 Nov 1844 (with number 5).
No 7: Christian doctrine and practice in the second century. 1845, Philadelphia 1846 (with nos 5, 6, 8), 2nd edn 1857 (with new postscript).
No 8: An exposition of vulgar and common errors, adapted to the year of grace MDCCCXLV, by Thomas Brown redivivus, whilome Knt and M. D. 1845 (imitation of Thomas Browne's Pseudodoxia epidemica, 1646; some material supplied by others). Philadelphia 1846 (with nos 5–7), 2nd edn 1854.
REVIEW: Athenaeum 27 Sep 1845.
No 10: On the principles of criminal law. 1846, Philadelphia 1846.
No 11: Christian sects in the nineteenth century. In a series of letters to a lady. 1846 (some material supplied by others), 2nd edn 1850.
REVIEW: Athenaeum 31 Oct 1846.
No 12: General principles of grammar. 1847, Philadelphia 1847, micro Cambridge MA 1994.
No 13: Sketches of geology. 1848 (some material supplied by others), 2nd edn 1854 (rev and enlarged).
No 14: On the state of man before the promulgation of Christianity. 1848, 2nd edn 1854.
No 15: Thoughts and opinions of a statesman. 1849 (mostly tr from German of Baron von Humboldt; some material supplied by others).
No 17: Christian doctrine and practice in the twelfth century. 1850, Micro Evanston IL 1991.
No 18: The philosophy of Ragged Schools. 1851.
Nos 19–22: On the state of man subsequent to the promulgation of Christianity. No 19 1851, 2nd edn 1854, reviewed in the Athenaeum, 27 Sep 1851, and by James Martineau in the Westminster Rev n.s. 1, Jan 1852. No 20 1852, reviewed in the Athenaeum, 17 Apr 1852. No 21 1852, reviewed in the Athenaeum, 31 July 1852. No 22 1854.
Pericles: a tale of Athens in the eighty-third Olympiad. 2 vols 1846 (anon).
REVIEW: Athenaeum, 20 June 1846; (John Conington) Edinburgh Rev 92, July 1850.
On the treatment of the dangerous and perishing classes of society, in Two prize essays on juvenile delinquency. By C. F. Cornwallis and Micaiah Hill. 1853, micros Princeton NJ [19?] and Woodbridge CT 1990. *The prizes were offered by Lady Byron.*

Contributions to periodicals

Young criminals. Westminster Rev n.s. 4, July 1853.
Wycliffe and his times. Westminster Rev n.s. 6, July 1854.
The naval school on board the Illustrious. Fraser's Mag 51 Apr 1855.
Self-education. Westminster Rev n.s. 8, July 1855.
History of the House of Savoy. Westminster Rev n.s. 9, Jan 1856.
The property of married women. Westminster Rev n.s. 10, Oct 1856.
Capabilities and disabilities of women. Westminster Rev n.s. 11, Jan 1857.
Naval education. Fraser's Mag 56 Sep 1857.

Published letters

Selections from the letters of Caroline Frances Cornwallis. Also some unpbd poems, original and translated, and an Appendix, containing 'Philosophical theories and philosophical experience'. Ed M. C. Power 1865, micro New Haven CT 1975.
REVIEW: [Louisa A. Merivale] North British Rev 42 June 1865.

§2

May, Mrs. In DNB.
Power, M. C. Preface to Selections from the letters of Caroline Frances Cornwallis, 1865. [JW]

Charles Robert Darwin 1809–82

The chief ms collection is in the Cambridge Univ Library, including letters, annotated books and pamphlets, working library and ms of publications. Important collections of unpbd letters are in the American Philosophical Assoc and Natural History Museum. Some ms relating to Beagle voyage in Darwin Museum, Down House, Kent.

Bibliographies

Rutherford, H. W. Catalogue of the library of Darwin now in the botany school Cambridge (subsequently divided between Cambridge Univ Lib and Down House). Cambridge 1908.

Peckham, M. The origin of species: a variorum text. Philadelphia 1959.

Handlist of Darwin papers at the University Library Cambridge. Cambridge 1960.

Osborne, E. A. The first edition of On the origin of species. Book Collector 9 1960.

Todd, W. B. Variant issues of On the origin of species. Book Collector 9 1960.

Darwin Library: list of books received in the University Library Cambridge Mar–May 1961 (see also Marginalia, below). Cambridge 1961.

Freeman, R. B. The works of Darwin: an annotated bibliographical handlist. 1965; rev 1977.

Darwin, Huxley and the natural sciences: a listing and guide to the Research Publications International Collection units 3, 4 and 5. Scientific papers and correspondence of Darwin c. 1830–82 from the Univ Lib Cambridge. Reading 1990.

History of the archive in Calendar *below.*

Collections and selections

Gesammelte Werke, tr J. V. Carus 13 vols Stuttgart 1875–81.

Darwinism stated by Darwin himself. Ed N. Sheppard, New York 1884.

Gesammelte kleinere Schriften, tr E. Krause 2 vols Leipzig 1885.

The living thoughts of Darwin. Ed J. Huxley and J. Fisher 1939.

The Darwin reader. Ed M. Bates and P. S. Humphrey 1957.

Darwin for today: the essence of his works. Ed S. E. Hyman, New York 1963.

What Darwin really said. Ed B. Farrington 1966.

Darwin. Ed P. Appleman, New York 1970.

The collected papers of Darwin. Ed P. H. Barrett, 2 vols Chicago 1977.

The works of Darwin. (Pickering Masters.) Ed P. H. Barrett, P. J. Gautrey and R. B. Freeman, 29 vols 1986–9.

The portable Darwin. Ed D. M. Porter and P. W. Graham, 1993.

§1

The zoology of the voyage of HMS Beagle, under the command of Captain Fitzroy RN, during the years 1832 to 1836, edited and superintended by Charles Darwin. 5 pts 1838–43.

Journal of researches into the geology and natural history of the various countries visited by HMS Beagle. 1839 (issued separately, and as vol 3: Journal and remarks, of Narrative of the surveying voyages of HM Ships Adventure and Beagle, ed R. Fitzroy), 1840, New York 1952; tr Ger 1844; 1845 (rev as Journal of researches into the natural history and geology), 1852, 1860 (with addns), 1870, 1872, 1873, 1876, 1879, 1882 etc; 2 vols New York 1846, 1855 etc; tr Rus 1870; Ital 1872; Ger 1875; Fr 1860 (selections), 1875; Danish 1876.

The structure and distribution of coral reefs, being the first part of the geology of the voyage of the Beagle. 1842, (rev) 1874, New York 1889, New York 1896, Berkeley CA 1962; tr Rus 1846 (selections); Ger 1876; Fr 1878; Ital 1888.

Geological observations on the volcanic islands visited during the voyage of HMS Beagle, being the second part of the geology of the voyage of the Beagle. 1844, 1876 (with third part), New York 1891 (with third part); tr Ger 1877.

Geological observations on South America, being the third part of the geology of the voyage of the Beagle. 1846; tr Ger 1878.

Geology. In A manual of scientific enquiry prepared for the use of Her Majesty's Navy and adapted for travellers in general, ed J. F. W. Herschel, 1849, 1851, 1859, 1871 (rev J. Phillips), 1886; rev and rptd separately as Geology, 1849; as Manual of geology, 1859; tr Rus 1860.

Geological observations on coral reefs, volcanic islands and on South America. 1851, 1890 (introd by J. W. Judd).

A monograph of the sub-class cirripedia. 2 vols 1851–4, 1 vol 1964.

A monograph of the fossil lepadidae. 2 vols 1851–4.

Darwin's natural selection: being the second part of his big species book written from 1856 to 1858. Ed R. C. Stauffer, Cambridge 1975 (transcript of ms from which Origin of species abstracted).

On the tendency of species to form varieties, and on the perpetuation of varieties and species by natural means of selection, by Charles Darwin and Alfred Wallace, communicated by Sir Charles Lyell and J. D. Hooker. Jnl of the Proceedings of Linnean Soc, Zoology 3, 1858; 1858 (offprint); rptd in Zoologist 16 1858; in The Darwin-Wallace celebrations, 1st July 1908, by the Linnean Society, 1908; in G. Sarton, Discovery of the theory of natural selection, Isis 14 1930; in The Darwin reader 1957, above; in B. J. Loewenberg, Darwin, Wallace and the theory of natural selection, New Haven CT 1957; in Evolution by natural selection, ed G. de Beer, Cambridge 1958.

On the origin of species by natural selection, or the preservation of favoured races in the struggle for life. 1859, 1901, 1902, 1906, 1910, 1950, Cambridge MA 1964; 1860 (2nd edn rev), 1861 (3rd edn rev), 1866 (4th edn rev), 1869 (5th edn rev), 1872 (as The origin of species) (6th edn rev), 1873, 1875, 1876 (with slight changes), 1878, 1880, 1882 etc; New York 1860 (with additions above not in 2nd English edn), 1868, 1870 etc; A variorum text, ed M. Peckham, 1959; tr Ger 1860 (with first form of Historical sketch, rev and expanded in 3rd English edn), 1863; Fr 1862, 1876; Rus 1864; Du 1863; Ital 1864; Swed 1869; Danish 1872; Polish 1873; Hungarian 1873–4; Sp 1877.

On the various contrivances by which British and foreign orchids are fertilised by insects. 1862, 1877 (rev as The various contrivances), 1882 etc, New York 1877, 1884; tr Ger 1862; Fr 1870; Ital 1883.

Recollections of Professor Henslow, in L. Jenyns (later Blomefield), Memoir of the Rev John Stevens Henslow, rector of Hitcham and professor of botany in the University of Cambridge, 1862.

On the movements and habits of climbing plants. Jnl of the Proceedings of Linnean Soc 9 1865, 1865 (offprint), 1875 (rev, much enlarged, and pbd separately), 1876, 1882 etc, New York 1876; tr Ger 1876; Fr 1877; Ital 1878.

The variation of animals and plants under domestication. 2 vols 1868, 1875 (rev), 1882 etc, New York 1868, 1876; tr Fr 1868; Ger 1868; Rus 1867 (selections), 1869; Ital 1876.

The descent of man, and selection in relation to sex. 2 vols 1871, 1871 (3 rev issues), 1874 (2nd edn rev), 1875 (rev), 1877 (rev), 1879, 1881, 1882 etc, New York 1871, 1872 etc; tr Du 1871–2; Ger 1871–2; Ital 1871; Rus 1871–2; Fr 1872; Swed 1872; Danish 1874–5; Polish 1874; Hungarian 1884.

The expression of the emotions in man and animals. 1872, 1873, 1890 (with addns by F. Darwin) etc, New York 1873, 1896, 1899; ed M. Mead, New York 1955; tr Ger 1872; Rus 1872; Du 1873; Fr 1874; Ital 1878.

Insectivorous plants. 1875, 1876, 1888 (2nd edn rev by F. Darwin) etc, New York 1875 etc; tr Ger 1876; Rus 1876; Fr 1877; Ital 1878.

The effects of cross and self fertilisation in the vegetable kingdom. 1876, 1878 (2nd edn rev), 1891 etc, New York 1877 (rev), 1892; tr Fr 1877; Ger 1877; Ital 1878.

A biographical sketch of an infant. Mind 2 1877; tr Fr 1877; Ger 1877; Rus 1877.

The different forms of flowers on plants of the same species. 1877, 1878, 1884 (2nd edn rev) (preface by F. Darwin) etc, New York 1877, 1896; tr Ger 1877; Fr 1878.

Erasmus Darwin. In E. Krause, Erasmus Darwin, tr from German by W. S. Dallas, 1879, 1887, (rev as The life of Erasmus Darwin) New York 1880; tr Ger 1880.

The power of movement in plants, assisted by Francis Darwin, 1880, 1882, New York 1881; tr Ger 1881; Fr 1882; Rus 1882; Ital 1884.

The formation of vegetable mould, through the action of worms, with observations on their habits. 1881, 1881 (rev), 1882 (rev), 1882 (corrected by F. Darwin) etc, New York 1882 etc; tr Fr 1882; Ital 1882; Ger 1882; Rus 1882.

Essay on instinct. In G. J. Romanes, Mental evolution in animals, 1883, 1885, New York 1884; tr Fr 1884; Ger 1885. Part of a chapter from unpbd Natural selection, above.

The foundations of The origin of species: two essays written in 1842 and 1844. Ed F. Darwin Cambridge 1909; rptd in Evolution by natural selection, above.

List of reviews of Origin of species in Correspondence ed Burkhardt et al *below and in* A. Ellegard, Darwin and the general reader, Chicago 1958, (rev) 1990.

Letters, diaries, notebooks and autobiography

The life and letters of Darwin, including an autobiographical chapter. Ed F. Darwin 3 vols 1887, 1887 (3 rev edns), 1888, 2 vols New York 1887, 1888 etc; tr Ger 1887; Fr 1888; Norwegian 1889.

Darwin: his life told in an autobiographical chapter, and in a selected series of his published letters. Ed F. Darwin 1892, 1902 etc, New York 1892, 1893, 1958; tr Ger 1893.

More letters. Ed F. Darwin and A. C. Seward 2 vols 1903, New York 1903, 1972.

Emma Darwin, wife of Charles Darwin; a century of family letters. Ed H. E. Litchfield, 2 vols Cambridge 1904 (priv ptd), 1915 (rev as Emma Darwin: a century of family letters, 1792–1896), New York 1915.

The complete correspondence between Wallace and Darwin 1857–81. In Alfred Russell Wallace, Letters and reminiscences, ed J. Marchant 2 vols 1916.

Autobiography of Darwin. Ed F. Darwin 1929 (first separate pbn), 1931, 1937 etc; ed N. Barlow 1958 ('with original omissions restored'), New York 1929, 1950 (introd G. G. Simpson), 1958 etc; tr Polish 1891; Rus 1896; Sp 1902; Ital 1919.

Darwin and Henslow: the growth of an idea. Letters 1831–60. Ed Nora Barlow 1967.

Diary of the voyage of HMS Beagle. Ed N. Barlow, Cambridge 1933, New York 1969; Darwin's Beagle diary. Ed R. D. Keynes, Cambridge 1988 (new transcription).

Darwin and the voyage of the Beagle. Ed N. Barlow 1945 (includes ms and letters).

Darwin's journal. Bull of BM (Natural History) historical ser 2 1959.

Ornithological notes. Ed N. Barlow, Bull of BM (Natural History) historical ser 2 1963.

Freeman, R. B. and P. J. Gautrey. Darwin's questions about the breeding of animals (1839). Jnl of Soc Bibl Natural History 5 1969; facs Sherborne Fund 3 1968.

Freeman, R. B. and P. J. Gautrey. Darwin's queries about expression (1867). Bull of BM (Natural History) historical ser 4 1972.

Darwin's early and unpbd notebooks. Transcribed by P. H. Barrett in H. E. Gruber, Darwin on man: a psychological study of scientific creativity, New York 1974.

Calendar of the correspondence, 1821–1882. Ed F. H. Burkhardt, S. Smith et al, New York 1985, Cambridge 1994 (rev).

Correspondence. Ed F. H. Burkhardt, S. Smith et al, 10 vols (continuing) Cambridge 1985– .

Darwin's notebooks, 1836–1844: geology, transmutation of species, metaphysical enquiries. Ed P. H. Barrett, P. J. Gautrey, S. Herbert, D. Kohn and S. Smith, Cambridge and London 1987.

Darwin's insects: Darwin's entomological notes. Ed K. G. V. Smith. Bull of BM (Natural History) historical ser 14 1987.

Darwin's notes on Beagle plants. Ed D. M. Porter. Bull of BM (Natural History) historical ser 14 1987.

Darwin's marginalia. 2 vols (vol 1 books, vol 2 pamphlets). Ed M. di Gregorio and N. Gill, New York 1990– .

Darwin's letters: a selection, 1825–1859. Ed F. H. Burkhardt, Cambridge 1996.

Other mss transcribed in Correspondence, ed Burkhardt et al, *above.*

§2

[Owen, R.] Darwin on the origin of species. Edinburgh Rev 3 1860.

[Jenkin, F.] The origin of species. North Br Rev 46 1867.

Müller, F. Facts and arguments for Darwin. Trs W. S. Dallas 1869.

[Mivart, St G. J.] Darwin's Descent of man. Quart Rev 131 1871.

Haeckel, E. The history of creation: a popular exposition of the doctrine of evolution. 2 vols New York 1874.

Müller, N. Lectures on Mr Darwin's philosophy of language. Fraser's Mag May–June 1876.

Gray, A. Darwiniana: essays and reviews pertaining to Darwinism. New York 1876, ed H. Dupree Cambridge MA 1963.

Butler, S. Evolution old and new. 1879.

Butler, S. Unconscious memory. 1880.

Aveling, E. B. The religious views of Darwin. 1882.

Canello, U. A. Letteratura e Darwinismo. Padua 1882.

Allen, G. Charles Darwin. 1885.

Butler, S. Luck or cunning as the main means of organic modification? [1886.]

Bettany, G. T. Life of Darwin. 1887.

Wallace, A. R. Darwinism: an exposition of the theory of natural selection with some of its applications. 1889.

Romanes, G. J. Darwin and after Darwin. 1892, 1893.

Huxley, T. H. Darwiniana. 1893.

Quatrefages, A. de. Les emules de Darwin. 2 vols Paris 1894.

Stirling, J. H. Darwinianism: workmen and work. Edinburgh 1894.

Tille, A. Von Darwin bis Nietzsche: ein Buch Entwicklungsethik. Leipzig 1895.

Poulton, E. B. Darwin and the theory of natural selection. 1896.

Johnston, W. W. Ill-health of Darwin: its nature and its relation to his work. Amer Anthropologist n.s. 3 1901.

Gould, G. M. In his Biographic clinics: the origin of the ill health of De Quincey, Carlyle, Darwin, Huxley and the Brownings, Philadelphia 1903.

Baldwin, J. M. Darwin and the humanities. Baltimore 1909.

Seward, A. C. Darwin and modern science. Cambridge 1909.

Bryce, J. B. Personal reminiscences of Darwin and of the reception of the Origin of species. Proc Amer Philosophical Soc 48 1909.

Judd, J. W. The coming of evolution. Cambridge 1912.

Huxley, L. Charles Darwin. 1921.

Atkins, H. Down, the home of the Darwins: the story of a house and the people who lived there. 1974, (rev) 1976.

Colp, R. To be an invalid: the illness of Darwin. Chicago 1977.

Freeman, R. B. Darwin: a companion. Folkestone 1978.

Biographies

Brent, P. Charles Darwin. London 1981.

Beer, G. Darwin's plots: evolutionary narrative in Darwin, George Eliot and nineteenth century fiction. London 1983.

Morton, P. The vital science: biology and the literary imagination 1860–1900. London 1984.

Young, R. M. Darwin's metaphor: nature's place in Victorian culture. Cambridge 1985.

Levine, G. Darwin and the novelists: patterns of science in Victorian fiction. Cambridge MA 1988.

Bowlby, J. Charles Darwin: a biography. London 1990.
Bowler, P. J. Charles Darwin: the man and his influence. Cambridge 1990.
Desmond, A. and J. R. Moore. Darwin. London and New York 1991.
Browne, J. Charles Darwin: voyaging. London and New York 1995.
[JB]

Thomas Davidson 1840–1900

§1

A short account of the Niobe group. New York 1875.
Longfellow. Boston 1882.
The Parthenon frieze and other essays. 1882.
The philosophical system of Rosmini-Serbati. 1882.
The place of art in education. Boston 1885.
The moral aspects of the economic question. Boston 1886.
The conditions, divisions, and methods of complete education. Orange NJ 1887.
A handbook to Dante. 1887.
Prolegomena to In memoriam. Boston 1889.
Bruno's thought. In Giordano Bruno: two addresses by D. G. Brinton and T. Davidson, Philadelphia 1890.
The evolution of scripture. New York 1891.
Aristotle and ancient educational ideals. New York 1892.
The education of the Greek people. New York 1894.
Rousseau and education according to nature. New York 1898.
A history of education. New York 1900.
The education of the wage-earners. Ed C. M. Bakewell, Boston [1904].
The philosophy of Goethe's Faust. Ed C. M. Bakewell, Boston 1906.
Education as world-building. Ed E. Moore, Cambridge MA 1925.

§2

Bakewell, C. M. A democratic philosopher and his work. International Jnl of Ethics 11 1901.
Knight, W. Memorials of Davidson. Boston 1907.
Blau, J. L. Rosmini, Domodossola, and Davidson. JHI 18 1958.
Lataner, A. Introduction to Davidson's Autobiographical sketch. JHI 18 1958.

Augustus De Morgan 1806–71

§1

The schoolmaster: essays on practical education. 1836.
Essay on probabilities. 1838, 1849.
First notions of logic. 1839.
The globes, celestial and terrestrial. 1845.
Formal logic: or the calculus of inference, necessary and probable. 1847; ed A. E. Taylor 1926.
Statement in answer to an assertion made by Hamilton, [1847].
On the syllogism [five papers with an appendix]. Trans Cambridge Philosophical Soc 8–10 1849–64.
On the difficulty of correct description of books. 1853, Chicago 1902.
Syllabus of a proposed system of logic. 1860.
A budget of paradoxes. Ed E. De Morgan 1872, 2 vols Chicago 1915, New York 1954.
Newton: his friend and his niece. Ed S. E. De Morgan and A. C. Ranyard 1885.
Essays on the life and work of Newton. Ed P. E. B. Jourdain 1914.
Also works on mathematics and education.

§2

Liard, L. In his Les logiciens anglais, Paris 1878.
De Morgan, S. E. Memoir of Augustus De Morgan 1882.
De Morgan, S. E. Threescore years and ten. Reminiscences of the late Sophia Elizabeth De Morgan. 1895.

Charles Lutwidge Dodgson, 'Lewis Carroll'

1832–98

§1

The game of logic. 1886.
A logical paradox. Mind n.s. 3 1894. Replies by A. Sidgwick, W. E. Johnson, ibid; A. Sidgwick, 4 1895; E. E. C. Jones, 'W', 14 1905; A. W. Burks, I. M. Copi, 59 1950; and A. J. Baker, 64 1955.
What the tortoise said to Achilles. Mind n.s. 4 1895. Replies by W. J. Rees, 60 1951; D. G. Brown, 63 1954.
Symbolic logic. 1897.

§2

Woolen, C. J. Lewis Carroll: philosopher. Hibbert Jnl 46 1948.
See also col 1492.

Robert Leslie Ellis 1817–59

The philosophical works of Francis Bacon. 1857. Ed with J. Spedding.
Mathematical and other writings. Ed W. Walton, with memoir by H. Goodwin, Cambridge 1863.

James Frederick Ferrier 1808–64

§1

Institutes of metaphysic: the theory of knowing and being. Edinburgh 1854, 1856.
Scottish philosophy: the old and the new. Edinburgh 1856.
Lectures on Greek philosophy and other philosophical remains. Ed A. Grant and E. L. Lushington, 2 vols Edinburgh 1866.
Philosophical works. 3 vols Edinburgh 1875–88. Vol 1, Institutes of metaphysic (3rd edn); vols 2 and 3, Lectures on Greek philosophy and other philosophical remains (2nd edn).

§2

Cairns, J. An examination of Ferrier's theory of knowing and being. 1856.
Cairns, J. The Scottish philosophy: a vindication and reply. Edinburgh 1856.
Fraser, A. C. In his Essays in philosophy, Edinburgh 1856.
Smith, J. An examination of Cairns's Examination. Edinburgh 1856.
Vera, A. An inquiry into speculative and experimental science, with special reference to Calderwood and Ferrier. 1856.
Deuchar, R. A brief review of ancient and modern philosophy, with refutations of Ferrier. Edinburgh 1864.
Grote, J. In his Exploratio philosophica, Cambridge 1865.
Fraser, A. C. Philosophical life of Ferrier. Macmillan's Mag Jan 1868.
Tulloch, J. In his Theories in philosophy and religion, Edinburgh 1884.
Haldane, E. Ferrier. Edinburgh 1894.
Segerstedt, T. T. In his Problem of knowledge in Scottish philosophy, Lund 1935.

Robert Flint 1838–1910

§1

The philosophy of history in France and Germany. Edinburgh 1874.
Theism: the Baird lecture for 1876. Edinburgh 1877, 1880 (3rd edn), London 1883, Edinburgh 1902 (10th edn).
Anti-theistic theories. Edinburgh 1879, 1885 (3rd edn).
Vico. Edinburgh 1884.
Historical philosophy in France, French Belgium and Switzerland. 1893.
Socialism. 1894, 1908 (rev).
Sermons and addresses. 1899.
Agnosticism. 1903.

Philosophy as scientia scientiarum. Edinburgh 1904.
On theological, Biblical and other subjects. Edinburgh 1905.
Also works on religion.

§2

MacLeod, N. Scottish divines. 1883.
Macmillan, D. Life of Flint. 1914.

Thomas Fowler 1832–1904

Elements of deductive logic. Oxford 1866. *See below.*
Elements of inductive logic. Oxford 1870, 2 pts Oxford 1895 (rev and combined with the previous as Logic, deductive and inductive, 10th rev edn of Elements of deductive logic, 6th rev edn of Elements of inductive logic).
Locke. 1880.
Bacon. 1881.
Shaftesbury and Hutcheson. 1882.
Progressive morality: an essay in ethics. 1884, 1895 (enlarged).
The principles of morals. 2 pts 1886–7. With J. M. Wilson.
Also works on Oxford.

Alexander Campbell Fraser 1819–1914

§1

Introductory lecture on logic and metaphysics. Edinburgh 1851.
Essays in philosophy. Edinburgh 1856.
Rational philosophy in history and in system. Edinburgh 1858.
Whately and the restoration of the study of logic. Cambridge [1863].
On mental philosophy. Edinburgh 1868.
Life and letters of Berkeley, and an account of his philosophy. Oxford 1871.
Berkeley. Edinburgh 1881.
Locke. Edinburgh 1890.
The philosophy of theism. 2 ser 1895–6, 1899 (rev).
Reid. 1898.
Biographia philosophica. Edinburgh 1904.
Locke as a factor in modern thought. Proc Br Acad 1 1904.
Berkeley and spiritual realism. 1908.

§2

Seth, A. Fraser. Proc Br Acad 6 1914.
Seth, A. Mind n.s. 24 1915.

Sir Francis Galton 1822–1911

§1

The telotype: a printing electric telegraph. 1850.
The narrative of an explorer in tropical South Africa. 1853, 1889 (with biographical introd).
The art of travel: or shifts and contrivances available in wild countries. 1855, 1856, 1860 (both rev and enlarged), 1867, 1872.
Meteorographica or methods of mapping the weather. 1863.
Hereditary genius: an enquiry into its laws and consequences. 1869, 1914, 1950.
English men of science: their nature and nurture. 1874.
Inquires into human faculty and its development. 1883, [1907] (EL).
Life history album 1884, 1902 (re-arranged). Ed Galton.
Record of family faculties. 1884.
Natural inheritance. 1889.
Finger prints. 1892. Supplementary ch on decipherment pbd separately 1893.
Fingerprint directories. 1895.
Index to achievements of near kinsfolk of some Fellows of the Royal Society. [1904.]
Eugenics: its definition, scope and aims. 1905, 1906.
Probability, the foundation of eugenics. Oxford 1907.
Galton also edited a ser of Vacation tourists and notes of travel, 1860–3.

§2

Memories of my life. 1908.
Pearson, K. Life, letters and labours of Galton. 1914.
Blacker, C. P. Eugenics: Galton and after. 1952.

William Graham 1839–1911

Idealism: an essay metaphysical and critical. 1872.
The creed of science, religious, moral and social. 1881, 1884 (rev).
The social problem. 1886.
Socialism, new and old. 1890, 1891.
English political philosophy from Hobbes to Maine. 1899.

Thomas Hill Green 1836–82

§1

Liberal legislation and freedom of contract. Oxford 1881.
Prolegomena to ethics. Ed A. C. Bradley, Oxford 1883, 1907 (5th edn).
The witness of God, and faith: two lay sermons. Ed A. and C. Toynbee 1883.
Works. Ed R. L. Nettleship 3 vols 1885–8 (with memoir), 1889–90.
An essay of the value and influence of works of fiction. Ed F. N. Scott, Ann Arbor MI 1911.

§2

Hodgson, J. R. Green as a critic. Contemporary Rev Dec 1880. Replies by Green Jan 1881; and Spencer, Feb 1881.
Nettleship, R. L. and J. Bryce. Professor T. H. Green: In memoriam. Contemporary Rev May 1882.
Caird, E. Green's last work. Mind 8 1883.
Balfour, A. J. Green's metaphysics of knowledge. Mind 9 1884.
Sidgwick, H. Green's ethics. Mind 9 1884.
Calderwood, H. Another view of Green's last work. Mind 10 1885.
Ritchie, D. G. Political philosophy of Green. Contemporary Rev June 1887.
Seth, A. Hegelianism and personality. Edinburgh 1887, 1893.
Chubb, P. The significance of Green's philosophical and religious teaching. Jnl of Speculative Philosophy 22 1888.
Chadwick, J. W. Green. Unitarian Rev 31 1889.
Conybeare, F. C. Political philosophy of Green. Nat Rev Aug 1889.
Dewey, J. Philosophy of Green. Andover Rev 11 1889.
Oxford metaphysics and ethics adapted to a natural system. Edinburgh 1889.
Eastwood, A. On thought-relations. Mind 16 1891.
Ritchie, D. G. The principles of state interference: essays on Spencer, Mill and Green. 1891.
Upton, C. B. Theological aspects of the philosophy of Green. New World 1 1892.
Dewey, J. Green's theory of the moral motive. Philosophical Rev 1 1892.
Dewey, J. Self-realization as the moral ideal. Philosophical Rev 2 1893.
Fairbrother, W. H. Green and his critics. Proc Aristotelian Soc 2 1894.
Haldar, H. Green and his critics. Philosophical Rev 3 1894.
James, G. F. Green und der Utilitarismus. Halle 1894.
Fairbrother, W. H. The philosophy of Green. 1896.
Laurie, S. S. The metaphysics of Green. Philosophical Rev 6 1897.
Johnson, R. B. C. The metaphysics of knowledge: an examination of Green's theory of reality. Princeton 1900.
Knox, H. V. Green's refutation of empiricism. Mind n.s. 9 1900.
McGilvary, E. B. 'The eternal consciousness'. Mind n.s. 10 1901.
Sidgwick, H. Lectures on the ethics of Green, Spencer and Martineau. 1902.
Bosanquet, B. Recent criticism of Green's ethics. Proc Aristotelian

Soc n.s. 2 1902. Replies by S. H. Hodgson, A. E. Taylor, and Bosanquet, ibid.
Bryce, J. In his Studies in contemporary biography, 1903.
Jones, E. E. C. Green's account of Aristotle's Ethics. Hibbert Jnl 1 1903.
Nettleship, R. L. Memoir of Green. 1906.
Barbour, G. F. Green and Sidgwick, on the community of the good. Philosophical Rev 17 1908.
Muirhead, J. H. The service of the state: four lectures on the political teaching of Green. 1908.
MacCunn, J. In his Six radical thinkers, 1910.
Knox, H. V. Has Green answered Locke? Mind n.s. 23 1914.
Townsend, H. G. The principle of individuality in the philosophy of Green. Ithaca NY 1914.
Sandelius, W. E. Liberalism in the political philosophy of Green. In Six studies in nineteenth-century English literature and thought, ed H. Orel and G. J. Worth, Lawrence KS 1962.
Le Chevalier, C. Ethique et idéalisme: le courant néo-Hegelian en Angleterre, Bosanquet et ses amis. Paris 1963.
Randall, J. H. Green: the development of English thought from Mill to Bradley. JHI 27 1966.

George Grote 1794–1871

See col 2429.

John Grote 1813–66

§1

A few notes on a pamphlet by Mr Shilleto entitled Thucydides or Grote? 1851.
Old studies and new. Cambridge 1856.
Essays and reviews. Cambridge 1862.
Exploratio philosophica. 2 pts Cambridge 1865, 1900.
An examination of the Utilitarian philosophy. Ed J. P. Mayor, Cambridge 1870.
Sermons. Cambridge 1872.
A treatise on the moral ideals. Ed J. P. Mayor, Cambridge 1876.
Plato's utilitarianism: a dialogue by Grote and H. Sidgwick. Classical Rev 3 1889.

§2

Whitmore, C. E. The significance of John Grote. Philosophical Rev 36 1927.

Sir William Hamilton 1788–1856

§1

Works of Reid. 2 vols Edinburgh 1846, 1 vol Edinburgh 1852 (3rd edn), 2 vols Edinburgh 1863 (6th edn). Ed Hamilton.
Letter to De Morgan on his claim to an independent rediscovery of a new principle in the theory of syllogism. 1847.
Discussions on philosophy and literature, education and university reform. 1852, 1853 (enlarged), 1866.
Collected works of Stewart. 11 vols Edinburgh 1854–60. Ed Hamilton.
Lectures on metaphysics and logic. Ed H. L. Mansel and J. Veitch, 4 vols Edinburgh 1859–60, London 1861–6 (rev).

Articles

On the philosophy of the unconditioned. Edinburgh Rev 50 1829.
Philosophy of perception. Edinburgh Rev 52 1830.
On logic: recent English treatises. Edinburgh Rev 56 1833.
On idealism: Collier. Edinburgh Rev 68 1839.

§2

Calderwood, H. Philosophy of the infinite. Edinburgh 1854, 1861 (enlarged).
Hare, J. C. Vindication of Luther against his recent English assailants. 1855 (2nd edn enlarged).
Ulrici, H. Englische Philosophie: Hamilton. Zeitschrift für Philosophie 27 1855.
Baynes, T. S. Spencer on Hamilton. In his Edinburgh essays, 1857.
McCosh, J. Hamilton's metaphysics. Dublin Univ Mag 54 1859.
Tyler, S. Philosophy of Hamilton. Biblical Repertory & Princeton Rev 31 1859.
Rémusat, C. de. Hamilton. Revue des Deux Mondes Apr 1859, Mar 1860.
Deuchar, R. A brief review of ancient and modern philosophy. Edinburgh 1864.
Jones, J. H. Know the truth: a critique on the Hamiltonian doctrine of limitation. New York 1865.
Masson, D. In his Recent British philosophy, 1865.
Mill, J. S. Examination of Hamilton's philosophy. 1865, 1865 (rev), 1867 (rev), 1872 (rev). *See col 2558.*
Stirling, J. H. Hamilton: being the philosophy of perception. 1865.
McCosh, J. Examination of Hamilton's logic. In his Philosophical papers, 1866.
Stirling, J. H. Was Hamilton a Berkeleian? Fortnightly Rev 1 Sep 1866.
Bolton, M. P. W. Inquisitio philosophica: an examination of the principles of Kant and Hamilton. 1866.
Bolton, M. P. W. The Scoto-Oxonian philosophy. 1869.
'Inquirer'. The battle of the two philosophers, Hamilton and Mill. 1866.
Mansel, H. L. The philosophy of the conditioned. 1866.
Ryan, M. The celebrated theory of parallels; with appendix refuting Hamilton's philosophy of the unconditioned. Washington 1866.
Veitch, J. Memoir of Hamilton. Edinburgh 1869.
Murray, J. C. Outline of Hamilton's philosophy. Boston 1870.
'An old student'. What do we know? 1872.
McCosh, J. In his Scottish philosophy, New York 1875.
Billing, M. Kritik öfver Hamilton's lära om det obetingade. Lund 1877.
Liard, L. In his Les logiciens anglais, Paris 1878.
Fink, W. C. An analysis of Hamilton's Lectures on metaphysics. Calcutta 1880.
Morris, G. S. In his British thought and thinkers, 1880.
Monck, W. S. H. Hamilton. 1881.
Green, T. H. The logic of the formal logicians. In his Works vol 2, 1886.
Veitch, J. Hamilton. Edinburgh 1882.
Veitch, J. Hamilton: the man and his philosophy. 1883.
Bourdillart, F. La réforme logique de Hamilton. Paris 1891.
Grote, J. Exploratio philosophica, pt 2. Cambridge 1900.

Thomas Norton Harper 1821–93

The metaphysics of the School. 3 vols 1879–84.

Frederic Harrison 1831–1923

Order and progress. 2 pts 1875.
Science and humanity: a lay sermon. 1879.
The social factor in psychology. [1879.]
The present and the future. 1880.
The ghost of religion. In 'E. L. Y.' (ed), The nature and reality of religion, 1885.
Politics and a human religion. 1885.
Moral and religious socialism. 1891.
The meaning of history and other historical pieces. 1894.
Tennyson, Ruskin, Mill and other literary estimates. 1900.
Positivism: its position, aims and ideals. 1901.
The religion of duty. Philadelphia 1901.

Herbert Spencer. Oxford 1905.
Collected essays. 4 pts 1907–8.
Bibliography of Harrison. Hawkhurst 1908. BM copy with ms notes.
Autobiographic memoirs. 2 vols 1911.
Among my books: centenaries, reviews, memoirs. 1912.
The positive evolution of religion. 1913.
On society. 1918.
See col 2356.

Sir John Frederick William Herschel 1792–1871

A preliminary discourse on the study of natural philosophy. 1831, 1842, 1851; tr Fr 1834; Ital 1840; Polish 1955.
The importance of literature to men of business. 1833, 1852.
Essays. 1857.
Familiar lectures on scientific subjects. 1866, 1871.
Also works on astronomy and mathematics.

James Hinton 1822–75

§1

Man and his dwelling place. 1859, 1872 (rev).
Life in nature. 1862; ed H. Ellis 1932.
The mystery of pain. 1866 (anon), 1874 etc; ed R. H. Hutton [1911].
Selections from manuscripts. 4 vols 1870–4.
Chapters on the art of thinking, and other essays. Ed C. H. Hinton 1879.
Others' needs. 1881.
Philosophy and religion. Ed C. Haddon 1881, 1884.
The lawbreaker and the coming of the law. Ed M. Hinton 1884.
Also works on medicine.

§2

Hopkins, J. E. Life and letters of Hinton. 1878, 1882 (4th edn).
Haddon, C. A law of development. 1883. Based on Hinton's unpbd writings.
Haddon, C. The larger life: studies in Hinton's ethics. 1886.
Ellis, E. M. O. In her Three modern seers, [1910].
Ellis, E. M. O. Hinton: a sketch. [1918.]

Shadworth Holloway Hodgson 1832–1912

§1

Time and space. 1865.
The theory of practice. 2 vols 1870.
Five idols of the theatre. [1872.]
The pre-suppositions of miracles. [1876.]
Is monism tenable? [1878.]
The philosophy of reflection. 2 vols 1878.
Philosophy in relation to its history. [1880.]
Outcast essays and verse translations. 1881.
The practical bearing of speculative philosophy. 1881.
The method of philosophy. 1882.
The two senses of 'reality'. 1883.
The relation of philosophy to science. 1884.
Philosophy and experience. 1885.
The reorganisation of philosophy. 1886.
The unseen world. 1887.
The metaphysic of experience. 4 vols 1898.
Inter-relation of the academical sciences. [1906.]
Some cardinal points in knowledge. [1911.]

§2

Dauriac, L. La méthode et la doctrine de Hodgson. L'Année Philosophique 1899.
Carr, H. W. Hodgson. Mind n.s. 21 1912.
Hicks, G. D. Hodgson. Proc Br Acad 6 1914.

Thomas Henry Huxley 1825–95

§1

On the educational value of the natural history sciences. 1854.
On races, species and their origin. 1860.
Evidence as to man's place in nature. Edinburgh 1863; tr Fr 1868.
On the methods and results of ethnology. 1865.
Lay sermons, addresses and reviews. 1870, 1871 (2nd edn), 1887 (3rd edn).
Critiques and addresses. 1873.
The evidence of the miracle of resurrection. 1876.
American addresses. 1877.
Hume. 1878.
Science and culture, and other essays. 1881.
The advance of science in the last half-century. New York 1887.
Social diseases and worse remedies. 1891, 1891 (2nd edn).
Essays on some controverted questions. 1892.
Evolution and ethics. 1893, 1893, 1893. With Prolegomena (1894) in Collected essays vol 9, *below*.
Collected essays. 9 vols 1893–4; tr Ital 1956 (in part).
Scientific memoirs. Ed M. Foster and E. R. Lankester 5 vols 1898–1903.
Religion without revelation. Ed J. Huxley 1957.

Articles

Almost all of Huxley's articles and some monographs are rptd in the vols of essays listed above. See also Wellesley 5 *1989.*
Time and life. Macmillan's Mag Dec 1859.
Bishop Berkeley on the metaphysics of sensation. Macmillan's Mag June 1871.
Balfour's attack on agnosticism. Nineteenth Century Mar 1895.
Also wrote extensively on scientific subjects.

§2

Young, G. R. Modern scepticism, viewed in relation to modern science. 1865.
Morris, F. O. Difficulties of Darwinism. 1869.
Lillie, J. Letter to Huxley. 1871.
Maschi, L. Confutazione delle dottrine trasformistiche di Huxley, Darwin. Parma 1874.
Porter, J. L. Science and revelation: their distinctive provinces. 1874.
Professor Huxley in America. New York 1876.
Hall, A. W. The problem of human life. 1880.
Jordan, W. L. Huxley on the laws of motion. 1882.
Denison, E. B. A review of Hume and Huxley on miracles. 1883.
McCosh, J. Agnosticism of Hume and Huxley. 1884.
Savile, B. W. Gladstone and Huxley on the Mosaic cosmogony. 1886.
Tafel, R. L. Huxley and Swedenborg. 1889.
Garbett, E. L. Huxley's mendacity on the effects of Noah's flood. 1891.
Garbett, E. L. Facts of the Jesus-Huxley case, on Noah's flood. 1893.
Hahn, G. Huxley. 1895.
White, F. E. Huxley on the relation of the ethical to the cosmic process. International Jnl of Ethics 5 1895. Replies by J. Royce, ibid; J. M. Baldwin and White, 6 1895.
Huxley, L. Life and letters of Huxley. 2 vols 1900, 1903. With bibliography.
Mitchell, P. C. Huxley. 1900, 1913.
Clodd, E. Huxley. 1902.
Wace, H. On agnosticism. 1902.
Clarke, W. N. Huxley and Brooks. 1903.
Thompson, W. H. Huxley and religion. 1905.
Davis, J. R. A. Huxley. 1907.
McGilvary, E. B. Huxley's epiphenomenalism. Jnl of Philosophy 7 1910.
Cadman, S. P. Darwin and other English thinkers. 1911.
Leighton, G. R. Huxley. 1912.

Huxley memorial lectures. Birmingham 1914.
Huxley, L. Huxley. 1920.
Gissing, G. R. Autobiographical notes, with comments on Tennyson and Huxley. 1930.
Huxley, L. Carlyle and Huxley: early influences. Cornhill Mag Mar 1932.
Huxley, L. An American student in Huxley's laboratory. Cornhill Mag June 1934.
Huxley, J. (ed). Huxley's Diary of the voyage of HMS Rattlesnake. 1935.
The Huxley papers: a descriptive catalogue. 1946.
Armytage, W. H. G. Arnold and Huxley: some new letters 1870–80. RES n.s. 4 1953.

Sir Henry Jones 1852–1922

§1

Morality as freedom. 1888.
Browning as a philosophical and religious teacher. Glasgow 1891, 1899.
Is the order of nature opposed to the moral life? Glasgow 1894.
A critical account of the philosophy of Lotze. Glasgow 1895.
The immortality of the soul in the poems of Tennyson and Browning. 1905.
The philosophy of Martineau. 1905.
Social responsibilities. Glasgow 1905.
Tennyson. 1905.
Idealism as a practical creed. 1909.
The working faith of the social reformer, and other essays. 1910.
The immanence of God and the individuality of man. Manchester 1912.
Social powers. Glasgow 1913.
Philosophical landmarks: being a survey of the recent gains and the present problems of reflective thought. Houston 1915.
The idealism of Jesus. 1919.
The obligations and privileges of citizenship: a plea for the study of social science. Houston 1919.
The principles of citizenship. 1919.
The life and philosophy of Edward Caird, with J. H. Muirhead. Glasgow 1921.
A faith that enquires. 1922.
Old memories: autobiography. Ed T. Jones [1923].
Essays on literature and education. Ed H. J. W. Hetherington [1924].

Articles

The nature and aims of philosophy. Mind n.s. 2 1893.
Idealism and epistemology. Mind n.s. 2 1893.
The present attitude of reflective thought towards religion. Hibbert Jnl 1–2 1902–4.
Balfour as sophist. Hibbert Jnl 3 1905.
Divine immanence. Hibbert Jnl 5 1907.
Robert Browning and Elizabeth Browning. CHEL 13 1907.
The ethical demand of the political situation. Hibbert Jnl 8 1910.

§2

Muirhead, J. H. Jones. [1923.]
Muirhead, J. H. Jones. International Jnl of Ethics 33 1923.
Hetherington, H. J. W. Life and letters of Jones. 1924.
Jones, H. M. Jones. 1953.

John Neville Keynes 1852–1949

Studies and exercises in formal logic. 1884, 1887 (enlarged), 1894 (enlarged), 1906 (rewritten and enlarged).
The scope and method of political economy. 1891, 1897 (rev), 1904 (rev), New York 1955, 1963.

Simon Somerville Laurie 1829–1909

§1

On the philosophy of ethics. Edinburgh 1866.
Notes expository and critical on certain British theories of morals. Edinburgh 1868.
Life and educational works of Comenius. Cambridge 1881.
Metaphysica nova et vetusta: a return to dualism. 1884; tr Fr 1901.
Ethica: or the ethics of reason. 1885, 1891 (rev and enlarged); tr Fr 1902.
Institutes of education: introduction to rational psychology. Edinburgh 1892, 1899 (rev), 1909.
Studies in the history of educational opinion from the renaissance. Cambridge 1903.
Synthetica: meditations epistemological and ontological. 2 vols 1906.
Also works on education.

§2

Remacle, G. La philosophie de Laurie. Brussels 1909.

George Henry Lewes 1817–78

Most G. H. Lewes mss are in the George Eliot–George Henry Lewes Collection, Beinecke Rare Book and Ms Lib, Yale Univ, and the Blackwood Papers, Nat Lib of Scotland.

§1

A biographical history of philosophy. 4 vols 1845–6, 1 vol 1857 (rev), 2 vols 1867 (as History of philosophy), 2 vols 1871 (rev), 2 vols 1880, Farnborough 1970 (rptd from 1857 edn); tr Ger 1871–6; Hungarian 1876–8; Rus 1889.
The Spanish drama: Lope de Vega and Calderón. 1846.
Ranthorpe. 1847, rptd Athens OH 1974 ed Barbara Smalley. A novel.
Rose, Blanche and Violet. 3 vols 1848. A novel.
The life of Maximilien Robespierre. 1849, 1899.
The noble heart: a tragedy. 1850.
The game of speculation, 1851; A chain of events, 1852; Taking by storm, 1852. Plays.
Comte's philosophy of the sciences. 1853, 1878, 1883, 1890. Rptd from articles in The Leader 1852.
The lawyers. 1853; A strange history in nine chapters, 1853; Buckstone's adventures with a Polish princess, 1855. Plays.
The life and works of Goethe. 2 vols 1855, 1864 (2nd edn rev), 1873 (abridged), 1875 (3rd edn rev), 1890 (4th edn), 1908, 1959; 2 vols Leipzig 1873, 1882; tr Ger 1857; Rus 1860; Fr 1866.
Sea-side studies at Ilfracombe, Tenby, the Scilly Isles and Jersey. Edinburgh 1858, 1860. Rptd from articles in Blackwood's Mag 1856–7.
The physiology of common life. 2 vols 1859–60. Rptd from articles in Blackwood's Mag 1858. Tr Ger 1860.
Captain Bland. 1860. A play.
Selections from the modern British dramatists. 2 vols Leipzig 1861, 1867 (new edn).
Studies in animal life. 1862. Rptd from articles in Cornhill Mag 1860.
Aristotle: a chapter from the history of science. 1864; tr Ger 1864.
Female characters of Goethe. 1867.
Problems of life and mind. 5 vols 1874[1873]–9.
The foundations of a creed. 2 vols 1874[1873]–5, (in Problems of life and mind, 1st ser); vol 1 tr Rus 1873.
On actors and the art of acting. 1875, 1968 (rptd from articles in the Pall Mall Gazette 1865), New York 1957; tr Ger [1875?].
The physical basis of mind. 1877 (in Problems of life and mind, 2nd ser).
The study of psychology. 2 vols 1879 (in Problems of life and mind, 3rd ser); tr Fr [1879?]; Ital 1907.

Mind as a function of the organism. 1879 (in Problems of life and mind, 3rd ser).

Contributions to periodicals

Collections

The principles of success in literature. Ed A. S. Cook, San Francisco 1885; ed F. N. Scott, Boston 1891; ed T. S. Knowlson, 1898; ed G. Tillotson, 1969 (rptd from articles in the Fortnightly Rev 1865).

Dramatic essays by John Forster and George Henry Lewes. Ed W. Archer and R. W. Lowe 1894 (rptd from articles in The Leader 1850–4).

Literary criticism. Ed A. R. Kaminsky, Lincoln NE 1964.

Versatile Victorian: selected critical writings of G. H. Lewes. Ed R. Ashton, Bristol 1992.

GHL's *literary receipts are pbd for the first time from the ms in the Berg Collection, New York Public Lib, in* The George Eliot letters vol 7, ed G. S. Haight, New Haven 1956, *and identify some anon articles. For his contributions to* Bentley's Misc, Blackwood's Mag, British and Foreign Rev, British Quart Rev, Contemporary Rev, Cornhill Mag, Edinburgh Rev, Foreign Quart Rev, Fortnightly Rev, Fraser's Mag, London Quart Rev, St Pauls Mag, *and* Westminster Rev *see* Wellesley 5 1989. *In addition, the following have been identified as his:*

The coming reformation. Douglas Jerrold's Shilling Mag May–Aug 1847.

François le Champi, by George Sand. Athenaeum May 1848.

The Agamemnon of Aeschylus and the Antigone of Sophocles. Athenaeum May 1848.

Vanity fair, by W. M. Thackeray. Athenaeum Aug 1848.

The apprenticeship of life. Leader Mar–June 1850.

Browning's new poem: Christmas Eve and Easter Day. Leader Apr 1850.

Tennyson's new poem: In memoriam. Leader June 1850.

Elizabeth Barrett Browning: poems. Leader Nov 1850.

Pendennis, by W. M. Thackeray. Leader Dec 1850.

Spontaneous generation. Once a Week July 1850.

Spencer's Social statics. Leader Mar–Apr 1851.

Lyell and Owen on development. Leader Oct 1851.

Herman Melville. Leader Nov 1851.

Spontaneous combustion in Bleak House. Leader Dec 1852–Feb 1853.

Heinrich Heine. Leader Dec 1854.

The tail of a tadpole. Once a Week July 1859.

Magic and science. All the Year Round Mar 1861.

Darwin on domestication and variation. Pall Mall Gazette Feb 1868.

The uniformity of nature. Mind 1, Apr 1876.

What is sensation? Mind 1, Apr 1876.

Consciousness and unconsciousness. Mind 2, Apr 1877.

Letters

The letters of George Henry Lewes. Ed W. Baker, 2 vols Victoria, British Columbia 1995.

§2

Boyd, A. K. H. Recent metaphysical works: Lewes, Maurice, Fleming. Fraser's Mag 56, Dec 1857. Review of Biographical history of philosophy.

Siegfried, H. An G. H. Lewes: eine Epistel. Berlin 1858. Criticism of Life of Goethe.

Biltz, C. Die dramatische Frage der Gegenwart. Potsdam 1859. Criticism of Life of Goethe.

Sidgwick, H. Lewes's History of philosophy. Academy Nov 1871.

Henderson, J. S. Lewes on Schelling and Hegel. Contemporary Rev Sep 1872.

Ribot, T. In his English psychology, 1873.

Harrison, F. Lewes's Problems of life and mind. Fortnightly Rev 16 n.s. July 1874.

Bain, A. Lewes on the postulates of experience. Mind 1 1876.

Carrau, L. La philosophie de Lewes. Revue Philosophique 2 1876.

Hodgson, S. H. In his Philosophy of reflection, 1878.

Hamilton, E. Lewes's doctrine of sensibility. Mind 4 1879.

Trollope, A. George Henry Lewes. Fortnightly Rev 25 n.s. Jan 1879.

Sully, J. Lewes. New Quart Mag n.s. 2 1879.

Read, C. Lewes's posthumous volumes. Mind 6 1881.

The new Phaedo. Blackwood's Mag 135, Feb 1884.

Cross, J. W. In his George Eliot's life, 3 vols 1885–6.

Green, T. H. Spencer and Lewes: their application of the doctrine of evolution to thought. In his Works, ed Nettleship vol 1, 1886.

Grassi Bertazzi, G. Esame critico della filosofia di G. H. Lewes, pt 1. Messina 1906. No more pbd.

Kitchel, A. T. George Lewes and George Eliot: a review of records. New York [1933].

Gary, F. Charlotte Brontë and Lewes. PMLA 51 1936.

Greenhut, M. Lewes and the classical tradition in English criticism. RES 24 1948.

Greenhut, M. Lewes as a critic of the novel. SP 45 1948.

Greenhut, M. Lewes's criticism of the drama. PMLA 64 1949.

Kaminsky, J. The empirical metaphysics of Lewes. JHI 13 1952.

The George Eliot letters. Ed G. S. Haight, 9 vols New Haven 1954–6, 1978.

Haight, G. S. Dickens and Lewes. PMLA 71 1956.

Haight, G. S. In his George Eliot: a biography, Oxford 1968, 1969.

Collins, K. K. G. H. Lewes revised: George Eliot and the moral sense. Victorian Stud 21 1978.

Ashton, R. G. H. Lewes: a life. Oxford 1991. [RA]

James McCosh 1811–94

Bibliographies

Dulles, J. H. McCosh bibliography. [Princeton 1895.]

§1

Method of the divine government physical and moral. 1850, 1856 (rev), 1867 (9th edn), New York 1880.

On the method in which metaphysics should be prosecuted. Belfast 1852.

Typical forms and special ends in creation, with G. Dickie. Edinburgh 1855; 1862.

The imagination: its use and abuse. 1857.

The intuitions of the mind inductively investigated. 1860, 1865 (rev), New York 1869, 1872 (rev).

The association of ideas. Dublin 1861.

The supernatural in relation to the natural. Cambridge 1862.

An examination of Mill's philosophy. 1866, 1871, 1877, New York 1880.

Philosophical papers: 1, Examination of Hamilton's logic; 2, Reply to Mill's 3rd edition [of his Examination of Hamilton's philosophy]; 3, Present state of moral philosophy in Britain in relation to theology. 1868, New York 1869.

The laws of discursive thought. 1870, New York 1881 (rev), 1891 (rev).

Christianity and Positivism. New York 1871, 1875.

Questions of modern thought. Philadelphia 1871. With others.

Scottish philosophy from Hutcheson to Hamilton. 1874, New York 1875, 1880.

Ideas in nature overlooked by Tyndall in his Belfast address. New York 1875.

The development hypothesis: is it sufficient? New York 1876.

The emotions. New York 1880.

The conflicts of the age. New York 1881.

The nature of development. Boston 1881.

Realistic philosophy defended. 2 vols New York 1887. Reprint of 8 papers in Philosophical series, New York and London 1882–5.

Psychology: the cognitive powers. New York 1886, 1891.

Psychology: the motive powers, emotions, conscience, will. New York 1887.
The religious aspect of evolution. New York 1888, New York 1890 (enlarged).
First and fundamental truths: a treatise on metaphysics. New York 1889.
The tests of the various kinds of truth. New York 1889. Enlargement of 1st of Philosophical series, earlier rptd in Realistic philosophy defended, *above*.
The prevailing types of philosophy: can they reach reality logically? New York 1890.
Our moral nature. New York 1892.
The philosophy of reality: should it be favored by America? New York 1894.

Articles

Typical forms: Goethe, Owen, Fairbairn. North Br Rev 15 1851.
Scottish metaphysicians. North Br Rev 27 1857.
Hamilton's metaphysics. Dublin Univ Mag 54 1859.
Intuitionalism and the limits of religious thought. North Br Rev 30 1859.
Mill's reply to his critics. Br & Foreign Evangelical Rev 17 1868; rptd in Amer Presbyterian & Theological Rev n.s. 6 1868.
Recent improvements in formal logic in Britain. Ibid.
Berkeley's philosophy. Presbyterian Quart & Princeton Rev n.s. 2 1873.
Elements involved in emotions. Mind 2 1877.
Contemporary philosophy: historical. Princeton Rev 1 1878.
Contemporary philosophy: mind and brain. Princeton Rev 1 1878.
Final cause. Princeton Rev 3 1879.
Law and design in nature. North Amer Rev 128 1879.
Development and growth of conscience. Princeton Rev 6 1880.
On causation and development. Princeton Rev 7 1881; rptd in Br & Foreign Evangelical Rev 30 1881.
The Concord school of philosophy. Princeton Rev 9 1881.
The Scottish philosophy as contrasted with the German. Princeton Rev 10 1882; rptd in Br & Foreign Evangelical Rev 32 1883.
A study of the mind's imagery, with H. F. Osborn. Princeton Rev 13 1884.
What an American philosophy should be. New Princeton Rev 1 1886.
Realism: its place in the various philosophies. New Princeton Rev 2 1886.
Recent works on Kant. Presbyterian & Reformation Rev 1 1890.
The office of induction in fundamental philosophy. Mind 16 1891.
Reality: what place it should hold in philosophy. In Addresses and proceedings of the International Congress of education of the World's Columbian exposition, New York 1894.
Also works on religion and education.

§2

Sloane, W. A. (ed). Life of McCosh: a record chiefly autobiographical. New York 1896.
Volbeda, S. De intuitieve philosophie van McCosh. Amsterdam [1914].

Sir James Mackintosh 1765–1832

§1

Disputatio physiologica inauguralis de actione musculari. Edinburgh 1787.
Vindiciae gallicae. Dublin 1791, London 1791 (rev), 1837 (new edn).
A discourse on the study of the law of nature and of nations. 1799, 1828, 1835 (enlarged); tr Fr 1830.
Dissertation on the progress of ethical philosophy. Edinburgh 1830; ed W. Whewell, Edinburgh 1836, 1862, 1872.
History of England. 3 vols 1830–2, 10 vols 1850, 2 vols 1853.
[Ripley, G.] Ethical philosophy of Mackintosh. Christian Examiner 13 1833.
History of the revolution in England in 1688, with life by Wallace. 1834.
Inaugural address as Rector of the University of Glasgow; Parting address. In Inaugural addresses, ed J. B. Hay 1839.
Tracts and speeches. 5 pts Edinburgh 1840 (25 copies).
Miscellaneous works. Ed R. J. Mackintosh 3 vols 1846, 1 vol 1851, 3 vols 1854.

§2

Hazlitt, W. In his Spirit of the age, 1825.
Everett, A. H. Mackintosh. North Amer Rev 35 1832.
De Quincey, T. Mackintosh's History of the revolution. Tait's Mag n.s. 1 1834.
[Croker, J. W.] Life of Mackintosh. Quart Rev 54 1835.
Mackintosh, R. J. Memoirs of the life of Mackintosh. 2 vols 1835.
Mill, James. A fragment on Mackintosh. 1835.
Macaulay, T. B. In his Critical and historical essays vol 2, 1843.
Peabody, A. P. Mackintosh. North Amer Rev 66 1848.
Carmichael, R. Notes and observations in reply to Mackintosh. In J. Butler, Fifteen sermons, 1856.
Meteyard, E. In his A group of eminent Englishmen, 1871.
See col 2441.

Sir Henry James Sumner Maine 1822–88

See col 2442.

Henry Longueville Mansel 1820–71

§1

The demons of the wind and other poems. 1838.
Prolegomena logica: an inquiry into the psychological character of logical processes. Oxford 1851, 1860 (enlarged).
Artis logicae rudimenta, from the text of Aldrich, with notes and marginal references. 1852, 1856, 1862.
The limits of demonstrative science: a letter to Whewell. Oxford 1853.
Man's conception of eternity. Oxford 1854.
Psychology, the test of moral and metaphysical philosophy. Oxford 1855.
A lecture on the philosophy of Kant. Oxford 1856.
The limits of religious thought examined. 1858, 1867 (5th edn); tr Danish 1888.
An examination of Maurice's strictures on the Bampton lectures of 1858. 1859.
Metaphysics, or the philosophy of consciousness. Edinburgh 1860, 1866.
A letter to Goldwin Smith concerning his postscript to his lectures on the study of history. Oxford 1861.
A second letter to Smith, with an examination of some passages in his Rational religion. Oxford 1862.
The philosphy of the conditioned. 1866.
Letters, lectures and reviews. Ed H. W. Chandler 1873.
The Gnostic heresies of the 1st and 2nd centuries. Ed J. B. Lightfoot 1875.

Contributions to periodicals

See Wellesley *5 1989.*
Also works on religion.

§2

Maurice, J. F. D. In his Theological essays, 1852.
Whewell, W. A letter to the author of the Prolegomena logica. Oxford 1852.
Calderwood, H. Philosophy of the infinite. Edinburgh 1854.
Maurice, J. F. D. What is revelation? 1859.

Maurice, J. F. D. Sequel to the inquiry, What is revelation? 1860.
McCosh, J. In his Intuitions of the mind, 1860.
Young, J. In his Province of reason, 1860.
Smith, G. In his Rational religion, Oxford 1861.
Spencer, H. In his First principles, 1862.
Jones, J. H. Know the truth. New York 1865.
Mill, J. S. Examination of Sir William Hamilton's philosophy. 1865 (2nd edn).
Deuchar, R. Review of Mill's Examination of Hamilton. Edinburgh 1865.
Bolton, M. P. W. Examination of the principles of the Scoto-Oxonian philosophy. 1869.
Green, T. H. In his Works vol 2, 1886.
Burgon, J. W. In his Lives of twelve good men, 2 vols 1888–9.
Martineau, J. In his Essays, reviews and addresses vol 3, 1891.

Harriet Martineau 1802–76

See col 1344.

James Martineau 1805–1900

§1

The rationale of religious inquiry. 1836, 1844, 1845, 1853, [1908] (as What is Christianity?).
The Christian view of moral evil. 1839.
Introductory lecture on mental and moral philosophy. 1841.
Endeavours after the Christian life. 2 vols 1843–7, 1 vol 1881 (6th edn); ed J. E. Carpenter 1907.
Miscellanies. Ed T. S. King, Boston 1852.
A plea for philosophic studies. 1854.
Essays philosophical and theological. Boston 1866, 2 vols 1868, New York 1879.
Is there any axiom of causality? Contemporary Rev Aug 1870.
The place of mind in nature, and intuition in man. 1872.
Religion as affected by modern materialism. 1874; tr Ger 1878.
Modern materialism in its relations to religion and theology. 1876, New York 1877.
The supposed conflict between efficient and final causation. 1877.
Ideal substitutes for God considered. 1878, 1879 (3rd edn).
The relation between ethics and religion. 1881.
A study of Spinoza. 1882, 1883 (rev).
Types of ethical theory. 2 vols Oxford 1885, 1886, 1889, 1891 (enlarged), 1898.
A study of religion, its sources and contents. 2 vols 1888, 1889 (rev), 1900.
Essays, reviews and addresses. 4 vols 1890–1.
National duties, and other sermons and addresses. Ed G. and E. Martineau 1903.
Also specifically religious works; see col 2673.

§2

Tyndall, J. Materialism and its opponents. Fortnightly Rev Nov 1875.
Sidgwick, H. Martineau's defence of types of ethical theory. Mind 11 1886.
Dyde, B. W. A basis for ethics. Mind 13 1888.
Dyde, B. W. Martineau's idiopsychological ethics. Jnl of Speculative Philosophy 22 1888.
Rashdall, H. Martineau and the theory of vocation. Mind 13 1888.
Moore, A. L. Science and faith. 1889.
Stephens, H. A complete analysis of Martineau's Type of ethical theory. [1890.]
Spencer, H. Martineau on evolution. In his Essays, 1891.
Hertz, J. H. The ethical system of Martineau. New York 1894.
Wilkinson, J. J. Martineau's Ethik. Leipzig 1899.
Jackson, A. W. Martineau: a biography and study. 1900.
Mellone, S. H. Martineau as an ethical teacher. International Jnl of Ethics 10 1900.
Knight, W. A. Inter amicos: letters between Martineau and Knight. 1901.
Drummond, J. and C. B. Upton. Life and letters of Martineau. 2 vols 1902.
Mellone, S. H. In his Leaders of religious thought in the nineteenth century, 1902.
Sidgwick, H. Lectures on the ethics of Green, Spencer and Martineau. 1902.
Crauford, A. H. G. Recollections of Martineau. 1903.
Seth, A. Martineau's philosophy. Hibbert Jnl 1 1903. Reply by G. Galloway, ibid.
Watson, J. Martineau: a saint of theism. Hibbert Jnl 1 1903.
Carpenter, J. E. Martineau: theologian and teacher. 1905.
Jones, H. The philosophy of Martineau in relation to the Idealism of the present day. 1905.
Upton, C. B. Martineau's philosophy. 1905.
Walker, L. J. Martineau and the humanists. Mind n.s. 17 1908. Replies by F. C. S. Schiller and Walker, n.s. 18 1909.
Cadman, S. P. In his Charles Darwin and other English thinkers, with reference to their religious and ethical value, [1911].
Mukerji, N. C. Martineau on the object and mode of moral judgment. International Jnl of Ethics 24 1913.

John Frederick Denison Maurice 1805–72

See col 2240.

James Mill 1773–1836

Mill's Common place books, *4 vols, are in the London Library. The Mill-Taylor Collection in the British Library of Political and Economic Science London School of Economics contains much material concerning James as well as John Stuart Mill. The BL holds mss collections of Grote, Napier and Place. Other material can be found in the Sir James Stuart mss collection in the National Library of Scotland as well as in the Mill Collection at Somerville College Oxford. There is a small collection of letters in the Horton Papers Central County Library Derby.*

Bibliography

Fenn, R. Concise list of the works of James Mill. In his James Mill's political thought, New York and London 1987.

Selections

Selected economic writings. Ed D. Winch, Edinburgh 1966. Selected bibliography appended.
Political writings. Ed T. Ball, Cambridge 1992.

§1

Outline of the course of lectures. Glasgow 1802, 1804, 1806, 1828.
An essay on the impolicy of a bounty on the exportation of grain; and on the principle which ought to regulate the commerce of grain. 1804.
Commerce defended: an answer to the arguments by which Mr Spence, Mr Cobbett, and others, have attempted to prove that commerce is not a source of national wealth. 1807, 1808; New York 1966; Edinburgh 1966. Tr Jap 1959.
Schools for all, not schools for churchmen only. 1812.
Proposals for establishing in the metropolis a day school for the application of the methods of Bell, Lancaster and others to the higher branches of education. 1815. Written with F. Place.
History of British India. 3 vols 1817, 1820, 6 vols 1826, 9 vols 1840–8 (with notes and continuation by H. H. Wilson), 1856, 10 vols 1858, 1872; 4 vols New York 1968. Tr Ger 1839–40.
An account of the maison de force at Ghent. 1817, rptd from Philanthropist 25, 1817.

Elements of political economy. 1821, 1824 (2nd edn rev and enlarged), 1826 (rev and enlarged), 1844, New York 1963, Edinburgh 1966. Tr Fr 1823, Ger 1824, 1826, 1921, Sp 1827, 1831, Ital 1830, 1844, 1854, Jap 1923, 1940, 1948.
An essay on government. 1821, Cambridge 1937, Indianapolis IN 1835, New York 1955. Tr Ital 1848 (see Essays on government etc. below).
Statement of the question of parliamentary reform. 1821.
Essays on government jurisprudence, liberty of the press, prisons and prison discipline, colonies, 1820 (separately issued), law of nations and education. [1825], [1828], rptd from 1824 suppl to 4th, 5th, 6th edns of Encyclopaedia Britannica.
Analysis of the phenomena of the human mind. 2 vols 1829; ed J. S. Mill 1869; 1878, New York 1967, rptd with notes ed J. M. Robson, Toronto 1989. In Collected works of J. S. Mill vol 31.
On the ballot: from the Westministe Review, for July 1830. 1830.
A fragment on Mackintosh. 1835, 1870.
Objections to the ballot answered. 1837.
The principles of toleration. 1837, New York 1971, rptd from Westminster Rev 6, 1826.
Extract from Mill's History on the double government; and observations given before the parliamentary committees in 1852, by John Sullivan. [1853]. From History of British India 4th edn.

Contributions to periodicals

Fenn (Bibliography, *above*) *lists approximately 600 articles from* St James's Chron, Literary Jnl, Eclectic Rev, Edinburgh Rev, Annual Rev and History of Lit, Monthly Rev, Philanthropist, Br Rev, Westminster Rev, Parliamentary History and Rev, London Rev *and* London and Westminster Rev.

Letters

There is no collected correspondence. Letters and lengthy excerpts from letters can be found in the following.

Bentham, J. The works of Jeremy Bentham. Ed J. Bowring vol 11 1843.
Constable, A. Archibald Constable and his literary correspondents. Ed T. Constable vol 2 Edinburgh 1873.
Napier, M. Selection from the correspondence of the late Macvey Napier. Ed M. Napier 1879.
Holland, M. J. Life and letters of Zachary Macaulay. 1900.
Wallas, G. The life of Francis Place. 1925.
Robertson, W. S. The life of Miranda. 1929.
Burr, A. The private journals of Aaron Burr. Ed M. L. Davis vol 2 New York 1938.
Miranda, F. Archivo del General Miranda. Vols 22–3 Havana 1950.
Ricardo, D. The works and correspondence of David Ricardo. Ed P. Saffra, Cambridge 1952.
Mill, J. S. John Mill's boyhood visit to France. Ed A. J. Mill, Toronto 1960.
Hamburger, J. James Mill on universal suffrage and the middle class. Jnl of Politics 24, 1962.
Mill, J. S. The earlier letters of John Stuart Mill. Ed F. Mineka vol 1 Toronto 1963.
Ghosh, R. N. The colonization controversy: Wilmot-Horton and the classical economists. Economica 31, 1964.
Robson, J. M. J. S. Mill and Bentham, with some observations on James Mill. In Essays in English literature from the Renaissance to the Victorian age, ed M. MacLure and F. W. Watt, Toronto 1964.
Bentinck, W. C. The correspondence of Lord William Cavendish Bentinck. Ed C. H. Phillips vol 1 Oxford 1977.
Bentham, J. The correspondence of Jeremy Bentham. Ed S. Conway vols 8–9 Oxford 1988–9.

Translation

Villers, C. Essay on the spirit and influence of the reformation of Luther ... with a sketch of the history of the church from its founder to the reformation. Introd and notes. 1805; abridged W. Marsh 1836.

§2

Spence, W. Agriculture the source of the wealth of Britain: a reply to the objections urged by Mill. 1808.
Thompson, W. Appeal of one half the human race: women: against the pretensions of the other half: men: to retain them in political, and thence in civil and domestic, slavery in reply to a paragraph of Mr Mill's celebrated 'Article on government'. 1825, rptd New York 1970, with introd J. Lee Castletownroche 1975.
Thompson, T. P. An exposition of the fallacies on rent, tithes etc. in the form of a review of Mill's Elements. 1826, 1832; (as The true theory of rent) 1826, 1830, 1832. Rptd from Pamphleteer 27, 1823.
Smith, L. Remarks upon An essay on government by Mill. 1827.
Maurice, F. D. James Mill: sketches and contemporary authors, xiii. Athenaeum 34, 1828, rptd in his Sketches of contemporary authors, 1828; ed A. J. Hartley, Hamden CT 1970.
Bentham, J. and T. P. Thompson. Greatest happiness. Westminster Rev 11–12, 1829, rptd in Thompson's Exercises [c. 1845]. Reply to Macaulay's review (*below*) of Essay on government almost entirely by Thompson; *see* Wellesley vol 3.
Macaulay, T. B. Mill's Essay on government: utilitarian logic and politics. Edinburgh Rev 49 1829.
Macaulay, T. B. Bentham's defence of Mill: utilitarian system of philosophy. Edinburgh Rev 49 1829.
Macaulay, T. B. Utilitarian theory of government, and the 'greatest happiness principle'. Edinburgh Rev 50 1829.
Cotterill, C. F. An examination of the doctrines of value, as set forth by Smith, Ricardo, McCulloch and Mill. 1831.
Mill, J. S. In E. L. Bulwer, England and the English vol 2, 1833 (altered by Bulwer).
Mill, J. S. Letter to the editor. Edinburgh Rev 79 1844.
Rumbold, E. A. A vindication of the character and administration of Rumbold from the misrepresentations of Mill. 1868.
Ribot, T. A. In his La psychologie anglaise, Paris 1870; tr 1873, New York 1874.
Bisset, A. In his Essays on historical truth, 1871.
Mill, J. S. In his Autobiography, 1873, New York 1924; early draft of J. S. Mill's Autobiography, ed J. Stillinger, Urbana IL 1961; Collected works of John Stuart Mill, vol 1 Autobiography and literary essays, ed J. M. Robson and J. Stillinger. Toronto 1981.
Bower, G. S. Hartley and Mill. 1881.
Bain, A. James Mill: a biography. 1882.
Morley, J. Life of Mill. Fortnightly Rev ns 31, 1882. Review of Bain.
Quesnel, L. Les deux Mill. Bibliothèque Universelle 13 1882.
Stuart-Glennie, J. S. James and John Stuart Mill. Macmillan's Mag 45 1882.
McCosh, J. In his Scottish philosophy, New York 1885.
Marion, H. Mill d'après les recherches de Bain. Revue Philosophique 16 1886.
Stephen, L. In his English utilitarians, 3 vols 1900.
Halévy, E. In his La formation du radicalisme philosophique, 2 vols Paris 1901–4; tr 1928, 1952.
Müller, K. von E. James Mill und die historische Methode. Berne 1908.
Davidson, W. L. In his Political thought in England: the utilitarians from Bentham to J. S. Mill, 1915. [ML]

John Stuart Mill 1806–73

The principal mss resources are to be found in the Mill-Taylor Collection at the British Library of Political and Economic Science, London School of Economics. There is also an important collection at Somerville College Oxford. Extensive collection of letters can be found in the Mill-Taylor Collection and at Johns Hopkins University Baltimore MD, the London School of Economics, the Nat Lib of Scotland, in the Osborn Collection Yale University, the Brotherton Collection Leeds, University College London, the India Office Library and at Kokugakuin University Osaka. The headnotes and textual introductions in Collected works *provide information regarding mss locations as well as extensive textual data.*

Bibliographies

Primary

Macminn, N., J. R. Hinds and J. M. McCrimmon. Bibliography of the published writings of John Stuart Mill. Evanston IL 1945; New York 1970.

Secondary

Amano, K. Vol 3 pt 4 of his Bibliography of the classical economists. Tokyo 1964.

Hascall, D. and J. M. Robson. Bibliography of writings on Mill. Mill News Letter, 1965–70.

Goehlert, R. John Stuart Mill: a bibliography. Monticello IL 1982.

Laine, M. Bibliography of works on John Stuart Mill. Toronto 1982.

Collections

Gesämmelte werke. 12 vols Leipzig 1869–80.

Collected works. Ed F. E. L. Priestley, F. E. Mineka, J. M. Robson et al 32 vols plus 1 vol indexes Toronto 1965–91. Vol 1 Autobiography and literary essays, 1981; vols 2–3 Principles of political economy, 1965; vols 4–5 Essays on economics and society, 1967; vol 6 Essays on England and the empire, 1982; vols 7–8 A system of logic: ratiocinative and inductive, 1973; vol 9 An examination of Sir William Hamilton's philosophy, 1979; vol 10 Essays on ethics, religion and society, 1969; vol 11 Essays on philosophy and the classics, 1978; vols 12–13 The earlier letters, 1812–1848, 1963; vols 14–17 The later letters, 1848–1873, 1972; vols 18–19 Essays on politics and society, 1977; vol 20 Essays on French history and historians, 1985; vol 21 Essays on equality, law and education, 1984; vols 22–5 Newspaper writings, 1986; vols 26–7 Journals and debating speeches, 1988; vols 28–9 Public and parliamentary speeches, 1988; vol 30 Writings on India, 1990; vol 31 Miscellaneous writings, 1989; vol 32 Additional letters, 1991; vol 33 Indexes, 1991.

Selections

Chapters and speeches on the Irish land question. 1870. Rptd from Principles of political economy.

Views on the subject of a double standard and subsidiary coins. Philadelphia 1876. Bk III ch x of Principles of political economy.

Early essays. Ed J. W. M. Gibbs 1897 (Bohn's Standard Lib).

Utilitarianism, On liberty, and Representative government. Introd A. D. Lindsay 1910, rptd New York 1954.

On liberty, Representative government, The subjection of women. Introd M. G. Fawcett 1912.

§1

With the exception of the People's edns, edns lacking textual authority are not listed.

The history of Rome. Ed J. M. Robson and J. Stillinger, Toronto 1981. Childhood exercise. In Collected works vol 1.

Ode to Diana. Ed J. M. Robson and Jack Stillinger, Toronto 1981. Poem. In Collected works vol 1.

Jeremy Bentham. Rationale of judicial evidence. 5 vols 1827. Ed Mill, with notes and addns, ed J. M. Robson, Toronto 1989. In Collected works vol 31.

A system of logic, ratiocinative and inductive. 2 vols 1843, 1846 (rev, significant alterations also pbd separately as Two chapters of A system of logic), 1851 (rev), 1856 (rev), 1862 (rev), 1865 (rev), 1868 (rev), 1872 (rev), 1884 (People's edn), ed. J. M. Robson, Toronto 1973. Collected works vols 7–8. Tr Ger 1849, 1852, 1862–3, 1868, 1872–3, 1877, 1884–6, Rus 1865–7, Fr 1866, 1880, 1889, 1896, 1897 (bk 6), Hungarian 1874–7, Sp 1897, Jap 1949–59, Ital 1957 (bks 2–3).
REVIEWS: A. Bain Westminster Rev 39, 1843; (W. H. Smith) Blackwood's Mag 54, 1843; Br Critic 4th ser 34, 1843; U.S. Mag and Democratic Rev ns 15, 1844; (J. Brazer) N. Amer Rev 61, 1845; [W. Bagehot] Prospective Rev 6, 1850; Sat Rev 2, 1856.

Essays on some unsettled questions of political economy. 1844, 1874, 1877, 1948 (photo facs of 1844), ed J. M. Robson, Toronto 1967. In Collected works vol 4. Tr Ital 1878, Jap 1936.
REVIEW: Spectator 17, 1844.

Principles of political economy. 2 vols 1848, 1849 (rev), 1852 (rev), 1857 (rev), 1862 (rev), 1865 (rev), 1865 (People's edn), 1871 (rev); ed W. J. Ashley 1909, ed J. M. Robson, Toronto 1965. Collected works vols 2–3. Tr Ital 1851, 1953, Ger 1852, 1864, 1869–81, 1881–5, 1913–21, 1924, Fr 1854, 1861, 1873, Rus 1860, 1865, 1874, 1875, 1897, Du 1876, Jap 1875, 1939, 1949, 1955, Sp 1943.
REVIEWS: (W. H. Smith) Blackwood's Mag 64, 1848; (N. W. Senior) Edinburgh Rev 88, 1848; Fraser's Mag 38, 1848; N. Amer Rev 67, 1848. [W. Bagehot] Prospective Rev 4, 1848; (G. Grote) Spectator 21, 1848; [W. E. Hickson] Westminster Rev 49, 1848; (A. De Vere) Edinburgh Rev 91, 1850; (G. Holmes) Southern Quart Rev 1, 1856.

Remarks on Mr Fitzroy's Bill. 1853 (pamphlet with Harriet Taylor Mill), ed J. M. Robson, Toronto 1984. In Collected works vol 21.

Report to the General Court of Proprietors drawing attention to the two bills now before Parliament relating to the government of India. 1858. In Collected works vol 30.

On liberty. 1859, 1859, 1864, 1865 (People's edn), 1869, ed J. M. Robson, Toronto 1977. In Collected works vol 18. Tr Du 1859, 1870, Fr 1860, 1861, 1864 (introd Dupont-White), 1877, 1925, Ger 1860, 1869, 1896, 1928, 1945, 1948, Cz 1861, Rus 1861, 1864, 1866–9, 1882, Ital 1865, 1890, 1895, 1921, 1924, 1946, Jap 1871, 1877, 1895, 1914, 1925, 1928, 1929, 1933, 1946, 1948, 1950, 1952, Danish 1875, Icelandic 1886, Swed 1881, 1889, 1917, 1948, Sp 1890, 1965, Finnish 1891, Chinese 1905, Yiddish 1909, Serbo-Croat 1918, 1921, Hebrew 1946, Norwegian 1947, Persian 1959.
REVIEWS: Br Quart 31, 1859; Dublin Univ Mag 54, 1859; [R. H. Hutton] Nat Rev 8, 1859; (P. L. Lavrov) Ocherk Teorii Lichnossti: Otechestvennyye Zapisti 11–12, 1859; Sat Rev 7, 1859; Universal Rev 1, 1859; [R. W. Church: Mill] Bentley's Quart Rev 2, 1860; (M. L. Milhailov) Sovremennik 11, 1860.

Thoughts on parliamentary reform. 1859 (pamph), 1859 (with addns), 1867 (in Dissertations and discussions vol 3), ed J. M. Robson, Toronto 1977. In Collected works vol 19.

Dissertations and discussions. 2 vols 1859, 3 vols 1867, 4 vols 1875, 5 vols Boston 1864–8, New York 1874–82. Tr Rus 1864–5, Ger 1874.
REVIEWS: Sat Rev 8, 1859; [R. H. Hutton] Economist 18, 1860.

Considerations on representative government. 1861, 1861 (rev), 1865, 1865 (People's edn), ed J. M. Robson, Toronto 1977. In Collected works vol 19. Tr Fr 1862, 1865 (introd Dupont-White), 1877 (introd Dupont-White), Ger 1862, 1873, Rus 1863 1866, Ital 1865, 1886, 1946, Sp 1865, 1878, 1965, Danish 1876, Jap 1871, 1890, 1921, 1955.
REVIEWS: [W. Bagehot] Economist 19, 1861, rptd in his Collected works, 1965–; (R. Cecil) Quart Rev 110, 1861; (H. Fawcett) Macmillan's Mag 4, 1861; (T. Hare) Fortnightly Rev 4, 1861; [R. H. Hutton] Economist 19, 1861; [A. Johnson] Westminster Rev ns 20, 1861; (J. Lorimer) N. Br Rev 35, 1861; Sat Rev 11, 1861; Spectator 34, 1861; (A. P. Peabody) N. Amer Rev 95, 1862, rptd in True and false democracy, Boston 1862.

Utilitarianism. 1863, 1864 (rev), 1867 (rev), 1871 (rev), ed J. M. Robson, Toronto 1969. In Collected works vol 10. Tr Ital 1866, 1946, Rus 1866–9, 1882, Jap 1877, 1880, 1923, 1928, 1935, 1946, 1954, Fr 1883, 1889, 1903, 1906, 1919, 1922, 1925, 1964, Sp 1891, 1945, 1955, Hebrew 1933, Turkish 1946, Polish 1959.
REVIEWS: [R. H. Hutton] Spectator 36, 1863; Westminster Rev ns 24, 1863.

Auguste Comte and Positivism. 1865, 1866 (rev), ed J. M. Robson,

Toronto 1969. In Collected works vol 10. Tr Fr 1868, 1879, 1885, 1890, 1893, 1898, 1903, Ger 1871, 1874, Ital 1903, Jap 1923.
REVIEWS: (G. H. Lewes) Fortnightly Rev 3, 1866; (W. Whewell) Macmillan's Mag 13, 1866; (C. Wright) Nation 2, 1866; (J. Fiske) N. Amer Rev 102, 1866, rptd in his Darwinism and other essays, Boston and New York 1885; (P. L. Lavrov) Sovremennoye Obozreniye 5, 1868.

An examination of Hamilton's philosophy. 1865, 1865 (rev), 1867 (rev), 1872 (rev), ed J. M. Robson, Toronto 1979. In Collected works vol 9. Tr Fr 1869, Ger 1908.
REVIEWS: [O. B. Frothingham] Christian Examiner 79, 1865; Eclectic Rev 9, 1865; (C. Wright) Nation 1, 1865; N. Amer Rev 103, 1866; [A. C. Fraser] N. Br Rev ns 4, 1865; (M. Pattison) Reader 5, 1865; [R. H. Hutton] Spectator 38, 1865; [H. B. Wilson] Westminster Rev ns 28, 1865; (H. B. Smith) Amer Presbyterian and Theological Rev 1, 1866; (J. Cunningham) Edinburgh Rev 124, 1866; (G. H. Emerson) Universalist Quart Rev 23, 1866.

Inaugural address delivered to the University of St Andrews. 1867, 1867; ed J. M. Robson, Toronto 1984. In Collected works vol 21. Tr Ger 1859, Hungarian 1874, Jap 1885, 1948.
REVIEWS: [W. G. Ward] Dublin Rev ns 8, 1867; (J. Morley), Fortnightly Rev 7, 1867; (E. P. Evans) N. Amer Rev 105, 1867; Sat Rev 23, 1867; [H. B. Wilson] Westminster Rev ns 31, 1867.

England and Ireland. 1868 (pamph, 5 edns), ed J. M. Robson, Toronto 1982. In Collected works vol 6.
REVIEWS: Sat Rev 25, 1868; The Times, 20 Feb 1868.

James Mill, Analysis of the phenomena of the human mind. 2 vols 1869 (2nd edn). Ed Mill, with notes; ed J. M. Robson, Toronto 1989. In Collected works vol 31.

The subjection of women. 1869, 1869, 1870, ed J. M. Robson, Toronto 1984. In Collected works vol 21. Tr Fr 1869, 1876, Ger 1869, 1872, 1880, 1891, Ital 1870, 1883, 1926, Rus 1869, 1870, 1871, 1896, 1906, Swedish 1869, Sp 1892, 1965, Jap 1878, 1921, 1923, 1928, 1929, 1948, 1950, 1957, 1959, Icelandic 1900.
REVIEWS: [A. Mozley] Blackwood's Mag 106, 1869; [M. Oliphant] Edinburgh Rev 130, 1869; (E. L. Godkin) Nation, 1869; ('J. R.') Nat Reformer 24, 1869; Sat Rev 27, 1869; (F. P. Cobbe) Theological Rev 6, 1869; [W. B. Rands] (Matthew Browne (pseud)) Contemporary Rev 14, 1870; Lippincott's 5, 1870; (A. D. Mayo) Monthly Rev and Religious Mag 43, 1870; [S. Amos] Westminster Rev 93, 1870.

Autobiography. 1873, 1873, 1874, 1874, 1879, 1908; ed. H. J. Laski, Oxford 1924 (with appendix of speeches) (WC); ed R. Howson, New York 1924 (from holograph ms); London 1926, 1944, 1957, 1960; ed J. M. Robson and J. Stillinger, Toronto 1988. In Collected works vol 1. Tr Danish 1874, Fr 1874, 1885, 1894, 1907, Ger 1874, Rus 1874, 1896, Sp 1892, 1939, Ital 2 vols 1921, Jap 1922, 1928, 1948, 1958, Polish 1931, 1948, Chinese nd. Early draft ed. J. Stillinger, Urbana 1961.
REVIEWS: Daily News, 18 Oct 1873; [A. Hayward] The Times, 10 Nov 1873; (A. Hayward) Fraser's Mag ns 8, 1873 and The Times 4, 10 Nov 1873; [W. E. Ellis?] The Times 4, 10 November 1873; [H. Cowell] Blackwood's Mag 114, 1873; La Critique Philosophique 2, 1873; [R. H. Hutton] Spectator 46, 1873; (W. R. Browne) Christian Evidence Jnl, 1874; Br Quart Rev 59, 1874; (J. M. Capes) Contemporary Rev 23, 1874; (A. L. Chapin) New Englander 33, 1874; Christian Observer 74, 1874; (A. V. Dicey) Nation 18, 1874; (E. E. Hale) Old & New 9, 1874; (H. Lincoln) Baptist Quart 1, 1874; (J. Morley) Fortnightly Rev ns 15, 1874, rptd in his Critical miscellanies, 1877; New England 33, 1874; [F. T. Palgrave] Quart Rev 136, 1874; (T. S. Perry) N. Amer Rev 118, 1874; Popular Science Monthly 4, 1874; (H. Reeve) Edinburgh Rev 139, 1874; Sat Rev 36, 1873, rptd Eclectic Mag ns 19, 1874; Scribner's Monthly 7, 1874; (J. L. Spalding) Catholic World 18, 1874; ('L. T.') Southern Mag 14, 1874; (J. Rickaby) Month ns 4, 5 1875.

Three essays on religion. Ed H. Taylor 1874, 1874, 1885, 1904, 1923; ed J. M. Robson, Toronto 1969. In Collected works vol 10. Tr Fr 1875, 1884, Ger 1875, Du 1875, Jap 1878, 1927, Swedish [1883], Ital 1946, 1958.
REVIEWS: Daily Free Press, 20 Oct 1874; Daily Telegraph 20, 22 Oct 1874; Morning Post, 20 Oct 1874 (rptd from Manchester Guardian), 22 Oct 1874; Dublin Morning Mail, 21 Oct 1874; The Times, 21 Oct 1874; Pall Mall Gazette 22, 29 Oct 1874; (J. Morley) Fortnightly Rev ns 16, 1874; ns 17, 1875, rptd in his Critical miscellanies, 1877; [R. H. Hutton] Spectator 47, 1874; (J. E. Cabot) N. Amer Rev 120, 1875; (A. V. Dicey)Nation 20, 1875; [W. H. Ward] Dublin Rev ns 24, 1875; (H. Reeve) Edinburgh Rev 141, 1875; (J. Rickaby) Month ns 4, 1875; Westminster Rev ns 47, 1875.

Socialism. Chicago 1879, rptd from Fortnightly Rev, 1879, ed. H. Taylor; ed. W. D. Porter, New York 1891. ed J. M. Robson, Toronto 1967. In Collected works vol 5. Tr Fr 1879; Ger 1880; Ital 1880, 1899.

The spirit of the age. Ed F. A. von Hayek, Chicago 1942.

Four dialogues of Plato. Ed R. Borchard 1946.

Prefaces to liberty. Ed B. Wishy, Boston 1959.

Contributions to periodicals

Mill wrote some 500 articles for newspapers which have been collected in Newspaper writings, ed J. M. and A. Robson, Toronto 1986 (Collected works vols 22–5). *His contributions to periodicals (quarterly, monthly, weekly) have been collected in the appropriate volumes of* Collected works.

Speeches

Mill's speeches have been reprinted in Journals and debating speeches, ed J. M. Robson, *and* Public and parliamentary speeches, ed J. M. Robson introd B. L. Kinzer (Collected works vols 26–9).

Letters, journals etc

Correspondence between John Stuart Mill and the Metropolitan Sanitary Association in public agency or trading companies. Memorials on sanitary reform, and on the economical and administrative principles of water supply for the metropolis. London 1851.

The letters of John Stuart Mill. Ed H. S. R. Elliot with note on Mill's private life by M. Taylor 2 vols 1910.

Bonar, J. John Stuart Mill and the protection of infant industries. 1911. Selection of letters introd by Bonar with preface by Hugh Elliot.

The earlier letters, 1812–1848. Ed F. E. Mineka 2 vols Toronto 1963. Collected works vols 14–17.

The later letters. Ed F. E. Mineka and D. N. Lindley 4 vols Toronto 1972. Collected works vols 14–17.

Journals and debating speeches. Ed J. M. Robson, Toronto 1988. Collected works vols 26–7.

Additional letters. Ed M. Filipiuk, M. Laine and J. M. Robson, Toronto 1991. Collected works vol 32.

List of letters to Mill. Collected works vol 32 appendix C.

John Mill's boyhood visit to France: being a journal and notebook written by John Stuart Mill in France, 1820–21. Ed A. J. Mill, Toronto 1960, rptd as Journal and notebook of a year in France, 1820–1821; ed J. M. Robson, Toronto 1988. In Collected works vol 26.

§2

[Empson, W.]. Bentham's Rationale of evidence. Edinburgh Rev 48, 1828. Critical of Mill's editorship.

Torrens, R. The budget, on commercial and colonial policy. With an introduction applying Mill's deductive method. 1844.

Hill, T. Fundamental laws of reasoning. Christian Examiner 40 (4th ser 5), 1846.

Disraeli on Mill. Spectator 19, 1846.

Opinions on the admission of dissenters and on university reform: Lord Palmerston, Lord John Russell, Sir William Hamilton, J. S. Mill, and others. [London?] 1847.

[Ellis, W.?] Causes of poverty. Westminster Rev 50, 1848. Signed W. E.
Senior, N. W. Relief of Irish distress in 1847 and 1848. Edinburgh Rev 89, 1848, rptd in his Journals, conversations and essays relating to Ireland, 1868.
McMahon, P. T. Tillage – waste lands – fixity of tenure. Dublin Rev 25, 1848.
[Scrope, G. P.]. Irish clearances, and improvement of waste lands. Westminster Rev 50, 1848.
[Hickson, W. E.]. Malthus. Westminster Rev 52, 1849.
Whewell, W. Of induction, with especial reference to Mr J. Stuart Mill's System of logic. 1849, rptd rev in his On the philosophy of discovery, 1860.
[Hutton, R. H.]. Mill and Whewell on the logic of induction. Prospective Rev 6, 1850.
Examination of Mill's philosophy of necessary truth and of causation. New Englander 8, 1850.
Ballantyne, J. R. On the philosophy of induction. Allahabad 1851.
Mansel, H. L. Appendix D to his Prolegomena logica. 1851.
Ballantyne, J. R. The method of induction. Mirzapore 1852.
Gouraud, C. Tendences de l'économie politique en France et en Angleterre. Revue des Deux Mondes ns 14, 1852.
Senior, N. W. Four introductory lectures on political economy. 1852.
Mansel, H. L. The limits of demonstrative science considered: a letter to the Rev. William Whewell. 12 April 1853. In his Letters, lectures and reviews, 1873.
Bowen, F. J. S. Mill on the theory of causation. N. Amer Rev 78, 1854.
[Jennings, W.]. Tendencies of modern logic. Dublin Rev 36, 1854.
Jennings, R. Natural elements of political economy. 1855.
Reybaud, L. John Stuart Mill et l'économie politique en Angleterre. Revue des Deux Mondes 10, 1855.
Fitzhugh, G. Slavery and political economy. DeBow's Rev 21, 1856.
Lyall, A. Mill's system of logic. In his Agonistes: or philosophical strictures, 1856.
Torrens, R. The principles and practical operation of Sir Robert Peel's bill of 1844. 1848, 1857 (2nd edn rev and enlarged).
[Abbot, T. K.]. Logic of induction – Mill. N. Br Rev 28, 1858.
[Arnold, T. jr]. Mill on liberty. Rambler os 25, 1859–60, rptd in Political thought in perspective, ed W. Ebenstein, New York 1957 (signed 'A.' Ebenstein and mistakenly attributed to Lord Acton).
Buckle, H. T. Mill on liberty. Fraser's Mag 59, 1859, rptd in his Essays, New York 1863, and in Miscellaneous and posthumous works, ed H. Taylor vol 1 1872. Tr Rus in Etudy, St Petersburg 1867.
Herzen A. I. 'Dzhon-Styuart Mill' i yevo kniga 'On liberty'. Kolokol, 15 Apr 1859. In his My past and thoughts, 6 vols 1924–27.
[Martineau, J.]. John Stuart Mill. Nat Rev 9, 1859, rptd in his Essays, reviews, and addresses, 2 vols New York 1879.
Rémusat, C. de. De la liberté civile et politique, à propos des ouvrages de MM. Jules Simon et Stuart Mill. Revue des Deux Mondes 22, 1859.
J. S. Mill: Über die Freiheit. Stimmen der Zeit, Nov 1859.
Who is the reformer: John Stuart Mill or John Bright? 1859.
Fitzhugh, G. The English reviews. DeBow's Rev 28, 1860. Critical of On liberty.
Lees, F. R. Law and liberty, with especial relation to the temperance question, the prohibition of liquor traffic, and the objections of J. S. Mill. Leeds 1860.
Lees, F. R. Relations of liberty to the temperance question. 1860.
Ward, W. G. In his On nature and grace, 1860.
J. S. Mill on parliamentary reform. Nat Reformer 1, 1860.
Mr Mill and the ladies. Sat Rev 11, 1860.
Chernyshevesky, N. G. Ocherki iz politicheskoy ekonomii (po Millyu). Sovremenik 6–10, 12 1861, rptd in his Collected works, Geneva 1870 and subsequently. Tr Fr, Brussels [1874?].
Taine, H. A. Mill et son Système de logique. Revue des Deux Mondes 32, 1861. Tr Rus, Vremya 3, 1861.
Mr Mill on double chambers. Spectator 34, 1861.
Baudrillart, H. J. L. J. S. Mill. In his Publicistes modernes, Paris 1862.
[Hutton, R. H.]. John Stuart Mill on the civil war. Spectator 35, 1862.
Whewell, W. Six lectures on political economy. Cambridge 1862.
Kirkman, T. P. On a so-called theory of causation, vide System of logic by J. S. Mill, bk 3 ch 5. Liverpool [1862].
Parker, J. Job's comforters: or scientific sympathy. 1862; 2nd edn 1876 and subsequently.
Reybaud, M. R. L. In his Economistes modernes, Paris 1862.
John Stuart Mills politische Schriften. Preussische Jarhrbücher 10, 1862.
True and false democracy: representation of all, and representation of the majority only. A brief synopsis of recent publications on this subject, by John Stuart Mill and Thomas Hare. Boston 1862.
Cummings, C. A. The later writings of John Stuart Mill. Christian Examiner 74, 1863.
Leslie, T. E. C. Utilitarianism and the common good. Macmillan's Mag 8, 1863.
Napier, J. The miracles: Butler's argument on miracles, explained and defended, with observations on Hume, Baden Powell and Mill. Dublin 1863.
Schérer, E. H. A. In his Études critiques sur la littérature contemporaine, vol 1 Paris 1863; tr as Essays on English literature, New York 1891.
Taine, H. A. In his Histoire de la littérature anglaise, vol 4 Paris 1863–4; tr 2 vols Edinburgh 1871.
Courage in belief. Christian Examiner 74, 1863.
Mr Mill on America. Sat Rev 15, 1863. Comment on letter of Mill's supporting North in the war against slavery.
[Bagehot, W.]. Mr John Stuart Mill on the increase of corruption. Economist 22, 1864, rptd in his Collected works, 6 1965.
Fiske, J. Principles of political economy. N. Amer Rev 98, 1864.
Stebbing, W. Analysis of Mr Mill's System of logic. 1864.
Taine, H. A. Le positivisme anglais: étude sur Stuart Mill. Paris 1864; tr 1870.
[Tennant C.]. Utilitarianism explained and exemplified in moral and political government. 1864.
Utilitarianism and the Saturday Review. Spectator 34, 1864.
Utilitarianism explained and exemplified in moral and political government: being a reply to J. S. Mill's Utilitarianism. 1864. Reviewed anon, Westminster Rev ns 25, 1864.
Antonovich, M. A. Dobrosovestnyye mysliteli i nedbrosovestneyye zhurnalisty. Sovremennik 2, 1865.
Bain, A. A letter to Westerton, chairman of Mill's committee. [1865].
Christie, W. D. Mill for Westminster. Macmillan's Mag 12, 1865.
Conway, M. D. The great Westminster canvass. Harper's Mag 31, 1865.
Dickson, W. M. The absolute equality of all men before the law... with an appendix containing John Stuart Mill's letter on reconstruction, and the correspondence herewith connected. Cincinnati OH 1865.
Deuchar, R. Review of An examination of Hamiltonian philosophy by J. S. Mill, M.P. Including strictures on Dr Mansell and Dr Candlish's modern theology. Edinburgh 1865.
Fothergill, S. Liberty, liquor, licence and prohibition. In answer to the argument of John Stuart Mill in his work On liberty. Swindon [1865].
Godkin, E. L. Aristocratic opinions of democracy. N. Amer Rev 100, 1865. Review essay on Tocqueville and Mill.
Grote, J. In his Exploratio philosophica pt 1, Cambridge 1865.
Guillaume, E. H. Mr John Stuart Mill. Nat Reformer 6, 1865.
[Guy, R. E.]. Calderwood and Mill on Hamilton. Dublin Rev ns 5, 1865. Signed R.E.G.
[Hutton, R. H.]. Mr John Stuart Mill as a politician. Spectator 38, 1865.
'J. P. A.' William Maccall and John Stuart Mill. Nat Reformer 6, 1865.

Lewes, G. H. Public affairs. Fortnightly Rev 6, 1865.
Maccall, W. Mill's refutation of Hamilton. Nat Reformer 6, 1865, rptd in his The newest materialism: sundry papers on the books of Mill, Comte, Bain, Spencer, Atkinson and Feuerbach, 1873.
McCosh, J. Supplement and questions. In D. Stewart's Outlines of moral philosophy, 1865.
Masson, D. Recent British philosophy. Including some comments on Mr Mill's answer to Hamilton. 1865, 1877.
Maurice, F. D. Mr Maurice on the satanic school. Spectator 38, 1865.
Parker, J. John Stuart Mill on liberty: a critique. 1865.
[Plummer, J.]. Remarkable men: members of the new parliament. No 1: John Stuart Mill. Cassel's Illustr Family Paper, 16 Sep 1865.
[Rands, W. B.]. Henry Holbeach (pseud). In his Henry Holbeach: student in life and philosophy: a narrative and discussion, 2 vols 1865.
Schiel, J. Die Methode der inductiven Forschung als die Methode der Naturforschung in getränger Darstellung, hauptsächlich nach J. S. Mill. Braunschweig 1865.
Schoelcher, V. Mr Mill and his clergymen supporters. Nat Reformer 6, 1865.
Spencer, H. Mill versus Hamilton – the test of truth. Fortnightly Rev 1, 1865.
Stephen, J. F. Mr Spencer on Mr Mill. Sat Rev, 12 Aug 1865.
Thayer, J. B. Mill's Dissertations and discussions. N. Amer Rev 100, 1865.
Thirwall, C. The bishop of St David's on Mr Mill's heresy. Spectator 38, 1865. *See also* Record 2, 1865, Spectator 38, 1865, *and* Sanger 1866, *below*.
Beer and bigotry. Nat Reformer 6, 1865.
The forthcoming election in Westminster. Ibid 1865.
John Stuart Mill als Philosoph und Nationalökonom. Unsere Zeit 1, 1865.
John Stuart Mill. Harper's Weekly 9, 1865. Short summary of career complimenting Mill on his election, with portrait.
Mr J. S. Mill and his supporters. Record 2, 14 June 1865.
Mr John Stuart Mill for Westminster. Nat Reformer 6, 1865.
Mr John Stuart Mill on marriage. Public Opinion, 15 July 1865. Substantial reprinting of anon leader in Standard, 10 July 1865.
Mr John Stuart Mill's atheism. Nat Reformer 6, 1865.
Mr Mill. Sat Rev 20, 1865. Comment on Mill's election campaign.
Mr Mill's indictment of Sir William Hamilton. Eclectic Rev 9, 1865.
Mr Mill's plan of reform. Spectator 38, 1865.
Mneniya Boklya o sochineniyakh Millya [Buckle's opinions of Mill's works]. Otechestvennyye Zapiski 1, 2 1865.
Mysli Dzhona-Styuarta Millya o pozitivnoy filosofii Ogyusta Konta [Mill's thoughts on the positive philosophy of Auguste Comte], Otechestvennyye Zapiski 7, 9 1865.
Parliament and reform. Westminster Rev ns 27, 1865. Includes review of Mill's Representative government.
The Record on the Westminster election. Spectator 38, 1865.
Religion and politics. Nat Reformer 6, 1965.
The religious views of Mr Mill – representation of Westminster. Morning Advertiser, 3 June 1865.
The Westminster election. Nat Reformer 6, 1865.
Alexander, P. O. Mill and Carlyle: an examination of Mr John Stuart Mill's doctrine of causation in relation to moral freedom. Edinburgh 1866.
[Atwater, L. H.]. McCosh on J. S. Mill and fundamental truth. Biblical Repertory and Princeton Rev 38, 1866.
Bagehot, W. The House of Commons [pt 4 of The English constitution]. Fortnightly Rev 6, 1866, rptd 1867 and in his Collected works 5, 1965.
Bascom, J. Utilitarianism. Bibliotheca Sacra 23, 1866.
Bolton, M. P. W. Inquisitio philisophica: an examination of the principles of Kant and Hamilton. 1866.
Bridges, J. H. The unity of Comte's life and doctrine: a reply to strictures on Comte's later writings, addressed to John Stuart Mill. 1866.
Cairnes J. E. University education in Ireland: a letter to J. S. Mill, Esq., M.P. 1866.
Calderwood, H. The sensational philosophy – Mr J. S. Mill and Dr McCosh. Br and Foreign Evangelical Rev 15, 1866.
'Charactacus'. Political letters II: the national debt. Nat Reformer 7, 1866. About Mill's speech on the malt tax.
'Charactacus'. Political letters VI: the rights of women. Ibid. About Mill's petition of 7 June 1866.
[Drysdale, G.]. Logic and utility: the tests of truth and falsehood, and of right and wrong. 1866. Signed G.R.
Grote, G. John Stuart Mill on the philosophy of Sir William Hamilton. Westminster Rev vol 29 ns 1866, rptd in his Minor works, ed. A. Bain, and as Review of the work of Mr John Stuart Mill, entitled Examination of Sir William Hamilton's philosophy, 1867 (pamphlet).
Grote, H. The philosophical radicals of 1832. 1866.
[Hayward, A.]. Parliamentary reform and the government. Fraser's Mag 73, 1866.
[Hutton, R. H.]. Mr Mansel's reply to Mill. Spectator 39, 1866. *See also* Mansel, *above*.
Lange, F. A. Mill's Ansichten über die sociale Frage und die angebliche Umwälzung der Socialwissenschaft durch Carey. Duisberg 1866.
Littré, E. Auguste Comte et Stuart Mill; G. Wyrouboff, Stuart Mill et la philosophie positive. Paris 1866.
Longe, F. D. A refutation of the wage-fund theory of modern political economy as enunciated by Mr Mill M.P. and Mr Fawcett M.P. 1866; ed with introd and notes by J. H. Hollander, Baltimore 1904, 1934.
Longe, F. D. A critical examination of George's Progress and poverty and Mill's theory of wages. [1883].
Mansel, H. L. The philosophy of the conditioned: comprising some remarks on Hamilton's philosophy and on Mill's examination of that philosophy. 1866.
McCosh, J. An examination of Mr J. S. Mill's philosophy, being a defence of fundamental truth. 1866, 1877 (rev).
Mellor, E. An examination of some of the points in Mr Mill's critique of the philosophy of Sir William Hamilton. Liverpool [1866].
O'Hanlon, H. F. A criticism of Mill's pure idealism, and an attempt to shew that, if logically carried out, it is pure nihilism. Oxford 1866.
[Oliphant, M.]. The great unrepresented. Blackwood's Mag 100, 1866.
[Plummer, J.]. Philosophical politicians. Working Man 2, 1866.
Phillipps, L. F. M. The battle of two philosophers, by an inquirer. 1866.
Sangar, J. M. Episcopal vows: what do they mean? A letter to the bishop of St David's on his recent endorsement of the alleged infidelity of J. S. Mill, Esq., M.P. 1866.
Shedden, T. On Sir William Hamilton and Mr Mill. In his Three essays on philosophical subjects, 1866.
Simon, T. C. Hamilton versus Mill: a thorough discussion of each chapter in Mill's examination of Hamilton. 2 pts Edinburgh 1866, 1868.
Smith, W. H. J. S. Mill on our belief in the external world. Blackwood's Mag 99, 1866.
Tyler, M. C. Mr Mill in the House of Commons. Nation 2, 1866.
Ward, J. H. John Stuart Mill. Boston Rev 6, 1866.
Ward, J. H. Political writings of John Stuart Mill. Ibid.
'W. G. D.' Mill and the inductive origin of first principles. Jnl of Sacred Lit ns 9, 1866.
Wyrouboff, G. Stuart Mill et la philosophie positive: E. Littré. Auguste Comte et Stuart Mill. Paris 1866.

John Stuart Mill, M.P. Eclectic Mag 67, 1866. With portrait. Brief laudatory biographical sketch on Mill's entry into Parliament; quotes Mr John Stuart Mill, Illus London News 48, 1866.
The malt tax and the national debt. Sat Rev 21, 1866.
Mr J. S. Mill and the inductive origin of first principles. Jnl of Sacred Lit, 4th ser 9, 1866.
Mr John Stuart Mill. Illus London News 48, 1866, rptd Nat Reformer 7, 1866. With portrait.
Mr Mill as a politician. Sat Rev 22, 1866.
Mr Mill in Parliament. Nat Reformer 7, 1866, rptd from Star.
Mr Mill in Parliament. Sat Rev 21, 1866.
Mr Mill's plan for London. Spectator 39, 1866.
Observations on the Royal Commission. By Jamaica. 1866.
Odd bricks from a tumbledown private building: by a retired constructor. 1866. On Sir William Hamilton's philosophy.
Women's rights. Sat Rev 1866.
Blakesley, G. H. A review of Mill's essay on liberty. Cambridge 1867.
Bledsoe, A. J. John Stuart Mill and Dr Lieber on liberty. Southern Rev 2, 1867.
Bonatelli, F.[?] Intorno al system di logica di J. S. Mill. Revista Bolognese di Scienze, Lettre, Arti e Scuole 1, 1867.
Brewster, D. The radical party: its principles, objects and leaders – Cobden, Bright and Mill. Manchester 1867.
Fitzhugh, G. John Stuart Mill on political economy. DeBow's Rev After the War ser 3, 1867.
Godkin, E. L. The tyranny of the majority. N. Amer Rev 104, 1867.
[Guy, R. E.]. Dr McCosh's Intuitions of the mind and Examination of Mill's philosophy. Dublin Rev ns 8, 1867. Signed R.E.G.
Hayes, W. Remarks, with reference to the land-laws of England, on some passages in Mill's Principles and Blanc's Letters on England. 1867.
[Hutton, R. H.]. Mr Mill's case for women. Spectator 40, 1867.
Mansel, H. L. Supplementary remarks on Mill's criticism of Hamilton. Contemporary Rev 6, 1867.
Millet, J. An Millius veram mathematicorum axiomatum originem invenirit. Paris and London 1867.
Purnell, T. Literary men in Parliament. In his Literature and its professors, 1867.
Romilly, H. Public responsibility and vote by ballot. 1867 (2nd edn).
Rozhdestvensky, M. N. O znachenii Dzhona Styuarta Millya v ryadu sovremennykh ekonomistov. St Petersburg 1867.
Shairp, J. C. Moral theories and Christian ethics. N. Br Rev ns 8, 1867.
[Vasey, G.]. Individual liberty, legal, moral and licentious: in which the political fallacies of Mill's essay on liberty are pointed out. 1867, 1877 (by 'Index').
Wright, C. Mansel's reply to Mill. Nation 4, 1867, rptd in his Philosophical discussions. New York 1877.
Female suffrage. Sat Rev 23, 1867.
J. S. Mill's psychological theory. By a philosophical conservative. [London] 1867.
Recent discussions concerning liberal education. Biblical Repertory and Princeton Rev ser 3, 39, 1867. Reviews Youmans's The culture demanded by modern life and Mill's inaugural address.
A review of Mr J. S. Mill's essay On liberty and an investigation of his claim to be considered one of the leading philosophers and thinkers of the age; also a refutation of his two statements: I. that Christian morality teaches us to be selfish. II. that the working classes of this country are mostly habitual liars. By a liberal. 1867.
Alexander, P. O. Moral causation: or notes on Mr Mill's notes to the chapter on freedom in the 3rd edition of his Examination of Sir W. Hamilton's philosophy. Edinburgh 1868.
Bain, A. Mental and moral science. 1868.
Beggs, T. The deterrent influence of capital punishment: a reply to the speech of J. S. Mill Esq M.P. 1868, 1868 (rev).
Blackwood, F. T. H. T. Mr Mill's plan for the pacification of Ireland examined. 1868.
Bunge, N. K. Styuart Mill: kak ekonomist Zhurnal Ministerstva Narodnovo Prosveshcheniya 140, 1868, rptd in his Ocherki politcheskoy-ekonomicheskoy literatury, St Petersburg 1895; tr as John Stuart Mill envisagé comme économist in his Esquisse de littérature politico-économique, Geneva 1900.
Fiske, J. Dissertations and discussions: political, philosophical, and historical. N. Amer Rev 106, 1868.
Godkin, E. L. Mr J. S. Mill on the Irish difficulty. Nation 6, 1868.
Godkin, E. L. Political philosophers in the legislature. Ibid 7, 1868.
Haven, J. Mill versus Hamilton. Bibliotheca Sacra 25, 1868.
Holyoake, G. J. A new defence of the ballot in consequence of Mr Mill's objections to it. 1868.
[Hutton, R. H.]. Mr J. S. Mill. Spectator 41, 1868.
Laurie. S. S. New utilitarianism – Mr Mill. In his Notes expository and critical on certain British theories of morals, Edinburgh 1868.
McCosh, J. Philosophical papers. 1868.
Morley, J. A political prelude. Fortnightly Rev ns 4, 1868.
[Villard, H.]. John Stuart Mill visited by an American. Chicago Tribune, 16 Mar 1868.
Watts, R. Utilitarianism, as expounded by J. Stuart Mill, Alex Bain, and others. Belfast [1868] (2nd edn rev).
John Stuart Mill. Br Quart Rev 48, 1868.
Mr Mill and the infallible. Sat Rev 26, 1868.
Mr Mill and Mrs M'Laren. Ibid.
The philosophy of John Stuart Mill. Theological Eclectic 4, 1868.
Althaus, F. Englische Charakterbilder. 2 vols Berlin 1869.
Bledsoe, A. J. What is liberty? Southern Rev 5, 1869.
Bowen, F. J. S. Mr Mill and his critics. Amer Presbyterian Rev 18, 1869.
Cairnes J. E. The character and logical method of political economy. Dublin 1869.
Chernyshevesky, N. G. Dopolneniya i primchaniya na pervuyu knigu politicheskoy economii Dzhona Styuarta Millya. Geneva 1869.
Davies, J. L. Universal morality and the Christian theory of duty. Fortnightly Rev 6, 1869.
Eccarius, J. G. Eines Arbeiters Widerlegung der National-ökonomischen Lehren J. S. Mills. Berlin 1869.
English, W. W. An essay on moral philosophy. 1869.
Finlason, W. F. A history of the Jamaica case. 1868, 1869 2nd edn (rev and enlarged).
Goggia, P. E. La mente di Mill: saggio di logica positiva applicata specialmente alla storia. Livorno 1869.
Hazard, R. G. Two letters on causation and freedom in willing, addressed to J. S. Mill. Boston 1869.
[Hutton, R. H.]. The latest phase of the utilitarian controversy. Br Quart Rev 50, 1869.
James, W. Bushnell's Women's suffrage and Mill's Subjection of women. N. Amer Rev 109, 1869.
Janet, P. Mill et Hamilton: la problème de l'existence des corps. Revue des Deux Mondes 83, 1869.
Lecky, W. E. H. History of European morals from Augustus to Charlemagne. 2 vols 1869; rev 1877; rptd 1920 and 1st chap as Survey of English ethics, ed W. A. Hurst 1903.
[Lucas, E.]. Mill on liberty. Dublin Rev ns 13, 1869.
Lucas, E. Mr Mill on liberty of the press. In Essays on religion and literature, ed H. E. Manning 3rd ser 1874.
McCarthy, J. The English positivists. Galaxy 7, 1869.
McCarthy, J. The liberal triumvirate. Ibid.
Morley, J. Mr Lecky's first chapter. Fortnightly Rev ns 5, 1869.
Ritchie, J. E. John Stuart Mill. In his British senators: or political sketches, past and present. 1869.
Stephen, J. F. Utilitarianism. Pall Mall Gazette, 1869, rptd shortened in his Liberty, equality, fraternity, 1873.
Stephen, L. The Comtist utopia. Fraser's Mag 80, 1869.

Williams, R. A few words on utilitarianism. Ibid.
[Williamson, E. S.]. William Kirkus (pseud). Mr John Stuart Mill. In her Miscellaneous essays, 2nd ser 1869.
An answer to Mr J. Stuart Mill's Subjection of women. The advance of transcendentalism. Female suffrage: an answer to Mrs H. Fawcett on the electoral disabilities of women. Grosvenor Papers nos 1–3, 1869, 1870.
The autobiography of consciousness: or the experiences of an indoor servant. Fraser's Mag 80, 1869.
Gneist und Mill: alt-englische und neu-englische Staatsanschauungen. Berlin 1869.
Mill and the ballot: a criticism of his opinions as expressed in thoughts on parliamentary reform. By a Westminster elector. 1869.
Mr Mill on endowments. Sat Rev 27, 1869.
Mr Mill's speech on capital punishment. Westminster Rev ns 35, 1869.
M. Mill et le droit politique des femmes. Revue Britannique 1, 1869.
Positivism in England. Southern Rev 5, 1869.
Recent discussions on the representations of minorities. Biblical Repertory and Princeton Rev ser 3 1869.
Kell, S. C. The ballot. Shall the vote be free or watched? The voter's own or some one's else? Bradford [186?] (pamphlet).
Davies, J. L. Professor Grote on utilitarianism. Contemporary Rev 15, 1870.
Jevons, W. S. Elementary lessons in logic. 1870; London and New York 1876 (new edn).
[Jordan, W.]. Nachrichten über das Schuljahr, 1869–70. In Programm des Königlichen Gymnasiums in Stuttgart. Stuttgart 1870.
[Jordan, W.]. Die Zweideutigkeit der Copula bei Stuart Mill. Ibid.
Grote, J. An examination of the utilitarian philosophy. Cambridge 1870.
Keynes, J. N. Studies and exercises in logic. 1870, 1906 (4th edn rev and enlarged), rptd 1928.
Killick, A. H. The student's handbook, synoptical and explanatory, of Mr J. S. Mill's System of logic. 1870.
MacCaig, D. A reply to John Stuart Mill, on the subjection of women. Philadelphia 1870.
McLaren, C. B. B. Hamilton's natural dualism, Mill's psychological theory and Berkeley's spiritual realism. In his University lectures in metaphysics, moral philosophy and English composition, Edinburgh 1870.
Ribot, T. A. In his La psychologie anglaise contemporaine, Paris 1870; tr 1873.
[Ribot, T. A.]. La philosophie contemporaire en Angleterre: M. John Stuart Mill (1841–1846). Revue Politique et Littéraire 11, 1873.
Stirling, J. Mr Mill on trades unions: a criticism. In Recess studies, ed A. Grant, Edinburgh 1870; tr Fr, Jnl des Economistes 20, 1870.
Stuart-Glennie, J. S. The principle of the conservation of force and Mr Mill's System of logic. Nature 7 Apr 1870.
Taylor, H. Mr Mill on the subjection of women. Fraser's Mag ns 1, 1870.
Thornton, W. T. Anti-utilitarianism. Fortnightly Rev ns 8, 1870.
White, C. Ecce femina: an attempt to solve the women question: an examination of arguments in favour of female suffrage by J. Stuart Mill. Hanover NH 1870.
John Stuart Mill. Appleton's Jnl 3, 1870.
Mr Mill's Subjection of woman from a woman's point of view. 1870.
Blackie, J. S. In his Four phases of morals, Edinburgh 1871.
Greeley, H. Mill on protection. New York Tribune, 13 Feb 1871.
Greeley, H. Mill's logic. Ibid, 15 Feb 1871.
Greeley, H. Intentions in statesmanship. Ibid, 17 Feb 1871.
[Hickson W. E.]. Life and immortality. Westminster Rev 56, 1871.
Jevons, W. S. The theory of political economy. London and New York 1871.
Newman, F. H. Epicureanism, ancient and modern. Fraser's Mag 84, 1871, rptd in his Miscellanies, 5 1891.
[Price, B.]. Mr Mill on land. Blackwood's Mag 110, 1871.
Stephen, L. Mr Mill on the land question. Nation 12, 1871.
Strakov, N. N. Zhensky vopros: razbor sochineniya Dzhona Styuarta Millya o podchinenii zhenchiny. St Petersburg 1871.
Ward, W. G. Mr Mill's denial of necessary truth. Dublin Rev ns 17, 1871, rptd in his Essays on the philosophy of theism, 2 vols 1884.
An alphabetical list of the philosophers and discoverers of Mill's System of logic. Oxford 1871.
Mr Mill on property in land. Sat Rev 31, 1871.
Mr Mill on women's suffrage. Ibid.
Calderwood, H. Handbook of moral philosophy. 1872.
Creg, W. R. In his Enigmas of life, 1872.
[Mozley, J. R.]. Mr John Stuart Mill and his school. Quart Rev 133, 1872.
Sidgwick, H. J. S. Pleasure and desire. Contemporary Rev 19, 1872.
Ward, W. G. Mr Mill on the foundation of morality. Dublin Rev ns 18, 1872, rptd in his Essays on the philosophy of theism, 2 vols 1884.
'A.' Mr Mill and his critics. Spectator 46, 1873.
'B.' John Stuart Mill. Examiner, 10 May 1873.
Bagehot, W. The late Mr Mill. Economist 31, 1873, rptd in his Collected works, 3 1965.
Blecky, H. A colloquy on the utilitarian theory of morals presented in Mr W. E. H. Lecky's history of European morals from Augustus to Charlemagne. 1873.
Bourne, H. R. Fox. John Stuart Mill: a sketch of his life. Examiner, 17 May 1873, rptd as John Stuart Mill: his education and marriage, Popular Science Monthly 3, 1873 and in his (ed) John Stuart Mill: notices of his life and works, 1873.
Bowne, B. P. Moral intuition vs utilitarianism. New Englander 32, 1873.
Brace, C. L. A reminiscence of John Stuart Mill. Victoria Mag 21, 1873.
Cairnes J. E. John Stuart Mill: his work in political economy. Examiner, 17 May 1873, rptd Popular Science Monthly 3, 1873, in Fox Bourne and in Bain, John Stuart Mill, 1882.
[Cazelles, E.]. John Stuart Mill: l'influence général de Mill. Démocratie du Midi, 24 May 1873. Signed E.C.
[Cazelles, E.]. John Stuart Mill: le philosophie. Ibid, 25 May 1873.
[Cazelles, E.]. John Stuart Mill: l'homme politique. Ibid, 28 May 1873.
[Cazelles, E.]. John Stuart Mill: le réformateur. Ibid, 28, 30 May, 4 June 1873.
Christie, W. D. Mill and Hayward. 1873. Also as Reply to Hayward, 1873 (without correspondence).
Conway, M. D. In memoriam: a memorial discourse in honour of John Stuart Mill, May 25, 1873. 1873.
Conway, M. D. John Stuart Mill. Harper's 47, 1873.
Courcelle-Seneuil, J.-G. L'oeuvre de John Stuart Mill. Jnl des Economistes 31, 1873.
Davin, N. F. John Stuart Mill. Canadian Monthly 3, 1873.
[Ellis, W.]. The founder of social science. The Times, 12 Nov 1873.
Fawcett, H. John Stuart Mill: his influence at the universities. Examiner 17 1873, rptd in Popular Science Monthly 3, 1873 and in Fox Bourne.
Fawcett, M. G. John Stuart Mill: his influence as a practical politician. Examiner 17 May 1873, rptd in Popular Science Monthly 3, 1873 and in Fox Bourne.
[Godkin, E. L. and C. Wright]. John Stuart Mill. Nation 16, 1873.
Harrison, F. John Stuart Mill: his relation to positivism. Examiner, 17 May 1873, rptd in Fox Bourne.
Harrison, F. The religion of inhumanity. Fortnightly Rev ns 13, 1873. Review of J. F. Stephen's Liberty, equality, fraternity.
[Hayward, A.]. John Stuart Mill. The Times, 10 May 1873 (obituary notice of special importance).

[Hayward, A.]. The personal life of George Grote. Quart Rev 135, 1873. Extract rptd The Times, 17 July 1873 (review).
Holyoake, G. J. John Stuart Mill as some of the working classes knew him. 1873.
Hooker, I. B. Correspondence with John Stuart Mill. In her Womanhood: its sanctities and fidelities. Boston [1873], 1888.
Hunter, W. A. John Stuart Mill: his position as a philosopher. Examiner, 17 May 1873, rptd Popular Science Monthly 3, 1873, and Fox Bourne.
Hunter, W. A. John Stuart Mill: his studies in morals and jurisprudence. Ibid.
Laugel, A. Les confessions de John Stuart Mill. Revue des Deux Mondes 108, 1873, rptd in his Grandes figures historiques, Paris 1875.
Levy, J. H. John Stuart Mill: his work in philosophy. Examiner 17 May 1873, rptd Popular Science Monthly 3, 1873, and Fox Bourne.
Mansel, H. L. On utility as a ground for moral obligation. In his Letters, lectures and reviews, 1873.
Marston, M. Life of John Stuart Mill, politician, philosopher, critic and metaphysician. [1873].
Minto, W. John Stuart Mill: his place as critic. Examiner, 17 May 1873, rptd Popular Science Monthly 3, 1873, and Fox Bourne.
Morley, J. The death of Mr Mill. Fortnightly Rev ns 13, 1873, rptd in his Critical miscellanies, 1877.
Pillon, F. John Stuart Mill, socialiste. Critique Philosophique 2, 1873.
Pillon, F. L'origine de la justice selon Bentham et M. Stuart Mill. Ibid.
Pillon, F. Mill au point de vue religieux. Ibid.
Pillon, F. Polémique de Mahaffy contre l'école associationiste. Ibid.
Pillon, F. Polémique de Mahaffy contre Stuart Mill au sujet des jugements mathématiques. Ibid.
[Rands, W. B.]. Mr Mill's Autobiography and Mr Fitzjames Stephen on 'liberty'. Saint Paul's Mag 13, 1873.
Renouvier, C. De l'esprit de la philosophie anglaise: utilitarianism – Robert Owen and Stuart Mill. Critique Philosophique 2, 1873.
Renouvier, C. La mort de Mill. Ibid.
Renouvier, C. Les rapports du criticisme avec la philosophie de Mill. Ibid.
Renouvier, C. Le principe du socialisme d'après l'Autobiographie de Mill. Ibid.
Sidgwick, H. J. S. John Stuart Mill. Acad, 15 May 1873.
Simcox, E. The influence of J. S. Mill's writings. Contemporary Rev 22, 1873.
Spencer, H. John Stuart Mill: his moral character. Examiner, 17 May 1873, rptd Popular Science Monthly 3, 1873, and Fox Bourne.
Sprague, A. P. [Mill and Agassiz]. Nat Quart Rev 28, 1873.
Stephen, J. F. Liberty, equality, fraternity. 1873.
Stephen, L. Mr Mill and the land laws. Nation 16, 1873.
Stephen, L. The late Stuart Mill. Ibid.
Taylor, H. Old-fashioned ethics and commonsense metaphysics, with some of their applications. 1873.
Taylor, H. John Stuart Mill: his career in the India House. Examiner, 17 May 1873, rptd Popular Science Monthly 3, 1873, and Fox Bourne.
Trimen, H. John Stuart Mill: his botanical studies. Examiner, 17 May 1873, rptd Popular Science Monthly 3, 1873, and Fox Bourne.
Ward, W. G. Mr Mill's reply to the Dublin Review. Dublin Rev ns 21, 1873, rptd in his Essays on the philosophy of theism, 2 vols 1884.
[Wilson, J.]. Liberty, equality, fraternity: John Stuart Mill. Quart Rev 135, 1873. Review of, inter alia, Fox Bourne and Stephen.
Wright, C. John Stuart Mill – a commemorative notice. Proc Amer Acad of Arts and Sciences 9, 1873–4, rptd Boston 1873 (pamphlet) and in his Philosophical discussions, New York 1877.
The death of Mr Mill. Pall Mall Gazette, 10 May 1873.
L'éducation de Stuart Mill d'après son Autobiographie. Critique Philosophique 2, 1873.
John Stuart Mill. Church Herald 4, 1873.
John Stuart Mill. Harper's Mag 47, 1873. Obituary, with portrait.
John Stuart Mill. Harper's Weekly 17, 1873. Obituary with portrait.
John Stuart Mill. Illus London News 62, 1873. Obituary with portrait.
John Stuart Mill. Nature 8, 1873.
John Stuart Mill. Revue Britannique 6, 1873.
J. S. Mill's Autobiography. Victoria Mag 22, 1873.
Mr John Stuart Mill. Athenaeum, 17 May 1873.
Mr John Stuart Mill. Spectator 46, 1873, rptd Every Saturday 3rd ser 3, 1873. Obituary.
Mr Mill. Sat Rev 35, 1873. Obituary.
Mr Mill and the land-laws. Nation 16, 1873.
Mr Mill on land tenure. The Times, 19 Mar 1873.
Mr Mill on landed property. Sat Rev 35, 1873.
Mr Mill's autobiography. Daily News, 18 Oct 1873.
News of week. Spectator 46, 1873.
Althaus, F. John Stuart Mill. Unsere Zeit Nf Jg 10 1874.
'B.V.' John Stuart Mill on religion. Nat Reformer 24, 1874.
Becker, L. E. Liberty, equality, fraternity: a reply to Stephen's strictures on Mr J. S. Mill's Subjection of women. Manchester 1874.
Browne, W. R. The Autobiography of John Stuart Mill: a lecture. 1874.
Birks, R. T. Modern utilitarianism: or the systems of Paley, Bentham and Mill examined and compared. 1874.
Cairnes J. E. Some leading principles of political economy newly expounded. 1874.
[Cowell, H.]. Liberty, equality, fraternity. Blackwood's Mag 115, 1874.
Crane, C. B. John Stuart Mill and Christianity. Baptist Quart 8, 1874.
[Fraser, A. C.]. Biographical notice of J. S. Mill. By Professor Fraser. Proc Royal Soc of Edinburgh, session 1873–74. Edinburgh 1874.
Grote, H. The personal life of George Grote. 1874.
Hale, E. E. Stuart Mill's history of Rome. Old & New 9, 1874. Wrongly attributes A. Mill's children's history to J. S. Mill.
[Hare, T.]. John Stuart Mill. Westminster Rev ns 45, 1874.
Henshaw, S. E. John Stuart Mill and Mrs Taylor. Overland Monthly 13, 1874.
Hinsdale, B. A. A history of a great mind: a survey of the education and opinions of John Stuart Mill. Cincinnati OH 1874.
[Hutton, R. H.]. Mr J. S. Mill's religious confession. Spectator 47, 1874, rptd in his Aspects of religious and scientific thought, 1899.
[Hutton, R. H.]. The Dublin Review on free will. Spectator 47, 1874. *See also* W. G. Ward, 1884, *below*.
Ierson, H. The religious views of John Stuart Mill. Unitarian Rev 1, 1874.
'J.R.' A visit to the tomb of Mill. Nat Reformer 24, 1874.
Jevons, W. S. Principles of science. 1874.
Morley, J. Mr Mill's doctrine of liberty. Fortnightly Rev ns 14, 1874; rev in The works of Lord Morley, vol 3 1921.
Musgrave, A. Capital: Mill's fundamental propositions. Contemporary Rev 24, 1874, rptd in his Studies in political economy, 1875.
Musgrave, A. Some thoughts on value. In his Studies in political economy, 1875.
Noble, F. A. Obedience and liberty. Presbyterian Quart and Princeton Rev ns 3, 1874.
Pillon, F. La science de la morale selon Bentham et M. Stuart Mill. Critique Philosophique 3, 1874.
'Rossel', Y. A. Dzhon Styuart Mill i yevo shkola. Vestnik Yevropy 221–4, 1874.
Russell, E. R. On the Autobiography of John Stuart Mill, etc. Liverpool 1874.
Porter, N. John Stuart Mill. International Rev 1, 1874.
Renouvier, C. L'opinion de Mill sur la liberté et la nécessité des actes. Critique Philosophique 3, 1874.

Sidgwick, H. J. S. Methods of ethics. 1874, 1901 (6th edn rev, preface especially).
Stork, C. A. Mr Mill's Autobiography as a contribution to Christian evidence. Quart Rev of Evangelical Lutheran Church 4, 1874.
Vladislavlev, M. Dzhon Styuart Mill. Zhurnal Ministerstva Narodnovo Prosveshcheniya 175, 1874.
Ward, W. G. Mr Mill's denial of free will. Dublin Rev ns 22, 1874, rptd in his Essays on the philosophy of theism, 2 vols 1884.
Wordsworth, W. Letter to the editor. Spectator 47, 1874. Responding to review of Three essays; probably by the poet's son.
La crise du développement mental de Stuart Mill d'après son Autobiographie. Critique Philosophique 2, 1874.
Fitzjames Stephen's answer to Mill. Church Eclectic 2, 1874.
Goethe and Mill: a contrast. Westminster Rev ns 46, 1874.
John Stuart Mill. Leisure Hour 23, 1874.
John Stuart Mill et ses doctrines. Revue Britannique 2, 1874.
John Stuart Mill's Autobiography. New England 33, 1874.
Mill, education, and science. Popular Science Monthly 4, 1874.
Mr J. S. Mill's religious confession. Spectator 47, 1874, rptd Littell's Living Age 123, 1874; Eclectic Mag ns 21, 1875.
A visit to the late Mr Mill's grave. Daily News, 29 July 1874.
Woman's duties and rights. Nat Quart Rev 28, 1874.
'Antichrist'. The Jesus Christ of Mill. 1875.
Brown, J. A. The religious opinions of John Stuart Mill. Lutheran Quart 5, 1875.
Carrau, L. Stuart Mill. In his La morale utilitaire, Paris 1875.
[Irons, W. J]. An examination of Mr Mill's Three essays on religion. 1875.
Leslie, T. E. C. John Stuart Mill. Acad 1, 1875, rptd in his Essays in political and moral philosophy, 1879.
Pillon, F. La raison profonde de la crise mentale de Stuart Mill: contradiction entre l'éducation intellectuelle et l'éducation morale dans la doctrine associationniste. Critique Philosophique 4, 1875.
Rickaby, J. Free will and four English philosophers. 1906, rptd New York 1969.
Seccombe, J. T. Science, theism and revelation considered in relation to Mr Mill's essay on nature. 1875.
Upton, C. B. Mill's Essays on religion. Theological Rev 12, 1875.
John Stuart Mill's Essays. Leisure Hour 24, 1875.
Mill et M. J. Morley: note sur l'introduction des possibilités dans les analyses de Stuart Mill. Critique Philosophique 4, 1875.
La personnalité divine et la création dans la pensée de Stuart Mill. Ibid.
La question de l'immortalité dans la philosophie de Stuart Mill. Ibid.
Ce qu'il y a de possible en fait d'attributs de la Divinité, selon Stuart Mill. Ibid.
Religious opinions of John Stuart Mill. Lutheran Quart 5, 1875.
La révélation de les espérances chrétiennes dans la philosophie de Stuart Mill. Critique Philosophique 4, 1875.
Bagehot, W. Indian government. Economist 34, 1876, rptd in his Collected works 8, 1965– .
Blatchford, Lord. The reality of duty as illustrated by the Autobiography of Mill. Contemporary Rev 28, 1876.
Bradley, F. H. In his Ethical studies, 1876, 1935 (2nd edn).
Cannegieter, T. De nuttigheidsleer van Stuart Mill en Prof. van der Wijck. Groningen 1876.
Kaspary, J. In his Natural laws: or the infallible criterion, 1876.
Mahaffy, J. P. Anticipation of Mill's theory of the syllogism by Locke. Mind 1, 1876. Reply by C. J. Munro, ibid.
'N.N.' Thirteen pages on intellectual property written with special reference to a doubtful doctrine of the late John Mill, by one of his pupils. Manchester [1876].
Rogers, F. The reality of duty: as illustrated by the autobiography of Mr John Stuart Mill. Contemporary Rev 28, 1876.
Sidgwick, H. J. S. Philosophy at Cambridge. Mind 1, 1876.
Ward, W. G. Mr Mill on causation. Dublin Rev ns 27, 1876, rptd in his Essays on the philosophy of theism, 2 vols 1884.
Leaving us an example: is it living – and why? an inquiry suggested by certain passages in John Stuart Mill's Essays on religion. [1876], 1880 (2nd, 3rd & 4th edns as The gospel for the nineteenth century).
Adams, L. John Stuart Mill. New Englander 36, 1877.
Hill G. Theism and Christianity. Universalist Quart and General Rev 34 (ns 14), 1877.
Jevons, W. S. John Stuart Mill's philosophy tested. Contemporary Rev 31, 1877–79; abridged in his Pure logic, London and New York 1890.
Paoli, A. Dei concetti direttivi di J. S. Mill nella logica e nella psicologia. Rome 1877.
Sidgwick, H. J. S. Bentham and Benthanism in politics and ethics. Fortnightly Rev ns 21, 1877, rptd in his Miscellaneous essays and addresses, 1904.
Is theism immoral? an examination of Mr J. S. Mill's arguments against Mansel's view of religion. Swansea 1877.
John Stuart Mill. Western (St Louis MO) ns 3, 1877.
Modern ideals and the liberty of the press. Dublin Review ns 29, 1877. Review of, inter alia, On liberty and Milton's Areopagitica.
Science of political economy. Nat Quart Rev 34, 1877.
Adamson, R. Professor Jevons on Mill's experimental methods. Mind 3, 1878.
Bain, A. Mill's theory of the syllogism. Mind 3, 1878, rptd in his Dissertations on leading philosophical subjects, 1903.
Edwards, T. The relativity, the unconditioned, belief and knowledge: some remarks on Mill's Examination of Hamilton. Calcutta 1878.
Gregory, D. A. J. S. Mill and the destruction of theism. Princeton Rev ns 2, 1878.
Jevons, W. S. J. S. Mill's philosophy tested by Professor Jevons. Mind 3, 1878. *See also* G. C. Robertson, 1878, *below*.
Liard, L. Les logicians anglais contemporains. Paris 1878.
Moffatt, R. S. The economy of consumption. 1878.
Moffatt, R. S. The principles of a time policy: . . . containing a re-criticism of the theories of Ricardo and Mill on rent, value and cost of production. 1878. Rptd from his The economy of consumption, *above*.
Robertson, G. C. J. S. Mill's philosophy tested by Jevons. Mind 3, 1878. Replies by A. Strachey and W. S. Jevons, ibid.
The ethics of utilitarianism. Nat Quart Rev 39, 1878.
Carrau, L. Le dualisme de St. Mill. Revue Philosophique 8, 1879.
Courtney, W. L. The metaphysics of John Stuart Mill. 1879.
Fontpertius, A. F. de. Un écrit posthume de John Stuart Mill sur le socialisme. Jnl des Economistes 8, 1879.
Funck-Bretano, T. In his Les sophistes grecs et les sophistes contemporains. Paris 1879.
George, H. Progress and poverty. San Francisco 1879, New York 1880.
[Hutton, R. H.]. Mr Courtney on Mill. Spectator 52, 1879. *See also* W. L. Courtney, 1879, *above*.
Leslie, T. E. C. On the philosophical method of political economy. In his Essays in political and moral philosophy, 1879.
'N.I.' Vorazheniya na ekonomicheskoye ucheniye Dzhona Styuarta Millya. Slovo 7, 1879.
Robertson, G. C. Courtney's metaphysics of John Stuart Mill. 1879.
Wägner, S. John Stuart Mills logiska system och dess kunskapsteoretiska förut sättninger. Lund Universitets Års-skligt 16, 1879–80.
The doctrine of perception. Nat Quart Rev 39, 1879.
Cobbe, F. P. The hopes of the human race, hereafter and here: essays on the life after death: with an introduction having special reference to Mr Mill's Essay on religion. 1880. 1st edn 1874.
Gnocci-Viani, O. Preface to sul socialismo. Milan 1880.

Karinsky, M. I. Klassifikatsiya vuvodov. St Petersburg 1880.
Morris, G. S. John Stuart Mill. In his British thought and thinkers, 1880.
Thompson, D. G. President Porter on Mill. Nat Quart Rev 41, 1880.
Armstrong, R. A. In his Latter-day teachers: six lectures, 1881.
Brochard, V. La logique de J. Stuart Mill. Revue Philosophique 12, 1881.
Gorodsev, P. D. Positivizm i khristianstvo: religiozno-filosofskiya vozzreniya Dzhona Styuarts Millya i ikh otnosheniye k khristianstvu. St Petersburg 1881.
Hodgson, S. H. De Quincey as political economist: or De Quincey and Mill on supply and demand. In his Outcast essays and verse translations, 1881.
Janet, P. De la valeur du syllogisme. Revue Philosophique 12, 1881.
Kohn, B. Untersuchengen über das Causalproblem auf dem Boden einer Kritik der einschlägigen Lehren J. S. Mills. Vienna 1881.
Laveleye, E. de. Les tendances nouvelles de l'économie politique en Angleterre. Revue des Deux Mondes 44, 1881.
Bain, A. John Stuart Mill: a criticism with personal recollections. 1882.
Bain, A. In his James Mill: a biography, 1882.
Blind, K. Stuart Mill über Irland. Gegenwar 21, 1882.
Brandes, G. M. C. John Stuart Mill. In his moderne geister, Frankfurt 1882; tr as Eminent authors of the nineteenth century, New York 1886, as Creative spirits of the nineteenth century, 1924, and as Dzhon Styuart Mill, Severny Vestnik 8, 1887.
Carruthers, J. Communal and commercial economy: with an examination of the correlated theorems of the pseudo-science of wealth as taught by Ricardo and Mill. 1882.
Dicey, A. V. John Stuart Mill. Nation 34, 1882. Review of Bain's biography.
Fawcett, H. In his Free trade and protection, 1822 (4th edn).
Fox, C. Memories of old friends. Ed H. N. Pym 2 vols 1882. 2nd edn, with 14 Mill letters.
Froude, J. A. Thomas Carlyle: a history of the first forty years of his life, 1795–1835. 2 vols 1882.
Gast, H. La religion dans Stuart Mill. Montauban 1882.
Morley, J. Valedictory. Fortnightly Rev ns 32, 1882.
Quesnel, L. Les deux Mill. Bibliothèque Universitaire et Revue Suisse 13, 1882.
Stuart-Glennie, J. S. James and John Stuart Mill: traditional and personal memorials. Macmillan's Mag 45, 1882.
'W. C.' Wealth: definitions by Ruskin and Mill compared. Glasgow [1882].
[Whitehurst, E. C.]. Caroline Fox, John Sterling, and John Stuart Mill. Westminster Rev ns 62, 1882. Review of Fox, Memories.
Bregmann, F. W. E. J. Über den utilitarianismus. Marburg 1883. *See also* Gizycki, 1884, *below*.
Galasso, A. Della conciliazione dell'egoismo coll'altruismo secondo Mill. Naples, 1883.
Green, T. H. In his Prolegomena to ethics, ed A. C. Bradley, Oxford 1883.
Hobhouse, L. T. Mill and Mazzini: a contrast. Marlburian 18, 1883.
Cole, H. Fifty years of public work. Ed and completed A. S. and H. L. Cole 2 vols 1884.
Clough, J. S. On Mill's position as a moralist. Cambridge 1884.
Fouillée, A. Les études récentes sur la propriété. Revue des Deux Mondes 63, 1884.
Frege, G. In his Die Grundlagen der Arithmetik. Breslau 1884; tr J. L. Austin, Oxford 1950.
Froude, J. A. Thomas Carlyle: a history of his life in London, 1834–1881. 2 vols 1884.
Gizycki, G. Über den Utilitarisimus. Vierteljahrsschrift für Wissenschaftliche Philosophie 8, 1884. *See also* Bregmann, 1883, *above*.
Olivier, S. H. John Stuart Mill on socialism. To-day ns 2, 1884.
Ward, W. G. Mr Mill's philosophical position. Ibid, rptd in his Essays on the philosophy of theism, 2 vols 1884.
Ward, W. G. The rule and motive of certitude. Ibid, rptd in his Essays on the philosophy of theism, 2 vols 1884.
Zuccante, G. Del determinismo di John Stuart Mill. Filosofia delle Scuole Italiane 2, 1884.
Beattie, F. R. An examination of the utilitarian theory of morals. Brantford 1885.
Harris, W. The history of the radical party in parliament. 1885.
Horney, F. Mills Vorschäge zur Hebung der arbeitenden Klasse. Vierteljahrsschrift für Volkswirtschaft, Politik und Kulturgeschichte 88, 1885.
Hunter, W. A. Etude sur Stuart Mill. Paris 1885.
Guyau, J.-M. La morale anglaise contemporaine. Paris 1885.
Levin, T. W. Notes on inductive logic, book I: being an introduction to Mill's System of logic. Cambridge 1885.
Levy, J. H. Mill's propositions and inferences of mere existence. Mind 10, 1885.
Löchen, A. Om Mills Logik. Christiania 1885.
Paepe, C. Mill, socialiste. Société Nouvelle 1, 1885.
Stephen, L. In his The life of Henry Fawcett, 1885.
Taylor, H. Autobiography. 2 vols 1885.
Dunbar, C. F. The reaction in political economy. Quart Jnl of Economics 1, 1886.
Green, T. H. The logic of Mill. In his Works vol 2, 1886.
Lauret, H. Philosophie de Stuart Mill. Paris 1886.
Sutherland, J. An alleged gap in Mill's utilitarianism. Mind 11, 1886.
Wilson, J. M. and T. Fowler. Principles of morals, pt II. Oxford 1886–7.
Foote, G. W. What was Christ? a reply to John Stuart Mill. 1887.
Garnet, R. Life of Thomas Carlyle. 1887.
Towry, M. H. On the doctrine of natural kinds. Mind 12, 1887. Replies by W. H. S. Monck, ibid; F. and C. L. Franklin, ibid 13, 1888.
Fox, L. A. Utilitarianism. Lutheran Quart ns 18, 1888.
[Horton, S. D.]. The parity of moneys as regarded by Adam Smith, Ricardo and Mill. 1888. Signed Amicus Curiae.
[Hutton, R. H.]. Carlyle and Mill. Spectator 61, 1888. Review of Jenks, 1888, *below*.
Jenks, E. Thomas Carlyle and John Stuart Mill. Orpington 1888.
Michaëlis, C. T. Stuart Mills Zahlbegriff. Berlin 1888.
Taylor, H. Correspondence of Henry Taylor. 1888.
Blyth, E. K. Life of William Ellis. 1889.
Courtney, W. L. Life of John Stuart Mill. 1889.
Donisthorpe, W. In his Individualism: a system of politics, 1889.
Gomperz, T. John Stuart Mill: ein Nachruf. Vienna 1889.
Hansen, S. Versuch einer Kritik des Mill'schen Subjectivismus. Vierteljahrsschrift für Wissenschaftliche Philosophie 13, 1889.
Lilla, V. Critica della doctrina etica-giuridica di J. S. Mill. Naples 1889.
Michaëlis, C. T. On some applications of the theory of international trade. Quart Jnl of Economics 4, 1889.
Störring, G. W. J. Stuart Mills Theorie über den psychologischen Ursprung des Vulgärglaubens an die Aussenwelt. Halle 1889.
'Ye. V.' Zhizn Dzhona Styuarta Millya. Severny Vestnik 3, 1889.
Some aspects of the tariff question. Harvard Quart Jnl of Economics 3, 1889.
Graham, W. Socialism: new and old. 1890.
James, W. Principles of psychology. 2 vols New York 1890.
Levy, J. H. The outcome of individualism. 1890. *See also* R. K Wilson [1912].
Martineau, J. John Stuart Mill's philosophy. In his Essays, reviews, and addresses, 4 vols London 1890–1.
Pikler, J. J. S. Mill's Theory of the belief in an external world. In his The psychology of the belief in objective existence, 1890.
Stout, G. F. The genesis of the cognition of physical reality. Mind 15,

1890. Replies by J. Pikler and Stout, ibid; J. M. Baldwin, ibid 16, 1891.
Keynes, J. N. The scope and method of political economy. London and New York 1891.
Martineau, J. In his Essays, reviews and addresses vol 3, 1891.
Stout, G. F. Belief. Mind 16, 1891.
Orr, J. J. S. Mill and Christianity. Theological Monthly 6, 1891.
Price, L. L. John Stuart Mill, 1806–1873: the theory of value. In his A short history of political economy in England, 1891.
Ritchie, D. G. In his Principles of state interference, 1891.
Walker, F. The wages question. New York 1891.
Ward, J. J. S. Mill's science of ethology. International Jnl of Ethics 1, 1891.
Bowne, B. P. The principles of ethics. New York 1892.
Čáda, F. Mill: pojema a obor logiky. Prague 1892.
[Carus, P.]. Nature and morality: an examination of the ethical views of John Stuart Mill. Open Court 6, 1892. Signed P. C.
Drysdale, C. R. The population question according to T. R. Malthus and J. S. Mill. 1892.
Ferri, F. L'utilitarismo di Stuart Mill. Milan 1892.
Holyoake, G. J. Sixty years of an agitator's life. 1892.
Towers, C. M. D. Mill and the London and Westminster Review. Atlantic Monthly 69, 1892.
Tugan-Baranovsky, M. I. Dzhon Styuart Mill: Yevo zhizn i uchono-literaturnaya deyatel nost. St Petersburg 1892.
Bonar, J. In his Philosophy and political economy, 1893.
Minto, W. J. S. Mill. In Encyclopaedia Britannica, 1893; with J. M. Mitchell, ibid, 1911.
Canna, E. In his History of the theories of production and distribution in English political economy from 1776 to 1848, 1893.
Laurie, H. Methods of inductive inquiry. Mind ns 2, 1893.
Pick, G. V. Digest of political economy: the Principles of John Stuart Mill. 1893.
Shee, W. A. My contemporaries. 1893.
Edgeworth, F. Y. The theory of international values. Economic Jnl 4, 1894, rptd in his Papers relating to political economy, 1925.
Edgeworth, F. Y. John Stuart Mill. In Palgrave's dictionary of political economy, 3 vols London and New York 1894–9.
Henrici, J. Einführung in die induktive Logik an Bacons Beispiel (der warme) nach Mills Regeln. In Festschrift zur Grosshertzogliche Gymnasium im Heidelberg, Leipzig 1894.
Seth, J. A study of ethical principles. Edinburgh and London 1894.
Stephen, L. John Stuart Mill. In DNB vol 37, 1894.
Čáda, F. Noetická záhada u Herbata a Milla. Prague 1894; tr Ger 1895.
Douglas, C. John Stuart Mill: a study of his philosophy. Edinburgh 1895.
Høffding, H. John Stuart Mill. In his Geschichte der neueren Philosophie, 2 vols Leipzig 1895–6; tr 1900.
Michel, H. De Millii individualismo. Paris 1895.
Payot, J. Quid apud Millium Spencerumque de exteris rebus disserentes sit reprehendum. Orléans 1895.
Robertson, J. M. John Stuart Mill. In his Modern humanists, 1895.
Sidgwick, H. J. S. The economic lessons of socialism. Economic Jnl 5, 1895, rptd in his Miscellaneous essays and addresses, 1904.
Taylor, A. In his Memories of a student, 1895.
Watson, J. Comte, Mill and Spencer. Glasgow 1895.
Carlile, W. W. The humanist doctrine of causation. Philosophical Rev 5, 1896.
Harrison, F. John Stuart Mill. Nineteenth Cent 40, 1896, rptd in his Tennyson, Ruskin, Mill and other literary estimates, 1899; tr Fr, Revue Occidentale 17, 1898.
McKechnie, W. S. In his State and the individual, Glasgow 1896.
Sänger, S. John Stuart Mill als Philosoph. Archiv für Geschichte der Philosophie 9, 1896.
Taussig, F. W. In his Wages and capital, 1896.
Dilke, C. W. John Stuart Mill, 1869–1873. Cosmopolis 6, 1897.
Douglas, C. The ethics of John Stuart Mill. Edinburgh 1897.
Folghera, P. Le syllogisme: Stuart Mill et M. Rabier. Revue Thomiste 3, 1897.
George, H. The science of political economy. New York and London 1897; ed and expanded H. George jr, New York 1898.
Kriegel, F. J. St. Mills Lehre vom Wert, Preis und der Bodenrente. Berlin 1897.
Leader, R. E. (ed). Life and letters of John Arthur Roebuck P. C. Q. C. M.P.: with chapters of autobiography. 1897.
Neatby, W. B. The existential import of propositions. Mind ns 6, 1897.
Pira, C. Framställning och kritik af J. St. Mills, Lotzes, och Sigwarts läror om begreppsbildingen i logiken. Stockholm 1897.
Seal, H. The individual always the unit. Westminster Rev 147, 1897.
White, W. The inner life of the House of Commons. Ed J. McCarthy 2 vols 1897.
Polozhitel'naya logika Dzh. St. Millya: yevo osnovnyye nachala i nauchnaya postanovka. St Petersburg 1897.
Zuccante, G. Alcune idee del Comte e dello Stuart Mill: intorno alla Psicologia Rendiconti 2nd ser 30, 1897.
Zuccante, G. Intorno alle origini della morale utilitaria dello Stuart Mill. Rendiconti ser 2 30 1897, rptd in his Giovanni Stuart Mill e l'utilitarismo, Florence 1922.
[Bellot, H. H. L.]. Contemporary literature: philosophy and theology. Westminster Rev 150, 1898.
Betham-Edwards, M. B. Reminiscences. 1898. Contains description of Mill at a women's suffrage meeting.
Hibben, J. G. The heart and the will in belief – Romanes and Mill. N. Amer Rev 166, 1898.
Lévy-Bruhl, L. A. Comte et Stuart Mill d'après leur correspondance. Revue Philosophique 23, 1898.
Pringle, G. O. S. Mill's humanity. Westminster Rev 150, 1898.
Wallas, G. The life of Francis Place. 1898.
Mill. Gunton's Mag 15, 1898.
Zuccante, G. Intorno all'utilitarismo dello Mill. Rivista Italiana del Filosofia, 1898.
Bonsanquet, B. The philosophical theory of the state. 1899.
Ely, R. T. Mill. Progress 4, 1899.
Faguet, E. Comte et Mill. Revue Bleue 14, 1899.
Graham, W. In his English political philosophy from Hobbes to Maine, 1899.
Kent, C. B. R. The English radicals: an historical sketch. 1899.
Makato, T. Japanese notions of English political economy. Glasgow 1899.
Rutkovsky, L. V. Kritika metodov induktivnovo dokazatel'stva. Zhurnal Ministerstva Narodnovo Prosveshcheniya 6, 7 1899.
Venn, J. The principles of empirical or inductive logic. 1899.
West, Mrs M. A boy's education. Education 19, 1899.
Zuccante, G. Ancora genesi della dottrina: i precursori dello Mill in Inghilterra. Memorie del Real Instituto Lombard di Scienze e Morale 20, 1899, rptd in his Giovanni Stuart Mill e l'utilitarismo, Florence 1922.
Zuccante, G. La morale utilitaria dello Stuart Mill: exposizione della dottrina, 21 1899, rptd in his Giovanni Stuart Mill, 1922.
Balmforth, R. John Stuart Mill and political education. In his Some social and political pioneers of the nineteenth century, 1900.
Daniels, W. M. Letter to John Stuart Mill. Atlantic Monthly 86, 1900.
Sänger, S. Mill's Theodizee. Archiv für Geschichte der Philosophie 13, 1900.
Stephen, L. In his The English utilitarians, 3 vols, 1900.
Veblen, T. B. Preconceptions of economic science. Quart Jnl of Economics 14, 1900, rptd in his Place of science in modern civilization, New York 1919, and in Veblen on Marx, race, science and economics, New York 1969.

McMahan, A. B. An interesting memorial of two great authors. Dial 31, 1901. On Mill and Browning.
Sänger, S. John Stuart Mill: sein Leben und Lebenswerk. Stuttgart 1901.
Albee, E. In his History of English utilitarianism, 1902.
Lubac, J. J. S. Mill et le socialisme. Paris 1902.
Überweg, F. In his Grundriss der Geschichte der Philosophie vol 4, Berlin 1902.
Ashley, M. L. The nature of hypothesis. In Studies in logical theory, ed J. Dewey, Chicago 1903.
Hanschmann, A. B. Bernard Palissy der Künstler, Naturforscher und Schriftsteller als Vater der induktiven Wissenschaftsmethode des Bacon von Verulam: mit der Darstellung der Inductionstheorie Francis Bacons und John Stuart Mills. Leipzig 1903.
Lewels, M. John Stuart Mill: die Stellung eines Empiristen zur Religion. Münster 1903.
Moore, G. E. In his Principia ethica, Cambridge 1903.
Reichel, H. Darstellung und Kritik von J. St. Mills: Theorie der induktiven Methode. Zeitschrift für Philosophie und Philosophische Kritik 122–3, 1903–4.
Stephen, L. Some early impressions. Nat Rev 42, 1903.
Bain, A. In his Autobiography, 1904.
Hobhouse, L. T. Liberalism and socialism. In his Democracy and reaction, 1904
Simon, D. John Stuart Mill und Pestalozzi. Vienna 1904.
Whitaker, A. C. History and criticism of the labor theory of value. New York 1904.
Dicey, A. V. In his Lectures on the relations between law and public opinion in England during the nineteenth century, 1905, 1914 (rev).
Gomperz, T. Zur Erinnerungen an Mill. In his Essays und Erinnerungen, Stuttgart and Leipzig 1905.
Holyoake, G. J. Bygones worth remembering. 2 vols 1905.
Jevons, W. S. Principles of economics. 1905.
Martinazzoli, A. La teorica dell'individualismo secondo Mill. Milan 1905.
Marx, K. Auflösung deer Ricardoschen schule: s. 7, John Stuart Mill. In his Theorien über den Mehrwert, 3 vols, Stuttgart 1905; tr as Theory of surplus value, 1969.
Thouverez, E. Stuart Mill. Paris 1905.
Vissac, M. de. John-Stuart Mill. Mémoires de l'Académie de Vaucluse 2nd ser 5, 1905.
Wellington, S. John Stuart Mill, the saint of rationalism. Westminster Rev 163, 1905.
Abb, E. Kritik des Kantischen Apriorismus vom Standpunkte des reinen Empirismus aus, unter besonderer Berücksichtigung von Mill und Mach. Zurich 1906.
Barth, P. Zu J. St. Mills 100. Geburtstage. Vierteljahrsschrift für Wissenschaftliche Philosophie und Soziologie 30, 1906.
Becher, S. Erkenntnistheorestische Untersuchungen zu Stuart Mills Theorie der Kausalität. Halle 1906.
Benn, A. W. In his History of English rationalism in the nineteenth century vol 1, 1906.
Bicknell, P. F. An apostle of clear thinking. Dial 40, 1906.
Bicknell, P. F. John Stuart Mill. Popular Science Monthly 69, 1906.
Boyd, W. F. John Stuart Mills Utilitarismus im Vergeleich mit dem seiner Vorgänger. Leipzig 1906.
Crozier, J. B. John Stuart Mill. In his The wheel of wealth, 1906.
Ellis, M. A. Variations in the editions of Mill's Principles. Economic Jnl 16, 1906.
Gribble, F. John Stuart Mill. Fortnightly Rev 86, 1906.
Hubbard, E. Mill and Harriet Taylor. In his Little journeys to the homes of great lovers, 18 East Aurora NY 1906.
Kualla, R. John Stuart Mill. In his Die geschichtliche Entwicklung der modernen Werttheorien. Tübingen 1906.
Moskowitz, H. Das moralische Beurteilungsvermögen in der englischen Ethik von Hobbes bis Mill. Erlangen 1906.
Renner, H. John Stuart Mill. Philosophische Wochenschrift und Literatur-Zeitung 2, 1906.
Sidgwick A. and E. M. Henry Sidgwick: a memoir. 1906.
Sidgwick, R. The library of John Stuart Mill. Cornhill Mag ns 21, 1906.
Kantzer, E. M. La religion de J. Stuart Mill. Caen 1906.
John Stuart Mill als Politiker und Sozialist. Vorwärts 20, 1906.
Mill, Spencer and socialism. Independent 61, 1906.
The recreation of John Stuart Mill. Sat Rev 101, 1906. On Mill's botanising.
The saint of rationalism. Current Lit 41, 1906.
MacCunn, J. In his Six radical thinkers, 1907.
Mallock, W. H. In his Socialism, New York 1907.
Schatz, A. In his L'individualisme économique et social, Paris 1907.
Seth, A. [A. Seth Pringle Pattison]. The philosophical radicals. Edinburgh 1907.
[Account of Mill's death and funeral.] Literary Guide and Rationalist Rev 1 July 1907.
Education, personally supervised. N. Amer Rev 184, 1907.
John Stuart Mill: ein karaktaristik. Forkskaren Jg 15 3, 1907.
John Stuart Mill: son politiker och sozialist. Forkskaren Jg 13 3, 1907.
Social freedom. Littell's Living Age 254, 1907.
Ashley, W. J. The present position of political economy in England. In Die Entwicklung der deutschen Volkswirtschaftslere im neunzehnten Jahrhundert vol 1, Leipzig 1908.
Davenport, H. J. In his Value and distribution, Chicago 1908.
Johnson, A. S. Protection and capital. Political Science Quart 23, 1908.
McCabe, J. Life and letters of George Jacob Holyoake. 2 vols 1908.
Morley, J. John Stuart Mill: an anniversary. TLS, 18 May 1906, rptd in his Critical miscellanies, 1908.
Read, C. A posthumous chapter by J. S. Mill. Mind ns 17, 1908.
Seth, J. A. The alleged fallacies in Mill's utilitarianism. Philosophical Rev 17, 1908, rptd in his Essays in ethics and religion, 1926.
Steglich, A. Mills Logik der daten. Leipzig 1908.
Whittaker, T. W. Comte and Mill. 1908, rptd in his Reason, Cambridge 1934.
Dicey, A. V. Letters to a friend on votes for women. 1909.
Gide, C. L'apogée et le décline de l'école classique: Stuart Mill. In Gide and C. Rist, Histoire des doctrines économiques depuis les physiocrates jusqu' à nos jours, Paris 1909; tr 1948.
Guskar, H. Der Utilitarismus bei Mill und Spencer: in kritischer Beleuchtung. Archiv für Systematisch Philosophie 15, 1909.
Tawney, G. A. John Stuart Mill's theory of inductive logic. Cincinnati OH 1909.
Winsløw, C. Mills Etik: et forsog til en fremstilling og kritik. Copenhagen 1909.
Chapman, E. M. English literature and religion, 1800–1900. 1910.
Fabbricatti, C. A. Positivismo? John Stuart Mill. Florence 1910.
Garnet, R. Life of W. J. Fox. 1910.
Haney, L. H. Rent and price: 'alternative use' and 'scarcity value'. Quart Jnl of Economics 25, 1910.
Hobhouse, L. T. John Stuart Mill. Nation 7, 1910.
Thieme, E. Die Sozialethik John Stuart Mills. Leipzig 1910.
Ward, W. John Stuart Mill and the mandate of the people. Dublin Rev 147, 1910.
Ward, W. John Stuart Mill. Quart Rev 213, 1910, rptd in his Men and matters, 1914.
Musings without method. Blackwood's Mag 187, 1910. Review of Elliott.
The political faith of John Stuart Mill. Current Lit 49, 1910.
The testimony of John Stuart Mill to mysticism. Outlook 95, 1910.
John Stuart Mill. Nation 91, 1910.
Bonar, J. The economics of John Stuart Mill. Jnl of Political Economy 19, 1911.

Cadman, S. P. In his Darwin and other English thinkers, 1911.
Finkelstein, F. Die allgemeinen Gesetze bei Comte und Mill. Heidelberg 1911.
Haney, L. H. In his History of economic thought, New York 1911; rev 1920, 1936.
Harrison, F. Autobiographic memoirs. 2 vols 1911.
Hobhouse, L. T. Gladstone and Mill. In his Liberalism, 1911.
Williams, T. A. Intellectual precocity: comparison between John Stuart Mill and the son of Boris Sidis. Pedagogical Seminary 18, 1911.
Famous autobiographies. Edinburgh Rev 214, 1911. *See also reply by* M. Taylor, 1912, *below*.
Archambault, P. Stuart Mill: choix de textes et étude du système philosophique. Paris [1912].
Beus, L. Der Begriff des Belief bei Mill. Bonn 1912.
Green, T. H. Lectures on the principles of political obligation. 1912.
Patten, S. N. Interpretation of John Stuart Mill. Annals of Amer Acad of Political and Social Science 44 suppl, 1912.
Phillips, M. A. John Stuart Mill and Browning's Pauline. Cornhill Mag ns 32, 1912.
Prichard, H. A. Does moral philosophy rest on a mistake? Mind ns 21, 1912, rptd in Mill: utilitarianism, ed S. Gorovitz, Indianapolis IN and New York 1971.
Seth, J. A. The English development of Hume's empiricism. In his English philosophers and schools of philosophy, 1912.
Taylor, M. Mrs Mill: a vindication by her granddaughter. Nineteenth Cent and After 71, 1912. Reply to Famous autobiographies, 1911.
Wilson, R. K., J. Levy et al. Individualism and the land question: a discussion. [1912].
Charles-Roux, J. J. H. Fabre en Avignon. Paris 1913.
Freundlich, E. Mills Kausaltheorie. Düsseldorf [1913].
Krumme, E. Du libéralisme classique à l'individualisme social: la place de John Stuart Mill dans l'histoire des doctrines économiques. Revue Internationale de Sociologie 21, 1913.
Legros, G. V. La vie de J. H. Fabre, naturaliste. Paris 1913, rptd 1924 as Fabre, poet of science, London 1913.
Norton, S. and M. A. DeWolfe (eds). The letters of Charles Eliot Norton. 2 vols Boston 1913.
Rey, L. The romance of John Stuart Mill. Nineteenth Cent 74, 1913, rptd 1913; also pbd as Le roman de John Stuart Mill, Paris 1913.
Trevelyan, G. M. In his The life of John Bright, 1913.
West, J. John Stuart Mill. 1913, 1933. (Fabian tract).
Degenfeld-Schonburg, F. G. von. Die Lohntheorie von Smith, Ricardo, Mill und Marx. Munich 1914.
Dugas, L. In his Penseurs libres et liberté de pensée. Paris 1914.
Gehrig, H. Mills als Sozialpolitiker. Jahrbücher für Nationalökonomie und Statistik 3rd ser 47, 1914.
Karinsky, M. I. Raznoglasiye v shkole novovo empiarizma po voprosu ovb istinakh samoochevidnakh. Zhurnal Ministerstva Narodnovo Prosveshcheniya, 1901–14, rptd Moscow 1914.
Gotthelft, F. E. Mills sozialpolitische Wandlungen. Munich [1914], rptd in Schmollers Jahrbuch 41, 1917.
Ray, J. La méthode de l'économie politique d'après J. S. Mill. Paris 1914.
Wust, P. J. Mills Grundlegung der Geisteswissenschaften. Bonn 1914.
Davidson, W. L. In his Political thought in England: the utilitarians from Bentham to Mill, 1915.
Holt, W. A beacon for the blind: being a life of Henry Fawcett. 1915.
Kotarbinski, T. Utylitaryzm w etyce Milla y Spencera. Cracow 1915, rptd as L'utilitarianisme dans la morale de Mill et de Spencer. In Mysliodziataniu, vol 1 of Wybór pism Warsaw 1957.
Lesevich, V. V. Dzhon Styuart Mill. In Sobraniye sochineni V. V. Lesevicha, Moscow 1915.
Oldershaw, L. R. F. Analysis of Mill's Principles of political economy. Oxford 1915.
Politics: woman's special sphere. Everybody's Mag 33, 1915.
Ashworth, M. The marriage of John Stuart Mill. Englishwoman 30, 1916.
Crawford, J. F. The relation of inference to fact in Mill's logic. Chicago 1916.
Thwing, C. F. Education according to John Stuart Mill. School and Society 3, 1916.
Barr, N. C. Mill and Comte. In Philosophical essays in honour of James Edward Creighton, ed G. H. Sabine, New York 1917.
Leeuw, H. J. van der. 700 stellingen van Mill, door een oudfabrikant. Rotterdam 1917.
Morley, J. In his Recollections, 2 vols 1917.
Harrison, F. Comte and Mill. In his On society, 1918, rptd Freeport NY 1971.
Chouville, L. Un article de J. Stuart Mill sur Vigny. Fr Quart 1, 1919.
Garnier, H. K. Mill and the philosophy of mediation. New York 1919.
Beer, M. In his History of British socialism, 2 vols 1920.
Dunning, W. A. In his History of political theories from Rousseau to Spencer, New York 1920.
Sorley, W. R. In his History of English philosophy, Cambridge 1920.
Hayek, F. A. John Stuart Mill and Harriet Taylor: their friendship and subsequent marriage. 1951.
Packe, M. St J. The life of John Stuart Mill. 1954, rptd New York 1970.
Robson, J. M. Principles and methods in the Collected works of John Stuart Mill. In Editing nineteenth-century texts, ed Robson, Toronto 1967.
O'Grady, J. 'Congenial vocation': J. M. Robson and the Mill project. In A cultivated mind: essays presented to John M. Robson, ed M. Laine, Toronto 1991.

Verse

Lush against Mill. Punch 49, 1865.
Philosophy and Punch. Ibid.
The power of pens. By a Westminster Boy. Ibid.
The tribulation of the "Tizer. Ibid.
'F.W.C.' Mill-iania Press 14, 1866.
Neaves, C. Buridan's Ass: or liberty and necessity. Blackwood's Mag 99, 1866, rptd Littell's Living Age 89, 1866.
Neaves, C. Stuart Mill on mind and matter. Blackwood's Mag 99, 1866, rptd Nat Reformer 7, 1866.
Neaves, C. Stuart Mill again: or the examiner examined. Blackwood's Mag 100, 1866.
Smith, E. G. Written in commemoration of the great reform demonstration held August 27th, 1866. Commonwealth, 15 Sep 1866.
Weston, J. A. [Untitled]. Commonwealth, 28 Apr 1866.
Weston, J. A. A Whit-Monday political poem. Ibid 19 May 1866.
Abacus Politicus. [Untitled]. Blackwood's Mag 99, 1866.
Pegasus in parliament. Fun ns 3, 1866.
Anacreontic. Fun ns 4, 1866.
The ladies in Parliament: a fragment after the manner of an old Athenian comedy. Macmillan's Mag 15, 1866.
The leading members . . . Punch 50, 1866. With drawing by C. H. Bennet.
Mr J. S. Mill's debut. Press 14, 1866.
What Lord Russell may be saying. Punch 50, 1866.
Extension of the franchise to women: notes of a speech delivered by J. S. Mill, Esq, MP, during the debate on the New Reform Bill. Fun ns 4, 1867.
Double acrostic no 6, verse 51. Fun ns 5, 1867. Answer ibid.
Dreams. Ibid.
The gladiators' muster. Punch 52, 1867. With cartoon.
Judy's opening speech, Women of England. Judy 1, 1867.
A Mill-ody. Fun ns 5, 1867.
The progress of reform. Ibid.

Song of head centre. Punch 52, 1867.
A vision of the future. Ibid.
Why, at last, I believe in reform. By a sceptic. Ibid.
After the mêlée. Punch 55, 1868.
Black and white. Tomahawk 2, 1868.
Cox for Finsbury! Punch 55, 1868.
The drawbacks of Jamaica ginger beer. Judy 3, 1868.
Election amenities. Punch 55, 1868.
Election ballads, 3: Air – 'The mistletoe bough'. Judy 4, 1868.
Elections' eve: A song of the future (?). Tomahawk 3, 1868.
Female patriotism. Judy 3, 1868.
The female franchise. Fun ns 8, 1868.
A Fenian on his friends. Punch 54, 1868.
Gladstone's dream. Judy 3, 1868. With cartoon.
The handing committee. Ibid. With cartoon.
John Stuart Mill. Owl, 18 Mar 1868.
Mill joins the ladies. Judy 4, 1868. With cartoon.
No third class! Ibid. With cartoon.
No thoroughfare: a monologue addressed by Mr Gladstone to Miss Mill. Judy 2, 1868. With cartoon.
'Overboard!' or the 'Liberal' privateersman. Ibid 3, 1868. With cartoon.
The power of speech. Fun ns 6, 1868.
Raising the wind: or the modern Iphigenia. Judy 2, 1868. With cartoon.
The revolt league against Eyre. Punch 54, 1868.
Rhymes of the rejected ones. Judy 4, 1868.
Robinson's reverie. Punch 54, 1868.
To Mr Robertson Gladstone. Judy 3, 1868. With cartoon.
A triple hurrah for Mill. William Gladstone Papers, BL Add. mss 44756 fol 55. Priv ptd and set to music.
'Wired': or political croquet. Judy 3, 1868. With cartoon.
'R.' To Mr Mill. Spectator 45, 1872.
'B.E.' John Stuart Mill. Examiner 13, 1873.
Elder, W. Acrostic. Nat Reformer 21, 1873.
'G.E.' John Stuart Mill. Examiner 13, 1873.
Murphy, J. J. John Stuart Mill. Macmillan's Mag 28, 1873.
Shore, A. To John Stuart Mill. Examiner 13, 1873.
[Bentley, E. C.]. John Stuart Mill. In his Biography for beginners, 1905. [ML]

John Daniel Morell 1816–91

Historical and critical view of the speculative philosophy of Europe in the nineteenth century. 2 vols 1846, Edinburgh 1847 (rev and enlarged).
On the philosophical tendencies of the age. 1848.
The philosophy of religion. 1849.
Elements of psychology, pt 1. 1853. All pbd.
Handbook of logic. [1855.]
Modern German philosophy. [Manchester 1856.]
Fichte's contributions to moral philosophy. 1860.
An introduction to mental philosophy on the inductive method. 1862.
Philosophical fragments, written during intervals of business. 1878.
Manual of the history of philosophy. [1884.]
Also works on religion and education.

Frederic William Henry Myers 1843–1901

See col 797.

Richard Lewis Nettleship 1846–92

Philosophical lectures and remains. Ed A. C. Bradley and G. R. Benson 2 vols 1897, 1901.
Memoir of T. H. Green. 1906.
The theory of education in Plato's Republic. Ed S. Leeson, Oxford 1935; tr Sp 1945.

John Henry Newman 1801–90

An essay on the development of Christian doctrine. 1845, 1846; ed C. F. Harrold, New York 1949.
An essay in aid of a grammar of assent. 1870, 1892; ed C. F. Harrold, New York 1947.
See col 2246.

Karl Pearson 1857–1936

Bibliographies

Morant, G. M. A bibliography of the statistical and other writings of Pearson. 1939.

§1

The Trinity: a nineteenth-century passion play. 1882. In verse.
Matter and soul. 1886.
The moral basis of Socialism. [1887.]
Socialism: its theory and practice. [1887.]
The ethic of freethought: a selection of essays and lectures. 1888, 1901 (rev).
The positive creed of freethought. [1888.]
The grammar of science. 1892, 1900 (rev and enlarged), 1911 (rev and enlarged), 1937, New York 1957.
Reaction! a criticism of Balfour's attack on rationalism. [1895.]
The chances of death and other studies in evolution. 2 vols 1897.
National life from the standpoint of science. 1901, 1905 (with appendices).
Nature and nurture: the problem of the future. 1910.
Social problems. 1912.
The life, letters and labours of Galton. 4 vols Cambridge 1914–30. Ed Pearson.
The science of man. 1920.
Galton: an appreciation. [1922.]
Darwin: an appreciation. [1923.]
Also works on statistics and biology.

§2

Pearson, E. S. Pearson. 1938. With bibliography.

James Allanson Picton 1832–1910

The mystery of matter, and other essays. 1873.
The religion of the universe. 1904.
Spinoza: a handbook to the Ethics. 1905, 1907.
Also works on religion.

Carveth Read 1848–1931

On the theory of logic. 1878.
Logic: deductive and inductive. 1898, 1906 (enlarged), 1914 (4th edn enlarged and rewritten).
The metaphysics of nature. 1905, 1908 (with appendices).
Natural and social morals. 1909.
The origin of man and of his superstitions. Cambridge 1920, 2 vols Cambridge 1925 (rev).
Also works on psychology.

David George Ritchie 1853–1903

The rationality of history. In Essays in philosophical criticism, ed A. Seth and R. B. Haldane 1883.
Darwinism and politics. 1889, 1891 (enlarged), 1895, 1901.

The ultimate value of social effort. [1890.]
Principles of state interference. 1891, 1896, 1902.
Darwin and Hegel, with other philosophical studies. 1893.
Natural rights. [1894.]
Evolution and democracy. In Ethical democracy, ed S. Coit 1900.
Studies in political and social ethics. 1902.
Plato. New York 1902.
Philosophical studies. Ed R. Latta 1905. With memoir.

George Croom Robertson 1842–92

The senses. 1866.
Hobbes. Edinburgh 1886.
Philosophical remains. Ed A. Bain and T. Whittaker 1894.
Elements of general philosophy. Ed C. A. F. R. Davids 1896. From lecture notes.
Elements of psychology. Ed C. A. F. R. Davids 1896. From lecture notes.

George John Romanes 1848–94

§1

A candid examination of theism. Boston 1878, 1892 (3rd edn). By 'Physicus'.
Darwin. 1882.
The scientific evidences of organic evolution. 1882.
Animal intelligence. New York 1883, London 1886 (4th edn).
Mental evolution in animals. 1883; tr Ger 1885.
Mental evolution in man. 1888; tr Fr 1891; Ger 1895.
Poems. 1889.
Darwin and after Darwin. Chicago 3 vols 1892–7.
An examination of Weismannism. 1893.
Mind and motion and monism. 1895.
Thoughts on religion. Ed C. Gore, Chicago 1895, 1897 (3rd edn).
Essays. Ed C. L. Morgan 1897.
Also works on psychology.

§2

Romanes, E. Life and letters of Romanes. 1896, 1902 (5th edn).

Sir John Robert Seeley 1834–95

David and Samuel, with other poems. 1859. By 'John Robertson'.
Classical studies as an introduction to the moral sciences. 1864.
Ecce homo: a survey of the life and work of Jesus Christ. 1866 (for 1865) etc; tr Ger 1867; Ital nd.
Liberal education in universities. In F. W. Farrar, Essays on a liberal education, 1867.
Lectures and essays. 1870.
Natural religion. 1882, Boston 1882.
Goethe reviewed after sixty years. Boston 1893, London 1894.
Introduction to political science. Ed H. Sidgwick 1896.
Ethics and religion. 1900.
Also works on history; *see col 2449.*

Andrew Seth, later Pringle-Pattison 1856–1931

§1

The development from Kant to Hegel. 1882.
Essays in philosophical criticism. Ed Seth and R. B. Haldane 1883.
Scottish philosophy: a comparison of the Scottish and German answers to Hume. Edinburgh 1885.
Hegelianism and personality. Edinburgh 1887, 1893.
The present position of the philosophical sciences. Edinburgh 1891.
Two lectures on theism. New York 1897.
Man's place in the cosmos. Edinburgh 1897, 1902 (rev).
Philosophical works of Calderwood. In W. Calderwood and D. Woodside, Calderwood 1900.
The philosophical radicals, and other essays. Edinburgh 1907.
The idea of God in the light of recent philosophy. Aberdeen and Oxford 1917, 1920 (rev).
The idea of immortality. Oxford 1922.
The philosophy of history. [1924.]
Haldane. 1930.
Studies in the philosophy of religion. Oxford 1930.
The Balfour lectures on realism. Ed G. F. Barbour, Edinburgh 1933. With memoir.

Articles

Hegel: an exposition and criticism. Mind 6 1881.
Contemporary records: mental philosophy. Contemporary Rev Feb 1884, Aug 1887.
Alexander's Moral order and progress. Mind 14 1889.
Hegel and his recent critics. Mind 14 1889.
Psychology, epistemology and metaphysics. Philosophical Rev 1 1892.
The problem of epistemology. Philosophical Rev 1 1892.
Epistemology in Locke and Kant. Philosophical Rev 2 1893.
The epistemology of neo-Kantianism and subjective idealism. Philosophical Rev 2 1893.
The new psychology and automatism. Contemporary Rev Apr 1893.
Man's place in the cosmos: Huxley on nature and man. Blackwood's Mag Dec 1893.
Epistemology and ontology. Philosophical Rev 3 1894.
Some epistemological conclusions. Philosophical Rev 3 1894.
Hegelianism and its critics. Mind n.s. 3 1894. Reply by D. G. Ritchie, ibid.
A new theory of the absolute. Contemporary Rev Nov–Dec 1894.
The term 'naturalism' in recent discussion. Philosophical Rev 5 1896.
Nietzsche. Blackwood's Mag Oct 1897.
The standpoint and method of ethics. Philosophical Rev 6 1897.
The opinions of Nietzsche. Contemporary Rev May 1898.
Scottish moral philosophy. Philosophical Rev 7 1898.
The venture of theism. Quart Rev 187 1898.
The utilitarian estimate of knowledge. Philosophical Rev 10 1901.
Martineau's philosophy. Hibbert Jnl 1 1903. Reply by G. Galloway, ibid.
A. C. Fraser. Proc Br Acad 6 1914.
The free man's worship: a consideration of Bertrand Russell's views on religion. Hibbert Jnl 12 1914.
Balfour's Theism and humanism. Hibbert Jnl 14 1916.
Do finite individuals possess a substantive or an adjectival mode of being? (symposium). Proc Aristotelian Soc 18 1918.
The idea of God: a reply to some criticisms. Mind n.s. 28 1919.
Pragmatism and idealist ethics. Philosophical Rev 32 1923.

§2

Jones, A. H. Seth Pringle-Pattison's epistemological realism. Philosophical Rev 20 1911.
Rashdall, H. The religious philosophy of Pringle-Pattison. Mind n.s. 27 1918.
Galloway, G. Idealism and the external world. Mind n.s. 29 1920.

Alfred Sidgwick 1850–1942

Fallacies. 1883.
Distinction and the criticism of beliefs. 1892.
The process of argument. 1893.
The use of words in reasoning. 1901.
The application of logic. 1910.
Elementary logic. Cambridge 1914.

Henry Sidgwick 1838–1900

The largest and most significant group of Sidgwick's papers so far located is housed in the Wren Lib, Trinity College, Cambridge. Sidgwick's letters are held by the Beinecke Lib, Yale; the Berg Collection, NYPL; the Bancroft Lib, Univ of California, Berkeley; the J. A. Symonds papers, Bristol Univ Lib; the BL; Bulwer-Lytton papers, Hertfordshire Record Office; Cambridge Univ Lib; the Butler Lib, Columbia Univ; the Ely Papers, Madison WI; Glasgow Univ Lib; the Houghton Lib, Harvard; the Brynmor Jones Lib, Hull Univ; the Hutzler Collection, Eisenhower Lib, Johns Hopkins Univ; Tennyson Research Centre, Lincoln; Dr William's Lib, London; Bodleian; Univ College London; Univ of London Lib; Wilfrid Ward papers, St Andrews Univ Lib. Other collections which contain Sidgwick material, including correspondence, are King's College, Cambridge; the Balfour of Whittinghame papers, Scottish Record Office; the T. H. Green papers, Balliol College, Oxford; Manchester College, Oxford (papers of the Metaphysical Soc); Newnham College, Cambridge; and various private collections. See also NRA.

Bibliographies

Hayward, F. H. The ethical philosophy of Sidgwick: nine essays, critical and expository. 1901.

Sidgwick, E. M. The Society for Psychical Research: a short account of its history and work on the occasion of the Society's jubilee, 1932. Proc of the Soc for Psychical Research 41 1932–3.

Sturges, R. P. Economists' papers: 1750–1950. 1975.

Schneewind, J. B. Sidgwick's ethics and Victorian moral philosophy. Oxford 1977.

§1

The methods of ethics. 1874, 1877, 1884, 1890, 1893, 1901, 1907; tr Jap 1898, Ger 1909, Ital 1995, Fr 1999.

A supplement to the first edition of The methods of ethics. 1878. Contains changes made for the second edn.

A supplement to the second edition of The methods of ethics. 1884. Contains changes made for the third edn.
REVIEWS: Athenaeum 1 1875; Sully, J. Examiner 20, 27 Feb 1875; Stephen, L. Fraser's Mag 91, Mar 1875; Caird, E. Acad 12 June 1875; Bain, A. Mind o.s. 1 1876; Cabot, J. E. North Amer Rev 122 1876; Dicey, A. Nation 22, 1 and 16 Mar 1876; Acad 27 Oct 1877 (review of 2nd edn and suppl to 1st edn); Bradley, F. H. Mr Sidgwick's hedonism, 1877; von Gizycki, G. Vierteljahrsschrift für wissenschaftliche Philosophie 4 1880–1 and 9 1885–6 (review of 3rd edn); Courtney, W. L. Edinburgh Rev 157, Apr 1883; von Gizycki, G. Mind o.s. 9 1884 (review of 3rd edn and suppl to 2nd edn); von Gizycki, G. International Jnl of Ethics 1 1891 (review of 4th edn); Barry, W. Quart Rev 172 1891; Mackenzie, J. S. International Jnl of Ethics 4 1893 (review of 5th edn).

The principles of political economy. 1883, 1887, 1901.
REVIEWS: Athenaeum 1 1883; Nation 36 1883; Quart Rev 78 1883; Westminster Rev n.s. 64 1883; Richards, H. Acad 19 May 1883; Synott, N. J. Dublin Rev 3rd ser 2 1884; Westminster Rev n.s. 129 1888; Nicholson, J. S. Quart Rev 219 1913.

The scope and method of economic science. 1885, rptd Miscellaneous essays, 1904.
REVIEWS: Edgeworth, F. Y. Acad 13 Mar 1886; Seligman, E. R. A. Political Science Quart 1 1886; Westminster Rev n.s. 69 1886.

Outlines of the history of ethics for English readers. 1886, 1888, 1892, 1896, 1902; tr Ital 1902.
REVIEWS: Athenaeum 2 1886; Wallace, W. Mind o.s. 11 1886; Westminster Rev n.s. 70 1886; Stanley, H. M. Dial Oct 1886.

The elements of politics. 1891, 1897, 1908, 1919.
REVIEWS: Benn, A. W. Acad 10 Oct 1891; Edgeworth, F. Y. Economic Jnl 1 1891; Ritchie, D. G. International Jnl of Ethics 2 1891–2; Nation 53 1891; Westminster Rev 136 1891; Wilson, W. Dial Nov 1891; Robinson, J. H. Annals of the Amer Acad of Political and Social Science 3 1892–3; Athenaeum 1 1892; Rashdall, H. Economic Rev 2 1892; Jnl of Education n.s. 14 1892; Jenks, J. Philosophical Rev 1 1892; Dunning, W. A. Political Science Quart 7 1892; Walpole, S. Edinburgh Rev 175, Jan 1892.

Practical ethics: a collection of addresses and essays. 1898, 1909.
REVIEWS: Bosanquet, B. International Jnl of Ethics 8 1897; Athenaeum 1 1898; Ritchie, D. G. Mind n.s. 7 1898; Nation 66 1898; Westminster Rev 149 1898; Acad 5 Feb 1898; Jnl of Education n.s. 20 Mar 1898; Ward, W. Quart Rev 189 Jan 1899.

Philosophy: its scope and relations. Ed J. Ward 1902.
REVIEWS: Athenaeum 2 1902; Jnl of Education n.s. 14 1902; Nation 75 1902; Creighton, J. E. Philosophical Rev 11 1902; Knight, W. Hibbert Jnl 2 1903–4; Pringle-Pattison, A. S. Mind n.s. 12 1903; Rogers, A. K. Dial July 1903.

Lectures on the ethics of T. H. Green, H. Spencer and J. Martineau. Ed E. E. C. Jones 1902.
REVIEWS: Moore, G. E. Cambridge Rev 20 Nov 1902; Taylor, A. E. Hibbert Jnl 1 1902–3; Mellone, S. H. International Jnl of Ethics 14 1903–4; Jnl of Education n.s. 15 1903; Bosanquet, B. Mind n.s. 12 1903.

The development of European polity. Ed E. M. Sidgwick 1903.
REVIEWS: Hodgson, W. E. Acad 21 Nov 1903; Rankin, G. C. International Jnl of Ethics 14 1903–4; Athenaeum 1 1904; Rait, R. S. Economic Rev 14 1904; Nation 78 1904; Dunning, W. A. Political Science Quart 19 1904; Dublin Figaro 14 May 1904.

Miscellaneous essays and addresses. Ed E. M. and A. Sidgwick 1904.
REVIEWS: Muirhead, J. H. Hibbert Jnl 1904–5; Athenaeum 1 1905; Jnl of Education n.s. 17 1905; Taylor, A. E. Philosophical Rev 15 1906; Seager, H. R. Political Science Quart 21 1906.

Lectures on the Philosophy of Kant and other philosophical lectures and essays. Ed J. Ward 1905.
REVIEWS: Moore, G. E. Hibbert Jnl 4 1905–6; Mackenzie, J. S. International Jnl of Ethics 16 1905–6; Taylor, A. E. Philosophical Rev 15 1906; Acad 3 Mar 1906; Hicks, G. D. Mind n.s. 22 1913.

Sidgwick, A. and E. M. Henry Sidgwick, a memoir. 1906.
REVIEWS: Athenaeum 1 1906; Jones, E. E. C. Hibbert Jnl 5 1906–7; Jnl of Education n.s. 28 1906; Maitland, F. W. Independent Rev June 1906; Acad 3 Mar 1906; Dewey, J. Political Science Quart 22 1907; Pringle-Pattison, A. S. Mind n.s. 17 1908; Edgeworth, F. Y. (rptd in Papers relating to political economy 3 1925).

National and international right and wrong. Ed J. Bryce 1920. A reprint of Public morality and The morality of strife from Practical ethics.
REVIEW: Taylor, A. E. Mind n.s. 29 1920.

Articles, prefaces etc

Goethe and Fredericka. Macmillan's Mag Mar 1860. Verses, rptd in Memoir 1906.

Eton. Macmillan's Mag Feb 1861.

Letter to The Times 20 Feb 1861, rptd in Memoir 1906.

The despot's heir. Macmillan's Mag Mar 1861. Verses, rptd in Memoir 1906.

Ranke's History of England. Macmillan's Mag May 1861.

Alexis de Tocqueville. Macmillan's Mag Nov 1861; rptd in Miscellaneous essays, 1904.

Ecce Homo. Westminster Rev July 1866; rptd in Miscellaneous essays, 1904.

Liberal education. Macmillan's Mag Apr 1867.

The prophet of culture. Macmillan's Mag Aug 1867; rptd in Miscellaneous essays, 1904.

The theory of classical education. In Essays on a liberal education, ed F. W. Farrar, 1867; rptd in Miscellaneous essays, 1904.

Mr Roden Noel's Poems. Spectator 13 Feb 1869.

Review of Courthope's Ludibria lunae. Spectator 7 Aug 1869.

Poems and prose remains of A. H. Clough. Westminster Rev Oct 1869; rptd in Miscellaneous essays, 1904.

Review of Baring-Gould's Origin and development of religious belief. Cambridge Univ Gazette 6 Jan 1870.

Clerical engagements. Pall Mall Gazette 6 Jan 1870.
Review of Broome's Stranger of Seriphos. Spectator 19 Feb 1870.
The verification of beliefs. Paper read to the Metaphysical Soc 27 Apr 1870.
Review of Grote's Examination of the Utilitarian philosophy. Cambridge Univ Reporter 8 Feb 1871.
Review of Courthope's Paradise of birds. Spectator 18 Feb 1871.
Review of Swinburne's Songs before sunrise. Cambridge Univ Reporter 22 Feb 1871.
Review of Maguire's Essays on the platonic ethics. Cambridge Univ Reporter 1 Mar 1871.
Review of Grote's Examination of the Utilitarian philosophy. Acad 1 Apr 1871.
Review of Conway's Earthly pilgrimage. Acad 15 Apr 1871.
Critique of Fraser's Berkeley. Athenaeum 17 and 24 June 1871.
Review of Hutton's Essays, theological and literary. Acad 1 July 1871.
The verification of beliefs. Contemporary Rev July 1871.
Review of Maguire's Essays on the platonic ethics. Acad 15 Sep 1871.
Beale's life theories and their influence on religious thought. Acad 15 Oct 1871.
Lewes's History of philosophy. Acad 15 Nov 1871.
Obituary of Prof Trendelenberg. Acad 1 Feb 1872.
Review of Zimmerman's Samuel Clarke's life and doctrine. Acad 1 Apr 1872.
Review of Leifchild's Higher ministry of nature. Athenaeum 6 Apr 1872.
Critique of Lord Ormathwaite's Astronomy and geology compared. Athenaeum 20 Apr 1872.
Pleasure and desire. Contemporary Rev Apr 1872.
Review of Cobbe's Darwinism in morals. Academy 15 June 1872.
Review of Barzellotti's La morale nella filosofia positiva. Acad 1 July 1872.
Review of Spicker's Die philosophie des Grafen von Shaftesbury. Acad 15 Aug 1872.
Review of Mahaffy's Kant's critical philosophy for English readers. Acad 15 Sep 1872.
Review of Jödl's Leben und philosophie David Hume. Acad 15 Oct 1872.
Monck's Space and vision. Athenaeum 18 May 1872.
Bree's Exposition of fallacies in Darwin's hypothesis. Athenaeum 20 July 1872. Replies by Bree, ibid.
Review of Bikker and Hatton's Ethics for undenominational schools. Athenaeum 27 July 1872.
Note in reply to Bree. Athenaeum 3 Aug 1872.
The sophists. I. Jnl of Philology 4 (8) 1872; II Jnl of Philology 5 (9) 1873; rptd in Lectures on the philosophy of Kant, 1905.
Review of Spencer's Principles of psychology. Acad 1 Apr 1873.
J. S. Mill. Acad 15 May 1873.
Review of Spencer's Principles of psychology. Spectator 21 June 1873.
Review of Tuke's Effect of the mind upon the body. Athenaeum 12 July 1873.
Review of Mansel's Letters, lectures, and reviews. Acad 15 July 1873.
Review of J. F. Stephen's Liberty, equality, fraternity. Acad 1 Aug 1873.
Review of Cairnes's Political essays. Spectator 8 Nov 1873.
Utilitarianism. Paper read to Metaphysical Soc 16 Dec 1873.
On a passage in Plato's Republic. Jnl of Philology 5 (10) 1874.
Review of Green and Grose's edn of Hume's Treatise. Acad 30 May 1874.
Review of Green and Grose's edn of Hume's Essays. Spectator 27 Mar 1875.
The theory of evolution in its application to practice. Paper read to Metaphysical Soc 13 July 1875.
The late Professor Cairnes. Spectator 31 July 1875.
Review of Green and Grose's edn of Hume. Acad 7 Aug 1875.
The Eton dispute. Spectator 27, Nov 1875.
The theory of evolution in its application to practice. Mind o.s. 1 (1) 1876.
Philosophy at Cambridge. Mind o.s. 1 (2) 1876.
Bradley's Ethical studies. Mind o.s. 1 (4) 1876. Replies by Bradley and Sidgwick, 2 (7) 1877.
Prof Calderwood on Intuitionism in morals. Mind o.s. 1 (4) 1876.
Idle fellowships. Contemporary Rev Apr 1876; rptd in Miscellaneous essays, 1904.
Hedonism and ultimate good. Mind o.s. 2 (5) 1877. Reply by T. H. Green, ibid.
Grote's treatise on moral ideals. Mind o.s. 2 (6) 1877.
Reply to Barratt on The suppression of egoism. Mind o.s. 2 (7) 1877.
Bentham and Benthamism. Fortnightly Rev May 1877; rptd in Miscellaneous essays, 1904.
The relation of psychogony to metaphysics and ethics. Paper read to Metaphysical Soc 15 Jan 1878.
Ethics. Encyclopaedia Britannica 9th edn 1878. Expanded to Outlines of the history of ethics for English readers.
Dr Georg von Gizycki on Hume's Ethics. Acad 5 Oct 1878.
The establishment of ethical first principles. Mind o.s. 4 (13) 1879.
Incoherence of empirical philosophy. Paper read to Metaphysical Soc 14 Jan 1879.
The so-called idealism of Kant. Mind o.s. 4 (15) 1879.
Review of Guyau's La morale d'épicure. Mind o.s. 4 (16) 1879.
Economic method. Fortnightly Rev Feb 1879.
What is money? Fortnightly Rev Apr 1879.
The wages fund theory. Fortnightly Rev Sep 1879.
The scope of metaphysics. Paper read to Metaphysical Soc 10 Apr 1879.
On historical psychology. Nineteenth Cent Feb 1880.
Kant's refutation of idealism. Mind o.s. 5 (17) 1880.
Review of Fouillée's L'Idée moderne du droit. Mind o.s. 5 (17) 1880.
Mr Spencer's ethical system. Mind o.s. 5 (18) 1880.
Inaugural address to the Society for Psychical Research. Proc of the Soc for Psychical Research 1 1882; Address to the Soc for Psychical Research, ibid.
On the fundamental doctrines of Descartes. Mind o.s. 7 (27) 1882.
The incoherence of empirical philosophy. Mind o.s. 7 (28) 1882; rtpd Lectures on the philosophy of Kant 1905.
Review of L. Stephen's The science of ethics. Mind o.s. 7 (28) 1882.
A criticism of the critical philosophy. I. Mind o.s. 8 (29) 1883; II. Mind o.s. 8 (31) 1883. Reply by R. Adamson, ibid.
Kant's view of mathematical premisses and reasonings. I. Mind o.s. 8 (31) 1883; II. Mind o.s. 8 (32) 1883.
Address to the Society for Psychical Research. Proc of the Soc for Psychical Research 1 1883; Ibid, Proceedings 2 1884.
Green's Ethics. Mind o.s. 9 (34) 1884.
Review of Fowler's Progressive morality. Mind o.s. 10 (38) 1885.
Review of Martineau's Types of ethical theory. Mind o.s. 10 (39) 1885.
The scope and method of economic science. Paper read to the Br Assoc 1885; rptd in Miscellaneous essays, 1904.
Dr Martineau's defence of Types of ethical theory. Mind o.s. 11 (41) 1886.
The historical method. Mind o.s. 11 (41) 1886.
Bluntschli's Theory of the state. EHR Apr 1886.
The possibilities of mal-observation. Proc of the Soc for Psychical Research 4 1886. Discussion with C. C. Massey.
Bi-metalism (no. 1): theory of international bi-metalism. Fortnightly Rev Oct 1886.
Economic socialism. Contemporary Rev Nov 1886. Rptd in Miscellaneous essays, 1904.
Idiopsychological ethics. Mind o.s. 12 1887. Reply to J. Martineau, 10 1885. Further discussion of Martineau.
The Kantian conception of free will. Mind o.s. 13 (51) 1888; rptd in The method of ethics, 1901, 1907.
Review of Pulszky's Theory of law and civil society. EHR Oct 1888.

Preface to Aschrott's English poor law system. 1888.
Address to the Society for Psychical Research. Proc of the Soc for Psychical Research 5 1888.
The scope and limits of the work of an ethical society. Paper read to the Cambridge Ethical Soc 18 May 1888. Rptd in Practical ethics, 1898.
Address to the Society for Psychical Research on the physical phenomena of spiritualism. Proc of the Soc for Psychical Research 5 1889.
Canons of evidence in psychical research. Proc of the Soc for Psychical Research 6 1889.
Ad interim report on The census of hallucinations. Proc of the Soc for Psychical Research 6 suppl 1889.
Experiments in thought transference. Proc of the Soc for Psychical Research 6 1889. With E. M. Sidgwick.
Plato's Utilitarianism: a dialogue by J. Grote and Sidgwick. Classical Rev 3 1889.
Some fundamental ethical controversies. Mind o.s. 14 (56) 1889. Replies by T. Fowler and L. A. Selby-Bigge, o.s. 15 1890.
Shakespeare's methods, with special reference to Julius Caesar and Coriolanus. 1889; rptd in Miscellaneous essays, 1904. Lecture.
Shakespeare and the romantic drama, with special reference to Macbeth. Rptd in Miscellaneous essays, 1904. Lecture.
A lecture against lecturing. New Rev May 1890; rptd in Miscellaneous essays, 1904.
Letter to the editor, Prof Sidgwick on lecturing. Jnl of Education n.s. 12 July 1890.
Second address on the census of hallucinations. Proc of the Soc for Psychical Research 6 1890.
Second ad interim report on the census. Proc of the Soc for Psychical Research 6 suppl 1890.
The morality of strife. International Jnl of Ethics 1 1890; rptd in Practical ethics, 1898.
The feeling-tone of desire and aversion. Mind n.s. 1 (1) 1892.
Spencer's Justice. Mind n.s. 1 (1) 1892.
Aristotle's classification of forms of government. Classical Rev Apr 1892.
Is the distinction between 'is' and 'ought' ultimate and irreducible? Proc Aristotelian Soc n.s. 1 1892. Symposium.
Unreasonable action. Mind n.s. 2 (6) 1893. Reply by H. R. Marshall, 3 1894; rptd in Practical ethics, 1898.
My station and its duties. International Jnl of Ethics 4 1893; rptd in Practical ethics, 1898, under the title The aims and methods of an ethical society.
Note to the Report of the Gresham University Commission. Jan 1894.
Luxury. International Jnl of Ethics 5 1894; rptd in Practical ethics, 1898.
A dialogue on time and common sense. Mind n.s. 3 (12) 1894; rptd in Lectures on the philosophy of Kant, 1905.
Political prophecy and sociology. National Rev Dec 1894; rptd in Miscellaneous essays, 1904.
The trial scene in the Iliad. Classical Rev Feb 1894.
Note on the term ἑκτημόροι or ἑκτημόριοι. Classical Rev July 1894.
Conjectures on the constitutional history of Athens. Classical Rev Oct 1894.
Economic science and economics. Dictionary of political economy vol 1, ed R. Palgrave 1894.
Report on the census of hallucinations. Proc of the Soc for Psychical Research 10 1894. With A. Johnson, F. W. H. Myers, F. Podmore and E. M. Sidgwick.
Disinterested deception. Jnl of the Soc for Psychical Research 6 1894.
The philosophy of common sense. Mind n.s. 4 (14) 1895; rptd in Lectures on the philosophy of Kant, 1905.
Theory and practice. Mind n.s. 4 (15) 1895.
Ritchie's Natural rights. Mind n.s. 4 (15) 1895.
The ethics of religious conformity. International Jnl of Ethics 6 1895; rptd in Practical ethics, 1898.
The economic lessons of socialism. Economic Jnl Sep 1895; rptd in Miscellaneous essays, 1904.
Note on the memorandum of Sir R. Giffen to the Royal Commission on the Financial Relations of Great Britain and Ireland. Report of the Commission 2 1895.
Memorandum in answer to questions from the Royal Commission on Secondary Education. Report of the Commission 6 1895.
Prefatory note to V. Solovev's A modern priestess of Isis. Abridged and tr Walter Leaf 1895.
Review of Gidding's Principles of sociology. Economic Jnl Sep 1896.
The ethics of religious conformity. International Jnl of Ethics 8 1896; rptd in Practical ethics, 1898.
Preface to J. R. Seeley's Introduction to political science. Ed Sidgwick 1896.
Involuntary whispering considered in relation to experiments in thought transference. Proc of the Soc for Psychical Research 12 1897.
Public morality. Paper read to the Eranus Soc 26 Jan 1897; rptd in Practical ethics, 1898.
The pursuit of culture. Paper read to the London School of Ethics and Social Philosophy 24 Oct 1897; rptd in Practical ethics, 1898.
Comments on Tennyson. In H. Tennyson, Life of Tennyson vol 1, 1897; rptd in Memoir, 1906.
Concessions and questions for the Synthetic Society. In The Wilfrid Wards and the transition, ed M. Ward, 1934.
Clerical veracity. Rptd in Practical ethics, 1898.
On the nature of the evidence for theism. Paper read to the Synthetic Soc 25 Feb 1898; rptd in Memoir, 1906.
Review of Gidding's Elements of sociology. Economic Jnl Sep 1899.
Authority, scientific and theological. Paper read to the Synthetic Soc 24 Feb 1899; rptd in Memoir, 1906.
The relation of ethics to sociology. International Jnl of Ethics 10 1899; rptd in Miscellaneous essays, 1904.
Memorandum to the Royal Commission on Local Taxation. Report of the Commission 1899.
Political economy, its scope; Political economy, its method; Political economy and ethics. In Dictionary of political economy vol 3, ed R. Palgrave, 1899.
Criteria of truth and error. Mind n.s. 9 (33) 1900; rptd in Lectures on the philosophy of Kant, 1905, with an appendix.
The philosophy of T. H. Green. Mind n.s. 10 38 1901; rptd in Lectures on the philosophy of Kant, 1905.
Prof. Sidgwick's ethical view: an auto-historical fragment. Mind n.s. 10 (38) 1901; rptd in The method of ethics, 1901, 1907.

Pamphlets

On the classical tripos exam (in support of the alteration proposed by W. G. Clark and R. Burn). Cambridge 1866.
The ethics of conformity and subscription. 1870; rptd in part only and with several textual alterations in Practical ethics, 1898.
The pursuit of culture as an ideal. An inaugural lecture delivered to the students of the Univ College of Wales, Aberystwyth, 13 Oct 1897; rptd in part in Miscellaneous essays, 1904.

§2

Obituaries

Jnl of Education Oct 1900; Economic Jnl 10 1900; Proc of the Soc for Psychical Research 15 1900–1 (rptd in F. W. H. Myers, Fragments of prose and poetry, ed E. Myers 1904); Cambridge Rev 25 Oct 1900; Pilot 15 Sep 1900; International Jnl of Ethics 11 1900–1; Mind n.s. 10 38 1901.

Criticism

Arnold, M. Culture and anarchy. 1869.
Spencer, H. Replies to criticisms. Fortnightly Rev n.s. 14 1873; rptd

in Essays, scientific, political, and speculative vol 2, New York 1891.
Bain, A. The emotions and the will. 3rd edn 1875.
Bradley, F. H. Ethical studies. 1876.
Calderwood, H. Sidgwick on intuitionism in morals. Mind o.s. 1 1876.
Barratt, A. Ethics and politics. Mind o.s. 2 1877.
Edgeworth, F. Y. New and old methods of ethics, or 'physical ethics' and 'methods of ethics'. 1877.
Magoun, G. F. Recent English thought in ethics. Jnl of Speculative Philosophy 11 1877.
Pollock, F. Happiness or welfare. Mind o.s. 2 1877.
Barratt, A. Ethics and psychogony. Mind o.s. 3 1878.
Carrau, L. Moralistes anglais contemporains: M. H. Sidgwick. Revue Philosophique 5 1878.
Pollock, F. The 'suppression' of egoism. Mind o.s. 2 1878.
Guyau, J. La morale anglaise contemporaine. Paris 1879.
Caird, E. Reply on Kant's idealism. Mind o.s. 4 1879; Ibid. Mind o.s. 5 1880.
Edgeworth, F. Y. Mathematical psychics: an essay on the application of mathematics to the moral sciences. 1881.
Spencer, H. Replies to criticisms on The data of ethics. Mind o.s. 6 1881; rptd in Appendix to Principles of ethics vol 2.
Bain, A. On some points in ethics. Mind o.s. 8 1883.
Green, T. H. Prolegomena to ethics. Oxford 1883.
Fowler, T. Professor Sidgwick on 'progressive morality'. Mind o.s. 10 1885.
Martineau, J. Professor Sidgwick on 'types of ethical theory'. Mind o.s. 10 1885.
Martineau, J. Types of ethical theories. 2 vols Oxford 1885.
Rashdall, H. Professor Sidgwick's Utilitarianism. Mind o.s. 10 1885.
Bradley, F. H. Mr Sidgwick on ethical studies. Mind o.s. 12 1887.
Green, T. H. Hedonism and ultimate good. Mind o.s. 12 1887.
Calderwood, H. Handbook of moral philosophy. 1888.
Seth, J. The evolution of morality. Mind o.s. 14 1889.
Dewey, J. Outlines of a critical theory of ethics. Rptd in The early works, 1882–1898, Carbondale IL 1967–72.
Marshal, T. Reply on definition of desire. Mind n.s. 1 1892.
Jones, E. E. C. Rational hedonism. International Jnl of Ethics 1894–5.
Jones, E. E. C. Discussion on Rational hedonism. International Jnl of Ethics 1894–5.
Marshal, T. Reply on unreasonable action. Mind n.s. 3 1894.
Seth, J. A study of ethical principles. 1894.
Seth, J. Is pleasure the summum bonum? International Jnl of Ethics 6 1895–6.
Rashdall, H. Professor Sidgwick on the ethics of religious conformity: a reply. International Jnl of Ethics 7 1896–7.
MacMillan, M. Sidgwick and Schopenhauer on the foundation of morality. International Jnl of Ethics 8 1898.
Magill, R. Der rationale Utilitarismus Sidgwicks. Jena 1899.
Rashdall, H. Can there be a sum of pleasures? Mind n.s. 8 1899.
Hayward, F. H. The real significance of Sidgwick's 'Ethics'. International Jnl of Ethics 11 1900–1.
Hayward, F. H. A reply to E. E. C. Jones. International Jnl of Ethics 11 1900–1.
Jones, E. E. C. Mr Hayward's evaluation of Professor Sidgwick's ethics. International Jnl of Ethics 11 1900–1.
Albee, E. An examination of Professor Sidgwick's proof of Utilitarianism. Philosophical Rev 10 1901.
Hayward, F. H. Constructive elements in the ethical philosophy of Sidgwick. Ethical World 15 Dec 1901.
Hayward, F. H. The ethical philosophy of Sidgwick: nine essays, critical and expository. 1901.
Seth, J. The ethical system of Henry Sidgwick. Mind n.s. 10 1901.
Albee, E. A history of English Utilitarianism. 1902.
Albee, E. Rejoinder to Barker's recent criticisms. Philosophical Rev 11 1902.
Barker, H. A recent criticism of Sidgwick's Methods of ethics. Philosophical Rev 11 1902.
Moore, G. E. Principia ethica. 1903.
Seth, A. Sidgwick's philosophy: its scope and relations. Mind n.s. 12 1903.
Jones, E. E. C. Professor Sidgwick's ethics. Proceedings of the Aristotelian Society n.s. 4 1904.
Winter, E. S. F. Henry Sidgwick's moralphilosophie. Flensburg 1904.
McTaggart, J. M. E. The ethics of Henry Sidgwick. Quart Rev 205 1906.
Rashdall, H. The theory of good and evil; a treatise on moral philosophy. Vol 1 1907.
Sinclair, A. G. Der utilitarismus bei Sidgwick und Spencer. Heidelberg 1907.
Barbour, G. F. Sidgwick and Green and the community of the good. Philosophical Rev 17 1908.
Jones, E. E. C. Henry Sidgwick's philosophical intuitionism. Bericht uber den III internationalen Kongress für Philosophie. Ed Th. E. Heidelberg 1909.
Bernays, P. Das moralprinzip bie Sidgwick und bei Kant. Abhandlung der Fries'schen Schule n.s. 3 1910. Also issued in pam 1910.
Maitland, F. W. Collected papers. Cambridge 1911.
Jones, E. E. C. Practical dualism. Proc of the Aristotelian Soc n.s. 18 1918.
Jones, E. E. C. Henry Sidgwick. Hastings Encyclopedia of Religion and Ethics 11 1920.
Sorley, W. R. A history of English philosophy. 1920.
Ward, James. The realm of ends or pluralism and theism. 3rd edn Cambridge 1920.
Broad, C. D. Five types of ethical theory. 1930.
Westermark, E. Ethical relativity. 1932.
Broad, C. D. Henry Sidgwick and psychical research. Proc of the Soc for Psychical Research 45 1938.
Havard, W. C. Henry Sidgwick and later utilitarian philosophy. Gainesville FL 1959.
Symonds, J. A. The letters of John Addington Symonds. Ed H. M. Schueler and R. L. Peters, Detroit 1969.
Rawls, J. A theory of justice. Cambridge MA 1971.
Symposium: Henry Sidgwick. The Monist 58 July 1974.
Schneewind, J. B. Sidgwick's ethics and Victorian moral philosophy. 1977.
Williams, B. The point of view of the universe. Cambridge Rev 7 May 1982.
Parfit, D. Reasons and persons. Oxford 1984.
Oppenheim, J. The other world. Cambridge 1985.
Skidelsky, R. Henry Sidgwick, between reason and duty. Sidgwick lecture, Newham College, 31 May 1988.
Essays on Henry Sidgwick. Ed B. Schultz, New York 1992.
Harrison, R. Henry Sidgwick. Philosophy 71 1996.
Schultz, B. The complete works and select correspondence of Henry Sidgwick, on CD-ROM. Charlottesville VA 1997.

Biographies

Benson, A. C. The life of Edward White Benson. New York 1899. Contains an autobiographical note by Sidgwick.
Stephen, L. Henry Sidgwick. DNB.
Bryce, J. Henry Sidgwick. In Studies in contemporary biography, 1903.
Ward, W. Some characteristics of Henry Sidgwick. In Ten personal studies, 1908.
Benson, A. C. The leaves of the tree: III Henry Sidgwick. Cornhill

Mag n.s. 102 Dec 1910; rptd in Leaves of the tree: studies in biography, 1911.
Lord Rayleigh. Some recollections of Henry Sidgwick. Proc of the Soc for Psychical Research 45 1938–9.
Sidgwick, Mrs. E. Henry Sidgwick, a memoir. 1938.
Broad, C. D. Henry Sidgwick. In Ethics and the history of philosophy, 1952.
Gauld, A. The founders of psychical research. 1968.
James, D. E. Henry Sidgwick, Science and faith in Victorian England. 1970.
Blanshard, B. Four reasonable men. Middleton CT 1984. [BS, JBS]

William Henry Smith 1808–72

See col 2657.

Mary Somerville née Fairfax later Greig 1780–1872

The Somerville Collection containing mss, letters and documents is in the Bodleian.

§1

A preliminary dissertation to 'The mechanism of the heavens'. 1831 (for private circulation), Philadelphia 1832.
The mechanism of the heavens. 1831.
REVIEWS: Literary Gazette 778 1831; Athenaeum 221 1832; Edinburgh Rev 55 1832; Monthly Rev n.s. 1 1832, Quarterly Rev 47 1832.
On the connexion of the physical sciences. 1834, Philadelphia 1834, London 1835 (2nd edn), 1836 (3rd edn), 1840 (5th edn), 1842 (6th edn), 1846 (7th edn), New York 1846, London 1849 (8th edn), New York 1853, 1857, London 1858 (9th edn completely rev), New York 1871 (from 7th London edn), London 1877 (10th edn corrected and rev by A. B. Buckley); tr Fr 1839; Ital 1841, 1861.
REVIEWS: Athenaeum 333 1834; British Critic 16 1834; Edinburgh Rev 59 1834; Literary Gazette 894 1834; Mechanics Mag 29 Mar 1834; Quart Rev 51 1834.
Physical geography. 2 vols 1848, 1 vol Philadelphia 1848, 2 vols London 1849, 2 vols Philadelphia 1849, 2 vols London 1849 (rev), 1 vol Philadelphia 1850 (2nd American edn from new and rev London edn), 2 vols London 1851 (3rd edn rev), 1 vol Philadelphia 1853 (new American edn from 3rd rev London edn with notes and glossary by W. S. Ruschenberger), Philadelphia 1854, 1855, 1 vol London 1858 (4th edn rev), Philadelphia 1859 (from 3rd rev London edn), London 1862 (5th edn), New York 1867, London 1870 (6th edn rev H. W. Bates), Philadelphia 1871 (from 3rd rev London edn), London 1877 (7th edn); tr Ger 1851; Ital 1856, 1861.
Physical geography. Mirzapore 1855 (extracted from the work of M. Somerville and including an account of the Himalaya by B. H. Hodgson. Ed J. R. B[allantyne]).
REVIEWS: Athenaeum 1088 1848, Quart Rev 83 1848, Blackwood's Mag 66 1849.
On molecular and microscopic science. 2 vols 1869 (illus).
REVIEWS: Edinburgh Rev 265 1869; Saturday Rev 27 1869.

Contributions to periodicals and collaborative works

On the magnetizing power of the more refrangible solar rays. Philosophical Trans of the Royal Soc 116 1826.
Astronomy: the comet. Quart Rev 1835.
Experiments on transmission of the chemical rays of the solar spectrum across different media. Comptes rendus 3 1836.
Electro-magnetism. History of Davenport-invention of the application of electro-magnetism to machinery . . . by Prof Silliman. Also, extracts from other public journals, and information on electricity, galvanism, electro-magnetism etc. By Mrs Somerville. New York 1837.
On the action of the rays of the spectrum on vegetable juices. Communicated by Sir J. Herschel. Philosophical Trans of the Royal Soc 4 1845.
An unpbd letter of Mary Somerville. With a comment by F. E. Hutchinson. Oxford 1929. (Rptd from The Oxford Mag.)

§2

Proctor, R. A. Monthly notices of the Royal Astronomical Soc Feb 1873. (Rptd in Light science for leisure hours, 1873.)
Somerville, M. Personal recollections from early life to old age of Mary Somerville. With selections from her correspondence. By her daughter. 1873, Boston 1874, London 1874, Boston 1876, 1879, 1885.
REVIEWS: Fortnightly Rev 21 1874; Quart Rev 136 1874.
Walford, L. B. Mary Somerville. Blackwood's Mag 143 1888. Rptd in Four biographies from 'Blackwood', Edinburgh and London 1888.
DNB
Patterson, E. C. Mary Somerville 1780–1872. Oxford 1979.
Patterson, E. C. Mary Somerville and the cultivation of science, 1815–1840. The Hague 1983.
McKinlay, J. Mary Somerville 1780–1872. Edinburgh 1987.
Blain, V., P. Clements and I. Grundy. The feminist companion to literature in English. 1990.

William Ritchie Sorley 1855–1935

§1

The historical method. In A. Seth and R. B. Haldane, Essays in philosophic criticism, 1883.
On the ethics of naturalism. Edinburgh 1885, 1904 (rev).
Recent tendencies in ethics. Edinburgh 1904.
Agnosticism: its meanings and claims. 1908.
The moral life and moral worth. Cambridge 1911.
The interpretation of evolution. [1912.]
The state and morality. In The international crisis: the theory of the state, 1916.
Moral values and the idea of God. Aberdeen and Cambridge 1918.
Spinoza. 1918.
A history of English philosophy. Cambridge 1920, 1965 (as A history of British philosophy to 1900). Based on CHEL.
Value and reality. In Contemporary British philosophy, ed J. H. Muirhead vol 2, 1925.
Tradition. Oxford 1926.

Articles

The morality of nations. International Jnl of Ethics 1 1891.
The philosophy of Herbert of Cherbury. Mind n.s. 4 1895.
Betting and gambling. International Jnl of Ethics 13 1903.
The knowledge of good. Hibbert Jnl 3 1905.
The method of a metaphysic of ethics. Philosophical rev 14 1905.
Ethical aspects of economics. International Jnl of Ethics 17 1907.
The interpretation of evolution. Proc Br Acad 4 1910.
The philosophical attitude. International Jnl of Ethics 20 1910.
Does religion need a philosophy? Hibbert Jnl 11 1913.
Time and reality. Mind n.s. 32 1923.
Also works on religion and contributions on philosophy to CHEL.

§2

Tennant, F. R. Sorley. Proc Br Acad 22 1935.
Muirhead, J. H. Sorley. Philosophy 11 1936.
Stout, G. F. Sorley. Mind n.s. 45 1936.

William Spalding 1809–59

See col 2302.

Herbert Spencer 1820–1903

The BL has most of Spencer's book mss. Senate House Lib, Univ of London, holds on permanent loan the substantial Athenaeum collection of Herbert Spencer's papers. For details of these, along with several less important collections, mostly letters, see Perrin, below.

Bibliographies

Duncan, D. In his Life and letters of Herbert Spencer, 1908, 2 vols New York 1908.

Rumney, J. In his Herbert Spencer's sociology, 1937, rptd New York 1966.

Schmid, M. and M. Weihrich. Bibliographie der werke von Herbert Spencer. Munich 1991.

Perrin, R. G. Herbert Spencer: a primary and secondary bibliography. 2 vols New York and London 1993. Includes detailed annotations of all Spencer's known pbns.

Collections and selections

Readings from Herbert Spencer on education. Comp Rev J. B. Young, New York 1883.

An epitome of the synthetic philosophy: the philosophy completed and in part revised. Abridged F. H. Collins 1889, New York 1889, London 1890 (2nd edn), 1894 (3rd edn), 1897 (4th edn), 1901 (5th edn), rptd Ann Arbor MI 1975; New York 1901 (2nd Amer edn); tr Fr 1891, 1894 (2nd edn), 1901 (3rd edn), Rus 1892, 1897 (2nd edn), Ger 1899, Hungarian 1903, 1905 (2nd edn).

Aphorisms from the writings of Herbert Spencer. Comp J. R. Gingell, New York 1894, 1894 (2nd edn, rev); tr Rus 1896.

[Works.] 15 vols New York 1896, 1897, 15 vols in 7 [190?] (author's edn), 19 vols London 1902, 18 vols New York and London 1910 (New Uniform edn), 1914, 1915 (Popular Uniform edn).

Selections from The data of ethics, Social statics, Education, and Progress...: also two complete essays: The development hypothesis and The use of anthropomorphism. New York and London [1902] (S & S Little Classics).

Seven essays selected from the works of Herbert Spencer. 1907.

Essays on education and kindred subjects. Introd by C. W. Eliot. New York 1910 (EL), London 1911 (as Essays on education, etc), New York 1919 (rev edn), ptd until at least 1946, rptd 1963, 1977. Incorporates Education: intellectual, moral, and physical (*see below*) plus 5 other previously pbd essays.

Passages from the philosophy of Herbert Spencer. Comp C. H. Stevens, Portland ME 1910.

Herbert Spencer: choix de textes et étude du système philosophique. Comp Edmond Parisot, Paris [1912].

The gist of Herbert Spencer. Ed Haldeman-Julius, Girard KS 1924.

Readings from Herbert Spencer. Comp O. Barnstorff, Frankfurt 1925.

Prophecy come true: some thoughts on political and social questions from the writings of Herbert Spencer. Comp E. H. Blakeney 1949.

Literary style and music, including short essays on gracefulness and beauty. 1950 (Thinker's Lib), New York 1951, London 1970, Port Washington NY 1970.

The works of Herbert Spencer. 21 vols Osnabrück 1966. Reprints edns pbd from '1884' [1880] to 1907.

The evolution of society: selections from Herbert Spencer's Principles of sociology. Ed with introd by R. L. Carneiro, Chicago 1967, rptd 1974 (Midway).

Herbert Spencer. Ed with introd by A. Low-Beer 1969.

Herbert Spencer: structure, function and evolution. Ed with introd by S. Andreski 1971.

Herbert Spencer on social evolution: selected writings. Ed with introd by J. D. Y. Peel, Chicago and London 1972, rptd 1974 (Midway).

Political writings. Ed with introd by J. Offer, Cambridge 1994.

Collected works of Herbert Spencer. Ed M. Taylor 12 vols 1996.

§1

With the 1867 pbn of the 2nd edn of First principles *and the 2nd vol of his* Principles of biology, *Spencer directed that his publishers (Williams and Norgate of London, and D. Appleton of New York) should no longer provide review copies of his books. (He was aggrieved by the frequent misconstruction and generally careless treatment of his ideas in the pages of the periodical reviews.) Spencer held to this policy for nearly 10 years. Had he not interdicted the normal review process, much more would have been written about the 2nd vol of the 1st edn of* The principles of biology, *the 2nd and 3rd edns of* First principles, *the 2nd edn of* The principles of psychology, *and the 3rd ser of* Essays.

The proper sphere of government: a reprint of a series of letters, originally published in the Nonconformist. 1843; contained in The man versus the state, Indianapolis 1981, and Political writings (ed J. Offer), Cambridge 1994. First pbd 15 June 1842–11 Jan 1843 in Nonconformist 62–88 and 92, and rev for pbn as a pam.

Social statics: or the conditions essential to human happiness specified, and the first of them developed. '1851' [1850], rptd Clifton NJ 1969, New York 1969, Brookfield VT 1970; London 1861, New York 1865 (with introductory notice and author's preface to Amer edn), ptd until at least 1890 (with author's 2nd preface added 1877), rptd New York 1954, 1970; London 1868 (stereotyped–3rd thousand), 1876, 1892 (abridged and rev, pbd with Man versus the state), New York 1892, ptd until at least 1915, including New York and London 1910 (New Uniform edn), 1915 (Popular Uniform edn); Osnabrück 1966 (abridged and rev etc; 1st pt of vol 11 of The works of Herbert Spencer). Tr Jap 1881–4; (in pt) Du 1883; (in pt) Ital [1921?]; (in pt) Fr 1923. *Imprint is 1851 but Spencer reports pbn in Dec 1850.*

REVIEWS: [T. Hodgskin], Economist 9, 8 Feb 1851; Literary Gazette 1780, 1 Mar 1851; [G. H. Lewes], Leader 2, 15 Mar–12 Apr 1851; Athenaeum 1224, 12 Apr 1851; North Br Rev 15, Aug 1851; Br Quart Rev 14, 1 Aug 1851; [R. H. Hutton], Ethics of the voluntary system, Prospective Rev 8, Jan 1852; Quart Rev of the Methodist Episcopal Church, South n.s. 10, Apr 1856; [C. A. Cummings], North Amer Rev 86, Jan 1858; [E. E. Hale], Christian Examiner 5th ser 17, Sep 1865; [J. P. Quincy], Atlantic Monthly 16, Sep 1865; [W. J. Youmans], Popular Science Monthly 41, Aug 1892; Monist 3 Oct 1892.

State-education self-defeating: a chapter from Social statics.... 1851, 1851 (8th thousand). First pbd as ch 26 of Social statics, *above.* Tr Du 1883.

A new theory of population, deduced from the general law of animal fertility. Introd by T. R. Trall. 1852, New York 1852, 1853, London 1857. First pbd in Westminster Rev n.s. 1 Apr 1852.

Over-legislation. 1854 (with addns, and as pt of Chapman's Lib for the People). First pbd in Westminster Rev n.s. 4 July 1853. Tr Sp 1895.

The principles of psychology. (Numerous printings of 2nd–4th edns; US edns often unnumbered.) 1855, rptd Brookfield VT 1970; 1865; recast in 2 vols to form vols 4–5 of A system of synthetic philosophy, 1860–96. Vol 1 1870 (2nd edn), New York 1871, London 1881 (3rd edn), rptd Boston 1977; New York 1881, London 1899 (4th edn); vol 2 1872 (2nd edn), New York 1873, London 1881 (3rd edn), New York 1881, London 1899 (4th edn); 2 vols in 3 New York 1872–80 (Westminster edn), 1896, [1900?], [1901?] (Westminster edn); 2 vols New York 1903, New York and London 1910 (New Uniform edn), 1915 (Popular Uniform edn), 1920, Osnabrück 1966 (vols 4–5 of The works of Herbert Spencer). Second edn first pbd Dec 1867–Mar 1872 in 16 fascicules. Tr Ger 1874–5, 1882–6, 1903; Fr 1875, 1898 (new edn); Rus 1876; Du 1898; Hungarian 1903; Ital 1907, 1909; (in pt) Sp 1910.

REVIEWS: Br Quart Rev 22, Oct 1855; [G. H. Lewes], Leader 6, 20 Oct–3 Nov 1855; New Quart Rev and Digest of Current Lit 5 no 1 1856; [R. H. Hutton], Atheism, Nat Rev 2, Jan 1856; Nonconformist 16 no 532, 9 Jan 1856; Theology and philosophy,

Westminster Rev n.s. 9, Jan 1856; G. E. Lewes, Saturday Rev 1, 1 Mar 1856; Athenaeum 1483, 29 Mar 1856; J. D. Morell, Br and Foreign Medico-Chirurgical Rev (US edn) 17 Apr 1856; D. A. Spalding, Nature 7, 20 Feb–13 Mar 1872; Saturday Rev 35, 18 Jan 1873; H. Sidgwick, Acad 4, 1 Apr 1873; Spectator 46, 21 June 1873; B. P. Bowne, New Englander 32, July 1873; St G. Mivart, Dublin Rev n.s. 23, 25, 28, 30–3rd ser 3 Oct 1874, July 1875, Jan, Apr 1877, Jan 1878–Jan 1880; L. Adams, New Englander 34, July 1875; Critique Philosophique May 1877–Sep 1878; A. Bain, Mr Spencer's psychological 'congruities', Mind 6, Apr–July 1881; T. C. Laws, Open Court 8, 12 Apr 1894; J. M. Baldwin, Amer Naturalist 31, June 1897.

Railway morals and railway policy. With addns and postscript by the author. 1855, 1856 (Traveller's Lib), 1858. First pbd in Edinburgh Rev 100, Oct 1854. With addns and postscript by the author.

Essays: scientific, political, and speculative. First ser (or vol) 1857, 1858, 1868 (stereotyped edn); 2nd ser (or vol) 1863, New York 1864, London 1868 (stereotyped edn); 3rd ser (or vol) 1874, 1875 (new edn), 1878 (3rd edn); vols 1–2 1883 (4th thousand), 3 vols 1885 (4th edn), 1891 (Lib edn containing 7 essays not previously repbd), New York 1891, 1901 (Lib edn containing 10 essays not previously repbd), New York 1901, ptd until at least 1916, including New York and London 1910 (New Uniform edn), 1915 (Popular Uniform edn); Osnabrück 1966 (vols 13–15 of The works of Herbert Spencer). Final edn includes more than four dozen of Spencer's previously pbd essays. Tr Rus 1866; Fr 1885, 1889–91 (3rd edn), 1898 (4th edn), 1904 (5th edn); Sp 1885, [1895], [1904], 1908, [1908] (new edn), [1943]; (in pt) Ger 1889; (in pt) Ital 1894.
REVIEWS: C. Wright, North Amer Rev 99, July 1864; E. Caird, Acad 5, 2 May 1874; Saturday Rev 38, 4 July 1874; J. Sully, Examiner 4 July 1874; Saturday Rev 71, 11 Apr 1891; Nation 53, 8 Oct 1891; Critic o.s. 20, 2 Apr 1892.

Education: intellectual, moral, and physical. (Multiple US publishers and numerous printings.) New York 1860 (author's edn), 1860 (International Science Lib), London 1861, [1861?] (stereotyped–3rd thousand); New York 1861, ptd by D. Appleton until at least 1898; London 1878 (Cheap edn), New York [c. 1880], 1880 (Cheap edn), New York and Chicago [188?], London and Edinburgh 1881 (5th thousand of the Cheap edn), New York 1883 [new edn?], 1884, London 1888 (14th thousand of the Cheap edn), Boston 1889, New York 1892 (new edn, with topic headings), London and Edinburgh 1893, Syracuse NY 1894 (Reading-Circle edn, with notes, criticism, and a topical index for reviews), New York and Chicago [1898], Akron OH [190?], New York 1900 [reissue of author's edn?], ptd by D. Appleton until at least 1929, including New York and London 1910 (New Uniform edn), 1915 (Popular Uniform edn); [1901?] (Westminster edn), London 1903 (Sixpenny edn), New York [1904], London 1910 (with corrections), New York [1912?], [1914?], London 1929 (Thinker's Lib), rptd 1935; ed F. A. Cavenagh, Cambridge 1932 (as Herbert Spencer on education, Landmarks in the History of Education, with introd and notes by Cavenagh); Girard KS [19–?] (4 bks, as What knowledge is of most worth? How to improve yourself intellectually, How to improve yourself morally, and How to improve yourself physically, Little Blue Bk ser nos 1613–16), London 1949 (Thinker's Lib, 2nd edn), Totowa NJ 1963; ed with introd and notes by A. M. Kazamias, New York 1966 (as Herbert Spencer on education, Classics in Education); Osnabrück 1966 (vol 16 of The works of Herbert Spencer). Four chs of Education first pbd as review articles in Westminster Rev n.s. 16 July 1859 (What knowledge is of most worth?), North Br Rev 21 May 1854 (The art of education), and Br Quart Rev 27, 29, Apr 1858, Apr 1859 (Moral discipline of children, and Physical training). Book includes separately pbd What knowledge is of most worth? (*below*). Tr Ger 1874, 1881 (improved edn), 1888, 1892, 1898, 1905, 1910, 1921, 1927, 1947, 1987; Danish 1876; Greek 1876, 1910; Ital 1876, 1912; Fr 1877, 1878, 1880 (Popular edn), 1885 (6th edn), 1888, 1890 (8th edn), 1897, 1912; Sp 1879, 1884 (2nd edn), [1906]; Icelandic 1884; Du 1887; Swed 1890; Hebrew 1894, 1908, [1910]; Hungarian [1895?]; Romanian [c. 1895]; Ital 1901; Polish 1960.
REVIEWS: NY Teacher n.s. 2 Dec 1860; A. P. Peabody, North Amer Rev 92, Jan 1861; Princeton Rev 33, Apr 1861; [E. Cary], Univ Quart Rev 4, July 1861; Eclectic Rev o.s. 114, 8th ser 1 Aug 1861; Pennsylvania School Jnl (Harrisburg) 9 1861; Amer Catholic Quart Rev 5, Oct 1880; E. R. Sill, Atlantic Monthly 51, Feb 1883; Amer Catholic Quart Rev 9, Oct 1884; S. S. Laurie, Educational Rev 4, Dec 1892; W. M. Payne, Educational Rev 10, Sep 1895; J. J. Tracy, Education 24, Feb 1904.

A system of philosophy. 1860, 1862 (also titled Prospectus of a system of philosophy). Priv ptd and circulated outline (to enlist subscribers) of what would become A system of synthetic philosophy (1860–96), *below*.

A system of synthetic philosophy. 10 vols 1860–96. *See individual works below:* First principles of a new system of philosophy, The principles of biology, The principles of psychology, The principles of sociology, and The principles of ethics.

First principles of a new system of philosophy. Vol 1 of A system of synthetic philosophy. (Multiple US publishers and numerous printings, many, especially US, lacking edn no. Title also rendered as First principles.) 1862, 1863 (2nd thousand), New York 1864, London 1867 (2nd edn), New York 1868, London 1870 (3rd edn), 1880 (4th edn), Chicago [1880], New York 1880 (4th edn, with added appendix), Philadelphia [1880], London 1884 (5th edn), 1893 (5th edn containing an appendix), rptd New York 1958; 1900 (6th and final edn, rev by author), New York 1900, 1900 (International Science Lib), New York 1901 (Lib of Universal Lit), 1902 (Astor Prose ser), London 1904 (6th edn rptd with additional appendix and new index), New York 1904, London 1908 (Popular edn), Chicago [1910?]; 2 vols London 1910, 1911; 1 vol New York and London 1910 (New Uniform edn), 1912, 1915 (Popular Uniform edn), 1926, London 1937 (Thinker's Lib), reissued 1945 (introd by T. W. Hill), rptd Westport CT 1976; Osnabrück 1966 (6th edn rptd etc; vol 1 of The works of Herbert Spencer). First pbd Oct 1860–June 1862 in 6 fascicules. Tr Rus 1867, 1886; Fr 1871, 1883 (3rd edn), 1888 (5th edn), 1902 (6th edn); Ger 1875, 1895, 1901; Sp 1879; Greek 1896; Du 1898; Ital 1901 (2nd edn); Hungarian 1903; (in pt) Hebrew 1910; Yiddish 1937.
REVIEWS: C. C. Everett (rev of fascicule nos 1–4), Christian Examiner 5th ser 10 May 1862; Athenaeum 1823, 4 Oct 1862; Br Quart Rev 37, Jan 1863; W. D. Wilson, Church Rev 16, Oct 1864–Jan 1865; H. L. Atwater, Princeton Rev 37, Apr 1865; [F. E. Abbot], Christian Examiner 6th ser 1 Mar 1866, reply by E. L. Youmans, Christian Examiner 6th ser 3 Mar 1867; R. P. Stebbings, Old and New 2 Oct 1870; B. P. Bowne, New Englander 31–2, Jan 1872–Jan 1873; O. A. Brownson, Catholic World 14 Feb 1872; J. B. Dalgairns, Contemporary Rev 20, Oct 1872; Dublin Rev n.s. 22, Jan 1874; J. W. Means, Bibliotheca Sacra 31, Apr 1874; J. P. Bland, Unitarian Rev and Religious Mag 3, Jan 1875; C. C. Everett, Unitarian Rev and Religious Mag 3, May 1875; W. H. Wynn, Quart Rev of the Evangelical Lutheran Church 7, Apr 1877; J. S. Patterson, Radical Rev 1 Aug 1877; [E. Beckett], Edinburgh Rev 159, Jan 1884, replies by R. A. Proctor, Knowledge 5, 1, 8 Feb, 14 Mar 1884, Beckett, 8 Feb, 14 Mar 1884, and E. L. Youmans and W. J. Youmans, Popular Science Monthly 24, Apr 1884; J. Ming, Amer Catholic Quart Rev 10, July 1885; Scottish Rev 9 1887; W. Barry, Dublin Rev 3rd ser 19 Apr 1888; Living Age n.s. 9 Oct 1900; B. P. Bowne, Methodist Rev n.s. 64, July 1904; F. C. Becker, Jnl of Philosophy, Psychology, and Scientific Methods 3, 24 May 1906.

The classification of the sciences: to which are added reasons for dissenting from the philosophy of M[onsieur] Comte. 1864, New York 1864, rptd (facs) Ann Arbor MI 1973; London 1867, 1869 (2nd edn, with preface), New York 1870 (2nd edn, with appendix), London 1871 (3rd edn, with postscript and appendix). Pt 2 rev and pbd separately as Reasons for dissenting from the philosophy of M[onsieur] Comte. Tr Fr 1872, 1901, 1905; Sp 1889, [1908?].

Illustrations of universal progress: a series of discussions [with a notice of Spencer's New system of philosophy]. New York 1864, 1883 (new and rev edn). Republishes 13 essays, 12 previously collected in Essays: scientific etc.
REVIEW: [J. P. Qũincy], Atlantic Monthly 13 June 1864.

The principles of biology. Vols 2–3 of A system of synthetic philosophy. (Numerous printings.) Vol 1 1864, New York 1864, London 1898 (rev and enlarged edn), New York 1898; vol 2 1867, New York 1867, London 1899 (rev etc), New York 1900; 2 vols New York 1901–4, New York and London 1910 (New Uniform edn), 1915 (Popular Uniform edn), Osnabrück 1966 (vols 2–3 of The works of Herbert Spencer). First pbd Jan 1863–Mar 1867 in 12 fascicules. Tr Ger 1876–7, 1903–6 (rev); Fr 1877, 1893–4 (4th edn), 1910 (6th edn); Du 1898; Hungarian 1903; Ital 1905, 1906.
REVIEWS: Reader 4, 19 Nov 1864; Popular Science Rev 4 no 2 1865; Natural History Rev n.s. 5, July 1865; Westminster Rev n.s. 28, July 1865; [O. A. Brownson], Catholic World 3 June 1866; [C. Wright], Nation 2, 8 June 1866; F. E. Abbot, North Amer Rev 107, Oct 1868, reply by Spencer, Appleton's Jnl of Lit, Science and Art 1, 31 July–7 Aug 1869; C. L. Morgan, Natural Science 13 Dec 1898; C. A. Kofoid, Dial 28, 16 Apr 1900.

Essays: moral, political and aesthetic. New York 1865, 1866 (new and enlarged edn), ptd until at least 1890. Republishes 11 essays previously collected in Essays: scientific etc.

The nebular hypothesis. [1865 or 1866], [1891?]. Revises and reissues 2 essays (Recent astronomy . . ., and The constitution of the sun) first pbd in Westminster Rev n.s. 14 July 1858 and Reader 5, 25 Feb 1865.

On circulation and the formation of wood in plants. In Trans of the Linnaean Soc 25 1866.

On political education. In Modern culture: its true aims and requirements; a series of addresses and arguments on the claims of scientific education, ed E. L. Youmans, 1867, New York 1867, 1871 (as The culture demanded by modern life). Excerpts Representative government: what is it good for? (previously pbd in Westminster Rev n.s. 12 Oct 1857).

The right to the use of the earth. Melbourne 1870, New York 1889, Cedar Rapids IA [189?] (Junior Why ser), Brooklyn [1913?]. First pbd as pt 2, ch 9 of Social statics.

Spontaneous generation, and the hypothesis of physiological units: a reply to the North American Review. New York 1870. First pbd in Appleton's Jnl of Lit, Science and Art 1, 31 July–7 Aug 1869.

Recent discussions in science, philosophy and morals. New York 1871, 1873 (new and enlarged edn), ptd until at least 1890.

Descriptive sociology: or groups of sociological facts, classified and arranged by Herbert Spencer. With D. Duncan, R. Scheppig and J. Collier. 8 nos (or vols) London and Edinburgh 1873–81, New York 1873–81. No 1 English; no 2 Ancient Mexicans, central Americans, Chibchas, and ancient Peruvians; no 3 Types of lowest races, Negrito races, and Malayo-Polynesian races, rptd Ann Arbor MI 1973; no 4 African races; no 5 Asiatic races; no 6 American races; no 7 Hebrews and Phoenicians; no 8 French. Series discontinued after 1881 because of mounting financial losses. Nos 9–17 (London 1910–34) were pbd under a provision in Spencer's will. Tr Rus 1878; (in pt) Sp 1896, 1898, 1980.
REVIEWS: Saturday Rev 36, 16 Aug 1873; Br Quart Rev 58, Oct 1873; E. B. Tylor, Nature 8, 30 Oct 1873; A. Gibson, Acad 5, 10 Jan 1874, replies by Spencer, J. Collier, S. R. Gardiner, and an unnamed ed, Acad 5, 24 Jan 1874, and E. L. Youmans, Popular Science Monthly 4 Mar 1874; E. Simcox, Fortnightly Rev n.s. 15 Jan 1874; [Youmans], Popular Science Monthly 4 Feb 1874; W. G. Sumner, Independent 26, 14 May 1874; Saturday Rev 38, 8 Aug 1874; [E. L. Godkin], Nation 19, 29 Oct 1874; B. M. Cordery, Acad 21, 1 Apr 1882.

His moral character. Examiner 17 May 1873. Included in John Stuart Mill: his life and works; twelve sketches, 1873, Boston 1873, rptd 1977.

Philosophy of style: an essay (with notes by the editor). (Multiple US publishers and numerous printings.) New York 1873, ptd by D. Appleton until at least 1933; [1882] (Humboldt Lib of Science), 1884, [1890] (Eng Classic ser); ed F. N. Scott, Boston 1892 (with introd and notes), 2nd edn 1895, rptd 1917; 1901, in Representative essays on the theory of style, ed W. T. Brewster, New York 1905; 1959 (with companion essay by E. A. Poe). First pbd in Westminster Rev n.s. 2 Oct 1852. Tr Ital 1987.

The study of sociology. (Numerous edns and printings, many lacking edn no.) 1873, New York 1873, London 1874 (2nd edn), 1874 (3rd edn), New York 1875, London 1878 (7th edn), 1880 (9th edn, with postscript), New York 1883, London 1887 (13th edn), 1888 (14th edn), New York 1889 (Amer edn), London 1892 (16th edn), 1897 (18th edn), New York 1899 (with preface by E. L. Y[oumans]), ptd until at least 1924; London 1904 (21st edn), New York and London 1910 (New Uniform edn), 1915 (Popular Uniform edn), Ann Arbor MI 1961 (introd by T. Parsons), Osnabrück 1966 (9th edn rptd; vol 12 of The works of Herbert Spencer), Philadelphia 1985. First pbd in 18 pts in Contemporary Rev 19–22 Apr 1872–Oct 1873 and Popular Science Monthly 1–4, May 1872–Dec 1873 (E. L. Youmans [1821–87] founded Popular Science Monthly as an Amer outlet for Spencer's writings). Tr Fr 1874, 1885 (7th edn), 1894 (11th edn); Rus 1874–5; Ger 1875, 1896; Swed 1880.
REVIEWS: Saturday Rev 36, 29 Nov 1873; O. W. Holmes, Sr, Boston Medical and Surgical Jnl 89, 11 Dec 1873; J. R. Amberley, Examiner 10 Jan 1874; [A. V. Dicey], Nation 18, 22 Jan 1874; Atlantic Monthly 33, Feb 1874; W. H. Brewer, Nature 9, 23 Apr 1874; A. Gibson, Acad 6, 11 July 1874; International Rev 1 no 3 1874; R. Bell, Theological Rev 11 Oct 1874; J. E. Cairnes, Fortnightly Rev n.s. 17, Jan–Feb 1875, reply by Spencer, Feb 1875; N. Porter, Princeton Rev n.s. 6 Sep 1880.

The morals of trade (together with Sins of trade and business; a sermon, by W. H. Lyttleton). 1874, 1891. First pbd in Westminster Rev n.s. 15 Apr 1859.

Replies to criticisms. 1874. First pbd in Fortnightly Rev n.s. 14, Nov–Dec 1873 and Popular Science Monthly 4, Jan–Mar 1874.

The principles of sociology. Vols 6–8 of A system of synthetic philosophy. (Numerous printings in various formats.) Vol 1 1876, New York 1877, London 1877 (2nd edn), 1885 (3rd edn, rev and enlarged [with appendix]), New York 1885; vol 2, pt 4 London 1879, New York 1880, London 1883 (2nd edn), pt 5 1882, New York 1882, 1886 (2nd edn); vol 3, pt 6 1883, New York 1883, 1886 (2nd edn), pts 7–8 (with completed vol 3) London 1896, New York 1896; 3 vols London 1876–96, rptd Westport CT 1975; 3 vols in 4 London 1876–96, 3 vols in 5 1877–96, 3 vols in 4 New York 1877–97, 3 vols in 5 1880–96, 3 vols in 4 1880–97, [3] vols in 5 1885–96 (Westminster edn), 3 vols 1896, 3 vols in 5 1897, 3 vols London 1897–1904, London and Oxford 1897–1906, New York 1900–5, 1905–7, New York and London 1910 (New Uniform edn), 1915 (Popular Uniform edn), New York 1923, 1925–9, Osnabrück 1966 (vols 6–8 of The works of Herbert Spencer), 1 vol abridged edn (ed with introd by S. Andreski) London 1969. Vol 1 first pbd June 1874–Dec 1876 in 9 fascicules, a tenth and 'supplementary' fascicule being added to printings after June 1877. An appendix to the 'Principles of sociology', vol 1, incorporated in the 3rd edn (1885), was priv and separately pbd in London. Excerpts of pts 1–6 appear in periodical lit. Pt 7 first pbd May 1895–Apr 1896 in Contemporary Rev 67–9 and Popular Science Monthly 47–8. Pt 8 first appears in completed vol 3 (1896). Principles of sociology includes separately pbd Ceremonial institutions (pt 4), Political institutions (pt 5, only 1st edn pbd separately), and Ecclesiastical institutions (pt 6), *below*. Tr Greek 1876; Rus 1876, 1880, 1899; Ger 1877–97; Fr 1878–98; Sp 1883, [1894], 1938 (abridged); (in pt) Ital 1884; Du 1898; Hungarian 1903.

REVIEWS: [E. L. Youmans] (rev of fascicule no 35), Popular Science Monthly 6, Jan 1875; A. Bain, Mind 1 Jan 1876; Saturday Rev 43, 10 Feb 1877; [F. M. Müller?], Pall Mall Gazette 3747, 21 Feb 1877; E. B. Tylor, Mind 2 Apr 1877, Spencer–Tylor exchange (or controversy), Mind 2 July 1877; [E. L Youmans and W. J. Youmans], Popular Science Monthly 11, May 1877; J. F. McLennan, Fortnightly Rev n.s. 21, May 1877, reply by Spencer, June 1877; J. F. McLennan, Fortnightly Rev n.s. 21, June 1877; reply by Spencer, ibid; Popular Science Monthly 11, June 1877 (rptd from Examiner, nd cited); [M. W. Hazeltine], North Amer Rev 125, July 1877; Amer Catholic Quart Rev 2, July 1877; [J. H. Allen], Radical Rev 1 Aug 1877; Spectator 50, 13 Oct 1877; Saturday Rev 49, 3 Jan 1880; Acad 17, 24 Jan 1880; Spectator 53, 10 Apr 1880; Dial 1 May 1880; [A. G. Sedgwick], Nation 31, 5 Aug 1880; Amer Catholic Quart Rev 6 Jan 1881; Saturday Rev 54, 1 July 1882; W. R. Barnes, Dial 3 Sep 1882; E. B. Tylor, Acad 23, 27 Jan 1883; C. Pellarin, Critique Philosophique Nov 1883–Jan 1884; Knowledge 2nd ser 1, 1 Nov 1885; Dublin Rev 3rd ser 15, Jan 1886; J. Bascom, Dial 5 Feb 1886; Athenaeum 3045, 6 Mar 1886; Mind 11 Apr 1886; É. Durkheim, 1886, tr and rptd in Sociological Inquiry 44 no 3 1974; Salay Villaret, Revista de España Dec 1886; W. J. Youmans, Popular Science Monthly 47, May 1895; Spectator 75, 6 July 1895; K. Vorländer, Zeitschrift für Philosophie und philosophische Kritik 108 1896; Acad 50, 5 Dec 1896; Athenaeum 3608, 19 Dec 1896; Critic o.s. 30, 9 Jan 1897; C. R. Henderson, Dial 22, 16 Jan 1897; A. W. Small, Amer Jnl of Sociology 2 Mar 1897; [W. J. Youmans], Popular Science Monthly 50, Mar 1897; Nation 64, 11 Mar 1897; W. D. Morrison, Mind n.s. 6 Apr 1897; F. H. Giddings, Science n.s. 5, 7 May 1897; [G. Gunton?], Gunton's Mag 12 May 1897; S. Ball, International Jnl of Ethics 8 Jan 1898; G. H. Trever, Methodist Rev n.s. 64, Nov 1904.

Note from Herbert Spencer. In W. G. Spencer, Inventional geometry; a series of problems, New York [1876], 1877.

Prison-ethics. New York 1877. First pbd in Br Quart Rev 32, July 1860; rptd in Jnl of the Amer Inst of Criminal Law and Criminology 1 Mar 1911; tr Sp 1895.

Ceremonial institutions. Pt 4 of The principles of sociology. 1879, New York 1880, London 1883 (2nd edn). *See* The principles of sociology, *above*.

The data of ethics. Pt 1 of The principles of ethics. (Multiple US publishers and numerous printings; no US-numbered edns.) 1879, Boston [1879], Chicago [1879]; New York 1879, ptd by D. Appleton until at least 1891, including Cheap Amer edn; Philadelphia [nd], London 1879 (2nd edn), 1881 (3rd edn, with appendix containing an additional ch and replies to criticisms), London and Edinburgh 1884 (4th thousand, with appendix etc), 1887, 1890; New York 1894 [enlarged from Appleton's 1879 edn], ptd until 1901; reprint of 1897 edn Ann Arbor MI 1977; New York 1902, London 1907 [1906], Chicago [1911?], New York [1912?]. *See* The principles of ethics, *below*.

Laws, and the order of their discovery, Origin of animal worship, and Political fetichism. New York [c. 1879 (Humboldt Lib of Science)]. Reprints (under altered title) ch from 1st edn of First principles and 2 essays first pbd in Fortnightly Rev n.s. 7 May 1870 and Reader 5, 10 June 1865. Tr (in pt) Sp 1895.

The principles of ethics. Vols 9–10 of A system of synthetic philosophy. (Numerous printings in various formats.) Vol 1, pt 1 1879, New York 1879, London 1879 (2nd edn), 1881 (3rd edn), pts 2–3 New York 1892; vol 2, pt 4 London 1891, New York 1891, pts 5–6 1893; London 2 vols in 3 1884–93, New York 2 vols 1892–3, 1896, 1897, 1899, London 1900–4, New York 1901 (Westminster edn), New York and London 1910 (New Uniform edn), 1915 (Popular Uniform edn), New York 1919, Osnabrück 1966 (vols 9–10 of The works of Herbert Spencer); Indianapolis 1978 (follows the text of New York 1897 edn; introd by T. R. Machan). Pt 4 pbd before pts 2–3. Excerpts of pt 4 appear in periodical lit. Principles of ethics includes separately pbd The data of ethics (pt 1), The inductions of ethics; and The ethics of individual life (pts 2–3), Justice (pt 4), and Negative beneficence and positive beneficence (pts 5–6), *above and below*. Tr Fr 1879–96, 1903 (3rd edn), 1905; Ger 1879–95, 1902; Rus 1880, 1896; (in pt) Ital 1881, 1905, 1909, 1920 (3rd edn); Sp 1881, 1893–7, (pt 4) 1947; Du 1898; (in pt) Polish 1898; Hungarian 1903.

REVIEWS: [E. L. Youmans], Popular Science Monthly 15, Aug 1879; Athenaeum 2705, 30 Aug 1879; W. James, Nation 29, 11 Sep 1879; J. Sully, Acad 16, 27 Sep 1879; Amer Catholic Quart Rev 4, Oct 1879; A. Bain, Mind 4, Oct 1879, also pbd in Popular Science Monthly 16, Dec 1879; Saturday Rev 48, 11 Oct 1879; J. McCosh, Princeton Rev n.s. 4, Nov 1879; G. Batchelor, Unitarian Rev and Religious Mag 12 Dec 1879; A. W. Gundry, Rose-Belford's Canadian Monthly and Nat Rev 3 Dec 1879; H. Calderwood, Contemporary Rev 37, Jan 1880; W. T. Stott, Baptist Quart Rev 2, Jan 1880; C. C. Everett, Unitarian Rev and Religious Mag 13 Jan 1880; Spectator 53, 21 Feb 1880; H. Sidgwick, Mind 5 Apr 1880; D. M'G. Means, Mind 5 July 1880; H. Wace, Contemporary Rev 38, Aug 1880; A. W. Benn, Mind 5 Oct 1880; T. G. Apple, Reformed Quart Rev 28, Apr 1881; J. T. Bixby, Mod Rev 3 no 1 1882; G. Smith, Contemporary Rev 41, Feb 1882, replies by Spencer, Mar 1882, and W. D. Le Sueur, Popular Science Monthly 22, Dec 1882; A. C. Sewell, New Englander 42, Jan 1883; Modern ethics, Edinburgh Rev 157, Apr 1883; E. Gould, New-Church Rev 1 no 2, July 1883; A. S. Hobart, Baptist Quart Rev 5, July 1883; A. C. Armstrong, Jnl of Christian Philosophy 3 Oct 1883; Spectator 64, 12 Apr 1890; Saturday Rev 72, 25 July 1891; Science 18, 7 Aug 1891; J. Brough, Acad 40, 22 Aug 1891; Athenaeum 3331, 29 Aug 1891; Critic o.s. 19, 5 Sep 1891; [W. J. Youmans], Popular Science Monthly 39, Oct 1891; J. Royce, International Jnl of Ethics 2 Oct 1891; J. Bascom, Dial 12 Oct 1891; St G. Mivart, Dublin Rev 3rd ser 26, Oct 1891; [D. M'G. Means], Nation 53, 29 Oct 1891; J. Gordon, North Amer Rev 154, Jan 1892; J. G. Schurman, Philosophical Rev 1 Jan 1892; H. Sidgwick, Mind n.s. 1 Jan 1892; J. Iverach, Critical Rev of Theological and Philosophical Lit 2 no 1 1892; Church Quart Rev 34, July 1892; R. R. Marett, Economic Rev 2 July 1892; Westminster Rev [o.s.] 138, Aug 1892; [W. J. Youmans], Popular Science Monthly 42, Nov 1892; J. Iverach, Critical Rev of Theological and Philosophical Lit 2 no 4 1892; S. Alexander, Mind n.s. 2 Jan 1893; Philosophical Rev 2 Jan 1893; J. S. Mackenzie, International Jnl of Ethics 3 Jan 1893; W. A. Dunning, Political Science Quart 8, Mar 1893; [W. J. Youmans], Popular Science Monthly 43, Aug 1893; Westminster Rev [o.s.] 140, Sep 1893; Athenaeum 3436, 2 Sep 1893 (2 reviews); W. Barry, Dublin Rev 4th ser 4, Oct 1893; J. S. Mackenzie, International Jnl of Ethics 4 Oct 1893; Science 22, 13 Oct 1893; Nation 57, 19 Oct 1893; J. G. Schurman, Philosophical Rev 2 Nov 1893; F. I. Herriott, Annals of the Amer Acad of Political and Social Science 3 Nov 1893; P. Shorey, Dial 15, 16 Dec 1893; S. Alexander, Mind n.s. 3 Jan 1894; V. Benini, Rivista Italiana di Filosofia 1 1894; Church Quart Rev 37, Oct 1894; V. B. Denslow, Social Economist 8 Feb 1895; T. B. Stork, Lutheran Quart 30 Jan 1900. *See also* Spencer, Replies to criticisms ..., Mind 6 Jan 1881; E. L. and W. J. Youmans, Reception of the 'Data of ethics', Popular Science Monthly 16, Jan 1880; M. J. Savage, Three recent utterances concerning ethics, Unitarian Rev and Religious Mag 13, Mar 1880.

The rights of children, and the true principles of family government. In Aid to family government: or from cradle to the school, ed B. Meyer, New York 1879. First pbd as ch 17 of Social statics.

Progress: its law and cause. New York 1881 (Humboldt Lib of Science), 1882 (subtitled With other disquisitions). Title essay first pbd in Westminster Rev n.s. 11 Apr 1857. Bks include other previously pbd essays. Tr Ger 1967.

Manners and fashion. In Sir W. H. Fowler, Fashion in deformity, as illustrated in the customs of barbarous and civilized races, [New York 1882]. First pbd in Westminster Rev n.s. 5 Apr 1854.

Political institutions: being part 5 of The principles of sociology. 1882, New York 1882, London 1885. *See* The principles of sociology, *above*.

Ecclesiastical institutions. Pt 6 of The principles of sociology. 1883, 1885, New York 1886 (2nd edn). *See* The principles of sociology, *above*.

The gospel of relaxation. In W. G. Moody, Land and labor in the United States, New York 1883. Republishes (under altered title) Spencer's address to the Americans, *see below*.

Report of Mr Spencer's interview and Mr Spencer's address. In Herbert Spencer on the Americans, and the Americans on Herbert Spencer, 1882 (comp E. L. Youmans), New York 1883, rptd 1973; 1887. Includes text of 20 Oct 1882 interview (retitled Spencer's impressions of America for pbn in Popular Science Monthly 22 Dec 1882) and his public address (retitled The gospel of work for pbn in Popular Science Monthly 22 Jan 1883). Also pbd in Contemporary Rev 43, Jan 1883.
REVIEWS: [E. L. Godkin and A. G. Sedgwick], Nation 35, 26 Oct 1882; [R. E. Thompson], Amer 5, 28 Oct 1882; Saturday Rev 54, 28 Oct 1882; Critic o.s. 2, 4 Nov 1882; Spectator 55, 4 Nov 1882; M. B. Martin, A text from Herbert Spencer, Dial 3 Jan 1883; Knowledge 3, 19 Jan 1883; M. J. Savage, Knowledge 3, 16 Feb 1883.

The coming slavery. New York 1884 (Elzevir Lib), 1888 (with other essays). First pbd in Contemporary Rev 45, Apr 1884. Tr Rus [1884]. *See* The man versus the state, *below*.

The man versus the state: containing The new toryism, The coming slavery, The sins of legislators and The great political superstition. With a postscript. London and Edinburgh 1884, New York 1884, London 1885 (8th thousand), London and Edinburgh 1892 (12th thousand), London 1892 (minor corrections and added note; pbd with abridged and rev Social statics); 1907 (original edn reissued), 1909, New York 1916 (ed T. Beale, with W. H. Taft et al), Caldwell ID 1940 (introd by A. J. Nock), ptd until at least 1954, rptd 1960; London 1940 (Thinker's Lib), Boston 1950, London 1950 (Thinker's Lib, 2nd edn), Osnabrück 1966 (2nd pt of vol 11 of The works of Herbert Spencer), Baltimore 1969 (ed with introd by D. MacRae), Indianapolis 1981 (republishes introd by A. J. Nock, with new foreword by E. Mack); contained in Political writings (ed J. Offer), Cambridge 1994. Reprints 4 essays previously pbd Feb–July 1884 in Contemporary Rev 45–6 and Popular Science Monthly 24–5. Includes separately pbd The coming slavery, *above*. Tr Fr 1885, 1892, 1895 (4th edn); Sp 1885, 1886, [1904], [1930], 1945, 1963; Du 1886; Ger 1886; Ital 1886; Swed [1912].
REVIEWS: J. A. Jameson, Dial 5 Oct 1884; G. P. Macdonell, Acad 26, 20 Dec 1884; London Quart Rev n.s. 3, Jan 1885; Spectator 58, 28 Mar 1885; É. de Laveleye, Contemporary Rev 47, Apr 1885, reply by Spencer, ibid; Nation 41, 9 July 1885; Dial 13 May 1892; J. S. Mackenzie, International Jnl of Ethics 3, Oct 1892.

Reasons for dissenting from the philosophy of M[onsieur] Comte. London and Edinburgh 1884, Berkeley CA 1968; tr Rus 1897.

What knowledge is of most worth? New York [1884]. First pbd in Westminster Rev n.s. 16 July 1859. Incorporated in Education, *above*.

An appendix to the Principles of sociology [3rd edn], vol 1. [1885?]. Ptd separately for private distribution. *See* The principles of sociology, *above*.

Essays speculative and practical. New York [1885]. Reprints 5 essays previously collected in Essays: scientific etc, *above*.

The nature and reality of religion. 1885. *See* Religion: a retrospect and prospect, etc, *below*.

Religion: a retrospect and prospect, Retrogressive religion, and Last words about agnosticism and the religion of humanity. In The nature and reality of religion: a controversy between Frederic Harrison and Herbert Spencer [with introd, notes and appendix by Count d'Alviella], ed E. L. Y[oumans], 1885, New York 1885; suppressed by Spencer June 1885, illegally repbd Boston 1885 (as The insuppressible book: a controversy between Herbert Spencer and Frederic Harrison, ed [with comments and addns] G. Hamilton [M. A. Dodge]). Reprints 3 essays first pbd in Nineteenth Cent 15–16, Jan–Nov 1884 and Popular Science Monthly 24–6, 1884–1885. Includes rejoinders by Harrison first pbd in Nineteenth Cent 15, Mar 1884 (The ghost of religion) and 16, Sep 1884 (Agnostic metaphysics), and Pall Mall Gazette 6144, 18 Nov 1884 (Mr Herbert Spencer and agnosticism). Pbn of The nature etc provoked a new controversy between Spencer and Harrison, whose letters were pbd in The Times, 29 May–10 June 1885, and rptd in The insuppressible book and Popular Science Monthly 27, Aug 1885. The latter source also includes E. L. Youmans's account of the pertinent events. *See also* E. L. Youmans and W. J. Youmans, Popular Science Monthly Jan 1885.

The insuppressible book. 1885. *See* Religion: a retrospect and prospect, etc, *above*.

The factors of organic evolution [with addns]. 1887, New York 1887, [1888?] (with The genesis of science [and addns]). First pbd in Nineteenth Cent 19, Apr–May 1886 and Popular Science Monthly 28–9, Apr–June 1886. Tr Ger 1886.
REVIEWS: G. J. D. Campbell, Nature 34, 12 Aug 1886; G. J. Romanes, Nature 35, 17 Feb 1887; Mind 12 Apr 1887. *See also* Romanes, The factors of organic evolution, Nature 36, 25 Aug 1887.

The genesis of science [with essay by T. H. Huxley]. New York 1887 (Humboldt Lib of Science), [1888?], nd (with The factors of organic evolution [and addns], *see above*).

Preface. In F. H. Collins, An epitome of the synthetic philosophy, 1889.

[Letter to The Times of 7 Nov 1889 on the land question]. In A symposium on the land question, ed J. H. Levy, 1890.

State-tamperings with money and banks. With introd and notes by T. F. Brownell, New York 1890. First pbd in Westminster Rev n.s. 13 Jan 1858.

From freedom to bondage. In A plea for liberty: an argument against socialism and socialistic legislation, ed T. Mackay, 1891, Indianapolis 1981 (with new foreword by J. Paul). Essay also pbd in Popular Science Monthly 38, Apr 1891. Tr Ger 1891; Romanian 1893.

Justice: being part 4 of The principles of ethics. 1891, New York 1891, 1892. *See* The principles of ethics, *above*.

The inductions of ethics; and The ethics of individual life: being parts 2 and 3 of The principles of ethics. New York 1892, 1893. *See* The principles of ethics, *above*.

Social statics, abridged and revised; together with The man versus the state. 1892. *See above*, Social statics, and The man versus the state.

The inadequacy of natural selection [together with Professor Weismann's theories]. [1893], New York 1893, 1894, 1897, Osnabrück 1966 (1st pt of vol 17 of The works of Herbert Spencer). First pbd in Contemporary Rev 63, Feb–May 1893; Popular Science Monthly 42–3, Apr–Aug 1893.

Negative beneficence and positive beneficence. Pts 5–6 of The principles of ethics. New York 1893. *See* The principles of ethics, *above*.

Professor Weismann's theories. [1893], Osnabrück 1966 (incorporated in 1st pt of vol 17 of The works of Herbert Spencer). First pbd in Contemporary Rev 63, May 1893 and Popular Science Monthly 43, Aug 1893. Incorporated in The inadequacy of 'natural selection', *above*.

A rejoinder to Professor Weismann. 1893, Osnabrück 1966 (2nd pt of vol 17 of The works of Herbert Spencer). First pbd in Contemporary Rev 64, Dec 1893.

Mr Herbert Spencer on the land question: being a reprint (by permission) of chapter 9 of Social statics (1851) together with certain extracts from Justice (1891) (Land Restoration Tracts no '2' [1]). 1894.

Mr Herbert Spencer and the Land Restoration League: correspondence between Mr Spencer and the general secretary of the League (Land Restoration Tracts no '1' [2]). 1894 (issued without Spencer's consent).

Prefatory note. In W. G. Spencer, A system of lucid shorthand, 1894.

Weismannism once more. With a postscript. 1894, Osnabrück 1966 (3rd pt of vol 17 of The works of Herbert Spencer). First pbd in Contemporary Rev 66, Oct 1894.

Mr Herbert Spencer on the Land Question: a correction of current misconceptions of his views, including a reprint, in parallel columns, of chapter ix of Social statics (1851) and pertinent extracts from Justice (1891). With a preface and postscript. New York 1895. Includes letters first pbd in the Daily Chron 20 Aug–8 Sep 1894.

Against the metric system. 1896, 1901 (2nd edn), 1904 (3rd edn, with addns), New York 1906. Incorporates letters first pbd in The Times 4–25 Apr 1896, 28 Mar–13 Apr 1899. Letters of 1896 rptd in Popular Science Monthly 49, June 1896. *See also* reply by T. C. Mendenhall, Oct 1896.

Various fragments. 1897, New York 1898, 1898 [enlarged], London 1900 (enlarged edn), 1907, New York and London 1910 (New Uniform edn [enlarged from 1898 edn]), 1915 (Popular Uniform edn), Osnabrück 1966 (vol 18 of The works of Herbert Spencer); tr Ger 1904.

REVIEWS: Athenaeum 3660, 18 Dec 1897; [F. F. Browne], Dial 25, 1 Aug 1898; E. Rathbone, International Jnl of Ethics 9, Oct 1898.

Facts and comments. 1902, New York 1902, 1902 [enlarged edn with appendix], rptd Freeport NY 1970, North Stratford NH 1977; New York and London 1910 (New Uniform edn), 1915 (Popular Uniform edn), Osnabrück 1966 (vol 19 of The works of Herbert Spencer); tr Fr 1903, 1904 (2nd edn), Sp 1903, Ger 1904.

REVIEWS: TLS 9 May 1902; Nation 74, 29 May 1902; Athenaeum 3893, 7 June 1902; W. Rice, Dial 33, 1 July 1902; Nation 75, 17 July 1902; S. W. Boardman, Independent 54, 21 Aug 1902; S. FitzSimons, Amer Catholic Quart Rev 27, Oct 1902; H. A. P. Torrey, Philosophical Rev 12 Mar 1903; E. B. McCormick, Westminster Rev [o.s.] 159, June 1903; L. Hearn, Atlantic Monthly 96, Aug 1905.

An autobiography. 2 vols 1904, New York 1904, London 1908 (Cheap edn), 1926, Osnabrück 1966 (vols 20–1 of The works of Herbert Spencer); tr Ger 1905, (in pt) Rus 1905, Fr 1907.

REVIEWS: TLS 22 Apr 1904; C. W. Saleeby, Acad and Lit 66, 23 Apr 1904; F. H. Giddings, Independent 56, 28 Apr 1904; Blackwood's Edinburgh Mag 175, May 1904; J. W. Chadwick, Current Lit 36, May 1904; W. M. Payne, Dial 36, 1 May 1904; Athenaeum 3993, 7 May 1904; Spectator 92, 21 May 1904; J. L. Gilder, Critic o.s. 44, June 1904; Contemporary Rev 85, June 1904; F. Gribble, Fortnightly Rev n.s. 75, June 1904; Knowledge and Scientific News 3rd ser 1, June 1904; L. F. Ward, Science n.s. 19, 10 June 1904; E. M. Colie, Bookman (New York) 19 June 1904; H. [C.] Macpherson, Bookman 26 June 1904; J. Finley, Lamp 28 June 1904; W. H. Hudson, Independent Rev 3 July 1904; W. James, Atlantic Monthly 94, July 1904; Reader Mag 4 July 1904; Outlook 77, 9 July 1904; [Bryce, James], Nation 79, 14 July 1904; W. A. White, Saturday Evening Post 177, 23 July 1904; F. Tracy, Amer Jnl of Theology 8 Oct 1904; F. C. S. Schiller, Mind n.s. 13 Oct 1904; Edinburgh Rev 208, July 1908; London Quart Rev [o.s.] 110, Oct 1908; Edinburgh Rev 214, Oct 1911. *See also* M. von Bulow, Spencer and his critics: a reply, Westminster Rev [o.s.] 162, Oct 1904.

The filiation of ideas (dated March, 1899), The nebular hypothesis (dated 18 April 1900), and Physical traits and some sequences ('[w]ritten in the autumn of 1902'). In D. Duncan, Life and letters of Herbert Spencer, 1908, vol 2 New York 1908.

The comparative psychology of man. Washington 1977. Reprints essay previously pbd in Jnl of the Anthropological Inst of Great Britain and Ireland 5 (1876) and rptd in Mind 1 Jan 1876 and Popular Science Monthly 8 Jan 1876.

Articles

This section includes many – but not all – of Spencer's more important contributions to periodical lit. Most are rptd in his Essays: scientific etc. *Five kinds of articles are excluded from the following list: (1) articles representing instalments (serialisation) of books and pts of books; (2) articles representing chs or selective excerpts of forthcoming books; (3) articles that were collected and rev to form books; (4) articles that later appeared – rev, enlarged, or sometimes unchanged – as separate books or pams; and (5) articles that are primarily replies to book reviews and other pbd criticism. Information about articles falling into the first four categories is given in the appropriate book entries, above; a few of the many articles replying to book reviews and other pbd criticism are noted along with the book reviews, above, and in §2, below. See Perrin, above, for full details on all Spencer's major and minor pbns (including rejoinders) in periodicals and newspapers.*

Poor laws: reply to T.W.S. . . . Bath and West of England Mag 3, Mar 1836.

Use and beauty. Leader 3, 3 Jan 1852.

The development hypothesis. Leader 3, 20 Mar 1852.

Origin of architectural types. Leader 3, 23 Oct 1852.

A theory of tears and laughter. Leader 3, 11 Dec 1852.

Gracefulness. Leader 3, 25 Dec 1852.

The value of evidence. Leader 4, 25 June 1853.

The universal postulate. Westminster Rev n.s. 4 Oct 1853.

The use of anthropomorphism. Leader 5, 5 Nov 1853.

Personal beauty. Leader 5, 15 Apr–13 May 1854.

The origin and function of music. Fraser's Mag 56, Oct 1857. Postscript added (and separately pbd in Mind 15 Oct 1890 and Popular Science Monthly 38, Nov 1890) for inclusion of article in 1891 edn of Essays: scientific etc.

The ultimate laws of physiology. Nat Rev 5 Oct 1857.

Representative government – what is it good for? Westminster Rev n.s. 12 Oct 1857.

Illogical geology. Universal Rev 2 July 1859.

The social organism. Westminster Rev n.s. 17 Jan 1860.

Bain on the emotions and the will. Br and Foreign Medico-Chirurgical Rev (US edn) 25 Jan 1860.

The physiology of laughter. Macmillan's Mag 1 Mar 1860.

Parliamentary reform: the dangers and the safeguards. Westminster Rev n.s. 17 Apr 1860.

The collective wisdom. Reader 5, 15 Apr 1865.

Mill versus Hamilton – the test of truth. Fortnightly Rev 1 July 1865.

Specialized administration. Fortnightly Rev n.s. 10, Dec 1871.

The ethics of Kant. Fortnightly Rev n.s. 44, July 1888; also pbd in Popular Science Monthly 33, Aug 1888.

Absolute political ethics. Nineteenth Cent 27, Jan 1890; also pbd in Popular Science Monthly 36, Mar 1890.

Lord Salisbury on evolution. Nineteenth Cent 38, Nov 1895.

The relations of biology, psychology, and sociology. Appleton's Popular Science Monthly 50, Dec 1896.

§2

Only a very small sampling of some of the more important (and mostly general) books and articles on Spencer up to 1920 is included here. For a comprehensive listing of both pre-1920 and post-1920 criticism of Spencer, as well as an intellectual biography (Remembering Spencer), see Perrin, above.

Jones, J. H. In Know the truth: a critique on the Hamiltonian theory of limitation, including some strictures upon the theories of Rev Herbert L. Mansel and Mr Herbert Spencer, Boston and New York 1865.

Harris, W. T. Herbert Spencer. Jnl of Speculative Philosophy 1 1867. Harris (1835–1909) founded and edited this jnl as an outlet for articles critical of Spencer's philosophy.

Quick, R. B. In Educational reformers, 1868, rptd Cincinnati 1885.

Martineau, J. The place of mind in nature, and intuition in man. Contemporary Rev 19 Apr 1872. Reply by Spencer, Contemporary Rev 20 June 1872.
[Mivart, St G.] Herbert Spencer. Quart Rev 135, Oct 1873. Reply by Spencer, Replies to criticisms, *above*.
[Moulton, J. F.] Herbert Spencer. Br Quart Rev 58, Oct 1873. Reply by Spencer, Replies to criticisms, *above*.
Birks, T. R. Modern physical fatalism, including an examination of Mr H. Spencer's First principles. 1876, 1882 (2nd edn with preface in reply to the strictures of Mr H. Spencer, by C. Pritchard). Reply by Spencer, Popular Science Monthly 18, Jan 1881.
Kirkman, T. P. In his Philosophy without assumptions, 1876. Reply by Spencer, Popular Science Monthly 17, Oct 1880.
Leitch, J. In his Practical educationists and their systems of teaching, Glasgow 1876.
Watson, J. The relativity of knowledge. (An examination of the doctrine as held by Mr Herbert Spencer.) Jnl of Speculative Philosophy 11 Jan 1877.
Wright, C. In his Philosophical discussions, New York 1877.
James, W. Remarks on Spencer's definition of mind as correspondence. Jnl of Speculative Philosophy 12 Jan 1878.
Watson, J. The world as force. (With especial reference to the philosophy of Mr Herbert Spencer.) Jnl of Speculative Philosophy 12 Apr 1878.
Guthrie, M. On Mr Spencer's formula of evolution as an exhaustive statement of the changes of the universe, followed by a résumé of criticisms of Spencer's First principles. 1879. Reply by Spencer, Popular Science Monthly 18, Jan 1881.
Youmans, E. L. Spencer's evolution philosophy. North Amer Rev 129, Oct 1879.
Denslow, V. B. In his Modern thinkers, principally upon social science, with introd by R. G. Ingersoll, Chicago 1880.
Morris, G. S. In his British thought and thinkers, Chicago 1880.
Guthrie, M. On Mr Spencer's unification of knowledge. 1882.
Ground, W. D. An examination of the structural principles of Mr Herbert Spencer's philosophy. Oxford 1883.
Lacy, W. M. An examination of the philosophy of the unknowable as expounded by Herbert Spencer. Philadelphia 1883, rptd 1912.
Morey, W. C. Herbert Spencer in the light of history. Baptist Quart Rev 5 July 1883.
McCosh, J. Herbert Spencer's philosophy as culminated in his ethics. Philosophic ser no 8. Edinburgh 1884, New York 1885.
Parsons, J. C. Bearings of the Spencerian philosophy, pt 1: on religion; [and] pt 2: on morality. Unitarian Rev and Religious Mag 22–3, Oct 1884–June 1885.
Sewall, H. Herbert Spencer as a biologist. Ann Arbor MI 1886.
Drey, S. Herbert Spencer's theory of religion and morality. London and Edinburgh 1887, Boston 1887 (as The moral and religious aspects of Herbert Spencer's philosophy).
Savage, M. J. Herbert Spencer: his influence on religion and morality. Liverpool 1887.
Bixby, J. T. In Crisis in morals, Boston 1891, 1900 (2nd edn; pbd as The ethics of evolution: the crisis in morals occasioned by the doctrine of evolution).
Ritchie, D. G. In Principles of state interference, 1891, 1896 (2nd edn).
Robertson, J. M. In Modern humanists, 1891.
Underwood, B. F. Herbert Spencer's synthetic philosophy. Brooklyn NY 1891.
Parsons, F. Government and the law of equal freedom: an examination of Herbert Spencer's theories of government and individual liberty. Boston 1892.
Huxley, T. H. Evolution and ethics. 1893 Romanes lecture. Included in Collected essays vol 9, 1894. Reply by Spencer, Athenaeum 3432, 5 Aug 1893.
Hudson, W. H. An introduction to the philosophy of Herbert Spencer, with a biographical sketch. New York 1894, 1904 (3rd edn).
Character sketch: Mr Herbert Spencer, by one who knows him. Rev of Revs 12 Oct 1895; Dec 1895 (US edn).
Watson, J. In his Hedonistic theories from Aristippus to Spencer, Glasgow, London and New York 1895.
Gaupp, O. Herbert Spencer. Stuttgart 1897, 1900 (2nd edn), 1906 (3rd edn).
Mackintosh, R. In his From Comte to Benjamin Kidd: the appeal to biology or evolution for human guidance, 1899.
Ward, J. In his Naturalism and agnosticism: the Gifford lectures, 1899, 1915 (4th edn). Replies by Spencer, Fortnightly Rev n.s. 66–7, Dec 1899–Apr 1900; and by Ward, 67, Mar 1900.
Collins, F. H. In his Philosophers and scientists, New York 1900 (Warner Classics ser).
Macpherson, H. C. Herbert Spencer: the man and his work. 1900, New York 1900 (as Spencer and Spencerism).
Waite, C. B. Herbert Spencer and his critics. Chicago 1900.
Compayré, G. Spencer et l'éducation scientifique. Paris 1901; tr 1907.
Derry, G. H. The personal side of Herbert Spencer. Sewanee Rev 10 Jan 1902.
Mellone, S. H. In his Leaders of religious thought in the nineteenth century, Edinburgh and London 1902.
Sidgwick, H. In his Lectures on the ethics of T. H. Green, Mr Herbert Spencer and J. Martineau, 1902.
Death of Mr Herbert Spencer. Daily Telegraph 9 Dec 1903.
Death of Mr Herbert Spencer. The Times 9 Dec 1903.
Giddings, Franklin H. The greatness of Herbert Spencer. Independent 55, 17 Dec 1903.
Herbert Spencer. Athenaeum 3972, 12 Dec 1903.
Herbert Spencer. Nature 69, 17 Dec 1903.
James, W. Herbert Spencer dead: passing of one of England's great thinkers. Evening Post (New York) 8 Dec 1903, rptd in Nation 77, 10 Dec 1903 and Critic o.s. 44, Jan 1904.
Ormond, A. T. Herbert Spencer. Booklover's Mag 1 June 1903.
Bonar, J. Herbert Spencer. Economic Jnl 14 Mar 1904.
Brabrook, E. W. Herbert Spencer. Man 4 no 3 1904.
Collier, J. In Royce, *below*.
Cranford, W. I. Herbert Spencer and his work. SAQ 3 Apr 1904.
Davison, W. T. The life and work of Herbert Spencer. London Quart Rev 3rd ser 12 July 1904.
Dewey, J. The philosophical work of Herbert Spencer. Philosophical Rev 13 May 1904.
Fairbairn, A. M. Herbert Spencer. Contemporary Rev 85, June 1904.
Herbert Spencer. Westminster Rev [o.s.] 161, Jan 1904.
Herbert Spencer: a portrait. Blackwood's Edinburgh Mag 175, Jan 1904.
Hobson, J. A. Herbert Spencer. South Place Mag 9 Jan 1904.
Hubbard, E. Little journeys to the homes of great philosophers: Spencer. East Aurora NY 1904.
Iverach, J. Herbert Spencer. Critical Rev of Theological and Philosophical Lit 14 nos 2–3 1904.
Lane, M. A. Herbert Spencer as scientist, moralist and reformer. Nat Mag 19 Jan 1904.
McPherson, L. G. The breadth of Herbert Spencer's teaching. Cosmopolitan 36, Feb 1904.
Mr Herbert Spencer. TLS 1 Jan 1904.
Pattison, A. S. P. [also A. S. Pringle-Pattison]. The life and philosophy of Herbert Spencer. Quart Rev 200, July 1904.
The philosophy of Herbert Spencer. Edinburgh Rev 199, Apr 1904.
Royce, J. Herbert Spencer: an estimate and a review, together with a chapter of personal reminiscences by James Collier. New York 1904.
Tönnies, F. Herbert Spencer, 1820–1903. Deutsche Rundschau 118, June 1904.

Woodbridge, F. J. E. Herbert Spencer. Amer Monthly Rev of Revs 29 Jan 1904.
Bishop, W. S. Philosophy of Herbert Spencer. Sewanee Rev 13 Jan 1905.
Harrison, F. Herbert Spencer. Oxford 1905.
Sidgwick, H. In his Philosophy of Kant and other philosophical lectures and essays, 1905.
Thouverez, É. Herbert Spencer. Paris 1905.
Thomson, J. A. Herbert Spencer. 1906, New York 1906.
Burke, J. B. B. Herbert Spencer and the master key. Contemporary Rev 89, June 1906.
'Two' [the Misses Baker]. Home life with Herbert Spencer. Bristol and London 1906, 1910 (new edn).
Duncan, D. The Life and letters of Herbert Spencer. 1908, 2 vols New York 1908.
Hudson, W. H. Herbert Spencer. 1908.
Eliot, C. W. Introduction. In Spencer, Essays on education and kindred subjects, New York 1910, London 1911 (as Essays on education, etc).
Shelton, H. S. Herbert Spencer as an ethical teacher. International Jnl of Ethics 20 July 1910.
Shelton, H. S. Spencer's formula of evolution. Philosophical Rev 19 May 1910.
Schiller, F. C. S. Spencer, Herbert. In Encyclopaedia Britannica vol 25, 11th edn, Cambridge 1911.
Shelton, H. S. The Spencerian formula of justice. International Jnl of Ethics 21 Apr 1911.
Bowne, B. P. Kant and Spencer. Boston and New York 1912.
Elliot, H. S. R. In DNB suppl 1901–1911, 1912.
Royce, J. In The Americana vol 19, New York 1912.
Morgan, C. L. Spencer's philosophy of science. Oxford 1913.
Werner, E. T. C. Herbert Spencer. Shanghai 1913.
Tillett, A. W. Spencer's synthetic philosophy. 1914.
Tillett, A. W. Militancy versus civilization: an introduction to, and epitome of, the teaching of Herbert Spencer concerning permanent peace as the first condition of progress. 1915.
Elliot, H. [S. R.] Herbert Spencer. 1917, New York 1917.
Holt, H. Herbert Spencer. Unpopular Rev 8 Oct 1917.
Bridge, J. H. Work and play with Herbert Spencer. Unpartizan Rev 14 July 1920.
Sarton, G. Herbert Spencer, 1820–1920. Scribner's Mag 67, June 1920, rptd (with addns) in Isis 3 Summer 1921. [RGP]

Sir James Fitzjames Stephen 1829–94

See col 2303.

Sir Leslie Stephen 1832–1904

See col 2394.

James Hutchinson Stirling 1820–1909

§1

The secret of Hegel. 2 vols 1865, 1 vol Edinburgh [1897] (rev).
Hamilton: being the philosophy of perception. 1865.
De Quincey and Coleridge upon Kant. Fortnightly Rev Oct 1867.
Jerrold, Tennyson and Macaulay, with other critical essays. Edinburgh 1868.
Lectures on the philosophy of law. 1873.
Textbook to Kant, with commentary. 1881.
The community of property. Edinburgh 1885.
Of philosophy in the poets. Edinburgh 1885.
A brief estimate of Carlyle. In T. Carlyle, Counsels to a literary aspirant, 1886.
Philosophy and theology. Edinburgh 1890.
Darwinism: workmen and work. Edinburgh 1894.
What is thought? Edinburgh 1900.
The categories. Edinburgh 1903, 2 pts 1907.
Also works on biology.

§2

Stirling, A. H. Stirling: his life and work. 1911.

George Frederick Stout 1860–1944

§1

Analytic psychology. 2 vols 1896.
A manual of psychology. 1899; ed C. A. Mace 1938 (5th rev and enlarged).
The groundwork of psychology. 1903, 1943 (3rd edn rev).
Studies in philosophy and psychology. 1930.
Mind and matter. Cambridge 1931. Partly rewritten in God and nature, below.
God and nature. Ed A. K. Stout, with memoir by J. A. Passmore. Cambridge 1952. With bibliography.

Articles

Many of Stout's articles are rptd in Analytic psychology *and* Studies in philosophy and psychology, *above.*
Is mind synonymous with consciousness? Proc Aristotelian Soc 1 1888.
The scope and method of psychology. Proc Aristotelian Soc 1 1888.
Ladd on body and mind. Mind 13 1888.
Remarks on mental association. Mind 13 1888.
Herbart compared with English psychologists and Beneke. Mind 14 1889.
The psychological work of Herbart's disciples. Mind 14 1889.
Romanes's Mental evolution in man. Mind 14 1889.
The genesis of the cognition of physical reality. Mind 15 1890. Replies by J. Pikler and Stout, ibid; and J. M. Baldwin, 16 1891.
Is the distinction between feeling, cognition and conation valid as an ultimate distinction of the mental functions? (symposium). Proc Aristotelian Soc 1 1891.
Does our knowledge or perception of the ego admit of being analyzed? (symposium). Proc Aristotelian Soc 1 1891.
A general analysis of presentations, with a view to their interaction. Proc Aristotelian Soc 2 1892.
Is the distinction between is and ought ultimate and irreducible? (symposium). Proc Aristotelian Soc 2 1892.
Is human law the basis of morality or morality of human law? (symposium). Proc Aristotelian Soc 2 1892.
The philosophy of Hodgson. Proc Aristotelian Soc 2 1892.
The relation between thought and language (symposium). Proc Aristotelian Soc 2 1894.
Is the knowledge of space a priori? (symposium). Proc Aristotelian Soc 3 1895.
Relative suggestion. Proc Aristotelian Soc 3 1895.
In what sense, if any, is it true that psychical states are extended? (symposium). Proc Aristotelian Soc 4 1896.
Reply to Angell's criticism of Analytic psychology. Philosophical Rev 7 1898.
Perception of change and duration. Mind n.s. 9 1900. Replies by S. H. Hodgson and T. Loveday, ibid.
Alleged self-contradictions in the concept of relation: a criticism of Bradley. Proc Aristotelian Soc n.s. 2 1902. Replies by H. W. Carr, S. H. Hodgson, J. Lindsay, ibid; by A. J. Finberg and Carr, 3 1903.
Error. In Personal idealism, ed H. Sturt 1903.
Primary and secondary qualities. Proc Aristotelian Soc n.s. 4 1904.
Neo-Kantism as represented by Hicks. Proc Aristotelian Soc n.s. 6 1906. Reply by G. D. Hicks, ibid.
Prichard's criticism of psychology. Mind n.s. 16 1907.
The nature of mental activity (symposium). Proc Aristotelian Soc n.s. 8 1908.

Are presentations mental or physical? Proc Aristotelian Soc n.s. 9 1909.
Instinct and intelligence (symposium). Br Jnl of Psychology 3 1910.
Philosophy. In Votiva tabella, St Andrews 1911.
Can there be anything obscure or implicit in a mental state? (symposium). Proc Aristotelian Soc n.s. 13 1913.
The status of sense data. Proc Aristotelian Soc n.s. 14 1914.
Instinct and emotion (symposium). Proc Aristotelian Soc 15 1915.
Russell's theory of judgment. Proc Aristotelian Soc 15 1915.
War and hatred. In The international crisis in its ethical and psychological aspects, ed E. M. Sidgwick 1915.
Do finite individuals possess a substantive or an adjectival mode of being? (symposium). Proc Aristotelian Soc n.s. 18 1918.
Alexander's theory of sense perception. Mind n.s. 31 1922. Replies by S. Alexander and J. E. Turner, 32 1923.
Are the characteristics of particular things universal or particular? (symposium). Proc Aristotelian Soc (suppl) 3 1923.
The nature of universals and propositions. Proc Br Acad 10 1923.
J. Ward on sense and thought. Mind n.s. 35 1926. With M. Ward.
Ward as a psychologist. Monist 36 1926.
The nature of introspection (symposium). Proc Aristotelian Soc 7 (suppl) 1927.
Truth and falsity. Mind n.s. 41 1932.
Self-evidence and matter of fact. Philosophy 9 1934.
Mechanical and teleological causation (symposium). Proc Aristotelian Soc (suppl) 14 1935.
Shand: a memoir. Proc Br Acad 22 1936.
Universals again. Proc Aristotelian Soc 15 (suppl) 1936.
Sorley. Mind n.s. 45 1936.
Phenomenalism. Proc Aristotelian Soc n.s. 39 1938.
Alexander: personal reminiscences. Mind n.s. 49 1940.
The philosophy of Alexander. Mind n.s. 49 1940.
Things, predicates and relations. Australasian Jnl of Psychology & Philosophy 18 1940.
A criticism of Alexander's theory of mind and knowledge. Australasian Jnl of Psychology & Philosophy 22 1944.
Distributive unity as a category. Australasian Jnl of Psychology & Philosophy 25 1947.

§2

Broad, C. D. Stout. Mind n.s. 54 1945.
Mace, C. A. Stout. Proc Br Acad 31 1945.
Mace, C. A. Stout. Oxford 1948.

Isaac Taylor 1787–1865

Elements of thought. 1822.
Physical theory of another life. 1836.
The world of mind. 1857.
Logic in theology and other essays. 1859.
Ultimate civilization and other essays. 1860.
See col 447.

Thomas Taylor 1758–1835

Bibliographies

'J. J. W.' A brief notice of Taylor, with a complete list of his published works. 1831.
Axon, W. E. A. Taylor: a biographical and bibliographical sketch. 1890.
Balch, R. Taylor the Platonist: a list of his original works and translations. 1917.

§1

Proclus Diadochus: the philosophical and mathematical commentaries translated. 2 vols 1778, 1779.
A dissertation of the Eleusinian and Bacchic mysteries. Amsterdam [1790], 2 pts 1813; ed A. Wilder, New York 1875, 1891 (4th edn).
A vindication of the rights of brutes. 1792.
Plato's works. 5 vols 1804. Tr with F. Sydenham.
Miscellanies in prose and verse. 1805.
Collectanea: miscellanies from the European and Monthly Magazines. 1806.
Aristotle's works translated and illustrated. 10 vols 1806–12.
A dissertation on the philosophy of Aristotle. 1812.
Theoretic arithmetic. 1816.
Elements of a new arithmetical notation. 1823.
Also trns of many other classical works.

§2

Notopoulos, J. A. Shelley and Taylor. PMLA 51 1936.
Evans, F. B. Taylor: Platonist of the Romantic period. PMLA 55 1940.
Politella, J. 'Plato Taylor': a Greek born out of his time. Serif 3 1966.

William Thomson 1819–90

§1

An outline of the laws of thought. 1842, 1849 (enlarged), 1853 (enlarged).
Inaugural lecture, Yorkshire Philosophical Society. 1866.
The limits of philosophical inquiry. Edinburgh 1868.
Will and responsibility. [1875.]
Word, work and will: collected papers. 1879.

§2

Thomson, E. H. Life and letters. 1919.

John Tulloch 1823–86

§1

Theism. 1855.
Rational theology and Christian philosophy in England in the seventeenth century. 2 vols Edinburgh 1872.
Pascal. 1878.
Modern theories in philosophy and religion. Edinburgh 1884.
Movements of religious thought in Britain during the nineteenth century. 1885.

§2

Oliphant, M. O. W. Memoir. 1888.
Also works on religion and education.

John Veitch 1829–94

§1

The Method, Meditations and selections from the Principles of Descartes translated. 1853, 1879 (6th edn with introd).
Speculative philosophy. 1864.
Memoir of Hamilton. Edinburgh 1869.
Lucretius and the atomic theory. Glasgow 1875.
The Tweed and other poems. Glasgow 1875.
The history and poetry of the Scottish border. Glasgow 1878.
Hamilton. Edinburgh 1882, 1883.
Institutes of logic. Edinburgh 1885.
The feeling for nature in Scottish poetry. 2 vols Edinburgh 1887.
Knowing and being: essays in philosophy, 1st series. Edinburgh 1889.
Merlin, and other poems. 1889.
Dualism and monism: essays in philosophy, 2nd series. Ed R. M. Wenley 1895.
Border essays [from Blackwood's Magazine]. 1896.

§2

Bryce, M. A. L. Memoir. 1896.

John Venn 1834–1923

§1

The logic of chance. 1866, 1876 (rev and enlarged), 1888 (rev and enlarged), New York 1962.
On some of the characteristics of belief. 1870.
Symbolic logic. 1881, 1894 (rev).
The principles of empirical or inductive logic. 1889.
Also works on Cambridge.

§2

Francis, H. T. In memoriam John Venn. 1923.

William Wallace 1843–97

Logic of Hegel. 1874, Oxford 1894 (2nd edn rev as Prolegomena to the study of Hegel's philosophy and especially of his logic).
Epicureanism. 1880.
Kant. Edinburgh 1882.
Schopenhauer. 1890.
Hegel's Philosophy of mind, translated with introductory essays. 1894.
Lectures and essays on natural theology and ethics. Ed E. Caird, Oxford 1898.

James Ward 1843–1925

Bibliographies

Titchener, E. B. and W. S. Foster. A list of the writings of Ward. Monist 36 1926.

§1

Naturalism and agnosticism. 2 vols 1899.
The realm of ends: or pluralism and theism. Cambridge 1911, 1912, 1920.
Heredity and memory. Cambridge 1913.
Psychological principles. Cambridge 1918, 1920.
A study of Kant. Cambridge 1922.
Psychology applied to education. Ed G. D. Hicks, Cambridge 1926.
Essays in philosophy. Ed W. R. Sorley and G. F. Stout, with memoir by O. Ward Campbell, Cambridge 1927.

Articles

An attempt to interpret Fechner's law. Mind 1 1876.
A general analysis of mind. Jnl of Speculative Philosophy 16 1882.
Objects and their interaction. Jnl of Speculative Philosophy 17 1883.
Psychological principles. Mind 8 1883, 12 1887.
Bradley's analysis of mind. Mind 12 1887.
The psychological theory of extension. Mind 14 1889.
The progress of philosophy. Mind 15 1890.
Mill's science of ethology. International Jnl of Ethics 1 1891.
Modern psychology: a reflexion. Mind n.s. 2 1893.
Assimilation and association. Mind n.s. 2–3 1893–4.
Bradley's Appearance and reality. Mind n.s. 3 1894. Replies by Bradley and Ward, ibid.
On the definition of psychology. Br Jnl of Psychology 1 1904.
The present problems of general psychology. Philosophical Rev 13 1904.
Is black a sensation? Br Jnl of Psychology 1 1905.
Mechanism and morals. Hibbert Jnl 4 1906.
The nature of mental activity (symposium). Proc Aristotelian Soc n.s. 8 1908.
Purpose and mechanism (discussion). Proc Aristotelian Soc n.s. 12 1912.
Reconstruction: personality the final aim of social eugenics. Hibbert Jnl 15 1917.
Are the materials of sense affections of the mind? (symposium). Proc Aristotelian Soc n.s. 17 1917.
Sense knowledge. Mind n.s. 28–9 1919–20.
In the beginning.... Proc Aristotelian Soc n.s. 20 1920.
Kant. Proc Br Acad 10 1923.
Bradley's doctrine of experience. Mind n.s. 34 1925.
A theistic monadism. In Contemporary British philosophy, ed J. H. Muirhead, vol 2 1925. With partial bibliography.
The Christian ideas of faith and eternal life. Hibbert Jnl 24 1926.
An introduction to philosophy. Monist 36 1926.

§2

Bain, A. Ward on free will. Mind 5 1880.
Bain, A. Ward's psychology. Mind 11 1886.
Bain, A. Ward's Psychological principles. Mind 12 1887.
Jones, E. E. C. Ward's refutation of dualism. Mind n.s. 9 1900.
Perry, R. B. Ward's philosophy of science. Jnl of Philosophy 1 1904.
Perry, R. B. Recent philosophical procedure with reference to science. Jnl of Philosophy 1 1904. Reply by Ward, ibid.
Creighton, J. E. Perry's references to Ward's Naturalism and agnosticism. Jnl of Philosophy 1 1904.
Muirhead, J. H. The last phase of Ward's philosophy. Mind n.s. 22 1913.
Prasanna-Kumára, A. Second paper on Ward's psychology. 1919.
Hicks, G. D. Ward's Psychological principles. Mind n.s. 30 1921.

William George Ward 1812–82

§1

Can experience prove the uniformity of nature? [1872.]
Essays on the philosophy of theism. Ed W. Ward 2 vols 1884.

§2

Ward, W. P. W. G. Ward and the Oxford movement. 1889.
— W. G. Ward and the Catholic revival. 1893.
Ward, M. W. G. Ward and W. P. Ward. Dublin Rev 198 1936.
See col 2669.

Richard Whately 1787–1863

§1

Elements of logic. 1826, 1832 (4th edn rev), 1836 (6th edn rev), 1840 (rev), 1844 (rev), 1848 (rev).
Elements of rhetoric. 1828, 1836 (5th edn rev), 1846 (7th edn rev); ed D. Ehninger, Carbondale 1963.
Easy lessons on reasoning. 1843.
Address to the members of the Manchester Athenaeum. In The importance of literature to men of business, 1852.
Paley's Works. 1859. A lecture.
Miscellaneous lectures and reviews. 1861.

§2

Bentham, G. Outline of a new system of logic, with a critical examination of Whately's Elements. 1827.
Mill, J. S. Whately's Elements of logic. Westminster Rev 9 1828.
Whately, E. J. Life and correspondence. 2 vols 1866, 1875 (rev and enlarged).
See col 2203.

William Whewell 1794–1866

§1

Boadicea: a poem. Cambridge 1820.
The history of the inductive sciences. 3 vols 1837, 1847 (rev, with suppl. 1857), 1857 (with addns), New York 1858; tr Ger 1840–1.
On the foundation of morals. Cambridge [1838?].
The philosophy of the inductive sciences founded on their history. 2 vols 1840, 1847 (enlarged), 3 vols 1858 (pt 1 as History of scientific ideas; pt 2 enlarged as Novum organon renovatum).

Two introductory lectures to two courses of lectures on moral philosophy. Cambridge 1841.
On the fundamental antithesis of philosophy. Cambridge 1844.
A letter to Herschel. Cambridge [1844].
The elements of morality, including polity. 2 vols 1845, 1854 (enlarged), 1864 (4th edn enlarged).
Of a liberal education in general. 3 pts 1845–52.
Lectures on systematic morality. 1846.
Of induction, with especial reference to Mill's System of logic. 1849.
Lectures on the history of moral philosophy in England. 1852, Cambridge 1862 (enlarged).
Of the plurality of worlds. 1853, 1854.
On the influence of the history of science upon intellectual education. In Royal Institute of Gt Britain lectures on education, 1855.
On the philosophy of discovery. 1860.
Also works on science, mathematics and education.

§2

Mill, J. S. In his Dissertations and discussions vol 2, 1859.
Stirling, J. H. Whewell and Hegel. In his Lectures on the philosophy of law, 1873.
Todhunter, I. Whewell: an account of his writings with selections from his correspondence. 1876.
Douglas, J. M. Life and selections from the correspondence. 1882.

John Wilson, 'Christopher North' 1785–1854

See col 2205.

10
Religion

GENERAL STUDIES

Stephen, J. Essays in ecclesiastical biography. 2 vols 1849, 1853, 1 vol 1860 (with a biographical notice of the author).
Gilfillan, G. In his Galleries of literary portraits, 2 vols 1856–7.
Stephen, L. History of English thought in the eighteenth century. 2 vols 1876, 1881 (for 1880), 1902, 1927.
Abbey, C. J. and J. H. Overton. The English church in the eighteenth century. 2 vols 1878, 1 vol 1887 (abridged), London and New York 1896, London 1902, 1906.
Stoughton, J. Religion in England from 1800 to 1850: a history, with a postscript on subsequent events. 2 vols 1884.
Tulloch, J. Movements of religious thought in Britain during the nineteenth century. 1885, 1971.
Overton, J. H. The English church in the nineteenth century, 1800–33. 1894.
Hunt, J. Religious thought in England in the nineteenth century. 1896, 1971.
White, A. D. A history of the warfare of science with theology in Christendom. 2 vols 1896, 1897, 1955, 1960.
Cornish, F. W. The English church in the nineteenth century. 2 vols 1910, New York 1968 (as vol 8 of A history of the English church), 1973 (as vol 8), 1977.
Storr, V. F. The development of English theology in the nineteenth century 1800–60. 1913.
Tatlow, T. The story of the student Christian movement of Great Britain and Ireland. 1933.
Webb, C. C. J. A study of religious thought in England from 1850. Oxford 1933.
Elliott-Binns, L. E. Religion in the Victorian era. 1936, 1946, Greenwich CT 1946, 1953, London 1964.
Kellett, E. E. Religion and life in the early Victorian age. 1938, Folcroft PA 1976, Norwood PA 1976, Philadelphia 1977, London 1978.
Elliott-Binns, L. E. The development of English theology in the later nineteenth century. 1952, [Hamden CT] 1972.
Elliott-Binns, L. E. English thought 1860–1900: the theological aspect. 1956.
Latourette, K. S. Christianity in a revolutionary age: a history of Christianity in the nineteenth and twentieth centuries. 5 vols 1958, New York 1958, Grand Rapids MI 1958, 1962, 1969, Exeter 1970, Westport CT 1973.
Davies, H. Worship and theology in England. 5 vols Princeton 1961–70, 2 vols (pts 1–4) Grand Rapids MI 1996. Vol 1 From Cranmer to Hooker, 1534–1603; vol 2 From Andrews to Baxter and Fox, 1603–1690; vol 3 From Watts and Wesley to Maurice, 1690–1850; vol 4 From Newman to Martineau, 1850–1900; vol 5 The ecumenical century, 1900–1965.
Sangster, P. Pity my simplicity, the evangelical revival and the religious education of children 1738–1800. 1963.
Best, G. F. A. Temporal pillars. Cambridge 1964.
Chadwick, O. The Victorian church, part 1. 1966, 1970, 1971.
Martin, D. A. A sociology of English religion. 1967, 1974.
Soloway, R. A. Prelates and people: ecclesiastical social thought in England, 1783–1852. 1969.
Chadwick, O. The Victorian church, part 2. London and New York 1970, 1972 (rev).
Symondson, A. (ed). The Victorian crisis of faith. 1970.
Gay, J. D. The geography of religion in England. 1971, 1976.
Harrison, B. Drink and the Victorians: the temperance question in England, 1815–1872. 1971, Keele 1994.
Ward, W. R. Religion and society in England, 1790–1850. 1972.
Welch, C. Protestant thought in the nineteenth century. 2 vols 1972, 1985.
Binfield, C. George Williams and the Y. M. C. A.: a study in Victorian social attitudes. 1973.
McLeod, H. Class and religion in the late Victorian city. 1974.
Newsome, D. Two classes of men: Platonism and English romantic thought. 1974.
Rowell, G. Hell and the Victorians: a study of nineteenth-century theological controversies concerning eternal punishment and the future life. Oxford 1974.
Anstey, R. The Atlantic slave trade and British abolition, 1760–1810. 1975.
Chadwick, O. The secularization of the European mind in the nineteenth century. Cambridge 1975.
Gilbert, A. D. Religion and society in industrial England: church, chapel and social change, 1740–1914. 1976.
Laqueur, T. W. Religion and respectability: Sunday schools and working class culture, 1780–1850. 1976.
Norman, E. R. Church and society in England, 1770–1970: a historical study. Oxford 1976.
Obelkevich, J. Religion and rural society: South Lindsey, 1825–1875. Oxford 1976.
Currie, R., A. Gilbert and L. Horsley. Churches and churchgoers: patterns of church growth in the British Isles since 1700. Oxford 1977.
Machin, G. I. T. Politics and the churches in Great Britain, 1832–1868. Oxford 1977, 1987.
Wolff, R. L. Gains and losses: novels of faith and doubt in Victorian England. 1977.
Carwardine, R. Trans-atlantic revivalism: popular evangelicalism in Britain and America, 1790–1865. 1978.
Oliver, W. H. Prophets and millennialists: the uses of biblical prophecy in England from the 1790s to the 1840s. Oxford 1978.
Harrison, J. F. C. The Second Coming: popular millenarianism, 1780–1850. 1979.

Moore, J. R. The post-Darwinian controversies: a study of the Protestant struggle to come to terms with Darwin in Great Britain and America 1870–1900. Cambridge 1979, 1981.
Boyd, K. M. Scottish church attitudes to sex, marriage and the family, 1850–1914. 1980.
Gilbert, A. D. The making of post-Christian Britain: a history of the secularization of modern society. 1980.
Prochaska, F. K. Women and philanthropy in nineteenth-century England. Oxford 1980.
Reardon, B. M. G. Religious thought in the Victorian age: a survey from Coleridge to Gore. 1980, 1995.
Cox, J. The English churches in a secular society: Lambeth, 1870–1930. Oxford 1982.
Hempton, D. and M. Hill. Evangelical Protestantism in Ulster society, 1740–1890. 1982.
Martin, R. H. Evangelicals united: ecumenical stirrings in pre-Victorian Britain, 1795–1830. 1983.
Eisen, S. and B. V. Lightman. Victorian science and religion: a bibliography. Oxford 1984.
Haig, A. The Victorian clergy. 1984.
McLeod, H. Religion and the working class in nineteenth-century Britain. 1984.
Cowling, M. Religion and public doctrine in modern England, II: assaults. Cambridge 1985.
Vance, N. The sinews of the spirit: the ideal of Christian manliness in Victorian literature and religious thought. Cambridge 1985.
Malmgreen G. (ed). Religion in the lives of English women, 1760–1930. 1986.
Valenze, D. Prophetic sons and daughters: female preaching and popular religion in industrial England. Princeton 1986.
Wright, T. R. The religion of humanity. 1986.
Brent, R. Liberal Anglican politics: whiggery, religion, and reform, 1830–1841. Oxford 1987.
Cameron, N. M. de S. Biblical and higher criticism and the defense of infallibilism in 19th century Britain. Lewiston NY 1987.
Norman, E. R. The Victorian Christian socialists. Cambridge 1987.
Parsons G. (ed). Religion in Victorian Britain. Manchester 1988.
Worrall, B. G. The making of the modern church. Christianity in England since 1800. 1988.
Cashdollar, C. D. The transformation of theology, 1830–1890: positivism and Protestant thought in Britain and America. Princeton 1989.
Stanley, B. The Bible and the flag: Protestant missions and British imperialism in the nineteenth and twentieth centuries. Leicester 1990.
Waterman, A. M. C. Revolution, economics and religion: Christian political economy, 1798–1833. Cambridge 1991.
Wolffe, J. R. The Protestant crusade in Great Britain, 1829–1860. Oxford 1991.
Ward, W. R. The Protestant evangelical awakening. Cambridge 1992.
Wolffe, J. R. God and Greater Britain. Religion and national life in Britain and Ireland, 1843–1945. 1994.
Lewis, D. M. (ed). Dictionary of evangelical biography: 1730–1860. 2 vols Oxford 1995.

1. THE ESTABLISHED CHURCHES: THE CHURCHES OF ENGLAND, IRELAND AND WALES; THE SCOTTISH EPISCOPAL CHURCH; THE CHURCH OF SCOTLAND (INCLUDING MEMBERS OF THE FREE CHURCH OF SCOTLAND)

General studies

Mathieson, W. L. Church and reform in Scotland: a history from 1797 to 1843. Glasgow 1916.
Webb, C. C. J. A century of Anglican theology, and other lectures. 1923.
Brose, O. J. Church and Parliament: the reshaping of the church of England 1828–1860. Stanford CA 1959.
Cockshut, A. O. J. Anglican attitudes: a study of Victorian religious controversies. 1959.
Mechie, S. The church and Scottish social development 1780–1870. Oxford 1960.
Brandreth, H. R. T. Episcopi vagantes and the Anglican church. 1961.
Newsome, D. The parting of friends, a study of the Wilberforces and Henry Manning. 1966.
Marsh, P. T. The Victorian church in decline: Archbishop Tait and the Church of England, 1868–1882. 1969.
Thompson, K. A. Bureaucracy and church reform, 1800–1965. Oxford 1970.
Akenson, D. H. The church of Ireland: ecclesiastical reform and revolution, 1800–1885. 1971.
Clark, G. K. Churchmen and the condition of England, 1832–1885: a study in the development of social ideas and practice from the old regime to the modern state. 1973.
Bentley, J. Ritualism and politics in Victorian Britain: the attempt to legislate for belief. Oxford 1978.
Cheyne, A. C. The transforming of the Kirk. Victorian Scotland's religious revolution. Edinburgh 1983.
Smith, D. C. Passive obedience and prophetic protest. A social criticism in the Scottish church 1830–1945. New York 1987.
Corsi, P. Science and religion: Baden Powell and the Anglican debate, 1800–1860. Cambridge 1988.
Heeney, B. The women's movement in the Church of England 1850–1930. Oxford 1988.
Gibson, W. Church, state, and society, 1760–1850. 1994.

1.A. THE EVANGELICALS

General studies

Seeley, Mary. The later Evangelical fathers: John Thornton, John Newton, William Cowper etc. 1879, 1914 (with preface by H. C. G. Moule).
Stock, E. The history of the Church Missionary Society. 4 vols 1899–1916.
Balleine, G. R. A history of the Evangelical party in the Church of England. 1908, 1911, 1933, 1951.
Russell, G. W. E. A short history of the Evangelical movement. 1915.
Baring-Gould, S. The evangelical revival. 1920.
Sloan, W. B. These sixty years: the story of the Keswick Convention. [1935].
Downer, A. C. A century of evangelical religion in Oxford. [1938].
Smyth, C. H. E. Simeon and Church Order: a study of the origins of the evangelical revival in Cambridge in the eighteenth century. Cambridge 1940.
Storr, V. F. Freedom and tradition: a study of liberal evangelicalism. 1940.
Bullock, F. W. B. The history of Ridley Hall, Cambridge. 2 vols Cambridge 1941–53.
Howse, E. M. Saints in politics: the 'Clapham sect' and the growth of freedom. 1952, 1960, 1971, Toronto 1981.
Reynolds, J. S. Evangelicals at Oxford. 1953, rev edn Abingdon 1975.
Davies, G. C. B. The first evangelical Bishop: some aspects of the life of Henry Ryder. 1958.
Bullock, F. W. B. Evangelical conversion in Great Britain 1696–1845. St Leonard's-on-Sea 1959, 1966.
Brown, F. K. Fathers of the Victorians: the age of Wilberforce. Cambridge 1961.
Orr, J. E. The light of the nations: evangelical renewal and advance in the nineteenth century. Exeter [1965], Grand Rapids MI 1965, Exeter 1966, Grand Rapids MI 1966.

Sandeen, E. The roots of fundamentalism. Chicago 1970.
Bradley, I. The call to seriousness: the evangelical impact on the Victorians. 1976.
Hennell, M. Sons of the prophets: evangelical leaders of the Victorian church. 1979.
Jay, E. The religion of the heart: Anglican evangelicalism in the nineteenth-century novel. Oxford 1979.
Toon, P. Evangelical theology 1833–1856: a response to Tractarianism. 1979.
Piggin, S. Making evangelical missionaries, 1789–1858. Abingdon 1984.
Rosman, D. Evangelicals and culture. 1984.
Lewis, D. M. Lighten their darkness: the evangelical mission to working-class London, 1828–1860. 1986.
Hilton, B. The age of atonement: the influence of evangelicalism on social and economic thought 1785–1865. Oxford 1988, 1991.
Hylson-Smith, K. Evangelicals in the Church of England, 1734–1984. 1988, 1989.
Bebbington, D. W. Evangelicalism in modern Britain: a history from the 1730s to the 1980s. 1989, 1993.

Biographies and memoirs

See also under Principal writers, *below.*

Scott, J. The life of Thomas Scott. 1822, Boston 1822, London 1823 (5th edn), Boston 1823, London 1824, New York 1824, London 1825 (8th edn), Lexington KY 1826, New Haven CT 1827, New York 1828, New York 1834, 1923.
Madden, S. Memoir of the Rev Peter Roe. Dublin 1842.
Hill, T. (ed). Letters and memoirs of the late Walter Augustus Shirley. 1849, 1850.
King, J. Memoir of the Rev Thomas Dykes. 1849.
Chatterton, H. G. Memorials personal and historical of Admiral Lord Gambier. 1861, 1861.
Marsden, J. Memoirs of the Rev Hugh Stowell. 1868.
Moody-Stuart, K. Brownlow North's records and recollections. 1878.
Knight, W. (ed). Memoir of Henry Venn. 1880, 1880, 1882.
Hodder, E. The life and work of the Seventh Earl of Shaftesbury. 2 vols 1886, 3 vols 1886, 3 vols 1887, 1890 (Popular edn), 1892 (Popular edn), New York and Toronto 1898, 3 vols Shannon, Eire 1971.
Bickersteth, M. C. A sketch of the life and episcopate of Robert Bickersteth. 1887.
Viscountess Knutsford. Life and letters of Zachary Macaulay. 1900.
Morris, H. The life of Charles Grant. 1904.
Darton, F. J. H. (ed). The life and times of Mrs Sherwood. 1910.
Padwick, C. E. Henry Martyn. 1922, New York 1922, London 1923, New York 1923, London 1925, 1953, Chicago 1950, 1980.
Woods, C. E. Memoirs and letters of Canon Hay Aitken. 1928.
Palmer, H. P. Joseph Wolff, his romantic life and travels. 1935.
Griggs, E. L. Thomas Clarkson. 1936, 1938, Westport CT 1970.
Forster, E. M. Marianne Thornton. 1956, New York 1973.
Hennell, M. M. John Venn and the Clapham sect. 1958.
Reynolds, J. S. Canon Christopher. Abingdon 1967.
Hopkins, H. E. Charles Simeon of Cambridge. Sevenoaks 1977.
Finlayson, G. B. A. M. The Seventh Earl of Shaftesbury. 1981.

Principal writers

Robert Aitken 1800–73

The Prayer Book unveiled. 1863, 1867.

Henry Alford 1810–71

The school of the heart and other poems. 2 vols Cambridge 1835.
The Greek Testament, with a critical commentary. 4 vols 1849–61, 1863, 1868, 1869, 1871, Boston 1872, New York 1873, Boston and New York 1874, London and Cambridge 1874, London 1877, Boston 1878, London 1880, Boston 1880, 1881, London 1883 (rev), Boston 1886, 1888, London 1894, London and Cambridge 1895, London 1899, Chicago 1958, 1968, Grand Rapids MI 1976, 1980.
The Queen's English: stray notes on speaking and spelling. 1864 (for 1863), 1864 (as A plea for the Queen's English), 1865, 1866, 1868, 1870 (rev and enlarged), 1878, 1888 (Bohn's Shilling Lib).
See F. Alford, Life, journals, and letters of Henry Alford, 1873, 1873, 1874.

James Begg 1808–83

Editor of and contributor to Bulwark *from 1851.*

Thomas Dehaney Bernard 1815–1904

The progress of doctrine in the New Testament. 1864 (2 edns), 1866, 1867, Boston 1867, New York 1867, Boston 1872, London 1873, New York 1877, London 1879, New York 1896, London and New York 1900, New York 1907, Grand Rapids MI 1937, 1939, New York 1939, Grand Rapids MI 1949, 1961, London 1968, Minneapolis 1970, New York 1971, Wenham MA 1972, Columbia SC 1994; tr Sp 1961.
The central teaching of Jesus Christ. 1892.

Edward Bickersteth 1786–1850

A scripture help. 1816, 1817, Boston 1817, New York 1817, London 1818, 1819, 1820 (2 edns), 1821, Trenton NJ 1822, 1823, London 1824, 1825, Richmond VA and New York 1828, London 1829, 1835, 1840, Philadelphia 1843, Nashville 1881.
Treatise on the Lord's Supper. 1822, 1823, 1824, 1825, Philadelphia 1825, London 1827, Philadelphia 1831, New York 1832, London 1835, Philadelphia 1836, London 1841, Philadelphia 1841, New York 1842, Philadelphia 1842, New York 1843, London 1847, New York 1849, London 1851, 1852, New York 1855, London 1857, New York 1858, 1862, Philadelphia 1863, 1868.
The Christian student. 1826, 1829, Boston 1830, London 1832, New York 1832 (in Works), 1844.
Christian psalmody. 1833 (3 edns), 1834, 1835, 1836 (3 edns), 1839, [1841] (enlarged), [c. 1855] (enlarged). One of the earliest church hymn-books, it formed the basis of his son, E. H. Bickersteth's Hymnal companion, 1870 etc.
The promised glory of the Church of Christ. 1844, 1845.
See T. R. Birks, Memoir of the Rev Edward Bickersteth, 2 vols 1851 (3 edns), 2 vols New York 1851, 2 vols London 1853 (4th edn), 2 vols New York 1855.

Thomas Tregenna Biddulph 1763–1838

Baptism a seal of the Christian covenant. 1816.
A search after truth. 1818, 1818 (rev).
Senior editor with Legh Richmond from 1798–c.1810 of Zion's Trumpet (The Christian Guardian *from 1801*).

Charles Smith Bird 1795–1862

The Oxford tract system considered with reference to the principle of reserve in preaching. 1838.
Transubstantiation tried by scripture and reason. 1839 (2 edns).
A plea for the reformed church. 1841.
A defence of the principles of the English Reformation from the attacks of the Tractarians, or, a second plea for the reformed church. 1843.
Romanism unknown to primitive Christianity. 1851.
The sacramental and priestly system examined. 1854.

Thomas Rawson Birks 1810–83

Horae Evangelicae. 1852, 1892 (ed H. A. Birks), 1902.
Modern rationalism, and the inspiration of the scriptures. 1853.
The Bible and modern thought. 2 pts [1861–2], 1862, Cincinnati 1864, 1867, Cincinnati and New York 1890?
A commentary on the book of Isaiah. 1871, 1878.
Scripture doctrine of creation. 1872, 1873, London and New York 1887.
The philosophy of human responsibility. 1872.
First principles of moral science. 1873.
Modern physical fatalism and the doctrine of evolution. 1876, 1882 (with a preface in reply to the strictures of H. Spencer and C. Pritchard).
Supernatural revelation. 1879.

Henry Blunt 1794–1843

Eight lectures upon the history of Jacob. 1828, 1830, 1831, 1833, 1835, 1836, Philadelphia 1839, London 1840, Philadelphia 1841, London 1845, Philadelphia 1848, 1851, London 1853, Philadelphia 1854, Greensboro NC 1956.

Andrew Alexander Bonar 1810–92

Narrative of a mission of inquiry to the Jews. Edinburgh 1842, 1844, 1845, Dundee 1846, Edinburgh 1846, 1847, 1849, Dundee 1849, Edinburgh 1852, Dundee 1856, Edinburgh 1857, 1862, 1865, 1866, 1867, London 1869, Edinburgh 1869, 1873, 1877, 1878, 1880, 1882, 1883, 1886, 1892, London 1892, Edinburgh 1894, 1913, London 1913, Edinburgh 1966, London 1966, Edinburgh 1973, 1988.
Memoir and remains of Robert Murray McCheyne. Philadelphia 1844, Dundee 1846, 1849, 1856, Edinburgh 1857, 1862, 1866, London 1869, Edinburgh 1869, 1873, 1877, 1880, Edinburgh and London 1882, Edinburgh 1883, 1886, London 1892, Edinburgh and London 1892, New York 1892, London 1894, Edinburgh 1894, New York 1899, Philadelphia 1912, London and Edinburgh 1913, Edinburgh and Carlisle PA 1966, 1973, Grand Rapids MI 1978, 1983; tr Gaelic 1865.
Commentary on the book of Leviticus, expository and practical. 1846.
Christ and His Church in the book of Psalms. 1859, New York 1860, 1861, 1877, Grand Rapids MI 1978.
Palestine for the young. 1865.
Diary and letters. Ed M. Bonar 1893, 1894, 1910, Edinburgh and Carlisle PA 1960, London 1984.

Horatius Bonar 1808–89

Hymns of faith and hope. 1857, 1858. 1st ser: 1865, 1866, 1871; 2nd ser: 1864, 1872, 1875; 3rd ser: 1866, 1869, 1871.
God's way of peace. 1862, New York 1862, London 1863, Philadelphia 1864, New York 1866, Richmond VA 1867, New York 1869, London 1874, New York 1878, Richmond VA 1879, London 1920 (excerpts), 1968; tr Gaelic 1874, Norwegian 1890?
See col 542, above.

Samuel Richard Bosanquet 1800–82

New system of logic. 1839, 1870.
The rights of the poor and Christian almsgiving vindicated. 1841.
Principia. 1843.

Patrick Brontë 1770–1861

Cottage poems. 1811 (2 edns), New York 1977.
The rural minstrel. 1813.
The cottage in the wood. 1815, 1818 (2 edns), 1859.
The maid of Killarney. 1818.
See W. W. Yates, The father of the Brontës, Leeds 1897; A. B. Hopkins, The father of the Brontës, [1927?], Baltimore 1958, New York 1968.
See also col 1118, above.

William Archer Butler 1814?–48

Sermons, doctrinal and practical. 1st ser: ed (with a memoir) T. Woodward, Dublin 1849, 1852, Cambridge 1855, Philadelphia 1856, Cambridge 1857, 1859, 1866; 2nd ser: ed J. A. Jeremie, Cambridge 1855, Philadelphia 1857, 1866.

Robert Smith Candlish 1806–73

Contributions towards the exposition of the book of Genesis. 3 vols Edinburgh 1843–62, 2 vols 1868 (rev).
The fatherhood of God. Edinburgh 1865, 1865, 1866, 1867, 2 vols 1870 (supplementary vol containing reply to T. J. Crawford etc).
The first epistle of John. Edinburgh 1866, 1869, 1870, Grand Rapids MI 1952, London 1973, Grand Rapids MI 1979.

Thomas Chalmers 1780–1847

A series of discourses on the Christian revelation, viewed in connection with the modern astronomy. Glasgow 1817 (6 edns), Edinburgh 1817 (2 edns), New York 1817, Hartford CT 1818, New York 1818, Glasgow and Edinburgh 1818, Andover MA 1818 (with 6 sermons occasioned by the death of the Princess Charlotte of Wales), Montpelier VT 1819, Glasgow 1822, London 1830, Glasgow 1830, [c. 1840] (as vol 7 of Works, with 6 additional discourses, entitled Astronomical discourses), New York 1845, 1848, London 1852, Edinburgh 1852, Edinburgh and London 1854, New York 1855, Glasgow and London 1862, London [1870] (as Christian revelation viewed in connexion with modern astronomy), Edinburgh and London 1871 (as Discourses on the Christian revelation viewed in connexion with the modern astronomy); tr Welsh, 1846. Commonly known as Astronomical discourses.
The application of Christianity to the commercial and ordinary affairs of life, in a series of discourses. Glasgow 1820 (4 edns), Boston 1821, New York 1821, Hartford CT 1821, Lexington KY 1822 (with other essays), Glasgow [c. 1840] (as vol 6 of Works, with 7 additional discourses, entitled Commercial discourses), New York 1845, 1848, Edinburgh 1850, Edinburgh and London 1852, New York 1857, Edinburgh 1862 (as Discourses on the application of Christianity to the commercial and ordinary affairs of life); tr Fr 1824. Commonly known as Commercial discourses.
The Bridgewater treatises on the power, wisdom and goodness of God as manifested in the Creation. Treatise 1: On the adaptation of external nature to the moral and intellectual constitution of man. 2 vols 1833, 1833, Philadelphia 1833, London 1834, 1835, Philadelphia 1835, 1836, Glasgow [c. 1836] (as vols 1 and 2 of Works, entitled On natural theology), London 1839, Glasgow 1839, London 1853, New York 1857, Edinburgh 1857 (as vol 5 of Select works), London 1869, 1871, 1884.
Works. 25 vols Glasgow [1836–42], New York 1841, 1844, Edinburgh 1848, Glasgow 1852.
Posthumous works. Ed W. Hanna 9 vols Edinburgh 1847–9, 1848–54, New York 1848–50, Edinburgh 1849, New York 1851–60, 1859–60, 1860.
Congregational sermons. 3 vols Edinburgh 1848, 3 vols Edinburgh and London 1852, 3 vols Glasgow 1899. Vols 8, 9 and 10 of Works, containing the Tron church sermons of 1819, with many additional sermons pbd for the first time.

Institutes of theology, with prelections on Hill's lectures in divinity etc. Ed W. Hanna 2 vols Edinburgh 1848, 1849, New York 1849, 1851, Edinburgh 1852, 1856.

See W. Hanna, Memoirs of Chalmers, 4 vols Edinburgh 1849–52, 1850, New York 1850, 1850–2, 1851–2, Edinburgh 1851–2, 1852, 2 vols Edinburgh and London 1854, 3 vols New York 1855, 4 vols New York 1857, 2 vols Edinburgh and London 1867, 4 vols New York 1871; ed J. C. Moffat Cincinnati 1853 (abridged).

See col 2474, above.

William Weldon Champneys 1807–75

The Spirit in the Word. 1862.
Facts and fragments. 1864.
Parish work. '1866' [1865].

Francis Close 1797–1882

The footsteps of error. 1863.
The stage, ancient and modern: its tendencies on morals and religion. 1877.

John William Cunningham 1780–1861

A world without souls. 1805, 1806, New Haven CT 1806, Boston 1808, 1809, Baltimore 1810, Boston 1810 (2 edns), 1815, Albany NY 1815, Philadelphia 1815 (with alterations), 1816, Boston 1832, New York 1845.
The velvet cushion. 1814 (6 edns), 1815 (3 edns), Albany NY 1815, Boston and New York 1815, New York 1815, Philadelphia 1815, New York 1853.
De Rancé, a poem. 1815 (2 edns), Elizabethtown NJ 1816, Newark NJ 1816, New York 1816, Middleboro MA 1857.
Sancho, or the proverbialist. 1816, 1817, Boston 1817, Philadelphia 1833.
Cautions to continental travellers. 1818, 1823.
On the practical tendency of Popery. 1828.
Editor of and contributor to Christian Observer, *1850–8.*

Andrew Bruce Davidson 1831–1902

Biblical and literary essays. Ed J. A. Paterson 1902, 1903.

James Denney 1856–1917

The epistle to the Thessalonians. 1892, New York 1892, London 1897, New York 1898, 1899, 1900, London 1902, New York 1905, Cincinnati 1971, 1972.
Studies in theology. 1894, 1895 (3 edns), New York 1895, 1896, 1897, London 1899, New York 1901, 1902, London 1904, New York 1906, London 1908, 1910, Grand Rapids MI 1976.
The second epistle to the Corinthians. 1894, New York 1894, 1899, 1900 (2 edns), 1903, 1905, 1908.
The death of Christ. 1902, 1903, New York 1903, 1904, Cincinnati and New York 1904, London 1905, 1907, New York 1907, 1911 (rev and pbd with The atonement and the modern mind), 1911, London 1920, 1950 (ed R. V. G. Tasker), Chicago 1952, 1956, 1961, 1964, London 1970, Chicago 1978, New Canaan CT 1981, Minneapolis 1982.
The atonement and the modern mind. 1903 (2 edns), Cincinnati and New York 1903, New York 1903, London 1908, 1910, New York 1911 (with The death of Christ).
Jesus and the Gospel. 1908, New York and Cincinnati 1908, New York 1908, London 1909 (2 edns), Cincinnati 1909, New York 1909, Philadelphia 1909, London 1913.
The way everlasting. 1911.
The Christian doctrine of reconciliation. 1917, London and New York 1917, New York 1918, London 1919, 1957, Minneapolis 1985.
Letters to William Robertson. 1920.
Letters. Ed J. Moffatt, London and New York 1922.

Nathaniel Dimock 1825–1909

The doctrine of the sacraments. 1871 (anon), London and New York 1908.
The doctrine of the death of Christ. [1890], 1903 (rev).

Alexander Duff 1806–76

Missionary addresses. Edinburgh and London 1850.
The Indian rebellion. 1858 (2 edns), New York 1858.

Charlotte Elliott 1789–1871

Editor of The Christian Remembrancer Pocket Book, *1834–59, and hymn writer.*

Thomas Erskine 1788–1870

Remarks on the internal evidence for the truth of revealed religion. Edinburgh 1820, 1821 (3rd edn), 1821 (5th edn), Philadelphia 1821, Edinburgh 1823 (6th edn), Andover MA 1823, Edinburgh and London 1823, Philadelphia 1823, Andover MA 1826, 1827, Edinburgh 1827 (8th edn), London 1829, Edinburgh 1829 (9th edn), Philadelphia 1829, 1831, Andover MA 1860, 1871, Edinburgh 1878 (10th edn).
An essay on faith. Edinburgh 1822 (2 edns), 1823, Philadelphia 1823, Edinburgh 1825, Portsmouth NH 1826, Edinburgh 1829, Philadelphia 1830.
The unconditional freeness of the Gospel. Edinburgh 1828 (2 edns), Boston 1828, Edinburgh 1829, 1831, Philadelphia 1831, Edinburgh 1870, 1873, 1879, 1892.
The brazen serpent; or life coming through death. Edinburgh 1831, 1879 (3rd edn), 1879.
The doctrine of election. 1837, Edinburgh 1878.
The spiritual order and other papers. Edinburgh 1871, 1876, 1884.
Letters. Ed W. Hanna 2 vols Edinburgh 1877, New York 1877, Edinburgh 1878, 1884.

George Stanley Faber 1773–1854

Prophecies relative to the period of 1260 years. 2 vols 1806, 1807 (rev), 1808, Boston 1808, London 1810, New York 1811, London 1814, 1818.
A view of the prophecies. 1808, 1809 (rev), Boston 1809.
The origin of pagan idolatry. 3 vols 1816, New York 1984.
A treatise on the genius and object of the Patriarchal, the Levitical and the Christian dispensations. 2 vols 1823.
The difficulties of infidelity. 1824, New York 1825, 1829, Philadelphia 1829, London 1833, Philadelphia 1835, New York 1853, 1866.
The difficulties of Romanism. 1826, Philadelphia 1829, London 1830, Philadelphia 1830, 1840, New York 1850, London 1853 (rev); tr Fr 1839.
The primitive doctrine of election. 1836, New York 1840, London 1842, New York 1843, 1852.
The primitive doctrine of justification. 1837, 1839.
The many mansions in the house of the Father, with a prefatory memoir by F. A. Faber. 1851, 1854, 1962.
The predicted downfall of the Turkish. 1853.
The revival of the French emperorship. 1853 (4 edns), 1859; as Napoleon III, the man of prophecy, New York 1859, 1865, Toronto 1865.

Patrick Fairbairn 1805–74

The typology of scripture. 2 vols Edinburgh 1845, 1847, Philadelphia 1852, Edinburgh 1854 (much enlarged), Philadelphia 1854, Edinburgh 1857, Philadelphia 1857, 1859, Edinburgh 1864, Philadelphia 1865, Edinburgh 1867, 1870, 1882, New York 1900, 1911, London 1953, 1 vol Grand Rapids MI 1960, 1969, 1975, 1989.
Commentary on Jonah. Edinburgh 1849, Grand Rapids MI 1964.
Commentary on Ezekiel. Edinburgh 1851, 1855, 1863, 1876, Evansville IN 1960, Grand Rapids MI 1960, Wilmington DE 1969, Grand Rapids MI 1971, Minneapolis 1979, Grand Rapids MI 1989.
The interpretation of prophecy. Edinburgh and Philadelphia 1856, Edinburgh 1865, New York 1866, 1874, London 1964, Grand Rapids MI 1976, 1993; tr Sp 1985.
Hermeneutical manual. Edinburgh, London and Dublin 1858, Philadelphia and New York 1859.
Imperial Bible dictionary. Ed Fairbairn 2 vols London and Glasgow 1866, 1870, 6 vols 1887, London and Glasgow 1888, London 1890, Grand Rapids MI 1957–8 (as Imperial Bible encyclopedia).
The revelation of the law in scripture. Edinburgh 1869, New York 1869, Grand Rapids MI 1957, Winona Lake IN 1979.
Commentary on the pastoral epistles. Edinburgh 1874, Grand Rapids MI 1956, 1976, Minneapolis 1980.
Pastoral theology. Edinburgh 1875, Audubon NJ 1992.

James Hatley Frere 1779–1866

Combined view of the prophecies. 1815 (2 edns), 1826.

William Goode 1762–1816

An entire new version of the book of Psalms. 1811.
Essays on all the scriptural names and titles of Christ. 1822.
The divine rule of faith and practice. 2 vols 1842, Philadelphia 1842, London 3 vols 1853 (rev and enlarged), 1855, ed A. E. Metcalfe 1906 (abridged).
The doctrine of the Church of England as to the effects of baptism in the case of infants. 1849, 1850, New York 1850, 1853, 1857.
A letter to the Bishop of Exeter. 1850 (4 edns).
The case of Archdeacon Wilberforce compared with that of Mr Gorham. 1854.

Thomas Guthrie 1803–73

The Gospel in Ezekiel. Edinburgh 1856, New York 1856, Edinburgh 1857, New York 1857, Edinburgh 1859, New York 1859, Edinburgh 1863, New York 1864, 1865, 1867, 1873, London 1874, 1877, 1878, New York 1883, 1891.

Alexander Haldane 1800–82

The lives of Robert Haldane of Airthrey and his brother James Alexander Haldane. 1852 (2 edns), 1853, New York 1853, 1854, London 1855, Edinburgh 1855, 1856, New York 1857, 1858, Edinburgh 1871, 1889, Edinburgh and Carlisle PA 1990.
Contributor to The Record *newspaper from 1828.*
See [Anon], A biographical sketch of Alexander Haldane, 1882.

Charles Abel Heurtley 1806–95

A history of the earlier formulations of the Western and Eastern Churches. 1892.
Wholesome words . . . with a prefatory memoir . . . by Rev William Ince. 1896.

Thomas Hartwell Horne 1780–1862

An introduction to the critical study and knowledge of the Holy Scriptures. 3 vols 1818–21, 4 vols 1821 (rev), 1822, 4 vols 1822 (corrected and enlarged), 4 vols 1823, 1825 (corrected), Philadelphia 1825, 4 vols New York and Philadelphia 1826, Boston 1827, Philadelphia 1827, London 1828 (corrected and enlarged), 4 vols Philadelphia 1831, New York 1833, 2 vols 1834, London 1834 (corrected and enlarged), 2 vols Philadelphia 1835, New York 1835, 2 vols Philadelphia 1836, New York 1837, London 1839 (corrected and enlarged), Philadelphia 1839, 1840, 1841, 2 vols New York and Pittsburgh 1844, 5 vols 1846 (corrected and enlarged), 2 vols New York and Pittsburgh 1846, 2 vols New York 1849, 2 vols 1850, 2 vols 1851, 2 vols 1852, 2 vols 1853, 2 vols 1854, 4 vols London 1856 (ed Horne, S. Davidson and S. P. Tregelles), 1857, 2 vols New York 1858, 1860 (enlarged), London 1863, 2 vols New York 1863, 2 vols 1864, 2 vols 1867, 4 vols Boston 1868, London 1869, 2 vols New York 1870, London 1872, 4 vols 1877, 2 vols New York 1878, New York and London 1888, New York 1899, Grand Rapids MI 1970 (rpt of 8th edn 1839).

Edward Irving 1792–1834

Collected writings. Ed G. Carlyle 5 vols 1864–5, London and New York 1866. *See* T. Carlyle, Fraser's Mag Jan 1835.

John Kitto 1804–54

The pictorial Bible. To which are added original notes [by J. Kitto]. Pbd in monthly pts anon. 3 vols 1836–8, 4 vols 1838–9, 1847–8, 1855–6, 58 pts [1871–6] (as The illustrated family Bible); tr Welsh (Old Testament only) 3 vols 1844–50. Kitto's notes were issued separately, anon, in 5 vols in 1840 as The illustrated commentary on the Old and New Testament.

Samuel Lee 1783–1852

A grammar of the Hebrew language. 1827, 1832, 1841, 1844 (rev).
The book of the patriarch Job. 1837.
An inquiry into the nature, progress, and end of prophecy. Cambridge 1849.

Edward Arthur Litton c. 1813–97

The Church of Christ, in its idea, attributes and ministry. 1851, Philadelphia 1856 (rev), Philadelphia and New York 1859, 1863, London 1898.
The Mosaic dispensation considered as introductory to Christianity. 1856.
A guide to the study of Holy Scripture. 1861, 1866.
Miracles. 1868.
Introduction to dogmatic. Pt 1 1882, pt 2 1892, 1902 (with introd by H. Wace), 1912 (ed H. G. Grey), 1960 (ed P. E. Hughes).

Zachary Macaulay 1768–1838

Editor of and contributor to The Christian Observer, *1802–16.*
See Viscountess Knutsford, Life and letters of Zachary Macaulay, 1900.

Robert Murray McCheyne 1813–43

The memoir and remains of Robert Murray McCheyne. Ed A. A. Bonar, Dundee 1843.
Additional remains of the Rev R. M. McCheyne. Edinburgh 1847.
A basket of fragments. Aberdeen 1848, 1860 (6th edn), Inverness 1975, 1979.
See also Andrew Alexander Bonar above.

Norman Macleod the younger 1812–72

Reminiscences of a highland parish. Edinburgh and London 1867, 1868, 1871, [1910] (illus).
Address on Christian missions to India. Edinburgh and London 1868.
Peeps at the Far East. 1871.
Editor of and contributor to Good Words *from 1860*.
See D. Macleod, Memoir of Norman Macleod, 2 vols London 1876, 2 vols New York 1876, 1 vol 1876, Toronto 1876, 2 vols New York 1877, 1 vol 1877, 1 vol Toronto 1877, 1 vol London 1877.

Hugh McNeile 1795–1879

The times of the Gentiles. 1828.
Lectures on the Church of England. 1840 (4 edns), 1842 (8th edn).

John Buxton Marsden 1803–70

History of the early Puritans. 1850, 1853, 1860.
History of the later Puritans. 1852, 1854, 1872.
History of Christian churches and sects from the earliest ages of Christianity. 2 vols 1856, 2 vols [1858] (new edn).
Editor of and contributor to The Christian Observer, *1859–69*.

Catherine Marsh 1818–1912

Memorials of Captain Hedley Vicars. 1856, New York 1856, Montreal 1856, New York 1857, 1858, London 1859, New York 1859, 1860, London 1861, New York 1864, 1867, 1869, 1874, 1880, 1899, 1956.
English hearts and English hands. 1857, 1858, New York 1858, London 1859, New York 1860, London 1866, 1869.
See L. E. O'Rorke, The life and friendships of Catherine Marsh, 1917, 1918.

Henry Martyn 1781–1812

Journals and letters. Ed S. Wilberforce 2 vols 1837, 1839.
See J. Sargent, Memoir of the Rev Henry Martyn, 1816; *and* C. E. Padwick, Henry Martyn, 1922, New York 1922, London 1923, New York 1923, London 1925, 1953, Chicago 1950, 1980.

Benjamin Williams Mathias 1772–1841

An inquiry into the doctrines of the Reformation. Dublin and London 1814.

Henry Melvill 1798–1871

The golden lectures 1850–7. 7 vols [1856–7], 1853 (selection), 1856 (as Golden counsels) (selection), 1876 (as Lectures etc) (selection).

Frederick Meyrick 1827–1906

Doctrine of the Church of England restated, with a preface by E. H. Browne. Oxford and London 1885, 1888 (enlarged), 1891, 1899, 1908; tr Ital 1891.
Memories of life at Oxford etc. 1905.

Hugh Miller 1802–56

Poems written in the leisure hours of a journeyman mason. Inverness 1829.
Letter from one of the Scotch people to the Right Honourable Brougham and Vaux. Edinburgh 1839, 1839.
Footprints of the Creator. Edinburgh and London 1849 (anon), New York 1850, ed L. F. F. Miller, Edinburgh and London 1861 (with memoir), Edinburgh 1869 (10th edn), 1869 (11th edn), 1870 (12th edn), Boston 1870, Edinburgh 1871 (13th edn), 1874 (16th edn), 1876 (18th edn), 1877 (19th edn), New York 1879, Edinburgh 1881 (21st edn), 1882 (22nd edn), New York 1892, 1899.
My schools and schoolmasters or, the story of my education. Edinburgh 1854 (2 edns), Boston 1854, Boston and New York 1855, 1856, Boston 1857, Edinburgh 1857, Boston 1858, London and Edinburgh 1858, Edinburgh 1859, Boston and New York 1859, Edinburgh 1860, Boston 1860, 1862, Edinburgh 1862, Boston 1863, 1864, 1865, Edinburgh 1869, New York 1870, Edinburgh 1870, 1871, Boston 1871, Boston and New York 1872, Edinburgh 1872, 1873, 1875 (25th edn), New York 1877, Edinburgh 1879, 1882, New York 1882, Edinburgh 1883, 1889, 1891, 1893, 1896, New York 1896, Edinburgh 1905, 1907, 1957, Farnborough 1971, Edinburgh 1993.
The testimony of the rocks. Edinburgh 1857 (2 edns), Edinburgh and London 1857, Boston, New York and Cincinnati 1857, New York 1857, Boston and New York 1858, Boston 1859, Boston and New York 1860, Boston 1862, Edinburgh 1866, Boston and New York 1866, Edinburgh 1869, 1870, Boston and New York 1870, Edinburgh 1871, 1872, New York and Boston 1872, Edinburgh 1873, London 1875, New York 1875, 1881, 1882, Edinburgh 1883, 1884, 1889, 1897, New York 1892, 1980.
See also col 2243.

Robert Moffatt 1795–1883

Missionary labours. 1840, 1842 (4th edn).

Favell Lee Mortimer 1802–78

The peep of the day. 1833, Boston 1836 (rev and corrected), New York 1840, 1842, 1844, Boston 1844, New York 1848, Nashville 1849, Boston 1849, New York 1849, London 1859, New York 1859, Philadelphia 1864, London 1877, 2 vols 1878, New York 1878, Philadelphia 1878, London 1884, 1886, Philadelphia 1890, 1897, New York 1906, London 1911, London and New York 1912, 1981; tr Chippewa 1844, Ojibway 1844, Arabic 1862, Hindi 1871, Cree 1898, Thai 1908, Swahili 1924.
Line upon line. 2 pts 1837–8, 2 pts 1841 (4th edn), Madras 1846, New York 1848, 1849, 1858, 1876, Philadelphia 1877, 2 vols London 1878, New York 1879, 1880, Philadelphia 1883, 2 vols London 1884–5, Nashville 1885, pt 1 London 1890, pt 2 [1890], pt 2 1893, 2 pts [1908], 1925 (as The new line upon line – a new and rev issue); tr Sinhalese 1846, Arabic 1866.
Precept upon precept. New York 1843, 1844, 1846, 1847, 1848, Boston 1849, New York 1850, 1854, 1859, Greenfield MA 1859, Boston 1864, New York 1869, Philadelphia 1870, 1874, London 1882, Boston 1883, Nashville 1885, Philadelphia 1897.
Reading without tears. 1857, 2 vols New York 1857–66, 1860, 1862, 1865, 1872.
Lines left out. 1862, New York 1863, 1872, London 1877.

Handley Carr Glyn Moule 1841–1920

Veni creator. 1890, New York 1890, 1892, 1895, 1902, 1906, [1928], Grand Rapids MI 1977.
Philippian studies. 1897, New York 1897, London 1898, London and New York 1899, New York 1900, London 1902, 1904 (5th edn), 1908 (6th edn), New York 1909, London 1927, Grand Rapids MI 1962, London 1975, Fort Washington PA 1975, New York 1978.
Colossian studies. 1898, New York 1898, London 1900 (3rd edn), 1903 (4th edn), London and New York 1917, London 1927 (for 1926), 1929.

Ephesian studies. 1900, 1900, New York 1900, London 1902, 1908, 1920, 1927 (for 1926), 1943, 1962, Grand Rapids MI 1962, London 1975, Fort Washington PA 1975, Westwood NJ 1978, London and New York 1983, London 1984.
Imitations and translations, English, Latin and Greek. 1905 (for 1904).

Frederick Myers 1811–51

Catholic thoughts on the Church of Christ and the Church of England. 1834–41 (anon) (priv ptd), 1874, 1878, ed F. W. H. Myers 1883.
Catholic thoughts on the Bible and theology. 1841–8 (anon) (priv ptd), 1874, 1879, 1883.

James Orr 1844–1913

The Christian view of God and the world. Edinburgh 1893 (2 edns), New York 1893, 1897, Edinburgh 1897, 1900, 1902, New York 1904, 1907, Edinburgh 1908 (10th edn), New York 1908, Grand Rapids MI 1947, 1948, 1954, 1989.
The progress of dogma. 1901, London and New York 1902, London 1907, New York 1907, London 1908, New York 1908, Grand Rapids MI 1952, Tappan NJ 1979.
God's image in man and its defacement. London and New York 1905, London 1906, New York 1906, London 1907, New York 1907, London 1908, New York 1908, Grand Rapids MI 1948, 1978.
The virgin birth of Christ. 1907, New York 1907, London 1908, New York 1912, London 1914, New York 1918, 1921, 1927, Joplin MO 1972; tr Korean 1931.
The resurrection of Jesus. 1908, New York 1908 (2 edns), Cincinnati and New York 1908, 1909, London 1909, Grand Rapids MI 1965, Joplin MO 1972, Minneapolis 1980; tr Norwegian 1913, Korean 1930.
The faith of a modern Christian. 1910, New York 1910.
Sin a problem of today. 1910, Toronto 1910, New York 1910, New York and Cincinnati 1978.

John Overton 1763–1838

The true churchmen ascertained. 1801, York 1802.

Josiah Pratt 1768–1844

Psalms and hymns adapted for public worship. 1835, 1836, 1839, 1854.
Editor of The Christian Observer, *1802, and editor of* Missionary Register, *1813–41*.
See J. and J. H. Pratt, Memoir of the Reverend Josiah Pratt, 1849.

Sir William Mitchell Ramsay 1851–1939

The church in the Roman Empire before AD 170. 1893, 1893 (rev), 1894, 1895, 1897, 1900, 1903, 1904, Boston 1904, London 1907, 1910, New York 1911, 1912, New York and London 1919, Grand Rapids MI 1954, 1979.
St Paul the traveller. 1895, London and New York 1896, London 1897, London and New York 1898, London 1900, London and New York 1901, London 1902, London and New York 1903 (7th edn), 1904, 1905, 1908 (10th edn), 1909, London 1910, London and New York 1912, London 1920 (14th edn), 1925 (15th edn), 1927, 1928, 1930, 1942 (19th edn), Grand Rapids MI 1949, 1951, 1960, 1966, Nashville 1979, Grand Rapids MI 1979, 1982, 1985.
The teaching of Paul in terms of the present day. London and New York 1913, 1914, Grand Rapids MI 1979.

Ellen Henrietta Ranyard 1810–79

Editor of The Book and Its Mission, *1856–65, changing its name to* The Missing Link Mag.

Legh Richmond 1772–1827

Co-editor with T. T. Biddulph of Zion's Trumpet, *1798–c. 1810* (The Christian Guardian *from 1802*).
The fathers of the English church. 8 vols 1807–12.
Annals of the poor. 1814, 1814, 1815, New York 1815, New Haven CT 1815, Baltimore 1815, 1816, London 1826 (5th edn), 1828 (enlarged and illus with introd sketch of author by J. Ayre), Philadelphia and New York 1828, Boston 1829, London 1830, Philadelphia 1830, 1831, 1834, New York 1841, London 1842, New York 1842, Edinburgh 1843, New York 1844, London 1845, 1846, Edinburgh 1847, Philadelphia 1849, London 1850, New York 1850, Halifax UK 1851, Springfield MA 1852, Halifax UK 1853, London 1856, New York and London 1859, New York 1859, Troy NY 1859, London and New York 1861, New York 1864, London 1869, New York and Philadelphia 1870, Edinburgh [1871], Philadelphia 1874, [c. 1875] (enlarged and illus), London 1877, [1878] (with memoir and illus), [1879], Philadelphia 1879, [1883] (ed J. S. Stallybrass); New York 1883, London 1886, 1899, Boston 1899, New York 1930, London 1970, 1983; tr Rus 1817 (partial), Ger 1899. Includes The dairyman's daughter, often ptd separately from 1809.
See T. S. Grimshawe, A memorial of the Rev Legh Richmond, 1829 (3rd and 4th edns), 1829 (5th and 6th edns), New York 1829, New York and Boston 1830, London 1833 (7th edn), 1834 (8th edn), 1837 (9th edn), 1840 (10th edn), New York 1844, 1845, London 1846 (11th edn), New York 1851, London 1853 (12th edn), New York 1857, 1859.

John Charles Ryle 1816–1900

Expository thoughts on the Gospels. 7 vols 1856–[1869?], 4 vols Ipswich 1856–9, 3 vols New York 1865–73, 2 vols London 1866, 2 vols New York 1867, 3 vols 1867, 3 vols 1869–73, 2 vols London 1872, 2 vols 1874, 3 vols New York 1874–5, 7 vols London 1875–83, 7 vols New York 1875, 3 vols 1876, 3 vols 1879, 3 vols 1881, 2 vols 1882, London 1887, 2 vols 1896, 3 vols 1896–7, 4 vols 1897, 3 vols 1904, 2 vols 1905, 3 vols 1908, 2 vols New York 1925, 2 vols Grand Rapids MI 1951, 7 vols London 1954–7, 1 vol Grand Rapids MI 1955, 4 vols 1956–7, 3 vols London 1957, 3 vols Cambridge 1969, 2 vols Grand Rapids MI 1971, 2 vols Cambridge 1975, 4 vols Grand Rapids MI 1977, 4 vols Welwyn 1985, 3 vols Edinburgh and Carlisle PA 1987.
Knots untied. 1874, 1883 (9th edn), 1885, 1896, 1898, 1899 (rev), 1900, 1902, 1927 (27th edn), 1932 (condensed and rev by C. S. Carter), 1954 (31st edn), New York 1959, 1959, Grand Rapids MI 1959, 1964, Cambridge 1977.
Holiness. 1877 (with preface) (2nd edn), 1879 (enlarged), 1883, 1889, 1900, Grand Rapids MI 1952, London 1952, Grand Rapids MI 1956, Greensboro NC 1956, Cambridge 1956, Westwood NJ 1956, Grand Rapids MI 1962, 1971, 1976, Greensboro SC 1977, Cambridge 1977, Old Tappan NJ 1979, Grand Rapids MI 1979, Welwyn 1979, Grand Rapids MI 1984, Darlington 1995.
Practical religion. 1879, 1900, New York 1959, Cambridge 1959, New York 1960, Grand Rapids MI 1977.

George Salmon 1819–1904

Introduction to the New Testament. 1885, 1886, London and Dublin 1888, London 1889, New York 1889, London 1891, 1892, 1894, 1897, 1899, 1904, 1913.

The infallibility of the church. 1888, 1890, Searcy AR 1890, London 1899, 1914, New York 1914, Searcy AR 1914, London 1923, Searcy AR 1948, London 1952 (5th edn) (rev), Grand Rapids MI 1952; abridged and ed H. F. Woodhouse London 1952; 1959, New York 1959; tr Sp 1985.
The human element in the Gospels. Ed N. J. D. White 1907, New York 1907, 1908.

James Scholefield 1789–1853

Scriptural grounds of union. Cambridge 1841, 1841.
The Christian altar. Cambridge 1842, 1843.

Robert Benton Seeley 1798–1886

Essays on the church, by a layman [R. B. Seeley]. 1834, 1834 (rev and enlarged), 1836, 1840, 1859 (7th edn).

Mary Martha Sherwood née Butt 1775–1851

See col 1072.

Charles Simeon 1759–1836

Horae homilecticae. 11 vols 1819–20, appendix, 6 vols 1828, 21 vols 1832, 1833, 1847 (8th edn), 21 vols Grand Rapids MI 1955 (as Expository outlines on the whole Bible), 1988. A long series beginning 1796.
An appeal to men of wisdom and candour. 1816, Baltimore 1817.
See W. Carus, Memoirs, 1847; H. C. G. Moule, Life of Simeon, 1892, ed J. R. S. Taylor 1948; H. E. Hopkins, Charles Simeon of Cambridge, Sevenoaks 1977.

Catherine Sinclair 1800–64

See col 1401.

George Smeaton 1814–89

Doctrine of the atonement as taught by Christ himself. Edinburgh 1868, 1871, Grand Rapids MI 1953.
Memoir of Alexander Thomson. Edinburgh 1869.
Doctrine of the atonement as taught by the apostles. Edinburgh 1870, Grand Rapids MI 1957, Winona Lake IN 1979, Peabody MA 1988, Edinburgh and Carlisle PA 1991.
Doctrine of the Holy Spirit. Edinburgh 1882, 1889, London 1958, Edinburgh and Carlisle PA 1974.
Editor of British and Foreign Evangelical Rev.

James Stephen 1789–1859

Essays in ecclesiastical biography. 2 vols 1849, 2 vols 1850, 2 vols 1853, 1860, 1867, 1868, 1872, 1891, 2 vols 1907, 2 vols New York 1907, 2 vols 1972, Freeport NY 1973.
See also col 2452.

Hugh Stowell 1799–1865

A model for men of business. 1854, 1855, New York 1855, London 1859, 1872.
See J. Marsden, Memoirs of the Rev Hugh Stowell, 1868.

Charles Richard Sumner 1790–1874

The ministerial character of Christ. 1824, 1835.

John Bird Sumner 1780–1862

A treatise on the records of creation. 2 vols 1816, 2 vols 1818 (corrected), 2 vols 1825 (3rd edn), 2 vols 1825 (4th edn), 2 vols 1833 (5th edn), 1 vol 1850 (6th edn).
The evidence of Christianity, derived from its nature and reception. 1824, Philadelphia 1825, London 1826, 1830 (4th edn), 1830 (5th edn), 1836, 1842 (7th edn), 1848 (8th edn), 1861 (rev with reference to current objections).

Henry Thornton 1760–1815

Family commentary. Ed R. H. Inglis 2 vols 1835–7.
See also col 484.

Charlotte Elizabeth (Phelan) Tonna 1790–1846

See L. H. J. Tonna, A memoir of Charlotte Elizabeth, New York 1847.
Editor of and contributor to Christian Ladies Mag. *See col 1413.*
See also col 1484.

Charlotte Maria (A. L. O. E.) Tucker 1821–93

Wings and stings. Edinburgh, London and New York 1855, London and New York 1856, Boston 1860, London 1863, New York 1869, Edinburgh and London 1870, London and Edinburgh 1872, London and New York 1872, 1880, London, Edinburgh and New York 1888.
The lady of Provence. 1871.
See A. Giberne, A lady of England, the life and letters of Charlotte Maria Tucker, 1895, New York 1895.
See also col 1738.

Henry Wace 1836–1924

Christianity and morality. London and Aylesbury 1876, London 1877 (rev), 1877, 1878 (4th edn), 1887 (7th edn), 1895 (8th edn).
The Gospel and its witnesses. 1883, 1884.
Christianity and agnosticism. Edinburgh and New York 1895, London and New York 1904, 1905.
Sermons on the sacrifice of Christ. 1898, New York 1898, London 1915 (with new introd), 1945.
The Bible and modern investigations. London and New York 1903, 1906.
An appeal to the first six centuries. 1905.

Samuel Waldegrave 1817–69

New Testament millenarianism. 1855, 1866.

Lewis Way 1772–1840

The latter rain. 1821, 1821.
Millenium. 1822.
Thoughts on the scriptural expectations of the Christian church. Gloucester 1823, 1826, 1828, Philadelphia 1840.
Palingenesia, the world to come. 1824, Paris 1824.

Thomas Webster c. 1783–1840

Editor of and contributor to Christian Guardian, *c. 1810–40.*

David Welsh 1793–1845

First editor of North British Rev.

William Wilberforce 1759–1833

A practical view of the prevailing religious system of professed Christians. 1797 (5 edns), Boston 1797 (2 edns), London 1798 (6th and 7th edns), Philadelphia 1798, Boston 1799, Dublin 1801, Boston 1803, London 1805 (8th edn), 1811 (9th and 10th edns), Boston 1815, London 1817 (12th edn), 1818 (13th edn), 1824 (15th edn), Glasgow 1826 (with introd by D. Wilson), Philadelphia 1826, Boston and New York 1829, London 1829 (17th edn), Glasgow 1829, London 1830 (18th edn), Baltimore 1833, London 1834, New York 1835, Philadelphia 1835, Glasgow 1838 (abridged) (with introd by D. Wilson), Boston 1839 (abridged), New York 1839, London 1841, Halifax UK 1841, New York 1851, Edinburgh [1854], New York 1856, London 1857 (22nd edn), New York 1859 (abridged), Edinburgh [1871], London 1880, 1886, 1888 (with a prefatory memoir by W. B.), New York 1899 (rev and abridged), London 1958 (abridged), 1989 (abridged); [1830?] (abridged as Nominal and real Christianity contrasted); Peabody MA 1996 (abridged as A practical view of Christianity); tr Fr 1821.

An appeal to the religion, justice and humanity of the inhabitants of the British Empire, in behalf of the negro slaves of the West Indies. 1823, 1823, 1962, New York 1969 (with another essay as Slavery in the West Indies).

§2

Isaac, Robert and Samuel Wilberforce (his sons). Life of William Wilberforce. 5 vols 1838, Philadelphia 1838, London 1839, 1 vol London 1839 (abridged by C. Morris), 2 vols Philadelphia 1841, 1 vol London 1843 (abridged), 2 vols Philadelphia 1846 (enlarged), 1 vol New York 1857 (abridged), 1 vol London 1868 (rev and condensed), 1872 (rev and condensed), 5 vols Freeport NY 1972; tr Ger 1840 (full text).

Colquoun, J. C. William Wilberforce. 1866, 1867,

Coupland, Sir R. Life of William Wilberforce. 1925, 1945.

Pollock, J. Wilberforce. 1977, New York 1978.

Samuel Charles Wilks 1789–1872

Editor of and contributor to The Christian Observer, *1816–50.*

Daniel Wilson 1778–1858

The evidences of Christianity. 2 vols 1828–30, Boston and New York 1829–30, London 1832, Boston 1834, Boston and New York 1838, London 1841 (4th edn), Boston and New York 1845, 1852, 1929.

The sufficiency of Holy Scripture as the rule of faith. 1841, Calcutta 1841 (with appendix on Tract 90 by J. H. Newman), London 1842.

Bishop Wilson's journal letters. Ed Daniel Wilson (his son) 1863.

See J. Bateman, Life of Rt Rev Daniel Wilson, *1859, 1860, Boston 1860, London 1861.*

William Carus Wilson 1791–1859

Editor of Christian Guardian *from 1840.*

See J. M. Ewbank, The life and times of William Carus Wilson, Kendal 1959, 1960.

Emma Jane Worboise 1825–87

See col 1441.

1.B. THE OXFORD MOVEMENT AND THE HIGH CHURCHMEN

General studies

Perceval, A. P. A collection of papers connected with the theological movement of 1833. 1842, 1843.

Palmer, W. A narrative of events connected with the publication of the Tracts for the times. Oxford 1843, 1843, 1843 (with postscript), New York 1843, London 1883 (with introd and suppl to 1883).

Bricknell, W. S. The judgment of the bishops upon Tractarian theology. Oxford 1845.

Newland, H. G. Three lectures on Tractarianism. 1852, 1853 (2nd edn), 1855 (4th edn), 1860.

Browne, E. G. K. History of the Tractarian movement. Dublin 1856, 1856, London 1861 (rev and priv ptd as Annals 1842 to 1860).

Oakeley, F. Historical notes on the Tractarian movement 1833–45. 1865.

Mozley, T. Reminiscences chiefly of Oriel College and the Oxford movement. 2 vols 1882, 1882, Boston and New York 1882, Boston 1884, Farnborough 1969.

Church, R. W. The Oxford movement: twelve years 1833–45. 1891, 1891, 1892, 1897, 1900, 1904.

Worley, G. The Catholic revival of the nineteenth century. 1894.

Overton, J. H. The Anglican revival. [1897], Chicago and New York 1898.

Cruttwell, C. T. Six lectures on the Oxford movement and its results on the Church of England. 1899.

Thureau-Dangin, P. La renaissance catholique en Angleterre au XIXe siècle. 3 pts Paris 1899–1906; tr W. Wilberforce 2 vols 1914 (rev and re-edited).

Bodington, C. Devotional life in the nineteenth century. 1905.

Holland, H. S. The mission of the Oxford movement. In his Personal studies, 1905; rptd from Lyra apostolica, ed H. C. Beeching, 1899.

Hall, S. A short history of the Oxford movement. 1906, 1907.

Hutchison, W. G. The Oxford movement: selections from Tracts for the times. [1906].

Guibert, J. Le revéil du Catholicisme en Angleterre au XIXe siècle. Paris 1907.

Ollard, S. L. The Oxford movement. 1909.

Tuckwell, W. Pre-Tractarian Oxford: a reminiscence of the Oriel 'Noetics'. 1909.

Ward, W. P. The Oxford movement. [1913].

Baring-Gould, S. The Church revival. 1914, 1914, New York 1914, London [1915].

Ollard, S. L. A short history of the Oxford movement. 1915, 1932, 1963, 1983.

Brémond, H. L'inquiétude religieuse. Ser 1, Paris 1919.

Knox, W. L. The Catholic movement in the Church of England. 1923, New York 1925, London 1930.

Webb, C. C. J. A century of Anglican theology and other lectures. 1923.

Brilioth, Y. T. The Anglican revival: studies in the Oxford movement. 1925, London and New York 1933.

Kaye-Smith, S. Anglo-Catholicism. 1925.

Ollard, S. L. The Anglo-Catholic revival. 1925.

Webb, C. C. J. Religious thought in the Oxford movement. 1928.

Stewart, H. L. A century of Anglo-Catholicism. 1929.

Shaw, P. E. The early Tractarians and the Eastern Church. [1930].

Embry, J. The Catholic movement and the Society of the Holy Cross. 1931.

Clarke, C. P. S. The Oxford movement and after. 1932.

Sparrow Simpson, W. J. The history of the Anglo-Catholic revival from 1845. 1932.

Dawson, C. H. The spirit of the Oxford movement. 1933, New York 1933, London 1934, 1945, New York 1976.

Donovan, M. F. G. After the Tractarians: from the recollections of Athelstan Riley. 1933.

Faber, G. Oxford apostles: a character study of the Oxford movement. 1933, New York 1934, London 1936, 1954, 1974, New York 1976.

Knox, E. A. The Tractarian movement 1833–45. 1933, 1934.

Morse-Boycott, D. The secret history of the Oxford movement. 1933.

Peck, W. G. The social implications of the Oxford movement. 1933.
Schaefer, P. Die katholische Wiedergeburt der englischen Kirche. Munich 1933; tr 1935.
Upton, W. P. The churchman's history of the Oxford movement. 1933.
Brandreth, H. R. T. The oecumenical ideals of the Oxford movement. 1947.
Reckitt, M. B. Maurice to Temple: a century of the social movement in the Church of England. 1947.
Matthews, W. R. The religious philosophy of Dean Mansel. Oxford 1956.
Allchin, A. M. The silent rebellion: Anglican religious communities 1845–1900. 1958.
Fox, A. Dean Inge. [1960].
Butler, P. Gladstone, church, state and Tractarianism: a study of his religious ideas and attitudes, 1809–1859. Oxford 1982.
Ellsworth, L. E. Charles Lowder and the ritualist movement. 1982.
Leonard, E. George Tyrrell and the Catholic tradition. 1982.
Rowell, G. The vision glorious: themes and personalities of the Catholic revival in Anglicanism. Oxford 1983, 1990.
Parry, J. P. Democracy and religion: Gladstone and the Liberal Party, 1867–1875. Cambridge 1986.
Imberg, R. In quest of authority. The 'Tracts for the Times' and the development of the Tractarian leaders, 1833–1841. Lund, Sweden, 1987.
Crumb, L. N. The Oxford movement and its leaders. A bibliography of secondary and lesser primary sources. 1988, suppl 1993.
Imberg, R. Tracts for the times. A complete survey of all the editions. Lund, Sweden, 1988.
Chadwick, O. Spirit of the Oxford movement: Tractarian essays. Cambridge 1990, 1992.

Magazines

The British Magazine. Ed H. J. Rose 1832–6; ed S. R. Maitland 1836–49.
The British Critic. Ed J. H. Newman et al 1836–8; ed Newman 1838–41; ed T. Mozley 1841–3. Founded 1793 by W. Jones of Nayland. *See* Wellesley vol 2.
The Christian Remembrancer. Ed William Scott and Francis Garden 1841–4; ed Scott and J. B. Mozley 1844–54; ed Scott 1854–68.
The Guardian. Founded Jan 1846 by R. W. Church, F. Rogers (Baron Blatchford) and M. Bernard.

Biographies and memoirs

Churton, E. Memoir of Joshua Watson. 2 vols 1861, 1 vol 1863.
Shutte, R. N. A memoir of Henry Newland. 1861.
Blomfield, A. A memoir of Charles James Blomfield, Bishop of London. 2 vols 1863, 1 vol 1864.
[Farrer, afterwards Lear, H. L. S.] Life of Robert Gray, Bishop of Capetown. Ed his son C. Gray 2 vols 1876 (for 1875), 1 vol 1883 (abridged).
Fowler, J. R. W. Sibthorp: a biography told chiefly in his own correspondence; with appendix containing fragments of his earlier teaching. 1880, 1880.
[Trench, M.] Charles Lowder: a biography, by the author of the Life of St Teresa. 1881, 1882 (3rd and 4th edns), New York 1883, London 1883 (9th edn), 1885 (11th edn), 1887 (12th edn), 1891 (13th edn), 1899 (14th edn).
Ornsby, R. Memoirs of James Robert Hope-Scott. 2 vols 1884.
Overton, J. H. and E. Wordsworth. Christopher Wordsworth, Bishop of Lincoln 1807–85. 1888, 1890.
T[owle], E. A. Alexander Heriot Mackonochie: a memoir. Ed F. F. Russell 1890, New York 1890, London 1891.
Bellasis, E. Memorials of Mr Bellasis 1800–73. 1893, 1895 (enlarged), 1923.
Carter, T. T. Richard Temple West: a record of life and work. 1895.
Marindin, G. E. Letters of Frederic, Lord Blachford. 1896.
B[utler], A. J. (ed). Life and letters of William John Butler, Dean of Lincoln. 1897, 1898.
Fowler, J. T. (ed). Life and letters of John Bacchus Dykes. 1897, 1899.
Purcell, E. S. Life and letters of Ambrose Phillipps de Lisle. Ed and finished by Edwin de Lisle 2 vols 1900.
Lake, K. Memorials of William Charles Lake, Dean of Durham 1869–94. Ed his widow Katharine Lake 1901.
Osborne, C. E. The life of Father Dolling. 1903, 1903, [1905].
Acland, J. E. A layman's life in the days of the Tractarian movement: in memoriam Arthur Acland Troyte. Oxford 1904.
Crouch, W. Bryan King and the riots of St George's-in-the-East, with a preface by G. W. E. Russell and a note by J. B. Knight. 1904.
Kelway, A. C. George Rundle Prynne: a chapter in the early history of the Catholic revival. 1905.
Kate, Mother. Old Soho days and other memories. 1906.
Paget, E. C. A year under the shadow of St Paul's. 1908.
Romanes, E. Charlotte Mary Yonge: an appreciation. 1908.
Bennett, F. The story of W. J. E. Bennett and of his part in the Oxford church movement of the nineteenth century etc. 1909.
Moberly, C. A. E. Dulce domum: George Moberly, his family and friends. 1911, 1916.
Hutton, W. H. et al. Robert Gregory 1819–1911: the autobiography. Ed W. H. Hutton 1912.
Mason, A. J. Life of William Edward Collins, Bishop of Gibraltar. 1912.
Russell, G. W. E. Edward King, sixtieth Bishop of Lincoln: a memoir. 1912 (3 edns), New York 1912, London 1913 (5th edn).
Watson, E. W. The life of Bishop John Wordsworth. 1915.
Congreve, G. and W. H. Longridge. Letters of Richard Meux Benson. 1916. *See* W. H. Longridge, Spiritual letters of Richard Meux Benson, 1924.
Russell, G. W. E. Arthur Stanton: a memoir. 1917.
Randolph, B. W. and J. W. Townroe. The mind and work of Bishop King. 1918.
Newbolt, W. C. E. Years that are past. [1921].
Paget, S. Henry Scott Holland: memoir and letters. 1921, 1921, New York 1921.
Benson, A. C. The trefoil. 1923, New York 1924. On early life of Archbishop Benson.
Hine, J. E. Days gone by. 1924.
Talbot, E. S. Memories of early life. 1924.
Denison, H. P. Seventy-two years' Church recollections. 1925.
Otter, J. L. Nathaniel Woodard: a memoir. 1925.
Fullerton, T. G. Father Burn of Middlesbrough. 1927.
Coles, V. S. S. Letters, papers, addresses, hymns and verses with a memoir [by G. W. Borlase]. Ed J. F. Briscoe 1930.
Briscoe, J. F. and H. F. B. Mackay. A Tractarian at work: a memoir of Dean Randall. 1932.
Crosse, G. Charles Gore: a biographical sketch. 1932.
Gore, J. F. Charles Gore: father and son. 1932.
Middleton, R. D. Keble, Froude and Newman: short essays in the early history of the Oxford movement. Canterbury [1933].
Mansbridge, A. Edward Stuart Talbot and Charles Gore. 1935.
Prestige, G. L. The life of Charles Gore: a great Englishman. 1935.
Lockhart, J. G. Charles Lindley, Viscount Halifax. 2 vols 1935–6.
Middleton, R. D. Magdalen studies. 1936, 1938. Biographical essays on 10 men associated with the Oxford movement.
Stephenson, G. Edward Stuart Talbot 1844–1934. 1936.
Clarke, C. P. S. Bishop Chandler: a memoir. 1940.
Cross, F. L. Darwell Stone: churchman and counsellor. 1943.
Middleton, R. D. Newman and Bloxam: an Oxford friendship. 1947.
Williams, T. J. Priscilla Lydia Sellon. 1950, 1965 (rev).
Nias, J. C. S. Gorham and the Bishop of Exeter. 1951.
Woodgate, M. V. Father Benson, founder of the Cowley Fathers. 1953.
Davies, G. C. B. Henry Phillpotts, Bishop of Exeter 1778–1869. 1954.

Meachem, S. Lord Bishop: the life of Samuel Wilberforce. 1970.
Baker, W. J. Beyond port and prejudice: Charles Lloyd of Oxford, 1784–1829. Orono ME 1981.
Matthew, H. C. G. Gladstone 1809–1874. Oxford 1986.
Dennis, B. Charlotte Yonge: novelist of the Oxford movement. Lewiston NY 1992.

Principal writings

Tracts for the times, The library of the Fathers, Plain sermons, The Anglo-Catholic library, The English saints, and Lyra apostolica.
Tracts for the times. Ed J. H. Newman 6 vols 1833–41. 90 tracts were issued anon between 9 Sep 1833 (3 tracts) and 27 Feb 1841 (Tract no 90). 5 lists of the Tracts and their authors are extant: (1) appendix to H. P. Liddon's Life of Pusey vol 3, 1897, pp. 473–80; (2) Sir G. Prevost, Whitaker's almanack, 1883; (3) F. H. Rivington [based on information supplied by Newman in 1869], John Bull Sep 1890; (4) J. R. Bloxam, ms at Magdalen College, Oxford; (5) W. J. Copeland (revision of list in Whitaker's almanack, 1883). In the case of 2 tracts further evidence has come to light modifying these lists slightly. The contributors were: J. W. Bowden (nos 5, 29, 30, 56, 58); A. Buller (no 61); C. P. Eden (no 32); R. H. Froude (nos 8 (with J. H. Newman), 9, 59, 63); B. Harrison (nos 16, 17, 24, 49, 74 (with Newman), 81 (with E. B. Pusey)); John Keble (nos 4, 13, 40, 52, 54, 57, 60, 89); T. Keble (nos 12, 22, 43, 84 (with Sir G. Prevost)); H. E. Manning and C. Marriott (no 78); A. Menzies (no 14); J. H. Newman (nos 1–3, 6, 8 (with R. H. Froude), 10–11, 15 (with Sir W. Palmer), 19–21, 31, 33–4, 38, 41, 45, 47, 71, 73–4 (with B. Harrison), 75–6, 79, 82–3, 85, 88, 90); Sir W. Palmer (no 15 (with Newman)); A. P. Perceval (nos 23, 35, 36); Sir G. Prevost (no 84 (with T. Keble)); E. B. Pusey (nos 18, 66–70, 77, 81 (with B. Harrison)); I. Williams (nos 80, 86–7); R. F. Wilson (no 51). The remaining 17 tracts were reprints from older Anglican divines. There is some confusion about the numbering of the tracts after the 1st edn, when no 70 was enlarged and ptd as part of no 65 and Tracts 67–9 were reckoned as no 70.
Lyra apostolica. 1836; ed H. S. Holland and H. C. Beeching 1899. Poems originally ptd in Br Mag. Of the 179 pieces, Newman wrote 109, Keble 46, I. Williams 9, R. H. Froude 8, J. W. Bowden 6 and R. I. Wilberforce one. The authors used Greek letters as signatures: α=Bowden, β=Froude, γ=Keble, δ=Newman, ϵ=Wilberforce, ζ=Williams.
The library of the Fathers of the Holy Catholic Church, anterior to the division of the East and West. Ed J. Keble, J. H. Newman, E. B. Pusey and (1843–57) C. Marriott, 48 vols 1838–85. Included the works of 13 Fathers, e.g. St Chrysostom (16 vols), St Augustine (12 vols), St Athanasius (5 vols), St Gregory (4 vols). The prefaces were contributed by: C. Marriott (15), E. B. Pusey (12), J. H. Newman (4), J. Keble (2), P. E. Pusey (2), H. P. Liddon (1), H. G. Wilberforce (1), H. Browne (1). The translators included Keble, Newman, Pusey, R. W. Church, T. Keble, Sir G. Prevost, W. J. Copeland, J. B. Morris, Macmullen, P. E. Pusey and W. Bright. A complete list of the Library, with the translator and editor of each vol, so far as they are known, is ptd as an appendix to H. P. Liddon, Life of Pusey vol 1, 1893, ch 18.
Plain sermons by the contributors to the Tracts for the times. [Ed I. Williams and W. J. Copeland] 10 vols 1839–48. Preface to vol 1 by I. Williams, H. Jeffreys et al. On last p. of vol 10 it is stated that the sermons were the work, in various proportions carefully set out, of 7 authors designated by the first 7 letters of the alphabet: A = John Keble; B = Isaac Williams; C = E. B. Pusey; D = J. H. Newman; E = Thomas Keble; F = Sir George Prevost; G = R. F. Wilson. But a ms note in W. J. Copeland's copy of vol 7 assigns sermons 221–6 to him; and in Pusey's copy the same sermons are assigned to H. Copeland who was not a contributor to the Tracts for the times and probably felt unable for that reason to appear among the authors of the series. It seems likely that the 6 sermons were substantially his but were adapted by J. Keble to enable them to be assigned to him. They appear among the contributions of A in the statement appended to vol 10.
The library of Anglo-Catholic theology. 88 vols 1841–63. Ed W. J. Copeland 1841–3, W. F. Audland 1843–7, C. L. Cornish 1847–54, J. Barrow 1854–63. The series was intended to include the principal post-Reformation divines, but the full programme was not carried out. The contributors included Keble, Edward Churton, W. H. Mill, C. P. Eden, A. W. Haddan, N. Pocock, J. Bliss and William Scott. Among the writers rptd were Bishop Andrewes, Archbishop Laud, Archbishop Bramhall, Bishop Cosin, Thorndike, Bishop Thomas Wilson and Bishop Hickes.
Lives of the English saints. 4 vols 1844–5; ed A. W. Hutton 6 vols 1900–1. Suggested by Newman, but he ceased to be editor after the first 2 Lives. The compilers of the 33 Lives were: R. W. Church (1), J. D. Dalgairns (7), T. Meyrick (4), M. Pattison (2), F. W. Faber (9), Newman (3), R. A. Coffin (1), R. Ornsby (1), J. A. Froude (1), J. Walker (1), F. Oakeley (1), J. Barrow (2). The list by Hutton in vol 6, Appendix 2 of the 1900 edn is correct except for its ascription of St Ninian (by Barrow) to Pattison and of St Bartholomew (by Dalgairns) to T. Mozley. A list corrected by Newman is among the Bloxam mss at Magdalen College, Oxford.

Principal writers

John James Blunt 1794–1855

Undesigned coincidences in the Old and New Testaments. 1847, 1847, New York 1847, London 1850, New York 1851, London 1853, New York 1854, London 1856, New York 1856, London 1859, 1860, 1863, 1865 (9th edn), New York 1871, London 1873 (12th edn), New York 1874, London 1876 (13th edn), 1881, 1884 (15th edn), New York 1891, London 1897, Birmingham 1965, 1983.

John William Bowden 1798–1844

St Bartholomew's Eve: a tale of the sixteenth century in two cantos. Oxford 1818 (anon) (for Canto I), 1820? (for Canto II), 1821. With J. H. Newman. The copy in BM contains ms notes by J. R. Bloxam, assigning the separate pts to the respective authors.
Tracts for the times. Nos 5, 29–30, 56, 58, 1833–5.
4 articles in Br Critic 1836, 1837, 1839, 1841. *See* Wellesley vol 2.
Lyra apostolica. 1836, 1864. Poems signed α.
Life and pontificate of Gregory the Seventh. 2 vols 1840, New York 1845.
Thoughts on the work of the six days of creation. Oxford 1845. The editor's preface is signed JHN, i.e. J. H. Newman.

John William Burgon 1813–88

Petra: a prize poem recited in the Theatre, Oxford, June IV MDCCCXLV. Oxford 1845, 1846 (with short poems).
Poems 1840 to 1878. 1885.
The lives of twelve good men. 2 vols 1888 (2 edns), New York 1888, London 1889 (3 edns), New York 1891, London 1891 (with portraits). *See* E. M. Goulburn, Burgon: a biography, with extracts from his letters and early journals, 2 vols 1892.

Richard William Church 1815–90

Lives of the English saints: life of St Wulstan. 1844 (anon), 1901.
Dante: an essay. Christian Remembrancer 1850, 1854 (in Essays and reviews), 1878 (with a trn of De Monarchia by F. J. Church), 1879, London and New York 1889 (with other essays), (with other essays) 1897, 1901, London [1906] (essay on Dante, without the trn, but with Church's essays St Anselm and William Rufus, and St

Anselm and Henry I), London and New York 1906, [1910] (essay on Dante only), Port Washington NY 1969, Folcroft PA 1973.
Essays and reviews, collected from the British Critic and the Christian Remembrancer. 1854.
Sermons preached before the University of Oxford. 1868, 1869, 1880 (in The gifts of civilisation), [1913] (with preface by the Bishop of London, as The gifts of civilisation).
Life of St Anselm. 1870, London and New York 1871, London 1873, 1877, 1879, 1881, 1884, 1885, 1888, 1888 (as vol 3 in Miscellaneous writings), 1892, New York 1895, London and New York 1895, London 1899, 1905, 1913, 1937. Civilization before and after Christianity: two lectures. 1872, 1880 (in The gifts of civilisation).
On some influences of Christianity upon national character: three lectures. 1873, 1880 (in The gifts of civilisation).
The sacred poetry of early religions: two lectures. 1874, 1880 (in The gifts of civilisation).
The beginning of the Middle Ages. 1877, New York 1878, 1883, 1885, 1886, London 1887, New York 1890, 1892, 1893, London 1895 (as vol 7 in Miscellaneous writings), New York 1898, London 1899 (with maps), 1900, New York 1900, 1901, 1902, London and New York 1903, London 1905, New York 1907, London 1908, 1910, London and New York 1914, New York 1916.
Human life and its conditions: sermons preached before the University of Oxford in 1876–8 etc. 1878, 1886, London and New York 1894.
Spenser. New York 1879 (Makers of Lit), 1879 (EML), London 1880 (EML), New York 1881, London and New York 1887 (EML), 1888, London 1888 (as vol 5 in Miscellaneous writings), 1894 (EML), New York 1899 (EML), London 1901 (EML), 1902, London and New York 1906 (EML), London 1909 (Pocket edn), 1923 (Pocket edn) London and New York 1926 (EML), London 1939 (EML), 1968 (Gale Lib ser), New York 1968, Folcroft PA 1973.
Bacon. London and New York 1884 (EML), London 1888 (as vol 4 in Miscellaneous writings), 1889 (EML), New York 1894 (EML) (Portrait edn), London and New York 1895 (EML), 1896 (EML), New York 1899 (EML), 1901 (EML), London 1902, New York 1902 (EML), London 1909 (EML pocket edn).
Discipline of the Christian character. 1885, 1886, 1890, 1894, London and New York 1900, 1913. Sermons.
Advent sermons. 1886.
[Miscellaneous writings.] 10 vols 1888 (Uniform edn).
The Oxford movement: twelve years 1833–45. 1888 (as vol 6 in Miscellaneous writings), 1891, London and New York 1891, London 1892, 1897, 1900, 1904, London 1909, 1922, 1932, Hamden CT 1966, Chicago 1970.
Cathedral and university sermons. 1892, London and New York 1893.
Village sermons preached at Whatley. (1st ser) 1892, London and New York 1899, (2nd ser) 1894, London and New York 1895 (with a new sermon added), 1902, (3rd ser) 1897; 1913 (as Sixteen village sermons: preached at Whatley) (Macmillan's Shilling Theological Lib).
Pascal and other sermons. London and New York 1895, 1896, 1900, 1909.
The message of peace and other Christmas sermons. London and New York 1895, London 1896, Philadelphia 1896, London and New York 1897, London 1978, New York 1979.
Occasional papers 1846–90. [Ed M. C. Church] 2 vols 1897 (as vols 8–9 in Miscellaneous writings).

§2

Church, M. C. (ed). Life and letters of Dean Church. 1894, 1895, 1888 (as vol 10 in Miscellaneous writings).
Donaldson, A. B. In his Five great Oxford leaders, 1900, 1902, 1905.
Holland, H. S. In his Personal studies, 1905.
Lathbury, D. C. Dean Church. 1905, 1912.
Cecil, A. In his Six Oxford thinkers, 1909.

William John Conybeare 1815–57, and John Saul Howson 1816–85

The life and epistles of St Paul. 2 vols 1852, 1855, 1856 (rev), 1857, New York 1857, London 1858, New York 1860, London 1861, 1862 (with maps and plates), 1863, New York 1863, London 1864 (2 edns), New York 1864, London 1867, New York 1868, 1869, London 1870, New York 1871, 1872, Hartford CT 1875, New York 1875, London 1877, New York 1877, Philadelphia 1877, New York 1880, London 1886, New York 1886, 1889, 1 vol London 1892, New York 1892, London 1893, 1896, Hartford CT 1896, New York 1897, Hartford CT 1898, New York 1899, Hartford CT 1900, London 1901, Hartford CT 1904, 1905, London and New York 1906, Hartford CT 1907, 1908, New York 1908, Hartford CT 1910, 1911, New York 1913, Hartford CT 1913, 1914, 1915, New York and Chicago 1917, Hartford CT 1920, 1920, Grand Rapids MI 1949, 1950, 1951, 1953, 1954, 1962, 1964, 1971, 1974, 1976, 1980, 1983, 1987.

John Davison 1777–1834

Discourse on prophecy. 1824, 1825, 1839 (4th edn).
An inquiry into the origin and intent of primitive sacrifice. 1825.

Aubrey Thomas De Vere 1814–1902

Essays, chiefly on poetry. 2 vols London and New York 1887.
Essays, chiefly literary and ethical. London and New York 1889.
Recollections. London and New York 1897.
See W. P. Ward, De Vere: a memoir, 1904.
See also col 605.

Digby Mackworth Dolben 1848–67

Poems. Ed R. Bridges, Oxford 1911 (with a memoir), 1915 (rev and enlarged), Aversham 1981.

Alexander Penrose Forbes 1817–75

Besides 4 vols of collected sermons, many pbd separately, Forbes pbd lectures, manuals of devotion and articles in Edinburgh Quart, North Br Rev *and* Christian Remembrancer. *See* Wellesley vol 5 1989.
A short explanation of the Nicene Creed. Oxford and London 1852, Oxford 1866, 1883, 1888, 1898.
Liber ecclesie Beati Terrenani de Arbuthnot: missale secundum usum ecclesiae Sancti Andrae in Scotia. [Ed A. P. Forbes] Burntisland, Fife 1864.
An explanation of the Thirty-nine Articles. 2 vols 1867–8, Oxford 1871, Oxford and New York 1875, Oxford 1878, London 1881, New York, Oxford and London 1887, 1890, 1903, 1906.
Kalendars of Scottish saints. Edinburgh 1872.
List of Forbes's works in D. J. Mackay, Memoir 1888.
See also J. O. Mowat, Bishop A. P. Forbes, 1925; R. Strong, Alexander Forbes of Brechin: the first Tractarian bishop, Oxford 1995.

James Anthony Froude 1818–94

See col 2425, above.

Richard Hurrell Froude 1803–36

Tracts for the times. Nos 9, 59, 63 and possibly part of 35, 1833–5.
Lyra apostolica. Derby 1836, 1838, 1864, 1915. Poems signed β.
Remains. Part 1 (ed J. Keble and J. H. Newman) 2 vols 1838; pt 2 (ed J. B. Mozley, preface by J. Keble) 2 vols 1839.
See L. I. Guiney, Hurrell Froude: memoranda and comments, 1904.

Elizabeth Furlong Shipton Harris

From Oxford to Rome, by a companion traveller. 1847 (anon), 1847 (rev), New York 1847.
Rest in the church, by the author of From Oxford to Rome. 1848.

Robert Stephen Hawker 1803–75

See col 617, above.

Reginald Heber 1783–1826

The personality and office of the Christian comforter. 1816, Oxford 1816, 1818.
Life of Bishop Jeremy Taylor. (With Works of Jeremy Taylor) 1822, 1828, 1839, 1847–54, 1847–56, 1848–65, 1850–6, 1851–9, 1852–61, 1854. Also pbd separately 1824, 1828, 1839.
Poetical works. 1841, 1852, 1854 (new edn with portrait), 1861, 1874 (with portrait and illus), [1881].
See also col 350, above.

Walter Farquhar Hook 1798–1875

Five sermons preached before the University of Oxford. Oxford 1837, Leeds and London 1847.
Hear the church: a sermon. Newcastle-upon-Tyne 1838 (29 edns), Burlington NJ 1838, London 1839 (30th edn), Colombo 1839, London 1841 (31st edn).
An ecclesiastical biography, containing the lives of the ancient Fathers and modern divines etc. 8 vols Leeds and London 1845–52.
Lives of the Archbishops of Canterbury (to Archbishop Juxon). 12 vols 1860–76.
The church and her ordinances (sermons). Ed W. Hook 2 vols 1876.
Parish sermons. Ed W. Hook 1879.
And many other lectures, addresses and treatises.
See W. R. W. Stephens, Life and letters of Hook DD, FRS, 1878.

John Keble 1792–1866

See cols 392.

Thomas Keble 1793–1875

Plain sermons by contributors to the Tracts for the times. (Sermons signed E in vols 1–2, 4, 10.)
Tracts for the times. Nos 12, 22, 43, 84 (concluded by Sir G. Prevost), 1833–8.

Alexander Knox 1757–1831

Remains. [Ed J. J. Hornby] 4 vols 1834–7, 1836–7 (vols 1 and 2 only), 4 vols 1844.
Thirty years' correspondence with J. Jebb, Bishop of Limerick. Ed C. L. Forster 1834, 2 vols Philadelphia 1835, 2 vols 1836.

Henry Parry Liddon 1829–90

A list of Liddon's pbd works is given in the appendix to his Life and letters, 1904. *47 of these are sermons pbd separately between 1858 and 1890. Many of them appear to have been collected afterwards and rptd in various vols.*
Sermons preached before the University of Oxford: second series. *See* Some words for God, *below.*
Some words for God: being sermons preached before the University of Oxford 1863–5. 1865, 1869 (for 1868) (as Sermons preached before the University of Oxford), [1859–68], 1873, 1873, 1881, 1884; 2nd ser [1868–79], 1879, 1880, 1883, 1887; 1st and 2nd ser, 2 vols in 1, 1891 (for 1890).
The divinity of Our Lord and Saviour Jesus Christ: the Bampton lectures for 1866. London and Oxford 1867, 1868 (2nd edn), New York 1868, London and Oxford 1869, London 1869, New York 1869, London and Cambridge 1871 (5th edn), New York 1871, London and Cambridge 1872 (6th edn), New York 1873, London 1875 (7th edn), 1878 (8th edn), New York 1881 (9th edn), London 1882 (rev) (9th edn), 1884 (rev) (10th edn), 1885 (rev) (11th edn), 1888 (12th edn), 1889 (13th edn), 1890 (14th edn), London and New York 1891 (15th edn), London 1892 (16th edn), 1894 (17th edn), 1897 (18th edn), London and New York 1900, 1903, New York 1906, London 1908, 1934 (abridged by G. Goodman), 1968 (rpt of Goodman's abridged edn), Fort Washington PA 1968 (rpt of Goodman's abridged edn), Minneapolis 1978; tr Ger [1883?].
The priest in his inner life. 1869.
Some elements of religion: Lent lectures 1870. 1872, New York 1872, London 1873 (2nd edn), 1881 (for 1880) (3rd edn), London and Edinburgh 1883 (4th edn), London 1885 (5th edn), 1889 (6th edn), London and New York 1890 (7th edn), 1891, London 1892 (8th edn), London and New York 1898, 1899, New York 1901, London and New York 1904.
Thoughts on present church troubles [4 sermons]. 1881, New York 1881, Oxford and London 1882 (for 1881).
Easter in St Paul's: sermons. 2 vols 1885, New York 1885, 1889, London 1891 (for 1890), New York and London 1892, London and New York 1897, New York 1907.
Advent in St Paul's: sermons. 2 vols 1889 (for 1888), 1889 (rev), New York 1889, London 1 vol 1891 (for 1890), London and New York 1896, 1899, London 1906, 1912.
Christmastide in St Paul's: sermons. 1889, New York 1889, London 1891 (3rd edn), 1893 (4th edn), 1898 (5th edn), New York 1903.
The magnificat: sermons. 1889, 1890 (2nd edn), London and New York 1891 (3rd edn), 1895 (4th edn), 1898 (5th edn), London 1903, 1910.
Passiontide sermons. London and New York 1891, 1891 (2nd edn), 1892 (3rd edn), London 1895 (4th edn), London and New York 1898 (5th edn), 1903, 1906.
Sermons on Old Testament subjects. 1891, 1893 (3rd edn), London, New York and Bombay 1898, New York 1904 (5th edn).
Essays and addresses. London and New York 1892, 1901.
Sermons on some words of Christ. London and New York 1892, 1895, London 1898, London and New York 1899, London, New York and Bombay 1915.
Explanatory analysis of St Paul's epistle to the Romans. 1893, 1893, London and New York 1897 (3rd edn), 1899 (4th edn), Grand Rapids MI 1961, New York 1971, Minneapolis 1977 (rpt of 1899 edn).
Life of Edward Bouverie Pusey, by H. P. Liddon, J. O. Johnston and R. J. Wilson. Vols 1–2, 1893; vol 3, 1895; vol 4, ed J. O. Johnston and W. C. E. Newbolt, 1897.
Clerical life and work: a collection of sermons with an essay. 1894, 1895, London and Bombay 1903.
Explanatory analysis of St Paul's first epistle to Timothy. London and New York 1897, Minneapolis 1978.
Sermons preached on special occasions 1860–89. 1897.
Sermons on some words of St Paul. London and New York 1898, 1911.

§2

Donaldson, A. B. In Five great Oxford leaders, 1900, 1902.
Johnston, J. O. Life and letters of Liddon, with a concluding chapter by the Bishop of Oxford (Francis Paget). 1904.
Holland, H. S. In his Personal studies, 1905.
Russell, G. W. E. Dr Liddon. 1905, [1911].
Liddon: a centenary memoir [by various hands]. 1929.

Henry Longueville Mansel 1820–71

The limits of religious thought examined. London and Oxford 1858, 1858, London 1859, 1859, Boston 1859, 1860, London 1867 (5th edn), Boston and New York 1868, London 1870, New York 1973; tr Danish 1888.
See also col 2554, above.

Charles Marriott 1811–58

Tracts for the times. No 78, 1837.
Sermons preached for the University and in other places. Oxford 1843.
Sermons preached in Bradfield Church, Berks, Oriel College Chapel and in other places. Oxford and London 1850.

Edward Monro 1815–66

The dark mountains: an allegory. 1858, Philadelphia 1858, Boston 1867.

James Bowling Mozley 1813–78

The theory of development: a criticism of Dr Newman's Essay. Christian Remembrancer Jan 1847, 1878, New York 1879.
Eight lectures on miracles: the Bampton lectures for 1865. 1865, 1867, 1872, New York 1872, London 1878, New York 1878, London 1880, New York 1881, London 1883, New York 1883, London 1886, 1890, London and New York 1895, 1902.
Sermons preached before the University of Oxford and on various occasions. 1876, 1876, New York 1876, London 1877, New York 1877, London 1879, 1883, New York 1885, London 1886, London and New York 1895, London 1896, London and New York 1900, London 1906.
Ruling ideas in early ages etc. 1877, New York 1877, London 1878, New York 1878, 1879, 1880, 1881, London 1884, 1889, London and New York 1896, London 1900, 1906, London and New York 1907.
Essays, historical and theological. 2 vols 1878, 1879, 1884 (with memoir by his sister, Anne Mozley, and includes an anon notice by R. W. Church rptd from Guardian), 1892, 1972.
Sermons, parochial and occasional. 1879, 1879, New York 1879, 1880, London 1882, London and New York 1895, 1900.
Lectures and other theological papers. 1883, New York 1883, London and New York 1893.
Letters of the Rev J. B. Mozley DD. Ed his sister Anne Mozley 1885 (for 1884), New York 1885.

Thomas Mozley 1806–93

Reminiscences, chiefly of Oriel College and the Oxford movement. 2 vols 1882, 1882, Boston and New York 1882, Boston 1884, London 1885, Farnborough 1969.

John Mason Neale 1818–66

See col 643, above.

John Henry Newman 1801–90

See col 2246, above.

Francis Edward Paget 1806–82

Caleb Kniveton. Oxford 1833.
St Antholin's: or old churches and new. 1841.
The Warden of Berkingholt. Oxford 1843 (2 edns).
The Owlet of Owlstone Edge. By the author of St Antholin's. 1856 (for 1855), 1856, 1858 (4th edn).
A student penitent of 1695. 1875.
See E. Hill, Letters to the Elford Flock. Some account of the ministry of Francis Edward Paget, nd; and S. Paget and J. M. C. Crum, Francis Paget, Bishop of Oxford, 1912, 1913.
See also col 1376 above.

Sir William Palmer 1803–85

Origines liturgicae. 2 vols Oxford 1832, 1836, 1839, London 1845; suppl 1845.
Tracts for the times. No 15, 1833 (rev and completed by J. H. Newman).
A treatise on the Church of Christ. 2 vols 1838, 1839, 1840 (excerpt as The Church of Christ), 1841, New York 1841, London 1842 (rev and enlarged), 1857.
Letters to N. Wiseman DD on the errors of Romanism etc. Oxford 1842 (for 1841–2), Baltimore 1843, 1849, London 1851 (3rd edn).
A narrative of events connected with the publications of the Tracts for the times. Oxford 1843 (3 edns, 3rd with postscript), New York 1843, London 1883 (with introd and suppl).

William Palmer 1811–79

Harmony of Anglican doctrine with the doctrine of the Catholic and Apostolic Church of the East. Aberdeen 1846 (anon).
Dissertations on subjects relating to the Orthodox or Eastern Catholic Communion. 1853; tr Greek 1854.
Notes of a visit to the Russian church in 1840, 1841. Ed J. H. Newman 1882, 1895.

Arthur Philip Perceval 1799–1853

Tracts for the times. Nos 23, 35 (with R. H. Froude), 36, and possibly 17, 1833.
A vindication of the principles of the authors of the Tracts for the times. 1841, 1841.
A collection of papers connected with the theological movement of 1833. 1842, 1843.

Edward Bouverie Pusey 1800–82

Tracts for the times. Nos 18, 66, 67, 68, 69, 70, 71, 81, and possibly 76, 1834–7.
A letter to the Archbishop of Canterbury. Oxford 1842, London and Oxford 1842, Oxford [1843?] (with notes); tr Ger 1843.
A letter to the Bishop of London. Oxford 1851, London 1851, Oxford and London (4th edn), (5th edn), (6th edn), Hobart 1851.
Parochial sermons. 3 vols 1852–73, 1886 (rev).
The doctrine of the Real Presence. Oxford 1853, 1855, London 1883.
The Real Presence. Oxford 1857, 1869, 1885.
The minor prophets. Oxford 1860, London 1879, 1883, 2 vols New York 1886, 2 vols 1888–9, London 1891, 1895, 8 vols 1906–7, 2 vols New York 1907, 2 vols Grand Rapids MI 1950, 2 vols 1953, 2 vols 1957, 1985, 2 vols Buffalo NY 1986.
Daniel the prophet: nine lectures. Oxford, London and Plymouth 1864, London 1868, 1869, Oxford and New York 1876, London 1880, 1883 (7th edn), New York 1885, 1886, 1891, London 1892 (9th edn), Minneapolis 1978.
An eirenicon. Pt 1, Oxford 1865, New York 1866; pt 2 (1st letter to Dr Newman), London and Oxford 1869; pt 3 (Is healthful reunion impossible?), Oxford 1870, Oxford and London 1876.
Historical preface to J. H. Newman's Tract no 90. 1865, 1866, Oxford 1903 (with other essays).
Sermons preached before the University of Oxford 1859–72. Oxford 1872, 1884.

Lenten sermons 1858–74. Oxford 1874, London 1883, 1893.
What is of faith as to everlasting punishment? Oxford 1880, London 1880, 1880.
Parochial and cathedral sermons. Oxford 1882, Oxford and London 1883, 1887, 1892.

§2

See H. P. Liddon, Life of Pusey, ed J. O. Johnston, R. J. Wilson and W. E. Newbolt, 4 vols 1893–7; [M. Trench], The story of Dr Pusey's life, 1900; G. W. E. Russell, Dr Pusey, 1907, [1913]. *A complete bibliography by F. Madan of Pusey's pbd works is given as appendix A in vol 4 of his Life by Liddon. See also* G. L. Prestige, Pusey, 1933.

Hugh James Rose 1795–1838

The state of the Protestant religion in Germany, in a series of discourses. Cambridge 1825; 2 pts 1829 (enlarged and with an appendix, first pbd separately in 1828, replying to critiques of the 1st edn).

Martin Joseph Routh 1755–1854

Reliquiae sacrae: sive auctorum fere jam perditorum secundi tertiique saeculi post Christum natum quae supersunt. Vols 1–4, Oxford 1814–18, 5 vols Oxford 1846–8, 5 vols Hildesheim and New York 1979.
Scriptorum ecclesiasticorum opuscula praecipua quaedam. 2 vols Oxford 1832, 1840, 1858 (rev W. Jacobson).
Tres breves tractatus. [Ed M. J. Routh] 1854.

§2

See R. D. Middleton, Dr Routh, Oxford 1938.

Richard Chenevix Trench 1807–86

See col 687, above.

Joseph Blanco White, formerly Jose Maria Blanco 1775–1841

Night and death. 1828. A sonnet.
Second travels of an Irish gentleman in search of a religion. 2 vols Dublin 1833 (anon). In answer to T. Moore, Travels of an Irish gentleman, 1833.
The life of Joseph Blanco White, written by himself. Ed J. H. Thom 3 vols 1845.

Isaac Williams 1802–65

See col 693, above.

1. C. LIBERAL THEOLOGIANS

General studies

Raven, C. E. Christian socialism 1848–54. 1920, 1968, New York 1968.
Boulger, J. D. Coleridge as religious thinker. New Haven CT 1961.
Chadwick, H. The vindication of Christianity in [Brooke Foss] Westcott's thought. Cambridge 1961.
Reardon, B. M. G. From Coleridge to Gore: a century of religious thought in Britain. 1971.
Drummond, A. L. and J. Bulloch. The Scottish church 1688–1843; the age of the Moderates. Edinburgh 1973.
Ellis, I. Seven against Christ: a study of 'Essays and Reviews'. Leiden 1980.
Hinchliff, P. Benjamin Jowett and the Christian religion. Oxford 1987.

Biographies and memoirs

Davidson, R. T. and W. Bentham. Life of Archbishop Tait. 2 vols 1891.
The Dean of Windsor [A. V. Baillie] and H. Bolton. A Victorian dean: a memoir of Arthur Stanley, Dean of Westminster, with many new and unpublished letters. 1930.
Eden, G. R. and F. C. Macdonald (ed). Lightfoot of Durham: memories and appreciations. Cambridge 1932.
Sanders, C. R. Coleridge and the broad church movement: studies in S. T. Coleridge, Dr Arnold of Rugby, J. C. Hare, Thomas Carlyle and F. D. Maurice. Durham NC 1942.

Principal writings

Lux mundi: a series of studies in the religion of the Incarnation. 1889, 1890 (2nd–10th edns), New York 1890, London 1891 (12th edn), 1892 (13th edn), 1895 (14th edn), Chicago 1895, London and New York 1895, London 1898, New York 1898, London 1899 (reprint of 12th edn), 1902, 1904 (15th edn), London and New York 1905, London 1913, 1921. Charles Gore (ed), W. J. H. Campion, H. Scott Holland, W. Lock, A. Lyttelton, J. R. Illingworth, R. C. Moberly, Aubrey Moore, R. L. Ottley, F. Paget and E. S. Talbot.
Carpenter, J. A. Gore: a study in liberal catholic thought. 1960.

Principal writers

Edwin Abbott Abbott 1838–1926

Philochristus. 1878 (anon) (2 edns), Boston 1878, London 1916 (anon).
Onesimus: memoirs of a disciple of Paul. 1882, Boston 1882.
The kernel and the husk. 1886 (anon), Boston 1887.
The Anglican career of Cardinal Newman. 2 vols London and New York 1892.
The spirit on the waters. 1897.
Silanus the Christian. 1906.

Matthew Arnold 1822–88

St Paul and Protestantism. 1870 (2 edns), 1875, New York 1883 (with other essays), London 1887, 1888 (with other essays), 1889, 1892, New York 1894, London 1896, New York 1897, 1898, 1902, London 1904, New York 1908, 1912, 1924; ed R. H. Super, Ann Arbor MI 1968.
Literature and dogma. 1873 (3 edns), 1874, 1875, 1876, New York 1877, 1881, 1883, London 1884, 1887, 1888, London and New York 1889, London 1891, New York 1892, London and New York 1893, New York 1895, London and New York 1896, London 1897, New York 1898, 1899, London 1900, New York 1901, 1902, London 1903, 1904, New York 1906, 1908, London 1909, New York 1914, 1924; ed Super 1968 (with above); New York 1970; tr Fr 1876.
God and the Bible. 1875, New York 1875, Boston 1876, New York 1876, 1879, 1883, London 1884, 1887, 1888, 1889, New York 1893, 1895, London 1897, New York 1901, 1903, London 1904, 1906, New York 1913, 1924, 1970, Ann Arbor MI 1970 (in Complete prose works, ed R. H. Super vol 7).
Last essays on church and religion. 1877, 1903, New York 1983.
See also col 517, above.

Thomas Arnold 1795–1842

Sermons. 3 vols 1829–34; 2 vols 1845 (rev edn); 6 vols 1878 (rev Mrs W. E. Forster née Arnold).
Principles of church reform. 1833 (4 edns), 1962. Postscript to Principles of church reform, 1833 (in 4th edn).
Miscellaneous works. Ed A. P. Stanley 1845.
See also col 2410, above.

§2

Life and correspondence. Ed A. P. Stanley 2 vols 1844 (3 edns), New York 1845, New York and Philadelphia 1845, Boston 1860, London 1868, 1 vol 1901, 1903 (abridged); tr Ger 1847.

Stopford Augustus Brooke 1832–1916

Theology in the English poets. 1874 (2 edns), New York 1875, London 1880, New York 1880, London 1891, 1893, 1896, 1904, 1907, [1910] (EL), 1915.
See col 2324, above.

Edward Caird 1835–1908

The evolution of religion. 2 vols Glasgow and New York 1893, New York 1893, 1894, Glasgow 2 vols 1894, 1899, 1907, New York 1969.
The evolution of theology in the Greek philosophers. 2 vols Glasgow 1904, 1923, New York 1968.
See A. W. Benn, History of English rationalism in the nineteenth century, 1906, *and col 2527, above.*

John Caird 1820–98

An introduction to the philosophy of religion. Glasgow 1880, New York 1881, Glasgow 1889, New York 1889, Glasgow 1891, New York 1891, 1894, Glasgow 1901, 1904, 1910, 1920.
Fundamental ideas of Christianity, with memoir by Edward Caird. 2 vols Glasgow 1899, 1904.

George Douglas Campbell, 8th Duke of Argyll 1823–1900

The reign of law. 1867 (4 edns), New York 1868, 1869, London 1870, 1871, New York 1872, 1873, London 1877, New York 1879, 1882, London 1884, New York 1884, 1888, London 1890,
See also col 2517, above.

Robert Chambers 1802–71

Vestiges of the natural history of Creation. 1844.

Robert Henry Charles 1855–1931

A critical history of the doctrine of a future life. 1899, 1913 (rev and enlarged).

Thomas Kelly Cheyne 1841–1915

The origin and religious contents of the Psalter. 1891, New York 1892, 1895.
Founders of Old Testament criticism. 1893.
Encyclopedia biblica. 4 vols 1899–1903, 1914. Joint editor with J. S. Black.

John William Colenso 1814–83

The Pentateuch and Book of Joshua critically examined. 7 pts 1862–79, 1862–4 (rev); pt 1, 1863 (rev); [1863] extracts; 5 pts 1865, 1865 (preface and part of pt 5 only), 1870 (pts 1–4 only), 1894; 2 pts 1884, 1885, 1888, 1894, New York 1899.

Samuel Taylor Coleridge 1772–1834

Lectures 1795 on politics and religion. In The collected works of Samuel Taylor Coleridge vol 1, ed L. Patton and P. Mann, 1971.
Confessions of an inquiring spirit. Ed H. N. Coleridge 1840.
Notes on English divines. Ed D. Coleridge 2 vols 1853.
See col 298, above.

John Llewelyn Davies 1826–1916

Theology and morality. 1873, New York 1873.
Order and growth. London and New York 1891.

Samuel Rolles Driver 1846–1914

An introduction to the literature of the Old Testament. 1891, Edinburgh 1892, New York 1893, London 1894 (rev and with an appendix), 1897 (enlarged), New York 1898, 1902, 1903, 1906 (rev and enlarged), Edinburgh 1907, New York 1908 (rev and enlarged), London 1909 (rev), New York 1910, 1912, London and New York 1913 (rev), Edinburgh and New York 1913, New York 1916, 1923, 1925, 1928, 1931, 1942, 1948, Edinburgh 1950, Cleveland OH 1956, New York 1960, Edinburgh 1961, Cleveland OH 1963, 1967, Gloucester MA 1972; tr Ger 1896.

Henry Drummond 1851–97

Natural law in the spiritual world. 1883 (2 edns), 1884 (11th, 12th and 13th edns), New York 1884, London 1885 (15th, 16th, 17th edns), New York 1885, 1886, London 1887 (19th edn), New York 1887, London 1888 (22nd, 23rd edns), Albany NY 1888, New York 1888, 1889, London 1890 (25th edn), New York 1890, 1891, 1892, Philadelphia 1892, London 1893 (30th edn), New York 1893, Philadelphia 1893, London 1894 (31st edn), Chicago 1895, New York 1895, London 1896 (32nd edn), New York 1897, London 1899 (37th edn), Chicago 1900, 1901, London 1902, Chicago 1902, London 1910 (43rd edn), 1916, Albuquerque 1981, London 1989; tr Sp 1992.
The Lowell lectures on the ascent of man. 1894, New York 1894 (3 edns), 1895, London 1896, New York 1898 (8th edn), 1899, 1900, London 1901, New York 1901, 1902, 1903, 1904, London 1906, New York 1907, 1911; tr Fr 1909.

Alexander Ewing 1814–73

Present-day papers on prominent questions in theology. The Papers, originated and ed A. Ewing, were begun in Nov 1869 and the first 3 sers were pbd monthly until May 1871, then pbd in 4 vols 1870–4, 5 vols 1878. The 4th ser was by F. Myers and ed H. Whitehead.
Revelation considered as light: a series of discourses. 1873.

Frederic William Farrar 1831–1903

The life of Christ. 1874, 2 vols 1874, London and New York 1874, New York 1874, London 1876, Hartford CT 1876, London [1876–8] (illus), New York 1877, London [1878] (illus), Hartford CT 1878, 1 vol Albany NY 1878, London [1880], 1881, London and New York 1882, New York 1883, 5 vols London 1883, 1886, New York 1887, 1 vol London [1887–9], London and New York 1888, New York 1889, London 1890, [1890–1] (illus), 1891 (illus), Philadelphia 1891, New York 1893, London 1894 (illus), New York 1894, 1895, London 1896, New York 1897, London 1898, New York 1898, London and Paris 1900, London 1901; ed W. Lefroy 1903; London, Paris and New York 1903, ed A. F. W. Ingram, London 1906; London and Paris 1906, London 1907, London and New York 1909, New York 1911, London 1912, 1913, Grand Rapids MI 1949, Cleveland OH 1950, Portland OR 1960, London 1963 (reissue of edn of 1894), Portland OR 1964, Cleveland OH 1965, Portland OR 1972, 1976, 1980, Minneapolis 1982, London 1989, New York 1989, Salt Lake City 1994; tr Rus 1885, Fr 1888, Swed 1894.

Eternal hope. 1878, New York 1878, London and New York 1878, London 1879, 1880, New York 1880, London 1883, New York 1886, 1888, 1890, London 1892 (with new preface), London and New York 1892, New York 1894, 1899, New York and London 1904, London 1912.

See also col 1524, above.

Percy Gardner 1846–1937

Exploratio evangelica. 1899, 1907.
Evolution in Christian doctrine. 1918.

Thomas Hill Green 1836–82

The witness of God, and Faith: two lay sermons. 1883, 1886.

See also col 2544, above.

Renn Dickson Hampden 1793–1868

The scholastic philosophy in its relation to Christian theology. Oxford 1833, London 1837, Hereford and London 1848, 1852. *See* A concise history of the Hampden controversy, with documents, by H. Christmas, 1848.

Augustus William Hare 1792–1834, and Julius Charles Hare 1795–1855

Guesses at truth, by two brothers. 2 vols 1827, 1 vol 1838, ser 2 Cambridge and London 1848, London 1847, 1851–5, 1859, New York 1861, Boston 1861, 1865, London and New York 1866, London 1866, 1867, London and New York 1871, London 1874, London and New York 1876, New York 1877, London 1878, 1882, 1884, 1889, New York 1897.

See also col 2144, above.

James Hastings 1852–1922

A dictionary of the Bible. Ed Hastings et al, 5 vols Edinburgh 1898–1904, 1900–4, London 1903–4, New York and Edinburgh 1903, New York 1904, Edinburgh 1906, 1909, New York 1909, Edinburgh 1909, London 1910, New York 1911–12, 1914, 1916, 1919–23, 1921, Edinburgh 1923–7, New York 1924, Edinburgh 1936, New York 1937, 1939, 1942, 1944, 1947, 1948, Edinburgh and New York 1950, New York 1951, 1954, 1963; ed F. C. Grant and H. H. Rowley, New York 1963; New York 1988, Peabody MA 1988, 1989, 1996; tr Chinese 1916.

Edwin Hatch 1835–89

The organization of the early Christian churches. 1881, 1882, 1888, London and New York 1888, London 1892, London and New York 1895, 1901, London 1909, New York and London 1918, New York 1972.
The influence of Greek ideas and usages upon the Christian church. 1890, 1891, London and Edinburgh 1892, London 1895, 1897, 1898, 1901, London and Edinburgh 1901, 1904, 1907, 1914, New York 1957, 1966, Gloucester MA 1970, New York 1972; tr Ger 1892.

Fenton John Anthony Hort 1828–92

The way, the truth, the life: Hulsean lectures. 1871; ed B. F. Westcott, Cambridge, London and New York 1893, London and New York 1894, Cambridge 1894, London 1897, London and New York 1908, 1922.
Judaistic Christianity. 1894, 1898, 1904.
Life and letters. Ed A. F. Hort 2 vols 1896.
The Christian Ecclesia. Ed J. O. F. Murray 1897, 1898, 1900, 1908, 1914.

Richard Holt Hutton 1826–97

Essays theological and literary. 2 vols 1871, [1874], 2 vols 1877 (for 1876) (rev and enlarged), 1880, London and Edinburgh 1888 (theological essays only), 1888 (literary essays only) (enlarged), London and New York 1895 (theological essays only) (rev).
Essays on some of the modern guides of English thought in matters of faith. London, Edinburgh and New York 1887, London 1888, London and New York 1888, 1891, 1900, Freeport NY 1972.
Aspects of religious and scientific thought. London and New York 1899, London 1901, Farnborough 1971, London and New York 1971.

See also col 2237, above.

William Ralph Inge 1860–1954

Christian mysticism. 1899, New York 1899, London 1912, 1913, 1918, 1921, 1925, 1929, 1933, New York 1933, London 1948, New York 1948, 1956, 1960, 1964, Cleveland OH 1964, New York 1966.
The philosophy of Plotinus. 2 vols London and New York 1918, 1923, 1929, London 1941, London and New York 1948.
Outspoken essays. 1919; 2nd ser, 2 vols '1919' [1922], 1921, London and New York 1923, 1924, London 1925, London and New York 1926, London 1927, London and New York 1933, Westport CT 1968, New York 1969.
Christian ethics and modern problems. London and New York 1930, 1932 (5th edn), Westport CT 1970.

Benjamin Jowett 1817–93

Epistles of St Paul to Thessalonians, Galatians and Romans: translation and commentary with essays and dissertations. 2 vols 1855, 1859; ed L. Campbell 2 vols 1894 (the trn and commentary 'edited and condensed').

Charles Kingsley 1819–75

The good news of God: sermons. 1859, New York 1859, London 1860 (3rd edn), Boston 1865, London 1874, 1877 (6th edn), 1878 (8th edn), 1880 (9th edn), 1883, London and New York 1890, 1892, 1898, London 1908, 1913, 1969.
What, then, does Dr Newman mean? 1864 (3 edns); ed W. Ward, Oxford 1913 (in J. H. Newman, Apologia pro vita sua).
Letters and memories of his life. Ed by his wife, 2 vols 1877.

See also col 1311, above.

Joseph Barber Lightfoot 1828–89

Dissertations on the apostolic age. From his edns of St Paul's epistles, 1865–75, London and New York 1892.
Essays on the work entitled Supernatural religion. London, Cambridge and New York 1889, London and New York 1893.

Thomas Martin Lindsay 1843–1914

Religious life in Scotland, from the Reformation to the present day. 1888. With others.
A history of the Reformation in Europe. 2 vols Edinburgh 1906–7, 1907–8, New York 1907–8, 1910, 1911, 1912, 1913, Edinburgh 1914, New York 1914, 1917, 1920, Edinburgh 1922, New York 1922, 1925–6, Edinburgh 1933–4, New York 1936, 1936–8, 1941, Edinburgh 1948, New York 1949, 1950, Edinburgh 1956, 1959, 1964, Freeport NY 1972.

Robert William Mackay 1803–82

The progress of the intellect, as exemplified in the religious development of the Greeks and Hebrews. 2 vols 1850. *See* article by George Eliot, Westminster Rev 54 1851.
The Tubingen School and its antecedents. Edinburgh 1863.

Hugh Macmillan 1833–1903

Bible teachings in nature. 1867, New York 1867, London 1868, 1869, New York 1869, London 1870, 1871 (5th edn), 1872 (7th edn), New York 1873, London 1874 (9th edn), 1875 (10th edn), 1876 (11th edn), 1880, 1882, Rochester NY 1883, London 1885, 1889, 1899, 1893, 1903, 1912.
The ministry of nature. 1871, 1872, 1879, 1882, 1885, London and New York 1888, 1893.
The Isles and the Gospel, with memoir by George A. Macmillan. 1907.

John Frederick Denison Maurice 1805–72

The Kingdom of Christ, by a clergyman of the Church of England. [1837–8], 3 vols 1838, 2 vols 1842, 1843, New York and Philadelphia 1843, London 1883, 1891 (4th edn), [1906] (EL), London and New York 1938; ed A. R. Vidler 2 vols London 1958, 1959, [1960], 1964.
Moral and metaphysical philosophy. 1845, 1848 (rev), 4 vols 1850–7, 2 vols 1871–2, 2 vols 1872 (new edn with preface).
The religions of the world. Cambridge 1847, London 1848 (rev), Cambridge 1852, Boston 1854, Cambridge 1861, London 1877, Cambridge 1886, New York 1988 (vol 4 in The best in the literature of philosophy and world religions).
Theological essays. 1853, Cambridge and London 1853 (additions), 1854 (concluding essay and preface only), London 1871, 1957.
The doctrine of sacrifice. Cambridge 1854.
The epistles of St John: lectures on Christian ethics. Cambridge 1857.
The conscience: lectures on casuistry. London and Cambridge 1868, 1872, London 1883.
The friendship of books and other lectures. Ed T. Hughes 1874.
See Life of Maurice, chiefly told in his own letters, ed J. F. Maurice 2 vols 1884; *and* F. M. G. E. Higham, Frederick Denison Maurice, 1947.
See also col 2240, above.

Alfred Williams Momerie 1848–1900

Defects of modern Christianity. Edinburgh and London 1882, Edinburgh 1885 (rev) (3rd edn), 1888, 1890 (4th edn), 1894.
The religion of the future. Edinburgh and London 1893.

Mark Pattison 1813–84

Tendencies of religious thought in England 1688–1750. 1860 (in Essays and reviews), 1861, 1862, 1865, 1874.
Memoirs. Ed Mrs Pattison 1885, Farnborough 1969, 1988.
Sermons. London and Edinburgh 1885.
Essays, collected by H. Nettleship. 2 vols Oxford 1889, New York 1889, London [1908] (containing 16 of the original 21 essays); New York 1965.
See col 2265, above.

Baden Powell 1796–1860

Tradition unveiled. London and Oxford 1839, London 1839, 1840 (suppl), Philadelphia 1841.
Christianity without Judaism. 1856 (ptd for private circulation only), 1857, 1866 (rev).

Hastings Rashdall 1858–1924

The universities of Europe in the Middle Ages. 2 vols Oxford 1895; rev F. M. Powicke and A. B. Emden 3 vols 1936, 3 vols Oxford 1936, 2 vols London and New York 1942, 2 vols Oxford 1942, 3 vols 1951, 3 vols 1958, 3 vols 1964, 3 vols 1969, 3 vols Oxford and New York 1987; tr Jap 1966.
Doctrine and development. 1898.
The theory of good and evil. 2 vols Oxford 1907, 1924, 1948, New York 1971.
The idea of Atonement in Christian theology. 1919, 1920, 1925.
See P. E. Matheson, Life of Rashdall, 1928.

Frederick William Robertson 1816–53

Sermons preached at Trinity Chapel, Brighton. Ed S. E. Robertson 4 ser 1855–63, 1856–7 (ser 1–3), 1857–8 (ser 1–2), 1872 (4 ser); 5 ser 5 vols 1874–90 (ed C. B. Robertson); 1 vol 1898 (preface by C. B. Robertson, introd by I. Maclaren); 1904 (10 sermons); 1906 (12 sermons).
Lectures and addresses on literary and social topics. 1858, Boston 1859, London 1861, Boston 1865, London 1866, Boston 1869; ed S. A. Brooks, London 1876 (enlarged).
Expository lectures on St Paul's Epistles to the Corinthians. 1859, 1860, Boston 1860, 1862, 1863, 1864, London 1865, Boston 1866, 1868, 1868 (as vol 4 of Sermons preached at Trinity Chapel, Brighton), London 1870, 1872, 1874, 1877, 1879, 1883, 1885, 1889, 1892, 1902, 1907; tr Ger 1895.
See Life and letters, by S. A. Brooke, 2 vols 1865, 1866, 2 vols Boston 1867, 1 vol London 1868, 2 vols Boston 1869, 1870, 1871, London 1872, 1872, 2 vols 1873, 1877, 2 vols 1880, 2 vols 1882–3, 1884, 1887, 2 vols 1891, 2 vols 1901, London and New York 1903, London 1906; tr Ger 1888.

William Sanday 1843–1920

Inspiration. London and New York 1893, 1894, London 1896 (enlarged with new preface), London and New York 1903, London 1911, London and New York 1914.
Christologies, ancient and modern. Oxford and New York 1910, 1911 (in Christology and personality).

Sir John Robert Seeley 1834–95

Ecce homo. 1866 (for 1865) (anon), 1866 (5th and 6th edns), Boston 1866, Philadelphia 1866, Boston 1867, 1868, London 1868 (9th edn), 1869 (10th edn), Boston 1871, 1872, 1873, 1875, 1881, 1883, London and New York 1888, Boston 1888, 1890, 1893, London and New York 1895, Boston 1896, 1898, New York 1900, London and New York 1903, Boston 1903, London 1904, Boston 1907, Manchester UK 1907, London and New York 1907, 1908 (EL), London 1908, 1910, New York 1910, Boston 1913, New York 1915 (EL), London, Toronto and New York 1920 (EL), London and New York 1929, London, Toronto and New York 1932, London and New York 1969; ed O. Lodge [1908]; ed J. E. Odgers 1910; tr Ital 1940.
Natural religion, by the author of Ecce homo. 1882, 1882, Boston 1882, 1886, London and New York 1891, London 1895.
See also col 2449, below.

Henry Sidgwick 1838–1900

The ethics of conformity and subscription. 1870, 1898 (in his Practical ethics).
See col 2587, above.

Sydney Smith 1771–1845

Sermons preached at St Paul's. 1846.
See also col 2197, above, and A. Chevrillon, Smith et la renaissance des idées libérales en Angleterre, Paris 1894.

William Henry Smith 1808–72

Thorndale: or the conflict of opinions. Edinburgh 1857, 1858.
Gravenhurst: or thoughts on good and evil. Edinburgh and London 1862, 1875 (with memoir by his widow).

William Robertson Smith 1846–94

The Old Testament in the Jewish church. Edinburgh 1881, New York 1881, 1882, 1891, Edinburgh and London 1892 (enlarged), New York 1892, London 1895, New York 1900, London 1902, 1907, 1908, 1926; tr Ger 1894.
The Prophets of Israel. Edinburgh 1882, New York 1882, 1892, 1895 (with introd and additional notes by T. K. Cheyne), 1895, London 1897, New York 1897, London 1902, 1907, 1912, 1919, 1928, New York 1982; tr Du 1889.
Lectures on the religion of the Semites. Edinburgh 1889, New York 1889, London 1894 (rev and ed J. S. Black?), New York 1899, London 1901, 1907, 1914, New York 1923, 1956, 1969, 1972, London 1978, Sheffield 1995; ed S. A. Cook London 1927, New York 1927; tr Jap 1969.

Arthur Penrhyn Stanley 1815–81

Sermons and essays on the apostolical age. Oxford 1847, 1852 (rev), Oxford and London 1874, [1890].
Essays, chiefly on questions of Church and State. 1870, 1884, 1969.
Christian institutions. 1881, 1881, New York 1881, London 1882, 1884, 1890, 1906.
See G. G. Bradley, Recollections, 1883; R. E. Prothero, Life and correspondence, 1893.

John Sterling 1806–44

Essays and tales. Ed J. C. Hare 2 vols 1848, 2 vols Farnborough 1971. With memoir.
Twelve letters [to William Coningham]. Ed W. Coningham, London and Brighton 1851, London and Bath 1872.
See T. Carlyle, Life of Sterling, 1851, 1852; ed W. H. White, Oxford 1907 (WC). *See also col 2199, above.*

Connop Thirlwall 1797–1875

Remains, literary and theological. Ed J. J. S. Perowne 3 vols 1877–8.
Letters, literary and theological. Ed J. J. S. Perowne and L. Stokes 1881, 1882.
See J. C. Thirlwall, Connop Thirlwall, 1936. *See also col 2456, above.*

Mary Augusta Ward, née Arnold 1851–1920

Robert Elsmere. 3 vols 1888.
A writer's recollections. 2 vols 1918, London and New York 1918, 1919, Folcroft PA 1973.
See col 1713, above.

Brooke Foss Westcott 1825–1901

A general survey of the history of the canon of the New Testament. Cambridge 1855, 1866, Cambridge and London 1870, 1875 (with new preface), Cambridge 1881, Cambridge and London 1886, Cambridge, London and New York 1889, Joplin MO 1889, London and New York 1896, Grand Rapids MI 1980.
An introduction to the study of the Gospels. London and Cambridge 1860, Boston and New York 1862, Boston 1866, London and Cambridge 1867, 1872, Boston and New York 1872, London 1875, Boston and New York 1875, New York 1880, 1882, 1885, London 1887, New York 1887, London 1888, 1895, New York 1896, 1902.
A general view of the history of the English Bible. London, Cambridge and New York 1868, Cambridge 1872 (rev), London and New York 1905 (rev W. A. Wright), 1916, New York 1922, 1927, 1972.
Social aspects of Christianity. London, Cambridge and New York 1887, London and New York 1888, London 1910.
Essays in the history of religious thought in the West. London and New York 1891, London 1903, Freeport NY 1972.
See Life and letters, ed A. Westcott 2 vols 1903, 1 vol 1905 (abridged); *and* A. G. B. West, Memories of Brooke Foss Westcott, Cambridge 1936.

Richard Whately 1787–1863

Historic doubts relative to Napoleon Buonaparte. 1819 (anon), 1821, 1826, Oxford 1827, London 1831, Cambridge MA 1832, London 1833, 1841, Boston 1843, London 1846, Philadelphia 1846, London 1849 (9th edn) (rev and enlarged), 1852, 1853, New York 1853, Baltimore 1853, Boston 1853, London 1855, New York 1856, London 1859, New York 1860, London 1865, New York 1867, Andover MA 1870, New York 1871, Andover MA 1874, London 1881, 1886, 1887, New York [1895], Berkeley CA 1985; tr Ger 1836.
The use and abuse of party-feeling in matters of religion. Oxford 1822, London 1823, 1833, Dublin 1847, London 1859 (enlarged).
Letters on the Church, by an episcopalian. 1826, New York 1837.
The Kingdom of Christ delineated. 1841, 1842, 1842, New York 1842, 1843, Philadelphia 1843, London 1845, New York 1848, London 1851 (rev), New York 1853, 1854, 1859, 1864, London 1912.
See Life and correspondence, ed E. J. Whately 2 vols 1866, 1868, 1875 (enlarged). *See also col 2203, above.*

2. NONCONFORMIST WRITERS

General studies

Dale, R. W. The evangelical revival and other sermons. 1880.
Dale, R. W. The old evangelicalism and the new. 1889.
Sandall, R. The history of the Salvation Army. 3 vols 1947–55.
Orr, J. E. The second evangelical awakening in Britain. 1949, 1953.
Cowherd, R. G. The politics of English dissent: the religious aspects of liberal and humanitarian reform movement from 1815 to 1848. New York 1956, 1959.
Sykes, J. The Quakers: a new look at their place in society. 1958.
Escott, H. A history of Scottish Congregationalism. Glasgow 1960.
Routley, E. English religious dissent. Cambridge 1960.
Isichei, E. Victorian Quakers. Oxford 1970.
Everitt, A. The pattern of rural dissent, the nineteenth century. Leicester 1972.
Thompson, D. Nonconformity in the nineteenth century. 1972.
Bowmer, J. C. Pastor and people: a study of church and ministry in Wesleyan Methodism from the death of John Wesley to the death of Jabez Bunting. 1975.
Cunningham, V. 'Everywhere Spoken Against': dissent in the Victorian novel. Oxford 1975.
Ward, W. R. Early Victorian Methodism: the correspondence of Jabez Bunting. 1976.
Binfield, C. So down to prayers: studies in English nonconformity, 1780–1920. 1977.
Kent, J. Holding the fort: studies in Victorian revivalism. 1978.

Scotland, N. Methodism and the revolt of the field: a study of the Methodist contribution to agricultural trade unionism in East Anglia, 1872–96. Gloucester UK 1981.
Bebbington, D. W. The Nonconformist conscience: chapel and politics, 1870–1914. 1982.
Hempton, D. Methodism and politics in British society 1750–1850. 1984, 1987.
Werner, J. S. The primitive Methodist connexion: its background and early history. Madison WI 1984.
Bebbington, D. The Baptists in Scotland. Glasgow 1988.
Brown, K. D. A social history of the Nonconformist ministry in England and Wales, 1800–1930. Oxford 1988.
Lovegrove, D. Established church, sectarian people: itineracy and the transformation of English dissent, 1780–1830. Cambridge 1988.
Munson, J. The Nonconformists. 1991.
Watts, M. R. The expansion of evangelical nonconformity. Vol 2. The dissenters. Oxford 1995.

Biographies and memoirs

Gilbert, J. Memoir of the life and writings of the late Rev Edward Williams. 1825.
Bennett, J. Memoirs of the life of the Rev David Bogue. 1827.
Treffry, R. Memoirs of the Rev Joseph Benson. 1840, New York 1842, 1853, 1868.
Campbell, J. Memoir of David Nasmith. 1844.
Gadsby, J. Memoir of William Gadsby. Manchester 1844, 1847, London 1870, Salisbury MD 1990.
Allen, W. Life of William Allen with selections from his correspondence. 3 vols 1846–7.
Haldane, A. The lives of Robert Haldane of Airthrey, and of his brother, James Alexander Haldane. 1852, 1852 (rev and enlarged), 1853, New York 1853, 1854, London 1855, Edinburgh 1855, London 1856, New York 1857, 1858, Edinburgh 1871, 1889, Edinburgh and Carlisle PA 1990.
Redford, G. and James, J. A. The autobiography of . . . William Jay. 1854, 1855, New York 1855, 1856, Edinburgh and Carlisle PA 1874.
Pike, J. B. and J. C. A memoir and remains of Rev John Gregory Pike. 1855.
Alexander, W. L. Memoir of the life and writings of Ralph Wardlaw. Edinburgh 1856.
Bunting, T. P. The life of Jabez Bunting. 2 vols 1859–87.
Dale, R. W. The life and letters of John Angell James. 1861, 1861, 1862.
Oliphant, M. The life of Edward Irving. 2 vols 1862, New York 1862, London 1862 (rev and enlarged), 1864, 1865, 1869.
Thorne, J. Memoir of James Thorne. 1873.
Hood, E. P. Thomas Binney, his mind, life and opinions. 1874.
Chew, R. James Everett, a biography. 1875.
Hood, E. P. Christmas Evans. 1881, 1883, 1888, New York 1901.
Mursell, A. James Phillippo Mursell. 1886.
Watson, E. S. George Gilfillan, letters and journals. 1892.
Pierson, A. T. George Müller of Bristol. 1899, Westwood NJ 1899, New York 1899, London 1900, 1901, 1902, 1907, 1912, New York 1941, 1944, London 1972, Grand Rapids MI 1983; tr Swed 1909, Ger 1910.
Bennett, W. H. Robert Cleaver Chapman of Barnstaple. Glasgow 1902.
Hodder Williams, J. E. The life of Sir George Williams. 1906.
Wreford, H. Memoirs of the life and last days of William Kelly. 1906.
Stephenson, T. B. William Arthur. 1907.
Rees, E. E. Christmas Evans. 1936.
Wilkinson, J. T. William Clowes, 1780–1851. 1951.
Rupp, G. Thomas Jackson, Methodist patriarch. 1954.
Northcott, C. Robert Moffat, Pioneer in Africa. 1961.
Wilkinson, J. T. Samuel Drew 1765–1833. Redruth, Cornwall 1963.
Binfield, C. Sir George Williams and the YMCA. 1973.
Jones, R. T. John Elias. Bridgend 1974.
Holmes, R. F. G. Henry Cooke. Belfast 1981.

Principal writers

Joseph Angus 1816–1902

The voluntary system. 1839.
Christ our life. 1853, Philadelphia 1853.
Bible Hand-book. 1854, Philadelphia 1857, London 1860, Philadelphia 1865, 1866, London 1868, Philadelphia 1868, New York 1868 (rev F. S. Hoyt), New York and Cincinnati 1868 (2nd rev edn F. S. Hoyt), Philadelphia 1873, London 1874, Philadelphia 1883, New York, Chicago and Toronto 1890 (rev S. G. Green), London 1904 (rev S. G. Green), 1907, 1908, 2 edns '1952' [1953], Westwood NJ 1961; tr Fr 1857, Ital 1858, Welsh 1860, Sp 1985.
Christian churches. 1862, 1884, 1913.
Regeneration. 1897.

William Arthur 1819–1901

The tongue of fire. 1856, Nashville 1857, London 1859, New York 1863, 1865, Nashville 1869, New York 1870, London 1877, Nashville 1878, 1880, London 1885, 1886, Nashville 1888, Columbia SC 1891, New York 1893, London 1896, New York 1900, London 1901, 1902, Cincinnati 1903, London 1905, Cincinnati and New York 1905, 1907, Cincinnati 1908, Winona Lake IN 1912, London 1914, Nashville 1920 (rev), London 1949 (rev); tr Fr 1864, Du 1878, Kaffir 1907.

Thomas Binney 1798–1874

The ultimate objective of the evangelical dissenters. 1834.

John Brown 1784–1858

Expository discourses on 1 Peter. 3 vols 1848, 2 vols 1848, 2 vols Edinburgh 1849, 3 vols London 1866, 1 vol New York 1868, 2 vols Edinburgh 1975.
Discourses and sayings of Our Lord Jesus Christ. Edinburgh 1850 (3 vols), New York 1852, 1854 (2 vols), 1858, 1860, Edinburgh 1883, 1967, Winona Lake IN 1981, Edinburgh and Carlisle PA 1990 (rev and enlarged).
Commentary on Galatians. 1853, Edinburgh 1853, New York 1853, Evansville IN 1957, Grand Rapids MI 1963, Lafayette IN 1963, Marshallton DL 1970, Evansville IN 1978, Minneapolis 1979, 1981.
Parting counsels: an exposition of 2 Peter 1. Edinburgh 1856, Edinburgh and Carlisle PA 1980.
Commentary on Romans. Edinburgh and London 1857, New York 1857, Edinburgh 1869, 1883, Minneapolis 1979, Grand Rapids MI 1981.
Commentary on Hebrews. Edinburgh and London 1862, New York 1862, Evansville IN 1960, London 1961, 1964, 1973, Edinburgh and Carlisle PA 1976, London 1978.

Henry Bellenden Bulteel 1800–66

The doctrine of the miraculous interference of Jesus on behalf of believers. 1832, 1833 (rev).

Jabez Bunting 1779–1858

Sermons. 2 vols 1861–2, New York 1862–3, 1863, 1864.

John McLeod Campbell 1800–72

Christ the bread of life. Glasgow 1851, 1869.
The nature of the Atonement. Cambridge 1856, 1867 (with introd and notes), 1869, 1873, London 1878, London and New York 1886, 1895, 1915, Greenwood SC 1959, Edinburgh and Grand Rapids MI 1996.
Thoughts on Revelation. Cambridge 1862, 1874, Philadelphia 1874.
Reminiscences and reflections. Ed D. Campbell 1873.
Memorials. Ed D. Campbell 2 vols 1877.

Adam Clarke c. 1760–1832

The Holy Bible . . . With a commentary and critical notes. 8 vols 1810–25, 6 vols New York 1826–8, 1827, 1828, 1831–44, 1832, 1833, London 1836, New York 1837, Baltimore 1838, New York 1840, New York and Nashville 1842, New York 1843, 1845, London 1850, New York 1853, Cincinnati 1854, 6 vols New York 1854, 1856, 1857, Cincinnati 1857, 1860, New York 1873, 1881, Cincinnati 1882, New York 1883, 1911, Nashville 1976 (as Commentary on the Holy Bible); tr Sp 1980.
A short account of the introduction of the Gospel into the British Isles. 1815.
The love of God to a lost world. 1818, 1819, Philadelphia 1820, New York 1826, 1828, 1837.
Memoirs of the Wesley family. 1823, New York 1824, 1832, London 1836 (rev and enlarged), New York 1846 (rev and enlarged), 1848; ed G. Peck 1851, 1859, London 1860 (rev and considerably enlarged).
An account of the infancy, religious and literary life of Adam Clarke . . . partly written by himself and one of his daughters. 3 vols 1833, New York 1833 (2 edns), 1841.
The miscellaneous works of Adam Clarke. Ed J. Everett 13 vols 1836–7, 1843–4, 1868.
Christian missions. London and Glasgow 1837, 1844.

Thomas Coke 1747–1814

A commentary on the Holy Bible. 6 vols 1801–3, New York 1812; tr Sp 1980.
A history of the West Indies. 3 vols Liverpool 1808–11, 1971.
Extracts from the journals of the late Rev Thomas Coke. Dublin 1816.

Samuel Cox 1826–93

Salvator mundi. 1877, 1878, New York 1878, London 1879, 1880, 1884, 1888, 1890, 1904, 1908, 1979, Pittsburgh 1983.

Isaac Crewdson 1780–1844

Beacon to the Society of Friends. 1835 (2 edns).

Robert William Dale 1826–95

The atonement. 1875 (3 edns), 1876, 1877, 1880, 1881, 1884 (9th edn), 1887, 1888, 1889, 1891, 1892, 1894, 1895, 1896, 1897, 1900, 1902, 1904, 1905, 1909, 1914, 1924.
The living Christ and the four Gospels. 1890, 1890, Cincinnati 1890, New York 1890 (2 edns), London 1891, 1899, New York 1900, London 1901, 2 vols 1903 (14th edn), 1904, 1905, New York 1910, 1977; tr Jap 1892.
See A. W. W. Dale, Life of Dale, 1898.

John Nelson Darby 1800–82

The collected writings of J. N. Darby. Ed W. Kelly 34 vols 1867–1900, 1956–77, Winschoten, Netherlands 1971–2, Sunbury PA 1971.
Letters by J. N. D. 3 vols 1886–9, 1914–15, Oak Park IL 1971, Sunbury PA 1971, Winschoten, Netherlands 1971.

Samuel Davidson 1806–98

The text of the Old Testament considered. 1856, 1859 (rev).
Autobiography and diary, with an account of the Davidson controversy of 1857. Edinburgh 1899.

George Dawson 1821–76

The demands of the age upon the Church. 1847.
Biographical lectures. Ed G. St Clair 1886 (for 1885), 1887.

Samuel Drew 1765–1833

The life of the Rev Thomas Coke. 1817, New York 1818, 1837, 1847, 1853.
Editor of The Imperial Mag *from 1819*.

James Everett 1784–1872

Wesleyan takings. 2 vols 1820, 1834, 1840. With J. Beaumont.
Historical sketches of Wesleyan Methodism in Sheffield. 2 vols (only one pbd) Sheffield 1823.
Wesleyan Methodism in Manchester. Manchester 1827.
The village blacksmith. 1831, 1832, Toronto 1835, Baltimore 1836, London 1837, New York 1839, 1844, London 1845 (12th edn), Cincinnati 1853, New York 1853, 1856, London 1858, 1863, 1866, 1869, 1879 (18th edn), 1889, Nashville 1892.
Memoirs of the life, character, and ministry of William Dawson. 1842, Philadelphia 1843, 1844 (abridged edn).
Adam Clarke portrayed. 3 vols 1843–9, 2 vols 1866 (rev and enlarged).
Methodism as it is. 2 vols 1863–5.

Andrew Martin Fairbairn 1838–1912

The place of Christ in modern theology. 1893 (4 edns), New York 1893, London 1894 (2 edns), New York 1894, 1895, 1896, London 1897, New York 1897, 1899, 1900, London 1902, New York 1904, London 1905, 1907, New York 1911, London 1912, New York 1912, 1913, 1916.
See W. B. Selbie, Life of Fairbairn, 1914.

Peter Taylor Forsyth 1848–1927

The person and place of Jesus Christ. London and Boston 1909, 1911, Cincinnati and New York 1919, 1930, 1946, 1948, 1951, 1955, 1961, Grand Rapids MI 1964.
The principle of authority. [1912], New York 1912, 1952.
Religion in recent art. Manchester and London 1889, 1901, New York 1902, 1905, 1911.

John Foster 1770–1843

Essays in a series of letters to a friend. 2 vols 1805, 1806 (3rd edn), Hartford CT 1807, London 1808, Boston 1811, Oxford 1811, 1813, Hartford CT 1814, 1 vol Utica NY 1815, London 1819, 1823 (rev), Andover MA 1826, London 1826, 1830, Boston 1833, New York 1835, London 1838 (13th edn), Boston 1839, New York 1840, London 1844, New York 1847, London 1848, New York 1848, 1849, 1850, Hartford CT 1851, London 1851, New York 1853, 1854, London 1855, New York 1856, Nashville 1856, 1856, New York 1858, 1860, Nashville 1861, London 1861, 1863, New York 1864, London 1865, 1867, 1870, 1873, New York 1875, London 1876,

Nashville 1876, New York 1882, London and New York 1889, Nashville 1891, London and New York 1892, London 1894, Nashville 1896, London and New York 1908, 1912, London 1912.
Discourse. 1819, Trenton NJ 1822, Bristol 1833.
An essay on the evils of popular ignorance. 1820, 1821, Boston 1821, New York 1821, London 1834, Bristol 1839, London 1845 (rev and enlarged), 1847, 1850, New York 1850, London 1853, 1856, New York 1856, 1859, London 1863, 1865, New York 1866, London 1872, 1876, 1886, New York 1899.
Introductory essay to P. Doddridge's The rise and progress of religion in the soul. Glasgow 1825, [1839], 1873 (in Essays on a man's writing memoirs of himself).
The established church. 1834 (anon).
Critical essays contributed to the Eclectic Review. 2 vols 1844, New York and Philadelphia 1844, London 1856, 1858, 1860, 1868, 1875, 1877–9.
Fosteriana. Ed H. G. Bohn 1858, 1877.
An essay on the improvement of time and other literary remains. Ed J. E. Ryland 1863, New York 1874, 1876, London 1886.
See Life and correspondence, ed J. E. Ryland 2 vols 1846, New York 1846, London 1848, New York 1849, Boston 1850, 1851, London 1852, Boston and New York 1855, 1860, London 1861, 1866.
See also col 2143, above.

Elizabeth Fry 1780–1845

Memoir of Elizabeth Fry. Ed by her daughters 2 vols 1847, Philadelphia 1847, London 1848 (rev and enlarged), Philadelphia 1848, London 1853; tr Ger 1850, Fr 1852.

Alfred Ernest Garvie 1861–1945

The Ritschlian theology. Edinburgh 1899, 1902.

Philip Henry Gosse 1810–88

Omphalos: an attempt to untie the geological knot. 1857.

Joseph John Gurney 1788–1847

Notes of a visit made to some of the prisons in Scotland and the north of England in company with Elizabeth Fry. 1819 (2 edns), Edinburgh and London 1819, Norwich and London 1847.
Observations on the religious particularities of Friends. 1824 (4 edns), 1825, Philadelphia 1825, London 1826, Philadelphia 1832, Bradford 1834, London and Norwich 1834 (henceforth as Observations on the distinguishing views and practices of the Society of Friends), New York 1840, Norwich 1842, London 1848, New York 1854, 1856, London 1859, New York 1860, 1869, 1880, 1884, 1888, Richmond VA 1979 (as A peculiar people).
Essays on the evidence, doctrines, and practical operation of Christianity. 1825, 1826, Philadelphia 1829, London 1831, London and Norwich 1833, London 1840, Philadelphia 1856, 1884; tr Sp 1830.
Essay on the habitual exercise of love to God. 1834, 1835, 1835, Philadelphia 1835, New York 1839, Philadelphia 1840, 1844, 1848, Norwich 1856; tr Fr 1839, Ger 1843.
Familiar letters to Henry Clay. 1840 (as A winter in the West Indies) (2 edns), New York 1840, London 1841 (2 edns), New York 1969.

James Alexander Haldane 1768–1851

Journal of a tour through the northern counties of Scotland and the Orkney Isles. Edinburgh 1798 (3 edns).

Robert Haldane 1764–1843

The evidence and authority of divine revelation. 2 vols Edinburgh 1816, London and Edinburgh 1834 (rev and enlarged), 1839, Edinburgh 1843.
Commentary on the book of Romans. Edinburgh 1835, London 1839, Edinburgh 1842 (enlarged), New York 1847, 1849, Edinburgh 1852, New York 1853, 1855, 1858, London 1858, New York 1860, 1864, 1870, Edinburgh 1874, Evansville IN 1955, 1957, London 1958, Evansville IN 1958, McLean VA 1958, London 1966, Marshallton DL 1970, Grand Rapids MI 1988.
Works, with a memoir by Olinthus Gregory and observations on his character. Ed O. Gregory 6 vols 1832 (for 1831–2), 3 vols New York 1832–3 (with memoir by J. Mackintosh and a sketch of his character by J. Foster), 6 vols London (1836–41), New York 1838, London 1839, New York 1844, London 1845, 1846, 4 vols New York 1849, London 1850, 1851, 1853, 1854, 1855, New York 1858–60, London 1858, 1860, 1861, 6 vols 1866, 1868, 1870, 1875, 1878, 1889.

John Howard Hinton 1791–1873

Works. 7 vols 1864–5.

Thomas Jackson 1783–1873

A fourth letter to the Rev John Cockin. Leeds 1815.
Misrepresentations exposed. Leeds 1815.
The life of John Goodwin. 1822, 1872.
The works of the Rev J. Wesley. Ed Jackson 14 vols 1829–31, 7 vols New York 1831, 13 vols London 1846–7, 15 vols 1856, 15 vols 1865–6, 1872, 1873, 14 vols 1881, Salem OH 1978.
The church and the Methodists. 1834 (3 edns).
Expository discourses. 1839.
The centenary of Wesleyan Methodism. 1839, New York 1839, 1840.
The life of the Rev Charles Wesley. 2 vols 1841, 1842, New York 1842, 1844.
An answer to the question, 'Why are you a Wesleyan Methodist?' 1842 (5 edns) (anon), New York 1842, London 1850, 1860, New York and Cincinnati 1872.
The life of the Rev Robert Newton. 1854, 1855, New York 1855, Nashville 1855, London 1856, 1857, Nashville 1860.
The duties of Christianity. 1857, 1867.
The providence of God. 1862, 1866 (rev).
The institutions of Christianity. 1868.

John Angell James 1785–1859

The anxious enquirer after salvation directed and encouraged. London and Birmingham 1834 (2nd edn), New York 1834, London 1835 (5th edn), New York 1840, London [1850?], [1880], [1884], 1886, 1889; tr Welsh 1847, Malagasy 1853.
Works. 1860–4.
Autobiography. 1864.

William Jay 1769–1853

Works. Collected and rev by author. Baltimore 1833, 1835, 12 vols Bath 1842–8, 3 vols New York 1844, 1847, 1849, 1852, 1861.

Andrew John Jukes 1810–1901

The second death and the restitution of all things by M. A. [A. J. Jukes]. 1867, 1869, 1873, 1875, 1876, 1877, 1878, 1881, New York 1883, London 1885, New York 1886, London 1887, 1891, New York 1891, London 1897, Canyon Country CA 1976.

William Kelly 1821–1906

Lectures on the church of God. 1861, 1865, 1869 (rev), 1876 (rev), 1885, Denver 1900, London 1902 (rev) (8th edn), 1904 (rev) (9th edn), 1906 (10th edn), Sunbury PA 1918, London 1918 (rev), Orange CA 1959.
Lectures on the second coming. 1865, 1876, 1879, 1903, Sunbury PA 1970, Oak Park IL 1970.
Christ tempted and sympathising. 1871, 1906, Sunbury PA 1975, Charlotte NC 1975.

John Scott Lidgett 1854–1953

The spiritual principle of the atonement. 1897, 1898 (2nd edn), 1907 (4th edn), Cincinnati 1907, Minneapolis 1983.
The fatherhood of God. Edinburgh 1902, 1913, Minneapolis 1987.

Robert Mackintosh 1858–1933

Essays towards a new theology. Glasgow and Edinburgh 1889.

Alexander Maclaren 1826–1910

Sermons. [1869]–1908.

George Mueller 1805–97

A narrative of some of the Lord's dealings with George Mueller, written by himself. 4 vols 1837–86.

Baptist Wriothesley Noel 1798–1873

Essay on the union of Church and State. 1848, 1849 (corrected), 1849 (corrected), New York 1849, London 1867 (abridged).

John Deodatus Gregory Pike 1784–1854

Persuasives to early piety. Derby 1819, 1821, Limerick ME 1828, Derby 1829, 1830, New York 1830, Derby 1833, Derby and London 1834, [1835?], Derby 1837, New York 1839, London 1839 (abridged), New York 1843, Halifax UK 1860, London [1862], [1865], 1865, Morgan PA 1996.
Joint editor of The General Baptist Repository and Missionary Observer *from 1822–34.*

Henry Rogers 1806–77

Essays from the Edinburgh Review. 3 vols 1850–5, 1855, 1860, 2 vols 1874.
The eclipse of faith. 1852 (anon), 1852, Boston 1852, London 1853 (rev), Boston 1853, London 1854 (5th edn), Boston 1854, London 1855 (6th edn), 1855 (7th edn), Boston 1855, 1856, 1860, London 1861 (10th edn), 1877 (15th edn), Boston 1885, London 1885 (17th edn).

Frederic Seebohm 1833–1912

The spirit of Christianity. 1876 (priv ptd); ed H. E. Seebohm 1916.

John Pye Smith 1774–1851

Scripture testimony to the Messiah. 2 vols 1818–21, 3 vols 1829 (enlarged), 3 vols 1837 (enlarged), 2 vols 1847, 2 vols Edinburgh 1859, 2 vols 1872.
On the relation between the Holy Scriptures and some parts of geological science. 1834, 1839, 1840 (enlarged), New York 1840, London 1843, 1848, Philadelphia 1850, London 1852, 1852 (with a sketch of the author by J. H. Davies), London 1854, 1855.

Charles Haddon Spurgeon 1834–92

The treasury of David. 7 vols 1870–85, 7 vols Toronto and New York 1882–6, 7 vols London 1888, 7 vols 1890–5, 7 vols New York 1892, 7 vols Toronto and New York 1892, 7 vols London 1896–1900, 7 vols 1907, 7 vols 1908, 6 vols New York 1913, 2 vols Grand Rapids MI 1940, 6 vols 1950, 3 vols London 1963, 3 vols Grand Rapids MI 1966, 2 vols Bryon Center MI 1970, 2 vols Grand Rapids MI 1975, 7 vols 1976, 1 vol 1976 (condensed), 7 vols Welwyn 1977, 7 vols Grand Rapids MI 1978, 2 vols Lynchburg VA 1980, 7 vols Grand Rapids MI 1983, 7 vols Pasadena 1983, 2 vols Grand Rapids MI 1984, 2 vols Nashville 1984, 2 vols Lynchburg VA 1988, 3 vols Peabody MA 1990; tr Ger 1893, Swed 1898.

Isaac Taylor 1787–1865

The natural history of enthusiasm. 1829 (anon), 1830 (anon) (4th edn), Boston 1830 (anon), New York and Boston 1830 (anon), London 1831 (anon), New York 1831 (anon), London 1832 (anon), 1834 (anon), New York 1834, London 1842 (rev) (8th edn), New York 1843, London 1844, 1845, New York 1849, 1850, 1853, 1855, 1856, 1859, London 1867, 1868, New York 1868.
The physical theory of another life. 1836, New York 1836, London 1839, New York 1839, London 1847, New York 1852, 1853, London 1857, 1858, 1866, 1871.
The restoration of belief. [1852] (anon), 1853 (anon), Philadelphia 1853 (anon), Cambridge 1855 (anon), Philadelphia 1855 (anon), 1856 (anon), London 1864 (rev and enlarged), Boston 1867.
The spirit of Hebrew poetry. London and New York 1861, New York 1862, Philadelphia 1873, New York 1974.
See col 477, above.

Robert Vaughan 1795–1868

The age of great cities. 1843, 1843, 1969, Shannon 1972, New York 1985.
Founder and editor of and contributor to Br Quart Rev, *1845–65.*

Robert Alfred Vaughan 1823–57

Hours with the mystics. 2 vols 1856; ed R. Vaughan 2 vols 1860; 1 vol 1865, 2 vols 1879; ed W. Vaughan 2 vols [1880]; 2 vols 1888, 2 vols 1889, 1 vol 1891, 1 vol New York 1893, 1 vol London 1895, 1 vol 1900, 1 vol 1910, 1 vol 1917.
See col 2305, above.

Edward Williams 1750–1813

An essay on the equity of divine government and the sovereignty of divine grace. London and Shrewsbury 1809, London 1813, 1825.

Caroline Wilson, née Fry 1787–1846

The listener. 2 vols 1830, Philadelphia 1832, London 1833, Philadelphia 1833, London 1834, Philadelphia 1836, London 1839, 1842, Philadelphia 1844, 1849, New York 1852, London 1867, 1 vol 1856; tr Fr 1844.
Letters on the development of Christian doctrine, in reply to Mr Newman's Essay [i.e. An essay on the development of Christian doctrine]. Ed T. Woodward, Dublin 1850.

3. ROMAN CATHOLIC WRITERS

General studies

Knox, W. L. and A. R. Vidler. The development of modern Catholicism. 1933.
Norman, E. R. Anti-Catholicism in Victorian England. 1968.

McClelland, V. A. English Roman Catholics and higher education, 1830–1903. Oxford 1973.
Larkin, E. The Roman Catholic church and the creation of the modern Irish state, 1878–1886. Dublin 1975.
Chinnici, J. P. The English Catholic enlightenment: John Lingard and the Cisalpine movement, 1780–1850. Shepherdstown WV 1980.
Schoenl, W. J. The intellectual crisis in English Catholicism: liberal Catholics, modernists, and the Vatican in the late nineteenth and early twentieth centuries. 1982.
Chadwick, O. Newman. Oxford 1983.
Kerr, D. A. Peel, priests, and politics. Sir Robert Peel's administration and the Roman Catholic Church in Ireland, 1841–1846. Oxford 1983.
Earnest, J. D. and G. Tracey (ed). John Henry Newman. An annotated bibliography of his tract and pamphlet collection. 1984.
Norman, E. R. The English Catholic Church in the nineteenth century. Oxford 1984.
Schiefen, R. J. Nicholas Wiseman and the transformation of English Catholicism. Shepherdstown WV 1984.
Paz, D. G. Popular anti-Catholicism in mid-Victorian England. Stanford CA 1992.

Biographies and memoirs

Leslie, S. Henry Edward Manning. 1921.
Schultenover, D. G. George Tyrrell: in search of Catholicism. Shepherdstown WV 1981.
Ker, I. John Henry Newman. A biography. Oxford 1989.
Gilley, S. Newman and his age. 1990.
Sagovsky, N. 'On God's Side': a life of George Tyrrell. Oxford 1990.

Principal writers

Edward Caswall 1814–78

Lyra catholica: containing all the breviary and missal hymns, with others from various sources. Tr Caswall 1849, 1851, 1884, [1850?] (selected as A Catholic hymn-book for schools and private use).
See col 594, above.

John Dobrée Bernard Dalgairns 1818–76

Life of St Stephen Harding. 1844 (anon), 1900 (as vol 1 of The lives of the English saints); tr Fr 1848.
Life of St Gilbert. 1844 (anon), 1901 (as vol 4 of The lives of the English saints).
Life of St Aelred. 1845 (anon), 1901 (as vol 5 of The lives of the English saints).
Life of St Richard. 1845 (anon), 1901 (as vol 6 of The lives of the English saints).
Lives of St Waltheof and St Robert of Newminster. 1845 (anon), 1901 (as vol 5 of The lives of the English saints).
The devotion to the heart of Jesus. 1853, 1854, Philadelphia 1854 (rev), Baltimore 1855, 1857, 1867, 1870, 1875, London 1896, 1910; ed A. Ross [1910]; 1979.
The Holy Communion: its philosophy, theology and practice. London and Dublin 1861, Dublin 1861, 1865, 1868, New York 1868, Dublin 1897, 1908; ed A. Ross 2 vols 1911, Louisville KY 1980.

Frederick William Faber 1814–63

See col 610, above.

Henry Edward Manning 1808–92

Sermons. 4 vols 1842–50, 1 vol 1844, 3 vols New York 1856.
The unity of the Church. 1842, New York 1843, 1844, London 1845.
Sermons preached before the University of Oxford. Oxford and London 1844, 1845.
Sermons on ecclesiastical subjects. 3 vols 1863–73, 2 vols New York and San Francisco 1899.
The temporal mission of the Holy Ghost. 1865, 1866, New York 1866, London 1877, New York 1884, 1885, 1887, 1890, London 1892, New York 1896, London and New York 1899, New York 1901, 1905, London and New York 1909.
Miscellanies. 3 vols 1877–88, 1909.
See A. W. Hutton, Cardinal Manning, 1892; R. C. Jenkes, A few recollections of Cardinal Manning, [1892?] (priv ptd); E. S. Purcell, Life of Cardinal Manning, 2 vols 1895, 1896, 1896, 1896; S. Leslie, Manning: his life and labours, 1921.

Frederick Oakeley 1802–80

Sermons preached chiefly in the Chapel Royal at Whitehall. Oxford 1839.
Life of St Augustine of Canterbury. 1844 (anon), 1901 (in vol 3 of Lives of the English saints).
The order and ceremonial of the Mass. 1848, New York 1849, London 1859 (rev and corrected), New York 1859 (rev and corrected), London [1910?].
Historical notes on the Tractarian movement. 1865.
Also some 38 pbd works, including articles in Br Critic, Dublin Rev *and* The Month.

John Hungerford Pollen the elder 1820–1902

Letter to the parishioners of St Saviour's Leeds. Oxford 1851.
Narrative of five years at St Saviour's Leeds. Oxford 1851.
See A. Pollen, John Hungerford Pollen, 1912, *who lists Pollen's writings, pp. 377–8.*

William Sewell 1804–74

Sermons addressed to young men, preached chiefly in the chapel of Exeter College, Oxford. 1835.
Christian morals. 1840.
Popular evidences of Christianity. (Pt 1) 1843, 1845 (as Dialogues on the evidences of Christianity between a Brahmin and a Christian). No more pts pbd.
Christian politics. 1844.
The plea of conscience for seceding from the Catholic church to the Romish schism in England: a sermon to which is prefixed an essay on the process of conscience. Oxford 1845, 1845, 1845, 1846.
Journal of a residence at the college of St Columba in Ireland. Oxford 1847.
A year's sermons to boys, preached in the chapel of St Peter's College, Radley. 2 vols Oxford 1854–9. Vol 2 entitled Sermons to boys...
Christian vestiges of creation. Oxford 1861.
The microscope of the New Testament. Ed W. J. Chrichton 1878.
See also col 1400, above.

George Tyrrell 1861–1909

Nova et vetera: informal meditations. 1897, 1900 (3rd edn), London and New York 1902 (4th edn), London 1907; tr Ital 1912.
Hard sayings. London and New York 1898, 1899, 1900, London 1903, London and New York 1904, 1910; tr Fr 1907.
External religion: its uses and abuses. London and St Louis 1899, London 1900, St Louis 1900, 1901, London 1903, St Louis 1903, London, New York and Bombay 1906, London 1909, London and New York 1914.
The faith of the millions: essays. 2 ser London and New York 1901, 1902, 1904.

Oil and wine. 1902 (priv ptd), 1906, London and New York 1907 (with new preface).
Lex orandi: or prayer and creed. 1903, London, New York and Bombay 1904, London and New York 1907.
The Church and the future. 1903 (priv ptd), 1910.
A much-abused letter. London and New York 1906; tr Fr 1908.
Lex credendi: a sequel to Lex orandi. London, New York and Bombay 1906, London and New York 1907.
Through Scylla and Charybdis. London and New York 1907.
Medievalism: a reply to Cardinal Mercier. London and New York 1908, 1909 (with addns) (3rd edn), Tunbridge Wells 1994.
Christianity at the cross-roads. London and New York 1909, 1910, 1910, 1913, London 1963.
Versions and perversions of Heine and others. 1909.
Autobiography and life, arranged by M. D. Petre. 2 vols London and New York 1912.
Essays on faith and immortality, arranged by M. D. Petre. 1914, London and New York 1914.
Letters from a 'Modernist': the letters of George Tyrrell to Wilfrid Ward, 1893–1908. Ed M. J. Weaver 1981.

William George Ward 1812–82

The ideal of a Christian church considered in comparison with existing practice. 1844, 1844, 1844 (selections), Farnborough 1969, New York 1977.
See W. Ward, Ward and the Oxford movement, 1889, *and* Ward and the Catholic Revival, 1893, 1912.
Ward edited Dublin Rev, 1863–78.

Henry William Wilberforce 1807–73

Reasons for submitting to the Catholic church: a farewell letter. 1851, London and Derby 1855 (6th edn).
The Church and the empires. 1874. With memoir by J. H. Newman.
Owned and edited Catholic Standard *(later* Weekly Register*), 1854–63.*

Robert Isaac Wilberforce 1802–97

Lyra apostolica. Derby 1836, 1838, 1864 (13th edn). Poem signed ϵ.
The doctrine of the Incarnation of Our Lord Jesus Christ. London and Derby 1848, London 1849, Philadelphia 1849, London 1850, London and Derby 1852 (5th edn), London 1875, 1879, 1885, 1892, 1895.
The doctrine of Holy Baptism. Derby 1849, 1849, 1850, 1850.
The doctrine of the Holy Eucharist. Derby 1853, London and Oxford 1853, London 1854, Philadelphia 1853, London 1885, New York 1885.
An inquiry into the principles of Church-authority. London and Derby 1854, 1854, Baltimore 1855.

Nicholas Patrick Stephen Wiseman 1802–65

Lectures on the doctrines and practices of the Roman Catholic church. 1836 (ptd without the author's sanction), 2 vols 1836 (authorised edn as Lectures on the principal doctrines and practices etc), 2 vols New York 1836, Philadelphia 1837, 2 vols New York 1843, 2 vols London 1844 (rev and corrected), Baltimore 1846, 2 vols London 1847, 1851, 2 vols Baltimore 1851, 2 vols 1854, 2 vols London 1855, 2 vols Baltimore 1857, 1859, 2 vols New York 1862, 2 vols Baltimore 1862, 2 vols 1865, Dublin 1867, London 1888; tr Ger 2 vols 1838, Sp 2 vols 1851, Fr 2 vols 1854.
High Church claims: or a series of papers on the Oxford controversy. 1838, 1839, 1841, 1939.
Essays on various subjects. 3 vols 1853, 6 vols New York 1853, 1873, 1876; ed J. Murphy, London 1888; tr Ger 1854.
Fabiola: or the church of the catacombs. 1854 (anon), New York 1854, Philadelphia 1854, London 1855, [1855], New York 1855, 1856, 1861, New York and Montreal 1874, New York 1880, New York and Cincinnati 1885, New York 1886, 1889, [1896], New York and Cincinnati 1896, London 1897, 1898, [1904], [1906], New York 1913, 1920, 1928, London and New York 1929; ed J. R. and A. C. Hagan, London and New York 1932 (school edn); London 1936, New York 1951, Derby 1956, London 1962, New York 1976, Chicago 1978, Boston 1981; tr Ger 1854, Fr [1858], 1935, Ital 1864, Sp 1870, Hungarian 1888, Swed 1898, Esperanto 1911, Czech 1917, Du 1928, Ukrainian 1942, Sotho 1972, Polish 1974, Rus 1991.
Recollections of the last four Popes and of Rome in their times. 1858, New York 1858, Boston 1858, London 1859 (rev), New York 1875, London 1899 (rev), New York 1918, 1928, London 1936 (abridged); tr Ger 1858, Fr 1858.
See W. Ward, The life and times of Cardinal Wiseman, 2 vols 1897.

4. JEWISH WRITERS

General studies

Gartner, L. P. The Jewish immigrant in England, 1870–1914. 1960.
Gilam, A. The emancipation of the Jews in England, 1830–1860. New York 1982.
Cesarani, D. The making of modern Anglo-Jewry. Oxford 1990.
Endelman, T. M. Radical assimilation in English Jewish history, 1656–1945. Bloomington IN 1990.
Kershen, A. J. and J. A. Romain. Tradition and change: a history of reform Judaism in Britain, 1840–1995. 1995.

Biographies and memoirs

Montefiore, Sir M. Diaries of Sir Moses and Lady Montefiore. 1890, 1983.
Collard, G. Moses, the Victorian Jew. Oxford 1990. Study of Moses Montefiore.

Principal writers

Israel Abrahams 1858–1925

Aspects of Judaism. 1895, London and New York 1895. With C. G. Montefiore.
Studies in Pharisaism and the Gospels. 2 ser Cambridge 1917, 1924, New York 1967, Cambridge 1977.
See H. M. J. Loewe, Israel Abrahams: a biographical sketch, Royston 1944.
Co-editor with C. G. Montefiore of the Jewish Quart Rev, *from 1889–1907.*

Claude Joseph Goldsmid Montefiore 1858–1938

Lectures on the origin and growth of religion, as illustrated by the religion of the ancient Hebrews. London and Edinburgh 1892, London 1893, London and Edinburgh 1897, New York 1972.
Liberal Judaism. London and New York 1903, London 1918.
The Synoptic Gospels. Ed Montefiore 2 vols 1909, 1927 (rev and partly rewritten), New York 1968 (rpt of 1927 edn). A 3rd vol of additional notes by I. Abrahams was never pbd.
Rabbinic literature and Gospel teachings. 1930, New York 1970.
See M. G. Bowler, Claude Montefiore and Christianity, Atlanta 1988; *and* C. G. Montefiore, An English Jew: the life and writings of Claude Montefiore, 1989.

5. UNITARIANS AND 'FREE THINKERS'

General studies

Lecky, W. E. H. History of the rise and influence of the spirit of rationalism in Europe. 2 vols 1865, 1865, 1869, 1910; tr Ger 1874; Du 1894.

Robertson, J. M. A short history of freethought, ancient and modern. 1899, 2 vols 1906 (rewritten and greatly enlarged), 1915 (rev and expanded), 1936 (as A History of freethought).
Benn, A. W. The history of English rationalism in the nineteenth century. 2 vols 1900, 2 vols London and New York 1906, 2 vols New York 1962.
Stewart, H. L. Modernism, past and present. 1932.
Cockshut, A. O. J. The unbelievers: English agnostic thought 1840–1890. 1964, New York 1966.
Royle, E. Radical politics, 1790–1900; religion and unbelief. 1971.
Royle, E. Victorian infidels: the origins of the British secularist movement, 1791–1866. Manchester 1980.
Watts, M. R. The dissenters. Vol 2, The expansion of evangelical nonconformity. Oxford 1995.

Biographies and memoirs

Taylor, J. J. A retrospect of the religious life of England. 1845, 1876. With an introductory ch on recent developments by J. Martineau and a preface by H. E. Osler.
H. Martineau, Autobiography, 3 vols 1877, 1983.
Stephen, Sir L. George Eliot. 1902, New York 1902, London 1907, New York 1913, 1919, London 1924, 1926, 1940, New York 1972.
Duncan, D. The life and letters of Herbert Spencer. 1908, 1996.
Lafourcade, G. Swinburne, a literary biography. New York 1932.
Pichanick, V. K. Harriet Martineau, the woman and her work, 1802–76. Ann Arbor MI 1970.
Annan, N. Leslie Stephen the Godless Victorian. 1984.
Ashton, R. G. H. Lewes: a life. Oxford 1991.

Principal writings

Essays and reviews [by F. Temple, Rowland Williams, Baden Powell, H. B. Wilson, C. W. Goodwin, Mark Pattison, B. Jowett]. 1860, 1861 (3 edns), 1862, 1862, 1865; ed F. H. Hedge, New York 1874. *See also* J. L. Altholz, The anatomy of a controversy. Aldershot 1994.

Principal writers

Robert Aspland 1782–1845

Causes of the slow progress of Christian truth. [1825.]
Memoir of the life, works and correspondence of Robert Aspland. Ed R. B. Ashand 1850.

Charles Beard 1827–88

Port Royal. 2 vols 1861, 1873.
The Reformation of the sixteenth century in its relation to modern thought and knowledge. 1883 (2 edns), London and Edinburgh 1883, London 1885, London and Edinburgh 1897, London 1903; ed H. Gow, London 1906, 1907, 1927, Ann Arbor MI 1962, 1975, Westport CT 1980, New York 1981; tr Ger 1884.
Editor of Theological Rev, *1864–79.*

Thomas Belsham 1750–1829

A summary view of the evidence and practical importance of the Christian revelation. 1807.

Jeremy Bentham 1748–1832

Not Paul, but Jesus. 1823 (anon), Camden NJ 1917.
Church of Englandism and its Catechism examined. 1818.
See vol 3.

Charles Bray 1811–84

The philosophy of necessity. 2 vols 1841, 1863 (rev), 1889 (rev and abridged).
Christianity viewed in the light of our present knowledge. [1876].
Phases of opinion and experience during a long life. [1884].

Joseph Estlin Carpenter 1844–1928

The first three Gospels. 1890, 1904, 1906, 1909; tr Du [1892].
Studies in theology. 1903. With P. H. Wicksteed.
The Bible in the nineteenth century. London and Bombay 1903, 1903.

Walter Richard Cassels 1826–1907

Supernatural religion. 3 vols 1874–7 (anon), 1874–7, 2 vols 1874, 1874, 1875 (rev), 3 vols 1879, 1902, 1905.

James Drummond 1835–1918

The Jewish Messiah. 1877.
Philo Judaeus. 1888, Amsterdam 1888.
Via, veritas, vita. 1894, 1895.
The character and authorship of the Fourth Gospel. 1903, New York 1904.
Studies in Christian doctrine. 1908 (2 edns).

George Eliot (Mary Ann Evans) 1819–80

The life of Jesus critically examined, by D. F. Strauss. 3 vols 1846, 1 vol London and New York 1892. Anon trn.
The essence of Christianity, by Ludwig Feuerbach, translated by Marian Evans. 1854.
See G. S. Haight, George Eliot, 1968, New York 1985.
See also col 1282, above.

William Johnson Fox 1786–1864

Christ and Christianity. 2 vols 1831, Boston 1833.
On the religious ideas. 1849, 1907, 1975; tr Fr 1877.

William Rathbone Greg 1809–81

The creed of Christendom. 1851, New York 1855, London 1863, 1874 (for 1873) (with new introd), 1875, 2 vols Boston 1877, New York 1878, Toronto 1878, London 1879, Boston 1879, London 1880, 2 vols 1883 (with new introd), Chicago 1888, London 1892; ed W. R. W. Sullivan 1905, 1957.
Enigmas of life. 1872, 1873, Boston 1873, London 1874 (with postscript) (8th edn), Boston 1874, 1876, New York 1876, London 1877 (15th edn), New York 1880, London 1883, 1884, 1886, 1889, 1891 (with prefatory memoir) (18th edn), 1892, 1905.
See also col 2481.

Charles Christian Hennell 1809–50

An inquiry concerning the origin of Christianity. 1838, 1841, 1870 (enlarged); tr Ger 1840.

James Hinton 1822–75

The mystery of pain. 1866 (anon), 1870, New York 1872, London 1874 (rev), 1879 (rev), 1885, Boston 1886, 1887; ed J. R. Nichols 1890, New York 1892, London 1895, New York 1899, London 1899, 1903, 1905, [1909]; ed R. H. Hutton [1911], New York 1914.

Lawrence Pearsall Jacks 1860–1955

Authority in religious belief. 1893 (in Religion and modern thought and other essays [by various authors]); [1894] (pbd separately in

the Theological essays ser, vol 1 no 9); 1907 (in Authority in religious belief and other essays by L. P. Jacks et al). Previously separately pbd as Unitarian tracts.
The Hibbert journal. 1902– . Ed Jacks.
Writings. 6 vols 1916–17.
From authority to freedom. 1920.

James Martineau 1805–1900

The rationale of religious inquiry. 1836, 1844, 1845, 1853, [1908] (as What is Christianity?).
Endeavours after the Christian life. 2 ser 1843–7, Boston 1848, 1858, 1863, 1 vol London 1867 (4th edn), 1874 (5th edn), 1885 (8th edn), 1892 (9th edn), 1900, 1906, [1907]; ed J. E. Carpenter [1907], 1907, [1907].
Types of ethical theory. 2 vols Oxford 1885, Oxford and New York 1886 (rev), 1889, 1891 (enlarged), Oxford 1901 (rev).
A study of religion. 2 vols Oxford and New York 1888, Oxford 1889 (rev), 1900.
Essays, reviews and addresses. 4 vols 1890–1, 1901, New York 1901.
The seat of authority in religion. London and New York 1890, London 1890 (rev), 1891 (rev) (3rd edn), 1898 (4th edn), 1905 (5th edn).
See J. Drummond and C. B. Upton, Life and letters of James Martineau, 2 vols 1902; J. Estlin Carpenter, Martineau: theologian and teacher, 1905; *and* A. W. Jackson, James Martineau, 1900, Boston 1900, 1901.
See also col 2555, above.

John Stuart Mill 1806–73

Nature, the utility of religion and theism [3 essays on religion, with introductory notice by H. Taylor]. 1874, 1874 (2nd edn), 1874 (4th edn), New York 1884, London 1885, Girard KS 1900, London 1904, 1914, 1923, New York 1926, Eugene OR 1950, New York 1958, Indianapolis 1958, 1969.
See col 2558, above.

Francis William Newman 1805–97

The soul: her sorrows and her aspirations. 1849, 1852 (3rd edn), 1858 (6th edn), 1862 (7th edn), 1868, 1877, 1882, 1905 (with memoir by C. B. Upton).
Phases of faith. 1850, 1853, 1858 (5th edn), 1860 (6th edn), 1865, 1870, 1891 (rev), 1907, Leicester and New York 1970 (in Victorian Lib ser).
Memoir and letters. Ed I. G. Sieveking 1909.
See col 645, above.

Andrew Seth 1856–1931, from 1898 as A. S. Pringle-Pattison

Man's place in the cosmos. Edinburgh and London 1897, Edinburgh and New York 1902 (rev and enlarged).
The idea of God in the light of recent philosophy. Aberdeen, Oxford and New York 1917, London and New York 1920 (rev), New York 1971.
The idea of immortality. Oxford 1922, New York 1971.
See col 2585, above.

James Elimalet (Elishama) Smith 1801–57

Editor of The Shepherd, *1834*.
See W. A. Smith, 'Shepherd' Smith the Universalist, 1892.

John Hamilton Thom 1808–94

Laws of life after the mind of Christ. 2 ser 1883–6, 1901 (2nd ser only).
A spiritual faith, with memoir by J. Martineau. 1898, 1908 (abridged).

James Ward 1843–1925

Naturalism and agnosticism. 2 vols 1899, London and New York 1899, 2 vols London 1903, 2 vols London and New York 1906, 1 vol London 1915, 1 vol New York 1971.
The realm of ends: or pluralism and theism. Cambridge 1911, New York 1911, Cambridge 1912, New York 1912, Cambridge 1920.
See col 2615, above. [DML]

11
English Studies

Scholars are listed in alphabetical order. Cross-references have not been included to the general section on Prose or to the section on History, above, though both include many writers who in the 19th century contributed incidentally to the study of English literature, notably W. D. Adams, W. Barnes, S. A. Brooke, J. C. Collins, E. Dowden, W. Elwin, G. Gilfillan, Edmund Gosse, W. P. Ker, C. Kingsley, D. Masson, W. A. Raleigh, G. Saintsbury and Thomas Wright.

History and development of English Studies

Aarslef, H. From Locke to Saussure: essays on the study of language and intellectual history. 1982.

Aarslef, H. The study of language in England 1780–1860. 1983.

Arthur, S. A. Teaching the 'Secular Scriptures': an institutional history of English studies 1860–1910. Unpbd diss, Univ of Ohio 1992.

Bacon, A. English literature becomes an academic subject: King's College, London as pioneer. VS 29 1986.

Baldick, C. The social mission of English criticism 1848–1932. Oxford 1983.

Baron, D. Grammar and good taste. 1982.

Benzie, W. Dr F. J. Furnivall: Victorian scholar adventurer. Norman OK 1983.

Burchfield, R. Unlocking the English language. 1989.

Burrow, J. The uses of philology in Victorian Britain. In Ideas and institutions of Victorian Britain, ed R. Robson, 1967.

Cantor, N. F. Inventing the Middle Ages. Cambridge 1991.

Court, F. E. The social and historical significance of the first English literature professorship in England. PMLA 103 1988.

Court, F. E. Institutionalising English literature: the culture and politics of literary study. Stanford CA 1992.

Crowley, T. The politics of discourse, the standard language question in British cultural debates. 1989.

Crowley, T. Proper English? Readings in language, history and cultural identity. 1991.

Dixon, J. A schooling in 'English': critical episodes in the struggle to shape literary and cultural studies. Milton Keynes 1991.

Doyle, B. The invention of English. In Englishness. Ed R. Colls and P. Dodd 1989.

Eagleton, T. The function of criticism. 1984.

Faulkner, P. The paths of virtue and early English. In From medieval to medievalism, ed J. Simons, 1992.

Frantzen, A. J. Desire for origins: new language, Old English, and teaching the tradition. New Brunswick NJ 1990.

Ganzel, D. Fortune and men's eyes, the career of John Payne Collier. Oxford 1982.

Goodson, I. and P. Medway. Bringing English to order: the history and politics of English as school subject. 1990.

Graff, G. Professing literature: an institutional history. 1991.

Harris, R. English studies at Toronto. Toronto 1988.

Jasen, P. Arnoldian humanism and the Canadian university. Queen's Quart 95 1988.

Kearney, A. The first crisis in English studies. Br Jnl of Educational Stud 36 1988.

Kearney, A. Literary journalism and the English debate in the 1880s. Durham Univ Jnl 54 1993.

Kijinski, J. L. Securing literary values in an age of crisis: the early argument for English studies. ELT 31 1988.

Kijinski, J. L. John Morley's English Men of Letters series and the politics of reading. VS 34 1991.

Korsten, F. J. M. The English Men of Letters series, a monument of late-Victorian criticism. ES 73 1992.

McMurtry, J. English language, English literature: the creation of an academic discipline. 1985.

Matthews, D. 'Quaint Inglis': Walter Scott and the rise of Middle English studies. In Medievalism in England, second series, ed L. J. Workman and K. Verduin, Cambridge 1996.

Michael, I. The historical study of English as a subject: a preliminary enquiry into some questions of method. History of Education 8 1979.

Murray, K. M. E. Caught in the web of words: James Murray and the Oxford English dictionary. Oxford 1979.

Oates, J. C. T. Young Henry Bradshaw. In Essays in honour of Victor Scholderer, ed D. E. Rhodes, Mainz 1970.

Palmer, D. J. The rise of English studies. Oxford 1965.

Parrinder, P. Authors and authority: a study of English literary criticism and its relation to culture 1750–1900. 1977.

Plotkin, C. The tenth muse: Victorian philology and the genesis of the poetic language in the writings of Gerard Manley Hopkins. Carbondale and Edwardsville IL 1989.

Ruggiers, P. G. Editing Chaucer, the great tradition. Norman OK 1984.

Schafer, J. Documentation in the O. E. D.: Shakespeare and Nashe as test cases. Oxford 1980.

Simons, J. R. C. Trench and the development of English at King Alfred's College. In Winchester, history and literature, ed S. Barker and C. Haydon, Winchester 1991.

Small, I. and J. Guy. The literary, aestheticism and the founding of English as a discipline. ELT 33 1990.

Taylor, D. Hardy's literary language and Victorian philology. Oxford 1993.

Wawn, A. George Stephens, Cheapinghaven and old northern antiquity. In Medievalism in England, second series, ed L. J. Workman and K. Verduin, Cambridge 1996.

Williams, R. Cambridge English, past and present. In Writing in society, London nd.

George Atherton Aitken 1860–1917

The life of Richard Steele. 2 vols 1889.
The life and works of John Arbuthnot. Oxford 1892.
Poems and satires of Andrew Marvell. 2 vols 1892 (ML).
The poetical works of Robert Burns. Edited with a memoir, 3 vols 1893.
The poetical works of Thomas Parnell. Edited with a memoir and notes 1894.
Richard Steele. 1894 (Mermaid ser), 1903. Selected plays, with introd and appendixes.
Romances and narratives by Daniel Defoe. 16 vols 1895–6.
The critic by R. B. B. Sheridan. 1897.
The rivals by R. B. B. Sheridan. 1897.
The school for scandal by R. B. B. Sheridan. 1897.
The Spectator, with introduction and notes. 8 vols 1898.
The Tatler, with introduction and notes. 4 vols 1898–9.
The journal to Stella by J. Swift. 1901.
Journal of the plague year by Daniel Defoe. [1908].
Memoirs of a cavalier by Daniel Defoe. [1908].
Notes on the bibliography of Pope. 1914.

Henry Alford 1810–71

The Queen's English: stray notes on speaking and spelling. Cambridge 1864 [1863], rev and enlarged 1870 as The Queen's English: a manual of idiom and usage.
Alford wrote a large number of vols of poetry and works on Greek and theology. See also under Poetry 1835–1870, *above.*

Edward Arber 1836–1912

English reprints. 30 vols 1868–71.
The first printed English New Testament, translated by William Tyndale, photolithographed from the unique fragment now in the Grenville Collection, British Museum. 1871.
Annotated reprints. 3 vols 1872–5.
A transcript of the register of the company of stationers of London 1554–1640 AD. 5 vols 1875–94 (priv ptd).
An English garner: ingatherings from our history and literature. 8 vols 1877–96; ed and rearranged T. Seccombe 12 vols 1903. *See* H. Guppy, An analytical catalogue of the contents of the two editions of An English garner, 1909.
The English scholar's library of old and modern works. 16 vols 1878–84.
An introductory sketch to the Martin Marprelate controversy 1558–90. 1880. No 8 of The English scholar's library, *above.*
The first three English books on America? 1511–55 AD: being chiefly translations, compilations, etc by Richard Eden. Birmingham 1885.
The war library. 2 vols Birmingham 1894.
The story of the pilgrim fathers 1606–23 AD as told by themselves, their friends and their enemies. 1897.
British anthologies. 10 vols 1899–1901.
The term catalogues 1668–1709 AD; with a number for Easter term 1711 AD, from the quarterly lists issued by the booksellers. 3 vols 1903–6 (priv ptd).
A Christian library: a popular series of religious literature. 3 vols 1907 (priv ptd).

Thomas Arnold 1823–1900

A manual of English literature, historical and critical; with an appendix on English metres. 1862, 1867 (rev and enlarged), 1873, 1877, 1885, 1888, 1897 (all rev).
Chaucer to Wordsworth: a short history of English literature, from the earliest times to the present day. [1870], 2 vols 1875.
A Catholic dictionary. 1884, 1917, [1928], 1951. With W. E. Addis.

Editions

Select English works of John Wycliff. 3 vols Oxford 1869–71.
Selections from Addison's papers contributed to the Spectator. 1875.
Beowulf: a heroic poem of the eighth century; with translation, notes and appendix. 1876.
Pope, selected poems: the Essay on criticism, the Moral essays, the Dunciad. 1876.
Henrici, Archidiaconi Huntendunensis, Historia Anglorum: the history of the English by Henry, Archdeacon of Huntingdon, from AD 55 to AD 1154. 1879 (Rolls ser).
English poetry and prose: a collection of illustrative passages from the writings of English authors, commencing in the Anglo-Saxon period and brought down to the present time. 1882.
Symeonis monachi opera omnia. 2 vols 1882–5 (Rolls ser).
Clarendon, History of the rebellion, book vi. 1886.
Dryden, An essay of dramatic poesy. 1889, 1903.
Memorials of St Edmund's Abbey. 1890.

William Beloe 1756–1817

Poems and translations. 1788.
Incidents of youthful life: or the true history of William Langley. 1790, 1807. Children's tale.
Miscellanies: consisting of poems, classical extracts and oriental apologues. 3 vols 1795.
Julia: or last follies. 1795. Poems.
Anecdotes of literature and scarce books. 6 vols 1807–12.
The sexagenarian: or recollections of a literary life. 1817, 1818.

Editions and translations

The rape of Helen, from the Greek of Coluthus. 1786.
A free translation of the preface to Bellendenus. 1788.
Alciphron's epistles, now first translated. 1791. With T. Munro.
The history of Herodotus. 4 vols 1791, 6 edns by 1830.
The British critic: a new review. May 1793–Oct 1826. Vols 1–42 ed Robert Nares and Beloe.
The Attic nights of Aulus Gellius. 3 vols 1795.
A new and general biographical dictionary. 15 vols 1798–1810. In this (3rd) edn vols 7, 9, 11, 13 and 15 were ed Beloe.

William Blades 1824–90

The life and typography of William Caxton, England's first printer; with evidence of his typographical connection with Colard Mansion, the printer at Bruges. 2 vols 1861–3.
A catalogue of books printed by (or ascribed to the press of) William Caxton. 1865.
A list of medals, jettons, tokens, etc in connection with printers and the art of printing. 1869 (priv ptd).
How to tell a Caxton; with some hints where and how the same might be found. 1870.
A list of medals struck by order of the Corporation of London; with an appendix of other medals, struck privately or for sale, having reference to the same corporate body or its members. 1870 (priv ptd).
Typographical notes. [1870] (priv ptd).
Shakspere and typography: being an attempt to show Shakspere's personal connection with, and technical knowledge of, the art of printing; also remarks upon some common typographical errors, with especial reference to the text of Shakspere. 1872. *A jeu d'esprit.*
Some early type specimen books of England, Holland, France, Italy and Germany; with explanatory remarks. 1875.

The biography and typography of William Caxton. 1877. A different work from the Life, *above*.
The enemies of books. 1880, 1888 (rev and enlarged), 1896; tr Fr 1883.
Numismata typographica: or the medallic history of printing, reprinted from the Printers' Register. 1883.
An account of the German morality-play entitled Depositio cornuti typographici; with a rhythmical translation of the German version of 1648. 1885.
Bibliographical miscellanies. 5 pts 1890. Pt 1 Signatures; pt 2 The chained library at Wimborne Minster; pts 3–5 Books in chains.
The Pentateuch of printing, with a chapter on Judges, with a memoir of the author, and list of his works, by T. B. Reed. 1891.
Blades also contributed many essays on printing and bibliography to periodicals, and pbd several short papers; he edited Juliana Berners, Boke of St Albans; The dictes and sayings of the philosophers, Christine Pisan, Moral proverbes; *and he was a prime mover in the Caxton celebration of 1877.*

James Boswell 1778–1822

A biographical memoir of the late Edmond Malone. 1814 (priv ptd). Rptd from GM June 1813; reissued in Catalogue of early English poetry by E. Malone, 1836.
A Roxburghe garland. 1817.
The plays and poems of William Shakespeare comprehending an enlarged history of the stage, by the late E. Malone. 21 vols 1821. The 3rd variorum edn; ed Boswell from Malone's mss.
Boswell also pbd the 6th (rev) edn of his father's Life of Johnson.

Joseph Bosworth 1789–1876

Grammars and dictionaries

An introduction to Latin construing. 1821, 1846.
Latin construing. 1821, 1850.
The elements of Anglo-Saxon grammar. 1823.
A compendious grammar of the primitive English or Anglo-Saxon language. 1826.
Græcæ grammatices rudimenta by William Bosworth, with additions by Joseph Bosworth. 1830.
A dictionary of the Anglo-Saxon language. 1838, 4 vols Oxford 1898 (rev partly from Bosworth's mss by T. N. Toller), 1908–21.
A compendious Anglo-Saxon and English dictionary. 1848, 1881, 1888.

Editions, translations, etc

The origin of the Dutch. 1836.
Scandinavian literature. 1839. Anthology.
The origins of the English, Germanic and Scandinavian languages and nations. 1848.
A literal English translation of King Alfred's Anglo-Saxon version of the Compendious history of the world by Orosius. 1855, 1859.
A description of Europe, and the voyages of Ohthere and Wulfstan, with Anglo-Saxon text and a literal English translation and notes. 1855.
The history of the Lauderdale manuscript of King Alfred's Anglo-Saxon version of Orosius. Oxford 1858.
King Alfred's Anglo-Saxon version of the Compendious history of the world by Orosius, containing facsimile specimens of the Lauderdale and Cotton manuscripts. 1859. The Anglo-Saxon text with notes and various readings.
The Gothic and Anglo-Saxon Gospels in parallel columns with the versions of Wycliffe and Tyndale. 1865.

Henry Bradley 1845–1923

The Goths from the earliest times to the end of the Gothic dominion in Spain. 1888.
The making of English. 1904.
Changes in the language to the days of Chaucer. CHEL vol 1 1907.
The misplaced leaf of Piers the plowman. In J. M. Manly, Piers the plowman and its sequence, 1908 (EETS).
The authorship of Piers the plowman. 1910 (EETS).
The 'Cædmonian' Genesis. E & S 6 1910.
English place names. 1910 (Eng Assoc).
On the relations between spoken and written language, with special reference to English. 1914; Proc Br Acad 8 1919.
The numbered sections in Old English poetical manuscripts. 1916; Proc Br Acad 7 1918.
Shakespeare's English. In Shakespeare's England vol 2, 1916.
Sir James Murray 1837–1915. [1919]; Proc Br Acad 8 1919.
On the text of Abbo of Fleury's Quaestiones Grammaticales. Proc Br Acad 10 1921. [1922].
The collected papers, with a memoir by Robert Bridges. Oxford 1928. With bibliography.

Editions

A new English dictionary on historical principles, founded mainly on the materials collected by the Philological Society, edited by James A. H. Murray, Henry Bradley, William A. Craigie, C. T. Onions. 11 vols Oxford 1884–1933. Bradley was joint editor from 1889, and was responsible for E, F–G, L–M, S–SH, ST, W–WEZZON.
Stratmann, F. H. A Middle-English dictionary: new edition revised by Henry Bradley. Oxford 1894.
Morris, R. Historical outlines of English accidence, revised by L. Kellner with the assistance of Henry Bradley. 1895.
Morris, R. Elementary lessons in historical English grammar, revised by Henry Bradley. 1897.
Caxton, W. Dialogues in French and English. 1900 (EETS).
Stevenson, W. Gammer Gurton's Needle, edited with critical essay and notes. In Representative English comedies vol 1, ed C. M. Gayley, New York 1903.

Henry Bradshaw 1831–86

Discovery of the long lost Morland manuscripts in the library of the University of Cambridge. In J. H. Todd, The books of the Vaudois, 1865.
The printer of the Historia S Albani. 1868.
The skeleton of Chaucer's Canterbury tales: an attempt to distinguish the several fragments of the work as left by the author. 1868, [1871].
Notice of a fragment of the fifteen Oes and other prayers printed at Westminster by William Caxton about 1490, 91, preserved in the library of the Baptist College, Bristol. 1877.
The early collection of canons known as the Hibernensis: two unfinished papers. Ed F. J. H. Jenkinson, Cambridge 1893.
Bradshaw, who was Univ Librarian of Cambridge, also pbd other bibliographical papers, addresses and catalogues.

§2

Prothero, G. W. A memoir of Bradshaw. 1888.
Collected papers, comprising 1: Memoranda; 2: Communications read before the Cambridge Antiquarian Society: together with an article contributed to the Bibliographer and two papers not previously published. Ed F. J. H. Jenkinson, Cambridge 1889.
Leeper, A. A scholar-librarian. 1901.
Newcombe, C. F. Some aspects of the work of Bradshaw. 1905.
Crone, J. S. Bradshaw: his life and work. [1931].

Arthur Henry Bullen 1857–1920

Anthologies

A Christmas garland: cards and poems from the fifteenth century to the present time. 1885.

Lyrics from the song-books of the Elizabethan age. 1887; More lyrics from the song-books of the Elizabethan age, 1888; 1889 (selected from the 2 preceding vols).
Lyrics from the dramatists of the Elizabethan age. 1889.
Musa Proterva: love poems of the Restoration. 1889 (priv ptd).
Speculum amantis: love poems from rare song-books and miscellanies of the seventeenth century. 1889 (priv ptd).
Poems, chiefly lyrical, from romances and prose tracts of the Elizabethan age; with chosen poems of Nicholas Breton. 1890.
Shorter Elizabethan poems. 1903. Part of E. Arber, An English garner.
Some longer Elizabethan poems. 1903. Part of E. Arber, An English garner.

Editions and reprints
The works of John Day. 7 pts 1881 (priv ptd).
A collection of old English plays. 4 vols 1882–5 (priv ptd). 16 rare Elizabethan-Jacobean plays.
The English dramatists. 14 vols 1885–7 (priv ptd). Marlowe, 3 vols; Middleton, 8 vols; Marston, 3 vols.
A collection of old English plays: new series. 3 vols 1887–90 (priv ptd). Dramatic works of Nobbes, Davenport et al.
Robert Burton's The anatomy of melancholy, with introduction. 1893, 1904, 1923.
The works of Francis Beaumont and John Fletcher: variorum edition. Vols 1–4 (all pbd), 1904–12. Bullen was general editor, each play being ed by a different hand.
Sonnets by William Shakespeare. Stratford-on-Avon 1905, 1921 (rev with memoir of Bullen by H. F. B. Brett-Smith).
The works of William Shakespeare. 10 vols Stratford-on-Avon 1910 (Stratford Town edn). Includes contributions by other scholars.
Bullen also issued edns of Peele, Campion, William Browne, Arden of Feversham, *Davison's* Poetical rhapsody, England's Helicon (1600), *a selection from Drayton, etc. He contributed largely to* DNB *and* GM, *which he edited in 1906, and was general editor of* The Muses' Library.

Writings
The willow. Stratford-on-Avon 1916 (priv ptd). Poems.
Weeping-Cross. Stratford-on-Avon 1917 (priv ptd). Poems.
Weeping-Cross and other rimes. 1921.
Elizabethans. 1924. Critical essays.

Alexander Chalmers 1759–1834

A lesson in biography. 1798, Edinburgh 1887 (priv ptd). A parody of Boswell's Life of Johnson.
The Tatler, with prefaces, historical and biographical. 4 vols 1803.
The British essayists; with prefaces, historical and biographical. 45 vols 1803, 1817, 38 vols 1823, Boston 1856. With index.
The Spectator. 8 vols 1806.
The Guardian. 2 vols 1806.
Walker's classics. 45 vols 1808–12. Prefaces by Chalmers.
The British gallery of contemporary portraits. 2 vols 1809–16. Many lives by Chalmers.
A history of the colleges, halls and public buildings attached to the University of Oxford. 2 vols Oxford 1810.
The works of the English poets from Chaucer to Cowper. 21 vols 1810. A much expanded revision of Dr Johnson's collection, the additional lives all by Chalmers.
The Projector. 3 vols 1811. Periodical essays rptd from GM.
The general biographical dictionary. 32 vols 1812–17. Expanded by Chalmers from A new and general biographical dictionary, rev W. Tooke, R. Nares and W. Beloe, 15 vols 1798–1810.
A dictionary of the English language. 1820. Dr Johnson's dictionary abridged.
The life of Martin Luther. 1857.
Chalmers also supervised edns of the following, generally with memoirs of some length: Beattie, Burns, Cruden, Fielding, Gibbon, Johnson, Milton, Paley, Edward Reynolds, Shakespeare.

Derwent Coleridge 1800–83

Observations on the plan of the society's proposed New English Dictionary. Trans of the Philological Soc 1860.
Coleridge also wrote on education and edited the poems of W. M. Praed (1864).

Herbert Coleridge 1830–61

Glossarial index to the printed English literature of the 13th century. 1859, 1862 as Dictionary of the first, or oldest words in the English language.

Contributions to periodicals
On diminutives in letters. Trans of the Philological Soc 1857.
On the Scandinavian element in the English language. Trans of the Philological Soc 1859.
English etymology. Macmillan's Mag 1, Mar 1860.
On the exclusion of certain words from a dictionary. Trans of the Philological Soc 1860–1. With F. J. Furnivall.

Contributions to collaborative works
Prefatory essay to Le Morte Arthur, ed F. J. Furnivall. 1864 (EETS).

John Payne Collier 1789–1883

Ms autobiography, diaries and correspondence at the Folger Lib. Other letters are held by Edinburgh Univ Lib, BL, Bodleian, Houghton Lib, Harvard, Huntington and Univ of Newcastle.

§1

Criticisms on the bar, including strictures on the principal counsel, by Amicus Curiæ. 1819. Anon.
The poetical Decameron, or ten conversations on English poets and poetry, particularly of the reigns of Elizabeth and James I. 2 vols Edinburgh 1820.
The poet's pilgrimage: an allegorical poem. 1822, 1825.
Punch and Judy, accompanied by the dialogue of the puppet show, an account of its origin, and of puppet plays in England. 1828, 1844, 1859, 1870, 1873, 1881, 1944.
The history of English dramatic poetry to the time of Shakespeare, and annals of the stage to the Restoration. 3 vols 1831, 1879 (rev).
New facts regarding the life of Shakespeare. 1835.
New particulars regarding the works of Shakespeare. 1836.
A catalogue, biographical and critical, of early English literature, the property of Lord Francis Egerton. 1837.
Farther particulars regarding Shakespeare and his works. 1839.
The Egerton papers: a collection of public and private documents, chiefly illustrative of the times of Elizabeth and James I, the property of Lord Francis Egerton. 1840.
Reasons for a new edition of Shakespeare's works. 1841, 1842 (expanded).
Memoirs of Edward Alleyn, including some new particulars respecting Shakespeare. 1841 (Shakespeare Soc). Contains some of the forgeries ascribed to Collier.
Memoirs of the principal actors in the plays of Shakespeare. 1846 (Shakespeare Soc).
Notes and emendations to the text of Shakespeare's plays from early manuscript corrections in a copy of the folio 1632 in the possession of J. P. Collier. 1852, 1853 (with preface).
Reply to Mr N. E. S. Hamilton's Inquiry into the imputed Shakespeare forgeries. 1860.
Illustrations of early English popular literature. 2 vols 1863–4 (priv ptd).

A bibliographical and critical account of the rarest books in the English language. 2 vols 1865.
Illustrations of Old English literature. 3 vols 1866 (priv ptd).
Odds and ends. 1870 (priv ptd).
An old man's diary, forty years ago. 4 pts 1871 (priv ptd).
Trilogy on the emendations of Shakespeare's text contained in Mr Collier's corrected folio, 1632, and employed by recent editors of the poet's works. 3 pts [1874].

Editions

A select collection of old plays. 12 vols 1825–7. Dodsley's collection with additional plays by Collier.
Kynge Johan, by John Bale. 1838.
Patient Grisil, by Henry Chettle. 1841.
The school of abuse, by Stephen Gosson. 1841.
The works of William Shakespeare: the text formed from an entirely new collation of the old editions, with the various readings, notes, a life of the poet, and a history of the early English stage. 8 vols 1842–4, 1853, 1858, 1875–8.
Shakespeare's library: a collection of the romances [etc] used by Shakespeare. 2 vols [1843].
Extracts from the stationers' register relating to the drama and popular literature to 1586. 1848–9 (Shakespeare Soc).
The diary of Philip Henslowe, from 1591 to 1609. 1848.
The plays of Shakespeare: the text regulated by the old copies, and by the recently discovered folio of 1632, containing early manuscript emendations. 1853.
Seven lectures of Shakespeare and Milton by the late S. T. Coleridge. 1856. Collier's own manuscript notes, at first unjustly suspected to be forged.
Poems by Michael Drayton. 1856.
Shakespeare's comedies, histories, tragedies, and poems. 6 vols 1858.
The works of Edmund Spenser. 5 vols 1862.
The firste (second) part of Churchyard's Chippes, by Thomas Churchyard. [1870].
Foure letters, by Gabriel Harvey. [1870.]
Pierces supererogation, by Gabriel Harvey. [1870].
Have with you to Saffron-Walden, by Thomas Nash. [1870].
Epitaphes, epigrams, songs and sonetes, by George Turberville. [1870].
The plays and poems of William Shakespeare, with the purest text, and the briefest notes. 8 vols 1875–8 (priv ptd).
Collier also rptd, generally with introds, many Elizabethan and Stuart rarities (mainly dramatic and poetic), both independently and for the Camden, Percy and Shakespeare Socs and Roxburghe Club, including works by Thomas Heywood, Anthony Munday and Thomas Nash. The BM possesses a number of bks containing Collier's notes and annotations in ms.

Collier anonymously pbd some small vols of his own verse in 1822 (rptd 1825, authorship acknowledged, and 1828) and 1870. He also produced trns from Schiller (1824, 1825, rptd 1874, 1875) and, anonymously, from Casti (1850).

§2

Singer, S. W. The text of Shakespeare vindicated from the interpolations and corruptions advocated by J. P. Collier. 1853.
Wheatley, H. B. Notes on the life of John Payne Collier, with a complete list of his works and an account of such Shakespeare documents as are believed to be spurious. 1884.
Ganzel, D. Fortune and men's eyes. The career of John Payne Collier. Oxford 1982.
Ziegler, G. A Victorian reputation: John Payne Collier and his contemporaries. ShS 17 1985.

George Lillie Craik 1798–1866

Sketches of the history of literature and learning in England from the Norman conquest. 6 vols 1844–5. 2 vols 1861 as A compendious history of English literature and of the English language from the Norman conquest.
Outlines of the history of the English language for the use of junior classes in colleges and the higher classes in schools. 1851.
The English of Shakespeare illustrated by a philological commentary on his Julius Caesar. 1857.

Contributions to periodicals

The text of Shakespeare. North Br Rev 20, Feb 1854.
Curiosities of the English language. Dublin Univ Mag 50, Oct 1857.

Editions

Spenser and his poetry. 3 vols 1845.
Bacon: his writings and philosophy. 3 vols 1846–7.
Craik also wrote textbooks on history, and the celebrated Pursuit of knowledge under difficulties (1830). *See also col 2120 above.*

Peter Cunningham 1816–69

Poems upon several occasions. 1841 (priv ptd).
Westminster Abbey: its art, architecture and associations – a handbook for visitors. 1842.
Inigo Jones: a life of the architect by Peter Cunningham; remarks on some of his sketches for masques and dramas by J. R. Planché [etc]. 1848 (Shakespeare Soc).
A handbook for London, past and present. 2 vols 1849, 1851 (3rd edn, as Murray's handbook for modern London), [1866] (rev), [1867] (rev), 1879.
The story of Nell Gwynn, and the sayings of Charles II, related and corrected. 1852; ed H. B. Wheatley 1892; [1926], 1927.
Cunningham also wrote several annual handbooks on London.

Editions

The poems of William Drummond of Hawthornden, with life. 1833.
Extracts from the accounts of the revels at court, in the reigns of Queen Elizabeth and James I, from the original office books of the masters and yeomen, with an introduction and notes. 1842 (Shakespeare Soc).
Lives of the most eminent English poets, by Samuel Johnson; with notes, corrective and explanatory. 3 vols 1854.
The works of Oliver Goldsmith. 4 vols 1854.
The letters of Horace Walpole, now first chronologically arranged. 9 vols 1857–9, 1891.
Cunningham also edited 2 vols for the Percy Soc, Songs of England and Scotland, Specimens of the British poets, *and Pope's works; he was treasurer of the Shakespeare Soc and a contributor to* Fraser's Mag, GM, Athenaeum, *etc.*

Peter Augustin Daniel fl 1870–1904

Notes and conjectural emendations of certain doubtful passages in Shakespeare's plays. 1870.
Romeo and Juliet: parallel texts of the first two quartos. 1874 (New Shakespeare Soc).
Romeus and Juliet (written first in Italian by Bandell, and nowe in English) by A. Brooke; Rhomeo and Julietta (translated by W. Painter from the French paraphrase by P. Boasistuau, of Bandello's version of Romeo e Giulietta). 1875 (New Shakespeare Soc, originals and analogues pt 1).
The works of Francis Beaumont and John Fletcher: variorum edition. 4 vols 1904–12. General editor A. H. Bullen; Daniel edited The maid's tragedy and Philaster in vol 1 and The beggar's bush in vol 2.
Daniel also contributed introds to the following plays issued in the Shakespeare Quarto-Facs Ser: Romeo and Juliet, 1874; King Lear, 1885; Much ado, 1886; Henry V, 1887; Richard II, 1887; Richard III, 1888; Merry wives, 1888.

John Davies d. 1890

On Celtic words used by early English writers. Tenby 1855.

Contributions to periodicals

On the races of Lancashire as indicated by the local names and dialect of the county. Trans of the Philological Soc 1855.
On the connexion of the Keltic with the Teutonic languages and especially with the Anglo-Saxon. Trans of the Philological Soc 1857.
A comparison of Celtic words found in Old English literature and English dialects with modern Celtic forms. Archaeologia Cambrensis 1881–2.
The Celtic element in the Lancashire dialect. Archaeologia Cambrensis 1882–3.
The Celtic element in the dialect of the counties adjoining Lancashire. Archaeologia Cambrensis 1884.
The Celtic element in the dialectic words of the counties of Northampton and Leicester. Archaeologia Cambrensis 1885.
Davies was a member of the Royal Asiatic Soc and translated the Bhagavad Gita *as well as writing on Indian philosophy, theology and Sanskrit.*

Thomas Frognall Dibdin 1776–1847

Poems. 1797.
An introduction to the knowledge of rare and valuable editions of the Greek and Roman classics. Gloucester 1802, 1804 (enlarged), 2 vols 1808 (rev), 1827 (greatly enlarged).
The Director: a weekly literary journal. 2 vols 1807. Ed Dibdin.
Specimen bibliothecae britannicae. 1808.
The bibliomania or book-madness, in an epistle addressed to Richard Heber. 1809, 1811 (enlarged), 2 pts 1842 (improved), 1876, 1905.
The typographical antiquities of Great Britain. Vols 1–4 (all pbd), 1810–19. A partial revision of Ames.
Bibliography, a poem: book I. [1812].
Bibliotheca Spenceriana: or a descriptive catalogue of the library of Earl Spencer. 4 vols 1814–15.
The bibliographical Decameron. 3 vols 1817.
A bibliographical, antiquarian and picturesque tour in France and Germany. 3 vols 1821; tr Fr 1825.
Aedes Althorpianae: or an account of the mansion, books and pictures at Althorp. 2 vols 1822.
A descriptive catalogue of the books lately of the library of the Duke di Cassana Serra and now of the Earl Spencer. 4 vols 1823.
The library companion. 2 vols 1824.
The Sunday library: a selection of sermons from eminent divines. 6 vols 1831.
Bibliophobia: remarks on the present languid state of literature and the book trade, by Mercurius Rusticus. 1832.
Reminiscences of a literary life. 2 pts 1836.
The bibliographical, antiquarian and picturesque tour in the northern counties of England and Scotland. 3 vols 1838.
Cranmer: a novel, by a member of the Roxburghe Club. 3 vols 1839.
Dibdin also pbd reprints of Tudor and Stuart rarities, mainly for the Roxburghe Club, as well as sermons, pamphlets, etc.

Francis Douce 1757–1834

The dance of death. [1794?] (anon), 1833 (enlarged). Ed Douce with elaborate dissertation.
Illustrations of Shakespeare and of ancient manners, with dissertation on the clowns and fools of Shakespeare. 2 vols 1807.
A catalogue of the Harleian manuscripts in the British Museum. 1808–12. Revised by Douce.
A catalogue of the Lansdowne manuscripts in the British Museum. 1819. With Sir H. Ellis.

Contributions to periodicals

Dissertation on the runic jasper ring belonging to George Cumberland. Archaeologia Cambrensis 1827.
Douce also pbd edns of Arnold's Chronicle *(1811); and a few ME texts for the Roxburghe Club. The Bodleian possesses numerous bks annotated by Douce.*

Alexander Dyce 1798–1869

Editions

Specimens of British poetesses. 1825, 1827.
The poetical works of William Collins. 1827.
The works of George Peele. 3 vols 1828–39.
The works of John Webster. 4 vols 1830, 1857.
The dramatic works of Robert Greene. 2 vols 1831, 1861.
The dramatic works and poems of James Shirley. 6 vols 1833.
Specimens of English sonnets. 1833.
The works of Richard Bentley. 3 vols 1836–8.
The works of Thomas Middleton. 5 vols 1840.
The poetical works of John Skelton. 2 vols 1843, 1856.
The works of Beaumont and Fletcher. 11 vols 1843–6.
The works of Christopher Marlow. 3 vols 1850.
Recollections of the table talk of Samuel Rogers. 1856, 1887, 1903, 1952 (rev).
The works of Shakespeare: the text revised. 6 vols 1857, 9 vols 1864–7 (adds glossary), 1907.
The works of John Ford. 3 vols 1869.
Dyce also pbd the Aldine edns of Akenside, Beattie, Parnell, Pope and Shakespeare's poems, as well as several Elizabethan texts for the Camden, Percy and Shakespeare Socs.

Miscellaneous writings

Select translations from the Greek of Quintus Smyrnaeus. 1821.
Remarks on Mr J. P. Collier's and Mr Charles Knight's editions of Shakespeare. 1844.
A few notes on Shakespeare with occasional remarks on Mr Collier's copy of the folio 1632. 1858, 1859.

John Earle 1824–1903

Gloucester fragments, legends of St Swithun and Sancta Maria Aegyptiaca. 1861.
Guide to Bath, ancient and modern. 1864.
Two of the Saxon chronicles parallel, with supplementary extracts from the others, edited with introduction, notes and a glossarial index. 1865, 1889, 1892.
A book for the beginner in Anglo-Saxon. 1866, 1877, 1902.
The philology of the English tongue. 1866, 1871, 1892.
Rhymes and reasons: essays by J. E. 1871.
A word for the mother tongue: inaugural lecture for the chair of Anglo-Saxon at Oxford, Nov 17 1876. Oxford 1876.
The peace of Wedmore and how it touches the history of the English language. Oxford 1878.
English plant names. 1880.
Anglo-Saxon literature. 1884.
A handbook on the land charters and other Saxonic documents. 1888.
English prose: its elements, history and usage. 1890.
Deeds of Beowulf done into modern prose. 1892.
The Psalter of 1539. 1894.
Bath during British independence. 1895.
A simple grammar of English now in use. 1898.
Alfred as a writer. In Alfred the Great, ed A. Bowker, 1899.
The Alfred jewel. 1901.
The place of English in education. In An English miscellany presented to Dr Furnivall, Oxford misc, 1901.

Contributions to periodicals

An unnamed habit of language. Macmillan's Mag 31, Nov 1874.

On local names. Trans of the Bristol and Gloucestershire Archaeological Soc 1884.

Alexander John Ellis 1814–90

Phonetics: a familiar system of the principles of that science, by A. J. E. 1844.

The essentials of phonetics: containing the theory of a universal alphabet, together with its practical application. 1848.

An extension of phonography to foreign languages: containing a complete phonographic alphabet; and hints towards the construction of a phonographic short hand in French and German. 1848.

Phonetic spelling familiarly explained, for the use of romanic readers: with numerous examples. 1849.

On early English pronunciation, with especial reference to Shakespeare and Chaucer; containing an investigation of the correspondence of writing with speech in England, from the Anglo-Saxon period to the present day, including a re-arrangement of F. J. Child's memoirs on the language of Chaucer and Gower. 5 pts 1869–89 (Chaucer Soc, Philological Soc, EETS). Pt 5 a dialect survey of England.

On the sensations of tone as a physiological basis for the theory of music, by Hermann Ludwig von Helmholtz; translated from the third German edition, with additions and notes. 1875, 1885 (rev with addns). 'More than a third consisted of work by Ellis himself' – DNB.

The English, Dionysian and Hellenic pronunciations of Greek, considered in reference to school and college use. 1876.

An early English hymn to the Virgin, with notes on the Welsh phonetic copy. 1876 (English Dialect Soc).

The history of musical pitch, reprinted with corrections and an appendix, from the Journal of the Society of Arts. 1880.

Ellis also wrote many other papers and bks on phonetics, phonography, music, mathematics, philosophy, etc, and produced phonetic texts of the Bible, Macbeth, The Tempest, Bunyan's Pilgrim's Progress, *etc. He edited* The Fonetic Frend (1849) *and* The Spelling Reformer (1849–50), *and was a significant figure in the movement for spelling reform.*

Frederic Thomas Elworthy 1830–1907

The dialect of West Somerset. 1875–6.

An outline of the grammar of the dialect of West Somerset. 1877.

Specimens of English dialects. 1879.

The West-Somerset word-book: a glossary of dialectal and archaic words used in the west of Somerset and east Devon. 1886.

Horns of honour: and other studies in the by-ways of archaeology. 1900.

Contributions to periodicals

On West Somerset patois. Somersetshire Archaeological and Natural History Soc Proc 1876.

Devonshire speech the true classic English. Report and Trans of the Devonshire Assoc 1880.

On the Devonshire pronoun min or mun = them. Report and Trans of the Devonshire Assoc 1881.

Further unnoted grammatical peculiarities in the dialect of Somerset and Devon. Proc of the Philological Soc 1883–4.

On some fresh words and phrases in the Somerset dialect. Trans of the Philological Soc 1898.

Elworthy also wrote on folklore and traditional custom and belief.

Frederick Gard Fleay 1831–1909

Almond blossoms. 1857. Poems.

The poetry of Catullus rendered into English. 1864.

Shakespeare manual. 1876.

Guide to Chaucer and Spenser. 1877.

Introduction to Shakespearian study. 1877.

Marlow's tragedy of Edward the second, with introductory remarks and notes. 1877.

English sounds and English spelling. 1878.

The life and death of King John, by William Shakespeare, together with the troublesome reign of King John, edited with notes. 1878.

The logical English grammar. 1884.

A chronicle history of the life and work of William Shakespeare. 1886.

A chronicle history of the London stage 1559–1642. 1890.

A biographical chronicle of the English drama 1559–1642. 2 vols 1891.

Egyptian chronology: an attempt to conciliate the ancient schemes and to educe a rational system. 1899.

Fleay also produced several grammars and papers on education, etc. He was editor of Spelling Reformer (1880–1), *and contributed to* Trans of the New Shakespeare Soc *many important papers and edns of* Pericles *and* Timon *without the non-Shakespearian scenes.*

Harry Buxton Forman 1842–1917

Editions

The works of Percy Bysshe Shelley, in verse and prose, edited with prefaces, notes and appendices. 8 vols [1876]–80. Also poems only, 4 vols 1876, and with memoir 5 vols 1892 (Aldine edn).

Letters of John Keats to Fanny Brawne, written in the years 1819 and 1820, with introduction and notes. 1878, 1889 (rev and enlarged).

The poetical works and other writings of John Keats, edited with notes and appendices. 4 vols 1883; suppl 1890; [poems only] 1884.

The letters of John Keats: complete edition. 1895.

The complete works of John Keats. 5 vols Glasgow 1900–1.

The poetical works of John Keats, edited with an introduction and textual notes. Oxford 1906.

Note books of Percy Bysshe Shelley, deciphered, transcribed and edited, with a full commentary. 1911 (Boston Bibliophile Soc).

The life of Percy Bysshe Shelley, by Thomas Medwin, with an introduction and commentary. 1913.

Forman also supervised edns of separate poems by Shelley as well as works by Matthew Arnold, the Brownings et al.

Other works

Our living poets: an essay in criticism. 1871.

The Shelley library: an essay in bibliography. 1886.

The books of William Morris described, with some account of his doings in literature and in the allied crafts. 1897.

Forman also contributed to Literary anecdotes of the nineteenth century, ed Sir W. R. Nicoll and T. J. Wise, 2 vols 1895–6, *as well as publishing papers on Shelley, Chatterton et al.*

§2

Barker, N. and J. Collins. A sequel to an enquiry. The book forgeries of H. Buxton Forman and T. J. Wise re-examined. Newcastle DE 1992.

Collins, J. The two forgers: a biography of Harry Buxton Forman and T. J. Wise. Aldershot 1992.

Edward Augustus Freeman 1823–92

Contributions to periodicals

Literature and language. Contemporary Rev 52, Oct 1887.

Freeman wrote extensively on politics, geography and medieval history, and against blood sports. *See also col 2423 above.*

Frederick James Furnivall 1825–1910

Furnivall's unindexed papers are held in the ms lib, King's College, London.
Proposal for the publication of a New English Dictionary by the Philological Society. 1859.
Recent work at Chaucer. Macmillan's Mag 27, Mar 1873.

Editions for the Ballad Society (founded by Furnivall in 1868)
Ballads from manuscripts. 1868.
Captain Cox: his ballads and books. 1871.
Love poems and humerous ones 1614–19. 1874.

Editions for the Chaucer Society (founded by Furnivall in 1868)
A six-text print of Chaucer's Canterbury tales in parallel columns. [1868].
The Cambridge ms of Chaucer's Canterbury tales. 1868–79; The Corpus ms, 1868–79; The Ellesmere ms, 1868–79; The Hengwrt ms, 1868–79; The Lansdowne ms, 1868–79; The Petworth ms, 1868–79; The Harleian ms 7,334, 1885; The Cambridge ms Dd 4.24, completed by the Egerton ms 2726, 1901–2.
Essays on Chaucer: his words and works. [1868–94].
Odd texts of Chaucer's minor poems. 1868.
A parallel-text edition of Chaucer's minor poems. [1871]; Trial-forewords, 1871.
Supplementary parallel-texts of Chaucer's minor poems. [1871].
A one-text print of Chaucer's minor poems. [1871].
Originals of some of Chaucer's Canterbury tales. [1872].
Chaucer as valet and squire to Edward III. 1876.
Supplementary Canterbury tales. 1876.
Animadversions uppon the annotacions and corrections of some imperfections of impressiones of Chaucers workes reprinted in 1598 sett downe by F. Thynne. 1876.
Autotypes of Chaucer's manuscripts. 1877.
A parallel-text print of Chaucer's Troilus and Criseyde. [1881].
Chaucer's Boecce. 1886.
John Lane's continuation of Chaucer's Squire's tale. 1887.
A one-text print of Chaucer's Troilus and Criseyde. 1894.
The romaunt of the rose. 1911.

Editions for EETS (founded by Furnivall in 1864)
Arthur: a short sketch of his life and history in English verse. 1864.
Thynne on Speght's Chaucer. 1865. With G. Kingsley.
The Wrights chaste wife, by Adam of Cobsam. 1865.
Political, religious and love poems. 1866, 1903.
The book of quinte essence. 1866.
Hymns to the Virgin and Christ; the Parliament of Devils. 1867.
The staciouns of Rome; and The pilgrim's sea-voyage; with Clene maydenhod. 1867.
The babees book, Aristotle's ABC, Urbanitatis [etc]. 1868.
Caxton's Book of curtesye. 1868.
Queene Elizabethes Achademy [etc], [by Sir H. Gilbert]. 1869.
Awdeley's Fraternitye of vacabondes, Harman's Caveat etc. 1869. With E. Viles.
The fyrste boke of the introduction of knowledge made by A. Borde [etc.]. [1870].
The minor poems of William Lauder. 1870.
A supplicacyon for the beggars, by Simon Fish. 1871.
The history of the Holy Grail, by Henry Lovelich from the French of Sir R. de Borron. 1874–8.
Emblemes and epigrames, by Francis Thynne. 1878.
Adam Davy's 5 dreams about Edward II [etc]. 1878.
The fifty earliest English wills in the Court of Probate 1387–1439. 1882.
The anatomie of the bodie of man, by Vicary. 1888.
The Curial made by maystere A. Charretier, translated by Caxton. 1888.
Caxton's Eneydos. 1890.
Hoccleve's works. 1892–7.
The three king's sons, englisht from the French. 1895.
The English conquest of Ireland AD 1166–85. 1897.
Child-marriages, divorces and ratifications in the diocese of Chester AD 1561–6. 1897.
Lydgate's Deguileville's Pilgrimage of the life of man. 1899–1901.
Robert of Brunne's Handlyng synne. 1901–3.
Minor poems of the Vernon ms. 1901.
The Macro plays. 1904.
The tale of Beryn etc. 1909. With W. G. Stone.
The Gild of St Mary, Lichfield. 1920.

Editions for the New Shakespeare Society (founded by Furnivall in 1873)
Stafford's Compendious examination of certayne complaints of divers of our countrymen. 1876.
Spalding's A letter on Shakespeare's authorship of the Two noble kinsmen. 1876.
Tell-trothes new-yeares gift etc. 1876.
Harrison's description of England in Shakespeare's youth. 1877.
Stubbe's Anatomy of abuses. 1877.
The Digby mysteries. 1882.
A list of all the songs and passages in Shakspere which have been set to music. 1884. With J. Greenhill.
Some 300 fresh allusions to Shakspere. 1886.
Robert Laneham's letter. 1890, 1907.

Editions for the Roxburghe Club
Seynt Graal: or the Sank Ryal, partly in English verse by Henry Lovelich and wholly in French prose by Robiers de Borron. 2 vols 1861–3.
Robert of Brunne's Handlyng synne, William of Waddington's Le manuel des pechiez. 1862.
La queste del Saint Graal; in the French prose of Walter Map. 1864.
A royal historie of the excellent knight Generides. Hertford 1865.
The boke of nurture, by John Russell; The boke of kervynge, by Wynkyn de Worde; The boke of nurture, by Hugh Rhodes. 2 vols 1866.

Editions of Shakespeare
The Leopold Shakspere, in chronological order, from the text of Prof Delius. [1877].
Double text dallastype Shakespeare. 1895.
The works of William Shakespeare according to the orthography and arrangement of the more authentic quarto and folio versions. 1904 (Old Spelling Shakespeare).
The Century Shakespeare. 40 vols 1908. With introds and notes, and a vol on the life and work of Shakespeare, by Furnivall and J. J. Munro.
Cassell's illustrated Shakespeare. 1913.
Furnivall also edited a number of the plays separately.

Other editions
Le Morte Arthur, edited from the Harleian ms 2,252 in the British Museum. 1864.
Bishop Percy's folio manuscript: ballads and romances. 1867. With J. W. Hales.
The boke of nurture by H. Rhodes. [1868?]
Mannyng of Brunne, Robert. The story of England AD 1338. 1887 (Rolls ser).
Lamb's Tales from Shakespeare, with introduction and additions. 1901.
Many other works were written, edited or provided with introds by Furnivall, who founded the Wiclif Soc and the Browning Soc in 1881, and the same year compiled a Browning bibliography. In 1874 he contributed to Gervinus's commentaries on Shakspere an essay on metrical tests for the chronology of Shakespeare's works. In 1886 he founded the Shelley Soc. He was, as secretary of the Philological Soc, the proposer of the scheme for the New English Dictionary.

§2

An English miscellany presented to Dr Furnivall in honour of his seventy-fifth birthday. Oxford 1901.
Sidgwick, F. Frederick James Furnivall. Eng Illustr Mag 30 1904. A memoir with bibliography.
Dr Frederick James Furnivall. 1910. Obituary notices by Mrs C. C. Stopes and A. Brandl.
Ker, W. P. Memoir. Proc Br Acad 3 1909–10.
Furnivall: a volume of personal record. 1911. Reminiscences by 49 contributors, with a biography by J. J. Munro.
Benzie, W. Dr F. J. Furnivall: Victorian scholar adventurer. Norman OK 1983.
Myers, B. F. J. Furnivall. Lexicographer, philanthropist, oarsman. Jnl of the William Morris Soc 9 1992.

John Genest 1764–1839

Some account of the English stage from 1660 to 1830. 10 vols Bath 1832. Anon.

Sir Israel Gollancz 1863–1930

Pearl: an English poem of the fourteenth century, edited with a modern rendering. 1891, 1923 (EETS, with Cleanness, Patience and Sir Gawain).
Cynewulf's Christ, edited with a modern rendering. 1892.
Charles Lamb's Specimens of English dramatic poets, now first edited anew. 1893.
The Exeter book, edited with a translation, notes and introduction. 1895 (EETS).
The parlement of the thre ages, edited with introduction, notes. 1897.
Hoccleve's works, vol 2: The minor poems in the Ashburnham ms addit 133. 1897 (EETS).
Marlowe's The tragical history of Doctor Faustus. 1897.
Hamlet in Iceland: being the Icelandic Ambales Saga, edited and translated. 1898.
Otway's Venice preserved. 1899.
Select early English poems. 1913.
A book of homage to Shakespeare. 1916. Gollancz was general editor.
Ich dene: some observations on a manuscript of the life and feats of arms of Edward Prince of Wales, the Black Prince, a metrical chronicle in French verse by the Herald of Sir John Chandos. 1921.
The Middle Ages in the lineage of English poetry. 1921.
Sir Gawayne and the Greene Knight, re-edited by R. Morris, revised. 1925, 1940.
The sources of Hamlet. 1926.
The Cædmon manuscripts of Anglo-Saxon biblical poetry, Junius XI in the Bodleian Library. 1927.
Allegory and mysticism in Shakespeare: reports of three lectures. 1931 (priv ptd).
Gollancz was general editor of the following publishers' sers: The Temple Shakespeare, The Temple Classics, The King's Classics, The King's Novels, The Shakespeare Library. For memoir, see F. G. Kenyon, Proc Br Acad 18 1932.

Alexander Balloch Grosart 1835–99

Series of reprints

The Fuller worthies library. 39 vols Edinburgh and Blackburn 1868–76 (priv ptd). Works of Sir John Davies, Fulke Greville, Henry Vaughan, Marvell, George Herbert; poems of Fuller, Crashaw, Donne, Southwell, Sidney et al.
Miscellanies of the Fuller worthies library. 4 vols Blackburn 1870–6 (priv ptd). Works of minor 16th- and 17th-century writers.
Occasional issues of unique and very rare books. 18 vols 1875–83 (priv ptd). 16th- and 17th-century rarities such as Robert Dover's Annalia Dubrensia, Robert Chester's Love's martyr, Willobie his Avisa etc.
The Chertsey worthies library, edited with memorial-introductions, notes, illustrations and facsimiles. 14 vols [Blackburn] 1876–80 (priv ptd). Works of Nicholas Breton, John Davies of Hereford, Joshua Sylvester, Francis Quarles, Joseph Beaumont, Henry More, Cowley.
Early English poets, edited with memorial-introductions and notes. 9 vols 1876–7 (priv ptd). Herrick, Sidney, Giles Fletcher, John Davies of Hereford.
The Huth library: or Elizabethan-Jacobean unique or very rare books, largely from the library of Henry Huth, edited with notes, introductions and illustrations. 29 vols 1881–6 (priv ptd). Works of Greene, Nashe, Gabriel Harvey, and Dekker's prose works.
Grosart also issued The complete works of Edmund Spenser, 9 vols 1882–4 (priv ptd) *(with contributions by E. Dowden, F. T. Palgrave et al),* The complete works of Samuel Daniel, 5 vols 1885–96 (priv ptd), The poetical works of George Herbert, 1891 (Aldine), *edns for Camden Soc, Roxburghe Club and Chetham Soc, and numerous other reprints including a number of 17th-century Puritan divines.*

Writings

Hymns. Liverpool 1868 (priv ptd).
Songs of the day and night: or three centuries of original hymns. Edinburgh 1890 (priv ptd), 1891.
Robert Ferguson. 1898.
Also numerous theological works, contributions to A. H. Miles, The poets and the poetry of the century 1891–7, *and many articles in periodicals, etc. For an appreciation, see* O. Smeaton, A great Elizabethan, Westminster Rev 151 1899.

Edwin Guest 1800–80

A history of English rhythms. 2 vols 1838. 2nd edn ed W. W. Skeat, 1882.
On English pronouns personal. Proc Philological Soc 1844.
Guest also wrote extensively on Romano-British history and pbd numerous articles in Trans of the Philological Soc.

John Wesley Hales 1836–1914

Notes and essays on Shakespeare. 1884.
Folia litteraria: essays and notes on English literature. 1893.

Contributions to collaborative works

The teaching of English. In F. W. Farrar, Essays on a liberal education, 1867.

Contributions to periodicals

English dialects. Good Words 1867.
The study of the English language. Macmillan's Mag 15, Apr 1867.
Old English metrical romance. Fraser's Mag 92, Sep 1875.
Illustrations of Shakespeare's language. Antiquary 1884.
Hales also pbd edns of Bishop Percy's Folio ms with F. J. Furnivall, Milton's Areopagitica, *and various works by Goldsmith, Gray, Johnson, Spenser and Malory. He was general editor of the* Handbooks of English Literature ser 1895–1903.

Fitz-Edward Hall 1825–1901

Recent examples of false philology. New York 1872.
Modern English. 1873.
The English adjectives in -able, with special reference to reliable. 1877.
Doctor indoctus: some strictures on Professor John Nichol of Glasgow. 1880.

Contributions to periodicals

English rational and irrational. Nineteenth Cent 8, Sep 1880.

The English Philological Society's dictionary. Nation 1880.
On some points of usage in English. Amer Jnl of Philology 1882.
A brace of whims. Nation 1894.
A nice point of biblical English. Nation 1894.
Hall also wrote on Indian literature and philosophy and edited the works of Sir David Lindsay (with J. A. Murray, 1865–9) and William Lauder (with F. J. Furnivall, 1864–70) for the EETS.

James Orchard Halliwell, later Halliwell-Phillipps 1820–89

§1

Shakesperiana: a catalogue of the early editions of Shakespeare's plays and of the commentaries and other publications illustrative of his works. 1841.
A dictionary of archaic and provincial words, obsolete phrases, proverbs and ancient customs from the fourteenth century. 2 vols 1846–7, 6 edns by 1904.
The life of William Shakespeare; including many particulars respecting the poet and his family never before published. 1848.
Contributions to early English literature derived chiefly from rare books and ancient inedited manuscripts from the fifteenth to the seventeenth century. 6 pts 1849.
A new boke about Shakespeare and Stratford-on-Avon. 1850.
Observations on the Shakespeare forgeries at Bridgewater House, illustrative of a facsimile of the spurious letter of H. S. 1853 (priv ptd). On the John Payne Collier controversy.
A brief hand-list of books, manuscripts etc illustrative of the life and writings of Shakespeare, collected between the years 1842 and 1859. 1859 (priv ptd).
A dictionary of old English plays, existing either in print or in manuscript, from the earliest times to the close of the seventeenth century. 1860.
A brief hand-list of the records belonging to the Borough of Stratford-on-Avon showing their general character; with notes of a few of the Shakespearian documents in the same collection. 1862 (priv ptd).
A hand-list of upwards of a thousand volumes of Shakesperiana added to the three previous collections of a similar kind. 1862 (priv ptd).
A descriptive calendar of the ancient manuscripts and records in the possession of the corporation of Stratford-on-Avon; including notices of Shakespeare and his family, and of several persons connected with the poet. 1863 (priv ptd).
Illustrations of the life of Shakespeare in a discursive series of essays. 1874.
New lamps or old? a few additional words respecting the E and the A in the name of our national dramatist. Brighton 1880. Favours the spelling 'Shakespeare'.
Outlines of the life of Shakespeare. Brighton 1881 (priv ptd), 1882 (tripled in size), 2 vols 1887 (7th edn, enlarged). A different work from the Life of Shakespeare, above.
A calendar of the Shakespearean rarities, drawings and engravings, preserved at Hollingbury Copse. 1887 (priv ptd); ed E. E. Baker 1891 (enlarged).
Halliwell pbd many other bks and pamphlets, many of them in very small limited edns, dealing with Shakespearian topography, history, iconography, etc; with 16th- and 17th-century literature and earlier literature; also catalogues, inventories, etc.

Editions

The voiage and travaile of Sir John Maundevile, kt, reprinted from the edition of 1725, with an introduction, additional notes and glossary. 1839.
The harrowing of Hell: a miracle play, written in the reign of Edward the second, now first published from the original manuscript in the British Museum, with an introduction, translation and notes. 1840.
The first sketch of the Merry wives of Windsor. 1842 (Shakespeare Soc).
The nursery rhymes of England, obtained principally from oral tradition. 1842, 1843 (with addns), 1846 (4th edn, with addns) (Percy Soc).
Private diary of John Dee, and the catalogue of his library of manuscripts. 1842 (Camden Soc).
Nugae poeticae: select pieces of old English popular poetry, illustrating the manners and arts of the fifteenth century. 1844.
The Thornton romances: the early English metrical romances of Perceval, Isumbras, Eglamor and Degrevant, selected from manuscripts at Lincoln and Cambridge. 1844 (Camden Soc).
Letters of the kings of England, now first collected from the originals, edited, with an historical introduction and notes. 2 vols 1846.
Morte Arthure: the alliterative romance of the death of King Arthur, now first printed from a manuscript in Lincoln Cathedral. 1847.
The poetry of witchcraft illustrated by copies of the plays on the Lancashire witches by Heywood, [Brome] and Shadwell. 1853 (priv ptd).
The works of William Shakespeare: the text formed from a new collation of the early editions; to which are added all the original novels and tales on which the plays are founded, copious archaeological annotations on each play; an essay on the formation of the text; and a life of the poet. 16 vols 1853–65 (150 copies ptd for the editor).
A glossary or collection of words, phrases, names and allusions to customs, proverbs etc which have been thought to require illustration in the works of the English authors, particularly Shakespeare and his contemporaries, by Robert Nares: a new edition, with considerable additions. 2 vols 1859. With Thomas Wright.
A treatyse of a galaunt; with the maryage of the fayre Pusell, the bosse of Byllyngesgate unto London Stone, from the unique edition printed by Wynkyn de Worde. 1860 (priv ptd).
Shakespearian facsimiles: a collection of curious and interesting documents, plans, signatures & illustrative of the biography of Shakespeare and the history of his family, from the originals chiefly preserved at Stratford-on-Avon, facsimiled by E. W. Ashbee, selected by Halliwell. 1863 (priv ptd).
Stratford-upon-Avon in the times of the Shakespeares, illustrated by extracts from the Council books of the Corporation, selected especially with reference to the history of the poet's father. 1864–5.
Those songs and poems from the excessively rare first edition of England's Helicon, 1600, which are connected with the works of Shakespeare. 1865 (25 copies).
Halliwell edited some 150 works, mainly but not entirely in 17th-century literature, and did much work for the Camden, Percy and Shakespeare Socs. In 1841–2, with Thomas Wright, he edited Archaeologist *and* Jnl of Antiquarian Science, *of which only 10 issues appeared.*

§2

Winsor, J. Halliwelliana: a bibliography of the publications of James Orchard Halliwell-Phillipps. Cambridge MA 1881.
Wright, G. R. A brief memoir of the late Halliwell-Phillipps. 1889.
Obituary. Athenaeum 12 Jan 1889.

Nicholas Esterhazy Stephen Armitage Hamilton d. 1915

An inquiry into the corrections on Mr J. Payne Collier's Annotated Shakspere folio, 1632; and of certain documents likewise published by Mr Collier. 1860.

Hamilton also compiled a dictionary of English, French and German (1853), the National gazetteer of Great Britain and Ireland (1860), *and edited various medieval materials.*

Sir Thomas Duffus Hardy 1804–78

A review of the present state of the Shakespearian controversy. 1860.
Hardy edited numerous works for the Record Commission and wrote on medieval administrative documents and processes.

Joseph Haslewood 1769–1833

Editions

The book containing the treatises of hawking, hunting, coat-armour, fishing and blasing of arms [by Juliana Berners]. 1810.
Ancient critical essays upon English poets and poësy. 2 vols 1811–15.
The first [and second] tome of the palace of pleasure [by William Painter]. 2 vols 1813.
Mirror for magistrates; collated with various editions. 2 vols 1815.
Barnabae itinerarium: or Barnabee's journal [by Richard Brathwait]. 1818, 2 vols 1820 (enlarged).
Also various rarities for the Roxburghe Club, etc.

Miscellaneous writings

Some account of the life and publications of the late Joseph Ritson. 1824.
Roxburghe revels and other relative papers, including answers to the attack on the memory of the late Joseph Haslewood, with specimens of his literary productions. Ed J. Maidment, Edinburgh 1873 (priv ptd).
Haslewood also contributed largely to GM, *to* S. E. Brydges, Censura literaria, 1807–9, *and to* Bibliographer 1810–14.

William Carew Hazlitt 1834–1913

The history of the origin and rise of the Republic of Venice. 2 vols 1858, 1860 (enlarged).
Hand-book to the popular, poetical and dramatic literature of Great Britain, from the invention of printing to the Restoration. 1867.
Memoirs of William Hazlitt, with portions of his correspondence. 2 vols 1867.
Collections and notes. 4 ser and suppls 1876–1903. Catalogues of early English writings; general index by G. J. Gray 1893.
Schools, school-books and schoolmasters: a contribution to the history of educational development in Great Britain. 1888.
The livery companies of the City of London. 1892.
A manual for the collector and amateur of old English plays. 1892.
The coinage of the European continent. 2 vols 1893–7.
The coin collector. 1896.
The confessions of a collector. 1897.
Four generations of literary family: the Hazlitts 1725–1896. 2 vols 1897.
The Lambs: their lives, their friends and their correspondence. 1897.
Shakespeare. 1902, 1903 (rev), 1908 (recast and expanded).
The book-collector: a general survey of the pursuit. 1904.
The later Hazlitts. 1912 (priv ptd).
Hazlitt also pbd poems, essays, a novel, and several vols in H. B. Wheatley, The Book-lover's Lib 1886–1902.

Editions

Old English jest-books. 3 vols 1864.
The Roxburghe Library. 8 vols 1868–70. Includes inedited tracts illustrating the manners, opinions and occupations of Englishmen during the sixteenth and seventeenth centuries, 1867; The English drama and stage 1543–1664, illustrated by a series of documents, 1869.
English proverbs and proverbial phrases collected from the most authentic sources. 1869, 1882 (enlarged), 1907.
Warton, Thomas. History of English poetry, edited with new notes and other additions. 4 vols 1871.
Prefaces, dedications, epistles selected from early English books 1540–1701. [1874] (priv ptd).
Dodsley, Robert. A select collection of old English plays, revised and enlarged. 15 vols 1874–6.
Fairy tales, legends and romances, illustrating Shakespeare and other early English writers. 1875.
Poetical and dramatic works of Thomas Randolph, now first collected. 2 vols 1875.
Shakespeare's library: a collection of the novels, romances, poems and histories used by Shakespeare, second edition greatly enlarged. 6 vols 1875. 1st edn by J. P. Collier.
Letters of Charles Lamb: an entirely new edition. 2 vols 1886.
Lamb and Hazlitt: further letters and records. 1900.
Hazlitt's editorial works also included reprints of Herrick, Suckling, William Hazlitt (his grandfather), an anthology of early popular poetry of England, and a trn of Montaigne.

George Birkbeck Norman Hill 1835–1903

Dr Johnson, his friends and critics. 1878.
The life of Sir Rowland Hill. 2 vols 1880.
Footsteps of Dr Johnson (Scotland). 1890.
Writers and readers. 1892. 6 lectures: 1–4 on revolutions in literary taste; 5–6 on the study of literature as a part of education.
Harvard College, by an Oxonian. New York 1894.
Talks about autographs. Boston 1896. Reminiscences of Lamb, Arnold, Froude et al.
Letters written by a grandfather, selected by Lucy Crump. 1903.
Letters, arranged by Lucy Crump. 1906. Arranged to form a complete memoir.

Editions

Boswell's Life of Johnson, including Boswell's Journal of a tour to the Hebrides and Johnson's diary of a journey into North Wales. 6 vols Oxford 1887, 1934.
The history of Rasselas, Prince of Abyssinia. Oxford 1887.
Wit and wisdom of Samuel Johnson. Oxford 1888.
Letters of David Hume to William Strahan. Oxford 1888.
Goldsmith, The traveller. Oxford 1888.
Selected essays of Dr Johnson. 2 vols 1889.
Lord Chesterfield's Worldly wisdom: selections. Oxford 1891.
Letters of Dante Gabriel Rossetti to William Allingham. 1897.
Johnsonian miscellanies. 2 vols Oxford 1897.
Unpublished letters of Dean Swift. 1899.
The memoirs of the life of Edward Gibbon. 1900.
Lives of the English poets, by Samuel Johnson, edited by Hill, with brief memoir of Birkbeck Hill by Harold Spencer Scott. 3 vols Oxford 1905. Includes bibliography of Hill's writings.

Jennett Humphreys fl. 1880–1905

Contributions to periodicals

Among the dictionaries. Cornhill Mag 45, June 1881.
English: its ancestors, its progeny. Fraser's Mag 106, Oct 1882.
Dictionary making. Leisure Hour 1883.
Sir Thomas Bodley. Longman's Mag 33, Feb 1899.
Humphreys wrote many works in verse and prose for young children. She was an associate of J. A. H. Murray.

Joseph Hunter 1783–1861

Literary studies and editions

Who wrote Cavendish's Life of Wolsey? 1814, 1825.

Golden sentences [from Fuller, Sir Thomas Browne, Whichcote et al]. Bath 1826.
Life of Sir Thomas More by Cresacre More. 1828.
The diary of Ralph Thoresby. 2 vols 1830.
Boucher, J. Glossary of archaic and provincial words. 1832–3. Ed with Joseph Stevenson.
The Towneley mysteries. 1836 (Surtees Soc).
A disquisition on the scene, origin, date etc of Shakespeare's Tempest. 1839 (priv ptd).
The diary of Dr Thomas Cartwright. 1843 (Camden Soc).
New illustrations of the life, studies and writings of Shakespeare. 2 vols 1845.
Milton: a sheaf of gleanings after his biographers and annotators. 1850.
The great hero of the ancient minstrelsy of England, Robin Hood. 1852, Worksop 1883.
Pope: his descent and family connections. 1857.

Historical and antiquarian writings

Hallamshire: the history and topography of the parish of Sheffield. 1819.
South Yorkshire: the history and topography of the Deanery of Doncaster. 2 vols 1828–31.
The Hallamshire glossary. 1829.
English monastic libraries. 1831.
Gens Sylvestrina: memorials of some of my ancestors. 1846 (priv ptd).
Collections concerning the early history of the founders of New England. 1849.
Also edns of various rolls for the Public Records Commissioners. Hunter's contributions to Archaeologica *are listed in* Sylvester Hunter, A brief memoir of the late J. Hunter, 1861.

Clement Mansfield Ingleby 1823–86

The Shakespeare fabrications: or the manuscript notes of the Perkins folio shown to be of recent origin, with an appendix on the authorship of the Ireland forgeries. 1859. On the John Payne Collier controversy.
A complete view of the Shakespeare controversy, concerning the authenticity and genuineness of manuscript matter affecting the works and biography of Shakespeare, published by Mr J. Payne Collier as the fruits of his researches. 1861.
An introduction to metaphysics. 2 pts 1864–9.
Was Thomas Lodge an actor? An exposition touching the social status of the playwright in the time of Queen Elizabeth. 1868.
The still lion: an essay towards the restoration of Shakespeare's text, reprinted with additions from the second annual volume of the German Shakespeare Society. 1874, 1875 (enlarged as Shakespeare hermeneutics).
Shakespeare – the man and the book: being a collection of occasional papers on the bard and his writings. 2 pts 1877–81.
Shakespeare's bones: a proposal to disinter them, considered in relation to their possible bearing on his portraiture: illustrated by instances on visits of the living to the dead. 1883.
Essays by the late C. M. Ingleby, edited by his son [Holcombe Ingleby]. 1888.
Ingleby also pbd several shorter papers, mainly on Shakespeare, and a number of books on philosophy and logic.

Editions

Shakespeare allusion book, pt 1. 1874.
Shakespeare's Centurie of prayse: being materials for a history of opinion on Shakespeare and his works, culled from writers of the first century after his rise. 1874, 1879 (rev with addns for New Shakespeare Soc by L. T. Smith).
Shakespeare's Cymbeline: the text revised and annotated. 1886, 1889.

David Irving 1778–1860

The life of Robert Ferguson. Glasgow 1799.
Lives of Scottish authors, viz Fergusson, Falconer and Russell. Edinburgh 1801.
The elements of English composition. Edinburgh 1801, 11 edns by 1841.
The lives of the Scotish poets. 2 vols Edinburgh 1804, London 1810 (rev).
Memoirs of the life and writings of George Buchanan. Edinburgh 1807, 1817 (rev).
Observations on the study of civil law. Edinburgh 1815.
A catalogue of the law books in the Advocates' Library. Edinburgh 1831.
Lives of Scotish writers. 2 vols Edinburgh 1839. Rptd from Encyclopaedia Britannica 7th edn.
The history of Scottish poetry. Ed J. A. Carlyle, Edinburgh 1861. With memoir of Irving by David Laing.

Editions

The poetical works of R. Fergusson. Glasgow 1800.
Selden's table talk. 1819, 1854 (rev).
The poems of Alexander Montgomerie. Edinburgh 1821. With D. Laing.
The moral fables of Robert Henryson. Glasgow 1832 (Maitland Club).
Davidis Buchanani de scriptoribus scotis libri duo. Edinburgh 1837 (Bannatyne Club).
Also other works for the Maitland and Bannatyne Clubs. Irving contributed the article on the English language to the 7th edn of Encyclopaedia Britannica *(1842, rptd in the 8th edn 1860).*

John Jamieson 1759–1839

The use of sacred history. Edinburgh 1802, 2 vols Hartford 1810.
An etymological dictionary of the Scottish language. 2 vols Edinburgh 1808, 1818 (abridged by author), 1867 (rev by J. Longmuir), 4 vols Paisley 1879–87 (rev by J. Longmuir and D. Donaldson).
An historical account of the ancient culdees of Iona. Edinburgh 1811, Glasgow 1890.
Hermes Scythius: or the radical affinities of the Greek and Latin languages to the Gothic. Edinburgh 1814.
The Bruce [by Barbour] and Wallace [by Blind Harry]. 2 vols Edinburgh 1820.
Jamieson also pbd 3 long poems (1789–98), sermons and theological works.

Augustus Henry Keane 1833–1912

A handbook of the history of the English language. 1860, enlarged edn 1875.
Keane also wrote on geography, ethnology, history and anthropology.

Thomas Keightley 1789–1872

An account of the life, opinions and writings of John Milton with an introd to Paradise lost. 1855.
The Shakespeare expositor. 1867.

Editions

The poems of John Milton, with notes. 2 vols 1859.
The plays of William Shakespeare. 6 vols 1864, 4 vols 1892–4.
Keightley also wrote on classical literature, mythology and history.

John Mitchell Kemble 1807–57

History of the English language. First or Anglo-Saxon period. Cambridge 1834.
The names, surnames and nicnames of the Anglosaxons. 1846.

Contributions to periodicals

On Anglo-Saxon accents. GM 1835.
On the north Anglian dialect. Proc of the Philological Soc 1845–6.

Editions and translations

The Anglo-Saxon poems of Beowulf. 1833, 1835.
A translation of the Anglo-Saxon poem of Beowulf. 1837.
The poetry of the Codex Vercellensis, with an English translation. 1843 (Ælfric Soc).
Salomon and Saturn. 1845. All but 20 copies called in.
The dialogue of Salomon and Saturnus, with an historical introduction. 1848 (Ælfric Soc).
The Gospel according to Saint Matthew in Anglo-Saxon and Northumbrian. Cambridge 1858.
Kemble wrote or edited many other works of a historical and philological nature.

Charles Knight 1791–1873

Arminius, or the deliverance of Germany: a tragedy. Windsor 1814.
The bridal of the Isles: a mask. 1817 (2nd edn).
A glossary; the lives of Tasso and Fairfax. Prefixed to 5th edn of E. Fairfax's Tasso, 2 vols Windsor 1817.
The menageries: the quadruples. 3 vols 1829–40 (Soc for Diffusion of Useful Knowledge). Anon.
The working man's companion. Pt 1: The right of industry – capital and labour, 1831 (Soc for the Diffusion of Useful Knowledge) (2nd edn); pt 2: The results of machinery, namely cheap production and increased employment, 1831 (Soc for the Diffusion of Useful Knowledge). Anon.
Trades' unions and strikes. 1834. Anon.
The pictorial edition of the works of Shakspere. 7 vols [1839–]41, 5 vols 1867 (rev).
Shakspere and his writings. In Knight's Store of knowledge, 1841.
London. 6 vols 1841–4; rev E. Walford 6 vols [1875–7]. Ed Knight, and contains many articles by him.
William Shakspere: a biography. 1842, 1850 (as Studies and illustrations of Shakspere vol 1).
William Caxton: a biography. 1844.
Studies of Shakspere, forming a companion volume to every edition of the text. 1849. Rptd from Pictorial and Library edns.
Studies and illustrations of the writings of Shakspere. 3 vols 1850.
The struggle of a book against excessive taxation. [1850] (2nd edn).
Once upon a time. 2 vols 1854, 1859, 1865.
The English cyclopaedia. 22 vols 1854–70. With A. Ramsay and J. Thorne.
The old printer and the modern press. 1854. Partly based on biography of Caxton, 1844.
The popular history of England. 8 vols 1856–62.
Passages of a working life, with a prelude of early reminiscences. 3 vols 1864–5, 1873, 1874.
Shadows of old booksellers. 1865, 1905, 1927.
Begg'd at court: a legend of Westminster. 1867. A novel.
For life, see A. A. Clowes, Charles Knight: a sketch, 1892 (with bibliography). *Knight pbd many edns of Shakespeare, including a facs edn (1895), pbd and wrote some of* Knight's Weekly Vols, *pbd several cyclopaedias, and did much work for the Soc for the Diffusion of Useful Knowledge.*

David Laing 1793–1878

Select remains of the ancient popular poetry of Scotland. Edinburgh 1822; ed J. Small, Edinburgh 1885 (with a memoir of Laing).
Various pieces of fugitive Scottish poetry. 2 vols Edinburgh 1823–5.
Early Scottish metrical tales. Edinburgh 1826, Paisley 1889.
The poems of William Dunbar. 2 vols Edinburgh 1834. Suppl of selections from minor makars, 1865.
The letters and journals of Robert Abillie. 3 vols 1841–2 (Bannatyne Club).
The works of John Knox. 6 vols 1846–64 (Wodrow Soc and Bannatyne Club).
The poems and fables of Robert Henryson. Edinburgh 1865.
The poetical works of Sir David Lyndsay. 2 vols Edinburgh 1871, 3 vols Edinburgh 1879 (with bibliography).
In addition to over 100 papers in Proc Soc Antiquaries of Scotland, *and various antiquarian books and pams, Laing edited or assisted in editing many rarities (mainly Scottish) for the Abbotsford, Bannatyne, Hunterian and Spalding Clubs, and Shakespeare and Wodrow Socs, including 27 works for the Bannatyne Club alone. For details, see* T. G. Stevenson, Notices of David Laing with list of his publications, 1878 (priv ptd), *and* D. Murray, David Laing, antiquary and bibliographer, Scottish Historical Rev July 1914.

Robert Gordon Latham 1812–88

An address to the authors of England and America on the necessity and practicability of permanently remodelling their alphabet and orthography. Cambridge 1834.
An inaugural lecture delivered at University College, London, October 4th, 1839. 1840.
The English language. 1841.
An elementary English grammar. 1843.
First outlines of logic applied to grammar and etymology. 1847.
Elements of English grammar for the use of ladies schools. 1847.
The history and etymology of the English language for the use of classical schools. 1849.
A grammar of the English language for the use of commercial schools. 1850.
A handbook of the English language. 1851.
On the importance of the study of language as a branch of education for all classes. 1855.
A smaller English grammar for the use of schools. 1861.
Elements of comparative philology. 1862.
A defence of phonetic spelling. 1872.
Two dissertations on the Hamlet of Saxo Grammaticus and Shakespear. 1872.
Essential rules and principles for the study of English grammar. 1876.

Contributions to periodicals

The plot and dramatis personae of Shakespeare's Titus Andronicus. Fraser's Mag 82, Sep 1870.
Latham wrote many other works on ethnology and philology. He pbd an edition of Johnson's Dictionary *between 1866 and 1870.*

Sir Sidney Lee 1859–1926

§1

Stratford-on-Avon, from the earliest times to death of William Shakespeare. 1885, 1907.
The study of English literature: an address. 1893 (priv ptd).
A life of William Shakespeare. 1898, 1915 (rewritten and enlarged), 1925 (new preface).
Shakespeare's King Henry the Fifth: an account and an estimate. 1900, 1908.
Queen Victoria: a biography. 1902.
Great Englishmen of the sixteenth century. 1904. On Thomas More, Philip Sidney, Walter Ralegh, Spenser, Bacon, Shakespeare's career, foreign influences on Shakespeare.
Shakespeare and the modern stage, with other essays. 1906.
The French renaissance in England: an account of the literary relations of England and France in the sixteenth century. Oxford 1910.

Principles of biography: the Leslie Stephen lecture. Cambridge 1911.
The place of English literature in the modern university: a lecture. 1913.
King Edward VII: a biography. 2 vols 1925–7.
Elizabethan and other essays. Ed F. S. Boas, Oxford 1929 (with memoir).
Lee pbd other pams, mainly on Elizabethan topics. He contributed to CHEL, Cambridge Modern History, Year's Work in English Studies (1921–3), Trans New Shakespeare Soc *and other composite works.*

Editions

The boke of Duke of Huon of Burdeux, by Lord Berners. 4 pts 1882–7 (EETS).
The autobiography of Edward, Lord Herbert of Cherbury. 1886, 1906.
The dictionary of national biography, vol 27–end of suppl 2, 1891–1917. In addition to editing the Dictionary, Lee contributed 820 articles, exclusive of his work in the supplements.
Shakespeare's comedies, histories and tragedies: being a reproduction in facsimile of the first folio edition, with introduction and census of copies. Oxford 1902. Similar facs reprints of Pericles, Sonnets, Venus and Adonis, Lucrece, 1905. Census also pbd separately; Notes and additions to the census, 1906.
Elizabethan sonnets, with an introduction. 2 vols 1904. A rearrangement of parts of Arber's English garner.
Methuen's standard library. 40 vols 1905–6.
The works of William Shakespeare. 20 vols Cambridge MA 1907–10 (Caxton edn). General introd only by Lee.
The chronicle history of King Leir. 1909. With introd.
Shakespeare's England. 2 vols Oxford 1916. Planned and partly ed Lee.

§2

Pollard, A. F. Lee and the Dictionary of national biography. Bull Inst of Historical Research June 1926.
Harrison, G. B. Sir Sidney Lee. London Mercury June 1930.
Firth, C. H. Sir Sidney Lee. 1931.

Robert William Lowe fl. 1877–91

The fashionable tragedian. 1877. On Irving. Written with William Archer.
A bibliographical account of the English theatrical literature from the earliest times to the present day. 1888.
Thomas Betterton: a biography. 1891.
Lowe also edited Churchill's Rosciad *and* Apology, *Cibber's* Apology *and J. Doran's* Their Majesties' servants, *as well as a series of dramatic essays by Hazlitt, Hunt, Lewes, etc, with Archer.*

Samuel Lysons 1763–1819

Our vulgar tongue. 1868.
Lysons wrote extensively on theology, medieval history and the history of Gloucestershire.

George Campbell Macaulay 1852–1915

Francis Beaumont: a critical study. 1883.
The history of Herodotus, translated. 2 vols 1890.
Poems by Matthew Arnold, selected and edited. 1896, 1928.
The complete works of John Gower, edited from the manuscripts with introductions, notes and glossaries. 4 vols Oxford 1899–1902.
Gower: selections from Confessio amantis. Oxford 1903.
James Thomson. 1908 (EML).
Also German, Greek and Latin textbooks and edns of 4 of Tennyson's Idylls of the King *and of Lord Berners'* Froissart (Globe).

Sir Frederic Madden 1801–73

The ancient English romance of Havelok the Dane, accompanied by the French text; with an introduction, notes and a glossary. 1828 (Roxburghe Club).
Privy purse expenses of the Princess Mary, daughter of King Henry the eighth, afterwards Queen Mary, with a memoir of the Princess and notes. 1831.
The ancient English romance of William and the werewolf; edited, with an introduction and glossary. 1832 (Roxburghe Club). With 2 letters on werewolves by A. Herbert.
Illuminated ornaments, selected from manuscripts and early printed books from the sixth to the seventeenth centuries, drawn and engraved by H. Shaw; with descriptions by Madden. 1833.
The Olde English versions of the Gesta Romanorum, edited for the first time from manuscripts in the British Museum and University Library, Cambridge, with an introduction and notes. 1838 (Roxburghe Club).
Syr Gawayne: a collection of ancient romance-poems by Scottish and English authors, relating to that celebrated knight of the round table, with an introduction, notes and a glossary. 1839 (Bannatyne Club).
Lazamon's Brut, or chronicle of Britain: a poetical semi-Saxon paraphrase of the Brut of Wace, now first published from the Cottonian manuscripts in the British Museum; accompanied by a literal translation, notes and a grammatical glossary. 3 vols 1847 (Soc of Antiquaries).
The Holy Bible in the earliest English versions made from the Latin Vulgate by John Wycliffe and his followers; edited by the Rev Josiah Forshall and Madden. 4 vols Oxford 1850. Contains glossary, with 2 distinct texts throughout.
Universal palaeography: or facsimiles of writings of all periods and nations, by J. B. Silvestre; accompanied by an historical and descriptive text by Champollion-Figeac and A. Champollion, translated from the French, and edited, with corrections and notes. 2 vols 1850.
Matthei Parisiensis, Monach Sancti Albani, Historia Anglorum, sive, ut vulgo dicitur, historia minor: item, ejusdem abbreviato chronicorum Angliae. 3 vols 1866–9 (Rolls ser). To vol 3 is prefaced a life and criticism of Matthew Paris.
Madden was Keeper of mss at the BM from 1837, and produced various guides and catalogues for that department; his other edns included one of Warton's History of English poetry.

James Maidment 1795?–1879

A north countrie garland. Edinburgh 1824 (anon); ed T. G. Stevenson, Edinburgh 1868.
A [second; third] book of Scottish pasquils. 3 pts Edinburgh 1827–8, Edinburgh 1868 (enlarged).
Reliquiae Scoticae: Scotish remains in prose and verse. Edinburgh 1829. With R. Pitcairn.
Analecta Scotica: collections illustrative of the civil, ecclesiastical and literary history of Scotland. 2 vols Edinburgh 1834–7.
Fragmenta Scoto-dramatica 1715–58. Edinburgh 1835.
Bannatyniana: notices relative to the Bannatyne Club, including critiques on some of its publications. Edinburgh 1836.
Scotish elegiac verses on the principal nobility and gentry from 1629–1729. Edinburgh 1842.
A new book of old ballads. Edinburgh 1844; ed T. G. Stevenson, Edinburgh 1868, 1885.
Scotish ballads and songs. Edinburgh 1859, 1868.
Dramatists of the Restoration. 14 vols Edinburgh 1872–9. With W. H. Logan.
Maidment also pbd much, mainly Scottish antiquities, for the Abbotsford, Bannatyne, Hunterian and Maitland Clubs and the Spottiswoode Soc. For

details, see T. G. Stevenson, A bibliographical list of the various publications by James Maidment from 1817 to 1878, Edinburgh 1883.

George Perkins Marsh 1801–82

Lectures on the English language. New York 1860.
The origins and history of the English language and the early literature it embodies. 1862.

Contributions to periodicals
Notes on Mr Hensleigh Wedgwood's dictionary of English etymology. Trans of the Philological Soc 1865.
Old English literature. Nation 1865.
Notes on the new edition of Webster's dictionary. Nation 1866–7.
Marsh translated Rask's Old Icelandic grammar. *He wrote on history, geography and American affairs. A number of his speeches to the House of Representatives were printed.*

John Miller Dow Meiklejohn 1836–1902

An easy grammar for beginners. 1864.
The standard grammar. Edinburgh 1882.
The English language. Its grammar, history and literature. 1886.
A new grammar of the English tongue. 1887.
A short grammar of the English tongue with 300 exercises. 1890.
The book of the English language. 1891.

Contributions to periodicals
Plain English. All the Year Round 1868.
Meiklejohn also edited Chaucer and Shakespeare and wrote textbooks on geography. He translated Kant's Critique of pure reason (1862).

George Washington Moon 1823–1909

A defence of the Queen's English. In reply to 'a plea for the Queen's English' by the Dean of Canterbury. 2 pts 1863; 2nd edn as The Dean's English: a criticism of the Dean of Canterbury's essays on the Queen's English, 1864.
The bad English of Lindley Murray and other writers. 1868.
Common errors in spelling and writing. 1875.
Bad English exposed: a series of criticisms on the errors of Lindley Murray and other grammarians. 1876.
The King's English. 1881.
The reviser's English. 1882–6.
The Bishop's English. 2nd edn 1904.
Moon wrote a novel, poetry and numerous works on art and theology as well as a tract on shortcomings in semaphore and the morse code.

Richard Morris 1833–94

The etymology of local names. Pt 1 (all pbd) 1857.
Historical outlines of English accidence, comprising chapters on the history and development of the language, and on word-formation. 1872; rev H. Bradley 1893.
Elementary lessons in historical English grammar. 1874; rev H. Bradley 1897.
English grammar. 1875. One of J. R. Green's Literature primers.
Notes and queries [on Pali lexicography]. [1887].
Also minor philological writings.

Editions
Roll's Pricke of conscience. 1863.
Early English alliterative poems of the West Midlands dialect of the fourteenth century. 1864 (EETS), 1934.
Sir Gawayne and the Green Knight: an alliterative romance-poem. 1864 (EETS), 1925.
The story of Genesis and Exodus: an Early English song. 1865 (EETS), 1895.
Dan Michel's Ayenbite of Inwyt: or remorse of conscience. 1866 (EETS).
Specimens of early English AD 1250–AD 1400, with grammatical introduction, notes and glossary. Oxford 1867; rev W. W. Skeat, Oxford 1872.
Old English homilies and homiletic treatises of the twelfth and thirteenth centuries. EETS 2 ser 1868–73.
Chaucer's translation of Boethius's De consolatione philosophiae. 1868 (EETS), 1886.
Legends of the Holy Rood; symbols of the Passion and crosspoems. In Old English of the eleventh, fourteenth and fifteenth centuries, 1871 (EETS).
An Old English miscellany: containing a bestiary, Kentish sermons, Proverbs of Alfred, religious poems of the thirteenth century. 1872 (EETS).
Cursor mundi: the cursur of the world – a Northumbrian poem of the XIVth century in four versions. 6 pts 1874–93 (EETS).
The Blickling homilies of the tenth century. 3 pts [1874–80] (EETS).
Morris's other editorial work included the Aldine Chaucer (1866), and the Globe Spenser (1869).

Sir James Augustus Henry Murray 1837–1915

Outline of English language and literature. 1858 (priv ptd).

Editions
Sir David Lindesay's works: the minor poems. 1863 (EETS).
The complaynt of Scotlande, vyth ane exortatione to the thre estaits to be vigilante in the deffens of their public veil. 1872 (EETS).
The romance and prophecies of Thomas of Erceldoune, with illustrations from the prophetic literature of the 15th and 16th centuries. 1875 (EETS).
A new English dictionary on historical principles, founded mainly on materials collected by the Philological Society. 11 vols Oxford 1884–1933, 13 vols Oxford 1933 (a corrected re-issue, with introd, suppl and bibliography, as The Oxford English dictionary). Murray was chief of the NED, though his actual editorial responsibility covered only A–D, H–K, O, P and T.

Writings
The dialect of the southern counties of Scotland: its pronunciation, grammar and historical relations, with an appendix and a linguistical map of Scotland. 1873 (Philological Soc).
The Romanes lecture 1900: the evolution of English lexicography. Oxford 1900.

Contributions to periodicals
The Rushworth glosses. Academy 1874.
Old English verbs in -cgan and their subsequent history. Trans of the Philological Soc 1882–4.
The English diphthong -ay. Academy 1890.
Also a book on Orkney. For an appreciation, see H. Bradley, Sir James Murray, Proc Br Acad 8 1919 *and S. Baldwin,* The Oxford English Dictionary 1884–1928; an address, [1928] *and K. M. E. Murray,* Caught in the web of words: James Murray and the Oxford English Dictionary, *Oxford 1979.*

Murray contributed some of the notes to Zupitza's EETS edn of Guy of Warwick. *He was one of the founding members of the Hawick Archaeological Soc. His earliest lectures on philology are recorded in the Soc's minute book and were summarised in the* Hawick Advertiser. *He also contributed the article on the English language to the 9th edn (1879) of the* Encyclopaedia Britannica *(rptd with revisions in the 11th edn, 1910).*

Robert Nares 1753–1829

Elements of Orthoepy, containing the whole analogy of the English language so far as it relates to pronunciation, accent and quantity. 1784, 1792 (as General rules for the pronunciation of the English language).

The British critic: a new review. May 1793–Oct 1826. Vols 1–42 ed Nares and William Beloe.

A new and general biographical dictionary. 15 vols 1798–1810. In this 3rd edn vols 6, 8, 10, 12 and 14 were ed Nares.

Essays and other occasional compositions. 2 vols 1810.

A glossary, or collection of words, phrases, names and allusions to customs, proverbs etc which have been thought to require illustrations in the works of English authors, particularly Shakespeare and his contemporaries. 1822, 1825; rev J. O. Halliwell and T. Wright 2 vols 1859, 1882, 1905. For an appreciation, *see* A book of words, TLS 1 June 1922.

Nares also pbd sermons and theological and miscellaneous works.

Sir Nicholas Harris Nicolas 1799–1848

Life of William Davison, secretary of state to Queen Elizabeth. 1823.

The history of the battle of Agincourt. 2 pts 1827, 1832.

History of the orders of knighthood of the British Empire. 4 vols 1841–2.

A history of the Royal Navy. 2 vols 1847.

Memoirs of the life and times of Sir Christopher Hatton. 1847.

Also antiquarian and heraldic works. Nicolas was a frequent contributor to GM *and* Archaeologia.

Editions

The literary remains of Lady Jane Grey. 1825.

The poetical rhapsody of Francis Davison. 2 vols 1826.

Private memoirs of Sir Kenelm Digby. 1827.

The retrospective review: second ser. 1827–8. With H. Southern.

The letters of Joseph Ritson. 2 vols 1833. Includes memoir of Ritson by Nicolas.

The complete angler of Izaak Walton and Charles Cotton. 2 vols 1836.

In addition to various antiquarian edns and reprints, Nicolas was responsible for the Aldine edns of Burns, Chaucer, Collins, Cowper, Surrey and Wyatt, Thomson and Kirke White.

Thomas Park 1759–1834

Sonnets and other small poems. 1797.

Cupid turned volunteer; in a series of prints designed by the Princess Elizabeth, with poetical illustrations by Thomas Park. 1804.

Nugae modernae: morning thoughts and midnight musings in prose and verse. 1818.

Park also contributed to several of the literary and antiquarian works of Sir S. E. Brydges, G. Ellis, J. Nichols, J. Ritson, G. Steevens et al.

Editions and revisions

The works of the British poets, collated with the best editions. 42 vols 1805–8; suppl 6 vols 1809.

Heliconia: comprising a collection of English poetry of the Elizabethan age 1575–1604. 3 vols 1815.

Facetiae: musarum deliciae. 1817. With E. Dubois.

Park also re-edited Sir John Harington, Nugae antiquae, 2 vols 1804; Horace Walpole, A catalogue of royal and noble authors, 5 vols 1806; The Harleian miscellany, 10 vols 1808–13; Thomas Percy, Reliques of ancient English poetry, 3 vols 1812; Joseph Ritson, A select collection of English songs, 3 vols 1813 (2nd edn). *The BM possesses a number of his annotated bks.*

John Plant fl. 1863–83

Early English. Proc of the Manchester Literary Club 1873–4.

Plant pbd catalogues of the lib of the Manchester Geological Soc, the Salford Free Museum and of the paintings in the Salford Royal Museum and Gallery where he was curator.

Samuel Weller Singer 1783–1858

Researches into the history of playing cards, with illustrations of the origin of printing and engraving on wood. 1816.

Remarks on the glossary to the antient metrical romance of Havelok the Dane. In a letter addressed to Francis Douce 1829.

The text of Shakespeare vindicated from the interpolations and corruptions advocated by J. P. Collier. 1853.

Editions

Shakespeare's jest book. 3 pts 1814–15.

Diana: or the sonnets of H[enry] C[onstable]. 1818 (facs).

Anecdotes, observations and characters of books and men, by Joseph Spence. 1820.

The British poets. 100 vols Chiswick 1822. Many of the preliminary notices by Singer.

The dramatic works of William Shakespeare. 10 vols 1826, 4 edns by 1875.

Singer also issued edns and reprints of the poems of Chalkhill, Chapman, Fairfax, Griffin, Herrick, Lodge, Lovelace, Marlowe and Marmion, as well as Bacon's Essays, *Cavendish's* Life of Wolsey, *Selden's* Table-talk, *and some French and Italian rarities, etc.*

Walter William Skeat 1835–1912

Editions

The vision of William concerning Piers Plowman. 4 pts 1867–85. (EETS).

The Bruce, by John Barbour. EETS 4 pts 1870–89.

The Holy Gospels in Anglo-Saxon, Northumbrian and Old Mercian versions. 4 pts Cambridge 1871–87.

The poetical works of Thomas Chatterton. 1871, 1891.

Ælfric's Lives of the Saints. 2 pts 1881–1900 (EETS).

Wulfila's The gospel of Saint Mark. 1882.

Specimens of early English. 3 vols Oxford 1882. With R. Morris.

The Kingis quair. 1884, 1911 (Scottish Text Soc).

Twelve facsimiles of old English manuscripts. 1892.

The complete works of Geoffrey Chaucer. 7 vols Oxford 1894–7.

The student's Chaucer. Oxford 1895.

Skeat also edited many other early English texts, mainly for the Chaucer Soc, EETS, Scottish Text Soc, and English Dialect Soc, which he founded.

Dictionaries and philological works

A Mœso-Gothic glossary. 1868.

Questions for examination in English literature: with an introduction on the study of English. Cambridge 1873.

Glossaries of English dialects. 1876.

An etymological dictionary of the English language, arranged on an historical basis. Oxford 1882, 1884 (corrected), 4 edns by 1910.

A concise etymological dictionary of the English language. Oxford 1882, 1886 (rev), 6 edns by 1936.

Principles of English etymology. First series, The native element. Oxford 1887, 2nd edn 1892. A second series, The foreign element, was pbd in 1891.

A concise dictionary of Middle English. 1888. With A. L. Mayhew.

A primer of English etymology. Oxford 1892, 6 edns by 1920.

A student's pastime. Oxford 1896. Articles from N & Q, including Skeat's autobiography.

Notes on English etymology, chiefly reprinted from the transactions of the Philological Society. Oxford 1901.

A primer of classical and English philology. Oxford 1905.

The science of etymology. Oxford 1912.

English dialects from the 8th century to the present day. Cambridge 1912.

Contributions to periodicals

On the study of Anglo-Saxon. Macmillan's Mag 39, Feb 1879.
The proverbs of Alfred. Trans of the Philological Soc 1895–8.
Skeat also pbd pamphlets on spelling-reform, place-names etc.

Lucy Toulmin Smith 1838–1911

The Maire of Bristowe is Kalendar, by Robert Ricart. 1872 (Camden Soc).
Gorboduc, or Ferrex and Porrex: a tragedy by Thomas Norton and Thomas Sackville, edited. Heilbronn 1883.
The forthcoming English dictionary. Academy 1883.
York plays: the plays performed by the crafts or mysteries, edited with introduction and glossary. Oxford 1885.
A common-place book of the fifteenth century, edited with notes. 1886.
A manual of the English grammar and language. [1886].
Les contes moralisés de Nicole Bozon. Paris 1889 (Société des Anciens Textes Français). With P. Meyer.
Expeditions to Prussia and the Holy Land made by Henry, Earl of Derby, afterwards King Henry IV. 1894 (Camden Soc).
The itinerary of John Leland, with an appendix of extracts from Leland's Collectanea. 5 vols 1906–10.
Lucy Toulmin Smith also contributed to The Shakespeare allusion book *prepared by the New Shakespeare Soc, and translated* J. J. Jusserand, English wayfaring life.

Henry Sweet 1845–1912

Readers and editions

King Alfred's West-Saxon version of Gregory's Pastoral care. 2 pts 1871–2 (EETS).
An Anglo-Saxon reader in prose and verse, with grammatical introduction, notes and glossary. Oxford 1876, 8 edns by 1908 (rev C. T. Onions 1922).
The Epinal glossary, edited with transliteration. 1883.
King Alfred's Orosius. 1883 (EETS); [extracts] Oxford 1885.
Ælfric, grammaticus, Abbot of Eynsham: selected homilies. Oxford 1885.
The oldest English texts. 1885 (EETS).
A second Anglo-Saxon reader, archaic and dialectal. Oxford 1887.

Primers and miscellaneous writings

A history of English sounds. 1874 (English Dialect Soc). Rptd from Trans of the Philological Soc 1873–4.
A handbook of phonetics. Oxford 1877.
An Anglo-Saxon primer, with grammar, notes and glossary. Oxford 1882, 8 edns to 1896, 1953 (rev).
First Middle English primer: extracts from the Ancren Riwle and Ormulum; with grammar and glossary. Oxford 1884.
Elementarbuch des gesprochenen Englisch: Grammatik, Texte und Glossen. Oxford 1885; tr Oxford 1890 (as A primer of spoken English).
An Icelandic primer, with grammar, notes and glossary. Oxford 1886.
Second Middle English primer: extracts from Chaucer, with grammar and glossary. Oxford 1886.
A history of English sounds from the earliest period, with full word-lists. Oxford 1888.
A primer of phonetics. Oxford 1890, 4 edns by 1932.
A manual of current shorthand. Oxford 1892.
A new English grammar, logical and historical. 2 pts Oxford 1892–8.
A short historical English grammar. Oxford 1892.
A primer of historical English grammar. Oxford 1893.
First steps in Anglo-Saxon. Oxford 1897.
The student's dictionary of Anglo-Saxon. Oxford 1897.
The practical study of languages. 1899.
The history of language. 1900.
The sounds of English: an introduction to phonetics. Oxford 1908.
Collected papers, arranged by H. C. K. Wyld. Oxford 1913. Includes Words, logic and grammar; The practical study of language; Linguistic affinity; Progress of linguistic science (5 papers); History of English (4 papers); Shelley's nature-poetry; Phonetics and accounts of living languages (6 papers). Many rptd from Trans of the Philological Soc.

William John Thoms 1825–1910

The book of the court, exhibiting the origin, peculiar duties, and privileges of the several ranks of the nobility and gentry, more particularly of the great officers of state and members of the royal household. 1838, 1844.
Three notelets on Shakespeare: 1, Shakespeare in Germany; 2, Folk-lore of Shakespeare; 3, Was Shakespeare ever a soldier? 1865.
Hannah Lightfoot; Queen Charlotte and the Chevalier d'Eon; Dr Wilmot's Polish progress; Lord Chatham and the Princess Olive. 1867. Rptd with addns from N & Q.
Human longevity: its facts and fictions, including an inquiry into some of the more remarkable examples. 1873.

Editions

A collection of early prose romances. 3 vols 1827–8, 1858 (enlarged as Early English prose romances), 1904.
Lays and legends of various nations; illustrative of their traditions, popular literature, manners, customs and superstitions. 2 sers 1834. Ser 1 France, Spain, Tartary and Ireland; ser 2 Germany.
Anecdotes and traditions illustrative of early English history and literature from manuscript sources. 1839 (Camden Soc).
The history of Reynard the fox, from the edition printed by Caxton in 1481, with notes and an introductory sketch of the literary history of the romance. 1844 (Percy Soc).
Gammer Gurton's famous histories of Sir Guy of Warwick, Sir Bevis of Hampton, Tom Hickathrift, Friar Bacon, Robin Hood and the King and the cobbler, newly revised and amended by Ambrose Merton, Gent, FSA. [1846]. 'Merton' is Thoms.
Gammer Gurton's pleasant stories of Patient Grissel, the Princess Rosetta and Robin Goodfellow; and ballads of The beggar's daughter, The babes in the wood, and Fair Rosamund, newly revised and amended by Ambrose Merton, Gent, FSA. [1846].
Notes and Queries. Vol 1, no 1, 3 Nov 1849–Sep 1872. Planned and founded by Thoms, who had previously begun a similar series in Athenaeum 26 Aug 1846.
Thoms also pbd or edited various other papers, and translated J. J. A. Worsaal, Primeval antiquities of Denmark *from the Danish; he was Secretary of the Camden Soc 1838–73.*

Benjamin Thorpe 1782–1870

Cædmon's metrical paraphrase of parts of the Holy Scriptures, in Anglo-Saxon. 1832 (Soc of Antiquaries) (with trn).
The Anglo-Saxon version of the story of Apollonius of Tyre. 1834 (with trn).
Analecta Anglo-Saxonica: a selection in prose and verse from Anglo-Saxon authors. Oxford 1834, 1846 (corrected).
Libri psalmorum versio antiqua Latina cum paraphrasi Anglo-Saxonica. Oxford 1835. Also ptd in Appendix B to Cooper's report on Rymer's Foedera, 1835.
Ancient laws and institutes of England. 2 vols 1840.
Codex Exoniensis: a collection of Anglo-Saxon poetry. 1842 (Soc of Antiquaries) (with trn).
Da halgan godspel on Englisc. Oxford 1842, 1846, 1851.

The homilies of the Anglo-Saxon Church. 2 vols 1844–6 (Ælfric Soc) (with trn).
Florence of Worcester's chronicle. 2 vols 1848–9.
Northern mythology, comprising the principal traditions of Scandinavia, North Germany and the Netherlands. 3 vols 1851.
Yule tide stories: a collection of Scandinavian tales. 1853, 1888.
The Anglo-Saxon poems of Beowulf, the scöp or gleeman's tale, and the fight of Finnesburg, with a literal translation, notes and glossary. Oxford 1855.
The Anglo-Saxon chronicle. 2 vols 1861 (Rolls ser) (with trns).
Diplomatarium Anglicum aevi Saxonici: a collection of English charters. 1865.
Edda Sæmundar from the Old Norse. 2 pts 1866.
Thorpe also issued trns of Rask's Anglo-Saxon grammar, 1830, 1865, 1879; *Lappenberg's* A history of England under the Anglo-Saxon Kings, 2 vols 1845, *and* A history of England under the Norman Kings, 1857; *and Pauli's* Life of King Alfred, 1853 *(which includes Thorpe's own version of Alfred's* Orosius*).*

Henry John Todd 1763–1845

Some account of the Deans of Canterbury. Canterbury 1793.
A vindication of our authorized translation and translators of the Bible. 1819.
Memoirs of the life and writings of Bishop Brian Walton. 2 vols 1821.
The life of Archbishop Cranmer. 2 vols 1831.
Todd also pbd catalogues and minor theological works.

Editions
Comus: a mask by John Milton, with preliminary illustrations. 1798.
The poetical works of John Milton, with the principal notes of various commentators. 6 vols 1801, 1809, 1826. Vol 1 was also issued separately as An account of the life and writings of John Milton.
The works of Edmund Spenser, with the principal notes of the various commentators. 5 vols 1805, 1850.
Illustrations of the lives and writings of Gower and Chaucer. 1810.
Johnson's dictionary of the English language, with numerous corrections and additions. 4 vols 1818, 5 edns by 1839.
Cranmer's Defence of the true and Catholick doctrine of the Sacrament. 1825.
Selections from the metrical paraphrases on the Psalms by George Sandys. 1839.

Duncan Crookes Tovey 1842–1912

Gray and his friends. Cambridge 1890. Letters.
The poetical works of James Thomson. 1897. With memoir.
Reviews and essays in English literature. 1897. Teaching of English literature, More's Utopia, Fuller's Sermons, Letters of the Earl of Chesterfield, Arnold's Last essays, Waller, Gay, Ossian and his maker, Coventry Patmore, Elizabethan poetry, A Cambridge reminiscence (by M. T.).
Gray's English poems. 1898, 1922.
Verses. 1901.
The letters of Thomas Gray, including the correspondence of Gray and Masson. 3 vols 1909–12.

Richard Chenevix Trench 1807–86

On the study of words: five lectures. 1851. Many subsequent edns as Trench on words.
English, past and present: five lectures. 1855.
On teaching by words. 1855.
Some deficiencies in our English dictionaries. Trans of the Philological Soc 1857; 2nd edn as On some deficiencies in our English dictionaries to which is added a letter from Herbert Coleridge, esq on the progress and prospects of the society's New English Dictionary, 1860.
A select glossary of English words used formerly in senses different from their present. 1859.

Letters
Richard Chenevix Trench, letters and memorials. Ed M. Trench, 2 vols 1888.
Trench was a prolific poet and pbd numerous works on theology and history. *See col 687 above.*

Arthur Wilson Verity 1863–1937

The influence of Christopher Marlowe on Shakespere's earlier style: being the Harkness prize essay. Cambridge 1886.
The works of Sir George Etheredge. 1887.
Nero and other plays. 1888 (Mermaid ser). Verity edited Field's Woman is a weathercock and Amends for ladies.
Thomas Heywood. 1888 (Mermaid ser). 5 plays.
The Pitt Press Shakespeare for schools. 13 vols Cambridge 1890–1905. 13 plays.
The Cambridge Milton for schools. 11 vols Cambridge 1891–9.
The student's Shakespeare. 3 vols Cambridge 1902–5. 3 plays only.

William Sidney Walker 1795–1846

Gustavus Vasa and other poems. 1813.
The heroes of Waterloo: an ode. 1815.
Poems from the Danish, selected by Andreas Anderson Feldborg, translated into English verse. 1815.
The appeal of Poland: an ode. 1816.
Corpus poetarum latinorum. 1828, 1849, 1904.
The poetical remains of William Sidney Walker. Ed J. Moultrie 1852 (with memoir).
Shakespeare's versification and its apparent irregularities explained. Ed W. N. Lettsom 1854.
A critical examination of the text of Shakespeare, with remarks on his language and that of his contemporaries. Ed W. N. Lettsom 3 vols 1860.
Walker was also almost entirely responsible for the pbn of Milton's De ecclesia christiana, 1825, *though the ostensible editor was C. R. Sumner.*

Sir Adolphus William Ward 1837–1924

A history of English dramatic literature to the death of Queen Anne. 2 vols 1875, 3 vols 1899 (rev).
Chaucer. 1879 (EML).
Dickens. 1882 (EML).
The Counter-Reformation. 1886.
Sir Henry Wotton: a biographical sketch. 1898.
Great Britain and Hanover: being the Ford lectures. Oxford 1899; tr Ger 1906.
The Electress Sophia and the Hanoverian succession. 1903.
Germany 1815–90. 3 vols Cambridge 1916–18.
Collected papers, historical, literary, travel and miscellaneous. 5 vols Cambridge 1921. 97 rptd articles, 40 being literary (vols 3–4).

Editions
The poetical works of Alexander Pope. 1869.
Old English drama, select plays: Marlowe's Dr Faustus and Greene's Friar Bacon and Friar Bungay. Oxford 1887.
The spider and the flie. 1894 (Spenser Soc).
The poems of John Byrom. 3 vols 1894–1912 (Chetham Soc).
Heywood's A woman killed with kindness. 1897.
The Cambridge modern history, planned by Lord Acton. 14 vols

Cambridge 1902–12, 1934. General editors Ward, G. W. Prothero and S. Leathes; Ward contributed 16 chs.

The poems of George Crabbe. 3 vols Cambridge 1905–7.

The works of Mrs Gaskell. 8 vols 1906.

The Cambridge history of English literature. 14 vols Cambridge 1907–16. General editors Ward and A. R. Waller; Ward contributed 14 chs.

The London merchant, and Fatal curiosity, by George Lillo. Boston 1907.

For Ward's minor writings, see A bibliography of Sir Adolphus William Ward by A. T. Bartholomew, with memoir by T. F. Tout, Cambridge 1926.

Henry William Weber 1783–1818

The battle of Flodden field: a poem of the sixteenth century. 1808.

Metrical romances of the thirteenth, fourteenth and fifteenth centuries. 3 vols Edinburgh 1810.

The dramatic works of John Ford. 2 vols 1811. Also various correspondence relating to Ford.

Tales of the East. 3 vols Edinburgh 1812.

The works of Beaumont and Fletcher. 14 vols 1812.

Illustrations of northern antiquities, from the earlier Teutonic and Scandinavian romances. 1814. Assisted by Sir W. Scott and R. Jamieson.

Hensleigh Wedgwood 1803–91

Notices of English etymology. Trans of the Philological Soc 1844.

Dictionary of English etymology. 3 vols 1859–65.

On the origin of language. 1866.

Contested etymologies. 1882.

Wedgwood pbd numerous philological articles and also wrote on geometry.

Alfred Slater West 1846–1932

The elements of English grammar. Cambridge 1893.

English grammar for beginners. Cambridge 1895.

Editions

Bacon's essays. 1897.

Earle's Microcosmography. Cambridge 1897.

Henry Benjamin Wheatley 1838–1917

Of anagrams. 1862.

Samuel Pepys and the world he lived in. 1880.

The book-lover's library. 1886–1902. Wheatley was general editor of the series. His own contributions were: How to form a library, 1886; The dedication of books, 1887; How to catalogue a library, 1889; Literary blunders, 1893; How to make an index, 1902.

A handbook of art industries in pottery and the precious metals. 2 pts 1886.

Remarkable bindings in the British Museum. 1889.

London past and present, based on the handbook of London by the late Peter Cunningham. 3 vols 1891.

Historical portraits: some notes on the painted portraits of celebrated characters of England, Scotland and Ireland. 1897.

Prices of books: an inquiry into the changes in the prices of books which have occurred in England at different periods. 1898.

Hogarth's London: pictures of the manners of the eighteenth century. 1809.

Contributions to periodicals

A dictionary of reduplicated words in the English language. Appendix of Trans of the Philological Soc 1865.

Chronological notices of dictionaries of the English language. Trans of the Philological Soc 1865.

Spelling reformers. Academy 1877.

The story of Johnson's dictionary. Antiquary 1885.

John Wesley's English dictionary. Bookworm 1888.

The Early English Text Society and F. J. Furnivall. Library 1912.

Editions

Diary of John Evelyn, with a life of the author. 4 vols 1879.

Chap-books and folk-lore tracts. 1885. With G. L. Gomme.

Reliques of ancient English poetry, edited with general introduction, additional prefaces, notes, glossary etc. 3 vols 1891.

The diary of Samuel Pepys, with Lord Braybrooke's notes, edited with additions. 10 vols 1893–9.

Also minor bibliographical and topographical works, and edns of 17th-century rarities.

Richard Grant White 1822–85

Shakespeare's scholar: being historical and critical studies of his text, characters and commentators, with an examination of Mr Collier's folio of 1632. New York 1854.

Memoirs of the life of Shakespeare. Boston 1865.

Words and their uses: a study of the English language. Boston 1870.

Everyday English. 1880.

Editions

The complete works of Shakespeare. 1857.

Introductions

The confessions of W. H. Ireland. 1874.

White wrote numerous articles on English and American English for the periodicals Galaxy *and* Atlantic Monthly *between 1867 and 1881. He wrote many other works on Shakespeare, a novel, poetry and an anti-Darwinian tract. He also contributed the article on English lang and lit to Johnson,* Universal Cyclopedia 1877.

Simon Wilkin 1790–1862

A catalogue of the books belonging to the Public Library, and to the City Library of Norwich, methodically arranged. 4 pts Norwich 1825–32, 1 vol 1847.

A catechism of the use of the globes. 2 pts 1826.

Sir Thomas Browne's works, including his life and correspondence. 4 vols 1836, 3 vols 1852.

Joseph Kingdom of Norwich: a memoir. Norwich 1855. By M. H. Wilkin; preface and introductory ch by Simon Wilkin.

William Aldis Wright 1831–1914

Bacon's Essays and Colours of good and evil, with notes and glossarial index. 1862.

The works of William Shakespeare. 9 vols Cambridge 1863–6. Vol 1 ed W. G. Clark and J. Glover; vols 2–9 ed Clark and Wright.

The works of William Shakespeare. 1864, 1904 (Globe). With W. G. Clark.

The Bible word-book: a glossary of the Old English Bible words. 1866, 1884 (rev). With J. Eastwood.

Chaucer, The clerk's tale. 1867.

Shakespeare's select plays. 10 vols Oxford 1868–83. With W. G. Clark.

Bacon's Advancement of learning. 1869, 1875, 1880.

The pilgrimage of the lyf of the manhode, from the French of de Deguilleville. 1869 (Roxburghe Club).

Generydes: a romance in seven-line stanzas. EETS 2 pts 1873–8.

The metrical chronicle of Robert of Gloucester. 1887 (Rolls ser).

Letters and literary remains of Edward FitzGerald. 1889; Letters, 1894; Letters to Fanny Kemble, 1895; Rubáiyát, 1899; Miscellanies, 1900; More letters, 1901.
Facsimile of the manuscript of Milton's minor poems. 1899.
Milton's poetical works. 1903.
Roger Ascham, English works. Cambridge 1904.
The authorized version of the English Bible 1611. Cambridge 1909.
Femina, now first printed from a unique ms in the Library of Trinity College Cambridge. 1909 (Roxburghe Club).
The Hexaplar Psalter: being the Book of Psalms in six English versions. 1911.
Wright also pbd biblical studies and was editor of the Jnl of Philology 1868–1913. [JS]

12 Travel

(1) GENERAL

See Biography of the Library of Royal Commonwealth Society, *ed D. H. Simpson, 1961;* Cambridge history of the British Empire; *J. N. L. Baker,* History of geographical discovery and exploration, *1931.*

Blakiston, Major John (1785–1867). Twelve years' military adventure in three quarters of the globe 1802–14. 1829.

Boteler, Capt John Harvey (1796–1885). Recollections of my sea-life from 1808 to 1830. Ed D. Bonner-Smith 1942.

Clarke, Edward Daniel (1769–1822). Travels in various countries of Europe, Asia, Africa. 6 vols 1810–23.

Franklin, Sir John (1786–1847). Narrative of a journey to the shores of the Polar Sea 1819–22. 1823.

Franklin, Sir John (1786–1847). Narrative of a second expedition to the Polar Sea. 1828.

McCormick, Robert (1800–80). Voyages of discovery in the Arctic and Antarctic Seas, and round the world: being personal narratives of attempts to reach the North and South Poles [1827–]. 2 vols 1884.

Holman, James (1786–1857). Voyage round the world 1827–32. 1834–5.

Holman, James (1786–1857). Travels in China, New Zealand, New South Wales, Van Diemen's Land, Cape Horn etc. 2nd edn 1840.

Darwin, Charles Robert (1809–82). Journal of researches into the geology and natural history of the various countries visited by HMS Beagle from 1832–6. 1839. *See col 2537.*

Haley, Nelson Cole. Whale hunt: the narrative of a voyage 1849–53. 1950.

Page, Charlotte A. Under sail and in port in the glorious 1850s. Ed A. P. Johnson 1950.

Anson, George, Baron (1697–1762). A voyage round the world: in the years 1740, 1741, 1742, 1743, 1744. 1853.

Buckingham, James Silk (1786–1855). Voyages, travels, adventures. 2 vols 1855.

Armstrong, Alexander (1818–99). A personal narrative of the discovery of the north-west passage. 1857.

McClintock, Sir Francis Leopold (1819–1907). Voyage of the Fox: discovery of the fate of Franklin. 1859.

Atkinson, Thomas Witlam (1799–1861). Travels; in the regions of the upper and lower Amoor, and the Russian acquisitions on the confines of India and China. 1860.

Muter, Elizabeth McMullin. Travels and adventures of an officer's wife in India, China and New Zealand. 1864.

MacGregor, John (1825–92). A thousand miles in the Rob Roy canoe. 1866.

MacGregor, John. The Rob Roy on the Baltic. 1867.

MacGregor, John. The Rob Roy on the Jordan, Nile, Red Sea etc. 1869.

Frere, Alice M. (Mrs Godfrey Clerk). The antipodes and round the world, or travels in Australia, New Zealand, Ceylon, China, Japan and California. 1870.

Kennedy, David. Kennedy's colonial travel: a narrative of a four years' tour through Australia, New Zealand, Canada etc. [1876.]

Kent, S. H. Within the Arctic Circle: experiences of travel through Norway to the North Cape, Sweden and Lapland. 1877.

Brassey, Lady Anne (1839–87). A voyage in the Sunbeam. 1878.

Bridges, Mrs F. D. Journal of a lady's travels round the world. 1883.

Tangye, Richard (1833–1906). Reminiscences of travel in Australia, America and Egypt. Illustr E. C. Mountfort, Birmingham 1883.

Palgrave, William Gifford (1829–88). Ulysses: scenes and studies in many lands. 1887.

Haweis, Hugh Reginald (1839–1901). Travel and talk 1885–93–95. My hundred thousand miles of travel through America, Australia, Tasmania, Canada, New Zealand, Ceylon, and the paradises of the Pacific. 1896.

Dale, John. Round the world by doctors' orders. Being a narrative of a year's travel in Japan, Ceylon, Australia, China, New Zealand, Canada, the United States etc. 1894.

Bagot, A. G. Sport and travel in India and Central America. 1897.

Rees, Fred A. On peak, pyramid and prairie: travel scenes and stories in Europe, Africa and America. [1905?]

(2) AFRICA

Brucek, James (1730–94). Travels between the year 1768 and 1773, through part of Africa, Syria, Egypt and Arabia into Abyssinia to discover the source of the Nile. 1805.

Barnard, Lady Anne (1750–1825). The Cape of Good Hope 1797–1802. Ed D. Fairbridge 1924.

Barrow, Sir John (1764–1848). Travels into the interior of S. Africa. 2 vols 1801–4.

Park, Mungo (1771–1806). The journal of a mission to the interior of Africa in the year 1805. 1815.

Salt, Henry (1780–1827). A voyage to Abyssinia, and travels into the interior of that country 1809–10. 1814.

Burckhardt, John Lewis (1784–1817). Travels in Nubia. 1819.

Daniell, Samuel (1775–1811). Sketches representing the native tribes, animals and scenery of S. Africa [with descriptive letterpress by William Somerville and Sir John Barrow]. 1820.

Moffat, Robert (1795–1883) and Mary (1795–1871). Apprenticeship at Kuruman 1820–38. Ed I. Shapera 1951.

Moffat, Robert (1795–1883) and Mary (1795–1871). The Matabele journals 1829–60. Ed J. P. R. Wallis 2 vols 1945.

Burchell, William John (1781–1863). Travels in the interior of Southern Africa. 2 vols 1822–4.

Denham, Dixon (1786–1828). Travels and discoveries in Northern and Central Africa 1822–4. 1826.

Irby, Charles Leonard (1789–1845). Travels in Egypt and Nubia, Syria and the Holy Land. 1823. With J. Mangles.
Wilson, William Rae (1772–1849). Travels in Egypt and the Holy Land. 1823.
Laing, Major Alexander Gordon (1793–1826). Travels in Timannee, Kooranko and Sodima.
Laing, Major Alexander Gordon (1793–1826). Countries in Western Africa. 1825.
Laing, Major Alexander Gordon (1793–1826). Mission to Timbuktu. 1826.
Bain, Andrew Geddes (1797–1864). Journals [S. Africa 1826–]. Ed M. H. Lister 1949.
Clapperton, Hugh (1788–1827). Journal of a second expedition into the interior of Africa from the Bight of Benin to Soccatoo. 1829.
Lander, Richard Lemon (1804–34) and J. Lander (1807–39). Journal of an expedition to explore the course and termination of the Niger. 3 vols 1832.
Owen, Vice-Admiral William Fitzwilliam (1774–1857). Narrative of voyages to explore the shores of Africa, Arabia and Madagascar. 2 vols 1833.
Pringle, Thomas (1789–1834). Africa sketches. 1834.
St. John, James Augustus (1801–75). Egypt and Mohammed Ali, or, travels in the valley of the Nile. 1834.
Smith, Sir Andrew (1797–1872). The diary of Sir Andrew Smith, Director of the 'Expedition for exploring Central Africa' 1834–6. 2 vols 1939–40.
Hoskins, George Alexander (d. 1864). Travels in Ethiopia. 1835.
Pringle, Thomas (1789–1834). Narrative of a residence in S. Africa. 1835.
Owen, Francis (d. 1854). The diary of a mission with Dingaan in 1837–8. Ed Sir G. E. Cory 1926.
Davidson, John (1797–1836). Notes taken during travels in Africa. 1839.
Tindall, Rev Joseph (1807–61). Journeys in South West Africa 1839–55. Ed B. A. Tindall 1959.
Meyrick, Henry Howard (1822–47). Life in the Bush 1840–7. Ed F. J. Meyrick 1939.
Wilkinson, John Gardner (1797–1875). Modern Egypt and Thebes: being a description of Egypt including the information required for travellers in that country. 1843.
Yates, William Holt. The modern history and condition of Egypt. 1843.
Merriman, Nathaniel James (1810–82). The Cape journals 1848–55. Ed D. H. Varley and H. M. Matthew 1957.
Saleman, Sir William Henry (1788–1856). A journey through the kingdom of Oudi in 1849–50. 2 vols 1858.
Galton, Sir Francis (1822–1911). Narrative of an exploration in tropical South Africa. 1853.
Parkyns, Mansfield. Life in Abyssinia. 1853.
Baikie, William Balfour (1825–64). Narrative of an exploring voyage up the rivers Kwo'ra and Bi'nue [i.e. Niger and Tsadda] in 1854. 1856.
Price, Elizabeth Lees (1839–1919). Journals written in Bechuanaland, Southern Africa 1854–83 with an epilogue: 1889 and 1900. Ed U. Long 1956.
Murray, Emma (1834–1905). Bloemfontein 1856–60. Ed J. Murray 2 vols 1954.
Burton, Sir Richard Francis (1821–90). First steps in East Africa. 1856.
Burton, Sir Richard Francis (1821–90). The lake regions of central equatorial Africa, with notices of the Lunar mountains and sources of the White Nile 1857–9. 2 vols 1860.
Burton, Sir Richard Francis (1821–90). The Nile Basin. 1864.
Livingstone, David (1813–73). Narrative of an expedition to the Zambesi and its tributaries 1858–64. 1865; ed J. P. R. Wallis 1956.
Livingstone, David (1813–73). Livingstone's travels. Ed J. I. McNair 1954.
Livingstone, David (1813–73). Private journals. Ed I. Schapera 1960.
Moffat, John Smith (1835–1918). The Matabele mission: a selection from the correspondence of John and Fanny Moffat, David Livingstone and others 1858–78. Ed J. P. R. Wallis 1945.
Buchanan, Nathaniel (1826–1901). Packhorse and waterhole; with the first overlanders to the Kimberley [1859–]. Ed G. Buchanan 1933.
Tristram, Henry Baker (1822–1906). The Great Sahara. 1860.
Petherick, John (1813–82). Egypt, the Soudan and Central Africa, with explorations from Khartoum on the White Nile to the regions of the Equator. 1861.
Dobie, John Shedden (1819–1903). African journal 1861–6. Ed A. F. Hattersley 1945.
Stewart, Rev James (1831–1905). Zambesi journal 1862–3. Ed J. P. R. Wallis 1953.
Speke, John Hanning (1827–64). Journal of discovery of the source of the Nile. 1863.
Grant, Lt Col James Augustus (1827–92). A walk across Africa: or domestic scenes from my Nile journal. 1864.
Leask, Thomas Smith (1839–1912). The South African diaries of Thomas Leask 1865–70. Ed J. P. R. Wallis 1954.
Baker, Sir Samuel White (1821–93). The Albert Nyanza great basin of the Nile and exploration of the Nile sources. 1866.
Baker, Sir Samuel White (1821–83). The Nile tributaries of Abyssinia and the sword hunters of the Hamran Arabs. 1871.
Baker, Sir Samuel White (1821–83). Ismailia: a narrative of the expedition to Central Africa for the suppression of the slave trade, organised by Ismail, Khediv of Egypt. 2 vols 1874.
Wingfield, Lewis Strange (1842–91). Under the palms in Algeria and Tunis. 2 vols 1868.
Hinderer, Mrs Anna (1827–70). Seventeen years in the Yoruba country. 1872.
Stanley, Sir Henry Morton (1841–1904). How I found Livingstone. 1872.
Stanley, Sir Henry Morton (1841–1904). Through the dark continent. 2 vols 1878.
Stanley, Sir Henry Morton (1841–1904). In darkest Africa. 2 vols 1890.
Reade, William Winwood (1838–75). African sketchbook. 2 vols 1873.
Cunynghame, Arthur Augustus Thurlow (1812–84). My command in South Africa, 1874–1878; comprising experiences of travel in the colonies of South Africa and the independent states. 1879.
Kingston, William Henry Giles (1814–80). Great African travellers from Mungo Park to Livingstone and Stanley. [1874.]
McKiernan, Gerald (1844–92). Narrative and journal in S. W. Africa 1875–9. Ed P. Serton 1934.
Baines, Thomas (1822–75). Northern goldfield diaries of 1877. Ed J. P. R. Wallis 1946.
Cameron, Verney Lovett (1844–94). Across Africa. 2 vols 1877.
Edwards, Amelia Blandford (1831–92). A thousand miles up the Nile. 1877.
Hooker, Sir Joseph Dalton (1817–1911). Journal of a tour in Morocco and the Great Atlas. 1878. With J. Ball.
Trollope, Anthony (1815–82). S. Africa. 1878.
Thomson, Joseph (1858–95). To the central African Lakes and back: the narrative of the Royal Geographical Society's East Central African Expedition 1878–80. 2 vols 1881.
Thomson, Joseph (1858–95). Through Masai land: a journey of exploration among the snow-clad volcanic mountains and strange tribes of E. Equatorial Africa. 1885.
Mitchison, Alexander William. The expiring continent: a narrative of travel in Senegambia. 1881.
Williams, Josiah. Life in the Soudan: adventures amongst the tribes and travels in Egypt in 1881 and 1882. 2nd edn 1884.

Winstanley, William. A visit to Abyssinia; an account of travel in modern Ethiopia. 1881.
Oliphant, Laurence (1829–88). The land of Khemi: up and down the middle Nile. 1882.
Wilkinson, Mrs. A lady's life and travels in Zululand and the Transvaal during Cetewayo's reign: being the African letters and journals of the late Mrs Wilkinson. 1882.
Johnston, Sir Harry Hamilton (1858–1927). The River Congo from its mouth to Bolobo. 1884.
Johnston, Sir Harry Hamilton (1858–1927). The Kilima-njavo expedition: a record of scientific exploration in Eastern Equatorial Africa. 1886.
Bousfield, Henry Brougham (1832–1902). Six years in the Transvaal: notes of the founding of the Church there. 1886.
Hore, Annie. To Lake Tanganyika in a bath-chair. 1886.
Headley, Joel Tyler (1813–97). Great explorations in the wilds of Africa. Toronto 1886.
Smith, William Wilson Hind (b. 1869). A boy's scrambles: falls and mishaps in Morocco. 1886.
Bruce, George Windham Hamilton Knight (1852–96). Journey to the Zambesi in 1888. Ed C. E. Tripp 1939.
Anderson, Andrew A. Twenty-five years in a waggon: sport and travel in South Africa. Illus. New edn 1888.
Harris, Walter Burton. The land of an African sultan: travels in Morocco. 1889.
Budge, E. A. Wallis (Ernest Alfred Wallis 1857–1934). The Nile: notes for travellers in Egypt. 1890.
Bent, James Theodore (1852–97). The ruined cities of Mashonaland. 1892.
Bent, James Theodore (1852–97). The sacred city of the Ethiopians. 1893.
Bent, James Theodore (1852–97). Southern Arabia, Soudan and Sokoto. 1900.
Macdonald, Col Sir Claude Maxwell (1852–1915). Up the Niger. 1892.
Cook, Thomas. My mission tour in South Africa: a record of interesting travel and Pentecostal blessing. 1893.
Selous, Frederick Courteney (1851–1917). Travel and adventure in South-East Africa, being the narrative of the last eleven years spent by the author on the Zambesi. 1893.
Bailey, Henry. Travel and adventures in the Congo Free State and its big game shooting, by Bula N'Zau [pseud]. 1894.
Bryce, James Viscount (1838–1922). Impressions of S. Africa. 1897.
Kingsley, Mary Henrietta (1862–1900). Travels in West Africa. 1897.
Cunningham-Graham, Robert Bontine (1852–1936). Mogreb el Acksa: a journey in Morocco 1898. 1921 (rev).
Stevenson, James Hamilton. Barotseland journal 1898–9. Ed J. P. R. Wallis 1954.
Carnegie, David Wynford (1871–1900). Letters from Nigeria 1899–1900. Ed Lady H. M. Carnegie 1902.
Lloyd, Albert Bushnell. In swarf land and cannibal country; a record of travel and discovery in Central Africa. 1900.
Markham, Violet Rosa. South Africa, past and present, an account of its history, politics and native affairs followed by some personal reminiscences of African travel. 1900.
Powell-Cotton, Percy Horace Gordon. Into unknown Africa: a narrative of twenty months travel and sport in unknown lands and among new tribes. Illustr A. Forestier 1904.

(3) AMERICA

North America

Thompson, David (1770–1857). Explorations in Western America 1784–1812. Ed J. B. Tyrrell 1916.
Harmon, Daniel Williams (1778–1845). Ten years in the Indian country 1800–16. Ed W. K. Lamb 1957.
Selkirk, Thomas Douglas, 5th Earl of (1771–1820). Journal of travels in British N. America and the north-eastern United States 1803–4. Ed P. C. T. White 1958.
Clark, William (1770–1838). Journals [1804–6]. Ed B. de Voto 1954.
Lambert, John. Travels through lower Canada and the United States of N. America in the years 1806, 1807 and 1808. 3 vols 1810.
Nuttall, Thomas (1786–1859). Travels in the old North-west in 1810. Ed J. E. Graustein 1951.
Ross, Sir John (1777–1856). A voyage of discovery for the purpose of exploring Baffin's Bay, and enquiring into the probability of a North-West Passage. 2 vols 1819.
Parry, Sir William Edward (1790–1855). Journal of a voyage for the discovery of a North-West Passage 1819–20. 2 vols 1821–3. 1824.
Parry, Sir William Edward (1790–1855). Journal of a third voyage 1824–5. 1826.
Parry, Sir William Edward (1790–1855). Narrative of an attempt to reach the North Pole 1827. 1828.
Simpson, Sir George (1787–1860). Fur trade and empire 1824–5. Ed F. Merk 1931.
Ogden, Peter Skene (1794–1854). Snake country journals 1824–5 and 1825–6. Ed E. E. Rich and A. M. Johnson 1950.
Hall, Basil (1788–1844). Travels in North America in 1827 and 1828.
Hall, Mrs Basil. The aristocratic journey: being outspoken letters written during a fourteen months' sojourn in America 1827–8. Pope-Hennessy 1931.
Ross, Sir James Clark (1800–62). A second voyage in search of a north west passage 1829–33. 1835.
Simpson, Thomas (1808–40). Narrative of the discoveries on the N. coast of America [1829–]. 1843.
Domett, Alfred. Journal of a tour in Canada, the United States and Jamaica 1833–5. Ed E. A. Horsman and L. R. Benson 1955.
Murray, Charles Augustus (1806–95). Travels in North America during the years 1834, 1835 & 1836, including... a visit to Cuba and the Azore Islands. 1839.
Cather, Thomas (b. 1813). Voyage to America in 1836. Ed T. Yoseloff 1961.
Sheridan, Francis. Galveston Island 1839–46. Ed W. W. Pratt 1954.
Dickens, Charles (1812–70). American notes for general circulation. 2 vols 1842.
Harris, Edward (1799–1863). Up the Missouri with Audubon. Ed J. F. McDermott 1951.
Le Froy, Major Gen Sir John Henry (1817–90). In search of the magnetic North: a soldier-surveyor's letters from the North-West 1843–4. Ed C. F. G. Stanley 1955.
Gregg, Josiah. Excursions in Mexico and California 1847–50. Ed M. G. Fulton 1944.
Hepburn, George (1802–83). Journal on his voyage from Scotland to Otago in 1850. Ed W. D. Stewart 1934.
Taylor, John Glanville (1823–51). The United States and Cuba: eight years of change and travel. 1851.
Oliphant, Laurence (1829–88). Minnesota and the Far West. 1855.
Hind, Henry Youle (1823–1908). Narrative of the Canadian Red River exploring expedition of 1857 and of the Assinniboine and Saskatchewan exploring expedition of 1858. 2 vols 1860.
Palliser, John (1817–87). The exploration of that portion of British North America which lies between the western shore of Lake Superior and the Pacific Ocean 1857–60. 1863.
Carnegie, James 9th Earl of Southesk (1827–1905). Saskatchewan and the Rocky Mountains 1859–60. 1875.
Burton, Sir Richard Francis (1821–90). The city of saints and across the Rocky Mountains to California. 1861.
Cheadle, Walter Butler (1835–1910). Journal of a trip across Canada 1862–3, with introduction and notes by A. G. Doughty and G. Lanctot. 1931.
Cheadle, Walter Butler. The North-West passage by land. 1865.
Massie, James William (1799–1869). America: the origin of her

present conflict . . . illustrated by incidents of travel during a tour in the summer of 1863. 1864.

Shaw, James. Twelve years in America: being observations on the country, people, institutions and religion, with notices of slavery and the late war. 1867.

Butler, Sir William Francis (1838–1910). The great lone land; a narrative of travel in the North-West of America. 1872.

Butler, Sir William Francis. The wild North land. 1873.

Quin, Windham Thomas Wyndham, Earl of Dunraven (1841–1926). The Great Divide: travels in Upper Yellowstone in the summer of 1874. 1876.

Price, Major Sir Rose Lambart (1837–99). The two Americas; an account of sport and travel. With notes on man and manners in North and South America. 1877.

Bishop, Isabella Bird (1832–1904). A lady's life in the Rocky Mountains. 1879.

Gordon, Daniel M. (1845–1925). Mountain and prairie: a journey from Victoria to Winnipeg via Peace River Pass. 1880.

Baker, Sarah S. (Sarah Schoonmaker 1824–1906). The children on the plains; a story of travel and adventure in the great prairies of North America. London and New York 1885.

Latin America

Haynes, Gen Robert (1769–1851). Barbadian diary 1787–1836. Ed E. M. W. Cracknell 1934.

Nugent, Maria (1775–1834). Journal of a voyage to, and residence in, the island of Jamaica 1801–5. 2 vols 1839.

Mawe, John (1764–1829). Travels in the interior of Brazil . . . including a voyage to the Rio de la Plata. 1812.

Koster, Henry (1793–c. 1820). Travels in Brazil. 1816.

Caldcleugh, Alexander (d. 1858). Travels in South America during the years 1819–20–21 containing an account of the present state of Brazil, Buenos Ayres and Chile. 1825.

Hall, Basil (1788–1844). Extracts from journals written on the coasts of Chile, Peru and Mexico 1820–2. 2 vols 1824.

Hart, Miss. Letters from the Bahama Islands 1823–4. Ed R. Kent 1949.

Cochrane, Charles Stuart. Journal of a residence and travels in Colombia during the years 1823 and 1824. 1825.

Conder, Josiah (1789–1855). The modern traveller: a popular description, geographical, historical and topographical, of the various countries of the globe: Mexico and Guatemala. 1825.

Stevenson, William Bennet (b. 1787?). A historical and descriptive narrative of twenty years' residence in South America. 1825.

Waterton, Charles (1782–1865). Wanderings in S. America. 1825.

Miers, John (1789–1879). Travels in Chile and La Plata. 2 vols 1826.

Hamilton, John Potter (1777/8–1873). Travels through the interior provinces of Colombia. 1827.

Bickford, Rev James (1860–95). An autobiography of Christian labour in the West Indies, Demerara, Victoria, New South Wales and South Australia 1836–88. 1890.

Gardner, George (1812–49). Travels in the interior of Brazil . . . during the years 1836–1841. 1846.

Turnbull, David. Travels in the West. Cuba, with notices of Porto Rico, and the slave trade. 1840.

Stephens, John Lloyd (1805–52). Incidents of travel in Central America, Chiapas, and Yucatan. 1841.

Head, Sir Francis Bond (1793–1875). Rough notes taken during some rapid journeys across the pampas and among the Andes. 1846.

Wallace, Alfred Russel (1823–1913). Travels on the Amazon and Rio Negro. 1853.

De Bonelli, L. Hugh. Travels in Bolivia, with a tour across the pampas to Buenos Ayres. 1854.

Trollope, Anthony (1815–82). The West Indies and the Spanish Main. 1859.

Sill, Edward Roland. Around the Horn: December 1861 to March 1863. Ed T. Williams and B. Simison 1944.

Bates, Henry Walter (1825–92). The naturalist on the Amazons. 2 vols 1863.

Burton, Sir Richard Francis (1821–90). Explorations of the highlands of Brazil. 1869.

Burton, Sir Richard Francis. Letters from the battle-fields of Paraguay. 1870.

Kingsley, Charles (1819–75). At last: a Christmas in the West Indies. 2 vols 1871.

Musters, George Chaworth (1841–79). At home with the Patagonians. 1871.

Dixie, Lady Florence Caroline (1857–1905). Across Patagonia. 1880.

Simson, Alfred. Travels in the wilds of Ecuador, and the exploration of the Putumyo river. 1886.

Wells, James William. Exploring and travelling three thousand miles through Brazil from Rio de Janeiro to Maranhao. 1886.

Millican, Albert. Travels and adventures of an orchid hunter: an account of canoe and camp life in Colombia. 1891.

Hudson, William Henry (1841–1922). The naturalist in La Plata. 1892.

Hudson, William Henry. Idle days in Patagonia. 1893.

Whymper, Edward (1840–1911). Travels among the Great Andes of the Equator. 1892.

Brine, Lyndesay (1834–1906). Travels amongst American Indians . . . including a journey in Guatemala, Mexico and Yucatan. 1894.

Fitzgerald, Edward Arthur (1871–1931). The highest Andes. 1899.

Enock, Charles Reginald (1868–1970). The great Pacific coast, twelve thousand miles in the golden west, being an account of life and travel in the western states of North and South America, from California, British Columbia and Alaska to Mexico. 1909.

(4) ASIA

Daniell, Thomas (1749–1840) and William Daniell (1769–1837). Oriental scenery. 2 vols 1801.

Daniell, Thomas and William Daniell. A picturesque voyage to India, by way of China. 1810.

Mountnorris, George Annesley, Earl of (1769–1844). Voyages and travels in India, Ceylon, the Red Sea, Abyssinia, and Egypt, in the years 1802, 1803, 1804, 1805, and 1806. 1809.

Symes, Michael (1753?–1809). Journal of his second embassy to the court of Ava in 1802. [Burma.] Ed P. G. E. Hall 1955.

Barrow, Sir John (1764–1848). Travels in China. 1804.

Barrow, Sir John (1764–1848). Voyage to Cochin-China. 1806.

Buchanan, Francis (1762–1829). A journey from Madras through the countries of Mysore, Canava and Malabar 1807. 2 vols 1870.

Morier, James Justinian (1780–1849). Journey through Persia, Armenia, and Asia Minor to Constantinople 1808–9. 1812.

Morier, James Justinian (1780–1849). A second journey through Persia 1810–16. 1818.

Nugent, Maria (1775–1834). A journal from the year 1811 till the year 1815, including a voyage to and residence in India. 2 vols 1839.

Hall, Basil (1788–1844). Travels in India, Ceylon and Borneo [1812–]. Ed H. G. Rawlinson 1931.

Hall, Basil. Account of voyage of discovery to the W. Coast of Corea. 1818.

Hall, Basil. Fragments of voyages and travels. 9 vols 1831–3.

Light, Henry (1783–1870). Travels in Egypt, Nubia, Holy Land, Mount Lebanon and Cyprus in the year 1814. 1818.

Porter, Sir Robert Ker (1777–1842). Travels in Georgia, Persia, Armenia, Babylonia etc in 1817–20. 2 vols 1821–2.

Ouseley, William (1767–1842). Travels in various countries of the East, more particularly Persia, etc. 3 vols 1819–23. Quarto.

Gordon, Capt Peter (1790–1857). A tour through Persia in 1820. 1833, micro Cambridge 1990.

Burckhardt, John Lewis (1784–1817). Travels in Syria and the Holy Land. 1822.

Burckhardt, John Lewis. Travels in Arabia. 2 vols 1829.
Buckingham, James Silk (1786–1855). Travels in Palestine through the countries of Bashan and Gilead. 1822.
Irby, Charles Leonard (1789–1845). Travels in Egypt and Nubia, Syria and the Holy Land. 1823. With J. Mangles.
Leake, William Martin (1777–1860). Journal of a tour in Asia Minor. 1824.
Fenton, Mrs Michael (1800–75). Narrative of life in India 1826–30. 1901.
Fraser, James Baillie (1783–1856). Travels and adventures in the Persian Provinces on the southern banks of the Caspian Sea. 1826.
Brown, Samuel Sneade (1809–75). Home letters, written from India between the years 1828–41. 1848.
Crawford, John (1783–1868). Embassy to the Courts of Siam and Cochin-China. 2 vols 1828.
Malcolm, Sir John (1769–1833). Sketches of Persia. 1828.
Dobell, Peter (1772–1852). Travels in Kamtchatka and Siberia, with a narrative of a residence in China. 1830.
Webster, James. Travels through the Crimea, Turkey and Egypt performed during the years 1825–1828. 1830.
Tyerman, Daniel (1773–1828). Journal of voyages and travels by the Rev Daniel Tyerman and George Bennet, deputed from the London missionary society to visit their various stations in the South Sea Islands, China, India etc. 1831.
Madden, Richard Robert (1798–1886). Travels in Turkey, Egypt, Nubia and Palestine in 1824, 1825, 1826 & 1827. 2nd edn 1833.
Damer, G. L. (Mrs Dawson). Travels in the Holy Land, Greece, Turkey & Egypt. 2nd edn [184?].
Burnes, Lt Col Sir Alexander (1805–44). Cabool: being a personal narrative of a journey to, and residence in that city, in the years 1836, 1837 and 1838. 1842.
Burnes, Lt Col Sir Alexander. Travels into Bokhara. 3 vols 1834.
Rich, Claudius James (1787–1820). Narrative of a residence in Koordistan. 2 vols 1836.
Malcolm, Howard (1799–1879). Travels in Hindustan and China. Edinburgh 1840.
Wood, John (1811–71). A journey to the source of the Oxus. 1841.
Hofland, Barbara (1770–1844). Alfred Campbell, or, Travels of a young pilgrim in Egypt and the Holy Land. New edn 1841.
Hyde, Orson (1805–78). A voice from Jerusalem, or A sketch of the travels of the minister of Elder Orson Hyde to Germany, Constantinople and Jerusalem. Liverpool [1842].
Davidson, G. F. Trade and travel in the Far East; or Recollections of twenty-one years passed in Java, Singapore, Australia, and China. 1846.
Barber, James. The overland guide-book; a complete vademecum for the overland traveller to India via Egypt. 1845, 1850.
Griffith, William (1810–45). Journals of travels in Assam, Burma, Bootan, Afghanistan and the neighbouring countries. Calcutta 1847.
Smith, Rev George (1815–71). A narrative of an explanatory visit to each of the consular cities of China and to the islands of Hong Kong and Chusan 1844–6. 1847.
Curzon, Robert (1810–73). Visits to monasteries in the Levant. 1849.
Oliphant, Laurence (1829–88). A journey to Katmandu. 1852.
Oliphant, Laurence. The land of Gilead. 1880.
Oliphant, Laurence. A trip to the north-east of Lake Tiberias. 1885.
Layard, Sir Austen Henry. Discoveries in the ruins of Nineveh and Babylon; with travels in Armenia, Kurdistan and the desert. 1853.
Layard, Sir Austen Henry. Early adventures in Persia, Susiana and Babylonia. 2 vols 1887.
Moses, Henry. An Englishman's life in India, or Travel and adventures in the East. 1853.
Danvers, Robert William (1833–58). Letters from India and China during the years 1854–8. 1898.
Hooker, Sir Joseph Dalton (1817–1911). Himalayan journals. 1854.
Howe, Fisher (1798–1871). Oriental and sacred scenes from notes of travel in Greece, Turkey and Palestine. 1854.
Burton, Sir Richard Francis (1821–90). Personal narrative of a pilgrimage to El-Medinah and Meccah. 3 vols 1855.
Burton, Sir Richard Francis. Narrative of a year's journey through central and East Arabia. 1865.
Burton, Sir Richard Francis. Sind re-visited. 1877.
Burton, Sir Richard Francis. The gold-mines of Midian: a fortnight's tour in North West Arabia. 1878.
Aveling, T. W. Voices of many waters, or, Travels in the lands of the Tiber, the Jordan, and the Nile: with notices of Asia Minor, Constantinople, Athens. 2nd edn rev 1856.
Bowring, Sir John (1792–1872). The kingdom and people of Siam 1855. 1857.
Porter, Rev J. L. Five years in Damascus. 1855.
Porter, Rev J. L. The giant cities of Bashan. 1865.
Porter, Josias Leslie (1823–89). Five years in Damascus . . . with travels and researches in Palmyra, Lebanon and the Hauran. 1855.
Yule, Henry (1820–89). Narrative of the mission to the court of Ava in 1855 [Burma]. 1858.
Baker, Sir Samuel White (1821–93). The rifle and hound in Ceylon. 1857 (2nd edn).
Baker, Sir Samuel White. Eight years in Ceylon. 1884.
Falkland, Amelia Cary, Viscountess (1803–58). Chow Chow: being selections from a journal kept in India, Egypt and Syria. 2 vols 1857.
Elsmie, George Robert (1838–1909). Thirty five years in the Punjab 1858–93. 1908.
Smith, Albert Richard. To China and back. 1859.
Atkinson, Thomas Witlam (1799–1861). Travels in the regions of the upper and lower Amoor, and the Russian acquisitions on the confines of India and China. 1860.
Dixon, William Hepworth (1821–79). The Holy Land. 2 vols 1865.
Palgrave, William Gifford (1826–88). A year's journey through central and eastern Arabia. 2 vols 1865.
Tristram, Henry Baker (1822–1906). The land of Israel: a journal of travels in Palestine. 1865.
Tristram, Henry Baker. The land of Moab. 1873.
Wills, Charles James. In the land of the lion and sun: or modern Persia 1866–81. 1883.
Dennys, Nicholas Belfield. The treaty ports of China and Japan. 1867.
Freshfield, Douglas W. (1845–1934). Travels in the central Caucasus and Bashan, including visits to Ararat and Tabreez etc. 1869.
Freshfield, Douglas W. The exploration of the Caucasus. 2 vols 1896.
Matheson, John. England to Delhi, a narrative of Indian travel. 1870.
Cooper, Thomas Thornville (1839–78). Travels of a pioneer of commerce in pigtail and petticoats; or An overland journey from China towards India. 1871.
Vincent, Frank (1848–1916). The land of the white elephant: sights and scenes in southeastern Asia. A personal narrative of travel and adventures in Farther India, embracing the countries of Burma, Siam, Cambodia and Cochin-China 1871–2. New York 1874.
Bowring, Lewin Bentham (1824–1910). Eastern experiences. 1871.
Palmer, Edward Henry (1840–82). The desert of the Exodus. 1871.
Andrews, Emerson. Travels in Bible lands: Italy, Egypt, Asia Minor, Syria and Palestine. 1872.
Maughan, William Charles (d. 1914). The Alps of Arabia: travels in Egypt, Sinai, Arabia and the Holy Land by William Charles Maughan. 1873.
Goldsmid, Frederic John (1818–1908). Telegraph and travel; a narrative of the formation and development of telegraphic communication between England and India. 1874.
Burton, Lady Isabel (1831–96). Inner life of Syria. 2 vols 1875.

Burton, Lady Isabel. Arabia, Egypt and India. 1879.
Burnaby, Frederick Gustavius (1842–85). A ride to Khiva. 1876.
Burnaby, Frederick Gustavius. On horse-back through Asia Minor. 2 vols 1877.
Cumming, Constance. From the Hebrides to the Himalays. 1876.
Cumming, Constance. A lady's cruise in a French man-of-war. 1882.
Cumming, Constance. Wanderings in China. 1886.
Bryce, James, Viscount (1838–1922). Trans-Caucasia and Ararat. 1877.
Low, Sir Hugh (1824–1905). Journal of Perak. 1877.
Conder, Claude Reignier (1848–1910). Tent work in Palestine. 1878.
Gill, William John (1843–82). The river of golden sand: the narrative of a journey through China and Eastern Tibet to Burma. Illus. Introd by H. Yule. 2 vols 1880, 1883, Farnborough 1969.
O'Donovan, Edmund (1844–83). The Merv Oasis: travels and adventures east of the Caspian 1879–81. 2 vols 1882.
Bishop, Isabella Bird (1831–1904). Unbeaten tracks in Japan. 2 vols 1880.
Bishop, Isabella Bird. Journeys in Persia and Kurdistan. 2 vols 1891.
Bishop, Isabella Bird. Korea and her neighbours. 2 vols 1898.
Bishop, Isabella Bird. The Yangtze valley and beyond. 1899.
Blunt, Lady Anne Isabella (1837–1917). A pilgrimage to Nejd. 2 vols 1881.
Merrill, Selah. East of the Jordan: a record of travel and observation in the countries of Moab, Gilhead, and Bashan. 1881.
Baber, Edward Colborne (1843–90). Travels and researches in western China. 1882.
Hannington, James (1847–85). A journey through Palestine in 1884, and a journey through Masailand and U-Soga in 1885. Ed E. C. Dawson 1888.
Doughty, Charles Montagu (1843–1926). Travels in Arabia Deserta. 2 vols Cambridge 1888; ed T. E. Lawrence 2 vols 1921.
Little, Archibald John (1838–1908). Through the Yang-tse gorges; or Trade and travel in western China. 1888.
Younghusband, Sir George John. Eighteen hundred miles on a Burmese tat through Burmah, Siam and the E. Shan States. 1888.
Younghusband, Sir George John. On short leave to Japan. 1894.
Wingfield, Lewis Strange (1842–91). Wanderings of a globe-trotter in the Far East. 2 vols 1889.
Dilke, Charles Wentworth (1843–1911). Greater Britain: a record of travel in English-speaking countries. With additional chapters on English influence in Japan and China and on Hong Kong and the Straits settlements. 1890.
Browne, Edward Granville (1862–1925). A year amongst the Persians. 1893.
Harris, Walter Burton. Journey through the Yemen. 1893.
Marsden, Kate (1859–1931). On sledge and horseback to outcast Siberian lepers. 1893.
Conway, Sir Martin (1856–1937). Climbing and exploration in the Karakoram-Himalays. 1894.
Dunmore, Charles Adolphus, 7th Earl of (1841–1907). The Pamirs: being a narrative of a year's expedition on horseback and on foot through Kashmir, to Tibet, Chinese Tartary and Russian Central Asia. 2 vols 1894.
Gardner, Nora Beatrice, née Blyth, Hon. Rifle and spear with the Rajpoots: being the narrative of a winter's travel and sport in northern India. 1895.
Norman, Henry (1858–1939). The people and politics of the Far East: travels and studies in the British, French, Spanish and Portuguese colonies, Siberia, China, Japan, Korea, Siam and Malaya. 1895.
Hogarth, David George (1862–1928). A wandering scholar in the Levant. 1896.
Macgregor, John. Through the buffer state: a record of recent travels through Borneo, Siam and Cambodia. 1896.
Pollok, FitzWilliam Thomas. Fifty years' reminiscences of India; a retrospect of travel, adventure and shikar. Illus. 1896.
Halcombe, Charles J. H. The mystic flowery land: being a true account of an Englishman's travels and adventures in China. 1896, 1899.
Adair, Frederick Edward Shafto, 4th Baron. The big game of Baltistan and Ladakh. A summer in High Asia. 1899.
Cobbold, Ralph Patteson. Innermost Asia: travel and sport in the Pamirs. 1900.
Haggard, Henry Rider (1856–1925). A winter pilgrimage; being an account of travels through Palestine, Italy and the island of Cyprus, accomplished in the year 1900. 1901.
Savory, Isabel. A sportswoman in India; personal adventures and experiences of travel in known and unknown India. Illus. Philadelphia 1900.

(5) AUSTRALASIA AND THE PACIFIC

Flinders, Matthew (1774–1814). A voyage to Terra Australis 1801–3. 2 vols 1814.
Lockerby, William (1782–1853). Journal of a sandalwood trader in the Fijian Islands 1808–9. 1925.
MacQuarie, Lachlan (1761–1824). Tours in New South Wales and Van Diemen's Land 1810–22. 1956.
Oxley, John Joseph William Molesworth (1783–1828). Journals of two expeditions into the interior of New South Wales 1817–18. 1820.
Oxley, John Joseph William Molesworth (1783–1828). Journal of a second expedition into the interior or Terra Incognita of New South Wales. 1818.
Hovell, William Hilton (1786–1875). Journey of discovery to Port Philip, New South Wales, in 1824 and 1825. 1831.
Fenton, Mrs Michael (c. 1800–75). Tasmania during the years 1826–30. 1901.
Dillon, Peter (1785?–1847). Successful voyage in the South Seas to ascertain the actual fate of La Pérouse's expedition. 2 vols 1829.
Markham, Edward. Voyage to Van Diemen's Land 1833. Ed K. R. von Stieglitz 1952.
Banbury, Col Henry William St Pierre (1812–75). Early days in W. Australia: letters and journals [1834–7]. Ed Lt Col W. St Pierre Bunbury and W. P. Morrell 1930.
Bickford, Rev James (1806–95). An autobiography of Christian labour in the West Indies, Demarara, New South Wales and S. Australia 1836–88. 1890.
Franklin, Lady Jane (1792–1875). Visit to New South Wales 1839. 1943.
Eyre, Edward John (1815–1901). Journals of expeditions of discovery into central Australia and overland from Adelaide to King George's Sound in 1840–1. 1845.
Brooke, Sir James (1803–68). A letter from Borneo, with notices of the country and its inhabitants. 1842.
Brooke, Sir James (1803–68). The private letters of Sir James Brooke, Rajah of Sarawak, narrating the events of his life from 1838 to the present time. Ed C. Templar 3 vols 1853.
Sturt, Charles (1795–1869). Two expeditions into the interior of Southern Australia, during the years 1828–31. 2 vols 1833.
Sturt, Charles (1795–1869). Narrative of an expedition into Central Asia, performed under the authority of Her Majesty's Government, during the years 1844, 1845 and 1846. 2 vols 1849.
Brunner, Thomas. The great journey: an expedition to explore the interior of the Middle Island, New Zealand 1846–8. 1954.
Cheever, Henry Theodore (1814–97). The island world of the Pacific: being the personal narrative and results of travel through the Sandwich or Hawaiian Islands, and other parts of Polynesia. Glasgow [1850?].
Buckley, William (1780–1856). The life and adventures of Buckley, 32 years a wanderer amongst the aborigines of the then unexplored country round Port Philip, now the province of Victoria. 1852.

Baker, John Holland (1841–1930). A surveyor in New Zealand 1857–96. Ed N. Baker 1932.
Stuart, John McDouall (1815–66). Journals 1858–62 to fix the centre of the continent [Australia]. Ed W. Hardman 1865.
Bowring, Sir John (1792–1872). A visit to the Philippine islands. 1859.
Burke, Robert O'Hara (1821–61). The Australian exploring expedition of 1860. 1861.
Cracroft, Sophia. An account of the Hawaiian Kingdom 1861–6. Ed A. L. Korn 1958.
Turner, George (1817/8–91). Nineteen years in Polynesia: missionary life, travels, and researches in the islands of the Pacific. 1861.
Wallace, Alfred Russel (1823–1913). The Malay archipelago. 2 vols 1869.
Macdonald, D. A year in the New Hebrides, Loyalty Islands and New Caledonia. 1873.
Strutt, William (1825–1915). Australian journal. Ed G. Mackaness 1958.
Stack, Rev James West (1835–1919). Early Maoriland adventures. Ed A. H. Reed 1935.
Stack, Rev James West. More Maoriland adventures. Ed A. H. Reed 1935.
Stack, Rev James West. Further Maoriland adventures. Ed A. H. Reed 1938.
Anderson, John William. Notes of travel in Fiji and New Caledonia with some remarks on South Sea islanders and their languages. Illus. 1880.
Forbes, Henry Ogg (1851–1932). A naturalist's wanderings in the Eastern Archipelago. 1885.
Chalmers, James (1841–1901). Pioneering in New Guinea. 1887.
Bevan, Theodore Francis. Toil, travel and discovery in British New Guinea. 1890.
Stevenson, Mrs M. I. Letters from Samoa 1891–5. 1906.
Fitzgerald, Edward Arthur (1871–1931). Climbs in the New Zealand Alps. 1896.
Carnegie, David Wynford (1871–1900). Spinfex and sand: a narrative of five years' pioneering and exploration in W. Australia. 1898.
Passfield, Sidney James Webb, Baron (1859–1947) and Lady Beatrice (1858–1943). Visit to New Zealand in 1898: Beatrice Webb's diary with entries by Sidney Webb. 1959.
Verschuur, G. At the antipodes; travels in Australia, New Zealand, Fiji Islands, the New Hebrides, New Caledonia, and South America 1888–1889. Tr Mary Daniels. Illus. 1891, new edn 1900.

(6) EUROPE

The Continent

MacNevin, William James (1763–1841). A ramble through Swisserland in the summer and autumn of 1802. 1803. *See* G. R. de Beer, Travellers in Switzerland, 1949.
Coxe, William (1747–1828). Travels in Poland, Russia, Sweden and Denmark. 1802. Travels in Denmark rptd Philadelphia 1810, and extracted in Pinkerton, J. A general collection of the best and most interesting voyages and travels. 1808–14.
Philips, John Burton. Continental travel in 1802–3. 1904.
Greatheed, Bertie (1759–1826). An Englishman in Paris 1803. Ed J. P. T. Bury and J. C. Barry 1953.
Carr, John (1772–1832). A northern summer, or Travels round the Baltic, through Denmark, Sweden, Russia, Prussia and part of Germany in the year 1804. 1805.
Thornton, Thomas (1757–1823). A sporting tour in France. 1806.
Lemaistre, J. G. Travels after the peace of Amiens through parts of France, Switzerland, Italy and Germany. 1806.
Sansom, J. Travels from Paris through Switzerland and Italy. 1807.
Byron, George Gordon Noel, 6th Baron (1788–1824). Letters written from Portugal, Spain, Greece and the shores of the Mediterranean 1809–11. [1824.]
Byron, George Gordon Noel. The Ravenna journal 1821. Ed Lord Ernle 1928.
Porter, Sir Robert Ker (1777–1842). Travelling sketches in Russia and Sweden. 2 vols 1809.
MacDonald, James. Travels through Denmark and a part of Sweden during the winter and spring of the year 1809. 1810.
Galt, John (1779–1839). Voyages and travels, in the years 1809, 1810, and 1811 containing statistical, commercial and miscellaneous observations on Gibraltar, Sardinia, Sicily, Malta, Serigo and Turkey. 1812.
Forsyth, Joseph (1763–1815). On antiquities, arts, letters in Italy. 1813.
Hobhouse, John Cam, Baron Broughton (1786–1869). Journey through Albania. 1813.
Bridges, George Windham. Alpine sketches by a member of the University of Oxford. 1814.
Shelley, Percy Bysshe (1792–1822). Visits to France, Switzerland and Savoy 1814. Ed C. S. Elton 1894.
Eustace, John Chetwode (1762?–1815). A classified tour through Italy. 1815.
Southey, Robert (1774–1843). Journal of a tour in the Netherlands in the autumn of 1815. 1902.
Waldie, Jane (1793–1826). Sketches descriptive of Italy in 1816–17. 1817.
Stoppard, John (1785–1879). Letters after a tour through some parts of France, Switzerland and Germany. 1817.
Clifford, Lady de. A picturesque tour through France, Switzerland, on the banks of the Rhine and through parts of the Netherlands. 1817.
Milford, John. A tour through the Pyrenees, south of France, Switzerland, Italy and the Netherlands. 1818.
Hookham, Thomas. A walk through Switzerland in September 1816. 1818.
Raffles, Thomas (1788–1863). A tour through some parts of France, Savoy, Switzerland and Germany, and the Netherlands. 1818.
Baillie, Marianne. First impressions on a tour on the Continent. 1819.
Bowring, Sir John (1792–1872). Observations on the state of religion and literature in Spain. 1819.
Bowring, Sir John (1792–1872). Some account of the state of the prisons in Spain and Portugal. 1824.
Rose, Stewart. Letters from the north of Italy addressed to Henry Hallam. 1819.
Starke, Mrs Mariana (1762?–1838). Guide for travellers on the Continent. 1820.
Williams, Hugh William (1773–1829). Travels in Italy, Greece etc. 1820.
Cockburn, James Pattison (1779?–1847). Swiss scenery. 1820.
Hodgskin, Thomas (1787–1869). Travels in the north of Germany. Edinburgh 1820.
Journal of a tour in France, Switzerland and Lombardy. 1821. Anon.
Voyages and travels of Her Majesty Caroline, Queen of Great Britain including visits to various parts of Germany, France, Italy, Greece, Palestine etc. 1821.
Robinson, William (1804–27). Voyages up the Mediterranean and in the Indian seas [1821–6]. Ed J. A. Heraud 1837.
Scott, John (1783–1821). Sketches of manners, scenery etc in the French provinces, Switzerland and Italy. 1821.
Holman, James (1786–1857). Journey undertaken in 1819, 1820 and 1821 through France, Savoy, Switzerland etc. 1822.
Bakewell, Robert (1768–1843). Travels in the Tarentaisi and various parts of the Grecian and Pennine Alps and in Switzerland and Auvergne. 1823.
Tennant, Charles (1768–1838). A tour through parts of the

Netherlands, Holland, Germany, Switzerland, Savoy and France. 1824.
Forbes, Murray. The diary of a traveller over Alps and Appenines. 1824.
Downes, George. Letters from continental countries. 1825.
Duppa, Richard (1770–1831). Miscellaneous observations and opinions on the Continent. 1825.
Lion hunting: or a summer's ramble through parts of Flanders, Germany and Switzerland. 1826. Anon.
Hazlitt, William (1778–1830). A journey through France and Italy. 1826.
A tour to Great St Bernard and round Mont Blanc. 1827. Anon.
Jones, George Matthew (1785?–1831). Travels in Norway, Sweden, Finland, Russia and Turkey. 1827.
Stevenson, Seth William (1784–1853). Tour in France, Savoy, N. Italy, Switzerland, Germany and the Netherlands. 1827.
Granville, Augustus Bozzi (1783–1872). St Petersburgh. A journal of travels to and from that capital through Flanders, the Rhenich provinces, Prussia, Russia, Poland, Silesia, Saxony, the federated states of Germany and France. 1828, rptd New York 1971.
Walter, W. Letters from the Continent. 1828.
Sinclair, J. D. An autumn in Italy. 1829.
Murray, John (1808–92). A glance at some of the beautiful sublimities of Switzerland. 1829.
Cobbett, J. P. Journal of a tour in Italy. 1830.
Frankland, Charles Colville (1797–1876). Travels to and from Constantinople in 1827 and 1828, or Personal narrative of a journey from Vienna through Hungary, Transylvania, Wallachia, Bulgaria and Roumelia to Constantinople. 1830.
Inglis, Henry David (1795–1835). Spain in 1830. 1831.
Inglis, Henry David. Switzerland, the south of France and the Pyrenees. 1837.
Roscoe, Thomas (1791–1871). The tourist in Switzerland and Italy. 1830.
Elliott, Charles Boileau (1803–1866). Letters from the north of Europe, or, a Journal of travels in Holland, Denmark, Norway, Sweden, Finland, Russia, Prussia and Saxony. 1832.
Ritchie, Leitch (1800?–65). Travelling sketches in the north of Italy, the Tyrol and on the Rhine. 1832.
Liddiard, William (1774–1841). Three months' tour in Switzerland and France. 1832.
Forbes, James David (1809–68). Travels through the Alps [1832–50]. Ed W. A. B. Coolidge 1900.
Forbes, James David. Norway and its glaciers. 1853.
Wilder, F. The journal of an economical tourist to France, Switzerland and Italy. 1833.
Bateman, Mrs. A summer's tour through Belgium up the Rhine and to the lakes of Switzerland. 1834.
Beckford, William Thomas (1759–1844). Italy, Spain and Portugal with an excursion to the monasteries of Alcobaça and Batalha. 2 vols 1834.
Dyke, T. (1801?–66). Tour through Belgium, Rhenish Prussia, Germany, Switzerland. 1834.
Hayward, Abraham (1801–84). A journey across the Alps. 1834.
Stanhope, Philip Henry, 5th Earl (1805–75). Letters from Switzerland. 1834.
A peep at the Continent: or six weeks' tour through parts of Belgium, Rhenish Prussia, Savoy, Switzerland and France. 1835. Anon.
Leake, William Martin (1777–1860). Travels in N. Greece. 4 vols 1835.
Rickman, E. S. Sketch of a pedestrian tour through Switzerland. 1835.
Thomson, William. Two journeys through Italy and Switzerland. 1835.
Wilkley, E. A ramble through France, Italy, Switzerland etc. 1836.
Laing, Samuel (1780–1868). Journal in Norway. 1836.
Laing, Samuel (1780–1868). Tour in Sweden. 1839.
Laing, Samuel (1780–1868). Notes on the social and political state of France, Prussia etc. 1842.
Atkins, Henry Martin (1818–42). Ascent to the summit of Mont Blanc. 1837.
O'Connor, Matthew (1773–1844). A tour through Belgium, Germany, France and Switzerland. 1837.
Clarke, Edward Daniel (1769–1822). Travels in various countries of Scandinavia including Denmark, Sweden, Norway, Lapland and Finland. 1838.
Slade, Adolphus (1802–77). Travels in Germany and Russia including a steam voyage ... from Vienna to Constantinople in 1838–39. 1840.
Bremner, Robert. Excursions in Russia. 2 vols 1839.
Bremner, Robert. Excursions in Denmark, Norway and Sweden. 2 vols 1840.
Clarke, Andrew. Tour in France, Italy and Switzerland during the years 1840 and 1841. 1841.
Fry, Elizabeth (1780–1845). Journeys on the Continent 1840–1. Ed R. Johnson 1931.
Chambers, William (1800–83). A tour in Switzerland. 1841.
Sedgwick, Miss C. N. (1789–1807). Letters from abroad. 1841.
Davy, John (1790–1868). Notes and observations in the Ionian island and Malta. 2 vols 1842.
Strutt, Mrs Elizabeth. Domestic residence in Switzerland. 1842.
Holmes, Mrs Dalkeith. A ride on horseback to Florence through France and Switzerland. 1842.
Yates, Mrs Ashton. Letters written during a journey to Switzerland. 1843.
Borrow, George (1803–81). The Bible in Spain. 3 vols 1843; suppl in Hand-book for travellers in Spain, 1913 (priv ptd).
Shelley, Mary Wollstonecraft (1797–1851). Rambles in Germany and Italy. 1844.
Buckingham, James Silk (1786–1855). Belgium, the Rhine, Switzerland and Holland. 1844.
Lamont, Martha Macdonald. Two years in France and Switzerland. 1844.
Snow, Robert. Memorials of a tour on the Continent. 1845.
Alexander, William Lindsay (1808–84). Switzerland and the Swiss churches. 1846.
Cheever, George Barrell. Wanderings of a pilgrim in the shadow of Mont-Blanc and the Jungfrau Alp. 1846.
Ford, Richard (1796–1858). Handbook for travellers in Spain. 2 vols 1845.
Ford, Richard. Gatherings from Spain. 1846.
Lear, Edward (1812–88). Illustrated excursions in Italy. 1846.
Lear, Edward. A tour in Sicily May–June 1847. Ed G. Proby 1938.
Lear, Edward. Journals of a landscape painter in Albania, Illyria etc. 1851.
Lear, Edward. Journals of a landscape painter in S. Calabria. 1852.
Lear, Edward. Journal of a landscape painter in Corsica. 1870.
Lear, Edward. Indian journal 1873–5. Ed R. Murphy 1953.
Massie, James William (1799–1869). A summer's ramble in Belgium and Switzerland. 1846.
Wilkinson, Sir John Gardner (1797–1875). Dalmatia and Montenegro. 2 vols 1848.
Morgan, John Minter (1782–1854). A tour through Switzerland and Italy 1846–7. 1850.
Smith, Albert Richard. A month in Constantinople. 1850.
Townsend, Francis. Journal of a tour in Italy. 1850.
Sewell, Elizabeth Missing (1815–1906). Journal kept during a summer tour. 1851.
Spencer, Edmund. Travels in European Turkey in 1850, through Bosnia, Servia, Bulgaria, Macedonia, Thrace, Albania and Epirus with a visit to Greece and the Ionian Isles. 1851.

Cayley, George John (1826–78). Las Alforjas: or the bridle roads of Spain. 2 vols 1853.
Grant, James. Records of a run through continental countries. 1853.
Oliphant, Laurence (1829–88). The Russian shores of the Black Sea in the autumn of 1852. 1853.
Blackwell, Eardley, J. In Switzerland in 1854. 1855.
Headley, J. T. Travels among Alpine scenery. 1855.
Street, George Edmund (1824–81). Bricks and marble in the Middle Ages: notes of a tour in the north of Italy. 1855.
Street, George Edmund (1824–81). Some account of Gothic architecture in Spain. 1865.
Wills, Alfred. Wanderings among the High Alps. 1856.
White, Walter (1811–93). On foot through the Tyrol. 1856.
Pestalozzi, Mrs Conrad. My travels abroad. 1856.
Lowe, Helen. Unprotected females in Norway. 1857.
Travels in Switzerland, Italy and Dalmatia, by a lady. 1857. Anon.
Stephen, Sir Leslie (1832–1904). The playground of Europe [Switzerland 1857–69]. 1871.
Hinchcliff, Thomas Woodbine (1825–82). Summer months among the Alps. 1857.
Hinchcliff, Thomas Woodbine. Peaks, passes and glaciers. 1859.
Clark, William George (1821–78). Peloponnesus: notes of study and travel. 1858.
King, Samuel William (1821–68). The Italian valleys of the Pennine Alps. 1858.
Coleman, Edmund Thomas. Scenes from the snowfields. 1859.
Tyndall, John (1820–93). Glaciers of the Alps. 1860.
Tyndall, John (1820–93). Hours of exercise in the Alps. 1871.
Whymper, Edward (1840–1911). Scrambles amongst the Alps [1860–5]. 1871.
Barrow, Sir John (1764–1848). Expeditions on the glaciers, including an ascent of Mont Blanc, Monte Rose, Col du Géant 1862. 1864.
Mackenzie, Georgina Mary Muir. Across the Carpathians. 1862. With A. P. Irby.
Mackenzie, Georgina Mary Muir. Travels in the Slavonic provinces of Turkey in Europe. 1867.
Wordsworth, Christopher (1807–85). Journal of a tour in Italy. 1863.
Brocklebank, John. Continental and oriental travels: being excursions in France, Italy, Egypt and Sinai. 1865.
McTear, Robert. Notes of a continental tour. 1865.
Rivington, Alexander. Notes of a travel in Europe. 1865.
Bradbury, J. Three weeks from home through France and Switzerland. 1866.
Coolidge, William Augustus Brevoort (1850–1926). Alpine Studies [1868–1905]. 1912.
Dowsing, William. Rambles in Switzerland. 1868.
Butler, Samuel (1835–1902). Alps and sanctuaries of Piedmont and the Canton Ticino [1869–]. 1881.
Girdlestone, Rev A. G. (b. 1842). The high Alps without guides. 1870.
Taylor, George Ledwell (1788–1873). The autobiography of an octogenarian architect, being a record of his studies at home and abroad. 1870–2.
Evill, William. A winter journey to Rome and back. 1871.
Vizard, John. A tour through France, Italy and Switzerland. 1872.
Carr, Alfred. Adventures with my alpenstock and knapsack: or a five weeks' tour in Switzerland in 1874. 1875.
Jackson, Lady Catherine Hannah Charlotte (d. 1891). Fair Lusitana. 1874. On Portugal.
Plunket, Frederica. Here and there among the Alps. 1875.
Freshfield, Douglas (1845–1934). Across country from Thonon to Trent. 1865.
Freshfield, Douglas. Italian Alps. 1875.
Carter, Charles Rooking. Incidents of travel and sketches of remarkable places in England and other countries. 1875.
Green, John Richard (1837–83). Stray studies from England and Italy. 1876.
Rodwell, George Farrar (b. 1843). South by east: notes of travel in southern Europe. 1877.
A Briton abroad. 1878. Anon.
Mahaffy, Sir John Pentland (1839–1919). Rambles and studies in Greece. 1878.
Stevenson, Robert Louis (1850–94). An inland voyage. 1878.
Stevenson, Robert Louis. Travels with a donkey in the Cévennes. 1879.
Stevenson, Robert Louis. Swiss note. 1880. In his Essays and criticisms, Edinburgh 1903.
Dixon, William Hepworth (1821–79). British Cyprus. 1879.
Miller, William. Wintering in the Riviera, with notes of travel in Italy and France. 1879.
Mummery, Albert Frederick (1855–95). My climbs in the Alps and Caucasus [1879–]. 1895.
Farrer, Richard Ridley (b. 1856). A tour in Greece. 1880.
Knight, Edward Frederick (1852–1925). Albania, a narrative of recent travel. 1880.
Capper, Samuel James. Shores and cities of the Bodensee. 1881.
Havergal, Frances Ridley (1836–79). Swiss letters. 1882.
Holworthy, S. M. Alpine scrambles and classic rambles. 1882.
Bryce, James Viscount (1838–1922). Memories of travel [Switzerland 1884]. 1923.
Minchin, James George Cotton. The growth of freedom in the Balkan Peninsula. Notes of a traveller in Montenegro, Bosnia, Servia, Bulgaria and Greece. 1886.
Tissot, Victor. Unknown Switzerland. 1889.
Gosse, Sir Edmund William (1849–1928). In Switzerland poetical and pictorial. 1893.
Layard, Sir Austen Henry. A handbook of Rome and its environs. 1894.
Marsh, Herbert. Two seasons in Switzerland. 1895.

Great Britain

Colt-Hoare, Richard (1758–1838). Northern tour. 1800. Cardiff Public Lib MS 3.127.5.
Colt-Hoare, Richard (1758–1838). Tour in S. Wales 1801. 1802. Cardiff Public Lib MS 3.127.2.1.
Heath, Charles. The excursion down the Wye from Ross to Monmouth. 1800.
Bristed, John. A pedestrian tour through part of the Highlands of Scotland in 1801. 2 vols 1803.
Evans, Thomas. Cambrian itinerary: or Welsh tourist. 1801.
Campbell, Alexander (1764–1824). A journey from Edinburgh through parts of North Britain. 2 vols 1802.
Barber, J. T. A tour through South Wales and Monmouthshire. 1803.
Hutton, William (1723–1815). Remarks upon North Wales. 1803.
Malkin, Benjamin Heath (1769–1842). The scenery, antiquities and biography of South Wales. 1804.
Denholm, James (1772–1818). A tour to the principal Scotch and English Lakes. 1804.
Evans, Rev John. A tour through South Wales. 1804.
Evans, Rev John. North Wales. 1812.
Fenton, Richard. Tours in Wales 1804–13. 1917 (Cambrian Archaeological Soc).
Pratt, Samuel Jackson (1749–1814). Gleanings in England. 3 vols 1804.
Thornton, Thomas (1757–1823). A sporting tour through the northern parts of England and Scotland. 1804.
Travers, Benjamin (1783–1858). A descriptive tour to the Lakes. 1804.
Donovan, Edward (1768–1837). Descriptive excursions through South Wales and Monmouthshire, in the year 1804 and the four preceding summers. 2 vols 1805.
Mawman, Joseph. An excursion to the Highlands of Scotland and the English Lakes. 1805.

Duke of Rutland, John Henry Manners, 5th Duke (1778–1857). A tour round the Southern coasts of England. 1805.
Duke of Rutland, John Henry Manners, 5th Duke (1778–1857). A tour to the northern parts of Great Britain. 1813.
Duke of Rutland, John Henry Manners, 5th Duke (1778–1857). A tour through North and South Wales. 1848.
Woodward, George Moutard (1760?–1809). Eccentric excursions in different parts of England and S. Wales. 1807.
Hutchinson, John. Tour through the High Peak of Derbyshire. 1809.
Dennis, Alexander. Journal of a tour through a great part of England and Scotland in the year 1810. 1816.
Webb, Daniel Carless. Four excursions to various parts of Great Britain in 1810 and 1811. 1812.
Daniell, William (1769–1837). A voyage round Great Britain in the summer of 1813. 1814.
Ayton, Richard (1786–1823). A voyage round Great Britain in the summer of 1813. 2 vols 1814.
Horne, Thomas Hartwell (1780–1862). The Lakes of Lancashire, Westmorland and Cumberland. 1816.
Pugh, Edward. Cambria depicta. 1816.
Compton, Thomas. A tour through N. Wales. 1817.
Brown, John. Notes on an excursion into the Highlands of Scotland in autumn 1818. 1819.
Cromwell, Thomas Kitson (1792–1870). Excursions through England and Wales, Scotland and Ireland. 1818.
Sketch of a tour in the Highlands of Scotland, through Perthshire, Argyleshire and Inverness-shire. 1819. Anon.
Hassell, John (d. 1825). Tour of the Grand Junction Canal. 1819.
Southey, Robert (1774–1843). Tour in Scotland in 1819. Ed C. H. Herford 1929.
Selwyn, Mrs. Excursions through the most interesting parts of England, Wales and Scotland 1819–23. 1824.
Newell, Rev Robert Hasell. Letters on the scenery of Wales. 1821.
Wilkinson, Thomas. Tours to the British Mountains. 1824.
A summer ramble in the North Highlands. 1825. Anon.
Baines, Edward (1774–1848). A family tour to the Lakes of Cumberland, Westmorland and Lancashire. 1829.
Botfield, Beriah (1807–63). Journal of a tour through the Highlands of Scotland during the summer of 1829. 1830.
Cobbett, William (1762–1835). Rural rides. 1830.
Anderson, George. Guide to the Highlands and Islands of Scotland, including Orkney and Zetland. 1834.
Smith, B. P. A journal of an excursion round the south-eastern coast of England. 1834.
Head, Sir George. A home tour through the manufacturing districts of England in the summer of 1835. 1836.
Head, Sir George. A home tour through various parts of the United Kingdom. 1837.
Smith, C. L. Excursions through the Highlands and Isles of Scotland in 1835 and 1836. 1837.
Roscoe, Thomas (1791–1871). Wanderings and excursions in North Wales. 1836.
Holland, John (1794–1872). The tour of the Don. 2 vols 1837.
Lauder, Sir Thomas Dick (1784–1848). Highland rambles. 2 vols 1837.
Turner, Thomas. Narrative of a journey associated with a fly, from Gloucester to Aberystwyth, and through North Wales in 1837. 1840.
Bennett, G. J. A pedestrian tour through North Wales. 1838.
Onwhyn, Joseph. Guide to the Highlands of Scotland. 1839.
Townshend, Chauncey Hare (1798–1868). A tour through part of the Western Highlands of Scotland. 1839.
Mackay, Charles (1814–89). The Thames and its tributaries. 2 vols 1840.
Mackay, Charles (1814–89). The scenery and poetry of the English Lakes. 1846.
Ritchie, Leitch (1800?–65). The Wye and its associations. 1841.
Evans, F. Furness and Furness Abbey: or a companion through the Lancashire part of the Lake District. 1842.
Maxwell, William Hamilton (1792–1850). Wanderings on the Scottish Border. 2 vols 1844.
'Ramble, Reuben'. Reuben Ramble's travels in the southern counties of England. 1845.
Hicklin, John. Excursions in North Wales. 1847.
Thorne, James (1815–81). Rambles by rivers: the Thames. 2 vols 1847–9; Handbook to the environs of London, 1876.
A six weeks' tour in the Highlands of Scotland, by a pedestrian. 1851. Anon.
Collins, William Wilkie (1824–89). Rambles beyond railways: or notes in Cornwall taken a-foot. 1851; ed A. Rowe 1948.
Sidney, Samuel (1813–83). Rides on railways leading to the Lakes and Derbyshire. 1851.
Borrow, George (1803–81). An expedition to the Isle of Man in 1855. Douglas 1915.
Borrow, George (1803–81). Wild Wales: its people, language and scenery. 3 vols 1862.
King, J. W. Journeyings through England and Wales. 1856.
Boase, J. J. A. A ramble in Scotland in 1857, starting from Oxford. BM add MSS 35.051. Vol 7, ff. 251.
A fortnight's ramble through some of the more beautiful counties of old England, by a Manchester clerk. 1859. Anon.
Halliwell, James Orchard (1820–89). Notes of family excursions in North Wales. 1860.
Pinks, W. J. Country trips. 1860.
Bradley, Edward ('Cuthbert Bede'). A tour in tartan-land. 1863.
Oxford to John O'Groats: what we saw and what we paid. 1866. Anon.
Houlding, Henry. From Lancashire to London on foot. 1867.
Douglas, J. P. A run through South Wales via the London and North-Western railway. 1868.
Thornbury, George Walter (1828–76). A tour round England. 2 vols 1870.
Roger, James Cruickshank (1820–99). Journal of a summer tour. 1898.

13 Household Books

(Cookery, Domestic management, Domestic medicine and child-care, Etiquette, Food, Servants)

Special collections

See Blanche Leigh, Preston, and Swiss Cottage collections catalogued by card in Special Collections, Univ of Leeds. See also the catalogue of the Fuller Collection at Oxford Brooke Univ. Parts of the collections of Elizabeth David and Jane Grigson are held at the Guildhall Library, London. The BL and the National Lib of Scotland have good collections.

Bibliographies

Vicaire, G. Bibliographie gastronomique. 1890.
'The Epicure' directory of schools and teachers of cookery and domestic subjects. 1899.
'The Epicure' directory of schools and teachers of domestic economy. 1909.
Oxford, A. English cookery books to 1850. 1913.
Bitting, K. Gastronomic bibliography. 1939.
Rudolph, G. A. Kansas State University receipt book and household manual, bibliography series no. 4. 1968.
Noling A. W. Beverage literature: a bibliography. 1971.
Axford, L. English language cookbooks, 1600–1973. 1976.
Simon, A. Bibliotheca gastronomica. Rptd 1978.
Maclean, V. A short-title catalogue of household and cookery books published in the English tongue 1701–1800. 1981.
The André L. Simon/Eleanor Lowenstein collection of gastronomic literature: a preliminary bibliography. 1982.
Dyer, J. Vegetarianism: an annotated bibliography. 1982.
Wilson, C. Anne (ed). Leeds Food History Symposium Papers. 1986– .
Attar, D. A bibliography of household books published in Britain 1800–1914. 1987.
Driver, E. A bibliography of cookery books published in Britain 1875–1914. 1989.
Sales catalogues of: Cooks Books, Rottingdean, Sussex; Janet Clarke, Bath, Avon; John Lyle, 3 Faubourg Saint Roch, 34620 Puisserguier, France.

Major works

For authors spanning 1900, publications after 1900 have been included to offer a sense of the position of their writing. The distinctive feature of these books is the way they define an enormous mass market, with some authors selling literally millions of books. The first date in each entry indicates the first known edn; for books with very large print runs or many edns or impressions the date of the last known printing is given; together with an indication of the number of edns or highest known numbered edition; the sign + indicates 'more than'.

Acton, E. (1799–1859)
  Modern cookery, in all its branches: reduced to a system of easy practice, for the use of private families. 1845, 18+ edns to 1905.
  The English bread-book for domestic use, adapted to families of every grade. 1857.
See also col 2077.
Addison, Mrs Kate
  Economical cookery for the middle classes. 1879, 1912.
Adkins, Thomas Francis
  Alphabetical guide to sailors' cookery. 2nd edn 1899, 14th edn 1941.
Agogos (Day, Charles William)
  Hints on etiquette and the usages of society. 1836, 28+ edns 1946.
Alexander, Charles Wesley (1832–1927)
  The housewife's friend and family help. [1888].
Allbutt, Dr Henry Arthur. *See also* Attar and Driver, bibliographies, *above*.
  The wife's handbook 1886. 45th edn 1913.
  Every mother's handbook. 1897.
Allen, Miss Mary L.
  Breakfast dishes for every morning of three months. 1884, 24th edn 1915.
  Five-o'clock tea. 1886, 1896.
  Savouries and sweets. 1886, 24th edn 1915.
  Savoury dishes. 1886.
  Luncheon dishes. 1891.
  Soups, broths, purées. 1894.
Allinson, Dr Thomas Richard (1858–1918)
  Wholesome cookery. [1892].
  Dr Allinson's vegetarian cookery. 1905.
Andrew, Thomas
  A cyclopaedia of domestic medicine and surgery. [1842], 5+ edns 1847.
Appert, C.
  The art of preserving all kinds of animal and vegetable substances for several years. 1811.
Arcana Fairfaxiana manuscripts . . . introduction by G. Weddell. 1890.
Armstrong, John
  The young woman's guide to virtue, economy and happiness. [1825], 8th edn 1828.
Armstrong, Mrs Lucie Heaton
  Good form. 1889.
  The etiquette of party-giving. 1893.
  Letter to a bride. 1896.
  Etiquette and entertaining. 1903.
  Etiquette-up-to-date. [1908].
The art of feeding the invalid . . . by a medical practitioner and a lady professor of cookery. [1893], 4th edn 1923.
Arthur, Timothy Shay (1809–85)
  Advice to young ladies on their duties and conduct in life. 1855.

Austin, Thomas
  Two fifteenth-century cookery-books. 1888.
Baines, M. A.
  Domestic servants, as they are and as they ought to be. [1859].
Baker, Mrs
  The companion to the lying-in room. [1857].
Baker, Miss (d. 1876)
  The vegetist's dietary and manual of vegetable cookery . . . by Domestica. [1876 or 1877], 9th edn 1897.
Barker, Lady Mary Ann
  Houses and housekeeping. 1876.
  The bedroom and boudoir. 1878.
Barnett, Edith A.
  National Health Society's penny cookery book. 1879.
  The cookery instructor. [1881].
Barnett, Edith and Hannah Cox O'Neill
  Primer of domestic economy. 1892.
Baylis, Thomas Henry (1817–1908)
  The rights, duties and relations of domestic servants, their masters and mistresses. 1857, 6th edn 1906.
Beale, Lady Mary (Mrs W. Phipson Beale, née Thompson)
  Wholesome cookery. 1882, 6th edn 1895.
  Letters to young housekeepers by Marie de Joncourt. 1912.
Beard, Sidney Hartnoll (b. 1862)
  A simple guide to a natural and humane diet. 1898.
  A comprehensive guide-book to a natural, hygienic, and humane diet . . . [1900], 8th edn 1921.
Beaty-Pownall, Mrs S.
  A book of sauces. 1896.
  The 'Queen' cookery books: Soups, No 1 1899; Ices No 2 1899; Pickles and preserves, No 3 1899; Entrées, No 4 1900; Meats and game, No 5 1900; Sweets, No 6 1901; Sweets, Part II, No 7 1901; Breakfast and lunch dishes, No 8 1901; Salads, sandwiches and savouries, No 9 1901; Vegetables, No 10 1902; Bread, cakes, and biscuits, No 11 1902; Fish, No 12 1903; Fish, Part II, No 13 1903.
  Vegetarian cookery. 1907.
Beauvilliers, A.
  The art of French cookery. 1824.
Beeton, Isabella Mary (1836–65). *See Attar and Driver, bibliographies, above.*
  The book of household management. 1861.
  How to manage house and servants and to make the most of your means. [1866].
  The management of children in health and sickness. [1866].
  Beeton's housewife's treasury of domestic information. [1880].
See also col 2210.
Beeton, Samuel Orchart (1831–77). *See Attar and Driver, bibliographies, above.*
  All about everything. [1871].
  Beeton's book of the laundry. [1871].
  Beeton's dictionary of practical recipes and everyday information. [1871].
  Family etiquette. [1876].
  Beeton's housekeeper's guide. [1880].
  Beeton's shilling recipe book. [1883].
  Beeton's domestic recipe-book. [nd].
See also col 2211.
Bell, J.
  A treatise on confectionery in all its branches. 1817.
Bertram, James Glass (pseud Jenny Wren)
  Modern domestic cookery, including plans for dinner and supper parties. 1880.
  The 'Jenny Wren' series of cookery manuals: The art of preparing soups, stews, hashes and ragouts, [1888]; How to prepare dishes of fishes, [1888]; The art of preparing puddings, tarts, jellies and other sweets, [1890]; The art of preparing dainty dishes for dinners, luncheons and suppers, [1891]; The complete art of dinner-giving with notes on luncheons and suppers, 1891; A treatise on the cooking of big joints, 1891; Sauces, seasoning and salads, [1892].
Bishop, F.
  The illustrated London cookery book. 1852.
Bits about babies. 1870.
Black, George
  Sick-nursing. [1880].
  The young wife's advice book. [1880], 4+ edns 1910.
  Household medicine. [1882].
  The household doctor. 1889, 3+ edns 1948.
  The doctor. [1890].
  The doctor at home. 1891, 4+ edns 1927.
  Every-day ailments and accidents. 1892.
  The family health book. 1892.
Black, Mrs Margaret (1830–1903)
  Household cookery and laundry work. [1882], 151,000+ copies after 1897.
  Hints to young housekeepers. [1884].
  La bonne cuisine, a selection of high-class and household cookery recipes. [1893].
  Collins' school series: Cookery and domestic economy, [1891]; Cookery for schools, [1899].
  Superior cookery. 35,000 copies [1903].
Blunders in behaviour corrected. 1855.
Book of domestic duties. [1835].
Book of fashionable life. [1845].
Book of health: a compendium of domestic medicine. 1828.
Boorde, A.
  The fyrst boke of the introduction of knowledge made by Andrew Boorde . . . A compendyous regyment, or a dietary of helth, made in Mountpyllier, compiled by Andrew Boorde . . . Ed F. J. Furnivall 1870.
Bowman, A.
  The new cookery book. 1869.
Braidwood, Peter Murray
  The domestic management of children. 1874.
  The mother's help and guide. 1894.
The breakfast book. 1865.
Briggs, Miss E.
  School Board for London: Cookery book and general axioms for plain cookery. 1890, 1898.
Brillat-Savarin, Jean-Anthelme (1755–1826)
  The handbook of dining. Tr L. F. Simpson 1859.
  Gastronomy as a fine art . . . A translation of the 'Physiologie du Goût' by R. E. Anderson. 1877, 1889.
  Brillat-Savarin's 'Physiologie du Goût'. A handbook of gastronomy. New and complete tr with 52 original etchings by A. Lalauze 1884.
Brisse, Baron Leon (1813–76)
  366 menus and 1200 recipes of the Baron Brisse . . . Tr Mrs Matthew Clark 1882, 10th edn 1909.
Broadbent, Albert
  Science in the daily meal. [1899].
  Fruits, nuts and vegetables. 1900, 90,000 edns 1915.
  Recipes for forty vegetarian dinners. [1900]. 180,000+ copies, 14+ numbered edns.
  Simple and healthful food. [1903].
  A book about salads. 1905.
Brown, Matilda (1836–1936)
  Myra's cookery book. [1884].
Brown, Miss Rose
  Breakfast book, what to have for breakfast. [1898].
  Cakes, fancy and plain. [1900].
  Puddings, creams and jellies. [1901].

Daily kitchen tables. [1902].
Easy entrées and savouries. [1902].
Vegetables and salads. [1904].
Sweets, for bazaars and children's holidays etc [1905].
Pastry and preserves. [1906].
Dinner to-day. [1907].
Soups and fish. [1907].
Extra puddings. [1908].
Poultry and game. [1909].
The 101 series: One hundred and one little dinners. [1909]; One hundred and one recipes for cold meats. [1909]; One hundred and one dainties for afternoon tea. [1910]; One hundred and one luncheon dishes. [1910]; One hundred and one recipes for salads, sandwiches and savouries. [1913]; One hundred and one sweet dishes. [1913]; One hundred and one varieties for breakfast. [1913]; One hundred and one varieties for supper. [1913].

Buchan, William (1729–1805)
Advice to mothers. 1803.

Buckland, Anne Walbank
Our viands. 1893.

Buckmaster, John Charles (1819–1908)
Simple lessons for home use. Cookery 1877.
Buckmaster's domestic economy and cookery. [1880 or 1881].

Buckton, Catherine M.
Food and home cookery. 1879.
Our dwellings, healthy and unhealthy. 1885.
Comfort and cleanliness. 1898.

Bull, Thomas
Hints to mothers. 1839. 13+ edns 1877.
The maternal management of children. 1840. 7+ edns to 1877.

Burnett, Alexander
The medical adviser. 1825.

Butcher, John
Instructions in etiquette. 1847.

Butler, W. C.
Butler's modern practical confectioner. 1890.
The modern cook. 1894.

Caddy, Florence (b. 1837)
Household organization. 1877.

Callcott, Maria Hutchins
A few household hints, and lessons of conduct for female servants. 1856.

Campbell, Lady C. S. M.
The lady's own cookery book, and new dinner-table directory. 1844.

Carême, M. A. (1783–1833)
The royal Parisian pastrycook and confectioner. 1834.
French cookery. 1836.

Carnell, P. P.
A treatise on family wine making. 1814.

Carter, S.
The frugal housewife. Originally written by Susanna Carter; but now improved by an experienced cook in one of the principal taverns in the City of London. 1823.

Carter, W.
The cook and confectioner's guide. [1800?].

Cartwright, Thomas
Domestic science. 1900.

Cassell
Cassell's household guide. [1873–4], 11+ edns 1912.
Cassell's dictionary of cookery. [1875–6], 1912.
Cassell's family doctor. 1897. 5+ impressions 1955.

A catechism for servants. 1843.

Chambers, W. and R. Ltd.
Cookery and domestic economy, for young housewives. 1838.

Chase, A. W.
England and America's new and useful receipt book. 1868.

Chavasse, Pye Henry (Charles, C. H./George Carpenter) (1810–79)
Advice to mothers on the management of their offspring. 1839, 19+ edns to [1939].
Advice to wives. 1843, 17th edn [1921].
Counsel to a mother. 1869, 6th edn [1890].

Chevalley de Rivaz, Victor (pseud 'The G. C.')
'The Queen' recipes. 1881.
Practical dinners . . . by 'The G.C.'. 1887.

Child, Mrs Lydia Maria (1802–80)
The mother's book. 1832, 4+ edns to 1856.
The family nurse. 1837.

Chloe, Aunt
One hundred and one methods of poultry cookery. 1888.

Chubb, W. P.
The general receipt book; or, oracle of knowledge. 1825.

Clarke, Sir Arthur (1778–1857)
The mother's medical assistant. 1820.

Clarke, Mrs Edith (1844–1926)
National Training School of Cookery: Plain cookery recipes, 1883, 16th edn 1921; High-class cookery recipes, 1885, 12th edn 1912; Artizan recipes, 1895, 1921; New high-class cookery with game recipes, 1896, 1926.
Cheap recipes for fish cookery. 1883.
Recipes for cheap dinners. 1884.
Recipes for plain cookery. 1885.

Cobbett, A.
The English housekeeper. 1842.

Cobbett, William (1762–1835). *See Attar and Driver, bibliographies, above.*
Cottage economy. 1822, 17+ edns 1979.
See also col 2109.

Cole, Miss Rose Owen
The official handbook for the National Training School for Cookery. 1877, 1924.
Breakfast and savoury dishes. 1885.
How to cook fish. 1887.
Sickroom cookery. 1887.

Combe, Andrew (1797–1847)
Treatise on the physiological and moral management of infancy. 1840, 11+ edns 1896.

Cook, Millicent Whiteside
Tables and chairs. [1876].

Cooke, Mordecai Cubitt (1825–1914)
British edible fungi: how to distinguish and how to cook them. 1891.
Edible and poisonous mushrooms. 1894.

Cookery made easy. [1861].

The cookmaid's complete guide, and The art of cookery made easy. 1850.

Cooley, Arnold James
A cyclopaedia of practical receipts. 1845, 6th edn 1880.

Copley, E. *See* Hewlett, Esther.

Cosnett, T.
The footman's directory, and butler's remembrancer. 1825.

Cre-fydd's family fare. 1864.

A cup of coffee. Cup that cheers series, No 1 1883.

Cupples, Anne Jane
A book about house work. 1877.

Curious old cookery receipts. [1891].

Curtiss, Fred Hull
The comic cookery book and dyspeptics guide to the grave. 1891.

Dalgairns, Mrs
The practice of cookery, adapted to the business of every day life. 1829.

Dallas, Eneas Sweetland (1828–79)
Kettner's book of the table. 1877.
See also col 2222.

Davidson, Mrs J. E.
Dainties, English and foreign. 1888.
Eggs: English and foreign ways of cooking them. 1890.
Cold meat cookery. 1898.
Davies, Frederick
Cakes and biscuits. 1891.
Pastry and confectionery, creams, jellies and ices. 1891.
Temperance drinks for summer and winter. 1892.
D'Avigdor, Elm Henry (pseud Wanderer) (1841–95)
Dinners and dishes. 1885.
De Salis, Mrs Harriet Anne (née Bainbridge)
A la mode cookery: Savouries à la mode, 1886, 19th impression 1917; Entrées 1887, 8+ edns 1915; Dressed game and poultry, 1888; Dressed vegetables, 1888, 7th impression 1909; Oysters, 1888; Soups and dressed fish, 1888, 9th impression 1907; Sweets and supper dishes, 1888, 9th impression 1908; Cakes and confections, 1889, 8th impression 1910; Puddings and pastry, 1889; Drinks, 1891; Gardening, fruits, 1895; Gardening, vegetables, 1895; National viands, 1895; Up-to-date recipes, 1902.
Tempting dishes for small incomes. 1890, 9th impression 1908.
Wrinkles and notions for every household. 1890.
The art of cookery past and present. 1898.
The housewife's referee. 1898, 7th impression 1910.
Dewhurst, Henry W.
The new medical adviser and family physician. 1836.
Dinners and dinner-parties, or the absurdities of artificial life. 1862.
Docwra, Mrs Mary E.
The non-alcoholic cookery book. [1880].
Dodd, G.
The food of London. 1856.
Dods, Miss Matilda Lees
A handbook of cookery. 1881, 5+ edns 1906.
Cottage cookery. [1898].
Hints for the sickroom. [1899].
Dolby, R.
The cook's dictionary, and housekeeper's directory. 1830.
Domestic economy, and cookery, for rich and poor. 1827, 1837.
Domestic economy for the use of schools. 1878.
The domestic service guide to housekeeping. 1865.
Doncaster, Mary W.
Luxurious modern cookery. 1889.
Donovan, Michael
The cabinet of useful arts. 1830.
Doran, J.
Table traits, with something on them. 1854.
Duckitt, Miss Hildagonda Johanna (1840 [1839?]–1905)
Hilda's 'Where is it?' of recipes. 1891, 32,000 edns 1925.
Hilda's diary of a Cape housekeeper. 1902.
Earle, Mrs Maria Theresa (1836–1925)
Pot-pourri from a Surrey garden. 1897, 15+ edns 1919.
More pot-pourri from a Surrey garden. 1899.
Eastlake, Charles Lock (1836–1906)
Hints of household taste. 1868, 4th edn 1878.
Eaton, M.
The cook and housekeeper's complete and universal dictionary. 1823.
Economical cookery, for young housekeepers. 1835.
Edmunds, Mrs H.
Sweet, sweet home, or the mother's guide and servant's chart. [1897].
Edwards, F.
On the extravagant use of fuel in cooking operations. 1869.
The Englishwoman in India. 1864.
The epicure's almanac and directory. 1843.
Espoir (pseud)
How to live on a hundred a year. [1874].
Etiquette for gentlemen: with hints. 1838, 20+ edns after 1843.
Etiquette for the ladies. 1837, 18th edn 1840.
Etiquette for ladies. [1857].
Etiquette, politeness and good breeding. [1870].
The family cookery book. 1812.
The family economist. 1848.
The family hand-book. 1845.
Faunthorpe, Rev J. P.
Household science. 1881, 5th edn 1889.
Favourite cakes of rural England. The Cable series of farm and household books, no 2 [1899].
The female instructor; or, young woman's companion. 1811, 1812.
Fennings, Alfred
Every mother's book. [1856].
Fennings' everybody's doctor. [1864].
A few hints for home happiness and comfort. 1860.
Filippini, Allesandro (Fillipini, Alexander)
One hundred desserts. 1893.
One hundred ways of cooking eggs. 1893.
One hundred ways of cooking fish. 1893.
The table: how to buy food, how to cook it, and how to serve it (The Delmonico cook book). 1889, 6th edn 1893.
The international cookbook. 1906.
Finchley, Holy Trinity Church, National and Industrial Schools, Finchley manuals of industry, 1: Cooking; or, practical and economical training for those who are to be servants, wives, and mothers. 1849.
The flower, fruit and kitchen garden. [1853].
The footman. [1855].
Forward, Charles Walter
Practical vegetarian recipes. 1891.
Popular vegetarian cookery. [1905].
Francatelli, C. E. (1805–65)
The modern cook. 1846, 29th edn 1896, ed C. H. Senn 1911.
The cook's guide, and housekeeper's and butler's assistant. 1861, 1888.
Plain cookery. 1862, 1877.
The royal English and foreign confectioner. 1862.
Francis, L. M.
The frugal housewife. 1832.
French domestic cookery, combining economy with elegance. 1825.
Gardiner, Florence Mary
Furnishings and fittings for every home. [1894].
Garrett, Theodore Francis
The encyclopaedia of practical cookery. 8 vols [1892–4], 9+ edns to 1898.
A book of practical recipes for the use of Palmine. 1909.
The gentlewoman. 1864.
Gironci, Maria
Recipes of Italian cookery. [1892].
Italian recipes for food reformers. 1905.
Glenny, G.
The culture of fruits and vegetables. 1860.
Going to service. [1858].
Good servants make good places. [1871].
Good things made, said and done. 1879, 44+ edns to 1949.
Goodall's palatable cookery. 1881.
Gooding, Ralph
A manual of domestic medicine. 1867.
Gordon, Miss Martha H.
Cookery for working men's wives. [1888], 5+ edns to [1918].
Gouffé, J.
The royal cookery book, le livre de cuisine. 1868.
The book of preserves, le livre de conserves, containing instructions for preserving meat, fish, vegetables, and fruit. 1871.

Graham, Thomas John (1795?–1876)
Modern domestic medicine. 1827, 14+ edns 1882.
Green, D. R.
The housekeeper's friend. [1886].
Greville, Lady Beatrice Violet (1842–1932)
The gentlewoman in society. 1892.
The guide to service: The lady's maid, 1838; The maid-of-all-work, 1838; The housemaid, 1839; The nursery maid, 1839; The laundry-maid, 1842; The nurse, 1843. Authorship ascribed to Harriet Martineau+. *See also Attar and Driver, bibliographies, above.*
Gunter, W.
Gunter's confectioner's oracle, containing receipts for desserts on the most economical plan for private families. 1830.
The habits of good society. [1859], 4+ edns to [1890].
Hale, Mrs Sarah Josephina Buell (1788–1879)
The new household receipt-book. 1854.
Hall, A.
Good cookery illustrated. 1867.
Hall, H. B.
The oyster; where, how, and when to find, breed, cook, and eat it. 1861.
Hamer, Mrs Sarah Sharp (née Heaton) (1839–1927) (pseuds Phillis/Phyllis Browne; Olive Patch; A. G. Payne)
Common-sense housekeeping. [1877].
A year's cookery by Phillis Browne. [1879 or 1880], 14+ edns to 1910.
What girls can do. [1880.]
The girl's own cookery book by Phillis Browne. [1882 or 1883].
Diet and cookery for common ailments . . . by Phyllis Browne. 1894.
The dictionary of dainty breakfasts by Phyllis Browne. 1898.
Practical housekeeping. 1906.
Hammond, E.
Modern domestic cookery, and useful receipt book. 1815, 1816, 1826.
Hardships made easy. [1864].
Harrison, Miss Mary
Mary Harrison's guide to modern cookery. 1891, 7+ edns to 1929.
Cookery for busy lives and small incomes. 1892.
The skilful cook. 1884, 10th edn 1919.
The school cookery book. 1898.
Simple lessons in cookery. 1898.
Haslehurst, P.
The family friend, and young woman's companion. 1814.
Hassall, A. H.
Adulterations detected; or, plain instructions for the discovery of frauds in food and medicine. 1857.
Hassell, Joseph
Lessons in domestic economy for elder girls. 1874.
Hayward, A.
The art of dining; or, gastronomy and gastronomers. 1852.
See also col 2235.
Hazlitt, W. Carew (1834–1913)
Old cookery books and ancient cuisine. 1886.
See also col 2695.
Headdon, M. E.
Household object lessons. 1886.
Household and domestic economy. 1893.
Henderson, W. A.
The housekeeper's instructor: or, universal family cook. [1800].
Henry VIII, King of England
The privy purse expenses of King Henry the eighth, from November MDXXIX, to December MDXXXII. 1827.
Henry, Mrs May and Miss Edith B. Cohen
The economical cook: a modern Jewish recipe book. 1889, 5th edn 1937.
Herisse, Emile
The art of pastry making. 1893, 10+ edns to 1929.
Heritage, Miss Lizzie
Cookery for schools. 1891.
Cassell's new universal cookery book. 1894, 4th edn 1909.
Cookery for invalids. [1897].
Hervey, Henrietta A.
Anglo-Indian cookery at home. 1895.
Hewlett, E.
The cook's complete guide. 1834.
The housekeeper's guide. 1834.
The complete cottage cookery. 1858, 1862.
Hewlett, Esther (also known as Esther Copley)
Cottage comforts, with hints for promoting them. 1825, 23rd edn 1858.
The young servant's friendly instructor. 1827.
Catechism of domestic economy. 1851.
Hints for happy homes, or, family experiences. [1859].
The young wife. [1870].
Hints and helps for every-day emergencies. [1860].
Hints to domestic servants. 1854.
Holland, M.
The complete economical cook, and frugal housewife. 1825, 1829.
Holt, Vincent M.
Why not eat insects? [1885].
Home work and how to do it. [1886].
Homely letters on household things. [1879].
Hooper, Mary
Little dinners. 1874.
Cookery for invalids, persons of delicate digestion, and for children. 1876, 7th edn 1904.
Every day meals. 1877, 8th edn 1903.
Good plain cookery. [1882].
Houlston and sons
Houlston's housekeeper's assistant: or, complete family cook. 1828.
The household encyclopaedia. 1858.
Household work. [1849], 14th edn [1863].
The house-keeper's receipt book. 1813.
The housemaid; her duties, and how to perform them. [1877].
The housewife's cookery book. [1860].
How a schoolmistress may live upon seventy pounds a year. [1887].
How to behave. [1865].
How to make home happy. [1880].
Howard, Lady Constance
Etiquette: what to do, and how to do it. 1885.
Hughes, Joseph
Hughes's domestic economy. 1891.
Hughes, W.
A practical treatise on the choice and cookery of fish. 1854.
Hughson, D.
The new family receipt book. 1817.
Humelbergius, D.
Apician morsels; or, tales of the table, kitchen, and larder. 1834.
Humphry, Mrs Charlotte Eliza (Madge of 'Truth')
Housekeeping. 1893.
Manners for men. 1897.
Manners for women. 1897.
A word to women. 1898.
Manners for girls. 1901.
Etiquette for every day. [1902].
Hunter, A.
Culina famulatrix medicinae: or, receipts in modern cookery; with a medical commentary, written by Ignotus. 1804, rev Hunter 1806.
Hutton, Barbara
Monday morning: how to get through it. [1863].
The Indian cookery book. [1869].
Indian domestic economy and receipt book. 1852.

Instructions in household matters. 1845.
Irwin, D.
The housewife's guide. [1830].
Jack, Miss Florence B.
The art of cooking for invalids. 1896, 6th edn 1926.
The art of laundry work. 1896, 6+ edns 1913.
Fish and fish entrées. 1898.
Soups, stocks and purées. 1898.
Vegetables, salads and vegetable entremets. 1898.
Breakfast and savoury dishes. 1903.
Hot puddings, soufflés and fritters. 1903.
Cold sweets, jellies and creams. 1904.
Entrées of meat, game and poultry. 1904.
Cakes, one hundred tested recipes. 1907.
The woman's book. 1911.
Cookery for every household. 1914, 9th edn 1938.
James, Mrs Eliot
A guide to Indian household management. [1879].
Our servants. [1883].
Jarrin, G. A.
The Italian confectioner, or complete economy of desserts. 1820.
Jeaffreson, John Cordy (1831–1901)
A book about the table. 1875.
Jennings, James
The family cyclopaedia. [1822].
Two thousand five hundred practical recipes in family cookery. 1841.
Jerrold, Thomas Serle (1833–1907)
Our kitchen garden: the plants we grow and how we cook them. 1881 (1917 edn entitled Our war-time kitchen garden).
Jerrold, William Blanchard (1826–84) (pseud Fin-Bec)
The epicure's year book – and table companion, for 1868–9. 1868–9.
The book of menus. 1876.
The dinner bell. 1878.
The cupboard papers. 1881.
Jewry, M.
Warne's model cookery and housekeeping book. 1868.
Jex-Blake, Sophia Louisa (1840–1912). *See also Attar and Driver, bibliographies, above.*
The care of infants. 1884.
Johnson, Mrs
The bride elect. [1878].
Johnson, L.
Practical family cookery. 1839.
Johnstone, C. I.
The cook and housewife's manual. 1826, 1829.
Kenney-Herbert, Colonel Arthur Robert (1840–1916) (pseud Wyvern). *See also Attar and Driver, bibliographies, above.*
Culinary jottings. 1885.
Tinned food. 1893.
Common-sense cookery. [1894], 4+ edns to 1913.
Fifty breakfasts. [1894].
Fifty dinners. [1895].
Fifty lunches. [1896].
Picnics and suppers. 1901.
Vegetarian and simple diet. 1904.
Kilvert's book of economical cookery and useful household recipes. [1887].
Kingscote, Adeline Georgina Isabella (d. 1908)
The English baby in India and how to rear it. 1893.
Kingsford, Anna (1846–88)
Health, beauty and the toilet. Letters to ladies from a lady doctor. 1886.
Kirk, Mrs Eliza Walker
Book of tried favourites. 1900, 26th edn 1948.
Kirwan, A. V.
Host and guest. 1864.
Kitchiner, W. (1775?–1827)
Apicius redivivus; or, the cook's oracle. 1817, 1818, 1831.
The housekeeper's ledger. 1824.
The art of invigorating and prolonging life. 1828.
The housekeeper's oracle; or, art of domestic management. 1829.
Klickman, Flora (1867–1958). *See also Attar and Driver, bibliographies, above.*
Etiquette of today. [1902].
The knife and fork for 1849.
Kochheim, A. von
A handbook of foreign cookery. 1845.
Labourers' Friend Society.
The housekeeper's ledger. 1824.
The lady's maid. [1877].
Lake, Nancy
Menus made easy. [1884], 37+ edns [1954].
Daily dinners. [1892].
Lancashire cookery book. [1896], 22+ edns to 1929.
Landon, Major James Henry (1832–1915). *See also Attar and Driver, bibliographies, above.*
The Pytchley book of refined cookery and bills of fare. 1885, 5th edn 1891.
Breakfasts, luncheons, and ball suppers. 1887.
The laundry maid. [1877].
Laurie, Mrs J. W.
Home and its duties. [1870].
Laurie, Joseph (d. 1865)
The parent's guide. 1849.
Lear, Mrs Henrietta Louisa Sidney (née Farrer) (1824–96)
A Lenten cookery book. [1876].
Maigre cookery. 1884.
Lebour-Fawssett, Madame Emilie
Economical French cookery for ladies. 1887.
French cookery for ladies. 1890.
Leslie, E.
The Indian meal book. 1846.
Letters about missuses. 1854.
Letters to a mother on the watchful care of her infant. 1831.
London at table; or, how, when, and where to dine and order a dinner; and where to avoid dining. 1851.
Lord, Mrs E.
Laundry work (how to teach it). 1890.
The theory and practice of laundry work for scholars. 1894, 4+ edns to 1898.
Lovell, M. S.
The edible mollusks of Great Britain and Ireland. 1876.
Lyttelton, Mary Kathleen
Common sense for housewives. [1896].
MacDonald, D.
The new London family cook. [1800?]
Mackenzie, C.
Five thousand receipts in all the useful and domestic arts, constituting a complete and universal practical library, and operative cyclopaedia. 1823, 16th edn [1835].
Maitland, Miss Agnes Catherine (1849–1906). *See also Attar and Driver, bibliographies, above.*
The rudiments of cookery. [1883].
The afternoon tea book. 1887.
The cookery primer. [1888].
What shall we have for breakfast? 1889.
[Mallock, M. M.]
A younger sons' [*sic*] cookery book by a younger son's daughter. 1896, 9+ impressions 1935.
Mann, Miss Ellen E. *See also Attar and Driver, bibliographies, above.*
Manual of the principles of practical cookery. 1899.

Liverpool School of Cookery recipe book. 1900, 5+ impressions to 1917.
Invalid recipes. 1901.
Manners and tone of good society. [1879], 48+ copies to 1955.
Marshall, Mrs
The child's guide to good breeding. 1839.
Marshall, Mrs Agnes Bertha (d. 1905). *See also Attar and Driver, bibliographies, above.*
The book of ices. [1885], 24,000 copies 1976.
Mrs. A. B. Marshall's cookery book. [1888], 80,000+ copies to [1904].
Mrs. A. B. Marshall's larger cookery book. [1891], 11,000+ copies to [1902].
Fancy ices. [1894], 5th edn [1922].
Martin, S.
The new experienced English-housekeeper. 1800.
Massey, J. and W. J.
Massey and son's biscuit, ice, and compote book. 1866.
Masters, T.
The ice book. 1844.
[Mathew, Mrs Emily de Vere]
Supper dishes for people with small means. [1882], 16th edn 1891.
Cheap dinner dishes. [1883].
Cakes and other good things. [1886].
Cookery for our sick and invalid poor. [1887].
The Jubilee penny cookery book. [1887].
Tinned meats, fish, and fruits. [1887].
100 cheap dishes. [1891].
Mayhew, The Brothers [Athol and Henry] (Henry Mayhew 1812–87)
The greatest plague of life. [1847].
Mew, James and John Ashton (Mew b. 1837; Ashton b. 1834)
Drinks of the world. 1892.
Miles, Alfred H. (b. 1848)
The household guide. [1897].
The household oracle. [1897].
Look inside. [1897].
Millington, C.
The housekeeper's domestic library. 1810.
Millington, S. M. T.
The servant's companion and useful guide. 1864.
Modern cookery. 1856, 1918.
Mollard, J.
The art of cookery made easy and refined. 1801.
Moore, Margaret Jane (The Countess Dowager Mountcashell)
Advice to young mothers on the physical education of children. 1823.
Morewood, S.
A philosophical and statistical history of the inventions and customs of ancient and modern nations in the manufacture and use of inebriating liquors. 1838.
The mother's thorough resource-book. [1860].
Mott, Edward Spencer (1844–1910)
Cakes and ale. 1897, 6th edn [1925].
The flowing bowl. 1899, 6th edn [1925].
Murray, A.
The domestic oracle. [1850].
Muskett, Philip Edward and Mrs. H. F. Wicken
The art of living in Australia. [1893].
Nelson's home comforts. A new edition, revised and enlarged by Mary Hooper. [1882], 23rd edn after 1903.
Neville, G.
The new female instructor; or, young woman's guide to domestic happiness. [1825?]
The new family receipt book. 1811, 5+ edns to 1837.
The new home: or wedded life. 1862.
Nightingale, Florence (1820–1910). *See also Attar and Driver, bibliographies, above.*
Notes on nursing. [1859 or 1860], 13+ edns 1980.
Notes on nursing for the labouring classes. 1861.
Nourse, Mrs
Modern practical cookery, pastry, confectionery, pickling and preserving. 1811.
The nursery governess. 1845.
The nursery maid: her duties and how to perform them. [1877].
Oldfield, Dr Josiah (1863–1953)
'The Best' series: Best penny cookery vegetarianism, [1893]; Best way to begin vegetarianism, [1893]; Best 20c cookery, [nd].
The penny guide to fruitarian diet and cookery. 1902, 165,000 edns 1952.
Oram, G.
Masters and servants: their relative duties. 1858.
Orlebar, Miss Eleanor E.
Food for the people; or, lentils and other vegetable cookery. 1879.
P., P. O.
The nabob's cookery book. 1870.
Cookery-book for fasting. 1871.
The economical cook. [1886].
Paidagogos (pseud probably of Charles William Day)
More hints on etiquette. 1838.
Panton, Jane Ellen (1848–1923)
From kitchen to garret. 1888, 5th edn 1896.
Nooks and corners. 1889.
Homes of taste. 1890.
Suburban residences. 1896.
The way they should go. 1896.
Parkes, Mrs W.
Domestic duties; or, instructions to young married ladies, on the management of their households. 1825.
Pastry and sweets for the dinner and supper tables. 17th edn 1903, 26+ edns in total.
Payne, Arthur Gay
Common-sense papers on cookery. [1877], 5+ edns to 1912.
Choice dishes. 1882.
The housekeeper's guide to the use of preserved meats, fruits, vegetables. [1886].
Cassell's shilling cookery. 1888, 17+ edns to 1910.
Cassell's vegetarian cookery. 1891, 9+ edns to [1918].
Pease, S. E.
Hints on nursing the sick and other domestic subjects. [1871].
Peel, Mrs Dorothy Constance (1872–1934). *See also Attar and Driver, bibliographies, above.*
Ten shillings a head per week. 1899, 9+ edns to 1916.
The single handed cook. 1904.
Mrs C. S. Peel's cook-books: Entrées made easy, 1905; Puddings and sweets, 1905; Savouries simplified, 1905; Still room cookery, 1905; Dishes made without meat, 1907; Fish and how to cook it, 1907.
Meatless cookery. [1911].
Pennell, Mrs Elizabeth Robins (1855–1936). *See also Attar and Driver, bibliographies, above.*
The feasts of Autolycus. 1896.
The people's housekeeper. 1876.
Philip, J. M.
How to make home happy. 1864.
Philip, Robert Kemp (1819–82). *See also Attar and Driver, bibliographies, above.*
The young housekeeper as daughter. [1850].
The practical housewife. [1855].
Enquire within upon everything. 1856, 124th edn 1970.
The interview. [1856].
The housewife's reason why. [1857].
The corner cupboard. 1858.
The dictionary of daily wants. 1858–60, 63 edns after 1887.

The family cyclopaedia. [1859].
The family save-all. 1861.
The young woman's companion. 1863.
Consult me. [1866].
A journey of discovery. 1867.
Best of everything. 1870.
Take my advice. 1872.
The lady's every-day book. [1873].
New facts upon all subjects. [1874].
Pierce, C.
The household manager. 1856.
[Pillow, Mrs H.]
Nursery cookery . . . Ed Mrs Ada S. Ballin. *See also Attar and Driver, bibliographies, above.* [1900].
Pitney, Augusta Anne
Cottage economy, by a cottager. 1855.
Plumptre, A.
Domestic management; or, the healthful cookery-book. 1812.
Poole, W. H. and Mrs Poole
Cookery for the diabetic. 1891, 6+ edns to 1915.
Popular lessons on cookery. 1880, 11,000 copies to 1885.
Practical economy. 1821, 7+ edns to 1830.
Praga, Mrs Alfred
Appearances: how to keep them up on a limited income. 1899.
How to furnish. 1899.
Starting housekeeping. 1899.
How to keep a house on £200 a year. 1904.
Radcliffe, M.
A modern system of domestic cookery; or, the housekeeper's guide. 1823.
Read, G.
The complete biscuit and gingerbread baker's assistant. 1855.
The confectioner. [1860?]
Redding, C.
A history and description of modern wines. 1833.
Everyman and his own butler. 1839.
Reece, Richard (1775–1831)
The domestic medical guide. 1803, 17th edn 1850.
A practical dictionary of domestic medicine. 1808.
Reeve, Mrs Christina Georgina Jane (Gollop)
Cookery and housekeeping. 1882, 4th edn 1888.
Roberts, I.
The young cook's guide. 1836.
Roberts, W. H.
The British wine-maker, and domestic brewer. 1847.
Robinson, J.
The whole art of curing, pickling, and smoking meat and fish. 1847, 1864.
Ross, Mrs Janet Ann (1842–1927). *See also Attar and Driver, bibliographies, above.*
Leaves from our Tuscan kitchen or how to cook vegetables. 1899, 11+ impressions 1936.
Rumball, James Quilter
The mother's monitor, or nursery errors. 1829.
Rundell, M. E.
A new system of domestic cookery, formed upon principles of economy, and adapted to the use of private families. 1807, 22nd edn 1893.
The new family receipt-book. 1810.
Russell, E.
The complete family cook: being an entire system of cookery. 1800.
S. P. K.
What to do with cold mutton. 1863.
Sala, George Augustus Henry Fairfield (1828–95)
The thorough good cook. 1895.
See also col 1394.

Sandford, Mrs Henry (Mrs Margaret E.)
The girls' reading-book or chapters on home work and duties. 1876.
Santiagoe, Daniel (b. 1864?)
The curry cook's assistant. 1887.
Sarah, Aunt
Aunt Sarah's cookery book for a Jewish kitchen. 1872.
Aunt Sarah's directions for teaching economical cookery, in Jewish schools and families. 1877.
Sargeant, Anne Maria
The maid-of-all-work's complete guide. [1850].
The housemaid's complete guide. [1851].
Schulz, C.
The school of arts; or, fountain of knowledge. Containing several hundred truly valuable and useful receipts. [1830].
Senn, Charles Herman (1864–1934). *See also Attar and Driver, bibliographies, above.*
Practical gastronomy. 1892, 13+ edns to 1972.
Practical household recipes. [1892].
Recherche side dishes for breakfast, luncheon, dinner and supper. 1893, 5th edn [1899].
Ye art of cookery in ye olden time. [1896?]
Practical cookery manual of plain and middle class recipes. 1897, 7th edn 1920.
The Isobel handbooks: No 6 Breakfast and supper dishes. 1898.
Senn's culinary encyclopaedia. 1898, 10+ edns to 1973.
Ices, and how to make them. [1900].
The 'Main' cookery book. 1900.
Meatless fare and Lenten cookery. 1900, 6+ edns after 1935.
The new century cookery book. 1901, 10th edn 1933.
Cookery for the sick and convalescent. [1903], 8th edn 1928.
Savoury breakfast, dinner and supper dishes. 1904.
Chafing dish and casserole cookery. [1905], 5th edn [1927].
Cooking in stoneware. 1905 (Casserole cookery 1912, 10+ edns after 1928).
The popular cookery book of French and English dishes. [1905].
Senn's egg cookery. [1905], 8+ edns to [1935].
Recherche luncheon and dinner sweets. [1906], 6+ edns to 1922.
Emergency dinners. [1907].
Recherche entrées. [1907].
Manual for diabetic diet and cookery. [1908].
Popular breakfast dishes and savouries. [1908].
Simple cookery for the people. [1908], 11+ edns after 1925.
Ideal breakfast dishes, savouries and curries. [1910].
How to cook vegetables. 1911.
The paper-bag cookery manual. 1911.
Light fare recipes. [1914].
Servants defended, by one of their own class. 1847.
The servant's guide and family manual. 1830, 5+ edns to [1859].
The servant's practical guide. A handbook of duties and rules. [1880].
Shaw, T. G.
Wine, the vine, and the cellar. 1864.
Short
Dinners at home. 1878.
Breakfasts and luncheons at home. 1880.
Breakfasts, luncheons and dinners. 1886.
Sigmond, G. G.
Tea; its effects, medicinal and moral. 1839.
Simmonds, Peter Lund (1814–97)
The animal food resources of different nations. 1885.
The popular beverages of various countries. 1888.
Simpson, J.
A complete system of cookery, on a plan entirely new. 1806.
Sketches of the domestic manners, and institutions, of the Romans. 1821.

Smiles, Samuel (1812–1904). *See also Attar and Driver, bibliographies, above.*
Physical education; or, the nurture and management of children. 1838.
Smith, Mrs
The female economist: or, a plain system of cookery. 1810.
Smith, A.
Practical and economical cookery, with a series of bills of fare. 1858.
Smith, J.
The principles and practice of vegetarian cookery; founded on chemical analysis. 1860.
Smith, Louisa E.
Home washing. A practical guide to the housewife. 1890.
Souter, Helen Greig (pseud Aunt Kate)
Aunt Kate's cakes and candies book. [1900].
Aunt Kate's cookery book. 1902.
Aunt Kate's jams and jellies. [1910].
Aunt Kate's home-made drinks. [1911].
Aunt Kate's favourite recipes. [1912].
Aunt Kate's cookery book No 2. 1920.
Soyer, A. B. (1809–58)
The gastronomic regenerator: a simplified and entirely new system of cookery. 1846, 7th edn 1850.
Soyer's charitable cookery. 1847.
The modern housewife or ménagère, comprising one thousand receipts. 1849, 82,000+ copies to 1861.
The pantropheon; or, History of food, and its preparation, from the earliest ages of the world. 1851.
A shilling cookery for the people. 1855.
Soyer's culinary campaign. 1857.
Instructions for military hospitals. 1860.
Stables, William Gordon (1840–1910)
The mother's book of health. [1894].
The wife's guide to health and happiness. [1894].
See also col 1869.
Stacpoole, Florence
Advice to women on the care of the health. 1892, 5+ edns 1917.
Our sick. [1892].
The home doctor. [1895].
Handbook of housekeeping. [1898].
The care of little children. [1898].
Thrifty housekeeping. [1898].
A healthy home. [1905].
A book of simple remedies. [1907].
One hundred things. [1910].
The mother's book. [1912].
Standage, H. C.
Temperance and light drinks. 1893.
Stavely, S. W.
The new whole art of confectionery. 1815, 1828.
Steel, Flora Annie and Grace Gardiner (Flora Annie Steel 1847–1929)
The complete Indian housekeeper and cook. 1890, 12th edn 1921.
Stephenson, A.
Raffold's cookery improved: being a complete family cook. [1813].
Stewart, Lady Alice Margaret King and Ella Robertson Christie
Fare and physic of a past century. 1900.
Stewart, Andrew
The Scottish cookery book. [1878 or 1879].
The thrifty housewife. [1882].
Stewart, J. A.
The young woman's companion; or, the female instructor. [1814].
Stoddart, Miss L. W.
Cookery teachers' manual. 1893.
Plain cookery recipes. [1893 or 1894].
Sugg, Marie Jenny
The art of cooking by gas. 1890.
Sturgeon, L.
Essays, moral, philosophical, and stomachical, on the important science of good-living. 1823.
Tate, Mrs Louisa S.
The child's cookery book. [1887].
Taylor, Mrs Ann (1757–1830)
Practical hints to young females. 1815, 11th edn 1822.
The present of a mistress to a young servant. 1816.
See also col 473.
Tegetmeier, William Bernhard (1816–1912)
A manual of domestic economy. 4th edn 1858, 13th edn 1891.
The scholar's handbook. 1876, 5+ edns to 1905.
Tegg, Thomas (1776–1845)
Book of utility, or, repository of useful information. 1822.
Thomas, J. E.
The housewife's guide, or a complete system of modern cookery. 1831, 1833.
Thompson, Sir Henry (1820–1904)
Food and feeding. [1880], 12th edn after 1901.
'365' series of cookery books. *See also Attar and Driver, bibliographies, above.*
365 dinners. [1906].
Thudichum, John Louis William (1829–1901)
The spirit of cookery. 1895.
Timbs, John (1801–75). *See also Attar and Driver, bibliographies, above.*
Hints for the table: or, the economy of good living. 1838, 1859.
Lady Bountiful's legacy to her family and friends. 1868.
Trusler, Rev Dr John (1735–1820)
A system of etiquette. [1805].
Trusler's domestic management. 1819.
Tucker, William
The family dyer and scourer. 1817.
Tusser, T.
Five hundred pointed of good Husbandrie. 1590.
Ude, L. E.
The French cook; or, the art of cookery developed in all its branches. 1813, 14th edn 1841.
Urban, Felix
The first book of manners. 1856.
Vasey, G.
Illustrations of eating; displaying the omnivorous character of man. 1847.
Vegetable cookery, with an introduction recommending abstinence from animal food and intoxicating liquors. 1829.
Vegetarian cookery. 1852.
Volant, F. and J. R. Warren.
Memoirs of Alexis Soyer; witty unpublished receipts and odds and ends of gastronomy. 1859.
The economy of cookery, for the middle classes, the tradesman, and the artisan. 1860.
Wadd, W.
Comments on corpulency, lineaments of leanness, memoranda on diet and dietetics. 1829.
Walker, Thomas (1784–1836)
Aristology or the art of dining. 1881.
Wallace, J.
The confectioner's guide, and ladies' and housekeeper's instructor. 1831.
Wallace, Maria S.
Study and work at the Kensington School for Cookery. 1877.
Walsh, John Henry (1810–88). *See also Attar and Driver, bibliographies, above.*
A manual of domestic economy. 1857, 6+ edns to [1890].
The economical housekeeper. 1857.
The British housekeeper's book. 1860.
The English cookery book: uniting a good style with economy. 1860.

Ward and Lock's home book. [1880].
Warren, Mrs Eliza. *See also Attar and Driver, bibliographies, above.*
The economical cookery book for housewives. 1858, 1881.
How I managed my house on £200. 1864.
How I managed my children. 1865.
Comfort for small incomes. 1866.
A house and its furnishings. [1869].
Cookery cards for hanging in the kitchen. 1871.
My lady-help and what she taught me. 1877.
How the lady-help taught girls how to cook. 1879.
A young wife's perplexities. 1886.
Cookery for an income of £200 a year. 1887.
Watson, C.
The book of diet. [1913].
Watson, J. E.
The housewife's directory. 1825.
Webster, Thomas (1773–1844). *See also Attar and Driver, bibliographies, above.*
An encyclopaedia of domestic economy. 1844, 4th edn 1861.
Wells, Robert. *See also Attar and Driver, bibliographies, above.*
The bread and biscuit baker's and sugar-boiler's assistant. 1889, 7+ edns 1929.
The pastrycook and confectioner's guide. 1889, 6th edn 1929.
Ornamental confectionery. 1890.
The modern flour confectioner. 1891, 6th edn 1930.
Toffees and sweets. [1893 or 1894].
Wells' cakes and buns. [1897].
Bread, cakes, buns, and biscuits. [1904 or 1905].
Pleasant drinks. [1908].
Welter, H.
Essai sur l'histoire du café. 1868.
White, J.
A treatise on the art of baking. 1828.
Whiting, S.
Memoirs of a stomach. Written by himself, that all who eat may read. With notes, critical and explanatory, by a minister of the interior. 1853.
Wicken, Mrs H. F.
The Kingswood cookery book. 1885.
Australian table dainties and appetising dishes. 1897.
Wigg, Thomas Carter
The feeding of infants, . . . food for the sick and infirm. [1880].
Wigley, Mrs S. S. (Mrs W. H. Wigley)
Our home work. [1876].
Cookery and home comforts. [1877].
Simple lessons in domestic economy. [1878].
Workers at home. 1880.
Thoughts for mothers. 1881.
The Marshfield maidens. [1905].
Williams, James
The footman's guide. [1845 3rd edn], 6th edn 1856.
Williams, William Mattieu (1820–92)
Cantor lectures on the scientific basis of cookery. 1883.
The science of cookery. 1884.
The chemistry of cookery. 1885, 4th impression 1906.
Willis, M.
Cookery made easy. 1825.
Willy, Herr Theodore
All about piping. 1891.
A woman's secret. 1860.
Wright, Miss Christian E. Guthrie
The school cookery book. 1879, 10+ edns to 1930.
Young housekeepers. 1895.
Young nurses. 1896.
The young woman's companion, or female instructor. [1820].
The young woman's companion: or, frugal housewife. 1813.
Young, Mrs Hannah M. (1858–1949). *See also Attar and Driver, bibliographies, above.*
Choice cookery. 1888, 6th edn after 1893.
Domestic cookery . . . cooking by gas. 1886, 21st edn [1897].
Liebig Company's practical cookery book. 1893.
The housewife's manual. [pre 1900], 22nd edn [1913].
Home-made sweetmeats. [1902].
Home-made cakes and sweets. 1904. [LH]

14 Sport

Since the literature of nineteenth-century sport is large, it has not been possible to make this section comprehensive. Histories of particular sporting institutions, e.g. yacht clubs, books on physical training and wholly statistical works have, with one or two exceptions, been omitted.

(1) BIBLIOGRAPHIES

Howard, H. C., Earl of Suffolk and Berkshire, H. Peek and F. G. Aflalo (ed). In their Encyclopaedia of sport. 2 vols 1897–8, 4 vols 1911. Bibliographies under each main heading.
Slater, J. H. Illustrated sporting books: a descriptive survey. 1899.
Nevill, R. H. Old English sporting books. 1924.
Schwerdt, C. F. G. R. Hunting, hawking, shooting, illustrated in a catalogue of books, manuscripts, prints and drawings. 4 vols 1928–37.
Gee, E. R. The sportsman's library: being a descriptive list of the most important books on sport. New York 1940.
Darwin, B. Sporting writers of the nineteenth century. In Essays presented to Sir Humphrey Milford, Oxford 1948.
Cox, R. W. History of sport in Britain: a bibliography of historical publications, 1800–1988. Manchester 1991.

(2) PERIODICALS

The Sporting Magazine or Monthly Calendar of the Transactions of the Turf, the Chase etc. 1792–1870.
Annals of Sporting and Farming Gazette. 1822–8. Monthly.
Bell's Life in London and Sporting Chronicle. 1822–86. Weekly.
Pierce Egan's Life in London and Sporting Guide. 1824–7. Merged in 1827 with Bell's Life in London, *above*. Weekly.
New Sporting Magazine. 1831–70. Monthly. From July 1846 identical except for title page with The Sporting Magazine, *above*.
The Sportsman. 1834–70. Monthly. From July 1846 identical except for title page with The Sporting Magazine, *above*.
The Oracle of Rural Life: an Almanack for Sportsmen. 1839–44; 1841 as Sporting Oracle; 1842–4 as Sporting Almanack.
The Sporting Review. 1839–70. Monthly. From July 1846 identical except for title page with The Sporting Magazine, *above*.
The Field. 1853– . Weekly.
The Sporting Life. 1859– . Daily. Originally 24 Mar–27 Apr 1859 as Penny Bell's Life and Sporting News.
Baily's Monthly Magazine of Sports and Pastimes. 1860–1926. From 1889 as Baily's Magazine etc.
The Sporting Gazette. 1862–1905. Merged in 1905 with Land and Water, *below*. Weekly. From 1880 as The Country Gentleman.
The Sporting Times ['the pink 'un']. 1865– . Weekly. *See also* J. G. Booth, Old pink 'un days, 1924, *and* Master [i.e. J. Corlett, the paper's owner] and men, 1926.
The Sportsman. 1865–1924. Merged in 1924 with The Sporting Life, *above*. Daily.
Land and Water. 1866–1920. Merged in 1920 with The Field, *above*. Weekly. As The Country Gentleman and Land and Water 1905–15 apart from 2 nos, Aug 1914, appearing under original title.
Illustrated Sporting and Dramatic News. 1874– . Weekly.
The Badminton Magazine of Sports and Pastimes. 1895–1923. Monthly.
Country Life. 1895– . Weekly. Before 1897 appeared as Racing Illustrated.

(3) GENERAL STUDIES

Strutt, J. Glig-gamena angel-eeoe: or the sports and pastimes of the people of England. 1801, 1830; ed J. C. Cox [1903].
Taplin, W. The sporting dictionary and rural repository of general information upon every subject appertaining to the sports of the field. 2 vols 1803.
Taplin, W. The sportsman's cabinet: or a correct delineation of the various dogs used in the sports of the field. 2 vols 1803–4. Under pseudonym 'A veteran sportsman'.
Egan, P. Sporting anecdotes original and select. 1804, [1808], 1820, 1825, 1827 (as P. E.'s anecdotes, original and selected).
Thornton, T. A sporting tour through the northern parts of England and the Highlands of Scotland. 1804.
Thornton, T. A sporting tour through various parts of France. 2 vols 1805.
Howitt, S. et al. Foreign field sports, fisheries, sporting anecdotes. 1814. Plates with text.
'Needham, T. H.' (T. B. Johnson). The complete sportsman. 1817.
Mayer, J. The sportsman's directory. 1817.
Chafin, W. Anecdotes respecting Cranbourn Chase with the rural amusements it afforded our ancestors. 1818, 1818.
'Scott, W. H.' (J. Lawrence). British field sports. 1818.
'Careless, John'. The old English squire: a poem in ten cantos. 1821.
Hassell, J. Excursions of pleasure and sport on the Thames. 1823.
Armiger, C. The sportsman's vocal cabinet comprising original songs and ballads relative to field sports. 1830.
Johnson, T. B. The sportsman's cyclopaedia. 1831.
Egan, P. P. E.'s book of sports and mirror of life. 1832.
Maxwell, W. H. Wild sports of the west [of Ireland]. 1832; ed W. H. H. Quin, 4th Earl of Dunraven, 1924.
Maxwell, W. H. The field book: or sports and pastimes of the United Kingdom. 1833.
Walker, D. British manly exercises. 1834, 1835; ed 'Craven' (i.e. J. W. Carleton) 1847. Appendix as Games and sports, 1837.

Harewood, H. (pseud?). A dictionary of sports containing explanations of every item applicable to racing, shooting, hunting, fishing, hawking, archery etc. 1835.
Walker, D. Exercises for ladies. 1836, 1837.
'Nimrod' (C. J. Apperley) (ed). Sporting. 1838. Contributions by various well-known sporting writers.
Blaine, D. P. An encyclopaedia of rural sports. 1840; ed 'Harry Hieover' (C. Bindley) 1852.
Colquhoun, J. The moor and the loch, containing minute instructions in all Highland sports. 1840, 2 vols 1878 (4th edn), 1888 (7th edn).
Walker, D. Defensive exercises. 1840. Boxing, wrestling, fencing, shooting.
Carleton, J. W. (ed). The sporting sketch book: a series of characteristic papers by the most distinguished sporting writers of the day. 1842.
'Nimrod' (C. J. Apperley). Nimrod abroad. 2 vols 1842. Pbd under own name.
'Craven' (J. W. Carleton). Hyde Marston: or a sportsman's life. 3 vols 1844. A novel.
Maxwell, W. H. Wanderings in the Highlands and Islands. 2 vols 1844, 1853 (as Sports and adventures in the Highlands etc).
Mills, J. The sportsman's library. Edinburgh 1845. A general treatise on sport.
St John, C. W. G. Short sketches of the wild sports and natural history of the Highlands. 1846, 1893 (with memoir of the author); ed H. E. Maxwell 1919 as Sports and natural history of the Highlands.
Hall, H. B. Highland sports and Highland quarters. 2 vols [1847].
Lloyd, L. The English county gentleman: his sports and pastimes. 1849. Verse.
St John, C. W. G. A tour in Sutherlandshire with extracts from the field books of a sportsman. 2 vols 1849, 1884.
Hall, H. B. Scottish sports and pastimes. 1850.
Hall, H. B. The sportsman and his dog. 1850.
'Hieover, Harry' (C. Bindley). Sporting facts and sporting fancies. 1853.
'Stonehenge' (J. H. Walsh). Manual of British rural sports. 1856, 1859, 1875, 1886 (16th edn).
'Hieover, Harry' (C. Bindley). The sportsman's friend in a frost. 1857. Essays on various sports.
Lennox, Lord W. P. Merrie England: its sports and pastimes. 1857.
Colquhoun, J. Salmon-casts and stray shots. 1858. On field sports in general.
'Hieover, Harry' (C. Bindley). The sporting world. 1858.
Hamilton, J. P. Reminiscences of an old sportsman. 2 vols 1860. On field sports.
Lennox, Lord W. P. Pictures of sporting life and character. 2 vols 1860.
Miles, H. D. (ed). The book of field sports. 42 pts [1860–3].
Dougall, J. D. Scottish field sports. Glasgow 1861.
Lennox, Lord W. P. Recreations of a sportsman. 2 vols 1862.
Miles, H. D. The sportsman's companion. 12 pts [1863–4].
St John, C. W. G. Natural history and sport in Moray. Edinburgh 1863.
Corbet, H. Tales and traits of sporting life. 1864.
Colquhoun, J. Sporting days. 1866. On field sports.
Stretton, C. Sport and sportsmen: a book of recollections. 1866.
'Caw' (C. A. Wheeler) (ed). Sportascrapiana: cricket and shooting, pedestrian, equestrian, rifle and pistol doings, lion hunting and deer stalking. 1867.
Newton, G. W. Rural sports and how to enjoy them; with an appendix containing memories and characteristics of eminent sportsmen. 1867.
Egerton, T., Earl of Wilton. On the sports and pursuits of the English, as bearing upon their national character. 1868.
Miles, H. D. English country life: a work of reference for the gentleman, the sportsman, the farmer. [1868–9]. Largely sporting.
Trollope, A. (ed). British sports and pastimes. 1868.
Lennox, Lord W. P. Sport at home and abroad. 1872.
'Old Shekarry' (H. A. Leveson). Sport in many lands. 2 vols 1876.
'Bagatelle' (A. G. Bagot). Sporting sketches at home and abroad. 1879, 1881 (as Sporting sketches in three continents).
'Rockwood' (T. Dykes). Stories of Scottish sports. Glasgow 1881.
'Avon' (W. Kenrick). How I became a sportsman: being early reminiscences of a veteran sportsman. 1882.
Speedy, T. Sport in the Highlands and Lowlands of Scotland. Edinburgh 1884.
Bromley-Davenport, W. Sport. 1885. A treatise on field sports.
Gale, F. Modern English sports: their use and their abuse. 1885.
Somerset, H. C. F., 8th Duke of Beaufort, and A. E. T. Watson (ed). The Badminton library of sports and pastimes. 28 vols 1885–96; Motors and motor-driving, 1902. Various contributors. Sports covered are listed in vol on The poetry of sport, an anthology which also contains introd giving history of the series. Most vols rev in subsequent edns. Vols on archery, big-game shooting, driving, fencing, hunting and swimming contain bibliographies.
Reynardson, C. T. S. B. Sports and anecdotes of bygone days. 1887.
'Rockwood' (T. Dykes). All round sport with fish, fur and feather. 1887.
Gale, F. Sports and recreations in town and country. 1888.
'Ellangowan' (J. G. Bertram). Out of door sports in Scotland. 1889.
Stoddart, J. Sports and pastimes: men I have met. 2 vols Manchester [1889].
Corballis, J. H. Forty-five years of sport. Ed A. T. Fisher 1891.
Kennard, M. E. Sporting tales. 1893.
Pollock, W. H., F. C. Grove, C. Prevost, E. B. Michell and W. Armstrong. Fencing, boxing and wrestling. 1893 (Badminton Lib of Sports and Pastimes).
'Ubique' (P. Gillmore). Leaves from a sportsman's diary. 1893.
Watson, A. E. T. (ed). Fur, feather and fin series. 12 vols 1893–1906. Vols with sporting sections on the partridge, pheasant, hare, red deer, fox, salmon, grouse, trout, pike and perch, snipe and woodcock, rabbit, wildfowl.
Astley, Sir J. D. Fifty years of my life in the world of sport. 2 vols 1894.
Grimble, A. Highland sport. 1894.
Hartopp, E. C. C. Sport in England: past and present. 1894.
De Crespigny, Sir C. C. Memoirs. Ed G. A. B. Dewar 1896, 1910, 1925 (as Forty years of a sportsman's life). Includes accounts of ballooning, bull-fighting etc.
Pemberton, Sir M. (ed). The Isthmian library. 12 vols 1896–1902. Vols on Rugby football, ice sports, cycling, golf, rowing, boxing, figure-skating, croquet, hockey, tennis and racquets, small-boat sailing, athletics.
Howard, H. C., Earl of Suffolk and Berkshire, H. Peek and F. G. Aflalo (ed). The encyclopaedia of sport. 2 vols 1897–8, 4 vols 1911.
Binstead, A. M. A pink 'un and a pelican: some random reminiscences, sporting or otherwise. 1898.
Gibbs, J. A. A Cotswold village: or country life and pursuits in Gloucestershire. 1898. Includes chs on field sports.
Haydon, T. Sporting reminiscences. 1898.
Kipling, Rudyard. An almanac of twelve sports. 1898. Verse.
Slaughter, F. E. (ed). The sportswoman's library. 2 vols 1898.
Aflalo, F. G. (ed). The cost of sport. 1899.
Manners, H. J. B., 8th Duke of Rutland, and G. A. B. Dewar (ed). The Haddon Hall library. 9 vols 1899–1903. Vols on Fly-fishing, Our gardens, Wild life in Hampshire highlands [includes sport], Hunting, Our forests and woodlands [includes sport], Bird-watching, Outdoor games: cricket and golf, Shooting [includes ch on The literature of the gun], Farming.
Croome, A. C. M. et al (ed). Fifty years of sport at Oxford, Cambridge

and the great public schools. 3 vols 1913–22. Vols 1–2 Oxford and Cambridge; vol 3 Eton, Harrow and Winchester.
Darwin, B. (ed). The game's afoot: an anthology of sports. 1926.
Colquhoun, Sir I. and H. W. Machell. Highland gatherings. 1927. Contains much history.
Parker, E. (ed). The Lonsdale anthology of sporting prose and verse. 1932 (Lonsdale Lib vol 12).
Hare, C. E. The language of sport. 1939, 1949 (as The language of field sports). On etymology of sporting terms.
Hole, C. English sports and pastimes. 1949.
Tennyson, C. They taught the world to play. VS 2 1958–9.
Winn, W. E. Tom Brown's schooldays and the development of muscular Christianity. Church History 29 1960.
Brander, M. The hunting instinct: the development of field sports over the ages. 1964.
Harrison, B. H. Religion and recreation in nineteenth century England. Past and Present 38 1967.
Haley, B. E. Sports and the Victorian world. Western Humanities Rev 12 1968.
Margeston, S. Leisure and pleasure in the nineteenth century. 1969.
Harrington, H. R. Muscular Christianity: the study of the development of a Victorian idea. Unpbd PhD thesis, Stanford Univ 1971.
Kennard, J. A. Women, sport and society in Victorian England. Unpbd EdD thesis, Univ of North Carolina, Greensboro NC 1974.
Harris, H. A. Sport in Britain: its origins and development. 1975.
Parish, R. British sporting literature through the ages with special reference to the 19th century. Unpbd MA diss in librarianship, Univ of Sheffield 1975.
Lansbury, C. Sporting humour in Victorian literature. Mosaic 9 1976.
Bailey, P. C. A mingled mass of perfectly legitimate pleasures: the Victorian middle class and the problem of leisure. VS 21 Autumn 1977.
Harrington, H. R. Charles Kingsley's fallen athlete. VS 21 Autumn 1977.
Wright, C. J. Before Tom Brown: education and the sporting ethos in the early 19th century. Jnl of Educational Administration and History 9 1977.
Bailey, P. C. Leisure and class in Victorian England. 1978.
Haley, B. E. The healthy body and Victorian culture. Cambridge MA 1978.
Pointon, M. The growth of women's sport in late Victorian society as reflected in contemporary literature. Unpbd MEd thesis, Univ of Manchester 1978.
Redmond, G. The first Tom Brown's schooldays (1804) and others: origins of muscular Christianity in children's literature. Quest, Monograph 30 Summer 1978.
Walvin, J. Leisure and society, 1830–1950. 1978.
Baker, W. J. The leisure revolution in Victorian England: a review of recent literature. Jnl of Sport History 6 Winter 1979.
Crawford, S. A. G. M. Sporting sketches: a study of selected writings by Sir Walter Scott. Physical Education Rev 2 1979.
Mangan, J. A. Athleticism in the Victorian and Edwardian public school. Cambridge 1981.
Redmond, G. Before Hughes and Kingsley: the origins and evolution of muscular Christianity in English children's literature. In Sports fiction, ed C. Jenkins and M. Green, Centre for Contemporary Cultural Stud, Univ of Birmingham, Sep 1981.
Sandiford, K. A. P. The Victorians at play. Jnl of Social History 15 Winter 1981.
Redmond, G. Moral tales for manly boys: Christian sport in children's literature, 1783 to 1857. In Society, religion and sport, ed J. A. Mangan, Proc of the inaugural conference of the Br Soc of Sports History, Univ of Keele. Sep 1983.
Sandiford, K. A. P. Sport and Victorian England. Canadian Jnl of History 18 1983.
Tozer, M. Charles Kingsley and the muscular Christian idea of manliness. Physical Education Rev 8 1985.
Mangan, J. A. and R. J. Park (ed). From fair sex to feminism: sport and the socialization of women in the industrial and post industrial eras. 1986.
Mason, T. Sporting news 1860–1914. In The press in English society from the 17th to the 19th centuries, ed M. Harris and A. Lee, 1986.
Mangan, J. A. and J. Walvin (ed). Manliness and morality: middle class masculinity in Britain and America, 1800–1940. Manchester 1987.
Mason, T. Sport in Britain: a social history. Cambridge 1987.
Mangan, J. A. Pleasure, profit and proselytism. 1988.
Mason, T. Sport in Britain. 1988 (Faber Historical Handbooks).
McCrone, K. E. Sport and the physical emancipation of women, 1870–1914. 1988.
Vamplew, W. Pay up and play the game!: professional sport in Britain 1875–1914. Cambridge 1988.
Holt, R. Sport and the British: a modern history. Oxford 1989.
Tozer, M. Thomas Hughes' Tom Brown versus true manliness. Physical Education Rev 12 1989.
Holt, R. Sport and the working class in modern Britain. Manchester 1990.
Vertinsky, P. A. The eternally wounded woman: women, exercise and doctors in the late nineteenth century. Manchester 1990.
Bromhead, J. Harold Abrahams: athlete, author, amateur. In Leisure in art and literature, ed T. Winnifrith and C. Barrett, 1991.
Hyde, G. M. Up tails all: leisure, pleasure and paranoia in Kenneth Grahame's The wind in the willows. In Leisure in art and literature, ed T. Winnifrith and C. Barrett, 1991.
Ickringill, S. J. S. P. G. Woodhouse: the case of leisure as the sole topic of an author's output. In Leisure in art and literature, ed T. Winnifrith and C. Barrett, 1991.
Larrissy, E. Leisure and civilisation in English literature. In Leisure in art and literature, ed T. Winnifrith and C. Barrett, 1991.
Mangan, J. A. Lamentable barbarians and pitiful sheep: rhetoric of protest and pleasure in late Victorian and Edwardian Oxbridge. In Leisure in art and literature, ed T. Winnifrith and C. Barrett, 1991.
Mangan, J. A. Sport and the cultural bond. 1991.
Lowerson, J. R. Sport and the English middle class 1880–1914. Manchester 1993.
Hargreaves, J. Sporting females: critical issues in the history and sociology of women's sport. 1994.
Birley, D. Land of hope and sport. Manchester 1995.

(4) INDIVIDUAL SPORTS (in alphabetical order)

Angling

Bibliographies

[Ellis, Sir H.] A catalogue of books on angling. 1811; ed W. Pickering 1836 (as Bibliotheca piscatoria) (issued separately and as appendix to Boosey's Piscatorial reminiscences, *below*).
Westwood, T. and T. Satchell. Bibliotheca piscatoria: a catalogue of books on angling, the fisheries and fish-culture. 1883. Expanded from earlier edn by Westwood 1861, suppl 1869. Suppl by R. B. Marston to 1883 edn as Appendix C in English catalogue of books vol 6, 1901.
Hampton, J. F. Modern angling bibliography from 1881 to 1945. 1947.
Robb, J. Notable angling literature. [1947].

Periodicals

The Fishing Gazette. 1865– . Weekly.

§1

Taylor, S. Angling in all its branches. 1800.
Mackintosh, A. The Driffield angler. Gainsborough [1806], Derby

[1815?] (as The modern fisher). Treatise also contains sections on shooting and coursing.

Howitt, S. The angler's manual: or concise lessons of experience. Liverpool 1808.

Williamson, T. The complete angler's vade-mecum. 1808.

Salter, R. The modern angler. Oswestry [1811?].

Lascelles, R. A series of letters on angling, shooting and coursing. 3 pts 1813–14.

Salter, T. F. The angler's guide. 1814, 1815, [1823], 1833.

Charleton, T. W. The art of fishing: a poem. North Shields 1819.

'Piscator' (T. P. Lathy). The angler: a poem in ten cantos. 1819. Largely plagiarism of The anglers, a poem pbd anon 1758 and attributed to Thomas Scott.

Salter, T. F. The troller's guide. 1820, 1841.

'An angler' (Sir Humphrey Davy). Salmonia: or days of fly fishing. 1828, 1829, 1832; ed J. Davy 1851, 1869.

March, J. The jolly angler or waterside companion. [1831].

'Greendrake, Gregory' (J. Coad). The angling excursions of Gregory Greendrake esq [in Ireland]. Dublin 1832. Originally pbd in 3 pts Dublin 1824–6, this edn with addns by 'Geoffrey Greydrake' (T. Ettingsall) called the 4th.

Penn, R. Maxims and hints for an angler and miseries of fishing to which are added maxims and hints for a chess player. 1833 (anon), 1839, 1842 (as Maxims and hints on angling, chess, shooting and other matters).

Baddeley, J. The London angler's book. 1834.

[Bitton, W.] The angler in Ireland. 2 vols 1834. A description of a fishing tour.

[Chatto, W. A.] Scenes and recollections of fly-fishing. 1834. Under pseudonym 'S. Oliver'.

Hansard, G. A. Trout and salmon fishing in Wales. 1834.

Medwin, T. The angler in Wales: or days and nights of sportsmen. 2 vols 1834.

'An old angler and bibliopolist' (T. Boosey). Piscatorial reminiscences and gleanings; to which is added a catalogue of books on angling. 1835. *See* Ellis, A catalogue of books on angling, *above.*

[Chatto, W. A.] The angler's souvenir. 1835 (under pseudonym 'P. Fisher'); ed G. C. Davies [1877].

Stoddart, T. T. *See col 672, above.*

A collection of right merrie garlands, for North Country anglers. Newcastle-on-Tyne 1836, 1842; ed J. Crawhall 1864.

Jesse, E. An angler's rambles. 1836.

Ronalds, A. The fly-fisher's entomology. 1836; ed 'Piscator' (B. Smith) 1856 (5th edn); ed J. C. Carter 1901 (10th edn); ed H. E. Maxwell 2 vols Liverpool 1913; ed H. T. Sheringham 1921.

Hofland, T. C. The British angler's manual: or the art of angling in England, Scotland, Wales and Ireland, with some account of the principal rivers. 1839; ed E. Jesse 1848.

Younger, J. On river angling for salmon and trout. Edinburgh 1840, 1860, 1864.

Pulman, G. P. R. The vade mecum of fly-fishing for trout. London and Axminster 1841, London 1846, 1851.

Rustic sketches: being poems on angling. Taunton 1842.

Scrope, W. Days and nights of salmon fishing in the Tweed. 1843; ed H. T. Sheringham 1921.

Wayth, C. Trout fishing, or the river Darent: a rural poem. 1845.

Blakey, R. Hints on angling. 1846.

The angler's complete guide to the rivers and lakes of England. 1853, 1859.

The angler's complete guide to the rivers and lochs of Scotland. 1854.

Angling: or how to angle and where to go. 1854; ed W. Senior 1898 (with memoir of Blakey).

(ed). The angler's song book. 1855.

Historical sketches of the angling literature of all nations. 1856.

Akerman, J. Y. Spring-tide: or the angler and his friends. 1850. Fishing sketches.

Newland, Rev H. The Erne: its legends and its fly fishing. 1851. Fiction based on fact.

Forest scenes in Norway and Sweden: being extracts from the journal of a fisherman. 1854. Fiction based on fact.

'A North-Country angler' (T. Doubleday) (ed). The Coquet-Dale fishing songs. Edinburgh 1852. Mainly by R. Roxby with a memoir by Doubleday.

Badham, C. D. Prose halieutics: or ancient and modern fish tattle. 1854.

'Clericus' (W. Cartwright). Rambles and recollections of a fly-fisher. 1854.

Facts and fancies of salmon fishing. 1874.

Davy, J. The angler and his friend: or piscatory colloquies and fishing excursions. 1855.

The angler in the Lake District. 1857.

Stewart, W. C. The practical angler. Edinburgh 1857, 1861; ed W. E. Hodgson 1905.

A caution to anglers: or The practical angler and The modern practical angler compared. Edinburgh 1871. *See* Pennell, *below.*

Francis, F. The angler's register: a list of the come-at-able fisheries in England, Scotland, Ireland and Wales. 1858, [1859] (including Brittany and Belgium), [1860] (including Germany and the Tyrol).

A book on angling: being a complete treatise on the art of angling. 1867, 1867, 1872, 1880, 1885; ed H. E. Maxwell 1920.

By lake and river: an angler's rambles in the north of England and Scotland. 1874.

Hot pot: or miscellaneous papers [mainly on angling]. 1870.

Angling reminiscences. 1887.

Songs of the Edinburgh Angling Club. Edinburgh 1858, 1879; ed J. Smith 1900.

'Conway, James' (J. C. Walter). Letters from the Highlands: or two months among the salmon and the deer. 1859, 1861 (as Forays among salmon and deer).

Crawhall, J. The compleatest angling booke that ever was writ. Newcastle-on-Tyne 1859, 1881.

Chaplets from coquet-side. Newcastle 1873.

Border notes and mixty-maxty. Newcastle 1880.

Cliffe, J. H. Notes and recollections of an angler. 1860.

Smith, A. The Thames angler. 1860. Prose and verse.

Wilcocks, J. C. The sea-fisherman. Guernsey 1865, London 1868, 1875, 1884.

[Rooper, G.] The autobiography of the late Salmo Salar esq or Tweed salmon. 1867; rptd in his Flood, field and forest, 1869.

Thames and Tweed. 1870.

Pennell, H. C. The modern practical angler. [1870.] *See* Stewart, *above.*

(ed). Fishing gossip: or stray leaves from the notebooks of several anglers. Edinburgh 1866.

Knox, A. E. Autumns on the Spey. 1872.

Kingsley, C. Chalk-stream studies. In his Prose idylls, 1873.

Senior, W. Waterside sketches: a book for wanderers and anglers. 1875.

By stream and sea: a book for wanderers and anglers. 1877.

Travel and trout in the Antipodes: an angler's sketches in Tasmania and New Zealand. 1880.

Near and far: an angler's sketches of home and sport and colonial life. 1888.

Davies, G. C. Angling idylls. 1876. Prose.

Henderson, W. Notes and reminiscences of my life as an angler. 1876, 1879 (as My life as an angler).

Ellacombe, H. N. Shakespeare as an angler. 1883.

Froude, J. A. Cheneys and the house of Russell. In his Short studies on great subjects 4th ser, 1883.

International Fisheries Exhibition, London 1883. The Fisheries Exhibition literature [18 handbooks in 3 vols and index vol]. 1884. The following are relevant: vol 2, C. E. Fryer, The salmon fisheries; W. Senior, Angling in Great Britain; vol 3, J. P.

Wheeldon, Angling clubs and preservation societies; J. J. Manley, Literature of sea and river fishing.
'Isys, Cotswold' (Rev R. H. Glover). An angler's strange experiences. 1883. Verse.
Lyra piscatoria: original lyrics. 1895.
Roscoe, E. S. Rambles with a fishing-rod. 1883, 1906.
'The amateur angler' (E. Marston). An amateur angler's days in Dovedale. 1884.
Fresh woods and pastures new. 1887.
Days in clover. 1892.
By meadow and stream. 1896.
On a sunshine holyday. 1897.
An old man's holidays. 1900.
Each of the above contains a number of angling essays and recollections.
Westwood, T. In memoriam Izaak Walton: twelve sonnets and an epilogue. [1884.]
Bernnand, Sir F. C. (ed). The incomplete angler, after Master Izaak Walton. 1887.
'Bickerdyke, J.' (C. H. Cook). The book of the all-round angler. 1888, 1900, 1912, 1922 (5th edn).
Days in Thule with rod, gun and camera. 1894.
Days of my life on waters fresh and salt. 1895.
Practical letters to young sea fishers. 1898.
Roberts, Sir R. H. The silver trout and other stories. 1888.
Kennard, M. E. Landing a prize. 3 vols 1889. Novel.
Lang, A. Angling sketches. 1891.
Macvine, J. Sixty-three years angling, from the mountain streamlet to the mighty Tay. 1891.
Sandeman, F. By hook and by crook. 1892. Essays.
Angling travels in Norway. 1895.
Hopkins, F. P. Fishing experiences of half a century. 1893.
Shrubsole, E. S. Long casts and sure rises. 1893.
Armistead, J. J. An angler's paradise and how to obtain it. Scarborough 1895.
Buchan, John (ed). Musa piscatrix. 1896. Anthology.
Maxwell, Sir H. E. and F. G. Aflalo (ed). The angler's library. 6 vols 1897–9. C. H. Wheeley, Coarse fish; F. G. Aflalo, Sea-fish; A. Jardine, Pike and perch; Sir H. E. Maxwell, Salmon and sea trout; G. A. B. Dewar, South country trout streams; J. Watson, The English lake fisheries.
Cadman, H. Harry Druidale: fisherman from Manxland to England. 1898.
Dewar, G. A. B. In pursuit of the trout. 1898.
Taylor, J. P. Fishing and fishers. [1898.] Includes chs on the lit of fishing.
Grimble, A. The salmon rivers of Scotland. 4 vols 1899–1900.
Durnford, Rev R. The fishing diary 1809–19 of R. D. Ed H. Nicoll, Winchester 1911.

§2

Parker, E. (ed). An angler's garland. 1920. Anthology.
Hills, J. W. A history of fly fishing for trout. 1921. Includes ch on lit of fly-fishing.
Taverner, E. Salmon fishing. 1931 (Lonsdale Lib vol 10). Includes 3 chs on the literature of salmon fishing.
Dickie, J. M. (ed). Great angling stories. London and Edinburgh 1941. Includes verse.
Trench, C. P. C. A history of angling. St Albans 1974.
Lowerson, J. Angling in T. Mason, ed, Sport in Britain: a social history. Cambridge 1989.
See also Lang *under* Cricket, *below;* Grimble, Jeans, 'Wildfowler' *under* Shooting, *below.*

Archery

Bibliographies

Walrond, H. In C. J. Longman and H. Walrond, Archery, 1894 (Badminton Lib).
Lake, F. H. and H. A. Wright. Bibliography of archery. Manchester 1974.

Periodicals

The Archer's Register. 1864–6, 1877– . Annual.

§1

Roberts, T. The English bowman: or tracts on archery. 1801.
Waring, T. A treatise on archery. 1814.
Dodd, J. W. Ballads of archery, sonnets etc. 1818.
Hastings, T. The British archer. 1831.
'An old toxopholite'. The archer's guide; accompanied by a sketch of the history of the long-bow. 1833.
Harrison, A. P. The science of archery, showing its affinity to heraldry. 1834.
Warburton, R. E. E. The Hawkstone bow-meeting. Chester 1835. Verse.
Rhymes on the rules of the Cheshire bowmen. Northwich [1840?].
Hansard, G. A. The book of archery. 1840.
Ford, H. A. Archery: its theory and practice. 1856, 1859; ed W. Butt 1887 (as The theory and practice of archery).
'A toxopholite'. A history of the Royal Toxopholite Society. Taunton 1867 (priv ptd), 1870.
Paul, J. B. The history of the Royal Company of Archers. Edinburgh 1875.
Rushton, W. L. Shakespeare an archer. 1897.

§2

Burke, E. H. A history of archery. 1958.

Athletics

Bibliographies

Lovesey, F. and T. McNab. A guide to British track and field literature: 1275–1968. 1969.

Periodicals

Athletic News. Manchester 1875–1931. Merged with Sporting Chron. Weekly.

§1

Thorn, W. Pedestrianism: an account of the performances of celebrated pedestrians. Aberdeen 1813.

§2

Cook, Sir T. A. International sport: a short history of the Olympic movement. 1909.
Buchanan, I. An encyclopaedia of British athletic records. 1961.
Quercetani, R. L. A world history of track and field athletics. Oxford 1964.
Watman, M. Encyclopaedia of athletics. 1977 (4th edn).
Lovesey, P. The official centenary history of the Amateur Athletic Association. Enfield 1979.
Park, R. J. Athletes and their training in Britain and America 1800–1914. In Sport and exercise medicine: essays in the history of sports medicine, ed J. W. Berryman and R. J. Park, Urbana IL 1992.

Billiards

Bibliographies

'Crawley, Rawdon' (G. F. Pardon). Bibliographical catalogue of books on billiards. In his Billiard book, 1877 (2nd edn).

Periodicals

The Billiard Rev. 1895–8. Irregular.

§1

White, E. A practical treatise on the game of billiards. 1807.
Kentfield, E. The game of billiards. 1839.
Roberts, J. Roberts on billiards. Ed H. Buck [1869], [1870].
Bennett, J. Billiards. 1873. Includes short history of the game.

Let us to billiards: prize essays on billiards as an amusement for all classes. Manchester 1873.
Cook, W. Billiards. Ed A. G. Payne [1884].
Buchanan, J. P. Hints on billiards. 1895.

§2

Everton, C. History of snooker and billiards. 1986.

Boxing

Bibliographies

Magriel, P. D. Bibliography of boxing: a chronological check list of books in English published before 1900. New York 1948.
Hartley, R. A. History and bibliography of boxing books: a collector's guide to the history of pugilism incorporating a bibliography containing some 2,100 titles on all aspects of pugilism published in the English language. Acton? 1988.

Periodicals

The Fancy, or true Sportsman's Guide: being authentic memoirs of the lives, actions, prowess and battles of the leading pugilists. 55 nos 1821–5, 2 vols 1826. Irregular.

§1

A treatise on boxing. 1802.
Egan, P. Boxiana: or sketches of antient and modern pugilism. 1812, 1818–24 (with 3 additional vols).
Pancratia, or a history of pugilism: containing a full account of every battle of note from the time of Broughton and Slack down to the present day. 1812.
Mendoza, D. Memoirs of the life of Daniel Mendoza. 1816; ed P. D. Magriel 1951.
'One of the Fancy' (Thomas Moore). Tom Crib's memorial to congress. 1819. Boxing verse.
'Corcoran, Peter' (J. H. Reynolds). The fancy: a selection from the poetical remains of the late Peter Corcoran, with a brief memoir of his life. 1820; ed J. Masefield [1904].
Humphries, R. The memoirs of John Scroggins the pugilistic hero, with authentic annals of pugilism from the early days of Figg 1719 to those of Spring and Langan 1824. 1827.
Hazlitt, W. The fight. In his Literary remains vol 2, 1836.
[Dowling, F. D.] Fistiana or the oracle of the ring: comprising a defence of British boxing, a brief history of pugilism with chronological tables of prize battles from 1780–1840. 1841, 1842 etc (annual rev edn with suppl until 1870).
Borrow, G. H. In his Lavengro, 1851.
[Dowling, F. D.] Fights for the championship and celebrated prize battles from the days of Figg and Broughton to the present time. 1855, 1860 (as The championship of England).
'Walker, Johnny' (J. Badman). The life and adventures of the renowned Johnny Walker. Winchester [1857].
Sayers, T. Memoirs of Tom Sayers, champion of England. 1858.
History of the great international contest between Heenan and Sayers at Farnborough on the 17th April 1860. 1860.
The fight of Sayerius and Heenanus: a lay of ancient London. Punch 28 Apr 1860.
Miles, H. D. Pugilistica: the history of British boxing. 1866, 3 vols [1880–1], Edinburgh 1906.
Miles, H. D. Tom Sayers, sometime champion of England: his life and pugilistic career. 1866.
Donnelly, 'Ned'. Self defence: or the art of boxing. [1879].
Shaw, G. B. Cashel Byron's profession. 1886, [1889], 1901 (Novels of his nonage 4; also includes The admirable Bashville, a play from the novel, and Note on modern prize-fighting).
Henning, F. W. J. Some recollections of the prize ring. 1888.
Doyle, A. Conan. Rodney Stone. 1896. Novel.
'Thormanby' (W. W. Dixon). Boxers and their battles: anecdotal sketches and personal recollections of famous pugilists. 1900.
Henning, F. W. J. Fights for the championship: the men and their times. 2 vols [1902].

§2

Bettinson, A. F. and W. O. Tristram (ed). The National Sporting Club past and present. 1901.
Sayers, H. Fights forgotten: a history of some of the chief English and American prize fights since the year 1788. [1909].
Wignall, T. C. The story of boxing. 1923.
Shepherd, T. B. (ed). The noble art: an anthology. 1950.
Deghy, G. Noble and manly: the history of the National Sporting Club. 1956.
Brailsford, D. Bareknuckles: a social history of prize fighting. Cambridge 1988.
Shipley, S. Boxing. In Sport in Britain: a social history, ed T. Mason, Cambridge 1989.

Bowling

Haynes, A. H. The story of bowls. 1972.
Pilley, P. From Drake to Bryant: the story of bowls. 1987.

Cards

Bibliographies

Horr, N. T. A bibliography of card-games and of the history of playing cards. Cleveland 1892.
Jessel, F. A bibliography of works in English on playing cards and gaming. 1905.
Hargrave, C. P. Bibliography of cards and gaming. In her History of playing cards, New York [1930].

§1

Mathews, T. Advice to the young whist-player. Bath 1804 etc. Author given as 'Matthews' until 1822 (13th edn).
The Faro table: or the gambling mothers. 2 vols 1808.
Singer, S. W. Researches into the history of playing cards. 1816.
Read, W. Rouge et noir: a poem in 6 cantos. 1821.
'Elia' (Charles Lamb). Mrs Battle's opinions on whist. In his Elia: essays which have appeared under that signature in the London Magazine [first ser], 1823.
The St James' guide: or the sharper detected. 1825. Treatise exposing methods of cheating.
Garner, W. Garner's miscellaneous recitations: or whims of the loo table. 1827.
[Luttrell, H.] Crockford-house: a rhapsody in two cantos. 1827.
'An amateur' (G. F. Pardon). Whist: its history and practice. 1843.
Chatto, W. A. Facts and speculations on the origin and history of playing cards. 1848.
Pettigrew, J. J. On the origin and antiquity of playing cards. 1853.
'Cavendish' (H. Jones). The principles of whist. [1862], 1863 (5th edn as Laws and principles of whist), 1901 (24th edn).
Taylor, E. S. (ed). The history of playing cards. 1865.
'Cavendish' (H. Jones). Card essays. 1879.
Courtney, W. P. English whist and English whist players. 1894. Includes 3 chs on the lit of whist.
'Portland' (J. Hogg) (ed). The whist table: a treasury of notes on the royal game. [1895.]

Chess and other board games

Bibliographies

Simpson, R. Catalogue of books on the origin, history and practice of the game of chess. 1863.
Svendsen, K. Chess fiction in English to 1945: a bibliography. Langston, Hampshire 1950.
Bibliotheca Van der Linde-Niemeijeriana: a catalogue of the chess collection in the Royal Library, the Hague. Hague 1955.

Periodicals

The Chess-Monthly. 1879–96.
The Chess-Player's Chron. 1841–56, 1859–62. Monthly.
British Chess Mag. Huddersfield 1881– . Monthly.

§1

Sturges, J. Guide to the game of draughts. 1800.

[Pratt, P. (ed)]. Studies of chess. 2 vols 1803.

'An amateur' (Rev T. Pruen). An introduction to the history and study of chess. Cheltenham 1804.

Twiss, R. Pamphlets on chess and draughts. In his Miscellanies vol 2, 1805.

An easy introduction to the game of chess. 2 vols 1806.

Sarratt, J. H. A treatise on the game of chess. 1808; ed W. Lewis 1822.

Kenny, W. S. Practical chess grammar. 1817.

Peacock, Thomas Love. The chess dance. In his Melincourt vol 2 ch 28, 1817.

'An Oxford graduate'. Observations on the automaton chess player. 1819.

Playfair, P. The queen and her pawns against the king and his pieces: a poem. 1820.

Sarratt, J. H. A new treaties on the game of chess. 2 vols 1821, 1828.

Cochrane, J. A treatise on the game of chess. 1822. With a catalogue of writers on the game.

Lewis, W. Elements of the game of chess. 1822.

Dibdin, C. I. M. The Chessiad: a mock-heroic poem in five cantos. In his Comic tales and lyrical fancies, 1825.

Madden, F. Historical remarks on the introduction of the game of chess into Europe. Archaeologica 24 1832.

Walker, G. A new treatise on chess. 1832, 1833, 1841 (with full bibliography), 1846 (as The art of chess-play).

Lewis, W. A treatise on the game of chess. 1844.

Staunton, H. The chess-player's handbook. 1847.

Walker, G. Chess and chess-play: original stories and sketches. 1850.

'An amateur' (S. S. Boden). A popular introduction to the study and practice of chess. 1851.

[Tomlinson, C.] Chess: a poem. 1854.

'A member of the Cambridge University Chess Club'. Chess: a poem. 1858.

'An Englishman' (F. M. Edge). Paul Murphy, the chess champion; with a history of chess and chess clubs in England. 1859.

'Captain Crawley' (G. F. Pardon). Backgammon: its theory and practice with something of its history. [1860.]

Forbes, D. The history of chess. 1860.

Staunton, H. Chess praxis: a supplement to The chess-player's handbook. 1860.

Kennedy, H. A. Waifs and strays, chiefly from the chessboard. 1862, 1876.

'Carroll, Lewis' (C. L. Dodgson). Through the looking-glass, and what Alice found there. 1872.

Gossip, G. H. D. The chess-player's manual: a complete guide to chess. 1875.

MacDonnell, G. A. Chess life-pictures. 1883.

Gould, J. The game of draughts. 1884.

Winter-Wood, E. J. The unexpected guest: a chess tale. In Chess souvenirs, 1886.

Tylor, L. Chess: a Christmas masque. 1888.

Bird, H. E. Chess history and reminiscences. [1893].

MacDonnell, G. A. The knights and kings of chess. 1894. Essays on chess and chess-players.

§2

Murray, H. J. R. A history of chess. Oxford 1913.

Sergeant, P. W. A century of British chess. 1934.

Murray, H. J. R. A history of board-games other than chess. Oxford 1952.

Murray, H. J. R. A short history of chess. Oxford 1963.

See also Penn *under* Angling, *above.*

Cock-fighting

§1

Houston, T. The cock-fight. 1804.

The game cock, with an account of his origin. 1825.

Tregellas, J. T. The amusing adventures of Josee Cock, the Perran cock-fighter. 1857. Verse.

Cooper, J. W. Game fowls: their origin and history. 1869.

[Taylor, S. A.] Cocking and its votaries. 1885 (priv ptd).

Atkinson, H. The old English game-fowl. 1891, Idle 1899.

Atkinson, H. Cock-fighting and game-fowl. Bath 1938.

§2

Scott, G. R. The history of cock-fighting. [Hindhead 1957.] With bibliography.

Fitzbarnard, L. Fighting sports. Hindhead 1983.

Coursing

'Sportsman'. A treatise on greyhounds. 1819.

Goodlake, T. The courser's manual or stud-book. 1828. With a contribution by Sir Walter Scott and a history of coursing.

Continuation of The courser's manual. 1833.

Thacker, T. The courser's companion. Derby 1829, 2 vols 1834–5.

'Stonehenge' (J. H. Walsh). The greyhound: a treatise on breeding and training for public running. 1853, 1864, 1875.

Bullock, W. J. The coursing guide: or the Waterloo Cup made easy. [1873], [1874].

Brown, D. The history of coursing. In The greyhound stud book vol 3, 1884.

Jones, T. The courser's guide. 1896.

See also Lascelles and Mackintosh *under* Angling, *above;* 'The Druid' *under* Hunting, Racing, Riding, *below.*

Cricket

Bibliographies

Gaston, A. J. The bibliography of cricket. In Wisden's Cricketers' Almanack for 1892, 1894, 1900, 1923.

Bibliography of cricket. 1895 (priv ptd). A separate work from the above.

Taylor, A. D. The catalogue of cricket literature. 1906.

Waghorn, H. T. Bibliography of cricket. In his The dawn of cricket, 1906.

Britton, C. J. Cricket books: the 100 best old and new. Birmingham 1929.

Goldman, J. W. Bibliography of cricket. 1937 (priv ptd).

Brodribb, A. G. N. Cricket in fiction: a bibliography. Canford 1950 (priv ptd).

Padwick, E. A. (ed). A bibliography of cricket. 1984 (2nd edn).

Allen, D. R. Early books on cricket. 1987.

Eley, S. and P. Griffiths (ed), Padwick's bibliography of cricket. II 1991.

Periodicals

John Wisden's Cricketers' Almanack. 1864– . 1864–9 as Cricketers' Almanack; 1938 as Wisden Cricketers' Almanack. Index (to 1943) by R. Pogson, 1944.

Cricket. 1892–1914. Weekly. After 1913 as The World of Cricket.

§1

Boxall, T. Rules and instructions for playing at the game of cricket. [1800], [1801], 1804.

Lambert, W. Instructions and rules for playing the noble game of cricket. Lewes 1816, 1830 (12th edn). Later edns variously as The cricketer's guide or Lambert's cricketer's guide. The 20th edn was pbd in 1829 before the 12th. The 13th–19th edns have not been traced. Originally a plagiarism of T. Boxall, Rules and instructions, *above; see also* G. B. Buckley, Lambert's cricketer's guide in Cricketer spring annual 1942; R. S. Rait Kerr, Lambert's cricketer's guide in Cricketer spring annual 1949.

Bentley, H. A correct account of all the cricket matches played by the Mary-le-bone Club and all other principal matches 1786–1822 inclusive. 1823. With suppls for 1823, 1824–5.
Mitford, Mary Russell. A country cricket-match. In her Our village vol 1, 1824.
Maunder, S. The game of life: or death among the cricketers. In Death's doings: verse and prose [by] various writers, 1826. Ed and illustr R. Dagley.
Nyren, John. The young cricketer's tutor; to which is added the cricketers of my time or recollections of the most famous old players. Ed C. Cowden Clarke 1833. Subsequent edns until 1858 (11th) as Nyren's cricketer's guide; ed C. Whibley 1893 (under original title); ed F. S. Ashley-Cooper 1902; ed E. V. Lucas 1907 (as The Hambledon men); ed J. Arlott in his From Hambledon to Lords, 1948; ed N. Cardus 1948 (under original title). Original edn reviewed by John Mitford, GM July, Sep 1833.
Pycroft, Rev J. The principles of scientific batting. Oxford 1833. Under pseudonym 'A gentleman'.
The cricket field: or the history and science of cricket. 1851, 1873 (6th edn), 1887 (9th edn); ed F. S. Ashley-Cooper 1922; ed J. Arlott in his From Hambledon to Lords, 1948. *See also* L. E. S. Gutteridge, Bibliography of Pycroft's Cricket field in Cricket Soc News Letter 35 1954.
The cricket tutor. 1862.
Cricketana. 1865. Cricket articles rptd from London Soc Aug–Nov 1862, Jan, Mar, June 1863.
Cricket reminiscences of the old players and observations on the young ones. 1868.
Oxford memories. 2 vols 1886 (chs 21–5); ed J. Arlott in his Middle ages of cricket, 1949.
[Castelden, G.] Woburn Park: a fragment in rural rhyme. 1839, 1840. Pt 2 describes a match in some detail.
Lillywhite, F. W. Lillywhite's illustrated hand-book of cricket. 1844.
'Felix, N.' (N. Wanostrocht). Felix on the bat. 1845, 1850, 1855, 1962 (with memoir by G. Brodribb).
How to play Clarke. 1852; ed F. S. Ashley-Cooper 1922.
A cricket song. Ed F. S. Ashley-Cooper, Nottingham 1923. *See also* J. Arlott, Felix and some aspects of early cricket, in his Concerning cricket, 1949.
Denison, W. Cricket: sketches of the players. 1846; ed J. Arlott in his Middle ages of cricket, 1949.
Lillywhite, F. (ed). The guide to cricketers. Annual 1849–66. In 1867 merged with John Lillywhite's Cricketers' companion. 2 issues in 1849, 1860–1, 1861–2, 1862–3, 3 issues 1865–6. First 3 issues contain treatise by William Lillywhite; 2 issues of 1849 as The young cricketer's guide.
Bolland, W. Cricket notes. 1851.
Gale, F. The public school matches and those we meet there. 1853 (under pseudonym 'Wykehamist'), 1896 (as Public school cricket matches forty years ago).
Echoes from the old cricket fields: sketches of cricket and cricketers from the earliest history of the game. 1871, 1896.
The life of the Hon Robert Grimston. 1885.
The game of cricket. 1887.
'Chambers, C.' (T. Smith). The cricket match: a poem in two cantos. 1859.
Lillywhite, F. The English cricketers' trip to Canada and the United States. 1860.
'Old cricketer' (C. Box?). The cricket-bat and how to use it. 1861.
Prowse, W. J. In memoriam [of the Kent cricketer Alfred Mynn]. Bell's Life in London 10 Nov 1861. Verse.
Haygarth, A. Frederick Lillywhite's cricket scores and biographies from 1746 [to 1878]. 15 vols 1862–1925. Vols 3–4 as Lillywhite's cricket scores etc, vols 5–6 and 14 as Arthur Haygarth's Cricket scores etc, vols 7–13 as Marylebone Club cricket scores etc, vol 15 ed F. S. Ashley-Cooper as MCC cricket scores etc but consisting only of biographies. Index to all first-class matches in scores and biographies vols 1–14 by J. B. Payne, Harrogate 1903.
Grace, E. M. The trip to Australia: scraps from the diary of one of the twelve. 1864. *See also* F. S. Ashley-Cooper, E. M. G. cricketer, 1916.
Payne, J. B. Scores and analyses [of matches not in Wisden] 1864–81. Harrogate [1904].
The Canterbury cricket week. Canterbury 1865.
John Lillywhite's cricketers' companion. 1865–85. In 1886 merged with James Lillywhite's cricketers' annual.
Fitzgerald, R. A. Jerks in from short-leg. 1866. Under pseudonym 'Quid'.
Wickets in the west: or the twelve in America. 1873.
Selkirk, G. H. Guide to the cricket ground. 1867. Practical treatise with ch on the history of the game.
Box, C. The theory and practice of cricket. 1868.
The English game of cricket. 1877. With anthology of cricket verse.
Gale, F. Echoes from the old cricket fields: sketches of cricket and cricketers from the earliest history of the game. 1871, 1896.
The game of cricket. 1887.
'Thomsonby' (H. P. Thomas). Cricketers in council. 1871. Practical treatise which includes some verse.
James Lillywhite's cricketers' annual. 1871–1900.
Compton, H. A colonial cricket match. In his Semi-tropical trifles, 1875.
'An old cricketer'. A cricketer's notebook. 1881. Verse and prose.
Trollope, Anthony. The cricket-match. In his Fixed period, 2 vols Edinburgh 1882.
Geering, T. Cricket on our common fifty years ago. In his Our parish: a medley, Hailsham 1884, London 1925 (with memoir by A. Beckett as Our Sussex parish).
Sapte, W. Cricketers guyed for 1886. [1885]. Humorous articles.
Shaw, A. and A. Shrewsbury. Cricket: Shaw and Shrewsbury's team in Australia. Nottingham 1885.
Bowen, E. E. Willow the King [and other verses on cricket]. In his Harrow songs, 1886.
Glover, W. Reminiscences of half a century. 1889. Includes chs on cricket.
Hutchinson, H. G. Cricketing saws and stories. 1889.
Peter Steele the cricketer. [1895]. A novel.
[Gale, N. R.] Cricket songs. Rugby 1890.
Cricket songs. 1894.
More cricket songs. 1905.
Dale, B. Some statistics of cricket: or the influence of the weather on the wicket. [1891.]
Grace, W. G. Cricket. Bristol 1891.
Cricketing reminiscences and personal recollections. 1899.
W. G.'s little book. [1909.] Traces changes and developments in the game.
See also W. M. Brownlee, W. G. G.: a biography, *1887;* The memorial biography of W. G. G., *ed M. B. Hawke, 1919; B. R. M. Darwin,* W. G. G., *1934; C. Box,* W. G. G., *1934; C. Box,* W. G. G., *1952; A. A. Thomson,* The great cricketer, *1957.*
Nelson, A. Comic cricket. [1891.] Humorous articles.
Lucas, E. V. Songs of the bat. 1892.
Willow and leather: a book of praise. Bristol [1898]. Anthology.
Standing, P. C. Gentlemen v Players: with introduction and history of the contest since its origin in 1806. 1892.
Cricket of to-day and yesterday. 2 vols 1902.
The Hon F. S. Jackson [a biography]. 1906.
Anglo-Australian cricket 1862–1926. 1926.
Daft, R. Kings of cricket: reminiscences and anecdotes. Bristol [1893].
A cricketer's yarns. Ed F. S. Ashley-Cooper 1926.
Christian, E. B. V. At the sign of the wicket: essays on the glorious game. Bristol [1894]. Includes chs on cricket literature.
(ed). The light side of cricket: stories, sketches and verses. 1898.

Trew-Hay, J. The match of the season [Surrey v Lancs Aug 16–18 1894]: a lay of the Oval. [1894.]
Cobley, F. Black hats v white hats: or Ilkley tradesmen at the wickets and around the festive board. Otley 1895. Verse and prose.
Pentelow, J. N. England v Australia: the story of the test matches. 1895, 1904.
Cochrane, A. J. H. Lays from the pavilion and the links. In his Leviore plectro: occasional verses, 1896.
Told in the pavilion. Bristol 1896. Short stories.
Furniss, H. et al. How's that? Including A century of Grace by H—F—, verses by E. J. Milliken and cricket sketches by E. B. V. Christian. Bristol [1896].
Read, W. W. Annuals of cricket: a record of the game during the last twenty-three years. 1896.
Disney, T. Cricket lyrics. [1897.]
Holmes, R. S. The county cricket championship 1873–96. Bristol [1897].
Moffat, D. Crickety cricket. 1897. Verse.
Ranjitsinhji, K. S. The Jubilee book of cricket. 1897. Reviewed by Francis Thompson in Academy 4 Sep 1897.
With Stoddart's team in Australia. 1898.
See also P. C. Standing, Ranjitsinhji: prince of cricket, *1903; R. Wild,* The biography of Ranjitsinhji, *1934.*
Ashley-Cooper, F. S. Stoddart's team in Australia 1897–8. [1898.]
Curiosities of first-class cricket: descriptions of curious incidents arranged year by year from 1730–1901. 1901.
MCC match list: a summary of 8642 matches played in the UK by the MCC since 1787. 1930.
Bone, D. D. Fifty years' reminiscences of Scottish cricket. Glasgow 1898.
Giffen, G. With bat and ball: twenty-five years reminiscences of Australian and Anglo-Australian cricket. 1898.
Wells, H. G. The veteran cricketer. In his Certain personal matters, 1898.
Lyttelton, Hon R. H. Cricket. 1898.
Giants of the game. [1899.]
Newbolt, Sir H. In vitaï Lampada. In his Island race, 1898.
Pullin, A. W. Talks with old Yorkshire cricketers. Leeds 1898.
Talks with old English cricketers. Edinburgh 1900.
(ed). Alfred Shaw, cricketer: his career and reminiscences. 1902.
[Barrie, J. M.] The Allahakbarrie book of Broadway cricket for 1899. [1899] (priv ptd), 1950 (as Allahakbarrie's CC 1899).
Caffyn, W. Seventy-one not out: reminiscences. Ed 'Mid-on' (R. P. Daft) 1899.
Fry, C. B. (ed). The book of cricket: a gallery of famous players. [1899.]
Snaith, J. C. Willow the King: the story of a cricket match. [1899.] A novel.
Bayly, A. E. and W. Briscoe. Chronicles of a country cricket club. 1900. Fiction.
Bettesworth, W. A. The Walkers of Southgate: a famous brotherhood of cricketers. 1900.
Chats on the cricket field, with explanatory notes by F. S. Ashley-Cooper. [1910.] Interviews with c. 60 cricketers rptd from The Cricket Field and Cricket 1892–1906.
Ford, W. J. A cricketer on cricket. 1900.
Warner, Sir P. F. Cricket in many climes. 1900.
Lord's 1787–1945. 1946.
Gentlemen v Players 1806–1949. 1950.
Thompson, Francis. At Lords [and other cricketing verse]. In A rhapsodist at Lord's, in E. V. Lucas, One day and another, 1909.
Lang, Andrew. Games and sport: cricket, golf, fishing. Pt 9 vol 2 of his Collected poems, ed L. B. Lang 4 vols 1923.

§2

Gordon, H. S. C. M. Cricket form at a glance showing the batting and bowling of every cricketer who has played in first class matches in any two seasons between 1878–1902, with every run scored for or against the Australians in England, the elevens they met, the results and that of every county match. 1902.
Benson, E. F. and E. H. Miles. The cricket of Abel, Hirst and Shrewsbury. 1903.
Taylor, A. D. Annals of Lord's and history of the MCC. Bristol [1903].
Barlow, R. G. Forty seasons of first-class cricket: autobiography and reminiscences. Manchester [1908].
Toms, T. S. England v Australia in the tests 1877–1908. [1909.]
Harris, G. R. C. Baron Harris. Lord's and the MCC: a cricket chronicle of 137 years. 1914. With F. S. Ashley-Cooper.
Harris, G. R. C. A few short runs. 1921. Cricketing reminiscences.
Altham, H. S. A history of cricket [with select bibliography]. 1926, 1938 (with E. W. Swanton), 1947, 1948, 2 vols 1962.
Gordon, H. S. C. M. Eton v Harrow at Lord's: the story of the matches by Bernard Darwin and reminiscences of every match since 1861 by an actual player in each game. 1926.
Parker, E. Between the wickets: an anthology of cricket. 1926.
Lewis, W. J. The language of cricket with illustrative extracts from the literature of the game. Oxford 1934.
Buckley, G. B. Fresh light on pre-Victorian cricket: a collection of cricket notices from 1709 to 1837. Birmingham 1937.
The MCC 1787–1937. 1937 (rptd from The Times MCC no). Includes Edmund Blunden, Some cricket books.
Brodribb, G. The English game: a cricket anthology. 1948.
Brodribb and S. Brogden. The first test match: England v Australia 1877. 1950.
Joy, N. Maiden over: a short history of women's cricket. 1950.
Kerr, R. S. Rait. The laws of cricket: their history and growth. 1950. Including list of edns of laws pbd 1744–1835.
Martineau, G. D. Bat, ball, wicket and all: an account of the origin and development of the implements, dress and appurtenances of the national game. 1950.
Parker, E. The history of cricket. 1950 (Lonsdale Lib of Sports vol 30).
Meynell, L. Famous cricket grounds: a brief history of some of the famous grounds in England. 1951.
Arlott, J. Cricket. 1953. Includes much history with extensive quotations from early cricket literature.
Brodribb, G. The book of cricket verse: an anthology. 1953.
Martineau, G. D. The valiant stumper: a history of wicket-keeping. 1957.
Morrah, P. Alfred Mynn and the cricketers of his time. 1963. With bibliography.
Swanton, E. W. (ed). The world of cricket. 1966. With sections on lit.
Scott, P. Cricket and the religious world in the Victorian period. Church Quart 3 1970.
Mandle, W. F. The professional cricketer in the 19th century. Labour History 23 1972.
Sandiford, K. A. P. Cricket and the Victorians: a historiographical essay. Historical Reflections 9 1982.
Sandiford, K. A. P. English cricket crowds during the Victorian age. Jnl of Sport History 9 Winter 1982.
Sandiford, K. A. P. Amateurs and professionals in Victorian county cricket. Albion 15 Spring 1983.
Sandiford, K. A. P. Cricket and the Victorian society. Jnl of Social History 17 Winter 1983.
Sandiford, K. A. P. Victorian cricket technique and industrial technology. British Jnl of Sports History 1, Dec 1984.
Sissons, R. The players: a social history of the professional cricketer. 1988.
Williams, J. Cricket in T. Mason, ed, Sport in Britain: a social history. Cambridge 1989.
Sandiford, K. A. P. Women's cricket in Victorian England. Jnl of the Cricket Soc 15 Spring 1992.

Midwinter, E. Cricket in schoolboy literature. Jnl of the Cricket Soc 16 Autumn 1993.
Sandiford, K. A. P. Cricket and the Victorians. Aldershot 1994.

Croquet

Bibliographies

Prior, R. C. A. Notes on croquet: and some ancient bar and ball games related to it. 1872.
Rhoades, M. L. Croquet: an annotated bibliography. Metuchen NJ 1992.

§1

Lillie, A. Croquet: its history, rules and secrets. 1897.
Croquet up to date. 1900.
Pritchard, D. M. C. The history of croquet. 1986.
Smith, N. Queen of games: a history of croquet. 1991.
See also Lawn tennis *under* Tennis, *below.*

Cycling

Bibliographies

Lightwood, J. T. Bibliography of cycling literature. In his Cyclists' touring club: the romance of 50 years cycling, 1928.

§1

Davis, A. The velocipede and how to use it. 1868.
The velocipede: its history. 1869.
[Bottomley, J. F.] The velocipede: its past, its present and its future. 1869.
Jefferson, R. L. Awheel to Moscow and back: the record of a record cycle ride. 1895.
For details of the many books describing cycling tours pbd 1870–1900, see bibliography in Lightwood's Cyclists' touring club, *1928, above.*
The humours of cycling. 1897. A selection of cycling stories by H. G. Wells, Jerome K. Jerome et al.
Waugh, A. Legends of the wheel. Bristol [1898]. Verse.
Jerome, Jerome K. Three men on the bummel. Bristol [1900].
Alderson, F. Bicycling: a history. Newton Abbot 1972.
Demans, A. B. Victorian and Edwardian cycling and motoring from old photographs. 1977.
Rubenstein, D. Cycling in the 1880s. VS 21 Autumn 1977.

Driving

Bibliographies

Somerset, H. C. F., 8th Duke of Beaufort. The bibliography of driving. In his Driving, 1889 (Badminton Lib).

§1

Cross, T. The autobiography of a stage-coachman. 3 vols 1861.
Reynardson, C. T. S. B. Down the road: or reminiscences of a gentleman coachman. 1875.
Lennox, Lord W. P. Coaching: with anecdotes of the road. 1876.
Malet, H. E. Annals of the road: or notes on mail and stage coaching in Great Britain. 1876.
Harris, S. Old coaching days. 1882.
The coaching age. 1885.
Haworth, M. E. Road scrapings: coaches and coaching. 1882.
Maudsley, A. Highways and horses. 1888.
Tristram, W. O. Coaching days and coaching ways. 1888.
Corbett, E. An old coachman's chatter; with some practical remarks on driving. 1890.

§2

Shone, A. B. A century and a half of amateur driving. 1956.
See 'Cecil', 'Nimrod' *and* Whitehurst *under* Hunting, Racing, Riding, *below.*

Falconry and Hawking

Bibliographies

Harting, J. E. Bibliotheca accipitraria: a catalogue of books ancient and modern relating to falconry. 1891.
Barber, R. H. A supplementary bibliography of hawking: books published in England between 1891 and 1943, together with a list of the most important books published prior to that period. 1943 (priv ptd).
Wood, C. A. and F. M. Fyfe. An annotated bibliography of ancient, medieval and modern falconry. In their Art of falconry: being the De arte venandi cum avibus of Frederick II of Honenstaufen, Stanford CA 1943, Boston 1955.

§1

Sebright, Sir J. S. Observations upon hawking. 1826.
Belany, J. C. A treatise upon falconry. Berwick-on-Tweed 1841.
Burton, Sir R. F. Falconry in the valley of the Indus. 1852.
Salvin, F. H. and W. Brodrick. Falconry in the British Isles. 1855, 1873.
Salvin and G. E. Freeman. Falconry: its claims, history and practice. 1859.
Freeman, G. E. Practical falconry; to which is added, How I became a falconer. 1869.
Fisher, C. H., G. E. Freeman et al. Prize essays on falconry. 1871.
Harting, J. E. The ornithology of Shakespeare. 1871. Contains much on falconry and hawking.
Hints on the management of hawks. 1884, 1898 (with additional chs on falconry).
Mitchell, E. B. The art and practice of hawking. 1900.

Fencing

Bibliographies

Foster, F. W. A list of works on sword play. N & Q July–Dec 1875.
Castle, E. Bibliotheca artis dimicatoriae. In W. H. Pollock et al, Fencing; boxing; wrestling, 1889 (Badminton Lib).
Thimm, C. A. A complete bibliography of the art of fence. 1891.
Thimm, C. A. A complete bibliography of fencing and duelling. 1896.
Aylward, J. D. Some nineteenth-century fencing books. Connoisseur Oct 1950.

§1

Mathewson, T. Fencing familiarized. Salford 1805.
Roland, J. The amateur of fencing. 1809.
Angelo, H. C. W. A treatise on the utility and advantages of fencing. 1817.
Reminiscences. 2 vols 1828, 1904 (with notes and memoir by H. L. Smith).
Martelli, C. An improved system of fencing. 1819.
Roland, G. A treatise on the theory and practice of the art of fencing. Edinburgh 1823.
An introductory course of fencing. Edinburgh 1827.
Young, W. The fencer's manual. Chatham 1840.
Chapman, G. Foil practice: with a review of the art of fencing. 1861.
Notes and observations on the art of fencing: a sequel to Foil practice. 1864.
Burton, Sir R. F. The book of the sword. 1884. All pbd of 3 projected vols.
The sentiment of the sword: a country-house dialogue. Ed A. F. Sieveking 1911.
Castle, E. Schools and masters of fence. 1885, 1892.

§2

Aylward, J. de V. The house of Angelo: a dynasty of swordsmen. 1953.
Aylward, J. de V. The English master of arms. 1956.
Baldick, R. The duel: a history of duelling. 1965.

Football: Association and Rugby

Bibliographies

Young, P. M. In his Manchester United, 1960.
McLaren, D. A. Handbook of rugby literature. Dunedin 1990 (2nd edn).

Periodicals

The Football Annual. 1873–1908. Association and Rugby.

§1

Football: the first day of the sixth match. Rugby [1851].
'An old boy' (Thomas Hughes). In his Tom Brown's school days, Cambridge 1857.
Shearman, Sir M. and J. E. Vincent. Football: its history for five centuries. 1885.
Marshall, Rev F. (ed). Football: the Rugby union game. 1892, [1894]; ed L. R. Tosswill 1925.
The origin of Rugby football: report with appendices of the sub-committee of the Old Rugbeian Society. Rugby 1897.
'Tityrus' (J. A. H. Cotton). The rise of the Leaguers 1863–97. 1897.
The real football: a sketch of the development of the Association game. 1900.
Jackson, N. L. et al. Association football. 1899.
Weddell, A. J. Handy guide to English league football. Liverpool 1899.

§2

Gibson, A. and W. Pickford. Association football and the men who made it. 4 vols [1905–6].
Sutcliffe, C. E. et al. The story of the football league 1888–1938. Preston 1938.
Green, G. The official history of the FA cup. 1949, 1960.
Marshall, H. and J. P. Jordan. Oxford v Cambridge: the story of the University Rugby match. 1951.
Green, G. et al. The history of the Football Association. 1953.
Marples, M. A. History of football. 1954.
Owen, O. L. The history of the Rugby Football Union. 1955.
Pelmear, K. and J. E. Morpurgo. Rugby football: an anthology. 1958.
Green, G. and A. H. Fabian (ed). Association football. 4 vols 1960. Includes much on early history of the game.
Thomas, J. B. G. Great rugger clubs. 1962.
Delaney, T. A century of soccer: a centenary publication of the Football Association. 1963.
Titley, U. A. and R. McWhirter. Centenary history of the rugby football union. 1970.
Mandle, W. F. Games people played: cricket and football in England and Victoria in the late nineteenth century. Historical Stud 15 1973.
Walvin, J. The people's game: a social history of English football. 1975.
Mason, T. Association football and English society 1863–1915. Hassocks 1980.
Tischler, S. Footballers and businessmen: the origins of professional soccer in England. New York 1981.
Baker, W. J. William Webb Ellis and the origins of rugby football – the life and death of a Victorian myth. Albion 13 Summer 1981.
Williams, G. Rugby union. In Sport in Britain: a social history, ed T. Mason, Cambridge 1989.
Macrory, J. Running with the ball: the birth of rugby football. 1991.

Golf

Bibliographies

Lawless, P. A golfer's bibliography. In his Golfer's companion, 1937.
Hopkinson, C. Collecting golf-books 1743–1938. 1938.
Murdoch, J. S. K. and J. Seagle. Golf: a guide to information sources. Detroit MI 1979.

Periodicals

The Golfing Annual. 1887–1910.
Golf. 1890– . Weekly. From 16 June 1899 as Golf Illustrated.
Golfing. 1895– . Weekly. From 24 Feb 1897–30 June 1898 as Golfing and Cycling Illustrated. From 7 July–27 Oct 1898 as Golfing and Cycling.

§1

[Cundell, J.] Rules of the Thistle Golf Club; with some historical notices relative to the progress of golf in Scotland. Edinburgh 1824; rptd in R. Clark, Golf, 1875.
Carnegie, G. F. Golfiana: or niceties connected with the game of golf. Leith 1833, Edinburgh 1833, 1842, 1867 (in Poems on golf), 1875 (in R. Clark, Golf).
'A keen hand' (H. B. Farnie). The golfer's manual: being an historical and descriptive account of the national game of Scotland. Cupar 1857, London 1947.
Chambers, R. A few rambling remarks on golf. 1862.
'A golfer' (G. Robb). Historical gossip about golf and golfers. Edinburgh 1863.
Poems on golf. Edinburgh 1867.
[Brown, T.] Golfiana: or a day at Gullane. [Edinburgh?] 1869; rptd in J. Kerr, The golf-book of East Lothian, 1896.
Marsh, T. Blackheath golfing lays. 1873.
Clark, R. (ed). Golf: a royal and ancient game. Edinburgh 1875, London 1893. Mainly an anthology of golf lit.
Hogg, W. T. M. Gullane: a poem. Edinburgh 1875.
Forgan, R. The golfer's handbook. Cupar 1881, London [1890], [1897] (as The golfer's manual).
Hutchinson, H. G. Hints on the game of golf. Edinburgh 1886, Edinburgh and London 1891 (6th edn).
British golf links. 1897.
The golfing pilgrim on many links. 1898.
The book of golf and golfers. 1899.
Aspects of golf. Bristol 1900.
Fifty years of golf. [1919.]
Jackson, D. Golf songs and recitations. Cupar 1886, Leven 1895.
Simpson, Sir W. G. The art of golf. Edinburgh 1887.
Stewart, J. L. Golfiana miscellanea: being a collection of interesting monographs on golf. 1887.
Lang, A. Two rhymes on golf. In W. A. Knight and T. T. Oliphant, On the links, Edinburgh 1889.
Lang et al. A batch of golfing papers. London and St Andrews 1892.
'Flint, Violet' (J. E. Thomson). A golfing idyll. St Andrews 1892. Verse.
'J. A. C. K.' Golf in the year 2000: or what we are coming to. 1892. A novel.
Stobart, M. A. Won at the last hole: a golfing romance. 1893. A novel.
Thomson, J. Golfing and other poems and songs. Glasgow 1893.
Kennard, M. E. The sorrows of a golfer's wife. 1896. A novel.
Mackern, L. (ed). Our lady of the green: a book of ladies' golf. 1899.
Low, J. L. F. G. Tait: a record, being his life, letters and golfing diary. [1900.]

§2

Wood, H. B. Golfing curios and 'the like'. 1910. With bibliography.
Hilton, H. H. and G. G. Smith (ed). The royal and ancient game of golf. 1912.
Clapcott, C. B. The rules of golf of the ten oldest golf clubs 1754–1848. Edinburgh 1935.
Darwin, B. et al. A history of golf in Britain. 1952.
Mortimer, C. G. and F. J. C. Pignon. The story of the Open Golf Championship 1860–1950. 1952.
Browning, R. H.-K. A history of golf. 1955.
Cousins, G. Golf in Britain: a social history from the beginnings to the present day. 1975.
Henderson, I. T. and D. I. Stirk. Golf in the making. Bradford 1979.
Henderson, I. T. and D. I. Stirk. The compleat golfer: an illustrated history of the royal and ancient game. 1985.
Lowerson, J. Golf. In Sport in Britain: a social history, ed T. Mason, Cambridge 1989.
See also Cochrane *and* Lang *under* Cricket, *above.*

Hockey

Bibliographies

Malherbe, W. A. Bibliography of hockey. Kronsted 1956.

§1

Battersby, H. F. P. Hockey. 1895.

Solbé, F. de L. Hints on hockey. Edinburgh and London 1900.

Hunting, Racing, Riding

Bibliographies

Somerset, H. C. F., 8th Duke of Beaufort, and M. Morris. Bibliography of hunting and hunters. In their Hunting, 1885 (Badminton Lib).

Huth, F. H. Works on horses and equitation: a bibliographical record of hippology [including some racing bks]. 1887.

Higginson, A. H. British and American sporting authors: their writings and biographies, with a bibliography by S. R. Smith. 1951. Mainly concerned with hunting.

Allen, J. A. The steeplechaser's library: a bibliography. In Steeplechasing, ed J. H. P. Verney, Baron Willoughby de Broke 1954 (Lonsdale Lib vol 32).

Loder, E. P. Bibliography of the history and organisation of horse-racing and thoroughbred breeding in Great Britain and Ireland. 1975.

Beavan, W. F. Big game hunting, deer stalking, game shooting, wildfowling, gamekeeping, poaching and associated natural history: a chronological bibliography covering the years c. 1413 to 1939. Chester 1982.

Grimshaw, A. The horse: a bibliography of British books, 1851–1976. 1982.

Wells, E. B. Horsemanship: a bibliography of printed material from the sixteenth century through 1971. 1985.

Periodicals

The Racing Calendar. 1773– . Annual. *See also* C. M. Prior, The history of The Racing Calendar, 1926.

Racing Times. 1851–64, 1866–8. Weekly.

Horse and Hound. 1884– . Weekly.

The Racing World. 1887– . Weekly.

Bailey's Hunting Directory. 1897– . Annual.

§1

Chifney, S. The narrative or address of S— C— to the public in general, but more particularly to such of them as are connected with the turf. 1800.

Adams, J. The analysis of horsemanship: teaching the whole art of riding. 3 vols 1805.

Hawkes, J. The Meynellian science: or fox-hunting upon system. [1808?], 1848; ed L. H. Irvine, Leicester 1932.

Lawrence, J. The history and delineation of the horse with a particular investigation of the character of the race-horse and the business of the turf. 1809.

Morland, T. H. The genealogy of the English race horse; with observations upon the present improved method of breeding for the turf. 1810.

Songs of the chace: containing an extensive collection relative to the sports of the field. 1811 (2nd edn).

Beard, J. A diary of fifteen years hunting, viz from 1796 to 1811. Bath 1813.

Lloyd, G. and R. Symes. The improved art of riding. [1815?]

Steward, C. A new and complete guide to the art of riding. 1821.

Allen, J. Principles of modern riding for ladies. 1825.

Principles of modern riding for gentlemen. 1825.

Anecdotes on the origin and antiquity of horse-racing. 1825.

Cook, J. Observations on fox-hunting and the management of hounds. 1826; ed R. G. Verney 1922.

Johnson, T. B. The hunting directory. 1826. Prose work on all aspects of hunting.

Stanley, E. The young horsewoman's compendium of the modern art of riding. 1827.

Hood, Thomas. The Epping hunt. 1829. Verse.

Brown, T. Biographical sketches and authentic anecdotes of horses. 1830. Includes Charles Dibdin, The high-mettled racer, also pbd separately 1831.

'Nimrod' (Charles James Apperley). Remarks on the condition of hunters. 1831; ed C. Tongue 1855; ed F. T. Barton 1908.

Nimrod's hunting tours. 1835; ed W. S. Sparrow 1926.

Memoirs of the life of the late John Mytton. 1835, 1851 (with memoir of the author by Surtees).

The chace, the turf and the road. 1837; ed Sir H. E. Maxwell 1898; ed W. S. Sparrow 1927.

Nimrod's northern tour. 1838.

The horse and the hound. Edinburgh 1842.

Hunting reminiscences. 1843; ed W. S. Sparrow 1926.

My life and times. Ed E. D. Cuming 1927. Taken in part from articles in Fraser's Mag 1842.

My horses and other essays. Ed E. D. Cuming 1928. Miscellaneous contributions to periodicals.

Warburton, R. E. E. Hunting songs and ballads. Chester 1834, London 1846, 1859, 1860, 1873, 1877; ed H. Maxwell 1912.

'Caveat emptor' (Sir George Stephen). The adventures of a gentleman in search of a horse. 1835.

Hawke, Hon M. B. E. The Epwell hunt [and another hunting poem]. Cheltenham [1835?]; with two other hunting poems, [1840?].

Poems on hunting [with a sketch of Hawke's sporting career by Nimrod]. Pontefract? 1842.

Peters, J. G. A treatise on equitation. 1835.

Smith, T. Extracts from the diary of a huntsman. 1838, 1841, 1921, 1933.

The life of a fox written by himself. 1843 (under the pseud 'Wily'), 1896; ed R. G. Verney, Lord Willoughby de Broke, 1926.

[Surtees, R. S.] *See col 1403, above.*

'Quis'. Shelton gorse. Bedford 1839.

Radcliffe, F. P. D. The noble science: a few general ideas on fox-hunting. 1839; ed W. C. A. Blew 1893; ed Blew and C. Bradley 2 vols 1911.

Whyte, J. C. History of the British turf. 2 vols 1840.

Mills, J. *See col 1355, above.*

Vyner, R. T. Notitia venatica: a treatise on fox-hunting. 1841, [1871]; ed W. C. A. Blew 1892; ed Blew and C. Bradley 2 vols 1910. All edns illustr H. Alken.

Corbet, H. The steeple chase calendar: a consecutive chronicle of the sport in Great Britain 1826–44. 1845; suppl, 1846.

'Hieover, Harry' (C. Bindley). Stable talk and table talk. 1845–6.

The pocket and the stud. 1848.

The hunting-field. 1850.

Practical horsemanship. 1850.

Bipeds and quadrupeds. 1853.

'Gêlert'. Fores's guide to the foxhounds and staghounds of England to which are added the otter-hounds and harriers of several counties. [1849], 1908 (as A guide to the foxhounds etc).

Hall, H. B. Exmoor. 1849. Sporting reminiscences of the area.

Brooklands: a sporting biography. 2 vols 1852.

Rous, Hon H. J. The laws and practice of horse racing. 1850. *See also* T. H. Bird, Admiral Rous and the English turf 1795–1877, 1939.

Wayte, S. C. The equestrian's manual. 1850.

'Cecil' (Cornelius Tongue). The stud farm: or hints on breeding for the turf, the chase and the road. 1851, 1856, 1873.

Stable practice: or hints on training for the turf, the chase and the road. 1852.

Records of the chase and memoirs of celebrated sportsmen. 1854, 1877, 1922.

Hunting tours. 1864.

'Martingale' (J.? White). Turf characters: the officials and the subalterns. 1851.

'Scrutator' (K. W. Horlock). Letters on the management of hounds. 1852.

Horses and hounds: a practical treatise on their management. 1855.
The master of the hounds. 3 vols 1859. A novel.
Recollections of a fox-hunter. 1861.
The country gentleman. 3 vols 1862. A novel.
The science of foxhunting. 1868.
Berkeley, Hon G. C. G. F. Reminiscences of a huntsman. 1854.
'The Druid' (H. H. Dixon). The post and the paddock, with recollections of George IV, Sam Chifney and other turf celebrities. [1856], [1856], [1857].
Silk and scarlet. 1859.
Scott and Sebright. 1862.
Saddle and sirloin. 1870. Includes coursing.
The above 3 books all contain racing and hunting history and reminiscence. See also J. B. Booth, Bits of character: a life of H. H. D., *1936.*
Clarke, Mrs J. S. The habit and the horse: a treatise on female equitation. 1857.
Eardley-Wilmot, Sir J. E. Reminiscences of the late Thomas Assheton Smith esq, a famous fox-hunter. 1860, 1862; ed Sir H. E. Maxwell 1902 (6th edn).
Head, Sir F. B. The horse and his rider. 1860.
Whyte-Melville, G. J. *See col 1439, above.*
Collyns, C. P. Notes on the chase of the wild red deer in the counties of Devon and Somerset. 1862.
Clarke, C. A box for the season. 2 vols 1864. A hunting novel.
Which is the winner? 3 vols 1864. A racing novel.
Crumbs from a sportsman's table. 2 vols 1865. A hunting novel.
The flying scud. 2 vols 1867. A racing novel.
Trollope, A. Hunting sketches. 1865; ed J. Boyd 1934; ed L. Edwards 1952.
Lays of the Belvoir hunt. 1866, 1874.
'Meadows, Lindon' (C. B. Greatrex). Dame Perkins and her grey mare. 1866. Hunting verse.
Craven, W. G. The Margravine: a story of the turf. 2 vols 1870.
Bowers, G. Notes from a hunting box not in the shires. 1873.
'Old Calabor'. Over turf and stubble. 1873. A novel.
Won in a canter. 3 vols 1874. A novel.
Grey Abbey. 2 vols 1877. A novel with racing scenes.
Randall, J. Old sports and sportsmen, or the Willey country with sketches of Squire Forester and his whipper-in Tom Moody. 1873.
Sidney, S. The book of the horse and hints on horsemanship. 1874, 1881.
'Vieille Moustache' (R. Henderson). The barb and the bridle: a handbook of equitation for ladies. 1874.
Musters, J. C. The great run with J. C. M.'s foxhounds. Nottingham [1877]. Verse.
Hunting songs and poems. Nottingham 1885.
Sewell, A. Black Beauty: the autobiography of a horse. 1877.
Smart, H. Bound to win: a tale of the turf. 3 vols 1877.
'Triviator'. The West Union stag hounds and the Baytown run. [1877.] Verse.
'Brooksby' (E. P. Elmhirst). The hunting countries of England: their facilities, character and requirements. 2 vols 1878.
The cream of Leicestershire. 1883. Articles selected and rptd from Field.
Fitt, J. N. Covert-side sketches: or thoughts on hunting. 1878.
Whitehurst, F. F. Tally-ho: sketches of hunting, coaching etc. 1878.
Hark away: sketches of hunting, coaching etc. 1879.
Rice, J. History of the British turf. 2 vols 1879.
Webber, B. Pigskin and willow. 3 vols 1879.
'Blinkhoolie'. Angram, a hidden talent: the story of a wasted horse. York [1880].
The tale of a horse. 1884.
Watson, A. E. T. Sketches in the hunting field. 1880.
Racecourse and covert side. 1883. Sketches.
Types of the turf: anecdotes and incidents. 1883. Under pseud 'Rapier'.
Racing and 'chasing: a collection of sporting stories. 1897.
The turf. 1898.
Bagot, A. G. Men we meet in the field. 1881.
Hayes, M. H. Riding on the flat and across country: a guide to practical horsemanship. 1881, 1882.
O'Donoghue, Mrs N. P. Ladies on horseback. 1881, 1891.
The common sense of riding: riding for ladies with hints on the stable. 1887.
Mason, G. F. My day with the hounds and other stories. Cambridge [1882].
Sporting recollections. 1885.
Flowers of the hunt. 1889.
The white hat and other stories. Bristol [1891].
The tame fox, and other sketches. [1897.]
Heroes and heroines of the Grand National: containing a complete account of every race. 1907.
'Wanderer' (E. H. D'Avigdor). Across country. 1882. Short stories.
Fair Diana. 1884. A hunting novel.
Hunt-room stories and yachting yarns. 1885. Short stories.
A loose rein. 1887. A hunting novel.
Kennard, M. E. The right sort: a romance of the shires. 3 vols 1883.
The girl in the brown habit. 3 vols 1886.
Killed in the open. 3 vols 1886.
A real good thing. 3 vols 1887.
A glorious gallop. 1888.
Our friends in the hunting field. 1889. Prose sketches.
That pretty little horse-breaker. 3 vols 1891.
Wedded to sport. 3 vols 1892.
The hunting girl. 3 vols 1893.
The catch of the county. 3 vols 1894.
A crack county. 3 vols 1894.
At the tail of the hounds. 1897.
Morals of the Midlands. 1899.
Day, W. Reminiscences of the turf. 1886.
Turf celebrities I have known. 1891.
Hone, J. P. History of Newmarket and annals of the turf. 3 vols 1886.
Fortescue, Hon Sir J. W. Records of stag-hunting on Exmoor. 1887.
The story of a red deer. 1897.
Roberts, Sir R. H. In the shires: a sporting novel. [1887.]
Curb and snaffle. 1888. A novel.
Hard held. 1889. Sequel to preceding.
High-flyer hall: Joshua Blewitt's sporting experiences. [1893.] A novel.
Not in the betting. 1893. A novel.
Russell, F. Cross country reminiscences. 1887.
In scarlet or silk: recollections of hunting and steeplechase riding. 1896.
The Haughtyshire hunt. 1897. A novel.
Colonel Botcherby MSH. 1899. A novel.
Taunton, T. H. Portraits of celebrated racehorses 1702–1870, together with their respective pedigrees and performances recorded in full. 4 vols 1887–8.
'Thormanby' (W. W. Dixon). The horse and the rider: an anecdotic medley. 1888.
Kings of the turf: memoirs and anecdotes. 1898.
Kings of the hunting-field: memoirs and anecdotes. 1899.
Baden-Powell, R. S. S. Pigsticking: a complete account for sportsmen. 1889, 1924.
Thomson, J. A. Three great runs. 1889.
Eighty years reminiscences. 2 vols 1904.
'Curzon, L. H.' (J. G. Bertram). The blue ribbon of the turf: a chronicle of the race for the Derby. 1890.
A mirror of the turf: or the machinery of horse-racing revealed. 1892.
Black, R. The jockey club and its founders. 1891.
Horse-racing in England [a history]. 1893.

Chetwynd, Sir G. Racing reminiscences and experiences of the turf. 2 vols 1891.
Kent, J. Racing life of Lord George Cavendish Bentinck. Ed Hon F. C. Lawley 1892.
Custance, H. Riding recollections and turf stories. 1894.
Underhill, G. F. The helterskelter hounds. 1894. A novel.
 Hunting. 1897.
 Gone to ground: a hunting novel. 1899.
 A century of English fox-hunting. 1900.
Williams, W. P. Poems in pink. Salisbury and London 1894.
 Plain poems. Salisbury and London 1896.
 Over the open. 1897. A novel.
 Rhymes in red. Salisbury and London 1899.
Fothergill, G. A. A riding retrospect. 1895.
Lutyens, F. M. Mr Spinks and his hounds: a hunting story. [1896.]
Porter, J. Kingsclere. Ed B. Webber 1896. Trainer's reminiscences of famous stables.
Lister, T., 4th Baron Ribblesdale. The Queen's hounds and stag-hunting recollections. 1897.
Bradley, C. The reminiscences of Frank Gillard, huntsman, with the Belvoir hounds 1860–96. 1898.
Pease, Sir A. E. Hunting reminiscences. 1898.
Somerville, E. Œ. and Martin Ross (V. F. Martin). The silver fox. 1898.
 Some experiences of an Irish RM. 1899.
Anderson, T. S. Holloas from the hills. Jedburgh 1899. Verse.
Lyall, J. G. The merry gee-gee – how to breed, break and ride him for'ard away and the noble art of backing winners on the turf. 1899.
Cawthorne, G. J. and R. S. Herod. Royal Ascot: its history and its associations. 1900, 1902.
Dixon, W. S. The sport of kings. 1900. Articles on hunting.
Reeve, J. S. (ed). Lyra venatica: a collection of hunting songs [largely 19th century]. 1906.
Apperley, N. W. A hunting diary [1864–1920]. Ed E. D. Cuming 1926.
Osbaldeston, G. Squire Osbaldeston: his autobiography. Ed E. D. Cuming 1926.
Paget, G. and L. Irvine (ed). The flying parson and Dick Christian: incorporating chapters from Silk and scarlet and Post and paddock and letters from George Osbaldeston. 1934. With first pbn of hunting prose and verse by John Empson, the flying parson.

§2

Blew, W. C. A. A history of steeple-chasing. 1901.
Fletcher, J. S. The history of the St Leger stakes 1776–1901. 1902.
Aflalo, F. G. (ed). The hunting library: 1, Hare-hunting and harriers by H. A. Bryden; 2, Fox-hunting in the shires, by T. F. Dale; 3, The master of hounds by G. F. Underhill, with bibliography. 1903. All vols partly historical.
Cook, Sir T. A. A. A history of the English turf. 3 vols [1905].
Moorhouse, E. The romance of the Derby. 2 vols 1908.
Coaten, A. W. British hunting: a complete history of the national sport of Great Britain and Ireland. 1910.
Lattimer, R. B. The story of 'John Peel'. Cornhill Mag Oct 1919.
Verney, R. G., Lord Willoughby de Broke (ed). The sport of our ancestors: being a collection of prose and verse setting forth the sport of fox-hunting as they knew it. 1921.
Humphris, E. M. The life of Fred Archer. 1923.
Birkett, Lady D. N. Hunting lays and hunting ways: an anthology of the chase. 1924.
Machell, H. W. John Peel: famous in sport and song. 1926. Includes a history of the well known song with facsimiles of mss of words and music.
Humphris, E. M. The life of Mathew Dawson. 1928.
Munroe, D. H. The Grand National 1839–1931. 1931.
Higginson, A. H. The Meynell of the west: being a biography of James John Farquharson esqre, master of fox hounds 1806–58. 1936.
Higginson, A. H. Two centuries of foxhunting. 1946.
Biegel, P. (ed). Booted and spurred: an anthology of riding. 1949.
Orchard, V. R. Tattersalls: two hundred years of sporting history. 1953.
Eliot, Lady G. E. O. Portrait of a sport: a history of steeplechasing. 1957. With bibliography.
Mortimer, R. The Jockey Club. 1958. A history.
Mortimer, R. The history of the Derby Stakes. 1962.
Murphy, G. (ed). The horse lover's treasury: an illustrated anthology of verse and prose. 1963.
Longrigg, R. The history of fox-hunting. 1975.
Carr, R. English fox-hunting: a history. 1976.
Vamplew, W. The turf: a social and economic history of horse-racing. 1976.
Itzkowitz, D. C. Peculiar privilege: a social history of English fox-hunting 1753–1885. Hassocks 1977.
Whitehead, G. K. Hunting and stalking deer in Britain throughout the ages. 1980.
Munsche, P. B. Gentlemen and poachers – the English game laws 1671–1831. Cambridge 1982.
Brander, M. Deer stalking in Britain. Sportsmans Lib 1986.
Hill, C. R. Horse power: the politics of the turf. Manchester 1987.

Mountaineering

Bibliographies

Catalogue of books in the library of the Alpine Club. 1880, 1888, 1899, 1915.
Engel, C. E. La littérature alpestre en France et en Angleterre aux xviiie et xixe siècles. Paris 1931.
Engel, C. E. In his A history of mountaineering in the Alps, 1950.
Engel, C. E. In his They came to the hills [studies of famous mountaineers from Forbes to Smythe], 1952.
Smith, J. A. Mountaineering. 1995 (Readers' Guide ser).
Porter, E. C. Library of mountaineering and exploration and travel. Chicago 1959.
Bridge, G. Rock-climbing in the British Isles 1894–1970: a bibliography of guide books. Reading 1971.
Worsley, A. R. Readers' guide to books on mountaineering. 1972.
Read, B. J. Mountaineering, the literature in English: a classified bibliography. F. L. A. (Lib Assoc) thesis 1976.
Krawczyk, C. Mountaineering: a bibliography of books in English to 1974. Metuchen NJ 1977.
Neate, W. R. Mountaineering and its literature: a descriptive bibliography of selected works published in the English language 1744–1976. Milnthorpe 1978.

Periodicals

The Alpine Jnl: a record of mountain adventure and scientific observation. 1863– . Monthly.
Scottish Mountaineering Club Jnl. Edinburgh 1890– . Thrice yearly.

§1

Wilkinson, T. Tours to the British mountains. 1824.
Forbes, J. D. Travels through the Alps. 1843, 1845; ed W. A. B. Coolidge 1900.
 Norway and its glaciers visited in 1851; followed by Journals of excursions in the high Alps. 1853, 1900 (Journals only, in Travels through the Alps). *See* J. C. Shairp et al, Life and letters of J. D. Forbes, 1873.
Smith, A. R. The story of Mont Blanc. 1853, 1854, 1860 (as Mont Blanc with a memoir of the author by E. Yates).
Hudson, Rev C. and E. S. Kennedy. Where there's a will there's a way: an ascent of Mont Blanc by a new route and without guides. 1856, 1856 ('with two ascents of Monte Rosa').

Wills, A. Wanderings among the high Alps. 1856, 1858.
The eagle's nest: a summer home among the Alps, together with some excursions among the great glaciers. 1860.
Peaks, passes and glaciers: a series of excursions by members of the Alpine Club. Ed J. Ball 1859; ed E. S. Kennedy 2 vols 1862.
Tyndall, J. The glories of the Alps: being a narrative of excursions and ascents. 1860, 1896.
Mountaineering in 1861: a vacation tour. 1862.
Hours of exercise in the Alps. 1871; ed L. C. Tyndall 1899.
See also A. S. Eve and C. H. Creasey, The life and work of John Tyndall, *1945.*
Galton, Sir F. (ed). Vacation tourists and notes of travel in 1860 [1861 and 1862–3]. 3 vols 1861–4. Includes accounts of mountaineering.
Ball, J. The Alpine guide. 3 pts 1863–8; ed W. A. B. Coolidge et al 4 pts 1898–1911.
Browne, Rev G. F. Ice-caves of France and Switzerland: a narrative of subterranean exploration. 1865.
Freshfield, D. W. Across country from Thonon to Trent: rambles and scrambles in Switzerland and the Tyrol. 1865.
Travels in the central Caucasus, including ascents of Kazbek and Elbruz. 1869.
Italian Alps. 1875. Accounts of many ascents.
The exploration of the Caucasus. 2 vols 1896. Includes accounts of mountaineering.
Moore, A. W. The Alps in 1864. 1867; ed A. Kennedy, Edinburgh 1902; ed E. H. Stevens 2 vols Oxford 1939. Many ascents described.
The Caucasus in 1874: from the original ms in the library of the Alpine Club. [c. 1950.]
Girdlestone, Rev A. G. The high Alps without guides. 1870.
Stephen, Sir L. The playground of Europe. 1871, 1894, Oxford 1936.
Whymper, E. Scrambles amongst the Alps. 1871; ed H. E. G. Tyndale 1936 (6th edn) (with addns from Whymper's unpbd diaries).
The ascent of the Matterhorn. 1880.
Travels amongst the Great Andes of the Equator. 1892 (with separate pbn of appendix by various hands); ed F. S. Smythe 1949.
The Alps revisited. Graphic 29 Sep–20 Oct 1894.
Chamonix and the range of Mont Blanc: a guide. 1896.
The valley of Zermatt and the Matterhorn: a guide. 1897.
See F. S. Smythe, Edward Whymper, *1940; R. W. Clark,* The day the rope broke, *1965.*
Wilson, H. S. Alpine ascents and adventures. 1878.
Burnaby, Mrs E. A. F. (afterwards Main, afterwards Le Blond). The high Alps in winter: or mountaineering in search of health. 1883.
High life and towers of silence. 1886.
My home in the Alps. 1892. Includes chs on mountaineering.
Barrow, J. Mountain ascents in Westmoreland and Cumberland. 1886.
Cunningham, C. D. and W. de W. Abney. The pioneers of the Alps. 1887.
Dent, C. T. Above the snow line: mountaineering sketches between 1870 and 1880. 1887.
Can Mount Everest be ascended? Nineteenth Cent Oct 1892.
Conway, W. M., Baron Conway. Conway and Coolidge's climbers' guides. 17 vols 1890–1910. With W. A. B. Coolidge.
Climbing and exploration in the Karakoram-Himalayas. 3 vols 1894.
The Alps from end to end. 1895.
The first crossing of Spitsbergen: with descriptions of several mountain ascents. 1897.
The Bolivian Andes: a record of climbing and exploration in the Cordillera Real in the years 1898 and 1900. 1901.
Aconcagua and Tierra del Fuego: a book of climbing, travel and exploration [in 1898–9]. 1902.
Mountain memories. 1920.
Davies, Rev J. S. Dolomite strongholds: the last untrodden Alpine peaks. 1894.
Smith, W. P. H. Climbing in the British Isles: England. 1894.
Smith and H. C. Hart. Climbing in the British Isles: Wales and Ireland. 1895.
Mummery, A. F. My climbs in the Alps and Caucasus. 1895, [1913]. With introd by M. Mummery and appreciation by J. A. Hobson.
Fitzgerald, E. A. (ed). Climbs in the New Zealand Alps. 1896.
The highest Andes: a record of the first ascent of Aconcagua and Tupungato. 1899.
Weston, Rev W. Mountaineering and exploration in the Japanese Alps. 1896.
Wherry, G. E. Alpine notes and the climbing foot. Cambridge 1896.
Younghusband, Sir F. E. The heart of a continent: a narrative of travels in Manchuria, across the Gobi desert, through the Himalayas. 1896, 1937. Includes some mountaineering.
Jones, O. G. Rock climbing in the English Lake District. 1897, Keswick 1900 (with memoir of the author by W. M. Cook and an appendix by G. D. and A. Abraham), 1911.
Mathews, C. E. The annals of Mont Blanc. 1898.
Oppenheim, E. C. New climbs in Norway. 1898.
Gribble, F. H. The early mountaineers. 1899.
Slingsby, W. C. Norway, the northern playground: sketches of climbing in Norway between 1872 and 1903. Edinburgh 1904; ed E. Slingsby, Oxford 1941.
Coolidge, W. A. B. Alpine studies. 1912. Collection of mountaineering articles largely pbd before 1900.
See R. W. Clark, An eccentric in the Alps: the story of W. A. B. C. the great Victorian mountaineer, *1959.*

§2

Lunn, A. (ed). The Englishman in the Alps: being a collection of English prose and poetry relating to the Alps. Oxford 1913.
Carr, H. R. C. and G. A. Lister (ed). The mountains of Snowdonia in history, the sciences, literature and sport. 1925, 1948.
Spencer, S. (ed). Mountaineering. 1934 (Lonsdale Lib). With bibliography.
Lunn, A. Switzerland and the English. 1944.
de Beer, G. Travellers in Switzerland. Oxford 1949.
Clark, R. W. The Victorian mountaineers. 1953.
Irving, R. L. G. A history of British mountaineering. 1955.
Mason, K. Abode of snow: a history of Himalayan exploration and mountaineering. 1955.
Clark, R. W. and E. C. Pyatt. Mountaineering in Britain: a history from the earliest times to the present day. 1957.
Lunn, A. A century of mountaineering 1857–1957. 1957.

Polo

Miller, E. D. Modern polo. 1896.
Dale, T. F. The game of polo. [1897.]
Polo past and present. 1905.
Dryburgh, T. B. Polo. 1898, 1906.
Kipling, R. The Maltese cat. In his Day's work, 1898.
Dorling, T. The Hurlingham Club 1869–1953. Hurlingham 1953.

Rowing, Canoeing, Boating, Punting

Bibliographies

Brittain, F. Oar, scull and rudder: a bibliography of rowing. Oxford 1930.
International Canoe Federation. Bibliography of books and magazines on canoes and canoeing. 1979 (2nd edn).
Skilling, B. C. British canoeing literature, January 1866–January 1966: a bibliography and subject guide. Unpbd F. L. A. (Lib Assoc) thesis 1967.

Periodicals

The Rowing Almanack and Oarsman's Companion. 1861–1915, 1920–8. Annual.

§1

'A boating man'. A treatise on the art of rowing as practised at Cambridge. Cambridge 1842.

Shadwell, A. T. W. A treatise on steering. 1844.

'Oarsman' (A. T. W. Shadwell?). Principles of rowing. Cambridge 1846, Oxford [1857?].

[Bateman, J. F.] Aquatic notes: or sketches of the rise and progress of rowing at Cambridge. Cambridge 1852.

Mansfield, R. B. The log of the Water Lily. 1852. Account of a voyage on the Neckar, Maine, Moselle and Rhine.

The Water Lily on the Danube: being a brief account of the perils of a pair-oar during a voyage from Lambeth to Perth. 1853. Both works rev in 1 vol 1854, 5th edn as The log of the Water Lily during three cruises, [1873] (with account of a third voyage on the Saône and Rhone).

'Argonaut' (E. D. Brickwood). The arts of rowing and training. 1866, 1876 (as Boat racing or the arts of rowing).

Macgregor, J. A thousand miles in the Rob Roy canoe on rivers and lakes of Europe. 1866, 1871 (7th edn).

The Rob Roy on the Baltic. 1867.

The Rob Roy on the Jordan, Nile, Red Sea and Gennesareth. 1869, 1880 (6th edn).

See E. Hodder, J. M., 'Rob Roy', *1894.*

Macmichael, W. F. The Oxford and Cambridge boat races – from AD 1829 to AD 1869. Cambridge 1870.

Baden-Powell, W. Canoe travelling: log of a cruise on the Baltic. 1871.

Woodgate, W. B. Boating. Badminton Lib of Sports and Pastimes 1888.

Jerome, J. K. Three men in a boat (to say nothing of the dog). Bristol 1889.

Alcock, A. T. Hints on coxing. Cambridge 1895.

Squire, P. W. Punting. Badminton Lib of Sports and Pastimes 1898.

Peacock, W. The story of the inter-university boat race. 1900.

Sherwood, W. E. Oxford rowing: a history of boat-racing at Oxford. Oxford 1900.

Selwyn, T. K. Eton in 1829–30: a diary of boating and other events written in Greek edited with translation and notes by E. Warre. 1903.

Bourne, G. C. Memories of an Eton wet-bob of the seventies. [Ed R. C. Bourne], Oxford 1933.

§2

Steward, H. T. The records of Henley Royal Regatta from its institution in 1839 to 1902. 1903.

Cook, Sir T. A. and G. Nicholls. Thomas Doggett deceased. 1908. Pt 2 is a history of Doggett's 'Coat and badge' race.

Smith, L. C. (ed). Annals of public school rowing. Oxford 1919.

Burnell, R. D. The Oxford and Cambridge boat race 1829–1953. Oxford 1954.

Ross, G. The boat race: the story of the first hundred races. 1954.

Burnell, R. D. Henley Regatta: a history. Oxford 1957.

Cleaver, H. A history of rowing. 1957.

Rivington, R. T. Punting: its history and techniques. Oxford 1983.

Wigglesworth, N. (comp). Victorian and Edwardian boating from old photographs. 1987.

Dodd, C. Rowing. In Sport in Britain: a social history, ed T. Mason, Cambridge 1989.

Halladay, E. Rowing in England: a social history: the amateur debate. Manchester 1990.

Dodd, C. The story of world rowing. 1992.

Wigglesworth, N. The social history of English rowing. 1992.

Shooting

Bibliographies

Phillipps-Wolley, Sir C. A short bibliography of big game shooting. In his Big game shooting, 1894 (Badminton Lib of Sports and Pastimes).

'Gerrare, Wirt' (W. Greener). A bibliography of guns and shooting. 1896.

Riling, R. Guns and shooting: a selected chronological bibliography. New York 1951.

Periodicals

Shooting Times. 1882– . Weekly. 9 Sep 1882–11 Apr 1884 as Wildfowler's Illustrated Shooting Times; 18 Apr–19 Sep 1884 as Illustrated Shooting Times.

§1

Thornhill, R. B. The shooting directory. 1804.

Williamson, T. Oriental field sports. 1807.

Vincent, J. Fowling: a poem. 1808.

'Thomas, B.' (T. B. Johnson). The shooter's guide. 1809, 1814 (4th edn), 1832 (9th edn).

The shooter's companion. 1819, 1834.

The sportsman and gamekeeper's directory. [1835?]; ed J. B. Johnson 1851.

The shooter's preceptor. 1838.

'Markwell, Marmaduke'. Advice to sportsmen with anecdotes of the most renowned shots of the day. 1809.

Dobson, W. Kunopaedia: a practical essay on training the English spaniel with instructions for attaining the art of shooting, flying. 1814.

Hawker, P. Instructions to young sportsmen [on guns and shooting]. 1814, 1816, 1824, 1825 (with addns pbd separately), [1825?], 1826, 1830 (with Abridgement of the new game laws pbd separately), 1831; ed P. W. L. Hawker 1854 (10th edn), 1859; ed E. Parker 1922.

The diary of Colonel Peter Hawker. Ed R. Payne Gallwey 2 vols 1893; ed E. Parker 1931 (as Colonel Hawker's shooting diaries).

Alken, H. A cockney's shooting season in Suffolk. 1822.

Watt, W. Remarks on shooting to which are added a part of the game-laws both written in familiar verse. 1835, 1839.

'Oakleigh, Thomas' (A. K. Killmister). The Oakleigh shooting code: containing two hundred and twenty chapters of information relative to shooting. 1836.

The shooter's handbook. Edinburgh 1842.

Rawstorne, L. Gamonia: or the art of preserving game. 1837; ed E. Parker 1929.

Harris, Sir W. C. Narrative of an expedition into Southern Africa during the years 1836 and 1837. Bombay 1838, London 1839 (as The wild sports of Southern Africa).

Portraits of the game and wild animals of Southern Africa. 1840. Plates with extensive text. *See* E. C. Tabler, Captain Harris and his book: a biographical and bibliographical essay, Charleston 1944.

Peake, R. B. Snobson's seasons: being annals of cockney sports. [1838?], 1846 (as An evening's amusement).

Scrope, W. The art of deer-stalking. 1838, 1883 (as Days of deer stalking).

Webber, A. Shooting: a poem. 1841.

Lacy, R. The modern shooter: containing poetical instructions and directions for every description of inland and coast shooting. 1842.

'Craven' (J. W. Carleton). Recreations in shooting. 1846.

'John Sobieski and Charles Edward Stuart' (J. C. and C. M. Allen, afterwards J. H. and C. S. H. Allan). Lays of the deer forest. 2 vols Edinburgh 1848.

Cumming, R. G. G. Five years of a hunter's life in South Africa. 2 vols 1850, 1 vol 1856 (as The lion hunter of South Africa).

Knox, A. E. Game birds and wild fowl. 1850.

'Hieover, Harry' (C. Bindley). Bipeds and quadrupeds. 1853.

Dougall, J. D. Shooting simplified: a concise treatise on the art of shooting. Glasgow 1857, London 1865.

Folkard, H. C. The wild-fowler: a treatise on ancient and modern wild-fowling historical and practical. 1859.

'Stonehenge' (J. H. Walsh). The shot-gun and sporting rifle. 1859.
The modern sportsman's gun and rifle. 2 vols 1882–4.
Jeans, T. The Tommiebeg shootings: or a moor in Scotland. 1860. A novel about shooting and fishing.
'Marksman'. The dead shot or sportsman's complete guide: being a treatise on the use of the gun. 1860, 1892 (6th edn).
'Martingale' (C. White). Sporting scenes and country characters. 1860. Prose sketches mainly on shooting.
Baldwin, W. C. African hunting from Natal to the Zambesi. 1863.
[Robertson, W.] Forest sketches: deer-stalking in the Highlands fifty years ago. Edinburgh 1865.
Shirley, E. P. Some account of English deer parks with notes on the management of deer. 1867.
'Wildfowler' (L. Clements). Shooting and fishing trips in England [and other countries]. Ser 1, 2 vols 1876; ser 2, 2 vols 1879 (as Shooting adventures etc).
Modern wildfowling. 1880.
Public shooting quarters: being a descriptive list of localities where shooting can be obtained. 1881.
[Jefferies, J. R.] (Richard Jefferies). The gamekeeper at home. 1878.
The amateur poacher. 1879.
Sanderson, G. P. Thirteen years among the wild beasts of India. 1878.
Manley, J. J. Notes on game and game shooting. [1880.]
Greener, W. W. The gun and its development. [1881], [1884], [1885], 1896, 1907, 1910.
Modern shot guns. 1888, 1891.
Sharpshooting for sport and war. 1900.
Selous, F. C. A hunter's wanderings in Africa. 1881.
Travel and adventure in south-east Africa. 1893.
Phillipps-Wolley, Sir C. Sport in the Crimea and Caucasus. 1881.
A sportsman's Eden [British Columbia]. 1888.
Payne-Gallwey, Sir R. W. F. The fowler in Ireland. 1882.
Letters to young shooters. Ser 1, 1890, 1899 (5th edn); ser 2, 1892, 1894 (with index to 1st–2nd sers); ser 3, 1896.
Whitehurst, F. F. On the Grampian hills: grouse and ptarmigan shooting. 1882. Prose sketches.
Grimble, A. Deer stalking. 1886.
Shooting and salmon fishing: hints and recollections. 1892.
The deer forests of Scotland. 1896, 1901 (with Deer stalking).
Leaves from a game book. 1898.
Cookson, J. C. F. Tiger-shooting in the Doon and Ulwar. 1887.
Lancaster, C. An illustrated treatise on the art of shooting. 1889, 1924 (8th edn).
Macintyre, D. Hindu-Koh: wanderings and wild sport on and beyond the Himalayas. 1889.
'Purple heather' (W. A. Adams). Something about guns and shooting. 1890.
Watson, J. (ed). The confessions of a poacher. 1890.
Poachers and poaching. 1891.
Buxton, E. N. Short stalks. 2 sers 1892–8.
Crealock, H. H. Deer-stalking in the Highlands of Scotland. Ed J. N. Crealock 1892.
Millais, J. G. Game birds and shooting – sketches. 1892.
British deer and their horns. 1897. Includes chs on stalking.
Dixon, C. The game birds and wild fowl of the British islands. 1893.
Cornish, C. J. Nights with an old gunner. 1897.
Macpherson, H. A. A history of fowling. Edinburgh 1897.
Teasdale-Buckell, G. T. Experts on guns and shooting. 1900. On evolution of shooting in the 19th century.
Harris, J. E., 2nd Earl of Malmesbury. Half a century of sport in Hampshire [shooting jnls 1798–1840]. Ed F. G. Aflalo 1905 (with memoir by the 5th Earl).
See also Bickerdyke, Conway, Lascelles, Mackintosh *and* Penn *under* Angling, *above.*

Skating, Tobogganing, Curling
Bibliographies
Foster, F. W. A bibliography of skating. 1898.

§1

[Ramsey, J.] An account of the game of curling. 1811 (priv ptd).
Frostiana: or a history of the river Thames in a frozen state, to which is added the art of skating. 1814.
Clay, T. Instructions on the art of skating. 1828.
Crawford, H. A descriptive and historical sketch of curling. 1828.
Brown, Sir R. Memorabilia curliana mabenensia. Dumfries 1830.
'A member of the Skating Club'. A skater's manual. 1831.
'Dove, Walter' (M. Whitelaw). The skater's monitor, instructor and evening companion. Edinburgh 1846.
'Cyclos' (G. Anderson). The art of skating. 1852.
Vandervell, H. E. and T. M. Witham. A system of figure-skating: being the theory and practice of the art in England, with a glance at its origin and history. 1869, 1889, 1893 (by Witham only).
Harwood, J. A. Rinks and rollers. [1876.] Includes history of roller skating.
Pycroft, J. On roller skating. Brighton [1876?].
Idyls of the rink. 1877. Verse.
Goodman, N. and A. Handbook of fen skating. 1882.
[Macnair, J.] The channel-stone: or sweeping frae the rinks. 4 sers Edinburgh 1883–4.
Monier-Williams, M. S. F. and S. F. Combined figure skating. 1883, 1892 (as Figure skating: simple and combined).
Taylor, J. Curling: the ancient Scottish game. 1884.
Kerr, J. The history of curling. Edinburgh 1890.
Cook, Sir T. A. Notes on tobogganing at St Moritz. 1894, 1896.
Fowler, G. H. On the outside edge: diversions in the history of skating. 1897.

§2

Bloom, A. The skaters of the Fens. Cambridge 1958.
Brown, N. Ice-skating: a history. 1959.
Bird, D. L. Our skating heritage: a centenary history of the National Skating Association of Great Britain 1879–1979. 1979.
Smith, D. B. Curling: an illustrated history. Edinburgh 1981.

Swimming
Bibliographies
Thomas, R. H. Swimming: a bibliographical list of works. 1868, 1904.
Greenwood, F. A. Bibliography of swimming. New York 1940.

§1

Frost, J. Scientific swimming. 1816.
Hughes, R. The whole art of swimming. [1820.]
Familiar hints on sea-bathing. 1838.
Richardson, C. Instructions on the art of swimming. 1857.
Swimming and swimmers; with an account of the progress of the art during the last twenty years. 1861.
Pearce, P. H. A treatise and poem on swimming. 1868.
'Piscator'. How to swim, float, plunge, bathe and dive. 1871.
'Dolphin' (J. T. Latey). The channel feats of Captain Webb and Captain Boyton. [1875.]
Leahy, J. The art of swimming in the Eton style. 1875.
Randall, J. Captain Webb the intrepid champion Channel swimmer. Madeley 1875.
Webb, M. The art of swimming. Ed A. G. Payne [1875].
Wilson, W. Swimming, diving and how to save life. Glasgow 1876.
The swimming instructor: a treatise on the arts of swimming and diving. 1883.
Brewster, F. W. How to avoid being drowned. 1885.

§2

Hedges, S. G. Swimming in literature. Chambers's Jnl Aug 1933.
Orme, N. I. Early British swimming, 55 BC to AD 1719. Exeter 1983.

Spawson, C. Haunts of the black masseur: the swimmer as hero. 1992.

Tennis, Lawn Tennis, Fives, Badminton

Bibliographies

Foster, F. W. A bibliography of lawn tennis 1874–97. Richmond 1897.

Periodicals

The Lawn-Tennis Handbook 1888– . Annual.

Lawn Tennis. 1896– . Weekly. 17 June–14 Oct 1891 nos 1–18; then fortnightly as Lawn Tennis and Croquet 27 Apr 1896–1 Nov 1899; as Lawn Tennis and Croquet and Badminton 6 Dec 1899–25 Apr 1900.

§1

Hazlitt, W. Cavanagh the fives player. From The Indian jugglers. In his Table talk vol 1, 1821.

[Lukin, R.] A treatise on tennis. 1822.

Wingfield, W. C. The game of sphairistike: or lawn tennis. 1874.

'Cavendish' (Henry Jones). The games of lawn tennis and badminton. 1876, 1890 (9th edn).

Latouche, J. Lawn tennis. New Quart Mag 5 1876.

Marshall, J. The annals of tennis. 1878. Real tennis.

Tennis cuts and quips in prose and verse with rules and wrinkles. [1884.]

Smythe, J. Lawn tennis. [1878.]

Brownless, W. M. Lawn tennis: its rise and progress. Bristol 1889.

§2

Noel, E. B. and J. O. M. Clark. A history of tennis. 2 vols Oxford 1924. Real tennis; includes ch on the lit of tennis.

Myers, A. W. Fifty years of Wimbledon. 1926.

Burrow, F. R. The 'last eights' at Wimbledon 1877–1926. [1927.]

Aberdare, Lord. Rackets, squash, tennis, fives and badminton. 1936 (Lonsdale Lib of Sports, Games and Pastimes).

Bruce, M. G. L., 4th Baron Aberdare of Duffryn. The story of tennis. 1959. Real and lawn.

Adams, B. The badminton story. 1980.

Davis, P. The encyclopaedia of badminton. 1987.

Walker, H. Lawn tennis. In Sport in Britain: a social history, ed T. Mason, Cambridge 1989.

Yachting

Bibliographies

Hanson, H. J. (ed). The Cruising Assoc Lib catalogue. [1927], 1931, 1954.

Periodicals

Hunt's Universal Yacht List. 1851–1914. Annual.

Hunt's Yachting Mag. 1852–87. Monthly.

The Yachtsman. 1891–1913. Continued as Yachting, Sailing and Motor-Boating. Weekly.

The Yachting World. 1894– . Weekly.

§1

Folkard, H. C. The sailing boat: a description of English and foreign boats and practical directions for sailing. 1853, 1901 (5th edn).

Hughes, R. E. Two summer cruises with the Baltic fleet in 1854–5: being the log of the 'Pet' yacht. 1855.

Macmullen, R. T. Down channel. 1869; ed D. Kemp 1893; with biographical foreword by A. Ransome 1931.

Orion: or how I came to sail alone in a 19-ton yacht. 1878.

An experimental cruise single handed in the 'Procyon' 7-ton lugger. 1880. Rev edns of these 2 works were incorporated into the 1893 edn of Down channel, *above*.

Middleton, E. E. The cruise of the Kate. 1870. Description of one of the first single-handed voyages.

Robinson, C. E. The cruise of the Widgeon: 700 miles in a ten-ton yawl from Swanage to Hambury. 1876.

Kemp, D. A manual of yacht and boat sailing. 1878; ed B. H. Smith 1900 (9th edn).

Watson, G. L. Progress in yachting and yacht-building. In Lectures on naval architecture and engineering [given at the Glasgow naval and marine engineering exhibition 1880–1], 1881. A concise history of yachting and yacht-building in the 19th century.

Speed, H. F. Cruises in small yachts. 1883, 1926 (with More cruises by M. Speed).

Knight, E. F. The cruise of the Falcon: a voyage to South America in a 30-ton yacht. 2 vols 1884.

The Falcon on the Baltic: a coasting voyage from Hammersmith to Copenhagen in a 3-ton yacht. 1889.

The cruise of the Alerte [to Trinidad]. 1890.

Reminiscences: the wanderings of a yachtsman. 1923.

Cowper, F. Sailing tours: the yachtsman's guide to the cruising waters of the English coast. 5 vols 1892–6.

Jack-all-alone: his cruises. 1897.

§2

Gabe, J. Yachting: historical sketches of the sport. 1902. Includes short histories of the most important yacht clubs.

Guest, M. and W. B. Boulton. The Royal Yacht Squadron: memorials of its members, with an enquiry into the history of yachting and a complete list of members with their yachts from the foundation of the Club [in 1815] to the present time. 1903.

British yachts and yachtsmen: a complete history of British yachting from the middle of the sixteenth century to the present day. 1907.

Heaton, P. Yachting: a history. 1955.

Burnell, R. D. Races for the 'America's' cup. 1965.

Simper, R. Victorian and Edwardian yachting. Batsford 1978.

See also 'Wanderer' *under* Hunting, *above*. [RWC]

15 Education

A(I). GENERAL SOURCES

Trimmer, Sarah. The oeconomy of charity. 1787, 1801.
Reflections upon the education of children in Charity Schools. 1792.
The Charity School spelling book. 1800, 1808 (2nd edn). Pt 1 Words of one syllable; Pt 2 Polysyllables.
The guardian of education: a periodical work. 5 vols 1802–6.
A comparative view of the new plan of education promulgated by Mr J. Lancaster. 1805.
The Edgeworths: R. L. Edgeworth; Maria Edgeworth. *See col 901 above.*
Bell, Andrew. An experiment in education made at the Male Asylum of Madras, suggesting a system by which a school or family may teach itself under the superintendence of the master or parent. 1797, 1814 (5th edn enlarged), 1807 (3rd edn as An analysis of the experiment).
Instructions for conducting a school. 1808.
Sketch of a National Institution. 1808.
Elements of tuition, pt iii: Ludus literarius, the classical and grammar school. 1815.
The wrongs of children. 1819. A periodical of which only 3 pts were issued; very rare.
Letters to Sir John Sinclair on the Infant School Society at Edinburgh: the scholastic institutions of Scotland, with a scheme of a classical school for children of the richer classes. 1829.
See R. Southey (vol 1) and his son Charles Cuthbert (vols 2–3), Life of the Rev Andrew Bell, *1844.*
Meiklejohn, J. M. D. An old educational reformer, Dr Bell. 1891.
Salmon, D. The practical parts of Lancaster's improvements and Bell's experiment. Cambridge 1932.
Hamilton, Elizabeth. Letters on the elementary principles of education. 2 vols Bath 1801–2.
Letters addressed to the daughter of a nobleman on the formation of principles, religious and moral. 2 vols 1806.
Hints addressed to patrons and directors of schools to shew that the benefits derived from the new modes of teaching may be increased by a partial adoption of the plan of Pestalozzi. 1815.
Shaw, William. Suggestions respecting a plan of national education. Bath 1801.
Barrow, William. An essay on education particularly the merits and defects of the discipline and instruction in our academies. 2 vols 1802.
Bentham, Jeremy. Principles of penal law. 1802.
Chrestomathia. 1817. Rptd and ed M. J. Smith and W. H. Burston 1983.
Church of Englandism examined: strictures on the National Society's schools. 2 pts 1818. *See* Quart Rev 21 1819.
Works. Ed J. Bowring 11 vols Edinburgh 1843. Papers relative to codification and public instruction in vol 4; Chrestomathia in vol 8; Memoirs and correspondence in vols 10–11. *See* J. P. Potter, Letter to John Hughes on the system of education proposed by the popular parties, 1828, Pamphleteer 29 1828, a reply to the Benthamite Chrestomathic School proposal.
Stephen, L. The English Utilitarians, vol 1: Jeremy Bentham. 1900.
Halévy, E. The growth of philosophic radicalism. Tr 1928, 1934 (rev).
Crabb, G. The order and method of instructing children. 1802.
Harrison, G. Some remarks relative to the present state of education among the Quakers. 1802.
Education surest means to diminish crime. 1803.
Simons, T. Moral education the one thing needful. 1802; A sequel, 1805 (on Undenominationalism).
Lancaster, Joseph. Improvements in education as it respects the industrious classes. 1803.
A letter to John Foster on the means of educating and employing the poor in Ireland. 1805.
An appeal for justice in the case of ten thousand poor and orphan children. 1806.
Improvements in education abridged. 1808.
A remarkable establishment of education at Paris. 1809.
Instructions for forming a society for the education of the labouring classes. 1809.
Hints and directions for building, fitting up and arranging schoolrooms. 1809.
Address to the friends and superintendents of Sunday Schools. 1809.
The British system of education. 1810.
The school for girls on the Royal Lancasterian system. 1812.
Oppression and persecution. Bristol 1816.
Letters on national subjects. Washington 1820.
The Lancasterian system with improvements. Baltimore 1821.
See David Salmon, Joseph Lancaster, *1904. Supplemented by many articles in the* Educational Record *1905–29. See under Bell, above.*
Bartle, G. F. Joseph Lancaster and his biographers. History of Education Soc 1980.
Dickson, M. Teacher extraordinary: Joseph Lancaster 1778–1838. Lewes 1986.
Hogan, D. Joseph Lancaster and the psychology of the early classroom system. History of Education Quart 29 1989.
Benson, Maria. Thoughts on education. 1806.
Colquhoun, Patrick A. A new and appropriate system of education for the labouring people. 1806.
Bowles, John. A letter addressed to Samuel Whitbread. 1807; Second letter, 1808.

Ingram, Robert A. An essay on schools of industry and religious instruction. 1808.
Weyland, R. A. A letter to a country gentleman on the education of the lower orders. 1808.
Bernard, Sir Thomas. Of the education of the poor. 1809.
The New School. 1809.
The Barrington School. 1812.
See Reports of the Society for bettering the conditions and increasing the comforts of the poor, *under Official documents, below.*
Smith, Sydney. Essay: too much Latin and Greek. 1809.
Works. 2 vols 1859.
Also contributions to the Edinburgh Rev, *of which he was co-founder; see also under Education of women and girls, below.*
Bouyer, Renynold Gideon A. A comparative view of the two new systems of education for the infant poor. 1811.
Ensor, J. On national education. 1811. *See* Quart Rev 6 1811.
Marsh, H. The national religion the foundation of national education. 1811. A sermon rptd in the Pamphleteer 1 1813. *See* Quart Rev 6 1811; Edinburgh Rev 19 1811, 21 1813.
Vindication of Dr Bell's system. 1811.
The Philanthropist. Ed W. Allen 1811. Articles on Lancaster, popular education etc.
Hollingsworth, Nathaniel John. Address to the public in recommendation of the Madras system, with a comparison. 1812.
Mill, James. Schools for all, in preference to schools for Churchmen only. 1812.
Education. In Supplement to the Encyclopaedia Britannica, 4th, 5th and 6th edns, 1816–24.
State of the nation. Westminster Rev Oct 1826.
Analysis of the human mind. 1829.
Stephen, L. The English Utilitarians, vol 2: James Mill. 1900.
Halévy, E. The growth of philosophic radicalism. Tr 1928, 1934 (rev).
Burston, W. H. (ed). James Mill on education. 1969.
Burston, W. H. James Mill on philosophy and education. 1974.
O'Donnell, M. G. The educational thought of the classical economists. Lanham MD 1985.
Poole, Rev John. The village school improved etc. 1812.
Southey, Robert. Origin, nature and object of the new system of education. 1812.
See Lancaster, above; Quart Rev *6 1811, 8 1812, 19 1818, 39 1829, and* Edinburgh Rev *19 1811, 21 1813, 33 1820.*
Owen, Robert. A new view of society: or essays on the formation of the human character. 1813. *See* Edinburgh Rev 32 1819.
Macnab, H. G. The new views of Mr Owen impartially examined. 1819.
Owen, R. D. Outline of the system of education at New Lanark. Glasgow 1824. By his son.
Silver, H. The concept of popular education: a study of ideas and social movements in the early nineteenth century. 1965.
Harrison, J. F. C. 'The steam engine of the new moral world': Owenism and education. Jnl of Br Stud 6 1967.
Harrison, J. F. C. Utopianism and education. Robert Owen and the Owenites. 1968.
Harrison, J. F. C. (ed). Robert Owen on education. 1969.
McLaren, D. J. Robert Owen, William Maclure and New Harmony. History of Education 25 1996.
Babington, Thomas. Practical view of Christian education in its early stages. 1814.
Carpenter, Lant. Systematic education. 2 vols 1815. With J. Joyce and Shepherd.
Principles of education. 1820. By Carpenter only.
Pestalozzi, John Henry. Address to the British public to aid a plan of preparing school-masters for the people. Yverdun 1817.
Letters on early education addressed to J. P. Greaves, Secretary to the London Infant Society (with a memoir of Pestalozzi). 1827, 1850, 1851.
Many English trns and commentaries.
How Gertrude teaches her children. Tr 1894, 1915 (3rd edn rev).
Pullen, P. H. The Mother's book exemplifying Pestalozzi's plan of awakening the understanding of children. 1820.
de Prati, J. The principles and practice of education illustrative of the Pestalozzian and Chrestomathic systems. 1829.
Biber, G. E. Pestalozzi and his plan. 1831.
Mayo, Charles. Pestalozzi and his Principles. 1837.
Russell, J. The student's Pestalozzi. 1888.
Russell, J. Pestalozzi: his life and work. 1890, 1900, 1903. Trn of R. de Guimps, Histoire de Pestalozzi.
Green, J. A. Educational ideas of Pestalozzi. 1905.
Hayward, F. H. The educational ideas of Pestalozzi. 1905.
Green, J. A. Pestalozzi's educational writings. 1912.
Brown, S. A comparative view of the systems of Pestalozzi and Lancaster. 1925. *See E. Hamilton, above; R. Dunning, J. Payne, below.*
Brougham, Henry P. (Baron Brougham and Vaux). Letter to Sir Samuel Romilly. Pamphleteer 13 1818.
Speech on the education of the poor, June 1820. Pamphleteer 40–1 1820; Hansard n.s. vol 1 1820, col 39. *See* Edinburgh Rev 35 1821.
Practical observations upon the education of the people addressed to the working classes and their employers. 1825. *See E. W. Grinfield,* A reply to Mr Brougham's Practical observations, Edinburgh Rev 42 1825, 45 1826, Quart Rev 32 1825.
Inaugural discourse on being installed Lord Rector of Glasgow University. 1825. *See* Edinburgh Rev 42 1825.
Speech in the House of Lords on the education of the people, 21 May 1835. Hansard vol 27 cols 1293–1333. *See* 'M. A. Queen's College, Oxford', A letter to Henry Brougham on the best method of restoring decayed grammar schools, 1818. Pamphleteer 13 1818.
Ireland, J. A letter to Henry Brougham. 1819. Pamphleteer 14 1818, Edinburgh Rev 30–2 1818–19.
See Samuel Butler, below.
Dallaway, Miss R. C. Observations on the most important subjects in education. 1818.
Heberden, William. On education: a dialogue after the manner of Cicero. 1818.
Jardine, George. Outlines of philosophical education illustrated. Glasgow 1818, 1825.
Macnab, Henry Grey. Analysis and analogy recommended in education. Paris 1818.
See Robert Owen, above.
Myers, T. Remarks on a course of education. 1818.
Arrowsmith, Joseph P. Art of instructing the infant deaf and dumb, with method of educating deaf mutes, by the Abbé de L'Épée. 1819. *See* Quart Rev 26 1822, Edinburgh Rev 102 1855.
Hoare, Louisa. Hints for the improvement of early education and nursery discipline. 1819, 1820, 1824, 1826, 1877 (19th edn).
Butler, Samuel. Thoughts on education of the poor: letter to Henry Brougham on certain changes in the Education Bill. 1820. *See under Memoirs, below.*
Knox, Vicesimus, Headmaster of Tonbridge School 1781–1812. Remarks on the tendency of certain clauses in a Bill now pending in Parliament to degrade grammar schools etc. 1820.
See Liberal Education *1781, 1795;* Pamphleteer *19 1820.*
Pullen, P. H. *See Pestalozzi, above.*
Bamford, Robert Walker. Essays on the discipline of children, particularly as regards their education. 1822.
Hill, Matthew Davenport. Public education: plans for the government and liberal instruction of boys in large numbers, drawn from experience. 1822, 1825 (2nd edn rptd 1894, in which 'drawn from experience' was replaced by 'as practised at Hazelwood School'). Reviewed by Jeffrey, Edinburgh Rev 41 1825, and by De

Quincey, London Mag Apr–May 1824. The original scheme was started in 1817.
De Quincey, Thomas. Letters to a young man whose education has been neglected. London Mag 7 1823.
Pole, Thomas. Observations on infant schools. Bristol 1823. *See* Edinburgh Rev 38 1823 *and under Adult and technical education, below.*
Wilderspin, Samuel. The importance of educating the children of the poor. 1823, 1825 (as Infant education).
Early discipline illustrated: or the infant system progressive and successful. 1832.
A system for the education of the young. 1840, 1852 (8th edn rev as The infant system for developing the intellectual and moral powers of all children from one to seven years of age).
A manual for the religious and moral instruction of young children in nursery and infant schools. 1845. With T. J. Terrington.
McCann, P. and F. A. Young. Samuel Wilderspin and the infant school movement. 1982.
Goyder, David George. Manual of the system of instruction. Bristol 1824, 1825 (4th edn). Goyder complained that Stow had adopted his plan without acknowledgement.
Montgomery, James. The chimney-sweeper's friend and mining boy's album. 1824. Illustrated by Cruikshank.
A treatise on the management of infant schools. 1826.
Wilson, Rev William. The system of infants' schools. 2 vols 1825, 1826 (2nd edn).
A manual of instruction for infants' schools. 1829.
Advice to instructors of infant schools. nd. *See* Quart Rev 32 1825.
Daly, Robert. Observations upon the state of education in Ireland. Dublin 1826.
On the proposed system of non-scriptural education of the poor in Ireland. 1831. With R. J. McGhie.
Mayo, Charles. Observations on the establishment and direction of infant schools. 1826. *See Elizabeth Mayo, below.*
Newnham, W. The principles of physical, intellectual, moral and religious education. 1827.
Ward, Valentine. Observations on Sunday schools. Leeds 1827.
Pillans, J. Principles of elementary teaching, chiefly in reference to the Parochial schools of Scotland. Edinburgh 1828.
Three lectures. 1836.
The rationale of discipline as exemplified in the High School. Edinburgh 1852.
Contributions to the cause of education. 1856.
Educational papers read before the Education Department of the Social Science Association. Edinburgh 1862.
Wood, John. Account of the Edinburgh Sessional School and other parochial institutes for education established in that city in the year 1812, with strictures on education in general. Edinburgh 1828.
Biber, George E. Christian education. 1830.
Pestalozzi and his plan. 1831. *See Pestalozzi, above.*
Mayo, Elizabeth. Lessons on objects to children in the Pestalozzian school at Cheam. 1830, 1831, 1859 (16th edn). *See* Quart Jnl of Education 1831.
Practical remarks on infant education. 1831. Contains 2 articles by Dr Charles Mayo and practical comment by Miss Mayo.
Lessons on objects by lessons on shells. 1833.
See Quart Jnl of Education *1833, and Charles Mayo, above. The formal memorising of the Mayos was satirised by Charles Dickens in Mr Gradgrind of* Hard times.
Sewell, William. An essay on the cultivation of the intellect by the study of dead languages. 1830.
A speech at the meeting of Friends of National Education at Willis's rooms, 7 Feb 1850, 1850.
See Special subjects 1 and 6, below; L. James, A forgotten genius: Sewell of St Columba's and Radley, *1945.*
Stow, David. Physical and moral training. 1831, 1840 (enlarged as The training system in the Glasgow Normal Seminary), 1859 (as The training system, the moral training school and the Normal Seminary).
Arnold, Thomas. Letter on education of the middle classes. 1832.
Miscellaneous works. 1845.
Collected sermons. 3 vols 1850–3.
Stanley, A. P. Life of Thomas Arnold. 1844, 1904 (popular edn).
Hughes, Thomas. Tom Brown's schooldays. Cambridge 1857. Anon.
Findlay, J. J. Dr Arnold of Rugby. Cambridge 1897.
Fitch, J. Thomas and Matthew Arnold. 1897, 1905.
Strachey, L. Dr Arnold. In his Eminent Victorians, 1918. This account is severely criticised by R. L. Archer in his Secondary education in the nineteenth century, Cambridge 1932.
Trilling, L. In his Matthew Arnold, New York 1939, 1955 (rev).
Wymer, N. G. Dr Arnold of Rugby. 1953.
Bamford, T. W. Thomas Arnold. 1960.
Bamford, T. W. Thomas Arnold on education. 1970.
McCrum, M. Thomas Arnold, headmaster: a reassessment. 1989.
Frend, William. A plan of universal education. 1832.
Abbott, Jacob. The teacher; or moral influences employed in the instruction and government of the young. 1833. Revised by Rev Charles Mayo 1834.
Combe, George. Lectures on popular education. Edinburgh 1833.
Principles of physiology applied to physical and mental education. 1835.
Remarks on national education. Edinburgh 1847.
What should secular education embrace? Edinburgh 1848.
See Education: its principles and practice as developed by George Combe, collated and edited by W. Jolly, *1879; George Combe,* Discussions on education, The select works of George Combe *1893.*
Gibbon, Charles. The life of George Combe. 2 vols 1878.
Price, A. A pioneer of scientific education, George Combe (1788–1858). Education Rev 12 1960.
de Giustino, D. Conquest of mind: phrenology and Victorian social thought. 1975.
Shapin, S. and B. Barnes. Science, nature and control. In Dale, R. et al (ed), 1976, *under* A(ii), *below.*
Cooter, R. The cultural meaning of popular science. Cambridge 1984.
Tomlinson, S. Phrenology, education and the politics of human nature: the thought and influence of George Combe. History of Education 26 1997.
Roebuck, A. J. National education. 1833.
Duppa, Baldwin Francis. The education of the peasantry in England. 1834.
Industrial schools for the peasantry. 1837 (Central Soc of Education).
Lord Brougham's Bill for promoting education. 1838 (Central Soc of Education). First Bill proposing taxation for popular education.
Schools for the industrial classes: present state of education among the working classes. 1838 (Central Soc of Education).
Agricultural colleges: or schools for the sons of farmers. 1839.
Place, Francis. Improvement of the working people. 1834.
Simpson, James. Necessity of popular education as a national object. Edinburgh 1834.
Hull, J. The philanthropic repertory. 3 pts 1835. Pt 1: Hints and plans relating to popular education.
Maurice, Frederick Denison. The educational magazine. 1835– .
Has the Church or State power to educate the nation? 1839.
The Christian Socialist. 1851– .
National Education: a sermon at St Mark's College Chelsea. 1853.
Learning and working. 1855.

The workman and the franchise: chapters from English history on the representation and education of the people. 1866.
A few words on secular and denominational education. 1870.
See F. Maurice, Life of Maurice, *1884.*
Reiner, Charles. Lessons on number and lessons on form. 1835. Pam.
Whewell, William. Thoughts on the study of mathematics. Cambridge 1835. *See* Edinburgh Rev 62–3 1836.
See Universities, *below.*
Williamson, J. The diffusion of knowledge amongst the middle classes. 1835. *See* Edinburgh Rev 62 1836.
Gray, J. Thoughts on education with particular reference to the grammar school system. 1836.
Dunn, Henry. Popular education. 1837.
National education, the question of questions. 1837.
See Edinburgh Rev *66 1838.*
Calm thoughts on the recent Minutes of the Committee of Council. 1847.
Hoppus, J. Thoughts on academical education and degrees in arts. 1837.
Crisis of popular education. 1847.
Wyse, Sir Thomas. Educational reform or the necessity of a national system. 1837.
Education in the United Kingdom: its progress and prospects. 1837 (Central Soc of Education). Sir Thomas was one of the founders of the Soc. *See B. F. Foster,* Education reform: a review of Wyse, New York 1837.
Notes on education reform from the unpublished memoirs of Sir Thomas Wyse. Ed W. M. Wyse, Waterford 1901.
Boone, James S. The educational economy of England. Pt 1, 1838.
Horner, Leonard. On the state of education in Holland [with] measures to extend and improve education in Great Britain. 1838. A trn with addns of V. Cousin, De l'instruction publique en Hollande.
Brown, C. M. Leonard Horner, 1785–1864: his contribution to education. Jnl of Educational Administration and History 17 1985.
Martineau, Harriet. How to observe. 1838.
Household education. 1849, 1861, 1867, 1876.
Taylor, Isaac. Home education. 1838.
Austen, Mary. On national education. 1839.
Kay-Shuttleworth, Sir James. Recent measures for the promotion of education in England. 1839.
The school in relation to the State, the Church and the Congregation. 1847.
Public education. 1853.
Four periods of public education. 1862. A reprint of earlier bks and pams.
Memorandum on popular education. 1865.
Some of the results of the Education Act and Code of 1870. Fortnightly Rev May 1876.
See Official documents, below, contribution to the Minutes of the Committee of Council on Education 1839–49.
Smith, F. The life and work of Kay Shuttleworth. 1923, rptd Bath 1974.
Tholfson, T. G. (ed). Sir James Kay-Shuttleworth on popular education. 1974.
Paz, D. G. Sir James Kay-Shuttleworth: the man behind the myth. History of Education 14 1985.
Selleck, R. J. W. James Kay-Shuttleworth: journey of an outsider. 1994.
Phillpots, Henry. Charge to the clergy of Exeter, Triennial Visitation 1839. 1839. On the State and religious education.
Russell, Lord John. National education: parliamentary speeches by Russell and the Marquess of Lansdowne and recent measures for the promotion of education in England, with statistical tables (1826–39). 1839.
L[ord?], E. Discursive remarks on modern education. 1841.
Barwell, Mrs L. M. Letters from Hofwyl by a parent. 1842. *See* Pestalozzi, *above.*
Lovett, W. and J. Collins. Chartism: a new organisation for the people. 1842. Rptd with introd by Asa Briggs Leicester 1969.
Spencer, Herbert. State education. In his The proper sphere of government, 1843.
State education self defeating. 1851.
Education, intellectual, moral and physical. 1861; ed F. A. Cavanagh, Cambridge 1932.
Compayre, G. Spencer et l'éducation scientifique. Paris 1901. *See Memoirs, below.*
Tomlinson, S. From Rousseau to evolutionism: Herbert Spencer on the science of education. History of Education 25 1996.
Fenn, J. The school master's legacy and family monitor. 1843.
Hinton, J. H. Second letter to Sir James Graham on the educational clauses of the Factories Bill. 1843.
Owen, Sir Hugh. Letter to the Welsh people. 1843.
Shaftesbury, Lord. Moral and religious education of the working classes. 1843.
Wordsworth, W. The excursion. 1814. Bks 8–9, with Wordsworth's note in 1843 edn. *See J. Fotheringham,* Wordsworth's Prelude as a study in education, 1899.
Skinner, S. Educational essays: practical observations on instruction, discipline, physical training. 1844.
Wordsworth, C. Discussions on public education. 1844.
Diary in France mainly concerning education and the Church. 1845.
Parsons, B. Education the birthright of every human being. 1845.
Amos, Andrew. Four lectures on the advantages of a classical education as an auxiliary to a commercial education; with a letter to Whewell. 1846.
Angus, Joseph. Four lectures on the advantages of a classical education. 1846. 2 distinct essays written for 2 prizes offered by Henry Beaufoy; Angus won the first prize; James Pycroft, author of Oxford memories 1886, the second.
Baines, Sir Edward. Letters written to the Rt Hon Lord John Russell. 1846, 1848.
The late struggle for the freedom of education. 1846.
An alarm to the nation on the measure of State education. 1848.
On the progress and efficiency of voluntary education. 1848.
Strictures on the new Government Measure. 1853.
National education. 1856.
Our past educational improvement. 1857.
Voluntary and religious education. 1857.
Booth, James. Education and educational institutions considered with reference to the present state of society. 1846.
Examination the province of the State. 1847.
On the influence of examination as an instrument of education. 1854.
Systematic instruction and periodical examination. 1857. *See* Quart Rev 108 1860.
Foden, Frank. The examiner: James Booth and the origins of common examinations. Leeds 1989.
Hamilton, Rev Richard Winter. Institutions of popular education. Leeds 1846. *See R. V. Taylor,* Biographia Leodiensis, Leeds 1865.
Hook, Dean Walter F. On the means of rendering more efficient the education of the people: a letter to the Bishop of St David's. 1846. *See R. V. Taylor,* Biographia Leodiensis, Leeds 1865.
Kay, Joseph. Education of the poor in England and Europe. 1846.
Social conditions and education of the people in England and Europe. 2 vols 1850.
The condition and education of poor children in English and German towns. 1853.
Mann, Horace. Report of an educational tour in Germany and parts of Great Britain and Ireland. 1846. With preface by Hodgson.
Binney, Thomas. Education. 1847.

Dawes, Richard. Hints on improved self-paying national education. 1847.
Observations on the working of the Government scheme of education. 1847.
Suggestive hints towards improved secular instruction, making it bear on practical life. 1849.
Remarks occasioned by the present crusade against the Committee of Council on Education. 1850.
Schools and other similar institutions for the industrial classes. 1853.
Lessons on the phenomena of industrial life. 1854, 1867 (3rd edn).
See Minutes of the Committee of Council on Education 1847–8 (report by Rev H. Moseley, HMI) and the general report of Matthew Arnold for 1853.
Remarks on the reorganisation of the Civil Service and its bearing on educational progress. 1854.
Teaching of common things. 1854.
Address to the Huddersfield Mechanics' Institute. 1856.
Manual of educational requirements for the Civil Service, with a preface on its educational value and importance. 1856.
Educational values and importance. 1856.
Effective primary instruction the only sure road to success in secondary instruction. 1857.
Henry, W. C. A biographical notice of the late Very Rev Richard Dawes MA, Dean of Hereford. 1867 (priv pbd).
Adamson, J. W. The illiterate Anglo-Saxon, ch ix. Cambridge 1946.
Curtis, S. J. and M. E. A. Boultwood. An introductory history of English education since 1800. 1960, 1964 (rev). Richard Dawes and King's Somborne, pp. 63–8. Dawes used a Project Method.
Ball, N. Richard Dawes and the teaching of common things. Education Rev 17 1964.
Layton, D. Science in the schools: the first wave – a study of the influence of Richard Dawes. Br Jnl of Educational Stud 20 1972.
Dufton, J. National education: what it is and what it should be. 1847.
Kendall, Henry E. Designs for schools and school houses. 1847 (illus). Kendall was the pioneer of a succession of school architects.
Porter, G. R. The influence of education shown by facts in the Criminal Tables for 1845 and 1846. 1847 (Br Assoc Report).
Pycroft, J. Four lectures on classical education as auxiliary to commercial. 1847.
Willm, J. The education of the people. Glasgow 1847.
Lectures on education. 1848 (Crosby Hall).
Woodward, Nathaniel. A plea for the middle classes. 1848.
See under Memoirs, below.
Heeney, B. Mission to the middle classes, the Woodward schools 1848–1891. 1961.
Biggs, W. Lecture upon national education. Leicester 1849.
Emery, T. Educational economy: or State education vindicated. 1849.
Powell, B. State education. 1849.
Cooper, Thomas. Cooper's journal: or unfettered thinker. Jan–Oct 1850. A weekly.
Shirreff, Emily A. and M. G. Grey. Thoughts on self-culture. 2 vols 1850.
Intellectual education. 1858.
Watts, John. On national education considered as a question of political and financial economy. 1850.
Birley, W. A letter to Archdeacon Denison in reply to his strictures. 1851.
Couling, S. Our labouring classes, intellectual, social, moral condition. 1851.
Hare, Julius C. Education the necessity of mankind: sermon on the opening of Hurstpierpoint. 1851.
Inglis, Sir Robert H. The parochial schools of Scotland: a speech in the House of Commons, 4 June 1851.
Manchester and Salford Education Bill (1851–2).
Newland, H. Socinianism the inevitable result of the Manchester and Salford scheme of national education. 1851.
Richson, C. Sketch of some of the clauses which induced the abandonment of the voluntary system. 1851.
Educational facts and statistics: evidence before the House of Commons. 1852.
See Parliamentary papers under Official documents, below.
Close, F. National education: the secular system, the Manchester Bill and the Government scheme considered. 1852.
Denison, G. A. Supplement to Appendix B of a reply to the promoters of the Manchester and Salford Education Bill. 1852.
Facts and considerations on the Manchester and Salford Education Bill. 1853.
Hinton, J. H. A review of the evidence in relation to the state of education in Manchester and Salford. 1852.
A few plain words on the two Education Bills. 1852.
Case of the Manchester educationists: state of education in Manchester and Salford. 2 pts 1852–4.
Newman, Cardinal John Henry. *See under Universities: General works, below.*
Roth, Matthias D. Movements or exercises according to Ling's system for the due development and strengthening of the human body in childhood and in youth. 1852.
The Gymnastic Free Exercises of P. H. Ling, arranged by H. Rothstein. Tr with addns by Roth 1853.
A letter to the Earl of Granville, on the importance of rational gymnastics as a branch of national education. 1854.
A plea for the compulsory teaching of the elements of physical education in our national elementary schools: or the claims of physical education to rank with reading, writing and arithmetic. 1870.
On the neglect of physical education and hygiene by Parliament and the Education Department as the principal cause of the degeneration of the physique of the population. 1879.
On school hygiene and scientific physical education. 1880.
Wilkinson, J. Popular education. 1852.
Whately, Richard. Address to the clergy on the recent changes in Irish national education. 1853.
See also J. M. Goldstrom, Richard Whately and political economy in school books, *1833–80.* Irish Historical Stud *15 1967.*
Education of the blind. Edinburgh Rev 99 1854, 173 1891.
Nicholls, Sir George. History of the English Poor Law. 2 vols 1854, 1898. Vol 3, 'from 1834', by Mackay, 1899.
Tate, Thomas. The philosophy of education. 1854.
Conington, John. The academical study of Latin. 1855. *See* Edinburgh Rev 105 1857.
Morley, Henry. Infant Gardens: an article for Household Words. 1855. Written to draw attention to the work of Baroness von Bülow who visited England to introduce the Kindergarten system of Froebel.
Dickens, Charles. *See* his novels, especially Nicholas Nickleby, Dombey and Son, David Copperfield, Hard times.
See J. L. Hughes, Dickens as an educator, *New York 1906; J. Manning,* Dickens on education, *Toronto 1959; P. Collins,* Dickens and education, *1963.*
Hill, Alexander. Hints on the discipline appropriate to schools. 1855. *See* Hazelwood School, *under Special sources: schools, below, and G. B. Hill,* Life of Sir Rowland Hill, 2 vols 1880.
Miller, J. C. Which? or neither? an examination of the Education Bills of Lord John Russell and Sir J. S. Pakington. 1855.
Dunning, R. A series of works on education after the methods of Pestalozzi. 1856.
Macleod, N. The Home School: hints on home education. Edinburgh 1856.
Temple Archbishop Frederick. National education. In Oxford essays contributed by members of the University, 1856.

On apprenticeship and schools. 1858.
The education of the world. In Essays and reviews, 1860. *See* Quart Rev 109 1861.
Sermons preached in Rugby School Chapel in 1858, 1859, 1860. 3 further sermons, 1861–71.
National Schools. 1870.
The true ideal of the educator. 1898. *See* J. G. Sheppard, *below.*
Currie, J. The principles and practice of infant school education. 1857.
The principles and practice of common school education. Edinburgh 1861.
Hill, Alfred (ed). Essays upon educational subjects. 1857, rptd 1971.
McCombie, W. On education in its constituents and issues. Aberdeen 1857.
Sheppard, J. G. Remarks on the Rev F. Temple's scheme for the extension of middle-class education. 1857.
Skeats, H. S. Results of government education. 1857, 1858.
St John, James Augustus. The education of the people. 1858, rptd 1971.
Hawtrey, S. T. A letter containing an account of St Mark's School Windsor. 1859 (3rd edn).
A narrative essay on a liberal education chiefly embodied in an attempt to give a liberal education to children of the working classes. 1868.
Coleridge, J. T. Public school education. A lecture to the Athenaeum. 1860.
Arnold, Matthew. The popular education of France, with notices of that of Holland and Switzerland. 1861 (Report to Newcastle Commission).
A French Eton. 1864, 1892 (with Schools and universities in France).
Schools and universities on the Continent. 1868 (Report to the Schools Inquiry Commission).
Culture and anarchy. 1869, 1875; ed J. D. Wilson, Cambridge 1932.
Friendship's garland. 1871.
A Bible-reading for schools. Ed Arnold 1872.
Report on higher schools and universities in Germany. 1874.
'Ecce, convertimur ad Gentes'. Fortnightly Rev Feb 1879.
Special report on elementary education in Germany, Switzerland and France. 1886 (Cmd 4752). *See* Quart Rev 125 1868.
Reports on elementary schools 1852–82. Ed F. Sandford 1889; ed F. S. Marvin 1908.
Thoughts on education chosen from the writings of Arnold. Ed L. Huxley 1912.
Fitch, Sir J. Thomas and Matthew Arnold and their influence on English education. 1897.
Connell, W. F. The educational thought and influence of Arnold. 1950.
Palmer, Imelda. Matthew Arnold: culture, society and education. 1979.
See col 517, above.
Fitch, Sir Joshua. Public education: why is a new code wanted? 1861.
Charity schools and the endowed schools commission. 1873.
Lectures on teaching. 1881.
Notes on American schools and training colleges. 1888.
Educational aims and methods. 1900.
See under Thomas and Matthew Arnold, above.
Lilley, A. L. Sir Joshua Fitch. 1906.
Fraser, William. National education: reasons for the rejection in Britain of the Irish system – a brief exposition for Christian educationists. 1861. *See* Quart Rev 132 1872.
Hort, Rev F. J. A. Thoughts on the Revised Code of Education: its purposes and probable effects. 1861.
Senior, N. W. Suggestions on popular education. 1861.
Vaughan, Charles James. The revised code dispassionately considered. Cambridge 1861.
Coleridge, Derwent. The teachers of the people. 1862.
Garfit, A. Some points of the education question, with outline of the progress of popular education. 1862.
The conscience clause and the extension of education in the neglected districts practically considered. 1868.
Grant, A. R. Remarks on the revised code. Cambridge 1862.
Grote, John. A few words on the new educational code. 1862.
Grove, J. A few words on the new educational code and the report of the Education Commissioners. 1862.
Lowe, Robert (Viscount Sherbrooke). Speech of the Rt Hon Robert Lowe MP on the Revised Code of the Regulations of the Committee of the Privy Council on Education in the House of Commons, 13 Feb 1862.
Primary and classical education. Edinburgh 1867.
Middle class education: endowment or free-trade? 1868.
See Matthew Arnold, Reports on elementary education, *above, and under Memoirs, below, and D. Sylvester,* Robert Lowe and education *1960.*
'One of practical experience'. Remarks on popular education in reference to the New Code. Bradford 1862.
Randolph, E. J. The good properties of the Revised Code. 1862.
Gill, John. Introductory text-book to school education, method and school management. 1863 (9th edn).
Systems of education: a history and criticism. 1876.
Ruskin, John. *Seee col 2275, above.*
Walter, J. Correspondence relative to the Resolutions on the Educational Grant to be moved, May 5th 1863. On the unaided schools.
Hodgson, W. B. Exaggerated estimates of reading and writing. Trans Nat Assoc for the Promotion of Social Science 1864, rptd 1868.
Lectures on economic science. 1870.
See Harvey J. Graff in History of Education Quart *26 1986.*
The Museum and English journal of education. 5 vols 1864–9. Includes the Pupil teacher.
Thompson, D'A. W. Day-dreams of a schoolmaster. Edinburgh 1864.
Wayside thoughts: desultory essays on education. 1868.
Thring, Edward. Education and school. 1864.
Theory and practice of education. 1883.
Sermons preached at Uppingham School. 2 vols 1886.
Addresses. 1887.
See under Memoirs, below; and G. Hoyland, The man who made a school, *1946.*
Leinster-Mackay, D. The educational world of Edward Thring. 1988.
de Laspée, Henry. Calisthenics: or the elements of bodily culture on Pestalozzian principles. 1865.
Education of the mentally defective. Edinburgh Rev 122 1865.
Melville, D. The conscience clause; meaning, authority, use. 1865.
Menet, J. Letter on Mr Walter's motion. 1865. *See Walter, above.*
Sewell, Elizabeth M. Principles of education drawn from nature and revelation. 2 vols 1865.
Thompson, A. F. The English school-room: thoughts on private tuition. 1865.
Bruce, Henry Austin (Baron Aberdare). An address delivered to the National Association for the Promotion of Social Science. 1866.
Grant, P. The history of factory legislation 1802–50, with a warning by the Earl of Shaftesbury. Manchester 1866.
Pound, Rev William. Remarks upon English education in the nineteenth century. 1866.
Farrar, Dean Frederic William et al. Essays on a liberal education. 1867–8. By C. S. Parker, H. Sidgwick, J. Seeley, E. E. Bowen, F. W. Farrar, J. M. Wilson, H. W. Hales, W. Johnson and Lord Houghton.
Observations on mental education. 1868.
Laurie, Simon Somerville. On primary instruction in relation to education. 1867.
Institutes of education. Edinburgh 1868.
John Amos Comenius. Cambridge 1881.

Occasional addresses on educational subjects. 1888.
Studies in the history of educational opinion from the Renaissance. Cambridge 1888, 1903 (rev).
Training of teachers and methods of instruction. Cambridge 1902.
Almond, Hely Hutchinson. Mr Lowe's educational theories examined from a practical point of view. Edinburgh 1868.
Cooper, A. A. (Earl of Shaftesbury). Speeches relating to the labouring classes. 1868. *See P. Grant, above.*
Fraser, James, Bishop. National education: a sermon. 1868.
Hill, F. D. The children of the State: the training of juvenile paupers. 1868, 1889.
Markby, T. Practical essays on education. 1868.
Maxse, Frederick Augustus. The education of the agricultural poor. 1868.
National education and its opponents. 1877.
Quick, Robert Hibert. Essays on educational reformers. 1868, 1902, 1929.
Storr, F. Life and remains of Quick. 1899.
Roby, H. J. The present state of the schools: the Law of Charities as affecting Endowed Schools. Chs ii, iv of the Schools Inquiry Commission. 1868.
Arnott, Neil. Fundamental principles of national education. 1869, 1870.
Galton, Sir Francis. Hereditary genius: an enquiry into its laws and consequences. 1869, 1892.
English men of science: their nature and nurture. 1874.
Inquiries into human faculty and its development. 1883, 1907.
Maclaren, Archibald. A system of physical education. Oxford 1869, 1895.
Training in theory and practice. 1896.
Norris, John P. The education of our people: weak points and strength. 1869.
'Outis' (J. L. Tupper). Hiatus: the void in modern education. 1869.
Quain, R. On some defects in general education: the Hunterian Oration. 1869, 1870.
Campbell, H. Compulsory education. 1870.
Holland, H. W. Proposed national arrangements for primary education. 1870.
Playfair, Lyon. Primary education, technical education. Edinburgh 1870.
Rigg, G. H. History and present position of primary education in England and in connexion with Wesleyan Methodism. 1870.
Sproat, G. M. Education of the rural poor. 1870.
Wilson, James Maurice. Lecture on mathematical teaching. Rugby 1870.
Morality in public schools. 1882. Rptd from Jnl of Education Nov 1881.
Voluntary schools and State education. Manchester 1894.
Education and popular control. 1898.
The elementary education problem. Manchester 1898.
Education and crime: a sermon. 1905.
The day school and religious education: a sermon. 1907.
McCrie, J. Autopaedia: or instructions on personal education. 1871 (enlarged).
Fawcett, Henry and M. G. Essays and lectures on social and political subjects. Cambridge 1872. Contains 3 essays on educational subjects, all by M. G. Fawcett.
Jourdan, B. A. Essay on improvements in education during the eighteenth and nineteenth centuries. 1872.
Morley, John (Viscount). The struggle for national education. 1873.
See D. A. Hamer, John Morley, Liberal intellectual in politics, *1968.*
Payne, Joseph. The true foundation of science teaching. 1873.
The science and art of education. 1874.
Pestalozzi: influence on elementary education. 1875.
Froebel and the Kindergarten. 1876.
A visit to German schools. 1876.
Lectures on the science and art of education. 1880.
See Works of Payne, *ed Dr J. F. Payne, 2 vols 1883.*
Aldrich, R. Schools and society in Victorian Britain: Joseph Payne and the new world of education. New York 1995.
Todhunter, Isaac. The conflict of studies and other essays connected with education. 1873.
Grey, Mrs W. (Maria Georgina Shirreff). The study of education as a science: paper read at the British Association, Belfast. 1874.
The ruling principle of method applied to education, by Antonio Rosmini Serbati. 1887, Boston 1889. Tr Mrs Grey.
Last words to girls. 1889.
Mrs Grey was joint-author with her sister of Self-culture, *1850.*
See Emily A. Shirreff and M. G. Grey, above, and Special subjects (4), below. See also col 2301.
Kingsley, Charles. Health and education. 1874. *See col 1311, above.*
Norton, Lord (C. B. Adderley). A few thoughts on national education. 1874.
Robson, E. R. School architecture. 1874. Rptd with introd by M. Seaborne 1972.
Clarke, E. H. Sex in education. Boston 1875.
Leitch, J. H. Practical educationists and their systems of teaching. Glasgow 1875.
Fearon, Daniel Robert. School inspection. 1876. Also contributions to the Schools Inquiry Commission.
Lancaster, Henry Hill. Essays and reviews: prefatory notice by B. Jowett. Edinburgh 1876.
Stanley, Edward Lyulph (Baron Stanley). Three letters on Oxford University Reform. 1876.
Our national education. 1890.
Latham, H. On examinations as a means of selection. Cambridge 1877. *See* Quart Rev 108 1860, Edinburgh Rev 139 1874.
Bain, Alexander. Education as a science. 1879.
Williams, D. G. Alexander Bain as an educational psychologist. Aberdeen Univ Rev 45 1974.
Lyschinska, M. J. The Kindergarten principle: educational values and applications. 1880.
Rutherford, Mark. The autobiography of Mark Rutherford, dissenting minister. 1881. A novel.
The early life of Mark Rutherford, by himself. 1913. Autobiography.
Craik, Sir Henry. The State and its relation to education. 1882.
Acland, A. H. D. The education of citizens. Manchester 1883.
Eve, H. W. and A. Sidgwick. The practice of education. Cambridge 1883.
Farrar, F. W. and R. B. Poole. General aims of the teacher and form management. Cambridge 1883.
Kay, D. Education and educators. 1883.
Buxton, Sydney. Overpressure and elementary education. 1885.
Froebel, Freidrich W. A. (1782–1852)
English translations:
Jarvis, Miss J. Fundamental principles of the education of man. New York 1885.
Hailmann, W. N. Fundamental principles of the education of man. New York 1887.
Michaelis, E. and H. Keatly Moore. Froebel's letters on the Kindergarten. 1891.
Bowen, H. C. Froebel and education by self activity. 1893.
Jarvis, Miss J. Pedagogics of the Kindergarten. New York 1900.
Jarvis, Miss J. Education by development. New York 1905 (pt 2).
Fletcher, S. S. F. and J. Welton. Froebel's writings on education rendered into English. 1912.
English commentaries:
Ronge, J. and B. Practical guide to the English Kindergarten. 1855.
Minutes of the Committee of Council on Education. 1855–6.
Barnard, H. Papers on Froebel's Kindergarten. New York 1881.
Shirreff, E. The Kindergarten principle of Froebel's system. 1897.
Herford, W. H. The student's Froebel. 1901.

Murray, E. R. Froebel as a pioneer in modern psychology. 1914.
Kilpatrick, W. H. Froebel's Kindergarten principle. New York 1916.
Priestman, B. O. Froebel education today. 1946.
Lawrence, E. (ed). Froebel and English education. 1952.
See J. Payne and M. J. Lyschinska, above.
Bryant, Sophie. Educational ends. 1887.
The teaching of morality in the family and the school. 1897.
Harrison, F. Politics and education: an address. 1887.
Meath, Earl (ed). Prosperity or pauperism? Physical, industrial and technical training. 1888.
Sidgwick, Henry. On stimulus. Cambridge 1888.
Findlay, Joseph John. Teaching as a career for university men. 1889.
The principles of class teaching. 1898.
The school: an introduction to the study of education. 1912.
The children of England. 1923.
The aims and organisation of education. 1925.
Herford, William Henry. The school: essay towards humane education. 1889.
Landon, J. School management. 1889.
James, William. Principles of psychology. 1890.
Psychology: briefer course. 1892.
Talks to teachers. 1899.
Bryce, James. The teaching of civic duty. Contemporary Rev 1891.
Paget, E. The spirit of discipline. 1891.
'The thirteen'. Thirteen essays on education. 1891.
Acland, Arthur H. D. and H. L. Smith (ed). Studies in secondary education. 1892.
Herbart, J. F. (1776–1841)
English translations:
Felkin, H. M. and E. The science of education: its general principles deduced from its aims, and the aesthetic revelation of the world. 1892.
Felkin, H. M. and E. Letters and lectures on education. 1898, 1901 (corrected).
Mulliner, B. A. The application of psychology to the science of education. 1898.
English commentaries:
De Garmo, C. Herbart and the Herbartians. 1895.
Felkin, H. M. and E. An introduction to Herbart's science and practice of education. 1895, 1901 (corrected).
Hayward, F. H. The reform of moral and biblical instruction on the lines of Herbartianism. 1902.
The critics of Herbartianism. 1903.
Davidson, A. New interpretation of Herbart's psychology. 1906.
The meaning of education as interpreted by Herbart. 1907.
See Sir John Adams, below.
Lyttleton, Hon E. Mothers and sons: or problems in the home training of boys. 1892.
Solomon, O. Theory of educational Sloyd. 1892.
Huxley, Thomas Henry. Science and education. In his Collected essays vol 3, 1893–4. *See* Quart Rev 123 1867.
Jolly, William. Ruskin on education. 1894.
Religious instruction in Board Schools. Edinburgh Rev 180 1894.
Gregory, Robert. Elementary education: some account of its rise and progress in England. 1895, 1905 (with appendix).
Sully, James. Studies of childhood. 1895.
Formby, C. W. Education and modern secularism. 1896. *See* Quart Rev 132 1872.
Hawtrey, M. The co-education of the sexes. 1896.
Rooper, T. G. A pot of green feathers, school and home life. 1896.
On professional education. 1903.
Selective writings. Ed R. G. Tatton 1907.
Adams, Sir John. Herbartian psychology applied to education. 1897.
Exposition and illustration. 1909.
The evolution of educational theory. 1912.
The new teaching. 1918.
Modern developments in educational practice. 1922.
Errors in school. 1927.
Barnett, P. A. Teaching and organisation with special reference to secondary schools. 1897.
Tuer, Andrew W. History of the horn-book. 1897. Dedicated by command to HM the Queen-Empress. The author claimed that 3 real horn-books were stowed away in the cover of each copy. *See P. Stone*, When children read from horn-books, Country Life 19 Oct 1961.
Armstrong, Henry Edward. The heuristic method of teaching or the art of making children think for themselves. In Special reports on educational subjects vol 2, 1898.
The teaching of scientific method and other papers on education. 1903.
Cookson, C. (ed). Essays on secondary education. Oxford 1898.
Holman, Henry. English national education: a sketch of the rise of public elementary schools in England. 1898.
Churton, Annette. Kant on education. 1899.
Scott, R. P. What is secondary education? 1899.
Soulsby, L. H. M. Some thoughts for mothers and teachers. 1899.
Stray thoughts on character. 1900.
Welton, James. The logical bases of education. 1899.
Principles and methods of teaching. 1906.
Educational theory. *See under* Education, Encyclopaedia Britannica, 11th edn, 1910.
The psychology of education. 1911.
What do we mean by education? 1915.
MacCunn, J. The making of a character. 1900.
Ware, F. Education reform: the task of the Board of Education. 1900.
Educational foundation of trade and industry. 1901.
Winch, W. H. Educational problems. 1900.
Maltby, S. E. Manchester and the movement for national elementary education 1800–1870. 1918.
Dobbs, A. E. Education and social movements 1700–1850. 1919.
For modern commentaries on some of the writers noted above, see the following collections:
Silver, H. English education and the radicals 1780–1850. 1975.
Gordon, P. and J. White. Philosophers as educational reformers: the influence of idealism on British educational thought and practice. 1979.
Lowe, R. (ed). Biography and education: some eighteenth and nineteenth century studies. History of Education Soc 1980.
Reeder, D. A. Educating our masters. The Victorian Lib, Leicester 1980. Addresses and essays by G. Coombe, Sir James Kay-Shuttleworth, F. D. Maurice, Robert Lowe, Lyon Playfair, T. H. Green, Henry Solly, A. H. D. Acland and Michael Sadler.
Bantock, G. H. Studies in the history of educational theory, vol 2: The mind and the masses 1760–1980. 1984. Includes Pestalozzi, Froebel, Coleridge, Owen, Herbert and Arnold, amongst others.
Scott, P. and P. Fletcher (ed). Culture and education in Victorian England. 1990.

A(II). MODERN STUDIES

In addition to secondary sources on individual authors cited in the previous section, see also works listed under Special subjects, below.

Bibliographies and guides

Higson, C. W. J. Sources for the history of education. The Lib Assoc 1967 (Section C: books 1801–70; D: textbooks and children's books 1801–70; E: Government publications up to and including 1918); suppl The Lib Assoc 1976 (Section H: books, 1801–70; I: textbooks and children's books, 1801–70; J: Government publications up to and including 1918).

Silver, H. and S. J. Teague. The history of British universities 1800–1969: a bibliography. 1969.
Argles, M. British government publications in England during the nineteenth century. History of Education Soc 1971.
Vaughan, J. Board of Education circulars: a finding list and index. History of Education Soc 1972.
Brock, W. H. From Liebig to Nuffield: a bibliography of the history of science education, 1839–1974. Stud in Science Education 2 1975.
Cunningham, P. The local history of education in England and Wales: a bibliography. Leeds 1976.
Louden, L. Articles on education in three non educational periodicals 1866–1908: a bibliography. Victorian Soc Occasional Pbns No 3: Victorian education. 1976.
Thoms, D. W. The history of technical education in London 1904–1940. History of Education Soc 1976. A guide to sources.
Bartle, G. F. The records of the British and Foreign School Society. The Local Historian 16 1984.
Aldrich, R. and P. Gordon. Dictionary of British educationists. 1989. Includes short biographies of a number of nineteenth-century educationists.
Parker, F. and B. J. Parker. Education in England and Wales: an annotated bibliography. New York 1991. Includes a category on history of education.

Educational development

Adamson, J. W. English education 1789–1902. 1930.
Barnard, H. C. A short history of education 1760–1944. 1947.
Musgrove, F. Middle-class education and employment in the nineteenth century: a critical note. Economic History Rev 12 1959. *See also* 14 1961–2.
Curtis, S. J. and M. E. Boultwood. An introductory history of English education since 1800. 1960.
Simon, B. Studies in the history of education 1780–1870. 1960. Subsequently retitled The two nations and the educational structure 1780–1870, 1974.
Adamson, J. W. English education 1789–1902. Cambridge 1964.
Armytage, W. H. G. Four hundred years of English education. Cambridge 1964.
Baron, G. Society, schools and progress in England. Oxford 1965.
Archer, R. L. Secondary education in the 19th century. Bath 1966 (rptd).
Bone, T. R. (ed). Studies in the history of Scottish education, 1872–1939. 1967.
Sanderson, M. Education and the factory in industrial Lancashire 1780–1840. Economic History Rev 20 1967.
Sturt, M. The education of the people. A history of primary education in England and Wales. 1967.
Armytage, W. H. F. The French influence on English education. 1968.
Curtis, S. J. A history of education in Great Britain. 1968 (rptd).
Sanderson, M. Social change and elementary education in industrial Lancashire, 1700–1840. Northern History 3 1968.
Stewart, W. A. C. and W. P. McCann. The educational innovators 1750–1880. 1968; Vol 2, 1881–1967, 1969.
Atkinson, N. Irish education: a history of educational institutions. 1969.
Haines, G. Essays on the German influence upon English education and science, 1850–1919. Hamden CT 1969.
Musgrave, P. W. Society and education in England since 1800. 1969.
Scotland, J. The history of Scottish education. 2 vols 1969.
Simon, B. (ed). Education in Leicestershire 1540–1940. 1969.
Maclure, J. S. One hundred years of London education, 1870–1970. 1970.
Wardle, D. English popular education 1780–1970. 1970. 2nd edn 1976.
Hurt, J. Education in evolution: church, state, society and popular education 1800–1870. 1971.
Lawson, J and H. Silver. A social history of education in England. 1971. Chs 7, 8 and 9.
Murphy, J. Church, state and schools in Britain 1800–1970. 1971.
Sutherland, G. Elementary education in the nineteenth century. 1971.
Wardle, D. Education and society in nineteenth-century Nottingham. 1971.
Coleman, B. I. The incidence of education in mid century. In Nineteenth-century society, ed E. A. Wrigley, 1972.
Cook, T. G. (ed). Local studies and the history of education. 1972.
Goldstrom, J. M. The social content of education, 1808–1870. 1972.
Neuberg, V. E. (ed). Literacy and society. 1972.
Lawson, J. and H. Silver. A social history of education in England. 1973.
Saffin, N. W. Science, religion and education in Britain 1804–1904. Kilmore, Australia 1973.
Stephens, W. B. Early Victorian Coventry. Education in an industrial community, 1830–1851. In A. Everitt, Perspectives in English urban history, 1973.
Stephens, W. B. Regional variations in education during the industrial revolution, 1780–1870. The task of the local historian. Leeds 1973.
Evans, L. W. Studies in Welsh education. Cardiff 1974.
Wardle, D. The rise of the schooled society: the history of formal schooling in England. 1974.
West, E. G. Education and the industrial revolution. 1975.
Dale, R. Schooling and capitalism. 1976. Includes essays by R. Johnson and others on the schooling of the working class in nineteenth-century Britain.
Lowe, R. (ed). Victorian education. History of Education Soc 1976.
Middleton, N. and S. Weitzman. A place for everyone: a history of state education from the eighteenth century to the 1970s. 1976.
Orme, N. Education in the West of England. Exeter 1976.
Silver, H. Aspects of neglect: the strange case of Victorian popular education. Oxford Rev of Education 1976.
Stone, L. (ed). Schooling and society: studies in the history of education. 1976. Includes articles on elite attitudes towards mass education and the growth in demand for elementary education in England.
Lowe, R. Studies in the local history of education. History of Education Soc 1977.
McCann, P. (ed). Popular education and socialization in the nineteenth century. 1977. Local studies of educational development and schooling by P. McCann, B. Madoc-Jones, D. Rubinstein on London, S. Frith on Leeds, W. E. Marsden on Merseyside, plus chs by H. Silver on half-time schooling, and S. M. Goldstrom and J. S. Hurt on the content of elementary education.
Reeder, D. (ed). Urban education in the nineteenth century. History of Education Soc 1977. Chs by D. Fraser, W. B. Stephens, W. E. Marsden, D. Reeder and D. Smith on politics, social geography, literacy and social thought in relation to education, schooling and children in towns and cities.
Horn, P. Education in rural England, 1800–1914. 1978.
Lowe, R. New approaches to the study of popular education 1851–1902. History of Education Soc 1979.
Gordon, P. Selection for secondary education. 1980.
Hurt, J. S. Elementary education and the working classes. 1980.
Ringer, F. Education and society in modern Europe. 1980.
Coolahan, J. Irish education: its history and structure. 1981.
Davey, Ian E. Popular education and socialization. History of Education Quart 21 1981.
Aldrich, R. An introduction to the history of education. 1982.
McCann, P. Radicalism and education in Britain. History of Education Quart 22 1982.

Marsden, W. E. Diffusion and regional variation in elementary education in England and Wales 1800–1870. History of Education 11 1982.

Anderson, R. D. Education and opportunity in Victorian Scotland: schools and universities. Oxford 1983.

Humes, W. and H. Paterson (ed). Scottish culture and education, 1800–1980. Edinburgh 1983.

Kiesling, H. J. Nineteenth-century education according to West: a comment. Economic History Rev 36 1983. See also the reply by West in this vol.

Marsden, W. E. Education and urbanisation in nineteenth-century Britain. Paedigogica Historica 23 1983.

Sanderson, M. Education, economic change and society in England, 1780–1870. 1983.

Silver, H. Education as history. 1983. Includes a commentary on historical approaches to nineteenth-century education.

History of Education Soc. The churches and education. 1984.

Partington, G. Two Marxisms and the history of education. History of Education 13 1984. (A critique of Marxist interpretations of the educational history of the nineteenth and twentieth centuries).

Sutherland, G. Ability, merit and measurement: mental testing and English education, 1880–1940. 1984.

Marsden, W. E. Unequal educational provision in England and Wales: the nineteenth century roots. 1987.

Muller, D. K., F. Ringer and B. Simon (ed). The rise of the modern educational system: structural change and social reproduction 1870–1920. 1987. Includes chs on English educational development, endowed grammar schools, the reconstruction of secondary education, public schools and higher education by B. Simon, H. Steedman, D. Reeder, J. Honey and R. Lowe.

Stephens, W. B. Education, literacy and society, 1830–70: the geography of diversity in provincial England. Manchester 1987.

Hurt, J. S. Outside the mainstream: a history of special education. 1988.

Tulasiewicz, W. and C. Brock (ed). Christianity and educational provision in international perspective. 1988. See the essay by V. A. McClelland on the developing concept of Roman Catholic voluntary effort in education in England and Wales.

Vincent, D. Literacy and popular culture: England 1750–1914. 1989.

Steedman, C. Childhood, culture and class in Britain: Margaret McMillan 1860–1931. 1990.

Jones, G. E. (ed). Education, culture and society. Some perspectives on the nineteenth and twentieth centuries. 1991.

Goodenow, R. E. and W. E. Marsden (ed). The city and education in four nations. 1992. Includes a review of English research, mostly nineteenth century, by D. Reeder, and chs on English schooling by C. Heward and W. Marsden.

Rattansi, A. and D. Reeder (ed). Rethinking radical education. 1992. Includes historical chs by I. Davey on the origins of mass schooling; J. Purvis, a feminist critique; and R. Johnson on radical traditions.

Policymaking, government and administration

Graves, J. Policy and progress in secondary education. 1943.

Bingham, J. H. The period of the Sheffield School Board 1870–1903. Sheffield 1949.

Leese, J. Personalities and powers in English education. 1950.

Eaglesham, E. From school board to local authority. 1956.

Murphy, J. The religious problem in English education: the crucial experiment. Liverpool 1959.

Gosden, P. H. J. H. The Board of Education Act, 1899. British Jnl of Educational Stud 2 1962.

Ball, N. Her Majesty's Inspectorate 1839–49. Birmingham 1963.

Cruickshank, M. Church and state in English education 1870 to the present day. 1963.

Simon, B. Education and the labour movement 1870–1920. 1965.

Gordon, P. The Endowed Schools Act and the education of the poor, 1860–1900. Durham Research Rev 17 1966.

Gosden, P. H. J. H. The development of educational administration in England and Wales. Oxford 1966.

Balls, F. E. The Endowed Schools Act of 1869 and the development of the British grammar school. Durham Research Rev 19–20 1967.

Bone, T. R. School inspection in Scotland 1840–1966. 1968.

Akenson, D. H. The Irish education experiment: the national system of education in the nineteenth century. 1969.

Cowan, I. R. School board elections and politics in Salford 1870–1900. Durham Research Rev 23 1969.

McCann, W. P. Elementary education in England and Wales on the eve of the 1870 Act. Jnl of Educational Administration and History 2 1969.

Midwinter, E. C. The administration of public education in late Victorian Lancashire. Northern History 4 1969.

Roberts, K. O. The separation of secondary from technical education, 1889–1903. The Vocational Aspect of Education 21 1969.

Ward, J. T. and J. H. Treble. Religion and education in 1843: reaction to the Factories Education Bill. Jnl of Ecclesiastical History 20 1969.

Alwall, E. The religious trend in secular Scottish school books, with a survey of the debate on education in Scotland in the middle and late 19th century. 1970.

Bishop, A. S. The rise of a central authority for English education. 1970.

Bradshaw, D. C. A. (ed). Studies in the government and control of education since 1800. History of Education 1970.

Johnson, R. Educational policy and social control in early Victorian England. Past and Present 49 1970.

McCann, W. P. Trade unionists, artisans and the 1870 Education Act. British Jnl of Educational Stud 18 1970.

Roach, J. Public examinations in England 1850–1950. 1970.

Murphy, J. Church, state and schools in Britain 1800–1870. 1971.

Murphy, J. The Education Act 1870: text and commentary. 1972.

Rich, E. E. The Education Act of 1870. 1972.

Sutherland, G. (ed). Studies in the growth of nineteenth-century government. 1972. Chs on educational government and administration.

Keane, P. An English county and education: Somerset, 1889–1902. EHR 88 1973.

Marcham, A. J. Educating our masters: political parties and elementary education 1867–1870. British Jnl of Educational Stud 21 1973.

Sutherland, G. (ed). Policy-making in elementary education, 1870–1895. 1973.

Elton, E. A. Secondary education in the East Riding of Yorkshire 1944–1974. Leeds 1974.

Gordon, P. The Victorian school manager. A study in the management of education, 1800–1902. 1974.

Jones, D. K. The educational legacy of the anti corn law league. History of Education 3 1974.

MacLaren, A. A. Religion and social class: the disruption years in Aberdeen. 1974.

Parkin, R. The Central Society of Education 1836–40. 1975.

Roper, H. Administering the elementary education Acts, 1870–1885. Leeds 1976.

Balls, F. E. The endowment of education in the nineteenth century: the case of the Bedford Harpur Trust. History of Education 6 1977.

Fox, C. et al. Education: government and society in the nineteenth century. Dublin 1977.

Jones, D. K. The making of the education system, 1851–81. 1977.

Nelson, P. G. Leicester suburban school boards. History of Education 6 1977.

Paz, D. G. Working-class education and the state, 1839–1849: the sources of government policy. Jnl of British Stud 16 1977.

Gosden, P. H. J. H. and P. R. Sharp. The development of an education service: the West Riding 1889–1974. 1978.
Rimmington, G. T. Education, politics and society in Leicester 1883–1903. 1978.
Hurt, J. Elementary education and the working class. 1979.
Ward, L. O. The Liberation Society: an educational pressure group. Jnl of Educational Administration and History 11 1979.
Dunford, J. E. Her Majesty's inspectorate of schools in England and Wales 1860–1870. Leeds 1980.
Fidler, G. C. The Liverpool Labour movement and the school board: an aspect of education and the working class. History of Education 9 1980.
Aldrich, R. Peel, politics and education 1839–46. Jnl of Educational Administration and History 13 1981.
Cannell, G. Resistance to the Charity Commissioners: the case of St Paul's Schools, 1860–1904. History of Education 10 1981.
Elliott, A. The Bradford school board and the Department of Education, 1870–1902: areas of conflict. Jnl of Educational Administration and History 13 1981.
Fletcher, L. A further comment on recent interpretations of the Revised Code, 1862. History of Education 10 1981.
Paz, D. The politics of working-class education. 1981.
Bailey, K. B. The formation of school boards in Buckinghamshire. Jnl of Educational Administration and History 14 1982.
Evans, G. W. The Aberdare report and education in Wales, 1881. Welsh History Rev 11 1982.
Jones, G. E. Controls and conflicts in Welsh secondary education 1889–1944. Cardiff 1982.
Lewis, J. Parents, children, school fees and the London School Board 1870–1890. History of Education 11 1982.
Lilley, R. C. Attempts to implement the Bryce Commission's Recommendations – and the consequences. History of Education 11 1982.
Mason, D. M. Inspectors' Reports and the Select Committee of 1864. History of Education 11 1982.
Aldrich, R. 1870: a local government perspective. Jnl of Educational Administration and History 15 1983.
Griggs, C. The trades union congress and the struggle for education 1868–1925. 1983.
Leinster-Mackay, D. P. Private or public schools: the educational debate in laissez-faire England. Jnl of Educational Administration and History 15 1983.
Pritchard, P. B. Churchmen, Catholics and elementary education: a comparison of attitudes and policies in Liverpool during the school board era. History of Education 12 1983.
Richards, S. 'Masters of Arts and Bachelors of barley': the struggle for agricultural education in mid-nineteenth century Britain. History of Education 12 1983.
Griggs, C. and D. Wall. Eastbourne and the school board era that never was. History of Education 13 1984.
Allsobrook, D. I. Schools for the shires: the reform of middle-class education in mid-Victorian England. Manchester 1986.
Daglish, N. D. Planning the Education Bill of 1896. History of Education 16 1987.
Daglish, N. D. The politics of educational change: the case of the Higher Grade schools. Jnl of Educational Administration and History 19 1987.
Curtis, B. Patterns of resistance to public education: England, Ireland and Canada West, 1830–1890. Canadian Education Rev 32 1988.
Williams, H. G. The Foster Education Act and Welsh politics 1870–1914. Welsh History Rev 14 1988.
Miller, P. Historiography of compulsory schooling: what is the problem? History of Education 18 1989.
Green, A. Education and state formation: the rise of education systems in England, France and the USA. 1990.
Daglish, N. D. Sir John Gorst as an educational innovator: a reappraisal. History of Education 21 1992.
Davison, L. M. Delays to filling the gaps: evidence from school boards in the East Riding of Yorkshire. History of Education 22 1993.
Martin, J. Entering the public arena: the female members of the London School Board 1870–1904. History of Education 22 1993.
Taylor, T. Lord Cranbourne, the church party and Anglican education 1893–1902: from politics to pressure. History of Education 22 1993.
Brehony, K. J. The 'schoolmasters' parliament': the origins and formation of the Consultative Committee of the Board of Education 1868–1916. History of Education 23 1994.
Martin, J. Fighting down the idea that the only place for women was home? Gender and policy in elementary education, 1870–1914. History of Education 24 1995.
Daglish, N. D. Education policymaking in England and Wales. The crucible years, 1895–1911. 1996.
Stocks, J. C. Church and state in Britain: the legacy of the 1870s. History of Education 25 1996.
Williams, H. G. Longueville Jones, Ralph Lingen and inspectors' reports: a tragedy of Welsh education. History of Education 25 1996.
Cook, L. A. The contribution of nonconformity to elementary education in Swansea from the mid-Victorian era to the end of the nineteenth century. History of Education 26 1997.
Goodman, J. Constructing contradiction: the power and powerlessness of women in the giving and taking of evidence in the Bryce Commission, 1895. History of Education 26 1997.

Curriculum developments

McIntosh, P. C. Landmarks in the history of physical education. 1957. 2nd edn 1968.
Gilmour, R. The Gradgrind School: political economy in the classroom. VS 11 1967–8.
Selleck, R. J. W. The new education. 1968.
Layton, D. Science for the people. The origin of the school science curriculum in England. 1973.
Brock, W. H. (ed). H. E. Armstrong and the teaching of science, 1880–1930. 1973.
Inkster, I. Science instruction for youth in the Industrial Revolution. The Vocational Aspect of Education 23 1973.
van Praagh, G. (ed). H. E. Armstrong and science education. 1973.
Smith, H. The society for the diffusion of useful knowledge, 1826–46. 1974.
Layton, D. The educational work of the Parliamentary Committee of the British Association for the Advancement of Science. History of Education 5 1976.
Gordon, P. Commitments and developments in the elementary school curriculum 1870–1907. History of Education 6 1977.
Gordon, P. and D. Lawton. Curriculum change in the nineteenth and twentieth centuries. 1978.
Ball, F. The Taunton Commission and the maintenance of the classical curriculum in the Grammar Schools. Jnl of Educational Administration and History 11 1979.
Jenkins, E. W. From Armstrong to Nuffield. 1979.
Jenkins, E. W. Science, sentimentalism or social control? The nature study movement in England and Wales, 1899–1914. History of Education 10 1981.
Howson, A. G. A history of mathematics education in England. 1982.
MacLeod, R. Days of judgement. Science, examinations and the organization of knowledge in late Victorian England. 1982.
History of Education Soc. The fitness of the nation: physical and health education in the nineteenth century. 1983.
Newton, P. A French influence on nineteenth- and twentieth-century physics teaching in English secondary schools. 1983.

Price, M. H. Mathematics in English education 1860–1914: some questions and explanations in curriculum history. History of Education 12 1983.
Goodson, I. and S. Ball (ed). Defining the curriculum; histories and ethnographies. 1984. Some chs on the nineteenth-century curriculum and school experiences of working-class boys and girls.
Goodson, I. (ed). Social histories of the secondary curriculum. 1985. Some chs with a nineteenth-century content relating to elementary school science teaching, domestic subjects, and the sixth form curriculum.
Bailey, K. 'Plain and nothing fancy': Her Majesty's Inspectors and school needlework in the 1870s. Jnl of Educational Administration and History 18 1986.
Byrne, K. R. The Royal Dublin Society and the advancement of popular science in Ireland, 1731–1860. History of Education 15 1986.
Rainbow, B. The rise of popular music education in nineteenth century England. VS 30 1986.
Thistlewood, D. Social significance in British art education 1850–1950. Jnl of Art Education 20 1986.
White, R. The anatomy of a Victorian debate: an essay in the history of liberal education. British Jnl of Educational Stud 34 1986.
Michael, I. The teaching of English: from the sixteenth century to 1870. 1987.
Prophet, B. and D. Hodson. The science of common things: a case study in social control. History of Education 17 1988.
Bayley, S. N. Life is too short to learn German: modern languages in English elementary education, 1872–1904. History of Education 18 1989.
Goodson, I. and P. Medway (ed). The history and politics of English as a school subject. 1990. Includes an essay on the political history of English teaching from the early nineteenth century to the present day.
Shackleton, J. R. Jane Marcet and Harriet Martineau: pioneers of economics education. History of Education 19 1990.
Court, F. E. Institutionalising English literature: the culture and politics of literary study, 1750–1900. 1992.
Bayley, S. N. and D. Y. Ronish. Gender, modern languages and the curriculum in Victorian England. History of Education 21 1992.
Furlong, B. A. Alexander Alexander 1849–1928: building the foundations of health and strength in Liverpool and Southport. History of Education 21 1992.
Cox, G. A history of music education in England, 1872–1928. 1993.
Inkster, I. Science for all: studies in the history of Victorian science and education. 1996.

B. SPECIAL SUBJECTS

(1) THE UNIVERSITIES

Sources: general works

'A graduate'. Enquiry into the studies in the universities preparatory to Holy Orders. 1824.
Considerations on the injuries arising from the course of education pursued in the universities and public schools. 1832.
Blakesley, J. W. The studies of the universities essentially general. Cambridge 1836.
Thoughts on the recommendations of the Ecclesiastical Commission. 1836.
[Radnor, Earl]. An historical vindication of Earl Radnor's Bill to inquire respecting the statutes and administration of Oxford and Cambridge. 1837.
Whewell, William. Principles of English university education. 1837.
'A layman'. The independence of the universities and colleges. Oxford 1838.
Sewell, William. Collegiate reform: a sermon. Oxford 1838.
The nation, the Church and the University of Oxford: two sermons. Oxford 1849.
Huber, V. A. The English universities. 2 vols in 3 1843 (abridged trn). *See* Quart Rev 72 1843, Edinburgh Rev 81 1845.
Quart Rev 73 1843, 124 1868, 134 1873.
Lyell, Sir Charles. Travels in North America. 2 vols 1845. Oxford and Cambridge: historical and critical, vol 1 pp. 271–316.
Pillans, James. A word for the universities of Scotland. Edinburgh 1848.
English universities and their reforms. Blackwood's Mag Feb 1849.
University reform. Edinburgh Rev 89 1849.
Christie, William Dougal. Two speeches in the House of Commons on the universities [25 May 1843, 10 Apr 1845]. 1850.
Hamilton, Sir William. Discussions on philosophy and literature, education and university reform, chiefly from the Edinburgh Review. Edinburgh 1852, 1866 (3rd edn). *See* Education iii to vii, Appendix: Universities.
Newman, Cardinal John Henry. Discourses on the scope and nature of university education, addressed to the Catholics of Dublin. Dublin 1852, London 1859.
Office and work of the universities. 1856.
Lectures and essays on university subjects. 1859. All incorporated in The idea of a university defined and illustrated: 1, in nine discourses addressed to the Catholics of Dublin; 2, in occasional lectures and essays addressed to members of the Catholic University, 1873.
Lorimer, J. Universities of Scotland, past, present and possible. Edinburgh 1854.
See Scottish universities, Edinburgh Rev *81 1845, 143 1876; J. Pillans, above.*
British universities. Edinburgh Rev 107 1858.
Campion, W. M. Commissioners and colleges. 1858.
Roby, H. J. Remarks on college reform. Cambridge 1858.
Emery, William. Past and present expenses and social conditions of university education. In Br Assoc Report 1862.
Seeley, Sir John. Liberal education in universities. In his Essays on a liberal education, 1867.
Griffiths, J. Enactments in Parliament concerning the universities of Oxford and Cambridge. Oxford 1869.
Wilkins, A. Our national universities. 1871.
Fitch, Sir Joshua G. The universities and the training of teachers. Contemporary Rev Dec 1876. An anticipation of the Day Training Colleges.
Caird, J. University addresses on academic study. Glasgow 1899.
For the study of English and other modern literatures, see Quart Rev *156 1883, 164 1887; H. Nettleship,* Study of modern European languages and literatures in Oxford, *1887; J. C. Collins,* The study of English literature, *1891.*

Admission of Dissenters
to the universities of Oxford, Cambridge and Durham

An address to Dissenters. 1834.
Dalby, W. The real question at issue. 1834.
Gray, J. H. The admission of Dissenters into the universities considered. Oxford 1834.
Hamilton, Sir William A. Bill to remove certain disabilities. Edinburgh Rev 60 1834.
Moberly, George. A few remarks on the proposed admission of Dissenters. Oxford 1834.
Pearson, G. Abrogating religious tests and subscriptions. Cambridge 1834.
Sedgwick, Adam. Admission of Dissenters to academical degrees. Cambridge Chron 9 June 1834. *See* H. J. Rose, Letter, Cambridge Chron 10 June 1834.
Selwyn, William. College examinations in Divinity. Cambridge 1834.

Sewell, S. Thoughts on the admission of Dissenters to the University of Oxford. Oxford 1834.
Turton, Thomas. Thoughts on the admission of persons, without regard to their religious opinions, to certain degrees in the universities of England. Cambridge 1834, 1835 (with A review of the principal dissenting colleges).
Lee, Samuel. Some remarks on the Dean of Peterborough's tract. Cambridge 1834.
Thirwall, Connor. A letter to the Revd Thos Turton on the admission of Dissenters to academical degrees. Cambridge 1834. A second letter followed the above.
Whewell, William. Additional remarks on some parts of Mr Thirwall's two letters. Cambridge 1834.
See also Quart Rev *52 1834,* Edinburgh Rev *60 1834–5.*
Wordsworth, Christopher. On the admission of Dissenters to reside and graduate. Cambridge 1834.
Manning, William Oke. Remarks upon religious tests at the English universities. 1846.
Arnold, Thomas et al. Opinions on the admission of Dissenters to the universities and on university reform. 1847.
Opinions on the admission of Dissenters and on university reform. 1847. By Palmerston, Lord John Russell, Sir W. Hamilton, J. S. Mill et al.
Smith, G. Plea for the abolition of tests in the university. Oxford 1864.
Young, Sir G. Series of letters to the Guardian, later published as a pamphlet under the title University tests. 1868.
Select Committee on University Tests: report to Parliament. 1870. Summarised in Cambridge Chron 6 May 1871.

Modern studies: general works

The following are in addition to those cited in the previous section. See also under Individual universities, below.

Armytage, W. H. G. Civic universities: aspects of a British tradition. 1955.
Newsome, D. Godliness and good learning: four studies on a Victorian ideal. 1961.
Ashby, Sir Eric and M. Anderson. The rise of the student estate in Britain. 1970.
Sanderson, M. The universities and British industry 1850–1970. 1972.
Sanderson, M. (ed). The universities in the nineteenth century. 1974. Includes writings of Hamilton, Jowett, Whewell, Pattison, Huxley, Arnold, Mill and Newman.
Stone, L. (ed). The university in society. 2 vols 1974.
Rothblatt, S. Tradition and change in English liberal education: an essay in history and culture. 1976.
Burrow, J. W. The English tradition of liberal education. History of Education Quart 20 1980.
Newton, J. S. The liberationists and the universities: Edward Miall and the struggle for university reform in the mid-nineteenth century. Durham Univ Jnl 43 1981.
Heyck, T. W. The transformation of intellectual life in Victorian England. 1982.
Jarausch, C. H. (ed). The transformation of higher learning 1860–1930. 1983.
Slee, P. Learning and liberal education: the study of modern history in the Universities of Oxford, Cambridge and Manchester 1800–1914. Manchester 1986.
Heyck, T. W. The idea of a university in Britain 1870–1970. History of European Ideas 8 1987.
Mangan, J. A. Liberal education and the ancient universities: ideology and change in Victorian and Edwardian Oxbridge. International Jnl of the History of Sport 4 1987.
Jones, D. R. The origins of civic universities: Manchester, Leeds and Liverpool. 1988.
Brockliss, L. (ed). History of Universities No VIII. 1989. Ch on experimental sciences in early nineteenth-century Oxford.
Mangan, J. A. Lamentable barbarians and pitiful sheep: rhetoric of protest and pleasure in late Victorian and Edwardian 'Oxbridge'. VS 34 1991.
Anderson, R. D. Universities and elites in Britain since 1800. 1992.
Soffer, R. N. Discipline and power: the university, history and the making of an English elite, 1870–1930. Stanford CA 1994.

Individual universities: sources and modern studies

Aberdeen

Fasti Aberdonenses: selections from the records of the University and King's College of Aberdeen 1494–1854. 1854 (Spalding Club).
Grant Duff, Sir M. E. Inaugural addresses delivered to the University of Aberdeen. Edinburgh 1867.
Bulloch, J. M. History of the University of Aberdeen 1495–1895. 1895.
Aberdeen University studies. Aberdeen 1900.
Rectorial addresses delivered in the Universities of Aberdeen 1835–1900. Aberdeen 1902.
McLaren, C. A. P. J. Anderson and the history of the university. Aberdeen Univ Rev 51 1985.
McLaren, C. A. The process of educational change: Aberdeen 1875–1884. Aberdeen Univ Rev 51 1986.
Edwards, G. P. Aberdeen and its classical tradition. Aberdeen Univ Rev 51 1986.
Anderson, R. D. The student community at Aberdeen 1860–1939. 1988.

Birmingham

Smith, E. The educational work of the Birmingham and Midland Institute. 1870.
Lodge, Sir O. Addresses to students by the Principal. 1900.
Vincent, E. W. and P. Hinton. The University of Birmingham: its history and significance. Birmingham 1947.

Bristol

McQueen, J. G. and W. S. Taylor (ed). University and community: essays to mark the centenary of the founding of University College. Bristol 1976.

Cambridge

'Pembrochian'. Gradus ad Cantabrigiam: or a dictionary of the terms used at the University of Cambridge. 1803.
Wilson, J. Memorabilia Cantabrigiae. 1803.
Byron, Baron George Gordon. Thoughts suggested by a College examination, 1806; Granta: a medley, 1806. In his Hours of idleness, 1807.
Wainewright, L. The literary and scientific studies pursued, encouraged and enforced in the University of Cambridge. 1815.
Quart Rev 19 1818. On the chair of Botany.
'Eubulus' (Samuel Butler of Shrewsbury). Thoughts on the present system of academic education. 1822.
A letter to Philograntus. 1822.
'Philograntus' (J. H. Monk). A letter on the additional examination of students. 1822. *See* 'Eubulus', *above.*
[Gooch, R.] The Cambridge tart, by Socius. 1823.
'A brace of Cantabs'. Gradus ad Cantabrigiam: or a new university guide to the academic customs and colloquial or cant terms. 1824.
Dyer, G. The privileges of the University of Cambridge. 1824.
[Wright, J. M. F.] Alma mater: or seven years at the University of Cambridge by a Trinity-man. 1827. *See* London Mag Apr 1827.
Gunning, Henry. Letters from Cambridge illustrative of the studies, habits and peculiarities of the University. 1827.
Gunning, Henry. The ceremonies observed in the Senate House Cambridge. 1828.
Sedgwick, Adam. A discourse on the studies of the Universities. Cambridge 1833.

'Resident members of the University'. Hints for the introduction of an improved course of study in the University. Cambridge 1835.
Selwyn, William. Extracts from college examinations in divinity with a letter to the lecturers and examiners. Cambridge 1835.
[Le Grice, C. V.] Conversations at Cambridge: miscellaneous pieces. Cambridge 1836.
Walsh, B. D. A historical account of the University of Cambridge and its colleges, in a letter to the Earl of Radnor. 1837.
Cambridge University Magazine. Mar 1839–Nov 1840.
Peacock, George. Observations on the statutes of the University of Cambridge. 1841.
Whewell, William. Liberal education, with particular reference to the University of Cambridge. 1845.
Amos, A. Four lectures on the advantages of a classical education, with a letter to Whewell. 1846.
Alma mater: a satire dedicated to the collegiate dignitaries. 1848.
Bain, A. University education. Westminster Rev 69 1848. A review of Whewell, Liberal education, *above.*
Bristed, C. A. Five years in an English university. 2 vols New York 1852, 1 vol 1873.
Cambridge essays contributed by members of the University. 4 vols 1855–8.
Potts, Robert. Cantabrigiensis liber: aids afforded to poor students in the University, with maxims designed for learners. Cambridge 1855.
Mill, John Stuart. Dissertations and discussions. 4 vols 1859–75. On Adam Sedgwick, Discourse, *above.*
Everett, W. On the Cam: lectures on the University of Cambridge. 1866.
The Light Blue. 4 vols 1866–70.
Wilson, James Maurice. Letter to St John's College on sciences in relation to school and university. 1867.
[Rice, J.] The Cambridge freshman: or memoirs of Mr Golightly; by Martin Legrand. 1871.
Hilton, A. C. et al. The Light Green: a superior and high-class periodical. Cambridge 1872–3.
On the training of teachers. Cambridge Univ Reporter 2 Nov 1877, 20 Nov 1878; Teachers' training syndicate: first annual Report, 3 Dec 1880.
Burnand, F. C. Personal reminiscences of the ADC. 1880 (Univ Amateur Dramatic Club).
Whibley, C. In cap and gown: three centuries of Cambridge wit. 1889.
Lehmann, R. C. In Cambridge courts. 1891.
Atkinson, Thomas D. Cambridge described and illustrated. Cambridge 1897. Introd by J. W. Clark.
Stephen, J. K. Lapsus calami and other verses. Ed H. S., Cambridge 1898.
Stubbs, C. W. The story of Cambridge. 1905.
Leigh, A. A. A record of college reform. 1906.
Tillyard, A. I. A history of university reform from 1800. Cambridge 1913.
Winstanley, D. A. Early Victorian Cambridge. Cambridge 1940.
Winstanley, D. A. Later Victorian Cambridge. Cambridge 1947.
Hilken, T. J. N. Engineering at Cambridge University 1783–1965. Cambridge 1967.
Rothblatt, Sheldon. The revolution of the dons: Cambridge and society in Victorian England. 1968.
Reeve, F. A. (ed). Victorian and Edwardian Cambridge. 1971.
Rich, E. E. (ed). St Catharine's College, Cambridge. A volume of essays. 1973.
Simms, T. H. Homerton College, 1695–1978: from dissenting academy to approved society in the University of Cambridge. 1979.
Rashid, Salim. The growth of economic studies at Cambridge: 1776–1860. History of Education Quart 20 1980.
Garland, M. M. Cambridge before Darwin: the ideal of a liberal education. 1981.
Rupp, G. A. A Cambridge centenary: the Selwyn Divinity School, 1879–1979. Historical Jnl 24 1981.
Brooke, C. N. L. A history of Gonville and Caius College. 1982.
Porter, R. The natural science tripos and the Cambridge school of geology, 1850–1914. History of Universities 2 1982.
Deacon, R. The Cambridge apostles: a history of Cambridge University's elite intellectual secret society. 1985.
Allen, P. A Victorian intellectual elite: records of the Cambridge apostles, 1820–1877. VS 33 1989.
Twigg, J. A. A history of Queens' College Cambridge. 1987.
A history of the University of Cambridge, Vol IV, 1870–1990. 1993.

Canterbury

Gardner, W. J. et al. A history of the University of Canterbury, 1873–1973. 1973.

Dublin

Todd, James H. University of Dublin: remarks on some statements attributed to T. Wyse. 1844.
Taylor, W. B. S. History of the University of Dublin. 1845. *See* Edinburgh Rev 88 1848.
Vickers, R. Praelection on the university system of education. Dublin 1849.
Tyrrell, R. Y. et al. Kottabos: a college miscellany. Dublin 1869.
Hermathena: papers by members of T C D. Dublin 1874– .
Stubbs, J. M. History of the University of Dublin. Dublin 1889. *See* Quart Rev 175 1892.
Dixon, W. M. Trinity College Dublin. Dublin 1902.
Burtchaell, G. D. and T. U. Sadleir. Alumni dublienses 1593–1860. Dublin 1937.

Dundee

Southgate, D. University education in Dundee: a centenary history. 1982.

Durham

The Thorp letters. 5 vols 1831–62.
Durham University Journal. 1876– .
Embleton, Dennis. History of the Medical School, afterwards the Durham College of Medicine. Newcastle 1890.
Turner, George Grey. A short history of the Durham University College of Medicine. Durham Univ Jnl 1896.
The student's guide to the University of Durham. 1897.
Fowler, J. T. Durham University: earlier foundations and present colleges. 1904.
Whiting, C. E. The University of Durham 1832–1932. 1932.
Tudor, H. St Cuthbert's Society 1888–1988. Durham 1988.
Moyes, W. A. Hatfield 1846–1996. Durham 1996.

Edinburgh

Edinburgh essays. 1858.
Dazel, A. History of the University of Edinburgh. 2 vols Edinburgh 1862.
Geddes, P. et al. Viri illustres academiae Jacobi Sexti Scotiae regis anno CCCmo. Edinburgh 1884.
Grant, Sir Alexander. The story of the University of Edinburgh. 2 vols 1884.
Rectorial addresses delivered before the university 1859–99. Ed A. Stodart-Walker 1900.
Horn, D. B. A short history of the University of Edinburgh 1556–1889. Edinburgh 1967.
Anderson, R. G. W. The Playfair collection and the teaching of chemistry at the University of Edinburgh 1713–1858. Edinburgh 1978.
Donaldson, G. (ed). Four centuries: Edinburgh university life, 1583–1983. 1983.

Glasgow

Remarks on a pamphlet 'A memorial respecting the college of Glasgow'. Glasgow 1835.
Inaugural addresses by Lord Rectors of the University. Ed J. B. Hay 1839.
Macaulay, Thomas Babington, Baron. Inaugural address as Lord Rector. 1849.
Munimenta alme universitatis glasguensis: records of the University till 1727. 3 vols in 4 Glasgow 1854 (Maitland Club).
Disraeli, Benjamin (Earl of Beaconsfield). Inaugural address delivered to the University of Glasgow. 1873. *See* Edinburgh Rev 139 1874.
Addison, W. I. et al. Roll of the graduates of the University of Glasgow 1727–1897 with biographical notes. Glasgow 1898.
Primrose, A. P. Inaugural address 1900. *See* Edinburgh Rev 195 1902.
Couts, I. History of the University of Glasgow. Glasgow 1909.
Morgan, A. Scottish university studies. Oxford 1933.
Robertson, P. L. The development of an urban university, Glasgow, 1860–1914. History of Education Quart 30 1990.

Ireland

'Nemo'. A few words on the new Irish Colleges. 1845.
Corrigan, D. J. University education in Ireland. Dublin 1865.
Sullivan, W. K. University education in Ireland. Dublin 1866.
Andrews, T. Address on education to the Social Science Association. 1867.
Studium generale: a chapter of contemporary history. 1867. On the University of London, the new Irish universities, Maynooth.
Walsh, W. J. The Irish university question. Dublin 1890. *See* Quart Rev 148 1879, 187 1898, 197 1903; Edinburgh Rev 135 1872, 137 1873, 187 1898, 195 1902.

Leeds

The Yorkshire College of Science: scheme for the foundation of a college. 1869.
Report of the inauguration of the Yorkshire College of Science. 1875.
The inauguration of the University of Leeds: a special issue of the Gryphon, the journal of the University of Leeds. 1904.
Smithells, A. From a modern university. Oxford 1921.
Curtis, S. J. The University of Leeds. Universities Rev 22 1949.
Brown, E. J. The private donor in the history of the University of Leeds. 1954.
Shimmin, A. N. The University of Leeds: the first half century. Cambridge 1954.
Gosden, P. H. J. H. and A. J. Taylor. Studies in the history of a university to commemorate the centenary of the University of Leeds. 1975.
Anning, S. T. and W. K. Walls. A history of the Leeds School of Medicine 1831–1981. Leeds 1982.

London

Campbell, Thomas. The Times 9 Feb 1824. A letter.
Campbell, Thomas. Suggestions respecting the plan of an University in London. NMM 13 1825.
Edinburgh Rev 42 1825, 43 1826, 48 1828, 164 1886.
'An Oxonian'. Proposals for founding an University in London considered. 1825.
Quart Rev 33 1825.
London University: prospectus. London Mag Aug 1826.
'Christianus'. Letter to Robert Peel on the London University. 1828. *See* Quart Rev 39 1829.
The London University Press: remarks upon a popular system of classical instruction. Bath 1828.
The second statement of the Council explanatory of the plan of instruction. 1828. *See* Edinburgh Rev 48 1828.
Stähele, A. Letter to the Council of the University of London. 1828.
'A subscriber'. Remarks to the provisional committee for the intended establishment of King's College London. 1828. *See* London Mag July 1828.
Yates, James. Outlines of a constitution for the University of London. 1832.
Morgan, John M. Address to the proprietors of the University of London. 1833. Proposes a Chair of Education.
Sewell, William. A second letter to a dissenter on the opposition of the University of Oxford to the Charter of the London College. Oxford 1834. *See* Edinburgh Rev 42 1825.
London University. Quart Jnl of Education 7 1834.
Wetherall, Sir C. Substance for a speech on incorporating the University of London. 1834. In opposition, on behalf of Oxford.
E., E. (D. Edwards). The metropolitan university: remarks on a central university examining board. 1836.
De Morgan, Augustus. Thoughts suggested by the establishment of the University of London. 1837.
Hoppus, John. Thoughts on academic education and degrees in arts. 1837.
Letter to a member of the Senate relative to the BA examination. 1838.
Beattie, William. Life and letters of Thomas Campbell. 3 vols 1849. *See* vol 2 ch 14.
Jelf, Richard W. Grounds for laying before the Council of King's College London theological essays by F. D. Maurice. 1853.
Andrews, Thomas. Studium generale. 1867. *See* T. Andrews *under* Ireland, *above*.
Beard, C. University College and Mr Martineau. 1867.
Bagehot, Walter. Matthew Arnold on the London University. Fortnightly Rev June 1868.
Grote, Harriet. The personal life of George Grote. 1873.
Prospectus of the Association for Promoting a Teaching University for London. 1886. *See* Edinburgh Rev 164 1886.
Quart Rev 164 1887, 191 1900.
The proposed teaching university for London. The Times 31 Jan 1888.
London University Commission and Albert University Charter, by Sir J. G. Fitch. Quart Rev 174 1892.
Notes and memorials for the history of University College London. Ed W. P. Ker 1898.
Wilson, G. S. The University of London and its colleges. 1923.
Haldane, R. B. (Viscount). Birkbeck College centenary lectures. 1924.
Humberstone, T. L. University reform in London. 1926.
Bellot, H. H. L. University College London 1826–1926. 1929.
Hearnshaw, F. J. C. et al. The centenary history of King's College, London 1828–1928. 1929.
Collins, W. J. The University of London fifty years ago. Contemporary Rev Sep 1935.
Gledstone, M. Centenary of the Bedford College for Women. Universities Rev 21 1949.
Coats, A. W. Alfred Marshall and the early development of the London School of Economics. Economica 34 1967.
Kaye, E. A history of Queen's College, London, 1848–1972. 1972.
Harte, N. and J. North. The world of University College London, 1828–1978. 1978 (University College London).
Heulin, G. King's College London, 1828–1978. 1978 (King's College London).
Bacon, A. English literature as a subject: King's College London as a pioneer. VS 29 1986.
Marsh, N. The history of Queen Elizabeth College: one hundred years of university education in Kensington. 1986 (King's College).
Bender, T. (ed). The University and the city: from medieval origins to the present. Oxford 1987. Essay on University of London in the nineteenth century.
Bingham, C. The history of Royal Holloway College. 1987.

Manchester (including Owens College and the Victoria University)

Essays and addresses by Professors of Owens College. 1874.

Thompson, Joseph. The Owens College: its foundation and growth and its connection with the Victoria University Manchester. Manchester 1886.

Hartog, Sir Philip. Owens College Manchester: a brief history of the College. 1900.

Fiddes, E. Chapters in the history of Owens College and of Manchester University (1857–1914). Manchester 1937.

Charlton, H. B. Portrait of a university 1851–1951. Manchester 1951.

Newcastle

Bettenson, E. M. The University of Newcastle upon Tyne: a historical introduction 1834–1971. Newcastle 1971.

Nottingham

Tolley, B. H. The peoples' scientific university: science education in the East Midlands, 1860–1960. Midlands History 7 1982.

Oxford

Walker, J. Oxoniana. 4 vols 1807.

Edinburgh Rev 14 1809, 16 1810, 53 1831, 54 1831, 76 1843, 88 1848, 96 1852, 170 1889, 198 1903.

Copleston, E. A reply to the calumnies of the Edinburgh Review. Oxford 1810.

A second reply. Oxford 1810.

A third reply. Oxford 1811. *See* J. Davidson, *below*; Edinburgh Rev 14 1808, 16 1810; Quart Rev 4 1810; D. K. Sandford to P. Elmslie, Pamphleteer 21 1822.

'A Nobleman'. Letters to his son at Eton and Oxford. 2 vols 1810.

[Tatham, E.] A new address to members of Convocation. Oxford 1810.

An address to the Chancellor upon abuses. Oxford 1811. Both this and the preceding work by the Rector of Lincoln College.

'A gentleman of the University'. A poetical essay on the existing state of things. [1811?]

'A Cambridge Master of Arts'. Oxoniana: a didactic poem. 1812.

[Boone, James S.] The Oxford spy: a dialogue in verse. Oxford 1818. With a prose appendix on studies.

Townsend, W. C. The paean of Oxford: a reply to the charges against the University. 1826.

Skelton, J. Pietas oxoniensis or records of Oxford founders. Oxford 1828.

Whittock, N. The microcosm of Oxford. 1828.

Ingram, James. Apologia academica. Oxford 1831.

Memorials of Oxford. 3 vols 1837.

'A member of Convocation' (V. Thomas). The legality of the present academical system asserted against the new calumnies of the Edinburgh Review. Oxford 1831. *See* Edinburgh Rev 54 1831, *and under* Thomas, *below*.

Quart Jnl of Education 1–2, 4, 7 1831–4.

Academical abuses disclosed by Initiated. 1832.

'A member of Convocation' (V. Thomas). The legality [etc] reasserted. Oxford 1832.

Present state and future prospects of mathematical and physical studies in the University. Oxford 1832.

'A graduate'. Thoughts on reform at Oxford. Oxford 1833.

Quart Rev 52 1834, 61 1838, 137 1874.

Sewell, William. The attack upon the University of Oxford in a letter to Earl Grey. 1834 (2nd edn).

Suggestions for the extension of the University. Oxford 1850.

The university commission: or Lord John Russell's post-bag. Oxford 1850. Anon.

'A resident member of Convocation' (A. C. Tait). Hints on a plan for the revival of the professorial system. Oxford 1839.

Davidson, J. Remarks and occasional publications. Oxford 1840. Includes Review of replies to the calumnies of the Edinburgh Rev 1810. *See* J. H. Newman, Idea of a university: discourse vi, Liberal knowledge in relation to professional, 1852.

Bentham, Jeremy. Works. Ed J. Bowring 11 vols Edinburgh 1843. Vol 10 ch 2, Westminster School and Oxford.

[Caswell, E.] The art of pluck, by Scriblerus Redivivus. 1843.

Garbett, James. Dr Pusey and the University of Oxford. 1843.

Coleridge, John Duke (Baron). Memorials of Oxford. Oxford 1844. Verse.

Maurice, J. F. D. The New Statute and Mr Ward. Oxford 1845.

[Pycroft, J.] The collegian's guide: or recollections of college days, by the Revd – M A – College. 1845.

'Nema'. The Devil's return from Oxford. Oxford 1847.

'Country schoolmaster'. A letter to the authors of Suggestions for an improvement of the Examination Statute. Oxford 1848.

[Jowett, Benjamin and Arthur Penryn Stanley]. Suggestions for an improvement of the Examination Statute. Oxford 1848.

Walker, R. A letter on improvements in the present Examination Statute, and the studies of the University. Oxford 1848.

Grand university logic stakes. 1849.

'A member of the Oxford Convocation' [C. A. Row]. Letter to Lord John Russell on the constitutional defects of the University and Colleges of Oxford, with suggestions for a Royal Commission. 1850.

Price, B. Suggestions for the extension of professorial teaching. 1850.

Row, C. A. Letter to Sir Robert Inglis in reply to his speech on university reform. 1850.

Hamilton, Sir William. Discussions on philosophy and literature, education and university reform, chiefly from the Edinburgh Review. Edinburgh 1852, 1866 (3rd edn). *See under* Universities: general works, *above*; E. Moore, *below*.

'Bede, Cuthbert' (E. Bradley). The adventures of Mr Verdant Green, an Oxford freshman. 1853.

Thomas, V. The legality of the academic system asserted. 2 pts Oxford 1853. *See* Edinburgh Rev 96 1852, *and* 'A member of Convocation', *above*.

Tutors' Association Reports, Oxford 1853–4:

1. Recommendations respecting extension;
2. Recommendations respecting the constitution;
3. Recommendations relating to the professorial and tutorial systems;
4. Recommendations respecting College Statutes.

See F. H. Dickinson and E. A. Freeman, Suggestions with regard to certain proposed alterations, *Oxford 1854; J. W. Aud and J. Patteson,* Suggestions with regard to the possibility of legal education, *Oxford 1854.*

Barrow, T. The case of Queen's College Oxford. 1854.

Barry, H. B. Remarks on the three proposals for reforming the Constitution of the University. Oxford 1854.

Pusey, Edward Bouverie. Collegiate and professional teaching and discipline. 1854. *See* H. H. Vaugham, *below*.

Vaugham, H. H. Oxford reform and Oxford professors. 1854.

Wilson, H. B. A letter to the Chancellor of the University on university and college reforms. 1854.

'Members of the University'. Oxford essays. 1855, 1856, 1857.

Acland, Sir Thomas Dyke. Some account of the origin and objects of the new examinations for the title of Associate in Arts. 1858.

'Clericus' (A. Clissold). A letter to the Vice-Chancellor on theology. 1858.

Smith, G. Oxford University reforms. 1858.

Reorganisation of the University. Oxford 1868.

Oxford and her colleges. 1894.

Acland, H. W. and J. Ruskin. The Oxford Museum. 1859.

Rogers, J. E. T. Education in Oxford and its methods. 1861.

Moore, E. Frugal education attainable under the existing collegiate system. Oxford 1867.

'Beta' (Thomas E. Brown). Christ Church servitors in 1853 by one of them. Macmillan's Mag 19 1868.
Pattison, Mark. Suggestions on academical organisation. Edinburgh 1868.
Mansel, H. L. The Phrontisterion: or Oxford in the nineteenth century. Ed H. W. Chandler 1873. A skit on the Royal Commission of 1850–2.
Essays on the endowment of research. 1876. By various writers.
Mozley, Thomas. Reminiscences chiefly of Oriel College and the Oxford movement. 2 vols 1882. *See* Quart Rev 154 1882.
Brodrick, George Charles. A history of the University of Oxford. 1886.
English literature at the universities. Quart Rev 163 1886. Discusses Petition for a school of modern literature, Oxford 1886.
Burgon, John W. Historical notes of Oxford colleges. Oxford 1888.
Essays. Ed H. Nettleship 2 vols Oxford 1889.
Mackinder, H. J. and Sir M. E. Sadleir. University extension: has it a future? 1890, 1891 (enlarged as University extension past, present and future). *See* Quart Rev 172 1891.
Foster, Joseph. Alumni oxoniensis 1500–1886. Oxford 1891.
Wells, J. et al. Oxford and Oxford life. 1892.
Our memories: shadows of old Oxford. 2 ser 1893–5.
Thompson, L. Christ Church. 1900.
Tuckwell, W. Reminiscences of Oxford. 1900.
Pre-Tractarian Oxford: a reminiscence of the Oriel Noetics. 1909. *See* Quart Rev 156 1883.
See C. Mallet, A history of the University of Oxford *vol 3, 1927.*
Green, V. H. H. Oxford common room: a study of Lincoln College and Mark Pattison. 1957.
Ward, W. R. Victorian Oxford. 1967.
Lawson, F. H. The Oxford Law School 1850–1965. 1969.
Bill, E. G. W. and J. F. A. Mason. Christ Church and reform 1850–1867. Oxford 1970.
Bill, E. G. W. University reform in nineteenth-century Oxford. 1974.
Green, V. H. H. A history of Oxford University. 1974.
Rowse, A. L. Oxford in the history of the nation. 1975.
Green, V. H. H. The commonwealth of Lincoln College 1427–1977. Oxford 1979.
Bacon, A. Attempts to introduce a School of English Literature at Oxford: the national debate of 1886 and 1887. History of Education 9 1980.
Berard, R. N. Edward Augustus Freeman and university reform in Victorian Oxford. History of Education 9 1980.
Engel, Arthur. Political education in Oxford 1873–1914. History of Education Quart 20 1980.
Engel, Arthur. From clergyman to don: the rise of the academic profession in nineteenth century Oxford. 1983.
Howarth, J. Science education in late-Victorian Oxford: a curious case of failure. English Historical Rev [illegible] 1987.
Soffer, Reba N. Nation, duty, character and confidence: history at Oxford, 1850–1914. Historical Jnl 30 1987.
Jones, J. Balliol College, Oxford: a history, 1263–1939. 1988.
Slee, P. The Oxford ideal of a liberal education 1800–1860: the invention of tradition and the manufacture of practice. History of Universities 7 1988.
Turner, G. Experimental science in early nineteenth-century Oxford. History of Universities 8 1989.
Curthoys, M. C. and H. S. Jones. Oxford athleticism, 1850–1914: a reappraisal. History of Education 24 1995.

Reading

Childs, W. M. Making a university: an account of the university movement at Reading. 1933.

St Andrews

Rectorial addresses at St Andrews University 1863–1893. Ed W. Knight 1894.
Donaldson, Sir J. Addresses delivered in the University of St Andrews from 1886 to 1910. Edinburgh 1911.
Votiva tabella: memorial volume of St Andrews University 1411–1911. 1911.

Salford

Gordon, C. The foundation of the University of Salford. 1975.

Wales

Davies, W. C. and W. L. Jones. The University of Wales and its colleges. 1905.
Williams, J. The university movement in Wales. 1969.
Williams, J. The University of North Wales. 1987.

(2) SCHOOLS, TEACHERS AND COLLEGES

Sources

Ingram, Robert A. A sermon for the Charity School. Colchester 1788.
Parochial beneficence: the Baxted School of Industry. Colchester [1800].
An essay on Schools of Industry. [1808].
Cappe, C. An account of two Charity Schools in York. York 1800.
Cappe, C. Observations on Charity Schools in York. York 1805.
Royal Military College: HM Warrants and Statutes. 1802.
Vincent, Rev W., Head Master of Westminster School. A defence of public education with an attempt to state fairly the question whether the religious instruction and moral conduct of the rising generation, are sufficiently provided for and effectually secured in our schools and universities. 1802. *See* Remarks on Vincent's Defence by a layman, 1802; D. Morris, An attempted reply to the Master of Westminster School, 1802.
Byron, G. G. On a change of masters at a great public school. 1805.
On a distant view of Harrow. 1806.
In his Hours of idleness, 1807.
'A Carthusian' (Robert Smythe). Historical account of the Charterhouse. 1808.
Bernard, Sir Thomas. The new school. 1809.
Barrington School (Bishop Auckland): principles, practices and effects. 1812.
See Reports of the Society for bettering the conditions and increasing the comforts of the poor, *under Official documents, below.*
Smith, Sydney. Edinburgh Rev 16 1810. Review of Remarks on the system of education in public schools, 1809.
The public schools. Edinburgh Rev 16 1810, 51 1830, 53 1831, 113 1861, 120 1864, 146 1877, 185 1897; Quart Rev 25 1821, 39 1829, 52 1834, 102 1857, 108 1860, 177 1893, 187 1898, 189 1899. *See* Sir J. T. Coleridge, *below.*
Harrison, R. Sermons on various important subjects, with life of the author by W. Harrison. Manchester 1813.
Poole, J. The village schools improved: the new system explained. 1813, Oxford 1815 (2nd edn).
Hill, Thomas Wright. The pupils of Hill-Top School Birmingham. Birmingham 1815. Hill-Top, 1803–19, was the predecessor of the Hill's Schools, Hazelwood etc.
Ackermann, Rudolph. The history of the Colleges of Winchester, Eton and Westminster, with the Charter-House, the Schools of St Paul's, Merchant Taylors, Harrow and Rugby, and the Free School of Christ's Hospital. 1816.
Lauphier, W. H. Upper Sunbury School Middlesex, for a limited number of persons of distinction and respectability. 1816.
The Trifler: a periodical paper. Mar–Sep 1817. *See* Vincent, *above.*
Bowles, William Lisle. Vindiciae wykehamicae: or a vindication of Winchester College in a letter to Henry Brougham. 1818, 1819.
Carlisle, Nicholas. A concise description of the Endowed Grammar Schools in England and Wales. 2 vols 1818. On the state of grammar schools in the early nineteenth century.

Rules for the government of the Westminster New Charity. 1818.
Grammar Schools and the education of the poor. Edinburgh Rev 32 1819.
Vindication of the Enquiry into Charitable Abuses with an exposure of the misrepresentation contained in the Quarterly Review. 1819.
Butler, Samuel. A letter to Henry Brougham esq. 1820.
Edinburgh Academical Institution: Milton's plan of education with the plan of the EAI founded thereon, by William Scott. Pamphleteer 17 1820.
The Etonian: a magazine, 1820–1, 1821–2, 1824 (4th edn). *See* Quart Rev 25 1821.
Quart Rev 25 1821, 52 1834, 171 1890, 187 1898. On Eton.
[Hill, Matthew Davenport]. Plans for the government and liberal instruction of boys in large numbers as practised at Hazelwood School. 1822, 1825 (as Public education: plans etc), 1894. Ascribed to Arthur Hill et al. *See* F. Jeffrey, Edinburgh Rev 41 1825; T. De Quincey, London Mag Apr–May 1824.
Sheepshanks, Rev John. Brief history of Leeds Grammar School. 1822.
Churcher's College Petersfield and life of Churcher. Petersfield 1823.
The system pursued in the Pestalozzian Academy South Lambeth with some remarks on education. 1826. The author claims to have conversed daily with Pestalozzi at Yverdon.
Buckler, J. C. Sixty views of Endowed Grammar Schools. 1827.
Hill, Sir Roland and F. The laws of Hazelwood School. 1827.
Scots Parochial Schools. Edinburgh Rev 46 1827.
Ward, Valentine. Observations on Sunday Schools. Leeds 1827.
City of London Literary and Philosophical Institution. *See* Edinburgh Rev 47 1828.
History of the Foundations in Manchester of Christ's College, Chetham's Hospital and the Free Grammar School. 3 vols Manchester 1828–9.
Malet, Sir Alexander. Some account of the system of fagging at Winchester School, with remarks and a correspondence with Dr Williams, Head Master of that public school, on the late expulsions thence for resistance to the authority of the prefects. 1828. *See* Letter to Sir Alexander Malet by an old Etonian, 1829; Quart Rev 39 1829.
Gilbert, Richard. Liber scholasticus. 1829, 1843 (as Parents' school and college guide). On emoluments at Oxford, Cambridge, Durham, the public and other endowed schools and from City companies.
A very short letter from one Old Westminster to another. 1829.
'Etonensis'. Observations on an article in the last Edinburgh Review [51 1830] entitled Public schools of England. Eton 1830. *See* A few words in reply to Some remarks by Etonensis, 1834; The Eton system vindicated in reply to some recent publications, 1834; Quart Rev 52 1834.
A letter to the Edinburgh Review in answer to no CV [53 1831] respecting Westminster School. 1831.
Village schools of industry. 1831.
Eton College Magazine. Eton 1832 (8 issues).
[Hill, Arthur]. Sketch of the system of education at Bruce Castle, Tottenham and Hazelwood. 1833.
The kaleidoscope conducted by Eton boys. Eton 1833.
Statutes of Robert Johnson, Oakham and Uppingham. Uppingham 1837.
Coates, T. Visit to Borough Road Model School. In Central Society of Education, 1838 (2nd pbn).
Conciop apud scholae Hergensis gubernatores habita xj Kal Jul. 1838.
Fry, A. Bruce Castle, Tottenham Junior School. In Central Society of Education, 1838 (2nd pbn).
Bruce Castle Magazine. 1839.
Westminster School of Industry. [An Ackermann colourprint. c. 1840].
Smith, A. J. A concise history of Berkhampstead. Hertford 1842.
Charter, Act of Parliament, By-laws and Regulations of the Foundling Hospital. 1843.
Liverpool Collegiate Institution: origin and progress. 1843.
Sandford, John. Parochialia: or church, school and parish. 1845.
[Williamson, R.] A short account of the discipline, studies and examinations, prizes etc of Westminster School. 1845. Anon; rptd from Quart Jnl of Education.
Confessions of an Etonian, by J. E. M. 1846.
The legacy of an Etonian. Ed R. Nolands, Cambridge 1846.
Wordsworth, Charles. Christian boyhood at a public school: a collection of sermons and lectures delivered at Winchester College. 2 vols 1846.
Guthrie, Thomas. Plea for ragged schools. Edinburgh 1847.
  Seed-time and harvest of ragged schools. Edinburgh 1860. *See* Edinburgh Rev 85 1847.
[Roper, W. J. D.] Chronicles of Charterhouse, by a Carthusian. 1847.
Murray, A. M. Remarks on education. 1847. On Charity Schools. Miss Murray co-operated in founding Queen's College London, 1848.
Creasy, Sir Edward Shepherd. Some account of Eton. 1848. *See* Edinburgh Rev 113 1861.
  Memoirs of eminent Etonians, with notices on the early history of Eton College. 1850.
Hall, Peter. An historical guide to Wimborne, with a particular account of Queen Elizabeth's Free Grammar School. 1848, 1853 (2nd edn).
Manchester Free Grammar School, by an old scholar. 1849.
Steven, W. History of the High School of Edinburgh. 1849. *See* Edinburgh Rev 15 1812.
Notices on the early history of Eton College. 1850.
Reformatory schools. Edinburgh Rev 94 1851, 101 1855.
List of Queen's Scholars of St Peter's College Westminster since 1663. 1852.
Sarah Nowell's endowed charity school in Iffley. Oxford 1854.
Sewell, William. A year's sermons preached in St Peter's College Radley. 2 vols Oxford 1854–69.
Vaughan, Charles John. A letter to the Viscount Palmerston on the monitorial system of Harrow School. 1854. *See* Earl of Galloway, Observations on the abused reform of the monitorial system 1854; Remarks addressed to Dr Vaughan by Anti-Monitor, 1854; A few words on the monitorial system, by one who was a monitor, 1854.
Close, Francis. High Church education, delusive and dangerous: being an exposition of the system adopted by W. Sewell. 1855.
Goulburn, Edward Heyrick. The book of Rugby School: history and daily life. 1856. *See* Quart Rev 102 1857.
Harper, A. History of the Cheltenham Grammar School from 1851. Cheltenham 1856.
Hasenbeth, F. C. Sedgley Park School: history. 1856.
Farrar, F. W. On some defects in public school education. 1857.
K. H. [Herbert Kynaston]. Lays of the seven half centuries. 1859.
Coleridge, Sir John Taylor. Public school education: a lecture at Tiverton. 1860. *See* Edinburgh Rev 113 1861; Quart Rev 108 1860; Paterfamilias, *below*.
The Eton observer: a miscellany conducted by present Etonians. Eton 1860.
Paterfamilias [Matthew G. Higgins, alias Jacob Omnium?]. Letters. Cornhill Mag May, Dec 1860, Mar 1861.
Etonian. Thoughts on Eton suggested by Sir John Coleridge's speech at Tiverton. 1861.
Johnson, William [Cory]. Eton reform. 1861. *See* Edinburgh Rev 113 1861.
  Hints for Eton Masters. 1862, 1898.

Moberly, George. Five short letters to Sir William Heathcote on the studies and discipline of public schools. 1861.
Social science: Cassell's prize essays by working men and women. 1861.
The Eton College Chron. No 1, 14 May 1863–no 1,000, 5 Mar 1903.
Stapylton, H. E. C. Eton School lists 1791–1850. 1864; Appendix 1853–6–9, Eton 1868; Second appendix 1862–5–8, 1871–4–7, London and Eton College 1884.
School foundations and class education. 1865.
Sidebotham, J. S. Memorials of the King's School Canterbury. Canterbury 1865.
Staunton, Howard. The great schools of England. 1865.
[Collins, W. L.] The public schools; Winchester, Westminster, Shrewsbury, Harrow, Rugby. Edinburgh 1868.
'An old Cheltonian'. Reminiscences of Cheltenham College. 1868.
Haig Brown, W. (ed). Sertum Carthusainum floribus seculorum contextum 1620–1869. 1870.
Mansfield, R. B. School-life at Winchester College. 1870.
Recollections of Eton, by an Etonian. 1870.
Bedford, F. W. History of the George Heriot's Hospital. Edinburgh? 1872.
How not to do it as exemplified by the Skinners in their government of Tonbridge School, by an old Tonbridgean. [1873].
The endowed schools debate and the alleged neglect of the Skinners' scheme. [1874].
Maxwell Lyte, H. C. A history of Eton College. 1875.
Blanch, W. H. Dulwich College and Edward Alleyn. 1877.
Conybeare, J. C. To the Governors of Tonbridge School. [1877]. *See* Edinburgh Rev 36 1822.
Cox, T. History of the Heath Grammar School, Halifax. 1879.
Rowntree, T. S. A sketch of the history of Ackworth School. 1879.
Thompson, H. History of Ackworth School during its first hundred years. Ackworth 1879.
G[erard], J. Memorials of Stonyhurst College. 1881.
Rugby School Register 1675–1904. 3 vols 1881–1904.
Claridge, W. Origin and history of Bradford Grammar School from its foundation to Christmas 1882. Bradford 1882.
Gaskall, C. M. Records of an Eton schoolboy. 1883.
The leaflet, by members of Rugby School. Rugby 1883–7.
Seven years at Eton 1857–64. Ed J. B. Richards 1883.
Forshall, F. H. Westminster School, past and present. 1884.
Cotterell, C. C. Suggestive reforms in public schools. 1885.
Mozley, Rev Thomas. Reminiscences chiefly of towns, villages and schools. 2 vols 1885.
A short account of the Marylebone Charity School. 1885.
Thornton, Percy M. Harrow School and its surroundings. 1885.
Bowen, Edward E. Harrow songs. 1886.
Pearman, A. J. Ashford: its College and Grammar School. 1886.
Clifton College Register 1862–87, compiled by E. M. Oakley. 1887, 1890. With preface by J. M. Wilson.
Graham, J. W. Our need of a new public school. 1887.
Gibbs, A. E. Historical records of St Albans, containing the history of the Grammar School. 1888.
Wilkinson, C. A. Reminiscences of Eton. 1888. On Keate's period.
Great public schools, by various authors. 1889.
History of Shrewsbury School from the Blakeway manuscripts and many other sources. Shrewsbury 1889.
Young, W. The history of Dulwich College to 1857, with life of Edward Alleyn. 2 vols 1889.
Bousfield, W. et al. Elementary schools: how to increase their utility – six lectures. 1890.
Drage, Geoffrey. Eton and the Empire. Eton 1890.
 Eton and the Labour question. 1894.
Mansfield College Oxford: origin and opening, by various authors. 1890.
Marlborough College Register 1843–89. 1890.
Moore, T. The education brief on behalf of voluntary schools. 1890.
Recollections of schooldays at Harrow. Manchester 1890.
Wrench, R. G. Winchester word book. Winchester 1891.
Barker, G. F. R. and A. H. Stenning. Westminster School Register 1764–1883. 1892.
Peacock, Matthew Henry. History of the Free Grammar School of Queen Elizabeth at Wakefield. Wakefield 1892.
[Tucker, William Hill]. Eton of old: or eighty years since 1811–22, by an Old Colleger. 1892.
University College School London: register 1831–91, with historical introduction by T. Orme. 1892.
The Whitgift Foundation: a sermon by E. H. Genge. Croydon 1892.
Whitgift Grammar School: history and register. Croydon 1892.
Cowie, George. Wyggeston's Hospital, Hospital Schools and Grammar Schools 1511–1893. Leicester 1893.
Lockwood, E. Early days of Marlborough College. 1893.
Magell, E. H. Educational institutes of the Religious Society of Friends. 1893.
Ward, B. History of St Edmunds College. 1893.
Winchester College and the Quarterly Review. Quart Rev 177 1893.
Danvers, F. C. et al. Williams. 1894. *See* Edinburgh Rev 27 1816, Quart Rev 179 1894.
Hipkins, F. C. Repton: village, church, priory and school. Derby [1894], Repton 1899 (as Repton and its neighbourhood).
Uppingham School Roll 1824–94. 1894. *See* Statutes of Robert Johnson, *above*.
Eardley Wilmot, E. P. and E. C. Streatfield. Charterhouse, old and new. 1895.
Fitzgerald, P. H. Stonyhurst memories. 1895.
Coleridge, A. D. Eton in the forties, by an old Colleger. 1896, 1898 (2nd edn).
Watney, J. Some account of Mercers' School. 1896.
Garstang, J. A history of Blackburn Grammar School. 1897.
John, W. [Cory]. Extracts from the letters and journals of William Cory, selected by F. W. Cornish. Oxford 1897. On Eton 1832–42, 1845–72; King's College Cambridge 1842–5.
Matthews, J. H. D. and V. Thompson. Leeds Grammar School Register 1820–96. 1897.
Morley, S. R. Studies in London Board Schools. 1897.
Sedbergh School and its Chapel. Leeds 1897.
Ford, Lionel. Public School athletics. In Essays on secondary education, ed C. Cookson, Oxford 1898.
Holman, H. English national education. 1898.
Houson, E. W. and G. T. Warner. Harrow School. 1898.
Kingswood School: history, registers of Woodhouse Grove School, by three old boys. 1898.
Minchin, J. G. Old Harrow days. 1898.
Rouse, W. H. D. A history of Rugby School. New York 1898.
 Our public schools, their influence on English history: Charterhouse, Eton, Harrow, Merchant Taylors, Rugby, St Paul's, Westminster, Winchester. 1901.
St Botolph Aldgate: the story of a City parish. Ed A. G. B. Atkinson 1898. On Sir John Cass School.
Sargeant, John. Annals of Westminster School. 1898.
Sterry, W. Annals of Eton College. 1898.
Barletot, R. G. History of Crewkerne School. 1899.
Benson, Arthur C. Fasti Etonenses: a biological history of Eton. Eton 1899.
Butler, Henry Montague. Public school sermons. 1899.
Cardwell, J. H. Story of a charity school in Soho. 1899.
Cust, L. A history of Eton College. 1899.
Fisher, G. W. Annals of Shrewsbury School. 1899.
Leach, Arthur Francis. Early Yorkshire Schools. 2 vols 1899–1903.
 A history of Winchester College. 1899.
 A history of Bradfield College, Oxford. 1900.
 History of Warwick School. 1906.

Educational charters and documents 598–1909. Cambridge 1911.
The schools of medieval England. 1915. *See* Fortnightly Rev Nov 1892.
Lubbock, A. Memories of Eton and Etonians, with boys' chances at Eton by Robert Lubbock. 1899.
Meade, L. T. A public school boy. 1899.
Spalding, T. A. The work of the London School Board. 1899.
Mockler-Ferryman, A. F. Annals of Sandhurst: a chronicle of the Royal Military College, with a sketch of the history of the Staff College. 1900.
Tod, A. H. Charterhouse. 1900.
Warner, T. R. Winchester. 1900.

Modern studies: general

Robson, A. H. The education of children engaged in industry 1833–76. 1931. Factory schools.
Rich, R. W. Training of teachers during the nineteenth century. Cambridge 1933.
Tropp, Asher. The school teachers. 1957.
Bell, E. Moberley. A history of the Church Schools Company 1883–1958. 1958.
Newsome, David. Godliness and good learning. 1961. Ideals of the public school.
Sanderson, J. M. The grammar school and the education of the poor, 1786–1840. British Jnl of Educational Stud 11 1962.
Bamford, T. W. Rise of the public schools: a study of boys' boarding schools in England and Wales from 1837 to the present day. 1967.
Sellman, R. R. Devon village schools in the nineteenth century. 1968.
Clark, E. A. G. The early ragged schools and the foundation of the ragged school union. Jnl of Educational Administration and History 1 1969.
Kitching, J. The Catholic poor schools. Jnl of Educational Administration and History 1 and 2 1969.
Rubinstein, D. School attendance in London 1870–1904: a social history. 1969.
Barnard, H. C. Were those the days. A Victorian education. 1970.
Cruickshank, M. A history of the training of teachers in Scotland. 1970.
Frow, E. and R. The half time system of education. Manchester 1970.
Goldstrom, S. M. (ed). Education: elementary education 1780–1900. 1970.
Johnson, M. Derbyshire village schools in the nineteenth century. Newton Abbott 1970.
Seaborne, M. The English school: its architecture and organisation. Vol 1: 1370–1870, 1971; vol 2: 1870–1970, 1977.
Gosden, P. H. J. H. The evolution of a profession. Oxford 1972.
Whitbread, N. The evolution of the nursery-infant school. 1972.
Percival, A. Very superior men: some early public school headmasters and their achievements. 1973.
Wadsworth, A. P. The first Manchester Sunday schools. In Essays in social history, ed M. W. Flinn and T. Smout, 1974.
Simon, B. and I. Bradley (ed). The Victorian public school: studies in the development of an educational institution. 1975.
Davies, W. The intermediate school in rural Wales, 1897–1907: the problem of school organization. Nat Lib Wales Jnl 19 1976.
Laqueur, W. Religion and respectability: Sunday schools and working class culture 1780–1850. New Haven CT 1976.
Dent, H. C. The training of teachers in England and Wales 1800–1975. 1977.
Fraser, G. (ed). The world of the public school. 1977.
Gathorne-Hardy, J. The public school phenomenon 1597–1977. 1977.
Honey, J. R. de S. Tom Brown's universe: the development of the public school in the 19th century. 1977.
Fletcher, L. The teachers' press in Britain 1802–1880. Leeds 1978.
Phillips, T. R. The elementary schools and the migratory habits of the people 1870–1890. British Jnl of Educational Stud 26 1978.
Thomas, J. B. The day training college: a Victorian innovation in teacher training. British Jnl of Teacher Education 4 1978.
Horn, P. (ed). Village education in nineteenth-century Oxfordshire: the Whitchurch School log book and other documents. Oxford 1979.
Humphries, S. Hurrah for England: schooling and the working class in Bristol, 1870–1914. Southern History 1 1979.
Dick, M. The myth of the working class Sunday school. History of Education 9 1980.
Elliott, B. The provision of reformatory schools, the landed class and the myth of the superiority of rural life in mid-Victorian England. History of Education 9 1980.
Mangan, J. A. Images of Empire in the late-Victorian public school. Jnl of Educational Administration and History 12 1980.
Burnett, J. (ed). Destiny obscure: autobiographies of childhood, education and freedom: a study of nineteenth-century working class autobiography. 1981. Throws light on the schooling of the poor.
Digby, A. and P. Searby. Children, school and society in nineteenth-century England. 1981. Includes documentary extracts.
Humphries, S. Hooligans or rebels? An oral history of working-class childhood and youth 1889–1939. Oxford 1981. Oral recollections of elementary and reformatory schools.
Mangan, J. A. Athleticism in the Victorian and Edwardian public school: the emergence and consolidation of an educational ideology. Cambridge 1981.
Timmons, G. T. Secondary education in Coventry in the late 19th century. Jnl of Educational Administration and History 13 1981.
Bergen, B. H. Only a schoolmaster: gender, class and the effort to professionalise elementary teaching in England, 1870–1910. History of Education Quart 22 1982.
Clark, E. A. G. The last of the voluntaryists: the Ragged School Union in the school board era. History of Education 11 1982.
Searby, P. (ed). Educating the Victorian middle class. History of Education Soc 1982. Includes chs on girls' schools, preparatory schools, schools for lower middle class children, and the local boys at Harrow School.
Stephens, W. B. Schooling and literacy in rural England, 1800–1914. History of Education Quart 22 1982.
Ball, N. Educating the people. A documentary history of elementary schooling in England 1840–1870. 1983.
Brown, C. M. Lancashire industrialists and their schools 1833–1902. Jnl of Educational Administration and History 15 1983.
Chandos, J. Boys together: English public schools 1800–1864. 1983.
Clark, A. Victorian schools. 1983.
Gardner, P. W. The lost elementary schools of Victorian England: the people's education. 1984.
Hurt, J. Reformatory and industrial schools before 1933. History of Education 13 1984.
Leinster-Mackay, D. The rise of the English prep school. 1984.
McCrone, K. Play up! Play up! And play the game. Sport at the Victorian public school. Jnl of Br Stud 23 1984.
Anderson, R. Sunday schools and Scottish society in the 19th century. Past and Present 109 1985.
Ellis, A. Educating our masters. 1985. History of school reading books in the nineteenth century.
Mason, D. M. School attendance in 19th century Scotland. Economic History Rev 38 1985. *See also* the reply by R. D. Anderson, in this vol.
Unwin, R. W. Alternative educational establishments in an English market town, 1830–70. Jnl of Educational Administration and History 17 1985. Anglican and Wesleyan day schools.
Bryant, M. The London experience of secondary education. 1986. Chs 4–9 for London schools in the nineteenth century.
Clamp, P. G. Robert J. Saunders, factory inspector and his national factory schools experiment, 1841–1843. Jnl of Educational Administration and History 18 1986.

Davidson, L. M. School attendance and the school attendance committee: the East and North Ridings of Yorkshire, 1876–1880. Jnl of Educational Administration and History 18 1986.

Mitch, D. F. The impact of subsidies to elementary schools on enrolment rates in 19th century England. Economic History Rev 39 1986.

Roach, J. A. Boys and girls at school 1800–70. History of Education 15 1986.

Roach, J. A. A history of secondary education in England. 1986. (Endowed, private and public schools).

Rubinstein, W. D. Education and the social origins of the British elites 1880–1927. Past and Present 112 1986. Argument about the role of public schools.

Hills, P. Education and evangelisation: Presbyterian missions in mid nineteenth century Glasgow. Scottish History Rev 66 1987.

Piggot, D. Problems of staffing the nineteenth century rural school in England. History of Education 16 1987.

Chinn, C. Was separate schooling a means of class segregation in late-Victorian and Edwardian Birmingham? Midland History 13 1988.

Shrosbree, C. Public schools and private education. The Clarendon Commission, 1861–64 and the Public Schools Acts. Manchester 1988.

Heward, C. The class relations of compulsory school attendance: the Birmingham jewellery quarter 1851–86. History of Education Quart 29 1989.

Horn, P. The Victorian and Edwardian schoolchild. Gloucester 1989.

Marsden, W. E. 'Mrs Walker's merry games for little people': locating Froebel in an alien environment. British Jnl of Educational Stud 38 1989. Infant schools.

Rich, P. J. Elixir of Empire: the English public schools: ritualism, freemasonry and Imperialism. 1989.

Berghoff, Elmut. Public schools and the decline of the British economy, 1870–1914. Past and Present 129 1990.

Stannard, K. P. Ideology, education and social structure: elementary schooling in mid Victorian England. History of Education 19 1990.

Thomas, J. B. Victorian beginnings. In British universities and teacher education. A century of change, ed Thomas, 1990.

Gardner, P. W. 'Our schools'; 'their schools'. The case of Eliza Duckworth and John Stevenson. History of Education 20 1991.

Gibson, W. The social origins and education of an elite: the nineteenth-century episcopate. History of Education 20 1991. Includes an analysis of schools attended.

Griggs, C. The National Union of Teachers in the Eastbourne area 1874–1916: a tale of tact and pragmaticism. History of Education 20 1991.

Hirst, D. J. Public health and the public elementary schools, 1870–1907. History of Education 20 1991.

Martin, J. 'Hard-headed and large-hearted': women and the industrial schools, 1870–1885. History of Education 20 1991.

Roach, J. A. Secondary education in England 1870–1902: public activity and private enterprise. 1991.

Springhall, J. 'Boys of Bircham School': the penny dreadful origins of the popular English school story, 1867–1900. History of Education 20 1991.

Cale, M. Working for God? Staffing the Victorian reformatory and industrial school system. History of Education 21 1992.

Evans, W. G. Gender stereotyping and the training of elementary school teachers: the experience of Victorian Wales. History of Education 21 1992.

Seaborne, M. Schools in Wales: 1500–1900 – a social and architectural history. 1992.

Albissetti, J. C. The feminisation of teaching in the nineteenth century: a comparative perspective. History of Education 22 1993.

Bartle, G. F. The impact of the British and Foreign School Society on elementary education in the main textile areas of the industrial north. History of Education 22 1993.

Heward, C. Men and women and the rise of professional society: the intriguing history of teacher educators. History of Education 22 1993.

Leinster-Mackay, D. The origins of the incorporated association of preparatory schools and its early concerns: a centennial acknowledgement. History of Education 22 1993.

Robinson, W. Pupil teachers: the Achilles heel of the higher grade girls' schools 1882–1904? History of Education 22 1993.

Fletcher, J. Hiram's Hospital revisited: a further exploration of a byway of early Victorian history. History of Education 23 1994.

Taylor, T. As the old cocks crow, the younger ones learn: the school strikes of 1889 and the new union movement. History of Education 23 1994.

Thody, A. M. School management in nineteenth-century elementary schools: a day in the life of a headteacher. History of Education 23 1994.

Jenkins, E. (ed). Studies in the history of education. Leeds 1995. Nineteenth century topics include preparatory schools and the development of school management.

Betts, R. 'Tried as in a furnace': the National Union of Teachers and the abolition of the school boards, 1896–1903. History of Education 25 1996.

Copelman, Dina M. London's women teachers: gender, class and feminism 1870–1930. 1996.

Willis, R. Professional autonomy or state sponsorship: the dilemmas for private teachers in their campaign for registration in Victorian England. History of Education 25 1996.

Cook, L. A. The contribution of nonconformity to elementary education in Swansea from the mid-Victorian era to the end of the nineteenth century. History of Education 26 1997.

Coppock, D. A. Respectability as a prerequisite of moral character: the social and occupational mobility of pupil teachers in the late nineteenth and early twentieth centuries. History of Education 26 1997.

Modern studies: individual schools and colleges

Bates, H. and A. Wells. A history of Shrewsbury High School. 1962.

Zebedee, D. H. Lincoln Diocesan Training College 1862–1962. Lincoln 1962.

Stack, V. E. Oxford High School. 1963.

Bishop, T. J. H. Winchester and the public school elite. 1967.

Hope Simpson, J. B. Rugby since Arnold: a history of Rugby School from 1842. 1967.

Silver, P. and H. Silver. The history of a national school, 1824–1974. 1974.

Baker, D. Partnership in excellence: a late-Victorian educational venture: the Leys school, Cambridge, 1875–1975. Cambridge 1975.

Bradbury, J. L. Chester College and the training of teachers. Chester College 1975.

Cox, M. A history of Sir John Deans's grammar school, Northwich. Manchester 1975.

May, T. The history of the Harrow County School for Boys. Harrow School 1975.

Morris, J. A. A history of the Latymer School at Edmonton. Trustees of the Latymer Foundation 1975.

Bartle, G. F. A history of Borough Road College. 1976.

Berry, M. H. A. and J. H. Higginson (ed). Canterbury chapters: a Kentish heritage for tomorrow. Canterbury 1976.

Tozer, M. Physical education at Thrings Uppingham. Uppingham 1976.

Parsons, C. Schools in an urban community: a study of Carsbrook 1870–1965. 1978.

McGregor, G. P. Bishop Otter College and policy for teaching education, 1839–1980. 1981.
Rose, Martial. A history of King Alfred's College, Winchester, 1840–1980. 1981.
Thomas, D. H. The Chester industrial school 1863–1940. Jnl of Educational Administration and History 13 1981.
Allthorpe-Guyton, M. with J. Stevens. A happy eye. A school of art in Norwich 1845–1982. 1982.
Cowie, E. E. Stephen Hawtrey and a working-class Eton. History of Education 11 1982.
Seed, J. Manchester College, York: an early nineteenth century Dissenting Academy. Jnl of Educational Administration and History 14 1982.
Jenkins, E. W. 'A magnificent pile': a centenary history of the Leeds Central High School, Leeds. Leeds 1985.
Simpson, P. Education for profit: the proprietorial schools of Bath in the 19th and 20th centuries. Jnl of Educational Administration and History 18 1986.
Ball, J. and W. Ball. Stockport Grammar School, 1487–1987. Congleton 1987.
Lyon, N. B. Four centuries: the history of Wellingborough School. The School 1988.
Tozer, M. 'The readiest hand and most open heart': Uppingham's first mission to the poor. History of Education 18 1988.
Lewis, J. The village school. 1989.
Bentley, J. Dare to be wise. A history of the Manchester Grammar School. 1990.
Leach, C. A school at Shrewsbury. The four foundations. 1990.
Mead, A. H. A miraculous draft of fishes: a history of St Paul's School 1509–1990. 1990.
Hinde, T. Imps of promise: a history of King's School, Canterbury. 1991.
McGregor, G. P. A church college for the 21st century? 150 years of Ripon and York St John 1841–1991. A study of policy and its absence. York, 1991.
Quick, A. Charterhouse: a history of the school. 1991.
More, C. The training of teachers, 1847–1947: a history of the church colleges at Cheltenham. 1992.
More, C. 'A splendid college'. An illustrated history of teacher training in Cheltenham 1847–1990. 1992.
Harrison, M. M. and W. B. Marker (ed). Teaching the teachers: the history of Jordanhill College of Education, 1828–1993. 1996.

(3) ADULT AND TECHNICAL EDUCATION

Sources

Pole, Thomas. History of the origin and progress of Adult Schools. 1814, 1816 (enlarged).
Winks, J. F. History of Adult Schools. Gainsborough 1821. Only known copy in Leicester City Lib.
Place, Francis. Improvement of the working people. 1834.
Baker, C. Mechanics' Institutes and Libraries. 1837 (Central Soc of Education, 1st pbn). *See* Quart Rev 32 1825.
Duppa, B. F. A manual for Mechanics' Institutes. 1839. *See* T. Coates, *below*.
Coates, T. Report on the state of Mechanics' Institutes. 1841. *See* R. B. Litchfield, Working Men's College Mag 1860.
Ellis, William. Education as a means of preventing destitution, with exemplifications from the teaching of the conditions of well-being and the principles of economic science at the Birkbeck Schools. 1851.
Hudson, J. W. History of adult education. 1851. With reasons for decline of Mechanics' Institutes in some areas.
Hole, J. History and management of Literary, Scientific and Mechanics' Institutes. 1853.
Maurice, F. D. Learning and working. 1853.
On the representation and education of the People. 1866. *See* The Working Men's College 1854–1904, ed J. L. Davies 1904.
Report of the Society of Arts on industrial instruction. 1853.
Fitzwyram, J. Introduction of industrial work into village schools: an experiment at Shipsbourne Kent. 1859.
Jones, H. B. The Royal Institution: its founder and its first professors. 1871.
Galloway, R. Education, scientific and technical. 1881.
Godard, J. G. George Birkbeck: the pioneer of popular education. 1884.
Edwards, F. W. Technical education: its rise and progress, including recommendations to the Royal Commission. 1885. *See* Quart Rev 165 1887.
Industrial education. 1888.
Commercial education, including a review of commercial schools on the Continent. 1889.
Magnus, Sir Philip. Industrial education. 1888.
Mackinder, H. J. and M. E. Sadler. University extension, past, present and future. 1891.
Roberts, R. D. Eighteen years of university extension. 1891.
Sexton, A. H. The first Technical College. 1894.
White, W. (of Edgbaston). Our Jubilee year 1895: the story of the Severn Street and Priory Firstday schools, Birmingham. 1895. *See* Memoirs of Joseph Sturge; Alexander Peckover, Life of Joseph Sturge, in Memoirs, *below*.
Rowntree, J. W. and H. B. Binns. A history of the Adult School movement. 1903. Revised edn with introd by C. Charlton. Nottingham 1985.

Modern studies

Argles, M. South Kensington to Robbins: an account of English scientific and technical education since 1851. 1965.
Rowbotham, S. The call to University extension teaching 1873–1900. Univ of Birmingham Historical Jnl 12 1969.
Tyrell, A. Political economy, Whiggism and the education of working-class adults in Scotland 1817–40. Scottish History Rev 48 1969.
Kelly, T. A history of adult education in Great Britain. Liverpool 1970 (2nd edn), 1992 (3rd edn).
Roderick, G. W. and M. D. Stephens. Scientific and technical education in nineteenth-century England. Newton Abbot 1973.
Porter, J. (ed). Education and labour in the South-West. Exeter 1976.
Skingsley, T. A. Technical training and education in the English printing industry: a study of late nineteenth-century attitudes. Jnl of the Printing Historical Soc 13 1978–9, 14 1979–80.
Heward, C. Industry, cleanliness and Godliness: sources and problems in the history of scientific and technical education and the working classes 1850–1910. Stud in Science Education 7 1980.
Inkster, I. The public lecture as an instrument in science education for adults: Great Britain 1750–1850. Paedagogica Historica 20 1980.
Johnson, R. Really useful knowledge: radical education and working class culture, 1790–1848. In John Clarke, C. Cricher and R. Johnson, Working-class culture: studies in history and theory, 1980.
Stephens, W. B. Adult education and society in an industrial town: Warrington, 1800–1900. Exeter 1980.
Marriott, J. Stuart. A backstairs to a degree: demands for an open university in late Victorian England. Leeds 1981.
Rowbotham, S. Travellers in a strange country: responses of working-class students to the University extension movement, 1873–1910. History Workshop 12 1981.
Roderick, G. W. and M. D. Stephens (ed). Where did we go wrong? Industrial performance, education and the economy in Victorian Britain. 1981.
Ahlstrom, Goran. Engineers and industrial growth: higher techni-

cal education and the engineering profession during the nineteenth and early twentieth centuries: France, Germany, Sweden and England. 1982.
Devereux, W. A. Adult education in inner London 1870–1980. Inner London Education Authority 1982.
Floud, R. C. Technical education and economic performance: Britain, 1850–1914. Albion 14 1982.
Heward, C. Education, examinations and the artisans. In Days of judgement, ed R. McLeod, 1982.
Marriott, J. Stuart. The whisky money and the University extension movement. Jnl of Educational Administration and History 15 1983.
Harrop, S. A. Adult education and literacy: the importance of post-school education for literacy levels in the eighteenth and nineteenth centuries. History of Education 13 1984.
Marriott, J. Stuart. Extramural empires: service and self interest in English university adult education 1813–1983. Nottingham 1984.
Garner A. D. The Society of Arts and the Mechanics' Institutes: the co-ordination of endeavour towards scientific and technical education, 1851–54. History of Education 14 1985.
Inkster, I. (ed). The steam intellect society: essays on culture, education and industry c. 1820–1914. Nottingham 1985.
Marriott, J. Stuart. University extension lecturers: the organisation of extra mural employment in England 1873–1914. Leeds 1985.
Radcliffe, C. J. Mutual improvement societies in the West Riding of Yorkshire 1835–1900. Jnl of Educational Administration and History 18 1986.
Roderick, G. W. Education, culture and industry in Wales in the nineteenth century. Welsh History Rev 13 1987.
Lysons, K. Passport to employment: a history of the London Chamber of Commerce's education and industry scheme 1887–1987. 1988.
History of Education Soc. Education and employment: initiatives and experiences 1780 to the present. 1989.
Sharp, P. R. Victorian values and the private funding of education – the case of the schools of art in the 1860s. Jnl of Educational Administration and History 21 1989.
Watson, M. I. Mutual improvement societies in nineteenth century Lancashire. Jnl of Educational Administration and History 21 1989.
Evans, G. W. The Welsh Intermediate and Technical Education Act, 1889: a centenary appreciation. History of Education 19 1990.
Hennock, E. P. Technological education in England, 1850–1926: the uses of a German model. History of Education 19 1990.
Roderick, G. W. Industry, technical manpower and education: South Wales in the nineteenth century. History of Education 19 1990.
Summerfield, P. and E. J. Evans. Technical education and the state since 1850: historical and contemporary perspectives. Manchester 1990.
Flett, K. Sex or class revisited: the education of working class women and men in mid nineteenth-century England. History of Education 24 1995. *See also* the response by J. Purvis in this issue.
Green, A. Technical education and state formation in nineteenth-century England and France. History of Education 24 1995.
Donnelly, J. F. Getting technical: the vicissitudes of academic industrial chemistry in nineteenth-century Britain. History of Education 26 1997.

Modern studies: colleges and institutes

Harrison, J. F. C. A history of the London Working Men's College 1854–1954. 1954.
Tylecote, M. The Mechanics' Institutes of Lancashire and Yorkshire before 1851. 1957.
Salt, J. The creation of the Sheffield Mechanics' Institute: educational advance and social pressures in an industrial town. The Vocational Aspect of Education 18 1966.
Royle, E. Mechanics' Institutes and the working classes, 1840–1860. Historical Jnl 14 1971.
Cardwell, D. S. L. Artisan to graduate: essays to commemorate the foundation in 1824 of the Manchester Mechanics' Institute, now in 1974 the University of Manchester Institute of Science and Technology. Manchester 1974.
Thackray, Arnold. Natural knowledge in a cultural context: the Manchester model. American Historical Rev 79 1974.
Inkster, I. The social context of an educational movement: a revisionist approach to the English mechanics' institutes. Oxford Rev of Education 3 1976.
Silver, H. and S. J. Teague (ed). Chelsea College. 1977.
Abel, E. K. Toynbee Hall, 1884–1914. Social Service Rev 1979.
Attfield, J. With light of knowledge: a hundred years of education in the Royal Arsenal Co-operative Society, 1877–1977. 1981.
Evans, R. A. The University and the city: the educational work of Toynbee Hall. 1884–1914. History of Education 11 1982.
Hall, A. R. Science for industry: a short history of the Imperial College of Science and Technology and its antecedents. 1982.
Garner, A. D. and E. W. Jenkins. The English Mechanics' Institutes: the case of Leeds 1824–42. History of Education 13 1984.
Katoh, Shoji. Mechanics' Institutes in Great Britain to the 1850s. Jnl of Educational Administration and History 21 1989.
Bourne, R. and P. Latham. Artifex semper auxilio: a century of vocational education in south east London. Lewisham College 1991.
Cuddy, B. and T. Mansell. The Royal Engineering College at Cooper's Hill. History of Education 23 1994.

(4) EDUCATION OF WOMEN AND GIRLS

Sources

Lackington, James. Confessions. 1804.
[More, Hannah]. Hints towards forming the character of a young Princess. 2 vols 1805. *See* Edinburgh Rev 7 1805.
Broadhurst, T. Advice to young ladies on the improvement of the mind. 1808. *See* Edinburgh Rev 15 1810.
Smith, Sydney. Female education. 1810.
West, J. Letters to a young lady. 3 vols 1811.
'Domina' [Barbara Hofland?]. York House: conversations in a Ladies' School, principally founded on facts. 1813.
Remarks on female education adapted particularly to the regulation of schools. 1823.
Broadhurst, F. A word in favour of female schools. Pamphleteer 27 1826.
'An experienced teacher'. The complete governess: a course of mental instruction for ladies. 1826.
Sinclair, C. Modern accomplishments or the march of intellect. 1836, 1837.
 Modern society: conclusion of Modern accomplishments. 1837.
[Duppa, B. F.] Scottish Institution for the education of young ladies. 1837 (Central Soc of Education, 1st pbn).
Ellis, Lady M. The education of young ladies for other occupations than teaching. 1838 (Central Soc of Education, 2nd pbn).
By a lady. The young lady's friend: a manual of practical advice and instructions to young females on their entering upon the duties of life after quitting school. 1840 (3rd edn).
Maurice, J. F. D. Queen's College London: its object and method. 1848. *See* Quart Rev 84 1848, 86 1850.
 A letter to the Bishop of London in reply to the article in no 172 [96 1850] of the Quarterly Review. 1850.
 Plan of a female college. Cambridge 1855.
 Lectures to ladies on practical subjects. 1855. Introductory lecture.
Grey, Mrs W. and E. A. E. Shirreff. Thoughts on self-culture addressed to women. 2 vols 1850.
Parkes, B. R. Remarks on the education of girls. 1854.

Booth, James. On the female education of the industrious classes. 1855.
[Bülow, Baroness M. von]. Women's educational mission: an explanation of Froebel's infant gardens. 1855.
Shirreff, E. A. E. Intellectual education and its influence on women. 1858.
The work of the National Union. 1873.
The Kindergarten: principles of Froebel's system and their bearing on the education of women. 1876. *See* Mrs W. Grey, *below*.
Women's education. Edinburgh Rev 109 1859.
Shailer, W. The young woman's companion or female instructor. Halifax 1861.
Cobbe, F. P. Female education and how it would be effected by university examinations. 1862 (Social Science Congress).
Life as told by herself. 1904.
Davies, Emily. On secondary instruction relating to girls. 1864.
The application of funds to the education of girls. 1865.
Higher education of women. 1866.
Women in the universities of England and Scotland. Cambridge 1896.
Thoughts on some questions relating to women 1860–1908. 1910.
Stephen, B. Emily Davies and Girton College. 1927.
Bennett, D. Emily Davies and the liberation of women, 1830–1921. 1990.
Fitch, Sir Joshua. The education of women. Victoria Mag Mar 1864.
Address on the College for Working Women. 1872.
Women and the universities. Contemporary Rev Aug 1890.
Reports on women's training colleges. 1886–93.
Hodgson, William B. The education of girls considered in connexion with university local examinations: a lecture. 1864.
Ruskin, J. Queens' Gardens. In his Sesame and lilies, 1865.
Sewell, E. M. Principles of education applied to female education in the upper classes. 2 vols 1865, 1 vol 1914 (abridged).
The reign of pedantry in girls' schools. Nineteenth Cent 23 1888.
See P. Comenius, Innocent femina sensualis in unconscious conflict, *in* Suffer and be still: women in the Victorian Age, *ed M. Vicinus, Bloomington IN 1973*.
Beale, Dorothea. On the education of girls. Fraser's Mag 74 1866.
Reports issued by the Schools Inquiry Commission on the education of girls. 1869.
On the organisation of girls' day schools. 1873 (Social Science Congress).
Girls' schools past and present. Nineteenth Cent 23 1888.
Work and play in girls' schools. 1898, 1901. With L. H. M. Soulsby and J. F. Dove.
Addresses to teachers. 1908.
See Cheltenham Ladies' College Mag *1890–1*.
Raikes, E. Dorothea Beale of Cheltenham (1831–1905). 1908.
Shillito, E. H. Dorothea Beale. 1920.
Steadman, F. C. In the days of Miss Beale: a study of her work and influence. 1931.
Faithful, L. M. In the house of my pilgrimage. 1924. Lilian Faithful became headmistress of Cheltenham College in 1906.
Clarke, A. K. A history of the Cheltenham Ladies' College [1853–1953]. 1953.
Airy, George B. The history and position of the Blue Coat Girls' School, Greenwich. 1867.
Hill, Florence D. Children of the state: the training of juvenile paupers. 1868; ed F. Fowke 1889. *See* Edinburgh Rev 142 1875.
Education of girls and employment of women of the upper classes. 1869 (2nd edn).
Butler, J. E. (ed). Woman's work and woman's culture. 1869.
Mill, John Stuart. The subjection of women. 1869. *See* Edinburgh Rev 130 1869.
Wolstenholme, E. C. The education of girls: its present and future. In J. E. Butler, *above*.
Grey, Mrs W. (Maria Georgina Grey, née Shirreff). The education of women. 1871.
Fawcett, M. G. Free education in its economic aspect: Schools Inquiry Commission on the education of girls – education of women. In H. and M. G. Fawcett, Essays and lectures on social and political subjects, Cambridge 1872.
Gurney, M. Are we to have education for middle-class girls? The history of Camden Collegiate Schools. 1872.
Somerville, Mary. Personal recollections and selections from correspondence. 1873. *See* Quart Rev 136 1874.
Maudsley, H. Sex in mind and education. 1874.
Anderson, E. G. Sex in education: a reply 1874. *See* Edinburgh Rev 166 1887.
Alderley, Lady Stanley. Personal recollections of women's education. Nineteenth Cent 6 1879.
Bryant, Sophie. Over-work from the teachers' point of view. 1885.
An account of the North London Collegiate School. 1886. *See* Edinburgh Rev 166 1887.
Educational ends or the ideal of personal development. 1907.
Scrigmour, R. M. (ed). The North London Collegiate School 1850–1950. 1950.
Pfeiffer, E. Women and work: relation to health and physical development of the Higher Education. 1888.
Ridley, A. E. Frances Mary Buss and her work for education. 1895. *See* F. M. Buss, Leaves from her note-book, by S. G. Toplis 1896; E. M. Hill and S. Bryant, Frances Mary Buss Schools' Jubilee Record, 1900.
Bremner, G. S. Education of girls and women in Great Britain. 1897.
Frances, E. G. (Countess of Warwick) et al. Progress in women's education in the British Isles. In Report of the education section, Victorian era exhibition 1897–8.
Zimmern, Alice. Renaissance of girls' education in England. 1898.
Burstall, S. English high schools for girls. 1911.
(ed). Public schools for girls. 1911. With M. A. Douglas.
James, M. E. Alice Ottley, first headmistress of the Worcester High School for Girls, 1883–1912. 1914.

Modern studies (since 1960)

Kamm, J. Hope deferred: girls' education in English history. 1965.
Bradbrook, M. C. 'That infidel place': a short history of Girton College 1869–1969. 1969.
Burstyn, J. N. Education and sex. The medical case against higher education for women in England, 1870–1900. Past and Present 117 1973.
Richardson, J. The great revolution: women's education in Victorian times. History Today 24 1974.
McWilliams-Tullberg, R. Women at Cambridge: a men's university – though of a mixed type. 1975.
Pederson, J. S. The reform of women's secondary and higher education: institutional change and social values in mid and late Victorian England. History of Education Quart Spring 1975.
Dyehouse, C. Social Darwinist ideas and the development of women's education in England, 1880–1920. History of Education 5 1976.
Pederson, J. S. Schoolmistresses and headmistresses: elites and education in nineteenth-century England. Jnl of British Stud 15 1976.
Burstyn, J. N. Women's education in England during the nineteenth century: a review of the literature 1970–1976. History of Education 6 1977.
Dyehouse, C. Good wives and little mothers: social anxieties and the schoolgirl's curriculum, 1880–1920. Oxford Rev of Education 3 1977.
Delamont, S. The domestic ideology and women's education. In The nineteenth-century woman, ed S. Delamont and L. Duffin, 1978.
Bryant, M. The unexpected revolution: a study in the history of the

education of women and girls in the nineteenth century. Univ of London, Inst of Education 1979.
Burstyn, J. N. Victorian Education and the ideal of womanhood. 1980.
Fletcher, S. Feminists and bureaucrats: a study in the development of girls' education in the nineteenth century. Cambridge 1980.
Moore, L. Aberdeen and the higher education of women 1868–1977. Aberdeen Univ Rev 48 1980.
Watts, R. E. The Unitarian contribution to the development of female education, 1790. 1850. History of Education 9 1980.
Widdowson, F. Going up into the next class: women and elementary teacher training 1840–1914. Women's Research and Resources Centre Pbns 1980.
Dyehouse, C. Girls growing up in late Victorian and Edwardian England. 1981.
Kersey, S. N. (ed). Classics in the education of girls and women. 1981.
Pederson, J. S. Some Victorian headmistresses: a conservative tradition of social reform. VS 24 1981.
Purvis, J. The double burden of class and gender in the schooling of working class girls in nineteenth-century England. In Schools, teachers and teaching, ed L. Barton and S. Walker, Lewes 1981.
Purvis, J. Women and teaching in the nineteenth century. In Education and the state, ed R. Dale et al, 1981.
Purvis, J. 'Women's life is essentially domestic, public life being confined to men' (Comte): separate spheres and inequality in the education of working-class women, 1854–1900. History of Education 10 1981.
Digby, A. New schools for the middle class girl. In P. Searby, Educating the Victorian middle class. History of Education Soc 1982.
Fletcher, S. Co-education and the Victorian grammar school. History of Education 11 1982.
Aldrich, R. Educating our mistresses. History of Education 12 1983.
Purvis, J. Towards a history of women's education in nineteenth-century Britain. In Achievement and inequality in education, ed J. Purvis, M. Hale et al, 1983.
Fletcher, S. Women first: the female tradition in English physical education, 1880–1980. 1984.
Moore, L. Invisible scholars: girls learning Latin and Mathematics in the elementary public schools of Scotland before 1872. History of Education 13 1984.
Atkinson, P. Strong minds and weak bodies: sports, gymnastics and the medicalisation of women's education. British Jnl of Sports History 2 1985.
Fletcher, S. The making and breaking of female tradition: women's physical education in England, 1880–1980. British Jnl of Sports History 2 1985.
History of Education Soc. The education of women and girls. 1985.
Howarth, J. Public schools, safety nets and educational ladders: the classification of girls' secondary schools 1880–1914. Oxford Rev of Education 11 1985.
Montgomery, F. A. Edge Hill College: a history 1885–1985. 1985.
Purvis, J.(ed). The education of girls and women. History of Education Soc 1985.
Burns, J. From polite knowledge to useful knowledge. History Today 1986.
Cockerill, J. Second chance: the story of Hillcroft College, the residential working women's college. Hillcroft 1986.
Griffin, P. (ed). St Hugh's: one hundred years of women's education in Oxford. 1986.
Hunt, F. (ed). Lessons for life – the schooling of girls and women 1850–1950. Oxford 1987.
Pederson, J. S. The reform of girls' secondary and higher education in Victorian England: a study of elites and educational change. 1987.
Gomershall, M. Ideals and realities: the education of working-class girls, 1800–1870. History of Education 17 1988.
Harrop, S. The Merchant Taylors' school for girls, Crosby: one hundred years of achievement, 1888–1988. Liverpool 1988.
Horn, P. The education and employment of working-class girls, 1870–1914. History of Education 17 1988.
McCrone, K. E. Sport and the physical emancipation of English women 1870–1914. 1988.
Theobald, M. R. The accomplished woman and the propriety of intellect: a new look at women's education in Britain and Australia, 1800–1850. History of Education 17 1988.
Thomas, J. B. University College, Bristol: a pioneering teacher training for women. History of Education 17 1988.
Flett, K. Sex or class: the education of working class women, 1800–1870. History of Education 18 1989. *See also* the responses of J. Purvis and M. Gomershall in this vol.
Purvis, J. Hard lessons: the lives and education of working-class women in nineteenth-century England. Cambridge MA 1989.
Summerfield, P. (ed). Women, education and the professions. History of Education Soc 1989. Two nineteenth-century essays: Women university students and Sexual politics in the NUT.
Myers, G. Science for women and children: the dialogue of popular science in the nineteenth century. In Nature transformed: science and literature 1700–1900, ed J. Christie and S. Shuttleworth, 1989.
Evans, W. Gareth. Education and female emancipation: the Welsh experience, 1847–1914. 1990.
Evans, W. Gareth. The Welsh Intermediate Technical Education Act 1889 and the education of girls. Welsh History Rev 15 1990.
Paterson, F. M. S. and J. Fewell (ed). Girls in their prime. Scottish education revisited. Edinburgh 1990. Includes essays on the nineteenth century.
Avery, G. The best type of girl: a history of girls' independent schools. 1991.
Purvis, J. A history of women's education in England. 1991.
Gilbert, J. S. Women students and student life at England's civic universities before the first world war. History of Education 23 1994.
Stone, James S. Emily Faithfull: Victorian champion of women's rights. 1994.
Dyehouse, C. No distinction of sex? Women in British universities, 1870–1939. 1995.
Gomershall, M. Challenges and changes? The education of Lancashire factory women in the later nineteenth century. History of Education 24 1995.
Gallant, Mary P. Against the odds: Anne Jemima Clough and women's education in England. History of Education 26 1997.
Stevenson, J. Women and the curriculum at the Polytechnic at Regent Street, 1888–1913. History of Education 26 1997.

(5) OFFICIAL DOCUMENTS

Education Acts and Bills

England and Wales

Health, and morals of apprentices Act (Sir Robert Peel, the elder). 1802.
Parochial schools Bill (Samuel Whitbread). 1807.
Factory Bill to extend the provisions of the Act of 1802 (Sir Robert Peel, the elder). 1815. The Bill in a modified form was accepted as an Act, 1819.
Parish schools Bill (Henry Brougham). 1820. Withdrawn.
Act to make further provisions for the regulation of cotton mills and factories (Sir John Cam Hobhouse). 1825.
Factory Act (consolidating Act). 1831.
Reform Act. 1832.
University of Durham Act. 1832.
Education Bill (J. A. Roebuck). 1833.

Education Act [£20,000 per annum voted for building schools in Great Britain]. 1833.
Factory Act (Lord Ashley, later Earl of Shaftesbury). 1833.
Wood's Bill to open universities to Dissenters. 1834.
Act to facilitate the conveyance of sites for school rooms. 1836.
Grammar school Act. 1840.
School sites Act (to afford further facilities for the conveyance and endowment of sites for schools). 1841.
Mines regulation Act. 1842.
Factory Bill (Sir James Graham). 1843. Modified and accepted in 1844.
School sites Act (extending Act of 1841). 1844.
School sites Act (to extend and explain the provisions of earlier Acts). 1849.
Education Bill (W. J. Fox). 1850.
Factory Act (restricting hours of employment of women and young persons). 1850.
Act to amend the granting of sites for schools. 1851.
Charitable Trusts Act. 1853.
Factory Act (further regulations for the employment of children in factories). 1853.
The Literary and Scientific Institutions Act (to give greater facilities for procuring and settling sites and buildings in trust for institutions established for the promotion of literature, science, or the fine arts, or for the diffusion of useful knowledge). 1854.
Oxford University Act. 1854.
Education Bill (Sir John Pakington). 1855.
Act appointing a Vice-President of the Council of Education (repealed by the Board of Education Act 1899). 1856.
Cambridge University Act. 1856.
Act to bring the employment of women, young persons and children in bleaching works and dyeing works under the regulations of the Factory Acts. 1860.
Act to prohibit the employment of women and children during the night in certain operations connected with bleaching by the open-air process. 1862.
Act to amend the above Act. 1863.
The Factory Acts Extension Act. 1867.
Workshops Regulation Act (restricting age of employment of children to the age of 13 and obliging attendance at school for at least 10 hours a week). 1867.
Public schools Acts. 1868.
Endowed schools Act. 1869.
Elementary schools Act (W. E. Forster). 1870. *See* National Education Union: a verbatim report with indexes of the debates in Parliament during the progress of the Elementary Education Bill 1870, together with a reprint of the Act, 1870.
Factory and Workshop Act. 1870. Extension of earlier Acts.
Factory Act for Jews (restricting employment on Sundays). 1871.
Act to amend the Acts relating to factories and workshops. 1871.
University tests Act. 1871.
Metalliferous mines regulation Act (prohibiting employment of boys under 12, or of any female, below ground). 1872.
Agricultural children Act (prohibiting employment of a child under 10 unless he had attended 250 times at a certified school within 12 months; exemption granted to children who held a certificate of having passed the Fourth Standard). 1873.
Elementary education (amendment) Act. 1873.
Further Factory Act (repealing former Acts, fixing hours of employment of children and extending the obligation of school attendance). 1874.
Education Act (Lord Sandon). 1876.
Oxford and Cambridge Act. 1877.
The canal boats Act (securing the education of children on such boats). 1877.
Factory and workshop consolidation Act. 1878.
Elementary education (industrial schools) Act. 1879.
Act to make further provision as to bye-laws under the elementary education Acts (requiring every local authority to make bye-laws). 1880.
Education Act (Mr Mundella). 1880.
City parochial charities Act. 1883.
Factory and workshop Act (amendment Act). 1883.
Canal boats amendment Act. 1884.
Coal mines regulation Act (extension of previous regulations). 1887.
Mortmain and charitable uses Act. 1888.
Victoria University Act (to enable graduates of the Victoria University to hold offices where previously only graduates of Oxford, Cambridge or London were eligible). 1888.
Technical education Act. 1889.
Welsh intermediate education Act. 1889.
Education Code Act (permitting extension of the curriculum of evening schools and to make Parliamentary grants in certain cases). 1890.
Factory and workshop Act (employment of children raised to 11 years). 1891.
Free education Act (extra grants made to schools in which fees were abolished). 1891.
Schools for science and art Act (to facilitate transfer of such institutions to the School Boards). 1891.
Mortmain and charitable uses Act amended. 1891.
Technical and industrial institutions Act (freeing such public institutions from the operation of the Mortmain and charitable uses Act). 1892.
Elementary education (school attendance) Act (raising the leaving age to 12). 1893.
Elementary education blind and deaf children Act. 1893.
The prevention of cruelty to children Act (to prevent boys under 14 and girls under 16 from begging or receiving alms under pretence of singing, playing, performing or offering goods for sale). 1894.
Education Bill (Sir John Gorst). 1896.
School Board Conference Act (expense of travelling to conferences chargeable upon the rates). 1897.
Voluntary school Act (special grants to Voluntary schools, freeing them from the payment of rates). 1897.
Elementary school teachers (superannuation) Act. 1898.
University of London Act. 1898.
Board of education Act. 1899.
Elementary education (school attendance) Act (raising leaving age to 12). 1899.
Elementary education (amendment) Act (amending the Free education Act of 1891). 1900.
Mines regulation Act (prohibition of child labour underground). 1900.
University of Birmingham established by Act of Parliament. 1900.

Scotland

Most of the Factory Acts applied to Scotland.
Scottish education Act (James IV). 1496.
Education Act (Scotland) (fixing salaries). 1803.
Parochial schools Act. 1829.
Act for endowing schools in the Highlands. 1838.
University (Scotland) Act. 1858.
Parochial and burgh schoolmasters Act. 1861.
Education (Scotland) Act. 1872.
Act instituting the Scotch [later Scottish] Education Department. 1878.
Educational endowments Act. 1882.
Act reorganising the Scottish Education Department. 1885.
Universities (Scotland) Act. 1889.

Reports of Royal Commissions

England and Wales

Royal Commission to inquire into educational charities (Brougham). 1818–37; Report, 44 vols 1819–42.

State, discipline, studies and revenues of the University and colleges of Oxford. 2 pts 1852. *See* Edinburgh Rev 96 1852.

Documents relating to the University and colleges of Cambridge. 3 vols 1852.

State, discipline etc of Cambridge. 2 pts 1853.

On popular education in England (Newcastle Commission). 6 vols 1861. Including reports by J. Fraser, Matthew Arnold and M. Pattison. *See* Edinburgh Rev 114 1861; Inquiry into the truth of the report on the state of popular education in the County of Durham, Durham 1862.

To inquire into the revenues and management of certain colleges and schools, and the studies pursued (Public Schools or Clarendon Commission). 4 vols 1864. *See* Quart Rev 108 1860, 116 1864; Edinburgh Rev 120 1864.

Schools inquiry or Taunton Commission: to inquire into the education given in schools not comprised within the Commissions on popular education and on public schools 1864–8. Report, 21 vols 1868. Matthew Arnold, vol 6; *see* Quart Rev 126 1869.

Schools inquiry commission on technical education. 1867.

On scientific instruction and the advancement of science (Devonshire Commission). 10 pts 1870–5. Full information respecting the whole range of instruction in science.

Report of the Lord's Commission on safeguards for the maintenance of religious instruction and worship in Oxford, Cambridge and Durham. 4 pts 1870–1. *See* Edinburgh Rev 135 1872.

On the property and income of Oxford and Cambridge. 3 vols 1873.

On technical instruction. 5 vols 1882–4. Led to the Technical instruction Act, 1889.

On the working of the elementary education Acts (Cross Commission). 10 vols 1886–8. *See* Quart Rev 165 1887; Edinburgh Rev 180 1894. The Report led to the establishment of Day Training Colleges in universities and university colleges after 1890.

University of London (Selborne Commission). 1888–9.

University of London (Gresham Commission). 3 vols 1892–4.

On secondary education (Bryce Commission). 9 vols 1895. *See* Quart Rev 1897; Edinburgh Rev 185 1897. Eventually led to the Board of Education Act 1899, and to the Education Act 1902.

Scotland

Inquiry into Scottish universities. 1826.

State of universities and colleges of Scotland. 4 vols 1837. *See* Edinburgh Rev 59 1834.

Analysis and review: the universities of King's College and Marischal College, Aberdeen. 1839.

Inquiry into all types of schools in Scotland (Argyll Commission). 1867.

Inquiry into the endowed institutions in Scotland (Colebrooke Commission). 1872.

Scottish universities. 1876.

Reports other than those of Royal Commissions

Reports of the Society for bettering the conditions and increasing the comforts of the poor. 1797–1805. Leading supporters were Sir Thomas Bernard and Count Rumford. The reports contain the following dealing with English education:

44. Extracts from an account of the asylum or school of instruction for the blind at Liverpool by Sir Thomas Bernard;
50. Extracts from an account of a provision for chimney sweepers' boys at Kingston upon Thames, by the Bishop of Durham;
61. Extracts from an account of the benefits of the Charity Schools at Chester, by Sir Thomas Bernard;
64. Extracts from an account of the Mendip school by Sir Thomas Bernard;
89. Extracts from an account of the School of Industry at Kendal, by Sir Thomas Bernard, with a copy of the plan of instruction at the Kendal schools of industry;
97. Extracts from an account of the schools for poor children at Weston near Bath by Miss Masters;
100. Account of the Free-Chapel schools in West Street, Seven Dials, by John Dougan;
107. An account of the Ladies' Schools and some other Charities at Leeds, by Sir Thomas Bernard;
111. Account of a Sunday school at Kirkstall, Leeds by Mrs Carr;
112. Account of a school for poor children at Fincham;
118. Account of a school in the Borough road, by John Walker;
121. Account of a school near Hawkstone in the County of Salop, by Sir Thomas Bernard.

Appendices to vol 4, 1805:

6. Statement as to the reception and management of the children in the Foundling Hospital, London;
10. Copy of the agreement signed by the parents of the children learning the Straw Platt in the West-street schools;
12. Copy of a proposal for an enquiry into the present state of the schools for the education of the poor.

Poor Law Commission: annual reports. 1835 etc. *See* Sir W. Chance, Children under the Poor Law, 1897.

Committee of Council on Education (annual reports and minutes of the Committee, 1839–40 to 1857–8). *See* Edinburgh Rev 75 1842, 97 1853.

Report by H. Moseley. 1845.

Report of inquiry into the state of education in Wales. 1847. *See* Edinburgh Rev 97 1853.

Reports of Matthew Arnold on elementary schools 1852–82. Ed F. Sandford 1889, 1908 (enlarged).

Revised instructions to HM Inspectors. 1897.

Baines, Sir Edward. Second Report, Congregational Board of Education. 1846.

Annual reports of the Catholic Poor School Committee. 1848 etc.

The educational record of the British and Foreign School Society. 1848 etc. *See* H. B. Binns, A century of education: being the centenary history of the British and Foreign School Society 1808–1908, 1908.

National Society Church School Inquiry (1856–7).

Report of the Northamptonshire Society for promoting and extending education in accordance with the principles of the Established Church, embracing parochial, training, reformatory and middle schools. Northampton 1856–65.

Education Department Reports. 1858–9, 1898–9.

Report on religious teaching in Board Schools. 1895. *See* Edinburgh Rev 180 1894.

Special reports on educational subjects. Vol 1, 1896; vol 2, 1897; vol 3, 1898; vol 4, 1900. With reports by M. E. Sadler and Robert Morant.

Scientific instruction: report of committee of the British Association. 1867–8.

Technical education in various countries: letter from B. Samuelson to the Vice-President of the Education Department. 1867.

Chambers of Commerce on technical education: letter from J. Behrens. 1868.

Technical and primary education: circular to HM representatives abroad with replies. 1868.

National Education League: first general meeting, Birmingham, Oct 1869.

National Education Union: congress held in Manchester. 1869.

London School Board report by Professor Huxley on curriculum. 1871.

First report. 1873.

Final report. 1904 (rev).

See T. A. Spalding et al, The work of the London School Board, *[1900].*

International conference on education. 1884.

Report of a conference on secondary education held at Oxford. Oxford 1893.

Resolutions of the Bradford Independent Labour Party. 1893. These 2 reports led to the Bryce Commission, 1895.

Parliamentary Papers

Reports of a Select Committee to inquire into the education of the lower orders (Brougham's Committee). 12 pts 1816–18. *See* Quart Rev 19 1818, Edinburgh Rev 30–1 1818–19.

Education inquiry (1833–5) (Lord Kerry's return). 3 vols 1835. Many of the statistics were unreliable.

Committee on providing useful education for the poorer classes. 1838.

Manchester and Salford, educational facts and statistics: evidence before the House of Commons. *See* Edinburgh Rev 95 1852.

(6) MEMOIRS

Trimmer, Sarah. Some account of her life and writings with original letters. 2 vols 1814.

Edgeworth, Richard Lovell. Memoirs, begun by himself and concluded by Maria Edgeworth. 2 vols 1820.

Clarke, Edward Daniel. Life and remains, by W. Otter. 2 vols 1825.

Murray, Lindley. Memoirs in letters written by himself. York 1826.

Parr, Samuel. Aphorisms, opinions and reflections of the late Dr Parr. Ed E. B. H. 1826.

Pestalozzi, J. H. Memoir by C. Mayo. 1828 (2nd edn). Lecture delivered in 1826.

Parr, Samuel. Parriana. Ed E. H. Barker 2 vols 1828–9.

Lancaster, Joseph. Epitome of events and transactions in his life, and rise and progress of the Lancasterian system, by himself. New Haven CT 1833.

Romilly, Sir Samuel. Memoirs with selection of his correspondence, edited by his sons. 3 vols 1840.

Arnold, Thomas. Life and correspondence, by A. P. Stanley. 1844. *See* Edinburgh Rev 81 1845.

Findlay, J. J. Arnold of Rugby: his school life and contributions to education. Cambridge 1897.

Fitch, J. G. Thomas and Matthew Arnold and their influence on education. 1897.

Selfe, S. G. F. Dr Arnold of Rugby. 1899.

Strachey, L. In his Eminent Victorians, 1918.

Whitridge, A. Arnold of Rugby. 1928.

Trilling, L. In his Matthew Arnold, New York 1939, 1955 (rev).

Wymer, N. Dr Arnold of Rugby. 1953. Contains letters, diaries and journals written by Dr Arnold, Mrs Arnold and friends, relations and pupils.

Bell, Andrew. Life, comprising the history of the system of mutual tuition, by R. and C. C. Southey. 3 vols 1844.

An old educational reformer, Andrew Bell, by J. M. D. Meiklejohn. Edinburgh 1881.

Cooper, Thomas. Cooper's journal. 1850.

Copleston, Edward. Memoir with selections from his diary and correspondence, by W. I. Copleston. 1851.

Owen, Robert. Life written by himself, with selections from his writings and correspondence. 1857.

Podmore, F. Robert Owen. 2 vols 1906.

Cole, G. D. H. Robert Owen. 1925. Ch 8, Ideas on education.

Shelley, Percy Bysshe. Life, by T. J. Hogg. 4 vols 1858. *See col 436, above.* Syon House Academy; Eton 1804–10; Oxford 1810–11.

Hill, Thomas Wright. Remains, with notices of his life (1763–1851), by himself and M. D. Hill. 1859. Hill-Top School Birmingham. *See* The pupils of Hill-Top School, B (2), above.

William Sewell in Ireland. Quart Rev 108 1860.

Henslow, John Stevens. Memoir by L. Henyns (afterwards Blomefield). 1862.

Clough, Arthur Hugh. Letters and remains. 1865. Rugby 1829–36; Oxford 1837–48; University Hall London 1849–52. *See col 596, above.*

Lennox, Lord William Pitt. Drawn on my memory. 2 vols 1866. Westminster School 1808–14.

Dawes, Richard. Biographical notice by W. C. Henry. 1867.

Stow, David. Memoir by W. Fraser. 1868.

Pryme, George. Autobiographical recollections. Ed A. Bayne, Cambridge 1870.

Brougham, Henry (Baron). Life and times, written by himself. 3 vols Edinburgh 1871.

Cooper, Thomas. Life of Thomas Cooper written by himself. 1872.

Mill, John Stuart. Autobiography. Ed Helen Taylor [his step-daughter] 1873; ed R. Howson, New York 1924 (from ms). *See* Bentham, *below;* Quart Rev 136 1874; *col 2558, above.*

Owen, Robert Dale. Threading my way. 1874.

Lovett, William. Life and struggles of William Lovett in pursuit of bread, knowledge and freedom, by himself. 1876.

Macaulay, Thomas Babington (Baron). Life and letters, by G. O. Trevelyan. 2 vols 1876. Trinity College Cambridge 1818–24.

Denison, George A. Notes of my life 1805–78. Oxford 1878, 1879.

Whewell, William. Life and correspondence, by Mrs Stair Douglas. 1881. Cambridge 1812–66, Master of Trinity College 1841–66.

Denison, George A. Middle class schools and the conscience clause. Oxford 1883.

Hodgson, William B. Life and letters, by J. M. D. Meiklejohn. 1883.

Birkbeck, George. Memoir and review, by J. G. Godard. 1884.

Maurice, Frederick Denison. Life, chiefly told in his own letters. Ed F. Maurice 2 vols 1884.

Pattison, Mark. Memoirs. 1885.

Froebel, Friedrich W. A. Autobiography. Tr E. Michaelis and H. K. Moore 1886.

Jevons, W. Stanley: letters and journals, edited by his wife. 1886. University College School 1850–1; University College London 1851, 1859–80.

Fraser, James. Second Bishop of Manchester 1818–85, by Thomas Hughes QC. 1887.

Bradshaw, Henry. Memoir, by G. W. Prothero. 1888. Eton 1843–50; King's College Cambridge 1850; University Librarian 1875–86.

Thomas Poole and his friends, by Mrs Henry Sandford. 2 vols 1888.

Rogers, W. Reminiscences compiled by R. H. Hadden. 1888.

Ellis, William. Life and some account of his writings for the improvement of education, by E. K. Blyth. 1889.

Forster, William Edward. Life, by T. Wemyss Reid. 1889.

Greton, F. E. Memory's harkback through half-a-century 1808–58. 1889, Shrewsbury 1814, Cambridge 1822.

Thring, Edward. A memory, by H. Skrine. 1889.

Teacher and poet, by H. D. Rawnsley. 1889.

Toynbee, Arnold. F. C. Montague and P. L. Gell, in Johns Hopkins University studies, Baltimore 1889. On Toynbee Hall.

Milnes, Richard Monckton (Baron Houghton). Life, letters and friendships, by T. Wemyss Reid. 2 vols 1890.

Peel, Sir Robert. From private papers and correspondence, by C. S. Parker. 3 vols 1891–9. Harrow 1801–4; Oxford 1805–8.

Sedgwick, Adam. Life and letters, by J. W. Clark and T. M. Hughes. Cambridge 1890. *See* Quart Rev 172 1891.

Tait, Archibald Campbell, Archbishop of Canterbury. Life, by R. T. Davidson and W. Benham. 2 vols 1891. Edinburgh High School and Academy 1821–7; Glasgow University 1827–30; Oxford 1830–42; Rugby 1842–50; Oxford University Commission 1850 etc.

Wordsworth, Charles. Annals of my early life 1806–46. 1891. Harrow, Oxford, Winchester.

Butler, George. Recollections 1819–90, by Josephine E. Butler. Bristol 1892. Harrow, Cambridge, Oxford, Durham, Liverpool.

Manning, Cardinal, by A. W. Hutton. 1892. Voluntary schools, ch 7.

Lowe, Robert (Viscount Sherbrooke). Life and letters, by A. P. Martin. 2 vols 1893.

Stanley, Arthur Penrhyn. By R. E. Prothero and G. G. Bradley. 1893. Rugby 1829–34; Oxford 1834–63.

Wordsworth, Charles. Annals of my life 1846–56. Ed W. E. Hodgson 1893. Trinity College; Glenalmond 1846–54.

Hill, Frederic. An autobiography of fifty years in time of reforms. Ed C. Hill 1894.

Widgery, William Henry, schoolmaster. By W. K. Hill. 1894.

Freeman, Edward Augustus. Life and letters, by W. R. W. Stephens. 2 vols 1895. Cheam 1837–9; private tutor 1839–41; Oxford 1841; Regius Professor 1884–92.

Jowett, Benjamin. A personal memoir, by Lionel A. Tollemache. [1895.]

Manning, Cardinal. Life, by E. S. Purcell. 2 vols 1895. Harrow 1822–6; Oxford 1827–30. Vol 1, the Voluntary Schools in mid-century; vol 2, Education Act 1870; University College Kensington.

Stephen, Sir James Fitzjames. Life, by L. Stephen. 1895. Eton 1842–5; King's College London 1845–7; Cambridge 1847–51. On the 'Apostles'.

Butler, Samuel. Life and letters, by Samuel Butler [his grandson]. 2 vols 1896. *See* Quart Rev 187 1898, *and col 2327, above.*

Hare, Augustus J. C. The story of my life. 6 vols 1896–1900. Harrow 1847–8; Oxford 1853–7.

Jowett, Benjamin. Life and letters, by E. Abbott and L. Campbell. 2 vols 1897.

Hawtrey, Edmund Craven. Headmaster and afterwards Provost of Eton, by F. St J. Thackeray. 1896. *See* Quart Rev 187 1898.

Lee, Samuel. A scholar of a past generation: a brief memoir of Samuel Lee, by A. M. Lee. 1896.

Palmer, Roundell (Earl of Selborne). Memorials. 2 vols in 4 pts 1896–8. Rugby 1823–5; Winchester 1825–30; Oxford 1830–7. University tests and Education Act 1870 in vol 1 pt 2; Oxford reform 1854 in vol 2 pt 2.

Clough, Anne Jemima. A memoir, by B. A. Clough. 1897. First Principal of Newnham College, Cambridge.

Cory [Johnson], William. Extracts from his letters and journals. Ed F. W. Cornish, Oxford 1897. Eton 1832–42.

Roebuck, John Arthur. Life and letters. Ed R. E. Leader 1897.

Thring, Edward. Life, diary and letters, by Sir G. R. Parkin. 2 vols 1898, 1900 (abridged). *See* Quart Rev 187 1898.

Benson, Edward White, Archbishop of Canterbury. By A. C. Benson. 2 vols 1899. Wellington College.

Gladstone, William Ewart. Life. Ed T. Wemyss Reid 1899. Eton and Christ Church Oxford, by A. F. Robbins; Oxford Union Society, by F. W. Hirst; Gladstone as scholar, by A. J. Butler.

Liddell, Henry George. A memoir, by H. L. Thomson. 1899. Head Master, Westminster 1846–55; Dean of Christ Church, Oxford 1853–5.

Morris, William. Life, by J. W. Mackail. 2 vols 1899. Marlborough 1848–51; Exeter College Oxford 1853–5.

Playfair, Lyon. Memoirs and correspondence, by T. Wemyss Reid 1899.

Quick, Robert Herbert. Life and remains by F. Storr. 1899.

Brodrick, G. C. Memoirs and impressions 1831–1900. 1900. Balliol and Merton Colleges Oxford.

Huxley, Thomas Henry. Life and letters, by L. Huxley. 2 vols 1900.

Pearson, Charles Henry. Memorial by himself, his wife and his friends. Ed W. Stebbing 1900.

Besant, Sir Walter. An autobiography. 1902. Cambridge and the People's Palace.

Bowen, Edward Ernest. Memoir with essays, songs and verses, by W. E. Bowen. 1902. King's College London 1852–4; Harrow 1859–1901.

Acland, Sir Thomas Dyke. Memoir and letters. Ed A. H. D. Acland 1903.

Gladstone, William Ewart. Life, by John Morley. 3 vols 1903. Vol 1, Eton 1821–7; Oxford 1828–31.

Bain, Alexander. An autobiography. 1904.

Spencer, Herbert. An autobiography. 2 vols 1904. [DAR]

16 Newspapers and Magazines

A. Technical development: Advertising; Management and distribution; Wages and conditions; Techniques of journalism; Press and advertising periodicals; News agencies and press organisations.
B. The history of journalism: Memoirs and biographies of individual journalists, newspaper proprietors and publishers; The general history of the press; Lists of newspapers.
C. The daily and weekly press. The daily papers: London morning papers; London evening papers; Provincial daily papers; Scottish daily papers; Irish daily papers; London papers published more than once a week. The weekly papers: Sunday papers; General weekly papers; Illustrated papers; Unstamped and radical journals; Weekly literary reviews; Religious papers; Agricultural papers; Financial and commercial papers; Sporting papers; Humorous papers; Juvenile papers; Miscellaneous specialised papers; Accounts and studies of individual papers.
D. Magazines and reviews: Monthly magazines; Quarterly magazines; Accounts and studies of magazines and reviews.
E. School and university journalism.
F. Annuals and yearbooks.

A. TECHNICAL DEVELOPMENT

See also under Book Production and Distribution, col 1.

(1) ADVERTISING

Besides the returns of the Advertisement Duty (repealed in 1853) here listed, others issued together with the Stamp Duty will be found in col 2882 below. Important information may also be gleaned from the introductory matter to the Newspaper Advertisement Agents' Directories listed below.

[House of Commons: accounts and papers.] Abstract of account of sums paid for advertisements and proclamations in newspapers by the public offices. (470) xix 559 1822.
[House of Commons: accounts and papers.] Ireland: return of sums paid by the Stamp Office for advertisements. (588) xviii 465 1822.
[House of Commons: accounts and papers.] Amount of duty paid for advertisements by each provincial newspaper in England. (524) xxxii 617 1833.
[House of Commons: accounts and papers.] Ireland: sums paid by each newspaper in Ireland for stamps 1832–3, distinguishing sums paid for paper from those paid for advertisements. (658) xxxii 625 1833.
[House of Commons: accounts and papers.] Ireland: sums paid by the Irish Government to each newspaper in Ireland 1832–3, distinguishing sums paid to each for advertisements; duty or services for which paid, etc. (633) xxxii 629 1833.
[House of Commons: accounts and papers.] Number of advertisements which appeared in each of the newspapers published in London, 1831 to 1834; amount of duty paid by each during the period above-mentioned. (108) xxxvii 703 1835.
[House of Commons: accounts and papers.] Ireland: advertisement duty assessed on each paper in Ireland, 1834; sums paid monthly by each paper; arrears due for advertisement duty, Jan 5 1835. (265) xxxvii 695 1835.
Knight, C. Advertisements. In his London, 1843.
The advertising system. Edinburgh Rev 77 1843.
A guide to advertisers. 1852 (5 edns).
Advertisements. Quart Rev 97 1855.
Smith, W. Advertise: how? when? where? 1863.
Sampson, H. A history of advertising. 1874.
[Nicoll, D.] Publicity: an essay on advertising, by an adept of 35 years' experience. 1878.
Clay, A. The agony column of The Times 1800–70. 1881.
Teele, A. L. Ideal advertising. 1892.
Palmer, H. J. The march of the advertiser. Nineteenth Cent Jan 1897.
Sinclair, A. Fifty years of newspaper life 1845–95. [c. 1897] (priv ptd).
Smith, T. 21 years in Fleet Street. 1899.
Stead, W. T. The art of advertising. 1899.
Benson, S. H. Wisdom in advertising. 1901.
Moran, C. G. The business of advertising. 1905.
Richards, J. M. With John Bull and Jonathan. 1905. American advertising methods come to Britain.
Street, E. and L. Jackson. Advertising. Jnl of Royal Soc of Arts 24 Jan 1913.
Sparrow, W. S. Advertising and British art. 1924.
Presbrey, F. The history and development of advertisement. Garden City NY 1929.
Smith, W. Spilt ink. 1932. Appointed advertising manager of the Daily Mail in 1900.
'On the road' one hundred years ago. Ed J. Cannon, Publishers' Circular 9 Feb–13 Apr 1935.
Roll call 1910. Statistical review of press advertising. Apr 1935. A chronological list of advertising agents.
Mansfield, F. J. The story of the advertiser. Journalist 21 1938.
Agents who used the provincial press 100 years ago. Newspaper World 12 Sep 1942.
Aspinall, A. Statistical accounts of the London newspapers 1800–36. EHR 65 1950. Advertisement duty returns.
Turner, E. S. The shocking history of advertising. 1953.
Wood, J. P. The story of advertising. New York [1958].
Elliott, B. B. A history of English advertising. 1962. Contains a section on the trade press.
Smyth, A. L. Youde's billposting journal. Manchester Rev 10 1963. Publicity for an attempt to monopolise bill-posting in Manchester in 1897.

De Vries, L. Victorian advertisements: the art of the Victorian persuaders. [1968.] Introd by J. Laver.

Hindley, D. and G. Advertising in Victorian England, 1837–1901. 1972. Copious illustration – and valuable list of early advertising agents.

Asquith, I. Advertising and the press in the late 18th and early 19th centuries: James Perry and the Morning Chronicle, 1790–1821. Historical Jnl vol 18 no 4 1975.

Nevett, T. R. London's early advertising agents. Jnl of Advertising History Dec 1977.

Bennett, S. Victorian newspaper advertising: counting what counts. Publishing History 8 1980. Analysis based on The Times and Windsor and Eton Express.

Nevett, T. R. Advertising in Britain: a history. 1982.

Opie, R. Rule Britannia: trading in the British image. 1985.

Nevett, T. R. Advertising and editorial integrity in the 19th century. In The press and English society from the 17th to the 19th centuries, ed M. Harris and A. J. Lee, London and Toronto 1986.

Nevett, T. R. American influence on British advertising before 1920. In Historical perspectives in marketing: essays in honor of Stanley C. Hollander, ed Nevett and R. A. Fullerton, Lexington KY [1988].

Nevett, T. R. Thomas Barratt and the development of British advertising. International Jnl of Advertising vol 7 no 3 1988.

Richards, T. The commodity culture of Victorian England: advertising and spectacle, 1851–1914. Stanford CA 1990.

Nevett, T. R. Advertising. In Victorian periodicals and Victorian society, ed J. D. Van and R. Van Arsdel, Toronto and Aldershot 1994.

See also Press and Advertising Directories; Press and Advertising Periodicals.

(2) MANAGEMENT AND DISTRIBUTION

The commercial history of a penny magazine. Penny Mag Sep–Dec 1833.

[Grant, J.] Travels in town by the author of Random recollections. 2 vols 1839. Chs 7–8.

The bringing forth of the daily newspaper. Chambers's Jnl 26 Aug 1854.

King, J. Four and twenty hours in a newspaper office. Once a Week 26 Sep 1863, 6 Feb 1864.

Philbrick, F. A. and W. A. S. Westoby. The postage and telegraph stamps of Great Britain. 1881.

Sidman, W. A treatise on newspaper book-keeping. 1887.

Yeo, H. Newspaper management. Manchester 1891.

Maxwell, H. The life and times of the Rt Hon W. H. Smith MP. 2 vols Edinburgh 1893.

Newnes, George, Ltd. How popular periodicals are produced. [1894.]

Norton, B. T. and G. T. Feasey. Newspaper accounts: being a practical treatise on the books and accounts in use in large and small newspaper offices. 1895.

Harmsworth, A. C. (Viscount Northcliffe). Making a modern newspaper: some secrets revealed. Harmsworth's Mag July 1898.

[Hepworth, T. C.] All about a London daily from the paper mill to the breakfast table. [1898.]

Haywood, A. and Son. 1832–1899: a brief survey of the news trade. Manchester 1899.

Special newspaper trains, by Brunel Redivivus. Railway Mag Nov 1899.

Courtney, L. H. The making and reading of newspapers. 1901.

Ewen, H. L'E. Unadhesive postage stamps of the United Kingdom. 1905.

Ewen, H. L'E. Newspaper and parcel stamps issued by the railway companies of the United Kingdom. 1906.

Given, J. L. Making a newspaper. 1913.

Pocklington, G. R. The story of W. H. Smith and Son. 1921, 1932 (rev F. K. Foat) (priv ptd).

Kitchin, F. H. Moberly Bell and his times. 1925.

Bell, E. H. C. M. The life and letters of C. F. Moberly Bell. 1927.

Aspinall, A. The circulation of newspapers in the early nineteenth century. RES 22 1946. On reading-rooms, the hiring-out of papers, etc.

Colby, R. A. That he who rides may read: W. H. Smith and Son's railway library. Wilson Lib Bull 27 1952.

Bell, R. F. Gordon and Gotch, London: the story of the G. and G. century 1853–1953. 1953.

Haig, R. L. Circulation of some London newspapers, 1806–11: two documents. SB 7 1955.

Wadsworth, A. P. Newspaper circulations 1800–1954. Trans Manchester Statistical Soc 1955.

Chilston, Viscount. W. H. Smith. 1965.

(3) WAGES AND CONDITIONS

The earlier portion of the Library of the London Society of Compositors is deposited at the St Bride Foundation.

Memorial of London Compositors addressed to proprietors of newspapers with a report of a meeting of the employers. [1809.]

London Union of Compositors. The London scale of prices for compositors' work: agreed upon April 16th 1810, with explanatory notes, and the scales of Leeds, York, Dublin, Belfast and Edinburgh. [c. 1835] (4 edns).

London Trade Society of Compositors. Report of a committee appointed to draw up a statement of the regular mode of working on newspapers. 1820.

London Union of Compositors. Report of the proceedings of the delegated meeting of compositors, December 12 1833. [1833.]

London Union of Compositors. Report of the General Trade Committee to the Compositors of London, March 4 & 11 1834. [1834.]

London Union of Compositors. Report of the Trade Council on the mode of working of The Times newspaper. [1835.]

London Society of Compositors. Report of the journeymen members of the conference of master printers and compositors held in 1847. 1847, [1875], [1879], [1883].

London Association of Master Printers. The agreements made with the compositors, pressmen and machine-minders in Nov 1866. 1867.

London Society of Compositors. Report of the Special Committee appointed to revise the trade rules, examine the system of working in each office and frame a report upon the evidence that may come before them. 1868.

London Society of Compositors. Rules and regulations for news work. [1868.]

Manchester Typographical Society. Regulations for piece-work on daily papers. Manchester 1873.

London Society of Compositors. Report of the Special Committee appointed to consider the best means for improving the conditions of newspaper compositors. 1874.

Glasgow Typographical Society. Newspaper time and piece scales of prices. Glasgow 1884.

The Vigilance Gazette: a monthly journal devoted to the interests of the London Society of Compositors. Nos 1–11 May 1888–May 1890. Continued as London Printers' Circular.

London Society of Compositors. News department: workmen's memorial to the newspaper proprietors. 1889.

London Society of Compositors. Fair and unfair religious and temperance weekly newspapers. 1890.

London Printing and Allied Trades Association. The London scale of prices for compositors' work. 1891.

London Society of Compositors. News department: report of the

committee on the system of working in each office. 1891. Supplementary report of 1891 presented 11 Nov 1891.
The Institute of Journalists, by an old journalist. Nat Rev Oct 1892.
The Institute of Journalists. Proceedings. 1892–1912. Quarterly.
Society of Women Journalists. Annual report. [1894–5?]–1897–8–1914–15 (21st annual report)–?
London Society of Compositors. Rates and rules for working composing machines in London, agreed upon between representatives of the London newspapers and master printers and the London Society of Compositors. 1896.
Dickson, J. J. Manchester Typographical Society and Branch of the Typographical Association centenary 1797–1897. Manchester 1897.
London Society of Compositors. Jubilee. A brief record of events prior to and since 1848. Ed C. W. Bowerman 1898.
Glasgow Typographical Society. Scale of prices for the working of composing machines in newspaper offices. Glasgow 1898.
The economic position of women in journalism, by a woman journalist. Humanitarian July 1900.
London Association of Correctors of the Press. Jubilee. 1854–1904. [1904.]
MacDonald, J. R. Women in the printing trades: a sociological study, with a preface by F. Y. Edgeworth. 1904.
Murasken, E. Newswriters' unions in English-speaking countries. New York 1938.
Fifty years of Institute leadership. Inst of Journalists Jnl 27 1939.
Keefe, H. J. A century in print: the story of Hazell's 1839–1939. 1939.
Taylor, H. A. Through fifty years. Inst of Journalists Jnl 28 1940.
Howe, E. Newspaper printing in the nineteenth century. 1943.
Howe, E. The trade: passages from the literature of the printing craft 1550–1935. 1943.
Hutchinson, W. The printer's devil: an account of the history and objects of the Printers' Pension Corporation. 1943.
Aspinall, A. The social status of journalists at the beginning of the nineteenth century. RES 21 1945.
Howe, E. The London compositor: documents relating to wages, working conditions and customs of the London printing trade 1785–1900. 1947 (Bibl Soc).
Howe, E. and H. E. Waite. The London Society of Compositors. 1948.
Clowes, W. B. Family business 1803–1953. 1953.

(4) TECHNIQUES OF JOURNALISM

[Whitefoord, C.] Advice to the editors of newspapers. 1799.
[Copleston, E.] Advice to a young reviewer, with a specimen of the art. Oxford 1807.
Conder, J. Reviews reviewed: including an enquiry into the moral and intellectual effects of habits of criticism, and their influence on the general interests of literature; to which is subjoined a brief history of the periodical reviews published in England and Scotland by T. C. O'Reid. Oxford 1811.
Journalism. Westminster Rev 18 1833.
The newspapers. Metropolitan Mag Jan 1833.
Hughes, T. Anonymous journalism. Macmillan's Mag Dec 1861.
[Morley, J.] Anonymous journalism. Fortnightly Rev Sep 1867.
[House of Commons.] Special Report from the Select Committee on the Electric Telegraphs Bill. 1868.
Reed, T. A. The reporter's guide. 1869.
Modern newspaper enterprise. Fraser's Mag June 1876.
Whittaker, S. Parliamentary reporting in England, foreign countries and the colonies. Manchester 1877.
[House of Commons.] Report from the Select Committee on Parliamentary Reporting. 1878.
Bussey, H. F. and T. W. Reid. The newspaper reader: the journals of the 19th century on the events of the day. 1879.
[House of Lords.] Report from the Select Committee on Parliamentary Reporting. 1880.
Reade, A. A. Literary success: being a guide to practical journalism. [1880.]
Davies, E. P. The reporter's handbook. 1884.
Dawson, J. Practical journalism. 1885.
Pendleton, J. Newspaper reporting in olden times and today. 1890.
Russell, P. The author's manual: a complete and practical guide to all branches of literary work. [1891.]
Mackie, J. B. Modern journalism. 1894.
[Humboldt, W.] The compleat leader writer. Macmillan's Mag Sep 1894.
Baines, F. E. Forty years at the Post Office. 2 vols 1895.
Phillips, E. How to become a journalist. 1895.
Smith, L. A. Women's work in the London and provincial press. Newspaper Press Directory 1897.
Bennett, E. A. Journalism for women: a practical guide. 1898.
Kingston, A. Pitman's guide to journalism. 1898, 1904.
An Editor. How to write for the press: a practical handbook for beginners in journalism. 1899, 1904 (rev).
Pendleton, J. How to succeed as a journalist. 1902.
Lawrence, A. Journalism as a profession. 1903.
Wellcome, H. S. The evolution of journalism. 1909.
MacDonagh, M. The Reporters' Gallery. [1913.]
Salmon, L. M. The newspaper and the historian. New York 1923.
Coronation reporting a century ago. Newspaper World 22 May 1937.
Mansfield, F. J. Social and Personal. Journalist 20 1937. On the rise of gossip and the 'personal column' as a newspaper staple.
Pollard, H. G. Novels in newspapers: some unpublished letters of Captain Mayne Reid. RES 18 1942. On syndication.
Maurer, O. Anonymity vs signature in Victorian reviewing. SE 27 1948.
Jump, J. D. Weekly reviewing in the eighteen-fifties. RES 24 1948.
Snyder, L. and R. B. Morris. A treasury of great reporting. New York 1949.
Jump, J. D. Weekly reviewing in the eighteen-sixties. RES n.s. 3 1952.
Mathews, J. J. The genesis of newspaper war correspondence. Journalism Quart 29 1952.
Watson, M. R. Magazine serials and the essay tradition 1746–1820. Baton Rouge LA 1956. Includes a list of essay serials.
Fielding, K. J. The weekly serialisation of Dickens's novels. Dickensian 54 1958.
Fielding, K. J. Monthly serialisations of Dickens's novels. Dickensian 54 1958.

(5) PRESS AND ADVERTISING PERIODICALS

The newsmen's weekly chronicle. Nos 1–7, 2 July–13 Aug 1837.
Members' circular. Provincial newspaper society (from 1889, Newspaper society). 1840–1963. Quarterly to 1894, then monthly. Early issues are especially valuable in conveying confidential information and advice on advertising matters.
London, provincial and colonial press news. No 1, 15 Jan 1866–Dec 1912. Ed C. W. Dorrington. Monthly.
The newspaper press. W. Allen. No 1, 1 Dec 1866–1 July 1872. Ed A. Andrews. Monthly. Incorporated into The printers' register. Useful for circulation data.
The Fleet Street gazette: a journeyman's journal. Nos 1–7, 28 Feb–23 May 1874. Fortnightly.
The journalist: an illustrated phonographic magazine. Nos 1–21, Nov 1879–July 1881. Ed H. R. Evans. Monthly.
Press gazette and reporter's journal. J. Allen & Co. Croydon 1880– .
The Newsvendor. No 1, Jan 1873–Feb 1883. Weekly after first 9 nos.
Successful advertising. Smiths' advertising agency. 1879–1902,

1909, 1926. Ed T. Smith, then Smith and J. H. Osborne. Originally annual, with subtitle The secrets explained. Jubilee no, 1928. Ed P. Smith.
The journalist. No 1, 15 Oct 1886–Jan? 1902. Weekly, latterly as The journalist and newspaper proprietor. Continued under that title Feb 1902–May 1909. Monthly.
The advertising register. Nos 1–54, 12 Nov 1886–7 Oct 1887. Weekly.
Journalism. Nos 1–17, Nov 1887–Feb 1889.
The newsagent and advertisers' record. Nos 1–15, July 1889–Dec 1890. Continued as News and book trade review and stationers' gazette, vol 102, no 14 vol 61, no 17, 6 Apr 1940–29 Apr 1950. Continued as Newsagents' booksellers' review and stationers' gazette, vol 61, no 18 vol 67, no 30, 6 May 1950–28 July 1956. Continued as Retail newsagent, bookseller and stationer, vol 67 no 31, 4 Aug 1956; continued as Retail newsagent from vol 82 no 24, 12 June 1971; continued as Retail newsagent, tobacconist and confectioner from vol 87 no 7, 14 Feb 1976.
Advertising. Smiths' advertising agency. Oct 1891–Jan 1914. Ed J. H. Osborne. Monthly.
The advertisers' monthly circular. Nos 1–7, Jan–Nov 1895.
The newsagents' chronicle. Nos 1–75, 16 Feb 1895–26 Feb 1898. Fortnightly.
The advertiser's journal. No 1, June 1898.
Advertising notes. No 1, Jan–Dec 1898. Continued as Profitable advertising, Jan 1899–Dec 1904. Ed C. Vernon. Monthly.
The newspaper owner and manager. 5 Jan 1898–11 Oct 1899. Continued as Newspaper owner and modern printer, 18 Oct 1899–20 May 1903. Continued as Master printer and newspaper owner, 27 May 1903–1 Apr 1905. Continued as The newspaper owner, 8 Apr 1905–28 June 1913. Continued as The newspaper world, 5 July 1913–28 Dec 1935. Continued as The newspaper world and advertising review, 4 Jan 1936–12 Mar 1953. Prop and ed C. Baker, then Benn. Weekly.
Early days of The newspaper world. 3 Jan 1948.
The press, 1898–1948 (50th anniversary issue). 1948.
The advertiser's review. Lowe & Wyman. No 1, 8 Apr 1899–24 Dec 1904. Ed E. S. Day. Incorporated in Advertising News, nos 1–66, 5 Feb 1904–Nov/Dec 1905. Amalgamated with Progressive advertising and outdoor publicity, nos 1–13, 25 Oct 1901–Aug 1909.
Modern advertising. Nos 1–4, June 1900–Apr 1901.
Newspaper and poster advertising. Nos 1–18, 28 July 1900–21 Dec 1901. Incorporated in The advertiser's review.
Victorian periodicals newsletter. 1968–78. Continued as Victorian periodicals review, 1979– . Quarterly.
Journal of advertising history. Vol 1, no 1, Dec 1972–Vol 2, no 2, 1981. Ed I. Keil. Irregular.
Journal of newspaper and periodical history. 1984–93. London, then Westport CT. Ed M. Harris. 3 then 2 per year. Continued as Studies in newspaper and periodical history, 1994– . Annual.
Book and magazine collector. No 1, Mar 1984. Monthly.

(6) NEWS AGENCIES AND PRESS ORGANISATIONS

Wynter, A. Who is Mr Reuter? In his Our social bees: or, pictures of town and country life, 1863. Rptd from Once a Week 23 Feb 1861.
The grey book. National association of journalists, 1886–1890; thereafter Institute of Journalists. Annual.
Whorlow, H. The provincial newspaper society, 1836–1886: a jubilee retrospect. 1886. The title was shortened to Newspaper Society in 1889.
Through Reuter's agency. Cassell's Saturday Jnl 31 Aug 1889.
The institute of journalists. Sell's Dictionary of the World's Press. 1891.
FitzGerald, W. G. The romance of our news supply. The Strand Mag July/Dec 1895. Reuters, Exchange Telegraph, Press Assoc and Central News are all featured.
The National press agency. Our silver anniversary 1873–1898. 1898.
Something about the institute of journalists at the end of the century. Sell's Dictionary of the World's Press. 1901.
Collins, H. M. From pigeon post to wireless. 1925. A history of Reuters.
Pillars of the press. World's press news June–July 1929. 4 articles on press agencies.
Central news agency. Diamond jubilee souvenir. 1931.
[Davies, E. W.] The newspaper society 1836–1936: a centenary retrospect. 1936.
Through fifty years: an outline of the history of the Institute of Journalists. The Journal, Jubilee suppl 28 1940.
Storey, G. Reuters' century 1851–1951. 1951.
Boorman, H. R. P. (comp). The newspaper society: 125 years of progress. 1961.
Scott, G. Reporter anonymous: the story of the Press association. 1968.
Scott, J. M. Extel 100: centenary history of the Exchange telegraph. 1972.
Ewart, A. and V. Leonard (ed). 100 years of Fleet Street: as seen through the eyes of the Press Club. 1982.
Bainbridge, C. (ed). One hundred years of journalism: social aspects of the press. Macmillan, for Inst of Journalists. 1984.
The Journal: Institute of Journalists' centenary no. Nov/Dec 1984.
Brewer, R. (comp). Newspapers: past, present, future. 1985. To mark the 150th anniversary of the Newspaper Soc.
Read, D. The power of news: the history of Reuters. 1992.

B. THE HISTORY OF JOURNALISM

For further information on policy and achievements of individual journalists, editors and proprietors, see the sections dealing with the histories and studies of the appropriate journals, below. Many biographical studies of journalists are to be found in The newspaper press directory *and in* The world's press news.

(1) MEMOIRS AND BIOGRAPHIES OF INDIVIDUAL JOURNALISTS, NEWSPAPER PROPRIETORS AND PUBLISHERS

For additional material, see Madden and Dixon 1976 and Uffelman 1992 under General History of the Press, Bibliographies, below.
À Beckett, A. W. (1844–1909: Punch)
The à Becketts of Punch. 1903.
The recollections of a humorist. 1907.
À Beckett, Gilbert (1811–56: Punch). *See col 1988, above.*
Adams, W. E. (b. 1832: Newcastle Weekly Chron).
Memoirs of a social atom. 2 vols 1903.
Ainsworth, William Harrison (1805–82: Ainsworth's Mag; Bentley's Misc; NMM). *See col 1091, above.*
Aird, A.
Reminiscences of editors, reporters and printers during the last sixty years. Glasgow 1890.
Alford, Henry (1810–71: Contemporary Rev). *See col 513, above.*
Allingham, William (1824–89: Fraser's Mag). *See col 514, above.*
Allon, Henry (1818–92: Br Quart Rev)
Letters to a Victorian editor. Ed A. Peel 1929.
Annand, James (1843–1906: Newcastle Daily Leader)
Hodgson, G. B. From smithy to senate: the life story of James Annand, journalist and politician. 1908.
Appleton, Charles E. C. B. (1841–79: Acad)
Appleton, J. H. and A. H. Sayce. Dr Appleton, his life and literary relics. 1881.

Arnold, William T. (1852–1904)
Ward, M. A. and C. E. Montague. William Thomas Arnold, journalist and historian. Manchester 1907.
Austin, Alfred (1835–1913: Nat Rev). *See col 699, above.*
Crowell, N. B. Alfred Austin, Victorian. Albuquerque 1953.
Bagehot, Walter (1826–77: Economist). *See col 2468, above.*
Buchan, A. The spare chancellor: the life of Bagehot. 1959.
St John-Stevas, N. Walter Bagehot. 1959.
Tener, R. H. and N. St J. Stevas. Bagehot and Bailey. TLS 8 Feb 1963.
Baines, Edward (1774–1848: Leeds Mercury)
Baines, E. The life of Baines by his son. 1851.
Baldwin, Charles (1774–1869: Standard)
Register & Mag of Biography April 1869. Memoir.
Baldwin, Walter (Clapham Observer)
Mursell, A. and C. Woods. Walter Baldwin. 1903.
Barclay, Thomas (b. 1853: The Times)
Thirty years 1876–1906: Anglo-French reminiscences. 1914.
Barmby, J. Goodwin (1820–81: Promethean)
Armytage, W. H. G. The journalistic activities of J. Goodwin Barmby. N & Q 201, Apr 1956.
Barnes, Thomas (1785–1841: The Times)
Blunden, E. Thomas Barnes (1785–1841): literary diversions of an editor. TLS 10 May 1941.
Hudson, D. Thomas Barnes of The Times. Cambridge 1943.
Parker, W. M. Thomas Mitchell and Thomas Barnes. TLS 27 May 1944.
Aspinall, A. Thomas Barnes to Brougham: from friends to foes. TLS 27 July 1946. *See also* 7 Sep 1946.
Blunden, E. Thomas Barnes. TLS 3 Aug 1946. *See also* 24 Aug and 5 Oct 1946.
Beatty-Kingston, William (1837–1900: Daily Telegraph)
A journalist's jottings. 2 vols 1890.
Men, cities and events. 1895.
Beeton, Samuel (1831?–77: Englishwoman's Domestic Mag; Boy's Own Jnl etc). *See col 2211, above.*
Spain, N. Mrs Beeton and her husband. 1948.
Hyde, H. M. Mr and Mrs Beeton. 1951.
Bell, John (1745–1831: Bell's Weekly Messenger)
Morison, S. John Bell. Cambridge 1930 (priv ptd).
Bell, John Browne (1779–1855: News of the World)
Berrey, R. P. The romance of a great newspaper. [c. 1933.]
Bell, George (1814–90: Aunt Judy's Mag; N & Q etc)
Bell, E. George Bell, publisher. 1924 (priv ptd).
Bentley, Richard (1794–1871: Bentley's Misc; Temple Bar)
Gettmann, R. A. A Victorian publisher: a study of the Bentley papers. Cambridge 1960.
Bertram, J. G.
Some memories of books, authors and events. Westminster 1893.
Besant, Annie (1847–1933: Nat Reformer (1860); Link; Theosophist). *See col 2316, above.*
Nethercot, A. H. The first five lives of Annie Besant. 1961.
Nethercot, A. H. The last four lives of Annie Besant. 1963.
Dinnage, R. Annie Besant. 1986.
Taylor, A. Annie Besant: a biography. 1992.
Besant, Walter (1836–1901). *See col 1455, above.*
Autobiography. Ed S. Sprigge 1902.
Colby, R. A. Harnessing Pegasus: Walter Besant, The author and the profession of authorship. Victorian Periodicals Rev 23 1990.
Black, William (1841–98). *See col 1466, above.*
Reid, W. William Black, novelist: a biography. 1902.
Blanchard, E. L. Laman (1820–89: Chambers's London Jnl; Daily Telegraph etc). *See col 1994, above.*
Life and reminiscences. Ed C. Scott and C. Howard 1891.
Blanchard, Samuel Laman (1804–45: True Sun; Court Jnl; Courier; etc). *See col 541, above.*
Sketches from life; with a memoir of the author by Sir Edward Bulwer Lytton. 3 vols 1846.
Poetical works; with a memoir of Blanchard Jerrold. 1876.
Blatchford, Robert (1851–1943: Clarion)
My eighty years. 1931.
Thompson, L. Robert Blatchford: portrait of an Englishman. 1951.
Blowitz, Henri Stefan de (1832–1903: The Times)
My memoirs. 1903.
Giles, F. A prince of journalists: the life and times of Henri Stefan Opper de Blowitz. 1962.
Mullen, T. E. Henri de Blowitz: the foreign correspondent and international affairs. Emory Univ Quart 21 1965.
Blumenfeld, Ralph D. (1864–1948: Daily Express)
R. D. B.'s diary 1887–1914. 1930.
Bodkin, M. M'. D. (1850–1933)
Recollections of an Irish judge. 1914.
Boon, John (1859–1928: Exchange Telegraph Co)
Victorians, Edwardians and Georgians: the impressions of a veteran journalist extending over forty years. 2 vols 1928.
Borthwick, Algernon (Baron Glenesk) (1830–1908: Morning Post)
Lucas, R. Lord Glenesk and the Morning Post. 1910.
Bottomley, Horatio (1860–1933: Youth etc)
Symons, J. Horatio Bottomley. 1955.
Bowles, Thomas Gibson (1842–1922: Vanity Fair)
Naylor, L. E. The irrepressible Victorian. 1965.
Bowring, John (1792–1872: Westminster Review). *See col 238, above.*
Autobiographical recollections. 1877.
Boyd, Frank M. (1863–1950: Pelican)
A pelican's tale: fifty years of London and elsewhere. 1919.
Boyle, Frederick (1841–83)
The narrative of an expelled correspondent. 1877.
Bradlaugh, Charles (1833–91: National Reformer)
Autobiography. 1873.
Bonner, H. B. and J. M. Robertson. The life of Charles Bradlaugh. 2 vols. 1894.
Champion of liberty: Charles Bradlaugh. Ed J. P. Gilmour 1933.
Brodrick, G. C. (1831–1903)
Memories and impressions 1831–1900. 1900.
Brooks, C. W. Shirley (1816–74: Punch). *See col 1996, above.*
Layard, G. S. A great Punch editor: being the life, letters and diaries of Shirley Brooks. 1907.
Brougham, Henry (1778–1868: Edinburgh Rev). *See col 2412, above.*
Buchanan, William (1781–1863: Edinburgh Courant)
The editorship of the Edinburgh Daily Courant. Edinburgh 1860.
Buckingham, James Silk (1786–1855: Athenaeum etc)
Specimens of newspaper literature, with personal memoirs. 2 vols Boston 1850.
Autobiography. 2 vols 1855.
Turner, R. E. J. S. Buckingham. 1934.
Burnand, F. C. (1836–1916: Punch). *See col 2033, above.*
Records and reminiscences. 2 vols [1904].
Busby, Thomas (1755–1838: Morning Post; Monthly Musical Jnl)
Boyle, A. Portraiture in Lavengro. N & Q 13, 27 Oct 1951.
Bussey, H. Findlater (d. 1919)
Sixty years of journalism. Bristol 1906.
Byrne, Nicholas (1761?–1833: Morning Post)
Herd, H. Seven editors. 1955.
Cadett, Herbert
The adventures of a journalist. 1900.
Campbell, Duncan (1824–90: Northern Chron [Inverness])
Reminiscences and reflections of an octogenarian Highlander, who was for over 26 years editor of the Northern Chronicle, Inverness. Inverness 1910.
Campbell, Thomas (1777–1844: New Monthly Mag). *See col 283, above.*
Beattie, William. The life and letters of Thomas Campbell. 3 vols 1848.

Redding, C. Literary reminiscences and memoirs of Thomas Campbell. 2 vols 1860.

Carlile, Richard (1790–1843: Republican). *See col 2085, above.*

Holyoake, G. J. The Life and character of Richard Carlile. 1849.

Campbell, T. C. The battle of the press as told in the story of the life of Carlile by his daughter. 1899.

Centenary of Carlile, greatest fighter for press freedom. Journalism 26 1943.

Carnie, William (Aberdeen Herald)

Reporting reminiscences. 2 vols Aberdeen 1902–6 (priv ptd).

Carr, Emsley (1867–1941: News of the World)

Sir Emsley Carr: fifty years as editor. World's Press News 1 May 1941.

Cassell, The House of (Cassell's Mag; Quiver; Mag of Art etc)

Nowell-Smith, S. The house of Cassell 1848–1958. 1958.

Cassell, John (1817–65: Cassell's Illustr Family Paper; Quiver etc.)

Pike, G. H. John Cassell. 1894.

Catling, Thomas (1838–1920: Lloyd's Weekly Newspaper)

My life's pilgrimage. 1911.

Chambers, Robert (1802–71. Chambers's Jnl). *See col 2528, above.*

Chambers, W. Memoirs of Robert Chambers; with autobiographical reminiscences of William Chambers. Edinburgh 1872.

Chambers, William (1800–83: Chambers's Jnl)

The story of a long and busy life. Edinburgh 1882.

Chapman, John (1821–94: Prospective Rev; Westminster Rev)

Haight, G. S. George Eliot and John Chapman with Chapman's diaries. New Haven 1940.

Race, S. John Chapman. N & Q 26 April, 17 May 1941, May 1953.

Chatto & Windus, the house of (GM; Belgravia; Idler etc.)

Low, D. M. A century of writers 1855–1955. 1955.

Clarke, William (1852–1901: Spectator; Daily Chron)

A collection of his writings, with a biographical sketch. Ed H. Burrows and J. A. Hobson 1908.

Cobbe, Frances Power (1822–1904: Echo). *See col 2222, above.*

The life of Frances Power Cobbe by herself. 2 vols 1894.

Cobbett, William (1762–1835: Political Register). *See col 2109, above.*

The life of Cobbett. Manchester 1835.

Smith, E. Cobbett: a biography. 2 vols 1878.

Carlyle, E. I. William Cobbett. 1904.

'Melville, Lewis' (L. S. Benjamin). The life and letters of Cobbett. 2 vols 1913.

Cole, G. D. H. The life of Cobbett. 1924.

Pemberton, W. B. William Cobbett. 1949.

Pearl, M. L. Cobbett: a bibliographical account. 1953. With information on his journalistic ventures.

Coleridge, S. T. (1772–1834: Morning Post). *See col 298, above.*

Gillman, J. The life of Coleridge vol 1. 1838 (all pbd).

See replies by Daniel Stuart and H. N. Coleridge, GM May–Aug 1838.

Bourne, H. R. F. Coleridge among the journalists. GM Nov 1887.

See also under studies of the Morning Post, *below.*

Colles, Ramsay (1862–1919: Irish Figaro etc.)

In castle and courthouse: being the reminiscences of thirty years in Ireland. 1911.

Conder, Josiah (1789–1855: Patriot). *See col 324, above.*

Conder, E. R. Josiah Conder: a memoir. 1857.

Cook, Edward Tyas (1857–1919: Pall Mall Gazette; Westminster Gazette)

Literary recreations. 1918.

Mills, J. S. Cook: a biography. 1921.

Cooper, Charles A. (1829–1916: Scotsman)

An editor's retrospect. 1896.

Cooper, Frederick Fox (1806–79: John Bull; Colored News)

Cooper, F. R. Nothing extenuate: the life of Cooper. 1964.

Cooper, Thomas (1805–1892: Cooper's Jnl). *See col 603, above.*

The life of Cooper, written by himself. 1872.

Conklin, R. J. Cooper, the Chartist. Manila 1935.

Courtney, Leonard H. (Baron Courtney) (1832–1918: The Times etc.)

Gooch, G. P. The life of Courtney. 1920.

Courtney, W. L. (1850–1928: Murray's Mag; Daily Telegraph; Fortnightly Rev)

The making of an editor 1850–1928. 1930.

Cowen, Joseph (1831–1900: Newcastle Chron)

Jones, E. R. The life and speeches of Cowen. 1885.

Duncan, W. The life of Cowen. 1904.

Croal, David.

The early recollections of a journalist 1832–1859. Edinburgh 1898.

Croker, John Wilson (1780–1857: Quart Rev etc.). *See col 2121, above.*

Croly, George (1780–1860: Literary Gazette; Blackwood's Mag). *See col 326, above.*

Boyle, A. Portraiture in Lavengro. N & Q 27 Oct 1951.

Crosland, T. W. H. (1865–1924: Academy; Dome etc.). *See col 726, above.*

Brown, W. S. The life and genius of Crosland. 1928.

Crowe, Joseph (1825–96)

Reminiscences of thirty-five years of my life. 1895.

Dallas, Eneas Sweetland (1828–79: Once a Week etc.). *See col 2222, above.*

Dalziel, George (1815–1902 and Edward 1817–1905: Punch; Illustr London News; Cornhill Mag; Fun; Judy etc.)

The brothers Dalziel: a record of fifty years' work 1840–1900. 1901.

Dangerfield, Edmund (1864?–1938: Cyclist)

Armstrong, A. C. Bouverie Street to Bowling Green Lane: fifty-five years of specialized publishing. 1946.

Delane, J. T. (1817–79: The Times)

Dasent, A. I. John Thaddeus Delane, editor of The Times: his life and correspondence. 2 vols 1908.

Cook, E. T. Delane of The Times. 1915.

De Quincey, Thomas (1785–1859: Westmorland Gazette etc.) *See col 2123, above.*

Pollitt, C. De Quincey's editorship of the Westmorland Gazette, with selections from his work on that journal from July 1818 to November 1819. Kendal 1890.

New essays by De Quincy: his contributions to the Edinburgh Saturday Post and the Edinburgh Evening Post 1827–8. Ed S. M. Towe, Princeton 1966.

Dickens, Charles (1812–70: Daily News; Household Words; All the Year Round etc.). *See col 1181, above.*

Lehmann, R. C. Dickens as editor: being the letters written by him to William Henry Wills, his sub-editor. 1912.

Ley, J. W. T. When Dickens led a reporters strike. Journalist 25 1942.

Grubb, G. G. Dickens's influence as an editor. SP 42 1945.

Grubb, G. G. Dickens and the Daily News. In Booker memorial studies, Chapel Hill 1950; pts 2–4 in Nineteenth-Century Fiction 6–7 1952–3.

Grubb, G. G. 'Dickens rejects'. Dickensian 52 1956.

See also under studies of the appropriate journals, below.

Dickens, John (1785?–1851: Daily News)

John Dickens, journalist. Dickensian 53 1957.

Dicks, John (1818–81: Bow Bells)

Summers, M. John Dicks, publishers. TLS 7 Nov 1942.

Dilke, Charles Wentworth (1789–1864: Athenaeum) *See col 2139, above.*

The papers of a critic, with a biographical sketch by Sir Charles Wentworth Dilke. 2 vols 1875.

Dixon, W. W. The spice of life: a medley of memoirs, by 'Thormanby'. 1911.

Downey, Edmund (1856–1937: Waterford News)

Twenty years ago: a book of anecdote illustrating literary life in London. 1905.

Dunlop, Andrew

Fifty years of Irish journalism. Dublin 1911.

Edwards, H. Sutherland (1828–1906)
Personal recollections. 1900.
Edwards, J. Passmore (1829–1911: Echo)
A few footprints. 1905 (priv ptd).
'Eliot, George' (1819–80: Westminster Rev). *See col 1282, above.*
Pinney, Thomas. Essays of George Eliot. 1963. The introd describes her reviewing for several jnls and her editing for the Westminster.
Elwin, Whitwell (1816–1900: Quart Rev). *See col 2225, above.*
Some letters of Whitwell Elwin. TLS 18–25 Sep 1953.
Shattock, J. Showman, lion hunter, or hack: the quarterly editor at midcentury. In J. H. Wiener, ed. Innovators and preachers: the role of the editor in Victorian England. Westport CT 1985.
Escott, T. H. S. (1844–1924: Fortnightly Rev)
Platform, press, politics and play. Bristol 1895.
Espinasse, Francis (1823?–1912: Edinburgh Courant)
Literary recollections and sketches. 1893.
Ewing, Juliana (1841–85: Aunt Judy's Mag). *See col 1521, above.*
Juliana Ewing's world. TLS 9 Aug 1941.
Maxwell, C. Mrs. Gatty and Mrs Ewing. 1949.
Laski, M. Mrs Ewing, Mrs Molesworth and Mrs Hodgson Burnett. 1951.
Felbermann, Heinrich (1850–1925: Life)
The memoirs of a cosmopolitan life. 1936.
Finlay, George (1799–1875). *See col 2420, above.*
Miller, W. Finlay as a journalist. EHR 39 1924.
Fonblanque, Albany (1793–1872: Examiner)
Fonblanque, E. B. de. The life and letters of Fonblanque. 1874.
Forbes, Archibald (1838–1900)
Souvenirs of some continents. 1885.
Memoirs and studies of war and peace. 1895.
Forster, John (1812–76: Foreign Quart Rev; Daily News; Examiner). *See col 2225, above.*
Forsyth, William (1818–79: Aberdeen Jnl). *See col 2226, above.*
Selections from the writings of the late William Forsyth, with a memoir by Alexander Walker. Aberdeen 1882.
Foster, Ernest (1852–1919: Cassell's Saturday Jnl)
An editor's chair. 1909.
Fox, William Johnson (1786–1864: True Sun)
Garnett, R. The life of W. J. Fox. 1909.
Francis, John (1811–82: Athenaeum)
Francis, J. C. John Francis, publisher. 2 vols 1888.
Frost, John (1784?–1877: Welchman)
Williams, D. John Frost: a study in Chartism. Cardiff 1939.
Frost, Thomas (1821–1908)
Forty years' recollections: literary and political. 1880.
Reminiscences of a country journalist. 1886.
Froude, James Anthony (1818–94: Fraser's Mag etc.) *See col 2425, above.*
Maurer, O. Froude and Fraser's Magazine 1860–74. SE 28 1949.
Dunn, W. H. James Anthony Froude. 2 vols Oxford 1961–3.
Furniss, Harry (1854–1925: Punch)
Confessions of a caricaturist. 1901.
Fyfe, H. Hamilton (1869–1951)
Sixty years of Fleet Street. 1949.
Gallenga, Antonio (1810–95: The Times)
Episodes of my second life. 2 vols 1884.
Cerutti, T. Antonio Gallenga: an Italian writer in Victorian England. Oxford 1974.
Garrett, F. Edmund (1865–1907: Pall Mall Gazette; Westminster Gazette)
Cook, E. T. Garrett: a memoir. 1909.
Garvin, J. L. (1868–1947: Newcastle Chron)
Garvin, K. Garvin: a memoir. 1948.
Giffard, Stanley Lees (1788–1858: Standard; Morning Herald)
[Memoir.] Standard, 9 Nov 1858.
Gifford, William (1756–1826: Quart Rev)
Clark, B. R. Gifford, Tory satirist. New York 1930.
Gillies, R. P. (1788–1858)
Memoirs of a literary veteran. 3 vols 1851.
Greenwood, Frederick (1830–1909: Pall Mall Gazette)
[Memoir.] Blackwood's Mag Jan 1910.
See also J. W. Robertson Scott, The story of the Pall Mall Gazette, 1950.
Grove, George (1820–1900: Macmillan's Mag). *See col 2232, above.*
Hall, Anna Maria (1800–81: Juvenile Forget-me-not; Sharpe's Jnl; St James's Mag). *See col 1304, above.*
See under S. C. Hall, *below.*
Hall, Samuel Carter (1800–89; New Monthly Mag)
A book of memories. 1871, 1877.
Retrospect of a long life 1815–83. 2 vols 1883.
Hammerton, J. A. (1871–1949)
Books and myself: memoirs of an editor. [1944.]
Hannay, James (1827–73: Edinburgh Courant; Punch etc.). *See col 2234, above.*
Reminiscences of a provincial editor. Temple Bar May 1868. *See also* April 1873.
Worth, G. J. Hannay: his life and works. Lawrence KS 1964.
Hardman, William (1828–90: Morning Post)
[Memoir.] Sell's World's Press 1891.
Harland, John (1806–68: Manchester Guardian)
Read, D. Harland: the father of provincial reporting. Manchester Rev 8 1958.
Harris, Frank (c. 1855–1931: Evening News; Fortnightly Rev; Saturday Rev)
Tobin, A. I. and E. Gertz. Harris: a study in black and white. Chicago 1931.
'Kingsmill, Hugh' (H. K. Lunn). Frank Harris. 1932.
Frank Harris: his life and adventures. Ed G. Richards 1947.
Brome, V. Frank Harris. 1949.
Harris, Walter Burton (1866–1933: The Times)
Mathews, J. J. Harris, Times correspondent in Morocco. Journalism Quart 17 1940.
Harvey, D. W. (1786–1863: Sunday Times; True Sun)
Redding, C. [Memoir.] Newspaper Press 1 Sep 1869.
Harwood, Philip (1809–87: Saturday Rev)
[Memoir.] Saturday Rev 17 Dec 1887.
Haynie, Henry
The captains and the kings: intimate reminiscences of notabilities. 1905.
Hayward, Abraham (1801–84). *See col 2235.*
A selection from the correspondence of Abraham Hayward. Q.C. from 1834 to 1884, with an account of his early life. 2 vols 1886.
Hazlitt, William (1778–1830: Examiner etc.). *See col 2146, above.*
Howe, P. P. The life of Hazlitt. 1922.
Maclean, C. Born under Saturn. 1943.
Healy, Christopher
The confessions of a journalist. 1904.
Hedderwick, James (1814–97: Glasgow citizen)
Backward glances. Edinburgh 1891.
Helm, W. H. (1860–1936: Morning Post)
Memories. 1937.
Henley, William E. (1849–1903: Scots Observer; Mag of Art etc.). *See col 741, above.*
Buckley, J. H. Henley: a study in the 'Counter-Decadence' of the nineties. Princeton 1945.
Connell, J. W. E. Henley. 1949.
Henty, G. A. (1832–1902: Union Jack). *See col 1576, above.*
G. A. Henty. TLS 28 Nov 1952.
Hetherington, Henry (1792–1849: Poor Man's Guardian etc.)
Holyoake, G. J. The life of Hetherington. 1849.
Barker, A. G. Henry Hetherington 1792–1849. 1938.

Herzen, Alexander (1812–70)
Partridge, M. Herzen and the English press. Slavonic Rev 36 1958.
Hewlett, Henry G.
Autobiography, memoirs and letters. Ed H. F. Chorley 2 vols 1873.
Hibbert, H. G.
Fifty years of a Londoner's life. 1916.
Higgins, Matthew James (1810–68: New Monthly Mag; Morning Chron; Pall Mall Gazette etc.)
'Jacob Omnium'. Essays on social subjects with a memoir by W. S. Maxwell. 1875.
Hodder, George (d. 1870: Morning Post)
Memoirs of my time. 1870.
Hogg, James (1770–1835: Blackwood's Mag). *See col 363, above.*
Strout, A. L. Notes on Hogg. N & Q 2 April 1933, 29 Nov 1941.
Strout, A. L. Miscellaneous letters to, from and about Hogg. N & Q 13, 27 Dec 1941.
Strout, A. L. The life and letters of Hogg the Ettrick Shepherd. Vol 1 (1778–1825), Lubbock TX 1946.
Holland, John (1794–1872: Sheffield Mercury etc.)
Hudson, W. The life of Holland. 1874.
Hollingshead, John (1827–1904: Weekly Mail)
My lifetime. 2 vols 1895.
Holyoake, George Jacob (1817–1906: Reasoner etc.)
Sixty years of an agitator's life. 1892.
Goss, C. W. F. A descriptive bibliography of the writings of Holyoake. 1908.
McCabe, J. The life and letters of Holyoake. 2 vols 1908.
Hone, William (1780–1842: Reformist's Register; Patriot). *See col 2154, above.*
Hackwood, F. W. Hone: his life and times. 1912.
Plummer, A. Hone: a centenary memoir. Jnl of SW Essex Technical College 1 1941.
Peterson, T. The fight of Hone for British press freedom. Journalism Quart 25 1948.
Sikes, H. M. Hone: Regency patriot, parodist and pamphleteer. Newberry Lib Bull 5 1961.
Hood, Thomas (1799–1845: London Mag; New Monthly Mag etc.). *See col 367, above.*
Letters of Hood from the Dilke Papers in the British Museum. Ed L. A. Marchand, New Brunswick NJ 1945.
Hook, Theodore (1788–1841: John Bull, New Monthly Mag etc.). *See col 930, above.*
Barham, R. H. D. The life and remains of Hook. 2 vols 1849.
Hoaxer and wit: Hook. TLS 23 Aug 1941.
Howitt, William (1792–1879) and Mary (1799–1888): (Howitt's Jnl etc.). *See col 2157, above.*
Woodring, C. R. Victorian samplers: William and Mary Howitt. Lawrence KS 1952.
Lee, A. Laurels and rosemary: the life of William and Mary Howitt. Oxford 1955.
Dunicliff, J. Mary Howitt: another lost Victorian writer. 1992.
Hunt, J. H. Leigh (1784–1859: Examiner etc.). *See col 2159, above.*
Autobiography. 3 vols 1850: ed T. Hunt 1860 (by his eldest son); ed R. Ingpen 1903.
Blunden, E. Leigh Hunt: a biography. 1930.
Brewer, L. My Leigh Hunt library. Cedar Rapids IA 1932 (priv ptd).
Landré, L. Leigh Hunt. 2 vols Paris 1936.
Hunt's dramatic criticisms 1808–31. Ed L. H. and C. W. Houtchens, New York 1949.
Hunt's Literary criticism. Ed L. H. and C. W. Houtchens, New York 1956.
Hunt's political and occasional essays. Ed L. H. and C. W. Houtchens, New York 1962.
Hunt, Thornton (1810–73: Constitutional; Leader; Daily Telegraph etc.)
Blunden, E. Leigh Hunt's eldest son. Essays by Divers Hands new ser 19 1942.
See also N & Q 9, 23 Oct 1943.
Hunt, William (Eastern Morning News)
Then and now: or fifty years of newspaper work. Hull 1887.
Hutcheon, William (Morning Post)
Gentlemen of the press. 1933.
Hutton, Richard Holt (1826–97: Spectator; National Rev)
See col 2237, above.
Hogben, John R. Hutton: a monograph. Edinburgh 1899.
LeRoy, G. C. Richard Holt Hutton. PMLA 56 1 1941.
Tener, R. H. Hutton's Essays theological and literary: a bibliographical note. N & Q 205 1960.
Tener, R. H. More articles by Hutton. BNYPL Jan 1962.
Tener, R. H. The writings of Richard Holt Hutton: a checklist of identifications. Victorian Periodicals Newsletter 17 1972.
Livingstone, J. C. More published writings of Richard Holt Hutton. Victorian Periodicals Newsletter 20 1973.
Tener, R. H. R. H. Hutton: some attributions. Victorian Periodicals Newsletter 20 1973.
Jameson, Anna (1794–1860). *See col 2165, above.*
Johnston, J. Anna Jameson: Victorian, feminist, woman of letters. Aldershot 1997.
Jeffrey, Francis (1773–1850: Edinburgh Rev). *See col 2169, above.*
Greig, J. A. Jeffrey of the Edinburgh Review. 1948.
Jeffs, Harry (1860–1938: Evening Star (Wolverhampton); Christian World)
Press, preachers and politicians: reminiscences 1874–1932. 1933.
Jennings, H. J. (Birmingham Daily Mail; Financial News)
Chestnuts and small beer. 1920.
Jerdan, William (1782–1869: Sun; Literary Gazette)
Autobiography. 4 vols 1852–3.
Men I have known. 1866.
Ransom, H. Jerdan, editor and literary agent. SE 27 1948.
On a large collection of Jerdan papers, see Bodleian Lib Record 3 1950.
Jerome, Jerome Klapka (1859–1927: Idler; Today). *See col 1602, above.*
My life and times. 1926.
Jerrold, Douglas (1803–57: Lloyd's Illustr London News; Douglas Jerrold's Shilling Mag etc.). *See col 2002, above.*
Jerrold, W. B. The life of Jerrold. 1859.
Jerrold, W. C. Jerrold and Punch. 1910.
Jerrold, W. C. Jerrold: dramatist and wit. 2 vols [1914].
Jeyes, Samuel Henry (1857–1911: Standard)
Low, S. Jeyes. 1915.
Jones, Kennedy (1865–1921: Evening News etc.)
Fleet Street and Downing Street. [1920.]
Keene, Charles (1823–91: Punch)
Layard, G. S. The life and letters of Keene. 1892.
Kemble, John Mitchell (1807–57: British & Foreign Rev)
Kingsley, Charles (1819–75: Politics for the People). *See col 1311, above.*
Kingsley, Henry (1830–76: Edinburgh Daily Rev)
See col 1318, above.
Wolff, R. L. Henry Kingsley. Harvard Lib Bull 13 1959.
Kingston, W. H. G. (1814–80: Colonial Mag; Union Jack etc.). *See col 1319, above.*
Kingsford, N. R. The life, work and influence of Kingston. Toronto 1947.
Knight, Charles (1791–1873: Guardian; Knight's Quart Rev; Penny Mag etc.). *See col 2699, above.*
Passages of a working life during half a century: with a prelude of early reminiscences. 3 vols 1864–5.
Knight, Joseph (1829–1907: N & Q). *See col 2238, above.*
Francis, J. C. Notes by the way; with memoirs of Knight etc. 1909.
Hale, B. F. R. Joseph Knight. N & Q 19 Oct 1949.
Knowles, James Thomas (1831–1908: Contemporary Rev; Nineteenth Century)

Brown, A. W. The Metaphysical Society: Victorian minds in crisis 1869–80. New York 1947.
Labouchere, Henry (1831–1912: Truth)
Thorold, A. L. The life of Labouchere. 1913.
Pearson, H. Labby. 1936.
West, E. J. An unappreciated Victorian dramatic critic: Labouchere. Quart Jnl of Speech 29 1943.
Lane, John (1854–1925: Yellow Book)
May, J. L. Lane and the nineties. 1936.
Lang, Andrew (1844–1912: Longman's Mag etc.). *See col 2362, above.*
Salmond, J. B. Andrew Lang and journalism. 1950.
Latimer, Thomas (1803–88: Western Times)
Lambert, R. S. The Cobbett of the west: a study of Thomas Latimer and the struggle between pulpit and press at Exeter. 1939.
Leech, John (1817–64: Punch)
Frith, W. P. Leech's life and work. 2 vols 1891.
Kitton, F. G. John Leech. 1883, 1884 (rev).
Le Fanu, Joseph Sheridan (1814–73: Dublin Univ Mag)
See col 1323, above.
Lemon, Mark (1809–70: Punch etc.). *See col 2006, above.*
Hatton, J. With a show in the north. 1871.
Adrian, A. A. Mark Lemon: first editor of Punch. 1966.
Lennox, John (1794–1853: Greenock Newsclout)
Stewart, W. Lennox and the Greenock Newsclout. Glasgow 1918.
Levy, Joseph Moses (1812–88: Daily Telegraph)
[Memoir.] Daily Telegraph 13 Oct 1888.
Lewes, George Henry (1817–78: Cornhill Mag; Fortnightly Rev). *See col 2550, above.*
Lewis, George Cornewall (1806–63: Edinburgh Rev)
Linton, Eliza Lynn (1822–98: Saturday Rev etc.). *See col 1326, above.*
Layard, G. S. Mrs Lynn Linton: her life, letters and opinions. 1901.
Anderson, N. F. Woman against women in Victorian England: a life of Eliza Lynn Linton. 1987.
Linton, William James (1812–98). *See col 632, above.*
Memories. 1895.
Ward Lock, the house of (Temple Bar; Boys's Own Mag; Windsor Mag etc.)
Liveing, E. Adventures in publishing: the house of Ward Lock. 1954.
Longmans, Green etc., the house of (Edinburgh Rev; Longman's Mag etc.)
Cox, H. and J. E. Chandler. The house of Longman 1724–1924. 1925 (priv ptd).
Lockhart, John Gibson (1794–1854: Quart Rev). *See col 2189, above.*
Low, Sidney (1857–1932: St James's Gazette)
Chapman-Huston, D. The lost historian: a memoir of Sir Sidney Low. 1936.
Lowe, Charles (1848–1931; The Times)
The tale of a Times correspondent, Berlin 1878–1891. [1928.]
Lowe, Robert (Viscount Sherbrooke) (1811–92: The Times)
Martin A. P. Life of Lowe. 2 vols 1893.
Lucas, Frederick (1812–55: Tablet)
Riethmüller, C. Frederick Lucas. 1862.
Lucas, E. The life of Frederick Lucas. 2 vols 1886.
Lucas, Samuel (1818–68: The Times)
Mornings of the recess 1861–4. 2 vols 1864.
Lucy, Henry William (1845–1924: Daily News; Observer; Punch etc.)
Sixty years in the wilderness. 1909.
Sixty years in the wilderness: a second series. 1912.
Nearing Jordan: being the third and last volume of sixty years. 1916.
The diary of a journalist: later entries. 1922.
Lytton, Edward George Earle Lytton Bulwer (Baron Lytton) (1802–73: New Monthly Mag). *See col 1144, above.*
McCarthy, Justin (1830–1912: Morning Star). *See col 2440, above.*
An Irishman's story. 1904.
McCulloch, J. R. (1789–1864: Scotsman)
Reid, H. C. [Biographical notice.] In McCulloch's Dictionary of commerce, 1869.
Macdonell, James (1842–79)
Nicoll, W. R. Macdonell: journalist. 1890.
Mackay, Charles (1814–89: Morning Chron; Illustr London News).
See col 636, above.
Forty years' recollections of life, literature and public affairs from 1830–70. 2 vols 1877.
Through the long day: or memorials of a literary life during half a century. 2 vols 1887.
Mackay, William
Bohemian days in Fleet Street, by a journalist. 1913.
Mackintosh, Alexander (1858–1948: Aberdeen Free Press)
Fifty-seven years in the Press Gallery. World's Press News 7 Apr 1938.
Macmillan, the house of (Macmillan's Mag; Nature; Eng Illustr Mag etc.)
Morgan, C. The house of Macmillan 1843–1943. 1943.
Macmillan, Alexander (1818–96: Macmillan's Mag etc.)
Letters. Ed G. A. Macmillan 1908 (priv ptd).
Graves, C. L. (Life and letters of Macmillan. 1910.
Maginn, William (1793–1842: Blackwood's Mag etc.)
See col 2191, above.
Kenealy, E. V. William Maginn. Dublin Univ Mag Jan 1844.
Mahony, Francis Sylvester ('Father Prout'; 'Oliver Yorke') (1804–66: Fraser's Mag etc.). *See col 2239, above.*
The works of Father Prout. Ed C. Kent 1881.
Mannin, E. Two studies in integrity. 1954.
Martineau, Harriet (1802–76: Daily News; Household Words; Westminster Rev etc.). *See col 1344, above.*
Harriet Martineau's autobiography, with memorials by M. W. Chapman. 3 vols 1877.
Wheatley, V. The life and works of Harriet Martineau. 1957.
Webb, R. K. Harriet Martineau. 1960.
Hunter, S. Harriet Martineau: the poetics of moralism. Aldershot 1996.
Martineau, James (1805–1900: Prospective Rev; Nat Rev etc.). *See col 2555, above.*
Drummond, J. and C. B. Upton. The life and letters of J. Martineau. 2 vols 1902.
Massingham, H. W. (1860–1924: Daily Chron)
H. W. M.: a selection from the writings of Massingham. Ed H. J. Massingham 1925.
Masson, David (1822–1907: Reader; Macmillan's Mag)
See col 2239, above.
Maurice, J. Frederick Denison (1805–72: Athenaeum)
See col 2240, above.
Mayo, Isabella Fyvie (1843–1914)
Recollections. 1910.
Merle, Gibbons (d. 1855: White Dwarf: Galignani's Messenger etc.)
A newspaper editor's reminiscences. Fraser's Mag Nov 1839, Sep–Oct 1840, June 1841.
Miall, Edward (1809–81: Nonconformist)
Miall, A. The life of Edward Miall. 1881.
Mill, John Stuart (1806–73: London Rev; Westminster Rev). *See col 2258, above.*
Macminn, N., J. R. Hainds and J. M. McCrimmon. Bibliography of the published writings of Mill, edited from his manuscript. Evanston 1945. With a record of Mill's contributions to many periodicals.
Robson, A. P. and J. M. Robson, ed. John Stuart Mill: Newspaper Writings. Toronto 1986.
Miller, Hugh (1802–56: Witness). *See col 2243, above.*
Bayne, P. The life and letters of Miller. 2 vols 1871.

Mitchel, John (1815–75: United Irishman)
MacCall, S. Irish Mitchel: a biography. 1938.
Mitford, Mary Russell (1787–1855: New Monthly Mag; London Mag; Monthly Mag etc.). *See col 960, above.*
Coles, W. A. Magazine and other contributions by Mary Russell Mitford and Thomas Noon Talfourd. SB 12 1959.
Montague, C. E. (1867–1928: Manchester Guardian)
Elton, O. C. E. Montague: a memoir. 1929.
Montgomery, James (1771–1854: Sheffield Iris). *See col 408, above.*
Holland, J. and J. Everett. The life of Montgomery 7 vols 1854–6.
Moore, F. F. (1855–1931)
A journalist's note book. 1894.
Morley, John (1838–1923: Pall Mall Gazette; Fortnightly Rev; Macmillan's Mag). *See col 2373, above.*
My recollections. 2 vols 1917.
Hirst, F. W. The early life and letters of Lord Morley. 2 vols 1927.
Knickerbocker, F. W. Free minds: Morley and his friends. Cambridge MA 1943.
Staebler, W. The liberal mind of Morley. Princeton 1943.
Morris, Mowbray (1847–1911: Macmillan's Mag; The Times) Bolitho, H. A late Victorian man of letters. Blackwood's Mag Jan 1950.
Morris, W. O'Connor (1824–1904: The Times)
Memories and thoughts of life. 1895.
Mudie, George (fl. 1822: Economist 1821–2)
Armytage, W. H. G. Mudie: journalist and utopian. N & Q May 1957.
Murray, David Christie (1847–1907)
Recollections. 1908.
Murray, Henry
A stepson of fortune: the memoirs, confessions and opinions of Murray. 1909.
Murray, John, the house of (Quart Rev; Representative; Academy; Murray's Mag)
Smiles, S. A publisher and his friends. 2 vols 1891.
'Paston, George' (E. M. Symonds). At John Murray's 1843–92. 1932.
Murray, John, II (1778–1843: Quart Rev; Representative)
Elwin, M. The founder of the Quarterly Review. Quart Rev 281 1943.
John Murray 1778–1843: 'the Anax of publishers'. TLS 26 June 1943.
Napier, Macvey (1776–1847: Edinburgh Rev)
Selection from the correspondence edited by his son. 1879.
Shattock, J. Politics and reviewers: the Edinburgh and the Quarterly in the early Victorian age. Leicester 1989.
Nevinson, Henry W. (1856–1941: Daily Chron)
Changes and chances. 1923.
Newman, John Henry (1801–90: Rambler; Br Critic)
See col 2246, above.
Newnes, George (1851–1910: Tit-Bits; Rev of Reviews; Strand Mag; Westminster Gazette etc.)
Bookman (London) May 1899.
Friedrichs, H. The life of Sir George Newnes. 1911.
Nicoll, W. Robertson (1851–1923: Br Weekly; [London] Bookman)
A bookman's letters. 1913.
Parker, W. A. A great Scots journalist. Scots Mag 56 1951.
Northcliffe, Viscount (Alfred C. W. Harmsworth) (1865–1922: Daily Mail etc.)
Pemberton, M. Lord Northcliffe: a memoir. 1922.
Wilson, R. M. Lord Northcliffe. 1927.
Fyfe, H. H. Northcliffe: an intimate biography. 1930.
Ryan, A. P. Lord Northcliffe. 1953.
Greenwall, H. J. Northcliffe: Napoleon of Fleet Street. 1957.
Pound, R. and G. Harmsworth. Northcliffe. 1959.
Oastler, Richard (1789–1861: Ashton Chron)
Driver, C. Tory radical: the life of Oastler. 1946.
O'Connor, T. P. (1848–1929: Sun; T. P.'s Weekly etc.)
Memoirs of an old Parliamentarian. 2 vols 1929.
Fyfe, H. H. T. P. O'Connor. 1934.

O'Malley, William (1853–1939: Star)
Glancing backward. [1923.]
O'Shea, J. A. (1839–1905: Standard)
Leaves from the life of a special correspondent. 2 vols 1885.
Owen, Robert (1771–1858: New Moral World). *See col 2498, above.*
Podmore, F. The life of Owen. 1906, 2 vols 1923.
A bibliography of Robert Owen. Aberystwyth 1914, 1925.
Paterson, James (1805–76)
Autobiographical reminiscences. Glasgow 1871.
Patmore, Peter George (1786–1855: Court Jnl; New Monthly Mag). *See col 2194, above.*
My friends and acquaintances. 3 vols 1854.
Memoirs and correspondence of Coventry Patmore. Ed B. Champneys 2 vols 1900.
Patmore, D. Portrait of my family. 1935.
Payn, James (1830–98: Cornhill Mag; Chambers's Jnl). *See col 1380, above.*
Some literary recollections. 1884.
Pearson, C. Arthur (1866–1921: Daily Express; Pearson's Weekly etc.)
Dark, S. The life of Sir Arthur Pearson. 1922.
Phillips, Ernest (1870–1956)
[Reminiscences.] Newspaper World 12, 19 Nov 1938.
Phillips, Richard (1767–1840: Monthly Mag)
Memoirs of the public and private life of Sir Richard Phillips. 1808.
Timbs, J. Recollections of Sir Richard Phillips. In his Walks and talks about London, 1864.
Boyle, A. Portraiture in Lavengro. N & Q 12 May, 18 Aug, 15 and 29 Sep, 13 Oct 1951.
Prior, Melton (1845–1910: Illustr London News)
Campaigns of a war correspondent. Ed S. L. Bensusan 1912.
Ransome, Arthur (1884–1967)
Bohemia in London. 1907.
Redding, Cyrus (1785–1870: New Monthly Mag etc.)
Fifty years' recollections. 3 vols 1858.
Yesterday and today: being a sequel to fifty years' recollections. 3 vols 1863.
Reeve, Henry (1813–95: Edinburgh Rev)
Laughton, J. K. Memoirs of the life and correspondence of Reeve. 2 vols 1898.
The letters of Reeve and Charles Greville. Ed A. H. Johnson 1924.
Reid, T. Wemyss (1842–1905: Speaker; Leeds Mercury)
Memoirs of Sir Wemyss Reid. Ed S. J. Reid 1905.
Reynolds, G. W. M. (1814–79: Reynolds' Miscellany; Reynolds' Weekly Newspaper). *See col 1390, above.*
[Memoir.] Bookseller 8 July 1879.
Summers, M. G. W. M. Reynolds. TLS 4 July 1942.
Hunter, J. V. B. S. George Reynolds, sensational novelist and agitator. Book Handbook 4 1947.
Kausch, D. George W. Reynolds: a bibliography. Library 28 1973.
Richardson, J. Hall (1857–1945)
From the City to Fleet Street, 1927.
Rintoul, Robert Stephen (1787–1858: Dundee Advertiser; Spectator)
[Memoir.] Dundee Advertiser 27 April 1858; Spectator 1 May 1858.
Ritchie, Leitch (1800–65: Chambers's Jnl; Era). *See col 1392, above.*
Robinson, Henry Crabb (1775–1867: The Times). *See col 2195, above.*
The diary, reminiscences and correspondence of Crabb Robinson. Ed T. Sadler 3 vols 1869.
Baker, J. M. Crabb Robinson of Bury, Jena, The Times and Russell Square. 1937.
Crabb Robinson in Germany 1800–5. Ed E. J. Morley 1929. With material on his contributions to the Monthly Register.
Robinson, John Richard (1828–1903: Daily News)
Thomas, F. M. Fifty years of Fleet Street: being the life and recollections of Sir J. R. Robinson. 1904.
Roche, Eugenius (1786–1829: Courier; Morning Post)
London in a thousand years. 1830.

Runciman, James (1852–91)
Sidelights; with a memoir by Grant Allen. 1893.
Russell, Alexander (1814–76: Scotsman)
Alexander Russell. Edinburgh 1876 (priv ptd).
Graham, H. G. In his Literary and historical essays, 1908.
Russell, Edward (1834–1920: Liverpool Daily Post)
That reminds me. 1899.
Russell, William Howard (1820–1907): The Times)
The great war with Russia: a personal retrospect. 1895.
Atkins, J. B. The life of Russell. 2 vols 1911.
Furneaux, H. The first war correspondent, Russell of The Times. 1945.
Mathews, J. J. The father of war correspondents. Virginia Quart Rev 21 1945.
My diary north and south. Ed F. Pratt, New York 1954.
My Indian Mutiny diary, 1957.
Despatches from the Crimea 1854–6. Ed N. Bentley 1966.
Sala, George Augustus (1828–96: Temple Bar; Daily Telegraph). *See col 1394, above.*
Things I have seen and people I have known. 2 vols 1895 (2nd edn).
The life and adventures of Sala, written by himself. 2 vols 1895.
Strauss, R. Sala: the portrait of an eminent Victorian. 1942.
Edwards, P. D. Dickens' 'young men': George Augustus Sala, Edmund Yates and the world of Victorian journalism. Aldershot 1997.
Scott, C. P. (1846–1932: Manchester Guardian)
Hammond, J. L. C. P. Scott. 1934.
C. P. Scott 1846–1932: the making of the Manchester Guardian. 1946.
Scott, Clement (1841–1904: Theatre etc.)
The wheel of life: a few memories and recollections. 1898.
Scott, Constance Margaret
Old days in Bohemian London. 1919.
Scott, John (1783–1821: Champion; London Mag)
Zeitlin, J. The editor of the London Magazine. JEGP 20 1921.
Hughes, T. R. John Scott: editor, author and critic. London Mercury April 1930.
Scott, J. W. Robertson (1866–1963: Pall Mall Gazette; Westminster Gazette)
Faith and works in Fleet Street. 1947.
The day before yesterday: memories of an uneducated man. 1951.
Scott, William (1813–72: Saturday Rev; Christian Remembrancer)
Shand, Alexander I. (1832–1907: The Times)
Days of the past. 1905.
Shorter, Clement K. (1857–1929: Sphere etc.)
C. K. S.: an autobiography. Ed. J. M. Bulloch 1927 (priv ptd).
Simpson, Richard (1820–76: Rambler; Home & Foreign Rev)
Simpson, William (1823–99: Illustr London News)
Autobiography. Ed G. E. Todd 1903.
Sinclair, Alexander (Glasgow Herald)
Fifty years of newspaper life 1845–95. Glasgow [c. 1897] (priv ptd).
Smith, Charles Manby
The working man's way in the world: being the autobiography of a journeyman printer. 1854.
Smith, Ernest
Fields of adventure. 1923.
Smith, George Murray (1824–1901: Cornhill Mag; Pall Mall Gazette)
Lee, S. Memoir of George Smith. In DNB Suppl 1901.
Huxley, L. The house of Smith Elder. 1923 (priv ptd).
Glynn, J. Prince of publishers: a biography of George Smith. 1986.
Smith, Horatio (1779–1849: London Mag; New Monthly Mag)
A graybeard's gossip about his literary acquaintance. New Monthly Mag March–Dec 1847.
Smith, James Elimalet (1801–57: Shepherd)
Smith, W. A. 'Shepherd' Smith, the universalist. 1892.
Smith, Sydney (1771–1845: Edinburgh Rev). *See col 2197, above.*
Bullett, G. Sydney Smith: a biography and a selection. 1951.
Letters. Ed N. C. Smith 2 vols Oxford 1953.
Smith, Wareham (1874–1938)
Spilt ink. 1928.
Southey, Robert (1774–1843: Quart Rev). *See col 457, above.*
Graham, W. Southey as a Tory reviewer. PQ 2 1923.
Havens, R. D. Southey's contributions to the Foreign Review. RES 8 1932.
Spears, Robert (1825–99: Stockton Gazette; Christian Life)
Memorials of Robert Spears. Belfast 1903.
Spender, J. A. (1862–1942: Westminster Gazette)
Life, journalism and politics. 2 vols 1927.
Journalism in my time. Inst of Journalists' Jnl 28 1940.
Harris, W. J. A. Spender. 1946.
Stark, Malcolm (Glasgow Herald)
The pulse of the world. 1915.
Stead, William Thomas (1849–1912: Pall Mall Gazette; Rev of Reviews)
Waugh, B. William T. Stead: a life for the people. [1885.]
Stead, E. My father. 1913, 1918.
Harper, E. K. Stead the man: personal reminiscences. 1914.
Whyte, F. The life of Stead. 2 vols 1925.
Mansfield, F. J. Who started the New Journalism? World's Press News 3 March 1938.
Terrot, C. The maiden tribute: a study of the white slave traffic of the nineteenth century. 1959.
Baylen, J. O. George Meredith and Stead: three unpublished letters. HLQ 24, 1960.
Baylen, J. O. and R. B. Holland. Whitman, Stead and the Pall Mall Gazette. Amer Lit 33 1961.
Hogan, P. G. and J. O. Baylen. G. Bernard Shaw and Stead: an unexplored relationship. Stud in Eng Lit 1 1961.
Baylen, J. O. A Victorian's 'crusade' in Chicago 1893–4. Jnl of Amer History 51 1964.
Baylen, J. O. William Archer, Stead and the theatre: some unpublished letters. Univ of Mississippi Stud in Eng 5 1964.
Stafford, A. The age of consent. 1964.
Baylen, J. O. W. T. Stead and the New Journalism. Emory Univ Quart 21 1965.
Baylen, J. O. The Tsar's 'lecturer-general': W. T. Stead and the Russian revolution of 1905. Atlanta GA 1969.
Schults, R. L. Crusader in Babylon: W. T. Stead and the Pall Mall Gazette. Lincoln NE 1972.
Robson, A. The significance of The maiden tribute of modern Babylon. Victorian Periodicals Newsletter 11 1978.
Steed, Henry Wickham (1871–1956: The Times)
Through thirty years 1892–1922. 2 vols 1924.
Steevens, George Warrington (1869–1900). *See col 2392, above.*
Things seen, with a memoir by W. E. Henley. 1900.
Works: memorial edition. Ed G. S. Street and V. Blackburn 7 vols 1900–2.
Stephen, Leslie (1832–1904: Cornhill Mag). *See col 2394, above.*
Annan, N. Stephen: his thought and character in relation to his time. 1951.
Fenwick, G. Leslie Stephen's Life in Letters: a bibliographical study. Winchester 1993.
Stephenson, Albert Frederick (1854–1934: Southport Critic; Halifax Guardian etc.)
Stephenson, W. H. Albert Frederick Stephenson: a Lancashire newspaper man. Manchester 1937.
Sterling, Edward (1773–1847: The Times)
Carlyle, T. The life of John Sterling. 1851.
Sterling, John (1806–44: Blackwood's Mag etc.; Athenaeum etc.). *See col 2199, above.*
Carlyle, T. The life of John Sterling. 1851.

Stillman, W. J. (1828–1901: The Times)
The autobiography of a journalist. 2 vols 1901.
Strachey, John St Loe (1860–1927: Spectator)
The adventure of living. 1922.
Strachey, A. St Loe Strachey: his life and his paper. 1930.
Sanders, C. R. The Strachey family 1588–1932. Durham NC 1953.
Strahan, Alexander (Sunday Mag; Contemporary Rev; Good Words)
Twenty years of a publisher's life. Day of Rest Jan–Dec 1881.
Srebrnick, P. T. Alexander Strahan, Victorian publisher. Ann Arbor MI 1986.
Strauss, G. L. M. (1807–87: Grocer)
Reminiscences of an old Bohemian. 2 vols 1882.
Stuart, Daniel (1766–1846: Morning Post)
Reply to statements in James Gillman, Life of Coleridge, GM May, June, Aug 1838.
Woof, R. S. Wordsworth's poetry and Stuart's newspapers 1797–1803. SB 15 1962.
Talfourd, Thomas Noon (1795–1854: New Monthly Mag; London Mag). *See col 1985, above.*
Watson, V. Talfourd and his friends, TLS 20–27 Apr 1956.
Coles, W. A. Magazine and other contributions by Mary Russell Mitford and Talfourd. SB 12 1959.
Taylor, John (1757–1832: Morning Post; Sun)
Records of my life. 2 vols 1832.
Taylor, John Edward (1791–1844; Manchester Guardian)
[Memoir.] Manchester Guardian 10 Jan 1844.
Taylor, Tom (1817–80: Punch). *See col 2024, above.*
Thackeray, W. M. (1811–63: Constitutional; Cornhill Mag etc.). *See col 1406, above.*
Gulliver, H. S. Thackeray's literary apprenticeship. Valdosta GA 1934.
Dodds, J. W. Thackeray: a critical portrait. New York 1941.
The letters and private papers of Thackeray. Ed G. N. Ray 4 vols Cambridge MA 1945–6.
Stevenson, L. The showman of Vanity Fair. New York 1947.
Ray, G. N. Thackeray. 2 vols New York 1955–8.
Thomas, William Beach (b. 1868)
A traveller in news. 1925.
Thomas, William Luson (1830–1900: Graphic)
[Memoir.] Graphic 20 Oct 1900.
Tillotson, W. F. (1844–89: Bolton Evening News)
Bolton's newspaper family. Newspaper World 14 Jan 1939.
Singleton, F. Tillotsons 1850–1950. 1951.
Tinsley, William (1831–1902: Tinsley's Mag etc.)
Random recollections of an old publisher. 2 vols 1900.
Townsend, Meredith White (1831–1911: Spectator)
Asia and Europe. 1901.
Trollope, Anthony (1815–82: St Paul's Mag). *See col 1418, above.*
Letters. Ed B. A. Booth, New York 1951.
Troup, George (1811–79: North Br Daily Mail)
Troup, G. E. The life of Troup, journalist. Edinburgh 1881.
Tulloch, John (1823–86: Fraser's Mag). *See col 2614, above.*
Tweedie, Mrs Alec
Thirteen years of a busy woman's life. 1912.
Urquhart, David (1805–77: Free Press)
Robinson, G. L. The life of Urquhart. Oxford 1932.
Vaughan, Robert (1795–1868: Br Quart Rev)
Venables, George Stovin (1810–88: Saturday Rev)
[Memoir.] Saturday Rev 13 Oct 1888.
Villiers, Frederick (1852–1922)
Pictures of many wars. 1902.
Vizetelly, Henry (1820–94: Illustr Times etc.)
Glances back through 70 years. 2 vols 1893.
Wainewright, Thomas Griffiths (1794–1852: London Mag)
Wilde, O. Intentions. 1891, 1894.
Curling, J. Janus weathercock. 1938.
Lindsey, J. Suburban gentleman: the life of Wainewright: poet, painter and poisoner. 1942.
Wakeley, Thomas (1795–1862: Lancet)
Sprigge, S. The life and times of Wakeley. 1897.
Walford, Edward (1823–97: Once a Week; GM)
Buckler, W. E. Walford: a distressed editor. N & Q Dec 1953.
Watson, Aaron (1850–1926: Echo)
A newspaper man's memories. [1925.]
Watson, James (1799–1874)
Linton, W. J. Watson: a memoir. 1880 (priv ptd).
Watts, Alaric (1797–1864: United Services Gazette). *See col 488, above.*
Watts, A. A. The life of Watts by his son. 2 vols 1884.
White, Joseph Blanco (1775–1841: London Rev (1829) etc.). *See col 2649, above.*
Whiteing, Richard (1840–1928)
My harvest. 1915.
Wilde, Oscar (1854–1900: Woman's World). *See col 2060, above.*
Wilkinson, Henry Spenser (1853–1937)
Thirty-five years 1874–1909. 1933. Autobiography of a journalist and military expert.
Williams, F. C.
Journalistic jumbles. [1880?]
Wilson, John ('Christopher North') (1785–1854: Blackwood's Mag). *See col 2205, above.*
Wood, Ellen (Mrs Henry) (1814–87: Argosy). *See col 1440, above.*
Yates, Edmund (1831–94: World). *See col 1726, above.*
Recollections and experiences. 2 vols 1884.
Edwards, P. D. Dickens' 'young men': George Augustus Sala, Edmund Yates and the world of Victorian journalism. Aldershot 1997.
Yorke, Henry Redhead (1772–1813: H. R. Yorke's Political Rev)
Sykes, J. A. C. France in 1802. 1906.

(2) THE GENERAL HISTORY OF THE PRESS

Bibliographies and Reference Works

Burney collection of newspapers, 1603–1817: mss catalogue. BL. Newspapers in vol VI (1801–17) held in Newspaper Library.
Catalogue of a collection of early newspapers and essayists, formed by the late John Thomas Hope Esq., and presented to the Bodleian Library by the late Rev F. W. Hope. Ed J. H. Burn. Oxford 1865.
Poole, W. F. An index to periodical literature. Boston 1882, 6 suppls to 1907; rptd Gloucester MA 1963.
Peet, H. W. A bibliography of journalism: a guide to the books about the press and pressmen. 1915. Rptd from Sell's World's Press 1915.
[Muddiman, J. G.] Tercentenary handlist of English and Welsh newspapers, magazines and reviews, 1620–1920. The Times. 1920; rptd 1966.
Cannon, C. L. comp. Journalism: a bibliography. New York 1924. (New York Pub Lib).
Stewart, A. comp. Catalogue of the Press Club Library on journalism. 3 vols 1935, 1946, 1948.
LeFanu, W. R. British periodicals of medicine: a chronological list, 1640–1899. Baltimore MD 1938; rev Oxford 1984, ed J. Loudon.
Nafziger, R. O. comp. International news and the press. New York 1940. An annotated bibliography.
Egoff, S. A. Children's periodicals of the nineteenth century: a survey and bibliography. 1951.
Ward, W. S. comp. Index and finding list of serials published in the British Isles, 1789–1832. Lexington KY 1954; suppl BNYPL 77 1974.
British union-catalogue of periodicals. 4 vols, 1955–8. Ed B. D. Stewart. Suppls 1959–80. Lists holdings – including those of newspapers – in c. 400 British libraries. Succeeded by Serials in the British Library 1981–.

Ferguson, J. P. S. Scottish newspapers held in Scottish libraries. Edinburgh 1956. Rev as Directory of Scottish newspapers. 1984.
Price, W. C. The literature of journalism: an annotated bibliography. Minneapolis MN 1959. Continued by Price and C. M. Pickett. An annotated journalism bibliography, 1958–1968. 1970.
Blum, E. Reference books in the mass media. Urbana IL 1962. Rev as Basic books in the mass media. 1972, 1980; and by Blum and F. Wilhoit as Mass media bibliography: reference, research and reading. 1990.
Stratman, C. J. British theatrical periodicals, 1720–1960: a bibliography. New York 1962, rev 1972.
The Wellesley index to Victorian periodicals, 1824–1900. Toronto 1966–89, 5 vols. Vols 1–3 ed W. E. Houghton; vol 4 ed W. E. Houghton, E. R. Houghton and J. H. Slingerland: vol 5 Index ed J. H. Slingerland. Identification of contributors to selected quarterlies and monthlies with bibliographies of their articles and stories, an index of initials and pseudonyms, and detailed introductions to more than forty periodicals.
McCoy, R. E. Freedom of the press: an annotated bibliography. Carbondale IL 1968. Supplemented by Freedom of the press: a bibliocyclopedia: ten-year suppl (1967–1977). 1979.
Victorian Periodicals Newsletter 1968–78; continued as Victorian Periodicals Review 1979–. Quarterly, with annual bibliography.
The new Cambridge bibliography of English literature. Vol 3 (1800–1900). Cambridge 1969. Includes newspapers and magazines, ed H. M. and S. K. Rosenberg.
White, C. L. Women's magazines, 1693–1968. 1970.
Wiener, J. H. A descriptive finding list of unstamped British periodicals, 1830–1836. Bibliographical Soc 1970.
Gray, D. J. A list of comic periodicals published in Great Britain 1800–1900, with a prefatory essay. Victorian Periodicals Newsletter 15 1972.
Dixon, D. Local newspapers and periodicals of the nineteenth century: a checklist of holdings in provincial libraries. Leicester 1973, rev 1976.
Ward, W. S. comp. British periodicals and newspapers, 1769–1832: a bibliography of secondary sources. Lexington KY 1973.
Index of authors and titles of the publishers Kegan Paul, Trench, Trübner and Henry S. King 1853–1912. Bishop's Stortford 1974.
Index to the archives of George Allen & Co 1893–1915. Bishop's Stortford 1974.
Tye, J. R. Periodicals of the nineties: a checklist of literary periodicals published in the British Isles at longer than fortnightly intervals. Oxford 1974.
Bibliography of British newspapers. Ed C. A. Toase. Series of county vols. Library Association 1975; British Library 1982–.
Catalogue of the Newspaper Library, Colindale. Comp P. E. Allen. 8 vols 1975. Holdings as at 1971. Suppls to 1993.
Gifford, D. The British comic catalogue 1874–1974. Westport CT 1975.
Turner, M. L. Index and guide to the lists of the publications of Richard Bentley and Son 1829–1898. Bishop's Stortford 1975.
Madden, L. and D. Dixon. The nineteenth-century periodical press in Britain: a bibliography of modern studies, 1901–1971. New York 1976. First pbd as suppl to Victorian Periodicals Newsletter 8, Sep 1975. Contains (a) Bibliographies, finding lists; (b) General history of periodicals and newspapers; (c) Individual periodicals and newspapers; (d) Studies and memoirs of proprietors, editors, journalists and contributors. *See also* Uffelman, L. K. *below*.
Palmegiano, E. M. ed. Women and British periodicals, 1832–1867: a bibliography. Victorian Periodicals Newsletter 9 1976.
Sader, M. ed. Comprehensive index to English-language little magazines 1890–1970. Series one 8 vols. Millwood 1976.
The Waterloo directory of Victorian periodicals, 1824–1900. Ed M. Wolff, J. S. North and D. Deering. Waterloo Ont 1976.
The Warwick guide to British labour periodicals 1790–1970: a check-list. Ed R. Harrison, G. B. Woolven and R. Duncan. Hassocks Sussex and Atlantic Highlands NJ 1977.
White, R. B. ed. The English literary journal to 1900: a guide to information sources. Detroit 1977.
Boyce, G., J. Curran and P. Wingate ed. Newspaper history: from the seventeenth century to the present day. London and Beverly Hills CA 1978. Includes extensive bibliography.
Harrison, J. F. C. and D. Thompson. Bibliography of the Chartist movement, 1837–1976. Brighton and Atlantic Highlands NJ 1978.
Houfe, S. The dictionary of British book illustrators and caricaturists, 1800–1914. Woodbridge Suffolk 1978. Includes contributors to periodicals.
Vann, J. D. and R. Van Arsdel ed. Victorian periodicals: a guide to research. New York 1978.
Dixon, D. English juvenile periodical literature, 1870–1914: a bibliographical analysis. Leicester 1979. Unpbd M. Phil thesis.
Northern Ireland newspapers: a checklist with locations. Belfast 1979. Rev 1987. Ed J. R. R. Adams.
Stanton, M. N. English literary journals 1900–1950; a guide to information sources. Detroit 1982. Complements R. White's The English literary journal to 1900, above.
West. J. Town records. Chichester 1983. Includes locations of selected provincial newspapers.
Sullivan, A. ed. British literary magazines. 4 vols Westport CT 1983–6. Vol 2 The romantic age 1789–1836. 1983. Vol 3 The Victorian and Edwardian age 1837–1913. 1984. Profiles of individual periodicals with bibliographies.
Dixon, D. The provincial press: a decade of writings 1972–1981. Victorian Periodicals Rev 17 1984. Updates Madden Dixon bibliography 1976 above.
Journal of Newspaper and Periodical History 1984–1993. London, then Westport CT. Continued as Studies in Newspaper and Periodical History. 1994–. Annual.
Lake, B. British newspapers: a history and guide for collectors. 1984.
Nineteenth-century short-title catalogue. Newcastle upon Tyne, 1984–.
Fulton, R. D. and C. M. Colee ed. Union list of Victorian serials: a union list of selected nineteenth century British serials available in United States and Canadian libraries. New York 1985.
Gifford, D. The complete catalogue of British comics. Exeter 1985. *See also* Gifford 1976, *above*.
Lake, F. H. Regimental journals and other serial publications of the British Army, 1660–1981: an annotated bibliography. 4 vols [1986].
The Waterloo directory of Irish newspapers and periodicals, 1800–1900. Ed J. S. North. Waterloo Ontario 1986. Includes over 4000 titles.
Wells, R. Newsplan: reports of the pilot project in the south-west. British Library series, 1986–. Plans for storage techniques.
Doughan, D. and D. Sanchez. Feminist periodicals 1855–1984: an annotated bibliography of British, Irish, Commonwealth and international titles. Brighton 1987.
Gibson, J. S. W. comp. Local newspapers 1750–1920: a select location list. Birmingham 1987. Covers England and Wales, Channel Islands, Isle of Man.
Linton, D. and R. J. Boston. The newspaper press in Britain: an annotated bibliography. 1987.
Palmegiano, E. M. The British Empire in the Victorian press, 1832–1867: a bibliography. New York 1987.
Tarbert, G. C. ed. Periodical directories and bibliographies: an annotated guide. Detroit 1987. Includes directories, bibliographies etc. about periodicals from 1850 to the present.
Jones, P. H. A bibliography of the history of Wales. Cardiff 1989. Microfiche with explanatory booklet.
Vann, J. D. and R. T. Van Arsdel ed. Victorian periodicals: a second guide to research. New York 1989.

The Waterloo directory of Scottish newspapers and periodicals, 1800–1900. Ed J. S. North. 2 vols Waterloo Ontario 1989.
Zuckerman, M. E. comp. Sources on the history of women's magazines, 1792–1980. Westport CT 1991.
Griffiths, D. M. ed. The encyclopedia of the British press, 1442–1992. Basingstoke 1992. Includes a thematic bibliography.
Uffelman, L. K. The nineteenth-century periodical press in Britain: a bibliography of modern studies. 1972–1987. Edwardsville IL 1992. Contains (a) Bibliographies, finding lists; (b) General list of periodicals and newspapers; (c) Individual periodicals and newspapers; (d) Studies and memoirs of proprietors, editors, journalists and contributors.
Bryant, H. E. and S. Haneage comp. Dictionary of British cartoonists and caricaturists, 1730–1980. Aldershot 1994.
Richardson, R. and R. Thorne ed. The Builder illustrations index 1843–1883. 1994.
Vann, J. D. and R. T. Van Arsdel ed. Victorian periodicals and Victorian society. Aldershot 1994.

Histories of the Press

Oldmixon, John. Memoirs of the press, historical and political, for thirty years past, from 1710 to 1740. 1742.
Savage, J. An account of the London daily papers, and the manner in which they are conducted. 1811.
[Brougham, H.] Abuses of the press. Edinburgh Rev 22 1813.
Hankin, E. Letter to the Rt Hon the Earl of Liverpool on the licentiousness of the press. 1814.
Holt, F. L. The law of libel. 1816 (2nd edn).
[Poynder, J.] Observations on Sunday newspapers, tending to show the impiety of such a violation of the Sabbath, the religious and political evils consequent upon the practice, and the necessity which exists for its suppression. By a layman. 1820.
[House of Commons.] Return of the names of individuals sentenced for political libel (King's Bench and Scotland) 1808–21. Commons Journals 76 1821, pp. 1208–9.
[House of Commons: accounts and papers.] Return of persons prosecuted for libels, blasphemy and sedition. (379) xxi 399. 1821. [Ditto, 1823.] (562) xv 239 1823.
[House of Commons.] Return of details concerning nearly all prosecutions for libel (Great Britain without Ireland) 1813–22. Commons Journals, vol 78 1823, pp. 1082 ff.
[Salgues, J. B.] Les milles et une calomnies: ou extraits des correspondences privées insérés dans les journaux anglais et allemands pendant le ministère de M. le Duc Decazes. 2 vols Paris 1822.
[Hazlitt, W.] The periodical press. Edinburgh Rev 38 1823; rptd in Complete works of Hazlitt, ed P. P. Howe, vol 16 1933.
Stanhope, Leicester. Sketch of the history and influence of the press in British India. 1823.
The periodical press of Great Britain and Ireland. 1824.
[Mill, James.] Periodical literature. Westminster Rev 1 1824.
Newspapers. Westminster Rev 2 1824.
[Westmacott, C. M.] The spirit of the public journals 1823–5. 3 vols 1824–6.
[Mudie, R.] Babylon the great. 2 vols 1825.
[Merle, G.] Newspaper press. Westminster Rev 10 1829.
[Merle, G.] Weekly newspapers. Westminster Rev 10 1829.
[House of Commons: accounts and papers.] Return of prosecutions for libels or misdemeanours in the reigns of Geo. 3 and Geo. 4, against members of the Government, or persons acting in official capacity, conducted in the Department of the Solicitor to the Treasury. (608) xxx 211 1830.
D., R. K. Letter to Viscount Althorp on the proposed reduction in the Newspaper Stamp and Advertisement Duties. 1831.
[House of Commons: accounts and papers.] Return of persons in confinement for non-payment of Penalties; prosecutions connected with the Paper Duties; and drawbacks allowed on the exportation of paper. (346) xv 539 1831.
The influence of the newspapers. Fraser's Mag Sep–Oct 1831.
Lamb, C. Newspapers thirty-five years ago. Englishman's Mag Oct 1831; rptd in his Last essays of Elia, 1833.
[House of Commons: accounts and papers.] Number of persons committed for selling unstamped publications since Dec 10 1831. (4) xxxiv 103 and (711) xxxiv 107 1832.
The companion to the newspaper. No 1, Mar 1833–47. Monthly paper pbd by Charles Knight, with the number of duty stamps issued to each paper.
[House of Commons: accounts and papers.] Return of prosecutions for libel since the accession of His present Majesty William IV, either by ex officio informations or indictment, conducted in the Department of the Solicitor to the Treasury. (202) xlviii 267 1834.
[Alison, A.] The influence of the press. Blackwood's Mag Sep 1834.
[House of Commons: accounts and papers.] Return of the names of individuals prosecuted for political libel etc from March 17 1821; Convictions in Great Britain, 1821–1831, for offences of blasphemy and sedition; Number of informations filed by the Attorney-General against persons accused of blasphemy or sedition 1821–1834. (410) xlviii 269 1834.
Influence of the press. Westminster Rev 21 1834.
Fox, W. J. The morality of the press. 1835.
Roebuck, J. A. The stamped press of London and its morality. [1835.]
Advertising in Scotland. Tait's Mag Mar 1836.
Crawfurd, J. The Newspaper Stamp and the newspaper postage compared. 1836.
[Knight, C.] The Newspaper Stamp and the duty on paper, viewed in relation to their effects upon the diffusion of knowledge, by the author of the Results of machinery. 1836.
The morning and evening papers. Fraser's Mag May 1836.
[Westmacott, C. M.] The Stamp Duties: serious considerations on the proposed alteration of the Stamp Duty on newspapers. 1836.
[Grant, J.] The great metropolis. 2 vols 1837.
[House of Commons: accounts and papers.] Effect upon the revenue by reduction of Stamp Duty on newspapers, and of legal proceedings relating to Stamp Duty on newspapers, and sale of unstamped papers. (291) xxxiv 303 1837.
Newspapers and other publications found in the coffee, public and eating houses in Westminster. Jnl of Statistical Soc Dec 1838.
The religious periodical press. Fraser's Mag Sep 1838.
The fourth estate: or the moral influence of the press. 1839.
The spirit of the metropolitan conservative press: being a selection from the London conservative journals during the year 1839. 1840.
Simmonds, P. L. Statistics of newspapers in various countries. Jnl Statistical Soc July 1841.
[House of Commons: accounts and papers.] Numbers of newspapers to which stamps were issued, and the number issued to newspapers, 1836 to 1842; number of advertisements inserted in the London papers, the English provincial newspapers, the Irish papers etc 1836–42; amount of advertisement duty received in England, etc. Total for each year, rate of duty. (340) xxvi 613 1842.
Knight, C. London newspapers. [In his] London, 1843.
[Evans, D. M.] City men and City manners. 1845, 1852.
The newspaper and periodical press of London. London Jnl, Vols 1–2 1845–6.
The power of the press: is it rightly employed? Facts, inquiries and suggestions addressed to members of Christian churches. 1847.
The provincial press of the United Kingdom. In Reynold's miscellany, 1847.
Tisley, H. Treatise on the Stamp laws in Great Britain and Ireland. 1849 (2nd edn).
[House of Commons: accounts and papers.] Estimate of the annual

expense of collecting the Stamp Duty on newspapers; stating the number and wages of persons employed at Somerset House, and in Edinburgh and Manchester, in stamping the paper; the annual cost of machinery, and the expense of clerks, including those who receive the money for the stamps. (211) xxxiii 571 1850.
Hunt, F. K. The fourth estate: contributions towards a history of newspapers, and of the liberty of the press. 2 vols 1850.
Munsell, J. The British press. [In his] Typographical miscellany, Albany NY 1850.
Espinasse, F. 'Herodotus Smith'. The periodical and newspaper press. The Critic: Journal of British and Foreign Literature and the Arts 1851–2.
[House of Commons.] Report from the Select Committee on Newspaper Stamps. (558) xvii 1 1851.
Mayne, F. The perilous nature of the Penny Periodical Press. 1851.
Barnes, E. Newspapers and the Stamp question. Br Quart Rev 15 1852. *See also* Edinburgh Rev 98 1853.
[Schlesinger, M.] Sauntering in London. 1853.
Smith, A. Press orders: being the opinions of the leading journals on the abolition of the newspapers privileges. 1853.
Knight, C. The old printer and the modern press. 1854.
Urquhart, D. Public opinion and its organs. 1855.
[Greg, W. R.] The newspaper press. Edinburgh Rev 102 1855.
The London daily press. Westminster Rev 64, new ser 8, 1855.
Cockburn, H. Memorials of his time. Edinburgh 1856.
Clarigny, C. Histoire de la presse en Angleterre et aux États Unis. Paris 1857.
A Distinguished Writer. The press and the public service. 1857.
[House of Commons: accounts and papers.] Return of correspondence on the subject of the registration of newspapers, and securities on the publication of newspapers and pamphlets. xxxiv 199 1857–8.
[Murray, E. C. G.] The press and the public service, by a distinguished writer. 1857.
A quarterly reviewer. The newspaper press reviewed. 1857.
Andrews, A. The history of British journalism. 2 vols 1859.
Macintosh, C. A. Popular outlines of the press. 1859.
Amphlett, J. The newspaper press in part of the last century and up to 1860: recollections. 1860.
Fontane, T. Aus England: Studien und Briefe über Londoner Theater, Kunst und Presse. Stuttgart 1860.
Grattan, C. J. The gallery: a sketch of the history of Parliamentary reporting and reporters. 1860.
The newspaper press of the present day. 1860.
[Kirwan, A. V.] Editors and newspaper writers of the last generation, by an old apprentice of the law. Fraser's Mag Feb, May, July 1862.
Scott, J. A. The British newspaper: the penny theory and its solution. Dublin Univ Mag Mar 1863.
Bertrand, E. La régime régal de la presse en Angleterre. Paris 1868.
Reid, H. G. The press. In J. Samuelson, The civilisation of our day, 1868.
Holtzendorff, F. von. Englands Presse. In Sammlung-Wissenschaftliche Vorträge, Berlin 1870.
Grant, J. The newspaper press: its origin, progress and present history. 3 vols 1871, 1872.
[Marshall, T. W.] Protestant journalism, by the author of My clerical friends. 1874.
Murphy, A. The Tory press. Contemporary Rev Apr 1874.
Politics and the press. Fraser's Mag July 1875.
Routledge, J. Chapters in the history of popular progress, chiefly in relation to the freedom of the press and trial by jury 1660–1820, with an application to later years. 1876.
Webber, V. A. The English newspaper press and its influence. Ryde 1876.
[House of Commons.] Report from the Select Committee on the law of libel. 1879.
[Armstrong, R. A.] The story of nineteenth century reviewing. Modern Rev 1 1880.
English journalism. Nation (New York) 22–9 July, 12, 26 Aug, 16, 30 Sep, 14, 28 Oct 1880.
'Oldcastle, John' (Wilfred Meynell). Journals and journalism. 1880.
Paterson, J. The liberty of the press, speech and public worship. 1880.
The religious press. Dublin Rev 3rd ser 6 1881.
Hatton, J. Journalistic London. 1882.
Pebody, C. English journalism and the men who have made it. 1882.
R., G. The penny newspaper: the story of the cheap press. [1883.]
Bowles, T. G. Newspapers. Fortnightly Rev July 1884.
Croker, J. W. The Croker papers 1809–30. Ed L. J. Jennings 3 vols 1884.
Elliott, G. The newspaper Libel and Registration Act 1881. 1884.
Whorlow, H. The Provincial Newspaper Society: a jubilee retrospect. 1886.
Bourne, H. R. Fox. English newspapers: chapters in the history of journalism. 2 vols 1887.
Powell, A. The law specially affecting printers, publishers and newspaper proprietors. [1887.]
B., H. A. About newspapers: chiefly English and Scottish; with an appendix containing an account of the periodical publications issued in connection with the Anglican Communion in Great Britain and Ireland. Edinburgh 1888.
Fraser, H. The law of libel in its relation to the press. 1889.
Kelly, R. S. The law of newspaper libel. 1889.
O'Connor, T. P. The New Journalism. New Rev Oct 1889.
Greenwood, F. The newspaper press. Nineteenth Century May 1890.
Baker, A. The newspaper world: essays on press history and work, past and present. 1890.
Quail, J. Our journals and journalists. Hull 1890.
Robertson Nicholl, W. James Macdonnell, journalist. 1890.
Fisher, J. R. and J. A. Strahan. The law of the press: a digest of the law affecting newspapers in England, India and the Colonies. 1891.
Leader, J. D. Seventy-three years of progress. A history of the Sheffield Independent from 1819 to 1892. 1892.
Massingham, H. W. The London daily press. 1892.
Oliphant, M. O. W. and F. R. Oliphant. The Victorian age of literature. 2 vols 1892.
Archer, T. The highway of letters and its echoes of famous footsteps. 1893.
Blowitz, Henri. Journalism as a profession. Contemporary Rev Jan 1893.
Blowitz, Henri. Reminiscences of a journalist. Contemporary Rev Feb 1893.
Crawford, Emily. Journalism as a profession for women, Contemporary Rev Sep 1893.
Cust, Henry. Tory Press and Tory Party, Nat Rev May 1893.
March-Phillips, Evelyn. 'Women's Newspapers', Fortnightly Rev n.s. vol 56, 1894.
Gilzean-Reid, Sir Hugh and P. J. Macdonall, 'The Press', in John Samuelson ed, The civilisation of our day. A series of original essays on some of its more important phases at the close of the nineteenth century, by expert writers. 1896.
Lucy, H. W. The power of the British press. North Amer Rev Aug 1896.
Greenwood, Frederick. Forty Years of Journalism, The English Illus Mag vol 17, July 1897.
Rose, J. H. The unstamped press 1815–36. EHR 12 1897.
Smith, L. A. Woman's work in the London and provincial press. In Newspaper press directory, 1897.
Taylor, F. The newspaper press as a power both in the expression and formation of public opinion. The Chancellor's Essay 1898. Oxford 1898.
Wellsman, W. The local press of London. 1898.

Collet, C. D. History of the taxes on knowledge: their origin and repeal, with an introduction by G. J. Holyoake. 2 vols 1899, 1 vol 1933 (abridged).
Duckworth, L. A complete summary of the law relating to the English newspaper press. 1899.
Halewyck, M. Le régime régal de la presse en Angleterre. Louvain 1899.
Stead, W. T. A journalist on journalism. [1899.]
Walpole, G. Some old Parliamentary reporters. 1899.
'Delta'. A generation of Scottish literature and journalism. Bookman (London) May–June, Aug–Sep 1900.
Shadwell, A. 'Proprietors and Editors'. Nat Rev, Mar–Aug 1900.
Tinsley, W. Random recollections of an old publisher. 2 vols 1900.
The progress of British newspapers in the 19th century. [1901.] Supplement to Sell's World's press guide, 1901.
Bennett, E. A. A note on the revolution in journalism. Academy 10 Mar 1900; rptd in his Fame and fiction, 1901.
Millar, J. H. A literary history of Scotland. 1903.
Leach, H. Fleet Street from within. Bristol 1905.
Lorensz, T. Die englische Presse. Halle 1907.
Adams, E. D. Great Britain and the American Civil War. 2 vols 1908.
Couper, W. J. The Edinburgh periodical press. 2 vols Stirling 1908.
Francis, J. C. Notes by the way. 1909.
Borsa, M. Il giornalismo inglese. Milan 1910.
Escott, T. H. S. Masters of English journalism. 1911.
Bell, W. G. Fleet Street in seven centuries. 1912.
Chancellor, E. B. The annuals of Fleet Street. 1912.
Dibblee, G. B. The newspaper. 1912.
Scott-James, R. A. The influence of the press. 1913.
Bullard, F. L. Famous war correspondents. Boston 1914.
Symon, J. D. The press and its story: an account of the birth and development of journalism up to the present day, with the history of all the leading newspapers. 1914.
Mineau, G. Famous war correspondents. Madison WI 1915. With bibliography.
Philips, J. S. P. The growth of journalism. In CHEL vol 14 1916.
Simonis, H. The street of ink. 1917.
Birrell, A. Life, literature and literary journalism during the first half of the last century. London Mercury May 1920.
Martin, B. K. The triumph of Lord Palmerston. [1924.]
Herd, H. The making of modern journalism. [1927.]
Robbins, A. The press. [1928.]
Wickwar, W. H. The struggle for the freedom of the press 1819–32. 1928.
Cruse, A. The Englishman and his books in the early nineteenth century. 1930. Contains a chapter on periodicals and their readers.
Graham, W. English literary periodicals. 1930, rptd 1966.
Hammond, J. L. and B. The age of the Chartists. [1930.]
Jordan, D. and E. J. Pratt. Europe and the American Civil War. 1931.
Morrison, S. The English newspaper 1622–1932. Cambridge 1932.
Cavour e l'Inghilterra: Carteggio di V. E. d'Azeglio. 3 pts Bologna 1933.
Stutterheim, K. von. Die englische Presse. Berlin 1933; tr 1934.
Kellett, E. E. In Early Victorian England 1830–1965, ed G. M. Young 1934. Ch on the press.
Pollard, G. Serial fiction. In New paths in book collecting, ed J. Carter 1934; 1938 (separately).
Weil, G. Le journal. Paris 1934.
Maccoby, S. English radicalism 1832–52. [1935.]
Grünbeck, M. Die Presse Grossbritanniens: ihr geistiger und wirtschaftlicher Aufbau. 2 vols Leipzig 1936. Vol 1: Geschichte und allgemeine Gegenwartsstrucktur der britischen Presse.
Mansfield, F. J. Royal interest in the press. Newspaper World 8 May 1937.
Postgate, R. and A. Vallance. Those foreigners: the English people's opinions on foreign affairs as reflected in their newspapers since Waterloo (1815–1937). 1937.
Sper, F. The periodical press of London, theatrical and literary 1800–30. Boston 1937.
Lefanu, W. R. British periodicals of medicine. Baltimore MD 1938, rev by J. Loudon Oxford 1984.
Maccoby, S. English radicalism 1853–86. 1938.
Maitland, F. H. One hundred years of headlines 1837–1937. 1938.
Steed, H. W. The press. [1938.]
Glicksberg, C. I. Henry Adams and the English and American press in 1861. Journalism Quart 16 1939.
Steed, W. British newspaper history. Listener 9 Feb 1939.
Bentley, E. G. Those days. 1940.
Innis, H. A. The newspaper in economic development. Jnl of Economic History 2 (suppl) 1942.
Jaryc, M. Studies of 1935–42 on the history of the periodical press. Jnl of Modern History 15 1943.
Gohdes, C. The periodicals. [In his] American literature in nineteenth-century England, New York 1944. *See also* appendix, Representative articles on American literature appearing in British periodicals 1833–1901.
Hudson, D. British journalists and newspapers. 1945.
Innis, H. A. The English press in the nineteenth century: an economic approach. UTQ 15 1945.
Aspinall, A. Politics and the press 1780–1850. 1949.
Altick, R. D. Nineteenth-century English periodicals. Newberry Lib Bull 2nd ser 9 1952.
Dodds, J. W. The age of paradox: a biography of England 1841–51. New York 1952. Ch 3.
Herd, H. The march of journalism: the story of the British press from 1622 to the present day. 1952.
Shannon, E. F. jr. Tennyson and the reviewers 1827–51. Cambridge MA 1952.
Maccoby, S. English radicalism 1886–1914. 1953.
Symonds, R. V. The rise of English journalism. Exeter 1953.
Herd, H. Seven editors. 1955.
Webb, R. K. The British working class reader 1790–1848. 1955.
Andrews, J. S. The reception of Gotthelf in British and American nineteenth-century periodicals. MLR 51 1956.
Aspinall, A. The reporting and publishing of House of Commons debates 1771–1834. In Essays presented to Sir Lewis Namier, ed R. Pares and A. J. P. Taylor. 1956.
Altick, R. D. The English common reader: a social history of the mass reading public 1800–1900. Chicago 1957.
Arundell, D. The critic at the opera. 1957.
Dalziel, M. Popular fiction 100 years ago. 1957.
Ellegård, A. The readership of the periodical press in mid-Victorian Britain. Gothenburg 1957.
Perkin, H. J. The origins of the popular press. History Today 7 1957.
Webb, R. K. The Victorian reading public. Universities Quart 12 1957.
Cox, R. G. From Dickens to Hardy. 1958. Vol 6 of The Pelican guide to English literature. Contains a chapter on reviews and magazines.
Ellegård, A. Darwin and the general reader: the reception of Darwin's theory of evolution in the British periodical press 1859–72. Gothenburg Stud in Eng 1958.
Herd, H. A press gallery. 1958.
Appleman, P. W. A. Madden and M. Wolff. 1859: entering an age of crisis. Bloomington 1959. Includes R. D. Altick, The literature of an imminent democracy; and M. Wolff, Victorian reviewers and cultural responsibility.
Eye-witness: an anthology of British reporting. Ed J. Fisher 1960.
Andrews, J. S. The reception of Fritz Reuter in Victorian England. MLR 56 1961.
Read, D. Press and people 1790–1850: opinion in three English cities. 1961.

Worth, G. J. Popular culture and the seminal books of 1859. Victorian Newsletter no 19 1961.
Mayo, R. D. The English novel in the magazines 1740–1815. Evanston IL 1962.
Sowder, W. J. Emerson's early impact on England: a study in British periodicals. PMLA 77 1962.
James, L. Fiction for the working man 1830–50. Oxford 1963.
Stratman, C. J. Scotland's first dramatic periodical: the Edinburgh Theatrical Censor. Theatre Notebook 17 1963.
Gross, J. The rise and fall of the man of letters. 1969, rev 1991.
Hollis, P. The pauper press: A study in working-class Radicalism in the 1830s. 1970.
Knightley, P. The first casualty: the war correspondent as hero, propagandist and myth maker from the Crimea to Vietnam. 1975.
Kronick, David A. A history of scientific and technical periodicals. 2nd edn 1976.
Lee, A. J. The origins of the popular press in England, 1855–1914. 1976.
Williams, K. The English newspaper: an illustrated history to 1900. 1977.
Boyce, G., J. Curran, and P. Wingate ed. Newspaper history from the seventeenth century to the present day. 1978.
Roper, D. Reviewing before the Edinburgh, 1788–1802. 1978.
Meadows, A. J. ed. The development of science publishing in Europe. 1980. Includes chapters on periodicals.
Koss, S. J. The rise and fall of the political press in Britain. 2 vols 1981, 1983.
Shattock, J. and M. Wolff ed. The Victorian periodical press: samplings and soundings. Leicester and Toronto 1982.
Brown, L. Victorian news and newspapers. Oxford 1985.
Coover, J. Music publishing, copyright and piracy in Victorian England: a twenty-five year chronicle 1881–1906. 1985. Draws on music periodicals.
Wiener, J. H. ed. Innovators and preachers: The role of the editor in Victorian England. Westport CT 1985.
Williams, C. First with the news: the history of W. H. Smith 1792–1972. 1985.
Harris, M. and A. Lee ed. The press in English society from the seventeenth to nineteenth centuries. 1986.
Yearbook of English Studies 16 1986. Ed G. K. Hunter and C. J. Rawson. Special number on literary periodicals.
Black, J. The English press in the eighteenth century. 1987.
Wiener, J. H. ed. Papers for the millions: the new journalism in Britain 1850s to 1914. Westport CT 1988.
Shattock, J. Politics and reviewers: the Edinburgh and the Quarterly in the early Victorian age. Leicester 1989.
Brake, L., A. Jones and L. Madden ed. Investigating Victorian journalism. 1990.
Lund, M. and L. K. Hughes. The Victorian serial. Charlottesville VA 1991.
Griffiths, D. M. ed. The encyclopedia of the British press. Basingstoke 1992.
Jones, A. Press, politics and society. A history of journalism in Wales. 1993.
Brake, L. Subjugated knowledges: journalism, gender and literature in the nineteenth century. 1994.
Beetham, M. A magazine of her own? Domesticity and desire in the woman's magazine 1800–1914. 1996.
Jones, A. Powers of the press. Newspapers, power and the public in nineteenth-century England. Aldershot 1996.

(3) LISTS OF NEWSPAPERS

Lists of Files now extant

British Museum catalogue of printed books. Supplement: newspapers published in Great Britain and Ireland 1801–1900. 1905. Also separately ptd.
[Muddiman, J. G.] Tercentenary handlist of English and Welsh newspapers, magazines and reviews 1620–1920. The most complete list available, based on the BM holdings, but not innocent of serious misprints.
Crane, R. S. and F. B. Kaye. A census of British newspapers and periodicals 1620–1800. Chapel Hill NC 1927. Records the files in American libraries, with supplementary summary list of those lacking.
Gregory, W. Union list of serials in libraries of the United States and Canada. New York 1927, 1943; Supplement, ed G. B. Malikoff, New York 1945; Supplement, ed M. Franck, New York 1953.
Deutsches Institut für Zeitungskunde. Standortskatalog wichtiger Zeitungbestände in deutschen Bibliotheken. Leipzig 1933.
Stewart, A. The evolution of the English newspaper from its origins to the present day as illustrated by the catalogue of the Press Club collection. 1935 (priv ptd).
Haskell, D. A checklist of cumulated indexes to individual periodicals in the New York Public Library. New York 1942. A guide to existing indexes to weeklies, monthlies and quarterlies listed in CBEL.
Ward, W. S. Index and finding list of serials published in the British Isles 1789–1832. Lexington KY 1953.
British union catalogue of periodicals. 4 vols 1955–8; Suppl to 1960, 1962.
Library of Congress. Newspapers on microfilm. Washington 1953, 1963 (5th edn).

Government Returns of the Stamp Duties

The original returns of the Stamp Duty on Newspapers from about 1749 to 1855 were scheduled for destruction under the Public Record Office Act of 1877. Besides the official returns listed below from House of Commons Accounts & Papers, they were frequently cited in works on the press, e.g. Charles Knight's Companion to the Newspaper.

Account of all weekly newspapers published on Saturdays and Sundays. (445) xvi 387 and (579) xvi 391 1821.
Newspaper returns: an account of the number of stamps for newspapers for the year 1801; distinguishing the London from the provincial newspapers, and distinguishing the different London newspapers and the amount of duty received from each. (272) xxi 381 1822; rptd Inquirer Aug 1822, p. 300.
Account of stamps issued for newspapers, with the amount of the duties charged thereon from 1814 to 1824. (375) xxi 327 1825.
Ireland: account of the number of stamps issued to each newspaper from 1822 to 1826. (235) xxiii 383 1826.
Ireland: stamp duties on pamphlets, newspapers and advertisements in Ireland 1797–1826. (99) xvii 23 1827.
Stamps issued to each of the newspapers in England, Scotland and Wales (except those published in London) 1825 to 1829. (609) xxv 347 1830.
Ireland: stamp duties on newspapers and advertisements in Ireland, 1810 to 1830. (406) xxv 363 1830.
Ireland: stamps issued to each newspaper in Ireland 1826–9. (549) xxv 349 1830.
Stamps issued for the London newspapers, duty received, duty paid for advertisements, 1820 to 1829. (549) xxv 349 1830.
Ireland: stamps issued to each newspaper in Ireland 1830 to 1831. (242) xxxiv 123 1832.
Number of square feet of surface of one copy of each of the daily newspapers, 1831; amount of stamp duty actually paid; rate of payment for each hundred square feet. (188) xxxiv 117 1832.
Number of stamps issued for newspapers and other publications 1821–31; number issued for London newspapers 1830; duties on pamphlets and advertisements 1830. (30) xxxiv 127 1832.
Scotland: number of stamps issued to each of the newspapers in Scotland 1831; amount of advertisement duty. (465) xxxiv 121 1832.

Stamps issued for the London newspapers, duty received, duty paid for advertisements for 1831. (290) xxxiv 119 1832.

Number of stamps issued by the Stamp Office for London newspapers specifying each newspaper by name, and number of stamps issued to printers or publishers 1832–3. (758) xxxii 609 1833.

Number of stamps issued to each provincial newspaper in England 1832–3. (519) xxxii 613 1833.

Ireland: number of stamps issued to each newspaper in Ireland 1832–3. (503) xxxii 623 1833.

Ireland: a return of the number of stamps issued to each newspaper in Ireland respectively from 5 Jan 1833 to 5 April 1834; and the number of stamps cancelled by each newspaper respectively for the same period. (412) xlix 407. Ditto from 5 April to 5 July 1834 (510) xlix 400 1834.

Number of stamps issued to newspapers in the United Kingdom 1835–6; amount of advertisement duty by London newspapers 1836. (294) xlv 345 1836.

Number of stamps issued monthly to each of the London newspapers from January to April 1837, and of the advertisement duty in the same period. (232) xxxix 321 1837.

Number of stamps issued monthly to each of the provincial papers in England and Wales from 1 Jan to 20 June 1837; of the number of advertisements published in each newspaper for the same period; and the amount of duty on advertisements paid by each paper for the same period. (In 526) xxxix 305 1837. Ditto from 1836 to 1838. (307) xxxvi 413 1838.

Number of stamps issued by the Stamp Office for all newspapers in Great Britain and Ireland from 30 June to 1 Dec 1837, specifying each newspaper by name, and number of stamps issued each month during that period to each newspaper. (73) xxxvi 393. Ditto 1–31 Dec 1837; similar return for each month of the quarter ended 31 March 1838. (368) xxxvi 403 1838.

Ireland: number of stamps issued to Irish newspapers in each year since 1824, distinguishing those printed in Dublin; newspapers existing in Ireland in 1824; newspapers which have ceased to exist since 1824; newspapers established since 1824, and which still exist. (In 488) viii 235 1838.

Number of stamps issued at 1d in the United Kingdom 1838–9, specifying each newspaper, and the number of stamps issued each month. (213) xxx 483. Ditto from April to June 1839. (449) xxx 493 1839.

Number of stamps at 1d issued to the several newspapers 1838, specifying each newspaper by name, and the number of stamps issued each month during that period to each newspaper; similar returns for Ireland. (15) xxix 483 1840.

Number of stamps issued to the several newspapers in Great Britain 1839, specifying each newspaper by name, and the number of stamps issued each month during the period to each newspaper. (266) xxix 503 1840.

Number of stamps issued to each newspaper in England and Wales 1839–40, specifying also the amount of advertisement duty paid by each newspaper in each of the above years; similar returns for Ireland and Scotland. (294) xxix 523 1840.

Number of stamps issued to the several newspapers in the United Kingdom April to June 1840, specifying each newspaper by name. (525) xxix 513 1840.

Number of newspaper stamps at 1d and 1/2d issued to the several newspapers in Great Britain 1 July to 1 Sep 1840, specifying each newspaper by name; number of stamps each month; similar returns for Ireland; similar returns from 1 Oct to 31 Dec 1840. (14) xiii 461 1841.

Number of stamps issued to each newspaper in England and Wales during each of the three years ending 5 Jan 1841, and similar returns for Scotland and Ireland; also return of number of newspaper stamps issued from 5 Jan to 31 March 1841. (407) xiii 481 1841.

Number of stamps issued to each of the newspapers in the United Kingdom; amount of advertisement duty paid. (26) ii 45 1841 (Sess 2); (44) xxvi 561 1842; (257) xxvi 587 1842; (572) xxvi 601 1842; (98) xxx 513 1843; (174) xxx 537 1843; (282) xxx 559 1843; (611) xxx 571 1843; (55) xxxii 419 1844.

Return of papers published in the metropolis, which are registered as newspapers, a portion whereof is published without stamps. (78) xxxiii 567 1850.

Return of stamps at 1d issued to each newspaper published in London, Dublin and Edinburgh. Quarterly, 1851–4, xxxix 501 and 519 1854.

Return of names of newspapers in the United Kingdom to which halfpenny stamps were issued; number issued to each; and amount of duty paid, in 1852. lvii 573 1853.

Number of newspaper stamps at 1d issued to each newspaper in England, Ireland, Scotland and Wales in 1851, 1852 and 1853. xxxix 479 1854. Ditto in 1854 xxx 497 1855. Ditto, 1854 to 1 July 1855, xxx 509 1855; ditto, July–Dec 1855, xxxviii 511 1856.

Return of registered newspapers and publications in the United Kingdom, and of the number of stamps issued to each quarterly 1855 to 1857. xxxiv 259 1858.

Lists in General Directories

The Post Office London directory for 1805 by B. Critchett. [1804] (6th edn). This edn first includes the London papers with days of issue; from the 15th edn 1814 onwards it contains the country papers as well. Annually to 1839.

Holden's triennial directory for 1805, 1806, 1807. [1805] (4th edn). Contains a list of London and country newspapers: this did not appear in the earlier edns, nor is it in the 10th edn for 1817, 1818, 1819, which was the first issued by Underhill after Holden's death.

Pigot and Co's London and provincial new commercial directory for 1822–3. [1822.] 2nd edn for 1823–4; 3rd edn for 1827–8; 6th edn for 1836–7; 7th edn Dec 1839.

Robson's London commercial directory for 1823. Also for 1839, 1840, 1843 (24th edn); the first edn for 1819 has no list. The lists in the later edns seem to have been supplied by Newton and Co, Warwick Square, Newgate St.

W. Kelly and Co. The Post Office London directory for 1840. 1839 onwards. The issues for the years from 1840–7 have opposite each paper the number of stamps issued to it for the second quarter of the preceding year; for the years 1842–7 they have the amount of advertisement duty paid as well. Annual.

Press and Advertising Directories

Most of those publications which survived were annual.

The Advertisers' Guide, to the Newspaper Press of the United Kingdom. Lewis & Lowe. 1844 (3rd edn). Copy in John Johnson Collection, Bodleian. 'Shewing the average Circulations, and average Number of Advertisements of such Publications, the Political Character, and the price of each Paper'.

Curtis's Complete List of London Periodicals and Newspapers. J. E. Curtis. Newport Pagnel(l) [1845].

The Newspaper Press Directory (intermittently with subtitles: and Advertiser's Guide). C. Mitchell & Co. 1846, 1847, 1851, 1854, 1856–1900 on; Benn from 1949. Ed Mitchell 1846–59, W. H. Wellsman 1859–97. Included reviews of the year, editorial contributions, newspaper map (from 1860).

W. H. Wellsman. History of the Directory. 1895 (Jubilee edn).

W. H. Wellsman. Editorial address. 1905 (Diamond Jubilee edn).

S. Gliserman. Mitchell's Newspaper Press Directory, 1846–1907. Victorian Periodicals Rev 4 1969.

D. Linton. 'Mr Mitchell's "National Work"'. Journal of Advertising History 2 1979.

Classified and Priced Catalogue of London Periodicals, Current Law Reports, and Newspapers. Longman, Brown, Green and Longmans. 1846–.

A Guide to Advertisers. Effingham Wilson. 1850–2?

Scottish Newspaper Directory and Guide to Advertisers. T. C. Jack. Edinburgh. 1855. (2nd edn).

Deacon's Newspaper Handbook and Advertisers' Guide. S. Deacon & Co. 1863?–1904. Intermittent. Preceded as early as 1846 by S. Deacon's Correct List of All the English, Scottish, and Irish Newspapers.

Frederick May's London Press Dictionary and Advertiser's Handbook. May 1871–3. Continued as May's British and Irish Press Guide (with varying subtitles), 1874–89. Continued as Willing's British and Irish Press Guide. Willing. 1890–8. Continued as Willing's Press Guide. 1899 to date (continuing through both World Wars).

Street's List of Newspapers Published in Great Britain and Ireland. George Street & Co. 1872–3, 1890, 1892. Continued as Street's Newspaper Directory for Great Britain and Ireland. 1898–1917, 1920.

Eyre's Guide. 1873?–. 'Containing a list of all the newspapers and periodicals published throughout the United Kingdom and the Colonies'.

A List of the (Principal) Newspapers Published in the United Kingdom. R. F. White & Son. 1878–1912–. Intermittent. James White founded his advertising agency in 1800.

C. H. May & Co's Press Manual. 1878–.

The Philosophy of Advertising. Sell, 1881–2. Continued as Sell's Dictionary of the World's Press (with varying subtitles). 1883/4–1911/12 (including 2 vols in 1899). Continued as Sell's World's Press. 1914–15, 1919, 1921. Lists of newspapers etc. are of secondary significance to large and authoritative editorial sections. Featured Heads of the world's press, from 1886. Progress of British newspapers in the 19th century, illustrated, first appeared in a suppl to 1901 edn; and A bibliography of journalism, by H. W. Peet, in 1915.

D. Linton. Sell's publications: a hundred years and more. Sell's Directory: Products and Services 1985.

Everett's Directory of the Principal Newspapers of the World. W. H. Everett. 1881–.

The Advertisers' Guardian (originally with subtitles: and Advertisement Agents' Guide). T. Dixon. 1885, 1887–91. Ed L. Collins. 1900, 1902. Ed Dixon. 'Siftings' of newspapers and periodicals, with critical comment on other guides.

The Advertiser's ABC: T. B. Browne's Advertisement Press Directory and Provincial Newspaper Gazetteer. Browne. 1886–1918, 1920–31/2. The largest agency of its time also published T. B. Browne's Provincial Newspaper Circular. [1891.]

Newspaper Gazetteer and Guide to Advertisers. Newton & Co. 1886–.

An Advertiser's Guide to Publicity. Moody's Printing Works. Birmingham 1887–.

Shelley & Co's Complete Press Directory. 1887–.

The Annual Index of Periodicals and Photographs for 1890. Review of Reviews Office. 1891. Continued as Index to the Periodical Literature of the World 1892 (for 1891), 1893 (for 1892). Continued as Index to the Periodicals of 1894. Annually to 1901. Ed W. T. Stead.

Handy Newspaper List. C. & E. Layton. 1891?–1915.

Curtice's Index and Register of Periodical Literature. E. Curtice. [1893.] Continued as Curtice's Index to The Times (the London morning and evening papers, 120 weeklies, and 31 provincial newspapers). [1894.] Short-lived offshoots of the pioneer Romeike & Curtice press cuttings agency; indexes of contents rather than press guides.

Practical Advertising. Mather & Crowther. 1895, 1897, 1899, 1901–16, 1921–3. 'Handy guide by practical men'. First ed G. D. Sutherland.

Some of the Principal Newspapers and Journalists of London. Waterlow. 1896–.

Walker's Press Directory. H. T. Walker & Co. 1897.

Vicker's Newspaper Gazetteer. J. W. Vickers. 1900–16. 'An annual reference book to the press of the world'.

Smith's Advertisers' Handbook. Occasional suppl to Successful Advertising (see Press and Advertising Periodicals).

Linton, D. Mitchell's May's and Sell's newspaper directories of the Victorian era. Journal of Newspaper and Periodical History Spring 1987.

C. THE DAILY AND WEEKLY PRESS

Numbers and dates of periodicals in brackets are conjectural. Those without brackets are based on holdings recorded in Tercentenary handlist; Crane and Kaye; A census of British newspapers and periodicals; British Union catalogue of periodicals *or personal observation. In listing proprietors it has often been impossible to assign ultimate responsibility, especially in cases of multiple control.*

(1) DAILY PAPERS

London Morning Papers

The public ledger. No 1, 12 Jan 1760–14 Sep 1836. New ser no 1, 3 July 1837–11 July 1870. Continued as Public ledger evening report, 11 July 1870–2 May 1932. Continued as Evening report: the public ledger, 3 May 1932–27 July 1945. From 5 Sep 1836 to 1 July 1837 there appeared a separate paper, Constitutional and public ledger. *See col 2887, below.* Prop Lee Stevens. Ed Alexander Chalmers.

The morning chronicle. [No 1, 28 June 1769]–no 184, 3 Jan 1770–20 Dec 1862. Prop James Perry 1789–1821; William I. Clement 1822–34; John Easthope 1834–48(?); Duke of Newcastle, W. E. Gladstone, Sydney Herbert et al 1848 (?)–54; William Glover 1854–60(?); George Stiff 1860(?)–2. Ed James Perry 1789–1819, John Black 1819–43, Andrew Doyle 1843–8, J. D. Cook 1848–54, T. L. Holt, G. H. Francis.

The morning post. No 1, 2 Nov 1772–no 51561, 30 Sep 1937. Incorporated in Daily telegraph. Prop Daniel Stuart 1795–1803; Nicholas Byrne; C. E. Michele 1833–49; T. B. Crompton 1849–58; W. J. Rideout 1858–76; Algernon Borthwick 1876–1908. Ed Daniel Stuart 1795–1803, Nicholas Byrne (assisted by Eugenius Roche 1817–27) 1803–33, C. E. Michele 1833–49, Peter Borthwick 1849–52, Algernon Borthwick 1852–72, William Hardman 1872–90, Alexander Leys Moore 1890–4, Algernon Locker 1895–7, J. N. Dunn 1897–1905.

The morning herald. No 1, 1 Nov 1780–31 Dec 1869. Prop Henry Bate Dudley 1780–1824; ? Thwaites ?–1843; Edward Baldwin 1843–57; James Johnstone 1867–? Ed Alexander Chalmers, Thomas Wright (?), Edward Baldwin and S. L. Giffard 1843–6, Robert Knox 1846–57, Thomas Hamber 1857–?.

The times. No 940, 1 Jan 1788 onwards. Started as Daily universal register, no 1, 1 Jan 1785; the original title was continued as a subtitle from 1 Jan to 17 Mar 1788. Prop John Walter I 1785–1803; John Walter II 1803–47; John Walter III 1847–94; Arthur Fraser Walter 1894–1908. Ed William Combe 1797–1808, Henry Crabb Robinson 1808–9, John Walter II, J. H. Stoddart 1814–17, Thomas Barnes 1817–41, J. T. Delane 1841–77, Thomas Chenery 1878–84, G. E. Buckle 1884–1912.

The oracle. No 1, 1 June 1789–28 Feb 1794. Amalgamated with Public advertiser and continued as Oracle and public advertiser, 1 Mar 1794–8 Sep 1798. Incorporated in Daily advertiser and continued as Oracle and daily advertiser, 10 Sep 1798–24 Mar 1802. Continued as Daily advertiser and oracle, 25 Mar 1802–8 June 1809. Prop John Bell 1789–96; Peter Stuart. Ed James Boaden.

The true Briton. No 1, 1 Jan 1793–no 3437, 31 Dec 1803. Incorporated in Daily advertiser and oracle. Ed John Heriot 1793–1803.

The morning advertiser. No 1, 8 Feb 1794 onwards. Prop The Licensed Victuallers' Association. Ed ? Anderson, John Scott, ? Sheridan, James Grant 1850–70, Alfred B. Richards 1870–6, Thomas Hamber 1876–86, Thomas Wright 1886–94, Frank G. Dovey.

The porcupine. No 1, 30 Oct 1800–31 Dec 1801. Incorporated in True Briton. Pop and ed William Cobbett.

The British press or morning literary advertiser. No 1, 1 Jan 1803–31 Oct 1826. Ed George Lane, Robert Heron, J. B. Capes.

The advertiser's daily magazine. [No 1, 29 Jan 1805]–no 9, 8 Feb 1805–?.

The morning star. [1805]–no 58, 25 Jan 1806–?.

The aurora and British imperial reporter. No 1, 19 Jan–no 121, 8 June 1807–?. Ed William Jerdan.

The day. No 1, 2 Jan 1809–no 2057, 20 Apr 1815–[1817]. Incorporated in New times. Ed Eugenius Roche 1809–11, John Scott, ? Hogan.

The new times. [1817]–1 Jan 1818–4 Oct 1828. Continued as Morning journal 6 Oct 1828–13 May 1830. Started before Easter 1817 and soon absorbed in Day; continued as Day and new times, but the first part of the title was dropped before the end of 1817. Ed J. H. Stoddard 1817–26. Eugenius Roche 1827–8, Robert Alexander and J. M. Gutch 1828–30.

The British statesman. No 1, 10 Feb–no 262, 11 Dec 1819.

The representative. No 1, 25 Jan–29 July 1826. Prop John Murray.

The tatler. No 1, 4 Oct 1830–13 Feb 1832. Ed J. H. Leigh Hunt.

The daily politician. No 1, 25 Jan–no 24, 20 Feb 1836. Another paper of the same name ran for a few days in Sep of the same year.

The constitutional and public ledger. No 1, 15 Sep 1836–1 July 1837. *See* Public ledger, *above*. Prop The Metropolitan Newspaper Co, a group of Radical sympathisers. Ed S. L. Blanchard assisted by Thornton Hunt.

The morning gazette. No 1, 2 Oct–no 54, 2 Dec 1837.

The iron times. No 1, 7 July 1845–no 264, 11 May 1846. Prop and ed T. L. Holt.

The daily news. No 1, 21 Jan 1846–31 May 1930. Amalgamated with Daily chronicle and continued as News-chronicle, 2 June 1930–17 Oct 1960. Prop Bradbury and Evans, Joseph Paxton, Joshua Walmsley et al; George Smith; Samuel Morely, Henry Labouchere, Henry Oppenheim et al. Ed Charles Dickens Jan 1846, John Forster Feb–Oct 1846, E. E. Crowe Oct 1846–1851, F. Knight Hunt 1851–4, William Weir 1854–8, Thomas Walker 1858–69, Edward Dicey 1869, F. H. Hill 1870–85, H. W. Lucy Dec 1885–June 1887, John R. Robinson 1887–95, E. T. Cook 1895–1901.

The London telegraph. No 1, 1 Feb–8 July 1848. Prop H. Ingram. Ed Thomas Hodgkin.

The daily telegraph. No 1, 29 June 1855 onwards. First pbd at 2d but in 1856 was the first daily newspaper to be sold at 1d. Prop A. B. Sleigh 1855; family company under J. M. Levy, Edward Lawson (Lord Burnham), Henry Lawson (Viscount Burnham) 1856–1927. Ed A. B. Richards 1855, Edward Lawson (Lord Burnham) 1856–1916(?) assisted by Thornton Hunt 1856–72 and Edwin Arnold 1873–1901.

The morning news. No 1, 3 Mar 1856–no 924, 29 June 1859. Ed Henry Mayhew.

The morning star. No 1, 17 Mar 1856–no 4251, 13 Oct 1869. Prop Samuel Lucas 1856–65. Ed Samuel Lucas 1856–65, J. McCarthy, J. Morley June–Oct 1869.

The standard. 29 June 1857–16 Mar 1916. Founded as an evening paper in 1827 (*see col 2889, below*), it was for many years run in conjuction with Morning herald; in 1857 it became a morning paper, though an evening edn continued to be pbd. Prop James Johnstone 1857–76; W. H. Mudford. Ed Thomas Hamber 1857–70, John Gorst 1870–74, W. H. Mudford 1874–1900, G. B. Curtis 1900–4.

The morning mail. 23 Apr 1864–21 July 1865. Continued as London general advertiser, 22 July 1865–1 Dec 1866.

The day. No 1, 19 Mar–4 May 1867.

The London daily reporter. [1869]–no 376, 2 Jan 1871–16 June 1871. Continued as London daily recorder, 17 June 1871–31 Dec 1872.

The financier. No 1, 1 Mar 1870–23 May 1924. Incorporated in Financial times.

The daily chronicle. No 3320, 25 Nov 1872–31 May 1930. Incorporated in News chronicle. Started weekly in 1855 as Clerkenwell news and general advertiser, nos 73–1200, 8 Oct 1856–5 Feb 1866; continued for a few issues daily, then twice weekly as Clerkenwell news and London times, nos 1201–2394, 7 Feb 1866–Dec 1869; then continued daily as Clerkenwell news and London daily chronicle, nos 2395–2779, 11 Dec 1869–5 Mar 1871; continued as London daily chronicle and Clerkenwell news, nos 2780–3319, 6 Mar 1871–23 Nov 1872. Prop Edward Lloyd. Ed Robert Whelan Boyle 1876–89, Alfred Ewen Fletcher 1889–94, H. W. Massingham 1894–9, W. Fisher 1899–1903.

The hour. No 1, 24 Mar 1873–11 Aug 1876. Prop D. Morier Evans. Ed Thomas Hamber.

The circle. No 1, 29 Jan–no 87, 9 May 1874. Ed William Saunders.

The echo. No 1 (of morning edition), 4 Oct 1875–31 May 1876. Run in connection with Echo (*see below under evening papers*). The first halfpenny morning daily. Prop Albert Grant. Ed Horace Voules.

The sportsman. 20 Mar 1876–22 Nov 1924. Incorporated in Sporting life. No 1, 2 Aug 1865 (twice weekly); thrice weekly in 1867. Ed Charles Russell 1867–75, Thomas Whitefoot 1878–85, A. Allison, S. Downing 1889–?.

The daily express. Nos 1–101, 1 May–25 Aug 1877.

The continental times. [1878]–12 Mar 1881–15 Feb 1890. Pbd in London and Paris.

Sporting life. 23 Mar 1883 onwards. Started as Bell's penny life in London, no 1, 16 Mar 1859; continued twice weekly as Sporting life from no 12, 30 Apr 1859; in 1861 it absorbed Sporting telegraph (no 1, Feb 1860–6 Mar 1861); in Apr 1881 it was pbd 4 times weekly; on 23 Mar 1883 it became a daily paper; on 1 July 1886 it absorbed Bell's life in London, below. Prop George Maddick and S. O. Beeton; Edward Hulton 1885–?. Ed Henry Fiest 1859–74, Charles W. Blake 1874–91, George S. Lowe 1891–?.

The summary. No 1, 10 July 1883–11 Oct 1884. Pbd by Times.

The financial news. No 114, 1 July 1884 onwards. Absorbed Financial times and took over its title. Started as Financial and mining news, nos 1–113, 28 Jan–28 June 1884. Prop and ed Harry H. Marks.

The morning mail. Nos 1–69, 20 Apr–9 July 1885.

The journal. Nos 1–43, 1 Nov–20 Dec 1886.

The financial times. 13 Feb 1888 onwards. Started as London financial guide, no 1, Jan–Feb 1888. *See* Financial news, *above*.

The daily oracle. Nos 1–840, 21 Nov 1889–27 Aug 1892. Ed T. P. Whittaker.

Galignani's messenger. No 23515, 1 Jan 1890–31 Dec 1895. Continued as Daily messenger, no 25679, 1 Jan 1896–30 July 1904. Started in Paris in 1814, thrice weekly and became daily in 1821. Ed Cyrus Redding 1815–18, James S. Bowes, Gibbons Merle 1830–55, J. C. Mackenzie, Horatio Bottomley 1896, Norman Angell.

The daily graphic. No 1, 4 Jan 1890–16 Oct 1926. An illustrated paper. Incorporated in Daily sketch. Prop William L. Thomas.

Morning. No 1, 21 May 1892–4 Sep 1898. Continued as London morning, no 1968, 5 Sep 1898–22 Apr 1899. Continued as Morning herald, no 1, 24 Apr 1899–1 Sep 1900. Incorporated in Daily express. Halfpenny paper. Ed Chester Ives.

The morning leader. No 1, 23 May 1892–11 May 1912. Incorporated in Daily news. Halfpenny paper. Ed F. W. Wilson.

The daily courier. Nos 1–98, 23 Apr–15 Aug 1896. Prop George Newnes. Ed W. Earl Hodgson.

The daily mail. No 1, 4 May 1896 onwards. Prop and ed Alfred Harmsworth.

The daily express. No 1, 24 Apr 1900 onwards. Prop C. A. Pearson. Ed Pearson 1900–4.

London Evening Papers

The star. No 1, 3 May 1788–15 Oct 1831. Incorporated in Albion and star. Prop Peter Stuart; Alexander Tilloch. Ed Andrew Macdonald, Alexander Tilloch, John Mayne, Rowland Nash.

The courier. [Sep 1792]–no 86, 31 Dec 1792–6 July 1842. Prop James Perry; Daniel Stuart 1799–1822. Ed Daniel Stuart 1803–11, Peter Street 1811–22, William Mudford 1827?, Eugenius Roche 1828?, John Galt 1830, James Stuart 1830–6, Samuel Laman Blanchard 1837–9.

The sun. No 1, 1 Oct 1792–15 Apr 1876. No 16042, 24 Jan 1844 gives this information: 'The sun is published every morning at five o'clock in time for the early trains and town delivery; a second edition (Evening sun) is published in time for the afternoon trains, and a third edition at seven o'clock for Post, containing Parliamentary and all other news in London up to that hour.' Prop Patrick Grant Apr 1826–1831; Murdo Young 1832–1850; Charles Kent 1850–?. Ed John Heriot 1792–1806, Robert Clark 1806–7, William Jerdan 1813–17, John Taylor, Murdo Young, Patrick Grant, W. F. Deacon–? 1845, Charles Kent.

The albion and evening advertiser. [1799]–no 106, 7 Jan 1800–[1807]. Ed Allan M'Leod, John Fenwick.

The traveller. [1801]–no 5519, 1 Jan 1818–28 Dec 1822. Incorporated in Globe and traveller. Prop Robert Torrens. Ed Edward Quin, Walter Coulson.

The globe. [No 1, 1 Jan 1803]–no 1536, 8 Dec 1807–31 Dec 1922. Incorporated in Evening standard. It absorbed Traveller on 28 Dec 1822 and was called Globe and traveller, until 5 Feb 1921; it also absorbed Statesman, Feb 1824, Evening chronicle, Mar 1824, Nation, July 1824, and Argus, July 1828. Prop Richard Phillips and London booksellers; Robert Torrens 1822–64; Conservative syndicate under Stafford Northcote until 1866–75; George C. H. Armstrong 1875–1907. Ed George Lane 1803, Robert Heron 1803, Robert Torrens, Walter Coulson 1822–5, Gibbons Merle 1825–30, R. D. Hanson, George Stevenson, John Wilson 1834–?, [?] Westcomb, R. H. Patterson, H. N. Barnett, Marwood Tucker 1868, George C. H. Armstrong 1871–89, Ponsonby Ogle, Algernon Locker 1891, George Elliot Armstrong 1895–1907.

The statesman. [No 1, 26 Feb 1806]–no 107, 30 June 1807–18 Feb 1824. Incorporated in Globe and traveller. Ed John Hunt 1806–9, W. M. Willett 1809, John Scott 1809–14, Daniel Lovell 1814–17, Sampson Perry 1817–19, David Carey 1819–24.

The pilot. [No 1, 1 Jan 1807]–no 687, 15 Mar 1809–31 Oct 1815. Ed E. Samuel, Herbert Compton, ? Fitzgerald.

The Alfred and Westminster gazette. [No 1, 17 Apr 1810]–no 22, 12 May 1810–23 Apr 1833. The second part of the title was soon dropped.

Cobbett's evening post. Nos 1–55, 29 Jan–1 Apr 1820. Prop and ed William Cobbett.

The true Briton. No 1, 1 July 1820–13 Nov 1822. Incorporated in Traveller.

The British traveller. No 1, 19 July 1821–no 3703, 25 May 1833. Ed W. M. Willett.

The new globe. No 1, 3 Feb–no 132, 5 July 1823.

The evening chronicle. Nos 1–30, 4 Feb–19 Mar 1824. Incorporated in Globe and traveller. Ed J. S. Buckingham.

The nation. Nos 1–65, 10 May–24 July 1824. Incorporated in Globe and traveller. Ed T. J. Wooler.

The evening times. Nos 1–46, 14 Nov 1825–5 Jan 1826.

The standard. No 1, 21 May 1827–29 June 1857. Continued as Evening standard, no 11179, 11 June 1860–13 Mar 1905. Continued as Evening standard and St James's gazette, 14 Mar 1905–23 Oct 1916. Continued as Evening standard, 24 Oct 1916 onwards. It absorbed Albion and star 1 Jan 1836. Prop Charles and Edward Baldwin 1827–57; James Johnstone 1857–76. Ed S. L. Giffard (assisted by A. A. Watts and William Maginn) 1827–45, Robert Knox 1846–57, ? Pritchard, Charles Williams 1860–3, Thomas Hamber 1863–70, John Gorst 1870–4, W. H. Mudford 1874–1900.

The argus. Nos 1–24, 30 June–26 July 1828. Incorporated in Globe and traveller. Ed J. S. Buckingham.

The albion. 15 Nov 1830–15 Oct 1831. Continued as Albion and star 17 Oct 1831–31 Dec 1835. Incorporated in Standard.

The true sun. No 1, 5 Mar 1832–23 Dec 1837. Prop Patrick Grant 1832; John Bell; Daniel Whittle Harvey 1833–7. Ed Patrick Grant, Samuel Laman Blanchard, John Bell, Daniel Whittle Harvey, W. J. Fox 1833 (?)–7.

The shipping gazette. Nos 1–557, 4 Jan 1836–13 Oct 1837. Continued as Shipping gazette and commercial advertiser, 14 Oct 1837–9 Mar 1838. Ed William Carpenter 1836.

Shipping and mercantile gazette. No 1, 12 Mar 1838–30 June 1884. Continued as Shipping and mercantile gazette and Lloyd's list, 1 July 1884–30 June 1914. Continued as Shipping and mercantile gazette and daily index 1 July 1914–3 Feb 1916. Prop and ed William Mitchell.

The evening star. No 1, 25 July 1842–no 188, 28 Feb 1843.

The railway director. No 1, 3 Jan 1845–14 Mar 1846.

The express. No 1, 1 Sep 1846–30 Apr 1869. Run in conjunction with Daily news. Ed Thomas Elliott 1846–55, J. R. Robinson 1855–69.

The evening journal. No 1, 6 Oct 1851–14 Apr 1860.

The evening star. No 1, 17 Mar 1856–no 4251, 13 Oct 1869. Run in conjunction with Morning star. Ed F. W. Chesson.

The evening herald. No 1, 29 June 1857–no 2428, 27 May 1865. Run in conjunction with Standard.

The Pall Mall gazette. No 1, 7 Feb 1865–27 Oct 1923. Incorporated in Evening standard. Prop George Murray Smith 1865–May 1880; Henry Yates Thompson May 1880–1892; William Waldorf Astor 1892–1909. Ed Frederick Greenwood 1865–May 1880, Horace Voules May 1880–1, John Morley 1881–3, W. T. Stead 1883–9, E. T. Cook 1889–92, C. Kinloch Cooke 1892–3, H. C. Cust 1893–6, Douglas Straight 1896–1909.

The glow-worm. No 1, 5 June 1865–no 1152, 13 Feb 1869. Ed F. C. Burnand, A. W. à Beckett, T. H. S. Escott, T. W. Robertson.

The daily recorder (of commerce). [1866]–no 1982, 1 Jan 1873–20 Dec 1887. Incorporated in Evening post (i.e. Evening news).

The little times. No 1, 27 Apr–no 22, 22 May 1867. Ed Mayne Reid.

The echo. No 1, 8 Dec 1868–31 July 1905. In 1875 it ran a morning edn and its style was changed to Evening echo (*see col 2888, above*). The first halfpenny newspaper. Prop Cassell, Petter and Galpin 1868–75; Albert Grant 1875–6; J. Passmore Edwards 1876–1884; syndicate headed by Andrew Carnegie 1884–5; J. Passmore Edwards 1885–96. Ed Arthur Arnold 1868–75, Horace Voules 1875–6, J. Passmore Edwards 1876–84, Howard Evans, Aaron Watson, W. M. Crook 1898–?.

The London Figaro. No 1, 17 May 1870–no 263, 11 Mar 1871. Ed J. Mortimer.

The public ledger and evening report. 11 July 1870–2 May 1932. Continued as Evening report: the public ledger, 3 May 1932–27 July 1945. *See col 2885 above under morning papers*. Not pbd Saturdays.

The St James's gazette. No 1, 31 May 1880–13 Mar 1905. Incorporated in Evening standard. Prop H. Huck Gibbs 1880–8; E. Steinkopff 1888–?, Ed Frederick Greenwood 1880–8, Sidney Low 1888–97, Hugh Chisholm 1897–1900.

The evening news. No 1, 26 July 1881–Dec 1887. Continued as Evening post, no 1427, 21 Dec 1887–12 Jan 1889. Continued as Evening news and post, 13 Jan 1889–11 May 1889. Continued as Evening news, 12 May 1889 onwards. Halfpenny paper. Prop Coleridge Kennard ?–1894; Alfred Harmsworth 1894–?. Ed Charles Williams 1881–4, John R. K. Ralph, ? Coplestone, Frank Harris 1889–92, Percy White, Louis Tracy 1894, Kennedy Jones 1894–1900.

The star. No 1, 17 Jan 1888–17 Oct 1960. Incorporated in Evening news. Halfpenny paper. Prop T. P. O'Connor. Ed T. P. O'Connor 1888–July 1890, H. W. Massingham July 1890–Jan 1891, James Stuart 1892–7, E. Parke.

The Westminster gazette. No 1, 31 Jan 1893–31 Jan 1928. Incorporated in Daily news. Prop George Newnes Ltd 1893–1908. Ed E. T. Cook 1893–6, J. A. Spender 1896–1922.

The sun. No 1, 27 June 1893–11 Oct 1906. Prop T. P. O'Connor. Ed T. P. O'Connor 1893–6, W. S. Johnstone.

The evening mail. No 1, 1 Apr 1896–9 Oct 1901.

Provincial Daily Papers

An asterisk before an entry indicates that no copy of the paper has been located. A valuable source of information on the proprietors of the provincial, Scottish and Irish press is Newspaper press directory, 1846 onwards.

*The mercantile gazette, and Liverpool and Manchester daily advertiser (Liverpool). No 1, 6 Aug 1811–?; expired before 1812. *See* A. Andrews, History of British journalism, vol 2, 1859, p. 124. Ed ? Solomon.

*The northern express and Lancashire daily post (Manchester). No 1, 1 Dec 1821–Feb 1822. *See* A. Andrews, *above*. Pbd Henry Burgess.

Northern daily times (Liverpool). No 1, 24 Sep 1853–6 June 1857. Continued as Northern times, 7 June 1857–19 Feb 1860. Continued as Daily times, 20 Feb 1860–30 Jan 1861. Ed Charles Willmer.

The daily war telegraph (Manchester). No 2, 21 Oct 1854–29 Jan 1855. Continued as War telegraph, 30 Jan–20 Mar 1855. Continued as Daily telegraph, 22 Mar–7 Apr 1855. Continued as Manchester daily telegraph, 9 Apr–30 Nov 1855.

The war express and daily advertiser (Manchester). No 4, 24 Oct–no 46, 15 Dec 1854. Continued as Manchester express etc., 18 Dec 1854–8 June 1855.

The Manchester daily times. No 1, 12 Dec 1854–15 June 1855. Incorporated in Manchester examiner and times; *see below.*

The northern express (Darlington). No 1, 21 Apr–27 Oct 1855. Continued as Northern daily express (Newcastle), 30 Oct 1855–16 Oct 1886. Ed R. N. Worth 1866–7.

The Birmingham daily press. No 1, 7 May 1855–20 Nov 1858. Prop George Dawson, William Harris, James Freeman et al.

The Sheffield daily telegraph. No 1, 8 June 1855–14 July 1934. Continued as Sheffield telegraph, 16 July 1934–29 Oct 1938. Continued as Sheffield telegraph and daily independent, 31 Oct 1938–13 May 1939. Continued as Telegraph and independent, 15 May 1939–12 June 1942. Continued as Sheffield telegraph and independent, 13 June–14 July 1942. Continued as Sheffield telegraph, 15 July 1942 onwards. Prop William Leng and Frederick Clifford 1864; William Leng 1864–1902. Ed William Leng 1864–1902.

The daily post (Liverpool). No 1, 11 June 1855–28 Oct 1879. Continued as Liverpool daily post, 29 Oct 1879 onwards. Ed M. J. Whitty 1855–?, Edward R. Russell 1869–?, John Macleay.

The Birmingham daily mercury. No 1, 12 June 1855–22 Aug 1857. Incorporated in Birmingham daily press.

The Manchester examiner. 17 June 1855–10 Mar 1894. Started weekly, no 1, 10 Jan 1846; twice weekly at the beginning of 1854; and in Oct Manchester examiner extraordinary was issued on the four weekdays on which Manchester examiner itself did not appear; on 12 Dec this became Manchester daily times (*see above*); when this ceased 15 June 1855, Manchester examiner and times was continued daily under its old title; it was incorporated in Umpire (Manchester) in Mar 1894 (*see under Sunday paper below*). Prop Thomas Ballantyne, John Bright et al 1855–?. Ed Thomas Ballantyne 1846, A. W. Paulton 1846–64, H. Dunckley 1864–88, J. S. R. Phillips 1889–91, W. M. Leslie, A. Ireland.

The morning news (Sheffield). No 1, 19 June–14 Nov 1855.

The Manchester guardian. 2 July 1855–22 Aug 1959. Continued as Guardian, 24 Aug 1959 onwards. Started weekly, no 1, 5 May 1821; twice weekly in Sep 1836. Prop J. E. Taylor I 1821–44; J. E. Taylor II 1844–1905. Ed J. E. Taylor I 1821–44, R. S. Taylor 1844–8, Jeremiah Garnett 1848–61, J. E. Taylor II 1861–72, C. P. Scott 1872–1930.

Stevenson's daily express (Nottingham). No 1, 2 July 1855–29 May 1856.

North and South Shields gazette. Daily telegraphic edition (South Shields). No 1, 2 July 1855–20 Apr 1860. Continued as North and South Shields gazette and daily telegraph, 21 Apr 1860–30 Dec 1876. Continued as North and South Shields daily gazette and shipping telegraph, 2 Jan 1877–26 Jan 1884. Continued as Shields daily gazette and shipping telegraph, 28 Jan 1884–2 Apr 1932. Continued as Shields gazette and shipping telegraph, 4 Apr 1932 onwards. Started weekly, no 1, 24 Feb 1849. Prop James Stevenson 1849–54; James Cochrane Stevenson 1854–83; Northern Press Co Ltd (with J. C. Stevenson as head) 1883–1905. Ed W. K. Kelly, D. M. McLennan ?–Oct 1861, ? Finlay, William Duncan 1865–78, James Annand 1878–85, Aaron Watson 1885–92.

The Hull morning telegraph. [1855?]–no 4921, 12 July 1869–30 Apr 1880. Incorporated in Hull express.

The Sheffield daily news. No 1, 2 Dec 1856–27 Dec 1862.

The Liverpool daily mail. No 1, 17 Mar–no 19, 10 Apr 1857.

The Birmingham daily post. No 1, 4 Dec 1857–20 May 1918. Continued as Birmingham post, 21 May 1918–2 Nov 1956. Continued as Birmingham post and Birmingham gazette, 3 Nov 1956–23 Sep 1964. Continued as Birmingham post, 24 Sep 1964 onwards. Prop John F. Feeney and John Jaffray 1857–69; John Jaffray and John Feeney 1869–94; John Feeney 1894–1905. Ed John Jaffray 1857–61?, ? Silk, J. T. Bunce 1862–98, A. H. Poultney 1899–1905.

The Liverpool mercury. 1 Jan 1858–12 Nov 1904. Incorporated in Liverpool daily post. Started weekly, no 1, 5 July 1811; twice weekly in 1847. Ed Egerton Smith 1811–?, Thomas Ballantyne, John Maitland, John Lovell 1880–90, G. Wynne 1890–1904.

The daily chronicle and northern counties advertiser (Newcastle). No 1, 1 May 1858–30 Dec 1861. Continued as Newcastle daily chronicle and northern counties advertiser, 1 Jan 1862–16 Mar 1923. Continued as North mail and Newcastle daily chronicle, 19 Mar 1923–18 Sep 1939. Incorporated in Newcastle journal (*see below*, Newcastle daily journal). Started weekly as Newcastle chronicle, no 1, 24 Mar 1764. Prop Joseph Cowen 1858–1900. Ed Joseph Cowen, Langley Baxter, James Annand ?–1879, ? Ruddock, Aaron Watson 1885–93.

The western daily press (Bristol). No 1, 1 June 1858–30 Jan 1932. Continued as Western daily press and Bristol mirror, 2 Feb 1932 onwards. Incorporating Bristol times and mirror (*see below*, Daily Bristol times). Prop P. S. Macliver and Walter Reid 1858–91; Walter Reid 1891–?. Ed Walter Reid 1858–?.

The Sheffield daily argus. No 1, 11 May–no 20, 3 June 1859.

Willmer's Liverpool morning news. No 1, 16 July–no 104, 15 Nov 1859. Ed Charles Willmer.

The western morning news (Plymouth). No 1, 3 Jan 1860–31 Jan 1921. Continued as Western morning news and mercury, 1 Feb 1921 onwards. Ed William Saunders, Edward Spender 1860–78, Albert Groser 1878–94.

The Nottingham daily express. No 1, 4 Jan 1860–6 Apr 1918. Continued as Nottingham journal and express (incorporating the long dormant copyright of Nottingham journal which had been purchased from William Bradshaw in 1887), 8 Apr 1918–5 Sep 1953. Amalgamated with Nottingham guardian and subsequently pbd as Guardian journal. Prop John W. Jevons 1860–4; Jevons and E. Renals 1864–?. Ed J. Dods Shaw, D. Edwards 1891–7.

The Bristol daily post. No 1, 24 Jan 1860–26 Jan 1878. Absorbed Bristol mercury and was continued as Bristol mercury and daily post, 27 Jan 1878–19 Dec 1901. Continued as Bristol daily mercury, 21 Dec 1901–30 Nov 1909. Ed Harold Lewis.

The daily western mercury (Plymouth). No 1, 2 June–25 Sep 1860.

Continued as Western daily mercury, 26 Sep 1860–31 Jan 1921. Incorporated in Western morning news. Ed Isaac Latimer, Edwin Goadby 1866–74.

The Newcastle daily journal. 2 Jan 1861–29 Mar 1930. Continued as Newcastle journal, 31 Mar 1930–5 July 1958. Continued as Journal, 7 July 1958 onwards. Started weekly as Newcastle journal, no 1, 12 May 1832. Ed Robert Redpath, A. D. Murray.

The Cambrian daily leader (Swansea). No 1, 20–3 May 1861. Continued as Cambria daily leader, 24 May 1861–15 Mar 1930. Incorporated in South Wales daily post.

The Nottingham daily guardian. No 1, 1 July 1861–9 Oct 1905. Continued as Nottingham guardian, 10 Oct 1905–5 Sep 1953. Amalgamated with Nottingham journal and express and continued as Guardian journal. Ed J. R. Forman.

The Liverpool evening mercury. No 1, 26 Aug 1861–9 Jan 1863.

The Liverpool journal of commerce. No 1, Oct 1861–28 Feb 1873. Continued as Journal of commerce, Mar 1873–21 Aug 1880. Continued as Liverpool journal of commerce, 23 Aug 1880–Dec 1911. Continued as Journal of commerce, 1 Jan 1912 onwards. When it incorporated Liverpool shipping telegraph, no 11,908, 30 Dec 1899, was followed by no 22,846, 1 Jan 1900, as a result of its taking over the numbering of the latter. Prop Charles Birchall 1880–1905. Ed Thomas Ballantyne 1861 (?).

The Manchester courier. [1861]–28 Jan 1916. Started weekly, no 1, 1 Jan 1825. Prop Thomas Sowler 1871–Apr 1891. Ed A. A. Watts 1825–6, John Sowler, R. S. Sowler 1839, Thomas Sowler, Francis Hitchman.

The Leeds mercury. [1861]–19 Oct 1901. Continued as Leeds and Yorkshire mercury, 21 Oct 1901–4 Nov 1907. Continued as Leeds mercury, 5 Nov 1907–25 Nov 1939. Incorporated in Yorkshire post. Started weekly, no 1, May 1718; thrice weekly in July 1855. Prop Edward Baines I 1801–27; Edward Baines I and Edward Baines II 1827–37; Edward Baines I, Edward Baines II and Frederick Baines 1837–48; Edward Baines II and Frederick Baines 1848–?. Ed Edward Baines I, Edward Baines II, Thomas Baines ?–1887, T. Wemyss Reid May 1870–87, Talbot Baines 1887–97.

The Birmingham daily gazette. No 1, 12 May 1862–30 Jan 1904. Continued as Birmingham gazette and express, 1 Feb 1904–16 Nov 1912. Continued as Birmingham gazette, 18 Nov 1912–2 Nov 1956. Incorporated in Birmingham post. Started weekly as Aris's Birmingham gazette, no 1, 16 Nov 1741. Ed John Caldecott, J. T. Bunce, Dr J. A. Langford, Dr Sebastian Evans, A. W. Still 1860–1890–1904.

Exeter and Plymouth gazette daily telegrams. 7 Feb 1863–30 Apr 1885. Daily edition of Exeter and Plymouth gazette. Prop J. Salter.

The Sheffield daily advertiser. No 1, 24 Feb–no 60, 6 May 1863.

The daily courier (Liverpool). 21 Apr 1863–2 Oct 1882. Continued as Liverpool courier, 3 Oct 1882–2 Sep 1922. Continued as Daily courier, 9 Oct 1922–31 Dec 1929. Started weekly as Liverpool courier and commercial advertiser, no 1, 6 Jan 1808. Prop Thomas Kaye 1808–56; Charles Tinling 1856, subsequently joined by John A. Willox and R. Hadden to become C. Tinling & Co. Ed Thomas Kaye, Charles Tinling, John A. Willox.

The eastern morning news (Hull). No 1, 26 Jan 1864–8 Nov 1929. Ed William Saunders, William Hunt, J. A. Spender 1886–90.

The eastern evening news (Hull). No 1, 26 Jan 1864–30 Apr 1867.

The Shields daily news (North Shields). No 1, 22 Aug 1864–6 June 1933. Continued as Shields news, 7 June 1933–31 Dec 1937. Continued as Shields evening news, 1 Jan 1938–21 Aug 1959.

The Ipswich times. [1864]–no 380, 2 Mar 1866–9 Oct 1874. Continued as East Anglian daily times, 11 Oct 1874 onwards. Ed F. W. Wilson 1874–90.

The daily Bristol times and mirror. 5 Jan 1865–31 Dec 1883. Continued as Bristol times and mirror, 1 Jan 1884–29 Jan 1932. Incorporated in Western daily press. Started weekly as Bristol times and Bath advocate, no 1, 2 Mar 1839–26 Mar 1853; continued weekly as Bristol times and Felix Farley's Bristol journal, 2 Apr 1853–31 Dec 1864. Ed T. D. Taylor, Charles Pebody ?–1882.

The Sunderland daily shipping news. No 1, 6 Nov 1865–no 10,431, 31 Dec 1913.

The Sheffield evening star and daily times. [1865]–no 2,760, 21 Apr 1874–23 Jan 1888. Incorporated in Evening telegraph (Sheffield).

The Yorkshire post (Leeds). No 5,928, 2 July 1866 onwards. Amalgamated with Leeds intelligencer, 2 July 1754–no 5,927, 30 June 1866, a weekly. Prop Yorkshire Conservative Newspaper Company. Ed John R. K. Ralph 1866–82, Charles Pebody 1882–90, H. J. Palmer 1890–1903.

The northern evening express (Newcastle). No 1, 1 Aug 1866–16 Oct 1886. Ed William Saunders.

The western times (Exeter). [1866] onwards. Started as Exeter weekly times no 1, 6 Oct 1827; present title from 3 Jan 1829. Ed T. Latimer ?–23 Jan 1873, Hugh Latimer and Stephen Glanville.

The evening express of the Devon weekly times (Exeter). No 1, 19 Dec 1866–25 Oct 1873. Continued as Devon evening press, 27 Oct 1873–30 Sep 1904. Continued as Express and echo, 1 Oct 1904 onwards.

The Bolton evening news. No 1, 19 Mar 1867 onwards. Prop W. F. Tillotson 1867–1889; Tillotson and Son 1898–?. Ed W. Brimelow 1867–1913.

The Bradford daily telegraph. No 1, 16 July 1868–15 Dec 1926. Continued as Bradford telegraph and argus, 16 Dec 1926–10 May 1930. Continued as Telegraph and argus 12 May 1930–3 Nov 1956. Continued as Telegraph and argus and Yorkshire observer, and eventually as Telegraph and argus when it dropped the rest of its title, 5 Nov 1956 onwards.

The Manchester evening news. No 1, 10 Oct 1868–26 July 1963. Continued as Manchester evening news and chronicle, 29 July 1963 onwards. Prop W. Evans & Co. Ed John Astle.

The Brighton daily news. No 1, 2 Nov 1868–31 May 1880. Incorporated in Argus (Brighton).

The western counties daily herald (Plymouth). No 1, 12 Nov 1868–13 Feb 1869.

The Bradford daily times. [1868]–no 813, 1 Jan–14 Sep 1871.

The Sussex daily news (Brighton). [1868]–no 1147, 2 July 1872–3 Mar 1956. Incorporated in Evening argus (Brighton).

The Bradford observer. [1868]–16 Nov 1901. Continued as Yorkshire daily observer, 17 Nov 1901–15 Jan 1909. Continued as Yorkshire observer, 16 Jan 1909–3 Nov 1956. Started weekly, no 1, 6 Feb 1834. Prop William Byles; W. P. Byles. Ed William Byles 1834–?, W. P. Byles, W. Harrison.

The western daily standard (Plymouth). No 1, 2 Mar 1869–5 Mar 1870.

The Oldham evening express. No 1, 5 Apr 1869–10 July 1889.

The western mail (Cardiff). No 1, 1 May 1869 onwards. Prop and ed Lascelles Carr.

The Leicester daily mail. No 1, 3 May 1869–19 Feb 1870. Continued as Leicester weekly express, nos 1–33, 26 Feb–1 Oct 1870.

The Newcastle daily telegraph. No 1, 19 June 1869–19 Nov 1870. Continued as Newcastle morning telegraph, 23 Nov 1870–7 June 1871. Continued as Newcastle evening telegraph, 8 June–23 Dec 1871.

The evening gazette for Middlesbrough. [8 Nov 1869]–6 Dec 1872. Continued as Daily gazette for Middlesbrough, 7 Dec 1872–10 June 1881. Continued as North eastern daily gazette (Middlesbrough), 11 June 1881–7 Nov 1936. Continued as North eastern gazette, 9 Nov 1936–13 Nov 1940. Continued as Evening gazette, 14 Nov 1940 onwards. Ed Hugh Gilzean Reid.

The northern echo (Darlington). No 1, 1 Jan 1870 onwards. Until 17 June 1870 it emanated from Hartlepool. Ed W. T. Stead 1871–80.

The Newcastle evening courant. No 1, 5 Mar 1870–Nov 1874. Continued as Newcastle daily courant, 26 Nov 1874–5 Feb 1876.

The evening telegram (Newport, Mon). No 1, 1 Aug 1870–12 July 1872. Continued as South Wales evening telegram, 13 July 1872–29 June 1876. Continued as South Wales daily telegram, 1 July 1876–13 Feb 1891. Continued as South Wales evening telegraph, 17 Feb–27 Nov 1891.

The Bolton morning news. No 1, 8 Aug–12 Nov 1870.

The evening news (Hull). No 54, 1 Oct 1870–6 July 1876. Continued as Hull express, 7 July 1876–25 May 1891. Incorporated in Hull daily news.

The eastern counties daily press (Norwich). No 1, 10 Oct 1870–2 May 1871. Continued as Eastern daily press, 3 May 1871 onwards. Ed J. Spilling 1873–97, A. Cozens-Hardy 1897–1937.

The Bolton daily chronicle. [1870]–no 705, 5 May 1873–July 1907. Continued as Bolton evening chronicle, 1 August 1907–21 Dec 1917.

The Birmingham daily mail. [1870]–no 154, 6 Mar 1871–16 May 1918. Continued as Birmingham mail, 17 May 1918–8 Apr 1963. Continued as Birmingham evening mail and despatch, 9 Apr 1963 onwards. Prop John Feeney and John Jaffray 1870–94; John Feeney 1894–1905. Ed H. J. Jennings 1870–80.

The evening express (Liverpool). [1870]–no 692, 2 June 1873–13 Oct 1958.

The Birmingham morning news. No 1, 4 Jan 1871–27 May 1876. Ed George Dawson.

The Huddersfield daily examiner. No 1, 28 Jan 1871 onwards. Ed Joseph Woodhead, Ernest Woodhead.

The Huddersfield daily chronicle. No 1, 30 Jan 1871–31 Dec 1915.

The sporting chronicle (Manchester). No 1, 14 Feb 1871 onwards. Prop Edward Hulton and E. O. Bleackley. Ed Edward Hulton.

The Liverpool daily Albion. [1871]–no 539, 21 July 1873–30 June 1875. Continued as Liverpool evening Albion, 1 July 1875–21 June 1879. Continued as Liverpool Albion, 23 June 1879–30 June 1883. Continued as Liverpool daily Albion, [July]–5 Oct–25 Mar 1887.

The Bolton evening guardian. [1871]–no 825, 1 Jan 1874–26 May 1893. Incorporated in Bolton evening news. Prop Thomas Cunliffe 1868–92.

The northern counties daily mail (Newcastle). No 1, 1 May–no 88, 10 Aug 1872.

The Leicester daily post. No 1, 1 Aug 1872–31 Mar 1921. Ed Angus Galbraith.

The Leicester evening news. [1872]–no 982, 12 June 1875–28 June 1878.

The Bradford evening mail. No 1, 18 Sep 1872–1 May 1875. Incorporated in Bradford chronicle.

The Bradford chronicle. No 1, 1 Oct 1872–18 June 1882. Absorbed Bradford evening mail and became Bradford daily chronicle and mail, 19 June 1882–25 Aug 1883.

The Leeds daily news. [1872]–no 148, 1 May 1873–29 May 1905. Continued as Yorkshire evening news, 1 June 1905–3 Dec 1963. Amalgamated with Yorkshire evening post. Prop Charles and Frank Macaskie c. 1880–?. Ed Charles Macaskie c. 1880–c. 1900.

The South Wales daily news (Cardiff). No 1, 7 Feb 1872–8 Apr 1918. Continued as South Wales news, 9 Apr 1918–24 Aug 1928. Amalgamated with Western mail. Ed John Astle 1872–4.

The Staffordshire daily sentinel (Hanley). No 2, 10 Apr 1873–30 Dec 1881. Continued as Staffordshire sentinel, 1 Jan 1882–16 Mar 1929. Continued as Evening sentinel, 18 Mar 1929 onwards.

The Sheffield post. No 19, 17 May 1873–25 July 1882. Continued as Sheffield daily post, 26 July 1882–19 July 1884. Continued as Sheffield post, 21 July 1884–28 May 1887.

The Sunderland daily echo and shipping gazette. No 1, 22 Dec 1873–3 Dec 1928. Continued as Sunderland echo and shipping gazette, 4 Dec 1928–2 May 1959. Continued as Sunderland echo (Echo Sunderland), 4 May 1959 onwards. Prop Samuel Storey.

The York herald. 1 Jan 1874–31 Dec 1889. Continued as Yorkshire herald, 1 Jan 1890–31 Dec 1936. Started weekly, no 1, 2 Jan 1790; reverted to this frequency, 2 Jan 1937–18 June 1954. Amalgamated with the Yorkshire gazette and continued weekly as Yorkshire gazette and herald, 25 June 1954 onwards. Ed William Hargrove 1813–46. W. Wallace Hargrove, Edwin N. Goadby 1874–87, A. H. Fletcher 1899–?.

The Manchester evening mail. No 1, 4 May 1874–10 July 1916. Ed Thomas Sowler.

The evening express telegram (Cheltenham). No 70, 6 July 1874–20 Jan 1875. Continued as Evening telegram and express, 21 Jan 1875–30 Dec 1882.

The East Anglian daily times (Ipswich). No 1, 13 Oct 1874 onwards. Begun weekly as Ipswich express, no 1, 13 Aug 1839.

The Wakefield evening herald. [1874]–no 4555, 5 Jan 1889–24 Dec 1890.

The Midland counties evening express (Wolverhampton). No 1, 2 Nov 1874–15 Jan 1876. Continued as Evening express, 17 Jan 1876–28 June 1884. Continued as Evening express and star, 30 June 1884–23 Apr 1889. Continued as Express and star, 24 Apr 1889 onwards. Prop Thomas Graham. Ed A. Meikle.

The Southport daily news. 3 May 1875–17 Nov 1877. Continued as Liverpool and Southport daily news, 19 Nov 1877–18 Feb 1881. Begun weekly as Southport independent, no 1, 4 July 1861. Prop Frederick M. Jones.

The Bath argus evening telegram. Nos 1–208, 17 May 1875–19 Jan 1876. Continued as Evening argus, nos 209–646, 20 Jan 1876–30 Oct 1877. Continued as Bath argus and West of England advertising register (daily edn), 647, 31 Oct 1877–30 Apr 1892. Continued as Bath daily argus, 2 May 1892–28 July 1893. Continued as Bath argus and West of England advertising register, 29 July 1893–10 Apr 1897. Continued as Bath daily argus, 11 Apr 1897–31 Jan 1900. Amalgamated with Bath daily chronicle to appear as Bath daily chronicle and argus. The first 646 nos were daily edns of the weekly Bath argus and West of England advertising register which began 23 July 1870.

The Birmingham evening news. No 1, 16 Aug 1875–no 119, 15 Jan 1876. Incorporated in Birmingham morning news.

The Scarborough daily post. No 1, 21 Feb 1876–24 May 1887. Continued as Scarborough post, 25 May 1887–12 May 1910. Continued as two: Scarborough daily post, 13 May 1910–29 Sep 1921; and Scarborough weekly post, 13 May 1910–27 Jan 1922. Continued as Scarborough post and weekly pictorial, 3 Feb 1922–7 Jan 1932.

The Brighton and Sussex daily post. No 1, 1 July 1876–8 July 1885. Continued as Brighton and Sussex evening post, 9 July 1885–7 Feb 1886.

The Sunderland daily times. No 1, 3 July 1876–3 Aug 1878. Incorporated in Sunderland daily echo.

The Sunderland daily post. No 1, 21 July 1876–3 Sep 1891. Incorporated in Sunderland daily herald.

The northern times (Oldham). No 1, 19 Mar 1877–11 June 1880. Continued as Oldham evening standard, 1880–2. Continued as Oldham daily standard, 9 Jan 1882–8 June 1917. Continued as Oldham evening standard, 11 June 1917–28 Dec 1928. Incorporated in Oldham evening chronicle.

The daily telegram (Wisbech). No 1, 24 Apr–no 123, 15 Sep 1877.

The Bristol evening news. No 1, 29 May 1877–30 Jan 1932. Ed T. Watkins.

The Warrington evening post. No 1, 17 May 1877–6 Apr 1878. Continued as Evening post, 8 Apr 1878–31 Dec 1880.

The evening post (Worcester). No 1, 4 June 1877–21 May 1881. Continued as Worcestershire evening post, 30 May 1881–3 Mar 1883. Continued as Worcestershire echo, 5 Mar 1883–3 Jan 1930.

The evening news (Portsmouth). [1877]–no 211, 1 Jan 1878–17 Jan 1959. Continued as News, 19 Jan 1959 onwards.

The Bath evening chronicle. No 2, 12 June 1877–4 August 1883.

Continued as Bath daily chronicle, 7 Aug 1883–31 Jan 1900. Continued as Bath daily chronicle and argus, 1–14 Feb 1900. Continued as Daily chronicle and argus, 15 Feb 1900–7 Oct 1903. Continued as Bath daily chronicle and argus, 8 Oct 1903–15 Sep 1911. Continued as Bath and Wilts chronicle, 16 Sep 1911–11 Apr 1925. Continued as Bath and Wilts chronicle and herald, 14 Apr 1925–10 June 1961. Continued as Bath and Wilts evening chronicle, 12 June 1961 onwards.

The northern evening mail (West Hartlepool). [1877]–no 200, 18 Feb 1878–2 Oct 1883. Continued as Northern daily mail, 29 Oct 1883 onwards. Prop Samuel Storey.

The Swansea daily shipping register. [1877]–11 June 1888–3 July 1888. Continued as Swansea gazette, 4 July 1888–4 Jan 1913.

The evening star of Gwent and South Wales times (Newport, Mon). No 1, 10 Nov 1877–30 Mar 1889. Continued as South Wales daily times and star of Gwent, 1 Apr 1889–25 June 1892. Continued as South Wales daily star, 27 June 1892–6 Sep 1900. Continued as South Wales daily telegraph, 7 Sep 1900–24 Jan 1903. Continued as Newport and Monmouthshire evening telegraph, 12 Jan–10 July 1903. Between 12 and 24 Jan this existed as registration copies only.

The daily midland echo (Wolverhampton). No 1, 11 Dec 1877–2 Jan 1879. Continued as Midland echo, 8–15 Jan 1879.

The Grimsby express. No 1, 27 Apr 1878–25 May 1891. Incorporated in Hull daily news.

The Nottingham evening post. No 1, 1 May 1878–1 July 1963. Continued as Evening post and news, 2 July 1963 onwards.

The Gateshead and Tyneside echo (Gateshead). No 1, 24 Apr 1879–20 Jan 1880. Continued as Tyneside echo (Newcastle) until 30 Aug 1888.

The Derby daily telegraph and reporter. No 1, 28 July 1879–13 Oct 1881. Continued as Derby daily telegraph, 14 Oct 1881–29 Jan 1932. Continued as Derby daily telegraph and Derby daily express, 30 Jan–12 Mar 1932. Continued as Derby evening telegraph and Derby daily express, 14 Mar 1932–14 Aug 1933. Continued as Derby evening telegraph, 15 Aug 1933 onwards.

The Derby evening gazette. No 1, 28 July 1879–2 Oct 1880. Continued as Derby and Burton evening gazette, 4 Oct 1880–25 May 1881. Continued as Derby and Burton gazette, 27 May 1881–11 July 1884. Continued as Derby evening gazette, 12 July–30 Dec 1884.

The Liverpool echo. No 1, 27 Oct 1879 onwards. Ed Alexander G. Jeans.

The Worcester daily times and journal. No 1, 5 Jan 1880–30 Jan 1937. Continued as Worcester evening times, 1 Feb–30 Oct 1937. Continued as Evening news and times, 1 Nov 1937–21 Oct 1939. Continued as News and times, 23 Oct 1939–5 Oct 1941. Continued as evening news and times, 7 Oct 1941–20 Oct 1962. Continued as Worcester evening news, 22 Oct 1962 onwards. Ed C. H. Birbeck.

The Northampton mercury daily reporter. No 1, 9 Feb 1880–30 July 1885. Continued as Northampton daily reporter, 1 Aug 1885–6 Apr 1908. Continued as Northampton daily echo, 13 Apr 1908–22 Aug 1919. Continued as daily echo, 23 Aug 1919–31 Oct 1931. Continued as Chronicle and echo, 2 Nov 1931 onwards. Prop Mrs T. E. Dicey ?–1885; Samuel Smith Campion.

The evening herald (Northampton). No 1, 16 Feb 1880–31 July 1881. Continued as Northampton daily chronicle and evening herald, 1 Aug 1881–31 Oct 1931. Amalgamated with Daily echo (Northampton) and continued as Chronicle and echo, 2 Nov 1931 onwards.

The evening chronicle (Oldham). No 1, 17 Mar 1880–17 Mar 1882. Continued as Oldham evening chronicle, 20 Mar 1882 onwards. Prop ? Hirst and ? Rennie.

The argus (Brighton). No 1, 30 Mar 1880–24 Aug 1896. Continued as Evening argus, 25 Aug 1896 onwards.

The evening star (Wolverhampton). No 1, 28 June 1880–27 June 1884. Incorporated in Evening express (Wolverhampton). Ed Harry Jeffs.

The Sussex evening times (Brighton). No 1, 6 July 1880–30 Apr 1915.

The evening news (Norwich). No 1, 2 Jan–11 Feb 1882. Continued as Eastern evening news (Norwich), 13 Feb 1882 onwards.

The evening press (York). [1882]–20 Mar 1884–31 Dec 1904. Continued as Yorkshire evening press, 1 Jan 1905 onwards.

The Scarborough evening news. [1882]–no 908, 4 Jan 1886 onwards. Ed Meredith J. Whittaker.

The Stockport echo. No 1, 10 Feb 1883–25 June 1889. Continued as Cheshire echo, 1889–92; and as Cheshire evening echo, 1893–5; and as Cheshire daily echo, 1 Nov 1895–30 Sep 1939.

The Midland echo (Birmingham). No 1, 26 Feb 1883–1 Mar 1885. Incorporated in Evening express and star (Birmingham).

The evening times (Liverpool). No 1, 9 June 1883–9 June 1884. Continued as Liverpool and Bootle evening times, 10 June 1884–31 Dec 1894.

The evening mail (Portsmouth). No 1, 14 Jan 1884–8 June 1895. Continued as Mail, 1895–6; and as Southern daily mail, 23 Mar 1896–14 Jan 1905.

The Midland evening news (Wolverhampton). No 1, 3 Apr 1884–31 July 1915.

The Hull daily news. 21 Oct 1884–18 Mar 1914. Continued as Daily news, 19 Mar 1914–1 Feb 1916. Continued as Hull daily news, 2 Feb 1916–28 Apr 1923. Continued as Hull evening news, 30 Apr 1923–17 Apr 1930. Incorporated in Daily mail (Hull). Started weekly as Hull news, no 1, 3 Jan 1852.

The Derby express. No 1, 22 Oct 1884–27 Feb 1909. Continued as Derby daily express, 1 Mar 1909–29 Jan 1932. Incorporated in Derby daily telegraph.

The South Wales echo (Cardiff). [1884]–1 July 1889 onwards.

The Newcastle daily leader. No 1, 28 Sep 1885–31 Oct 1903. Ed James Annand, Aaron Watson.

The Hull daily mail. No 1, 29 Sep 1885–31 Dec 1895. Continued as Daily mail (Hull), Jan 1896 onwards.

The Nottingham evening news. No 1, 21 Oct 1885–30 Oct 1948. Continued as Evening news, 1 Nov 1948–23 Sep 1950. Continued as Nottingham evening news, 25 Sep 1950–1 July 1963. Incorporated in Nottingham evening post. Ed D. Edwards 1891–7.

The evening chronicle (Newcastle-on-Tyne). No 1, 2 Nov 1885 onwards.

The Birmingham daily times. No 1, 4 Nov 1885–31 Mar 1890.

The evening post (Exeter). No 1, 12 Nov 1885–6 June 1902.

The Derby morning post. No 1, 16 Nov 1885–5 July 1887.

The Norfolk daily standard (Norwich). [1886]–no 695, 15 Dec 1887–31 Jan 1903. Continued as Norfolk evening standard. Incorporated in Eastern evening mail in 1905.

The Lancashire evening post (Preston). No 1, 16 Oct 1886–31 Dec 1892. Continued as Lancashire daily post, Jan 1893–1 Jan 1949. Continued as Lancashire evening post, 3 Jan 1949 onwards. Ed John Toulmin.

The northern daily telegraph (Blackburn). No 1, 26 Oct 1886–13 Oct 1956. Continued as Northern evening telegraph, 15 Oct–11 Dec 1956. Continued as Evening telegraph, 12 Dec 1956–31 Aug 1963. Continued as Lancashire evening telegraph, 2 Sep 1963 onwards.

The Sheffield evening telegraph. No 1, 4 June 1887–23 June 1888. Continued as Evening telegraph and star, 25 June 1888–17 Jan 1898. Continued as Yorkshire telegraph and star, Jan 1898–7 Oct 1937. Continued as Telegraph and star, 8 Oct 1937–12 Nov 1938. Continued as Star, 14 Nov 1938 onwards.

The Blackburn evening express. No 1, 29 Aug 1887–5 Oct 1888. Continued as Evening express and standard, 6 Oct 1888–26 Apr 1890. Continued as Lancashire evening express and standard, 28 Apr 1890–8 June 1895. Continued as Lancashire daily express and standard, 10 June 1895–3 Mar 1899.

The Cambridge daily news. No 1, 28 May 1888–29 Sep 1962. Continued as Cambridge news, 1 Oct 1962 onwards. Prop William F. Taylor 1888–?.

The southern echo (Southampton). No 1, 20 Aug 1888–5 Sep 1891. Continued as Southern echo and Bournemouth telegraph, 7 Sep 1891–21 Feb 1901. Continued as Southern daily echo, 23 Feb 1901–30 June 1958. Continued as Southern evening echo, 1 July 1958 onwards. Prop J. Passmore Edwards Aug 1888–July 1891.

The Yorkshire evening post (Leeds). No 79, 1 Dec 1890 onwards. Ed Alexander Paterson, Alfred Turner.

The midland daily telegraph (Coventry). No 1, 9 Feb 1891–15 Nov 1941. Continued as Coventry evening telegraph, 17 Nov 1941 onwards.

The daily argus (Birmingham). No 1, 9 Nov 1891–30 June 1902. Incorporated in Birmingham evening dispatch.

The daily guardian (Warrington). No 1, 28 Nov 1891–8 Aug 1896. Continued as Warrington daily guardian, 10 Aug 1896–3 Oct 1903.

The daily independent press (Cambridge). No 1, 2 Jan–no 138, 31 July 1892.

The South Wales argus (Newport, Mon). No 1, 30 May 1892 onwards.

The Bradford daily argus. No 1, 16 June 1892–14 July 1923. Continued as Yorkshire evening argus, 16 July 1923–31 Dec 1925. Amalgamated with Bradford daily telegraph. Ed H. Fieldhouse.

The Leicester daily express. No 1, 20 June 1892–5 Oct 1895.

The Halifax evening courier. No 1, 21 June 1892–30 Apr 1921. Continued as Halifax daily courier and guardian, 2 May 1921 onwards.

The South Wales daily post (Swansea). No 1, 13 Feb 1893–12 Mar 1932. Continued as South Wales evening post, 14 Mar 1932 onwards.

The Newcastle evening news. No 1, 2 Oct 1893–27 Apr 1899.

The Barrow evening echo. No 1, 21 Mar 1894–30 June 1898.

The eastern daily telegraph (Grimsby). No 1, 27 Feb 1897–31 Dec 1898. Continued as Grimsby daily telegraph, Jan 1899–12 Mar 1932. Continued as Grimsby evening telegraph, 14 Mar 1932 onwards.

The Isle of Man daily times. No 1, 4 May 1897 onwards.

The Manchester evening chronicle. No 1, 10 May 1897–31 Mar 1914. Continued as Evening chronicle, 1 Apr 1914–26 July 1963. Incorporated in Manchester evening news. Founded by Edward Hulton and E. O. Bleackley.

The evening herald (Ipswich). No 1, 1 Sep–29 Dec 1897. Continued as Daily herald, 30 Dec 1897–30 July 1898. Incorporated in Evening star.

The north western daily mail (Barrow). No 1, 1 Jan 1898–31 Dec 1940. Continued as North-western evening mail, 1 Jan 1941 onwards.

The Newcastle morning mail. No 1, 23 May 1898–9 Feb 1901. Continued as Morning mail. 11 Feb–9 Aug 1901.

The Oxford and district morning echo. No 25, 22 Oct 1898–no 112, 3 Feb 1899. Continued as Oxford morning echo, 4 Feb 1899–30 Jan 1900.

The Sunderland morning mail. No 1, 14 Nov 1898–11 Feb 1901.

Scottish daily papers

An asterisk signifies that no copy has been found.

The day (Glasgow). Nos 1–112, 2 Jan–30 June 1832. Ed John Strang.

*The conservative (Edinburgh). No 1, 24 Feb 1837–?.

North British daily mail (Glasgow). No 1, 14 Apr 1847–31 Dec 1900. Continued as Glasgow daily mail, 1 Jan–8 June 1901. Incorporated in Daily record (Glasgow). Ed George Troup 1847–8, Robert Somers 1849–59, C. Cameron 1860–73, James R. Manners.

Daily mail (Glasgow). [1848]–no 217, 17 Mar 1849–12 July 1851.

War telegraph (Edinburgh). No 1, 9 Oct 1854–no 53, 8 Dec 1854. Continued as Northern telegraph, no 54, 9 Dec 1854–no 77, 6 Jan 1855. Ed J. W. Finlay.

Northern telegraphic news (Aberdeen). No 1, 23 Jan 1855–7 Oct 1876.

The Glasgow daily news. [No 1, 13 Apr 1855]–no 69, 30 June–no 111, 17 Aug 1855.

Morning bulletin (Glasgow). No 1, 26 May–no 12, 8 June 1855.

The daily express (Edinburgh). No 1, 23 June 1855–27 Aug 1859. Incorporated in Caledonian mercury. Ed W. H. Murray.

The Glasgow times. No 1, 25 June 1855–9 June 1869.

The Caledonian mercury (Edinburgh). 2 July 1855–20 Apr 1867. Incorporated in Scotsman. Started thrice weekly, no 1, 28 Apr 1720; later twice weekly; an evening paper from 14 July 1866. Prop Thomas Allan. Ed David Buchanan 1810–27, James Browne, J. G. Cochrane, J. D. White, W. D. Bruce, James Robie 1855–66, William Saunders 1866–7.

The daily Scotsman (Edinburgh). 2 July 1855–31 Dec 1859. Continued as Scotsman, 2 Jan 1860 onwards. Started weekly as Scotsman, no 1, 25 Jan 1817. Prop William Ritchie; John Ritchie 1847–70, J. R. Findlay 1870–98. Ed William Ritchie and Charles Maclaren 1817, J. R. McCulloch 1817–21, Charles Maclaren 1822–45, James Law 1845–9, Alexander Russel 1849–76, Robert Wallace 1876–80, Charles Cooper 1880–1906.

Daily bulletin (Glasgow). [July 1855]–no 1416, 9 Dec 1859–12 Feb 1861.

*The bawbee (Edinburgh). No 1, 19 Oct 1857–?. Halfpenny paper. Ed J. G. Bertram.

The Glasgow morning journal. No 1, 29 June–4 Sep 1858. Continued as Morning journal, 6 Sep 1858–11 Jan 1870. Continued as Daily express and morning journal, 12 Jan–19 Aug 1870. Incorporated in Star (Glasgow). Ed Robert Somers.

The Glasgow herald. 3 Jan 1859 onwards. Started weekly as Glasgow advertiser, no 1, 27 Jan 1783; twice weekly from 1 Nov 1802; thrice weekly in 1855. Present title adopted 23 Aug 1805. Ed John Mennons 1782–1803, Samuel Hunter 1803–37, George Outram 1837–56, James Pagan 1856–70, William Jack, J. H. Stoddart, Charles Russell 1887–1906.

The daily argus (Dundee). No 1, 23 May 1859–20 Apr 1861. Incorporated in Dundee courier.

The daily courant (Edinburgh). 2 Jan–31 Oct 1860. Continued as Edinburgh evening courant, 1 Nov 1860–15 Dec 1871. Continued as Edinburgh courant, 16 Dec 1871–6 Feb 1886. Incorporated in Scottish news (Glasgow). Started thrice weekly as Edinburgh evening courant, no 1, 15 Dec 1718. Ed George Houy 1826–7, David Buchanan 1827–48, Joseph Robertson 1849–53, William Buchanan 1853–60, James Hannay 1860–4, Francis Espinasse 1864–7, J. Scott Henderson 1867–72. James Mure, W. R. Lawson.

The daily review (Edinburgh). No 1, 2 Apr 1861–12 June 1886. Ed J. B. Manson 1861–8, Henry Kingsley 1868–71, T. B. Gillies 1871–4, George Smith 1874–7, William Mackie 1877–86.

The Dundee courier. 22 Apr 1861–15 Nov 1899. Continued as Courier and argus. 16 Nov 1899–4 May 1926. Incorporated in Dundee advertiser. Started as Dundee weekly courier, no 1, 20 Sep 1816. Ed ? Mitchell.

The Dundee advertiser. 1 May 1861–4 May 1926. Continued as Dundee advertiser and courier, 10 May–2 June 1926. Continued as Courier and advertiser, 3 June 1926 onwards. Started weekly, no 1, 16 Jan 1801; twice a week on 8 Apr 1845. Ed R. S. Rintoul, John Leng 1851–1900.

The Greenock telegraph. 24 Apr 1863 onwards. Started weekly in 1857. Prop J. F. Neilson and R. C. Mackenzie. Ed W. H. Wylie.

Evening citizen (Glasgow). No 1, 8 Aug 1864–7 Aug 1914. Continued as Glasgow citizen, 8 Aug 1914–27 Oct 1923. Continued as Evening citizen, 29 Oct 1923 onwards. Started weekly as Glasgow citizen in 1842. Ed James Hedderwick 1842–97, Edwin C. Hedderwick.

The Glasgow evening mail. No 1, 24 Apr–30 Dec 1865.

The Glasgow evening herald. No 1, 29 Apr–30 Dec 1865.

The Glasgow evening post. No 1, 9 July 1866–31 Dec 1868. Continued as Evening journal, 1 Jan 1869–11 Jan 1870. Continued as Star, no 1,

12 Jan 1870–16 Feb 1872. Continued as Evening star, 17 Feb 1872–13 Mar 1875. Continued as Evening news and star, 15 Mar 1875–10 Feb 1888. Continued as Glasgow evening news, 11 Feb 1888–23 Sep 1905. Continued as Glasgow news, 25 Sep 1905–3 Oct 1915. Continued as Evening news, 4 Oct 1915–17 Jan 1957. Initially run in conjunction with Morning journal (Glasgow). Ed Frederick Wicks, J. Murray Smith, James Stephen Jeans.

Evening news (Greenock). No 1, 17 July 1866–11 Jan 1868. Continued weekly as Greenock news, 18 Jan 1868–25 June 1870.

Greenock daily press. No 1, 5 Mar–27 Apr 1867. Continued weekly to 28 Dec 1867.

The Aberdeen daily free press. 4 May 1872–30 June 1874. Continued as Daily free press, 1 July 1874–31 Dec 1900. Continued as Aberdeen free press, 1 Jan 1901–30 Nov 1922. Amalgamated with Aberdeen journal and subsequently pbd as Aberdeen press and journal. Started weekly as North of Scotland gazette, no 1, 1 Apr 1845. Ed Henry Alexander.

The Edinburgh evening news. No 1, 27 May 1873 onwards. Ed Hector C. Macpherson.

The Glasgow news. No 1, 15 Sep 1873–6 Feb 1886. Continued as Scottish news, 7 Feb 1886–11 Feb 1888. Ed R. H. Patterson 1873–4.

The Paisley daily express. [No 1 Oct? 1874]–no 223, 1 June 1875 onwards.

Evening news (Dundee). No 1, 28 Mar 1876–12 Mar 1879.

Aberdeen journal, and general advertiser for the North of Scotland (daily edition). 24 Apr 1877–17 July 1901. Continued as Aberdeen daily journal, 18 July 1901–30 Nov 1922. Amalgamated with Aberdeen free press and subsequently pbd as Aberdeen press and journal. Started as Aberdeen journal and North-British magazine, no 1, 29 Dec 1747–5 Jan 1748. Ed William Forsyth 1849–79, David L. Pressly.

Evening telegraph (Dundee). No 1, 13 Mar 1877 onwards.

The Edinburgh evening telephone. No 1, 1 Nov 1878–no 79, 31 Jan 1879.

Aberdeen evening express. No 1, 20 Jan 1879–23 Mar 1899. Continued as Evening express, 24 Mar 1899 onwards. Ed David L. Pressly.

The evening express (Edinburgh). No 1, 6 Mar 1880–6 Feb 1886. Run in conjunction with Edinburgh courant.

Evening gazette (Aberdeen). No 1, 23 Jan 1882–30 Nov 1922. Incorporated in Evening express. Ed William Alexander 1882–94.

The Edinburgh evening dispatch. No 1, 4 Jan 1886–10 Dec 1921. Continued as Evening dispatch, 12 Dec 1921–18 Nov 1963. Incorporated in Edinburgh evening news. Run in conjunction with Scotsman.

The Scottish leader (Edinburgh). No 1, 3 Jan 1887–4 July 1894. Ed John Macfarlane, C. H. Hanson, J. H. Dalziel.

The daily record (Glasgow). No 1, 28 Oct 1895–8 June 1901. Continued as Daily record and daily mail, 10 June 1901–29 Mar 1902. Continued as Daily record and mail, 31 Mar 1902–12 Mar 1954. Continued as Record, 13 Mar 1954–.

Evening post (Dundee). No 1, 22 Jan 1900–16 May 1905.

Irish Daily Papers

Saunders's news-letter (Dublin). [June 1777]–4 June 1878. Continued as Saunders's Irish daily news, 5 June 1878–24 Nov 1879. Started thrice weekly in 1755. Prop James Potts, John Potts 1796–?. Ed John Potts, J. T. Potts 1846–71.

The freeman's journal. [Before 1820]–20 Dec 1924. Started as Public register: or freeman's journal, no 1, 10 Sep 1763, twice weekly. Prop Francis Higgins 1783–1802; Philip Whitfield Harvey 1802–26; Henry Grattan 1826–30; Patrick Lavelle 1830–7; Mary Lavelle 1837–41; John Gray. Ed Francis Higgins 1783–1802, Philip Whitfield Harvey, Henry Grattan, Patrick Lavelle, John Gray, Edmund Dwyer Gray, Edward Byrne 1884–91.

The Cork daily advertiser. No 1, 1 Oct 1836–1 Jan 1837.

The daily express (Dublin). No 1, 3 Feb 1851–10 Feb 1917. Continued as Daily express and Irish daily mail, 12 Feb 1917–18 June 1921. Ed G. H. Francis, J. Robinson.

The Belfast daily Mercury. 19 Apr 1854–2 Nov 1861. Started as Belfast Mercury, no 1, 29 Mar 1851.

The southern reporter (Cork). 12 June 1855–16 June 1871. Continued as Irish daily telegraph, 1 July 1871–11 Dec 1873. Started weekly in June 1807.

The Belfast news-letter. 2 July 1855–1 Sep 1962. Continued as News letter, 3 Sep 1862 onwards. Started weekly, no 1, 1 Sep 1737. Ed Alexander Mackay 1796–1844, James A. Henderson 1845–83, Sir James Henderson.

The mail and Waterford daily express. No 1, 13 July 1855–30 June 1860.

The northern whig (Belfast). 1 Feb 1858 onwards. Started weekly in 1824. Ed F. D. Finlay 1824–?, E. M. Whitty, Thomas MacKnight.

The Irish times (Dublin). No 1, 29 Mar 1859 onwards. Ed G. B. Wheeler 1859–77, J. A. Scott 1877–99, Arthur Locker.

The morning news (Dublin). No 6, 2 May 1859–31 Dec 1864. Ed A. M. Sullivan.

The evening freeman (Dublin). [1859]–30 June 1871. Continued as Evening telegraph, no 1, 1 July 1861–19 Dec 1924. Started thrice weekly, no 1, 18 Jan 1831.

The Cork constitution. 2 Jan 1860–14 Aug 1925. Started thrice weekly in 1822.

The Cork daily herald. 2 Mar 1860–19 July 1901. Started weekly as Cork herald, no 1, 21 June 1856. Ed David A. Nagle.

The Dublin evening mail. 4 Feb 1861–1 Feb 1928. Continued as Evening mail, 2 Feb 1928–19 July 1962. Started thrice weekly, no 1, 3 Feb 1823. Prop Thomas Sheehan; J. S. Lefanu 1839–73. Ed Joseph T. Haydn 1823–?, Remigius Sheehan, H. Maunsell.

The Cork examiner. [1861] onwards. Started thrice weekly, no 1, 30 Aug 1841.

The Dublin evening post. 23 Jan 1865–21 Aug 1875. Started twice weekly, no 1, 10 June 1732. Ed John Magee ?–1809 (?), James Magee jr ?–1814, F. W. Conway.

The evening Irish times (Dublin). [1865]–31 Oct 1921.

The morning mail (Dublin). [Feb 1870]–no 346, 17 Mar 1871–30 Aug 1912.

The Waterford daily mail. 24 May 1870–19 Sep 1908. Started weekly as Waterford mail, no 1, 16 Aug 1823. 'Daily' was omitted from the title from 30 Oct 1874 to 11 Dec 1886.

The Belfast evening telegraph. [Sep 1870]–no 171, 20 Mar 1871–18 Apr 1918. Continued as Belfast telegraph, 19 Apr 1918 onwards.

The daily examiner (Belfast). 16 Nov 1870–31 Dec 1872. Continued as Ulster examiner and northern star, 1 Jan 1873–22 July 1882. Incorporated in Morning news (Belfast). Started as Ulster examiner, no 1, 14 Mar 1868.

The evening press (Belfast). [July 1871]–no 520, 15 May 1873–21 May 1874.

The Belfast times. No 1, 1 Jan–31 May 1872. Continued as Belfast daily times, 1 June–10 Aug 1872.

The Belfast morning news. 20 Aug 1872–27 Apr 1882. Continued as Morning news, no 1, 1 May–no 72, 22 July 1882. Continued as Morning news and examiner, no 73, 24 July 1882–no 222, 18 Jan 1883. Continued as Morning news, vol 39, no 17, 19 Jan 1883–vol 39, no 8034, 27 Aug 1892. Incorporated in Irish news (Belfast). Started thrice weekly, no 1, 2 July 1855. Prop E. D. Gray May 1882–?. Ed Daniel Reed.

The Ulster echo (Belfast). No 1, 26 May 1874–8 June 1916.

The Dublin sporting news. No 1, 5 Feb 1889–31 Dec 1901.

The Belfast evening star. No 1, 29 Jan–31 May 1890.

The Irish news (Belfast). No 1, 15 Aug 1891–27 Aug 1892. Continued as Irish news and Belfast morning news, 29 Aug 1892–31 Aug 1925; 1 Jan–29 Mar, 19 July–30 Sep, 11 Oct 1926 onwards.

The Irish daily independent (Dublin). No 1, 18 Dec 1891–31 Dec 1904. Continued as Irish independent, 2 Jan 1905 onwards. Ed Edward Byrne.
The evening herald (Dublin). No 1, 19 Dec 1891 onwards.
The evening echo (Cork). [1893]–no 825, 6 May 1896 onwards.
The daily nation (Dublin). 5 June 1897–31 Aug 1900. Incorporated in Irish daily independent. Started weekly, no 1, 15 Oct 1842. Ed A. M. Sullivan 1858–76, C. G. Duffy.
The evening news (Waterford). [1898]–no 288, 1 June 1899–31 Dec 1957.

London papers published more than once a week

The most important entries in this section are those London evening papers which were pbd three times a week; they were for the most part founded in the 18th century and were nearly extinct by 1850. There are 3 other kinds of paper which were pbd more than once a week: the London suburban press, various technical and trade journals and numerous provincial papers which existed as weeklies in 1800 and were pbd more frequently until they finally became dailies.

Tri-weekly: Monday, Wednesday and Friday

Lloyd's evening post and British chronicle. No 1, 22 July 1757–30 Dec 1805–[1815?]. Ed Robert Heron.
London packet: or new Lloyd's evening post. [Oct 1769]–no 91, 28 May 1770–no 11584, 30 Dec 1836. Incorporated in St James's chronicle. Prop Charles Baldwin.
The evening mail. [Feb 1789]–no 62, July 1789–27 June 1868. Continued as Mail, 30 June 1868–11 Oct 1922. Incorporated in The Times weekly edition. Only twice a week from July 1868 to 1871. Run in conjunction with The Times.
The mercantile chronicle. No 1, 20 July 1821–10 Jan 1823. Incorporated in London packet; or new Lloyd's evening post.
The evening chronicle. No 1, 31 Jan 1835–no 1940, 23 July 1847. Prop John Easthope. Ed George Hogarth.
The Hackney and Kingsland gazette. [1864]–no 277, 10 July 1867–19 May 1929. Continued as Hackney gazette and north London advertiser, 21 May 1926 onwards.

Tuesday, Thursday and Saturday

The London evening post. No 1, 1 Dec 1727–13 Mar 1806.
The general evening post. No 1, 2 Oct 1733–1 Feb 1822. Incorporated in St James's Chronicle. Ed Stephen Jones.
The London chronicle. No 1, 1 Jan 1757–28 Apr 1823. Incorporated in London packet: or new Lloyd's evening post.
The St James's chronicle. No 1, 12 Mar 1761–2 Aug 1866. Incorporated in Press. Prop Henry Baldwin; Charles Baldwin; James Johnstone; Charles Newdigate. Ed John MacDiarmid 1802, S. L. Giffard 1819–?, Thomas Ballantyne.
The English chronicle. No 1, 2 Jan 1779–30 Dec 1843. Ed William Radcliffe.
The inquisitor. [No 1, 18 Oct 1808]–no 129, 15 Aug 1809–?. Ed John Browne Bell.

Bi-weekly (Tuesday and Friday unless otherwise noted)

The London gazette. No 1, 16 Nov 1665 at Oxford; from no 24, 5 Feb 1666 onwards in London. Ed Thomas Walker Oct 1869–Nov 1888.
The national adviser. No 1, 10 Aug 1811–no 138, 2 Dec 1812. Monday and Thursday.
The London evening chronicle. No 1, 2 Aug 1824–no 133, 7 Nov 1825.
The record. No 1, 1 Jan 1828–31 Dec 1948. Incorporated in Church of England newspaper and continued as Church of England newspaper and record, 7 Jan 1949 onwards. Frequency varied until it became a weekly 31 Mar 1882. *See below under* Religious Papers.
The patriot. No 1, 22 Feb 1832–27 Dec 1866. Continued as English independent, 3 Jan 1867–24 Dec 1879. Frequency varied until it finally settled as a weekly, 6 Jan 1859. *See below under* Religious Papers.
The City press. No 1, 18 July 1857 onwards. Wednesday and Saturday. Ed William Hill Collingridge.
The East End news. [1859]–no 509, 17 July 1869–13 Sep 1899. Continued as East End news and London shipping chronicle, 16 Sep 1899–26 Apr 1963.
The south London press. No 1, 7 Jan 1865 onwards.
The south London observer, Camberwell and Peckham times. No 295, 6 June 1874–3 Dec 1948. Continued as South London observer, 10 Dec 1948 onwards. Started weekly in 1868 as Camberwell and Peckham times, no 74, 2 Apr 1870–no 294, 20 May 1874. Wednesday and Saturday.

(2) WEEKLY PAPERS

Besides the various types of papers here listed, one or more weekly papers were pbd in nearly every provincial town of any importance throughout the century. No attempt has been made to list them here, but they may be traced in the Lists of newspapers, col 2881, above, and in The provincial press, col 2924, below.

Sunday Papers

E. Johnson's Sunday monitor and British gazette. [No 1, 26 Mar 1780]–no 66, 24 June 1781–22 Sep 1805. Continued as Johnson's Sunday monitor and British gazette, 29 Sep 1805–20 Feb 1814. Continued as Sunday monitor, 27 Feb 1814–25 Jan 1829.
The London recorder. [No 1], 27 July 1783–no 1152, 9 July 1809. In 1796 it absorbed Sunday reformer and universal register (founded by George Tipley in 1793) and became London recorder and Sunday reformer.
The review and Sunday advertiser. No 1, 22 June 1789–1796–(?). Continued as Sunday review (?)–no 574, 19 Aug 1798–19 Mar 1809.
The observer. No 1, 4 Dec 1791 onwards. Managed by Lewis Doxat 1804–57. Prop William I. Clement 1815–52; ? Beer ?–1880; F. A. Beer 1880–?. Ed Lewis Doxat 1804–57, Joseph Snowe, ? M'Dermott, C. Kinloch Cooke, Edward Dicey 1870–89, H. D. Traill 1889–91, J. H. MacCarthy 1892–3, F. A. Beer 1894–1901.
The selector: or Say's Sunday reporter. [?Nov 1795]–no 161, 9 Dec 1798–no 569, 27 Apr 1806.
Bell's weekly messenger. No 1, 1 May 1796–28 Mar 1896. Continued as Country sport and messenger of agriculture, 4 Apr 1896–31 Dec 1904. Prop John Bell; John Edmund Cox. Ed John Bell 1796–1825, F. L. Holt, Thomas Wade, J. N. Lee, John Edmund Cox.
The weekly dispatch. No 1, 27 Sep 1801–24 June 1928. Continued as Sunday dispatch, 1 July 1928–11 June 1961. Prop Robert Bell 1801–15 and 1816–?; James Harmer 1821 (?)–?; George Stiff 1869–74; A. W. Dilke Jan 1875–83; George Newnes. Ed Robert Bell 1801–15 and 1816–?, George Kent 1815–16, James Harmer, Joseph Wrightson 1838–56, Sydney French 1856–62, T. J. Serle 1862–75, A. W. Dilke 1875–6, H. R. Fox Bourne 1876–87, W. A. Hunter, Charles J. Tibbits 1896–?.
The British Neptune. [? Jan 1803]–1 Dec 1805–12 May 1823. Ed Robert Heron 1805–6.
The Englishman. [No 1, 29 May 1803]–no 32, 8 Jan 1804–20 Apr 1834. Prop William I. Clement 1821–34.
The news. No 1, 19 May 1805–no 1768, 26 Aug 1839. Absorbed Sunday herald, 1829 and Sunday evening globe 1837. Ed John Hunt, John Scott.
The independent Whig. [No 1, 5 Jan 1806]–no 6, 9 Feb 1806–no 793, 25 Mar 1821. Ed Henry White.
The Sunday advertiser. [1807?]–no 555, 4 Jan 1818–5 Aug 1821. Absorbed Weekly register, 12 Aug 1812 and continued as Sunday advertiser and weekly register, 12 Aug 1821–5 Jan 1823. Continued as Weekly register, 12 Jan 1823–no 1073, 30 Dec 1827. Continued as Sunday herald, no 1074, 6 Jan 1828–8 Feb 1829. Incorporated in News. In 1822 it was run in conjunction with Morning post. Ed W. R. Macdonald 1828–9.

The examiner. No 1, 3 Jan 1808–26 Feb 1881. Prop John Hunt and J. H. Leigh Hunt 1808–25; Robert Fellowes 1828–30?; Albany Fonblanque 1830?–65; William McCullagh Torrens 1865–70; H. R. Fox Bourne 1870–73?; P. A. Taylor 1873–8; Lord Rosebery 1878–81. Ed J. H. Leigh Hunt 1808–21, Albany Fonblanque 1830–47, John Forster 1847–55, M. W. Savage 1856–9, Henry Morley 1859–67, Robert Williams, William Minto 1874–8, Charles Williams.

The national register. No 1, 3 Jan 1808–12 May 1823. Prop John Browne Bell and J. de Camp; Eugenius Roche. Ed Eugenius Roche 1808–11.

The London and provincial Sunday gazette. [Aug 1808?]–no 488, 6 Jan 1818–no 589, 11 May 1823.

The anti-Gallican monitor and anti-Corsican chronicle. No 1, 27 Jan 1811–no 362, 4 Jan 1818. Continued as British monitor, 4 Jan 1818–10 Apr 1825. Incorporated in English gentleman. Ed Lewis Goldsmith.

The constitution. [Jan 1812?]–no 314, 4 Jan 1818–5 Jan 1823. Continued as Observer of the times and constitution, 12 Jan–6 Apr 1823. Incorporated in Englishman.

The champion. No 52, 2 Jan 1814–no 491, 2 June 1822. Started as Drakard's paper, no 1, 10 Jan–no 51, 26 Dec 1813. Continued as Investigator, 9 June 1822–(?). Prop J. Clayton Jennings; R. D. Richards 1817; John Thelwall 1818. Ed John Scott.

Bell's Sunday dispatch. No 1, 16 Apr 1815–[?]. Continued as Weekly dispatch, (?)–no 54, 21 Apr 1816–(?). Ed by Robert Bell on his exclusion from Weekly dispatch (1801), but dropped when he resumed control of the original paper.

The weekly intelligence. [Jan 1816?]–no 105, 4 Jan–no 143, 27 Sep 1818. Incorporated in British luminary and continued as Weekly intelligencer and British luminary, 30 July 1820–May 1821. Continued as British luminary and weekly intelligencer (*see below*).

The British luminary. [No 1, 4 Jan 1818]–no 3, 25 Jan 1818–8 June 1823. Absorbed Weekly intelligencer (*see above*). Ed George Glenny.

Wooler's British gazette (Manchester). No 1, 3 Jan 1819–no 259, 14 Dec 1823. Ed T. J. Wooler.

The guardian. No 1, 12 Dec 1819–25 Apr 1824. Prop Edward H. Locker; Edward H. Locker and Charles Knight June 1820–2. Ed Charles Knight June 1820–2.

John Bull. No 1, 17 Dec 1820–no 3739, 16 July 1892. Absorbed Britannia 19 Apr 1856. Prop ? Salomons and Samuel Phillips 1845–6, G. W. Turner, C. G. Prowett, G. H. Smith.

The representative. No 1, 6 Jan 1821–15 Apr 1823. Run in conjunction with the Sun. Prop Patrick Grant.

The observer of the times. No 1, 7 Jan 1821–no 103, 29 Dec 1822. Incorporated in Constitution.

The real John Bull. No 1, 21 Jan 1821–21 Mar 1824.

The Brunswick, or true blue. No 1, 28 Jan–no 18, 28 May 1821.

John Bull's British journal. No 1, 25 Feb–11 Mar 1821.

Aurora Borealis. No 1, 25 Mar–no 45, 30 Dec 1821. Incorporated in Observer of the times.

Life in London. No 1, 13 Jan–no 23, 16 June 1822. Incorporated in Bell's life in London. Ed W. R. Macdonald.

Bell's life in London and sporting chronicle. No 1, 3 Mar 1822–29 May 1886. Incorporated in Sporting life. Prop Robert Bell 1822–4; William I. Clement 1825–52; William Charles Clement; Edward Hulton 1885. Ed Robert Bell, W. R. Macdonald, V. G. Dowling 1824–52, F. L. Dowling 1852–67, R. B. Wormald.

The Sunday times. No 1, 20 Oct 1822 onwards. Started as New observer, nos 1–6, 18 Feb–25 Mar 1821. Continued as Independent observer, no 1, 1 Apr 1821–no 85, 13 Oct 1822. Prop Daniel Whittle Harvey; ? Valpy; Henry Colburn; T. K. Chapman 1842; J. M. Levy 1855–6; E. T. Smith 1956–8; Edward Wilmot Seale 1858–67; Mrs F. A. Beer. Ed Henry White 1821, Daniel Whittle Harvey 1822–?, ? Clarkson, Thomas Gaspey 1828, William Carpenter 1854, J. M. Levy 1855–6, E. T. Smith 1856–8, Henry N. Barnett, Joseph Knight and Ashby Sterry, Joseph Hatton 1874–81, Philip Robinson 1887–90, A. W. à Beckett 1890–4, Mrs F. A. Beer 1894–7, F. G. Smale 1897–1904.

The weekly globe. No 1, 4 Jan 1824–20 Mar 1825. Incorporated in Common sense.

Pierce Egan's life in London and sporting guide. No 1, 1 Feb 1824–28 Oct 1827. Incorporated in Bell's life in London. Ed Pierce Egan.

The colonist and commercial weekly advertiser. Nos 1–8, 24 Feb–21 Mar 1824. Continued as Colonist and weekly courier, no 9, 28 Mar–no 39, 24 Oct 1824. Continued as Sunday herald, no 1, 31 Oct 1824–no 69, 22 May 1825.

Common sense. No 1, 1 Aug 1824–no 80, 5 Feb 1826. Absorbed Weekly globe and continued as Common sense and weekly globe, 28 Mar 1825–5 Feb 1826.

Old England. No 1, 14 Nov 1824–no 52, 6 Nov 1825.

The telescope. No 1, 12 Dec 1824–no 53, 11 Dec 1825.

The English gentleman. No 1, 19 Dec 1824–no 153, 18 Nov 1827. Continued as Nimrod, 25 Nov 1827–13 Jan 1828. Absorbed British monitor 17 Apr 1825.

The age. 15 May 1825–7 Oct 1843. Absorbed Argus and continued as Age and argus 16 Oct 1843–26 Apr 1845. Continued as English gentleman, no 1, 3 May 1845–no 73, 12 Sep 1846. Prop Charles M. Westmacott 1825–c. 1843; Thomas Holt, H. Bronder and G. Bronder 1843; Charles M. Westmacott Oct 1843–Apr 1845 (?). Ed Charles M. Westmacott, A. B. Richards, J. H. Stocqueler.

The atlas. No 1, 21 May 1826–29 Jan 1869. Prop H. J. Slack 1852. Ed R. S. Rintoul 1826–8(?), Robert Bell, G. H. Francis, H. J. Slack 1852, Edmund Ollier 1859–60, J. B. Hopkins.

The weekly times. No 1, 3 June 1826–no 357, 5 May 1833. From 26 Apr–27 Dec 1829 it was called Liberal.

The sphynx. No 1, 8 July 1827–26 Apr 1829. Prop and ed J. S. Buckingham.

Pierce Egan's weekly courier. No 1, 4 Jan–26 Apr 1829. Ed Pierce Egan.

The United Kingdom. No 1, 30 Oct 1830–no 168, 12 Jan 1834–(?). Absorbed Town, 27 July 1834.

The satirist: or censor of the times. No 1, 10 Apr 1831–no 924, 15 Dec 1849. Ed Barnard Gregory.

Bell's new weekly messenger. No 1, 1 Jan 1832–no 1288, 25 Mar 1855. Incorporated in News of the world. Prop and ed John Browne Bell.

The town. No 1, 1 Jan 1832–no 134, 20 July 1834. Incorporated in United Kingdom.

The weekly true sun. No 1, 10 Feb 1833–no 331, 29 Dec 1839. Continued as Statesman, no 332, 5 Jan 1840–no 394, 28 Mar 1841. Continued as British queen and statesman, no 395, 4 Apr 1841–19 Aug 1843. Prop Daniel Whittle Harvey. Ed W. J. Fox, Thomas Ballantyne Jan 1840–Mar 1841.

The new weekly dispatch. No 1, 8 Sep 1833–no 72, 18 Jan 1835. Continued as British and American intelligencer, no 1, 25 Jan–no 11, 5 Apr 1835.

The weekly times. No 16, 27 Dec 1835–no 53, 11 Sep 1836. Continued as London weekly times, nos 1–13, 18 Sep–18 Dec 1836.

The Sunday evening globe. No 1, 11 Sep 1836–no 32, 30 Apr 1837. Incorporated in News.

The champion. No 1, 18 Sep–no 9, 14 Nov 1836. Continued as Champion and weekly herald, no 10, 20 Nov 1836–no 189, 26 Apr 1840. Incorporated in Northern liberator (Newcastle). Ed Henry Hetherington, Richard Cobbett.

The weekly chronicle. No 1, 18 Sep 1836–15 June 1851. Continued as Weekly news and chronicle, 21 June 1851–30 Dec 1854. Continued as Weekly chronicle, 6 Jan–1 Sep 1855. Continued as Weekly chronicle and register 8 Sep 1855–21 Dec 1867. Prop T. L. Holt and ? Marryat; H. G. Ward. Ed H. G. Ward 1836–49.

The London Mercury. No 1, 18 Sep 1836–no 53, 17 Sep 1837. Prop John Bell; J. B. Bernard; John Bell. Ed J. Bronterre O'Brien.

Cleave's London satirist and gazette of variety. No 1, 14 Oct–no 9, 9 Dec 1837. Continued as Cleave's penny gazette of variety, no 10, 16 Dec 1837–no 327, 20 Jan 1844. Unstamped. Ed John Cleave.

The Planet. No 1, 17 Dec 1837–no 310, 4 Feb 1844. Ed John Browne Bell.

The crown. No 1, 1 July 1838–no 42, 14 Apr 1839. Prop Renton Nicholson, Joseph Last and Charles Pitcher. Ed Renton Nicholson.

The operative. No 1, 4 Nov 1838–30 June 1839. Incorporated in London dispatch. Ed J. Bronterre O'Brien.

The charter. No 1, 27 Jan 1839–no 60, 15 Mar 1840. Incorporated in Statesman and weekly true sun. Ed William Carpenter.

The penny Sunday times and people's police gazette. [No 1, 5 Apr 1840]–no 2, 12 Apr 1840–(?). Continued as Lloyd's penny Sunday times etc. (?)–no 171, 9 July 1843–no 529, 27 Apr 1850–(?). Unstamped. Ed Edward Lloyd.

Tom Spring's life in London and sporting chronicle. [June? 1840]–no 17, 4 Oct 1840–18 June 1843–(?). Pbd by W. M. Clarke. Unstamped.

Bell's penny dispatch and penny Sunday chronicle. [Nov 1840?]–no 66, 27 Feb–no 97, 2 Oct 1842. Unstamped.

Lloyd's illustrated London newspaper. Nos 1–7, 27 Nov 1842–8 Jan 1843. Continued as Lloyd's weekly newspaper, no 8, 15 Jan 1843–26 May 1918. Continued as Lloyd's Sunday news, 2 June 1918–30 Sep 1923. Continued as Sunday news, 7 Oct 1923–9 Aug 1931. Incorporated in Sunday graphic. Prop Edward Lloyd. Ed Edward Lloyd, William Carpenter 1844, Douglas Jerrold 1852–7, Blanchard Jerrold 1857–84, Thomas Catling 1884–1907.

The news of the world. No 1, 1 Oct 1843 onwards. Absorbed Bell's new weekly messenger, Apr 1855. Prop John Browne Bell 1843–55; Lascelles Carr c. 1891. Ed John Browne Bell 1843–55, John William Bell 1855–77, Walter John and A. W. Bell 1877–91, Emsley Carr 1891–1941.

New Tom Spring's life in London and sporting times. No 1, 28 Oct 1843–no 59, 7 Dec 1844.

The family times. No 1, 6 June 1846–no 162, 26 June 1849.

The weekly times. No 1, 24 Jan 1847–27 Sep 1885. Continued as Weekly times and echo, no 1, 4 Oct 1885–29 Dec 1912. Prop George Stiff; John Hutton; J. Passmore Edwards. Ed F. G. Tomlins.

Reynolds's weekly newspaper. No 1, 5 May 1850–14 Sep 1924. Continued as Reynold's illustrated news, 21 Sep 1924–23 Feb 1936. Continued as Reynold's news, 1 Mar 1936–13 Aug 1944. Continued as Reynolds's news and Sunday citizen, 20 Aug 1944–16 Sep 1962. Continued as Sunday citizen, 23 Sep 1962–18 June 1967. Prop G. W. M. Reynolds. Ed G. W. M. Reynolds 1859–79, Edward Reynolds 1879–94 (assisted by Arthur Downing 1879–88 and William Thompson 1888–94), William Thompson 1894–?.

Bell's news. No 1, 24 Feb 1855–no 118, 16 May 1857. Incorporated in Weekly star.

The penny newsman and Sunday morning mail and telegraph. No 1, 28 Jan 1860–10 July 1864. Continued as Newsman, etc. no 234, 17 July 1864–12 Feb 1865.

The London halfpenny newspaper. No 1, 11 Aug–no 4, 1 Sep 1861.

The Sunday gazette. No 1, 7 Jan 1866–24 Nov 1867.

The referee. No 1, 19 Aug 1877–9 Sep 1928. Continued as Sunday referee, 16 Sep 1928–4 June 1932. Incorporated in Sunday chronicle. Ed Henry Sampson 1877–91.

The people. No 1, 16 Oct 1881 onwards. Prop W. T. Madge and George C. H. Armstrong. Ed Sebastian Evans, Joseph Hatton 1892–1907.

The umpire (Manchester). No 1, 4 May 1884–25 May 1917. Continued as Empire, 1 Apr–15 July 1917. Continued as Empire news, 22 July 1917–26 Nov 1944. Continued as Sunday Empire news, 3 Dec 1944–1 Oct 1950. Continued as Empire news and the umpire (Empire news incorporating Umpire), 8 Oct 1950–15 Feb 1953. Continued as The Empire news, 22 Feb 1953–6 Nov 1955. Continued as Empire news and Sunday chronicle, 13 Nov 1955–16 Oct 1960. Incorporated in News of the world. In Mar 1894 absorbed Manchester examiner and times, which was for a time a daily paper.

The Sunday chronicle (Manchester). No 1, 23 Aug 1885–4 June 1939. Continued as Sunday chronicle and Sunday referee, 11 June 1939–26 Dec 1943. Continued as Sunday chronicle, 2 Jan 1944–6 Nov 1955. Incorporated in Empire news. A London edition, Sunday chronicle and Sunday referee, ran from 11 June 1939–9 Mar 1952. Prop Edward Hulton and E. O. Bleackley.

The Sunday sun. No 1, 10 May 1891–3 Jan 1909. Style changed to Weekly sun, and back again. Ed T. P. O'Connor.

The Sunday Mercury. No 1, 25 Oct 1891–23 Apr 1893.

The Sunday graphic. No 1, 30 July 1893–31 Mar 1901.

The Sunday mail. No 1, 17 May 1896–29 Dec 1914.

The Sunday special. No 1, 5 Dec 1897–27 Dec 1903. Ed George Wedlake.

General weekly papers

The Westminster journal and old British spy. [1794 ?]–no 3,368, 7 Sep 1805–26 Dec 1812. Continued as Westminster journal and imperial weekly gazette, 2 Jan 1813–1 Jan 1814–(?). Continued as Imperial weekly gazette and Westminster journal, (?)–3 Jan 1818–22 Jan 1825. Started as New weekly miscellany, no 1, 18 July 1741 (*see vol 2*).

The craftsman: or Say's weekly journal. [July? 1758]–no 649, 5 Jan 1771–no 2,498, 16 June 1810. Incorporated in Baldwin's London journal, *below*. Pbd Charles Say, Mary Vint.

Baldwin's London journal or British chronicle. [No 1, 2 Jan 1762]–(?). Continued as London journal, (?)–no 309, 31 Dec 1768. Continued as Baldwin's London weekly journal, no 400, 6 Jan 1769–no 3,968, 31 Dec 1836. Prop Henry Baldwin, Charles Baldwin, Robert Baldwin.

The county chronicle and weekly advertiser. [No 1, 29 May ? 1787]–no 37, 12 Feb 1788–no 4,051, 2 Mar 1841. Continued as County chronicle, Surrey herald and weekly advertiser for Kent etc, no 4,052, 9 Mar 1841–no 9068, 25 Dec 1869. Continued as County chronicle and Mark Lane journal, no 9,070, 1 Jan 1870–30 Dec 1902. Pbd in London and Guildford from Jan 1858 to Dec 1878 and in Lewes from Jan 1879 onwards.

The county herald and weekly advertiser. [1791?]–no 1,186, 16 Apr 1814–4 Oct 1873. Variations in subtitle. Pbd Guildford 1858–73.

The mirror of the times. [Apr? 1796]–no 92, 6 Jan 1798–no 1,391, 23 Feb 1823.

The philanthropic gazette. No 1, 1 Jan 1817–27 Aug 1823. Incorporated in Baldwin's London weekly journal.

The Christian reporter. No 1, 3 Jan 1820–11 Feb 1822. Incorporated in Philanthropic gazette.

The British freeholder and Saturday evening journal. No 1, 5 Feb 1820–no 175, 10 May 1823.

The London weekly gazette. No 1, 13 Mar 1822–no 68, 2 July 1823.

The weekly press. 23 Aug 1823–2 Apr 1831.

The British guardian and Protestant advocate. No 1, 7 Jan 1824–no 116, 22 Mar 1826.

The world. No 1, 4 May 1827–28 Mar 1832.

The olio: or museum of entertainment. Vols 1–11, 12 Jan 1828–20 July 1833.

The spectator. No 1, 5 July 1828 onwards. Prop R. S. Rintoul 1828–58; ? Scott 1858–61; Meredith Townsend and R. H. Hutton 1861–97; J. St Loe Strachey 1897–1925. Ed R. S. Rintoul 1828–58, Thornton Hunt 1858–61, Meredith Townsend and R. H. Hutton 1861–97, J. St Loe Strachey 1897–1925.

The Court journal. No 1, 2 May 1829–13 Mar 1925. Prop Henry

Colburn. Ed P. G. Patmore 14 Oct 1831–32, William Carpenter 1848, Charles Taylor.

The country times. No 1, 4 Jan 1830–no 102, 26 Dec 1831.

Old England. 14 Apr 1831–21 Feb 1842. No issue from 12 Mar 1836–15 June 1839.

Chambers's Edinburgh journal. Vols 1–12, 4 Feb 1832–30 Dec 1843. New series, vols 1–20, 6 Jan 1844–31 Dec 1853. Continued as Chambers's journal of popular literature, science and arts, vols 1–20, 7 Jan 1854–26 Dec 1863. 4th series, vols 1–20, 2 Jan 1864–29 Dec 1883. 5th series, vols 1–14, 5 Jan 1884–27 Nov 1897. Continued as Chambers's journal, 6th series, vols 1–13, 4 Dec 1897–26 Nov 1910. 7th series, vols 1–21, 3 Dec 1910–28 Nov 1931. Continued monthly, 8th series, vols 1–15, Jan 1932–Dec 1946. 9th series, vols 1–10, Jan 1947–Dec 1956. Prop William and Robert Chambers 1832–71 (assisted by Thomas Smibert 1837–41(?), W. H. Wills 1842(?)–44(?), Leitch Ritchie 1845(?)–59, James Payn 1858–73, Robert Chambers Jr 1873–88, C. E. S. Chambers).

The penny magazine. No 1, 31 Mar 1832–27 Dec 1845. Prop Society for the Diffusion of Useful Knowledge. Ed Charles Knight.

The Parliamentary review and family magazine. Vols 1–4, 1833–4. Continued as Parliamentary review, vols 1–2, 8 Feb–30 Aug 1834. Ed J. S. Buckingham.

The London dispatch. No 1, 17 Sep 1836–no 160, 6 Oct 1839.

The London journal. No 1, 17 Sep 1836–no 47, 2 Aug 1837.

The metropolitan Conservative journal. No 1, 8 Oct 1836–no 117, 29 Dec 1838. Continued as Conservative journal and Church of England gazette, no 118, 5 Jan 1839–no 320, 31 Dec 1842.

The penny satirist. No 1, 22 Apr 1837–25 Apr 1846. Continued as London pioneer, 1846–8. Ed Barnard Gregory.

The town. No 1, 3 June 1837–26 Jan 1842. Ed Renton Nicholson 3 June 1837–23 May 1840.

The Court gazette. No 1, 7 Apr 1838–no 438, 4 Apr 1846. Ed J. B. Torr.

The argus. No 1, 3 Feb 1839–30 Sep 1843. Incorporated in Age and argus.

Britannia. No 1, 20 Apr 1839–12 Apr 1856. Incorporated in John Bull. Ed D. T. Coulton 1839–50.

Chambers's London journal of history, literature, poetry, biography and adventure. Vols 1–3, 1841–3. Prop H. & H. Chambers. Ed E. L. Blanchard.

The family herald. No 1, 17 Dec 1842–22 June 1940. Monthly supplement issued from 1877–1940. Ed Mark Lemon.

The sentinel. No 1, 7 Jan 1843–no 179, 7 June 1846. Prop and ed Jonathan Duncan.

Lloyd's monthly [weekly] volume of amusing and instructive literature. Vols 1–22, 1845–6. Continued as Lloyd's weekly volume of amusing and instructive literature, new series, vols 1–7, [1847].

The London journal. No 1, 1 Mar 1845–no 2,029, 29 Dec 1883. New ser no 1, 5 Jan 1884–28 Apr 1906. Continued as New London journal, 3rd ser no 1, 5 May 1906–8 May 1909. Continued as London journal, 15 May 1909–27 Jan 1912. Incorporated in Spare moments. Prop George Stiff 1845–57; Herbert Ingram Oct 1957; George Stiff Nov (?) 1857; ? Johnson. Ed G. M. W. Reynolds 1846, W. H. D. Adams, Mark Lemon 1858–9.

The people's journal. No 1, 3 Jan 1846–June 1849. Amalgamated with Howitt's journal and continued as People's and Howitt's journal, July 1849–June 1851. Prop John Saunders, ? Turrell, William Howitt. Ed John Saunders, William Howitt.

The national. No 1, 14 Mar 1846–no 157, 10 Mar 1849.

Douglas Jerrold's weekly newspaper. No 1, 18 July 1846–no 129, 30 Dec 1848. Continued as Douglas Jerrold's weekly news and financial economist, no 130, 6 Jan 1849–no 181, 29 Dec 1849. Continued as Weekly news and financial economist, no 182, 6 Jan 1850–no 255, 31 May 1851.

Reynold's miscellany. Vols 1–42, 7 Nov 1846–19 June 1869. Ed G. M. W. Reynolds.

Howitt's journal of literature and popular progress. 2 Jan 1847–24 June 1848. Amalgamated with People's journal (*see above*). Ed William and Mary Howitt.

The family friend. Begun monthly, vols 1–6, 1849–52. Continued weekly, new series, vols 1–21, 1852–Nov 1861. Enlarged series, vols 1–8, Jan 1862–Dec 1865. New series, 3 vols 1866–7. New series, with illustrations, vols 1–52, 1870–Sep 1921. New series, nos 1–8, 4 Feb–25 Mar 1929. Incorporated in Girls' mirror. Ed R. K. Philip 1849–52, W. Jones 1852–5.

The leader. No 1, 30 Mar 1850–no 536, 30 June 1860. Continued as Saturday analyst and leader, nos 537–557, 7 July–24 Nov 1860. Prop E. F. S. Pigott et al. Ed Thornton Hunt and G. H. Lewes 1850–Sep (?) 1854, Thornton Hunt, and Thomas Ballantyne.

Leigh Hunt's journal; a miscellany for the cultivation of the memorable, the progressive, and the beautiful. Nos 1–17, 7 Dec 1850–29 Mar 1851. Ed J. H. Leigh Hunt.

Chambers's papers for the people. Edinburgh. Vols 1–12, 1850–2.

The press. No 1, 7 May 1853–15 Nov 1884. Incorporated in English churchman. Prop B. Disraeli 1853–8; R. H. Patterson 1858–?. Ed Samuel Lucas 1853, D. T. Coulton 1854–7, R. H. Patterson 1858–?, G. H. Townsend.

The court circular. No 1, 26 Apr 1856–8 Feb 1911. Prop Edward Walford; W. H. Stephens. Ed H. Prendergast, Edward Walford June 1858–June 1859.

The Saturday review. No 1, 3 Nov 1856–23 July 1938. Prop A. J. B. Beresford Hope and J. D. Cook 1856–68, A. J. B. Beresford Hope 1868–87; P. Beresford Hope; Lewis H. Edmunds; Frank Harris 1894–8; 6th Earl of Hardwicke 1898–1904. Ed J. D. Cook 1856–68, Philip Harwood 1868–83, Walter H. Pollock 1884–94, Frank Harris 1894–8, Harold Hodge 1898–1913.

The welcome guest. No 1, 1 May 1858–Sep 1861. Prop John Maxwell Nov 1859–Sep 1861. Ed G. A. Sala, R. Brough, W. F. Ainsworth.

Town talk. No 1, 8 May 1858–no 56, 14 Nov 1859. Prop John Maxwell. Ed Edmund Yates.

Everybody's journal. No 1, 1 Oct 1859–no 18, 28 Jan 1860. Ed W. H. D. Adams.

The dial. No 1, 7 Jan 1860–2 June 1864. Ed David Thomas.

The London review and weekly journal. No 1, 7 July 1860–27 Mar 1869. Incorporated in Examiner. Ed Charles Mackay 1860, William Black.

Public opinion. No 1, 5 Oct 1861–22 June 1951. Ed Percy White 1880–90, P. Fisher.

Bow bells: a weekly magazine of general literature. Vols 1–2, 12 Nov 1862–27 July 1864. New series, vols 1–47, 3 Aug 1864–28 Dec 1887. Continued as Bow bells weekly: a journal of fiction, society, gossip, fashion, new series, vols 1–36, 6 Jan 1888–12 Feb 1897. Continued as Bow bells, a journal for the home, new series, 15–22 Feb 1897. Incorporated in Duchess novelette. Prop G. M. W. Reynolds and John Dicks. Ed G. M. W. Reynolds, Charles Shurey.

Happy hours. No 1, 16 Mar 1867–no 564, 29 Dec 1877.

Pall Mall budget. No 1, 3 Oct 1868–31 Dec 1920. Prop William Waldorf Astor. Ed C. L. Hind 1893–5.

Vanity Fair. No 1, 7 Nov 1868–June 1929. Ed T. Gibson Bowles.

The Queen's messenger. No 1, 21 Jan–no 25, 8 July 1869. Prop(?) and ed E. C. Grenville Murray.

The latest news. No 1, 28 Aug 1869–no 57, 25 Sep 1870. Ed Henry Sampson.

Figaro. No 1, 17 May 1870–31 Dec 1898. Ed James Mortimer.

The world. No 1, 8 July 1874–25 Mar 1922. Prop Edmund Yates and E. C. Grenville Murray July–Nov 1874; Edmund Yates Nov 1874–May 1894. Ed Edmund Yates July 1874–May 1894.

Light. No 1, 6 Apr–27 Oct 1876. Ed John Morley.

The Whitehall review. No 1, 20 May 1876–25 Oct 1912. Prop and ed Edward Legge.

Mayfair. 2 Jan 1877–14 Feb 1880. Ed H. W. Lucy.

Truth. No 1, 4 Jan 1877–27 Dec 1957. Prop Henry Labouchere 1877–1909. Ed Henry Labouchere assisted by Horace Voules 1877–97 (?), Horace Voules 1897(?)–1902.

The week. No 1, 5 Jan 1878–31 May 1879. Ed L. J. Jennings.

The citizen. No 1, 3 May 1878–24 June 1931. Incorporated in Insurance circular. Ed James Sutherland.

Life. No 1, 12 July 1879–15 Dec 1906. Prop Lord Rosebery. Ed H. P. Stephens, H. Felbermann, Charles Williams.

Society. [No 1, 2 May 1879]–no 45, 12 Mar 1880–31 Aug 1901. Prop and ed George Plant.

England. No 1, 27 Mar 1880–28 May 1898.

Tit-bits. No 1, 22 Oct 1881 onwards. Prop George Newnes. Ed George Newnes, P. Galloway Fraser.

St Stephen's review. No 1, 17 Mar 1883–no 502, 1 Dec 1892. Continued as Big Ben, 8 Dec 1892–30 Mar 1893.

Cassell's Saturday journal. No 1, 6 Oct 1883–19 Feb 1921. Ed E. Foster 1887–1907.

The outlook. No 1, 11 July 1885–Sep 1892. Incorporated in American settler.

The British weekly. No 1, 5 Nov 1886 onwards. From 1 Jan 1959 pbd in Edinburgh. Ed W. Robertson Nicoll.

The tattler. No 1, 7 July 1887–no 114, 26 Oct 1889. Continued as Pelican, 2 Nov 1889–Apr 1920. Ed F. M. Boyd.

Answers to correspondents. No 1, 2 June 1888–no 82, 21 Dec 1889. Continued as Answers, 28 Dec 1889–18 Feb 1956. Prop Alfred Harmsworth. Ed Alfred Harmsworth.

The Scots observer (Edinburgh). No 1, 24 Nov 1888–15 Nov 1890. Continued in London as National observer, 22 Nov 1890–16 Oct 1897. Ed W. E. Henley Oct 1888–Mar 1894.

The speaker. No 1, 4 Jan 1890–23 Feb 1907. Continued as Nation, 2 Mar 1907–21 Feb 1931. Incorporated in New statesman. Prop John Brunner 1890–9. Ed T. Wemyss Reid 1890–9.

Pearson's weekly. No 1, 26 July 1890–10 Sep 1938. Continued as New Pearson's and today, 17 Sep–19 Nov 1938. Continued as New Pearson's weekly, 26 Nov 1938–1 Apr 1939. Amalgamated with Tit-bits. Prop and ed C. A. Pearson.

To-day. No 1, 11 Nov 1893–19 July 1905. Ed Jerome K. Jerome 1893–7, Barry Pain 1897–9.

The new age. No 1, 4 Oct 1894–7 Apr 1938. Ed Frederick A. Atkins 1894–?, A. E. Fletcher.

Illustrated Papers

The mirror of literature, amusement and instruction. No 1, 22 Nov 1822–13 June 1847. Continued monthly to 1849. Ed John Timbs 1827–38, Thomas Byerley, P. B. St John.

The illustrated London news. No 1, 14 May 1842 onwards. Prop Nathaniel Cooke and Herbert Ingram 1842–8; Herbert Ingram 1848–60; William Ingram 1872–1900. Ed F. W. N. Bayley, William James Stewart, Charles Mackay 1848–58(?), John Latey 1858–90, C. K. Shorter 1891–1900. Sub-ed John Timbs 1842–58.

Lloyd's illustrated London newspaper. No 1, 27 Nov 1842–no 7, 8 Jan 1843. Continued as Lloyd's weekly newspaper.

The illustrated weekly times. No 1, 11 Mar–no 6, 15 Apr 1843.

Illustrated London life. [No 1, 12 Mar]–no 5, 9 Apr–13 Aug 1843. Ed Renton Nicholson.

The pictorial times. No 1, 18 Mar 1844–3 Jan 1848. Incorporated in Lady's newspaper. Prop Andrew Spottiswoode 1844–5; Herbert Ingram 1845–8. Ed Henry Vizetelly, F. Knight Hunt.

The lady's newspaper. No 1, 2 Jan 1847–Jan 1848. Continued as Lady's newspaper and pictorial times, 15 Jan 1848–26 Dec 1863. Incorporated in Queen. Prop Herbert Ingram.

The historic times. No 1, 19 Jan–no 13, 13 Apr 1849. Continued as Illustrated historic times, no 14, 20 Apr 1849–no 89, 26 Sep 1850.

The field. No 1, 1 Jan 1853 onwards. Prop Bradbury and Evans Jan–Nov 1853; Benjamin Webster Nov 1853–Nov 1854; Edward William Cox 1854–79. Ed Mark Lemon 1853, Benjamin Webster Nov 1853–Nov 1854, J. H. Walsh 1858–88, Frederick Toms 1888–99, William Senior 1900–10.

Cassell's illustrated family paper. No 1, 31 Dec 1853–9 Mar 1867. Continued as Cassell's magazine, Mar 1867–Nov 1874, *below*. Prop John Cassell 1853–4; Petter and Galpin 1854–8; Cassell, Petter and Galpin. Ed John Cassell 1854–9, George William Petter 1859, William M. Thomas 1867–8, John Lovell, 1868–9, H. R. Haweis 1869–70, George Manville Fenn 1870–4.

Pen and pencil. No 1, 10 Feb–31 Mar 1855. Ed W. J. Linton.

The illustrated times. No 1, 9 June 1855–no 885, 2 Mar 1872. Absorbed by Zig-zag. Prop David Bogue and Henry Vizetelly 1855–?; Herbert Ingram. Ed Henry Vizetelly.

The picture times. No 1, 30 June 1855–12 Apr 1856. Incorporated in Illustrated times.

The coloured news. No 1, 4 Aug–no 9, 29 Sep 1855.

The illustrated news of the world. No 1, 6 Feb 1858–no 300, 31 Oct 1863. Ed J. Moir, John Tallis, J. E. Ritchie 1860–3.

The halfpenny journal. No 1, 1 July 1861–29 Jan 1866.

The welcome guest. No 1, 31 Aug 1861–17 Dec 1864. Incorporated in Halfpenny journal.

The queen. No 1, 7 Sep 1861 onwards. Prop S. O. Beeton 1861; Edward William Cox. Ed P. S. Cox.

The penny illustrated paper. No 1, 12 Oct 1861–24 May 1913. Continued as London life 2 June 1913–July 1960. Title officially abbreviated to P. I. P., 4 Jan 1908–24 May 1913. Run in conjunction with Illustrated London news.

The illustrated weekly news. No 1, 12 Oct 1861–no 423, 30 Oct 1869.

The illustrated sporting news. [No 1, 15 Mar]–no 2, 22 Mar 1862–no 138, 29 Oct 1864. Continued as Illustrated sporting and theatrical news to 19 Mar 1870. Ed Henry Sampson 1869–70.

Land and water. No 1, 27 June 1866–16 Sep 1920. From 3 June 1905–30 Dec 1915 incorporated in County gentleman. Finally incorporated in Field.

The illustrated Midland news (Birmingham). No 1, 4 Sep 1869–no 80, 11 Mar 1871. Prop Joseph Hatton and R. W. Johnson.

The graphic. No 1, 4 Dec 1869–23 Apr 1932. Continued as National graphic, 28 Apr–14 July 1932. Incorporated in Sphere. Prop William L. Thomas. Ed Sutherland Edwards 1869–70, Arthur Locker 1870–91, Heath Joyce.

The illustrated newspaper. [1869]–no 81, 18 Mar–30 Dec 1871.

The illustrated sporting and dramatic news. [No 1], 28 Feb 1874–22 Jan 1943. Continued as Sport and country, 5 Feb 1943–16 Oct 1957. Continued as Farm and country, 30 Oct 1957 onwards.

The pictorial world. No 1, 7 Mar 1874–9 July 1892. Incorporated in Black and white. Ed H. W. Cutts.

The penny pictorial news. No 1, 1 Sep 1877–10 Nov 1888. Continued as Pictorial news, 17 Nov 1888–27 Sep 1891. Continued as Penny pictorial weekly, no 736, 3 Oct 1891–4 June 1892. Ed Charles P. Sisley.

The lady's pictorial. No 1, 5 Mar 1881–26 Feb 1921. Incorporated in Eve. Ed Alfred Gibbons.

The lady. No 1, 19 Feb 1885 onwards. Prop Thomas Gibson Bowles. Ed Miss Stewart.

The daily graphic. No 1, 4 Jan 1890–16 Oct 1926. Incorporated in Daily sketch. Prop William L. Thomas. The first illustrated daily paper.

Black and white. No 1, 6 Feb 1891–13 Jan 1912. Incorporated in Sphere. Ed Oswald Crawfurd.

The sketch. No 1, 1 Feb 1893–17 June 1959. Prop William Ingram. Ed C. K. Shorter, John Latey.

Country life. No 1, 8 Jan 1897 onwards. Prop Edward Hudson.

The illustrated mail. No 1, 17 June 1899–1 June 1907. Continued as Weekly illustrated.

The sphere. No 1, 27 Jan 1900–27 Jan 1964. Ed C. K. Shorter 1900–26.

Unstamped and Radical Journals

This type of periodical, often issued in octavo, has usually been associated with a single personality, and by far the greater bulk are of pronounced radical tendency; for this reason Chartist, Socialist and trade union weekly papers have also been included in this section. Some unstamped Sunday papers of a similar kind but with more space given to news have already been noted above.

Cobbett's political register. No 1, 16 Jan 1802–20 Feb 1836. Prop W. Cobbett. Ed W. Cobbett 1802–35, W. Cobbett Jr 1835–6.

Mr Redhead Yorke's weekly political review. No 1, 7 Dec 1805–6 July 1811. Continued as Weekly political and literary record, 13 July–28 Dec 1811. Ed H. R. Yorke.

The Phoenix. No 1, 14 Feb–no 46, 25 Dec 1808. Ed F. W. Blagdon.

The black dwarf. No 1, 29 Jan 1817–Dec 1824. Ed T. J. Wooler.

Hone's reformists' register and weekly commentary. No 1, 1 Feb–25 Oct 1817. Prop and ed William Hone.

The anti-Cobbett: or weekly patriotic register. No 1, 15 Feb–no 8, 5 Apr 1817.

The republican. No 1, 23 Feb–no 6, 30 Mar 1817. Continued as Sherwin's weekly political register, 5 Apr 1817–21 Aug 1819. Continued as Republican, vol 1, no 1, 28 Aug 1819–29 Dec 1826. Ed W. T. Sherwin, R. Carlile, J. A. St John.

The white dwarf. No 1, 29 Nov 1817–no 13, 21 Feb 1818. Tory. Ed Gibbons Merle 1817–18.

The yellow dwarf. No 1, 3 Jan–no 21, 23 May 1818. Ed John Hunt.

Shadgett's weekly review of Cobbett, Wooler, Sherwin and other democratic and infidel writers. No 1, 1 Feb 1818–no 78, 26 July 1819.

The Gorgon. No 1, 23 May 1818–24 Apr 1819. Ed J. Wade and Francis Place.

The Medusa or penny politician. No 1, 20 Feb 1819–28 Jan 1820. Unstamped.

The true Briton (Boston). No 1, 9 June–no 20, 20 Oct 1819.

Edmond's weekly recorder, and Saturday's advertiser (Birmingham). No 1, 26 June 1819–8 Aug 1819. Continued as Edmond's weekly register, 26 Aug–8 Jan 1820. Prop G. Edmonds.

The theological comet, or free thinking Englishman. No 1, 24 July–21 Aug 1819. Continued as Theological and political comet, 28 Aug–13 Nov 1819.

The cap of liberty. No 1, 8 Sep 1819–5 Jan 1820. Incorporated in Medusa. Ed J. Griffin.

The democratic recorder and reformer's guide. No 1, 2 Oct–no 4, Nov 1819. Ed E. Edmonds.

The white hat. No 1, 16 Oct–11 Dec 1819.

The blue dwarf (Yarmouth). Nos 1–6, 1820.

The economist: a periodical paper explanatory of the New System of Society projected by Robert Owen. No 1, 27 Jan 1821–no 52, 9 Mar 1822. Ed George Mudie.

The lion. No 1, 4 Jan 1828–25 Dec 1829. Ed R. Carlile.

The political letter and pamphlets, published for the avowed purpose of trying with the government the question of law, whether all publications containing news . . . are liable to the imposition of the stamp duty. No 1, 9 Oct 1830–14 May 1831. Ed William Carpenter.

The prompter. No 1, 13 Nov 1830–12 Nov 1831. Unstamped. Ed R. Carlile.

The poor man's guardian. No 1, 9 July 1831–26 Dec 1835. Prop Henry Hetherington. Ed T. Mayhew 1831–2, and J. Bronterre O'Brien 1832–5.

The poor man's advocate (Manchester). No 1, 21 Jan 1832–no 50, 5 Jan 1833. Ed J. Doherty and J. Hobson.

The working man's friend. No 1, 22 Dec 1832–no 33, 3 Aug 1833. Ed J. Cleave.

The Isis: a London weekly publication, edited by a lady. 1832. Ed Richard Carlile and Eliza Sharples Carlile.

The cosmopolite. No 1, 10 Mar 1832–19 May 1833. Unstamped.

The crisis. Vol 1, no 1, 14 Apr 1832–vol 4, no 20, 23 Aug 1834. Ed Robert Owen and J. E. Smith.

The 'destructive' and poor man's conservative. No 1, 2 Feb–7 Dec 1833. Continued as People's conservative and trades' union gazette, 14 Dec 1833–7 June 1834. Ed J. Bronterre O'Brien 1833–4.

The gauntlet; a sound weekly republican newspaper. No 1, 10 Feb 1833–30 Mar 1834. Ed R. Carlile.

Hetherington's twopenny dispatch, and people's police register. No 1, 14 June 1834–10 Sep 1836. Continued as London dispatch, no 1, 17 Sep 1836–no 160, 6 Oct 1839. Incorporated in Champion and weekly herald. Prop Henry Hetherington. Ed Augustus Beaumont, J. Bronterre O'Brien 1836–9.

The shepherd. No 1, 30 Aug 1834–3 Mar 1838. Ed J. E. Smith.

The new moral world. No 1, 1 Nov 1834–10 Jan 1846. Pbd successively at London, Manchester, Birmingham and Leeds. Ed Robert Owen, G. A. Fleming.

The weekly herald. 18 Sep–13 Nov 1836. Incorporated in Champion.

Bronterre's national reformer. No 1, 7 Jan–no 11, 18 Mar 1837. Ed J. Bronterre O'Brien.

The northern liberator (Newcastle-on-Tyne). No 1, 21 Oct 1837–no 137, 23 May 1840. Continued as Northern liberator and champion, 30 May–19 Dec 1840. Ed A. H. Beaumont.

The northern star, and Leeds general advertiser (Leeds). No 1, 18 Nov 1837–13 Mar 1852. Continued as Star and national trades journal, nos 750–5, 20 Mar–1 May 1852. Continued as Star of freedom, nos 1–6, 8 May–27 Nov 1852. Prop Feargus O'Connor; G. J. Harney 1852. Ed William Hill 1842, G. J. Harney 1847–50.

The national: a library for the people. No 1, 5 Jan–no 25, 29 June 1839. Ed W. J. Linton.

The Chartist. No 1, 2 Feb–no 23, 7 July 1839. 'Physical force'; Chartist.

The Chartist circular (Glasgow). No 1, 28 Sep 1839–9 July 1841. Ed W. Thompson.

The English Chartist circular, and Temperance Record for England and Wales. No 1, 23 Jan 1841–no 153, 10 Jan 1844. Ed James Harris.

The London phalanx. No 1, 3 Apr 1841–30 Apr 1842. Continued monthly, June 1842–May 1843. Fourierist. Ed Hugh Doherty.

The oracle of reason. No 1, 6 Nov 1841–no 103, 2 Dec 1843. Ed Charles Southwell, G. J. Holyoake, Thomas Paterson, William Chilton.

The British statesman. No 1, 13 Mar 1842–no 46, 21 Jan 1843. Incorporated in British queen and statesman. Prop and ed J. Bronterre O'Brien June–Dec 1842.

The league, No 1, 30 Sep 1843–4 July 1846. Organ of the Anti-Corn Law League. Ed A. W. Paulton.

The movement, and anti-persecution gazette. No 1, 16 Dec 1843–no 68, 2 Apr 1845. Ed G. J. Holyoake and M. Q. Ryall.

The national reformer, and Manx weekly review of home and foreign affairs. No 1, Nov 1844–no 75, Apr 1846. No 76 (n.s. no 1), 3 Oct 1846–no 110 (n.s. no 35), 29 May 1847. Ptd at Douglas, Isle of Man, where no stamp was needed. Prop and ed J. Bronterre O'Brien.

The herald of progress. No 1, 25 Oct 1845–no 16, 23 May 1846. Continued as Reasoner and herald of progress, no 1, 3 June 1846–no 788, 30 June 1861. Continued monthly as Secular world, no 789, June(?) 1863–no 826, Dec 1864. Continued as Reasoner and secular world, no 827, Jan 1865–no 838, Dec 1865–[no 910, 1872 irregularly]. Between Aug and Dec 1861 there appeared Counsellor on secular, co-operative and political questions. Ed G. J. Holyoake.

Politics for the people. No 1, 6 May–no 17, 29 July 1848. Christian Socialist. Prop J. W. Parker. Ed J. M. Ludlow and F. D. Maurice.

The spirit of the age. No 1, 1 July 1848–3 Mar 1849. Prop W. H. Ashurst. Ed A. Campbell, G. J. Holyoake.

The standard of freedom. No 1, 1 July 1848–no 171, 4 Oct 1851. Incorporated in Weekly news and chronicle. Prop John Cassell.

The spirit of the times. No 1, 10 Mar–29 Sep 1849. Continued as Weekly tribune, 6 Oct 1849–6 July 1850.

Reynolds's political instructor. No 1, 10 Nov 1849–11 May 1850. Ed G. W. M. Reynolds.

Cooper's journal or, Unfettered thinker and plain speaker for truth, freedom, and progress. No 1, 5 Jan–no 30, 26 Oct 1850. Ed Thomas Cooper.

Robert Owen's weekly letter to the human race. [No 1]–no 18, May 1850.

The red republican. No 1, 22 June–no 24, 30 Nov 1850. Continued as Friend of the people. No 1, 14 Dec 1850–no 33, 26 July 1851. n.s. no 1, 7 Feb–no 12, 24 Apr 1852. Ed G. J. Harney.

The Christian Socialist. No 1, 2 Nov 1850–27 Dec 1851. Ed J. M. Ludlow.

Robert Owen's journal. No 1, 2 Nov 1850–23 Oct 1852.

The operative. No 1, 4 Jan 1851–no 80, 10 July 1852.

The people's paper. No 1, 8 May 1852–4 Sep 1858. Ed Ernest Jones.

The friend of the people. No 1, 28 Jan 1860–20 Sep 1861.

The national reformer. No 1, 14 Apr 1860–vol 62, no 14 (n.s.), 1 Oct 1893. Prop Charles Bradlaugh. Ed Charles Bradlaugh, Annie Besant, J. M. Robertson.

The elector. No 1, 23 June 1860–no 142, 2 Aug 1862. Formerly Ballot, no 1, 19 Nov 1859–no 31, 16 June 1860.

The co-operator (Dewsbury and London). No 1, June 1860–Dec 1869. Continued as Co-operator and herald of health, 1 Jan–5 Feb 1870. Continued as Co-operator, anti-vaccinator and herald of health, 12 Feb–16 July 1870. Continued as Co-operator and anti-vaccinator, 23 July 1870–23 Sep 1871. Began as a monthly and continued as a fortnightly before becoming a weekly. Ed Edward Longfield 1869–?, Henry Pitman June 1861 (?)–1871.

The bee-hive. No 1, 19 Oct 1861–no 404, 10 July 1869–no 794, 30 Dec 1876. Continued as Industrial review, 6 Jan 1877–28 Dec 1878. Prop Trades Newspaper Co and George Potter 1861–9; Daniel Pratt 1869–Mar 1873; George Potter July 1873–1878. Ed George Stoup 1861–4, Robert Hartwell 1864–Dec 1868, George Potter Jan 1869–Feb 1870, Henry Solly assisted by George Potter Feb–Dec 1870, George Potter Jan 1871–Dec 1877.

British miner and general newsman. 13 Sep 1862–28 Feb 1863. Continued as Miner, 7 Mar–6 June 1863. Continued as Miner and workmen's advocate, 13 June 1863–Sep 1865. Continued as Workman's advocate, 9 Sep 1865–3 Feb 1866. Continued as Commonwealth, 10 Feb 1866–20 July 1867. Incorporated in Train (13 July 1866–?). The organ successively of British Miners' Benefit Assoc, International Working Men's Assoc and Reform League. Ed John Towers 7 Mar–6 June 1863, William Whitehorn.

The international herald. No 1, 2 Mar 1872–no 81, 18 Oct 1873. Continued as Republican herald, 1873–4. Organ of International Working Men's Assoc. Ed W. Harrison Riley.

The miners' advocate and record (Middlesbrough). No 1, 17 Jan 1873–31 Oct 1874.

The miners' weekly news (Coventry). No 1, 16 Aug 1873–no 23, 17 Jan 1874.

The union chronicle (Manchester, Leamington and Coventry). 1873–5. Continued as National agricultural labourers' chronicle, 1875–7. Continued as English labourers' chronicle, 1877–94.

Daylight (Norwich). No 1, 5 Oct 1878–25 Dec 1909. Pbd Edward Burgess.

The railway review. No 1, 16 July 1880 onwards.

The radical. 4 Dec 1880–8 July 1882. Ed Samuel Bennett, F. W. Souter.

The freethinker. No 1, May 1881 onwards. Ed G. W. Foote.

Justice. No 1, 19 Jan 1884–22 Jan 1925. Ed H. M. Hyndman 1884–6, H. Quelch 1886–1913.

The democrat. No 1, 15 Nov 1884–1 Sep 1890. Continued as Labour world, no 1, 21 Sep 1890–no 37, 22 Mar 1891. Continued as Sunday world, 29 Mar–31 May 1891. Ed Michael Davitt.

Commonweal: the official journal of the Socialist League. No 1, Feb 1885–12 May 1894. Ed William Morris.

Brotherhood. 22 Apr 1887–Apr 1903. Continued as a monthly. Organ of the Land Nationalization Soc. Ed J. Bruce Wallace.

The leaflet newspaper. 4 Feb–23 June 1888. Continued as Socialist, 7 July–1 Sep 1888. Continued monthly Feb–Apr 1889. Ed Thomas Bolas.

The link. No 1, 4 Feb–no 44, 1 Dec 1888. Organ of Law and Liberty League. Ed Annie Besant and W. T. Stead.

The Labour elector. No 10, 15 Dec 1888–July 1894. Started as a monthly, nos 1–5, June–Oct 1888. Continued fortnightly, nos 6–9, 1 Nov–3 Dec 1888. Suspended from Apr 1890–Jan 1893. Ed H. H. Champion.

The north and east London star. No 1, 30 Mar–11 May 1889. Continued as North London press and star, 18 May 1889–25 Jan 1890. Continued as People's press, 8 Mar 1890–Feb 1891. Prop Edward O. Adams Mar 1889–?; organ of several trade unions Mar 1890–Feb 1891. Ed Edward O. Adams.

The workman's times (Huddersfield). No 1, 29 Aug 1890–17 Mar 1894. Pbd in London 1892–3 and Manchester 1893–4. Ed Joseph Burgess.

The trade unionist. No 1, 4 Apr–22 Aug 1891. n.s. incorporating Dockers' record, 29 Aug 1891–19 Mar 1892. Incorporated in Workman's times. Ed Tom Mann.

The labour leader. No 1, 10 Oct 1891–28 Sep 1922. Incorporated in New Leader. Ed Keir Hardie, Bruce Glasier, H. N. Brailsford.

The clarion. No 1, 12 Dec 1891–June 1932. Continued as New clarion, 11 June 1932–10 Mar 1934. Pbd in Manchester 12 Dec 1891–6 May 1893. Prop Robert and Montagu Blatchford, Edward Francis Fay. Ed Robert Blatchford.

Weekly Literary Reviews

The director: a weekly literary journal. No 1, 24 Jan–4 July 1807. Ed T. F. Dibdin.

The literary gazette. No 1, 25 Jan 1817–26 Apr 1862. Incorporated in Parthenon. Ed H. E. Lloyd and Miss Ross, William Jerdan 1817–50, L. A. Reeve 1850–8, J. M. Jephson 1858, C. W. Shirley Brooks Nov 1858–9, H. Christmas, W. R. Workman, F. Arnold, John Morley 1861, C. W. Goodwin.

The literary journal. No 1, 29 Mar 1818–19.

The county literary chronicle and weekly review. [1819]–no 59, 1 July 1820–no 260, 8 May 1823. Continued as Literary chronicle and weekly review, no 261, 15 May 1823–no 471, 24 May 1828. Incorporated in Athenaeum. Ed J. W. Dalby 1826–8.

The indicator. No 1, 13 Oct 1819–no 99, 30 Aug 1821. Ed J. H. Leigh Hunt nos 1–76, 13 Oct 1819–21 Mar 1821.

The literary examiner. Nos 1–27, 1823. Ed J. H. Leigh Hunt.

The Somerset House gazette, and literary museum. No 1, 11 Oct 1823–no 52, 2 Oct 1824. Ed Ephraim Hardcastle.

The Palladium. No 1, 6 Feb 1825–no 98, 17 Dec 1826.

The athenaeum. No 1, 2 Jan 1828–11 Feb 1921. Incorporated in Nation. Prop J. S. Buckingham and Henry Colburn Jan–July 1828; J. Sterling, F. D. Maurice et al July 1828–Jan 1830; James Holmes Jan–June 1830; James Holmes and J. H. Reynolds June 1830–2; C. W. Dilke 1832–64; C. W. Dilke II 1864–9; C. W. Dilke III 1869–?. Ed J. S. Buckingham Jan–July 1828 (assisted by H. Stebbing), F. D. Maurice July 1828–May 1829, John Sterling May 1829–June 1830, C. W. Dilke June 1830–46, T. K. Hervey 1846–53, W. H. Dixon Jan 1853–Aug 1869, John Doran 1869–71, N. MacColl 1871–1900.

The companion. No 1, 9 Jan–no 29, 23 July 1828. Ed J. H. Leigh Hunt.

Leigh Hunt's London journal. No 1, 2 Apr 1834, no 61, 30 May 1835. Merged with Printing machine and continued as Leigh Hunt's London journal and printing machine, no 62, 6 June–no 91, 26 Dec 1835. Ed J. H. Leigh Hunt.

Notes and queries. No 1, 3 Nov 1849 onwards. Ed W. J. Thoms

1849–Sep 1872, John Doran 1872–8 (assisted by H. F. Turle 1873–8), H. F. Turle 1878–83, Joseph Knight 1883–1907.

Household words. No 1, 30 Mar 1850–28 May 1859. Prop C. Dickens and Bradbury and Evans. Ed C. Dickens.

All the year round. No 1, 30 Apr 1859–30 Mar 1895. Prop C. Dickens. Ed C. Dickens, C. Dickens Jr.

Once a week. No 1, 2 July 1859–May 1879. Prop Bradbury and Evans; James Rice ?–1873; George Manville Fenn 1873–?. Ed S. Lucas 1859–65, Edward Walford 1865–?, E. S. Dallas Jan 1868–July 1869, Mark Lemon, George Manville Fenn 1873–?.

The Parthenon. No 1, 3 May 1862–no 57, 30 May 1863. Ed C. W. Goodwin.

The reader. No 1, 3 Jan 1863–28 July 1866. Ed J. M. Ludlow, David Masson 1863–?, J. Dennis, T. Bendyshe.

The academy. No 1, 9 Oct 1869–11 Sep 1915. Began monthly and became weekly in 1874. Prop John Murray nos 1–12, 9 Oct 1869–10 Sep 1870; Charles Appleton et al Sep 1870–1873; Academy Co Ltd. 1873–8; Henry Villiers 1880–96; John Morgan Richards 1896–?. Ed Charles Appleton 1869–78, C. E. Dobell, 1878–81, James Sutherland Cotton Jan 1881–Nov 1896, Charles Lewis Hind 1896–Oct 1903.

Sala's journal. No 1, 30 Apr 1892–11 Apr 1894. Ed G. A. Sala.

Literature. No 1, 23 Oct 1897–11 Jan 1902. Ed H. D. Traill 1897–1900.

Religious Papers

The record. No 1, 1 Jan 1828–31 Dec 1948. Incorporated in Church of England newspaper and continued as Church of England newspaper and the record, 7 Jan 1949 onwards. Frequency varied until it became a weekly 31 Mar 1882. Prop James Evans and Andrew Hamilton. Ed Henry Blunt, Edward Garbett 1854–67.

The Catholic vindicator. 5 Dec 1818–4 Dec 1819. Ed W. E. Andrews.

The Catholic advocate. No 1, 3 Dec 1820–no 34, 22 July 1821.

The world. No 1, 4 May 1827–28 Mar 1832. Incorporated in Patriot. Prop and ed Stephen Bourne.

The Catholic journal. No 1, 1 Mar 1828–no 55, 15 Mar 1829.

The Christian advocate. No 1, 7 Jan 1830–no 505, 2 Sep 1839.

The patriot. No 1, 22 Feb 1832–27 Dec 1866. Continued as English independent, 3 Jan 1867–24 Dec 1879. Incorporated in Nonconformist. Frequency varied until it finally settled as a weekly, 6 Jan 1859. Ed Stephen Bourne 1832, Josiah Conder 1833–55.

The watchman. No 1, 7 Jan 1835–31 Dec 1889. Wesleyan. Ed J. C. Rigg 1848–64.

The witness (Edinburgh). No 1, 15 Jan 1840–27 Feb 1864. Twice weekly. Ed Hugh Miller 1840–56.

The tablet. No 1, 16 May 1840–23 July 1842. *See below under* True tablet. Ed F. Lucas 1840–2, M. J. Quin 1842.

The Nonconformist. 14 Apr 1841–24 Dec 1879. Continued as Nonconformist and independent, 1 Jan 1880–18 Sep 1890. Continued as Independent and nonconformist, 26 Sep 1890–30 Dec 1897. Continued as Independent, 6 Jan 1898–29 Mar 1900. Incorporated in Examiner. Ed Edward Miall 1841 (?)–81.

The Jewish chronicle. [No 1, 12 Nov 1841]–new ser 6–20 May 1842. Suspended until 18 Oct 1844 when it resumed as Jewish chronicle and working man's friend – 22 Dec 1954. Continued as Jewish chronicle and Hebrew observer – 2 Aug 1869. Continued as Jewish chronicle Aug 1869 onwards. Fortnightly Oct 1844–Oct 1847. From 3 July 1865–2 Aug 1869 a penny abridged edn was issued concurrently. Prop Isaac Valentine 1841–20 May 1842; Joseph Mitchell and Isaac Valentine 18 Oct 1844–Aug 1854; Marcus Bresslau Aug 1854–Jan 1855; Abraham Benisch Jan 1855–Aug 1869; Lionel Cohen, Samuel Montagu and Lionel Van Oven Aug 1869–June 1875; Abraham Benisch June 1875–July 1878; Anglo-Jewish association; Israel Davis, Sydney Montagu Samuel, Asher Myers. Ed Moses Angel and David Meldola 1841–May 1842, Marcus Bresslau Oct 1848–Jan 1855, Abraham Benisch Jan 1855–Aug 1869, Michael Henry Aug 1869–June 1875, Abraham Benisch June 1875–July 1878, Asher Myers 1878–1902.

The true tablet. 20 Feb–31 Dec 1842. Continued as Tablet, 7 Jan 1843 onwards. From 19 Mar–31 Dec 1842 True tablet has two sets of enumeration, one derived from Tablet (1840–42). From 5 Jan 1850–11 Sep 1858 Tablet was pbd in Dublin. Prop F. Lucas 1842–Oct 1855; John Wallis; Cardinal Herbert Vaughan Nov 1868–?. Ed. F. Lucas 1842–55, John Wallis 1855–68, Herbert Vaughan Nov 1868–93 (?), J. G. Snead-Cox 1893 (?)–1920.

The English churchman. No 1, 5 Jan 1843 onwards. Ed D. W. Godfrey 1843–63.

The guardian. No 1, 12 Jan 1846–30 Nov 1951. Anglican. Ed Thomas Henry Haddan, M. R. Sharp 1859–83, J. Sharp 1883–95, W. H. Lathbury 1896–9.

The Christian times. No 1, 12 Aug 1848–no 528, 11 Aug 1858. Continued as Beacon and Christian times, no 1, 18 Aug 1858–no 54, 24 Aug 1859. Ed William Leask.

The Wesleyan times. No 1, 8 Jan 1849–29 July 1867. Continued as Methodist times, 5 Aug 1867–31 Dec 1869.

The Catholic standard. No 1, 13 Oct 1849–12 May 1855. Continued as Weekly register, 19 May 1855–14 Mar 1902. Prop H. W. Wilberforce 1854–63; ? De Lacy Towle 1880; Cardinal Manning 1880–1; Wilfrid Meynell 1881–?. Ed H. W. Wilberforce 1854–63, Orby Shipley 1880–1, Wilfrid Meynell 1881–?.

The freeman. No 1, 24 Jan 1855–no 2297, 17 Feb 1899. Continued as Baptist times and freeman, 24 Feb 1899 onwards.

The Christian world. No 1, 9 Apr 1857–28 Sep 1961. Low Church. Ed J. Whittemore 1857–60, James Clarke 1860–88, James G. Clarke.

The revival. No 1, 30 July 1859–27 Jan 1870. Incorporated in Christian, no 1, 3 Feb 1870 onwards. Low Church.

The universe. 8 Dec 1860–17 Sep 1909. Continued as Universe and Catholic weekly, 24 Sep 1909–14 June 1912. Continued as Universe, 14 June 1912–1 June 1962. Continued as Universe and Catholic times, 8 June 1962 onwards.

The Methodist recorder. No 1, 4 Apr 1861 onwards.

The Church times. No 1, 7 Feb 1863 onwards. High Church. Ed G. J. Palmer 1863–92, T. A. Lacey.

Sunday magazine. Vols 1–7, Oct 1864–Sep 1871. New ser, vols 1–35, Nov 1871–Apr 1906. Incorporated in Good words. Prop Alexander Strahan. Ed T. Guthrie 1864–73, W. G. Blaikie 1873–80, B. Waugh 1881–94.

The methodist. No 1, 1 Jan 1874–no 580, 27 Dec 1884.

The secular review. No 1, 6 Aug 1876–28 Jan 1877. Ed G. J. Holyoake.

The secular review. 9 June 1877–29 Dec 1888. Continued as Agnostic journal, 5 Jan 1889–15 June 1907. Ed G. W. Foote.

The war cry and official gazette of the Salvation Army. No 1, 27 Dec 1880 onwards.

The Christian commonwealth. No 1, 20 Oct 1881–24 Sep 1919.

Agricultural Papers

The farmer's journal. 15 Aug 1807–15 Apr 1809. Continued as Evans and Ruffy's farmer's journal, 22 Apr 1809–16 July 1832. Incorporated in Bell's weekly messenger.

Fleming's weekly express. No 1, 4 May 1823–no 167, 9 July 1826. Continued as Fleming's British farmer's chronicle, 10 July 1826–26 Jan 1829.

Exley, Dimsdale and Hopkinson's Corn Exchange circular. No 1, 1 Jan 1824–no 306, 28 Dec 1829.

The corn trade circular. No 1, 24 Oct 1825–no 402, 24 June 1833.

The Mark Lane express. No 1, 2 Jan 1832–31 Mar 1924. Continued as Farmer's express, 7 Apr 1924–29 July 1929. Incorporated in Farm, field and fireside. Prop Walter Darkin. Ed Peter Lund Simmonds 1841, Joseph Robertson, William Shaw.

The universal corn reporter. No 1, 6 Feb 1832–14 Jan 1870.

The new farmer's journal. No 1, 11 Feb 1833–no 58, 21 May 1834. Incorporated in Mark Lane express.

The magnet. No 1, 13 Mar 1837–no 2616, 27 Aug 1888. Ed John Browne Bell.
The farmer's journal. No 1, 9 Dec 1839–no 362, 28 Dec 1848.
The Scottish farmer and horticulturalist. No 1, 3 Apr 1861–11 Oct 1865. Continued as Farmer, 18 Oct 1865–26 Dec 1881. Continued as Farmer and the chamber of agriculture journal, 2 Jan 1882–5 Oct 1889. Continued as Farmer and stockbreeder and chamber of agriculture journal, 9 Oct 1889–13 July 1925. Continued as Farmer and stock-breeder and agricultural gazette, 20 July 1925 onwards.
The agricultural gazette. No 1, Jan 1874–17 July 1925. Incorporated in Farmer and stock-breeder. Ed J. C. Morton 1874–88.

Financial and Commercial Papers
The bankers' circular. No 1, 25 July–no 7, 5 Sep 1828. Continued as Circular to bankers, no 8, 12 Sep 1828–no 1417, 31 Dec 1853. Continued as Bankers' circular, 7 Jan 1854–9 Jan 1858. Continued as Monetary times and bankers' circular, 16 Jan 1858–31 Dec 1859. Continued as Bankers' circular and monetary times, 7 Jan–24 Mar 1860.
The London mercantile journal. No 1, 13 July 1830–22 Mar 1870.
Nicholson's weekly register. No 1, 1 Jan 1842–no 130, 22 June 1844. Continued as London commercial record, no 1, 29 June 1844–28 June 1940. Incorporated in London corn circular.
The economist. No 1, 2 Sep 1843 onwards. Prop James Wilson 1843–60; then his family to 1928. Ed James Wilson 1843–59 (assisted by Herbert Spencer 1843–53), Walter Bagehot 1859–77, R. H. Inglis-Palgrave and Daniel C. Lathbury 1877–83, Edward Johnson 1883–1907.
The money market review. No 1, 9 June 1860–25 June 1921. Continued as Investors' chronicle and money market review, 2 July 1921 onwards.
The insurance record. No 1, 30 Jan 1863 onwards.
The investor's guardian. No 1, 22 Aug 1863 onwards.
The bullionist. No 1, 6 Jan 1866–5 Dec 1899. Continued as Daily bullionist, 7 Dec 1899–2 June 1900. Incorporated in Financier. Ed David Morier Evans, John Scott Henderson, Arthur Henry Evans 1883–?.
The commercial world. [1874]–no 179, 1 Jan 1878–1 Mar 1939.
The statist. No 1, 12 Mar 1878–28 Apr 1967. Prop Robert Giffen 1878–1910; Thomas Lloyd 1878–1920. Ed Arthur Ellis 1878–80, Robert Giffen, George Paish.
The shipping world. No 1, May 1883 onwards.
The financial chronicle. [No 1, 19 June 1883]–no 1, new ser 19 June 1886–20 May 1931.
The capitalist. No 1, 16 Nov 1885–25 Dec 1926. Continued as Investor, 1 Jan 1927–Mar 1943.
The financial world. [1886]–27 Apr 1887 onwards.

Sporting Papers
Kent's weekly dispatch and sporting mercury. [1816]–no 98, 5 Apr 1818–no 192, 23 Jan 1820.
The racing times. [Feb 1851]–no 8, 16 Apr 1851–10 Aug 1868.
The sporting gazette. No 1, 1 Nov 1862–no 920, 27 Dec 1879. Continued as County gentleman, no 921, 3 Jan 1880–30 Dec 1915. Incorporated in Land and water.
The sporting times. No 1, 11 Feb 1865–5 Dec 1931. Prop John Corlett 1874–1912. Ed J. H. Shorthouse, John Corlett.
The sporting clipper. [1872]–19 Apr 1874–30 June 1894.
The athletic news (Manchester). [June 1875]–no 92, 3 Mar 1877–23 Apr 1917. Incorporated in Sporting chronicle. Prop Edward Hulton and E. O. Bleackley. Ed T. R. Sutton 1875–95.
The fishing gazette. No 1, 26 Apr 1877 onwards.
The bicycling times. No 1, 24 May 1877–25 Dec 1883. Continued as Cycling times, 1 Jan 1884–25 Mar 1887.
The cyclist. [1879]–no 12, 7 Jan 1880–11 Nov 1903. Continued as Cyclist trade review, 1 Nov 1903–4 May 1905. Continued as Cycle and motor trades review, 11 May 1905–19 Jan 1911. Amalgamated with Cycle trader and review. Prop William Iliffe. Ed Edmund Dangerfield, Henry Sturmey.
The sportsman's weekly guide to the turf. No 1, 21 Feb 1880–15 Nov 1884.
Horse and hound. No 1, 29 Mar 1884 onwards.
The racing world. No 1, 26 Feb 1887–26 July 1929.
The jockey. No 1, 18 Apr 1890–29 Dec 1956. Not pbd 8 Aug 1914–22 Mar 1919. Registration copies only from 26 Dec 1936.
Cycling. No 1, 27 Jan 1891 onwards. Ed Charles Sisley.

Humorous Papers
The quizzical gazette and merry companion. No 1, 27 Aug 1831–no 21, 14 Jan 1832. Ed John Mitford.
Figaro in London. No 1, 10 Dec 1831–9. Prop Thomas Lyttleton Holt. Ed G. A. à Beckett 1831–27 Dec 1834.
Punch: or the London Charivari. No 1, 17 July 1841 onwards. Prop Ebenezer Landells and Joseph Last 1841; Ebenezer Landells 1842; Bradbury and Evans. Ed Mark Lemon 1841–70, C. W. Shirley Brooks 1870–4, Tom Taylor 1874–80, F. C. Burnand 1880–1906.
Fun. No 1, 21 Sep 1861–Aug 1901. Incorporated in Sketchy bits. Prop Dalziel brothers. Ed Thomas Hood the younger 1861–74, Henry Sampson 1874–8, Charles Dalziel.
The comic news. No 1, 13 July 1863–14 Mar 1865. Ed J. H. Byron, Charles Collins.
Judy: or the London serio-comic journal. 1 May 1867–23 Oct 1907. Prop Charles Ross Apr 1869–?; Dalziel brothers. Ed Charles Ross.
The tomahawk. No 1, 11 May 1867–no 164, 25 June 1870. Ed A. à Beckett, M. S. Morgan.
Moonshine. July 1879–Aug 1902. Ed Arthur Clements.
Ally Sloper's half holiday. 3 May 1884–9 Sep 1916. Incorporated in London society. Prop Dalziel brothers. Ed Charles Ross.
Sketchy bits. No 1, 25 Apr 1893–9 May 1910.

Juvenile Papers
Boys of England. No 1, 24 Nov 1866–23 June 1899. Continued under various titles, Up-to-date boys, Boys of the Empire, Boys of our Empire, Boys of England, until 22 Dec 1906. Ed Charles Stevens, Edwin J. Brett.
The young Englishman's journal. No 1, 13 Apr 1867–73. Ed W. L. Emmett.
Young men of Great Britain. No 1, 29 Jan 1868–17 June 1889. Ed Edwin J. Brett, Vane St John.
The young Briton. No 1, 18 Sep 1869–77. Ed W. L. Emmett.
The gentleman's journal. No 1, 1 Nov 1869–Oct 1872. Ed George Frederick Pardon.
Our young folks' weekly budget. No 1, 2 Jan 1871–no 447, 28 June 1879. Continued as Young folks, no 448, 5 July 1879–no 733, 20 Dec 1884. Continued as Young folks' paper, 27 Dec 1884–28 June 1891. Continued as Old and young, 4 July 1891–11 Sep 1896. Continued as Folks at home, no 1, 18 Sep 1896–29 Apr 1897. Ed James Henderson.
The boys' standard. No 1, 6 Nov 1875–18 June 1892. Ed Charles Fox.
The boys' own paper. No 1, 18 Jan 1879–Feb 1967. Prop Religious Tract Soc. Ed G. A. Hutchinson, J. Macaulay.
The boys' world. No 1, 14 Apr 1879–31 Jan 1883. Ed Ralph Rollington.
The Union Jack. No 1, 1 Jan 1880–25 Sep 1883. Prop Alfred Harmsworth. Ed W. H. Kingston, G. A. Henty.
The girl's own paper. No 1, 3 Jan 1880–26 Sep 1908.
The boys' newspaper. No 1, 15 Sep 1880–14 Aug 1882. Continued as Youth, 21 Aug 1882–25 Apr 1888. Prop Cassell Sep 1880–Apr 1881; William Ingram. Ed George Weatherly, Alfred Harmsworth.
The boys' illustrated news. No 1, 6 Apr 1881–no 61, 31 May 1882. Ed Mayne Reid.
The boys' comic journal. No 1, 17 Mar 1883–16 Apr 1898. Ed Edwin J. Brett.
Ching-Ching's own. No 1, 23 June 1888–17 June 1893. Ed E. Harcourt Burrage.

Comic cuts. No 1, 17 May 1890–12 Sep 1953. Incorporated in Knock-out. Prop Alfred Harmsworth. Ed Alfred Harmsworth.

Comic pictorial nuggets. No 1, 7 May–no 29, 19 Nov 1892. Continued as Nuggets, no 30, 26 Nov 1892–10 Mar 1905.

The world's comic. No 1, 6 July 1892–10 Nov 1908.

Chums. No 1, 12 Sep 1892–July 1932. Continued monthly to July 1934 and as an annual 1935–41. Prop Cassell. Ed Max Pemberton 1892–4, Ernest Foster 1894–1907.

Miscellaneous Specialized Papers

The military register. No 1, 30 Mar 1814–11 Apr 1821.

The united services gazette. No 1, 9 Feb 1833–29 Dec 1921. Ed A. A. Watts 1833–43.

The naval and military gazette. No 1, 9 Feb 1833–no 2774, 17 Feb 1886. Incorporated in Broad arrow.

The Civil Service gazette. No 1, 1 Jan 1853–Nov 1926. Ed John Bolger.

The army and navy gazette. No 1, 7 Jan 1860–26 Nov 1921. Continued as Army, navy and air force gazette, 3 Dec 1921–12 Nov 1936. Continued as United services review, 19 Nov 1936–Apr 1947. Continued as United services and Empire review, May 1947–Aug-Sep 1957. Not pbd between 28 Sep 1939 and Feb 1942. Ed W. H. Russell.

The broad arrow. No 1, 1 July 1868–18 Apr 1917.

The Admiralty and Horse Guards' gazette. No 1, 1 Nov 1884–19 Jan 1901.

The era. No 1, 30 Sep 1838–21 Sep 1939. Prop Licensed Victuallers' Association; Frederic Ledger 1850–74; E. Ledger. Ed William Carpenter 1838, William Henry Harrison 1845, Frederic Ledger 1850–74.

The London entr'acte. [1869]–no 27, 8 Jan 1870–no 137, 17 Feb 1872. Continued as Entr'acte, no 138, 24 Feb 1872–26 Apr 1907.

The stage. No 1, 25 Mar 1881 onwards. Begun monthly as Stage director, no 1, Feb 1880–no 14, 1 Mar 1881.

The auction register and law chronicle. No 1, 7 Jan 1813–no 146, 23 Feb 1815. Continued as Law chronicle and estate advertiser, no 147, 2 Mar 1815–no 2747, 30 Dec 1847.

The law gazette. No 1, 15 Aug 1822–no 1146, 23 Dec 1847.

The jurist. No 1, 14 Jan 1837–no 939, 6 Jan 1855. New ser no 1, 13 Jan 1855–67. Ed John Jervis.

The law times. No 1, 8 Apr 1843–25 Oct 1965. Amalgamated with Law journal and continued as New law journal. Prop Edward William Cox. Ed Basil Crump.

The solicitor's journal. 3 Jan 1857 onwards.

The law journal. No 1, 19 Jan 1866–25 Oct 1965. Amalgamated with Law times and continued as New law journal. Ed W. D. I. Foulkes 1879–90.

The lancet. No 1, 5 Oct 1823 onwards. Ed Thomas Wakley 1823–62, James Wakley 1862–86, Thomas H. Wakley 1886–1905.

The medical times. 28 Sep 1839–26 Dec 1885. Prop Frederick Knight Hunt. Ed F. Knight Hunt 1839–?, T. P. Healey, J. S. Bushman.

The provincial medical and surgical journal. 3 Oct 1840–22 Dec 1852. Continued as Association medical journal, 7 Jan 1853–27 Dec 1856. Continued as British medical journal, 3 Jan 1857 onwards. Ed J. R. Cormack, A. Wynter 1855–60, W. O. Markham 1860–6, E. A. Hart 1866–94, E. A. Hart and Dawson Williams 1894–97, Dawson Williams and C. L. Taylor 1897–1916.

Nature: a weekly illustrated journal of science. No 1, Nov 1869 onwards. Prop Macmillan. Ed J. N. Lockyer.

The gardener's gazette. 7 Jan 1837–26 June 1847. Ed George Glenny.

The gardener's chronicle. No 1, 2 Jan 1841 onwards. Prop Bradbury and Evans. Ed John Lindley 1841–65, Maxwell T. Masters.

Amateur gardening. No 1, 3 May 1884 onwards.

The railway times. No 1, 29 Oct 1837–28 Mar 1914.

Bradshaw's railway gazette. No 1, 12 July 1845–no 103, 28 Nov 1846. Continued as Railway gazette, 5 Dec 1846–20 Jan 1872.

The railway news. No 1, 2 Jan 1864–30 Nov 1918. Incorporated in Railway gazette.

The mining journal. No 1, 29 Aug 1835 onwards. Ed T. W. Robertson.

The mechanics' magazine. 30 Aug 1823–28 Dec 1872. Continued as Iron, no 1, 18 Jan 1873–9 June 1893. Incorporated in Industries and iron. Ed J. C. Robertson 1823–June 1852, R. A. Brooman July 1852–July 1857, E. J. Reed July 1857–1872.

The engineer. No 1, 4 Jan 1856 onwards. Ed Zerah Colburn 1859–66.

The colliery guardian. No 1, 2 Jan 1858 onwards. Ed H. K. Atkinson.

Engineering. No 1, 5 Jan 1866 onwards. Ed Zerah Colburn.

Griffith's iron trade exchange. 28 Mar 1873–June 1874. Continued as London iron trade exchange, 27 June 1874–24 Sep 1877. Continued as Iron and steel trades journal and mining engineer, no 1477, 1 Oct 1877–31 Dec 1920. Incorporated in Foundry trade journal.

The builder. No 1, 31 Dec 1842 onwards. Prop J. A. Hanson. Ed George Godwin 1842–83.

The builder's weekly reporter. No 2, 17 Mar 1856–23 July 1886. Continued as Builder's reporter and engineering times, 30 July 1886–31 Oct 1906. Incorporated in Building trade.

The freehold land times and building news. No 3, 1 Apr–no 20, 15 Dec 1854. Continued as Land and building news, 1 Jan 1855–27 Dec 1856. Continued as Building news, 2 Jan 1857–12 Mar 1926. Incorporated in Architect. Prop George Maddox; J. Passmore Edwards 1862–?.

The architect. No 1, 2 Jan 1869 onwards. Ed ? Hobart.

The educational times. 2 Oct 1847–Dec 1923. Continued as Educational outlook, Jan 1924–1937. Continued as Educational times, Sep 1946–Nov 1951. Continued as Education today, Jan 1952 onwards. Prop College of Preceptors.

The photographic news. No 1, 10 Sep 1858–8 May 1908. Incorporated in Amateur photographer. Prop Cassell; G. Wharton Simpson 1868–?. Ed William Crooks 1858–Jan 1860, G. Wharton Simpson Jan 1862–Jan 1880.

The grocer. No 1, 4 Jan 1862 onwards. Prop W. Reed and L. M. Reed. Ed G. L. M. Strauss.

The accountant. No 1, Oct 1874 onwards. Weekly from 2 Jan 1875.

The draper's record. No 1, 6 Aug 1887 onwards.

Weldon's ladies' journal of dress, fashion, etc. July 1879–Mar 1954. Continued as Weldon's home journal, Apr 1954–Sep 1955. Continued as Home, Oct 1955–Oct 1963. Incorporated in Homes and gardens.

Home chat. No 1, 23 Mar 1895–25 Apr 1959. Incorporated in Woman's weekly. Prop Alfred Harmsworth. Ed Maud Bown.

Woman. No 1, 3 Jan 1890–7 Aug 1912. Ed Arnold Bennett 1896–1900.

(3) ACCOUNTS AND STUDIES OF INDIVIDUAL PAPERS

Brief summaries of many centenary numbers by J. C. Francis are to be found in N & Q 1898–1914. *Useful notices, apart from those cited, may be found in* Newspaper world. *See also bibliographies by* Madden and Dixon, 1976, *and* Uffelman, 1992, *listed under Bibliographies and Reference Works above, and the annual bibliography in the* Victorian Periodicals Review.

London Morning Papers

Morning Chronicle [1769]

When Dickens quarrelled with the Morning Chronicle. World's Press News 23 June 1938.

Carlton, W. J. Charles Dickens, dramatic critic. Dickensian 56 1960.
Morning Post 1772
Francis, J. C. The Morning Post 1772–1916. N & Q 14–28 Oct, 25 Nov 1916.
Ferguson, M. T. The Morning Post 1772–1921. 1922.
Hindle, W. H. The Morning Post 1772–1937. 1937.
'Journalist'. The Morning Post. Nat Rev Sep 1937.
Colgate, W. Death at 164: the portrait of a newspaper. Queens Quart 45 1938.
Glickfield, C. W. Coleridge's prose contributions to the Morning Post. PMLA 69 1954.
The Times 1788
Stephen, L. The Times on the American war: a historical study. 1865, New York 1915.
Marchant, J. History through The Times: a collection of leading articles on important events 1800–1937. 1937.
The history of The Times. Vol 1, 'The Thunderer' in the making 1785–1841, 1935; vol 2, The tradition established 1841–84, 1939; vol 3, The twentieth century test 1884–1912, 1947; vol 4, The 150th anniversary and beyond, 2 pts 1952.
Morning Advertiser 1794
Centenary number. 8 Feb 1894.
Daily News 1846
McCarthy, J. and J. R. Robinson. The Daily News jubilee. 1896.
Cruickshank, R. J. The roaring century 1846–1946. 1946.
World's Press News 17 Jan 1946; Newspaper World 19 Jan 1946. Centenary articles.
Grubb, G. G. Dickens and the Daily News. In Booker Memorial studies. Chapel Hill 1950; pts 2–4 in Nineteenth-Century Fiction 6–7 1951–2.
Daily Telegraph 1855
Rhode, D. The social relationships of the Daily Telegraph. New Century Rev Apr 1898.
Jubilee number. 17 Sep 1905.
Burnham, Lord. Peterborough Court: the story of the Daily Telegraph. 1955.
Coulling, S. M. Matthew Arnold and the Daily Telegraph. RES new ser 12 1961.
Standard 1857
Notes on the history of the Standard. People Jan 1906.
Financial News 1884
Twentieth anniversary number 23 Jan 1904.
Daily Mail 1896
Harmsworth, A. C. (Viscount Northcliffe). The romance of the Daily Mail. 1903.
McKenzie, F. A. The mystery of the Daily Mail 1896–1921. 1921.
News in our time 1896–1946: Golden Jubilee book of the Daily Mail. 1946.

London Evening Papers

Sun 1792
Grant, P. Statement of facts regarding the Sun newspaper. [1832.]
Globe [1803]
Atlay, J. B. The Globe centenary: a sketch of its history. 1903.
True Sun 1832
Vivian, C. H. Dickens, the True Sun and Samuel Laman Blanchard. Nineteenth-Century Fiction 4 1950.
Pall Mall Gazette 1865
Stead, W. T. The Pall Mall Gazette. Rev of Reviews Feb 1893.
10,000th number. 14 Apr 1897.
Last number. 27 Oct 1923.
Booth, B. A. Trollope and the Pall Mall Gazette. Nineteenth-Century Fiction 4 1949.
Collins, J. P. The boy who saved a famous paper. Chambers's Jnl Sep 1951.
Scott, J. W. Robertson. The story of the Pall Mall Gazette. 1950.
Scott, J. W. Robertson. The life and death of a newspaper. 1952.
Scott, J. W. Robertson. 'We' and me: memoirs of four eminent editors. 1956. Includes material on J. A. Spender's editorship.
Laurence, D. H. Bernard Shaw and the Pall Mall Gazette: an identification of his unsigned contributions. Shaw Bull 5–6 1954.
Neiman, F. Some newly attributed contributions of Matthew Arnold to the Pall Mall Gazette. MP 55 1957.
Echo 1868
The staff of the Echo. Bookman (London) July 1898.
30th Birthday. Double no 8 Dec 1898.
St James's Gazette 1880
Green, R. L. Lewis Carroll and the St James's Gazette. N & Q 7 Apr 1945.
Star 1888
Shaw, G. B. London music in 1888–9 as heard by Corno di Bassetto. 1937. Musical criticisms first pbd in Star.
The story of the Star 1883–1938. 1938.

The Provincial Press: General Studies of more than one Paper

Hunt, W. Hull newspapers. Hull 1880.
Morley, J. C. The newspaper press and periodical literature of Liverpool. Liverpool 1887.
Wightman, H. A list of the newspapers in Lancashire, Yorkshire and Cheshire. Liverpool 1887.
Edwards, F. A. The early newspaper press of Hampshire. Southampton 1889.
Smith, C. F. The press of Essex 1837–97. Essex Rev July 1897.
The Gazette's precursors: Tyneside newspapers half a century ago. Shields Daily Gazette 24 Feb 1899.
Patterson, A. Yorkshire journalism past and present. Barnsley 1901.
Willox, J. The press of Liverpool. Liverpool Courier 6 Jan 1908.
Burton, G. H. Stamford Mercury 17, 24 Apr 1914. Articles on Lincolnshire newspapers and journalists.
Slade, J. J. and H. Richardson. Wiltshire newspapers past and present. Wiltshire Archaeological & Natural History Mag 40–1 1917–22.
Jones, I. A history of printers and printing in Wales to 1810 and of successive and related printers to 1923. Cardiff 1925.
Fenton, W. A. Cambridge periodicals 1750–1931. Cambridge Public Lib Record & Book List Mar 1931.
Sunderland and Portsmouth. Newspaper World 11 Feb 1939.
Cambridge's weekly newspapers. Newspaper World 12 Aug 1939.
Watson, S. F. Some materials for a history of printing and publishing in Ipswich. Proc Suffolk Inst of Archaeology & Natural History 24 1948.
Briggs, A. Press and public in nineteenth-century Birmingham. Dugdale Soc Occasional Papers 8 1950.
The Norwich Post: its contemporaries and successors. Norwich 1951. 250 years of Norwich newspapers.
Burton, K. G. The early newspaper press in Berkshire 1723–1855. Reading 1954.
Desmond, R. G. C. Our local press: a short historical account of the newspapers of Walthamstow. Walthamstow 1954.
Read, D. North of England newspapers c. 1700–c. 1900 and their value to historians. Proc Leeds Philosophical & Literary Soc, Literary & Historical Section 8 1957.
Laughton, G. E. and L. R. Stephen. Yorkshire newspapers: a bibliography with locations. 1960.
Read, D. Press and people 1790–1850: opinion in three English cities [Leeds, Manchester and Sheffield]. 1961.
Cranfield, G. A. The development of the provincial newspaper 1700–60. Oxford 1962. The early history of many nineteenth-century journals.

Sewell, G. Echoes of a century: the centenary history of Southern Newspapers Ltd 1864–1964. Southampton 1964.
Smith, R. E. G. Newspapers first published before 1900 in Lancashire, Cheshire and the Isle of Man. 1965.
Milne, M. The newspapers of Northumberland and Durham. Newcastle 1971.

Provincial Dailies

Sheffield Daily Telegraph 1855
Shepherdson, W. Reminiscences in the career of a newspaper. 1876.
Jubilee 1855–1905. Sheffield 1905.
Manchester Guardian 1855
Mills, W. H. A century of history. 1921.
Musson, A. E. Newspaper printing in the Industrial Revolution. Economic History Rev 10 1957–8. Material drawn exclusively from Guardian.
Shields Daily Gazette 1855
Jubilee number. 24 Feb 1899.
The oldest evening paper. Newspaper World 1 Apr 1939.
The Birmingham Post 1857
Jubilee number 4 Dec 1907.
Centenary supplement. 4 Dec 1957.
Whates, H. R. G. The Birmingham Post 1857–1957. Birmingham 1957.
Liverpool Daily Mercury 1858; Liverpool Daily Post 1855
Liverpool Daily Post jubilee number. 13 June 1905.
The centenary of the Liverpool Post and Mercury: a record of the progress of Liverpool and its leading newspaper. Liverpool 1911.
Trollope, A. Tireless traveller: twenty letters to the Liverpool Mercury. 1875. Ed B. A. Booth, Cambridge 1941.
Newcastle Chronicle 1858
Dolman, F. The Newcastle Chronicle and its editor, Joseph Cowen. Young Man Aug 1895.
Western Daily Press (Bristol) 1858
Great provincial newspapers II. Caxton Mag Oct 1901.
The first daily in the west. Newspaper World 22 Apr 1939.
Western Morning News (Plymouth) 1860
Great provincial newspapers IV. Caxton Mag Dec 1901.
Nottingham Daily Express 1860
The oldest provincial daily. Newspaper World 8 Apr 1939.
Bristol Mercury (Bristol Daily Post 1860)
Lewis, H. The history of the Bristol Mercury 1715–1886. Bristol [1887?].
Western Daily Mercury (Plymouth) 1860
Walling, R. A. J. The Western Daily Mercury. Cornish Mag Jan 1899.
Leeds Mercury [1861]
A champion of reform. Newspaper World 27 May 1939.
Liverpool Journal of Commerce 1861
Liverpool's shipping daily. Newspaper World 11 Mar 1939.
Birmingham Gazette 1862
Birmingham's oldest newspaper. Newspaper World 5 Aug 1939.
Liverpool Courier 1863
Centenary number. 6 Jan 1908.
Daily Bristol Times and Mirror 1865
Wells, C. The history of the Bristol Times and Mirror. 1913.
Yorkshire Post 1866
The Leeds Intelligencer–Yorkshire Post. Newspaper World 19 Aug 1939.
Gibb, M. A. and F. Beckwith. The Yorkshire Post: two centuries. [Leeds] 1954.
Yorkshire Observer (Bradford Observer 1868)
75 years retrospect. Yorkshire Observer 6 Feb 1909.
Huddersfield Examiner 1871
A fair name. Newspaper World 21 Jan 1939.
Yorkshire Herald (York) 1874
Jubilee number 2 Jan 1905.
Liverpool Echo 1879
Morning and evening at Liverpool. Newspaper World 25 Feb 1939.
Wolverhampton Express and Star 1880; Midland Counties Evening Express 1874
Wolverhampton's evening paper. Newspaper World 24 Dec 1938.

Provincial Weeklies

Berkshire Chronicle
The Berkshire Chronicle. Newspaper World 16 Aug 1939.
Berrow's Worcester Journal
The oldest English newspaper. Worcester 1890.
Britain's oldest weekly. Newspaper World 18 Mar 1938.
Griffiths, I. Berrow's Worcester Journal. Worcester 1941.
Blackburn Times
Jubilee number. 3 June 1905.
Blackpool Gazette
From visitors' list to daily paper. Newspaper World 17 Dec 1938.
Bury Times
Jubilee number. 8 July 1905.
Cardiff Times
Jubilee number. 15 Oct 1887.
Chester Courant
A nursery of journalists. Newspaper World 1 July 1939.
Coventry Mercury and Standard
The Coventry Mercury and Standard. Newspaper World 29 July 1939.
Derby Mercury
The chronicler of Derby. Newspaper World 8 July 1939.
Doncaster Gazette
Yorkshire Journal–Doncaster Gazette. Newspaper World 28 Oct 1939.
Falkirk Herald
The jubilee of the Falkirk Herald 1846–96. Falkirk 1896.
Gloucester Journal
Chance, H. G. The bicentenary of the Gloucester Journal. Gloucester 1922.
Grantham Journal
Quilter, H. H. Mid-Victorian Grantham: a commentary on the earliest numbers of the Grantham Journal. Grantham 1937.
Hampshire Advertiser (Southampton)
Centenary number. 28 July 1923.
Hereford Times
The British Chronicle–Hereford Times. Newspaper World 6 May 1939.
Huddersfield Examiner
Our jubilee: a brief sketch of the history of the Examiner. Huddersfield Examiner 6 Sep 1901.
Impartial Reporter (Enniskillen)
The Trimbles of Enniskillen. Newspaper World 2 Sep 1939.
Ipswich Journal
The history of the Ipswich Jnl for 150 years. [Ipswich 1875.]
Isle of Man Times (Douglas)
The jubilee of the Isle of Man Times: the story of its first half century. Douglas 1911.
Kentish Gazette
222 years in Canterbury. Newspaper World 20 May 1939.
Kentish Express and Ashford News (Ashford)
Jubilee. July 14 1855–July 15 1905. Ashford 1905.
Lancaster Guardian
History of the paper and reminiscences by 'Old Hands'. [Lancaster 1897] (priv ptd).
Lincoln, Rutland and Stamford Mercury
Burton, G. H. Notes on newspapers. Stamford Mercury 20 Mar 1914.
Evans, F. H. Brief sketch . . . Lincoln, Rutland and Stamford Mercury. 1938.

Newton, D. Mercury story: a brief record of the Lincoln, Rutland and Stamford Mercury. Stamford 1962.
Macclesfield Courier and Herald
Centenary number. 4 Feb 1911.
Middlesex Chronicle (Hounslow)
Jubilee number and supplement. 9 Jan 1909.
Newcastle Journal
228 years on Tyneside. Newspaper World 15 Apr 1939.
Norfolk News (Norwich)
Round a newspaper office: Norfolk News Co. [Norwich 1902.]
North British Advertiser (Edinburgh)
The case of Mr John Gray, the founder of the North British Advertiser. Edinburgh 1831.
Northampton Mercury
1720–1901. [Northampton 1901.]
Hadley, W. W. The bicentenary record of the Northampton Record. Northampton 1920.
It flourisheth by circulation. Newspaper World 3 June 1939.
Norwich Mercury
The Norwich Mercury. Newspaper World 13 May 1939.
Preston Chronicle
Spencer, J. H. The Dobson family of the Preston Chronicle. Preston Herald 29 Dec 1950.
Reading Mercury
Noble engine of freedom. Newspaper World 17 June 1939.
Rochdale Observer
Jubilee number. 17 Feb 1906.
Salisbury and Winchester Journal
Richardson, H. 1729–1929. Supplement 7 June 1929.
The Salisbury and Winchester Journal. Newspaper World 24 June 1939.
Scarborough Mercury
Jubilee number. 21 July 1905.
Shrewsbury Chronicle
The Shrewsbury Chronicle – Salop's first newspaper. Newspaper World 7 Oct 1939.
Staffordshire Advertiser (Stafford)
A centenary history of the Staffordshire Advertiser. Stafford 1895.
Stirling Observer
90 years' progress 1836–1926. Stirling 1926.
Trowbridge and Wiltshire Advertiser
Three generations at Trowbridge. Newspaper World 29 Apr 1939.
Wakefield Express
Jubilee 1852–1902. Souvenir. [Wakefield 1902.]
Wellington Journal
Advertising and literature. Newspaper World 10 June 1939.
Western Gazette
Flying Post–Western Gazette. Newspaper World 22 July 1939.
Windsor and Eton Express and General Advertiser
Bebbington, W. G. The most remarkable man of his age: Byron in the Windsor and Eton Express and General Advertiser. Keats–Shelley Memorial Bull 7 1956.

The Scottish Press: General Studies of more than one Paper

The newspaper press of Scotland. Fraser's Mag May, July–Aug 1838.
M'Bain, J. M. Bibliography of Arbroath periodical literature and political broadsides. Arbroath 1889.
Norrie, W. Edinburgh newspapers past and present. Earlestown 1891.
Concerning three northern newspapers: their rise and progress 1748–1900: Aberdeen Daily Journal, Aberdeen Weekly Journal, Aberdeen Evening Express. Aberdeen 1900.
Noble, J. A bibliography of Inverness newspapers and periodicals. Ed. J. Whyte, with appendix by W. Mackay, Stirling 1903.
Graham, M. The early Glasgow press. Glasgow 1906.
Couper, W. J. The Edinburgh periodical press. 2 vols Stirling 1908.
Stewart, W. The Glasgow press in 1840. Glasgow 1921 (priv ptd).

Scottish Daily Papers

Scotsman (Edinburgh) 1855
The story of the Scotsman. Edinburgh 1886 (priv ptd).
Centenary number. 25 Jan 1917.
Ritchie, Findlay and Law. Newspaper World 28 Jan 1939.
Jones, S. Hazlitt in Edinburgh: an evening with Mr Ritchie of the Scotsman. Études anglaises 17 1964.
150th anniversary supplement. 24 Jan 1967.
Glasgow Herald 1859
Stewart, W. The Glasgow Herald: the story of a great newspaper from 1783 to 1911. Glasgow 1911.
Dundee Advertiser 1861
Millar, A. H. The Dundee Advertiser 1801–1901: a centenary memoir. Dundee 1901.
Dundee Courier 1861
Great provincial newspapers I. Caxton Mag Aug 1901.
Edinburgh Evening News 1873
Fifty years 1873–1923. Edinburgh 1923.
Aberdeen Journal 1877
The Aberdeen Journal and its history; the men who made it. Aberdeen 1894.
Our 150th year. Aberdeen 1897.
Mitchell, W. A. Or was it yesterday? 1947.
The Evening Telegraph (Dundee) 1877
Silver Jubilee number. 13 Mar 1902.

The Irish Press: General Studies of more than one Paper

Madden, R. R. The history of Irish periodical literature from the end of the seventeenth to the middle of the nineteenth century. 2 vols 1867.
Proprietors for 143 years. Newspaper World 7 Jan 1939. Belfast papers.
Baird's. Newspaper World 4 Mar 1939. Belfast papers.
Dublin's Newspaper family. Newspaper World 15 July 1939.
Inglis, B. The freedom of the press in Ireland 1784–1841. 1954.

London Papers Published more than once a Week

City Press 1857
Jubilee number. 13 July 1907.
London Gazette 1865
The cost of printing and publishing the London, Edinburgh and Dublin Gazettes in each of the years 1846, 1847, 1848 and 1849, exclusive of stamps and paper, with balance sheets for each of the said years, showing the profit and loss. House of Commons Accounts & Papers (677) xxxiii 429 1850.
Handover, P. M. A history of the London Gazette 1665–1965. 1965.

Weekly Papers: Sunday

Observer 1791
1791–1921: a short record of 130 years. 1921.
175th anniversary supplement. 4 Dec 1966.
The Observer of the nineteenth century. Ed M. Miliband 1966.
Weekly Dispatch: Sunday Dispatch 1801
The Weekly Dispatch: special centenary number. 9 June 1901.
The Sunday Dispatch: 150th anniversary number. 23 Sep 1951.
Examiner 1808
Blunden, E. Leigh Hunt's Examiner examined: comprising an account of that celebrated newspaper's contents 1808–25. 1928.
Graham, W. Shelley's debt to Leigh Hunt and the Examiner. PMLA 40 1925.
Johnson, R. B. Shelley–Leigh Hunt: how friendship made history. 1929.
Stout, G. D. The political history of Leigh Hunt's Examiner together with an account of 'The Books'. Washington Univ Stud new ser (Lang & Lit) 19 1949.

Champion 1814
Parker, W. M. and D. Hudson. Thomas Barnes and the Champion. TLS 1, 15 Jan 1944.
Jones, L. M. Keats's theatrical reviews in the Champion. Keats–Shelley Jnl 3 1954.
Sunday Times 1822
100 years of history. 1920.
Newspaper World 16 Apr 1938.
Lloyd's Weekly News (Lloyds Illustrated Newspaper 1842)
Diamond jubilee number. 30 Nov 1902.
News of the World 1843
Through four reigns: the romance of a great newspaper. [1928.]
Berrey, R. P. The romance of a great newspaper. [c. 1933.]
Centenary article. World's Press News 30 Sep 1943.
Reynolds' Newspaper 1850
Jubilee number. 27 May 1900. *See* 1 Mar 1936.
Weekly Sun 1891
[Opinions on by eminent men. Ed T. P. O'Connor] 1896.

General Weekly Papers
Spectator 1828
Thomas, W. B. The story of the Spectator 1828–1928. 1928.
6,000th number. 25 June 1943.
125th anniversay number. 15 May 1953.
Colby, R. A. 'How it strikes a contemporary': the Spectator as critic. Nineteenth-Century Fiction 11 1957.
Tener, R. H. Swinburne as a reviewer. TLS 25 Dec 1959.
Tener, R. H. The Spectator records 1847–97. Victorian newsletter 1960.
Tener, R. H. Spectatorial Strachey. TLS 31 Dec 1964.
Paden, W. D. Swinburne, the Spectator in 1862 and Walter Bagehot: six studies in nineteenth century English literature and thought. Ed H. Orel and G. G. Worth, Lawrence KS 1962.
Waller, J. O. Edward Dicey and the American negro in 1862: an English working journalist's view. BNYPL Jan 1962.
Chambers's Journal 1832
Chambers, R. Essays familiar and humorous, reprinted from Chambers's Journal. [1866.]
Chambers, R. Tales from Chambers's Journal. 11 vols [1884–5].
Chambers, W. Our Jubilee year. Chambers's Jnl 28 Jan 1882.
Gray, W. F. A hundred years old. Chambers's Jnl Feb 1932.
Index to fiction in Chambers's Jnl 1854–1910. Victorian Fiction Research Guide 17 1989.
Press 1853
A sketch of the political history of the last three years in connection with the Press newspaper, and the part it has taken on the leading questions of the time. 1856.
Saturday Review 1856
Grant, J. The Saturday Review: its origin and progress. 1873.
Bevington, M. M. The Saturday Rev 1855–68: representative educated opinion in Victorian England. New York 1941.
Everybody's Journal
N & Q 30 Sep 1939.
London Rev 1860
Books, R. L. Matthew Arnold and the London Review. PMLA 76 1961.
Bow Bells 1862
Lloyd-Jones, A. Bow Bells. N & Q 22 Nov 1952.
Queen's Messenger 1869
G., A. M. The spleen of Mr Murray. Blackwood's Mag Feb 1951.
Truth 1877
Mr Labouchere and Truth. Bookman (London) Sep 1892.

Illustrated Papers
Jackson, M. The pictorial press: its origin and progress. 1885.
Blackburn, H. The Cantor lectures on the art of book and newspaper illustration. 1894.
Gamble, W. Newspaper illustrations. Penrose's Pictorial Annual 3 1897.
Gamble, W. Pictorial telegraphy. Penrose's Pictorial Annual 4 1898.
Shorter, C. K. Illustrated journalism: its past and future. Contemporary Rev Apr 1899.
Illustrated London News 1842
Centenary number. 16 May 1942. Historical material also in issue of 10 June 1951.
Field 1853
Centenary number. 22 Nov 1952.
Rose, R. N. The field 1853–1953: a centenary volume. 1953.
Daily Graphic 1890
21 years of progress of the pioneer illustrated daily newspaper. Daily Graphic 4 Jan 1911 (supplement).
County Life 1897
70th anniversary number. 12 Jan 1967.

Unstamped and Radical Journals
Berguer, L. T. A warning letter to HRH the Prince Regent. 1819 (3rd edn).
Standard 10 Sep 1833.
Gammage, R. G. The history of the Chartist movement 1837–54. Newcastle 1854, 1894 (rev).
Rose, J. H. The unstamped press 1815–36. EHR 12 1897.
Menger, A. The right to the whole produce of labour. Tr 1899.
Dierlamm, G. Die Flugschriftenliteratur der Chartistenbewegung in der öffentlichen Meinung. Tübingen 1909.
Kovalev, Y. V. The literature of Chartism. Victorian Stud 2 1958.
Cole, G. D. H. Chartist portraits. Ed A. Briggs 1965.
Cobbett's Political Register 1802
Birrell, T. A. The Political Register: Cobbett and English literature. English Stud 45 (Supplement) 1964.
Yellow Dwarf 1818
Marshall, W. H. Pulpit oratory I–III: essays by J. H. Reynolds in imitation of William Hazlitt. Lib Chron 28 1962.
Northern Star 1837
Glasgow, E. The establishment of the Northern Star newspaper. History 39 1954.
Bee-Hive [1861]
Coltham, S. The Bee-Hive newspaper: its origins and early struggles. In Essays in labour history, ed A. Briggs and J. Saville 1960.
Coltham, S. George Potter, the Junta and the Bee-Hive. International Rev of Social History 9–10 1964–5.

Weekly Literary Reviews
Literary Gazette 1817
Duncan, R. W. Byron and the London Literary Gazette. Boston Univ Stud in Eng 2 1956.
Duncan, R. W. The London Literary Gazette and American writers. Papers on English Lang & Lit Spring 1965.
Athenaeum 1828
See two special issues of the Victorian Periodicals Rev *devoted to the* Athenaeum, vol 23, nos 2 and 4, 1990.
An on-going project to index the contributors to the Athenaeum, *originally based at City University, London, is available on the world wide web.*
Francis, J. C. John Francis, publisher of the Athenaeum. 2 vols 1888.
Marchand, L. A. The Athenaeum: a mirror of Victorian culture. Chapel Hill NC 1940.
Fryckstedt, M. C. Geraldine Jewsbury's Athenaeum reviews: a mirror of mid-Victorian attitudes to fiction. Uppsala 1986.
Leigh Hunt's London Journal 1834
Marchand, L. A. Leigh Hunt's London Journal. Jnl Rutgers Univ Lib 6 1943.
Notes and Queries 1849
N & Q 29 June, 7 Sep 1946, 4 Oct 1947, 19 Aug 1950.
Periodical July 1947.

Household Words 1850: All the Year Round 1859
See also Dickens entry col 1181.
Grubb, G. G. Dickens's pattern of weekly serialization. ELH 9 1942.
Grubb, G. G. Dickens's editorial methods. SP 40 1943.
Grubb, G. G. The editorial policies of Charles Dickens. PMLA 58 1943.
Grubb, G. G. The American edition of All the Year Round. PBSA 47 1953.
Grubb, G. G. Dickens the paymaster once more. Dickensian 51 1955.
Hopkins, A. B. Dickens and Mrs Gaskell. HLQ 9 1946.
Gomme, G. J. L. T. B. Aldrich and Household Words. PBSA 42 1948.
Buckler, W. E. Dickens's success with Household Words. Dickensian 46 1950.
Buckler, W. E. Dickens the paymaster. PMLA 66 1951.
Buckler, W. E. Household Words in America. PBSA 45 1951.
Morley, M. Plays from the Christmas number of Household Words. Dickensian 51 1955.
Morley, M. All the Year Round plays. Dickensian 52 1956.
Collins, P. A. W. Keep Household Words imaginative. Ibid.
Collins, P. A. W. Dickens's periodicals: articles on education; an annotated bibliography. Univ of Leicester Vaughan College Papers 3 1957.
Collins, P. A. W. Dickens as editor: some uncollected fragments. Dickensian 56 1960.
Collins, P. A. W. The significance of Dickens's periodicals. REL 2 1961.
Collins, P. A. W. Inky fishing nets: Dickens as editor. Dickensian 61 1965.
Adrian, A. A. Dickens as verse editor. MP 58 1960.
Hunter, R. A. and I. Macalpine. Dickens and Conolly: an embarrassed editor's disclaimer. TLS 11 Aug 1961.
Lohrli, A. Dickens's Household Words on American English. Amer Speech 37 1962.
Lohrli, A. Household Words and its 'office book'. Princeton Univ Lib Chron 26 1964.
Easson, A. Dickens, Household Words and a double standard. Dickensian 60 1964.
Lohrli, A. comp. Household Words, a weekly journal 1850–1859: table of contributors and their contributions, based on the Household Words office book. Toronto 1973.
Oppenlander, E. A. Dickens' All the Year Round: descriptive index and contributor list. Troy NY 1984.

Once a Week 1859
Buckler, W. E. E. A. Dallas's appointment as editor of Once a Week. N & Q 24 June 1950.
Buckler, W. E. E. A. Once a Week under Samuel Lucas 1859–65. PMLA 67 1952.
Gettmann, R. A. Serialization and Evan Harrington. PMLA 64 1949.
Gettmann, R. A. Serialization of Reade's A good fight. Nineteenth-Century Fiction 6 1952.

Academy 1869
Roll-Hansen, D. Matthew Arnold and the Academy: a note on English criticism in the eighteen-seventies. PMLA 68 1953.
Roll-Hansen, D. The Academy 1869–79: Victorian intellectuals in revolt. Copenhagen 1957.

Religious Papers

Fletcher, J. R. Early Catholic periodicals in England. Dublin Rev 198 1936. Includes valuable biography of nineteenth-century Catholic papers.

The Tablet 1840
Walsh, M. The Tablet 1840–1990: a commemorative history. 1990.

Jewish Chronicle 1841
The Jewish Chronicle 1841–1941: a centenary of newspaper history. 1950.

Christian World 1857
Farningham, M. Some personal reminiscences. Christian World 11 Apr 1907.

Universe 1860
Seventieth anniversary. 5 Dec 1930.

Agricultural Papers

Mark Lane Express 1832
70th birthday number. 31 Mar 1902.

Financial and Commercial Papers

Skinner, J. The early background to financial journalism. World's Press News 20 July 1942.

Economist 1843
Centenary issue. 4 Sep 1943.
The Economist 1843–1943: a centenary volume. 1943.
Gordon, S. The London Economist and the high tide of laissez-faire. Jnl of Political Economy 63 1955.

Sporting Papers

Sporting Times 1865
3,000th number. 19 Mar 1921.
Booth, K. B. Sporting Times: the 'Pink 'Un' world. 1938.

Humorous Papers

Spielmann, M. H. The rivals of Punch: a glance at the illustrated comic press of half a century. Nat Rev July 1895.
Roe, F. G. The lighter side of collecting some 'comics' of yesteryear. Connoisseur 108 1941.

Punch 1841
Mr Punch: his origin and career, with a facsimile of his original prospectus in the handwriting of Mark Lemon. [c. 1870.]
Spielmann, M. H. The history of Punch. 1895.
Mr Punch's pageant 1841–1908: a souvenir catalogue. 1909.
Dickensian peeps into Punch. Dickensian 31–35 1935–39. Cartoons etc. with Dickensian associations.
Falconer, J. W. A hundred years of Punch. Dalhousie Rev 21 1941.
Horton-Smith, L. G. H. Punch: have you a complete set? N & Q 25 Jan, 15 Feb 1947. On the 'suppressed' issue of 7 Feb 1885.
Ray, G. N. Thackeray and Punch: 44 newly identified contributions. TLS 1 Jan 1949.
Darwin, B. Christmas and Mr Punch. Nat Rev Dec 1950. Christmas drawings 1864–1900.
Williams, R. E. A centenary of Punch. 1956. A collection of cartoons.
Price, R. G. G. A history of Punch. 1957.
Maurer, O. Punch on slavery and the Civil War in America. Victorian Stud 1 1957.
Maurer, O. Punch and the Opera War 1847–67. Texas Stud in Lang & Lit 1 1959.
Adburgham, A. A Punch history of manners and modes 1841–1940. 1961.
Pulling, C. Mr Punch and the police. 1964.
Altick, R. D. Our gallant colonel in Punch and Parliament. BNYPL Sep 1965.

Judy 1867
Peyrouton, N. C. Dickens and the Judy magazine. Dickensian 62 1966.

Moonshine 1879
The staff of Moonshine: portraits and facts concerning the celebrated weekly paper. 1900.

Juvenile Papers

Rollington, R. A brief history of boys' journals with interesting facts about the writers of boys' stories. Leicester 1913.
Dexter, W. Boys' periodicals of the nineties. Chambers's Jnl Dec 1943.
Turner, E. S. Boys will be boys. 1949.

Egoff, S. A. Children's periodicals of the nineteenth century: a survey and bibliography. 1951.
Enough of blood. TLS 4 Dec 1959. The battle to counter the penny-dreadfuls.
Young Folks 1871
McCleary, G. F. Stevenson in Young Folks. Fortnightly Rev Feb 1949.

Miscellaneous Specialized Papers

Ulrich, C. F. and K. Küp. Books and printing: a selected list of periodicals 1800–1942. Woodstock VT 1943.
Casson, H. One hundred years of architectural journalism. Builder 11 June 1948.
Lancet 1823
Centenary number 6 Oct 1923.
Builder 1842
Centenary issues 1–8 June 1943.
Richardson, R. and R. Thorne ed. The Builder illustrations index 1843–1883. 1994.

D. MAGAZINES AND REVIEWS

See headnote under C. The Daily and Weekly Press, above

(1) MONTHLY MAGAZINES

The gentleman's magazine: or monthly intelligencer. Vols 1–5, Jan 1731–Dec 1735. Continued as Gentleman's magazine and historical chronicle, vols 6–77, Jan 1736–Dec 1807. New series, vols 78–103, Jan 1808–Dec 1833. Continued as Gentleman's magazine: new series vols 1–45, Jan 1834–June 1956. Continued as Gentleman's magazine and historical review: new series, vols 1–19, July 1856–Dec 1865. New ser, vols 1–5, Jan 1866–May 1868. Continued as Gentleman's magazine, entirely new series, vols 1–16, June 1868–June 1876. From July 1876, vol 17, no 1747, returns to consecutive numbering from the beginning. Vols 240–72, Jan 1877–Sep (?) 1907. From Oct 1907 to 1922 covers only were ptd to retain copyright of the title. Gentleman's annual: being the New Year supplement of the Gentleman's magazine, 1870 etc. Indexes: General index to first 20 vols 1753. Index from 1731 to 1786, by S. Ayscough, 2 vols 1789. From 1787 to 1818, by J. Nichols, vol 34 1821. A list of the plates, maps etc from 1731 to 1813, 1814. A list of the plates and woodcuts from 1731 to 1818 by C. St Barbe jr, vol 5, 1821. Prop John Nicholas and J. B. Nichols 1792–1856; John Henry Parker 1856–65; Bradbury, Evans & Co 1865–May 1868; Chatto and Windus 1868–1906. Ed Edward Cave 1731–54, R. Cave 1754–66, D. Henry 1754–92, J. Nichols 1778–1826, J. B. Nichols 1826–33, John Mitford 1834–50, J. G. Nichols 1851–6, John Henry Parker 1856–65, Edward Walford 1866–7, Bolton Corney, Joseph Hatton 1867–74, Joseph Knight 1887–1905.
The Scots magazine. Vols 1–65, Jan 1739–Dec 1803. Continued as Scots magazine and Edinburgh literary miscellany, vols 66–79, Jan 1904–July 1817. Continued as Edinburgh magazine and literary miscellany: a new series of the Scots magazine, vols 1–18, Aug 1817–June 1826. Prop Constable. Ed Thomas Pringle and James Cleghorn 1817–?.
The universal magazine of knowledge and pleasure. Vols 1–113, June 1747–Dec 1803. Continued as Universal magazine: new series, vols 1–21, Jan 1804–June 1814. Continued as New universal magazine: new series, vols 1–3, July 1814–Sep 1815.
The monthly review. Vols 1–2, May 1749–Apr 1750. Continued as Monthly review: or new literary journal, vols 3–4, May 1750–May 1751. Continued as Monthly review; or literary journal, vols 5–81, June 1751–Dec 1789. Enlarged series, vols 1–108, Jan 1790–Nov 1825. Continued as Monthly review (new and improved series), vols 1–15, Jan 1826–Dec 1830. New and improved series, vols 1–?, Jan 1831–Dec 1844 (?). Indexes: A general index from the commencement to the end of the 70th vol, by S. Ayscough, 2 vols 1786. A continuation of the general index from the commencement of the new series [Jan 1790] to the end of the 81st volume [Dec 1816], [by J. C.], 2 vols 1818. Ed Ralph Griffiths 1749–1803, G. E. Griffiths 1803–25, M. J. Quin 1825–32.
The critical review: or annals of literature. 1756–1817: 1st ser, vols 1–70; 2nd ser extended and improved: a new arrangement, 39 vols 1791–1803; 3rd ser 24 vols 1804–11; 4th ser 6 vols 1812–14; 5th ser 5 vols 1815–17. Incorporated in Monthly review. Ed Tobias Smollett, ? Guthrie, Percival Stockdale, George Gregory, Samuel Hamilton.
The lady's magazine: or entertaining companion for the fair sex. Vols 1–50, 1770–Dec 1819. New ser vols 1–10, Jan 1820–9. Improved ser, vols 1–4, 1830–2. Incorporated in Ladies' museum and continued as Lady's magazine and museum of belles lettres: improved series, enlarged, vols 1–11, 1832–7. Incorporated in Court magazine and monthly critic, and continued as Court magazine and monthly critic and ladies' magazine and museum of belles lettres, vols 12–31, Jan 1838–47.
The Hibernian magazine: or companion of entertaining knowledge. Dublin. Feb 1771–Apr 1785. Continued as Walker's Hibernian magazine, May 1785–July 1812.
The Arminian magazine. Vols 1–20, Jan 1778–Dec 1797. Continued as Methodist magazine, vols 21–44, Jan 1798–Dec 1821. Continued as Wesleyan-Methodist magazine, 3rd ser vols 1–136, Jan 1822–Dec 1913. Continued as Magazine for the home, vol 137, Jan–Dec 1914. Continued as Magazine of the Wesleyan Methodist Church, vols 138–149, Jan 1915–Dec 1926. Continued as Methodist magazine, vol 150, Jan 1927 onwards. Wesleyan Methodist magazine, 6th edn, vols 1–5, 1861–5. Wesleyan Methodist magazine, abridged edn, new ser vols 1–5, 1866–70. Ed John Wesley 1778–91, George Story 1791–6(?), Joseph Benson 1796–1821, Jabez Bunting 1821–3, Thomas Jackson 1823–42, G. Cubitt, L. Thornton, W. H. Rule, Benjamin Frankland and Benjamin Gregory 1868–76, Benjamin Gregory 1876–93.
The European magazine and London review, by the Philological Society of London. Vols 1–87, Apr (?) 1782–July 1825. From vol 51, Jan–June 1807, 'by the Philological Society of London' omitted. New series, vols 1–2, 1825–6. Incorporated in Monthly magazine. Ed James Perry.
The Edinburgh magazine: or literary miscellany. Vols 1–13, June 1785–June 1791. New ser, vols 1–22, Jan 1793–Dec 1803. Incorporated in Scots magazine.
The botanical magazine: or, flower-garden displayed. Vols 1–14, 1787–1800. Continued as Curtis's botanical magazine, vols 15–53, 1801–26. New ser vols 1–70, 1827–44. 3rd ser vols 71–130, Jan 1845–1904. 4th series 1905 etc. onwards. Now quarterly. Indexes: A general index to the Latin names and synonyms for the plants depicted in vols 1–107 of Curtis's botanical magazine, by E. Tonks, 1883. A new and complete index to the Botanical magazine, 1787–1904, to which is prefixed a history of the magazine by I. W. B. Hemsley. 1906. Prop S. Curtis 1799–1846 (?). Ed William Curtis 1787–99, John Sims 1800–26, W. J. Hooker 1827–67, J. D. Hooker 1866–1904.
The sporting magazine: or monthly calendar of the transactions of the turf, the chace etc. Vols 1–50, Oct 1792–1817. New ser vols 51–75, 1817–29. 2nd (really 3rd) ser, vols 76–100, 1829–42. 3rd [4th] ser, 56 vols 1843–70. From July 1846 onwards this is identical, except for title-pages, with New sporting magazine, Sportsman and Sporting review. Index of engravings, 1792–1870. 1892.
The Evangelical magazine. Vols 1–20, July 1793–1812. Continued as Evangelical magazine and missionary chronicle, vols 21–30, 1813–Dec 1822. New ser vols 1–36, Jan 1823–Dec 1858. 3rd ser vols 1–10, Jan 1859–Dec 1868. New [4th] ser vols 1–21 (old ser vol 100),

Jan 1869–92. New [5th] ser vols 1–12 (old ser vols 101–12), 1893–1904. Index to first 24 vols, July 1793–Dec 1816. 1817. Ed John Eyre and Matthew Wilks 1793–?, ? Fuller, Dr Haweis, E. Williams, ? Greatheed ?–1823, George Burder, John Morison 1843–?, H. F. Burder. J. Stoughton, John Kennedy and Josiah Viney 1889–90, D. B. Hooke, 1891–1904.

The British critic: a new review. Vols 1–42, May 1793–Dec 1813. New series, 23 vols Jan 1814–June 1825. 3rd series, 3 vols Oct 1825–Oct 1826. Incorporated in Quarterly theological review and continued as British critic, quarterly theological review and ecclesiastical record. *See under quarterlies, col 2949, below*. Index: A general index to the first 20 vols, by S. Ayscough. 2 pts 1804. General index to vols 21–40, 1st ser, by F. W. Blagden 1815. Ed W. Beloe, R. Nares, T. F. Middleton, W. R. Lyall et al.

The repertory of arts and manufactures. Vols 1–16, 1794–1802. Continued as Repertory of arts, manufactures and agriculture, 2nd series, vols 1–46, June 1802–June 1825. Continued as Repertory of patent inventions and other discoveries and improvements in arts, manufactures and agriculture, vols 1–6, July 1825–June 1828. Continued as Repertory of patent inventions, and other discoveries and improvements in arts, manufactures and agriculture, vols 7–16, July 1828–Dec 1833. New ser, vols 1–18, Jan 1834–Dec 1842. Enlarged series, vols 1–40, Jan 1843–Dec 1862. Indexes: An analytical index to the sixteen vols of the 1st series of all patents granted for inventions 1795–1802. 1806. A general index to the 25 vols of the 2nd series, including all patents 1806–15. 1815. Index to all patents granted in England 1815–45. 1846. Appendix to index. 1815–45. 1849. Index to the Repertory 1846–50. 1851. Index for 1851. [1852.]

The monthly magazine and British register. Vols 1–63, Feb 1796–Jan 1826. Continued as Monthly magazine: or British register of literature, sciences and belles lettres, new series, vols 1–18, 1826–34. New ser vol 19, 1835. Continued as Monthly magazine of politics, literature and the belles lettres, vols 20–26, 1835–8. Continued as Monthly magazine, 9 vols 1839–43. Prop Richard Phillips; ? Holland. Ed John Aikin 1796–1806, George Gregory 1806–8, Richard Phillips, ? Holland ?–1836, James Grant 1836–?, Francis F. Barham and Abraham Heraud July 1839–May 1840, Abraham Heraud May 1840–?.

The Gospel magazine and theological review. 1796 onwards. Ed W. Row 1796–1839.

The journal of natural philosophy, chemistry and the arts. Vols 1–5, Apr 1797–Dec 1801. New ser vols 1–36, Jan 1802–Dec 1813. Incorporated in Philosophical magazine. Prop and ed William Nicholson.

The Anti-Jacobin review and magazine: or monthly political and literary censor. Vols 1–35, July 1798–April 1810. Continued as Antijacobin review, and true churchman's magazine: or monthly political and literary censor, vols 36–50, May 1810–Aug 1817. Continued as Antijacobin review; True churchman's magazine and Protestant advocate: or monthly political and literary censor, vols 51–5, Sep 1817–Feb 1819. Continued as Antijacobin review; and Protestant advocate: or monthly political and literary censor, vols 56–61, Mar 1819–Dec 1821. Ed 'John Gifford' (John Richards Green).

The philosophical magazine. Vols 1–68, June 1798–Dec 1826. Continued as Philosophical magazine: or annals of chemistry, mathematics, astronomy, natural history and general science, vols 1–11, Jan 1827–June 1832. Continued as London and Edinburgh philosophical magazine and journal of science, vols 1–16, July 1832–June 1840. Continued as London, Edinburgh and Dublin philosophical magazine and journal of science, vols 17–37, July 1840–Dec 1850. 4th ser, vols 1–50, Jan 1851–Dec 1875. 5th ser, vols 1–50, Jan 1876–Dec 1900. 6th ser, vols 1–50, Jan 1901–Dec 1925. 7th ser, vols 1–35, Jan 1926–Dec 1944. Continued as Philosophical magazine, vol 36, Jan 1945 onwards. Index: General index to vols 1–11 of 2nd ser 1827–32. 1835. Ed Alexander Tilloch 1797–Dec 1813, Alexander Tilloch and William Nicholson Jan 1814–June 1822, Alexander Tilloch, William Nicholson and Richard Taylor July 1822–June 1825, Richard Taylor July 1825–Dec 1826, Richard Taylor and Richard Phillips Jan 1827–June 1832, Richard Taylor, Richard Phillips and David Brewster July 1832–June 1840, Richard Taylor, Richard Phillips, David Brewster and Robert Kane July 1840–Dec 1850, Richard Taylor, Richard Phillips, David Brewster, Robert Kane and William Francis Jan–Dec 1851, Richard Taylor, David Brewster, Robert Kane and William Francis Jan 1852–Dec 1853, Richard Taylor, David Brewster, Robert Kane, William Francis and John Tyndall Jan 1854–Dec 1858, David Brewster, Robert Kane, William Francis and John Tyndall Jan 1859–Dec 1863, David Brewster, Robert Kane and William Francis Jan 1864–June 1868, Robert Kane and William Francis July–Dec 1868, Augustus Mathieson, Robert Kane and William Francis Jan 1869–June 1870, Robert Kane and William Francis July 1870–July 1871, Robert Kane, William Francis and William Thomson Aug 1871–1889, William Francis and William Thomson 1889–90, William Francis, William Thomson and George Fitzgerald 1890–1, William Francis, George Fitzgerald and Lord Kelvin 1892–1904.

The lady's monthly museum: or polite repository of amusement and instruction. Vols 1–16, July 1798–June 1806. New series, vols 1–17, July 1806–Dec 1814. Improved series vols 1–28, Jan 1815–Dec 1828. Continued as Ladies' museum, vols 1–3, 1829–32. Amalgamated with Ladies' magazine.

The general Baptist repository. Vols 1–10, Oct (?) 1802–1821. Continued as General Baptist repository and missionary observer, vols 1–6 [3rd] ser, Jan 1822–Dec 1859. Continued as General Baptist magazine and missionary observer, new ser [4th], vols 1–4, Jan 1860–Dec 1863. Continued as General Baptist magazine, Jan 1864–Dec 1891. Continued as Baptist Union magazine, vols 1–2, Jan–Dec 1893. New ser, vols 1–2, Jan 1894–Dec 1895. Continued as Church and household, Jan 1896–Dec 1901. Ed J. Goadby 1833–59, J. J. Goadby 1859–June 1867, W. Underwood, W. R. Stevenson, J. C. Pike July–Dec 1867, W. Underwood Jan 1867–Dec 1869, John Clifford Jan 1870–Dec 1883, R. W. Stevenson and J. Fletcher Jan 1884–Aug 1889, J. Fletcher Sep 1889–1891, J. Clifford and G. Hawker 1892–5, D. Davies 1896–1901.

The Christian observer. Vols 1–74, 1802–74. Continued as Christian observer and advocate, vols 75–77, 1875–7. Ed J. Pratt 1802, Z. Macaulay 1802–16, S. C. Wilks 1816–50, J. W. Cunningham 1850–8, J. B. Marsden 1859–69.

The literary journal: a review of literature, science, manners and politics. Vols 1–4, [Jan 1803]–Dec 1804. Continued as Literary journal; or universal review of literature domestic and foreign, vol 5 vols 1–2 (2nd ser), 1805–6. Ed James Mill.

The imperial review or London [Edinburgh] and Dublin literary journal. Vols 1–5, 1804–5. The last 2 vols only have 'Edinburgh' in the title.

The eclectic review. Vols 1–10, Jan 1805–Dec 1813. New ser vols 1–30, Jan 1814–Dec 1828. 3rd ser, vols 1–16, Jan 1829–Dec 1836. New [4th] ser, vols 1–28, Jan 1837–Dec 1850. New [5th] ser, vols 1–12, Jan 1851–Dec 1856. New [6th] ser, vols 1–4, Jan 1857–Dec 1858. New [7th] ser, vols 1–5, Jan 1859–June 1861. New [8th] ser July 1861–Dec 1868. Prop Josiah Conder 1814–36 ?. Ed S. Greatheed, D. Parker, T. Williams 1805–13, Josiah Conder 1814–36, T. Price 1837–50, T. Price and W. H. Stowell 1851–4, J. E. Ryland 1855–6, Edwin Paxton Hood 1850 (?)–8. See M. R. Hiller, Victorian Periodicals Review 27 1994. Identifies contributors.

La belle assemblée; or Bell's court and fashionable magazine. Vols 1–8, Feb 1806–1810. New and improved ser vols 1–30, 1810–24. 3rd ser, vols 1–15, 1825–June 1832. Continued as Court magazine and belle assemblée, vols 1–9, July 1832–1837. Continued as Court magazine and monthly critic, vols 10–11, 1837. Continued as Court magazine and monthly critic and lady's magazine, and museum of the belles-lettres, music etc., united series, Jan 1838. Prop John Bell 1806–21. Ed Mrs Norton 1832–7.

The monthly repository of theology and general literature. Vols 1–21, Jan 1806–Dec 1826. Continued as Monthly repository and review, new series, vols 1–11, Jan 1827–June 1837. Continued as Monthly repository, enlarged series, vols 1–2(?), July 1837–Apr 1838. Prop Robert Aspland 1806–26; British and Foreign Unitarian Association Book Committee 1827–31; W. J. Fox 1831–June 1837; J. H. Leigh Hunt July 1837–Apr 1838. Ed Robert Aspland 1806–26, W. J. Fox 1828–36, R. H. Horne June 1836–June 1837, J. H. Leigh Hunt July 1837–Apr 1838.

The literary panorama: a review of books, register of events, magazine of varieties. Vols 1–2, Oct 1806–Sep 1807. Continued as Literary panorama, being a review of books, magazine of varieties and annual register, vols 3–9, Oct 1807–June 1811. Continued as Literary panorama: being a compendium of national papers and Parliamentary reports . . . a review of books, and magazine of varieties, forming an annual register, vols 10–15, July 1811–Sep 1814. Continued as Literary panorama, and national register, new series, vols 1–9, Oct 1814–July 1819. Incorporated in New monthly magazine. Vols 1–4, new series, rptd Boston 1816–17.

Flower's political review, and monthly register. Vols 1–9, Jan 1807–July 1811. Ed B. Flower.

The cabinet: or monthly report of polite literature. Vols 1–4, Feb–Mar 1807–Dec 1808.

The satirist, or monthly meteor. Vols 1–14, Oct 1807–June 1814.

The Belfast monthly magazine. Vols 1–13, Sep 1808–Dec 1814.

The London review. Vols 1–2, Feb–Nov 1809. Ed Richard Cumberland.

The poetical magazine. Vols 1–4, May 1809–Apr 1811. Prop and ed Rudolph Ackermann.

The Baptist magazine. Vols 1–96, Jan 1809–Dec 1904. Prop Baptist Missionary Society; William Groser 1838–56; Samuel Manning Jan 1857–1860. Ed William Groser 1838–56, D. Katterns, W. G. Lewis, C. H. Spurgeon 1861–?, W. G. Lewis 1866–80, J. P. Barnett 1881–4, Stephen A. Swaine 1886(?)–Mar 1889, James Stuart 1890–1904.

The Edinburgh Christian instructor. Vols 1–30, July 1810–Dec 1831. New ser, vols 1–4, Jan 1832–Dec 1835. New ser [3rd] vols 1–2, Jan 1836–Dec 1837. Continued as Edinburgh Christian instructor, and Colonial religious register, new ser [4th] vols 1–3, Jan 1838–Dec 1840. Ed Andrew Thomson 1810–30 (?), Marcus Dods 1831 (?)–35, Archibald Bennie 1835–7.

The British review and London critical journal. Vols 1–23, Mar 1811–Nov 1825. Ed William Roberts.

The scourge: or monthly expositor of imposture and folly. Vols 1–10, Jan 1811–Dec 1815.

The entertaining magazine: or repository of general knowledge. Vols 1–3, Jan 1813–Dec 1815.

The annals of philosophy: or magazine of chemistry, mineralogy, mechanics, natural history, agriculture and the arts. Vols 1–16, Jan 1813–Dec 1820. New ser, 12 vols Jan 1821–Dec 1826. Incorporated in Philosophical magazine. Ed Thomas Thomson 1813–20, Richard Phillips and Edward William Brayley 1821–6.

The new monthly magazine, and universal register. Vols 1–14, Jan 1814–Dec 1820. Continued as New monthly magazine and literary journal, vols 15–48, Jan 1821–Dec 1836. Continued as New monthly magazine and humourist, vols 49–149, Jan 1837–Dec 1871. Continued as New monthly magazine, new series, vols 1–15, Jan 1872–June 1879. New [3rd] ser, vols 1–5, July 1879–Dec 1881. Continued as New monthly, vols 6–7, Jan ? 1882–1884. Prop Henry Colburn and Frederic Shoberl 1814–June 1845; W. H. Ainsworth 1845–79; W. F. Ainsworth 1879–84. Ed Frederic Shoberl, vol 1 Feb 1814–?; Dr John Watkins, vols 1–10, Feb 1814–Dec 1818; Alaric Watts, vol 11 Jan 1819–May or June 1819; Thomas Campbell Jan 1821–Dec 1830 (assisted by Cyrus Redding 1821–Aug 1830 and Samuel Carter Hall Sep–Dec 1830), Samuel Carter Hall Jan–Oct 1831, E. G. Bulwer-Lytton Nov 1831–Aug 1833 (assisted by Samuel Carter Hall), Samuel Carter Hall Sep 1833–Dec 1836, Theodore Hook Jan 1837–Aug 1841, Thomas Hood Oct 1841–Sep 1843 (assisted by Frederic Shoberl), R. F. Williams, P. G. Patmore 1841–5(?), W. H. Ainsworth 1845–70, W. F. Ainsworth 1871–9. *See* Wellesley index vol 3 1979.

The Asiatic journal and monthly register for British India and its dependencies. Vols 1–28, Jan 1816–Dec 1829. Continued as Asiatic journal and monthly register for British and foreign India, China and Australasia, new ser, vols 1–40, Jan 1830–Apr 1843. Continued as Asiatic journal and monthly miscellany, 3rd ser, vols 1–4, May 1843–Apr 1845. Continued as Asiatic quarterly review, vol 1, Jan 1886 onwards. Ed D. Boulger.

Blackwood's Edinburgh magazine. Begun as Edinburgh monthly magazine, nos 1–6, Apr–Sep 1817. Continued as Blackwood's Edinburgh magazine, Oct 1817–Dec 1905. Continued as Blackwood's magazine, Jan 1906 onwards. Index: General index to vols 1–50. Edinburgh 1855. Prop Blackwood (with John Murray summer 1818–winter 1819). Ed Thomas Pringle and James Cleghorn Apr–Sep 1817, William Blackwood Oct 1817–Sep 1834, Alexander Blackwood Oct 1834–Apr 1845 (Robert Blackwood 1836–7 during Alexander's illness), John Blackwood May 1845–Oct 1879, William Blackwood III Nov 1879–?. *See* Wellesley index vol 1.

The new bon ton magazine: or telescope of the times. Vols 1–6, May 1818–Apr 1821.

The pocket magazine of classic and polite literature. Vols 1–13, Jan 1818–June (?) 1824. Continued as Arliss' pocket magazine of classic and polite literature, new ser, vols 1–5, July (?) 1824–1826. Continued as Pocket magazine. Robin's series, 4 vols Jan 1827–Dec 1828. Continued as Pocket magazine, [1829–31]–Jan 1832–1883.

The tickler: or monthly compendium of good things. Vols 1–6, no 6, Dec 1818–June 1824.

The Christian remembrancer: or the churchman's biblical, ecclesiastical and literary miscellany. Vols 1–22, Jan 1819–Dec 1840. Continued as Christian remembrancer: a monthly magazine and review, new series, vols 1–8, Jan 1841–Dec 1844. Continued as Christian remembrancer: a quarterly review, vols 9–56, Jan 1845–Oct 1868. Ed William Scott and Francis Garden 1841–4, William Scott and J. B. Mozley 1844–54, William Scott 1854–68.

The Edinburgh monthly review. Edinburgh. Vols 1–5, Jan 1819–June 1821. Continued as New Edinburgh review, vols 1–4, July 1821–Apr 1823.

The London magazine. Vols 1–10, Jan 1820–Dec 1824. New ser, vols 1–10, Jan 1825–Mar 1828. 3rd ser, vols 1–3, Apr 1828–June 1829. Prop Baldwin, Cradock and Joy Jan 1820–June 1821; John Taylor and James Hessey July 1821–Sep 1825; Henry Southern Sep 1825–Mar 1828; Charles Knight Apr 1828–June 1829. Ed John Scott 1820–Jan 1821, John Taylor July 1821–1824, Henry Southern July 1825–Mar 1828, Charles Knight Apr 1828–June 1829.

The Newcastle magazine. Sep 1820–July 1921. New ser, vols 1–10, Jan 1822–Mar 1831. Ed William Andrew Mitchell.

The drama: or theatrical pocket magazine. Vols 1–7, May 1821–May 1824. New ser 1 vol 1825.

The annals of sporting and fancy gazette. Vols 1–13, Jan 1822–June 1828.

The new European magazine. Vols 1–4, July 1822–June 1824.

The world of fashion and continental feuilletons. Vols 1–28, 1824–51. Continued as Ladies' monthly magazine. The world of fashion, vols 29–56, 1852–79. Continued as Le monde élégant, or the world of fashion, vols 57–68, 1880–91. Prop and ed John Browne Bell 1824–51.

The Newgate monthly magazine: or calendar of men, things and opinions. 2 vols Sep 1824–Aug 1826. Ed William Campion.
The oriental herald and colonial review. Vols 1–23, Jan 1824–Dec 1829. Ed J. S. Buckingham.
The Dublin and London magazine. Vols 1–2, Mar 1825–Dec 1826. Continued as Robins's London and Dublin magazine, 1 vol Jan–June 1827. Continued as Dublin and London magazine, Feb–June 1828. Suspended from July 1827–Feb 1828. Ed M. J. Whitty.
The gardener's magazine. Vols 1–19, Mar 1826–1832. Ed J. C. Loudon.
The united service journal, and naval and military magazine. Jan 1829–Dec 1841. Continued as United service magazine and naval and military journal, Jan 1842–Apr 1843. Continued as Colburn's united service magazine and naval and military journal. May 1843–Mar 1890. Continued as United service magazine, Apr 1890–June 1920. Incorporated in Army quarterly. Prop Henry Colburn.
The magazine of natural history, and journal of zoology, botany, mineralogy, geology and meteorology. Vols 1–9, May 1829–Dec 1836. New ser, vols 1–4, Jan 1837–Aug 1840. From vol 2, new ser, title became Magazine of natural history. Ed J. C. Loudon 1829–31, John Denison 1831–6, Edward Charlesworth 1837–40.
The British magazine. Vols 1–2, Jan–Dec 1830.
Fraser's magazine for town and country. Vols 1–80, Feb 1830–Dec 1869. New ser, vols 1–26, Jan 1870–Oct 1882. Replaced by Longman's magazine below. Prop J. Fraser Feb 1830–Dec 1841; G. W. Nickisson Jan 1842–June 1847; J. W. Parker and Son 1847–63; Longman's 1863–82. Ed William Maginn 1830–6 (assisted by John Heraud 1830–3), Francis Mahony 1836–7(?), George William Nickisson 1841–7, J. W. Parker II 1847–60, J. A. Froude 1860–74, William Allingham 1874–9, John Tulloch 1879–81. *See* Wellesley index vol 2 1972.
The national magazine. Vol 1, July–Dec 1830. Continued as National magazine and Dublin literary gazette, vol 2, Jan–Apr 1831(?). Begun weekly as Dublin literary gazette: or weekly chronicle of criticism, belles lettres, and fine arts, 2 Jan–26 June 1830. Ed S. Lover 1830, P. D. Hardy 1831.
Cobbett's twopenny trash: or politics for the poor. Vols 1–2, July 1830–July 1832. Prop and ed W. Cobbett.
The diamond magazine. 2 vols 1831–2.
The magazine of the beau monde. Vols 1–12, 1831–42.
The metropolitan: a monthly journal of literature, science and the fine arts. Vols 1–5, May 1831–Dec 1832. Continued as Metropolitan magazine, vols 6–57, Jan 1833–Apr 1850. Prop Thomas Campbell(?); F. Marryat; James Grant. Ed Thomas Campbell, F. Marryat 1832–5, James Grant.
The ladies' cabinet of fashion, music and romance. [1832]–vol 5, Jan 1834–vol 14, Dec 1838. New ser vols 1–10, Jan 1839–Dec 1843. [New ser] vol 1, Jan 1844 [vol 17, June 1852]. Continued as Ladies cabinet of fashion (incorporated with New monthly belle assemblée), new ser, vols 1–37, July 1852–Dec 1870. From Oct 1852 this is identical, except for title-pages, with New monthly belle assemblée and Ladies' companion. Ed Margaret and Beatrice de Courcy.
Tait's Edinburgh magazine. Vols 1–4, Apr 1832–Jan 1834. New ser, vols 1–27, Feb 1834–Jan 1861. New ser, 1 vol May 1861. Absorbed Johnstone's Edinburgh magazine June 1834. Prop William Tait 1832–4; William Tait and Christian Isobel Johnstone 1834–46; George Troup and Archibald Alison 1847–8?; George Troup 1848?–50; John Smith Mansfield and John Hosack May 1850–Nov 1855?; George Troup Dec 1855–Nov 1861. Ed William Tait 1832–4; Christian Isobel Johnstone (principal editor) and William Tait (managing editor) May 1834–Dec 1846; George Troup Jan 1847–Apr 1850; Horatio Mansfield May 1850–Nov 1855; George Troup Dec 1855–Sep 1861. *See* Wellesley index vol 4.
Chambers's historical newspaper, a monthly record of intelligence. Nos 1–39, Nov 1832–Jan 1836. Prop and ed R. and W. Chambers.
The Dublin University magazine. Vols 1–90, Jan 1833–Dec 1877. Continued as University magazine: a literary and philosophic review, vols 1–5, Jan 1878–June 1882. 2 further quarterly nos pbd Sep and Dec 1882. Prop Isaac Butt, W. A. Butler et al Jan 1833–June 1833; James M'Glashan July 1833–Dec 1855; Hurst & Blackett Jan 1856–Mar 1856; Digby Pilot Starkey and Cheyne Brady Apr–Oct 1856; Cheyne Brady Nov 1856–July 1861; J. S. Le Fanu July 1861–Mar 1870; Charles F. Adams Apr 1870–May 1873; Durham Dunlop June 1873–Nov or Dec 1877; Keningale Cook May–Dec 1877. University Magazine Keningale Cook Jan 1878–Dec 1880. Editors: Charles S. Stanford Jan 1833–July 1834, Isaac Butt Aug 1834–Nov 1838; James M'Glashan Dec 1838–Mar 1842; Charles Lever Apr 1842–May 1845; James M'Glashan June 1845; John F. Waller July 1845–Dec 1855; Durham Dunlop Jan 1856–Oct 1856; Cheyne Brady Nov 1856–June 1861; J. S. Le Fanu July 1861–June 1869; Charles F. Adams July 1869–May 1873; Durham Dunlop June 1873–June 1877; Keningale Cook July 1877–Dec 1877. University Magazine Keningale Cook Jan 1878–Dec 1880. *See* Wellesley index vol 4.
The companion to the newspaper; and journal of facts in politics, statistics and public economy. Vols 1–4, Mar 1833–Jan 1837. Under the superintendence of Society for the Diffusion of Political Knowledge. Ed Charles Knight.
The sportsman. Began weekly, vol 1, Aug 1833–May 1834. Continued monthly, vol 2, June 1834–Jan 1835. Continued as Sportsman and veterinary recorder, vols 1–3, Jan 1835–July 1836. Continued as Sportsman, new series, vols 1–6, July 1836–June 1839. 2nd series, vols 1–53, July 1839–Dec 1870. From July 1846 the vols of this periodical are identical, with the exception of the title-pages, with New sporting magazine, Sporting magazine and Sporting review.
The Christian lady's magazine. Vols 1–31, Jan 1834–June 1849. Ed Charlotte Elizabeth Tonna [formerly Phelan] 1834–46.
The architectural magazine and journal of improvement in architecture, building and furnishing, and in the various arts and trades connected therewith. Vols 1–5, Mar 1834–Jan 1839. Ed J. C. Loudon.
The family magazine. Vols 1–4, Aug 1834–Dec 1837. Incorporated in Ward's miscellany. Ed J. Belcher.
Blackwood's lady's magazine and gazette of the fashionable world. Vols 1–49 1836–60.
Bentley's miscellany. Vols 1–64, Jan 1837–Dec 1868. Prop Richard Bentley 1837–54; W. H. Ainsworth 1854–68. Ed Charles Dickens Jan 1837–Feb 1839, W. H. Ainsworth Mar 1839–Dec 1841, Richard Bentley Jan 1842–Nov 1854, W. H. Ainsworth Dec 1854–Dec 1868. *See* Wellesley index vol 4.
The magazine of zoology and botany. Began bi-monthly. Vols 1–2, Feb 1837–1838. Continued as Annals of natural history; or magazine of zoology, botany and geology, vols 1–5, Mar 1838–Aug 1840. Continued as Annals and magazine of natural history, including zoology, botany and geology (including Charlesworth's magazine of natural history), vols 6–20, Sep 1840–Dec 1847. 2nd series, vols 1–20 (including supplementary number, Jan 1858), Jan 1848–Dec 1857. 3rd series, vols 1–20, Jan 1858–Dec 1867. 4th series, Jan 1868–Dec 1877. 5th ser etc., Jan 1878 onwards.
The monthly chronicle: a national journal of politics, literature, science and art. Vols 1–7, March 1838–June 1841. Prop D. Lardner and Bulwer Lytton. Ed D. Lardner, Bulwer Lytton and Robert Bell.
The servant's magazine, under the superintendence of Committee of the London Female Mission. Vols 1–3, Apr(?) 1838–1840. Continued as Servants' magazine, or female domestics' instructor, vols 4–25, 1841–Dec 1862. New ser, vols 1–4, Jan 1863–Dec 1866. Continued as Servants' magazine; or, the friend of the household workers, vols 1–3, Jan 1867–Dec 1869.

The Wesleyan Methodist Association magazine. Vols 1–20, [1838]–Dec 1857. Continued as United Methodist Free Churches' magazine, new ser, vols 1–34, Jan 1858–Dec 1891. Continued as Methodist monthly, new ser, vols 1–16, Jan 1892–Dec 1907. Ed M. Miller 1872–7, J. S. Withington.

The art-union. A monthly journal of the fine arts. Vol 1–5, Feb 1839–Dec 1843. Continued as Art-union, monthly journal of the fine arts, and the arts decorative and ornamental, vols 6–9, Jan 1844–Nov(?) 1847. Continued as Art-union monthly journal of the arts, vol 10, Jan–Nov 1848. Continued as Art-journal, vols 11–74, Jan 1849–Feb 1912. Prop Samuel Carter Hall 1839–51. Ed Samuel Carter Hall 1839–80, Marcus Huish.

The sporting review: a monthly chronicle of the turf, the chase and rural sports in all their varieties. Vols 1–54, Jan 1839–Dec 1870. From 1845 the vols of this periodical are identical, except for the title-pages, with New sporting magazine and Sportsman. Ed 'Craven' (John William Carleton).

Peter Parley's magazine. Vols 1–23(?), Jan 1840–Mar 1863.

The colonial magazine and commercial-maritime journal. Vols 1–8, 1840–June 1842. Ed Robert M. Martin.

Bradshaw's Manchester journal. Began weekly vol 1, May–Oct 1841. Continued as Bradshaw's journal: a miscellany of literature, science and art, vols 2–3, Nov 1841–Oct 1842. Continued as Bradshaw's journal: a monthly miscellany of literature etc., vol 4, Dec 1842–May 1843. Ed George Falkner Dec 1842–May 1843.

The north of England magazine: a monthly journal of politics, literature, science and art. Vols 1–2, Feb 1842–May 1843. Continued as North of England magazine, and Bradshaw's journal of politics, literature, science and art, vol 3, June–Sep 1843.

Magazine for the young. Vols 1–34, Jan 1842–Dec 1875. Ed John and Charles Mozley.

Ainsworth's magazine. Vols 1–26, Feb 1842–Dec 1854. Prop W. H. Ainsworth Feb 1842–Oct 1843; J. Mortimer Oct 1843–1845; W. H. Ainsworth 1845–Dec 1854. Ed W. H. Ainsworth Feb 1842–June 1845; F. Mahoney and J. Mortimer July–Nov 1845; W. H. Ainsworth Dec 1845–Dec 1854. *See* Wellesley index vol 3 1979.

The illuminated magazine. Vols 1–4, May 1843–Apr 1845. New ser, 1 vol (7 nos), 1845. Prop Ebenezer Landells. Ed Douglas Jerrold 1843–5, W. J. Linton 1845.

Tegg's magazine of knowledge and amusement. Vol 1, nos 1–12, May 1843–Apr 1844.

The English journal of education. Vols 1–4, Jan 1843–Dec 1846. New ser, Jan 1847–Feb 1864. Incorporated in Museum. Ed H. Moody 1843–7.

The national temperance chronicle. July 1843–Dec 1850. New ser, vols 1–4, July 1851–Dec 1856. Organ of National Temperance Society. Ed Thomas Spencer July 1851–Feb 1853.

Hood's magazine and comic miscellany. Vols 1–3, Jan 1844–June 1845. Continued as Hood's magazine, vols 4–10, July 1845–Dec 1848. Continued as Hood's magazine and literary scientific and dramatic journal, new ser, vol 1, Jan 1849. Ed Thomas Hood.

Simmonds's colonial magazine and foreign miscellany. Vols 1–15, Jan 1844–Dec 1848. Continued as Colonial magazine and East India review, vols 16–23, Jan 1849–June 1852. Continued as Colonial and Asiatic review, [new series], vols 1–2, July 1852–June 1853. Ed P. L. Simmonds 1844–8, W. H. G. Kingston 1849–52.

The Wesleyan juvenile offering: a miscellany of missionary information for young persons. Vols 1–23, Jan 1844–Dec 1866. New series, vols 1–12, Jan 1867–Dec 1878.

The musical times and singing class circular. June 1844–Dec 1902. Continued as Musical times, Jan 1903 onwards. Between Feb 1854 and July 1855, fortnightly.

Wade's London review: a critical journal and magazine. Vols 1–3, 16 nos Oct 1844(?)–Jan 1846. Ed T. Wade.

The British mothers' magazine. Vols 1–11, Jan 1845–Dec 1855. Continued as British mothers' journal, Jan 1856–Dec 1859. Continued as British mothers' journal and domestic magazine, 1860–Dec 1863. Continued as British mothers' family magazine, Jan–Dec 1864. Ed Mrs J. Bakewell.

Douglas Jerrold's shilling magazine. Vols 1–7, Jan 1845–June 1848. Prop and ed Douglas Jerrold.

Hogg's weekly instructor. [Vol 1, 1845]–vol 2, Aug 1845–21 Feb 1846. New series, vols 1–2, 1848–9. Continued as Hogg's instructor, vols 3–10, 1849–53. New series, vols 1–6, July 1853–June 1856. Continued as Titan, a monthly magazine. Conjoined series, vols 23–9, 1856–9.

The Oxford and Cambridge review. Vols 1–5, July 1845–Dec 1847.

Sharpe's London magazine: a journal of entertainment and instruction for general reading. Began weekly, 1 Nov 1845–vol 5 (no 113), 24 Dec 1847. Monthly, vols 5–8, Jan 1848–Feb 1849. Continued as Sharpe's London journal of entertainment and instruction, vols 9–15, Mar 1849–June 1852. Continued as Sharpe's London magazine of entertainment and instruction for general reading, new ser, vols 1–37, July 1852–Dec 1870. From 1858, this is identical, except for the title-pages, with Ladies' companion, New monthly belle assemblée, Ladies' cabinet and Illustrated London magazine. Prop Bethel Henry Strousberg. Ed 'Frank Fairlegh' (Francis E. Smedley) 1847–52, Mrs S. C. Hall 1852–3, Bethel Henry Strousberg 1854, Alfred W. Cole.

The almanack of the month: a review of everything and everybody. Vols 1–2, Jan–Dec 1846. Ed Gilbert à Beckett.

The labourer: a monthly magazine of politics, literature, poetry etc. Vols 1–4, 1847–8. Ed Feargus O'Connor and Ernest Jones.

The rambler: a journal of home and foreign literature, politics, science, music and the fine arts. Began weekly Jan–Aug (?) 1848. Continued monthly, vols 3–12, Sep 1848–Dec 1853. New series, vols 1–11, Jan 1854–Feb 1859. New ser, bi-monthly, vols 1–6, May 1859–May 1862. Continued as Home and foreign review. *See below, under quarterlies.* Prop John Moore Capes 1848–57; Richard Simpson, Frederick Capes and John Acton 1858–62. Ed John Moore Capes 1848–52, James Spencer Northcote 1852–4, John Moore Capes 1854–Oct 1857, Richard Simpson Nov 1857–Feb 1859, John Henry Newman Mar–July 1859, John Acton Sep 1859–May 1862. *See* Wellesley index vol 1 1968.

The democratic review. June 1849–Sep 1850. Ed G. J. Harney.

The ladies' companion at home and abroad. Vols 1–2, 29 Dec 1849–25 Dec 1850 (weekly). Continued monthly as Ladies' companion and monthly magazine, Feb 1951–Dec 1852–1870. From Oct 1852, this is identical, except for the title-pages, with Ladies' cabinet and New monthly belle assemblée. Ed Mrs Loudon 1850–1.

The household narrative of current events ('for the year 1850' etc.): being a monthly supplement to Household words. Vols 1–6, Jan 1850–Dec 1855. Prop C. Dickens and Bradbury and Evans. Ed C. Dickens.

The germ: thoughts towards nature in poetry, literature and art. Nos 1 & 2, Jan & Feb 1850. Continued as Art and poetry: being thoughts towards nature conducted principally by artists, nos 3 & 4, Mar & May 1850; rptd Portland ME 1898; ed W. M. Rossetti 1901 (facs).

Papers for the schoolmaster. Mar 1851–Dec 1864. New series, vols 1–7, Jan 1864–Dec 1871. Succeeded by Schoolmaster (organ of the National Union of Teachers) 6 Jan 1872 onwards. Now Teacher. Ed C. H. Bromby.

The gentleman's herald of fashion: containing all the newest French and English costumes with models and patterns. Oct 1851–Sep 1862.

The monthly packet of evening readings for the young members of the English church. Vols 1–30, Jan 1851–Dec 1865. Continued as Monthly packet of evening readings for the members of the English church, new series, vols 1–30, Jan 1866–Dec 1880. 3rd series, vols 1–20, Jan 1881–Dec 1890. 4th series, vols 1–17, Jan

1891–June 1899. Ed Charlotte M. Yonge 1871–91, Christabel R. Coleridge 1891–?, Arthur Innes.

The American magazine. Oct 1851–Feb 1852. Ed H. H. Paul.

The leisure hour: a family journal of instruction and recreation. Began weekly, Jan 1852–Dec 1880. Continued monthly, 1881–Oct 1905. Index to first 25 vols, 1852–76, [1878]. Ed W. H. Miller 1852–8, James Macaulay 1858–95, William Stevens 1895–1900.

Chambers's pocket miscellany. Edinburgh. Vols 1–24, 1852–3.

The Englishwoman's domestic magazine. 8 vols 1852–[9]. New series, 9 vols [1860–4]. New series, 25 vols [1865–77]. Continued as Illustrated household journal and Englishwoman's domestic magazine, 3 vols [1880–1]. Incorporated in Milliner, dressmaker and draper.

The charm: a magazine for boys and girls. May 1852–Apr 1854.

Chambers's repository of instructive and amusing tracts. Edinburgh. Vols 1–12, 1853–4.

Bentley's monthly review: or literary argus. 1 vol May 1853–Apr 1854. Continued as Bentley's monthly review, new series, May–June 1854. Continued as New monthly review, vol 1, July–Oct 1854.

The illustrated London magazine: a monthly journal. Vols 1–4, July 1853–1855. New series, vols 1–30, 1856–1870. From 1857, this is identical, except for the title-pages, with Ladies' companion, New monthly belle assemblée and Ladies' cabinet. Ed R. B. Knowles 1853–5.

The free press. Sheffield. Vols 1–14, 13 Oct 1855–June 1866. Continued as Diplomatic review vol 14 (no 6)–25 July 1866–Jan 1877. Frequency varies: began weekly, Oct 1855–Mar 1858; continued bi-weekly, Apr–May 1858; continued monthly, June 1858–July 1870; continued quarterly, Oct 1870–Jan 1877. Beginning Jan 1866 there were 2 edns, one entirely in English, the other including material in French. Ed D. Urquhart.

The boy's own magazine. Vols 1–8, Jan 1855–Dec 1862.

The national magazine. Vols 1–15, Nov 1856–May 1864. Ed John Saunders and John Westland Marston.

The train. Jan 1856–Jan 1858. Ed Edmund Yates.

Gossip for the garden, a handbook for the florist and suburban horticulturist. Vols 1–8, Mar 1856–Dec 1863. Ed E. S. Dodwell, J. Edwards, W. Dean, John Sladden.

The ladies' treasury: an illustrated magazine of entertaining literature, education, fine art, domestic economy etc. Vols 1–9, Apr 1857–Dec 1865. New ser, Jan 1866–1895. Ed Mrs Warren.

The Englishwoman's review and drawing-room journal of social progress, literature and art. Vol 1, Mar–Aug 1857. New series, vols 1–2, Sep 1857–Sep 1859.

The Englishwoman's journal. Vols 1–3, Mar 1858–Aug 1859.

The geologist: a popular monthly magazine of geology. Vols 1–7, Jan 1858–June 1864. Ed S. J. Mackie.

Macmillan's magazine. Cambridge and London. Vols 1–59, Nov 1859–Oct 1907. Prop Macmillan. Ed David Masson Nov 1859–Apr 1868, George Grove May 1868–Apr 1883, John Morley May 1883–Sep 1885, Mowbray Morris Oct 1885–1907. *See* Wellesley index vol 1 1968.

The what-not: or, ladies' handy-book and monthly magazine of literature. 1859–66.

The Cornhill magazine. Jan 1860–Dec 1939. Resumed Jan 1944–1946. Continued quarterly 1947 onwards. Prop George Murray Smith 1860–1901. Ed W. M. Thackeray Jan 1860–May 1862, Frederick Greenwood and G. H. Lewes and George Murray Smith 1862–4(?), Frederick Greenwood and George Murray Smith 1864(?)–8(?), Edward Dutton Cook and G. H. Lewes and George Murray Smith 1868(?)–Mar 1871, Leslie Stephen Apr 1871–Dec 1882, James Payn Jan 1883–June 1896, J. St Loe Strachey July 1896–Dec 1897, Reginald John Smith Jan 1898–Dec 1916. *See* Wellesley index vol 1.

Good words. Edinburgh. Jan 1860–Apr 1906. Amalgamated with Sunday magazine and continued weekly, May 1906–10 and pbd in London. Prop Alexander Strahan. Ed Norman Macleod, Donald Macleod.

Temple Bar: a London magazine for town and country readers. Vols 1–132, Dec 1860–Dec 1905. New series, vols 1–2, Jan–Dec 1906. Index: Alphabetical list of the titles of all articles appearing in the previous 99 vols, vol 100, Apr 1894. Prop George Sala 1860–6; Richard and George Bentley 1866–95; Richard Bentley II 1895–8, Macmillan 1898–1906. Ed George Sala Dec 1860–Nov 1863, Edmund Yates Dec 1863–Sep or Oct 1867, George Bentley Oct or Nov 1867–May 1895; Richard Bentley II June 1895–Aug 1898; Gertrude Townshend Mayer Sep 1898–Dec 1900?.

Duffy's Hibernian magazine: a monthly journal of literature, science and art. Vols 1–3, July 1860–Dec 1861. Continued as Duffy's Hibernian sixpenny magazine, new series, vols 1–5, Jan 1862–June 1864. Continued as Hibernian magazine, 3rd series, vol 1, July 1864.

Once a month: original tales by the most popular authors. Nos 1–14, 1861–2. New series, nos 15–17, 1862.

The quiver. Nos 1–6, Sep 1861–Sep 1864. New series, vols 1–2, Oct 1864–Oct 1865. New series, 1866–June 1956. Prop Cassell 1861–1926. Ed John Cassell, C. H. H. Wright, John Willis Clark 1864, Thomas T. Shore 1865, H. G. Bonavia Hunt 1865–1905.

The sixpenny magazine: a miscellany for all classes and seasons. Vols 1–14, July 1861–May 1867. New series, vols 1–2, June 1867–Mar 1868.

The St James's magazine. Vols 1–21, Apr 1861–Mar 1868. New series, Apr 1868–[1882]. Prop John Maxwell. Ed Mrs S. C. Hall 1861–2, Mrs Braddon, Mrs J. H. Riddell, Edward Walford 1870, W. J. Morgan.

The Victoria magazine. 1863–vol 28, Dec 1876–[1880]. Ed Emily Faithfull.

The month: an illustrated magazine of literature, science and art. Vols 1–11, July 1864–Dec 1869. New ser, vols 12 (new ser)–186, Jan 1870–Dec 1948. New ser, vol 1, Jan 1949 onwards. Issued twice monthly 1871–3, resumed monthly 1874 as Month and Catholic review, 1874–81; continued as Month, a Catholic magazine and review, 1882–90; continued as Month, a Catholic magazine 1890–1913; continued as Month 1914 onwards. Index 1864–1908. 1909. Prop Frances Taylor 1864–June 1865; Society of Jesus 1865 onwards. Ed Frances Taylor 1864–5, Henry J. Coleridge 1865–81, Richard F. Clarke 1882–Feb 1894, John Gerard 1894–97, Sidney F. Smith 1897–1901.

The shilling magazine. Illustrated: a miscellany of literature, social science, fiction, poetry etc. Vols 1–4, May 1865–[7]. Ed S. Lucas.

The fortnightly review. No 1, 15 May 1865–Dec 1954. Incorporated in Contemporary review. Pbd twice monthly to no 35, 15 Oct 1866. Thereafter monthly. Prop Chapman and Hall. Ed G. H. Lewes 1865–6, John Morley 1867–82, T. H. S. Escott 1882–6, Frank Harris 1886–94, W. L. Courtney 1894–1928. *See* Wellesley index vol 2.

The argosy, a magazine of tales, travels, essays and poems. Vols 1–75, Dec 1865–Dec 1901. Prop Mrs Henry Wood 1867–87. Ed Mrs Henry Wood 1865–June 1887, Charles W. Wood July 1887–?.

The young Englishwoman: a magazine of fiction and fashions. Vols 1–4, 1865–6. New series, 3 vols 1867–9. New series 8 vols 1870–7. Continued as Sylvia's home journal. 14 vols 1878–91. Continued as Sylvia's journal, 3 vols 1892–4. Prop Samuel Orchart Beeton. Ed John Tillotson.

Merry and wise: a magazine for young people edited by Old Merry. Vols 1–5, Jan 1865–Dec 1869. New series, vols 1–2, Jan 1870–Dec 1871. Continued as Old Merry's monthly, Jan–Dec 1872.

Gilead. Vols 1–7, June 1865–Dec 1876. Continued as Wayside words, vols 8–35, Jan 1877–Dec 1904. Ed T. H. Gregg 1865–Dec 1872, F. Harper Jan 1873–1904.

The contemporary review. Jan 1866 onwards. Prop Alexander Strahan 1866–Jan 1877; 'Strahan and Co Ltd' (Samuel Morley,

Francis Peek, John Paton Brown) Feb 1877–?. Ed Henry Alford Jan 1866–Mar 1870, James Thomas Knowles Apr 1870–Jan 1877, Alexander Strahan Feb 1877–1882, Percy William Bunting 1882–1911 (John Paton Brown 'consulting editor' 1882–8). *See* Wellesley index vol 1.

Belgravia. Nov 1866–June 1899. Prop John Maxwell. Ed M. E. Braddon. 1866–93.

The Englishwoman's review: a journal of woman's work. Began quarterly, Oct 1866–July 1869. New series, Jan 1870–Dec 1875. Continued monthly at least by Jan–Dec 1876. Continued as Englishwoman's review of social and industrial questions, Jan 1877–July 1910. Ed Jessie Boucherett, C. A. Biggs, Helen Blackburn.

Aunt Judy's magazine. Vols 1–19, May 1866–Oct 1881. New ser, vols 1–4, Nov 1881–Oct 1885. Ed Mrs Alfred Gatty 1866–73, H. K. F. Gatty and J. H. Ewing 1873–6, H. K. F. Gatty 1877–85.

Tinsley's magazine. Vols 1–42, Aug 1867–May 1889. New series, vols 43–8, June 1889–Mar 1892. Continued as Novel review: with which is incorporated Tinsley's magazine, 1 vol 1892. Ed Edmund Yates 1867–9.

The St Pauls: a monthly magazine. Vols 1–14, Oct 1867–March 1874. Prop James S. Virtue Oct 1867–May 1869; Alexander Strahan June 1869–Oct 1872; Henry S. King Nov 1872–Mar 1874. Ed A. Trollope Oct 1867–July 1870; Alexander Strahan Aug 1870–Oct 1872; Henry S. King Nov 1872–Mar 1874. *See* Wellesley index vol 3 1979.

The Broadway annual. Vol 1, Sep 1867–Aug 1868. Continued as Broadway, new series, vols 1–4, Sep 1868–July 1870. New series, vols 1–5, Aug 1870–Dec 1872.

Once a month: a monthly magazine of general and amusing literature. Vols 1–2, Nov 1868–Dec 1869. Continued as Once a month: a London magazine of romance, literature, politics, music and the drama, new series, vol 1, Jan 1871. Continued as Once a month: an illustrated magazine of romance, general literature etc. New series, vols 1–2, Mar 1872–Aug 1873. Ed Joseph Collins 1872–3.

The portfolio: an artistic periodical. Jan 1870–Dec 1893. 3rd series, vols 1–48, 1894–1907. Ed P. G. Hemerton.

Cope's tobacco plant: a monthly periodical interesting to the manufacturer, the dealer and the smoker. Liverpool. Mar 1870–Jan 1881. Ed John Fraser.

National Society for Women's Suffrage journal. Manchester. Vol 1, nos 1–6, Mar–Aug 1870. Continued as Women's suffrage journal, vol 1, no 7–vol 21, Sep 1870–June 1890. Ed Lydia E. Becker.

The traveller: an international monthly of real estate, agriculture, mineral, financial, educational, statistical, market and general reports in Great Britain and the United States. Birmingham. Vols 1–2, Apr 1871–Nov 1872.

The transatlantic: a magazine of American periodical literature conducted by the editor of 'The Anglo-American times'. Vols 1–4, Aug 1872–Aug 1875.

The Irish monthly magazine. Vols 1–2, July 1873–Nov 1874. Continued as Irish monthly, vols 3–83, Dec 1874–Sep 1954. Ed Father Matthew Russell.

The British architect: a national record of the aesthetic and constructive arts; and business journal of the building community. Vols 1–88, Jan 1874–Apr 1919. Incorporated in Builder.

The Argonaut: a monthly magazine. Vols 1–7, no 50, Jan 1874–1878. Ed George Gladstone 1874–7, Edwin Paxton Hood 1877–8.

Cassell's family magazine. Dec 1874–Nov 1897. Continued as Cassell's magazine, Dec 1897–Mar 1912. Continued as Cassell's magazine of fiction (and popular literature), Apr 1912–June 1919. Continued as Cassell's (magazine), July 1919–Dec 1932. Incorporated in Story-teller. Began weekly, 1853. *See col 000, above.* Prop Cassell. Ed H. G. Bonavia Hunt 1874–96, Max Pemberton 1896.

The Celtic magazine: a monthly periodical devoted to the literature, history, antiquities of the Celt at home and abroad. Inverness. Vols 1–13, Nov 1875–Oct 1888. Ed Alexander Mackenzie and Alexander Macgregor 1875–6, Alexander Mackenzie 1876–86, Alexander Macbain 1886–8.

The poet's magazine. Vols 1–6, 1876–9. Continued as Lloyd's magazine, with which is incorporated the poet's magazine, vols 7–11, 1879–81. Continued as Authors and artists, 1881. Continued as Lloyd's London magazine, 1882–6. Continued quarterly as Lloyd's quarterly magazine, 1886–8. Continued as Modern poets, 1892–4. Continued as Modern authors, 1895. Continued as Lloyd's magazine, 1895–June 1900. Ed L. Lloyd.

The quaver, with which is published 'Choral harmony'. Vols 1–6, Jan 1876–Mar 1885.

The nineteenth century. Vols 1–48, Mar 1877–Dec 1900. Continued as Nineteenth century and after, Jan 1901–Dec 1950. Continued as Twentieth century, Jan 1951 onwards. Index: Catalogue of contributors and contributions. 1877–1901. By James Knowles [1904]. Ed and prop James T. Knowles Mar 1877–1900. *See* Wellesley index vol 2 1972.

The theatre: a weekly critical review. 3 vols 1877–8. Continued as Theatre: a monthly review and magazine, new series, vols 1–3, Aug 1878–1879. New series, 6 vols, 1880–2. New series, 30 vols, 1883–Dec 1907. Ed Clement Scott 1880–9, B. E. J. Capes 1890, B. E. J. Capes and Charles Eglington 1891–2, Charles Eglington 1893, Addison Bright 1894–7.

The welcome hour: an illustrated monthly magazine. [1877]–vol 2, no 7, Jan 1878–vol 17, Sep? 1893. Ed Percy Russell 1891–3.

The magazine of art illustrated. Vols 1–25, May 1878–Oct 1902. New series, vols 1–2, Nov 1902–July 1904. Prop Cassell. Ed Arthur Trendell 1878–80, Eric Robertson 1880–1, W. E. Henley Oct 1881–Aug 1886, Sidney Galpin 1886, M. H. Spielmann 1887–1904.

Time: a monthly miscellany of interesting and amusing literature. Vol 1, Apr 1879–[1891]. Ed Edmund Yates 1879–81, E. M. Abdy Williams 1885–6, Walter Sichel 1888–9, E. B. Bax 1890–1.

Modern thought. Vols 1–6, Feb 1879–Jan 1884. Ed J. Westby-Gibson.

The biograph and review. Vols 1–6, Jan 1879–Dec 1881. New series, vol 1, Jan 1882–June 1882. Ed 'Guy Roslyn' (Joshua Hatton).

Celebrities of the day: British and foreign. Vols 1–3, Apr 1881–Dec 1882. Ed S. E. Thomas.

The national Temperance mirror. Vols 1–27, Jan 1881–Apr 1907.

Longman's magazine. Vols 1–46. Nov 1882–Oct 1905. Successor to Fraser's magazine. Prop Longman. Ed Charles J. Longman. *See* Wellesley index vol 4.

The English illustrated magazine. Vols 1–49, Oct 1883–Aug 1913. Prop Macmillan 1882–93; William Ingram. Ed J. W. Comyns Carr, C. Kinloch Cooke, Clement Shorter and William Ingram 1893–1900.

The national review. Vols 1–34, Mar 1883–May 1950. Continued as National and English review, vols 135–154, June 1950–June 1960. Prop Alfred Austin Mar 1883–July 1893; Leopold James Maxse 1893–1932. Ed Alfred Austin and W. J. Courthope Mar 1883–Aug 1887; Alfred Austin Sep 1887–July 1893; Leopold James Maxse 1893–1929. *See* Wellesley index vol 2 1972.

Merry England: an illustrated magazine. Vols 1–24, May 1883–Mar 1895. Ed Wilfred Meynell.

Progress: a monthly magazine of advanced thought. Vols 1–7, Jan 1883–Dec 1887. Ed G. W. Foote.

Eastward Ho! Vols 1–7, May 1884–Apr 1888. Ed Freeman Wills.

The monthly magazine of fiction. Nos 1–504, [1885–1927]. Continued as Magazine of fiction, series nos 505–22, [1927–8]. Continued as Magazine of fiction and complete story teller, nos 523–60, [1928–31]. Continued as Magazine of fiction: the complete story teller monthly, nos 561–79, [1931–3]. Continued as Complete story-teller etc., nos 580–673, [1933–41].

The lady's world: a magazine of fiction and society. 1 vol Nov 1886–Oct 1887. Continued as Woman's world, vols 1–3, Nov 1887–Oct 1890. Ed Oscar Wilde Nov 1887–autumn 1889.

Murray's magazine: a home and colonial periodical. Vols 1–2,

Jan–Dec 1887. Continued as Murray's magazine: a home and colonial periodical for the general reader, vols 3–10, Jan 1888–Dec 1891. Prop John Murray. Ed Edward Arnold.

Scottish notes and queries (Aberdeen). Vols 1–12, June 1887–June 1899. 2nd series, vols 1–8, July 1889–June 1907. 3rd series, vols 1–13, Jan 1923–Dec 1935. General index to 1st series 1887–1899. 1901. Ed John Bulloch.

Atalanta. [For girls.] Vols 1–11, Oct 1887–Sep 1898. Ed L. T. Meade and Alicia A. Leith 1887–8, L. T. Meade and John C. Staples 1888–91 (?), L. T. Meade 1891 (?)–2, L. T. Meade and A. B. Symington 1892–3, A. B. Symington 1893–6, Edwin Oliver 1896–8.

Beeton's boy's own magazine. [1888]–new series, vols 1–6, Dec 1888–Nov 1890. Ed G. A. Henty.

Lucifer: a theosophical monthly. Vols 1–11, 1887–97. Continued as Theosophical review, 11 vols 1897–1907. Ed H. P. Blavatsky, Mabel Collins, Annie Besant, G. R. S. Mead.

The universal review. Vols 1–8, May 1888–Dec 1890. Ed H. Quilter.

Art and letters; an illustrated review. 8 vols, Jan 1888–Dec 1889. English edn of Les lettres et les arts. Ed Frédéric Masson.

The new review. Vols 1–17, June 1889–Dec 1897. Ed Archibald Grove 1889–94, W. E. Henley Jan 1895–1897. *See* Wellesley index vol 3 1979.

The Newbery House magazine: a monthly review for churchmen and churchwomen. Vols 1–11, July 1889–Dec 1894.

The expository times. Oct 1889 onwards. Index to vols 1–20, 1889–1909. By James Donald. [1910.] Prop and ed James Hastings.

The monthly record of eminent men. Vols 1–4, Jan 1890–Dec 1891. Ed George Potter.

The review of reviews. Vols 1–87, Jan 1890–Feb 1936. Continued as World review of reviews, 1 vol, Mar–Aug 1936. Continued as World review, Sep 1936–May 1953. Prop George Newnes and W. T. Stead Jan–Apr 1890; W. T. Stead Apr 1890–1912. Ed W. T. Stead 1890–1912.

Lambert's monthly. Vols 1–2, Jan 1890–May 1891. Ed G. E. Campbell.

The author. Vols 1–29, May 1890–Apr 1919. Continued quarterly, vol 29, July 1919 onwards. Organ of the Incorporated Society of Authors. Ed Walter Besant 1890–1901.

The King's own: a monthly magazine for the study and the home. Vols 1–9, Jan 1890–Oct 1898. Prop and ed John Urquhart.

The Strand magazine: an illustrated monthly. Jan 1891–Mar 1950. Incorporated in Men only. Prop George Newnes. Ed George Newnes 1891–?, H. Greenough Smith.

The Ludgate monthly. Vols 1–6, May 1891–Jan 1894. Continued as Ludgate illustrated magazine, vols 6–9, Feb 1894–Oct 1895. Continued as Ludgate, new series, vols 1–11, Nov 1895–Feb 1901. Ed Phil May 1891–?, A. M. De Beck.

The bookman: a monthly journal for book readers. Vols 1–87, Oct 1891–Dec 1934. Amalgamated with London Mercury. Ed William Robertson Nicoll (assisted by Ernest Hodder-Williams 1899–1903).

The idler magazine. Vols 1–38, Feb 1892–Mar 1911. Prop Robert Barr and J. K. Jerome. Ed J. K. Jerome and Robert Barr Feb 1892–July 1894, J. K. Jerome Aug 1894–Nov 1897, Arthur Lawrence and S. H. Sime May 1899–Jan 1900, S. H. Sime Sep 1900–Jan 1901.

The Albemarle. Vols 1–2, Jan–Sep 1892. Ed Hubert Crackanthorpe and W. H. Wilkins.

The butterfly. Nos 1–10, May 1893–1894. New series, nos 1–12, 1899–1900. Ed L. Raven-Hill and Arnold Golsworthy.

The studio. Vol 1, Apr 1893 onwards. Index: General index to the first 21 vols, 1893–1901. 1911. Prop Charles Holme. Ed J. Gleeson White 1893, Charles Holme, C. Geoffrey Holme.

The Pall Mall magazine. Vols 1–54, May 1893–Sep 1914. New series, vols 1–5, May 1927–Sep 1929. From Oct 1914 to Apr 1927, and again from Oct 1929 to Sep 1937 amalgamated with Nash's magazine as Nash's and Pall Mall magazine. Incorporated in Good housekeeping. Prop William Waldorf Astor 1893–1910 (?). Ed Douglas Straight and Frederic Hamilton 1893–6, Frederic Hamilton 1896–1900.

The free review: a monthly magazine. Vols 1–7, Oct 1893–Mar 1897. Continued as University magazine and free review, vols 8–10, Apr 1897–Sep 1898. Ed John M. Robertson 1893–5, G. Astor Singer 1896–Mar 1897, 'Democritus' (George Bedborough?) 1897.

The Positivist review. Vols 1–31, Jan 1893–Dec 1923. Continued as Humanity, vols 32–3, Jan 1924–Dec 1925. Ed E. S. Beesly 1893–1900.

The Bohemian, a monthly magazine and review of literature, drama and art. Vols 1–6, June 1893–Oct 1899. Ed S. L. Bensusan 1893–June 1894(?), Charles W. Forward, H. S. Muller.

The Englishwoman. An illustrated magazine. Vols 1–10, Mar 1895–Dec 1899. Ed E. Hepworth Dixon.

The Windsor magazine. Vols 1–90, Jan 1895–Sep 1939. Ed David Williamson.

The Savoy. Nos 1–2, Jan and Apr 1896 (quarterly). Continued monthly, nos 3–8, July–Dec 1896. Prop Leonard Smithers. Ed Arthur Symons.

The architectural review for the artist and craftsman. Magazine issue of Builder's journal. July 1896 onwards.

The Temple magazine. Vols 1–3, Oct 1896–Sep 1899. Continued as Temple magazine for home and sundry reading, vol 4, Oct 1899–Sep 1900. Ed Frederick A. Atkins 1896–8, John Foster Fraser 1899–1900.

To-morrow: a monthly review. Vols 1–5, no 1, Jan 1896–Jan 1898. Ed J. T. Grein.

Pearson's magazine. Vols 1–88, 1896–Nov 1939. Prop C. A. Pearson.

The new century review. Vols 1–8, Jan 1897–Dec 1900. Ed Douglas Story Aug–Dec 1900.

The railway magazine. July 1897 onwards.

The royal magazine. Vols 1–44, Nov 1898–Nov 1930. Continued as New royal magazine, vols 1–2, Dec 1930–May 1932. Continued as Royal pictorial, vols 2–4, June 1932–Dec 1934. Continued as Royal screen pictorial, 1 vol, Jan–June 1935. Continued as Screen pictorial, July 1935–Sep 1939. Ed Peter Keary.

The wide world magazine. Vols 1–135, Apr 1898–Dec 1965. Incorporated in Geographical magazine. Prop George Newnes. Ed W. Fitzgerald.

The girl's realm. Vols 1–17, Nov 1898–Nov 1915.

The Harmsworth monthly pictorial magazine. Vols 1–4, July 1898–July 1900. Continued as Harmsworth magazine, vols 5–6, Aug 1900–July 1901. Continued as Harmsworth London magazine, vols 7–10, Aug 1901–July 1903. Continued as London magazine, vols 11–65, Aug 1903–Oct 1930. Continued as New London magazine, new series, vols 1–6, Nov 1930–May 1933. Incorporated in Story-teller.

The British Empire review. July 1899–Sep 1939.

The monthly review. Vols 1–27, Oct 1900–June 1907. Ed H. Newbolt 1900–7.

The imperial and colonial magazine and review illustrated. Vols 1–3, Nov 1900–[May] 1901. Ed 'Celt' and E. F. Benson.

(2) QUARTERLY MAGAZINES

The Edinburgh review: or critical journal. Edinburgh. Vol 1, Oct 1802–Oct 1929. Indexes: R. Ryland, vols 1–27, Oct 1802–Nov 1812, Edinburgh 1813; vols 28–50, Apr 1813–Jan 1830, Edinburgh 1832; vols 51–80, Apr 1830–Oct 1844, 1850; vols 81–110, Jan 1845–Oct 1859, 1862; vols 111–140, Jan 1860–Oct 1874, 1876. Prop Constable 1802–26; Longman 1826–1929. Ed Sydney Smith Oct 1802, Francis Jeffrey Jan 1803–June 1829, Macvey Napier Oct 1829–Jan 1847, William Empson Apr 1847–Oct 1852, George C. Lewis Jan 1853–Jan 1855, George C. Lewis and Henry Reeve Apr 1855, Henry Reeve July 1855–Oct 1895, Arthur R. D. Elliot Jan 1896–1923. *See* Wellesley index vol 1.

The quarterly review. Feb 1809 onwards. No issues between Apr 1824 and Mar 1825. Indexes: vols 1–19, Quart Rev 20 1820; vols 21–39, Quart Rev 40 1831; vols 41–59, Quart Rev 60 1839; vols 61–79, Quart Rev 80 1850; vols 81–99, Quart Rev 100 1858; vols 101–120, Quart Rev 121 1867; vols 122–139, Quart Rev 140 1876; vols 141–159, Quart Rev 160 1885; vols 161–180, Quart Rev 181 1895; vols 182–200, Quart Rev 201 1905 etc. Prop John Murray. Ed William Gifford Feb 1809–Apr 1824, John Taylor Coleridge Mar–Dec 1825, John G. Lockhart Mar 1826–June 1853, Whitwell Elwin Sep 1853–July 1860, William Macpherson Oct 1860–Jan 1867, William Smith Apr 1867–July 1893, John Murray (1851–1928) Oct 1893–Jan 1894, Rowland E. Prothero Apr 1894–Jan 1899, George W. Prothero Apr 1899–1922. *See* Wellesley index vol 1.

The reflector. Nos 1–4, 1811–2. Ed J. H. Leigh Hunt.

Annals of the fine arts. Vols 1–5, July 1817–Dec(?) 1820.

The quarterly musical magazine and review. Vols 1–10, 1818–28. Ed R. M. Bacon.

The Edinburgh philosophical journal. Edinburgh. Vols 1–14, June 1819–Apr 1826. Continued as Edinburgh new philosophical journal, vols 1–57, Apr 1826–July 1854. New series, vols 1–19, Jan 1855–Apr 1864. Ed David Brewster and Robert Jameson 1819–24, Robert Jameson 1824–Apr 1854, Laurence Jameson, J. Anderson, W. Jardine, J. H. Balfour 1855–64.

The retrospective review. Vols 1–14, 1820–6. New series vols 1–2, 1827–8. Ed Henry Southern 1820–6, Henry Southern and H. Nicholas 1827–8.

Ollier's literary miscellany in prose and verse. No 1, 1820.

The liberal: verse and prose from the south. 2 vols 1822–3. Ed J. H. Leigh Hunt.

The album. Vols 1–4, 1822–5. Ed F. B. St Leger.

Knight's quarterly magazine. Vols 1–3, June 1823–Nov 1824. Continued as Quarterly magazine, vol 1, no 1, Aug 1825. Ed Charles Knight.

The Westminster review. Vols 1–24, Jan 1824–Jan 1836. Continued as London and Westminster review, vols 25–33, Apr 1836–Mar 1840. Continued as Westminster review, vols 34–45, June 1840–June 1846. Continued as Westminster and foreign quarterly review, vols 46–56, Oct 1846–Oct 1851. Continued as Westminster review: new series, vols 1–71, Jan 1852–Apr 1887. Continued monthly, vols 128 (resumption of numbering from 1824)–181, Apr 1887–Jan 1914. General index Jan 1824–Jan 1836, Westminster Rev 24; July 1835–Mar 1840 (including 2 vols of London Rev), Westminster Rev 33. Prop Jeremy Bentham et al 1824–9; T. Perronet Thompson 1829–35; William Molesworth 1836–40; W. E. Hickson 1840–51; John Chapman 1852–60; George Manwaring 1860–1; Trubner & Co. Ed Henry Southern and John Bowring 1824–7, John Bowring 1827–9, T. Perronet Thompson 1829–35, John Stuart Mill 1836–40, W. E. Hickson 1840–51, John Chapman (assisted by George Eliot) 1852–July 1854), John Chapman 1854–1894, Mrs John Chapman 1894–1914. *See* Wellesley index vol 3 1979.

The Edinburgh journal of science. Edinburgh. Vols 1–10, Apr 1824–Apr 1829. New series, vols 1–6, July 1829–Apr 1832. Incorporated in Philosophical Magazine. Ed David Brewster.

The British critic, quarterly, theological review and ecclesiastical record. Vols 1–34, Jan 1827–Oct 1843. Prop Francis Rivington. Ed Edward Smedley Jan 1827–Oct 1833, James Shergold Boone Jan 1834–Nov 1837, S. R. Maitland Jan 1838, John Henry Newman July 1838–Apr 1841, Thomas Mozley July 1841–Oct 1843.

The foreign quarterly review. Vols 1–37, July 1827–July 1846. Incorporated in Westminster review. Ed Robert Pearse Gillies 1827 (nominal ed until June 1830), John George Cochrane 1827–34, Frederic Shoberl 1835–8, Benjamin Edward Pote 1838–Jan 1840, James William Worthington Apr 1840–Apr 1842, John Forster July 1842–Oct 1843, Walter Keating Kelly 1844–6. *See* Wellesley index vol 2 1972.

The foreign review and continental miscellany. Vols 1–5, 1828–30.

The law magazine: or quarterly journal of jurisprudence. Vols 1–55, Oct 1828–Feb 1856. Continued as Law magazine and law review, vols 1–31, May 1856–Nov 1871. Continued as Law magazine and review, vols 1–4, Feb 1872–Aug 1875. Continued as Law magazine and review and quarterly digest of all reported cases, vols 1–23, Nov 1875–Aug 1898. 5th series, vols 24–40, Nov 1898–Aug 1915.

The London review. Nos 1–2, 1829. Prop Nassau W. Senior. Ed Joseph Blanco White. *See* Wellesley index vol 2 1972.

The quarterly journal of education. Vols 1–10, Jan 1831–Oct 1835. Organ of the S. D. U. K.

The Freemasons' quarterly review. Vols 1–9, Apr 1834–Dec 1842. New series, vols 1–7, Mar 1843–Dec 1849. Continued as Freemasons' quarterly magazine and review, vols 1–3, Mar 1850–Dec 1852. Continued as Freemasons' magazine: new series, 2 vols Mar 1853–Oct 1854. Continued monthly as Freemason's monthly magazine, vol 1, Jan–Dec 1855. Continued as Freemasons' magazine and Masonic mirror, vols 2–6, Jan 1856–June 1859. New series, vols 1–25 (no 2), 9 July 1859–26 Aug 1871. Weekly from 6 Jan 1858.

The London review. Vols 1–2, Apr 1835–Jan 1836. Incorporated in Westminster review. Prop William Molesworth. Ed John Stuart Mill. *See* Wellesley index vol 3 1979.

The British and foreign review: or European quarterly journal. Vols 1–8, July 1835–1844. Prop Thomas Wentworth Beaumont. Ed William Wallace July 1835, G. A. Young Oct 1835–Jan 1836, Thomas Wentworth Beaumont Apr–July 1836, John Mitchell Kemble Dec 1836–Oct 1844. *See* Wellesley index vol 3 1979.

The Christian teacher. Vols 1–4, Jan 1835–June 1838 (monthly). New series, vols 1–6, July 1839–Oct 1844. Issued quarterly from vol 2, 1840. Continued as Prospective review, vols 1–10, Feb 1845–Aug 1854, plus a separate no 41, for Feb 1855. Ed John R. Beard, William Johns and G. Buckland 1835–8, J. H. Thom 1839–44, J. H. Thom, James Martineau, J. J. Tayler and Charles Wicksteed 1845–52; James Martineau, J. J. Tayler, J. H. Thom, Charles Wicksteed and W. C. Roscoe 1852–3; James Martineau, J. J. Taylor, J. H. Thom, Charles Wicksteed, W. C. Roscoe and R. H. Hutton 1853–4. *See* Wellesley index vol 3 1979.

The British and foreign medical review and quarterly journal of practical medicine and surgery. Vols 1–24, Jan 1836–Oct 1847. Index to first 25 vols. By R. Bower, vol 25, 1848. Ed J. Forbes and J. Conolly.

The Dublin review. May 1836 onwards. Index: complete list of articles pbd May 1836–Apr 1936. 1936. Prop Nicholas Wiseman 1837–62; Henry Edward Manning 1863–79; Herbert Vaughan 1879–1903(?). Ed M. J. Quinn May–July 1836, M. A. Tierney Dec 1836, James Smith Apr–July 1837, Nicholas Wiseman 1837–63 (assisted by C. W. Russell, with H. R. Bagshaw as sub-editor), W. G. Ward 1863–78 (with Cashel Hoey as sub-editor), J. C. Hedley 1879–84 (with W. E. Driffield as sub-editor), Herbert Vaughan 1885–91, James Moyes 1892–1900. *See* Wellesley index vol 2 1972.

The Church of England quarterly review. Vols 1–44, Jan 1837–Nov 1858. Ed E. Thompson.

The foreign and colonial quarterly review. Vols 1–3, Jan 1843–Apr 1844. Continued as New quarterly review: or home, foreign and colonial journal, vols 4–8, no 1, July 1844–July 1846. Ed James William Worthington.

The English review: or quarterly journal of ecclesiastical and general literature. Vols 1–19, Apr 1844–Apr 1853.

The North British review. Vols 1–53, May 1844–Jan 1871. No issue May 1857. Prop T. and T. Clark; group of liberal Catholics under John Acton 1869–71. Ed David Welsh 1844–May 1845, Edward F. Maitland Aug 1845–Nov 1846, William Hanna Feb 1847–Feb 1850, A. C. Fraser May 1850–Feb 1857, John Duns Aug 1857–May 1860, ? Forster Aug 1860, W. G. Blaikie Nov 1860–Aug 1863, David Douglas Nov 1863–July 1869, T. F. Wetherell Oct 1869–Jan 1871. *See* Wellesley index vols 1 and 2 1968, 1972.

The law review and quarterly journal of British and foreign jurisprudence. Vols 1–23, Nov 1844–Feb 1856. Incorporated in Law magazine.

The British quarterly review. Vols 1–53, Feb 1845–Apr 1886. Prop Robert Vaughan Feb 1845–Oct 1865; Henry Allon Jan 1866–Apr 1886. Ed Robert Vaughan 1845–65, Henry Robert Reynolds 1866–74, Henry Allon 1866–86. *See* Wellesley index vol 4.

The prospective review. 1845–55. *See above, under* Christian teacher.

The Irish quarterly review. Dublin. Vols 1–9, Mar 1851–Jan 1860.

The new quarterly review and digest of current literature. Nos 1–41, 1852–62.

The Scottish review: a quarterly journal of social progress and general literature. Glasgow. Vols 1–10 and one no, Jan 1853–Jan 1863. Organ of the Scottish Temperance League.

The London quarterly review. Sep 1853–Jan 1932. Continued as London quarterly and Holborn review, Apr 1832 onwards. Prop John Robinson Kay and James Smith Budgett 1853–62; London Quart Rev Company Ltd 1862–97; Wesleyan Methodist Book Room 1897–1900 and beyond. Ed Thomas M'Nicoll 1853–8, Thomas M'Nicoll Apr 1858–1860, William Burt Pope 1860–83, William Burt Pope and James Harrison Rigg 1883–6, James Harrison Rigg 1886–98, William L. Watkinson 1898–1904. *See* Wellesley index vol 4.

The national review. Vols 1–18, July 1855–Apr 1864. Ed Walter Bagehot and R. H. Hutton 1855–62, Walter Bagehot and C. H. Pearson 1862–4. *See* Wellesley index vol 3.

Meliora: a quarterly review of social science. Vols 1–12, Apr 1858–Oct 1869. Ed Henry Septimus Sutton 1859–69.

The Atlantis: a register of literature and science conducted by members of the Catholic University of Ireland. Vol 1, nos 1–2, Jan, July 1858; vol 2, nos 3–4, Jan, July 1859; vol 3, nos 5–6, Jan 1860, Jan 1862; vol 4, nos 7–8, 1863; vol 5, no 9, Feb 1870. Prop John Henry Newman. Ed John Henry Newman and W. K. Sullivan 1858, W. K. Sullivan and P. Le Page Renouf.

The ibis: a magazine of general ornithology. Vols 1–6, Jan 1859–Oct 1864. New series, 6 vols 1865–Oct 1870. 3rd series, 6 vols Jan 1871–Oct 1876. 4th series, Jan 1877–Oct 1882. 5th series, 6 vols Jan 1883–Oct 1888. 6th series, 6 vols Jan 1889–Oct 1894. 7th series, 6 vols Jan 1895–Oct 1900. 8th series, Jan 1901–Oct 1906 ... 14th series, vol 6, 1942. Then vol 85 1943 onwards. Indexes: Index of genera and species referred to, and to the plates [series 1–3] 1859–76, 1879; Index of genera etc. [series 4–6] 1877–94, 1897; Index of genera series 7–9, 1895–1912, 1916; General subject index series 1–6 1859–94. Ed O. Salvin 1871–6, O. Salvin and P. L. Sclater 1877–82, P. L. Sclater and H. Saunders 1883–8, P. L. Sclater 1889–94, P. L. Sclater and H. Saunders 1895–1900.

Bentley's quarterly review. Vols 1–2, Mar 1859–Jan 1860. Prop Richard Bentley. Ed John Douglas Cook ('director'), William Scott and Robert Cecil. *See* Wellesley index vol 2 1972.

The natural history review. Vols 1–5, Jan 1861–Oct 1865. Ed T. H. Huxley et al.

The home and foreign review. Vols 1–4, July 1862–Apr 1864. Prop John Acton and Richard Simpson July–Dec 1862; John Acton 1863–4. Ed John Acton (assisted by Thomas Wetherell 1862–4 and P. Le Page Renouf Oct 1863–Apr 1864). *See* Wellesley index vol 1 1968.

The fine arts quarterly review. Vols 1–3, May 1863–Jan 1865. New series, vols 1–2, July 1866–June 1867. Ed B. B. Woodward 1863–5.

The Alpine journal: a record of mountain adventure and scientific observation. [By members of the Alpine Club.] Mar 1863 onwards. Now twice a year. Index to vols 1–15. By F. A. Walroth, 1892. Ed H. B. George 1863–7, A. T. Malkin 1868, Leslie Stephen 1868–71, D. W. Freshfield, W. A. B. Coolidge, A. J. Butler, W. M. Conway, G. Yeld.

The quarterly journal of science. Vols 1–7, Jan 1864–Oct 1870. New series, vols 8–15, Jan 1871–Oct 1878. Continued as Journal of science, 3rd series, vols 1–7, Jan 1870–Dec 1885. Ed J. Samuelson and W. Crookes 1864–70, W. Crookes 1871–85.

The theological review: a journal of religious thought and life. Begun bi-monthly, vols 1–2, Mar 1864–Nov 1865. Continued quarterly, vols 3–12, Jan 1866–Dec 1875. Continued as Theological review: a quarterly journal of religious thought and life, vols 13–16, Jan 1876–Oct 1870. Ed C. Beard. *See* Wellesley index vol 3 1979.

The Friends' quarterly examiner. Jan 1867–Oct 1946. Continued as Friends' quarterly, new series, Jan 1947 onwards. Ed W. C. Westlake.

The new quarterly magazine. Vols 1–10, Oct 1873–Oct 1878. New series, vols 1–3, Jan 1879–Apr 1880. Ed O. J. F. Crawfurd 1873–Jan 1878, Francis Hueffer Apr–Oct 1878, C. Kegan Paul Jan 1879–Apr 1880. *See* Wellesley index vol 3 1979.

The church quarterly review. Oct 1875 onwards. Ed A. R. Ashwell 1876–9.

Mind: a quarterly review of psychology and philosophy. Jan 1876 onwards. Ed George Croom Robertson 1876–92, G. F. Stout 1892–1920.

Brain: a journal of neurology. Apr 1878 onwards. Index: General index to vols 1–23, 1878–1900. 1902. Prop Macmillan. Ed J. C. Bucknill, J. Crichton-Browne, D. Fevrier, J. Hughlings-Jackson 1878–83, J. C. Bucknill, J. Crichton-Browne, D. Fevrier, J. Hughlings-Jackson, A. de Watteville 1883–5, A. de Watteville plus editorial committee 1885–1900.

The modern review. Vols 1–5, Jan 1880–Oct 1884. Ed R. A. Armstrong.

The Downside review. July 1880 onwards. Originally 3 times a year, now quarterly. Index to vols 1–25, vol 25 1906. Ed Alfred Maskell, Dom Edmund Ford, Abbot Gasquet, Abbot Butler.

The law quarterly review. Jan 1885 onwards. Ed F. Pollock 1885–1919.

The English historical review. Jan 1886 onwards. Ed Mandell Creighton 1886–91, S. R. Gardiner 1891–5, S. R. Gardiner and R. L. Poole 1895–1901.

The centenary guild hobby horse. Vols 1–7, Jan 1886–Oct 1892. Continued as Hobby horse, 3 nos 1893–4. Ed H. P. Horne and A. H. Mackmurdo 1886–7, H. P. Horne 1888–91, A. H. Mackmurdo 1892, H. P. Horne 1893–4.

The Jewish quarterly review. Vols 1–20, Oct 1888–July 1908. New series edited for Dropsie College for Hebrew and Cognate Learning Philadelphia, 1910 onwards. Ed Israel Abrahams and Claude Montefiore Oct 1888–July 1908.

The archaeological review. Vols 1–4, Mar 1888–Jan 1890. Incorporated in Folklore. Ed G. L. Gomme.

Folklore. 1890 onwards.

The yellow book. Vols 1–13, Apr 1894–Apr 1897. Prop John Lane. Ed Aubrey Beardsley and Henry Harland.

The Savoy. *See col 2948, above, under Monthly magazines.*

The quarto. Irregular. 2 nos 1896; 3rd no 1897; 4th no 1898. Ed John Bernard Holborn.

The dome: a quarterly containing examples of all the arts. Nos 1–5, Mar 1897–May 1898. 1 issue gratis Aug 1898. Continued monthly, new series, vols 1–7, Oct 1898–July 1900. Prop and ed Ernest J. Oldmeadow.

Beltaine: the organ of the Irish literary theatre. Irregular. No 1, May 1899; no 2, Feb 1900; no 3, Apr 1900. Ed W. B. Yeats.

The Anglo-Saxon review. June 1899–Sep 1910. Ed Lady Randolph S. Churchill.

(3) ACCOUNTS AND STUDIES OF MONTHLY AND QUARTERLY MAGAZINES

Basic to the study of Victorian periodicals is W. E. Houghton ed, The Wellesley index to Victorian periodicals, 5 vols 1966–1989 *which includes identification of authorship, tables of contents and historical intro-*

ductions to British monthlies and quarterlies 1824–1900 with bibliographies of contributors. Evidence of authorship is cited for every attribution. Vol 1, 1966, *covers* Blackwood's Mag, Contemporary Rev, Cornhill Mag, Edinburgh Rev (with an initial section covering 1802–23), Home & Foreign Rev, Macmillan's Mag, North Br Rev, and Quart Rev. Vol 2 1972 *covers* Bentley's Quart, Dublin Rev, Foreign Quart Rev, Fortnightly Rev, Fraser's Mag, London Rev (1829), National Rev (1883–), New Quart Mag, Nineteenth Century, Oxford and Cambridge Mag (1856), Rambler (1848–62), Scottish Rev (1882–1900). Vol 3 1979 *covers* Ainsworth's Mag, Atlantis, British and Foreign Rev, London Rev (1835–6), London and Westminster Rev (1836–40), Modern Rev, Monthly Chronicle, National Rev (1855–64), New Monthly Mag (1821–54), New Rev, Prospective Rev, St Pauls, Temple Bar, Theological Rev, Westminster Rev. Vol 4 1987 *covers* Bentley's Miscellany, British Quart Rev, Dark Blue, Dublin University Mag, London Quart Rev, Longman's Mag, Tait's Edinburgh Mag, University Mag. Vol 5 *contains the* Epitome and index. *See also issues of the* Victorian Periodicals Rev *which correct and update the* Wellesley index, *including* vol 23 no 2 1990, vol 26 no 4 1993, vol 27 nos 3 & 4 1994, vol 28 no 4 1995, *and* vol 29 no 4 1996.

Accounts and Studies covering several Monthlies and Quarterlies

In addition to items listed below, see L. Madden and D. Dixon ed. The nineteenth century periodical press in Britain: a bibliography of modern studies. 1901–1971. New York 1976 *and* L. Uffelman, ed. The nineteenth century periodical press in Britain: a bibliography of modern studies 1972–1987. Edwardsville IL 1992. *See also the annual bibliographies in the* Victorian Periodicals Review.

Brown, A. W. The Metaphysical Society: Victorian minds in crisis 1869–80. New York 1947.

Lockhart, J. G. John Bull's letter to Lord Byron. Ed A. L. Strout, Norman OK 1947.

Houghton, W. E. British periodicals of the Victorian age: bibliographies and indexes. Lib Trends 7 1959.

Morrison, J. L. The Oxford Movement and the British periodicals. Catholic Historical Rev 45 1959.

Maurer, O. 'My squeamish public': some problems of Victorian magazine publishers and editors. SB 12 1959.

Amarasinghe, U. Dryden and Pope in the early nineteenth century: a study of changing literary taste 1800–30. Cambridge 1962.

Fielding, K. J. American notes and some English reviewers. MLR 59 1964.

Fetter, F. W. Economic controversy in the British reviews 1802–50. Economica 32 1965.

Gordon, B. J. Say's Law, effective demand and the contemporary British periodicals 1820–50. Economica 32 1965.

Roper, D. Reviewing before the Edinburgh 1788–1802. 1978.

Accounts and Studies of Monthly Magazines

Mayo, R. D. The Gothic short story in the magazines. MLR 37 1942.

Smith, J. Magazines of the nineties. Chambers's Jnl Jan 1945.

Ward, W. S. Some aspects of the conservative attitude towards poetry in English criticism 1798–1820. PMLA 60 1945.

Morgan, B. W. and A. R. Hohlfield. German literature in British magazines 1750–1860. Madison WI 1949.

Mayo, R. D. The Gothic romance in the magazines [1700–1820]. PMLA 65 1950.

Gentleman's magazine 1731

A selection of curious articles from the Gentleman's magazine. Ed J. Walker 4 vols 1814 (3rd edn).

The autobiography of Sylvanus Urban. GM July–Sep, Nov–Dec 1856, Jan–Apr 1857.

The Gentleman's magazine library: being a classified collection of the chief contents of the Gentleman's magazine from 1731 to 1868. Ed G. L. Gomme 1883.

Bullen, A. H. GM Feb 1906.

Blunden, E. The Gentleman's magazine 1731–1907. In his Votive tablets, 1931.

Buckley, W. E. Henry Kingsley and the Gentleman's Magazine. JEGP 50 1951.

Monthly review 1749

Robberds, J. W. A memoir of the life and writings of William Taylor. 1843.

Nangle, B. C. The Monthly review: second series 1790–1815. Indexes of contributions and articles. Oxford 1955.

Critical review 1756

Roper, D. The politics of the Critical review 1756–1817. Durham Univ Jnl 22 1961.

Roper, D. Reviewing before the Edinburgh, 1788–1802. 1978.

Arminian magazine 1778

Blacket, J. The oldest religious periodical in the world. Methodist Mag Jan–Mar 1927.

Botanical magazine 1787

Curtis's botanical magazine dedications 1827–1927: portraits and biographical notes by E. Nelmes and W. Cuthbertson. 1931.

A new and complete index, to which is prefaced a history of the magazine by I. W. B. Hemsley. 1906.

Hooker, W. J. Companion to the Botanical magazine: being a journal containing such interesting information as does not come within the limits of the magazine. Vols 1–2, 1835–7. Incorporated in the Annals of natural history.

Sporting magazine 1792

Index of engravings in Sporting magazine 1792–1870. [1892.]

Monthly magazine 1796

Dowden, W. S. A Jacobin journal's view of Lord Byron. SP 48 1951.

Carnall, G. The monthly magazine. RES new ser 5 1954.

Eclectic review 1805

Remarks on the principles of the Eclectic review with reference to civil and ecclesiastical subjects illustrated by extracts from that publication. 1817.

Foster, J. Contributions, biographical, literary and philosophical to the Eclectic review. 2 vols 1844.

The controversy between the Eclectic review and Mr James Grant: reprinted from the Morning Chronicle. 1856 (10 edns).

Hiller, M. R. The Eclectic Review 1805–1868. Victorian Periodicals Rev 27 no 3 1994. Index of articles and contributors to the review, based on work done for the Wellesley Index.

Monthly repository 1806

Mineka, F. E. The dissidence of dissent: the Monthly repository 1806–38. Chapel Hill NC 1944.

British review 1811

Ward, W. S. Lord Byron and 'my grandmother's review'. MLN 64 1949.

New monthly magazine 1814

Redding, C. Literary reminiscences and memoirs of Thomas Campbell. 2 vols 1860.

Sadleir, M. Bulwer and his wife. 1933.

Rollins, H. E. Letters of Horace Smith to his publisher Colburn. Harvard Lib Bull 3 1949.

Strickland, G. ed. Selected journalism from the English reviews by Stendhal, with translations of other critical writings. 1959. On his work as French correspondent of New monthly magazine.

Sikes, H. M. 'The infernal Hazlitt', the New Monthly Magazine and the Conversations of James Northcote RA. Essays in History and Lit 5 1965.

Blackwood's Edinburgh magazine 1817

Wilson, John. The recreations of Christopher North. 3 vols 1842.

Wilson, John. Essays critical and imaginative. 4 vols 1866.

Eagles, J. The sketcher. 1856.

Eagles, J. Essays contributed to Blackwood's magazine. 1857.

Tales from Blackwood. 12 vols Edinburgh 1858–61. New series, 12 vols Edinburgh 1878–80. 3rd series 6 vols Edinburgh 1889–90.

Travel, adventure and sport from Blackwood's Magazine. 6 vols Edinburgh 1889–90.
Gordon, M. Christopher North: a memoir. 1862.
Shand, A. I. Magazine writers. Blackwood's Mag Feb 1879.
Douglas, G. B. S. The Blackwood group. 1897.
Oliphant, M. O. Annals of a publishing house: William Blackwood and his sons: their magazine and friends. 2 vols 1897.
Porter, M. Annals of a publishing house: John Blackwood. Edinburgh 1898. A continuation of the previous entry.
Strout, A. L. Hunt, Hazlitt and Maga. ELH 4 1937.
Strout, A. L. Walter Scott and Maga. TLS 5 Feb 1938.
Strout, A. L. Blackwood's magazine, Lockhart and John Scott: a Whig satirical broadside. N & Q 11 Jan 1941.
Strout, A. L. 'Timothy Tickler' of Blackwood's magazine. N & Q 25 Jan 1941.
Strout, A. L. A study in periodical patchwork: John Wilson's re-creations of Christopher North 1842. MLR 38 1943. Compares original text in Blackwood's with that of the collected edn.
Strout, A. L. George Croly and Blackwood's magazine. TLS 6 Oct 1950.
Strout, A. L. Lockhart: champion of Shelley. TLS 12 Aug 1955.
Strout, A. L. William Maginn as gossip. N & Q June 1955.
Strout, A. L. A bibliography of articles in Blackwood's magazine 1817–25. Texas Technological College Lit Bull 5 1959. This important bibliography complements the section on Blackwood's in the Wellesley index, vol 1 giving attributions of articles 1817–1900. It also contains a select bibliography.
Strout, A. L. Some miscellaneous letters, concerning Blackwood's magazine. N & Q Mar, July 1954.
Wardle, R. M. The motive for Byron's George Russell of A. MLN 65 1950.
Parker, W. M. Anthony Trollope and Maga. Blackwood's Mag Jan 1945.
Nolte, E. A. Michael Scott and Blackwood's magazine: some unpublished letters. Library 5th ser 8 1953.
Tredrey, F. D. The House of Blackwood 1804–1954. Edinburgh 1954.
Cooke, Mrs A. K. William Maginn on John Keats. N & Q Mar 1956.
Fetter, F. W. The economic articles in Blackwood's Edinburgh magazine and their authors 1817–53. Scottish Jnl of Political Economy 7 1960.

London Magazine 1820

Blunden, E. Keats' publisher. 1936.
Wendland, I. Der Einfluss der Politik auf das London magazine und seine Hauptbeiträger. Emsdetten 1937.
Hennig, J. Early English translations of Goethe's essays on Byron. MLR 44 1949.
Brooks, E. L. Coleridge's second packet for Blackwood's magazine. PQ 30 1951. Speculates on Coleridge's authorship of certain articles in London magazine.
Brooks, E. L. Was William Hazlitt a news reporter? N & Q Aug 1954. On possibility that Hazlitt contributed more than Table Talk and dramatic criticism.
Brooks, E. L. Byron and the London magazine. Keats-Shelley Jnl 5 1956.
Bauer, J. The London magazine 1820–9. Copenhagen 1953.
Patmore, D. A literary duel. Princeton Univ Lib Chron 16 1954. On duel between John Scott and J. G. Lockhart.
House, J. In his All in due time, 1955.
Morgan, P. F. Taylor and Hessey: aspects of their conduct of the London Magazine. Keats-Shelley Jnl 7 1958.
Strickland, G. ed. Selected journalism from the English reviews by Stendhal, with translations of other critical writings. 1959. On his work as French correspondent of London Magazine.
Sikes, H. M. Hazlitt, the London magazine and the 'anonymous reviewer'. BNYPL Mar 1961.
Prance, C. A. Peppercorn papers. Cambridge 1964 (priv ptd).

Fraser's magazine 1830. *See* Wellesley index vol 2.

A gallery of illustrious literary characters 1830–8 drawn by D. Maclise, accompanied by notices chiefly by W. Maginn: republished from Fraser's magazine. Ed W. Bates [1873].
Mahony, F. S. (Father Prout). The works of Father Prout, edited with biographical introduction and notes by C. Kent. 1892.
Thrall, M. M. H. Rebellious Fraser's 1830–40. New York 1934.
Our past and our future. Fraser's Mag July 1879.
Sampson, M. Fraser's magazine: 'Regina'. N & Q 31 Aug 1940.
Maurer, O. Froude and Fraser's magazine 1860–74. SE 28 1949.
White, E. N. Thackeray's contributions to Fraser's magazine. SB 19 1966.

Dublin University magazine 1833. *See* Wellesley index vol 4.

Sadleir, M. The Dublin University magazine: its history, contents and bibliography. Pbns of Bibl Soc of Ireland 5 1938.

Bentley's miscellany 1837. *See* Wellesley index vol 4.

Tales from Bentley. 4 vols 1860, 1865.
Dexter, W. Bentley's Miscellany. Dickensian 33 1937.
Littlewood, L. M. A Victorian magazine. Contemporary Rev Mar 1937.
Rickels, M. The humorists of the old southwest in the London Bentley's miscellany. Amer Lit 27 1950.
Gettmann, R. A. Barham and Bentley. JEGP 56 1957.

Art Journal (Art-union 1839)

Fifty years of art 1849–99: being articles and illustrations selected from the Art journal. Ed D. C. Thomson 1900.

Musical times 1844

Scholes, P. A. The mirror of music 1844–1944: a century of musical life in Britain as reflected in the pages of the Musical Times. 2 vols 1948.

Sharpe's London magazine 1845

Boase, G. C. Sharpe's London Magazine. N & Q 12 Apr 1879.
'Bede, Cuthbert' (E. Bradley). Sharpe's London Magazine. N & Q 26 Apr 1879.

Rambler 1848. *See* Wellesley index vol 2.

Altholz, J. L. The liberal Catholic movement in England: the Rambler and its contributors. 1962.
Altholz, J. L. A bibliographical note on the Rambler. PBSA 56 1962.

Macmillan's magazine 1859. *See* Wellesley index vol 1.

Buckler, W. E. Tennyson's Lucretius bowdlerized? RES new ser 5 1954.
Gurr, A. J. Macmillan's magazine. REL 6 1965.
Parry, A. Theories of formation: Macmillan's Magazine vol 1 Nov 1859. Victorian Periodicals Rev 26 1993.
Worth, G. Alexander Macmillan and his magazine. Victorian Periodicals Rev 26 1993.

Cornhill Magazine 1860. *See* Wellesley index vol 1.

The Cornhill gallery, containing 100 engravings by F. Leighton, J. E. Millais etc. 1865.
Maurer, O. L. Stephen and the Cornhill Magazine 1871–82. SE 32 1953.
Scott, J. W. Robertson. The story of the Pall Mall Gazette. 1950.
Smith, P. The Cornhill Magazine number 1. REL 4 1963.

Temple Bar 1860. *See* Wellesley index vol 3.

The one hundredth volume of Temple Bar magazine: being an alphabetical list of all articles appearing in the previous ninety-nine volumes. Temple Bar Apr 1894.
de Baun, V. C. Temple Bar: index of Victorian middle-class thought. Jnl Rutgers Univ Lib 19 1955.

Month 1864

Gerard, J. A 'century' and a retrospect. Month Dec 1902.
Jubilee issues. Month Jan, June 1914.
75th anniversary issue. Month July 1939.
Martindale, C. C. Newman and the Month. Month Dec 1950.
Thomas, A. The Month: attribution of articles. N & Q June 1954.

Fortnightly Review 1865. *See* Wellesley index vol 2.
Waugh, A. The biography of a periodical. Fortnightly Rev Oct 1929.
Waugh, A. A hundred years of publishing. 1930.
Everett, E. M. The party of humanity: the Fortnightly Review and its contributors 1865–74. Chapel Hill NC 1939.
Contemporary review 1866. *See* Wellesley index vol 1.
Strahan, A. Account in Day of Rest Jan–Dec 1881.
Lowe, R. L. Matthew Arnold and Percy William Bunting: some new letters 1884–7. SB 7 1955.
Aunt Judy's Magazine 1866
Twenty years with Aunt Judy. TLS 7 Dec 1946
Belgravia 1867
Indexes to fiction in Belgravia 1867–1899. Ed P. D. Edwards, I. G. Sibley, M. Versteeg. Victorian Fiction Research Guide 14 St Lucia Queensland 1988.
Tinsley's magazine 1867
Index to fiction in Tinsley's magazine. Ed S. Thomas. Victorian Fiction Research Guide 7 St Lucia Queensland 1981.
Cope's tobacco plant 1870
Altick, R. D. Cope's tobacco plant: an episode in Victorian journalism. PBSA 45 1951.
Cassell's family magazine 1874
Index to fiction in Cassell's family magazine 1874–1910. Ed S. Thomas. Victorian Fiction Research Guide 12 1987.
Nineteenth century 1877. *See* Wellesley index vol 2.
Sixty years ago. Nineteenth Century. Mar 1937.
Fairchild, H. N. 'La Saisiaz' and the Nineteenth Century. MP 48 1950. On a symposium in the magazine 1877.
75th anniversary number. Twentieth Century Mar 1952.
Goodwin, M. Nineteenth century opinion: an anthology of extracts from the first fifty volumes of the Nineteenth century 1877–1901. 1952 (Pelican).
Brake, L. Theories of formation, the Nineteenth Century: volume 1 no 1 Mar 1877. Victorian Periodicals Rev 25 1992, rptd in her Subjugated knowledges 1994.
Time 1879
Mumby, F. A. and F. H. Stallybrass. From Swann Sonnenschein to George Allen and Unwin Ltd. 1955.
Index to fiction in Time 1879–91, Murray's magazine and the Quarto. Ed S. Thomas. Victorian Fiction Research Guide 4 1980.
Longman's magazine 1882. *See* Wellesley index vol 4.
Reid, F. Andrew Lang and Longman's. London Mercury Mar 1938.
Parker, W. M. Lang and Longman's. Scots Mag new ser Mar 1944.
Maurer, O. Andrew Lang and Longman's Magazine 1882–1905. SE 34 1955.
Blagden, C. Longman's Magazine. REL 4 1963.
National review 1883
Milner, V. Fifty-five years: an historical note. Nat Rev Oct 1948. *See* historical material in last issue, June 1960.
Murray's magazine 1887
Index to fiction in Time, Murray's magazine and the Quarto. Ed S. Thomas. Victorian Fiction Research Guide 4 1980.
Woman's world 1887
Wyndham, H. When Oscar Wilde was editor. Life & Letters Dec 1947.
Wyndham, H. 'Edited by Oscar Wilde'. Lib Rev 12 1949.
Brake, L. Oscar Wilde and the Woman's World. In her Subjugated knowledges 1994.
Expository times 1889
Jubilee number. Oct 1939.
Strand magazine 1891
The 100th number of the Strand magazine: a chat about its history by Sir George Newnes, Bart. Strand Mag Apr 1899.
Dawson, A. An interview with Sir George Newnes. Bookman (London) May 1899.
Pound, R. The Strand magazine 1891–1950. 1966.
Whitt, J. F. The Strand magazine 1891–1950: a selective checklist. 1979. Lists material relating to Conan Doyle, P. G. Wodehouse and other writers, mainly of detective, mystery or fantasy fiction.
Pall Mall Magazine 1893
Indexes to fiction in the Pall Mall Magazine 1893–1914. Ed S. Thomas. Victorian Fiction Research Guide 9 1983.
Savoy 1896
Garbáty, T. The French coterie of the Savoy 1896. PMLA 75 1960.
Harris, W. Innocent decadence: the poetry of the Savoy. PMLA 77 1962.
Brake, L. The savoy: 1896. Gender in crisis. In her Subjugated knowledges 1994.
The Harmsworth monthly pictorial magazine 1898
Indexes to fiction in the Harmsworth magazine, later the London magazine 1898–1915. Ed S. Thomas. Victorian Fiction Research Guide 10 1984.

Accounts and Studies of Quarterly Magazines

Cox, R. G. The great reviews. Scrutiny 6 1937.
Welker, J. J. The position of the quarterlies on some classical dogmas. SP 37 1940.
Lloréns, V. Colaboraciones de emigrados españoles en revistas inglesas 1824–34. Hispanic Rev 19 1951.
Edinburgh Review 1802. *See* Wellesley index vol 1.
'Scipio, C.' A sketch of the politics of the Edinburgh Review. 1807.
Selections from the Edinburgh Review comprising best articles in that journal from its commencement to the present time, and explanatory notes. Ed M. Cross 4 vols 1833, 6 vols Paris 1835–6.
Macaulay, T. B. Critical and historical essays contributed to the Edinburgh Review. 3 vols 1843, 1887 (complete); ed F. C. Montague 3 vols 1903.
Jeffrey, F. Contributions to the Edinburgh Review. 4 vols 1844, 1853.
Rogers, J. Essays selected from contributions to the Edinburgh Review. 3 vols 1850–5.
Brougham, J. Contributions to the Edinburgh Review. 3 vols 1856.
Smith, S. Essays rptd from the Edinburgh Review 1802–18. 1874, 1880 (with addns up to 1827).
Constable, T. Archibald Constable and his literary correspondents. 3 vols Edinburgh 1873.
Eliot, A. R. D. The Edinburgh Review. Edinburgh Rev 196 1902.
Griggs, E. L. Southey and the Edinburgh Review. MP 30 1933.
Schneider, E. Thomas Moore and the Edinburgh review. MLN 61 1946.
Schneider, E. Tom Moore and the Edinburgh review of Christabel. PMLA 77 1962. Contains an account and bibliography of the whole controversy.
Clive, J. The Earl of Buchan's kick: a footnote to the history of the Edinburgh review. Harvard Lib Bull 5 1951.
Clive, J. The Scotch reviewers: the Edinburgh Review 1802–15. 1957.
Karminski, A. The Edinburgh Review after 150 years. Listener 30 Oct 1952.
Fetter, F. W. The authorship of economic articles in the Edinburgh Review 1802–47. Jnl of Political Economy 61 1953.
Crawford, T. The Edinburgh Review and romantic poetry 1802–29. Auckland Univ Coll Bull no 47 (Eng ser no 8). 1955.
Collins, P. Dickens and the Edinburgh Review. RES 14 1963.
Alexander, J. H. Edinburgh reviewers and the English tradition. Salzburg 1976.
Fontana, B. Rethinking the politics of commercial society: the Edinburgh Review 1802–1832. Cambridge 1985.
Shattock, J. Politics and Reviewers: The Edinburgh and the Quarterly in the early Victorian Age. Leicester 1989.
Quarterly review 1809. *See* Wellesley index vol 1.
Centenary article. Quart Rev 210 1909.
Graham, W. Tory criticism in the Quarterly review 1809–53. New York 1921.

Strout, A. L. Lockhart and Croker. TLS 30 Aug, 13 Sep 1941. Letters on Lockhart's appointment as editor.
Strout, A. L. Unpublished letters of Lockhart to Croker. N & Q 11 Sep 1943, 9 and 23 Mar, 20 Apr, 4 and 18 May, 1 and 15 June 1946.
Shine, H. and H. C. The Quarterly review under Gifford: identification of contributors 1809–24. Chapel Hill 1949.
Lochhead, M. Lockhart, and Quarterly review and the Tractarians. Quart Rev 291 1953.
Lochhead, M. Miss Rigby and the Quarterly review: pioneer woman journalist. Quart rev 298 1960.
Johnson, R. V. Pater and the Victorian anti-Romantics. EC 4 1954.
Parker, W. M. Dean Milman and the Quarterly Review.
Parker, W. M. Gladstone as a Quarterly review contributor. Quart Rev 293 1955.
Fetter, F. W. The economic articles in the Quarterly Review and their authors. Jnl of Political Economy 66 1958.
Shattock, J. Politics and reviewers: the Edinburgh and the Quarterly in the early Victorian age. Leicester 1989.
Cutmore, J. The Quarterly Review under Gifford: some new attributions. Victorian Periodicals Rev 24 1991.
Cutmore, J. Sir John Barrow's contributions to the Quarterly Review 1809–24. N&Q 239 1994.
Cutmore, J. Wellesley Index I's Quarterly Review Identifications: was the Murray register a reliable source?; The early Quarterly Review 1809–24: New attributions and sources; Further Quarterly Review Attributions Wellesley Index vol 1. Victorian Periodicals Rev 27 1994.
Cutmore, J. The early Quarterly Review: new attributions of authorship. Victorian Periodicals Rev 28 1995.

Liberal 1822
A critique on the Liberal. 1822.
Lord Byron, Leigh Hunt and the Liberal. Ed L. P. Pickering 1925. Selections.
Dilke, C. W. The Liberal. N & Q 1 July 1893. On C. A. Browne's marked file.
Marshall, W. H. Byron, Shelley, Hunt and Liberal. Philadelphia 1960.

Knight's quarterly magazine 1823
Sadleir, M. Bulwer and his wife. 1933.

Westminster review 1824. *See* Wellesley index vol 3.
Blyth, E. K. Life of William Ellis. 1889.
Nesbitt, G. L. Benthamite reviewing: the first twelve years of the Westminster Review 1824–36. New York 1934.
Fraiberg, L. The Westminster Review and American literature 1824–85. Amer Lit 24 1952.
Johnson, L. G. General T. Perronet Thompson 1783–1869. 1957.
Haight, G. S. George Meredith and the Westminster Review. MLR 53 1958.
Daniels, E. A. Collaboration of Mazzini on an article in the Westminster Review. BNYPL Nov 1961.
Fetter, F. W. Economic articles in the Westminster Review and their authors 1824–51. Jnl of Political Economy 70 1962.
Morgan, P. F. Francis Place's copy of the Westminster Review. N & Q Sep 1966.
Rosenberg, S. The financing of radical opinion: John Chapman and the Westminster Review, in J. Shattock and M. Wolff, ed. The Victorian periodical press. Leicester 1982.

British critic 1827
Mozley, T. Reminiscences chiefly of Oriel College and the Oxford Movement. 2 vols 1882.
Houghton, E. R. The British critic and the Oxford Movement. SB 16 1963.

British and Foreign Review 1835. *See* Wellesley index vol 3.
Winegarner, L. Thackeray's contributions to British and foreign review. JEGP 47 1948.

Dublin review 1836. *See* Wellesley index vol 2.
Centenary article 198 1936.
McLaughlin, P. J. Dr Russell and the Dublin review. Studies 41 1952.

North British review 1844. *See* Wellesley index vol 1.
The story of the North British Review. Scottish Rev 3 Jan 1907.
Shattock, J. Problems of parentage: the North British Review and the Free Church of Scotland, in J. Shattock and M. Wolff, ed. The Victorian periodical press. Leicester 1982.

British quarterly review 1845. *See* Wellesley index vol 4.
Osbourn, R. V. The British quarterly review. RES new ser 1 1950.

London quarterly review 1853. *See* Wellesley index vol 4.
See historical material. Oct 1943.

Yellow book 1894
The Yellow book: a selection. Ed N. Denny 1950.
Townsend, J. B. The Yellow book. Princeton Univ Lib Chron 16 1955.
Egerton, G. and T. de V. White. A leaf from the Yellow book: the correspondence of George Egerton. 1958.
Mix, K. L. A study in yellow: the Yellow book and its contributors. 1960.
Huntley, J. Aline and Henry Harland, Aubrey Beardsley and the Yellow book: a verification of some evidence. N & Q Mar 1962.
Weintraub, S. The Yellow book: a reappraisal. Jnl of General Education 16 1964.
Harrison, F. F. The Yellow book: an anthology. Woodbridge 1982.
Dowling, L. Letterpress and picture in the literary periodicals of the 1890s. YES 16 1986.

Quarto 1896
Index to fiction in Time, Murray's magazine and the Quarto. Ed S. Thomas. Victorian Fiction Research Guide 4 1980.

Dome 1897
West, P. The Dome: an aesthetic periodical of the 1890's. Book Collector 6 1957.
Ziegler, A. P. The Dome and its editor publisher: an exploration. Amer Book Collector 15 1965.

E. SCHOOL AND UNIVERSITY JOURNALISM

Cambridge

The Galvanist, by Hydra Polycephalus Esq. Nos 1–11, 1804. By W. D. Whittington et al.
The Cambridge monthly repository or literary miscellany. No 1, Dec 1819.
The Cambridge quarterly review and academical register. Nos 1–3, Mar–Oct 1824.
The snob: a literary and scientific journal, not conducted by members of the University. Nos 1–11, 9 Apr–18 June 1829. Continued as Gownsman, vol 2, no 17, 5 Nov 1829–25 Feb 1830. By W. M. Thackeray, Edward FitzGerald et al.
Punch in Cambridge. Vols 1–3, 7 Feb 1832–30 Dec 1834.
Toby in Cambridge. Vols 1–4, Oct 1832–12 Sep 1836.
The Cambridge quarterly review and magazine of literature, arts, sciences. Nos 1–3, 1 July 1833–Jan 1834. By Sheridan Knowles, Douglas Jerrold et al.
The Cambridge University magazine. Nos 1, 2, 1835.
The freshman. Nos 1–6, 5 Mar–9 Apr 1836.
The fellow. Nos 1–11, 6 Oct–15 Dec 1836.
The individual. Nos 1–16, 25 Oct 1836–11 Apr 1837.
The Cambridge University magazine. Vol 1, no 1–vol 3, no 1, 1840–3. The wrappers of the first 5 nos bore the title 'The symposium'. Ed George Brimley, C. B. Wilcox, W. M. W. Call.
Cambridge essays contributed by members of the University. 4 vols, 1855–8.
Academica. No 1, May 1858. Ed R. P. O'Hara.
The lion university magazine. Nos 1–3, May–Oct 1858. Ed H. R. Haweis.

The bear university magazine. No 1, Oct 1858. By G. O. Trevelyan.
The Cambridge terminal magazine. Nos 1–3, Dec 1858–Apr 1859.
The light blue. Vol 1, no 1–vol 4, 1866–71. Ed J. C. Ross, C. Greene, E. S. Shuckburgh, R. K. Miller.
Momus: a semi-occasional university periodical. Nos 1–3, 1866–9. Ed E. H. Palmer, G. A. Critchett, W. H. Pollock.
The Cambridge undergraduates' journal. No 1, 14 Oct 1868–6 Nov 1874. Incorporated in Oxford and Cambridge undergraduates' journal.
The Cambridge University gazette. Nos 1–33, 28 Oct 1868–15 Dec 1869.
The Cambridge University reporter. No 1, 19 Oct 1870 onwards.
The Moslem in Cambridge. Nos 1–3, Nov 1870–Apr 1871. Ed G. S. Davies.
The lantern of the Cam. Nos 1–4, 1871.
The tatler in Cambridge. Nos 1–80, 26 Apr 1871–15 June 1872.
The light green. Nos 1–2, May, Nov 1872; rptd 1882, 1890. Ed A. C. Hilton.
The Cantab. Nos 1–2, 1873.
The light blue incorporated with the light green. Nos 1–4, May 1873–May 1874.
Light greens. No 1, July 1875.
The Cambridge tatler. Nos 1–10, 6 Mar–29 May 1877.
The Cambridge review. No 1, 15 Oct 1879 onwards.
The Cambridge meteor. Nos 1–7, 7–14 June 1882. Ed G. N. Bankes, J. A. Fabb, J. K. Stephen.
Ye true blue. Nos 1–2, [1883]. Ed G. M. Maxwell.
The blue 'un. Vol 1, no 1, 31 May 1884.
The May bee. Nos 1–7, 4–11 June 1884.
The Cambridge University magazine. Nos 1–13, 6 May–7 Dec 1886. Ed J. J. Withers.
The reflector. Vol 1, nos 1–4, 1–22 Jan 1888. Ed J. K. Stephen.
The Cambridge fortnightly. Vol 1, nos 1–5, 24 Jan–13 Mar 1888. Ed N. Wedd and Roger Fry.
The gadfly. No 1, 15 Nov 1888. By W. M. Guthrie and R. B. Ross.
The Granta. No 1, 18 Jan 1889 onwards. In term time. Suspended from June 1914 to May 1919 and from June 1939 to Mar 1946. Ed R. C. Lehmann 1889–95, C. F. G. Masterman 1898.
The wasp. Nos 1–4, 12–16 June 1891.
The Cambridge observer. Nos 1–21, 3 May 1892–7 Mar 1893. Ed S. Makower.
The Cambridge A. B. C. Nos 1–4, 8–12 June 1892. Ed R. Austen Leigh and H. Warre Cornish.
The 'K. P.' illustrated. No 1, 1 Feb 1893–1894(?).
The Cantab. Jan 1898–Dec 1899.
The bubble. No 0, 10 June 1898.
The Cambridge gazette. No 1, 15 Oct 1898–6 Oct 1900.
The Cambridge magazine. Nos 1–15, 27 Apr–30 Nov 1899.
The snarl. Nos 1–2, 31 Oct, 14 Nov 1899.
Alma mater. Nos 1–5, 1900.

College magazines

St John's
The eagle. Lent term 1858 onwards.
Christ's
Fleur-de-lys. Nos 10–11, 20 May, 7 June 1871.
The Christ's College magazine. No 1, Easter term 1886 onwards. Ed J. R. Seeley.
Girton
The Girton review. No 1, 1882 onwards.
Jesus
The chanticleer. No 1–21, Oct 1885–1892. Continued as Chanticlere no 22, 1892 onwards.
The rag. 6 nos 1896.
Corpus Christi
The benedict. Nos 1–59, 1898–1928.
Trinity
The trident. Nos 1–6 (7 nos), June 1889–Nov 1892.
Emmanuel
Emmanuel College magazine. Nos 1–31, May 1889–1938.
Trinity Hall
The silver crescent. Nos 1–48, Nov 1890–1907.
The brass halo. Nos 1–3, 1893–4. Ed J. W. Murison.
Gonville and Caius
The Caian. 1891 onwards.
Pembroke
The Pem. Nos 1–13, Mar 1893–1897. New series, no 1, Mar 1897 onwards.
Peterhouse
The Peterhouse magazine. No 1, Mar 1893.
The sex. 1897 onwards. Organ of the Peterhouse sexcentenary club.
King's
Basileona. No 1, June 1900–Mar 1903. Continued as Basileon, 1907–14, 1919–25, 1928–9, 1931, 1934–5, 1937, 1940 onwards.

London

The London University magazine. Vols 1–2, 1829–30.
The London University chronicle. No 1, 26 Apr 1830–?. Ed F. Lucas.
The marauder. 1830.
The London University inquirer. 1833.
The adventurer or London University magazine. 1833.
The London University magazine. Nos 1–3, 1842.
The King's College magazine, conducted by the students of King's College, London. 1842.
The London University College magazine. Vol 1, 1849.
The King's College literary and scientific magazine. 1849–50. Continued as King's College magazine, 1850–1.
The London University magazine. Vols 1–3, 1856–9. New series, nos 1–5, 1859.
The London student. Vol 1, nos 1–5, Apr–Oct 1868. Ed J. R. Seeley.
The London students' gazette: a monthly chronicle of student opinion and student news. Nos 1–8, 1872.
The King's College magazine. Vols 1–4, 1877–81.
The University College London gazette. Vol 1, nos 1–12, Oct 1886–Nov 1887(?)–[1889?]. Ed Henry Morley.
The privateer. Nos 1–11, 1892–3. Ed E. V. Lucas.
The University College gazette. No 1, 30 Nov 1895–1904. Continued as UCL Union magazine. 1904–19. Continued as University College magazine, 1919 onwards.
The King's College magazine (ladies' dept). Nos 1–52. Michaelmas term, 1896–1914.

Oxford

The Oxford review: or literary censor. Vols 1–3, no 3, 1807–8.
The farrago: or the lucubrations of Councillor Bickerton Esquire. Nos 1–2, 1816.
Il vagabondo: a terminal miscellany. Nos 1–8, 1816.
The Oxonian. Nos 1–3, 1817.
The undergraduate. Nos 1–6, 1819.
The Oxford miscellany. Nos 1–2, [1820].
The Oxford quarterly magazine. Vol 1, 1825.
The Oxford literary gazette, and classical and foreign journal. Nos 1–4, 11 Mar–20 May 1829.
The Oxford University magazine. Vol 1, 1834.
The Oxford magazine. No 1, 1845.
The Oxonian. No 1, 1847.
Oxford essays, contributed by members of the University. 1855–8.
The Oxford and Cambridge magazine, conducted by members of the two universities. Nos 1–12, 1856. Ed William Fulford.
Undergraduate papers. Nos 1–2 (4 pts), 3 Dec 1857–Apr 1858. Ed John Nichol.
The Oxford critic and university magazine (contributed chiefly by undergraduate members of the University). Nos 1–3, [1857].

Great Tom: a university magazine. Nos 1–4, [1861]. Ed Bertram Montgomery.
College rhymes, contributed by members of the universities of Oxford and Cambridge. Vols 1–14, 1861–74. Ed R. E. Coles, C. L. Dodgson, F. E. Weatherly.
The Milton magazine. Nos 1–2, 1866.
The Oxford undergraduates journal. No 1, 31 Jan 1866–Oct 1875. Continued as Oxford and Cambridge undergraduates journal, 21 Oct 1875–30 Nov 1882. Continued as Oxford review, 7 Dec 1882–14 June 1883. Continued as Oxford and Cambridge undergraduates journal, 18 Oct 1883–4 Dec 1884. Continued as Oxford review, Jan 1885–19 June 1914.
Dark blue: an Oxford University magazine. No 1, [1867].
The Oxford spectator. 1868. By R. S. Copleston, E. Nolan, T. H. Ward.
The Radcliffe. Nos 1–10, 27 Feb–9 June 1869.
The Oxford University magazine and review. Nos 1–2, 1869.
The Oxford University gazette. No 1, 28 Jan 1870 onwards.
The dark blue. Vols 1–14, 1871–3. Prop J. C. Freund Mar 1871–Jan 1873. Ed J. C. Freund. *See* Wellesley index vol 4.
The Shotover papers: or echoes from Oxford. Vol 1, 1874–5. Ed W. E. W. Morrison, F. G. Stokes, F. S. Pulling.
The public schools magazine: conducted by the university men. Vol 1, nos 1–4, 1875.
Ye roonde table: an Oxford and Cambridge magazine. Vol 1, nos 1–6, 2 Feb–June 1878.
Waifs and strays: a terminal magazine of Oxford poetry. Nos 1–10, [1879–82].
The Oxford magazine: a weekly newspaper and review. 1883 onwards. Ed R. Lodge, P. E. Matheson, C. Cannan, J. E. King, A. D. Godley, D. G. Hogarth, R. Carter, J. Fischer Williams, A. J. Carlyle, C. G. Robertson.
The rattle. Vol 1, no 1–vol 3, no 6, 25 Feb 1886–30 May 1888.
The undergraduate. Nos 1–21, 24 Jan–6 Dec 1888.
The new rattle. Vol 1, no 1, 1890–1893. Annual.
The Isis. No 1, 27 Apr 1892 onwards. Ed M. H. M. T. Pigott, W. K. Stride.
The spirit lamp. Vol 1, no 1–vol 4, no 2 (15 nos), 6 May 1892–6 June 1893. Ed Sandys Mason, Lord Alfred Douglas.
Fritillary: magazine of the Oxford women's colleges. Nos 1–37, 1893–June 1931.
The ephemeral. Nos 1–6, 1893. Ed Lord Alfred Douglas.
The chameleon. Vol 1, no 1, Dec 1894. Ed J. F. Bloxam.
The octopus. Nos 1–6, May 1895. Ed Comyns Carr.
The procter. No 1, 5 Mar 1896.
The bulldog. Vol 1, no 1, 28 Feb 1896.
The JCR. Vol 1, no 1, Feb 1897–June 1899.
Ye tea-potte. Vol 1, 1898. Ed A. F. R. Abbott and L. L. Morell.
The bump. Vol 1, no 1, 21 May 1898.
The X: an unknown quantity. Vol 1, no 1, 10 Nov 1898–6 Dec 1900.
The quad. Nos 1–4, 1900–1. Ed C. Scott Moncrieff.

College magazines

Jesus
The druid. Nos 1–6, 1862–3.
Corpus Christi
The Pelican record. 1891 onwards.
Wadham
The Wadham College gazette. 1897 onwards. Ed F. E. Smith et al.

Edinburgh

The new lapsus linguae: or the college tattler, session 1824–5, edited by Criticus, student of medicine and Justus, student of law. 1825.
The cheiliad, or university coterie: being violent ebullitions of graphomaniacs affected by cacoethes scribendi and famae sacra fames. Nos 1–16, 1827.
The university squib. Nos 1–2, 1833.
The Edinburgh University journal and critical review. Nos 1–12, 1833. Ed A. Miller.
The university maga. Vols 1–2, Jan–Mar 1835, 1 Dec 1837–23 Mar 1838.
The Edinburgh University souvenir. 1835.
The Edinburgh University magazine. Nos 1–3, 1839.
Edinburgh essays by members of the University. 1857.
The Edinburgh University magazine. Nos 1–3, 1866.
The Edinburgh University magazine. Vol 1, nos 1–4, Jan–Apr 1871. Ed R. L. Stevenson, J. W. Ferrier et al.
The student: a casual. 1887. Continued as Student, 1887.

Aberdeen

The Aberdeen University magazine. Vol 1, Jan–Aug 1836.
The King's College miscellany. Nos 1–8, 1846–7.
The Aberdeen Universities' magazine. Dec 1849–Apr 1850.
The academic. Nos 1–7. New series, nos 1–8, 1877–8.
Alma mater. 28 Nov 1883 onwards.

St Andrews

St Andrews University magazine. Nos 1–12, Cupar 1863–4.
The tomahawk. Nos 1–4, Cupar [1874].
St Andrews University news sheet. 1886–9.
College echoes. 1889 onwards.

Glasgow

The collegian, conducted by students in the University of Glasgow. 13 Dec 1826–7 Mar 1827.
The college album: a selection of original pieces edited by students in the University of Glasgow. 1828, 1830, 1832. Continued as Glasgow University album for 1836 (1838–40, 1843, 1845, 1847, 1851, 1854, 1858, 1859), edited by the students. Continued as Old college, being the Glasgow University album for MDCCCLXIX, edited by students. 1869. Continued as New college: Glasgow University album. 1874.
The Glasgow University magazine. 1889 onwards.

Dublin

The Dublin University review and quarterly magazine. Vol 1, pts 1–3, Jan–June 1833.
The Dublin University magazine. 90 vols Jan 1833–Dec 1877. Continued as University magazine: a literary and philosophical review. 5 vols Jan 1878–June 1882. Monthly; two further quarterly nos pbd in Sep and Dec 1882. *See col 2940, above*, under Monthly Magazines.
The Catholic University gazette. Vol 1, 1854–6.
Kottabos: a college miscellany. Vols 1–3, 1868–81. 2nd series, 1881–91. 3rd series, 1895. Ed R. Y. Tyrrell 1868–81, J. B. Bury 1888–95.
Hermathena: a series of papers on literature, science and philosophy by members of Trinity College, Dublin. 1873 onwards. Index of contributors to Hermathena 1873–1943, by J. G. Smyly [1944]. Ed J. K. Ingram, B. Williamson, J. P. Mahaffy, R. Y. Tyrrell. Annual; postgraduate.
The Dublin University review. 1885–7.

Eton

The microcosm: a periodical by Gregory Griffin. 2 vols 6 Nov 1786–30 July 1787. Various edns to 1827. By R. Smith, George Canning, J. H. Frere et al.
The miniature: a periodical paper, by Solomon Grildrig of the college of Eton. Nos 1–34, 23 Apr 1804–1 Apr 1805. By T. Rennell, H. G. Knight, G. Canning the younger et al.
The college magazine. 1819. Ed W. B[lunt].
The salt-bearer: a periodical work by an Etonian [T. W. Helps]. May 1820–Apr 1821.
The Etonian. 2 vols Oct 1820–Aug 1821. Ed W. Blunt and W. M. Praed.
The Eton miscellany, by Bartholomew Bouverie. 2 vols 1827. By W. E. Gladstone, G. A. Selwyn, P. A. Pickering et al.

The oppidan. Nos 1–2, Oct 1828.
The Eton College magazine. Nos 1–8, June–Nov 1832. By J. Wickens, G. W. Lyttelton, C. G. Wynne et al.
The kaleidoscope. Nos 1–9, 1833. By A. J. Ellis, T. B. Charlton, G. W. Lyttelton, F. H. Doyle et al.
The Eton bureau. Nos 1–7, 1842. By C. W. Johnson, W. Johnson (later Cory), J. D. Coleridge et al.
The Eton School magazine. Vol 1, nos 1–6, 1847–8.
Porticus etonensis. Nos 1–2, 1859. Ed M. Lubbock and M. Hankey.
The Eton observer: a miscellany conducted entirely by present Etonians. Vol 1, no 1–vol 2, no 10, 21 Feb–21 Sep 1860. By V. S. Coles, V. C. Amcotts, W. Pollock et al.
The phoenix. Nos 1–5, [1860–1]. Ed V. C. Amcotts.
Etonensia. Nos 1–2, 1862. By V. S. Coles, V. C. Amcotts and Lord Francis Hervey.
The Eton College chronicle. 14 May 1863 onwards.
The Eton scrap book. Nos 1–7, 1865. Ed H. Maxwell Lyte and E. H. Primrose.
The adventurer. Nos 1–29, 1867–72. By R. Shute, C. W. Bell, A. A. Tilley, E. C. Selwyn, G. C. Macaulay et al.
The Eton review. Nos 1–6, 1867–8.
The phœnix. No 1, 1874.
The salt-hill papers: or vindiciae Etonenses by two Etonians. 4 June 1875. By J. K. Stephen and E. H. Ryle.
The sugar-loaf papers, by three Etonians. 1875. By J. K. Stephen, E. H. Ryle and M. T. Tatham.
The Etonian. Nos 1–30, 19 May 1875–2 Aug 1876. By G. N. Curzon, S. Sandbach, H. St C. Feilden, J. K. Stephen et al.
The Eton rambler. Nos 1–6, 1880. By A. C. Benson and S. Leathes.
The Mosleian. Nos 1–2, 1882. Continued as Vanitas, no 3, 1882. By A. W. M. Bosville.
The rambler. No 1, 27 Jan 1883. By A. W. M. Bosville.
The Etonian. Nos 1–29, 1883–5. By E. D. Hildyard, W. J. Seton, R. C. Devereux et al.
The Eton review. Nos 1–10, 1886. By H. C. Dawkins and J. H. Hope.
The Eton fortnightly. Nos 1–10, 1887. By A. Clutton Brock, J. A. C. Tilley, A. B. Lowry et al.
The Eton observer. Nos 1–2, 1887. By I. Z. Malcolm and M. M. MacNaughten.
The present Etonian. Nos 1–15, 1888. Ed J. R. L. Rankin.
The Eton review. Nos 1–10, 1889. Ed Lord Elmley (Earl Beauchamp).
The parachute. Nos 1–3, 22 June–30 July 1889. By R. S. Bosanquet, F. M. S. Parker and Lord Warkworth.
The rocket. No 1, 31 Mar 1890. Ed J. S. Arkwright.
The student's humour. No 1, 4 June 1891. By V. R. Hoare, C. C. Bigham, J. S. Arkwright, H. F. G. Watkins et al.
The mayfly. Nos 1–3, 16 May–24 June 1891. By A. B. Ramsay and H. F. G. Watkins.
The Eton idler. Nos 1–7, 22 May–1 Aug 1893. By H. E. S. Fremantle and C. W. E. Cotton.
The Eton spectator. Nos 1–3, 1893. Ed A. S. Ward.
The new Etonian. Nos 1–4, 1895. Ed A. S. Ward.
The amphibian. Nos 1–9, 1898–9.
The bantling. Nos 1–9, 1900.
The gnat. Nos 1–3, 1900.

Harrow

The Harrovian. Nos 1–6, 1828. A collection of poems, essays and trns.
The triumvirate. Vols 1–2, [1860–1].
The Harrovian. Vols 1–3, 16 Oct 1869–6 July 1872.
The Harrovian. Nos 1–26, 21 Nov 1878–30 July 1881.
Harrow notes: a school newspaper, edited by an old Harrovian. Vols 1–5, 1883–7. Continued as Harrovian, vol 1, 2 Feb 1888 onwards.

Rugby

The Rugby magazine. 2 vols 1835–7. Ed A. H. Clough.
The Rugbaean. Vol 1, 1840.
The Rugby miscellany. Nos 1–10, 1846.
The new Rugbeian. Vols 1–3, 1858–Dec 1861.
The meteor. Vol 1, 1867(?) onwards.
The leaflet, edited by members of Rugby School. Nos 1–6; new series nos 1–26, 1883–7.
The sibyl. Nos 1–24, 1890–5.

Rossall

Rossall news. Nos 1–14, 1850.
Rossall herald. Nos 1–6, 1850.
The Rossallian. Vol 1, 1870 onwards.

Marlborough

The Marlburian. 20 Sep 1865 onwards.

Winchester

The Wykehamist. Oct 1866 onwards.
The Winchester review. Nos 1–2, 1880.

Wellington

Wellingtonia. Vol 1, nos 1–6, 1866–7.
The Wellingtonian. 1868 onwards.

Repton

The Reptonian. May 1866 onwards.

Clifton

The Cliftonian. Dec 1867 onwards.

Haileybury

The Haileyburyian. Mar 1868 onwards.

Cheltenham

The Cheltenham College magazine. Vols 1–4, 1869–74. Continued as Cheltonian, 1874 onwards.

Malvern

The Malvernian. Nov 1869 onwards.

Shrewsbury

The Salopian. 1876 onwards.

Working Men's College

The Working Men's College magazine. Nos 1–37, Jan 1859–Jan 1862. Ed R. B. Litchfield.
The Working Men's College journal: the monthly organ of the Working Men's College. Vols 1–22, Feb 1890–1932. Continued as Journal, vol 23, 1933 onwards.

School and University Journalism: Accounts and Studies

Marillier, H. C. University magazines and their makers. 1899 (priv ptd), 1902 (enlarged).
Russell, G. W. E. Collections and recollections. 1903 (new edn).

Cambridge

Gray, G. J. Cambridge University periodicals. Cambridge Rev 10 Mar 1886.
Bowes, R. A catalogue of the books printed at, or relating to the University, town and county of Cambridge 1521–1893. Cambridge 1894. Index by E. J. Worman, 1894.
Bartholomew, A. T. Catalogue of books and papers bequeathed to the University of Cambridge by J. W. Clark. Cambridge 1912.
The Cambridge tart: epigrammatic and satiric poetical effusions etc. Dainty morsels served up by Cantabs on various occasions, dedicated to members of the University of Cambridge by Socius. 1823.
Calverly, C. S. Verses and translations. 1862.
[Bankes, G. N.] Cambridge trifles. 1881.
Seaman, O. Paulopostprandials. 1883.
Calverly, C. S. The literary remains with a memoir by W. J. Sendall. 1885.
Seaman, O. Horace at Cambridge. 1894.

Trevelyan, G. The ladies in Parliament and other pieces. 1888; rev in Interludes in prose and verse, 1905.
In cap and gown. Ed C. Whibley 1889, 1898 (3rd edn with new preface).
S[tephen], J. K. Quo musa tendis? 1891.
S[tephen], J. K. Lapsus calami. 1891, 1896 (enlarged).
Pain, B. In a Canadian canoe. 1891, 1898.
Pain, B. Playthings and parodies. 1892, 1896.
Lehmann, R. C. In Cambridge courts. 1891, 1897.
Kellett, E. E. Book of Cambridge verse. 1911.
Nicholson, R. A. The don and the dervish: a book of verse, original and translated. 1911.
Cambridge University Magazine
Characters of freshmen and other papers, reprinted from the Cambridge University magazine. 1848.
Cambridge Review
The book of the Cambridge review 1879–97. 1898.
Light Green
Hilton, A. C. Works. Ed R. P. Edgecumbe 1904.
Granta
Rice, F. A. The Granta and its contributors 1889–1914. 1924.
Philip, J., J. Simpson and N. Snowman. The best of Granta 1889–1966. 1967.

London

Hawgood, J. A. University College and its magazine. Univ College Mag June 1927.
Bellot, H. H. University College London 1826–1926. 1929.
University College London Gazette
Solly, H. S. The Life of Henry Morley. 1898.
Sleuth
'Sleuth'. King's College magazine. N & Q 10 Mar 1945.

Oxford

G[odley], A. D. Verses to order. 1892, 1904 (enlarged).
G[odley], A. D. The casual ward: academic and other oddments. 1912.
Seccombe, T. and H. S. Scott. In praise of Oxford: an anthology in prose and verse. Vol 2, 1912.
Symon, J. D. The earlier Oxford magazines. Oxford & Cambridge Rev 13 1911.
Oxford Magazine
Echoes from the Oxford magazine: being reprints of seven years. 1890.
More echoes from the Oxford Magazine: being a second series of reprints of seven years. 1896.
Oxonian 1817
Fair-play: or no 1 of the Oxonian exposed by a member of the University of Oxford. 1817.
Isis
Pigott, T. M. Two on a tour and other papers from the Isis. 1895.

Edinburgh

Edinburgh University Magazine
The new Amphion: being the book of the Edinburgh University Union Fancy Fair. 1886.
Student
Famous Edinburgh students. 1914. Mainly rptd from Student.

Aberdeen

Smith, R. H. A village propaganda. 1889.
Donaldson, J. The Aberdeen Universities' magazine 1849–50. Aberdeen Univ Rev 1 1913.
Leask, W. K. The story of the University magazine 1836–1914. Aberdeen Univ Rev 4 1914.

St Andrews

Murray, R. F. The scarlet gown. 1891, 1932 (with memoir by Andrew Lang).

Dublin

Kottabos
Echoes from Kottabos. Ed R. Y. Tyrell and E. Sullivan 1906.

Eton

Harcourt, L. V. An Eton bibliography. 1902.

Rugby

C., G. A. F. M. Matthew Arnold and the Rugby Magazine 1837. N & Q 28 Mar 1942. Evidence that Arnold did not contribute.

F. ANNUALS AND YEAR BOOKS

(1) LITERARY ANNUALS

The spirit of the public journals: being an impartial selection of the most exquisite essays and jeux d'esprit etc. 29 vols 1798 (for 1797) to 1823 (for 1822). New series, 3 vols 1824 (for 1823) to 1826 (for 1825).
The annual anthology. 2 vols 1799–1800. Bristol. Ed Robert Southey.
The poetical register, and repository of fugitive poetry for 1801, 1802, 1803, 1804, 1805, 1806–7, 1808–9, 1810–11. 8 vols 1802–14.
Flowers of literature for 1801 & 1802: or characteristic sketches of human nature and modern manners. 1803, 1804, 1805, 1806, 1807. 6 vols 1803–8. Ed F. Prevost and Francis W. Blagdon vols 1–2, Francis W. Blagdon vols 3–6.
The annual review: and history of literature for 1802, 1803, 1804, 1805, 1806, 1807, 1808. 7 vols 1803–9.
Forget me not: a Christmas and New Year's present. 25 vols 1823–47. Prop Rudolph Ackermann. Ed Frederic Shoberl.
Friendship's offering. 21 vols 1824–44. In 1833 absorbed Winter's wreath and continued as Friendship's offering and winter's wreath: a Christmas and New Year's present, until 1843. Continued as Friendship's offering of sentiment and mirth, 1844. Ed T. K. Hervey 1826, T. K. Hervey and B. E. Pote 1827, Charles Knight 1828, Thomas Pringle 1829–33, H. Inglis 1834; W. H. Harrison 1825, Leitch Ritchie 1842–4.
The Graces: or literary souvenir for 1824. 1824.
Blossoms at Christmas and first flowers of the New Year. 2 vols 1825–6.
Homage aux dames. 1825.
The literary souvenir: or cabinet of poetry and romance. 10 vols 1825–34. Continued as Literary souvenir and cabinet of modern art. New series, 1 vol 1835. Continued as Cabinet of modern art and literary souvenir, 2nd–3rd series, 1836, 1837. Prop Alaric A. Watts 1826–37. Ed Alaric A. Watts.
The amulet: or Christian and literary remembrancer. 11 vols 1826–36. Ed Samuel Carter Hall.
The every day book forming a complete history of the year, months and seasons. 2 vols 1826–7. Each vol issued in weekly pts during the preceding year. Ed William Hone.
Janus: or the Edinburgh literary almanac. 1826. Ed John Wilson and J. G. Lockhart.
The ladies' pocket magazine. 15 vols 1826–39.
The pledge of friendship. 3 vols 1826–8.
A wreath from the Emerald Isle: a New Year's gift. Dublin 1826. Ed P. D. Hardy.
The bijou: or annual of literature and the arts. 3 vols 1828–30. Ed W. Fraser.
The keepsake. 30 vols 1828–57. Ed W. H. Ainsworth 1828, F. M. Reynolds 1829–35, Caroline Norton 1836, Lady E. Stuart Wortley 1837, F. M. Reynolds 1839, Lady E. Stuart Wortley 1840, Countess of Blessington 1841–50, Marguerite Power 1851–7.
The table book. 1828. Issued in weekly pts for the preceding year. Successor to the Every day book. Ed William Hone.
The winter's wreath: or a collection of original contributions in

prose and verse. 5 vols 1828–32. Absorbed in Friendship's offering. Ed W. B. Chorley.
Affection's offering: designed as a Christmas and New Year's gift. 4 vols 1829–[32].
The anniversary: or poetry and prose for 1829. Ed Allan Cunningham.
The gem: a literary annual. 4 vols 1829–32. Ed Thomas Hood 1829.
Le petit bijou. 1829. Ed H. D'Emden.
The talisman. 2 vols 1829–31. Ed Elam Bliss, Zillah Watts.
The treasure of knowledge, literature, instruction and amusement. 2 vols 1829–30.
Affection's gift. 5 vols 1830–3, 1844.
The anthology: an annual reward book for Midsummer and Christmas. 1830. Ed J. D. Parry.
The comic annual. 11 vols 1830–9. 1842. Ed Thomas Hood.
The landscape annual. 5 vols 1830–4. Continued as Jennings' landscape annual: or tourist in Spain. 3 vols 1835–7. Continued as Jennings' landscape annual, 1838. Continued as Jennings' landscape annual: or tourist in Portugal, 1839. Ed T. Roscoe 1835–8, W. H. Harrison 1839.
Mr Mathew's comic annual for 1830, with humorous cuts and other embellishments; as published (1830; 'performed', 1831–3) by him at the Adelphi Theatre. 4 vols 1830–3.
The zoological keepsake: or zoology, and the garden and museum of the Zoological Society. 1830.
The cabinet annual register, and historical, political, biographical and miscellaneous chronicle. 3 vols 1831–3.
The cameo. 1831. Largely rptd from Bijou, above. Ed William Pickering.
The comic offering: or ladies' melange of literary mirth. 5 vols 1831–5. Ed Louisa H. Sheridan.
The iris: a literary and religious offering. 2 vols 1831(?)–2(?). Ed Thomas Dale.
The new comic annual. 1831. Dedication and preface refer to it as Falstaff's annual.
The remembrance. 13(?) vols 1831–[43]. Only vols for 1831, 1834, 1838 and 1843 have been noted. Ed T. Roscoe 1831 and 1834, T. Albin 1843.
The sacred offering: a poetical annual. 8 vols Liverpool 1831–8. Ed M. A. Jevons.
The talisman. 1831. Largely rptd from Iris, above. Ed Zillah Watts.
Fisher's drawing-room scrap book. 21 vols 1832–52. Ed L. E. Landon 1832–9, L. E. Landon and Mary Howitt 1840, Mary Howitt 1841, Sarah Ellis 1844–5, Caroline Norton 1846–9, Charles Mackay 1850–2.
Heath's picturesque annual. 14 vols 1832–45. The vols for 1844 and 1845 were also issued as Cattermole's historical annual. Ed Leitch Ritchie 1832–9, Catherine Gore 1840, T. Roscoe 1841, Jules Janin and Catherine Gore 1842, Catherine Gore 1843, R. Cattermole 1844–5.
The amethyst: or Christian's annual. 3 vols 1832–4. Ed Richard Huie and R. K. Greville.
The musical gem. 3(?) vols 1832[–45]. Ed N. Mori and W. Ball.
The bouquet: a collection of tales, essays and poems, original and select. 3 vols 1832[–4].
The pocket album and literary scrap book. 1832.
The botanic annual. 1832. Ed Robert Mudie.
The year book of daily recreation and information. 1832. Ed William Hone.
The Continental annual and romantic cabinet. 1832. Ed W. Kennedy.
The Yorkshire literary annual. Leeds. 1832. Ed C. F. Edgar.
The Easter gift. 1832, [1836], 1838. Ed L. E. Landon.
The Easter offering. 1832. Ed Joseph Booker.
The landscape album. [2 vols 1832–4.] Written by Thomas Moule; illustr W. Westall. Ed Charles Tilt.
Heath's book of beauty. 15 vols 1833[–47]. Continued as Book of beauty; or regal gallery, 2 vols 1848[–9]. Ed L. E. Landon 1833, Countess of Blessington 1834–47.
The Christian keepsake and missionary annual. 8 vols 1833[–40]. Ed W. Ellis.
Turner's annual tour. 3 vols 1833[–5]. Written by Leitch Ritchie; illustr J. M. W. Turner.
The aurora borealis. Newcastle-on-Tyne. 1833. Ed William Howitt.
The oriental annual, or scenes in India: containing a series of tales, legends and historical romances. 3 vols 1834–6. New series 2 vols 1837–8; 1839–40. Ed Hobart Caunter 1834–6, T. Bacon 1839–40; illustr W. Daniell 1834–6, and by engravings by W. and E. Finden after T. Bacon and Meadows Taylor 1839–40.
The album wreath and bijou littéraire. 1834. Ed J. Francis.
The white rose of York: a midsummer annual. 1834. Ed G. Hogarth.
The Continental landscape annual. 3 vols 1835, [1837–8]. Ed F. Fergusson.
Gems of beauty. 5 vols 1836[–40]. Ed Countess of Blessington; illustr E. Corbould.
The squib annual of poetry, politics and personalities. 1836.
Affection's keepsake: original poetry. 11(?) vols 1836–46. Ed T. Albin.
The Scottish annual. Glasgow 1836. Ed W. Weir.
The sportsman's annual: 1st series, Dogs. 1836. Illustr E. Landseer, A. Cooper and C. Hancock.
Flowers of loveliness. 1836–41(?). Ed Countess of Blessington et al.
Findens' tableaux. 5 vols 1837–41. Ed Mrs S. C. Hall 1837, Mary Russell Mitford 1838–41; illustr with engravings by W. and E. Finden after W. Perring etc.
The pictorial album: or cabinet of painting. 1837. Illustr George Baxter.
The scenic annual for 1838. Ed Thomas Campbell.
Portraits of the children of the nobility. 3 vols 1838[–41]. Ed Louisa Fairlie. Parodied in Children of the mobility, 1841; illustr John Leech.
The hunter's annual. 2 vols 1838[–9]. Ed A. H. Baily.
The Christmas library: birds and flowers, and other country things. 1838. Ed Mary Howitt.
The amaranth: a miscellany of original prose and verse. 1839. Ed T. K. Hervey.
The annual of British landscape scenery. 1839. Ed L. A. Twamley; illustr with engravings after Fielding, Cox, Warren and Radclyffe.
Album wreath of music and literature. 1840.
The Lilliputian picturesque annual. 1841. Ed B. Crecerelle.
The Protestant annual. 1841. Ed Charlotte Elizabeth Tonna (formerly Phelan).
The Renfrewshire annual. 2 vols Paisley 1841–2. Ed Mrs Maxwell.
A love gift. 4 vols 1842[–5].
The Christian souvenir. 1842. Ed C. B. Tayler.
The comic album: a book for every table. 2 vols 1843–4.
The holly branch. 1843. Ed E. Davis.
The gem of loveliness. 1843. Ed H. I. and W. Stevens.
The Catholic keepsake. 1843.
The Victoria annual. 1844.
The ball room annual. 1844.
George Cruikshank's table book. 1845. Ed Gilbert à Beckett.
The comic miscellany. 1845. Ed J. Poole.
The coronal. 1846. Ed E. Lacey.
The golden annual. 1848.
The annual miscellany. 1848.
Portraits of the female aristocracy. Vols 1–2, 1849.
The Christian keepsake. 1850. Ed Mrs Ellet.
The Cheltenham literary annual. 1857. Ed Mrs H. Chetwynd.
The Scottish annual. Glasgow 1859. Ed C. R. Brown.
Many annuals were issued from 1860 onwards which form an integral part of many of the weekly and monthly periodicals listed in the preceding sections. These were either extra numbers or enlarged forms of the June and Dec issues.

Accounts and Studies of Literary Annuals

Tales of adventure and stories of travel [from the annuals] of fifty years ago. 1893.

Tallent-Bateman, C. T. Drawing room annuals. Papers of Manchester Literary Club 1897.

Faxon, F. W. Literary annuals and gift-books. Boston 1912, rptd Pinner 1973. The bibliography of English annuals draws on the work of Tallent-Bateman; it contains many items not listed above.

A cabinet of gems: short stories from the English annuals. Ed B. A. Booth, Berkeley 1938.

Weitenkampf, F. The keepsake in 19th century art. Boston Public Lib Quart 4 1952.

Bose, A. The verse of the English annuals. RES new ser 4 1953.

Renier, A. Friendship's offering: an essay on the annuals and gift books of the 19th century. 1964.

Boyle, A. An index to the annuals 1820–50. Vol 1: Authors. Worcester 1967. *See* K. Ledbetter, Boyle's An Index to the Annuals: some proofing suggestions. Victorian Periodicals Rev 26 1993.

A partial list of the French annuals of the same period, many of which were trns from the English and vice versa, will be found in J. Brivois, Bibliographie des ouvrages illustrés du 19me siècle, Paris 1883; *and* L. Carteret, Le trésor du bibliophile romantique et moderne, 3 vols and index, Paris 1924–7. *The American annuals are listed by* Faxon, *above, and* R. Thompson, American literary annuals and gift-books 1825–65, New York 1936.

Annual Anthology 1799

Curry, K. The contributors to the Annual anthology. PBSA 42 1948.

Annual Review 1803

Curry, K. Southey's contributions to the Annual review. Bull of Bibl 16 1939.

Table book 1827

Barnett, G. L. Dating Lamb's contributions to the Table book. PMLA 60 1945.

Drawing-room scrap book 1832

The drawing-room scrap book: being a selection edited by the Hon Mrs Norton and Charles Mackay. 4 vols [1853–4].

(2) JUVENILE ANNUALS

The Christmas box: an annual present for children. 1828–9. Continued as Christmas box and annual present for young persons, 1829. Ed T. C. Croker.

The juvenile keepsake. 2 vols 1829–30. Ed T. Roscoe.

The juvenile forget me not. 9 vols 1829–37. Ed Mrs S. C. Hall. Juvenile. Forget-me-not, 1833–7.

The New Year's gift and juvenile souvenir. 8 vols 1829–36. Ed Zillah Watts.

Ackermann's juvenile forget me not. 3 vols 1830–2. Absorbed in Juvenile forget-me-not in 1833. Ed Frederic Shoberl.

The excitement: or a book to induce young people to read. 8 vols Edinburgh [1830–7]. *See also* New excitement, 8 vols 1838–[45]. Ed Robert Jamieson.

Marshall's Christmas box: a juvenile annual. 2 vols 1831–2. Ed W. Marshall.

The infant annual. Liverpool 1835. Ed H. M. Marshall.

The New Year's token: or Christmas present. 2 vols 1835 [–6].

The nursery offering: or children's gift. 2 vols Edinburgh 1835–6.

Fisher's juvenile scrapbook. 15 vols 1836–50. Ed Bernard Barton 1836, Bernard Barton and Agnes Strickland 1837–9, Sarah Ellis 1840–8, Jane Strickland 1849, Mrs Milner 1850.

The new juvenile keepsake. 1839. Ed L. E. Landon.

Peter Parley's annual: a Christmas and New Year's present for young people. 1839–89(?). Ed W. Martin.

The recreation: a gift book for young readers. 6 vols Edinburgh 1842[–8].

The child's own annual. 2 vols 1843[–4].

The juvenile missionary keepsake. 1846.

The juvenile offering. 1848.

My own treasury: a gift book for boys and girls. [1850.] Ed Mark Merriwell.

Beeton's annual: a book for the young. 1866. Ed S. O. Beeton and J. G. Wood.

The children's annual. 3 vols 1869[–71].

Numerous juvenile annuals were issued from 1860 onwards as an integral part of juvenile magazines. Thus Boys own annual *and* Girls own annual *are the issues of each paper for the whole year put up in cloth bindings. Other magazines issued an extra number at Christmas which is described as annual, sometimes under a totally different title. Frequently, however, the annuals of this period are enlarged or double numbers of the December issue in an elaborately coloured cover.*

(3) YEAR BOOKS

General

The annual register: or a view of the history, politicks and literature of the year 1758 onwards. In 1790 the stock and copyright were sold: the first was bought by Otridge and the second by Rivington; each party issued a distinct continuation. Rivington's ran from 1791 to 1800, new series 1801 to 1827. General index 1758–80, 1783; 2nd edn 1784; 3rd edn with addns; General index 1781–92, 2 vols 1799. General index 1758–1819, 1826.

The new annual register: or general repository of history, politics and literature for the year 1780–1825. Vols 1–45.

The Asiatic annual register for the year 1799–1811. Vols 1–12. Ed L. D. Campbell 1804–6, E. Samuel 1810–11.

The Edinburgh annual register. 1808–27. Vols 1–19. Ed Robert Southey 1809–15.

The annual chronology and historical record of important and interesting events in 1827, by Tell-Tale Time. 1828.

Arcana of science and art. 6 vols 1828–38. Continued as Year-book of facts in science and art. 29 vols 1839–1880 (for 1879). Ed John Timbs 1839–73, C. W. Vincent 1874–5, J. Mason 1876–9.

The British almanac of the Society for the Diffusion of Useful Knowledge. 1828–1914. Ed Charles Knight.

The companion to the [British] almanack 1828–56. A complete index to the Companion to the almanack, 1828–43, 1843.

The annual historian: a sketch of the chief historical events of the world for the year 1831. 1832. Ed J. Cobbin.

The British annual and epitome of the progress of science for 1837–9. 3 vols Ed R. D. Thomson.

The annual scrap book: a selection of paragraphs which have appeared in the newspapers and periodicals. 1838–41.

The annual mirror for 1845: an historical register. Vol 1. Ed W. Lurcott.

The British year book for the country for 1856. Ed C. MacIntosh and T. L. Kemp.

The photographic news almanac for 1860 with which is included Photographic almanac. 1859(?)–63. Continued as Year-book of photography, 1864–1907/8. Ed G. W. Simpson 1865–80, H. B. Pritchard 1881–4, T. Bolas 1885–9, T. C. Hepworth 1892–5, E. J. Wall 1897–1900, P. R. Salmon 1901–?.

The statesman's year book: a statistical, genealogical and historical account of the states and sovereigns of the civilised world for 1864 onwards. Ed Frederick Martin 1864–82, J. S. Keltie 1883–? (assisted by I. Renwick from 1895).

Whitaker's almanack for 1869. [1868] onwards. Ed Joseph Whitaker 1868–95.

The Era almanack. Annual register of dramatick and musical events 1868–1919. Ed Edward Ledger 1868–1905.

The year book of women's work. 6 vols 1875–80. Continued as Englishwoman's year book for 1881. 35 vols 1881–1916. Ed L. M. Hubbard 1875–98, E. Jones 1899–1916.

The annual summary: a complete chronicle of events at home and abroad. 2 vols 1875–6 (also for 1876–7). Ed J. Mason.
The year's art. 1880 onwards. Ed Marcus Huish.
The constitutional year book and politician's guide. 1885–1939.

Biographical
The annual necrology for 1797–8; including also various articles of neglected biography. 1800.
Public characters of 1798–1810. 10 vols. Vol 1 rptd 4 times.
The annual biography and obituary for the years 1817–37. Vols 1–21.
The annual biography: being lives of eminent or remarkable persons who have died within the year 1842. 1843. Ed C. R. Dod.
Who's who in 1849. 1849 onwards. Ed H. R. Addison 1849, C. H. Oakes 1851–64, W. J. Lawson 1865–9, Douglas Sladen 1897–9.
Men of the time. 1852, 1853, 1856, 1857, 1862, 1865, 1868, 1872, 1875, 1879, 1884, 1887. Continued as Men and women of the time, 1891, 1895, 1899 (15th edn). Ed A. A. Watts 1856, E. Walford 1862, G. H. Townsend 1868, Thompson Cooper 1872–84, T. H. Ward 1887, G. W. Moon 1891, V. G. Plarr 1895–9.
The biographical magazine. Vols 1–7, 1852–7. Monthly. Ed J. P. Edwards.
The military obituary for 1853, 1854. Continued as The annual military obituary for 1855, 1856. 4 vols. Ed H. S. Smith.
The annual Royal Naval obituary for 1855.
Hardwicke's annual biography for 1856–7: containing memoirs of celebrated characters who have died during the year 1855–6. 2 vols. Ed E. Walford.
Celebrities of the day, British and foreign: a monthly repertoire of contemporary biography. Vols 1–3, 1881–2. Monthly. Ed S. E. Thomas.

The Peerage
The present peerage of the United Kingdom. 25 vols 1808–32. Pbd by Stockdale.
The royal blue book: or fashionable directory, and canvassing guide for 1822. 1822–1940. In 1900 Royal blue book, court and parliamentary guide.
A general and heraldic dictionary of the peerage and baronetage of the United Kingdom. Triennial. 1826 onwards. Continued also as Burke's genealogical and heraldic dictionary etc. Ed John Burke 1826–46, John B. Burke 1840–?.
The annual peerage of the British Empire. 4 vols 1827–9. Prop and ed Anne, Eliza and Maria Innes.
The peerage of the British Empire: to which is added the baronetage of the three kingdoms. Vols 1–27, 1832–58. Continued as Peerage and baronetage of the British Empire, vols 28–81, 1859–1912. Edmund Lodge lent his name; in reality prop and ed Anne, Eliza and Maria Innes to death of survivor, Maria, in 1862.
Webster's royal red book: or court and fashionable register. 1847–1939. From May 1925 incorporated Boyle's court guide and fashionable register.
Debrett's illustrated baronetage and knightage of the United Kingdom of Great Britain and Ireland. 1865 onwards. Ed R. H. Mair.
Debrett's illustrated peerage of the United Kingdom of Great Britain and Ireland. 1865 onwards. For the years 1866, 1867 and 1868 this and the previous entry were issued in one volume. Ed R. H. Mair.
The upper ten thousand: an alphabetical list of all members of noble families. 3 vols 1875–7. Continued as Kelly's handbook of the upper ten thousand for 1878–9, 2 vols. Continued as Kelly's handbook to the titled, landed and official classes. 1880 onwards. Ed A. B. Thom 1875–7.

Official
[Perrin, W. G.] Admiralty library: subject catalogue of printed books. Pt 1, 1912.
A list of the general and field officers as they rank in the army. 1754–1868.
List of the officers of the several regiments and corps of militia. 1793–1825.
The monthly army list. Jan 1798–Feb 1809. Continued as Army list etc., Mar 1809 onwards.
The new annual army list (and militia list). 1840–1916. A quarterly edn was started in 1897. Ed H. G. Hart.
The official army list etc. 1880 onwards. Quarterly from 1913; semi-annual from 1923.
An alphabetical list of the commission officers of His Majesty's Fleet etc. 1748–1846.
A list of the flag officers of HM Fleet. 1749–1846.
Steel's original and correct list of the Royal Navy. 1783–1816. Monthly during war, and quarterly during peace.
The Navy list. Feb 1814 onwards. Quarterly; then monthly.
The new Navy list. 1839–56. Quarterly; half-yearly from 1846. Ed Charles Haultain 1839–45, J. Allen 1846–56.
The Royal Navy list. 1878 onwards. Quarterly; annual since 1914. Ed C. E. Warren 1878–81, Francis Lean 1878–1906.
The Naval annual 1886–1911. Ed Lord Brassey 1886–9, T. A. Brassey 1890–1911.
The East India register and directory for 1803–44. Semi-annual. Continued as East India register and army list for 1845–60. Continued as Indian Army and Civil Service List, 1861–76. Continued as India list, civil and military, 1877–95. Replaced by India Office list and Indian Army list. Ed J. Mathison, A. W. Mason, J. S. Kingston, G. Owen, G. H. Brown, F. Clark.
The British imperial calendar and Civil Service list. 1810 onwards. Suspended from 1920 to 1925. Ed B. P. Capper 1810–14, R. Capper 1816–17, J. Debrett 1818–22.
The parliamentary pocket companion for 1833 onwards. Now styled Dod's parliamentary pocket companion. Ed C. R. Dod 1841–55, R. P. Dod 1856–?.
A general police and constabulary list and analysis of criminal and police statistics. Sep 1844.
Shaws' union officers' manual of duties etc. 1846 onwards. Now Local government manual.
The mercantile navy list. 1850 onwards. Ed J. H. Brown 1850–62, I. I. Mayo 1863–?.
The Foreign Office list for 1852 onwards. Ed F. W. H. Cavendish and E. Hertslet.
The Colonial Office list: or general register of the colonial dependencies of Great Britain. 1862–1925. Continued as Dominions Office and Colonial Office list for 1926. 1926–40. Ed W. C. Sargeaunt and A. N. Birch.

Religious
The ecclesiastical and university annual register. 3 vols 1809–11.
The missionary register for the year 1813[–55] containing an abstract of the proceedings of the principal missionary and Bible societies throughout the world. 43 vols.
The annual monitor: or new letter case memorandum book. Nos 1–30, York 1813–41. New ser, Annual monitor: or obituary of the members of the Society of Friends. York 1842 onwards. Index for the years 1813–32, York 1833.
Minutes of several conversations between the Methodist Ministers at their 86th annual conference. 1829 onwards.
The Catholic directory etc. 1838 onwards.
The clergy list for 1841. 1841–1917.
The Congregational year book for 1846 onwards. Ed J. Blackburn 1846–7, R. Ashton and W. S. Palmer 1848–52, R. Ashton.
The Churchman's year book for 1852[–7]: or ecclesiastical annual register. 6 vols.
The clerical directory: a biographical and statistical book of reference for facts relating to the clergy and the Church. 2 vols

1858–9. Continued as Crockford's clerical directory for 1860 onwards.
General Baptist year book for 1866. 1865–91.
The Christian year book. 2 vols 1867–8.
The clergy directory and parish guide: an alphabetical list of the clergy of the Church of England. 1872.
The official year book of the Church of England. 1883 onwards.

Educational

The Cambridge University calendar. 1796 onwards. Ed John Beverley, B. C. Raworth, J. W. Clark.
The Oxford University calendar for the year 1810 onwards. Ed J. Walker, P. Bliss.
The London University calendar for the year 1844 onwards.
The literary and educational year book for 1859 and 1860. 2 vols.
Crockford's scholastic directory for 1861.
The public schools calendar. 2 vols 1865[–6]. Ed C. E. Pascoe.
The institute register and handbook of reference. 1868.
A practical handbook to the principal schools of England. 2 vols 1877–8. Ed C. E. Pascoe.
Year-book of the scientific and learned societies of Great Britain and Ireland. 1884–1939; 1950 onwards.

Professional

The new law list. 5 vols 1798–1802. Continued as Clarke's new law list, 38 vols 1803–40. Continued as Law list, 1841 onwards. Ed J. Hughes 1798–1802, S. Hill 1803–19, T. Cockell 1820–48, W. Powell 1849–58, W. W. Dalbaic 1859–71, W. H. Cousins 1872–83, J. S. Purcell.
The Lawyer's companion for 1848, containing a list of the English Bar. 1848 onwards. Ed W. F. Finlason 1855–60, H. Moore.
The medical annual for 1831–4. 4 vols. Ed R. Reece.
The medical directory of Great Britain and Ireland for 1845.
The London medical directory. 3 vols 1845–7. Incorporated in Provincial medical directory and continued as London and provincial medical directory, 1848 onwards. In 1861 it absorbed Medical directory for Scotland and Medical directory for Ireland.
The provincial medical directory. 1847.
The medical directory for Scotland. 9 vols 1852–60.
The medical directory for Ireland. 9 vols 1852–60.
The London medical guide: containing a complete directory of the names of all qualified medical practitioners residing in London and the suburbs. 1872.

Miscellaneous Commercial

The Post Office London directory for 1799–1839. 41 vols. Continued as W. Kelly and Co, The Post Office London directory for 1840 onwards.
The British postal guide: containing the chief public regulations of the Post Office. 1856–79. Quarterly. Continued as Post Office guide, 1880 onwards. Quarterly.
Bradshaw's railway time tables. No 1, 19 Oct–no 3, 18 Nov 1839. Continued as Bradshaw's railway companion, 1 Jan 1840–Nov 1840. Continued as Bradshaw's railway guide, [no 1] Dec 1841–no 6, May 1842. Continued as Bradshaw's monthly general railway and steam navigation guide etc., no 7, June 1842–June 1961.
Osborne's railway time table and literary companion. Birmingham Nov 1839–1867.
The ABC: or alphabetical railway guide. Oct 1853 onwards. Monthly.
Cook's excursionist and international tourist advertiser. 1864–70. Ed Thomas Cook.
The municipal corporations directory, 1866; or official guide to the counties and municipal boroughs of England and Wales. 1866.
Cook's continental time tables and tourist's handbook. 1873 onwards.
Dickens's dictionary of continental railways, steamboats, diligences etc: being an easy guide for travellers. 1880–1. Continued as Dickens's continental ABC railway guide, 1881–7. Ed Charles Dickens Jr.
The British tariff for 1829–30[1862–3]. 34 vols. Ed R. Ellis 1829–47, E. Beedell 1847–63.
The yearly journal of trade for 1836–46. 11 vols. Ed Charles Pope.
The exporter's directory: an index to merchandise shipped to Australia, New Zealand, India, Africa, N. and S. America etc. 1878–81.
The international mercantile directory (Collingwood's). 1881–1930.
The banking almanac, directory and year book. 1845–1919. Continued as Banker's almanac, 1920 onwards. Ed D. Morier Evans 1856–?, R. H. Inglis Palgrave 1876(?).
The Stock Exchange year book. 1874 onwards.
The directory of directors. 1880 onwards. Ed T. Skinner.
The newspaper press directory. 1846 onwards. Ed C. Mitchell. *See col 2884, above.*
The brown book: a book of ready reference to the hotels, libraries, post offices, cab stands, in the metropolis. 3 vols 1864–7.
London in 1880 [etc.] illustrated with birds-eye views of the principal streets; also its chief suburbs and environs. 1880–9. Ed H. Fry.
The municipal corporations companion, diary and year book of statistics. 1877–1914. At end: County councils, municipal corporations and local authorities companion. Ed J. R. S. Vine 1877–89.
The brewer's annual for 1841–3. 3 vols. Ed G. Amsinck.
The Licensed victualler's year book for 1874–1940. Ed H. D. Miles.
Duncan's manual of British and foreign brewery companies. 1889–1900. Continued as Manual of British and foreign brewery companies for 1902 onwards. Known as Brewery manual. Ed W. W. Duncan 1889–?.

Sport

The racing calendar; containing an account of the plates, matches and sweepstakes run for in 1773 etc onwards. Since 1846 there have been 2 vols for each year with the same serial no; Races past and races to come. Ed J. Weatherby 1773–93, E. and J. Weatherby 1794–1830, E. and C. Weatherby 1831–5, E., C. and J. Weatherby 1836–9, C. and J. Weatherby 1840–58, E., C. and J. Weatherby 1859–67, C. J., E. and J. P. Weatherby.
Guide to the turf: or pocket racing companion. 1842–53. Continued as Ruff's guide to the turf, 1854 onwards. In 1869 including Baily's turf guide. Ed W. Ruff 1842–53, W. H. Langley 1854–6.
The cricketer's manual for 1849, by 'Bat'.
The guide to cricketers. 14 vols 1853–66. Incorporated in John Lillywhite's cricketers' companion. Ed F. Lillywhite.
The cricket chronicle for the season 1863. 1864. Ed W. Bayly.
The archer's register: a year book of facts for 1864. 1864–6, 1877–1915. Ed J. Sharp 1864–88, F. T. Follett 1889–97, H. Walrond 1898–1915.
The cricketer's almanack. 1864–9. Continued as John Wisden's cricketer's almanack. 1870 onwards.
Mantz's cricket directory, with the laws of cricket as revised by the Marylebone Club. [1865.]
The cricketer's handbook for 1865. Manchester 1865.
J. Lillywhite's cricketer's companion for 1865–73. 9 vols. Continued as J. Lillywhite's cricketer's annual for 1874–85. Ed J. Lillywhite 1865–73, C. W. Alcock 1873–85.
The football annual. 1873–1908. Ed C. W. Alcock.
The football calendar, containing laws of both sections of the game, list of clubs, playing grounds, and fixtures for the season 1875–6. 1875–94. Ed G. H. West.
The bicycle annual for 1879–83. 5 vols. Continued as cycling annual for 1884–?. Ed C. W. Nairn 1879–83, and C. J. Fox 1879–?.
The lawn tennis annual. 1882. Ed L. S. F. Winslow.
The Field lawn tennis calendar. 1882–91. Ed B. C. Evelegh.
The year's sport: a review of British sports and pastimes for 1885. 1886. Ed A. E. T. Watson.

The golfing annual. 1888–1910. Ed C. R. Bauchope, John Bauchope.

The yachting racing calendar and review for 1888. 1888–95. Ed Dixon Kemp.

Baily's fox-hunting directory. 1897–8. Continued as Baily's hunting directory 1898–9 onwards.

Studies of year books

Dring, E. H. Early railway time tables. Library 4th ser 2 1921.

Gosse, C. W. F. The London directories 1677–1855. 1932.

Annual Register 1758

H., A. M. The annual register: a bibliographical note. N & Q 13 Feb 1943.

Todd, W. B. A bibliographical account of the Annual Register 1758–1825. Library 5th ser 16 1961. [AJ, DL, JSHK AND JW]

Index